W9-CYE-387

The New York Times
Directory of the Theater

The New York Times
Directory of the Theater

Introduction by
CLIVE BARNES

**An ARNO PRESS BOOK published in Cooperation with
QUADRANGLE / THE NEW YORK TIMES BOOK CO.**

Copyright © 1928, 1929, 1930, 1931, 1932, 1933, 1934, 1935,
1936, 1937, 1938, 1939, 1940, 1941, 1942, 1943, 1944, 1945,
1946, 1947, 1948, 1949, 1950, 1951, 1952, 1953, 1954, 1955,
1956, 1957, 1958, 1959, 1960, 1961, 1962, 1963, 1964, 1965,
1966, 1967, 1968, 1969, 1970, 1971 by The New York Times Company

Copyright © renewed 1956, 1957, 1958, 1959, 1960, 1961,
1962, 1963, 1964, 1965, 1966, 1967, 1968, 1969, 1970, 1971,
1972 by The New York Times Company

Introductory material Copyright © 1973
by Arno Press, Inc.

Library of Congress Catalog Card Number 73-3054
ISBN 0-8129-0364-1

Manufactured in the United States of America

Introduction

By Clive Barnes

A man who is tired of the theater is tired of life—Dr. Johnson might have said, had he not been so terrified of the backstage bosoms of David Garrick's actresses, that he felt impelled to apply the remark to London. But seriously, theater is fun. It is an art of the most surprising diversity. It ranges from the unquestioned to the questionable. It keeps a man's mind lively and his heart open.

A theater is a temple for a pagan as well as a religious man. It is a place to come together and talk about hopes, fears, and the future of mankind and the banana-skin. To me and many other people, the state of the theater is the state of the town. There are cities I have adored, towns that have enraptured me, even villages that I felt I could live in forever, but fundamentally there are only two towns in the entire world that can support an addict's habit—theater. The towns, of course, are New York and London. I was born in the latter, and I have chosen the former. Partly, I suppose, for The New York Times. It is, let me make clear my preference, a paper I love, immoderately, even while seeing with a possibly skeptical lover's eye, its faults.

On theater, we have as a newspaper done fairly well, I think and hope. We have always tried to record the theater in a way and perhaps to a depth, that no other newspaper has quite been able to. We have pretty well covered the field. Whenever a curtain opens we try to be there—at least in spirit. Nowadays where so many curtains open, figuratively at least, in attics, basements and assorted gymnasia, we do sometimes miss out. But we watch for the best. Our aim has always been the same. We are trying to present a consecutive, instant-style opinion of the New York theater as it happens. You may not like our views, but for future theatrical historians we have at least done our best in recording such facts that are not subject to the necessary whims and fancy of opinion.

When Arno Press a few years ago approached the idea of reprinting every Times notice and every Times theater story from 1920 to 1970, I thought it was a wild, crazy and quite lovely idea. As a bibliomaniac and a collector, I really longed for the volumes and couldn't wait for them to come off the press. I could understand completely the interest it had for me but I wondered what interest it had for other people.

However, when I finally got my copies and started to browse through them I fell totally in love with the concept.

This is a unique history of the American theater. With space sufficient to the purpose and, just about, time sufficient to the need, the Times critics, helped by the generous editors now accustomed to eccentricity, have produced a curious subjective history of 50 years of the American theater.

There have not been too many New York Times theater critics—only nine since 1920. And of the nine only four of us have served more than five years, while Brooks Atkinson, the grandaddy of us all, was the critic from 1925 to 1960, with only four years off for good behavior as a war correspondent. One of the pleasanter aspects of the complete collection is to read Mr. Atkinson, at length and at depth.

Personally I am as amazed now at the value of these volumes as I was initially skeptical of their production. At first I felt in all humanity, or at least civilized humanity, who would want to read the wanderings of critics and their henchmen (some of our henchmen have been very distinguished, such as George S. Kaufmann—whatever became of that guy?—Arthur Gelb, Dan Sullivan and Mel Gussow) spread over unremitting acres of critical print. Looking at drama notices with even the respite of turning a page or two to find the baseball score did not seem my idea of most people's fun. When I saw them I realized that these were not just for me and a few friends (known and unknown) but, forgive me if this sounds pompous, a major contribution to the history of the American theater. Wow!

The series was planned in ten volumes. The first eight volumes provided the complete review and news coverage from 1920 until 1970. These eight were published—or, let me be accurate, at least certain staff people got copies—about three months before the final two volumes. At first it seemed no great loss. These were the reviews—the final two volumes were merely the Appendix and the Index. Who needed them? Everyone. The volumes were certainly fun to thumb through—Good Grief did that Woolcott really say *that* about *that*—but for any kind of research it was totally useless.

I would be trying to find for half-an-hour a review of a play subject to revival, before giving up and asking Clara Rotter, our drama secretary, to unearth it for me. Then finally the Appendix and the Index at last appeared—and the Golden Gates opened. Now I could use scientifically volumes that I could only have used previously with merely

hope and intelligence. The two volumes that I imagined would be the most boring and the most useless of the series, in fact, proved the most invaluable of them all.

Now Arno Press and Quadrangle have decided to issue the Appendix and Index of our Theater Reviews as a separate entity. Why? Probably because it realizes that the play is the thing, and that what Brooks, or Walter Kerr, or whoever, says about any play or a player is totally fascinating but of not absolute importance. Walter and myself, for example, write beautifully—although to be honest I can only speak for Walter—but we don't, any of us, affect the remorseless march of statistics.

What this volume—a rather unwieldy volume I am afraid—gives you is simply the clear facts of 50 years of the American theater. Who did what, and when did they do it. As a supplement, did they win any prizes for it?

What you have got here is the bare bones of half a century of the American theater—the half century, incidentally, that mattered. You can settle bets with this book—okay, when was "The Glass Menagerie" first produced—and you can wander through it with a theater buff's addictive pleasure of spiritual name-dropping.

A theater buff is a man who wants to know everything about the theater. What was Hume Cronyn's first role in New York, what was Albee's first play? When did Olivier and Richardson with the Old Vic first venture into New York? And how about Brando?

Fans are able to establish every role an actor or actress have ever been seen in New York—you can get an instant and complete directory of, say, Julie Harris and Antony Perkins.

Lists appeal to us. I sometimes, on a plane (openly) or at a tedious dinner party (surreptitiously) will write down all the names of the actors and actresses I have seen play Hamlet, or Macbeth or Desdemona. It may not be particularly intellectual as a pastime, but it is beguiling and there is always a point in life when memories live longer than dreams.

Give me the name Gielgud, for example. I will recall my first horrified brush with him in London, seeing his first King Lear as an undemanding, uncomprehending, but thrilled, urchin-nine-year-old. Then the rest of his roles as

time went on, as my love affair with the theater progressed to that glorious point where lifelong marriage is an adolescent state of ecstasy.

This book gives you those names. It jogs your remembrances, it fills in very inevitable gaps. If you know your subject you can look at these lists and suddenly reconstruct a complete career. Theater historians and drama critics always live on nostalgia, we continually survive in the past. It is no accident that all daily drama reviewers have the words "last night" thrown around their necks like an albatross. Never tonight. Always last night. Lovers of the theater are continually looking back, trying to capture in our hands the swift flying arrow of art. It is always gone before we noticed it—and our remembrances of theater-time past are blurred.

This volume, fat and authoritative, will give you many legitimate facts. But pray do not give too much value of the awards. In this book you will find the meticulously entered records of more than 50 years of awards. Accept them as facts—yes, we actually have got them all right—but please, please do not regard them as anything else.

Look carefully at these awards. Awards are suspect. Art is not a matter of democratic process, which is an intellectual concept related solely and rightly to government. People get the government they deserve, which is fair, but they also get the arts they deserve, which is a pity. The Oscars are by no means a record of the greatest films, nor are the Tonys a true record of the best plays or the best performances. You don't vote for art, you respond to it. I am personally skeptical of all awards. As a journalist, however, I often need a record of them. Here they all are—50 years of losers and winners. But when you use these lists, please, please remember that some of the winners turned out losers, and some of the losers are surviving.

This book is at one level a simple record of careers and achievement. But, at an obviously deeper level, it is a key that can lead you to the complete compilation of what one particular New York newspaper has thought, worried and pondered over, and even once in a while merely announced. This is the New York theater, and we at the New York Times over a long 50 years have tried to love it. We have succeeded—and have the bouquets and scars to prove it. This book is our battle insignia—but please look deeper.

Contents

Theater Critics of The New York Times 1920-1970

Alexander Woollcott • 1914-1922

John Corbin • 1902; 1917-1919; 1923

Stark Young • 1924-1925

Brooks Atkinson • 1925-1942; 1946-1960

Lewis Nichols • 1942-1946

Howard Taubman • 1960-1965

Stanley Kauffmann • 1966

Walter Kerr • 1966-1967

Clive Barnes • 1967 to present

Clive Barnes
Critic 1967 to present
Born London, England 1927
King's College, London; Oxford (B.A.)

Left pre-medical studies to join Royal Air Force (1946-1947), but finished college with honors in English; administrative officer in town planning for London County Council (1952-1961); also freelance journalist, with articles on music, dance, theater, films and television appearing in The New Statesman, The Spectator, London Daily Express and The New York Times; chief dance critic of The Times of London and executive editor of three periodicals: Dance and Dancers, Music and Musicians, and Plays and Players (1961-1965); came to The New York Times in 1965 as dance critic and added duties of drama critic in 1967; author of six books on dance; critical writing instructor at New York University since 1968.

Walter Kerr
Critic 1966-1967; Sunday critic
1966 to present
Born Evanston, Illinois 1913
DePaul University; Northwestern
University (B.S. and M.A.)

Film critic for two hometown newspapers while in high school; member of drama faculty at Catholic University (1938-1949), during which time he directed some fifty plays; wrote or collaborated on several plays and books for musicals produced on Broadway; drama critic for Commonweal (1950-1952) and The New York Herald-Tribune (1951-1966).

Stanley Kauffmann
Critic 1966
Born New York, New York 1916
New York University (B.F.A.);
Ford Foundation Fellow

Spent ten years with Washington Square Players in New York as actor and stage manager; author of more than forty published plays and seven novels; directed plays for stage and radio; film critic for The New Republic beginning in 1958; theater critic for WNET-TV in New York since 1963 and conductor of that station's "The Art of Film" program (1963-1967); after leaving The Times, returned to The New Republic as film critic and associate literary editor; visiting professor of drama at Yale (1967-1968).

Howard Taubman
Critic 1960-1965
Born New York, New York 1907
Cornell University (A.B.),
Phi Beta Kappa

While in college worked on copy desk of The New York Post; joined The New York Times as reporter after graduation in 1929; moved to music department in 1930; became music editor in 1935 and returned to that post after year and a half with Mediterranean edition of Stars and Stripes during World War II; music critic (1955-1960); critic-at-large since 1966; author of seven books on music and musicians.

Lewis Nichols
Critic 1942-1946
Born Lock Haven, Pennsylvania 1903
Harvard (A.B.)

Took a summer reporting job with The New York Times in 1925 and, upon graduation from college the following summer, returned as a general news reporter; drama editor (1932-1942); Sunday Book Review columnist ("In and Out of Books") from 1957 until his retirement from The Times in 1969; short story writer.

Brooks Atkinson
Critic 1925-1942, 1946-1960
Born Melrose, Massachusetts 1894
Harvard (A.B.)

Printed and edited his own news pamphlets in his early teens; briefly worked as reporter for The Springfield Daily News, served in infantry in World War I, taught English at Dartmouth; joined The Boston Evening Transcript in 1919 as police reporter, later assistant to drama critic; joined The New York Times in 1922 and served as Sunday Book Review editor until 1925; took leave as drama critic to be war correspondent in China-Burma-India military theater (1942-1944) and news correspondent in Moscow (1945-1946); critic-at-large (1960-1965); retired from The Times in 1965; awarded Pulitzer Prize for series of articles on Soviet Union in 1947; author of eight books.

Stark Young
Critic 1924-1925
Born Como, Mississippi 1881
University of Mississippi (B.A.),
Phi Beta Kappa; Columbia (M.A.)

Taught English (1904-1922) at the University of Mississippi, University of Texas and Amherst College; on editorial staff of The New Republic and also associate editor of Theatre Arts Monthly (1921-1924); returned to The New Republic as drama editor after two years with The New York Times; lecturer at New School for Social Research in New York (1925-1928); translated three Chekhov plays; poet, best-selling novelist, playwright and painter; died at age 81.

John Corbin
Critic 1902, 1917-1919, 1923
Born Chicago, Illinois 1870
Harvard (A.B. and A.M.); Oxford

Combined teaching English composition at Harvard (1895-1907) with being assistant editor of Harper's Magazine (1897-1900), drama critic of Harper's Weekly (1899-1900), on editorial staff of Encyclopaedia Britannica (1900-1902) and drama critic of The New York Sun (1905-1907); literary manager of the New Theater in New York (1908-1910); editorial writer for The New York Times (1919-1929); wrote voluminously on drama, government, democracy, public affairs and education, including twelve books; died at age 89.

Alexander Woollcott
Critic 1914-1922
Born Phalanx, New Jersey 1887
Hamilton College (A.B.)

Acting debut at age 5; joined The New York Times as cub reporter in 1909; covered World War I battles for Stars and Stripes; left The Times for The New York Herald in 1922; moved to The New York Sun in 1924 and then to The World (1925-1928); added radio to his media in 1929; prolific writer of books and articles and collaborator on several plays; appeared on the New York stage in the 1930s; weakened by a heart attack in 1940 while acting in a road company and died three years later from a heart attack suffered during a radio broadcast.

Awards

NOTE: In this section will be found listings of the five principal theater awards: The Nobel Prize for Literature (when awarded to a writer whose major work was in the drama), the Pulitzer Prizes, the New York Drama Critics Circle Awards, the Antoinette Perry (Tony) Awards, and the off-Broadway Obie Awards. The awards are listed by year and within each year by category. It should be noted, however, that the awards started in different years, that the categories varied over the years, and that not in every year was an award given in each category.

Nobel Prizes
in Literature awarded to a dramatist

1922

Jacinto Benavente (Spanish Dramatist)

1923

William Butler Yeats (Irish Poet & Playwright)

1925

George Bernard Shaw (Irish Playwright)

1932

John Galsworthy (British Novelist and Dramatist)

1934

Luigi Pirandello (Italian Playwright)

1936

Eugene O'Neill (American Dramatist)

1951

Par Lagerkvist (Swedish Novelist, Poet and Playwright)

1953

François Mauriac (French Novelist and Playwright)

1957

Albert Camus (French Novelist and Playwright)

1964

Jean-Paul Sartre (French Novelist, Philosopher and Playwright)

1969

Samuel Beckett (Irish Novelist and Playwright)

Pulitzer Prizes
for original American Plays

1919 - 1920

Beyond The Horizon (by Eugene O'Neill)

1921

Miss Lulu Bett (by Zona Gale)

1922

Anna Christie (by Eugene O'Neill)

1923

Icebound (by Owen Davis)

1924

Hell-Bent fer Heaven (by Hatcher Hughes)

1925

They Knew What They Wanted (by Sidney Howard)

1926

Craig's Wife (By George Kelly)

1927

In Abraham's Bosom (by Paul Green)

1928

Strange Interlude (by Eugene O'Neill)

1929

Street Scene (by Elmer Rice)

1930

The Green Pastures (by Marc Connelly)

1931

Alison's House (by Susan G. Glaspell)

1932

Of Thee I Sing (by George S. Kaufman, Morrie Ryskind, George Gershwin, Ira Gershwin)

1933

Both Your Houses (by Maxwell Anderson)

1934

Men in White (by Sidney Kingsley)

1935

The Old Maid (by Zoë Akins)

1936

Idiot's Delight (by Robert E. Sherwood)

1937

You Can't Take It with You (by Moss Hart and George S. Kaufman)

1938

Our Town (by Thornton Wilder)

1939

Abe Lincoln in Illinois (by Robert E. Sherwood)

1940

The Time of Your Life (by William Saroyan)

1941

There Shall Be No Night (by Robert E. Sherwood)

1942

(No Award)

1943

The Skin of Our Teeth (by Thornton Wilder)

1944

(No Award)

1945

Harvey (by Mary Cole Chase)

1946

State of the Union (by Russel Crouse and Howard Lindsay)

1947

(No Award)

1948

A Streetcar Named Desire (by Tennessee Williams)

1949

Death of a Salesman (by Arthur Miller)

1950

South Pacific (by Richard Rodgers, Oscar Hammerstein II, Joshua Logan)

1951

(No Award)

1952

The Shrike (by Joseph Kramm)

1953

Picnic (by William Inge)

1954

The Teahouse of the August Moon (by John Patrick)

1955

Cat on a Hot Tin Roof (by Tennessee Williams)

1956

The Diary of Anne Frank (by Frances Goodrich, Albert Hackett)

1957

Long Day's Journey into Night (by Eugene O'Neill)

1958

Look Homeward, Angel (by Ketti Frings)

1959

J. B. (by Archibald MacLeish)

1960

Fiorello! (by George Abbott, Jerome Weidman, Sheldon Harnick, Jerry Bock)

1961

All The Way Home (by Tad Mosel)

1962

How to Succeed in Business Without Really Trying (by Abe Burrows, Jack Weinstock, Willie Gilbert, Frank Loesser)

1963

(No Award)

1964

(No Award)

1965

The Subject Was Roses (by Frank D. Gilroy)

1966

(No Award)

1967

A Delicate Balance (by Edward Albee)

1968

(No Award)

1969

The Great White Hope (by Howard Sackler)

1970

No Place to Be Somebody (by Charles Gordone)

1971

The Effect of Gamma Rays on Man-in-the-Moon Marigolds (by Paul Zindel)

1972

(No Award)

New York Drama Critics Circle Awards

1936

Best American Play: Winterset (by Maxwell Anderson)

1937

Best American Play: High Tor (by Maxwell Anderson)

1938

Best American Play: Of Mice and Men (by John Steinbeck)
Best Foreign Play: Shadow and Substance (by Paul Vincent Carroll)

1939

Best American Play: (No Award)
Best Foreign Play: The White Steed (by Paul Vincent Carroll)

1940

Best American Play: The Time of Your Life (by William Saroyan)
Best Foreign Play: (No Award)

1941

Best American Play: Watch on the Rhine (by Lillian Hellman)
Best Foreign Play: The Corn Is Green (by Emlyn Williams)

1942

Best American Play: (No Award)
Best Foreign Play: Blithe Spirit (by Noel Coward)

1943

Best American Play: The Patriots (by Sidney Kingsley)
Best Foreign Play: (No Award)

1944

Best American Play: (No Award)
Best Foreign Play: Jacobowsky and the Colonel (by S. N. Behrman; written originally in German by Franz Werfel)

1945

Best American Play: The Glass Menagerie (by Tennessee Williams)
Best Foreign Play: (No Award)

1946

Best American Play: (No Award)
Best Foreign Play: (No Award)
Best Musical Production: Carousel (by Richard Rodgers, Oscar Hammerstein)

1947

Best American Play: All My Sons (by Arthur Miller)
Best Foreign Play: No Exit (by Jean-Paul Sartre)
Best Musical Production: Brigadoon (by Alan Jay Lerner, Frederick Loewe)

1948

Best American Play: A Streetcar Named Desire (by Tennessee Williams)
Best Foreign Play: The Winslow Boy (by Terence Rattigan)

1949

Best American Play: Death of a Salesman (by Arthur Miller)
Best Foreign Play: The Madwoman of Chaillot (by Jean Giraudoux)
Best Musical Production: South Pacific (by Richard Rodgers, Oscar Hammerstein II)

1950

Best American Play: The Member of the Wedding (by Carson McCullers)
Best Foreign Play: The Cocktail Party (by T. S. Eliot)
Best Musical Production: The Consul (by Gian-Carlo Menotti)

1951

Best American Play: Darkness at Noon (by Sidney Kingsley)
Best Foreign Play: The Lady's Not for Burning (by Christopher Fry)
Best Musical Production: Guys And Dolls (by Abe Burrows - Jo Swerling - Frank Loesser)

1952

Best American Play: I Am a Camera (by John Van Druten)
Best Foreign Play: Venus Observed (by Christopher Fry)
Best Musical Production: Pal Joey (by Richard Rodgers - Lorenz Hart - John O'Hara)

1953

Best American Play: Picnic (by William Inge)
Best Foreign Play: The Love of Four Colonels (by Peter Ustinov)
Best Musical Play: Wonderful Town (by Joseph Fields - Jerome Chodorov - Betty Comden - Adolph Green - Leonard Bernstein)

1954

Best American Play: The Teahouse of the August Moon (adapted by John Patrick from a book by Vern Sneider)
Best Foreign Play: Ondine (adapted by Maurice Valency from a book by Jean Giraudoux)
Best Musical Production: The Golden Apple (book and lyrics by John Latouche - music by Jerome Moross)

1955

Best American Play: Cat on a Hot Tin Roof (by Tennessee Williams)
Best Foreign Play: Witness for the Prosecution (by Agatha Christie)
Best Musical Production: The Saint of Bleecker Street (by Gian-Carlo Menotti)

1956

Best American Play: The Diary of Anne Frank (dramatization by Frances Goodrich and Albert Hackett)
Best Foreign Play: Tiger at the Gates (Jean Giraudoux's French play as translated by Christopher Fry)
Best Musical Production: My Fair Lady (music & lyrics by Frederick Loewe and Alan Jay Lerner adapted from G.B. Shaw's "Pygmalion")

1957

Best American Play: Long Day's Journey into Night (by Eugene O'Neill)
Best Foreign Play: The Waltz of the Toreadors (by Jean Anouilh)
Best Musical Production: The Most Happy Fella (music & lyrics by Frank Loesser) (adapted from Sidney Howard's play "They Knew What They Wanted")

1958

Best American Play: Look Homeward, Angel (by Ketti Frings)
Best Foreign Play: Look Back in Anger (by John Osborne)
Best Musical Production: The Music Man (music & lyrics by Meredith Wilson)

1959

Best American Play: A Raisin in the Sun (by Lorraine Hansberry)
Best Foreign Play: The Visit (adapted by Maurice Valency from a play by Friedrich Duerrenmatt)
Best Musical Production: La Plume de Ma Tante (by Robert Dhery)

1960

Best American Play: Toys in the Attic (by Lillian Hellman)
Best Foreign Play: Five Finger Exercise (by Peter Shaffer)
Best Musical Production: Fiorello! (by Jerome Weidman, George Abbott, Jerry Bock, Sheldon Harnick)

1961

Best American Play: All The Way Home (Tad Mosel's dramatization of "A Death In The Family" by James Agee)
Best Foreign Play: A Taste of Honey (by Shelagh Delaney)
Best Musical Play: Carnival! (by Michael Stewart, Helen Deutsch, Bob Merrill)

1962

Best American Play: The Night of the Iguana (by Tennessee Williams)

Best Foreign Play: A Man for All Seasons
(by Robert Bolt)
Best Musical Play: How to Succeed in Business Without Really Trying (by Abe Burrows, Jack Weinstock, Willie Gilbert, Frank Loesser)

1963

Best Play: Who's Afraid Of Virginia Wolf?
(by Edward Albee)
Best Foreign Play: (No Award)
Best Musical Play: (No Award)
Special Citation: Beyond The Fringe

1964

Best Play: Luther (by John Osborne)
Best Musical Play: Hello Dolly! (book by Michael Stewart, music & lyrics by Jerry Herman)
Special Citation: The Trojan Women (by Euripides, translated by Edith Hamilton)

1965

Best Play: The Subject Was Roses (by Frank D. Gilroy)
Best Musical Play: Fiddler on the Roof (by Joseph Stein, Sheldon Harnick, Jerry Bock)

1966

Best Play: Marat/Sade (by Peter Weiss)
Best Musical Production: Man of La Mancha (by Dale Wasserman, Mitch Leigh, and Joe Darion)
Special Citation: Hal Holbrook's one man show "Mark Twain Tonight!"

1967

Best Play: The Homecoming (by Harold Pinter)
Best Musical Play: Cabaret (by Joe Masteroff, John Kander, and Fred Ebb)

1968

Best Play: Rosencrantz and Guildenstern Are Dead (by Tom Stoppard)
Best Musical Play: Your Own Thing (by Donald Driver, Hal Hester, and Danny Apolinar)

1969

Best Play: The Great White Hope (by Howard Sackler)
Best Musical Play: 1776 (by Peter Stone and Sherman Edwards)

1970

Best Play: Borstal Boy (by Frank McMahon, an adaptation of Brendan Behan's autobiography)
Best American Play: The Effect of Gamma Rays on Man-in-the-Moon Marigolds (by Paul Zindel)
Best Musical Play: Company (book by George Furth; music & lyrics by Stephen Sondheim)

1971

Best Play: Home (by David Storey)
Best American Play: The House of Blue Leaves (by John Guare)
Best Musical Play: Follies (book by James Goldman; music and lyrics by Stephen Sondheim)

1972

Best Play: That Championship Season (by Jason Miller)
Special Citation: Sticks and Bones (by David Rabe)
Best Foreign Play: The Screens (by Jean Genet)
Best Musical Play: Two Gentlemen of Verona (adapted from Shakespeare by John Guare and Mel Shapiro; music by Galt MacDermot)

Antoinette Perry (Tony) Awards

1947

Director: Elia Kazan (All My Sons)

Actor, Dramatic Star: Jose Ferrer (Cyrano de Bergerac), Fredric March (Years Ago)

Actress, Dramatic Star: Ingrid Bergman (Joan of Lorraine), Helen Hayes (All My Sons)

Actress-Featured or Supporting: Patricia Neal (Another Part of the Forest)

Costume Designer: Lucinda Ballard (Happy Birthday, Another Part of the Forest, Street Scene, John Loves Mary, The Chocolate Soldier), David Ffolkes (Henry VIII)

Actor-Featured or Supporting: David Wayne (Finian's Rainbow)

Choreographer: Agnes de Mille (Brigadoon) Michael Kidd (Finian's Rainbow)

1948

Play: Mister Roberts (Authors, Thomas Heggen and Joshua Logan; Producer, Leland Hayward)

Actor, Dramatic Star: Henry Fonda (Mister Roberts), Paul Kelly (Command Decision), Basil Rathbone (The Heiress)

Actress, Dramatic Star: Judith Anderson (Medea), Katharine Cornell (Anthony and Cleopatra), Jessica Tandy (A Streetcar Named Desire)

Scenic Designer: Horace Armisted (The Medium)

Costume Designer: Mary Percy Schenck (The Heiress)

Actor, Musical Star: Paul Hartman (Angel in the Wings)

Actress, Musical Star: Grace Hartman (Angel in the Wings)

Choreographer: Jerome Robbins (High Button Shoes)

1949

Play: Death of a Salesman (Author, Arthur Miller; Producers, Kermit Bloomgarden and Walter Fried)

Director: Elia Kazan (Death of a Salesman)

Actor, Dramatic Star: Rex Harrison (Anne of the Thousand Days)

Actress, Dramatic Star: Martita Hunt (The Madwoman of Chaillot)

Actor-Featured or Supporting: Arthur Kennedy (Death of a Salesman)

Actress-Featured or Supporting: Shirley Booth (Goodbye, My Fancy)

Scenic Designer: Jo Mielziner (Sleepy Hollow, Summer and Smoke, Anne of the Thousand Days, Death of a Salesman, and South Pacific)

Costume Designer: Lemuel Ayers (Kiss Me, Kate)

Musical Play: Kiss Me, Kate (Author, Bella and Samuel Spewack; Composer and Lyricist, Cole Porter)

Producer, Musical Play: Saint-Subber and Lemuel Ayers (Kiss Me, Kate)

Actor, Musical Star: Ray Bolger (Where's Charley?)

Actress, Musical Star: Nanette Fabray (Love Life)

Choreographer: Gower Champion (Lend An Ear)

1950

Play: The Cocktail Party (Author, T. S. Eliot; Producer, Gilbert Miller)

Director: Joshua Logan (South Pacific)

Actor, Dramatic Star: Sidney Blackmer (Come Back, Little Sheba)

Actress, Dramatic Star: Shirley Booth (Come Back, Little Sheba)

Scenic Designer: Jo Mielziner (The Innocents)

Costume Designer: Aline Bernstein (Regina)

Musical Play: South Pacific (Authors, Oscar Hammerstein II and Joshua Logan; Composer, Richard Rodgers; Lyrics, Oscar Hammerstein II)

Producer, Musical Play: Oscar Hammerstein II, Richard Rodgers, Joshua Logan, and Leland Hayward (South Pacific)

Actor, Musical Star: Ezio Pinza (South Pacific)

Actress, Musical Star: Mary Martin (South Pacific)

Actor-Featured or Supporting: Myron McCormick (South Pacific)

Actress-Featured or Supporting: Juanita Hall (South Pacific)

Choreographer: Helen Tamiris (Touch and Go)

1951

Play: The Rose Tattoo (Author, Tennessee Williams; Producer, Cheryl Crawford)

Director: George S. Kaufman (Guys and Dolls)

Actor, Dramatic Star: Claude Rains (Darkness at Noon)

Actress, Dramatic Star: Uta Hagen (The Country Girl)

Actor-Featured or Supporting: Eli Wallach (The Rose Tattoo)

Actress-Featured or Supporting: Maureen Stapleton (The Rose Tattoo)

Scenic Designer: Boris Aronson (The Rose Tattoo, The Country Girl, and Season in the Sun)

Costume Designer: Miles White (Bless You All)

Musical Play: Guys and Dolls (Authors, Jo Swerling and Abe Burrows; Composer and Lyricist, Frank Loesser)

Producer, Musical Play: Cy Feuer and Ernest Martin (Guys and Dolls)

Actor, Musical Star: Robert Alda (Guys and Dolls)

Actress, Musical Star: Ethel Merman (Call Me Madam)

Actor-Featured or Supporting: Russell Nype (Call Me Madam)

Actress-Featured or Supporting: Isabel Bigley (Guys and Dolls)

Choreographer: Michael Kidd (Guys and Dolls)

1952

Play: The Fourposter (Author, Jan de Hartog; Producer, Playwrights Company)

Director: Jose Ferrer (The Shrike, Stalag 17, and The Fourposter)

Actor, Dramatic Star: Jose Ferrer (The Shrike)

Actress, Dramatic Star: Julie Harris (I Am a Camera)

Actor-Featured or Supporting: John Cromwell (Point of No Return)

Actress-Featured or Supporting: Marian Winter (I Am a Camera)

Scenic Designer: Jo Mielziner (The King and I)

Costume Designer: Irene Sharaff (The King and I)

Musical Play: The King and I (Author and Lyricist, Oscar Hammerstein II; Composer, Richard Rodgers)

Producer, Musical Play: Richard Rodgers and Oscar Hammerstein II (The King and I)

Actor, Musical Star: Phil Silvers (Top Banana)

Actress, Musical Star: Gertrude Lawrence (The King and I)

Actor-Featured or Supporting: Yul Brynner (The King and I)

Actress-Featured or Supporting: Helen Gallagher (Pal Joey)

Choreographer: Robert Alton (Pal Joey)

1953

Play: The Crucible (Author, Arthur Miller; Producer, Kermit Bloomgarden)

Director: Joshua Logan (Picnic)

Actor, Dramatic Star: Tom Ewell (The Seven Year Itch)

Actress, Dramatic Star: Shirley Booth (Time of the Cuckoo)

Actor-Featured or Supporting: John Williams (Dial "M" for Murder)

Actress-Featured or Supporting: Beatrice Straight (The Crucible)

Scenic Designer: Raoul Pène du Bois (Wonderful Town)

Costume Designer: Miles White (Hazel Flagg)

Musical Play: Wonderful Town (Authors, Joseph Fields and Jerome Chodorov; Composer, Leonard Bernstein; Lyrics, Betty Comden and Adolph Green)

Producer, Musical Play: Robert Fryer (Wonderful Town)

Actor, Musical Star: Thomas Mitchell (Hazel Flagg)

Actress, Musical Star: Rosalind Russell (Wonderful Town)

Actor-Featured or Supporting: Hiram Sherman (Two's Company)
Actress-Featured or Supporting: Sheila Bond (Wish You Were Here)
Choreographer: Donald Saddler (Wonderful Town)

1954

Play: The Teahouse of the August Moon (Author, John Patrick; Producers, Maurice Evans and George Schaefer)
Director: Alfred Lunt (Ondine)
Actor, Dramatic Star: David Wayne (The Teahouse of the August Moon)
Actress, Dramatic Star: Audrey Hepburn (Ondine)
Actor-Featured or Supporting: John Kerr (Tea and Sympathy)
Actress-Featured or Supporting: Jo Van Fleet (The Trip to Bountiful)
Scenic Designer: Peter Larkin (Ondine and The Teahouse of the August Moon)
Costume Designer: Richard Whorf (Ondine)
Musical Play: Kismet (Authors, Charles Lederer and Luther Davis; Composer, Aleksandr Borodin; Lyrics, Robert Wright and George Forrest)
Producer, Musical Play: Charles Lederer (Kismet)
Actor, Musical Star: Alfred Drake (Kismet)
Actress, Musical Star: Dolores Gray (Carnival in Flanders)
Actor-Featured or Supporting: Harry Belafonte (Almanac)
Actress-Featured or Supporting: Gwen Verdon (Can-Can)
Choreographer: Michael Kidd (Can-Can)

1955

Play: The Desperate Hours (Author, Joseph Hayes; Producers, Howard Erskine and Joseph Hayes)
Director: Robert Montgomery (The Desperate Hours)
Actor, Dramatic Star: Alfred Lunt (Quadrille)
Actress, Dramatic Star: Nancy Kelly (The Bad Seed)
Actor-Featured or Supporting: Francis L. Sullivan (Witness for the Prosecution)
Actress-Featured or Supporting: Patricia Jessel (Witness for the Prosecution)
Scenic Designer: Oliver Messel (House of Flowers)
Costume Designer: Cecil Beaton (Quadrille)
Musical Play: The Pajama Game (Authors, George Abbott and Richard Bissell, Composers, Richard Adler and Jerry Ross)
Producer, Musical Play: Frederick Brisson, Robert Griffith, and Harold S. Prince (The Pajama Game)
Actor, Musical Star: Walter Slezak (Fanny)
Actress, Musical Star: Mary Martin (Peter Pan)
Actor-Featured or Supporting: Cyril Ritchard (Peter Pan)
Actress-Featured or Supporting: Carol Haney (The Pajama Game)
Choreographer: Bob Fosse (The Pajama Game)

1956

Play: The Diary of Anne Frank (Authors Frances Goodrich and Albert Hackett; Producer, Kermit Bloomgarden)
Director: Tyrone Guthrie (The Matchmaker)
Actor, Dramatic Star: Paul Muni (Inherit the Wind)
Actress, Dramatic Star: Julie Harris (The Lark)
Actor-Featured or Supporting: Ed Begley (Inherit the Wind)
Actress-Featured or Supporting: Una Merkel (The Ponder Heart)
Scenic Designer: Peter Larkin (No Time for Sergeants and Inherit the Wind)
Costume Designer: Alvin Colt (Pipe Dream)
Musical Play: Damn Yankees (Authors, George Abbott and Douglass Wallop; Composers, Richard Adler and Jerry Ross)
Producer, Musical Play: Frederick Brisson, Robert Griffith, and Harold S. Prince in association with Albert B. Taylor (Damn Yankees)
Actor, Musical Star: Ray Walston (Damn Yankees)
Actress, Musical Star: Gwen Verdon (Damn Yankees)
Actor-Featured or Supporting: Russ Brown (Damn Yankees)
Actress-Featured or Supporting: Lotte Lenya (The Threepenny Opera)
Choreographer: Bob Fosse (Damn Yankees)

1957

Play: Long Day's Journey into Night (Author, Eugene O'Neill; Producers, Leigh Connell, Theodore Mann and Jose Quintero)
Director: Moss Hart (My Fair Lady)
Actor, Dramatic Star: Fredric March (Long Day's Journey into Night)
Actress, Dramatic Star: Margaret Leighton (Separate Tables)
Actor-Featured or Supporting: Frank Conroy (The Potting Shed)
Actress-Featured or Supporting: Peggy Cass (Auntie Mame)
Scenic Designer: Oliver Smith (My Fair Lady)
Costume Designer: Cecil Beaton (My Fair Lady)
Musical Play: My Fair Lady (Author, Alan Jay Lerner; Composer, Frederick Loewe)
Producer, Musical Play: Herman Levin (My Fair Lady)
Actor, Musical Star: Rex Harrison (My Fair Lady)
Actress, Musical Star: Judy Holliday (Bells Are Ringing)
Actor-Featured or Supporting: Sydney Chaplin (Bells Are Ringing)
Actress-Featured or Supporting: Edith Adams (Li'l Abner)
Choreographer: Michael Kidd (My Fair Lady)

1958

Play: Sunrise at Campobello (Author, Dore Schary; Producers, Lawrence Langner, Theresa Helburn, Armina Marshall, Dore Schary)
Director: Vincent J. Donehue (Sunrise at Campobello)
Actor, Dramatic Star: Ralph Bellamy (Sunrise at Campobello)
Actress, Dramatic Star: Helen Hayes (Time Remembered)
Actor-Featured or Supporting: Henry Jones (Sunrise at Campobello)
Actress-Featured or Supporting: Anne Bancroft (Two for the Seesaw)
Scenic Designer: Oliver Smith (West Side Story)
Costume Designer: Motley (The First Gentleman)
Musical Play: The Music Man (Author, Meredith Wilson and Frank Lacey; Composer and Lyricist, Meredith Wilson)
Producer, Musical Play: Kermit Bloomgarden and Herbert Greene in association with Frank Productions (The Music Man)
Actor, Musical Star: Robert Preston (The Music Man)
Actress, Musical Star: Thelma Ritter (New Girl in Town); Gwen Verdon (New Girl in Town)
Actor-Featured or Supporting: David Burns (The Music Man)
Actress-Featured or Supporting: Barbara Cook (The Music Man)
Choreographer: Jerome Robbins (West Side Story)

1959

Play: J. B. (Author, Archibald Macleish; Producer, Alfred de Liagre, Jr.)
Director: Elia Kazan (J. B.)
Actor, Dramatic Star: Jason Robards, Jr. (The Disenchanted)
Actress, Dramatic Star: Gertrude Berg (A Majority of One)
Actor-Featured or Supporting: Charles Ruggles (The Pleasure of His Company)
Actress-Featured or Supporting: Julie Newmar (Marriage-Go-Round)
Scenic Designer: Donald Oenslager (A Majority of One)
Costume Designer: Rouben Ter-Arutunian (Redhead)
Musical Play: Redhead (Authors, Herbert and Dorothy Fields, Sidney Sheldon, and David Shaw; Composer, Albert Hague; Lyrics, Dorothy Fields)
Producer, Musical Play: Robert Fryer and Lawrence Carr (Redhead)
Actor, Musical Star: Richard Kiley (Redhead)
Actress, Musical Star: Gwen Verdon (Redhead)
Actor-Featured or Supporting: Russell Nype (Goldilocks) tied with the cast of La Plume de Ma Tante
Actress-Featured or Supporting: Pat Stanley (Goldilocks) tied with the cast of La Plume de Ma Tante
Choreographer: Bob Fosse (Redhead)

1960

Play: The Miracle Worker (Author, William Gibson; Producer, Fred Coe)
Director: Arthur Penn (The Miracle Worker)
Actor, Dramatic Star: Melvyn Douglas (The

Best Man)

Actress, Dramatic Star: Anne Bancroft (The Miracle Worker)

Actor-Featured or Supporting: Roddy MacDowall (The Fighting Cock)

Actress-Featured or Supporting: Anne Revere (Toys in the Attic)

Scenic Designer: Howard Bay (Toys in the Attic); Oliver Smith (The Sound of Music)

Costume Designer: Cecil Beaton (Saratoga)

Musical Play: Fiorello! (Authors, Jerome Weidman and George Abbott; Composer, Jerry Bock; Lyrics, Sheldon Harnick); tied with The Sound of Music (Authors, Howard Lindsay and Russell Crouse; Composer, Richard Rodgers; Lyrics, Oscar Hammerstein II)

Producer, Musical Play: Robert Griffith and Harold S. Prince (Fiorello!); Leland Hayward and Richard Halliday (The Sound of Music)

Actor, Musical Star: Jackie Gleason (Take Me Along)

Actress, Musical Star: Mary Martin (The Sound of Music)

Actor-Featured or Supporting: Tom Bosley (Fiorello!)

Actress-Featured or Supporting: Patricia Neway (The Sound of Music)

Choreographer: Michael Kidd (Destry Rides Again)

1961

Play: Becket (Author, Jean Anouilh (translated by Lucienne Hill); Producer, David Merrick)

Director: John Gielgud (Big Fish, Little Fish)

Actor, Dramatic Star: Zero Mostel (Rhinoceros)

Actress, Dramatic Star: Joan Plowright (A Taste of Honey)

Actor-Featured or Supporting: Martin Gabel (Big Fish, Little Fish)

Actress-Featured or Supporting: Colleen Dewhurst (All the Way Home)

Scenic Designer: Oliver Smith (Becket and Camelot)

Costume Designer: Motley (Becket); Tony Duquette and Adrian (Camelot)

Musical Play: Bye Bye Birdie (Author, Michael Stewart); no award for composer

Producer, Musical Play: Ed Padula (Bye Bye Birdie)

Actor, Musical Star: Richard Burton (Camelot)

Actress, Musical Star: Elizabeth Seal (Irma La Douce)

Actor-Featured or Supporting: Dick Van Dyke (Bye Bye Birdie)

Actress-Featured or Supporting: Tammy Grimes (The Unsinkable Molly Brown)

Choreographer: Gower Champion (Bye Bye Birdie)

1962

Play: A Man for All Seasons (Author, Robert Bolt; Producers, Robert Whitehead and Roger L. Stevens)

Director: Noel Willman (A Man for All Seasons)

Actor, Dramatic Star: Paul Scofield (A Man for All Seasons)

Actress, Dramatic Star: Margaret Leighton (The Night of the Iguana)

Actor-Featured or Supporting: Walter Mathau (A Shot in the Dark)

Actress-Featured or Supporting: Elizabeth Ashley (Take Her, She's Mine)

Scenic Designer: Will Steven Armstrong (Carnival!)

Costume Designer: Lucinda Ballard (The Gay Life)

Musical Play: How to Succeed in Business Without Really Trying (Authors, Abe Burrows, Jack Weinstock and Willie Gilbert; Composer, Frank Loesser)

Composer, Musical Play: Richard Rodgers (No Strings)

Producer, Musical Play: Cy Feuer and Ernest Martin in association with Frank Productions (How to Succeed in Business Without Really Trying)

Actor, Musical Star: Robert Morse (How to Succeed in Business Without Really Trying)

Actress, Musical Star: Anna Maria Alberghetti (Carnival!); Diahann Carroll (No Strings)

Actor-Featured or Supporting: Charles Nelson Reilly (How to Succeed in Business Without Really Trying)

Actress-Featured or Supporting: Phyllis Newman (Subways Are for Sleeping)

Choreographer: Agnes De Mille (Kwamina) Joe Layton (No Strings)

1963

Play: Who's Afraid of Virginia Woolf? (Author, Edward Albee; Producers, Theatre '63, Richard Barr, and Clinton Wilder)

Director: Alan Schneider (Who's Afraid of Virginia Woolf?)

Actor, Dramatic Star: Arthur Hill (Who's Afraid of Virginia Woolf?)

Actress, Dramatic Star: Uta Hagen (Who's Afraid of Virginia Woolf?)

Actor-Featured or Supporting: Alan Arkin (Enter Laughing)

Actress-Featured or Supporting: Sandy Dennis (A Thousand Clowns)

Scenic Designer: Sean Kenny (Oliver!)

Costume Designer: Anthony Powell (The School for Scandal)

Musical Play: A Funny Thing Happened on the Way to the Forum (Authors, Bert Shevelove and Larry Gelbart; Music & Lyrics, Steven Sondheim)

Composer, Musical Play: Lionel Bart (Oliver!)

Producer, Musical Play: Harold S. Prince (A Funny Thing Happened on the Way to the Forum)

Actor, Musical Star: Zero Mostel (A Funny Thing Happened on the Way to the Forum)

Actress, Musical Star: Vivien Leigh (Tovarich)

Actor-Featured or Supporting: David Burns (A Funny Thing Happened on the Way to the Forum)

Actress-Featured or Supporting: Anna Quayle (Stop the World—I Want to Get Off)

Choreographer: Bob Fosse (Little Me)

1964

Play: Luther (Author, John Osborne)

Producer: Herman Shumlin (The Deputy)

Director: Mike Nichols (Barefoot in the Park)

Actor, Dramatic Star: Alec Guiness (Dylan)

Actress, Dramatic Star: Sandy Dennis (Any Wednesday)

Actor-Featured or Supporting: Hume Cronyn (Hamlet)

Actress-Featured or Supporting: Barbara Loden (After the Fall)

Scenic Designer: Oliver Smith (Hello, Dolly!)

Costume Designer: Freddy Wittop (Hello, Dolly!)

Musical Play: Hello, Dolly! (Author, Michael Stewart; Composer and Lyricist, Jerry Herman)

Producer, Musical Play: David Merrick (Hello, Dolly!)

Actor, Musical Star: Bert Lahr (Foxy)

Actress, Musical Star: Carol Channing (Hello, Dolly!)

Actor-Featured or Supporting: Jack Cassidy (She Loves Me)

Actress-Featured or Supporting: Tessie O'Shea (The Girl Who Came to Supper)

Choreographer: Gower Champion (Hello, Dolly!)

1965

Play: The Subject Was Roses (Author, Frank D. Gilroy; Producer, Edgar Lansbury)

Director: Mike Nichols (Luv, The Odd Couple)

Actor, Dramatic Star: Walter Matthau (The Odd Couple)

Actress, Dramatic Star: Irene Worth (Tiny Alice)

Actor-Featured or Supporting: Jack Albertson (The Subject Was Roses)

Actress-Featured or Supporting: Alice Ghostley (The Sign in Sidney Brustein's Window)

Scenic Designer: Oliver Smith (Baker Street, Luv, The Odd Couple)

Costume Designer: Patricia Zipprodt (Fiddler on the Roof)

Musical Play: Fiddler on the Roof (Author, Joseph Stein; Composer, Jerry Bock; Lyricist, Sheldon Harnick)

Producer, Musical Play: Harold Prince (Fiddler on the Roof)

Actor, Musical Star: Zero Mostel (Fiddler on the Roof)

Actress, Musical Star: Liza Minnelli (Flora, The Red Menace)

Actor-Featured or Supporting: Victor Spinetti (Oh What a Lovely War)

Actress-Featured or Supporting: Maria Karnilova (Fiddler on the Roof)

Choreographer: Jerome Robbins (Fiddler on the Roof)

1966

Play: Marat/Sade (Author, Peter Weiss; Producer, David Merrick Arts Foundation)

Director: Peter Brook (Marat/Sade)

Actor, Dramatic Star: Hal Holbrook (Mark Twain Tonight!)
Actress, Dramatic Star: Rosemary Harris (The Lion in Winter)
Actor-Featured or Supporting: Patrick Magee (Marat/Sade)
Actress-Featured or Supporting: Zoe Caldwell (Slapstick Tragedy)
Scenic Designer: Howard Bay (Man of La Mancha)
Costume Designer: Gunilla Palmstierna-Weiss (Marat/Sade)
Musical Play: Man of La Mancha (Author, Dale Wasserman; Composer and Lyricist, Mitch Leigh and Joe Darion)
Producer, Musical Play: Albert W. Selden and Hal James (Man of La Mancha)
Actor, Musical Star: Richard Kiley (Man of La Mancha)
Actress, Musical Star: Angela Lansbury (Mame)
Actor-Featured or Supporting: Frankie Michaels (Mame)
Actress-Featured or Supporting: Beatrice Arthur (Mame)
Choreographer: Bob Fosse (Sweet Charity)

1967

Play: The Homecoming (Author, Harold Pinter; Producer, Alexander H. Cohen)
Director: Peter Hall (The Homecoming)
Actor, Dramatic Star: Paul Rogers (The Homecoming)
Actress, Dramatic Star: Beryl Reid (The Killing of Sister George)
Actor-Featured or Supporting: Ian Holm (The Homecoming)
Actress-Featured or Supporting: Marian Seldes (A Delicate Balance)
Scenic Designer: Boris Aronson (Cabaret)
Costume Designer: Patricia Zipprodt (Cabaret)
Musical Play: Cabaret (Author, Joe Masteroff; Composer and Lyricist, John Kander and Fred Ebb)
Producer, Musical Play: Harold Prince (Cabaret)
Actor, Musical Star: Robert Preston (I Do! I Do!)
Actress, Musical Star: Barbara Harris (The Apple Tree)
Actor-Featured or Supporting: Joel Grey (Cabaret)
Actress-Featured or Supporting: Peg Murray (Cabaret)
Choreographer: Ron Field (Cabaret)

1968

Play: Rosencrantz and Guildenstern Are Dead (Author, Tom Stoppard; Producer, David Merrick Arts Foundation)
Director: Mike Nichols (Plaza Suite)
Actor, Dramatic Star: Martin Balsam (You Know I Can't Hear You When the Water's Running)
Actress, Dramatic Star: Zoe Caldwell (The Prime of Miss Jean Brodie)
Actor-Featured or Supporting: James Patterson (The Birthday Party)
Actress-Featured or Supporting: Zena Walker (A Day in the Death of Joe Egg)
Scenic Designer: Desmond Heeley (Rosencrantz and Guildenstern Are Dead)
Costume Designer: Desmond Heeley (Rosencrantz and Guildenstern Are Dead)

Musical Play: Hallelujah, Baby! (Author, Arthur Laurents; Composer and Lyricist, Jule Styne, Betty Comden, Adolph Green)
Producer, Musical Play: Albert Selden, Hal James, Jane Nusbaum, Harry Rigby (Hallelujah, Baby!)
Actor, Musical Star: Robert Goulet (The Happy Time)
Actress, Musical Star: Patricia Routledge (Darling of the Day) tied with Leslie Uggams (Hallelujah, Baby!)
Actor-Featured or Supporting: Hiram Sherman (How Now, Dow Jones)
Actress-Featured or Supporting: Lillian Hayman (Hallelujah, Baby!)
Choreographer: Gower Champion (The Happy Time)

1969

Play: The Great White Hope (Author, Howard Sackler; Producer, Herman Levin)
Director: Peter Dews (Hadrian VII)
Actor, Dramatic Star: James Earl Jones (The Great White Hope)
Actress, Dramatic Star: Julie Harris (Forty Carats)
Actor-Featured or Supporting: Al Pacino (Does a Tiger Wear a Necktie?)
Actress-Featured or Supporting: Jane Alexander (The Great White Hope)
Scenic Designer: Boris Aronson (Zorba)
Costume Designer: Loudon Sainthill (Canterbury Tales)
Musical Play: 1776 (Author, Peter Stone; Composer and Lyricist, Sherman Edwards)
Producer, Musical Play: Stuart Ostrow (1776)
Actor, Musical Star: Jerry Orbach (Promises, Promises)
Actress, Musical Star: Angela Lansbury (Dear World)
Actor-Featured or Supporting: Ronald Holgate (1776)
Actress-Featured or Supporting: Marian Mercer (Promises, Promises)
Choreographer: Joe Layton (George M!)

1970

Play: Borstal Boy (Author, Frank McMahon adapting Brendan Behan's autobiography; Producers, Michael McAloney and Burton C. Kaiser in association with the Abbey Theater of Dublin)
Director: Joseph Hardy (Child's Play);
Actor, Dramatic Star: Fritz Weaver (Child's Play)
Actress, Dramatic Star: Tammy Grimes (Private Lives)
Actor-Featured or Supporting: Ken Howard (Child's Play)
Actress-Featured or Supporting: Blythe Danner (Butterflies Are Free)
Scenic Designer: Jo Mielziner (Child's Play)
Costume Designer: Cecil Beaton (Coco)
Musical Play: Applause (Book, Betty Comden and Adolph Green, based on original story by Mary Orr and the movie All About Eve; Composer, Charles Strouse; Lyrics, Lee Adams)
Producer, Musical Play: Joseph Kipness and Lawrence Kasha in association with Nederlander Productions and George M. Steinbrenner III (Applause)
Actor, Musical Star: Cleavon Little (Purlie)

Actress, Musical Star: Lauren Bacall (Applause)
Actor-Featured or Supporting: Rene Auberjonois (Coco)
Actress-Featured or Supporting: Melba Moore (Purlie)
Choreographer: Ron Field (Applause)

1971

Play: Sleuth (Author, Anthony Shafer; Producers, Helen Bonfils, Morton Gottlieb and Michael White)
Director: Peter Brook (A Midsummer Night's Dream)
Actor, Dramatic Star: Brian Bedford (The School for Wives)
Actress, Dramatic Star: Maureen Stapleton (The Gingerbread Lady)
Actor-Featured or Supporting: Paul Sand (The Story Theater)
Actress-Featured or Supporting: Rae Allen (And Miss Reardon Drinks a Little)
Scenic Designer: Boris Aronson (Company)
Costume Designer: Raoul Pene du Bois (No, No, Nanette)
Musical Play: Company (Book by George Furth; music and lyrics by Stephen Sondheim)
Director, Musical: Harold Prince (Company)
Producer, Musical Play: Harold Prince (Company)
Actor, Musical Star: Hal Linden (The Rothschilds)
Actress, Musical Star: Helen Galagher (No, No, Nanette)
Actor-Featured or Supporting: Keene Curtis (The Rothschilds)
Actress-Featured or Supporting: Patsy Kelly (No, No, Nanette)
Choreographer: Donald Sadler (No, No, Nanette)

1972

Play: Sticks and Bones (Author, David Rabe; Producer, Joseph Papp)
Director: Mike Nichols (Prisoner of Second Avenue)
Actor, Dramatic Star: Cliff Gorman (Lenny)
Actress, Dramatic Star: Sada Thompson (Twigs)
Actor-Featured or Supporting: Vincent Gardenia (Prisoner of Second Avenue)
Actress-Featured or Supporting: Elizabeth Wilson (Sticks and Bones)
Scenic Designer: Boris Aronson (Follies)
Costume Designer: Florence Klotz (Follies)
Special Awards: Richard Rodgers, Ethel Merman
Musical Play: Two Gentlemen of Verona (adapted from Shakespeare by John Guare and Mel Shapiro; music by Galt MacDermot)
Director, Musical: Harold Prince and Michael Bennett (Follies)
Producer, Musical Play: Joseph Papp (Two Gentlemen of Verona)
Score: Stephen Sondheim (Follies)
Actor, Musical Star: Phil Silvers (A Funny Thing Happened on the Way to the Forum)
Actress, Musical Star: Alexis Smith (Follies)
Actor-Featured or Supporting: Larry Blyden (A Funny Thing Happened on the Way to the Forum)
Actress-Featured or Supporting: Linda Hopkins (Inner City)
Choreographer: Michael Bennett (Follies)

Obie (Off-Broadway) Awards

1956

Best Over-All Production: Uncle Vanya
Best Director: Jose Quintero (The Iceman Cometh)
Best Actor: Jason Robards, Jr. (The Iceman Cometh), tied with George Voskovec (Uncle Vanya)
Best Actress: Julie Bovasso (The Maids)
Best New Play: Absalom (by Lionel Abel)

1957

Best Over-All Production: Exiles
Best Director: Gene Frankel (Volpone)
Best Actor: William Smithers (The Seagull)
Best Actress: Colleen Dewhurst (The Taming of the Shrew, The Eagle Has Two Heads, and Camille)
Best New Play: A House Remembered (by Louis A. Lippa)

1958

Best Over-All Production: No Award
Best Director: No Award
Best Actor: George C. Scott (Richard III, As You Like It, and Children of Darkness)
Best Actress: Anne Meacham (Suddenly Last Summer)
Best New Play: Endgame (by Samuel Beckett)

1959

Best Over-All Production: Ivanov
Best Director: William Bell (Ivanov) tied with Jack Ragotzy (Time of the Cuckoo and A Clearing in the Woods)
Best Actor: Alfred Ryder (I Rise in Flame, Cried the Phoenix)
Best Actress: Kathleen Maguire (Time of the Cuckoo)
Best New Play: The Quare Fellow (by Brendan Behan)

1960

Best Over-All Production: The Connection
Best Director: Gene Frankel (Machinal)
Best Actor: Warren Finnerty (The Connection)
Best Actress: Eileen Brennan (Little Mary Sunshine)
Best New Play: The Connection (by Jack Gelber)

1961

Best Over-All Production: Hedda Gabler
Best Direction: Gerald A. Freedman (The Taming of the Shrew)
Best Actor: Khigh Dhiegh (In the Jungle of Cities)
Best Actress: Anne Meacham (Hedda Gabler)
Best New Play: The Blacks (by Jean Genêt)

1962

Best Over-All Production: No Award
Best Direction: John Wulp (Red Eye of Love)
Best Actor: James Earl Jones (N.Y. Shakespeare Festival, Clandestine on the Morning Line, The Apple, and Moon on a Rainbow Shawl)
Best Actress: Barbara Harris (Oh Dad, Poor Dad, Mamma's Hung You in the Closet and I'm Feelin' So Sad)
Best New Play: No Award

1963

Best Over-All Production: Six Characters in Search of an Author (Play), The Boys From Syracuse (Musical)
Best Direction: Alan Schneider (The Pinter Plays)
Best Actor: George C. Scott (Desire Under the Elms)
Best Actress: Colleen Dewhurst (Desire Under the Elms)
Best New Play: No Award

1964

Best Over-All Production: The Brig (Play), What Happened (Musical)
Best Director: Judith Malina (The Brig)
Best Actor: (No Award)
Best Performance: Gloria Foster (In White America)
Best New Play: Play (by Samuel Beckett)

1965

Best Play: The Old Glory
Best Musical Production: The Cradle Will Rock
Best Director: Ulu Grosbard (A View From the Bridge)
Best Performances: Roscoe Lee Brown, Frank Langella, Lester Rawlins (The Old Glory)

1966

Best Play: The Journey of the Fifth Horse
Best Actor: Dustin Hoffman (The Journey of the Fifth Horse)
Best Actress: Jane White (Coriolanus and Love's Labor's Lost)

1967

Distinguished Plays: Futz (by Rochelle Owens), Eh? (by Henry Livings), La Turista (by Sam Shepard)
Best Actor: Seth Allen (Futz)
Best Director: Tom O'Horgan (Futz)

1968

Best Actress: Billie Dixon (The Beard)
Best Actor: Al Pacino (The Indian Wants The Bronx)
Best Director: Michael A. Schultz (Song of the Lusitanian Bogey)
Best Musical: In Circles
Best Foreign Play: The Memorandum

1969

Off-Broadway Excellence; categories unspecified. *The Living Theater* (Frankenstein), *Jeff Weiss* (International Wrestling Match), *Julie Bovasso* (Gloria & Esperanza), *Judith Malina* and *Julian Beck* (Antigone), *Arlene Rothlein* (The Poor Little Match Girl), *Nathan George* and *Ron O'Neal* (No Place To Be Somebody), *Theater Genesis* (sustained excellence), *Jules Feiffer* (Little Murders), *Ronald Tavel* (Boy on the Straight-Back Chair), *Israel Horovitz* (The Honest-To-God Schnozzola), *Open Theater* (The Serpent), *Performance Group* (Dionysius in '69), and *Boston Om Theater* (Riot).

1970

Best Play: The Effect of Gamma Rays on Man-in-the-Moon Marigolds
Tied with: Approaching Simone
Best Foreign Play: What The Butler Saw
Best Musical: The Last Sweet Days of Isaac
Tied with: The Me Nobody Knows
Best Performance: Sada Thompson (The Effect of Gamma Rays on Man-in-the-Moon Marigolds)

1971

Best Play: The House of Blue Leaves
Distinguished Foreign Plays: Boesman and Lena; AC/DC; Dream on Monkey Mountain
Distinguished Production: Trial of Catonsville Nine
Special Citation: Orlando Furioso

1972

Best Theater Piece: The Mutation Show
Special Citation: Free the Army
Best Music and Lyrics: Micki Grant (Don't Bother Me, I Can't Cope)
Best Score: Elizabeth Swados (Medea)
Best Visual Effects: Allen Ginsberg (Kaddish)

Theater Awards and Prizes 1920-1972

Included in this section are Times articles covering the following awards and prizes:

Nobel Prizes
in Literature awarded to a dramatist

Pulitzer Prizes
for original American plays

New York Drama Critics Circle Awards

Antoinette Perry (Tony) Awards

Obie (Off-Broadway) Awards

Theater Awards and Prizes

1920

PULITZER PRIZE

COLUMBIA TO HONOR LEADERS IN THE WAR

Pershing, Sims, Hoover, Davison, and Bishop Brent to Receive Degrees Today.

BUTLER'S GUESTS AT DINNER

Degrees to be Given to 2,632 Students at Exercises in Gymnasium.

PRIZE WINNERS ANNOUNCED

Medal for Meritorious Service to Science Goes to Albert Einstein of Switzerland.

In recognition of their great service in organizing and commanding the national effort for America's co-operation in the World War, Columbia University, at its 166th annual commencement today, will confer the honorary degree of Doctor of Laws on Henry P. Davison, Chairman of the War Council, American Red Cross; Herbert Hoover, Chairman of the Commission of Relief in Belgium and of the United States Food Administration; the Right Rev. Charles Henry Brent, Chief of the Chaplain's Service in the A. E. F. and former Protestant Episcopal Bishop of the Philippine Islands; Rear Admiral William S. Sims, Commander of the United States Naval Forces operating in European waters during the war, and General John J. Pershing, Commander in Chief of the American Expeditionary Forces.

The aid rendered by those whom Columbia chose to honor this year is classed as military, naval, relief, religious and educational. The decision to award but one honorary degree instead of honorary degrees of several kinds and grades to a number of candidates was said to be a noteworthy departure from the annual custom of the university.

President Nicholas Murray Butler's Commencement dinner in honor of the distinguished men who are to receive the honorary degrees today, was given last night at his residence, 60 Morningside Drive. The guests invited to meet General Pershing, Admiral Sims, Bishop Brent, Mr. Hoover and Mr. Davison, included Colonel William Barclay Parsons, John G. Milburn, Dr. Walter B. James, Rev. Dr. William T. Manning, Stephen Baker, Benjamin B. Lawrence, Alfred E. Marling, Professors F. J. E. Woodbridge, E. D. Perry, Franklin H. Giddings and Charles T. Terry and A. H. Thorndike of the University Faculties; Franklin K. Lane, Frank A. Munsey, Chauncey M. Depew, James R. Sheffield, Charles D. Hilles and Alfred Holman of San Francisco.

Degrees for 2,632 Students.

Degrees will be awarded today to 2,632 students of Columbia, Barnard and Teachers College and of the graduate Schools of Columbia University. The Commencement Day exercises will be held in the gymnasium, Broadway and 119th Street, at 11 o'clock this morning. The candidates for degrees will be presented to President Butler by the deans of the respective schools.

The candidates for the honorary degree will be presented to President Butler by William Barclay Parsons, Chairman of the Trustees. Following the exercises there will be alumni luncheons and in the afternoon the annual costume parade on South Field, the Columbia-Pennsylvania baseball game and class reunions and entertainments.

Following are the prizes, medals and honors that have been awarded for 1920, it was announced:

Barnard Medal, for meritorious service to science, to Albert Einstein, Zurich, Switzerland, in recognition " of his highly original and fruitful development of the fundamental concepts of physics through application of mathematics."

Butler Medals. Gold medal to Senator Benedetto Croce, Senator of Italy, in recognition of the completion of his " Filosofia dello Spirito." The gold medal is awarded every five years for the most distinguished contribution made during the preceding five-year period anywhere in the world to philosophy or educational theory, practice or administration.

The silver medal, awarded annually to the graduate of Columbia University who has during the preceding year shown the most competence in philosophy or in educational theory, practice or administration, to Henry R. Marshall, '73, of New York City.

Class of 1889 Medal, in recognition of his extraordinary effective service during the war as engineer to the Fuel Administrator, to Robert Van A. Norris, '85S.

Class of 1882, Residence Hall Scholarship, School of Mines, Lincoln T. Work, Yonkers, N.Y.

Earle prize in Classics to Andre Mesnard, 1920, of New York City.

Prizes in Journalism.

Pulitzer prize in Journalism, for the best editorial written during the year, the test of excellence being clearness of style, moral purpose, sound reasoning and power to influence public opinion in the right direction. $500. To Harvey E. Newbranch, of the Evening World-Herald, Omaha, for an editorial, "Law and the Jungle."

Pulitzer prize in Journalism, for the best example of a reporter's work during the year; the test being strict accuracy, terseness, the accomplishment of some public good commanding public attention and respect, $1,000. To John J. Leary, Jr., for the series of articles written during the national coal strike in the winter of 1919, which appeared in the New York World.

Pulitzer prize in letters. For the original American play, performed in New York, which shall best represent the educational value and power of the stage in raising the standard of good morals, good taste and good manners, $1,000, awarded to "Beyond the Horizon " by Eugene O'Neil. Produced at the Little Theatre during the season 1919-1920.

The Advisory Board recorded their appreciation of Abraham Lincoln by John Drinkwater and regretted that by reason of its foreign authorship this play was not eligible for consideration in connection with this award.

For the best book of the year upon the history of the United States, $2,000, awarded to " The War With Mexico " by Justin H. Smith.

For the best American biography, teaching patriotic and unselfish service to the people, awarded to " The Life of John Marshall " by Albert J. Beveridge.

Alumni Association medal, for proficiency in advanced design, to John A. Takajian.

American Institute of Architects Medal, for the best general standard in all departments of work, to Donald G. Mixsell.

Alumni Association prize, to the most faithful and deserving student of the graduating class, to Charles E. Shaw, Louisville, Ky.

Brainard Memorial Prize, to the student adjudged by his classmates as most worthy of distinction, to Samuel Weinstein, New York.

Medals for Excellence in Oratory.

Curtis Medals, for excellence in oratory. Gold medal to Archie O. Dawson. Silver medal to Julius Sherwin.

Deutscher Verein Prize of $40 for proficiency in German, to Alexander Lipsky.

Elsberg Prize of a medal and $50 for excellence in modern history, to Laurence A. Kahn.

Green Prize of $50 for the student making the best record in his undergraduate work, to Alfred M. Michaelis.

Rolker Prize, income of $1,000, to the member of the graduating class deemed by his classmates the most worthy of special distinction, to Samuel Weinstein.

Van Amringe Prize, income of $5,000, to the student most proficient in mathematic subjects, to Edward H. Reimer.

Van Buren Prize, income of $5,000, to the student passing the best examination in analytical geometry, differential and integral calculus, to Joseph Feld.

Ordronaux Prize, annual income of $3,000, for general proficiency in legal study, to Clarence M. Tappin.

Convers prize, annual income of $1,000 for the best essay on an assigned legal subject, to Sylvan Lehmayer.

Darling prize, to the most faithful and deserving student in mechanical engineering, to Horace H. Nahm.

Illig medals, for proficiency in regular studies, Frederick H. Melzer, Stephen P. Burke and Harry H. Meyer.

Toppan Prize, $150, for best paper on constitutional law, to John F. Wharton.

Squires prize, for original investigation of a sociological nature, to Thomas J. Jones.

Montgomery prize, income of $1,000, for most proficient student in courses in school of business, Henry W. Sweeney and Robert E. Knodel.

Winners in Barnard.

Duror Memorial Graduate Fellowship, $600, to student in Barnard showing most promise of distinction in chosen line of work, to Sylvia B. Kopald.

Gerard Medal, to Barnard undergraduate most proficient in American Colonial history, to Esther Schwartz.

Herrman prize, $50, to the most proficient undergraduate in botany, to Carolyn Oldenbusch.

Kohn prize, $50, for excellence in mathematics, to Florence L. Schaeffer.

Reed prize, income of $1,000, for special study in origin of Christianity, to Louise G. H. Meixell.

Speranza prize, $50, for excellence in Italian, to Catharine R. Santelli.

Tatlock prize, income of $1,250 fund, for proficiency in Latin, to Katherine H. Shea.

Von Wahl prize, income of $1,300 fund, for excellence in zoology, to Lillian Sternberg.

Breitenbach prize, $200 for highest proficiency in junior university course, to Herbert C. Kassner.

Kappa Psi prize, for highest proficiency throughout the entire university course, to Gerschen Cohen.

Isaac Plaut fellowship, for a year of study at a foreign school or university, to Moritz A. Dittmar.

Seabury Scholarship, providing tuition during senior year, for the highest standing during three years, to Louis Ensler.

1921

PULITZER PRIZE

SIMS'S BOOK WINS COLUMBIA PRIZE

Zona Gale Receives $1,000 Award for Original American Play, "Miss Lulu Bett."

BOSTON POST GETS MEDAL

University's Commencement Exercises Begin With Baccalaureate Sermon by Chaplain Knox.

Commencement exercises at Columbia University began yesterday with the annual baccalaureate services in St. Paul's Chapel, with a sermon by the Rev. Raymond C. Knox, Chaplain of the university. The service was conducted by the Rev. Duncan H. Browne, an alumnus, who was chaplain of the 305th Infantry and is now Dean of the Denver Cathedral, and the lesson was read by Stephen Baker, one of the Trustees of the university.

President Nicholas Murray Butler headed the academic procession, and following him were the candidates for bachelor's degrees in Columbia College, Barnard, Teachers College, the School of Journalism, and the School of Business. An augmented choir also was in the procession.

Taking his text from Revelations 3:8 —" Behold I have set before thee an open door, and no man can shut it "— the Chaplain also reminded the classes of 1921 of one of the sayings of Alexander Hamilton, one of the most famous of the graduates of Columbia: " Never aim at the second best." He urged all the graduates to do their work, " however trivial and unnoticed it may seem, for the sake of doing it well."

" We look out upon a world devastated by the angry hand of man in war," Chaplain Knox continued. " Ours is the task of reconstruction; to provide bread and homes for the millions left starving and shelterless; to bind up the wounds and restore the waste places and to knit together the torn tissues of humanity.

" And who shall do it, if it be not you? Beneath the unrest and the clash of class, more fundamental than any scheme for industrial reorganization, the foremost problem now to be solved is, who shall do the world's work, and what shall be the reward for which men toil?

Reward in Work Well Done.

" If college education and college training mean anything, if they are to justify the cost and the sacrifice that have made them possible, then every one who is their privileged possessor must find his incentive and reward in work well done, that thereby he may have the power to do it better and in ever greater amount. The distinctive mark of the college graduate is not in his degree, nor even in his culture. It is found in the way he responds to his task. Who asks, not 'how little can I do?' or ' Have I done enough?' but ' Let me do more.'

" You go to join the company of those who, having seen the vision, shall ever hereafter not be disobedient unto it. For to make supreme and dominant the life of the spirit is the highest mission of Columbia herself. The university is not composed of bricks and stones, dear as they are in treasured memories. The true Columbia is invisible, devoted to truth; believing in imperishable ideals; setting her standard by the scale of the eternal; ever seeking new contacts with a world unseen; drawing her creative power from the fountains of the deep; inspiring a faith by which the spirit of man is made unconquerable; consecrated to the service of God and man—this is the university whose name you bear!

" We want America first in service. To lose sight of this standard would be to accept a view of our nation which was Germany's downfall. We would see America a nation to whom much has been given, and from whom much shall therefore be required; a nation that accepts for itself, as we accept for ourselves, the rule of life, 'The greatest among you shall be he that serves.' "

Columbia College class day exercises will be held at 2 o'clock today on the Green. The program includes the announcement of the elections to Phi Beta Kappa and the awarding of the Alumni, Rolker and Brainard prizes, as well as the traditional events of ivy planting, the class prophecy, valedictorian address and the presentation. A baseball game on South Field between Yale and Columbia will follow the exercises.

Teachers College class day exercises will begin at 3:30 o'clock in the Whittier Hall Garden. The Barnard College senior dance will be given in Students' Hall, Barnard, tonight.

Awards of Prizes and Honors.

Columbia University yesterday announced the award of prizes and honors for the year 1921, including the prizes and medals in journalism and letters established under the will of Joseph Pulitzer, founder of the School of Journalism. The honors will be conferred at the commencement exercises.

The Pulitzer gold medal for the most disinterested and meritorious public service rendered by any American newspaper during the war was awarded to The Boston Post for its part in the exposure of the Ponzi frauds. Other awards were:

For the best example of a reporter's work during the year, the test being strict accuracy, terseness, the accomplishment of some public good commanding public attention and respect, $1,000, awarded for an interview with President Wilson published in The New York World on June 18, 1920, to Louis Seibold.

For the American novel published during the year which shall best present the wholesome atmosphere of American life and the highest standard of American manners and manhood, $1,000, "The Age of Innocence," by Edith Wharton.

For the original American play, performed in New York, which shall best represent the educational value and power of the stage in raising the standard of good morals, good taste and good manners, $1,000, "Miss Lulu Bett," by Zona Gale, produced at the Belmont Theatre during the season of 1920-21.

Sims's Book Wins Prize.

For the best book of the year upon the history of the United States, $2,000, "The Victory at Sea," by Rear Admiral William S. Sims, in collaboration with Burton J. Hendrick.

For the best American biography teaching patriotic and unselfish services to the people, illustrated by an eminent example, excluding, as too obvious, the names of George Washington and Abraham Lincoln, $1,000, "The Americanization of Edward Bok," by Edward Bok.

General awards were made in Columbia University as follows:

Nicholas Murray Butler Medal, in silver or bronze, awarded annually to the graduate of Columbia University in any of its parts who has during the year preceding shown the most competence in philosophy or in educational theory, practice or administration, awarded in silver, in recognition of the publication in 1920 of his volume entitled "The Psychology of Functional Neuroses," to Harry Levi Hollingworth, Ph. D., Associate Professor of Psychology in Columbia University.

A gold medal, known as the Chandler Medal, awarded annually to the person appointed Chandler lecturer on the Charles Frederick Chandler Foundation, established by the alumni and former students of Professor Chandler, to Frederick Gowland Hopkins, D. Sc., F. C. S., F. I. C., F. R. C. P., F. R. S., Professor of Biological Chemistry in the University of Cambridge.

Department honors were awarded as follows:

Botany, Ruth Clendenin; chemistry, Anna Josephine Eisenman (high honors); economics, Dorothy Louise Falk, Marie Rose Mayer; English, Ruth Adele Ehrich, Marjorie Cecile Mars (high honors), Beryle May Siegbert; French, Mary Wingfield Scott; Latin, Thelma Beryl DeGraff (high honors); mathematics, Theodosia Catherine Bay, Margaret Kimmich Bush, Lovilla Laura Butler, Edris Elizabeth Cannon, Grace Heloise Green, Elizabeth Gertrude Hoffman, Beatrice Ethel Kafka, Dorothy Aline Lind; philosophy, Sarah Kitay; physics, Lois Adele Gurnee; psychology, Eloise May Becker; Spanish, Margaret Ada Beney, Elsie May Guerdan.

Awards in School of Law.

Awards in the School of Law were:

Ordronaux Prize in Law, the annual income of $3,000, to a candidate for the degree of Bachelor of Laws of at least one year's standing, for general proficiency in legal study, divided between Edward Gluck, 1921, New York City, and Loring Whiting Post, 1921, Chicago, Ill.

E. B. Convers Prize, the annual income of $1,000, to the member of the graduating class of the Law School who writes the best essay on an assigned legal subject, to Theodore Houston Solley, 1921, of New York.

In the School of Mines, Engineering and Chemistry, the Edward A. Darling Prize in Mechanical Engineering was won by William Spencer Bowen, 1921, of New York. The William C. Ellig Medals for commendable proficiency were awarded to Thomas P. Clendenin of Mount Vernon; Edwin Florance, New Brunswick, N. J., and Lincoln Thomas Work of Yonkers, all members of the senior class.

The Faculty of Political Science awarded the James Gordon Bennett Prize for the best essay on some subject of contemporaneous interest in the domestic or foreign policy of the United States to Arthur Harry Schawartz, 1923, of Brooklyn. The Robert Noxon Toppan Prize of $150, for the best examination on a paper prepared by the Professor of Constitutional Law, was awarded to Leonard Acker, 1922, of Poughkeepsie, N. Y.

In Barnard College the Duror Memorial Graduate Fellowship of $600 was awarded to Marjorie Cecile Marks, 1921, of New York. The Jenny A. Gerard Gold Medal for proficiency in American Colonial history was won by Eleanor Mix Phelps, 1923, of New York. The Herman Prize of $50 in botany was awarded to Kathryn Wheller Small, 1921, of New York. The Kohn Prize of $50 for excellence in mathematics was won by Dorothy Aline Lind, 1921, of New York.

The Reed Prize for distinction in special study of the origin of Christianity and early church history, and established by Mrs. William Barclay Parsons in memory of her mother, Mrs. Sylvanus Reed, was won by Olga Marie Autenrieth, 1923, of New York. The Speranza Prize, established in memory of the former Professor of Italian as an award for proficiency in that laanguage, was won by Margarete Ada Beney, 1921, New York. The Jean Willard Tatlock Memorial Prize for proficiency in Latin was won by Helen Margaret Matzke, 1924, of New York. The Constance Bon Wahl Memorial Prize in zoology was won by Mary Agnes Jennings, 1921, of New York.

Prizes Won by Seniors.

In Columbia College the Alumni Prize of $50 for the most faithful and deserving member of the Senior Class was won by Archie Owen Dawson, '21, of Hartsdale, N. Y. The Edward Sutliffe Brainard Memorial Prize, awarded to a senior "who is adjudged by his classmates as most worthy of distinction on the ground of his qualities of mind and character," was won by Lawrence Robert Condon, '21, of New York.

The Chanler Historical Prizes for award in Columbia College for the best essays on civil government were conferred as follows: First prize, $500, John Storck, '21, of New York; second prize, $100, Edward Pendleton Howard, '21, of Dallas Texas, and third prize, $50, Samuel Sherman, '21, of Brooklyn, N. Y. The George William Curtis medals for delivery of original orations were awarded to Gustav Peck, '21, of New York, and Louis Nizer, '22, of Brooklyn. The Deutscher Verein prize of $50 went to Joseph Leon Wainer, '23, of Brooklyn.

The Albert Marion Elsberg Memorial prize for excellence in modern history in Columbia College went to William John Shultz of Brooklyn. The Albert Asher Green Memorial Prize for scholarship was won by Mayer Edel Ross, '21, of 669 Gates Avenue, Brooklyn. Other Columbia College prizes were awarded as follows:

Charles M. Rolker Jr. Prize, annual income of $1,000, the gift of Mrs. C. M. Rolker, in memory of her son, Charles M. Rolker Jr., of the Class of '07, awarded to the member of the graduating class in Columbia College deemed by his classmates the most worthy of special distinction as an undergraduate student because of scholarship, participation in student activities, or pre-eminence in athletic sports, or in any combination of these, to Lawrence Robert Condon, '21, of New York City.

The Professor Van Amringe Mathematical Prize, annual income of $5,000, given by George G. De Witt of the class of '67 in honor of Professor John Howard Van Amringe, and awarded annually to the student of Columbia College deemed most proficient in the mathematical subjects designated during the year of award for freshmen and sophomores in the college, to Wilfred Francis Skeats, '23, of Orange, N. J.

Prize in Mathematics.

The John Dash Van Buren Jr. Prize in Mathematics, annual income of $5,000, the gift of Mrs. Louis P. Hoyt in memory of her nephew, John Dash Van Buren Jr. of the class of '05, and awarded to the candidate for an academic degree in Columbia College who passes the best examination in analytical geometry, differential and integral calculus, and in such additional subjects as the Department of Mathematics may prescribe, to Ralph De Laer Kronig, '22, of New York City.

The Class of '92 Residence Halls Scholarships for college spirit were awarded for the next academic year to Carl Richard Moszczenski, Columbia College, '22, of Brooklyn, and Horatio Porter, School of Mines, '22, of St. Louis, Mo. The Earle Prize of $50 in the classics was won by Thelma Beryl De Graff, '21, of New York. The Philolexian Prizes were awarded as follows: First, Henry Ernst Obermeyer, '21, New York City; second, Horace Campbell Coon, '22, Glen Ridge, N. J.; third, Frank Fraser Bond, '21, St. John's, N. F.

These awards were made in the College of Pharmacy:

Breitenbach Prize, a cash prize of $200 given annually by Max J. Breitenbach for the highest proficiency in the junior university course, to Rose Lein, '21, Jersey City, N. J.

Kappa Psi Prize, a gold medal presented annually by the Gamma Chapter of the Kappa Psi Fraternity for the highest proficiency throughout the university course, to Harry Taub, '21, New York City.

Isaac Plaut Fellowship, founded by Albert Plaut in memory of his father, Isaac Plaut, provides for a year of study at a foreign school or university, awarded to that student who shall have shown during his full course of study the greatest taste and aptitude for original investigation, to Herbert Carl Kassner, '21, Jamaica, N. Y.

Seabury Scholarship, founded by Dr. Henry C. Lovis in memory of George J. Seabury, providing tuition during the senior year of the university course for the highest standing during the three years, to Abraham Taub, '22, New York City.

These prizes were awarded in he School of Architecture: Alumni Association Medal, offered by the Alumni Association of the School of Architecture, for proficiency in advanced design, to George Wolcott Trofast-Gillette, '21, of Garden City, N. Y. American Institute of Architects Medal, offered by the American Institute of Architects to that student of the School of Architecture who has during his course maintained the best general standard in all departments of his work, to Duane Reginald Everson, '21 of New York City.

1922

NOBEL PRIZE

NOBEL PRIZE FOR EINSTEIN.

Bonavente, Spanish Dramatist, Gets Literary Section Award.

STOCKHOLM, Nov. 9.—The Nobel Committee has awarded the physics prize for 1921 to Professor Dr. Albert Einstein of Germany, identified with the theory of relativity, and that for 1922 to Professor Neils Bohr, Copenhagen.

The prize for outstanding achievement in literature for the present year has been awarded to the Spanish dramatist, Jacinto Benavente. It amounts to 500,000 francs.

Jacinto Benavente began his career as a clown in pantomime. Later he became an actor, winning a not inconsiderable reputation. In 1894 he started writing for the stage, his early efforts consisting mainly of drama and farce. By some critics he is considered the most important figure in present day Spanish literature.

PULITZER PRIZE

'UNKNOWN SOLDIER' THEME WINS PRIZES

News Story and Editorial on Arlington Burial Receive 1921 Pulitzer Awards.

TARKINGTON NOVEL PICKED

"Alice Adams" His Second Work So Selected—"Anna Christie" the Best Play.

The theme of the burial of the "Unknown Soldier" in Arlington Cemetery on last Armistice Day won two of the annual prizes in journalism established under the will of Joseph Pulitzer and awarded by juries selected from the teaching staff of the Columbia School of Journalism. Winners of the journalism prizes, as well as the Pulitzer prizes in letters and several scholarships, were announced yesterday by Frank D. Fackenthal, Secretary of Columbia University.

Kirke L. Simpson of The Associated Press won the prize of $1,000 "for the best example of a reporter's work during 1921, the test being strict accuracy, terseness, and the accomplishment of some public good commanding public attention and respect." His news reports on the ceremonies attending the burial of the "Unknown Soldier" were printed in The Associated Press newspapers on Nov. 9, 10 and 11.

After The Associated Press had received "hundreds of tributes to the beauty of its news dispatches about the 'Unknown Soldier,'" all the articles were reprinted in a supplement to the Service Bulletin of the association and widely distributed. Mr. Simpson's stories continuously covered the arrival of the body on the Olympia, the solemn watch in the Capitol and the ceremony of burial in the National Cemetery.

The writer has been for years a member of the Washington staff of The Associated Press.

The $500 prize for the best editorial of the year went to Frank M. O'Brien of The New York Herald for his editorial entitled "The Unknown Soldier," published on Nov. 11, 1921.

For the second time in the history of the Pulitzer prizes in letters, Booth Tarkington won the prize of $1,000 for the best novel of the year. A jury of three, appointed by Columbia University, picked Mr. Tarkington's "Alice Adams" as the best novel of 1921. His novel, "The Magnificent Ambersons," won the same prize for 1918.

The prize is offered "for the American novel published during the year which shall best present the wholesome atmosphere of American life and the highest standard of American manners and manhood." The members of the jury were Professor Stuart P. Sherman, the Rev. Dr. Samuel M. Crothers and Professor Jefferson B. Fletcher. Mr. Tarkington's novel was published by Doubleday, Page & Co.

Eugene O'Neill's play, "Anna Christie," won the prize of $1,000 "for the best original American play performed in New York, which shall best represent the educational value and power of the stage in raising the standard of good morals, good taste and good manners."

The prize of $2,000 for the best book of the year on the history of the United States was awarded by a jury of historians to James Truslow Adams for his history, "The Founding of New England," published by the Atlantic Monthly Company.

The prize of $1,000 "for the best American biography teaching patriotic and unselfish services" was awarded to Hamlin Garland for his book, "A Daughter of the Middle Border," published by the MacMillan Company.

The prize of $1,000 for the best volume of verse published during the year by an American author went to Edwin Arlington Robinson for his "Collected Poems," published by the MacMillan Company.

Among the journalism prizes, the gold medal "for the most disinterested and meritorious public service rendered by any American newspaper during the year" went to The World. The recommendation of the jury was based on "articles exposing the operations of the Ku Klux Klan, published during September and October, 1921."

The prize of $500 for the best cartoon of 1921 was awarded to Rollin Kirby of The World. The work, "On the Road to Moscow," was published on Aug. 5, 1921.

Three traveling scholarships of $1,500 each, awarded to graduates of the School of Journalism, also were announced. The winners, who will spend a year studying in Europe the press and the "social, political and moral conditions of the people," are Robert Arthur Curry of Nassau, L. I.; Zilpha Mary Carruthers of Denver, Col., and Robert Henry Best of Spartanburg, S. C. All are members of the graduating class of the School of Journalism.

The annual scholarship of $1,500 to enable a student to study music in Europe was won by Sandor Harmati of Hollis, L. I., A symphonic tone poem was the basis of the recommendation. He is a graduate of the Royal Academy of Budapest.

A similar scholarship for a student of art was awarded to Miss Edith Bell of Des Moines, Iowa, a student in the school of the National Academy of Design.

1923

NOBEL PRIZE

NOBEL PRIZE AWARDED TO WILLIAM B. YEATS

Free State Senator Has Long Been Distinguished as an Irish Poet and Playwright.

STOCKHOLM, Nov. 14 (Associated Press).—The Nobel Prize for literature has been awarded to William Butler Yeats, the Irish author, it was announced today.

William Butler Yeats, poet and playwright, is one of the best known of the literary lights of the new Irish nationalist school. In his numerous lyrical poems, essays, sketches and works for the stage he has drawn widely upon his native Irish legend and life for material, giving it an original turn of treatment in which both critical judgment and lay opinion have frequently been blended with great charm.

Yeats has been especially active in an effort to build up an Irish literary theatre, and figured largely on the platform and in his writings as an advocate of the fulfillment of Ireland's national aspirations. In 1922 he was appointed a member of the new Irish Free State Senate, and took his place as a member of that body at the Senate's first meeting last December.

Yeats was born in 1865. In 1917 he married Georgia Hyde Lees, and has two children.

PULITZER PRIZE

PULITZER PRIZES FOR 1922 AWARDED

Alva Johnston Receives $1,000 for Reports of Scientists' Convention in The Times.

MEDAL TO MEMPHIS PAPER

Commercial Appeal Selected for Disinterested and Meritorious Public Service in Ku Klux Attitude.

The Memphis Commercial Appeal has received the gold medal for the most disinterested and meritorious public service rendered by any American newspaper during the last year, according to the award of the juries on the Pulitzer prizes and traveling scholarships of the School of Journalism, Columbia University, made public yesterday.

Alva Johnston received the $1,000 prize for the best example of a reporter's work during the year for his reports of the proceedings of the convention of the American Association for the Advancement of Science, published in THE NEW YORK TIMES on Dec. 27 to 30, 1922. William Allen White of Emporia, Kan., received the $500 prize for the best editorial article for an editorial entitled "To an Anxious Friend" in The Emporia Gazette on July 27, 1922.

The prize for the best American novel of the year went to "One of Ours," by Willa Cather; for the best play, to "Icebound," by Owen Davis; for the best book on history, to "The Supreme Court in United States History," by Charles Warren; for the best book of American biography, to "The Life and Letters of Walter H. Page," by Burton J. Hendrick, and for the best volume of verse, to Edna St. Vincent Millay.

No awards were made for the best history of the services rendered to the public by the American press during the preceding year or for the best cartoon. The announcement of the awards follows:

Prizes in Journalism.

For the most disinterested and meritorious public service rendered by any American newspaper during the year, a gold medal costing $500. Jury: Professor John W. Cunliffe, Professor Roscoe C. E. Brown, Henry W. Sackett.

The medal was awarded to The Memphis Commercial Appeal, Memphis, Tenn., for its courageous attitude in the publication of cartoons and the handling of news in reference to the operations of the Ku Klux Klan.

For the best editorial article written during the year, the test of excellence being clearness of style, moral purpose, sound reasoning and power to influence public opinion in the right direction, $500. Jury: Professor Roscoe C. E. Brown, Professor John W. Cunliffe, Associate Harold de W. Fuller.

The prize was awarded to William Allen White for an editorial entitled, "To an anxious Friend," in The Emporia Gazette, Emporia, Kan., July 27, 1922.

For the best example of a reporter's work during the year; the test being strict accuracy, terseness, the accomplishment of some public good commanding public attention and respect, $1,000. Jury: Professor Charles Phillips Cooper, Associate Carl Dickey, Associate Allen Sinclair Will.

The recommendation of the jury, confirmed by the teaching staff, is that the prize be awarded to Alva Johnston for his reports of the proceedings of the Convention of the American Association for the Advancement of Science held in Cambridge, Mass., in December, 1922, published in THE NEW YORK TIMES Dec. 27 to 30, 1922.

Prizes in Letters.

For the American novel published during the year which shall best present the wholesome atmosphere of American life, and the highest standard of American manners and manhood, $1,000. Jury—Jefferson B. Fletcher, Samuel M. Crothers, Bliss Perry.

The jury recommends for the award of the Prize in the Novel, "One of Ours," by Willa Cather, published by Alfred Knopf, Inc., New York, 1922.

For the original American play performed in New York, which shall best represent the educational value and power of the stage in raising the standard of good morals, good taste and good manners, $1,000. Jury: William Lyon Phelps, Clayton Hamilton, Owen Johnson.

The jury recommends for the award of the Prize in the Drama, "Icebound," by Owen Davis, produced at the Sam H. Harris Theatre in New York during the season 1922-1923.

For the best book of the year upon history of the United States, $2,000. Jury: Worthington C. Ford, John B. McMaster, Charles Downer Hazen.

The jury recommends for the award of the Prize in History, "The Supreme Court in United States History," by Charles Warren, published by Little, Brown & Company, Boston, Massachusetts, 1922.

For the best American biography teaching patriotic and unselfish services to the people, illustrated by an eminent example, excluding, as too obvious, the names of George Washington and Abraham Lincoln, $1,000. Jury: Maurice Francis Egan, William Roscoe Thayer, William Allen White.

The jury recommends for the award of the Prize in Biography, "The Life and Letters of Walter H. Page," by Burton J. Hendrick, published by Doubleday, Page & Company, Garden City, New York, 1922.

For the best volume of verse published during the year by an American author, $1,000. Jury: Wilbur L. Cross, Richard Burton, Ferris Greenslet.

The jury recommends for the award of the Prize in Verse, the following by Edna St. Vincent Millay: "The Ballad of the Harp-Weaver," printed for Frank Shay, New York, 1922; "A Few Figs from Thistles," published by Frank Shay, New York, 1922; "Eight Sonnets in American Poetry, 1922: A Miscellany," published by Harcourt, Brace & Co., New York.

Traveling Scholarships.

Three traveling scholarships, having the value of $1,500 each, to graduates of the School of Journalism, who shall have passed their examinations with the highest honor and are otherwise most deserving, to enable each of them to spend a year in Europe, to study the social, political and moral conditions of the people, and the character and principles of the European press. On the nomination of the teaching staff of the School of Journalism, the following were appointed:

1. Geneva Bertha Seybold, Topeka, Kan.; 2. Lee Mills Merriman, Chicago, Ill.; 3. Roswell Sessoms Britton, Soochow, China.

Alternates: 1. Paul Friederichsen, Clinton, Iowa; 2. Charles Ruggles Smith, Cambridge, Mass.; 3, Josephina Lula Chase, Bakersfield, Cal.

An annual scholarship, having the value of $1,500, to the student of music in America who may be deemed the most talented and deserving, in order that he may continue his studies with the advantage of European instruction, on the nomination of a jury composed of members of the teaching staff of the Department of Music in Columbia University and of the teaching staff of the Institute of Musical Art. Jury: Professor Daniel Gregory Mason, Professor Walter Henry Hall, Frank Damrosch.

The jury recommends for the award of the music scholarship, Mr. Wintter Watts of Brooklyn, New York, for a suite for orchestra entitled "Etchings," and for a dramatic ballad for voice and orchestra entitled "The Vinegar Man."

An annual scholarship, having the value of $1,500, to an art student in America, who shall be certified as the most promising and deserving by the National Academy of Design, with which the Society of American Artists has been merged.

The Society of American Artists and the National Academy of Design recommend for this scholarship, Mr. Henry Hensche of Chicago, Ill., a student of the National Academy of Design Schools.

1924

PULITZER PRIZE

PULITZER AWARDS FOR 1924 GIVEN OUT

San Diego (Cal.) Reporter Gets $1,000 for Story on Eclipse, the Best of the Year.

WOMAN WROTE BEST NOVEL

"Hell-Bent Fer Heaven" Captures Drama Prize—Several Educators Are Among Winners.

Nicholas Murray Butler, President of Columbia University, yesterday announced the awards of the Pulitzer prizes and traveling scholarships for 1924. The awards were made at the recent annual meeting of the Advisory Board of the School of Journalism, out of funds provided by the late Joseph Pulitzer, publisher of The New York World.

The prizes in journalism follow:

1. For the most disinterested and meritorious public service rendered by any American newspaper during the year, a gold medal, costing $500—Awarded to The New York World for its work in connection with the exposure of the Florida peonage evil.

2. For the best history of the services rendered to the public by the American press during the preceding year, $1,000. No competition.

3. For the best editorial article written during the year, the test of excellence being clearness of style, moral purpose, sound reasoning and power to influence public opinion in the right direction, $500—Awarded to The Boston Herald, for an article entitled "Who Made Coolidge?" published September 14, 1923.

In addition, a special prize of $1,000 was awarded to the widow of Frank I. Cobb in recognition of the distinction and influence of her husband's editorial writing and services.

4. For the best example of a reporter's work during the year; the test being strict accuracy, terseness, the accomplishment of some public good commanding public attention and respect, $1,000—Awarded to Magner White for his story on the eclipse of the sun, published in The San Diego Sun, San Diego, Cal., September 10, 1923.

5. For the best cartoon published in any American newspaper during the year, the determining qualities being that the cartoon shall embody an idea made clearly apparent, shall show good drawing and striking pictorial effect, and shall be helpful to some commendable cause of public importance, $500. Awarded to J. N. Darling for the cartoon entitled "In Good Old U. S. A.," published in the New York Tribune on May 6, 1923.

Prizes in Letters.

1. For the American novel published during the year which shall best present the wholesome atmosphere of American life and the highest standard of American manners and manhood, $1,000. Awarded to "The Able McLaughlins," by Margaret Wilson, published by Harper & Brothers, New York, 1923.

2. For the original American play, performed in New York, which shall best represent the educational value and power of the stage in raising the standard of good morals, good taste and good manners, $1,000. Awarded to "Hell-Bent Fer Heaven," by Hatcher Hughes, produced at the Klaw Theatre in New York during the season 1923-1924.

3. For the best book of the year upon the history of the United States, $2,000. Awarded to the "American Revolution: A Constitutional Interpretation," by Charles Howard McIlwain, published by the Macmillan Company, New York, 1923.

4. For the best American biography teaching patriotic and unselfish services to the people, illustrated by an eminent example, excluding, as too obvious, the names of George Washington and Abraham Lincoln, $1,000. Awarded to "From Immigrant to Inventor," by Michael Pupin, published by Charles Scribner's Sons, New York, 1923.

5. For the best volume of verse published during the year by an American author, $1,000. Awarded to "New Hampshire, a Poem with Notes and Grace Notes," by Robert Frost, published by Henry Holt & Co., New York, 1923.

Traveling Scholarships.

1. Three traveling scholarships, having the value of $1,500 each, to graduates of the School of Journalism who shall have passed their examinations with the highest honor and are otherwise most deserving, to enable each of them to spend a year in Europe, to study the social, political and moral conditions of the people, and the character and principles of the European press. Marian Elizabeth Robinson, Orlando, Fla.; Herbert Brucker, East Orange, N. J., and Phelps Haviland Adams, New York City. Alternates: Joshua Garrison Jr., Virginia Beach, Va.; Hilda Juanita Couch, Nyack, N. Y., and Alfred DeGroff Walling, Keyport, N. J.

2. An annual scholarship, having the value of $1,500, to the student of music in America who may be deemed the most talented and deserving, in order that he may continue his studies with the advantage of European instruction, on the nomination of a jury composed of members of the teaching staff of the Department of Music in Columbia University and of the teaching staff of the Institute of Musical Art. No award.

3. An annual scholarship, having the value of $1,500, to an art student in America, who shall be certified as the most promising and deserving by the National Academy of Design, with which the Society of American Artists has been merged. Philip Bower, New York City, a student of the National Academy of Design Schools. Mr. Bower is 28 years of age and has been a student of the Academy Schools for four years, having studied under Ivan G. Olinsky for nearly three years and then under Francis C. Jones and Charles W. Hawthorne. He has served as monitor in both night and day classes.

Awards Based on Recommendations.

The awards by the Advisory Board followed reports from various juries appointed to make recommendations. The members of the Advisory Board are: Solomon B. Griffin, formerly of The Springfield (Mass.) Republican; John L. Heaton, The New York World; Victor F. Lawson, The Chicago Daily News; Ralph Pulitzer, The New York World; Melville E. Stone, The Associated Press; Robert Lincoln O'Brien, The Boston Herald; Arthur M. Howe, The Brooklyn Daily Eagle; Joseph Pulitzer, The St. Louis Post Dispatch; John Stewart Bryan, The Richmond News Leader; Rollo Ogden, THE NEW YORK TIMES and Alfred Holman, The San Francisco Argonaut.

All members of the board participated in making the awards, except Mr. Stone, who was absent because of illness.

Margaret Wilson, author of "The Able McLaughlins," is a Chicago short story writer. She won first prize of $2,000 with the same novel in a contest conducted by Harper & Brothers, book publishers. The story deals with the life of Scotch settlers in a pioneer Iowa community. It is her first novel. Miss Wilson was graduated from the University of Chicago in 1904.

Four Winners Are Educators.

Hatcher Hughes, author of "Hell-Bent fer Heaven," lectures on modern drama at Columbia University. He was graduated from the University of South Carolina in 1907. "Hell-Bent fer Heaven," is a drama of the Blue Ridge Mountain country, of which Mr. Hughes is a native. Mr. Hughes is also the author of "Wake Up, Jonathan," in which Mrs. Fiske appeared two years ago.

Charles Howard McIlwain, author of "The American Revolution: A Constitutional Interpretation," is professor of History and Government at Harvard University. He was graduated from Princeton in 1894. He has written several other historical books.

Michael Pupin, author of "From Immigrant to Inventor," was born in Hungary in 1858. He is Professor of Electro-Mechanics at Columbia University. He has made many inventions, especially in electricity and wireless.

Robert Frost, author of "A Poem With Notes and Grace Notes," was born in San Francisco in 1875, studied at Dartmouth and Harvard and has been a teacher of English and psychology. He lives at South Shaftsbury, Vt., and has been known particularly for his poems interpreting New England life. The popularity of free verse was attributed in large part to his poetry. He resumed last Fall the post in the English department at Amherst College which he held some years ago.

1925

PULITZER PRIZE

SIDNEY HOWARD PLAY WINS PULITZER PRIZE

'They Knew What They Wanted' Had Been Pronounced Moral by Play Jury.

AWARD TO CUB REPORTERS

Two Chicago Men Get $1,000 Apiece for Bringing Loeb and Leopold to Justice.

EDNA FERBER HONORED

Edwin Arlington Robinson, Rollin Kirby, Frederic L. Paxson and Others on List.

"So Big," a novel by Edna Ferber; "They Knew What They Wanted," a play by Sidney Howard, and "The Man Who Died Twice," a volume of poetry by Edwin Arlington Robinson, are among the winners of the Pulitzer prizes for 1924, it was announced yesterday.

The prize for reporting went to James W. Mulroy and Alvin H. Goldstein for their work as members of the staff of The Chicago Daily News, in bringing Richard Loeb and Nathan F. Leopold to justice for the murder of Robert Franks.

The full announcement by the Advisory Board of the School of Journalism of Columbia University follows:

Prizes in Journalism.

"1. For the most disinterested and meritorious public service rendered by any American newspaper during the year, a gold medal costing $500.

"No award.

"2. For the best history of the services rendered to the public by the American press during the preceding year or for the publication and distribution through the Columbia University Press of publications of service to American journalism. One thousand dollars.

"No competition.

"3. For the best editorial article written during the year, the test of excellence being clearness of style, moral purpose, sound reasoning and power to influence public opinion in the right direction, due account being taken of the whole volume of the writer's editorial work during the year. Five hundred dollars ($500).

"Awarded to The Charleston (S. C.) News and Courier, for the editorial entitled "The Plight of the South," published Nov. 5, 1924.

"4. For the best example of a reporter's work during the year, the test being strict accuracy, terseness, the accomplishment of some public good commanding public attention and respect. One thousand dollars ($1,000).

"Awarded in duplicate to Messrs. James W. Mulroy and Alvin H. Goldstein for their services, while members of the staff of The Chicago Daily News, toward the solution of the murder of Robert Franks Jr. in Chicago on May 22, 1924, and the bringing to justice of Nathan F. Leopold and Richard Loeb.

"5. For the best cartoon published in any American newspaper during the year, the determining qualities being that the cartoon shall embody an idea made clearly apparent, shall show good drawing and striking pictorial effect, and shall be helpful to some commendable cause of public importance, due account being taken of the whole volume of the artist's newspaper work during the year. Five hundred dollars ($500).

"Awarded to Mr. Rollin Kirby of The New York World, for the cartoon entitled 'News From the Outside World,' published Oct. 5, 1924.

Prizes in Letters.

"1. For the American novel published during the year which shall best present the wholesome atmosphere of American life, and the highest standard of American manners and manhood. One thousand dollars ($1,000).

"Awarded to 'So Big,' by Edna Ferber, published by Doubleday, Page & Co., Garden City, N. Y., 1924.

"2. For the original American play, performed in New York, which shall best represent the educational value and power of the stage in raising the standard of good morals, good taste and good manners. One thousand dollars ($1,000).

"Awarded to 'They Knew What They Wanted,' by Sidney Howard, produced at the Klaw Theatre in New York during the season 1924-25.

"3. For the best book of the year upon the history of the United States. Two thousand dollars ($2,000).

"Awarded to 'A History of the American Frontier,' by Frederic L. Paxon, published by Houghton Mifflin Company, Boston, Mass., 1924.

"4. For the best American biography teaching patriotic and unselfish services to the people, illustrated by an eminent example, excluding as too obvious, the names of George Washington and Abraham Lincoln, one thousand dollars ($1,000).

"Awarded to 'Barrett Wendell and His Letters,' by M. A. De Wolfe Howe, published by the American Monthly Press, Inc., Boston, Mass., 1924.

"5. For the best volume of verse published during the year by an American author, one thousand dollars ($1,000).

"Awarded to 'The Man Who Died Twice,' by Edwin Arlington Robinson, published by the MacMillan Company, New York, 1924.

Traveling Scholarships.

"1. Three traveling scholarships, having the value of $1,500 each, to graduates of the School of Journalism, who shall have passed their examinations with the highest honor and are otherwise most deserving, to enable each of them to spend a year in Europe, to study the social, political and moral conditions of the people, and the character and principles of the European press. on the nomination of the teaching staff of the School of Journalism, the following were appointed:

"1. Daniel Robert Maue, Monticello, Minn.

"2. William G. Worthington, Providence, R. I.

"3. Richmond B. Williams, Brooklyn, N. Y.

"Alternates:

"1. Theodore Bernstein, New York City.

"2. Dorothy Dodd, Tallahassee, Fla.

"3. Cicely Applebaum, New York City.

"2. An annual scholarship, having the value of $1,500, to the student of music in America who may be deemed the most talented and deserving, in order that he may continue his studies with the advantage of European instruction, on the nomination of a jury composed of members of the teaching staff of the Department of Music in Columbia University and of the teaching staff of The Institute of Musical Art.

"In view of the great merit of the works presented, two scholarships, having the value of $1,500 each, were awarded to Douglas Moore of Cleveland, Ohio and to Leopold D. Mannes of New York City."

Members of the Advisory Board who made the awards were Ralph Pulitzer of The New York World, Solomon B. Griffin, The Springfield (Mass.) Republican; Victor F. Lawson, The Chicago (Ill.) Daily News; Melville E. Stone, The Associated Press; Alfred Holman, The San Francisco (Cal.) Bulletin; Arthur M. Howe, The Brooklyn (N. Y.) Daily Eagle; Robert Lincoln O'Brien, The Boston (Mass.) Herald; Rollo Ogden, The New York Times; Joseph Pulitzer, The St. Louis Post-Dispatch, and Edward Page Mitchell, The New York Sun.

The Advisory Board had before it the reports of the juries, composed, as to the Prizes in Journalism, of members of the teaching staff of Columbia University and members of the American Society of Newspaper Editors, designated by the President of that society, and, as to the Prizes in Letters, of members chosen from the National Institute of Arts and Letters.

"They Knew What They Wanted" was the first play to be tried by a play jury. A complaint had been made to the authorities that it was immoral. Police Commissioner Enright and District Attorney Banton sent a play jury to try it. The jury acquitted it on the first ballot.

Feat of "Cub" Reporters.

James W. Mulroy and Alvin H. Goldstein had been in newspaper work less than a year before they performed the feat for which they were awarded the Pulitzer prize. Mulroy is 25 years old and Goldstein 23. They were in the cub or beginner class when they were sent out from The Chicago Daily News office on a vague tip that there had been a kidnapping.

They found that Robert Franks was the kidnapped boy, and talked with his father who had then received the blackmailing letter demanding a ransom of $10,000. At that time the evening papers had accounts of the discovery of the body of an unidentified boy. Mulroy suggested that it might be the body of Franks, and Goldstein hurried to the the place where the body had been found. Mulroy obtained a photograph of young Franks and sent it to Goldstein and the identification of the murdered boy was made.

That was half of their achievement. The second part was to find evidence copper-rivetting the case against Loeb and Leopold. An expert had reported that the typewritten demand for ransom had been written on a certain make of portable typewriter. Both Loeb and Leopold denied that they had ever used such a machine. Mulroy and Goldstein, who were both University of Chicago men, went to work among the former associates of Loeb and Leopold and took to Police Headquarters specimens of typewriting by Leopold. The expert found that these specimens were done on the same machine used in writing the blackmailing letter.

Mulroy is now a star on The Chicago Daily News. Goldstein is on the staff of the St. Louis Post Dispatch. They received $1,500 each as shares in the reward for solving the Franks case.

CHARLESTON, S. C., April 26.—Robert Lathan, who wrote the Pulitzer prize-winning editorial, The Plight of the South, has been editor of The News and Courier since the Spring of 1910.

1926

NOBEL PRIZE

SHAW IS MYSTIFIED BY HIS NOBEL PRIZE

Suggests He Was Chosen for Literature Award Because He Wrote Nothing in 1925.

IN POLITICAL NEWS AGAIN

Author Finds Two Parties in Parlia- and Wants Liberals to Join With Labor Party.

Copyright, 1926, by The New York Times Company.
Special Cable to THE NEW YORK TIMES.

LONDON, Nov. 11.—"It is a great mystery to me. I suppose it is given to me because I wrote nothing at all this year," was Bernard Shaw's characteristic comment today in reply to the news that the Nobel Prize for literature for 1925 had been awarded to him. He added that he had received no official intimation of the award.

Shaw also figured in the political news today. Commander Kenworthy, a former Liberal Member of Parliament who joined the Labor Party and is a Labor candidate in Central Hull, received a letter from the sage containing this interesting passage:

"Now that the Irish Party is gone from the House of Commons it is a two-party House, and all sensible Liberals must recognize that they must be represented by the Labor Party or not at all. I am naturally glad you have formally joined the Labor Party, being a member of it myself."

STOCKHOLM, Sweden, Nov. 11 (AP).—The Nobel prize for chemistry, 1925, was awarded today to Dr. Richard Zsigmondy, Professor of Inorganic Chemistry of the University of Goettingen, Germany. The chemistry prize for 1926 went to Professor Theodore Svedberg of the University of Upsala, Sweden.

The Swedish Academy of Sciences, which awards the honors, decided to divide the Nobel prize for physics for 1925 between Professor James Franck, University of Goettingen, and Professor Gustav Hertz of Halle University. The 1926 physics award was made to Professor Jean Baptiste Perrin of the University of Paris.

Professor Svedberg lectured at Wisconsin University in 1923. He was mentioned for the Nobel prize in 1915.

Professor Jean B. Perrin is an authority on transmutation of matter. He was French exchange Professor at Columbia University in 1913.

The Nobel Prizes are awarded in the fields of physics, chemistry, medicine or physiology, literature and preservation peace. In addition to their recognition of world-wide pre-eminence in the respective fields of endeavor for the year specified, they carry with them cash prizes averaging about $35,000.

The prizes are financed by a fund established by the late Alfred B. Nobel, Swedish scientist and inventor of dynamite. The first awards were distributed on Dec. 10, 1901, the fifth anniversary of his death.

PULITZER PRIZE

PULITZER PRIZES AWARDED FOR 1925

'Arrowsmith,' by Sinclair Lewis, and 'Craig's Wife,' by George Kelly, Are Among Winners.

A TIMES EDITORIAL WINS

E. M. Kingsbury's Neediest Cases Appeal Gets $500 Award—Poetry Prize Is Given to Amy Lowell.

The Pulitzer prizes in journalism and letters for 1925, as established in the will of Joseph Pulitzer, former publisher of The World, were announced yesterday at Columbia University.

Sinclair Lewis's "Arrowsmith" won the $1,000 prize "for the American novel published during the year which shall best present the wholesome atmosphere of American life and the highest standard of American manners and manhood."

The drama, "Craig's Wife," by George Kelly, won the $1,000 prize "for the original American play performed in New York, which shall best represent the educational value and power of the stage in raising the standard of good morals, good taste and good manners."

The sixth volume of the "History of the United States," by Edward Channing, won the $2,000 prize "for the best book of the year upon the history of the United States."

Harvey Cushing's "The Life of Sir William Osler," won the $1,000 prize "for the best American biography teaching patriotic and unselfish services to the people, illustrated by an eminent example, excluding, as too obvious, the names of George Washington and Abraham Lincoln."

The late Amy Lowell's "What's O'Clock" won the $1,000 price "for the best volume of verse published during the year by an American author."

Prizes in Journalism.

Prizes in journalism were awarded as follows:

"For the most disinterested and meritorious public service rendered by an American newspaper during the year, a gold medal costing $500, awarded to The Enquirer Sun, Columbus, Ga., for the service which it rendered in its brave and energetic fight against the Ku Klux Klan, against the enactment of a law barring the teaching of evolution, against dishonest and incompetent public officials, and for justice to the negro and against lynching.

"For the best editorial article written during the year, the test of excellence being clearness of style, moral purpose, sound reasoning and power to influence public opinion in the right direction, due account being taken of the whole volume of the writer's editorial work during the year, $500 awarded to THE NEW YORK TIMES for the editorial entitled 'The House of a Hundred Sorrows,' by Edward M. Kingsbury, published Dec. 14, 1925.

"For the best example of a reporter's work during the year, the test being strict accuracy, terseness, the accomplishment of some public good commanding public attention and respect, $1,000, awarded to William Burke Miller of The Louisville (Ky.) Courier-Journal for his work in connection with the story of the trapping in Sand Cave, Ky., of Floyd Collins.

"For the best cartoon published in any American newspaper during the year, the determining qualities being that the cartoon shall embody an idea made clearly apparent, shall show good drawing and striking pictorial effect, and shall be helpful to some commendable cause of public importance, due account being taken of the whole volume of the artist's newspaper work during the year: $500, awarded to B. R. Fitzpatrick of The St. Louis Post-Dispatch, St. Louis, Mo., for the cartoon entitled, 'The Laws of Moses and the Laws of Today,' published April 12, 1925."

Traveling Scholarships Awarded.

There was no competition for and therefore no award of the $1,000 prize "for the best history of the services rendered to the public by the American press during the preceding year or for the publication and distribution through the Columbia University Press of publications of service to American journalism."

Three traveling scholarships, worth $1,500 each, open to "graduates of the School of Journalism who shall have passed their examinations with the highest honor and are otherwise most deserving, to enable each of them to spend a year in Europe, to study the social, political and moral conditions of the people, and the character and principles of the European press," were awarded to Lawrence Hopkins Odell of White Plains, N. Y.; Miss Dorothy Ducas of New York City and Leif Eid of Everett, Wash. Their alternates are Gordon Neander Havens of Brooklyn, N. Y.; Lawrence Robert Goldberg of Revere, Mass., and Francis Lincoln Grahlfs of Jamaica, N. Y.

Miss Lucille Crews of Redlands, Cal., won the $1,500 scholarship for "the student of music in America who may be deemed the most talented and deserving, in order that he may continue his studies with the advantages of European instruction, on the nomination of the teaching staff of the Department of Music and of the teaching staff of the Institute of Musical Art." Her winning composition was a sonata for viola and piano and a symphonic elegy for orchestra, entitled "To the Unknown Soldier."

Art Announcement Tonight.

The National Academy of Design at its annual meeting tonight will announce the winner of the $1,500 scholarship for "an art student in America who shall be certified as the most promising and deserving by the National Academy of Design, with which the Society of American Artists has been merged."

The awards were ratified yesterday at a meeting of the trustees of Columbia University in accordance with action taken on April 22 by the Advisory Board of the School of Journalism, which was established at Columbia by the late Mr. Pulitzer.

The members of the Advisory Board are Melville E. Stone, Associated Press; Edward Page Mitchell; Ralph Pulitzer, The World; Robert Lincoln O'Brien, Boston Herald; Arthur M. Howe, Brooklyn Daily Eagle; John L. Heaton, The World; Joseph Pulitzer, St. Louis Post Dispatch; Rollo Ogden, THE NEW YORK TIMES; Alfred Holman, San Francisco; Casper S. Yost, St. Louis Globe-Democrat, and President Nicholas Murray Butler of Columbia University.

The Advisory Board in making its decisions had before it recommendations from members of the National Institute of Arts and Letters in the case of awards in letters, and from members of the teaching staff of the School of Journalism and members of the American Society of Newspaper Editors, in the case of awards in journalism.

The award in drama was recommended unanimously by a jury consisting of A. E. Thomas, Chairman; Owen Davis and Walter Prichard Eaton.

Dr. Butler authorized a statement that in the opinion of the jury the "most worthy book" was Bernard Fay's "L'Esprit Revolutionnaire en France et aux Etats-Unis à la Fin du 18 Siècle," but it was "held to be ineligible under the terms of the award," so that the prize went to Channing's volume on the "History of the United States."

Lewis's Book About Doctors.

Sinclair Lewis, author of "Arrowsmith," is also the creator of "Main Street" and "Babbitt," novels which created much discussion. "Main Street" was the first of his satirical interpretations of American life, and "Babbitt" gave the world a new word.

In "Arrowsmith," which the novelist published last year after a three years' silence, he contrasted the life of research workers in the field of medical science with that of those physicians and surgeons who go in solely for commercial success, and in the character of Leora, the wife of Dr. Martin Arrowsmith, he drew what is regarded as a masterly portrait of a woman. Mr. Lewis wrote "Arrowsmith" with the assistance of Dr. Paul H. De Kruif, author of "Microbe Hunters," to whom the novelist gives credit for the accuracy of the technical detail of the medical profession in his novel.

Mr. Lewis was born in 1885 in Sauk Center, Minn., and was graduated from Yale College in 1907. His first job was as a reporter on The New Haven Journal-Courier. He also worked as a reporter for The San Francisco Bulletin, The Associated Press and elsewhere, and was a writer and editor in the magazine field for several years.

Kelly Just Missed 1924 Prize.

George Kelly, whose "Craig's Wife" won the drama prize, just missed winning the Pulitzer prize for 1924 with his play, "The Show-Off." The play jury, consisting of Professor William Lyon Phelps of Yale, Clayton Hamilton, the playwright, and Owen Johnson, the novelist, recommended "The Show-Off" for the prize, but was overruled by the Advisory Board in favor of "Hell-Bent Fer Heaven," a play by Hatcher Hughes, a lecturer on the drama at Columbia.

The Theatre Club, Inc., recently awarded a gold medal to Mr. Kelly for having written the best American play of 1925 in "Craig's Wife." The play is a study of a married woman to whom the possession of material things seems so vital that she finally wrecks the spiritual happiness of her marriage.

Mr. Kelly was born in Philadelphia thirty-four years ago. Beginning his theatrical career as an actor in juvenile parts in road companies, Mr. Kelly later went into vaudeville, where he began to write his own one-act plays several years ago. One of these sketches was the nucleus of "The Torch-Bearers," his first full-length play, which made a hit on Broadway three years ago.

Channing a Harvard Professor.

Edward Channing, author of the prize-winning historical work, is Professor of Ancient and Modern History at Harvard. He was born in Dorchester, Mass., in 1856 and was graduated from Harvard in 1878, taking his Ph.D. degree two years later.

Dr. Harvey Cushing is a surgeon who has written much on surgery. He was born in Cleveland in 1869, was graduated from Yale in 1891 and Harvard Medical School in 1895. During the war he served as a Colonel in the Medical Corps in France. He is now Professor of Surgery at Harvard.

Miss Amy Lowell, the poet, died in May, 1925. She was a sister of A. Lawrence Lowell, President of Harvard. Born in Brookline, Mass., in 1874, she was educated in private schools. Her first volume of poems was published in 1912, after which she gradually won recognition as one of the chief exponents of "the new verse." Her book, "What's O'Clock," the prize-winner, was published posthumously.

The Columbus (Ga.) Enquirer-Sun, which won the prize for public service, is published by Julian Harris, son of Joel Chandler Harris, creator of Uncle Remus. Mr. Harris began newspaper work in 1890 as a reporter on The Atlanta (Ga.) Constitution, of which he later became managing editor. In 1911 he came to New York as Sunday editor of The New York Herald. He was formerly in charge of The Herald's Paris edition. In 1921 he returned to Georgia and bought The Enquirer-Sun, in which he has consistently fought the Ku Klux Klan.

Kingsbury on Times Since 1915.

Edward M. Kingsbury, author of the editorial, "The House of a Hundred Sorrows," has been a member of the editorial staff of THE NEW YORK TIMES since 1915. He was born in 1854, was graduated from Harvard in 1875 and was admitted to the bar in Massachusetts in 1879. In 1881 he became a member of the staff of The New York Sun under Charles A. Dana. In the book, "Dana and His People," Edward P. Mitchell, former editor-in-chief of The Sun, wrote about Mr. Kingsbury as follows:

"For a third of a century Kingsbury was a prime factor in making the paper's editorial page what it was said by the kind-hearted to be. He had most of the talents except that of self-promotion. He caught speedily the inherited characteristics and added to these the rich qualities of a personality almost unique for exquisite humor, fine wit, broad literary appreciation and originality of idea and phrase. From 1881 to 1915 many of the notable articles and casual essays on subjects a little apart from the more obvious actualities were due to that very accomplished and exceedingly modest artist of the pen."

William Burke Miller, whose stories of the Floyd Collins case in The Louisville Courier-Journal won the prize for reporting, received a bonus of $1,000 from his newspaper for his work on that assignment. In addition to getting and writing all the news, he led rescue parties into the cave and was the only man, because of his small size, who was able to crawl all the way to the place where Collins was trapped. Miller has left the newspaper profession and is now en-

gaged in the ice cream business in Florida. Miller is in his early twenties.

D. R. Fitzpatrick, cartoonist of The St. Louis Post-Dispatch, is about 35 years old. He attended the Superior (Wis.) High School and the Chicago Art Institute, and then obtained employment with The Chicago Daily News as a comic artist for one year and a cartoonist for one year. Thirteen years ago he went to The Post-Dispatch as cartoonist. He is also staff cartoonist on Collier's Weekly.

Miss Lucille Crews of Redlands, Cal., who won the musical scholarship, was born in Pueblo, Col., and was graduated from Dana Hall School, Wellesley. She studied music at the New England Conservatory of Music, in Boston, and the Northwestern University School of Music, in Evanston, Ill., as well as with private teachers.

Youngest Girl Winner.

Miss Dorothy Ducas is the youngest girl winner of a traveling scholarship since the prizes were established. She is 20 years old and lives at 536 West 113th Street.

Lawrence Hopkins Odell is the son of Isaac Odell, a merchandise broker of 287 South Lexington Avenue, White Plains, N. Y. He is 21 years old and received the Bachelor of Arts degree from Columbia in 1924.

Leif Eid is 25 years old and is from Everett, Wash. He came to Columbia from Washington State University, and won the Katherine MacMahon Memorial Scholarship, valued at $150, for the year 1925-26. He also is a member of Sigma Delta Chi.

MR. KINGSBURY'S EDITORIAL.

It Was Written for Neediest Cases Appeal of The Times.

Following is the editorial, "The House of a Hundred Sorrows," written by Edward M. Kingsbury and now awarded a Pulitzer prize. It was published in THE NEW YORK TIMES on Dec. 14, 1925, in connection with The Hundred Neediest Cases appeal:

THE HOUSE OF A HUNDRED SORROWS.

The walls are grimy and discolored. The uneven floors creak and yield under foot. Staircases and landings are rickety and black. The door of every room is open. Walk along these corridors. Walk into this room. Here is a sickly boy of 5, deserted by his mother, underfed, solitary in the awful solitude of starved, neglected childhood. "Seldom talks." Strange, isn't it? Some, many children, never "prattle," like your darlings. They are already old. They are full, perhaps, of long, hopeless thoughts. There are plenty of other "kids" in this tenement. Here is one, only three. Never saw his father. His mother spurned and abused him. He is weak and "backward." How wicked of him when he has been so encouraged and coddled! Doesn't know any games. How should he? Do children play? Not his kind. They live to suffer.

In Room 24 is Rose, a housemother of 10. Father is in the hospital. Mother is crippled with rheumatism. Rose does all the work. You would love Rose if she came out of Dickens. Well, there she is, mothering her mother in Room 24. In Room 20 age has been toiling for youth. Grandmother has been taking care of three granddaughters who lost their mother. A brave old woman; but what with rheumatism and heart weakness, threescore-and-ten can't go out to work any more. What's going to happen to her and her charges? Thinking of that, she is ill on top of her physical illness. A very interesting house, isn't it, Sir? Decidedly "a rum sort of place." Madam? Come into Room 23. Simon, the dollmaker—but handmade dolls are "out"—lives, if you call it living, here. Eighty years old, his wife of about the same age. Their eyesight is mostly gone. Otherwise they would still be sewing on buttons and earning a scanty livelihood for themselves and two little girls, their grandchildren. The girls object to going to an orphan home. Some children are like that.

You must see those twin sisters of 65 in Room 47. True, they are doing better than usual on account of the coming holidays; making as much as $10 a month, whereas their average is but $6. Still, rents are a bit high; and the twins have been so long together that they would like to stay so. In Room—but you need no guide. Once in The House of a Hundred Sorrows you will visit every sad chamber in it. If your heart be made of penetrable stuff, you will do the most you can to bring hope and comfort to its inmates, to bring them Christmas and the Christ:

"For I was a hungered, and ye gave me meat: I was thirsty, and ye gave me drink: I was a stranger, and you took me in.

"Naked, and ye clothed me: I was sick, and ye visited me: I was in prison, and ye came unto me."

1927

PULITZER PRIZE

PULITZER AWARDS ARE MADE FOR 1926

Bromfield's 'Early Autumn' and Green's 'In Abraham's Bosom' Get Novel and Play Prizes.

MRS. SPEYER'S POETRY BEST

S. F. Bemis Captures Honors in History and Prof. Emory Holloway in Biography.

BROOKLYN CARTOONIST WINS

Journalism Laurels Go to Boston Herald for Sacco Editorial and Canton News for Crime Drive.

The Pulitzer prizes in journalism and letters for 1926 were announced yesterday by President Nicholas Murray Butler for the Advisory Board of the School of Journalism of Columbia University. The prizes were established in the will of Joseph Pulitzer, former publisher of The World.

The prize of $1,000 for a novel was awarded to Louis Bromfield for "Early Autumn," his third published book. The terms of the award require that it be given for "the American novel published during the year which shall best present the whole atmosphere of American life and the highest standard of American manners and manhood." Last year Sinclair Lewis, who won the prize with "Arrowsmith," refused to accept it.

"In Abraham's Bosom," written by Paul Green, assistant professor of philosophy in the University of North Carolina, was voted the prize play. The award is made for an "original play, performed in New York, which shall best represent the educational value and power of the stage in raising the standard of good morals, good taste and good manners." The drama prize is for $1,000.

The $2,000 prize for the best book of the year upon the history of the United States went to "Pinckney's Treaty, a Study of America's Advantage from Europe's Distress, 1783-1800," the author of which was Samuel Flagg Bemis. The prize of $1,000 for the best American biography, teaching patriotic and unselfish services to the people, went to Professor Emory Holloway, for "Whitman, an Interpretation in Narrative." The best volume of verse by an American author, carrying a prize of $1,000, was voted to be "Fiddler's Farewell," by Leonora Speyer.

Awards in Journalism.

The awards in journalism were as follows:

"1. For the most disinterested and meritorious public service rendered by any American newspaper during the year, a gold medal costing $500.

"Awarded to The Canton Daily News, Canton, Ohio, for its brave, patriotic and effective fight for the purification of municipal politics and for the ending of a vicious state of affairs brought about by collusion between city authorities and the criminal element, a fight which had a tragic result in the assassination of the editor of the paper, Don R. Mellet.

"2. For the best history of the services rendered to the public by the American press during the preceding year or for the publication and distribution through the Columbia University Press of publications of service to American journalism, $1,000.

"No competition.

"3. For the best editorial article written during the year, the test of excellence being clearness of style, moral purpose, sound reasoning and power to influence public opinion in the right direction, due account being taken of the whole volume of the writer's editorial work during the year, $500.

"Awarded to The Boston Herald, Boston, Mass., for the editorial entitled 'We Submit—,'" by F. Lauriston Bullard, published Oct. 26, 1926.

St. Louis Reporter a Winner.

"4. For the best example of a reporter's work during the year, the test being strict accuracy, terseness, the accomplishment of some public good commanding public attention and respect, $1,000.

"Awarded to John T. Rogers of The St. Louis Post-Dispatch, St. Louis, Mo., for the inquiry leading to the impeachment of Judge George W. English of the United States Court for the Eastern District of Illinois.

"5. For the best cartoon published in any American newspaper during the year, the determining qualities being that the cartoon shall embody an idea made clearly apparent, shall show good drawing and striking pictorial effect, and shall be helpful to some commendable cause of public importance, due account being taken of the whole volume of the artist's newspaper work during the year, $500.

"Awarded to Nelson Harding of The Brooklyn Daily Eagle, Brooklyln, for the cartoon entitled 'Toppling the Idol,' published Sept. 19, 1926."

Three traveling scholarships, each having a value of $1,500, were awarded to three high ranking graduates of the School of Journalism. They will study journalism in Europe, as well as general conditions, for a year. They are Gordon Neander Havens of Brooklyn, Orrin Tisdale Pierson of Denver and Jacob S. Hohenberg of Jamaica, L. I. Two students were nominated as alternates. They were Paul Douglas Gesner of Marshall, Mich., and Miss Frances Bernice Schiff of 290 Riverside Drive, New York.

Music and Art Awards.

Two other scholarships were announced. They were:

"An annual scholarship of $1,500 to the student of music in America who may be deemed the most talented and deserving, in order that he may continue his studies with the advantage of European instruction, on the nomination of a jury composed of members of the teaching staff of the Department of Music in Columbia University and of the teaching staff of the Institute of Musical Art. Awarded to Quinto E. Maganini of California.

"An annual scholarship of $1,500 to an art student in America who shall be certified as the most promising and deserving by the National Academy of Design, with which the Society of American Artists has been merged. Awarded to Olindo M. Ricci of 3,661 Bronxwood Avenue, the Bronx."

Playwright Worked in Fields.

Paul Green, author of the prize play, is also a youngster. He was born on a farm near Lillington, N. C., on March 17, 1894, and working in the fields became the champion cotton-picker of his county. It was during these farm days that he gained his insight into the negro, which he has transplanted faithfully to his plays. He was a student at the University of North Carolina in 1917, when he enlisted. He later saw four months' service on the Western front.

Mr. Green's "In Abraham's Bosom," was his first full length play. Previous to it he had written from thirty-five to forty one-act plays, which were largely produced and acted by Professor Koch's Carolina Playmakers at Chapel Hill, N. C. His plays were all devoted to studies of the "poor whites" and the negroes. A one-act play called

PAUL GREEN,
Author of Prize-Winning Play.

"The No 'Count Boy," won the Belasco Cup in the Little Theatre Tournament in 1925. He has another play in the present tournament, entitled "The Last of the Lowries." Another full length play, "The Field God" is current at the Greenwich Village Theatre and will move on Monday to an uptown playhouse.

"In Abraham's Bosom" opened last Dec. 30 at the Provincetown Playhouse, later going into the Garrick Theatre. It was well received and continued its run until March 5.

The Provincetown Playhouse announced last night that the play would be revived beginning next Sunday night at its theatre in MacDougal Street. The same cast which presented it at the Garrick Theatre will again be seen, with Frank Wilson in the leading rôle.

Mr. Green is the second alumnus of the University of North Carolina to capture the Pulitzer prize for the drama. The 1924 prize went to Hatcher Hughes for his play, "Hell-Bent Fer Heaven." Mr. Green is at work on more plays and on a novel.

1928

PULITZER PRIZE

WILDER NOVEL WINS PULITZER AWARD

Young Author's Book "The Bridge of San Luis Rey" Adjudged Best of the Year.

O'NEILL TAKES PLAY PRIZE

'Strange Interlude' His Third Winner—E. A. Robinson Also Three-Time Victor—Other Awards.

The Pulitzer awards in journalism and letters for 1927 were announced yesterday by President Nicholas Murray Butler of Columbia. The awards were made by the Trustees of Columbia University on the recommendation of the Advisory Board of the School of Journalism.

The prize of $1,000 for the novel considered the best of the year by the jury goes to Thornton Wilder, a young writer, for his second novel, "The Bridge of San Luis Rey." The

story is of old Peru and has been called by a reviewer a metaphysical study of love. The prize is given under the terms of the award "for the American novel published during the year which shall best represent the whole atmosphere of American life, and the highest standard of American manners and manhood." Last year the same prize went to Louis Bromfield for "Early Autumn," and in the preceding year to Sinclair Lewis for "Arrowsmith," but Mr. Lewis refused to accept it.

Eugene O'Neill, who has been called America's foremost playwright, receives the $1,000 prize awarded annually for a play, his winning play being "Strange Interlude." The award is made for "the original American play performed in New York which shall best represent the educational value and power of the stage in raising the standard of good morals, good taste and good manners."

After complaints against the prize-winning play and another play had been made to District Attorney Banton recently he sent two assistants to see them. Mr. Banton passed "Strange Interlude" and the other play on the basis of their report that the plays did not follow the author's texts in their entirety.

The District Attorney's reviewers further reported that "many of the lines in the manuscript and the plays which might offend good taste are not read by the actors." They reported that there were some coarse lines which offend good taste in each play, "but the District Attorney, as an official, is not concerned with matters affecting good taste," Mr. Banton explained.

O'Neill has won the prize twice previously, the first time in 1920, for his play "Beyond the Horizon" and the second time in 1922 with his "Anna Christie." First prize went last year to Paul Green, Assistant Professor of Philosophy, University of North Carolina, for "In Abraham's Bosom."

Parrington Wins $2,000 Prize.

Vernon Louis Parrington is winner of the $2,000 prize for the best book of the year upon the history of the United States. His winning book is entitled "Main Currents in American Thoughts," and is in two volumes, "The Colonial Mind, 1620-1800," and "The Romantic Revolution in America, 1800-1860." This prize was awarded last year to Samuel Flagg Bemis for "Pinckney's Treaty; a Study of America's Advantage from Europe's Distress, 1783-1800."

The prize of $1,000 for the best American biography teaching patriotic and unselfish services to the people was awarded to Charles Edward Russell, journalist and author and at one time and another Socialist candidate for Governor of New York, Mayor of New York City and United States Senator from New York. Mr. Russell's prize-winning book is "The American Orchestra and Theodore Thomas." The prize was awarded last year to Professor Emory Holloway for "Whitman, an Interpretation in Narrative."

Edwin Arlington Robinson, the poet who was praised for his first efforts by Theodore Roosevelt, received for the third time the $1,000 award for "the best volume of verse published during the year by an American author. His winning volume bears the title "Tristram" and has been described by critics as first among modern versions of the old love story of Tristram and Isolt. This prize last year was awarded to Leonora Speyer for "Fiddler's Farewell."

Two of the prizes in journalism were not awarded this year. The prize of $1,000 for the best example of a reporter's work during the year, the test being strict accuracy, terseness, the accomplishment of some public good, was not awarded, because the jury believed that no specimen submitted in the contest was up to standards set for the award.

Likewise the announcement discloses that there was "no competition" for the $1,000 prize for "the best history of services rendered to the public by the American press during the preceding year or for the publication and distribution through Columbia University Press of Publications of service to American journalism."

Awards in Journalism.

The awards in journalism were as follows:

"For the most disinterested and meritorious public service rendered by an American newspaper during the year, a gold medal costing $500—Awarded to The Indianapolis Times for its work in exposing political corruption in Indiana, prosecuting the guilty and bringing about a more wholesome state of affairs in civil government."

"For the best editorial article written during the year, the test of excellence being clearness of style, moral purpose, sound reasoning and power to influence public opinion in the right direction, due account being taken of the whole volume of the writer's editorial work during the year, $500—Awarded to Grover Cleveland Hall for his editorials in The Montgomery Advertiser, Montgomery, Ala., against gangism, floggings and racial and religious intolerance.

"For the best cartoon published in any American newspaper during the year, the determining qualities being that the cartoon shall embody an idea made clearly apparent, shall show good drawing and striking pictorial effect, and shall be helpful to commendable cause of public importance, due account being taken of the whole volume of the artist's newspaper work during the year, $500—Awarded to Nelson Harding, of The Brooklyn Daily Eagle, for the cartoon entitled, 'May His Shadow Never Grow Less,' published Dec. 15, 1927."

Mr. Harding won the same prize last year with his cartoon, "Topping the Idol."

Scholarship in Journalism.

Three traveling scholarships of $1,800 each, to graduates of the School of Journalism who shall have passed their examinations with the highest honor to enable each of them to spend a year in Europe, to study the social and political conditions were awarded to Philip Seckler, Brooklyn; Alfred Dudley Britton Jr., New York, and Mary D. Ronan, New York. Alternates—Haig Gordon Garbedian, West New York, N. J.; Margaret C. Lloyd, Bradford, Pa., and Elliott A. Crooks, Alma, Mich.

Two other scholarship awards were announced as follows:

"An annual scholarship, having the value of $1,500, to the student of music in America who may be deemed the most talented and deserving, in order that he may continue his studies with the advantage of European instruction, on the nomination of a jury composed of members of the teaching staff of the Department of Music in Columbia University and of the teaching staff of the Institute of Musical Art. Awarded to Lamar Stringfield. Mr. Stringfield was born at Raleigh, N. C., and received his academic education at Mars Hill and Wake Forest (N. C.) colleges. He started the study of the flute and composition while serving in the army and has studied with Emil Medicus, George Barrere, Percy Goetschius, Henry Hadley and Chalmers Clifton. Mr. Stringfield's compositions (at present numbering to opus 41) include vocal and instrumental solos, chamber music of various combinations and compositions for small and large orchestras, many of which have been constructed by the use of folk music that has been preserved by the mountaineers of Western North Carolina.

"An annual scholarship, having the value of $1,500, to an art student in America who shall be certified as the most promising and deserving by the National Academy of Design, with which the Society of American Artists has been merged. Awarded to Gordon Samstag of New York City."

The members of the Advisory Board of the School of Journalism are:

President Nicholas Murray Butler, Columbia University; Melville E. Stone, The Associated Press; Ralph Pulitzer, The World; Arthur M. Howe, Brooklyn Daily Eagle; John L. Heaton, The World; Robert Lincoln O'Brien, Boston Herald; Joseph Pulitzer, St. Louis Post-Dispatch; Rollo Ogden, NEW YORK TIMES; Alfred Holman, San Francisco, Cal.; Casper S. Yost, St. Louis Globe-Democrat; Stuart H. Perry, Adrian (Mich.) Evening Telegram; Julian Harris, Columbus (Ga.) Enquirer-Sun; Frank R. Kent, Baltimore Sun.

The Advisory Board, in making these awards, had before them the reports of the several juries designated to pass upon the competitors for the several prizes. The juries for the prizes in journalism are chosen from the staff of the School of Journalism of Columbia University and from the American Society of Newspaper Editors. The juries for the prizes in letters are chosen from the National Institute of Arts and Letters.

The juries in the letters awards were:

Novels—Richard Barton, Robert M. Lovett, Jefferson B. Fletcher.

Drama—A. E. Thomas, Walter Prichard Eaton, Clayton Hamilton.

History—Worthington C. Ford, James Truslow Adams, Charles Downer Hazen.

Biography—Royal Cortissoz, George M. Harper, Van Wyck Brooks.

Poetry—Wilbur L. Cross, John Erskine, Robert Frost.

Nikolas Murray Photo.
EUGENE O'NEILL,
Writer of the Prize Play.

Wilder Only 30 Years Old.

Thornton Wilder, who has been described by Professor William Lyon Phelps of Yale as "a star of the first magnitude," has just passed 30 and is unmarried. His father is Amos Parker Wilder, one of the editors of The New Haven Journal and a graduate of Yale. Thornton was born at Madison, Wis., and spent his early years in Hong Kong, where his father then was Consul General. He later prepared for college in California and was graduated from Yale in 1920. Following his graduation he spent two years at the American Academy in Rome and his visit there inspired his first book, "Cabala," published in 1926. He is the author of several plays.

His mother, to whom he dedicated "The Bridge," was Miss Isabel Niven of Dobbs Ferry, daughter of the Rev. Dr. Niven, pastor of the Presbyterian Church of that place.

Eugene O'Neill was born in New York City on Oct. 16, 1888, the son of James and Ella (Quinlan) O'Neill. He was a student at Princeton in 1906-7, Harvard 1914-15. He married Kathleen Jenkins of New York in 1909 and they were divorced in 1912. He married Mrs. Agnes Boulton Burton in 1918.

O'Neill engaged in various lines of business in the United States, Central and South America, and appeared in a vaudeville version of "Monte Cristo." He spent two years at sea. He was a reporter on the New London (Conn.) Telegraph and since 1914 has devoted his time to playwriting.

Charles Edward Russell was born at Davenport, Ia., on Sept. 25, 1860, the son of Edward and Lydia (Rutledge) Russell. He was graduated from St. Johnsbury (Vt.) Academy in 1881. He entered upon a newspaper career and from 1894-7 was city editor of The New York World, and from 1897 to 1899 managing editor of The New York American. From 1900 to 1902 he published The Chicago American.

Nelson Harding was born in Brooklyn in 1875. He was educated in the public schools there before he studied at the Chase School, the Greenwich (Conn.) Academy and the Art Students' League. He has been connected with The Eagle since 1908. He had been apprenticed to an architect at the age of 18.

Edward Arlington Robinson, who received the Pulitzer prize for poetry in 1922 for his "Collected Poems," and again in 1925 for his volume, "The Man Who Died Twice," was born at Head Tide, Me., on Dec. 22, 1869, the son of Edward and Mary E. (Palmer) Robinson. He was educated at Gardiner, Me., and studied at Harvard from 1891 to 1893. Yale awarded him the degree of Litt. D. in 1922.

1929

PULITZER PRIZE

1928 PULITZER PRIZE FOR PETERKIN NOVEL

Award Goes to "Scarlet Sister Mary"—Elmer Rice's "Street Scene" Adjudged Best Play.

STEPHEN V. BENET HONORED

For Poem "John Brown's Body"—Rollin Kirby and B. J. Hendrick Win Third Time.

Pulitzer Prize winners for 1928-29 were announced yesterday. Julia Peterkin's "Scarlet Sister Mary" was adjudged the best novel; Elmer Rice's "Street Scene," the best play; Fred Albert Shannon's "The Organization and Administration of the Union Army, 1861-1865," the best book on history; Burton J. Hendrick's "The Training of an American," the best biography, and Stephen Vincent Benet's "John Brown's Body," the best book of verse.

The Evening World won the prize for the most meritorious public service rendered by an American newspaper during the year. Honorable mention went to The Brooklyn Daily Eagle, The Chicago Tribune and The St. Paul (Minn.) Dispatch and Pioneer Press. Paul Scott Mowrer of The Chicago Daily News won the prize for the best example of correspondence; Louis Isaac Jaffe of The Norfolk Virginian-Pilot, for the best editorial; Paul Y. Anderson of The St. Louis Post-Dispatch for the best reporter's work, and Rollin Kirby of The World for the best cartoon.

Two Win for Third Time.

It was the third time Mr. Kirby and Mr. Hendrick had won Pulitzer awards. Mr. Kirby's award, which carries a $500 prize, was for his cartoon, "Tammany," published Sept. 24, 1928, and adjudged on the following qualifications: "For the best cartoon published in any American newspaper during the year, the determining qualities being that the cartoon shall embody an idea made clearly apparent, shall show good drawing and striking pictorial effect, and shall be intended to be helpful to some commendable cause of public importance, due account being taken of the whole volume of the artist's newspaper work during the year."

Mr. Hendrick, "for the best American biography teaching patriotic and unselfish services to the people, illustrated by an eminent example, excluding, as too obvious, the names of George Washington and Abraham Lincoln," received a $1,000 prize.

His winning biography, "The Training of an American; The Earlier Life and Letters of Walter H. Page," was published by the Houghton, Mifflin Company. Mr. Hendrick won the biography prize for 1922 with "The Life and Letters of Walter H. Page," and he was the co-author with Admiral William S. Sims of "The Victory at Sea," which won a $2,000 Pulitzer prize as the best book on the history of the United States published in 1920.

A change was made this year in

the qualifications for the prize play which broadens the field for the award, although the judges have never adhered too strictly to the letter of the specifications. The citation formerly read:

"For the original American play performed in New York which shall best represent the educational value and power of the stage in raising the standards of good morals, good taste and good manners."

This year the qualifications end with the word "stage."

List of the Awards.

The list of awards is announced as follows:

PRIZES IN JOURNALISM:

For the most disinterested and meritorious public service rendered by an American newspaper during the year, a gold medal costing $500. Awarded to The New York Evening World, for its effective campaign to correct evils in the administration of justice, including the fight to curb "ambulance chasers," support of the "fence" bill and measures to simplify procedure, prevent perjury and eliminate politics from municipal courts; a campaign which has been instrumental in securing remedial action.

Honorable mention is given to The Brooklyn Daily Eagle, for its campaign against "ambulance chasers" which supplemented the work of The New York Evening World; to The Chicago Tribune for its work in connection with the primary election, and to The St. Paul Dispatch and Pioneer Press, Minn., for its campaign for conservation of forests.

For the best example of correspondence during the year, the test being clearness and terseness of style, preference being given to fair, judicious, well-balanced and well-informed interpretative writing, which shall make clear the significance of the subject covered in the correspondence or which shall promote international understanding and appreciation, $500. Awarded to Paul Scott Mowrer, of The Chicago Daily News.

For the best editorial article written during the year, the test of excellence being clearness of style, moral purpose, sound reasoning and power to influence public opinion in what the writer conceives to be the right direction, due account being taken of the whole volume of the writer's editorial work during the year, $500. Awarded to Louis Isaac Jaffé of The Norfolk Virginian-Pilot, Norfolk, Va., for his editorial entitled "An Unspeakable Act of Savagery," published June 22, 1928, which is typical of a series of articles written on the lynching evil and in successful advocacy of legislation to prevent it.

For the best example of a reporter's work during the year; the test being strict accuracy, terseness, the preference being given to articles that achieve the accomplishment of some public good commanding public attention and respect, $1,000. Awarded to Paul Y. Anderson of The St. Louis Post-Dispatch, St. Louis, Mo., for his highly effective work in bringing to light a situation which resulted in revealing the disposition of Liberty bonds purchased and distributed by the Continental Trading Company in connection with naval oil leases.

PRIZES IN LETTERS.

For the American novel published during the year, preferably one which shall best present the whole atmosphere of American life, $1,000. Awarded to "Scarlet Sister Mary," by Julia Peterkin, published by The Bobbs-Merrill Company, Indianapolis, Ind., 1928.

For the original American play, performed in New York, which shall best represent the educational value and power of the stage, $1,000. Awarded to "Street Scene," by Elmer L. Rice, produced at The Playhouse in New York, during the season 1928-1929, published by Samuel French, New York, 1928.

For the best book of the year upon the history of the United States, $2,000. Awarded to "The Organization and Administration of the Union Army, 1861-1865," by Fred Albert Shannon, published by the Arthur H. Clark Company, Cleveland, 1928.

For the best volume of verse published during the year by an American author, $1,000. Awarded to "John Brown's Body," by Stephen Vincent Benet, published by Doubleday, Doran & Co., 1928.

TRAVELING SCHOLARSHIPS.

Three traveling scholarships, having the value of $1,800 each, to graduates of the School of Journalism, who shall have passed their examinations with the highest honor and are otherwise most deserving, to enable each of them to spend a year in Europe, to study the social, political and moral conditions of the people, and the character and principles of the European press. On the nomination of the teaching staff of the School of Journalism, the following were apointed: Helen R. Fairbanks of Great Neck, L. I.; Prescott Freese Dennett of Bangor, Me.; and Will Cramer Weng of Terre Haute, Ind. The following were appointed alternates: Wayne William Parrish of Decatur, Ill.; Herbert Anderson Yocom of Arcata, Cal., and Josephine Russell of New York City.

An annual scholarship, having the value of $1,500 to the student of music in America who may be deemed the most talented and deserving, in order that he may continue his studies with the advantage of European instruction, on the nomination of a jury composed of members of the teaching staff of the Department of Music in Columbia University and of the teaching staff of the Institute of Musical Art. Awarded to Carl Bricken. Mr. Bricken was a student at the Mannes School of Music from 1923 to 1928 and studied piano with Ralph Leopold from 1923 to 1925.

An annual scholarship, having the value of $1,500, to an art student in America, who shall be certified as the most promising and deserving by the National Academy of Design, with which the Society of American Artists has been merged. Awarded to Herbert Sanborn of New York. Mr. Sanborn has been studying at the National Academy of Design since 1923. In 1927 he was awarded honorable mention for his drawing of the figure in the day class and also for drawing of the figure in the night class. In 1928, he was awarded the Hallgarten School Prize for painting from life and during the current school year, 1928-1929, he received eight prizes for monthly compositions.

White Studio.

ELMER RICE,
Winner of the Prize for the Best Play.

RICE WAS PLAYWRIGHT AT 21.

Author of "Street Scene" Caused a Sensation With "On Trial" in 1914.

Elmer L. Rice, whose play "Street Scene" won the $1,000 Pulitzer award, has had plays produced on Broadway since 1914, when he was 21 years old. Last April 23, at a meeting at the Hotel Astor, where William A. Brady lauded Mr. Rice's skill both as a playwright and director, "Street Scene" received the prize medal of the Theatre Club, Inc.

Mr. Rice's first play, "On Trial," was a sensational success, the more unusual since he had never before written a play. He was just out of law school and was unknown in the theatre.

His other plays include "Morningside Plays," 1917; "Iron Cross," 1917; "Home of the Free," 1917; "For the Defense," 1919; "It Is the Law," 1922; "The Adding Machine," 1923; "Close Harmony," 1924, and "Cock Robin," 1927, which was written in collaboration with Philip Barry.

Mr. Rice was born in this city on Sept. 28, 1892, and received his preparatory education in the public schools.

In 1912 he was graduated from the New York Law School with the degree of Bachelor of Laws cum laude and in the following year he was admitted to the New York bar. He was married to Hazel Levy of this city on June 16, 1915. They have two children.

1930

PULITZER PRIZE

LA FARGE NOVEL WINS 1930 PULITZER PRIZE

"Laughing Boy" Gets Award for Fiction—Connelly's "Green Pastures" Held Best Play.

POETRY HONOR FOR AIKEN

Van Tyne, Historian, and James, Biographer, in List—Owen and Stowe Win in Journalism.

The Pulitzer awards in journalism and letters for 1930 were announced yesterday by Columbia University. The awards were made by the trustees of the university on the recommendation of the advisory board of the School of Journalism.

The prize of $1,000 for the best American novel published during the year, the novel which best presents "the whole atmosphere of American life," was given to Oliver La Farge for his "Laughing Boy."

The prize of $1,000 for "the original American play, performed in New York, which shall best represent the educational value and power of the stage," was awarded to Marc Connelly for his play, "The Green Pastures."

Claude H. Van Tyne won the prize of $2,000 "for the best book of the year upon the history of the United States" with "The War for Independence." The award in this case is posthumous. Dr. Van Tyne died last March.

The prize of $1,000 for the best American biography was given to Marquis James for "The Raven, a Biography of Sam Houston." The condition of this prize required the portrayal of "patriotic and unselfish services to the people, illustrated by an eminent example, excluding, as too obvious, the names of George Washington and Abraham Lincoln."

For the best volume of verse published during the year by an American author, the prize of $1,000 went to Conrad Aiken for his "Selected Poems."

Prizes Given in Journalism.

The journalism prizes were as follows:

"For the best example of correspondence during the year, the test being clearness and terseness of style, judicious, well-balanced and well-informed interpretative writing, which shall make clear the significance of the subject covered in the correspondence or which shall promote international understanding and appreciation, $500, awarded to Leland Stowe, of The New York Herald Tribune, for the series of articles covering the conference on reparations and the establishment of the international bank."

"For the best example of a reporter's work during the year, the test being strict accuracy, terseness, the preference being given to articles that achieve the accomplishment of some public good commanding public attention and respect, $1,000, awarded to Russell D. Owen of The New York Times, for his reports by radio of the Byrd Antarctic Expedition."

A special award of $500 was made to W. O. Dapping of The Auburn (N. Y.) Citizen for his report of the outbreak at Auburn prison in December, 1929.

"For the best cartoon published in any American newspaper during the year, the determining qualities being that the cartoon shall embody an idea made clearly apparent, shall show good drawing and striking pictorial effect, and shall be intended to be helpful to some commendable cause of public importance, due account being taken of the whole volume of the artist's newspaper work during the year, $500, awarded to Charles R. Macauley of The Brooklyn Daily Eagle, for the cartoon entitled 'Paying for a Dead Horse.'"

Two Awards Not Bestowed.

No awards were made this year for "the most disinterested and meritorious public service rendered by an American newspaper during the year" and for the best editorial article written during the year. Each of these awards consists of $500. The test of excellence for the best editorial article is "clearness of style, moral purpose, sound reasoning and power to influence public opinion in what the writer conceives to be the right direction."

The jury was unable to find a single editorial in any American newspaper during the year which could stand this test and deserve the prize, and was unable to pick any paper which performed the service perscribed for the other award.

On the nomination of the teaching staff of the School of Journalism, three students were appointed to receive traveling scholarships, of a value of $1,800 each, for having passed their examination with the highest honor and being otherwise most deserving. The students are:

WAYNE WILLIAM PARRISH, Decatur, Ill.
GEORGE WORTHINGTON POST, 17 East Eleventh Street, New York.
RICHARD H. CUNNINGHAM, 52 Lanam Road, Stamford, Conn.

The scholarships were awarded "to enable each of them to spend a year in Europe to study the social, political and moral conditions of the people and the character and principles of the European press."

An annual scholarship, having the value of $1,800, to the student of music in America deemed the most talented and deserving, to allow continuance of studies with the advantage of European instruction, was awarded to Mark Wessel of Chicago, Ill. The nomination for this scholarship was made by a jury of the teaching staff of the Department of Music in Columbia University and of the teaching staff of the Institute of Musical Art.

Sidney Fischman of New York received the $1,800 scholarship awarded annually to "an art student in America who shall be certified as the most promising and deserving by the National Academy of Design, with which the Society of American Artists has been merged."

Connelly Began in Journalism.

Marc Connelly, author of "The Green Pastures," was born in McKeesport, Pa., forty years ago. He

Pulitzer School of Journalism Awards for 1931

CHOSEN AS THE WINNERS OF THE PULITZER PRIZES.

All photos by The Times Wide World.

MARC CONNELLY,
(Play)

entered journalism at the age of 20 in Pittsburgh. He came to New York in 1915 and sold some lyrics to a musical comedy producer. He also contributed to Life, wrote magazine articles and contributed lyrics and sketches for the theatre. His first successful play was "Dulcy," in which he collaborated with George S. Kaufman, with whom he wrote other plays as well. "The Wisdom Tooth," which he wrote independently in 1927 was a moderate success. His next play, "The Wild Man of Borneo," which he wrote in collaboration with H. J. Mankiewicz, was a failure. Then came his big success with "The Green Pastures," this year.

Claude H. Van Tyne, winner of the historic book prize, was born in Tecumseh, Mich., in 1869, was graduated from the University of Michigan, studied at Leipzig, Heidelberg and Paris and took his Ph. D. at the University of Pennsylvania in 1900. Three years later he joined the history department of the University of Michigan and acted as head of the department from 1911 until his death in March of this year.

In writing "The War for Independence," he had at his command at the University of Michigan the rich resources of the Clements library, to which had recently been added the important historical papers of Sir Henry Clinton and Lord George Germaine. The scholarship of Professor Van Tyne is illustrated by the fact that on the basis of these collections he altered his own opinions in certain important respects and frankly acquainted the public with the fact that he had done so.

1931

PULITZER PRIZE

'Years of Grace,' by Margaret Ayer Barnes, Is Adjudged Foremost Novel of 1930.

'ALISON'S HOUSE' BEST PLAY

Written by Susan G. Glaspell— Awards Made in Journalism and Scholarship.

The Pulitzer awards for 1931, made to fourteen persons and one newspaper for outstanding achievements in letters, journalism and scholarship, were announced yesterday by

SUSAN GLASPELL,
For the Best Play.

HENRY JAMES,
For the Best Biography.

CHARLES S. RYCKMAN,
For the Best Editorial.

ROBERT FROST,
For the Best Volume of Verse.

BERNADOTTE E. SCHMITT,
For the Best American History.

MARGARET AYERS BARNES,
For the Best Novel.

A. B. MacDONALD,
For the Best Reporting.

H. R. KNICKERBOCKER,
For Foreign Correspondence.

EDMUND DUFFY,
For the Best Cartoon.

Columbia University.

Contrasting with the list of 1930, in which New Yorkers were largely represented, this year's prize winners were drawn principally from other parts of the country. The awards, made by the trustees of Columbia

University on the recommendation of the Advisory Board of the School of Journalism, were announced in three groups of five each, as follows:

In the group devoted to letters the award for the year's best novel is

given to "Years of Grace," by Margaret Ayer Barnes; that for the best play goes to "Alison's House," by Susan G. Glaspell, produced by Eva Le Gallienne at the Civic Repertory Theatre; that for the best book of the year dealing with the history of

the United States to "The Coming of the War," by Bernadotte E. Schmitt; that for the best American biography to "Charles W. Eliot," by Henry James; and that for the best volume of verse to the "The Collected Poems of Robert Frost," by Robert Frost.

The literary awards, for which funds are provided by the will of Joseph Pulitzer, are for $1,000, with the exception of the prize for the best treatment of a historical topic, which is $2,000.

Journalistic Awards.

In the recognitions of journalistic achievements, $1,000 is awarded to A. B. MacDonald of The Kansas City (Mo.) Star for the best reporter's work of the year, the prize being case at Amarillo, Texas. Other prizes of $500 each are given to H. R. Knickerbocker of The Philadelphia Public Ledger and New York Evening Post for the best example of foreign correspondence, the award being based on a series of articles concerning the Soviet five-year plan; to Charles S. Ryckman of The Fremont (Neb.) Tribune for the year's best editorial, and to Edmund Duffy of The Sun (Baltimore, Md.) for the year's best cartoon.

All the prize winners were notified about a week ago, and most of them have already signified their acceptance, it was said at the office of the secretary of Columbia University. The only instance in which a Pulitzer prize has been refused is that of Sinclair Lewis, who announced that he would not accept the literary award after it had been offered to him in 1926.

A gold medal costing $500 is given to The Atlanta (Ga.) Constitution for the most disinterested and meritorious public service rendered by an American newspaper, the award being based on a successful campaign against municipal graft, which has led to date to fifty-three indictments and to the conviction of nineteen persons.

The third group of prizes comprises five traveling scholarships of $1,800, three for students in journalism, one in art and one in music. The journalism prize winners, whose names also had been announced by their respective schools previously, are Frederick Daniel Sink of Zanesville, Ohio; David A. Davidson, New York, and Winston Phelps, New York City, all of the School of Journalism. Elliot Griffis, received the music scholarship and Samuel Klein that for art. Both the latter are of New York.

Because of the choice of his collected works for the verse award, Mr. Frost achieves the honor of having won two Pulitzer prizes. In 1924 the poetry prize went to his "New Hampshire, a Poem with Notes and Grace Notes." Mr. Frost makes his home near South Shaftsbury, Vt. In 1922 the Vermont Women's Club chose him poet laureate of that State. Aside from his literary work, he has taught at Amherst and at the University of Michigan.

Mrs. Barnes Has 3 Children.

Margaret Ayer Barnes, winner of the prize for the best novel, is the wife of Cecil Barnes, a Chicago lawyer, and the mother of three sons. During the past five years she also has written a book of short stories under the title "Prevailing Winds" and three plays. She began to write in 1926 while she was convalescing from serious injuries sustained in a motor accident in France. In a recent interview she was quoted as saying she lay flat on her back and wrote with paper on a plaster-cast chest.

She later dramatized Edith Wharton's "Age of Innocence," produced in New York in 1928. Her plays, "Jenny" and "Dishonored Lady," written in collaboration with Edward Sheldon, were produced with Jane Cowl and Katharine Cornell in the name parts.

Mrs. Barnes was born in Chicago, where she still lives, on April 8, 1886. She was graduated from Bryn Mawr College in 1907 and was married in 1910. She is a member of the Society of Midland Authors, the Dramatists' Guild of the Authors' League of America and the Fortnightly and Friday Clubs.

Miss Glaspell, author of the prize play, had been known previously for her novels and short stories. Since her prize play was written she has produced another novel, "Ambrose Holt and Family," a tragi-comedy.

She began her career as a journalist, writing political news for a Des Moines newspaper before she went to Chicago and thence to New York. "The Glory of the Conquered," "The Visioning" and "Fidelity" were three of her novels before her first play, "Suppressed Desires," was written in 1915 with her husband, George Cram Cook, who died in 1923.

She has been identified with the little theatre movement through the Provincetown Players, and makes her home in the Cape Cod town. Her other works include "Inheritors," 1921; "Verge," 1922; "The Road to the Temple," 1926; "The Comic Artist" (in collaboration with Norman Matson, whom she married in 1925), produced in London in 1929; "Brook Evans," 1928, and "Fugitive's Return," 1929.

Miss Glaspell was born at Davenport, Iowa, July 1, 1882. She was graduated from Drake University and did post-graduate work at the University of Chicago.

Dr. Schmitt Has Lectured Here.

Dr. Schmitt, recipient of the history award, is a professor of modern history at the University of Chicago. He is known in New York through his other historical works, through his editorship of the Journal of Modern History, and the lectures he has given to Summer students at Columbia and New York Universities. Other colleges at which he has lectured include the University of Tennessee, the University of Wisconsin, Cornell University and Stanford University.

Born at Strasburg, Va., in 1886, Dr. Schmitt lived in the South during his early years and boyhood. He is graduated from the University of Tennessee in 1904, and was a Rhodes Scholar at Oxford, receiving his B. A. and M. A. degrees from Merton College. In addition, he holds a doctor's degree from the University of Wisconsin. He is unmarried.

The remaining members of the literary group, Mr. James, who received the biography award, is a son of the late William James, the philosopher, and in 1920 edited an edition of his father's letters. Although born in Boston and best known for his practice of law there and for his connection with Harvard University, from which he graduated in 1899 and of which he is an overseer, Mr. James also has many acquaintances in New York, partly as a result of his work as a member of the Regional Plan Commission.

Mr. Ryckman, who wrote the prize-winning editorial is 32 years old, has been editor of the paper in which his editorial appeared for the last nine years. Others of his editorials have been quoted by New York, Chicago and San Francisco newspapers. He was married in 1922 to Miss Mary Redmond of Fremont.

Solved "The Perfect Crime."

The reportorial award to Mr. MacDonald was based upon his investigation of the so-called "perfect crime" in which A. D. Payne, lawyer, murdered his wife by blowing up the family automobile at Amarillo, Texas, on June 27 last. Mr. MacDonald was assigned to the case by The Kansas City Star after local authorities had admitted they were unable to trace the killer. Uncovering a secret love affair between Payne and his former stenographer, the reporter showed this to have furnished a motive for the slaying and be produced evidence which ultimately led to a confession by the husband.

Mr. MacDonald has been a reporter and special writer for forty years, beginning his journalistic work on The Kansas City Times. He is married and the father of five children. Much of his other newspaper work has been devoted to exposure of lotteries and of individuals whom his paper regarded as dangerous to the community. The Pulitzer award is the second recognition given to him for solving the Payne murder, the staff of The Star having previously presented $500 to him at a testimonial dinner.

Mr. Knickerbocker, winner of the correspondence award, is 32 years old. He has been in newspaper work for eleven years, five of which have been spent abroad. As Berlin correspondent of The Public Ledger and of The New York Evening Post, Mr. Knickerbocker published a series of twenty-four articles on Soviet Russia in December, 1930, and January, 1931, following a survey of that country. In 1929 he uncovered a story leading to the arrest and conviction of two men for forging documents linking Senators Borah and Norris with the Soviet régime.

He is a Texan and has worked on The Newark Morning Ledger, The New York Sun and the International News Service. He is a graduate of the Columbia University School of Journalism.

Mr. Duffy, creator of the prize cartoon, was born in New Jersey and studied art in New York and Paris. He has contributed illustrations and cartoons to Scribners, Century and Collier's magazines and to several New York newspapers, including The World and The Tribune. For a time he was a cartoonist on the staff of The New York Leader, no longer in existence. He joined the staff of The Baltimore Sun in September, 1924. His wife, Ann Rector Duffy, also is an artist.

The traveling scholarships in journalism, music and art are awarded, it is explained in the university's announcement, to students who have shown the most promise in their studies and are deemed most talented and deserving. In the case of the journalism students three alternates were named—Valerie A. Fite of Bridgeburg, Ont.; Milton Bracker of 611 West 158th Street and Lincoln K. Barnett of 325 East Seventy-fourth Street. Mr. Davidson lives at 518 West 148th Street, Mr. Phelps at 384 West 253d Street and Mr. Sink in Zanesville, Ohio.

The art and music awards to Mr. Klein and to Mr. Griffis were announced through the National Academy of Design and the department of music in Columbia University, respectively, at about the same time as the journalism scholarships. The conditions of the art and music scholarships are roughly the same as those governing the journalism grants, that the recipient shall use the $1,800 provided for a year of advanced study abroad.

Last year's winners in the letters and journalism groups included Oliver La Farge, novelist, Marc Connelly, playwright; Marquis James, biographer; Conrad Aiken, poet; the late Claude H. Van Tyne, historian; Russell Owen and W. O. Dapping, reporters; Leland Stowe, correspondent, and C. R. MacCauley, cartoonist.

Tells of Atlanta Paper's Service.

Commenting on the award to The Atlanta Constitution of the gold medal "for the most disinterested and meritorious public service rendered by an American newspaper during the year," Julian Harris, news director of The Constitution, visiting New York on business, said:

"The municipal corruption in Atlanta which The Atlanta Constitution fought and exposed was the worst in the history of the city. The wisdom of the paper's campaign is fittingly exhibited in the fact that a large percentage of the city's former officials were convicted of graft and malfeasance and now are serving terms in the penitentiary.

"My own connection with the success of The Constitution's fight is wholly secondary. The credit for the entire thing should and will go to Clark Howell, the editor and owner of the paper. His interest in the affair has been the afflatus for the city exposure and his devotion to clean journalism has been unflagging. The Pulitzer committee's decision in favor of The Constitution is a fitting climax, and one richly deserved, to Mr. Howell's long and splendid career in the South."

Julian Harris and his wife, Julia Collier Harris, received the award in 1926, as editors and owners of The Columbus Enquirer-Sun of Columbus, Ga., for that paper's campaign against the Ku Klux Klan. A year ago the Harrises sold The Enquirer-Sun, and Mr. Harris joined The Atlanta Constitution. Prior to the World War he was managing editor of The New York Herald and was twice editor of its affiliate, The Paris Herald. More recently he became the centre of the "cornpone and potlikker controversy." He is a Watch Tower correspondent for THE NEW YORK TIMES.

THE PRIZE-WINNING EDITORIAL

It Says Norris Is Kept in Senate to Annoy the East.

The Pulitzer prize-winning editorial, "The Gentleman From Nebraska," appearing in The Fremont (Neb.) Daily Tribune on Nov. 7 last, was written by Charles S. Ryckman. In it, Mr. Ryckman tells why, in his opinion, Nebraska has returned George W. Norris to the United States Senate for term after term, regardless of all opposition to him. The editorial read in part:

"The State of Nebraska has elected Norris to the United States Senate this year, as it has many times in the past, mainly because he is not wanted there. If his return to Washington causes discomfiture in official circles, the people of Nebraska will regard their votes as not having been cast in vain. They do not want farm relief or any other legislative benefits a Senator might bring them; all they want is a chance to sit back and gloat.

"This grouch is cultural as much as political. Nebraska and its people have been the butt of Eastern jokesters so long they are embittered. Every major Federal project of the last half century has been disadvantageous to them. The building of the Panama Canal imposed a discriminatory rate burden upon them. Various reclamation projects have increased agricultural competition. Federal tariff policies increase the cost of living in Nebraska without material benefit to Nebraska producers.

"George Norris is the burr Nebraska delights in putting under the Eastern saddle. He is the reprisal for all the jokes of vaudevillists, the caricatures of cartoonists and the gibes of humorists that have come out of the East in the last quarter of a century."

1932

NOBEL PRIZE

NOBEL SCIENCE PRIZE WON BY DR. LANGMUIR

Chemistry Award, Announced in Stockholm, Goes to Inventor of Gas-Filled Tungsten Lamp.

PIONEER IN RADIO FIELD

He Has Also Contributed New Methods of Welding and Given New Atomic Theories.

GALSWORTHY GETS PRIZE

British Novelist and Dramatist Receives Award in Literature—Expresses His Delight.

Wireless to THE NEW YORK TIMES.

STOCKHOLM, Nov. 10.—The Nobel Prize in Chemistry was awarded today to Dr. Irving Langmuir of Schenectady, N. Y.

The Nobel Prize in Literature was awarded to John Galsworthy, British novelist and dramatist. The value of the prize this year is about 172,000 kroner [$30,000 at the current exchange].

The prize in physics has not been awarded, and the money is now in reserve both for this year and last year.

Galsworthy "Very Pleased."

Wireless to THE NEW YORK TIMES.

LONDON, Nov. 10.—When John Galsworthy received the news today, at his Sussex home near Arundel, that he had won the Nobel prize in Literature, he said:

"I am very pleased and very proud."

Rudyard Kipling and George Bernard Shaw are the only other British writers who have received the Nobel Prize.

WIN NOBEL PRIZES.

Times Wide World Photo.
Dr. Irving Langmuir.

Times Wide World Photo.
John Galsworthy.

Dr. Langmuir Native of Brooklyn.

Dr. •Irving Langmuir, associate director of the General Electric Company laboratories at Schenectady and one of the most distinguished research scientists of the day, was born in Brooklyn in 1881. He was educated at Columbia University and in Germany. He joined the General Electric Company in 1909.

Dr. Langmuir has made researches in many branches of science and has received many honors. In 1919 he propounded a new theory on the arrangement of electrons in atoms and molecules, for which, the following year, he received the William H. Nichols Gold Medal, presented by the New York section of the American Chemical Society. He next advanced a new theory of matter, in which he said that "space and time have a structure analagous to that of matter."

In 1922 Dr. Langmuir turned his attention to radio; and he is credited with inventing and developing many types of the vacuum tube. These tubes, the results of Dr. Langmuir's studies of the forms of the electron, were first developed by him in 1912.

In 1922 he developed the radio tube to a power of 1,000 kilowatts.

Others of Dr. Langmuir's inventions are the nitrogen-filled incandescent electric light bulb and the atomic hydrogen welding arc. The latter process was perfected by him in 1927,

and by it previously unweldable metals were melted and fused without the slightest trace of oxidization.

In 1929 Princeton University presented to Dr. Langmuir the honorary degree of Doctor of Science. The citation said in part:

"He has for twenty years attacked fundamental problems with the freedom of an academician, yet with all the powerful resources of the industrial engineer. Langmuir's is the accepted concept of absorption and orientation of molecules at surfaces; his studies have furnished us a mechanism of gas reactions at the surface of the metal tungsten, universally used in electric illumination, long-distance telephony and radio."

Last March Dr. Langmuir received the $10,000 award and gold medal offered annually by Popular Science Monthly for notable scientific achievement. In 1929 he was president of the American Chemical Society.

Galsworthy's First Books.

John Galsworthy's first book to attract considerable attention was "The Island Pharisees," which was published in 1904 and was followed two years later by "The Man of Property."

His stature as a figure in English literature began to grow with the publication of those two books, but, aside from his novels, he wrote a number of plays, four of which achieved unusual distinction. These were "The Silver Box," "Justice," "Loyalties' and "Escape." "The Silver Box," the first of his plays, was produced in London on Sept. 25. 1906, under the management of Granville-Barker.

Mr. Galsworthy, the son of a distinguished legal practitioner of London, whose first name was also John, was born at Coombe, in Surrey, on Aug. 14, 1867. He went to Harrow and Oxford, where he took honors in law and was called to the bar in 1890.

He met Joseph Conrad, whom he afterward championed, in 1893 while on a cruise in the South Seas. Conrad was then mate of the Torrens and Mr. Galsworthy, weary of legal work which made him unhappy, was by traveling making use of the fortune his father had amassed.

Mr. Galsworthy at one time said that he had written fiction for five years before he had even mastered its primary technique.

He was the author of at least twenty novels, including the formidable "The Forsyte Saga," which has taken its place as his greatest work. These included, among the later ones, "Captures," "The White Monkey," "Caravan," "Swan Song," "On Forsyte 'Change" and "Maid in Waiting."

PULITZER PRIZE

Musical Play Gets the Pulitzer Award

Sixteen persons and one newspaper were included in the 1932 Pulitzer awards for outstanding achievements in letters, journalism and scholarship, which were announced yesterday by Columbia University.

The awards, made on the recommendation of the advisory board of the School of Journalism, were announced by the trustees of the university in three groups.

In the group devoted to letters the award for the novel adjudged the best of those published in 1931 was given to "The Good Earth," by Pearl S. Buck; that for the best play to "Of Thee I Sing," by George S. Kaufman, Morrie Ryskind and Ira Gershwin, produced by Sam H. Harris at the Music Box Theatre; that for the best book of the year dealing with the history of the United States to "My Experiences in the World War," by General John J. Pershing; that for the best American biography to "Theodore Roosevelt," by Henry F. Pringle, and that for the best volume of verse published during the year to "The Flowering Stone," by George Dillon. "Of Thee I Sing" is the first musical comedy to win a Pulitzer prize.

The literary awards, for which funds are provided by the will of Joseph Pulitzer, are $1,000 each, with the exception of the work dealing with a historical topic, which carries a prize of $2,000.

Heading the list of awards in the journalism group is the one for the best correspondence during the year, given to Walter Duranty, Moscow correspondent of THE NEW YORK TIMES, for his articles on Russia, especially those dealing with the Five-Year Plan.

"Mr. Duranty's dispatches show profound and intimate comprehension of conditions in Russia and of

the causes of those conditions," the announcement said. "They are marked by scholarship, profundity, impartiality, sound judgment, and exceptional clarity, and are excellent examples of the best type of foreign correspondence."

Charles G. Ross of The St. Louis Post-Dispatch receives a prize for his article entitled "The Country's Plight—What Can Be Done About It?" a discussion of the economic situation of the United States, published Nov. 29, 1931. John T. McCutcheon of The Chicago Tribune receives a prize for his cartoon "A Wise Economist Asks a Question," published Aug. 19, 1931.

The prizes awarded in the journalism group are $500 each.

No award was made for the best editorial article written during the year, while the award of $1,000 for the best example of a reporter's work during the year was deferred.

A gold medal costing $500 for the most disinterested and meritorious public service rendered by an American newspaper during the year was awarded to The Indianapolis News. An editorial in The News, published on Aug. 1, 1930, was held to have been a powerful contributing force in the elimination of waste in city management and reduction of taxes in eighty-six counties in Indiana.

Traveling Scholarships.

The third group of prizes awarded consists of three traveling scholarships of $1,800 each to graduates of the School of Journalism. These awards were made on the nomination of the teaching staff of the School of Journalism to enable the recipients to spend a year in Europe to study conditions and the character and principles of the European press.

The awards were given to Frank R. Kelley, 1,519 Union Street, Brooklyn; Selma Hautzik, 1,955 Grand Concourse, the Bronx, and Jonathan D. Springer, Port Chester, N. Y. Alternates named for these awards are Michael J. Caplan, 2,940 Broadway; Betty Ballantine, Berkeley, Cal., and William Harrison, 422 East Seventeenth Street, Brooklyn.

An annual scholarship having a value of $1,800 was awarded to Ernest Bacon of San Francisco, Cal., by a jury composed of members of the teaching staff of the Department of Music of Columbia University. This scholarship is awarded to enable the recipient to continue his studies in Europe. Another scholarship with a value of $1,800 was awarded to Francesco Roggeri of New York City on the nomination of the National Academy of Design, with which the Society of American Artists has been merged.

White Studio.
GEORGE S. KAUFMAN,
American Play.

Blackstone Studio.
MORRIE RYSKIND,
American Play.

New York Times Studio.
IRA GERSHWIN,
American Play.

Of the award for the best novel the announcement said:

"Preference has been given to 'The Good Earth' for its epic sweep, its distinct and moving characterization, its sustained story interest, its simple and yet richly colored style. Also, so far as may be gathered, Mrs. Buck gives an undistorted picture of the life described."

An "Unusual" Award.

Referring to the award to Kaufman, Ryskind and Gershwin for "Of Thee I Sing," it declared:

"This award may seem unusual, but the play is unusual. Not only is it coherent and well knit enough to class as a play, aside from the music, but it is a biting and true satire on American politics and the public attitude toward them. Its effect on the stage promises to be very considerable, because musical plays are always popular and by injecting genuine satire and point into them a very large public is reached. The spirit and style of the play are topical and popular, but, of course, the work is all the more spontaneous for that, and has a freshness and vitality which are both unusual and admirable. The play is genuine, and it is felt the prize could not serve a better purpose than to recognize such work."

The award to General Pershing carried the following comment:

"General Pershing has not only written the most authoritative, the most penetrating and the most decisive account of our own part in the war, but he has presented a finer spirit in narration than any of the others, more objectivity, more fullness and more balance. The book is epic in the sense that it is a great national story, displaying the American character in its finest aspects."

Mr. Pringle's "Theodore Roosevelt" was commended as follows:

"Mr. Pringle's book presents vitalized portrait of an outstanding American. It seeks to strike a fair balance where that—in a time so near to the subject—is difficult to achieve. It is well documented and well written. It is especially valuable for its candor and its human quality."

Of Mr. Dillon's "The Flowering Stone" the announcement said:

"Of the four or five volumes which received most serious consideration, Mr. Dillon's verse seemed most original and authentic. Some of his poems are exceedingly beautiful. The prize is awarded to him as a young poet of very great promise."

Board Recommending Winners.

The advisory board of the School of Journalism, upon whose recommendations the Pulitzer awards and traveling scholarships were made, has the following membership:

President NICHOLAS MURRAY BUTLER.
KENT COOPER, Associated Press.
JULIAN HARRIS, Atlanta Constitution.
JOHN L. HEATON, formerly of The World.
ARTHUR M. HOWE, formerly of The Brooklyn Daily Eagle.
FRANK R. KENT, Baltimore Sun.
ROBERT LATHAN, Asheville (N. C.) Citizen and Times.
ROBERT L. O'BRIEN, formerly of The Boston Herald.
ROLLO OGDEN, THE NEW YORK TIMES.
STUART PERRY, Adrian (Mich.) Daily Telegram.
JOSEPH PULITZER, St. Louis Post Dispatch.
RALPH PULITZER, formerly of The World.
WALTER WILLIAMS, president of the University of Missouri.

George S. Kaufman

Mr. Kaufman, co-winner of the play award, is a native of Pittsburgh who has won a place high in the list of Broadway playwrights and directors. He has collaborated with others in the writing of numerous hits. Mr. Kaufman entered journalistic work as a columnist on The Washington Times and later succeeded Franklin P. Adams on The Evening Mail in New York. He then became a reporter on The Tribune and subsequently assistant and then dramatic editor on THE NEW YORK TIMES.

He has written only one play by himself—"The Butter and Egg Man." He won his first big successes in collaborations with Marc Connelly—"Dulcy," "To the Ladies," "Merton of the Movies" and "Beggar on Horseback." Later he collaborated with Edna Ferber in "Minick" and "The Royal Family"; with Ring Lardner in "June Moon," and with Moss Hart in "Once in a Lifetime." He collaborated with Mr. Ryskind, in addition to "Of Thee I Sing," in "The Cocoanuts," "Animal Crackers" and "Strike Up the Band."

Morrie Ryskind

Mr. Ryskind was born on the east side on Oct. 20, 1895. His father kept a cigar store on Washington Heights and he started out in life with the ambition of being a professional baseball pitcher. Six weeks before he was to have taken his degree at the Columbia School of Journalism in 1917 he was expelled from the university for writing some anti-war articles in The Jester, the school journal, of which he was the editor. He joined the staff of The World, from which he resigned to write scenarios. In addition to collaborating with Mr. Kaufman he has been a silent collaborator in several musical pieces and plays. He is the author of two volumes of light verse.

Ira Gershwin

Ira Gershwin is the brother of George Gershwin, the composer. The former wrote the lyrics for "Of Thee I Sing" and the latter the music. Ira Gershwin has for many years written the lyrics of all the shows composed by his brother. He was born on the east side and spent two years at City College. He has written the lyrics for the following shows: "Lady, Be Good," "Tell Me More," "Tip Toes," "The Song of the Flame," "Strike Up the Band," "Girl Crazy," "Funny Face" and "Treasure Girl."

George Dillon

George Dillon was born in Jacksonville, Fla., in 1906. In 1923 he entered the University of Chicago and began his career as a poet in the same group in which Glenway Wescott and Elizabeth Madox Roberts had been active. While at the university he started a poetry magazine called The Forge. Shortly thereafter Harriet Monroe, the editor of Poetry, invited him to become associate editor. He has had poems in many magazines and in a number of anthologies and has taken several important prizes for poetry.

"Boy in the Wind," his first published volume of verse, was the first selection of the Poetry Book Club. This was followed by "The Flowering Stone," which won him a Guggenheim award and the Pulitzer prize.

1933

PULITZER PRIZE

ANDERSON DRAMA

'Both Your Houses' Chosen— Stribling Takes Award for the Best Novel.

DEAD HISTORIAN HONORED

F. J. Turner's Last Volume, Biography by Nevins and MacLeish Poetry Cited.

In a setting of literary personages, gathered at the dinner of the Friends of the Princeton Library at the Hotel Plaza last night, the Pulitzer Prizes for Literature in 1932 were awarded.

The $1,000 prize for the best novel of the year was given to T. S. Stribling, for "The Store," a story of life in an inland Southern community in the middle '80s of the last century. The novel was published by Doubleday, Doran Company.

Maxwell Anderson was adjudged to have written the play that best represents "the educational value and power of the stage," in "Both Your Houses," now playing at the Royale Theatre under the imprimatur of the Theatre Guild, which has been the producer of two other prize winners.

The award for the best volume dealing with the history of the United States was made posthumously to the late Frederick Jackson Turner, for "The Significance of Sections in American History," published by Henry Holt & Co.

Allan Nevins won the prize for the best American biographical work with his "Grover Cleveland," published by Dodd, Mead & Co. The poetry prize was awarded to "Conquistador," by Archibald MacLeish, published by Houghton, Mifflin Company.

The history prize is $2,000. All the others are for $1,000. The winners were announced by Frank D. Fackenthal, secretary of Columbia University.

Two Winners Speak.

Mr. Nevins and Mr. Stribling were the only ones of this year's prize winners present at the dinner. Both made brief speeches into the microphone which carried their voices over the coast to coast network of the National Broadcasting Company.

Advising the audience, which included most of the "crowned heads of literature," as Herbert Putnam, librarian of Congress, had pointed out earlier, that "only the husband of the wife of an author understands the stress and strain she undergoes about the time the Pulitzer Prizes are awarded," Mr. Stribling attributed his success to the fact that his home is in the South.

The author of "The Store," said that with the sharply defined and contrasting strata of life in the South for material a novelist would have to make a real effort to "jumble things up" in order to do a bad book. The South had a real past, he declared, while the past of the North was "only the present extended backward."

Mr. Nevins said that the effect

of winning the prize was to produce a feeling of humility rather than of elation. He was peculiarly aware of the significance of the Pulitzer Prize, he declared, because in the years he spent working "under the gilded dome of the World Building," he learned to "hold the deepest regard for the ideals and aims of Joseph Pulitzer."

Earlier Winners Speak.

Dr. William Lyon Phelps, as toastmaster, introduced winners of prizes in other years for brief addresses. Fiction was represented by Willa Cather, the drama by Elmer Rice, history by James Truslow Adams, poetry by Robert Frost and biography by Henry James. Edward D. Duffield, president of Princeton University, discussed the importance of literature in contemporary life. In a short address, he said:

"Is it not well that in a time of uncertainty, when doubt and questioning leads to confusion, that men should turn to literature in order that their interest should be awakened in the happenings of the past and encouragement given them to a thoughtful investigation of the present? May it not be that in some quiet spot like Princeton men may turn again to those finer things in life, which, seemingly, we have lost, and as they read the pages on which the great minds have recorded their thoughts of living value, find once more the faith in the eternal verities from which we have been swept away?

"If we are to steer our course to a safe harbor, we must regain our vision, through the fog and mist of the present, so that we may see the eternal stars by which to guide our course. If faith and trust and honor and integrity are to again be controlling factors in life, what better method can be devised than to learn once more from those who have found the solution of their problems in spiritual strength?"

Pershing Is Introduced.

Just before the formal announcement of the prize winners Dr. Phelps introduced "the greatest prize winner of all, our beloved chief, General John J. Pershing," who declared he would rather face a battery of artillery than a microphone and said that, nevertheless, he was glad to have an opportunity of "meeting so many authors whom I have not read."

The literary fête came to an end after Dr. Nicholas Murray Butler had delivered an address in which he said that the evening's experience had served to weaken his conviction that the real need of the country is "a constitutional amendment requiring universal illiteracy." It had occurred to him, he said, that if the citizenry were prohibited

Photo by Florence Vandamm.
**Maxwell Anderson,
Drama.**

from reading "it might have time to think."

"But here we are," he continued, "dealing with the intangible and imponderable of immeasurable value and being happily and fortunately diverted, for the time being, from the more material aspects which are engrossing the attention of the whole civilized world."

Second Political Satire.

"Both Your Houses" is the second successive political satire to win the Pulitzer Prize. Last year the award went to "Of Thee I Sing." While the latter dealt with the absurdities of campaigning, Mr. Anderson's play concerns itself with the active operation of the Federal Government.

Its theme is of the padding of a deficiency bill, which starts out as a $40,000,000 measure and ends at $400,000,000. The characters range from charming scamps to unscrupulous plunderers and the idealists have a very hard time. It opened in Pittsburgh last Feb. 27 and came to the Royale on March 6. It was received warmly by the critics.

Although the other prizes are awarded for the year 1932, the prize for the best drama was given to the best play produced in the 1932-33 season. "Both Your Houses" is scheduled to close Saturday night after that evening's performance and move to Philadelphia for two weeks.

Following are brief biographical sketches of the prize winners:

Maxwell Anderson.

Maxwell Anderson entered the theatre by way of school teaching and newspaper work. In the latter capacity he was on the staffs of the old New York Globe and The World. His first play was "The White Desert," back in 1923. After that came "The Feud," and in 1924 the famous "What Price Glory," which he wrote with Laurence Stallings. Then followed "Outside Looking In," "First Flight" (with Stallings), "The Buccaneer" (with Stallings), "Forfeits," "Saturday's Children," "Gods of the Lightning" (with Harold Hickerson), "Gypsy," "Elizabeth the Queen" and "Night Over Taos."

Mr. Anderson lives in New York City, but just now he is in Hollywood.

1934

NOBEL PRIZE

Italian Playwright's General Contribution to Literature Is Basis of Award.

HIS PLAYS METAPHYSICAL

Author Long Interested in What He Terms Man's Need to Deceive Himself.

Wireless to THE NEW YORK TIMES.
STOCKHOLM, Nov. 8.—The Nobel Prize in literature was awarded today to the Italian playwright Luigi Pirandello.

By The Associated Press.
STOCKHOLM, Nov. 8.—The award of the Nobel Prize of $41,318 to Luigi Pirandello was based on the author's general contribution to literature, there being no mention

Times Wide World Photo.
NOBEL PRIZE WINNER.
Luigi Pirandello.

of any particular work.

Last year's prize was awarded to the Russian, Ivan Alexeyevich Bunin, poet and novelist.

Author Expresses Pleasure.
By The Associated Press.

ROME, Nov. 8.—The little white beard of Luigi Pirandello bobbed in lively fashion today as he chuckled over his success in winning the Nobel prize in literature.

Italy's premier playwright, now that Gabriel d'Annunzio's sun is setting, received an interviewer in the library of his small apartment in a suburb. He read with great interest a telegram from Stockholm announcing the award. Smiling broadly, he said:

"Of course, I'm going to keep it. There are poor authors, too.

"Certainly I'm going to keep on working. I have dozens of ideas just crying to be put on paper."

Signor Pirandello said one of the greatest disappointments he has had in recent years was in connection with the United States. He had a contract with the Shubert Theatre Corporation, which failed. Consequently he has not sent to America the play "Giants of the Mountain," which was especially written to be produced in the United States because of the grandiose stage setting required.

"In order to find out something about the situation," he related, "I wrote to a New York lawyer, but he replied that merely to study the situation he wanted $500. At this rate the only one who would have realized a profit would have been the lawyer."

He said he now was putting his latest comedy, "One Doesn't Know How," on the Italian stage.

He is greatly interested in the project of the Italian Government to create a State theatre.

Asked when he intended to visit America next, he replied, "I'm waiting for better times."

Chooses Metaphysical Themes.

Throughout his literary career Luigi Pirandello has been juggling with the philosophical problem of reality. In his plays, short stories, essays, poems and novels the question "What is reality?" is an ever-recurring theme.

Signor Pirandello's predilection for metaphysics is probably bound up with his early education. He was

born on June 28, 1867, on a country estate near Girgenti, Sicily. He first went to Rome at the age of 19. In 1891 he entered the University of Bonn in Germany and there came into contact with professors of philosophy. At Bonn he received his doctorate in philosophy. Ever since that time he has been influenced by the impressions he received during his student days in Germany.

His first volume, in verse, was published in 1889. Luigi Capuana, a Sicilian contemporary of Signor Pirandello, persuaded him to try his pen at fiction, and in 1894 he published his first novel, "L'Esclusa" (The Outcast). From that time on novels and short stories flowed from his pen. One of his best-known novels, "The Late Mattia Pascal," appeared in 1904.

Wrote His Play at 45.

It was not until he was 45 years old that he turned to the theatre. In his plays he gave vigorous expression to the despairing outlook on life that had characterized his novels and short stories.

Despite their concentration on metaphysical problems, Signor Pirandello's plays are frequently sprinkled with brilliant wit. His comedies and other plays reveal his ability to vitalize philosophical questions through the medium of characters who are intensely alive. Their conversation is always marked by sensibility and wit. His play "Tonight We Improvise" is a half-humorous, half-serious attempt to set forth in dramatic terms the answer to the riddle of reality.

Signor Pirandello's plays have been successful both in Italy and in many foreign countries. They have been translated into fifteen languages.

In 1925 he opened in Rome a theatre where his own and new foreign plays are produced.

Signor Pirandello's plays include "Henry IV," "Right You Are," "Six Characters in Search of an Author," "Each in His Own Way," "The Pleasure of Honesty," "Naked," "As You Desire Me," "Tonight We Improvise" and a volume of one-act plays. His novels include "The Old and the Young," "Shoot," "The Outcast," "One, None and a Hundred Thousand" and "The Late Mattia Pascal." He has also brought out two well-known volumes of short stories, "The Naked Truth" and "Horse in the Moon."

In January of this year an Italian opera, "Legend of a Changeling Son," composed by Francesco Malipiero, to which Signor Pirandello contributed the libretto, received its world première in Brunswick, Germany. When it was produced in Rome three months later, in the presence of Premier Mussolini, critics received it coolly, calling it "half a disaster."

Signor Pirandello is a member of the Italian Academy. After the World War he received the Cross of the Legion of Honor from the French Government.

PULITZER PRIZE

The Pulitzer Prize winners for 1933, outstanding among whom are Caroline Miller for her novel "Lamb in His Bosom" and Sidney Kingsley for his play "Men in White," were announced last night at a dinner at the Columbia University Men's Faculty Club, 400 West 117th Street.

Frederick T. Birchall of THE NEW YORK TIMES won the award for distinguished service as a newspaper correspondent, the selection being based on his news stories sent from Europe.

The prize for the best book of the year on the history of the United States went to Herbert Agar, an attaché at the American Embassy in London, for "The People's Choice," and Tyler Dennett of Princeton University won the award in American biography with "John Hay." The poetry prize was presented to Robert Hillyer of Harvard for his "Collected Verse."

Controversy over the decision of the Advisory Board of the School of Journalism, which exercises final judgment, was under way even before the awards were announced.

Along with the formal statement of the prize winners, there were issued two announcements setting forth that the juries which assisted in selecting the prize-winning play and historical work had not recommended the winners finally selected.

The drama jury, composed of Clayton Hamilton, Walter Prichard Eaton and Austin Strong, voted unanimously for Maxwell Anderson's "Mary of Scotland," produced by the Theatre Guild.

Two members of the history jury, on which Charles D. Hazen, Burton J. Hendrick and M. A. DeWolfe Howe served, voted for "Over Here," the fifth volume of Mark Sullivan's "Our Times," and the third expressed the opinion that no award should be made. The names of the two who favored the Sullivan book were not made public.

Secretary Frank D. Fackenthal of Columbia explained that the members of the two juries "always understood that they were retained in an advisory capacity and consequently they do not question the right of the Advisory Board of the School of Journalism to exercise their own judgment." Mr. Fackenthal said that the members of the two juries had asked that the public be informed of their decisions "in justice to themselves."

At the annual dinner of the Columbia School of Journalism Alumni, at which the awards were announced, there was no mention of the controversy, although Dr. Nicholas Murray Butler, president of the university, explained in great detail the method of selection.

"The prizes are awarded," he said, "by the trustees of the university on the recommendations of the advisory board of the School of Journalism, which, in turn, has the benefit of the suggestions and recommendations made to it by the juries.

"But the responsibility for choice between these recommendations rests primarily upon the advisory board. This board made its recommendations to the Columbia University trustees, and that body, in a stated meeting this afternoon, has awarded the prizes as follows."

Thereupon Dr. Butler read the list of winners. Several of the winners of the newspaper prizes, he pointed out, represented small-town newspapers, "showing that there is opportunity for the small man in the new deal."

Mrs. Miller, winner of the novel award, who hails from a small town in Southern Georgia, said in a brief speech that "no one who ever won this award was so deeply grateful as I am."

Dean Carl W. Ackerman of the School of Journalism read the following cablegram from Mr. Birchall:

"Please express my great appreciation of having been admitted to the distinguished company of Pulitzer Prize winners. I take it as acknowledgment of honest effort to tell the truth without fear or malice

about happenings of interest and importance to the whole world. That effort I have made and I am grateful for this recognition thereof."

In addition to the award for distinguished newspaper correspondence, there were several other prizes in the field of journalism. These included:

For meritorious public service, The Medford (Ore.) Mail Tribune. This newspaper was credited with stemming a rising tide of public insurrection which was the outgrowth of a bitter political fight. An organization led by Llewellyn Banks, defeated candidate for the United States Senate, was defying the courts and threatening that "blood is likely to be spilled." The Mail Tribune, under the editorship of Robert W. Ruhl, took the leadership in pleading for straight-thinking and peace.

For distinguished editorial writing, E. P. Chase, editor of The Atlantic (Iowa) News Telegraph. In an editorial titled "Where Is Our Money?" he held the American people themselves responsible for the economic crisis because of their excessive spending in the boom days. He urged old-fashioned thrift as the way out.

For distinguished work as a reporter, Royce Brier of The San Francisco Chronicle. Mr. Brier worked sixteen continuous hours covering the San Jose lynchings; blinded by tear gas, menaced by flying bricks and manhandled by the mob, he and four assistants telephoned a running story from a garage.

For distinguished work as a cartoonist, Edmund Duffy of The Baltimore Sun, for his cartoon, "California Points With Pride—!"

Music Scholarship.

An annual scholarship of $1,500, for the music student who is considered the most talented and deserving of the advantages of European instruction, went to Frank Percival Price, carillonneur at the Rockefeller Memorial carillon. A similar scholarship in art was awarded to Cathal O'Toole, Dublin-born artist now living in Long Island City.

The award for distinguished service by a newspaper carries with it a $500 gold medal. Awards of $500 cash went to the winners of the prizes for newspaper correspondence, editorial writing, and best cartoon. The prize-winning reporter, novelist, playwright, biographer and poet received $1,000 each. The award in history carried a $2,000 prize.

The advisory board which made the awards is composed of the following: Dr. Nicholas Murray Butler, president of Columbia; Kent Cooper, general manager of The Associated Press; Julian Harris, editor of The Atlanta Constitution; John L. Heaton, formerly of The New York World; Arthur M. Howe of The Brooklyn Eagle; Frank R. Kent of The Baltimore Sun; Robert Lathan of The Asheville Citizen and Times; Robert Lincoln O'Brien, head of the United States Tariff Commission; Rollo Ogden, editor of THE NEW YORK TIMES; Stuart H. Perry, publisher of The Adrian (Mich.) Daily Telegram; Marlen E. Pew, editor of Editor and Publisher; Joseph Pulitzer, publisher of The St. Louis Post-Dispatch, and Ralph Pulitzer, former publisher of The New York World.

Honorable Mention Awards.

In addition to awarding first prizes the Pulitzer committee selected several persons for honorable mention in various categories. They follow:

For distinguished service as a newspaper correspondent:

John E. Elliott of The New York Herald Tribune for his correspondence from Germany.

Harry Carr of The Los Angeles Times for his series of dispatches from Australia, Japan, China, the Philippines and Europe.

For distinguished editorial writing:

To "Why We Still Have Lynchings in the South," by Osborn Zu-

ber, published in The Birmingham News, Sept. 13, 1933;

To "The Strategic Gains," by Geoffrey Parsons in The New York Herald Tribune, April 21, 1933;

To "The Governor Sends Troops to Gallup," by E. H. Shaffer in The Albuquerque Tribune, Aug. 31, 1933;

To "The Freedom of the Press," by Casper S. Yost in The St. Louis Globe Democrat, Nov. 2, 1933;

To "The Newspapers and the Code," by Douglas W. Swiggett in The Milwaukee Journal, July 25, 1933;

To "Freedom of the Press," by Bainbridge Colby in The New York American, Oct. 9, 1933;

To "Iowa's Disgrace," by James E. Lawrence in The Lincoln (Neb.) Star, April 28, 1933;

To "Some Aspects in the Administration's Program," by William R. Mathews in The Arizona Daily Star (Tucson), July 16, 1933.

Reportorial Work Honored.

For distinguished reportorial work:

Eben A. Ayers, Andrew J. Clarke and Edward J. Kelley of the Boston bureau of The Associated Press, for their vigilance and accuracy in covering the kidnapping of Margaret McMath at Harwichport, Mass.;

Edward J. Donohue of The Times Leader (Wilkes-Barre, Pa.) for his able and convincing work setting forth corruption in office on the part of members of the public school boards in Luzerne County.

H. Ellwood Douglass of The St. Louis Post-Dispatch for his accounts of the epidemic of encephalitis in St. Louis;

Meigs O. Frost of The New Orleans Times-Picayune for his reporting of the case of Pearl Ledet, accused of causing a death in an automobile accident case.

Charles J. Truitt, correspondent of The Philadelphia Evening Bulletin, in covering the district of Ocean City and Salisbury, Md., after the severest storm in the history of the Eastern Shore had severed all communications;

Frederick Woltman of The New York World-Telegram for clear, exact and understanding writing in reporting the status of various closed banks in the suburban areas of New York after the national bank holiday.

Three traveling scholarships of $1,500 each were awarded to graduates of the School of Journalism at Columbia "who shall have passed their examinations with highest honor and are otherwise most deserving, to enable each of them to spend a year in Europe to study the social, political and moral conditions of the people and the character and principles of the European press." The winners were:

Fred Gruin, 1,011 Bergenline Avenue, North Bergen, N. J.; Harold A. Bezazian, 6,215 Winthrop Avenue, Chicago, and Betty Turner, 5,747 County Club Drive, Oakland, Calif.

Alternates named were: Mark J. Ginsbourg, Shanghai, China; Jerome I. Myerberg, 30 Dophin Road, Newton, Mass., and Mary J. Durham, Greencastle, Ind.

SIDNEY KINGSLEY.

Mr. Kingsley, actor and playwright, won his award with his first play to reach Broadway. "Men in White" had its opening at the Broadhurst Theatre Sept. 26, 1933. It was presented by the Group Theatre in association with Sidney Harmon and James R. Ullman.

The prize-winner is a native New Yorker, having been born in 1907. He got his schooling at Townsend Harris Hall and Cornell University, being graduated from the latter in 1928. After college he appeared briefly with a stock company at the Tremont Theatre in the Bronx and in a small rôle in the Broadway production, "Subway Express." At present he is traveling in Europe.

"Men in White" aroused critical comment ranging from high praise to disapproval. Brooks Atkinson wrote in THE NEW YORK TIMES:

"It is a good, brave play, despite a certain austerity in the writing and a slavish fondness for medical

Sidney Kingsley
For Best Play.

terms. * * * You may question the logic of the story. You may criticize the continuity and the writing. But 'Men in White' has force in the theatre. It is warm with life and high in aspiration, and it has a contagious respect for the theme it discusses."

1935

PULITZER PRIZE

PULITZER AWARDS GO TO 'THE OLD MAID' AND A FIRST NOVEL

Zoe Akins Play and Josephine Johnson's 'Now in November' Receive Annual Prizes.

LISTS KEPT CLOSE SECRET

Arthur Krock, William H. Taylor and Sacramento Bee Get Honors in Journalism.

The annual announcement of the Pulitzer prize winners in journalism and letters, made last night in the Hotel Commodore at a dinner of the Columbia University School of Journalism alumni, had the added fillip of being surrounded by mystery which was dispelled only at the last minute.

Even the winners were kept in the dark, theoretically at least, until Dr. Nicholas Murray Butler, president of Columbia, gave the signal that released the news to them and to the public. At the signal from Dr. Butler, a messenger boy hurried from the dining room bearing telegrams addressed to the

chosen authors, playwrights and newspaper men.

As the best play of the 1934 season the advisory committee selected Zöe Akins's "The Old Maid," dramatized from a story of old New York by Edith Wharton.

"Now in November," a first novel by Josephine Winslow Johnson, was adjudged the outstanding work in that category.

Correspondent Takes Prize.

In journalism Arthur Krock, Washington correspondent of THE NEW YORK TIMES, received the Pulitzer Prize for the best correspondence for his articles reflecting scenes in the nation's capital under the New Deal.

William H. Taylor of the sports staff of The New York Herald Tribune won the prize for the best example of a reporter's work with his stories on the America's Cup races.

The prize for verse went to Audrey Wurdemann, wife of Joseph Auslander, for her volume of poems, "Bright Ambush."

Professor Charles McLean Andrews of Yale University, former president of the American Historical Association, received the history prize for "The Colonial Period in American History," and the prize for the best American biography went to Douglas Southall Freeman, editor of The Richmond (Va.) News Leader, for "R. E. Lee," a four-volume study of the Civil War hero into which the author put twenty years of research. David S. Muzzey received honorable mention for his "James G. Blaine."

Award for Public Service.

In addition to the awards to Mr. Krock and Mr. Taylor, there were other awards in journalism. The gold medal for the "most disinterested and meritorious service by an American newspaper" was given to The Sacramento (Calif.) Bee for publishing a series of articles by Arthur B. Waugh.

Mr. Waugh, associate editor of The Bee, was sent to Nevada to investigate complaints his newspaper had received against President Roosevelt's nomination of Federal District Judge Frank H. Norcross for the Circuit Court of Appeals and of William Woodburn as a Federal District judge. The committee held that the articles written by Mr. Waugh led to the dropping of the nominations after an investigation.

The Sheboygan Press, of Sheboygan, Wis., received honorable mention, for an investigation of conditions in State hospitals, resulting in a legislative investigation and correction of evils. Walter J. Pfister, an alumnus of the Class of 1924, now city editor of the Sheboygan Press, attended the dinner.

No editorial published in 1934 was deemed sufficiently distinguished to merit an award. The prize for the best example of a cartoonist's work went to Ross A. Lewis of The Milwaukee Journal for a cartoon, published in that newspaper Sept. 1, under the caption, "Sure, I'll Work for Both Sides."

Two scholarships in music and art, each worth $1,500 for study abroad, were announced at the dinner. The former was awarded

to Samuel Barber of New York and the latter to Eileen Ortlip of Fort Lee, N. J., who was certified by the National Academy of Design as the "most promising and deserving" candidate.

Three traveling scholarships for journalism students also were awarded to Elwood M. Thompson of Lincoln, Neb.; August Loeb of Shreveport, La., and Joseph P. Ciszek of Brooklyn. Donald Reynolds of Brooklyn, Marie F. Sauer of Elizabeth, N. J., and Leo M. Friedman of Brooklyn were named as alternates.

Board That Made Awards.

Members of the advisory board that recommended the awards last Friday were Dr. Butler; Julian Harris of The Atlanta Constitution; Kent Cooper, general manager of The Associated Press; Arthur M. Howe, editor emeritus, The Brooklyn Daily Eagle; Frank R. Kent, The Baltimore Sun; Robert Lathan, The Asheville (N. C.) Citizen and Times; Robert Lincoln O'Brien Sr., United States Tariff Commission; Rollo Ogden, editor of The New York Times; Stuart H. Perry, Adrian (Mich.) Telegram; Marlen Pew of Editor and Publisher; Joseph Pulitzer, St. Louis Post-Dispatch, and Ralph Pulitzer, formerly publisher of The New World.

To guard against such premature publication of the winners as has occurred in recent years, the committee adopted unusual precautions to keep the names of the prize winners secret until they were announced formally at the dinner. No printed releases were distributed in advance of the dinner and the usual practice of notifying the winners in advance was abandoned.

Through the early courses of the dinner the tables buzzed wtih gossip and speculation over the probable awards, and seating lists were studied eagerly in search of cryptograms that might shed light on winners of the coveted awards. Not until 9 o'clock, when Dean Carl W. Ackerman of the School of Journalism interrupted the diners to introduce Dr. Butler was the mystery dispelled.

Claude A. Jagger of the class of 1925 presided at the dinner with Dean Ackerman as toastmaster. Julian Harris in a brief speech commenting on "freedom of the press," which other speakers declared was "dear to the hearts of us all," said "90 or 95 per cent of the editors of the country never would know it" if they were deprived of that heritage.

Dean Ackerman praised Joseph Pulitzer's ideal of a free and outspoken press and predicted that the time would soon come when all the graduates of the Pulitzer School of Journalism would be placed in jobs immediately upon graduation. Another speaker was Robert Lathan of The Asheville Citizen.

The prize-winning reporter, novelist, playwright, biographer, poet and historian received $1,000 each. Awards of $500 each went to the winners of the prizes for newspaper correspondence and best cartoon. The award for distinguished service by a newspaper carries with it a medal worth $500.

Award for Correspondence.

The basis of the award to Mr.

Krock was set forth in the following language:

"For distinguished service as foreign or Washington correspondent during the year, the test being clearness and terseness of style; and the preference being given to fair, judicious, well-balanced and well-informed, interpretive writing, which shall make clear the significance of the subject covered in the correspondence or which shall promote international understanding and appreciation."

The citation that went with the $1,000 award to Mr. Taylor follows:

"For a distinguished example of a reporter's work during the year; the test being strict accuracy, terseness and the preference being given to articles that achieve the accomplishment of some public good, commanding public attention and respect."

The following excerpt is from the report of the committee in support of its recommendation that The Sacramento Bee receive the medal for distinguished public service:

"The award of the Public Service prize to The Sacramento Bee of Sacramento, Calif., recognizes the work of Arthur B. Waugh, associate editor, who was sent to Nevada to investigate complaints the newspaper had received against the nominations by President Roosevelt of Federal District Judge Frank H. Norcross to the United States Circuit Court of Appeals, and William Woodburn to the place to be vacated by Norcross.

"Mr. Waugh discovered that much more was involved than the mere appointment of two Federal judges. His investigation convinced him that the situation affected the future welfare of the citizens of Nevada and he spent two weeks going through the records of Reno and Carson City, and interviewing various persons.

"This investigation covered the activities of the Wingfield political machine in Nevada over a period of years and included the events leading up to the tragic bank crash of November, 1932. Because of the influence of the Wingfield organization over State and county officials and influential Nevadans, every fact was secured only through great persistence.

"The publication of these articles created such a sensation in Nevada that Congress was overwhelmed with petitions demanding that the nomination not be approved. The hearings held by a subcommittee of the Senate Judiciary Committee substantiated Mr. Waugh's articles published in January, 1934, in The Sacramento Bee and the appointments were dropped by common consent.

"The effect of the exposé was apparent in last Fall's elections when the Nevadans completely overthrew the Wingfield machine."

At its May 3 meeting the advisory board changed its term of membership to four years and rearranged the date of expiration of terms so that elections would be more equalized. Joseph Pulitzer was elected for a four-year term ending June 30, 1939, to succeed himself, and Harold Stanley Pollard of The New York World-Telegram was elected for a four-year term to succeed the late John L. Heaton.

Brief sketches of the principal winners follow:

Zoe Akins.

With her first winning of the Pulitzer Prize, Zöe Akins reaches the climax of a career not quite like that of any contemporary American playwright. She has run a full gamut of themes and dra-

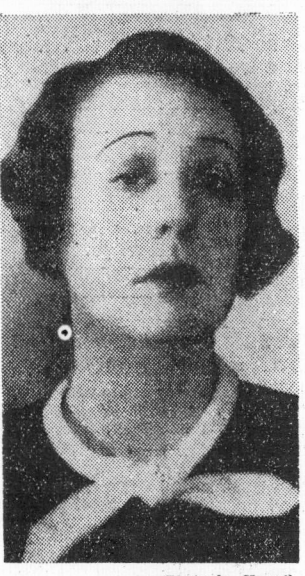

Photo by Hurrell.

Zöe Akins,
for best play.

matic treatment, from the extravagant glamour of "Déclassée," in which Ethel Barrymore starred in 1919, to the restraint of "The Old Maid," adapted from Edith Wharton's story of New York a hundred years ago.

Even more than is the case with most plays, the critical and public response to Miss Akins's work has been unpredictable. "Déclassée" was a popular success. "The Texas Nightingale," considered a worthy successor in 1922, failed. "The Furies," starring Laurette Taylor in 1928, was generally liked by the reviewers but not at the box office. On the other hand, "The Greeks Had a Word for It," which raised critical eyebrows in 1930, enjoyed a solid financial success.

Several years later, while in Hollywood as a scenario writer, Miss Akins wrote her next play, "The Old Maid." It continued the puzzling Akins tradition.

Because of an impending conflict in Broadway openings, Harry Moses, the producer, invited the New York critics to the out-of-town première in Baltimore on Saturday, Jan. 5. Those who saw it there wrote what the theatre calls "mixed notices." At least two New York papers waited until Jan. 7 to review the play at its opening here at the Empire Theatre, and even then sent "second-string" critics.

"The Old Maid" is the story of a bitter struggle through the years between two sisters for the love of an illegitimate child of one of them. Co-starring Judith Anderson and Helen Menken, and staged by Guthrie McClintic, the play has been known on Broadway as "a matinee show." That is, its principal appeal has been to feminine audiences. The Theatre Club, an organization of women theatregoers, presented its annual gold medal to Miss Akins on April 23 as the author of their favorite play of the season.

Miss Akins was born on Oct. 30, 1886, in Humansville, Mo. Her first plays to be produced on Broadway were "Papa" and "The Magical City," the latter in collaboration with Pierre Patelin. Her subsequent plays, several of them adaptations, have included:

"Foot-Loose," 1920 (adapted from her own earlier work, "Forget-Me-Not"); "Daddy's Gone-a-Hunting," 1921; "The Varying Shore," 1921; "Greatness," 1922; "A Royal Fandango," 1933; "The Moon-Flower," 1924; "First Love," 1926; "Thou Desperate Pilot" and "The Crown

Prince," 1927, and "The Love Duel," 1929. She is the author also of a number of poems and a novel, "Cake Upon the Waters."

Miss Akins was married in March, 1932, to the late Hugo Rumbold, British painter and theatrical designer.

1936

NOBEL PRIZE

NOBEL PRIZE IS WON BY EUGENE O'NEILL

By The Associated Press.

STOCKHOLM, Sweden, Nov. 12.— The Nobel Prize in Literature was awarded today to Eugene O'Neill, noted American dramatist.

Professor Carl David Anderson of the California Institute of Technology shared the prize for physics with Professor V. G. Hess of Innsbruck University, Austria.

Professor Peter Debye of the Kaiser Wilhelm Institute for Physics in Berlin, will receive the chemistry prize for his studies of the structure of the molecule.

Mr. O'Neill became the second American to win the literature prize. Sinclair Lewis, novelist, received it in 1930.

Mr. O'Neill will receive the prizes for 1935 and 1936, totaling about $45,000, as no award was made last year in literature.

Professor Anderson and Professor Hess will receive about $20,000 each.

The Nobel Foundation's managing board of directors, as is customary, did not cite any specific work by the winner of the literature prize.

Professor Anderson's award was granted for his discovery in 1933 of positrons—positive electrons—by the bombardment of atoms with a high voltage current.

Professor Hess's prize was for his research in cosmic radiation.

King Gustav will present the awards Dec. 10 at a ceremony in connection with the anniversary of the death of Alfred B. Nobel, Swedish discoverer of dynamite, who left the $9,000,000 fund from which the prizes are given.

Mr. O'Neill is considered by the Scandinavian public as the world's leading playwright. "Mourning Becomes Electra," will be staged in connection with the Nobel festival.

Special to THE NEW YORK TIMES.

SEATTLE, Wash., Nov. 12.—Eugene O'Neill awoke this morning in a house on a bluff overlooking fog-curtained Puget Sound to have his wife tell him that he was the winner of the Nobel Prize for letters.

The announcement was not a complete surprise. Mr. O'Neill said today that friends in New York had telegraphed rumors of the award.

"But I didn't think the award would go to an American so soon after Sinclair Lewis received it in 1930," he said, talking before a cheerfully blazing fireplace and

wearing a gray sweater and flannels. "I thought perhaps it might go to Dreiser. He deserves it."

The playwright is in Seattle getting the "feel" of the Northwest for background of the play which he is writing.

The drama, which he hopes to have finished for an October opening next year in New York, is written as eight plays in one. It is the history of an American family from 1806 to 1932 and the scene shifts from the East to the West coast, to the East again and ends in the Middle West. Five generations will be chronicled.

"It has a general theme, with a subordinate psychological theme, which deals in the recurrence of family traits under different conditions," he explained.

"I am trying to show the development of psychological characterization in relation to the changing times—what the railroads, what the panics did to change people's lives."

The playwright said if the first play of the series is produced in October, the next one will open in February.

"People will be seeing it for years," he said, "it will go on and on. And I hope, after all eight plays have been produced once, somebody will take a chance and run them off on successive nights. That will knock the audience cold and they'll never want to see another play."

Mr. O'Neil was notified formally that he was a Nobel Prize winner by the Swedish Consul in Seattle. But he said he would be unable to arrange his affairs in time to be in Stockholm for the presentation ceremony Dec. 10.

Message Sent to O'Neill

Formal announcement of the award of the Nobel Prize in letters was contained in a cable message from Stockholm received here yesterday by Richard Madden, play agent for Eugene O'Neill.

Mr. Madden forwarded the message to Mr. O'Neill in Seattle.

The only dramatist to receive the Pulitzer Prize three times, Mr. O'Neill won those awards for "Beyond the Horizon," "Anna Christie" and "Strange Interlude."

He was born forty-eight years ago at the Barrett House, Broadway and Forty-third Street. His father was James O'Neill, the actor, who starred for many years in "The Count of Monte Cristo." After a year in Princeton young O'Neill was suspended. He worked for a mail-order house for a year, and then went to sea, gaining the experience which he later used in his plays.

Later he was a newspaper reporter. His health failing, he was sent to a sanitarium, from which he brought back material for a play about tuberculosis. He began to write one-act plays, but found himself deficient in technique. Accordingly, he studied for a time with Professor Baker's famous "47 Workshop" class at Harvard. Then he went to Provincetown, where he wrote his early plays. They were produced by the Provincetown Players. The plays were then produced in the little theatres of Greenwich Village, and finally on Broadway.

This first Broadway production of a full-length drama was "Beyond the Horizon" in 1920. From that time on his reputation as one of the world's leading dramatists has grown steadily. His plays have been produced not only in this country, but also in London, Paris, Berlin, Moscow, Dublin, Vienna, Stockholm, Budapest, Tokyo, Melbourne and practically everywhere else that the theatre flourishes.

Shaw Pleased by Award

Wireless to THE NEW YORK TIMES.

LONDON, Nov. 12.—The award of the Nobel Prize to Eugene O'Neill came as a surprise to most theatregoers in London, who have never been enthusiastic over his work. Except in intellectual circles here

his dramas are not widely appreciated. Although not popular with the mass of the British people, who are inclined to prefer levity, Mr. O'Neill's plays generally were received favorably by critics but most of them had short runs.

The notable exception to this rule was "Anna Christie" which was a great success years ago.

In literary circles, however, the choice was praised. George Bernard Shaw was delighted when the news was conveyed to him by THE NEW YORK TIMES.

"An excellent decision," he said. "I always thought that this year's prize should go either to Upton Sinclair or O'Neill, so America would have received it in either case. Of course, I am very pleased. I don't remember whether any play writer has had the prize since I got it ten or eleven years ago."

In this, Mr. Shaw's memory lapsed, for Luigi Pirandello received it in 1934 and John Galsworthy in 1932.

J. B. Priestly said:

"I cannot count myself a great admirer or close student of O'Neill's work, but I am sincerely glad to learn that a man who has devoted himself with such deep seriousness to our English-speaking theatre has been awarded the prize. I think such an award may increase the seriousness and responsibility of our theatre."

PULITZER PRIZE

'IDIOT'S DELIGHT' A PULITZER WINNER

Veiled in secrecy to the latest possible moment, the annual announcement of the Pulitzer Prize awards in letters and journalism was made last night at the annual dinner of the alumni of the Columbia University School of Journalism, at the Hotel Commodore.

After Dr. Nicholas Murray Butler, president of Columbia, had read the citations of the winners to the eager audience, he handed to a waiting messenger boy telegrams apprising each winner of his selection. This year, for the first time, the winners had been kept completely in the dark until the public announcement.

As the best play of the current season the advisory board of the school, which recommended the winners, and the trustees of Columbia University, which confirmed their selections, chose "Idiot's Delight," the anti-war play by Robert E. Sherwood in which Lynn Fontanne and Alfred Lunt are now appearing.

The advisory board disclosed that it had lifted its restriction excluding previous drama winners from consideration both for the season 1935-36 and for succeeding seasons. This restriction had aroused wide discussion and was believed to be a factor in the formation of the New York Drama Critics Circle, which last month awarded its first annual prize to Maxwell Anderson for "Winterset." Mr. Anderson, who won in 1933 with "Both Your Houses," had been believed to be excluded by the board's restriction.

"Honey in the Horn," a first novel by H. L. Davis, former cow-

puncher, won the award as the best novel of the year. A story of life in Oregon, it had previously won the seventh annual $7,500 Harper prize novel contest.

Andrew C. McLaughlin, Professor Emeritus of History at the University of Chicago, won the history award with "A Constitutional History of the United States," which appeared last Spring.

Professor Ralph Barton Perry of Harvard University won the biographical prize for "The Thought and Character of William James." Robert Peter Tristram Coffin received the poetry prize for "Strange Holiness."

In journalism, Lauren D. Lyman of THE NEW YORK TIMES won the prize for distinguished reporting, for his exclusive story on the sailing of Colonel Charles A. Lindbergh and his family for England to take up their residence there.

The prize for the best foreign or Washington correspondence was awarded posthumously to Will Barber of The Chicago Tribune, who died of malarial fever in Addis Ababa while covering the Italo-Ethiopian War.

Felix Morley of The Washington Post and George B. Parker, editor-in-chief of the Scripps-Howard newspapers, divided the prize for the best editorial writing of the year.

The award annually made "for the most disinterested and meritorious public service rendered by an American newspaper during the year" went to The Cedar Rapids (Iowa) Gazette for "its crusade against corruption and misgovernment in the State of Iowa."

St. Paul Paper Is Named

Honorable mention in this division went to The St. Paul (Minn.) Daily News "for its campaign against corruption and misgovernment in St. Paul."

Four newspaper men received honorable mention in the field for distinguished correspondence. They were Webb Miller of The United Press, for his stories of the Italo-Ethiopian War; Ashmun Brown of The Providence Journal, for his Washington correspondence; Jay G. Hayden of The Detroit News, for a series of political articles written on a tour of the country, and James A. Mills of The Associated Press, for his story of the granting of an oil concession in Ethiopia to an American company.

Photographers Irk Butler

While Dr. Butler was reading the list of awards he became annoyed at the activities of news photographers, who were busy snapping pictures with the aid of flash bulbs from a point directly in front of the dais. He halted a moment and with a sweeping gesture in their direction declared:

"If they were awarding a prize for a nuisance, there it would go."

The photographers continued their activities and Dr. Butler, plainly showing his indignation, stopped again.

"Why don't you leave off bread and butter and learn manners," he said to them.

The audience, many members of which recalled the temporary blinding of Arturo Toscanini by a photographer's flash bulb at his farewell concert at Carnegie Hall last week, applauded Dr. Butler's rebuke of the picture-takers.

After the interruptions, Dr. Butler went on with the announcements of the awards. No award was made for the best example of a cartoonist's work published in an American newspaper during the year, the committee presumably feeling that none of the nominations before it were of sufficiently

high caliber to merit the prize.

Dr. Butler announced the three traveling scholarships in journalism, which carry stipends of $1,500 each to permit their holders to study in Europe for a year. They went to:

Sevellon Brown of Providence, R. I.
Helen Beal of Delaware, Ohio.
Louis H. Birnbaum of Cleveland.

The alternates selected were:
John A. McWethy of Aurora, Ill.
Philip D. Taylor of Bloomington, Ind.
Wirt McClintic Mitchell of Fayette, Mo.

Two scholarships in art and music, each worth $1,500 and providing for study abroad, also were awarded. That for music was won by Samuel Barber of New York City, and that for art by Sigmund Kozlow of Maspeth, Queens.

It was announced that at a meeting of the advisory board on Friday Kent Cooper and Julian Harris had been elected to four-year terms to succeed themselves.

Several Meetings Held

Before making its recommendations, the advisory board of the School of Journalism held several meetings over the week-end in Dr. Butler's office. The members of the board, all of whom were pledged to secrecy about their recommendations, are:

Dr. Butler, Kent Cooper of The Associated Press; Julian Harris, The Chattanooga Times; Harold S. Pollard, The New York World-Telegram; Arthur M. Howe, 205 Rugby Road, Brooklyn; Frank R. Kent, The Baltimore Sun; Robert Lathan, The Asheville (N. C.) Citizen and Times; Robert Lincoln O'Brien, United States Tariff Commission; Rollo Ogden, THE NEW YORK TIMES; Stuart H. Perry, The Adrian (Mich.) Daily Telegram; Marlen E. Pew of Editor and Publisher; Joseph Pulitzer, The St. Louis Post-Dispatch; Ralph Pulitzer, 450 East Fifty-second Street, New York, and Dean Carl W. Ackerman.

The drama jury which assisted the advisory board this year was reported to have consisted of Professor William Lyon Phelps of Yale, Mrs. Padraic Colum and a third person whose name was not learned. Elmer Rice announced in December that he had refused an invitation to serve on it.

Reporting Standard Revised

The advisory board has changed the terms of the prize for reporting, giving preference to "news stories prepared under the pressure of edition time, that redound to the credit of journalism."

The recommendations of the advisory board were laid before the trustees of Columbia University at a meeting in Dr. Butler's office at 4 P. M. yesterday. The trustees have always maintained a veto power over the awards, and it has been exercised on several occasions in the past.

Every possible precaution was taken against the premature publication of the names of the winners between the close of the trustees' meeting and the announcement by Dr. Butler at 9 o'clock. The grand ballroom of the Commodore, where nearly 400 persons had gathered for the dinner, buzzed with conjecture.

Hugh W. Robertson of the Westchester County Publishers, president of the Journalism Alumni, presided at the dinner.

The prize-winning playwright, novelist, historian, biographer, poet and reporter receive $1,000 each. Awards of $500 each went to the winners of the prizes for the best newspaper correspondence and the best editorial. The award for distinguished service by a newspaper carried with it a medal worth $500.

The prize for distinguished correspondence was awarded on the following basis:

"For distinguished service as a

foreign or Washington correspondent during the year, the test being clearness and terseness of style, preference being given to fair, judicious, well-balanced and well-informed interpretative writing, which shall make clear the significance of the subject covered in the correspondence, or which shall promote international understanding and appreciation."

Basis for Editorial Prize

The conditions under which the editorial prize was awarded are these:

"For distinguished editorial writing during the year, limited to the editorial page, the test of excellence being clearness of style, moral purpose, sound reasoning and power to influence public opinion in what the writer conceives to be the right direction, due account being taken of the whole volume of the writer's editorial work during the year."

Mr. Lyman's selection for the reporting prize was made in accordance with the following stipulations:

"For a distinguished example of a reporter's work during the year, the test being strict accuracy, terseness, the preference being given to news stories prepared under the pressure of edition time, that redound to the credit of the profession of journalism."

After Dr. Butler had finished, Dean Ackerman spoke briefly of the progress that had been made by the School of Journalism, predicting that all members of the current graduating class would be employed by Summer. He paid a tribute to Professor Roscoe C. E. Brown, who is retiring at the end of the current academic year. The audience rose and applauded Professor Brown.

Laurence H. Sloan of the class of 1913 was elected president of the Alumni Association to succeed Mr. Robertson.

NEW YORK DRAMA CRITICS CIRCLE AWARDS

Anderson's Poetic Play Voted Best of Season by Newly Organized Circle.

COMPANY IS NOW ON TOUR

Plaque Will Be Presented in Washington—'Idiot's Delight' Said to Be Runner-Up.

"Winterset," Maxwell Anderson's poetic play—the theme of which had been suggested by the Sacco-Vanzetti case—won yesterday the first annual prize awarded by the New York Drama Critics Circle.

Of the seventeen newspaper and magazine writers entitled to choose the season's best drama fourteen ultimately agreed on the winner's superior merit. Several ballots were taken before the other finalist—said to have been "Idiot's Delight," by Robert E. Sherwood—became the semi-official runner-up.

The prize is a silver plaque depicting a scene of the old John Street Theatre, designed by Henry Varnum Poor. It will be given formally to Mr. Anderson on the stage of the National Theatre in Washington a week from tonight. "Winterset," now in Philadelphia on a tour, moves to the capital on

Photo by Vandamm Studios.
WINS CRITICS AWARD
Maxwell Anderson

Monday. Members of the Circle, Guthrie McClintic, the play's director and producer, and others will go down to take part in the ceremony.

The award carries the following citation:

"The Circle's decision is based on the conviction that in 'Winterset' the author accomplished the notably difficult task of interpreting a valid and challenging contemporary theme dealing with the pursuit of human justice in terms of unusual poetic force, realizing a drama of rich meaning and combining high literary distinction with compelling theatrical effect.

Points to "Courage and Wisdom"

"While this award is primarily to the play and its author, the Circle feels that, since the production of 'Winterset' so admirably projected Mr. Anderson's conception, special appreciation must also be expressed to Guthrie McClintic, the producer and director; to Jo Mielziner, the designer, and to the members of the cast. Courage and wisdom were clearly required in both the writing and presenting of 'Winterset'—and the Circle thinks it is a proof of the vitality and dignity of the New York theatre that his play was produced and so widely appreciated."

Mr. Anderson's capture of the critics' prize completes a cycle that began two years ago. At that time the drama judges for the Pulitzer Prize committee agreed unanimously that Mr. Anderson's "Mary of Scotland" had been the season's best offering. The general Pulitzer committee thereupon over-ruled its own judges and gave the award to "Men in White."

Last year, Mr. Anderson's "Valley Forge" was prominently mentioned for the season's prize, which ultimately went to "The Old Maid." The city's drama critics, discouraged by the last two awards, then decided to get together and give their own prize.

The meeting at which "Winterset" was chosen took place at the Algonquin Hotel. At first, five plays were under discussion—"Winterset"; "Idiot's Delight," which had opened just the evening before; "Dead End," by Sidney Kingsley; "First Lady," by Katharine Dayton and George S. Kaufman, and "End of Summer," by S. N. Behrman. One by one, advocates of other plays switched their votes until Mr. Anderson's had fourteen. It had been agreed in advance that thirteen provided the necessary majority; anything less than that would bring no decision.

Line-Up of the Critics.

Of the seventeen, the following voted for "Winterset": Kelcey Allen, Brooks Atkinson, Robert Benchley, Whitney Bolton, John Mason Brown, Rowland Field, Gilbert Gabriel, Joseph Wood Krutch, Richard Lockridge, Burns Mantle, George Jean Nathan, Arthur Pollock, Walter Winchell and Stark Young. The following voted for other plays: John Anderson, Percy Hammond and Robert Garland. Under the by-laws of the Circle, the dissenters are not prohibited from writing minority opinions.

Mr. Anderson entered the theatre by way of school teaching and newspaper work. His first play was "The White Desert," in 1923. After that came "The Feud," the famous "What Price Glory?" which he wrote with Laurence Stallings; "Outside Looking In," "First Flight" and "The Buccaneer," both with Mr. Stallings; "Forfeits," "Saturday's Children," "Gods of the Lightning" (this also was about the Sacco-Vanzetti case, and was written in collaboration with Harold Hickerson); "Gypsy," "Elizabeth the Queen," "Night Over Taos," "Both Your Houses" (which won the Pulitzer Prize in 1923), "Mary of Scotland," "Valley Forge" and "Winterset."

1937

PULITZER PRIZE

The Pulitzer Prizes in letters and journalism for the current year were announced last night by Dr. Nicholas Murray Butler, president of Columbia University, at the annual dinner of the alumni of the School of Journalism. About 250 persons attended the dinner, but because of the secrecy surrounding the awards in recent years only one of the prize winners was present.

The $1,000 award for the "most distinguished" novel of the last year went to Margaret Mitchell, author of "Gone With the Wind," a best seller published by the Macmillan Company. The prize for the most distinguished play was awarded to George S. Kaufman and Moss Hart, co-authors of "You Can't Take It With You," now playing at the Booth Theatre. Mr. Kaufman won the prize once before, for "Of Thee I Sing," a political satire with music.

For the most distinguished book on the history of the United States, the committee selected the "Flowering of New England," written by Van Wyck Brooks and published by E. P. Dutton & Co., for the $1,000 prize. Allan Nevins's "Hamilton Fish, the Inner History of the Grant Administration," published by Dodd, Mead & Co., was adjudged the most distinguished biography "teaching patriotic and unselfish services to the people."

It was the second time that Mr. Nevins, a Professor of History at Columbia, had been honored with a Pulitzer Prize for his work in biography, his "Grover Cleveland" having won the award in 1933. Robert Frost received the poetry award for the third time in his career, with "A Further Range," published by Henry Holt & Co.

Anne O'Hare McCormick, a member of the editorial staff of THE NEW YORK TIMES, received the $500

prize for the most distinguished foreign correspondence for her "dispatches and feature articles from Europe in 1936." The terms covering this award read:

"For distinguished services as a foreign or Washington correspondent during the year, the test being clearness and terseness of style, preference being given to fair, judicious, well-balanced and well-informed interpretive writing, which shall make clear the significance of the subject covered in the correspondence or which shall promote international understanding and appreciation."

It was the first time that a woman received a major Pulitzer Prize in journalism.

Five reporters who covered the tercentenary celebration of Harvard University shared the $1,000 award for the most distinguished example of a reporter's work, "the test being strict accuracy, terseness, the preference being given to stories prepared under the pressure of edition time, that redound to the credit of journalism." The five reporters who won this prize were:

John J. O'Neill of The New York Herald Tribune, William L. Laurence of THE NEW YORK TIMES, Howard W. Blakeslee of The Associated Press, Gobind Behari Lal of Universal Service and David Dietz of the Scripps-Howard newspapers.

The St. Louis Post-Dispatch received the $500 gold medal for "the most disinterested and meritorious public service" rendered by an American newspaper during the year for its exposure of "wholesale fraudulent registration in St. Louis." The citation accompanying the award read:

"By a coordinated news, editorial and cartoon campaign, this newspaper succeeded in invalidating upward of 40,000 fraudulent ballots in November and brought about the appointment of a new election board."

Other Newspapers Named

Four other newspapers received honorable mention for public service. The citations as read by Dr. Butler follow:

"To The Daily News of New York City, for its public health campaign covering venereal diseases and prophylaxis.

"To The Providence Journal and Evening Bulletin, Rhode Island, for a research study of direct and indirect taxes, based upon one year's detailed expenditures of three families of working people.

"To The Cleveland Press, Cleveland, for its investigation and exposé by news, editorials and cartoons of a cemetery racket.

"To The Atlanta Journal, Atlanta, Ga., for its campaign by news, editorials and radio to end corruption and inefficiency in the Police Department."

John W. Owens, editor of The Sun, Baltimore, received the $500 award for the most distinguished editorial writing of the year. The prize was given for his year's work but it was understood that his editorial, "The Opposition," which appeared after the election, carried the most weight. Honorable mention was given to W. W. Waymack, associated editor of The Des Moines Register and Tribune of Des Moines, Iowa. Mr. Owens was the only one of the prize winners who attended the dinner.

C. D. Batchelor of The New York Daily News received the $500 prize for the most distinguished example of the cartoonist's art published during the year. The prize-winning cartoon was entitled "Come on In, I'll Treat You Right. I Used to Know Your Daddy." It depicted a disheveled harridan in a kimono at the foot of a staircase talking to a youth. Upon her breast was inscribed the word "War." On the young man's back were the words, "Any European Youth."

John Francis Knott of The Dal-

Van Damm Studio Photo.

The final scene of the prize-winning play, "You Can't Take It With You"

White Studio Photo.

George S. Kaufman (left) and Moss Hart, co-authors of "You Can't Take It With You."

las News and Quincy Scott of The Portland Oregonian received honorable mention for cartoons published in their newspapers during the year.

Three traveling scholarships worth $1,500 each were awarded to Richard T. Baker of Cedar Falls, Iowa; Fred J. Pannwitt of Nokomis, Ill., and Robert W. Root of Ames, Iowa. They were selected from among the students of the school of journalism as completing the course with the "highest honor" and deemed "most deserving," to enable them to spend a year abroad to "study the social, political and moral conditions of the people and the character and principles of the foreign press."

The three graduates chosen as alternates were Jack Steele of Rockaway, N. J.; Elizabeth Ryan of South Hadley, Mass., and Vance Packard of State College, Pennsylvania.

A $1,500 scholarship in music was awarded to Ross Lee Finney of Smith College, Northampton, Mass., and a scholarship of equal value in art was awarded to David P. Swasey of 19 East Fifty-ninth Street.

At a meeting of the trustees of Columbia in the afternoon before the dinner, William Allen White, publisher of The Emporia Gazette, Emporia, Kan., and Walter Lippmann, columnist of The New York Herald Tribune, were elected to the Pulitzer Prize advisory committee. They were chosen to fill the vacancies on the board caused by the death of Rollo Ogden, editor of The New York Times, and Marlen E. Pew, editor of Editor and Publisher.

Members of the advisory board which selected this year's winners with the approval of the trustees of Columbia University were:

Dr. Butler, Julian L. Harris, editor of The Chattanooga Times; Harold S. Pollard, editorial writer for The New York World-Telegram; Arthur M. Howe, editor emeritus of The Brooklyn Eagle; Frank R. Kent, vice president of the Sun Papers, Baltimore; Robert Lathan, editor of The Asheville (N. C.) Citizen and Times; Robert Lincoln O'Brien, chairman of the United States Tariff Commission; Stuart H. Perry, publisher of The Adrian (Mich.) Daily Telegram; Joseph Pulitzer, publisher of The St. Louis Post-Dispatch; Ralph Pulitzer, life representative of the Pulitzer estate, and Kent Cooper, general manager of The Associated Press.

None of the winners was advised in advance of his selection. Simultaneously with Dr. Butler's announcement at the dinner, however, telegrams of notification were sent to each of them.

Dr. Butler interrupted the dinner as the fish course was being served to make the announcement for which the journalistic and literary world had been waiting.

He was introduced by Dean Carl W. Ackerman of the School of Journalism, who was toastmaster. Dr. Butler noted that this year marked the twentieth year in which the prize awards had been announced by the president of Columbia University.

George S. Kaufman, Moss Hart

George S. Kaufman, the modern American theatre's best known collaborator, won a Pulitzer Prize once before. With Morrie Ryskind, he was the author of the book for "Of Thee I Sing," which in 1931 satirized politics and has since become almost a part of the country's folklore.

"You Can't Take It With You" is Moss Hart's first experience of the prize, although not his first as a collaborator with Mr. Kaufman. Together they wrote "Once in a Lifetime," in 1930, and "Merrily We Roll Along," in 1934. At the moment they are on the Coast working on a musical show for the Fall.

Mr. Kaufman was born in Pittsburgh and in his earlier career worked on newspapers in Washington and New York, at one time being the drama editor of The New York Times. His first success, written with Marc Connelly, was "Dulcy," in 1921. Since that year he has had at least one new show on Broadway every year, his collaborators including Mr. Connelly, Mr. Ryskind, Ring Lardner, Edna Ferber, Alexander Woollcott and others.

The list of his plays is a history of theatrical success, some of the names being "To the Ladies," "Merton of the Movies," "Beggar on Horseback," "Animal Crackers," "June Moon," "Minick," "The Royal Family," "Dinner at Eight," "The Cocoanuts," "Strike Up the Band," "Once in a Lifetime," "The Bandwagon," "Of Thee I Sing," "Let 'Em Eat Cake," "Merrily We Roll Along," "First Lady" and this year's "Stage Door."

Mr. Kaufman also is well known as a director.

Mr. Hart is a New Yorker, who entered the theatre as a stenographer in the office of Augustus Pitou. His first success was the Kaufman collaboration, "Once in a Lifetime." Since then he has written the books for "Face the Music," "As Thousands Cheer" and "Jubilee," as well as adapting the book for "The Great Waltz." Mr. Hart is 32 years old and Mr. Kaufman is 48.

In giving its award to "You Can't Take it With You," the committee has followed the public—the play has been the most popular one of the season. Opening on Dec. 14 of last year, to date it has had not one empty seat, and at each performance there usually are between ten and thirty persons standing.

The play is the story of a mad family living up near the seat of the prize—Columbia University. The grandfather, a part played by Henry Travers, attends college commencements and collects snakes; the father makes fireworks in the cellar; the mother writes plays because some years before a typewriter was delivered to the house by mistake; the children all have their hobbies and ride them through the three acts.

Two years ago, the New York drama reviewers, dissatisfied with the Pulitzer awards, formed their own circle to pick the "best play" of the year. Last season, their first, they chose Maxwell Anderson's "Winterset," while the Pulitzer Prize went to Robert E. Sherwood's "Idiot's Delight." This year the critics chose "High Tor," also by Mr. Anderson.

NEW YORK DRAMA CRITICS CIRCLE AWARDS

Maxwell Anderson for Second Time Hailed as Author of Best Play of Year

"High Tor," Maxwell Anderson's fantasy of the Hudson Highlands, is "the best American play of the 1936-37 season," in the opinion of a majority of the New York Drama Critics Circle, it was announced yesterday. Meeting on Friday at

DRAMA CRITICS CIRCLE AWARD FOR "BEST AMERICAN PLAY"

Vandamm Studio Photo.

The silver plaque, designed by Henry Varnum Poor and representing a scene from the John Street Theatre of 1790, which goes to Maxwell Anderson. Since the prize was established in 1936 Mr. Anderson has made a clean sweep of it. Last year he won it for "Winterset"; this year for "High Tor."

the Hotel Algonquin, the newspaper and magazine reviewers reached that decision after eleven ballots, the final vote reading "High Tor," fourteen; "Johnny Johnson," three; "Daughters of Atreus," one.

It is the critics' second annual award—the prize is a silver plaque by Henry Varnum Poor, depicting a scene from the old John Street Theatre—and it is the second time that Mr. Anderson has won it. His "Winterset" was last year's victor.

After a dinner on Thursday night at the Algonquin, Mr. Anderson will receive his prize at the ceremonies to be broadcast from 8 P. M. to 8:30 over WJZ and the other stations of the Blue network. Guthrie McClintic, producer and director of the play, also will be a guest, and the program will include a scene from "High Tor" and speeches by several of the critics.

Play Praised for Fantasy

The circle's award carries the following citation:

"The Drama Critics Circle awards its annual prize for 1936-37 to Maxwell Anderson's fantasy, 'High Tor.' In its decision the circle celebrates the advent of the first distinguished fantasy by an American in many years. Imaginative and as comic as it is poetic in both spirit and expression, 'High Tor' is a singular accomplishment, giving rare grace to this theatrical season in New York. For a second successive year the circle felicitates both Mr. Anderson and his perceptive producer, Guthrie McClintic."

At his home in New City yesterday Mr. Anderson deferred until Thursday any comment on the award other than to remark, "I'm glad to get it."

Mr. McClintic, who also produced "Winterset," said happily:

"Naturally, I'm delighted. I think it's a very good choice. I agree with the critics, and I congratulate them."

Busiest of American playwrights of the day, Mr. Anderson is represented by two other productions on Broadway, "The Wingless Victory," at the Empire and "The Masque of Kings," at the Shubert.

Mountain Is Setting

"High Tor" opened on Jan. 9 at the Martin Beck, where it is playing now with Burgess Meredith and Peggy Ashcroft in the featured rôles. Like Mr. Anderson's other recent plays it is in blank verse, and the inspiration for it was virtually at the backdoor of his country home. Its setting is the mountain, High Tor, towering above the Hudson River just below Haverstraw, and for at least part of its plot it returns to the legends of the days of Henry Hudson.

Members of the circle voting for "High Tor" were: Kelcey Allen, Women's Wear; Brooks Atkinson, THE NEW YORK TIMES; Robert Benchley, The New Yorker; Whitney Bolton, The Morning Telegraph and The Literary Digest; John Mason Brown, The Evening Post; Gilbert Gabriel, The American; Douglas Gilbert, The World-Telegram; Mrs. Edith J. R. Isaacs, Theatre Arts Monthly; Joseph Wood Krutch, The Nation; Richard Lockridge, The Sun; Burns Mantle, The News; Arthur Pollock, The Brooklyn Eagle; Ruth Sedgwick, Stage Magazine, and Richard Watts Jr., The Herald Tribune.

Still dissenting at the final ballot were John Anderson, The Evening Journal; Stark Young, The New Republic; John W. Gassner, New Theatre and Film Magazine, and George Jean Nathan, Esquire and The Saturday Review of Literature. Of this quartet the first three voted for Paul Green's "Johnny Johnson," while Mr. Nathan favored "Daughters of Atreus," by Robert Turney. Both plays had short runs on Broadway.

Plays mentioned in the early ballots but later dropped were "You Can't Take It With You," "Having Wonderful Time," "Marching Song," "Yes, My Darling Daughter," "The Masque of Kings" and "The Wingless Victory."

Vandamm Studio Photo.
Maxwell Anderson

1938

PULITZER PRIZE

'OUR TOWN' WINS PULITZER AWARD

The year's awards of the Pulitzer Prizes in letters and journalism were announced last night by Dr. Nicholas Murray Butler, president of Columbia University, at the annual dinner of the alumni of the Graduate School of Journalism, which was held at the Columbia Men's Faculty Club.

Thornton Wilder's drama "Our Town," now playing at the Morosco Theatre, won the prize of $1,000 "for the original American play, performed in New York, which shall represent in marked fashion the educational value and power of the stage, preferably dealing with American life."

The prize of the same amount for "a distinguished novel published during the year by an American author, preferably dealing with American life," went to "The Late George Apley," by John Phillips Marquand, published by Little, Brown & Co. of Boston.

For "a distinguished book of the year upon the history of the United States" the judges awarded a prize of $1,000 to "The Road to Reunion, 1865-1900," by Professor Paul Herman Buck of Harvard University. This book, also published by Little, Brown, deals with the reconciliation of the North and the South after the Civil War.

The prize for American biography was divided between Odell Shepard for his "Pedlar's Progress: The Life of Bronson Alcott," published by Little, Brown, and Marquis James for his two-volume biography of Andrew Jackson, of which Volume I, "The Border Captain," was published previously, and Volume II, "Portrait of a President," was published last year by the Bobbs Merrill Company of Indianapolis.

The terms of this award provide that it shall go to "a distinguished American biography teaching patriotic and unselfish services to the people, illustrated by an eminent example, excluding, as too obvious, the names of George Washington and Abraham Lincoln."

Marya Zaturenska won the prize of $1,000 for "a distinguished volume of verse published during the year by an American author" for her "Cold Morning Sky," published by the Macmillan Company of New York.

In the field of journalism, Arthur Krock, Washington correspondent of THE NEW YORK TIMES, won the prize of $500 "for distinguished service as a foreign or Washington correspondent during the year." In announcing the award, Dr. Butler said that it had been made to Mr. Krock "for his exclusive, authorized interview with the President of the United States on Feb. 27, 1938."

Pittsburgh Reporter a Winner

Raymond Sprigle of The Pittsburgh Post-Gazette won the prize of $1,000 for the best reporting of the year, by "his series of articles, supported by photostats of the essential documents, exposing the one-time membership of Mr. Justice Hugo L. Black in the Ku Klux Klan."

Vaughn Shoemaker of The Chicago Daily News won an award of $500 "for distinguished service as a cartoonist, as exemplified by his cartoon 'The Road Back,' published Nov. 11, 1937." This cartoon pictured a soldier retracing his steps toward another war, while a figure of "The World" exclaimed with astonishment, "You're going the wrong way!"

The award of $500 for distinguished editorial writing was made to W. W. Waymack, associate editor of The Des Moines (Iowa) Register and Tribune. The award was

made in recognition of the high standard of editorial writing maintained through the year by Mr. Waymack, and no one of his editorials was singled out by the judges for specific mention.

The Bismarck (N. D.) Tribune won the gold medal costing $500 awarded annually "for the most disinterested and meritorius public service rendered by an American newspaper during the year," for a series of news reports and editorials entitled "Self-Help in the Dust Bowl."

A special public service prize, which took the form of a bronze plaque, was awarded to The Edmonton (Alberta) Journal "for its leadership in defense of the freedom of the press" during a controversy with the Social Credit provincial government. Engraved certificates were voted to each of the six daily and ninety weekly papers in the province which joined in the fight.

Three Are Previous Winners

Mr. Wilder, Mr. James and Mr. Krock had each won a Pulitzer Prize previously, while Mr. Waymack had received honorable mention only last year in editorial writing. Mr. Wilder won the novel prize for 1928 with "The Bridge of San Luis Rey"; Mr. James received the 1930 biography prize for "The Raven," a biography of Sam Houston, and Mr. Krock won the award for the best Washington or foreign correspondence in 1934.

The awards were formally voted by the trustees of Columbia University at a meeting late yesterday afternoon. Unlike the last few years, no attempt was made to preserve secrecy about the winners until the actual announcement was made by Dr. Butler at the dinner.

The trustees acted on the recommendation of the Advisory Board of the Graduate School of Journalism, the members of which, in addition to Dr. Butler, are Dean Carl W. Ackerman of the School of Journalism, Kent Cooper of The Associated Press, Julian LaRose Harris of The Chattanooga Times, Chattanooga, Tenn.; Arthur M. Howe, editor-in-chief emeritus of The Brooklyn Daily Eagle, Frank R. Kent of The Baltimore Sun, Robert Lincoln O'Brien, chairman of the United States Tariff Commission; Stuart H. Perry of The Adrian (Mich.) Telegram, Harold Stanley Pollard of The New York World-Telegram, Joseph Pulitzer, publisher of The St. Louis Post-Dispatch, Ralph Pulitzer of New York and William Allen White of The Emporia (Kan.) Gazette.

Student Winners Named

Dr. Butler also announced at the dinner the award of three traveling scholarships of $1,500 each to graduates of the School of Journalism to permit them to spend a year in study abroad. Those selected, on nomination of the teaching staff of the school, were Robert Weston Martin of Pasco, Wash.; Elizabeth E. Hewit of Spokane, Wash., and Dana A. Schmidt of Los Angeles. Jane Davis of Minneapolis, Robert D. McMillen of Hopewell, N. J., and William W. Cook of Detroit were named alternates.

The scholarship of $1,500 usually awarded to "the student of music in America who may be deemed the most talented and deserving" for study in Europe was not awarded this year.

Norman Thomas of Portland, Me., won a scholarship of $1,500 awarded annually to an art student certified as the most promising and deserving by the National Academy of Design, with which the Society of American Artists has been merged.

The announcement of awards by Dr. Butler, acknowledgments by a number of the prize winners, and two excerpts from "Our Town" by members of its cast were broadcast over WEAF and the red network of

Times Wide World from Vandamm

A scene from "Our Town," by Thornton Wilder. Left to right: Martha Scott, John Craven and Frank Craven.

the National Broadcasting Company. Dean Ackerman introduced the prize winners.

"Our Town" was the runner-up to John Steinbeck's "Of Mice and Men" for this year's award by the New York Drama Critics Circle. The Steinbeck play received twelve votes and Mr. Wilder's four. The Circle, composed of active newspaper and magazine reviewers, was founded three years ago in part as a protest against the type of play that had been winning the Pulitzer prize.

Recalls Drought Conditions

The statement of the university announcing the award of the medal for public service to The Bismarck Tribune recalled "the dismal and discouraging conditions" that have prevailed in North Dakota as the result of drought and soil exhaustion.

"Under the leadership of The Tribune a State-wide effort has been made to restore the confidence of a people who had become apathetic; to spread the doctrine of self-help and common sense in a land where grasping for political panaceas has been an inevitable result of the devastation which has affected both the land and the people," it said.

"The Tribune by reporting the private activities and experiences of farmers and by editorial guidance and encouragement succeeded in developing State-wide interest in self-help projects.

"The Tribune pioneered and fought for a detailed program of agricultural self-help, requiring a sharp change in the outlook and methods which characterized the State's two preceding generations.

"This is an outstanding example of newspaper leadership and public service which is possible only in a country where the press is free from official control and not dependent upon governmental patronage or financial subsidies."

The award to The Edmonton Journal was the first ever made to

a newspaper outside the United States. The announcement pointed out that there was no constitutional guarantee of the freedom of the press in Canada, but that until the Social Credit government took office in Alberta this right had been assumed.

"The present nomination revolved about the Alberta Press Act of 1937, which would have abolished freedom of the press in the Province," the university's statement said.

"Under the leadership of John M. Imrie of The Edmonton Journal, largest Albertan daily, the six dailies and ninety weeklies in the Province were organized against the act. Their efforts led provincial government to modify it, although in amended form it still abolished press freedom as we know it.

"Their campaign led to widespread opposition to the act, not only in Alberta but in all Canada. The Lieutenant Governor of Alberta referred the act to the Dominion government, whose Supreme Court declared it unconstitutional on March 4, 1938. The act will be reviewed again this Summer by the Judicial Committee of the Privy Council in London, highest tribunal in the British Empire."

NEW YORK DRAMA CRITICS CIRCLE AWARDS

'OF MICE AND MEN' WINS CRITICS' PRIZE

The New York Drama Critics Circle, the association of newspaper and magazine play reviewers, desig-

nated John Steinbeck's "Of Mice and Men" yesterday as the best American play of the current season. At the same time Paul Vincent Carroll's "Shadow and Substance" won a citation as the best theatrical importation of the year. Both plays are running on Broadway.

Mr. Steinbeck, who adapted the play from his own novel of the same name, will receive a plaque designed for the Circle by Henry Varnum Poor. There have been two previous awards, both to Maxwell Anderson for his "Winterset" and "High Tor." The citation for a distinguished foreign play is being given this year for the first time. The presentations will be made at a dinner Sunday night at the Hotel Algonquin, where yesterday's meeting also took place.

Four Ballots Required

"Of Mice and Men" won its citation on the fourth ballot, with twelve critics voting for it and four dissenting in behalf of Thornton Wilder's "Our Town." "Shadow and Substance" won on the first ballot and by unanimous vote. The citation in behalf of "Of Mice and Men" reads:

"For its direct force and perception in handling a theme genuinely rooted in American life; for its bite into the strict quality of its material; for its refusal to make this study of tragical loneliness and frustration either cheap or sensational, and finally for its simple, intense and steadily rising effect on the stage."

To make the award, it was necessary for twelve of the Circle's members to agree on a play. The dozen who decided on "Of Mice and Men" were Robert Benchley (represented by proxy), Richard Watts Jr., George Jean Nathan, Stark Young, Burns Mantle, John Anderson, John W. Gassner, Mrs. Edith Isaacs, Sidney Whipple, Arthur Pollock, Kelcey Allen and Richard Lockridge. The four who voted for "Our Town" were Joseph Wood Krutch (proxy), John Mason Brown, Mrs. Ruth Sedgwick and Brooks Atkinson.

On the first ballot the voting was "Of Mice and Men," 9; "Our Town," 4; "Golden Boy," "The Cradle Will Rock" and "Prologue to Glory," 1 each. The second ballot showed "Of Mice and Men," 9; "Our Town," 5; "Golden Boy" and "The Cradle Will Rock," 1 each. The third ballot: "Of Mice and Men," 11; "Our Town," 5. Members of the circle who did not vote because they had not seen enough plays, were Whitney Bolton and Walter Winchell.

Winning Play Opened Nov. 23

The winning play opened at the Music Box Theatre on Nov. 23. Sam H. Harris is the producer; George S. Kaufman the director. The latter is reported to have given Mr. Steinbeck a number of suggestions for his dramatization. In the cast are Wallace Ford, Broderick Crawford, John F. Hamilton and Claire Luce, with Mr. Ford playing the role of George and Mr. Crawford that of the ponderous, slow-witted Lennie. Mr. Steinbeck never has seen his play, although Mrs. Steinbeck came to New York some time ago to attend a performance.

"Shadow and Substance" opened at the John Golden Theatre on Jan. 26, with Sir Cedric Hardwicke, Julie Haydon, Sara Allgood and Lloyd Gough in the chief roles. It is produced by Eddie Dowling and directed by Peter Godfrey. Mr. Carroll is now in this country on a visit.

Guests at the dinner on Sunday will be Mr. Steinbeck—if he comes East, or his representative, if he does not—Mr. Harris, Mr. Kaufman, Mr. Carroll and Mr. Dowling. George Jean Nathan, president of the Circle, will make the awards

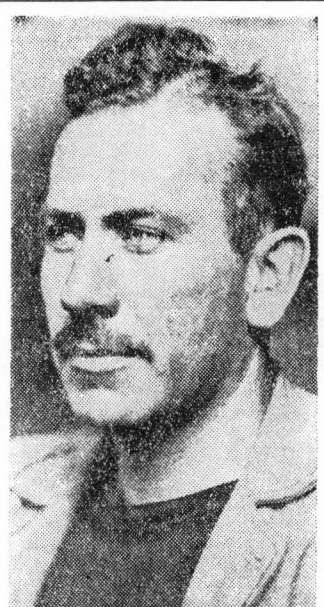

HIS DRAMA WINS AWARD
John Steinbeck

and the proceedings, along with a scene or so from the winning American play, will be broadcast.

The Critics Circle was formed three years ago to protest some of the Pulitzer Prize awards.

1939

PULITZER PRIZE

LINCOLN PLAY WINS A PULITZER AWARD

Sherwood Is Honored Again— Mrs. Rawlings, Van Doren and Mott Also Named

The annual award of the prizes in letters and journalism established under the will of Joseph Pulitzer was announced yesterday afternoon by the trustees of Columbia University after they had acted on the recommendations of the advisory board of the Graduate School of Journalism.

Robert E. Sherwood's play, "Abe Lincoln in Illinois," now playing at the Plymouth Theatre, won the prize of $1,000 awarded "for the original American play, performed in New York, which shall represent in marked fashion the educational value and power of the stage, preferably dealing with American life."

The prize of $1,000 for "a distinguished novel published during the year by an American author, preferably dealing with American life," was awarded to "The Yearling" by Marjorie Kinnan Rawlings, published by Charles Scribner's Sons.

For "a distinguished book of the year upon the history of the United States," a prize of $1,000 was

awarded to "A History of American Magazines" by Frank Luther Mott, published by the Harvard University Press.

Van Doren's Book a Winner

Carl Van Doren's widely acclaimed biography, "Benjamin Franklin," won the prize of $1,000 for "a distinguished American biography teaching patriotic and unselfish services to the people, illustrated by an eminent example, excluding, as too obvious, the names of George Washington and Abraham Lincoln." It was published by the Viking Press, Inc.

The prize of $1,000 for "a distinguished volume of verse published during the year by an American author" went to "Selected Poems," by John Gould Fletcher, published by Farrar & Rinehart, Inc.

Louis P. Lochner, correspondent of The Associated Press in Berlin, won the prize of $500 awarded for "distinguished service as a foreign or Washington correspondent during the year, the test being clearness and terseness of style, preference being given to fair, judicious, well-balanced and well-informed interpretative writing which shall make clear the significance of the subject covered in the correspondence or which shall promote international understanding and appreciation."

A gold medal costing $500 was awarded to The Miami (Fla.) Daily News "for the most disinterested and meritorious public service rendered by an American newspaper during the year." It was in recognition of a successful campaign for the ousting of a majority of the Miami City Commissioners.

Honorable mention in the field of public service was awarded to The Waterbury (Conn.) Republican and American for its exposure of municipal graft in that city.

Oregon Editorial Chosen

R. G. Callvert of The Portland (Ore.) Oregonian won the prize of $500 for editorial writing for his work during the year, as exemplified by his editorial "My Country 'Tis of Thee . . . ." published Oct. 2.

The terms of this prize provide that it shall be awarded for "distinguished editorial writing during the year limited to the editorial page, the test of excellence being clearness of style, moral purpose, sound reasoning and power to influence public opinion in what the writer conceives to be the right direction, due account being taken of the whole volume of the writer's editorial work during the year."

Thomas L. Stokes of the Scripps-Howard Newspaper Alliance won the prize of $1,000 for "a distinguished example of a reporter's work during the year, the test being strict accuracy, terseness, the preference being given to news stories prepared under the pressure of edition time that redound to the credit of the profession of journalism." The announcement specified that the prize was given to Mr. Stokes for his investigation of WPA conditions in Kentucky.

Charles George Werner of The Daily Oklahoman, Oklahoma City, received an award of $500 for his cartoon, "Nomination for 1938," published last Oct. 6. It portrayed a grave marked by a headstone bearing the inscription "Grave of Czecho-Slovakia, 1919-1938." On the grave rested the Nobel Peace Prize.

This prize is awarded for "a distinguished example of a cartoonist's

work published in an American newspaper during the year, the determining qualities being that the cartoon shall embody an idea made clearly apparent, shall show good drawing and striking pictorial effect, and shall be intended to be helpful to some commendable cause of public importance, due account being taken of the whole volume of the artist's newspaper work during the year."

Usual Dinner Omitted

Departing from the practice of the last few years, when the awards were announced at the annual dinner of alumni of the Graduate School of Journalism, they were made public without ceremony after the meeting of the trustees of Columbia. The dinner will not be held this year.

The trustees made the awards on the recommendation of the Advisory Board of the School of Journalism, which consists of the following:

Dr. Nicholas Murray Butler, president of Columbia; Robert Lincoln O'Brien, former publisher of The Boston Herald; Ralph Pulitzer, Joseph Pulitzer, publisher of The St. Louis Post-Dispatch; Arthur M. Howe, editor emeritus of The Brooklyn Eagle; Julian LaRose Harris, executive editor of The Chattanooga Times; William Allen White, editor of The Emporia Gazette; Kent Cooper, general manager of The Associated Press; Stuart H. Perry, publisher of The Adrian (Mich.) Telegram; Harold Stanley Pollard, chief editorial writer of The New York World-Telegram; Frank R. Kent, columnist of The Baltimore Sun; Sevellon Brown, editor of The Providence Journal, and Walter M. Harrison, managing editor of The Daily Oklahoman.

The trustees also announced the award of three traveling scholarships with a value of $1,500 each to graduates of the School of Journalism to enable them to spend a year abroad "to study the social, political and moral conditions of the people and the character and principles of the foreign press."

Bernard S. Redmont of New York City, Patricia Bradford Rey of Elmhurst, Queens, and John Earnshaw Leard of West Roxbury, Mass., received the scholarships on nomination of the faculty of the School of Journalism. James Dean Allen of New York City, Margaret E. Miller of San Diego, Calif., and J. Whitford Dolson of New York City were named as alternates.

Music and Art Prizes

Dante Fiorillo of Westwood, N. J., received a scholarship of $1,500 awarded "to the student of music in America who may be deemed the most talented and deserving, in order that he may continue his studies with the advantage of European instruction, on the nomination of a jury composed of members of the teaching staff of the Department of Music in Columbia University and of the teaching staff of the Institute of Musical Art."

Peter Cook of Kingston, N. J., won a scholarship of $1,500 given each year "to an art student in America, who shall be certified as the most promising and deserving by the National Academy of Design, with which the Society of American Artists has been merged."

Mr. Sherwood, who won the prize for the best play of the year with "Abe Lincoln in Illinois," had previously won the award in the same category in 1936 with "Idiot's Delight." His current play received five votes on the final ballot when the New York Critics Circle was unable to agree on the best American play of the season on April 19.

"Abe Lincoln in Illinois" was second to Lillian Hellman's "The Little Foxes," which received six votes in this year's balloting of the critics, but under the constitution

of the circle the winning play must receive at least twelve votes. The circle was founded four years ago, partly as a protest against previous awards of the Pulitzer Prize in the drama field.

Pach Bros., 1939
Robert E. Sherwood
Play

As a result of the selection of "Abe Lincoln in Illinois," Robert Emmet Sherwood becomes a twice-winner of the Pulitzer prize in playwrighting, having received the honor in 1936 for "Idiot's Delight." Only Eugene O'Neill, who won the award three times, and George S. Kaufman, who collaborated on two prize winners, have achieved a comparable station among American dramatists. Mr. Sherwood, who passed his forty-third birthday last month, is in England.

"Abe Lincoln in Illinois," heralded by the critics as an unusually forceful plea for continuance of the democratic way of life, marked a departure in Broadway production methods. Last season four Pulitzer prize-winners—Mr. Sherwood, Maxwell Anderson, Sidney Howard and Elmer Rice—and S. N. Behrman formed the Playwrights Company to produce their own works without the services of the usual intermediary, the producer.

Mr. Sherwood's play, directed by Mr. Rice, was the company's first production. By coincidence one of the company's proposed productions of next season is a dramatization by Mr. Howard of "Benjamin Franklin," by Carl Van Doren, which won the biography prize yesterday.

In addition to his work as a playwright, Mr. Sherwood is one of the foremost figures working for the advancement of the theatre as a whole. He is president of the Dramatists Guild, representing the organized playwrights in the United States, and of the American National Theatre and Academy, the only theatrical body ever to receive a Federal charter from Congress.

Mr. Sherwood was born in New Rochelle, N. Y. While a student at Harvard University he left his academic studies to enlist in the Forty-second Highlanders — the Black Watch—of the Canadian Expeditionary Force, the United States being a neutral power at the time. After his honorable discharge in February, 1919, he was made drama editor of Vanity Fair. Later he was an associate editor of Life. He wrote on motion pictures for The

New York Herald until its merger with The New York Tribune and for The New York Evening Post syndicate.

Mr. Sherwood's first success was "The Road to Rome." Besides "Idiot's Delight," his other works include "The Queen's Husband," "Waterloo Bridge," "This Is New York," "Reunion in Vienna," "The Petrified Forest," "Acropolis" and an adaptation from the French of "Tovarich." "Abe Lincoln in Illinois" opened last Oct. 15 with Raymond Massey in the title role. It is current at the Plymouth Theatre.

Mr. Sherwood's wife is the former Madeline Hurlock. He was separated by divorce from his first wife, Mary Brandon.

NEW YORK DRAMA CRITICS CIRCLE AWARDS

DRAMA CRITICS FAIL TO NAME 'BEST PLAY'

Circle's Award Is Passed for First Time as Annual vote Is Split Four Ways

'FOXES' AND 'LINCOLN' LEAD

Proponents of Both Are Firm —'White Steed' Is Adjudged Leading Foreign Work

Members of the New York Drama Critics Circle were unable to agree yesterday on the best American play of the season and unexpectedly passed their annual award for the first time in the circle's four-year history. The critics met at the Hotel Algonquin.

On the tenth and final ballot "The Little Foxes," by Lillian Hellman, received six votes; "Abe Lincoln in Illinois," by Robert E. Sherwood, five; "Rocket to the Moon," by Clifford Odets, two, and "My Heart's in the Highlands," by William Saroyan, two. Under the Circle's constitution the winning play has to receive twelve of the fifteen votes cast.

The action of the critics was a surprise to the theatrical profession, because the Broadway predictions almost unanimously favored "Abe Lincoln in Illinois" to win the prize. The general objection of many of the critics to the Sherwood play, however, was that it was not the best example of creative playwrighting and relied too much on the letters and speeches of Lincoln.

"The White Steed," by Paul Vincent Carroll, was unanimously chosen on a single ballot as the season's best play by a foreign author. Mr. Carroll, an Irish dramatist, won the honorary citation last year for "Shadow and Substance."

The four plays that survived the final ballot were also the only ones officially proposed during the afternoon's voting, a ballot for "Awake and Sing!" by Mr. Odets, being declared invalid since the play is not a work of this season. On the first vote "The Little Foxes" had six and one-third votes; "Abe Lincoln in Illinois," five and one-third; "My Heart's in the Highlands," one and one-third, and

"Rocket to the Moon," two.

Nathan Generous on Ballot

The split vote was cast by George Jean Nathan, president of the Circle, who decided to indicate his critical approval of three shows at once. The other critics overruled their president and decided he would have to vote for only one show. As a result "The Little Foxes" picked up an extra vote on the second ballot. Thereafter the race was limited to "The Little Foxes" and "Abe Lincoln in Illinois."

On the fifth and ninth ballots the Sherwood play led by a one-vote margin but dropped back to second place on the final tally. "Rocket to the Moon" had two supporters on all ballots. "My Heart's in the Highlands" disappeared from the list of candidates on several ballots, showing its greatest strength—two votes—on the last poll.

The final vote by the critics follows:

"The Little Foxes"—Kelcey Allen, Women's Wear Daily; John Anderson, Journal and American; Robert Benchley, New Yorker; John W. Gassner, Forum; Arthur Pollock, Brooklyn Daily Eagle, and Mrs. Ruth Woodbury Sedgwick, Stage Magazine.

"Abe Lincoln in Illinois"—Brooks Atkinson, THE NEW YORK TIMES; Burns Mantle, Daily News; Richard Watts, Herald Tribune; Sidney B. Whipple, World-Telegram, and Walter Winchell, Daily Mirror.

"Rocket to the Moon"—Richard Lockridge, Sun, and Joseph Wood Krutch, Nation.

"My Heart's in the Highlands"—John Mason Brown, Post, and George Jean Nathan, Newsweek, Esquire and Scribner's.

Stark Young of The New Republic and Mrs. Edith J. R. Isaacs of Theatre Arts Monthly were ineligible to cast votes, not having reviewed a sufficient number of plays during the season.

All Four to Be Honored

After the final vote the Circle issued the following statement:

"Inasmuch as the failure to reach a decision was the result of a difference of opinion, rather than any feeling that no play was worthy of the award, the Circle decided to honor the four plays responsible for the disagreement by inviting their authors to the annual dinner, which will be held on Sunday night at the Algonquin Hotel, in token of the general critical regard for their work."

Whether all the authors would be present at the dinner was uncertain. Mr. Sherwood has already booked passage on the Queen Mary for tomorrow and Mr. Odets is in Mexico City.

1940

PULITZER PRIZE

John Steinbeck's "The Grapes of Wrath," the controversial book about the migratory workers of California, yesterday was announced by the trustees of Columbia University as the winner of the Pulitzer Prize for the most distinguished novel published during 1939 by an American author.

Although the book was presumably judged solely on the basis of literary values, it was expected that because of the sociological and political significance it has attained since publication a year ago April 14 the selection would be attacked from some quarters as a tacit approval of the novel's disclosures that recommended it

and the trustees who approved the recommendation.

Dr. Nicholas Murray Butler, president of the university, in announcing the award, did not say whether the selection was a unanimous one.

"The Grapes of Wrath" was one of five recipients of Pulitzer Prizes in the field of letters, the others being for the best biography of the year, the best book of poetry, the best history and the best play. The journalism awards were for the best job of domestic reporting, the best foreign correspondence, the most disinterested public service by a newspaper, the best editorial writing and the best cartoon.

The other awards in the field of letters were:

Play—William Saroyan's "Time of Your Life."

Biography—Ray Stannard Baker's "Woodrow Wilson: Life and Letters," Vols. VII and VIII.

History—Carl Sandburg's "Abraham Lincoln: The War Years."

Poetry—Mark Van Doren's "Collected Poems."

The awards in journalism were:

Distinguished public service by a newspaper—The Waterbury (Conn.) Republican and American for exposure of graft in the city administration that resulted in trial and conviction of several city officials.

Domestic reporting—S. Burton Heath of The New York World-Telegram for his series of articles on Federal Judge Martin T. Manton that were followed by the latter's resignation, indictment and conviction for accepting financial favors from companies whose affairs were up before him for judicial decision.

Foreign correspondence—Otto D. Tolischus, THE NEW YORK TIMES, for his articles from Berlin explaining the economic and ideological background of war-engaged Germany.

Distinguished editorial writing—Bart Howard of The St. Louis Post-Dispatch.

Distinguished cartoon—Edmund Duffy of The Baltimore Sun for his cartoon "The Outstretched Hand," which depicted Hitler standing in smoking ruins about a group of smaller figures "Minorities" and stretching out to them a hand dripping with blood while in the other were crumpled papers titled "broken promises." The bloody hand was labeled "peace offer."

Honorable mention for foreign correspondence was given to Lloyd Lehrbas of The Associated Press, who was in Warsaw at the time of the first German bombing attacks last September. The San Francisco Chronicle won honorable mention in the category of public service for its part in "settling the waterfront and warehouse strike" in that city last year.

The literary awards were all "firsts" for their recipients as, with one exception, were those in journalism. The one person of the nine individuals who had won previously was Mr. Duffy, the cartoonist, who received the awards in 1931 and 1934. The prize-winner in 1931 also was on foreign affairs, showing a Russian Communist pulling a cross from a mosque. His cartoon in 1934 was "California Points With Pride." It showed the two San José lynch victims hanging from a gallows with a figure labeled "Governor Rolph" in the foreground.

The selection of the most distinguished play should not provoke

the controversy this year that it has in times past, as it agrees with that of the Critics Circle. The organized newspaper and magazine critics selected Mr. Saroyan's play as their "best" for the year on Friday. The play closed a run of 185 performances on April 6, but after announcement of the award yesterday the producers, the Theatre Guild and Eddie Dowling said it would be revived for a Fall run.

S. Burton Heath, winner of the reporting prize, has been a New York newspaperman for more than thirteen years, the last twelve on The New York World-Telegram, where he has done much notable work in addition to his exposure of judicial corruption.

Otto Tolischus, whose correspondence from Germany for THE NEW YORK TIMES has been outstanding for many years, now is stationed in Stockholm, where he has been reporting from that neutral vantage point developments of the German invasion of Norway.

Mr. Tolischus's work had been under fire from German authorities for some time when in March he was advised that his permit to remain in Germany was to be rescinded. Subsequently he was told that if he would leave the country for a period of six weeks he would be readmitted. He went to Copenhagen, to Oslo and then to Stockholm. When permission was sought for his return the Berlin authorities rescinded their former ruling and agreed to his return for an eight-day period only, just sufficient for him to obtain whatever personal belongings he might have left behind and settle any business affairs. Mr. Tolischus remains as correspondent for THE TIMES in Stockholm.

The award to The Waterbury Republican and American, morning and afternoon newspapers jointly published by William J. Pape and edited by E. Robert Stevenson, culminated a campaign of several years to "drive the rascals out." Their disclosures of misuse of city funds to a probable total of between $1,000,000 and $3,000,000 resulted in May, 1939, in the indictment of Mayor T. Frank Hayes, at that time also Lieutenant Governor of Connecticut, and twenty-one other public officials, contractors and auditors. They were convicted last August, Mayor Hayes receiving a sentence of not less than ten years in prison.

Among the literary awards, that to Mark Van Doren for his "Collected Poems" marked an unusual sequence in Pulitzer awards. Last year his older brother, Carl, won the award for the most distinguished biography, his work of "Benjamin Franklin."

Ray Stannard Baker, former editor of The Chicago Record and one of the so-called muckraking editors

William Saroyan
Drama

of the old McClure's Magazine, was press chief of the American commission at Versailles in 1919. His close contacts with President Wilson there inspired him to start to work on his monumental history of the life and times of the United States' World War President.

Carl Sandburg long has been noted as one of America's most gusty poets. His venture into historical and biographical writing has won him, in recent years, even higher literary praise, and his studies of Lincoln have been hailed as among the great literary works of the present century.

In addition to prizes in letters and journalism, the three annual traveling scholarships provided for by the Pulitzer Prize fund also were announced yesterday. Each is worth $1,500 and is intended to give the recipients a year's foreign travel. They were won by David D. Newsom of Richmond, Calif.; Ross P. Schlabach Jr. of Newport News, Va., and Miss Nona P. Baldwin of Montclair, N. J. All are students in the Graduate School of Journalism at Columbia. Whereas previous winners generally have gone to Europe, it was said this year's winners probably would travel in South America.

Three alternates were chosen for the scholarship awards. They were Miss Ann C. Hicks of Boston, Miss Anne Boyer of Palo Alto, Calif., and Peter B. Greenough of Brookline, Mass.

Two other annual scholarships, in music and art, also were awarded. Also worth $1,500 each, they are for study wherever the student selects. The music scholarship was awarded to Paul Noroff of Moylan, Pa., and the art scholarship to Albert Wasserman of New York City.

The monetary awards in journalism and letters are for $1,000 and $500, except for that to a newspaper, which consists only of a medal, although its intrinsic value approximates the lesser figure. The domestic reporting award is $1,000. The others are $500 each. The literary awards all are $1,000 each.

The prizes are awarded from a fund set up by the late Joseph Pulitzer, for many years publisher of The New York World and The St. Louis Post-Dispatch. Selections are made by the trustees of Columbia University, who are aided by an advisory board of the School of Journalism.

The advisory board this year was composed of Dr. Butler, acting ex-officio; Walter M. Harrison of The Oklahoma City (Okla.) Daily Oklahoman; Arthur M. Howe of Brooklyn, Frank R. Kent of The Sun Papers, Baltimore; Robert Lincoln O'Brien of Washington, D. C., former publisher of The Boston Herald; Stuart H. Perry of The Adrian (Mich.) Telegram; Kent Cooper, general manager of The Associated Press; Harold Stanley Pollard of The New York World-Telegram; Sevillon Brown of The Providence (R. I.) Journal; Joseph Pulitzer of The St. Louis Post-Dispatch; Julian LaRose Harris of The Chattanooga (Tenn.) Times; William Allen White of The Emporia (Kan.) Gazette, and Carl W. Ackerman, dean of the Pulitzer School of Journalism, who serves as executive secretary.

To fill a vacancy on the board created by the death of Ralph Pulitzer, former publisher of The World, Arthur Krock, Washington correspondent of THE NEW YORK TIMES, was elected. Mr. Krock twice has won the Pulitzer award for the best Washington correspondence. His term runs to June 30, 1943.

Three of the board members whose terms expired this year—Messrs. Cooper, Brown and Harris—were re-elected for four-year terms.

Following a custom begun last year, the prizes were announced without ceremony at 4 o'clock yesterday afternoon, immediately following the formal voting of the

trustees. In previous years they had been announced at the annual alumni dinner of journalism school graduates.

William Saroyan

"The Time of Your Life" and its author, William Saroyan, now have won both major prizes in the theatre for the current season. Last Friday the New York Drama Critics Circle—association of the local newspaper and magazine reviewers—voted its annual prize to the play. The award will be made Sunday night. "The Time of Your Life" is the first play to have won both prizes since the critics a few years ago decided to give their own award because of growing resentment on their part at the choices made by the Pulitzer committee.

Mr. Saroyan was born in Fresno, Calif., in 1908. He was educated in public schools and did odd jobs, and in his 'teens began his writing career by submitting a short story to Hairenik, an Armenian daily paper published in Boston. In the Winter of 1934 his story "The Daring Young Man on the Flying Trapeze" was published by Story. The magazine instantly received a deluge of other Saroyan offerings. Story published some and others went to the American Mercury and other magazines. His first book, "The Daring Young Man on the Flying Trapeze and Other Stories," came out in the Fall of 1934.

He entered the theatre as the author of "My Heart's in the Highlands," which the Group Theatre offered experimentally last season. After a few special performances the Theatre Guild took it over for its subscribers. "The Time of Your Life" was produced by Eddie Dowling in association with the Theatre Guild, with Mr. Dowling playing a leading role. A third Saroyan play, "Love's Old Sweet Song," opened on Broadway last Thursday.

"The Time of Your Life" played 185 performances on Broadway—ending April 6—but despite its length of run it lost almost $25,000 for its two producers and for Lee Shubert, who also was involved financially. It is to be taken on the road to cities as far west as Chicago, after reopening here for a few weeks in the Fall.

Mr. Saroyan is believed to be at work on a number of other plays—"Sweeney in the Trees" and a group of one-acters.

NEW YORK DRAMA CRITICS CIRCLE AWARDS

'TIME OF YOUR LIFE' WINS CRITICS' PRIZE

Saroyan Play Chosen as Best by an American to Appear on Broadway This Season

SHERWOOD DRAMA SECOND

Dowling Says Prize-Winner May Be Revived—No Award for a Foreign Work

New York's drama reviewers decided yesterday that William Saroyan's "The Time of Your Life" had been the best play by an American

HIS PLAY WINS

William Saroyan, author of "The Time of Your Life." *Vandamm*

to open on Broadway this season. Meeting at the Algonquin under their formal title of New York Drama Critics Circle, the newspaper and magazine critics voted the citation and accompanying silver plaque to Mr. Saroyan by a vote of eleven to seven, the seven being divided among three other plays with Robert E. Sherwood's "There Shall Be No Night" getting four of them.

In the citation, the critics noted: "To William Saroyan, whose 'The Time of Your Life' is an exhilarating demonstration of the fresh, original and imaginative talent he has brought into our American theatre, for the provocation of the play's unconventionality, and for the depth of its honest joy."

The winning play is not now running, having closed an engagement of 185 performances on April 6. Late yesterday afternoon, Eddie Dowling, who in association with the Theatre Guild was producer and who also was the leading player, said that it might be revived on Broadway for a few weeks. At all events, it is scheduled to visit the road next season, playing in various towns as far west as Chicago. It was reported on Broadway that despite its long run the show ended its local career on the bad side of the financial ledger.

Seven Ballots Required

In all, seven ballots were cast before the Saroyan play was chosen. According to the by-laws of the Circle, a three-quarters majority is required until after five ballots have been cast, when the members can, by a three-quarters vote, agree that a simple majority will do. This ballot barely passed, and with the next vote "The Time of Your Life" was elected.

The critics this year did not award a prize to the best foreign play seen on Broadway.

Voting for the Saroyan play were Sidney Whipple of The World-Telegram, Stark Young of The New Republic, Brooks Atkinson of THE NEW YORK TIMES, Joseph Wood Krutch of The Nation, Richard Watts Jr. of The Herald Tribune, John Anderson of The Journal-American, John Mason Brown of The Post, George Jean Nathan of Newsweek, Arthur Pollock of The Brooklyn Daily Eagle, Grenville Vernon of The Commonweal and John W. Gassner of The One-Act

Play Magazine.

Dissenting were Burns Mantle of The Daily News, Walter Winchell of The Mirror, Kelcey Allen of Women's Wear and Rosamond Gilder of Theatre Arts Magazine, who wanted "There Shall Be No Night"; Richard Lockridge of The Sun and Robert Rice of The Morning Telegraph, who voted for Maxwell Anderson's "Key Largo"; and Louis Kronenberger of Time, who favored "The Man Who Came to Dinner." Robert Benchley of The New Yorker did not vote.

The critics usually meet in mid-April, but this year postponed the decision until after "There Shall Be No Night" and another Saroyan play, "Love's Old Sweet Song," could open. "The Time of Your Life" led throughout, starting with ten votes and never falling below nine. "There Shall Be No Night" at one time had seven votes, but thereafter dwindled to four. Aside from the plays mentioned, "The World We Make" received a favorite son vote in the first ballot.

Author Proud of Honor

Some time ago, Mr. Saroyan remarked that if one of his dramas should win the Pulitzer Prize for the drama he would send it back. Not so with the Critics Prize, he said last night, terming it "a great distinction, which I am very proud to accept." He will do so the evening of May 12 when, over the radio, will be heard scenes from the play and speeches by the Messrs. Saroyan, Mantle, Nathan, Dowling and Krutch and Theresa Helburn of the Theatre Guild.

"The Time of Your Life" is Mr. Saroyan's second play, "My Heart's in the Highlands," his first, having been produced last season. During its preliminary tryout it had difficulty shaking into shape, with Mr. Dowling and Mr. Saroyan finally directing it themselves. Julie Haydon, Charles de Sheim, Gene Kelly, Len Doyle and others were in it. Its merits and demerits caused discussion all through the Winter.

Mr. Saroyan is believed to be at work on several new plays, including one called "Sweeney in the Trees," which he hopes to produce and direct himself, and a handful of one-acters.

1941

PULITZER PRIZE

The annual awards of the Pulitzer prizes in letters and journalism, which were announced yesterday by the trustees of Columbia University, acting upon the recommendation of the advisory board of the Graduate School of Journalism, contained a special citation to THE NEW YORK TIMES.

This precedent-breaking award was made "to THE NEW YORK TIMES for the public educational value of its foreign news report, exemplified by its scope, by excellence of writing and presentation, and supplementary background information, illustration and interpretation," according to the announcement by the trustees.

"Upon recommendation of the advisory board stating that a supreme journalistic achievement of this kind does not clearly fall into any of the present categories defined for awards, the trustees take this means of recognizing THE NEW YORK TIMES," the announcement added.

No award was made by the trustees in the field of the novel. Rob-

ert E. Sherwood's "There Shall Be No Night" won the $1,000 award for "the original American play, performed in New York, which shall represent in marked fashion the educational value and power of the stage, preferably dealing with American life."

The award in United States history went to "The Atlantic Migration," published last year by the Harvard University Press, although its author, Marcus Lee Hansen, died in 1938. The prize in biography went to Ola Elizabeth Winslow for her study of Jonathan Edwards, published by the Macmillan Company, and the prize for verse went to "Sunderland Capture," by Leonard Bacon, published by Harper and Brothers.

A gold medal costing $500 was awarded to The St. Louis Post-Dispatch for "the most disinterested and meritorious public service rendered by an American newspaper during the year," in recognition of that newspaper's successful campaign against the smoke nuisance in its home city.

In place of awarding an individual Pulitzer prize for foreign or Washington correspondence, the trustees approved a suggestion by the advisory board to have the names of all American news reporters in the war zones of Europe, Asia and Africa since the beginning of the present war engraved on a bronze plaque or scroll to be mounted in the Journalism Building of Columbia University.

Reuben Maury of The New York Daily News won the annual award of $500 "for distinguished editorial writing during the year, limited to the editorial page, the test of excellence being clearness of style, moral purpose, sound reasoning and power to influence public opinion in what the writer conceives to be the right direction."

Westbrook Pegler, whose column, "Fair Enough," appears daily in The New York World-Telegram and more than 100 other newspapers throughout the United States, received the prize of $1,000 for reporting in recognition of his articles on scandals in the ranks of organized labor that led to the exposure and conviction of George Scalise, president of the Building Service Employes Union.

The prize of $500 awarded annually for "a distinguished example of a cartoonist's work" was given to Jacob Burck of The Chicago Times for a cartoon entitled "If I Should Die Before I Wake." It represented a small girl kneeling in prayer at the side of her bed in a room torn by jagged bomb-holes.

The selections of the trustees in the fields of history, biography and poetry, and their failure to make any award in the field of the novel, were decidedly at variance with the choices named recently by a panel of thirty-nine literary critics, which were gathered and made public by The Saturday Review of Literature. The prize awards ignored the first and second choices of the critics in each of these four categories.

The critics had selected Ernest Hemingway's "For Whom the Bell Tolls," with twenty-one votes to six for their second choice, Kenneth Robert's "Oliver Wiswell." They had selected also "As I Remember Him" by Hans Zinsser in the field of biography; "New England: Indian Summer," by Van Wyck Brooks, in the field of history, and tied on two poems, "And in the Human Heart," by Conrad Aiken,

and "The White Cliffs" by Alice Duer Miller.

No explanation of their failure to select any novel for the award was made public by the trustees. The terms of the award are "for a distinguished novel published during the year by an American author, preferably dealing with American life." It was pointed out that the final qualification might have weighed against Mr. Hemingway's novel, which dealt with the Spanish Civil War.

Novels Passed in 1917, 1920

The regulations for the award of the prizes, as revised last May, provide that "if in any one year no book or play written for a prize offered shall be of sufficient excellence in the opinion of the advisory board * * * then in that case the amount of such prize or prizes may be withheld in such year." No award was made to a novel in 1917 and again in 1920.

The Advisory Board recommended to the trustees that the prizes that have been awarded for distinguished service as a foreign or Washington correspondent during the year, and for a distinguished example of a reporter's work during the year, should be divided in the future into four categories in order to draw a clearer line between the reporting of spot news in Washington and abroad, and editorial correspondence.

The classifications they recommended to the trustees would each carry a prize of $500, and would be: local and regional news reporting, reporting of national affairs or events, reporting of international affairs or events, and "newspaper correspondence." It was learned that this recommendation is now being studied by counsel for the university to determine whether it is in accord with the will of Joseph Pulitzer, who set up the prizes.

The members of the Advisory Board were Dr. Nicholas Murray Butler, president of Columbia; Sevellon Brown of The Providence Journal; Kent Cooper of The Associated Press; Julian La Rose Harris of The Chattanooga Times; Walter M. Harrison of The Daily Oklahoman, Oklahoma City, Okla.; Arthur M. Howe, editor emeritus of The Brooklyn Eagle, and Frank R. Kent of The Baltimore Sun.

Also Arthur Krock, Washington correspondent of THE NEW YORK TIMES; Robert Lincoln O'Brien, formerly editor of The Boston Herald; Stuart H. Perry of The Adrian (Mich.) Telegram; Harold Stanley Pollard of The New York World Telegram; Joseph Pulitzer of The St. Louis Post-Dispatch; William Allen White of the Emporia (Kan.) Gazette, and Dean Carl W. Ackerman of the School of Journalism.

Fellowship Winners Named

The trustees also announced yesterday the award of three traveling fellowships with a value of $1,500 each to members of the graduating class of the School of Journalism, to enable them to spend a year in travel and study abroad. The awards went to Pat Mayo Holt of Gatesville, Texas; Richard K. Pryne of La Crescenta, Calif., and Alvadee Eugenia Hutton of New Cumberland, Pa.

As alternates, the trustees named Vernon De Long Groff of Sellersville, Pa., Helene Kazanjian of Belmont, Mass., and Helen Markel of New York.

Mr. Holt is 20 years old, and was graduated last year from the University of Texas. He spent the Summers from 1935 to 1938 working for The Gatesville Messenger, and from 1938 to 1940 was a part-time member of the editorial staff of The (Austin) Daily Texan.

Mr. Pryne, who is 22, received his Bachelor of Arts degree from the University of California at Los Angeles last year. He was editor of The Daily Bruin.

Miss Hutton is 23. She received her degree of Bachelor of Science

from Temple University last year. She was a member of the staff of The Temple University News and the "Templar," senior yearbook.

A scholarship of $1,500 awarded annually "to the student of music in America who may be deemed the most talented and deserving, in order that he may continue his studies with the advantage of European instruction" was awarded by to Edmund Haines of the Eastman School of Music, Rochester, N. Y.

An annual scholarship of $1,500 for an art student in America "who shall be certified as the most promising and deserving by the National Academy of Design," was awarded to Ariane Beigneux of Roxbury, Conn., and New York.

Mr. Haines, 27 years old, is a native of Ottumwa, Iowa, and is now studying for the degree of Doctor of Philosophy in music. He received the Pulitzer prize in music for his "Symphony No. 1." Miss Beigneux, 22, lives at 390 Central Park West, and for six years has been a student at the National Academy of Design.

Robert E. Sherwood
Drama

Biographical sketches of Pulitzer Prize winners in letters and journalism follow:

Robert E. Sherwood

With "There Shall Be No Night," Robert Emmet Sherwood has won his third Pulitzer Prize for the drama, a record equaled only by Eugene O'Neill. Further, Mr. Sherwood has won the award on three of his last four produced shows, with the odd one, an adaptation, not being eligible. "Idiot's Delight," which won for the season of 1935-1936, and "Abe Lincoln in Illinois," in 1938-1939, were the other winners; "Tovarich," of the season of 1936-1937, was the adaptation.

"There Shall Be No Night," in which Alfred Lunt and Lynn Fontanne played the leading roles, opened on Broadway April 29, 1940, and thus was too late for the Pulitzer Prize last year, although the New York Drama Critics Circle gave it second place. One hundred and seventy-nine performances were given on Broadway and the play closed Nov. 2, thereafter taking to the road. The road tour

ended last Saturday in New Haven, with the Playwrights Company and the Theatre Guild, the producers, saying they will bring it back to Broadway in the Fall before starting a second tour.

Mr. Sherwood was born in New Rochelle, N. Y., on April 4, 1896. He was a student at Harvard from 1914 to 1917, but left to join the Black Watch of the Canadian Expeditionary Force. In 1919 he became dramatic editor of Vanity Fair and from there went to Life as assistant editor, editor, motion-picture critic—various capacities from 1920 to 1928. He wrote on films for The New York Herald and also for The New York Evening Post syndicate.

His first play was "The Road to Rome" in 1926, his output since then being "The Love Nest," "The Queen's Husband," "Waterloo Bridge," "This Is New York," "Reunion in Vienna," "The Petrified Forest," "Idiot's Delight," "Tovarich," "Abe Lincoln in Illinois" and "There Shall Be No Night." A play called "Acropolis" was done in London, never in New York.

"There Shall Be No Night" had its inspiration in a radio broadcast from Helsinki, Finland, while Russia was marching into that country. The broadcast, by W. L. White, inspired Mr. Sherwood to set down in drama form his convictions about the invasion, about all invasions against liberty. Its characters are a Finnish scientist and his family; one by one they go out to fight. Mr. Sherwood wrote the play rapidly and the Lunts, who were just ending a tour in "The Taming of the Shrew" started rehearsing practically before the pages were out of the typewriter.

Mr. Sherwood is a member of the Free Company, which has been dramatizing the Bill of Rights for the radio, and is a member of the Committee to Defend America by Aiding the Allies. He is a member also of the Joint Army and Navy Committee on Welfare and Recreation and recently has been organizing hows to tour the training camps. He is a member—along with Maxwell Anderson, Elmer Rice and S. N. Behrman—of the Playwrights Company.

NEW YORK DRAMA CRITICS CIRCLE AWARDS

CRITICS' PRIZE GOES TO 'WATCH ON RHINE'

Lillian Hellman's Play Wins Annual American Award— Saroyan Is Second

'CORN IS GREEN' HONORED

Emlyn Williams's Production Named Best Importation —Seven Ballots Cast

Lillian Hellman won the annual award of the New York Drama Critics Circle yesterday for her American play, "Watch on the Rhine." The local newspaper and magazine reviewers decided on the winner after seven ballots had been cast, sec-

ond place going to William Saroyan's "The Beautiful People."

Emlyn Williams's "The Corn Is Green" won the prize for the best importation, the vote in that case being virtually unanimous. Herman Shumlin is the producer of both plays—the first double winner in the circle's history. Both are current on Broadway, "Watch on the Rhine" having opened April 1, and "The Corn Is Green" last Nov. 26.

Of the nineteen critics present, the following voted for "Watch on the Rhine" on the final ballot: Rosamund Gilder of Theatre Arts, Arthur Pollock of The Brooklyn Daily Eagle, Wolcott Gibbs of The New Yorker, Richard Lockridge of The Sun, Louis Kronenberger of PM, John W. Gassner, Walter Winchell of The Daily Mirror, Richard Watts of The Herald-Tribune, Oliver Claxton of Cue, Sidney B. Whipple of The World-Telegram, Kelcey Allen of Women's Wear Daily, and Brooks Atkinson of The New York Times. Voting for "The Beautiful People" were George Jean Nathan of Esquire, Joseph Wood Krutch of The Nation, John Anderson of The Journal-American, Grenville Vernon of The Commonweal, John Mason Brown of The Post and Stark Young of The New Republic. Burns Mantle of The Daily News voted for "Native Son."

To Be Presented Sunday

The awards—in the case of the American play a plaque of the old John Street Theatre and for the importation a scroll—will be presented Sunday evening at a dinner at the Algonquin Hotel, where yesterday's meeting was held. Scenes from the winning plays will be broadcast, and accompanying the prizes will be these citations:

"To Lillian Hellman for 'Watch on the Rhine,' a vital, eloquent and compassionate play about an American family suddenly awakened to the danger threatening its liberty.

"To Emlyn Williams for 'The Corn Is Green,' a simple and sincere play describing how a devoted teacher helps a young Welsh miner to intellectual fulfillment."

The Critics Circle has a house rule that awards shall be given on the basis of a three-quarters majority, if possible. If five ballots are taken without a decision the circle may vote to suspend that rule and make a decision on the basis of simple majority. After the fifth ballot it was necessary to take three votes on the question of simple majority, one before the sixth ballot and two before the final seventh.

On the first ballot nine of the members wanted "Watch on the Rhine," three were for "The Beautiful People," two each for "Native Son" and "The Talley Method" and one each for "Arsenic and Old Lace" and "Claudia." During subsequent ballots two other plays were mentioned, "Lady in the Dark" and "Flight To the West," each of which got a vote. For the best foreign or imported play "The Corn Is Green" got sixteen votes, with two critics having no choice and with Mr. Winchell not voting.

Setting Outside Capital

The winning play has its setting outside Washington. Into a typical American home comes the daughter of the family, her three children and her husband who has been fighting Nazism through Europe. During the course of the play the husband, played by Paul Lukas, decides to go back into Germany, with all its risks, to carry on his work in the underground movement.

"The Corn Is Green" is about a school teacher, played by Ethel Barrymore, and the development of a young poetic Welsh miner. The play was successful in London before it was produced here.

Of the authors: Miss Hellman wrote "The Children's Hour" and "The Little Foxes," which Mr. Shumlin also produced. Mr. Williams, an actor as well as author,

was last seen on Broadway in 1936 in "Night Must Fall," which he wrote.

The circle was founded in 1933 by the local reviewers who had become discouraged over previous Pulitzer Prize awards for the drama. Maxwell Anderson won the prize the first two years—for "Winterset" and "High Tor"; John Steinbeck got it in the season of 1937-38 for his dramatization of his novel, "Of Mice and Men"; there was no award the following season; and William Saroyan won both the Critics and the Pulitzer Prizes last year for "The Time of Your Life." This year's meeting was delayed until after Monday evening's opening of Mr. Saroyan's latest play.

1942

NEW YORK DRAMA CRITICS CIRCLE AWARDS

NO AMERICAN PLAY HONORED BY CRITICS

Drama Circle Finds Season's Theatre Offerings Not 'Up to Standards of Award'

COWARD FARCE ACCLAIMED

'Blithe Spirit' Is Cited as the Best Foreign Play—Annual Dinner to Be Abandoned

---

The New York Drama Critics Circle decided yesterday to make no award for the best American play of the season and chose Noel Coward's "Blithe Spirit" as the best foreign play.

Meeting in the afternoon at the Hotel Algonquin, the critics took five ballots before reaching a decision for no award. This was the second time since it was founded in 1935 that the Critics Circle failed to honor an American play.

Unlike the situation in 1939, when the vote was hopelessly divided, the seventeen critics had little difficulty yesterday in making up their minds. On the first ballot John Steinbeck's "The Moon Is Down" received four ballots and "In Time to Come," by Howard Koch and John Huston, received three, while "no choice" was the decision of ten. On the second ballot the vote between the two runners-up to "no choice" was reversed. On the third vote "The Moon Is Down" dropped to two and "In Time to Come" rose to four.

"No Choice" Gets 11 Votes

On the final ballot eleven members voted "no choice." They were Wilella Waldorf of The New York Post, Richard Lockridge of The Sun, Louis Kronenberger of PM, Joseph Wood Krutch of The Nation, Wolcott Gibbs of The New Yorker, Richard Watts Jr. of The Herald Tribune, George Jean Nathan of

The American Mercury and Esquire, Arthur Pollock of The Brooklyn Eagle, John Anderson of The Journal-American, John Mason Brown of The World-Telegram and John Gassner of Current History and Direction.

Four members — Burns Mantle of The News, George Freedley of The Morning Telegraph, Kelcey Allen of Women's Wear and Stark Young of The New Republic—voted for "In Time to Come" on the final ballot. Two members—Brooks Atkinson of THE NEW YORK TIMES and Rosamond Gilder of Theatre Arts Monthly—remained faithful to "The Moon Is Down.".

The critics required only two ballots to agree to cite "Blithe Spirit," by Noel Coward, as the best foreign play. On the second Mr. Watts, Mr. Gassner, Mr. Gilder, Mr. Gibbs, Mr. Lockridge, Mr. Waldorf, Mr. Mantle, Mr. Atkinson, Mr. Allen, Mr. Freedley, Mr. Anderson and Mr. Krutch selected "Blithe Spirit." Mr. Brown, Mr. Nathan, and Mr. Pollock had no choice, and Mr. Young voted for "Angel Street."

Citation for Coward Play

In citing "Blithe Spirit" the Critics Circle said: "To Noel Coward, for the skill and adroitness with which he has concocted a farce comedy of gayety and wit."

In announcing the Circle's choice the critics pointed out that while the Circle was "organized to encourage native playwrights and honor native dramatists, it has also the third obligation of maintaining the standards of the theatre and of dramatic criticism," and that it felt it would cause "a serious confusion of standards if it merely made a selection from a group of plays none of which seemed up to the standards of the previous awards."

The critics also voted to abandon their annual dinner and radio broadcast, at which time the awards would have been made, and also to donate the money, which they would have spent for a scroll and a plaque for the winning plays, to the British War Relief and to the American Theatre Wing.

1943
PULITZER PRIZE

Wilder Play, Sinclair Novel Are Pulitzer Prize Winners

The trustees of Columbia University announced yesterday that the Pulitzer Prize for the best original American play of 1942 had been awarded to "The Skin of Our Teeth," by Thornton Wilder, and that the prize for a distinguished novel had gone to "Dragon's Teeth," by Upton Sinclair. The awards were made by the trustees on the recommendation of the advisory board of the Graduate School of Journalism.

Prizes in journalism were awarded to The Omaha (Neb.) World-Herald for its campaign for the collection of scrap metal; to Forrest W. Seymour of The Des Moines (Iowa) Register and Tribune for editorial writing; to Hanson W. Baldwin, military and naval editor of THE NEW YORK TIMES, for his series of articles reporting his tour of the South Pacific battle areas, and to Jay Norwood Darling of The New York Herald Tribune for distinguished service as a cartoonist.

Mr. Baldwin, whose prize-winning articles appeared in THE TIMES from Oct. 23 through Oct. 30 of last year, has just returned to this country from Tunisia and is now preparing a series of articles for THE TIMES on his observations there.

Frank Noel of The Associated Press won the prize for news photography, Ira Wolfert of the North American Newspaper Alliance received the prize for telegraphic reporting of international affairs by virtue of his series of three articles on the sea battle off Guadalcanal last Nov. 13 and 14 and George Weller of The Chicago Daily News received the award for a distinguished example of a reporter's work on a story of local or regional interest.

No award was made for a distinguished example of telegraphic reporting on national affairs published in daily newspapers of this country, for which a prize of $500 is usually awarded.

In the field of letters, in addition to the Wilder play and the Sinclair novel, the history award was made to "Paul Revere and the World He Lived In," by Esther Forbes, and the biographical award went to "Admiral of the Ocean Sea," by Samuel Eliot Morison. Robert Frost won the poetry prize for "A Witness Tree."

A prize in music, which was authorized by the trustees of the university last March and was awarded yesterday for the first time, went to William H. Schuman, Professor of Music at Sarah Lawrence College, Bronxville, N. Y., for his "Secular Cantata No. 2, a Free Song," which was performed by the Boston Symphony Orchestra.

The annual award of three traveling scholarships to graduates of the School of Journalism, which in the past has usually been announced with the Pulitzer prizes, was withheld yesterday, but university officials said the winners might be announced today.

As has often been the case in the past, the trustees provided several surprises in their selections. The award to "The Skin of Our Teeth," which carries with it a prize of $500, was not particularly surprising, but that to "Dragon's Teeth" in the field of the novel was a decided departure from the general expectation.

Last month the New York Drama Critics Circle, after a hard-fought contest in which the supporters of "The Skin of Our Teeth" fought a steadfast but losing battle, voted their annual prize to "The Patriots" by Sidney Kingsley.

The terms of the Pulitzer award provide that the prize shall go to "the original American play, performed in New York, which shall represent in marked fashion the educational value and power of the stage, preferably dealing with American life."

The novel award, which likewise carries with it a prize of $500, is made "for a distinguished novel published during the year by an American author, preferably dealing with American life." Mr. Sinclair's novel, published by the Viking Press, was hardly considered in advance speculations about the award.

The annual award for "the most disinterested and meritorious public service rendered by an American newspaper during the year" is a gold medal costing $500. It went to The Omaha World-Herald "for its initiative and originality in planning a State-wide campaign for the collection of scrap metal for the war effort."

"The Nebraska plan was adopted on a national scale by the daily newspapers, resulting in a united effort which succeeded in supplying our war industries with necessary scrap material," the trustees pointed out.

The prize of $500 won by Mr. Seymour for distinguished editorial writing was made for his work throughout the year and not for a single editorial. The regulations governing the award specify that "the test of excellence being clearness of style, moral purpose, sound reasoning, and power to influence public opinion in what the writer conceives to be the right direction, due account being taken of the whole volume of the writer's editorial work during the year."

Mr. Baldwin's prize of $500 was won "for distinguished correspondence during the year, the test being clearness and terseness of style, preference being given to fair, judicious, well-balanced and well-informed interpretative writing, which shall make clear the significance of the subject covered in the correspondence or which shall promote international understanding and appreciation."

The cartoon award to Mr. Darling was made for distinguished service as a cartoonist as exemplified by the cartoon entitled "What a Place for a Wastepaper Salvage Campaign," published on Sept. 13, 1943. It depicted the Capitol in Washington being overwhelmed by a flood of bureaucratic regulations and other paper work.

The $500 prize for a news photograph, which is open to amateurs as well as professional newspaper photographers, was won by Mr. Noel for a picture entitled "Water," which was serviced by The Associated Press on April 17, 1942.

It was a photograph of an Indian sailor in a lifeboat four days after being torpedoed in the Indian Ocean, 270 miles off Sumatra, while the ship was en route from Singapore to Rangoon. The picture was taken by Mr. Noel, a victim of the same torpedoing, from an adjoining lifeboat. The Indian's boat was later lost at sea and Mr. Noel's story, filed from Padang, Sumatra, after his rescue, was the first warning that Japanese submarines were operating in the Indian Ocean.

The $500 prize won by Mr. Wolfert was "for a distinguished example of telegraphic reporting on international affairs published in daily newspapers in the United States," while that of a similar amount awarded to Mr. Weller was "for a distinguished example of a reporter's work during the year, the test being accuracy and terseness, the preference being given to news stories published in a daily newspaper prepared under the pressure of edition time relating to matters of special interest of a local or regional character."

Mr. Weller won the award for his story of how a pharmacist's mate aboard a United States submarine under enemy waters performed an operation for appendicitis, thereby saving a sailor's life. It was not made clear how this story came to be included in the category of those of local or regional interest.

Thornton Wilder

The award for the best drama of the year to Thornton Wilder, now a major in the Army Air Forces, marks the third Pulitzer prize to be won by the author of "The Skin of Our Teeth." Previous awards were for his novel "The Bridge of San Luis Rey," published in 1928, and for his play "Our Town," which was produced just a decade later.

This year's winner has been at the center of a controversy since its opening last Nov. 18. A play about how the Antrobus family of Excelsior, N. J., survived the Ice Age, it was described by Lewis Nichols of THE NEW YORK TIMES as "the best the Forties have seen in many months, the best pure theatre."

Later two writers for The Saturday Review of Literature attempted to show that Major Wilder had "lifted" great portions of the play from James Joyce's novel "Finnegans Wake." Major Wilder never replied to the charges. When the New York Critics Circle met to choose the best play of the year, the award went to Sidney Kingsley's "The Patriots" after the controversy over the alleged "plagiarism" was aired. Five critics, including Mr. Nichols, voted to the end for "The Skin of Our Teeth."

While at Yale Major Wilder wrote plays, but his first success was as a novelist.

Prior to "The Skin of Our Teeth," which was produced by Michael Myerberg only after several noted producers had shied away from it, with Tallulah Bankhead, Fredric March and Florence Eldridge in the leading roles, his last Broadway production was "The Merchant of Yonkers." With Jane Cowl and Percy Waram in the cast, the play ran for thirty-nine performances late in 1938.

Major Thornton Wilder
Play

To the general public Mr. Wilder is perhaps best known for his play "Our Town," in which Frank Craven was starred. This was later made into a moving picture. In both "Our Town" and "The Skin of Our Teeth" Major Wilder used new and unusual stage techniques.

NEW YORK DRAMA CRITICS CIRCLE AWARDS

Sergeant Sidney Kingsley

CRITICS PRIZE WON BY 'THE PATRIOTS'

Kingsley Drama of Jefferson, Hamilton Gets 13 Votes as Season's Best Play

The New York Drama Critics Circle celebrated Jefferson Day yesterday by voting its award for the best play of the season to Sidney Kingsley's "The Patriots," a drama in which Thomas Jefferson and Alexander Hamilton are the two leading characters. Thornton Wilder's "The Skin of Our Teeth" was the runner-up, although "The Patriots" led from the start of the balloting and the competition at the end was not close. The final vote was 13 for "The Patriots," 4 for "The Skin of Our Teeth," 1 for "This Is the Army."

Mr. Kingsley's drama, which was produced by the Playwrights Company and Rowland Stebbins, received its award on the seventh ballot cast by the newspaper and magazine play reviewers who comprise the circle and after suspension of rules which call for a three-quarters majority to decide the winner. Previously the circle had decided no foreign play had been good enough to merit recognition and receipt of the prize the group usually gives for the best importation.

On the last ballot the following were in favor of "The Patriots": John Anderson of The Journal-American, Joseph Wood Krutch of The Nation, George Jean Nathan of Esquire, Stark Young of The New Republic, Arthur Pollock of The Brooklyn Eagle, George Freedley of The Morning Telegraph, Ward Morehouse of The Sun, Kelcey Allen of Women's Wear Daily, Wilella Waldorf of The Post, Burns Mantle of The Daily News, Wolcott Gibbs of The New Yorker, Jesse Zunser of Cue and John Gassner of Direction. "The Skin of Our Teeth" received votes from Howard Barnes of The Herald Tribune, Burton Rascoe of The World-Telegram, Rosamond Gilder of Theatre Arts Monthly and Lewis Nichols of THE TIMES. Louis Kronenberger of PM voted for "This Is the Army."

In the citation accompanying the award—the more tangible part being a plaque designed by Henry Varnum Poor—the circle noted the winning play's "dignity of material, its thoughtful projection of a great American theme, its vigorous approach to the characters portrayed and, in spite of certain limitations, its driving final effect on the stage." The plaque and scroll will be given to Mr. Kingsley at the circle's annual dinner to be held May 2 at the Algonquin, when a scene from the play is to be broadcast. Irving Berlin also was invited to be a guest, this in recognition of his work for "This Is the Army."

Beside the three shows named in the final ballot, "Harriet," "The Eve of St. Mark" and "Oklahoma" also were mentioned by a vote or so at various times.

Mr. Kingsley now is a sergeant in the Army, and his play is the first by an outsider to be produced by the Playwrights Company.

1944

NEW YORK DRAMA CRITICS CIRCLE AWARDS

Unable to agree on the best American play of the season, the members of the New York Drama Critics Circle decided yesterday to omit their annual award this spring. Lillian Hellman's "The

Searching Wind" came close to winning, receiving seven votes and lacking only one for a majority. John Van Druten's "The Voice of the Turtle" received two votes; "Tomorrow the World," one, and four critics had no choice. "Jacobowsky and the Colonel" received a citation as the best foreign play of the year, the circle agreeing that since it was written originally by Franz Werfel in German it should be in that category.

This year for the first time the members of the circle contented themselves with a single ballot. Those favoring Miss Hellman's play were Ward Morehouse of The Sun, John Gassner of Decision, Jesse Zunsser of Cue, Howard Barnes of The Herald Tribune, Kelcey Allen of Women's Wear Daily, T. H. Wenning of Newsweek and Arthur Pollock of The Brooklyn Eagle. George Freedley of The Morning Telegraph and Lewis Nichols of THE TIMES favored "The Voice of the Turtle," and John Chapman of The Daily News voted for "Tomorrow the World." Wilella Waldorf of The Post, Rosamond Gilder of Theatre Arts Monthly, Wolcott Gibbs of The New Yorker and Louis Kronenberger of PM voted for no award.

The only discussion in advance of voting centered around the definition of a foreign play. In the case of "Jacobowsky and the Colonel" it was decided that while the play as now seen is by S. N. Behrman, it was based on Mr. Werfel's.

The circle decided to hold no annual dinner this year. Mr. Barnes, as president, presided.

1945

PULITZER PRIZE

'HARVEY' IS WINNER OF PULITZER PRIZE

1944 Award for Distinguished Novel Goes to John Hersey's 'A Bell for Adano'

JAMES B. RESTON HONORED

Coverage of Dumbarton Oaks Conference for The Times Cited —War Feats Rewarded

Pulitzer prizes for 1944 were awarded yesterday to "A Bell for Adano," the novel by John R. Hersey, to "Harvey," the play by Mary Chase, and to James B. Reston of THE NEW YORK TIMES, whose news dispatches and interpretative articles on the Dumbarton Oaks Security Conference were cited as "a distinguished example of telegraphic reporting on national affairs published in daily newspapers in the United States."

The trustees of Columbia University, in announcing fifteen

awards, gave the music prize to Aaron Copland for his "Appalachian Spring," a ballet written for and presented by Martha Graham and her company. It was commissioned by Mrs. E. S. Coolidge and first presented at the Library of Congress in Washington last October.

The other awards in the field of letters were: For history, to "Unfinished Business," by Stephen Bonsal; for biography, to "George Bancroft: Brahmin Rebel," by Russell Blaine Nye; for verse, to "V-Letter and Other Poems," by Karl Shapiro.

Detroit Free Press Honored

The prize for "the most disinterested and meritorious public service rendered by an American newspaper during the year" was awarded to The Detroit Free Press for its investigation of legislative graft and corruption at Lansing, Mich. The citation noted that "numerous indictments were found; more than 100 persons are awaiting trial; sixteen have been convicted; five have pleaded guilty and four persons are serving sentence." This award was a gold medal costing $500. Other awards in journalism, letters and music were $500 each.

The photograph of Marines raising the American flag on Mount Surabachi on Iwo, taken by Joe Rosenthal, photographer of The Associated Press, received the award for an "outstanding example of news photography." The trustees recognized the exceptional merit of this famous photograph, which is being used as a poster for the Seventh War Loan, by lifting the deadline rule of the advisory board. The photograph was taken in February of this year, the announcement said, "but the board moved by resolution that the rule be suspended for this distinguished example."

George W. Potter, chief editorial writer of The Providence Journal-Bulletin, received a prize for his editorials published during 1944, especially for those on the freedom of the press. The announcement said that the advisory board of the School of Journalism, which recommends all the awards, had indicated its satisfaction with the large number of editorials on this important subject that appeared in the American press during the year.

Harold V. (Hal) Boyle, war reporter and columnist of The Associated Press, received an award for "distinguished correspondence during the year."

Mauldin Gets Cartoon Prize

Sgt. Bill Mauldin, cartoonist of the United Feature Syndicate, Inc., won the prize for distinguished service as a cartoonist. The cartoon selected from his series "Up Front With Mauldin," as exemplifying his work, showed a single GI Joe slogging through mud and rain conducting three German prisoners back to the rear, with this caption: "Fresh, spirited American troops, flushed with victory, are bringing in thousands of hungry, ragged, battle-weary prisoners.' (News item.)"

The prize for a "distinguished example of telegraphic reporting on international affairs" was awarded to Mark S. Watson, military correspondent of The Baltimore Sun "for his distinguished reporting during the year 1944 from Washington, London and the fronts in Sicily, Italy and France."

The prize for a distinguished example of a reporter's work in matters of special interest of a local or regional character was given to

Jack S. McDowell of The San Francisco Call Bulletin. Mr. McDowell gave a blood donation, flew to the front in the Southwest Pacific to see it utilized and then returned home to write a series of five articles that greatly stimulated blood donations in both San Francisco and Los Angeles.

In a special journalism citation, the advisory board commended the work of the "cartographers of the American press, whose maps of the war fronts have helped notably to clarify and increase public information on the progress of the armies and navies engaged."

Novel and Play Award Terms

The terms of the novel award prescribe that it be "a distinguished novel published during the year by an American author, preferably dealing with American life." Mr. Hersey's novel was published by Alfred A. Knopf, Inc.

Terms of the play award are "for an original American play, performed in New York, which shall represent in marked fashion the educational value and power of the stage, preferably dealing with American life." "Harvey" was produced by Brock Pemberton, who also produced "Miss Lulu Bett," by Zona Gale, which won the Pulitzer award for the 1920-21 season. The 1944-45 season covered by the current award included all plays produced up to April 1.

Doubleday, Doran & Co., Inc., published Mr. Bonsal's "Unfinished Business," which received the award for a distinguished book of the year upon the history of the United States. Alfred A. Knopf, Inc., published Mr. Nye's "George Bancroft: Brahmin Rebel," which won the prize "for a distinguished American biography teaching patriotic and unselfish service to the people, illustrated by an eminent example, excluding, as too obvious, the names of George Washington and Abraham Lincoln." Reynal & Hitchcock, Inc., published Mr. Shapiro's "V-Letter and Other Poems," who won the prize for a "distinguished volume of verse by an American author."

The trustees gave an annual scholarship, having a value of $1,500, to Vincent de Gregorio of 201 West 106th Street. The terms of the award require that it be given to an art student in America certified by the National Academy of Design, with which the Society of American Artists has been merged. Mr. de Gregorio, now a sergeant in the Army serving in the Pacific, began studying at the National Academy of Design in 1933, after his graduation from George Washington High School.

The trustees announced that awards would be made later of three traveling scholarships, valued at $1,500 each, to graduates of the school of journalism.

Mary Coyle Chase

Mary Coyle Chase, author of "Harvey," is a former newspaper woman, who has been represented on Broadway only once before. Brock Pemberton, producer of "Harvey," presented a comedy by her called "Now You've Done It," in 1937. That play closed after a brief run. In contrast, "Harvey" opened at the Forty-eighth Street Theatre last Nov. 1 and has played to capacity audiences ever since.

The playwright was born thirty-seven years ago in Denver, Col., and went into newspaper work at an early age. She covered the usual work of women reporters of the time, writing society notes and

Mary Chase
Play

"sob" stories. She gave up newspaper work when she married Robert L. Chase, now city editor of The Rocky Mountain News in Denver. They have three children, all boys.

After the production of her first play, she tried several plays, none of which found a producer, and wrote short stories before scoring with "Harvey." She now is writing her first book.

NEW YORK DRAMA CRITICS CIRCLE AWARDS

Tennessee Williams' Hit Wins on First Ballot—'Harvey' Is Second—'Remember Mama,' 'Bell for Adano' Get 1 Vote

Tennessee Williams' "The Glass Menagerie" is the season's best American play, in the opinion of the New York Drama Critics Circle. The drama won the annual award on the first ballot cast by the local newspaper and magazine reviewers, meeting yesterday afternoon at the Hotel Algonquin. No award was made this season for "best foreign play," since none was deemed worthy of it.

Of the fourteen votes cast "The Glass Menagerie" won nine. Two votes went for "Harvey" and one each for "I Remember Mama" and "A Bell for Adano." One critic voted for no award. Those in favor of the winner were John Chapman of The Daily News, Ward Morehouse of The Sun, Kelcey Allen of Women's Wear Daily, Wilella Waldorf of The Post, John Gassner of Forum, Tom Wenning of Newsweek, George Freedley of The Morning Telegraph, Wolcott Gibbs of The New Yorker and Rosamond Gilder of Theatre Arts Magazine. Joseph Wood Krutch of The Nation and Howard Barnes of the Herald-Tribune held out for "Harvey," Arthur Pollock of The Brooklyn Daily Eagle for "A Bell for Adano" and Lewis Nichols of THE NEW YORK TIMES for "I Remember Mama." Louis Kronenberger of PM voted for no award.

In the words of the citation, the award was offered "To Tennessee Williams for his play 'The Glass Menagerie' and its sensitive understanding of four troubled human beings." According to the rules of the Critics Circle, the proceedings start with one unofficial, unsigned, nominating ballot, with Mr. Wil-

liams' play receiving eight votes at that time. On this preliminary ballot Mr. Gibbs voted for "Trio," but swung into line on the first official voting. Mr. Gibbs said he stood out for "Trio" as a protest against License Commissioner Paul Moss, who closed the show in a cause célèbre earlier in the season.

"The Glass Menagerie" also is eligible for this year's Pulitzer Prize for the drama. The entries for that close April 1 and Mr. Williams' play came in from the West

Tennessee Williams
Conway Studios

the night of March 31. It is his first play to receive Broadway attention, although the Theatre Guild once tried out his "Battle of the Angels," abandoning it on the road. Prior to its Broadway opening "The Glass Menagerie" had a successful run in Chicago.

The play has only four characters; its cast is composed of Laurette Taylor, Eddie Dowling, Julie Haydon and Anthony Ross. It concerns an aging woman, now impoverished, who looks back on a happy youth before she married the wrong man; her son, her crippled daughter and the Gentleman Caller who visits the house. Mr. Dowling and Margo Jones receive credit for the direction, and Mr. Dowling and Louis J. Singer are the producers. The play is at the Playhouse, where since its opening it has been in the category of a "smash hit."

Mr. Williams, members of the cast and others connected with the production will be guests of the circle at the annual dinner, April 22 at the Algonquin. The circle made no award last season.

1946

PULITZER PRIZE

Pulitzer Prizes Awarded; 'State of Union' the Play

"State of the Union," by Russel Crouse and Howard Lindsay, won yesterday the Pulitzer prize for the best original American play of the 1945-46 season. The trustees of Columbia University, who annually award the Pulitzer prizes in letters and journalism on the recommendation of the Advisory Board of the Graduate School of Journalism, omitted the award for the best American novel of the year.

Four newspaper men won prizes of $500 each for distinguished reporting during the year. They were Arnaldo Cortesi of THE NEW YORK TIMES for his dispatches from Buenos Aires; William L. Laurence of THE TIMES for his eye-witness account of the atom-bombing of Nagasaki; Homer Bigart of The New York Herald Tribune for his war correspondence from the Pacific theatre, and Edward A. Harris of The St. Louis Post-Dispatch for his articles on the tidewater oil situation.

A gold medal costing $500 was awarded to The Scranton (Pa.) Times for its fifteen-year investigation of judicial practices, which resulted in the resignation and subsequent indictment of United States District Court Judge Albert W. Johnson of the Middle District of Pennsylvania. He now is awaiting trial on a charge of conspiracy to obstruct justice.

The $500 prize for editorial writing went to Hodding Carter of The Delta Democrat-Times of Greenville, Miss., for a group of editorials on the subject of racial, religious and economic intolerance, as exemplified by an editorial entitled "Go for Broke," published on Aug. 27, 1945. The prize of similar value for distinguished work as a cartoonist went to Bruce Russell of The Los Angeles Times, for a cartoon entitled "Time to Bridge That Gulch." The award in the field of news photography was omitted.

"The Age of Jackson," by Arthur M. Schlesinger Jr., won the $500 prize for a distinguished work on American history, and "Son of the Wilderness," a biography of John Muir, the naturalist, by Linnie Marsh Wolfe, won the $500 prize for biography. This award was posthumous, as Mrs. Wolfe died on Sept. 15, 1945.

The prize for a distinguished volume of verse by an American author was not awarded. It was the first time since the poetry prize was instituted, in 1922, that this award was omitted, although similar omissions in other fields have not been unusual. The failure to award the novel prize this year was the fourth instance in that category.

Leo Sowerby won the $500 prize for distinguished musical composition, for "The Canticle of the Sun," which was commissioned by the

Co-authors of "State of the Union"

Alice M. Ditson Fund, and was first performed by the Schola Cantorum in this city last month.

An annual scholarship of $1,500 to the American art student certified as the most promising and deserving by the National Academy of Design, with which the Society of American Artists has been merged, was awarded to Iris Maragliotti of Ardsley and Fort Hill Roads, Scarsdale, N. Y.

The four prizes for reporting were awarded in four different fields of news coverage. That won by Mr. Cortesi for his reports from Buenos Aires was "for distinguished correspondence during the year, the test being clearness and terseness of style, preference being given to fair, judicious, well-balanced and well-informed interpretative writing, which shall make clear the significance of the subject covered in the correspondence or which shall promote international understanding and appreciation."

Mr. Harris won the prize for "a

distinguished example of telegraphic reporting on national affairs"; for his articles, which, the Columbia announcement said, "contributed to the nation-wide opposition to the appointment and confirmation of Edwin W. Pauley as Under-Secretary of the Navy."

Mr. Bigart's prize was conferred for "a distinguished example of telegraphic reporting on international affairs," while that won by Mr. Laurence was "for a distinguished example of a reporter's work during the year, the test being accuracy and terseness, the preference being given to news stories published in a daily newspaper prepared under the pressure of edition time relating to matters of special interest of a local or regional character." This award, the

announcement said, was not only for Mr. Laurence's eye-witness account of the dropping of an atom bomb on Nagasaki but for his subsequent ten articles, published in THE TIMES, on the development, production and significance of the atomic bomb.

The members of the Advisory Board who made the recommendation were Dr. Frank D. Fackenthal, acting president of Columbia University; Sevellon Brown, The Providence Journal; Robert Choate, The Boston Herald; Kent Cooper, The Associated Press; Walter M. Harrison, Oklahoma City, Okla.; Frank R. Kent, The Baltimore Sun; John S. Knight, Knight Newspapers, Inc.; Arthur Krock, THE NEW YORK TIMES; William R. Mathews, The Arizona Star, Tucson, Ariz.; Stuart R. Perry, The Adrian (Mich.) Daily Telegram; Harold S. Pollard, The New York World-Telegram; Joseph Pulitzer, The St. Louis Post-Dispatch; Roy A. Roberts, The Kansas City Star. Three members were elected to

the Advisory Board to replace three who resigned. Mr. Knight, whose term expired this year, was elected to succeed Mr. Roberts, who resigned. Gardner Cowles Jr., editor and publisher of The Des Moines Register and Tribune, succeeded Arthur M. Howe of Brooklyn, who resigned, and Palmer Hoyt, editor and publisher of The Denver Post, succeeded Mr. Harrison, also resigned. The Board adopted resolutions expressing appreciation of the services of Mr. Roberts, Mr. Howe and Mr. Harrison and regretful acceptance of the resignations.

It was announced that the winners of the three traveling scholarships of $1,500 awarded annually to graduates of the School of Journalism for foreign study would be revealed later in the year.

Lindsay and Crouse

Howard Lindsay and Russel Crouse authors of "State of the Union," are Broadway's most successful collaborators. Their twelve-year association began auspiciously in 1934 when they joined forces to write the book for the hit musical "Anything Goes." Since then they have provided the book for "Red Hot and Blue" and "Hooray for What!" and dramatized "Life With Father," now in its seventh year, from the writings of the late Clarence Day. Mr. Lindsay played the role of Father until 1944. In addition, they have produced "Arsenic and Old Lace," "Strip For Action," (in association with Oscar Serlin) which the team also wrote, and "The Hasty Heart."

Mr. Lindsay was born in Waterford, N. Y., on March 29, 1899, and was graduated from the Boston Latin School in 1907. He was a student at Harvard for a year and made his first appearance on the stage in 1909 touring with "Polly of the Circus." Later he appeared in silent pictures, vaudeville, tent shows, burlesque and toured with McKee Rankin. In 1913 he joined Margaret Anglin as stage manager, remaining with her five years.

He served in the United States infantry in the first World War and returned to show business in 1919.

Mr. Crouse was born in Findlay, Ohio, on Feb. 20, 1893, and attended school in Toledo, Ohio. Before entering the theatre he worked as a reporter, sports writer and columnist on The Cincinnati Commercial-Tribune, The Kansas City Star, The New York Globe, The New York Evening Mail and The New York Evening Post from 1910 to 1931. He served as an enlisted man with the United States Navy in World War I and as a member of the Writers War Board in World War II.

He has written several books, among them "Mr. Currier and Mr. Ives," "It Seems Like Yesterday," "Murder Won't Out," "The American Keepsake." He wrote the libretto for the musical comedy "The Gang's All Here" and "Hold Your Horses," with Corey Ford. His screen work includes scripts for "Mountain Music," "The Big Broadcast of 1938," "Artists and Models Abroad" and "The Great Victor Herbert." He is president of the Authors League of America.

"State of the Union," regarded as one of the theatrical season's outstanding productions, opened last November at the Hudson Theatre, co-starring Ralph Bellamy and Ruth Hussey. It is a study of a struggle for the 1948 Presidential nomination and tells of the failure of reactionary elements in the Republican party to convert a liberal candidate, who gives up a chance to run for President rather than sacrifice his political ideals. Leland Hayward is the producer.

NEW YORK DRAMA CRITICS CIRCLE AWARDS

PLAY CRITICS VOTE NO AWARD FOR YEAR

Decide Also Against Selecting Best Importation From Europe —'Carousel' Gets Citation

The New York Drama Critics' Circle decided yesterday to make no award for the best American play this year, and none for the best importation from Europe. Its members voted a special citation to "Carousel," however, after that musical had been ruled from the "American" classification because of its basis in Ferenc Molnar's "Liliom." The meeting was held at the Algonquin.

Although no play was regarded as "best" by the majority, the two winning the highest number of votes were "State of the Union," by Howard Lindsay and Russel Crouse, and "Born Yesterday," by Garson Kanin. Both are hits. Harry Brown's "A Sound of Hunting" won one vote in the final tabulation, as did Elmer Rice's "Dream Girl." Four reviewers voted against giving an award. Ten votes constituted a majority.

Those newspaper and magazine reviewers favoring "State of the Union" were Tom Wenning of Newsweek, Howard Barnes of The Herald Tribune, Joseph Shipley of New Leader, Irene Kittle Kamp of Cue, John Gassner of Column Review, Kelcey Allen of Women's Wear Daily and John Chapman of The Daily News. Followers of "Born Yesterday" were Arthur Pollock of The Brooklyn Daily Eagle, Woolcott Gibbs of The New Yorker, Richard Watts Jr. of Go, Joseph Wood Krutch of The Nation and Ward Morehouse of The Sun. John Mason Brown of the Saturday Review of Literature voted for "A Sound of Hunting" and Harry Bull of Town and Country for "Dream Girl." Those wishing no award were Louis Kronenberger of PM, Rosamond Gilder of Theatre Arts Monthly, George Freedley of The Morning Telegraph and Lewis Nichols of THE TIMES.

Before it was ruled from the "American" classification, "Carousel" received three votes as the best play of the year, and at the close of the meeting it won its citation on the first ballot, with eleven votes to three for "Lute Song" and three for "no award." Written by Oscar Hammerstein 2d and Richard Rodgers, "Carousel" was cited because its "various elements are freshly and charmingly combined into an unusual contribution" and offer an advancement in the musical field.

The "no award" decision on the best foreign importation came on the second ballot, when eleven members so voted, with five voting for "Antigone" and one for "O Mistress Mine."

As is the custom at Critics' Circle meetings, the balloting on the "best American play" opened with an unsigned, testing vote. At that time, "State of the Union" received four; "Carousel," "A Sound of Hunting" and "Home of the Brave," three each; "Born Yester-

day," two; "Dream Girl" and "Deep Are the Roots," one each, and no award, one.

Mr. Brown, president of the Circle, presided, and it was voted to omit the annual dinner this year, since there is to be no award. This marks the fourth time since 1936 that the critics have decided against making an award.

1947

NEW YORK DRAMA CRITICS CIRCLE AWARDS

'ALL MY SONS' WINS CRITICS' LAURELS

Arthur Miller's Play Is Named Best of Season—'No Exit' Tops Foreign Imports

By LOUIS CALTA

Arthur Miller's "All My Sons" was selected as the best American play of the season yesterday by the New York Drama Critics Circle. Eugene O'Neill's "The Iceman Cometh" was runner-up, although "All My Sons" led from the start of the balloting. The local newspaper and magazine reviewers voted "No Exit" the best foreign importation and "Brigadoon" the best in the musical comedy field.

Because it failed last season to find a play worthy of its annual award (and thereby provoked open dissatisfaction among the members), the Critics Circle made it mandatory for an award to be given. The group decided that the selection be made at the end of each season "without regard to any absolute critical standard."

In the words of the citation the award was given to "All My Sons" "Because of the frank and uncompromising presentation of a timely and important theme; because of the honesty of the writing and the accumulative power of the scenes, and because it reveals a genuine instinct for the theatre in an intelligent and thoughtful new playwright."

According to the rules of the Critics Circle, the proceedings started with every reviewer noting anonymously his personal choice. "All My Sons" received twelve votes; "The Iceman Cometh," 7; "Another Part of the Forest," four; "Joan of Lorraine," one, and "Brigadoon," one. These included proxy votes for Wolcott Gibbs and Joseph Wood Krutch, both of whom were unable to attend because of illness.

Holds on Second Ballot

In the second ballot, which called for a signed vote, "All My Sons" polled twelve votes again, while "The Iceman Cometh" lost an adherent garnering six votes. "Another Part of the Forest" received four, "Joan of Lorraine" picked up two and "Brigadoon" received one vote.

Those in favor of Mr. Miller's drama in the second balloting were Kelcey Allen of Women's Wear Daily, Brooks Atkinson of THE

TIMES, George Freedley of The Morning Telegraph, Robert Garland of The Journal-American, Rosamond Gilder of Theatre Arts Magazine, Joseph Wood Krutch of The Nation, Ward Morehouse of The Sun, Arthur Pollock of The Brooklyn Daily Eagle, Joseph Shipley of The New Leader and Stark Young of The New Republic.

The six who voted for the O'Neill play were John Chapman of The Daily News, Harry Bull of Town and Country Magazine, Robert Coleman of The Daily Mirror, John Gassner of Current Hostory, George Jean Nathan of American Mercury and Richard Watts of The New York Post. "Another Part of the Forest" received support from Howard Barnes of The Herald Tribune, Otis L. Guernsey of Cue, Louis Kronenberg of PM and T. H. Wenning of Newsweek.

In the so-called preferential voting, which ultimately decided the winners, all five plays nominated on the first ballot had to be listed by each critic in order of his preference with the first choice getting five points and the last one point. Under this system, "All My Sons" polled 86, "The Iceman Cometh", 80; "Another Part of the Forest," 72; "Joan of Lorraine," 55, and "Brigadoon," 53.

16 Votes for "No Exit"

"No Exit," written by Frenchman Jean-Paul Sartre, received sixteen votes on the straight one-vote-to-critic ballot while Konstantine Simonov's "The Whole World Over" got 4. In the musical field "Brigadoon" got 8, "Annie Get Your Gun," 6, "Finian's Rainbow," 6; "Call Me Mister," 2, and "Street Scene," 1. The preferential balloting for musicals saw "Brigadoon" winning 89 points, "Finian's Rainbow," 73; "Annie Get Your Gun," 65; "Call Me Mister," 56, and "Street Scene," 47.

"All My Sons" opened on Broadway at the Coronet Theatre on Jan. 29 under the auspices of Harold Clurman, Elia Kazan and Walter Fried in association with Herbert H. Harris. The play tells the story of a war profiteer who made his money selling defective munitions to the Army and the reaction of his family when they learn about it. It is told against a single setting of an ordinary American backyard. The playwright has been represented on Broadway only on one other occasion when he wrote "The Man Who Had All the Luck" in 1944. He also is the author of "Focus," the novel about anti-Semitism.

The presentations will be made on Sunday at a cocktail party to be held at the Algonquin Hotel.

TONY AWARDS

20 STAGE NOTABLES GET PERRY AWARDS

Authors, Producers, Others Honored Along With Actors to Start Annual Event

New York's theatre honored twenty men and women early today with the first presentation of the annual Antoinette Perry Awards for outstanding contributions to the current theatrical season. Twelve hundred persons, including many theatrical celebrities, cheered the winners at a midnight ceremony in the Waldorf-Astoria.

Two current Broadway shows were represented by two award winners each. "All My Sons" produced prizes for its author, Arthur Miller, and its director, Elia Kazan. "Finian's Rainbow" was represented by its dance director, Michael Kidd, and David Wayne, who plays and sings the role of Og, a leprechaun.

Five other performances won awards for actors and actresses. Frederic March, who received a Hollywood "Oscar" on March 13, carried off a Perry Award for his performance in "Years Ago." He became the first actor to win the film award and, in the same season, one of its Broadway counterparts.

The other acting awards went to Ingrid Bergman, also an "Oscar" winner, for her performance in "Joan of Lorraine," Jose Ferrer for "Cyrano de Bergerac," Helen Hayes for "Happy Birthday" and Patricia Neal for her first Broadway appearance in "Another Part of the Forest."

Unlike the prizes awarded annually by the Motion Picture Academy of Arts and Sciences, the Perry Awards do not designate their recipients as "best" or "first," but the classifications in which they are given will be elastic from year to year. The awards are made by directors of the American Theatre Wing in memory of the actress and director who was chairman of the Wing's wartime board.

The award already has been dubbed a "Tony," as her associates called Miss Perry, who died last year. Brock Pemberton, representing the Wing, handed out the awards. For the women, each "Tony" was an initialed sterling silver compact case. The men received engraved gold bill clips.

The winners also included some persons within the theatrical orbit but not of the theatre itself. Among these were Ira Katzenberg, a retired shoe manufacturer, and his wife, Rita, who were cited for "enthusiasm as inveterate first-nighters." They have been attending opening nights for three decades. Another prize went to Vincent Sardi Sr. "for providing a transient home and comfort station for theatre folk at Sardi's for twenty years."

Other prizes went to Lucinda Ballard for her costume designing in six current Broadway productions; Dora Chamberlain for "unfailing courtesy as treasurer of the Martin Beck Theatre"; Agnes de Mille for dance direction in "Brigadoon"; David Ffolkes for designing the settings of "Henry VIII";

Burns Mantle for his annual publication, "The Ten Best Plays"; Jules J. Leventhal as "the season's most prolific backer and producer"; P. A. McDonald for his intricate construction for the production of "If the Shoe Fits," and to Kurt Weill for his score for "Street Scene."

The presentation came as a climax to an evening of entertainment by dozens of Broadway performers. It was announced that the Waldorf's ballroom would be engaged by the Wing for a similar party every Easter Sunday evening.

1948

PULITZER PRIZE

The 1948 Pulitzer Prize for the best original American play was awarded yesterday to "A Streetcar Named Desire," by Tennessee Williams. The award for the most distinguished fiction in book form went to "Tales of the South Pacific," by James A. Michener.

Dr. Frank D. Fackenthal, acting president of Columbia University, announced fourteen awards in the fields of journalism, letters and music. It was the thirty-first year of the Pulitzer Prizes, which are awarded annually by the trustees of Columbia University on recommendation of the Advisory Board of the Graduate School of Journalism.

Dr. Fackenthal himself received from the Advisory Board, meeting for the last time before his forthcoming retirement as acting president of Columbia on June 7, a scroll in recognition of his long services in connection with the development of the Pulitzer Prizes. The scroll assured him of "the Pulitzer Prize of our friendship in perpetuity."

The gold medal awarded annually "for the most disinterested and meritorious public service rendered by an American newspaper during the year," went to The St. Louis Post-Dispatch for its coverage of the mine disaster at Centralia, Ill., and its subsequent campaign for reforms in mine safety laws.

Four prizes were awarded for reporting. George E. Goodwin of The Atlanta Journal, won the prize for local reporting, for an exposé of vote frauds. Two awards were made in the field of national reporting, to Bert Andrews of The New York Herald Tribune, and Nat S. Finney of The Minneapolis Tribune. Paul W. Ward of The Baltimore Sun won the prize for reporting international affairs. Virginius Dabney of The Rich-

mond (Va.) Times-Dispatch won the prize for distinguished editorial writing; Reuben L. (Rube) Goldberg of The New York Sun received the similar award for a distinguished cartoon, and Frank Cushing of The Boston Traveler was named the winner of the $500 prize for the best news photograph.

The prizes in letters included awards to "Across the Wide Missouri," by Bernard DeVoto, in the field of American history; to "Forgotten First Citizen: John Bigelow," by Margaret Clapp, in the field of biography, and to "The Age of Anxiety," by W. H. Auden, in poetry.

Piston Wins Music Prize

The prize for distinguished musical composition was awarded to Walter Piston for his Symphony No. 3, which had its first performance by the Boston Symphony Orchestra last January.

Each of the individual prizes carries an award of $500. The gold medal for The St. Louis Post-Dispatch is valued at the same amount.

An annual scholarship of $1,500 to the art student in America who is certified as "the most promising and deserving" by the National Academy of Design, with which the Society of American Artists has been merged, was awarded to Philip Anthony Moose of 139 West Ninety-fifth Street.

In accordance with their custom in recent years, the trustees deferred the awards of the three traveling scholarships for graduates of the School of Journalism until the completion of the academic year. These scholarships have a value of $1,500 each and are conferred upon the three highest ranking students in the class.

The Advisory Board re-elected three of its members to serve terms lasting until 1952. They were Sevellon Brown of The Providence (R. I.) Journal-Bulletin; Kent Cooper of The Associated Press, and William R. Mathews of The Arizona Daily Star of Tucson, Ariz.

The other members of the Advisory Board are Robert Choate, The Boston Herald; Gardner Cowles, The Des Moines (Ia.) Register and Tribune; Palmer Hoyt, The Denver Post; Frank R. Kent, The Baltimore Sun; John S. Knight, Knight Newspapers, Inc.; Arthur Krock, THE NEW YORK TIMES; Stuart H. Perry, The Adrian (Mich.) Telegram; Harold S. Pollard, The New York World-Telegram, and Joseph Pulitzer, The St. Louis Post-Dispatch.

Newspaper's Campaign Through

The award to The St. Louis Post-Dispatch was the result of a long campaign begun by that newspaper after the mine disaster at Centralia, Ill., which cost 111 lives on March 25, 1947. The newspaper assigned a staff of seven reporters to investigate the many ramifications of the situation, in the minefield, in Springfield, the Illinois State capital, and in the Bureau of Mines in Washington.

As a result of their news stories and the editorials and cartoons with which The Post-Dispatch followed up their efforts, the Illinois Legislature enacted two laws strengthening mine inspections; the Centralia Coal Company, operator of the mine, was indicted and fined $1,000 after it had pleaded nolo contendere, and the director of the Illinois Mines and Minerals Department resigned. He was later indicted and is awaiting

trial.

Mr. Goodwin, a 30-year-old former naval officer, won the prize for local reporting by an extensive investigation of vote frauds in Telfair County, Georgia, at the general election on Nov. 5, 1946. He spent several weeks investigating the frauds before writing his stories, which appeared in The Atlanta Journal beginning March 2, 1947.

2 National Affairs Awards

Mr. Andrews received one of the two awards for reporting on national affairs for his stories on the State Department's loyalty inquiry, the first of which appeared in The New York Herald Tribune on Nov. 1. They told in detail of the way in which an unnamed State Department employe had been dismissed as a bad security risk, without having had an opportunity to defend himself.

The award to Mr. Finney was for a series of articles charging the Truman Administration with planning to put the ordinary affairs of Federal civilian agencies under a system of censorship. His first story on this subject appeared in The Minneapolis Tribune Oct. 19.

Mr. Ward won the prize for international reporting for a series of stories on daily life in the Soviet Union, for which he conducted research while he was in Moscow for the meeting of the Council of Foreign Ministers early in 1947. After his return to this country he wrote a series of nineteen articles that appeared in The Baltimore Sun between April 30 and May 18, 1947.

The award of the prize for editorial writing to Mr. Dabney was made on the basis of his entire volume of work during 1947. The terms of this award provide that the test of excellence shall be "clearness of style, moral purpose, sound reasoning and power to influence public opinion in what the writer conceives to be the right direction."

Mr. Goldberg, veteran cartoonist of the New York Sun, won the prize for cartoons for a drawing that appeared in that newspaper on July 22. It showed a huge atomic bomb, with a house and family on top, perched precariously on a cliff labeled "World Control," but threatening to topple into a gulf marked "World Destruction."

Picture of Fight with Police

The prize for news photography was won by Mr. Cushing through a picture captioned "Boy Gunman at Bay," which appeared in The Boston Traveler of June 23, 1947. It showed a youthful gunman who was engaged in a pistol fight with the police, holding a school boy in front of him as a shield. Mr. Cushing heard of the battle over a police radio while on another assignment in the vicinity, and took the picture before the police overpowered the thug.

The victory of "A Streetcar Named Desire" marked the second time that the Pulitzer Prize and the New York Drama Critics Award have gone to the same play. The only other time was in 1940, when William Saroyan's "The Time of Your Life," received both awards. Mr. Saroyan rejected the Pulitzer prize, but Columbia informed him that the award would remain in the Pulitzer records, notwithstanding his attitude.

Mr. Michener's book is not a novel, but a collection of short stories. It was published by the Macmillan Company. Mr. DeVoto's prize-winning history was published by Houghton Mifflin Company; the prize-winning biography

by Margaret Clapp was published by Little Brown & Co., and Mr. Auden's volume of verse was published by Random House.

A musical version of "Tales of the South Pacific" is being prepared by the well-known collaborating team of Richard Rodgers and Oscar Hammerstein 2d. They also will present the show in the fall in conjunction with Leland Hayward and Joshua Logan.

Tennessee Williams
Play

Tennessee Williams was born Thomas Lanier Williams in Columbus, Miss., in 1914. He abandoned his given name when he felt he had "compromised" it by the imperfection of his early writing, and he took Tennessee as a gesture to his pioneer ancestors in that state. His first play to reach Broadway, "The Glass Menagerie," won the New York Drama Critics Circle Prize in 1945.

Five years earlier his "Battle of Angels" had failed in a Boston tryout. In the interval, Mr. Williams worked as a waiter, an elevator operator, a movie usher and at other odd jobs to stay alive while continuing to write. He got a job writing scripts for the movies but it lasted only six months.

After the success of "The Glass Menagerie," he obtained a production for "You Touched Me," a play he had written earlier in collaboration with Donald Windham. This play failed, and Mr. Williams' next entry on Broadway was "A Streetcar Named Desire."

Before "Streetcar" was produced, another Williams play, "Summer and Smoke," received its first production in the Dallas (Tex.) Theatre '47 last summer under Margo Jones' direction. Miss Jones will put the play on here next season. At present Mr. Williams is continuing to write while on a visit to Italy.

FRANK S. ADAMS

NEW YORK DRAMA CRITICS CIRCLE AWARDS

By an overwhelming vote, "A Streetcar Named Desire" received the accolade of the New York Drama Critics Circle yesterday afternoon as the best new American play of the year produced in New York. Its author, Tennessee Williams, won the same prize for his play, "The Glass Menagerie," in 1945. The Circle, which met at the Hotel Algonquin, also selected "The Winslow Boy," by Terence Rattigan, as the best of the foreign crop.

Twenty-one critics voted. "A Streetcar Named Desire" was chosen by seventeen; "Mister Roberts," two; "Command Decision" and "Medea," one each. In the foreign category, ten supported "The Winslow Boy"; five, "The Respectful Prostitute"; three, "The Old Lady Says 'No!'"; two, "Where Stars Walk," and one "Galileo." The award to a musical was dispensed with because none was deemed worthy. Also dropped were the customary citations to the winners.

Yesterday's voting was considerably simplified in comparison to the complicated system of preferential voting followed in the past. One signed ballot, based on the simple plurality arrangement, answered the purpose quickly. Wrangling was thus avoided and everything went along amicably.

Votes for "Streetcar"

The seventeen who voted for "A Streetcar Named Desire" were: Brooks Atkinson, THE NEW YORK TIMES; Howard Barnes, Herald Tribune; Louis Kronenberger, PM; Ward Morehouse, The Sun; Richard Watts Jr., New York Post; John Chapman, Daily News; William Hawkins, World-Telegram; John Mason Brown, Saturday Review of Literature; Wolcott Gibbs, The New Yorker; George Freedley, The Morning Telegraph; Joseph Shipley, The New Leader; Richard P. Cooke, The Wall Street Journal; Kelcey Allen, Women's Wear; Kappo Phelan, The Commonweal; Rosamond Gilder, Theatre Arts; John Gassner, Forum, and Joseph Wood Krutch, The Nation.

The remaining four votes were distributed to "Mister Roberts," "Command Decision" and "Medea." Tom Wenning and Robert Coleman of Newsweek and The Daily Mirror, respectively, gave their votes to "Mister Roberts"; Robert Garland, Journal-American, to "Command Decision," and George Jean Nathan, American Mercury, to "Medea," the Greek classic in a new adaptation by Robinson Jeffers.

Adherents of "The Winslow Boy" were: Freedley, Brown, Gibbs, Shipley, Allen, Hawkins, Wenning, Chapman, Krutch and Gilder. For "The Respectful Prostitute": Atkinson, Barnes, Morehouse, Cooke, Phelan. For "The Old Lady Says 'No!'"; Watts, Nathan, Gassner. For "Where Stars Walk": Garland, Coleman. For "Galileo": Kronenberger.

Awards to Be Made Sunday

Next Sunday afternoon (2-2:30) several scenes from "A Streetcar Named Desire" will be broadcast over WOR. Elia Kazan, director of the play, formally will receive the award from Mr. Brown, president of the circle, in the absence of the author, who is in Rome. Later that afternoon the circle will be host at a cocktail party to the performers in both companies.

The authors of the prize-winning plays are young men—Mr. Williams, 33; Mr. Rattigan, 35. Born in Mississippi, Mr. Williams persevered in his struggle to reach the top rung of the ladder. A graduate of the University of Missouri, he majored in drama at the State University of Iowa. "A Streetcar Named Desire," which deals with two Southern sisters and the disintegration of one of them, is the first play to be presented on Broadway by Irene M. Selznick, daughter of the film magnate, Louis B. Mayer. For Mr. Williams it marks his third local offering. The first was "The Glass Menagerie"; the second, "You Touched Me," a collaboration.

The Rockefeller Foundation gave him a fellowship and he was granted a prize of $1,000 by the American Academy of Arts and Letters. His next play, "Summer and Smoke," will be sponsored by Margo Jones next season.

Result Announced at Show

No sooner was the final curtain lowered at yesterday's matinee of "A Streetcar Named Desire" than Jessica Tandy, who has the central feminine role, stepped to the footlights and relayed the news to the audience. Applause greeted the announcement.

Mr. Rattigan had an easier road to travel than Mr. Williams. Born in London, Mr. Rattigan attended Harrow and Trinity Colleges. On this side he hasn't been as successful as abroad. Over there two of his works, "French Without Tears" and "While the Sun Shines," were performed more than 1,000 times. Only two of his seven plays seen here were rated hits. "O Mistress Mine," in which the Lunts starred, and "The Winslow Boy." The latter won the 1946 Ellen Terry Prize as the best British play.

Jointly sponsored here by the Theatre Guild, H. M. Tennent, Ltd., and John C. Wilson, "The Winslow Boy" concerns a teen-aged British naval cadet, who is unjustly accused of stealing. As the result of a furor, the case is finally adjudicated by Parliament. The plot was suggested by an actual incident of that description. On May 1 the run will close at the Empire and the attraction, the cast of which was brought over from London, will begin a transcontinental tour.

TONY AWARDS

'MISTER ROBERTS' WINS PERRY AWARD

'Outstanding Play' Also Gains Prizes for Henry Fonda and Joshua Logan, Director

---

KELLY, RATHBONE HONORED

Judith Anderson, Katharine Cornell and Jessica Tandy Rewarded for Roles

---

"Mister Roberts," the play about the waiting war in the back areas of the Pacific, carried off top honors last night at the second annual presentation of the Antoinette Perry Awards for outstanding contributions to the arts, crafts and business of the theatre during the current season.

The hit show, based by its co-authors, Thomas Heggen and Joshua Logan, on Mr. Heggen's novel of the same title, was named the season's "outstanding" play. It also won a "Tony," as the prizes are nicknamed, for its star, Henry Fonda, cited for a distinguished performance by an actor, and it captured a double honor for Mr. Logan, who also received an award for directing it.

The awards—twenty-five in all, in twenty categories—were presented at the Waldorf-Astoria before a gathering of nearly 1,000 persons, including many theatrical celebrities. The citations refrained from using the words "best" or "first," employing such terms as "outstanding" and "disinguished" instead. The winners were chosen by the board of the American Theatre Wing, which was headed throughout the war by the late Antoinette Perry, for whom the awards are named.

In addition to Mr. Fonda, two other actors were honored for "distinguished performances" — Paul Kelly, the star of "Command Decision," and Basil Rathbone, co-star of "The Heiress." All three, it was noted, are well-known film performers and all have appeared previously on Broadway.

Three actresses were similarly named for "distinguished performances." They were Judith Anderson of "Medea," Jessica Tandy of "A Streetcar Named Desire" and Katharine Cornell of "Antony and Cleopatra," which is now touring.

Awards for "outstanding performances by newcomers" went to June Lockhart of "For Love or Money" and James Whitmore of "Command Decision."

For the women, the awards were gold bracelets, each with a disc inscribed with the actress' initials and the name of the prize. The men got gold bill clips, similarly inscribed.

John Garfield represented the Experimental Theatre in accepting a "Tony" for "experiment in theatre." Mr. Garfield starred in the Experimental Theatre's production of "Skipper Next to God."

For "spreading theatre to the country while the originals perform in New York," prizes went to Mary Martin, who heads the national company of "Annie Get Your Gun," and Joe E. Brown, starring in the first road company of "Harvey." Awards for a "distinguished musical stage performance" went to Paul and Grace Hartman of "Angel in the Wings."

The "outstanding foreign company" was judged to be the cast of "The Importance of Being Earnest." In the absence of John Gielgud, the director, the award was accepted by Theresa Helburn, co-administrator of the Theatre Guild, one of the play's sponsors. Although the play was presented during the 1946-47 theatrical season, according to generally accepted statistical reckoning, the season for the purpose of the Perry Awards runs from March to March, thus enabling "Importance" to qualify.

Awards for scene design were won by Horace Armistead for "The Medium;" for costumes by Mary Percy Schenck, "The Heiress;" dance direction by Jerome Robbins, "High Button Shoes," and orchestra conducting by Max Meth, "Finian's Rainbow." George Gebhart, whose services as a production electrician have been employed by four shows so far this season, won a "Tony" as the outstanding backstage technician.

For twenty-five years of courteous and efficient service as a backstage doorman, George Pierce of the Empire Theatre received a "Tony" and took a bow. Robert W. Dowling, president of the City Investing Company, which owns several legitimate theatres in New York, and Paul Beisman, operator of the American Theatre in St. Louis, were named as "progressive theatre operators."

Rosamond Gilder, who edited Theatre Arts before its recent merger with Stage Magazine, was honored for her "contribution to theatre through a publication." Robert Porterfield, head of the Virginia Barter Theatre, won an award for his "contribution to development of regional theatre."

A special award, for "a distinguished Wing volunteer worker through the war and after," went to Vera Allen, who replaced Miss Perry as chairman and secretary of the Wing board, a post she held until last November.

1949

PULITZER PRIZE

'Salesman' Is Pulitzer Play; Sherwood, Cozzens Cited

By CHARLES GRUTZNER

Arthur Miller's "Death of a Salesman" won the Pulitzer Prize yesterday as the best American play of the 1948-49 season and Robert E. Sherwood received the biography prize for his "Roosevelt and Hopkins." The award for the best novel by an American author went to "Guard of Honor," by James Gould Cozzens.

The award to "Death of a Salesman" gave Mr. Miller's modern tragedy a clean sweep of the three major drama prizes. The play, which opened at the Morosco Theatre on Feb. 10, has also received the New York Drama Critics Circle award and the Antoinette Perry award. It is the first play to take all three honors.

Mr. Sherwood's award for "a distinguished American biography teaching patriotic and unselfish services to the people, illustrated by an eminent example," made him a four-time Pulitzer Prize winner. Mr. Sherwood's previous Pulitzer Prizes were for plays—"Idiot's Delight" in 1936; "Abe Lincoln in Illinois" in 1939, and "There Shall Be No Night" in 1941.

Fourteen Pulitzer Prize awards in the fields of journalism, letters and music were announced by Provost Albert C. Jacobs of Columbia University, acting in behalf of Gen. Dwight D. Eisenhower, president, who will return to the university later this month. The awards are made annually by the trustees of Columbia University on recommendation of the advisory board of the Graduate School of Journalism.

The individual awards, made for the thirty-second year, carried cash prizes of $500 each, and the award to an American newspaper for the most disinterested and meritorious public service was a gold medal costing $500. The medal winner was The Nebraska State Journal, for its campaign leading to the establishment of an "all-star" Presidential preference primary in Nebraska that spotlighted the issues early in last year's campaign.

With one exception all the awards were for works published or produced in the 1948 calendar year. The drama prize was for a play produced between April 1,

Arthur Miller
Play

1948, and March 31, 1949.

The music prize went for the first time to a work composed for a motion picture. It was awarded to Virgil Thomson for his music for "Louisiana Story," a documentary film on the drilling of an oil well and the reactions of a "Cajun" family.

The poetry award winner was Peter Viereck, for his book "Terror and Decorum," published by Charles Scribner's Sons. One of the groups of poems is about the African campaign, in which Mr. Viereck served with the United States Army. Mr. Viereck is a son of George Sylvester Viereck, former Nazi propagandist, with whose views he voiced disagreement.

Prizes in journalism went to Malcolm Johnson of The New York Sun for a series of twenty-four articles entitled "Crime on the Waterfront"; to C. P. Trussell of THE NEW YORK TIMES for "consistent excellence in covering the national scene from Washington"; to Price Day of The Baltimore Sun for "a distinguished example of reporting of international affairs";

to John H. Crider of The Boston Herald and Herbert Elliston of The Washington Post for "distinguished editorial writing during the year"; to Lute Pease of The Newark Evening News for "a distinguished example of a cartoonist's work"; and to Nathaniel Fein of The New York Herald Tribune for "an outstanding example of news photography."

The prize for a volume on American history went to "The Disruption of American Democracy," by Dr. Roy Franklin Nichols. The book, published by the Macmillan Company, covers the political crisis in the years 1856 to 1861, leading to the Civil War.

"Guard of Honor," Mr. Cozzens' prize-winning novel, was published by Harcourt, Brace & Co. Mr. Sherwood's biographical work was based on forty boxes of material accumulated by the late Harry Hopkins during his close association with the late President Franklin D. Roosevelt and upon the author's intimate knowledge of both men whom he served as adviser during much of the New Deal era. The book was published by Harper & Bros.

Mr. Johnson's series on waterfront crime in New York was described in the award announcement as a distinguished example of local reporting that was accurate and terse and prepared under the pressure of edition time.

The awards to Mr. Crider and Mr. Elliston marked the first time since 1936 that two awards have been made for editorial writing.

The cartoon that won the prize for Mr. Pease was titled "Who, Me?" It showed John L. Lewis, a pickaxe behind his broad back, standing in front of a broken display window labeled "U. S. Economy." The gaping hole was marked "Coal Strike." A black-robed figure marked "Court Order" pointed an accusing finger at the leader of the mine workers. The cartoonist, 80 years old, is the oldest person to win one of the Pulitzer Prizes since they were established by the will of Joseph Pulitzer.

Mr. Fein's prize photograph, captioned "Babe Ruth Bows Out," showed the late home run king, cap in hand, acknowledging the ovation of the crowd at Yankee Stadium, where he made his last appearance in baseball uniform.

The award to Mr. Day for international reporting was based on his series of twelve articles entitled "Experiment in Freedom—India and Its First Year of Independence," which formed part of a world-wide study undertaken by The Baltimore Sun on the strengths and weaknesses of the British Commonwealth in a changing world.

Announcement was made that the three traveling scholarships awarded annually to graduates of the Columbia University School of Journalism would be bestowed at the end of the school year. The scholarships, to enable a year's study abroad, have a value of $1,500 each.

Rudolph Franz Zallinger of 102 Leonard Road, Hamden, Conn., won the annual art scholarship, also with a value of $1,500. The 29-year-old winner, a student last year at the Yale University Art School, is now a teacher there. The art scholarship winner is selected by the National Academy of Design in a national competition open to all art students in this country.

The election of Hodding Carter, editor of The Delta Democrat-Times, at Greenville, Miss., to the advisory board of the Graduate School of Journalism at Columbia was announced at the same time as the Pulitzer Prizes. Mr. Carter succeeds Palmer Hoyt of The Denver Post. Re-election of Frank R. Kent of The Baltimore Sun and Stuart H. Perry of The Adrian (Mich.) Telegram to three-year terms on the advisory board was announced.

The advisory board met at the university last Thursday and Friday to make its recommendations for the prizes. Provost Jacobs presided in the absence of General Eisenhower. Members of the board present were Sevellon Brown, The Providence (R. I.) Journal-Bulletin; Kent Cooper, The Associated Press; William R. Matthews, The Arizona Daily Star, Tucson; Robert Choate, The Boston Herald; Gardner Cowles, The Des Moines Register and Tribune; Mr. Hoyt, Mr. Kent, John S. Knight, Knight Newspapers, Inc.; Arthur Krock, THE NEW YORK TIMES; Stuart H. Perry, The Adrian (Mich.) Telegram; Harold S. Pollard, The New York World-Telegram, and Joseph Pulitzer, The St. Louis Post-Dispatch.

Arthur Miller

The Pulitzer Prize to Arthur Miller for his drama, "Death of a Salesman," follows a series of awards that the 33-year-old New York playwright and novelist has received since he was an undergraduate at the University of Michigan.

This season "Death of a Salesman" brought prizes to Mr. Miller from the New York Drama Critics Circle, the American Theatre Wing (Antoinette Perry Award), the Theatre Club and the American Newspaper Guild. An earlier play, "All My Sons," produced in 1947, won him Critics Circle and Donaldson awards. He also got the Avery Hopwood Award for two successive years, as an undergraduate playwright, and a prize of the Theatre Guild Bureau of New Plays.

"Death of a Salesman," which won critical acclaim after it opened here on Feb. 10 at the Morosco Theatre, is the first play ever to be chosen as a Book-of-the-Month Club selection. It tells the tragic story of Willy Loman, a veteran Brooklyn traveling man who, after years on the road with "a smile and a shoeshine," discovers that he has been a failure as a father and has outlived his usefulness. It has been described as a drama that appeals primarily to male theatregoers. Men in the audience at the Morosco have wept.

It is scheduled for production beginning this summer in Chicago, London, Stockholm, Prague, Paris, Rome, Budapest and Mexico City.

Rangy and raw-boned, Mr. Miller was born in Harlem, on West 111th Street (he does not remember the exact address) and was brought up in Brooklyn, where he still resides. He is married to the former Mary Slattery, whom he met when they were classmates at the University of Michigan. They have two children, Jane, 4, and Robert, 1.

Mr. Miller has held jobs as a dishwasher, stock clerk, truck driver, waiter, seaman and ship fitter. He continues to take periodic turns as a factory worker, explaining:

"Anyone who doesn't know what it means to stand in one place eight hours a day doesn't know what it's all about."

A skilled carpenter and mechanic, he practices these avocations on his farm in Roxbury, Conn., where he also does some of his writing. In Brooklyn Mr. Miller attended Abraham Lincoln High School, where he played end on the football team. Injuries to his knees on the gridiron later caused his rejection for military service.

Other writings of Mr. Miller include "Focus," a novel about anti-Semitism; "Situation Normal," a war story that was the basis for his screen play, "GI Joe," and "The Man Who Had All the Luck," his first Broadway play.

NEW YORK DRAMA CRITICS CIRCLE AWARDS

MILLER PLAY WINS CRITICS' PLAUDITS

'Death of a Salesman' Is Voted Top New U. S. Drama—'South Pacific,' 'Madwoman' Cited

By SAM ZOLOTOW

By a preponderance of votes, "Death of a Salesman," "The Madwoman of Chaillot" and "South Pacific" were selected yesterday by the New York Drama Critics Circle as the outstanding Broadway shows of the 1948-49 season.

"Death of a Salesman," written by Arthur Miller, was chosen at the meeting of the critics, held in the Hotel Algonquin, as the best new American play. It marks the second time Mr. Miller has received the award, his "All My Sons" having been similarly cited for the 1946-47 season.

Picked as the best new foreign play, "The Madwoman of Chaillot" is the work of the late French author Jean Giraudoux and was adapted for local consumption by Maurice Valency. "South Pacific," which was voted the best new musical, had its première as recently as Thursday night. It represents the combined product of Richard Rodgers, Oscar Hammerstein 2d and Joshua Logan.

One signed ballot in each case clearly indicated a virtual unanimity of opinion. The results of the tally were: "Salesman," 23 votes; "Chaillot," 22, and "Pacific," 18. Other offerings voted upon in each of the foregoing categories were: "Anne of the Thousand Days" (2), 'Summer and Smoke" (1) and "The Silver Whistle" (1); "Edward, My Son" (3), "The Victors" (2) and no vote (1); "Kiss Me, Kate" (6), "Love Life" (1) and no vote (1).

Tally of Votes Recorded

Here's how the critics voted on "Salesman": Brooks Atkinson (THE NEW YORK TIMES), Howard Barnes (Herald Tribune), John Chapman (Daily News), Ward Morehouse (The Sun), Richard Watts Jr. (Post), William Hawkins (World - Telegram), Robert Coleman (Mirror), Harold Clurman (New Republic), George Freedley (Morning Telegraph), John Mason Brown (Saturday Review of Literature), Thomas R. Dash (Daily News Record), George Jean Nathan (weekly reviewer for The Journal - American and critic for a number of magazines), Wolcott Gibbs (The New Yorker),

Thomas Felder (Cue), Kappo Phelan (Commonweal), Louis Kronenberger (Time), Robert Garland (Journal-American), Richard Cook (Wall Street Journal), George Currie (Brooklyn Eagle), John Gassner (Forum), Tom Wenning (Newsweek), Kelcey Allen (Women's Wear), Gilbert Gabriel (Theatre Arts). John Lardner (of the defunct Star) did not cast a vote.

"Anne of the Thousand Days": Lawrence Perry (North American Newspaper Alliance), Jack Gaver (United Press). "Summer and Smoke": Joseph Wood Krutch (The Nation). "The Silver Whistle": Joseph Shipley (New Leader).

Foreign Play Vote

"The Madwoman of Chaillot": Atkinson, Shipley, Felder, Krutch, Hawkins, Wenning, Currie, Cook, Gassner, Phelan, Kronenberger, Perry, Allen, Dash, Brown, Clurman, Barnes, Freedley, Chapman, Gibbs, Lardner, Gabriel. For "Edward, My Son": Coleman, Gaver, Garland. "The Victors": Watts, Morehouse. No vote: Nathan.

Ballot on Musicals

"South Pacific": Atkinson, Clurman, Dash, Freedley, Gibbs, Morehouse, Nathan, Krutch, Coleman, Hawkins, Wenning, Gassner, Currie, Cook, Perry, Felder, Allen, Watts. "Kiss Me, Kate": Brown, Chapman, Barnes, Garland, Shipley, Kronenberger. "Love Life": Phelan. No vote: Gaver.

Critics who voted by proxy were Atkinson, Gabriel and Lardner.

Two Hits in Three Plays

A story of an aging commercial traveler, "Death of A Salesman" is the third of Mr. Miller's plays to be produced on Broadway. The second, "All My Sons," was a hit, but the first one, "The Man Who Had All the Luck," expired after only four performances.

In his review of "Salesman," Mr. Atkinson paid Mr. Miller the following tribute: "Arthur Miller has written a superb drama. From every point of view, 'Death of A Salesman' is rich and memorable drama. It is so simple in style and so inevitable in theme that it scarcely seems like a thing that has been written and acted."

Almost gaunt in appearance, Mr. Miller is a tall, lanky playwright. Born in Harlem thirty-three years ago, he was reared in Brooklyn. Winning prizes are nothing new to Mr. Miller. At the University of Michigan he captured two successive Avery Hopwood Playwriting Awards. Before tackling Broadway, he won the Theatre Guild's Bureau of New Plays prize of $1,200.

Besides "The Madwoman of Chaillot," two other Giraudoux plays have been seen here. They were "Amphitryon 38" and "Siegfried." The adapter of "Chaillot" is Maurice Valency, associate professor of comparative literature at Columbia University. It marks his first Broadway attempt.

Mr. Atkinson's praise for the play ran like this: "M. Giraudoux is dead, but the luster of a fine mind still shines in this original fantasy, which has been admirably adapted. Alfred de Liagre Jr. deserves a word of thanks for appreciating the quality of Giraudoux's work and for having the courage to install it on Broadway."

"South Pacific" emanates from James Michener's Pulitzer Prize book, "Tales of the South Pacific." Responsible for its conversion into a musical are Oscar Hammerstein 2d and Joshua Logan, authors of the libretto; Richard Rodgers, score, and Mr. Hammerstein, lyrics. Each has had a number of consecutive hits to his credit. The

attraction was presented by the same trio plus Leland Hayward.

Reporting on its qualities, Mr. Atkinson said: "One thing that makes 'South Pacific' so rhapsod-

WIN DRAMA AWARDS

For the best American play: Arthur Miller, who wrote "Death of a Salesman."

For the best foreign play: The late Jean Giraudoux, original author of "The Madwoman of Chaillot."

ically enjoyable is the hard work and organization that has gone into it under Mr. Logan's spontaneous direction."

At the first intermission of Saturday's matinee at "Death of A Salesman," a scroll will be presented to Mr. Miller by Mr. Brown, president of the Circle. Between 7:30 and 8 that evening, a radio program will be broadcast over WJZ on a coast to coast network. It will include a twenty-minute scene from the play and brief speeches by the Messrs. Miller and Brown and Kermit Bloomgarden, co-producer with Walter Fried. The next membership meeting of the Circle is scheduled for September, at which time resignations will be considered.

'SALESMAN,' 'KATE' WIN PERRY AWARDS

Rex Harrison and Martita Hunt Also Get 'Tonys' for Roles in Broadway Shows

Arthur Miller's drama, "Death of a Salesman" and the Cole Porter-Sam and Bella Spewack musical, "Kiss Me, Kate," won Antoinette Perry awards for outstanding contribution to the theatre here last night. Two British performers, Rex Harrison and Martita Hunt won prizes for their respective roles in "Anne of the Thousand Days" and "The Madwoman of Chaillot."

The awards, in twelve categories, were presented at a dinner at the Waldorf-Astoria, attended by almost 1,000 persons, including many noted theatre representatives. Winners were chosen by the American Theatre Wing. During the second World War the Wing's board was headed by the late Antoinette Perry, for whom the awards are named. The prizes have been described as "the only citation which the professional theatre gives to its own."

Ray Bolger, star of "Where's Charley?", and Nanette Fabray, featured in "Love Life," received awards for performances in musicals. Prizes for supporting roles in dramas went to Arthur Kennedy, of "Death of a Salesman," and Shirley Booth of "Goodbye, My Fancy."

There was an award for scene designing to Jo Mielziner, and one for costume designing to Lemuel Ayers. These were presented for their work during the 1948-49 season. Mr. Ayers also is co-producer of "Kiss Me, Kate."

Award to Elia Kazan

Elia Kazan got a prize for directing "Death of a Salesman." Another went to Gower Champion for his dance direction in the revue, "Lend An Ear."

Each award, nicknamed a "Tony," was a silver medallion, four inches in diameter, executed from an original casting by Herman Rosse. The face of the medallion carried an adaptation of the traditional comic and tragic masks and the reverse side, a relief profile of Miss Perry with the engraved citation and the name of the winner.

In connection with the awards for play and musical, Kermit Bloomgarden and Walter Fried, co-producers of "Death of a Salesman," and Saint Subber and Mr. Ayers, co-sponsors of "Kiss Me, Kate," received scrolls.

These were the third annual presentations to be made by the American Theatre Wing. The organization emphasized that it avoids any "firsts" or "bests" and presents the prizes for a "notable contribution to the current season." A spokesman for the Wing declared:

"In order to promote vitality and originality, categories are chosen to represent valuable innovations or trends to be encouraged. Anything that enlivens the theatre may win a 'Tony.' And, in theory at least, they may be given for any contribution to the art, craft or business of the theatre."

Second Prize to 'Salesman'

Earlier this month "Death of a Salesman" also won the Critics' Circle award for the best play of the current season. "South Pacific," the Richard Rodgers-Oscar Hammerstein 2d-Leland Hayward-Joshua Logan musical play which won the Critics' Circle prize for a musical was not eligible for the Perry award which was confined to presentations seen up to March 1. "South Pacific" opened here on April 7. It will be eligible for an award next year.

Mr. Miller, whose modern tragedy about Willy Loman the Brooklyn salesman, was selected as a winner, received a "Tony" in 1947 as "a promising new playwright" for his "All My Sons." Mr. Kazan won a prize as the director of that play. Mr. Fried was its co-producer.

Last night's dinner included entertainment by a score of stage, screen and radio performers. Brock Pemberton, permanent chairman of the dinner, and James E. Sauter, entertainment chairman, were masters of ceremonies.

Mrs. Kazan accepted the award for her husband who is in Hollywood. Pembroke Davenport, the conductor, represented Mr. Porter.

1950

PULITZER PRIZE

'SOUTH PACIFIC' WINS 1950 PULITZER PRIZE

'The Way West' Ruled Best Novel—Berger of The Times Gets Reporting Award

By RICHARD H. PARKE

The 1950 Pulitzer Prize for the best original American play was won yesterday by the musical production "South Pacific," and the award for the best novel by an American author went to A. B. Guthrie Jr. for his "The Way West."

The award to "South Pacific" marked the second time in the thirty-three-year history of the prize that it had gone to a musical. The show "Of Thee I Sing" received the prize in 1932.

Richard Rodgers wrote the music and Oscar Hammerstein 2d the lyrics for "South Pacific," which is based on James A. Michener's book, "Tales of the South Pacific." Mr. Michener received the Pulitzer Prize for the novel in 1948. Mr. Rodgers and Mr. Hammerstein won a special Pulitzer "citation" in 1944 for "Oklahoma!"

Reporter Receives Award

Among the awards announced in the field of journalism was one to Meyer Berger of THE NEW YORK TIMES for his account on Sept. 7, 1949, of an insane rampage on a Camden, N. J., street during which Howard B. Unruh, 28-year-old war veteran, shot and killed thirteen persons.

Mr. Berger was cited for "a distinguished example of local reporting during the year, the test being accuracy and terseness, the preference being given to news stories published in a daily newspaper prepared under the pressure of edition time."

Fourteen Pulitzer Prizes in the fields of journalism, letters and music were announced by Gen. Dwight D. Eisenhower, president of Columbia University. The awards are made annually by the trustees of the university on recommendation of the Advisory Board of the Graduate School of Journalism.

The individual awards carry cash prizes of $500 each, while an award to an American newspaper for the most disinterested and meritorious public service is in the form of a gold medal costing $500.

The medal was won by two newspapers, The Chicago Daily News and The St. Louis Post-Dispatch, for articles exposing the presence of Illinois newspaper men on state pay rolls. Each paper received a separate Pulitzer Prize. The St. Louis Post-Dispatch also won the 1948 medal for its coverage of the mine disaster at Centralia, Ill., and its subsequent campaign for reforms in mine safety laws.

All of the awards were based on works published or produced in the 1949 calendar year, with the exception of the drama and music prizes. These covered the period from April 1, 1949, to March 31, 1950.

Prizes in the journalism field, in addition to those given to Mr. Berger and the two newspapers, went to Edmund Stevens of The Christian Science Monitor for his series entitled, "This is Russia—Uncensored;" to Edwin O. Guthman of The Seattle Times for his stories clearing Prof. Melvin Rader of the University of Washington of charges of communism, and to Carl M. Saunders, editor of the Jackson (Mich.) Citizen Patriot for an editorial that later resulted in the designation of Memorial Day as a day of "Prayer for Peace."

Also in the journalism field were a prize to James T. Berryman, cartoonist of The Washington Evening Star, for a cartoon entitled, "All Set for a Super-Secret Hearing in Washington," and one to Bill Crouch, a photographer of The Oakland (Calif.) Tribune, for his picture of a near-collision between a B-29 and a stunt flier at an air show. Mr. Berryman's father, the late Clifford K. Berryman, won a Pulitzer Prize six years ago for a cartoon in The Star.

Biographer's Second Prize

The award for biography went to Samuel Flagg Bemis for the book, "John Quincy Adams and the Foundtions of American Foreign Policy," published by Alfred A. Knopf. Mr. Bemis won a Pulitzer Prize in 1927 for his "Pinckney's Treaty, a Study of America's Advantage From Europe's Distress."

Oliver W. Larkin, Professor of Art at Smith College since 1931, received the prize in history for his "Art and Life in America," published by Rinehart & Co. Gwendolyn Brooks, young Chicago poet, won the prize in poetry for "Annie Allen," published by Harper and Brothers. Her work has been described as "a small Spoon River anthology of the Negro."

The award in music was won by Gian-Carlo Menotti, author and composer of "The Consul," which is now playing on Broadway. "The Consul," which recently won the New York Drama Critics Circle Award, is a three-act musical drama that tells the story of human desperation in a police state.

"The Way West," Mr. Guthrie's prize-winning novel, was published by William Sloane Associates. It is the tale of a trek of a hundred-odd men, women and children from Independence, Mo., to the new promised land of Oregon. The author, who teaches writing at the University of Kentucky, is 49 years old.

The award to Mr. Stevens for reporting on international affairs was based on a series of forty-four articles that were filed from Berlin immediately after his departure from Moscow. In the series he analyzed and described the Russian people, their customs, their lives and their leaders.

Cleared University Professor

Mr. Guthman of The Seattle Times, whose award was won in the field of reporting on national affairs, was assigned by his paper to clear up a dispute over testimony given before the Washington State Legislature's Un-American Activities Committee. This testimony indicated that Professor Rader had attended a school for Communists. Mr. Guthman's articles led to the professor's exoneration by Dr. Raymond B. Allen, president of the University of Washington.

The editorial that won the prize for Mr. Saunders was written on the strength of the author's conviction that Memorial Day should be devoted to prayers for peace because the holiday was dedicated to those who had lost their lives in war.

Mr. Berryman's prize-winning cartoon shows a vacant table in what is presumably a Congressional hearing room. Around the table is a battery of television and newsreel cameras, microphones and a typewriter—all in readiness for the hearing that is about to start.

The prizes to The Chicago Daily News and The St. Louis Post-Dispatch were for a series written by George Theim and Roy J. Harris, which exposed the names of fifty-one Illinois newspaper editors and publishers who had been on the Illinois state pay roll. The articles aroused nation-wide attention and caused several newspapers over the country to undertake similar investigations to determine if the practice applied to their own areas.

Announcement also was made of the award of an art scholarship of $1,500 to Leonard Everett Fisher of 4810 Beach Forty-eighth Street, Brooklyn. Mr. Fisher was selected by the National Academy of Design.

It was announced at the same time that three traveling scholarships, with a value of $1,500 each, would be given on the completion of the current school year to graduates of the Columbia School of Journalism. The nominations will be made by the journalism faculty.

Members of the Advisory Board of the Graduate School of Journalism who participated in the Pulitzer recommendations were:

Sevellon Brown, The Providence (R. I.) Journal-Bulletin; Kent-Cooper, The Associated Press; William R. Matthews, The Arizona Daily Star, Tucson; Robert Choate, The Boston Herald; Gardner Cowles, The Des Moines Register and Tribune; Hodding Carter, The Delta Democrat-Times, Greenville, Miss.; John S. Knight, Knight Newspapers, Inc.; Arthur Krock, THE NEW YORK TIMES; Harold S. Pollard, The New York World-Telegram and Sun, and Joseph Pulitzer, The St. Louis Post-Dispatch.

Mr. Choate, Mr. Knight and Mr. Cowles were re-elected to serve four-year terms.

NEW YORK DRAMA CRITICS CIRCLE AWARDS

By J. P. SHANLEY

"The Member of the Wedding," "The Cocktail Party" and "The Consul" were chosen yesterday by the New York Drama Critics Circle as the best stage productions of their kind on Broadway during the 1949-50 season.

Each show was named by a substantial plurality at the balloting session in the Hotel Algonquin. "The Member of the Wedding," by

WINNERS OF ANNUAL DRAMA CRITICS CIRCLE AWARDS

T. S. Eliot

Carson McCullers

Gian-Carlo Menotti

Carson McCullers, received seventeen votes as the best American play. In the same category, four votes went to "Come Back, Little Sheba"; three to "The Consul" and one to "The Innocents."

"The Cocktail Party," written by T. S. Eliot, won twenty votes as the best foreign play. The only other show to gain support under this heading was "The Enchanted," with four votes.

As the best musical play, Gian-Carlo Menotti's "The Consul" got twenty votes. Three went to "Lost in the Stars" and three to "Regina."

"The Member of the Wedding," a story of the poignant efforts of a motherless, adolescent girl to find a social structure to which she can belong, is Mrs. McCullers' first play. It is a dramatization of her successful novel of the same title.

Author's Fourth Award

Mrs. McCullers, who was born in Columbus, Ga., is 32 years old. Two other books she has written, "The Heart Is a Lonely Hunter" and "Reflections in a Golden Eye," were on best-seller lists. Their tall, slender author decided to turn to playwriting after she had been urged to do so by Tennessee Williams. Mrs. McCullers has won two Guggenheim Fellowships and an award from the American Academy of Arts and Letters.

A play in verse about the trials of a group of frustrated moderns, "The Cocktail Party" has been a subject of intense controversy among theatregoers since it had its Broadway première. Champions of Mr. Eliot find its philosophical and mystic qualities profound and inspiring. His opponents regard the play as superficial and pretentious.

Best known for his poetry, which brought him the Nobel Prize for Literature in 1948, Mr. Eliot, born in St. Louis in 1888, went to England thirty-six years ago and became a British subject. His other plays include "Murder in the Cathedral," "Sweeney Agonistes" and "The Family Reunion."

"The Consul," officially labeled a "musical drama," also can be described as an "opera." As such it is a unique addition to the list of Broadway attractions that have been selected in the best musical category by the critics. It is the story of the attempts of a family, residing in a European police state, to get away to a democracy.

Menotti Also Was Director

Mr. Menotti not only is the author and composer of "The Consul" but also directed the presentation. Thirty-eight years old, he is a native of Cadigliano on Lake Lugano in Italy. He came to this country in 1928 and, five years later, completed his first opera, "Amelia Goes to the Ball," later presented by the Metropolitan Opera. Among his more recent works is the musical drama, "The Medium."

The voting of the critics in the three categories follows:

American Play

"The Member of the Wedding": Brooks Atkinson (THE NEW YORK TIMES), Richard Watts Jr. (Post), John Chapman (Daily News) Robert Coleman (Mirror), Arthur Pollock (Compass), Kelcey Allen (Women's Wear), Wolcott Gibbs (The New Yorker), Ethel Colby (Journal of Commerce), Lawrence Perry (North American Newspaper Alliance), Tom Dash (Women's Wear), John Gassner (Forum), John Mason Brown (Saturday Review of Literature), Whitney Bolton (Morning Telegraph), Tom Wenning (Newsweek), Gilbert Gabriel (Cue), Joseph Shipley (New Leader) and Richard Cook (Wall Street Journal).
Harold Clurman (New Republic), represented by proxy, also voted for "The Member of the Wedding," but was disqualified because he had directed the play.
"Come Back, Little Sheba": William Hawkins (World Telegram-Sun), Robert Garland (Journal-American), George Jean Nathan (Journal-American) and Jack Gaver (United Press).
"The Consul": Howard Barnes (Herald Tribune), Louis Kronenberger (Time) and Kappo Phelan (Commonweal).
"The Innocents": Ward Morehouse (World Telegram-Sun).

Foreign Play

"The Cocktail Party": Atkinson, Barnes, Watts, Chapman, Morehouse, Coleman, Garland, Bolton, Gibbs, Kronenberger, Allen, Dash, Colby, Gabriel, Cook, Brown, Shipley, Gassner, Gaver and Wenning.
"The Enchanted": Hawkins, Pollock, Nathan and Clurman.
Not voting: Phelan and Perry.

Musical

"The Consul": Atkinson, Watts, Morehouse, Hawkins, Garland, Coleman, Nathan, Kronenberger, Cook, Pollock, Gibbs, Bolton, Phelan, Colby, Gabriel, Wenning, Allen, Dash, Brown and Gassner.
"Lost in the Stars": Barnes, Chapman and Perry.
"Regina": Gaver, Clurman and Shipley.

Joseph Wood Krutch, the critic of The Nation, disqualified himself from voting in any of the categories because he had been unable to see enough plays during the season. Proxies voted also for Mr. Gibbs and Mr. Hawkins.

On Saturday, the producers and authors of the winning plays will receive scrolls from Mr. Chapman, the president of the Critics Circle, in a ceremony to be carried by the American Broadcasting Company from 6:45 to 7:15 P. M. There also will be dramatizations of highlights from the productions.

After yesterday's voting, Mr. Coleman proposed that the Critics Circle hold regular luncheon meetings and invite guest speakers. The motion was defeated with what one observer described as "a roar of shock and horror."

TONY AWARDS

8 PERRY AWARDS GO TO 'SOUTH PACIFIC'

Hit Musical Sweeps the Field —T. S. Eliot's 'Cocktail Party' Captures 'Tony'

T. S. Eliot's verse play, "The Cocktail Party," and the Richard Rodgers-Oscar Hammerstein 2d-Joshua Logan musical, "South Pacific," were named winners of Antoinette Perry awards last night for outstanding contributions to the theatre in their respective fields. The prizes were presented

at a dinner in the Waldorf-Astoria Hotel attended by 1,500 persons, including many of the theatre's foremost celebrities.

Sponsored by the American Theatre Wing, the awards honor the memory of Antoinette Perry, who served as chairman of the board of that war-born organization. The prizes, called "Tonys" in show business, are regarded as similar to the movie industry's "Oscars." Technically, however, they are not given for "firsts" or "bests," but rather, for "notable contributions to the theatre.".

Selection of "South Pacific" was almost a foregone conclusion, the fabulous musical having arrived at the Majestic Theatre last April 7, too late to be considered for the 1949 prize which went to "Kiss Me, Kate." Deadline for the Perry awards is March 1.

Altogether seventeen "Tonys" were given out in fifteen categories by Helen Hayes, newly elected president of the Wing, and Mrs. Martin Beck, chairman of the board. Of these, creators and cast members of "South Pacific" carted off eight, one of the largest sweeps ever made since the institution of the prizes four years ago.

Honored for Libretto

The Messrs. Logan and Hammerstein were honored for the libretto, while Mr. Rodgers was named for his score. In addition, Mr. Logan received a prize for his direction of the musical. Mary Martin, Ezio Pinza, Juanita Hall and Myron McCormick completed the coup, being designated for distinguished performances in a musical.

Shirley Booth and Sidney Blackmer of "Come Back, Little Sheba" were chosen for distinguished performances in a play, and Jo Mielziner, who scored with his scene-designing last year, received another "Tony" for the sets he drew for this season's "The Innocents," the melodrama fashioned by William Archibald from Henry James' "The Turn of the Screw." The prize for outstanding choreography went to Helen Tamiris for her dance creations in the revue "Touch and Go," seen earlier this season.

Aline Bernstein, the celebrated costume designer, garnered a "Tony" for her costumes in "Regina," the musical which Marc Blitzstein created out of Lillian Hellman's "The Little Foxes." Maurice Abravanel, also associated with "Regina" during its run here earlier this season, was hailed for outstanding musical direction.

Since the American Theatre Wing's board, composed of representatives of various phases of the legitimate theatre, has flexibility in making its selections, prizes also are given for significant service wherever recognized. Hence, a "Tony" also went to Joe Lynn of the "Miss Liberty" production as an outstanding stage technician.

Evans Gets Citation

Maurice Evans received special recognition for the work he did in guiding the City Center theatre company through a highly successful season.

Gilbert Miller received a scroll as the producer of "The Cocktail Party" and a similar prize also was given to the Messrs. Rodgers, Hammerstein, Logan and Leland Hayward for offering "South Pacific."

In addition, the Wing took heed of the thousands of entertainers who have served veterans since 1943. Mrs. Franklin D. Roosevelt was to have presented a special scroll of appreciation to Philip Faversham, whose name was

drawn from a bowl in which were the names of those who had done a minimum of thirty hours of hospital work outside of New York. In Mr. Faversham's absence, the scroll was accepted by Miss Esther Hawley of the Theatre Wing.

A posthumous award went to the late Brock Pemberton, founder of the Perry awards and its original chairman. Mr. Pemberton, who designed the plan by which the awards are decided, died last month.

Included in the program was entertainment by performers from several of the current Broadway productions and elsewhere. James E. Sauter presided. Barbara Luna and Michael de Leon, the children in "South Pacific," accepted the "South Pacific," accepted the prizes for Miss Martin and Mr. Pinza, who will return from a week's vacation tomorrow, when the show will reopen. Mr. Miller represented Mr. Eliot.

And You Can't Get Tickets

Sidney Blackmer and Shirley Booth were happy to be voted Antoinette Perry awards Saturday night for their performances in "Come Back, Little Sheba." After they received the medallions, however, they were surprised to note that the engraver had been guilty of an error in inscribing them. In the case of Mr. Blackmer, the legend read: "To Sidney Blackmer for his distinguished performance in 'South Pacific'." Miss Booth's prize identified her also with the Rodgers-Hammerstein-Logan-Hayward musical.

On behalf of the engraver, it might be said that "South Pacific" took eight of the fifteen awards given by the Perry committee for the 1949-50 season. Apparently the title just got to be a habit with him.

1951

NOBEL PRIZE

STOCKHOLM, Sweden, Nov. 15 —Four nuclear scientists—including two young chemists from the University of California—were announced today as winners of the Nobel Prize, along with Par Lagerkvist, 60-year-old Swedish author.

The Nobel award for chemistry was divided between Professors Edwin M. McMillan, 44, and Glen T. Seaborg, 39, of the University of California. Sir John Douglas Cockcroft, 54, of Harwell Institute, England, and Dr. Ernest Thomas Sinton Walton, 48, of Dublin University, shared the physics prize.

The value of the awards was given as $32,517.

Mr. Lagerkvist, the winner of the prize for literature, is Sweden's foremost novelist, poet and playwright of the moment. He is the fourth Swede to win this distinction since 1901 when the Nobel foundation was established under the will of the dynamite inventor Alfred Nobel, who died five years earlier.

The McMillan-Seaborg team— the first time in Nobel prize history that one American institution, in this case the University of California, produced two prize winners in the same year— won

the honor because of its discoveries in chemistry of the transuranium elements.

The Cockcroft-Walton citation reads: "For their pioneer work on the transmutation of atomic nuclei by artificially accelerated atomic particles."

The American prize-winning pair has been described as a team of superdetectives of the cosmos. Both scientists had significant roles in the development of the atom bomb (as had Professor Cockcroft, the physics co-winner).

When Dr. McMillan and Dr. Seaborg accept the prize from King Gustaf Adolf Dec. 10, the anniversary of the death of the donor, they will be accompanied by Prof. Ernest O. Lawrence of the University of California, their mentor, and by their wives.

Sir John (he was knighted in 1948) was born at Todmorden, on the border of Lancashire and Yorkshire, on May 27, 1897, of a family long engaged in the textile industry. He was graduated as an electrical engineer from the Manchester College of Technology in 1922, after two years service with the Royal Field Artillery in France during World War I. He entered St. John's College, Cambridge, in 1924, and received his Doctorate of Philosophy in 1928.

In the spring of 1939, Dr. Cockcroft succeeded Sir Edward Appleton as Jacksonian Professor of Natural Philosophy at Cambridge but within a few months, following the outbreak of World War II, he joined the Ministry of Supply as assistant director of research. Since then he has served in various important capacities in the national service, including the development of radar and the atomic bomb.

Dr. Cockcroft served as the director of the atomic energy division, National Research Council of Canada, from 1944 to 1946, when he became director of the British Atomic Energy Establishment, a position he still holds. He is a chevalier of the Legion of Honor, France, and the recipient of numerous other high honors.

Dr. Cockcroft married Eunice Elizabeth Crabtree in 1925. They have one son and four daughters.

Walton Born in Belfast

Dr. Walton was born in Belfast, Ireland, Oct. 6, 1903, son of the Rev. J. A. Walton. He was educated at Methodist College, Belfast, Trinity College, Dublin, and Cambridge University. He has been a Fellow of Trinity College since 1934, and professor of natural and experimental philosophy since 1946.

Dr. Walton married Winifred Isabel Wilson in 1934. They have two sons and two daughters.

Dr. McMillan was born at Redondo Beach, Calif., Sept. 18, 1907. He was graduated from the California Institute of Technology in 1928 and received his Ph.D. in physics at Princeton in 1932, when he joined the faculty of the University of California. He became a full professor in 1946.

In 1941 he married Elsie W. Blumer, a sister of the wife of Prof. Lawrence who won the Nobel Prize for his invention of the cyclotron. They have three children.

Seaborg of Swedish Parentage

Dr. Seaborg was born at Ishpeming, Mich., April 19, 1912, of Swedish parentage. He was graduated from the University of Cali-

fornia, Los Angeles, in 1934, and received his Ph. D. in chemistry at the University of California in 1937, when he joined the California faculty. He became a full professor in 1945.

In 1942 he married Helen L. Griggs, student secretary of Professor Lawrence. They have three sons and one daughter.

Professor Seaborg was one of the key figures in the atomic bomb project from 1942 to 1946. In addition to his war work on microwave radar, Dr. McMillan also worked on sonar at the Navy Radio and Sound Laboratory at San Diego, Calif., and later joined the Los Alamos Atomic Bomb Laboratory in New Mexico.

The official citation accompanying the Lagerkvist award reads: "For the artistic power and deep-rooted independence he demonstrates in his writings in seeking an answer to the eternal questions of humanity."

Mr. Lagerkvist's work best known internationally is his most recent novel, "Barabbas," about the robber that the multitude chose that Pontius Pilate should release in preference to Jesus. "Barabbas" has been translated and published in the United States, and has met with exceptional praise.

Mr. Lagerkvist, the youngest of seven children, was born in 1891 in the southern province of Smaland. He came from a long line of farmers and perhaps the influence of radical trends and movements, which was strongly reflected in Mr. Lagerkvist's output of thirty-five volumes of prose, verse and drama, was a reaction against the deeply religious, staid and conservative spirit of his family home.

He studied at the University of Upsala for two years and published his first novel, "People," in 1912. "Two Tales About Life," his second, appeared in 1913. Both novels were old-fashioned, but they exhibited a spirit of opposition to the conventional use of language.

In describing his work, Swedish critics most frequently refer to him as an expressionist. His early dramas bear out this characterization. In "Difficult Hour" written in 1918, "Chaos" and "Secret of Heaven," both written in 1919, and "The Invisible" in 1923, Mr. Lagerkvist preached the indestructibility of the soul as a protest against the might-is-right mentality.

Among Mr. Lagerkvist's most noteworthy novels are: "Evil Tales," "Guest of Reality," "Life Vanquished," "Fighting Spirit," "The Executioner," "The Mailed Fist," all written between 1924 and 1934. His later plays include "Man Who Relived His Life" and "The Dwarf."

When Mr. Lagerkvist was told that he had won the Nobel Prize, he said: "I have no particular message, it is all in my books."

NEW YORK DRAMA CRITICS CIRCLE AWARDS

By J. P. SHANLEY

"Darkness at Noon," "The Lady's Not for Burning" and "Guys and Dolls" were selected yesterday by the New York Drama Critics Circle as the best stage productions of the 1950-51 season on Broadway.

In a balloting session at the

Hotel Algonquin, "Darkness at Noon," Sidney Kingsley's drama based on Arthur Koestler's novel, won the designation of best American play. "The Lady's Not for Burning," Christopher Fry's romantic comedy in blank verse, was chosen as the best foreign play, and "Guys and Dolls," the Abe Burrows-Jo Swerling-Frank Loesser work, as the best musical.

In the first category the voting among the twenty-one critics and four proxy representatives who participated was unusually close. "Darkness at Noon" got ten votes to eight for "Billy Budd," three each for "The Rose Tattoo" and "The Autumn Garden" and one for "The Country Girl."

The strong showing of "Billy Budd" was regarded as particularly interesting, since the Louis O. Coxe-Robert Chapman drama, based on a Herman Melville novel, almost closed because of poor business soon after its première on Feb. 10. It is continuing after three reprieves.

Seventeen for "Guys and Dolls"

"The Lady's Not for Burning" received twenty-three votes in its category. "Black Chiffon" and "The House of Bernarda Alba" got one vote each.

In the musical group, seventeen votes went to "Guys and Dolls" and seven to "The King and I." Before the balloting in this category, however, there was a vote on a motion to give joint recognition to the two musical productions. The motion was defeated by the narrow margin of eleven votes to ten.

Before the vote for the best American play, the critics agreed that "Darkness at Noon" qualified for that category even though Mr. Koestler is a native of Hungary.

Mr. Kingsley, who is 44 years old, also won a Critics' award for his play, "The Patriots," presented during the 1942-43 season, and a Pulitzer Prize for his 1933-34 drama, "Men in White." Like the Messrs. Burrows and Loesser, he is a native of New York and attended public school here. He was graduated from Cornell University in 1928 and appeared as an actor in the play, "Subway Express," before turning to playwriting. His successful dramas also include "Dead End" and "Detective Story."

"Darkness at Noon" is an anti-Soviet drama, having as its central character an old-line Bolshevik who has fallen into disfavor with Communist party authorities.

Christopher Fry, 44 years old, is a native of Bristol, England. He left school at the age of 17 to go on the stage. His plays include "A Boy With a Cart," "A Phoenix Too Frequent," "Thor With the Angels," "The First Born" and "Venus Observed." He also adapted Jean Anouilh's "Ring Round the Moon" and wrote music and lyrics for London productions including one edition of "Charlot's Revue."

"The Lady's Not for Burning" is a frothy fable about the love of a disillusioned man for a woman under sentence of death for witchcraft. After closing here, the production went to Washington and to Philadelphia, where it is nearing the end of its American run.

Mr. Burrows, who is 40 years old, attended City College and New York University. He has been an accountant, bank runner and salesman of maple syrup, wallpaper and woven labels. He has achieved success as a Hollywood scenarist and as a radio script writer and video comic. "Guys and Dolls" was the first Broadway production on which he worked.

Jo Swerling, a native of Russia, is 53 years old. After coming to the United States, he worked as a newspaper and magazine writer.

DRAMA CRITICS CIRCLE AWARD WINNERS

Sidney Kingsley

Frank Loesser

In 1929, he and Edward G. Robinson collaborated on the comedy, "Kibitzers," in which Mr. Robinson subsequently appeared on the Broadway stage. Later, Mr. Swerling became one of Hollywood's most successful screen writers, his credits including the films, "Lifeboat," "Pride of the Yankees" and "Leave Her to Heaven."

Frank Loesser, who is 40 years old, entered City College at the age of 15. He worked as an errand boy and did newspaper work before turning to songwriting. His compositions have included "Praise the Lord and Pass the Ammunition," "Rodger Young" and many other song hits. His first score for the stage was in the musical, "Where's Charley?" "Guys and Dolls" was his second Broadway assignment.

"Guys and Dolls," based on stories by the late Damon Runyon, is about the life and times of some Manhattan tinhorns, night-club chorines, Salvation Army workers and police.

The voting in the three categories follows:

AMERICAN PLAY

"Darkness at Noon": Mark Barron (The Associated Press), Whitney Bolton (Morning Telegraph), John Chapman (Daily News), Robert Coleman (Daily Mirror), Thomas R. Dash (Daily News Record), Jack Gaver (The United Press), Wolcott Gibbs (The New Yorker), William Hawkins (World-Telegram and Sun), Ward Morehouse (World-Telegram and Sun), and Joseph T. Shipley (New Leader).

"Billy Budd": Kelcey Allen (Women's Wear), John Mason Brown (Saturday Review of Literature), Richard Oooke (Wall Street Journal), Gilbert W. Gabriel (Cue), Louis Kronenberger (Time), George Jean Nathan (American Mercury), Richard Watts (Post), and Thomas H. Wenning (Newsweek).

"The Rose Tattoo": Brooks Atkinson (The New York Times), Lawrence Perry (North American Newspaper Alliance), and Arthur Pollock (Compass).

"The Autumn Garden": Harold Clurman (New Republic), John Gassner (Current History), and Louis Sheaffer (Brooklyn Eagle).

"The Country Girl": Ethel Colby (Journal of Commerce).

FOREIGN PLAY

"The Lady's Not for Burning": Allen, Atkinson, Barron, Bolton, Brown, Colby, Coleman, Cooke, Dash, Gabriel, Gassner, Gaver, Gibbs, Hawkins, Kronenberger, Morehouse, Nathan, Perry, Pollock, Sheaffer, Shipley, Watts and Wenning.

"Black Chiffon": Chapman.

"The House of Bernarda Alba": Clurman.

MUSICAL

"Guys and Dolls": Allen, Atkinson, Barron, Chapman, Clurman, Colby, Cooke, Dash, Gaver, Gibbs, Hawkins Nathan, Perry, Pollock, Sheaffer, Watts, and Wenning.

"The King and I": Bolton, Brown, Coleman, Gabriel, Gassner, Kronenberger, Morehouse and Shipley.

Mr. Clurman's vote for "The Autumn Garden," which he staged, was authorized after a discussion by the critics.

The Journal-American was not represented in the voting. Because of illness, Robert Garland, the Critics Circle member from that newspaper, had not seen enough productions to participate.

The Herald Tribune also was without a representative at the voting. Howard Barnes, its critic, resigned his post recently. The Circle yesterday accepted with regret the resignation of Mr. Barnes as an active member of the group and made him an honorary member.

On Sunday evening, Mr. Chapman, president of the Circle, will present scrolls to the authors and producers of the winning shows as part of a variety program to be carried on television Channel 2, beginning at 8 P. M.

TONY AWARDS

'DOLLS,' 'TATTOO' GET PERRY PRIZES

Hit Musical and Play Sweep 'Tonys' for Contributions to Current Drama Season

Tennessee Williams' play, "The Rose Tattoo," and the Abe Burrows-Jo Swerling-Frank Loesser musical, "Guys and Dolls," received Antoinette Perry awards for outstanding contributions to the current theatre season last night at the Waldorf-Astoria Hotel. Many stage celebrities attended the dinner, at which the prizes were presented to twenty-three individuals, representing eighteen categories.

The awards, called "Tonys," are bestowed annually by the American Theatre Wing in honor of the late Miss Perry, formerly chairman of the organization. The first major theatre prizes of the season, they will be followed soon by the Critics' Circle, Donaldson, Pulitzer and Derwent awards. In the theatre, the "Tonys" are regarded as the equivalent of "Oscars" in the motion-picture industry.

Nine individuals connected with "Guys and Dolls" received recognition for their contributions to the musical hit, which is based on stories by the late Damon Runyon. Silver plaques were awarded to Mr. Burrows and Mr. Swerling, who did the book for the show, and to Frank Loesser, for his score.

Robert Alda Cited

Robert Alda received a plaque for a distinguished star performance in the musical and Isabel Bigley for a distinguished featured portrayal. Awards went also to George S. Kaufman, the director of the production, and to Michael Kidd, its choreographer. Cy Feuer and Ernest Martin, producers of "Guys and Dolls," received scrolls.

The plaques for "The Rose Tattoo" were distributed to Mr. Williams, to Maureen Stapleton and Eli Wallach for distinguished featured performances, and to Boris Aronson for his set in that play, as well as those he designed for "The Country Girl" and "Season in the Sun." Cheryl Crawford, sponsor of "The Rose Tattoo," received a scroll.

For the "outstanding musical score of the season" a "Tony" was presented to Irving Berlin, who composed the score for "Call Me Madam." Ethel Merman, the star, and Russell Nype, a featured player in the same production, also won awards.

Uta Hagen of "The Country Girl" and Claude Rains of "Darkness at Noon" won plaques for distinguished star performances in dramas.

Other recipients of awards were Miles White, for his costumes for "Bless You All"; Lehman Engel, for his musical direction of "The Consul" and Richard Raven, master electrician of "The Autumn Garden," as an "outstanding stage technician."

Special Plaque to Ruth Green

A "special recognition" plaque went to Ruth Green for her volunteer work in arranging reservations and seating for the five Perry award dinners.

Ilka Chase, acting for Helen Hayes, president of the Wing, who is in Hollywood, made the presentations. She was assisted by Mrs. Martin Beck, chairman of the organization's board.

Another feature of the program was the presentation of a citation to the Wing for its work on behalf of veterans. The award was made by Maj. Gen. Carl R. Gray Jr., Veterans Administrator in Washington.

James Sauter was master of ceremonies at an entertainment to honor the "Tony" winners. Among the performers who appeared were Celeste Holm, Anne Jeffreys, Herb Shriner, Joan Edwards, Lucy Monroe, Lois Hunt, Eugene Conley, Nancy Donovan, Barbara Ashley, Dorothy Greener, Arthur Blake and Juanita Hall. Miss Hall won a "Tony" last year for her performance as Bloody Mary in "South Pacific."

1952

NOBEL PRIZE

Nobel Prize Is Given To Novelist Mauriac

By GEORGE AXELSSON
Special to The New York Times.

STOCKHOLM, Sweden, Nov. 6 —François Mauriac, French novelist and journalist, won this year's Nobel Prize in literature today. He was selected for the award by the Swedish Academy of Literature.

Two teams of American and British scientists shared the physics and chemistry prizes, respectively.

Prof. Edward Mills Purcell of Harvard University, 40 years old, and Prof. Felix Bloch, 47, Swiss-born nuclear scientist at Stanford University, won the physics prize for their development of new methods for nuclear magnetic precision measurements and their discoveries in this field.

As had been revealed earlier, two British biochemists, Drs. Archer John Porter Martin, 42, and Richard Laurence Milling-

Associated Press
Francois Mauriac

ton Synge, 38, shared the chemistry prize for their invention of the partition chromatography process, a method of coloring and thus identifying particles originally discovered by a Russian, Michael Tswett. The process made possible great strides in bacteriological and other research.

M. Mauriac, 67-year-old French academician, has attracted attention since World War II by his fiery anti-Communist editorials in the Paris newspaper Le Figaro. However, his non-journalistic writ-

ings won him the Nobel Prize in literature—in European eyes the most coveted of the year's crop of Nobel awards.

Dr. Purcell and Dr. Bloch each led a group of researchers at Harvard and Stanford, respectively. The two groups worked independently of each other, but published at about the same time papers on a new important discovery in their mutual field.

The methods developed by the two scientists for nuclear magnetic precision measurements constitute a vast improvement over past practices and, in the opinion of world experts, spelled an immense advance for atomic science.

'Greatest Honor,' Mauriac Says

Special to THE NEW YORK TIMES.

PARIS, Nov. 6—François Mauriac said today that the Nobel prize for literature was "the greatest honor I have ever received."

The honor was particularly important, coming from a foreign country, M. Mauriac remarked, because it gave him "a foretaste of posterity's judgment" and "the hope of having created human types that have an echo in the most diverse countries."

Declaring that the award will be interpreted as an honor for France, the writer said it was a very moving thing "to incarnate, however unworthy he may be, his country."

M. Mauriac's contribution to the ever-present political controversy in France during the last few years has taken the form mostly of editorials appearing once or twice a week in the conservative Paris paper Le Figaro.

His deep Roman Catholic faith and his abhorrence of communism and atheism are always expressed in beautiful French.

M. Mauriac was born in Bordeaux on Oct. 11, 1885, and was educated in Catholic schools before attending the University of Bordeaux. His literary career began when he came to Paris in 1906. His first published work, a book of poems, appeared in 1909.

His great success as a novelist came after World War I. He averaged almost a novel a year during the Nineteen Twenties and Thirties. Most had as a background the Bordeaux region, a great agricultural and commercial center.

M. Mauriac's novels and later his plays have been hailed as brilliant psychological studies of individuals tortured or led astray by earthly temptations and passions.

PULITZER PRIZE

"The Shrike" by Joseph Kramm won the 1952 Pulitzer Prize yesterday for the best original American play, and "The Caine Mutiny" by Herman Wouk was judged the best novel by an American author.

The thirty-fifth annual awards were announced by the trustees of Columbia University through Dr. Grayson Kirk, vice president and acting head of the university. The awards are made on the recommendation of the Advisory Board of the Graduate School of Journalism.

In the field of journalism, The St. Louis Post-Dispatch won a gold medal for "distinterested and meritorious public service rendered by a United States newspaper." The

newspaper was honored for its investigations and disclosures of widespread corruption in the Internal Revenue Bureau and other departments of the Government. This was its fifth Pulitzer Prize, the paper having won previously in 1937, 1941, 1948 and 1950.

Starting with the revelation in March, 1951, of the effect of "influence" wielders on the prosecution of income tax frauds, the work of The Post-Dispatch led to the indictment and prosecution of James P. Finnegan, St. Louis head of the Internal Revenue Bureau. It led also to the dismissal or resignation of revenue bureau employes in all parts of the country.

The journalism awards also included one to Anthony Leviero, White House correspondent of THE NEW YORK TIMES, for his exclusive article of April 21, 1951, in which he disclosed the record of conversations between President Truman and General of the Army Douglas MacArthur at their Wake Island conference in October, 1950.

Mr. Leviero was cited for a "distinguished example of reporting on national affairs." This year the award to journalists was set at $1,000 instead of $500 as in recent years.

George de Carvalho of The San Francisco Chronicle won the award for distinguished local reporting for his stories of a "ransom racket" by which money was extorted from Chinese in the United States for relations held in Red China. The award for a distinguished example of reporting of international affairs went to John M. Hightower of the Washington Bureau of The Associated Press.

The editorial writing award was won by Louis LaCoss of The St. Louis Globe-Democrat for his editorial entitled, "The Low Estate of Public Morals." The test of excellence, the announcement explained, was "clearness of style, moral purpose, sound reasoning and power to influence public opinion in what the writer conceives to be the right direction."

Fred L. Packer of The New York Mirror won the cartoon award for his drawing entitled, "Your Editors Ought to Have More Sense Than to Print What I Say!" The editorial depicts President Truman addressing a White House press conference.

Two photographers, John Robinson and Don Ultang, both of The Des Moines Register and Tribune, shared the photography prize for their sequence of six photographs of the Drake-Oklahoma A. & M. football game of Oct. 20, 1951, in which player Johnny Bright's jaw was broken.

Two Special Citations

The advisory board adopted two special resolutions containing journalism citations. One was to The Kansas City Star for the editorial planning, organization and execution of the news coverage of the 1951 floods in Kansas and northwestern Missouri.

The resolution called the newspaper's work a "distinguished example of editing and reporting that also gave the advance information that achieved the maximum of public protection."

The second citation went to Max Kase of The New York Journal-American for his exposures of

"bribery and other forms of corruption in the popular American sport of basketball, which exposures tended to restore confidence in the game's integrity."

Prizes in the field of letters, in addition to the awards for the play and novel, included one for a "distinguished book of the year upon the history of the United States." The winner was "The Uprooted" by Oscar Handlin. "Charles Evans Hughes" by Merlo J. Pusey won the award for biography, while "Collected Poems" by Marianne Moore was the winner in the poetry division.

The prize in music went to Gail Kubic for his "Symphony Concertante" performed at Town Hall on Jan. 7, 1952. In its announcement, the trustees pointed out that the prizes are for work done in 1951 except for the music and drama awards, which cover work accomplished in the year ending March 31.

No award was given last year in the field of drama, and there was no explanation for the omission. This year's winner, "The Shrike," which concerns a man who is taken to the psychiatric ward of a city hospital after a suicide attempt, is at the Cort Theatre. The management had advertised that it would run only four more weeks, but a spokesman said yesterday after the award was announced that the decision to close would be reconsidered.

The $1,500 scholarship awarded annually to the art student certified as the most promising and deserving by the National Acamedy of Design was won by James N. Wines of 105 Bonnie Hill Road, Towson 4, Md.

Three traveling scholarships of $1,500 each will be awarded at the close of the school year to graduates of the Columbia Journalism School who shall have passed their examinations with the highest honors and be considered otherwise most deserving.

Members of the advisory board who participated in the recommendations included Dr. Kirk; Sevellon Brown, The Providence (R. I.) Journal-Bulletin; Kent Cooper, The Associated Press; Hodding Carter, The Delta Democrat-Times, Greenville, Miss.; Robert Choate, The Boston Herald; Gardner Cowles, Cowles Magazines, Inc.; John S. Knight, Knight Newspapers, Inc.; Arthur Krock, THE NEW YORK TIMES; William R. Mathews, The Arizona Daily Star, Tucson, Ariz.; Benjamin M. McKelway, The Evening Star, Washington; Stuart H. Perry, The Adrian (Mich.) Telegram, and Joseph Pulitzer, The St. Louis Post-Dispatch.

In the absence of Dean Carl W. Ackerman of the Graduate School of Journalism, who is ill, Prof. Richard T. Baker of the journalism faculty acted as chairman of the board.

RICHARD H. PARKE

NEW YORK DRAMA CRITICS CIRCLE AWARDS

John van Druten's "I Am A Camera" was voted "the best new American play" of the 1951-52 season yesterday by the New York Drama Critics' Circle. Mary Chase's comic fantasy, "Mrs. McThing," was runner-up.

In a single round of balloting, ten of the drama reviewers voted for "I Am a Camera," while five cast their ballots for "Mrs. McThing." Joseph Kramm's drama, "The Shrike," received three

votes, a similar number went to Paul Osborn's play, "Point of No Return," and Maxwell Anderson's 'Barefoot in Athens" obtained two. One critic voted for Truman Capote's "The Grass Harp." Altogether, twenty-four votes were cast.

Christopher Fry's comedy in modern dress, "Venus Observed," won the designation of the "best new foreign play" of the season. It received fifteen votes. Jan de Hartog's "The Fourposter" drew eight votes in this category and one of the critics abstained.

The revival of "Pal Joey," the musical by Richard Rodgers, Lorenz Hart and John O'Hara, won the designation of "the best musical of the season." The entertainment won twenty of the twenty-four votes. "Three Wishes for Jamie" and "Paint Your Wagon" got one vote each, while two members of the critics' circle abstained from voting in this group.

In an unusual action, the drama appraisers voted unanimously to cite Bernard Shaw's "Don Juan in Hell" as "a distinguished and original contribution to the theatre." The Shaw work, now in its third visit to the local scene, has had extraordinary success with the team of Charles Boyer, Charles Laughton, Sir Cedric Hardwicke and Agnes Moorehead reading the dream sequence from "Man and Superman." It is now playing at the Plymouth Theatre.

The balloting session was held at the Hotel Algonquin, with Gilbert Gabriel, president, presiding. Robert Garland, who resigned as drama critic for The Journal-

Christopher Fry

American, was made an honorary member of the critics' circle. Louis Kronenberger, drama critic for Time, who did not attend the session, voted by proxy for "Don Juan in Hell" as the best play of the season. However, the vote was not considered acceptable by the critics because they felt it did not comply with the official categories. Absent members who did not participate in the voting were Wolcott Gibbs and Joseph Wood Krutch.

Adapted from the autobiographical "Berlin Stories" of Christopher Isherwood, "I Am a Camera," is the story of the noted English-American novelist's student days

The New York Times
John van Druten

in 1930 Berlin, during which time he made a series of photographic impressions of life in the pre-Hitler German capital as through the lens of "a camera, with its shutter open."

Specifically, "I Am a Camera" revolves around the curious friendship of young Isherwood for Sally Bowles, an English girl who has fled the respectability of her home to an amoral existence in Berlin's bohemia. "I Am a Camera" represented the start of Mr. van Druten's twenty-seventh year as a major contributor to the American stage. His playwriting credits include "There's Always Juliet," "The Voice of the Turtle," "I Remember Mama" and, more recently, "Bell, Book and Candle."

"Venus Observed" is a play in blank verse by the 44-year-old English playwright-poet. It is one of four plays by Mr. Fry denoting the various seasons. "Venus" is supposed to exemplify autumn. In it the author tells the story of a widowed duke who invites his son to choose a stepmother from several of his father's fair friends. The action takes place in an observatory.

TONY AWARDS

'FOURPOSTER,' 'KING' WIN PERRY AWARDS

Named Outstanding Play and Musical—Jose Ferrer Gets Prizes for Acting, Directing

Jan de Hartog's "The Fourposter" and "The King and I," by Richard Rodgers and Oscar Hammerstein 2d, were named winners of the sixth annual Antoinette Perry Memorial Trophies as the season's outstanding play and musical, respectively, last night at the Waldorf-Astoria. Two prizes, one for acting and the other for

direction, were taken by José Ferrer. Presentation of the medallions was made by Helen Hayes, president of the sponsoring American Theatre Wing.

The awards—called Tonys in the trade—are given in honor of the late Miss Perry, actress-director-producer, who was the organization's wartime secretary and board chairman.

Mr. Ferrer, a triple-threat man in the theatre, won his performance accolade for his portrayal of a patient in a ward for the mentally ill in "The Shrike." He was named the campaign's leading director on the basis of his staging of "The Shrike," "The Fourposter" and "Stalag 17," all hits.

Other Prizes for Musical

Of the Perry prizes in the sixteen regular divisions, "The King and I" carried off the major share. In addition to the musical's creators, other winners were Gertrude Lawrence for her "distinguished performance" in the starring role of the English schoolmistress who undertakes to bring Western culture to the court of Siam; Yul Brynner, playing Siam's king, for his "distinguished supporting" performance; Jo Mielziner, who designed the sets, and Irene Sharaff, designer of the costumes.

The Messrs. Rodgers and Hammerstein, their trophy room already laden from past honors, received a scroll as the show's producers.

Jessica Tandy and Hume Cronyn, the husband-and-wife team co-starring in "The Fourposter," accepted the Tony in behalf of Mr. de Hartog, a Dutch writer who resides abroad. The Playwrights Company, producer of the two-character comedy dealing with the joys and sorrows of thirty-five years of wedded life, also received a scroll, which was accepted on its behalf by Roger Stevens.

Julie Harris of "I Am a Camera" was the "distinguished performance" winner among the actresses in the straight play category, with Marian Winters of the same production being named for her "distinguished supporting performance."

Three in Revival Honored

The revival of the musical, "Pal Joey," for which Mr. Rodgers also contributed the score, won prizes for three of the company's members: Robert Alton for choreography; Max Meth, conductor and musical director, and Helen Gallagher, "distinguished supporting performance by an actress in a musical."

Phil Silvers, energetic comedian of "Top Banana," took the Tony in the "distinguished musical performance, star male" division; John Cromwell of "Point of No Return" scored for his supporting performance in a dramatic play, while Peter Feller, master carpenter with the musical, "Call Me Madam," was chosen "outstanding stage technician."

Three special Perry prizes were presented. The winners were Edward Kook—himself a donor of prizes to playwrights through his Arts of the Theatre Foundation—for his "contributing to and encouraging the development of stage lighting and electronics"; Judy Garland, "for an important contribution to the revival of vaudeville" through her recent stint at the Palace, and Charles Boyer, "for a distinguished performance in 'Don Juan in Hell,' thereby assisting in a new theatre trend."

1953

PULITZER PRIZE

'Old Man and the Sea' and Inge Play Named—The Times Gets a Citation

By MILTON BRACKER

Ernest Hemingway, a major novelist since the Nineteen Twenties, and William Inge, whose first play on Broadway was produced only three years ago, won the 1953 Pulitzer Prize for fiction and drama—for "The Old Man and the Sea" and "Picnic," respectively—it was announced at Columbia University yesterday.

Mr. Hemingway, who became world-famous with the publication of "A Farewell to Arms" a generation back, was honored for a short novel about a simple Cuban fisherman. It was published originally in Life magazine last September and was brought out subsequently in book form by Charles Scribner's Sons.

Mr. Inge, whose achievement in "Come Back, Little Sheba" caused him to be highly regarded in 1950, won the $500 drama award for a play that he set in his native Kansas. Now running at the Music Box, "Picnic" had previously won the prize of the Drama Critics Circle.

The thirty-sixth annual awards were formalized at a regular meeting of the trustees of Columbia after a luncheon at the Morn-

Lee Samuels
Ernest Hemingway

ingside Drive residence of President Grayson Kirk. As usual, the action of the trustees served to confirm the recommendations of the Advisory Board of the Pulitzer Prizes.

Repeaters on the new list included Archibald MacLeish, who won the prize for poetry for the second time, Don Whitehead of The Associated Press, and THE NEW YORK TIMES, which received a special citation for its News of

the Week in Review in the Sunday paper.

Mr. MacLeish was honored this time for "Collected Poems, 1917-52." In 1933, he won for "Conquistador." The citation for THE TIMES—which had previously won more awards than any other newspaper—declared that News of the Week in Review for seventeen years "has brought enlightenment and intelligent commentary to its readers." The Review was founded by Lester Markel, Sunday Editor of THE TIMES.

An innovation this year was the breakdown of the award for local reporting into two categories.

One of these went to the full reportorial and photographic staffs of The Providence (R. I.) Journal and Evening Bulletin for "their spontaneous and cooperative coverage of a bank robbery and police chase, leading to the capture of the bandit" on Sept. 30, 1952. Twelve individuals were named as sharers of the $1,000 award, because their work had appeared under by-lines, but it was explained that their fellow staff members were being honored equally.

While the Providence award was for a "distinguished example of local reporting * * * the test being the quality of local news stories written under the pressure of edition time," the other local award applied to distinguished work where the pressure of edition time was not a factor, but where the "initiative and resourcefulness and * * * constructive purpose" of the writer counted most.

The winner was Edward J. Mowery of The New York World-Telegram and Sun, for his reporting of facts that brought vindication and freedom to Louis Hoffner, a man who had been sentenced to life imprisonment in 1941.

Last November, largely because of the efforts of Mr. Mowery and his newspaper to bring new evidence to the courts, Mr. Hoffner regained his freedom. Both The World-Telegram and The Sun had won previous Pulitzer awards, but this was the first for the combined paper.

For "disinterested and meritorious public service rendered by a United States newspaper, published daily, Sunday or at least once a week," gold medals were awarded for the first time to two weeklies.

These were The Whiteville (N. C.) News Reporter and The Tabor City (N. C.) Tribune. They were cited "for their successful campaign against the Ku Klux Klan, waged on their own doorstep at the risk of economic loss and personal danger, culminating in the conviction of over 100 Klansmen and an end to terrorism in their communities."

Don Whitehead of The Associated Press won the 1953 prize for a distinguished example of reporting on national affairs. Mr. Whitehead, a lanky Southerner with wide experience as a war correspondent, was honored for his 4,400-word account of "The Great Deception" —the Eisenhower trip to Korea just after the Presidential election.

This year's $1,000 for a distinguished example of reporting on international affairs went to Austin Wehrwein of The Milwaukee Journal. He had written a series of twenty-six articles that ran over a two-month period beginning last October. Titled "Canada's New Century," the series sought to interpret post-war Canada to the average American. It was popular on both sides of the border.

A writer for The Wall Street Journal will receive the $1,000 for distinguished editorial writing. He is Vermont C. Royster, senior associate editor of the downtown

daily.

Mr. Royster was honored for his comments that appear under the heading "Review and Outlook," a regular feature of his newspaper. The test of excellence, according to the advisory committee, is "clearness of style, moral purpose, sound reasoning and power to influence public opinion in what the writer conceives to be the right direction." No one piece was singled out, but Mr. Royster's "warmth, simplicity and understanding of the basic outlook of the American people" were said to be well illustrated by his closing pararaphs on Nov. 12.

"We do not think Americans are immune to human frailties," he wrote. "Other things being equal they can be grateful for bread and circuses and express their gratitude at the polls. But present them with a moral issue and nothing else is equal * * * Long is the list —and now longer—of the would-be buyers of the electorate who have had their power snatched from them by the people's moral indignation."

Cartoonist of the year, in Pulitzer terms, was Edward D. Kuekes of The Cleveland Plain Dealer. He won $1,000 for a drawing front-paged by his paper on Nov. 9, under the title "Aftermath."

Previously the recipient of various other honors for more than thirty years of work, Mr. Kuekes' prize-winning effort showed two stretcher-bearers carrying away a corpse in Korea. One asked, "Wonder if he voted?" The other replied, "No—he wasn't old enough."

William M. Gallagher of The Flint Journal won the photography award of $1,000. His prize-winning picture caught Adlai E. Stevenson, Democratic candidate for President, baring a worn sole by way of indicating how much heavy campaigning he was doing. Mr. Gallagher explained last night that "it was a blind shot"—taken with his camera rigged on the stage in such a position that he was not looking through it when the shutter snapped. Published on Sept. 2, it proved one of the outstanding pictures of the campaign—and incidentally brought the candidate an avalanche of new shoes.

In the category of letters, the year's $500 award for a distinguished book on the history of the United States went to George Dangerfield for "The Era of Good Feelings," published by Harcourt, Brace & Co. The 47-year-old author, a native of Great Britain, presented a study of the Administrations of James Monroe and John Quincy Adams. The book had previously won the 1953 Bancroft Prize, annually awarded by Columbia for "distinguished writings in American history."

The biography award went to "Edmund Pendleton 1721-1803" by David J. Mays, published by the Harvard University Press. Pendleton was a Virginian who, with Jefferson and Wythe, revised the Statutes of the Old Dominion. As a Revolutionary leader he took part in the Continental Congress. Jefferson thought Pendleton "the ablest man in debate I have ever met with" and also "one of the most virtuous and benevolent of men." Mr. Mays is a lawyer, 56, born in Richmond.

The music award, initiated in 1943, was not included this year. There have been similar omissions in other categories at various times in the past.

The annual $1,500 art scholarship for a student judged most promising and deserving by the National Academy of Design, with which the Society of American

Artists has been merged, went to Richard Joseph Anuszkiewiez of Erie, Pa. The annual Pulitzer traveling scholarships in journalism will be announced separately at the close of the academic year at the Graduate School of Journalism.

Mr. Hemingway's first Pulitzer Prize, $500, was awarded because the judges found "The Old Man and the Sea" the most "distinguished fiction published in book form during the year by an American author, preferably dealing with American life." Hemingway's previous novels have had European settings—Spain and Italy, for examples. The Cuban background of his prize-winner is "American" in the sense that the other twenty republics of the Western Hemisphere are American, too.

Mr. Inge's play was cited for being an "original American play, which shall represent in marked fashion the educational value and power of the stage, preferably dealing with American life." Mr. Inge has said that in future work he may use the same background he has used in his first plays.

Re-election of the following members of the advisory board for a four-year term was announced: Hodding Carter, The Delta Democrat-Times, Greenville, Miss.; Stuart H. Perry, The Adrian Telegram, Adrian, Mich., and J. D. Ferguson, The Milwaukee Journal, Milwaukee, Wis.

Members of the board who participated in the recommendations are:

Dr. Kirk.

Sevellon Brown, Providence Journal-Bulletin.

Kent Cooper, Associated Press.

William R. Mathews, Arizona Daily Star, Tucson, Ariz.

Robert Choate, Boston Herald.

Gardner Cowles, Des Moines Register and Tribune.

Hodding Carter, Delta Democrat-Times, Greenville, Miss.

John S. Knight, Knight Newspapers, Inc.

Arthur Krock, THE NEW YORK TIMES.

Joseph Pulitzer, St. Louis Post-Dispatch.

Stuart H. Perry, Adrian (Mich.) Telegram.

B. M. McKelway, Evening Star, Washington, D. C.

J. D. Ferguson, Milwaukee Journal.

Dean Carl W. Ackerman of the Graduate School of Journalism is secretary of the board. He was in the Harkness Pavilion of the Columbia-Presbyterian Medical Center for a checkup yesterday.

William Inge

The author of "Picnic," which received the Pulitzer drama prize, is a relative newcomer to the Broadway playwriting ranks. William Inge's first drama to be produced in New York was "Come Back, Little Sheba," presented in 1950 by the Theatre Guild. It had a run of 190 performances and won for Mr. Inge the designation of "most promising new playwright" in a poll among drama critics. "Picnic" is his second Broadway play.

Born in 1913 in Independence, Kan., Mr. Inge was the youngest of five children. His father was a traveling salesman. After receiving the degree of Bachelor of Arts at the University of Kansas, Mr. Inge won his master's degree at George Peabody College for Teachers in Nashville, Tenn.

He taught high school in Columbus, Kan., and then served in the English Department at Stephens College in Columbia, Mo., where Maude Adams, the celebrated actress, also was a member of the faculty.

Later, while critic on The St. Louis Star-Times, he interviewed

William Inge
Drama

Tennessee Williams, whose play, "The Glass Menagerie," was in rehearsal for a Chicago opening. Mr. Inge went to Chicago to see it and three months later completed his play, "Farther Off From Heaven." It was produced in 1947 at Margo Jones Theatre '47 in Dallas.

"Picnic," which opened at the Music Box on Feb. 19, under the sponsorship of the Theatre Guild and Joshua Logan, is the story of the impact on a group of women and girls of the arrival in a Kansas town of a braggart male. The drama was chosen by the New York Drama Critics Circle last month as the "best new American play" of the 1952-53 season.

NEW YORK DRAMA CRITICS CIRCLE AWARDS

'PICNIC' IS CHOSEN BEST NATIVE PLAY

'Crucible' 2d in Critics Circle Ballot—'Wonderful Town,' '4 Colonels' Also Win

William Inge's play, "Picnic," was named yesterday "the best new American play" of the 1952-53 season by the New York Drama Critics Circle. Arthur Miller's drama, "The Crucible," was runner-up.

The Circle, composed of drama reviewers from newspapers, news agencies and magazines, met at the Algonquin Hotel. Fourteen members cast their ballots personally, while eight voted by proxy. The award winners were decided on a plurality basis.

In a single round of balloting, eleven of the critics voted for "Picnic," while four cast ballots for "The Crucible." Tennessee Williams' controversial play, "Camino Real," won two votes, and "The Climate of Eden," the Moss Hart play based on Edgar Mittelholzer's novel, "Shadows Move Among Them," drew one ballot.

In this round, four of the aisle-sitters abstained from passing judgment, apparently holding the opinion that none of the season's stage products merited the accolade.

Ustinov Comedy Named

"The Love of Four Colonels," the Peter Ustinov comedy, co-starring Lilli Palmer and Rex Harrison, took top honors as "the best foreign play." It received thirteen votes. Frederick Knott's English melodrama, "Dial M For Murder," starring Maurice Evans, won eight votes in this category. There was one abstention.

"Wonderful Town" practically won the race by itself for honors in the musical department. It garnered twenty votes to emerge as the "best new musical." "Hazel Flagg" obtained a single vote. One critic refrained from voting in this classification.

The citations to "Picnic" and "The Love of Four Colonels" places the Theatre Guild in the enviable position of having participated in the production of two prize-winning attractions this season. The Guild co-produced the Inge play with Joshua Logan, and the Ustinov play with Richard Aldrich and Richard Myers.

The session, which lasted about an hour, was presided over by Joseph T. Shipley. Absent members who voted by proxy were: Brooks Atkinson, Mark Barron, John Mason Brown, Richard Cooke, Walter F. Kerr, Louis Kronenberger, Thomas H. Wenning and George Jean Nathan. Wolcott Gibbs did not participate in the voting. Scrolls, symbolic of the honors, will be presented to the winners by the organization at a date to be announced soon.

Brown's Bid Rejected

A proposal made by Mr. Brown, in a letter, that a special citation be given to "John Brown's Body," the Stephen Vincent Benet epic poem, adapted and directed by Charles Laughton, was rejected.

"Picnic" is the second Broadway play by Mr. Inge to prove a hit. His previous work, "Come Back, Little Sheba," produced in 1950, also won critical and popular support. The action of "Picnic" takes place in a small Kansas town. It is the story of the forces let loose by a visit to this community of a braggart vagrant.

This newspaper's reviewer made the following comment about Mr. Inge's current hit: "An original, honest play with an awareness of people. Most of the characters in 'Picnic' do not know what is happening to them. But, Mr. Inge does, for he is an artist."

Mr. Ustinov's "Four Colonels," which opened last January at the Shubert Theatre, is a romantic fantasy dealing with four Allied officers in a disputed zone in Europe, who are confronted with a mysterious castle that defies their efforts to enter it. The author is starred in the current London version, now in its fourth year. It is Mr. Ustinov's first play here, although he has contributed five plays to the West End. American audiences may recall him for his portrayal of Nero in the film, "Quo Vadis."

"Wonderful Town," which brought Rosalind Russell back to the Broadway stage after many years, was written by Joseph Fields and Jerome Chodorov, who based the book on their play, "My Sister Eileen." The lyrics were provided by Betty Comden and Adolph Green, and the music by Leonard Bernstein.

TONY AWARDS

DRAMA, MUSICAL WIN PERRY PRIZES

'Crucible,' 'Wonderful Town' Get 'Tonys' for Service to Current Stage Season

Arthur Miller's drama, "The Crucible," and the musical, "Wonderful Town," received Antoinette Perry awards here last night for "distinguished contributions to the current theatre season."

Shirley Booth, Tom Ewell, Rosalind Russell and Thomas Mitchell were among the performers who were honored at the seventh annual bestowal of "Tonys" by the American Theatre Wing after a dinner in the Waldorf-Astoria Hotel.

The "Tonys," silver gilt medallions with a bas-relief portrait of the late Miss Perry, wartime chairman of the board and secretary of the Wing, were presented to the winners by Faye Emerson before an audience of 1,000 persons, including many leading representatives of the entertainment world.

In making an award to "The Crucible," the board of the Wing, composed of authorities from all segments of the theatre, including managements and unions, honored Mr. Miller for the third time. He won "Tonys" in 1947 for his drama, "All My Sons," and in 1949 for "Death of a Salesman."

Producers Receive Scrolls

Kermit Bloomgarden and Robert Fryer, the respective producers of "The Crucible" and "Wonderful Town," received scrolls in recognition of their achievements. The book for "Wonderful Town" was by Joseph Fields and Jerome Chodorov; the score by Leonard Bernstein and the lyrics by Betty Comden and Adolph Green.

Miss Booth and Mr. Ewell won their prizes for their performances in a "dramatic play." Miss Booth, the star of "The Time of the Cuckoo," also is a three-time winner, having been chosen for performances in "Goodbye, My Fancy," in 1949, and in "Come Back, Little Sheba," in 1950. Earlier this month she won an "Oscar" from the Academy of Motion Picture Arts and Sciences for her performance in the screen version of "Come Back, Little Sheba," which marked her motion picture debut.

Mr. Ewell's "Tony" was for his performance in the comedy, "The Seven Year Itch," in which he is starred. Miss Russell, the star of "Wonderful Town," and Mr. Mitchell, who is co-starred in "Hazel Flagg," were selected for performances in musicals.

Awards for featured performances in non-musical attractions went to Beatrice Straight of "The Crucible" and John Williams of "Dial M for Murder." Sheila Bond of "Wish You Were Here" and Hiram Sherman, who appeared in the revue, "Two's Company," won "Tonys" for featured performances in musical presentations.

Other Winners Are Listed

Other winners were Raoul Pène du Bois, set designer ("Wonderful Town"); Miles White, costume designer ("Hazel Flagg"); Joshua Logan, director ("Picnic"); Donald Saddler, choreographer ("Wonderful Town"); Lehman Engel, musical director ("Wonderful Town" and the S. M. Chartock Gilbert and Sullivan series), and Abe Kurnit, property man ("Wish You Were Here").

There were three special awards for "contributions to the theatre not covered by regular categories." The winners were Beatrice Lillie, the star of "An Evening With Beatrice Lillie;" Danny Kaye, who heads the variety bill at the Palace Theatre, and the Equity Community Theatre, represented by Miss Lyn Ely and Mark A. McCloskey, director of the Board of Education's Bureau of Community Education.

A program of entertainment preceded the awards. The presentation ceremonies were broadcast nation-wide by the National Broadcasting Company.

1954

PULITZER PRIZE

By CHARLES GRUTZNER

The Pulitzer Prize for drama was awarded yesterday to "The Teahouse of the August Moon." This gives a clean sweep of the year's three top drama awards to John Patrick's light satire of the American occupation of Okinawa. The play has already won the Antoinette Perry and New York Drama Critics Circle awards.

The trustees of Columbia University, who made public the annual awards in belles-lettres, journalism and music, announced there was no award this year for fiction. It was learned that the advisory board on the Pulitzer Prizes felt the year 1953 had produced no novel by an American author that merited such distinction.

All the awards are for works produced in the previous calendar year, except those for drama and music, for which the juries consider works produced up to March 31 of the current year.

"The Teahouse of the August Moon," playing at the Martin Beck Theatre, where it opened Oct. 15, was adapted by Mr. Patrick from a novel by Vern Sneider.

The Pulitzer drama prize, $500 in cash, is for "the original American play which shall represent in marked fashion the educational value and power of the stage, preferably dealing with American life." In addition to sweeping the "Big Three" drama awards, "Teahouse" has been honored also with the Theatre Club and Aegis Theatre Club awards.

Charles A. Lindbergh's autobiography, "The Spirit of St. Louis," published by Charles Scribner's Sons, won the $500 prize for an American biography "teaching patriotic and unselfish services to the people."

Mr. Lindbergh, recently made a reserve brigadier general in the Air Force, won fame as the first man to fly the Atlantic alone. He has received many honors for his aviation achievements.

The $500 prize for a United States history was awarded to Bruce Catton's "A Stillness at Appomattox," published by Doubleday & Co., Inc. The book is the final volume of Mr. Catton's Civil War trilogy, following "Mr. Lincoln's Army" and "Glory Road." "A Stillness at Appomattax" has also won the 1954 National Book Award.

A gold medal for disinterested and meritorious public service by a newspaper, published daily or at least once a week, went to Newsday, of Garden City, L. I., for its exposé of trotting track scandals and labor racketeering.

John Patrick
Drama

The daily, of which Alan Hathway is managing editor and Alicia Patterson, editor and publisher, turned the first dirt in the scandals that led eventually to a state-wide investigation of harness racing by a Moreland Act Commission appointed by Governor Dewey, and to the conviction of William DeKoning, Nassau County labor racketeer, of extortion and grand larceny.

$1,000 Prizes in Journalism

Other awards in journalism, each with a $1,000 cash prize, are:

For a distinguished example of local reporting, under the pressure of edition time, to The Vicksburg (Miss.) Sunday Post-Herald for covering in accurate detail the tornado that struck Vicksburg last Dec. 5, a Saturday, at 5:35 P. M., shortly before edition time.

For distinguished local reporting, where edition time was not a factor, to Alvin Scott McCoy of The Kansas City (Mo.) Star, for a series of exclusive stories that led to the resignation under fire of C. Wesley Roberts as Republican National Chairman.

For national affairs reporting, to Richard L. Wilson of The Cowles Newspapers for his exclusive publication of the Federal Bureau of Investigation report to the White House in the Harry Dexter White case before it was put before the Senate by J. Edgar Hoover.

For international reporting, to Jim G. Lucas of the Scripps-Howard newspapers for his human interest reporting, much of it from the front lines, during most of the three years of the Korean war.

For editorial writing, to The Boston Herald for editorials by Donald M. Murray on the "new look" in national defense, analyzing changes in American military policy. The test of excellence in this category was "clearness of style, moral purpose, sound reasoning and power to influence public opinion in what the writer conceives to be the right direction."

For cartooning, to Herbert L. Block (Herblock) of The Washington Post—now The Washington Post and Times-Herald—for a cartoon showing the robed figure of death saying to the shade of Premier Joseph Stalin of Russia, after his death, "You Were Always a Great Friend of Mine, Joseph."

For news photography, to Mrs. Walter M. Schau, amateur photographer of San Anselmo, Calif., for her pictures of a rescue of two men from a trailer cab hanging off the side of a bridge from which the vehicle later fell.

Mrs. Schau's photographs of the rescue were published first in The Akron (Ohio) Beacon Journal and distributed nationally by The Associated Press. She is the first winning woman photographer in the twelve years of the picture award, and the second amateur to have won out over the nation's professional news photographers.

Mr. Block was the only Pulitzer Prize repeater among this year's winners. He also won the Pulitzer Prize for cartooning in 1942.

The award of dual prizes for local reporting, one under deadline pressure and the other for less hurried writing, was an innovation last year that was continued this year.

Poetry, Music, Art Awards

The $500 prize in poetry was awarded to Theodore Roethke's "The Waking: Poems 1933-1953," published by Doubleday & Co. Mr. Roethke, an associate professor of English at the University of Washington, was twice a Guggenheim Fellow, has held a fellowship of the Fund for the Advancement of Education, and has won the Tietjens Prize and the Levinson Prize.

The prize in music, also $500, went to Quincy Porter's Concerto for Two Pianos and Orchestra. Dr. Porter, Professor of Music at Yale University, has been the recipient of several medals and citations for his compositions, which include chamber and instrumental music as well as the larger forms. The Concerto for Two Pianos and Orchestra was performed on March 17 of this year by the Louisville Symphony Orchestra.

A traveling fellowship in art, having a value of $1,500, was given to Henry E. Niese of Montclair, N. J.

Yesterday's awards were the thirty-seventh annual Pulitzer Prizes. The advisory board acceded to the request of Dean Carl W. Ackerman of the Graduate School of Journalism that he be permitted to retire as board secretary after twenty-three years' service. The board elected Prof. John Hohenberg of the Graduate School as secretary for the 1954-55 year.

The advisory board received this year a record number of nominations for the Pulitzer Prizes, 530 in all, compared with 418 last year.

Members of the advisory board on Pulitzer Prizes are Dr. Grayson Kirk, president of Columbia University; Sevellon Brown, The

Providence Journal-Bulletin; Kent Cooper, The Associated Press; William R. Mathews, The Arizona Daily Star, Tucson, Ariz.; Robert Choate, The Boston Herald; Gardner Cowles, The Des Moines Register and Tribune; Hodding Carter, The Delta Democrat-Times, Greenville, Miss.; John S. Knight, Knight Newspapers, Inc.; Arthur Krock, The New York Times; Joseph Pulitzer, The St. Louis Post-Dispatch; Stuart H. Perry, The Adrian (Mich.) Telegram; B. M. McKelway, The Evening Star, Washington; J. D. Ferguson, The Milwaukee (Wis.) Journal.

John Patrick

John Patrick, who combines writing with agriculture and sheep breeding on his Suffern, N. Y., farm, was born in Louisville, Ky., on May 17, 1906. He received his early education in several Southern boarding schools and subsequently at Holy Cross College of New Orleans and at Harvard and Columbia.

After leaving Columbia he took to writing in earnest. He wrote a play, which remains unidentified, and provided radio adaptations, among them "Arrowsmith," for Helen Hayes. For a while the screen demanded his attention.

Hollywood still calls upon his services quite frequently. Among the scenarios he is responsible for are "The President's Lady" and "Coins in the Fountain." He is now converting "Mister Roberts" for the screen.

His Broadway bow as a playwright with "Hell Freezes Over" (1935) was not auspicious. It was a failure and so was the second, "The Willow and I" (1942). However, the third, "The Hasty Heart," catapulted him into the limelight and gave him the recognition for which he had been striving.

The plot emanated from his experiences as an ambulance driver with the American Field Service in Africa, India and Burma. On a transport carrying him back to the United States, he wrote the script. As soon as it was submitted to Howard Lindsay and Russel Crouse, they produced it for a run of 204 performances.

Mr. Patrick's next three plays lacked the stamina of "The Hasty Heart" and were short-lived: "The Story of Mary Surrat" (1947), which marked his debut as a director; "The Curious Savage" (1950) and "Lo and Behold" (1950).

Until Mr. Patrick came to grips with the dramatization of Vern Sneider's novel, "The Teahouse of the August Moon," all of his previous plays were originals. His handiwork did not meet with Mr. Sneider's approval.

Reporters who knew about the strained relationship between Mr. Patrick and Mr. Sneider were reluctant to use the information in advance of the New York première, which took place on Oct. 15, 1953, at the Martin Beck Theatre under the auspices of Maurice Evans, in association with George Schaefer.

Mr. Sneider's fears turned out to be groundless, the critics were unanimous in their approbation. Credit was reflected not only on Mr. Patrick, but also on the cast, headed by David Wayne and John Forsythe; the director, Robert Lewis, and the scenic designer, Peter Larkin.

Two weeks ago "The Teahouse of the August Moon" duplicated its success not only in London, but also on the distant island of Okinawa, where the story develops. All the action stems from the attempts of the American oc-cupation forces there to inculcate the ideals of democracy in an oriental village. Although Washington had blueprinted the transformation, the humorous results are far from the anticipation of the high brass.

NEW YORK DRAMA CRITICS CIRCLE AWARDS

'TEAHOUSE' PICKED BY DRAMA CRITICS

Voted Best Play—'Ondine' Is the Leading Import and 'The Golden Apple' Top Musical

"The Teahouse of the August Moon," "Ondine" and "The Golden Apple" were chosen yesterday by the New York Drama Critics Circle as the best presentations of the 1953-54 stage season here.

In a voting session at the Algonquin Hotel, "Teahouse," John Patrick's comedy from Vern Sneider's novel of the same name, was designated as the best American play. "Ondine," the "romance" by the late Jean Giraudoux, adapted from the French by Maurice Valency, was named as the best foreign play. "The Golden Apple," with book and lyrics by John Latouche and music by Jerome Moross, was picked as the best musical.

Seventeen members of the circle attended the meeting and the votes of six others were submitted by proxies. In its category, "Teahouse" received fourteen ballots. There were four votes for "The Caine Mutiny Court Martial," two for "Tea and Sympathy," one each for "The Girl on the Via Flaminia" and "Ladies of the Corridor" and one abstention.

"Ondine" won sixteen votes and "The Confidential Clerk" five in the foreign play balloting. There were two abstentions.

'Beautiful Sea' Second

In the votes for the musical "The Golden Apple" received thirteen, "By the Beautiful Sea" three and "John Murray Anderson's Almanac" and "The Threepenny Opera" one each. Five of the critics abstained.

Louis Kronenberger, the critic for Time, was registered as abstaining in each category. Mr. Kronenberger, who was represented by proxy, proposed that the usual designations be waived and that a single award go to the Phoenix Theatre for its outstanding work during the season. The motion was defeated.

The Phoenix, which is located at Twelfth Street and Second Avenue, is currently the showcase for "The Golden Apple." Since it began its policy of presenting major stage productions in December it also has housed "Madam, Will You Walk" and "Coriolanus." "The Golden Apple" will move uptown to the Alvin Theatre next Tuesday after completing its run at the Phoenix.

Before the voting Joseph T. Shipley, the drama critic for The New Leader, and president of the circle, pointed out that "The Golden Apple" was eligible for votes because the organization's rules did not confine it to "Broadway," but only to New York in making selections.

Another proposal from Mr. Kronenberger—to give a special citation to the Phoenix—and one by Robert Coleman, critic of The Mirror, to present a citation to Victor Borge for his one-man show, "Comedy in Music," also were disapproved.

"Teahouse" and "Ondine" also were the recipients of Antoinette Perry Awards here last month. The Perry prizes were voted by the board of the American Theatre Wing for outstanding productions, performers, writers, directors and technicians.

A story about the American occupation of Okinawa after World War II, "Teahouse" was described by Brooks Atkinson, the drama critic of The New York Times as "a light and sagacious comedy . . . completely captivating."

"Ondine," which is about a love affair between a water nymph and a knight, was described by the same critic as "ideal from every point of view."

"The Golden Apple," is a satirical musical in which the legend of Helen and Ulysses is applied to a mythical American town at

Honored by Drama Critics Circle

Maurice Valency, adapter of French play, "Ondine," chosen as best foreign play.

John Patrick, adapter, "The Teahouse of the August Moon," best American play.

John Latouche, who wrote book and lyrics for "The Golden Apple," best musical.

Jerome Moross, who wrote the music for "The Golden Apple," top presentation.

the turn of the twentieth century.

M. Giraudoux and Mr. Valency also were the author and adaptor of "The Madwoman of Chaillot," which the critics selected as the best foreign play of the 1948-49 season.

The winning authors will receive scrolls from Mr. Shipley on Thursday at the Columbia Broadcasting System studio at 49 East Fifty-second Street. The ceremony and excerpts from yesterday's meeting, recorded on tape, will be broadcast by C. B. S. on Sunday from 5 to 6 P. M. on the radio program, "Stage Struck."

TONY AWARDS

"The Teahouse of the August Moon" and "Kismet" won Antoinette Perry Awards last night as the outstanding play and musical of the current Broadway stage season.

Audrey Hepburn, David Wayne,

A scene from the prize-winning play "The Teahouse of the August Moon." In the center foreground is David Wayne, who was selected as the best dramatic actor in a starring role.

Alfred Drake and Doretta Morrow in a scene from "Kismet," adjudged best musical. Mr. Drake won "Tony" for interpretation of stellar part. Louis Adrian, director, also won award.

Audrey Hepburn, who was chosen best dramatic star for her portrayal in "Ondine."

Dolores Gray, best feminine musical star, selected for part in "Carnival in Flanders."

Dolores Gray and Alfred Drake were among the performers who received "Tonys" (silver medallions) for their performances.

The presentations were made at the eighth annual Perry awards dinner at the Plaza Hotel under the sponsorship of the American Theatre Wing. The prizes are named for the late Miss Perry, who was the Wing's chairman and secretary during World War II.

Miss Hepburn, chosen for her portrayal of a water nymph in "Ondine," was the winner Thursday of an Academy Award for her acting in the film "Roman Holiday." Her Perry prize was for "a distinguished performance in a dramatic play by a female star."

Mr. Wayne won in the dramatic category for his performance as Sakini, the quixotic Okinawan in "The Teahouse of the August Moon." He received a "Tony" in 1947 for his work in "Finian's Rainbow."

Jo Van Fleet, John Kerr Cited

Miss Gray, who appeared in "Carnival in Flanders," and Mr. Drake, who heads the cast of "Kismet," were selected for outstanding performances by stars in musical presentations.

Jo Van Fleet, who was seen in "A Trip to Bountiful," and John Kerr of "Tea and Sympathy" won awards for featured performances in dramas. Corresponding recognition in the musical category was given to Gwen Verdon of "Can-Can" and Harry Belafonte of "John Murray Anderson's Almanac."

Other "Tonys" went to Peter Larkin for sets in "Ondine" and "Teahouse," Richard Whorf for costumes in "Ondine," Alfred Lunt for direction of "Ondine," Michael Kidd for choreography in "Can-Can," John Davis, now with "Picnic," for "consistently good work as a theatre electrician," and Louis Adrian for musical direction of "Kismet."

Mr. Kidd's award was the third he has won for his dance creations, the others having been for "Finian's Rainbow" and "Guys and Dolls" in 1951.

Altogether, there were nineteen "Tonys" and three scrolls in the sixteen categories covered by the awards. In the case of "Teahouse," a "Tony" went to John Patrick, who wrote the play from a novel by Vern Sneider, and scrolls were presented to Maurice Evans and George Schaefer, the producers.

Voting This Year Close

The "Tonys" for "Kismet" went to Charles Lederer and Luther Davis, who wrote the book, and to Robert Wright and George Forrest, who adapted the music from Alexander Borodin and wrote the lyrics. Charles Lederer, who produced the musical, got a scroll.

Management and the performer and craft unions of the entertainment field are represented on the Wing's board that chooses the Perry Award winners. The voting this year was so close that it appeared for a while that—for the first time since the prizes were instituted—a second ballot might be required.

Helen Hayes, president of the Wing, headed the dinner committee. Russell Nype, Jean Swetland, Joseph Scandur, Frances Greer and the Meyer Davis orchestra participated in an entertainment program. James Sauter was the master of ceremonies.

The Messrs. Lunt, Belafonte, Evans and Schaefer were unable to attend the dinner. Mr. Whorf accepted the award for Mr. Lunt; Mrs. Belafonte for her husband, and Mariko Niki of the cast of "Teahouse" for the show's producers.

1955

PULITZER PRIZE

Pulitzer Winners: 'Fable' And 'Cat on Hot Tin Roof'

By CHARLES GRUTZNER

"Cat on a Hot Tin Roof" won for Tennessee Williams yesterday his second Pulitzer Prize for drama. The Mississippi playwright had taken the 1948 award for "Streetcar Named Desire."

Tennessee Williams

A dramatist with a poetic command of the theatre, Tennessee Williams has won five major playwriting awards since his first work opened on Broadway ten seasons ago.

Yesterday's award for "Cat on a Hot Tin Roof" was his second Pulitzer Prize, the first having been given to him in 1947 for "A Streetcar Named Desire." He is also a three-time winner of the New York Drama Critics Circle honors— for "Cat on a Hot Tin Roof," "A Streetcar Named Desire" and "The Glass Menagerie." The last-named play, which made him, at 31, one of the best-known dramatists, started Mr. Williams on his Broadway career. It opened to a fine set of notices on March 31, 1945.

Shy and sensitive, Mr. Williams received his southern accent and background for most of his plays from Columbus, Miss., where he was born on March 26, 1914. In his early teens, his family moved to St. Louis, where Thomas Lanier Williams, as his parents named him, attended high school. In his spare time, he tried his hand at writing poems and short stories. In his school years, he began to dislike his given name, feeling it was more suited to "an author of sonnets to spring." He adopted the name Tennessee in honor of his pioneer ancestors in that state.

As a student at the University of Missouri and later at Iowa, Mr. Williams turned to playwriting. In 1936, his first play to be produced, a farce called "Cairo, Shanghai, Bombay!" was shown in Memphis. The next year, his first serious plays, "Candles to the Sun," about coal miners, and "Fugitive Kind," about a flophouse, were put on by an amateur theatrical group in St. Louis.

Mr. Williams kept at his writing all through college, but economic necessity forced him to work as a clerk in a shoe factory. For two years he would return home from work, drink black coffee and pound his typewriter until dawn. He was graduated from Iowa in 1938.

His first break came when he won first prize in a Group Theatre play contest a year later. This led to a Theatre Guild production of his "The Battle of the Angels," which closed on the road, never reaching Broadway. Then came a period of wanderlust. He worked at various jobs —as an all-night elevator operator in a hotel, a waiter, teletype operator, restaurant cashier and a movie house usher. While employed as a $17-a-week usher, in 1943, he managed to get a job as a Hollywood scenario writer for $250. After spending six months in Hollywood, he wrote "The Glass Menagerie."

The 1955 Pulitzer Prize for the best American work of fiction went to "A Fable," William Faulkner's allegory based on life in the trenches of World War I. Mr. Faulkner, also a Mississippian, had won the 1949 Nobel Prize for Literature.

The opera "The Saint of Bleecker Street" brought its composer, Gian-Carlo Menotti, his second Pulitzer Prize. Mr. Menotti had received the 1950 award for his opera "The Consul."

"Cat on a Hot Tin Roof," which deals with a warped family on a Mississippi Delta plantation, is playing at the Morosco. "The Saint of Bleecker Street" closed April 2 at the Broadway Theatre after ninety-two performances. It will have its television premiere on May 15 as the season's last production of the N. B. C. Opera Theatre.

Both "Cat" and "The Saint" have also won the 1955 awards of the New York Drama Critics Circle.

The trustees of Columbia University announced fourteen prizes in drama, belles-lettres, journalism and music. The announcement marked the thirty-eighth annual awards under the will of Joseph Pulitzer, publisher of The New York World.

Paul Horgan's "Great River, the Rio Grande in North American History," received the prize for a distinguished book on United States history.

The prize for a "distinguished patriotic and unselfish service

Tennessee Williams
Drama

to the people" went to William S. White, a member of the Washington Bureau of The New York Times, for "The Taft Story"—the life of the late Senator Robert A. Taft.

The poetry prize went to "The Collected Poems of Wallace Stevens." The collection includes poems written in the last quarter century by Mr. Stevens, who won the Bollingen Prize in Poetry of the Yale University Library for 1949, and the National Book Award in 1950.

Among eight journalism awards, the prize "for disinterested and meritorious service" went to The Columbus (Ga.) Ledger and Sunday Ledger-Enquirer for complete news coverage and fearless editorial attack on corruption in neighboring Phenix City, Ala.

The prize for local reporting under the pressure of deadline time went to Mrs. Caro Brown, a reporter for The Alice (Tex.) Daily Echo for a series on the successful attack upon one-man political rule in Duval County.

The prize for local reporting, without having to write for a deadline, was won by Roland Kenneth Towery, managing editor of The Cuero (Tex.) Record, for a series exposing a scandal in the administration of the Veterans Land Program in Texas.

The award for national reporting was given to Anthony Lewis of The Washington Daily News for a series of articles. The series resulted in the clearing of Abraham Chasanow, dismissed unjustly by the Navy Department as a security risk, and brought his restoration to duty with an acknowledgment by the Navy that it had been mistaken.

The prize for distinguished reporting of international affairs was awarded to Harrison E. Salisbury of The New York Times for his series of articles, "Russia Re-viewed." This was based on his six years as correspondent in the Soviet Union.

Editorial on Strike

The Detroit Free Press received the editorial writing prize for an editorial by Royce Howes, associate editor, who "impartially and clearly" analyzed the responsibility of both labor and management for an unauthorized strike that made idle 45,000 Chrysler auto workers.

The prize for cartooning went to Daniel R. Fitzpatrick of The St. Louis Post-Dispatch for a cartoon on Indochina titled "How Would Another Mistake Help,?" published June 8, 1954, and also for "the distinguished body of Mr. Fitzpatrick's work both in 1954 and his entire career."

John L. Gaunt Jr., photographer for The Los Angeles Times, received the news photography prize for his picture of a tragic young couple standing beside the angry sea in which their infant son had perished only a few minutes earlier.

The award to The Columbus Ledger and Sunday Ledger-Enquirer for disinterested and meritorious public services took the form of a gold medal. The other journalism awards were $1,000 cash each.

The prizes for drama, music and letters were $500 each.

Several selections were made by special juries in each field and passed on to the Advisory Board on Pulitzer Prizes, which recommended one winner in each field to the Columbia University trustees. The trustees met yesterday afternoon and accepted the advisory board's recommendations.

Pulitzer Is Extolled

The Advisory Board made public a memorial to Joseph Pulitzer, editor and publisher of The St. Louis Post-Dispatch, who died March 30. Mr. Pulitzer was a son of the founder of the Pulitzer awards. The memorial noted that the editor of The St. Louis Post-Dispatch had inherited a great newspaper tradition, which he "steadily enhanced throughout his professional career, elevating and protecting the standards of publication implicitly imposed by the First Amendment on American journalism as its special responsibility to the people."

The Advisory Board adopted a resolution honoring Arthur Krock of The New York Times, who retired as a member of the board under a rule, which he had proposed, limiting membership to three terms of four-years each.

The Columbia trustees announced the award of the Pulitzer art scholarship, of $1,500, to Jack W. Henderson, 25-year-old student at the Art Students League. Mr. Henderson of Kansas City, Mo., is residing while in New York at 125 West Sixty-ninth Street.

Three traveling scholarships in journalism, each having a value of $1,500, will be awarded at the end of the school year to graduates of the Columbia School of Journalism.

The Advisory Board elected Joseph Pulitzer Jr., new editor and publisher of The St. Louis Post-Dispatch, to a four-year term, succeeding his late father. Benjamin M. McKelway, editor of The Washington Star, was re-elected to a four-year term. Turner Catledge, managing editor of The New York Times, was elected to succeed Mr. Krock. Prof. John Hohenberg of the Columbia School of Journalism was re-elected board secretary.

The present board is:
Dr. Grayson Kirk, president of Columbia University; Sevellon Brown, The Providence (R. I.) Journal; Hodding Carter, The Delta Democrat-Times, Greenville, Miss.; Robert Choate, The Boston Herald; Kent Cooper, The Associated Press, New York; Gardner Cowles, Cowles Magazines, Inc., New York; J. D. Ferguson, The Milwaukee Journal; John S. Knight, Knight Newspapers, Inc., Chicago; Turner Catledge, The New York Times; William R. Mathews, The Arizona Daily Star, Tucson, Ariz.; Benjamin M. McKelway, The Evening Star, Washington; Stuart H. Perry, The Adrian (Mich.) Telegram; Joseph Pulitzer Jr., The St. Louis Post-Dispatch; John Hohenberg, secretary, Columbia University.

NEW YORK DRAMA CRITICS CIRCLE AWARDS

The annual awards of the New York Drama Critics Circle were presented last evening on the stage of the Morosco Theatre. Walter F. Kerr, president of the organization, handed scrolls to the winners.

Tennessee Williams accepted the citation for his "Cat On a Hot Tin Roof," chosen as the best American play. The scroll for Agatha Christie's "Witness for the Prosecution," designated as the best foreign play, was accepted by Francis L. Sullivan, a member of the cast. Miss Christie is in Baghdad. The award for Gian-Carlo Menotti's "The Saint of Bleecker Street," chosen as

Drama Critics Circle Makes Awards

Tennessee Williams, left, accepts scroll from Walter F. Kerr

the best musical, was accepted by producer Chandler Cowles. Mr. Menotti is in Italy.

After the presentations, a benefit performance of "Cat On a Hot Tin Roof" was given for the Actors Fund of America.

TONY AWARDS

Hayes Drama Chosen Best Play—Musical Prize to 'Pajama'

By ARTHUR GELB

"The Desperate Hours," which Joseph Hayes tossed off in less than eleven weeks, won the Antoinette Perry Award last night as the outstanding play of the Broadway season ended March 1.

A chilling suspense story about three escaped convicts who terrorize an Indiana home, the melodrama earned an additional "Tony"—as the silver medallion is known—for its director, Robert Montgomery. He was cited for the season's most distinguished job of staging.

In the musical sphere, "The Pajama Game," the hit show that spoofs labor-management relations in a pajama factory, nosed out such attractions as "Fanny," "Peter Pan" and "Silk Stockings" for the top song-and-dance honors. The musical also won "Tonys" in two other categories.

Nancy Kelly, Alfred Lunt, Mary Martin and Walter Slezak were honored for their performances in starring roles.

Miss Kelly, who drew warm

notices for her acting in "The Bad Seed," portrays the terrified mother of a 9-year-old girl who commits murders almost as casually as she consumes ice cream.

Mr. Lunt collected critical raves earlier in the season for his polished portrayal in "Quadrille" of a married American railroad executive who elopes with an equally committed marchioness.

Singing and Flying Award

Mary Martin earned her honors for singing and flying through the recent musical version of "Peter Pan."

And Mr. Slezak, who long ago tried and failed to make the

Walter Slezak, for performance in musical, "Fanny."

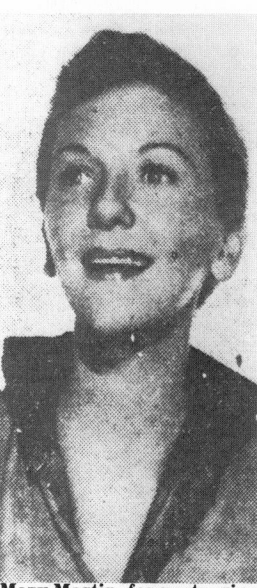

Mary Martin, for portraying title role in "Peter Pan."

Alfred Lunt, for his role in dramatic play, "Quadrille."

Nancy Kelly, cited for her acting in "The Bad Seed."

Paul Newman, left, Malcolm Brodrick, center, and Karl Malden in "The Desperate Hours," which last night was named outstanding dramati; play at a dinner at the Plaza.

grade as an opera star in Vienna, currently is delighting audiences for his miming in "Fanny."

The awards—given in honor of the late Miss Perry, who was the secretary of the American Theatre Wing during World War II—were presented by Helen Hayes at a dinner in the Plaza Hotel's grand ballroom. One thousand persons, many of them important figures in the entertainment field, witnessed the event, which marked the beginning of the annual prize-granting season on Broadway. Soon to follow will be the Critics

Circle awards and the Pulitzer prizes.

"Tonys" are to the professional theatre what "Oscars" are to the motion-picture industry. What makes them so much hankered after is the fact that the recipients are selected by top-ranking members of their own profession. Performer and craft unions of the entertainment field as well as management were represented on the American Theatre Wing's board that chose this year's winners.

Since prizes were granted for productions that opened before March 1, "Bus Stop" and "Cat

on a Hot Tin Roof," both of which were highly praised by the critics, were excluded from

this season's competition. They will be eligible, however, for the balloting in 1956.

Proscenium Group Wins

There were seventeen categories of awards, a new one having been added this year for consistently good work by an off-Broadway group. The "Tony" in this category went to Prescenium Productions, now presenting Anouilh's "Thieves' Carnival" at the Cherry Lane Theatre. Earlier in the season, it put on a successful revival of Congreve's "The Way of the World."

The quartet of winners for outstanding featured performances were:

Francis L. Sullivan, for his interpretation of the crafty defense attorney in the triple-twist murder thriller, "Witness for the Prosecution"; Patricia Jessel, as the dubious witness in the same play; Cyril Ritchard, for his dual impersonation of Mr. Darling and the timorous pirate in "Peter Pan," and Carol Haney, who slithers and mugs her way exuberantly through "The Pajama Game."

Other awards went to Oliver Messel, for his "House of Flowers" settings; Cecil Beaton, for his "Quadrille" costumes; Robert Fosse, for his choreography in "The Pajama Game"; Richard Rodda, a stage technician, for his backstage work in "Peter Pan," and Thomas Schippers, conductor of the orchestra for "The Saint of Bleecker Street."

1956

PULITZER PRIZE

By MILTON BRACKER

The 1956 Pulitzer Prizes in letters, journalism, music and art were announced yesterday by Columbia University. The novel honored was "Andersonville," by MacKinlay Kantor, and the winning play was "The Diary of Anne Frank," by Frances Goodrich and Albert Hackett.

In history, the award went to Richard Hofstadter for "The Age of Reform: From Bryan to F. D. R."

In biography, the work chosen was "Benjamin Henry Latrobe," by Talbot F. Hamlin.

Elizabeth Bishop was named the year's Pulitzer poet. She had published a collection called "Poems: North and South—A Cold Spring."

Eight individuals and two publications without reference to individuals were honored in seven categories of journalism prizes.

The winners included: for meritorious public service, The Watsonville (Calif.) Register-Pajaronian; for local reporting under deadline conditions, Lee Hills of The Detroit Free Press; for local reporting under conditions not usually subject to deadline, Arthur Daley, sports columnist of The New York Times; for distinguished national reporting, Charles L. Bartlett of The Chattanooga Times.

Also, for international reporting, William Randolph Hearst Jr., Kingsbury Smith and Frank

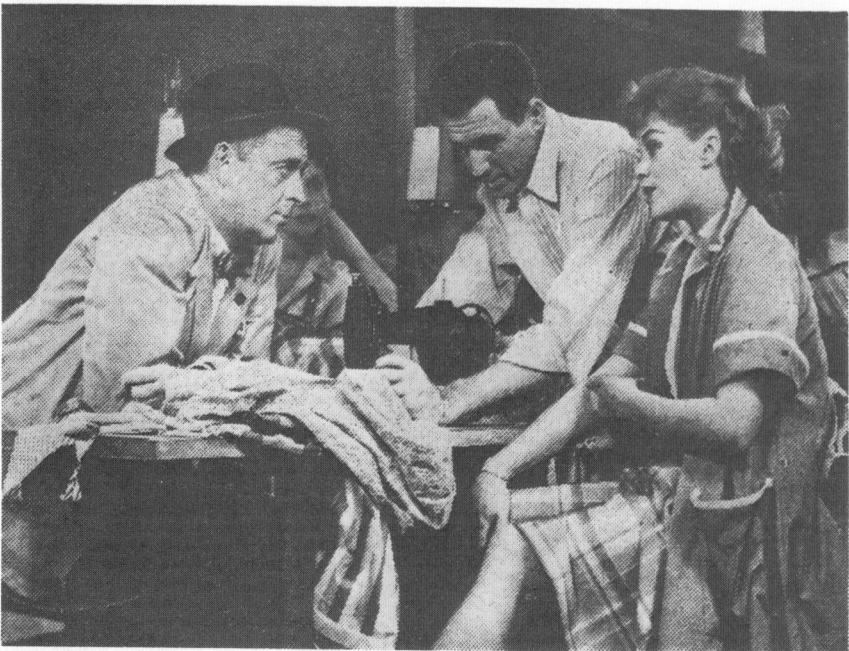

Eddie Foy Jr., left, John Raitt and Janis Paige as they appear in "The Pajama Game," chosen the outstanding musical of the theatre season from March 1, 1954 to March 1, 1955.

Conniff of the Hearst newspapers; for distinguished editorial writing, Lauren K. Soth of The Des Moines Register and Tribune; for the year's best cartoon, Robert York of The Louisville Times, and for photography, The New York Daily News. The music award went to Ernst Toch for his Symphony No. 3, and the traveling scholarship in art to Mrs. Carol Maringer Benson of Cleveland.

The letters awards are $500 each. Those in journalism are $1,000 each. The music award is of $500 and the art scholarship is valued at $1,500. Three traveling scholarships in journalism will be awarded separately.

The announcement marked the thirty-ninth annual awards under the will of Joseph Pulitzer, publisher of The New York World.

The stage version of "The Diary of Anne Frank," depicting the life of a group of Jewish refugees in Nazi-occupied Netherlands, had already won two top theatrical honors.

These were the American Theatre Wing's Antoinette Perry Award for the outstanding play of the year, and the New York Drama Critics Circle Award for the best new American play.

Based on "Anne Frank: The Diary of a Young Girl," a 1952 best seller, the play opened at the Cort Theatre on Oct. 5. Susan Strasberg has won acclaim in the title role of the child whose spirit illumined the days of terror. The real Anne Frank eventually lost her life after the hideaway was discovered.

Mr. Kantor's prize novel told the story of thousands of Union prisoners of the Confederacy in the Civil War. Published last Oct. 26 by the World Publishing Company, "Andersonville" was hailed as a tremendous work on a tremendous theme. It involved a feat of research and has been awarded by many critics an important place in the steadily growing literature of the Civil War.

Mr. Hofstadter's "The Age of Reform: From Bryan to F. D. R." has been considered by some authorities to represent a landmark in American political thought. Published by Alfred A. Knopf, it examined the half-century between 1890 and 1940.

Mr. Hamlin's study of Benjamin Henry Latrobe was the first full-length account of the life of the nation's first professional architect. It was published by the Oxford University Press.

Miss Bishop became the latest woman to enter the ranks of Pulitzer Prize poets, others having included Audrey Wurdemann and Marianne Moore. Her collection was published by Houghton Mifflin Company. A former Guggenheim fellow, and poetry consultant at the Library of Congress, she has been living in Brazil since late 1951.

Daily News Is Winner

The New York Daily News, rather than any one of its camera men, was honored for photography. The tabloid was cited "for its consistently excellent news picture coverage in 1955, an outstanding example of which was its photograph, 'Bomber Crashes in Street.'"

Published on Nov. 3, the picture referred to was taken from a plane by George Mattson, who flew in a News plane over the scene of a B-26 crash in East Meadow, L. I.

The $500 music award went to Dr. Toch, whose honored "Symphony No. 3" was first performed by the Pittsburgh Symphony Orchestra on Dec. 2, with William Steinberg conducting. Dr. Toch was born in Vienna in 1887. He came here in 1934.

The drama prize of $500 is awarded "for the American play, preferably original in its source and dealing with American life, which shall represent in marked fashion the educational value and power of the stage."

To the extent that "The Diary of Anne Frank" does not deal with American life, the award is unusual but not without precedent. Some previous winners— "Idiot's Delight" and "There Shall Be No Night," both by Robert E. Sherwood for example —were set abroad, although both, unlike the 1956 winner, had American characters.

The award for meritorius public service went to a daily newspaper with a circulation of 7,800. It was cited for its "courageous exposure of corruption in public office, which led to the resignation of a district attorney and the conviction of one of his associates."

The incident dated to last Oct. 26, at 1 A.M. William Kennedy, a reporter, and Sam Vestal, a photographer, of the Watsonville newspaper were held at pistol point when they discovered District Attorney Charles L. Moore Jr.'s car in the driveway of a home owned by a known gambler.

In the "deadline" category of local reporting, Mr. Hills, executive editor of his newspaper, won $1,000 for what the official citation called his "aggressive, resourceful and comprehensive front-page reporting" of the United Automobile Workers' negotiations with the Ford Motor Company and General Motors for a guaranteed annual wage.

Where a deadline was not generally a factor, the winner in the same category was Mr. Daley, who in 1942 took over the column "Sports of The Times" from John Kieran.

Mr. Daley was cited for the column in general and for six sample pieces. They had dealt with baseball, boxing, horse-racing and the question of amateurism in track.

Mr. Daley is a Fordham University graduate remembered by many of his colleagues as a center fielder who was death on left-handed batters pulling to right center. He was usually there before the ball.

In general, the award of Pulitzer Prizes for sports writing has been rare. The last one was to Max Kase of The New York Journal-American in 1952; the first to William H. Taylor of The Herald Tribune in 1935.

The award for national reporting went to Mr. Bartlett, who is Washington correspondent of The Chattanooga Times. The paper is published by the Times Printing Company, of which Arthur Hays Sulzberger, president and publisher of The New York Times, is publisher.

Mr. Bartlett was honored for a series of stories that disclosed the continued interest of Secretary of the Air Force Harold E. Talbott in a business management concern that had obtained fees from companies with Government contracts.

The upshot of the stories, and others that Mr. Bartlett's pieces touched off, was Mr. Talbott's resignation last Aug. 1. In a let-

Frank Conniff, left, William Randolph Hearst Jr., center, and Kingsbury Smith, who shared award for international reporting, as they appeared yesterday after announcement.

ter to President Eisenhower, the Secretary said he did not wish to embarrass either the President or the Administration.

The Associated Press log for July 14, 1955, shows the impact of Mr. Bartlett's first story:

"We had missed the boat Tuesday night," the log said, "by failing to pick up a Chattanooga Times exclusive from its Washington correspondent, reporting a Senate committee vote to look into the business connections of Air Force Secretary Talbott. (Chattanooga sent a detailed advisory message but nobody acted on it.) Tonight (Thursday) The New York Times got into the story in a big way and we reported it then. Later * * * the lesson was applied; we acted quickly to pick up fresh developments reported by the Chattanooga member."

The three members of the Hearst organization won the prize for a "distinguished example of reporting on international affairs."

Mr. Hearst is editor in chief of the Hearst newspapers; Mr. Smith is vice president and general manager of International News Service; and Mr. Conniff is editorial assistant to Mr. Hearst.

The three men went to Moscow as a team. There at the time of the shake-up that ousted Premier Georgi M. Malenkov in favor of Nikolai A. Bulganin, they obtained a series of exclusive interviews with the Soviet leadership, including Marshal Bulganin.

For distinguished editorial writing, the prize awarded to Mr. Soth was primarily for one piece, titled "If the Russians Want More Meat * * *" published on Feb. 10, 1955. It invited a Soviet farm delegation to this country. When the invitation was acceped, Mr. Soth pursued the subject editorially; his subsequent comments in The Des Moines Register and Tribune were also cited in the award.

The year's best cartoon was deemed to be by Mr. York. The work was called "Achilles." Published in The Louisville Times last Sept. 16, it showed the sym-

bolic figure of American prosperity tapering to a weak heel labeled "Farm Prices."

The jurors for the Pulitzer Prizes were appointed early in the year by the university. They were invited to exercise their independent and collective judgment and to submit from two to five recommendations in each category without necessarily indicating an order of preference.

The Pulitzer jurors met on March 12 and 13, reviewing hundreds of entries. Their recommendations were for the consideration of the Advisory Board.

This met on April 26 and 27 at the Graduate School of Journalism. The final step was taken yesterday afternoon by the trustees of the university, who acted on the recommendations of the Advisory Board.

Columbia University announced yesterday that three editors and a publisher had been elected to the Advisory Board on the Pulitzer Awards.

These included Norman Chandler, president and publisher of The Los Angeles Times, who replaces Stuart H. Perry, publisher of The Adrian (Mich.) Telegram. Mr. Perry, whose term would have expired next year, resigned.

The editors chosen for regular three-year terms, were Barry Bingham of The Louisville Courier-Journal; Paul Miller of The Rochester (N. Y.) Times Union; and Louis B. Seltzer of The Cleveland (Ohio) Press. They fill vacancies created by the retirement under a three-term retirement rule of Sevellon Brown, former editor and publisher of The Providence (R. I.) Journal; Kent Cooper of The Associated Press, and William R. Mathews of The Arizona Daily Star, Tucson.

Prof. John Hohenberg of the Columbia University Graduate School of Journalism was elected for a third one-year term as secretary of the board.

The Advisory Board now com-

prises: Dr. Grayson Kirk, president of Columbia University; Hodding Carter, The Delta Democrat - Times, Greenville, Miss.; Turner Catledge, The New York Times; Robert Choate, The Boston Herald; Gardner Cowles, Cowles Magazines, Inc., New York; J. D. Ferguson, The Milwaukee Journal; John S. Knight, Knight Newspapers, Inc., Chicago; Benjamin M. McKelway, The Washington Evening Star; Joseph Pulitzer Jr., The St. Louis Post-Dispatch; Mr. Chandler, Mr. Bingham, Mr. Miller, Mr. Seltzer, and Professor Hohenberg, secretary.

NEW YORK DRAMA CRITICS CIRCLE AWARDS

'ANNE FRANK' GETS AWARD OF CRITICS

Play Draws 11 Votes as Best U. S. Entry—'My Fair Lady' and 'Tiger' Also Named

"The Diary of Anne Frank" was named yesterday by the New York Drama Critics Circle as the best new American play presented during the current Broadway season. Frances Goodrich and Albert did the dramatization of the best-seller.

The Circle members voted unanimously for the first time in the twenty-one year history of the organization in choosing "My Fair Lady" as the best musical of the 1955-56 season. The Frederick Loewe-Alan Jay Lerner hit was adapted from Shaw's "Pygmalion." "Tiger at the Gates" was selected as the best foreign play.

The drama reviewers, representing local newspapers, news agencies and magazines, met at the Algonquin Hotel. Eighteen members cast their ballots personally, while three voted by proxy. The award winners were decided on a plurality basis.

"The Diary of Anne Frank" came out on top in its division by a margin of almost 2 to 1. It drew eleven votes against the six cast for the next contender, "Inherit the Wind." Several weeks ago, "Diary" also captured the highly coveted American Theatre Wing Antoinette Perry Award as "the outstanding play of the season."

Dispute on Category

Before the balloting began there was a spirited discussion as to whether or not the Goodrich-Hackett dramatization rightly could be considered an American work. The argument against it stemmed from the fact that while the authors are Americans the source material was of foreign origin. The play is an adaptation of Anne Frank's extraordinary account of her adolescence, which she spent hiding from hte Nazis in a loft in Amsterdam during World War II.

By a vote of, 9 to 4, however, the critics ruled that "any play written by an American based on a foreign work, but not on a foreign play, could be considered as an American play in the

voting."

Five of the critics present did not vote on the question. In the vote for the awards, one critic continued to regard "Diary" as a foreign play

In the best play category, single votes were won by "Time Limit!." A View From the Bridge" and "The Chalk Garden." One critic refrained from voting in this clasification.

"Tiger at the Gaets," the French play of Jean Giraudoux as translated by Christopher Fry, garnered approval from fourteen of the aisle-sitters in the foreign division. The the foreign division. "The Lark," Lillian Hellman's adaptation of Jean Anouilh's drama about Joan of Arc was runner-up with four ballots. "The Chalk Garden" and "The Diary of Anne Frank" won single votes in this category.

The critics' session was presided over by Walter Kerr. Absent members who voted by proxy were Brooks Atkinson, Louis Kronenberger and Wolcott Gibbs.

Scrolls, symbolic of the honor, will be presented to the winners by the organization at a date to be announced later.

The list of the votes cast in the three categrories follows:

BEST PLAY

"The Diary of Anne Frank": Brooks Atkinson, The Times; William Hawkins, World-Telegram and Sun; Ethel Colby. Journal of Commerce; Richard Watts Jr., The Post; Thomas H. Wenning, Newsweek; John McClain. Journal - American; Walter Kerr, Herald Tribune; Wolcott Gibbs. New Yorker; Robert Coleman, Mirror; Richard Cooke, Wall Street Journal; John Keatting. Cue.
"Inherit the Wind": Ward Morehouse. North American Newspaper Alliance; John Chapman. Daily News; Jack Gaver, United Press; Joseph Shipley, New Leader; Whitney Bolton. Morning Telegraph; Mark Barron, Associated Press.
"Time Limit": Thomas R. Dash, Women's Wear Daily.
"A View From the Bridge": Henry Hewes, Saturday Review.
"The Chalk Garden": Louis Kronenberger, Time.
Abstained from voting: George Jean Nathan.

BEST MUSICAL

"My Fair Lady": All of the twenty-one critics.

BEST FOREIGN PLAY

"Tiger at the Gates": Dash, Cooke. Hawkins, Bolton, Shipley. Kerr, Atkinson, Kronenberger, Watts, Coleman, Wenning. Keating, Gibbs and Nathan.
"The Lark": Colby, Morehouse, Gaver, Barron.
"The Chalk Garden": Hewes and McClain.
"The Diary of Anne Frank": Chapman.

TONY AWARDS

'Damn Yankees' and 'Anne Frank' Cited as Top Offerings

By SAM ZOLOTOW

"Damn Yankees" led the field in six of eighteen categories last night as the outstanding musical

Gwen Verdon and Ray Walston, outstanding feminine and male stars, in a scene from "Damn Yankees." This production also won a "Tony" as the top musical of the year.

in the American Theatre Wing's tenth annual sweepstakes for the "Tony" awards. "The Diary of Anne Frank" was named the top play of the season.

The prizes, which were distributed at a dinner in the Plaza Hotel, are in memory of Antoinette Perry, the wing's World War II chairman. Broadway looks upon them as the counterpart of Hollywood's "Oscars."

Julie Harris won a "Tony" as the feminine star in the drama branch for her interpretation of Joan of Arc in "The Lark," the Jean Anouilh - Lillian Hellman play. Miss Harris had received a "Tony" in 1952 for her portrayal in "I Am a Camera."

Two of the leading performers in "Inherit the Wind" were honored. They were Paul Muni, star, and Ed Begley, who is featured.

In the musical category, Gwen Verdon and Ray Walston, stars of "Damn Yankees," were chosen as the top actor and actress.

Producing Trio Scores Again

"Damn Yankees" is the second consecutive winner in the musical classification for the producers—Frederick Brisson, Robert E. Griffith and Harold S. Prince. Last year the trio captured the same prize for their production of "The Pajama Game."

"Damn Yankees" was inspired by Douglas Wallop's novel "The Year the Yankees Lost the Pennant." It was adapted by George Abbott (also the director) and Mr. Wallop to the music and lyrics of Richard Adler and the late Jerry Ross. Mr. Abbott figured as co-author and co-director of "The Papama Game," for which the team of Adler and Ross supplied the songs.

More awards that went to

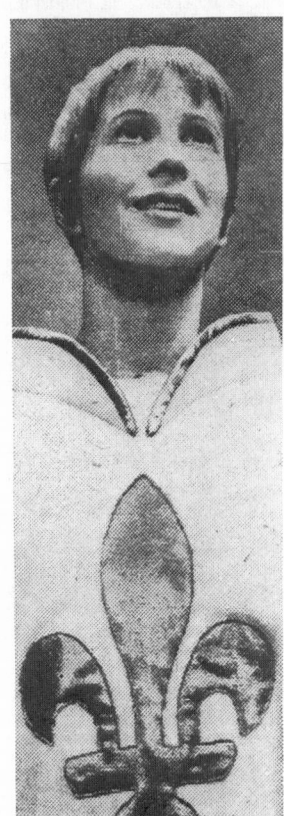

Julie Harris, who was chosen as the outstanding dramatic actress for her distinguished performance in "The Lark."

Paul Muni, who was selected as the foremost dramatic actor for his portrayal in "Inherit the Wind."

"Damn Yankees": Russ Brown, featured actor in a musical; Robert Fosse, choreographer, and Hal Hastings, musical director, who served in the same capacity in "The Pajama Game."

Two years ago, Miss Verdon won a "Tony" for her performance in "Can-Can." Last year Mr. Fosse was picked for his choreography in "The Pajama Game."

"The Diary of Anne Frank," which co-stars Joseph Schildkraut and Susan Strasberg, was dramatized by Frances Goodrich and Albert Hackett from the book "Anne Frank: The Diary of a Young Girl." The producer is Kermit Bloomgarden.

The Theatre Collection of the New York Public Library and "The Threepenny Opera" were singled out for special citations.

George Freedley is the curator and founder of the theatre collection, which will celebrate its twenty-fifth anniversary on Sept. 1. This year's Kelcey Allen Memorial Award also will be presented to Mr. Freedley at a luncheon today in Sardi's Restaurant.

"The Threepenny Opera" was cited as "a distinguished off-Broadway production." The Bert Brecht-Kurt Weill-Marc Blitzstein musical was revived by Carmen Capalbo and Stanley Chase at the Theatre de Lys, where it has been running since last Sept. 20.

Lotte Lenya, appearing in "The Threepenny Opera," earned a "Tony" as a featured actress in a musical. Miss Lenya, who is the widow of Mr. Weill, created the role of Jenny in the 1928 Berlin production.

Other Award Winners

Other awards were presented to the following:

Una Merkel of "The Ponder Heart" for her performance as a featured actress in a drama; Tyrone Guthrie for his direction of "The Matchmaker;" Peter Larkin for designing the scenery of "No Time for Sergeants," and "Inherit the Wind"; Alvin Colt for his costumes in "Pipe Dream," and Harry Green for his services as electrician and sound man in "Middle of the Night." Mr. Larkin won a similar prize in 1954 for his scenery in "Ondine" and "The Teahouse of the August Moon."

Nominations were restricted to the period between March 1, 1955, and Feb. 29 of this year. The winners were selected from sixty-nine nominees by the Wing's board.

More than 500 persons attended the dinner dance. The presentations were made by Helen Hayes, president of the wing, and some of the nominees. Jack Carter was master of ceremonies for the first half of the program, and Miss Hayes took over for the second. The program was televised on Channel 5.

1957

NOBEL PRIZE

Albert Camus Wins Nobel Letters Prize

By FELIX BELAIR Jr.

Special to The New York Times.

STOCKHOLM, Sweden, Oct. 17—The Nobel Prize in Literature for 1957 was awarded today to Albert Camus, French novelist and playwright. The Swedish Academy of Literature cited him as the world's foremost literary antagonist of totalitarianism.

The official Nobel citation, which carries with it an honorarium of $42,000, said M. Camus had been selected for the distinction because of "his important literary production, which with clear-sighted earnestness illuminated the problems of the human conscience in our times."

M. Camus, aged 43, becomes the youngest winner of the Nobel literature prize since Rudyard Kipling, who was about a year younger when he received the honor in 1907. M. Camus also becomes the ninth French writer to win the award since it was established in 1901. Other French laureates were René François Sully Prudhomme, Frederic Mistral, Romain Rolland, Anatol France, Henri Bergson, Roger Martin du Gard, André Gide and François Mauriac.

The sentiments of the Academy members, who voted unanimously for M. Camus as laureate, were expressed in superlatives tonight by Dr. Anders Osterling, permanent secretary of the awarding group:

"There is in his writings a genuine moral pathos which impels him to attack boldly and in his own markedly personal way the great fundamental problems of life—an effort which can unhesitatingly be said to conform with the idealistic aim which is the very base of the Nobel Prize."

Dr. Osterling said that M. Camus had come a long way from the nihilism that marked his earlier preoccupation with the so-called existentialist philosophy.

"Camus has left nihilism far behind him and his existentialism can reasonably be called a forme of humanism," Dr. Osterling observed.

"If one wanted to characterize his attitude, it would be enough to quote one of his pronouncements from the war years:

"'We have to patch together what has been torn asunder, to make justice conceivable in an obviously unjust world, to make happiness meaningful for people who have been poisoned by the unhappiness of the age. Of course, this is a superhuman effort. But what we call a superhuman task is simply one that mankind needs a long time to carry out.'"

War Brought Disillusionment

M. Camus was born in Algeria and went to France for the first time at the age of 25 as a newspaper man. Then came World War II, which brought temporary disillusionment. M. Camus has said that he was a Communist for a year, until he learned better.

His ideals came to the fore again in "La Peste" (The Plague), published in 1947. In this the chief character remarks at one point: "In these times it takes courage to be reasonable."

Speaking for the Academy, Dr. Osterling said of "The Plague": "This symbolic novel, with its calm and precise objectivity, is irresistibly convincing as a realistic description. But it is also inspired by the experiences of the French Resistance movement against an evil and an all-powerful authority."

The Nobel award group's thinking was further reflected by Dr. Osterling when he said: "As an author Camus is now

This is a scene from the prize-winning play, "The Diary of Anne Frank." Left to right: Gusti Huber, Joseph Schildkraut, Susan Strasberg, Eva Rubinstein and Jack Gilford.

in the full tide of his development. He has recently completed two works of importance, the monologue "La Chute" [The Fall] and the collection of short stories "The Exile and The Kingdom," both worthy additions to earlier proofs of his mastery as a narrator."

The literary award is one of the Nobel prizes given from a fund set up by Alfred Nobel, Swedish explosives manufacturer and philanthropist.

Camus Expresses Surprise

Special to The New York Times.

PARIS, Oct. 17—M. Camus said today that if the decision had been up to him, he would have given the Nobel Prize to his French literary senior, André Malraux.

He named M. Malraux, who is 56 years old, as one of his two mentors. The other, he said, is Jean Grenier, his philosophy teacher in Algiers, who was present with hundreds of newspaper men and literary figures at an open house reception given by his publisher today.

M. Camus expressed surprise that he had been chosen. "I thought that the Nobel Prize should crown an already completed life's work or at least one more advanced than mine," M. Camus declared.

PULITZER PRIZE

By HARRISON E. SALISBURY

President Grayson Kirk of Columbia University announced yesterday the 1957 Pulitzer awards for letters, journalism and music. The drama award went to "Long Day's Journey Into Night" by Eugene O'Neill.

It was the fourth Pulitzer Prize for the works of O'Neill, who died Nov. 27, 1953.

In the forty-year history of the prizes no other playwright had ever been honored four times. The only other person to win four Pulitzer prizes is Robert Frost, the poet.

No award was made this year in the field of fiction. However, a special citation was given to Kenneth Roberts for his distinguished series of historical novels.

The history prize went to George F. Kennan, former United States Ambassador to Moscow, for "Russia Leaves the War." The biography award was voted to Senator John F. Kennedy, Democrat of Massachusetts, for his "Profiles in Courage." The poetry prize went to Richard Wilbur for his "Things of This World."

8 Journalism Prizes

Eight prizes were awarded in the field of journalism, two to newspapers and six to individuals.

The winners: for meritorious public service, The Chicago Daily News; for local reporting under deadline conditions, The Salt Lake City, Utah; for local re-

porting under conditions not usually subject to deadline, Wallace Turner and William Lambert of The Portland (Ore.) Oregonian; for national reporting, James Reston of The New York Times; for international reporting, Russel Jones of The United Press; for editorial writing, Buford Boone of The Tuscaloosa (Ala.) News; for cartoons, Tom Little of The Nashville Tennessean; for news photography, Harry T. Trask of The Boston Traveler.

The music award went to Norman Dello Joio for "Meditations on Ecclesiastes." The traveling scholarship in art was not awarded for 1957.

The awards in the field of letters and music are $500. Those in journalism carry a prize of $1,000. Three traveling scholarships in journalism will be announced later.

The prizes were started in 1917 under the will of Joseph Pulitzer, publisher of The New York World. They are made by the trustees of Columbia University, acting on the recommendations of an advisory board.

The award to "Long Day's Journey Into Night" gives the drama a clean sweep of the year's honors. It had already won the New York Drama Critics Circle Award and the American Theatre Wing's Antoinette Perry award.

The first Pultzer award to O'Neill was made in 1920 for "Beyond the Horizon". He won again in 1922 with "Anna Christie" and with "Strange Interude" in 1928. O'Neill won the Novel prize for literature in 1936.

"Long Day's Journey Into Night" is generally regarded as is an autobiographical fragment, dealing with the playwright's family in his early manhood. The play encompasses a tragic day in the summer home of the Tyrone family. James Tyrone, like O'Neill's father, is an actor. His wife Mary is a narcotics addict. They play centers on the family's antagonisms and attraction.

O'Neill wrote his play in 1941 but did not want it published in his lifetime nor produced, at east in the United States, until twenty-five years after his death.

However, Carlotta Monterey, O'Neill's widow, released the script for production by the Royal Dramatic Theatre in Stockholm where it was given a world première in February, 1956.

The work was then given to José Quintero, Ted Mann and Leigh Connell for a Broadway production which opened Nov. 7, 1956, at the Helen Hayes Theatre with a cast starring Frederic March and Florence Eldridge.

No Explanation Given

No explanation for the failure to award a fiction prize was made. However, this action is customary when the advisory board feels that no work produced in the year meets the requisite standards of excellence. No prizes were awarded in this category in 1941, 1946 and 1954.

The special citation to Mr. Robers was given "for his historical novels which have long contributed to the creation of greater interest in our early

American history."

Mr. Roberts is the author of seven historical novels, the first, "Arundel," published in 1930 and the latest, "Lydia Bailey," published in 1947. He is 72 years old and a resident of Kennebunk Me.

Mr. Kennan's work, published by the Princeton University Press, had previously won the National Booksellers Award. It is the first of a project three-volume study of American relations with Russia in the period of the Bolshevik seizure of power in Russia and the period immediately thereafter.

Mr. Kennedy's book, published by Harper & Bros., deals with decisive moments in the live of John Quincy Adams, Daniel Webster, Thomas Hart Benton, Sam Houston, Edmund G. Ross, Lucius Q. C. Lamar, George Norris, Robert A. Taft and other American political figures.

Mr. Wilbur is Professor of English at Wesleyan University. His collection of poems, a selection of his work over the past five years, was published by Harcourt, Brace & Co. He is considered one of the most talented of younger American poets.

The prize for "disinterested and meritorious public service" was won by The Chicago Daily News for its "determined and courageous" action in exposing a $2,500,000 fraud centering in the office of the State Auditor of Illinois.

The Daily News exposé, in which twenty-one reporters, desk men and rewrite men participated resulted in the indictment and conviction of State Auditor Orville E. Hodge, his assistant, Edward Epping, and Edward Hintz, president of a Chicago bank involved in the fraud.

Under the pressure of developing the story two city editors on the staff of The Chicago Daily News suffered heart attacks. One of the principal reporters working on the exposé was George Thiem, who was a major participant in the exposé of an Illinois state payroll scandal that in 1950 won a joint Pulitzer award for The Daily News and The St. Louis Post-Dispatch.

Air Crash Story Cited

The award to the Salt Lake Tribune for reporting against the pressure of edition time was given for coverage by its staff of the crash of a United Airlines DC-7 and a Trans-World Airline Super Constellation, twenty-two miles northeast of Grand Canyon, Ariz., on June 30, 1956. It was the worst commercial air disaster ever to occur and 128 persons were killed.

"This was a team job that surmounted great difficulties in distance, time and terrain," the citation said.

The non-deadline reporting award won by Mr. Turner and Mr. Lambert of The Portland Oregonian concerned a series of articles revealing vice and corruption in Portland, involving municipal officials and officers of the International Brotherhood of Teamsters, Chauffeurs, Warehousemen and Helpers of America, Western Conference.

The two reporters, said the citation, "fulfilled their assignments despite great handicaps and the risk of reprisal from lawless elements."

Mr. Reston was honored for "his distinguished national correspondence, including both news dispatches and interpretive reporting."

A series of five dispatches

written by Mr. Reston in June, 1956, analyzing the effects of President Eisenhower's illness on the functioning of the Federal Executive Branch, was cited as an outstanding example of his work.

This was Mr. Reston's second Pulitzer prize. His first, also for national reporting, was won in 1945 for his dispatches and analyses of the Dumbarton Oaks conference. Mr. Reston is the chief correspondent of The New York Times in Washington. He has held this post since 1953.

Hungarian Coverage

The prize to Mr. Jones was awarded for his "excellent and sustained" coverage of the Hungarian revolt last autumn. Working at considerable personal risk, Mr. Jones wrote eyewitness reports of the Hungarian rising and its brutal suppression by Soviet force. He stayed on the scene until he was expelled from Budapest in December after five weeks in the thick of the trouble.

Mr. Jones' prize is the first in the history of the awards to go to The United Press or one of its correspondents.

Mr. Boone's editorial award was give nfor his "fearless and reasoned editorials in a community inflamed by a segregation issue." The issue concerned the application of Miss Autherine J. Lucy, a Negro, for admission as a student at the University of Alabama, located in Tuscaloosa.

Mr. Boone, president and publisher of the newspaper, wrote a series of editorials that were credited with demonstrating the willingness of a community to follow sober and enlightened leadership despite mob impulses.

Mr. Little won the cartoon award for a drawing published Jan. 12, 1956, depicting a little boy in braces and crutches, watching a football game played by youngsters of his age. The title is "Wonder Why My Parents Didn't Give Me Salk Shots?"

The photography award was made to Mr. Trask for his dramatic sequence of pictures of the sinking liner Andrea Doria after her collision with the Stockholm.

The winner of the prize for music, Mr. Joio, teaches musical composition at Sarah Lawrence College, Bronxville, N. Y. He has composed in almost all musical media. This "Meditations on Ecclesiastes" was originally designed as music for a ballet. It is contemporary in character and was first performed at the Juilliard School of Music April 20, 1956.

761 Enrties for Awards

The journalism prizes were awarded from a record total of 761 entries. These were examined by a panel of twenty-two jurors in March. This panel then made its recommendations to the fourteen-member Advisory Board on Pulitzer Prizes.

The board also received similar recommendations from jurors in the fields of letters, music and art. The board noted on the recommendations April 25 and 28, submitting final choices to the Columbia University trustees. Yesterday, the trustees approved the selections which were announced by Dr. Kirk.

The advisory board comprises: Dr. Kirk, Barry Bingham, The Louisville (Ky.) Courier-Journal; Hodding Carter, The Delta Democrat-Times, Greenville, Miss.; Turner Catledge, The New York

Times; Norman Chandler, The Los Angeles Times; Robert Choate, The Boston Herald; Gardiner Cowles, Cowles Magazines, Inc.; J. D. Ferguson, The Milwaukee Journal; John S. Knight, Knight Newspapers, Inc., Chicago; Benjamin M. McKelway, The Evening Star, Washington; Paul Miller, Gannett Newspapers, Inc., Rochester, N. Y.; Louis B. Seltzer, The Cleveland Press; John Hohenberg, Columbia University, secretary.

NEW YORK DRAMA CRITICS CIRCLE AWARDS
'Journey' Best U. S. Work—'Toreadors,' 'Fella' Also Cited

By ARTHUR GELB

The fabled power of woman had a slight setback yesterday when "Long Day's Journey Into Night" received the Drama Critics Circle award as the best American play of the season.

The Eugene O'Neill drama won the votes of nineteen unchivalrous gentlemen, despite a ballot cast by Ethel Colby for Tennessee Williams' "Orpheus Descending." Miss Colby, representing The Journal of Commerce, is the only woman mem-

Arthur Cantor

Best musical: "The Most Happy Fella," by Frank Loesser. In a scene are, from the left, Ralph Farnworth, Rico Froelich and Arthur Rubin. "Candide" was runner-up in this class.

ber of the circle.

The critics also selected Jean Anouilh's "The Waltz of the Toreadors" as the best foreign play and, with six of the members refusing to vote, chose "The Most Happy Fella" as the best musical. "The Most Happy Fella" was adapted by Frank Loes-

ser from Sidney Howard's play "They Knew What They Wanted."

The meeting took place at the Algonquin Hotel. Whitney Bolton of The Morning Telegraph was chairman. Fifteen members were present, while five cast their votes by proxy. The latter

were Brooks Atkinson of The Times, Louis Kronenberger of Time, Henry Hewes of The Saturday Review, Robert Coleman of The Mirror and Ward Morehouse of the S. I. Newhouse newspapers.

The award to "Long Day's Journey Into Night" is just one

Gjon Mili

Best U. S. play: "Long Day's Journey Into Night," by Eugene O'Neill. In scene are Florence Eldridge and Fredric March, seated; Bradford Dillman, left, and Jason Robards Jr.

Best foreign play: "The Waltz of the Toreadors," by Jean Anouilh. In a scene from the importation from France are Sir Ralph Richardson, who is starred, and Mildred Natwick.

more indication of the Nobel Prize dramatist's powerful resurgence after a decade of near neglect. The last new O'Neill play produced on Broadway was "The Iceman Cometh," in 1946. "Long Day's Journey Into Night" was completed in 1941 --twelve years before the author's death—and received its first production in Stockholm, Sweden, in February of last year. It opened at the Helen Hayes Theatre here on Nov. 7, 1956.

In the foreign play category, runners-up to "The Waltz of the Toreadors," which received twelve votes, were Graham Greene's "The Potting Shed," five votes; Terence Rattigan's "Separate Tables," two votes, and George Bernard Shaw's "In Good King Charles's Golden Days," one vote.

Before the balloting began on the best musical, nine critics went on record as being opposed to selection of a prize-winner in that category this season. When it was decided to go ahead with the voting, nine ballots were cast for "The Most Happy Fella," three for "Candide" and one each for "Bells Are Ringing" and "Cranks." The vote for "Cranks," a revue that had a short run earlier this season at the Bijou, was cast by Mr. Hewes, who through the years has established a reputation as a rugged individualist.

During the meeting yesterday, the critics also decided to voice objection to a plan by the League of New York Theatres to change opening-night curtain time from 8 to 8:30 P. M. The circle maintained that a later curtain would interfere with deadline schedules for critics writing their reviews for morning newspapers.

A committee—comprised of Walter Kerr of The Herald Tribune, Mark Barron of the Associated Press and John McClain of The Journal-American —was appointed to explain the critics' stand to James F. Reilly, executive director of the league.

The list of the votes cast in the three production categories follows:

BEST PLAY

Long Day's Journey Into Night: Atkinson, Kerr, John Chapman of The News, Coleman, Richard Watts Jr. of The Post, Tom Donnelly of The World-Telegram and Sun, McClain, Morehouse, Wolcott Gibbs of The New Yorker, Kronenberger, Thomas H. Wenning of Newsweek, Tom Dash of Women's Wear Daily, Fred Keating of Cue, Hewes, Bolton, Joseph Shipley of The New Leader, Barron, Jack Gaver of The United Press and Richard Cooke of The Wall Street Journal.

Orpheus Descending: Miss Colby.

BEST FOREIGN PLAY

Waltz of the Toreadors: Atkinson, Kerr, Chapman, McClain, Watts, Coleman, Kronenberger, Gibbs, Hewes, Dash, Keating, Bolton.

The Potting Shed: Donnelly, Morehouse, Wenning, Barron, Gaver.

Separate Tables: Miss Colby, Cooke.

In Good King Charles' Golden Days: Shipley.

BEST MUSICAL

The Most Happy Fella: Coleman, Dash, Keating, McClain, Barron, Bolton, Gaver, Morehouse, Miss Colby.

Candide: Atkinson, Chapman Donnelly.

Bells Are Ringing: Cooke.

Cranks: Hewes.

Abstained from voting: Watts

Kerr, Gibbs, Kronenberger, Wenning, Shipley.

TONY AWARDS

'FAIR LADY' WINS 6 'TONY' AWARDS

'Long Day's Journey Into Night' Voted Top Drama by the Theatre Wing

KIDD IS CITED 4TH TIME

Harrison, March, Margaret Leighton and Judy Holliday Take Acting Awards

By SAM ZOLOTOW

By capturing more than one-third of the seventeen categories embraced in the annual Antoinette Perry or "Tony" awards, "My Fair Lady" easily won the designation as the outstanding musical for the term between March 1, 1956, and last Feb. 28.

The spotlight was focused on Michael Kidd, choreographer of "Li'l Abner," for achieving a feat. He is the first to get four "Tonys" since the prizes were initiated in 1947. He was named previously for his work in "Finian's Rainbow," "Guys and Dolls" and "Can-Can."

Winners of the competition, conducted each year by the American Theatre Wing, were made known at the group's dinner last night in the Waldorf-Astoria.

The "Tonys" are named in memory of Miss Perry, actress-director and World War II chairman of the wing. They are recognized on Broadway as the equivalent of Hollywood's "Oscar" and television's "Emmy" and are bestowed for "distinguished contributions" to the theatre.

O'Neill Play Honored

Eugene O'Neill's "Long Day's Journey Into Night" and its star, Fredric March, were cited in the drama classification. The play received the Critics Circle prize last week.

Last year's Critics Circle award went to "My Fair Lady," which opened here March 15, 1956. Based on George Bernard Shaw's "Pygmalion," "My Fair Lady" was written by Alan Jay Lerner (book and lyrics) and Frederick Loewe (score).

By garnering six citations in all, "My Fair Lady" equals the mark held by "South Pacific" (1950) and "Damn Yankees" (1956). The following members of "My Fair Lady's" entourage shared in the distribution:

Rex Harrison, musical star; Oliver Smith, scenic designer; Cecil Beaton, costume designer; Moss Hart, director, and Franz Allers, musical director.

Besides "Long Day's Journey," two "Tonys" also were given to "Bells Are Ringing" and "Li'l Ab-

Winners of Annual 'Tony' Awards

Fredric March
Dramatic star

Margaret Leighton
Dramatic star

Judy Holliday
Musical star

Rex Harrison
Musical star

ner." Judy Holliday was chosen as the top feminine musical star in "Bells Are Ringing" and Sydney Chaplin, her leading man, as best supporting actor in a musical. "Li'l Abner's" second "Tony" was acquired by Edith Adams for her portrayal as a featured musical player.

Other Winners Listed

The other winners were:
Margaret Leighton ("Separate Tables"), dramatic star; Peggy Cass ("Auntie Mame"), supporting actress; Frank Conroy ("The Potting Shed"), supporting actor; American Shakespeare Festival, special award, and the late Howard McDonald (stage technician), who had been on Kermit Bloomgarden's staff. Mr. McDonald's posthumous honor was accepted by his widow.

On hand to make the presentations were Bert Lahr, Beatrice Lillie, Tom Ewell, Nancy Kelly, Lillian Gish, Cornelia Otis Skinner, Cliff Robertson and Nancy Olson.

The "Tony," which was de-

signed by Herman Rosse, is a silver medallion decorated on one side with the masks of Thespis and Thalia. The reverse side contains a raised profile of Miss Perry and an inscription to the winner.

Katharine Cornell and her husband, Guthrie McClintic, officiated as co-chairmen while Mrs. Martin Beck, the wing's first vice president, served as co-ordinator.

1958
PULITZER PRIZE

Three of the 1958 Pulitzer prizes in Journalism were awarded yesterday for coverage of last autumn's school integration crisis in Little Rock, Ark. Two of the three prizes

were won by the same newspaper, The Arkansas Gazette, an unusual honor designed to record the high esteem felt by the awards committee for the excellence of this Little Rock newspaper's achievement.

The third prize was awarded to Relman Morin, an Associated Press reporter, for his coverage of integration violence in Little Rock.

Agee Novel Honored

The year's award for the best novel went to "A Death in the Family" by the late James Agee. Thus, the Pulitzer committee, like the National Book Awards committee, passed up James Gould Cozzens' best-selling novel, "By Love Possessed." The National Book Awards prize went to John Cheever's "The Wapshot Chronicle."

The 1958 drama award went to "Look Homeward, Angel," Ketti Frings' dramatization of the famous novel by the late Thomas Wolfe. None of Mr. Wolfe's novels ever received a Pulitzer prize.

The following prizes were awarded in journalism:

For meritorious public service— The Arkansas Gazette, Little Rock.

For international reporting— The New York Times.

For local reporting under deadline conditions—The Fargo (N. D.) Forum.

For local reporting under non-deadline conditions — George Beveridge of The Evening Star, Washington.

For national reporting (two awards)—Relman Morin of The Associated Press and Clark Mollenhoff of The Des Moines Register and Tribune.

For editorial writing—Harry S. Ashmore of The Arkansas Gazette.

Cartoons—Bruce M. Shanks of The Buffalo Evening News.

News photography—William C. Beall of The Washington Daily News.

Special citation—Walter Lippmann of The New York Herald Tribune.

The prize biography was given to the late Douglas Southall Freeman's multi-volume "George Washington," which was completed after his death in 1953 by John Alexander Carroll and Mary Wells Ashworth. Dr. Freeman won a Pulitzer Prize in 1935 for his biography of Robert E. Lee.

The history prize went to Bray Hammond for his "Banks and Politics in America: From the Revolution to the Civil War." The poetry prize was awarded to Robert Penn Warren for "Promises: Poems 1954-1956," and the prize for music went to Samuel Barber for the score of the opera "Vanessa."

The announcement of ten Pulitzer awards for journalism

and six awards in arts and letters was made by Grayson Kirk, president of Columbia University. The awards are given by the trustees of Columbia on recommendation of the Advisory Board on Pulitzer prizes.

Prizes Are $500 and $1,000

The awards in arts and letters are $500. Those in journalism carry a prize of $1,000. The prizes have been given since 1917 under the will of Joseph Pulitzer, publisher of the old New York World.

The double award to The Arkansas Gazette was made for its public service and editorial coverage of the explosive Little Rock integration crisis.

The newspaper was cited for "demonstrating the highest qualities of civic leadership, journalistic responsibility and moral courage."

"The newspaper's fearless and completely objective news coverage, plus its reasoned and moderate policy, did much to restore calmness and order to an overwrought community," the citation said.

Mr. Ashmore, executive editor of The Arkansas Gazette, was cited "for the forcefulness, dispassionate analysis and clarity of his editorials" on the integration situation.

A check of Pulitzer Prize annals disclosed that The Arkansas Gazette was the first newspaper to win the public service prize and the editorial prize for its work on the same news story.

Report on Mob Cited

In the third Pulitzer award growing out of the Little Rock crisis, Mr. Morin was cited for "his dramatic and incisive eyewitness report of mob violence on Sept. 23. 1957, during the integration crisis" in Little Rock.

It was the second time Mr. Morin was honored by the Pulitzer committee. In 1951, he shared with five other reporters a Pulitzer award for coverage of the Korean War. Mr. Morin, long a foreign and domestic correspondent for The Associated Press, is now stationed in New York, assigned to special coverage.

Ordinarily only one prize is given for national affairs reporting. This year, however, a second prize was awarded. This went to Mr. Mollenhoff for a lengthy inquiry into labor union racketeering. Mr. Mollenhoff's stories were credited with assisting Congressional investigations into James R. Hoffa, Dave Beck, Frank Brewster and other Teamsters union figures.

The New York Times, winner of the Award for International Reporting, was cited for "its distinguished coverage of foreign news, which was characterized by admirable initiative, continuity and high quality during the year."

This was the first time that the international reporting award was given to a newspaper staff, although collective staff awards have been made in other fields.

In 1941, The Times won a special Pulitzer citation "for the public educational value of its foreign news report, exemplified by its scope, by excellence of writing, presentation and supplementary background infor-

mation, illustration and interpretation."

The special citation given this year to Mr. Lippmann was voted "for the wisdom, perception and high sense of responsibility with which he has commented for many years on national and international affairs."

Tornado Coverage Noted

The award to The Fargo Forum was given for its swift and vivid news and picture coverage of a tornado that struck the city June 20, 1957. The award to Mr. Beveridge was for his study of urban problems of Washington. The report was cited as having stimulated "widespread public consideration" of the situation.

Mr. Shanks, award was given for a cartoon depicting the dilemma of union members confronted by racketeering union leaders. The phootgraphy award to Mr. Beall was given for a picture of a policeman talking with a 2-year-old boy who wanted to get closer to a parade.

Mr. Agee's Pulitzer award was posthumous. He died three years ago at the age of 45 as he was completing "A Death in the Family." The novel, published by McDowell, Obolensky, Inc., New York, is said to be to some extent autobiographical.

The Pulitzer Prize for drama is made "for the American play, preferably original in its source and dealing with American life, which shall represent in marked fashion the educational value and power of the stage." The fact that the prize-winning play, "Look Homeward, Angel," was adapted from a novel did not therefore bar it from consideration.

3 Elected to Board

Three new members were elected to the Advisory Board on Pulitzer Prizes. They are Erwin D. Canham, editor of The Christian Science Monitor; Kenneth MacDonald, editor of The Des Moines Register and Tribune, and W. D. Maxwell, editor of The Chicago Tribune.

They will replace Gardner Cowels of Cowles Magazines, Inc., New York; Robert Choate, The Boston Herald, and John S. Knight of Knight Newspapers, Inc., Chicago. The members retire after serving four-year terms.

Members of the 1958 advisory board, in addition to Messrs. Cowles, Choate and Knight, were Dr. Kirk Barry Bingham, The Louisville Courier-Journal; Hodding Carter, The Delta Democrat-Times, Greenville, Miss.; Turner Catledge, The New York Times; Norman Chandler, The Los Angeles Times; J. D. Ferguson, The Milwaukee Journal; Benjamin M. McKelway, The Washington Evening Star; Paul Miller, Gannett Newspapers, Inc., Rochester, N. Y.; Joseph Pulitzer Jr., The St. Louis Post-Dispatch; Louis B. Seltzer, The Cleveland Press, and John Hohenberg, Professor of Journalism, Columbia University Graduate School of Journalism, secretary.

Harrison E. Salisbury

NEW YORK DRAMA CRITICS CIRCLE AWARDS

"Look Homeward Angel" and "Music Man" Win Awards

By LOUIS CALTA

"Look Homeward, Angel," Ketti Frings' adaptation of Thomas Wolfe's turbulent autobiographical novel, yesterday won the Drama Critics Circle award as the best American play of the season.

The intensely moving drama of North Carolina life in 1916, which opened at the Ethel Barrymore Theatre last November, came out on top in its division by the handsome margin of fifteen votes of the total of nineteen cast. Runners-up in this category were William Inge's "The Dark at the Top of the Stairs," with three ballots, and William Saroyan's "The Cave Dwellers," with one.

The Circle members, noted for their independent-mindedness, were momentarily stymied in their initial attempt to choose the season's best musical. "The Music Man" and "West Side Story" were tied for top honors with nine votes each in the first round of balloting. Louis Kronenberger, who voted by proxy, had abstained on the grounds that no musical was worthy of the award.

After a short deliberation during which John Chapman of The Daily News volunteered to change his selection, it was generally agreed to conduct a second closed ballot. This time "The Music Man" was declared the winner with ten votes as opposed to the eight of "West Side Story."

"The Music Man," a warm cartoon of provincial life in Iowa in 1912, has book, music and lyrics by Meredith Willson. The selection of "Look Homeward, Angel" and "The Music Man" represents a feather in the cap of Kermit Bloomgarden, producer of both attractions.

The critics also bestowed their annual best foreign play award to "Look Back in Anger," the John Osborne drama about Britain's angry young men. It received thirteen votes against the three cast for the next contender, "Time Remembered."

The drama reviewers, representing local newspapers, news agencies and magazines, met at the Algonquin Hotel. Seventeen members cast their ballots personally, while two voted by proxy.

Before the meeting, the Circle members adopted the following resolution in memory of George Jean Nathan, drama critic and author who died yesterday morning:

"The New York Drama Critics Circle regrets the passing of one of its founders, George Jean Nathan, who undoubtedly did more than any single critic to raise the standards of playwriting in America, its level of theatrical production and in influencing the growth of intelligent playgoing in our country."

Three scrolls, symbolic of the honors, will be presented to the winners at a date to be announced soon. For the first time, the critics affixed their

Best U. S. play—Anthony Perkins, Jo Van Fleet, Hugh Griffith in "Look Homeward, Angel."

Best foreign play—Mary Ure, left, and Vivienne Drummond in scene from "Look Back in Anger."

Best musical—Barbara Cook, Robert Preston are shown as they appear in "The Music Man."

signatures to the scrolls despite an objection raised by one critic that they implied general endorsement. However, it was determined that the over-all John Hancocks represented the plurality vote.

The list of votes cast in the three production categories follows:

BEST PLAY

Look Homeward, Angel: Wolcott Gibbs of The New Yorker, Tom Dash of Women's Wear Daily, Chapman of The Daily News, Frank Aston of The World-Telegram, Robert Coleman of The Mirror, Jack Gaver of The United Press, Kronenberger of Time, Mark Barron of The Associated Press, Thomas H. Wenning of Newsweek, Whitney Bolton of The Morning Telegraph, Emory Lewis of Cue Magazine, Richard Watts of The Post, Ward Morehouse of the S. I. Newhouse newspapers, Richard Cooke of The Wall Street Journal and John McClain of The Journal-American.

The Dark at the Top of the Stairs: Brooks Atkinson of The Times, Walter Kerr of The Herald Tribune and Ethel Colby of The Journal of Commerce.

The Cave Dwellers: Henry Hewes of The Saturday Review.

BEST MUSICAL

The Music Man: Watts, McClain, Chapman, Kerr, Barron, Gibbs, Aston, Morehouse, Cooke, Gaver.

West Side Story: Coleman, Bolton, Wenning, Atkinson, Lewis, Dash, Hewes, Colby.

BEST FOREIGN PLAY

Look Back in Anger: Gibbs, Watts, Cooke, Chapman, McClain, Kronenberger, Wenning, Kerr, Morehouse, Barron, Colby, Bolton, Lewis.

Time Remembered: Atkinson Dash, Coleman.

The Entertainer: Hewes, Aston.

Romanoff and Juliet: Gaver.

TONY AWARDS

By SAM ZOLOTOW

"The Music Man" waltzed off last night with five of the eighteen Tony awards, Broadway counterpart of the Hollywood "Oscars" and the television Emmys.

The prizes were distributed at the twelfth annual dinner-dance of the American Theatre Wing in the Waldorf-Astoria Hotel. More than 885 persons attended.

Close behind Meredith Willson's song-and-dance entertain-

Ralph Bellamy and Mary Fickett in "Sunrise at Campobello," which won in dramatic category. Mr. Bellamy was also honored for portrayal of President Roosevelt.

ment, singled out last week by the Drama Critics Circle as the top musical of the season, was "Sunrise at Campobello."

Four Tonys were captured by the Dore Schary drama dealing with a critical phase in the life of Franklin Delano Roosevelt.

Named for the late Antoinette Perry, actress-director and World War II chairman of the wing, the awards are presented for "distinguished contributions" to the theatre. Eighty nominations, covering the period between March 1, 1957, and last Feb. 28, were considered by the wing.

In the musical field, "The Music Man" had received nine nominations in various categories while those for "Sunrise at Campobello," in the drama division, numbered five, one less than "Look Homeward, Angel," "The Rope Dancers" or "Time Remembered."

Personnel connected with "The Music Man" were declared the winners in these classifications:

Musical star (male), Robert Preston; David Burns and Barbara Cook, both featured performers, and Herbert Greene, musical director. A scroll was given to Kermit Bloomgarden, producer of the show in association with Mr. Greene and Frank Productions, Inc., one of the many enterprises conducted by Frank Loesser.

In the male dramatic star grouping, Ralph Bellamy was chosen for his impersonation of the late President Roosevelt. Others rewarded with Tonys in this offering were Vincent J. Donehue, director, and Henry Jones, a supporting player in the role of Louis McHenry Howe, President Roosevelt's confidant. The Theatre Guild and Mr. Schary, co-sponsors, received scrolls.

For the first time in the

twelve-year history of the Tonys, two musical actress stars appearing in the same offering were designated for awards. This distinction was shared by Gwen Verdon and Thelma Ritter of "New Girl in Town." Miss Verdon is now a three-time winner. She was cited previously for "Can Can" (1954) and "Damn Yankees" (1956).

Others who have achieved three awards are Mary Martin, Shirley Booth, Jose Ferrer, Jo Mielziner and Arthur Miller. Thus far, the record established by Michael Kidd, choreographer, with four Tonys remains unequaled.

Attractions garnering two winners each were "Time Remembered" and "West Side Story." A Tony went to Helen Hayes, co-star of "Time Remembered," and to Harry Romar, the production's electrician. "West Side Story" was represented by Jerome Robbins, choreographer, who won an award in 1948, and Oliver Smith, scenic designer.

The other winners were Anne Bancroft, a Broadway newcomer, for her supporting performance in "Two for the Seesaw"; Motley, for designing the costumes of "The First Gentleman," and a special award to the New York Shakespeare Festival, of which Joseph Papp is the founder and producer.

A surprise award was made. The recipient was Mrs. Martin Beck, first vice president of the wing, who has been associated with the organization since 1939. For her "devoted service," she received a gold bracelet, attached to which was a gold charm inscribed with an appropriate insigne. It was presented by Helen Menken, the wing's president.

For the second year in a row, the Tony program was not televised. Last year, the telecast by the Columbia Broadcasting System was blocked by a jurisdictional dispute between two unions, Theatrical Protective Union (Local 1) and the International Brotherhood of Electrical Workers.

Despite the cancellation, the sponsor, the Pepsi-Cola Metropolitan Bottling Company,

Barbara Cook, Eddie Hodges, center, and David Burns in a scene from Meredith Willson's "The Music Man," which captured the honors in the musical classification.

Helen Hayes, whose performance in "Time Remembered" won her an award.

Mrs. Martin Beck, first vice president of Theatre Wing, who was given a surprise award for devoted service.

donated $5,000 to the wing's activities. Last night, the telecast was called off as a result of the strike by the I. B. E. W. against WCBS-TV.

Serving as co-chairmen of the dinner dance were Mary Martin, Fredric March and Mrs. Albert D. Lasker. Entertainment was provided by Mindy Carson and Bill Hayes. Music was furnished by Meyer Davis' orchestra.

1959
PULITZER PRIZE

Robert Lewis Taylor's 'Jaimie McPheeters' Gets Fiction Award

By PETER KIHSS

Archibald MacLeish won the 1959 Pulitzer Prize for drama yesterday for his verse play, "J. B.," a modern retelling of the Book of Job.

It was his third Pulitzer Prize; the others were for poetry, in 1933 and 1953.

The fiction award went to Robert Lewis Taylor for "The Travels of Jaimie McPheeters," a story about a wagon-train journey to California in 1849.

Other prizes in letters went to "The Republican Era: 1869-1901," by the late Leonard D. White, with the assistance of Miss Jean Schneider, for history; "Woodrow Wilson, American Prophet," by Arthur Walworth, for biography, and "Selected Poems, 1928-1958," by Stanley Kunitz, for poetry.

A newspaper campaign against corruption, gambling and vice won the 1959 Pulitzer Prize medal for meritorious public service for The Utica (N. Y.) Observer-Dispatch and The Utica Daily Press.

Other prizes in journalism were as follows:

For local reporting under deadline conditions — Mary Lou Werner of The Washington Evening Star.

For local reporting under non-deadline conditions — John Harold Brislin of The Scranton Tribune and The Scrantonian.

For national reporting—Howard Van Smith of The Miami News.

For international reporting— Joseph Martin and Philip Santora of The New York Daily News.

For editorial writing—Ralph McGill of The Atlanta Constitution.

For cartoons—William H. (Bill) Mauldin of The St. Louis Post-Dispatch, his second such Pulitzer prize.

For news photograph—William Seaman of The Minneapolis Star.

The Pulitzer prize for music went to Concerto for Piano and Orchestra, by John La Montaine of New York.

Prizes Are 43d

The forty-third annual prizes were awarded by the trustees

The New York Times

Archibald MacLeish

'A Raisin in the Sun' and 'Visit' Cited by Critics

Best American Play: Sidney Poitier and Claudia McNeil in scene from "A Raisin in the Sun," by Lorraine Hansberry.

Best Musical: A scene from "La Plume de ma Tante," French revue. It is first revue so honored by drama critics.

of Columbia University on recommendation of the Advisory Board on Pulitzer Prizes. The prizes have been given since 1917 under the will of Joseph Pulitzer, publisher of the old New York World.

Those for journalism, except for the medal, carry $1,000 cash awards, while those in letters and music provide $500 apiece.

In announcing the prizes, Dr. Grayson Kirk, president of Columbia, made public a statement by the Advisory Board. This noted that there had been 556 nominations for the journalism prizes and said that this was evidence to refute "the sometimes generalized criticism of a 'complacent press.'"

Mr. McLeish and Mr. Mauldin are among thirty-four individuals who have won Pulitzer Prizes more than once. Three have won four prizes each — Robert Frost, the poet; Eugene O'Neill, the playwright, and Robert E. Sherwood, as playwright and biographer.

Besides Mr. MacLeish, other three-time winners include Carl Sandburg, as poet and historian; Thornton Wilder, as novelist and playwright, and Rollin Kirby and Edmund Duffy, cartoonists.

Arthur Krock of The New York Times won prizes for general correspondence in 1935 and 1938 and was credited by the Advisory Board with the outstanding national reporting of 1950. However, no award was made in that category because he was then a member of the board.

Taylor's Ninth Book

Mr. MacLeish, who will be 67 years old Thursday, won the Pulitzer Prize for poetry for his "Conquistador" in 1933 and "Collected Poems, 1917-1952," in 1953.

"J. B." has had a successful run since opening at the ANTA Theater Dec. 11. On April 12, it won the thirteenth annual Antoinette Perry award—the Tony—given by the American Theatre Wing for the outstanding Broadway dramatic production of the season.

Mr. Taylor's prize-winning novel was his ninth book. A 46-year-old resident of Sharon, Conn., he has written considerably for The New Yorker, among other magazines.

The $500 history prize fund will be divided between the estate of the late Dr. White and Miss Schneider, his research assistant. Dr. White, a University of Chicago professor of public administraion, died on Feb. 23, 1958, shortly before his book—the last of four volumes on the evolution of the United States system of government from 1789 to 1901—was published.

Mr. Walworth worked for ten years on his two-volume prize-winning life of Wilson. Mr. Kunitz, the prize-winning poet, had won previous prizes from Poetry magazine and The Saturday Review.

The two prize-winning Utica newspapers, members of the Gannett group, were cited for "their successful campaign against corruption, gambling and vice in their home city and the achievement of sweeping civic reforms in the face of political pressure and threats of violence."

"By their stalwart leadership of the forces of good government," the citation added, "these newspapers upheld the best traditions of a free press."

Virginia Coverage Cited

Miss Werner, 32 years old, was honored for her year-long coverage of the school integration crisis in Virginia. Mr. Brislin, who was for six years an American Newspaper Guild district council president, was acclaimed for a four-year campaign to halt labor violence in Scranton, Pa., that helped to send ten union officials to jail.

Mr. Smith received the national reporting prize for a series on deplorable conditions in a migrant labor camp at Immokalee, Fla.

Messrs. Martin and Santora won the international reporting prize for a ten-article series in The New York Daily News on brutality in Cuba under Fulgencio Batista, who was then President.

Mr. McGill was honored for "long, courageous and effective editorial leadership," including particularly an editorial attacking synagogue and school bombing as "the harvest of defiance of courts."

Mr. Mauldin's latest prize was for a cartoon resulting from the way Boris Pasternak, Soviet novelist, had to give up the Nobel prize for literature. Mr. Mauldin's 1945 award was for World War II cartoons for the United Feature Syndicate, Inc.

The photographic prize to Mr. Seaman was for a dramatic picture of the traffic death of a 9-year-old boy.

A $1,500 annual traveling scholarship to an art student certified as most promising and deserving by the National Academy of Design went to Jerome Paul Witkin, a Cooper Union student. He lives at 61-14 Bleecker Street, Ridgewood, Queens.

Broader Concepts Noted

The advisory board's statement, an innovation, noted that exposures of corruption had won more Pulitzer Prizes since 1917 than any other newspaper activity. But it cited "broadening concepts" of journalism, and expressed the hope that future entries would emphasize as well "science, education, cultural undertakings and international efforts designed to advance the well-being of mankind."

A Columbia spokesman reported that the board had considered but "took no action" on a proposal by Robert W. Sarnoff, chairman of the National Broadcasting Company, to add television prizes. He said it was the sense of the board at its annual meeting April 23 "that TV drama is included in prizes currently available to television."

Members of the 1959 advisory board were:

Dr. Kirk; Barry Bingham, The Louisville Courier-Journal; Erwin D. Canham, The Christian Science Monitor, Boston; Hodding Carter, The Delta Democrat-Times, Greenville, Miss.; Turner Catledge, The New York Times; Norman Chandler, The Los Angeles Times; J. D. Ferguson, The Milwaukee Journal; Kenneth MacDonald, The Des Moines Register and Tribune.

W. D. Maxwell, The Chicago Tribune; Benjamin M. McKelway, The Washington Evening Star; Paul Miller, Gannett Newspapers, Inc., Rochester, N. Y.; Joseph Pulitzer Jr., The St. Louis Post-Dispatch; Louis B. Seltzer, The Cleveland Press, and John Hohenberg, Professor of Journalism, Columbia University Graduate School of Journalism, secretary.

Messrs. Catledge, McKelway and Pulitzer were re-elected to four-year terms. Professor Hohenberg, who last month edited a Columbia University Press anthology, "The Pulitzer Prize Story," was re-elected secretary for a sixth successive one-year term.

NEW YORK DRAMA CRITICS CIRCLE AWARDS

A first effort by a woman playwright yesterday nosed out by one vote two other major contenders for the Drama Critics Circle Award for the best American play.

The winner, "A Raisin in the Sun," written by Lorraine Hansberry, also has the distinction of being the first play by a Negro writer to earn the award.

Oddly enough, although the play was favorably reviewed by all seven of the major newspaper critics when it opened on March 11, none of the seven voted for it yesterday. Their votes were divided instead among "Sweet Bird of Youth," "J. B." and "A Touch of the Poet."

"A Touch of the Poet," by Eugene O'Neill, received three votes: "Sweet Bird of Youth," by Tennessee Williams, and "J. B.," by Archibald MacLeish, five each, and "A Raisin in the Sun," six.

After debating the possibility of withholding any award to a musical of the current season, twelve of the nineteen critics finally cast their votes for "La Plume de Ma Tante," the revue from France. This is the first time the Circle has ever smiled on a revue and is an indication of the poverty of good musicals now running on Broadway.

Runners-up in the musical category were "Redhead," three votes, and "Flower Drum Song," two. Maintaining his reputation as a rugged individualist, Henry Hewes, of The Saturday Review, cast his ballot for "The Seven Deadly Sins," a ballet that was done earlier this season at the City Center.

10 Critics Cite 'Visit'

"The Visit" won the award as the best foreign play, with ten critics voting in its behalf. Adapted by Maurice Valency from a play by Friedrich Duerrenmatt, it closed on Broadway on May 6, 1958, after 190 performances. The other plays cited in the foreign category were John Osborne's "Epitaph for George Dillon," six votes, and "The Power and the Glory" and "Rashomon," each winning one.

"The Power and the Glory," which was produced off Broadway earlier this season, was adapted by Denis Cannan and Pierre Bost from a book by Graham Greene. "Rashomon" was adapted by Fay and Michael Kanin from several Japanese stories.

The critics met at the Algonquin Hotel, where they have been getting together for discussion, argument and balloting since 1936. John McClain of The Journal-American was chairman. Fourteen members were present while five cast their votes by proxy. The latter were Brooks Atkinson of The Times; Richard Cooke of The Wall Street Journal; Ward Morehouse of the S. I. Newhouse newspapers; Kenneth Tynan of The New Yorker, and Thomas H. Wenning of Newsweek.

The list of the votes cast in the three production categories follows:

BEST PLAY

A Raisin in the Sun: Whitney Bolton of The Morning Telegraph; Jack Gaver of United Press International; Henry Hewes of The Saturday Review;

Emory Lewis of Cue; Joseph T. Shipley of The New Leader, and Kenneth Tynan of The New Yorker.

J. B.: Brooks Atkinson of The Times; John Chapman of The News; Ethel Colby of The Journal of Commerce; Richard Cooke of The Wall Street Journal, and Thomas H. Wenning of Newsweek.

Sweet Bird of Youth: Frank Aston of The World Telegram and The Sun; Thomas R. Dash of Women's Wear Daily; Walter F. Kerr of The Herald Tribune; John McClain of The Journal American, and Ward Morehouse of the S. I. Newhouse newspapers.

A Touch of the Poet: Robert Coleman of The Mirror; Mark Barron of The Associated Press and Richard Watts Jr. of The Post.

BEST FOREIGN PLAY

The Visit: Aston, Atkinson, Bolton, Chapman, Dash, Gaver, Hewes, Kerr, McClain, Wenning.
Epitaph for George Dillon: Barron, Coleman, Lewis, Morehouse, Tynan and Watts.
The Power and the Glory: Shipley.
Rashomon: Colby.
Abstention: Cooke.

BEST MUSICAL

La Plume de ma Tante: Aston, Atkinson, Bolton, Chapman, Colby, Dash, Kerr, Lewis, McClain, Morehouse, Tynan, Watts.
Redhead: Cooke, Shipley, Wenning.
Flower Drum Song: Barron, Coleman.
The Seven Deadly Sins: Hewes.
Abstention: Gaver.

ARTHUR GELB

Best Foreign Play: Lynn Fontanne and Alfred Lunt, foreground, in "The Visit," adapted by Maurie Valency from Freidrich Durrenmatt's play. It closed on Broadway last May.

TONY AWARDS

By SAM ZOLOTOW

For the first time since the inception of the Antoinette Perry awards in 1947, the entire cast of a show has been singled out for a collective prize. The special Tony went to "La Plume de ma Tante" at the American Theatre Wing's annual distribution last night in the Waldorf-Astoria Hotel.

In behalf of the imported troupe, numbering fourteen, the prize was accepted by Robert

Archibald MacLeish, author of "J. B.," selected in dramatic play category.

Dhéry, star of the revue, which he wrote, devised and directed. The revue earned the accolade of the Drama Critics Circle last week as the best musical of the season.

The Wing cited "Redhead" and "J. B." as the outstanding musical and dramatic offerings, respectively. Altogether "Redhead," the product of Herbert and Dorothy Fields, Sidney Sheldon, David Shaw and Albert Hague, captured six Tonys, the high mark of the year.

Included in that number are Gwen Verdon and Richard Kiley, the stars; Bob Fosse, choreographer; Leonard Stone, featured player, and Rouben Ter-Arutunian, costume designer.

Other Tonys have been won by Miss Verdon in 1954 ("Can-Can"), 1956 ("Damn Yankees") and 1958 ("New Girl in Town"). As a four-time winner, she has equaled the record held by Michael Kidd, choreographer. Mr. Fosse has advanced a step, too. He was chosen twice in a row previously—in 1955 ("The Pajama Game") and 1956 ("Damn Yankees").

Stone and Nype in Tie

Inasmuch as Mr. Stone and Russell Nype, who appeared in "Goldilocks," were involved in a tie vote, the latter, a former winner, also received a Tony. In the musical featured-actress contingent, Pat Stanley of "Goldilocks" was selected.

"J. B.," Archibald MacLeish's modern counterpart of the story of Job, emerged with a second Tony. Elia Kazan, director, was named as the recipient. He was rewarded previously for his staging of "All My Sons" (1947) and "Death of a Salesman" (1949).

In a scene from "La Plume de ma Tante" are Jean Lefevre, left, and Colette Brosset with Robert Dhéry, who is holding Pierre Olaf on his shoulders and Roger Caccia by the neck. Jacques Legras is at the lower right. Cast was honored with special Tony.

Gwen Verdon and Richard Kiley, honored for their work in musical "Redhead."

In the Critics Circle sweepstakes, "J. B." and "Sweet Bird of Youth" had five votes each. The winner was "A Raisin in the Sun," with six votes. The Tony regulations apply to entries for the year ended Feb. 28. Consequently, "Sweet Bird" and "A Raisin" were ineligible for this year's prize because the former opened March 10 and the latter on the next night.

Chosen for special citations were John Gielgud for "his extraordinary insight into the writings of Shakespeare" and the team of Howard Lindsay and Russel Crouse for "having outlasted Gilbert and Sullivan as collaborators." Mr. Gielgud's recent solo performance in "Ages of Man" was hailed by the critics. Messrs. Lindsay and Crouse are currently represented by "Tall Story."

Delineations by stars in dramas brought Tonys to Gertrude Berg, "A Majority of One," and Jason Robards Jr., "The Disenchanted." "A Majority" obtained another Tony for the design of its scenery by Donald Oenslager. The Tonys to Miss Verdon and Mr. Robards were presented by Ingrid Bergman.

Designated for their acting in supporting roles were Charlie Ruggles, "The Pleasure of His Company," and Julie Newmar, "The Marriage-Go-Round." Although Mr. Ruggles' billing indicates he is co-starred, Helen Menken, the Wing's president, contended that Mr. Ruggles' assignment could be construed as of the supporting type.

For the musical direction of "Flower Drum Song," a Tony was presented to Salvatore Dell'Isola. Sam Knapp was honored as a stage technician. Mr. Knapp is the supervisor of six electricians at "The Music Man." He has been employed in the electrical field for twenty-seven years.

Of the eighty-two nominations, twenty awards were made in seventeen categories. The winners are never labeled "best" or "first." Broadway considers them, however, the equivalent of the Hollywood Oscar and the television Emmy. The yearly event is a memorial to Miss Perry, the Wing's World War II chairman, who died in 1946.

During the program, Miss Menken commended Dorothy Sands, who has been teaching acting at the Wing's Professional Training Center since 1946. As a token of the occasion, Miss Sands received a charm bracelet containing Tony facsimiles.

More than 1,000 persons were present. From 11:15 P. M. to 12:10 A. M. the proceedings were tlevised over Channel 2 under the sponsorship of the Pepsi-Cola Metropolitan Bottling Company. For the last two years, union disputes have prevented the telecast.

Money raised from the dinner dance will be devoted to the Wing's Professional and Student Hospital units. Music was furnished by Meyer Davis' orchestra.

Gertrude Berg, who was chosen for her performance in "A Majority of One."

Jason Robards Jr. in "The Disenchanted." He won the top dramatic actor award.

OBIE AWARDS

VILLAGE VOICE GIVES 'OBIE' STAGE AWARDS

"Obie" awards, originated by The Village Voice to designate achievement in the off-Broadway theatre, were made yesterday afternoon by the weekly Greenwich Village newspaper at the Village Gate, 185 Thompson Street.

Scrolls were presented by Kim Stanley, Broadway star, to the following winners of the 1958-59 season:

Actress, Kathleen Maguire ("The Time of the Cuckoo"); actor, Alfred Ryder ("I Rise in Flame, Cried the Phoenix"); direction of a foreign play, William Ball ("Ivanov"); direction of American plays, Jack Ragotzy ("The Time of the Cuckoo" and "A Clearing in the Woods"); over-all production, "Ivanov;" new play, Brendan Behan's "The Quare Fellow."

Also, musical, "A Party With Betty Comden and Adolph Green;" revue, Steven Vinaver's "Diversions;" open - stage set, David Hays ("The Quare Fellow"); proscenium set, Will Steven Armstrong ("Ivanov"); lighting, Nikola Cernovich (many productions); music, David Amram (many productions).

'Fiorello!' Authors

The four authors of "Fiorello!", the Broadway musical based on the flamboyant career of the late Fiorello H. La Guardia, plunged into work on Oct. 15, 1958, and were ready to put the finished product into rehearsal ten months later.

Jerry Bock, who composed the score, and Sheldon Harnick, who wrote the lyrics, had worked together once before, on a 1958 flop called "The Body Beautiful." But for Jerome Weidman and George Abbott, who wrote the book, it marked the first association as a team.

Mr. Abbott is the senior member of the team. In the last forty years, he has directed seventy-seven plays and musicals; produced thirty-eight shows; co-produced a half dozen; written four himself and written fifteen with other people. He has also played fifteen roles.

Mr. Abbott was born in Forestville, N. Y., in 1889. He entered the University of Rochester in 1907 with the vague idea of becoming a newspaperman but rapidly became interested in the theatre. Before he had graduated from Rochester, two of his plays had been performed by the dramatic club there. Encouraged by this, he enrolled in George Pierce Baker's 47 Workshop at Harvard,

'FIORELLO!' Prize-winners in drama division are the men responsible for the musical. From left: George Abbott and Jerome Weidman, who wrote the book; Sheldon Harnick, who wrote lyrics; Jerry Bock, at piano, who wrote music.

where he won a $100 prize for writing a play called "The Man in the Manhole."

After Harvard, Mr. Abbott came to New York and, by November, 1913, had made his acting debut in a play called "The Misleading Lady." "The Fall Guy," which he wrote with James Gleason, was his first playwriting success. He then directed and wrote, with Philip Dunning, the successful melodrama, "Broadway."

First for Weidman

Although Jerome Weidman has written fifteen books, including such best sellers as "I Can Get It for You Wholesale" and "The Enemy Camp," his first association with Broadway was "Fiorello!" He was born in 1913 on the Lower East Side. He went to DeWitt Clinton High School, City College and New York University Law School.

It was during his last year at law school that he began to write. He was 22 when his first novel, "I Can Get It for You Wholesale," was accepted for publication by Simon & Schuster. Mr. Weidman quickly switched from law to writing.

Mr. Harnick, a 35-year-old Chicagoan, had his first work, a Thanksgiving poem, published in the newspaper of the Portage Park Grammar School in Chicago when he was in the fifth grade.

After leaving the Army in 1946, he entered Northwestern University, where he majored in violin, but also did a great deal of writing. Finally, in 1950, he decided to give up the violin. His first song for Broadway was contributed to "New Faces of 1952"; it was called "The Boston Beguine" and was an immediate hit.

The youngest member of the "Fiorello!" team is Mr. Bock, who was born thirty-two years ago in New Haven. He was reared on Long Island, attended Flushing High School, where he wrote an original musical in his senior year, and then went to the University of Wsiconsin.

His apprenticeship in song writing was served at Camp Tamiment in the Poconos. It was there that he worked under the supervision of Max Liebman, writing the score of a new one-act revue every week for three summers.

His Broadway debut came in 1955 with the revue called "Catch a Star"; he contributed three songs. His first full score for a Broadway musical was "Mr. Wonderful," in 1956.

1960

PULITZER PRIZE

'Fiorello!' Is Pulitzer Play; 'Advise and Consent' Wins

By FOSTER HAILEY

Allen Drury's best-selling novel of Washington political life, "Advise and Consent," and the musical play "Fiorello!", based on the life of the late Mayor La Guardia of New York, were selected yesterday as Pulitzer Prize winners for 1960.

They were among thirteen awards and one citation in the fields of letters, music and journalism made by the trustees of Columbia University.

Awards were not made in two categories, newspaper cartooning and art.

A. M. Rosenthal of The New York Times foreign staff, who was expelled from Poland last year for his "probing" reporting, won the award in the field of international correspondence.

McKinley Work Cited

The other awards in letters were:

History—"In The Days of McKinley," by Margaret Leech, published by Harper & Brothers.

Biography — "John Paul Jones," by Samuel Eliot Morison, published by Little, Brown & Co.

Poetry—"Heart's Needle," by W. D. Snodgrass, published by Alfred A. Knopf, Inc.

Special citation—"The Armada," by Garrett Mattingly, published by Houghton, Mifflin.

The prize in music was given to Elliott Carter for his Second String Quartet, which was performed for the first time at the Juilliard School of Music on March 25.

Other awards in journalism were:

Public Service—The Los Angeles Times for a series by Gene Sherman on narcotics traffic across the border with Mexico.

Local reporting under pressure of a deadline—Jack Nelson of The Atlanta Constitution for a series on mental institutions in Georgia.

Exposé on Car Sales

Local reporting not under pressure—Miriam Ottenberg of The Washington Evening Star for a series exposing sharp practices in used-car sales.

National Affairs — Vance Trimble of the Scripps-Howard Newspaper Alliance, for a series of articles exposing relatives carried on Congressional payrolls.

Editorial writing — Lenoir Chambers, editor of The Norfolk Virginian-Pilot for editorials on school segregation.

News photography—Andrew Lopez of United Press International, for a series of four photographs of a condemned Cuban Army corporal before a

Castro firing squad.

The journalism awards each carried a monetary prize of $1,000. The money prizes in letters and music were $500 each.

The award to Mr. Drury for his novel detailing the pressures exerted on a Senator investigating a nominee for a Cabinet post came as no surprise.

"Advise and Consent" has been on all best-seller lists since its publication last year. It has been serialized and sold to the movies and is being dramatized for the New York stage.

Mr. Drury wrote his novel while on the staff of The New York Times as its Congressional correspondent.

The award to "Fiorello!" was a surprise to Broadway. It was only the third time the drama award had been won by a musical play.

The first was the musical satire "Of Thee I Sing," in 1932, and the second, "South Pacific," in 1950. The musical "Oklahoma!" won a special citation in 1944 but not the award.

"Fiorello!" had, however, already won one major award in its own category—musical play —and shared another. The New York Drama Critics Circle placed it first. It shared the Antoinette Perry award as best musical of the year with "The Sound of Music."

The award to Mr. Carter for his Second String Quartet was considered in music circles to be well-deserved. The only surprise was that the award went to a work of chamber music.

When the work was presented in March, Howard Taubman, The New York Times music critic, called it one of the best things of its kind and Mr. Carter "one of the outstanding composers of our time."

The award to Mr. Rosenthal in international correspondence was the fourth he has won this year for his reporting from Poland.

He had been honored previously by the Overseas Press Club, the New York Newspaper Guild and Long Island University's Polk Award.

27th to The Times

The prize was the twenty-seventh won by The New York Times or by a member of its staff. The newspaper also has won two special citations and C. L. Sulzberger, editorial columnist, one.

Arthur Krock, Washington columnist of The Times, also was honored in 1951, when his interview with President Truman was cited by the advisory board, of which he then was a member, as the "outstanding instance" of national reporting for that year. As a board member he was ineligible for an award, so none was made in that category.

The Pulitzer awards were set up in the will of the first Joseph Pulitzer almost half a century ago. They first were made in 1917.

Mr. Pulitzer was publisher of the old New York World for many years. The prizes are administered by the Graduate School of Journalism of Columbia University, which Mr. Pulitzer endowed.

The nominations for the awards are made by individuals or newspapers. The final selection is made by the advisory board, whose members this year were:

Dr. Grayson Kirk, president of Columbia; Barry Bingham, The Louisville Courier-Journal; Erwin D. Canham, The Christian Science Monitor; Hodding Carter, The Delta Democrat-Times, Greenville, Miss.; Turner Catledge, The New York Times; Norman Chandler, The Times-Mirror Company, Los Angeles; J. D. Ferguson, The Milwaukee Journal; Kenneth MacDonald, The Des Moines Register-Tribune; W. D. Maxwell, The Chicago Tribune; Benjamin M. McKelway, The Evening Star, Washington; Paul Miller, Gannett Newspapers; Joseph Pulitzer Jr., The St. Louis Post-Dispatch; and Louis Selzer, The Cleveland Press.

Members of the advisory board whose own newspapers are involved in any category do not participate in the discussion or the voting on the award in that division.

NEW YORK DRAMA CRITICS CIRCLE AWARDS

'5 Finger Exercise' Is Named by Critics Circle

By SAM ZOLOTOW

The New York Drama Critics Circle yesterday voted "Toys in the Attic" as the best American drama of the 1959-60 season, "Fiorello!" as the leading musical and "Five Finger Exercise" as the top foreign play.

Each won by a wide margin. Twenty reviewers participated in the voting at the circle's annual meeting in the Algonquin Hotel.

"Toys in the Attic," which was written by Lillian Hellman, staged by Arthur Penn and produced by Kermit Bloomgarden, garnered a dozen votes. It was Miss Hellman's third original work to be done by Mr. Bloomgarden. The other two were "Another Part of the Forest" and "The Autumn Garden."

"Toys" opened Feb. 25 at the Hudson Theatre, with Jason Robards Jr., Maureen Stapleton and Irene Worth starred. Set in New Orleans, the story concerns two hard-working spinster sisters and their love for a shiftless brother.

It was the selection of Frank Aston, The World-Telegram and The Sun; Mark Barron, The Associated Press; Whitney Bolton, The Morning Telegraph; Ethel Colby, The Journal of Commerce; Robert Coleman, The Mirror; Thomas R. Dash, Women's Wear Daily; Walter F. Kerr, The Herald Tribune; Louis Kronenberger, Time magazine; John McClain, The Journal American; Ward Morehouse, S. I. Newhouse newspaper chain; Richard Watts Jr., The Post, and Thomas H. Wenning, Newsweek.

Mr. Kronenberger and Mr. Coleman voted by proxy. No vote was filed by the former in the musical and foreign-play categories.

3 Name 'Miracle Worker'

The nearest to "Toys" was "The Miracle Worker," with three votes, from John Chapman, The Daily News, who was not present but telephoned his selections; Richard Cooke, The Wall Street Journal, and Jack Gaver, United Press International. "The Best Man" received two votes, from Emory Lewis,

'Toys in the Attic,' 'Fiorello!'

Maureen Stapleton, left, Irene Worth and Jason Robards Jr. in a scene from "Toys in the Attic." Lillian Hellman's drama was cited as the best American play of season.

Tom Bosley, left, Patricia Wilson and Howard da Silva as they appear in "Fiorello!," named best musical by critics.

In dramatic scene of Peter Shaffer's play, "Five Finger Exercise," chosen as best foreign play of the season, are Juliet Mills, left, Roland Culver and Jessica Tandy.

Cue magazine, and Joseph T. Shipley, The New Leader. The same number went to "The Connection." Voting for it were Henry Hewes, The Saturday Review, and Kenneth Tynan, The New Yorker. One vote was cast for "The Tenth Man" —by Brooks Atkinson of The Times.

"Fiorello!" the musical comedy by Jerome Weidman, George Abbott, Jerry Bock and Sheldon Harnick, emerged with ten votes. The plot deals with Mayor Fiorello H. La Guardia from the time he was a struggling lawyer until his first successful mayoralty campaign on the fusion slate.

That role is portrayed by Tom Bosley. Robert E. Griffith and Harold S. Prince produced the show under Mr. Abbott's direction at the Broadhurst. It opened Nov. 23.

Votes for Five Musicals

"Fiorello!" won the support of Barron, Bolton, Chapman, Colby, Coleman, Dash, Hewes, Lewis, McClain and Wenning. "Bye Bye Birdie" received three votes, from Aston, Cooke and Gaver, as did "Gypsy," from Kerr, Tynan and Watts. Those who named "The Sound of Music" were Morehouse and Shipley. "Greenwillow" had one vote, from Atkinson.

"Five Finger Exercise," a London hit, represents the local debut of its author, Peter Shaffer. Starred in the study of family relationship in a British home are Roland Culver and Jessica Tandy. It was staged by John Gielgud and has been running at the Music Box since Dec. 2 under the banner of Frederick Brisson and The Playwrights Company.

Thirteen critics were in favor of "Five Finger Exercise,": Aston, Barron, Bolton, Colby, Cooke, Dash, Gaver, Kerr, McClain, Morehouse, Shipley, Watts and Wenning.

"The Fighting Cock" was backed by Atkinson and Coleman. "The Balcony" was supported by Hewes and Tynan. "At the Drop of a Hat" was picked by Chapman and "Krapp's Last Tape" by Lewis.

TONY AWARDS

'Fiorello!,' 'Sound of Music' Tie—Mary Martin Gets 4th

The Antoinette Perry theatre awards went last night to "The Miracle Worker," among the plays for last year, and to two musical productions, "Fiorello!" and "The Sound of Music."

At the fourteenth annual Tony presentation ceremonies, attended by 1,200 persons in the Astor Hotel, the two musicals finished in a tie. "The Sound of Music," a musical play about the Trapp family of singers, received a total of five silver Tonys, and "Fiorello!" the musical comedy dealing with Mayor Fiorello H. La Guardia, captured three prizes.

The book for "Fiorello!" was written by George Abbott and

Anne Bancroft holds Patty Duke in a scene from "The Miracle Worker," selected for dramatic play prize. Miss Bancroft was honored as dramatic actress star.

Jerome Weidman, the lyrics by Sheldon Harnick and the music by Jerry Bock. "The Sound of Music" libretto was written by Howard Lindsay and Russel Crouse, the lyrics by Oscar Hammerstein 2d and the music by Richard Rodgers.

Mary Martin, the star of "The Sound of Music," was cited as the outstanding actress in a musical. The award marked the fourth time that Miss Martin has received a Tony. Jackie Gleason, one of the stars of "Take Me Along," a musical based on Eugene O'Neill's "Ah, Wilderness!," was selected as the year's outstanding male musical performer.

4 for "Miracle Worker"

To "The Miracle Worker," the story of Annie Sullivan's first week as a teacher to the blind, deaf and mute Helen Keller, the American Theatre Wing gave a total of four accolades.

Anne Bancroft, who plays the role of the teacher in "The Miracle Worker," received top prize as the dramatic actress, and Melvyn Douglas, who is the Presidential candidate reputedly modeled on Adlai E. Stevenson in "The Best Man," won a Tony as the outstanding male dramatic star. It was Miss Bancroft's second Tony.

The prize for the featured or supporting actress and actor in drama went to Anne Revere, for "Toys in the Attic," and Roddy McDowall, for "The Fighting Cock." The Tonys for the featured actress and actor in a musical were awarded to Patricia Neway of "The Sound of Music" and Tom Bosley, who portrays the title role in "Fiorello!"

The play director's prize went to Arthur Penn for "The Miracle Worker," which was written by William Gibson. Mr. Abbott received the top citation for musical director for his work on "Fiorello!"

Michael Kidd achieved a record for number of Tonys received by getting one this year for his choreography on "Destry Rides Again." It was his fifth.

Special awards were presented to Burgess Meredith and James Thurber, director and author, respectively, of "A Thurber Carnival." John D. Rockefeller 3d also received a special Tony for his leadership in plans for the Lincoln Center for the Performing Arts.

In addition to the Tonys for the best musical, the best musical actress and the outstanding featured actress, "The Sound of Music" accounted for Tonys

Melvyn Douglas in "The Best Man." He received the top dramatic actor award.

Jackie Gleason was named for his performance in musical "Take Me Along."

Tom Bosley, left, Patricia Wilson and Howard da Silva in "Fiorello!" also picked for a musical play award.

Mary Martin was chosen in the musical actress category for "The Sound of Music," co-winner as musical play.

given to Oliver Smith, the musical's scenic designer, and to Frederick Dvonch, its musical conductor. The fourth Tony accorded "The Miracle Worker" went to John Walters, the chief carpenter.

Howard Bay was honored for his work as scenic designer for "Toys in the Attic" and Cecil Beaton received a prize for costume design in "Saratoga."

Although the prizewinners, chosen from eighty-nine nominations in nineteen categories, were not officially labeled "best" or "first," Broadway has come to regard the Tonys as the equivalent of the Hollywood Oscar and the television Emmy. The Tonys are named in memory of the late Miss Perry, wartime chairman of the American Theatre Wing.

OBIE AWARDS

'CONNECTION' GETS 3 THEATRE 'OBIES'

Theatre achievements off Broadway were recognized last night with the fifth annual presentation of prizes, known as "Obies." They were distributed at the Village Gate, 185 Thompson Street, by the newspaper The Village Voice.

"The Connection" was the recipient of three awards. One went to its author, Jack Gelber; the second for being classified as the best all-round production, and the third to its leading actor, Warren Finnerty. Eileen Brennan of "Little Mary Sunshine" was chosen as the best actress.

Jean Genet's "The Balcony" was named as the best foreign play. David Hays, who designed the production, also received an award. Gene Frankel, who staged "Machinal," was chosen as the best director.

Cited for distinguished performances were William Daniels, "The Zoo Story"; Donald Davis, "Krapp's Last Tape"; Vincent Gardenia, "Machinal"; John Heffernan, "Henry IV, Part 2"; Jock Livingston and Nancy Marchand, "The Balcony"; Patricia Falkenhain, "Peer Gynt" and "Henry IV, Part 2," and Elisa Loti, "Come Share My House."

Named as distinguished plays were "Krapp's Last Tape," "The Prodigal" and "The Zoo Story."

A special citation went to Brooks Atkinson, drama critic of The New York Times, "for having put off-Broadway on the map."

SPECIAL AWARDS

Theatres Give Atkinson One on the Aisle for Life

Brooks Atkinson, drama critic for The New York Times, who is vacating the post at the end of this theatrical season, yesterday was given a lifetime pass to all the attractions of Broadway's legitimate theatres. He is the first person to be honored in this way.

The pass, lettered on a gold plate, was given to Mr. Atkinson by a committee of producers and theatre operators. It included Louis A. Lotito, president of the League of New York Theatres; John Shubert, representing the Shubert Theatres, and producers Robert Griffith, Kermit Bloomgarden and Herman Shumlin.

The inscription on the gold plate reads:

"To Brooks Atkinson, a life pass to all Broadway legitimate theatres, in deep admiration for his many years of service."

It is dated May 31, 1960.

The last day of May is traditionally the end of the theatre year.

THEATRE TO ADOPT ATKINSON'S NAME

Former Mansfield Will Be Furbished and Renamed in Honor of Retired Critic

Beginning next fall, the name of Brooks Atkinson will adorn a Broadway theatre.

Mr. Atkinson, who retired last month as drama critic of The New York Times, will be the city's, and perhaps the country's, first theatre reviewer to be thus honored. The only other newspaper man, though not a critic, to be honored nightly on Broadway in neon is the late columnist Mark Hellinger, after whom the Hellinger Theatre was named.

A sign bearing Mr. Atkinson's name will be installed outside the theatre that formerly was designated the Mansfield. Built and owned by Irwin and Henry Chanin in 1927, it is at 256 West Forty-seventh Street. The playhouse was named after Richard Mansfield, the American actor (1854-1907) who was considered the greatest exponent of Shakespearean drama of his day.

Like many of Broadway's legitimate theatres in the Thirties, the Mansfield went into foreclosure. It was purchased in 1942 by its present owner, Michael Myerberg.

Mr. Myerberg said yesterday that he would spend $200,000 to refurbish the theatre and that it would open Sept. 12 as the Brooks Atkinson Theatre. Its first attraction will be an intimate revue, "Vintage '60," to be produced by David Merrick in association with Zev Bufman, George Skaff and Max Perkins.

Mr. Myerberg said he had decided to rename the theatre "after much thought and consultation" with the former reviewer's "friends and colleagues." He had intended to make the announcement without Mr. Atkinson's "advice or comment" because of "his great modesty."

Apprised late yesterday afternoon of the honor, Mr. Atkinson, who was reached at his home in Durham, N. Y., said:

"It would certainly be a great honor not only to me but to the profession of drama criticism, which, as far as I know, has never been recognized in this fashion. It's a lucky thing that since I am now a retired critic, I shall never have to review a play in a theatre that bears my name."

Mr. Myerberg said:

"Mr. Atkinson has long been the great force in American theatre criticism—his influence reaching far beyond our city. The honors flowing toward him at his retirement have been a natural concomitant of the integrity, intelligence and self-

lessness which he brought to this immense responsibility.

"The Brooks Atkinson Theatre will lend distinction and honor and a constant reminder of high principle to the theatre as a whole."

For the last ten years, the Mansfield has been used for Columbia Broadcasting System telelvision programs.

1961

PULITZER PRIZE

Tad Mosel

FULL name is George Ault Mosel Jr. . . . won drama prize for first Broadway play, "All the Way Home," based on the late James Agee's Pulitzer Prize novel, "A Death in the Family" . . . 39 years old yesterday . . . one of television's leading writers . . . wrote "Star in the Summer Night," "My Lost Saints" and "The Lawn Party" . . . born Steubenville, Ohio . . . grew up in Larchmont, N. Y., graduated from Amherst College . . . attended Yale Drama School . . . master's degree in drama from Columbia . . . acted on Broadway in "At War With the Army" . . . from 1951 to 1953 sold tickets for an airline .

PULITZER DRAMA ALMOST CLOSED

Trucks Arrived for Sets 3 Days After Opening

By MILTON ESTEROW

"All the Way Home," which yesterday became the first Pulitzer Prize play based on a Pulitzer Prize novel, is the Cinderella story of many Broadway seasons.

Tad Mosel's dramatization of the late James Agee's "A Death in the Family," which won the novel prize in 1958, had planned to close three days after its

opening—trucks were ready to cart away the scenery. It has had two additional reprieves since then and has become known as "The Miracle on Forty-fourth Street."

Two weeks ago, it won the Drama Critics Circle Award for the best American play of the season.

"All the Way Home" opened at the Belasco Theatre Nov. 30 to critical approval. It is now in its twenty-third week but not many theatregoers have rushed to the box office.

Royalties Waived

To keep the play from closing, Mr. Mosel, the author; Arthur Penn, the director, and Fred Coe and his co-producer-press agent, Arthur Cantor, have waived their royalties, partly or completely, for many weeks.

The Shuberts, who own the theatre, have reduced the rental, according to Mr. Cantor.

"All the Way Home" recounts the effect of a father's sudden death on members of the family, especially the wife and young son. Mr. Agee, a poet, critic and writer, completed "A Death in the Family" in 1955, shortly before he died at the age of 45.

Mr. Agee's own father had died when he was a boy in Knoxville, Tenn., the locale of the story.

The novel, published in 1957 by McDowell, Obolensky (now Ivan Obolensky, Inc.) was on the best-seller lists for some time. The hard-cover edition had five printings and sold about 40,000 copies; the paperback sold 450,000.

One of the times the play's future was in doubt was the middle of last month. The closing had been set for last Saturday. Then, on April 18, the Drama Critics award was made. Business has increased considerably since then.

There are those who say Georgia Simmons' "conjure pennies" are a significant part of the play's success story.

When the play opened, Miss Simmons, a member of the cast, sewed leather casings partly around pennies, attached them to safety pins and gave them to all concerned with the production.

"You wear it if you want something special to happen," Miss Simmons said.

Mr. Mosel, who was 39 years old yesterday, said: "What with all those forces for good working for us, here we are."

'All Way Home' Pulitzer Play; Novel Is 'To Kill a Mockingbird'

By PHILIP BENJAMIN

"All the Way Home," a play based on the Pulitzer Prize novel for 1958, won the 1961 Pulitzer Prize for drama yesterday.

It was the first time in the forty-five-year history of the awards that a play based on a Pulitzer novel had received a Pulitzer in its own right.

The fiction prize was won by "To Kill a Mockingbird," by Harper Lee, a young Southern woman. It was published by the J. B. Lippincott Company.

Twelve other awards and a special citation were made in the fields of letters, music and journalism by the trustees of Columbia University. At the same time, the university announced that a new Pulitzer Prize for general nonfiction would be added to the established prizes next year.

In the journalism category, Lynn Heinzerling of The Associated Press won in the field of international reporting for his coverage of the Congo crisis and other African affairs.

In letters, the other awards were:

History—"Between War and Peace: The Potsdam Conference" by Herbert Feis, published by the Princeton University Press.

Biography—"Charles Sumner and the Coming of the Civil War" by David Donald, published by Alfred A. Knopf, Inc.

Poetry—"Times Three: Selected Verse From Three Decades" by Phyllis McGinley, published by the Viking Press.

Special citation—"The American Heritage Picture History of the Civil War."

In music, the prize was given to Walter Piston for his Symphony No. 7, first performed by the Philadelphia Orchestra on Feb. 10. Mr. Piston had previously won a Pulitzer Prize in 1948 for his Symphony 3.

Other Prizes Listed

The other awards in journalism were:

Public service—The Amarillo (Tex.) Globe-Times for exposing a breakdown in local law enforcement. The exposure resulted in resignations, indictments and the election of a reform slate.

Local reporting under deadline pressure—Sanche de Gramont of The New York Herald Tribune for his account of the death of Leonard Warren on the stage of the Metropolitan Opera House.

Local reporting not under pressure—Edgar May of The Buffalo Evening News for a series on New York State's public welfare services.

National affairs—Edward R. Cony of The Wall Street Journal for his analysis of a timber transaction that drew the attention of the public to problems of business ethics.

Editorial writing—William J. Dorvillier of The San Juan Star for editorials on clerical interference in the 1960 governorship election in Puerto Rico.

Cartoons—Carey Orr of The Chicago Tribune for his work as an editorial cartoonist.

News photography — Yasushi Nagao of the newspaper Main-ichi in Tokyo for his photograph of the fatal stabbing of the Japanese Socialist leader Inejiro Asanuma.

Awards of $1,000 and $500

In journalism, the individual winners were awarded $1,000 each. The award for public service by a newspaper was a gold medal. In the categories of music and letters, the prizes were $500 each.

The play "All the Way Home" had previously won the award of the New York Drama Critics Circle as the best American play of the season.

The play nearly foundered shortly after its opening on Nov. 30, 1960. It was a critical success, but it did not attract audiences. When the producers announced that the play would close, the public at last responded.

Written by Tad Mosel, "All the Way Home" was based on the novel "A Death in the Family," by the late James Agee, who died in 1955 at the age of 45. The play and novel tell of the impact of a man's sudden death on his wife and son. Mr. Agee himself left a wife and three children. His Pulitzer Prize for the novel was posthumous.

Novelist's First

"To Kill a Mockingbird" is the first novel by Miss Lee. It tells of life in a small Southern town. Its protagonist is a small girl named Scout Finch. The novel was a Reader's Digest Condensed Book selection and a Literary Guild selection.

The prize to Mr. Piston for his Symphony No. 7 was not unexpected among music critics. The symphony is regarded as a conservative work by a middle-of-the-road composer.

Mr. Nagao is the first foreign photographer to win a Pulitzer Prize. He became eligible for the prize when his picture was published in newspapers here.

The new Pulitzer Prize in general nonfiction will be given

"for a distinguished book by an American which is not eligible for consideration in any other existing category."

Created in Will

The Pulitzer awards were created in the will of Joseph Pulitzer, the publisher of The New York World. The first prizes were given in 1917. They are administered by the Graduate School of Journalism of Columbia University. The school was endowed by Mr. Pulitzer.

The prizes in letters go to American novelists; to American plays; to books on the history of the United States; to American biographies teaching patriotic and unselfish services to the people, and to volumes of verse by American authors.

In music the prizes go to composers of established residence in the United States.

The final selection for the awards is made by the advisory board upon nominations by individuals or newspapers.

This year's board members were:

Dr. Grayson Kirk, president of Columbia; Barry Bingham, The Louisville Courier-Journal; Erwin D. Canham, The Christian Science Monitor; Hodding Carter, The Delta Democrat-Times, Greenville, Miss.; Turner Catledge, The New York Times; Norman Chandler, The Times-Mirror Company, Los Angeles; J. D. Ferguson, The Milwaukee Journal; Kenneth MacDonald, The Des Moines Register-Tribune.

Also, W. D. Maxwell, The Chicago Tribune; Benjamin M. McKelway, The Evening Star, Washington; Paul Miller, Gannett Newspapers; Joseph Pulitzer Jr., The St. Louis Post-Dispatch; Louis B. Seltzer, The Cleveland Press, and Prof. John Hohenberg, Columbia Graduate School of Journalism.

Members of the board whose own newspapers are up for consideration in a particular category are required to leave the conference room during the discussion and voting on that category

NEW YORK DRAMA CRITICS CIRCLE AWARDS

'All the Way Home' Is Chosen Top U.S. Play by Drama Critics

By LOUIS CALTA

"All the Way Home," which had announced its closing the day after it opened, yesterday made it all the way home to the Drama Critics Circle Award for the best American play of the season. The voting took place at the Algonquin Hotel.

Tad Mosel's drama captured first place by virtue of eight votes. Twenty reviewers participated in the balloting, three by proxy. They also awarded top honors to "A Taste of Honey" as the best foreign play and to "Carnival!" as the best musical.

"All the Way Home," a dramatization of the late James Agee's Pulitzer Prize-winning novel, "A Death in the Family," opened Nov. 30 at the Belasco Theatre. The notices which ranged from outright recommendation to respectful approval, were not regarded as of box-office value.

When it was announced that it would close after five performances, a surge of popular support kept it going. Its new lease on life was termed in theatrical circles as "The Miracle of Forty-fourth Street."

The drama critics award imparted an additional fateful note to the play with the disclosure yesterday that it had intended to close in a fortnight. Such plans have now been set aside.

"All the Way Home" deals with the story of a young father killed in an automobile accident and with the shattering impact it has on his wife and 5-year-old son. The principal roles were

Aline MacMahon, left, with Colleen Dewhurst in a scene from "All the Way Home," chosen best American play.

Anthony Quinn, left, Dran Seitz and Laurence Olivier in a scene from "Becket," selected in the dramatic category.

created by Colleen Dewhurst as the mother, Arthur Hill as the father and John Megna as the boy.

It was the selection of Whitney Bolton, The Morning Telegraph; William H. Glover, The Associated Press; Walter Kerr, The Herald Tribune; Emory Lewis, Cue; John McCarten, The New Yorker; Howard Taubman, The New York Times; Richard Watts Jr., The New York Post, and Thomas H. Wenning, Newsweek.

The runner-up was "The Devil's Advocate," with five votes. It won the support of John Chapman, The Daily News; Ethel Colby, The Journal of Commerce; Richard Cook, The Wall Street Journal; Thomas R. Dash, Women's Wear Daily, and Joseph T. Shipley, New Leader.

"Advise and Consent" polled four votes, from Frank Aston, The World-Telegram and The Sun; Robert Coleman, The Daily Mirror; John McClain, The Journal-American, and Ward Morehouse of the S. I. Newhouse Chain.

3 Single Choices

Single ballots were cast for "Period of Adjustment," "A Far Country" and "Big Fish, Little Fish" by, respectively, Henry Hewes, The Saturday Review; Alan Pryce-Jones, Theatre Arts, and Jack Gaver, United Press International.

"Carnival!" the musical derived from the film, "Lili," dealing with the eager and sensitive young women overwhelmed by the tinsel and flamboyance of a European circus, emerged with thirteen votes—the widest margin of the three categories. Voting for it were Miss Colby and Aston, Messrs. Bolton, Chapman, Coleman, Dash, Gaver, Glover, Lewis, Morehouse, McClain, Watts and Wenning.

Its nearest competitors were "The Unsinkable Molly Brown" and "Irma la Douce," with two votes each. Messrs. McCarten

and Pryce-Jones cast their ballots for "Molly," while Messrs. Shipley and Taubman favored "Irma." "Do-Re-Mi" garnered a single vote from Mr. Kerr, "The Fantasticks" from Mr. Hewes and "Camelot" from Mr. Cooke.

"A Taste of Honey," a first playwriting effort by Shelagh Delaney, written when she was 19, garnered seven ballots. They were cast by Miss Colby and Messrs. Cooke, Bolton, Kerr, Morehouse, Pryce-Jones and Wenning. Five critics who favored "Becket" were Messrs. Chapman, Coleman, Hewes, McClain and Shipley. "Rhinoceros" received the support of Messrs. Aston, Glover, McCarten and Taubman. "The Hostage" drew votes from Messrs. Dash, Gaver and Watts. And "Roots" attracted a ballot from Mr. Lewis.

Every winner was named on the first ballot. Presentation of the scrolls, symbolic of the honors, will be made April 27 at the Algonquin. Louis Kronenberger, critic for Time, did not vote.

TONY AWARDS

Elizabeth Seal, Joan Plowright, Mostel and Burton Cited

By MILTON ESTEROW

Jean Anouilh's "Becket" and the musical "Bye Bye Birdie" each won four Tony Awards last night for "distinguished achievement" on the Broadway stage.

"Becket" was named the outstanding play of the season be-

Richard Burton, who plays in "Camelot," was given award for his performance.

Elizabeth Seal in "Irma La Douce." She was honored for her work in musical.

Zero Mostel, who was chosen for his performance in the drama "Rhinoceros."

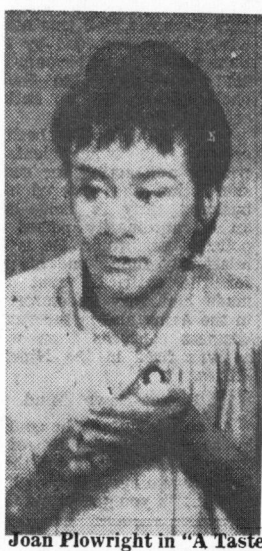

Joan Plowright in "A Taste of Honey." She won the top dramatic actress award.

In scene from "Bye Bye Birdie," honored in the musical comedy category, are Chita Rivera and Dick Van Dyke.

tween April 1 of last year and March 24. Oliver Smith received an award for scenic design, Motley for costume design and Teddy Van Bemmel as stage technician.

"Bye Bye Birdie" was cited as the outstanding musical, Dick Van Dyke won a prize for musical featured or supporting actor and Gower Champion won two—choreographer and director in a musical.

"Camelot" also received four Tonys.

Among the other players who received Tonys were Zero Mostel, Tammy Grimes and three British stars — Richard Burton, Joan Plowright and Elizabeth Seal.

The Tonys were presented at the fifteenth annual American Theatre Wing awards dinner attended by more than 1,000 persons at the Waldorf-Astoria Hotel. The Tony is a silver medallion named in memory of Antoinette Perry, the wing's wartime chairman.

The play director's prize went to Sir John Gielgud for "Big Fish, Little Fish."

Named for 'Rhinoceros' Role

Mr. Mostel was cited as male dramatic star for his role in "Rhinoceros." Miss Plowright of "A Taste of Honey" was named female dramatic star. Miss Seal ("Irma La Douce") got the prize for female musical star and Mr. Burton ("Camelot") as male musical star.

Miss Grimes received the Tony for musical featured or supporting actress in "The Unsinkable Molly Brown." Colleen Dewhurst of "All the Way Home" received an award as featured or supporting actress and Martin Gabel of "Big Fish, Little Fish" got one as featured or supporting actor.

Mr. Smith also was cited as scenic designer in a musical— "Camelot." These were his fourth and fifth Tonys. He was previously cited for his work in "The Sound of Music," "West Side Story" and "My Fair Lady."

Tony Duquette and the late Adrian were named winners of the award for costume designer, musical, in "Camelot." The show's musical conductor, Franz Allers, also won an award.

Special awards went to David Merrick, the producer and the Theatre Guild. The award to Mr. Merrick was "in recognition of a fabulous production record over the past seven years." The Guild was cited "for organizing the first repertory to go abroad for the State Department."

Equivalents of Oscars

Broadway regards the Tonys as equivalent to Hollywood Oscars. In previous years the balloting for them was confined to fifty members of the Wing's board of governors. This year about 500 members of the Wing voted.

In previous years a Wing committee counted the ballots. Although there were no official announcements of the winners, word leaked out before the actual presentations.

This year the ballots were mailed to Peat, Marwick, Mitchell & Co., accounting firm, which tabulated them. There was no announcement of the winners until the actual presentation.

"Becket" deals with the love-hate relationship of Henry II of England and a courtier who became Archbishop of Canterbury. It was translated by Lucienne Hill, starred Laurence Olivier and Anthony Quinn and was produced by Mr. Merrick. It closed last month after a run of 194 performances and is now on tour.

"Bye Bye Birdie" was written by Michael Steward (book), Charles Strouse (music) and Lee Adams (lyrics). The producer was Edward Padula in association with L. Slade Brown. Mr. Van Dyke and Chita Rivera were the stars when the show opened last April. They have been replaced by Gene Rayburn and Gretchen Wyler.

OBIE AWARDS

"Hedda Gabler" and "The Blacks" each received three Obie awards for achievement in the off-Broadway theatre at the sixth annual presentation on Saturday at the Village Gate, 185 Thompson Street. Obie is the phonetic abbreviation of Off Broadway.

"Hedda Gabler," which was revived and directed by David Ross at the Fourth Street Theatre, was termed the best all-around production. Anne Meacham, who plays the title role, was named as the best actress. Another member of that cast, Lester Rawlins, received one of six distinguished performance citations for his interpretation of George Tesman.

Each was the winner of similar Obie prizes previously. Mr. Ross for his 1956 revival of "Uncle Vanya"; Miss Meacham

for her 1958 portrayal in "Suddenly Last Summer," and Mr. Rawlins for his acting in "The Quare Fellow" in 1958.

Jean Genet's "The Blacks" at the St. Marks Playhouse was voted the best new play (European and American). A special citation was won by Bernard Frechtman for his translation of the French work. Godfrey M. Cambridge, who is appearing in the play, shared a prize in the distinguished performance category.

Khigh Dhiegh of Bertolt Brecht's "In the Jungle of Cities" was named as the best actor; Gerald A. Freedman as the best director for his staging of "The Taming of the Shrew"; "The Premise" as the best "off-off-Broadway production," and Teiji Ito for his music in "In the Jungle of Cities," "Three Modern Japanese Plays" and "King Ubu."

Besides Mr. Rawlins and Mr. Cambridge, others honored for distinguished performances were Joan Hackett ("Call Me by My Rightful Name"), Gerry Jedd ("She Stoops to Conquer"), Surya Kumari ("The King of the Dark Chamber") and James Coco ("The Moon in the Yellow River").

Scrolls were presented by Julie Harris, Broadway star. The contest was conducted by the Village Voice, a Greenwich Village newspaper. The judges were Harold Clurman, Tom Driver and Jerry Tallmer.

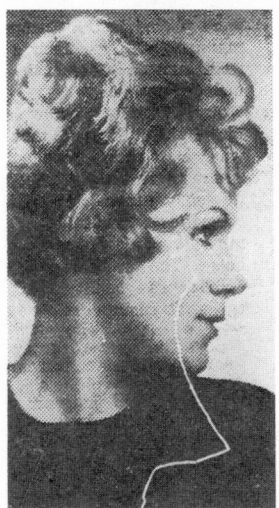

Tammy Grimes, honored for her featured role in "The Unsinkable Molly Brown."

'Hedda Gabler' and 'The Blacks' Each Win Three Obie Awards

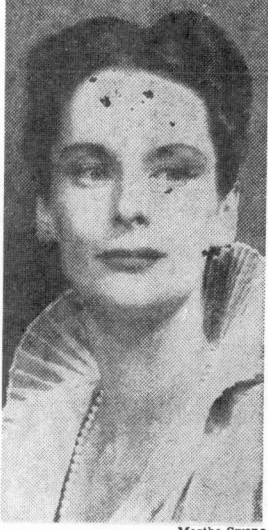

Martha Swope

Anne Meacham as she looks in Ibsen's "Hedda Gabler."

Khigh Dhiegh in Brecht's "In the Jungle of Cities."

1962

PULITZER PRIZE

Columbia Trustees Block Pulitzer Prize for 'Hearst'

By PETER KIHSS

The trustees of Columbia University yesterday turned down a Pulitzer Prize recommendation by the prize advisory board, rejecting an award for biography to "Citizen Hearst" by W. A. Swanberg. It was believed to have been the first time in the forty-six years of Pulitzer Prizes that the university trustees had rejected a recommendation by the advisory board. No award was made for a biography.

There was no formal announcement of the recommendation or the rejection. The prize terms call for $500 "for a distinguished American biography or autobiography teaching patriotic and unselfish services to the people, illustrated by an eminent example."

Speculation on Motive

There was speculation that some trustees might have questioned whether the life story of William Randolph Hearst, the often-controversial publisher of a nation-wide chain of newspapers, might have fitted into this definition. The university declined to comment.

Of the fourteen Pulitzer Prizes awarded for 1962, the honors for best play went to the musical comedy "How to Succeed in Business Without Really Trying" by Frank Loesser and Abe Burrows. The best novel was adjudged to be Edwin O'Connor's "The Edge of Sadness."

For the first time a general nonfiction category was set up, and the $500 award went to "The Making of the President 1960" by Theodore H. White. In journalism, the prize for public service by a newspaper went to The Panama City (Fla.) News and The Herald for a three-year campaign against corruption.

The prize for editorial writing went to Thomas M. Storke, 85-year-old editor and publisher of The Santa Barbara (Calif.) News Press for calling attention to what the paper said was a "campaign of hate and vilification" by the John Birch Society.

The letters prizes, all carrying $500 honorariums, also included the following:

For a distinguished history of the United States: "The Triumphant Empire, Thunder-Clouds Gather in the West," by Lawrence H. Gibson, an 81-year-old Research Professor of History Emeritus at Lehigh University.

For a distinguished volume of verse: "Poems," by Alan Dugan, a 39-year-old New York molder of anatomical models for medical instruction.

A $500 prize for distinguished musical composition went to "The Crucible," an opera by Robert Ward, a Nyack, N. Y., music editor.

Journalism prizes, which provide for $1,000 awards except for a gold medal in the case of the public-service category, also included:

For local reporting under the pressure of edition time: Robert D. Mullins, of The Deseret News, Salt Lake City, for resourceful coverage of a murder and kidnaping at Dead Horse Point, Utah.

For local reporting in which the pressure of edition time is not a factor: George Bliss, of The Chicago Tribune, for initiative in uncovering scandals in the Metropolitan Sanitary District of Greater Chicago, which led to the dismissal of several hundred public employes as incompetent, among other things.

For national reporting: Nathan G. Caldwell and Gene S. Graham, of The Nashville Tennessean, for six years' reporting of undercover management-labor activities that led to a conviction of the United Mine Workers for violating antitrust laws in conspiring with major coal companies to drive some small concerns out of business.

For reporting of international affairs: Walter Lippmann of The New York Herald Tribune Syndicate, now 72 years old, for his long and distinguished contribution to American journalism, an illustration being his 1961 interview with Premier Khrushchev of the Soviet Union.

For a cartoonist's work: Edmund S. Valtman of The Hartford Times, a former Estonian displaced person, for distinguished editorial cartooning during the year, as exemplified by a drawing of Premier Fidel Castro of Cuba leading a chained Cuba and telling a Brazilian peasant: "What You Need, Man, Is A Revolution Like Mine."

For news photography: Paul Vathis of The Associated Press bureau in Harrisburg, Pa., for a photograph of President Kennedy and former President Dwight D. Eisenhower, their heads bowed, as they conferred after the failure of the American-aided invasion of Cuba.

Rejection Reported

Four members of the Advisory Board on the Pulitzer Prizes reported last night that their group had recommended that the biography prize go to Mr. Swanberg's life of Mr. Hearst. They said this was after a vote in which Mark Schorer's biography of the late author Sinclair Lewis was the runner-up.

Erwin D. Canham, editor of The Christian Science Monitor, remembered "some criticism" within the board about the

Swanberg book, although he personally favored it. Norman Chandler, president of The Los Angeles Times-Mirror Company, said that he had first voted for Mr. Schorer's book, but that the Swanberg selection had been made unanimous after an overwhelming vote in its favor.

Others reporting the recommendation for the Swanberg book included W. D. Maxwell, vice president and editor of The Chicago Tribune, and Benjamin M. McKelway, vice president and editor of the Washington Evening Star.

The action by the Columbia University trustees was simply announced by Grayson Kirk, president of the university, as "no award" in the field of biography. A university spokesman, in response to questions, would say only:

"The proceedings of the Columbia trustees and of the advisory board are not matters of public record, and therefore no comment can be made on what went on inside these meetings."

Mr. Swanberg said last night that he had expected the Sinclair Lewis biography to win. Now 54 years old, he has written three earlier books: "Sickles the Incredible," "First Blood: The Story of Fort Sumter," and "Jim Fisk: The Career of an Improbable Rascal."

Book Described

In his summing up of Mr. Hearst's life, Mr. Swanberg wrote that the late newspaper publisher's influence on journalism was mostly bad, and "while he spoke piously of ideals in journalism, he left no gutter unexplored."

On the other hand, Mr. Swanberg added, Mr. Hearst's "sympathies were so aroused by the plight of the Cubans that he insisted on saving them" with the Spanish-American war, and and "he was so indignant at the exploitation of the common people that he became their defender against privilege."

The other members of the advisory board are:

Dr. Kirk; Barry Bingham, The Louisville Courier-Journal and The Times; Sevellon Brown, editor of The Providence (R. I.) Journal and The Evening Bulletin; Turner Catledge, managing editor of The New York Times; Kenneth MacDonald, vice president and editor of The Des Moines Register and Tribune; Ralph McGill, publisher of The Atlanta Constitution; Paul Miller, president of The Gannett Newspapers, Rochester, N. Y.; Joseph Pulitzer Jr., president and publisher of The St. Louis Post-Dispatch; Louis B. Seltzer, editor of The Cleveland Press; and John Hohenberg, Professor of Journalism at the Columbia Graduate School of Journalism, secretary.

Trustees Listed

Columbia University would not disclose which trustees attended yesterday's decisive meeting at the Low Memorial Library, but there were twenty-three active trustees eligible to vote. They are:

Dr. Kirk; Maurice T. Moore, chairman; Robert W. Watt, vice chairman; George E. Warren, clerk; Lester D. Egbert, associate clerk; Adrian M. Massie, Frank D. Fackenthal, Walter D. Fletcher, Douglas M. Black, William S. Paley, William A. M.

Burden, Roscoe C. Ingalls, Walter H. Sammis, Ronald M. Craigmyle, Thomas O'Gorman Fitz-Gibbon, William T. Gossett, Samuel R. Walker, Abram J. Abeloff, Alan H. Temple, Benjamin J. Buttenwieser, Harold F. McGuire, Percy Uris and Frederick van Pelt Bryan.

The university also has four emeritus trustees who would ordinarily not take part. They are former President Dwight D. Eisenhower, M. Hartley Dodge, Arthur Hays Sulzberger and John Heuss.

Ordinarily, the university's trustees meet to act on the advisory board's recommendation announced at 3 P. M. on the first Monday of each May. Last week, Professor Hohenberg had said "the trustees have accepted the recommendations of the advisory board all these years without question."

The deliberations usually last about half an hour, with a telephone call then authorizing release of the awards. Once the announcement was delayed until after 5 P. M. but this was attributed to somebody's forgetting to make the call from the closed meeting, while the trustees went on to other matters.

It was not until 4:23 P. M. yesterday that the prizes were announced, which led to a suspicion that something unusual had occurred. The university notified members of the advisory board by telegram about what had happened.

Along Broadway there was some discussion yesterday about the singling out of Mr. Loesser and Mr. Burrows to receive the prize for "How to Succeed" and share the $500 cash award.

The hit show, a jibe at the ways of big business, was an adaptation by Mr. Burrows with Dr. Jack Weinstock and Willie Gilbert of a book by Shepherd Mead; Mr. Loesser wrote the music and lyrics; Mr. Burrows directed the show.

The advisory board had recommended Mr. Loesser and Mr. Burrows as principally responsible, and these findings were confirmed by the university trustees.

It was the fourth time in the history of the prizes that a musical had carried off the award. Previous winners were "Of Thee I Sing" in 1932, "South Pacific" in 1950, and "Fiorello!" in 1960. In 1944, "Oklahoma!" won a special citation.

Mr. Ward's opera "The Crucible" had its first performance Oct. 26 by the New York City Opera Company under a Ford Foundation grant. It had mixed notices. The work was based on a play by Arthur Miller, and Harold C. Schonberg's review in The New York Times said "the action was strong enough to come right through. Mr. Ward's frequently noncommittal music." He termed the opera "musical platitudes."

The university announced that Mr. Canham, Mr. MacDonald and Mr. Maxwell had been re-elected unanimously to their second four-year terms on the advisory board, with Professor Hohenberg re-elected secretary for a one-year term.

The Pulitzer Prizes were set up by Joseph Pulitzer, an immigrant from Hungary, who became publisher of The St. Louis

Post-Dispatch and The New York World. Mr. Pulitzer in 1903 donated $2,000,000 to Columbia University to establish a school of journalism, and provided that the income from $500,000 of this be used for prizes or scholarships.

Mr. Pulitzer died Oct. 29, 1911. The first prizes were given in 1917. Awards have been omitted in a number of categories in the past, but yesterday was the first time there had been no award for a biography.

Abe Burrows

Joint winner with Frank Loesser of drama award for "How to Succeed in Business Without Really Trying" . . . Born in New York City in 1910 . . . Educated at New York University and the College of the City of New York. . . Employed as a Wall Street runner, board boy, coat and label peddler, accountant, salesman. . . . In the amusement field had chores as a radio and TV writer, playwright, play doctor, director, songwriter, piano player, radio and TV player and performer at night clubs, summer hotels and house parties . . . "A wit's wit" and "a clown's clown." . . . Had a hand in writing "Guys and Dolls," "Three Wishes for Jamie," "Can-Can," "Silk Stockings," "Say, Darling" and "First Impressions." . . .

Frank Loesser

Joint winner of drama award with Abe Burrows for "How to Succeed in Business

Without Really Trying," which also has received New York Drama Critics Circle award as well as seven Tonys. . . . 52-year-old composer-lyricist was born in New York. . . . Attended City College of New York. . . . Began to write songs there. . . . Worked as a reporter, pianist, singer, caricaturist in vaudeville act, reporter, editor of trade paper . . . Song hits include "Rodger Young," "Jingle Jangle Jingle," "Praise the Lord and Pass the Ammunition." . . . Among Broadway shows he furnished songs for were "Where's Charley?", "Guys and Dolls" (winner of Critics Circle award), "The Most Happy Fella" (adapted libretto from 1925 Pulitzer Prize play, "They Knew What They Wanted").

NEW YORK DRAMA CRITICS CIRCLE AWARDS

'IGUANA' IS CITED BY CRITICS CIRCLE

'How to Succeed' Best Show and 'Seasons' Top Import

By SAM ZOLOTOW

"The Night of the Iguana" was designated yesterday as the best American play of the 1961-62 season and "A Man for All Seasons" as the best foreign work by the New York Drama Critics Circle. "How to Succeed is Business Without Really Trying" came within one vote of being the unanimous selection of the Circle as the best musical.

The voting took place in the Algonquin Hotel. The winners will receive scrolls on Thursday or Friday of next week at a cocktail party at the Algonquin.

Seventeen of the eighteen reviewers who voted cast their ballots for "How to Succeed." They were Ted Kalem (Time), Henry Hewes (The Saturday Review), Whitney Bolton (The Morning Telegraph), Walter Kerr (The Herald Tribune), Richard Watts Jr. (The Post), Emory Lewis (Cue), Ethel Colby (The Journal of Commerce), Norman Nadel (The World-Telegram and The Sun).

Also, Ward Morehouse (S. I. Newhouse Chain), John Chapman (The Daily News), Thomas H. Wenning (Newsweek), Richard Cooke (The Wall Street Journal), Robert Coleman (The Mirror), Jack Gaver (United Press International), William H. Glover (The Associated Press), Thomas R. Dash (Women's Wear Daily) and Howard Taubman (The Times).

Shipley Is Dissenter

The lone dissenter was Joseph Shipley of Radio Station WEVD, who supported "No Strings." Mr. Cooke and Mr. Coleman voted by proxy. There were two abstentions, John McClain (The Journal American) and John McCarten (The New Yorker).

A dozen critics voted for Tennessee Williams' "The Night of the Iguana." They included Messrs. Kalem, Hewes, Bolton, Kerr, Watts,

Lewis, Nadel, Morehouse, Chapman, Wenning, Taubman and Miss Colby.

Paddy Chayefsky's "Gideon" ran second with six votes from Messrs. Cooke, Coleman, Shipley, Gaver, Glover and Dash.

Robert Bolt's "A Man for All Seasons" garnered fifteen votes from Messrs. Morehouse, Nadel, Chapman, Wenning, Lewis, Gaver, Bolton, Glover, Dash, Cook, Coleman, Shipley, Watts, Kerr and Miss Colby. The runner-up in the foreign division was Harold Pinter's "The Caretaker", which was chosen by Messrs. Kalem, Hewes, and Taubman.

Robert Morse and Rudy Vallée are starred in "How to Succeed," which stems from Shepherd Mead's book. The lampoon of big business was written by Abe Burrows, Jack Weinstock and Willie Gilbert. Music and lyrics were supplied by Frank Loesser, recipient of previous Circle prizes for "Guys and Dolls" and "The Most Happy Fella." Mr. Burrows also was involved with "Guys and Dolls" as co-author.

The attraction was put on by Cy Feuer and Ernest Martin. Of the seven shows produced by them, "How to Succeed" represents their sixth hit. The other five were "Guys and Dolls," "Where's Charley?," "Can-Can," "The Boy Friend" and "Silk Stockings." A suit has been brought against the producers by Herbert Greene, who alleges he is "the rightful owner of the production rights" of "How to Succeed."

Won Other Awards

Besides "Iguana," the Circle's accolade was bestowed

Friedman-Abeles

SCENE FROM AWARD-WINNING PLAY: Margaret Leighton and Patrick O'Neal as they appeared in Tennessee Williams' "The Night of the Iguana," chosen the best American play by the New York Drama Critics Circle.

upon Mr. Williams for "The Glass Menagerie," "A Streetcar Named Desire" and "Cat on a Hot Tin Roof." He also received Pulitzer Prizes for the last two.

Charles Bowden is the sponsor of "Iguana," in which Margaret Leighton, Shelley Winters and Alan Webb are starred. Screen rights were purchased by Seven Arts Productions before the play, a study of compassion, went into rehearsal. The down payment was $250,000 plus 10 per cent of the gross for every profitable week of the attraction's engagement until the ceiling price of $400,000 is reached.

It took thirteen days for "A Man for All Seasons," which opened Thanksgiving Eve at the ANTA Theatre, to become a sell-out. It is Mr. Bolt's second play to be done here. The first was "Flowering Cherry," which closed after its fifth performance.

The story concerns Sir Thomas More, who refused to compromise his principles and was hanged by Henry VIII. Starred in it are Paul Scofield, who will be replaced on June 25 by Emlyn Williams; Thomas Gomez, George Rose and Albert Dekker.

Sharing in the receipts are Robert Whitehead and Roger L. Stevens, producers and the American National Theatre and Academy, a nonprofit organization, which owns the ANTA Theatre. ANTA gets 25 per cent of the gross and because of its status retains the 10 per cent Federal ticket tax.

TONY AWARDS

'A Man for All Seasons' Wins Tony as Best Play

"How to Succeed in Business Without Really Trying" and "A Man for All Seasons" ran away with the 1962 Tony Awards last night.

"Howto Succeed" won seven awards, including that for the best musical.

"A Man For All Seasons," Robert Bolt's drama about the martyrdom of Sir Thomas More, won five awards, including that for the season's best play. Earlier it had been chosen by the New York Drama Critics Circle as the best foreign play. The critics also named "How to Succeed" as the best musical and "The Night of the Iguana" as the best American play.

Paul Scofield, in the role of Sir Thomas More, was named best starring actor in a drama.

Margaret Leighton of "Night of the Iguana" was named best actress starring in a drama.

Honors for female musical stars were tied by Anna Maria Alberghetti of "Carnival" and Diahann Carroll of "No Strings."

Robert Morse, the brash young hero of "How to Succeed," was named best male star in a musical.

The awards were presented at a dinner dance in the Waldorf-Astoria Hotel, attended by 1,100

'How to Succeed in Business' Is Top Musical—Schofield and Miss Leighton Cited

persons, for the benefit of the American Theatre Wing's training school and student troupes, which perform in schools and hospitals.

The Tony Award, the Broadway equivalent of Hollywood's Oscar, is named in honor of the late Antoinette Perry, wartime chairman of the Wing.

Only productions presented on Broadway between March 30, 1961, and March 30, 1962, were eligible for this year's awards. A committee made up of John Chapman, Richard Watts Jr., Jean Dalrymple, Radie Harris and Sidney Kingsley chose eighty-nine nominees in twenty-one categories. All members of the Wing—about 1,000—received ballots.

Special silver medallions, for over-all contributions to the stage, were presented to Richard Rodgers, the composer; Brooks Atkinson, former drama critic of The New York Times, and Franco Zeffirelli. Signor Zeffirelli designed and directed

the Old Vic production of "Romeo and Juliet" that appeared here last winter.

Other award winners were:
SUPPORTING ACTOR IN A DRAMA—Walter Matthau of "A Shot in the Dark."
SUPPORTING ACTRESS IN A DRAMA — Elizabeth Ashley of "Take Her, She's Mine."
SCENIC DESIGNER—Will Steven Armstrong, for "Carnival."
COSTUME DESIGNER—Lucinda Ballard, "The Gay Life."
SUPPORTING ACTOR IN A MUSICAL—Charles Nelson Reilly of "How to Succeed."
STAGE TECHNICIAN—Michael Burns, chief electrician for "A Man for All Seasons."
PRODUCER OF PLAY—Robert Whitehead and Roger L. Stevens, "A Man for All Seasons."
DIRECTOR OF PLAY—Noel Willman, "A Man for All Seasons."
CHOREOGRAPHER — Tie: Agnes de Mille, "Kwamina," and Joe Layton, "No Strings."
SUPPORTING ACTRESS IN A MUSICAL—Phyllis Newman, Subways Are for Sleeping."
DIRECTOR OF MUSICAL—Abe Burrows, "How to Succeed."
AUTHOR OF MUSICAL PLAY —Abe Burrows, Jack Weinstock and Willie Gilbert, "How to Succeed."
PRODUCER OF MUSICAL PLAY—Cy Feuer and Ernest Martin, "How to Succeed."
COMPOSER OF MUSICAL — Richard Rodgers, "No Strings."
MUSICAL DIRECTOR - CONDUCTOR—Elliott Lawrence, "How to Succeed."

group's annual meeting in the Algonquin Hotel. They also awarded a special citation to "Beyond the Fringe," the satirical English revue.

"Who's Afraid of Virginia Woolf?," written by Edward Albee, staged by Alan Schneider and produced by Richard Barr and Clinton Wilder, received nine votes. It is Mr. Albee's first Broadway play.

The previous works by the 34th year-old playwright — "The American Dream," "The Death of Bessie Smith," "The Zoo Story" and "The Sandbox" —all one-acters, have been presented Off Broadway.

The controversial comedy-drama opened Oct. 13 at the Billy Rose Theater and was an immediate success. Uta Hagen, Arthur Hill, George Grizzard and Melinda Dillon originally starred in the four-character play.

Second Unit Formed

Since it runs almost three and a half hours, a second company, featuring Kate Reid, Sheppard Strudwick, Bill Berger and Avra Petrides, was engaged to appear at the Wednesday and Saturday matinees. Several members of the two casts have been replaced.

Mr. Albee's play deals with two married couples whose lives are altered during an evening of drinking after a faculty party at a New England college. The playwright said his work was "probably about the ways we get through life."

Questioned about his provocative title, he recently explained: "'Who's Afraid of Virginia Woolf?' means 'Who's afraid of the Big, Bad Wolf' means 'Who's afraid of living life without illusions'?"

"Beyond the Fringe," received a special citation from the critics by "an overwhelming majority." Written and performed by Alan Bennett, Peter Cook, Jonathan Miller and Dudley Moore, the revue opened Oct. 27 at the Golden Theater.

The nine critics who cast their ballots for the Albee play were Whitney Bolton (The

1963

NEW YORK DRAMA CRITICS CIRCLE AWARDS

Award Given to 'Virginia Woolf'

The New York Drama Critics Circle yesterday voted "Who's Afraid of Virginia Woolf?" the best play of the 1962-63 season.

Seventeen reviewers participated in the voting at the

From left are: Dudley Moore, Alan Bennett, Jonathan Miller and Peter Cook, the authors and cast of "Beyond the Fringe," the British satirical show that was also cited.

Arthur Hill and Uta Hagen in a scene from "Who's Afraid of Virginia Woolf?" which was honored by Critics Circle.

Morning Telegraph), Richard Cooke (The Wall Street Journal), William Glover (The Associated Press), Theodore Kalem (Time), Walter Kerr (The Herald Tribune), Norman Nadel (The World-Telegram and The Sun), John McClain (The Journal American), Howard Taubman (The Times), and Richard Watts Jr. (The Post).

"Mother Courage" received three votes from Ethel Colby (The Journal of Commerce), Emory Lewis (Cue), and Henry Hewes (The Saturday Review).

"The Hollow Crown" won two votes from John McCarten (The New Yorker), who voted by proxy, and Joseph Shipley of radio station WEVD.

Three plays received one vote each. They were "The Milk Train Doesn't Stop Here Anymore," Robert Coleman (The Mirror), who voted by proxy; "Tchin-Tchin," John Chapman (The Daily News); and "Photo Finish," Jack Gaver (United Press-International).

Two critics did not vote. They were Leslie Hanscom, the new Newsweek critic, and Thomas R. Dash, who retired as critic of Women's Wear Daily on Jan. 1. His successor, Martin Gottfried, was elected to the circle. Mr. Taubman, president of the group, presided.

Last October, the critics decided to change their procedure for the selection of the season's best works. By a vote of 9 to 8 they provided that "there shall be one ballot cast for the best play — drama or musical — regardless of the country of its origin."

Until this change was made, the circle gave prizes to the best American play, the best foreign play and the best musical. The amendment was a victory for Mr. Chapman, who had waged a campaign for "one award only."

TONY AWARDS

'Funny Thing' Wins Tony as Musical— Uta Hagen Cited

The play "Who's Afraid of Virginia Woolf?" and the musical show "A Funny Thing Happened on the Way to the Forum" were named last night as the best stage productions of this year.

Tonys, Broadway's counterpart of Hollywood's Oscars, were awarded to the drama and the musical play during the 17th annual dinner of the American Theater Wing in the Americana Hotel.

"Who's Afraid of Virginia Woolf?," a comedy-drama dealing with the lives of two married couples, was written by Edward Albee. The first Broadway entry by the 34-year-old playwright had already been chosen by the New York Drama Critics Circle as the best play of the season.

The play accounted for a total of five awards, including

prizes in the important categories of best actress, best actor, director and producer.

"A Funny Thing Happened on the Way to the Forum," a musical based on the works of Plautus, is set in Rome in 200 B.C. The story concerns a wily slave intent on getting his freedom. The book is credited to Burt Shevelove and Larry Gelbart; the music and lyrics to Stephen Sondheim.

A total of six Tonys went to the musical.

Uta Hagen Honored

For her performance as an aggressive wife in "Who's Afraid of Virginia Woolf?," Uta Hagen was voted the best actress starring in a drama.

Arthur Hill, who plays the tormented husband in "Who's Afraid," was named best starring actor in a drama.

Because the four-character drama is exhausting, Miss Hagen and Mr. Hill are seen only in evening performances, and a separate cast gives matinees.

Zero Mostel, who is appearing in "A Funny Thing Happened on the Way to the Forum," was the winning musical star.

Vivien Leigh, co-star of "Tovarich," won the Tony for the best female musical star. She plays an expatriated Russian in Paris, a former Grand Duchess.

An unplanned performance by an amateur marked the ceremony of prize-giving to professionals. A man who later identified himself as Ronnie Mills, 27 years old, interrupted Abe Burrows on the stage.

Mr. Mills ran up to the platform and shouted that he could not make a living because he could not get his advertisements printed in newspapers. Ushered out of the chamber, he distributed cards indicating that he operated a dating service.

Three special Tony awards were distributed at the annual dinner.

One went to Irving Berlin, songwriter, now represented by "Mr. President," who will mark his 75th birthday on May 11, "for his distinguished contribution to the musical theater for these many years."

The second was presented to W. McNeil Lowry, director of the Ford Foundation's program in the Humanities and the Arts, "in behalf of the Ford Foundation for his and their distinguished support of the American theater."

The recipient of the third was the "Beyond the Fringe" troupe, consisting of Alan Bennett, Peter Cook, Jonathan Miller and Dudley Moore, "for their brilliance, which has shattered all of the old conceptions of comedy." The revue received a special citation last week from the New York Drama Critics Circle.

More than 1,100 persons attended the dinner, proceeds of which go to the wing's scholarship fund. Eighty nominees for "distinguished contributions to the theater" were named in 24 categories. The candidates include performers, writers, producers, directors, technicians and other creative members of the Broadway stage, who were connected with productions that arrived between April 1, 1962, and March 30, 1963.

The awards are named in

The New York Times

Four Tony winners display award at Americana Hotel, from left: Zero Mostel, best actor starring in a musical; Vivien Leigh, best actress starring in a musical; Uta Hagen, the best actress starring in a drama, and Arthur Hill, the best actor starring in a drama.

Friedman-Abeles
Edward Albee

honor of the late Antoinette Perry, World War II wing chairman. The Tonys are silver medallions three inches in diameter.

Members of the nominating committee included John Chapman, Richard Watts Jr. and Norman Nadel, drama critics of The Daily News, The New York Post and The World-Telegram and Sun, respectively; Sidney Kingsley, playwright-director-producer, and Jean Dalrymple, producer. The committee's chairman was Helen Menken, president of the wing.

Other awards were as follows:

SUPPORTING ACTOR, DRAMA: Alan Arkin, "Enter Laughing."

SUPPORTING ACTRESS, DRAMA: Sandy Dennis, "A Thousand Clowns."

SUPPORTING ACTOR, MUSICAL: David Burns, "A Funny Thing Happened on the Way to the Forum."

SUPPORTING ACTRESS, MUSICAL: Anna Quayle, "Stop the World—I Want to Get Off."

PRODUCER, PLAY: Richard Barr and Clinton Wilder, "Who's Afraid of Virginia Woolf?"

DIRECTOR, PLAY: Alan Schneider, "Who's Afraid of Virginia Woolf?"

PRODUCER, MUSICAL: Harold Prince, "A Funny Thing Happened on the Way to the Forum."

DIRECTOR, MUSICAL: George Abbott, "A Funny Thing Happened on the Way to the Forum."

AUTHOR, MUSICAL PLAY: Burt Shevelove and Larry Gelbart, "A Funny Thing Happened on the Way to the Forum."

COMPOSER AND LYRICIST, MUSICAL PLAY: Lionel Bart, "Oliver!"

MUSICAL DIRECTOR-CONDUCTOR: Donald Pippin, "Oliver!"

CHOREOGRAPHER: Bob Fosse, "Little Me."

SCENIC DESIGNER: Sean Kenny, "Oliver!"

COSTUME DESIGNER: Anthony Powell, "The School for Scandal."

STAGE TECHNICIAN: Solly Pernick, "Mr. President."

OBIE AWARDS

Off Broadway Awards Given

Colleen Dewhurst and George C. Scott received "Obie" awards on Saturday for their performances in "Desire Under the Elms." The "Obie's" are given annually by The Village Voice for outstanding achievement Off Broadway. The two "best productions" were "Six Characters in Search of an Author" and "The Boys From Syracuse." Alan Schneider was cited for his direction of "The Dumb Waiter" and "The Collection." The selections were made by John Gassner, Norman Nadel and Michael Smith.

1964

NOBEL PRIZE

Sartre Awarded Nobel Prize, but Rejects It

Existentialist Thinks His Writings Would Be Compromised

Special to The New York Times

STOCKHOLM, Oct. 22—The Nobel Prize for Literature was awarded today to Jean-Paul Sartre, who promptly refused the honor and the $53,000 that accompanies it.

The 59-year-old French writer, philosopher and exponent of existentialism took time out from luncheon in a Paris bistro to issue his refusal.

[In a statement in Paris, Sartre said a writer must not accept official awards, because to do so would add the influence of the institution that

honored his work to the power of his pen. That is not fair to the reader, he said.]

Sartre had forewarned the Swedish Academy, which makes the literature award, that he did not want it. Nevertheless, the academy members felt that he was the only possible recipient this year.

He is the first to turn down the award fully and freely.

In 1925, George Bernard Shaw rejected the prize, then decided to accept, with the money going toward the translating of Swedish literature. Boris Pasternak refused the 1958 award under evident Soviet pressure.

The academy's secretary, Karl-Ragnar Gierow, said: "If Sartre does not collect the prize, the money will be returned to the Nobel Prize funds. The academy's award is not guided by the possible winner's wishes but only by the decision of the academy's 18 members."

The academy chose Sartre for his "authorship, which has always been rich in ideas and which has had a vast influence on our times, mainly through its spirit of liberty and quest for truth."

After the award was announced, academy members refused to comment on Sartre's letter to the academy two days ago, in which he is said to have renounced the prize before he won it.

Sartre, born in Paris in 1905, is known as the "pope of existentialism." His first work was a novel published in 1938 and called "La Nausée" ("Nausea"). He has since written a number of novels, plays and philosophical works as well as a vast number of journalistic articles.

His book "Being and Nothingness" summarized the ideas behind existentialism in these words:

"Man can will nothing unless he has first understood that he must count on no one but himself; that he is alone, abandoned on earth in the midst of his infinite responsibilities, without help, with no other aim than the one he sets himself, with no other destiny than the one he forges for himself on this earth."

For the existentialist God does not exist and the world is just a phenomenon without any meaning other than what man may attach to it. Man is always faced with the responsibility of choice between good and evil, and man makes that choice not only for himself but for all humanity.

Sartre has taken a vigorous part in most of the great contemporary controversies. He has dealt, for example, with the American Negro problem, what he considers to be unnecessary fears of Communism, French treatment of Algerian freedom fighters and West German prosperity.

The chairman of the Swedish Academy's Nobel Committee,

Paris Match

Jean-Paul Sartre, the French author, in his Paris apartment. He refused to accept the Nobel Prize for Literature.

Anders Oesterling, hailed Sartre as "the father of the existentialist doctrine, which became this generation's intellectual self-defense."

In 1963 the literature prize went to Giorgos Seferiades, a former Greek diplomat whose poetry appears under the penname George Seferis.

Dr. Martin Luther King Jr., American Negro civil rights leader, was designated for 1964 peace prize. A Harvard professor, Konrad E. Bloch, and a West German researcher, Feodor Lynen, were the co-winners of the prize in physiology or medicine for studies on cholesterol. The winners in chemistry and physics are yet to be announced.

___

He suggests Advance Word

STOCKHOLM, Oct. 22 (Reuters)—Jean-Paul Sartre, in a statement to the Swedish press explaining his rejection of the Nobel award, said today:

"I very much regret that the affair has taken on the appearance of a scandal. That is because I was not sufficiently well-informed about what was happening. I did not know that the Nobel Prize is awarded without asking the opinion of the candidate."

___

Sartre Explains Stand

Special to The New York Times

PARIS, Oct. 22—Jean-Paul Sartre, who rejected the Nobel Prize for Literature today, cited literary and political reasons for his stand. He expressed his views in a lengthy statement that summed up his creed.

"A writer who takes political, social or literary positions must act only with the means that are his," Sartre said. Those means, he continued, "are the written word.

A writer must not accept official awards because he would be adding the influence of the institution that crowned his work to the power of his pen, he declared. "That," he said, "is not fair to the reader.

"It is not the same thing if I sign Jean-Paul Sartre or if I

sign Jean-Paul Sartre, Noble Prize winner," he said in the statement, which was given to newspapermen.

For the same reason, he said, he turned down appointment to the French Legion of Honor in 1945 and has no desire to enter the Collège de France, a high scholarly distinction.

"A writer must refuse to allow himself to be transformed into an institution, even if it takes place in the most honorable form," he said.

In expounding the political grounds for his action, Sartre, long a supporter of left-wing causes, put the Nobel Prize into the context of relations between East and West. The award, he declared, is one that goes only to Westerners "or to rebels of the East."

"It is regrettable," Sartre declared, "that the only Soviet work honored was one that was published abroad and forbidden in its own country."

Boris Pasternak's novel, "Dr. Zhivago," was first published in Italy and has not been issued in the Soviet Union.

Sartre listed Mikhail Sholokhov, the Soviet novelist; Pablo Neruda, the Chilean poet; and Louis Aragon, the French poet, as writers meriting the prize. All are Communists.

In the last decade the Swedish Academy has awarded the literature prize to Halldor Laxness of Iceland, Salvatore Quasimodo of Italy and Vio Andric of Yugoslavia, all of whom have expressed sympathies with left-wing causes.

If the prize had been awarded to him during the Algerian war. Sartre said, when he signed a manifesto favoring the rebel's cause, "I would have accepted it with gratitude because it would have honored not only me but the liberty for which we were all fighting."

In the present East-West confrontation, he said, "my sympathies go undeniably to Socialism and to what is called the Eastern bloc."

"But I believe that that is a false problem," Sartre said.

"Obviously I am renouncing the 250,000 [Swedish] crowns because I do not want to be institutionalized, neither in the East nor in the West."

NEW YORK DRAMA CRITICS CIRCLE AWARDS

"Luther" was voted the "best new work in any category" of the 1963-64 season yesterday by the New York Drama Critics Circle. "Hello, Dolly!" was chosen as the best musical.

A special presentation for excellence in production was given to the off Broadway drama, "The Trojan Women."

"Luther," by John Osborne, opened on Broadway in September and closed its run at the St. James Theater after 212 performances. It won the critics' award by a slim margin. Only 6 of the 18 critics who participated voted for "Luther."

They were Ethel Colby (The Journal of Commerce), Richard Cooke (The Wall Street Journal), John Gaver (United Press International), John McCarten (New Yorker), John McClain (The Journal-American and Whitney Bolton (The Morning Telegraph).

"Luther" deals with the implacable schismatic, Martin Luther, and his strength and weaknesses. Albert Finney played the title role. Tony Richardson staged it and David Merrick produced it by arrangement with the English Stage Company and Oscar Lewenstein.

Seven Others Share Votes

Mr. Osborne, one of England's earlier "angry young men," also

is the author of "Look Back in Anger," "The Entertainer" and "Epitaph for George Dillon," all of which have been presented here during the last seven years. "Look Back in Anger" was a runner-up for the critics' award during the 1957-58 season to "Look Homeward, Angel."

The rest of the votes in the best new work category were shared by seven productions, one of them being an Off Broadway play.

"After the Fall," the Arthur Miller play, received three votes from Martin Gottfried (Women's Wear Daily); Otis Guernsey (Show magazine) and Norman Nadel (The World-Telegram and The Sun.

"The Rehearsal," by Jean Anouilh, won three votes from Theodore Kalem (Time), Walter Kerr (The Herald Tribune) and Richard Watts Jr. (The Post).

Two Votes for 'Chips'

Two votes from Henry Hewes (The Saturday Review) and Emory Lewis (Cue) went to "Chips With Everything," by Arnold Wesker.

Four plays were given one vote each. They were James Baldwin's "Blues for Mr. Charlie," William Glover (The Associated Press); Neil Simon's "Barefoot in the Park," Ward Morehouse (Newhouse newspapers); Sidney Michaels's "Dylan," John Chapman (The Daily News", and Atholl Fugard's "The Blood Knot," Howard Taubman (The New York Times).

The vote for "The Blood Knot," now playing at the Cricket Theater, marks the second time an Off-Broadway production has been cited for first honors. "The Connection" was the first.

"Hello, Dolly!", the musical based on Thornton Wilder's "The Matchmaker," won by a large margin. Thirteen critics cast ballots for it. They were Chap-

David Burns and Carol Channing in musical "Hello, Dolly!"

Osborne Drama Is Adjudged 'Best in Any Category' for 1963-64 Stage Season —Off Broadway Work Also Cited

Albert Finney in title role of John Osborne's "Luther"

man, Nadel, Hughes, Glover, Kerr, Bolton, McCarten, Morehouse, Watts, Cloby, Cooke McClain and Taubman.

The musical, one of the season's biggest hits, also was produced by Mr. Merrick. Staged and choreographed by Gower Champion, it opened at the St. James Theater on Jan, with Carol Channing starred as the resourceful widow, Mrs. Dolly Gallagher Levi, the matchmaker

Single votes were cast for "Funny Girl," "High Spirits" and "Anyone Can Whistle," by Lewis, Glover and Gottfried. Two reviewers, Kalem and Guernsey, abstained from voting in this category. Five of the critics voted by proxy. They were Nadel, Bolton, McCarten, Morehouse and Guernsey.

The resolution for a special citation to "The Trojan Women" was proposed by Kerr. It was approved, 7 to 4, with 2 abstaining. Those who voted for it were Hughes, Kalem, Colby, Lewis, Watts, Kerr and Taubman.

The awards will be presented at a cocktail party to be held at the Algonquin Hotel on May 7 by Mr. Taubman, president of the critics' group. Mr. Taubman served as chairman of yesterday's award meeting.

TONY AWARDS

By SAM ZOLOTOW

The musical "Hello, Dolly!" and the drama "Luther" were named the season's best shows by the American Theater Wing last night.

The two productions by David Merrick won the Drama Critics

"Hello, Dolly!," which had been nominated for 11 Tonys in the various categories, received 10.

In addition to the selections of the musical itself, awards went to Carol Channing (musical star, actress), Gower Champion (a double award as director and choreographer), Mr. Merrick (producer), Michael Stewart (author), Jerry Herman (composer and lyricist), Oliver Smith (scenic designer), Freddy Wittop (costume designer) and Shepard Coleman (musical director).

For Mr. Smith this was the fifth Tony. His designs won him the award in 1957, 1958, 1960 and 1961. Mr. Champion previously won a dual award for directing and choreographing "Bye Bye Birdie" and one as the choreographer of "Lend an Ear."

"Hello, Dolly!" is Broadway's leading hit. Its plot was derived from Thornton Wilder's "The Matchmaker."

"Luther" was written by John Osborne. Albert Finney made his local stage debut in the title role. Tony Richardson staged the drama, which had a run of 212 performances under the auspices of the David Merrick Foundation. Mr. Merrick formed the foundation in 1959 to provide scholarships for college students in the creative arts.

Other awards were made as follows:

DRAMATIC STAR, ACTOR: Alec Guinness, "Dylan."

DRAMATIC STAR, ACTRESS: Sandy Dennis, "Any Wednesday." Miss Dennis won a Tony last year for her supporting performance in "A Thousand Clowns."

MUSICAL STAR, ACTOR: Bert Lahr, "Foxy."

DRAMATIC FEATURED OR SUPPORTING ACTOR: Hume

Herman Shumlin, left, best producer for "The Deputy" and Mike Nichols, best director for "Barefoot in the Park."

Cronyn, "Hamlet."

DRAMATIC FEATURED OR SUPPORTING ACTRESS: Barbara Loden, "After the Fall."

MUSICAL FEATURED OR SUPPORTING ACTOR: Jack Cassidy, "She Loves Me."

MUSICAL FEATURED OR SUPPORTING ACTRESS: Tessie O'Shea, "The Girl Who Came to Supper."

PLAY DIRECTOR: Mike Nichols, "Barefoot in the Park."

PRODUCER: Herman Shumlin, "The Deputy."

Eva Le Gallienne, who is celebrating her golden jubilee as an actress this year, was honored for her work with the National Repertory Theater.

She received a special Tony for her "distinguished contribution to the theater." The presentation was made by Richard Burton, star of "Hamlet."

Last month, Miss Le Gallienne won an award from the American National Theater and Academy for her "outstanding con-

Awards last month. At the New York Hilton Hotel last night, they received the Theater Wing's Tonys, Broadway's counterpart to Hollywood's Oscars.

Tony award winners for best performances after presentations at New York Hilton. They are, from left, Alec Guinness, male dramatic star; Sandy Dennis, female dramatic star, and Carol Channing and Bert Lahr, musical stars.

The New York Times

Named as best featured or supporting actress and actor in musical category were Tessie O'Shea and Jack Cassidy.

tribution to the art of the living theater and her leadership in the cause of repertory in America."

Miss Le Gallienne, who made her first stage appearance in 1914 at the age of 14, is the honorary president of the National Repertory Theater, a non-profit organization established in 1961. She was the founder of the Civic Repertory Theater in 1926 and one of the founders of the American Repertory Theater in 1946.

She said earlier yesterday at her home in Westport, Conn., that she would not act on the road next season. She may direct one or two plays for the National Repertory Theater's proposed program of three plays.

The winners of the Tonys awarded last night were determined through votes cast by members of the Theater Wing and by drama critics, editors and writers on the first and second night press lists.

They chose from 80 nominations on 20 categories, made by a committee of five: John Chapman and Richard Watts Jr., drama critics of The Daily News and The New York Post, respectively; Al Hirschfeld, caricaturist; Norton Mockridge, columnist of The World-Telegram and The Sun, and Jean Dalrymple, head of the City Center's light opera and drama divisions.

Eligible were shows that opened on Broadway between April 1, 1963, and April 30, 1964. The Tonys were named in memory of Antoinette Perry, wartime chairman of the Theater Wing. The award is a silver medallion three inches in diameter. Engraved on one side are the theater masks of comedy and tragedy; on the other side is the name of the winner. Tonys have been presented since 1947.

About 1,200 persons attended the dinner last night. The award ceremony was broadcast from 8 to 9 over Channel 9.

Proceeds of the event will be used by the Theater Wing to provide scholarships for aspiring actors and actresses. Helen Menken, president of the organization, was in charge of the arrangements. Sidney Blackmer was the master of ceremonies.

OBIE AWARDS

JONES'S 'DUTCHMAN' WINS DRAMA AWARD

LeRoi Jones has won a $500 prize for his short, two-character drama, "Dutchman," which was named the best American play done Off Broadway during the 1963-64 season. It is being performed with Edward Albee's "The American Dream" at the Cherry Lane Theater.

In addition to the prize, which came from Mr. Albee, Mr. Jones won an "Obie" one of a series of annual awards given by the Village Voice, a Greenwich Village newspaper. "Obie" is a phonetic abbreviation for Off Broadway.

"Obies" went to Kenneth H. Brown's "The Brig," produced by the Living Theater, for the best production; best design by Julian Beck, and best direction by Judith Malina. Samuel Beckett's "Play" was cited as the best play and Gloria Foster of "In White America" for giving the best performance. A special citation was given to the Judson Memorial Church for experimentation in the performing arts.

Other "Obie" winners were Rosalyn Drexler and Adrienne Kennedy for their plays, "Home Movies" and "Funnyhouse of a Negro," respectively; Lawrence Kornfeld for directing "What Happened," which was designated as the best production of a musical; and Al Carmines for his music for "Home Movies" and "What Happened."

Players receiving "Obies" for their performances were Philip Bruns, "Mr. Simian"; Joyce Ebert, "The Trojan Women"; Lee Grant, "The Maids"; David Hurst, "A Month in the Country"; Taylor Mead, "The General Returns From One Place to Another"; Estelle Parson, "Next Time I'll Sing to You" and "In the Summer House"; Diane Sands, "The Living Premise"; Marian Seldes, "The 'Ginger Man'"; Jack Warden, "Epiphany," and Ronald Weyand, "The Lesson."

1965
PULITZER PRIZE

Frank D. Gilroy
Drama

TALL, handsome and soft-spoken.... Made his theater debut in 1962 when his drama "Who'll Save the Plowboy?" was presented Off Broadway.... "The Subject Was Roses" is his first Broadway play.... Was turned down by 15 producers.... Borrowed $10,000 to keep it running.... 39 years old.... He is married and lives with his wife and three sons in Monroe, N. Y.... Born and educated in the Bronx; graduated from DeWitt Clinton High School.... Served in the Army for two and a half years.... Attended Dartmouth and studied at the Yale Drama School.... Has written for Hollywood and for television.

'Subject Was Roses' Wins Pulitzer Prize for Drama

By PHILIP BENJAMIN

Fiction and drama came back into their own in the awarding of the 1965 Pulitzer Prizes yesterday. Shirley Ann Grau's novel "The Keepers of the House" was awarded the fiction prize, and Frank D. Gilroy's "The Subject Was Roses" received the award for drama.

But for the second straight year music was ignored.

Last year, fiction, drama and music all were shut out—the first time since drama and fiction were added to the list of prizes in 1918 that no awards were given in these art categories. The prizes in music were established in 1943.

"The Subject Was Roses" is a three-character play about the painful adjustment a middle-class Bronx couple have to make when their son returns after three years in the Army. "The Keepers of the House" is a violent history of a Deep South family.

Of the eight categories of journalism, only editorial cartoons received no award yesterday.

J. A. Livingston, financial editor of The Philadelphia Bulletin, won the prize for international reporting for his articles on the growth of economic independence in Soviet-bloc satellite countries and for his analysis of their desire to resume trade with the West.

Louis M. Kohlmeier of the Washington bureau of The Wall Street Journal won the prize for national reporting for his articles on the growth of the fortune of President Johnson and his family.

Horst Faas of The Associated Press won the photography prize for his pictures of the war in South Vietnam.

It was the second year in a row that The Wall Street Journal and The Philadelphia Bulletin have won Pulitzer Prizes. Last year The Journal won the local general reporting award and The Bulletin won the local special reporting award. The Associated Press won an international reporting prize last year.

Melvin H. Ruder, publisher, editor, and reporter of The Hungry Horse News at Columbia Falls, Mont., received the award for local general reporting. He was cited for his coverage of the disastrous floods that hit Northwestern Montana last year.

The Hungry Horse News is a weekly with an average circulation fo 4,271. Mr. Ruder, who is 50 years old, founded it in 1946 on a G. I. loan. The paper was first put out on Aug. 8, 1946, in a two-story log cabin. It is now housed in a new building and has a staff of two printers, an apprentice, three part-time office workers, and Mr. and Mrs. Ruder.

Mr. Ruder was in a barnyard yesterday when someone shouted to him that he had won a Pulitzer Prize. He had been taking some children on a conservation tour.

"I lost money on the flood edition," he said in a telephone interview. "We just forgot all about advertising."

Likes the Mountains

The paper has only one linotype machine, Mr. Ruder said. "I work like hell," he went on. "I worked until 1 o'clock this morning and then got up at 7."

He said he would stay in Columbia Falls. "It's a beautiful area," he said. "I'm sitting right here at my desk and I look out the window and I see the mountains. And if I got up on top there'd be some elk and deer."

Gene Goltz of The Houston Post won the award for local special reporting with his exposé of government corruption in Pasadena, Tex. The exposé resulted in reforms.

The gold medal for public service was given to The Hutchinson (Kan.) News. This was for its successful effort to bring about reapportionment in Kansas, in the face of powerful local opposition. The newspaper won a suit in the state courts that forced the Kansas Senate to be apportioned on a population basis.

The Pulitzer Prize Advisory Board recognized that other papers have been active in the reapportionment field, but gave the prize to The Hutchinson News because of its early efforts in the field and because of the strong opposition it faced.

The Hutchinson News, which started as a weekly on July 4, 1872, has a circulation of 52,500, most of it in 40 sparsely populated counties in southwestern Kansas. Although politically independent, the newspaper supported Republicans from U. S. Grant until 1960, when it backed John F. Kennedy for President. John P. Harris, present chairman of the board, purchased The News and companion Tribune in 1933.

John R. Harrison of The Gainesville (Fla.) Sun won the prize for editorial writing. He conducted a successful campaign to improve housing conditions in his community, and helped bring about municipal approval for a minimum housing code.

With the exception of the gold medal award for public service, each journalism prize carries a $1,000 award.

In the field of letters, the prize for history went to Irwin Unger for "The Greenback Era," a study of the United States in the post-Civil War period.

'Henry Adams' Hailed

Dr. Ernest Samuels won the prize in biography for his three-volume work. "Henry Adams." The second volume. "Henry Adams—The Middle Years," had previously won the Bancroft Prize and the Parkman Prize in 1959.

John Berryman won the po-

etry prize with his volume of verse, "77 Dream Songs," and Howard Mumford Jones received the award for a general nonfiction book not eligible for consideration in any other category. The book was "O Strange New World," which portrayed America in its formative years.

Mr. Berryman's volume focuses on a hero named Henry who reacts with hopeless merriment to the brutality and stupidity of his times. It portrays a philosophical acceptance that elevates and even ennobles the character.

The prizes in letters and music carry $500 awards.

An official of the advisory board said yesterday that no musical composition had been recommended by the board, which submits its recommendations for Pulitzer Prizes to the board of trustees of Columbia University. The university's Graduate School of Journalism administers the prizes.

More than 600 nominations in the field of journalism alone were received this year. The nominations are generally made by the newspapers themselves.

Juries in each of the prize categories can make two to five recommendations, which then go to the advisory board, which accepts or rejects the recommendations. The board of trustees has the final word.

In 1962 in what was believed to be the first such instance, the board of trustees rejected the advisory board's recommendation of a prize for a biography of William Randolph Hearst by W. A. Swanberg.

The prizes were established by the will of Joseph Pulitzer, publisher of The St. Louis Post-Dispatch and of the old New York World. Mr. Pulitzer—whose competitor was Mr. Hearst—gave $550,000 to endow the prizes when he died in 1911. The first awards were made in 1917.

NEW YORK DRAMA CRITICS CIRCLE AWARDS

Gilroy's Play Best of 1964-65—'Fiddler' Is Top Musical

By MILTON ESTEROW

The New York Drama Critics Circle yesterday voted Frank D. Gilroy's "The Subject Was Roses" as the best play of the 1964-65 season. "Fiddler on the Roof," based on stories by Sholem Aleichem, was chosen overwhelmingly as the top musical.

Five of the 19 participating critics voted for "The Subject Was Roses," which has already become something of a theatrical legend. "Luv" and "The Odd Couple" each received four votes.

"Roses" was turned down by at least 15 producers. It opened on Broadway with a producer who had never pro-

duced a Broadway play; a director who had never directed one; a scenic artist who had never designed one; a general manager who had never managed one, and three actors who were not well known.

The three-character play deals with a 21-year-old veteran and his parents, to whose middle-class Bronx apartment he returns after three years in the Army. Howard Taubman, drama critic of The New York Times, wrote that "with simplicity, humor and integrity," the author had "looked into the hearts of three decent people and discovered, by letting them discover, the feelings that divide and join them."

Opened at 'Unwise' Time

The play opened last May 25, which is late in the Broadway season and which is considered by many experienced producers as unwise. It was unheralded and unsung. Its advance sale totaled $162. Despite enthusiastic notices, the producer, Edgar Lansbury, had to borrow $10,000 after the opening to keep the play running.

The cast includes Jack Albertson, Irene Dailey and Martin Sheen. Ulu Grosbard directed.

Mr. Gilroy, the 39-year-old Bronx-born playwright, was graduated from De Witt Clinton High School and served in the Army for two years. Later he attended Dartmouth College and wrote for television and Hollywood. He is married and lives with his wife and three sons in Monroe, N. Y. "Roses" is his first Broadway play. An earlier drama, "Who'll Save the Plowboy?" was presented off Broadway.

The playwright is also the author of a book, "About Those Roses, or How Not to Do a Play and Succeed." It was published with the text of the play itself by Random House.

Mr. Gilroy said that the total outlay for the play was $50,000, and that "we have been in the black for several weeks." His reaction to the award was: "It's just glorious. It's the final frosting on a wonderful cake."

The critics who voted for the play were Ted Kalem (Time magazine) and chairman of the circle; John McClain (The Journal-American), Emory Lewis (Cue magazine), Otis Guernsey (Show magazine) and Ethel Colby (The Journal of Commerce).

Four Love 'Luv'

The following voted for "Luv," a comedy by Murray Schisgal: Richard Watts (The Post), Walter Kerr (The Herald Tribune), William Glover (The Associated Press) and Richard Cooke (The Wall Street Journal).

Neil Simon's comedy, "The Odd Couple" was selected by John McCarten (The New Yorker), Whitney Bolton (The Morning Telegraph), John Chapman (The Daily News) and Ward Morehouse (Newhouse newspapers).

Five plays received one vote each. They were Arthur Miller's "Incident at Vichy," Mr. Taubman; Edward Albee's "Tiny Alice," Norman Nadel (The World-Telegram and The Sun); Robert Lowell's "The Old Glory," Richard Gilman (Newsweek); Eugene O'Neill's "Hughie," Henry Hewes (Saturday Review), and Ann Jellicoe's "The Knack,"

Irene Dailey, Martin Sheen, center, and Jack Albertson in "The Subject Was Roses," voted best play of season.

Zero Mostel, Maria Karnilova and supporting players in "Fiddler on the Roof," selected as outstanding musical.

Martin Gottfried (Women's Wear Daily).

Jack Gaver of United Press International abstained from voting for the best play.

Three productions staged by Mike Nichols—"Luv," "The Odd Couple" and "The Knack—received a total of nine votes.

Ayes for 'Fiddler'

Those who cast ballots for "Fiddler on the Roof," which is now at the Imperial Theater, were: Morehouse, Bolton, Taubman, Watts, McClain, Chapman, Nadel, Gottfried, Lewis, Colby, Glover, Guernsey, Gaver and Cooke.

The show, which was pro-

duced by Harold Prince and opened on Sept. 22, stars Zero Mostel. Joseph Stein wrote the book; the lyrics were by Sheldon Harnick and the music by Jerry Bock. Jerome Robbins did the staging and choreography.

"Oh What a Lovely War" received votes from Hewes, Gilman, McCarten and Kalem. Mr. Kerr abstained from voting for a musical. Messrs. Gaver and McCarten voted by proxy. The critics declined to vote for a foreign play.

The balloting took place at the Algonquin Hotel. The award, a scroll, will be presented at the hotel in a few weeks.

TONY AWARDS

Zero Mostel Shares Best Musical's 9 Honors

By SAM ZOLOTOW

"Fiddler on the Roof" was selected as the best musical of the 1964-65 season and "The Subject Was Roses" as the best play and winners of the Tony awards at the American Theater Wing's dinner last night in the Astor Hotel.

The Tony is Broadway's equivalent of the Hollywood Oscar.

"Fiddler on the Roof," based on Sholem Aleichem's stories, won 9 of the 20 categories. Tonys went to Zero Mostel, its star; Maria Karnilova, actress in a featured role; Jerome Robbins' (two awards), choreographer and director; Harold Prince, producer; Joseph Stein, adapter; Jerry Bock and Sheldon Harnick, composer and lyricist, and Patricia Zipprodt, costumer.

The show, which opened last Sept. 22 at the Imperial Theater, became an immediate hit. It tells the story of a dairyman (Mr. Mostel) in a Russian village at the turn of the century, his sharp-tongued wife (Miss Karnilova) and their five marriageable daughters.

"The Subject Was Roses," the first Broadway play for its author, Frank D. Gilroy, celebrated its first birthday on May 25. The story concerns a soldier who returns after serving three years in the army and his orientation with his father and mother.

It took more than two years to find 36 backers, who were willing to finance Edgar Lansbury's production for $40,000. Jack Albertson, who portrays the father, won a Tony for his performance as a featured dramatic player. In the attraction's advertisement, he is listed as one of the stars.

"The Subject was Roses" was the winner of the Pulitzer Prize as well as the New York Drama Critics Circle's award. The circle also named "Fiddler on the Roof" as the best musical.

"The Odd Couple" won four Tonys: Neil Simon, author; Mike Nichols, director; Walter Matthau, star; Oliver Smith, scenic designer.

Murray Schisgal's "Luv" won three Tonys: Mr. Nichols, director; Claire Nichtern, producer; Mr. Smith, scenery.

Other Tonys were presented to:

Irene Worth, dramatic star of Edward Albee's "Tiny Alice"; Liza Minnelli, musical star, who is making her first Broadway appearance in "Flora, the Red Menace"; Alice Ghostley, supporting actress in the drama, "The Sign in Sidney Brustein's Window"; Victor Spinetti, featured player in the musical "Oh What a Lovely War."

Gilbert Miller, dean of Broadway producers, who is 80 years old, was honored for "his distinguished career and contributions to the theater."

Mr. Miller, who produced 88 plays over a span of 43 years, is spending the summer abroad.

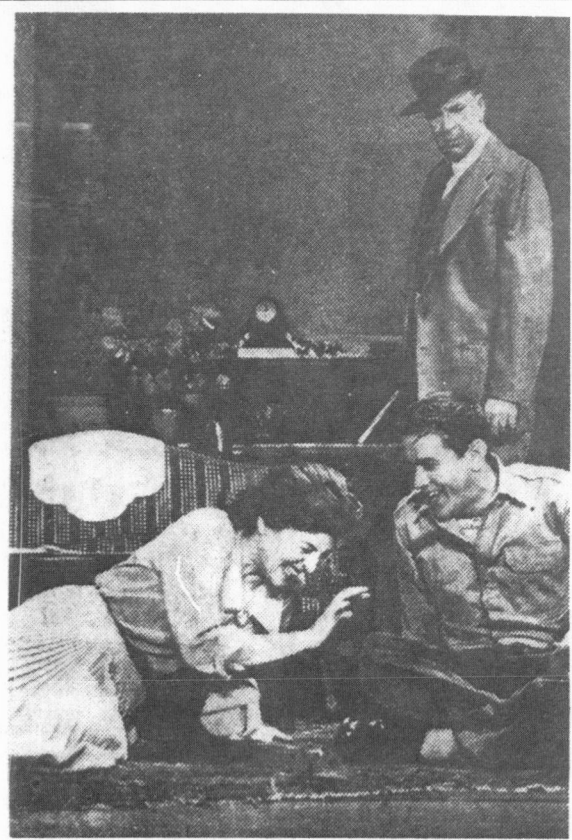

Irene Dailey, Martin Sheen and Jack Albertson, rear, in "The Subject Was Roses," which won Tony as best drama.

In his absence, the special Tony prize was accepted by George Cukor, film director. Mr. Cukor, before he went to Hollywood in 1929, was associated with Mr. Miller as a stage director.

Last September, Mr. Miller confirmed reports that he was planning to sell for $1 million the 940-seat Henry Miller's Theater, named for his father, at 124 West 43rd Street, between Broadway and the Avenue of the Americas. The reasons he gave were the dwindling supply of Broadway entries and his own desire to slow down as a producer.

In the spring, it looked as if the Tony awards might be abandoned as the result of differences over the selection of nominees. However, Helen Menken, president of the Theater Wing, arranged to have a committee select the nominees. Asked yesterday whether the Tonys would be distributed in 1966, Miss Menken said the decision was in the hands of the Theater Wing's board.

Seventy - six nominees in 19 categories were voted on by members of the Theater Wing, the League of New York Theaters, the organization of producers and theater owners, drama critics and drama editors.

The Tonys were established in 1947 as a memorial to Antoinette Perry, wartime chairman of the Theater Wing. They are silver medallions 3 inches in diameter. Each is inscribed on one side with the masks of comedy and tragedy and on the other side with the winner's name.

More than 1,200 people attended the dinner. Among them were 400 members of the chorus who were Miss Menken's guests. Proceeds will go to the Theater Wing's scholarship fund.

1966

NEW YORK DRAMA CRITICS CIRCLE AWARDS

'MARAT' IS NAMED BY DRAMA CRITICS

'Man of La Mancha' Is Best Musical—Holbrook Cited

By SAM ZOLOTOW

The New York Drama Critics Circle yesterday followed the lead by the Pulitzer Prize jury by deciding not to name an American play as the best of the 1965-66 season.

Instead, the circle selected "Marat/Sade," by the German-born Swede Peter Weiss, as the winner by one point over another imported work, the Irish Brian Friel's "Philadelphia, Here I Come!". It took three ballots to decide the winner.

"Man of La Mancha" was chosen on the first ballot as the winning musical. A special citation was awarded to Hal Holbrook's one-man show "Mark Twain Tonight!"

Mr. Weiss will receive the first cash award to accompany the critics' citation. Harry Kahn, a Wall Street investment broker, recently donated enough for a $1,000 prize in each of five years.

Mr. Weiss's drama was known

abroad under the title of "The Persecution and Assassination of Marat as Performed by the Inmates of the Asylum of Charenton Under the Direction of the Marquis de Sade."

A Popular Success

When the play opened Dec. 27 at the Martin Beck Theater, it received four enthusiastic reviews, one that was considered in-between and one that was unfavorable.

It proved popular and the run was extended several times. It finally closed April 30 after 145 performances. The offering was brought over from London, where it was presented by the Royal Shakespeare Company under the direction of Peter Brook.

The circle voted at the Algonquin Hotel under a new procedure. The change was designed to discourage the fractional voting under which, as in the last two seasons, the top award could go to plays supported by only a minority of members.

The amendment stipulates that the award be determined by a majority of those casting ballots. If no majority is reached on the first ballot, the members, again by majority, will vote whether to give an award at all. If yes, each voting member will assign points to his first, second and third choices, and the play with the largest total will receive the award.

How Votes Added Up

"Marat/Sade" was decided on the point system (three points for the critic's preference, two points for his second choice, and one point for the third choice).

The final tally was as follows: "Marat/Sade," 21 points; "Philadelphia, Here I Come!," 20; "The Royal Hunt of the Sun," 17; "Inadmissible Evidence," 12; "Entertaining Mr. Sloane," 5; "Mark Twain Tonight!", 3; "The Caucasian Chalk Circle," 3; "Serjeant Musgrave's Dance," 3; "Hogan's Goat," 2; "You Can't Take It With You," 2; "The Condemned of Altona," 2; the double bill of "Day of Absence" and "Happy Ending," 2; "The Journey of the Fifth Horse," 1.

No list of each of the critics' choices was available.

Four plays, each with three votes, were involved in a tie on the first ballot. Voting for "Philadelphia, Here I Come!" were William Glover (Associated Press), Ethel Colby (Journal of Commerce) and Walter Kerr (The New York Herald Tribune).

"The Royal Hunt of the Sun" was picked by John Chapman (The Daily News), Jack Gaver (United Press International) and John McCarten (The New Yorker).

"Inadmissible Evidence" was voted on by Henry Hewes (The Saturday Review), Theodore E. Kalem (Time Magazine) and Richard Cooke (The Wall Street Journal).

"Marat/Sade" obtained votes from Norman Nadel (World Journal), Richard Watts Jr. (The New York Post) and Emory Lewis (Cue Magazine).

"The Caucasian Chalk Circle," Stanley Kauffmann (The New York Times); "Entertaining Mr. Sloane," Martin Gottfried (Women's Wear Daily); "Serjeant Musgrave's Dance," Richard Gilman (Newsweek Magazine); "Mark Twain Tonight!," Ward Morehouse (S. I. Newhouse

Newspaper Chain); "The Lion in Winter," George Freedley (honorary member).

The 21 winning votes for "Marat/Sade" came from Mr. Lewis (3), Mr. Nadel (3), Mr. Watts (3), Mr. Kalen (2), Mr. Gottfried (2), Mr. Gilman (2), Miss Colby (2) and Messrs. Chapman, Gaver, Hewes and Kauffmann (1 each).

Voting for the runner-up, "Philadelphia, Here I Come!," with 20 votes, were Mr. Kerr (3), Mr. Glover (3), Miss Colby (3), Mr. Chapman (2), Mr. Cooke (2), Mr. Gaver (2), Mr. McCarten (2) and Messrs. Nadel Kalen and Watts (1 each).

On May 2, for the third time in four years, no play was named for the annual Pulitzer Prizes. The terms of the prizes call for "a distinguished play by an American author, preferably original in its source and dealing with American life."

For many years, the circle, founded in 1936, gave awards for the best American and foreign plays as well as for the best musical production. In 1963, the award was changed to "best play." "Luther," a British import, won the award in 1964.

For best musical, "Man of La Mancha" was voted for by: Miss Colby, Mr. Cooke, Mr. Gaver, Mr. Glover, Mr. Hewes, Mr. Lewis, Mr. Nadel and Mr. Watts. Three votes were cast for "Mame," by Mr. Kalem, Mr. McCarten and Mr. Morehouse. "Superman," "The Mad Show" and "Marat/Sade" each received one vote, from Mr. Kauffmann, Mr. Gilman and Mr. Gottfried, respectively. Abstaining from voting were Mr. Chapman and Mr. Kerr.

"Man of La Mancha," written by Dale Wasserman, Mitch Leigh and Joe Darion, is based on the life and works of Miguel de Cervantes. The show had a pedestrian start but has become a rousing hit at the downtown ANTA Washington Square Theater.

Mr. Kahn, who is 49 years old, is a general partner in the Wall Street brokerage firm of Neuberger & Berman. He has been a theater buff and a backer of a number of plays, one of which is the current "Luv." He explained that he was giving the prize money "to show the importance with which I regard the Broadway theater."

No date for the presentation has been set as yet.

A Correction

The new annual award of $1,000 given to the author of a play designated by the New York Drama Critics Circle as the best play of the season is provided by the Institute for Advanced Studies in the Theater Arts in conjunction with the Harry and Margery G. Kahn Foundation and not by Mr. Kahn as reported yesterday in The New York Times.

TONY AWARDS

'Marat/Sade' Wins 4—Lansbury and Holbrook Cited

By SAM ZOLOTOW

Five Tonys, emblematic of the best of the Broadway season of 1965-66, were awarded yesterday to the musical "Man of La Mancha" and its creators. Four went to "Marat/Sade," a drama. A posthumous award was made to Helen Menken, president of the American Theater Wing since 1956, who had supervised arrangements for the prizes until last year.

This year's distribution of awards at the Rainbow Room was sponsored by the League of New York Theaters, a group of producers and theater owners, in conjunction with the wing, which has been inactive. Yesterday was the first time the Tonys had been presented in the afternoon. From 1947 to 1965, they were awarded at a dinner given by the wing.

Starting the proceedings as co-master of ceremonies with Ginger Rogers, George Abbott, veteran producer, playwright and director, welcomed 664 persons to "the Tony matinee."

"Next year," he told them, "we are planning an elaborate ceremony on a nationwide television hookup over the National Broadcasting Company and Columbia Broadcasting System. Suggestions should be made to the committee—if you can find them."

Both Honored Earlier

"Man of La Mancha" and "Marat/Sade" were previously named by the New York Drama Critics Circle as the best in their respective fields. "Marat/Sade" won the circle's prize by one point over "Philadelphia, Here I Come!" Both were presented by the David Merrick Arts Foundation.

"Man of La Mancha," starring Richard Kiley, was written by Dale Wasserman, Mitch Leigh and Joe Darion, Mr. Kiley enacts the dual role of Cervantes and Don Quixote. It has been running since last November at the downtown ANTA Washington Square Theater. After a slow start, it developed into a rousing hit. It was produced by Albert W. Selden and Hal James.

"Marat/Sade," the work of Peter Weiss, was produced by the Royal Shakespeare Company and directed by Peter Brook. It was described as "a drama with Brechtian overtones that confronts the uncompromising individualist with the relentless revolutionary." The demand for tickets forced the management to extend its limited run several times before closing it April 30 after the 145th performance.

"Man of La Mancha" received the awards for best musical, best composer and lyricist, best musical star (Mr. Kiley), best musical director (Albert Marre) and best scenic designer (Howard Bay).

"Marat/Sade" won in the categories of best play, best director of a play, best dramatic

Bob Golby

Richard Kiley, left, with Irving Jacobson playing a scene from the musical, which won five Tony awards yesterday.

actor in a featured or supporting role (Patrick Magee) and best costume designer (Gunilla Palmstierna-Weiss).

Winners in the other categories were:

ACTOR (DRAMATIC STAR): Hal Holbrook in his one-man program, "Mark Twain Tonight!" (He also was cited by the Drama Critics Circle.)

ACTRESS (DRAMATIC STAR): Rosemary Harris, in "The Lion in Winter."

ACTRESS (MUSICAL STAR): Angela Lansbury, as "Mame."

FEATURED OR SUPPORTING DRAMATIC ACTRESS: Zoe Caldwell, "Slapstick Tragedy."

FEATURED OR SUPPORTING MUSICAL ACTOR: Frankie Michaels, the 10-year-old performer in "Mame."

FEATURED OR SUPPORTING MUSICAL ACTRESS: Beatrice Arthur, in "Mame."

CHOREOGRAPHER: Bob Fosse, "Sweet Charity."

The Tonys were named in memory of Antoinette Perry, the wing's wartime chairman. They are silver medallions three inches in diameter inscribed on one side with the masks of comedy and tragedy and on the reverse with the winner's name.

The award honoring the late Miss Menken for "a lifetime of devotion and dedicated service to the Broadway theater" was received by her husband, George N. Richard.

The presentation of prizes was changed this year. Awards went automatically to the author and the producer of the best play and of the best musical.

The balloting also underwent revision. Members of the wing did not vote. Those who did were members of the league, the first-night and second-night press list and the governing bodies of the Dramatists Guild, Actors Equity and the Society of Stage Directors and Choreographers.

The nominating committee was represented by Judith Crist, critic for the National Broadcasting Company and The New York Herald Tribune; Donald Flamm, broadcasting executive; Lee Jordan, critic for the Columbia Broadcasting System; Edward F. Kook, president of the Century Lighting Company; Norman Nadel, critic of former New York World-Telegram and The Sun, and Tom Prideaux, Life magazine reviewer.

1967

PULITZER PRIZE

By PETER KIHSS

Edward Albee, whose failure to get a Pulitzer prize in 1963 caused the drama prize jurors to resign in protest, won the 1967 Pulitzer prize yesterday for his latest play, "A Delicate Balance."

The prize for fiction went to Bernard Malamud for "The Fixer," whose theme is the anti-Jewish persecutions in Czarist Russia. The book was selected even though the prize rules urge a preference for a work dealing with American life.

Yesterday's awards at Columbia University of 15 prizes in journalism, letters and music created controversy, as has happened frequently over the years.

The award for reporting on international affairs went to R. John Hughes of The Christian Science Monitor for dispatches from Indonesia.

It was disclosed in The St. Louis Post-Dispatch that a split vote on the Advisory Board on the Pulitzer Prizes had recommended Mr. Hughes, overruling a 4-to-1 vote by a journalism jury that would have given the prize to Harrison E. Salisbury, an assistant managing editor of The New York Times, for his dispatches from North Vietnam.

The Post-Dispatch, whose editor and publisher is Joseph Pulitzer Jr., grandson of the donor of the prizes, said that opponents had emphasized Mr. Salisbury's initial failure to cite sources for casualty figures in his dispatches. But it added that the jury's recommendation said his work showed "enterprise, world impact and total significance (that) outweighs some demerits in the on-the-spot reporting."

The prize for biography went to Justin Kaplan for "Mr. Clemens and Mark Twain." Mr. Kaplan took the occasion of the award to voice "distress over the course we are following in Vietnam," to urge "positive alternatives" and to say he would turn the $500 prize money over to the American Friends Service Committee.

The other prizes in letters were as follows:

For history, William H. Goetzmann, for "Exploration and Empire: the Explorer and Scientist in the Winning of the American West"; for poetry, Anne Sexton, for "Live or Die," and for general nonfiction, "The Problem of Slavery in Western Culture," by David Brion Davis.

The prize for music went to Leon Kirchner, for his Quartet No. 3.

In journalism, gold medals for public service went to both The Louisville Courier-Journal, for a successful campaign to control the Kentucky stripmining industry, and The Milwaukee Journal, for a successful campaign to stiffen Wisconsin laws against water pollution.

The other prizes in journalism were as follows:

Local reporting, Robert V. Cox of The Chambersburg (Pa.) Public Opinion, for valid deadline reporting of a mountain manhunt.

Local investigative reporting: Gene Miller of The Miami Herald, for helping to free two persons wrongfully convicted of murder in separate cases.

National reporting: Stanley Penn and Monroe Karmin of The Wall Street Journal, for investigative reporting of a connection between United States crime and gambling in the Bahamas.

Editorial writing: Eugene Patterson of The Atlanta Constitution, for editorials during the year, including a protest over the Georgia Legislature's refusal to seat Julian Bond, who had criticized the draft and the Vietnam war.

Cartooning: Patrick B. Oliphant of The Denver Post, for cartoons during the year, including one questioning any desire for peace negotiations on the part of Ho Chi Minh, the North Vietnamese leader.

Photography: Jack R. Thornell of The Associated Press's New Orleans bureau, for a picture of the shooting of James Meredith in Mississippi during his march on behalf of Negro voter registration.

Every Category Represented

This was the first year since 1961 that the Pulitzer prizes—awarded by the trustees of Columbia University on recommendation of the 14-member advisory board—were given in every eligible category.

The drama prize had been omitted three times in the preceding four years before it was carried off by Mr. Albee yesterday. Broadway observers had generally agreed that the quality of works by American playwrights had sagged in that period.

In "A Delicate Balance," which opened at the Martin Beck Theater last Sept. 22, Mr. Albee showed how the lives of a middle-aged couple in an Eastern suburban community were upset by the advent of another couple, fleeing from some nameless menace.

In his review of the play in The New York Times, the drama critic Walter Kerr wrote:

"'A Delicate Balance' is the sort of play that might be written if there were no theater. It exists outside itself, beside itself, as detached from the hard floor of the Martin Beck where it opened last night as its alarmed characters are detached from themselves."

Mr. Kerr also commented that it was "offered to us on an elegantly lacquered empty platter the moment the curtain goes up."

When Mr. Albee's "Who's Afraid of Virginia Woolf?" was rejected for the 1963 drama prize by the advisory board, several board members contended it did not conform to the terms set for the award. "Virginia Woolf" dealt with the lacerating self-revelations of two couples on a college campus. The former terms for the drama award specified "the American play, preferably original in its source and dealing with American life, which shall represent in marked fashion the educational value and power of the stage."

The current terms have dropped the words "which shall represent in marked fashion the educational value and power of the stage."

Denial of the 1963 drama award to Mr. Albee led John Mason Brown, critic and author, and John Gassner, theater historian and critic, to resign as the drama jury, which they had constituted for six or seven years up to then.

Mr. Brown charged at that time that the advisory board had "made a farce out of the drama award." Asked if he considered yesterday's selection a vindication of his 1963 judgment, Mr. Brown replied:

"Well, not exactly a vindication. It's just that we were right then and we're right now. Edward Albee is a demonstrated career talent—as opposed to the fly-by-night boys—and I found 'A Delicate Balance' the most fascinating new American play of the season."

Mr. Gassner died in New Haven on April 2. Mr. Brown said he was sure Mr. Gassner would have shared his delight at the current award for Mr. Albee.

"I talked with him about the play before his death," Mr. Brown said, "and he took the trouble to send me a written review of it. A favorable one, as I recall."

"A Delicate Balance" is the ninth play by Mr. Albee, a 39-year-old New Yorker. It starred Jessica Tandy, Hume Cronyn and Rosemary Murphy, and closed here Jan. 14 to go on national tour.

The prize for fiction goes to a work "by an American author, preferably dealing with American life." Before yesterday's award to Mr. Malamud's "The Fixer," several other works on non-American themes had won the award.

These included Thornton Wilder's "The Bridge of San Luis Rey," set in Peru, in 1928; Pearl S. Buck's "The Good Earth," (China) in 1932; Ernest Hemingway's "The Old Man and the Sea," (Cuba) in 1953; and William Faulkner's "A Fable," (France) in 1955.

Prizes have also gone to John Hersey's "A Bell for Adano," with an Italian setting and dealing with American soldiers, in 1945; and James A. Michener's "Tales of the South Pacific," which also dealt with American servicemen, in 1948.

Mr. Malamud's novel parallels what happened to Mendel Beilis, who was vindicated after a false accusation of ritual murder in Russia in 1911. The novel describes the spiritual growth of a Jewish handyman who has refused to confess to a trumped-up charge of the same kind.

War Book Awards Too

Both "The Fixer" and Mr. Kaplan's "Mr. Clemens and Mark Twain" received this year's National Book Awards in their categories. Mr. Malamud, who is 33 ears, is a native of Brooklyn and former high-school teacher here. He has been on the faculty of Bennington College, in Vermont, since 1961.

Mr. Kaplan, who is 41, interrupted his career as an editor in a book publishing house in 1959 to begin working on his Mark Twain biography. He said yesterday in Cambridge, Mass.:

"I wish in turn to honor the American tradition of constructive dissent Mark Twain served so nobly, to voice my distress over the course we are following in Vietnam and to express also my faith and hope that we are capable of devising positive alternatives to that course."

Dr. Goetzmann, director of the American studies program at the University of Texas, began his prize-winning work in history more than a decade ago with his doctoral dissertation, dealing with Army exploration in the West.

The poetry prize winner, Mrs. Sexton, has published three books of poems. She now lives in Weston, Mass. The winner of the general nonfiction prize, Professor Davis, of Cornell University's history department, is now in India teaching under a Fulbright award.

Music With Electronics

The music winner, Professor Kirchner, of Harvard University, wrote his quartet for strings with an electronic extension—the use of a tape-recorder.

The two co-equal gold medals for public service in journalism recalled dual awards in 1951, when The Miami Herald and The Brooklyn Eagle each re-

ceived prizes for crime reporting in unconnected campaigns, and in 1953, when two North Carolina weeklies, The Whiteville News Reporter and The Tabor City Tribune, were cited for crusades against the Ku Klux Klan.

The Louisville Courier-Journal's campaign to save the Kentucky countryside began in 1964, and was credited with last year's passage by the state's Legislature of what had been called "the nation's toughest strip-mining control law."

The Milwaukee Journal has carried on a campaign for several years that was termed influential in the Wisconsin Legislature's passage of a $300-million water-pollution control law. Secretary of the Interior Stewart Udall said it was one of the country's strongest such measures.

Mr. Cox, winner of the local reporting prize, has become city editor of his 16,000-circulation daily since his coverage of the hunt that led to the killing of a mountain sniper who abducted 17-year-old Peggy Ann Bradnick. Mr. Cox was covering criminal court poceedings yesterday when the award was announced.

The work that led to Mr. Miller's award for local investigative reporting began in 1963, when he took up the case of Mary Katherin Hampton, sentenced to life imprisonment in Louisiana.

After his investigation showing that she had been several hundred miles from the scene of two slayings, she was finally set free by the state parole board last Nov. 30. Mr. Miller also obtained a retrial and acquittal in iMami on Feb. 19, 1966, of Joseph Shea, an airman convicted of murder in 1959.

The Wall Street Journal reporters' expose of gambling has been cited as being responsible for the overthrow of the ruling party in the Bahamas in the islands' election last Jan. 10.

The awards in all categories were for work done during the calendar year 1966, except for drama and music, which involve the year ending last March 31. The 40 editors who made up juries in the eight journalism categories had inspected 528 exhibits.

The procedure calls one the jurors to submit several recommendations—in the past, two to five used to be suggested—without necessarily indicating their order of preference.

The advisory board has the power to select, accept or reject jurors' recommendations. The Columbia trustees sin turn may acccept the advisory board recommendations or reject them completely, but may not pick substitutes.

Yesterday's meeting of the trustees was one of the longest in years. It started at 3 P.M. behind closed doors and announced the prizes at 4:29 P.M.

The journalism prizes carry with them $1,000 apiece, except for the public service award, while the prizes in letters and music provide $500 each.

Grayson Kirk, president of Columbia University, announced yesterday that James Reston, an associate editor of The New York Times, had been elected a member of the Advisory Board. He succeeds Turner Catledge, executive editor of The Times, who had served three terms and

was ineligible for re-election.

Newbold Noyes Jr., editor of The Washington Star, was re-elected to his second four-year term. Mr. Pulitzer, board chairman, was re-elected to continue in that post without termination date.

The prizes had been set up by Joseph Pulitzer, his grandfather, publisher of The St. Louis Post-Dispatch and The New York World, and these were the 51st awards since they were begun in 1917.

NEW YORK DRAMA CRITICS CIRCLE AWARDS

Musical and Pinter Play Honored by Drama Critics

By SAM ZOLOTOW

"The Homecoming" and "Cabaret" were chosen yesterday by the New York Drama Critics Circle as the best play and best musical, respectively, of the 1966-67 theatrical season. Both also won Tony awards this year.

Neither presentation received the required 15 votes on the first ballot, so the 19 members voted to proceed on the point system. The first choice by each critic received three points, the second two points and the third one point. "The Homecoming" won with 32 points and "Cabaret" polled 28.

"A Delicate Balance," by Edward Albee, which won the Pulitzer Prize last week, was voted the second-best play and "I Do! I Do!," the second-best musical. Both scored 19 points.

"The Homecoming," a British play written by Harold Pinter, was successfully presented in London by the Royal Shakespeare Company. With a British cast of six, it was imported by Alexander H. Cohen and opened here Jan. 5 at the Music Box.

The play depicts an eccentric British family, consisting of a father, three sons and one of their wives.

Although the actors were commended for their performances, the play was not enthusiastically received by the four daily reviewers. Two were against it and two were on the fence.

Business Favorable

Despite the critical reception, business was favorable. Mr. Cohen reported that the largest receipts were $42,757 for the week ended April 1; the lowest were last week's $22,194. The potential weekly capacity at the Music Box is $47,479.

"It's a tribute to the public, whose interest in good theater caused the play to survive in spite of the divided reviews," Mr. Cohen said.

The play will remain at the Music Box during the summer. A tour has been booked to start Oct. 2 in Wilmington and end May 18, 1968 in Baltimore. It will cover 19 cities.

"Cabaret," the work of Joe

Friedman-Abeles

Principals in "The Homecoming" are, standing from left, Terence Rigby and Michael Craig; seated from left, Paul Rogers, John Normington, Michael Jayston, Lynn Farleigh.

Friedman-Abeles

Lotte Lenya and Jack Gilford in a scene from "Cabaret"

Masteroff, John Kander and Fred Ebb, derives from the John van Druten play, "I Am a Camera," which was adapted from Christopher Isherwood's sketches in his "Berlin Diary." It tells what happened in the Berlin of 1930, then on the brink of Nazi domination.

The show was presented by Harold Prince at the Broadhurst Theater on Nov. 20 and subsequently moved to the larger Imperial Theater. It is Mr. Prince's second current Broadway hit. The other is "Fiddler on the Roof," which

will give its 1,100th performance tonight.

Mr. Masteroff said:

"The shows that won the Drama Critics Circle and Tony awards for the last three years —"Fiddler on the Roof," "Man of La Mancha" and "Cabaret" —each was, commercially speaking, the least likely to succeed. Maybe that might be a guide to people planning musicals."

Among the plays voted on were "You Know I Can't Hear You When the Water's Running," "America Hurrah," "The

Killing of Sister George" and "Black Comedy."

Other musicals considered were "You're a Good Man, Charlie Brown" and "The Apple Tree."

Scrolls will be presented to the winners at a luncheon on May 18 at the Algonquin.

In addition, Mr. Pinter will receive a prize of $1,000 from the Harry and Margery G. Kahn Foundation through the Institute for Advanced Studies in the Theater Arts.

TONY AWARDS

Robert Preston and Barbara Harris Get Star Prizes

By DAN SULLIVAN

"Cabaret" was voted the best musical of the 1966-67 Broadway season and "The Homecoming" the best dramatic play at last night's Tony Awards ceremonies in the Shubert Theater.

Robert Preston of "I Do! I Do!" and Barbara Harris of "The Apple Tree" won Tonys for their starring musical roles.

Paul Rogers of "The Homecoming" was voted best actor in a nonmusical play. Beryl Reid won the best-actress award for "The Killing of Sister George."

The ceremonies were televised nationally, over the American Broadcasting Company's network, for the first time since the Tony Awards were instituted in 1947. David Merrick, who appeared on the program, facetiously congratulated his TV audience for "not watching 'Bonanza.'"

More for 'Cabaret'

"Cabaret" garnered seven other "bests"—supporting actor, to Joel Grey; supporting actress, Peg Murray; director, Harold Prince; composer and lyricist, John Kander and Fred Ebb; set design, Boris Aronson; costume design, Patricia Zipprodt, and choreography, Ronald Field.

Ian Holm of "The Homecoming" was voted best supporting actor in a nonmusical play.

Peter Hall, who staged "The Homecoming," was voted best nonmusical director.

The nonmusical supporting-actress award went to Marian Seldes of Edward Albee's "A Delicate Balance." Miss Seldes also contributed the most modest acceptance speech of the evening—"I have this prize because Edward Albee wrote the part."

Miss Reid's speech was more exuberant. "I do hope this is habit forming."

Mr. Prince's fell somewhere between modesty and pardonable pride: "I have to thank the producers of my 'Cabaret' for hiring me as director—I don't know anyone else who'd have

me." (He is one of the producers.)

The award ceremonies, scheduled from 9:30 to 10:30 P.M. on A.B.C., ran eight minutes overtime, even though awards were announced and received at a fairly rapid clip.

Between awards and commercials for American Airlines, the sponsors, four numbers from contending musicals were staged.

Gate-Crasher's Coup

Mr. Grey opened the program on a somewhat sardonic (and, for television, rather racy) note with the "Willkommen" number from "Cabaret." Miss Harris sang "I Wanna Be a Movie Star" from "The Apple Tree." Mr. Preston and Mary Martin, the masters of ceremonies, sang "Nobody's Perfect" from

"I Do! I Do!" And Norman Wisdom sang and danced the title song from "Walking Happy."

The program did not proceed without a hitch. A man identified as Stan Berman, who makes a specialty of gate-crashing, managed to get on-stage and kissed the flustered Miss Harris as she accepted her prize. And Mr. Preston had a little trouble remembering the lyrics of the verse to end the show. (Miss Martin, who plays his wife in "I Do! I Do!" dutifully helped him out.)

The program was seen by a home audience estimated at 40-million. Inside the Shubert, television equipment made it necessary to reduce the seating capacity from 1,435 to 1,200. Seats cost from $10 to $35, and everyone attending, including

Mr. Berman wore formal clothes.

After the show, 600 persons paying $25 a ticket, attended a supper ball at the Plaza Hotel.

One of the first figures to appear on the Shubert stage last night was Mayor Lindsay, who told the crowd that "Broadway is more than just a street."

Certainly, 44th Street looked spiffier than usual for the Tony Awards. An 800-square-yard red-tweed carpet stretched from Sardi's Restaurant across to the Shubert, and an 800-million-candlepower spotlight illuminated the exterior of the theater in true Academy Awards style.

Alexander Cohen, who produced the show for about $500,-000 (most of it supplied by

American Airlines), said that he was trying to glamorize the Tonys in the way that Hollywood's Oscars, Television's Emmys and the recording industry's Grammys have been glamorized.

The Tonys were established in 1947 as a memorial to Antoinette Perry, wartime chairman of the American Theater Wing.

Presenting the awards were Lee Remick, John Forsythe, Lauren Bacall, Kirk Douglas, Mr. Merrick, Gower and Marge Champion, Harry Belafonte, Carol Burnett, Zero Mostel, Angela Lansbury and Barbra Streisand.

The New York Times

Barbara Harris after being honored as the best female star in a musical play.

OBIE AWARDS

VILLAGE GATE SCENE OF VOICE OBIES FETE

The Village Voice's annual prizes for off Broadway excellence were presented Saturday by the Greenwich Village weekly at the Village Gate, 160 Bleecker Street. The awards, known as Obies (an abbreviation for Off Broadway), were divided almost equally between Off Broadway and its offshoot, off Off Broadway.

Rochelle Owens's "Futz," Henry Livings's "Eh?" and Sam Shepard's "La Turista" were cited as distinguished plays. Seth Allen and Tom O'Horgan, both of "Futz," were chosen best actor and best director.

Other prizes follow:
Distinguished performances: Tom Aldredge and Bette Henritze of "Measure for Measure"; Robert Bonnard, "The Chairs"; Alvin Epstein, "Dynamite Tonight"; Neil Flanagan, "The Madness of Lady Bright"; Stacy Keach, "MacBird!"; Terry Kiser, "Fortune and Men's Eyes"; Eddie McCarty, "Kitchenette"; Robert Salvio, "Hamp," and Rip Torn, "The Deer Park."
Joseph Cino Memorial Award: Jeff Weiss for his plays, "And That's How the Rent Gets Paid" and "A Funny Walk Home."
Other citations: The La Mama Troupe for presenting repertory to European audiences; The Open Theater for its Laboratory work; Tom Sankey for writing "The Golden Screw," in which he acted; the Second Party Players for superior production standards, and John Dood for lighting.

1968

NEW YORK DRAMA CRITICS CIRCLE AWARDS

By SAM ZOLOTOW

"Rosencrantz and Guildenstern Are Dead" and "Your Own Thing" were named yesterday by the New York Drama Critics Circle as the best play and the best musical for the 1967-68 season.

It was the second prize for "Rosencrantz," a British play, which received a Tony Sunday night as the best play of the season. "Your Own Thing" was the first Off Broadway offering to win a competitive citation from the circle. The Off Broadway production of "The Trojan Women" was given a special citation by the circle in 1964.

The circle's rules permit the naming of a best American play if a foreign one wins by a majority. "Rosencrantz" received 13 votes out of 20. But no American play obtained a clear majority, and so it was voted not to give an award to an American play.

'The Price' Had 7 Votes

The voting for an American play was as follows:
Arthur Miller's "The Price" (seven votes): Clive Barnes, The New York Times; John Chapman, The Daily News; Harold Clurman The Nation; Richard P. Cooke, The Wall Street Journal; Jack Gaver, United Press International; William Glover, Associated Press and George Oppenheimer, Newsday.
Neil Simon's "Plaza Suite" (three votes): Ethel Colby, The Journal of Commerce; Hobe Morrison, Variety, and Richard Watts Jr., The New York Post.
Jay Allen's "The Prime of Miss Jean Brodie" (three votes): Walter Kerr, The New York Times; Emory Lewis, Cue magazine, and William Raidy, the S. I. Newhouse newspaper chain.
Robert Anderson's "I Never Sang for My Father" (two votes): Whitney Bolton, The Morning Telegraph, and Edward Sothern Hipp, The Newark News.
One vote each was received by Michael McClure's "The Beard" (Jack Kroll, Newsweek); Ron Cowen's "Summertree" (Brendan Gill, The New Yorker); Jerome Kass's "Saturday Night" (Martin Gottfried, Women's Wear Daily); Eugene O'Neill's "More Stately Mansions" (Henry Hewes, Saturday Review).
Ted Kalem of Time magazine did not vote in this category because he did not consider any American play worthy to be selected.

Voting for the best play was as follows:
"Rosencrantz" (13 votes); Mr. Barnes, Mr. Chapman, Mrs. Colby, Mr. Cooke, Mr. Gaver, Mr. Gottfried, Mr. Hewes, Mr. Hipp, Mr. Kalem, Mr. Kroll, Mr. Oppenheimer, Mr. Raidy and Mr. Watts.
Peter Nichols's "Joe Egg" (four votes): Mr. Gill, Mr. Glov-

Friedman-Abeles

Scene from "Cabaret," best musical, has Jack Gilford, left, Lotte Lenya and Bert Convy

At Sardi's, after receiving Tony Awards, are Robert Preston, left, voted best musical actor; Beryl Reid, voted best dramatic actress, and Paul Rogers, best dramatic actor.

er, Mr. Kerr and Mr. Lewis.

Scores on the Musicals

One vote each was cast for "The Price" (Mr. Clurman); "Plaza Suite" (Mr. Morrison) and "I Never Sang for My Father" (Mr. Bolton).

"Your Own Thing," written by Donald Driver, Hal Hester and Danny Apolinar, received nine votes, a majority, on the first ballot for the best musical. Voting for it were Mr. Barnes, Mr. Bolton, Mr. Cooke, Mr. Gill, Mr. Glover, Mr. Kerr, Mr. Oppenheimer Mr. Raidy, and Mr. Watts.

"George M!," by George M. Cohan, Michael Stewart and John and Fran Pascal (two votes): Mr. Chapman and Mr. Gaver.

"Hair," by Gerome Ragni, James Rado and Galt MacDermot (two votes): Mr. Hewes and Mr. Kroll.

"The Happy Time," by N. Richard Nash, John Kander and Fred Ebb (two votes): Mr. Morrison and Mrs. Colby.

"In Circles," by Gertrude Stein and Al Carmines (one vote): Mr. Lewis.

There were three abstentions in voting for the best musical: Mr. Gottfried, Mr. Hipp and Mr. Kalem. None thought any musical this season sufficiently outstanding. Mr. Clurman was not present for this vote.

There was a discussion about whether the abstentions were to be counted as votes in opposition. If they had been, there would have been no majority. The rules in that case call for a point system of balloting, where the first choice receives three points, the second choice, two points the third choice, one point. It was finally decided by vote not to count abstentions, as had been the circle's practice.

The awards will be presented Wednesday at 4:30 P.M. at a cocktail party at the Algonquin Hotel, where the critics met yesterday. Tom Stoppard, author of "Rosencrantz," will receive $1,000 contributed by Harry Kahn, a Wall Street broker interested in theater.

TONY AWARDS

Zoe Caldwell and Balsam Capture Acting Honors

By DAN SULLIVAN

A musical no longer running on Broadway was judged Broadway's best at the 22d annual Ar toinette Perry Awards ceremony last night at the Shubert Theater.

"Hallelujah, Baby!," which closed Jan. 13 after 292 performances at the Martin Beck Theater, won Tony awards in four categories—best musical, best score (Jule Styne, Betty Comden and Adolph Green), best female supporting actress (Lillian Hayman) and best female star (Leslie Uggams).

Brian Murray, left, and John Wood in "Rosencrantz and Guildenstern Are Dead." Work won award as best drama.

Friedman-Abeles

Robert Hooks and Leslie Uggams in "Hallelujah Baby!" It was judged best musical. Awards were given at Shubert.

Miss Uggams shared her honor with Patricia Routledge of "Darling of the Day," a short-lived musical, but "Hallelujah, Baby!" with book by Arthur Laurents, took more Tonys than any other show at last night's ceremony.

Far From Dead

Tom Stoppard's gloss on "Hamlet," "Rosencrantz and Guildenstern Are Dead," was judged the best straight play of the season. Desmond Heeley received separate awards for his sets and costumes for the show.

Selected as best actor in a straight dramatic role was Martin Balsam, who starred in three of the four one-act plays that comprised Robert Anderson's "You Know I Can't Hear You When the Water's Running."

Zoe Caldwell, the tempestuous heroine of "The Prime of Miss Jean Brodie," won the Tony for best actress in a dramatic role.

Robert Goulet, as the not-so-shy photographer of "The Happy Time," was best actor in a musical. Gower Champion won two awards as director and choreographer of the French-Canadian musical.

Mike Nichols, who had received his second Academy Award in two years on April 8 for having directed the film "The Graduate," picked up his fourth directional Tony in five years for Neil Simon's comedy "Plaza Suite."

Patterson a Winner

Best supporting actor in a straight play was James Patterson in Harold Pinter's "The Birthday Party." Best supporting actress was Zena Walker in "Joe Egg."

Hiram Sherman of "How Now, Dow Jones" was judged best supporting actor in a musical.

For the second year, the awards were televised nationally from the stage of the 1,469-seat Shubert. Seats cost $5 to $20, and there were few empty ones.

Acceptance speeches were short, sweet and sometimes misty. Mr. Nichols, speaking by videotape from Rome, started on a mock-conceited note by saying that he and his colleagues deserved "full credit," but then resumed the traditional humility: "for choosing Maureen Stapleton and George C. Scott for this show."

The closest thing to asperity came from Mr. Champion, receiving the choreography award: "I don't know how to break this to Clive Barnes." Mr. Barnes, dance and drama critic of The New York Times, was not enthusiastic over Mr. Champion's choreography for the show.

Alexander H. Cohen produced the evening for the League of New York Theaters with his usual brass-band-and-klieglights flair.

Red Carpet Missing

The red carpet that covered 44th Street at last year's ceremony, Mr. Cohen's maiden effort, was missing: a wag said it was still being cleaned. But the lineup of live talent, including such Hollywood-based celebrities as Jack Benny, Groucho Marx and Gregory Peck, was even longer.

Mr. Cohen had decreed that everyone at the Shubert wear formal clothes, but this—like the bleachers that were to have been erected outside the theater and the electronic onstage marquee that was to have blazed the names of the nominees and winners—failed to come to pass.

The National Broadcasting Company's cameramen and backstage crew wore what they always wear to work, the former site of the Astor Hotel was considered too weak to hold the bleachers and the awards were announced in the traditional the-envelope-please fash-

on.

Thirty-two private detectives were on hand to prevent such incidents as the appearance at last year's show of Stanly Berman, the noted gate-crasher. Mr. Berman ran out on the stage to kiss a nonplussed Barbara Harris on the cheek after she had received an award. Mr. Berman died on Feb. 25.

There were no unofficial interruptions last night, although Mr. Marx rather flustered Miss Uggams by interrupting the opening line of her acceptance speech ("I don't know where my feet are tonight") with: "Want me to look?"

The proceedings were officially interrupted by six commercials for Eastern Airlines, sponsor of the $1-million show (Mr. Cohen's estimate), and seven production numbers from "The Happy Time," "Man of La Mancha," "Cabaret," "Hello Dolly!," "How Now, Dow Jones," "Golden Rainbow" and "Hallelujah, Baby!"

There was also time out for special awards—to Carol Channing, the original star of "Hello Dolly!" and Pearl Bailey, the current one; David Merrick, the producer; the A.P.A.-Phoenix Company (which earlier had protested the league's decision not to consider its productions for Tonys this year); Audrey Hepburn; Maurice Chevalier and Marlene Dietrich.

Harold Prince's presentation of the A.P.A.'s award was conciliatory. He called the company's work "equal to the best of Broadway." Helen Hayes, accepting, said she hoped the company would be eligible next year "but meanwhile, we will cherish this."

The evening ended with a supper-ball at the Rainbow Room.

Among those who stayed home were David Black, a producer of the musical "George M!" Mr. Black, a member of the league's board, is suing Mr.

Cohen and the league for having ruled "George M!" out of this year's "best-musical" category.

The musical, which opened April 10, was excluded when the league moved the cut-off date for Tony nominations from April 11 back to March 19 on the grounds that the additional time was needed to prepare the telecast.

Also absent was Isabelle Stevenson, president of the American Theater Wing, which founded the Tony Awards in 1947. Mrs. Stevenson has protested the "George M!" decision, too, saying the awards were not created "for the convenience of a television program." She said she would stay home to see that the wing got proper mention on the program credits. It did.

The Tonys—small silver medallions with the ancient masks of comedy and tragedy on one side, and the winner's name on the other—are given in memory of Antoinette Perry, wartime chairman of the American Theater Wing.

The theater wing sponsored the awards until 1965. On the death of the group's president, Helen Menken, the wing authorized the League of New York Theaters to assume sponsorship.

An undisclosed portion of the receipts from last night's show —in 1967 it amounted to about $5,200—will go to the wing's scholarship fund, Mr. Cohen said. The league's share, he said, will be "in excess of $50,000."

Voting for the Tonys this year were 445 professional theater people members of the League of New York Theaters, drama critics, and members of the governing boards of Actors Equity, the Dramatists Guild and the Society of Stage Directors and Choreographers.

The nominating committee was composed of seven critics: Harold Clurman of The Nation

'Rosencrantz' and 'Hallelujah, Baby!' Garner Tonys

The New York Times (by Larry Morris)

Gathered after Tony awards were winners, from left; Patricia Routledge, who shared best musical actress award with Leslie Uggams; Robert Goulet, best actor, musical; Miss Uggams; Martin Balsam, best actor in drama, and Zoe Caldwell, best actress, drama. They are holding an award.

and New York magazines; William Glover, The Associated Press; Otis Guernsey, Best Plays of the Year series; Allen Jefferys, WABC-TV; Leo Lerman, Mademoiselle; George Oppenheimer, Newsday, and Tom Prideaux, Life.

OBIE AWARDS

WORKERS' THEATER LEADS OBIE WINNERS

El Teatro Campesino of Del Ray, Calif., and the San Francisco Mime Troupe won special Obie citations and prizes of $200 each, it was announced yesterday by The Village Voice, Greenwich Village's weekly newspaper. Obie is the phonetic condensation for Off Broadway.

El Teatro was cited for creating a workers' theater. The mime troupe obtained its citation for "uniting theater and revolution."

Two other special citations, without cash awards, went to the Negro Ensemble Company and the Fortune Society. The former was designated for "excellence in repertory theater." The Fortune Society was described as the first social agency to evolve from an Off Broadway production that considered the problems of the ex-

convict and the prison system.

Obies also were awarded to:

Billie Dixon, actress, "The Beard."
Al Pacino, actor, "The Indian Wants the Bronx."
Michael A. Schultz, director, "Song of the Luisitanian Bogey."
Robert LaVigne, designer, "A Midsummer Night's Dream" and "Endecott and the Red Cross."
"In Circles," the Gertrude Stein-Al Carmines musical.
"The Memorandum," Vaclav Havel's foreign play.
John Hancock, director, "A Midsummer Night's Dream."
Rip Torn, director, "The Beard."
Israel Horovitz, author, "The Indian Wants the Bronx."
John Guare, author, "Muzeeka."
Sam Shepard, author, "Forensic and the Navigators" and "Melodrama Play."

The following players also received Obies:

John Cazale, "Line" and "The Indian Wants the Bronx."
James Coco, "Fragments."
Jean David, "Istanboul."
Cliff Gorman, "The Boys in the Band."
Mari Gorman, "The Memorandum" and "Walking to Waldheim."
Moses Gunn, Negro Ensemble Company's repertory.
Peggy Pope, "Muzeeka."
Roy R. Schneider, "Stephen D."

1969

NOBEL PRIZE

By JOHN M. LEE
Special to The New York Times

STOCKHOLM, Oct. 23— Samuel Beckett, the avant-garde writer acclaimed for

his plays and novels of loneliness, despair and human degradation, was announced today as the winner of the 1969 Nobel Prize in Literature.

The selection committee, comprising members of the Swedish Academy, cited him "for his writing, which—in new forms for the novel and drama—in the destitution of modern man acquires its elevation."

Mr. Beckett, who was born in Dublin 63 years ago, but now lives in Paris, is best known for his play "Waiting for Godot," published in 1952, which evoked the futility of modern life.

Mr. Beckett could not be reached for comment on the prize. He was reported by his Paris publisher to be out of touch in Tunisia, and Nobel officials were unable to say whether he had received word of the award.

There was conjecture here that Mr. Beckett would refuse to come to Stockholm to accept the award, as is customary, at formal ceremonies on Dec. 10. The Nobel laureate in literature has traditionally addressed the Nobel banquet, but Mr. Beckett has rarely granted so much as an interview.

Jean-Paul Sartre, winner of the Nobel Prize in Literature in 1964, declined the award.

This year, the prize carries a cash award of about $73,-000.

There are five Nobel Prizes established under the will of Alfred Nobel, the Swede who invented dynamite, and a sixth prize established in economics through a grant by the Bank of Sweden. The first economics prize is to be announced on Monday.

Last week, three United States scientists were awarded the Nobel Prize in Physiology or Medicine for their discoveries concerning viruses and viral diseases. On Monday, the International Labor Organization won the Nobel Peace Prize. Prizes for chemistry and physics will be announced next Thursday.

Yeats and Shaw Cited

It was not immediately clear whether Mr. Beckett should be regarded as an Irish or a French winner, although Nobel officials recognize the country of work and residence. Mr. Beckett has lived in Paris since 1937, and he has written mostly in French.

The only Irish Nobel winner in literature was William Butler Yeats, the poet, in 1923. George Bernard Shaw, born in Ireland, was honored a few years later but as a British author.

The choice of Mr. Beckett delighted Stockholm literary

circles, which had derided the literature award in recent years as being influenced more by political, geographic and religious factors than by literary merit and influence.

The winner is selected by the 18-member Swedish Academy, which represents the literary Establishment. In the past, the awards have gone to long-established authors, many beyond their prime.

In a radio commentary on the choice of Mr. Beckett, Karl Ragnar Gierow, secretary of the academy, possibly mindful of the injunction in Alfred Nobel's will to honor uplifting literary works, seemed at pains to bring out the positive aspects of the deeply pessimistic Beckett.

"The degradation of humanity is a recurrent theme in Beckett's writing," Dr. Gierow said, "and to this extent his philosophy, simply accentuated by elements of the grotesque and of tragic farce, can be said to be a negativism that knows no haven."

But, using a photographic analogy, Dr. Gierow said that when a negative was printed, it produced "a positive, a clarification, with the black proving to be the light of day, the parts in deepest shade, those which reflect the light sources."

The academy official continued: "The perception of human degradation is not possible if human values are

denied. This is the source of inner cleansing, the life force in spite of everything, in Beckett's pessimism."

Praising Mr. Beckett for "a love of mankind that grows in understanding as it plumbs further into the depths of abhorrence," Dr. Gierow concluded rhapsodically:

"From that position, in the realms of annihilation, the writing of Samuel Beckett rises like a miserere from all mankind, its muffled minor key sounding liberation to the oppressed and comfort to those in need."

His Own Translator

The award covered Mr. Beckett's novels as well as his plays. He was a novelist before he became a playwright and he continues writing in both forms.

His first two novels, "Murphy" (1938) and "Watt" (1942), were written in English, and his trilogy, "Molloy" (1950), "Malone Dies" (1951), and "The Unnamable" (1952), and "How It Is" (1961), were written in French. Mr. Beckett translated them into English.

In his novels, as in his plays, there is a search for the self, and an achieving of nothing. Murphy, an Irishman living in London, finally dies in a fire. Malone also dies after undergoing nightmares and hallucinations. "The Unnamable" is a novel about a blob "whose identity is unproved, dying, or being born — it could be either," according to Stephen Spender in The New York Times Book Review.

In "How It Is," a humanoid looks for meaning while crawling through primeval ooze and discovers another creature, called Pim. Each may be the other's victim.

Lutfi Ozkok

Samuel Beckett

Impact

Bert Lahr, at left, and E. G. Marshall in the 1956 Broadway production of Samuel Beckett's play "Waiting for Godot."

vaudeville play," he said acerbically.

The true "Godot," he went on, was the one produced in a German prison, with the convicts as actors. "They [and the audience] understood that 'Godot' is not despair, but hope," he said. "'Godot' is life — aimless, but always with an element of hope."

Although Mr. Beckett is often associated with the dispossessed, he is no Bohemian. His dress is neat but simple — usually corduroy trousers, a white shirt, a four-in-hand tie and jacket. His apartment, which overlooks the exercise yard of the Santé Prison, is immaculate and filled with books and paintings. It contains a piano on which he sometimes plays for his own enjoyment, mostly Haydn and Scarlatti.

Mr. Beckett and the woman who has shared his life for many years also have a small house in the country, where he likes to stroll and watch the hawks.

To Paris in the 20's

Born in Ireland, April 3, 1906, and educated at Trinity College, Dublin, Mr. Beckett went to Paris for the first time in the 1920's. Then he taught briefly at Trinity, resigning abruptly in 1932 because "I had a big impulse to write." His first poem, "Whoroscope," had meanwhile been published and had won a £10 prize.

Returning to Paris, he met James Joyce, a fellow expatriate, wrote an essay on him and worked on a French translation of "Anna Livia Plurbella." Mr. Beckett was not, as some stories have it, Mr. Joyce's secretary.

Mr. Beckett has made one visit to the United States, in 1964 for the filming, by Grove Press, his publishers here, of "Film," a 22-minute movie featuring Buster Keaton.

Upset and dismayed by the frenetic pace of New York, he quickly fled back to Paris. Recalling the incident, he said of his return to the anonymity he enjoys in "my beloved France."

"A frightful experience, New York! Never again! Jamais encore!"

light together reaching minimum in about 10 seconds and immediately cry as before. Silence and hold for five seconds."

PULITZER PRIZE

Howard Sackler
Drama

WON award for "The Great White Hope," a play based on the life and stormy career of the former Negro heavyweight boxing champion, Jack Johnson. . . . Previously had won grants from the Rockefeller and Littauer Foundations, and had received both the Maxwell Anderson and Sergei Awards for his work as a playwright. . . . Director for the 1964 National Broadcasting television special, "Shakespeare, Soul of an Age." . . . Born in New York City in 1929 and graduated from Brooklyn College in 1950 with a bachelor of arts degree. . . . Has had plays produced in London's Hamstead Playhouse, San Francisco's American Conservatory Theater, the Poets' Theater of Boston and Washington's Arena Stage, where "The Great White Hope" was first seen in tryout. . . . Lives with wife and two children in London.

Beckett Wins Nobel for Literature

'In the Wilderness for 20 Years'

By ALDEN WHITMAN

A man with only a few close friends who leads a reclusive, although far from furtive, life, Samuel Beckett has gone out of his way to avoid literary fame and the necessity for explaining himself to importunate interviewers.

Indeed, it is typical of the writer that he has never met his nominator for the Nobel Prize, Prof. William York Tindall of Columbia University, though they have corresponded from time to time.

Typically, when a reporter sought out Mr. Beckett in Paris two years ago, he at first declined a meeting, then agreed to have a drink (but no serious talk) at La Closerie des Lilas, a restaurant in Montparnasse. After a while, however, he relaxed his stricture and chatted animatedly for several hours about himself, his life philosophy and his writings.

Mr. Beckett, Sam to intimates, is lanky and cadaverous. His face, which is long and lined, is topped by brows that wrinkle as he talks. He has blue eyes, which, behind steel-rimmed spectacles, can be merry or pensive. Failing sight makes it difficult for him to read for sustained periods.

As Mr. Beckett talked, in a musical tenor, his long fingers and spatulate thumbs often curled around his cigarette lighter, when they did not grasp his glass of Scotch.

'Writing Was Never Easy'

"Writing was never easy for me," Mr. Beckett remarked with a wry laugh. "I never thought of myself as a writer and I don't now. I was in the wilderness for 20 years until 'Godot' brought attention to my novels and short stories and poems. There was no trace of success until 'Godot,' which was written in 1948, was produced in 1953.

"Then I received a French Government grant of 700,-000 old francs that permitted a month's run in Paris."

Mr. Beckett felt strongly that the "Godot" produced in the United States in 1956 was not his "Godot."

"Bert Lahr, a musical-hall type, dominated the play, which is not supposed to have a dominant character and is not supposed to be a

'Calcutta!' Sketch Gives A Glimpse of Writings

Samuel Beckett is one of the 12 authors of "Oh! Calcutta!" the hit Off Broadway revue whose cast members appear in the nude for most of the performance. His contribution, entitled "Prologue," runs for 35 seconds.

Here are Mr. Beckett's stage directions for his material:

"There's a faint light on stage littered with miscellaneous rubbish, including naked people. Then there is a faint brief cry and immediately inspiration and slow increase of light reaching maximum in 10 seconds. Expiration and slow decrease of

By PETER KIHSS

Norman Mailer, with his report of a four-day protest against the war in Vietnam in "The Armies of The Night," shared a Pulitzer Prize yesterday for general nonfiction with Dr. Rene Jules Dubos, the microbiologist, as author of a study, "So Human an Animal: How We Are Shaped by Surroundings and Events." Mr. Mailer, who is currently soliciting petitions to run in the June 17 Democratic primary for nomination as Mayor of New York, said he was very pleased and would use his $1,000 prize money as "the first contribution" to the campaign fund for himself and the writer, Jimmy Breslin, seeking the Council presidency.

"The Great White Hope," written by Howard Sackle, won the Pulitzer Prize for drama. It was Broadway's version of the story of the first Negro heavyweight boxing champion, Jack Johnson, who prompted the search for a challenger. This was only the third time in seven years that the drama award has been given.

Indian and Negro Win

An American Indian and a Negro also won Pulitzer Prizes. N. Scott Momaday, a Kiowa who wrote the novel "House Made of Dawn," was perhaps the first American Indian so honored since the prizes started in 1917. Moneta J. Sleet Jr., Ebony magazine photographer, was preceded by at least one other Negro winner — Gwendolyn Brooks, the poet, in 1950.

The Los Angeles Times received the annual gold medal for disinterested and meritorious public service by a newspaper for exposing "wrongdoing within the Los Angeles city government commissions." One of its correspondents, William Tuohy, won the Pulitzer prize in international reporting for his coverage of the war in Vietnam.

Columbia University's acting president, Andrew W. Cordier, announced the awards in 16 categories after the 53d annual decision by the Columbia trustees on recommendations of the Advisory Board on the Pulitzer Prizes, as provided by the will of the late Joseph Pulitzer, publisher of The New York World and The St. Louis Post-Dispatch.

Dr. Dubos, a 68-year-old French-born professor at Rockefeller University, as co-winner of the general nonfiction prize receives $1,000 as does Mr. Mailer, the amount of the prize award in each category except that the newspaper public service prize consists of the medal.

Other Journalism Awards

The other journalism awards were:

Local Reporting, General — John Fetterman, of The Louisville Courier-Journal, for his story on how "the body of Pfc. James Thurman (Little Duck) Gibson came home from Vietnam."

Local Reporting, Special —

Albert L. Delugach and Denny Walsh of The St. Louis Globe-Democrat for a campaign against fraud and abuse of power in Local 562, St. Louis Steamfitters Union, resulting in convictions of the union and three officers for conspiracy to violate a ban on union contributions in Federal elections.

National Reporting — Robert Cahn, of The Christian Science Monitor, for a series on the need for saving national parks.

Editorial Writing—Paul Greenberg of The Pine Bluff (Ark.) Commercial, for editorial writing during 1968 for the newspaper in a community of fewer than 70,000 persons, a post for which he left Hunter College as a history lecturer in 1962.

Cartoons — John Fischetti, of The Chicago Daily News, for editorial cartooning during 1968 for the newspaper he joined after five years on The New York Herald Tribune until that daily ceased publication.

Spot News Photography — Edward T. Adams, of The Associated Press, for his picture of Brig. Gen. Nguyen Ngoc Loan, South Vietnam's national police chief, executing with his revolver, a Vietcong prisoner whose hands were tied behind his back.

In letters, the history prize went to "Origins of the Fifth Amendment," by Leonard W. Levy, chairman of the department of history at Brandeis University, a study of the constitutional protection against self-incrimination.

The biography prize was awarded to "The Man from New York: John Quinn and His Friends," by Benjamin Lawrence Reid, a professor of English at Mount Holyoke College, on the life of a New York lawyer who was an art patron and collector.

The poetry prize was captured by "Of Being Numerous," by George Oppen, a 61-year-old resident of Brooklyn who has been a member of the "Objectivist Group" of poets, such as William Carlos Williams and Ezra Pound.

Karel Husa, 47, a native of Czechoslovakia who left his country in 1946 after liberation from the Nazis appeared likely to be followed by a Communist takeover, won the prize for music with his "String Quartet No. 3." He is professor of composition and director of the symphony at Cornell University.

Mr. Mailer had won the National Book Award last March for the same report as the Pulitzer one on the October, 1967, antiwar demonstrations at the Pentagon.

Members of the Advisory Board indicated that both his book and Dr. Dubos's study of how man was "shaped by surroundings and events" had

been recommended jointly by the jury in their field.

Mr. Sackler's little-disguised play about Jack Johnson and his bitter defeat by Jess Willard was the winner of an Antoinette Perry award, one of Broadway's "Tony" prizes. It was understood to have had strong competition in the Pulitzer contests from "1776," a muscial play by Peter Stone, with music and lyrics by Sherman Edwards.

Dr. Momaday, the prize-winning novelist who grew up on southwestern Indian reservations and attended Indian schools is associate professor of English at the University of California in Santa Barbara.

In an essay in The New York Times Book Review last Sunday, he recalled how he brought Kiowa tales together in "The Way to Rainy Mountain." His novel on the reservation as a "House Made of Dawn" was reviewed in about 25 publications, above average for a first novel, according to Harper & Row, its publisher. The Times Book Review was among these.

Mr. Sleet's prize in the Feature Photography category was earned by a picture of Mrs. Coretta Scott King at the funeral service for her husband, the Rev. Dr. Martin Luther King Jr. A resident of Baldwin, L. I., Mr. Sleet was one of several photographers representing the nation's press in Ebenezer Baptist Church in Atlanta on a pool basis.

The public service campaign by The Los Angeles Times included six months' work by George Reasons, a reporter, investigating the city's Planning and Zoning Commission. For four months thereafter, Mr. Reasons, aided by four other reporters, Art Berman, Gene Blake, Robert L. Jackson and Ed Meagher, developed another series on zoning and hospital contracts.

The team of reporters then put in six months more investigating the Harbor Commission and the Recreation and Park Commission.

William F. Thomas, metropolitan editor, was in over-all charge of the project, which is continuing. Mayor Sam Yorty announced his candidacy for a third term by charging The Los Angeles Times with attempting to smear his administration; he said he sought vindication at the polls. He finished behind Councilman Thomas Bradley in the first round of the mayoral selection in April and The Times is supporting Mr. Bradley against Mayor Yorty in the May 27 runoff.

Two commissioners resigned and two were transferred in the planning and zoning inquiry. In the harbor investigation, two commissioners were convicted of bribery, one was found guilty of bribery and conflict of interest, and a $12-million city contract was canceled.

The recreation and park study saw two commissioners resign and a golf-course contract canceled. The over-all campaign led to a study of the entire structure of the Los Angeles city government, looking to possible charter reform.

Mr. Tuohy, The Los Angeles Times's prize-winner for reporting from Vietnam, had been covering the war for four years, initially as a correspond-

ent for Newsweek. He is now assigned to reporting from Beirut, Lebanon.

Mr. Walsh, who shared the special local reporting award with Mr. Delugach, left The St. Louis Globe-Democrat last November. He then went to Life magazine as an editor and investigative reporter, and now lives in Manhattan.

More than 650 entries were received and judged in the journalism categories, on which there were 43 jurors. The juries submit three to six entries to the Advisory Board. The prizes are for work during 1968, except for drama and music in which the year under scrutiny ended last March 31.

Yesterday was the first time since 1962 that women were left out of the Pulitzer honors. It was the 15th time in the 53 years of the prizes that no woman won an award.

NEW YORK DRAMA CRITICS CIRCLE AWARDS

By SAM ZOLOTOW

"The Great White Hope," winner of the Pulitzer Prize and Tony award as the best American play of the year, added the New York Drama Critics Circle prize yesterday to its list of honors.

"1776," winner of a Tony as best musical, won the same designation from the critics.

"The Great White Hope," based on the career of Jack Johnson, the first Negro heavyweight boxing champion, is the first Broadway work by Howard Sackler.

Only four other plays have made a clean sweep of Broadway honors: "Death of a Salesman" (1949); "The Teahouse of the August Moon" (1954); "The Diary of Anne Frank" (1956) and "Long Day's Journey Into Night" (1957).

Sackler was playing softball in the Show League in Central Park. Later, informed of the awards, he said:

"While I'm really delighted and honored, I'm even more relieved to be past the prizegiving period. The attention and nail-biting surrounding these prizes make the undertaking of any new work seem completely overwhelming in prospect.

"Now that I'm a member of The Great White Hope base-ball team in center field, I feel there's more of a group spirit than ever before. I'll use the money to give the cast a party next month."

The play did better than the baseball team. The Great White Hope" team lost to the "Little Murders" team 9 to 4.

In addition to a scroll, the author will receive $1,000. Harry Kahn, a Wall Street broker who is a senior partner in the firm of Neuberger & Berman, contributed the money.

"1776," based on the signing of the Declaration of Independence, was written by Peter Stone and Sherman Edwards. It was Mr. Edwards's first Broadway venture.

"The Great White Hope," which received 6 votes on the first ballot, failed to get the required majority of 10. The second ballot used a point system of 3, 2 and 1 for first, second and third choices.

This procedure gave "The Great White Hope" 25 points; "Hadrian VII" 19 and Cere-

The New York Times

Sherman Edwards

monies in Dark Old Men" 14.

Those voting for "The Great White Hope" were Harold Clurman (The Nation), Ethel Colby (Journal of Commerce), Richard Cooke (Wall Street Journal), Jack Gaver (United Press International), William Glover (Associated Press), Martin Gottfried (Women's Wear), Hobe Morrison (Variety), Walter Kerr (The New York Times), Jack Kroll (Newsweek), Emory Lewis (The Record) and William Raidy (Newhouse chain).

The circle voted not to select a best foreign play inasmuch as an American play had been chosen. The critics also decided to name the best musical on one ballot, requiring a majority of 9 of the 13 critics present.

John Chapman (Daily News), Edward S. Hipp (Newark News), George Oppenheimer (Newsday), Messrs. Gaver, Glover, Kerr, Morrison, Raidy and Mrs. Colby voted for "1776."

A motion introduced by Mrs. Colby to give Neil Simon, author of "Plaza Suite" and "Promises, Promises," a special citation because of "a succession of happy comedies that have given theatergoers the pleasure of laughter," was defeated.

The presentations will be made at 4 P.M. next Thursday at the Algonquin Hotel, where the circle held its annual meeting.

TONY AWARDS
'Great White Hope' and '1776' Win Tonys

By LEWIS FUNKE

"1776," the last eligible musical of the season, came out first last night in the 23d annual competition for the Antoinette Perry Awards at the Mark Heilinger Theater.

Arriving at the 46th Street Theater on March 16, unheralded and with many comparatively unknowns involved in its execution, it proved to be the season's sleeper, turning into an instant hit. Telling of the men and events connected with the writing of the Declaration of Independence, "1776" was written by Peter Stone based on an idea conceived by Sherman Edwards, who wrote the music and the lyrics. Mr. Edwards had never done a musical before.

The musical, produced by Stuart Ostrow, topped three other nominees, "Promises, Promises," "Hair" and "Zorbá." It also won a Tony for Peter Hunt as the best director of a musical. A third member of the company, Ronald Holgate, as the ebullient Richard Henry Lee of Virginia, was named the winner in the featured or supporting role category of a musical.

'White Hope' Scores

"The Great White Hope," by Howard Sackler, another newcomer to the Broadway theater, was named the best play, while its star, James Earl Jones, won a Tony as the best actor in a straight play. Mr. Jones, a tall, powerfully built man, with a booming voice, portrays Jack Jefferson, a role based on the late Jack Johnson, once world heavyweight champion. It is a taxing, almost completely virtuoso part that Mr. Jones enacts on the Alvin stage. Jane Alexander, as his white mistress, took honors in the featured or supporting category in a play.

Two performers in "Promises, Promises" beat out the competition in their respective categories. Jerry Orbach, as the ambitious insurance accountant who lends his apartment to superiors in the hope of advancement, took the Tony for best actor in a musical. Marian Mercer, playing an amusing pickup in a bar, triumphed in the featured or supporting cate-

gory in a musical.

Julie Harris carted off her third Tony, being named best actress in a play, this being the comedy "Forty Carats," by Jay Presson, adapted from a French hit by Pierre Barillet and Jean Pierre Gredy. Miss Harris won Tonys in "I Am a Camera" (1952) and "The Lark" (1956). Her current roles sees her as a woman of 40 who falls in love with a 22-year-old.

Angela Lansbury was judged the best actress in a musical, for her role as the madwoman in "Dear World," derived from the play "The Madwoman of Chaillot."

Al Pacino was named best in a supporting or featured role in a straight play. He appeared in "Does a Tiger Wear a Necktie?"

The best director of a play was the Englishman Peter Dews, who took the honor for "Hadrian VII."

Joe Layton was judged the winner among choreographers, for his dances in the musical "George M!"

The prize for costume design went to Louden Sainthill, whose work appears in the musical "Canterbury Tales."

Boris Aronson, one of the theater's leading scenic artists, won this third Tony for his sets in the musical "Zorbá."

The Tonys—small silver medallions with the traditional masques of comedy and tragedy on one side and the winner's name on the other—are the equivalent of Hollywood's Oscars. The winners represent the choices of those involved with the theater industry.

This season 434 ballots were sent to drama critics as well as other members of the press who report on the theater, members of the councils of Actors Equity Association, the Society of Stage Directors and Choreographers, the Dramatists Guild, the scenic artists' union and members of the league. How many ballots were returned was not divulged.

This was the third year the show was presented by the League of New York Theater under authorization from the American Theater Wing, which founded the Tonys in 1947 in honor of its wartime chairman, Antoinette Perry. The wing sponsored the annual presentation until 1965. On the death of the organization's president, Helen Menken, the wing authorized the league to take over.

As in the previous two seasons of the league's stewardship, Alexander H. Cohen master-minded the ceremonies. The imaginative producer who has worked hard to earn a reputation as a latter-day Barnum, put the show on with his accustomed razzmatazz.

As has been practice for these affairs, Mr. Cohen in-

Martha Swope

"1776," stars William Daniels, left, and Howard Da Silva

sisted on black tie for the patrons who paid from $5 to $35 to be in on the festivities. The 1,554-seat Hellinger was sold out. Following the show, 1,000 guests, who paid $25 a ticket, took over four rooms at the Plaza for the gala supper ball. Dining and dancing took place in the Grand Ballroom, the French Suite and the Crystal and Savoy Rooms.

In addition to the presentations last night, there were special awards to Sir Laurence Olivier of England's National Theater, Carol Burnett, stage and television star, Leonard Bernstein, conductor and composer, Rex Harrison, stage and screen star, and the Negro Ensemble Company, which leaves shortly for London where it will be the sole American representative at the World Theater Festival.

Between awards the audience was treated to excerpts from the musicals, "1776," "Promises, Promises," "Zorbá," and "Hair." There also were scenes from two plays, "Lovers," seen early in the season at the Vivian Beaumont and at present on tour, and "The Great White Hope."

Hosts for the program, directed by Clark Jones, were Alan King and Diahann Carroll.

Originally scheduled as a 1½-hour televised program over the National Broadcasting Company's national network, the ceremonies ran an additional 35 minutes. Two sponsors, Eastern Airlines and Virginia Slims, picked up the bill, paying an amount reported to be $1-million. Half the cost was for the show itself, the remainder for air time.

"The Great White Hope," with James Earl Jones and Jane Alexander, was judged the best play. Mr. Jones was named best actor and Miss Alexander, best supporting actress.

Steve Wasserman

Howard Sackler

Friedman-Abeles

Julie Harris
Best Actress

OBIE AWARDS

OFF BROADWAY BEST GIVEN OBIE AWARDS

The 14th annual Off Broadway theater awards (Obies) by The Village Voice, a weekly newspaper, were presented Saturday at the Village Gate. The judges refused to designate categories. The winners were: The Living Theater ("Frankenstein"), Jeff Weiss ("International Wrestling Match"), Julie Bovasso ("Gloria & Esperanza"), Judith Malina and Julian Beck ("Antigone"), Arlene Rothlein ("The Poor Little Match Girl"), Nathan George and Ron O'Neal ("No Place to be Somebody").

Also, Theater Genesis (sustained excellence), Jules Feiffer ("Little Murders"), Ronald Tavel ("The Boy on the Straight Back Chair"), Israel Horovitz ("The Honest-to-God Schnozzola"), Open Theater ("The Serpent"), Performance Group ("Dionysus in '69") and Boston Om Theater ("Riot").

The judges were Elizabeth Hardwick, The New York Review of Books; Robert Pasolli and Ross Wetzteon, The Village Voice, and Jerry Talmer, The New York Post.

1970

PULITZER PRIZE

By PETER KIHSS

A report on the alleged Songmy massacre of Vietnamese civilians by United States soldiers won the 1970 Pulitzer prize in international reporting yesterday for Seymour Hersh, a free-lance reporter whose article was circulated through the Dispatch News Service.

A black playwright, Charles Gordone, won the drama prize for an Off Broadway play, "No Place to be Somebody"—the first Off Broadway production so honored.

A musical composition on an electronic synthesizer won the music prize for the first time, the award going to "Time's Encomium," by Charles Wuorinen.

Ada Louise Huxtable, architecture critic of The New York Times, became the winner of the first Pulitzer prize for distinguished criticism. This was a new category, set up for criticism or commentary, and was divided in the judging, with Marquis W. Childs of The St. Louis Post-Dispatch taking the award for distinguished commentary.

The gold medal for meritorious public service went to

Songmy Incident Report Wins Pulitzer; Black Writer's Off-Broadway Play Takes Drama Prize

Steve Starr, of the Associated Press bureau in Albany, won the Pulitzer Prize in spot news photography for this photograph of armed students leaving Cornell University's student center after occupying the building last spring.

Newsday of Garden City, L. I., for a three-year investigation and exposé of secret land deals and zoning manipulations by public and political party officeholders.

With 17 individuals named Pulitzer prize-winners in the 54th year of the awards, the laurels for history were carried off by former Secretary of State Dean G. Acheson. This was for his book, "Present at The Creation: My Years in the State Department."

The prizes were announced by Dr. Andrew W. Cordier, president of Columbia University, after approval by the Columbia trustees, who had received recommendations by the 13-member Advisory Board on the Pulitzer Prizes.

A discussion of perhaps five minutes was disclosed to have taken place during the April 9 Advisory Board meeting on the music award and "whether a computer could compose," as one member put it.

The board decided to endorse a jury's recommendation after a few bars of the 12-tone piece composed by Mr. Wuorinen on the RCA Mark II Synthesizer were sung by Vermont C. Royster, editor and vice president of The Wall Street Journal.

Asked about this by telephone yesterday, Mr. Royster first said in a drawl, "You hear such wild rumors these days." But then he confirmed the report, and in response to urging, repeated the performance—"it goes something like this, 'bum, beep, deetely doot.'"

Yesterday's prizes for letters included:

Fiction—"Collected Stories," by Jean Stafford, a novelist who has written for many magazines. A prior winner for short stories was James A. Michener, with "Tales of the South Pacific," in 1948.

Biography—"Huey Long," by T. Harry Williams, professor of history at Louisiana State University, whose subject was the assassinated Senator from Louisiana.

Poetry—"Untitled Subjects," by Richard Howard, the third book of poems by the New York poet and translator.

General Nonfiction—"Gandhi's Truth," by Erik H. Erikson, professor of developmental psychology at Harvard University, whose book was a study of the origins of the assassinated Indian leader's theory of militant nonviolence.

The journalism prizes included:

Local Reporting, General—Thomas Fitzpatrick of The Chicago Sun-Times, for his article published last Oct. 9

against edition deadline pressure, giving his eyewitness account of a battle by the Weatherman faction of Students for a Democratic Society with the Chicago police.

Local Reporting, Special—Harold Eugene Martin of The Montgomery (Ala.) Advertiser, for articles exposing and halting a commercial scheme for using Alabama prisoners for testing drugs.

National Reporting—William J. Seton of The Chicago Daily News, for disclosures on the background of Judge Clement F. Haynsworth Jr., whose nomination to the Supreme Court by President Nixon was rejected by the Senate.

Editorial Writing—Philip L. Geyelin, editor of the editorial page of The Washington Post since 1967, for editorials during 1969.

Cartoons—Thomas F. Darcy, editorial cartoonist for Newsday since September, 1968, for cartoons during 1969.

Spot News Photograph—Steve Starr of the Albany Bureau of The Associated Press, for his photograph of demonstrating black students at Cornell University as they left a university building they had

occupied.

Feature Photography—Dallas Kinney of The Palm Beach Post for a portfolio of pictures of black migrant workers illustrating an eight-part series on their lives in poverty amid surrounding wealth.

Second Award for Newsday

The public service award to Newsday was its second Pulitzer gold medal—the first having been in 1954, for exposing state race track scandals and labor racketeering.

The Times Mirror Company, owner of The Los Angeles Times, announced a definitive agreement yesterday to take control of Newsday. The Times' publisher, Otis Chandler, was touring the Newsday plant when the prize was announced.

With a smile, Mr. Chandler posted a notice, "I'm proud of my staff." Bill D. Moyers, who is expected to leave this week the post of Newsday publisher, which he had held through the three years of the prize-winning inquiry, told a friend he was thinking of adding, "And I'm proud of MY staff."

Newsday's investigations since 1967 have led to convictions of three persons, indictment of five others, discharge of one public official, suspension of four public or party officials and resignation of four others. The articles have also been

credited with leading to a new state law requiring full disclosure of all zoning applications.

Mr. Gordone is apparently the third black to win a Pulitzer prize, following Moneta J. Sleet Jr., photographer, last year, and Gwendolyn Brooks, poetess, in 1950.

Yesterday's announcement of the prizes was moved to the Men's Faculty Club at Columbia from its traditional site at the Graduate School of Journalism. Students claiming to represent 60 of the 100 journalism students had urged delay because of yesterday's student strike in protest against United States military operations in Cambodia.

Two new members of the Advisory Board were named yesterday. They were Price Day, editor in chief of The Baltimore Sun, and Robert J. Donovan, Washington bureau chief of The Los Angeles Times. They were elected to four-year terms, succeeding Erwin D. Canham, editor in chief of The Christian Science Monitor, and Kenneth MacDonald, editor and publisher of The Des Moines Register & Tribune, who had completed a statutory limit of three terms.

Each individual Pulitzer prize carries with it a $1,000 cash award.

NEW YORK DRAMA CRITICS CIRCLE AWARDS

By LOUIS CALTA

The New York Drama Critics Circle yesterday voted "Borstal Boy" the best play of the 1969-70 season, "The Effect of Gamma Rays on Man-in-the-Moon Marigolds" as the best American play and "Company" as the best musical.

"Borstal Boy," Frank McMahon's adaptation of Brendan Behan's autobiography dealing with the late Irish playwright's early prison years in England, also won this year's Tony award for best dramatic work. Although it was written by an American living in Dublin, the critics decided that it was a foreign play since it came from the Abbey Theater and was an adaptation of the writings of Mr. Behan. The circle therefore determined to vote for "the best American play."

"The Effect of Gamma Rays," an Off Broadway play by Paul Zindel, which is now playing at the Mercer-O'Casey Theater, 240 Mercer Street, was judged the best American play.

"Company," the new musical about modern marriage, which has music and lyrics by Stephen Sondheim and a book by George Furth, garnered 13 votes to 7 for "Applause," which had walked

off with top honors at the 24th annual Antoinette Perry (Tony) awards this season.

"Borstal Boy" won the citation on the second ballot, after it failed to get an overall majority on the first. In this event, the circle uses a point system (three points for the critic's preference, two points for his second choice, and one point for the third choice) to name the winner.

The tally on the second ballot for best play was as follows: "Borstal Boy," 26 points; "Marigold," 22; "Indians," 19; "Child's Play," 16; "Last of the Red Hot Lovers," 15; "The Whitehouse Murder Mystery," 6; "Approaching Simone," 6; "The Constant Prince," 6; "Butterflies Are Free," 2; "Operation Sidewinder," 2; "A Scent of Flowers," 2; "Terminal," 2; "Who's Happy Now," 1, and "Whisper in the Dark," 1.

"Marigold" and "Indians" were deadlocked on the first vote for best American play, but the former was proclaimed the winner on a show of hands by 10 to 7 votes. Twenty-one critics participated in the voting, while one was absent.

The presentations will be made next Thursday afternoon at the Algonquin Hotel, where the circle held its annual meeting.

TONY AWARDS

By GEORGE GENT

"Applause" and Lauren Bacall, its star, walked off with top honors as best musical and best actress in a musical last night at the 24th annual presentations of the Antoinette Perry Awards at the Mark Hellinger Theater.

The musical, based on the film "All About Eve" and the Mary Orr story, opened March 30 at the Palace Theater and, despite a few critical reservations about Charles Strouse's music, was marked an instant hit."

"Applause" edged out "Coco" and "Purlie." Miss Bacall, appearing in her first musical on Broadway, won over another Hollywood luminary, Katharine Hepburn, who starred in "Coco," and Dilys Watling of "Georgy."

"Applause" had a book by Betty Comden and Adolph Green and lyrics by Lee Adams. It was produced by Joseph Kipness and Lawrence Kasha, in association with Nederlander Productions.

Captures 4 Awards

The musical about the efforts of a scheming young starlet to supplant an aging star captured four Tonys, including those for direction and choreography, both won by Ron Field.

"Borstal Boy," Frank McMahon's adaptation of Brendan Behan's book about the late Irish playwright's early prison years, was judged best dramatic play

Lauren Bacall in "Applause"

Tammy Grimes
Best dramatic actress

over "Child's Play," "Indians" and "Last of the Red Hot Lovers."

Tammy Grimes, who plays the lovable phony Amanda Prynne in the revival of Noël Coward's 1929 comedy "Private Lives," was named best dramatic actress, topping two-time winner Helen Hayes in "Harvey" and Geraldine Brooks in "Brightower," which has closed.

Fritz Weaver, the martinet master in a Roman Catholic boys' school in Robert Marasco's melodrama, "Child's Play," was named best dramatic actor. His co-star, Ken Howard, who plays the idealistic young teacher, was also named as best actor in a supporting or featured role.

Cleavon Little, who plays Purlie, the little minister with big dreams of a new church and freedom for his people in "Purlie," the musical adapted from Ossie Davis's play "Purlie Victorious," was named best actor in a musical. Blythe Danner, the kooky girl who befriends the blind youth in "Butterflies Are Free," was named best supporting actress in a dramatic role.

For supporting roles in musicals, top awards were won by René Auberjonois, who plays the gay designer in "Coco," and Melba Moore, who drew raves in her Broadway debut as the

knowingly innocent girlfriend in "Purlie."

Joseph Hardy was named best director for his taut handling of "Child's Play," and Jo Mielziner picked up two new Tonys —for scenic and lighting design in "Child's Play"—to add to his three previous awards. Cecil Beaton, who designed the costumes for "Coco," won his fourth Tony, adding to those he won in 1955, 1957 and 1960.

The Tonys—the theater's equivalent of Hollywood's Oscars—are small silver medallions with the traditional masks of comedy and tragedy on one side and the winner's name on the reverse.

The season 453 bollots were sent to drama critics and other members of the press who report on the theater, members of the councils of Actors Equity Association, the Society of Stage Directors and Choreographers, the Dramatists Guild and the scenic artists' union and members of the League of New York Theaters, which sponsors the show under authorization from the American Theater Wing, which founded the Tonys in 1947 in honor of its wartime chairman, Antoinette Perry.

As in the previous three years of the league's sponsorship, Alexander H. Cohen, the producer, planned and organized the ceremonies. The black-tie affair at the 1,554-seat Hellinger was sold out, with patrons paying $5 to $35 to view the procedings.

Award to Miss Streisand

Following the show, the guests, who paid $25 more a ticket, repaired to the Grand Ballroom of the Waldorf-Astoria Hotel for the gala supper ball.

Richard Barr, president of the League of New York Theaters and chairman of its executive committee, announced just prior to the telecast the formation of the National Academy of the Living Theater Foundation and the presentation of its first "On Stage Hall of Fame Award" to Barbra Streisand.

The academy, he said, will publicize, merchandise and promote live theater on a national scale. It will disseminate and gather information about the theater, including surveys on audience demographics, and will study such problems as automated ticket distribution and the feasibility of commercial subsidy for the theater.

Miss Streisand was on hand to receive the award from David Frost.

In addition to these presentations, there were special awards to Noël Coward whose Private Lives brought Tammy Grimes her Tony; Alfred Lunt and Lynne Fontanne, and the New York Shakespeare Festival Public Theater, with Joseph Papp, director.

Between awards, the audience was treated to excerpts from the three musicals nominated — "Applause," "Coco" and "Purlie"—as performed by their respective female leads, Miss Bacall, Miss Hepburn and Melba Moore.

The hosts for the telecast, directed by Clark Jones, were Julie Andrews, Walter Matthau and Shirley MacLaine. The presentations were made by Clive Barnes, drama critic of The New York Times; Michael Caine, Jack Casidy, Claire Bloom, Cary Grant, James Stewart and Robert Stephens, actors, and Mia Farrow, Patricia Neal and Maggie Smith, actresses.

The ceremonies were televised nationally over the network of the National Broadcasting Company. Scheduled to run from 10 to 11:30 P.M., the presentations ran 15 minutes overtime.

Last year, according to estimates by the A. C. Nielsen Company's rating service, 37 million people watched some part of the Tony telecast.

OBIE AWARDS

'Simone' and 'Gamma Rays' Share Off Broadway Prize

Winners of the 15th annual Village Voice Obie awards for the best Off Broadway works and performances were announced yesterday.

The best play award for 1969-70, which carries a cash prize of $1,000, will be shared by Megan Terry's "Approaching Simone" and Paul Zindel's "The Effect of Gamma Rays on Man-in-the-Moon Marigolds." Each year, the Plumsock Foundation makes a cash grant to the best new play.

The best performance award went to Sada Thompson for her portrayal of the mother in the Zindel play. "The Last Sweet Days of Isaac" and "The Me Nobody Knows" were tied for best honors in the musical category. Joe Orton's "What the Butler Saw" was cited as the best foreign play.

1971

PULITZER PRIZE

2d Off Broadway Play Wins Pulitzer

By PETER KIHSS

An Off Broadway play, "The Effect of Gamma Rays on Man-in-the-Moon Marigolds," by Paul Zindel, won the 1971 Pulitzer prize for drama yesterday. The first Pulitzer prize for an Off Broadway play was awarded last year.

For the first time since 1964, there was no Pulitzer prize for fiction. Fiction jurors were understood to have offered three candidates — "Mr. Sammler's Planet," by Saul Bellow; "Losing Battles," by Eudora Welty, and "The Wheel of Love and Other Stories," by Joyce Carol Oates.

The Advisory Board on the Pulitzer Prizes, which receives jury recommendations but may substitute choices of its own, decided in a closed-door meeting, however, that no work qualified under the standard for a distinguished book of fiction by an American author published in 1970. The trustees of Columbia University, who have the ultimate responsibility, upheld the board's view.

Among 17 prizes announced in the 55th yearly awards in journalism, letters and music, the prize for distinguished criticism went to Harold C. Schonberg, music critic of The New York Times. The prize for criticism was first awarded last year, going to Ada Louise Huxtable, architecture critic of The Times.

The gold medal for meritorious public service by a newspaper went to The Winston-Salem (N. C.) Journal and Sentinel for coverage of environmental problems that included blocking of proposed strip mining for aluminum ore endangering thousands of acres of Blue Ridge mountain country.

The Kent State University disorders in which four students were killed by Ohio National Guardsmen's bullets just a year ago today led to two Pulitzer prizes.

One for general local reporting went to the staff of The Akron (Ohio) Beacon Journal for its coverage of the tragedy. The other—for spot news photography—went to a student photographer, John Paul Filo, now 22 years old, of The Valley Daily News and Daily Dispatch of Tarentum and New Kensington, Pa., for a picture

of a distraught girl kneeling over one stain student's body.

The four prizes in letters were:

History — "Roosevelt: The Soldier of Freedom," by James McGregor Burns, the second of two volumes on the life of Franklin D. Roosevelt by the Williams College professor of government.

Biography — "Robert Frost: The Years of Triumph, 1915-1938," by Lawrance R. Thompson, who carried on research since 1939 as the poet's companion with the understanding that the work would not be published during Mr. Frost's lifetime.

Poetry—"The Carrier of Ladders," by William S. Merwin, the seventh volume of his own poetry by an author who has also translated poetry from French, Spanish, Latin and Portuguese.

General Nonfiction — "The Rising Sun," by John Toland, the story of Japan during World War II.

Electronic Music Honored

The Pulitzer prize in music went to "Synchronisms No. 6 for Piano and Electronic Sound," by Mario Davidowsky, associate professor of music at City College and lecturer in music at Columbia. The prize for the mixed-medium work followed last year's Pulitzer prize given for the first time to a composition on an electronic synthesizer.

Among the 11 journalism prizes were:

Special Local Reporting — William Hugh Jones of The Chicago Tribune for exposing bribery of policemen to refer sick poor people to certain private ambulance companies—an investigation in which he trained as a first-aid man and then obtained a job as ambulance driver. Sixteen indictments, including 10 of policemen, resulted.

National Reporting—Lucinda Franks and Thomas Powers of United Press International for a five-article, 12,000-word study on the life and death of Diana Oughton, "The Making of a Terrorist."

International Reporting—Jimmie Lee Hoagland of The Washington Post for reporting on South Africa's apartheid system of racial separation and its effects.

Editorial Writing — Horance G. Davis Jr., a professor at the University of Florida, for more than 30 editorials for The Gainesville (Fla.) Sun in support of peaceful desegregation of Gainesville schools. It was the second Pulitzer prize for editorials by a writer for the newspaper, purchased from Cowles Communications by The New York Times last October.

Cartoons — Paul Conrad of The Los Angeles Times for his editorial cartooning during 1970. It was the second Pulitzer Prize for Mr. Conrad, who won the 1964 award for work for The Denver Post. The most recent two-time winner for different newspapers was Anthony Lewis for national reporting, in 1955 for The Washington Daily News and in 1963 for The New York Times.

Feature Photography — Jack Dykinga of The Chicago Sun-Times for pictures of children in the Lincoln and Dixon State Schools for the Retarded in Illinois.

Prize for Jersey Column

Commentary — William A. Caldwell of The Record, Hackensack, N. J., for his daily column on local affairs, "Simeon Stylites," which he has been writing for more than 40 years.

The prizes provide for $1,000 awards in each category, aside from the gold medal for public service. The two United Press International writers, Miss Franks and Mr. Powers, will each receive $500.

Wallace Carroll, editor and publisher of the Winston-Salem newspapers, said the entire news and editorial staff of both his morning and afternoon dailies had participated in an aggressive effort for "protecting the environment."

He said they had found the Gibbsite Corporation of Rochester, N. Y., had obtained liens on thousands of acres to develop strip mining in an area whose great asset was tourism. The newspapers' campaigns, he said, aroused community and

business opposition, and the company withdrew its plans.

Rumors Corrected

Mr. Carroll said the newspapers were currently crusading to save Bald Head Island as a subtropical wilderness area. The island is threatened by developers' proposals for a luxury beach community. Gov. Robert Scott, Mr. Carroll said, has declared his determination to save the island.

The Akron Beacon Journal's coverage of the Kent State University turmoil under deadline pressure was credited with describing both what happened and why, in a balanced presentation despite wild rumors.

The prize-winning "Marigolds" drama has been running at the New Theater, 154 East 54th Street, since April 7, 1970, when it opened just a week past the deadline for plays to be considered for the 1971 prizes.

Mr. Zindel's play centers on a teen-age girl and her faith in humanity, despite discouraging life with a slattern mother and epileptic sister. The title comes from her school essay on experiments with atomic energy.

This year's members of the Advisory Board were:

Dr. William J. McGill, president of Columbia University; Mr. Carroll; Benjamin C. Bradlee, The Washington Post; John Cowles Jr., The Minneapolis Star & Tribune; Price Day, The Baltimore Sun; William B. Dickinson, The Philadelphia Bulletin; Robert J. Donovan, The Los Angeles Times; Lee Hills, Knight Newspapers.

Also Sylvan Meyer, The Miami News; Newbold Noyes Jr., The Washington Star; Joseph Pulitzer Jr., The St. Louis Post-Dispatch; James Reston, The New York Times; Vermont C. Royster, retired editor of The Wall Street Journal, and Prof. John Hohenberg, prize administrator.

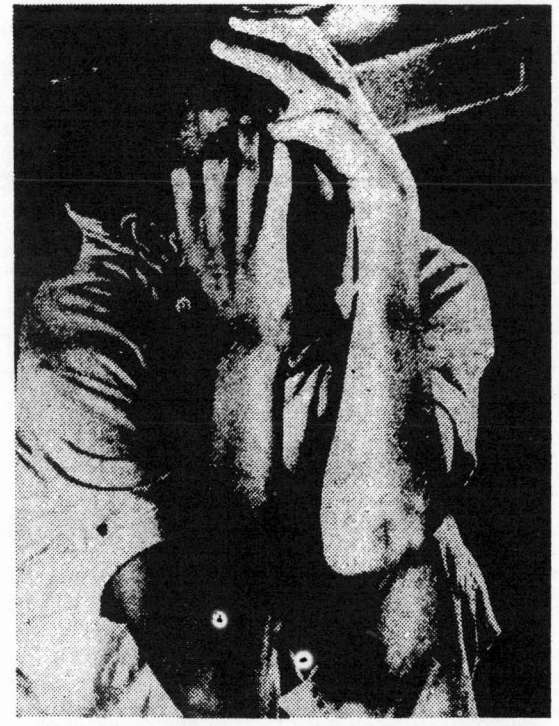

Jack Dykinga of Chicago Sun-Times won Feature Photography award for series on schools for retarded children.

NEW YORK DRAMA CRITICS CIRCLE AWARDS

Drama Critics Circle Selects 'Home' and 'Follies' as Bests

By LOUIS CALTA

The New York Drama Critics Circle yesterday picked "Home," a British import, as the best play of the 1970-71 season and "Follies" as the best musical.

An award for the best American play went to "The House of Blue Leaves," the Off Broadway comedy by John Guare, currently at the Truck & Warehouse Theatre, 79 East Fourth Street.

"Home," written by David Storey, also won The London Evening Standard award for best play of this season. It was produced here by Alexander H. Cohen and the Royal Court Theater in association with Clinton Wilder. A play about one day in the lives of four mental patients in a home, it opened at the Morosco Theater on Nov. 17, 1970, and closed after 111 performances.

Sir John Gielgud, Sir Ralph Richardson, Dandy Nichols and

Mona Washbourne played the leading parts in "Home," which was directed by Lindsay Anderson.

"Follies," with a book by James Goldman and music and lyrics by Stephen Sondheim, opened at the Winter Garden April 4 under the producing banner of Harold Prince.

"Home" won the citation on the second ballot, after it failed to get an over-all majority on the first. In this event, the circle uses a point system (three points for the critics' first preference, two points for his second choice and one point for the third choice) to name the winner.

"Follies" won top honors in its field on the first ballot, receiving 11 votes. "The Me Nobody Knows" received five, "No, No, Nanette" got one and "Two by Two" also got one.

"The House of Blue Leaves," which deals with a Queens composer and his problems

with his wife and mistress, won 6 votes out of 19 on the first ballot for the best play category. "Home" and "All Over" received four each, "Subject to Fits" 2, "The Philanthropist" 2 and "Sleuth" and "The Trial of the Catonsville Nine" one each.

The tally on the second ballot for best play was as follows: "Home," 24 points, "The House of Blue Leaves," 23 points; "The Philanthropist," 19; "All Over," 13; "Subject to Fits," 11; "The Trial of the Catonsville Nine," 11; "Sleuth," 5; "Alice in Wonderland," 3; "Father's Day," 3; "Place Without Doors." 2; "Les Blancs," 2; "Story Theater." 2; "Steambath," 2; "The Fabulous Miss Maria," 1, and "The Gingerbread Lady," 1.

TONY AWARDS

'Sleuth' and 'Company' Voted Tonys; Miss Stapleton and Bedford Winners

By McCANDLISH PHILLIPS

A constellation of talents that created the diamond-bright fire of "Company" won top honors last night in the theater's Antoinette Perry Awards, better known as Tonys.

"Company" took 6 of the 19 prize medallions and thus outdid "The Me Nobody Knows" and "The Rothschilds" as Broadway's best musical. "Sleuth," the British import, captured the award for the best play.

Another musical, the revival of the 46-year-old "No, No, Nanette," was not nominated in the best-musical category but it gathered four other Tonys and became a big winner of the evening.

"Sleuth," Anthony Shaffer's inricately and cleverly plotted mystery thriller, prevailed over "Home," "Story Theater" and "The Philanthropist." It was produced by Helen Bonfils, Morton Gottlieb and Michael White.

The British had gained a monopoly in the best dramatic actor field by taking all four nominations.

3 Formidable Losers

Brian Bedford captured the honor for portraying the aging Arnolphe in Molière's "The School for Wives," now at the Lyceum Theater. Mr. Bedford triumphed in a formidable class, over Alec McCowen, Sir John Gielgud and Sir Ralph Richardson.

Maureen Stapleton took a Tony as the best actress for her acrid comedy performance in Neil Simon's "The Gingerbread Lady."

The award for the best actress in a musical went to the indominably sparkling Helen Gallagher of "No, No, Nanette." When Patsy Kelly of the same show won as the best supporting actress in a musical, she said, "I'm going home now and faint."

Hal Linden, looking as patriarchial as his role, triumphed as the best actor in a musical as the kindly progenitor of the wealth-accumulators, "The Rothschilds."

The awards for the best supporting actor and the best supporting actress in plays went to Paul Sand of "Story Theater" and Rae Allen of "And Miss Reardon Drinks A Little."

Two for Sondheim

Stephen Sondheim made two consecutive appearances

Dennis Breck from Black Star

Anthony Quayle and Keith Baxter in "Sleuth," best play

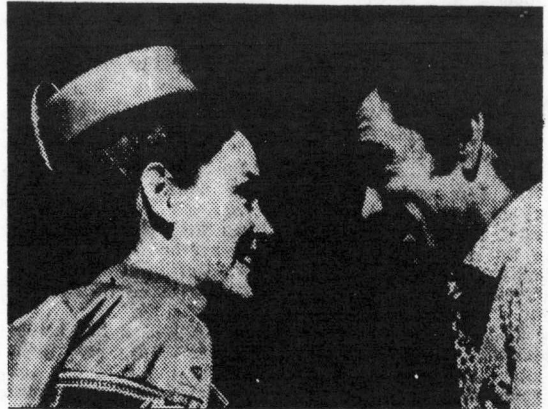

Susan Browning and Dean Jones in "Company," which was voted best musical play in Tony Awards last night.

in the gleam of the winner's spotlight, first as the composer of the best music and then as the writer of the best lyrics, both for "Company."

He made his remarks on the first round and said simply, "It's even nice to win two," when called the second time. George Furth took the award for the writing best book for a musical, again for "Company."

The stars were out last night on Broadway, not in private orbits but in dazzling droves, for the annual presentation.

A sellout audience of 1,597 persons, who had paid a $35 top for what an agent described as "the hottest ticket in town," filed into the Palace Theater through a throng of eager star-gazers who had gathered early to get a glimpse of the event.

The show ran 17 minutes past its scheduled two-hour cutoff at 11 P.M. on the American Broadcasting Company's TV network. Acceptance speeches were limited to 15-second effusions of gratitude and "I-couldn't-have-done-it-with-out-Jones" disclaimers. A few took longer.

Lauren Bacall and Angela Lansbury, both past winners, were the hostesses for the Palace ceremony. They were joined by two hosts with identical initials, Anthony Quayle and Anthony Quinn.

Tension built through the first hour as several entries shared the early honors. By 9:45 P.M., "No, No, Nanette" had taken a 3-to-1 lead over both "Company" and "The Rothschilds" in total awards won.

Moments later, "Company" gained its second Tony when Harold Prince, the prolific creator of musical hits, went forward to say a quiet word of thanks for designation as the "best director—musical."

"The Rothschilds" gained its first award when Keene Curtis took the "best supporting actor-musical prize for his tour de force in filling four roles, including those of Prince William of Hesse and Prince Metternich. Mr. Curtis, who has a shining pate, said he was grateful to follow the famously bald Yul Brynner onto the stage. "Touché," a spectator said, "Or toupée."

One major category, that for the best director of a play, was announced before the ceremony went on the air. It went to Peter Brook for "A Midsummer Night's Dream."

Brian Bedford
Best dramatic actor

Maureen Stapleton, awarded best dramatic actress, with Ayn Ruyman in play, **"The Gingerbread Lady."**

Hal Linden
Best actor, musical

Vernon L. Smith from Scope

Helen Gallagher
Best actress, musical

Silver and diamonds set a brilliant motif for the evening. Women swept into the theater from limousines, appropriately bejeweled and gowned. Men wore black-tie attire. It was the silver anniversary of the Tony Awards, first presented in 1947.

Even 14-year-old Gerry Cohen, son of Alexander H. Cohen, the producer of the two-hour spectacular, was commanded to appear in the correct dress by his father.

The production was directed by Clark Jones. It was written by Mr. Cohen's wife, Hildy Parks. The ceremony had the look of a Tony-award-winning musical or, more exactly, of 25 of them.

In the past, songs from the nominated musicals supplied a melodic bridge from award to award. Last night, top songs from 25 best musicals,

one for each year, were performed in solos and duets by a roster of star performers.

Gwen Verdon sang "Whatever Lola Wants" from "Damn Yankees" of 1956; Robert Preston voiced his ominous warning of "Trouble in River City" from "The Music Man" of 1958, and Yul Brynner and Patricia Morison exulted in a joyous moment of East-meets-West accord, leaping through the "Shall We Dance?" number from "The King and I" of 1952, in this revue-like review of hits.

The Tonys are given in memory of Antoinette Perry, actress and executive director of the American Theater Wing, who died in 1946.

The Tony itself is a 3-inch silvered medallion bearing the masks of comedy and tragedy. It cannot betray any secrets because it is not in-

scribed in advance. Tonys are handed out as unfilled blanks.

"It upsets some of the winners when they have to give their Tonys back almost as soon as they get them," a member of the production staff acknowledged. The medallions are engraved with the specifics and returned to winners later.

Others who suffered this sweet deprivation were Boris Aronson, judged the best scenic designer, for "Company"; Raoul Pene du Bois, the best costume designer, for "No, No, Nanette"; R. H. Poindexter, the best lighting designer, for "Story Theater," and Donald Saddler, the best choreographer, for "No, No, Nanette."

TONY AWARDS

By McCANDLISH PHILLIPS

The work of Joseph Papp, Off Broadway's gift to Broadway, ran off with the top honors last night in the theater's Antoinette Perry Awards, as two of his productions—one originating uptown, the other downtown—swept to victory in a surprise outcome.

"Two Gentlemen of Verona," which opened last July in the Delacorte Theater in Central Park and reopened on Broadway on Dec. 2, was judged the best musical of the year. And "Sticks and Bones" was named best play.

It was believed to be the first time that any producer had swept both categories, straight play and musical, in one year, making the triumph all the sweeter for the prolific Mr. Papp.

Cliff Gorman was named best actor in a play for his brilliant evocation of the late Lenny Bruce in "Lenny." The award for best actress in a play went to an artistic and sentimental favorite on Broadway, Sada Thompson, for her tour de force in four roles in "Twigs."

Phil Silvers, a veteran Broadway and motion picture comic who has often been second banana in Hollywood and top banana on Broadway, won the award as best actor in a musical for his performance in the revival of "A Funny Thing Happened on the Way to the Forum."

Alexis Smith won in a field of four nominees as best actress in a musical for her role in "Follies."

The surprise of the evening was the victory of "Two Gentlemen of Verona" as the

best musical play. It came near the end of the more than two-hour ceremony. televised nationally from the Broadway Theater, and it drew "oohs" from a capacity audience of 1,758, which had watched "Follies" rack up seven awards in early returns.

Sada Thompson
Best Actress in a Play

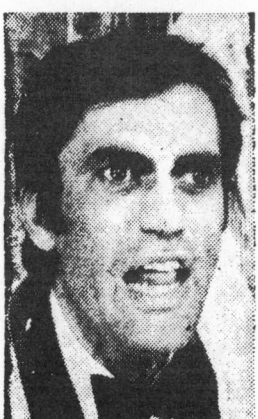
Cliff Gorman
Best Actor in a Play

1972

NEW YORK DRAMA CRITICS CIRCLE AWARDS

Critics Vote 2 Papp Shows Best of Year

By LOUIS CALTA

The New York Drama Critics Circle yesterday selected "Sticks and Bones" as the best play and "Two Gentlemen of Verona" as the best musical of the 1971-72 season.

Both productions, the work of Joseph Papp, founder-producer of the New York Shakespeare Festival, garnered top honors in the Antoinette Perry Awards last month.

"Sticks and Bones" by David Rabe, said to be an autobiographical play, opened in October at the Public Theater and was moved to the John Golden on March 1. "Two Gentlemen of Verona"

opened last July at the Delacorte Theater in Central Park and reopened Dec. 2 at the St. James.

The critics designated Jean Genet's "The Screens," which was produced last November by the Chelsea Theater Center of Brooklyn, in residence at the Brooklyn Academy of Music, as the best foreign play. The drama, set against the French-Algerian war, won 35 votes.

In the voting for best play, Jason Miller's "That Championship Season" also a product of the New York Shakespeare Festival, was runner-up with 27 votes to 35 for "Sticks and Bones." Mr. Genet's "The Screens" received 18.

The critics also passed a resolution noting that "certain producers have denied press tickets to the membership of the circle" and "censured such practices." In the future," the critics noted, "instances of this kind will be brought to the attention of the entire membership of the circle."

Some critics, it was reported, already favor "more decisive and more specific steps taken against such producers," but no further action was included in the resolution.

The presentations will be made next week at the Algonquin Hotel, where the Critics Circle held its meeting.

Drama Critics' Recount Deposes 'Winning' Play

The New York Drama Critics Circle erred on Monday in adding up the votes for the best play of the 1971-72 season.

Henry Hewes, circle president, said "That Championship Season" by Jason Miller, had won the critics' award with 37 votes and not "Sticks and Bones," by David Rabe, which received 36, as the circle previously reported. The error was discovered by Mr. Hewes when he tabulated voting for publication in the Saturday Review, the weekly magazine for which he serves as drama critic.

Mr. Hewes said he could not recall of a similar instance in the history of the circle.

Special Citation Voted By Critics to Rabe Play

The New York Drama Critics Circle will give a special citation to David Rabe's "Sticks and Bones," which erroneously had been adjudged the best drama of the 1971-72 season because of a mistake in the tabulation of the critics' votes.

A recheck by Henry Hewes, circle president, revealed that Jason Miller's "That Championship Season" had won the award.

The circle also is warding a special citation to Harold Pinter's "Old Times," which lost by one vote to Jean Genet's "The Screens" in the best foreign play category.

Zodiac
Jonelle Allen as Silvia in "Two Gentlemen of Verona"

Drew Snyder, left, and Tom Aldredge in a scene from "Sticks and Bones"

'Friedman-Abeles

one for best supporting actor in a play to Vincent Gardenia, who brought a touch of ethnic novelty to the event by making his acceptance speech in Italian.

The scene outside the theater before the big show began was, in the words of one observer, "crowded, crushed and chaotic" and, he might have added, almost comic in its confusion.

Twenty policemen tried to sort the ticket-holders from the gawkers and, finally, one of them said, "All right — anybody who has tickets, up against the wall." It was an earnest, if not elegantly stated, appeal designed to get a line of ingress organized and moving.

John Braswell, "The Only Jealousy of Emer."

Distinguished Performance: Elizabeth Wilson, "Sticks and Bones"; Marilyn Sokol and Kathleen Widdoes, "The Beggar's Opera"; Danny Sewell, "The Homecoming," and Marilyn Chris, "Kaddish."

Also, Jeanne Hepple and Ed Zang, "The Reliquary of Mr. and Mrs. Potterfield"; Ron Faber, "And They Put Handcuffs on the Flowers"; Alex Bradford, "Don't Bother Me, I Can't Cope"; Maurice Blanc, "The Celebration: Jooz/Guns/Movies/The Abyss," and Salome Bey, "Love Me, Love My Children."

Alexis Smith
Best Actress in a Musical

the two categories had become one—best score. Mr. Sondheim won it for "Follies." That show was also honored for having the best lighting, costumes, scenic design, choreography, actress and director.

Boris Aronson, scenic designer for "Follies," professed to be "speechless" in taking his fifth Tony award, named for the wartime chairman of the American Theater Wing.

The house was roused to standing ovations twice at the appearance of the special award winners, Richard Rodgers and Ethel Merman, two of the fixed stars of the musical theater. The program was produced by Alexander H. Cohen.

"Sticks and Bones" came to Broadway from Off Broadway, where it had opened in the Public Theater last October. The drama moved uptown on March 1 to the John Golden Theater.

The play tells of the experience of a soldier who returns, blinded, from Vietnam to his family and comes tap-tap-tapping back into their lives, a kind of specter representing things they do not want to know.

It is a somewhat autobiographical statement for David Rabe, its 31-year-old author, who served in Vietnam 11 months in 1966, came home, told of it, or tried to, and later said: "People didn't want to listen. It was a kind of closed-mindedness that made you feel like you were talking to walls."

Mr. Rabe tried to get away with his Tony without making any remarks, but he was detained on stage long enough to spill out a brief statement of his surprise.

"I really didn't think it was possible, I really didn't," he said in apparent reference to the triumph of a play that is essentially an expression of protest against a populace that cares too little about the hell its sons are raising in a small distant land.

For her work in the Rabe play, Elizabeth Wilson was voted best supporting actress. The Tony for best supporting actor in a musical went to Larry Blyden of "Forum."

In most of its first hour, the awards ceremony had the look of a no-surprise party for Hal Prince, the ranking genius of the musical form on Broadway, who collects Tonys almost as easily as some men collect wide ties.

By 9:18 P.M., 15 minutes after the program had started, his "Follies" had waltzed away with the first three Tonys and into a 3-0 lead against the entire field.

Then the producer's endurance champion, "Fiddler on the Roof," which has run seven and a half years on the Great White Way, received a special award.

A few moments later, Michael Bennett took a fourth award for "Follies" as best choreographer, later to be joined by Forence Klotz, for the costumes and Tharon Musser for the lighting.

Mr. Prince and Mr. Bennett made a joint appearance to receive the award for best director of a musical, for "Follies."

Mr. Prince is the owner of nine previous Tonys, seven as a producer and two as a director.

The monopolistic feeling of the evening knew a moment's early relief when Linda Hopkins took the award as the best supporting actress in a musical for her role in "Inner City."

Crowded and Chaotic

It was not until after 10 o'clock that a semblance of suspense was introduced into the proceeding — essentially a race to see which show would win the right to post the highest number of Tonys on its marque—when "Prisoner of Second Avenue" took two awards, one to Mike Nichols as best director and

OBIE AWARDS

'MUTATION SHOW' AWARDED TOP OBIE

Prizes Given for Merit in Off Broadway Theater

"The Mutation Show," produced by the Open Theater, won the Obie Award and $500 cash prize last night as the best theater piece of the Off Broadway season.

Jane Fonda's antiwar troupe received a special citation for its "Free the Army" show. The 17th annual awards were announced at the Village Gate, Bleecker and Thompson Streets. Groucho Marx was host at the ceremonies.

The awards, whose name is taken from O.B. for "Off Broadway," are presented by The Village Voice, the weekly newspaper.

Micki Grant was cited for her music and lyrics for "Don't Bother Me, I Can't Cope," and Elizabeth Swados won an Obie for her score for the Cafe La Mama production of "Medea."

The award for best visual effects went to Allen Ginsberg and Video Free America for "Kaddish."

The judges this year were Dick Brukenfeld, Michael Feingold, John Lahr, Julius Novick, Arthur Sainer, Michael Smith and Martin Washburn, all of The Voice staff.

Other awards included:

Special citations to Theater of Latin America for "Latin American Fair of Opinion; Meredith Monk for "Vessel," and Charles Stanley for his "all-around contribution" to Off Broadway.

Distinguished Direction: Tom Sydorick for "20th Century Tar"; Michael Smith, "Country Music"; Mel Shapiro, "Two Gentlemen of Verona," and Wilford Leach and

Phil Silvers
Best Actor in a Musical

"Two Gentlemen," a light-hearted romp through the Shakespeare comedy, with a New York accent added to the Bard's iambic pentameter, moves to rock and Latin American beats and bluesy jazz. John Guare and Mel Shapiro shared honors for the best book.

Stephen Sondheim, who won two Tonys last year for the music and lyrics to "Company," could not have hoped to repeat this time, because

Indexes

How To Use The Index

This index covers all the theater reviews printed in The New York Times during the period 1920-1970. It is divided into two sections: Titles and Persons.

The Title Index includes some 21,000 entries, listing each play reviewed by title. The Persons Index lists by name every performer, producer, director, playwright, etc., mentioned in the reviews, with the function in parentheses following the name, and the titles of the plays with which the person was connected, in chronological order. Additional explanations for each section are given on the sectional title page.

Citations in this index are by year, month, section of newspaper (if applicable), day, page and column; for example, 1928, Ap 1, IX 1:1. The citations also serve to locate the reviews in bound volumes and microfilm editions of The Times as well as in the volumes containing exclusively the reprints of all Times theater reviews.

In the citations, the months are abbreviated as follows:

Ja—January	My—May	S—September
F—February	Je—June	O—October
Mr—March	Jl—July	N—November
Ap—April	Ag—August	D—December

Titles

NOTE: All plays reviewed in The Times are listed here alphabetically by title. Titles are inverted only if they begin with an article ("Dr. Faustus" is listed under D, not F, but "The Dover Road" is listed under D, not T). Titles beginning with a number are alphabetized as though the number were spelled out. Wherever possible, foreign plays are entered under both the English and the foreign-language title. Plays reviewed more than once and plays with identical titles are given multiple listings; hence, "Hamlet" includes almost 150 listings.

For an explanation of the Index generally and of the citations, see facing page.

A

A Farkas 1928,O 28,IX,2:1
A la Carte 1927,Ag 18,25:3; 1927,Ag 28,VII,1:1
A la Mode de Chez Nous 1929,My 26,IX,4:1
A l'Ombre de la Guillotine 1928,D 30,VIII,1:3
A Nagyasszony 1927,O 30,IX,4:1
A Quoi Penses-Tu? 1928,O 28,IX,2:7
A Tabornok 1928,D 2,X,4:7
A Vol d'Oiseau 1926,D 5,VIII,8:7
Aaron Slick From Punkin Crick 1935,Ap 6,11:4
Abbe et la Ministre, L' 1927,O 2,VIII,2:4
Abdication 1948,S 28,32:5
Abe Lincoln in Illinois 1938,O 4,20:1;
 1938,O 17,12:2; 1938,O 23,IX,1:1;
 1939,Ap 23,X,1:1; 1939,Jl 30,IX,1:1; 1963,Ja 23,5:2
Abi Gezunt 1949,O 10,19:4
Abide With Me 1935,N 22,19:2
Abie's Irish Rose 1922,My 24,22:4;
 1926,Ag 29,VII,1:1; 1927,Mr 29,23:3;
 1927,Ap 12,24:5; 1927,My 8,VII,1:5;
 1927,Jl 31,VII,1:3; 1927,S 18,VII,1:1;
 1927,S 30,29:3; 1927,O 23,VIII,2:4;
 1928,Je 10,VIII,2:8; 1928,D 20,24:5;
 1937,My 13,30:2; 1954,N 19,19:1
Abisso 1920,O 10,VI,1:8
Abortion 1959,O 28,40:4
Abraham 1926,Mr 29,24:2
Abraham Cochrane 1964,F 18,26:1
Abraham Lincoln 1920,Mr 14,V,5:1;
 1920,My 23,VI,8:2; 1927,Ja 21,12:3; 1928,N 13,31:2;
 1929,O 22,26:3; 1934,D 1,8:6; 1940,Ap 28,IX,1:7;
 1940,My 5,X,1:2
Abraham's Offering 1938,D 18,IX,4:2
Absalom 1956,My 17,37:2
Absconders, The 1931,Ja 25,VIII,4:1
Absence of a Cello 1964,S 22,45:1; 1965,S 9,36:3
Absent Father 1932,O 18,23:5
Absolutely Freeee 1967,My 25,58:1
Accent on Youth 1934,D 26,19:1; 1935,Jl 2,24:3;
 1935,Jl 9,24:5; 1935,Jl 9,24:4; 1935,Jl 11,24:3;
 1935,Ag 13,20:3; 1935,S 29,X,1:6
Accordeur, L' 1928,D 30,VIII,1:3
According to Law 1940,Mr 20,36:2; 1944,Je 2,20:3
Accounting for Love 1954,D 2,37:6
Accumulator 1970,F 4,36:1
Accused 1925,S 20,VIII,2:4; 1925,S 30,20:1;
 1925,O 11,VIII,1:1
Ace, The 1933,Ag 25,12:4; 1933,S 17,X,1:6
Ace of Clubs 1950,Jl 8,7:2; 1950,Ag 13,II,1:5
Acheteuse, L' 1930,My 4,XI,2:6
Achilles Had a Heel 1935,Ap 28,X,1:1;
 1935,O 14,20:2
Acid Wine 1964,My 23,15:2
Acquisition, The 1968,D 31,19:1; 1969,Ja 12,II,1:1
Acquittal, The 1920,Ja 6,18:2; 1920,Ja 11,VIII,2:1
Acropolis 1933,N 24,25:8; 1933,D 10,X,3:6;
 1968,Ag 24,24:3; 1969,N 5,40:1; 1969,N 30,II,1:4
Across the Blue 1937,Je 1,27:1
Across the Board on Tomorrow Morning
 1942,Mr 21,13:5; 1942,Ag 18,17:1;
 1942,Ag 23,VIII,1:1; 1961,O 23,22:5
Across the Street 1924,Mr 16,VII,2:1;
 1924,Mr 25,24:1; 1924,Mr 30,VIII,1:1
Actis 1961,N 23,50:2
Actors Fund Fete 1942,F 23,24:5
Actress, The 1947,D 29,21:5
Actresses Will Happen 1941,Je 15,IX,2:6
Acts of St Peter 1934,Ap 22,IX,1:6
Ada Beats the Drum 1930,My 9,20:4
Adam et Eve et Cie 1928,Je 17,VIII,1:4
Adam Had Two Sons 1932,Ja 17,VIII,3:5;
 1932,Ja 21,17:1
Adam Solitaire 1925,N 7,19:2; 1925,N 15,VIII,1:1
Adam's Apple 1929,Je 11,27:5
Adams' Wife 1931,D 29,27:1
Adaptation 1969,F 11,27:1; 1969,F 23,II,1:1;
 1970,Mr 12,46:1
Adding Machine, The 1923,Mr 20,24:1;
 1923,Mr 25,VIII,1:1; 1923,Ap 1,VII,1:1;
 1924,Mr 23,VIII,1:3; 1928,Ja 29,VIII,2:6;
 1948,N 18,35:2; 1956,F 10,17:1; 1970,D 5,40:1
Adieux, Les 1957,F 19,36:1
Admirable Bashville, The 1956,F 21,38:1
Admirable Crichton, The 1920,F 29,V,5:3;
 1931,Mr 10,23:2; 1931,Mr 29,VIII,1:1
Admiral, The 1924,Ap 25,20:2; 1924,My 4,VIII,1:1;
 1929,Ja 23,21:1
Adoption, The 1965,N 14,132:1
Adorable Julia 1954,N 28,II,3:1
Adorable Liar, The 1926,Ag 31,15:2

Adrienne 1923,My 29,10:4
Adventure 1928,S 26,25:2
Adventure Story 1949,Mr 19,11:2
Adventurer, The 1935,N 11,21:1
Adventures of Huckleberry Finn 1968,Ap 15,41:1
Adventures of Marco Polo, The 1941,D 28,I,31:7
Adventures of the Black Girl in Her Search for God,
 The 1969,Mr 22,24:4
Adventures of the Worthy Soldier Schwejk, The
 1928,Mr 4,IX,2:1
Adventurous Age, The 1927,F 8,20:1
Advertising April 1923,F 4,VII,1:4
Advertising of Kate, The 1922,My 9,22:2;
 1922,My 14,VII,1:1
Advise and Consent 1960,O 19,57:3; 1960,N 18,25:1;
 1960,N 27,II,1:1
Advocate, The 1963,O 15,46:7; 1963,O 27,II,1:1
Affair, The 1962,S 21,34:2; 1962,O 7,II,1:1
Affair of Honor 1956,Ap 7,12:3
Affair of State, An 1930,N 20,30:3
Affaire, Une 1931,D 13,VIII,2:2
Affaires Sont les Affaires, Les 1924,Mr 11,17:1;
 1924,Mr 16,VIII,1:1
Affairs of State 1950,S 26,37:2; 1950,O 1,II,1:1;
 1952,Ag 22,12:2
Affranchis, Les 1927,N 6,IX,4:1
Afgar 1920,N 9,13:2; 1920,N 14,VI,1:1
Afore Night Come 1964,Je 26,34:1
Africana 1927,Jl 12,29:2; 1927,S 4,VII,1:1;
 1934,N 27,26:3
After All 1929,My 26,IX,1:3; 1930,Mr 12,32:7;
 1931,D 4,28:4
After All That 1931,F 22,VIII,3:5
After Dark 1926,O 10,VIII,2:1; 1928,D 11,35:2
After Dark: or, Neither Maid, Wife nor Widow
 1929,F 10,IX,1:1
After-Dinner Evening With Oskar Werner, An
 1967,Mr 27,39:1
After Holbein 1931,Je 17,32:3
After October 1936,F 22,13:3; 1936,My 17,IX,2:2
After Such Pleasures 1934,Ja 6,18:6; 1934,F 8,15:2
After the Angels 1961,F 11,27:5
After The Ball 1954,Je 11,19:3; 1954,Jl 18,II,1:6
After the Dance 1939,Jl 16,IX,2:3
After the Fall 1964,Ja 24,18:1; 1964,F 2,II,1:1;
 1965,Ja 25,21:6; 1966,F 1,26:1
After the Rain 1966,S 3,13:5; 1967,O 10,54:1;
 1967,O 22,II,3:7
After the Theatre 1942,S 28,13:1
After Tomorrow 1930,Ag 10,VIII,2:3;
 1931,Ag 27,22:4
Afternoon Storm 1948,Ap 12,24:2
Afterwards 1933,N 26,IX,3:6
Agamemnon 1936,N 2,25:6; 1967,Jl 24,23:1
Agamemnon's Death 1962,N 11,82:4
Agatha Calling 1935,O 1,27:5
Agatha Sue, I Love You 1966,D 15,61:1
Age and Grace 1956,F 21,38:2
Age de Juliette, L' 1935,Ja 13,IX,2:1
Age du Fer, L' 1932,N 13,IX,2:5
Age of Innocence, The 1928,N 18,IX,2:6;
 1928,N 28,24:2
Aged 26 1936,D 22,32:1
Agent 666, L' 1923,My 30,10:5
Ages of Man 1958,S 22,26:1; 1958,D 29,21:1;
 1959,Jl 10,28:2; 1963,Ap 15,36:1
Aglavaine and Selysette 1922,Ja 4,11:1
Ah, Wilderness! 1933,S 26,26:3; 1933,O 3,28:2;
 1934,My 1,26:3; 1934,O 30,23:1; 1935,Ag 20,25:1;
 1936,My 5,26:1; 1936,Je 7,IX,2:1; 1936,Je 28,IX,1:6;
 1940,Ag 20,23:2; 1941,O 3,26:2; 1941,O 12,IX,1:1;
 1953,F 7,10:6; 1953,F 15,II,1:1; 1954,Ag 21,20:4;
 1967,Mr 19,II,7:1; 1969,N 9,86:1
Ah! Wah! 1932,My 11,15:2
Aiglon, L' 1924,O 21,21:1; 1925,O 31,20:3;
 1926,O 3,29:5; 1927,D 27,24:3; 1934,N 5,22:2
Ain't It the Truth 1921,D 20,20:3
Air-Minded 1932,F 11,17:3
Airways, Inc 1929,F 21,30:5
Akokawe 1970,Je 5,21:1
Aladdin and His Wonderful Lamp 1963,O 21,39:1
Alarm Clock, The 1923,D 25,26:2
Alba, Il Gioro, La Notte, L' 1931,My 18,21:4
Alcestiade 1956,Je 29,11:5; 1957,N 6,43:1
Alcestis 1927,My 22,II,8:4
Alcestis Comes Back 1962,Ap 24,33:1
Alchemist, The 1931,Je 5,27:1; 1932,Ag 28,IX,1:1;
 1948,My 7,31:4; 1962,N 29,44:1; 1964,S 15,33:1;
 1966,O 14,48:1; 1966,O 30,II,1:1; 1969,Je 12,51:1;
 1969,Je 22,II,1:7; 1970,Ag 26,36:1
Alcide Pepis 1923,O 30,17:2
Alexander 1938,Ag 5,11:2; 1938,Ag 14,IX,2:2
Alexander Hamilton 1949,Mr 30,29:2

Alexander Pushkin 1928,Ja 27,14:2
Alfie 1964,D 18,27:1
Ali Baba 1951,Mr 27,34:2
Ali Baba and the Forty Thieves 1926,D 23,23:2;
 1927,D 23,16:7; 1956,S 3,10:1; 1970,D 29,40:1
Alias Jimmy Valentine 1921,D 9,20:3
Alibi 1928,Je 10,VIII,1:3
Alice Adams 1946,Mr 9,9:4; 1947,Ag 5,26:1
Alice in Arms 1945,F 1,18:4
Alice in Wonderland 1920,Ap 13,12:1;
 1930,D 25,31:3; 1932,D 12,18:3; 1932,D 25,IX,1:1;
 1933,F 2,21:2; 1935,N 10,43:5; 1947,Ap 7,19:2;
 1947,Ap 13,II,1:1; 1967,Mr 20,27:1; 1970,O 9,43:1;
 1970,O 18,II,3:1
Alice Sit-By-The-Fire 1932,Mr 8,19:3
Alice Takat 1930,F 23,III,7:2; 1936,F 11,19:2
Alice Through the Glass Lightly 1968,Ap 15,41:1
Alien Corn 1933,F 14,19:5; 1933,F 21,17:2;
 1933,F 26,IX,1:1; 1935,Ja 20,X,3:8; 1939,Jl 6,26:8;
 1939,Jl 23,IX,2:3
Alien Shadow 1949,Jl 22,16:5
Alison's House 1930,D 2,31:2; 1931,My 10,VIII,1:1;
 1931,My 12,29:2; 1932,N 13,IX,3:4
Alive and Kicking 1950,Ja 18,25:5
All Alone Susie 1923,N 4,VIII,2:7
All American 1962,Mr 20,44:1; 1962,Ap 8,II,1:2
All Around the Town 1952,Mr 26,33:2
All Bow Down 1935,Ag 6,20:4
All by Myself 1964,Je 16,47:1
All Desirable Young Men 1936,Jl 22,22:5
All Dressed Up 1925,S 10,28:1
All Editions 1936,D 23,17:2
All for All 1943,S 30,25:2
All for Love 1938,Ap 5,19:4; 1949,Ja 24,16:5
All Gaul Is Divided 1947,Je 24,27:3
All God's Chillum Got Shoes 1932,Ap 23,11:3
All God's Chillun Got Wings 1924,My 16,22:3;
 1924,My 18,VII,1:1; 1924,Ag 19,9:1;
 1924,Ag 24,VII,1:1; 1932,Mr 27,VIII,3:3;
 1933,Mr 14,19:4
All Good Americans 1933,D 6,29:2
All Gummed Up 1923,Ja 29,11:2
All in a Lifetime 1934,Ap 2,12:5
All in Favor 1942,Ja 21,20:6
All in Fun 1940,N 22,26:2; 1940,D 28,11:2
All in Good Time 1965,F 19,25:1
All in Love 1961,N 11,15:2
All in Marriage 1936,O 29,31:3
All in One 1955,Ap 20,40:3; 1955,Ap 24,II,1:1
All in the Family 1935,Jl 24,20:4
All Kinds of Giants 1961,D 19,40:1
All Kinds of Men 1957,S 20,20:3
All Men Are Alike 1941,O 7,27:2
All My Pretty Little Ones 1964,F 5,30:1
All My Sons 1947,Ja 30,21:2; 1947,F 9,II,1:1;
 1947,S 7,II,1:1; 1948,My 12,33:3; 1949,O 18,34:4
All Paris Knows 1934,Jl 24,20:1
All Rights Reserved 1934,N 7,33:5
All Soul's Eve 1920,My 13,9:1
All-Star Idlers of 1921, The 1921,Jl 16,5:2;
 1921,Ag 9,16:3
All-Star Jamboree 1921,Jl 14,18:1
All-Star Special 1931,Jl 18,16:4
All Summer Long 1953,Ja 29,23:1; 1954,S 24,26:2;
 1954,O 3,II,1:1
All That Fall 1957,O 8,41:2
All That Glitters 1938,Ja 20,18:2
All the Comforts of Home 1942,My 26,24:5
All the King's Horses 1928,Je 17,VIII,1:6;
 1934,Ja 31,21:3
All the King's Men 1929,F 5,27:1; 1948,Ja 19,19:2;
 1950,Jl 19,25:6; 1959,O 17,27:2; 1959,O 25,II,1:1;
 1963,Jl 12,12:1
All the Living 1938,Mr 25,14:4
All the Way From Texas 1926,Ag 8,VII,3:1
All the Way Home 1960,D 1,42:1; 1960,D 18,II,3:1;
 1960,D 27,26:7
All This While 1935,Jl 30,17:2
All Wave 1936,N 25,18:3
All Wet 1925,Jl 7,24:1
All Women Are One 1965,Ja 8,21:1
All You Need Is One Good Break 1950,F 10,20:3
Allah Be Praised! 1944,Ap 21,14:2
Allegro 1947,O 11,10:2; 1947,N 2,II,1:1;
 1948,Ja 18,II,3:5; 1952,S 18,36:3
Alles Fuer Marion 1931,F 15,VIII,3:1
Alles Nackt 1927,D 18,IX,1:8
Alles Schwindel 1931,Je 7,VIII,2:5
Alley Cat 1934,S 18,18:1
Alley of the Sunset 1959,D 31,11:1
Allez-Opp! 1927,Ag 3,29:3
Alligation, The 1970,S 23,43:1
Alligators, The 1960,N 15,47:1

Alloy 1924,O 12,VIII,2:1; 1924,O 28,27:1
All's Over, Then? 1934,Je 10,IX,1:1
All's Well That Ends Well 1927,Ap 17,17:6;
  1928,Ap 1,IX,2:4; 1929,Je 3,27:1; 1940,O 13,IX,1:5;
  1953,Jl 16,18:2; 1953,Jl 19,II,1:1; 1955,Je 7,37:4;
  1959,Ap 22,30:3; 1959,Ag 3,20:4; 1966,Je 17,39:1;
  1970,Je 16,53:1; 1970,Je 21,II,3:2
Allure 1934,O 30,22:6
Almanac 1954,Ja 3,II,1:1
Almost Crazy 1955,Je 21,37:1
Almost Faithful 1948,Je 5,9:2
Almost in Confidence 1936,F 18,26:7
Aloma of the South Seas 1925,Ap 21,18:1
Along Came a Spider 1963,My 28,33:1
Along Fifth Avenue 1949,Ja 14,28:2
Alouette, L' 1953,N 29,II,3:1
Als der Krieg zu Ende War (A House in Berlin)
  1950,D 27,32:3
Alt Heidelberg 1924,D 8,23:2; 1926,My 31,10:5;
  1932,N 20,IX,3:3
Alternate Current 1939,D 23,8:3
Altona 1961,Je 25,II,3:5
Always Afternoon 1929,F 24,IX,4:3
Always You 1920,Ja 6,18:2
Amahl and the Night Visitors 1970,D 24,10:2;
  1970,D 26,11:1
Amant de Madame Vidal, L' 1928,Mr 25,IX,4:6
Amants 1928,Mr 4,IX,4:5
Amants de Paris, Les 1927,N 6,IX,4:1
Amateur Hour 1936,Jl 21,13:1
Amazing Dr. Clitterhouse, The 1937,Mr 3,26:4
Amazing Grace 1967,D 10,82:1
Ambassador Extraordinary 1948,Jl 11,II,1:2
Ambush 1921,O 11,22:1; 1921,O 16,VI,1:1;
  1923,S 2,VI,1:7
Ame en Peine, L' 1928,F 12,VIII,2:1;
  1937,N 14,XI,3:1; 1950,My 31,25:2
Amedee: or, How to Disentangle Yourself
  1955,N 1,27:3
Amen Corner, The 1965,Ap 16,35:1;
  1965,Ap 25,II,1:2; 1965,Je 13,82:4; 1965,Ag 9,19:5
America Hurrah 1966,N 27,II,1:1; 1967,Ag 13,II,3:6;
  1967,O 10,55:2
American, Very Early 1934,Ja 31,21:2
American Aunt's Will, The 1936,Mr 23,22:4
American Born 1925,S 27,VII,2:1; 1925,O 6,31:3
American Chasidim 1928,Mr 17,8:8
American Dream 1933,F 22,24:5; 1933,Mr 5,IX,1:1
American Dream, The 1961,Ja 25,28:1;
  1961,O 25,33:5; 1963,My 29,39:6; 1965,F 13,10:7;
  1968,O 3,55:1
American Gothic 1953,N 11,35:6
American Hamburger League, The 1969,S 17,51:1
American Holiday 1936,F 22,13:3
American Jubilee 1940,My 13,20:5
American Landscape 1938,D 5,19:2; 1938,D 11,X,3:1
American Legend 1941,My 12,13:2
American Mime Theatre 1958,S 25,28:4
American Primitive 1937,Ag 13,12:5
American Theatre Highlights 1949,My 11,34:5
American Tragedy, An 1926,O 12,31:2;
  1926,O 24,VIII,1:1; 1931,F 21,15:5;
  1932,Ap 17,I,19:1
American Way, The 1939,Ja 23,9:2;
  1939,Ja 29,IX,1:1
Americana 1926,Jl 27,15:3; 1926,D 5,VIII,5:1;
  1928,O 14,X,2:1; 1928,O 14,X,1:6; 1928,O 31,28:2;
  1932,S 25,IX,1:6; 1932,O 6,19:3; 1932,O 16,IX,11:2
Americana Pastoral 1968,D 11,51:1
Americans Chez Nous, Les 1920,F 15,VIII,2:1;
  1920,Mr 7,V,6:1
Americans in France, The 1920,Ag 4,14:1
Americans on the Rhine 1934,O 11,28:4
America's Sweetheart 1931,Ja 25,VIII,2:4;
  1931,F 11,23:1
Ami d'Argentine, Un 1930,N 30,IX,3:3
Amis Comme Avant 1930,Ja 26,VIII,2:1
Amitie 1932,F 14,VIII,2:5
Among the Married 1929,O 4,24:3; 1929,D 8,X,2:7
Among Those Sailing 1936,F 12,24:4
Amor 1937,Ap 22,18:6
Amor Vincit Omnia 1936,N 15,XI,2:4
Amorous Antic, The 1929,D 3,29:2
Amorous Flea, The 1964,F 18,26:1
Amour a la Blague, L' 1929,Mr 10,X,1:8
Amour a l'Americaine, L' 1930,Ap 13,X,2:7
Amour Gai, L' 1933,N 12,IX,3:4
Amour Magicien, L' 1926,D 26,VII,2:1
Amourette 1933,S 28,25:2
Amoureuse 1924,N 28,13:1
Amoureuse Aventure, L' 1929,F 10,IX,4:6
Amours 1929,Ja 13,VIII,2:7
Amphitryon 1926,O 24,VIII,2:1; 1938,Ja 23,XI,1:6
  1952,N 21,21:2; 1970,F 4,38:1; 1970,My 29,13:1,
  1970,N 18,40:1
Amphitryon 38 1929,D 1,X,4:1; 1931,Mr 15,IX,2:4;
  1934,F 11,IX,3:7; 1937,Je 24,30:2; 1937,N 2,32:2;
  1937,N 7,XI,1:1; 1938,My 18,17:2; 1938,Je 5,IX,2:6;
  1939,Jl 16,IX,1:1
An und Aus 1926,D 5,VIII,8:7
Anastasia 1954,D 30,13:1; 1955,Ja 16,II,1:1
Anatevka 1966,D 22,40:5; 1968,F 2,28:1

Anathema 1923,F 9,10:2; 1923,Ap 11,16:2;
  1923,Ap 15,VII,1:1
Anatol 1922,F 5,VI,1:7; 1931,Ja 17,23:3
Anatomist, The 1931,O 25,VIII,2:6; 1932,O 25,24:3;
  1957,F 27,21:5
Ancient Mariner, The 1924,Ap 7,15:5;
  1924,Ap 13,VIII,1:1
And Be My Love 1934,Ja 19,25:2; 1945,F 22,30:4
And Him Stretched 1962,S 26,33:1
And I Met a Man 1970,Ap 11,20:3
And Life Burns On 1938,Jl 31,IX,1:4
And Now Goodbye 1937,Ja 19,29:1; 1937,F 3,26:4
And On We Go 1937,Ap 22,19:5
And People All Around 1966,Ag 7,II,1:1;
  1968,F 12,46:1
And Puppy Dog Tails 1969,O 20,60:1;
  1969,O 26,II,3:7
And So to Bed 1927,N 10,23:1
And Stars Remain 1936,S 29,35:2; 1936,O 4,IX,2:1;
  1936,O 13,32:2
And Still They Fight 1944,N 30,3:1
And the Wind Blows 1959,Ap 29,28:1;
  1959,My 17,II,1:1
And Things That Go Bump in the Night
  1965,Ap 27,27:5; 1965,My 9,II,1:2
Andersh 1922,S 26,18:2
Andersonville Trial, The 1959,D 30,15:1;
  1960,Ja 10,II,1:1; 1960,N 25,33:3
Andorra 1963,F 11,5:5; 1963,F 25,7:5
Androcles and the Lion 1925,N 24,28:1;
  1925,N 29,VIII,1:1; 1938,D 17,10:5; 1946,D 20,29:2;
  1946,D 29,II,1:1; 1958,F 22,8:3; 1961,N 22,24:2;
  1968,Je 27,47:1
Andromaque 1964,F 29,13:2
Angel 1933,D 8,31:1; 1933,D 24,IX,2:2
Angel Comes to Babylon, An 1962,S 29,15:2
Angel in the Pawnshop 1951,Ja 19,20:3
Angel in the Wings 1947,D 12,36:4; 1947,D 21,II,3:1;
  1948,F 8,II,2:1; 1948,Ag 29,II,1:1
Angel Island 1937,O 21,26:2
Angel Street 1941,D 6,15:2; 1944,Jl 9,II,1:1;
  1948,Ja 23,26:6
Angela 1928,D 4,28:2; 1969,O 31,33:1;
  1969,N 9,II,1:1
Angela Is Twenty-Two 1938,D 31,6:3
Angelic Doctor 1953,Ap 14,30:2
Angelica 1937,Ap 13,31:2
Angeline Moves In 1932,Ap 20,27:5
Angelo 1923,Mr 30,14:4
Angels Don't Kiss 1932,Ap 6,22:5
Angels Kiss Me 1951,Ap 18,37:6
Angels of Anadarko 1962,O 11,47:1
Angels on Earth 1929,D 11,34:7
Animal Crackers 1928,O 24,26:2
Animal Kingdom, The 1932,Ja 3,VIII,3:1;
  1932,Ja 13,26:4; 1932,Ja 24,I,1:1; 1938,Jl 27,14:5
Ankles Aweigh 1955,Ap 19,27:1; 1955,Ap 24,II,1:1
Ann Adams, Spinster 1933,Mr 27,12:4
Ann Veronica 1949,My 21,9:2
Ann Vroome 1930,Jl 27,VIII,2:3
Anna 1928,My 17,25:2
Anna Ascends 1920,S 23,14:1
Anna Christie 1921,N 3,22:1; 1921,N 6,VI,1:1;
  1921,N 13,VI,1:1; 1922,Ja 15,III,3:1;
  1923,Ap 11,16:2; 1923,Ap 15,VII,2:4;
  1923,N 18,VIII,2:8; 1924,My 11,VIII,1:4;
  1924,Je 24,18:4; 1930,My 4,XI,3:1; 1930,Je 11,33:3;
  1930,Je 12,30:2; 1941,Ag 10,IX,1:8; 1952,Ja 10,33:1;
  1952,Ja 20,II,1:1; 1955,N 22,41:1
Anna Karenina 1937,Ap 25,IV,4:5
Anna Kleiber 1965,Ja 20,33:1
Anna Lucasta 1944,Je 17,10:1; 1944,Ag 31,15:1;
  1944,S 24,II,1:5; 1945,Je 7,II,1:1; 1947,O 30,31:3;
  1947,N 9,II,3:7; 1956,Ap 13,21:8
Anna Russell and Her Little Show 1953,S 8,27:2
Anne 1965,Ag 22,82:2
Anne of England 1941,O 8,26:2
Anne of Green Gables 1969,Ap 18,39:1;
  1969,Ag 25,41:1
Anne of the Thousand Days 1948,D 9,49:2;
  1948,D 19,II,3:1; 1949,S 18,II,1:1
Anne-One Hundred 1927,Je 26,VIII,1:3
Anneliese von Dessau 1926,F 26,24:3
Annie 1924,O 12,VIII,2:1
Annie Dear 1924,N 5,25:3
Annie Get Your Gun 1946,Mr 29,18:2;
  1946,My 17,14:2; 1946,My 26,II,1:1;
  1946,S 29,II,1:1; 1947,Je 8,I,63:2; 1947,Je 9,26:6;
  1957,F 28,18:6; 1957,Mr 9,15:5; 1957,Ag 31,18:2;
  1958,F 20,29:2; 1966,Je 1,42:2
Annina 1934,Mr 12,21:6
Anniversary, The 1955,My 26,34:1; 1961,Ap 21,26:2
Anniversary Waltz 1954,Ap 8,34:1; 1954,Ap 25,II,1:1;
  1955,D 2,31:3; 1955,D 11,II,7:1
Annonce Faite a Marie, L' 1927,N 6,IX,4:1;
  1942,My 21,24:1; 1965,Ap 6,33:2
Another Chance 1969,Je 4,37:1
Another City, Another Land 1968,O 9,42:1
Another Evening With Harry Stoones
  1961,O 23,22:2
Another Language 1932,Ap 26,25:3;
  1932,My 15,VIII,1:1; 1932,D 25,IX,1:6;
  1933,My 9,20:2

Another Love 1934,Mr 20,26:3
Another Love Story 1943,O 13,29:2
Another Part of the Forest 1946,N 21,42:2;
  1946,D 1,II,1:1; 1949,O 17,19:1; 1949,O 18,34:4;
  1949,N 13,83:4
Another Room for Rent 1929,My 7,28:1
Another Sun 1940,F 24,8:6
Another Way Out 1923,My 12,15:4; 1923,My 26,8:4
Answered the Flute 1940,Mr 10,37:4
ANTA Album 1950,Ja 30,13:2; 1951,My 7,22:7
Anteroom, The 1936,Ag 15,6:7; 1936,S 6,IX,1:1
Anthony and Anna 1934,N 13,22:2; 1935,N 9,18:2;
  1935,D 8,X,5:1
Anthony on Overtime 1961,O 21,13:2
Antigone 1923,My 4,18:4; 1923,My 25,28:1;
  1930,Ap 25,28:4; 1946,Ja 10,28:2; 1946,F 19,21:3;
  1946,F 24,II,1:1; 1956,Ap 3,32:2; 1959,S 16,46:2;
  1960,D 14,52:1; 1962,D 29,5:5; 1967,Ja 14,18:1;
  1967,Je 19,43:1; 1968,O 11,36:1
Antoinette Sabrier 1929,Je 16,VIII,2:3
Antonia 1925,O 11,VIII,2:6; 1925,O 21,20:1
Antony and Cleopatra 1924,F 20,22:1;
  1924,F 24,VII,1:1; 1924,Mr 2,VIII,1:1;
  1924,Mr 9,VIII,1:1; 1930,D 14,IX,3:1;
  1932,F 7,VIII,1:5; 1934,S 18,18:2; 1935,Ap 16,26:7;
  1936,O 15,32:8; 1936,N 1,X,3:7; 1937,O 14,23:2;
  1937,N 11,30:2; 1945,Ap 25,26:5; 1947,N 27,49:2;
  1947,D 7,II,5:1; 1951,D 21,22:2; 1951,D 30,II,1:1;
  1953,My 10,II,1:1; 1959,Ja 14,28:1; 1960,Ag 1,19:1;
  1963,Je 21,33:1; 1963,S 14,12:4; 1967,Ag 2,25:1;
  1967,S 17,II,1:1; 1967,O 29,83:4; 1969,Ag 30,10:3
Anvil, The 1961,Ag 8,32:2; 1962,O 31,33:3
Any Day Now 1941,Je 10,28:2
Any Moment Now 1939,N 25,13:6
Any Wednesday 1964,F 19,34:1
Any Woman 1934,Ag 28,24:4
Anya 1965,N 30,48:1
Anybody Home 1949,F 26,10:5
Anybody's Game 1932,D 22,21:4
Anyone Can Whistle 1964,Ap 6,36:1
Anything Goes 1934,N 18,IX,1:7; 1934,N 22,26:1;
  1935,Je 15,20:5; 1935,S 15,IX,1:1; 1937,Ag 17,23:4;
  1937,Ag 26,24:3; 1962,My 16,35:1
Anything Might Happen 1923,F 21,22:3;
  1923,F 25,VII,1:1
Anzor 1930,Ag 10,VIII,2:3
Apache, The 1923,My 9,14:3
Apartment to Let 1924,Ap 1,18:1
Apocalypsis cum Figuris 1969,N 20,60:2;
  1969,N 30,II,1:4
Apollo of Bellac, The 1954,My 29,12:1;
  1954,Je 6,II,1:1; 1957,Ap 10,39:1; 1958,Mr 7,17:2
Apology 1943,Mr 23,14:2
Apothecary, The 1925,S 5,11:4; 1926,Mr 17,28:1
Apparition Theater of Prague, The 1966,N 17,56:2
Appearances 1925,O 15,27:3; 1929,Ap 2,28:1;
  1930,Mr 30,VIII,2:6
Applause 1970,Mr 31,35:1; 1970,Ap 5,II,1:1
Apple, The 1961,D 8,44:1; 1962,Ap 20,22:1;
  1962,Ap 23,33:3
Apple a Day, An 1936,My 25,23:5
Apple Cart, The 1929,Je 15,6:2; 1929,Ag 20,30:2;
  1929,S 8,IX,1:8; 1929,S 18,35:1; 1930,F 25,30:1;
  1930,Mr 2,IX,1:1; 1930,Mr 9,IX,4:3;
  1930,N 23,IX,1:3; 1953,My 8,29:3; 1956,O 19,23:1;
  1956,O 28,II,1:1
Apple of His Eye 1946,F 6,18:2
Apple Tree, The 1966,O 30,II,1:1; 1967,O 12,56:1;
  1967,N 10,61:1
Applesauce 1924,S 7,VII,1:4; 1924,O 12,VIII,2:1;
  1925,S 29,31:2
Applicant 1969,N 4,55:2
Apprentices, The 1968,Ag 21,40:5
Apres l'Amour 1924,N 2,VIII,1:3
Apricot Season, The 1952,O 4,43:8
Apron Strings 1930,F 18,28:2; 1931,Je 7,VIII,8:1;
  1937,Jl 13,22:3
Aqua Carnival 1962,Je 29,15:1
Aquacade 1939,My 5,26:2; 1939,My 14,XI,1:1
Aquacircus 1958,Je 30,24:6
Aquarama 1960 1960,Jl 1,14:6
Aquashow 1952,Je 25,25:1; 1953,Je 24,29:2;
  1954,Je 23,20:4
Arabesque 1925,O 11,VIII,2:6; 1925,O 21,20:2
Arabian, The 1926,Ap 25,VIII,1:8; 1927,N 1,20:5
Arabian Nightmare, The 1927,Ja 11,36:3
Arabian Nights 1954,Je 25,15:2; 1955,Je 24,16:1;
  1967,Jl 3,12:1
Archangel, The 1925,Mr 26,21:5
Archdupe 1931,D 27,VIII,4:1
Architect and the Emperor of Assyria, The
  1970,Jl 24,17:2; 1970,Ag 9,II,1:5; 1970,S 20,II,1:2
Architruc 1970,Ap 16,55:1
Ardele 1958,Ap 9,39:4
Arden of Faversham 1970,F 17,33:1
Are You Decent? 1934,Ap 20,16:2
Are You With It? 1945,N 12,17:3
Arena Conta Zumbi 1969,Ag 19,31:1
Arena Conte Bolivar 1970,Mr 31,33:1
Arenas of Lutetia 1968,D 1,II,3:5
Aren't Men Beasts? 1936,My 15,29:1

Aren't We All? 1923,Ap 15,VII,2:4; 1923,My 22,14:2; 1923,My 27,VII,1:1
Arf 1969,My 28,36:1
Aria Da Capo 1923,My 13,16:2; 1950,My 25,36:2; 1958,My 21,40:1; 1958,Je 27,18:5
Aria del Continente, L' 1927,O 5,30:2
Ariadne 1925,F 24,17:1; 1925,My 3,VIII,2:1
Aries Is Rising 1939,N 22,16:5
Aristocrat, The 1929,My 8,34:4
Aristocrats 1935,My 2,16:2; 1936,S 13,X,1:1; 1936,O 11,X,1:4
Arlecchino, the Servant of Two Masters 1956,Ag 28,31:1
Arlene Adair 1926,Jl 4,VII,3:2
Arlequin Poli par l'Amour 1955,N 9,40:1; 1955,N 20,II,1:1
Armer Columbus 1928,Ap 22,IX,6:7
Armlet of Jade 1936,Ap 15,25:3
Armor of Light 1950,F 24,26:4
Armored Train No 1469 1931,N 28,20:3
Arms and the Girl 1950,F 3,28:2
Arms and the Man 1921,Mr 6,VI,1:7; 1921,Ap 10,VI,1:1; 1925,S 15,28:1; 1925,O 4,IX,1:1; 1926,Ja 21,18:3; 1929,Ag 13,23:4; 1937,Jl 20,19:3; 1938,Ag 10,14:1; 1944,O 1,II,1:3; 1950,O 20,34:2; 1956,O 2,39:4; 1964,Ap 28,41:1; 1965,Je 24,32:5; 1967,Je 23,44:2; 1970,Jl 10,18:1; 1970,Ag 26,36:1
Arms for Venus 1937,Mr 12,18:7
Armseligen Besenbinder, Die 1928,N 19,16:2
Armstrong's Last Goodnight 1965,Jl 7,26:1
Army Play by Play, The 1943,Je 15,16:1; 1943,Je 20,II,1:1; 1943,Ag 3,13:3
Around the Corner 1936,D 29,17:2
Around the World 1946,Je 1,9:5; 1946,Je 9,II,1:1
Around the World in 80 Days 1963,Je 24,22:1; 1964,Je 29,33:2
Arrest That Woman 1936,S 19,20:4
Arrow-Maker, The 1956,O 5,20:1
Arsenic and Old Lace 1941,Ja 11,13:2; 1941,F 23,IX,1:1; 1941,Mr 25,26:7; 1942,My 11,18:6; 1943,Ja 1,26:5; 1943,Ja 10,VIII,1:6; 1943,D 13,18:6; 1944,Jl 3,7:3; 1970,N 5,59:1
Art and Craft 1936,D 1,30:4
Art and Mrs Bottle 1929,Nr 13,25:2; 1929,D 8,X,2:5; 1930,N 19,19:3; 1936,S 2,18:1
Art Antics of 1926 1926,Ap 19,24:2
Art of Living, The 1960,Ag 20,16:4
Arthur 1923,Mr 18,VII,1:1; 1929,S 29,IX,4:7
Article 330, L' 1930,N 23,IX,1:1
Artist and the Shadow, The 1930,Ap 6,IX,2:1
Artisten 1928,Je 10,17:2; 1928,S 23,IX,2:2
Artistic Temperament 1924,D 10,20:2
Artists and Models 1923,Ag 21,12:2; 1924,O 16,33:3; 1925,Je 25,16:2; 1926,Mr 22,16:2; 1926,Ap 4,VIII,1:1; 1927,N 16,28:2; 1930,Je 11,33:2; 1930,S 28,VIII,2:5; 1943,N 6,16:6; 1943,N 21,II,1:1
Arturo Ui 1963,N 12,49:1; 1963,N 24,II,1:1
Arzigogolo, L' 1931,Ap 27,24:4
As a Matter of Fact 1921,My 29,VI,1:7
As Bad as I Am 1935,S 29,X,1:6
As Far as Thought Can Reach (Back to Methuselah, Part V) 1922,Mr 14,11:2
As Good As New 1930,O 19,IX,3:4; 1930,N 4,37:3
As Husbands Go 1931,Mr 6,26:5; 1931,Mr 15,IX,1:1; 1933,Ja 20,20:5; 1935,Jl 2,24:3; 1935,Jl 10,24:1
As Long as They're Happy 1953,Ag 9,II,1:2
As the Earth Turns 1938,Ag 7,IX,2:1
As the Girls Go 1948,N 15,21:2
As Thousands Cheer 1933,S 10,II,5:3; 1933,O 2,22:1; 1933,O 15,IX,1:1; 1934,Jl 10,24:2
As-tu du Coeur? 1926,O 31,VIII,2:4
As We Forgive Our Debtors 1936,Ag 11,24:6; 1947,Mr 11,37:2
As You Desire Me 1930,N 30,IX,3:6; 1931,Ja 29,21:2; 1934,O 2,18:3; 1934,O 28,IX,3:4
As You Like It 1923,Ap 24,24:1; 1923,Ap 29,VII,1:1; 1930,Ap 3,32:5; 1930,S 19,18:5; 1934,N 11,IX,3:6; 1936,Ap 24,18:4; 1937,Ja 3,X,3:6; 1937,N 1,25:2; 1937,N 8,18:2; 1938,Jl 31,IX,6:8; 1939,Ap 23,X,2:5; 1939,My 9,28:4; 1941,O 21,29:2; 1945,Jl 4,10:4; 1947,F 21,16:2; 1950,Ja 27,27:2; 1950,F 19,II,1:1; 1955,O 29,12:2; 1958,Ja 21,33:6; 1959,Jl 1,27:1; 1959,Jl 5,II,1:1; 1961,Je 17,13:2; 1961,Je 25,II,1:1; 1961,Jl 5,30:1; 1963,Jl 17,19:2; 1966,Je 4,19:1; 1967,O 6,33:4; 1967,O 15,II,9:3; 1968,Je 24,42:3; 1968,Jl 6,9:1
As You Were 1920,Ja 28,22:3
Ascendancy 1935,Ja 31,22:3
Ascending Dragon, The 1935,O 1,27:6
Ascension de Virginie, L' 1929,N 3,IX,4:2
Ascent of F 6, The 1937,Mr 28,XI,2:2
Ashes 1924,Je 1,VII,4:3; 1924,O 21,21:2
Ashes of Love 1926,Mr 16,23:1; 1926,Mr 23,24:3
Asie 1932,Ja 10,VIII,3:1
Asino di Buridano, L' 1936,N 30,25:2
Ask My Friend Sandy 1943,F 5,16:2
Ask Your Wife 1929,O 14,20:4
Asleep 1927,Je 12,VII,2:1
Asmodee 1938,Je 12,X,2:3; 1939,Mr 12,XI,3:5; 1939,My 28,X,1:6; 1958,Mr 26,42:2
Aspern Papers, The 1959,Ag 13,21:5; 1962,F 8,26:1; 1962,F 18,II,1:1

Aspidistras 1927,Ja 2,VII,2:5; 1927,Ag 14,VII,1:7
Assalto, L' 1929,My 20,23:2
Assassin, The 1945,Mr 23,13:6; 1945,Ap 1,II,2:3; 1945,O 18,20:2
Assommoir, L' 1927,O 16,IX,4:7
Assorted Nuts 1940,Ap 7,I,44:6
Assumption of Hannele, The 1924,F 16,16:2
Astonished Heart, The 1935,O 17,28:3; 1936,Ja 10,16:1; 1936,F 2,IX,3:4; 1936,O 27,30:7; 1936,N 25,17:2; 1936,D 6,XII,5:1; 1940,Ag 6,15:3
Astonished Ostrich, The 1936,D 18,30:3; 1937,Ja 17,X,2:1
Astrakhan Coat, The 1967,Ja 13,18:1
At an Art Exhibition 1947,D 29,21:5
At Eight AM 1935,F 12,25:4
At Home Abroad 1935,S 4,22:3; 1935,S 8,IX,1:1; 1935,S 20,17:4; 1935,O 27,IX,1:1; 1935,O 27,IX,8:1
At Home at the Palace 1967,Ag 1,23:1
At Home With Ethel Waters 1953,S 23,36:1
At Mrs Beam's 1923,Mr 11,VIII,2:4; 1926,Ap 26,24:3; 1926,My 2,VIII,1:1; 1937,Jl 27,24:2
At Sea 1962,Ap 24,33:1
At the Bottom 1930,Ja 10,24:3
At the Drop of a Hat 1959,O 9,22:2
At the Drop of Another Hat 1966,D 28,30:2; 1967,Ja 8,II,1:5
At the Gate of the Kingdom 1927,D 9,28:5
At the Grand 1958,Ag 13,24:3
At the Silver Swan 1936,F 20,22:2; 1936,Mr 15,X,2:1
At the Stroke of Eight 1940,My 21,29:2
At the Theatre 1937,Ag 4,14:1
At War With the Army 1949,Mr 9,32:2; 1949,Mr 20,II,1:1
At Your Service 1937,Ag 17,23:1
Athalie 1939,My 14,XI,6:5; 1942,Mr 18,29:2
Athenian Touch, The 1964,Ja 15,25:4
Atlas and Eva 1928,F 7,30:2
Atlas-Hotel 1931,My 10,VIII,2:6
Atmosphere 1925,Ap 4,17:1
Atom Doctor, The 1950,S 10,II,3:1
Atout... Coeur 1936,Mr 27,25:4
Atrocities of 1932 1932,Ag 22,20:3
Attachee, L' 1929,My 19,IX,2:1
Attack 1942,S 8,13:4
Attore, L' 1929,Mr 11,29:5
Au Bagne 1929,Jl 21,VIII,2:1
Au Clair de la Lune 1929,N 10,X,4:1
Au Coin Joli 1923,O 23,16:1
Au Rat Mort, Cabinet No 6 1923,O 16,18:1
Au Soleil de l'Instinct 1932,Mr 20,VIII,2:2
Aube, le Jour Et la Nuit, L' 1929,Je 9,VIII,2:4
Aucassin et Nicolette 1921,Ap 9,9:3; 1921,Ap 17,VI,1:1; 1937,F 14,II,3:6; 1947,Ap 28,26:2
Audacious Mr Squire, The 1924,F 24,VII,1:4
Audition, The 1968,Je 19,38:2; 1968,Jl 8,45:1; 1968,Jl 14,II,4:5
Audition of the Apprentice Theatre 1939,Je 2,26:2
August for the People 1961,S 5,41:6
Augustus Does His Bit 1958,F 22,8:3
Aunt Caroline's Will 1954,Ag 11,21:1
Aunt of England 1935,Mr 28,25:4; 1935,Ap 21,IX,2:2
Auntie Mame 1956,N 1,47:2; 1956,N 11,II,1:1; 1958,Je 8,II,1:1; 1958,Ag 12,33:2
Aurelie 1932,D 18,X,3:6
Auslandreise 1932,N 20,IX,3:5
Autobiography 1956,O 3,29:2
Autocrat, The 1929,Je 9,VIII,2:4
Automobile Graveyard, The 1961,N 14,46:2
Autres, Les 1931,N 1,VIII,2:7
Autumn Crocus 1931,Ap 26,VIII,2:4; 1932,N 21,20:2; 1934,Ja 21,X,1:6; 1954,Je 22,24:7; 1954,Jl 7,23:7
Autumn Fire 1926,Ap 15,25:1; 1926,O 27,25:3; 1932,D 29,16:3
Autumn Garden, The 1951,Mr 8,36:2; 1951,Mr 18,II,1:1
Autumn Hill 1942,Ap 14,17:4
Autumn Manoeuvers 1938,N 27,IX,3:6
Autumn Violins 1929,F 10,IX,2:1
Autumn's Here 1966,O 26,40:1
Avalanche 1932,F 14,VIII,1:8
Avanti 1968,F 1,29:1
Avare, L' 1924,Mr 12,17:3; 1930,F 2,VIII,4:1 1966,F 9,32:1
Aventuriere, L' 1922,N 14,16:1; 1926,D 17,27:3
Avons-Nous Tuee?, L' 1927,F 13,VII,4:1
Avril 1932,O 16,IX,2:2
Awake and Sing! 1935,F 20,23:2; 1935,Mr 10,VIII,1:1; 1938,F 21,15:1; 1938,D 23,16:6; 1939,Mr 8,18:2; 1939,Mr 26,X,1:2; 1942,My 31,VIII,2:3; 1970,My 28,35:1; 1970,Je 7,II,1:1; 1970,Jl 5,II,1:2
Awakening of Spring, The 1964,My 13,50:1
Awful Mrs Eaton, The 1924,Jl 20,VII,1:7
Awful Truth, The 1922,S 19,14:3; 1922,S 24,VI,1:1
Awhile to Work 1937,Mr 20,23:1
Ayeya Vietnam 1966,D 21,2:4
Az Ego Szoknya 1928,S 30,IX,4:4
Azrael 1946,S 16,9:7
Azuma Kabuki Dancers and Musicians 1954,F 19,22:3; 1954,F 28,II,4:1; 1954,Mr 10,29:4; 1955,D 27,31:4; 1956,Ja 8,II,3:1

B

B J One 1930,Ap 11,24:6; 1930,Ap 27,IX,1:8; 1931,My 7,21:3
Baa, Baa, Black Sheep 1929,My 12,IX,2:3
Baal 1965,My 7,33:2; 1965,Je 6,II,1:1
Bab 1920,O 19,12:1
Babbling Brookes 1927,F 26,13:2
Babes Don't Cry Anymore 1968,F 21,55:1
Babes in Arms 1937,Ap 15,18:4; 1951,Mr 10,7:3
Babes in the Wood 1939,Ja 29,IX,1:3; 1964,D 29,21:2
Babes in the Zoo 1932,My 15,26:2
Babes in Toyland 1929,D 24,15:3; 1930,D 22,17:1
Babies a La Carte 1927,Ag 16,31:1
Babu 1967,D 23,28:1
Baby Cyclone, The 1927,Ag 14,VII,2:1; 1927,S 13,37:4; 1928,Ap 11,25:1
Baby-Foot 1962,O 11,48:5
Baby Mine 1921,S 4,13:2; 1927,Ap 3,VIII,2:1; 1927,Je 10,21:2
Baby Pompadour 1934,D 28,24:2
Baby Want a Kiss 1964,Ap 20,32:1
Baby With a Knife 1969,My 15,41:2
Baccara 1927,Ap 3,VIII,4:7
Bacchae, The 1962,Je 19,30:1; 1963,Ap 25,39:5; 1969,Mr 15,24:1; 1969,Mr 23,II,11:1
Bacchants, The 1967,F 25,14:1
Bachelor Born 1938,Ja 26,26:3; 1938,Ag 17,23:1
Bachelor Father, The 1928,F 29,28:2; 1929,O 20,IX,1:4
Bachelor's Brides 1925,My 29,20:2
Bachelor's Night, A 1921,O 18,20:1
Back Fire 1932,Je 14,26:3
Back Here 1928,N 27,36:3
Back Pay 1921,Ag 21,VI,1:8; 1921,Ag 31,8:2
Back Seat Drivers 1928,D 26,14:4
Back Streets 1933,My 18,17:4
Back to Methuselah 1923,O 14,VIII,1:8; 1923,O 21,VIII,2:2; 1924,F 3,VII,1:4; 1924,F 23,12:2; 1958,Mr 27,41:5; 1958,Ap 6,II,1:1; 1969,Ag 31,46:3
Back to Methuselah (Part I: In the Beginning) 1922,F 28,17:2
Back to Methuselah (Part II: The Gospel of the Brothers Barnabas) 1922,F 28,17:2
Back to Methuselah (Part III: The Thing Happens) 1922,Mr 7,11:1
Back to Methuselah (Part IV: The Tragedy of an Elderly Gentleman) 1922,Mr 7,11:1
Back to Methuselah (Part V: As Far as Thought Can Reach) 1922,Mr 14,11:2
Backlane Center 1961,N 23,51:1
Backslapper, The 1925,Ap 13,25:2
Bad Bad Jo-Jo 1969,Mr 20,53:1
Bad Girl 1930,O 3,30:2
Bad Habits of 1925 1925,F 9,17:1
Bad Habits of 1926 1926,My 1,11:1
Bad Man, The 1920,Ag 31,7:1; 1921,S 25,VI,1:1; 1921,O 2,VII,1:3; 1923,F 25,VII,1:7; 1923,Mr 11,VIII,2:4
Bad Manners 1933,Ja 31,15:5
Bad Penny, A 1931,Ag 23,VIII,2:4
Bad Place to Get Your Head, A 1970,Jl 16,38:1
Bad Seed, The 1954,D 9,42:1; 1954,D 19,II,3:1; 1955,My 1,II,3:1
Badges 1924,D 4,25:1
Bagels and Yox 1951,S 13,38:2
Bagrovyostrov 1928,D 16,III,3:5
Baigneuse du Lido, La 1928,Jl 1,VIII,1:8
Bajadere, Die 1925,O 2,26:2
Bajour 1964,N 24,42:1
Baker Street 1965,F 17,36:1; 1965,F 28,II,1:1
Bal des Voleurs, Le 1938,N 29,26:4
Balalaika 1936,D 23,17:4
Balcony, The 1960,Mr 4,21:1; 1960,Mr 20,II,1:1
Bald Soprano, The 1958,Je 4,39:2; 1963,S 18,35:4
Ball at the Savoy 1933,F 19,IX,3:1; 1933,S 9,9:7
Ballad for a Firing Squad 1968,D 12,64:2
Ballad for Bimshire 1963,O 16,54:1
Ballad of Jazz Street, The 1959,N 12,28:1
Ballad of John Ogilvie, The 1968,O 9,42:4
Ballad of the Sad Cafe, The 1963,O 31,27:1; 1963,N 10,II,1:1
Ballerina 1933,O 11,26:3; 1933,O 29,IX,1:6
Ballerina des Koenigs, Die 1921,Jl 24,VI,1:7; 1921,D 11,VI,1:4; 1922,Jl 23,VI,1:1
Balloon 1946,Ag 13,30:3
Ballots Up 1960,Ag 24,34:4
Balls 1965,F 11,45:1
Ballyhoo 1927,Ja 5,18:1; 1930,D 14,IX,3:1; 1930,D 23,24:1
Ballyhoo of 1932 1932,S 7,14:2
Bamboo Cross 1955,F 22,17:2
Bananas 1968,D 5,60:1
Banco 1922,S 21,18:1
Band Wagon, The 1931,My 17,VIII,3:2; 1931,Je 4,31:3; 1931,Je 7,VIII,8:1; 1931,Je 14,VIII,1:1; 1931,S 27,VIII,3:7
Banjo Eyes 1941,N 8,10:6; 1941,D 26,20:2
Banker's Daughter, The 1962,Ja 23,37:1
Banque Nemo, La 1931,D 13,VIII,2:2

Banquet for the Moon, A 1961,Ja 20,24:2
Banshee, The 1927,D 6,26:2
Bapteme, Le 1928,Mr 11,VIII,2:7
Baptiste 1952,N 13,34:2
Barbara 1929,N 18,24:5
Barbara's Wedding 1927,S 11,VIII,2:4; 1931,O 9,21:1
Barber Had Two Sons, The 1943,F 2,22:2
Barbier de Seville, Le 1939,Mr 7,19:2; 1955,N 9,40:1; 1955,N 20,II,1:1
Barchester Towers 1937,N 19,26:6; 1937,D 1,27:1
Bare Facts 1926,Jl 19,13:3; 1927,Je 30,35:1; 1927,Ag 17,27:5
Bare Facts of Today 1930,Ap 17,24:4
Barefoot 1925,O 20,29:2
Barefoot Boy With Cheek 1947,Ap 4,20:2
Barefoot in Athens 1951,N 1,35:2; 1951,N 11,II,1:1
Barefoot in the Park 1963,O 24,36:2
Bargold Lacht 1932,N 6,IX,3:2
Barker, The 1927,Ja 19,20:6; 1927,Ja 23,VII,1:1; 1928,Je 10,VIII,1:3
Barnet's Folly 1935,F 15,22:2; 1935,Mr 10,VIII,2:1
Barnum Was Right 1922,N 12,VIII,1:6; 1923,Mr 13,19:3
Baronet and the Butterfly, The 1924,Je 8,VII,1:8
Barranca Abajo 1963,Je 1,16:2
Barretts of Wimpole Street, The 1930,Ag 21,13:4; 1930,S 7,IX,2:1; 1931,F 1,VIII,3:5; 1931,F 10,25:1; 1931,F 15,VIII,1:8; 1931,F 22,VIII,1:1; 1934,N 11,IX,3:6; 1935,F 26,16:2; 1944,S 17,II,1:3; 1945,Mr 27,23:6; 1945,Ap 1,II,1:1
Barricou 1930,Ap 20,VIII,2:8
Barrier, The 1950,N 3,32:2
Barrister, The 1932,N 22,25:2
Barroom Monks, The 1962,My 29,21:1
Bartleby 1961,Ja 25,28:1
Basalik 1935,Ap 8,22:5
Basement, The 1967,O 3,56:1; 1967,O 15,II,3:3; 1968,O 16,40:1; 1968,N 3,II,7:4
Bassa Moona 1936,D 9,35:4
Bat, The 1920,Ag 24,6:1; 1920,N 14,VI,1:1; 1922,Ja 24,11:1; 1922,Ap 30,VII,1:1; 1937,Je 1,27:5; 1953,Ja 21,28:2
Bataille de la Marne 1931,D 20,VIII,2:7; 1932,F 21,VIII,1:8
Bathsheba 1947,Mr 27,40:2
Bats in the Belfry 1937,Mr 12,19:4; 1937,Ap 4,X,2:4
Battle Hymn 1936,My 23,12:1
Battle of Angels 1940,D 31,18:6; 1941,Ja 5,IX,1:7
Battle of Shrivings, The 1970,F 7,23:1
Battle Royal 1934,Ap 19,33:4
Battleship Gertie 1935,Ja 19,9:2
Battling Buttler 1923,O 9,17:2
Bauerngeneral, Der 1931,Ap 19,VIII,2:4
Baumeister Solness 1927,O 30,IX,4:1
Bavu 1922,F 27,16:1; 1922,My 14,VII,1:1
Bawdy Party 1968,F 3,20:1
Be Good Till You Die 1929,D 29,VIII,4:1
Be So Kindly 1937,F 9,19:4
Be Your Age 1929,F 5,27:1; 1953,Ja 15,24:2
Be Yourself! 1924,Ag 24,VII,1:8; 1924,S 4,13:3
Bead-Tangle 1970,Jl 16,38:1
Bear, The 1948,F 6,29:2
Beard, The 1967,O 25,40:1; 1967,N 5,II,3:1
Beast in Me, The 1963,My 17,29:1
Beast's Story, A 1969,Ja 13,26:1
Beat the Band 1942,O 15,26:1
Beaten Track, The 1926,F 9,23:2
Beau Austin 1929,N 17,IX,2:4
Beau Brummell 1924,Ap 4,19:2; 1933,Ag 9,20:6
Beau Danube Rouge 1931,My 17,VIII,1:5
Beau Gallant 1926,Ap 6,26:3
Beau Geste 1929,F 17,IX,2:1
Beau Metier, Le 1930,Ja 12,VIII,4:1
Beau Reve, Un 1928,Je 3,VIII,2:5
Beau-Strings 1926,Ap 27,22:2; 1926,My 2,VIII,1:1
Beautiful Bait, The 1962,N 13,44:1
Beautiful Changes, The 1956,Mr 24,15:2
Beautiful Dreamer 1960,D 28,22:1
Beautiful Jailer, The 1957,My 17,19:2
Beautiful Mariposa, The 1952,Jl 2,22:8
Beautiful People, The 1941,Ap 22,27:2; 1941,My 4,IX,1:1
Beauty and the Beast 1932,Ja 10,I,29:2
Beauty Part, The 1962,D 28,5:2; 1963,Ja 5,5:1; 1969,S 7,II,1:2
Beaux Jours, Les 1970,My 20,32:1
Beaux' Stratagem, The 1927,F 13,VII,2:1; 1928,Je 5,20:1; 1928,Je 10,VIII,1:1; 1930,Ap 13,X,2:7; 1935,Jl 17,22:5; 1957,Jl 9,25:4; 1959,F 25,35:4; 1959,Mr 1,II,1:1; 1970,F 10,50:2; 1970,F 22,II,1:1
Beaver Coat, The 1956,Mr 29,22:5
Because of Helen 1920,N 14,VI,1:4
Because We Must 1937,F 6,14:4
Becket 1960,O 6,50:1; 1960,O 16,II,1:1; 1960,O 18,36:3; 1961,My 9,44:1; 1961,Jl 12,35:6
Becky Sharp 1929,Je 4,29:1
Beclch 1968,D 17,59:1
Bed Bug, The 1931,Mr 20,28:6
Bed of Roses, A 1934,Ap 1,X,7:5
Bed Time 1958,Ap 11,20:2
Bedfellows 1929,Jl 3,19:2
Bedlam Galore, for Two or More 1965,Mr 8,34:1

Bedrock 1934,N 18,II,6:3
Bedtime Story 1952,My 8,35:6; 1957,Ap 1,21:2; 1958,Mr 11,33:1; 1958,Mr 16,II,1:1; 1959,Ap 16,28:1; 1959,Ap 26,II,1:1
Beekman Place 1964,O 8,50:1
Bees and the Flowers, The 1946,S 27,19:3
Bees on the Boat Deck 1936,My 6,27:2; 1936,Je 7,IX,2:1
Before Breakfast 1929,Mr 6,33:1; 1958,Mr 12,36:1; 1963,Je 11,29:4
Before I Wake 1968,O 14,56:1
Before Morning 1933,F 10,13:4
Before Sundown 1962,Mr 14,43:1
Before Sunset 1932,F 17,19:3; 1932,Mr 13,VIII,2:7; 1933,S 29,10:7; 1933,S 30,18:2; 1933,O 15,IX,1:6
Before You Go 1968,Ja 12,20:1; 1969,Ap 9,51:1
Before You're 25 1929,Ap 17,30:2
Beg, Borrow or Steal 1960,F 11,39:4
Beggar on Horseback 1924,F 13,17:2; 1924,F 17,VII,1:1; 1925,My 8,22:4; 1970,My 15,47:2; 1970,My 24,II,1:1
Beggar Student, The 1921,Ja 8,9:3; 1942,S 26,11:4
Beggarman, Thief 1935,Jl 16,24:1
Beggars Are Comming to Town 1945,O 29,16:2
Beggar's Holiday 1946,D 27,13:3; 1947,Ja 26,II,1:1
Beggar's Opera, The 1934,Jl 17,24:5; 1940,Mr 17,X,1:8; 1941,Ag 12,14:6; 1952,S 26,17:4; 1957,Mr 14,35:1; 1963,Jl 17,20:1; 1965,Mr 21,II,13:1
Beginner's Luck 1935,Jl 23,24:4
Beginning to End 1970,Ap 25,32:3
Behavior of Mrs Crane, The 1928,Mr 21,30:1; 1928,My 27,VIII,1:1
Behind the Red Lights 1937,Ja 14,17:4
Behind the Second Front 1949,My 9,3:3
Behind the Wall 1960,N 1,47:1
Behind Your Back 1937,F 14,X,3:1
Behold the Bride 1939,My 24,28:3; 1939,Je 11,IX,2:5
Behold the Bridegroom 1927,D 27,24:1; 1928,Ja 1,VIII,1:1
Behold This Dreamer 1927,O 16,IX,2:4; 1927,N 1,20:4
Behold We Live 1932,Ag 17,13:2; 1932,S 11,IX,1:1
Behold Your God 1936,Ap 22,28:3
Bei Mir Bistu Schoen 1961,O 23,22:2
Bela Is 26 1930,Mr 9,IX,8:5
Belafonte at the Palace 1959,D 16,55:1
Believers, The 1968,My 10,57:4
Belinda 1922,Jl 30,VI,1:7
Bell, Book and Candle 1950,N 15,37:4; 1950,D 17,II,3:1; 1954,O 6,30:8
Bell for Adano, A 1944,N 10,24:6; 1944,D 7,21:2; 1944,D 17,II,3:2; 1945,S 20,31:1
Bella 1961,N 17,40:1
Bellairs 1933,Ap 23,X,1:3
Bellamy Trial, The 1928,Ag 20,21:1; 1931,Ap 23,28:6
Belle au Bois, La 1932,Ap 3,VIII,2:1
Belle de Nuit, La 1932,Ap 10,VIII,2:5
Belle Helene, La 1941,Jl 8,14:1
Belle Mariniere, La 1929,D 8,X,2:2
Belle of New York, The 1942,O 4,VIII,2:3; 1948,D 2,36:6
Belle Starr 1969,My 3,40:2
Bellow Plays, The 1966,Je 8,42:2
Bells, The 1926,Ap 14,20:3; 1933,O 22,IX,2:2
Bells Are Ringing 1956,N 29,43:4; 1956,N 30,18:2; 1956,D 16,II,3:1; 1957,N 15,37:1
Belmont Varieties 1932,S 29,17:2
Beloved Augustine, The 1931,Ap 26,VIII,2:6
Below the Surface 1932,Ja 31,VIII,2:1
Belt, The 1927,O 20,33:1
Ben Bagley's New Cole Porter Revue 1965,D 23,20:1
Ben Bagley's Shoestring Revues 1970,O 24,22:1
Ben Franklin in Paris 1964,O 28,52:1
Bench, The 1968,Mr 5,35:2
Benefit of the Doubt, The 1935,Ag 4,IX,1:3
Benito Cereno 1964,N 2,62:2
Bequest to the Nation, A 1970,S 25,36:1
Beranger 1923,Ap 20,20:3
Berdichever Bridegroom, The 1930,S 24,26:2
Berenice 1963,O 30,46:1
Bergbahn 1929,My 26,IX,2:3
Berkaszarnya 1928,O 28,IX,2:1
Berkeley Square 1926,O 7,19:6; 1926,O 24,VIII,2:1; 1929,Mr 24,X,4:5; 1929,N 5,32:4; 1929,D 1,X,1:1; 1935,Ag 20,25:1
Berl and Shmerl Corporation 1934,Ap 2,12:5
Berlin 1931,D 31,16:1
Berlin 1945 1956,S 22,20:6
Berlioz 1927,F 20,VII,2:1
Bernard Shaw Story, The 1965,N 19,31:1
Bernardine 1952,O 17,33:4; 1952,N 9,II,1:1
Berretto a Songali, Il 1931,N 30,16:3
Bertha 1962,F 12,27:1
Bertha, the Sewing Machine Girl 1935,N 6,32:6
Besserer Herr, Ein 1927,My 29,VII,2:1
Best Foot Forward 1941,S 12,24:4; 1941,O 2,28:2; 1941,O 26,IX,1:3; 1956,Mr 3,16:1; 1963,Ap 3,43:1
Best House in Naples, The 1956,O 27,16:2
Best Laid Plans, The 1966,Mr 26,15:2
Best Man, The 1960,Ap 1,39:1; 1960,Ap 10,II,1:1; 1960,O 5,44:6
Best of Burlesque 1957,S 30,27:2

Best of Everything, The 1952,My 8,35:4
Best of Friends 1970,F 21,22:1
Best People, The 1924,Ag 20,8:1; 1933,Mr 16,21:5
Best Sellers 1933,My 4,20:2
Best Years 1932,S 8,16:2
Bet Your Life 1937,Ap 6,20:2; 1952,F 19,26:6
Bete Noire, La 1934,My 13,IX,2:2
Bethlehem 1926,D 21,20:1
Betrayal 1931,Ja 25,VIII,2:7
Betrayal, The 1928,Je 6,23:4
Betrothal, The 1959,F 16,52:2
Betrothed, The 1934,O 22,13:2
Betsy 1926,D 29,24:3
Better Luck Next Time 1966,Ja 28,21:1
Better 'Ole, The 1927,Ag 23,29:3
Better Times 1922,S 4,14:2
Betty, Be Careful 1931,My 5,33:3
Betty, Be Good 1920,My 5,14:2
Betty Behave 1927,Mr 9,28:4
Betty Lee 1924,D 26,18:2
Between the Devil 1937,O 15,19:1; 1937,O 24,XI,2:1; 1937,D 23,24:5
Between Two Thieves 1960,F 12,23:1
Between Two Worlds 1934,O 26,24:2
Between Us Two 1935,Ja 31,22:4; 1935,F 17,VIII,3:1
Beux Billes de Cadix, Les 1923,Ja 21,VII,1:3
Beverly Hills 1940,N 8,24:2
Beware of Dogs 1921,O 4,10:1
Beware of the Bull 1933,My 30,13:7
Beware of Widows 1925,N 8,VIII,2:1; 1925,D 2,22:3
Bewitched 1924,O 2,26:3; 1924,O 5,VIII,1:1; 1924,O 19,VIII,1:1
Beyond 1925,Ja 27,14:1; 1925,F 1,VII,1:1
Beyond Desire 1967,O 11,36:1
Beyond Evil 1926,Je 8,23:2
Beyond the Fringe 1961,Je 25,II,3:5; 1962,O 29,36:1
Beyond the Fringe, '65 1964,D 16,49:2
Beyond the Fringe 1964 1964,Ja 10,18:1
Beyond the Horizon 1920,F 4,12:1; 1920,F 8,VIII,2:1; 1920,Mr 10,9:2; 1926,D 1,24:2; 1926,D 26,VII,1:1; 1938,Mr 20,XI,3:1; 1962,O 26,27:2
Beyond the Ocean 1970,Ag 19,30:1
Bezauberndes Fraeulein 1933,N 19,IX,3:1
Biarritz 1929,Ag 11,VIII,2:1
Bible Salesman, The 1960,F 22,12:2; 1961,F 21,40:1
Bicentennial 1939,Ag 29,18:2
Bichon 1936,D 31,20:5
Bicycle Ride to Nevada 1963,S 25,38:1
Bidding High 1932,S 29,17:2
Biddy 1927,D 7,32:1
Biff, Bing, Bang 1921,My 10,20:1
Bifur 1932,F 28,VIII,1:1
Big Ben 1939,S 10,IX,2:2; 1946,Ag 4,II,1:4
Big Blow 1938,O 3,11:2
Big Boy 1925,Ja 8,28:2; 1925,Ag 25,12:2; 1925,S 6,VII,1:1
Big Business 1937,F 19,15:3
Big Claus and Little Claus 1931,Mr 1,VIII,3:1
Big Deal, The 1953,Mr 7,13:6
Big Fight, The 1928,Ag 31,23:1; 1928,S 19,33:1; 1928,S 23,IX,1:1
Big Fish, Little Fish 1961,Mr 16,42:2; 1961,Mr 26,II,1:1
Big Game 1920,Ja 22,23:1; 1920,Ja 25,VIII,2:2
Big Hearted Herbert 1934,Ja 2,17:3
Big House, The 1933,Ja 5,19:3; 1934,F 22,24:4; 1934,Mr 18,IX,2:3
Big Knife, The 1949,F 25,27:5; 1949,Mr 6,II,1:1; 1954,Ja 3,I,64:4; 1954,Ja 17,II,4:4; 1959,N 13,25:1
Big Lake 1927,Ap 9,17:2
Big Man 1966,My 20,41:1
Big Mogul, The 1925,My 12,26:3
Big Night 1933,Ja 18,16:2
Big Pond, The 1928,Ag 22,25:1; 1928,S 9,IX,1:1
Big Surprise, The 1932,O 17,18:3
Big Time Buck White 1968,D 9,58:1; 1968,D 15,II,5:1; 1968,D 29,II,1:1; 1969,D 7,II,5:1
Big Top 1942,My 9,11:1; 1942,My 17,VIII,1:3
Big Two, The 1947,Ja 9,21:2
Big White Fog 1940,O 23,26:2
Biggest Thief in Town 1949,Mr 31,31:2
Bil and Cora Baird's Marionette Theater 1955,D 27,29:2; 1956,S 3,10:1; 1963,Ap 12,34:2
Bill Noname 1970,Mr 3,37:1
Bill of Divorcement, A 1921,O 11,22:2; 1921,O 16,VI,1:1; 1924,S 7,VII,1:1
Billeted 1922,My 10,22:4
Billie 1928,O 2,34:2
Billion Dollar Baby 1945,D 30,II,1:1
Billy 1969,Mr 24,56:1
Billy Barnes People, The 1961,Je 14,10:3
Billy Barnes Revue, The 1959,Je 10,42:2; 1959,Ag 30,II,1:2
Billy Budd 1951,F 12,18:3; 1951,F 18,II,1:1; 1951,Ap 15,II,1:1; 1951,My 6,II,1:1; 1951,My 20,II,1:1; 1955,My 4,35:1; 1959,F 28,13:3
Billy Draws a Horse 1939,D 22,14:5
Billy Liar 1965,Mr 18,26:1
Billy the Kid 1951,Ag 21,23:2
Billygoat Eddie 1964,Ap 21,43:2
Bing Boys Are Here, The 1934,D 19,26:6

Biography 1932,D 13,25:3; 1933,Ja 22,IX,1:1;
  1934,F 6,24:4; 1934,My 20,IX,2:4;
  1937,Ap 11,II,12:8; 1938,Ag 3,14:7
Bird Cage, The 1925,Je 3,26:2; 1950,F 23,32:2
Bird in Hand 1928,My 13,IX,2:7; 1929,Ap 5,28:2;
  1929,Ap 14,X,1:1; 1942,O 20,24:2
Bird of Time 1961,Je 25,II,3:5
Birdbath 1966,Ap 12,43:1
Birds, The 1928,F 19,VIII,4:4; 1935,Jl 21,II,3:2;
  1966,Jl 1,40:1; 1967,My 7,67:1
Birth 1932,Mr 20,VIII,2:4
Birthday 1934,D 27,24:2
Birthday Party, The 1961,My 15,34:6; 1967,O 4,40:2;
  1967,O 15,II,1:1
Birthright 1920,My 25,14:2; 1932,N 4,25:1;
  1933,N 22,22:3
Biscuit 1966,My 17,51:2
Bishop Misbehaves, The 1935,F 21,22:4;
  1935,Ag 27,23:4
Bishop's Bonfire, The 1955,Mr 1,22:8;
  1955,Mr 6,II,3:1; 1961,Jl 27,22:2
Bit o' Love, A 1925,My 13,24:2
Bitch of Waverly Place, The 1965,Ap 2,26:1
Bitter Harvest 1936,Mr 1,IX,3:6; 1936,My 13,28:1
Bitter Oleander 1935,F 12,24:3
Bitter Stream 1936,Mr 31,16:6
Bitter Sweet 1929,Jl 19,14:2; 1929,O 27,IX,2:1;
  1929,N 6,30:2; 1929,D 29,VIII,4:1; 1930,N 4,37:3;
  1934,My 8,28:4; 1936,Ag 26,17:3
Bitter Tulips 1936,Mr 5,24:6
Bivouac at Lucca 1957,O 30,26:1
Black Ace, The 1929,Je 2,VIII,2:7
Black and White Revue, The 1923,O 28,VIII,2:1
Black Boy 1926,S 26,VIII,2:7; 1926,O 7,30:2
Black Chiffon 1949,Je 12,II,3:1; 1950,S 28,39:2;
  1950,O 15,II,1:1
Black Cockatoo, The 1926,D 31,11:1
Black Comedy 1965,Jl 29,19:1; 1967,F 13,42:1;
  1967,F 26,II,1:5; 1967,O 19,58:1
Black Crook, The 1929,Mr 12,26:5;
  1929,Mr 17,X,8:1; 1929,Ap 7,X,1:1
Black Diamond 1933,F 24,12:2
Black Divan 1921,Ap 10,VI,1:1
Black Eye, The 1935,O 12,13:5; 1935,N 10,IX,3:1;
  1938,Mr 8,22:4
Black-Eyed Susan 1954,D 24,7:5
Black Limelight 1936,N 10,31:1; 1937,My 2,XI,2:1
Black Magic 1931,S 6,VIII,2:1
Black Monday 1962,Mr 7,29:1
Black Nativity 1961,D 12,54:1
Black Oliver 1927,Je 5,VII,2:3
Black Pit 1935,Mr 21,26:6
Black Quartet, A 1969,Jl 31,28:1; 1969,Ag 3,II,1:4;
  1969,S 22,36:1
Black Rhythm 1936,D 21,19:2
Black Scandals 1928,O 27,23:2
Black Sheep 1932,O 14,22:6
Black Souls 1932,Mr 31,25:1
Black Swans 1938,Mr 6,XI,3:6
Black Tower 1932,Ja 12,29:2
Black Vanities 1941,My 4,IX,1:7
Black Velvet 1927,S 28,28:1
Black Widow 1936,F 13,24:3
Blackberries of 1932 1932,Ap 5,27:5
Blackbirds 1926,S 25,21:5; 1928,My 10,31:3;
  1933,D 4,22:3; 1934,Ag 26,II,6:5; 1934,S 16,X,2:1;
  1936,Jl 10,15:1; 1938,N 13,IX,2:2
Blackmail 1924,S 7,VII,1:4
Blackouts of 1949 1949,S 7,39:2
Blacks, The 1961,My 5,23:1; 1961,My 14,II,1:1
Blanchette 1924,Mr 19,19:4
Blancs, Les 1970,N 16,48:4; 1970,N 29,II,3:1;
  1970,N 29,II,3:5
Blaue Boll, Der 1931,Ja 25,VIII,4:1
Blaue Hemd von Ithaka, Das 1931,Mr 15,IX,2:4
Blaue Mazur, Der 1921,My 15,VI,1:6
Blaue vom Himmel, Das 1930,Ap 20,VIII,2:1
Bleak House 1952,S 4,24:7; 1953,Ap 21,33:2
Bless the Bride 1947,My 5,31:2; 1947,My 11,II,3:7
Bless the Child 1968,My 5,II,16:1
Bless You, Sister 1927,N 27,IX,2:1; 1927,D 27,24:5
Bless You All 1950,D 15,42:2; 1951,My 20,II,1:1
Blessed Event 1932,Ja 31,VIII,1:6; 1932,F 13,23:2;
  1932,F 21,VIII,1:1
Blind Alley 1935,S 25,19:6; 1939,Ag 23,18:8;
  1940,O 16,28:2
Blind Alleys 1924,N 18,23:3
Blind Angel, The 1965,Ap 2,26:1
Blind Heart, The 1927,My 8,30:2
Blind Man's Buff 1953,N 15,II,3:1
Blind Mice 1930,S 7,IX,2:4; 1930,O 16,28:2
Blind Wolf, The 1928,My 27,VIII,2:7
Blithe Spirit 1941,Jl 3,13:1; 1941,Jl 13,IX,1:4;
  1941,N 6,26:2; 1941,N 16,IX,1:1; 1943,S 12,II,1:1;
  1946,Je 5,17:3; 1952,F 23,7:5; 1970,S 17,57:1
Blitz 1962,My 8,5:6
Blitzstein! 1966,D 1,58:2
Bloch de Chicago 1933,O 1,IX,1:3; 1933,O 15,IX,1:8
Blonde Beast, The 1923,Mr 3,9:3
Blonde Sinner, The 1926,Jl 15,21:2
Blood, Sweat & Stanley Poole 1961,O 6,31:1
Blood and Sand 1921,S 21,16:2; 1921,S 25,VI,1:4
Blood Bugle, The 1961,Je 29,26:1

Blood Knot, The 1964,Mr 3,30:2
Blood Money 1925,N 1,VIII,1:3; 1927,Ag 23,29:2
Blood of the Bambergs, The 1962,Jl 20,15:3
Blood on the Moon 1934,S 30,IX,3:1
Blood Red Roses 1970,Mr 23,48:1
Blood Wedding 1949,F 7,16:2; 1949,F 13,II,1:1;
  1958,Ap 1,35:1
Bloodstream 1932,Mr 31,25:1
Bloody Laughter 1931,D 5,20:6
Bloomer Girl 1944,O 6,18:5; 1944,O 8,II,1:1;
  1947,Ja 7,33:2
Bloomfield 1930,O 12,VIII,4:2
Blossom Time 1921,S 30,10:1; 1921,O 9,VI,1:1;
  1922,O 24,18:2; 1923,My 22,14:3; 1923,Je 1,22:2;
  1931,Mr 5,32:1; 1936,Jl 29,23:1; 1936,Ag 30,II,5:8;
  1938,D 27,12:2; 1943,S 6,21:2
Blow the Man Down 1929,Ag 25,VIII,3:1
Blow Ye Winds 1937,S 8,20:5; 1937,S 24,17:4
Blow Your Own Trumpet 1943,S 19,II,1:6
Blue and the Gray, The 1929,D 27,26:4
Blue Bandanna, The 1924,Je 24,18:4
Blue Beard 1929,Jl 7,VIII,2:1
Blue Bird, The 1923,D 26,13:3; 1923,D 30,VII,1:1;
  1925,Ja 30,10:2; 1925,F 8,VII,1:1;
  1931,My 24,VIII,2:1; 1932,Ap 22,23:2
Blue Blood 1924,Ap 3,21:2
Blue Bonnet 1920,Ag 30,12:1
Blue Boy in Black, The 1963,My 1,32:1
Blue Butterfly, The 1929,F 17,29:3; 1929,My 4,17:2
Blue Comedy 1968,O 23,36:1
Blue Denim 1958,F 28,17:1; 1958,Ap 20,II,1:1
Blue Eyes 1921,F 22,11:2
Blue Flame, The 1920,Mr 16,18:1
Blue Fox 1957,D 5,47:2
Blue Ghost, The 1930,Mr 11,24:5
Blue Holiday 1945,My 22,13:3
Blue Jeans 1933,Ap 9,31:5
Blue Kitten, The 1922,Ja 14,9:3; 1926,Ja 3,VII,2:8
Blue Lagoon, The 1921,S 15,16:1
Blue Monday 1932,Je 3,23:2
Blue Peter, The 1924,O 19,VIII,2:7; 1925,Mr 25,25:3
Blue Train, The 1927,Je 5,VII,2:1
Blue Widow, The 1933,Ag 31,20:2
Bluebeard 1970,My 5,58:1
Bluebeard's Eighth Wife 1921,S 20,12:2
Blueprints 1969,F 25,36:1
Blues, Ballads and Sin-Songs 1954,O 5,23:4
Blues for Mister Charlie 1964,Ap 24,24:1;
  1964,My 3,II,1:1; 1965,My 5,52:1
Bluestone Quarry 1931,N 29,VIII,2:2
Bluff 1932,Ja 3,VIII,2:4
Bluffing Bluffers 1924,D 23,17:2
Blume von Hawaii, Die 1931,O 4,VIII,4:1
Blushing Bride, The 1922,F 7,12:1
Bob and Ray-The Two and Only 1970,S 25,36:1;
  1970,O 4,II,3:1
Bobard 1930,My 4,XI,2:6
Bobino 1944,Ap 7,33:3
Boccacco's Untold Tale 1923,My 8,22:3
Body and Soul 1922,O 8,VI,1:7
Body Beautiful, The 1935,N 1,24:3; 1958,Ja 24,15:2
Boeing-Boeing 1961,Ja 3,35:2; 1965,F 3,30:1
Boeuf sur le Toit, Le 1930,Ap 25,28:4
Bohemian Girl, The 1933,Jl 28,18:5
Bohikee Creek 1966,Ap 29,39:1
Bois Sacre, Le 1924,Mr 23,VIII,1:3
Bolls of Cotton 1925,D 22,18:3
Bolsheviks, The 1969,F 3,3:1
Bombasters Furioso 1924,Jl 19,10:4
Bombo 1921,O 7,20:2; 1923,My 15,22:2
Bomboola 1929,Je 27,17:3
Bon-bon 1920,Mr 1,16:2
Bon Garcon, Un 1929,Mr 19,36:2
Bon Voyage 1929,D 29,VIII,4:3; 1949,Ap 26,28:2
Bonaparte 1927,My 15,VIII,1:3
Bonaventure 1950,Ja 8,II,3:7
Bonds of Interest, The 1929,O 15,34:2; 1951,D 1,7:2;
  1958,My 7,43:1
Bonehead, The 1920,Ap 13,12:1; 1920,Ap 18,VI,2:4
Bonfire, The 1962,My 31,23:6
Bonfire to Glory 1936,Jl 28,23:4
Bonheur 1933,My 14,IX,1:4
Bonheur, Impair et Passe 1964,Ja 17,23:3
Bonheur, Le 1923,N 20,23:3
Bonheur du Jour, Le 1926,D 5,VIII,6:1
Bonita 1927,S 4,VII,2:4
Bonnes, Les 1963,S 4,34:3
Bonnet Over the Windmill 1937,S 9,19:4;
  1937,S 26,XI,2:5
Boo Hoo! East Lynne 1959,S 9,50:4
Book, The 1965,Ja 6,32:1
Book of Charm, The 1925,S 4,26:3;
  1925,S 13,VIII,1:1; 1936,Je 30,15:1
Book of Job, The 1922,O 31,11:1; 1936,Mr 5,24:6;
  1962,F 10,13:1
Boom Boom 1929,Ja 29,26:4
Boom-Boom Clopper 1940,Ja 6,8:7
Booster, The 1929,O 25,26:2
Bootleggers, The 1922,N 28,24:1
Borak 1960,D 14,51:1
Border-Land 1932,Mr 30,15:5
Borderer, The 1923,Mr 18,VII,1:1

Borderline 1937,F 10,18:6
Borgia, Les 1938,Je 12,X,2:3
Boris and Bessie 1937,D 23,24:6
Boris Godunoff 1925,F 27,14:1
Born Yesterday 1946,F 5,18:2; 1946,F 10,II,1:1;
  1946,N 5,32:1; 1947,F 9,II,3:7; 1947,My 18,II,1:1;
  1948,Ap 9,26:3; 1954,Ja 1,16:6; 1958,Mr 22,12:6
Borned in Texas 1950,Ag 22,30:6
Borrowed Life, The 1931,Ja 4,VIII,2:6
Borrowed Love 1929,Je 18,29:2
Borscht Capades 1951,S 18,38:3
Borstal Boy 1967,O 11,39:2; 1967,O 12,55:2;
  1970,Ap 1,38:1; 1970,Ap 12,II,9:6
Boston Story, A 1968,S 21,26:2
Boswell's Life of Johnson 1970,S 4,19:1
Both Ends Meet 1954,Jl 18,II,1:7
Both Kooney Lemels 1964,O 12,37:2
Both Your Houses 1933,Mr 7,20:3;
  1933,Mr 12,IX,1:1; 1933,My 23,22:2
Bottled 1928,Ap 11,25:1
Bottom of the Cup, The 1927,F 1,24:2
Bottomland 1927,Je 28,29:3
Boubouroche 1921,N 29,20:1; 1921,D 4,VII,1:2
Boucheur N'Est Pas de ce Monde, Le
  1926,D 26,VII,2:1
Boudoir 1941,F 8,18:4
Bough Breaks, The 1937,N 20,21:4
Bought and Paid For 1921,D 8,17:5
Boulevard Durand 1961,O 8,II,3:4
Bound East for Cardiff 1929,Ja 27,IX,1:1;
  1937,O 30,23:2; 1948,My 21,21:2;
  1948,My 30,II,1:1; 1961,My 11,43:1
Boundry Line, The 1930,F 6,21:1
Bourgeois Gentilhomme, Le 1924,N 20,21:2;
  1928,O 7,IX,1:1; 1929,Mr 17,30:4;
  1929,Mr 24,X,2:3; 1954,Ap 14,26:7; 1955,O 26,26:1;
  1955,O 30,II,1:1; 1964,Je 18,28:2
Bourgeois Gentleman, The 1949,Ag 31,27:2
Bourgeoise, La 1927,O 2,VIII,2:4; 1927,O 16,IX,4:7
Boutique Fantasque, La 1928,D 27,26:6;
  1929,D 28,10:6
Box 1968,Mr 8,48:1; 1968,O 1,39:1; 1968,O 13,II,5:1
Box and Cox 1956,My 24,27:2
Box-Mao-Box 1968,Mr 8,48:1; 1968,Mr 17,II,1:6
Box of Watercolors, A 1957,F 18,22:2
Box Seats 1928,Ap 20,27:2
Boy 1964,Ag 1,13:1
Boy David, The 1936,N 22,VI,7:1; 1936,D 13,XI,5:3;
  1936,D 15,30:6; 1939,Ag 6,IX,2:1
Boy Friend, The 1932,Je 8,22:3; 1954,O 1,20:1;
  1954,O 10,II,1:1; 1958,Ja 27,24:4; 1970,Ap 15,54:1;
  1970,Ap 26,II,5:7
Boy Growing Up, A 1957,O 8,41:1
Boy Meets Girl 1935,N 19,27:2; 1935,N 28,38:2;
  1935,D 15,XI,3:1; 1936,My 28,18:8;
  1936,Je 28,IX,1:8; 1937,Jl 6,23:1; 1943,Je 23,15:5
Boy on the Straight-Back Chair 1969,Mr 18,36:1
Boy Who Lived Twice, A 1945,S 12,31:2;
  1945,S 23,II,1:1
Boy Who Would Not Grow Up, The 1928,N 27,36:3
Boy With a Cart, The 1954,Ap 5,19:2
Boyd's Daughter 1940,O 12,20:2
Boyd's Shop 1936,F 21,20:5
Boys and Girls Together 1940,S 5,28:6;
  1940,O 2,19:2; 1940,O 13,IX,1:1
Boys From Syracuse, The 1938,N 13,IX,2:2;
  1938,N 24,36:1; 1963,Ap 16,31:1; 1963,Je 2,II,1:1;
  1963,N 9,14:3
Boys in Brown 1940,Je 23,IX,2:5
Boys in the Band, The 1968,Ap 15,48:1;
  1968,Ap 28,II,1:6; 1969,F 13,52:2; 1969,F 18,36:1;
  1969,S 20,21:2; 1970,Ap 18,34:1
Brain Sweat 1934,Ap 5,24:4
Brains 1926,My 4,30:2
Brandy Is My True Love's Name 1953,Je 18,38:5
Brass Ankle 1931,Ap 24,26:4
Brass Butterfly, The 1970,Ja 31,34:1
Brass Buttons 1927,D 6,26:3
Brass Door Knob, The 1926,My 8,21:2
Brass Paperweight, The 1928,N 4,IX,2:4
Brass Ring, The 1952,Ap 11,19:2
Braut von Lucullus, Die 1921,D 11,VI,1:4
Braut von Torozko, Die 1932,Je 19,IX,1:6
Brave and the Blind, The 1937,Mr 22,26:5
Bravo Giovanni 1962,My 21,41:2; 1962,My 27,II,1:1
Bravo! 1948,N 12,31:2
Breach of Marriage 1949,Ja 27,20:5
Bread 1932,D 14,27:3
Breadwinner, The 1930,O 1,26:3; 1930,O 19,IX,4:1;
  1931,S 23,19:4
Breakfast at Tiffany's 1966,D 15,60:1
Breakfast in Bed 1920,F 4,12:1
Breaking Point, The 1923,Jl 1,VI,1:4; 1923,Ag 17,8:4;
  1923,Ag 26,VI,1:1
Breaking Wall, The 1960,Ja 26,27:5
Breaks, The 1928,Ap 17,26:3
Breakspear on Gascony 1959,Ag 26,25:3
Brecht on Brecht 1961,N 15,52:2; 1962,Ja 4,26:1;
  1962,Ja 14,II,1:1
Brest-Litovsk 1930,N 30,IX,2:1
Bridal Crown, The 1938,F 7,11:2
Bridal Night, The 1966,N 8,45:1
Bridal Quilt 1934,O 11,28:5

Bridal Veil, The 1928,Ja 27,15:2
Bridal Wise 1932,My 31,15:5
Bride, The 1924,F 24,VII,2:5; 1924,My 6,25:1;
  1924,My 11,VIII,1:1; 1931,F 22,VIII,3:5
Bride for the Unicorn, A 1934,My 3,15:5;
  1936,Jl 26,IX,1:3
Bride Got Farblondjet, The 1967,N 6,61:6
Bride in the Morning, A 1960,My 26,38:2
Bride of Messina, The 1933,D 10,X,5:1
Bride of the Lamb 1926,Mr 31,20:3;
  1926,Ap 4,VIII,1:1; 1934,Mr 29,26:1
Bride of Torozko, The 1934,Jl 10,24:7;
  1934,S 14,24:2
Bride Retires, The 1925,My 18,12:3
Bride the Sun Shines On, The 1931,D 28,20:2;
  1936,Jl 1,29:2
Bridge, The 1930,My 6,33:1; 1939,My 28,X,1:3
Bridge of Distances, The 1925,S 29,30:1;
  1925,O 4,IX,1:1
Bridge of Sighs 1939,Jl 2,IX,1:4
Bridgehead 1934,Je 20,24:1; 1935,Ag 7,22:3
Brief Lives 1967,D 19,60:4
Brief Moment 1931,O 25,VIII,2:1; 1931,N 10,28:2;
  1932,F 28,VIII,1:1
Brig, The 1963,My 16,40:1; 1964,S 4,18:4
Brigadoon 1947,Mr 14,28:2; 1947,Mr 23,II,1:1;
  1949,Ap 16,11:1; 1950,My 3,36:2; 1957,Mr 28,37:1;
  1962,My 31,21:4; 1963,F 1,6:2; 1964,D 24,9:1;
  1967,D 14,59:2
Bright Boy 1944,Mr 3,19:5
Bright Honor 1936,S 28,14:1
Bright Rebel 1938,D 28,24:2
Bright Star 1935,O 13,IX,1:6; 1935,O 16,26:2;
  1936,F 17,21:4
Bright Sun at Midnight 1957,N 29,32:4
Brighten the Corner 1945,D 13,33:2
Brighter London 1923,Ap 8,VIII,1:7
Brightower 1970,Ja 29,32:1
Brights Lights of 1944 1943,S 17,27:4
Brigitta, La 1962,S 25,30:1
Bring Me a Warm Body 1962,Ap 17,29:3
Bring on the Girls 1934,O 23,23:2
Bringers of Offerings, The 1967,Jl 24,23:1
Bringing Up Father 1925,Mr 31,16:1
Britannicus 1958,N 29,17:2; 1961,Mr 3,17:1
Brittle Heaven 1934,N 14,22:5
Broadway 1926,S 17,19:3; 1926,S 26,VIII,1:1;
  1926,D 23,23:1; 1927,Ja 9,VII,2:1;
  1927,O 23,VIII,2:4; 1928,Mr 11,5:3;
  1928,Ap 15,IX,4:7; 1928,O 12,34:2
Broadway Boy 1932,My 4,23:5
Broadway Brevities, 1920 1920,S 30,12:2
Broadway Interlude 1934,Ap 20,16:3
Broadway Nights 1929,Je 23,VIII,2:4; 1929,Jl 16,23:2
Broadway Shadows 1930,Ap 1,34:6
Broadway Sho-Window 1936,Ap 13,14:5
Broadway Whirl, The 1921,Je 9,10:4
Broke 1925,My 3,VIII,2:1
Broken Branches 1922,Mr 7,11:1
Broken Chain, The 1929,F 21,30:4
Broken Dishes 1929,N 6,28:3
Broken Engagement, The 1921,My 12,20:2
Broken Heart, The 1962,Jl 10,28:2
Broken Hearts of Broadway 1944,Je 13,16:2
Broken Journey 1942,Je 24,22:2
Broken Jug, The 1958,Ap 2,36:1
Broken Wing, The 1920,N 30,14:1; 1920,D 5,VII,1:1
Brontes, The 1933,Ap 21,24:8; 1933,My 7,IX,1:4;
  1963,D 21,17:2
Bronx Express 1922,Ap 27,12:2; 1922,Ap 30,VII,1:1;
  1927,D 4,31:4
Bronx Express, 1968 1968,N 16,43:3
Brook 1923,Ag 20,14:3
Brooklyn, U S A 1941,D 22,24:2; 1941,D 28,IX,1:1;
  1942,Ja 11,IX,1:1
Brooklyn Biarritz 1941,F 28,16:2
Broomsticks Amen! 1934,F 10,20:4
Brother Cain 1941,S 13,21:5
Brother Elks 1925,S 15,29:2
Brother Rat 1936,D 8,30:6; 1936,D 17,34:5
Brother to Dragons 1968,D 8,86:1
Brotherhood 1970,Mr 18,39:1; 1970,Mr 29,II,1:1
Brothers 1928,D 26,14:3
Brothers Ashkenazi, The 1937,S 21,28:6;
  1955,N 12,24:4; 1970,N 17,53:2
Brothers Karamazov, The 1923,F 27,14:2;
  1923,Mr 4,VII,1:1; 1923,N 20,23:4; 1924,My 6,25:2;
  1926,D 12,VIII,3:4; 1927,Ja 4,20:1;
  1927,Ja 9,VII,1:1; 1928,My 6,IX,2:4; 1957,D 9,39:4;
  1957,D 22,II,3:1
Brouhaha 1958,Ag 28,18:8; 1960,Ap 27,31:2
Brout 1928,N 11,X,2:7
Brown Buddies 1930,O 8,29:1
Brown Danube, The 1939,My 18,30:4
Brown Sugar 1937,D 3,29:2
Browning 1930,D 14,IX,2:7
Browning Version, The 1948,O 10,II,3:7;
  1949,O 13,32:2; 1949,O 23,II,1:1; 1958,Mr 7,17:2
Brownstone Urge, The 1969,D 18,63:1
Brownsville Grandfather, The 1935,Ap 19,24:6
Bruder Straubinger 1921,N 16,22:3
Bruno and Sidney 1949,My 4,38:2

Bryllupsdager 1930,D 28,VIII,3:5
Bubble Along 1930,Je 3,27:3
Bublitchki 1938,Ja 17,11:2
Buccaneer, The 1925,S 20,VIII,2:4; 1925,O 3,10:2
Bucharest-Moscow 1941,O 12,I,25:1
Buck White 1969,D 3,63:1
Buckaroo 1929,Mr 18,31:1
Budget, The 1932,S 21,26:4
Buds of 1927 1927,F 22,22:5
Buffalo Skinner, The 1959,F 20,18:1
Bug 1929,Mr 3,III,3:6
Bugle in the Blood, The 1949,Mr 15,34:5
Bugles at Noon 1936,Jl 18,18:4
Bugs 1965,N 19,31:1
Building Blocks 1954,My 8,14:4
Building Fund, The 1928,Je 6,23:4
Building 222 1950,F 3,28:2
Bulldog Drummond 1921,D 27,10:2
Bulldog Drummond Hits Out 1937,D 22,33:2
Bullfight 1954,Ja 13,25:2
Bulls, Bears and Asses 1932,My 7,11:3
Bulls and Belles 1931,Ap 18,17:2
Bully, The 1924,D 26,18:1
Bunch and Judy, The 1922,N 12,VIII,1:6;
  1922,N 29,20:1
Bungler, The 1968,Ag 2,24:1
Bunk of 1926 1926,F 17,12:3; 1926,Ap 23,25:2
Buoyant Billions 1949,Ag 14,58:3; 1949,O 24,18:3;
  1959,My 27,32:2
Bureau-Crazy 1935,Ag 29,25:4
Burgomaster of Stilemonde, The 1923,N 16,15:3
Burial of Esposito, The 1969,D 8,60:4
Burlesk 1927,S 4,VII,1:1
Burlesque 1927,S 2,15:3; 1927,S 11,VIII,1:1;
  1928,Je 10,17:2; 1928,Jl 1,VIII,3:5; 1928,S 23,IX,2:2;
  1946,D 26,30:3; 1947,Ja 5,II,1:1
Burlesque As You Expect 1965,D 18,35:1
Burlesque-Mostly Girls 1931,F 13,20:2
Burlesque on Parade 1963,D 12,48:1
Burmese Pwe, A 1926,Mr 17,28:1
Burn Me to Ashes 1963,N 20,48:1
Burning, The 1963,D 4,57:1
Burning Bright 1950,O 19,40:2; 1950,O 29,II,1:1;
  1959,O 17,27:2
Burning Bush, The 1949,D 17,15:5
Burning Deck, The 1940,Mr 2,9:2
Burning Glass, The 1954,Mr 5,15:2;
  1954,Mr 14,II,1:1; 1954,Ap 11,II,2:1
Burning of the Lepers, The 1962,Ap 5,29:1
Bursting the Barriers 1930,My 7,25:1
Bury the Dead 1936,Mr 16,21:2; 1936,Ap 20,17:4;
  1936,Ap 26,IX,1:1
Bus Stop 1955,Mr 3,23:2; 1955,Mr 13,II,1:1
Business 1930,Ap 13,X,2:7
Business Widow, The 1923,D 11,27:1
Business With America 1933,Ja 1,IX,1:3
Buskers, The 1961,O 31,28:1
Busman's Honeymoon, A 1936,D 17,35:2;
  1937,Ja 10,X,1:8; 1937,Jl 13,22:3
Busybody, The 1924,S 30,27:5
But, Seriously... 1969,F 28,29:1
But for the Grace of God 1923,S 9,VII,2:4;
  1937,Ja 13,21:4; 1946,S 4,27:2; 1946,S 17,5:5
But for Whom Charlie 1964,Mr 13,42:2
But Never Jam Today 1969,Ap 24,40:1
But Not for Love 1934,N 27,26:2
But Not Goodbye 1944,Ap 12,19:2
Butter and Egg Man, The 1925,S 24,28:1;
  1927,Ag 23,28:3; 1927,Ag 31,19:3; 1949,Ap 29,27:1;
  1966,O 18,49:1
Butterflies 1927,F 2,22:4
Butterflies Are Free 1969,O 22,30:1; 1969,N 2,II,1:1;
  1970,N 5,60:4; 1970,D 3,60:2
Butterfly Dream, The 1966,My 20,41:1
Butterfly on the Wheel 1935,N 10,IX,3:1
Button, Button 1929,O 24,26:1; 1970,O 20,41:1;
  1970,N 1,II,26:1
Button Your Lip 1943,Je 15,16:1
Buttrio Square 1952,O 15,40:2
Buy, Buy Baby 1926,O 8,26:2
Buy Me Blue Ribbons 1951,O 18,33:2
Buzzard, The 1928,Mr 15,29:1
Buzzin' Around 1920,Jl 7,14:1
By Appointment 1934,O 13,10:4
By Candle Light 1928,O 7,IX,2:7
By George 1967,O 13,33:1
By Hex 1956,Je 19,25:1
By Jupiter 1942,Je 4,22:1; 1942,Ag 16,VIII,2:1;
  1942,Ag 30,VIII,1:1; 1967,Ja 20,28:2
By Pigeon Post 1940,My 19,IX,1:4
By Request 1928,Ag 26,VII,2:1; 1928,S 28,30:2;
  1928,O 7,IX,1:1
By the Beautiful Sea 1954,Ap 9,20:1;
  1954,Ap 18,II,1:1
By the Way 1925,N 22,VIII,1:8; 1925,D 29,20:3;
  1926,Ap 4,VIII,1:1; 1926,Ap 16,20:3
By Your Leave 1934,Ja 25,15:3
Bye Bye, Barbara 1924,Ag 26,6:3
Bye Bye Birdie 1960,Ap 15,13:4; 1961,Je 25,II,3:5
Bye Bye Bonnie 1927,Ja 14,15:3
Byron 1929,F 10,IX,4:7
Bystander 1931,F 1,VIII,3:4; 1937,S 15,27:1

C

Ca. . . C'Est Paris 1927,F 6,VII,4:1
Ca, C'Est Montmartre! 1927,F 6,VII,4:1
Cabalgata 1949,Jl 8,14:2
Cabaret 1966,N 21,62:1; 1966,D 4,II,5:1;
  1968,Ja 12,19:1; 1968,Mr 1,32:1; 1969,F 2,74:2
Cabaret Rive Gauche 1969,S 5,30:1
Cabbages and Kings 1933,Je 28,24:5; 1933,N 22,22:3
Cabin in the Sky 1940,O 26,19:2; 1940,N 3,IX,1:1;
  1940,N 10,IX,2:1; 1964,Ja 22,32:1
Cabrioles 1932,N 20,IX,2:1
Cactus Flower 1965,D 9,60:2; 1967,D 16,48:1
Caducee, Le 1922,Jl 30,VI,1:7
Caesar and Cleopatra 1925,Ap 14,27:1;
  1925,Ap 19,IX,1:1; 1927,N 6,IX,2:1;
  1929,Ja 6,VIII,4:7; 1932,O 16,IX,3:7;
  1935,Ag 22,21:1; 1949,D 22,28:2; 1950,Ja 8,II,1:1;
  1951,My 12:8; 1951,D 20,43:2; 1951,D 30,II,1:1;
  1963,Ag 1,18:2
Caesar Julius 1933,Mr 1,13:3
Cafe 1930,Ag 29,11:1
Cafe Crown 1942,Ja 24,12:5; 1964,Ap 18,32:1
Cafe de Danse 1928,D 30,VIII,1:6; 1929,Ja 6,VIII,4:4;
  1929,Ja 16,22:2
Cage, The 1927,Ag 14,VII,1:7; 1961,Mr 6,30:1;
  1970,Je 19,25:1; 1970,Jl 5,II,1:3
Cage Me a Peacock 1948,Jl 11,II,1:2
Cages 1963,Je 14,36:1
Caine Mutiny Court-Martial, The 1953,O 14,35:1;
  1953,D 15,52:8; 1954,Ja 21,27:2; 1954,Ja 31,II,1:1;
  1956,Je 14,40:1
Cajun, The 1926,My 6,23:3
Calculated Risk 1962,O 17,33:3; 1962,N 1,35:1
Calico Wedding 1945,Mr 8,18:6
California 1953,Je 18,38:5
Caligula 1949,Ap 23,10:2; 1950,D 31,II,3:7;
  1960,F 17,31:1; 1960,F 28,II,1:1
Call Home the Heart 1947,Ap 13,I,54:2
Call It a Day 1935,O 31,17:2; 1935,N 24,IX,1:2;
  1936,Ja 21,26:7; 1936,Ja 29,15:2; 1936,F 9,X,1:1
Call It Virtue 1963,Mr 28,8:2
Call Me by My Rightful Name 1961,F 1,31:1
Call Me Georges 1928,Je 10,VIII,1:3
Call Me Madam 1950,O 13,25:1; 1950,O 22,II,1:1;
  1951,My 20,II,1:1; 1952,Mr 16,84:3;
  1952,Mr 17,17:3; 1952,D 16,44:4
Call Me Mister 1946,Ap 19,26:2; 1946,Ap 28,II,1:1
Call Me Ziggy 1937,F 13,9:6
Call of Life, The 1925,O 10,10:1
Call on Kuprin, A 1961,My 26,29:3; 1961,Je 4,II,1:1
Call the Doctor 1920,S 1,14:1
Callimachus 1926,Mr 29,24:2
Calling All Stars 1934,D 22,26:1; 1934,D 14,28:2
Calling in Crazy 1969,O 7,42:2
Calvary 1960,Jl 22,13:1
Cambridge Circus 1964,O 7,53:1
Camel Through the Needle's Eye, The
  1929,Ap 16,32:2; 1929,Ap 28,IX,1:1
Camels Are Coming, The 1931,O 3,20:4
Camel's Back, The 1923,N 4,19:2; 1923,N 11,VIII,2:6;
  1923,N 18,VIII,1:1; 1924,F 10,VII,2:4
Camera Obscura 1968,My 9,55:2
Camilla States Her Case 1925,F 1,VII,2:1
Camille 1928,Ja 29,VIII,4:1; 1931,F 15,VIII,1:1;
  1932,O 28,23:2; 1932,N 2,23:3; 1934,O 22,13:2;
  1935,Jl 31,21:1; 1956,S 19,33:1
Camino Real 1953,Mr 20,26:1; 1953,Mr 29,II,1:1;
  1955,Mr 21,21:3; 1957,Ap 9,41:1; 1960,My 17,42:2;
  1960,My 29,II,1:1; 1970,Ja 9,42:1; 1970,Ja 18,II,1:1
Campo di Maggio 1931,Je 5,4:3; 1932,F 7,VIII,3:7
Can-Can 1953,My 8,28:1; 1953,My 17,II,1:1;
  1954,O 24,II,3:1; 1959,Ag 26,25:4; 1962,My 17,32:2
Can the Leopard...? 1932,Ja 3,VIII,2:1
Can We Tell? 1938,O 9,X,3:2
Canaries Sometimes Sing 1929,O 22,26:3;
  1929,N 10,X,2:1; 1930,O 21,34:2
Canary Dutch 1925,S 9,22:1
Candaules, Commissioner 1970,My 29,15:1
Candida 1922,Mr 23,11:1; 1924,D 13,12:3;
  1924,D 21,VII,1:1; 1925,Ja 11,VII,1:2;
  1925,Ap 5,IX,1:2; 1925,Ap 26,VIII,1:1;
  1925,N 10,23:4; 1925,D 19,14:2; 1926,Mr 17,28:3;
  1926,O 24,VIII,2:1; 1927,Ag 31,19:4;
  1935,Ag 20,25:1; 1935,O 27,IX,2:5; 1937,F 11,19:3;
  1937,F 28,XI,1:5; 1937,Mr 11,20:2;
  1937,Mr 21,XI,1:1; 1937,Ag 4,14:5;
  1938,Ag 31,13:2; 1942,Ap 28,24:4;
  1942,My 3,VII,1:1; 1945,Ag 7,25:3; 1946,Ap 4,33:2;
  1946,Ap 14,II,1:1; 1946,D 4,44:2; 1952,Ap 23,23:6;
  1957,F 9,14:1; 1957,Mr 29,18:5; 1961,Ap 27,26:1;
  1962,N 12,35:5; 1969,F 3,29:1; 1970,Ap 7,41:1
Candide 1933,My 16,15:6; 1956,D 3,40:2;
  1956,D 9,II,5:1; 1959,My 1,35:4
Candle in the Wind 1941,S 16,19:6; 1941,O 23,26:2;
  1941,N 2,IX,1:1
Candle-Light 1929,S 22,IX,2:6; 1929,O 1,28:2
Candyapple, The 1970,N 24,33:1
Cannibal Crackers 1969,N 25,52:2

Cannibals, The 1968,N 4,60:1; 1968,N 10,II,5:1
Cant 1931,D 20,VIII,1:6
Cantatrice Chauve, La 1962,Ja 16,30:1
Canteen Show, The 1942,S 4,18:1
Canterbury Tales 1968,S 7,23:3; 1969,F 4,34:1;
   1969,F 16,II,1:1
Cantico dei Cantici, Il 1931,Ap 13,17:3;
   1931,My 18,21:4
Cantilevered Terrace, The 1962,Ja 18,24:1;
   1962,Ja 28,II,1:1
Canto Della Vita, Il 1932,Ap 4,13:3
Cap des Tempetes 1937,N 14,XI,2:1
Cap With Bells, The 1931,N 30,16:3
Capacity for Wings 1957,Ja 10,25:2
Cape Cod Follies 1929,S 19,37:2
Cape Forlorn 1930,Ap 20,VIII,2:1
Cape Smoke 1925,F 17,19:1
Caponsacchi 1926,O 27,24:2; 1927,F 20,VII,1:1;
   1928,Ja 25,20:3
Caprice 1928,D 23,VIII,4:1; 1929,Ja 1,61:1;
   1929,Ja 13,VIII,1:1; 1929,Je 23,VIII,1:3
Caprice, Un 1924,N 25,26:2; 1938,F 8,17:2;
   1955,N 16,42:4
Caprices de Marianne 1936,Ja 12,IX,3:7
Captain Applejack 1921,D 31,14:2
Captain Brassbound's Conversion 1950,D 28,21:1
Captain Briquet 1923,S 16,VII,2:8
Captain Jinks 1925,S 9,22:1
Captain Jinks of the Horse Marines 1938,Ja 28,16:2
Captain of Koepenick, The 1931,Ap 26,VIII,1:4;
   1964,D 2,60:1
Captains and the Kings, The 1962,Ja 3,25:2
Captive, The 1926,S 30,23:1; 1926,O 10,VIII,1:1;
   1926,O 24,VIII,2:1
Caravan 1928,Ag 30,13:3; 1932,My 1,VIII,2:2
Card Players, The 1922,Ap 27,17:4;
   1922,My 21,VI,1:6
Cardinal, The 1931,Ja 12,24:2
Cardinal of Spain, The 1960,D 22,16:6
Cardinale, Il 1931,Ja 12,24:2; 1933,Ja 9,24:2
Cardinale Giovanni de Medici, Il 1935,D 9,24:8
Career 1943,O 29,22:6; 1957,My 1,42:6;
   1957,My 19,II,1:1
Career Angel 1943,N 19,24:2; 1944,My 24,23:7
Carefree Tree, The 1955,O 12,37:2
Careless Rapture 1936,S 12,20:6
Caretaker, The 1961,O 5,42:3; 1961,O 15,II,1:1;
   1963,N 25,23:2; 1964,Ja 31,16:1
Carib Song 1945,S 28,17:2
Caribbean Carnival 1947,D 6,12:2
Carine, ou la Jeune Fille Folle de son Ame
   1930,Ja 19,VIII,4:1
Carmen Jones 1943,O 20,17:2; 1943,D 3,26:2;
   1943,D 12,II,3:1; 1943,D 19,II,9:1; 1945,My 3,26:5;
   1946,Ap 8,32:2; 1946,Ap 14,II,1:2; 1951,S 22,8:6;
   1956,Je 1,28:2; 1959,Ag 18,25:1
Carmilla 1970,D 1,61:2
Carnaval 1924,D 30,15:1
Carnaval de l'Amour, Le 1928,Mr 11,VIII,2:7
Carnaval des Enfants, Le 1923,Mr 18,VII,1:1;
   1930,Mr 2,IX,4:2
Carnival 1924,N 30,VIII,2:1; 1925,Ja 4,VII,1:1;
   1929,Ap 25,32:5; 1962,Je 6,37:1
Carnival in Flanders 1953,S 9,38:2
Carnival! 1961,Ap 14,22:2; 1961,Ap 23,II,1:1;
   1968,D 13,58:1
Caroline 1923,F 1,13:2
Carolinian, The 1925,N 3,34:2
Carousel 1945,Ap 20,24:2; 1945,Ap 29,II,1:1;
   1949,Ja 26,28:2; 1949,F 6,II,1:1; 1950,Je 8,37:2;
   1953,My 6,38:1; 1954,Je 3,32:2; 1954,Je 13,II,1:1;
   1957,S 12,38:2; 1965,Ag 11,39:1; 1966,D 16,56:2
Carpenters, The 1970,D 22,40:1; 1970,D 27,II,1:1
Carpet Slippers 1931,Ja 18,VIII,2:6
Carricknabauna 1967,Mr 31,30:1
Carrida 1922,Ag 2,22:2
Carrie and Cleopatra 1939,My 14,XI,1:8
Carrosse du Saint-Sacrement, Le 1926,O 3,VIII,2:1;
   1930,Mr 9,IX,2:7
Carry Me Back to Morningside Heights
   1968,F 28,41:1
Carry Nation 1932,O 31,18:2
Carry On 1928,Ja 24,26:1; 1929,N 3,IX,1:7
Cartney and Kevney 1928,Ja 1,VIII,2:8
Carving a Statue 1964,S 18,25:1; 1968,My 1,43:1
Casa di Tutti, La 1932,D 5,21:4
Casablan 1954,N 13,13:1
Case History 1938,O 22,15:2
Case of Clyde Griffiths 1936,Mr 14,10:4
Case of Libel, A 1963,O 11,43:2; 1963,O 27,II,1:1
Case of Philip Lawrence, The 1937,Je 9,31:1
Case of Poisons, The 1935,Ja 21,18:2
Case of the Frightened Lady, The 1931,S 6,VIII,2:1
Case of the Noszty Boy and Mary Toth, The
   1927,Mr 20,VIII,4:3
Case of Youth, A 1940,Mr 25,10:3
Casey Jones 1938,F 21,14:2
Casino Varieties 1934,Ap 3,26:4
Cast of Characters 1959,Je 11,37:2
Caste 1927,D 24,8:1; 1929,F 24,IX,4:3;
   1935,Ag 13,20:3

Castiglione, La 1929,Je 2,26:5
Castle Adamant 1934,S 28,26:3
Castle in the Air 1950,Ja 8,II,3:7
Castle Irish 1938,Mr 21,20:1
Castlereagh 1935,F 20,22:4
Castles in the Air 1926,S 7,19:2
Casualties 1927,Mr 5,12:2
Cat and the Canary, The 1922,F 8,13:1;
   1935,Jl 9,24:4; 1935,Ag 13,20:3; 1937,Je 15,26:3;
   1965,Ja 5,26:1
Cat and the Fiddle, The 1931,S 27,VIII,3:1;
   1931,O 16,26:4
Cat and the Moon, The 1931,N 8,VIII,4:3;
   1959,Ja 27,27:5
Cat-Bird, The 1920,F 17,18:1; 1920,F 22,III,6:1
Cat Comes Back, The 1923,Ja 29,11:2
Cat on a Hot Tin Roof 1955,Mr 25,18:2;
   1955,Ap 3,II,1:1; 1958,Ja 31,24:2
Cat Screams, The 1942,Je 17,26:5
Catch a Star! 1955,S 7,35:2
Catch Me if You Can 1965,Mr 10,50:1
Cathedral, The 1930,D 28,VIII,2:6; 1932,D 18,X,5:6
Catherine 1923,S 30,II,1:6
Catherine Empereur 1938,Je 12,X,2:3
Catherine Goulden 1929,N 6,22:1
Catherine Was Great 1944,Jl 11,18:2; 1944,Ag 3,16:1
Cathleen ni Houlihan 1932,O 31,18:1
Catiline 1936,Ja 28,14:6
Cats' Pajamas, The 1962,Je 1,16:2
Catskill Dutch 1924,My 4,VIII,2:1; 1924,My 7,18:1;
   1924,My 11,VIII,1:1
Caucasian Chalk Circle, The 1961,N 1,35:1;
   1962,Mr 30,28:1; 1966,Mr 25,35:1;
   1966,Ap 10,II,1:1
Caught 1925,O 6,31:2
Caught Wet 1931,N 5,29:1
Caukey 1944,F 18,15:4
Causes Unknown 1936,O 5,24:1
Caution: A Love Story 1969,Ap 4,45:1
Cautious Campbell 1927,Ag 14,VII,1:7
Cavalcade 1931,O 14,26:4; 1931,N 1,VIII,2:1
Cave at Machpelah, The 1959,Jl 1,25:1
Cave Dwellers, The 1957,O 21,29:2; 1957,O 27,II,1:1;
   1961,O 16,34:2
Cave Girl, The 1920,Ag 19,12:2; 1920,Ag 22,VI,1:2
Cave Man, The 1928,Ja 1,VIII,1:3
Cave of Salamanca, The 1930,Mr 25,34:6
Caviar 1934,Je 8,19:2
Caviar and Wine 1932,Ap 17,VIII,2:6
Caviar to the General 1947,Ja 14,30:3
Cayenne Pepper 1961,D 13,55:5
Ce Que Femme Veut 1924,F 3,VII,1:4
Ce Soir on Improvise 1935,F 17,VIII,3:7
Ceiling Zero 1935,Ap 2,24:3; 1935,Ap 11,26:2;
   1935,Ap 21,IX,1:1; 1935,Ag 17,18:4
Celebration 1948,Ap 12,24:2; 1969,Ja 23,55:2;
   1969,F 2,II,3:1
Celebre Histoire, La 1928,My 13,IX,2:2
Celebrity 1927,D 11,IX,2:5; 1927,D 27,24:3
Celebrity, The 1928,Ag 26,VII,2:5
Cellar and the Well, The 1950,D 11,30:2
Cena Delle Beffe, La 1930,N 24,26:4
Cenci, The 1935,Je 16,X,1:1; 1935,Ag 18,IX,1:4
Censored 1938,F 28,18:2
Centuries, The 1927,N 30,23:1
Century Review, The 1920,Jl 22,9:5
Century Revue and the Midnight Rounders, The
   1920,Jl 13,9:1
Ceremonial Dance to Which There Is No End, A
   1969,My 26,55:2
Ceremonies in Dark Old Men 1969,F 6,33:1;
   1969,F 23,II,5:1; 1969,O 11,42:1
Ceremony of Innocence, The 1968,Ja 2,33:1;
   1968,Ja 14,II,1:1
Certain Young Man, A 1967,D 27,45:1
Certainly, Sir 1936,S 18,19:5
C'est Jeune 1927,O 2,VIII,2:4
Cette Vieille Canaille 1930,D 7,IX,4:2
Chacun Sa Verite 1939,Ja 24,17:1
Chagrins d'Amour 1926,N 14,VIII,2:1
Chaine, La 1931,My 10,VIII,2:4
Chains 1923,S 20,5:2; 1930,F 23,29:2; 1937,Ja 22,25:1
Chains of Dew 1922,Ap 28,20:2; 1922,Ap 30,VII,1:1
Chair, La 1930,O 19,IX,2:2
Chair, The 1930,O 4,15:4
Chair Endowed 1954,Jl 7,23:1
Chairs, The 1958,Ja 10,20:3; 1958,F 16,II,1:1
Chaises, Les 1970,My 6,49:1
Chaleur du Sein, La 1938,Je 12,X,2:3
Chalk Circle, The 1928,Ja 15,VIII,2:1;
   1933,Ag 22,20:5
Chalk Dust 1936,Mr 5,24:5
Chalk Garden, The 1955,O 27,29:1; 1955,N 13,II,1:1;
   1956,Ap 12,26:8; 1956,My 13,II,3:1
Chalked Out 1937,Mr 26,24:2
Challenge of Youth 1930,Ja 21,28:5
Chambre d'Hotel 1932,Mr 20,VIII,2:2
Chameleon, The 1932,Jl 19,20:4; 1949,F 7,16:2
Champ-Blays 1936,O 9,30:4
Champagne, Sec 1933,O 16,20:2
Champagne Complex 1955,Ap 13,33:1

Champion, The 1921,Ja 4,11:1; 1921,Ja 9,VI,1:1;
   1925,Ap 24,16:4
Chance Acquaintance 1927,N 27,IX,4:1
Chances, The 1962,Jl 4,11:2
Chandelier, Le 1939,Mr 19,XI,3:1
Change 1970,O 13,52:2
Change Your Luck 1930,Je 7,10:2
Changeling, The 1956,My 4,20:3; 1964,O 30,32:2
Changelings, The 1923,Ag 26,VI,2:1; 1923,S 18,16:3;
   1923,S 30,II,1:1
Channel One: Underground Television 1968,Je 3,55:4
Channel Road, The 1929,O 18,24:2;
   1929,O 27,IX,1:1
Chanson d'Asie 1937,My 16,X,2:6
Chanson du Bonheur, La 1935,N 24,IX,6:4
Chantecler 1927,N 6,IX,4:1; 1937,D 10,33:6
Chaparral 1958,S 10,38:2
Chapeau Chinois, Le 1930,Ap 27,IX,2:1
Char-A-Bang 1935,My 5,IX,1:7
Characters and Caricatures 1935,F 1,17:2;
   1937,Mr 8,22:1
Characters and Chicanery 1956,Ja 24,26:2
Charlatan, The 1922,Ap 25,14:2; 1922,Ap 30,VII,1:1
Charlatans 1962,Ap 27,26:1
Charles and Mary 1930,F 23,VIII,2:1
Charles Aznavour 1970,F 5,32:4
Charles the King 1936,O 10,20:6
Charley's Aunt 1925,Je 2,16:2; 1940,O 18,24:2;
   1941,Jl 31,12:4; 1953,D 23,22:2; 1970,Jl 6,38:1
Charlot's Masquerade 1930,S 5,30:7
Charlot's Revue 1924,Ja 10,18:1; 1924,Ap 6,VIII,1:1;
   1924,Ap 15,25:2; 1925,N 11,27:1;
   1925,N 15,VIII,1:1; 1925,D 27,VII,1:1
Charlotte Corday 1936,O 27,31:1; 1936,N 15,XI,3:2
Charm 1929,N 29,24:5
Charm School, The 1920,Ag 3,12:1; 1921,F 27,VI,1:6
Charmante Fille, Une 1927,O 2,VIII,2:4
Chase, The 1952,Ap 16,30:2
Chase the Ace 1935,Ap 21,IX,2:2
Chase the Ace 1935,Mr 26,23:3
Chastening, The 1923,F 17,9:2
Chastity, My Brother 1936,My 9,27:3
Chateau de Cartes, Le 1937,F 14,X,2:3
Chateau des Papes, Le 1932,N 13,IX,2:5
Chateaux en Espagne 1933,Ap 30,IX,2:3
Chatelaine de Shenstone, La 1930,Mr 23,IX,2:1
Chatiment, Un 1929,My 5,IX,2:4
Chatterton 1926,O 3,VIII,2:1
Chaud et Froid 1935,Ja 6,IX,2:1
Chauve-Souris 1921,Ap 10,VI,1:1; 1922,F 6,9:2;
   1922,F 12,VI,1:1; 1922,Mr 26,VI,1:2; 1922,Je 6,17:4;
   1922,O 11,22:2; 1922,O 22,VIII,1:1; 1923,Ja 5,12:2;
   1923,S 4,12:1; 1924,O 2,26:4; 1924,O 12,VIII,1:6;
   1924,D 14,VIII,6:1; 1925,Ja 15,25:1;
   1925,Ja 25,VII,1:1; 1927,O 23,VIII,1:1;
   1928,N 25,X,4:7; 1929,Ja 23,20:2; 1931,O 22,27:1
Chauve-Souris of 1943 1943,Ag 13,13:2
Chaver, Nachman 1939,O 2,15:2
Chayim Lederer 1932,N 15,24:4
Che! 1969,Mr 24,56:1; 1969,My 4,II,3:5;
   1970,Ja 18,II,1:1; 1970,S 20,II,1:2
Cheaper to Marry 1924,Ap 16,26:1;
   1924,Ap 20,VIII,1:1
Cheapside 1938,F 28,18:2
Checkerboard, The 1920,Ag 20,7:2;
   1920,Ag 22,VI,1:2; 1920,Ag 29,VI,1:2
Chee-Chee 1928,S 26,25:1
Chef, Le 1935,Ja 6,IX,2:1
Chemmy Circle, The 1968,Ag 10,17:2
Cher Antoine 1969,O 3,40:1
Cheri 1921,D 25,VI,1:8; 1930,N 16,VIII,4:1;
   1959,O 13,44:1
Cherokee Night, The 1932,Je 21,19:4;
   1932,Je 26,IX,1:1
Cherries Are Ripe 1930,O 19,IX,3:4
Cherry Blossoms 1927,Mr 29,22:3
Cherry Lane Follies, The 1930,Je 30,22:4
Cherry Orchard, The 1923,Ja 23,18:1;
   1923,Ja 28,VII,1:1; 1923,F 4,VII,1:1;
   1926,O 17,VIII,2:1; 1928,Mr 6,20:1;
   1928,My 6,IX,2:4; 1928,O 16,28:5; 1928,N 8,26:8;
   1928,N 18,IX,1:2; 1929,Je 2,VIII,1:1;
   1933,Mr 7,20:3; 1941,S 7,IX,2:5; 1944,Ja 26,22:1;
   1944,F 6,II,1:1; 1955,O 19,38:1; 1958,My 16,22:2;
   1960,Je 4,17:2; 1961,D 15,49:1; 1962,N 15,46:2;
   1964,Ja 29,29:5; 1965,F 10,46:1; 1965,Ag 2,17:2;
   1968,Mr 20,41:1; 1968,Ap 7,II,3:7; 1970,My 7,63:2
Cherry Pie 1926,Ap 15,24:4
Chevaliers de la Table Ronde 1938,Je 12,X,2:3
Chiaroscuro 1963,Je 6,40:8
Chic 1959,My 19,28:2
Chicago 1926,D 31,11:1; 1927,Ja 9,VII,1:1;
   1927,D 18,IX,1:8; 1935,Mr 14,19:6;
   1966,Ap 13,36:1
Chicago 70 1970,My 26,33:1; 1970,Je 7,II,3:1
Chicago/Conspiracy 1970,Ag 26,35:1
Chicken Every Sunday 1944,Ap 6,27:2;
   1944,Ap 16,II,1:1
Chicken Feed 1923,S 25,10:2
Chief Thing, The 1926,Mr 23,24:2;
   1926,Mr 28,VIII,1:1; 1963,Ap 30,27:2
Chien du Jardinier, Le 1957,F 19,36:1
Chiffon Girl, The 1924,F 20,23:2

Child and the Dragon, The 1966,Je 24,30:2
Child Buyer, The 1962,My 14,35:1; 1964,D 22,35:1
Child of Fortune 1956,N 14,41:1
Child of Manhattan 1932,Mr 2,15:1
Child of the Morning 1951,N 17,9:7;
  1958,Ap 22,40:2
Child of the World, The 1922,Ap 29,18:3
Childhood 1962,Ja 12,28:1; 1962,Ja 21,II,1:1
Children From Their Games 1963,Ap 12,33:1
Children in the Rain 1970,O 3,14:1
Children of Darkness 1930,Ja 8,25:1;
  1930,Ja 19,VIII,1:1; 1958,Mr 1,11:4
Children of the Don, The 1923,Mr 30,14:2
Children of the Moon 1923,Ag 18,10:3;
  1923,Ag 26,VI,1:1; 1923,S 9,VII,1:1;
  1923,S 16,VII,1:1; 1926,N 7,VIII,1:3;
  1930,My 4,XI,3:1
Children of the Shadows 1964,F 27,26:1
Children of the Sun 1963,Ag 11,56:3
Children's Hour, The 1934,N 21,23:2; 1934,D 2,X,1:1;
  1936,Je 7,IX,1:1; 1936,N 13,27:3;
  1936,N 29,XII,2:1; 1952,D 19,35:2;
  1952,D 28,II,1:1
Children's Party, A 1947,D 29,21:5
Children's Tragedy, The 1921,O 12,18:2;
  1921,O 16,VI,1:1; 1931,D 27,VIII,3:1
Child's Play 1970,F 18,39:1; 1970,Mr 1,II,1:4
Chiltern Hundreds, The 1947,S 14,II,3:8
Chimes of Corneville, The 1934,Je 29,16:2
Chimes of Normandy, The 1926,D 14,24:4;
  1931,N 3,31:3
Chimin de Damas, Le 1921,N 20,VI,1:3
China Marches On 1939,O 22,IX,2:1
China Rose 1925,Ja 20,18:1
Chinese, The 1970,Mr 11,42:2; 1970,Mr 22,II,3:1
Chinese Bungalow, The 1929,F 3,VIII,2:1
Chinese Lily, A 1925,Mr 24,26:5
Chinese Love 1921,Mr 1,18:1
Chinese Nightingale, The 1934,O 6,20:4
Chinese O'Neill 1929,My 23,27:1
Chinese Prime Minister, The 1964,Ja 3,14:1;
  1964,Ja 12,II,1:1; 1965,My 21,21:1
Chip, The 1960,My 17,42:2
Chip Woman's Fortune, The 1923,My 8,22:2;
  1923,My 16,22:5; 1923,My 20,VII,1:1
Chippies 1929,My 30,23:3
Chips With Everything 1963,O 2,49:1
Chivalry 1925,D 16,22:3
Chocolate Dandies, The 1924,S 2,22:2
Chocolate Soldier, The 1921,D 13,24:2;
  1930,Ja 28,28:1; 1931,S 22,33:3; 1932,F 9,30:3;
  1934,My 3,15:3; 1942,Je 24,22:2; 1947,Mr 13,34:2
Chocolates 1967,Ap 11,51:1
Choephori 1961,S 27,32:4
Choice, The 1930,My 9,20:5
Choir Rehearsal, The 1921,Mr 1,18:1
Chotard et Cie 1928,N 11,X,2:7
Christ 1928,D 25,6:1
Christian 1936,D 13,XI,5:1; 1937,F 25,18:6
Christine 1932,N 27,IX,3:2; 1960,Ap 29,27:1
Christmas Carol, A 1921,D 23,18:3; 1967,D 23,28:1
Christmas Eve 1939,D 28,17:2
Christmas in the Market Place 1960,D 10,26:1
Christmas Story 1967,D 23,28:1
Christophe Colomb 1957,Ja 31,20:5
Christopher Blake 1946,D 2,33:2; 1946,D 8,II,5:1
Christopher Columbus 1953,N 29,II,3:1
Christopher Comes Across 1932,Je 1,19:2
Christopher's Wonders 1960,S 27,41:1
Christus 1922,My 28,VI,1:6
Chronicles of Hell, The 1969,O 19,II,12:1
Chrysalis 1932,N 16,15:2
Chuck 1968,My 9,55:2; 1968,My 19,II,1:1
Chuckles of 1922 1922,My 2,22:2
Church Mouse, A 1927,D 4,X,2:3;
  1931,My 3,VIII,2:1; 1931,O 13,26:4;
  1933,Je 27,13:7
Church Street 1934,My 23,15:5; 1934,N 20,24:5;
  1948,F 10,27:2; 1948,F 15,II,1:3
Chushingura 1960,Je 10,37:1; 1960,Je 17,35:4;
  1969,S 11,53:1
Ciao, Rudy 1966,Ja 8,15:3; 1966,Ja 11,19:6
Ciboulette 1926,O 31,VIII,2:4
Cicero 1961,F 9,37:2
Cid 1934,O 24,24:2
Cid, Le 1958,O 31,35:2; 1963,N 8,36:2;
  1966,F 12,17:1
Cigarette Girl, The 1962,Je 21,26:2
Cinderelative 1930,S 19,18:4
Cinderella 1928,D 27,26:4; 1935,Ja 13,IX,3:1
Cinderella on Broadway 1920,Je 25,18:1
Cinderella's Brothers 1933,Ja 30,9:6
Cinders 1923,Ap 4,22:1
Cindy 1964,Mr 20,24:1; 1964,S 25,33:1
Circe 1929,Mr 31,VIII,2:7
Circle, The 1921,S 13,12:1; 1921,S 18,VI,1:1;
  1938,Ap 19,24:2; 1939,Jl 12,17:2; 1939,Jl 13,17:1;
  1944,N 19,II,2:4; 1946,Mr 17,II,1:3
Circle of Chalk, The 1929,Mr 31,VIII,2:6;
  1941,Mr 27,28:4; 1950,D 2,8:3
Circus Aimee 1932,My 22,VIII,2:2
Circus Girl, The 1928,O 21,IX,1:1
Circus-Madison Square Garden 1939,Ap 6,23:5

Circus Princess, The 1926,Mr 28,23:5;
  1927,Ap 26,32:2; 1937,Ag 31,26:6
Cissy 1932,D 24,10:5
Cities in Bezique 1969,Ja 13,26:1; 1969,Ja 19,II,3:5
Citta Morta, La 1923,N 28,14:1; 1935,S 22,X,7:7
City Chap, The 1925,O 27,21:1
City Haul 1929,D 31,14:4
City of Kings 1949,F 18,27:2
Civic Death 1936,N 9,23:4
Civil Death, The 1932,Ja 25,20:3
Civilian Clothes 1923,Jl 26,13:2
Clair de Lune 1921,Ap 10,VI,1:1; 1921,Ap 19,15:1;
  1921,Ap 24,VI,1:1
Claire Adams 1929,N 20,26:3
Clandestine Marriage, The 1954,O 4,23:2;
  1954,O 17,II,1:1
Clandestine on the Morning Line 1959,D 5,18:2;
  1961,O 31,28:1
Clap Hands 1934,Ag 21,12:7
Clara Gibbings 1928,D 9,X,2:1
Clara's Ole Man 1968,Mr 9,23:2
Clarence 1923,My 14,18:4
Claudia 1941,F 13,24:2; 1941,Mr 9,IX,1:1;
  1942,My 25,11:3; 1942,S 27,VIII,2:2;
  1942,O 4,VIII,2:1
Claw, The 1921,O 2,VII,1:8; 1921,O 18,20:1;
  1927,Ja 13,28:4
Clean Beds 1939,My 26,21:2
Clear All Wires! 1932,S 15,19:1; 1932,S 25,IX,1:1
Clearing in the Woods, A 1957,Ja 11,20:2;
  1957,Ja 20,II,1:1; 1959,F 13,32:1
Clerambard 1957,N 8,22:3; 1957,N 17,II,1:1
Client Serieux, Un 1927,Mr 27,VII,4:8
Climate of Eden, The 1952,N 7,20:2;
  1952,N 16,II,1:1; 1953,N 21,11:2
Climax, The 1926,My 18,29:3; 1927,S 25,VIII,2:1;
  1933,Je 14,22:2
Climbing 1937,Ja 20,18:2
Clinging Vine, The 1922,D 25,20:2;
  1922,D 31,VII,1:1
Clinton Street 1939,O 13,27:2
Clive of India 1934,F 18,IX,3:7
Clizia 1939,Jl 23,IX,6:3
Cloches de Cornville, Les 1926,D 14,24:4
Clock, The 1923,My 10,22:3; 1923,My 13,16:2
Clod, The 1923,My 26,8:4
Clog Dance, The 1960,Je 17,35:4
Cloister, The 1921,Je 6,16:3
Close Harmony 1924,D 2,23:1
Close Quarters 1937,Ap 18,II,3:5; 1939,Mr 7,19:2;
  1941,Ag 17,IX,1:8
Closed Door, The 1923,N 21,23:1
Closed Room, The 1934,Jl 24,20:2
Closing Door, The 1949,D 2,36:2
Clotture, Le 1927,Ja 23,VII,2:1
Cloud 7 1958,F 15,15:2
Clouds 1925,S 3,32:1
Clouds of the Sun 1922,My 6,11:2
Cloudy With Showers 1931,Ag 23,VIII,2:5;
  1931,S 2,17:5
Club Bedroom, The 1967,D 6,41:1
Club des Loufoques 1927,O 30,IX,4:7
Clubs Are Trumps 1924,O 5,VIII,1:3; 1924,O 15,27:1
Clutching Claw, The 1928,F 15,20:1
Clutterbuck 1949,D 5,29:2
Co-Respondent Unknown 1936,F 12,24:4;
  1936,Ag 19,18:5
Coach With the Six Insides, The 1962,N 27,44:1;
  1967,My 12,50:1
Coast of Illyria, The 1949,Ap 5,37:4; 1949,Ap 13,39:2
Coastwise 1923,D 1,23:1
Cobra 1924,Ap 6,VIII,2:1; 1924,Ap 23,24:1;
  1924,Ap 27,VIII,1:1; 1925,Ag 23,VII,1:8
Cochran's 1930 Revue 1930,Mr 28,22:7;
  1930,Ap 13,X,1:6
Cock-A-Doodle Dandy 1949,D 12,29:4;
  1950,F 1,26:2; 1955,N 4,26:5; 1958,N 13,39:2;
  1958,N 23,II,1:1; 1959,S 8,43:5; 1969,Ja 21,40:1;
  1969,F 2,II,1:1
Cock-A-Doodle-Doo 1949,F 28,16:5
Cock o' the Roost 1924,O 14,23:1
Cock Robin 1928,Ja 13,26:6
Cockeyed Kite 1961,S 14,27:1
Cocks and Hens 1927,Ap 3,VIII,1:4
Cocktail 1928,F 5,VIII,2:1; 1931,F 15,VIII,3:2
Cocktail Impromptu 1927,Ja 13,28:4
Cocktail Party, The 1949,Ag 23,28:6; 1949,S 11,II,2:1;
  1950,Ja 23,17:2; 1950,Ja 29,II,1:1; 1950,My 4,33:2;
  1950,My 7,II,2:5; 1950,My 14,II,1:1;
  1950,My 21,II,3:2; 1968,O 8,42:1; 1968,O 20,II,1:1
Cocktail 328 1930,Ap 13,X,2:7
Cocktails of 1934 1934,My 5,22:1
Coco 1969,D 19,66:1; 1969,D 28,II,1:1;
  1970,Ag 7,28:1
Cocoanuts, The 1925,D 9,30:1; 1925,D 13,IX,3:1;
  1926,Ap 18,VIII,1:1; 1926,Je 11,25:2
Coeur 1930,O 26,VIII,2:1
Coeur, Le 1936,Mr 8,IX,3:7; 1936,O 4,IX,1:1
Coeur a Gauche 1929,F 3,VIII,2:3
Coeur Ebloui, Le 1926,N 21,VIII,2:1
Coeur Partage, Le 1927,Ja 9,VII,2:5

Coeur Tout Neuf, Un 1928,F 12,VIII,1:3
Coffee Lace, The 1968,Jl 5,20:1; 1969,D 4,71:2
Coggerers, The 1939,Ja 21,18:4; 1960,Mr 23,33:1
Coiffeur Pour Dames 1928,Ja 1,VIII,2:3
Coincidence 1935,N 6,32:3; 1935,D 1,XI,5:3
Coiner, The 1934,N 22,26:2
Cold Comfort Farm 1936,Mr 2,13:7
Cold Feet 1923,My 22,14:2; 1923,My 22,14:3
Cold in Sables 1931,D 24,20:7
Cold Wind and the Warm, The 1958,D 9,55:1;
  1959,Ja 18,II,1:1
Colette 1925,S 29,31:2; 1970,My 7,60:1;
  1970,My 17,II,1:1; 1970,O 15,58:1
Colleagues, The 1962,Je 21,26:1
Collection, The 1962,N 27,44:1; 1962,D 9,II,5:1
Collector's Item 1952,F 9,11:2
Collision 1932,F 17,19:2
Collision Course 1968,My 9,55:2; 1968,My 19,II,1:1
Colombe 1951,D 15,13:2; 1965,F 24,33:1
Colonel Kusmin 1947,N 12,34:3
Colonel Satan 1931,Ja 12,24:1; 1931,Ja 18,I,28:6;
  1931,Ja 19,25:2; 1931,F 8,VIII,3:3
Colonello Bridall, L' 1934,Ap 16,20:3
Colonnade, The 1925,My 3,VIII,2:1
Color of Darkness: An Evening in the World of
  James Purdy 1963,O 1,34:1; 1963,O 1,24:1;
  1963,O 1,34:1
Com Zaa 1945,Ja 10,28:2
Come Across 1937,Ap 10,7:7; 1938,S 15,28:3
Come Angel Band 1936,F 19,17:1
Come as You Are 1970,Ag 12,32:1
Come Back, Little Sheba 1950,F 16,28:5;
  1950,F 26,II,1:1; 1950,My 14,II,1:1
Come Blow Your Horn 1961,F 23,31:3;
  1961,Mr 5,II,1:1
Come Easy 1933,Ag 30,22:5
Come Home to Roost 1936,O 11,X,3:1
Come In 1924,My 11,VIII,1:4
Come Into the Garden, Maud 1966,Ap 27,38:1
Come Live With Me 1967,Ja 27,29:1; 1967,F 5,II,1:1
Come Marching Home 1946,My 20,18:6
Come of Age 1934,Ja 13,16:6; 1952,Ja 24,22:2
Come-On Man, The 1929,Ap 23,26:2
Come on Strong 1962,O 5,29:1
Come Out, Carlo! 1962,My 4,27:2
Come Out of the Kitchen 1920,Mr 16,17:7
Come Out to Play 1937,F 10,18:5
Come Play With Me 1959,My 1,33:5
Come Seven 1920,Jl 20,10:1
Come Share My House 1960,F 19,20:2
Come Slowly, Eden 1966,D 7,56:1
Come Summer 1969,Mr 19,43:1
Come What May 1934,My 16,23:4
Come With Me 1928,My 20,VIII,2:3
Comedian, The 1923,Mr 14,14:1;
  1923,Mr 25,VIII,1:1; 1923,Ap 8,VIII,1:1;
  1956,O 18,36:4
Comedie du Bonheur, La 1926,D 12,VIII,3:4
Comedienne 1924,F 24,VII,1:4; 1924,O 22,18:1;
  1938,Jl 3,IX,2:1
Comedy in Music 1953,O 3,15:2; 1964,N 22,II,1:1
Comedy in Music, Opus 2 1964,N 10,54:1
Comedy of Crooks, A 1936,Je 8,22:3
Comedy of Errors, The 1923,My 16,22:5;
  1923,My 20,VII,1:1; 1932,My 22,25:3;
  1939,My 9,28:4; 1962,S 12,34:2; 1963,Je 13,28:1;
  1963,Je 21,35:3; 1964,My 21,43:1; 1967,Je 15,58:4;
  1968,F 28,40:2
Comedy of Good and Evil, A 1938,Ap 8,16:3
Comedy of the Changing Years, A 1969,Mr 4,37:5
Comedy of Women, A 1929,S 14,17:4
Comes a Day 1958,N 7,22:1
Comes the Revelation 1942,My 27,26:2
Comforter, The 1964,O 22,42:1
Comic, The 1927,Ap 20,28:2
Comic Artist, The 1928,Jl 22,VII,1:3; 1929,N 23,19:3;
  1933,Ap 20,20:3
Comic Strip 1958,My 15,26:2
Comic Supplement, The 1925,Ja 25,VII,1:4
Coming Forth by Day of Osiris Jones, The
  1961,Mr 15,45:2
Coming of Christ, The 1928,My 29,6:2;
  1957,D 23,29:8
Coming Spring 1934,S 23,X,2:4
Command Decision 1947,S 21,I,59:7; 1947,O 2,30:2;
  1947,O 12,II,1:1
Command Performance 1933,O 18,24:3
Command Performance, The 1928,S 23,IX,2:2;
  1928,O 4,27:1
Command to Love, The 1927,S 11,VIII,1:3;
  1927,S 21,27:1
Comme le Temps Passe 1927,O 30,IX,4:7
Comme les Autres 1932,Jl 3,IX,1:1
Commedia Dell' Arte 1927,Ap 6,24:3; 1957,Jl 5,13:2
Comment l'Esprit Vient aux Garcons
  1929,O 6,IX,2:2
Comment Reussir Dans les Affaires Sans Vraiment
  Se Fatiguer 1964,F 12,30:1
Committee, The 1964,S 17,53:1; 1964,S 27,II,1:1
Commodore Marries, The 1929,S 5,26:3;
  1929,S 15,IX,1:1
Common Glory, The 1947,Jl 19,11:2;
  1947,Jl 27,II,1:1

Common Ground 1945,Ap 26,27:2; 1945,My 6,II,1:1
Common Sense 1923,D 2,VIII,2:1
Common Sin, The 1928,O 16,28:2
Commune 1970,D 21,50:1; 1970,D 27,II,1:1
Commuting Distance 1936,Je 30,15:1
Company 1970,Ap 27,40:1; 1970,My 3,II,1:4; 1970,Jl 29,31:1
Company's Coming! 1931,Ap 21,35:5
Complaisant Lover, The 1959,Je 19,28:3; 1961,N 2,43:2
Complex, The 1925,Mr 4,17:2
Composite Man, The 1936,S 9,32:2; 1936,S 27,X,3:5
Compromising Daphne 1927,O 2,II,7:2; 1927,O 16,23:2:7
Compulsion 1957,O 25,21:1; 1957,N 3,II,1:1
Comrades 1956,Je 6,38:1
Comte Obligado 1929,Mr 12,26:2
Concept, The 1968,My 7,51:1; 1968,Je 2,II,1:1
Concert Varieties 1945,Je 2,10:7
Concerto for Fun 1949,My 10,28:3
Condemned of Altona, The 1966,F 4,21:1; 1966,F 13,II,1:1
Conditioned Reflex 1967,Ja 11,51:1
Conduct Unbecoming 1969,Jl 26,14:1; 1970,O 13,50:1; 1970,O 25,II,16:2
Conerico Was Here to Stay 1965,Mr 4,37:1; 1965,My 9,II,1:2; 1969,Mr 11,39:1
Coney Island Play 1970,O 31,34:2
Confederacy, The 1958,Jl 3,20:1; 1958,Jl 13,II,1:1
Confederates, The 1959,S 29,45:1
Confession 1927,My 3,24:3
Conspiracy and Tragedy of the Duke of Byron, The 1929,Ag 18,VIII,1:3
Conspiracy of the Doomed, The: or, In a Certain Country 1949,Ap 10,6:1
Constant Heckler, The 1948,Ag 21,8:5
Constant Nymph, The 1926,O 3,VIII,2:1; 1926,D 10,31:1; 1926,D 19,VII,3:1; 1927,Mr 6,VIII,1:4; 1927,Ap 24,VII,2:1
Constant Prince, The 1969,O 18,36:1; 1969,O 26,II,1:1
Constant Sinner 1937,Ap 6,21:2
Constant Sinner, The 1931,Ag 30,VIII,1:6; 1931,S 15,30:1
Constant Wife, The 1926,N 14,VIII,5:1; 1926,N 30,26:3; 1926,D 12,VIII,3:1; 1927,My 1,VIII,2:7; 1928,My 20,VIII,2:1; 1928,D 30,VIII,4:4; 1929,F 3,VIII,2:1; 1935,Jl 3,20:2; 1937,Je 6,XI,1:5; 1951,D 10,34:3; 1951,D 16,II,6:1
Consul, The 1950,Mr 2,32:3; 1950,Mr 16,41:1; 1950,Mr 26,II,1:1; 1950,Ap 2,II,7:1; 1950,My 14,II,1:1; 1951,Mr 4,II,3:7; 1951,Mr 4,82:4; 1951,My 4,30:8; 1951,S 8,9:3; 1951,S 23,II,1:1; 1952,O 30,41:2; 1957,S 4,40:3
Consulesa, La 1929,Ja 15,22:3
Conte di Monte Cristo, Il 1934,Ja 22,13:2; 1935,Ap 1,17:6
Continental Varieties 1934,O 4,18:3; 1934,N 15,24:3; 1935,D 27,15:3
Contractor, The 1970,Ag 17,32:1
Contrast, The 1926,O 1,26:2; 1940,Mr 26,17:2
Contribution 1969,Ap 2,37:1; 1969,Ap 13,II,1:1; 1970,Mr 10,53:1
Contributions 1970,Mr 10,53:1; 1970,Mr 29,II,1:1
Conversation at Midnight 1964,N 13,27:1
Conversation Piece 1934,F 17,20:5; 1934,Mr 11,X,3:6; 1934,O 24,24:1; 1934,N 18,IX,1:1; 1957,N 19,38:2
Conversion of the Jews 1970,Jl 31,14:1
Convict, The 1935,F 5,23:2
Cook for Mr General, A 1961,O 20,39:1
Cool World, The 1960,F 23,38:2
Coop, The 1966,Mr 2,48:1
Cop-Out 1969,Ap 8,42:1; 1969,Ap 20,II,11:4
Copper and Brass 1957,O 18,19:2
Cops and Horrors 1970,Ag 11,27:1
Coquette 1927,O 16,IX,2:4; 1927,N 9,23:1; 1927,N 13,IX,1:1; 1928,Jl 1,VIII,3:5; 1935,My 22,23:4; 1935,Jl 10,24:1

Coriolanus 1927,Je 18,8:3; 1933,D 17,IV,2:4; 1937,O 10,VI,4:7; 1938,F 2,14:5; 1952,Mr 14,26:2; 1952,Ap 13,II,3:8; 1953,Ag 21,9:2; 1954,Ja 20,34:2; 1954,Ja 24,II,1:1; 1959,Jl 8,24:5; 1961,Je 21,31:2; 1961,Jl 5,30:1; 1963,D 17,52:1; 1965,Je 21,36:1; 1965,Jl 15,23:1; 1968,My 26,II,7:1
Corn Is Green, The 1938,O 9,X,3:1; 1940,N 27,27:2; 1940,D 1,X,1:1; 1943,My 4,18:3; 1943,My 9,II,1:1; 1950,Ja 12,33:2; 1954,F 27,10:2
Cornelius 1935,Mr 21,27:4; 1935,Ap 14,IX,1:1
Corner of the Bed, A 1969,F 27,35:2
Cornered 1920,D 9,18:2
Corona, La 1932,Ap 19,23:3
Coronation at Mrs. Beam's 1938,Ag 4,14:4
Corps a Corps 1932,O 30,IX,3:8
Corruption in the Palace of Justice 1963,O 9,49:2
Corsican Brothers, The 1970,Mr 20,56:2
Cortez 1929,N 5,32:2
Cosi Sia 1923,N 14,29:2
Cosmonaute Agricole, Le 1970,Ap 8,38:3
Cottage to Let 1940,Ag 11,IX,2:5; 1941,My 18,IX,1:5
Cotton Club Revue of 1957 1957,Jl 10,23:4
Cotton Stockings 1923,D 19,16:2
Couchette No 3 1929,Mr 3,VIII,4:8
Coucou 1930,Je 1,VIII,2:1
Council of Love 1970,Ag 21,21:2; 1970,S 12,32:2
Counsellor-at-Law 1931,N 7,17:2; 1932,Mr 27,VIII,3:2; 1932,S 13,17:2; 1934,Ap 11,24:3; 1934,My 6,IX,2:5; 1942,N 25,17:2
Counsel's Opinion 1931,S 13,IX,2:5; 1932,Ap 17,VIII,2:6; 1932,D 14,27:3
Count Me In 1942,O 9,24:2
Count of Luxembourg, The 1930,F 18,28:2
Count X 1921,My 29,VI,1:7
Counterattack 1943,F 4,27:2; 1943,F 14,II,1:1
Countess Eva 1928,Mr 4,IX,2:7
Countess Maritza 1926,Mr 30,20:3; 1926,S 20,21:1; 1927,Ja 30,VII,4:3; 1936,Ag 19,18:2
Country Boy, The 1963,O 28,20:1
Country Girl, The 1950,N 11,10:6; 1950,N 19,II,1:1; 1952,Ap 4,21:1; 1952,Ap 13,II,3:7; 1966,S 30,55:1
Country People 1970,Ja 19,35:1
Country Scandal, A 1960,My 6,21:8; 1960,My 15,II,1:1
Country Wife, The 1926,D 19,VII,6:4; 1927,Ja 2,VII,2:5; 1931,Ap 19,31:5; 1935,Jl 2,24:2; 1936,O 7,32:3; 1936,O 25,X,2:4; 1936,D 2,34:1; 1936,D 13,XI,3:1; 1940,Ap 21,IX,1:6; 1955,Ap 6,35:1; 1957,Je 27,22:1; 1957,N 28,56:1; 1964,Ag 3,16:1; 1965,D 10,58:2; 1969,Ag 30,10:3
County Chairman, The 1936,My 26,26:5
Coup de Roulis 1928,O 21,IX,5:6
Coup du Deux-Decembre, Le 1928,Ap 15,IX,2:2
Courage 1927,Ja 20,20:1; 1928,O 9,34:2
Courageous One, The 1958,Ja 21,33:6; 1958,F 2,II,1:1
Course a l'Etoile, La 1928,D 9,X,2:7
Court Cards 1934,N 9,24:3
Court Circuit, Le 1923,O 16,18:1
Courtesan 1930,Ap 30,29:3
Courtesan, The 1960,Je 3,26:1
Courtin' Time 1951,Je 14,30:2; 1951,Jl 1,II,1:1
Courting 1925,S 14,17:1; 1925,S 20,VIII,1:1
Courtyard 1960,Mr 1,28:1
Cousin Muriel 1940,Mr 17,X,1:6
Cousin Sonia 1925,D 8,28:3
Couturiere de Luneville, La 1924,Mr 26,16:2
Covent Garden Tragedy, The 1968,Jl 9,30:2; 1968,Jl 14,II,4:5
Coward, The 1935,Jl 16,24:1
Cowboy Crazy 1926,Ag 1,VII,4:1
Cowboy in Israel, A 1962,O 29,36:2
Cox and Box 1934,S 7,24:3; 1936,S 29,34:2; 1939,Ja 17,27:5; 1942,F 20,20:2; 1944,F 18,15:5; 1948,Ja 20,26:2; 1951,F 20,21:2
Crab Apple 1936,Jl 8,14:2
Crabbed Youth and Age 1932,N 4,25:1
Cracks 1963,O 1,24:1
Cradle Call 1930,N 23,IX,1:3
Cradle of Willow, The 1941,D 16,20:2
Cradle Snatchers 1925,S 8,28:2; 1927,Ap 15,27:2; 1928,Ja 31,28:6; 1932,N 17,23:2
Cradle Song 1921,Mr 1,18:2; 1921,Mr 6,VI,1:2; 1926,N 21,VIII,4:1; 1927,Ja 25,18:2; 1927,Ja 30,VII,1:1; 1927,My 10,24:4; 1929,O 22,26:4; 1934,D 11,28:4; 1936,Je 7,IX,1:1; 1955,D 2,32:2
Cradle Will Rock, The 1937,D 6,19:4; 1938,Ja 4,19:3; 1947,N 25,38:3; 1947,D 27,11:2; 1964,N 9,40:4
Craig's Wife 1925,O 4,IX,2:1; 1925,O 13,21:2; 1925,O 18,IX,1:2; 1947,F 13,35:2; 1947,Mr 30,II,1:1
Cranks 1956,My 14,23:1; 1956,N 27,32:1
Cranmer of Canterbury 1959,D 4,36:1
Crashing Through 1928,O 30,26:5
Crazy Quilt 1931,My 20,28:4
Crazy With the Heat 1940,D 26,22:1; 1941,Ja 15,18:2; 1941,Ja 31,15:2
Creaking Chair, The 1924,Jl 27,VII,1:8; 1926,F 23,26:1
Cream in the Well, The 1941,Ja 21,19:2
Creditors 1949,N 22,36:5; 1949,N 27,II,1:1; 1962,Ja 26,19:1

Creeper, The 1965,Jl 15,21:1
Creeping Fire 1935,Ja 17,22:3
Creoles 1927,S 23,33:3
Crest of the Wave 1937,S 19,XI,3:1
Cretan Woman, The 1954,My 21,17:2; 1954,Jl 8,18:2; 1954,S 5,II,1:1
Cricket on the Hearth, The 1925,My 29,20:2
Crime 1927,F 23,27:3; 1927,O 19,24:2; 1927,N 6,IX,2:5; 1928,My 13,IX,2:2; 1928,My 19,7:4; 1928,Je 3,VIII,1:1; 1928,Je 24,VIII,1:4
Crime, The 1936,Mr 2,12:3
Crime and Crime 1963,D 17,51:2
Crime and Punishment 1927,Mr 6,VIII,2:1; 1931,Ja 26,20:5; 1935,Ja 23,20:3; 1946,Jl 21,II,1:5; 1947,D 23,29:3; 1948,Ja 4,II,1:1
Crime at Blossoms, The 1931,Je 7,VIII,2:1; 1933,D 17,IX,4:2; 1937,Jl 17,12:8
Crime in the Whistler Room, The 1924,O 10,22:2
Crime Marches On 1935,O 24,19:1
Crime Passionel 1948,Je 18,19:4
Crime Wave, The 1927,F 13,VII,1:4
Crimes and Crimes 1970,Ja 19,35:1
Crimes of Burke and Hare, The 1932,Ja 10,VIII,2:4
Crimes of Passion 1969,O 27,54:1; 1969,N 9,II,1:1
Criminal at Large 1932,O 11,26:3
Criminal Code, The 1929,O 3,28:2; 1929,O 13,IX,1:1
Criminals 1929,D 29,VIII,2:6
Criminals, The 1941,D 22,24:3; 1967,O 15,II,9:3; 1970,F 26,33:2
Cris des Coeurs 1928,Je 3,VIII,2:5; 1936,Ja 12,IX,3:7
Crisis in Heaven 1944,Je 25,II,1:4
Criss Cross 1926,O 13,20:2
Criss-Crossing 1970,Ja 22,30:1
Cristilinda 1925,N 1,VIII,1:3
Critic, The 1925,My 9,12:4; 1928,N 11,X,4:1; 1931,F 22,VIII,3:5; 1945,N 11,II,2:5; 1946,N 21,19:2; 1965,Jl 26,15:2; 1969,Mr 9,76:5
Critic's Choice 1960,D 15,61:3; 1961,D 7,53:2
Crocodile Chuckles, The 1929,F 24,IX,4:1
Cromwell 1926,N 7,VIII,4:3
Crooked Billet, The 1927,N 6,IX,2:5
Crooked Cross 1937,Ja 14,16:4; 1937,F 7,X,3:5
Crooked Friday, The 1925,My 21,26:3; 1925,O 9,27:3; 1925,O 18,IX,1:2
Crooked Gamblers 1920,Ag 2,12:1
Crooked Square, The 1923,S 11,10:2; 1923,S 16,VII,1:1
Crooks' Convention, The 1928,O 21,IX,2:1; 1929,S 19,37:4
Cross and the Sword, The 1965,Je 28,32:6
Cross My Heart 1928,S 18,32:7
Cross Roads 1929,N 12,34:2
Cross Ruff 1935,F 20,23:3
Cross-Town 1937,Mr 18,21:5
Crossing the Gap 1970,Je 18,54:2
Crossroads 1969,Ag 7,28:1
Crown Prince, The 1927,F 27,VII,4:6; 1927,Mr 24,23:2
Crowns 1922,N 10,20:3
Crow's Nest, The 1923,My 10,22:3; 1923,My 13,16:2
Cruce de Vias 1969,N 2,86:5
Crucible 1933,S 5,22:4
Crucible, The 1953,Ja 23,15:2; 1953,F 1,II,1:1; 1953,Mr 15,II,1:1; 1953,Jl 2,20:2; 1956,Ap 11,28:3; 1958,Mr 12,36:1; 1958,Mr 17,21:1; 1958,Je 1,II,1:1; 1964,Ap 7,30:2; 1965,Ja 20,35:1; 1968,Je 9,II,1:1
Crucified, Les 1923,Ap 8,VIII,1:7
Crucifies, Les 1923,O 30,17:2
Cruising Speed 600 MPH 1970,Ja 6,48:3
Crusaders, The 1929,Mr 3,VIII,2:1
Crusts 1962,N 30,28:1
Cry for Us All 1970,Ap 9,48:2
Cry Havoc 1942,N 8,VIII,1:7
Cry of Players, A 1968,N 15,40:1; 1968,N 24,II,9:4
Cry of the Peacock 1950,Ap 12,33:2
Cry of the Raindrop 1961,Mr 8,38:1
Cry of the Wild Ram 1960,Jl 16,10:8
Crystal Heart, The 1957,F 20,37:1; 1960,F 16,31:2
Cuando Los Hijos De Eva No Son Los Hijos De Adan 1932,Ap 23,11:2; 1937,My 1,17:4
Cuba Si 1968,D 10,53:1
Cuban Thing, The 1968,S 25,36:2
Cuckoo Clock, The 1927,O 30,IX,4:1
Cuckoos on the Hearth 1941,S 17,26:2
Cue for Passion 1940,D 20,33:4; 1958,N 26,25:2; 1958,D 7,II,5:1
Culbin Sands 1935,Mr 23,10:3
Cup, The 1923,N 13,25:1
Cup of Trembling, The 1948,Ap 21,33:5; 1959,My 1,33:5
Cupboard Love 1929,D 1,X,4:4
Curate's Play, The 1961,D 18,41:3
Cure For Love, The 1945,Ag 5,II,1:4
Cure for Matrimony 1939,O 26,26:3
Curioso Accidente, Un 1933,Mr 6,16:3
Curious Evening With Gypsy Rose Lee, A 1961,My 10,53:1
Curious Savage, The 1950,O 25,44:3; 1956,Mr 17,12:3
Curley McDimple 1967,N 23,59:2; 1969,N 25,53:1
Curse You, Jack Dalton 1935,Jl 16,24:1
Curtain Call 1937,Ap 23,24:7

Curtain Rises, The 1933,O 20,15:2
Curtains Up! 1959,N 3,26:3
Curtmantle 1962,S 5,44:3
Custom, The 1946,Je 29,22:6
Cut of the Axe 1960,F 2,38:2
Cute Gata.....Oute Zhmia 1957,D 20,31:1
Cyanamide 1954,Mr 26,17:6
Cyankali 1929,N 24,X:4
Cyclone 1934,D 2,X,2:1
Cyclone, Le 1931,O 25,VIII,1:6
Cyclone Lover, The 1928,Je 6,23:3
Cyclones, Les 1955,F 27,II,3:1
Cymbeline 1923,O 3,12:1; 1923,O 7,IX,2:2;
    1923,O 14,VIII,1:1; 1937,N 17,26:4;
    1937,D 5,XII,5:8; 1957,Ag 25,II,1:5; 1962,Jl 18,21:2;
    1970,Jl 24,17:2; 1970,Ag 23,II,1:6
Cynara 1930,Jl 13,VIII,1:3; 1931,N 3,31:1
Cyrano de Bergerac 1920,Mr 20,14:3; 1923,N 2,14:1;
    1923,N 11,VIII,1:1; 1926,Ja 24,II,8:5;
    1926,F 19,18:1; 1926,F 28,VIII,1:1;
    1927,N 27,IX,4:1; 1928,D 26,14:4;
    1932,N 13,IX,1:6; 1932,D 27,11:2; 1936,Ap 28,17:1;
    1946,O 9,33:2; 1946,N 3,I,54:6; 1946,N 3,II,1:1;
    1946,N 10,II,3:2; 1947,Ja 17,27:2; 1953,N 13,24:3;
    1962,Ag 1,21:1; 1963,Je 20,30:1; 1968,Ap 26,30:1
Czar Feodor 1922,O 22,VIII,1:6; 1922,D 6,3:2
Czarina, The 1922,F 1,22:1

D

Daddalums 1920,Jl 11,VI,1:6
Daddy Come Home 1963,Ap 17,33:1
Daddy Dumplins 1920,N 23,11:1; 1920,D 12,VI,1:3
Daddy Goodness 1968,Je 5,37:1
Daddy's Gone A-Hunting 1921,S 1,18:3;
    1921,S 4,VI,1:1; 1921,S 25,VI,1:1; 1921,O 2,VII,1:1
Daffy Dill 1922,Ag 23,14:5; 1922,Ag 27,VI,1:1
Dagger, The 1925,S 10,28:1
Dagmar 1923,Ja 23,18:2; 1923,F 11,VII,1:1
Daisy 1921,O 23,22:2
Daisy Mayme 1926,O 17,VIII,2:4; 1926,O 26,24:2;
    1926,O 31,VIII,1:4
Dallas, Nov 22, 1963 1966,N 13,80:1
Dallas-November 22d 1965,N 12,54:1
Dama Boba, La 1935,S 22,X,2:5
Damaged Goods 1937,My 18,27:2
Damask Cheek, The 1942,O 23,24:2;
    1942,N 8,VIII,1:1
Damask Drum, The 1961,F 4,15:1
Dame aux Camelias, La 1922,N 16,22:2;
    1922,N 19,VII,1:1; 1926,N 21,VIII,2:1;
    1926,D 7,24:2; 1934,Je 10,IX,2:5; 1937,O 9,16:3
Dame de Chambre, La 1924,Je 1,VII,1:7
Dame du Promenoir, La 1933,O 1,IX,1:3
Dame Nature 1938,S 27,24:3
Dames at Sea 1968,D 21,46:1; 1969,Ja 5,II,1:3;
    1969,Ag 29,24:3; 1970,Ja 5,46:3; 1970,S 24,60:1
Damn Deborah 1937,Ag 17,23:1
Damn the Tears 1927,Ja 22,11:1; 1927,Ja 30,VII,1:1
Damn Yankees 1955,My 6,17:1; 1957,Mr 29,15:7
Damn You, Scarlett O'Hara 1964,F 5,30:1
Damn Your Honor 1929,D 31,14:3
Damsel in Distress, A 1928,S 2,VII,2:1
Dance Me a Song 1950,Ja 21,10:5
Dance Night 1938,O 15,20:5
Dance of Death, The 1923,D 17,23:3;
    1928,F 5,VIII,4:7; 1932,Ja 11,29:5; 1935,O 2,26:2;
    1936,My 20,24:5; 1960,S 14,51:1; 1966,Je 3,31:1;
    1967,O 20,50:1; 1967,O 29,II,5:1; 1969,My 26,53:1
Dance of Life, The 1927,N 27,IX,4:7
Dance With No Music 1930,Ag 24,VIII,2:7
Dance With Your Gods 1934,O 8,14:3
Dancer, The 1946,Je 6,16:5
Dancers, The 1923,F 25,VII,1:7; 1923,O 18,17:2;
    1923,O 28,VIII,1:1
Dancing Girl, The 1923,Ja 25,16:2
Dancing Mothers 1924,My 4,VIII,2:1;
    1924,Ag 12,12:2; 1927,N 6,IX,4:1
Dancing Partner 1930,Jl 27,VIII,2:3; 1930,Ag 6,24:2
Dancing Years, The 1939,Ap 16,X,2:3
Dandelion 1969,D 24,12:1
Dandy Dick 1956,Ja 11,37:2
Dandy Dolls, The 1970,Ag 10,34:1
Danger 1921,D 23,18:3; 1935,Ag 27,23:4
Danger-Men Working 1936,F 7,14:4
Dangerous Age, The 1937,O 6,29:1
Dangerous Corner 1932,My 11,15:3; 1932,Je 5,X,2:2;
    1932,O 28,23:1; 1933,Jl 18,20:4
Daniel Boone 1967,D 23,28:1
Daniel Deronda 1969,Ja 11,22:2
Danny Dick 1925,Ap 11,28:2
Danny Kaye's International Show 1953,Ja 19,20:2;
    1953,Ja 25,II,1:1
Danny La Rue at the Palace 1970,Ag 31,24:1
Danny Larkin 1948,My 10,26:3
Dans Le Noir 1937,F 11,18:3
Dans l'Ombre du Harem 1927,My 29,VII,2:7
Danse de Minuit, La 1924,Mr 23,VII,1:3
Danseur Inconnu, Le 1928,S 23,IX,2:1
Danton's Death 1928,Ja 1,VIII,1:1; 1938,N 3,26:2;
    1938,N 13,IX,1:1; 1965,O 22,46:1; 1965,O 31,II,1:1
Dantons Tod 1927,D 21,28:3; 1928,Ja 1,VIII,3:1

Daphne in Cottage D 1967,O 16,56:1;
    1967,N 5,II,3:1
Daphne Laureola 1950,S 19,38:6; 1950,S 24,II,1:1
Dardamelle 1935,Je 30,X,1:4
Dare Devil, The 1924,F 3,VII,1:4
Dark, The 1925,Ag 9,VII,1:8; 1927,F 2,22:5
Dark Angel, The 1925,Ja 18,VII,2:8; 1925,F 11,19:2
Dark at the Top of the Stairs, The 1957,D 6,38:1;
    1957,D 15,II,3:1
Dark Corners 1964,My 6,43:1
Dark Eyes 1943,Ja 15,20:2; 1943,Ja 31,II,1:1;
    1948,Mr 25,34:4; 1948,Ap 11,II,3:1
Dark Halo 1959,Ap 15,28:4
Dark Hester 1931,My 17,VIII,1:3
Dark Horizon 1934,Ap 21,13:3
Dark Hours, The 1932,N 15,24:2
Dark Is Light Enough, The 1954,My 1,12:4;
    1955,F 24,20:1; 1955,Mr 6,II,1:1
Dark Isle 1930,Ja 26,VIII,4:3
Dark Lady of the Sonnets, The 1956,F 21,38:1;
    1956,Mr 4,II,1:1; 1959,Ag 21,13:1; 1961,D 15,48:1
Dark Legend 1952,Mr 25,24:2
Dark Little People, The 1924,Mr 2,VIII,2:7
Dark of the Moon 1945,Mr 15,27:2;
    1945,Mr 25,II,1:1; 1949,Ap 3,II,3:1; 1958,F 27,22:2;
    1970,Ap 4,21:2
Dark Red Island 1928,D 23,III,3:8
Dark River 1943,D 5,II,5:1
Dark Roads 1935,O 6,XI,3:7
Dark Saint, The 1932,F 21,VIII,1:6
Dark Sonnet 1958,Mr 12,36:1
Dark Tower, The 1933,N 27,20:3; 1934,Je 10,IX,1:1
Darker Flower, A 1963,Mr 11,7:2
Darkness at Noon 1951,Ja 15,13:4; 1951,Ja 21,II,1:1
Darling of the Day 1968,Ja 29,26:2; 1968,F 11,II,3:1
Darwin's Theories 1960,O 19,53:2
Date With April, A 1953,Ap 16,36:2
Daughter of Iorio 1927,S 12,6:4
Daughter of Silence 1961,D 1,28:1
Daughters of Atreus 1936,O 15,33:1
Daughters of Music 1926,S 26,VIII,2:7
Daughters of the Late Colonel, The 1951,O 15,21:2
Dave 1927,Je 5,VII,2:3
David and Bethsabe 1932,D 25,IX,1:6
David and Esther 1938,O 12,34:3
David Garrick 1929,Ag 2,17:5
David Show, The 1968,My 14,32:1; 1969,Je 11,43:1
David's Crown 1948,My 10,26:2
Davy Jones's Locker 1959,Mr 30,25:1;
    1959,D 28,18:1; 1966,D 25,48:5
Dawn 1924,O 19,VIII,2:6; 1924,N 25,27:1
Dawn, Noon, Eve 1930,Mr 9,IX,8:5
Dawn, the Day, the Night, The 1931,My 18,21:4
Dawn of Ireland, The 1920,O 1,14:2
Dawn's Early Light 1950,O 25,44:3; 1959,Ag 9,76:4
Day After Tomorrow 1950,O 27,25:2
Day Before Spring, The 1945,N 23,27:2;
    1945,D 2,II,1:1
Day by the Sea, A 1953,N 27,22:3; 1953,D 20,II,4:2;
    1955,S 27,42:1; 1955,O 2,II,1:1
Day I Forgot, The 1933,My 13,16:6
Day in the Sun 1937,Jl 27,24:3; 1939,My 17,29:2
Day of Absence 1965,N 16,56:1; 1970,Mr 18,39:1
Day of Glory, The 1946,D 22,II,2:1
Day of Judgement, The 1941,O 9,27:3
Day of Surprises, A 1921,My 1,VII,1:7
Day of the Prince 1963,My 15,33:4
Day the Money Stopped, The 1958,F 21,19:4
Day the Whores Came Out to Play Tennis, The
    1965,Mr 16,45:1
Day Will Come, The 1944,S 8,17:2
Daylight Saving 1929,Ja 13,VIII,2:4
Days and Nights of Beebee Fenstermaker, The
    1962,S 18,33:1
Days Between, The 1965,Je 4,39:1; 1965,Je 27,II,1:1
Days of Our Youth, The 1941,N 29,15:2
Days of the Commune, The 1956,N 20,44:4
Days of the Turbins 1926,N 7,20:1; 1926,N 14,17:2;
    1935,Mr 7,27:5
Days to Come 1936,D 16,35:1
Days Without End 1933,D 31,IX,2:2; 1934,Ja 9,19:1;
    1934,Ja 14,IX,1:1; 1934,F 4,IX,1:1; 1934,Ap 24,26:7;
    1935,F 5,23:2; 1935,Mr 3,VIII,1:3
Dazzling Prospect 1961,Je 25,II,3:5
De Luxe 1935,F 20,22:1; 1935,F 24,VIII,3:4;
    1935,Mr 6,22:2
De Muy Buena Familia 1932,Ap 29,13:3
De Sade Illustrated 1969,My 13,42:4
Deacon, The 1925,N 25,14:3
Dead Aunt, The 1931,N 30,16:3; 1933,F 13,11:3
Dead City, The 1923,N 28,14:1
Dead End 1935,O 29,17:2; 1935,N 3,X,1:1;
    1936,S 20,IX,3:7; 1937,Je 29,18:3; 1937,Ag 17,23:1
Dead Heat 1939,Ag 27,IX,1:6
Dead Pigeon 1953,D 24,10:2
Dead Queen, The 1966,F 9,32:1
Dead Ride Fast, The 1931,D 6,VIII,4:5
Dead Souls 1936,S 27,X,1:1; 1965,F 5,34:1
Deadfall 1955,O 28,20:1
Deadlock 1928,O 28,IX,1:3

Deadly Game, The 1960,Ja 31,II,1:7; 1960,F 3,27:2;
    1966,F 14,34:1
Dear Barbarians 1952,F 22,15:2
Dear Brutus 1926,Jl 15,21:3
Dear Charles 1952,D 21,44:5; 1953,Ap 20,22:4;
    1954,S 16,37:2; 1954,S 26,II,1:1
Dear Departed Mother-in-Law 1957,F 12,31:1
Dear Father 1924,D 21,VII,1:8
Dear Jane 1932,N 15,24:3
Dear Janet Rosenberg, Dear Mr Kooning
    1970,Ap 6,46:1; 1970,Ap 26,II,5:7
Dear Judas 1947,Ag 5,26:1; 1947,O 6,26:4
Dear Liar 1959,O 6,44:6; 1960,Mr 18,19:2;
    1960,Mr 27,II,1:1; 1962,Mr 19,36:1
Dear Love 1930,My 18,VIII,3:1
Dear Me 1921,Ja 18,14:1; 1921,Ja 23,VI,1:1;
    1921,Ja 30,VI,1:1
Dear Me, the Sky Is Falling 1963,Mr 4,9:1
Dear Miss Phoebe 1950,O 14,13:8
Dear Nobody 1963,My 8,47:4
Dear Octopus 1938,O 2,IX,2:1; 1939,Ja 12,22:2;
    1939,N 12,IX,2:5; 1940,My 19,IX,1:4
Dear Old Darling 1935,D 31,10:1; 1936,F 2,IX,1:3;
    1936,Mr 3,25:1
Dear Old England 1930,Ja 19,VIII,2:6;
    1930,Mr 26,24:6
Dear Ruth 1944,D 14,29:2; 1944,D 31,II,1:1;
    1946,Mr 1,17:3
Dear Sir 1924,S 24,21:3
Dear World 1969,F 7,33:1; 1969,F 16,II,1:1
Dearest Enemy 1925,S 19,9:2
Death and Resurrection of Mr Roche, The
    1968,O 11,44:4
Death Asks a Verdict 1937,Ja 10,X,1:8
Death of a Salesman 1949,F 11,27:2; 1949,F 20,II,1:1;
    1949,Mr 27,II,1:2; 1949,My 15,II,1:1;
    1949,Jl 29,12:5; 1949,Ag 7,II,1:4;
    1949,Ag 28,VI,11:1; 1950,Mr 4,10:7;
    1950,Mr 12,II,1:1; 1950,My 16,41:4;
    1950,Ap 28,25:4; 1950,S 21,20:5; 1963,Jl 20,11:2
Death of Bessie Smith, The 1961,Mr 2,19:1;
    1961,O 25,33:5; 1963,Je 11,29:2; 1968,O 3,55:1
Death of Cuchulain, The 1959,Ap 13,34:4
Death of Danton, The 1928,O 28,IX,2:1
Death of Odysseus, The 1953,N 4,30:5
Death of Pazukhin, The 1924,F 12,20:1
Death of Satan, The 1960,Ap 6,49:1;
    1960,Ap 17,II,1:1
Death of the Well-Loved Boy, The 1967,My 16,48:1
Death Takes a Holiday 1929,N 24,X,4:5;
    1929,D 27,26:4; 1931,F 17,29:1
Deathless, The 1943,Jl 11,II,1:2
Deaths and Entrances 1970,Je 3,51:2
Deathwatch 1957,Mr 7,25:4; 1958,O 10,34:2
Debauche 1929,Mr 24,X,2:1
Debonair 1930,Ap 24,29:2
Deburau 1920,D 24,14:3; 1921,Ja 2,VI,3:1;
    1921,Ja 16,VI,1:1; 1921,Ja 30,VI,1:1;
    1926,N 14,VIII,2:1; 1926,D 28,16:1
Debut 1956,F 23,32:1
Decameron, The 1961,Ap 13,32:1
Decameron Nights 1922,Ap 21,14:5
Deceased, The 1962,Mr 21,36:2
Decent People Frighten Me 1964,Ja 26,82:3
Decision 1929,My 28,37:3; 1944,F 3,23:2;
    1944,F 13,II,1:1; 1944,My 21,II,1:1; 1949,O 18,34:4
Declassee 1935,Ag 6,20:3
Decline and Fall of the Entire World As Seen
    Through the Eyes of Cole Porter Revisited, The
    1965,Mr 31,24:2
Decoy, The 1927,Ag 21,VII,1:8; 1932,Ap 2,13:4
Decree Nisi 1936,N 11,54:4
Dede 1921,N 20,VI,1:3
Deep Are the Roots 1945,S 27,24:4; 1945,O 7,II,1:1;
    1947,Ap 28,26:3; 1947,Jl 10,17:1; 1947,Ag 24,II,1:5;
    1960,O 4,47:1
Deep Blue Sea, The 1952,Mr 16,II,3:7; 1952,N 6,38:3;
    1952,D 7,II,7:2; 1952,D 14,II,3:1; 1953,Ap 4,8:6
Deep Channels 1929,O 19,22:3
Deep Harlem 1929,Ja 8,35:2
Deep Mrs Sykes, The 1945,Mr 20,22:6;
    1945,Mr 25,II,1:1
Deep River 1926,S 26,VIII,2:7; 1926,O 5,26:2;
    1926,O 10,VIII,1:1; 1926,O 10,VIII,4:8
Deep Tangled Wildwood, The 1923,N 6,22:1
Deer Park, The 1967,F 1,27:2; 1967,F 12,II,1:4
Defender of the Faith 1970,Jl 31,14:1
Defense d'Afficher 1931,S 27,VIII,2:7
Deferential Prostitute, The 1946,D 22,II,4:2
Defraudanten, Die 1931,Ja 25,VIII,4:1
Deirdre of the Sorrows 1920,S 26,VI,1:4;
    1949,D 15,51:2; 1959,O 15,46:1
Dejeuner d'Amoureux, Un 1929,My 5,IX,2:4;
    1936,N 26,38:2
Delicate Balance, A 1966,S 23,44:1; 1966,O 2,II,1:1;
    1967,O 28,35:2
Delicate Justice 1927,N 27,IX,2:1
Delicate Story 1940,D 5,32:2
Delightful Season, A 1960,S 29,30:1
Delila 1937,S 18,15:1
Delilah 1930,O 12,VIII,1:8
Delitto e Castigo 1931,Ja 26,20:5
Delta Wife, The 1927,My 6,20:3

Deluge, The 1922,Ja 28,14:2; 1927,Ja 11,36:2; 1935,Mr 26,23:7
Delusion 1935,Mr 29,26:4
Demi-Monde, Le 1922,N 15,22:3
Demi-Virgin, The 1921,O 19,22:1
Democratic Body, A 1942,F 13,24:7
Demon de la Chair, Le 1927,N 20,IX,4:4
Demon Mirror, The 1968,Mr 13,42:1
Demonstration, The 1967,O 2,54:2; 1969,N 20,60:1
Deodat 1931,Ap 19,VIII,2:8
Departs 1928,D 23,VIII,2:1
Depositaire, La 1924,My 25,VIII,1:8
Depths, The 1925,Ja 28,15:3; 1925,F 8,VII,1:1
Depths of the Heart, The 1930,D 8,27:1
Deputy, The 1964,F 27,26:1; 1964,Mr 8,II,1:1
Deputy of Paris, The 1947,Mr 22,9:5
Deraillement du T P 33 1927,F 13,VII,4:1
Dernier Empereur, Le 1926,D 19,VIII,3:3
Derryowen 1946,O 29,34:2
Desert Flower, The 1924,N 19,18:2
Desert Highway 1944,Ja 2,II,1:5
Desert Incident, A 1959,Mr 25,40:1
Desert Sands 1922,F 14,20:1
Desert Song, The 1926,D 1,24:2; 1927,My 8,VII,1:5; 1946,Ja 9,20:2; 1955,Jl 1,13:1
Deserteuse, La 1926,N 21,VIII,2:1; 1928,S 23,IX,2:1
Design For A Stained Glass Window 1950,Ja 24,26:2
Design for Living 1933,Ja 3,19:5; 1933,Ja 8,IX,3:2; 1933,Ja 25,13:2; 1933,Ja 29,IX,1:1; 1933,N 19,IX,2:5; 1935,Ap 21,IX,2:1
Desire 1927,My 29,VII,2:7; 1930,Jl 27,VIII,1:8
Desire Caught by the Tail 1950,F 18,9:8
Desire Under the Elms 1924,N 12,20:7; 1924,D 7,VIII,5:1; 1925,N 1,VIII,1:3; 1930,Ag 3,23:4; 1933,N 12,IX,1:1; 1951,N 22,45:1; 1952,Ja 17,23:4; 1952,Ja 20,II,1:1; 1953,N 29,II,3:1; 1963,Ja 11,5:6
Desk Set, The 1955,O 25,36:7
Desperate Hours, The 1955,F 11,20:2; 1955,F 20,II,1:1; 1955,My 1,II,3:1
Desperate Lovers, The 1927,F 20,VII,1:4
Destination Unknown 1937,Jl 6,23:4
Destinies 1929,D 29,VIII,2:6
Destiny Rag 1968,My 28,41:1
Destruction 1932,Jl 1,19:5
Destruction of Europe, The 1925,Ja 11,VII,2:7
Destry Rides Again 1959,Ap 24,24:1; 1959,My 3,II,1:1
Detective Story 1949,Mr 24,32:2; 1949,Ap 3,II,1:1; 1950,Mr 27,18:2; 1954,F 13,11:2
Detour, The 1921,Jl 17,VI,1:1; 1921,Ag 24,12:2; 1921,S 4,VI,1:1
Detour After Dark 1959,Je 9,11:4
Detra, Les 1921,Ap 17,VI,1:8
Deuces Wild 1962,Ap 25,31:1
Deutsche Passion 1933 1934,S 16,X,1:6
Deux Amis, Les 1927,Je 12,VII,2:1
Deux Paires d'Amis 1926,O 3,VIII,2:1
Deux Sous de Fleurs 1933,O 1,IX,1:3
Devil, The 1921,My 15,VI,1:6; 1930,F 2,VIII,2:4
Devil and Daniel Webster, The 1939,My 19,26:1; 1939,My 21,X,1:1
Devil and the Lady, The 1930,Ag 10,VIII,1:3
Devil Came From Dublin, The! 1955,Je 3,27:2
Devil in the Cheese, The 1926,D 30,22:4
Devil in the Mind 1931,My 2,23:2
Devil Is a Good Man, The 1940,Mr 20,36:2
Devil of Pei-Ling 1936,F 21,20:4
Devil Passes, The 1932,Ja 5,20:3; 1932,Ja 10,VIII,1:1
Devil Takes a Bride, The 1938,O 8,10:3
Devil to Pay, The 1925,D 4,26:2; 1925,D 13,IX,3:1; 1939,Jl 21,11:1; 1939,Ag 13,IX,2:4
Devil Within, The 1925,Ja 25,VII,1:4; 1925,Mr 17,19:4
Devils 1926,Mr 18,26:4
Devils, The 1961,F 21,41:1; 1963,N 5,25:1; 1963,N 17,II,1:1; 1965,N 17,51:2; 1965,N 28,II,1:1
Devil's Advocate, The 1961,Mr 10,20:1; 1961,Mr 19,II,1:1
Devil's Disciple, The 1923,Ap 24,24:1; 1923,My 6,VII,1:1; 1930,S 21,IX,2:1; 1941,S 11,20:6; 1950,Ja 26,23:2; 1950,F 5,II,1:1; 1970,Je 30,48:1; 1970,Jl 12,II,1:3
Devils Galore 1945,S 13,27:2; 1945,S 23,II,1:1
Devil's Game, A 1959,N 9,35:6
Devil's General, The 1953,O 11,II,3:7
Devil's Host, The 1928,S 9,IX,2:7; 1931,N 20,27:2
Devil's Little Game, The 1932,Ag 2,20:4
Devil's Mistress, The 1929,Mr 10,X,4:5
Devonshire Cream 1924,D 28,VII,2:2
Dew Drop Inn 1923,My 18,26:4
Diable 1926,O 31,VIII,2:4
Diable a Paris, Le 1927,N 13,IX,4:2
Diable et le Bon Dieu, Le 1951,Je 8,32:6; 1951,Ag 19,II,1:6
Dial 'M' for Murder 1952,O 14,41:5; 1952,O 30,41:2; 1952,N 30,II,1:1; 1953,N 8,II,1:1; 1957,Ja 9,27:4; 1958,F 8,12:2
Diamond Lil 1928,Ap 10,32:1; 1929,Ja 27,IX,1:3; 1948,Ja 26,16:6; 1948,F 15,II,3:2; 1948,N 30,33:2; 1949,F 7,16:2; 1951,S 15,8:2
Diamond Orchid 1965,F 11,44:4
Diana 1929,D 10,37:1

Diana e la Tuda 1927,Mr 13,II,9:3
Diarmuid and Grainne 1928,D 16,IX,4:6
Diary, The 1966,N 27,159:3
Diary of a Madman 1964,Ap 17,29:2; 1967,Mr 24,25:1
Diary of a Scoundrel 1956,N 5,41:1
Diary of Adam and Eve, The 1966,O 19,53:1
Diary of Anne Frank, The 1955,O 6,24:2; 1955,O 16,II,1:1; 1956,O 3,30:1; 1956,O 6,18:6; 1956,O 14,II,3:1; 1956,O 14,II,1:1; 1956,N 29,43:1; 1957,Ja 20,II,3:7; 1957,Ja 23,23:5; 1962,Jl 31,19:2; 1963,Ap 12,33:1
Dice of the Gods, The 1923,Ap 6,20:2; 1923,Ap 15,VII,1:1
Dick Whittington 1928,Ja 15,VIII,4:6
Dick Whittington and His Remarkable Cat 1950,N 25,10:5
Dictateur, Le 1926,N 7,VIII,2:7
Dictator, The 1926,O 5,26:4; 1928,Ap 29,IX,1:3
Did I Say No? 1931,S 23,19:4
Diener Zweier Herren 1928,Ja 10,28:3
Different Kick, A 1969,Ja 5,76:2
Difficult Woman, The 1962,Ap 26,22:7
Difficulty of Getting Married, The 1936,Jl 7,22:1
Diff'rent 1920,D 29,8:1; 1921,Mr 20,VI,1:1; 1925,F 11,19:3; 1925,Mr 1,VII,1:1; 1937,N 21,II,10:7; 1938,Ja 26,26:4; 1961,O 18,52:1
Digging for Apples 1962,S 28,29:4
Diloy le Chemineau 1926,N 14,VIII,2:1
Dindon, Le 1961,Mr 8,38:1
Ding and Company 1934,N 20,24:2; 1934,D 9,X,3:1
Dinner at Eight 1932,O 24,18:2; 1932,N 6,IX,1:1; 1933,Ja 7,11:5; 1933,Ja 29,IX,1:3; 1933,Ap 9,IX,1:7; 1933,O 17,26:2; 1966,S 28,38:1; 1966,O 9,II,1:1
Dinner Is Served 1929,Ag 16,18:4; 1930,F 8,13:4
Dinny and the Witches 1959,D 10,53:3
Dinosaur Wharf 1951,N 9,23:2
Dionysus in 69 1968,Je 7,35:3; 1968,Je 16,II,1:1; 1968,N 19,52:1
Diplomacy 1924,Mr 16,VIII,1:7; 1928,My 29,16:3; 1928,Je 3,VIII,1:1
Director Riggs' Crime 1949,O 18,34:4
Dirtiest Show in Town, The 1970,My 2,21:1; 1970,Je 29,42:2; 1970,Jl 5,II,14:5
Dirty Old Man, The 1964,My 5,53:1
Disciple, The 1931,S 27,VIII,2:8
Discours des Prix 1934,D 2,X,2:1
Disenchanted, The 1958,D 4,53:4; 1959,Ja 11,II,1:1
Dishonored Lady 1930,Ja 26,VIII,2:1; 1930,F 5,27:1; 1930,My 25,IX,2:4
Disintegration of James Cherry, The 1970,Ja 30,33:3; 1970,F 8,II,1:6
Dismissal, The 1923,Ap 24,10:3
Disney on Parade 1970,S 24,63:1
Displaced Person, The 1966,D 30,15:1
Disraeli 1921,S 25,VI,1:1; 1927,My 4,29:1
Distaff Side, The 1933,S 6,24:5; 1933,S 24,X,1:6; 1934,S 26,17:2
Distant Bell, A 1960,Ja 14,29:1
Distant City, The 1941,S 23,27:5
Distant Drum, A 1928,Ja 21,13:1
Distant Drums 1932,Ja 19,24:3; 1932,Ja 31,VIII,1:1
Distant Point 1941,N 9,IX,3:6
Distant Shore, The 1935,F 22,26:2
Distinguished Gathering 1935,O 8,26:3; 1935,N 3,X,1:7
Distinguished Villa, A 1926,Jl 14,19:4
Diversion 1927,Ag 14,VII,2:1; 1928,Ja 6,26:3; 1928,Ja 12,25:1
Diversions 1958,N 8,14:4
Divided by Three 1934,S 28,26:3; 1934,O 3,24:2
Divided Honors 1929,O 1,28:2
Divin Aretin, Le 1930,O 5,IX,4:3
Divin Mensonge 1926,N 14,VIII,2:1
Divina Pastora, La 1931,Mr 4,33:2
Divine Drudge 1933,Jl 4,16:4; 1933,O 27,22:3
Divine Moment, A 1934,Ja 8,21:8
Divorce a la Carte 1928,Mr 27,30:3
Divorce Me, Darling 1965,F 2,29:6
Divorce Me, Dear 1930,Ag 3,VIII,3:4; 1931,O 7,29:2
Dixie to Broadway 1924,O 30,22:1
Dizzy 1932,O 30,IX,2:2
Do, Mi, Sol, Do 1935,F 3,VIII,3:3
Do I Hear a Waltz? 1965,Mr 19,28:1; 1965,Mr 28,II,1:1
Do Not Pass Go 1965,Ap 20,44:1
Do Re Mi 1960,D 27,23:2; 1961,Ja 8,II,1:1
Do You Know the Milky Way? 1961,O 17,45:1
Dock Brief, The 1961,N 22,24:2
Doctor and the Devils, The 1959,Ja 21,27:8; 1962,Ag 22,28:1
Dr Cook's Garden 1967,S 26,52:1
Doctor Cupid 1952,Ag 14,19:6
Dr David's Dad 1924,Ag 14,10:3
Doctor Faustus 1926,O 27,25:5; 1937,Ja 9,21:2; 1957,F 19,35:7; 1961,Ap 26,36:1; 1961,Ag 22,23:1; 1966,F 16,49:1; 1968,Je 29,20:1
Doctor Faustus Lights the Lights 1951,D 3,23:4
Dr Fish 1970,Mr 11,42:2; 1970,Mr 22,II,3:1
Dr Galley 1970,Ja 23,25:1
Dr Harmer 1931,Mr 22,VIII,4:3
Doctor Herzl 1945,D 21,25:4

Doctor in Spite of Himself, The 1949,Ap 23,10:2; 1957,F 28,18:4
Dr Jeckyll and Mr Hyde 1927,Ap 24,VII,2:3
Doctor Knock 1928,F 24,15:2; 1936,Jl 14,22:1
Dr med Hiob Praetorius 1934,My 6,IX,2:2
Doctor Monica 1933,N 7,29:3
Dr Pygmalion 1932,Ap 24,VIII,1:1
Doctor Social 1948,F 12,29:5
Dr Willy Nilly 1959,Je 5,18:2
Doctor X 1930,Jl 31,12:4; 1931,F 10,25:1
Doctored Wife, The 1950,Jl 12,33:2
Doctor's Dilemma, The 1927,N 22,33:1; 1927,D 4,X,1:1; 1941,F 18,26:6; 1941,Mr 12,18:2; 1941,Mr 30,IX,1:1; 1942,Mr 15,VIII,1:1; 1955,Ja 12,22:1; 1955,Ja 23,II,1:1; 1969,Je 24,37:1
Doctors Disagree 1943,D 29,15:2
Doctors of Philosophy 1962,O 3,46:8
Dodo Bird, The 1967,D 9,62:1
Dodsworth 1934,F 26,20:4; 1934,Ag 21,12:3; 1938,F 23,26:2; 1938,Mr 13,XI,3:1
Does a Tiger Wear a Necktie? 1967,F 4,17:1; 1969,F 26,38:1; 1969,Mr 9,II,1:1; 1969,Mr 16,II,4:5
Dog Beneath the Skin, The 1936,F 23,X,1:3
Dog in the Manger, The 1944,Je 18,II,1:1
Doing Nicely 1940,D 4,34:3
Dole Brothers 1932,Mr 26,17:7
Dollar Princess 1949,Je 2,32:1
Dolle Hans 1930,My 4,XI,1:3
Doll's House, A 1928,Ap 22,IX,2:7; 1936,Mr 3,25:2; 1937,Jl 18,II,6:8; 1937,Jl 25,X,2:3; 1937,D 28,28:6; 1954,N 15,32:2; 1956,My 8,29:2; 1963,F 4,5:6
Dolly Jordan 1922,O 4,26:1
Dominant Sex, The 1934,D 4,23:1; 1935,Ap 2,24:5; 1937,O 24,XI,3:2
Domino 1932,F 28,VIII,1:1; 1932,Ag 7,IX,1:1; 1932,Ag 17,13:2
Dompteur, Le, ou L'Anglais Tel Qu' On La Mange 1926,Ja 10,VII,1:3
Don Carlos 1962,F 28,27:5; 1964,N 25,40:1
Don Juan 1921,S 8,14:2; 1927,Ap 10,VIII,4:7; 1930,D 28,VIII,3:5; 1932,N 13,IX,2:5; 1934,F 27,16:5; 1956,Ja 4,21:4; 1958,O 29,29:1; 1970,F 7,24:2; 1970,My 26,32:1; 1970,My 31,II,1:6
Don Juan in Hell 1951,O 23,34:4; 1951,N 4,II,1:1; 1960,O 4,47:3
Don Juan in the Russian Manner 1954,Ap 23,23:2
Don Juan Tenorio 1939,Jl 16,IX,1:1; 1953,N 20,18:5
Don Juan's Raincoat 1933,O 22,IX,2:3
Don Karlos 1935,Jl 28,X,1:6
Don Q Jr 1926,Ja 28,16:3
Don Quixote 1922,D 12,22:2
Don Quixote, Esquire 1920,My 7,12:6
Don Quixote Meets the Puppet-Master 1959,Ja 27,27:5
Dona Maria de Castilla 1933,Mr 19,IV,2:2
Donna Del Mare, La 1923,O 30,17:1
Donna Diana 1936,Je 28,IX,2:1
Donnybrook! 1961,My 19,23:1; 1961,My 28,II,1:1
Dono Maria la Brava 1926,My 18,29:1
Donogoo 1930,N 16,VIII,2:6; 1961,Ja 19,25:3
Donovan Affair, The 1926,Ag 31,15:2
Don't, George! 1944,N 4,18:6
Don't Bother Me, I Can't Cope 1970,O 8,60:3
Don't Bother Mother 1925,F 4,18:2
Don't Call Me By My Right Name 1963,O 1,34:1
Don't Drink the Water 1966,N 18,37:1; 1966,D 25,II,1:1
Don't Go Away Mad 1949,My 10,28:2
Don't Listen, Ladies 1948,D 29,16:2
Don't Look Now! 1936,N 4,41:3
Don't Shoot Mable It's Your Husband 1968,O 23,34:1
Don't Tell 1920,S 29,12:1
Don't Tell George 1928,Jl 22,VII,1:1
Don't Throw Glass Houses 1938,D 28,24:4
Don't Worry Brother! 1963,O 14,35:2
Doodle Dandy of the U S A 1942,O 19,15:2
Doomat, The 1922,D 8,36:3
Dope 1926,Ja 4,16:3
Dora Mobridge 1930,Ap 21,20:2
Dorian Gray 1928,My 22,18:4; 1936,Jl 21,13:3
Dorothea Angermann 1926,N 22,28:2; 1928,F 19,VIII,2:1
Dorothy Crawford - Recital 1939,Mr 13,12:1
Dorottya 1929,F 3,VIII,2:1
Dossers 1962,S 27,31:5
Dossier, The 1961,Ja 14,15:2
Dostigayev 1935,Ja 14,10:5
Douaumont 1929,D 2,VIII,4:3
Double 1929,Ja 13,VIII,2:7
Double Dan 1927,Je 5,VII,2:1
Double Dealer, The 1969,My 25,36:2; 1969,Ag 7,29:1
Double Door 1933,S 22,15:5; 1934,Mr 22,24:6; 1934,Ap 15,X,2:2; 1935,Ag 21,22:2
Double Dublin 1963,D 27,16:2
Double Dummy 1936,N 12,30:1
Double Exposure 1937,Ag 18,15:2
Double Harness 1933,Ja 13,18:5
Double in Hearts 1956,O 17,41:7
Double-Or Quit 1922,O 8,VI,1:7
Doughgirls, The 1942,D 31,19:2; 1943,Ja 10,VII,1:1
Douglas Once 1950,S 10,II,3:1

Dove, The 1925,F 12,17:3; 1925,F 22,VIII,1:1;
  1925,Ag 25,12:2; 1926,My 7,12:2
Dover-Calais 1927,My 1,VIII,1:3
Dover Road, The 1921,D 24,7:2; 1924,My 4,VIII,2:4;
  1924,D 20,18:2; 1926,Ap 29,20:3
Down in the Dumps 1937,Mr 7,II,1:1
Down to Miami 1944,S 12,23:5
Downstream 1926,Ja 12,28:1
Doyen, The 1962,Mr 11,41:4
Dozens, The 1969,Mr 14,51:1
Dracula 1927,Mr 11,24:3; 1927,S 25,VIII,4:8;
  1927,O 6,29:1; 1931,Ap 14,33:3; 1970,Ag 11,27:1
Dracula Sabbat 1970,O 2,28:2
Drag, The 1927,F 1,3:6
Dragon, The 1922,D 27,12:1; 1929,Mr 26,34:2;
  1963,Ap 10,32:1
Dragon's Mouth 1952,Je 8,II,3:1; 1955,N 17,45:1
Drake's Drum 1923,D 26,17:7
Drama at Inish 1933,F 12,II,2:8; 1934,N 15,24:2;
  1937,D 14,33:2
Drapier Letters, The 1927,S 18,VII,2:1
Drat! the Cat! 1965,O 11,54:2
Draw the Fires 1935,Je 9,IX,1:1
Dread 1929,O 27,IX,2:1
Dream Child 1934,Jl 31,20:2; 1934,S 28,26:2
Dream Girl 1945,D 15,13:2; 1945,D 23,II,3:1;
  1951,My 10,39:1
Dream Girl, The 1924,Ag 21,12:2
Dream Maker, The 1921,N 22,17:1
Dream of a Blacklisted Actor 1969,D 18,64:1
Dream of Peter Mann, The 1960,S 6,40:1
Dream of Sganarelle, The 1933,O 17,26:5
Dream of Swallows, A 1964,Ap 15,46:1
Dream Out of Time, A 1970,N 9,52:1
Dream Play 1926,Ja 21,18:2; 1933,Ap 23,X,1:3;
  1935,D 8,X,4:5; 1936,Je 28,IX,1:6; 1960,N 23,22:1;
  1970,Ap 17,45:1
Dream Queen 1930,F 23,III,7:2
Dream With Music 1944,My 19,15:2
Dreaming Dust, The 1955,D 8,46:5
Dreams 1970,Je 3,51:2
Dreams for Sale 1922,S 14,24:1
Dreigroschenoper, Die 1965,Mr 12,24:1;
  1965,Mr 21,II,13:1
Dreimal Hochzeit 1929,Ap 28,IX,1:4
Dreyfus Affair, The 1930,Mr 30,VIII,4:1
Drift 1925,N 25,15:3
Drifting 1922,Ja 3,20:3; 1922,Ja 22,VI,1:1
Drifting Apart: or, The Fisherman's Child
  1941,Ag 20,16:6
Drink to Me Only 1958,O 9,47:4
Druid Circle, The 1947,O 23,29:5; 1947,N 16,II,1:1
Drum and Bell 1932,Ap 21,25:4
Drums Begin, The 1933,N 25,10:5
Drums in the Night 1967,My 18,54:1
Drums of Jeopardy, The 1922,My 30,8:4
Drums of Oude, The 1927,My 3,24:3
Drums Professor, The 1935,Jl 30,17:2
Drums Under the Windows 1960,O 14,26:1
Drunkard, The 1929,D 31,14:6; 1934,Ap 1,X,1:1;
  1934,N 27,27:2; 1934,D 6,26:3; 1936,S 20,IX,3:4;
  1959,Je 24,37:2; 1970,Ap 14,54:1
Du Barry 1931,S 20,VIII,2:7; 1932,My 8,VIII,1:6;
  1932,N 13,IX,1:8; 1932,N 23,15:2; 1939,N 19,X,3:4;
  1939,D 24,IX,1:1; 1942,N 1,VIII,2:2
Du Barry Was a Lady 1939,D 7,34:2
Dual Marriage Way 1965,Ag 19,34:3
Duchess Misbehaves, The 1946,F 14,32:2
Duchess of Chicago, The 1928,Ap 15,II,2:4;
  1929,N 17,IX,4:1
Duchess of Malfi, The 1946,S 26,33:4;
  1946,O 16,35:2; 1957,Mr 20,33:1; 1962,Mr 5,27:1
Ducks and Drakes 1941,D 14,IX,4:3
Ducks and Lovers 1961,O 20,39:1
Due Orfanelle, Le 1936,O 5,24:4
Duel, Le 1922,N 16,22:2
Duel, The 1968,Ap 18,56:1
Duel of Angels 1960,Ap 20,42:2; 1960,My 1,II,1:1
Duet by Accident 1938,Mr 27,X,1:3
Duet for Solo Voice 1970,Ap 5,76:4
Duet for Three 1966,My 20,41:1
Duet for Two Hands 1947,O 8,28:3
Duet in Floodlight 1935,F 14,24:3; 1935,Je 5,22:1
Duke in Darkness, The 1942,O 18,VIII,1:4;
  1944,Ja 25,15:2
Dulcitus 1926,Mr 29,24:2
Dulcy 1921,Ag 15,14:1; 1921,Ag 21,VI,1:1
Dumb as a Fox 1924,N 30,VIII,2:1
Dumb-Bell 1923,N 27,23:2
Dumbbell People in a Barbell World 1962,F 15,25:1
Dumbwaiter, The 1962,N 27,44:1; 1962,D 9,II,5:1
Dunce Boy, The 1925,Ap 4,20:2
Dunnigan's Daughter 1945,D 27,16:1;
  1946,Ja 6,II,1:1
Dunungen 1939,F 26,IX,2:3
Duo 1970,F 4,36:1
Durand, Bijoutier 1930,F 2,VIII,4:1
Dust Heap, The 1924,F 24,VII,2:5; 1924,Ap 25,20:2
Dusty Ermine 1935,S 25,19:6; 1936,Mr 7,11:6
Dutch Uncle 1969,Mr 28,41:1
Dutchman 1964,Mr 25,46:2; 1965,N 17,53:7
Dutchman's Farm, A 1941,My 11,I,43:3
Dwarf, The 1963,S 19,21:1

Dybbuk, The 1921,S 2,9:2; 1922,Ja 29,VI,1:3;
  1924,Ja 29,17:7; 1925,D 16,22:2; 1925,D 20,VII,3:1;
  1926,Ja 6,16:2; 1926,Ja 17,VIII,1:1;
  1926,N 21,VIII,1:3; 1926,D 14,24:2; 1926,D 17,27:2;
  1926,D 26,VII,1:1; 1927,My 1,VIII,2:7;
  1928,F 26,VIII,4:1; 1937,F 24,18:4;
  1937,D 5,XII,5:8; 1948,My 3,26:3; 1954,O 27,33:6;
  1964,F 4,30:2
Dylan 1964,Ja 20,18:1
Dynamite Tonight 1964,Mr 16,36:2; 1967,Mr 16,52:2
Dynamo 1929,F 12,22:1; 1929,F 17,IX,1:1

E

E & O E 1935,Jl 12,15:3
E-MC2 1948,Je 16,36:2
Each Had Six Wings 1964,Mr 12,39:1
Eagle Has Two Heads, The 1946,S 16,9:7;
  1947,Mr 20,39:2; 1956,D 14,37:2
Earl Carroll's Vanities 1923,Jl 6,8:2; 1924,S 11,23:6;
  1925,Jl 7,24:1; 1925,D 29,20:3; 1926,Ag 25,19:4;
  1927,Ja 5,18:1; 1928,Ag 7,25:2; 1930,Jl 2,28:3;
  1931,Ag 28,18:7; 1940,Ja 15,11:2
Early Morning 1968,Ap 9,58:1; 1970,N 26,57:1
Early to Bed 1943,Je 18,16:2
Earth 1927,Mr 10,23:1; 1927,Mr 20,VIII,1:1
Earth Between, The 1929,Mr 6,33:1
Earth Journey 1944,Ap 28,24:2
Earth Spirit 1950,Je 7,33:4; 1970,Mr 28,32:1
Earthlight Theater 1970,N 4,38:2
Easiest Way, The 1921,N 14:1; 1921,S 11,VI,1:1
East Lynne 1926,Mr 11,18:4
East Lynne Goes West 1931,My 3,I,26:5
East of Broadway 1932,Ja 27,19:3
East of Suez 1922,S 22,16:3
East Side Professor, The 1938,F 12,19:7
East Side Wedding, An 1935,Ja 21,18:2
East Wind 1931,O 28,19:1; 1931,D 11,VIII,4:3
East Wind, The 1967,F 10,30:1
Easter 1926,Mr 19,24:3; 1928,O 28,IX,1:3;
  1957,Ja 17,35:2; 1957,F 3,II,1:1
Easter Man, The 1964,Jl 1,39:1
Eastward in Eden 1947,N 19,33:2; 1956,Ap 18,25:4
Eastwood Ho 1936,Jl 8,14:2
Easy Come, Easy Go 1925,O 27,20:2
Easy Mark, The 1924,Ag 27,14:2; 1924,Ag 31,VII,1:1
Easy Street 1924,Ag 15,16:4
Easy Terms 1925,S 23,22:2
Easy Virtue 1925,D 8,28:2; 1926,Je 10,29:2;
  1939,D 31,18:4
Eau Fraiche, L' 1931,Je 7,VIII,3:5
Ebb Tide 1931,Je 9,33:6
Eccentricities of Davy Crockett, The 1961,Ja 4,26:1
Echec a la Reine 1928,D 23,VIII,2:1
Echmiadzin 1946,O 21,27:3
Ecole des Charlatans, L' 1930,Ap 27,IX,2:1
Ecole des Contribuables, L' 1934,Ap 29,IX,2:2
Ecole des Femmes, L' 1930,N 2,VIII,3:1;
  1936,N 21,IX,2:4; 1951,Mr 19,22:1;
  1961,Ap 28,23:1
Ecole des Maris, L' 1939,Mr 19,XI,3:1
Ed Wynn's Carnival 1920,Ap 6,18:2;
  1920,Ap 18,VI,2:3
Eddie Fisher at the Winter Garden 1962,O 3,47:1
Eden End 1934,S 15,20:7; 1934,S 30,IX,3:1;
  1935,O 22,17:1
Edgar Allan Poe 1925,O 6,31:1; 1925,O 11,VIII,1:1
Edge of the Sword, The 1949,N 10,40:3
Edith Piaf 1947,O 30,30:2
Edna 1929,My 11,22:2
Edna His Wife 1937,D 8,30:3
Education of H*Y*M*A*N K*A*P*L*A*N, The
  1968,Ap 5,57:1; 1968,Ap 14,II,1:1
Edward, My Son 1948,O 1,30:2; 1948,O 10,II,1:1
Edward and Agrippina 1962,Mr 21,36:2
Edward II 1958,F 12,32:5; 1968,My 2,58:4;
  1969,Ja 19,II,30:5; 1969,S 4,50:1
Edwardians, The 1937,Ap 20,28:4; 1937,My 9,XI,1:4
Edwin Booth 1958,N 25,37:1; 1958,N 30,II,1:1
Edwina Black 1950,N 22,20:5
Effect of Gamma Rays on Man-in-the-Moon
  Marigolds, The 1965,Je 7,48:1; 1965,Je 27,II,1:1;
  1970,Ap 8,32:1; 1970,Ap 19,II,1:1
Egares, Les 1929,My 26,IX,4:1
Egerfogo 1958,Ja 30,18:6
Egg, The 1962,Ja 9,23:2
Egg and I, The 1958,S 11,43:4
Egg in Your Beer 1945,My 13,II,1:3
Egghead, The 1957,O 10,39:1
Egmont 1929,Mr 24,X,2:3; 1932,Je 19,IX,1:3
Egoists 1959,O 14,52:2
Egotist, The 1922,D 27,12:1; 1922,D 31,VII,1:1
Eh? 1966,O 17,47:1; 1966,N 6,II,1:1
Ehen Werden im Himmel Geschlossen
  1929,Ap 7,X,4:4
Eight Bells 1933,O 30,14:2; 1933,N 5,IX,1:1
Eight O'Clock Tuesday 1941,Ja 7,18:2
1849 1933,F 22,24:5
1860, or an Interrupted Festival 1931,O 22,27:1
1860: or, Aris 1931,O 22,27:1
Eileen 1922,Je 18,VI,1:6
Eisrevue 1969,O 23,55:1

El Alcalde De Zalamea 1953,N 23,32:5
El Cristo 1926,My 8,21:2; 1926,My 9,II,1:4
Elder Statesman, The 1958,Ag 20,21:5;
  1958,Ag 26,35:1; 1958,Ag 31,II,3:1
Eldest, The 1935,F 12,24:3
Eldorado 1930,S 4,26:3; 1931,O 25,VIII,2:5
Electra 1927,My 4,28:3; 1927,My 15,VIII,1:1;
  1927,D 2,20:6; 1927,D 18,IX,6:1; 1930,D 27,16:1;
  1931,My 24,VIII,3:5; 1932,Ja 9,21:4; 1937,Jl 4,X,2:1;
  1939,Jl 9,IX,1:6; 1952,N 20,38:2; 1952,N 30,II,8:3;
  1958,My 10,17:7; 1959,F 14,15:1; 1961,S 20,23:4;
  1962,Mr 22,42:1; 1962,Ag 30,34:1; 1962,N 11,82:4;
  1964,Ag 12,42:1; 1964,S 8,33:1; 1969,Ag 8,14:1
Electronic Nigger, The 1968,Mr 9,23:2
Eleventh Hour, The 1956,Jl 10,26:7
Eleventh Inheritor, The 1962,N 22,43:5
Elisabeth of Austria 1938,N 20,IX,1:8
Elisabeth von England 1930,D 14,IX,4:1
Elizabeth, la Femme Sans Hommes 1935,N 24,IX,3:7
Elizabeth and Essex 1930,Mr 2,IX,4:7; 1935,N 9,18:8
Elizabeth of England 1931,O 18,VIII,1:3
Elizabeth Sleeps Out 1935,Ag 27,23:4;
  1936,Ap 21,27:6
Elizabeth the Queen 1930,O 5,IX,4:6; 1930,N 4,37:1;
  1930,N 9,IX,1:1; 1936,Jl 28,23:4; 1936,Ag 4,15:2;
  1937,Ag 25,24:3; 1941,O 17,27:2; 1966,N 4,30:1
Elizabethans, The 1962,Ja 22,19:1
Elliott Murphy's Aquashow 1955,Je 23,25:1;
  1956,Je 20,26:2
Elmer Gantry 1928,Ag 10,9:4
Elmer the Great 1928,S 25,29:1; 1928,S 30,IX,1:1;
  1940,N 1,32:2
Elopement, The 1923,S 2,VI,1:7
Elsa Lanchester-Herself 1961,F 6,28:1
Elsie 1923,Ap 3,26:1
Elsie Janis and Her Gang 1922,Ja 17,13:2
Elton Case, The 1921,Jl 5,15:1; 1921,Jl 17,VI,1:1;
  1921,S 12,16:2
Elvire 1940,F 11,IX,2:5
Embers 1926,F 2,20:3; 1960,O 26,44:1
Embezzled Heaven 1944,O 22,VI,24:3; 1944,N 1,20:2;
  1944,N 5,II,1:2
Emerald Slippers, The 1970,S 2,31:2
Emlyn Williams 1952,F 5,25:2
Emlyn Williams as Charles Dickens 1970,N 4,41:1
Emma Hamilton 1929,O 13,IX,4:1
Emmanuel 1960,D 5,42:2
Emperor, The 1963,Ap 17,30:1
Emperor Jones, The 1920,N 7,VII,1:3; 1920,D 28,9:1;
  1921,Ja 2,VI,3:1; 1923,N 1,24:1; 1923,N 18,VIII,2:8;
  1924,Ja 10,18:2; 1924,My 7,18:1; 1925,S 11,20:1;
  1926,My 18,28:3; 1927,F 13,VII,4:6;
  1927,Ag 28,VII,1:1; 1930,Ap 1,10:1;
  1930,My 25,IX,1:8; 1930,S 14,VIII,2:1;
  1933,Mr 15,21:4; 1933,D 26,18:6; 1936,Ag 11,24:6;
  1939,Je 20,25:2; 1945,Ja 18:4; 1945,Ja 28,II,1:1;
  1964,Ag 6,20:4; 1964,Ag 16,II,5:1
Emperor of Make-Believe, The 1936,Mr 17,25:5;
  1936,Je 4,27:2; 1936,Jl 5,IX,1:8
Emperor's Clothes, The 1953,F 10,24:2;
  1953,O 23,19:7
Emperor's New Clothes, The 1941,D 27,15:5;
  1950,Je 20,23:2
Empire Builders, The 1968,O 2,34:1
Empress Eugenie, The 1932,N 23,15:4
Empress of Destiny 1938,Mr 10,16:2
En Attendant Godot 1968,Ap 23,38:1
Enchaines 1965,Mr 13,17:1
Enchanted, The 1950,Ja 19,34:2; 1958,Ap 23,41:1
Enchanted April, The 1925,Ag 25,12:3
Enchanted Cottage, The 1922,Mr 2,21:4;
  1923,Ap 2,22:3; 1923,Ap 8,VIII,1:1
Enchanted Isle 1927,S 20,33:2
Enchanted Maze, The 1935,D 14,10:4;
  1935,D 15,XI,5:4
Enchanted Prince, The: A 1932 Musical Fantasy
  1931,D 29,27:1
Enchanting Melody 1964,N 25,40:1
Enchantment 1927,Ap 28,27:3; 1953,Jl 1,24:3
Encore 1963,O 1,34:1
End As a Man 1953,S 16,39:1; 1953,S 27,II,1:1
End of All Things Natural, The 1969,S 12,38:1
End of Summer 1936,Ja 31,17:1; 1936,F 9,X,2:3;
  1936,F 18,26:4; 1936,Mr 1,IX,1:1
End of the Beginning, The 1961,My 11,43:1
End of the Dance, The 1929,My 11,22:2
Endecott and the Red Cross 1968,My 7,50:1
Endgame 1958,Ja 29,32:4; 1958,F 16,II,1:1;
  1962,F 12,27:1; 1964,F 21,32:1; 1970,My 6,47:1
Endless Chain, The 1922,S 5,21:2
Endlich Allein 1932,Ja 17,VIII,2:1
Endlose Strasse, Die 1932,Mr 27,VIII,3:1
Enemies 1935,Mr 19,24:7
Enemies Don't Send Flowers 1957,F 20,38:1
Enemy 1969,D 19,65:6
Enemy, The 1925,O 21,20:1; 1928,Ag 19,VII,1:1
Enemy of the People, An 1920,S 7,19:3;
  1923,D 4,25:1; 1927,O 4,32:5; 1928,Ap 22,IX,2:7;
  1928,N 6,34:3; 1937,F 16,19:1; 1950,D 29,14:1;
  1951,Ja 7,II,1:1; 1958,F 26,24:2; 1959,F 5,24:4
Enemy Within 1931,O 6,35:3
Enfant Prodigue, L' 1925,Mr 7,8:1

Engaged! or Cheviot's Choice 1925,Je 19,24:2;
　1965,Ap 24,19:2
Engagement Baby, The 1970,My 22,40:1
Engel Unter Uns 1933,Ja 22,IX,1:1
England Expects 1936,Ap 14,18:5
Enlevement, L' 1927,O 2,VIII,2:4
Ennemie, L' 1929,Ap 28,IX,2:4
Enough Stupidity in Every Wise Man 1923,D 6,23:1
Enter a Free Man 1968,Ap 7,II,8:1
Enter Laughing 1963,Mr 15,8:1; 1963,Je 16,II,1:1
Enter Madame 1920,Ag 17,11:2; 1920,Ag 22,VI,1:1;
　1920,O 17,VI,1:1; 1921,Mr 6,VI,1:2
Enterrement, L' 1939,F 7,17:2
Entertain a Ghost 1962,Ap 10,48:1
Entertainer, The 1958,F 13,22:2; 1958,F 23,II,1:1
Entertaining Mr Sloane 1964,Ja 30,21:1;
　1965,O 13,41:1; 1965,O 24,II,1:1
Envers d'une Sainte, L' 1932,F 21,VIII,1:6
Epinard Gagne le Grand Steeple 1926,D 19,VII,3:3
Epiphany 1963,Je 14,36:1
Episode 1925,F 5,23:2; 1925,F 8,VII,1:1;
　1925,F 15,VIII,1:1
Epitaph for George Dillon 1958,F 12,33:8;
　1958,N 5,44:1; 1958,N 16,II,1:1; 1960,D 29,17:1
Epstein 1970,Jl 31,14:1
Equipage, L' 1930,Ap 13,X,2:7
Er Ist an Allem Schuld 1928,Ja 10,28:3
Erb 1970,Ap 9,49:1
Eretz Israel 1930,N 27,32:3
Ergo 1968,Mr 4,29:1
Erminie 1921,Ja 4,11:1
Ernest in Love 1960,My 5,39:4
Erogenous Zones 1969,Ap 8,41:1
Erpingham Camp, The 1969,O 27,54:1;
　1969,N 9,II,1:1
Errant Lady 1934,S 18,18:2
Es Liegt in der Luft 1928,S 23,IX,2:2
Escapade 1929,S 29,IX,5:1; 1953,F 15,II,2:1;
　1953,Ap 8,37:2; 1953,N 19,40:1; 1953,N 29,II,1:1
Escape 1926,Ag 22,VII,1:2; 1926,Ag 29,VII,2:4;
　1926,S 12,VIII,2:1; 1926,D 12,VIII,3:4;
　1927,O 27,33:1; 1927,N 6,IX,1:1;
　1928,My 20,VIII,2:1
Escape Into Glory 1941,Mr 20,24:2
Escape Me Never! 1934,Ja 7,X,3:5; 1935,Ja 22,22:2;
　1935,F 10,VIII,1:1; 1936,Je 21,IX,2:4
Escape Me Not 1933,D 9,18:6
Escape This Night 1938,Ap 23,18:1
Escort 1942,S 6,VIII,1:8
Escurial 1956,O 3,29:2; 1960,Jl 22,13:1;
　1968,Mr 6,34:1
Eskimo, The 1926,Je 20,VII,3:1
Espanola 1921,D 30,13:1
Espionage 1935,O 16,27:5; 1935,N 10,IX,3:1
Espoir 1935,Ja 6,IX,2:1; 1935,F 3,VIII,3:3
Esta Noche... Teatro 1968,O 15,40:1
Esterke 1940,O 18,24:2
Et l'Enfer, Isabelle 1963,S 21,13:3
Et Vive le Theatre! 1930,Ap 20,VIII,2:8
Ete, L' 1934,D 2,X,2:1
Eternal Cage 1945,Mr 22,19:7
Eternal Husband, The 1962,O 18,46:4
Eternal Jew, The 1926,D 21,21:2
Eternal Problem, The 1937,Ap 12,14:5
Eternal Road, The 1937,Ja 8,14:2; 1937,Ja 24,X,1:1;
　1937,Ap 25,X,1:6
Eternal Sabbath 1963,O 19,17:2
Eternal Spring, The 1924,F 3,VII,1:4
Eternal Triangle 1966,N 8,45:1
Ethan Frome 1936,Ja 7,24:7; 1936,Ja 22,15:2;
　1936,F 2,IX,1:1; 1936,N 15,XI,2:1
Ethiopia 1936,Ja 25,18:1
Etienne 1930,Ap 27,IX,2:1
Etoile au Front, L' 1924,My 11,VIII,1:4
Etouffe Chretien, L' 1960,N 5,28:1
Eugenia 1957,Ja 31,20:1
Eumenides 1961,S 27,32:4
Eunuque, L' 1927,Ap 3,VIII,4:7
Europa A G 1932,O 2,IX,1:2
Eurydice 1948,O 17,I,67:4
Eusebe 1928,N 25,X,4:7
Eva the Fifth 1928,Jl 22,VII,1:7; 1928,Ag 29,19:3;
　1928,S 9,IX,1:1
Evangeline 1952,O 3,17:1
Evangelist, The 1967,Ap 28,30:3
Eve of St Mark, The 1942,O 8,30:2;
　1942,O 18,VIII,1:1; 1943,Ja 10,VIII,3:5
Eve Serves a Term of Childhood 1937,Je 20,X,2:1
Eve Toute Nue 1927,O 30,IX,4:7
Evelyne 1928,F 19,VIII,2:1
Even in Egypt 1930,Ja 19,VIII,2:6
Evening Dress Indispensable 1934,Mr 22,24:6
Evening for Merlin Finch, An 1968,D 30,25:1;
　1969,Ja 26,II,1:1
Evening in Cathay, An 1939,F 2,16:2
Evening of European Theatre, An 1960,Ap 26,41:1
Evening of Pantomime, An 1955,S 21,38:1
Evening of Rare Pleasures, An 1959,Je 4,26:2
Evening With Beatrice Lillie, An 1952,O 3,17:2;
　1952,O 12,II,1:1; 1954,N 26,26:7; 1954,D 12,II,5:1
Evening With Cecilia Loftus, An 1938,Mr 28,19:2
Evening With Ethel Waters, An 1959,Ap 9,36:1
Evening With G B S, An 1957,F 19,35:7

Evening With Max Morath at the Turn of the
　Century, An 1969,F 18,35:1; 1969,Ap 3,47:1;
　1969,My 4,II,3:1
Evening With Mike Nichols and Elaine May, An
　1960,O 10,37:1
Evening With Shaw, An 1955,Ag 13,6:6
Evening With the Times Square Two, An
　1967,My 21,83:6
Evening With Will Shakespeare, An 1952,D 7,86:5
Evening With Yves Montand, An 1959,S 23,45:1;
　1961,O 25,30:1
Evening's Frost, An 1965,O 12,56:1
Evensong 1932,Jl 1,19:6; 1932,Jl 24,IX,2:1;
　1933,F 1,13:4
Ever Green Lady, The 1922,O 12,25:2
Ever Since Paradise 1957,Jl 12,18:4
Ever the Twain 1929,O 9,31:3; 1929,O 20,III,3:5;
　1929,O 27,IX,1:1; 1933,D 17,IX,4:2
Evergreen 1930,O 14,31:2; 1930,D 4,30:4;
　1930,D 21,VIII,1:6
Every Man for Himself 1940,D 10,32:3
Every Man in His Humour 1937,Ag 7,7:3
Every Other Evil 1961,Ja 23,20:2
Every Thursday 1934,My 11,25:5
Everybody Loves Opal 1961,O 12,40:2
Everybody's Home 1932,D 5,21:4
Everybody's Welcome 1931,S 20,VIII,3:2;
　1931,O 14,26:3
Everyday 1921,N 17,15:1
Everyman 1926,Ag 9,1:1; 1927,Ag 1,4:3;
　1929,Ag 5,25:1; 1931,Jl 19,III,8:6; 1941,My 9,19:2;
　1953,O 12,30:2
Everyman Today 1958,Ja 16,32:4
Everything in the Garden 1967,N 30,60:1;
　1967,D 10,II,5:1; 1968,Ja 25,32:4
Everything Under the Sun 1963,O 1,34:1
Everything's Jake 1930,Ja 17,20:4
Everywhere I Roam 1938,Ap 22,15:1;
　1938,D 30,10:4; 1939,Ja 8,IX,1:1; 1939,Ja 22,IX,8:1
Eve's Complaint 1928,My 20,VIII,1:3
Eve's Leaves 1925,Mr 27,22:2
Evil Doers of Good, The 1923,Ja 17,22:2
Ewiges Volk 1933,Ap 30,IX,2:2; 1933,Je 25,IX,1:2
Ex-Napoleon 1960,D 29,16:3
Exaltation, L' 1929,Mr 10,X,1:8
Exceeding Small 1928,O 23,32:2; 1928,N 4,IX,1:1
Excelsior 1928,S 30,IX,1:3
Exception and the Rule, The 1965,My 21,19:1;
　1965,Je 6,II,1:1
Excerpts From Shaw 1955,Ag 13,6:6
Excess Baggage 1927,D 27,24:2; 1928,Ja 29,VIII,1:1
Exchange 1970,F 9,47:2
Exciters, The 1922,S 23,10:4
Excursion 1937,Ap 10,11:4; 1937,Ap 18,XI,1:1;
　1937,Jl 27,24:3
Exercise, The 1968,Ap 25,54:1; 1968,My 12,II,1:1
Exhaustion of Our Son's Love, The 1965,O 19,51:1
Exhibition 1969,My 16,41:1
Exile, The 1923,Ap 10,24:2
Exiled 1929,Je 21,17:5; 1929,Jl 7,VIII,1:3
Exiles 1925,F 20,20:2; 1957,Mr 13,27:1;
　1970,N 19,42:4
Exit the King 1963,S 13,19:4; 1968,Ja 10,48:1;
　1968,Ja 21,II,1:2
Exorcism 1920,Ap 4,VI,6:1
Expedition 1936,O 13,32:4
Expeditions One 1964,Jl 3,13:2
Experience Unnecessary 1931,D 31,16:2;
　1932,Mr 28,10:2
Experiment, The 1967,My 9,54:2
Expressing Willie 1924,Ap 17,22:1;
　1924,Ap 27,VIII,1:1; 1924,My 4,VIII,1:1
Extra 1923,Ja 24,22:3
Eye on the Sparrow 1938,My 4,26:3
Eyes 1930,My 10,25:1
Eyvind of the Hills 1921,F 2,14:1

F

Fabian, Der Elephant 1933,Ap 30,IX,2:2
Fables 1922,F 7,12:2
Fabulous Invalid, The 1938,O 10,15:1
Face, The 1941,N 29,15:3
Face of a Hero 1960,O 21,29:5
Face the Music 1932,F 4,25:4; 1932,F 18,24:5;
　1932,Mr 20,VIII,1:1; 1933,F 1,13:4
Face Value 1921,Jl 24,VI,1:1; 1921,D 27,10:2
Facon de Se Donner, La 1925,D 27,VII,2:1
Fade Out--Fade In 1964,My 27,45:1;
　1964,Je 21,II,1:1; 1965,F 16,40:2
Fading Mansion 1949,S 1,25:4
Failures, The 1923,N 23,20:1; 1923,D 2,VIII,1:1;
　1959,Ja 6,30:2
Fair Circassian, The 1921,D 7,22:3
Fair Game 1957,N 4,39:1
Fair Game for Lovers 1964,F 11,43:2
Fair Helen 1928,Ap 1,IX,2:4; 1931,Ag 30,VIII,2:1;
　1932,Jl 17,IX,1:2
Fairy, The 1931,F 8,VIII,2:1
Fairy Tales of New York 1961,Ja 26,33:1
Faiseur, Le 1936,Ja 12,IX,3:7; 1938,D 27,12:3
Faith and Prudence 1952,O 15,40:2

Faith of Our Fathers 1950,Ag 6,72:2;
　1950,Ag 13,II,1:1
Faithful, The 1935,Ja 20,X,3:8
Faithful Heart, The 1921,D 4,VII,1:3; 1922,O 11,22:1;
　1922,O 15,VIII,1:1; 1932,Ja 17,VIII,2:6
Faithfully Yours 1951,O 19,22:5
Fake, The 1924,Mr 23,VIII,1:3; 1924,O 7,26:3
Fall and Rise of Susan Lenox, The 1920,Je 11,11:2
Fall Guy, The 1924,Jl 20,VII,1:7; 1925,Mr 11,19:1;
　1926,O 10,VIII,2:1
Fall of Berg-Op-Zoom, The 1930,Je 8,IX,2:7
Fall of Eve, The 1925,S 1,18:1; 1925,S 6,VII,1:1
Fallen Angels 1925,My 10,VIII,1:3; 1927,D 2,20:4;
　1956,Ja 18,27:1
Fallen Saved, The 1929,D 31,14:6; 1959,Je 24,37:2
Falling Leaves 1924,N 30,VIII,2:1
Fallout 1959,My 21,36:2
False Dreams, Farewell 1934,Ja 16,18:3
False Flame, The 1931,N 16,22:4
Falstaff 1928,D 26,14:2; 1965,Jl 1,35:1;
　1966,Je 20,27:1
Fam and Yam 1960,O 26,44:1
Fame 1929,Mr 10,X,4:6
Famiglia Barrett, La 1933,N 19,IX,1:3
Familiar Pattern 1943,S 3,15:6
Familie, Eine 1946,N 11,44:1
Famille 1938,Je 12,X,2:3
Famille Lavolette, La 1926,O 10,VIII,2:1
Family, The 1943,Mr 31,22:4
Family Affair, A 1946,N 28,41:2; 1962,Ja 29,17:1
Family Affairs 1929,D 1,X,4:7; 1929,D 11,34:6;
　1934,Ag 23,13:3; 1934,S 16,X,2:1
Family Album 1936,Ja 10,16:1; 1936,F 2,IX,3:4;
　1936,D 1,31:1; 1948,F 21,8:2
Family Carnovsky, The 1943,O 19,16:7
Family Exit, The 1932,D 14,27:3
Family Man, A 1921,Je 26,VI,1:1; 1936,Jl 8,14:2
Family Mishmash, A 1958,O 20,36:1
Family Portrait 1939,Mr 9,18:4; 1939,Mr 19,XI,1:1;
　1946,N 11,44:1; 1948,Mr 14,II,2:5; 1959,My 6,48:2
Family Reunion, The 1939,Ap 9,X,1:5; 1947,N 29,9:2;
　1956,Je 9,13:6; 1958,O 21,39:1; 1958,O 26,II,1:1;
　1960,D 10,26:1
Family Upstairs, The 1925,My 3,VIII,2:1;
　1925,Ag 18,14:2; 1925,Ag 23,VII,1:1;
　1933,O 28,20:6
Family Way, The 1965,Ja 14,44:5; 1965,Ja 24,II,1:1
Famous Mrs Fair, The 1920,Ap 24,20:4
Famous Tragedy of the Queen of Cornwall, The
　1923,D 2,VIII,2:8
Fan, The 1921,O 4,10:1
Fanatics, The 1927,Ap 10,VIII,1:3; 1927,N 8,32:4
Fancy Free 1929,My 9,34:3
Fancy Meeting You Again 1952,Ja 15,23:2
Fanfare 1932,Je 24,15:2
Fanny 1926,S 22,30:1; 1931,D 27,VIII,3:4;
　1954,N 5,16:1; 1954,N 21,II,1:1; 1955,D 17,19:6;
　1956,N 17,17:7; 1956,D 2,II,3:1
Fanny Hawthorn 1922,My 12,22:2
Fanny's First Play 1926,O 10,VIII,2:1; 1956,S 5,22:6
Fanshastics 1924,Ja 17,13:2
Fantasia 1933,Ja 4,22:4
Fantasio 1938,F 8,17:2
Fantasmi 1937,Mr 22,26:5
Fantastic Fricassee, A 1922,S 12,24:1
Fantasticks, The 1960,My 4,55:2; 1961,S 8,36:5
Far Away 1936,O 11,X,1:4
Far-Away Corner, A 1939,F 15,15:2
Far Away Horses 1933,Mr 22,21:6
Far Country, A 1961,Ap 5,32:1; 1961,Ap 16,II,1:1
Far Cry, The 1924,S 28,VII,2:1; 1924,O 1,24:1;
　1924,O 5,VIII,1:1
Far Fetched Fables 1950,S 7,39:7
Far-Off Hills, The 1928,N 11,X,4:8; 1932,O 19,22:4;
　1937,O 12,30:4
Farandula, La 1930,Mr 25,34:6
Faraway Princess, The 1922,D 6,3:2
Farblondjete Honeymoon 1955,S 27,42:1
Farewell, Farewell Eugene 1960,S 28,35:1
Farewell Performance 1936,S 11,28:3;
　1936,S 27,X,3:5; 1936,O 4,IX,1:1
Farewell Summer 1937,Mr 30,20:2
Farewell to Arms, A 1930,S 23,30:3
Farm of Three Echoes 1935,D 2,19:4; 1939,N 29,18:3;
　1939,D 3,IX,5:4
Farmer General, The 1931,Mr 31,24:8
Farmer Takes a Wife, The 1934,O 9,17:2;
　1934,O 28,IX,3:1; 1934,O 31,17:1;
　1934,N 11,IX,1:1
Farmer's Wife, The 1924,Mr 16,VIII,1:7;
　1924,O 10,22:3
Farther Off From Heaven 1947,Je 4,33:3
Fashion 1924,F 5,21:2; 1924,F 10,VII,1:1;
　1937,Mr 21,II,7:8; 1959,Ja 21,27:1
Fashions for Men 1922,D 6,22:1; 1922,D 24,VII,1:1
Fashions of 1924 1923,Jl 19,18:2
Fast Life 1928,S 16,IX,2:4; 1928,S 27,35:2
Fast Service 1931,N 18,26:3
Fata Morgana 1924,Mr 4,16:3; 1924,Mr 9,VIII,1:1;
　1924,Ag 24,VIII,1:1; 1924,O 12,VIII,1:1;
　1931,D 26,15:3
Fatal Alibi, The 1932,F 10,26:6

Fatal Lady, The 1936,Mr 19,23:7
Fatal Wedding, The 1924,Je 3,22:3
Fatal Witness, The 1946,N 20,43:2
Fatal Woman, The 1930,Mr 2,IX,4:7
Fate's Messenger 1927,Ja 4,21:2
Father, The 1927,S 4,VII,2:1; 1927,S 11,VIII,2:4;
    1928,My 12,9:4; 1931,O 9,21:1; 1937,Ap 21,18:5;
    1949,Ag 21,II,1:1; 1949,N 17,36:2; 1949,N 27,II,1:1;
    1962,My 15,49:1
Father and Son 1956,O 20,17:4
Father Holds Court 1957,D 12,35:3
Father Malachy's Miracle 1937,N 18,26:4;
    1937,D 5,XII,5:1; 1938,Ja 23,XI,1:6
Father of Lies 1935,Ja 27,VIII,3:1
Father Returns, The 1929,My 7,28:1
Father Uxbridge Wants to Marry 1967,O 30,57:1
Faun 1935,N 25,23:5; 1935,D 1,XI,6:3
Faun, The 1924,F 6,19:2; 1924,Mr 28,17:2
Fausses Confidences, Les 1948,S 11,13:3;
    1952,N 13,34:2
Faust 1927,Ja 4,20:1; 1928,O 9,34:1; 1928,N 4,IX,4:1;
    1930,Mr 23,4:3; 1932,Je 19,IX,1:3;
    1933,Ja 22,IX,1:1; 1937,Ag 29,X,1:3;
    1938,Ag 28,IX,2:5; 1947,N 29,9:2
Faust, Part I 1961,F 5,27:2
Faustina 1952,My 26,19:5
Faut Que Chacun Soit a Sa Place, Il
    1924,F 24,VII,1:4
Feast of Panthers 1961,Mr 21,32:1
Feast With the Statue, The 1956,Ja 4,21:4
Feather in the Breeze 1936,Jl 14,22:2
Feather in the Wind 1932,Ag 2,13:4
Feathers in a Gale 1943,D 22,26:2
Fedora 1922,F 11,18:1; 1924,Ja 24,14:2
Fee, Die 1931,F 8,VIII,2:1
Felix 1926,O 10,VIII,2:1
Femme au Chat, La 1929,Je 9,VIII,2:4
Femme d'Amour, La 1927,Je 5,VII,2:1
Femme Dans un Lit, Une 1928,Ja 15,VIII,2:3
Femme en Blanc, La 1933,My 7,IX,2:5
Femme en Fleur, La 1936,F 23,X,2:3
Femme Libre, Une 1934,D 2,X,2:1
Femme Qu'a le Coeur Trop Petit, Une
    1934,F 11,IX,3:2
Femme Sous la Pluie, LIne 1929,My 26,IX,4:1
Femmes Savantes, Les 1967,F 7,34:2; 1970,F 14,12:1
Fencing Master, The 1936,Ap 1,29:1
Fessee, La 1937,Ja 24,X,2:1
Fest Fuer Boris, Ein 1970,O 13,52:2
Festa Italiana 1966,S 30,55:1
Festival 1930,Mr 5,26:7; 1955,Ja 19,22:1
Festival of the Saviour of the Seamen, The
    1925,Ap 26,VIII,1:3
Feu du Ciel 1930,Mr 16,IX,4:3
Feu la Mere de Madame 1957,F 12,31:1
Feu Marquis de Sade, Le 1921,Ap 17,VI,1:8
Feu Qui Reprend Mal, Le 1929,N 10,X,4:1
Feu sur la Terre, Le 1950,D 31,II,3:7
Feudalism or the Lowland 1937,Mr 8,22:2
Feudalismo Oppure La Terra Bassa 1937,Mr 8,22:2
Feuer aus Den Kesseln 1930,O 19,IX,2:4
Fever of Youth, The 1926,Ag 8,VII,3:1
Few Are Chosen 1935,S 18,19:3
Few Wild Oats, A 1932,Mr 25,22:6
Fiaccola Sotto il Moggio, La 1927,D 25,VIII,4:3
Fiddler on the Roof 1964,S 23,56:2; 1964,O 4,II,1:1;
    1964,O 6,36:5; 1965,Je 9,40:1; 1965,Ag 15,II,2:5;
    1966,D 22,40:5; 1967,F 17,50:1; 1967,S 7,50:1;
    1967,S 28,59:2; 1967,N 16,61:5; 1968,F 2,28:1;
    1968,F 22,36:2; 1969,Je 26,47:1; 1969,Ag 8,10:2;
    1969,N 16,82:6; 1970,F 28,20:1; 1970,Jl 8,34:1
Fiddler's House, The 1941,Mr 28,27:5
Field God, The 1927,Ap 22,18:2; 1927,My 1,VIII,1:1
Field of Ermine 1935,F 9,10:4
Fields Beyond, The 1933,F 14,19:5; 1936,Mr 7,11:2
Fiesco 1931,Jl 13,VIII,2:1
Fiesta 1928,D 13,25:2; 1929,S 18,35:1;
    1933,D 16,12:2
Fiesta in Madrid 1969,My 29,49:1
Fifth Column, The 1940,Ja 27,9:1; 1940,F 4,IX,1:6;
    1940,Mr 7,18:2; 1940,Mr 17,X,1:1
Fifth Commandment, The 1965,N 15,48:4
Fifth Horseman, The 1949,Je 14,26:6
Fifth Season, The 1953,Ja 24,13:2; 1954,F 25,24:5
Fifty-Fifty 1937,N 20,21:1; 1937,D 5,II,3:4
Fifty Million Frenchmen 1929,N 28,34:4;
    1930,Ja 5,VIII,1:8
57 Bowery 1928,Ja 27,14:3
Fig Leaf in Her Bonnet, A 1961,Je 15,50:1
Fig Leaves Are Falling, The 1969,Ja 3,19:1
Fighting Cock, The 1959,D 9,57:3; 1959,D 20,II,3:1
Fighting the Waves 1929,Ag 14,15:6;
    1929,S 22,IX,4:1
Fight's On, The 1937,Ag 4,14:1
Figlia Brutta, La 1937,Ag 30,24:6
Figlia del Dragone Rosso, La 1933,D 10,11:7
Figuro in the Night 1962,O 31,33:1
Fil a la Patte, Un 1962,Jl 8,II,1:1; 1966,F 18,25:1
Fils de Don Quichotte, Le 1930,N 2,VIII,2:1
Fin du Monde, La 1930,F 2,VIII,4:1; 1935,N 3,X,3:8
Final Balance, The 1928,O 31,28:3
Final Fling, The 1928,O 7,IX,2:3
Final Solution, The 1964,N 21,32:4

Find Daddy 1926,Mr 9,21:3
Find the Fox 1930,Je 21,20:4
Finders 1967,S 24,II,1:4
Fine and Dandy 1930,S 7,IX,2:4; 1930,S 24,26:1;
    1930,O 5,IX,1:1
Finian's Rainbow 1947,Ja 11,23:2; 1947,Ja 26,II,1:1;
    1947,O 22,38:4; 1947,N 9,II,3:7; 1948,Ag 29,II,1:1;
    1949,O 19,36:3; 1953,Mr 7,13:2; 1955,My 19,25:1;
    1960,Ap 28,31:1; 1967,Ap 6,44:1
Finis for Oscar Wilde 1964,F 15,15:1
Finished Abroad 1934,Mr 7,23:7
Finta Giardiniera, La 1927,Ja 19,20:5;
    1927,F 6,VII,1:1
Fiole, La 1923,N 20,23:3
Fiorello! 1959,N 24,45:3; 1959,N 29,II,1:1;
    1962,Je 14,24:1; 1962,O 10,60:1
Fioretta 1929,Ja 6,VIII,4:6; 1929,F 6,30:3
Fire in the Opera House 1930,Ap 6,IX,2:1
Fire to the Sea 1961,N 15,20:5
Fire-Weed 1950,Mr 30,38:2
Fire! 1968,My 12,II,7:1; 1969,Ja 29,26:1
Firebird 1932,Ap 17,VIII,3:8; 1932,S 25,IX,1:3;
    1932,N 22,25:2; 1932,D 18,X,4:5
Firebird of Florence 1945,Mr 23,13:4
Firebrand, The 1924,O 16,33:1
Firebugs, The 1963,F 13,7:2; 1963,N 22,41:1;
    1968,Jl 2,36:1; 1969,N 27,52:1
Firefly, The 1931,D 1,23:2; 1937,Ag 4,14:1;
    1938,Jl 12,15:4
Fireman, The 1938,Ap 24,II,2:8
Fireman's Flame, The 1937,O 11,26:2
Fires in the Night 1928,D 2,X,4:7
Fires of Spring 1929,O 13,IX,5:1
Fireworks 1969,Je 12,51:1
Fireworks for a Hot Fourth 1969,Je 12,51:1
Fireworks on the James 1940,My 15,30:2
First American Dictator 1939,Mr 15,18:2
First and the Last, The 1921,Je 26,VI,1:1
First Apple, The 1933,D 17,IX,4:2; 1933,D 28,25:1
First Cousins 1943,Je 15,16:1
First Crocus, The 1942,Ja 3,14:6
First Episode 1934,S 18,18:1
First Fifty Years, The 1922,Mr 14,11:2
First Flight 1925,S 18,26:2; 1925,S 27,VII,1:1
First Gentleman, The 1945,Jl 19,18:8;
    1945,Ag 5,II,1:2; 1957,Ap 26,22:2; 1957,My 5,II,1:1
First Impressions 1959,Mr 20,28:1; 1959,Mr 29,II,1:1
First in Heart, The 1947,N 14,29:2
First Lady 1935,N 11,21:3; 1935,N 27,17:4;
    1935,D 8,X,3:1; 1936,O 11,X,3:1; 1937,O 9,17:2;
    1952,My 23,16:5; 1952,My 29,18:5
First Law, The 1929,My 7,28:4
First Legion, The 1934,O 2,18:2; 1937,Je 8,30:7;
    1937,Ag 15,X,2:3
First Love 1926,S 19,IX,1:3; 1926,N 9,31:2;
    1961,D 26,20:2
First Man, The 1922,Mr 6,9:2; 1927,O 30,IX,4:1
First Million, The 1943,Ap 29,27:4
First Mortgage 1929,O 11,36:1
First Mrs Fraser, The 1929,Jl 21,VIII,1:4;
    1929,O 20,10:1; 1929,N 17,X,4:1; 1929,D 30,16:2;
    1930,Mr 9,IX,4:3; 1947,N 6,36:2
First Night 1930,N 27,32:3
First One Asleep, Whistle 1966,F 28,19:1
First Person Singular 1952,Mr 16,II,3:7
First Stone, The 1928,Ja 14,12:2
First Stop to Heaven 1941,Ja 6,10:7
First Wife, The 1928,Mr 28,21:5
First Year, The 1920,O 21,11:2; 1920,O 31,VI,1:1;
    1921,N 27,VI,1:1; 1926,D 19,VII,6:4
Firstborn, The 1952,Ja 26,IX,5:7; 1952,F 10,II,2:1;
    1957,Ja 7,29:2; 1958,My 1,35:1; 1958,My 11,II,1:1;
    1958,Jl 4,16:3
Fisher of Shadows, The 1921,My 1,VII,1:7
Fisherman, The 1965,Ja 27,24:6
Fishing for Wives 1966,Mr 16,50:1
Fitz 1966,My 17,51:2
Five Alarm Waltz 1941,Mr 14,16:2
Five Evenings 1963,My 10,37:3
Five Finger Exercise 1958,Ag 17,II,1:7;
    1959,D 3,45:4; 1959,D 13,II,3:1
Five From the Jazz Band 1927,N 20,IX,4:7
Five Kings 1939,F 28,16:4; 1939,Mr 5,X,3:1
Five Little Peppers, The 1952,My 19,13:1
Five O'Clock Girl, The 1927,O 11,26:3
Five on the Black Hand Side 1970,Ja 2,32:2;
    1970,Ja 11,II,1:1
Five Posts in the Market Place 1961,Mr 6,30:1
Five Queens 1963,S 11,46:2
Five Star Final 1930,D 31,11:1; 1931,Jl 18,16:4
Five Star Saint 1970,F 11,41:2
Flag Is Born, A 1946,S 7,10:6; 1946,S 15,II,21:1
Flahooley 1951,My 15,39:1; 1951,My 20,II,1:1;
    1952,Ag 13,17:7
Flair-Flair the Idol of Paree 1935,Mr 13,16:1
Flambeaux de la Noce, Les 1937,Ap 17,VII,2:3
Flame of Love 1924,Ap 22,19:2
Flamingo Road 1946,Mr 20,18:2
Flare Path 1942,Ag 23,VIII,1:6; 1942,D 24,20:2
Flashing Stream, The 1938,S 2,21:4; 1938,S 18,X,1:4;
    1939,Ap 11,19:2; 1939,Ap 16,X,1:1
Flat to Let 1931,D 20,VIII,3:6

Flea in Her Ear, A 1967,O 29,II,5:1; 1967,O 30,59:1;
    1969,O 4,25:1; 1969,O 12,II,9:1
Fledermaus, Die 1929,Jl 14,IX,2:1; 1929,N 1,23:3;
    1930,Ap 20,VIII,7:7; 1933,My 14,II,3:8;
    1937,Jl 14,17:1; 1942,O 29,26:5; 1954,My 20,38:5
Fledgling 1940,N 28,29:2
Flesh 1925,My 8,22:3
Fleur des Pois, La 1932,O 30,IX,3:7
Fleurs de Luxe 1930,Mr 23,IX,2:1
Flies, The 1947,Ap 18,26:3; 1948,F 29,II,2:1;
    1954,S 10,18:2
Flight 1929,F 10,IX,2:1; 1929,F 19,22:3;
    1929,Mr 24,X,1:1
Flight Into China 1939,S 12,28:1
Flight Into Egypt 1952,Mr 19,33:2; 1952,Mr 30,II,1:1
Flight of Lindbergh, The 1969,My 26,55:2
Flight to the West 1940,D 15,I,59:5; 1940,D 31,19:1;
    1941,Ja 19,IX,1:1; 1941,Mr 7,16:3
Flint 1970,Jl 26,49:2
Flip Side, The 1968,O 11,36:1
Flirting 1923,My 31,12:5
Flood Tide 1938,Mr 24,20:8
Floodlight 1937,Je 24,30:3
Flora 1935,O 30,17:4
Flora, the Red Menace 1965,My 12,41:2
Florentine Tragedy, A 1927,F 2,22:4; 1956,F 14,24:4
Florestan Ier, Prince de Monaco 1933,D 31,IX,2:2
Floriani's Wife 1923,O 1,10:1; 1923,O 7,IX,1:1
Florida Girl 1925,N 3,34:1
Florodora 1920,Ap 6,18:1; 1920,Ap 18,VI,2:4;
    1936,Ag 23,II,8:2
Flossie 1924,Je 4,25:2
Flouers O' Edinburgh, The 1957,Ag 22,22:8
Flower Drum Song 1958,D 2,44:1; 1958,D 7,II,5:1;
    1960,Mr 25,20:4
Flower of Cities All 1962,Jl 12,21:2
Flower of Hawaii 1931,O 4,VIII,4:1
Flowering Cherry 1959,O 22,46:1
Flowering Peach, The 1954,D 29,19:2;
    1955,Ja 9,II,1:1
Flowers of Progress, The 1957,F 27,21:1
Flowers of the Forest 1934,N 21,23:2;
    1934,D 9,X,3:1; 1935,Ap 5,21:6; 1935,Ap 9,25:2;
    1935,Ap 14,IX,1:1
Flowers of Virtue, The 1942,F 6,22:2
Floydada to Matador 1955,D 22,19:1
Flutter of Wings, A 1931,Ja 4,VIII,3:4
Fly Away Home 1935,Ja 16,20:4; 1936,Jl 21,13:1;
    1937,Ap 27,18:1; 1937,Jl 27,24:3; 1937,Jl 28,15:1
Fly Blackbird 1962,F 6,26:2; 1962,Ap 29,II,1:1
Fly by Night 1933,Je 3,16:2
Fly Paper 1970,Ag 11,27:1
Fly With Me 1920,Mr 25,11:4
Flying Blind 1930,My 16,20:2
Flying Colors 1932,S 16,24:2; 1932,O 9,IX,1:1
Flying Gerardos, The 1940,D 30,21:4
Flying Ginzburgs, The 1938,N 13,IX,2:2
Flying High 1930,F 9,VIII,4:2; 1930,Mr 4,24:4
Flying Trapeze, The 1935,Je 2,IX,2:3
Foemen of the Yard 1935,Ap 6,10:4
Foenix in Choir 1958,O 28,40:2
Fog 1927,F 8,20:1
Fog-Bound 1927,Ap 2,21:2
Fol-De-Rol 1937,D 11,22:4
Folies Bergere 1939,D 25,28:2; 1964,Je 3,36:1;
    1964,Je 21,II,1:1
Folk Festival 1932,My 16,19:1
Folle de Chaillot, La 1945,D 20,17:4
Folle de son Corps 1932,My 1,VIII,2:6
Folle du Ciel, La 1936,My 31,X,2:1
Folle Jeunesse 1927,O 9,VIII,2:4
Follies 1923,Je 26,14:5; 1924,Je 19,25:7;
    1924,O 31,19:3; 1925,Mr 11,19:2; 1925,Jl 7,24:3;
    1927,Ag 7,VII,1:8; 1927,Ag 28,VII,1:1;
    1932,O 13,22:2; 1933,N 19,IX,2:5
Follies, The 1923,D 23,VII,1:1
Follies of 1910, The 1960,Ja 15,37:3
Follow a Star 1930,S 18,28:2
Follow Me 1932,D 11,IX,5:3
Follow the Girls 1944,Ap 10,15:2; 1944,Ap 16,II,1:2
Follow the Sun 1935,D 24,10:3; 1936,F 5,15:8
Follow Thru 1928,D 23,VIII,4:1; 1929,Ja 10,24:3
Follow Your Saint 1936,S 25,20:3; 1936,O 11,X,3:1
Folly Town 1920,My 18,9:2
Fontaines Lumineuses, Les 1935,D 29,IX,2:1
Food for Midas 1942,Ja 31,12:7
Fool, The 1922,Jl 30,VI,1:3; 1922,O 24,18:1;
    1922,O 29,VII,1:1; 1923,Ja 15,18:4
Foolish Gentlewoman, The 1949,Ap 3,II,3:1
Foolish Notion 1945,Mr 14,23:2; 1945,Mr 18,II,1:1
Foolish Virgin, The 1924,Mr 22,12:2
Fools Are Passing Through 1958,Ap 3,24:2
Fool's Bells 1925,D 24,8:3
Fool's Errand, The 1927,My 3,24:3
Fools Errant 1922,Ag 22,12:3
Fools Rush In 1934,D 26,19:2
Foolscap 1933,Ja 12,21:2
Foot-Loose 1920,My 11,12:1; 1920,Ag 15,VI,1:1
Football 1969,Je 12,51:1
Footlights 1927,Ag 20,8:2
Footsteps of Doves, The 1967,Mr 14,54:1
For All of Us 1923,O 16,19:4
For Better or Worse 1927,F 1,24:3

For Charity 1937,Ag 25,24:3
For Goodness Sake 1922,F 22,13:1
For Heaven's Sake Mother 1948,N 17,33:4
For Keeps 1944,Je 15,17:5
For Love or Money 1947,N 5,36:2
For Services Rendered 1932,N 2,23:5;
  1932,N 27,IX,1:3; 1933,Ap 13,15:5
For the Defense 1935,F 27,17:3; 1935,Mr 24,VIII,2:3
For the Time Being 1957,D 18,42:7
For Valor 1935,N 12,24:4; 1935,N 19,27:5
For Value Received 1923,My 8,22:3
For Your Pleasure 1943,F 6,9:2
Forbidden 1923,O 2,10:2
Forbidden Melody 1936,O 13,30:3; 1936,N 3,33:1
Forbidden Roads 1928,Ap 17,26:4
Forced Wedding, The 1958,My 7,43:1
Forcing Bed, The 1929,Ag 4,VIII,1:6
Foreign Affairs 1932,Ap 14,25:5
Foreign Specter 1949,Je 5,15:3
Foreigners 1939,D 6,30:2
Forensic and the Navigators 1968,Ja 20,22:2;
  1970,Ap 2,43:1
Foreplay 1970,D 11,58:2
Forest, The 1924,Mr 16,VIII,1:7
Forest Ring, The 1930,Ap 26,11:2
Forest Rose, The 1928,F 26,VIII,2:7;
  1928,Mr 18,IX,1:1
Forever 1934,N 27,27:2
Forever This Land 1951,Jl 29,II,1:1; 1952,Je 30,14:6;
  1952,Jl 6,II,1:1
Forgotten Factor, The 1948,Ap 20,6:5
Forrigan Reel, The 1945,N 11,II,2:6
Forsaking All Others 1933,Mr 2,21:2
Fortress of Glass 1952,S 5,19:2
Fortuna 1962,Ja 4,26:1
Fortunato 1928,N 11,X,4:1; 1956,Mr 24,15:2
Fortune 1920,Ap 22,11:3
Fortune and Men's Eyes 1967,F 24,29:1;
  1969,O 23,55:1; 1970,Ja 18,II,1:1
Fortune Teller, The 1929,N 5,32:3
Fortuno 1925,D 23,22:1
Forty Carats 1968,D 27,45:1; 1969,Ja 5,II,1:3;
  1970,Ja 6,48:1
40 CV du Roi, La 1927,O 23,VIII,2:2
Forty-Eight Hour's Leave 1941,S 28,IX,1:4
Forty-Four Below 1935,Jl 23,24:3
49ers, The 1922,N 7,14:1; 1922,N 12,VIII,1:1
49th Cousin, The 1960,O 28,22:1
Forty-Ninth State, The 1947,My 27,30:4
41 in a Sack 1960,Mr 26,15:2
Forty-Seven 1930,F 4,29:1
Forty-Seven Ronin, The 1960,Je 10,37:1;
  1960,Je 17,35:4
Forty Years in Show Business 1950,O 2,19:5
Forty Years On 1968,N 5,53:3; 1969,Jl 26,14:1
  1970,Ag 30,II,1:1
Forward March 1932,O 23,IX,3:5
Forward the Heart 1949,Ja 29,9:2
Foudroye 1963,Je 6,40:6
Founders, The 1957,My 14,39:1
Fountain, The 1925,D 11,26:1; 1925,D 20,VII,3:1
Fountania 1926,Ja 17,II,8:8
Four Brawlers, The 1928,Mr 4,IX,2:7
Four Flights Up 1948,Ja 8,29:1
Four Flusher, The 1925,Ap 5,IX,2:4; 1925,Ap 14,27:4
417 1961,Mr 6,30:1
Four in Hand 1923,S 7,10:2
Four O'Clock 1933,F 14,19:6
Four One-Act Plays 1921,Mr 1,18:1;
  1921,Mr 6,VI,1:2
Four Pieces sur Jardin 1969,F 18,35:1
Four Saints in Three Acts 1952,Ap 17,35:1
Four Seasons, The 1968,Mr 15,32:1
Four Twelves are 48 1951,Ja 18,30:2
Four Walls 1927,S 20,33:1; 1927,O 2,VIII,1:1
Four Winds 1957,S 26,21:2
Fourberies de Scapin, Les 1938,D 13,30:3;
  1952,N 21,21:2; 1961,F 22,30:1
Fourposter, The 1951,O 25,34:2; 1951,N 25,II,1:1;
  1955,Ja 6,23:3
Foursome 1965,Mr 8,34:1
Fourteenth of July, The 1928,Mr 11,VIII,1:3
Fourth Avenue North 1961,S 28,50:2
Fourth of June, The 1964,F 1,12:1
Fourth Pig, The 1965,Ja 27,24:6
Fourth Wall, The 1928,Mr 25,IX,1:3; 1968,S 5,53:1;
  1968,S 29,II,1:1
Foxhole in the Parlor 1945,My 24,15:4
Foxy 1962,Jl 4,12:2; 1964,F 17,26:1; 1964,Mr 20,30:1
Fractured Follies of 1966 1965,D 18,35:1
Fraeulein Elsa 1932,D 18,X,5:8
Fragila Rosina 1927,My 10,24:4
Fragile 1929,F 10,IX,4:6
Fragile Fox 1954,O 13,27:1
Fragments 1967,O 3,56:1; 1967,O 15,II,3:3
Frail Emma 1928,S 16,IX,2:4
Frailties 1931,Ja 30,18:3
Francerie 1933,Ap 30,IX,2:3
Francesca da Rimini 1927,D 3,19:1; 1967,S 12,54:1
Frank Fay's Vaudeville 1939,Mr 3,20:4
Frankenstein 1968,O 3,54:1
Frankie and Johnny 1930,S 26,16:5; 1952,O 29,37:2
Frans Hals 1931,Ap 26,VIII,2:5

Franziska 1927,Ja 30,VII,4:3
Frasquita 1924,Mr 2,VIII,2:1; 1925,My 3,VIII,2:1
Fratricide Punished 1925,Ap 21,19:1; 1959,S 1,21:1
Frau Die Weiss Was Sie Will, Eine 1932,O 9,IX,3:7
Frau Flinz 1962,Jl 8,II,1:1
Frau Jitta's Suehne 1930,My 18,VIII,2:6
Freddy 1929,Jl 17,23:4
Frederika 1937,F 5,16:5; 1937,Jl 28,15:2
Free and Easy 1959,D 15,51:4; 1959,D 20,II,3:2
Free for All 1931,Ag 16,VIII,1:1; 1931,S 9,25:1;
  1947,S 18,28:2
Free Soul, A 1928,Ja 13,26:5
Freedom of the Press 1937,D 13,22:8
Freidel Becomes a Bride 1936,F 10,14:3
Freight 1949,F 4,30:2; 1950,Ap 27,36:2
Fremde Frau, Die 1921,D 11,VI,1:4
French Doll, The 1922,F 21,20:2
French for Love 1939,N 12,IX,1:8
French Leave 1920,N 9,13:1
French Touch, The 1945,D 10,18:2
French Way, The 1962,Mr 21,36:2
French Without Tears 1937,S 26,II,4:3;
  1937,S 29,19:1
Frenesie 1938,Mr 27,X,2:1
Frenetiques, Les 1935,Ja 13,IX,2:1
Frenzy 1948,Ap 22,35:2
Frere Jacques 1968,Je 8,23:2
Fresh Fields 1933,F 5,IX,3:5; 1934,Jl 15,X,1:1;
  1935,Jl 24,20:4; 1936,F 11,19:2; 1936,Je 23,27:3;
  1936,Je 30,15:1
Fresh Fruit 1927,S 11,VIII,2:4
Friars Club Frolic 1921,Je 13,16:2; 1922,Je 5,16:1;
  1933,My 15,16:4
Fric Frac 1936,N 29,XII,2:4
Friday Night 1965,F 9,42:5
Friedens Tragoedie 1936,N 17,34:4
Friederike 1929,F 17,IX,2:3
Friend Indeed 1926,Ap 27,22:3
Friends, The 1970,My 22,41:2; 1970,Jl 24,17:2;
  1970,Ag 30,II,1:1
Friends and Lovers 1961,My 11,43:1
Friendship 1931,My 10,VIII,2:5; 1931,S 1,30:2;
  1931,S 13,IX,1:1
Fritzi 1935,D 21,10:3
Frivolities of 1920 1920,Ja 9,22:2
Frog, The 1936,Ap 12,II,8:4
Frogs, The 1941,N 14,25:3; 1966,Jl 25,22:5
Frogs of Spring, The 1953,O 21,36:2
Frolic Wind 1935,Mr 14,19:7
From A to Z 1960,Ap 21,23:2
From Eight to Twelve 1926,N 9,30:3
From Here to There 1958,Ap 24,37:3
From Israel With Laughter 1969,O 17,34:1
From Morn to Midnight 1922,My 22,17:2;
  1931,S 22,30:4; 1931,S 26,25:5; 1948,D 7,41:6
From the Second City 1961,S 27,32:1;
  1961,O 8,II,1:1; 1969,O 15,34:1; 1969,O 26,II,31:5
From This Hill 1963,Ap 2,54:2
From Vienna 1939,Je 21,26:2; 1939,Je 25,IX,1:3;
  1939,Jl 2,IX,1:1
Front, The 1942,N 7,8:3
Front of the House 1936,S 21,26:3
Front Page, The 1928,Ag 15,19:2; 1928,Ag 26,VII,1:1;
  1928,S 9,IX,1:1; 1929,Ja 6,VIII,4:4;
  1929,Jl 14,IX,2:1; 1935,Jl 9,24:4; 1937,N 12,27:2;
  1946,S 5,22:4; 1946,S 15,II,21:1; 1968,O 20,85:5;
  1969,My 12,54:2; 1969,My 25,II,1:1;
  1969,O 26,II,1:1; 1969,N 2,86:1
Front Page Stuff 1926,D 29,24:4
Front Seat, The 1921,My 22,VI,1:6
Frozen Glory 1938,F 11,27:6
Fruehlingsluft 1921,N 29,17:4
Frugal Noon 1964,My 23,15:2
Fruits of Enlightenment, The 1928,N 25,X,2:3
Frying Pan, The 1966,N 8,45:1
Fuenf von der Jazzband 1927,N 20,IX,4:7
Fuente Ovejuna 1936,My 3,II,4:1
Fuenteovejuna 1935,S 22,X,2:5
Fuerza Ciega, La 1927,D 6,26:1
Fugitive, The 1936,Je 28,IX,1:8
Fulgens and Lucrece 1936,Mr 24,26:5
Full House 1935,Ag 22,20:3; 1935,S 22,X,3:3
Full Moon in March, A 1960,S 20,48:1
Full Swing 1942,My 3,VIII,1:7
Fulton of Oak Falls 1937,Ja 2,15:3; 1937,F 11,18:2
Fumed Oak 1935,O 22,16:5; 1936,Ja 14,25:1;
  1936,F 16,IX,3:1; 1936,N 28,13:1; 1963,D 6,XII,5:1;
  1937,Ag 24,24:5; 1948,F 24,20:4; 1967,My 4,34:1
Fun and Games 1941,Ag 31,IX,1:4
Fun and Magic 1957,D 30,19:4
Fun City 1968,Mr 7,53:2
Fun Couple, The 1962,O 27,15:2
Fun With Music 1946,N 25,38:5
Fundamental George, The 1949,Ag 17,19:4
Funny Face 1927,N 23,28:2; 1928,N 9,22:3
Funny Girl 1964,Mr 27,15:1; 1966,Ap 15,46:1
Funny Kind of Evening With David Kossoff, A
  1967,Ja 31,52:1
Funny Thing Happened on the Way to the Forum,
  A 1962,My 9,49:1; 1962,My 20,II,1:1;
  1962,Jl 6,22:5; 1962,O 14,83:4; 1963,Je 2,II,1:1
Funnyhouse of a Negro 1964,Ja 15,25:3
Funzapoppin 1949,Jl 1,16:2

Furies, The 1928,Mr 8,23:1; 1928,Mr 18,IX,1:1;
  1967,Jl 24,23:1
Furnished Rooms 1934,My 30,14:6
Fursey 1962,O 3,47:2
Fussballspieler, Der 1927,N 13,IX,2:1
Future That Was, The 1936,Ap 23,21:3
Futz 1968,Je 14,39:1; 1968,Je 30,II,1:1;
  1968,O 22,37:1

G

G-II 1948,My 28,27:3
Gabriel Schillings Flucht 1932,D 4,IX,1:6
Gabrielle 1941,Mr 26,26:2
Gainsborough Girls, The 1951,Jl 17,31:5;
  1951,Ag 12,II,1:4
Gala Night 1930,F 26,22:4
Galerie des Glaces, La 1924,N 16,III,7:4
Galician Rabbi, The 1937,F 13,9:7
Galileo 1947,Ag 1,21:4; 1947,D 8,34:2; 1963,Ja 5,5:2;
  1967,Ap 14,31:1; 1967,Ap 23,II,1:1; 1968,D 1,88:4
Gallant Cassian 1934,N 14,22:2
Galloper, The 1924,D 19,26:2
Gallows Glorious 1933,My 1,10:5;
  1933,My 21,IX,1:3
Gallows Humor 1961,Ap 19,35:1
Gambler, The 1952,O 14,40:1
Gambling 1929,My 19,IX,2:1; 1929,Ag 27,31:2;
  1929,S 22,IX,1:1
Game 1968,S 9,57:7
Game of Heroes, The 1966,F 22,14:2
Game of Love, A 1934,O 25,26:6
Game of Love and Death, The 1929,N 26,28:4
Game Without Rules 1961,D 29,4:4
Gamester 1935,Jl 9,24:4
Gammer Gurton's Needle 1959,S 1,21:1
Gandhi 1970,O 21,37:1
Gang War 1928,Ag 12,VII,1:2; 1928,Ag 21,27:2;
  1928,S 9,IX,1:1
Gang zum Weiher, Der 1931,Ap 5,VIII,1:6
Gang's All Here, The 1931,F 19,21:3; 1959,O 2,23:1;
  1959,O 11,II,1:1
Gantry 1970,F 16,44:1; 1970,S 6,II,1:1
Garden District 1958,Ja 8,23:4; 1958,Ja 19,II,1:1;
  1958,S 17,44:2
Garden of Allah, The 1920,Ag 29,VI,1:1
Garden of Eden, The 1927,Je 26,VIII,1:3;
  1927,Ag 14,VII,2:1; 1927,S 28,28:1; 1927,O 26,26:2
Garden of Sweets, The 1961,N 1,35:1
Garden of Time 1945,Mr 10,13:7
Garden of Weeds 1924,Ap 29,12:3;
  1924,My 4,VIII,1:1
Gardener's Dog, The 1927,O 21,27:1; 1957,F 19,36:1
Gardiens de Phare 1923,N 13,24:2
Garey Divorce Case, The 1929,My 12,IX,2:3
Garrick Gaieties 1925,My 18,12:2; 1925,Je 9,16:5;
  1925,Je 28,VIII,1:1; 1926,My 11,25:2;
  1926,Je 13,VII,1:1; 1930,Je 5,29:2; 1930,O 17,21:2
Garrison Theatre 1940,My 26,IX,2:1
Gartenlaube, Die 1930,Mr 30,VIII,4:1
Gas Light 1939,F 19,IX,3:1; 1939,Ag 30,20:8
Gasoline Gypsies 1931,Je 8,21:3
Gates of Summer, The 1970,Je 16,53:2
Gather Ye Rosebuds 1934,N 29,33:2; 1934,D 2,X,1:1
Gawpy Ballet, The 1928,D 17,25:1
Gay Adventure, The 1932,Ja 24,VIII,3:5
Gay Apprentice, The 1960,F 3,27:2
Gay Blades 1937,N 12,26:6; 1937,N 16,27:1
Gay Divorce 1932,N 13,IX,1:7; 1932,N 30,23:4;
  1933,N 19,IX,3:7; 1937,Jl 20,19:4; 1937,Ag 11,27:2;
  1960,Ap 4,37:1
Gay Invalid, The 1951,F 11,II,3:1
Gay Life, The 1961,N 20,38:1
Gay Lord Quex 1923,Ap 8,VIII,1:7
Gay Masquerade 1935,My 15,26:1
Gay Paree 1925,Ag 19,14:3; 1926,N 10,24:2;
  1927,Mr 22,31:1
Gayden 1949,My 11,34:4
Gazebo, The 1958,D 13,2:7
Geese 1969,Ja 13,26:6
Gefesselte Phantasie, Die 1936,N 8,X,2:1
Geisha, The 1931,O 6,35:4
General John Regan 1930,Ja 30,16:5
General Percy Gruendet ein Koenigreich
  1932,N 6,IX,3:1
General Seeger 1962,Mr 1,26:2
General's Daughter, The 1966,Mr 16,50:1
Generation 1965,O 8,5:6
Generations of Men, The 1962,My 31,23:6
Geneva 1938,Ag 2,15:6; 1938,Ag 7,IV,5:3;
  1938,Ag 21,IX,2:1; 1938,N 23,25:1; 1940,Ja 31,15:2
Genevieve 1936,O 25,X,3:8
Genius and the Crowd 1920,S 7,20:1
Genius and the Goddess, The 1957,D 11,41:1
Genius at Home 1934,Ja 16,18:3; 1934,F 11,IX,3:1
Gentle Grafters 1926,O 17,VIII,2:4; 1926,O 28,23:1
Gentle Jack 1963,N 29,50:7
Gentle People, The 1939,Ja 6,25:1; 1939,Jl 7,12:6;
  1939,Jl 30,IX,1:3; 1950,Ap 15,10:5
Gentle Rain 1936,S 2,18:2; 1936,S 20,IX,1:4

Gentleman Caller, The 1969,Ap 13,II,3:3;
1969,Ap 27,92:1; 1969,My 4,II,1:5; 1969,Jl 31,28:1;
1969,Ag 3,II,1:4
Gentleman From Athens, The 1947,N 30,I,78:2;
1947,D 10,42:4
Gentleman Unknown 1938,N 17,29:2; 1938,D 4,X,7:5
Gentlemen, the Queen 1927,Ap 23,14:3
Gentlemen of the Press 1928,Ag 28,27:2;
1928,S 2,VII,1:1
Gentlemen Prefer Blondes 1926,Ap 25,VIII,1:8;
1926,S 29,23:1; 1926,O 3,VIII,1:1; 1928,Ap 3,32:3;
1949,D 9,35:3; 1949,D 18,II,3:1
Gentlemen Unafraid 1938,Je 5,II,6:8
Gentlewoman 1934,Mr 23,28:4
Gently Does It 1953,O 29,43:4; 1953,N 8,II,1:1
George and Margaret 1937,F 26,25:2; 1937,S 23,32:2
George Barnwell 1928,O 2,34:3
George Dandin 1924,Ap 7,15:5; 1968,Je 28,36:1;
1968,Jl 7,II,1:1; 1970,O 19,50:1
George M! 1968,Ap 11,48:1; 1968,Ap 21,II,1:5
George Washington 1920,Mr 2,9:1
George Washington Crossing the Delaware
1962,Mr 2,24:1
George Washington Slept Here 1940,S 24,27:3;
1940,O 19,20:3; 1940,O 27,IX,1:1
George White's Scandals 1921,Jl 12,14:1;
1922,Ag 29,10:1; 1923,Je 19,22:5; 1925,Je 23,24:2;
1926,Je 15,23:2; 1928,Jl 3,19:1; 1929,S 24,29:1;
1931,S 15,30:1; 1935,D 26,20:2
Georgy 1970,F 15,II,1:1; 1970,F 27,26:1
Geranium Hat, The 1959,Mr 18,45:1
Geraniums in My Window 1934,O 27,20:6
German Tragedy, The; or, Bismarck and William II
1926,D 6,4:2
Germany Aflame 1933,O 28,20:5
Gertie 1926,N 16,24:2; 1952,Ja 31,23:1
Gertie Maude 1937,Ag 18,14:5; 1937,S 5,X,2:1
Gertrude 1970,N 13,29:1
Gertrude Stein's First Reader 1969,D 16,56:1
Gerts Have 1930,D 28,VIII,3:5
Geschichten aus dem Wienerwald 1931,D 27,VIII,1:4
Gespenster, Die 1928,F 8,28:6; 1929,F 6,30:3
Gestaendris 1921,Jl 24,VI,1:7
Gestern und Heute 1931,My 24,VIII,2:1
Get a Load of This 1941,N 30,IX,3:1
Get Away Old Man 1943,N 25,40:2
Get Me in the Movies 1928,My 22,18:3;
1928,My 27,VIII,1:1
Get Thee to Canterbury 1969,Ja 26,74:1
Get Together 1921,S 5,12:2; 1921,S 11,VI,1:6
Getaway, The 1925,S 27,VII,2:1
Getting Even 1929,Ag 20,31:1
Getting Gertie's Garter 1921,Ag 2,16:2
Getting Married 1927,D 25,VIII,1:4; 1931,Mr 31,25:5;
1950,Je 14,41:2; 1951,My 14,28:5; 1959,Je 5,18:2;
1970,Ja 20,46:1; 1970,Ja 21,34:1
Ghetto Sounds 1968,My 21,42:1
Ghost Bereft 1933,F 1,13:5
Ghost Between, The 1921,Mr 23,11:2
Ghost for Sale 1941,S 30,27:4
Ghost of Elsinore, The 1949,Ap 16,10:2
Ghost of Yankee Doodle, The 1937,O 28,28:5;
1937,N 7,XI,2:4; 1937,N 23,26:3
Ghost Parade, The 1929,O 31,28:4
Ghost Train, The 1926,Ag 26,17:2; 1929,Je 9,VIII,2:4
Ghost Writer, The 1933,Je 20,22:4
Ghosts 1922,F 7,12:1; 1923,N 7,14:1; 1925,D 2,23:2;
1926,Mr 17,28:2; 1927,Ja 11,36:3;
1927,Ja 16,VII,1:1; 1928,F 8,28:6; 1929,Ja 6,VIII,4:4;
1929,F 6,30:3; 1929,F 17,IX,1:1; 1933,My 24,24:5;
1935,D 13,30:6; 1936,My 12,26:8; 1937,N 28,XI,2:1;
1948,F 17,31:2; 1961,S 22,29:1; 1961,O 1,II,1:1
Gianni Schicci 1969,F 25,36:1
Giants, Sons of Giants 1962,Ja 8,26:2
Giants' Dance, The 1964,N 17,48:2
Giant's Stair, The 1927,My 4,29:1
Giant's Strength, A 1948,Je 19,8:5; 1948,D 13,18:6
Gideon 1961,N 10,38:1; 1961,N 19,II,1:1
Gift, The 1924,Ja 23,15:4; 1963,Jl 9,27:2
Gift Horse, The 1926,N 21,VIII,4:1
Gift of Fury, A 1958,Mr 24,21:4
Gift of Time, A 1962,F 23,34:1; 1962,Mr 4,II,1:1
Gigi 1951,N 26,20:4; 1956,My 24,27:1
Gilbert Becaud on Broadway 1966,N 1,35:1
Gilbert Becaud Sings Love 1968,O 7,53:5
Gimpel the Food 1970,O 21,40:1
Ginger 1923,O 17,14:1
Ginger Man, The 1963,N 22,42:1
Ginger Snaps 1930,Ja 1,30:5
Gingerbread Lady, The 1970,D 14,58:3;
1970,D 20,II,3:7
Gingham Dog, The 1968,O 13,II,18:6;
1969,Ap 24,41:1; 1969,My 4,II,1:5; 1969,Jl 13,II,1:1
Gingham Girl, The 1922,Ag 29,15:5
Gioconda 1926,N 14,VIII,2:1
Gioconda Smile, The 1948,Je 20,II,2:3; 1950,O 9,21:2;
1950,O 15,II,1:1
Girl and the Cat, The 1927,My 6,21:2
Girl Can Tell, A 1953,O 30,28:2
Girl Could Get Lucky, A 1964,S 21,36:1
Girl Crazy 1930,O 5,IX,4:6; 1930,O 15,27:1;
1930,D 28,VIII,1:1

Girl Friend, The 1926,Mr 18,26:5; 1928,O 28,IX,2:1
Girl From Childs, The 1935,Ap 16,27:5
Girl From Home, The 1920,My 4,9:2
Girl From Nantucket, The 1945,N 9,17:2
Girl From Samos, The 1954,N 24,17:1
Girl From Warsaw, The 1931,S 14,15:5
Girl From Wyoming, The 1938,O 31,12:1
Girl in Pink Tights, The 1954,Mr 6,13:2
Girl in the Coffin, The 1920,F 16,10:2
Girl in the Freudian Slip, The 1967,My 19,34:3
Girl in the Spotlight, The 1920,Jl 13,9:3
Girl of Good Family, The 1932,N 13,IX,3:7
Girl of the Golden West, The 1957,N 6,44:1
Girl of Yesterday, The 1930,S 27,21:2
Girl on the Via Flaminia, The 1954,F 10,37:1;
1954,Ap 6,35:5; 1954,O 13,26:5
Girl Outside, The 1932,O 25,24:3
Girl Trouble 1928,O 7,IX,2:3; 1928,O 26,22:3
Girl Unknown 1936,S 17,18:2; 1936,O 4,IX,3:7
Girl Who Came to Supper, The 1963,D 9,49:1
Girl With Carmine Lips, The 1920,Ag 11,6:1;
1920,Ag 15,VI,1:1
Girlfriend 1970,F 19,59:1
Girls Against the Boys, The 1959,N 3,26:1;
1959,N 8,II,1:1
Girl's Best Friend, A 1929,N 10,X,2:1
Girls in Uniform 1932,D 31,10:3
Girls in 509, The 1958,O 16,47:1
Girls of Summer 1956,N 20,45:1
Girls of Today 1935,N 20,26:5
Girofle-Girofla 1926,N 23,26:3; 1926,N 24,26:2
Girouette 1935,My 5,IX,2:4
Giuditta 1934,Ja 21,30:1
Giuochi di Prestigio 1931,N 2,26:1
Give a Dog. . . 1929,Je 9,VIII,3:5
Give and Take 1922,D 10,VIII,1:5; 1923,Ja 19,13:1
Give Me Back My Heart 1937,O 4,17:6
Give Me Yesterday 1931,Mr 5,32:1;
1931,Mr 15,IX,1:1
Give My Regards to Off Off Broadway
1966,D 9,57:1
Give Us This Day 1933,O 28,20:6
Glad Tidings 1951,O 12,33:2
Glamorous Night 1935,My 3,23:6
Glamour, Glory and Gold 1967,O 4,43:1
Glamour Preferred 1940,N 16,13:2
Glass Cage, The 1957,Mr 11,21:2
Glass Menagerie, The 1945,Ja 14,II,2:4;
1945,Ap 2,15:5; 1945,Ap 8,II,1:1; 1948,Jl 29,17:2;
1956,N 22,50:1; 1956,D 2,II,1:1; 1961,Mr 6,30:1;
1961,Ap 1,11:2; 1961,Ap 11,43:5; 1961,Ap 21,29:1;
1961,My 1,35:3; 1961,My 19,22:2; 1961,My 31,28:1;
1961,Je 16,27:3; 1961,Ag 21,20:7; 1964,Jl 20,18:3;
1965,My 5,53:2; 1965,My 16,II,1:1
Glass of Water, A 1930,Mr 6,16:3
Glass Slipper, The 1925,O 20,29:1;
1925,O 25,VIII,1:1
Glass Wall, The 1933,F 21,17:2
Glass Wasser, Das 1934,D 30,IX,2:1;
1935,Jl 28,X,1:6
Gli Spettri 1930,D 22,16:4
Glimpse of the Domesticity of Franklyn Barnabas, A
1960,Mr 7,24:2
Gloire, La 1921,O 23,22:2
Gloria and Esperanza 1969,Ap 5,30:1;
1969,Ap 7,51:2; 1970,F 5,32:1; 1970,F 15,II,7:5
Gloriana 1938,N 26,18:4
Glorious Morning 1938,Je 12,X,2:4; 1938,N 28,10:3
Glorious Ruler, The 1969,Jl 1,31:1
Glory 1922,D 26,10:1; 1936,Ja 27,20:1
Glory Be 1935,Mr 8,25:6
Glory for All 1937,F 9,18:2
Glory Hallelujah 1926,Ap 7,26:2; 1926,Ap 11,VIII,1:1
Glory in the Flower 1959,D 9,57:5
Glueck im Winkel 1921,Jl 24,VI,1:7
Glueck in Haus 1933,My 7,IX,2:5
Glueckliche Reise 1933,Ja 1,IX,1:1
Gnadiges Fraulein, The 1966,F 23,42:1;
1966,Mr 6,II,1:1
Go, Go, Go, God is Dead! 1966,O 12,37:1
Go Back for Murder 1960,Mr 24,40:2
Go Easy Mabel 1922,My 9,22:2
Go Fight City Hall 1961,N 3,28:5
Go Fly a Kite! 1969,O 20,60:1
Go-Go 1923,Mr 13,19:4
Go on Smoking Ladany! 1927,Mr 20,VIII,4:3
Go Show Me a Dragon 1961,O 28,18:1
Go West, Young Man 1923,N 13,25:2
Goa 1968,F 23,46:1
Goat Alley 1921,Je 21,20:2; 1927,Ap 21,24:3
Goat Song 1926,Ja 26,18:1; 1926,F 7,VII,1:1
Goats, The 1923,N 4,VIII,2:7
God, Man & You, Baby! 1963,O 30,47:1
God and Kate Murphy 1959,F 27,21:2
God Bless 1968,N 3,II,1:1
God Bless Our Home 1924,N 23,VIII,2:4
God Bless You, Harold Fineberg 1969,Mr 31,30:2
God Innis 1937,Ag 25,24:3
God Is a (Guess What?) 1968,D 18,56:1;
1968,D 19,63:6; 1968,D 29,II,1:1; 1969,My 13,41:1
God Is Back, Black and Singing Gospel at the
Fortune Theater 1969,N 19,48:1
God Loves Us 1926,O 20,22:2; 1926,O 31,VIII,1:4

God Man and Devil 1928,D 22,14:8; 1935,Mr 6,22:3
God of Revenge, The 1921,N 4,15:2
God of Vengeance, The 1922,D 20,22:5
God Slept Here, A 1957,F 20,38:1
God Strikes Back 1943,F 27,11:2
Goddesses of Athens, The 1955,D 14,52:4
Godless, The 1926,Ja 10,VII,1:3
Gods Are Wise, The 1930,My 6,33:1
Gods of the Lightning 1928,O 25,27:2;
1931,F 19,21:4
Gods of the Mountain, The 1925,Ap 4,20:2;
1925,Ap 26,VIII,1:1; 1930,My 25,36:2
God's Thieves 1930,O 27,17:4
God's Trombones 1960,F 10,43:4; 1960,F 21,II,1:1
Gods We Make, The 1934,Ja 4,16:4
Goetz von Berlichingen 1930,D 14,IX,4:1
Gogo Loves You 1964,O 10,19:2
Goin' Home 1928,Ag 24,23:2; 1928,S 2,VII,1:1
Going Gay 1933,Ag 4,18:5
Going Greek 1937,S 17,28:4
Going Places 1936,O 9,30:5; 1936,O 25,X,2:4
Going to America 1961,O 30,33:7
Gold 1921,Je 2,14:2
Gold Braid 1930,My 14,31:2
Gold Diggers, The 1926,D 19,VII,6:4;
1926,D 26,VII,4:3; 1927,D 3,19:2
Gold Eagle Guy 1934,N 18,IX,1:7; 1934,N 29,33:4;
1934,D 9,X,1:1
Gold Fields 1920,Jl 11,VI,1:6
Golden Age, The 1928,Ap 25,31:3; 1963,N 19,49:2
Golden Apple, The 1954,Mr 12,15:2;
1954,Mr 21,II,1:1; 1962,F 13,38:2
Golden Bat 1970,Je 27,18:2; 1970,Ag 16,II,1:1
Golden Book of Love, The 1923,N 22,21:4
Golden Boy 1937,N 5,18:5; 1937,N 21,XI,1:1;
1938,Ja 23,XI,1:6; 1938,Je 22,27:5;
1938,Jl 10,IX,1:5; 1938,O 23,IX,3:5;
1952,Mr 13,24:3; 1952,Mr 23,II,1:1; 1964,O 21,56:1;
1964,N 1,II,1:1
Golden Calf, The 1927,O 2,VIII,1:3
Golden Cinderella, A 1931,O 4,VIII,2:2
Golden Dawn 1927,O 2,VIII,4:6; 1927,D 1,32:3
Golden Days 1921,N 2,20:1; 1921,N 6,VI,1:1
Golden Dog, The 1929,D 25,21:2
Golden Falcon, The 1948,Mr 26,25:4
Golden Fleece, The 1969,Je 11,43:1
Golden Fleecing 1959,O 16,24:5
Golden Harp, The 1933,O 16,20:4
Golden Journey, The 1936,S 16,28:6
Golden Rainbow 1968,F 5,27:1; 1968,Mr 3,II,3:1
Golden Ring, The 1930,F 1,14:7
Golden Screw, The 1967,Ja 31,52:1;
1967,Mr 26,II,1:2
Golden Six, The 1958,My 2,31:5; 1958,O 27,31:2
Golden State, The 1950,N 27,29:3
Golden Stream, The 1936,F 13,25:1
Golden Streets, The 1970,Ag 14,21:1
Golden Wings 1941,N 25,33:3; 1941,D 9,46:6
Goldfish, The 1922,Ag 18,15:3
Goldilocks 1958,O 13,33:1; 1958,O 19,II,1:1
Goldne Meisterin, Die 1927,S 16,21:1;
1927,O 25,33:4
Golem, The 1927,F 5,13:2; 1931,N 6,28:5;
1931,D 13,VIII,3:4; 1948,My 17,22:3;
1959,F 26,38:2
Gondoliers, The 1929,O 22,26:3; 1931,Je 2,34:4;
1932,Ja 12,29:1; 1934,S 4,23:1; 1934,S 9,IX,1:1;
1935,Ag 6,20:5; 1936,Jl 19,12:5; 1936,S 8,23:1;
1939,Ja 20,14:2; 1940,O 1,29:2; 1942,Mr 4,22:3;
1944,F 22,26:3; 1948,Ja 27,31:2; 1951,F 13,27:2;
1954,Ap 14,24:3; 1957,My 29,34:2; 1960,F 7,II,1:1;
1961,Ja 26,33:2; 1961,D 8,44:1; 1962,Ap 19,34:2;
1962,Jl 7,9:4; 1962,N 16,25:2; 1963,Je 5,33:2;
1964,Mr 28,14:1; 1967,O 29,83:1; 1969,My 10,35:1
Gone Hollywood 1930,D 28,VIII,2:1
Gone Tomorrow 1948,My 12,34:6
Gone With the Wind 1941,O 21,28:3
Good, The 1938,O 6,27:2
Good as Gold 1957,Mr 8,22:2
Good Bad Woman, A 1925,F 10,21:1
Good Boy 1928,S 6,23:2
Good-Bye Please 1934,O 25,26:6
Good-Bye to Love 1940,Je 8,18:1
Good-Bye to Yesterday 1937,N 21,XI,3:6
Good Companions, The 1931,My 15,20:8;
1931,My 31,VIII,2:6; 1931,O 2,31:1;
1931,O 11,VIII,1:1
Good Day 1965,O 19,51:1
Good Earth, The 1932,S 25,IX,1:6; 1932,O 18,23:4;
1932,O 23,IX,1:1
Good Fairy, The 1930,O 13,31:2; 1930,D 23,24:2;
1931,N 15,VIII,4:1; 1931,N 25,17:1; 1932,N 18,22:3;
1937,My 15,23:3; 1939,Ag 30,15:5
Good Fellow, The 1926,Je 27,VII,3:1; 1926,O 6,22:1
Good Friday 1934,Ap 22,IX,1:6
Good Girl, The 1934,Je 26,22:5
Good Gracious, Annabelle 1923,F 15,23:2;
1923,F 25,VII,1:7
Good Hope, The 1927,O 19,24:2; 1927,O 23,VIII,1:1
Good Housekeeping 1949,Ag 17,19:3
Good Hunting 1938,N 22,26:5
Good Luck 1923,O 7,IX,2:2; 1964,O 19,38:3
Good Men and True 1935,O 26,12:4

Good Morning 1937,D 4,20:7
Good Morning, Bill! 1927,D 25,VIII,1:4
Good Morning, Corporal 1944,Ag 9,13:7
Good Morning, Dearie 1921,N 2,20:2;
  1921,N 6,VI,1:1; 1921,N 27,VI,1:1
Good Morning, Night 1968,Ap 15,41:1
Good Neighbor 1941,O 22,26:2
Good News 1927,Ag 14,VII,2:1; 1927,S 7,35:4
Good Night, Children 1942,F 15,VIII,3:6
Good Night Ladies 1945,Ja 18,16:2; 1945,Ja 28,II,1:1
Good Old Days, The 1923,Ag 15,21:2;
  1923,Ag 19,VI,1:1; 1925,N 1,VIII,1:3;
  1935,F 19,27:3; 1951,Jl 18,21:2
Good Road, The 1948,N 11,36:2
Good Soldier Schweik, The 1937,D 22,33:2;
  1963,Ap 9,57:1
Good Soup, The 1960,Mr 3,26:4
Good Times 1920,Ag 10,10:1
Good Woman, Poor Thing, A 1932,D 11,IX,5:1;
  1933,Ja 10,27:3
Good Woman, The 1921,Je 14,15:2
Good Woman of Setzuan, The 1956,D 19,41:2;
  1956,D 30,II,1:1; 1960,D 25,II,5:1; 1970,N 6,51:1;
  1970,N 15,II,1:5
Goodbye Again 1932,D 29,16:4; 1937,S 1,15:1;
  1943,N 10,28:4; 1956,Ap 25,38:1
Goodbye Charlie 1959,D 17,50:1
Goodbye in the Night 1940,Mr 19,31:2
Goodbye My Fancy 1948,N 18,35:2;
  1948,N 28,II,1:1
Goodbye People, The 1968,D 4,52:1;
  1968,D 15,II,3:1
Goodness, How Sad 1938,O 19,18:6; 1938,N 6,IX,3:5
Goodwill Ambassador 1959,Mr 3,39:2
Goose, The 1960,Mr 16,44:1
Goose-Feather Bed 1935,D 17,30:7
Goose for the Gander, A 1945,Ja 24,16:4
Goose Hangs High, The 1924,Ja 30,16:1;
  1924,F 3,VII,1:1
Gooseberry Fool 1929,N 2,14:8
Gordon Reilly 1952,N 26,20:5
Gore's Hell 1933,S 25,1:5
Gorilla, The 1925,Ap 19,IX,2:1; 1925,Ap 29,24:2
Gorilla Queen 1967,Mr 20,26:1; 1967,Mr 26,II,1:2;
  1967,Ap 25,36:1
Gospel Glow 1962,O 28,87:5
Gospel of the Brothers Barnabas, The (Back to
  Methuselah, Part II) 1922,F 28,17:2
Gosseline 1921,Je 19,VI,1:8
Gossipy Sex, The 1927,Ap 20,28:3
Gosta Berling's Saga 1936,Je 28,IX,1:6
Gott mit Uns 1928,D 30,VIII,1:3
Government Inspector, The 1967,Je 15,55:1;
  1967,Je 25,II,1:2; 1967,O 28,34:1
Grab Bag, The 1924,S 7,VII,1:4; 1924,O 7,26:2;
  1968,N 5,53:2
Gramercy Ghost 1951,Ap 27,20:2
Grand Duc, Le 1922,Jl 30,VI,1:7
Grand Duchess 1929,D 17,29:2
Grand Duchess and the Waiter, The 1925,O 14,31:1
Grand Duke, The 1921,Ap 17,VI,1:8; 1921,N 2,20:1;
  1921,N 6,VI,1:1; 1921,N 27,VI,1:1;
  1961,My 12,24:1
Grand Hotel 1930,D 22,VIII,4:6; 1930,N 14,30:4;
  1930,N 23,IX,1:1; 1931,S 4,22:7; 1931,S 27,VIII,1:4
Grand Kabuki 1960,Je 12,II,1:1
Grand Music Hall of Israel, The 1968,F 7,42:1
Grand Prize, The 1955,Ja 27,17:1
Grand Street Follies, The 1924,My 21,22:2;
  1925,Je 19,24:1; 1925,Je 28,VIII,1:1;
  1926,Je 16,23:2; 1927,My 20,22:3; 1927,Je 1,24:2;
  1927,Jl 3,VII,1:1; 1928,My 29,16:2;
  1928,Je 3,VIII,1:1; 1929,My 2,20:4;
  1929,My 12,IX,1:2; 1929,Je 19,34:3
Grand Tour, The 1951,D 11,45:2
Grand Vizier, The 1961,D 13,55:5; 1962,Mr 21,36:2
Grand Vizir, Le 1970,Ap 8,38:3
Grande Duchesse et la Garcon d'Etage, La
  1924,My 25,VIII,1:8
Grande Enfant, La 1931,D 13,VIII,2:2
Grandee Penitence, La 1926,N 14,VIII,2:1
Grandma's Diary 1948,S 23,36:2
Granite 1926,Je 20,VII,1:1; 1927,F 12,13:1;
  1936,Ja 14,24:6
Granite Fires 1936,Jl 22,22:4
Granny 1927,Ja 2,VII,2:5
Grass Harp, The 1952,Mr 28,26:2; 1952,Ap 6,II,1:1;
  1953,Ap 28,32:2; 1953,My 24,II,1:1
Grass Is Always Greener, The 1955,F 16,25:2
Gratefully Yours 1942,Ap 8,22:3
Gray Shadow 1931,Mr 11,23:4
Great Adventure, The 1921,F 26,9:2; 1926,D 23,23:1
Great Airplane Snatch, The 1969,My 28,36:1
Great American Family, The 1939,D 10,X,5:6
Great Barrington, The 1931,F 20,18:1
Great Big Doorstep, The 1942,N 27,26:2;
  1950,Mr 18,8:6
Great Broxopp, The 1921,N 16,22:1;
  1921,N 27,VI,1:1; 1923,Mr 11,VIII,2:4
Great Campaign, The 1947,Ap 1,33:2
Great Career, A 1968,D 30,25:1
Great Catherine, The 1927,Ap 3,VIII,4:7
Great Day 1945,Mr 25,II,2:4

Great Day in the Morning 1962,Mr 29,29:1
Great Day! 1929,Je 9,VIII,1:2; 1929,O 18,24:3
Great Expectations 1939,D 17,IX,4:5
Great Experiment, The 1936,Ap 22,28:4
Great Fortune, The 1922,D 9,11:1
Great Gatsby, The 1926,F 3,22:1; 1926,F 7,VII,1:1
Great God Brown, The 1926,Ja 25,26:1;
  1926,Ja 31,VII,1:1; 1926,Ap 11,VIII,1:1;
  1927,Jl 24,VII,1:7; 1936,Je 28,IX,1:6; 1959,O 7,48:1;
  1959,O 18,II,1:1
Great Goodness of Life (A Coon Show)
  1969,Ap 27,92:1; 1969,My 4,II,1:5; 1969,Jl 31,28:1;
  1969,Ag 3,II,1:4; 1969,S 22,36:1
Great Guns 1939,N 18,23:4
Great Indoors, The 1966,F 2,23:1
Great Lady 1938,D 2,26:6
Great Love, The 1935,O 22,17:3; 1935,D 24,11:5
Great Lover, The 1932,O 12,27:3
Great Magician, The 1951,N 22,45:1
Great Magoo, The 1932,D 3,20:7
Great Man, The 1931,Ap 8,20:6
Great Miracle, The 1931,D 12,23:5
Great Music 1924,O 6,24:1; 1924,O 12,VIII,1:1
Great Necker, The 1928,Mr 7,28:2
Great Possessions 1937,F 9,18:3
Great Power, The 1928,Jl 8,VII,1:2; 1928,S 12,25:1
Great Romancer, The 1937,Je 16,26:3;
  1937,Jl 4,X,1:4
Great Scot! 1965,N 12,56:3
Great Scott! 1929,S 3,25:1
Great Sebastians, The 1956,Ja 5,27:1;
  1956,Ja 15,II,1:1
Great Shakes 1931,Mr 12,22:2
Great Temptations, The 1926,My 19,29:1;
  1926,My 23,VIII,1:1
Great to Be Alive! 1950,Mr 24,28:2
Great Van Dyn, The 1935,Mr 6,22:2
Great Waltz, The 1934,S 24,14:4; 1934,S 30,IX,1:1;
  1935,Ag 6,20:5; 1935,N 3,X,1:5
Great Way, The 1921,N 8,28:2; 1921,N 13,VI,1:1
Great Western Union, The 1965,F 10,45:1
Great White Hope, The 1967,D 14,58:1;
  1967,D 24,II,3:1; 1968,O 4,40:1; 1968,O 13,II,1:1;
  1969,S 27,26:1
Greater Love 1931,Mr 3,39:1
Greater Love, The 1927,Ap 3,VIII,1:4
Greater Lust, The 1936,Jl 14,22:4
Greatest Man Alive!, The 1957,My 9,37:2
Greatest Show on Earth, The 1938,Ja 6,22:2
Greatness Comes to the Maronies 1937,Ag 18,15:2
Greatshot 1969,My 18,II,3:1
Greed for Gold, The: or, Wide Awake Lil
  1934,N 24,18:3
Greeks Had a Word for It, The 1930,S 26,16:5;
  1934,N 23,22:2
Green Bay Tree, The 1933,O 21,11:5;
  1933,O 29,IX,1:1; 1951,F 2,18:2
Green Beetle, The 1924,Jl 20,VII,1:7; 1924,S 3,12:3
Green Cockatoo, The 1930,O 10,20:5
Green Fields 1920,Mr 26,11:2
Green Goddess, The 1921,Ja 19,14:1;
  1921,Ja 23,VI,1:1; 1921,Ja 30,VI,1:1; 1923,S 7,10:2
Green Grow the Lilacs 1930,D 14,IX,3:1;
  1931,Ja 27,21:2; 1931,F 8,VIII,1:1
Green Hat, The 1925,Ap 5,IX,2:4; 1925,S 16,23:2;
  1925,S 20,VIII,1:1
Green Pastures, The 1930,F 27,26:1;
  1930,Mr 2,IX,1:1; 1930,Mr 9,IX,1:1;
  1931,Mr 1,VIII,1:1; 1932,O 11,26:6;
  1932,O 30,IX,2:4; 1933,O 5,24:5; 1933,O 22,IX,1:6;
  1935,F 27,16:2; 1935,Mr 24,VIII,1:1;
  1951,Mr 16,35:2; 1951,Ap 1,II,1:1
Green Ring, The 1922,Ap 5,22:1
Green Stick 1934,O 10,21:2
Green Table, The 1942,Ja 22,12:2; 1942,F 1,IX,2:2
Green Waters 1936,N 5,34:4
Greengrocer's Daughter, The 1966,Mr 16,50:1
Greenwich Village Follies 1920,Ag 31,7:3;
  1921,S 1,18:3; 1922,S 13,18:2; 1923,S 21,4:6;
  1924,S 17,16:1; 1924,S 21,VII,1:1; 1924,S 28,VII,1:1;
  1924,N 25,26:2; 1925,S 25,23:3; 1926,Ja 10,VII,1:1;
  1926,Mr 16,22:2; 1926,My 23,VIII,1:1;
  1928,Ap 10,32:2
Greenwich Village U S A 1960,S 29,30:5
Greenwich Villagers, The 1927,Ag 19,20:2
Greenwillow 1960,Mr 9,38:1; 1960,Mr 20,II,1:1;
  1970,D 8,60:1
Grey-Eyed People, The 1952,D 18,41:2
Grey Farm 1940,My 4,12:7
Grey Fox, The 1928,O 23,32:3
Grey Heir, The 1926,Ap 6,29:2
Grief Goes Over 1935,Je 7,24:5; 1935,Jl 28,X,1:1
Griffe, La 1923,N 27,23:5
Grin and Bare It 1970,Mr 17,36:1
Gringa, La 1928,Ja 22,VIII,4:7; 1928,F 2,17:1
Gringo 1922,D 15,26:3; 1922,D 24,VII,1:1
Grisou 1935,Je 30,X,1:4
Groove Tube 1969,O 12,88:3
Grosse Valise, La 1965,D 15,52:1
Grosses Welttheater 1933,Ap 16,IX,2:5
Grounds for Divorce 1924,Mr 2,VIII,2:7;
  1924,S 24,20:1; 1924,O 5,VIII,1:1
Group Theatre Sketches 1935,F 11,14:5

Growing Pains 1933,N 24,24:2
Gualtier l'Oyseau 1926,D 5,VIII,6:1
Guardsman, The 1924,O 14,23:1; 1924,O 19,VIII,1:1;
  1969,Ag 17,II,5:1
Guepe, La 1928,O 21,IX,5:6
Guernica 1969,My 1,50:1
Guerre de Troie N'Aura pas Lieu, La
  1935,D 29,IX,2:1
Guerrillas 1970,My 17,91:3
Guest in the House 1942,F 25,25:2
Guest of Honor, The 1920,S 21,12:1
Guest Room, The 1931,O 7,29:2
Guests at Lancaster Gate 1937,My 4,28:6
Guests of the Nation 1958,My 21,40:1;
  1958,Je 27,18:5; 1958,Ag 31,II,1:1
Guide, The 1968,Mr 7,50:1
Guignol 1930,Mr 30,VIII,2:4
Guilty One, The 1922,Ag 13,VI,1:3; 1923,Mr 21,19:1;
  1923,Mr 25,VIII,1:1
Guimpes and Saddles 1967,O 11,36:3
Guinea Pig, The 1929,Ja 8,35:1
Guitar 1959,N 11,42:5
Guns 1928,Ag 7,25:2
Guns of Carrar, The 1968,D 10,53:1
Gustav Vasa 1930,N 2,VIII,3:2
Gutta Iconoclast 1921,Je 14,15:2
Guys and Dolls 1950,N 25,11:2; 1950,D 3,II,1:1;
  1951,O 7,II,1:1; 1953,My 29,17:5; 1953,Je 7,II,1:3;
  1955,Ap 21,32:2; 1959,Jl 22,22:2; 1965,Ap 29,39:1;
  1966,Je 9,55:2; 1968,S 2,14:2
Gypsy 1929,Ja 15,22:2; 1929,Ja 27,IX,1:1;
  1959,My 22,31:6; 1959,My 31,II,1:1;
  1959,Je 7,II,1:3
Gypsy April 1927,Jl 31,VII,1:7
Gypsy Baron, The 1930,Ap 22,22:8; 1942,Je 20,8:5;
  1942,Ag 7,12:4; 1944,Je 15,17:3; 1944,N 15,20:3
Gypsy Blonde 1934,Je 26,22:5
Gypsy Fires 1925,D 8,28:3
Gypsy Jim 1924,Ja 6,VII,1:4; 1924,Ja 15,17:4;
  1924,Ja 20,VII,1:1
Gypsy Lady 1946,S 18,25:6
Gypsy Love 1934,Ap 16,21:6

H

H 1969,F 14,34:2
H M S Pinafore 1920,Ja 13,10:2; 1926,Ap 7,26:3;
  1931,My 19,25:2; 1931,My 31,II,1:2;
  1931,Jl 28,17:6; 1933,My 9,20:3; 1934,Ap 17,27:2;
  1934,S 14,24:3; 1935,Ag 13,20:6; 1935,Ag 17,18:4;
  1936,Ap 28,17:2; 1936,S 29,34:2; 1939,Ja 17,27:5;
  1942,Ja 22,12:2; 1942,F 1,IX,2:2; 1944,F 15,14:4;
  1948,Ja 20,26:2; 1949,Jl 29,13:2; 1949,O 18,34:2;
  1951,F 6,24:2; 1952,N 4,32:2; 1954,My 19,36:8;
  1955,O 18,48:1; 1957,My 1,42:6; 1957,Jl 29,16:1;
  1960,Ja 29,14:1; 1960,Jl 17,51:1; 1960,S 8,41:1;
  1961,F 2,26:6; 1961,Je 9,29:5; 1962,N 23,32:4;
  1964,Mr 21,13:4; 1964,N 20,40:1; 1965,Ap 15,39:1;
  1966,Je 8,41:2; 1966,N 24,64:1; 1967,N 1,40:1;
  1968,Ap 29,47:2; 1968,O 30,35:1; 1969,D 8,61:2
Ha-Ha, The 1968,Je 15,38:2
Habit 1926,N 4,VIII,4:7
Habit Vert, L' 1927,Ja 16,VII,2:1
Habitual Husband, The 1924,D 25,27:3
Hades, the Ladies 1934,Mr 29,25:3
Hadrian VII 1968,Jl 4,14:1; 1969,Ja 9,22:1;
  1969,Ja 19,II,1:2; 1969,S 20,20:1
Haessliche Maedchen, Das 1930,N 2,VIII,3:1
Hail and Farewell 1923,F 20,12:1
Hail Scrawdyke! 1966,N 29,50:1
Hair 1967,O 30,55:1; 1967,N 14,50:1;
  1967,N 19,II,1:1; 1967,D 22,38:1; 1968,Ap 30,40:2;
  1968,My 19,II,3:3; 1968,S 29,76:3; 1969,F 5,36:1;
  1969,Je 2,53:1; 1969,Je 7,26:1; 1969,S 13,30:1;
  1970,Ja 13,39:1; 1970,S 5,10:2; 1970,S 27,II,1:2
Hairpin Harmony 1943,O 2,18:5
Hairy Ape, The 1922,Mr 10,18:2; 1922,Ap 16,VI,1:1;
  1928,F 19,VIII,4:1; 1928,Je 10,VIII,2:8;
  1928,D 2,X,2:1; 1929,S 23,27:2; 1929,IX,4:7;
  1931,Ap 15,24:4; 1931,My 12,29:4
Haiti 1938,Mr 3,16:1
Hajj Malik, El 1970,O 4,II,5:1
Half a Loaf 1926,N 28,VIII,1:4
Half a Sixpence 1965,Ap 26,38:2
Half a Widow 1927,S 13,37:3
Half an Hour 1926,My 7,12:2
Half-Caste, The 1926,Mr 30,20:4
Half Gods 1929,D 23,18:5
Half Horse, Half Alligator 1964,S 20,120:3;
  1966,Mr 14,37:2
Half-Moon, The 1920,N 2,15:2
Half Moon Inn 1923,Mr 21,19:2; 1925,Mr 10,14:1
Half-Naked Truth, The 1926,Je 8,23:1
Half-Past Wednesday 1962,Ap 7,16:2
Halfway to Hell 1934,Ja 3,22:3
Halfway up the Tree 1967,N 8,52:1; 1967,N 19,II,1:1;
  1967,N 24,60:4
Hall of Healing 1952,My 8,35:6
Hallams, The 1948,Mr 5,18:2
Hallelujah, Baby! 1967,Ap 27,51:1; 1967,My 7,II,1:1
Hallowe'en 1936,F 21,20:3
Hamhocks 1968,Ag 24,24:2

Hamlet 1920,Mr 17,14:2; 1920,D 28,9:3;
  1921,Je 21,20:2; 1922,N 17,14:1;
  1922,N 26,VIII,1:1; 1922,D 17,VII,1:1;
  1923,Ja 14,VII,1:1; 1923,F 6,14:1;
  1923,Ap 22,VII,1:1; 1923,Ag 19,VI,9:2;
  1923,O 31,12:1; 1923,N 20,23:3; 1923,N 25,VIII,1:1;
  1923,N 27,23:6; 1924,Mr 18,25:2;
  1925,Ja 11,VII,2:7; 1925,F 20,20:1;
  1925,Mr 29,VIII,1:1; 1925,Ag 26,19:4;
  1925,Ag 27,19:4; 1925,O 12,19:2; 1925,O 24,18:3;
  1925,N 10,23:1; 1925,N 22,VIII,1:1; 1925,D 8,29:2;
  1926,Ja 3,VII,1:1; 1927,Ja 23,VII,2:1;
  1927,F 13,VII,2:3; 1927,Mr 12,13:1;
  1927,Mr 27,VII,2:6; 1927,Ap 7,23:3;
  1927,O 30,IX,4:7; 1927,D 9,28:2; 1928,Ja 5,33:2;
  1928,Ja 15,VIII,1:8; 1928,Je 2,11:3;
  1930,Mr 25,34:4; 1931,Mr 22,VIII,2:1;
  1931,Ap 24,26:4; 1931,O 25,VIII,2:2; 1931,N 6,28:4;
  1931,N 15,VIII,1:1; 1931,N 19,26:6;
  1931,N 22,VIII,8:3; 1932,Je 12,X,1:1;
  1932,Je 26,IX,1:3; 1932,Jl 3,IX,1:1;
  1932,N 13,IX,3:8; 1934,F 11,IX,3:7; 1934,N 15,25:1;
  1934,D 2,X,3:6; 1934,D 26,19:3; 1936,O 1,28:3;
  1936,O 9,30:2; 1936,O 11,X,1:4; 1936,O 18,X,1:1;
  1936,O 20,31:3; 1936,O 25,X,1:5; 1936,N 11,54:2;
  1937,Ja 6,19:4; 1937,Je 4,26:6; 1937,Ag 8,X,1:7;
  1937,Ag 24,24:4; 1938,O 13,28:1; 1938,O 30,IX,1:1;
  1938,N 8,26:1; 1939,Jl 7,12:2; 1939,Jl 9,IX,1:6;
  1939,Jl 16,IX,2:1; 1939,D 5,35:2; 1939,D 10,X,3:1;
  1942,D 18,1:6; 1944,N 19,II,2:4; 1945,D 14,25:2;
  1945,D 23,II,3:1; 1946,Je 4,18:4; 1947,Ja 8,26:2;
  1947,F 27,27:2; 1947,Jl 13,I,47:2; 1948,My 9,II,2:5;
  1948,S 11,13:3; 1948,D 4,9:2; 1949,Je 18,9:6;
  1951,Jl 20,13:6; 1952,D 2,39:1; 1953,Ag 25,18:6;
  1953,Ag 30,II,2:1; 1954,Ap 24,15:2; 1954,My 31,9:1;
  1955,Ja 4,24:5; 1955,N 24,40:7; 1956,Ap 11,28:1;
  1956,My 8,28:5; 1956,O 29,34:1; 1957,Ja 29,27:1;
  1957,Jl 3,15:2; 1957,Jl 7,II,1:1; 1957,O 29,34:2;
  1958,Je 21,11:1; 1958,D 17,2:7; 1959,Ag 19,34:1;
  1959,S 11,21:4; 1961,Mr 17,17:1; 1961,Mr 26,II,1:1;
  1961,Ap 12,46:1; 1961,Ag 30,II,1:1; 1963,My 9,41:1
  1963,My 19,II,1:1; 1963,O 23,37:2; 1964,F 28,17:5;
  1964,Ap 10,30:1; 1964,Ap 19,II,1:1; 1964,Je 2,32:8;
  1964,Je 17,49:1; 1964,Je 18,28:1; 1964,Jl 4,9:1;
  1965,Ja 23,15:4; 1965,Ag 20,18:2; 1967,F 17,44:1;
  1967,D 27,45:1; 1968,Ja 7,II,1:5; 1968,My 12,II,1:1;
  1968,Je 9,II,1:1; 1968,Je 10,59:1; 1968,Jl 4,15:1;
  1968,Jl 21,II,21:2; 1968,Ag 21,40:2; 1969,F 19,38:1;
  1969,Mr 2,II,3:1; 1969,Mr 4,34:1; 1969,Mr 5,40:3;
  1969,Mr 14,51:1; 1969,Mr 23,II,3:1;
  1969,My 2,38:1; 1969,My 11,II,1:1; 1969,Je 11,37:1;
  1969,Je 22,II,1:7; 1969,Je 30,33:1; 1969,Jl 6,II,1:1;
  1970,Je 5,23:1; 1970,Ag 3,37:3; 1970,O 19,51:1;
  1970,O 27,54:2; 1970,D 28,40:1
Hamlet in Wittenberg 1936,N 15,XI,2:4
Hamlet of Stepney Green 1958,N 14,21:1
Hamp 1964,Ag 18,25:1; 1967,Mr 10,32:1
Hand in Glove 1944,D 5,19:1; 1944,D 10,II,5:1
Hand Is on the Gate, A 1966,S 22,54:1
Handful of Fire 1958,O 2,45:3
Hands Across the Sea 1935,O 22,16:5;
  1936,Ja 14,25:1; 1936,F 16,IX,3:1; 1936,O 27,30:7;
  1936,N 25,17:2; 1936,D 6,XII,5:1; 1937,Ag 24,24:5;
  1948,F 24,20:4
Handy Man, The 1925,Mr 10,19:2
Hang Down Your Head and Die 1964,O 19,38:1
Hanging Judge 1952,S 24,40:4; 1952,O 12,II,3:8
Hangman, The 1935,O 23,18:6
Hangman's House 1926,D 17,27:2
Hangman's Whip 1933,F 25,20:2
Hanjo 1960,N 16,51:4
Hannibal Ante Portas 1929,Ap 15,22:2;
  1929,Jl 7,VIII,2:4
Hans Sonnenstoessers Hoellenfahrt 1937,Ja 3,X,2:6
Hansel and Gretel 1929,D 25,21:1
Hans's Crime 1961,F 4,15:1
Happiest Days, The 1939,Ap 12,26:2;
  1939,Ap 16,X,1:2
Happiest Girl in the World, The 1961,Ap 4,42:1
Happiest Millionaire, The 1956,N 21,21:3;
  1956,D 2,II,1:1; 1957,N 16,16:5
Happiest Years, The 1949,Ap 26,29:8
Happily Ever After 1945,Mr 16,21:2
Happily Never After 1966,Mr 11,37:1
Happiness 1967,N 11,25:2
Happiness Cage, The 1970,O 5,56:4; 1970,O 11,II,1:1
Happiness Is Just a Little Thing Called a Rolls
  Royce 1968,My 13,54:5
Happiness of Probity, The 1930,N 10,16:4
Happy 1927,D 6,26:3
Happy and Glorious 1931,N 21,21:4
Happy Apple, The 1970,Jl 26,49:2
Happy as Larry 1950,Ja 7,11:2; 1961,Ap 26,36:1
Happy Birthday 1946,N 1,31:2; 1946,N 10,II,1:1
Happy Birthday, Wanda June 1970,O 8,58:2;
  1970,O 18,II,1:1
Happy Days 1934,Ap 2,12:5; 1941,My 14,24:2;
  1961,S 18,36:1; 1961,O 1,II,1:1; 1965,S 14,45:2;
  1968,O 14,54:1
Happy End 1929,O 27,IX,4:1
Happy Ending 1936,Jl 15,14:3; 1942,S 28,13:1;
  1965,N 16,56:1
Happy Faculty, The 1967,Ap 19,50:1

Happy Family, A 1934,S 24,15:2
Happy-Go-Lucky 1920,Ag 25,6:1; 1920,Ag 29,VI,1:1;
  1926,O 1,27:2
Happy Haven, The 1963,My 10,40:6
Happy Hunting 1956,D 7,30:1; 1956,D 16,II,3:1
Happy Husband, The 1927,Jl 19,VII,2:3;
  1928,My 8,25:2; 1928,My 27,VIII,1:1
Happy Hypocrite, The 1936,Ap 9,21:6;
  1936,My 10,X,1:1; 1968,S 6,38:1
Happy Journey to Trenton and Camden, The
  1948,Mr 21,II,1:1; 1949,Jl 9,9:2; 1966,S 7,53:1
Happy Landing 1932,Mr 28,10:5; 1942,D 6,VIII,1:6
Happy Marriage, The 1952,Ag 8,9:2
Happy Medium 1936,My 4,17:7
Happy Returns 1938,My 20,16:6
Happy Time, The 1950,Ja 25,24:1; 1952,F 10,II,2:1;
  1968,Ja 19,32:2; 1968,Ja 28,II,3:1
Happy Town 1959,O 8,49:2
Happy Valley, Limited 1936,Je 30,15:1
Happy With Either 1948,Ap 23,28:1
Harangues, The 1970,Ja 14,42:1; 1970,Ja 25,II,1:4;
  1970,S 13,II,1:1
Harbor Light, The 1932,Ag 7,IX,2:2
Harbor Lights 1956,O 5,20:1
Hard Travelin' 1965,Je 17,25:1; 1965,Je 27,II,1:1
Harem, The 1924,N 16,VIII,2:8; 1924,D 3,24:1;
  1925,S 14,17:4
Harlem 1929,F 21,30:3; 1929,Mr 3,VIII,1:1
Harlem Cavalcade 1942,My 2,11:2
Harlequinade 1921,My 11,20:3; 1948,O 10,II,3:7;
  1949,O 13,32:2; 1949,O 23,II,1:1; 1959,F 14,15:1
Harmony 1932,N 13,IX,3:7
Harold 1928,Ap 29,IX,1:3; 1962,N 8,50:7;
  1962,N 30,27:1; 1967,My 10,39:1
Harold Arlen Songbook, The 1967,Mr 1,48:1
Harold Muggins Is a Martyr 1968,Jl 14,II,4:5
Harpers Ferry 1967,Je 6,52:2
Harriet 1943,Ja 29,22:1; 1943,Mr 4,24:2;
  1943,Mr 14,V,1:1; 1944,S 28,26:1
Harry, Noon and Night 1965,My 6,44:1
Harry Delmar's Revels 1927,N 29,30:2
Harvest 1925,Ap 19,IX,2:1; 1925,S 21,16:2
Harvest of Years 1948,Ja 13,29:2
Harvey 1944,N 2,23:2; 1944,N 12,II,1:1;
  1945,My 8,16:1; 1947,Jl 15,27:3; 1947,S 14,II,1:6;
  1949,Ja 6,29:2; 1949,F 13,II,3:7; 1949,Mr 24,34:1;
  1950,O 21,10:4; 1950,D 31,II,3:7; 1970,F 25,41:1;
  1970,Mr 8,II,1:1
Hassan 1923,S 30,II,1:6; 1923,O 14,VIII,2:6;
  1924,S 23,23:1; 1924,S 28,VII,1:1;
  1931,Mr 8,VIII,2:6
Hassard Short's Ritz Revue 1924,S 18,19:1
Haste To The Wedding 1954,My 6,44:6
Hasty Heart, The 1945,Ja 4,14:2; 1945,Ja 14,II,1:1;
  1954,Mr 13,10:1; 1959,S 15,45:2
Hat, a Coat, a Glove, A 1934,F 1,15:2
Hate Planters 1933,My 26,24:5
Hatfields & McCoys 1970,Je 23,34:1
Hatful of Rain, A 1955,N 10,44:1; 1955,D 4,II,1:1
Hats Off to Ice 1944,Je 23,15:2
Hau-Ruck 1934,My 6,IX,2:2
Haunted, The 1931,O 27,22:1; 1932,My 10,25:2
Haunted Host, The 1969,O 28,43:1
Haunted House, The 1924,S 3,12:1
Hauptmann von Koeepenick, Der
  1931,Ap 26,VIII,1:4
Haus Dazwischen, Das 1933,F 19,IX,3:1
Have I Got a Girl for You! 1963,D 3,53:2
Have I Got One for You 1968,Ja 8,32:1
Have You Heard This One 1953,N 9,23:4
Haven, The 1946,N 14,39:4
Having Wonderful Time 1937,F 22,12:5;
  1937,F 28,XI,1:1
Havoc 1924,Ja 27,VII,2:4; 1924,S 2,22:2;
  1924,S 7,VII,1:1
Hawk, The 1968,Ap 18,54:1
Hawk Island 1929,S 17,34:7
Hay Fever 1925,O 5,25:1; 1928,O 7,IX,5:3;
  1931,D 6,VIII,2:8; 1931,D 30,25:1; 1935,Jl 24,20:4;
  1935,Ag 6,20:3; 1970,N 10,55:1; 1970,N 22,II,18:6
Hay-Foot, Straw-Foot 1942,O 24,11:6
Hayride 1954,S 14,24:2
Hazel Flagg 1953,F 12,22:2
He 1931,My 3,VIII,1:1; 1931,S 22,33:1
He, She and the Ox 1934,F 21,22:7
He and She 1920,F 13,16:3; 1920,F 22,III,6:2
He Is to Blame for Everything 1928,Ja 10,28:3
He Loved the Ladies 1927,My 11,29:2
He Sits in a Crucible 1939,Ap 2,X,2:4
He Understood Women 1928,Ag 16,25:1
He Walked in Her Sleep 1929,F 3,VIII,2:1;
  1929,Ap 5,28:2
He Was Born Gay 1937,My 27,20:5;
  1937,Je 13,XI,1:7
He Who Gets Slapped 1922,Ja 10,15:1;
  1922,F 26,VI,1:6; 1927,N 27,IX,4:1;
  1946,Mr 21,31:4; 1946,Mr 31,II,1:1; 1956,F 2,18:1
Head First 1926,Ja 7,22:4
Head in the Noose 1931,D 27,VIII,2:6
Head-On Crash 1933,F 26,IX,3:1
Head or Tail 1926,N 10,24:1
Headless Horseman, The 1937,Mr 6,10:4

Headquarters 1929,N 24,X,4:5; 1929,D 5,32:4
Heads or Tails 1947,My 3,10:6
Heads Up! 1929,N 12,34:1
Healthy, Wealthy and Wise 1930,Mr 2,26:3;
  1930,Mr 23,IX,2:3
Hear That Trumpet 1946,O 8,19:2
Hear! Hear! 1955,S 28,38:1
Heart of a City 1942,F 13,24:6; 1942,Mr 1,VIII,1:1
Heart of Cellini, The 1923,O 21,VIII,2:1
Heart of Frances, The 1923,Ja 29,11:2
Heart of His Mystery, The 1933,Ap 24,10:1
Heart Was Not Burned, The 1938,D 11,X,5:3
Heartbreak House 1920,N 11,11:1; 1920,N 21,VI,1:2;
  1921,N 18,20:3; 1928,F 12,VIII,1:3; 1935,Jl 23,24:3;
  1938,Ap 30,18:2; 1938,My 8,X,1:1;
  1950,Mr 22,33:2; 1959,O 19,37:1; 1959,O 25,II,1:1;
  1963,Je 8,14:2; 1963,Je 28,24:1; 1967,Ag 27,II,1:1;
  1968,Jl 6,9:1
Heart's a Wonder, The 1958,S 19,23:2
Hearts Are Trumps! 1927,Ap 8,21:1
Heart's Content 1936,D 24,22:2; 1937,Ja 24,X,3:1
Heat Lightning 1933,S 16,9:6
Heat Wave 1931,F 18,14:6
Heaven 1920,Je 13,VI,1:8
Heaven & Hell, Inc 1927,O 23,VIII,1:3
Heaven and Charing Cross 1939,Ap 16,X,2:4;
  1939,Ap 16,X,2:3
Heaven Grand in Amber Orbit 1969,N 16,II,7:5
Heaven on Earth 1935,O 8,26:2; 1948,S 17,29:2;
  1948,S 26,II,1:1
Heaven-Tappers, The 1927,Mr 9,28:3
Heavenly Express 1940,Ap 19,24:2;
  1940,Ap 28,IX,1:1
Heavenly Twins, The 1955,N 5,23:2
Heavy Traffic 1928,S 6,23:3
Hector 1932,Mr 20,VIII,2:2
Hecuba 1926,My 31,19:1
Hedda Gabler 1920,O 5,12:2; 1924,My 17,18:4;
  1926,Ja 27,16:5; 1926,Ja 31,VII,1:1;
  1926,F 21,VII,1:2; 1928,Mr 27,30:2; 1929,F 4,20:3;
  1929,F 17,IX,1:1; 1931,Ap 5,VIII,4:1;
  1934,Je 5,28:3; 1934,D 4,22:5; 1936,Ag 19,18:5;
  1936,O 25,X,1:5; 1936,N 17,34:4; 1942,Ja 30,22:2;
  1948,F 25,27:2; 1954,O 24,II,3:3; 1954,D 12,II,5:1;
  1960,N 10,61:1; 1960,N 25,24:3; 1962,D 13,8:5;
  1968,Je 5,39:1; 1970,Ja 18,78:1; 1970,Ja 25,II,3:1;
  1970,Je 12,28:1; 1970,Je 21,II,1:1; 1970,Jl 18,12:1
Heel, The 1954,My 27,33:2
Heigh-Ho, Everybody 1932,My 26,31:2
Heilige aus U.S.A., Die 1931,D 13,VIII,3:5
Heilige Crispin, Der 1933,Je 25,IX,1:2
Heimkehr aus der Fremde, Die 1949,S 2,14:1
Heiress, The 1947,S 30,22:2; 1947,O 5,II,1:1;
  1949,F 3,26:2; 1949,F 13,II,3:7; 1950,F 9,34:2;
  1950,F 12,II,1:1
Heldenleben, Ein 1929,Ap 27,16:4
Helen 1932,Ja 31,I,5:2; 1952,D 15,22:6;
  1964,D 11,55:4
Helen Goes to Troy 1944,Ap 25,17:2;
  1944,Ap 30,II,1:1
Helen of Troy, New York 1923,Je 20,22:6
Helena's Boys 1924,Ap 6,VIII,2:1; 1924,Ap 8,22:2;
  1924,Ap 13,VIII,1:1
Hell-Bent Fer Heaven 1924,Ja 5,10:1;
  1924,F 10,VII,1:1
Hell for Leather 1936,N 27,27:2
Hell Freezes Over 1935,D 30,14:2
Hello, Daddy! 1928,D 27,26:5
Hello, Dolly! 1964,Ja 17,22:1; 1964,Ja 26,II,1:1;
  1965,Ag 10,17:2; 1965,S 11,17:1; 1965,O 10,3:3;
  1965,D 3,43:1; 1967,Mr 2,30:4; 1967,Je 14,38:1;
  1967,N 13,61:1; 1967,N 26,II,3:1; 1970,Ja 25,70:6;
  1970,Mr 30,52:1; 1970,Ap 12,II,3:7
Hello, Lola! 1926,Ja 13,30:1
Hello, Yourself 1928,O 31,28:2
Hello Again 1934,Je 14,28:4
Hello and Goodbye 1968,N 13,36:2; 1969,S 19,54:1
Hello Charlie 1965,O 25,47:2
Hello Grandpa! 1931,Ja 2,25:3
Hello Out There 1941,S 11,20:6; 1942,S 30,28:2;
  1955,D 22,19:1
Hello Paris 1930,N 17,29:3
Hello Solly! 1967,Ap 6,44:3
Hello Yourself! 1929,Ja 27,IX,1:3
Hell's Bells! 1925,Ja 27,14:2
Hellseherei 1931,Je 7,VIII,2:5
Hell'z-A-Splashin' 1959,Je 25,22:2
Hellzapoppin 1938,S 23,34:2; 1938,O 2,IX,1:1;
  1948,F 25,27:2
Heloise 1958,S 25,28:4; 1958,O 5,II,1:1
Help Stamp Out Marriage 1966,S 30,50:1
Help Yourself! 1936,Jl 15,15:1
Help! Help! the Globolinks 1970,D 24,10:2
Hen Upon a Steeple 1927,Ap 24,VII,2:3
Henky 1924,Ap 27,VIII,2:3
Henri Christophe 1945,Je 7,24:5; 1945,Je 17,II,1:1
Henrietta the Eighth 1935,Je 25,15:4
Henry, Sweet Henry 1967,O 24,51:2; 1967,N 5,II,3:1;
  1967,D 22,38:1
Henry-Behave 1926,Ag 24,19:4

Henry IV 1920,Je 20,II,9:2; 1939,F 5,IX,1:1;
1945,O 14,II,2:3; 1946,My 12,II,1:1;
1955,My 15,II,1:1; 1960,Mr 2,42:1;
1960,Mr 13,II,1:1; 1960,Ap 19,41:1; 1968,F 7,40:1;
1969,My 11,4:1
Henry IV, Part I 1926,Je 1,29:1; 1926,Je 6,VIII,1:1;
1935,Mr 1,16:1; 1935,Mr 24,VIII,2:3;
1939,Ja 31,17:2; 1945 S 27,24:5; 1946,My 7,25:2;
1955,S 22,34:2; 1958,Je 25,23:3; 1962,Je 18,20:4;
1962,Je 24,II,1:1; 1965,Je 30,42:1; 1968,Je 30,54:7
Henry IV, Part II 1946,My 8,33:4; 1960,Ap 24,II,1:1;
1965,Jl 1,35:1; 1968,Jl 2,33:1; 1968,Jl 14,II,1:1
Henry V 1928,Mr 16,26:2; 1928,Ap 1,IX,1:1;
1934,Ja 28,II,3:4; 1936,N 30,24:6; 1951,F 11,II,3:1;
1951,Ag 12,II,1:4; 1956,Je 20,27:2; 1956,Je 24,II,1:1;
1956,Jl 7,11:2; 1956,Ag 29,25:3; 1958,D 26,2:7;
1960,F 26,22:1; 1960,Je 30,23:1; 1963,Je 14,37:1;
1964,My 13,52:1; 1965,Je 29,27:2; 1966,Je 8,38:1;
1969,Je 9,57:1; 1969,Je 15,II,3:1; 1969,N 11,43:1
Henry VI 1953,Ag 9,II,1:2; 1963,Jl 18,14:1;
1964,Ja 14,24:7; 1966,Je 9,55:2
Henry VI, Part I 1964,Jl 21,29:1; 1964,Jl 23,18:1
Henry VI, Parts I, II, III 1970,Jl 5,II,3:1
Henry VI (Part III) 1957,O 18,19:5
Henry VIII 1926,Ja 3,VII,2:8; 1930,Jl 13,VIII,2:1;
1946,N 7,42:2; 1961,Je 22,22:1; 1961,Jl 2,II,1:1;
1969,O 11,42:1
Henry's Harem 1926,S 14,25:2
Her Cardboard Lover 1927,Mr 22,30:5;
1928,S 9,IX,2:7
Her Dearest Friend 1923,My 15,22:2
Her Family Tree 1920,D 28,9:2
Her First Affaire 1927,Ag 23,29:2
Her First Roman 1968,O 21,53:3; 1968,N 3,II,1:1
Her Friend the King 1929,O 8,34:5
Her Great Mistake 1940,F 5,12:6
Her Happiness 1922,O 8,VI,1:6
Her Last Adventure 1936,Mr 31,17:1
Her Majesty the Widow 1934,Je 19,24:5;
1937,Jl 14,16:2
Her Man of Wax 1933,O 12,32:3
Her Master's Voice 1933,O 24,24:3; 1933,D 10,X,3:1;
1964,D 28,33:2
Her Past 1929,F 10,IX,4:7
Her Salary Man 1921,N 29,20:1
Her Shop 1929,F 24,IX,4:3
Her Supporting Cast 1931,My 5,33:3
Her Temporary Husband 1922,S 1,16:2;
1923,My 13,VIII,3:5
Her Tin Soldier 1933,Ap 7,22:6
Her Unborn Child 1928,Mr 7,28:3
Her Way Out 1924,Je 24,18:3
Her Week-End 1936,Mr 20,28:5
Here Be Dragons 1970,D 21,52:1
Here Come the Clowns 1938,D 8,36:2;
1938,D 20,30:2; 1954,My 5,36:2; 1960,S 20,48:1
Here Comes Santa Claus 1962,My 18,34:1
Here Goes the Bride 1931,N 4,31:2
Here Lies Truth 1934,Ag 28,24:6
Here Runs the Bride 1934,S 20,21:3; 1934,N 4,IX,2:1
Here Today 1932,S 7,14:2; 1932,S 18,IX,1:1
Here Today, Gone Tomorrow 1940,D 5,32:6
Here's How 1934,F 23,22:4
Here's Home 1923,Ap 26,19:3
Here's Howe! 1928,My 2,19:3
Here's Josephine Premice 1966,Ap 26,54:4
Here's Love 1963,S 20,28:3; 1963,O 4,28:1
Here's Where I Belong 1968,Mr 4,32:1
Heritage 1933,Je 4,IX,1:3
Heritage and Its History, A 1965,My 19,42:1
Hermine, L' 1932,My 29,VIII,1:7
Hermonie 1929,Mr 3,VIII,4:8
Hernani 1930,Mr 2,II,1:5; 1930,Mr 23,IX,2:1
Herne's Egg, The 1960,S 20,48:1
Hero, The 1921,Mr 15,14:1; 1921,Mr 20,VI,1:1;
1921,S 6,13:2; 1921,S 11,VI,1:1
Hero Is Born, A 1937,O 2,18:6
Hero of Santa Maria, The 1926,My 1,10:1
Hero Rises Up, The 1968,N 9,26:2
Herod and Mariamne 1938,O 27,27:2
Herodienne, L' 1924,S 7,III,12:4
Heroes, The 1963,My 22,36:1
Heroic Years 1934,Ja 12,28:4
Heroine, The 1963,F 21,5:5; 1963,Je 16,II,1:1
Hershel, The Jester 1948,D 14,39:2
Hervey House 1935,My 18,21:2
Herzogin von Chicago, Die 1929,F 17,IX,2:3
He's Mine 1929,N 17,IX,2:4
Hetaerengespraeche 1927,Ja 9,VII,4:1
Heure du Berger, L' 1936,N 12,30:1
Heure H, L' 1936,My 31,X,2:1
Hey, Nonny, Nonny! 1932,Je 7,22:3
Hey Diddle Diddle 1937,Ja 22,24:2
Hey You, Light Man! 1963,Mr 2,5:2
Hi, Paisano 1961,O 2,36:2
Hi Ho Figaro 1947,Jl 23,18:8
Hi-Ya Gentlemen 1940,D 4,34:2
Hi Yank 1944,Ap 8,14:2
Hias 1925,Je 25,IX,1:2
Hickory Stick 1944,My 9,15:6
Hidden 1927,S 25,VIII,4:8; 1927,O 5,30:4
Hidden Horizon 1946,S 20,42:2
Hidden King, The 1957,Ag 21,21:1

Hidden River, The 1957,Ja 24,32:1; 1959,Ap 14,41:2
Hidden Stranger 1963,Ja 10,5:5; 1963,Ja 15,8:5
Hidden Years, The 1948,F 15,II,3:1
Hide and Seek 1934,Ag 7,20:2; 1957,Ap 3,26:1
High as a Kite 1940,N 23,12:8
High Button Shoes 1947,O 10,32:2; 1947,N 23,II,1:1;
1948,D 23,23:7; 1955,Mr 12,10:6
High Cost of Loving, The 1928,D 16,IX,2:1
High Flyers 1927,Je 26,VIII,1:1
High Gear 1927,O 7,24:3
High Ground, The 1951,F 21,31:2
High Hatters, The 1928,My 11,28:2
High John De Conquer 1969,Ap 23,39:1
High Kickers 1941,O 12,I,54:3; 1941,N 1,21:2
High Named Today 1954,D 11,11:2
High Road, The 1927,S 25,VIII,2:1; 1928,S 11,31:1
High Spirits 1964,Ap 8,34:1; 1964,N 4,46:4
High Stakes 1924,S 10,21:3
High Tor 1936,D 31,20:3; 1937,Ja 11,15:2;
1937,Ja 17,X,1:1
High Treason 1928,N 9,52:2; 1928,N 25,X,2:3
Higher and Higher 1940,Mr 17,X,2:5; 1940,Ap 5,24:3;
1940,Ag 6,15:4; 1940,Ag 11,IX,1:1
Highest Tree, The 1959,N 5,41:1
Highland Call, The 1939,N 21,19:1
Highland Fling, A 1944,Ap 29,13:2
Highway Robbery 1955,N 8,36:1
Hilarities 1948,S 10,20:2
Hilda Cassidy 1933,My 5,18:3
Hilda Crane 1950,N 2,38:2
Hill Between, The 1938,Mr 12,12:5
Him 1928,Ap 19,23:3; 1928,Ap 29,IX,1:1
Hindu, The 1922,Mr 22,13:3
Hinkeman 1924,Mr 2,VIII,2:1
Hipper's Holiday 1934,O 19,26:2
Hippolytus 1935,F 12,25:4; 1935,Je 15,20:4;
1948,N 22,25:5; 1968,N 20,38:3
Hired Husband 1932,Je 4,9:5
Hirsh Lekert 1936,Mr 11,23:2
His and Hers 1954,Ja 8,18:2
His Children 1926,My 4,30:2
His Chinese Wife 1920,My 18,9:3
His Excellency the Governor 1930,My 18,VIII,2:6
His Excellency's Last Will and Testament
1931,O 11,VIII,4:5
His House in Order 1951,Ag 12,II,1:4
His Jewish Girl 1936,D 9,34:1
His Majesty the Queen 1926,Mr 9,8:1
His Majesty's Car 1930,O 24,30:1
His Queen 1925,My 12,26:1
His Wife's Castle 1929,O 1,IX,2:2
His Wife's Lover 1929,O 21,30:6
His Wild Oat 1926,D 1,24:1
Hiss-Boom-Blah 1936,Ap 18,18:3
Histoire du Crocodile, L' 1926,O 3,VIII,2:1
Histoires de France 1929,O 27,IX,2:4
History as Was 1927,My 5,30:1
Hit the Deck! 1927,Ap 26,32:1; 1960,Je 24,32:1
Hit the Road 1941,Ap 4,18:3
Hit the Trail 1954,D 3,31:2
Hitch Your Wagon! 1937,Ap 9,18:2
Hitchy-Koo, 1920 1920,O 20,11:3
Hobo 1931,F 12,24:4; 1961,Ap 11,41:2
Hoboes in Heaven 1919,O 29,31:4
Hoboken Blues 1928,F 18,10:1; 1928,F 26,VIII,1:1;
1930,Ap 1,10:1
Hoboken Hoboes 1929,D 28,10:8
Hochste Eisenbahn 1932,O 23,IX,3:1
Hofmeister, Der 1963,Ag 10,9:1
Hogan's Goat 1965,N 12,56:1; 1965,N 21,II,1:2
Hokus Pokus 1928,Ja 29,VIII,4:1
Hold Everything 1928,S 2,VII,4:4; 1928,O 11,24:2
Hold It! 1948,My 6,31:5
Hold On to Your Hats 1940,Jl 17,25:3;
1940,S 12,30:3; 1940,S 29,IX,1:1
Hold Your Horses 1933,Ag 31,20:4; 1933,S 26,26:4;
1933,O 15,IX,1:1
Hole, The 1961,Ap 4,42:2
Hole in the Head, A 1957,Mr 1,15:1;
1957,Mr 10,II,1:1; 1958,N 26,25:2
Hole in the Wall, The 1920,Mr 27,11:1
Holiday 1928,N 27,36:1; 1928,D 9,X,1:1;
1930,F 6,21:2; 1941,Jl 23,15:2
Holiday for Lovers 1957,F 15,20:1
Holiday in Israel 1968,O 14,55:2
Holiday in Town, A 1935,S 30,12:3
Holiday on Broadway 1948,Ap 28,33:3
Holiday on Ice 1965,S 2,38:4; 1966,S 1,30:1;
1967,Ag 31,29:2; 1968,Ag 29,44:1; 1969,Ag 28,44:1
Holiday on Ice International 1955,Ag 29,17:5
Holka Polka 1925,O 15,27:2
Hollow Crown, The 1963,Ja 31,5:1
Holly and the Ivy, The 1950,My 21,II,3:2
Hollywood Holiday 1931,N 8,VIII,4:1
Hollywood Ice Revue 1942,Ja 20,26:4;
1943,Ja 24,II,1:1; 1950,Ja 21,13:4; 1953,Ja 16,17:2;
1954,Ja 15,16:2; 1955,Ja 14,16:1; 1956,Ja 13,17:1
Hollywood Music Box Revue, The 1929,Ja 6,VIII,4:4
Hollywood Party, A 1927,D 11,IX,2:5
Hollywood Pinafore 1945,Je 1,20:1; 1945,Je 10,II,1:1;
1945,Je 17,II,4:5
Holmeses of Baker Street, The 1936,D 10,34:3
Holy Night 1936,D 24,20:2; 1941,D 22,23:3

Holy Terror, A 1925,S 29,31:2
Homage to Shakespeare 1964,Mr 16,36:2
Home 1970,Je 20,23:1; 1970,Ag 17,32:1;
1970,N 18,41:1; 1970,N 29,II,1:1
Home and Beauty 1937,F 3,26:2; 1937,F 21,X,2:1
Home at Seven 1950,Mr 8,34:5
Home Away From, A 1969,Ap 29,40:3
Home Chat 1927,N 13,IX,2:1; 1932,F 7,VIII,3:1
Home Fires 1923,Ag 21,12:1; 1923,S 2,VI,1:1;
1969,Ap 8,42:1
Home Free! 1965,F 11,45:1
Home Is the Hero 1945,Ja 20,16:4; 1954,S 23,42:2
Home Is the Hunter 1945,D 21,25:4
Home Is Tomorrow 1948,N 22,25:4; 1948,D 12,II,4:7;
1950,Je 2,27:2
Home Life of a Buffalo 1948,My 12,34:6
Home Movies 1964,My 12,32:1
Home of the Brave 1945,D 28,13:2; 1946,Ja 6,II,1:1
Home on the Range 1968,My 21,42:1
Home Sweet Home 1936,Jl 1,29:2
Home Towners, The 1926,My 16,VIII,2:2;
1926,Ag 24,19:3; 1926,Ag 29,VII,1:1;
1926,S 5,VII,1:1
Homecoming 1931,O 27,22:1; 1932,My 10,25:2;
1942,N 17,28:5
Homecoming, The 1958,Ap 22,38:6; 1965,Je 4,38:8;
1967,Ja 6,29:1; 1967,Ja 15,II,1:1; 1967,Ja 22,II,1:4;
1967,O 5,47:3
Homeward Look, The 1954,Je 4,26:2
Homme, L' 1934,F 25,IX,2:3
Homme, la Bete et la Vertu, L' 1931,D 13,VIII,2:2
Homme a la Rose, L' 1921,S 11,VI,1:1
Homme au Foulard Bleu, L' 1935,My 26,XI,2:2
Homme Comme les Autres, Un 1937,F 28,XI,2:3
Homme de Joie, L' 1929,Mr 17,X,2:7
Homme d'Hier, L' 1929,My 19,IX,2:1
Homme En Or, Un 1927,Mr 13,VII,2:7
Homme et Ses Fantomes, L' 1924,Je 29,VII,1:8;
1924,N 14,16:1
Homme nu, L' 1932,Ap 3,VIII,2:1
Homme Que J'ai Tue, L' 1930,F 9,VIII,2:6;
1936,D 10,34:3
Homme Qui Assassina, L' 1924,N 11,20:1
Homme Qui Jouait du Banjo, L' 1926,O 24,VIII,2:1
Homme Qui N'est Plus de ce Nonde
1924,Mr 23,VIII,1:3
Homo 1969,Ap 12,40:2
Honest Liars 1926,Jl 20,17:2
Honest-to-God Schnozzola, The 1969,Ap 22,40:2
Honey Girl 1920,My 4,9:1
Honeydew 1920,S 7,20:1
Honeymoon 1932,D 11,IX,5:1; 1932,D 24,11:2
Honeymoon for Three, A 1933,Ja 30,9:6
Honeymoon in Israel, A 1962,O 15,33:5
Honeymoon Lane 1926,S 21,32:3
Honeymooning 1927,Mr 18,25:3
Honeymooning on High 1927,F 27,VII,4:6
Honeys, The 1955,Ap 29,26:1
Honor and Obey 1947,N 20,40:1
Honor and Offer 1968,D 1,II,3:1; 1969,My 14,36:1
Honor Be Damned! 1927,Ja 27,17:1
Honor Code, The 1931,My 19,25:3
Honor of the Family, The 1926,D 27,21:1
Honors Are Even 1921,Ag 11,8:2
Hoofers, The 1969,Jl 30,23:4
Hook-Up, The 1935,My 9,24:6
Hook'n Ladder 1952,Ap 30,31:2
Hoopla! 1929,Mr 10,X,4:6
Hooray for What! 1937,N 7,XI,2:4; 1937,D 2,32:5
Hooray!! It's a Glorious Day. . .And All That
1966,Mr 10,28:1
Hoosiers Abroad 1927,O 2,VIII,4:6
Hoot Mon, or Clans Across the Sea 1927,My 8,29:4
Hop, Signor! 1962,My 8,45:2
Hop Aboard 1936,Ag 16,II,3:4
Hopalong--Freud 1953,Je 18,38:5
Hope for a Harvest 1941,Ap 5,18:4; 1941,N 27,28:2;
1941,D 7,X,5:1
Hope for the Best 1945,F 8,14:4; 1945,F 18,II,1:1
Hope Is the Thing With Feathers 1948,Ap 12,24:2;
1948,My 12,34:6
Hope's the Thing 1948,My 12,34:6
Hoppla, Wir Leben! 1927,D 11,IX,4:1
Horrible Experience, L' 1923,O 23,16:1
Horse Eats Hat 1936,S 28,14:2
Horse Fever 1940,N 25,21:2
Horse Play 1937,Ag 28,8:3
Horse-Thief, The 1924,Ap 27,VIII,2:3
Horseman, Pass By 1964,Jl 16,46:4
Horses in Midstream 1953,Ap 3,18:7
Hortense, to Bed With You 1949,Jl 9,9:2
Hospitality 1922,N 14,16:1; 1922,D 3,VIII,1:1
Hostage, The 1960,S 21,42:1; 1960,O 2,II,1:1;
1960,O 30,II,1:1; 1961,D 13,55:4; 1962,N 30,28:1
Hostile Witness 1966,F 18,26:1
Hot-Cha! 1932,F 21,VIII,2:1; 1932,Mr 9,17:3;
1932,Mr 20,VIII,1:1
Hot Chocolates 1929,Je 21,17:4
Hot Corner, The 1956,Ja 26,25:2
Hot Feet 1970,D 22,38:1
Hot Mikado, The 1939,Mr 24,26:2; 1939,Ap 2,X,1:3;
1939,Je 23,23:4
Hot Money 1931,N 9,22:2

Hot Pan 1928,F 16,14:1; 1928,F 26,VIII,1:1
Hot Rhythm 1930,Ag 22,18:5
Hot Spot 1963,Ap 20,17:2
Hot Water 1929,Ja 22,22:3
Hotbed 1928,N 10,20:7
Hotel Alimony 1934,Ja 30,16:2
Hotel des Masques 1935,N 24,IX,3:7
Hotel in Amsterdam, The 1968,Jl 21,II,12:1;
1968,Ag 17,17:1
Hotel Mouse, The 1922,Mr 14,11:3
Hotel Paradiso 1956,My 3,34:8; 1957,Ap 12,22:2;
1957,Ap 21,II,1:1
Hotel Passionato 1965,O 23,16:1
Hotel Universe 1930,Ap 15,29:1; 1930,Ap 20,VIII,1:1;
1930,N 23,IX,1:3
Hotheads, The 1921,Je 12,VI,1:6
Hottentot, The 1920,Mr 2,9:1
Hour Glass, The 1930,O 26,VIII,4:6; 1955,O 17,33:1
House Afire 1930,Ap 1,34:7
House Beautiful, The 1931,Mr 13,20:4;
1931,Mr 22,VIII,1:1
House Divided, The 1923,N 12,14:1
House in Berlin, A (Als der Krieg zu Ende War)
1950,D 27,32:3
House in Paris, The 1944,Mr 21,17:1
House in the Country, A 1937,Ja 12,18:3
House in the Square 1940,Ap 14,IX,1:6
House of Atreus, The 1967,Jl 24,23:1;
1968,D 18,55:1
House of Bernarda Alba, The 1951,Ja 8,14:6;
1963,N 25,23:2
House of Borgia, The 1935,S 10,26:1;
1935,O 6,XI,3:1
House of Breath, The 1957,Ap 15,23:2
House of Connelly, The 1931,S 29,22:4;
1931,O 4,VIII,1:1
House of Doom, The 1932,Ja 26,20:4
House of Fear, The 1929,O 8,34:2
House of Flowers 1954,D 31,11:2; 1968,Ja 29,26:2
House of Leather, The 1969,My 18,II,3:1;
1970,Mr 19,56:1
House of Regrets 1942,O 18,VIII,1:5;
1948,Mr 14,II,2:4
House of Remsen 1934,Ap 3,26:4
House of Rothschild 1931,Mr 8,VIII,2:7
House of Shadows, The 1927,Ap 22,18:4
House of Ussher 1926,Ja 14,18:4
House of Women, The 1927,S 11,VIII,1:3;
1927,O 4,32:2; 1927,O 9,VIII,1:1
House on Cristo Street, The 1959,Ag 31,15:2
House on Grand Street, A 1953,O 10,12:6
House on the Lane, The 1949,My 9,3:3
House Remembered, A 1957,F 7,20:2
House Unguarded 1928,D 30,VIII,1:6;
1929,Ja 16,22:2
House With the Twisty Windows, The
1929,My 8,34:4; 1930,My 8,32:5
Houseboat on the Styx, The 1928,D 16,IX,2:1;
1928,D 26,14:3
Housekeeper, The 1957,N 18,36:5
Housemaster 1936,N 14,22:6
Houseparty 1929,S 10,26:5
Houses by the Green, The 1968,O 4,42:3
Houses of Sand 1925,F 18,17:1
Housewarming 1932,Ap 8,25:1
How a Nice Girl Named Janet Contracted Syphilis
1970,N 28,22:1
How Are They at Home? 1944,My 28,II,1:3
How Beautiful With Shoes 1935,N 29,24:1
How Come Lawd? 1937,O 1,18:5
How Come? 1923,Ap 17,26:1
How Do You Do? 1968,My 21,42:1;
1969,Ap 13,II,3:3
How D'you Do? 1933,Ap 26,13:4
How He Lied to Her Husband 1924,S 30,27:5;
1956,My 24,27:2
How I Wonder 1947,O 1,34:2
How Long Till Summer 1949,D 28,30:3
How Long Will You Love Me? 1931,Jl 19,VIII,2:3
How Much, How Much? 1970,F 15,II,1:1;
1970,Ap 21,49:1
How Now, Dow Jones 1967,D 8,53:1;
1967,D 22,38:1; 1967,D 24,II,3:2
How Pleasant to Know Mr Lear 1968,S 2,14:2
How Revolting! 1932,Mr 11,14:6
How the Other Half Loves 1970,Ag 7,23:1;
1970,S 11,33:2
How to Be a Jewish Mother 1967,D 29,18:1
How to Get Tough About It 1938,F 9,16:2
How to Make a Man 1961,F 3,16:1
How to Steal an Election 1968,O 14,56:1
How to Succeed in Business Without Really Trying
1961,O 16,34:1; 1963,Mr 30,5:4; 1964,F 12,30:1;
1964,Jl 18,10:1; 1966,Ap 21,45:1
Howdy, Mr Ice 1948,Je 25,28:5
Howdy, Mr Ice of 1950 1949,My 27,24:2
Howdy King 1926,O 17,VIII,2:4; 1926,D 14,24:4
Howdy Stranger 1937,Ja 15,17:5
Howie 1958,S 18,35:2
How's the World Treating You? 1966,O 25,50:1
How's Your Health? 1929,N 27,30:3
Hoy 1929,Ja 3,25:2
Hubby in Distress 1921,Ap 17,VI,1:1

Huckleberry 1962,Je 3,43:1
Hughie 1958,S 9,24:5; 1959,O 15,48:1;
1963,Je 11,29:4; 1964,D 23,21:2
Huis Clos 1962,Ja 16,30:1
Huitieme Femme de Barbe-Bleue, La 1936,Ja 27,20:5
Human Nature 1925,S 25,24:3
Humble, The 1926,O 14,22:2
Humbug, The 1929,N 28,34:5
Hummin' Sam 1933,Ap 10,8:8
Humming Bird, The 1923,Ja 16,16:2
Humoresque 1923,F 28,13:2; 1923,Mr 4,VII,1:1
Humours of the Court, The 1930,Ja 26,VIII,1:8
Humpty Dumpty 1932,S 18,IX,2:1
Hundert Meter Glueck 1933,F 19,IX,3:1
Hundred Days 1931,N 17,31:3; 1932,F 7,III,3:7;
1934,Ap 29,IX,2:3
Hundred Years Old, A 1928,D 9,X,2:1;
1929,Ap 19,27:5; 1929,O 2,28:2
Hunger und Durst 1965,Ja 19,28:6
Hungerers, The 1955,D 22,19:1
Hunky Dory 1921,My 29,VI,1:7; 1922,S 5,21:2
Hunted, The 1931,O 27,22:1; 1932,My 10,25:2
Hunter's Moon 1958,Mr 16,II,3:1
Hunting the Jingo Birds 1965,Mr 26,27:1
Hurricane 1923,D 26,13:4; 1934,D 23,IX,1:8
Husband Habit, The 1929,Mr 24,X,4:7
Husbands Are a Problem 1922,Ag 27,VI,1:5
Hush Money 1926,Mr 16,22:3
Hut a Yid a Landele 1968,O 19,28:1
Huui, Huui 1968,N 25,58:1; 1968,D 8,II,5:4
Hyde Park Corner 1934,O 6,20:1; 1934,O 28,IX,3:4
Hymn to the Rising Sun 1936,Ja 13,14:4;
1937,My 7,28:2

I

I Accuse 1937,O 26,19:1
I Am a Camera 1951,N 29,39:6; 1951,D 9,II,5:1;
1954,Mr 13,11:1; 1954,Ap 11,II,2:1; 1956,O 10,47:2;
1961,Jl 10,26:1
I Am Different 1938,Ag 28,IX,2:5
I Am My Youth 1938,Mr 8,22:4
I Can Get It for You Wholesale 1962,Mr 23,29:1;
1962,Ap 8,II,1:2
I Capture the Castle 1954,Ap 11,II,2:1
I Do! I Do! 1966,D 6,58:1; 1966,D 18,II,3:1;
1967,N 28,54:1
I Dream of Jeanie 1963,Je 25,23:1
I Dreamt I Dwelt in Bloomingdale's 1970,F 13,26:1
I Feel Wonderful 1954,O 19,22:5
I Forgot 1935,Mr 12,24:8; 1942,S 28,13:1
I Got Shoes 1963,Ja 25,12:2
I Gotta Get Out 1947,S 26,27:2
I Had a Ball 1964,D 16,50:1
I Have Been Here Before 1937,S 23,32:3;
1937,O 10,XI,1:4; 1938,O 14,26:2
I Hear It Kissing Me Ladies 1970,N 28,22:1
I Killed the Count 1937,D 11,23:4; 1942,S 4,18:1
I Knock at the Door 1956,Mr 19,27:5; 1957,S 30,27:2;
1964,N 26,53:2
I Know My Love 1949,F 24,29:2; 1949,Ap 23,10:2;
1949,N 3,36:1; 1949,N 20,II,1:1
I Know What I Like 1939,N 25,13:5
I Like It Here 1946,Mr 23,8:6
I Lived With You 1932,Ap 24,VIII,1:1
I Love an Actress 1931,S 18,29:2
I Love You and You'll Be Mine 1932,Mr 21,19:4
I Loved You Wednesday 1932,O 12,27:1
I Married an Angel 1938,My 12,26:2;
1938,My 22,XI,1:1
I Must Be Talking to My Friends 1967,N 17,59:1
I Must Love Someone 1939,F 8,18:7
I Myself 1934,My 10,24:6
I Never Sang for My Father 1968,Ja 26,30:1;
1968,F 4,II,1:1
I Only Want an Answer 1968,F 6,36:1
I Remember Mama 1944,O 20,16:2; 1944,O 29,II,1:1;
1948,Ap 11,II,3:1
I Rise in Flame, Cried the Phoenix 1959,Ap 15,30:1
I Saw a Monkey 1968,N 4,57:3
I Serve 1922,O 8,VI,1:7
I Shall Have a Child 1939,Ap 2,X,2:4
I Take Care of My Friends 1936,Jl 21,13:2
I Want a Policeman! 1936,Ja 15,15:5
I Want My Wife 1930,Mr 21,30:7
I Want to Go Home 1949,Je 5,15:3
I Want You 1961,S 15,29:1
I Was Dancing 1964,N 9,40:4
I Was Waiting for You 1933,N 14,23:3
I Will If You Will 1922,Ag 30,10:4
Ice-Bound 1923,Ja 21,VII,1:6; 1923,F 12,16:2;
1923,F 18,VII,1:1
Ice Capades 1952,S 12,18:1; 1953,S 11,25:1;
1954,S 16,37:1; 1955,S 15,38:1; 1956,S 13,41:2;
1957,S 5,33:2; 1958,S 4,33:2; 1959,S 4,12:1;
1960,S 1,30:1; 1961,Ag 31,24:4; 1962,Ag 30,34:1;
1963,Ag 29,37:2; 1964,Ag 27,27:2; 1966,Je 2,50:2;
1967,Je 2,33:1; 1969,Ja 8,42:1; 1970,Ja 7,35:1

Ice Follies 1937,D 22,29:1; 1939,D 5,38:2;
1941,D 2,32:2; 1957,Ja 16,36:1; 1958,Ja 15,26:2;
1959,Ja 14,30:1; 1960,Ja 13,20:1; 1961,Ja 11,25:2;
1962,Ja 10,24:6; 1963,Ja 10,5:2; 1964,Ja 8,41:2;
1965,Ja 13,35:1; 1966,Ja 12,27:6; 1967,Ja 11,51:1;
1969,My 23,38:1; 1970,My 23,27:1
Iceman Cometh, The 1946,O 10,31:3;
1946,O 20,II,1:1; 1946,O 27,II,1:1; 1948,Je 9,35:1;
1956,My 8,38:1; 1956,My 20,II,1:1; 1958,Ja 30,18:3;
1968,Ja 1,58:1
Icetime 1946,Je 21,20:5; 1947,My 29,28:2
Ich Tanze um die Welt mit Dir 1930,Ag 31,VIII,2:1
I'd Rather Be Right 1937,O 12,27:6;
1937,O 17,XI,2:1; 1937,O 26,18:2; 1937,N 3,28:2;
1937,N 14,XI,1:1; 1938,Ja 23,XI,1:6; 1939,F 21,15:4
Ideal Husband, An 1921,Mr 6,VI,1:7;
1946,Ap 14,II,2:1
Ides of March, The 1962,N 17,16:4; 1963,Ag 9,12:1
Idiot, The 1926,S 26,VIII,2:1; 1960,S 26,38:1;
1970,Jl 17,18:1; 1970,Jl 30,39:1
Idiote, L' 1960,S 16,39:4
Idiot's Delight 1936,Mr 10,26:7; 1936,Mr 25,25:2;
1936,Ap 12,IX,1:1; 1936,S 1,24:5; 1937,Ag 10,22:7;
1938,Mr 23,19:3; 1938,Ap 10,X,2:1;
1951,My 24,46:3; 1957,F 23,14:2; 1970,Mr 24,39:1
Idle Inn, The 1921,D 21,26:2; 1922,Ja 22,VI,1:1
If 1921,Je 26,VI,1:1; 1927,O 26,26:2;
1927,O 30,IX,1:1
If a Body 1935,Ap 21,II,8:3; 1935,My 1,25:3
If Booth Had Missed 1931,My 14,27:1; 1932,F 5,24:2;
1932,F 14,VIII,1:1
If Five Years Pass 1962,My 11,37:1
If Four Walls Told 1922,My 21,VI,1:6
If I Was Rich 1926,S 3,15:2; 1926,S 12,VIII,1:1
If I Were Rothschild 1940,Ja 1,28:7
If I Were You 1931,S 24,21:1; 1938,Ja 9,II,3:2;
1938,Ja 25,24:2
If I Wished To 1937,Ja 28,22:5
If in the Green Wood 1947,Ja 17,27:6
If Love Were All 1931,N 14,14:5
If the Rabbi Wants 1929,D 23,18:5
If the Shoe Fits 1946,D 6,29:4
If This Be Treason 1935,Jl 30,17:1; 1935,S 24,28:2;
1935,S 29,X,1:1
If Winter Comes 1923,F 4,VII,1:4; 1923,F 11,VII,1:4;
1923,Ap 3,26:1; 1923,Ap 8,VIII,1:1
If You Get It, Do You Want It? 1938,D 1,28:2
Ignorants Abroad, The 1960,My 24,43:2
Ihr Erster Ball 1930,N 25,30:3
IIIe Chambre, La 1929,N 24,X,2:1
'Il Tesoro D'Isacco 1928,Ja 26,17:1
I'll Be Home for Christmas 1967,Mr 14,54:1
I'll Say She Is 1924,My 20,15:1
I'll Take the High Road 1943,N 10,28:3
Illusion, L' 1928,D 16,IX,2:1
Illusioniste, L' 1927,Ja 11,36:5; 1933,D 3,IX,7:7
Illustrators' Show, The 1936,Ja 23,25:3
Illya Darling 1967,Ap 12,37:1; 1967,Ap 30,II,1:1;
1967,N 2,58:1
I'm Herbert 1967,Mr 14,54:1
I'm Solomon 1968,Ap 24,51:1
Im Weissen Roessel 1930,D 28,VIII,2:4;
1931,Ja 4,VIII,3:5
Image, L' 1928,Ja 1,VIII,2:3
Imaginary Cuckold, The 1958,My 7,43:1
Imaginary Invalid, The 1922,Jl 26,26:2;
1958,Ap 30,28:2; 1967,My 2,53:1; 1968,My 28,41:1
Imaginative Girl, The 1926,Ag 8,VII,3:1
Imbecile 1923,N 1,24:1
Immaculate Misconception, The 1970,O 28,63:3
Immodest Violet 1920,Ag 25,6:2; 1920,Ag 29,VI,1:1
Immoral Isabella 1927,O 28,20:3
Immoral Support 1935,S 3,24:3
Immoralist, The 1954,F 2,18:7; 1954,F 9,22:1;
1954,F 14,II,1:1; 1954,N 4,39:5; 1963,N 8,36:2
Immortal Beloved, The 1927,My 5,30:1
Immortal Garden 1934,O 19,26:3
Immortal Husband, The 1955,F 15,32:2
Immortal Thief, The 1926,O 4,21:1
Immortality, Ltd 1934,Mr 6,II,2:3
Imperatrice aux Rochers, L' 1927,Mr 20,VIII,2:4
Imperturbable Spirit, The 1955,Mr 8,23:2
Importance of Being Dressed, The 1963,N 3,87:3
Importance of Being Earnest, The 1925,Jl 28,24:2;
1926,My 4,30:1; 1926,O 3,VIII,2:1;
1930,Jl 27,VIII,1:8; 1936,O 22,31:2; 1939,Ja 13,16:2;
1939,S 17,X,2:3; 1947,Ja 24,18:6; 1947,Mr 4,30:2;
1947,Mr 9,II,1:1; 1963,F 27,5:2; 1968,Jl 6,9:1
Importance of Being Oscar, The 1961,Mr 15,45:2
Importance of Wearing Clothes, The 1951,D 11,44:7
Imported Wife, The 1924,N 2,VII,2:3
Impossible Years, The 1965,O 14,55:1
Impresario From Smyrna 1935,D 24,10:3
Impromptu, L' 1965,Mr 8,34:1
Impromptu at Versailles 1964,Mr 10,43:1
Impromptu de Versailles, L' 1961,F 22,30:1
Improper Duchess, The 1931,Ja 23,28:1;
1931,F 8,VIII,3:3
Improvisations in June 1928,F 27,16:5
In a Garden 1925,N 17,29:1; 1925,N 22,VIII,1:1
In a Jewish Grocery 2,15:2
In a Tenement House 1932,Ja 25,20:4

In Abraham's Bosom 1926,D 31,10:2;
  1927,F 20,VII,1:1
In and Out 1924,My 18,VII,2:4
In Any Language 1952,O 9,40:2; 1952,O 19,II,1:1
In April Once 1955,Mr 14,29:3
In Bamville 1924,Mr 16,VIII,2:1
In Bed We Cry 1944,N 15,20:2
In Circles 1967,O 14,12:1; 1967,N 5,II,1:7;
  1968,Je 28,36:1
In Clover 1937,S 21,29:1; 1937,O 14,23:1
In Command 1930,Mr 9,IX,4:3
In County Kerry 1947,D 29,21:5
In der Sache J Robert Oppenheimer 1964,N 3,27:2
In Dutch 1924,O 26,VIII,2:1
In Fondo Al Cuore 1930,D 8,27:1
In Gold We Trust 1936,S 1,24:1
In Good King Charles's Golden Days
  1939,Ag 13,28:1; 1939,Ag 20,IV,2:7;
  1939,S 3,IX,2:1; 1940,My 19,IX,1:4; 1952,D 11,46:2;
  1957,Ja 25,16:1; 1957,F 3,II,1:1
In Heaven and Earth 1936,Mr 27,24:8
In Heidelberg 1924,N 2,VII,2:3
In His Arms 1924,O 14,23:1
In His Own Write 1968,Je 20,50:5; 1968,Jl 9,30:2;
  1968,Jl 14,II,4:5
In-Laws 1934,O 25,28:2; 1960,O 17,32:4
In Love With Love 1923,Ag 7,20:1;
  1923,Ag 12,VI,1:1
In Old Kentucky 1935,Ag 27,23:4
In Splendid Error 1954,O 27,33:6
In the Bag 1936,D 18,30:2
In the Bar of a Tokyo Hotel 1969,My 12,54:1;
  1969,My 25,II,5:4
In the Beginning (Back to Methuselah, Part I)
  1922,F 28,17:2
In the Best of Families 1931,F 3,29:1; 1937,Jl 1,32:5
In the Claws of Life 1923,N 30,23:4; 1923,D 9,IX,1:1
In the Counting House 1962,D 15,5:5
In the Dark 1937,F 11,18:3
In the Days of the Turbins 1934,Mr 7,22:5
In the Groove 1938,Ap 22,14:5
In the Heat of the Night 1969,F 6,12:3
In the Jungle of Cities 1960,D 21,39:1;
  1961,Ja 15,II,1:1
In the Land of the Midnight Sun 1930,Ja 7,27:4
In the Matter of J Robert Oppenheimer
  1968,My 27,55:1; 1968,Je 7,31:1; 1968,Je 9,II,1:1;
  1969,Mr 7,28:1; 1969,Mr 16,II,1:3
In the Meantime 1930,D 7,IX,1:6
In the Near Future 1925,Mr 11,19:1
In the Next Room 1923,O 3,15:3; 1923,N 28,14:1;
  1923,D 23,VII,1:1; 1924,Je 7,16:5
In the Nick of Time 1967,Je 2,36:1
In the Night Watch 1921,Ja 31,10:1
In the Penal Colony 1962,My 4,27:2
In the Shadow of the Glen 1957,Mr 7,24:1;
  1957,Mr 17,II,1:1
In the Snare 1924,Jl 13,VII,1:6
In the Summer House 1953,D 30,17:1;
  1954,Ja 10,II,1:1; 1964,Mr 26,43:1
In the Train 1937,N 22,14:5
In the Wine Time 1968,D 22,II,7:1
In the Zone 1929,Ja 27,IX,1:1; 1930,F 9,VIII,2:1;
  1937,O 30,23:2; 1948,My 21,21:2;
  1948,My 30,II,1:1; 1961,My 11,43:1;
  1963,Je 11,29:4
In Theatre Street 1937,Ap 29,17:5; 1937,My 16,X,2:2
In 3 Zones 1970,N 3,28:1
In Time to Come 1941,D 29,20:2; 1942,Ja 4,IX,1:1
In Times Square 1931,N 24,29:3
In White America 1963,N 1,26:1; 1965,F 9,42:5
Inadmissible Evidence 1964,S 10,31:1; 1965,D 1,52:1
Incendio Doloso, L' 1931,N 16,22:4
Incident at Vichy 1964,D 4,44:1; 1964,D 20,II,3:1;
  1966,Ja 27,28:5
Inconnue d'Arras 1935,D 29,IX,2:1
Inconstant Moon, The 1937,Ag 18,15:2
Increased Difficulty of Concentration, The
  1969,D 5,48:1; 1969,D 21,II,3:1
Incubator 1932,N 2,23:3
India 1928,Ja 17,23:3
Indian Captive, The 1949,Ja 31,15:2
Indian Summer 1929,Ja 13,VIII,2:4; 1936,Ap 20,17:5;
  1936,My 17,IX,2:2
Indian Wants the Bronx, The 1968,Ja 18,47:2;
  1968,Je 30,II,1:1
Indiana 1935,D 29,IX,2:1
Indians 1968,Jl 9,30:2; 1968,Jl 21,II,12:1;
  1969,My 18,II,3:5; 1969,My 27,43:1;
  1969,O 14,51:1; 1969,O 19,II,1:1
Indifferent Shepherd, The 1948,Mr 14,II,2:4
Indiscretion 1929,Mr 5,28:1
Indoor Fireworks 1934,Mr 30,26:6
Infancy 1962,Ja 12,28:1; 1962,Ja 21,II,1:1
Infantry, The 1966,N 15,51:1
Infernal Machine, The 1937,D 13,22:7;
  1954,Mr 22,22:2; 1958,F 4,33:1
Infinite Shoeblack, The 1929,My 5,IX,1:3;
  1929,D 1,X,4:7; 1930,F 18,28:1; 1930,Mr 2,IX,1:1
Information Bureau, The 1962,Ja 31,21:1
Ingeborg 1933,D 11,23:3
Inherit the Wind 1955,Ja 12,24:1; 1955,Ap 22,20:2;
  1955,S 25,II,1:1; 1967,Je 23,50:1

Inheritors 1921,Mr 27,VII,1:2; 1925,S 28,24:3;
  1926,Ja 3,VII,2:8; 1927,Mr 8,23:1;
  1927,Mr 20,VIII,1:1
Injunction Granted! 1936,Jl 25,16:3
Injury Sustained 1940,O 24,30:3
Ink 1927,O 23,VIII,1:3; 1927,N 2,24:2
Inner Journey, The 1969,Mr 21,42:1
Innkeepers, The 1956,F 3,19:1
Innocent as Hell 1960,Je 30,2:6
Innocent Eyes 1924,My 21,22:2
Innocent Idea, An 1920,My 26,9:4
Innocent Party, The 1938,F 13,X,3:3
Innocent Voyage, The 1943,N 16,27:2
Innocente, L' 1928,Jl 1,VIII,1:8
Innocents, The 1950,F 2,30:2; 1950,F 12,II,1:1;
  1952,Jl 4,9:7; 1959,Ap 21,41:2
Inquest 1931,Jl 19,VIII,1:8; 1970,Ap 24,38:1;
  1970,My 3,II,3:1
Insect Comedy, The 1922,N 5,VIII,1:1;
  1923,My 13,VIII,3:5; 1936,Jl 26,IX,1:3
  1948,Je 4,26:3
Inside Out 1969,D 2,64:1
Inside Stand, The 1935,N 22,18:1
Inside Story 1942,O 30,22:2
Inside Story, The 1932,F 23,23:2
Inside the Room 1934,D 23,15:3
Inside U S A 1948,Mr 30,27:3; 1948,My 1,19:2;
  1948,My 23,II,1:1; 1948,Je 13,II,6:6;
  1948,Ag 29,II,1:1
Inspector Calls, An 1946,O 13,II,2:3; 1947,O 22,38:2
Inspector General, The 1922,O 9,15:4;
  1923,My 1,24:1; 1930,D 24,19:2; 1935,F 18,19:6;
  1935,F 24,VIII,3:1
Inspector Kennedy 1929,D 21,16:3
Instructions for the Running of Trains, etc on the
  Erie Railway to Go Into Effect January 1,1862
  1970,Ja 7,36:2; 1970,Ja 11,II,1:1
Insult 1930,My 4,XI,1:3; 1930,S 16,30:2
Interference 1927,F 20,VII,1:4; 1927,F 27,VII,1:3;
  1927,O 2,VIII,4:6; 1927,O 19,24:3;
  1927,D 18,IX,1:1; 1928,My 8,25:4
Interlock 1958,F 7,18:1
Intermezzo 1933,Mr 26,IX,2:1; 1957,F 15,20:4
International, The 1928,Ja 16,24:4
International Ice Frolics, The 1938,My 7,18:3
International Incident, An 1940,Mr 21,30:3;
  1940,Ap 3,18:2
International Playgirls '64 1964,My 22,40:2
International Revue 1930,F 9,VIII,4:2; 1930,F 26,22:2
International Set, The 1953,Je 12,19:3
International Soiree 1958,Mr 13,25:1
Intervention 1936,O 11,X,1:4
Interview 1966,N 7,66:1; 1967,Ag 13,II,3:6;
  1967,O 10,55:2; 1969,N 4,55:2
Intimate Relations 1932,Mr 29,23:2; 1962,N 2,27:1;
  1962,N 25,II,1:1
Intimate Strangers, The 1921,N 8,28:1
Into Thin Air 1955,My 25,39:1
Intruder, The 1928,Jl 26,25:4
Invasores, Los 1970,D 12,20:1
Investigation, The 1965,O 21,55:3; 1966,O 5,40:1;
  1966,N 13,II,1:1
Invitation au Voyage, L' 1928,O 5,17:1;
  1930,Ja 26,VIII,1:8
Invitation to a Beheading 1969,Mr 18,36:1;
  1969,Mr 30,II,1:1
Invitation to a March 1960,O 31,27:2
Invitation to a Murder 1934,My 18,26:3
Invites de Bon Dieu, Les 1953,N 29,II,3:1
Iolanthe 1920,Ja 6,13:3; 1926,Ap 20,24:2;
  1926,Ap 25,VIII,1:1; 1927,N 15,26:3;
  1931,Jl 14,21:5; 1932,Ja 5,20:2; 1934,My 1,26:4;
  1934,S 11,24:3; 1936,My 5,26:2; 1936,S 22,30:3;
  1939,Ja 13,16:3; 1942,F 24,26:4; 1944,F 23,17:1;
  1948,Ja 13,29:3; 1951,F 16,22:1; 1952,N 11,26:3;
  1954,Ap 28,36:8; 1955,S 28,38:1; 1961,My 26,9:6;
  1962,Ap 12,42:4; 1962,Ag 8,34:2; 1962,N 28,42:1;
  1964,N 18,52:1; 1965,My 19,42:1; 1967,O 18,40:1;
  1968,N 9,37:3
Iphigenia 1931,Ja 6,24:1
Iphigenia in Aulis 1921,Ap 8,18:2; 1921,Ap 17,VI,1:1;
  1962,N 11,82:4; 1967,N 22,40:2; 1967,D 3,II,1:1;
  1968,Ap 6,43:1; 1968,N 13,40:1
Iphigenia in Delphi 1962,N 11,82:4
Iphigenie in Tauris 1915,Je 1,15:5; 1949,Ap 9,8:1;
  1949,O 22,11:2
Irish Faustus, An 1963,D 19,40:1
Irkutsk Story, An 1961,Ap 18,44:1
Irma la Douce 1960,S 30,31:2; 1960,O 16,II,1:1;
  1960,O 30,II,1:1
Iron Flowers 1933,Je 13,22:2; 1933,Je 18,VIII,5:2
Iron Men 1936,O 20,30:6
Irregular Verb to Love, The 1963,S 19,22:2;
  1963,S 29,II,1:1
Irving Berlin's Music Box Revue 1921,S 23,18:2
Irving Berlin's New Music Box Revue
  1922,O 24,18:1
Is It Murder? 1951,Je 3,54:5
Is Life Worth Living? 1933,S 17,X,1:6;
  1933,N 10,24:6
Is This a Zither? 1935,Je 11,24:3
Is Your Honeymoon Really Necessary?
  1944,S 10,II,2:6

Is Zat So? 1925,Ja 6,23:4; 1925,F 1,VII,1:1;
  1925,Ap 25,18:2
Isabel 1925,Ja 14,19:1
Isabel, Edward and Anne 1923,Ap 8,VIII,1:7
Isabel's a Jezebel 1970,D 27,II,3:1
Island, The 1938,F 11,27:5
Island of Goats 1955,O 5,40:1
Isle of Children 1962,Mr 17,16:2
Ist Geraldine ein Engel? 1946,N 4,33:4
Istruttoria, L' 1933,F 13,11:3
It All Depends 1925,Ag 11,16:4
It Can't Happen Here 1936,O 28,30:3;
  1936,O 28,30:1; 1936,N 8,X,1:1; 1936,N 29,XII,3:3;
  1938,Jl 26,22:2
It Could Happen to You 1957,O 28,30:5
It Happened One Night 1944,Je 21,23:4
It Happened to Adam 1934,N 10,18:6;
  1934,N 25,IX,3:1
It Happened Tomorrow 1933,My 6,11:5
It Happens on Ice 1940,O 11,24:3; 1941,Ap 5,13:2;
  1941,Ag 31,IX,1:1
It Is the Law 1922,N 30,28:2
It Is to Laugh 1927,D 27,24:2
It Makes a Difference 1928,Ja 22,VIII,4:7
It Never Rains 1929,N 20,26:4; 1931,D 25,29:3
It Pays to Advertise 1924,F 10,VII,2:4
It Pays to Sin 1933,N 4,18:6
It Takes Two 1947,F 4,33:4
Italian Girl, The 1968,Jl 4,14:1
Italian Straw Hat, The 1957,O 1,37:2
Italienische Nacht 1931,My 10,VIII,1:5
Itche Mayer of Warsaw 1935,Ja 31,22:4
It's a Bird . . . It's a Plane . . . It's Superman
  1966,Mr 30,34:1
It's a Boy! 1922,Jl 23,VI,1:6; 1922,S 20,18:3
It's a Funny World 1956,O 22,24:1
It's A Gift 1945,Mr 13,18:7
It's a Grand Life 1930,F 2,VIII,2:7; 1930,F 11,30:3
It's a Small World 1938,N 7,22:4
It's a Wise Child 1929,Jl 28,VIII,1:6; 1929,Ag 7,29:1;
  1929,Ag 25,VIII,1:1; 1933,My 17,15:2
It's About Time 1942,Mr 31,28:3
It's All Yours 1942,Mr 26,26:2; 1962,Ap 25,31:1
It's an Ill Wind 1957,Ap 24,28:1
It's Called the Sugar Plum 1968,Ja 18,47:2
It's Never Too Late for Happiness 1968,O 21,59:3
It's Only Natural 1922,Ap 21,13:2
It's the Valet 1933,D 15,25:4
It's Up to You 1921,Mr 29,20:1; 1943,Ap 1,19:1
It's You I Want 1933,Mr 19,IX,2:2; 1935,F 6,23:3
Ivan the Terrible 1944,N 12,II,1:6
Ivanoff 1923,N 27,23:2
Ivanov 1958,O 8,42:1; 1958,O 19,II,1:1;
  1966,My 4,50:1; 1966,My 15,II,1:1
I've Got Sixpence 1952,D 3,44:2; 1952,D 7,II,5:1
Ivory Branch, The 1956,My 25,27:1
Ivory Door, The 1927,O 19,24:5; 1929,My 5,IX,1:3
Ivy Green, The 1949,Ap 6,37:2
Izzy 1924,S 17,16:2

J

J B 1958,Ap 24,37:1; 1958,My 4,II,1:1; 1958,D 12,2:7;
  1959,My 10,II,1:1; 1964,N 11,38:6
Jack 1958,Je 4,39:2
Jack and Jill 1923,Mr 23,17:2
Jack and the Beanstalk 1947,N 3,28:2
Jack Benny 1963,Mr 1,10:5
Jack in the Box 1960,My 19,43:3
Jack in the Pulpit 1925,Ja 7,33:1
Jack Jack 1968,Je 23,74:5
Jack MacGowran in the Works of Samuel Beckett
  1970,N 20,32:1; 1970,N 27,46:1; 1970,N 29,II,1:1
Jack o' Diamonds 1935,F 26,17:3
Jackass, The 1960,Mr 24,39:2
Jackhammer, The 1962,F 6,26:2
Jackknife 1958,S 23,36:2
Jackpot 1944,Ja 14,15:2
Jack's Up 1930,N 23,IX,3:5
Jackson White 1935,Ap 22,14:6
Jacob 1942,Je 14,VIII,1:7
Jacob and the Angel 1965,Ja 6,32:1
Jacob Slovak 1927,O 6,28:4
Jacobowsky and the Colonel 1944,Mr 15,17:2;
  1944,Mr 19,II,1:1; 1944,My 21,II,1:1;
  1945,Je 24,II,1:3
Jacob's Dream 1926,N 21,VIII,1:3; 1927,Ja 4,20:2;
  1927,N 14,21:1
Jacqueline 1921,N 20,VI,1:3
Jacques Bergson 1936,O 31,24:6; 1936,N 29,XII,3:3
Jacques Brel Is Alive and Well and Living in Paris
  1968,Ja 23,25:2; 1970,Ja 21,34:1; 1970,F 15,II,1:1
Jade God, The 1929,My 14,28:3
J'ai tue 1928,O 28,IX,2:7
J'Aime 1927,Ja 23,VII,2:1
Jakey Fat Boy 1970,Ap 6,46:1
Jalousie, La 1930,N 23,IX,1:1; 1932,Jl 3,IX,1:3;
  1932,D 4,IX,3:6
Jalousie du Barbouille, La 1937,D 28,28:7;
  1958,My 7,43:1
Jam Today 1942,Mr 1,VIII,1:3
Jamaica 1957,N 1,32:2; 1957,N 10,II,1:1

Jamboree 1932,N 25,18:4
Jane 1947,Ja 30,19:6; 1947,F 9,II,3:7; 1952,F 2,10:2;
  1952,F 10,II,1:1
Jane Brady-Editor 1935,Jl 2,24:3
Jane Clegg 1920,F 25,14:1; 1920,F 29,V,5:1;
  1920,Mr 28,V,6:1; 1926,D 12,VIII,4:7
Jane Eyre 1936,F 28,19:2; 1936,O 14,31:3;
  1936,N 8,X,3:4; 1937,Ja 3,X,2:1; 1937,F 7,X,1:1;
  1958,My 2,31:1
Jane-Our Stranger 1925,O 9,27:2
Jane's Legacy 1930,D 17,30:4; 1935,Ag 13,20:3
Janie 1942,S 11,24:2
January Thaw 1946,F 5,18:2
Janus 1955,N 25,37:2; 1956,Je 12,39:6;
  1957,Ap 25,34:2
Jar, The 1969,Ap 23,42:1; 1969,My 4,II,3:1
Jardin des Delices, Le 1969,N 4,54:1
Jardin des Supplices, Le 1929,Ap 21,X,2:7
Jarnegan 1928,S 16,IX,2:4; 1928,S 25,29:2
Jaselka 1965,Ja 6,32:1
Jason 1942,Ja 22,12:2
Javelin 1966,N 10,63:1
Jay Walker, The 1926,F 9,23:1
Jayhawker 1934,O 16,31:4; 1934,N 6,34:2
Jazz 1927,Ja 23,VII,2:1
Jazz a La Carte 1922,Je 3,8:3
Jazz Age 1937,Jl 20,19:3
Jazz and Minuet 1927,My 6,20:3
Jazz King, The 1924,Ap 6,VIII,2:1
Jazz Singer, The 1925,S 15,29:2
Jazz Train 1955,Ap 28,26:4
Je Serai Seule Apres Minuit 1927,O 23,VIII,2:2
Je T'Attendais 1929,Ja 20,VIII,1:8
Je Veux d'Etre Heureux 1928,My 13,IX,2:2
Je Vivrai un Grand Amour 1935,Jl 21,IX,1:6
Jealous God, The 1939,Mr 26,X,3:1
Jealous Moon, The 1928,O 21,IX,2:1; 1928,N 21,32:2
Jealous Wife, The 1930,N 16,VIII,4:1
Jealousy 1928,O 23,32:2; 1928,D 6,31:2;
  1934,D 20,31:4; 1936,S 28,14:3
Jealousy of the Barbouille, The 1958,My 7,43:1
Jean Christophe 1924,D 28,VII,1:1
Jean de la Lune 1929,My 12,IX,5:3; 1937,D 14,33:3
Jean le Mauranc 1927,Ja 2,VII,2:1
Jeanne 1932,N 27,IX,3:1
Jeanne d'Arc 1922,Ap 22,9:3
Jeanne de Pantin 1933,D 17,IX,5:8
Jeannette 1960,Mr 25,20:2
Jeannie 1940,F 18,IX,2:5; 1940,Ap 14,IX,1:7;
  1940,N 13,29:2
Jeb 1946,F 22,20:2; 1946,Mr 3,II,1:1
Jedermann 1927,D 8,33:2; 1927,D 18,IX,6:1
Jeff Chandler 1970,N 28,22:1
Jefferson Davis 1936,F 19,17:2
Jeg Skal Ha' et Barn 1939,Ap 2,X,2:4
Jehanne d'Arc 1925,Je 13,10:1; 1925,Jl 12,VII,1:1
Jehovah Joe 1929,Ag 25,VIII,3:1
Jemand 1931,D 13,VIII,3:6; 1932,Ja 17,VIII,2:2
Jennie 1963,O 18,35:2
Jenny 1929,Je 2,VIII,1:2; 1929,O 9,34:4
Jenny Kissed Me 1948,D 24,12:2
Jeppe vom Berge 1932,S 4,IX,2:1
Jeremiah 1939,F 4,11:2
Jericho-Jim Crow 1964,Ja 13,25:3; 1968,Mr 23,22:2
Jerry for Short 1929,Ag 13,23:4
Jerry Lewis' Variety Show 1957,F 8,18:5
Jest, The 1920,F 1,VIII,2:2; 1926,F 5,22:2;
  1926,F 14,VIII,1:1; 1930,N 24,26:4
Jesters, The 1938,Mr 14,13:3
Jeu de l'Amour et de la Mort, Le 1928,F 19,VIII,4:4
Jeu de l'Amour et du Hasard, Le 1955,N 16,42:4
Jeune Fille a Marier, La 1970,My 6,49:1
Jeune Fille a Reve, Une 1935,My 5,IX,2:4
Jeune Homme Venait de Se Pendre, Un
  1926,O 31,VIII,2:4
Jew of Malta, The 1965,Ap 17,9:1
Jew Suss 1929,O 6,IX,1:3; 1929,O 19,22:3;
  1931,N 8,VIII,4:4; 1936,Ag 16,X,2:5
Jew! 1968,My 9,55:2
Jewel of the South, The 1957,N 18,36:5
Jewel Robbery 1932,Ja 14,17:2; 1932,F 10,27:1;
  1932,F 21,VIII,2:3
Jeweled Tree, The 1926,O 8,26:2
Jewish Heart, The 1939,Ja 25,16:6
Jewish Melody, The 1933,Mr 27,12:4
Jewish Wife 1961,N 15,52:2
Jezebel 1933,D 20,26:3
Jig Saw 1934,My 1,26:3
Jill Darling 1934,D 20,29:8
Jim Cooperkop 1930,O 18,23:1
Jim Dandy 1941,N 8,10:5
Jim Jam Jems 1920,O 5,13:2
Jim the Penman 1928,D 2,X,4:2
Jimmie 1920,N 18,15:3
Jimmie's Women 1927,S 27,30:3
Jimmy 1969,O 24,38:1; 1969,N 9,II,1:1
Jimmy Roselli Show, The 1969,My 3,39:1
Jimmy Shine 1968,D 6,52:1; 1968,D 22,II,3:1
Jitta's Atonement 1923,Ja 18,16:3; 1925,F 1,VII,2:1;
  1935,Ja 31,22:3
Jo 1964,F 13,25:1
Joan At The Stake 1954,Je 25,15:3

Joan of Arc 1925,Je 21,VIII,1:2; 1926,Ap 24,21:2;
  1927,Ap 15,26:2
Joan of Arc-The Warrior Maid 1931,N 9,21:6
Joan of Arkansas 1925,Ap 5,16:1
Joan of Lorraine 1946,N 19,40:2; 1946,N 24,II,1:1;
  1947,N 14,29:1; 1955,Mr 26,12:2
Job, The 1964,Ag 1,13:1
Job's Kinfolks 1929,N 24,31:1
Joe Egg 1968,F 2,26:1; 1968,F 11,II,1:1;
  1968,Ap 27,43:2
Joe et Cie 1932,Je 12,X,1:2
Johannes Kreisler 1922,D 25,20:3; 1923,Ja 21,VII,1:1
John 1927,N 5,16:4
John Brown 1934,Ja 23,22:3; 1950,My 4,32:7
John Brown's Body 1931,Ja 12,24:2;
  1931,F 1,VIII,2:4; 1952,N 3,25:8; 1952,D 16,43:5;
  1953,F 16,17:2; 1953,F 22,II,1:1; 1960,Je 22,31:1;
  1964,Je 29,33:1; 1968,F 13,49:2
John Bull's Other Island 1948,F 11,33:4
John Ferguson 1921,My 24,20:1; 1921,Je 21,20:2;
  1928,Ja 18,23:1; 1933,Jl 11,15:7
John Gabriel Borkman 1926,Ja 30,13:1;
  1926,Ja 31,VII,1:1; 1946,N 13,33:2; 1959,N 26,57:4
John Hawthorne 1921,Ja 24,16:1; 1921,Ja 30,VI,1:1
John Henry 1939,D 12,36:4; 1939,D 17,IX,5:6;
  1940,Ja 11,18:2
John Loves Mary 1947,F 5,29:2
John Murray Anderson's Almanac 1953,D 11,42:2
John Turner Davis 1958,Jl 2,25:1
Johnny Belinda 1940,S 19,26:2
Johnny Doodle 1942,Mr 19,28:2
Johnny Johnson 1936,N 19,XII,1:1; 1936,N 20,26:3;
  1941,My 3,20:2; 1956,O 22,24:1
Johnny No-Trump 1967,O 9,60:2
Johnny on the Spot 1942,Ja 9,24:2
Johnny Spielt Auf 1928,Ap 15,IX,4:1
Johnny Summit 1957,S 25,23:4
Johnny 2X4 1942,Mr 17,24:6
Johnson Over Jordan 1939,Mr 12,XI,3:5;
  1939,Ap 2,X,1:6
Joies du Capitole, Les 1935,Ap 21,IX,2:1
Joint Owners in Spain 1929,My 7,28:1
Joker, The 1925,N 17,29:1
Joker Wild 1955,My 20,19:4
Jolly Joker, The 1928,O 28,IX,2:1
Jolly Orphan, The 1929,D 23,18:6
Jolly Roger 1933,Mr 26,IX,1:1
Jolly Roger, The 1923,Ag 31,10:4; 1923,S 9,VII,1:1
Jolly Tailors, The 1923,N 3,13:3
Jolly Village, The 1937,N 15,15:5
Jolly Wedding, The 1937,N 17,26:3
Jolly World, A 1931,Ja 24,15:3
Jollyanna 1952,Ag 13,17:7
Jolly's Progress 1959,D 7,42:2
Jonah and the Whale 1933,Ja 8,IX,3:3;
  1940,My 5,II,8:4
Jonah! 1966,F 16,52:1; 1967,S 22,52:2
Jonesy 1929,F 24,IX,4:1; 1929,Ap 10,32:2
Jonica 1930,Mr 30,VIII,2:7; 1930,Ap 8,27:1
Jonny's Busenfreund 1921,D 11,VI,1:4
Josef Suss 1930,Ja 21,28:5
Joseph 1930,F 13,25:3
Josephine 1934,S 26,17:5; 1934,O 14,X,3:1
Josephine Baker and Her Company 1964,F 5,30:1
Josephus 1933,D 1,22:5
Jotham Valley 1951,F 7,37:2
Journalisten, Die 1932,Jl 17,IX,1:1
Journees Entieres dans les Arbres, Des 1965,D 4,20:1
Journey by Night, A 1935,Ap 7,IX,2:1;
  1935,Ap 17,26:3
Journey in the Night, A 1932,Ja 31,VIII,2:1
Journey of Benjamin III, The 1928,Je 24,VIII,1:4
Journey of the Fifth Horse, The 1966,Ap 22,36:1;
  1966,My 8,II,1:1
Journey to Jefferson 1964,Jl 9,24:3
Journey to Jerusalem 1940,O 7,21:2
Journey to Pressburg, The 1931,Mr 8,VIII,2:7
Journey to the Day 1963,N 12,49:1
Journey With Strangers, A 1958,N 27,53:1
Journeyman 1938,Ja 31,14:2
Journey's End 1928,D 30,VIII,4:1; 1929,Ja 23,20:3;
  1929,F 10,IX,4:7; 1929,Mr 23,23:1;
  1929,Mr 31,VIII,1:1; 1929,Jl 14,IX,5:1;
  1929,S 15,IX,2:6; 1929,S 22,IX,4:1; 1930,Ja 27,24:7;
  1930,Mr 23,4:3; 1930,Mr 30,VIII,3:4;
  1930,Ag 5,26:4; 1930,Ag 24,VIII,2:7;
  1939,S 19,29:2; 1939,S 24,IX,1:1; 1968,O 28,55:3
Joy 1927,Ag 14,VII,1:7; 1970,Ja 28,50:1
Joy Forever, A 1946,Ja 8,20:2
Joy of Living 1931,Ap 7,31:1
Joy of Serpents 1930,Ap 4,22:4
Joy to the World 1948,Mr 19,28:2; 1948,Mr 28,II,1:1
Joy Will Come Back 1937,Mr 22,27:3
Joyce Grenfell 1958,Ap 8,32:1
Joyce Grenfell Requests the Pleasure 1955,O 11,48:1
Joyful Noise, A 1966,D 16,57:1
Joyous Season, The 1934,Ja 30,16:3; 1934,F 4,IX,1:1;
  1935,N 24,II,9:2
Juan de Manara 1927,Ag 28,VII,2:1
Juarez and Maximilian 1925,My 27,26:3;
  1926,O 12,31:1; 1926,O 17,VIII,1:1

Jubilee 1935,S 23,20:3; 1935,S 29,X,1:1;
  1935,O 14,20:1; 1935,O 27,IX,1:1;
  1935,N 24,IX,8:1
Jud Suess 1930,N 30,IX,2:1
Judas 1929,Ja 25,20:4
Judas Applause, The 1969,My 4,II,1:5
Judge, The 1954,My 14,36:2
Judges, The 1963,Je 6,40:8
Judge's Husband, The 1926,S 19,IX,1:3;
  1926,S 28,31:1
Judgment Day 1934,S 13,26:4; 1934,S 23,X,1:1;
  1937,My 20,16:1; 1937,Je 20,X,1:7; 1939,D 3,IX,7:6
Judicial Inquiry 1933,F 13,11:3
Judgment of Dr Johnson, The 1932,F 7,VIII,2:4
Judith 1922,O 13,14:2; 1924,Mr 2,VIII,2:7;
  1931,N 29,VIII,3:1; 1962,Je 21,25:4;
  1965,Mr 25,42:2; 1965,Ap 4,II,1:1
Judith of Israel 1928,F 17,24:2; 1928,Mr 18,IX,4:8
Judy 1927,F 8,20:2
Judy Drops In 1924,O 6,24:2
Judy Garland 1959,My 12,40:1; 1961,Ap 24,36:1
Judy Garland's New Variety Show 1956,S 27,43:2
Jugend im Mai 1927,Ja 23,VII,4:5
Juggernaut 1929,My 19,IX,3:2
Juice 1969,D 9,67:2
Jules, Juliette et Julien, ou L'Ecole du Sentiment
  1929,Je 9,VIII,2:4
Julia 1936,D 27,X,7:8
Julia, Jake, and Uncle Joe 1961,Ja 30,19:1
Julie 1927,My 10,24:4
Julie the Great 1936,Ja 15,15:3
Juliet and Romeo 1921,My 17,20:3
Juliette, ou La Cle des Songes 1930,Mr 30,VIII,2:4
Julius Caesar 1923,F 9,10:4; 1926,S 19,28:5;
  1927,Je 7,27:2; 1928,Ap 8,VIII,4:3; 1929,N 19,26:5;
  1930,Ap 4,22:3; 1931,N 18,26:3; 1932,F 9,30:7;
  1932,F 28,VIII,2:4; 1934,O 24,25:2; 1937,N 12,26:6;
  1937,N 28,XI,1:1; 1938,Ja 30,X,3:1; 1950,Je 21,30:1;
  1955,Je 29,23:3; 1955,Jl 13,20:1; 1955,Jl 17,II,1:1;
  1957,O 24,39:1; 1959,Ag 4,30:1; 1959,Ag 16,II,1:1;
  1962,F 22,19:6; 1962,My 12,14:1; 1965,Jl 2,18:1;
  1966,Je 24,29:2
Julius Caesar's Circus 1928,D 27,26:4
Jumbo 1935,N 18,20:2; 1935,N 24,IX,1:1
Jumping Fool, The 1970,F 10,53:1
June Days 1925,Ag 7,12:5; 1925,Ag 23,VII,1:1
June Love 1921,Ap 26,20:1
June Moon 1929,Ag 4,VIII,1:6; 1929,O 10,34:5;
  1933,My 16,15:5
Junebug Graduates Tonight! 1967,F 27,35:1
Jungle of Cities 1970,Mr 1,75:2
Junior Miss 1941,N 19,28:2; 1941,N 30,IX,1:1;
  1943,Ap 18,II,1:1
Junk 1927,Ja 6,25:1
Juno 1959,Mr 10,41:1; 1959,Mr 15,II,1:1
Juno and the Paycock 1925,N 22,VIII,1:8;
  1926,Mr 16,22:1; 1926,Mr 21,VIII,1:1;
  1927,D 20,32:2; 1932,O 20,24:3; 1937,Ag 29,X,2:1;
  1937,D 7,32:5; 1940,Ja 17,24:2; 1940,Ja 21,IX,1:2;
  1940,Ja 28,IX,1:1; 1950,D 31,II,3:7; 1955,F 24,20:4;
  1964,My 6,41:1; 1966,Ag 3,40:1
Jupiter Laughs 1940,S 10,27:1; 1941,N 9,IX,3:5
Just a Minute 1928,S 16,IX,2:4; 1928,O 9,34:3
Just Because 1922,Mr 23,11:1
Just Beyond 1925,D 2,22:4
Just Fancy! 1927,O 12,30:2
Just for Love 1968,O 18,40:1
Just Life 1926,S 15,33:3; 1926,S 19,IX,1:1
Just Married 1921,Ap 27,21:1; 1924,D 16,29:6;
  1924,D 21,VII,1:8
Just Suppose 1920,N 2,15:1; 1920,N 7,VII,1:1;
  1935,Jl 2,24:3
Just to Remind You 1931,S 8,39:1
Just Wild About Harry 1963,Jl 5,14:1
Juwelenraub am Kurfurstendamm 1932,F 21,VIII,2:3
Jux Will Er Sich Machen, Einen 1968,Ap 3,41:1

K

K Guy, The 1928,O 16,28:4
Kabale und Liebe 1928,Ja 17,22:3; 1931,N 1,VIII,4:2;
  1933,O 18,24:3
Kagami-Jishi 1969,S 11,53:1
Kage-No-Chikara 1930,Mr 5,26:7
Kagotsurube 1960,Je 3,26:1
Kai Khosru 1925,Ap 27,14:2; 1925,My 3,VIII,1:2
Kaisers Kulis, Des 1930,O 19,IX,2:4
Kaleidoscope 1957,Je 14,20:2
Kallol 1966,D 21,2:4
Kama Sutra, Le 1923,N 13,24:2
Kanjincho 1960,Je 3,26:1
Kansas City Kitty 1929,S 26,27:4
Kapores 1936,S 28,14:3
Karabash 1939,Ag 27,IX,3:1
Karl and Anna 1929,O 8,34:1; 1935,O 13,IX,3:1
Karl Gerhard's Revue 1930,Jl 13,VIII,2:1
Karl und Anna 1929,Mr 10,X,2:1; 1929,My 9,IX,2:4
Karussell 1922,F 5,VI,1:7
Kasimir und Karoline 1932,D 18,X,4:5
Kat 1931,O 4,VIII,4:1
Kataki 1959,Ap 10,24:1; 1959,D 16,55:1
Kate 1924,Mr 2,VIII,2:7

Katerina 1929,F 26,30:3
Katharina 1932,O 2,IX,3:1
Katharina Knie 1929,Mr 10,X,2:1
Kathleen 1948,F 4,26:2
Kathleen ni Houlihan 1920,Je 29,9:2
Katie Roche 1937,O 4,17:4
Katinka 1923,Ag 31,15:4; 1923,S 2,VI,1:7
Katja 1926,O 19,27:3
Katy Did 1927,My 10,24:3
Katy Did So What? 1935,N 6,32:3
Kean 1921,D 11,VI,1:4; 1961,N 3,28:2;
  1961,N 12,II,1:1
Keating 1927,D 26,26:6
Keep 'Em Laughing 1942,Ap 25,9:2;
  1942,My 10,VIII,8:3
Keep It Clean 1929,Je 25,35:5
Keep It in the Family 1967,S 28,59:1; 1967,O 8,II,1:6;
  1968,Ja 25,32:4
Keep Kool 1924,My 23,16:4
Keep Moving 1934,Ag 24,10:2
Keep Off the Grass 1940,My 5,X,1:6;
  1940,My 24,22:6; 1940,Je 16,IX,1:1
Keep Shufflin' 1928,F 28,18:3
Keep Your Eyes on Amelie 1952,N 25,35:2
Keeper of the Keys 1933,O 19,23:2
Keepers of Youth 1929,Je 9,VIII,2:4
Keeping Expenses Down 1932,O 21,25:2
Kek Roka 1957,D 5,47:2
Kelly 1965,F 8,28:2
Kelly's Vacation 1924,Mr 16,VIII,2:1
Kempy 1922,My 16,14:2; 1927,My 12,25:2;
  1927,My 22,VIII,1:1
Kept 1926,S 18,13:3
Kernel and the Shell, The 1965,Ja 6,32:1
Key, The 1933,S 7,17:5
Key Largo 1939,O 31,26:6; 1939,N 19,X,3:4;
  1939,N 28,30:2; 1939,D 3,IX,5:3; 1939,D 10,X,3:1;
  1942,Je 21,VIII,1:8
Keyhole, The 1962,Ja 31,21:1
Khaki Blue 1969,Mr 27,54:2
Kibbetzers, Inc 1935,My 13,18:5
Kibitzer, The 1929,F 10,IX,2:1; 1929,F 19,22:5;
  1931,N 7,17:3
Kick Back, The 1936,Je 23,27:3
Kicking the Castle Down 1967,Ja 19,43:1
Kid, The 1961,Mr 15,45:2
Kid Boots 1923,D 16,IX,2:4; 1924,Ja 1,21:3
Kid Himself, The 1925,D 25,23:2
Kid Mother 1927,F 27,VII,1:1; 1927,Mr 6,VII,1:6
Kidders, The 1957,N 13,40:6
Kidding Kidders 1928,Ap 24,28:3
Kiddish Hashem 1928,S 30,IX,1:1
Kiki 1921,N 30,13:1; 1921,D 4,VII,1:2;
  1921,D 11,VI,1:4
Kilgo Run, The 1953,D 13,105:1
Kill That Story 1934,Ag 30,22:2
Kill the One-Eyed Man 1965,O 21,56:1
Killer, The 1960,Mr 23,33:1; 1960,Ap 3,II,1:1
Killers 1928,Mr 14,28:3
Killing of Sister George, The 1965,Je 18,28:5;
  1966,O 6,57:1; 1966,O 16,II,1:1
Kilpatrick's Old-Time Minstrels 1930,Ap 21,20:2
Kinangozi 1924,F 10,II,3:7
Kind Lady 1935,Ap 24,24:5; 1935,Ap 28,X,1:1;
  1935,Jl 23,24:4; 1935,N 19,27:3; 1936,Je 12,19:3;
  1937,Jl 6,23:1; 1937,Jl 21,19:3; 1938,Jl 11,14:2;
  1940,S 4,28:3
Kind Sir 1953,S 28,21:2; 1953,N 5,41:2;
  1953,N 15,II,1:1
Kinder 1924,Mr 2,VIII,2:1
Kindertragoedie 1931,D 27,VIII,3:1
Kindischen Verliebten, Die 1924,Mr 2,VIII,2:1
Kindred 1939,O 8,IX,3:5; 1939,D 27,17:2;
  1940,Ja 7,IX,1:1
King, Queen, Knave 1932,F 18,24:4;
  1932,Mr 6,VIII,2:4
King and I, The 1951,Mr 30,26:2; 1951,Ap 8,II,1:1;
  1952,Ap 14,23:1; 1952,O 5,II,1:1; 1953,O 9,33:3;
  1953,O 18,II,3:1; 1955,My 17,33:4; 1956,Ap 19,35:4;
  1960,My 12,40:1; 1960,My 22,II,1:1;
  1961,Mr 19,22:5; 1963,Je 13,30:2; 1964,Jl 7,26:1;
  1968,My 24,39:1
King and Mistress Shore, The 1936,N 6,28:5;
  1936,N 22,XI,1:3
King And the Cobbler, The 1954,D 13,33:6
King and the Duke, The 1955,Je 2,25:2
King Arthur 1968,N 3,87:1
King Can Do No Wrong, The 1927,N 17,28:4
King for a Day, A 1923,D 2,VIII,2:1
King John 1929,Je 23,VIII,2:1; 1941,Ag 3,IX,2:2;
  1956,Je 28,33:5; 1960,Je 29,26:2; 1967,Jl 14,19:1;
  1970,Je 19,27:2
King Kong 1961,F 24,24:1

King Lear 1923,Mr 10,9:4; 1925,O 12,18:1;
  1927,Mr 13,VII,1:4; 1930,Ap 1,34:6;
  1930,D 26,18:2; 1934,N 4,IX,3:1; 1936,Ap 21,27:4;
  1940,Ap 28,IX,1:7; 1940,D 16,27:2; 1946,S 25,39:4;
  1946,O 13,II,2:3; 1947,F 19,32:2; 1950,Jl 19,26:7;
  1950,Ag 30,26:2; 1950,D 26,18:1; 1950,D 31,II,1:1;
  1953,Ag 9,II,1:2; 1955,Jl 28,19:2; 1956,Ja 13,17:1;
  1956,Ja 22,II,1:1; 1959,Ja 3,11:2; 1959,Ja 19,34:7;
  1961,My 15,34:6; 1962,Ag 14,35:1; 1962,N 7,49:3;
  1963,Je 10,37:1; 1963,N 23,22:1; 1964,Ap 3,28:1;
  1964,My 19,43:2; 1964,My 31,II,1:1;
  1964,Je 19,36:1; 1964,Jl 23,18:1; 1964,Jl 28,18:2;
  1965,Je 25,39:1; 1968,Ap 12,42:5; 1968,Je 3,55:4;
  1968,N 8,43:1; 1968,N 17,II,1:3
King Midas and the Golden Touch 1948,O 25,28:3
King Oedipus 1933,Ja 16,12:4
King of Friday's Men, The 1951,F 22,26:2
King of Hearts 1954,Ap 2,23:1; 1954,Ap 11,II,1:1
King of Nowhere, The 1938,Ap 3,XI,1:8
King of Rome, The 1935,My 15,26:1
King of the Dark Chamber 1961,F 10,21:1;
  1961,Ap 9,II,1:1
King of the Golden River, The 1929,D 27,26:5
King of the Whole Damn World 1962,Ap 16,32:2
King Saul 1925,S 18,26:3
King Solomon's Song of Songs 1923,Ap 4,22:2
Kingdom of God, The 1927,N 20,IX,2:7;
  1928,O 14,X,1:3; 1928,D 21,30:2;
  1928,D 30,VIII,1:1
Kingdom of God in Bohemia, The
  1931,Mr 8,VIII,2:7
King's Breakfast, The 1937,D 13,22:8
King's Coat, The 1933,Ja 12,21:4
King's Darling, The 1951,Jl 25,17:2
King's Leisure, The 1936,My 31,II,6:8
King's Maid, The 1941,Ag 27,15:3
King's Mare, The 1966,Jl 21,23:1
King's Messenger, The 1935,Ag 14,16:3
King's Pirate, The 1937,Je 11,26:1; 1937,Je 27,X,1:3
King's Standards, The 1958,F 14,19:1
Kismet 1953,D 4,2:4; 1955,My 1,II,3:1;
  1955,My 17,33:4; 1965,Je 23,45:1
Kiss and Tell 1943,Mr 18,22:1; 1943,Mr 28,II,1:1
Kiss Before the Mirror, The 1932,N 13,IX,3:7
Kiss for Cinderella, A 1930,F 1,14:6;
  1942,Mr 11,22:2; 1942,Mr 15,VIII,1:1
Kiss in a Taxi, The 1925,Ag 26,14:1;
  1925,Ag 30,VII,1:1
Kiss Mama 1964,O 2,30:1
Kiss Me, Kate 1948,D 31,10:3; 1949,Ja 16,II,1:1;
  1949,Ja 30,II,6:5; 1951,My 9,30:5; 1952,Ja 9,24:6;
  1954,Mr 27,13:2; 1956,F 15,27:6; 1956,F 19,94:1;
  1956,My 10,27:2; 1958,My 31,7:4; 1959,Ag 10,24:1;
  1963,D 1,184:3; 1964,F 16,29:1; 1965,My 13,31:1;
  1966,F 5,32:1; 1970,D 26,10:4
Kiss Me! 1927,Jl 22,17:1
Kiss of Importance, A 1930,D 2,31:3
Kiss the Boys Goodbye 1938,S 29,30:2
Kiss Them for Me 1945,Mr 21,27:2;
  1945,Mr 25,II,1:1
Kissing Time 1920,O 12,18:2
Kit Marlowe 1936,My 24,35:1
Kitchen, The 1966,Je 14,50:1
Kith and Kin 1930,My 14,31:1
Kittiwake Island 1960,O 13,43:1
Kitty, I Hardly Knew You 1963,Je 6,40:8
Kitty's Kisses 1926,My 7,12:2
Kleinburgerhochzeit, Die 1970,N 25,25:1
Kleine Komodie 1928,D 2,X,4:7
Knack, The 1964,My 28,42:2; 1964,Je 7,II,1:1
Knack With Horses, A 1970,D 21,52:1
Knickerbocker Holiday 1938,O 2,IX,3:3;
  1938,O 16,I,3:3; 1938,O 20,26:2; 1938,N 20,IX,1:1
Knight Errant 1928,S 2,VII,2:1
Knight From Olmedo, The 1962,N 26,36:2
Knight of Columbus, The 1922,O 27,17:1
Knight of the Burning Pestle, The 1927,Ap 23,15:1;
  1953,O 24,13:2
Knights of Song 1938,O 18,29:2
Knock 1937,N 17,26:3
Knock on Wood 1935,My 29,16:2
Knock Out 1927,Mr 27,VII,4:8
Koenigs Befehl, Des 1933,Je 25,IX,1:2
Koi No Yozakura 1930,Mr 5,26:7
Kommt ein Vogel Geflogen 1931,My 10,VIII,1:4
Komparserie 1933,Mr 19,IX,2:2
Konflikt 1933,Ap 16,IX,2:5
Kongi's Harvest 1968,Ap 15,49:1; 1968,Ap 21,II,5:3
Kongo 1926,Mr 31,20:5
Konjunktur 1933,D 10,X,5:1
Konto X 1930,N 2,VIII,3:1
Konzert, Das 1968,Mr 25,52:1
Kopf in der Schlinge 1931,D 27,VIII,2:6
Kosher Kitty Kelly 1925,Je 16,24:2
Kosher Widow, The 1959,N 2,40:2
Kossuth 1927,D 4,X,2:3
Krapp's Last Tape 1960,Ja 15,37:2; 1960,Ja 31,II,1:1;
  1960,Mr 29,47:6; 1965,Je 9,42:3; 1968,O 11,41:1
Krasch 1930,N 2,VIII,3:2
Kreatur, Die 1930,My 25,IX,1:8
Kremlin Chimes 1964,Je 23,26:3; 1965,F 25,23:1;
  1965,Mr 7,II,1:1

Kreutzer Sonata, The 1920,O 3,VI,1:7;
  1924,My 15,22:3; 1961,F 16,24:2
Kreuzabnahme 1929,My 26,IX,2:3
Kukla, Burr and Ollie 1960,N 1,47:2
Kultur 1933,S 27,24:3
Kumagai Jinya 1969,S 18,64:1
Kumquat in the Persimmon Tree, The
  1962,Je 19,27:2
Kurve, Die 1970,N 25,25:1
Kurzy of the Sea 1920,Ap 4,VI,6:1
Kuss-und Sonst Gar Nichts, Ein 1933,N 19,IX,3:1
Kwamina 1961,O 24,42:1; 1961,N 12,II,1:1
Kykunkor 1934,D 22,21:3
Kyrill Reist ins Abendland 1933,Ja 8,IX,2:1
Kyskhet 1939,Jl 9,IX,2:1

L

L A Under Siege 1970,Ag 16,II,1:7
Laboratoire des Hallucinations, Le 1923,N 20,23:3
Laburnum Grove 1933,N 29,23:4; 1933,D 17,IX,4:2;
  1935,Ja 15,23:5; 1935,Ja 20,X,1:1
Lac Sale, Le 1926,S 5,II,6:5; 1926,O 3,VIII,2:1
Lace on Her Petticoat 1951,S 5,40:3
Lace Petticoat 1927,Ja 5,18:2
Lacune, La 1970,My 6,49:1
Lad, The 1929,Ja 13,VIII,4:5
Ladder, The 1926,Je 27,VII,3:1; 1926,S 26,VIII,2:7;
  1926,O 23,15:1; 1927,O 7,24:2•
Ladies All 1930,Jl 20,VIII,2:1; 1930,Jl 29,25:2
Ladies and Gentlemen 1937,My 19,26:6;
  1939,S 24,IX,2:5; 1939,O 18,30:2; 1939,O 22,IX,1:3;
  1939,O 29,IX,1:3; 1949,O 17,19:1; 1949,O 18,34:4;
  1949,N 13,83:4
Ladies Don't Lie 1929,O 11,36:3
Ladies in Retirement 1939,D 24,IX,1:7;
  1940,Mr 27,24:3; 1941,Ag 17,IX,1:8
Ladies-in-Waiting 1934,Je 10,IX,1:1
Ladies Into Action 1940,Ap 21,IX,1:6
Ladies Leave 1929,O 2,28:3
Ladies' Money 1934,N 2,26:6
Ladies' Night 1920,Ag 10,10:1; 1920,Ag 15,VI,1:1;
  1933,N 19,IX,3:7
Ladies Night in a Turkish Bath 1961,Mr 22,38:1
Ladies of Creation 1931,Ag 30,VIII,1:7;
  1931,S 9,25:1
Ladies of the Corridor, The 1953,O 22,33:5;
  1953,N 1,II,1:1
Ladies of the Evening 1924,D 24,11:2
Ladies of the Jury 1929,O 6,IX,1:4; 1929,O 22,26:2
Ladro, Il 1932,F 22,23:4
Lady, The 1923,D 5,23:2; 1923,D 16,IX,1:1
Lady Akane, The 1960,N 16,51:4
Lady Alone 1927,Ja 16,VII,2:4; 1927,Ja 21,12:5
Lady Be Good 1924,D 2,23:4; 1924,D 28,VII,1:1;
  1926,Ap 15,25:1
Lady Behave 1941,Ag 3,IX,2:2; 1943,N 17,30:1
Lady Beyond the Moon 1931,Ap 1,36:5
Lady Billy 1920,D 15,18:2
Lady Bug 1922,Ap 18,15:3
Lady Butterfly 1923,Ja 23,18:1
Lady Clara 1930,Ap 18,28:7
Lady Comes Across, The 1942,Ja 10,10:2
Lady Cristilinda, The 1922,D 26,11:2
Lady Dedlock 1929,Ja 1,61:2
Lady Detained, A 1935,Ja 10,23:3
Lady Do 1927,Ap 19,24:2
Lady Fingers 1929,Ja 13,VIII,2:4; 1929,F 1,22:4
Lady for a Night, A 1928,Ap 17,26:4
Lady Frederick 1970,S 17,57:1
Lady From Alfaqueque, The 1928,N 11,X,4:1;
  1929,Ja 15,22:3
Lady From Maxim's, The 1970,Je 1,41:1
Lady From Paris, The 1950,S 27,36:1
Lady From the Provinces, The 1923,F 27,14:2;
  1923,Mr 4,VII,1:1
Lady From the Sea, The 1923,O 30,17:1;
  1929,Mr 19,36:1; 1934,My 2,25:2; 1935,D 14,11:3;
  1950,Ag 8,23:2; 1956,D 13,49:5
Lady Hamilton 1929,N 17,IX,2:6
Lady Has a Heart, The 1937,S 27,24:1;
  1937,O 3,XI,1:1
Lady in Danger 1945,Mr 30,18:6
Lady in Ermine, The 1922,O 3,22:2
Lady-in-Law, The 1927,O 23,VIII,4:1
Lady in Love, A 1927,F 22,22:1; 1927,F 27,VII,1:1
Lady in the Dark 1940,D 31,18:6; 1941,Ja 5,IX,1:7;
  1941,Ja 24,14:2; 1941,F 2,IX,1:1; 1941,S 3,26:6;
  1941,S 7,IX,1:1; 1943,Mr 1,14:2; 1952,Mr 8,11:3
Lady in Waiting 1940,Mr 28,19:1
Lady Inger of Ostrat 1927,N 27,IX,4:1
Lady Jane 1934,S 11,24:2
Lady Killer, The 1924,F 24,VII,2:5; 1924,Mr 13,14:2
Lady Lies, The 1928,N 11,X,2:4; 1928,N 27,36:2
Lady Luck 1936,Ap 16,21:2
Lady Maria, The 1947,Ag 5,26:1
Lady of Belmont, The 1931,F 1,VIII,3:3
Lady of Fatima 1948,F 13,27:4
Lady of Larkspur Lotion, The 1949,Jl 9,9:2
Lady of Letters 1935,Mr 29,26:6
Lady of Mexico 1962,O 20,13:2

Lady of the Camellias, The 1930,Mr 6,16:4;
1930,Mr 23,IX,2:3; 1931,Ja 27,21:2; 1963,Mr 22,7:1
Lady of the Lamp, The 1920,Ag 18,6:4;
1920,Ag 22,VI,1:2
Lady of the Orchids, The 1928,D 14,37:3
Lady of the Rose 1925,My 20,26:4
Lady of the Sea 1923,N 3,8:2; 1923,N 4,VIII,1:2;
1945,S 9,II,1:5
Lady or the Tiger?, The 1966,O 19,53:1
Lady Precious Stream 1934,D 29,11:4;
1936,Ja 28,15:2; 1936,F 23,X,1:1
Lady Refuses, The 1933,Mr 8,18:6
Lady Remembers, The 1932,My 11,15:3
Lady Says Yes, A 1945,Ja 11,18:5
Lady Screams, The 1927,My 3,24:2
Lady Who Came to Stay, The 1941,Ja 3,13:2
Lady Windermere's Fan 1927,F 27,VII,2:3;
1930,Jl 27,VIII,1:8; 1932,Ja 27,19:3; 1946,O 15,29:2
Lady With a Lamp, The 1929,Ja 27,IX,2:1;
1931,N 20,27:2
Lady XX 1928,O 28,IX,2:1
Lady's Gentleman, A 1937,D 24,20:5
Lady's Not for Burning, The 1949,Je 12,II,3:1;
1950,N 9,42:2; 1950,N 26,II,1:1; 1957,F 22,26:2;
1959,Ja 31,13:2
Lady's Virtue, A 1925,N 24,28:2; 1925,D 16,VIII,5:1
Laff That Off 1925,N 3,34:2
Laffing Room Only 1944,D 25,15:4; 1945,S 20,31:1
Lake, The 1933,Mr 26,IX,1:1; 1933,D 19,26:3;
1933,D 27,24:2; 1934,Ja 7,X,1:1
Lally 1927,F 9,16:3
Lamara 1930,Ag 10,VIII,2:3
Lambent Flame, The 1935,Jl 16,24:2
Lambs Gambol 1922,Ja 30,16:1; 1925,Ap 27,15:1;
1932,Ap 25,18:2; 1933,Ap 24,10:1
Lamentation of the Virgin Mary, The 1933,F 6,11:3;
1933,F 12,IX,2:1
Lamp at Midnight 1947,D 22,29:2
Lancashire Lass, The 1931,D 31,16:3
Lancelot and Elaine 1921,S 13,12:1
Lanceurs des Graines 1933,Jl 23,IX,1:3
Land Beyond the River, A 1957,Mr 29,15:7;
1957,Je 2,II,1:1
Land des Laechelns, Das 1929,D 8,X,4:4
Land Is Bright, The 1941,O 21,28:5; 1941,O 29,26:2;
1941,N 9,IX,1:1
Land of Bells, The 1935,My 10,25:4
Land of Fame 1943,S 22,31:5
Land of Promises, The 1933,N 5,IX,2:2
Land of Smiles 1931,My 9,15:2; 1942,Jl 5,VIII,1:7
Land's End 1946,D 12,37:5
Landscape 1969,Jl 13,II,8:1; 1969,Jl 25,34:1;
1970,Ap 3,43:1; 1970,Ap 12,II,3:1
Langrevin Pere et Fils 1930,Je 8,IX,2:4
Lantern, The 1935,O 6,XI,3:7
Laquelle 1927,O 16,IX,4:7; 1927,N 20,IX,4:4
Larger Than Life 1936,Mr 17,25:3; 1950,F 8,33:2;
1950,Mr 12,II,3:7
Lark, The 1955,My 13,21:2; 1955,My 29,II,1:1;
1955,N 18,20:1; 1955,N 27,II,1:1; 1956,Ja 8,II,3:1
Las Que Tienen Gue Servir 1962,D 18,5:1
Lash, The 1926,N 4,VIII,4:7
Lass O' Laughter 1922,My 21,VI,1:6;
1924,N 16,VIII,2:8; 1925,Ja 9,13:2
Lassie 1920,Ap 7,9:2
Last Analysis, The 1964,O 2,30:1; 1964,O 11,II,1:1
Last Christmas, The 1940,Ap 26,24:2
Last Dance, The 1948,Ja 28,27:2
Last Days of Lincoln, The 1961,O 19,39:7
Last Defensive, The 1931,S 27,VIII,3:2
Last Enemy, The 1930,Ja 5,VIII,2:2; 1930,O 31,21:1;
1934,Jl 13,14:4
Last Hour, The 1929,Ja 6,VIII,1:4
Last Love of Don Juan, The 1955,N 24,40:1
Last Man In, The 1926,My 6,23:3; 1930,My 8,32:5
Last Masks 1920,Ap 4,VI,6:1
Last Mile, The 1930,F 14,21:2; 1930,Mr 2,IX,1:1;
1930,D 21,VIII,3:1; 1931,F 8,VIII,3:3;
1932,Ap 3,VIII,2:1
Last Minstrel, The 1963,My 9,40:2
Last Night of Don Juan, The 1925,N 10,23:2
Last of Mrs Cheyney, The 1925,N 1,VIII,2:4;
1925,N 10,23:5
Last of the Ladies, The 1936,Mr 26,26:7
Last of the Red Hot Lovers 1969,D 29,37:1;
1970,Ja 4,II,1:1
Last Pad, The 1970,D 8,61:1
Last Stand 1970,D 31,8:3
Last Stop 1944,S 6,17:2
Last Straw, The 1970,Ap 5,76:4
Last Sweet Days of Isaac, The 1970,Ja 27,49:1;
1970,F 8,II,1:6; 1970,F 15,II,1:1
Last to Go 1969,N 4,55:2
Last Torture, The 1927,Ja 13,28:4
Last Train South 1938,S 4,X,2:2
Last Triangle, The (An Embroidered Camp)
1968,Mr 19,41:1
Last Trump, The 1938,Ag 6,7:1; 1938,Ag 14,IX,2:1
Last Waltz, The 1921,My 11,20:3
Last Warning, The 1922,O 25,23:1;
1922,O 29,VII,1:1; 1927,Ap 3,VIII,2:1
Late Arrival 1953,O 20,35:5

Late Christopher Bean, The 1932,N 1,24:3;
1933,My 17,15:2; 1935,Ag 28,13:1
Late George Apley, The 1944,O 20,16:4;
1944,N 22,26:2; 1944,N 26,II,1:3; 1944,D 3,II,1:1
Late Late Show, The 1968,N 4,57:3
Late Love 1953,O 14,35:2
Late Night Final 1931,Je 26,26:3
Late One Evening 1933,Ja 10,27:3
Late Wisdom 1934,Ap 24,27:4
Latent Heterosexual, The 1968,Mr 22,52:1;
1968,Mr 31,II,3:1
Laterna Magika 1964,Ag 4,21:1; 1964,Ag 16,II,5:1
Lauf ins Glueck 1935,My 19,IX,2:5
Laugh, Clown, Laugh! 1923,O 28,VIII,2:1;
1923,N 29,30:1; 1923,D 9,IX,1:1
Laugh, Town, Laugh! 1942,Je 20,9:1; 1942,Je 23,22:2;
1942,Jl 23,15:3
Laugh It Off 1925,Ap 25,18:4; 1934,Ap 5,24:2
Laugh Night 1936,S 14,25:1
Laugh Parade, The 1931,S 20,VIII,3:1; 1931,N 3,31:2;
1931,D 6,VIII,1:1
Laugh Time 1943,S 9,35:2; 1943,S 19,II,1:1
Laughing Lady, The 1923,F 13,25:1;
1923,F 18,VII,1:1; 1934,My 6,IX,2:5
Laughing Woman, The 1934,Ap 8,33:6; 1936,Jl 8,14:7;
1936,O 14,30:1
Laughs, Etc 1969,Mr 20,53:1
Laughs and Other Events 1960,O 11,57:1
Laughter in Court 1936,S 10,29:4; 1936,S 27,X,3:5
Laughter Over Broadway 1939,Ja 16,10:3
Laughter Over London 1936,D 8,31:3
Laughwind 1966,Mr 3,27:1
Launcelot and Elaine 1930,Mr 10,24:3
Laundry, The 1963,F 19,5:2
Launzi 1923,O 11,16:3
Laura 1947,Je 27,16:1
Laura Garnett 1934,Jl 17,24:4
Lauter Luegen 1937,O 24,XI,3:1
Lawbreaker, The 1922,F 7,12:1
Lawful Larceny 1922,Ja 3,20:2
Lawrence d'Arabie 1961,O 8,II,3:4
Lawrence of Arabia 1954,D 10,35:3
Lawyers' Dilemma, The 1928,Jl 10,17:2
Laying the Devil 1933,Jl 23,IX,1:3
Lazarus Laughed 1928,Ap 10,33:1; 1928,Ap 22,IX,2:3;
1948,Ap 9,27:4
Lazybones 1924,Je 1,VII,4:3; 1924,S 23,23:1
Lazzaro 1929,Jl 10,31:1; 1929,Ag 4,VIII,1:7;
1931,F 22,VIII,4:1
Leader, The 1965,Mr 8,34:1; 1969,Ap 22,40:2
Leading Lady 1948,S 15,38:1; 1948,O 19,33:1
Leaf and Bough 1949,Ja 22,10:2
League of Youth 1928,Mr 17,9:1
Leah Kleschna 1924,Ap 22,19:2; 1924,Ap 27,VIII,1:1
Lean Harvest 1931,My 8,20:2; 1931,O 4,VIII,2:2;
1931,O 14,26:3
Leap, The 1924,My 23,16:5
Leave Her to Heaven 1940,F 28,16:2
Leave It to Jane 1959,My 26,30:2
Leave It to Me! 1938,O 23,IX,3:5; 1938,N 10,32:2;
1938,N 20,IX,1:1; 1939,S 10,IX,1:1; 1940,Ja 18,27:2
Lebende Leichnam, Der, Der 1928,Ja 24,26:2
Lecon de Talma, La 1926,N 14,VIII,2:1
Ledge, A 1929,N 19,26:3
Lee Harvey Oswald: A Far Mean Streak of
Independence Brought on by Negleck
1968,Ap 19,35:1
Left Bank, The 1931,O 6,35:3; 1931,O 18,VIII,1:1
Left Turn 1936,Jl 7,22:3
Legal Grounds 1940,D 2,18:4
Legal Murder 1934,F 16,16:2
Legend 1930,My 7,25:1
Legend of Leonora, The 1926,My 1,10:1;
1927,Mr 30,22:4; 1927,Ap 3,VIII,1:1
Legend of Lizzie, The 1959,F 10,39:1
Legend of Lovers 1951,D 27,17:1; 1959,O 28,40:3
Legend of Sarah 1950,O 12,42:4
Legend of the Golem, The 1931,My 27,25:2
Legitimate Steal, The 1958,Ap 1,35:1
Lelia 1928,D 2,X,2:1
LeMaire's Affairs 1927,Mr 29,22:4
Lemon Sky 1970,My 18,40:1
Lemonade 1968,D 14,60:1
Lend an Ear 1948,D 17,38:2; 1959,S 25,20:5;
1969,O 29,32:1
Lend Me Your Ears! 1936,O 6,28:5
Lenin's Dowry 1932,My 13,17:3
Lenore 1920,Mr 1,16:3
Lenz 1926,Ap 29,20:4
Leonard Bernstein's Theater Songs 1965,Je 29,27:2
Leonard Sillman's New Faces of 1968
1968,My 3,43:1
Leopold le Bien-Aime 1927,O 30,IX,4:7
Leper, The 1970,Ap 24,40:1
Lesson, The 1956,O 3,29:2; 1958,Ja 10,20:3;
1958,F 16,II,1:1; 1963,S 18,35:4
Lesson in Consent, A 1969,My 26,55:2
Lesson in Love, A 1923,S 25,10:1; 1923,S 30,II,1:1
Let and Sub-Let 1930,My 20,32:2
Let 'Em Eat Cake 1933,O 3,26:5; 1933,O 23,18:1;
1933,N 12,IX,1:1
Let Freedom Ring 1935,N 7,26:2
Let Freedom Sing 1942,O 6,18:2

Let It Ride 1961,O 13,27:4
Let the Credit Go 1930,O 26,VIII,4:6
Let Them Down, Gently 1968,Ja 31,28:2
Let Them Say 1939,Ag 27,IX,1:4
Let Us Be Gay 1929,F 22,19:1; 1930,S 14,VIII,2:1;
1937,Je 29,18:3
Let Us Divorce 1932,Ap 17,VIII,2:6
Let's Face It 1941,O 10,27:1; 1941,O 30,26:2;
1942,N 29,VIII,2:1
Let's Get Married 1937,Ja 11,16:2
Let's Go 1924,My 20,15:1; 1927,Ap 18,18:2
Let's Laugh Again 1937,Ag 24,24:5
Let's Make an Opera 1950,D 14,50:2
Let's Move 1927,N 21,20:1
Let's Play Fair 1938,Ja 19,26:4
Let's Raise the Curtain 1936,S 29,34:3
Let's Sing Yiddish 1966,N 10,63:1
Letter, The 1927,Mr 6,VII,4:5; 1927,Mr 27,VII,2:6;
1927,S 27,30:1; 1927,O 2,VIII,1:1; 1927,O 30,IX,4:1;
1929,N 17,IX,2:6
Letter From Paris 1952,O 11,17:8; 1952,N 9,II,3:1
Letter of the Law, The 1920,F 24,11:1;
1920,F 29,V,5:1
Letter to the Times, A 1966,D 5,63:1
Letters to Lucerne 1941,D 9,47:6; 1941,D 24,14:2
Lettre Morte 1960,Mr 29,47:6; 1970,Ap 16,55:1
Letty Pepper 1922,Ap 11,22:2
Lew Leslie's Blackbirds of 1930 1930,O 23,34:5
Lew Leslie's Blackbirds of 1939 1939,F 13,12:2
Leyenda del Beso, La 1942,N 20,26:4
Liane, Le (Ties That Bind) 1929,Ap 22,22:1;
1933,Je 12,20:3
Liar, The 1950,My 19,30:2
Libel! 1935,D 3,32:8; 1935,D 8,X,5:8; 1935,D 21,10:5
Liberace's Variety Bill 1957,Ap 22,29:5
Liberte Provisoire 1934,My 27,X,2:1
Liberty Jones 1941,F 6,24:2
License, The 1969,Ap 23,42:1; 1969,My 4,II,3:1
Lido Girl, The 1928,Ag 24,23:2
Lid's Off, The 1936,Ap 4,11:6
Lie, The 1923,O 21,VIII,2:2
Liebe, Mord und Alkohol 1931,Mr 29,VIII,3:2
Liebestrank 1927,Ja 30,VII,4:3
Liebling Adieu 1931,N 29,VIII,4:2
Lied der Liebe, Das 1932,F 7,VIII,1:3
Lieutenant Comma 1932,N 13,IX,3:7
Life, Laughter And Tears 1942,F 26,15:2
Life and Death of an American 1939,My 20,11:2
Life and Death of Sir John Falstaff, The
1938,Mr 15,19:5
Life and Times of J Walter Smintheus, The
1970,D 10,59:1
Life Begins 1932,Mr 20,VIII,2:4; 1932,Mr 29,23:2
Life Begins Again 1935,F 26,16:2
Life Begins at 8:40 1934,Ag 7,20:7;
1934,Ag 12,IX,1:1; 1934,Ag 28,24:2;
1934,S 2,IX,1:1
Life Begins in '40 1940,Ap 5,24:2
Life I Gave You, The 1931,My 12,29:3
Life in the Sun, A 1955,Ag 24,24:7;
1955,Ag 28,II,1:6
Life Is a Dream 1962,Ja 15,22:3; 1964,Mr 20,24:1
Life Is Like That 1930,D 23,24:3
Life Line, The 1930,D 29,19:3
Life Marches On 1940,Ja 4,18:2
Life of Man, The 1923,Ap 17,26:1
Life of Reilly, The 1942,Ap 30,13:2
Life Price 1969,Ja 14,36:2
Life Size 1970,Je 18,54:2
Life That I Gave Him, The 1934,O 28,IX,3:4
Life With Father 1939,Ag 15,14:4; 1939,N 9,26:2;
1939,N 19,X,1:1; 1940,Mr 3,X,2:5;
1940,Ag 18,IX,1:1; 1947,Je 6,27:3; 1967,O 20,53:2
Life With Mother 1948,Je 9,36:3; 1948,O 21,32:2;
1948,O 31,II,1:1; 1949,Mr 27,II,1:1
Lifeline 1942,Jl 12,VIII,1:4; 1942,D 1,20:3
Life's Too Short 1935,S 21,18:5
Light, Lively and Yiddish 1970,O 28,58:1
Light Behind the Shadow, The 1936,Ja 21,26:6
Light of Asia, The 1928,O 10,32:2
Light of Heart, The 1940,Mr 3,X,3:4;
1941,Je 15,IX,2:5
Light of the World, The 1920,Ja 7,17:1;
1920,Ja 11,VIII,2:1
Light on the Mountain, The 1926,Ag 22,VII,1:2;
1926,S 2,15:4
Light Under the Bushel, The 1927,D 7,32:2
Light Up the Sky 1948,N 19,34:2; 1948,D 5,II,5:1
Light Wines and Beer 1930,N 11,28:6
Lightnin' 1920,Jl 27,11:2; 1921,S 11,VI,1:6;
1925,F 1,VII,2:1; 1938,S 16,17:2
Lights Out 1922,Ag 18,8:4
Lights Up 1940,F 18,IX,2:5
Ligne du Coeur, La 1931,O 25,VIII,1:7
Like a King 1921,O 4,10:1
Likely Tale, A 1956,Ap 8,II,3:1
Li'l Abner 1956,N 16,24:2; 1956,N 25,II,1:1
Lilies of the Field 1921,O 5,20:1
Liliom 1921,Ap 21,18:1; 1921,Ap 24,VI,1:1;
1921,My 1,VII,1:1; 1921,S 10,12:3;
1921,N 27,VI,1:1; 1927,Ja 2,30:1; 1927,Ja 9,VII,2:1;
1932,O 27,23:2; 1940,Mr 26,17:2;
1940,Mr 31,IX,1:1; 1956,F 18,12:5

Lilla 1928,Mr 4,IX,2:7
Lilly Turner 1932,S 20,26:1
Lily, The 1927,Ag 2,19:1
Lily Maid, The 1937,Ja 13,20:4
Lily of Little India, A 1966,Ja 22,17:2
Lily of the Valley 1942,Ja 27,25:2
Lily Sue 1926,N 17,22:2; 1926,N 28,VIII,1:1
Lily White 1930,My 18,VIII,3:1
Limb of Snow 1967,D 13,55:1
Lime Green 1969,Mr 27,54:2
Limelight 1936,O 13,32:3
Limits 1968,F 19,52:1
Limping Devil, The 1948,Ja 22,36:4
Linden Tree, The 1947,S 14,II,3:7; 1948,Mr 3,28:2
Line Engaged 1934,O 25,28:5
Line of Least Existence, The 1968,Mr 25,53:1
Lingering Past, The 1932,Je 30,26:5
Liola 1964,S 9,30:3
Lion et la Poule, Le 1923,N 21,23:2
Lion in Love, The 1960,D 31,10:7; 1963,Ap 26,28:3
Lion in the Square 1948,Mr 27,9:4
Lion in Winter, The 1966,Mr 4,23:1;
   1966,Mr 13,II,1:1
Lion Tamer, The 1926,O 8,26:1; 1926,O 17,VIII,1:1
Lionel Touch, The 1969,N 6,57:2
Liselott 1932,My 22,VIII,2:3
Listen Professor! 1943,D 23,22:1
Listen to the Quiet 1958,O 28,40:2
Listeners 1928,Mr 11,VIII,1:3
Listening In 1922,D 5,24:1
Little A 1947,Ja 16,31:2
Little Accident 1928,S 16,IX,2:4; 1928,O 10,32:3;
   1929,Ap 28,IX,1:4; 1929,S 22,IX,4:1
Little Angel, The 1924,S 29,10:3; 1924,O 5,VIII,1:1;
   1924,O 12,VIII,1:1
Little Baloney, A 1968,Ja 9,34:1
Little Bandit 1935,Ap 19,24:2
Little Bit of Fluff, A 1923,F 25,VII,1:7
Little Black Book, The 1932,D 27,11:2
Little Blue Light, The 1951,Ap 30,17:2
Little Boxes 1968,Jl 5,20:1; 1969,D 4,71:2;
   1969,D 14,II,3:3; 1970,F 15,II,1:1
Little Brown Jug 1946,Mr 7,32:2
Little Cantor, The 1930,S 24,26:2
Little Catherine 1931,Ja 19,27:2; 1931,D 6,VIII,2:7
Little Clay Cart, The 1924,D 6,13:3;
   1924,D 14,VIII,3:1; 1953,Jl 1,25:1
Little Clown, The 1930,Mr 15,23:3
Little Dark Horse 1941,N 17,14:4
Little Darling 1942,O 28,26:2
Little Dear 1936,D 31,20:5
Little Eyolf 1926,Ja 31,VII,1:1; 1926,F 3,22:1;
   1930,N 2,VIII,2:6; 1964,Mr 17,31:1
Little Father of the Wilderness, The 1930,Je 3,27:1
Little Foxes, The 1939,F 16,16:2; 1939,F 26,IX,1:1;
   1942,N 1,VIII,2:1; 1962,D 6,56:1; 1967,O 27,53:1;
   1967,N 5,II,1:1; 1968,Ja 6,24:4
Little Giants 1933,D 2,9:5
Little Glass Clock, The 1954,D 12,II,5:1;
   1956,Mr 27,40:2
Little Hut, The 1953,O 8,37:2; 1961,Jl 26,34:2
Little Inn, The 1935,Ag 20,25:1
Little Is Big 1968,Ap 15,41:1
Little Italy 1928,My 10,31:1
Little Jessie James 1923,Ag 16,10:4
Little King 1932,My 25,23:4
Little Ladyship 1939,F 26,IX,3:5
Little Malcolm and His Struggle Against the
   Eunuchs 1966,F 5,32:3
Little Man, The 1934,Je 20,24:3
Little Mary Sunshine 1959,N 19,49:3;
   1959,N 29,II,1:1; 1962,My 18,35:8
Little Me 1962,O 10,58:2; 1962,N 19,41:3;
   1962,D 2,II,1:1
Little Minister, The 1925,Mr 24,21:1
Little Miss Bluebeard 1923,Ag 29,12:1;
   1923,S 2,VI,1:1; 1923,S 9,VII,1:1
Little Miss Charity 1920,S 3,6:3
Little Miss Door-Step 1924,Ap 1,18:1
Little Moon of Alban 1960,D 2,34:1
Little Mouse, The 1925,S 8,21:5
Little Murders 1967,Ap 26,38:1; 1967,Je 4,II,1:1;
   1967,Jl 23,II,5:4; 1969,Ja 6,38:1; 1969,Ja 26,II,1:1;
   1969,O 2,54:1
Little Nellie Kelly 1922,Ag 6,VI,1:7; 1922,N 14,16:1;
   1923,Jl 3,25:2; 1923,Jl 8,VI,1:1; 1923,S 30,II,1:6
Little Ol' Boy 1933,Ap 25,15:5; 1936,My 11,16:1
Little Old New York 1920,S 9,9:2; 1920,S 19,VI,1:1
Little Orchard Annie 1930,Ap 22,33:1
Little Poor Man, The 1925,Ag 6,14:1;
   1925,Ag 23,VII,1:1
Little Princess, The 1931,F 7,11:3
Little Private World of Arthur Morton Fenwick,
   The 1967,O 31,38:2
Little Racketeer, The 1931,O 11,VIII,4:7;
   1932,Ja 19,24:4
Little Red Riding Hood 1948,Ja 12,15:3
Little Saint, The 1931,D 14,16:4
Little Shot 1935,Ja 18,28:4
Little Show, The 1929,My 1,28:5; 1929,My 12,IX,1:2
Little Spitfire, The 1926,Ag 17,15:2
Little Stone House, The 1923,My 11,20:3;
   1923,My 13,16:2

Little Stranger 1938,Jl 14,16:2; 1938,Jl 31,IX,1:3
Little Tailor, The 1938,Mr 21,18:2
Little Theatre Tournament 1926,My 4,30:2;
   1926,My 5,24:5; 1926,My 6,23:3; 1926,My 7,12:2;
   1926,My 8,21:2; 1928,My 10,31:1; 1928,My 10,31:1;
   1928,My 11,28:1; 1929,My 7,28:1; 1929,My 8,34:4;
   1929,My 9,34:3; 1929,My 10,32:2; 1929,My 11,22:2
Little Town of Bethlehem, The 1920,D 27,11:1;
   1922,D 26,15:4
Little Women 1931,D 8,36:2; 1944,D 13,29:2;
   1945,D 24,18:2
Littlest Circus, The 1957,O 14,32:4; 1959,D 26,5:6
Littlest Crown, The 1968,Ap 15,41:1
Littlest Revue, The 1956,My 23,37:2
Live and Learn 1930,Ap 10,24:6
Live Life Again 1945,O 1,14:7
Live Like Pigs 1965,Je 8,48:2
Live Wire, The 1950,Jl 19,26:2; 1950,Ag 18,16:2;
   1950,Ag 27,II,1:1
Livin' the Life 1957,Ap 29,20:1
Living Corpse, The 1924,Mr 18,25:2; 1928,Ja 24,26:2;
   1928,N 20,28:2; 1928,N 25,X,4:7; 1929,D 7,19:1
Living Dangerously 1934,Je 8,19:3; 1935,Ja 14,10:3
Living Mask, The 1924,Ja 22,15:1
Living Premise, The 1963,Je 14,34:1
Living Room, The 1953,Ap 17,29:5; 1954,N 18,41:1;
   1954,N 28,II,1:1; 1962,N 22,43:5
Livree de M le Comte, La 1927,N 20,IX,4:4
Liza 1922,N 28,24:1
Ljusnande Tid, Den 1939,S 17,X,2:4
Lo and Behold! 1951,D 13,45:2
Local Angle, The 1952,Ja 26,9:2
Local Stigmatic, The 1969,N 4,55:2
Locandiera, La 1923,N 1,24:1; 1923,N 22,16:1;
   1923,D 9,IX,1:1; 1926,N 23,26:1
Locked Door, The 1924,Je 20,17:2
Locked Room, The 1933,D 26,18:5
Loco 1946,O 17,29:2
Locus Solus 1922,D 9,11:4
Lodging for the Night, A 1922,O 2,10:2
Loggerheads 1925,F 10,21:1
Logia a la Natividad de Nuestro Senor Jesucristo, El
   1937,D 14,33:4
Logneren og Nonnen 1930,D 28,VIII,3:5
Lollipop 1924,Ja 22,15:3
Lolly 1929,O 17,26:2
Lombardi, Ltd 1927,Je 7,27:3
London, Paris and New York 1926,Je 8,23:1
London After Dark 1937,Ap 8,21:2
London Assurance 1932,Ag 28,IX,1:1; 1937,F 19,14:5;
   1970,Je 25,55:2; 1970,Ag 7,26:1
London Calling 1923,S 2,VI,1:7; 1930,S 28,VIII,4:1;
   1930,O 20,29:1
London Merchant, The 1928,O 2,34:3
London Prodigal, The 1928,D 23,VIII,4:1
London Wall 1931,My 2,23:2; 1931,My 24,VIII,1:6
Lone Valley 1933,Mr 11,18:6
Lonely Lee 1923,N 11,VIII,2:6
Lonely Way, The 1931,F 22,VIII,4:1
Lonesome Ship, The 1956,D 7,32:6
Lonesome Train, The 1965,Je 17,25:1;
   1965,Je 27,II,1:1
Lonesome West, The 1936,Je 30,15:1
Long and the Short and the Tall, The
   1962,Mr 30,28:2
Long Christmas Dinner, The 1966,S 7,53:1
Long Days, The 1951,Ap 21,10:5
Long Day's Journey Into Night 1956,F 11,12:6;
   1956,F 19,II,1:6; 1956,O 17,40:1; 1956,N 8,47:2;
   1956,N 18,II,1:1; 1957,J 3,14:1; 1957,Jl 6,9:5;
   1958,S 9,40:4; 1958,S 26,21:2; 1959,Ap 29,30:2;
   1962,My 16,35:4; 1962,S 30,85:8; 1963,Je 27,25:1
Long Dream, The 1960,F 18,36:2
Long Frontier, The 1935,Jl 23,24:4
Long Gallery, The 1958,Mr 7,17:2
Long Island Love 1926,Ag 1,VII,4:1
Long Live America 1939,Ja 2,28:3
Long Live Spain! 1937,Ja 10,X,3:3
Long Moment, The 1950,My 22,16:6
Long Road, The 1930,Jl 20,VIII,2:1; 1930,S 10,30:2
Long Voyage Home, The 1929,Ja 27,IX,1:1;
   1937,O 30,23:2; 1948,My 21,21:2;
   1948,My 30,II,1:1; 1961,D 5,49:1
Long Watch, The 1952,Mr 21,19:5
Long Way From Home, A 1948,F 9,25:2
Longing for Home 1923,S 22,15:1
Look, Ma, I'm Dancin' 1948,Ja 30,20:2;
   1948,F 8,II,2:1; 1948,F 8,II,1:1
Look After Lulu 1959,Mr 4,35:1; 1959,Jl 30,20:1
Look at the Heffernans 1934,N 17,13:2
Look Back in Anger 1957,O 2,28:2; 1957,O 13,II,1:1;
   1968,N 1,38:1
Look Homeward, Angel 1957,N 29,33:1;
   1957,D 8,II,5:1; 1958,Ag 31,II,1:1; 1962,Ap 4,38:3
Look to the Lilies 1970,Mr 30,59:1;
   1970,Ap 12,II,3:7
Look Who's Here 1920,Mr 3,12:2; 1932,O 31,18:5
Look: We've Come Through 1961,O 26,40:1
Loose Ankles 1926,Ag 17,15:1; 1926,Ag 29,VII,1:1
Loose Ends 1926,N 2,34:2
Loose Moments 1935,F 5,22:3
Loot 1968,Mr 19,40:2; 1968,Mr 31,II,1:1
Lord Adrian 1937,Ap 17,14:8

Lord Blesses the Bishop, The 1934,N 28,24:5
Lord Byron's Cain 1925,Ap 9,20:3
Lord Byron's Love Letter 1955,Ja 19,23:2
Lord of the Manor, The 1928,O 14,X,2:1
Lord Pengo 1962,N 20,41:2
Lorelei 1938,N 30,21:2
Lorenzaccio 1958,O 15,44:2
Lorenzo 1963,Ja 25,12:5; 1963,F 16,5:2
Lorsqu'on Aime 1921,D 25,VI,1:8
Los Angeles 1927,D 20,32:3
Losers 1967,S 24,II,1:4; 1968,Jl 26,21:4
Loss of Roses, A 1959,N 30,27:1; 1959,D 6,II,5:1
Lost 1927,Mr 29,22:2
Lost Boy 1932,Ja 6,24:4
Lost Child's Fireflies, A 1954,Jl 16,11:4
Lost Colony, The 1937,Jl 11,X,2:1
Lost Horizons 1934,O 16,31:2; 1934,O 21,IX,1:1
Lost in the Stars 1949,O 31,21:2; 1949,N 6,II,1:1
Lost Melody, The 1936,Je 28,IX,1:6
Lost Paradise 1934,D 14,28:3
Lost Sheep 1930,My 6,33:2
Lotte Goslar's Pantomime Circus-For Humans Only
   1957,D 17,45:1
Lottery, The 1930,N 23,IX,3:5; 1936,N 9,23:4
Lottie Dundass 1941,Ag 22,19:5; 1943,Ag 22,II,1:8
Lottie Gathers No Moss 1931,F 24,26:4
Loud Red Patrick, The 1956,O 4,28:1;
   1956,O 14,II,1:1
Loud Speaker 1927,Mr 3,27:2; 1927,Mr 20,VIII,1:1
Louder, Please! 1931,N 13,26:4
Louie the 14th 1925,Mr 4,17:1; 1925,N 17,29:3
Louisiana 1933,F 28,15:5; 1961,O 8,II,3:4
Louisiana Lady 1947,Je 3,35:2
Louisiana Purchase 1940,My 29,19:2;
   1940,Je 16,IX,1:1
Love 1921,Mr 6,VI,1:2
Love, Honor and Betray 1930,Mr 13,22:2
Love, Honor and Oh Baby 1940,Mr 29,25:2
Love Among the Paint Pots 1921,My 29,VI,1:7
Love Among the Ruins 1963,My 5,85:6
Love and Babies 1933,Ag 23,21:4
Love and How to Cure It 1937,F 11,19:3
Love and Kisses 1963,D 19,39:1
Love and Land 1931,F 1,VIII,3:3
Love and Let Love 1935,Mr 26,23:4; 1951,O 20,11:2;
   1968,Ja 4,30:1
Love and Libel 1960,D 8,44:1
Love and Maple Syrup 1970,Ja 8,47:1
Love and Politics 1929,O 21,30:7
Love at Second Sight 1927,S 11,VIII,2:4
Love Birds 1921,Mr 16,12:1
Love Call, The 1927,O 25,33:1
Love Chef, The 1921,Je 12,VI,1:6
Love Child, The 1922,N 15,22:1
Love City, The 1926,Ja 26,18:2
Love Doctor, The 1959,O 14,52:4
Love Dreams 1921,O 11,22:2; 1921,O 16,VI,1:1
Love Duel, The 1929,Ap 16,32:3
Love 'Em and Leave 'Em 1926,F 4,20:4;
   1926,F 14,VIII,1:1
Love Expert, The 1929,S 24,29:1
Love for Love 1925,Ap 1,21:2; 1925,Ap 5,IX,1:2;
   1925,S 15,29:3; 1936,Je 30,15:4; 1940,Je 4,19:5;
   1944,N 19,II,2:4; 1947,My 27,30:2; 1947,Je 1,II,1:1;
   1967,O 21,17:1; 1967,O 29,II,5:1; 1967,O 30,59:1
Love for Sale 1932,D 5,21:4; 1936,Ja 24,14:2
Love From a Stranger 1936,F 3,20:7; 1936,Ap 1,28:7;
   1936,Ap 26,IX,2:2; 1936,S 22,31:5; 1936,S 30,28:1
Love Goes to Press 1946,Je 19,16:2; 1947,Ja 2,22:2
Love Habit, The 1923,Mr 15,17:1;
   1923,Mr 25,VIII,1:1
Love in a Garden 1926,Je 16,23:3
Love in a Mist 1926,Ap 13,28:3; 1941,N 30,IX,3:1
Love in Albania 1949,Jl 17,II,1:6
Love in E Flat 1967,F 14,38:1
Love in Humble Life 1937,Mr 10,27:2
Love in Idleness 1944,D 22,13:2; 1945,Ja 7,II,2:3
Love in My Fashion 1937,D 4,21:4
Love in Our Time 1952,O 4,14:3
Love in Pawn 1923,Ap 8,VIII,1:7
Love in the Country 1930,S 28,VIII,4:4
Love in the Tropics 1927,O 19,24:3
Love Is a Time of Day 1969,D 23,21:3;
   1970,Ja 4,II,5:1
Love Is Like That 1927,Ap 19,24:1
Love Is No Heaven 1943,Mr 16,15:3
Love Is Not So Simple 1935,N 5,33:1;
   1935,N 10,IX,1:6; 1935,N 20,26:7
Love Kills 1934,My 2,25:3
Love Letter, The 1921,O 5,20:1
Love Life 1948,O 8,31:2
Love Me Little 1958,Ap 15,42:2
Love Me Long 1949,N 8,34:5
Love Nest, The 1927,D 23,17:1; 1928,My 27,VIII,1:1;
   1963,Ja 28,7:6
Love of Don Perlimplin and Belisa in the Garden,
   The 1953,N 4,30:5
Love of Four Colonels, The 1953,Ja 16,17:2
Love of Two Hours, The 1962,O 27,16:2
Love of Women 1937,D 14,33:2
Love on an Island 1934,Jl 24,20:5
Love on Leave 1944,Je 21,23:4

Love on the Dole 1935,F 17,VIII,3:1; 1936,F 25,23:3;
1936,Mr 8,IX,1:1
Love Scandal, A 1923,N 7,14:1
Love Set, The 1923,Mr 20,24:2
Love Song, The 1925,Ja 14,19:4
Love Spell, The 1925,N 25,14:2
Love Thief, The 1931,Ja 19,24:5
Love Your Crooked Neighbor 1969,D 30,40:1
Lovebound 1929,My 19,IX,2:1
Lovecraft's Follies 1970,Ap 19,II,12:1
Lovely Ladies, Kind Gentlemen 1970,D 29,38:1
Lovely Lady 1925,S 20,VIII,2:4; 1925,O 15,27:1;
1927,D 30,22:1; 1932,Mr 20,VIII,1:8
Lovely Light, A 1960,F 9,27:4; 1964,Ja 21,24:2
Lovely Me 1946,D 26,30:4
Lover, The 1963,S 19,21:1; 1964,Ja 6,35:1
Lovers 1956,My 11,23:1; 1967,S 24,II,1:4;
1968,Jl 26,21:4; 1968,N 24,II,9:4; 1968,N 26,43:1
Lovers, Villains and Fools: A Shakespearean Variety
Show 1956,O 24,44:7
Lovers and Enemies 1927,S 21,27:1
Lovers and Friends 1943,N 21,VI,16:1;
1943,N 30,23:2; 1943,D 5,II,5:1
Lovers and Other Strangers 1968,S 19,63:1;
1968,S 29,II,1:1
Lovers Breakfast, A 1936,N 26,38:2
Lovers in the Metro, The 1962,Ja 31,21:1
Lover's Leap 1934,O 26,24:3
Lovers' Meeting 1931,Je 17,32:3; 1937,Je 3,23:1
Love's Call 1925,S 11,20:1
Love's Labour's Lost 1932,Ag 7,IX,1:7;
1949,O 24,18:3; 1953,F 5,20:3; 1953,F 8,II,1:1;
1961,Je 23,19:1; 1961,Jl 2,II,1:1; 1964,Ap 8,36:2;
1965,Je 16,46:1; 1968,Je 28,36:1; 1968,D 22,54:3;
1969,Ja 5,II,3:1
Loves of Cass McGuire, The 1966,O 7,36:1;
1967,Je 4,II,1:1
Loves of Charles II, The 1933,D 28,25:2;
1937,Mr 29,15:1
Loves of Lulu, The 1925,My 12,26:1
Love's Old Sweet Song 1940,Ap 7,I,44:6;
1940,Ap 14,IX,3:3; 1940,My 3,16:3
Lovey 1965,Mr 26,27:1
Lovka Maladetz 1935,Mr 27,25:5
Low Bridge 1933,F 10,13:4
Low Tide 1924,Ag 17,VII,1:8
Lower Depths, The 1923,Ja 16,16:1;
1923,Ja 21,VII,1:1; 1923,D 9,IX,1:1;
1928,My 13,IX,2:7; 1956,O 3,29:2; 1964,Mr 31,30:1;
1964,Ap 12,II,1:1
Lower North 1944,Ag 26,15:4
Loyalties 1922,Mr 26,VI,1:2; 1922,Jl 9,VI,1:1;
1922,S 28,18:1; 1922,O 8,VI,1:1; 1928,Ag 26,VII,1:3
Luana 1930,S 18,28:1
Luck of the Devil 1936,Ja 14,25:1
Luckee Girl 1928,S 17,28:6
Lucky 1927,Mr 23,28:3
Lucky Boy 1935,D 2,19:5
Lucky Break 1925,Ag 12,16:2; 1934,O 3,25:3;
1934,O 28,IX,3:4
Lucky Dip 1930,N 16,VIII,4:1
Lucky Finger, The 1948,Ja 21,30:5
Lucky Night, The 1931,S 14,15:5
Lucky One, The 1922,N 21,15:2; 1922,D 3,VIII,1:1
Lucky Sam McCarver 1925,O 22,22:1;
1925,N 1,VIII,1:1; 1950,Ap 15,10:6
Lucky Sambo 1925,Je 8,19:4; 1926,My 26,24:2
Lucrece 1932,N 30,22:8; 1932,D 4,IX,3:3;
1932,D 21,22:2; 1933,Ja 1,IX,1:1
Lucrezia Borgia 1937,Mr 8,22:2
Ludlow Fair 1966,Mr 23,42:1
Ludo 1932,Je 12,X,1:3
Lui 1929,N 17,IX,2:6; 1929,N 24,X,2:1
Lullaby 1954,F 4,21:2
Lullaby, The 1923,S 9,VII,2:4; 1923,S 19,5:3;
1923,O 7,IX,1:1; 1923,D 16,IX,1:1
Lulu 1927,Ja 30,VII,4:3; 1927,O 2,VIII,2:4;
1928,O 28,IX,2:1; 1958,S 30,24:1; 1970,Mr 28,32:1
Lulu Belle 1926,F 10,20:1; 1926,F 14,VIII,1:1
Lunatic the Secret Sportsman and the Woman Next
1968,D 5,58:4
Lunatics and Lovers 1954,D 14,44:2
Lunchtime Follies, The 1942,Je 23,22:3
Lupa, La 1965,Ja 11,VII,2:7; 1969,Je 5,54:1
Lure, The 1924,My 18,VII,2:8
Lusitania 1926,Ja 20,22:1
Lute Song 1946,F 7,29:2; 1946,F 17,II,1:1;
1948,O 12,32:3; 1959,Mr 13,24:1
Luther 1961,Jl 8,9:2; 1961,Jl 28,10:2; 1963,S 11,46:3;
1963,S 26,41:1; 1963,O 6,II,1:1; 1965,F 15,30:4
Luv 1964,N 12,43:1; 1964,N 22,II,1:1;
1965,N 16,56:4
Lyle 1970,Mr 21,16:2
Lysistrata 1925,Ja 11,VII,2:7; 1925,O 17,18:3;
1925,D 15,28:2; 1925,D 20,VII,3:1;
1930,Ap 29,30:5; 1930,Je 1,VIII,1:1; 1930,Je 6,20:1;
1930,D 14,IX,2:7; 1937,Jl 20,19:3; 1938,Ag 7,IX,1:5;
1946,O 18,27:5; 1959,My 20,40:2; 1959,N 25,19:4;
1959,D 6,II,5:1; 1968,N 15,42:1

M

Ma Femme 1927,D 18,IX,4:4
Ma Liberte 1936,D 13,XI,5:1
Ma Soeur de Luxe 1933,Je 4,IX,1:6
Ma Soeur et Moi 1928,Ap 29,IX,2:3
Ma Tante d' Honfleur 1920,Ja 27,18:3
Macbeth 1920,N 3,14:2; 1921,F 18,16:1;
1921,F 20,VI,1:1; 1921,F 27,VI,1:1;
1921,Ap 20,11:1; 1921,Ap 24,VI,1:1; 1921,Je 7,20:2;
1921,D 27,10:3; 1923,F 11,VII,1:1; 1924,Mr 17,18:1;
1924,Mr 23,VIII,1:1; 1927,Ja 2,30:1;
1927,Ja 16,VII,4:3; 1928,F 7,30:7; 1928,N 4,IX,1:3;
1928,N 20,28:3; 1930,F 13,9:6; 1930,Mr 2,IX,2:4;
1930,Mr 26,24:6; 1931,O 11,VIII,4:5;
1934,Ap 3,26:4; 1935,S 17,26:3; 1935,O 8,26:4;
1936,Ap 5,IX,1:4; 1936,Ap 15,25:3;
1936,Ap 15,25:4; 1936,Jl 22,17:5; 1937,Mr 7,XI,2:1;
1937,O 11,26:3; 1937,N 27,21:3; 1937,D 19,XI,3:7;
1939,Je 4,IX,2:5; 1941,N 12,30:2; 1941,N 23,IX,1:1;
1942,Je 3,26:4; 1942,Jl 26,VIII,1:7; 1946,D 1,II,3:7;
1947,My 30,25:1; 1947,D 19,34:3; 1948,Ap 1,30:2;
1948,Ap 11,II,1:1; 1952,Jl 6,II,1:7; 1954,S 5,II,3:7;
1955,Je 19,II,1:1; 1955,O 8,12:6; 1955,O 20,42:2;
1956,My 24,27:1; 1956,O 30,42:2; 1956,N 4,II,1:1;
1957,Ag 16,11:2; 1959,Je 7,124:3; 1959,Ag 1,9:2;
1961,Ja 10,28:1; 1961,F 1,5:7; 1961,Je 19,31:1;
1961,Je 25,II,1:1; 1962,F 7,32:2; 1962,F 25,II,1:1;
1962,Je 6,35:2; 1962,Je 20,41:1; 1962,N 17,16:2;
1964,Jl 27,22:3; 1966,Je 29,38:1; 1966,Jl 14,27:2;
1966,Ag 29,23:4; 1966,Ag 30,34:1; 1967,Jl 31,21:1;
1968,N 30,49:3; 1969,Je 1,II,4:5; 1969,D 14,87:1;
1969,D 23,25:1
MacBird! 1967,F 23,38:1; 1967,Mr 12,II,1:1;
1967,Ap 11,54:5; 1967,Ap 16,II,3:6;
1967,Ap 16,II,1:1
Machen Sie Das Nicht Mit Ihrer Frau
1932,Je 19,IX,1:5
Machiavel 1931,O 18,VIII,4:4
Machinal 1928,S 8,10:3; 1928,S 16,IX,1:1;
1960,Ap 8,27:1; 1960,Ap 17,II,1:1
Machine Infernale, La 1934,My 13,IX,2:2;
1935,Ap 21,IX,2:2
Machine Wreckers, The 1923,My 13,VIII,3:5;
1937,Ap 12,14:2
Machines 1930,N 7,32:1; 1930,N 23,IX,2:4
Mackerel Skies 1934,Ja 24,20:4
Macushla 1920,My 18,9:3
Mad Dog, The 1921,N 9,20:1
Mad Honeymoon, The 1923,Ag 8,10:1;
1923,Ag 12,VI,1:1
Mad Hopes, The 1932,My 29,VIII,2:2; 1932,D 2,26:3
Mad Morning 1935,Je 25,14:1
Mad Show, The 1966,Ja 10,16:1
Madam Will You Walk 1939,N 14,20:3; 1953,D 2,2:4;
1953,D 20,II,3:1
Madame Alias 1927,S 4,VII,2:4
Madame Aphrodite 1961,D 30,13:1
Madame Bovary 1936,N 8,X,3:6; 1937,O 6,28:4;
1937,N 17,26:2
Madame Capet 1938,O 26,26:2
Madame Est Avec Moi 1937,My 16,X,2:6
Madame Is Served 1949,F 15,28:1
Madame Lafayette 1960,Mr 4,21:1
Madame Pagliacci 1935,S 30,12:3
Madame Pepita 1931,Mr 7,17:1
Madame Pierre 1922,F 16,11:1; 1922,F 19,VI,1:1
Madame Plays Nap 1929,D 18,31:2
Madame Pompadour 1924,N 2,VII,2:3;
1924,N 12,20:6
Madame Quinze 1935,Ap 21,IX,2:1
Madame Sans-Gene 1924,N 4,30:1
Madame X 1927,Mr 11,24:3; 1927,Ap 3,VIII,1:4;
1927,Jl 7,29:3
Madcap, The 1928,F 1,31:2
Made for Each Other 1924,S 30,27:2
Made in America 1925,O 15,27:2
Made in France 1930,O 19,IX,3:4; 1930,N 12,21:1
Made in Heaven 1946,O 25,28:2
Madeleine and the Movies 1922,Mr 7,11:1
Mademoiselle 1932,Ja 31,VIII,3:1; 1932,O 9,IX,3:6;
1932,O 19,22:4; 1936,O 4,IX,3:7
Mademoiselle Bourrat 1923,F 4,VII,1:4;
1926,N 21,VIII,2:1; 1929,O 8,34:3
Mademoiselle Colombe 1954,Ja 7,26:1;
1954,Ja 17,II,1:1
Mademoiselle Flute 1927,Je 12,VII,2:1
Mademoiselle Jockey 1926,D 5,VIII,6:1
Mademoiselle Josette Ma Femme 1924,Je 1,VII,1:7
Mademoiselle le Feu 1924,My 18,VII,2:8
Madmen and Specialists 1970,Ag 3,38:1
Madness of Lady Bright, The 1966,Mr 23,42:1
Madone des Sleepings, La 1928,O 14,X,5:1
Madonna Wo Bist Du? 1932,Jl 17,IX,1:3
Madras House, The 1921,O 30,VI,1:1;
1921,O 31,18:2; 1921,N 6,VI,1:1
Madre 1923,D 31,9:6
Madre, La 1959,F 12,24:1
Madrigal of Shakespeare, A 1968,F 14,56:2

Madwoman of Chaillot, The 1948,D 26,II,3:1;
1949,Ja 9,II,1:1; 1949,S 11,II,1:1; 1950,Je 14,41:2;
1951,Mr 4,II,3:7; 1970,Mr 23,48:3
Maedchen in Uniform 1932,N 6,IX,1:3
Mafro, Darling! 1929,Mr 17,X,1:4
Magda 1925,D 22,18:4; 1926,Ja 27,16:2;
1930,Je 1,VIII,2:8
Magdalen, The 1933,F 6,11:3; 1933,F 12,IX,2:1
Magdalena 1948,Jl 28,27:2; 1948,S 21,31:2;
1948,S 26,II,1:1; 1948,S 26,II,7:1; 1948,N 7,II,6:5
Maggie 1924,N 2,VII,2:3; 1953,F 19,20:2
Maggie, the Magnificent 1929,O 22,26:1;
1929,N 3,IX,1:1
Maggie Flynn 1968,O 24,52:1; 1968,N 3,II,1:1
Maggie French Understands 1963,Je 6,40:8
Magic 1929,D 17,28:5; 1935,Mr 14,19:2;
1942,S 30,28:2
Magic and Mimicry 1929,D 23,18:6
Magic and the Loss, The 1954,Ap 10,10:3
Magic Crystal, The 1924,Jl 13,VII,1:6
Magic Hours 1925,My 3,VIII,2:1
Magic Ring, The 1923,O 2,10:1
Magic Touch, The 1947,S 4,30:1; 1947,S 14,II,1:1
Magistrate, The 1959,My 14,30:6
Magnanimous Lover, The 1920,F 10,10:2;
1933,F 1,13:5
Magnificent Hugo, The 1961,Ap 8,12:2
Magnificent Yankee, The 1946,Ja 2,23:6;
1946,Ja 23,21:2; 1946,F 3,II,1:2
Magnolia 1923,Je 24,VII,1:4; 1923,Ag 28,12:3;
1923,S 2,VI,1:1
Magnolia Alley 1949,Ap 19,29:2
Magnolia Lady, The 1924,N 26,17:2
Magnolia Street 1934,Mr 9,22:6; 1934,Ap 1,X,1:7
Mahabharata 1970,N 28,22:1
Mahagonny 1970,Ap 29,51:1; 1970,My 10,II,15:1;
1970,My 10,II,1:1
Mahogany Hall 1934,Ja 18,18:5
Maid Errant 1926,Ag 8,VII,3:1
Maid in Japan 1939,F 20,12:5
Maid in the Ozarks 1946,Jl 16,20:3
Maid of All Work 1927,Ja 13,28:4
Maiden at the Dojo Temple, The 1960,Je 10,37:1;
1960,Je 17,35:4
Maidens and Mistresses at Home at the Zoo
1958,O 29,31:1
Maids, The 1963,N 15,29:1
Mail Call 1943,Je 15,16:1
Main Line, The 1924,Mr 26,19:4;
1924,Mr 30,VIII,1:1
Main Street 1921,Jl 24,VI,1:1; 1921,O 6,21:1
Mainly for Lovers 1936,F 11,19:5; 1936,F 22,13:2
Mains Sales, Les 1948,Ap 18,II,1:6; 1948,D 12,II,3:1
Mais n'te Promene Donc pas Toute Nue
1930,Mr 30,VIII,2:4
Maison de la Nuit, La 1953,N 29,II,3:1
Maitlands, The 1934,Jl 22,IX,1:3
Maitre Bolbec et son Mari 1926,N 14,VIII,2:1
Maitre de Son Coeur, Le 1931,F 22,VIII,4:1
Maitresse de Roi 1926,D 1,24:1
Major Barbara 1928,N 20,28:4; 1928,D 2,X,1:1;
1935,Mr 5,23:2; 1951,F 24,10:2; 1954,Je 30,23:2;
1956,O 31,27:1; 1965,My 18,33:1
Major Noah 1929,F 23,17:2
Majority of One, A 1959,F 17,28:2; 1959,F 22,II,1:1;
1960,Mr 10,37:5
Makbeth 1969,N 21,51:1; 1969,N 30,II,3:1
Make a Million 1958,O 24,39:2
Make a Wish 1951,Ap 19,38:1; 1951,My 20,II,1:1
Make-Believe 1930,N 8,21:1
Make It Snappy 1922,Ap 14,20:2
Make Like a Dog 1966,Mr 7,22:1
Make Me Disappear 1969,My 14,34:1
Make Me Know It 1929,N 5,32:5
Make Mine Manhattan 1948,Ja 16,26:2;
1948,F 8,II,2:1
Make Way for Lucia 1948,D 23,23:5
Make Yourself at Home 1945,S 14,21:2;
1945,S 23,II,1:1
Maker of Dreams, The 1920,Ap 28,9:3
Maker of Images, The 1927,Mr 5,12:2
Makers of Light 1922,My 24,22:3
Making of an Immortal, The 1928,Ap 3,32:4;
1928,Ap 29,IX,1:3
Making of Moo, The 1958,Je 12,34:1
Makropoulos Secret, The 1926,Ja 22,12:4;
1957,D 4,52:4
Mal de Test, Le 1965,S 9,36:3
Malade Imaginaire, Le 1926,N 14,VIII,2:1;
1929,Ap 14,X,2:1; 1958,Ap 30,28:2; 1970,F 18,40:2
Malcochon 1969,Ap 2,37:1
Malcolm 1966,Ja 12,29:1
Male Animal, The 1940,Ja 10,17:2; 1940,Ja 21,IX,1:1;
1941,Jl 9,24:6; 1952,My 1,35:1; 1952,My 18,II,1:1
Malia 1921,S 10,12:3
Malice Domestic 1942,Jl 21,22:1
Malice in Wonderland 1953,D 17,51:3
Malinda 1929,D 4,37:2
Malvaloca 1922,O 3,22:1
Mama 1930,Mr 30,VIII,4:8
Mama Loves Papa 1926,F 23,26:2
Mama's Affair 1920,Ja 25,VIII,2:1

Mamba's Daughters 1939,Ja 4,24:2; 1939,Ja 15,IX,1:1;
  1940,Mr 25,10:4; 1953,Mr 21,12:6
Mame 1966,My 25,41:1; 1967,Ag 15,31:2;
  1968,Ap 20,25:1; 1969,Ja 5,79:4; 1969,F 22,35:5;
  1969,Je 20,36:1
Mamma's Affair 1920,Ja 20,10:1
Man, The 1950,Ja 20,28:2; 1953,Ja 25,II,3:1;
  1953,F 15,II,2:1
Man About Town, A 1921,Mr 22,15:1
Man Alive 1965,My 23,13:1
Man and Boy 1963,S 5,28:1; 1963,N 13,34:1;
  1963,D 1,II,1:1
Man and Dog 1967,O 2,54:2
Man and Superman 1947,O 9,31:2; 1947,O 19,II,1:1;
  1949,My 17,28:6; 1953,F 21,11:2; 1960,Ag 17,35:3;
  1960,N 7,46:2; 1964,D 7,45:2; 1965,Ja 31,II,1:1;
  1970,F 24,48:1
Man and the Masses 1924,Ap 15,25:1;
  1924,Ap 20,VIII,1:1; 1924,My 25,VIII,1:8
Man Better Man 1969,Jl 3,22:1; 1969,Jl 13,II,1:1;
  1969,Jl 13,II,3:6
Man Bites Dog 1933,Ap 26,11:2
Man Dies, A 1968,Jl 16,35:1
Man-Eating Tiger, The 1927,S 25,VIII,4:8
Man for All Seasons, A 1961,N 23,51:1;
  1961,D 3,II,1:1; 1962,S 23,II,1:1; 1963,My 11,15:1;
  1964,Ja 28,24:2
Man From Cairo, The 1938,My 5,26:5
Man From Earth, The 1923,Ja 3,6:2
Man From Home, The 1927,O 2,VIII,4:6
Man From Toronto, The 1926,Je 18,27:2
Man Higher Up, The 1926,N 23,27:3
Man-Hunt 1940,D 4,34:3
Man in Dress Clothes, The 1922,Ap 30,VII,1:8;
  1937,Ag 24,24:4
Man in Evening Clothes, The 1924,D 6,13:4
Man in Half Moon Street, The 1939,Ap 9,X,1:8
Man in Possession, The 1930,F 9,VIII,2:1;
  1930,O 12,VIII,4:1; 1930,N 3,19:1; 1936,S 2,24:5;
  1939,S 26,21:4
Man in the Dog Suit, The 1958,O 31,34:2
Man in the Glass Booth, The 1967,Jl 29,12:1;
  1967,Ag 27,II,1:1; 1968,S 27,41:1; 1968,O 6,II,5:1;
  1969,Ap 17,58:1; 1969,Ap 18,37:3
Man in the Making, The 1921,S 21,16:2;
  1921,O 2,VII,1:1
Man in the Raincoat, The 1949,S 11,II,2:1
Man in the Stalls, The 1929,My 8,34:4
Man Is Man 1962,S 19,31:1
Man of Destiny, The 1925,N 24,28:1;
  1926,My 1,10:1; 1956,Ag 26,38:1; 1957,Ap 1,21:2
Man of Distinction 1957,Ag 27,33:7
Man of Gold, A 1929,My 6,30:2
Man of La Mancha 1965,N 23,52:1; 1966,O 5,42:5;
  1967,N 24,61:1; 1968,D 12,61:1; 1969,My 3,38:4;
  1970,Ja 25,70:6
Man of the People, A 1920,S 8,9:2
Man of Wax, The 1933,Ag 6,X,1:6
Man of Yesterday 1935,F 20,22:5;
  1935,Mr 17,VIII,1:4
Man on Stilts, The 1931,S 10,23:2
Man or Devil 1925,My 22,22:4
Man Out Loud, Girl Quiet 1962,Ap 4,38:1
Man Platonof, The 1929,Mr 3,VIII,3:1
Man Proposes 1933,D 24,IX,2:2
Man Under the Bridge, The 1933,N 5,IX,2:2
Man Who Ate the Popomack, The 1924,Mr 25,24:1;
  1924,Mr 30,VIII,1:1; 1924,Ap 6,VIII,1:1;
  1924,My 11,VIII,1:1; 1937,Jl 28,15:1
Man Who Came to Dinner, The 1939,S 26,21:3;
  1939,O 1,IX,2:5; 1939,O 17,31:1; 1939,O 22,IX,1:1;
  1940,F 10,19:5; 1940,F 18,IX,3:6;
  1941,Mr 23,IX,1:1; 1941,Jl 29,13:5;
  1941,D 14,IX,4:3
Man Who Changed His Name, The 1932,My 3,25:3
Man Who Died at Twelve O'Clock, The
  1929,My 11,22:2
Man Who Died Twice, The 1925,D 14,19:1
Man Who Had All the Luck, The 1944,N 24,18:5
Man Who Had Nothing, The 1937,Je 8,30:1
Man Who Is Getting Gray, The 1932,F 21,VIII,2:3
Man Who Killed Lincoln, The 1939,D 30,9:1;
  1940,Ja 18,26:4
Man Who Married a Dumb Wife, The
  1923,My 10,22:3; 1923,My 26,8:4; 1930,My 9,20:5
Man Who Never Died, The 1958,N 22,27:2
Man Who Pays the Piper, The 1931,Mr 1,VIII,2:4
Man Who Reclaimed His Head 1932,S 9,17:3
Man Who Washed His Hands, The 1967,F 16,33:1
Man Whom I Have Killed, The 1936,D 10,34:3
Man With a Load of Mischief, The 1925,O 27,20:1;
  1925,N 1,VIII,1:1; 1966,N 7,65:1
Man With Blonde Hair, The 1941,N 5,30:2
Man With Red Hair, A 1928,Mr 25,IX,1:3;
  1928,Je 17,VIII,1:6; 1928,N 9,22:7
Man With the Flower in His Mouth, The
  1969,Ap 23,42:1; 1969,My 4,II,3:1
Man With the Golden Arm, The 1956,My 22,28:1
Man With the Portfolio, The 1931,F 12,24:6
Man Without Money, A 1929,N 3,27:4
Mandarin, The 1920,N 10,18:2
Mandate 1926,F 15,19:1
Mandingo 1961,My 23,43:6

Mandragola 1930,F 2,VIII,4:1; 1949,Ja 25,26:6;
  1956,Mr 1,36:4; 1958,My 29,23:2; 1970,Ap 19,74:3
Manhattan 1922,Ag 16,7:5; 1922,Ag 20,VI,1:1
Manhattan Mary 1927,S 4,VII,2:4; 1927,S 27,30:3;
  1927,O 30,IX,1:1
Manhattan Medley 1932,S 25,IX,1:6
Manhattan Nocturne 1943,O 27,26:2
Manhattan Varieties 1932,O 22,18:3
Manhatters, The 1927,Jl 19,27:3; 1927,Ag 4,25:4
Manikin and Minikin 1927,My 4,29:1
Mann Ist Mann 1928,Ap 15,IX,4:7
Mann mit den Grauen Schlafen, Der
  1932,F 21,VIII,2:3
Mannequins 1925,D 27,VII,2:1
Manon 1929,Je 2,VIII,2:6
Manor House 1953,D 27,53:4
Manquait un Homme, Il 1929,Ap 14,X,2:1
Man's a Man, A 1962,S 20,30:2
Man's Estate 1929,Ap 2,28:2; 1929,Ap 28,IX,1:1
Man's House, A 1934,S 13,26:3; 1943,Ap 3,10:4;
  1943,Ap 4,II,2:1
Man's Man, A 1925,O 14,31:2; 1925,O 25,VIII,1:1;
  1931,Je 5,27:1
Man's Name, The 1921,N 16,22:1
Mansion on the Hudson 1935,Ap 3,20:4
Many a Slip 1930,F 4,29:2; 1940,N 16,12:7
Many Happy Returns 1945,Ja 6,15:5
Many Loves 1959,Ja 14,28:1; 1961,Je 16,29:1
Many Mansions 1937,Ag 3,20:5; 1937,O 28,28:6
Many Moons 1947,D 15,35:2
Many Things 1940,F 3,8:4
Many Waters 1928,Ag 5,VII,1:1; 1929,S 26,27:1;
  1929,O 6,IX,1:1
Marathon 1933,Ja 28,8:8
Marathon '33 1963,D 23,20:1
Marcel Marceau 1956,F 2,18:1; 1963,Ja 3,5:7;
  1965,N 18,56:1; 1970,Ap 8,38:3
March Hares 1921,Ag 12,8:3; 1921,Ag 21,VI,1:1;
  1923,Mr 13,19:5; 1928,Ja 1,VIII,1:3; 1928,Ap 3,32:6
March Heir, The 1932,D 14,27:3
March Indienne, La 1927,Mr 27,VIII,4:8
March March, The 1966,N 15,51:4
Marchands de Canons, Les 1933,Je 4,IX,1:6
Marchese di Priola, Il 1931,Mr 2,19:3
Marching By 1931,N 15,VIII,4:2; 1932,Mr 4,17:1
Marching Song 1937,F 18,18:2; 1959,D 29,20:1
Marching With Johnny 1943,N 23,28:2
Marco Millions 1928,Ja 10,28:2; 1928,Ja 22,VIII,1:1;
  1928,Ap 22,IX,1:1; 1929,Ja 6,VIII,4:4;
  1930,Mr 4,24:4; 1938,N 24,36:2; 1939,Ja 15,IX,3:1;
  1964,F 21,33:1; 1964,Mr 1,II,1:1
Marco Polo and the Drum of Ahmad 1950,D 18,34:2
Marcus in the High Grass 1960,N 22,38:6
Mardi Gras! 1965,Je 28,33:2; 1966,Jl 11,32:2
Marge des Tombes, En 1927,Ja 16,VII,2:1
Margin for Error 1939,O 15,48:7; 1939,N 4,11:3;
  1939,N 12,IX,1:1; 1940,Ag 11,IX,2:4
Margrave, La 1932,D 18,X,3:6
Marguerite Divided by Three 1930,S 28,VIII,4:4
Mari Que J'ai Voulu, Le 1934,Ap 29,IX,2:2
Maria 1933,O 29,IX,2:5
Maria Golovin 1958,N 6,43:1; 1958,N 30,II,11:1
Maria Stuart 1932,Je 19,IX,1:3; 1933,D 10,X,5:1;
  1968,Mr 27,38:1
Mariage de Figaro, Le 1964,F 26,41:2
Mariage Force, Le 1958,My 7,43:1
Mariage of Victorine, Le 1926,D 19,VII,3:3
Marie Antoinette 1921,N 23,16:1
Marie Antoinette in Pennsylvania 1949,My 12,26:2
Marie Tudor 1958,O 22,39:1
Marie Vison, La 1970,Jl 15,29:1
Mariee Eperdue, La 1935,My 26,XI,2:2
Mariette 1928,O 21,IX,5:6; 1929,D 8,X,4:4;
  1937,Je 29,18:3
Marigold 1927,My 29,VII,1:3; 1930,O 9,23:1
Marilyn's Affairs 1933,Mr 16,21:5
Mariners 1927,Mr 29,22:2; 1927,Ap 3,VIII,1:1;
  1929,My 19,IX,1:8
Marinka 1945,Jl 19,19:2
Marion, or the Hero of Lake George
  1932,Ap 23,11:3
Marion Show, The 1923,My 8,22:3
Marionette Man, The 1924,Ja 27,VII,2:7
Mariposa que Volo Sobre el Mar, La 1926,D 24,19:1;
  1927,My 8,VII,2:3
Marius 1929,Mr 31,VIII,2:7; 1930,N 9,IX,3:2;
  1956,F 6,27:4
Marjolaine 1922,Ja 25,16:1
Marjorie 1924,Ag 12,12:2
Mark Twain Tonight! 1959,Ap 7,40:2;
  1959,Ap 19,II,1:1; 1960,S 2,17:6; 1960,N 13,1:2;
  1962,O 11,48:4; 1966,Mr 24,48:2
Marks and Mabel 1945,S 9,II,1:4
Markurells in Wadkoeping 1930,N 2,VIII,3:2
Marlene Dietrich 1967,O 10,52:1; 1968,O 4,36:1
Marneschlacht, Die 1933,Mr 19,IX,2:2
Marquise, The 1927,Mr 20,VIII,2:7; 1927,N 15,26:4
Marquise 1931,N 1,VIII,4:3; 1935,F 24,VIII,3:1;
  1935,Mr 12,24:8
Marriage a la Mode 1930,O 26,VIII,2:1
Marriage Bed, The 1928,D 30,VIII,1:6;
  1929,Ja 8,35:1

Marriage By Instalments 1923,Ap 8,VIII,1:7
Marriage by Purchase 1931,Je 21,VIII,1:3
Marriage for Three 1931,N 12,30:5
Marriage-Go-Round, The 1958,O 30,37:1;
  1958,N 9,II,1:1
Marriage Has Been Disarranged, A 1930,D 10,28:2
Marriage Is for Single People 1945,N 22,38:2
Marriage Is No Joke 1934,F 7,16:2
Marriage of Cana, The 1932,F 3,22:4
Marriage of Fredaine, The 1924,Mr 2,VIII,1:3
Marriage of Kitty, The 1923,Mr 18,VII,1:1
Marriage of Mr Mississippi 1969,N 20,60:5
Marriage of St Francis, The 1935,D 1,XI,6:4
Marriage on Approval 1928,Mr 2,28:2
Marriage Proposal, The 1966,Je 28,51:1
Marriage Recipe, The 1930,Ag 4,13:2
Marriage Royal 1937,Jl 15,16:2
Married-And How! 1928,Je 15,30:2
Married Woman, The 1921,D 26,21:1;
  1922,F 5,VI,1:1
Marry the Man! 1929,Ap 23,26:3
Marry the Poor Girl 1920,S 27,18:3
Marrying Maiden, The 1960,Je 23,18:3
Marseilles 1930,N 9,IX,3:2; 1930,N 18,28:2
Marshal, The 1929,N 17,IX,4:7
Marshall 1930,My 10,25:1
Martine 1928,Ap 5,19:3; 1936,N 26,38:2
Martinique 1920,Ap 27,18:2; 1920,My 2,VI,2:2
Martyr Without Tears 1942,N 23,19:2
Marvellous History of Saint Bernard, The
  1958,F 24,16:3
Mary 1920,O 19,12:1
Mary, Mary 1961,Mr 9,24:2
Mary, Mary, Quite Contrary 1923,S 2,VI,2:6;
  1923,S 12,14:1; 1923,S 16,VII,1:1
Mary Agnes Is Thirty-Five 1965,F 9,42:5
Mary and the Fairy 1956,Mr 24,15:2
Mary Goes to See 1938,Mr 6,XI,3:6
Mary Jane McKane 1923,D 26,13:2
Mary of Magdala 1946,Mr 26,24:5
Mary of Scotland 1933,N 19,IX,2:5; 1933,N 28,28:3;
  1933,D 3,IX,5:1
Mary Queen of Scots 1921,F 6,VI,1:2
Mary Read 1934,N 22,26:7; 1934,D 16,XI,3:4
Mary Rose 1920,My 16,VI,1:7; 1920,Ag 8,VI,1:1;
  1920,D 23,9:2; 1920,D 26,VI,3:1; 1951,Mr 5,25:2;
  1951,Mr 11,II,1:1
Mary Stuart 1921,Mr 22,15:1; 1921,Ap 3,VII,1:1;
  1921,Ap 17,VI,1:1; 1956,Ap 28,10:2; 1957,O 9,39:1;
  1957,O 20,II,1:1; 1958,S 3,38:1; 1959,Jl 30,21:3
Mary Stuart in Scotland 1960,S 1,31:1
Mary the 3d 1923,F 6,14:2; 1923,F 11,VII,1:1
Mary Tudor 1935,D 13,30:6; 1936,Ja 12,IX,1:5
Mary Wants to Go on the Stage 1930,Mr 9,IX,8:5
Mascaiada 1929,D 28,10:6
Maschinentstuermer, Die 1922,Jl 23,VI,1:1
Mask and Gown 1957,S 11,29:1
Mask and the Face, The 1924,S 11,27:3;
  1933,My 9,20:2
Mask of Hamlet, The 1921,Ag 23,10:3
Mask of Virtue, The 1935,My 16,20:1;
  1935,Je 9,IX,1:1
Masked Woman, The 1922,D 23,14:2
Masks and Faces 1933,Mr 20,18:5
Masks of Angels 1965,Ja 20,33:1
Masque et Visage 1927,Ap 3,VIII,4:7
Masque of Kings, The 1937,Ja 19,28:3;
  1937,Ja 31,XI,2:1; 1937,F 9,19:4
  1938,My 8,X,1:7
Masque of Mercy, The 1962,My 31,23:6
Masque of Reason, The 1959,N 25,19:4;
  1962,My 31,23:6
Masque of Venice, The 1926,Mr 3,27:3;
  1926,Mr 7,VIII,1:2; 1928,F 12,VIII,2:1
Masquerade 1959,Mr 17,42:1
Massachusetts Trust 1968,S 1,II,1:1
Masse Mensch 1922,Ap 2,VI,1:2; 1924,Ap 20,VIII,1:1
Master, The 1928,Ap 1,IX,2:1
Master Builder, The 1925,N 11,27:1;
  1925,N 15,VIII,1:1; 1926,Ja 31,VII,1:1;
  1928,O 21,IX,1:3; 1955,Mr 2,23:2;
  1955,Mr 20,II,1:1; 1957,D 18,42:7; 1964,Je 10,50:2;
  1968,Je 22,26:1
Master Builder Solness 1950,My 26,19:3
Master of the Inn, The 1925,D 23,22:2
Master of the Revels 1935,Ag 14,16:2
Master Pierre Patelin 1949,Ap 23,10:2
Master Puntila and His Valet, Matti 1964,N 21,34:1
Masters, The 1963,Je 1,16:8
Match-Play 1966,O 12,37:1
Matchmaker, The 1954,Ag 24,18:1; 1954,S 5,II,3:7;
  1954,N 5,16:4; 1954,N 14,II,3:1; 1955,My 8,II,1:1;
  1955,D 6,45:6; 1955,D 18,II,3:1
Matinata 1920,N 14,VI,1:4
Matinee Girl, The 1926,F 2,20:3
Matinee Wife 1936,Ap 25,21:3
Mating Dance 1965,N 4,58:1
Mating Season, The 1927,Jl 19,27:6
Matriarch, The 1929,My 26,IX,1:3;
  1930,Ja 26,VIII,2:1; 1930,Mr 19,24:5
Matrimonial Bed, The 1927,O 13,23:2
Matrimony, PFD 1936,N 6,28:4; 1936,N 13,26:3
Matsuri 1930,Mr 5,26:7

Mattathias of Modin 1968,Ap 15,41:1
Matter of Days, A 1969,My 20,40:1
Matter of Like Life and Death, A 1963,O 3,28:2
Matty and the Moron and Madonna
　1965,Mr 30,53:1
Maud et Son Banquier 1928,Ap 1,IX,4:7
Maurice Chevalier 1932,F 10,26:6; 1947,Mr 11,37:2;
　1948,Mr 1,16:2; 1963,Ja 30,7:2
Maurice Chevalier at 77 1965,Ap 2,26:1
Mauvais Ange, Le 1927,Je 5,VII,2:1
Max and Mr Max 1932,Ja 24,VIII,3:5
May Night 1926,My 5,24:5
May Wine 1935,N 23,23:1; 1935,D 6,30:3
Maya 1927,F 13,VII,4:1; 1927,D 11,IX,2:1;
　1928,F 22,19:1; 1951,Ag 9,17:4; 1953,Je 10,35:1
Maybe Tuesday 1958,Ja 30,18:3
Mayfair 1930,Mr 18,30:5
Mayflowers 1925,N 25,14:2
Mayor Answers the Newspapers! Wow!
　1935,Je 19,23:3
Mayor of Casterbridge, The 1926,S 9,20:1;
　1926,O 3,VIII,2:1
Mayor of Zalamea, The 1946,Ja 28,15:5
Maytime 1937,Jl 6,23:4
Mazal Darf Men 1938,My 18,16:5
Mazal Tov 1938,My 23,21:3
Mazel Tov, Molly 1950,O 2,18:1
Mazel Tov, Rabbi 1938,N 28,10:4
Me 1925,N 24,28:1
Me, Candido! 1956,O 16,36:2
Me, The Sleeper 1949,My 16,18:6
Me and Harry 1942,Ap 3,24:6
Me and Juliet 1953,My 29,17:1; 1953,Je 7,II,1:1;
　1970,My 15,42:1
Me and Molly 1948,F 27,27:2; 1948,Mr 7,II,1:1
Me and Thee 1965,D 8,58:4
Me for You 1929,S 22,IX,2:6
Me Nobody Knows, The 1970,F 15,II,1:1;
　1970,My 19,42:1; 1970,My 31,II,1:6
Meanest Man in the World, The 1920,O 8,14:4;
　1920,O 13,18:2; 1920,O 24,VI,1:1
Measure for Measure 1927,S 18,VII,2:2;
　1931,Ag 9,VIII,1:3; 1946,Ag 24,6:8;
　1950,Mr 10,33:5; 1954,Je 30,23:1; 1954,Jl 4,II,1:1;
　1956,Je 29,16:1; 1957,Ja 23,24:1; 1957,F 3,II,1:1;
　1957,N 20,42:8; 1960,Jl 27,33:1; 1962,Ap 11,47:4;
　1964,Jl 27,22:3; 1966,Jl 14,27:1; 1967,F 15,37:1;
　1967,Ag 27,II,4:8; 1969,Je 13,41:3; 1969,Je 22,II,1:7;
　1970,Ap 5,71:1
Mecca 1920,O 5,12:2
Medal for Willie, A 1951,O 16,35:2
Medea 1920,Mr 23,12:2; 1926,D 19,VII,3:3;
　1941,Ag 3,IX,2:2; 1947,O 21,27:2; 1947,O 26,II,1:1;
　1948,S 30,32:4; 1949,My 3,31:2; 1951,S 14,22:5;
　1951,S 23,II,3:1; 1955,Ja 16,35:4; 1960,Jl 26,25:2;
　1964,S 1,31:1; 1965,N 29,46:1; 1966,D 21,42:1
Medecin de Son Honneur 1935,Mr 3,VIII,2:3
Medecin Malgre Lui, Le 1937,D 28,28:7
Medicine Man, The 1927,O 16,IX,2:4
Medicine Show 1940,Ap 13,20:6
Medico Delle Pazze, Il 1937,S 27,24:2
Mediterranee 1926,O 10,29:4; 1926,N 7,VIII,2:7
Medium, The 1947,My 2,28:2; 1947,My 11,II,1:1;
　1948,Ap 30,26:3; 1948,D 8,41:6; 1949,N 7,32:4;
　1950,Jl 20,22:5; 1950,S 3,II,1:1
Meek Mose 1928,F 7,30:1
Meet a Body 1944,O 17,19:5
Meet Lady Clara 1930,Mr 30,VIII,2:7
Meet My Sister 1930,D 31,11:1
Meet Peter Grant 1961,My 11,41:4
Meet the People 1940,O 20,IX,3:3; 1940,D 26,22:2;
　1941,Ja 12,IX,1:1
Meet the Prince 1929,F 26,30:5; 1929,Mr 10,X,1:1;
　1935,H 9,24:5; 1935,Ag 6,20:4
Meet the Wife 1923,N 27,23:4; 1923,D 16,IX,1:1;
　1927,Jl 3,VII,1:4; 1928,D 3,30:6; 1937,Jl 6,23:1
Meeting, The 1967,D 13,55:1
Meeting at Night 1934,Je 15,19:1; 1934,Jl 15,X,1:3
Megere Apprivoisee, La 1922,N 20,21:2
Megilla of Itzik Manger, The 1968,O 10,60:1;
　1969,Ap 21,55:1
Mei Lan-Fang 1930,F 17,18:2
Melians, The 1931,O 11,VIII,4:8
Melo 1929,Ap 7,X,1:3; 1929,Ap 14,X,2:1;
　1931,Ap 17,26:6; 1931,O 20,29:3
Melody 1933,F 15,17:4
Melody Lingers On, The 1969,N 17,55:1
Melody Man, The 1924,My 14,14:2;
　1924,My 18,VII,1:1
Melody That Got Lost, The 1938,F 6,X,1:2
Melusina 1930,My 11,IX,3:1
Member of the Wedding, The 1950,Ja 6,26:6;
　1950,Ja 15,II,1:1; 1950,My 14,II,1:1;
　1950,S 17,II,1:1; 1957,F 6,20:7
Memorandum, The 1968,My 6,55:1
Memory 1934,My 13,IX,2:6
Memory Bank, The 1970,Ja 12,24:3; 1970,Ja 25,II,1:4
Memory of Two Mondays, A 1955,S 30,21:1;
　1955,O 9,II,1:1
Memphis Bound 1945,My 25,23:2; 1945,Je 10,II,1:1
Men and Dreams 1966,S 7,51:2
Men in Shadow 1942,S 27,VIII,2:1; 1943,Mr 11,16:2

Men in White 1933,S 27,24:2; 1933,O 1,IX,1:1;
　1934,Je 29,16:3; 1955,F 26,13:2
Men Must Fight 1931,Ap 12,IX,2:1; 1932,O 15,13:4
Men of Distinction 1953,My 1,18:4
Men She Married 1928,S 30,IX,2:7
Men to the Sea 1944,O 4,25:2
Men We Marry, The 1948,Ja 17,11:2
Menace 1927,Mr 15,28:2
Menaechmi 1925,Je 9,16:2
Menagerie 1935,Jl 2,24:3
Mendel, Inc 1929,S 1,VIII,1:1; 1929,N 26,28:5
Menonite 1936,Mr 20,29:6
Mens Vi Venter 1939,Ap 9,X,2:3
Mensch aus Erde Gemacht 1933,N 5,IX,3:1
Menschen im Hotel 1930,Mr 16,IX,4:1
Mercenary Mary 1925,Ap 14,27:3; 1927,Ap 17,II,8:2;
　1927,D 4,X,2:3
Merchant of Berlin, The 1929,O 27,IX,4:1
Merchant of Venice, The 1920,My 9,VI,1:7;
　1920,N 12,15:5; 1920,D 30,16:2; 1921,Ap 2,14:2;
　1921,My 14,10:4; 1921,Je 9,10:2; 1921,N 22,17:1;
　1922,D 22,13:1; 1923,Ja 7,VII,1:1;
　1923,Ja 21,VII,1:1; 1923,N 6,22:2; 1924,N 18,23:2;
　1924,N 23,VIII,1:1; 1925,D 28,12:1;
　1926,Ja 3,VII,1:1; 1928,Ja 10,38:6; 1928,Ja 17,22:2;
　1928,Ap 1,IX,2:4; 1929,Ja 27,IX,1:3; 1929,S 24,28:4;
　1930,Mr 27,24:7; 1930,Ap 21,20:7;
　1930,N 16,VIII,3:1; 1930,N 23,IX,1:3;
　1930,D 3,29:2; 1931,F 1,VIII,3:3; 1931,N 4,31:1;
　1931,N 9,22:2; 1931,N 17,31:1; 1932,Ja 10,II,6:4;
　1932,Ap 29,13:4; 1932,N 24,34:5;
　1934,Ag 12,IX,5:5; 1938,Ja 15,18:8;
　1938,My 15,X,1:5; 1947,F 24,16:2; 1950,My 3,37:2;
　1953,Mr 5,20:2; 1953,My 10,II,1:1; 1955,Ja 8,9:7;
　1955,F 23,23:2; 1955,Jl 1,13:1; 1957,Jl 11,19:5;
　1957,Ag 18,II,1:1; 1960,Ap 13,46:5; 1962,F 3,13:2;
　1962,Je 22,1:4; 1964,Jl 23,18:1; 1965,Ap 17,9:1;
　1967,Je 24,46:2; 1970,My 10,II,3:1; 1970,Je 10,39:1;
　1970,Je 21,II,1:1; 1970,Jl 30,39:1
Merchant of Yonkers, The 1938,D 13,30:1;
　1938,D 18,IX,3:2; 1938,D 29,14:2
Merchants of Glory 1925,D 15,28:3;
　1925,D 27,VII,1:1
Merchants of Venus 1928,S 28,14:2
Merchant's Tale, The 1969,F 4,34:1
Mercy Street 1969,O 28,43:1; 1969,N 2,II,3:1
Merely Murder 1937,N 16,26:1; 1937,D 4,21:4
Mermaid's Holiday 1961,Jl 1,8:1
Mermaids Singing, The 1945,N 29,26:6;
　1945,D 9,II,5:1
Merrileon Wise 1926,D 19,VII,6:4
Merrily We Roll Along 1934,O 1,14:1;
　1934,O 7,IX,1:1; 1936,Je 30,15:1
Merry Andrew 1929,Ja 13,VIII,2:4; 1929,Ja 22,22:2
Merry Death, A 1959,N 10,55:3
Merry Duchess, The 1943,Je 24,25:1
Merry-Go-Round 1927,Je 1,25:4; 1927,Jl 5,19:4;
　1932,Ap 23,11:2; 1932,My 1,VIII,1:1;
　1932,My 11,15:3; 1932,N 27,IX,1:1
Merry-Go-Rounders, The 1956,N 22,50:1
Merry Malones, The 1927,S 11,VIII,1:3;
　1927,S 27,30:2; 1927,N 20,IX,1:1
Merry Merry 1925,S 25,24:3
Merry Widow, The 1921,S 6,13:1; 1929,F 17,IX,2:3;
　1929,D 3,29:1; 1931,S 8,39:1; 1931,O 11,VIII,4:4;
　1932,F 21,VIII,23:3; 1932,N 27,IX,1:2;
　1933,Ag 13,IX,1:3; 1942,Jl 16,22:1; 1943,Ag 5,19:2;
　1943,Ag 22,II,5:1; 1943,Ag 29,II,5:3;
　1943,S 26,II,1:5; 1944,O 9,17:1; 1957,Ap 11,36:6;
　1961,O 27,28:2; 1964,Ag 18,24:2
Merry Wives of Gotham 1924,Ja 27,VII,1:1
Merry Wives of West Point, The 1932,Mr 20,II,7:7
Merry Wives of Windsor, The 1928,Mr 20,20:1;
　1928,Ap 1,IX,1:1; 1928,O 2,24:5; 1929,Mr 24,X,2:3;
　1929,O 27,IX,2:4; 1938,Ap 15,22:3; 1954,F 17,27:1;
　1956,Je 21,34:4; 1959,Mr 14,23:1; 1959,Jl 9,23:2;
　1967,Ag 4,18:1; 1968,My 4,45:5; 1968,Jl 31,29:1
Merry Wives of Windsor, The: 1929 Version
　1929,Jl 27,7:2
Merry World, The 1926,Je 9,18:3; 1926,Je 13,VII,1:1
Merrye Playe, A 1956,My 24,27:2
Merton of the Movies 1922,N 14,16:2;
　1922,N 19,VII,1:1; 1968,S 26,62:1
Mes Amours 1940,My 3,16:5
Message for Margaret 1946,S 2,13:2; 1947,Ap 17,34:2
Messager, Le 1933,D 31,IX,2:2
Messin' Around 1929,Ap 23,26:3
Metamorphoses 1969,D 12,69:1; 1970,F 15,II,1:1
Metamorphosis 1957,F 20,38:1; 1957,Mr 17,II,8:5
Metaphors 1968,My 9,55:2
Meteor 1929,D 8,X,2:1; 1929,D 24,15:1
Metier d'Amant, Le 1928,Ap 29,IX,2:3
Metropole 1949,D 7,43:2
Mexican Hayride 1944,Ja 29,9:6; 1944,F 6,II,1:1
Mexican Mural 1942,Ap 27,19:2
Mexicana 1939,Ap 22,14:4; 1939,My 7,X,3:1
Michael and Mary 1929,D 14,23:3;
　1929,D 29,VIII,2:4; 1930,F 2,5:1; 1930,F 23,VIII,2:1
Michael Drops In 1938,D 28,24:3
Michael Kramer 1932,D 4,IX,1:4; 1938,F 20,XI,2:1
Michael Todd's Peep Show 1950,Je 29,37:2
Michel 1932,Ap 3,VIII,2:1
Michel Auclair 1925,Mr 5,23:1

Mid-Channel 1928,S 16,IX,1:4
Mid-Summer 1953,Ja 22,19:1; 1953,Mr 15,II,1:1
Mid-West 1936,Ja 2,21:2; 1936,Ja 5,IX,3:1;
　1936,Ja 8,22:4
Middle Man 1936,S 8,23:1
Middle of the Night 1956,F 9,39:1; 1956,F 19,II,1:1
Middle Watch, The 1929,S 1,VIII,1:3; 1929,O 17,27:1
Middle Years, The 1955,Mr 8,23:2
Middletown 1934,Ap 23,24:6
Midgie Purvis 1961,F 2,25:3; 1961,F 12,II,1:1
Midnight 1930,D 30,25:1
Midnight Caller, The 1958,Jl 2,25:1
Midnight Frolic 1920,Ag 4,7:1; 1921,N 19,11:3
Midnight Love 1931,S 13,IX,2:5
Midsummer Madness 1924,Jl 13,VII,1:6
Midsummer Night Scream, A 1960,D 9,39:2;
　1960,D 16,45:1
Midsummer Night's Dream, A 1921,My 15,VI,1:6;
　1925,Mr 8,VII,2:1; 1927,Je 27,25:1; 1927,Ag 8,6:1;
　1927,N 18,21:1; 1927,N 27,IX,1:1; 1927,D 4,X,6:1;
　1930,D 28,VIII,3:5; 1931,Ag 19,19:3;
　1932,Jl 13,15:1; 1932,N 18,22:2; 1934,S 19,15:1;
　1937,Je 2,21:2; 1939,My 9,28:4; 1939,My 14,XI,1:1;
　1939,Jl 23,IX,1:3; 1942,Ap 12,VIII,1:7;
　1945,Mr 25,II,2:4; 1950,Je 22,33:2; 1954,S 1,31:3;
　1954,S 19,VI,26:1; 1954,S 22,33:1; 1954,D 16,50:2;
　1956,Ja 14,12:2; 1956,Jl 20,9:5; 1957,Je 27,21:3;
　1958,Je 23,19:1; 1959,Je 3,30:1; 1959,Je 5,16:5;
　1959,Jl 29,34:1; 1960,Je 30,23:5; 1961,Ag 3,13:1;
　1962,Ap 18,30:3; 1962,Jl 2,22:2; 1963,Jl 1,19:2;
　1964,Je 30,23:2; 1964,Jl 12,II,1:1; 1965,N 21,123:1;
　1967,Je 19,42:1; 1967,Je 30,23:1; 1968,Je 13,54:1;
　1968,Je 23,II,1:1; 1968,D 9,59:1; 1970,Ag 28,15:1;
　1970,S 13,II,7:1
Migawari Zazen 1960,Je 10,37:1
Might-Have-Beens, The 1927,Je 19,VII,2:3
Mighty Conlon 1933,F 21,17:3
Mighty Man Is He, A 1960,Ja 7,25:2
Mighty Nimrod, The 1931,My 13,23:1
Mikado, The 1924,Jl 29,9:1; 1925,Ag 13,25:1;
　1926,S 22,13:1; 1926,O 10,VIII,2:1; 1927,S 19,30:1;
　1927,S 25,VIII,1:1; 1927,O 30,IX,4:6;
　1931,My 5,33:2; 1931,Ag 25,17:7; 1932,Jl 29,18:4;
　1933,Ap 18,13:4; 1934,Ap 3,26:3; 1934,Ap 24,27:5;
　1934,My 22,28:2; 1934,S 18,18:1; 1935,Jl 16,24:4;
　1935,Ag 24,17:5; 1936,Ap 11,18:4; 1936,Ag 21,13:2;
　1939,Ja 10,16:3; 1939,Mr 11,15:6; 1942,F 4,22:2;
　1944,F 12,11:3; 1946,Ag 12,9:2; 1947,D 30,18:2;
　1949,O 5,35:2; 1951,Ja 30,21:2; 1952,O 21,35:2;
　1954,Mr 24,31:1; 1955,S 30,20:2; 1957,Ap 24,28:2;
　1959,O 2,24:1; 1961,Ja 18,26:1; 1961,My 5,23:1;
　1962,N 14,43:1; 1964,N 27,43:1; 1965,Ap 17,11:3;
　1966,N 18,36:1; 1967,O 25,42:2; 1967,D 4,65:3;
　1968,My 2,59:1; 1968,N 2,29:4
Mike Angelo 1923,Ja 9,26:2
Mike Downstairs 1968,Ap 19,35:1
Mike The Angel 1943,Ap 6,25:3
Mile Away Murder 1937,Ap 3,17:2;
　1937,Ap 18,XI,1:4
Miles of Heaven, The 1937,Ag 31,27:4
Milestones 1930,Je 3,27:1
Milgrim's Progress 1924,N 30,VIII,2:1;
　1924,D 23,17:1
Milk and Honey 1961,O 11,52:1
Milk Train Doesn't Stop Here Anymore, The
　1962,Jl 12,19:8; 1963,Ja 18,7:1; 1963,S 18,32:1;
　1964,Ja 2,33:1; 1965,Jl 27,25:1
Milky Way, The 1934,My 9,23:2; 1934,My 20,IX,1:1;
　1943,Je 10,17:2
Mill Shadows 1932,F 29,20:7
Miller's Tale, The 1969,F 4,34:1
Milliarden-Souper, Das 1921,My 15,VI,1:6
Million Dollar Baby 1945,D 22,17:2
Million Torments, A 1936,Ja 16,24:5
Millionairess, The 1936,Ja 5,39:3; 1936,N 18,30:3;
　1936,D 13,XI,5:3; 1938,Ag 16,22:5; 1949,Ap 7,38:5;
　1952,Je 28,12:2; 1952,Jl 6,II,1:5; 1952,O 18,17:2;
　1952,O 26,II,1:1; 1969,Mr 3,28:1
Millions 1930,O 3,30:4
Mima 1928,D 13,24:2; 1928,D 23,VIII,1:1
Mime and Me, The 1960,Ap 8,27:3
Mime Theatre of Etienne Decroux, The
　1959,D 24,15:1
Mimic World of 1921, The 1921,Ag 18,9:2
Mimie Scheller 1936,O 1,28:4
Minick 1924,S 25,20:1; 1924,O 5,VIII,1:1
Minister-Praesident, Der 1936,Je 28,IX,2:1
Minna von Barnhelm 1968,N 13,37:1
Minnie and Mr Williams 1948,O 28,37:2
Minnie's Boys 1970,F 15,II,1:1; 1970,Mr 27,27:1;
　1970,Ap 5,II,3:1
Minor Adjustment, A 1967,O 7,33:3
Minor Miracle 1965,O 8,4:3
Minskey the Magnificent 1936,D 26,14:3
Minstrel Boy, The 1948,O 15,28:2
Minuet, A 1927,Mr 5,12:2
Minute's Wait, A 1920,Je 22,9:1
Mira 1970,Je 3,51:1

Miracle, The 1924,Ja 16,17:1; 1924,Ja 20,VII,1:1;
1924,Ja 26,10:1; 1924,Ja 27,VII,1:1;
1924,F 3,VII,1:1; 1924,F 17,4:3; 1924,My 22,14:3;
1924,Ag 19,9:1; 1925,Ag 17,10:4; 1925,S 29,31:6;
1925,O 29,29:1; 1926,D 28,16:2; 1927,F 1,24:5;
1927,Ap 15,27:1; 1927,My 29,II,2:5; 1927,Je 8,23:2;
1932,Ap 10,1,18:1; 1932,My 8,VIII,2:2;
1960,D 5,42:3
Miracle, Un 1927,D 25,VIII,4:3
Miracle at Tsubosaka Temple, The 1960,Je 3,26:1
Miracle at Verdun 1931,Mr 17,34:6; 1932,O 9,IX,3:8;
1932,O 16,IX,3:7
Miracle in America 1934,O 2,18:4
Miracle in Brooklyn 1966,Je 24,30:2
Miracle in the Mountains 1936,My 9,11:4;
1947,Ap 26,10:2
Miracle Man, The 1935,My 14,17:5; 1935,Je 9,IX,1:1
Miracle Painting 1942,Ap 27,19:2
Miracle Worker, The 1959,O 20,44:1; 1959,N 1,II,1:1;
1959,D 20,II,5:1; 1961,F 7,40:2; 1961,Mr 10,19:4;
1961,Mr 10,22:4; 1961,Ap 1,11:2; 1961,Ap 11,43:5;
1961,Ap 21,29:1; 1961,My 1,35:3; 1961,My 19,22:2;
1961,My 31,28:1; 1961,O 8,II,3:4
Miraculous Birth and the Midwives, The
1933,F 6,11:3; 1933,F 12,IX,2:1
Mirage, The 1920,O 1,14:1
Mirele Efros 1967,O 20,55:1; 1969,D 26,41:1
Miroir Qui Fait Rire, Le 1927,My 1,VIII,2:4
Mirror Lion Dance, The 1969,S 11,53:1
Mirrors 1928,Ja 19,17:1
Mis-Guided Tour 1959,O 13,44:7
Misalliance 1953,F 19,20:1; 1953,Mr 22,II,1:1;
1955,F 12,10:6; 1961,S 26,32:2
Misanthrope, Le 1922,N 22,18:2; 1926,D 10,31:2;
1957,Ja 8,26:1; 1957,F 8,19:1; 1960,Mr 9,38:3
Misanthrope, The 1937,F 24,18:6; 1956,N 13,44:1;
1968,O 10,59:1; 1968,O 20,II,1:1
Mischief 1928,Ag 5,VII,1:1
Misdoings of Charley Peace, The 1929,S 29,IX,2:1
Miser, The 1924,Mr 12,17:3; 1950,Mr 27,19:5;
1955,Mr 18,34:2; 1963,My 10,39:1;
1963,My 19,II,1:1; 1966,F 9,32:1; 1969,My 9,35:1;
1969,My 25,II,1:1
Miserabili I, 1934,S 24,15:1; 1934,O 1,14:2
Mismates 1925,Ap 14,27:2
Miss Ba 1934,N 11,IX,3:6
Miss Emily Adam 1960,Mr 30,43:1
Miss France 1930,Ap 13,X,2:7
Miss Gulliver Travels 1931,N 26,36:4
Miss Isobel 1957,D 27,22:1
Miss Julie 1927,O 30,IX,2:1; 1954,Mr 29,24:3;
1956,F 22,23:2; 1956,Mr 4,II,1:1; 1961,Jl 10,26:1;
1962,My 17,31:1; 1965,Jl 29,19:1; 1965,N 11,59:1
Miss Liberty 1949,Je 14,26:6; 1949,Jl 16,6:5;
1949,Jl 24,II,1:1; 1949,Ag 7,II,6:4
Miss Lonelyhearts 1957,O 4,26:2
Miss Lulu Bett 1920,D 28,9:1; 1921,Ja 2,VI,3:1;
1921,Ja 9,VI,1:1; 1921,Ja 23,VI,1:1;
1921,F 20,VI,1:1
Miss Mabel 1948,D 12,II,4:8
Miss Quis 1937,Ap 2,18:5; 1937,Ap 8,20:5
Miss Smith 1936,Jl 5,IX,1:8
Miss Swan Expects 1939,F 21,15:2
Miss Temple Is Willing 1936,Jl 21,13:1
Mission Mary 1925,O 4,IX,2:1
Mission Play, The 1925,F 1,IV,20:3
Mississippi 1929,Ap 14,X,2:1; 1931,Ja 11,VIII,1:6
Missouri Legend 1938,S 20,27:2; 1938,S 25,IX,1:1;
1951,F 10,10:4
Missouri Waltz 1950,F 15,23:2
Mr Adam 1949,My 26,34:6
Mr and Mrs Lyman 1968,Mr 6,35:1
Mr and Mrs North 1941,Ja 13,11:2; 1941,F 23,IX,1:1
Mr Banks of Birmingham 1939,Ja 21,18:4
Mr Barry's Etchings 1950,F 1,26:2
Mr Big 1941,S 7,I,51:3; 1941,S 14,IX,2:5;
1941,O 1,24:2
Mr Bolfry 1943,Ag 22,II,1:8
Mr Eno: His Birth, Death and Life 1930,N 9,IX,2:1
Mr Faust 1922,Ja 31,11:2
Mr Fox of Venice 1959,Ap 16,28:1
Mr Gilhooley 1930,O 1,26:1
Mr Gillie 1950,Mr 10,31:2
Mr Gladstone 1937,O 1,18:4; 1937,O 17,XI,3:5
Mr Grossman 1964,My 6,43:1
Mr Jiggins of Jigginstown 1936,D 18,30:2
Mister Johnson 1956,Mr 30,11:1; 1956,Ap 8,II,1:1
Mister Malatesta 1923,F 27,14:2
Mister Mayor! 1967,Ap 4,36:3
Mr Moneypenny 1928,S 30,IX,2:7; 1928,O 17,26:2;
1928,O 28,IX,1:1
Mr Montoe Holds the Fort 1955,Mr 8,23:2
Mister Noah 1933,Ja 18,16:2
Mr Papavert 1932,Ja 23,18:6
Mr Peebles and Mr Hooker 1946,O 11,29:2
Mr Perkins' Mission to the Land of the Bolsheviks
1944,D 17,I,7:2
Mr Pickwick 1927,F 20,VII,2:6; 1931,Ja 11,VIII,3:5;
1952,S 18,36:3; 1952,S 28,II,1:1
Mr Pim Passes By 1921,Mr 1,18:1; 1921,Mr 6,VI,1:2;
1927,Ap 19,24:1; 1927,My 22,VIII,1:1;
1935,Ag 7,22:2
Mister Pitt 1924,Ja 6,VII,1:4; 1924,Ja 23,15:3

Mr President 1962,Ag 29,18:4; 1962,S 26,36:1;
1962,O 14,II,1:7; 1962,O 22,34:2
Mr Prohack 1927,D 4,X,1:3; 1928,Ja 1,VIII,1:3
Mister Roberts 1948,F 19,27:2; 1948,F 29,II,1:1;
1950,My 21,II,1:1; 1950,Jl 20,22:4; 1950,Jl 22,11:4;
1950,Jl 23,II,1:6; 1951,F 9,20:7; 1956,D 6,46:2;
1962,O 12,27:2
Mister Romeo 1927,S 6,35:3
Mr Sampson 1927,My 6,20:3; 1927,My 8,30:1
Mr Samuel 1930,O 26,VIII,3:5; 1930,N 11,28:4
Mr Shaddy 1936,Jl 15,14:4
Mr Simian 1963,O 22,44:1
Mr Strauss Goes to Boston 1945,S 7,20:2
Mr Sycamore 1942,N 14,13:2; 1942,N 29,VIII,1:1
Mr What's-His-Name 1927,My 29,VII,1:3;
1927,S 4,VII,2:4
Mr Whistler 1931,D 6,VIII,2:6
Mr Whittington 1934,F 2,21:4
Mr Wonderful 1956,Mr 23,23:2
Mistletoe Bough, The 1923,My 12,15:4
Mrs Bumpstead-Leigh 1929,Ap 2,28:3
Mrs Dally 1965,S 25,5:7
Mrs Dally Has a Lover 1962,O 2,47:1
Mrs Dane's Defense 1928,F 7,30:1
Mrs Fischer's War 1931,Ag 9,VIII,1:3
Mrs Gibsons' Boys 1949,My 5,35:2
Mrs January & Mr Ex 1944,Ap 1,10:2
Mrs Jimmie Thompson 1920,Mr 30,9:1;
1920,Ap 18,VI,2:3
Mrs Kimball Presents 1944,Mr 1,17:3
Mrs McThing 1952,F 21,22:1; 1952,Mr 2,II,1:1
Mrs Moonlight 1928,D 23,VIII,4:7; 1930,S 30,24:3;
1936,Je 16,21:3; 1952,N 21,21:1
Mrs Mouse Are You Within? 1968,Ap 5,51:4;
1968,Je 2,II,3:6; 1968,Jl 8,45:1
Mrs Nobby Clark 1935,F 28,16:2
Mrs O'Brien Entertains 1939,F 9,16:3
Mistress of the House, The 1950,Ja 31,19:1
Mistress of the Inn, The 1923,N 22,16:1;
1926,N 23,26:1; 1937,Je 22,26:3
Mrs Partridge Presents 1925,Ja 6,23:3;
1925,Ja 11,VII,1:2; 1936,F 29,10:1
Mrs Patterson 1954,D 2,37:1; 1957,F 6,20:2
Mrs Snow 1970,Ja 6,48:3
Mrs Warren's Profession 1950,O 26,39:2;
1956,Je 7,35:2; 1958,Je 26,22:1; 1963,Ap 25,39:1
Mrs Wilson's Diary 1967,O 8,II,13:5
Mitschuldigen, Die 1966,Ap 6,34:1
Mixed Doubles 1927,Ap 27,22:3; 1969,Ap 12,43:2
Mixed Marriage 1920,D 15,18:2; 1920,D 26,VI,3:3
Mixture 1927,N 20,IX,4:4; 1929,N 10,X,4:1
Mkhumbhane 1960,Mr 31,29:2
Mlle Modiste 1929,O 8,34:1; 1937,My 5,28:5
Mob, The 1920,O 11,18:1; 1920,D 12,VI,1:3
Moby Dick 1955,Ap 26,25:3; 1955,Je 17,18:8;
1955,Jl 24,II,1:6; 1961,Ap 11,41:2; 1962,N 4,82:6;
1962,N 29,45:1; 1970,Je 3,52:1
Mock Emperor, The 1929,F 17,IX,2:1
Mocking Bird, The 1933,Je 23,18:2
Mod Donna 1970,My 4,48:1; 1970,My 10,II,1:1
Modern Statuary 1968,My 28,41:1
Modern Virgin, A 1931,My 21,33:4
Mogul of the Desert 1932,F 7,VIII,3:2
Moke Eaters, The 1968,O 28,55:3
Molly Darling 1922,S 2,10:2
Moloch 1929,Ja 27,IX,2:8
Moment Difficile, Le 1926,D 26,VII,2:1
Moment Musical 1943,Je 1,18:1
Moment of Truth 1951,D 9,II,7:7
Momiji-Gari 1969,S 18,64:1
Mon Coeur au Ralenti 1927,Je 12,VII,2:1
Mon Depute et sa Femme 1930,S 21,IX,2:8
Mon Heritier 1930,O 26,VIII,2:1
Mon Pere Avait Raison 1936,Je 21,IX,2:4
Money Business 1926,Ja 21,18:1
Money From Home 1927,Mr 1,30:2
Money in the Air 1932,Mr 8,19:3
Money Lender, The 1924,N 23,VIII,2:4;
1928,Ag 28,27:3
Money Mad 1937,My 25,32:5
Money Talks 1938,My 29,X,1:2
Money! Money! 1931,Mr 15,IX,2:8
Mongolia 1927,D 27,24:5
Mongrel, The 1924,D 16,28:2
Monique 1957,My 23,38:1
Monkey 1932,F 12,25:2
Monkey Talks, The 1925,D 29,20:1; 1926,Ja 3,VII,1:1
Monkey's Paw, The 1922,Jl 3,VII,1:1;
1923,My 12,15:4; 1929,My 10,32:2
Monsieur Beaucaire 1924,Mr 2,VIII,2:7
Monsieur Brotonneau 1923,Ap 8,VIII,1:7;
1924,Mr 13,14:1; 1930,O 5,IX,2:4
Monsieur de Cinq Heures 1924,O 12,VIII,1:6
Monsieur de Cleopatre, Le 1927,Ja 16,VII,2:1
Monsieur le Comte 1933,F 12,IX,3:4
Monsieur Qui Se Regrette, Un 1928,D 9,X,2:7
Monster, The 1922,Ag 10,20:3; 1933,F 11,11:5
Month in the Country, A 1930,Mr 18,30:5;
1930,N 23,IX,1:3; 1956,Ap 4,23:1;
1956,Ap 15,II,1:1; 1959,Mr 2,32:2;
1963,My 29,39:2
Month of Sundays 1968,S 17,50:1
Montmarte aux Nues 1926,O 3,VIII,2:1

Montmartre 1922,F 14,20:1; 1924,Je 15,VII,1:4
Montserrat 1949,O 31,21:4; 1952,My 11,II,3:8;
1954,My 26,34:2; 1961,Ja 9,30:5
Moon and Sixpence, The 1933,D 17,IX,4:3
Moon Besieged, The 1950,N 4,13:1; 1962,D 6,54:1
Moon-Flower, The 1924,Ja 27,VII,2:7; 1924,F 26,15:1;
1924,Mr 2,VIII,1:1
Moon for the Misbegotten, A 1947,F 21,16:2;
1957,My 3,21:2; 1957,My 12,II,1:1; 1958,Je 7,10:6;
1960,Ja 22,14:8; 1968,Je 13,55:2; 1968,Je 30,II,1:1
Moon in Capricorn 1953,O 28,37:2
Moon in the Yellow River, The 1931,My 17,VIII,3:3;
1931,S 27,VIII,2:8; 1932,F 21,VIII,2:1;
1932,Mr 1,19:3; 1932,Mr 13,VIII,1:1; 1961,F 7,40:2;
1961,Mr 19,II,1:1
Moon Is a Gong, The 1926,Mr 13,21:3;
1926,Mr 21,VIII,1:1
Moon Is Blue, The 1951,Mr 9,29:2; 1953,Jl 8,24:1;
1953,Ag 9,II,1:2; 1961,Ag 9,29:1
Moon Is Down, The 1942,Ap 8,22:2;
1942,Ap 12,VIII,1:1; 1942,My 10,VIII,1:1;
1943,Jl 11,II,1:5; 1963,N 15,5:2
Moon Is Red, The 1934,D 5,29:1; 1934,D 23,IX,1:8
Moon of the Caribbees 1929,Ja 27,IX,1:1;
1937,O 30,23:2; 1948,My 21,21:2;
1948,My 30,II,1:1
Moon on a Rainbow Shawl 1962,Ja 16,30:i;
1962,Ja 28,II,1:1; 1969,Ag 29,25:1; 1970,D 18,52:1
Moon Over Mulberry Street 1935,S 5,24:6
Moon Rises, The 1934,Ap 16,21:6;
1934,Ap 22,IX,1:1
Moon Shines on Kylenamoe, The 1962,O 31,33:1
Moon Vine, The 1943,F 12,22:2
Moon Walk 1970,N 27,52:1
Moonbirds 1959,O 10,13:1
Moondreamers, The 1969,D 9,68:1; 1969,D 21,II,3:1
Mooney and His Caravans 1968,My 17,50:3
Moonflowers 1936,Ap 6,19:4
Moonlight 1924,Ja 31,13:7
Moonlight Is Silver 1934,S 20,21:1; 1934,O 7,IX,3:7
Moonlight Scene 1942,Ap 27,19:2
Moor Born 1934,Ap 4,26:4; 1934,Ap 8,X,2:7
Moral Fabric 1932,N 22,25:3
Morals 1925,D 1,22:2; 1925,D 6,VIII,5:1
More Stately Mansions 1962,N 10,16:4;
1967,S 14,54:1; 1967,N 1,40:1; 1967,N 12,II,1:1
More the Merrier, The 1941,S 16,19:3
Morgen Wieder Lustig 1921,Je 5,VI,1:3
Morgue, The 1927,F 2,22:4
Morn to Midnight 1922,Je 27,16:4
Morning 1968,N 29,52:1; 1968,D 8,II,5:4
Morning After, The 1925,Jl 28,24:2
Morning Star, The 1940,Ap 17,26:4;
1941,D 28,IX,2:3; 1942,F 15,VIII,3:6
1942,S 15,18:4; 1942,S 20,VIII,1:1
Morning Sun 1963,O 7,36:2
Morning's at Seven 1939,N 7,30:2; 1939,N 12,IX,2:3;
1939,D 1,26:2; 1939,D 10,X,5:6; 1939,D 17,IX,3:1;
1955,Je 23,25:1; 1956,Ja 8,II,3:1
Moroni 1936,Ag 19,19:1
Morphia 1923,Mr 7,20:2
Morris, the Fiddler 1920,Ap 9,11:4
Morte Civile, La 1936,N 9,23:4
Morts Sans Sepulture 1946,D 22,II,4:1
Moscow Art Theatre 1924,My 13,25:2
Moscow Circus on Ice 1970,D 9,63:1
Moskvo Cheremushki 1959,Ja 25,27:7
Most Happy Fella, The 1956,My 4,20:1;
1956,My 13,II,1:1; 1956,Je 10,II,7:1; 1959,F 11,50:2;
1960,Ap 22,25:3; 1966,My 12,55:1
Most Immoral Lady, A 1928,N 11,X,2:4;
1928,N 27,36:1
Most of the Game 1935,O 2,27:4
Most Unwarrantable Intrusion, A 1968,Jl 9,30:2;
1968,Jl 14,II,4:5
Mot de Cambronne, Le 1936,O 25,X,3:8
Motel 1966,N 7,66:1; 1967,Ag 13,II,3:6;
1967,O 10,55:2
Motel Peissi, The Contor's Kid 1934,N 29,33:3
Mother, The 1935,N 20,26:3; 1937,Ag 29,X,1:3;
1939,Mr 19,XI,3:3; 1939,Ag 26,26:2
Mother Courage 1967,N 17,55:1; 1967,N 19,83:1
Mother Courage and Her Children 1963,Mr 30,5:5;
1964,My 12,32:2
Mother Lode 1934,D 24,16:5
Mother Lover, The 1969,F 3,28:1
Mother Martyr 1935,Ja 28,10:3
Mother of Pearl 1933,F 26,IX,3:1
Mother Said No 1951,Ap 17,34:2
Mother Sings 1935,N 13,24:1
Mother's Sabbath Days 1960,N 21,33:2
Mother's Son 1931,N 26,36:4
Moths, The 1970,My 12,46:1
Motke From Slobodke 1930,Ap 12,23:3
Motke Ganef 1932,D 30,15:2; 1935,Mr 18,15:2
Mouches, Les 1947,Ap 18,26:3
Moulin de la Galette, Le 1923,Ja 28,VII,2:7
Mount Holyoke Milestones 1933,Ap 9,II,3:4
Mountain, The 1933,S 12,28:6
Mountain Dew 1929,Mr 31,VIII,4:2
Mountain Fury 1929,S 26,27:2
Mountain Giants, The 1961,Ap 5,32:3

Mountain Man, The 1921,D 13,24:2
Mountebank, The 1923,My 8,22:2;
  1923,My 13,VIII,1:1
Mountebanks, The 1955,D 2,32:3
Mourners' Bench, The 1950,S 22,35:7
Mourning Becomes Electra 1931,O 27,22:1;
  1931,N 1,VIII,1:1; 1932,F 26,22:6;
  1932,Ap 10,VIII,1:1; 1932,My 10,25:2;
  1932,My 22,VIII,1:1; 1933,My 7,IX,2:3;
  1937,D 12,XI,3:8; 1938,Ja 30,X,1:3; 1961,N 22,24:3;
  1969,S 7,II,1:2
Mousetrap, The 1952,D 7,II,7:1; 1958,Ja 30,18:6;
  1960,N 7,46:1
Mouthpiece, The 1929,Je 16,VIII,2:1
Move On 1926,Ja 19,30:1
Move on, Sister 1933,O 25,22:4
Movie Man 1959,O 28,40:4
Moving Finger, The 1928,S 16,IX,1:4
Mozart 1925,D 27,VII,2:1; 1925,D 27,VII,6:7;
  1926,Jl 4,VII,1:3; 1926,N 23,26:2; 1926,D 28,16:1;
  1927,Ja 2,VII,1:1
Mr Winkle's Holliday 1946,Je 24,27:6
Mu Lan 1921,F 25,16:2
Much Ado About Nothing 1927,N 19,14:6;
  1928,N 18,IX,2:6; 1929,N 17,30:4;
  1933,Ap 30,IX,2:2; 1934,N 9,24:3;
  1941,Ap 20,IX,3:3; 1952,F 10,II,2:1;
  1952,My 2,20:1; 1955,Ag 20,20:4; 1957,Ag 8,15:2;
  1957,Ag 18,II,1:1; 1958,Je 22,21:1; 1958,Ag 27,34:6;
  1959,S 18,25:2; 1959,S 27,II,1:1; 1961,Ap 5,31:1;
  1961,Jl 7,17:1; 1963,Jl 15,25:2; 1964,Je 11,26:2;
  1964,Jl 24,15:2; 1964,Jl 27,22:3; 1968,O 16,33:1;
  1969,Je 16,57:1; 1969,S 1,13:1; 1970,S 4,19:1
Mud 1924,Jl 4,14:3
Mud Turtle, The 1925,Ag 21,8:2; 1925,S 6,VII,1:1
Mulatto 1935,Ag 8,13:2; 1935,O 25,25:2;
  1967,N 16,61:4
Mulberry Bush, The 1927,O 27,33:1;
  1930,My 18,VIII,2:6; 1955,S 28,38:3
Mummers and Men 1962,Mr 27,41:6
Mum's the Word 1940,D 6,28:5
Mundy Scheme, The 1969,D 12,75:1
Murder at the Vanities 1933,Ag 31,20:1;
  1933,S 13,22:4
Murder Gang 1935,N 16,19:2; 1935,D 15,XI,5:6
Murder Has Been Arranged, A 1930,N 30,IX,1:8;
  1931,D 12,23:5
Murder in Mayfair 1934,S 6,23:5; 1934,S 23,X,3:6
Murder in the Cathedral 1935,N 2,12:2;
  1935,D 21,11:3; 1936,Ja 12,IX,1:5; 1936,Mr 21,13:5;
  1936,Mr 29,IX,1:1; 1938,F 17,16:2;
  1953,Ap 26,II,1:1; 1958,Mr 22,12:4; 1966,Je 21,38:1
Murder in the Old Red Barn, The 1936,F 3,20:4
Murder Mistaken 1952,D 7,II,7:1
Murder on Account 1936,My 25,23:1; 1936,S 26,11:2
Murder on the Nile 1946,Mr 21,32:2
Murder on the Second Floor 1929,S 12,35:1;
  1929,S 22,IX,1:1
Murder Tonight 1937,Jl 3,18:6
Murder With Pen and Ink 1935,Jl 30,17:2;
  1935,Ag 20,25:1
Murder Without Crime 1942,Ag 9,VIII,1:8;
  1943,Ag 19,24:6
Murderer Among Us, A 1964,Mr 26,43:1
Murderous Angels 1970,F 8,70:1; 1970,Mr 15,II,1:4
Murray Anderson's Almanac 1929,Ag 4,VIII,1:6;
  1929,Ag 15,20:3
Murray Hill 1927,Ag 21,VII,1:8; 1927,S 30,29:1
Music at Night 1938,Ag 3,14:8; 1938,Ag 21,IX,2:1
Music Box Revue 1923,My 20,VII,1:3; 1923,S 24,5:3;
  1924,D 2,23:3
Music Hall Varieties 1932,N 23,15:3; 1933,Ja 3,19:4
Music Hath Charms 1934,D 31,8:2
Music in May 1928,N 4,IX,1:3; 1929,Ja 27,IX,1:3;
  1929,Ap 2,29:1
Music in My Heart 1947,O 3,30:2
Music in the Air 1932,O 23,IX,3:3; 1932,N 9,28:2;
  1932,N 20,IX,1:1; 1933,My 20,11:3; 1951,O 9,32:2;
  1951,O 21,II,1:1
Music Man, The 1957,D 20,31:1; 1958,S 28,II,1:1;
  1961,Mr 18,17:3; 1963,Ag 15,24:1; 1965,Je 17,26:4
Music Master, The 1927,S 7,34:4; 1927,S 15,34:4;
  1927,S 25,VIII,2:1
Music Shop, The 1962,F 16,35:2
Musical Chairs 1931,D 6,VIII,2:7; 1934,Jl 31,20:7
Musical Mishaps 1949,Mr 21,18:2
Musical World of Bertolt Brecht, The
  1968,My 14,39:1
Musik um Susi 1933,Ja 1,IX,1:1
Musk 1920,Mr 15,13:1
Musse 1930,D 14,IX,2:7
Musume Dojoji 1960,Je 10,37:1; 1960,Je 17,35:4
Mute, The 1920,Ap 9,11:4
Muted Strings 1936,N 11,54:4
Mutilated, The 1966,F 23,42:1; 1966,Mr 6,II,1:1
Mutiny 1936,My 11,16:2
Muzeeka 1968,Ap 29,47:2
My Aunt From Ypsilanti 1923,My 2,22:6
My Baby's Wedding 1938,O 10,15:3
My Beginning 1962,Ja 31,21:1
My Country 1926,Ag 1,VII,4:1; 1926,Ag 10,19:1;
  1926,Ag 29,VII,1:1
My Darlin' Aida 1952,O 28,36:4

My Daughter, Your Son 1969,My 14,36:2
My Dear Children 1939,Mr 25,19:6; 1939,My 3,26:4;
  1939,S 10,IX,1:6; 1940,F 1,16:2; 1940,F 11,IX,1:1;
  1941,Jl 22,22:6
My Dear Public 1943,S 10,28:1
My Fair Ladies 1941,Mr 24,12:7
My Fair Lady 1956,Mr 16,20:2; 1956,Mr 25,II,1:1;
  1956,Ap 29,II,17:1; 1956,Je 3,II,1:1;
  1956,Je 10,II,7:1; 1956,Ag 12,II,1:1;
  1956,O 28,II,1:1; 1957,F 5,27:2; 1957,Mr 26,33:4;
  1958,Mr 9,II,1:1; 1958,My 1,34:5; 1958,My 4,II,3:1;
  1959,Ja 19,24:6; 1959,Ja 27,26:1; 1959,F 16,24:1;
  1959,F 21,25:6; 1959,Ap 4,12:5; 1961,O 26,40:1;
  1962,Je 14,24:1; 1962,Ag 23,24:6; 1962,S 7,34:1;
  1963,S 2,19:4; 1963,S 21,13:1; 1963,N 16,16:1;
  1964,F 20,24:4; 1964,My 21,43:2; 1964,D 29,22:1;
  1968,Je 14,42:1
My Fiddle Is Broken 1928,D 2,X,4:7
My Forty Years in Show Business 1950,Mr 22,33:2
My Girl 1924,N 25,27:2
My Girl Friday! 1929,F 13,20:2
My Golden Girl 1920,F 3,18:2; 1927,S 11,VIII,1:3
My Heart's in the Highlands 1939,Ap 14,29:2;
  1939,My 7,X,1:1; 1949,N 22,36:7; 1950,F 18,8:4
My House Is Your House 1970,O 16,53:2
My Kinsman, Major Molineux 1964,N 2,62:2
My L A 1951,D 9,87:1
My Lady's Mill 1928,Jl 22,VII,1:3
My Little Girl 1931,F 2,22:4
My Magnolia 1926,Jl 13,19:2
My Malkele 1937,S 20,18:6
My Maryland 1927,S 13,37:2; 1936,Ag 12,14:2
My Mother, My Father and Me 1963,Mr 25,5:5
My Name is Aquilon 1949,F 10,38:2
My Name Is Legion 1952,Ap 21,23:7
My Pal Sasha 1941,O 23,24:4
My Place 1962,F 14,40:2
My Princess 1927,O 7,24:2
My Romance 1948,O 20,38:5
My Sister Eileen 1940,D 27,23:2; 1941,Ja 5,IX,1:1
My Son 1924,S 18,18:2; 1924,S 28,VII,1:1
My Son and I 1960,O 24,24:2
My Son's My Son 1936,My 27,26:4
My Sweet Charlie 1966,D 7,56:1; 1966,D 25,II,1:1
My Wife and I 1966,O 11,53:2
My Wife Is Different 1931,Ap 27,24:4
My Wife With Conditions 1963,O 21,39:1
My Wife's Perfume 1932,Ja 11,29:5
My 3 Angels 1953,Mr 12,23:2; 1956,F 4,24:2
Myrtie 1924,F 5,21:2
Myself and I 1929,Ag 31,13:6
Mysteries and Smaller Pieces 1966,F 26,14:1;
  1968,O 10,95:1
Mysterious Way, The 1923,O 28,VIII,2:1
Mystery Man, The 1928,Ja 27,14:2
Mystery Moon 1930,Je 24,23:4
Mystery of the Finding of the Cross, The
  1959,Ja 16,35:2
Mystery of Theodosia Burr, The 1947,Mr 10,24:7
Mystery Ship, The 1927,Mr 15,28:2
Mystery Square 1929,Ap 5,28:3

N

Nach Damaskus 1937,My 30,X,2:5
Nacht zum 17. April, Die 1932,D 18,X,4:5
Naked 1924,O 28,27:2; 1924,N 2,VII,1:1;
  1926,N 9,31:2; 1927,Ap 17,VII,1:4; 1950,S 7,39:2
Naked Genius, The 1943,O 22,20:5; 1943,O 31,II,1:1;
  1943,N 7,II,1:6
Naked Man, The 1923,D 16,IX,2:4;
  1925,N 8,VIII,2:1; 1935,Jl 2,24:3
Name Your Poison 1936,Ja 21,27:4
Nancy Ann 1924,Mr 9,VIII,2:3; 1924,Ap 1,18:1;
  1924,Ap 6,VIII,1:1
Nancy's Private Affair 1930,Ja 14,24:3
Nantucket Follies 1927,Jl 30,13:2
Naomi 1920,My 7,12:2
Nap Hand 1940,Mr 10,XI,2:6
Napi 1931,Mr 12,22:5
Napoleon 1928,Mr 9,21:1; 1934,S 4,23:2
Napoleon Greift Ein 1930,Je 1,VIII,2:1
Napoleon IV 1928,O 7,IX,5:3
Napoleon Passes 1927,D 21,29:2
Napoleon Unique 1936,N 13,27:3; 1936,N 29,XII,2:4
Napoleon Will Make Order 1930,F 23,III,7:2
Napoleon: The Hundred Days 1932,Ap 19,25:2;
  1932,My 8,VIII,1:3
Napoleon's Barber 1927,F 2,22:4
Narrow Road to the Deep North 1968,Je 27,49:2;
  1969,D 2,64:1; 1970,F 11,39:2
Nass Oder Trocken? 1929,Jl 7,VIII,2:1
Nat Turner 1960,N 7,46:3
Nathan der Weise 1936,D 10,45:2
Nathan the Wise 1942,Mr 12,25:4; 1942,Ap 4,18:4;
  1944,F 22,26:3; 1962,Mr 7,29:1; 1962,Mr 23,29:1
Nathan Weinstein, Mystic, Connecticut
  1966,F 26,15:2
National Anthem, The 1922,Ja 24,16:3;
  1922,F 5,VI,1:1
National Health 1969,O 19,75:1
Nationale 6 1935,N 24,IX,3:7; 1938,Ja 11,26:6

Native Ground 1937,Mr 24,28:4
Native Son 1941,Mr 25,26:5; 1941,Ap 6,IX,1:1;
  1942,O 24,10:6; 1942,N 1,VIII,1:1
Nativite, La 1933,F 6,11:3; 1933,F 12,IX,2:1
Nativity, The 1965,D 3,44:2
Nativity Play, The 1937,D 21,29:1
Natja 1925,F 17,19:2
Natural Affection 1963,F 2,5:2
Natural Look, The 1967,Mr 13,45:2
Natural Man 1941,My 8,20:4
Nature of the Crime 1970,Mr 24,41:1
Nature's Nobleman 1921,N 15,23:2
Nature's Way 1957,O 17,42:2
Naughty Cinderella 1925,O 4,IX,2:1; 1925,N 10,23:6
Naughty Marietta 1929,O 22,26:2; 1931,N 17,31:2;
  1936,S 2,19:5
Naughty-Naught ('00) 1937,Ja 25,23:2;
  1937,Jl 13,22:3; 1946,O 21,27:5
Naughty Riquette 1926,S 14,25:2; 1926,S 19,IX,1:1
Nautical but Nice 1931,Ap 19,31:6
Nautical Knot, A 1927,F 27,30:2
Ne Reveillez pas Madame 1970,O 24,29:5
Near Santa Barbara 1921,F 1,14:1
Near to the Stars 1932,F 23,23:2
Nearly Married 1929,S 22,IX,4:1
Nebeneinander 1924,Mr 2,VII,2:1
Ned McCobb's Daughter 1926,N 30,26:2;
  1926,D 5,VIII,5:1
Ned Wayburn's Gambols 1929,Ja 16,22:3
Neidhardt von Gneisenau 1927,Ja 23,VII,4:5
Neighborhood Playhouse Program 1930,F 21,23:1
Neighbors 1923,D 27,11:1; 1924,Je 18,23:3;
  1966,N 15,51:4; 1966,D 3,45:3; 1969,Ja 15,38:2
Neither Cat . . . Nor Damage 1957,D 20,31:1
Nekrassou 1957,Ag 20,22:1
Nekros 1960,O 26,44:1
Nellie Bly 1946,Ja 22,32:2; 1946,Ja 27,II,1:1
Nelson Touch, The 1931,S 20,VIII,2:6
Nem Elhetek Muzsikaszo Nelkul 1928,D 30,VIII,4:4
Nemesis 1921,Ap 5,24:3; 1921,Ap 10,VI,1:1
Nemica, La 1926,S 7,24:6
Nerves 1924,S 2,22:2; 1924,S 7,VII,1:1
Nervous Set, The 1959,My 13,43:1
Nervous Wreck, The 1923,O 10,16:1;
  1923,O 21,VIII,1:1; 1924,O 19,VIII,2:1
Nest, The 1922,F 2,20:1; 1970,Ap 10,46:1
Nether-World 1938,O 22,15:2
Neue Paradies, Das 1933,Ja 22,IX,1:1
Neveile, The 1924,F 9,16:2
Never Come Back 1932,O 29,18:6
Never Live Over a Pretzel Factory 1964,Mr 30,37:1
Never No More 1932,Ag 8,27:1; 1932,Ja 17,VIII,1:1
Never Say Horses 1951,D 7,34:4
Never Say Never 1951,N 21,21:2
Never Too Late 1962,N 28,42:1; 1963,S 25,48:1
Never Trouble Trouble 1937,Ag 18,15:2
Nevertheless 1920,D 28,9:1
New Americana 1928,N 30,32:4
New Aquacade Revue, The 1940,My 13,20:5
New Brooms 1924,N 18,23:5
New Cambridge Circus, The 1965,Ja 15,22:2
New Englander, The 1924,F 8,22:2
New Faces 1934,Mr 16,24:5; 1934,Ap 1,X,1:1
New Faces of 1936 1936,My 20,24:5
New Faces of 1943 1942,D 23,22:2
New Faces of 1952 1952,My 17,23:2;
  1952,My 25,II,1:1
New Faces of 1956 1956,Je 15,32:1
New Faces of 1962 1962,F 2,25:1
New Faces of 1968 1968,My 2,II,7:1
New Freedom, The 1930,My 15,32:4;
  1930,My 17,21:4
New Gallantry, The 1925,S 25,24:2
New Girl in Town 1957,My 15,40:1;
  1957,My 26,II,1:1
New Gossoon, The 1930,My 11,IX,2:7;
  1931,Ap 27,24:5; 1932,O 22,18:2; 1937,N 30,26:2
New Hellzapoppin, The 1939,D 12,36:4
New Life, A 1943,S 12,VI,14:4; 1943,S 16,26:6
New Man, The 1932,Ap 22,23:2
New Meet the People, The 1943,Ag 22,II,1:6
New Men, The 1962,S 7,35:2
New Moon, The 1928,S 2,VII,4:4; 1928,S 20,33:1;
  1942,Ag 19,14:2; 1944,My 18,16:2; 1955,Jl 1,13:1
New Morality, The 1921,Ja 31,10:1
New Music Hall of Israel, The 1969,O 3,40:1
New Pins and Needles 1939,N 21,19:2
New Poor, The 1923,D 30,VII,2:1; 1924,Ja 8,26:1;
  1924,Ja 20,VII,1:1
New Priorities of 1943 1942,S 16,28:2
New School for Scandal 1937,My 5,28:2
New Sin, The 1923,My 28,18:3
New Tenant, The 1964,My 28,40:2
New Toys 1924,Ja 20,VII,2:8; 1924,F 19,12:1;
  1924,F 24,VII,1:1
New Worlds 1922,S 26,18:2
New York 1927,N 15,26:2
New York Exchange 1926,D 31,11:2
New York Idea, The 1948,Ag 18,29:2;
  1963,Jl 13,12:2
New York to Cherbourg 1932,F 20,11:4

New Yorkers, The 1927,Mr 11,24:3;
  1930,N 16,VIII,3:1; 1930,D 9,31:1;
  1930,D 28,VIII,1:1
Newcomers 1923,Jl 15,VI,1:2
News Item 1935,Ag 6,20:3
Next 1969,F 11,27:1; 1969,F 23,II,1:1;
  1970,Mr 12,46:1
Next Half Hour, The 1945,O 30,14:6; 1945,N 4,II,1:1
Next Phase, The 1957,Ag 4,38:3
Next President, The 1958,Ap 10,34:3
Next Time I'll Sing to You 1963,N 28,69:2
Nic-Nax of 1926 1926,Ag 5,19:1
Nica 1926,Ja 26,19:1
Nice People 1921,Mr 3,11:1; 1921,Mr 6,VI,1:2;
  1958,O 20,36:1
Nice Women 1929,Je 11,27:4
Nicole et Sa Vertu 1927,O 30,IX,4:7
Nifties of 1923 1923,S 26,10:1
Nigger Rich 1929,S 21,16:7
Niggerlovers, The 1967,O 2,54:2; 1967,O 15,II,3:3;
  1968,Jl 7,II,1:1
Night 1923,My 26,8:4; 1968,N 29,52:1;
  1968,D 8,II,5:4
Night Arrival 1938,D 25,IX,5:4
Night at an Inn, A 1930,My 10,25:1
Night Before Christmas, The 1941,Mr 30,I,48:2;
  1941,Ap 11,25:2
Night Boat, The 1920,F 3,18:1
Night Call, The 1922,Ap 27,12:2; 1922,Ap 30,VII,1:1
Night Circus, The 1958,D 3,44:1
Night Club Queen 1933,D 3,IX,7:6
Night Conspirators 1963,My 23,31:4
Night Duel, The 1926,F 16,22:3
Night Hawk 1925,F 25,16:4; 1926,D 27,21:3
Night Hostess 1928,Jl 29,VII,2:2; 1928,S 13,31:2
Night in Budapest, A 1936,N 3,33:2
Night in Paris, A 1926,Ja 6,16:3; 1926,Jl 27,15:4
Night in Spain, A 1927,My 4,28:2;
  1927,My 22,VIII,1:1; 1927,Jl 3,VII,1:1;
  1949,Ag 28,II,1:1
Night in Spring, A 1935,Ag 7,22:2
Night in the House 1935,N 8,19:5
Night in the Woods, A 1931,Mr 2,19:3
Night in Venice, A 1929,Ap 7,X,2:1;
  1929,My 22,30:2; 1952,Je 27,18:6; 1952,Jl 13,II,1:1;
  1953,Je 26,15:2
Night Is Black Bottles, The 1962,D 5,56:1
Night Life 1962,O 2,45:2; 1962,O 24,44:1
Night Like This, A 1930,Mr 9,IX,4:1
Night Lodging 1920,Ap 14,18:2; 1920,Ap 18,VI,2:1
Night Music 1940,F 23,18:2; 1940,Mr 3,X,1:1;
  1951,Ap 9,29:6
Night Must Fall 1935,Jl 7,IX,1:7; 1936,S 29,34:1;
  1947,F 13,33:6
Night of January 16 1935,S 10,26:1; 1935,S 17,26:4;
  1935,S 22,X,1:1; 1935,D 16,22:5; 1936,S 30,29:3;
  1937,Jl 20,19:3
Night of Love 1940,O 29,32:6; 1941,Ja 8,14:2
Night of the Auk 1956,D 4,50:2; 1956,D 16,II,3:1;
  1963,My 22,35:2
Night of The Ball, The 1955,Ja 13,31:8;
  1955,F 13,II,3:1
Night of the Dunce 1966,D 29,21:1
Night of the Iguana, The 1961,D 29,10:1;
  1962,Ja 7,II,1:1
Night of the Party, The 1921,Jl 17,VI,1:8
Night Over Taos 1932,Mr 10,25:3
Night Remembers, The 1934,N 28,24:3
Night Sky 1937,Ja 7,28:7; 1937,Ja 31,XI,3:1
Night Thoreau Spent in Jail, The 1970,N 2,66:1
Night Watch In Syria 1943,Ja 5,15:5
Nightcap, The 1921,Ag 16,18:3; 1922,Ja 24,11:1
Nighthawks 1967,D 30,14:2
Nightingale, The 1927,Ja 4,20:4; 1947,Jl 17,16:4
Nightmare, The 1965,Ja 6,32:1
Nightmare Abbey 1952,Mr 16,II,3:8
Night's Candles 1933,Je 25,IX,1:3; 1933,S 21,22:1
Nights of Fury 1957,F 12,31:1
Nights of Wrath 1947,D 1,26:4
Nightshade 1920,Je 8,9:2
Nightstick 1927,N 11,20:4
Nikki 1931,S 30,23:4
Nina 1932,Ja 24,VIII,1:3; 1935,S 18,19:6;
  1935,O 13,IX,3:1; 1935,N 3,X,3:8; 1951,D 6,44:3
Nina Rosa 1929,O 27,IX,2:1; 1930,My 31,19:3;
  1930,S 22,22:5; 1937,Ag 26,24:3
9 by Six: A Cry of Players 1956,D 5,49:2
Nine Fifteen Revue, The 1930,F 12,26:2
Nine Girls 1943,Ja 14,26:2
Nine O'Clock Revue 1921,F 9,7:5; 1923,O 5,22:1;
  1936,Jl 8,14:3
Nine Pine Street 1933,Ap 28,15:5
Nine Sharp 1938,Ap 24,X,2:1
Nine Till Six 1930,S 29,17:2; 1936,Mr 14,10:3
Nine to Eleven, The 1925,Jl 12,VII,1:1
Nine to Six 1930,Ja 31,24:3
1935 1936,My 13,28:2
1931- 1931,D 11,34:3; 1931,D 20,VIII,1:1
1933 1933,F 22,24:5
1928 1928,Ap 8,VIII,4:1
1927 1927,Mr 6,VII,4:4
Nineteenth Hole, The 1927,O 2,VIII,4:6;
  1927,O 12,30:3; 1929,Ja 6,VIII,4:4

Nineteenth Hole of Europe, The 1949,Mr 28,16:2
Nineties 1934,Mr 22,24:6
Ninety Day Mistress, The 1967,N 7,49:1;
  1967,N 19,II,1:1
90 Horse Power 1926,Mr 16,22:4
Ninety Sail 1937,D 1,27:2
Ninth Month Midnight 1949,F 17,28:2
9th Street Guest, The 1930,Ag 26,24:3
Nirvana 1926,Mr 4,19:1; 1926,Ap 11,VIII,1:1
No, No, Nanette 1925,Mr 12,17:2; 1925,S 17,20:2
No Count Boy, The 1954,Jl 7,23:1
No Exit 1936,Ja 22,15:3; 1946,N 27,21:1;
  1956,Ag 15,23:1; 1967,O 31,38:2
No Foolin' 1926,Je 25,25:1
No for an Answer 1941,Ja 6,10:6
No Hard Feelings 1965,Ap 5,33:8
No Laughter in Heaven 1938,My 17,26:5
No Medals 1944,N 19,II,2:4
No More Blondes 1920,Ja 8,22:1
No More Frontier 1931,O 22,27:1
No More in Dust 1961,S 14,26:8
No More Ladies 1934,Ja 24,20:3; 1934,S 4,23:2;
  1934,S 19,14:4; 1934,O 7,IX,3:7
No More Peace 1936,Je 12,19:4; 1937,F 27,9:1;
  1937,Je 4,26:7; 1938,Ja 29,13:2
No More Women 1926,Ag 4,17:2
No Mother to Guide Her 1933,D 26,18:5
No Orchids For Miss Blandish 1942,Ag 9,VIII,1:8
No Ordinary Lady 1936,O 1,28:3
No Other Girl 1924,Ag 14,10:4
No Place to Be Somebody 1969,My 5,53:3;
  1969,My 18,II,1:1; 1969,My 18,II,22:1;
  1969,D 31,17:1
No Questions Asked 1934,F 6,24:3
No Sign of a Dove 1953,D 20,II,4:2
No Sleep for the Wicked 1937,Jl 1,32:5;
  1937,Jl 18,X,1:5
No Strings 1942,Je 14,VIII,2:1; 1962,Mr 16,24:1;
  1962,Mr 25,II,1:1; 1964,Ja 1,17:1; 1964,Jl 18,10:1
No Tears for Tony 1954,Je 3,32:6
No Time for Comedy 1939,Mr 31,18:4;
  1939,Ap 18,26:4; 1939,Ap 30,XI,1:1
No Time for Sergeants 1955,O 21,32:2;
  1955,N 6,II,1:1; 1956,F 26,II,1:1; 1956,Ag 24,15:8
No Trespassing! 1926,S 8,19:1; 1926,S 12,VIII,1:1
No Trifling With Love 1959,N 10,55:3;
  1968,Mr 5,35:1
No Way Out 1944,O 31,23:1
Noah 1935,F 14,25:2; 1935,Ag 4,IX,1:3;
  1935,N 6,32:2; 1935,D 1,XI,6:4; 1954,O 11,32:2
Nobel Prize, The 1933,Jl 4,16:4
Noble Experiment, The 1930,O 28,21:4
Noble Rogue, A 1929,Ag 20,31:2
Nobody Hears A Broken Drum 1970,Mr 20,55:1
Nobody Loves an Albatross 1963,D 20,20:1;
  1964,Ja 5,II,1:1
Nobody's Business 1923,O 23,17:1;
  1923,O 28,VIII,1:1
Nobody's Child 1956,Ag 23,25:2
Nobody's Money 1921,My 22,VI,1:6; 1921,Ag 18,9:3
Noces d'Argent, Les 1928,Ap 8,VIII,4:1;
  1930,D 28,VIII,3:5
Nocturne 1925,F 17,19:1
Noe 1931,Jl 5,VIII,1:3
Noel Coward's Sweet Potato 1968,S 30,59:1;
  1968,O 13,II,5:1
Noisy Passenger, The 1970,D 31,8:3
Noix de Coco 1936,Ja 12,IX,3:7
Non si Sa Come 1934,D 20,29:4
Nona 1932,S 18,IX,2:1; 1932,O 5,26:4
None Are So Blind 1923,My 9,14:4
Noon 1968,N 29,52:1; 1968,D 8,II,5:4
Noontide 1961,Je 2,37:1
Noose, The 1926,O 21,23:3
Norman, Is That You? 1970,F 20,30:1;
  1970,Mr 1,II,1:4
Norrtull Gang, The 1930,N 2,VIII,3:2
North and South 1930,O 5,IX,4:1
Not a Way of Life 1967,Mr 23,28:1
Not Enough Rope 1962,Mr 2,24:1
Not for Children 1935,N 25,23:8; 1935,D 22,IX,3:3;
  1935,D 29,IX,2:1; 1936,Mr 1,IX,2:2; 1951,F 14,35:2
Not Herbert 1926,Ja 27,16:2
Not in Our Stars 1924,F 10,VII,2:4; 1941,Ap 20,20:5
Not Now Darling 1970,O 30,33:1
Not Now-Later 1928,Ap 14,25:1
Not on the Lips 1929,Mr 26,34:3
Not so Fast 1923,My 23,18:4
Not So Long Ago 1920,My 5,14:1;
  1920,Ag 29,VI,1:3
Not While I'm Eating 1961,D 20,37:1
Notes From the Underground 1960,Ja 20,26:1
Notre Amour 1926,O 31,VIII,2:4
Notre Dame du Cinema 1936,Ja 19,IX,3:4
Nounouche 1923,O 23,16:1
Nous ne Sommes Plus des Enfants
  1927,My 29,VII,2:7
Nouveau Testament 1934,N 11,IX,3:6
Nouvelle Heloise, La 1923,Ap 8,VIII,1:7
Novice and the Duke, The 1929,D 11,37:2
Now 1968,Je 6,53:1

Now-A-Days 1929,Ag 6,29:3
Now Barabbas 1947,Ap 20,II,3:7
Now I Lay Me Down to Sleep 1949,Jl 23,7:3;
  1950,Mr 3,21:2; 1950,Mr 19,II,1:1
Now Is the Time for All Good Men 1967,S 27,42:1;
  1967,O 27,49:1
Now You See It 1954,Ap 20,35:2; 1967,N 20,59:1
Now You've Done It 1937,Mr 6,10:4
Nowhere Bound 1935,Ja 23,20:2
Nowhere to Go But Up 1962,O 9,46:6;
  1962,N 12,36:2
Noye's Fludde 1959,Mr 17,41:2
Nude in Washington Square, The 1934,Ag 7,20:1
Nude With Violin 1956,S 25,30:1; 1956,D 2,II,3:1;
  1957,N 15,36:1
Nuit, Une 1935,Je 16,X,1:1
Nuit au Bouge, Une 1923,O 16,18:1
Nuit d'Auberge, La 1929,N 10,X,4:1
Nuit du 12 au 13, La 1928,D 30,VIII,1:3
Nuit Venitienne, La 1930,F 2,VIII,4:1
Nuits de la Colere, Les 1947,D 1,26:4;
  1957,F 12,31:1
Numance 1937,Je 13,XI,2:1
Number, The 1951,O 31,33:2
Number 7 1926,S 9,21:3
Nuns, The 1970,Je 2,35:1
Nurse Cavell 1934,Ap 1,X,1:7
Nut Farm, The 1929,O 15,34:3
Nutmeg Tree 1941,O 19,IX,2:5
Nyckelromanen 1931,Mr 1,VIII,3:1
Nymph Errant 1933,O 7,18:2; 1933,O 29,IX,1:6

───────────

O

O, Oysters! 1961,Ja 31,23:1
O Evening Star 1935,D 26,20:1; 1936,Ja 9,24:6
O H M S 1931,Mr 29,VIII,2:1
O K 1925,My 4,16:1
O Marry Me 1961,O 28,13:1
O Mistress Mine 1936,D 4,30:3; 1936,D 20,XI,3:3;
  1946,Ja 24,25:2; 1946,F 3,II,1:1; 1946,S 1,II,1:1
O Nightingale 1925,Ap 16,25:2
O Say Can You See! 1962,O 9,45:1
Obbligato 1958,F 19,22:2
Object of Virtue, An 1930,N 5,28:3;
  1930,N 23,IX,2:4
Obratsov Russian Pupper Theater in an Unusual
  Concert 1963,O 3,28:1
O'Brien Girl, The 1921,O 4,10:2
Obsession 1946,O 2,39:2
Occasion, L' 1939,Ja 10,16:4
Occupe-Toi d'Amelie 1952,N 25,35:2
Octoroon, The 1929,Mr 13,28:3; 1936,S 1,24:2;
  1961,Ja 28,13:1
O'Daniel 1947,F 25,32:2
Odd Couple, The 1965,Mr 11,36:1; 1965,Mr 21,II,1:1
Odd Man In 1957,Jl 17,21:3
Odd Man Out 1925,My 26,24:3
Odds on Mrs Oakley, The 1944,O 3,18:8
Ode to Liberty 1934,D 11,28:2; 1934,D 22,20:2;
  1935,Jl 2,24:3; 1935,Jl 9,24:4; 1935,Ag 6,20:3;
  1937,Ag 18,15:2
Odeon-Revue 1927,My 22,VIII,2:7
Ododo 1970,N 25,26:1; 1970,D 6,II,5:1
Oedipe a Colone 1924,S 7,III,12:4
Oedipus 1946,My 21,19:2; 1968,Mr 31,II,5:1;
  1968,Ap 2,54:1; 1968,Jl 31,29:1; 1970,F 23,30:1
Oedipus and the Sphinx 1928,Mr 11,VIII,2:7
Oedipus on Colonos 1929,Mr 24,X,2:3
Oedipus Rex 1923,O 26,14:1; 1929,Mr 24,X,2:3;
  1936,O 18,X,3:8; 1937,My 9,XI,7:5;
  1945,N 11,II,2:5; 1945,D 17,16:7; 1948,My 24,23:2;
  1954,Jl 17,6:6; 1956,S 4,32:6; 1959,Ap 30,36:1;
  1960,Ap 30,15:2; 1965,Jl 9,17:1
Oedipus the King 1926,D 26,VII,4:8
Oedipus Tyrannus 1941,My 10,13:8; 1952,N 25,35:2
Of Love Remembered 1967,F 20,46:5
Of Mice and Men 1937,N 24,20:5; 1937,D 12,XI,3:1;
  1938,Ja 23,XI,1:6; 1939,Ap 30,XI,3:5;
  1958,D 5,38:1
Of One Mother 1937,Ja 18,21:3
Of Thee I Sing 1931,D 13,VIII,2:4; 1931,D 28,20:1;
  1932,Mr 20,VIII,1:1; 1932,My 8,VIII,1:1;
  1937,Ag 10,22:3; 1937,Ag 18,14:4; 1952,My 6,34:2;
  1952,My 11,II,1:1; 1969,Ap 8,19:1
Of V We Sing 1941,O 26,I,39:1; 1942,F 16,20:3
Of Very Good Family 1932,Ap 29,13:3
Ofay Watcher, The 1969,S 16,40:1; 1969,S 21,II,1:2
Off Key 1927,F 9,16:2
Off the Record 1935,Je 19,23:3; 1940,D 1,63:5
Off to Buffalo! 1939,F 22,18:2
Off Your Marx 1936,Ap 2,28:2
Offence, The 1925,N 16,25:1
O'Flaherty, V C 1920,Je 22,9:1; 1931,Ap 11,17:6;
  1957,F 19,35:7
O'Flynn, The 1934,D 28,24:1
Oh, Ernest! 1927,My 10,24:3
Oh, Hector! 1929,Mr 6,33:2
Oh, Henry! 1920,My 6,14:2
Oh, Herbert! 1945,Je 20,26:3
Oh, Johnny: or, Jonny Spielt Auf 1970,Mr 15,88:4

Oh, Kay! 1926,N 9,31:3; 1927,Jl 3,VII,1:1; 1927,S 22,33:3; 1960,Ap 18,37:2
Oh, Les Beaux Jours 1970,Ap 25,32:3
Oh, Men! Oh, Women! 1953,D 18,37:2
Oh, Mr Meadowbrook! 1948,D 27,17:2
Oh, Pioneers 1969,N 12,41:1
Oh, Please! 1926,D 22,24:3
Oh, Professor 1930,My 2,19:6
Oh, Promise Me 1930,N 25,31:1; 1930,D 7,IX,1:1
Oh, Say Can You See L A 1968,F 9,50:1
Oh, What a Life! 1942,O 13,19:2
Oh, You Girls! 1935,D 2,19:5
Oh Captain! 1958,F 5,21:2
Oh Dad, Poor Dad, Mamma's Hung You in the Closet and I'm Feelin' So Sad 1961,Jl 6,19:2; 1962,F 27,28:1; 1962,Mr 11,II,1:1; 1962,Ap 29,II,3:1; 1963,Ag 28,28:2
Oh What a Lovely War 1964,O 1,30:1; 1964,O 11,II,1:1
Oh What a Wedding! 1969,O 20,60:1
Oh! Calcutta! 1969,Je 18,33:1; 1969,Je 29,II,1:7; 1970,Jl 29,30:1
Oh! Mama 1925,Ag 20,22:2; 1925,Ag 30,VII,1:1
Oh! Oh! Nurse 1925,D 8,28:4
Oklahoma! 1943,Ap 1,27:1; 1943,Ap 11,II,1:1; 1943,My 9,II,6:4; 1943,N 14,II,1:1; 1945,F 4,II,5:1; 1947,My 1,35:3; 1947,My 11,II,3:7; 1951,My 30,15:2; 1951,S 13,38:2; 1951,S 23,II,3:1; 1953,S 1,19:1; 1953,S 6,II,1:1; 1955,Je 21,37:7; 1955,Jl 11,19:7; 1955,Ag 15,19:1; 1958,Mr 8,15:2; 1958,Mr 20,32:3; 1963,F 28,8:2; 1963,My 16,40:1; 1965,Jl 16,62:1; 1969,Je 24,37:1; 1969,Jl 6,II,1:1
Oktobertag 1928,D 2,X,4:4
Ol' Man Satan 1932,O 4,26:3
Old Acquaintance 1940,D 10,33:5; 1940,D 24,18:3; 1941,Jl 28,IX,2:3
Old Bill, M P 1922,Ag 13,VI,1:8; 1926,N 11,22:2
Old Bucks and New Wings 1962,N 6,39:4
Old English 1924,O 26,VIII,1:1; 1924,N 9,VIII,2:3; 1924,D 24,11:2; 1924,D 28,VII,1:1
Old Folks at Home 1934,Ja 14,IX,1:8
Old Foolishness, The 1940,D 21,20:2
Old Glory, The 1964,N 15,II,1:1
Old House, The 1920,Jl 11,VI,1:6
Old Judge Mose Is Dead 1969,Ag 29,25:1
Old King's 1924,Mr 12,19:3
Old Ladies, The 1935,Ap 4,21:2; 1935,Ap 28,X,2:3
Old Lady Says No, The 1935,Jl 28,X,1:1; 1948,F 18,35:1; 1948,F 22,II,1:1
Old Lady Says No!, The 1929,Ag 11,VIII,2:1
Old Lady Shows Her Medals, The 1926,O 31,VIII,2:4; 1928,My 11,28:1; 1932,Mr 8,19:3
Old Maid, The 1935,Ja 8,26:1; 1937,F 24,19:3; 1949,Ja 27,20:6
Old Maid and the Thief, The 1949,N 7,32:4
Old Man Minick 1924,Ag 24,VII,1:8
Old Man Murphy 1931,My 19,25:2
Old Music 1937,Ag 19,22:2; 1937,S 5,X,2:1
Old Rascal, The 1930,Mr 25,34:4; 1930,N 23,IX,1:3
Old Soak, The 1922,Ag 23,14:5; 1922,S 3,VI,1:1
Old Spain 1927,My 8,VII,2:3
Old Timer 1929,Ap 30,33:4
Old Tune, The 1961,Mr 24,37:1
Old Women, The 1935,Jl 12,15:3
Oldest Trick in the World, The 1961,F 21,40:1
Oliver 1962,S 27,32:3; 1963,Ja 8,5:5; 1966,F 5,32:2
Oliver Cromwell 1923,F 25,VII,1:7; 1923,My 30,10:5
Oliver Cromwells Sendung 1933,Mr 19,IX,2:2
Oliver Oliver 1934,Ja 6,18:5
Oliver Twist 1934,Ag 11,16:5; 1937,F 21,II,4:4
Olivia Bows to Mrs Grundy 1932,Ap 3,VIII,2:5
Ollapotrida 1927,My 1,VIII,1:3
Olympia 1928,Mr 3,6:3; 1928,Mr 25,IX,4:1; 1928,O 17,26:1
On a Clear Day You Can See Forever 1965,O 18,44:1
On an Open Roof 1963,Ja 30,7:3
On Approval 1926,O 19,27:1; 1927,My 15,VIII,2:6; 1942,Mr 1,VIII,1:5
On Baile's Strand 1959,Ap 13,34:4
On Board 1927,Mr 16,28:6
On Borrowed Time 1938,F 4,16:4; 1938,O 6,27:5; 1938,N 6,IX,1:1; 1953,Ja 1,19:1; 1953,F 11,34:1
On Call 1928,N 10,20:7
On Circe's Island 1962,Ap 27,26:1
On Foreign Soil 1927,D 24,8:2
On Location 1937,S 28,19:1
On Ne Badine Pas Avec l'Amour 1968,Mr 5,35:1
On Ne Roule pas Antoinette 1927,Ap 10,VIII,2:7
On Stage 1935,Jl 23,24:4; 1935,O 30,16:6
On Strivers' Row 1946,Mr 1,17:2
On the Brighter Side 1961,S 25,II,3:5
On the Double 1944,Ap 28,24:2
On the Harmful Effects of Tobacco 1948,F 6,29:2; 1956,Ap 26,38:1; 1959,Ap 16,28:1; 1959,Ap 26,II,1:1; 1968,Mr 6,34:1; 1969,Mr 9,76:5
On the High Road 1929,Ja 15,22:3; 1961,Ap 21,26:2
On the Level 1937,Mr 26,24:4
On the Make 1932,My 24,23:2

On the Necessity of Being Polygamous 1964,D 9,61:1
On the Road to New York 1944,Je 21,23:4
On the Rocks 1933,N 25,10:1; 1933,N 26,II,2:8; 1933,D 17,IX,4:2; 1934,Jl 11,20:4; 1938,Je 16,20:2
On the Spot 1930,Ap 3,32:6; 1930,Ap 20,VIII,2:1; 1930,O 30,33:3; 1931,Ja 18,VIII,3:1
On the Stairs 1922,S 26,18:2
On the Town 1944,D 29,11:4; 1945,Ja 7,II,1:1; 1945,F 4,II,5:1; 1959,Ja 16,36:1; 1959,Ja 25,II,1:1; 1959,F 14,15:1; 1963,My 31,30:7
On to Fortune 1935,Ja 15,23:2; 1935,F 5,22:2
On Trial 1949,D 9,35:5
On Vacation 1968,Ja 31,28:2
On Whitman Avenue 1946,My 9,28:2
On With the Dance 1925,My 1,22:4
On Your Toes 1936,Mr 23,22:4; 1936,Ap 13,14:4; 1937,F 6,15:2; 1937,Ag 3,21:2; 1954,O 12,24:4
Once a Crook 1940,S 1,IX,2:4
Once a Husband 1932,N 20,IX,3:6
Once an Actor 1950,Ag 1,19:8
Once Around the Block 1950,My 25,36:2; 1956,O 29,34:1
Once for the Asking 1963,N 21,42:2
Once in a Lifetime 1930,S 7,IX,2:4; 1930,S 25,22:3; 1930,D 7,IX,1:1; 1931,F 1,VIII,1:3; 1933,F 24,13:1; 1933,Mr 19,IX,2:2; 1962,O 30,30:1; 1964,Ja 29,20:1
Once Is Enough 1938,Ja 28,17:2; 1938,F 16,16:2
Once More With Feeling 1958,O 22,39:1; 1959,Jl 10,30:1
Once Over Lightly 1938,D 10,13:4; 1938,D 17,10:8; 1942,N 20,26:2; 1955,Mr 16,39:1
Once There Was a Russian 1961,F 20,32:2
Once Upon a Mattress 1959,My 12,40:1; 1959,My 17,II,1:1; 1960,S 21,43:4
Once Upon a Tailor 1955,My 24,36:2
Once Upon a Time 1933,S 22,15:1; 1939,D 21,28:2
Onda e lo Scoglio, L' 1931,Ap 13,17:3
Ondine 1954,F 19,23:1; 1954,F 28,II,1:1
One 1920,S 15,12:2
One, Two, Three! 1929,O 5,22:4; 1929,N 17,IX,4:7 1930,S 30,24:2
One-Act Plays of the Sea 1937,O 30,23:2
One-Act Variety Theatre 1940,Mr 20,36:2
One Bright Day 1952,Mr 20,37:2; 1956,Ap 8,II,3:1
One by One 1964,D 2,60:1
One Can't Marry a Penniless Girl 1928,D 2,X,4:7
One Chaste Man 1930,Je 11,33:5
One Day More 1926,Mr 19,24:3; 1933,F 1,13:5
One Eye Closed 1954,N 25,45:2
One Flew Over the Cuckoo's Nest 1963,N 14,40:2; 1963,D 1,II,1:1
One Flight Down 1937,D 14,32:4
One for All 1927,My 14,25:5
One for the Money 1939,F 6,9:2
One Glorious Hour 1927,Ap 15,27:2
One Good Year 1935,N 28,38:3
One Heluva Night 1924,Je 5,18:1
110 in the Shade 1963,S 12,33:2; 1963,O 25,37:1
One in a Million 1934,N 17,13:2
One Is a Lonely Number 1964,Je 19,37:3
One Kiss 1923,N 28,14:2
One Life for Another 1920,D 18,11:2
One-Man Show 1945,F 9,21:2; 1945,F 18,II,1:1
One Man's Woman 1926,My 26,25:1
One Mile Up 1928,D 30,VIII,1:6
One More Genius 1936,Ag 11,24:6
One More Honeymoon 1934,Ap 2,13:5
One More River 1960,Mr 19,12:2
One Night in Rome 1920,Ap 30,1:2; 1920,My 4,14:1
One Night Stands of a Noisy Passenger 1970,D 31,8:3
One of the Family 1925,D 23,22:3
One of the Finest 1927,O 16,IX,2:4
One of the Many 1921,O 4,10:3
One on the House 1941,Mr 30,I,47:3
One Over the Eight 1961,Je 25,II,3:5
One Sabbath Afternoon 1939,Ja 17,27:5
One Shot Fired 1927,N 8,32:5
One Sunday Afternoon 1933,F 16,23:5; 1933,Mr 19,IX,1:1; 1933,S 17,X,2:4; 1933,D 17,IX,4:2
One Thing After Another 1937,D 29,17:2
One-Third of a Nation 1937,Jl 31,6:4; 1938,Ja 18,27:2; 1938,Ja 30,X,1:1
One Touch of Venus 1943,O 8,14:1; 1943,O 17,II,1:1
One Trip of the Silver Star 1925,Jl 12,VII,1:8
One Tuesday Morning 1957,N 18,36:5
One Way Pendulum 1961,S 19,38:2
One Way Street 1928,D 25,31:2
One Way to Heaven 1936,S 29,35:1
One Wife or Another 1933,F 7,23:6
One Woman 1931,D 14,16:4
One-Woman Show, A 1962,My 22,31:1
One Woman's Husband 1920,Mr 23,9:3
Only a Countess May Dance When She's Crazy (An Almost Historical Camp) 1968,Mr 19,41:1
Only Game in Town, The 1968,My 21,42:1
Only Girl, The 1934,My 22,28:2
Only in America 1959,N 20,35:1
Only Jealousy of Emer, The 1970,Mr 25,36:4; 1970,Ap 26,II,1:3
Only the Heart 1942,D 7,22:3; 1944,Ap 5,17:2

Only the Young 1932,S 22,25:2
Only 38 1921,S 14,22:2
Onzieme Commandement 1932,My 15,VIII,2:2
Open Door, The 1928,Je 26,29:4; 1930,Ja 28,28:1
Open Fire, The 1921,Ag 21,VI,1:8
Open House 1925,N 1,VIII,2:4; 1925,D 15,28:3; 1947,Je 4,33:4
Open Season at Second City 1964,Ja 23,25:1
Open 24 Hours 1969,F 12,31:1
Opening Night 1963,O 3,28:2
Opening of a Window, The 1961,S 26,32:2
Opera Opera 1955,D 22,19:1
Operation Sidewinder 1970,Mr 13,33:1; 1970,Mr 22,II,1:4
Operetta 1970,Mr 9,42:1
Operette 1938,F 18,22:3; 1938,Mr 17,17:4; 1938,Ap 3,XI,1:8
Opium 1970,O 6,58:1
Oppenheimer File, The 1964,D 15,56:1
Opportunity 1920,Jl 31,5:1
Optimists, The 1928,Ja 31,28:2
Ora di Diana, L' 1937,My 17,22:3
Orage Mystique 1927,D 18,IX,4:4
Orange Blossoms 1922,S 20,18:1
Orange Souffle 1966,Je 8,42:2; 1966,Jl 16,14:6
Orchard Walls 1937,F 4,17:3; 1937,F 21,X,2:1
Orchids Preferred 1937,Ap 29,16:6; 1937,My 12,26:5
Order Please 1934,O 10,21:2
Ordinary Man, An 1968,S 10,39:1
Oresteia 1926,D 12,VIII,4:7; 1961,N 8,43:5; 1966,Je 30,29:1
Orestes 1926,Je 20,II,3:6; 1968,F 17,32:5
Organ Grinder, The 1934,Ja 1,28:3
Originale 1964,S 9,46:1
Orlando Furioso 1970,N 5,59:1; 1970,N 27,46:1
Oroonoko 1932,Ag 28,IX,1:1
Orphee 1935,Mr 23,10:3
Orpheus Descending 1957,Mr 22,28:1; 1957,Mr 31,II,1:1; 1959,Mr 18,44:6; 1959,My 15,23:3; 1959,O 6,45:2; 1961,Ag 28,21:2
Orpheus in der Unterwelt 1922,F 5,VI,1:7
Orpheus in Hades 1930,D 16,30:1
Orthee 1962,D 29,5:5
Oscar Wilde 1936,S 30,29:4; 1936,O 18,X,3:8; 1938,O 11,20:2; 1938,O 16,IX,1:1; 1957,Ap 20,21:3
Ostriches 1925,Mr 31,16:1
Otage, L' 1959,O 27,42:1
Othello 1921,Je 9,10:2; 1925,Ja 12,11:1; 1925,Ja 18,VII,1:1; 1929,F 4,21:2; 1930,My 20,33:1; 1932,Mr 6,VIII,2:1; 1932,My 1,VIII,2:2; 1934,Jl 22,23:4; 1934,Jl 29,IX,1:3; 1935,S 13,19:2; 1935,S 22,X,2:5; 1935,S 28,13:2; 1936,N 27,26:5; 1936,D 6,XII,6:1; 1937,Ja 7,16:4; 1938,F 27,X,1:4; 1942,Ag 9,VIII,1:7; 1942,Ag 16,VIII,1:7; 1943,O 3,VI,15:1; 1943,O 20,18:1; 1943,O 24,II,1:1; 1943,O 31,II,1:1; 1945,My 23,25:4; 1946,D 4,44:2; 1949,My 16,17:4; 1953,O 30,28:2; 1955,S 8,27:2; 1955,S 18,II,1:1; 1956,Mr 11,II,3:1; 1957,Je 24,19:2; 1957,Je 30,II,1:1; 1958,Jl 4,16:1; 1959,Ap 8,41:3; 1959,Ap 12,II,3:1; 1959,Jl 2,17:2; 1959,Jl 5,II,1:1; 1960,S 11,II,7:1; 1961,O 1,53:6; 1962,S 28,27:1; 1963,Ap 13,10:4; 1964,Ap 22,56:1; 1964,Jl 15,29:1; 1964,Jl 23,18:4; 1964,Ag 3,16:6; 1964,O 13,48:1; 1965,S 8,51:4; 1970,Je 22,43:1; 1970,Je 28,II,1:1; 1970,S 15,51:1
Other Heart, The 1952,My 11,II,3:7
Other Lives 1921,S 11,VI,1:6
Other Man, The 1968,F 9,50:1
Other Men's Wives 1929,N 13,24:4
Other One, The 1932,O 4,26:3
Other People's Houses 1941,N 9,IX,3:6
Other People's Lives 1932,D 4,IX,3:6; 1933,Ag 6,X,1:3
Other Rose, The 1923,D 16,IX,2:4; 1923,D 21,15:2; 1923,D 30,VII,1:1
Otherwise Engaged 1958,Ap 24,37:3
Ouija Board, The 1920,Mr 30,9:1
Our Betters 1923,S 14,22:2; 1928,F 21,18:2; 1928,Mr 4,IX,1:1; 1937,Jl 22,16:2; 1946,N 10,II,3:1
Our Eighteen-Year-Olds 1929,N 17,IX,4:7
Our Honor and Our Power 1936,Je 28,IX,1:6
Our Lan' 1947,Ap 19,11:2; 1947,S 29,16:5
Our Little Wife 1927,My 10,25:3
Our Man Crichton 1964,D 23,21:1
Our Man in Madras 1968,Ja 31,28:2
Our Nell 1922,D 5,24:1
Our Stage and Stars 1933,N 13,20:6
Our Town 1938,Ja 23,II,10:6; 1938,Ja 26,27:4; 1938,Ja 30,X,3:1; 1938,F 13,F,1,X,1:1; 1938,S 16,17:3; 1940,Je 30,35:5; 1944,Ja 11,24:5; 1944,Ja 16,II,1:1; 1946,My 2,27:3; 1946,O 27,II,2:4; 1955,Mr 18,32:8; 1959,Mr 24,46:2; 1959,Ap 5,II,1:1; 1961,Ap 4,34:3; 1961,N 4,14:7; 1968,S 29,77:4; 1968,D 14,62:1; 1969,N 28,50:1; 1969,D 7,II,7:1
Our Vivid Rustics 1922,Ap 30,VII,1:1
Our Wife 1933,Mr 3,13:2
Out-A-Luck 1924,O 5,VIII,1:3
Out From Under 1940,My 6,13:2; 1966,Je 8,42:2; 1966,Jl 16,14:6
Out Goes She 1928,D 30,VIII,4:1
Out O' Luck 1925,D 19,15:1
Out of a Blue Sky 1930,F 10,20:6
Out of My House 1942,Ja 8,28:6

Out of Sight 1937,Mr 5,17:6; 1937,Mr 28,XI,2:2
Out of Step 1925,Ja 30,12:1
Out of the Frying Pan 1941,F 12,24:2
Out of the Night 1927,O 18,32:3
Out of the Sea 1927,D 6,26:2
Out of the Seven Seas 1923,N 4,VIII,2:7;
  1923,N 20,23:3
Out of This World 1950,D 22,17:3;
  1951,My 20,II,1:1; 1955,O 13,35:2; 1955,N 10,44:2
Out West of Eighth 1951,S 21,20:3
Outlaw, The 1937,O 6,28:1; 1937,N 8,18:2
Outrageous Fortune 1943,N 4,28:5
Outrageous Mrs Palmer, The 1920,O 13,18:1;
  1920,O 24,VI,1:2
Outside Looking In 1925,S 8,28:1; 1925,S 13,VIII,1:1;
  1929,Je 23,VIII,2:1
Outside the Door 1949,Mr 2,33:2
Outsider, The 1923,Je 10,VII,1:4; 1924,F 17,VII,2:8;
  1924,Mr 4,16:4; 1924,Mr 9,VIII,1:1;
  1928,Ap 10,32:2
Outward Bound 1923,O 21,VIII,2:2;
  1923,D 2,VIII,2:8; 1924,Ja 8,26:1;
  1924,Ja 13,VII,1:1; 1927,Ja 30,VII,2:4;
  1927,Mr 16,28:3; 1938,D 23,16:5; 1939,Ja 1,IX,1:1
Over Here 1936,Mr 16,21:2
Over She Goes 1936,S 24,28:7
Over Twenty-One 1944,Ja 4,20:2
Overcoat, The 1960,S 7,45:1
Overruled 1959,My 27,32:2; 1959,Ag 21,13:1
Overtons, The 1945,F 7,16:6
Overture 1925,My 3,VIII,2:1; 1930,N 25,31:2;
  1930,D 8,26:4; 1930,D 14,IX,1:1
Overzealous Youth, The 1928,D 2,X,4:7
Owl and the Pussycat, The 1964,N 19,48:1;
  1966,Mr 4,25:5
Owl Answers, The 1969,Ja 13,26:1
Ox Cart, The 1966,D 20,58:1
Oy, Is Dus a Leben! 1942,O 13,19:2

P

P S I Love You 1964,N 20,40:1
Pacific 1860 1946,D 20,30:4; 1947,Ja 12,II,3:6
Pacifique 1937,N 14,XI,2:1
Pack Up Your Troubles 1943,Je 15,16:1
Paddy the Next Best Thing 1920,Ag 28,5:5
Padlocks of 1927 1927,Jl 6,23:4
Padre, The 1926,D 28,16:3
Padrone Delle Ferriere, Il 1934,Mr 19,13:5
Paese dei Campanelli, Il 1935,My 10,25:4
Pagan Lady 1930,S 28,VIII,4:1; 1930,O 21,34:2
Paganini 1925,N 22,VIII,1:8; 1935,F 10,VIII,3:1;
  1937,My 21,18:6; 1937,Je 6,XI,1:2
Pagans 1921,Ja 5,11:1
Page From a Diary 1936,Ja 17,14:6; 1936,F 9,X,3:1
Page Miss Glory 1934,N 28,24:2
Page Pygmalion 1932,Ag 4,17:5
Pageant of the Nativity of Christ 1948,D 25,6:7
Paging Danger 1931,F 27,19:2
Paid 1925,N 26,32:1
Paid Companions 1931,Je 23,28:4
Paid Off 1928,Jl 8,VII,1:2
Pain' Dur, Le 1949,My 1,II,3:1
Paint Your Wagon 1951,N 13,32:2; 1951,N 18,II,1:1
Painted Days, The 1961,Ap 7,24:1
Painted Smile, The 1938,My 8,X,1:7
Painted Veil, The 1931,O 11,VIII,2:4
Paisley Convertible, The 1967,F 13,42:1
Paix, La 1933,Ja 15,IX,2:1
Pajama Game, The 1954,My 14,20:2;
  1954,My 15,12:1; 1954,My 30,II,1:1;
  1955,N 13,II,3:1; 1957,My 16,27:1;
  1957,My 26,II,1:1
Pajama Lady, The 1930,O 12,VIII,4:1
Pajama Tops 1963,Je 1,15:1
Pajtashazassag 1928,D 30,VIII,4:4
Pal Joey 1940,D 26,22:2; 1940,Mr 7,17:2;
  1952,Ja 4,17:6; 1952,Ja 13,II,1:1; 1952,F 17,II,13:5;
  1954,Ap 1,40:5; 1954,Ap 11,II,2:1; 1961,Je 1,32:1;
  1963,My 30,21:1
Palace aux Femmes 1926,O 10,VIII,2:1
Pale Horse, Pale Rider 1957,O 30,26:1
Palm Tree in a Rose Garden, A 1957,N 27,26:2
Pan Pipes and Donkeys' Ears 1929,D 27,26:5
Panama Hattie 1940,O 4,28:4; 1940,O 31,28:2;
  1940,N 10,IX,1:1; 1943,D 5,II,5:1
Panic 1935,Mr 16,18:4; 1936,N 26,38:5
Pansy 1929,My 15,36:3
Pansy's Arabian Night 1924,Ag 24,VII,1:3
Pantagleize 1967,D 1,54:1; 1967,D 17,II,3:7
Paolo and Francesca 1924,D 3,24:2;
  1924,D 7,VIII,5:1; 1929,Ap 2,28:2
Papa Is All 1942,Ja 7,22:2; 1942,Ja 18,IX,1:1
Papavert 1931,O 11,VIII,2:1; 1931,D 30,25:1
Paper Tigers in Their True Colors 1958,N 5,41:8
Papers 1968,D 3,54:1
Papirossen 1936,S 18,19:3
Papp 1969,My 6,39:1; 1969,Je 8,II,1:7
Paquebot Tenacity, Le 1920,Ag 15,VI,1:1;
  1930,Mr 9,IX,2:7; 1939,Ja 10,16:4
Par le Temps Qui Court 1930,O 5,IX,4:3

Parade 1929,S 1,VIII,1:1; 1935,My 7,26:1;
  1935,My 12,X,2:5; 1935,My 21,22:2;
  1935,My 26,XI,1:1; 1960,Ja 21,27:4
Parade at the Devil's Bridge 1957,F 19,35:7
Parade of the Nude, The 1930,S 7,IX,1:3
Paradis Perdu, Le 1923,D 12,VIII,3:4
Paradise 1927,D 26,26:4; 1931,My 12,29:2
Paradise Alley 1924,Mr 16,VIII,2:1; 1924,Ap 2,17:3
Paradise Gardens East 1969,Mr 11,39:1
Paradise Island 1961,Je 24,11:1; 1962,Je 28,22:1
Paradise Lost 1935,D 10,31:5; 1935,D 29,IX,1:1;
  1939,Ja 8,IX,1:4
Paradise Now 1968,Ag 22,47:4; 1968,O 15,39:4;
  1969,Je 10,52:3
Parasite, The 1965,D 17,43:2
Parasites 1924,N 20,21:1; 1924,N 23,VIII,1:1
Paravents, Les 1966,Ap 22,36:3
Parce Que Je T'Aime 1928,S 30,IX,2:1
Pardon, Madame 1930,F 9,VIII,2:6
Pardon Me 1927,O 2,VIII,4:6
Pardon My Back 1937,Ag 4,14:1
Pardon My English 1932,D 11,IX,5:2;
  1933,Ja 21,11:4
Pardon My Glove 1926,My 23,VIII,1:1
Pardon Our French 1950,O 6,22:4
Parents and Children 1969,Ja 13,26:6
Pariah 1927,O 30,IX,2:1
Paris 1928,O 9,34:3; 1932,F 14,VIII,2:5
Paris-Boulevards 1926,N 21,VIII,2:1
Paris Bound 1927,D 28,26:3; 1928,Ja 1,VIII,1:1;
  1928,Ja 15,VIII,1:1; 1928,Jl 1,VIII,3:5;
  1929,My 1,28:6; 1929,My 19,IX,1:8; 1929,Jl 20,8:3
Paris-Capucines 1927,Ja 16,VII,2:1
Paris Is Out! 1970,F 3,35:1; 1970,F 15,II,1:1;
  1970,F 22,II,5:5
Paris Qui Charme 1929,Je 16,VIII,2:3
Paris '90 1952,Mr 5,33:2; 1952,Mr 16,II,1:1;
  1954,Mr 5,14:4
Pariser Platz 13 1931,Mr 1,VIII,1:3
Parisian Love 1927,Ja 28,15:5
Parisiana 1928,F 10,26:3
Parisienne, La 1924,N 25,26:2; 1929,Mr 10,X,4:6;
  1950,Jl 25,24:2
Park 1970,Ap 23,47:1
Park Avenue 1946,N 5,31:2
Park Avenue, Ltd 1932,Mr 4,17:1
Parlor Story 1947,Mr 5,29:2
Parmi les Loups 1926,N 7,VIII,2:7
Parnell 1935,N 12,24:2; 1936,Mr 1,IX,3:6;
  1936,Ap 24,19:5; 1936,My 5,26:2;
  1936,My 24,IX,1:7; 1936,My 31,X,1:5;
  1936,N 8,X,3:4; 1936,N 22,XI,1:3
Parnell of Avondale 1934,O 3,24:4
Parnosseh 1935,F 16,8:8; 1939,F 20,12:5
Parson's Bride, The 1929,Ja 22,22:3
Parted 1927,Je 5,VII,2:3
Partition 1948,O 29,31:2
Partners 1927,Jl 26,16:5
Partners Again 1922,My 2,22:2; 1922,My 14,VII,1:1;
  1923,Mr 1,10:3
Party, A 1932,Jl 10,IX,1:2; 1933,Ag 24,18:4;
  1933,S 3,IX,1:1
Party, The 1958,My 30,13:1
Party for Divorce, A 1966,O 12,37:1
Party Line, The 1937,Ag 30,25:4
Party on Greenwich Avenue, The 1967,My 11,52:1
Party With Betty Comden and Adolph Green, A
  1958,D 24,2:7
Party's Over, The 1933,Mr 28,23:3
Pas Avec l'Amour 1926,Ap 14,20:2
Pas Sur La Bouche 1929,Mr 26,34:3
Pasquale Never Knew 1938,Mr 31,14:2
Passage, Un 1970,D 31,8:3
Passage de Venus, Le 1928,Mr 18,IX,2:1
Passage to E M Forster, A 1970,O 28,62:1
Passage to India, A 1960,Ap 21,23:1; 1962,F 1,23:1;
  1962,F 11,II,1:1
Passenger to Bali, A 1940,Mr 15,26:2
Passing Brompton Road 1928,Ag 5,VII,1:2
Passing of Chow-Chow, The 1929,O 4,24:4
Passing of the Essenes, The 1930,O 19,IX,4:1
Passing of the Third Floor Back, The 1924,F 8,19:4;
  1928,Ja 17,22:7; 1928,F 21,18:2; 1937,Ag 3,20:6
Passing Present, The 1931,N 29,VIII,2:1;
  1931,D 8,36:2
Passing Show of 1921, The 1920,D 30,16:2
Passing Show of 1922, The 1922,S 21,18:2
Passing Show of 1923, The 1923,Je 15,24:6
Passing Show of 1924, The 1924,S 4,13:4
Passing Through From Exotic Places 1969,D 8,60:4;
  1969,D 21,II,3:1
Passion, La 1930,My 11,IX,2:4
Passion, Poison and Petrifaction 1959,Ag 21,13:1
Passion Flower, The 1920,Ja 14,12:1
Passion of Christ, The 1960,My 18,46:1
Passion of Gross, The 1955,Ja 24,20:2
Passion of Josef D, The 1964,F 12,29:1;
  1964,F 23,II,1:1
Passion of Judas, The 1930,D 2,31:2

Passion Play 1922,Je 15,4:5; 1922,My 10,21:3
  1925,Mr 2,5:6; 1925,Ag 17,8:1; 1926,Mr 30,20:2;
  1927,Jl 31,VII,1:6; 1930,My 9,9:1; 1930,My 12,1:5;
  1933,Jl 16,II,4:7; 1934,My 18,12:1; 1936,Mr 2,4:3;
  1936,Je 10,19:3; 1950,My 19,29:6; 1950,My 22,23:5
Passion Play, The 1929,Ap 30,32:1; 1929,My 5,IX,1:1;
  1931,F 23,36:2; 1932,My 2,13:1; 1934,F 12,15:1;
  1937,Mr 22,26:6; 1938,Mr 7,11:2; 1940,F 12,2:7
Passionate Pilgrim, The 1932,O 20,24:3
Passionate Prince, The 1925,O 11,VIII,2:6
Passionately 1929,Mr 8,31:4
Passionella 1966,O 19,53:1
Passionement 1928,Ja 15,VIII,2:1; 1929,Mr 8,31:4
Passions de Fantoches 1927,Ap 3,VIII,4:7
Passions of 1926 1926,Ag 3,19:4
Passport 1965,F 9,42:5
Passy-08-45 1927,F 20,VII,2:1
Pasteur 1923,Mr 13,19:1; 1923,Mr 18,VII,1:1;
  1923,Mr 25,VIII,1:1
Pastoral 1939,N 2,26:2
Pastorale 1936,Mr 5,24:6
Pastores, Los 1935,Ja 21,IX,1:7
Pastry Shop, The 1970,Je 12,28:1
Patchouli 1930,F 16,IX,4:4
Path of Flowers, The 1936,S 18,19:3
Paths of Glory 1935,S 19,29:1; 1935,S 27,24:2
Patience 1924,D 30,15:1; 1925,Ja 4,VII,1:1;
  1925,F 1,VII,1:1; 1927,My 24,23:2; 1928,Je 26,29:3;
  1929,D 16,34:5; 1931,Je 16,30:4; 1933,My 23,22:6;
  1934,O 12,32:2; 1935,S 3,24:4; 1936,O 6,28:6;
  1939,Ja 27,16:3; 1944,F 26,11:4; 1948,F 10,27:2;
  1954,Ap 7,41:1; 1964,Mr 26,42:1; 1965,Ap 16,34:1;
  1966,N 30,58:1; 1967,O 13,32:1; 1968,My 16,52:1;
  1968,N 1,34:1; 1970,My 10,72:4
Patio With Flamingo 1942,Ap 27,19:2
Patissiere du Village, La 1932,Ap 3,VIII,2:1
Patrasket 1932,Je 12,X,1:2
Patriarch, The 1926,D 11,15:1; 1929,N 26,28:5
Patrick--The First 1965,F 19,25:1
Patriot, The 1928,Ja 20,15:1; 1928,Ja 29,VIII,1:1
Patriot for Me, A 1965,Jl 11,II,1:4; 1969,O 6,58:1;
  1969,O 12,II,1:1
Patriots, The 1943,Ja 30,11:2; 1943,Ja 31,V,16:1;
  1943,F 7,II,1:1; 1943,My 9,II,1:1; 1943,D 21,22:5
Patsy, The 1925,D 24,8:5; 1929,Ja 6,VIII,1:4;
  1930,My 11,IX,3:1; 1935,Jl 16,24:1
Paul Among the Jews 1928,Ag 5,VII,1:1
Paul Bunyan 1941,My 6,25:1
Paul Draper Dance Program 1955,Ap 20,40:3
Paul I 1927,O 23,VIII,4:1
Pauvre Napoleon 1929,My 5,IX,2:4
Payment Deferred 1931,O 1,24:2
Peace 1967,Ap 27,II,4:8; 1968,N 10,87:1;
  1969,Ja 28,49:1; 1969,F 16,II,1:1; 1970,S 2,30:2
Peace Comes to Peckham 1947,Ap 20,II,3:7
Peace Harbor 1925,My 3,VIII,2:1
Peace in Our Time 1947,Jl 23,18:5; 1947,Ag 24,II,1:6
Peace on Earth 1933,N 30,39:2
Peace Palace 1933,Je 6,30:2
Peace Ship, The 1927,F 6,8:2
Peace Tragedy 1937,Ja 3,X,3:1
Peacock 1932,O 12,27:1
Peacocks 1924,Mr 2,VIII,2:7
Pearl of Great Price, The 1926,N 2,34:3
Pearls 1921,Je 14,15:2
Pearly Gates 1931,S 1,30:3
Peau d'Espagne 1933,Ap 30,IX,2:3
Peche, Le 1930,F 2,VIII,4:1
Pecheresse Innocent, La 1927,Ja 9,VII,2:5
Peddler, The 1967,D 9,62:1
Pedestrian, The 1965,O 10,11:1
Peek-A-Boo 1921,My 17,20:3
Peep Show 1950,Je 7,34:5; 1950,Jl 9,II,1:1;
  1950,Ag 27,II,1:1
Peepshow 1944,F 4,12:2
Peer Gynt 1923,F 6,14:1; 1923,F 11,VII,1:1;
  1928,Mr 24,4:6; 1928,Ap 1,IX,2:4; 1928,D 2,X,2:1;
  1935,S 24,28:2; 1935,O 20,XI,3:7; 1937,Mr 14,II,7:8;
  1944,O 1,II,1:3; 1951,Ja 29,15:2; 1951,F 4,II,1:1;
  1960,Ja 13,21:1; 1960,Ja 24,II,1:1; 1962,S 27,33:7;
  1969,Jl 17,56:1; 1970,D 23,12:5
Peg o' My Dreams 1924,My 6,25:3
Peg o' My Heart 1921,F 15,7:1; 1921,F 20,VI,1:1;
  1921,S 4,13:2; 1948,Ag 25,29:2
Peggy-Ann 1926,D 28,16:3; 1927,Jl 3,VII,1:1
Peh Shuh Tchuwan 1963,Ja 4,5:2
Pelerin, Le 1925,N 10,23:2
Pelerin Sentimental, Le 1930,N 23,IX,1:1
Pelican, The 1924,O 26,VIII,1:1; 1925,S 22,23:2;
  1925,S 27,VII,1:1; 1929,N 14,25:1
Pelleas and Melisande 1923,D 5,23:2;
  1923,D 16,IX,1:1; 1957,F 20,38:1
Pelleas et Melisande 1939,Ap 2,X,7:4
Penal Law 2010 1936,Ap 19,14:2
Penny Arcade 1930,Mr 11,24:5
Penny Change 1963,O 25,37:1
Penny Friend, The 1966,D 27,46:1
Penny Wars, The 1969,O 16,52:1; 1969,O 26,II,1:1;
  1970,F 15,II,1:1
Penny Wise 1935,Jl 2,24:2; 1937,Ap 20,28:6
People and Puppets 1959,Ja 27,27:5
People at Sea 1937,N 25,38:2; 1937,D 19,XI,3:7

People Don't Do Such Things 1927,N 24,28:3
People in Love 1937,My 28,17:5
People Is the Thing That the World Is Fullest Of
  1967,F 21,53:1
People of our Class 1938,My 13,16:6
People on the Hill 1931,S 26,25:5
People vs Ranchman, The 1968,O 28,56:1;
  1968,N 10,II,5:1
Pepper Mill 1937,Ja 6,19:4
Pequod 1969,Je 30,33:1
Peregrinus 1968,Ap 29,49:1
Perfect Alibi, The 1928,N 28,24:2
Perfect Fishel, The 1935,S 30,12:4
Perfect Fool, The 1921,N 8,28:2; 1921,N 27,VI,1:1
Perfect Marriage, The 1932,N 17,23:2;
  1944,O 27,17:6; 1944,N 5,II,1:2
Perfect Match, The 1970,N 18,41:1
Perfect Party, The 1969,Mr 21,42:1
Perfect Setup, The 1962,O 25,47:1
Perfectly Scandalous 1931,My 14,27:2
Perfumed Lady, The 1934,Mr 13,27:2
Pericas, Las 1969,N 2,86:5
Perichole, La 1926,D 28,12:2; 1926,D 29,24:4;
  1970,Mr 9,42:1
Pericles 1953,Ag 21,9:2; 1969,Ap 11,36:1;
  1969,Je 1,II,4:5
Period of Adjustment 1960,N 11,34:1;
  1960,N 20,II,1:1; 1962,Ja 3,25:1; 1962,Je 4,24:2
Peripherie 1926,O 2,40:6; 1926,D 19,VII,4:4;
  1928,Ja 3,29:1
Perlenkomoedie 1929,Ap 7,X,4:4
Persecution and Assassination of Marat As
  Performed by the Inmates of the Asylum of
  Charenton Under the Direction of the Marquis de
  Sade, The 1964,My 1,42:1; 1964,Ag 21,14:2;
  1965,D 28,35:1; 1966,Ja 9,II,1:1; 1967,Ja 4,34:1;
  1967,Ja 15,II,1:1
Persians, The 1927,F 27,VII,2:3; 1970,F 15,II,1:1;
  1970,Ap 16,53:1; 1970,Ap 26,II,1:3
Personal Appearance 1934,O 18,26:7; 1935,D 8,X,5:8;
  1936,Je 16,23:4; 1936,Je 23,27:3; 1936,Jl 9,17:4
Personality 1921,Ag 29,14:3
Persons Unknown 1922,O 26,12:1; 1929,Je 2,VIII,2:7
Peter 1930,Mr 2,IX,4:4
Peter, the Liar 1931,Mr 22,VIII,3:1
Peter and the Wolf 1969,N 30,85:5
Peter Flies High 1931,S 20,VIII,3:1; 1931,N 10,28:3
Peter Ibbetson 1926,Mr 26,24:7; 1931,Ap 9,30:3
Peter Pan 1924,N 7,16:2; 1928,Ja 15,VIII,4:6;
  1928,N 27,36:3; 1935,D 27,14:4; 1936,Ja 19,IX,1:3;
  1941,D 31,22:3; 1950,Ap 25,27:2; 1950,Ap 30,II,1:1;
  1954,Jl 20,15:3; 1954,O 21,30:2; 1954,O 31,II,1:1
Peter Petrolus 1937,Ap 5,16:5; 1937,Ap 25,X,1:1
Peter Rabbit 1928,D 27,26:4
Peter Weston 1923,S 20,5:2; 1923,S 30,II,1:1;
  1924,Je 15,VII,1:4
Peterpat 1965,Ja 7,27:1; 1965,Ag 19,34:3
Petit Choc, Le 1928,O 28,IX,2:1
Petit Peche 1926,O 24,VIII,2:1
Petite Bonnie Serieuse 1923,N 27,23:5
Petite Catherine, La 1930,O 26,VIII,2:1;
  1930,N 2,VIII,2:1
Petite Lili, La 1951,Mr 11,7:1
Petite Main Qui Se Place, Une 1922,Jl 2,VI,1:1
Petrified Forest, The 1934,D 21,31:6;
  1934,D 30,IX,1:6; 1935,Ja 8,26:1; 1935,Ja 13,IX,1:1;
  1935,Ja 20,X,1:3; 1935,N 24,II,9:3; 1935,D 8,X,5:8;
  1936,Mr 1,II,12:7; 1942,Ag 19,14:3;
  1943,Ja 10,VIII,1:6; 1943,N 2,30:6; 1943,N 7,II,1:1;
  1955,Mr 19,6:2
Petrus 1933,D 31,IX,2:2
Pets 1969,My 15,41:2
Petticoat Fever 1935,Mr 5,22:2; 1935,Je 25,14:5;
  1935,Jl 2,24:4; 1935,Ag 13,20:3; 1936,F 21,21:1;
  1937,Mr 21,II,7:3; 1937,Jl 6,23:1; 1937,Jl 20,19:3
Petticoat Influence 1930,D 16,34:6
Peu de Musique, Un 1923,N 6,22:1
Peyches et Cie de Bordeaux 1933,Ag 20,IX,1:3
Phaea 1930,Ag 31,VIII,2:1
Phaedra 1967,My 22,50:2; 1967,Je 11,II,1:1
Phantom Lover, The 1928,S 5,25:1
Phantom Ship, The 1926,Je 27,VII,3:1
Phantoms 1930,Ja 14,24:3
Phedre 1930,F 2,VIII,4:1; 1930,Mr 23,IX,2:3;
  1930,N 30,IX,3:3; 1963,O 21,39:1; 1966,F 11,36:1;
  1967,Ap 2,II,1:1; 1969,Mr 1,20:1
Philadelphia 1929,S 17,34:5
Philadelphia, Here I Come! 1966,F 17,28:1
Philadelphia Story, The 1939,F 17,14:2;
  1939,Mr 19,XI,2:6; 1939,Mr 29,21:1;
  1939,Ap 2,X,1:1; 1949,Je 28,32:4; 1967,Je 21,40:2;
  1967,Je 22,46:4
Philanderer, The 1958,My 13,26:2
Philanthropist, The 1970,Ag 5,20:1; 1970,S 10,59:1
Philip Goes Forth 1931,Ja 4,VIII,2:2; 1931,Ja 13,35:4;
  1931,Ja 18,VIII,1:1
Philipp Hotz 1969,N 27,52:1
Philippine 1937,N 14,XI,7:5
Philoctetes 1959,Ja 14,28:1; 1961,Ap 25,41:1;
  1964,Ag 19,29:1
Philomel 1932,D 4,IX,3:8
Philosopher, A - A Drunkard 1936,S 28,14:3
Philosophy in the Boudoir 1969,My 22,55:2

Phoebe of Quality Street 1921,My 10,20:1
Phoenix, The 1923,Ja 11,21:4; 1923,Ja 21,VII,1:3
Phoenix Too Frequent, A 1950,Ap 27,36:2;
  1958,Mr 11,33:1; 1958,Mr 16,II,1:1
Phoenix '55 1955,Ap 25,20:2
Photo Finish 1962,Mr 28,35:3; 1962,Ap 26,23:7;
  1963,Ja 23,5:5; 1963,F 14,5:2
Physician of Mad Woman, The 1937,S 27,24:2
Physicists, The 1964,O 14,52:1; 1964,O 25,II,1:1
Piacere Dell 'Onesta, Il 1929,Mr 25,33:1;
  1930,N 10,16:4
Piano Dans l'Herbe, Un 1970,S 17,56:1
Pibe de Corralon, El 1927,D 23,16:4
Picara Molinera, La 1929,Ja 3,25:2
Piccoli, The 1933,Ja 20,20:5
Piccolo Santo, Il 1931,D 14,16:4
Pick-Up Girl 1944,My 4,25:2
Pickwick 1927,F 16,17:4; 1927,Mr 13,VII,1:1;
  1927,S 6,35:2; 1927,S 11,VIII,1:1; 1927,O 2,VIII,1:1;
  1963,Jl 5,13:2; 1965,O 6,5:3
Pickwick Club, The 1936,S 27,X,1:1; 1936,O 4,IX,1:8
Picnic 1934,My 3,15:2; 1953,F 20,14:7;
  1953,Mr 1,II,1:1; 1953,Ag 30,II,1:1; 1957,F 21,32:1
Picnic on the Battlefield 1960,My 17,42:2;
  1967,S 9,25:2
Picture of Dorian Gray, The 1956,Ag 18,15:5;
  1963,Ag 29,37:4
Pictures in the Hallway 1956,My 28,23:1;
  1956,S 17,23:2; 1956,S 23,II,1:1; 1959,D 28,19:1;
  1964,D 17,51:1
Pie-Eyed Piper, The 1932,D 5,21:4;
  1942,Je 14,VIII,2:1
Pie in the Sky 1941,D 23,26:5
Pied Piper of Hamelin, The 1950,Ap 3,19:2
Pierre of the Plains 1929,Ja 6,VIII,4:4
Pierre ou Jack? 1931,Ap 19,VIII,2:7
Pierrot the Prodigal 1925,Mr 7,8:1;
  1925,Mr 15,VIII,1:1
Pierrot's Journey 1944,Ag 5,23:1
Pieton de L'Air, Le 1964,Mr 4,33:2
Pietro 1920,Ja 20,10:2; 1920,Ja 25,VIII,2:2
Pig Pen, The 1970,My 21,47:1; 1970,My 31,II,1:6
Pigeon, The 1922,F 3,13:1; 1930,O 15,26:2;
  1957,My 17,19:2
Pigeons 1965,Mr 4,37:1
Pigeons and People 1933,Ja 1,IX,2:5; 1933,Ja 17,22:3
Piggy 1927,Ja 12,22:2
Pigs 1924,Je 8,VII,1:8; 1924,S 2,22:5
Piker, The 1925,Ja 16,14:1
Pikvikski Klub 1936,O 4,IX,1:8
Pilate's Daughter 1927,Mr 7,17:2
Pile ou Face 1936,Jl 5,IX,1:8
Pilgrimage, The 1925,N 10,23:2
Pilgrims, The 1969,F 4,34:1
Pilgrim's Progress 1948,Jl 20,27:5; 1962,Mr 21,36:2
Pillar to Post 1943,D 11,11:2
Pillars of Society, The 1931,O 15,19:1
Pimpernel! 1964,Ja 7,26:6
Pin to See the Peepshow, A 1953,S 18,17:2;
  1953,N 8,II,1:1
Pin Up 1966,Je 24,30:2
Pinch Hitter, A 1922,Je 2,20:4
Ping-Pong 1959,Ap 17,22:1
Pink and Patches 1948,My 11,28:1
Pink Elephant, The 1953,Ap 23,37:2
Pink Slips on Parade 1937,F 1,14:4
Pink String and Sealing Wax 1943,S 19,II,1:5;
  1957,S 6,13:1
Pinocchio 1939,Ja 3,19:2; 1940,Mr 25,10:4;
  1968,Ap 15,41:1
Pins and Needles 1922,F 2,20:1; 1936,Je 15,24:6;
  1937,N 29,18:6; 1938,Ja 23,XI,1:1; 1939,Ap 21,26:2;
  1967,Je 9,51:2
Pinwheel 1927,F 4,16:4; 1927,F 13,VII,1:1
Pinwheel Revel 1922,Je 16,20:6; 1922,Ag 1,14:2
Pinye of Pinchev 1936,S 21,27:5
Pioneers 1932,F 26,22:5
Pioniere in Ingolstadt 1929,My 12,IX,1:8
Pipe Dream 1955,D 1,44:1; 1955,D 11,II,5:1
Pipe in the Fields, The 1927,O 23,VIII,4:4;
  1931,Mr 14,23:4
Piper, The 1920,Mr 20,14:2
Piper Paid 1934,D 26,19:1
Pique-Nique en Campagne 1969,My 1,50:1
Pirate, The 1929,Ap 21,IX,1:4; 1942,S 15,18:6;
  1942,N 26,39:2; 1942,D 6,VIII,1:1
Pirate Mallory 1935,O 8,26:3
Pirates of Penzance, The 1926,D 7,25:1;
  1926,D 12,VIII,3:1; 1931,Je 30,23:6; 1933,Ag 8,22:4;
  1934,Ap 10,26:5; 1934,S 7,24:3; 1935,Jl 23,24:2;
  1936,Ap 21,27:5; 1936,S 1,24:4; 1938,Je 3,16:2;
  1939,Ja 6,25:1; 1942,F 18,22:2; 1942,F 20,20:2;
  1944,F 18,15:5; 1946,My 17,14:6; 1946,S 21,19:2;
  1948,Ja 6,27:2; 1948,Ja 11,II,1:1; 1949,O 11,41:2;
  1951,F 20,21:2; 1952,O 28,36:4; 1954,Mr 31,32:5;
  1955,O 7,21:1; 1957,My 8,43:1; 1960,O 7,29:1;
  1961,Ja 20,24:5; 1961,S 7,41:1; 1961,S 17,II,1:1;
  1962,N 21,28:1; 1964,N 27,43:1; 1965,Ap 21,50:6;
  1966,My 24,54:1; 1966,N 16,54:1; 1967,Ag 7,34:2;
  1968,Ap 26,32:1; 1968,N 7,54:1; 1970,Jl 26,49:5;
  1970,D 6,84:6
Pitter Patter 1920,S 29,12:2
Place for Chance, The 1964,My 15,44:2

Place for Polly, A 1970,Ap 20,45:1
Place of Our Own, A 1945,Ap 3,23:7
Place Without Doors, A 1970,D 1,60:1
Places, Please 1937,N 13,10:6
Plain and Fancy 1955,Ja 28,14:2; 1955,F 6,II,1:1;
  1955,F 6,II,6:6; 1956,F 5,II,3:1
Plain Dealer, The 1929,My 23,27:1
Plain Jane 1924,My 13,24:2
Plaisir, Le 1927,Ja 9,VII,2:5
Plan for a Hostess 1938,Mr 27,X,1:3
Plan M 1942,F 21,15:2; 1942,Mr 1,VIII,1:1
Plancher des Vaches, Le 1932,Mr 20,VIII,2:2
Planctus Mariae 1968,Ap 29,49:1
Plant in a Sun 1937,D 13,22:8; 1938,Ja 31,14:2
Plantation 1970,Mr 10,53:1
Plantation Revue, The 1922,Jl 18,18:4
Platon Krechet 1936,O 4,IX,1:8
Play 1964,Ja 6,35:1; 1964,Mr 25,46:2;
  1969,O 19,II,12:1
Play, A 1925,F 11,19:2
Play, Genius, Play! 1935,O 31,17:2
Play, The 1961,F 5,27:2
Play by Aleksandr Solzhenitsyn, A 1970,O 18,94:1;
  1970,O 25,II,1:3
Play It Again, Sam 1969,F 13,52:3; 1969,F 23,II,1:1;
  1969,Jl 13,II,1:1; 1970,F 7,25:2
Play of Daniel, The 1958,Ja 3,15:3; 1958,Ja 26,II,1:1;
  1959,Ja 6,30:2; 1959,D 28,17:6; 1960,Jl 13,30:6;
  1960,D 27,23:6; 1961,D 28,22:6; 1966,Ja 2,64:4
Play of Herod, The 1963,D 10,55:2; 1965,D 29,24:2;
  1968,D 27,40:1
Play of Risen Christ, The 1970,Mr 9,44:1
Play of the Adoration of the Magi, The
  1923,D 26,15:4
Play of the Offering of the Shepherds, The
  1923,D 26,15:4
Play of the Shepherds, The 1923,D 26,15:4
Play on Love 1970,Ja 16,31:1
Play That on Your Old Piano 1965,O 15,49:1
Play With a Tiger 1964,D 31,14:2
Play Without a Name, A 1928,N 26,30:5
Playboy of Newark, The 1943,Mr 20,11:2
Playboy of the Western World, The 1930,Ja 3,20:4;
  1932,O 21,25:1; 1937,N 22,14:5; 1946,O 28,18:3;
  1958,My 9,19:2; 1968,S 4,40:1
Player Queen, The 1923,O 17,14:2
Players' Masque for Marie Tempest, The
  1935,Je 23,IX,1:3
Playing the Game 1927,D 20,32:5
Playing With Love 1929,F 27,16:4
Playroom, The 1965,D 6,49:1
Plays for Bleecker Street 1962,Ja 12,28:1;
  1962,Ja 21,II,1:1
Play's the Thing, The 1926,N 4,25:1;
  1926,N 14,VIII,1:1; 1927,Mr 20,VIII,4:3;
  1928,D 23,VIII,4:7; 1935,Jl 24,20:4;
  1948,Ap 29,19:2; 1948,My 9,II,1:1
Plaza Suite 1968,F 15,49:1; 1968,F 25,II,1:1;
  1968,D 14,61:2; 1970,Mr 22,90:3
Please 1933,N 17,22:2; 1933,D 3,IX,7:6
Please, Mrs. Garibaldi 1939,Mr 17,24:3
Please Do Not Disturb 1936,Je 23,27:1
Pleased to Meet You 1928,O 30,27:2
Pleasure 1931,D 28,20:2
Pleasure Bound 1929,F 10,IX,2:1; 1929,F 19,22:4
Pleasure Cruise 1932,My 15,VIII,1:1
Pleasure Man 1928,O 2,34:7
Pleasure of His Company, The 1958,O 23,36:1;
  1958,N 2,II,1:1; 1959,Ap 24,22:3
Plebeians Rehearse the Uprising, The 1968,S 8,II,11:1;
  1970,Jl 23,26:1
Plebejer Proben Den Aufstand, Die 1966,Ja 18,32:1
Plein aux As 1926,O 31,VIII,2:4
Plot Against the Chase Manhattan Bank, The
  1963,N 27,29:1
Plot Thickens, The 1922,S 6,16:1
Plot Twenty-One 1937,N 6,3:4
Plough and the Stars, The 1926,Mr 21,VIII,2:6;
  1927,N 29,30:2; 1927,D 4,X,1:1; 1934,N 13,22:2;
  1934,N 25,IX,1:1; 1937,O 8,26:5; 1950,Ap 2,II,1:1;
  1956,Ap 6,14:1; 1960,D 7,56:2
Plum Hollow 1935,Je 16,II,6:7
Pluma en el Viento 1932,Ap 2,13:4
Plume de Ma Tante, La 1958,N 12,42:1;
  1958,N 16,II,1:1; 1959,S 13,II,1:1
Plumes in the Dust 1936,O 26,21:3; 1936,N 7,14:2;
  1936,N 15,XI,1:1
Plunder 1928,Jl 22,VII,1:3
Plus Beaux Yeux du Monde, Les 1925,D 27,VII,2:1
Plus ca Change 1930,F 26,22:3
Plus Jamais ca 1932,My 29,VIII,1:7
Plutocrat, The 1930,F 21,23:3
Pocket Edition 1940,Ap 26,24:2
Pocket Watch, The 1966,Ja 6,18:1
Poet's Follies of 1955 1955,My 15,II,3:1
Point of Departure 1951,F 11,II,3:1
Point of Honor, A 1937,Ja 31,II,10:4; 1937,F 12,26:2
Point of No Return 1951,O 31,32:2; 1951,D 14,35:2;
  1951,D 23,II,3:1; 1957,Mr 23,17:2
Point Valaine 1934,D 26,19:3; 1934,D 30,IX,1:6;
  1935,Ja 17,22:2; 1935,F 3,VIII,1:1
Poison Gas Over Berlin 1929,Mr 6,12:3
Poison Pen 1937,Ag 10,22:3

Poisoned by Pictures 1926,S 1,27:3
Poisoned Kiss, The 1936,Je 7,IX,5:1; 1937,Ap 22,19:1
Poissons Rouges, Les 1970,F 3,39:1
Poker Session, The 1964,F 12,30:4; 1967,S 20,42:2
Poldekin 1920,S 10,12:1; 1920,S 19,VI,1:1
Policeman's Holiday 1936,Ap 6,18:7
Policemen, The 1961,N 22,24:2
Policy Kings 1938,D 31,6:2
Polish Rabbi, The 1939,Mr 20,13:3
Political Party, A 1963,S 27,17:5
Polly 1923,Ap 8,VIII,1:7; 1925,O 12,19:1;
   1928,N 11,X,2:4; 1928,D 23,VIII,4:1; 1929,Ja 9,28:3
Polly of Hollywood 1927,F 22,22:3
Polly Preferred 1923,Ja 12,13:3; 1924,Ap 13,VIII,1:3
Polly With a Past 1921,Mr 3,13:6
Polonaise 1945,O 8,20:2; 1945,O 14,II,1:1
Pom' Pom' ! 1928,Ap 1,IX,4:7
Pomeroy's Past 1926,Ap 20,24:4; 1926,My 2,VIII,1:1;
   1936,Ag 4,15:2
Ponder Heart, The 1956,F 17,14:2; 1956,F 26,II,1:1
Pony Cart, The 1954,S 15,39:2
Poor Bitos 1964,N 16,40:2
Poor Little Ritz Girl 1920,Jl 29,7:1
Poor Millionaire, The 1966,O 24,48:2
Poor Nut, The 1925,Ap 19,IX,2:1; 1925,Ap 28,18:1
Poor Old Jim 1929,My 10,32:2
Poor Richard 1924,N 16,VIII,2:8; 1930,Ja 18,2:7;
   1964,D 3,59:1
Popolo Senza Dio 1934,F 19,19:2
Poppa 1928,D 25,31:1; 1928,D 30,VIII,1:1
Poppa Is Home 1961,D 20,37:1
Poppy 1923,S 4,14:2; 1924,S 6,14:2;
   1924,D 21,VII,1:8
Poppy God, The 1921,Ag 30,10:1; 1921,S 4,VI,1:1
Popsy 1941,F 11,26:2
Porgy 1927,O 11,26:2; 1927,O 16,IX,1:1;
   1928,Jl 1,VIII,3:5; 1929,Ap 28,IX,1:4;
   1929,S 14,17:3
Porgy and Bess 1935,O 1,27:2; 1935,O 11,30:2;
   1935,O 20,XI,7:1; 1936,F 2,IX,1:3; 1942,Ja 23,16:2;
   1942,F 1,IX,1:1; 1943,S 14,26:2; 1944,F 8,13:2;
   1945,Je 17,II,4:3; 1950,N 26,II,7:8; 1952,Ag 6,17:7;
   1952,S 8,18:2; 1952,S 18,36:5; 1952,S 28,VI,20:1;
   1952,O 10,21:4; 1953,F 17,21:1; 1953,Mr 10,25:5;
   1953,Mr 15,II,1:1; 1954,Jl 15,24:2; 1954,S 23,42:6;
   1954,D 17,36:7; 1954,D 22,30:2; 1955,Ja 13,31:1;
   1955,Ja 21,19:6; 1955,F 8,23:4; 1955,F 16,26:4;
   1955,F 23,23:8; 1955,Ap 22,20:6; 1955,Jl 9,9:5;
   1955,Ag 5,14:5; 1955,O 13,37:4; 1955,D 27,29:1;
   1956,Ja 11,36:1; 1956,Ja 15,II,3:1; 1961,My 18,40:1;
   1964,My 7,32:1; 1965,Mr 6,17:1; 1965,O 20,53:3
Port O' London 1926,F 10,20:2
Port-Royal 1955,F 27,II,3:1; 1960,Ap 26,41:1
Port Said 1931,N 22,VIII,2:1
Porta Chiusa, La 1923,N 21,23:1
Portofino 1958,F 22,8:3
Portrait in Black 1947,My 15,30:2
Portrait of a Lady 1954,D 22,27:6
Portrait of a Madonna 1957,Ap 1,21:2;
   1959,Ap 16,28:1; 1959,Ap 26,II,1:1
Portrait of a Queen 1965,My 7,35:5; 1968,F 29,29:1
Portrait of Gilbert 1934,D 29,11:5
Portrait of the Artist as a Young Man, A
   1962,My 29,21:1
Portugalische Schlacht, Die 1931,Je 7,VIII,2:5
Possessed, The 1939,O 25,26:2; 1959,Ja 31,13:7
Possession 1925,F 1,VII,2:1; 1928,Jl 22,VII,1:7;
   1928,S 23,IX,2:2; 1928,O 3,35:1
Possibilities 1927,F 19,13:3; 1968,D 5,60:1
Post Mortem 1931,Ap 28,31:6; 1938,Ap 3,II,3:7
Post Office, The 1920,D 11,11:2; 1965,Ja 6,32:1
Post Road 1934,D 5,28:3; 1935,Jl 23,24:3;
   1936,Ag 5,15:4; 1937,Ap 21,18:2; 1949,Ap 28,27:3
Postcards 1927,D 6,41:1; 1970,Mr 17,36:1
Postman Always Rings Twice, The 1936,F 7,14:4;
   1936,F 26,17:2
Postmark Zero 1965,N 2,28:1
Postmistress, The 1928,Ja 15,VIII,2:1
Pot Boiler, The 1923,My 11,20:3
Pot-Luck 1921,S 30,10:1
Potash und Perlmutter 1921,Je 5,VI,1:3
Potash and Perlmutter 1926,N 14,VIII,2:1;
   1935,Ap 6,11:3
Potash and Perlmutter, Detectives 1926,S 1,27:3;
   1926,S 5,VII,1:1; 1929,Ap 28,IX,1:4
Potenza, La 1926,Je 29,21:3
Potiphar's Wife 1927,Ag 19,20:6; 1927,S 4,VII,2:1;
   1928,D 24,10:7
Potters, The 1923,O 28,VIII,2:1; 1923,D 10,21:4;
   1923,D 16,IX,1:1
Potter's Field 1934,Ap 22,IX,1:1
Potting Shed, The 1957,Ja 30,32:1; 1957,F 10,II,1:1;
   1958,Mr 16,II,3:1; 1958,N 3,49:2
Poudre d'Or, La 1928,Je 17,VIII,1:4
Poulette et Son Poulain 1924,Je 15,VII,1:4
Pound on Demand, A 1946,D 20,29:3;
   1959,Ap 16,28:1; 1959,Ap 26,II,1:1
Poupees de Paris, Les 1962,D 13,8:2;
   1964,My 16,11:1
Pour Lucrece 1953,N 29,II,3:1
Pousse-Cafe 1966,Mr 19,19:2
Poverty Is No Crime 1928,My 13,IX,2:7;
   1928,Je 3,VIII,2:1; 1935,F 21,22:5

Power 1937,F 24,18:5
Power and Glory 1938,My 1,X,2:5
Power and the Glory, The 1956,Ap 6,14:3;
   1956,My 13,II,3:1; 1958,D 12,2:7
Power of Darkness, The 1920,Ja 22,22:1;
   1920,Ja 25,VIII,2:1; 1948,O 11,28:2; 1959,S 30,33:1;
   1962,Je 21,26:1
Power of Dreams, A 1958,Mr 11,33:1
Power of the Press 1936,Ap 6,19:2
Power That Builds, The 1935,Mr 9,18:4
Power Without Glory 1948,Ja 14,30:2
Practical Cats 1954,Ag 27,11:5
Praise Of Folly 1954,F 24,23:2
Prayer Meeting: or, The First Militant Minister
   1969,Ap 27,92:1; 1969,Jl 31,28:1; 1969,Ag 3,II,1:4
Praying Curve 1927,Ja 16,VII,2:4; 1927,Ja 25,18:2
Pre-Honeymoon 1936,My 1,19:4
Precedent 1931,Ap 15,24:5; 1931,Ap 26,VIII,1:1
Precieuses Ridicules, Les 1938,D 13,30:3
Precious 1929,Ja 15,22:5
Precious Bane 1932,Ap 24,VIII,1:1
Precipice 1934,Je 6,24:4
Prelude 1935,Je 27,17:4; 1936,Ap 20,17:4
Prelude in the Theater 1961,F 5,27:2
Prelude to Exile 1936,N 17,34:6; 1936,N 22,XI,3:2;
   1936,D 1,31:1
Premise, The 1962,Jl 27,15:5
Prenez Ma Dame 1923,N 27,23:5
Prescott Proposals, The 1953,D 17,53:1;
   1953,D 27,II,3:1
Prescription for Happiness 1957,My 19,34:1
Present Arms 1928,Ap 27,16:2; 1928,Jl 22,VII,6:1
Present From Margate, The 1933,D 15,28:1
Present Laughter 1943,My 9,II,1:1; 1943,My 23,II,1:7;
   1946,O 30,31:2
President's Daughter, The 1970,N 4,41:2
Press Cuttings 1957,F 19,35:7
Press Time 1938,N 28,10:4
Pressing Business 1930,N 18,28:5
Pretender, The 1960,My 25,42:1
Pretty Little Parlor 1944,Ap 18,24:8
Price, The 1968,F 8,37:1; 1968,F 18,II,1:1;
   1968,O 19,29:1; 1968,O 30,39:1; 1969,Mr 6,36:2
Pride 1923,My 3,22:3
Pride and Prejudice 1935,O 23,19:2; 1935,N 3,X,1:5;
   1935,N 6,32:4; 1935,N 10,IX,2:5; 1935,N 17,IX,1:1;
   1936,F 28,19:2; 1936,Mr 29,IX,1:2;
   1936,Ag 30,IX,1:1; 1937,Ag 3,20:5
Pride's Crossing 1950,N 21,37:5
Priere Pour les Vivants 1933,O 29,IX,2:5
Priest in the Cellar, The 1969,F 19,39:1
Prima Donna 1929,S 22,IX,2:6; 1929,D 12,36:4
Prime of Miss Jean Brodie, The 1968,Ja 17,39:1;
   1968,Ja 25,32:4; 1968,Ja 28,II,1:1
Primer for Lovers 1929,N 19,26:5
Primrose Path, The 1939,Ja 5,16:3; 1939,Ja 16,11:2
Prince and the Pauper, The 1920,N 2,15:1;
   1920,N 7,VII,1:1; 1920,N 21,VI,1:4
Prince Charlie and Flora 1931,Ag 29,16:5
Prince Charming 1930,O 14,31:1
Prince Chu Chang 1930,O 12,VIII,4:1
Prince of Liederkranz, The 1963,O 1,34:1
Prince of Peasantmania 1970,F 22,88:1
Prince of Pilsen, The 1930,Ja 14,24:3
Prince of Wisdom, The 1932,Jl 10,IX,1:4
Prince Reuvaini 1967,N 19,83:1
Princess, The 1929,Mr 10,X,4:6
Princess April 1924,D 2,23:2
Princess Flavia 1925,N 3,34:3; 1925,N 8,VIII,1:1
Princess Ida 1925,Ap 14,27:2; 1934,S 28,26:3;
   1936,O 13,32:2; 1955,O 14,22:3; 1961,My 19,23:1;
   1967,Ap 17,46:2
Princess in the Cage, The 1933,Mr 19,IX,2:2
Princess Liana 1929,Jl 14,IX,6:8
Princess of Trapezunt 1933,F 19,IX,3:1
Princess Rebecca Birnbaum 1966,Mr 7,22:1
Princess Turandot, The 1934,N 13,14:2; 1937,Ag 3,20:5
Princess Virtue 1921,My 5,20:2
Princesse Isabelle 1935,N 10,IX,1:1
Princesse Lointaine, La 1929,N 17,IX,2:6
Printemps 1929,Ap 21,X,2:7
Prinzessin Olala 1921,D 11,VI,1:4
Priorities of 1942 1942,Mr 13,23:2;
   1942,Mr 29,VIII,1:1; 1942,My 10,VIII,8:3
Priscilla and the Profligate 1920,O 31,VI,1:4
Prison Bars 1928,My 10,31:1
Prisoner, The 1927,D 30,22:2
Prisoners of War 1935,Ja 29,24:1
Prisonniere, La 1928,Ja 1,VIII,1:3
Prisons de Femmes 1931,O 4,VIII,2:4
Private Affair, A 1936,My 15,28:7
Private Company 1936,F 11,19:3
Private Ear, The 1963,O 10,51:1
Private Enterprise 1947,D 7,II,7:1
Private Hicks 1936,Ja 13,14:4
Private Life of the Master Race, The 1945,Je 13,28:3;
   1945,Je 17,II,1:1; 1956,Ja 31,33:3
Private Lives 1930,S 25,14:2; 1930,O 12,VIII,1:8;
   1931,Ja 28,24:1; 1931,My 12,29:3;
   1935,Ap 21,IX,2:1; 1935,Je 26,18:3; 1937,Jl 14,17:4;
   1948,O 5,30:2; 1948,N 7,II,1:1; 1963,Jl 4,8:5;
   1968,My 20,59:1; 1969,D 5,52:1; 1969,D 14,II,3:3
Privilege Car 1931,Mr 4,33:1

Proces, Le 1952,N 18,36:2
Processional 1925,Ja 13,17:1; 1925,Ja 18,VII,1:1;
   1925,Ja 25,VII,1:1; 1937,O 14,23:1;
   1937,O 24,XI,1:1
Processo dei Veleni, Il 1935,Ja 21,18:2
Prochaine, La 1932,My 1,VIII,2:6
Procureur Hallers, Le 1924,N 13,18:1;
   1927,F 13,VII,4:1
Prodigal, The 1960,F 12,23:1; 1960,F 21,II,1:1
Prodigal Father, The 1935,Jl 2,24:2; 1937,Ag 17,23:1
Prodigal Son, The 1942,F 18,22:2; 1965,My 21,19:1
Prof' d'Anglais, Le 1930,My 25,IX,2:8
Professeur Klenow, Le 1933,Je 4,IX,1:6
Professor Bernhardi 1936,Jl 12,IX,1:8;
   1968,Mr 20,38:1
Professor From Peking, The 1939,Ag 27,IX,1:5
Professor Klenow 1924,Mr 2,VII,2:1
Professor Mamlock 1937,Ap 14,30:3
Professor Schelling 1939,Jl 2,IX,1:6
Professor Tim 1927,Ap 17,VII,1:4
Profile 1947,Ag 12,26:1
Profound Bow to Memory 1939,S 25,16:2
Profumo di Mia Moglie, Il 1932,Ja 11,29:5
Progress 1924,Ja 27,VII,2:4
Progress of Bora, The Tailor, The 1968,Je 27,49:2
Projection Room, The 1969,Ja 15,38:2
Projimos, Los 1966,Je 29,38:5
Prologue in Heaven 1961,F 5,27:2
Prologue to Glory 1938,Mr 18,22:2;
   1938,Mr 27,X,1:1
Promenade 1969,Je 5,56:1; 1969,Je 15,II,1:1
Promessi Sposi I, 1934,O 22,13:2
Prometheide 1926,N 21,VIII,2:1
Prometheus Bound 1957,Ag 9,11:6; 1967,My 11,52:1;
   1967,Je 11,II,1:1
Prometheus Unbound 1927,My 29,VII,6:7
Promis' Lan', De 1930,My 28,31:2
Promise 1936,Mr 22,XI,1:7; 1936,D 31,20:4
Promise, The 1967,N 15,38:1; 1967,N 26,II,1:1
Promised Valley 1947,Jl 23,18:3
Promises, Promises 1968,D 2,59:3; 1968,D 15,II,3:1;
   1969,O 4,26:4; 1970,Ja 18,VII,7:1
Promises to Keep 1965,Jl 22,25:1
Promoter, The 1938,D 27,12:3
Proof Thro' the Night 1942,D 26,14:2
Propitious Moment, The 1936,N 12,30:1
Proposal, The 1961,My 11,43:1; 1970,Ag 26,36:1
Proposition, The 1968,Ap 20,25:3
Proscenium 1933,Je 15,21:2
Prosit Gypsy 1929,Je 2,VIII,2:6
Prosper 1935,Ja 13,IX,2:1
Protective Custody 1956,D 29,8:7
Proud Accent 1949,Ap 23,10:2
Proud Princess, The 1924,F 17,VII,2:8
Proud Woman, A 1926,N 16,24:1
Province 1936,Ap 4,10:4
Provincetown Follies, The 1935,N 4,24:3
Provoked Wife, The 1936,O 25,X,2:4
Prowling Death 1923,Ja 21,VII,1:3
Prunella 1926,Je 16,23:3; 1929,Ap 10,23:3
PS 193 1962,O 31,33:1
Psychological Moment, The 1931,Mr 4,33:2
Public Eye, The 1963,O 10,51:1
Public Relations 1944,Ap 7,23:3
Public Savior Number One 1935,Je 11,23:2
Pudding on the Ritz 1932,Ap 9,18:3
Pueblo 1928,Mr 1,29:3
Puffy 1928,Jl 29,VII,2:2
Puisque Je T'Aime 1929,My 26,IX,4:1
Puissance des Mots, La 1928,F 12,VIII,1:3
Pullman Car Hiawatha 1962,D 4,46:2
Punch for Judy, A 1921,Ap 19,15:1
Punch Without Judy 1939,D 17,IX,4:3
Punchinello 1932,Mr 27,VIII,2:1
Punk, or the Amateur Rehearsal 1923,My 10,22:3
Puntila 1959,My 15,26:2
Puppet-Play, A 1926,My 8,21:2
Puppet Show 1930,O 29,26:5
Puppet Theater of Don Cristobal, The 1964,S 3,23:2
Puppets 1925,Mr 10,19:1
Puppets of Passion 1927,F 25,24:4;
   1927,Mr 6,VIII,1:1
Puppy Love 1925,O 4,IX,2:1; 1926,Ja 28,16:3
Pure in Heart, The 1932,O 9,IX,3:7; 1934,Mr 21,24:3
Purgatory 1960,S 20,48:1
Purification, The 1954,My 29,12:1; 1954,Je 6,II,1:1;
   1959,D 9,57:5
Puritan, The 1936,Ja 24,14:3
Purity 1930,D 7,IX,1:6; 1930,D 26,18:2
Purlie 1970,F 15,II,1:1; 1970,Mr 16,53:1
Purlie Victorious 1961,S 29,29:1; 1961,O 8,II,1:1;
   1962,Ap 29,II,1:1; 1970,Mr 22,II,3:1
Purple Canary, The 1963,Ap 23,31:1
Purple Dust 1956,D 28,15:1; 1957,Ja 6,II,1:1
Purple Mask, The 1920,Ja 6,18:1; 1920,Ja 11,VIII,2:1
Pursuit of Happiness, The 1933,O 10,24:4;
   1934,Je 24,IX,1:4; 1935,Jl 16,24:2; 1936,Jl 15,14:1;
   1952,Mr 22,9:2
Put and Take 1921,Ag 24,12:3
Put Down That Whip 1945,My 23,25:5
Put It in Writing 1963,My 14,31:1
Putain Respectueuse, La 1946,D 22,II,4:2
Puzzles of 1925 1925,F 3,25:3

Pygmalion 1926,N 16,24:1; 1926,N 21,VIII,1:1;
  1927,Ap 11,21:1; 1927,My 12,25:2; 1937,Jl 7,26:3;
  1938,Ja 27,16:3; 1945,D 27,16:1; 1946,Ja 6,II,1:1;
  1947,F 6,29:4; 1952,F 9,11:2
Pygmalion and Galatea 1920,Ap 28,9:3
Pyramids 1926,Jl 20,17:2

Q

Quadrature of the Circle 1931,D 13,VIII,3:1
Quadrille 1952,Jl 17,20:4; 1952,S 13,10:7;
  1952,O 12,II,3:7; 1953,Ap 5,II,1:1; 1954,N 4,39:2;
  1954,N 14,II,1:1
Quand Je Voudrais 1924,Je 29,VII,1:8
Quand Jouons-Nous La Comedie? 1935,O 27,IX,2:1
Quarantine 1924,N 23,VIII,2:4; 1924,D 17,19:7
Quare Fellow, The 1956,Jl 25,24:1; 1958,N 28,34:1
Quatrieme, Le 1928,Ap 29,IX,2:3
Quatuor 1928,N 11,X,2:7
Que Vida de Perro 1968,Ag 2,24:1
Queen After Death 1956,Mr 13,33:2
Queen and the Rebels, The 1956,F 5,II,3:1;
  1965,F 26,16:1
Queen at Home 1930,N 2,VIII,3:5; 1930,D 30,25:2
Queen Bee 1929,N 13,25:1
Queen Christina 1937,N 29,18:1
Queen High 1926,S 9,21:2
Queen Mab 1925,My 3,VIII,2:1
Queen Mother 1938,D 26,29:4
Queen O' Hearts 1922,O 11,22:1
Queen of Greece, The 1969,Ap 12,40:2
Queen of Scots 1934,Je 9,18:5; 1934,Jl 15,X,1:3
Queen of Spades, The 1931,O 22,27:1
Queen Victoria 1923,N 16,15:1; 1923,N 25,VIII,1:1
Queen Who Kept Her Head, The 1934,F 21,23:4
Queen's Comedy, The 1950,S 10,II,3:1
Queen's Husband, The 1928,Ja 26,17:2;
  1928,F 12,VIII,1:1; 1931,N 15,VIII,2:1;
  1936,Je 2,33:2
Queens of France 1966,S 7,53:1
Queen's Taste, The 1928,S 30,IX,2:7
Queer Adventure, A 1930,O 27,17:6
Queer Cattle 1932,My 19,24:2
Queer People 1934,F 16,16:2
Quem Quaeritis 1954,My 2,II,1:1
Quest 1928,Ja 8,VIII,2:3
Question of Fact, A 1954,Ja 17,II,4:4
????? 1939,Ja 2,28:2
Quick 1930,N 23,IX,1:1
Quick Years, The 1953,N 26,51:2
Quicksand 1928,F 14,26:3
Quiet, Please! 1940,O 20,IX,2:3; 1940,N 9,20:3
Quiet Wedding 1938,N 6,IX,3:5
Quiet Weekend 1941,Ag 3,IX,1:8
Quince Bush, The 1932,Ag 21,IX,1:1
Quitter, The 1934,F 6,24:4
Quo Vadis 1932,O 17,18:2
Quodlibet 1970,O 13,52:2
Quotations From Chairman Mao Tse-Tung
  1968,Mr 8,48:1; 1968,O 1,39:1; 1968,O 13,II,5:1

R

R U R 1922,O 10,16:1; 1922,O 15,VIII,1:1;
  1922,O 22,VIII,1:1; 1922,D 24,VIII,1:1;
  1930,F 18,28:1; 1942,D 4,30:2; 1950,My 7,IV,13:6
Rabbit Race, The 1963,Ag 28,39:3
Rabbit's Foot, The 1924,Ap 27,VIII,2:3
Rabelais 1968,D 20,63:1; 1970,My 20,32:1;
  1970,My 31,II,1:6
Race Errante, La 1932,Ap 10,VIII,2:5
Race of Hairy Men!, A 1965,Ap 30,42:1;
  1965,My 9,II,1:2
Race With the Shadow, The 1924,Ja 21,20:5;
  1927,Ap 7,23:1
Rachel Cowan 1929,My 9,34:3
Racket, The 1927,N 23,28:3; 1927,D 18,IX,1:1;
  1930,N 20,30:6
Racketty Packetty House 1931,N 7,16:1
Radio Carnival 1932,Mr 14,13:3
Radio Girl, The 1929,O 19,22:4
Raetzel um Beate 1936,N 8,X,2:1
Rag Picker of Paris, The: or, Modest Modiste
  1935,N 12,23:7
Ragged Army 1934,F 27,16:5
Ragged Edge, The 1927,F 13,VII,1:4; 1935,N 26,28:3
Rags 1922,Ja 29,VI,1:3
Railroads on Parade 1939,My 14,XI,1:2
Rain 1922,O 15,VIII,1:8; 1922,N 8,18:2;
  1922,N 12,VIII,1:1; 1925,My 13,24:2;
  1925,S 27,28:6; 1925,N 25,23:5; 1926,O 12,27:1;
  1927,F 13,VII,4:1; 1927,Mr 3,23:2;
  1927,Mr 27,VII,4:8; 1929,My 11,22:2;
  1935,F 13,24:1; 1935,F 17,VIII,1:1; 1935,Ag 27,23:4;
  1944,N 12,VI,28:4; 1948,F 2,15:2;
  1952,Ag 3,VI,20:1
Rain Before Seven 1935,Ag 13,20:3
Rain From Heaven 1934,D 11,26:5; 1934,D 16,XI,2:1;
  1934,D 25,28:4; 1935,Ja 6,IX,1:1
Rain or Shine 1928,F 10,26:3; 1928,F 19,VIII,1:1;
  1929,Ja 6,VIII,4:4

Rainbow 1928,N 4,IX,1:3; 1928,N 22,25:1;
  1928,D 16,IX,1:1
Rainbow, The 1923,Ap 8,VIII,1:7
Rainbow Revue, The 1924,F 24,VII,1:4
Rainbow Rose 1926,Mr 17,28:2
Rainbow's End 1928,D 26,14:6
Rainmaker, The 1954,O 29,28:1; 1954,N 7,II,1:1;
  1956,Je 1,26:7
Rainy Day, The 1923,O 14,VIII,2:4
Rainy Day in Newark, A 1963,O 23,35:1
Raisin' Hell in the Son 1962,Jl 3,13:2
Raisin in the Sun, A 1959,Mr 12,27:1;
  1959,Mr 29,II,1:1; 1959,Ag 5,32:3
Rally 'Round The Girls 1942,Mr 29,VIII,2:2
Ralph Roister Doister 1932,Ag 28,IX,1:1
Ramayana 1931,Ja 13,35:4; 1970,N 29,83:4
Ramblers, The 1926,S 21,32:2; 1926,N 28,VIII,1:1
Ramshackle Inn 1944,Ja 6,17:5
Rang Tang 1927,Jl 13,20:1
Rap, The 1931,Ap 7,31:2
Rapacino 1927,D 23,16:4
Rape of Lucretia, The 1948,D 30,24:2
Rape of the Belt, The 1960,N 7,46:1
Rape of the Sabine Women, The 1949,F 5,10:5
Rapid Transit 1927,Ap 8,21:2
Rapide de Minuit, Le 1932,Ap 3,VIII,2:1
Rapunzel and the Wicked Witch 1968,Ap 15,41:1
Raquel Meller 1926,Ap 15,24:1; 1926,O 26,25:1
Rashomon 1959,Ja 28,36:2; 1959,F 8,II,1:1;
  1959,F 22,II,1:1
Rasputin 1927,N 11,6:5; 1929,My 12,IX,2:3
Rat, The 1924,Je 15,VII,1:4; 1924,Je 29,VII,1:8;
  1925,F 11,19:3
Rat Race, The 1949,D 23,16:2
Rat Trap, A 1926,N 7,VIII,1:3
Rate of Exchange 1968,Ap 2,50:1
Rates, Les 1927,Je 19,VII,2:3
Rats 1968,My 9,55:2; 1968,Je 30,II,1:1
Rat's Mass, A 1969,N 1,39:1
Rats of Norway, The 1933,Ap 30,IX,1:7;
  1948,Ap 16,27:6
Ratten, Die 1932,D 4,IX,1:5; 1966,Ap 13,36:1
Rattle of a Simple Man 1963,Ap 18,39:1
Rauhnacht 1932,F 21,VIII,2:1
Raw Meat 1933,Mr 23,13:2
Razzle Dazzle 1951,F 20,21:1
Re-Echo 1934,Ja 12,28:4
Ready When You Are, C. B.! 1964,D 8,55:1
Real Inspector Hound, The 1968,Je 19,38:2;
  1968,Jl 8,45:1; 1968,Jl 14,II,4:5
Real McCoy, The 1928,Jl 15,VIII,2:1
Real Strange One, A 1958,Ap 24,37:3
Reaper 1940,D 4,34:3
Reapers, The 1930,Ap 6,IX,2:1; 1935,O 7,11:4
Rebecca 1942,Ap 14,1:6; 1942,My 31,VIII,2:3;
  1944,Ap 30,II,1:1; 1945,Ja 19,17:2; 1945,Ja 28,II,1:2
Rebel, The 1964,F 22,14:5
Rebound 1930,Ap 4,29:1; 1930,F 16,IX,1:1;
  1931,N 1,VIII,4:1
Recapture 1930,Ja 19,VIII,2:6; 1930,Ja 30,16:4
Reckoning, The 1969,S 5,28:1; 1969,S 14,II,1:3;
  1969,S 14,II,1:1; 1969,S 22,36:1
Reclining Figure 1954,O 8,26:5
Recluse, The 1966,Ap 13,36:1
Reconstruction 1969,Jl 8,36:1
Recruiting Officer, The 1931,O 18,I,30:1;
  1937,N 27,20:3; 1958,F 8,12:2
Recruits 1934,O 13,10:4; 1935,Ja 20,X,3:1
Red, Hot and Blue! 1936,O 8,26:1; 1936,O 11,X,3:1;
  1936,O 30,26:3
Red, White and Maddox 1968,O 5,71:4;
  1968,N 3,87:1; 1969,Ja 27,27:1; 1969,F 2,II,3:1
Red and Black 1929,F 10,IX,2:1
Red Blinds 1926,O 1,27:1
Red Cat, The 1934,S 20,21:1
Red Cross 1968,Ap 29,47:2
Red Dragon's Daughter, The 1933,D 10,11:7
Red Dust 1928,Ja 3,29:2
Red Eye of Love 1961,Je 13,28:1
Red Falcon, The 1924,O 8,22:1
Red Geranium, The 1922,My 9,22:3
Red Gloves 1948,D 6,28:2; 1948,D 12,II,3:1
Red Harvest 1937,Mr 31,29:2
Red Hawk, The 1923,D 2,VIII,2:1
Red-Headed Blonde 1953,Ap 20,22:4
Red Horse Animation, The 1970,N 20,32:1
Red Letter Day, The 1952,F 22,14:4;
  1952,Mr 16,II,3:7
Red Light 1931,D 6,VIII,2:7
Red Light Annie 1923,Ag 22,10:3
Red Mill, The 1945,O 17,16:2; 1945,O 28,II,1:1
Red Night 1936,Mr 5,25:1; 1936,Ap 5,IX,1:2
Red Pepper 1922,My 30,8:3
Red Peppers 1935,O 17,28:3; 1936,Ja 10,16:1;
  1936,F 2,IX,3:4; 1936,O 27,30:7; 1936,N 25,17:2;
  1936,D 6,XII,5:1; 1940,Ag 6,15:3; 1948,F 21,8:2
Red Planet 1932,D 19,19:2
Red Poppy, The 1922,D 21,18:2
Red Rainbow, A 1953,S 15,37:4
Red Rhumba 1936,Ap 14,18:1
Red River, The 1961,Ja 10,27:2
Red Robe, The 1928,My 2,18:5; 1928,D 26,15:1;
  1929,Ja 13,VIII,1:1

Red Roses for Me 1946,Mr 10,II,2:1;
  1951,Ap 26,35:8; 1955,D 29,15:2; 1956,Ja 8,II,1:1;
  1961,F 11,26:5; 1961,N 28,41:1
Red Rover's Revenge 1934,D 22,21:3
Red Rust 1929,Mr 17,X,1:4; 1929,D 18,31:1
Red Velvet Goat, The 1939,Ja 21,18:4
Red White and Blue 1950,O 8,64:5
Redemption: Lebende Leichnam, Der 1928,N 20,28:2;
  1929,F 5,27:2
Redemptor, The 1959,My 5,40:1
Redhead 1959,F 6,21:1; 1959,F 15,II,1:1
Reflected Glory 1936,Jl 22,23:1; 1936,S 18,19:5;
  1936,S 22,30:2
Regatta 1928,F 5,VIII,4:7
Regina 1949,N 1,32:2; 1949,N 13,II,1:1;
  1952,Je 2,25:4
Regular Guy, A 1931,Je 5,27:1
Rehearsal, The 1952,My 27,30:5; 1952,N 28,22:2;
  1963,S 24,45:2; 1963,O 20,II,1:1
Reigen 1921,Jl 24,VI,1:7
Reincarnation of Christ Show, The 1966,D 4,II,5:1
Reine Flammette, La 1928,N 11,X,2:7
Reine Morte, La 1964,F 16,52:1
Reise I Natten, En 1932,Ja 31,VIII,2:1
Rejected Loyalty 1932,F 7,VIII,3:2
Rejouissance, La 1929,F 24,IX,1:8
Relapse, The 1948,F 15,II,3:2; 1950,N 23,54:2
Relations 1928,Ag 21,27:3
Relative Values 1951,N 29,41:2; 1951,D 9,II,7:7
Release 1926,My 4,30:2
Religione e Patria 1936,Mr 23,22:4
Reluctant Debutante, The 1956,O 11,50:1;
  1956,O 21,II,1:1
Reluctant Dragon, The 1931,D 12,23:5
Reluctant Peer, The 1964,Ja 16,30:2
Remains, The 1928,Jl 15,VIII,2:1
Remains to Be Seen 1951,O 4,37:1; 1952,D 17,44:4;
  1953,Ja 25,II,3:1
Remarkable Mr Pennypacker, The 1953,D 31,11:2
Remember the Day 1935,Jl 9,24:3; 1935,S 26,19:3;
  1935,O 13,IX,1:1; 1936,Je 30,15:1
Remolienda, La 1968,F 3,20:1
Remote Asylum 1970,D 13,II,3:1
Remote Control 1929,S 11,24:5; 1929,S 22,IX,1:1
Renard 1970,Mr 25,36:4; 1970,Ap 26,II,1:3
Rendez-Vous, Le 1930,O 26,VIII,2:1
Rendezvous 1932,O 13,22:3
Rendezvous at Senlis 1961,F 28,39:2
Rendezvous in Wien 1956,S 5,23:1
Reno 1937,Ag 10,22:7
Repetition, La 1952,N 28,22:2; 1957,S 3,23:2
Report, The 1969,Je 12,51:1
Reprise 1935,My 2,16:2
Republic, The 1970,Ap 28,49:1
Republic Frolics 1932,O 13,22:2
Request Stop 1969,N 4,55:2
Requiem for a Nun 1956,S 24,23:6; 1959,Ja 31,13:2;
  1959,F 8,II,1:1
Reseda 1933,Ja 15,IX,2:1
Resistible Rise of Arturo Ui, The 1960,N 16,51:2;
  1960,D 25,II,5:1; 1968,Ag 8,25:1; 1968,Ag 30,22:2;
  1968,S 2,14:2; 1968,D 23,44:1; 1969,Ag 18,28:1
Resounding Tinkle, The 1961,Ap 4,42:2
Respect for Riches, The 1920,My 12,9:1
Respectful Prostitute, The 1948,F 10,27:2;
  1948,F 15,II,1:1; 1948,Mr 21,II,1:1
Respectfully Yours 1947,My 14,29:4
Restless Flame, The 1952,Ap 15,30:6
Restless Heart 1957,My 9,37:4
Restless Women 1927,N 27,IX,2:1; 1927,D 27,24:1
Resurrection 1930,Je 8,IX,3:1; 1934,N 20,24:5
Retabilillo de Don Cristobal, El 1964,S 3,23:2
Retablo de Maese Pedro, El 1925,D 30,10:1
Retour de Jerusalem 1929,F 3,VIII,1:2
Retreat From Folly 1937,F 25,18:2; 1937,Je 29,18:3
Retreat to Pleasure 1940,D 18,32:2
Return, The 1923,Jl 22,VI,1:1
Return Engagement 1940,N 2,19:2
Return Journey, The 1928,S 9,III,3:5;
  1928,S 23,IX,1:3
Return of Hannibal, The 1937,F 2,21:1
Return of Peter Grimm, The 1921,S 22,12:2
Return of Second City in "20,000 Frozen
  Grenadiers," The 1966,Ap 22,36:1
Return of Sherlock Holmes 1923,O 11,23:7
Return of the Soldier, The 1928,Jl 8,VIII,1:7
Return of the Vagabond, The 1940,Ap 13,20:1;
  1940,Ap 21,IX,1:8; 1940,My 14,27:2
Return of Ulysses, The 1943,Ja 28,22:2;
  1943,F 7,II,1:6
Return to Folly 1935,Jl 23,24:3
Return to Tyassi 1950,D 1,31:4
Return to Yesterday 1936,Ap 29,19:1;
  1936,My 31,X,1:5
Reunion 1938,Ap 12,26:4
Reunion in New York 1940,F 22,28:4;
  1940,Mr 3,X,1:3
Reunion in Vienna 1931,O 11,VIII,4:6;
  1931,N 17,31:1; 1931,N 29,VIII,1:1; 1934,Ja 4,17:1;
  1934,Ja 28,IX,3:4
Reunion of Sorts 1969,O 15,40:1
Revelry 1927,S 4,VII,2:4; 1927,S 13,37:1;
  1927,S 25,VIII,1:1

Revels of 1935 1934,O 3,24:2
Revels of 1936 1935,S 30,12:4
Revenge With Music 1934,N 29,33:5
Revenger's Tragedy, The 1966,O 7,37:1;
    1970,D 2,58:1; 1970,D 6,II,5:1
Revisor 1927,My 1,II,6:8; 1927,My 1,VIII,2:4;
    1935,F 18,19:6; 1935,O 6,XI,3:7
Revolt 1928,O 21,IX,2:1; 1928,N 1,25:3;
    1933,Ja 12,21:3
Revolt of the Beavers, The 1937,My 21,19:2
Revolt of the Mummies, The 1923,My 8,22:3
Revolte in Erziehungshaus 1929,Mr 10,X,2:1
Revue des Femmes Nouvelles, La 1926,D 5,VIII,6:1
Revue Russe, The 1922,O 6,28:1
Rhapsody 1944,N 23,37:2
Rhapsody, The 1930,S 16,30:3
Rhapsody in Black 1931,My 5,33:2
Rhinoceros 1959,N 2,41:1; 1960,Ap 30,15:3;
    1961,Ja 10,27:1; 1961,Ja 22,II,1:1
Rhondda Roundabout 1939,Je 18,IX,1:7
Rhythm of the City, The 1929,My 7,28:1
Riceyman Steps 1926,D 12,VIII,4:7
Rich Full Life, The 1945,N 10,9:2
Rich Man, Poor Man 1916,F 13,15:4
Rich Paupers 1932,Mr 14,13:4
Richard II 1934,N 4,IX,3:1; 1937,F 6,14:2;
    1937,F 14,X,1:1; 1937,S 7,16:3; 1937,S 16,28:2;
    1937,S 26,XI,1:1; 1940,Ap 2,31:2;
    1947,My 11,II,3:7; 1951,Ja 25,21:2;
    1951,Mr 25,75:3; 1953,Ja 1,19:1; 1953,Ja 25,II,3:1;
    1956,Jl 4,15:1; 1956,O 24,44:1; 1956,N 4,II,1:1;
    1961,Ag 30,25:1; 1962,Je 18,20:2; 1962,Je 24,II,1:1;
    1962,Ag 8,36:1; 1964,Je 17,47:1; 1968,Je 24,42:3;
    1968,Jl 7,II,1:1; 1969,S 4,50:1
Richard III 1920,Mr 8,7:1; 1920,Mr 21,VI,6:1;
    1930,Mr 31,24:1; 1930,S 21,IX,2:1; 1933,D 3,IX,7:7;
    1934,D 28,24:3; 1937,My 30,X,2:2; 1943,Mr 27,8:3;
    1944,O 1,II,1:3; 1949,F 9,33:2; 1949,F 13,II,1:1;
    1953,My 10,II,1:1; 1953,Jl 15,22:2; 1953,Jl 19,II,1:1;
    1953,D 10,65:2; 1957,N 26,41:1; 1961,My 25,32:3;
    1961,Je 25,II,3:5; 1963,Ag 21,37:5; 1964,Ja 14,24:7;
    1964,Je 12,44:2; 1965,Je 3,26:1; 1966,Ag 11,26:1;
    1967,Je 14,43:1; 1967,Je 25,II,1:2; 1970,Jl 4,11:1;
    1970,Ag 3,37:3
Richard of Bordeaux 1933,F 26,IX,3:1;
    1934,F 4,IX,2:2; 1934,F 15,16:2; 1934,F 25,IX,1:1
Richelieu 1929,D 26,20:3; 1934,My 22,28:1
Riddle Me This! 1932,F 26,22:5; 1933,Mr 15,21:3
Ride a Cock Horse 1937,Ap 4,II,9:7; 1965,Je 25,36:1
Riders to the Sea 1937,F 15,13:2; 1949,F 4,30:2;
    1957,Mr 7,24:1; 1957,Mr 17,II,1:1
Ridgeway's Late Joys 1939,O 22,IX,3:5
Riding Hood Revisited 1961,Ja 4,26:1
Riff-Raff 1926,F 9,18:6
Right Age to Marry, The 1926,F 7,VII,2:3;
    1926,F 16,22:3
Right Girl, The 1921,Mr 16,12:1
Right Honourable Gentleman, The 1965,O 20,50:2
Right Next to Broadway 1944,F 22,26:2
Right of Happiness 1931,Ap 3,34:2
Right of Possession 1930,My 9,20:5
Right This Way 1938,Ja 6,22:3
Right to Dream, The 1924,My 27,14:2
Right to Kill, The 1926,F 16,22:2
Right to Love, The 1925,Je 9,16:4
Right to Strike, The 1920,O 31,VI,1:4;
    1921,O 25,20:1; 1921,O 30,VI,1:1
Right You Are (If You Think You Are)
    1927,F 24,27:1; 1927,Mr 6,VIII,1:1; 1950,Je 29,37:2;
    1957,Mr 5,37:1; 1964,Mr 5,37:1; 1966,N 23,34:2;
    1966,D 11,II,3:1
Righteous Are Bold, The 1946,O 27,II,1:3;
    1955,D 23,12:1
Rimers of Eldritch, The 1967,F 21,53:1
Rinaldo in Campo 1962,My 12,14:5
Ring Around Elizabeth 1941,N 18,32:2
Ring Around the Moon 1950,Ja 27,29:2;
    1950,N 24,30:1; 1968,N 2,28:1
Ring Two 1939,N 14,20:3; 1939,N 23,38:2
Ringer, The 1929,Mr 24,X,4:7
Ringmaster, The 1935,Mr 12,24:5; 1935,Ap 7,IX,1:6
Rings on Her Fingers 1932,My 22,VIII,1:3
Ringside 1928,Ag 30,13:2; 1928,S 9,IX,1:1
Ringside Seat 1938,N 23,24:5
Rio Rita 1927,F 3,18:3; 1927,F 13,VII,1:1;
    1927,Jl 3,VII,1:1
Riot 1968,D 20,64:1; 1968,D 29,II,1:1
Riot Act, The 1963,Mr 9,5:2
Rip Van Winkle 1920,D 14,22:3; 1925,N 24,28:5;
    1925,D 6,VIII,5:1; 1929,D 21,22:7; 1935,Ag 7,22:2;
    1947,Jl 16,28:2; 1967,D 23,28:1
Ripples 1930,F 2,VIII,2:7; 1930,F 12,26:1
Rise Above It 1941,Je 15,IX,2:6
Rise and Shine 1936,My 8,21:4
Rise of Rosie O'Reilly, The 1923,D 26,13:4
Rising Heifer, The 1952,D 24,12:4
Rising of the Moon, The 1920,Je 22,9:1;
    1920,Je 29,9:2; 1928,Je 6,23:4; 1932,O 21,25:1;
    1937,F 15,13:2
Rising Son, The 1924,O 26,VIII,2:1; 1924,O 28,27:2
Rising Sun, The 1929,O 27,IX,2:2
Risk, The 1922,Jl 30,VI,1:7
Rita Coventry 1923,F 20,12:2

Ritornell 1927,Ap 6,24:3
Ritzy 1930,F 11,30:4
Rivalry, The 1959,F 9,24:2; 1959,F 15,II,1:1
Rivals, The 1922,Je 6,18:2; 1923,My 9,14:2;
    1923,My 13,VIII,1:1; 1930,Mr 14,24:4;
    1930,Mr 23,IX,1:1; 1935,S 25,19:6; 1941,N 18,32:2;
    1942,Ja 15,24:2; 1942,Ja 25,IX,1:1;
    1956,Mr 11,II,3:1; 1969,O 18,37:1
River, The 1965,F 9,42:5
River Line, The 1952,S 7,II,3:1; 1952,N 9,II,3:2;
    1957,Ja 3,29:2
River's End, The 1924,Mr 16,VIII,2:1
Riverside Drive 1931,Ja 6,24:2
Riverwind 1962,D 14,5:5
Riviera 1925,D 25,22:2
Road House 1932,O 30,IX,2:3
Road to Damascus, The 1937,My 30,X,2:5
Road to Happiness, The 1927,My 3,24:1
Road to Paradise, The 1935,Jl 16,24:2
Road to Rio, The 1930,My 7,25:1
Road to Rome, The 1927,F 1,24:2; 1927,F 6,VII,1:1;
    1928,Je 10,VIII,1:3; 1928,Je 10,VIII,2:8;
    1929,N 10,X,4:8; 1929,N 23,19:1;
    1929,D 29,VIII,2:6
Road to Ruin 1937,F 12,26:2
Road Together, The 1924,Ja 18,21:2
Roads and Rain 1926,My 6,23:3
Roadside 1930,S 27,21:1
Roamin' Gentleman, A 1930,F 23,VIII,2:5
Roaming Stars 1930,Ja 25,12:2
Roar China! 1930,O 28,23:1; 1930,N 9,IX,1:1
Roar Like a Dove 1964,My 22,40:2
Roar of the Greasepaint-the Smell of the Crowd
    1965,My 17,46:2
Robbers, The 1926,N 21,VIII,1:3; 1928,Ag 10,9:2
Robbery, The 1921,Mr 1,18:1
Robe de Perles, La 1928,Ja 15,VIII,2:3
Robe Rouge, La 1920,F 24,11:1; 1922,F 5,VI,1:7
Robert E Lee 1923,Je 21,22:4; 1923,Jl 8,VI,1:1;
    1923,N 11,VIII,2:6; 1923,N 21,23:1;
    1923,N 25,VIII,1:1
Roberta 1933,N 20,18:4; 1935,Ag 18,II,3:2;
    1937,Je 27,II,6:1; 1937,S 7,16:4
Robert's Wife 1937,N 24,20:2; 1937,D 19,XI,3:7
Robin Hood 1929,N 20,26:5; 1932,Ja 28,25:4;
    1935,Jl 15,20:6; 1944,N 8,28:2; 1950,N 6,32:2
Robin Landing 1937,N 19,26:4
Rock Me, Julie 1931,Ja 4,VIII,2:3; 1931,F 4,21:1
Rockbound 1929,Ap 20,23:2
Rockefeller and the Red Indians 1968,O 25,37:1
Rocket to the Moon 1938,N 25,18:2; 1938,D 4,X,5:1;
    1948,Mr 23,30:4; 1948,Ap 11,II,3:1
Roger Bloomer 1923,Mr 2,18:3; 1923,Mr 11,VIII,1:3;
    1923,Ap 1,VII,1:1
Rogues and Vagabonds 1930,My 8,32:5
Roi, Deux Dames et un Valet, Un 1935,Mr 3,VIII,2:3
Roi, Le 1931,Ap 5,VIII,3:1
Roi Cerf, Le 1937,O 27,28:7; 1937,N 30,26:3
Roi Dagobert, Le 1926,N 14,VIII,2:1
Roi Masque, Le 1932,Ja 17,VIII,1:6
Roi Pausole, Le 1931,Ja 25,VIII,8:8
Rolf's Revue 1930,Jl 13,VIII,2:1
Roll Sweet Chariot 1934,O 3,24:3; 1934,O 14,X,1:1
Rollo's Wild Oat 1920,N 24,14:1; 1921,Ja 9,VI,1:1;
    1921,Ja 23,VI,1:1
Rolls-Royce, La 1929,Ap 28,IX,2:4
Roman Candle 1960,F 4,34:2
Roman Holiday 1937,Ap 14,31:5
Roman Servant, A 1934,D 3,14:5
Romance 1921,Mr 1,18:2; 1921,Mr 6,VI,1:2;
    1926,N 4,VIII,4:7; 1935,Ag 27,23:4;
    1937,Ag 17,23:1
Romance, Inc 1929,Mr 24,X,4:7
Romance in Cherry Blossom Lane 1930,Mr 5,26:7
Romance of Ida, The 1929,F 3,VIII,2:1
Romance of the Western Chamber 1936,F 23,X,1:1
Romancing 'Round 1927,O 4,32:4
Romanesques, Les 1930,Mr 2,IX,4:2
Romanoff and Juliet 1956,My 19,12:5;
    1956,Jl 1,II,1:6; 1957,O 11,24:1
Romantic Adventure of an Italian Ballerina and a
    Marquis, A 1931,O 22,27:1
Romantic Age, The 1922,N 15,22:1;
    1922,N 19,VII,1:1
Romantic Mr Dickens 1940,D 3,33:2
Romantic Young Lady, The 1926,My 5,24:3;
    1927,My 5,30:2
Romanticismo 1933,My 1,10:5; 1934,My 14,20:2
Romany Love 1947,Mr 10,25:1
Romanzo di un Giovane Povero, Il 1935,F 25,12:3
Romeo and Jeanette 1969,D 16,53:1

Romeo and Juliet 1922,D 28,20:1; 1923,Ja 25,16:1;
    1923,F 4,VII,1:1; 1923,Ap 22,VII,1:1;
    1923,N 13,25:2; 1927,Ja 2,VII,2:5; 1928,D 2,X,4:4;
    1930,Ap 22,33:1; 1932,F 28,VIII,2:4; 1933,F 3,21:5;
    1933,N 30,38:5; 1934,D 4,23:2; 1934,D 21,30:3;
    1934,D 30,IX,1:1; 1935,O 18,27:5;
    1935,N 17,IX,2:4; 1935,D 24,10:2;
    1935,D 29,IX,1:3; 1940,Ap 16,28:4;
    1940,My 10,27:1; 1947,Ap 7,18:5; 1949,O 17,19:2;
    1951,Ja 23,24:8; 1951,Mr 12,21:2; 1951,Mr 25,II,1:1;
    1952,S 17,34:6; 1952,O 12,II,3:8; 1953,My 29,17:5;
    1955,D 16,36:3; 1956,F 24,20:4; 1956,Mr 4,II,1:1;
    1956,Je 13,45:8; 1956,S 19,34:6; 1956,O 25,41:1;
    1956,N 4,II,1:1; 1957,Je 28,30:2; 1959,Je 15,31:1;
    1959,Je 21,II,1:1; 1960,Jl 1,14:1; 1961,F 24,24:1;
    1961,Ag 16,36:3; 1962,F 14,39:1; 1962,F 25,II,1:1;
    1962,Ap 3,42:1; 1965,Je 21,36:3; 1967,F 22,18:1;
    1968,Je 11,55:2; 1968,Je 23,II,1:1; 1968,Ag 16,19:1;
    1970,My 28,28:1
Romeo y Julieta 1965,Ag 28,13:3
Romio and Julietta 1925,Ap 21,19:1
Romulus 1962,Ja 11,27:1
Romulus the Great 1964,Ag 25,24:3; 1964,Ap 30,29:1
Ronde, La 1932,O 30,IX,3:7; 1955,Je 28,24:2;
    1960,My 10,44:2
Rondelay 1969,N 6,55:1
Roof, The 1929,N 6,30:4; 1929,N 24,X,1:6;
    1930,Je 14,9:2; 1931,O 31,22:4; 1931,N 8,VIII,1:1
Roof and Four Walls, A 1923,Ja 21,VII,1:3
Rookery Nook 1942,My 31,VIII,2:3
Room, The 1964,D 10,62:1
Room in Red and White, A 1936,Ja 20,23:3
Room of Dreams 1930,N 6,22:4
Room Service 1935,N 17,II,7:7; 1937,My 20,16:1;
    1937,My 30,X,1:1; 1937,D 16,35:4;
    1938,Ja 16,X,1:6; 1953,Ap 7,34:1; 1970,My 13,49:1;
    1970,My 24,II,1:1; 1970,Jl 5,II,1:2
Room V 1941,S 28,IX,1:4
Room 349 1930,Ap 23,24:5
Roomful of Roses, A 1955,O 18,48:1
Rooming House, The 1970,Ja 23,25:1
Roosty 1938,F 15,21:2
Roots 1961,Mr 7,40:2; 1961,Mr 19,II,1:1
Rope 1928,F 23,18:3; 1928,Mr 4,IX,1:1
Rope Dancers, The 1957,N 21,39:1; 1957,D 1,II,1:1;
    1957,D 22,II,1:1; 1959,Mr 14,26:1; 1959,Jl 15,26:2
Rope's End 1929,S 20,34:5
Rosa Machree 1922,Ja 10,15:2
Rosalie 1927,D 18,IX,2:3; 1928,Ja 11,26:3;
    1929,Ja 27,IX,1:3; 1957,Je 26,28:2
Rosalinda 1942,O 29,26:5; 1943,F 14,II,1:4
Rose 1969,O 29,30:1
Rose, The 1922,D 30,13:4
Rose and Glove 1934,S 9,35:5
Rose and the Ring, The 1931,D 24,20:7
Rose Bernd 1922,S 27,17:1; 1922,O 1,VII,1:1;
    1922,O 1,VII,1:6; 1922,O 1,VII,1:1; 1922,O 8,VI,1:2;
    1922,O 8,VI,1:1; 1932,D 4,IX,1:3
Rose Briar 1922,D 26,11:3
Rose Burke 1942,Ja 25,IX,2:5
Rose Girl, The 1921,F 12,II,1:1
Rose in the Wilderness 1949,Ja 5,21:2
Rose Marie 1924,Ag 24,VII,1:8; 1924,S 3,12:2;
    1925,Mr 21,16:2; 1925,D 4,26:1; 1927,Ap 17,II,8:2;
    1928,Mr 31,23:2; 1928,Ap 29,IX,2:8;
    1936,Jl 22,22:6
Rose of Florida, The 1929,F 23,17:1
Rose of France 1933,O 29,II,3:3
Rose of Persia 1935,Mr 1,17:4
Rose of Stamboul, The 1922,Mr 8,11:2
Rose Tattoo, The 1951,F 5,19:2; 1951,F 11,II,1:1;
    1966,O 21,36:2; 1966,N 20,II,1:1
Rose Without a Thorn 1932,Ap 3,VIII,1:5
Roseanne 1923,D 31,9:5; 1924,Mr 11,16:3
Rosemary 1960,N 15,47:1
Rosen 1921,My 15,VI,1:6
Rosencrantz and Guildenstern Are Dead
    1967,O 17,53:1; 1967,O 29,II,1:1; 1970,N 19,39:3
Rosenkavalier, Der 1927,Mr 6,VII,4:4
Rosenmontag 1921,Jl 24,VI,1:7
Roses Are Real, The 1964,Ja 23,27:1
Rosmersholm 1924,F 8,22:3; 1925,My 6,27:2;
    1935,D 3,32:5; 1946,N 23,11:5; 1962,Ap 12,42:1;
    1962,Ap 22,II,1:1
Ross 1960,My 13,26:4; 1961,O 8,II,3:4;
    1961,D 27,20:2; 1962,Ja 7,II,1:1
Rosse 1933,My 7,IX,2:5
Rote General, Der 1928,D 23,VIII,4:1
Rothschild Siegt bei Waterloo 1937,Ja 3,X,2:5
Rothschilds, The 1970,O 20,40:1; 1970,N 1,II,1:1
Rotters, The 1922,My 23,12:4
Rough Diamond, A 1926,D 19,VII,6:1
Rouille, La 1929,D 29,VIII,2:6
Roulette 1932,Ja 17,VIII,2:2; 1932,Mr 27,VIII,3:1;
    1935,Je 16,X,1:1
Round Table, The 1927,Ag 28,VII,1:1;
    1930,F 28,20:5
'Round the Family Table 1938,O 8,10:3
Round the Town 1924,My 22,14:3
Round Trip 1945,My 30,16:4
Round-Up, The 1932,Mr 8,19:4
Round With Ring, A 1969,O 30,56:1
Route 1 1964,N 18,52:3

Roy de Malousie, Le 1928,Jl 1,VIII,1:8
Royal Baggage 1934,O 27,20:5
Royal Box, The 1928,N 21,32:3
Royal Exchange 1935,D 7,22:3
Royal Family, The 1927,D 29,26:4; 1928,Ja 8,VIII,1:1;
   1928,Jl 1,VIII,3:5; 1931,Ap 12,IX,1:3;
   1934,O 24,24:2; 1935,Je 25,14:5; 1936,Jl 16,15:4;
   1936,Ag 12,15:1; 1940,Ag 13,15:3; 1951,Ja 11,28:2
Royal Fandango, A 1923,N 11,VIII,2:6;
   1923,N 13,25:1; 1923,N 18,VIII,1:1
Royal Gambit 1959,Mr 5,34:2; 1959,Mr 15,II,1:1
Royal Highness 1949,Ap 14,29:3
Royal Hunt of the Sun, The 1964,Jl 8,40:6;
   1965,O 27,36:2; 1965,N 14,II,1:1
Royal Koko 1937,Ja 10,X,2:5
Royal Virgin, The 1930,Mr 18,30:5
Royal Visitor, The 1924,O 5,VIII,2:2
Rubicon, Le 1926,O 3,VIII,2:1
Rubicon, The 1922,F 22,13:1
Ruddigore 1920,Ja 20,11:2; 1920,F 1,VIII,2:2;
   1927,My 21,25:2; 1931,Ag 11,28:3; 1934,S 25,25:2;
   1936,O 23,26:4; 1944,Mr 3,19:5; 1954,Ap 21,36:4;
   1955,O 21,32:2; 1964,D 4,44:1; 1965,Ag 27,16:1;
   1966,N 23,28:1
Rudolph of Austria 1932,Ap 10,VIII,3:7
Ruffian on the Stair, The 1969,O 27,54:1;
   1969,N 9,II,1:1
Rufus Le Maire's Affairs 1926,Jl 18,VII,1:7;
   1927,Ap 10,VIII,1:1
Rugantino 1964,F 2,II,1:4; 1964,F 7,34:1
Rugged Path, The 1945,N 12,17:2; 1945,N 18,II,1:1
Ruined Lady, The 1920,Ja 21,10:2;
   1920,Ja 25,VIII,2:2
Ruint 1925,Ap 8,24:2
Rules of the Game, The 1960,D 20,44:1
Ruling Class, The 1969,F 28,31:1
Rumanian Rhapsody, No 1 1929,Ap 27,16:4
Rumpelstiltskin 1948,Mr 15,27:3
Rumple 1957,N 7,42:2
Run, Little Chillun! 1933,Mr 2,21:3;
   1933,Mr 12,IX,7:1; 1939,Ap 30,XI,2:1;
   1943,Ag 14,6:1
Run, Thief, Run 1957,My 2,27:1
Run Sheep Run 1938,N 4,26:2
Runaway Road, The 1926,N 14,VIII,5:1
Runaways, The 1928,D 2,X,4:1
Rune of Healing, The 1931,Mr 22,VIII,3:1
Runnin' Wild 1923,O 30,17:3
Russell Patterson's Sketch-Book 1960,F 8,35:1
Russet Mantle 1936,Ja 17,15:5; 1936,Ja 26,IX,1:1;
   1936,Ag 18,15:2
Russian Bank 1940,My 25,20:2
Russian Isba 1920,F 17,19:2; 1920,F 29,V,5:2;
   1920,Mr 12,18:4
Russian Love 1930,N 27,32:3
Russian People, The 1942,Jl 18,8:2; 1942,D 16,21:3;
   1942,D 30,17:2
Russian Question, The 1946,D 14,18:2;
   1947,My 4,I,54:3
Rust 1924,F 1,12:1
Rut, The 1923,My 8,22:3
Ruth and Paul Draper 1940,D 27,23:2
Ruth Draper 1928,D 26,14:5; 1954,Ja 26,21:2
Rutherford and Son 1927,Ap 13,29:2
Ruy Blas 1933,O 10,24:4; 1938,Jl 24,IX,2:1;
   1957,D 14,16:3
Ryan Girl, The 1945,S 25,28:2; 1945,S 30,II,1:2

S

S A D M P, La 1937,N 14,XI,7:5
S S Glencairn 1924,N 4,31:4; 1924,D 28,VII,1:1;
   1929,Ja 10,24:5; 1929,Ja 27,IX,1:1;
   1948,My 21,21:2; 1948,My 30,II,1:1
Sabbati Zebi 1923,O 22,19:2
Sable Brush, The 1956,N 28,41:1
Sable Coat, The 1924,Jl 6,VII,1:1
Sabrina Fair 1953,N 12,37:1; 1953,N 22,II,1:1;
   1954,Ag 5,18:1
Sacco and Vanzetti 1929,Ap 23,26:5
Sacco-Vanzetti 1969,F 9,78:1
Sacred and Profane Love 1920,F 24,11:1;
   1920,F 29,V,5:2
Sacred Flame, The 1928,N 20,28:2;
   1929,Mr 3,VIII,2:5; 1952,O 8,35:2
Sacrifice 1920,D 11,11:2
Sacrifice of Isaac, The 1933,N 22,22:4
Sacrilege, The 1921,My 3,20:1
Sadie Is a Lady 1950,Ja 28,9:2
Sadie Thompson 1944,N 17,25:2; 1944,N 26,II,1:1
Safari 1955,My 12,32:6
Sage of Rottenburg, The 1963,N 20,48:1
Sagra del Signore Della Nave 1925,Ap 4,20:2
Sail Away 1961,Ag 10,17:7; 1961,O 4,48:5;
   1962,Je 23,14:3
Sailor, Beware! 1933,S 29,24:4; 1934,Ja 21,X,1:6;
   1935,My 7,28:4; 1955,Mr 6,II,3:1
Sailors of Cattaro 1934,D 11,28:4
Saint, The 1924,O 13,20:3
Saint and Sinners 1935,D 30,15:2
Saint From USA, The 1931,D 13,VIII,3:5

St Helena 1936,F 5,15:8; 1936,Mr 8,IX,1:1;
   1936,S 29,35:1; 1936,O 7,32:1; 1936,O 11,X,1:1
Saint in a Hurry, A 1935,D 29,IX,2:1
Saint Joan 1923,D 29,8:4; 1924,Ja 6,VII,1:1;
   1924,Mr 27,16:2; 1924,O 26,30:2; 1924,N 9,VII,2:3;
   1925,Ja 11,VII,2:7; 1930,Je 29,VIII,1:4;
   1934,N 27,27:2; 1936,Mr 10,27:4; 1936,Mr 15,X,1:1;
   1936,Jl 26,II,1:3; 1940,Mr 11,10:6; 1948,Ja 11,II,3:7;
   1949,Ap 23,10:2; 1950,Mr 4,10:6; 1951,O 5,23:2;
   1951,O 14,II,1:1; 1954,S 18,12:1; 1955,F 13,II,3:1;
   1955,My 29,II,1:1; 1956,S 12,42:1; 1956,S 16,II,1:1;
   1956,D 15,20:3; 1962,F 21,57:4; 1963,Je 25,23:1;
   1964,My 14,41:1; 1968,Ja 5,42:1; 1968,Ja 14,II,1:1
St Joan of the Stockyards 1964,Je 12,45:1
Saint Julian the Hospitaler 1970,O 21,40:1
St Louis Woman 1946,Ap 1,22:2
St Moritz 1937,Jl 16,22:5
Saint of Bleecker Street, The 1954,D 28,21:1;
   1955,Ja 2,II,1:1; 1965,Mr 19,28:1
St Simeon Stylites 1926,My 7,12:2
Saint Wench 1933,Ja 3,19:3
Sainte Jeanne 1925,D 27,VII,2:1
Saintliness of Margery Kempe, The 1959,F 3,35:6
Saint's Parade 1930,N 1,23:4
Saison au Congo, Une 1967,D 3,II,10:6
Saison d'Amour 1926,O 31,VIII,2:4
Sakura 1928,D 26,14:4
Salad Days 1955,N 13,II,3:1; 1958,N 11,24:1
Salad of the Mad Cafe, The 1964,Ap 1,43:1
Sale and a Sailor, A, or Glory! What Price!
   1926,Ap 25,30:4
Sally 1920,D 22,16:1; 1921,S 11,20:2; 1948,My 7,31:2
Sally, Irene and Mary 1922,S 5,21:2; 1938,Jl 5,13:4
Salome 1922,My 23,12:4; 1923,My 8,22:2;
   1923,My 20,VII,1:1; 1931,Je 21,VIII,1:4;
   1956,F 14,24:4
Saloon Bar 1939,N 26,IX,3:6
Salt and Pepper 1933,Ap 24,10:2
Salt Water 1929,N 27,30:3
Salut a Moliere 1964,Mr 4,33:2
Saluta 1934,Ag 29,13:4
Salute to Spring 1937,Jl 14,16:2
Salvage 1957,Ap 10,39:2
Salvation 1928,F 1,31:1; 1928,F 12,VIII,1:1;
   1939,S 29,19:2; 1969,Mr 13,53:1; 1969,S 25,55:1;
   1969,O 5,II,1:1; 1970,F 15,II,1:1
Salvation on a String 1954,Jl 7,23:1
Sam, The Highest Jumper of Them All
   1960,Ag 8,24:3
Sam Abramovitch 1926,D 19,VII,6:1; 1927,Ja 20,20:5
Sam Ego's House 1947,N 1,11:3; 1954,N 11,43:1
Samarkand 1926,D 22,24:4
Sambo 1969,D 22,42:1; 1970,Ja 11,II,1:1;
   1970,Ja 11,II,3:7; 1970,Jl 23,24:1
Samson 1931,F 9,25:1; 1936,N 30,25:2
Samson and Delilah 1920,N 18,18:1;
   1920,N 28,VI,1:1; 1920,D 5,VII,1:1;
   1920,D 12,VI,1:3; 1920,D 26,VI,3:2
San Toy 1932,Mr 20,VIII,1:8
Sancho Panza 1923,O 21,VIII,2:1; 1923,N 27,23:1;
   1923,D 2,VIII,1:1
Sancho's Master 1927,Ap 10,VIII,4:7
Sand 1967,Mr 26,II,1:2
Sandalwood 1926,S 23,23:1; 1926,O 3,VIII,1:1
Sandbox, The 1960,My 17,42:2
Sandhog 1954,N 24,17:1
Sandro Botticelli 1923,Mr 27,24:2; 1923,Ap 1,VII,1:1
Sands of the Negev 1954,O 20,32:1
Sandy Hooker, The 1929,N 10,X,4:8
Sang de Danton, Le 1931,Je 28,VIII,1:8
Sangen om Skrapuken 1967,Ap 9,II,1:3
Sansone 1931,F 9,25:1; 1936,N 30,25:2
Santa Claus 1957,D 18,42:7; 1960,Jl 22,13:1
Sap, The 1924,D 16,28:3
Sap of Life, The 1961,O 3,44:1
Sap Runs High, The 1936,F 1,9:4; 1936,F 5,15:3
Sapphire Ring, The 1925,Ap 5,IX,2:4;
   1925,Ap 16,25:2
Sappho 1935,Mr 22,26:4; 1960,Ja 12,22:1;
   1961,Ag 23,28:5
Sarah Adler Testimonial 1939,Mr 15,18:2
Sarah and the Sax 1964,My 5,53:1
Sarah Simple 1937,My 5,28:4; 1937,My 23,X,2:1;
   1940,N 18,22:5
Saratoga 1959,D 8,59:4
Sardanapale 1926,N 7,VIII,2:7; 1926,N 21,VIII,2:1
Sari 1930,Ja 29,27:1
Satan 1927,N 27,IX,4:7
Satellite 1935,N 21,27:5
Satiric Evening 1963,O 24,36:2
Satisfaction Guaranteed 1969,F 12,31:1
Saturday It Rained 1932,D 14,27:3
Saturday Night 1924,F 11,18:1; 1926,O 26,25:1;
   1926,N 7,VIII,1:1; 1928,Jl 31,13:5; 1933,Mr 1,13:2;
   1933,Mr 19,IX,1:1; 1968,F 26,43:1
Saturday Night Kid, The 1958,My 16,22:1
Saturday's Children 1927,Ja 27,13:1; 1927,F 6,VII,1:1;
   1935,Jl 30,17:2; 1936,Jl 7,22:5
Satyr 1937,Je 17,18:5; 1937,Jl 4,X,1:4
Sauce for the Gander 1928,F 19,VIII,4:1
Sauvage, La 1938,Mr 27,X,2:1
Savage Rhythm 1932,Ja 1,30:4
Savages Under the Skin 1927,Mr 25,25:2

Save It for Your Death Bed 1968,N 4,57:3
Save Me a Place at Forest Lawn 1963,My 9,40:2
Save Me the Waltz 1938,Mr 1,19:2
Save Your Face 1970,My 28,28:1
Saved 1970,O 29,57:1; 1970,N 1,II,10:1
Saving Grace, The 1963,Ap 19,28:1
Savonarola 1942,Ap 24,20:2
Savonarola Brown 1930,F 26,22:3
Say Darling 1958,Ap 4,17:1; 1958,Ap 13,II,1:1;
   1959,F 26,38:2
Say It With Flowers 1926,D 6,29:1;
   1931,D 13,VIII,2:2
Say Nothing 1965,Ja 28,21:2
Say When 1928,Je 27,29:3; 1934,O 28,IX,3:1;
   1934,N 9,24:2
Scaffold for Marionettes, A 1968,Mr 24,II,16:5
Scalawag, The 1927,Mr 30,22:3
Scandal in Assyria 1939,My 28,X,2:5
Scandals 1920,Je 8,9:1; 1924,Jl 1,16:1;
   1927,Jl 3,VII,1:1; 1931,Ag 11,28:4;
   1931,Ag 16,VIII,1:1; 1931,S 27,VIII,3:7;
   1935,O 30,17:1; 1939,Ag 20,IX,2:1;
   1939,Ag 29,17:2; 1939,S 3,IX,1:1
Scapegoat, The 1950,Ap 20,36:5
Scapin 1964,Mr 10,43:1
Scaramouche 1923,O 25,14:2
Scarecrow, The 1953,Je 17,31:1
Scarlet Coat, The 1924,D 24,11:1
Scarlet Fox, The 1928,Mr 28,31:1
Scarlet Lady, The 1926,O 17,VIII,2:1
Scarlet Letter, The 1926,Ja 8,16:5
Scarlet Lily, The 1927,Ja 31,12:3
Scarlet Lullaby 1968,Mr 11,48:1   \
Scarlet Man, The 1921,Ag 23,10:3
Scarlet Pages 1929,S 1,VIII,1:1; 1929,S 10,26:3;
   1929,S 22,IX,1:1
Scarlet Sister Mary 1930,O 5,IX,4:6; 1930,N 26,19:2
Scarlet Woman, The 1929,Ja 27,IX,1:3
Scarlett 1970,Ja 3,19:1
Scars 1929,F 10,IX,2:1
Scatterin', The 1960,S 15,44:2
Scene of the Crime, The 1940,Mr 29,24:1
Scenes From the Lives of the Romanoffs
   1927,F 16,4:6
Scent of Flowers, A 1969,O 21,42:1; 1969,N 2,II,3:1;
   1970,F 15,II,1:1
Schemers 1924,S 16,27:1
Scherz, List und Rache 1928,Ap 22,IX,6:7
Schicksal Nach Wunsch 1932,O 23,IX,3:1
Schlageter 1933,My 28,IX,1:3; 1933,Je 25,IX,1:2
Schlemihl 1936,S 19,20:4
Schloss, Das 1968,N 20,35:3
Schoen ist die Welt 1931,Ja 11,VIII,1:8
Schoen und Schick 1928,Ag 26,II,1:2;
   1928,N 4,IX,2:1
Schon Ist die Welt 1932,Ja 17,VIII,2:1
School for Brides 1944,Ag 2,19:4
School for Husbands, The 1933,O 17,26:5;
   1933,D 3,IX,6:5
School for Scandal, The 1923,Mr 13,19:2;
   1923,Je 5,24:3; 1925,O 24,19:1; 1925,D 7,18:2;
   1925,D 13,IX,3:1; 1929,D 15,X,4:2; 1931,N 11,26:4;
   1931,N 22,VIII,3:1; 1940,Je 18,29:5;
   1940,Je 23,IX,1:1; 1949,Ja 21,24:5; 1953,Je 24,29:2;
   1962,Mr 19,36:1; 1962,Ap 6,31:3; 1962,My 18,34:2;
   1962,N 30,27:1; 1963,Ja 26,5:2; 1966,N 22,33:2;
   1966,D 11,II,3:1; 1970,Je 11,51:1; 1970,Je 21,II,1:1
School For Slavery 1942,Mr 29,VIII,2:2
School for Virtue 1931,Mr 11,23:4; 1931,Ap 22,29:2
School for Wives 1934,N 14,22:2; 1951,Mr 19,22:1;
   1957,Je 20,23:4
Schoolgirl 1930,N 2,VIII,3:5; 1930,N 21,31:1
Schoolhouse on the Lot 1938,Mr 23,18:4
Schoolmaster, The 1928,Mr 21,30:1
Schwartse Mamme 1939,Ja 16,11:3
Schweiger 1926,Mr 24,20:4; 1926,Mr 28,VIII,1:1
Schweik in the Second World War 1959,My 23,18:3;
   1967,N 12,II,17:1
Schwierige, Der 1930,N 30,IX,2:1
Score 1970,O 29,57:4
Scorpion, The 1933,N 28,28:4
Scotch Mist 1926,S 21,32:3
Scotland Yard 1929,S 28,16:6
Scott of Abbotsford 1933,Mr 30,20:2
Scrambled Wives 1920,Ag 6,16:1
Scrap 1931,S 27,VIII,2:8
Scrap Book 1932,Ag 2,20:3
Scrapbooks 1953,N 6,24:2
Scrapped 1927,O 16,IX,2:7
Screwball, The 1957,My 25,24:7
Scribby's Suppen Sind die Besten 1929,D 22,VIII,4:6
Scuba Duba 1967,N 10,36:1; 1967,O 22,II,3:7;
   1968,Ja 7,II,1:5; 1969,Ap 7,51:1
Sea Dogs 1939,N 7,30:3
Sea Gull, The 1929,Ap 10,32:2; 1929,S 17,34:1;
   1930,F 23,III,7:2; 1930,F 26,22:2; 1930,My 4,XI,1:1;
   1938,Mr 17,16:5; 1938,Mr 29,19:2;
   1938,Ap 3,XI,1:1; 1949,Ap 23,10:2;
   1954,My 12,38:1; 1954,My 23,II,1:1; 1954,Jl 7,22:1;
   1956,O 23,38:1
Sea Legs 1937,My 19,26:5
Sea Shells 1935,Jl 16,24:2

Sea Woman, The 1923,Ja 21,VII,1:6; 1925,Ag 25,12:2; 1925,Ag 30,VII,1:1
Sea-Woman's Cloak, The 1925,N 5,28:1
Seagull, The 1936,My 21,19:2; 1936,Je 21,IX,1:5; 1936,Ag 30,IX,1:1; 1960,Je 2,26:4; 1960,Ag 24,33:2; 1961,Ja 8,48:5; 1962,Mr 22,42:1; 1962,Ap 1,II,1:1; 1964,Ap 6,36:1; 1968,Jl 25,27:2
Seagulls Over Sorrento 1952,S 12,18:4; 1952,S 21,II,1:1
Searching for the Sun 1936,F 20,22:6
Searching Sun, The 1952,My 8,37:3
Searching Wind, The 1944,Ap 13,25:2; 1944,Ap 23,II,1:1
Season Changes, The 1935,D 24,10:2
Season in the Sun 1950,S 29,31:2; 1950,O 8,II,1:1
Season of Choice 1959,Ap 14,40:1
Season of the Beast 1958,Mr 14,29:2
Second Act, The 1927,My 5,30:1
Second Best Bed 1946,Je 42,20:2
Second City 1962,Ja 12,30:2
Second Comin', The 1931,D 9,32:4
Second Guesser 1946,F 20,29:2
Second Hurricane 1937,Ap 22,18:4
Second Little Show, The 1930,Ag 17,VIII,2:2; 1930,S 3,36:1
Second Man, The 1927,Ap 12,24:3; 1927,Ap 24,VII,1:1; 1928,F 12,VIII,2:1; 1930,My 2,23:2; 1930,My 25,IX,2:3
Second Marriage 1953,O 12,30:1
Second Mate, The 1930,Mr 25,34:5
Second Mrs Aarons, The 1969,Je 4,37:1
Second Mrs Tanqueray, The 1922,Jl 9,VI,1:1; 1924,S 28,VII,2:1; 1924,O 19,VIII,1:1; 1924,O 28,27:1; 1924,N 2,VII,1:1; 1950,O 8,II,3:7
Second Shot, The 1937,Ap 20,28:4
Second String, A 1960,Ap 14,36:2
Second Threshold 1951,Ja 3,23:2; 1951,Ja 14,II,1:1; 1952,S 25,38:8; 1952,O 12,II,3:7; 1952,N 9,II,3:2
Second Time Around, The 1962,Ap 21,14:1
Secret 1946,O 10,33:2
Secret, Le 1928,Mr 25,IX,4:6
Secret Concubine, The 1960,Mr 22,29:2
Secret Garden, The 1931,N 8,31:4
Secret Life of Walter Mitty, The 1964,O 27,44:5
Secret of Love, The 1936,F 24,15:2
Secret of Suzanne, The 1920,Ja 13,10:2
Secret of the Sphinx 1924,Mr 2,VIII,1:3
Secret Room, The 1945,N 8,16:2
Secret Service Smith 1927,S 4,VII,2:4
Secretary Bird, The 1968,O 18,40:5; 1969,S 14,94:4
Secrets 1922,O 8,VI,1:7; 1922,D 26,11:1; 1922,D 31,VII,1:1
Security 1929,Mr 10,X,4:5; 1929,Mr 29,20:1
See My Lawyer 1939,S 28,29:1
See Naples and Die 1929,S 27,30:4
See the Jaguar 1952,D 4,46:2
Seed of the Brute 1926,O 17,VIII,2:4; 1926,N 2,34:3; 1926,N 7,VIII,1:1
Seeds in the Wind 1948,Ap 26,27:2; 1948,My 26,29:2
Seeing Stars 1935,N 1,25:5
Seeing Things 1920,Je 18,19:2
Seen But Not Heard 1936,Jl 22,23:4; 1936,S 18,19:2
Seeniaya Ptitza 1924,D 29,11:1
Seidman and Son 1962,O 16,32:2
Sellout, The 1933,S 7,17:2
Semele's Bar Mitzvah 1938,Ja 17,11:2
Semi-Detached 1960,Mr 11,20:2; 1962,D 6,54:3; 1963,O 8,49:1; 1963,O 20,II,1:1
Send for Dr O'Grady 1923,Jl 29,VI,1:6
Send Me No Flowers 1960,D 6,54:1
Sensations 1970,O 26,48:2
Sentenced 1932,Mr 6,VIII,2:4
Sentimental Scarecrow 1934,Mr 22,24:6
Sentinels 1931,D 26,15:1
Separate Tables 1954,S 23,42:1; 1954,O 24,II,3:3; 1955,My 22,II,1:1; 1956,O 26,33:1; 1956,N 4,II,1:1; 1957,S 15,II,1:1
Seperate Rooms 1940,Mr 25,10:3
September Tide 1948,D 16,39:5; 1949,Ja 9,II,3:7
Sequestres d'Altona, Les 1961,Je 25,II,3:5
Serata D'Inverno 1929,Ap 8,32:5
Serena Blandish 1929,Ja 13,VIII,2:4; 1929,Ja 24,30:3; 1929,F 3,VIII,1:1
Serenade, The 1930,Mr 5,26:7
Serjeant Musgrave's Dance 1966,Mr 9,44:1; 1966,Mr 20,II,1:1; 1968,Je 16,52:4
Sermon 1963,O 1,34:1
Serpent, The 1969,F 9,II,1:4; 1970,My 24,II,3:1; 1970,Je 2,35:1
Serpent in the Orchard, The 1949,Ap 24,II,1:1
Serpent's Tooth, A 1922,Ag 25,8:5
Servant in the House, The 1921,My 3,20:1; 1925,Ap 8,24:2; 1925,Ap 12,VIII,1:1; 1926,My 4,30:1
Servant of Two Masters, The 1928,Ja 10,28:3; 1928,Ja 22,VIII,6:1; 1958,F 11,35:2; 1960,F 24,42:2; 1960,F 29,31:5; 1966,Je 28,51:1
Service 1932,N 13,IX,3:4
Service for Two 1926,Ag 31,15:1; 1926,S 5,VII,1:1; 1935,Ag 20,25:1
Serving Folk 1920,Ap 22,11:3
Set a Thief 1927,F 22,22:1
Set My People Free 1948,N 4,38:2; 1948,N 14,II,1:1

Set to Music 1939,Ja 19,16:2
Settled Out of Court 1960,O 20,44:4
Seul 1923,N 13,24:2
Seven 1929,D 28,10:5
Seven Against One 1930,My 7,25:1
Seven at Dawn, The 1961,Ap 18,43:1
Seven Days of Mourning 1969,D 17,64:1; 1970,Ja 4,II,5:1
Seven Descents of Myrtle, The 1968,Mr 28,54:1; 1968,Ap 7,II,1:5
Seven Keys to Baldpate 1930,Ja 8,25:2; 1935,My 28,30:2
Seven Lively Arts 1944,D 8,26:6; 1944,D 17,II,3:1
Seven Mirrors 1945,O 26,17:2
7 Rue de la Paroisse 1927,Ap 3,VIII,4:7
Seven Scenes for Yeni 1963,My 13,36:2
Seven Year Itch, The 1952,N 21,21:2; 1952,N 30,II,1:1; 1953,My 18,26:8
Seven Year Love 1929,O 27,IX,2:1
Seventeen 1924,Ap 12,18:2; 1926,My 1,10:1; 1951,Je 22,16:6; 1951,Jl 1,II,1:1; 1951,Jl 1,II,9:5
1776 1926,Ap 24,11:2; 1969,Mr 17,46:2; 1969,Mr 23,II,1:1; 1970,Je 18,54:4
Seventh Heart, The 1927,My 3,24:4
Seventh Heaven 1922,O 31,11:1; 1922,N 5,VIII,1:1; 1927,S 3,13:1; 1927,S 25,VIII,2:1; 1955,My 27,16:2
Seventh Trumpet, The 1941,N 22,10:6
Severed Cord, The 1929,My 9,34:3
Severed Head, A 1963,Je 28,22:1; 1964,O 29,40:1
Sex 1926,Ap 27,22:4; 1930,S 28,VIII,2:5
Sex Appeal Paris 32 1932,My 29,VIII,1:6
Sex Fable, The 1931,O 21,26:1
Sexe Faible, La 1929,D 29,VIII,2:6
Sexe Fort, Le 1927,F 13,VII,4:1; 1937,Ja 14,17:4
Sextet 1958,N 27,53:1
Sganarelle 1958,My 7,43:1; 1970,Ja 13,41:1
Sh! The Octopus 1928,F 22,19:2
Shabtai Tavi 1932,D 7,28:8
Shadow, The 1922,Ap 25,14:2; 1922,Ap 30,VII,1:1; 1923,D 15,16:2; 1930,N 17,21:2; 1936,Ap 26,II,12:6
Shadow and Substance 1938,Ja 23,XI,1:6; 1938,Ja 27,16:2; 1938,F 6,X,1:1; 1938,O 23,IX,3:5; 1956,Mr 14,38:1; 1959,N 4,42:1
Shadow Man, The 1930,Mr 5,26:7
Shadow of a Gunman, The 1927,Je 26,VIII,1:3; 1932,O 31,18:1; 1958,N 21,26:1; 1958,N 30,II,1:1
Shadow of Heroes 1961,D 6,59:1
Shadow of My Enemy, A 1957,D 12,35:4
Shadow of the Glen, The 1932,N 4,25:1
Shadow of the Rockies, The 1929,Ja 29,26:4
Shadow Play 1935,O 22,16:5; 1936,Ja 14,25:1; 1936,F 16,IX,3:1; 1936,N 28,13:1; 1936,D 6,XII,5:1; 1939,Ag 15,14:5; 1948,F 24,20:4
Shadow Years, The 1957,Ja 9,26:2
Shadows of the Evening 1966,Ap 27,38:1
Shady Lady 1933,Jl 6,26:3
Shake Hands With the Devil 1949,O 21,30:4
Shakes Versus Shaw 1959,Ja 27,27:5
Shakespeare and Company 1925,O 22,22:5
Shakespeare in Harlem 1959,O 28,40:7; 1960,F 10,43:4; 1960,F 21,II,1:1
Shakespeare Revisited 1962,Jl 19,19:2
Shakespeare's Merchant 1939 1939,Ja 10,16:3
Shakuntala 1959,S 10,41:2
Shall We Join the Ladies? 1921,Je 26,VI,1:1; 1922,Mr 26,VI,1:2; 1925,Ja 14,19:1; 1929,Mr 17,30:4; 1929,My 9,34:3; 1929,My 12,28:3
Shame Woman, The 1923,O 17,14:1; 1923,O 21,VIII,1:1
Shanghai Gesture, The 1925,D 20,VII,4:1; 1926,F 2,20:2; 1929,My 14,28:4; 1929,Je 2,VIII,2:7
Shangri-La 1956,Je 14,40:1
Shannons of Broadway, The 1927,S 11,VIII,1:3; 1927,S 27,30:4; 1927,O 9,VIII,1:1
Sharlee 1923,N 23,20:1
Sharon's Grave 1961,N 9,39:2
Shatter'd Lamp, The 1934,Mr 22,26:3
Shaughraun, The 1968,My 22,54:1
Shavings 1920,F 17,18:1; 1920,F 22,III,6:1
She, Too, Was Young 1938,S 4,X,2:1
She Couldn't Say No! 1926,S 1,27:3; 1926,S 12,VIII,1:1
She Cried for the Moon 1935,Jl 23,24:3
She Gave Him All She Had 1939,D 2,20:7
She Got What She Wanted 1929,Mr 5,28:1
She Had to Know 1925,F 3,25:3; 1925,F 8,VII,1:1
She Lived Next to the Firehouse 1931,F 11,23:1
She Loves Me 1963,Ap 24,39:1; 1963,My 5,II,1:1
She Loves Me Not 1933,N 21,22:4; 1933,N 26,IX,1:1; 1934,My 2,25:1; 1934,My 27,X,2:5
She Means Business 1931,Ja 27,21:2
She Shall Have Music 1959,Ja 23,18:4
She Stoops to Conquer 1924,Je 10,24:3; 1928,My 15,17:1; 1928,My 20,VIII,1:1; 1928,S 2,VII,2:1; 1949,D 29,21:3; 1950,Je 18,34:4; 1960,N 2,42:5; 1960,N 13,II,1:1; 1960,N 15,36:3; 1968,Ja 1,11:1; 1968,Ap 1,58:3; 1969,Ag 18,28:1
She Wanted to Know 1925,Ja 25,VII,1:4
Sheep on the Runway 1970,F 2,28:3; 1970,F 8,II,5:5
Sheep Well, The 1936,My 3,II,4:1
Shelf, The 1926,Jl 4,VII,3:2; 1926,S 28,31:1
Shelter 1926,Ja 26,18:2
Shephard's Pie 1941,My 18,IX,1:5

Shepherd King, The 1955,O 13,36:2
Shepherd of Avenue B, The 1970,My 16,30:1
Shepherd's Chameleon, The 1960,N 30,41:1
Sheppey 1933,S 15,22:2; 1933,O 1,IX,2:2; 1944,Ap 19,27:2
Sherlock Holmes 1928,F 21,18:4; 1929,N 26,28:3; 1953,O 31,11:2; 1953,N 8,II,1:1
Sherry! 1967,Mr 29,39:1; 1967,Ap 9,II,1:1
She's My Baby 1928,Ja 4,22:2
Shewing-Up of Blanco Posnet, The 1923,O 17,14:2; 1926,D 26,VII,4:8; 1959,S 19,26:7; 1959,O 4,II,1:1
Shinbone Alley 1957,Ap 15,23:2; 1957,Ap 28,II,1:1
Shining Hour, The 1934,F 14,22:6; 1934,F 25,IX,1:1; 1934,S 5,25:4; 1934,S 23,X,3:6; 1936,Ag 12,15:3
Ship, The 1929,F 17,IX,2:1; 1929,N 21,24:7
Ship Comes Home, A 1937,My 18,27:1; 1937,Je 6,XI,1:3
Ship Comes in, A 1934,S 20,21:1
Shipwrecked 1924,N 2,VII,2:3; 1924,N 13,18:1
Shock of Recognition, The 1967,Mr 14,54:1
Shock Troops 1969,F 22,36:1
Shoemaker and the Peddler, The 1960,O 15,27:4
Shoemaker's Holiday, The 1938,Ja 3,17:2; 1938,Ja 9,X,1:1; 1938,Ja 23,XI,1:6; 1967,Mr 3,25:1; 1967,Je 3,19:1
Shoemaker's Prodigious Wife, The 1949,Je 15,38:2; 1962,S 2,44:4; 1964,S 3,23:2
Shoes 1970,Mr 10,53:1
Shoestring Revue 1929,N 23,19:2; 1955,Mr 1,22:2
Shoestring '57 1956,N 6,31:1
Shoot 1922,Je 8,14:2
Shoot Anything With Hair That Moves 1969,F 3,29:1
Shoot the Works! 1931,Jl 22,19:5; 1931,Jl 26,VIII,2:1; 1931,Ag 21,20:2
Shooting Shadows 1924,Je 27,16:5
Shooting Star 1933,Je 13,22:2
Shop at Sly Corner, The 1949,Ja 19,35:2
Shore Leave 1922,Ag 9,20:2
Short Cut, The 1930,Ja 28,28:2
Short Story 1935,N 5,33:2; 1935,D 1,XI,5:3
Shorty 1948,N 14,I,70:6
Shot in the Dark, A 1961,O 19,40:1
Should a Mother Tell? 1938,N 25,18:3
Should I Marry, or Shouldn't I? 1936,S 28,14:3
Shout From the Rooftops 1964,O 29,40:1
Show, The 1925,Jl 12,VII,1:1
Show Boat 1927,D 28,26:1; 1928,Ja 8,VIII,1:1; 1928,My 4,31:3; 1928,My 27,VIII,1:8; 1928,Je 10,VIII,1:3; 1932,My 20,22:2; 1932,My 29,VIII,5:6; 1938,Je 30,21:1; 1946,Ja 7,17:2; 1946,Ja 13,II,1:1; 1948,S 9,33:2; 1948,S 19,II,1:1; 1952,Je 6,19:5; 1954,My 6,44:1; 1954,O 29,28:4; 1956,Je 22,16:1; 1957,Je 28,30:2; 1961,Ap 13,32:1; 1966,Jl 20,48:1
Show Booth, The 1923,Ap 4,22:2; 1923,Ap 8,VIII,1:1
Show Girl 1929,Jl 3,19:3; 1929,Ag 8,29:4; 1929,Ag 25,VIII,1:1; 1961,Ja 13,37:1; 1961,Ja 29,II,1:1
Show Is On, The 1936,N 9,22:2; 1936,N 15,XI,2:1; 1936,D 26,14:2; 1937,Ja 10,X,1:1; 1937,S 20,18:4
Show Me Where the Good Times Are 1970,Mr 6,32:1
Show-Off, The 1924,Ja 20,VII,2:8; 1924,F 6,16:2; 1924,F 17,VII,1:1; 1924,Mr 16,VIII,1:1; 1924,S 7,VII,1:1; 1924,O 21,21:1; 1924,O 26,VIII,1:1; 1925,F 15,VII,1:1; 1932,D 13,25:4; 1950,Je 1,24:5; 1950,Je 11,II,1:1; 1967,D 6,40:2; 1967,D 17,II,3:7
Show Time 1942,S 17,20:2; 1942,O 4,VIII,1:1
Showboat Revue 1934,Je 6,24:2; 1935,Ag 18,13:2
Shrike, The 1952,Ja 16,20:2; 1952,Ja 27,II,1:1; 1953,N 26,51:2
Shroud My Body Down 1934,D 9,II,1:6
Shuffle Along 1921,My 23,16:2; 1952,My 9,20:5
Shuffle Along of 1933 1932,D 27,11:3
Shulamith 1931,O 14,26:4
Shunned 1960,D 21,39:1
Shylock and His Daughter 1947,S 30,22:2; 1947,N 30,II,1:1
Shylock '47 1947,My 28,30:5
Si Je Voulais 1937,Ja 28,22:5
Siberia 1928,Ap 15,IX,4:1
Side-Show 1931,My 16,13:1
Sidewalks and the Sound of Crying 1956,O 29,34:1
Sidewalks of New York 1927,O 4,33:1
Sidna 1926,Jl 23,11:2
Siebenstein 1933,My 28,IX,1:3
Siege 1937,D 9,31:4
Siege of Besztercze, The 1929,F 3,VIII,2:1
Siege of Numancia 1966,O 5,42:5
Siegfried 1928,My 20,VIII,1:3; 1930,O 21,34:1; 1939,F 21,15:2
Sigh No More 1945,Jl 12,8:4; 1945,Ag 24,15:1; 1945,S 2,II,1:2
Sightseers 1929,My 8,34:4
Sign in Sidney Brustein's Window, The 1964,O 16,32:1; 1964,N 1,II,1:1
Sign of Jonah, The 1957,My 2,27:1; 1960,S 9,35:1
Sign of the Leopard 1928,D 2,X,4:2; 1928,D 12,34:4; 1928,D 24,17:7
Sign of Winter 1958,My 8,35:1
Signature 1945,F 15,25:2

Signo Della Croce, Il 1935,O 7,11:1
Signor Bracoli 1932,O 2,IX,2:3
Signora Dalle Camelie, La 1934,O 22,13:2;
  1937,O 9,16:3
Signora Morli-One and Two 1928,D 16,IX,2:1
Signori, Il Figlio E' Nato 1935,Je 8,13:7
Signs Along the Cynic Route 1961,D 15,49:5
Silence 1924,F 17,VII,2:8; 1924,N 13,18:2;
  1969,Jl 13,II,8:1; 1969,Jl 25,34:1; 1970,Ap 3,43:1;
  1970,Ap 12,II,3:1
Silence of Lee Harvey Oswald, The 1966,N 25,47:1
Silent Forces 1920,Ag 30,12:1
Silent House, The 1927,Jl 3,VII,1:4; 1928,F 8,28:5;
  1928,F 12,VIII,1:1; 1932,N 9,28:3; 1935,Ag 7,22:2
Silent Knight, The 1937,N 17,26:4; 1937,D 5,XII,5:8
Silent Night, Lonely Night 1959,D 4,36:1;
  1959,D 13,II,3:1
Silent Witness, The 1931,F 22,VIII,4:4;
  1931,Mr 24,31:5; 1931,My 10,VIII,3:5
Silhouettes 1969,S 9,41:1
Silk Hat Harry 1943,Ag 22,II,1:6
Silk Stockings 1955,F 25,17:3; 1955,Mr 27,II,1:1
Silks and Satins 1920,Jl 16,19:1
Silver Box, The 1928,Ja 18,23:1; 1928,My 20,VIII,2:1;
  1928,N 25,X,2:3; 1935,Jl 16,24:2
Silver Cord, The 1926,D 21,21:1; 1927,Ja 16,VII,1:1;
  1927,S 14,29:2; 1927,O 2,VIII,1:3;
  1928,F 19,VIII,2:1
Silver Fox, The 1921,S 6,13:1
Silver Grey Toy Poodle 1969,My 15,41:2
Silver Swan, The 1929,Ap 7,X,2:1; 1929,N 3,IX,1:7;
  1929,N 28,34:5
Silver Tassie, The 1929,O 25,26:1; 1929,N 3,IX,4:1;
  1929,N 10,X,1:1; 1935,Ag 14,16:1; 1949,Jl 22,16:5
Silver Tassle, The 1949,S 4,II,1:1; 1969,S 12,35:2
Silver Whistle, The 1948,N 25,49:2
Sim Sala Bim 1940,S 10,27:1; 1940,S 15,IX,1:1
Simon And Laura 1954,D 12,II,5:1
Simon Called Peter 1924,My 4,VIII,2:1;
  1924,N 11,20:2
Simon's Hour 1926,My 6,23:3
Simon's Wife 1945,Mr 9,16:4
Simple Life, A 1964,My 18,36:1
Simple Simon 1930,F 2,VIII,2:7; 1930,F 19,22:1;
  1930,Mr 2,IX,1:1; 1930,Mr 16,IX,1:1;
  1930,N 23,IX,1:3; 1931,Mr 10,23:2
Simple Woman, The 1937,Mr 29,14:1
Simpleton of the Unexpected Isles, The
  1935,F 19,27:5; 1935,F 24,VIII,1:1; 1935,Jl 30,17:3;
  1935,Ag 25,X,1:3; 1954,Ja 12,19:1
Simply Heavenly 1957,My 22,38:2; 1957,Je 2,II,1:1
Sin of Pat Muldoon, The 1957,Mr 14,35:1
Sinbad the Sailor 1929,D 27,26:5
Sing and Whistle 1934,F 12,18:3
Sing for Your Supper 1939,Ap 25,18:6
Sing High, Sing Low 1931,N 13,26:4
Sing Israel Sing 1967,My 12,50:1
Sing Me No Lullaby 1954,O 15,17:2;
  1954,O 24,II,1:1
Sing Muse 1961,D 7,52:1
Sing Out, Sweet Land! 1944,Ja 7,II,1:1;
  1944,D 28,24:2; 1945,F 4,II,5:1
Sing Out the News 1938,S 26,12:5; 1938,O 2,IX,1:1
Sing Till Tomorrow 1953,D 29,17:2
Sing to Me Through Open Windows
  1965,Mr 16,45:1
Singapore 1932,N 15,24:2
Singer, The 1920,My 25,14:2
Singin' the Blues 1931,Ap 12,IX,2:1; 1931,S 17,21:3
Singing Girl, The 1952,Je 4,31:8
Singing Jailbirds 1928,My 20,VIII,2:1; 1928,D 5,34:4;
  1930,F 10,20:8
Singing Rabbi, The 1931,S 11,24:4
Singing Thief, The 1933,D 4,22:4
Single Man at a Party 1959,Ap 22,30:4
Sinner 1927,F 8,20:2
Sins of Mothers 1937,Mr 30,20:2
Sirena 1931,S 22,33:4
Sirena Varada, La 1937,O 23,15:3
Sirocco 1927,N 25,24:4; 1927,D 18,IX,4:1
Sissy the Rose of Bavaria 1933,Ja 15,IX,8:6
Sister Oakes 1949,Ap 25,19:4
Sisters 1927,D 11,IX,2:5; 1927,D 26,26:5
Sisters of the Chorus 1930,My 18,VIII,3:1;
  1930,O 21,34:3
Sisters' Tragedy, The 1930,My 6,33:1
Sitting on the Fence 1935,Mr 12,25:4
Sitting Pretty 1924,Mr 30,VIII,2:7; 1924,Ap 9,24:2
Sive 1959,S 6,II,1:3
Six Characters in Search of an Author
  1922,O 31,11:2; 1922,N 5,VIII,1:1; 1925,Je 16,26:4;
  1928,Je 24,VIII,4:2; 1931,Ap 16,29:2; 1934,D 5,29:1;
  1955,D 12,38:1; 1955,D 25,II,3:1; 1961,My 11,43:1;
  1963,Mr 11,7:2
Six-Cylinder Love 1921,Jl 24,VI,1:1; 1921,Ag 26,8:2
Six Feet Under 1928,Ja 22,VIII,4:7
Six-Fifty, The 1921,O 2,VII,1:8; 1921,O 25,20:1;
  1921,O 30,VI,1:1
Six Flights Up 1939,F 26,IX,2:3
Six Miracle Plays 1933,F 6,11:3; 1933,F 12,IX,2:1
Six of Calais, The 1934,Jl 18,20:3; 1934,Ag 12,IX,1:3
Sixieme Etage 1938,Je 12,X,2:3
1650 1933,F 22,24:5

Sixth Finger in a Five Finger Glove 1956,O 9,31:4
Sixth Floor 1939,Je 11,IX,2:5
60,000 Heroes 1935,Ja 28,11:5
Sketch Book 1929,Jl 2,33:5; 1935,Je 5,22:2
Skidding 1928,My 22,18:5
Skin Deep 1927,O 18,32:1
Skin Game, The 1920,My 23,VI,1:3; 1920,O 21,11:1;
  1920,O 31,VI,1:2
Skin of Our Teeth, The 1942,N 19,29:5;
  1942,N 22,VIII,1:1; 1943,Ja 3,VIII,1:1;
  1943,My 9,II,1:1; 1945,Mr 20,22:8;
  1945,My 27,II,1:3; 1945,N 18,II,2:5;
  1955,Je 29,25:3; 1955,Ag 18,16:1; 1955,Ag 28,II,1:1;
  1960,O 14,24:1; 1961,Mr 6,30:1; 1961,Mr 20,32:6;
  1961,Mr 28,40:2; 1961,Ap 1,11:2; 1961,Ap 11,43:5;
  1961,Ap 21,29:1; 1961,My 1,35:3; 1961,My 19,22:2;
  1961,My 31,28:1; 1966,Je 2,51:1; 1968,S 12,55:1
Skipper Next to God 1948,Ja 5,14:5
Skirt, The 1921,N 8,28:1
Skits-Oh-Frantics 1967,Ap 3,39:2
Skull, The 1928,Ap 24,28:3
Sky Drift 1945,N 14,25:2
Sky High 1925,Mr 3,21:4
Skylark 1921,Jl 26,10:6; 1939,Mr 19,XI,2:5;
  1939,O 12,32:2; 1939,O 22,IX,1:3;
  1942,Ap 12,VIII,1:6
Skyrocket, The 1929,Ja 12,14:7
Sky's the Limit, The 1934,D 18,25:5
Skyscraper 1965,N 15,48:1
Skywriting 1968,My 9,55:2; 1968,My 19,II,1:1
Slapstick Tragedy 1966,Mr 6,II,1:1
Slave, The 1964,D 17,51:1; 1965,N 17,53:7
Slave of Duty, The 1926,D 7,25:1; 1931,Je 30,22:6;
  1934,S 7,24:3
Slave Ship 1969,N 22,46:1; 1969,N 23,II,1:1;
  1969,N 23,II,3:1; 1970,S 13,II,1:1
Slaves All 1926,D 7,24:4
Slaves of Luxury 1930,F 8,13:3
Slaves of the Public 1934,Mr 10,18:6
Sleep, My Pretty One 1944,N 3,26:8
Sleep No More 1944,S 1,11:5
Sleep of Prisoners, A 1951,My 16,46:6;
  1951,O 17,36:2; 1951,O 28,II,1:1; 1952,Ja 2,21:7;
  1955,Ja 15,10:5; 1955,F 27,II,3:1
Sleeping Clergyman, A 1933,S 21,24:2;
  1933,O 8,X,2:4; 1934,O 9,16:1
Sleeping Prince, The 1953,S 29,25:1; 1953,N 6,24:4;
  1953,D 20,II,4:2; 1954,F 9,22:8; 1956,N 2,31:1
Sleepy Hollow 1948,Je 4,26:3
Sleuth 1970,N 13,25:1; 1970,N 22,II,18:1
Slice It Thin 1945,My 11,22:5
Slight Ache, A 1964,D 10,62:1
Slight Case of Murder, A 1935,S 12,28:5;
  1935,S 22,X,1:1
Slightly Delinquent 1954,O 26,32:5
Slightly Delirious 1935,Ja 1,25:3
Slightly Married 1943,O 26,19:2
Slightly Scandalous 1944,Je 14,16:2
Slow Dance on the Killing Ground 1964,D 1,50:1;
  1968,N 3,87:1; 1970,My 14,43:1
Slow Dusk 1958,Ap 24,37:3
Slow Memories 1970,N 18,41:1
Small Hours, The 1951,F 16,22:1
Small Miracle 1934,S 27,24:3
Small Timers, The 1925,Ja 28,15:3
Small War on Murray Hill 1957,Ja 4,19:1;
  1957,Ja 13,II,1:1
Small Wonder 1948,S 16,33:5; 1948,S 26,II,1:1
Smarty's Party 1928,S 25,29:4
Smell the Sweet Savor 1940,F 3,8:4
Smile at Me 1935,Ag 24,18:4
Smile of the World, The 1949,Ja 13,26:5
Smiles 1930,N 2,VIII,1:3; 1930,N 19,19:2
Smilin' Through 1920,Ja 4,IX,2:1
Smiling Faces 1931,D 13,VIII,2:5; 1932,Ag 31,12:3
Smiling Madame Beudet 1921,My 1,VII,1:7
Smiling the Boy Fell Dead 1961,Ap 20,28:1
Smiling Through 1932,Ja 3,VIII,3:1; 1935,Jl 30,17:2
Smith's Daughters, The 1922,Ja 29,VI,1:3
Smokeweaver's Daughter, The 1959,Ap 15,30:1
Smoky Cell 1930,D 17,30:2
Smooth as Silk 1921,F 23,18:3
Smyth With a Y 1937,Je 30,19:5
Snafu 1944,O 26,19:5
Snapshots of 1921 1921,Je 3,19:2
Snark Was a Boojum, The 1943,S 2,14:4
Sniper, The 1959,O 28,40:4
Snookie 1941,Je 4,26:2
Snow Maiden, The 1960,Ap 5,43:3
Snowangel 1963,Je 14,36:1
So Am I 1928,Ja 28,9:1
So English! 1938,N 27,IX,1:7
So Far and No Father 1932,F 17,19:4;
  1932,Mr 6,VIII,2:4
So Many Paths 1934,D 7,26:5
So Proudly We Hail 1936,S 23,28:4; 1938,Mr 30,18:5;
  1938,Ap 9,11:1
So That's That 1925,D 15,28:3
So This Is London 1922,Ag 31,18:2; 1923,Ap 12,22:1
So This Is Love 1928,D 2,X,4:2
So This Is Paris 1930,Ap 27,IX,2:3
So This Is Politics 1924,Je 17,22:2
So Was Napoleon 1930,Ja 9,22:2

Soap Opera 1968,My 10,54:7
Social Register, The 1931,O 4,VIII,2:3;
  1931,N 10,28:2
Society Girl 1931,D 31,16:1
Socrates 1930,Ap 13,X,1:6
Soeurs Guedonee, Les 1931,D 13,VIII,2:2
Soeurs Hortensias, Les 1934,My 13,IX,2:1
Soft Shoulders 1940,Jl 18,22:5
Softly, and Consider the Nearness 1964,My 12,32:1
Soif, La 1949,F 9,33:2
Soif et la Faim, La 1966,Mr 2,47:5
Soiled Hands 1948,Ap 18,II,1:6
Soir des Noces, Le 1930,N 30,IX,3:3
Sojourner Truth 1948,Ap 22,35:2
Sol Hyam's Brocanteur 1923,N 27,23:5
Sold to the Movies 1970,Je 18,54:2
Soldier and the Gentlewoman, The 1933,My 7,IX,1:4
Soldiers 1967,O 10,14:3; 1967,O 11,37:1;
  1968,Mr 3,88:2; 1968,Mr 10,II,1:1; 1968,My 2,58:1;
  1968,My 12,II,3:1; 1968,Jl 7,II,1:1; 1968,D 14,62:5;
  1969,Ja 5,II,3:1
Soldiers and Women 1929,Ag 25,VIII,3:1;
  1929,S 3,25:1; 1929,S 22,IX,1:1
Soldier's Tale, A 1955,Jl 13,21:2
Soldier's Wife 1944,O 5,18:6; 1944,O 15,II,1:1;
  1946,S 2,13:2
Soles Truncos, Los 1959,Ag 31,15:2
Solid Gold Cadillac, The 1953,N 6,24:2;
  1953,N 15,II,1:1; 1954,Ag 16,13:4
Solid Ivory 1925,N 17,29:3
Solid South 1930,My 11,IX,2:6; 1930,O 15,27:1
Soliloquy 1938,N 29,26:4
Solitaire 1929,Mr 10,X,4:5; 1929,Mr 13,28:3;
  1942,Ja 28,22:2; 1942,F 8,IX,1:1
Solo 1962,Ap 27,26:1
Some Girl 1927,D 24,8:2
Some of the People 1937,Mr 11,20:1
Some Party 1922,Ap 17,22:1
Somebody 1931,D 13,VIII,3:6
Somebody Knows 1932,My 29,VIII,1:1
Somebody's Lion 1921,Ap 13,20:1
Someone From Assisi 1962,Ja 12,28:1;
  1962,Ja 21,II,1:1
Someone to Talk To 1956,Jl 19,30:2
Someone Waiting 1953,N 26,51:7; 1956,F 15,26:1
Someone's Comin' Hungry 1969,Ap 1,51:1
Something About a Soldier 1962,Ja 5,36:2
Something Different 1967,N 29,52:1;
  1967,D 10,II,15:6; 1968,Ja 7,II,1:5
Something for Nothing 1937,D 10,33:5
Something for the Boys 1943,Ja 17,VIII,1:1;
  1944,Ap 30,II,1:5
Something Gay 1935,Ap 30,12:2
Something More Important 1935,Jl 12,15:3
Something More! 1964,N 11,36:1
Something to Brag About 1925,Jl 12,VII,1:8;
  1925,Ag 14,14:3
Something to Live For 1935,Ja 20,X,2:4
Something Unspoken 1958,Ja 8,23:4
Sometime Jam Today 1967,F 13,41:1
Somewhere in France 1941,Ap 29,16:8
Son, Come Home, A 1968,Mr 9,23:2
Son, The 1950,Ap 1,12:4; 1950,Ag 16,24:6
Son Mari 1936,Ap 17,17:3
Son of Cock-Strong 1970,Mr 9,43:1
Son of Man 1933,O 22,IX,2:2
Son of the Grand Eunuch 1937,Ja 15,17:8
Son of the Man, The 1934,D 4,22:1
Son to Dorothy, A 1951,N 20,37:2
Son Who Hunted Tigers in Jakarta, The
  1969,D 8,60:4
Sondra 1967,My 10,39:1
Song and Dance Man, The 1924,Ja 1,21:2;
  1930,Je 17,25:5
Song at Twilight, A 1966,Ap 17,86:5
Song for a Certain Midnight 1959,S 17,49:1
Song of Bernadette 1944,Jl 27,15:3; 1946,Mr 27,22:2
Song of Daphnis, The 1938,Je 23,26:5
Song of Dnieper 1946,O 26,10:5
Song of Life, The 1932,Ap 4,13:3
Song of Love, The 1928,S 25,31:2
Song of Norway 1944,Ag 22,20:2; 1944,Ag 27,II,1:1;
  1946,Mr 8,17:1; 1951,Ja 11,28:5; 1958,Je 23,19:2;
  1959,Je 26,16:2
Song of Sixpence, A 1930,Ap 6,IX,2:1
Song of Songs 1931,Ap 13,17:3; 1931,My 18,21:4;
  1958,O 29,31:1
Song of the Bridge 1942,Ap 7,27:5
Song of the Flame 1925,D 11,26:4; 1925,D 20,VII,4:1;
  1925,D 31,10:2
Song of the Ghetto, The 1932,O 3,15:5
Song of the Grasshopper 1967,S 29,52:2
Song of the Lusitanian Bogey, The 1968,Ja 3,52:1;
  1968,Ja 14,II,1:1; 1969,My 13,41:1
Song Out of Sorrow 1941,D 12,34:5; 1955,N 1,27:3
Song Writer, The 1928,Ag 14,15:2
Songs and Impressions 1955,S 29,38:2
Songs From Milk Wood 1970,Ja 13,41:1
Sonitchka 1930,Mr 8,21:3
Sonny 1921,Ag 17,12:2
Sons, The 1922,D 13,28:3
Sons and Soldiers 1943,My 5,22:2
Sons o' Fun 1941,N 1,20:1; 1941,D 2,28:2

Sons o' Guns 1929,N 27,30:4; 1930,Ja 12,VIII,1:1; 1930,Ag 24,VIII,1:1
Sonya 1921,Ag 16,18:3
Sonya's Search for the Christmas Star 1929,D 14,24:6
Sophie 1920,Mr 3,12:2; 1944,D 26,22:7; 1963,Ap 16,32:1
Sophisticrats, The 1933,F 14,19:5
Sorcerer, The 1928,Je 24,VIII,1:1; 1954,My 26,34:3
Sorcieres de Salem, Les 1955,F 27,II,3:1
Sorrow of Frederick, The 1967,Jl 8,14:2
Sorry You've Been Troubled 1929,O 13,IX,4:1
Sortileges 1932,N 13,IX,2:5
So's Your Old Antique 1930,My 8,32:5
So's Your Old Manhattan 1927,My 5,30:5
Sotoba Komachi 1961,F 1,15:1
Soul Gone Home 1959,O 28,40:7
Soul of a Woman, The 1930,F 22,13:1
Souls for Sale 1936,S 21,27:6
Sound of Hunting, A 1945,N 21,16:6; 1945,D 2,II,1:1; 1954,Ap 7,41:1
Sound of Music, The 1959,N 17,40:2; 1959,N 22,II,1:1; 1961,My 19,22:6; 1967,Ap 27,52:1; 1970,Jl 3,13:1
Sound of Silence, A 1965,Mr 9,30:1
Sour Grapes 1926,Jl 4,VII,3:2; 1926,S 7,19:1; 1926,S 12,VIII,1:1
Sourball 1969,Ag 6,29:2
South 1955,My 2,17:4
South Pacific 1943,D 30,11:2; 1949,Ap 8,30:2; 1949,Ap 17,II,1:1; 1949,Je 5,II,1:1; 1950,Ap 26,36:5; 1951,Jl 10,30:5; 1951,S 2,II,1:1; 1951,N 2,19:1; 1951,N 11,II,3:1; 1955,My 5,39:5; 1957,Ap 25,35:1; 1961,Ap 27,26:3; 1965,Je 3,25:1; 1967,Je 13,56:1; 1968,Je 30,54:2; 1969,Jl 7,27:1
South Sea Bubble 1956,Ap 26,37:6; 1956,My 13,II,3:1
Southern Exposure 1950,S 27,36:3
Southwest Corner, The 1955,F 4,18:2; 1955,F 13,II,1:1
Souviens-Toi, Mon Amour 1954,N 28,II,3:1
Spanische Nachtigall, Die 1920,D 12,VI,1:4
Spanish Armada, The 1962,Ap 4,38:1
Spanish Love 1920,Ag 18,6:1; 1920,Ag 22,VI,1:2
Sparkin' 1931,Mr 4,33:2
Sparviero, Lo 1934,N 12,16:1
Speak of the Devil! 1939,O 7,21:7
Speakeasy 1927,S 27,30:1
Speaking of Murder 1956,D 20,37:1
Speckled Band, The 1926,N 14,VIII,2:1
Spell, The 1930,Mr 23,4:3
Spellbound 1927,F 16,17:2; 1927,N 15,26:2; 1927,N 20,IX,1:1; 1931,F 22,VIII,4:1
Spice of 1922 1922,Jl 7,12:4
Spider, The 1927,F 13,VII,1:4; 1927,Mr 23,29:1; 1927,Mr 27,VII,1:1
Spider's Web, The 1954,D 15,41:1; 1955,Ja 9,II,3:1
Spiegel, Der 1932,Ja 17,VIII,2:1
Spiro Who? 1969,My 19,55:1; 1969,Je 15,II,3:6
Spite Corner 1921,Jl 17,VI,1:1; 1922,S 26,18:1
Spithead 1969,N 22,46:3
Spitting Image 1968,S 11,42:1; 1969,Mr 3,28:1
Spofford 1967,D 15,54:3; 1967,D 24,II,3:2
Spoken English and Broken English 1959,Ja 27,27:5
Sponge Room, The 1964,F 25,24:1
Sponono 1964,Ap 3,28:1; 1964,Ap 12,II,1:1
Spook House 1930,My 25,IX,3:1; 1930,Je 4,33:3
Spook Sonata, The 1924,Ja 7,23:3; 1924,Ja 13,VII,1:1; 1927,Jl 10,VII,2:3
Spooks 1925,Je 2,16:4
Spoon River Anthology 1950,Ja 16,18:5; 1963,My 2,40:5; 1963,S 30,23:2; 1963,O 8,40:5; 1964,F 15,14:7; 1964,Je 27,15:2
Sport 1930,F 16,IX,4:4
Sport of Kings, The 1926,My 5,24:2; 1928,Ag 26,VII,1:3
Sporting Blood 1929,Jl 28,VIII,1:6
Sporting Thing to Do, The 1923,F 20,12:2; 1923,F 25,VII,1:1
Sposa e la Cavalla, La 1937,Mr 22,26:5
Spot of Bother 1937,Jl 7,26:2
Spot on the Sun, The 1927,Jl 24,VII,1:7; 1927,D 25,VIII,2:3
Spots of the Leopard, The 1963,S 25,38:1
Spread Eagle 1927,Ap 5,30:2; 1927,Ap 10,VIII,1:1; 1928,Jl 22,VII,1:3; 1929,N 10,X,4:8; 1935,N 5,33:6
Spread It Abroad 1936,Ap 2,29:5; 1936,My 3,X,1:2
Spree de Corps 1955,D 9,33:8
Spretti 1923,N 7,14:1
Spring, The 1921,F 6,VI,1:2
Spring, 1600 1934,F 1,14:1; 1934,Mr 4,IX,3:8
Spring Again 1941,O 28,28:3; 1941,N 11,28:2
Spring Cleaning 1923,N 10,16:3; 1923,N 18,VIII,1:1
Spring Dance 1936,Jl 7,22:2; 1936,Ag 26,17:4
Spring Fever 1925,Ag 4,14:2
Spring Freshet 1934,O 5,28:3
Spring-Heeled Jack 1970,Ag 27,41:2
Spring in Autumn 1933,O 25,22:5; 1937,Ag 17,23:1
Spring Is Here 1929,Mr 12,26:1
Spring Meeting 1938,Je 19,IX,2:1; 1938,D 9,30:4
Spring Production 1944,My 20,12:4
Spring Song 1927,D 22,26:3; 1932,Ag 14,IX,1:6; 1934,O 2,18:2

Spring Thaw 1938,Mr 22,18:1
Spring Tide 1936,Ag 9,IX,1:5
Spring Tonic 1936,My 11,16:1
Spring 3100 1928,F 16,14:2
Springboard, The 1927,O 2,VIII,4:6; 1927,O 13,23:1
Spring's Awakening 1955,O 10,30:2
Springtime 1924,My 11,VIII,1:4
Springtime Folly 1951,F 27,23:4
Springtime for Henry 1931,D 10,29:2; 1932,Ja 10,VIII,1:1; 1932,D 4,IX,3:8; 1933,My 2,20:5; 1936,Je 23,27:6; 1936,Je 30,15:1; 1938,Ag 31,12:5; 1940,F 27,16:3; 1951,Mr 15,36:2
Springtime of Youth 1922,O 27,15:1
Squall, The 1926,N 12,20:1; 1927,D 4,X,1:3
Square, The 1961,Mr 24,37:1
Square Crooks 1926,Mr 2,23:2
Square in the Eye 1965,My 20,54:1; 1965,Je 6,II,1:1
Square Peg, A 1923,Ja 29,10:2; 1923,F 11,VII,1:1
Square Root of Wonderful, The 1957,O 31,40:1; 1970,Mr 12,47:1
Squaring the Circle 1931,Ap 27,24:4; 1931,D 13,VIII,3:1; 1935,S 22,X,3:2; 1935,O 4,24:6; 1936,Ag 12,15:3; 1941,S 7,IX,2:5
Squaring the Triangle 1921,Je 14,15:2
Squat Betty 1964,F 25,24:1
Squaw Man, The 1921,D 27,10:3
Squeaker, The 1928,Je 24,VIII,4:2
Squealer, The 1928,N 13,36:3
Stag, The 1929,Ap 21,IX,2:1
Stag at Bay, The 1935,Jl 30,17:1
Stage Affair, A 1962,Ja 17,30:2
Stage Door 1936,S 29,35:1; 1936,O 4,IX,2:1; 1936,O 23,26:3; 1936,N 1,X,1:1
Stags at Bay 1934,D 15,9:2
Staircase 1968,Ja 11,41:2; 1968,Ja 21,II,3:7
Staircase, The 1923,Ja 29,11:2
Stairs, The 1927,N 8,32:7
Stairs to the Roof 1947,F 26,35:4
Stalag 17 1951,My 9,41:2; 1953,Ap 6,24:2
Star and Garter 1942,Je 25,26:2; 1942,S 13,VIII,1:1
Star of Bengal 1929,S 26,27:2
Star Spangled 1936,Mr 6,25:4; 1936,Mr 11,23:1
Star Spangled Family 1945,Ap 11,18:6
Star-Spangled Girl, The 1966,D 22,38:1; 1967,Ja 8,II,1:5
Star Time 1944,S 13,16:2; 1944,S 17,II,1:1
Star Turns Red, The 1940,Mr 24,IX,2:5
Star-Wagon, The 1937,S 17,28:5; 1937,S 30,18:5; 1937,O 10,XI,1:1
Starcross Story, The 1954,Ja 14,25:2
Stardust 1935,Jl 17,22:4
Starlight 1924,O 5,VIII,1:3; 1925,Mr 4,17:2; 1925,Mr 8,VII,1:1; 1925,Mr 15,VIII,1:1
Stars and Stripes 1968,My 9,55:2
Stars in Your Eyes 1939,F 10,18:2; 1939,Mr 5,X,1:2
Stars on Ice 1942,Jl 3,12:2
Stars on Ice (2d Edition) 1943,Je 25,13:2
Stars Turn Red, The 1962,O 25,47:1
Starweed 1926,S 19,IX,1:3
State of the Union 1945,N 7,21:3; 1945,N 15,25:2; 1945,N 25,II,1:1; 1946,S 8,II,1:1; 1947,Jl 15,26:2
Statisterna 1931,O 11,VIII,4:6
Stay Down Miner 1936,My 11,16:4
Steadfast 1923,O 31,12:1
Steal the Old Man's Bundle 1970,My 16,30:1
Steam Roller, The 1924,O 26,VIII,2:1; 1924,N 11,20:2
Steambath 1970,Jl 1,49:1; 1970,Jl 2,30:3; 1970,Jl 12,II,1:3; 1970,O 11,II,1:1
Steamship Tenacity 1922,Ja 3,20:2
Steel 1931,N 19,26:5; 1939,D 20,30:2
Stella Brady 1931,O 11,VIII,4:3
Stella Dallas 1924,Ja 20,VII,2:8
Stellvertreter, Der 1963,F 23,7:8; 1963,S 10,46:1; 1963,S 26,41:4; 1963,S 27,19:3
Stempellbrueder 1929,N 24,X:2:4
Stempenu, the Fiddler 1929,Mr 9,24:7
Step a Little Closer 1948,My 28,26:6
Step on a Crack 1962,O 18,48:1
Stepdaughters of War 1930,O 7,27:1
Stephen D 1962,S 25,31:3; 1962,D 21,7:2; 1963,F 14,5:2; 1966,Ag 5,17:1; 1967,S 25,58:1; 1967,O 8,II,1:6
Steppe Around 1922,Mr 29,17:4
Stepping Out 1929,My 21,29:1
Stepping Sisters 1930,Ap 23,24:2
Stepping Stone, The 1963,My 24,16:2
Stepping Stones 1923,N 7,14:3
Steps Leading Up 1941,Ap 19,20:6
Stepsisters 1936,O 13,32:3
Stevedore 1934,Ap 19,33:2; 1934,Ap 29,IX,1:1; 1934,O 2,18:2; 1935,My 7,26:2; 1949,F 23,30:2
Steward's Tale, The 1969,F 4,34:1
Stewed Prunes 1960,N 15,47:1
Stick-in-the-Mud 1935,D 2,18:2
Stiffkey Scandals of 1932, The 1969,Je 14,24:3
Stigma 1927,F 11,19:1
Still Life 1936,D 1,31:1; 1937,Ag 24,24:5; 1937,D 13,22:8; 1958,Mr 11,33:1; 1958,Mr 16,II,1:1; 1967,My 4,34:1
Still Waters 1925,S 8,21:5; 1926,F 26,24:2; 1926,Mr 2,23:1; 1926,Mr 7,VIII,1:2
Stockade 1954,F 5,14:2

Stockholm Is Stockholm 1930,N 2,VIII,3:2
Stolen Fruit 1925,O 8,31:4; 1925,N 8,VIII,1:1
Stomp 1969,N 17,60:1; 1969,N 23,II,1:1
Stone for Danny Fisher, A 1954,O 22,24:2
Stone Tower, The 1962,Ag 24,14:2
Stop, You're Killing Me 1969,Mr 20,53:1
Stop-Over 1938,Ja 12,16:5
Stop Press 1935,F 22,26:4; 1935,Mr 17,VIII,1:4; 1939,Mr 20,13:2
Stop the World-I Want to Get Off 1962,S 17,39:3; 1962,O 4,45:4; 1962,O 14,II,1:1
Stories From the Vienna Woods 1931,D 27,VIII,1:4
Stork, The 1925,Ja 27,14:2; 1930,N 2,VIII,3:2
Stork Is Dead, The 1932,S 24,18:2
Stork Mad 1936,O 1,28:4
Storm 1924,Ag 24,VII,1:3
Storm, The 1929,D 29,VIII,2:1; 1962,Mr 31,17:2
Storm Center 1927,D 1,33:2
Storm Child 1935,Jl 16,24:1; 1936,Ap 18,18:4
Storm in a Teacup 1936,F 6,23:1
Storm Operation 1944,Ja 12,28:2
Storm Over Patsy 1937,Mr 2,16:4; 1937,Mr 9,26:4; 1937,Mr 14,XI,1:1
Storm Song 1931,Ja 4,VIII,2:2; 1936,Jl 7,22:1
Story for a Sunday Evening, A 1950,N 18,10:5
Story for Strangers, A 1948,S 22,39:2
Story of Mary Surratt, The 1947,F 10,25:2
Story of Miss N N, The 1942,S 28,13:1
Story of the Glorious Resurrection of Our Lord, The 1962,Je 10,II,1:1
Story of the Wolf 1932,N 6,IX,3:4
Story Teller, The 1951,D 15,11:3
Story Theater 1970,O 27,54:1; 1970,N 8,II,1:1
Story Theater Repertory 1970,O 21,40:1
Story to Be Whispered, A 1942,Ag 20,21:4
Strada, La 1969,D 15,63:1
Straight Thru the Door 1928,O 5,17:2
Straight Up 1970,S 2,30:2
Strana Avventura, Una 1930,O 27,17:6
Strange Bedfellows 1948,Ja 15,27:3
Strange Case of Martin Richter, The 1968,N 6,34:2
Strange Child 1935,F 26,16:1
Strange Fruit 1945,N 30,18:6
Strange Gods 1933,Ap 17,16:6
Strange Interlude 1928,Ja 31,28:1; 1928,F 5,VIII,1:1; 1928,Jl 1,VIII,3:5; 1928,D 18,37:3; 1929,O 1,34:8; 1931,F 4,21:2; 1931,F 22,VIII,1:3; 1937,Ja 5,19:1; 1963,Mr 13,5:2; 1963,Je 18,34:6; 1964,Mr 1,II,1:1
Strange Orchestra 1932,O 23,IX,1:1; 1933,N 29,23:2
Strange Play, A 1944,Je 2,20:3
Strange Prince, The 1926,D 8,24:2
Strange Rhythm 1937,Ap 20,29:2
Strange Shadow 1949,Jl 20,30:4
Stranger, The 1935,N 7,26:2; 1945,F 13,21:2; 1945,F 18,II,1:2; 1949,S 2,14:1
Stranger in the Hills 1949,O 10,19:2
Strangers at Home 1934,S 15,20:5
Strangler Fig, The 1940,My 7,31:2
Straw, The 1921,N 11,16:2
Straw Hat, The 1926,O 15,20:2; 1937,D 31,8:2; 1939,S 30,10:6
Straw Hero, The 1936,N 24,35:1
Strawberry Blonde, The 1927,F 8,20:3
Streamline 1934,S 29,13:1; 1934,O 21,IX,1:3
Street Scene 1929,Ja 11,20:4; 1929,Ja 20,VIII,1:1; 1929,My 19,IX,1:1; 1929,N 17,IX,2:6; 1929,N 29,24:5; 1930,Mr 16,IX,4:1; 1930,S 10,14:2; 1930,S 28,VIII,2:4; 1947,Ja 10,17:2; 1947,Ja 19,II,1:1
Street Singer, The 1929,Jl 28,VIII,1:6; 1929,S 18,35:2
Street Singers 1938,D 12,25:6
Street Sounds 1970,O 23,32:1
Street Wolf, The 1929,Ja 1,61:1
Streetcar Named Desire, A 1947,D 4,42:2; 1947,D 14,II,3:1; 1949,Je 12,II,1:1; 1949,S 29,38:1; 1949,O 13,33:6; 1949,N 29,36:6; 1949,D 11,II,3:1; 1950,My 24,36:1; 1955,Mr 4,18:2; 1956,F 16,24:1; 1965,F 19,27:1
Streets Are Guarded, The 1944,N 21,19:7; 1944,N 26,II,1:1
Streets of New York, The 1931,O 7,29:1; 1934,Jl 21,14:5; 1963,O 30,47:1
Streets of Paris, The 1939,Je 20,25:2; 1939,Je 25,IX,1:1
Strega, La 1939,Jl 23,IX,5:3
Strictly Dishonorable 1929,S 19,37:1; 1929,S 29,IX,1:1; 1929,D 17,29:2; 1931,Mr 11,23:5; 1931,Mr 29,VIII,2:1; 1931,Ap 12,IX,1:3
Strike Me Pink 1933,Mr 6,16:3
Strike Up the Band 1929,D 29,VIII,4:3; 1930,Ja 15,29:1
String 1969,Ag 2,37:1; 1969,Ap 13,II,1:1
Stringing Broadway 1932,Mr 7,13:2
Strings, My Lord, Are False, The 1942,Mr 18,29:3; 1942,My 20,24:2
Strip for Action 1942,O 1,26:2; 1942,O 11,VIII,1:1
Strip Girl 1935,O 21,22:6
Stripped 1929,Je 9,VIII,1:2; 1929,O 13,IX,5:1; 1929,O 22,26:1
Strong, The 1924,F 27,15:3
Strong Are Lonely, The 1953,S 30,38:3; 1956,F 5,II,3:1
Strong Breed, The 1967,N 10,60:1; 1967,N 26,II,1:1

Strong Man's House, A 1929,Je 30,VIII,1:2; 1929,S 17,34:3
Strong Sex, The 1937,Ja 14,17:4
Stronger, The 1949,Je 15,38:2; 1956,F 22,23:2; 1965,N 11,59:1
Stronger Than Love 1925,D 20,VII,4:1; 1925,D 29,20:2
Struggle for the Negev 1953,D 14,45:5
Strut Miss Lizzie 1922,Je 20,22:6
Stubble Before Swords 1936,Mr 24,26:8
Student Gypsy, The 1963,O 1,34:1
Student of Vich 1929,Ja 3,25:2
Student Prince, The 1924,D 3,25:3; 1931,Ja 30,18:1; 1932,N 20,IX,3:3; 1936,Jl 12,II,5:2; 1937,Jl 28,15:1; 1943,Je 9,16:2; 1961,Jl 14,14:1
Study in Color 1964,Ag 1,13:1
Sturm im Wasserglas 1930,D 28,VIII,2:4
Styles in Acting 1932,Ap 3,VIII,13:3
Stylish Stouts 1926,S 19,IX,1:3
Subject Was Roses, The 1964,My 26,45:1; 1964,Je 7,II,1:1
Submarine S-4 1929,My 26,IX,2:3
Subscriber, The 1968,N 5,53:2
Subscription List, The 1960,Je 3,26:1
Substitute, The 1960,Je 10,37:1
Substitute for Murder 1935,O 23,18:6
Suburban Tragedy 1966,Mr 7,22:1
Subway, The 1929,Ja 26,15:1; 1929,Jl 15,25:4
Subway Express 1929,S 25,34:3
Subway in the Sky 1957,F 28,19:1
Subways Are for Sleeping 1961,D 28,22:1
Success 1923,Jl 8,VI,1:1
Success Story 1932,S 27,24:4; 1932,O 2,IX,1:1; 1934,Ja 2,17:4
Successful Calamity, A 1921,Mr 19,11:2
Successor, The 1964,F 26,43:2
Such a Nice Young Man 1920,Jl 11,VI,1:6
Such Is Life 1927,S 1,27:3
Such Men Are Dangerous 1928,O 7,IX,2:7
Sudden and Accidental Re-education of Horse Johnson, The 1968,D 19,63:1
Sudden End of Anne Cinquefoil, The 1961,Ja 11,25:2
Suddenly a Stranger 1936,Ag 4,15:2
Suddenly Last Summer 1958,Ja 8,23:4; 1958,Ja 19,II,1:1
Suds in Your Eye 1944,Ja 13,15:5
Sue, Dear 1922,Jl 11,16:2
Sugar Hill 1931,D 26,15:2
Sugar Plum 1939,Ap 2,X,1:7
Suicide Club, The 1929,Mr 10,X,4:5
Suicide Love 1924,S 7,VII,1:4
Suit Tragicue de Raspoutine 1924,Je 15,VII,1:4
Sujet de Roman, Un 1923,Ja 14,VII,1:1; 1923,Je 10,VII,1:4
Summer and Smoke 1947,Jl 9,18:5; 1947,Ag 10,II,1:1; 1948,O 7,33:2; 1948,O 17,II,1:1; 1950,O 29,II,3:7; 1951,N 23,32:7; 1952,Ja 25,13:5; 1952,F 10,II,2:3; 1952,Ap 25,19:5; 1952,My 4,II,1:1
Summer Day's Dream 1949,S 9,28:5; 1949,O 9,II,3:7
Summer Ghost, A 1962,Ap 27,26:1
Summer Night 1939,N 3,17:1
Summer of Daisy Miller, The 1963,My 28,33:1
Summer of the Seventeenth Doll 1958,Ja 23,23:2; 1959,O 14,52:1; 1968,F 21,59:1; 1968,Mr 3,II,3:1
Summer Pygmies, The 1960,D 13,24:6
Summer Wives 1936,Ap 14,18:1
Summertree 1968,Mr 4,29:1; 1968,Mr 17,II,1:6; 1969,D 10,60:1
Sun and I, The 1933,Ap 4,15:2; 1937,F 27,9:5; 1949,Mr 21,18:4
Sun Field, The 1942,D 10,33:2
Sun Kissed 1937,Mr 11,20:2
Sun-Kist 1921,My 24,20:2
Sun Never Sets, The 1938,Je 26,IX,2:1
Sun Showers 1923,F 6,14:2
Sun-Up 1923,My 25,28:1; 1925,My 5,25:1; 1925,Ag 14,13:4; 1928,S 18,34:6; 1928,O 23,33:1; 1929,F 19,22:6; 1930,My 10,25:1
Sunday Breakfast 1952,My 30,12:2
Sunday Dinner 1970,N 3,28:1; 1970,N 8,II,1:1
Sunday in New York 1961,N 10,40:1
Sunday Man, The 1964,My 14,41:3
Sunday Nights at Nine 1933,N 13,20:7; 1934,Mr 5,18:5; 1934,N 19,12:1; 1935,N 11,21:1; 1936,D 7,27:3
Sundown Beach 1948,S 8,37:1; 1948,S 12,II,1:1
Sunken Bell, The 1932,O 9,IX,1:8
Sunny 1925,S 23,22:1; 1925,S 27,VII,1:6
Sunny Days 1928,F 9,29:1
Sunny River 1941,D 5,28:2
Sunrise at Campobello 1958,Ja 31,25:1; 1958,F 9,II,1:1
Sunset 1966,My 13,34:1
Sunshine 1926,Ag 18,15:2
Sunshine Sisters 1933,N 26,IX,3:6
Sunstroke 1969,D 8,60:4
Sunup to Sundown 1938,F 2,14:3
Supper for the Dead 1954,Jl 7,23:1
Suppressed Desires 1920,F 10,10:2
Suprise for the Countess, A 1930,Mr 25,34:6
Sur la Dalle 1923,O 30,17:2
Sur le Banc 1923,O 16,18:1
Surcouf 1926,N 7,VIII,2:7; 1926,N 14,VIII,2:1

Sure Fire! 1926,O 21,23:1
Surgeon, The 1932,O 28,23:1
Surmise 1927,O 23,VIII,1:3
Survival of the Fittest 1921,Mr 15,14:1; 1921,Mr 20,VI,1:1
Survivors, The 1948,Ja 20,27:2; 1948,Ja 25,II,1:1
Susan and God 1937,Ap 11,II,12:3; 1937,Ap 25,X,2:6; 1937,O 8,26:4; 1937,O 17,XI,1:1; 1938,Ja 23,XI,1:6; 1943,D 14,30:2
Susan Slept Here 1961,Jl 12,35:2
Susanna, Don't You Cry 1939,My 23,27:2
Susannah 1955,F 25,18:4
Susannah and the Elders 1937,N 21,XI,3:6; 1938,Ag 2,15:5; 1940,O 13,47:7; 1940,O 30,28:2; 1959,O 19,37:3
Susie Is a Good Girl 1968,N 5,53:2
Suspect 1937,F 17,16:2; 1937,Mr 7,XI,2:1; 1940,Ap 10,30:4
Suspense 1930,Ap 10,24:5; 1930,Ap 27,IX,1:8; 1930,Ag 13,22:3
Suzanne 1929,F 17,IX,4:2
Suzette 1921,N 25,18:3; 1921,D 4,VII,1:2
Swan, The 1923,O 14,VIII,2:4; 1923,O 24,15:3; 1923,O 28,VIII,1:1; 1930,Jl 27,VIII,1:8; 1936,Je 30,15:1; 1954,Ag 17,16:6
Swan Song 1946,My 16,29:2; 1951,O 16,35:2
Swanee River 1923,S 15,VI,1:2
Swedenhielms 1931,Mr 1,VIII,3:1
Sweeney Agonistes 1935,O 2,26:2
Sweeney Todd 1924,Jl 19,10:4; 1957,Ag 28,21:4
Sweet Adeline 1929,Ag 25,VIII,3:1; 1929,S 4,33:1; 1929,S 15,IX,1:8
Sweet Aloes 1934,N 1,24:1; 1936,F 25,23:5; 1936,Mr 5,24:5
Sweet and Low 1930,N 18,28:5
Sweet Bird of Youth 1956,Ap 17,27:2; 1959,Mr 11,39:2; 1959,Mr 22,II,1:1
Sweet Chariot 1930,O 12,VIII,4:1; 1930,O 24,30:2
Sweet Charity 1942,D 29,26:4; 1966,Ja 31,22:1; 1967,Jl 1,13:1; 1967,O 13,34:3
Sweet Confession 1959,Ap 15,30:1
Sweet Enemy, The 1965,F 16,39:1
Sweet Eros 1968,N 22,38:1
Sweet Genevieve 1945,Mr 21,27:3
Sweet Land of Liberty 1929,S 24,29:2
Sweet Little Devil 1924,Ja 22,15:4
Sweet Miani 1962,S 26,33:2
Sweet Mystery of Life 1935,O 12,13:3
Sweet Nell of Old Drury 1923,My 19,16:4
Sweet Peggy Clive 1924,F 12,20:2
Sweet River 1936,O 29,30:2
Sweet Seventeen 1924,Mr 18,24:2
Sweet Shadow 1935,Ag 7,22:2
Sweet Stranger 1930,O 22,23:3
Sweet William 1921,My 29,VI,1:7
Sweetheart Shop, The 1920,S 1,13:4
Sweetheart Time 1926,Ja 20,23:2
Sweethearts 1929,S 23,25:1; 1947,Ja 22,31:2; 1947,F 2,II,1:1
Swifty 1922,O 17,14:1
Swing Along 1936,S 20,IX,1:4
Swing It 1937,Jl 23,17:2
Swing Mikado, The 1939,Mr 2,18:2; 1939,Mr 12,XI,1:1
Swing Out, Sweet Land! 1944,N 10,24:6
Swing Sister Wac Swing 1944,Ja 4,20:4
Swing Your Lady 1935,N 16,19:4; 1936,O 19,22:4
Swingin' the Dream 1939,N 30,24:2
Switch in Time, A 1955,My 26,34:1
Swords 1921,S 2,9:3; 1921,S 11,VI,1:1; 1921,N 20,VI,1:1
Sylvia 1923,Ap 26,22:1
Symphony 1935,Ap 27,20:3
Symphony in Two Flats 1930,S 17,30:4
Synthetic Sin 1927,O 11,26:2
System du Docteur Goudron et du Professeur Plume, Le 1923,N 13,24:2

T

Ta Bouche 1929,Mr 15,28:5
Tableau, Le 1963,S 4,34:3
Tableaux 1961,D 18,41:3
Tabloid 1929,S 29,IX,5:1
Taboo 1922,Ap 5,22:1
Tabula Rasa 1970,O 13,52:2
Taciturne, Un 1931,N 22,VIII,1:6
Tadpole, The 1931,D 9,VIII,2:7
Tailor Becomes a Storekeeper, The 1938,Ap 14,26:3
Tailor-Made Man, A 1929,O 22,26:3
Takatsuki 1960,Je 17,35:4
Take a Bow 1944,Je 16,15:3
Take a Brace 1923,Ap 20,20:3
Take a Chance 1932,N 28,11:2
Take a Gander 1956,D 14,36:4
Take a Giant Step 1953,O 4,II,1:1; 1956,S 26,30:1
Take Back Your Freedom 1940,S 1,IX,2:2
Take Her, She's Mine 1961,D 22,19:1
Take It As It Comes 1944,F 11,17:2
Take It Away 1936,D 15,30:5; 1936,D 22,32:3
Take It Easy 1950,D 25,23:6
Take It From the Top 1967,N 23,59:2

Take Me Along 1959,O 23,22:2; 1959,N 1,II,1:1
Take Me to Bed 1969,Je 14,24:1
Take My Advice 1927,N 2,24:3
Take My Tip 1932,Ap 12,25:2
Take One Step 1968,Jl 5,17:1
Take the Air 1927,N 23,28:2
Take Two From One 1931,O 4,VIII,2:6
Taken From Life 1938,Ja 29,34:4
Tale of Kasane, The 1969,F 25,36:1
Tale of the Soldier, The 1927,Ag 14,VII,1:7
Tale of the Wolf, The 1925,S 27,VII,2:1; 1925,O 8,31:2; 1925,O 18,IX,1:2
Tale Retold, A 1928,My 10,31:1
Talent '49 1949,Ap 13,39:4
Talent '54 1954,Ap 13,40:1
Tales of Hoffmann 1932,Ja 10,VIII,1:6
Tales of Rigo 1927,My 31,25:3
Talk About Girls 1927,Je 15,31:3
Talking Parrot, The 1923,D 4,25:3
Talking to You 1942,Ag 18,17:1; 1961,O 23,22:5
Tall Kentuckian, The 1953,Je 17,30:1
Tall Story 1959,Ja 30,33:2
Talley Method, The 1941,F 25,26:3; 1941,Mr 2,IX,1:1
Tambor y Cascabel 1932,Ap 21,25:4
Tambourine 1925,D 30,10:2
Tambourines to Glory 1963,N 4,47:1
Tamburlaine the Great 1951,O 14,II,3:7; 1956,Ja 20,19:1; 1956,Ja 29,II,1:1
Tame Cat, The 1926,Ja 10,VII,1:3
Taming of the Shrew, The 1921,My 12,20:2; 1923,O 16,19:3; 1924,N 25,27:3; 1925,D 19,14:1; 1925,D 27,VII,1:1; 1927,My 4,29:1; 1927,O 26,26:4; 1927,N 13,IX,1:1; 1928,My 27,VIII,1:8; 1930,Mr 28,22:8; 1933,N 5,IX,3:1; 1935,Ap 23,24:1; 1935,S 22,X,3:2; 1935,S 29,X,3:1; 1935,O 1,27:3; 1935,O 20,X,1:1; 1936,Ap 14,18:4; 1937,Ap 11,XI,2:1; 1939,Ap 23,X,2:4; 1939,My 9,28:4; 1940,F 6,17:2; 1941,Ag 17,IX,1:8; 1947,D 7,II,7:1; 1951,Ap 26,35:2; 1951,N 18,II,3:1; 1954,Jl 1,22:2; 1954,Jl 4,II,1:1; 1956,Ag 6,20:1; 1956,Ag 11,11:2; 1956,Ag 26,II,1:1; 1957,F 21,30:2; 1960,Je 22,29:1; 1960,Ag 20,17:1; 1962,Ap 24,33:3; 1962,Je 21,25:1; 1963,Mr 8,9:1; 1965,Je 24,32:2; 1965,Jl 3,10:5; 1966,F 5,32:1
T'Amo E Sarai Mia 1932,Mr 21,19:4
Tancred 1923,Jl 17,14:4
Tangerine 1921,Ag 10,8:2
Tangletoes 1925,F 18,17:1
Tango 1968,Ja 1,11:1; 1969,Ja 20,33:1; 1969,F 9,II,12:1
Tantrum, The 1924,My 18,VII,2:4; 1924,S 5,20:2
Tanyard Street 1941,F 5,16:2
Tanzgraefin, Die 1925,S 18,26:3
Tap Happening 1969,Je 20,36:1
Tapestry in Gray 1935,D 28,10:2
Taps 1925,Ap 15,16:2
Tarnish 1923,O 2,10:1
Tarot 1970,D 12,19:1
Tars and Spars 1944,Ap 7,23:1
Tartuffe 1922,N 23,21:3; 1930,F 2,VIII,4:1; 1957,O 9,39:1; 1961,Mr 1,28:1; 1964,Mr 10,42:2; 1965,Ja 15,23:1; 1967,S 18,60:1; 1968,Je 12,39:1; 1968,Je 23,II,1:1; 1968,Jl 3,28:2
Tarzan of the Apes 1921,S 8,14:3
Taste of Honey, A 1959,F 12,24:7; 1959,Mr 15,II,3:1; 1960,O 5,46:1; 1960,N 6,II,1:1; 1961,My 17,43:1
Tattar-Adel 1939,S 17,X,2:4
Tattle Tales 1930,Jl 20,VIII,2:1; 1933,Je 2,22:6
Tattooed Countess, The 1961,My 4,40:2
Tavern, The 1920,S 28,14:1; 1920,O 10,VI,1:1; 1921,Ja 23,VI,1:1; 1921,My 24,20:1; 1930,My 20,32:1; 1962,Ap 5,29:1; 1964,Mr 6,39:2
Tchin-Tchin 1962,O 9,37:3; 1962,O 26,26:2; 1962,N 25,II,1:1
Tea and Sympathy 1953,O 1,35:1; 1953,O 11,II,1:1; 1954,Ag 15,II,1:1; 1956,D 4,50:1; 1957,Ap 26,22:5
Tea for Three 1935,Jl 9,24:4
Tea Party 1968,O 16,40:1; 1968,N 3,II,7:4
Teahouse of the August Moon, The 1953,O 16,32:1; 1953,O 25,II,1:1; 1954,Mr 10,30:2; 1954,Ap 23,23:6; 1954,Ap 23,23:5; 1954,My 2,II,3:1; 1954,My 20,37:1; 1954,S 12,II,1:1; 1954,S 18,13:4; 1955,F 17,22:1; 1955,My 10,24:1; 1955,Ag 7,60:3; 1955,Ag 14,II,1:5; 1956,Ap 20,22:1; 1956,My 7,31:8; 1956,My 29,32:1; 1956,Je 4,25:4; 1956,N 9,33:2
Teaser, The 1921,Jl 28,8:3
Teaspoon Every Four Hours, A 1969,Je 16,57:1
Technique 1931,My 15,21:1
Teddy and Partner 1933,F 12,IX,3:4
Telemachus Clay 1963,N 16,17:2
Telephone, The 1947,My 2,28:2; 1947,My 11,II,1:1; 1948,Ap 30,26:3; 1948,D 8,41:6; 1950,Jl 20,22:5
Tell Her the Truth 1932,O 29,18:2
Tell Me More 1925,Ap 14,27:3
Tell Me Pretty Maiden 1937,D 17,33:5
Tell My Story 1939,Mr 16,26:6
Temoin, Le 1936,F 23,X,2:3
Temper the Wind 1946,D 28,10:2; 1947,Ja 12,II,1:1
Temperance Town, A 1929,Ag 11,VIII,2:1

Tempest, The 1929,D 30,16:2; 1934,F 4,IX,3:4;
1934,Ap 17,26:6; 1940,Ap 1,14:2; 1945,Ja 26,17:2;
1945,F 4,II,1:1; 1945,N 13,24:6; 1950,S 17,II,3:7;
1952,Ap 13,II,3:8; 1955,Ag 2,18:2; 1955,Ag 7,II,1:1;
1955,S 3,8:6; 1957,Ag 14,21:1; 1959,D 28,19:2;
1960,Je 20,35:1; 1960,Je 26,II,1:1; 1962,Je 22,14:1;
1962,Jl 17,18:2; 1963,Ap 3,43:1; 1970,F 15,67:1;
1970,Ag 29,14:1
Tempest, The: or, The Enchanted Forest
1959,Je 10,42:2
Tempest in a Top Hat, A 1938,Ap 24,II,2:8
Temporary Island, A 1948,Mr 15,27:3
Temps d'Aimer, Le 1926,D 12,VIII,3:4
Temps Difficiles, Le 1934,Mr 11,X,2:4
Ten Little Indians 1944,Je 28,21:2
Ten Million Ghosts 1936,O 24,23:7
Ten Minute Alibi 1933,O 18,24:3; 1935,Je 11,24:4;
1937,Jl 20,19:3
Ten Nights in a Barroom 1927,Ja 16,VII,1:1;
1928,Mr 28,31:2; 1930,My 25,IX,2:3;
1932,Ja 21,17:1
Ten Per Cent 1927,S 14,29:3
Ten Sixty-Six and All That 1935,My 26,XI,2:5;
1938,Mr 11,14:2
Tender Trap, The 1954,O 14,37:2; 1961,Ag 26,15:1
Tenderloin 1960,O 18,47:2; 1960,O 30,II,1:1
Tendresse, La 1921,Ap 10,VI,1:1; 1922,S 26,18:1;
1922,O 1,VII,1:1
Tenth Avenue 1927,Ag 16,31:1
Tenth Commandment, The 1926,N 18,27:1
Tenth Man, The 1929,Mr 21,29:2; 1959,N 6,24:2;
1959,N 15,II,1:1; 1961,Ap 14,23:4; 1962,O 3,46:1;
1966,Ap 23,15:6; 1967,N 9,54:1
Tenth of an Inch Makes the Difference, A
1962,N 13,44:1
Tenting Tonight 1947,Ap 3,32:2
Tents of Israel 1929,My 26,IX,1:3
Teresa of Avila 1961,S 13,55:1
Terminal 1970,Ap 15,51:2; 1970,My 24,II,3:1
Terminus 1928,S 30,IX,2:1
Terrain Vague 1931,Mr 1,VIII,2:6
Terre d'Israel 1930,O 12,VIII,4:2
Terrible Jim Fitch 1969,Mr 20,53:1
Terrible Meek, The 1930,My 4,XI,3:1
Terrible Swift Sword, The 1955,N 16,42:1
Terrible Turk, The 1934,F 25,IX,1:6
Terzett zu Viert 1933,O 22,IX,2:3
Tess of the d'Urbervilles 1929,Ag 18,VIII,1:3
Tessa 1935,Ja 6,IX,2:1
Testamento della Zia d'America, Il 1936,Mr 23,22:4
Tevye and His Daughters 1957,S 17,38:2
1957,S 29,II,1:1
Tevye the Dairyman 1935,O 25,25:1; 1970,D 6,84:8
Texas Li'l Darlin' 1949,N 26,10:5
Texas Nightingale, The 1922,N 21,15:2;
1922,D 3,VIII,1:1
Texas Steer, A 1968,N 13,39:1
Texas Town 1941,Ap 30,22:3
Thais 1931,Je 19,21:3
Thank You 1921,O 4,10:2; 1921,O 16,VI,1:1
Thank You, Miss Victoria 1966,Ap 12,43:1
Thank You, Mr Pepys 1937,D 1,27:2
Thank You Svoboda 1944,Mr 2,13:2
Thanks for Tomorrow 1938,S 28,28:2
Thark 1927,Jl 24,VII,1:7
That Awful Mrs Eaton! 1924,S 30,27:1
That Day 1922,Jl 9,VI,1:4; 1922,O 4,27:3
That Ferguson Family 1928,D 24,10:7
That 5 A.M. Jazz 1964,O 20,42:2
That French Lady 1927,Mr 16,29:3
That Girl at the Bijou 1956,N 10,15:4;
1956,N 18,II,11:2
That Hat! 1964,S 24,45:1
That Lady 1949,O 20,38:8; 1949,N 23,18:4;
1949,D 4,II,5:1
That Old Devil 1944,Je 6,14:2
That Smith Boy 1926,F 20,13:1
That Sort 1926,Ap 20,24:6
That Summer-That Fall 1967,Mr 17,33:1
That Thing Called Love 1965,My 19,42:1
That's All 1969,N 4,55:2
That's Gratitude 1930,S 12,28:1; 1930,S 21,IX,1:1;
1932,Je 17,24:3
That's That 1924,Ap 30,19:2
That's the Woman 1930,S 4,27:2
That's Your Trouble 1969,N 4,55:2
Theater of Peretz, The 1963,N 6,35:2
Theatre 1941,O 26,IX,2:3; 1941,N 13,34:2
Theatre of Angna Enters, The 1955,Ja 25,22:2
Theatre of Robert Frost, The 1962,My 31,23:6
Theatre of the Piccoli 1940,Mr 22,22:2
Theatre of the Soul 1942,Mr 21,13:5
Theatre Royal 1934,O 24,24:2; 1934,N 11,IX,1:1
Them's the Reporters 1935,My 30,21:4
Then Came the Dawn 1935,Ag 29,25:4
Theodora, the Queen 1934,F 1,15:3
Theophilus 1942,Ja 7,23:2
There Go All of Us 1935,Mr 24,VIII,2:3
There Is a Play Tonight 1961,F 16,24:2
There Is No End 1950,F 17,27:4
There Shall Be No Night 1940,Mr 30,11:2;
1940,Ap 30,25:2; 1940,My 5,X,1:1; 1940,S 10,27:3;
1940,S 22,IX,1:1; 1943,D 16,34:5; 1944,Ja 2,II,1:5

There Was a Little Girl 1960,Mr 1,28:1
There Was a Young Man 1940,F 27,17:4
There Was an Old Woman... 1969,O 16,56:4
There You Are! 1932,My 17,25:4
There'll Be Some Changes Made 1969,O 2,56:2
There's a Girl in My Soup 1967,O 19,58:1;
1967,N 12,II,5:6
There's Always a Breeze 1938,Mr 3,16:2
There's Always Juliet 1931,O 13,26:5; 1932,F 16,24:2;
1932,F 28,VIII,1:1; 1932,O 28,23:2
There's Always Tomorrow 1934,My 13,IX,2:6
There's Wisdom in Women 1935,Jl 16,24:1;
1935,O 31,17:1
Therese 1945,O 10,24:2; 1945,O 28,II,1:1
Theresina 1927,My 8,II,1:8
These Are My Loves 1960,Ap 19,41:2
These Are the Times 1950,My 11,37:2
These Charming People 1925,O 7,31:2;
1925,O 11,VIII,1:1
These Days 1928,N 4,IX,1:3; 1928,N 13,36:2
These Few Ashes 1928,O 31,28:1; 1929,My 5,IX,1:3
These Modern Women 1928,F 14,26:2
These Mortals 1936,Ja 5,IX,1:1
These People 1938,Ap 5,19:2
These Tender Mercies 1948,Je 7,16:4
These Two 1933,Mr 5,IX,1:6; 1934,My 8,28:3
Thesmophoriazusae, The 1955,D 14,52:4
Thespis 1953,Ja 17,13:5
They All Come to Moscow 1933,My 12,20:6
They All Want Something 1926,O 13,20:2
They Came by Night 1937,Jl 8,21:1; 1937,Jl 25,X,1:3
They Came to a City 1943,Je 6,II,1:6
They Can't Get You Down 1941,N 2,IX,3:5
They Don't Grow on Trees 1968,D 7,63:1
They Don't Mean Any Harm 1932,F 24,25:2;
1932,D 4,IX,3:6; 1933,Ag 6,X,1:8
They Had to See Paris 1930,Ap 27,IX,2:3
They Knew What They Wanted 1924,N 25,27:1;
1924,N 30,VIII,1:2; 1936,Jl 7,17:2; 1936,Jl 8,14:2;
1936,Jl 21,13:1; 1936,Jl 28,23:4; 1939,O 3,19:1;
1949,F 17,28:2
They Never Come Back 1920,D 19,I,22:3
They Never Grow Up 1930,Ap 8,27:1
They Shall Not Die 1934,F 22,24:4;
1934,Mr 4,IX,1:3; 1934,Mr 11,X,1:1
They Should Have Stood in Bed 1942,F 14,18:5
They Walk Alone 1939,F 5,IX,3:2; 1941,Mr 13,24:2
Thief, The 1927,Ap 23,15:2; 1927,My 1,VIII,1:1;
1932,F 22,23:4
Thieves 1920,Ap 9,11:4; 1926,Je 8,23:1
Thieves' Carnival 1955,F 2,21:1; 1955,F 13,II,1:2;
1967,Je 5,52:1
Thin Ice 1922,O 2,20:1
Things That Are Caesar's, The 1932,S 18,IX,1:6;
1932,O 18,23:4; 1933,Ja 29,IX,1:3
Third Best Sport 1958,D 31,15:3
Third Day, The 1929,Ag 13,23:4
Third Ear, The 1964,My 29,16:1
Third Little Show, The 1931,My 10,VIII,2:4;
1931,Je 2,34:3; 1931,Je 14,VIII,1:2
Third Parade, The 1933,O 23,18:2
Third Party Risk 1939,My 28,X,2:5
Third Person 1951,N 1,35:3; 1955,D 30,13:4
Third Time Lucky 1929,D 8,X,2:5
Thirst 1929,My 10,32:2
Thirsty Soil 1937,F 4,16:2
13 Belgrave Square 1931,Je 14,VIII,2:2
13 Daughters 1961,Mr 3,17:2
30th of August, The 1969,F 3,3:1
30 Days Hath September 1938,O 1,10:5
39 Steps 1938,Mr 12,13:1
37 Sous de M Montaudoin, Les 1939,F 7,17:2
Thirty Pieces of Silver 1951,Mr 18,42:1
This, Too, Shall Pass 1946,My 1,32:4
This Bird of Dawning Singeth All Night Long
1968,D 31,19:1; 1969,Ja 12,II,1:1
This Earth Is Ours 1940,Ap 26,24:2
This Fine-Pretty World 1923,D 27,11:1
This for Remembrance 1937,Mr 17,31:1
This Happy Breed 1943,My 9,II,1:1; 1952,Ap 4,23:2
This Here Nice Place 1966,N 2,35:2
This Inconstancy 1933,Mr 25,13:6;
1933,Ap 16,IX,1:3
This Is Edwin Booth 1958,Ag 27,32:7
This Is New York 1930,N 29,21:1; 1930,D 7,IX,1:1
This Is the Army 1942,Jl 5,28:2; 1942,Jl 12,VII,6:1;
1942,Ag 16,VIII,1:1; 1943,N 11,30:3;
1943,D 5,II,5:1
This Is the Rill Speaking 1966,Ap 12,43:1
This Is Today 1935,Jl 30,17:2
This Island Is Mine 1959,Jl 1,26:4
This Mad Whirl 1937,Ja 10,II,4:8
This Man's Town 1930,Mr 2,IX,4:7; 1930,Mr 11,24:4
This Marriage 1924,My 18,VII,2:8
This Music Crept by Me Upon the Waters
1953,O 23,20:8; 1959,N 25,19:4
This Night or Never 1930,My 11,IX,3:1
This One Man 1930,O 22,32:3; 1933,Ap 23,X,1:3
This Our House 1935,D 12,33:3
This Property Is Condemned 1956,O 29,34:1;
1960,Ag 26,13:1
This Queen of Sheba 1928,D 2,X,4:2
This Rock 1943,F 19,23:2
This Side Idolatry 1933,O 20,15:4; 1933,N 5,IX,1:3

This Side of Paradise 1962,F 22,19:6
This Story of Yours 1968,D 14,60:4
This Thing Called Love 1928,S 18,32:7;
1929,Ja 27,IX,1:3; 1935,Jl 2,24:4
This Time Tomorrow 1947,N 4,31:2
This Was a Man 1926,N 24,27:1; 1926,N 28,VIII,1:1;
1928,My 20,VIII,2:1
This Was a Woman 1944,Ap 30,II,1:3
This Was Burlesque 1962,Mr 7,29:1; 1965,Mr 17,55:3;
1970,F 12,31:1
This Way Out 1929,Ap 28,24:4
This Way to Paradise 1930,Ja 31,24:2;
1930,F 16,IX,2:1
This Way to the Tomb 1961,D 9,21:1
This Woman Business 1926,D 8,25:1
This Year of Grace 1928,Mr 23,14:2; 1928,N 8,27:1;
1928,N 25,X,1:1; 1929,Ap 21,IX,1:6
Thistle in My Bed 1963,N 20,48:1
Thomas Paine 1927,Ap 10,II,9:4; 1930,Mr 21,30:7;
1938,S 20,27:1
Thor, With Angels 1956,O 15,29:4
Thorntons, The 1956,F 15,26:1
Thoroughbred 1933,N 7,29:2
Thoroughbreds 1924,S 9,12:1
Those Endearing Young Charms 1943,Je 17,16:3
Those Naughty Nineties 1931,S 13,IX,2:7
Those That Play the Clowns 1966,N 25,48:1
Those We Love 1930,F 20,22:2; 1930,Mr 2,IX,1:1
Thou Art the Man 1937,Ap 9,18:5
Thou Desperate Pilot 1927,Mr 8,23:1
Thou Shalt Not- 1938,S 25,IX,3:5
Thoughts on the Instant of Greeting a Friend on the
Street 1968,My 9,55:2; 1968,My 19,II,1:1
Thousand and One Nights 1959,D 16,53:2
Thousand Clowns, A 1962,Ap 6,31:2;
1962,Ap 15,II,1:1
Thousand Generations and One, A 1923,My 9,14:4
Thousand Summers, A 1932,My 25,23:4
Thracian Horses, The 1961,S 28,58:2
Three 1928,D 4,28:2
Three After Three 1939,N 25,13:5
Three and One 1933,O 26,22:6
Three and the Man 1923,Ja 3,9:3
3 Bags Full 1966,Mr 7,22:1
Three Barrows, The 1926,N 28,VIII,1:4
Three Breakfasts 1947,D 29,21:5
Three by Ferlinghetti 1970,S 23,43:1
Three by Thurber 1955,Mr 8,23:2
Three Cheers 1928,O 7,IX,2:3; 1928,O 16,28:1;
1928,O 21,IX,1:1
Three Cities 1938,O 11,20:3
Three-Cornered Moon 1933,Mr 17,20:6;
1934,N 27,27:2; 1935,Je 25,14:5
Three Doors 1925,Ap 24,16:4
Three Estates, The 1959,Ag 26,25:3
3 for Tonight 1955,Ap 7,23:2; 1955,Ap 17,II,1:1
Three Graces, The 1924,F 3,VII,1:4
Three Guardsmen, The 1936,F 17,21:3
Three in Love 1931,S 26,25:5; 1933,N 8,32:5
Three Little Business Men, The 1923,S 4,12:1
Three Little Girls 1930,Mr 30,VIII,2:7;
1930,Ap 15,29:1; 1930,S 28,VIII,2:5
Three Live Ghosts 1920,S 30,12:1; 1920,O 10,VI,1:2
Three Love Affairs 1958,Mr 11,33:1;
1958,Mr 16,II,1:1
Three Men and a Girl 1939,F 6,9:3
Three Men and a Woman 1932,Ja 12,29:2
Three Men on a Horse 1935,Ja 22,22:7;
1935,Ja 31,22:3; 1936,F 19,16:2; 1936,Mr 15,X,2:1;
1936,Mr 24,26:4; 1936,Je 7,IX,1:1; 1942,O 10,10:2;
1969,O 17,35:1; 1969,O 26,II,1:1
Three Months Gone 1970,S 10,59:1
Three Musketeers, The 1921,My 20,18:5;
1928,Mr 4,IX,2:3; 1928,Mr 14,28:1;
1928,Mr 25,IX,1:1; 1929,O 13,IX,4:7;
1968,Je 26,43:1; 1968,Jl 7,II,1:1; 1968,Jl 24,49:2
Three Philip Roth Stories 1970,Jl 31,14:1
Three Pills in a Bottle 1923,My 12,15:4
Three Plays of the Sea 1970,Ag 20,39:1
Three Set Out 1937,Je 23,29:3
Three Showers 1920,Ap 6,18:1
Three Sisters, The 1923,Ja 30,12:2; 1923,F 4,VII,1:1;
1926,O 27,24:1; 1926,N 7,VIII,1:1;
1927,Mr 13,VII,2:4; 1929,F 17,IX,4:2;
1930,Ja 9,22:2; 1938,F 13,X,3:3; 1939,O 16,23:1;
1942,D 22,31:2; 1942,D 27,VIII,1:1; 1955,F 26,13:2;
1955,Mr 20,II,1:1; 1959,S 22,46:1; 1959,O 4,II,1:1;
1963,Je 20,30:7; 1963,Jl 22,19:2; 1964,Je 23,24:1;
1964,Jl 5,II,1:1; 1964,Jl 28,26:7; 1965,F 12,15:1;
1965,My 15,19:4; 1968,Mr 18,56:1; 1969,Ap 4,29:1;
1969,Ag 10,II,3:1; 1969,Ag 31,II,4:1;
1969,O 10,38:1; 1969,O 19,II,3:1; 1970,F 12,30:1;
1970,F 22,II,1:1
Three Thousand Red Ants 1970,S 23,43:1
Three Times the Hour 1931,Ag 26,15:5
Three Times Three 1956,My 24,27:2; 1962,Mr 2,24:1
Three to Make Ready 1946,Mr 8,16:2;
1946,Mr 17,II,1:1
Three Waltzes 1937,N 15,15:6; 1937,D 27,10:2;
1938,Je 26,II,7:5
Three Wise Fools 1936,Ja 14,25:2; 1936,F 2,IX,1:3;
1936,Mr 2,12:2
Three Wishes for Jamie 1952,Mr 22,9:2

Three Women and Mr Clifford 1931,Ja 4,VIII,1:1
Three Young Maids From the Folies Bergere
   1929,Mr 5,28:2
Threepenny Opera, The 1928,D 2,X,4:4;
   1933,Ap 14,22:4; 1954,Mr 11,26:5;
   1954,Mr 21,II,1:1; 1954,Ap 4,II,7:1; 1955,S 21,38:1;
   1956,F 12,83:1; 1956,Mr 11,II,1:1; 1956,Ap 8,II,3:1;
   1956,D 30,II,1:1; 1960,S 15,44:3; 1966,O 28,33:1
Three's a Crowd 1923,F 4,VII,1:4; 1930,O 5,IX,4:6;
   1930,O 16,28:3; 1930,O 26,VIII,1:1
Three's a Family 1943,My 6,24:2; 1943,N 19,24:3
Three...With Women in Mind 1970,N 28,22:1
Thrills 1925,Ap 17,24:3
Throng a' Scarlet 1947,D 2,37:2; 1950,F 6,20:5
Through the Night 1930,Ag 19,19:1
Through the Years 1932,Ja 29,13:3
Thumbs Down 1923,Ag 7,20:1
Thumbs Up! 1934,D 28,24:1; 1935,S 8,IX,1:1
Thunder in the Air 1928,My 6,IX,2:4;
   1929,N 12,34:3
Thunder on the Left 1928,Ag 19,VII,1:1;
   1928,O 21,IX,1:3; 1933,N 1,25:2
Thunder Rock 1939,N 15,18:1; 1939,N 19,X,3:6;
   1940,Jl 29,10:4; 1940,Ag 11,IX,2:4; 1956,F 27,18:1
Thurber Carnival, A 1960,F 27,13:2; 1960,Mr 6,II,1:1;
   1960,S 13,41:1; 1962,Ap 12,42:1
Thursday Evening 1923,My 9,14:4
Thus 1962,Ap 25,31:1
Thy Kingdom Come 1957,Je 25,24:6
Thy Name Is Woman 1920,N 16,19:1;
   1926,Ag 22,VII,1:2
Thy People 1935,Ag 13,20:3
Thy Will be Done 1929,N 14,29:2
Ti-Coq 1951,F 10,10:2; 1951,F 25,II,1:1
Tia Juana 1927,N 16,28:4
Tiara, The 1932,D 12,18:3
Tick-Tack-Toe 1920,F 24,11:2
Ticket-of-Leave Man, The 1933,Jl 4,16:4;
   1934,Je 25,18:5; 1961,D 23,15:1
Tickets, Please! 1950,Ap 28,25:2; 1950,My 7,II,1:1
Tickle Me 1920,Ag 18,9:1
Tickless Time 1918,D 28,9:1
Tidbits of 1946 1946,Jl 9,17:2
Tide Rising 1937,Ja 26,17:2
Tidings Brought to Mary, The 1922,D 25,20:1;
   1922,D 31,VII,1:1; 1929,Ap 7,X,2:7;
   1942,My 21,24:1
Tiefstapler, Der 1932,S 4,IX,2:1
Tierra Baja 1937,My 8,22:4
Ties That Bind (Le Liane) 1929,Ap 22,22:1
Tiger, The 1936,S 15,36:5; 1936,O 4,IX,3:7;
   1963,F 6,5:2
Tiger and the Horse, The 1960,Ag 25,26:5
Tiger at the Gates 1955,Je 3,27:1; 1955,Je 12,II,1:1;
   1955,O 4,35:1; 1955,O 23,II,1:1; 1968,Mr 1,30:1;
   1968,Mr 10,II,1:1
Tiger Cats 1924,Ag 17,VII,1:8; 1924,O 19,VIII,2:6;
   1924,O 22,18:1
Tiger Rag, The 1961,F 17,20:2; 1961,Mr 5,II,1:1
Tiger Smiles, The 1930,D 18,29:1
Tiger Tiger Burning Bright 1962,D 24,5:2
Tight Britches 1934,S 12,26:2
Tightwad, The 1927,Ap 18,18:2
Till the Cows Come Home 1936,O 28,30:6;
   1936,N 15,XI,3:2
Till the Day I Die 1935,Mr 27,24:5
Timber 1936,Jl 29,11:5
Timber House 1936,S 21,27:5
Time 1923,O 14,VIII,2:4; 1923,N 27,23:3
Time, Place and the Girl, The 1942,O 22,24:3
Time and the Conways 1937,Ag 27,23:3;
   1937,S 12,XI,2:1; 1938,Ja 4,19:2
Time and the Hour 1936,O 5,24:1
Time and the Yellow Roses 1961,Je 25,II,3:5
Time for Bed 1969,Je 14,24:1
Time for Elizabeth 1948,S 28,32:3
Time for Singing, A 1966,My 23,48:2
Time for the Gentle People, A 1967,My 26,50:1
Time Gentlemen Please! 1961,N 9,40:4
Time Is a Dream 1924,Ap 23,24:2
Time Limit! 1956,Ja 25,27:2; 1956,F 5,II,1:1
Time of Storm 1954,F 26,14:2
Time of the Cuckoo, The 1952,O 16,37:4;
   1952,N 2,II,1:1; 1953,Ja 4,II,1:1; 1958,O 28,40:2
Time of the Key, A 1963,S 12,33:3
Time of Their Lives 1937,O 26,19:1
Time of Vengeance 1959,D 11,39:1; 1959,D 27,II,1:1
Time of Your Life, The 1939,O 26,26:2;
   1939,N 5,IX,1:1; 1939,N 26,IX,1:1; 1940,S 24,27:2;
   1955,Ja 20,34:1; 1955,Ja 30,II,1:1; 1969,N 7,37:1;
   1969,N 16,II,1:4
Time Out for Ginger 1952,N 27,50:4
Time Out of Mind 1970,Jl 15,29:1
Time Present 1968,My 25,38:1; 1968,Je 2,II,3:6;
   1968,Jl 5,20:1
Time Remembered 1955,My 4,35:1; 1957,N 13,41:2;
   1957,N 24,II,1:1
Time to Burn 1940,D 4,34:3
Time to Go 1952,My 8,35:6; 1960,Mr 23,33:1
Time to Laugh, A 1962,Ap 25,31:4
Times Have Changed 1935,F 19,28:2; 1935,F 26,16:1
Times Square 1968,Ja 27,16:3
Timon 1932,Mr 6,VIII,2:1

Timon of Athens 1935,D 15,XI,5:6; 1952,Je 8,II,3:1;
   1963,Jl 31,19:2
Tin Gods 1928,F 19,VIII,4:1
Tin Pan Alley 1928,N 2,29:1
Tin Top Valley 1947,Mr 1,11:2
Tin Waltz 1954,Ap 23,23:2
Tinguely Machine Mystery, or the Love Suicide at
   Kaluka, The 1965,D 24,15:5
Tinker's Dam 1943,Ja 29,22:2
Tinker's Wedding, The 1957,Mr 7,24:1;
   1957,Mr 17,II,1:1
Tiny Alice 1964,D 30,14:2; 1965,Ja 10,II,1:1;
   1969,S 30,42:1; 1969,O 12,II,9:1; 1970,Ja 17,24:1;
   1970,F 15,II,1:1
Tio Ch'an 1962,N 13,44:1
Tip-Toes 1925,D 29,20:2; 1926,S 1,27:4;
   1929,My 19,IX,2:1
Tip-Top 1920,O 6,13:2
Tipsy Sisters, The 1957,Je 29,11:5
Tired Business Man, The 1929,Je 5,32:5
Tirena 1959,Ag 19,34:1
'Tis of Thee 1940,O 28,21:3
'Tis Pity She's a Whore 1926,Ja 24,VII,1:3;
   1934,My 13,IX,2:2; 1958,D 6,21:1; 1967,O 21,15:2
Title, The 1921,N 15,23:3
Titus Andronicus 1956,D 3,40:2; 1957,Jl 2,33:8;
   1967,Ag 10,43:2
Tivoli Pantomine 1968,S 9,57:2
To Account Rendered 1931,Ja 24,15:3;
   1931,F 15,VIII,2:5
To Be Continued 1952,Ap 24,37:2
To Be or Not to Be-What Kind of a Question Is
   That? 1970,O 20,39:1
To Be Young, Gifted and Black: The World of
   Lorraine Hansberry 1969,Ja 3,15:1;
   1969,My 25,II,1:5; 1969,S 22,36:1
To Broadway With Love 1964,Ap 30,28:6
To Bury a Cousin 1967,My 17,38:3
To Clothe the Naked 1967,Ap 28,30:1
To Damascus 1933,N 12,IX,1:1; 1961,F 15,40:2
To Have and to Hold 1937,Je 9,31:2;
   1937,Je 27,X,1:3
To Have the Honor 1924,My 11,VIII,2:7
To Kill a Cat 1939,Jl 2,IX,1:6
To Love 1922,O 18,16:2
To My Husband 1936,Je 2,35:2
To My Love 1956,Je 7,35:3
To Quito and Back 1937,S 21,29:1; 1937,S 26,XI,3:6;
   1937,O 7,30:4
To See Ourselves 1930,D 28,VIII,2:6; 1935,My 1,25:2
To Tell You the Truth 1948,Ap 19,28:6
To the Chicago Abyss 1965,O 10,11:1
To the Ladies! 1922,F 21,20:1; 1922,Mr 12,VI,1:1
To What Red Hell 1928,N 18,IX,2:3;
   1940,My 5,I,54:8
Toad of Toad Hall 1929,D 23,5:2; 1931,Ja 4,VIII,2:5
Tobacco Road 1933,D 5,31:2; 1934,Je 20,24:1;
   1934,D 4,22:5; 1937,My 20,16:2; 1938,N 27,IX,3:4;
   1940,S 32:3; 1942,S 7,34:2; 1943,S 6,21:3;
   1949,Ag 11,27:5; 1950,My 7,23:2; 1960,My 11,44:2
Tobias and the Angel 1932,Ap 3,VIII,1:4;
   1937,Ap 29,16:5; 1950,Ap 26,36:3; 1957,O 21,29:5
Tobias the Milkman 1930,Je 21,20:4
Todo un Hombre 1937,Ap 28,19:2
Toilet, The 1964,D 17,51:1
'Toinette 1961,N 21,46:1
Tom Paine 1967,N 12,II,17:6; 1968,Mr 26,38:1;
   1968,My 12,II,1:1; 1968,Je 30,II,1:1;
   1969,Mr 30,71:2
Tom Sawyer 1931,D 26,15:3; 1947,D 27,11:3;
   1958,Jl 15,21:8
Tom Thumb the Great 1932,Ag 28,IX,1:1
Tombeau Sous l'Arc de Triomphe 1929,Je 16,VIII,2:3
Tombola, La 1936,N 9,23:4
Tommy 1927,Ja 11,36:4; 1927,Mr 27,VII,1:1;
   1933,Ag 8,22:5; 1969,O 26,82:1
Tomorrow 1928,D 29,20:2
Tomorrow and Tomorrow 1931,Ja 14,26:3;
   1931,Ja 25,VIII,1:1; 1931,F 1,VIII,2:1
Tomorrow the World 1943,Ap 15,22:2;
   1943,Ap 25,II,1:1; 1944,S 10,II,2:6
Tomorrow Will Be Friday 1932,S 18,IX,1:1
Tomorrow With Pictures 1960,Je 3,26:3
Tomorrow's a Holiday! 1935,D 31,10:2
Tomorrow's Harvest 1934,D 6,26:5
Tomorrow's Monday 1936,Jl 16,15:6
Tone Pictures and the White Peacock 1927,Ap 6,24:3

Tongue in Cheek 1949,Ap 23,10:2
Toni 1924,My 18,VII,2:8
Toni aus Wien, Die 1931,Ag 30,VIII,2:2
Tonight at Seven-Thirty 1935,O 17,28:3;
   1935,O 22,16:5
Tonight at 12:00 1928,N 16,28:1
Tonight at 8:30 1936,Ja 10,16:1; 1936,Ja 11,9:4;
   1936,O 27,30:7; 1936,D 6,XII,5:1; 1939,Ag 15,14:5;
   1940,Ag 6,15:3 1940,Ag 11,IX,11:2; 1948,F 21,8:2;
   1948,F 21,8:2; 1948,F 24,20:4
Tonight in Living Color 1969,Je 11,43:1
Tonight in Samarkand 1955,F 17,22:2
Tonight or Never 1930,N 9,IX,3:2; 1930,N 19,19:3
Tonight We Improvise 1936,D 20,XI,3:8;
   1959,N 7,27:4

Tons of Money 1922,My 21,VI,1:6
Too Close for Comfort 1960,F 3,27:2
Too Famous for Words 1936,My 21,19:4
Too Hot for Maneuvers 1945,My 3,26:5
Too Late the Phalarope 1956,O 12,35:1
Too Many Boats 1934,S 12,26:3
Too Many Girls 1939,O 19,26:2; 1939,O 29,IX,1:6
Too Many Heroes 1937,N 16,26:2
Too Much Johnson 1964,Ja 16,29:1
Too Much Party 1934,Mr 6,28:4
Too True to Be Good 1932,Mr 1,19:2;
   1932,Mr 6,VIII,1:1; 1932,Ap 5,27:5;
   1932,Ap 10,VIII,1:1; 1932,Ag 7,I,23:2;
   1932,Ag 28,IX,1:1; 1937,Jl 27,24:2;
   1937,Ag 15,II,5:8; 1963,Mr 14,8:2; 1963,Mr 23,5:6;
   1963,Ap 9,28:1
Toothbrush, The 1970,S 27,84:5
Top Banana 1951,N 2,19:2; 1951,N 18,II,1:1
Top Hole 1924,S 2,22:3
Top-Notchers 1942,My 30,8:5
Top O' the Hill 1929,N 27,30:4
Top Secret 1960,S 6,40:1
Top Speed 1929,N 17,IX,4:1; 1929,D 26,20:1
Topaze 1928,N 4,IX,4:4; 1930,F 13,25:3;
   1930,Mr 2,IX,1:1; 1931,F 17,29:1; 1947,D 29,21:5
Topics of 1923 1923,N 21,23:2
Toplitzky of Notre Dame 1946,D 27,13:4
Topsy and Eva 1924,D 24,11:1
Topsy-Turvy 1939,F 13,12:3
Torch, The 1922,O 8,VI,1:7
Torch Bearers, The 1922,Ag 30,10:2; 1922,S 3,VI,1:1;
   1929,Mr 22,30:4
Torch Song 1930,Ag 3,VIII,3:4; 1930,Ag 28,23:1;
   1930,S 7,IX,1:1
Torches, The 1923,My 11,20:3
Tortilla Flat 1938,Ja 13,16:2
Total Eclipse 1968,S 13,42:1
Totentanz 1923,D 17,23:3
Toto 1921,Mr 22,15:2
Touch 1970,N 9,52:1
Touch and Go 1949,O 14,34:2; 1949,O 30,II,1:1;
   1950,My 20,9:2
Touch of Brimstone, A 1935,S 23,20:1
Touch of the Poet, A 1957,Mr 30,12:5;
   1957,Ap 7,II,3:1; 1958,O 3,23:2; 1958,O 12,II,1:1;
   1961,My 15,34:6; 1962,S 30,85:8; 1967,My 3,38:2
Touch Wood 1934,Jl 1,X,1:3
Touche-A-Tout 1929,O 20,IX,4:4
Touchstone 1953,F 4,33:2
Tough at the Top 1949,Jl 17,58:5; 1949,Ag 7,II,1:4
Tour 1968,My 9,55:2
Tour au Paradis, Un 1933,D 3,IX,7:7
Tour De Four 1963,Je 19,41:1
Tour de Nesle, La 1930,S 7,IX,1:3; 1932,S 25,IX,2:5
Toussaint L'Ouverture 1936,Mr 16,21:6
Tout Paris 1928,N 18,IX,2:1
Tovarich 1933,D 3,IX,7:7; 1935,Ap 25,19:8;
   1935,My 19,IX,1:1; 1936,S 29,35:2; 1936,O 4,IX,2:1;
   1936,O 16,31:4; 1936,O 25,X,1:1; 1937,Ap 25,X,2:4;
   1952,My 15,39:2; 1953,N 29,II,3:1; 1963,Ja 23,5:6;
   1963,Mr 20,5:1; 1963,Mr 21,8:3
Tower Beyond Tragedy, The 1950,N 27,29:1;
   1950,D 10,II,5:1
Town and Country Jig, A 1937,D 13,22:8
Town Boy 1929,O 5,22:4
Town Hall Tonight 1927,N 27,IX,2:1
Town House 1948,S 24,31:2
Town Lunatics 1933,F 6,11:4
Town of Titipu, The 1927,S 19,30:1; 1931,My 5,33:2;
   1934,S 18,18:1
Town's Woman, The 1929,Mr 12,26:2
Toy Box 1955,D 18,95:3
Toy Cart, The 1930,D 7,IX,2:7
Toy for the Clowns, A 1962,S 13,31:2
Toys in the Attic 1960,F 26,23:2; 1960,Mr 6,II,1:1
Trachiniae 1931,Ja 27,21:2
Traffic Signals 1937,Ag 7,7:4
Tragedia del Faro, La 1932,Je 3,23:2
Tragedian in Spite of Himself, A 1948,F 6,29:2
Tragedy of an Elderly Gentleman, The (Back to
   Methuselah, Part IV) 1922,Mr 7,11:1
Tragedy of Nan, The 1920,F 18,9:1; 1920,F 22,III,6:1
Tragedy of the Ages, The 1933,Ap 7,22:7
Tragedy of the Lighthouse, The 1932,Je 3,23:2
Tragic Muse, The 1928,Jl 22,VII,1:3
Tragic 18 1926,O 11,18:2
Tragical Historie of Doctor Faustus, The
   1937,Ja 31,XI,1:1; 1964,O 6,34:2
Tragicomedy of Don Cristobita and Dona Rosita,
   The 1958,My 30,12:2
Traite d'Auteuil, Le 1921,Jl 17,VI,1:8
Traitor, The 1930,My 3,23:4; 1949,Ap 1,30:2;
   1949,Ap 10,II,1:1
Traitor's Gate 1938,D 4,X,7:5
Transatlantic Rhythm 1936,O 2,16:3
Transfers 1970,Ja 23,25:1; 1970,F 1,II,7:2
Transfuges, Les 1929,N 10,X,4:1
Transgressor Rides Again, The 1969,My 21,42:1
Transit of Venus, The 1927,My 22,VIII,2:1
Transplanting Jean 1921,Ja 4,11:2; 1921,Ja 9,VI,1:1
Trapped 1928,Ag 26,VII,2:1; 1928,S 12,25:3
Travails of Sancho Panza, The 1969,D 20,35:1
Traveler's Track 1936,Jl 21,13:5

Traveling Lady 1954,O 28,45:2
Traveling Salesman, The 1932,N 1,24:4
Traveller Without Luggage 1964,S 18,26:2
Travelling Light 1965,Ap 9,18:1
Tread Softly 1935,N 8,19:6; 1935,D 8,X,5:1
Tread the Green Grass 1932,Jl 24,IX,1:3;
  1950,Ap 21,19:4
Treasure, The 1920,O 5,13:1; 1920,O 24,VI,1:1;
  1934,D 18,25:5
Treasure Girl 1928,O 21,IX,2:1; 1928,N 9,22:1
Treasure Island 1925,D 23,22:5; 1938,My 15,II,2:3
Treasure of Isaac, The 1928,Ja 26,17:1
Treasury of Loyal Retainers, The 1969,S 11,53:1
Treat 'Em Rough 1926,My 23,VIII,1:1; 1926,O 5,26:2
Treat Her Gently 1941,Mr 30,I,48:1
Treatment, The 1968,My 10,54:7
Tree, The 1932,Ap 13,23:5
Tree Grows in Brooklyn, A 1951,Ap 20,24:3;
  1951,Ap 29,II,1:1; 1951,My 20,II,1:1
Tree of Aphrodite, The 1926,Jl 18,VII,1:7
Tree of Eden 1938,O 30,IX,1:2
Tree Witch, The 1961,Je 5,39:4
Trees Die Standing, The 1969,O 13,52:1
Trelawney of the 'Wells' 1925,Je 2,16:2;
  1927,F 1,24:4; 1927,F 6,VII,1:1; 1935,Jl 16,24:1;
  1970,O 12,48:1; 1970,O 25,II,16:1
Trespass 1947,Ag 24,II,1:7
Trevor 1968,Jl 5,20:1; 1969,D 4,71:2
Trial, The 1947,N 2,II,3:7; 1950,Ap 13,34:3;
  1952,N 18,36:2; 1955,Je 15,35:2
Trial by Fire 1947,D 5,31:5
Trial by Jury 1931,Jl 28,17:6; 1933,My 9,20:3;
  1934,Ap 17,27:2; 1934,S 14,24:3; 1935,Ag 13,20:6;
  1936,Ap 28,17:2; 1936,S 1,24:4; 1939,Ja 6,25:1;
  1944,F 15,14:4; 1948,Ja 6,27:2; 1949,O 18,34:2;
  1951,F 6,24:2; 1952,N 4,32:2; 1955,O 18,48:1;
  1957,Jl 29,16:1; 1962,N 23,32:4; 1964,N 20,40:1;
  1966,Je 8,41:2
Trial Divorce 1927,Ja 9,30:2; 1927,Ja 16,VII,2:4
Trial Honeymoon 1947,N 4,31:2
Trial Marriage 1927,F 1,24:3
Trial of Dmitri Karamazov, The 1958,Ja 28,30:1
Trial of Dr Beck, The 1937,Ag 10,22:2;
  1937,Ag 22,X,2:3
Trial of Jesus, The 1932,Ap 17,VIII,3:1
Trial of Joan of Arc, The 1921,Mr 28,8:2;
  1921,Ap 17,VI,1:1
Trial of Lee Harvey Oswald, The 1967,N 6,64:1
Trial of Mary Dugan, The 1927,S 20,33:1;
  1927,O 9,VIII,1:1; 1928,Mr 7,28:3; 1928,My 4,31:3;
  1928,Je 24,VIII,1:4; 1928,S 30,IX,4:4;
  1929,F 24,IX,1:8
Trial of Oscar Wilde, The 1935,Ap 21,IX,2:1
Trial of the Catonsville Nine, The 1970,Ag 16,II,1:7
Trials of Brother Jero, The 1967,N 10,60:1;
  1967,N 26,II,1:1
Tricheurs, Les 1932,Ap 3,VIII,2:2
Trick for Trick 1932,F 19,14:2
Trifles 1927,F 13,VII,4:6; 1928,My 11,28:1;
  1932,Ja 30,13:6
Trigger 1927,D 7,32:1
Trigon, The 1965,O 11,62:2
Trilby 1921,D 24,7:2; 1958,Ja 9,40:3
Trimmed in Scarlet 1920,F 3,18:1
Trio 1929,Mr 17,X,2:7; 1930,N 2,VIII,3:2;
  1932,F 8,21:1; 1944,D 30,13:4
Triomphe de l'Amour, Le 1958,O 17,32:1
Trios Henry, Les 1930,Ag 13,X,2:7
Trio's Wedding The 1930,Jl 13,VIII,2:1
Trip to Bountiful, The 1953,N 4,30:3;
  1953,N 15,II,1:1; 1956,Jl 5,25:1; 1959,F 27,20:4
Trip to Pressburg, A 1933,Mr 12,IX,2:7
Trip to Scarborough, A 1929,Mr 18,31:2
Triple-A Plowed Under 1936,Mr 16,21:1
Triple Crossed 1927,My 6,21:2
Triple Play 1937,Ag 24,24:4; 1959,Ap 26,II,1:1
Triplepatte 1926,N 14,VIII,2:1
Triplets 1932,S 22,25:2
Tristan and Isolt 1927,Mr 30,VIII,2:7
Tristi Amori 1930,O 27,17:6
Tristram 1962,O 29,36:1
Triumph 1935,O 15,18:5
Triumph of Delight 1965,My 1,19:1
Triumph of Robert Emmet, The 1969,My 8,54:1
Triumph of the Egg, The 1925,F 11,19:3
Triumph of X, The 1921,Ag 25,8:2
Triumphant Bachelor, The 1927,S 16,21:1
Troika 1928,Mr 4,IX,2:7; 1930,Ap 2,32:6
Troilus and Cressida 1927,N 20,IX,4:7;
  1932,Je 7,22:3; 1953,Ag 19,25:2; 1956,Ap 4,22:7;
  1956,D 27,21:1; 1957,Ja 6,II,1:1; 1961,Jl 24,15:1;
  1963,Je 19,40:2; 1965,Ag 13,17:1; 1968,Ag 9,30:5;
  1969,Jl 31,26:1
Trois, Six, Neuf 1936,Je 21,IX,2:4
Trois Chambres, Les 1931,Mr 15,IX,1:6
Trois et Une 1933,Ja 1,IX,3:4
Trois Jeunes Filles Nues 1926,N 7,VIII,2:7;
  1929,Mr 5,28:2
Trois Maries, Les 1933,F 6,11:3; 1933,F 12,IX,2:1
Trois Masques, Les 1923,N 6,22:1
Trois Rois, Les 1933,F 6,11:3; 1933,F 12,IX,2:1
Trojan Horse, The 1940,O 31,28:3

Trojan Incident 1938,Ap 22,15:2; 1938,My 1,X,8:3
Trojan Women, The 1923,My 27,10:2; 1923,N 8,17:6;
  1938,Ja 25,24:2; 1941,Ap 9,32:5; 1957,Mr 19,42:7;
  1963,D 24,7:6; 1965,Mr 18,25:1; 1967,Ag 27,II,4:8
Trojaner 1929,My 26,IX,2:3
Trompeur de Seville, Le 1937,My 16,X,2:5
Troth, The 1920,Je 29,9:2
Trotsky in Exile 1970,F 1,II,5:1
Trou Dans le Mur, Le 1929,F 24,IX,1:8
Trouble, Le 1928,Ap 29,IX,2:3
Trouble in July 1949,D 2,36:2
Trouble in Mind 1955,N 5,23:2
Trouble in Tahiti 1955,Ap 20,40:3
Trouble in the Works 1969,N 4,55:2
Troubled Waters 1965,Je 4,40:2
Troublemakers, The 1952,N 9,II,3:2; 1954,D 31,11:3
Troupe Du Roi, La 1970,F 4,38:1
Trouper, The 1926,Mr 9,21:1
Truce of the Bear 1957,O 24,39:1
Truckline Cafe 1946,F 28,19:4
True to Form 1921,S 13,12:1
Truly Valiant 1936,Ja 10,17:3
Trumpet Shall Sound, The 1926,D 11,15:2
Trumpeter of Sakkingen 1921,Ja 15,11:3
Trumpets and Drums 1969,O 13,52:1
Trumpets of the Lord 1963,D 23,22:3; 1967,Je 1,51:3;
  1969,Ap 30,37:1
Truth About Blayds, The 1922,Ja 15,VI,1:7;
  1922,Mr 15,22:1; 1922,Mr 26,VI,1:2;
  1932,Ap 12,25:2; 1936,Ag 19,18:5
Truth Game, The 1928,O 21,IX,1:3; 1930,D 29,19:1
Try and Get It 1943,Ag 3,13:2
Try It With Alice 1924,Je 24,18:4
Trysting Place, The 1933,My 8,22:3
Tsar Fyodor Ivanovitch 1923,Ja 9,26:1;
  1923,Ja 11,25:1; 1923,Ja 14,VII,1:1;
  1923,My 22,14:3; 1929,F 19,22:3
Tsar Lenin 1937,Jl 18,X,1:4
Tsubosaka Reigenki 1960,Je 3,26:1
Tu m'ePouseras 1927,Mr 13,VII,2:7
Tudor Wench, The 1933,N 12,IX,3:6
Tulip Tree, The 1962,N 30,25:5
Tulips Are Blooming, The 1935,D 4,27:6
Tumbler, The 1960,F 25,32:2
Tunnel of Love, The 1957,F 14,31:4; 1957,D 5,47:2
Tunnel Trench 1929,N 26,28:7; 1929,D 15,X,4:2
Turandot 1929,Ja 12,14:4
Turcaret 1928,Mr 4,IX,4:5
Turista, La 1967,Mr 26,II,1:2; 1969,Ap 13,II,3:3
Turlututu 1962,S 29,14:2
Turn in the Road, A 1921,Je 12,VI,1:6
Turn of the Screw 1946,O 28,19:2
Turpentine 1936,Je 27,21:6
Tutto Per Bene 1929,Je 3,27:1
TV 1966,N 7,66:1; 1967,Ag 13,II,3:6; 1967,O 10,55:2
Twang 1965,D 22,24:8
Tweedles 1923,Ag 14,10:1; 1923,Ag 19,VI,1:1
Twelfth Disciple, The 1930,My 17,21:4
Twelfth Night 1921,N 1,17:1; 1921,N 6,VI,1:1;
  1923,O 23,17:1; 1925,O 25,VIII,1:1; 1926,D 21,21:4;
  1927,Je 12,VII,2:1; 1930,Mr 27,24:7;
  1930,S 14,VIII,2:8; 1930,O 16,28:2;
  1930,O 19,IX,4:5; 1930,N 2,VIII,1:1;
  1932,Ag 7,IX,1:6; 1932,O 23,IX,3:1;
  1932,N 19,20:5; 1934,Jl 17,24:5; 1934,Ag 21,12:4;
  1938,D 18,IX,5:6; 1940,O 18,26:7;
  1940,O 27,IX,1:5; 1940,N 20,26:3;
  1940,N 24,IX,1:1; 1941,D 3,32:2; 1949,O 4,33:2;
  1949,O 8,9:4; 1949,O 9,II,1:1; 1950,D 3,II,3:1;
  1954,N 10,42:2; 1954,D 12,II,3:1; 1955,My 1,II,3:1;
  1955,Je 7,37:4; 1957,Ja 5,12:2; 1957,Jl 4,16:4;
  1957,Jl 7,II,1:1; 1958,Ag 7,21:4; 1958,Ag 27,32:1;
  1958,D 10,54:2; 1959,Jl 11,10:2; 1960,My 18,48:6;
  1960,Je 9,29:4; 1963,O 9,47:1; 1964,Jl 23,18:1;
  1966,Je 10,51:2; 1966,Je 23,28:1; 1968,Je 15,40:1;
  1969,Ag 14,29:2; 1969,S 1,13:1; 1970,Ja 1,18:1
Twelfth Night's Tune, A 1967,D 23,28:1
Twelve Miles Out 1925,N 17,29:2; 1927,F 20,VII,1:4
Twelve Pound Look, The 1921,Je 14,18:2;
  1934,F 6,24:4
Twelve Thousand 1928,Mr 13,23:1;
  1928,Mr 18,IX,1:1
Twentieth Century 1932,D 30,15:1; 1933,F 12,IX,1:1;
  1950,D 25,23:6
Twenty-Five Cent White Cap, The 1962,Mr 2,24:1
$25 an Hour 1933,My 11,14:4
Twenty-four Inventions 1964,Ag 11,37:5
27 Wagons Full of Cotton 1955,Ja 19,23:2;
  1955,Ap 20,40:3
Twenty to One 1935,N 13,24:3
Twice 100,000 1931,N 22,VIII,3:1; 1934,N 23,22:6
Twilight Walk 1951,S 25,25:4
Twin Stars 1928,Ja 15,VIII,2:1
Twinkle Twinkle 1926,N 17,22:2
Twist of Sand, A 1969,F 22,36:1
Twisting Road, The 1957,N 18,36:5
Two Angry Women of Abingdon 1936,S 14,25:1
Two Blind Mice 1949,Mr 3,32:2; 1949,Mr 20,II,1:1
Two Blocks Away 1921,Ag 31,8:3
Two Bouquets, The 1936,S 13,X,1:5; 1938,Je 1,19:2
Two by Two 1925,F 24,17:1; 1970,N 11,37:1;
  1970,N 22,II,1:1
Two Character Play, The 1967,D 13,54:5

Two Cities 1969,Mr 1,22:1
Two Executioners, The 1960,My 17,42:2;
  1964,Mr 25,46:2
Two Fellows and a Girl 1923,Jl 20,8:2
2 for Fun 1955,My 26,34:1
Two for Fun 1961,F 14,45:3
Two for the Seesaw 1958,Ja 17,15:1; 1958,Ja 26,II,1:1;
  1963,S 4,34:1
Two for the Show 1940,F 9,14:2; 1940,F 18,II,1:1;
  1940,F 18,IX,2:1
Two Gentlemen of Soho, The 1928,N 11,X,4:1
Two Gentlemen of Verona 1936,Je 28,IX,2:1;
  1957,Jl 23,21:5; 1958,Mr 19,35:1; 1960,Ap 6,47:3
Two Hearts 1934,My 6,22:2
245 1930,D 28,VIII,3:5
200,000 1936,O 14,30:2; 1936,N 29,XII,3:3;
  1966,F 15,33:5
200 Were Chosen 1936,N 21,21:1; 1936,N 29,XII,1:1
Two Kingdoms 1934,N 20,24:2
Two Little Girls in Blue 1921,My 4,10:3
Two Married Men 1925,Ja 14,19:1
Two Misers, The 1943,D 9,30:5
Two Mothers, The 1937,F 24,19:3
Two Mrs Carrolls, The 1935,Ja 13,26:1;
  1935,Ag 4,IX,1:3; 1943,Ag 4,14:1; 1943,Ag 8,II,1:1
Two Neck-Ties 1929,O 13,IX,4:7
Two Noble Kinsmen, The 1928,Ap 8,VIII,2:7
Two of Us, The 1970,Ag 1,13:2; 1970,S 11,33:2
Two on an Island 1940,Ja 16,18:4; 1940,Ja 23,17:2;
  1940,Ja 28,IX,1:2; 1940,F 4,IX,1:1
Two on the Aisle 1951,Jl 20,13:6; 1951,Jl 29,II,1:1
Two Orphans, The 1926,Ap 6,26:2;
  1926,Ap 11,VIII,1:1; 1936,O 5,24:4
2 + 2 = 5 1927,N 29,30:3
Two Seconds 1931,O 10,20:6
Two Share a Dwelling 1935,O 9,26:3; 1935,N 3,X,1:7
Two Shepherds, The 1935,F 12,25:4
Two Story House 1941,S 2,20:3
Two Strange Women 1933,Ja 11,23:3
Two Strangers From Nowhere 1924,Ap 8,22:3
Two Time Mary 1937,Ag 3,20:5
Two Times One 1970,Ap 5,76:4
Two Weeks With Pay 1940,Je 25,28:3
Two Worlds 1926,Je 27,VII,3:1
Two's Company 1952,D 16,43:5; 1952,D 21,II,3:1
Tyger!Tyger! and Other Burnings 1969,Mr 9,76:5
Type 424 Meet Type Oh-Oh, No! 1970,Je 18,54:2
Typewriter, The 1955,Jl 29,8:3
Typists, The 1963,F 6,5:2
Tyranny of Love, The 1921,Mr 2,7:3;
  1921,Mr 6,VI,1:2; 1921,My 3,20:2;
  1921,My 8,VI,1:1; 1921,My 15,VI,1:7
Tyrant, The 1930,N 13,33:1
Tyrants 1924,Mr 5,14:1

U

U S A 1956,D 19,41:4; 1959,O 29,38:1;
  1959,N 8,II,1:1
Ubu Roi 1968,Je 29,20:1; 1968,Jl 14,II,1:1;
  1970,F 17,33:1
Ugly Daughter, The 1937,Ag 30,24:6
Ugly Duchess, The 1930,Je 1,VIII,2:8
Ugly Runts, The 1935,Je 11,24:4
Ulysses in Nighttown 1958,Je 6,30:1;
  1958,Je 15,II,1:1
Umbrella, The 1965,My 27,31:1
Unburied Dead, The 1946,D 22,II,4:1
Unchastened Woman, The 1926,F 17,12:1;
  1926,F 21,VII,1:2
Uncle Harry 1942,My 21,24:1; 1944,Ap 30,II,1:4
Uncle Moses 1930,N 29,21:3
Uncle Sam in Israel 1952,D 8,38:5
Uncle Tom's Cabin 1928,O 21,IX,1:3;
  1932,Ja 24,III,5:7; 1933,My 30,13:4; 1933,O 10,24:3;
  1934,F 19,19:2; 1934,Jl 6,15:1; 1945,S 30,II,1:2;
  1949,Ap 18,13:3
Uncle Vanya 1924,Ja 29,16:2; 1929,My 25,17:1;
  1930,Ap 16,26:5; 1930,Ap 20,VIII,1:1;
  1930,My 4,XI,1:1; 1930,S 23,30:3;
  1945,Mr 25,II,2:4; 1946,My 14,18:2;
  1946,My 19,II,1:1; 1956,F 1,25:2; 1956,F 12,II,1:1;
  1956,Mr 4,II,1:1; 1960,F 13,33:4; 1960,F 14,19:1;
  1962,Jl 17,18:4; 1963,Jl 2,16:2; 1969,Ag 31,II,4:1;
  1970,Mr 15,II,7:3
Uncle Willie 1956,D 21,17:1
Uncommon Denominator, The 1963,My 8,35:2
Unconquered, The 1940,F 14,25:2
Under Conviction 1923,My 9,14:4
Under Glass 1933,O 31,24:3
Under Milk Wood 1953,My 29,17:1; 1956,Ag 22,25:3;
  1957,O 16,42:5; 1957,N 10,II,1:1; 1961,Mr 30,25:1;
  1961,Ap 9,II,1:1; 1962,O 6,13:4
Under One Roof 1932,F 8,21:2; 1941,My 4,IX,1:6
Under Plain Cover 1962,Jl 10,25:3
Under the Counter 1947,O 4,10:2
Under the Gaslight 1929,Ap 3,27:1
Under the Lilacs 1934,N 19,13:3
Under the Sycamore Tree 1952,Ap 24,38:4;
  1952,My 11,II,3:7; 1960,Mr 8,37:2
Under the Weather 1966,O 28,35:1; 1966,D 25,II,1:1

Under the Yum-Yum Tree 1960,N 17,45:1;
  1964,My 29,18:1
Undercover Man 1966,Je 3,30:2
Undercurrent, The 1925,Ja 18,VII,2:8; 1925,F 4,18:2;
  1929,Ja 21,18:3
Underground 1952,F 13,33:2
Undertow 1929,N 10,X,4:8
Underwrite Your Husband 1923,O 14,VIII,2:4
Undesirable Lady, An 1933,O 10,24:4
Uneasy Virtue 1937,Ag 4,14:1
Unentbehrliche, Der 1937,O 24,XI,3:1
Unexpected Husband 1931,Je 3,29:4
Unexpurgated Memoirs of Bernard Mergendeiler,
  The 1968,My 9,55:2
Unfair to Goliath 1970,Ja 26,27:1
Unguarded Hour, The 1935,Ag 25,X,1:3
Unhappy Loves 1930,O 27,17:6
Uniform of Flesh 1949,Ja 31,15:2
Uninvited Guest, The 1927,S 28,28:2
United States vs Julius and Ethel Rosenberg, The
  1969,Ap 20,II,3:1; 1969,Ap 27,92:1
Universal Nigger, The 1970,Mr 21,18:1
Unknown, The 1920,Ag 10,17:7; 1920,Ag 29,VI,1:4
Unknown Lady, The 1923,N 6,22:1
Unknown Soldier and His Wife, The 1967,Jl 7,22:1
Unknown Warrior, The 1928,Mr 4,IX,4:7;
  1928,O 30,26:6; 1931,O 23,28:4
Unnaturliche Tochter, Die 1932,Je 19,IX,1:3
Unquiet Spirit, The 1937,N 14,XI,3:1
Unseen Hand, The 1970,Ap 2,43:1
Unshaven Cheek, The 1963,Ag 20,38:2
Unsinkable Molly Brown, The 1960,N 4,28:1
Unsophisticates, The 1926,Ag 8,VII,3:1;
  1929,D 31,14:5
Until the Monkey Comes 1966,Je 21,38:1
Untitled-Benefit 1920,My 2,VI,2:2; 1921,My 2,12:3;
  1922,My 8,14:5; 1926,Je 6,VIII,1:1; 1933,Ja 25,13:3;
  1935,Je 23,IX,1:3
Untitled-Dance 1930,F 13,25:2
Untitled-Dramatic Reading 1933,Mr 6,16:4;
  1955,O 7,21:1
Untitled-Judy Garland 1967,D 26,45:1
Untitled-Magic Show 1925,D 15,4:6;
  1926,My 24,24:2
Untitled-Magician 1927,Ap 19,25:2
Untitled-Marionettes 1923,S 11,10:2; 1928,D 21,30:3;
  1932,D 23,22:2; 1957,D 24,11:6
Untitled-Nativity Play 1941,D 25,28:5;
  1946,D 25,46:1; 1950,D 25,15:2
Untitled-One Man Show 1926,Ap 12,18:1;
  1928,D 12,34:5; 1930,Mr 31,24:1; 1930,D 2,31:2;
  1949,Ap 26,30:4; 1949,My 4,38:2; 1952,O 31,30:6;
  1955,My 25,39:1; 1963,Ja 12,5:2; 1967,N 20,61:1;
  1970,O 31,34:1
Untitled-One Woman Show 1921,Ja 28,16:2;
  1921,N 12,18:2; 1921,N 19,11:2; 1921,N 28,16:2;
  1921,D 4,VII,1:2; 1922,Mr 17,20:2; 1923,Ja 15,15:3;
  1923,O 29,18:2; 1923,N 4,VIII,1:2; 1923,N 19,19:1;
  1925,N 9,25:2; 1926,Ap 12,18:1; 1926,Ap 19,24:4;
  1926,Ap 25,VIII,1:1; 1926,Je 20,VII,1:1;
  1926,S 25,21:3; 1926,O 18,18:2; 1928,Mr 4,IX,2:1;
  1928,Je 10,VIII,1:3; 1928,Je 24,VIII,4:2;
  1928,D 17,25:3; 1929,Ja 6,VIII,1:1;
  1929,My 19,IX,2:1; 1929,N 18,22:6; 1929,D 27,26:6;
  1930,D 27,16:3; 1931,Je 21,VIII,1:3;
  1932,N 15,24:2; 1934,D 27,24:3; 1936,Ja 20,23:3;
  1936,D 28,13:1; 1937,D 1,27:1; 1938,O 31,12:2;
  1938,D 27,12:2; 1942,D 26,14:3; 1947,Ja 13,18:2;
  1949,Je 29,33:5; 1951,Ap 23,20:2; 1952,D 13,18:6;
  1956,Ap 9,23:5; 1956,D 26,32:1
Untitled-Pageant 1929,Jl 18,14:4; 1933,Je 25,IX,1:3
Untitled-Pantomime 1921,Ap 3,VII,1:1;
  1955,Je 5,48:1; 1958,Ja 22,23:1
Untitled-Play 1921,D 25,VI,1:8; 1923,O 7,IX,2:2;
  1924,F 3,VII,1:4; 1924,Jl 5,14:4; 1925,O 27,VII,2:1;
  1927,O 2,II,7:2; 1927,D 18,IX,4:4; 1928,F 5,VIII,2:1;
  1928,Mr 18,IX,2:1; 1928,Je 10,VIII,1:3;
  1928,Je 17,VIII,1:4; 1928,N 11,X,2:7;
  1928,N 18,IX,2:6; 1928,D 9,III,3:8;
  1929,Mr 3,VIII,4:8; 1929,N 10,X,1:8;
  1929,D 29,VIII,4:1; 1930,Jl 13,VIII,2:1;
  1931,Ap 6,24:4; 1931,Ap 7,31:2; 1931,N 15,VIII,2:1;
  1932,Ja 31,VIII,3:1; 1933,Ap 2,IX,2:4;
  1933,Je 4,IX,1:6; 1933,N 12,IX,3:4;
  1934,Mr 18,IX,2:3; 1935,O 27,IX,2:1;
  1935,N 24,31:7; 1936,Je 7,IX,1:1;
  1937,Ja 24,X,2:1; 1950,Ja 8,II,3:7
Untitled-Poetry Reading 1964,Je 22,23:4;
  1967,Jl 18,29:1
Untitled-Puppet Show 1929,Mr 4,20:4;
  1932,My 25,23:4; 1934,Ja 9,19:2
Untitled-Reading 1952,Ja 30,20:2; 1952,F 17,II,1:1;
  1957,Ja 23,24:6; 1957,Ap 17,35:1
Untitled-Recital 1923,D 29,8:2; 1930,Mr 10,24:4;
  1931,Mr 23,24:3; 1931,Ap 13,17:4; 1932,F 8,21:1;
  1954,D 27,21:2; 1955,Ja 9,II,7:1; 1970,S 3,36:1

Untitled-Revue 1922,Jl 9,VI,1:1; 1922,S 16,18:2;
  1922,O 3,22:4; 1923,My 12,15:4; 1924,F 19,12:1;
  1924,My 25,VIII,1:8; 1924,Je 15,VII,1:4;
  1926,O 26,18:3; 1926,O 31,VIII,2:4;
  1926,N 21,VIII,2:1; 1927,O 9,VIII,2:4;
  1928,Ja 15,VIII,2:3; 1928,Mr 11,VIII,2:7;
  1928,Mr 18,III,3:1; 1928,S 23,IX,2:1;
  1928,N 18,IX,2:1; 1928,N 19,16:2; 1929,F 24,IX,1:8;
  1929,O 20,IX,4:4; 1930,Ap 22,33:2;
  1930,N 30,IX,3:3; 1931,My 3,VIII,1:7;
  1933,O 22,IX,2:2; 1933,D 19,26:3; 1935,S 23,20:2;
  1935,N 11,21:2; 1939,Ja 16,11:3; 1939,Ap 5,31:2;
  1941,My 18,IX,1:1; 1947,N 23,II,1:1;
  1950,Mr 29,36:2; 1957,Ja 20,II,3:7;
  1961,Ja 18,II,1:1; 1962,Ja 12,30:2; 1962,Je 7,31:1;
  1964,N 10,56:2; 1965,Je 25,38:1; 1966,O 3,62:5;
  1967,Ag 29,26:1; 1968,O 21,55:4
Unto Such Glory 1936,Ja 13,14:4; 1937,My 7,28:2
Unto the Third 1933,Ap 21,24:8
Unto Thee a Garden 1968,O 28,55:3
Unwritten Chapter, The 1920,O 12,18:1
Uomo d'Oro, Un 1929,My 6,30:2
Up and Up, The 1930,S 9,25:2; 1930,S 14,VIII,1:1
Up Eden 1968,N 27,42:1
Up in Central Park 1945,Ja 29,17:2; 1947,My 20,29:2;
  1947,My 25,II,1:1
Up in the Clouds 1922,Ja 3,20:3
Up Pops the Devil 1930,S 2,19:1; 1930,S 14,VIII,1:1
Up She Goes 1922,N 7,14:2
Up the Alley 1931,Jl 24,20:3
Up the Garden Path 1937,Jl 7,26:2
Up the Ladder 1922,Mr 7,11:2
Up the Line 1926,N 23,26:1
Up the Rebels 1941,O 31,21:1
Up to Thursday 1965,F 11,45:1
Upon My Soul 1927,Ap 22,19:1
Ups-A-Daisy 1928,O 9,34:2
Uptown West 1923,Ap 4,22:2
Uri Muri 1928,Ap 15,IX,4:1
Uriel Acosta 1939,D 31,18:3
Ursache, Die 1929,My 12,IX,1:8
US 1966,O 15,32:1; 1966,N 6,II,1:5
Utbu 1966,Ja 5,24:1
Utopia, Limited 1936,My 23,10:6; 1957,F 27,21:1;
  1957,Mr 17,II,1:1; 1960,Ap 8,27:2
Utopia! 1963,My 7,47:4

V

Vacances de Paques, Les 1927,Ja 2,VII,2:1
Vacant Possession 1933,O 22,IX,2:2
Vacation Follies 1939,Ag 30,15:6
Vaches Maigres, Les 1936,Je 7,IX,1:1
Vagabond, The 1923,D 28,13:4
Vagabond King, The 1925,S 22,23:3; 1935,N 29,22:7;
  1943,Je 30,24:2; 1961,N 24,36:1
Vagrant, The 1962,F 16,35:2
Valentin le Desosse 1932,N 20,IX,2:2
Valiant, The 1926,My 5,24:5; 1927,F 22,22:5;
  1929,S 22,24:6
Valley Forge 1934,N 27,26:4; 1934,D 11,28:3;
  1934,D 23,IX,1:1
Valley of Content, The 1925,Ja 14,19:2
Valliere, La 1933,Ap 16,IX,2:5
Valmouth 1960,O 7,29:1
Values 1927,My 5,30:1
Vamp, The 1955,N 11,30:1
Van Dyck, The 1921,O 12,18:2
Vanderbilt Revue, The 1930,O 26,VIII,3:5;
  1930,N 6,22:6
Vanities 1926,Ja 10,VII,1:1; 1927,F 22,19:1;
  1931,Ag 11,28:4; 1931,Ag 16,VIII,1:1;
  1931,S 6,VIII,1:1; 1932,S 18,IX,2:1; 1932,S 28,22:4
Vanity Fair 1946,N 3,I,54:6; 1946,N 10,II,3:1;
  1962,N 28,44:8
Variations of 1940 1940,Ja 29,12:1
Variations on a Theme 1958,My 9,16:5
Variety Anthology 1932,Mr 21,19:4
Various Heavens 1936,Mr 8,IX,1:1
Varying Shore, The 1921,D 6,24:1; 1921,D 11,VI,1:1
Vatzlav 1970,Ag 23,II,1:6
Vaudeville (Belmont) 1931,Ja 6,24:1
Vaudeville (Broadway) 1932,D 27,11:4
Vaudeville (Carnegie Hall) 1932,Ja 12,I,30:4
Vaudeville (Central) 1922,S 19,14:1; 1922,S 24,VI,1:1
Vaudeville (Forty-Fourth Street Theatre)
  1921,S 20,12:2
Vaudeville (Hippodrome) 1923,D 18,16:1;
  1924,Ja 1,21:1; 1924,Ja 22,15:6; 1924,F 12,20:2;
  1924,F 19,12:1; 1924,Mr 18,25:1; 1924,Ap 1,18:1;
  1924,Ap 29,12:2; 1924,S 30,27:5; 1924,O 21,21:2;
  1925,S 1,18:3; 1925,O 20,29:2; 1925,D 8,28:6;
  1925,D 29,21:2; 1926,F 23,26:2; 1926,Mr 16,22:2;
  1926,Mr 23,24:3; 1926,Mr 30,20:4; 1926,Ap 13,28:2;
  1926,Ap 20,24:6; 1926,Ap 27,22:3; 1926,My 4,31:2;
  1926,My 8,29:2; 1926,My 11,25:3
Vaudeville (Hollywood) 1932,F 16,24:3;
  1932,Mr 22,17:5; 1932,Ap 19,25:5
Vaudeville (Knickerbocker) 1928,F 19,VIII,1:1
Vaudeville (Lexington) 1921,O 18,20:2
Vaudeville (Loew's State) 1927,F 1,24:6;
  1932,Je 13,19:7; 1932,Jl 18,9:7; 1932,O 3,15:5

Vaudeville (New Amsterdam Theatre)
  1931,Je 22,17:3
Vaudeville (Palace Theatre London) 1931,Ja 6,24:6
Vaudeville (Palace) 1921,Ja 25,14:2; 1921,My 17,20:3;
  1921,Je 14,18:2; 1921,Jl 5,15:1; 1922,F 14,21:1;
  1923,Ja 16,16:3; 1923,Ja 23,18:2; 1923,Ja 30,21:1;
  1923,F 13,25:1; 1923,Mr 6,26:1; 1923,Mr 13,19:2;
  1923,Ap 3,26:4; 1923,My 15,22:2; 1923,O 23,18:2;
  1923,O 30,16:1; 1923,N 13,24:2; 1923,N 20,23:4;
  1924,Ja 1,21:1; 1924,Ja 15,17:3; 1924,Ja 22,15:6;
  1924,F 12,20:2; 1924,F 19,12:1; 1924,Mr 18,25:1;
  1924,Ap 1,18:1; 1924,Ap 29,12:2; 1924,S 16,26:5;
  1924,S 30,27:5; 1924,O 21,21:2; 1925,Ap 7,16:3;
  1925,Ap 21,18:1; 1925,Je 7,VIII,1:1;
  1925,Je 28,VIII,1:1; 1925,S 29,31:2; 1925,O 6,31:3;
  1925,O 20,29:2; 1925,D 8,28:6; 1925,D 29,21:2;
  1926,Mr 16,22:2; 1926,Mr 23,24:3;
  1926,Mr 30,20:4; 1926,Ap 13,28:3; 1926,Ap 20,24:6;
  1926,Ap 27,22:3; 1926,My 4,31:2; 1926,My 8,29:2;
  1926,My 11,25:3; 1926,Je 1,29:5; 1926,Je 8,23:1;
  1926,Je 15,23:3; 1926,Je 22,21:3; 1926,Je 29,21:3;
  1926,Jl 6,19:3; 1926,Jl 13,19:4; 1926,Jl 20,17:4;
  1926,Jl 27,15:4; 1926,Ag 3,19:2; 1926,Ag 10,19:4;
  1926,Ag 17,21:2; 1926,Ag 24,19:3; 1926,Ag 31,15:3;
  1926,S 7,24:6; 1926,S 14,25:3; 1926,S 21,32:5;
  1926,S 28,30:4; 1926,O 19,27:5; 1926,O 26,24:2;
  1926,N 2,35:2; 1926,N 9,30:3; 1926,N 16,24:3;
  1926,N 23,27:3; 1926,N 30,27:2; 1926,D 7,24:3;
  1926,D 21,20:5; 1926,D 28,12:3; 1927,Ja 4,21:2;
  1927,Ja 18,23:2; 1927,Ja 23,VII,1:1; 1927,Ja 25,18:3;
  1927,F 8,20:3; 1927,F 13,VII,1:1; 1927,Mr 1,31:2;
  1927,Mr 22,31:1; 1927,Mr 29,22:6; 1927,Ap 5,30:2;
  1927,Ap 12,25:4; 1927,Ap 19,24:3; 1927,Ap 26,33:1;
  1927,My 3,25:2; 1927,My 10,25:3; 1927,My 17,27:4;
  1927,My 24,23:1; 1927,My 31,25:1; 1927,Je 7,27:3;
  1927,Je 14,33:3; 1927,Je 28,29:2; 1927,Jl 5,19:3;
  1927,Jl 12,29:3; 1927,Jl 19,27:6; 1927,Jl 26,16:5;
  1927,Ag 2,19:1; 1927,Ag 23,29:3; 1927,S 13,36:3;
  1927,S 20,33:3; 1927,S 27,31:3; 1927,O 4,34:3;
  1927,O 11,27:2; 1927,O 18,32:4; 1927,O 25,33:2;
  1927,N 1,20:3; 1927,N 8,33:3; 1927,N 15,27:2;
  1927,N 22,33:2; 1927,N 29,30:4; 1927,D 6,26:3;
  1927,D 13,33:5; 1927,D 20,33:4; 1927,D 27,25:2;
  1928,Ja 3,29:3; 1928,Ja 10,28:5; 1928,Ja 17,23:3;
  1928,Ja 24,26:4; 1928,Ja 31,29:2; 1928,F 7,30:5;
  1928,F 14,26:2; 1928,F 21,19:2; 1928,F 28,18:7;
  1928,Mr 6,20:5; 1928,Mr 13,23:2; 1928,Mr 20,20:2;
  1928,Mr 27,30:5; 1928,Ap 3,32:5; 1928,Ap 10,32:4;
  1928,Ap 17,26:2; 1928,Ap 24,29:2; 1928,My 1,33:2;
  1928,My 8,25:2; 1928,My 15,17:1; 1928,My 29,17:4;
  1928,Je 5,21:3; 1928,Je 26,29:4; 1928,Jl 3,19:2;
  1928,Jl 10,17:3; 1928,Jl 17,15:5; 1928,Jl 24,13:4;
  1928,Jl 31,13:5; 1928,Ag 7,25:5; 1928,Ag 14,15:5;
  1928,Ag 21,27:5; 1928,Ag 28,27:3; 1928,S 4,21:3;
  1928,S 18,34:6; 1928,S 25,29:4; 1928,O 2,35:1;
  1928,O 9,35:2; 1928,O 23,32:5; 1928,O 30,27:3;
  1928,N 6,35:2; 1928,N 12,18:7; 1928,N 19,16:3;
  1928,N 26,31:2; 1928,D 3,30:6; 1928,D 17,23:3;
  1928,D 24,10:8; 1928,D 31,9:3; 1929,Ja 14,20:3;
  1929,Ja 21,18:3; 1929,F 4,21:4; 1929,F 11,26:2;
  1929,F 18,29:1; 1929,Mr 11,22:5; 1929,Mr 18,30:5;
  1929,Mr 25,33:2; 1929,Ap 8,32:7; 1929,Ap 22,22:6;
  1929,My 13,26:3; 1929,My 20,22:8; 1929,Je 3,27:4;
  1929,Je 10,22:6; 1929,Je 17,29:3; 1929,Je 24,27:4;
  1929,Jl 1,31:4; 1929,Jl 8,17:6; 1929,Jl 15,25:4;
  1929,Ag 19,23:1; 1929,S 2,16:3; 1929,S 9,30:5;
  1929,S 16,30:4; 1929,S 23,24:6; 1929,S 30,22:3;
  1929,O 7,22:4; 1929,O 14,20:4; 1929,O 21,31:2;
  1929,N 4,29:1; 1929,N 11,20:5; 1929,N 18,22:4;
  1929,N 25,22:4; 1929,D 2,28:6; 1929,D 9,33:2;
  1929,D 16,34:4; 1929,D 23,19:1; 1929,D 30,16:3;
  1930,F 10,20:3; 1930,F 17,18:4; 1930,Mr 3,18:5;
  1930,Mr 7,21:2; 1930,Mr 10,24:4; 1930,Mr 24,24:5;
  1930,Mr 31,24:2; 1930,Ap 21,20:7; 1930,My 5,27:5;
  1930,My 26,25:2; 1930,Jl 7,22:2; 1930,Ag 4,13:2;
  1930,Ag 11,13:3; 1930,Ag 18,24:3; 1930,S 8,17:3;
  1930,S 15,29:2; 1930,S 22,23:2; 1930,S 29,19:1;
  1930,O 13,31:3; 1930,O 20,29:1; 1930,N 3,19:2;
  1930,N 10,17:1; 1930,N 17,21:2; 1930,N 24,26:3;
  1930,D 1,19:1; 1930,D 8,27:2; 1930,D 22,16:5;
  1930,D 29,19:3; 1931,Ja 5,20:3; 1931,Ja 19,25:3;
  1931,Ja 26,21:5; 1931,F 2,23:3; 1931,F 16,16:3;
  1931,Mr 2,19:2; 1931,Mr 9,25:7; 1931,Ap 6,24:3;
  1931,Ap 13,17:2; 1931,Ap 20,16:2; 1931,My 4,15:2;
  1931,My 11,15:5; 1931,My 18,21:1;
  1931,My 25,17:4; 1931,Je 8,21:2; 1931,Je 15,23:5;
  1931,Je 22,17:2; 1931,Je 29,20:1; 1931,Jl 6,24:6;
  1931,Jl 13,13:4; 1931,Jl 20,20:3; 1931,Ag 3,15:7;
  1931,S 7,9:2; 1931,S 28,17:5; 1931,O 19,28:5;
  1931,O 26,23:3; 1931,N 2,26:2; 1932,Ja 4,27:4;
  1932,F 15,13:3; 1932,Mr 7,13:4; 1932,Ap 4,13:4;
  1932,Ap 18,19:5; 1932,Ap 25,18:3;,1932,My 2,13:2;
  1932,My 9,19:3; 1932,My 16,19:2; 1932,My 23,18:7;
  1932,My 30,16:7; 1932,Je 6,18:2; 1932,Je 13,19:7;
  1932,Jl 4,14:5; 1932,Jl 11,11:6; 1932,Jl 18,9:7;
  1932,Ag 1,11:5; 1932,S 12,13:5; 1932,O 3,15:5;
  1933,Ja 16,13:2; 1949,My 20,32:4; 1950,My 25,36:2;
  1951,O 17,36:6; 1951,N 17,9:6; 1952,F 27,22:2;
  1952,Mr 12,31:2; 1952,Mr 16,II,1:1;
  1952,Ap 14,23:2; 1952,Ap 27,II,1:1; 1953,O 15,42:1
Vaudeville (Palladium) 1931,My 12,28:4;
  1935,O 30,16:8; 1949,Ag 17,19:3; 1953,Ap 24,29:4
Vaudeville (Pavilion) 1931,Mr 20,29:3

Vaudeville (Proctor's) 1927,My 17,27:4
Vaudeville (Winter Garden) 1922,F 14,21:1
Vaudeville Marches On 1938,D 30,11:1
Veau Gras, Le 1924,Mr 23,VIII,1:3
Vegetable, The, or From President to Postman 1929,Ap 11,32:3
Veilchen von Montmartre 1931,Mr 29,VIII,3:1
Veils 1928,Mr 14,28:5
Veldt, The 1965,O 10,11:1
Velvet Glove, The 1949,D 27,26:2
Veneer 1929,N 13,24:5; 1929,N 24,X,1:1
Venetian, The 1931,Mr 15,IX,4:3; 1931,O 11,VIII,4:5; 1931,N 2,26:1
Venetian Glass Nephew, The 1931,F 24,26:3
Venetian Hour, A 1934,Mr 22,24:6
Venetian Twins, The 1968,My 29,23:1
Venice Preserv'd 1955,D 13,54:4
Vent de Folie, Un 1926,D 5,VIII,6:1; 1927,Ap 24,VII,2:2
Ventose 1927,D 18,IX,4:4
Ventres Dores, Les 1929,N 17,IX,2:6
Venturi, The: A Squeeze Play 1970,Mr 21,17:1
Venus 1927,D 26,26:5
Venus at Large 1962,Ap 13,30:1
Venus et Adonis 1933,Jl 23,IX,1:3
Venus Observed 1950,Ja 19,35:2; 1950,N 26,II,1:1; 1952,F 14,24:2; 1952,F 24,II,1:1
Venus-Shot 1966,Je 24,30:2
Vera Cruz Interior 1942,Ap 27,19:2
Verbrecher, Die 1928,D 23,VIII,4:1
Verdict, The 1934,S 22,12:5; 1958,My 24,19:8
Verfl--- Geld, Das 1931,N 15,VIII,4:1
Verge, The 1921,N 15,23:2; 1921,N 20,VI,1:1
Verhoer von Habana, Das 1970,O 13,52:2
Veritable Histoire de Mignon, La 1927,F 20,VII,2:1
Vermont 1928,D 30,VIII,1:6; 1929,Ja 9,28:1
Veronica 1965,N 19,31:1
Veronica's Veil 1925,Mr 2,5:6; 1927,Mr 7,17:2; 1930,Mr 10,14:3; 1931,F 23,36:2; 1933,F 20,11:7; 1934,F 19,20:7; 1935,Mr 11,14:2; 1936,F 10,19:6; 1936,Mr 2,4:3; 1940,F 12,2:7; 1950,F 12,II,1:5; 1954,F 28,I,78:5
Versailles 1931,Ja 25,I,14:2; 1932,O 20,19:5
Versunkene Glocke, Die 1924,N 3,21:2; 1936,N 20,26:3
Vertrag von Nizza, Der 1922,Ap 2,VI,1:2
Very Rich Woman, A 1965,O 5,5:8
Very Special Baby, A 1956,N 15,43:2
Very Warm for May 1939,N 12,IX,2:3; 1939,N 18,23:2
Very Wise Virgin, A 1927,Je 3,25:3
Vetter aus Dingsda 1921,Je 5,VI,1:3
Via Crucis 1923,F 11,VII,1:4; 1923,N 13,25:2
Viceroy Sarah 1934,Je 24,IX,1:4; 1935,F 13,27:4; 1935,Mr 10,VIII,2:1; 1939,Ag 15,14:4
Vickie 1942,S 23,28:1
Victim, The 1952,My 3,17:5
Victims, The 1968,Mr 6,34:1
Victims of Amnesia, The 1970,S 23,43:1
Victims of Duty 1960,Ja 20,26:1; 1964,My 28,40:2; 1968,Mr 6,34:1
Victims of Life 1931,O 21,26:2
Victor, or The Children Take Over 1968,Jl 10,22:4
Victoria and Her Hussar 1930,S 21,IX,2:6
Victoria Regina 1935,D 13,30:5; 1935,D 27,15:2; 1936,Ja 5,IX,1:1; 1936,Mr 8,IX,1:1; 1936,S 1,24:5; 1937,Je 22,26:2; 1937,Jl 11,X,1:7; 1937,S 26,XI,3:6; 1938,Ap 17,X,2:1; 1938,O 4,20:2; 1938,O 9,X,1:3
Victors, The 1948,D 27,17:2; 1949,Ja 2,II,1:1
Victory 1937,N 14,XI,2:5
Victory Belles 1943,O 27,26:3
Vida es Sueno, La 1964,Mr 18,49:1
Vie Athenienne, La 1931,D 13,VIII,2:2
Vie en Rose, La 1931,D 20,VIII,2:7
Vie Est Belle, La 1928,Je 3,VIII,2:5
Vie Parisienne, La 1941,N 6,20:3; 1945,Ja 13,14:5; 1964,Mr 11,34:2
Vie Que Je T'Ai Donnee, La 1930,Ap 6,IX,2:3
Vie Secrete, Une 1929,Mr 24,X,2:1
Vieille Maman, La 1927,N 6,IX,4:1
Vielgeliebte, Die 1935,My 19,IX,2:5
Vienna at Night 1945,Ap 30,12:4
Viens Avec Nous Petit! 1927,F 20,VII,2:1
Vient de Paraitre 1927,D 11,IX,2:2; 1928,S 23,IX,2:1
Vierge Folle, La 1924,Mr 22,12:2
Viet Rock 1966,O 12,34:1; 1966,N 11,38:1; 1966,N 27,II,1:1
Vietnam Discourse 1968,Mr 31,II,22:6
View From the Bridge, A 1955,Ag 31,16:8; 1955,S 30,21:1; 1955,O 9,II,1:1; 1956,O 12,35:3; 1956,N 9,34:4; 1965,Ja 29,24:1
Viewing, The 1967,Ja 11,51:1
Vigil 1932,D 11,IX,4:5
Vigil, The 1948,My 11,28:1; 1948,My 22,8:6
Vikings, The 1930,My 13,27:3
Vilaine Femme, Une 1933,Ja 1,IX,3:4
Villa Franca 1932,Mr 17,16:5
Villa of Madame Vidac, The 1959,O 1,40:1
Village, The 1927,Ag 14,VII,1:7
Village, The: A Party 1968,N 13,39:1
Village Green 1941,Je 17,24:7; 1941,Ag 27,15:3; 1941,S 4,24:4; 1941,S 14,IX,1:1
Village Wedding, A 1930,S 24,26:2

Village Wooing 1934,Ap 18,22:5; 1934,Je 20,24:3; 1935,O 27,IX,2:5; 1955,Ag 13,6:6; 1956,S 5,22:6
Villana, La 1928,Ja 1,VIII,8:3
Villano En Su Rincon, El 1935,S 22,X,2:5
Ville Sans Amour, Le 1928,D 16,IX,4:7
Vincent 1959,O 1,40:1; 1959,O 11,II,1:1
Vinegar Tree, The 1930,N 20,30:3; 1930,D 7,IX,1:1; 1931,N 15,VIII,4:1; 1932,Je 9,27:7; 1932,Jl 10,IX,1:3; 1935,Ag 14,16:1
Vingt ans, Madame 1928,Ap 8,VIII,4:1
Vintage Wine 1934,My 30,14:2; 1934,Je 24,IX,1:4
Vintage '60 1960,S 13,41:1
Viol de Lucrece, Le 1931,Jl 5,VIII,1:6
Violet 1944,O 25,16:1
Violet, The 1930,S 30,24:2
Virgin, The 1926,F 23,26:1
Virgin and the Fawn, The 1949,Mr 18,33:2
Virgin Man, The 1927,Ja 19,20:4
Virgin of Bethulia, The 1925,F 24,17:2
Virgin With a Big Heart, The 1925,F 1,VII,2:1
Virginia 1937,S 3,13:2; 1937,S 12,XI,1:1; 1937,O 5,29:1
Virginian, The 1937,Ag 10,22:7
Virtue (?) 1922,N 17,14:1
Virtue's Bed 1930,Ap 16,26:5
Virtuous Island, The 1957,Ap 10,39:1
Visit, The 1958,My 6,40:1; 1958,My 18,II,1:1; 1958,S 7,II,1:1; 1958,N 16,II,1:1; 1960,Mr 9,38:3; 1960,Je 25,13:5; 1967,S 13,41:1
Visit to a Small Planet 1957,F 8,18:1; 1957,F 24,II,1:1
Visit With the Family, A 1957,O 17,42:5
Visitatio Sepulchri 1968,Ap 29,49:1
Visitor, The 1944,O 18,24:5
Visitor From Forest Hills 1968,F 15,49:1
Visitor From Hollywood 1968,F 15,49:1
Visitor From Mamaroneck 1968,F 15,49:1
Vita Nuova 1935,F 26,16:2
Viva Madison Avenue 1960,Ap 7,42:1
Viva O'Brien 1941,O 10,27:2
Vivat! Vivat Regina! 1970,My 24,80:1; 1970,Jl 20,21:2
Vive la Femme 1927,My 29,VII,2:1
Vive la Libe 1964,Ja 9,36:3
Vive le Roi 1935,N 24,IX,3:7
Vive l'Empereur 1921,N 21,VIII,2:1
Viveuse et le Moribond, La 1926,F 14,III,11:1
Vocation, La 1926,D 19,VII,3:3
Vogue 1921,O 23,22:2
Vogues and Frolics 1924,Je 26,21:7
Vogues of 1924 1924,Mr 28,14:3
Voice From the Minaret, The 1922,Ja 31,11:2; 1922,F 5,VI,1:1
Voice of Israel, The 1948,O 26,40:2
Voice of the Turtle, The 1943,D 9,30:3; 1943,D 19,II,3:1; 1944,D 10,II,6:4; 1944,D 19,27:2; 1947,Jl 10,17:1; 1947,Ag 24,II,1:5; 1961,Je 28,41:1
Voie Lactee, La 1933,F 26,IX,2:2
Voix Humaine, La 1930,Mr 9,IX,2:7
Volpone 1928,Ap 10,32:1; 1928,Ap 22,IX,1:1; 1928,D 9,X,2:7; 1930,Mr 11,24:5; 1937,N 16,26:4; 1947,F 25,32:2; 1948,Ja 9,24:6; 1957,Ja 8,27:1; 1957,Ja 13,II,10:1; 1957,F 3,II,1:1; 1957,F 5,27:2; 1964,Jl 20,18:3; 1967,Je 30,29:1
Voltaire 1922,Mr 21,17:1
Von Mund zu Mund 1926,D 5,VIII,8:7
Vor Sonnenuntergang 1932,Mr 13,VIII,2:7
Vortex, The 1924,N 30,VIII,2:1; 1925,S 8,21:5; 1925,S 17,20:1; 1925,S 27,VII,1:1; 1926,Ja 3,VII,1:1
Voyage, Le 1937,F 28,XI,2:1
Voyage Circulaire 1934,D 2,X,2:1
Voyage de Monsieur Perrichon, Le 1937,N 2,32:3
Voyage Round My Father, A 1970,N 28,20:2
Voyageur et l'Amour, Le 1932,Ap 3,VIII,2:2
Voyageur Sans Bagage, Le 1938,Ja 2,X,3:5
Vrai Mistere de la Passion, Le 1935,Jl 21,IX,1:6; 1937,S 5,X,5:3
Vray Proces de Jehane d'Arc, Le 1929,Je 16,VIII,2:3

W

Wade in de Water 1929,S 14,17:2
Wait a Minim! 1966,Mr 8,43:1
Wait Till We're Married 1921,S 27,14:1
Wait Until Dark 1966,F 3,21:1
Waiting For Gillian 1954,Ap 22,36:2
Waiting for Godot 1955,N 13,II,3:1; 1956,Ap 20,21:2; 1956,Ap 29,II,1:2; 1957,Ja 22,25:1; 1958,Ag 6,22:1; 1968,Ag 23,38:1
Waiting for Lefty 1935,F 11,14:5; 1935,Mr 27,24:5; 1967,D 19,58:2
Waiting in the Wings 1960,Ag 9,31:4; 1960,S 8,40:3
Wake Up, Darling 1956,My 3,34:2
Wake Up, Jonathan 1921,Ja 18,14:1; 1921,Ja 23,VI,1:1; 1921,Ja 23,VI,1:6
Wake Up and Dream 1929,Ap 14,X,1:8; 1929,D 31,14:3; 1930,Ja 5,VIII,1:8; 1930,Ja 12,9:1; 1930,Ja 12,VIII,1:1
Walk a Little Faster 1932,D 8,24:4
Walk Down Mah Street! 1968,Je 13,54:1

Walk Hard 1944,D 1,28:2; 1946,Mr 28,34:2
Walk in Dark Places, A 1966,Ja 28,21:1
Walk in Darkness 1963,O 29,30:2
Walk Into My Parlor 1941,N 20,38:2
Walk Together Children 1968,N 12,54:1
Walk Together Chillun 1936,F 5,15:2
Walk-Up 1961,F 24,24:1
Walk With Music 1940,Je 5,33:2
Walking Gentleman, The 1942,My 8,26:2
Walking Happy 1966,N 28,47:1; 1966,D 18,II,3:1
Walking to Waldheim 1967,N 11,25:2; 1967,N 19,II,1:1
Wall, The 1960,O 12,44:4; 1960,O 23,II,1:1; 1961,N 9,40:3
Wall Street 1927,Ap 21,24:4
Wall Street Scene 1937,O 19,29:2
Wallace, The 1960,Ag 23,26:4
Wallflower 1944,Ja 27,14:2
Walrus and the Carpenter, The 1941,N 10,20:2
Waltz in Goose Step 1938,N 2,26:2
Waltz Invention, The 1969,Ja 12,II,20:4
Waltz King, The 1943,N 28,II,1:1
Waltz of the Dogs, The 1928,Ap 26,31:3
Waltz of the Toreadors, The 1956,Mr 11,II,3:1; 1956,D 22,14:8; 1957,Ja 18,17:2; 1957,Ja 27,II,1:1; 1958,Mr 5,37:1
Walzer aus Wien 1930,N 25,30:3
Wandering 1968,My 9,55:2
Wandering Jew, The 1921,O 27,22:1; 1921,O 30,VI,1:1; 1927,F 2,22:4
Wandering Stars 1946,D 14,18:2; 1966,N 14,52:2
Wanhope Building, The 1947,F 11,36:5
Wann und Wo 1927,D 18,IX,1:8
Wanted 1928,Jl 3,19:2
Wanted for Murder 1937,Je 29,18:1; 1937,Ag 26,25:3
War 1929,S 19,37:3; 1966,Ap 13,36:1
War and Peace 1942,My 22,26:3; 1943,Ag 22,II,1:8; 1962,Je 16,10:1; 1965,Ja 12,32:1; 1965,Ja 31,II,1:1; 1967,Mr 22,42:1; 1967,Ap 2,II,1:1
War Games 1969,Ap 18,37:1
War Is Hell Gray, The 1929,D 27,26:4
War President 1944,Ap 25,17:3
War Song, The 1928,S 25,29:3
Warhol Machine, The 1967,O 4,43:1
Warm Body, A 1967,Ap 17,44:2
Warm Peninsula, The 1959,O 21,46:2
Warn That Man 1942,Ja 1,IX,1:4
Warning, The-A Theme for Linda 1969,Ap 27,92:1; 1969,Jl 31,28:1; 1969,Ag 3,II,1:4; 1969,S 22,36:1
Warrior's Husband, The 1932,Mr 12,19:4
Wars of the Roses, The 1963,Jl 18,14:1; 1964,Ja 14,24:7
Wars of the Roses, The (Part I) 1970,Jl 2,30:1
Wars of the Roses, The (Part II) 1970,Jl 3,15:1
Warson at Night 1938,Ja 31,14:3
Washington-All Change! 1939,N 14,19:2
Washington Heights 1931,S 30,23:4
Washington Jitters 1938,My 3,19:1
Washington Square College Varsity Show 1931,Ap 19,31:6
Wasp, The 1923,Mr 28,14:3
Wasp's Nest, The 1927,O 26,26:3
Waste 1936,D 20,XI,3:3
Watch on the Rhine 1941,Mr 25,26:7; 1941,Ap 2,26:2; 1941,Ap 13,IX,1:1; 1941,Ag 24,IX,1:1; 1942,Ap 24,20:6; 1942,My 3,VIII,1:7
Watch-Pit 1969,Ja 30,39:1
Watched Pot, The 1933,My 5,13:7; 1947,O 29,31:4
Water Carrier, The 1936,D 25,20:2; 1939,Jl 2,IX,1:6
Watercolor 1970,Ja 22,30:1
Watering Place, The 1969,Mr 13,51:1
Waterloo Bridge 1929,D 1,X,4:7; 1930,Ja 7,29:2; 1931,N 29,VIII,4:1
Waters of the Moon 1951,My 6,II,3:7; 1953,Ap 2,34:3
Wave and the Rock, The 1931,Ap 13,17:3
Way, The 1940,O 12,20:3
Way Back, The 1949,Ja 29,9:5
Way of the Cross, The 1959,Ja 16,35:2
Way of the World, The 1924,N 18,23:4; 1931,Je 2,34:3; 1948,N 7,II,3:1; 1950,Ap 9,73:5; 1953,Ap 10,17:1; 1954,S 30,38:2; 1954,O 17,II,1:1; 1965,Je 2,40:1; 1969,Ag 7,29:1
Way Out, The 1932,D 14,27:3
Way Things Go, The 1950,Mr 3,19:8; 1950,Mr 12,II,3:7
Way Things Happen, The 1923,D 30,VII,2:1; 1924,Ja 29,17:5; 1924,F 3,VII,1:1
Way to the Stars, The 1932,O 2,IX,2:5
Ways and Means 1936,D 1,31:1; 1948,F 21,8:2; 1967,My 4,34:1
Wayside 1957,Ap 18,34:1
Wayward Saint, The 1955,F 18,17:1; 1955,F 27,II,1:1
Wayward Stork, The 1966,Ja 20,27:1
We All Do 1927,Mr 1,30:3
We Americans 1926,S 26,VIII,2:7; 1926,O 13,20:4
We Are No Longer Children 1932,Ap 1,17:2
We at the Cross Roads 1939,Mr 26,X,3:1
We Bombed in New Haven 1967,D 7,58:1; 1967,D 17,II,3:7; 1968,S 26,64:2; 1968,O 17,51:1; 1968,O 27,II,1:1
We Comrades Three 1962,O 12,26:1; 1966,D 21,46:1

We Girls 1921,N 10,26:3
We Have Always Lived in the Castle 1966,O 20,53:1
We Live and Laugh 1936,My 9,10:3
We Moderns 1923,D 30,VII,2:1; 1924,Mr 12,17:2;
1924,Mr 16,VIII,1:1
We Never Learn 1927,D 25,VIII,2:3; 1928,Ja 24,26:1
We Real Cool 1965,Jl 3,10:5
We the People 1933,Ja 23,9:5; 1933,F 5,IX,1:1
We Were Dancing 1935,O 17,28:3; 1936,N 28,13:1;
1936,D 6,XII,5:1; 1940,Ag 6,15:3
Weak Link, The 1940,Mr 5,19:2
Weak Sisters 1925,O 14,31:3
Weak Woman, A 1926,Ja 27,16:3
Weaker Sex, The 1931,Mr 1,VIII,1:3
Weather Clear, Track Fast 1927,O 19,24:5
Weather Clear-Track Fast 1927,O 2,VIII,4:6
Weather Permitting 1935,My 24,24:5
Weathercock, The 1948,Ag 6,22:3
Weavers, The 1921,Jl 24,VI,1:7; 1928,Ap 1,IX,2:4
Web, The 1932,Je 28,24:4
Web and the Rock, The 1950,Ag 20,II,1:1
We'd Rather Switch 1969,D 20,35:1
Wedding, The 1948,F 6,29:2; 1961,Ap 21,26:2
Wedding Breakfast 1954,N 22,29:2; 1954,D 5,II,5:1
Wedding Chains 1932,Mr 28,10:5
Wedding in Japan 1949,N 11,29:1; 1957,Mr 12,37:7
Wedding in Paris 1954,Ap 6,35:2
Wedding March, The 1955,O 17,33:1
Wedding Night 1930,N 2,VIII,3:2
Wednesday's Child 1934,Ja 17,23:2;
1934,Ja 28,IX,1:1
Week-end 1929,O 23,26:4
Weekend 1968,Mr 14,50:2; 1968,Mr 31,II,1:1
Weep for the Virgins 1935,D 2,18:1
Weh dem der Luegt 1928,Ap 1,IX,2:4
Weibsteufel, Der 1927,My 8,VII,1:5
Weisse Laemmchen, Das 1921,Mr 6,VI,1:7
Welcome Stranger 1920,S 14,12:1; 1921,O 21,18:2
Welcome to Our City 1962,O 13,17:1
Welded 1924,Mr 9,VIII,2:3; 1924,Mr 18,24:1;
1924,Mr 23,VIII,1:1; 1965,Mr 13,17:1
Well of Romance, The 1930,N 8,21:2
Well of the Saints, The 1932,Ja 22,15:2;
1934,N 22,26:2; 1959,Ap 11,15:4; 1970,Ag 10,34:1
Welttheater 1933,Je 25,IX,1:2
Wen, The 1966,Je 8,42:2; 1966,Jl 16,14:6
Wer Will Unter die Soldaten? 1931,My 10,VIII,3:2
We're All in the Gutter 1927,Mr 5,12:2
We're Civilized? 1962,N 9,30:1
Werewolf, The 1922,Jl 23,VI,1:1; 1924,Je 8,VII,1:8;
1924,Ag 26,6:1; 1924,Ag 31,VII,1:1
West of the Moon 1961,Je 29,26:1
West Side Story 1957,S 27,14:4; 1957,O 6,II,1:1;
1957,O 13,II,9:1; 1957,O 27,II,15:3;
1960,Ap 28,31:1; 1960,My 8,II,1:1;
1961,Mr 31,22:3; 1961,Je 17,13:2; 1964,Ap 9,24:2;
1964,D 31,12:1; 1965,Je 25,37:2; 1968,Je 25,32:1;
1968,S 1,II,20:4
Western Chamber, The 1936,F 23,X,1:1
Western Union 1937,Ag 10,22:7
Western Waters 1937,D 29,17:1
Western Wind 1949,Ag 9,20:6
Wet Paint 1965,Ap 13,33:1
Wetter Fuer Morgen-Veranderlich 1932,Je 19,IX,1:3
Wetward Ho 1921,Ap 22,13:2
We've Got to Have Money 1923,Ag 21,12:1
What a Killing 1961,Mr 28,41:1
What a Life 1938,Ap 14,26:2; 1939,Ag 2,17:5
What a Question 1930,F 23,VIII,2:5
What a Relief 1935,D 14,10:6; 1935,D 19,34:4
What Ann Brought Home 1927,F 22,22:2
What Big Ears! 1942,Ap 21,18:5
What Can Money Buy 1923,O 7,IX,2:2
What D' You Call It? 1940,Mr 20,36:2
What Did We Do Wrong? 1967,O 23,56:1;
1967,N 12,II,5:6; 1967,N 19,II,1:1
What Did You Say "What" For? 1959,My 5,40:1
What Do We Know 1927,D 24,8:1
What Does the Public Want? 1923,Jl 16,14:3
What Every Woman Knows 1926,Ap 14,20:2;
1926,Ap 18,VIII,1:1; 1928,D 2,X,4:4;
1936,Jl 21,13:1; 1938,Ag 30,14:5; 1946,N 9,13:2;
1954,S 29,23:4; 1954,D 23,16:2
What Girls Do 1935,Ja 14,10:4
What It Is to Be Young 1937,Ap 27,18:6
What Makes Sammy Run? 1964,F 28,19:1
What Might Happen 1926,Je 20,VII,1:1
What Never Dies 1926,D 19,VII,6:1; 1926,D 29,24:2;
1927,Ja 16,VII,1:1
What Next 1920,Ja 27,7:2
What of It? 1929,Mr 9,24:2
What Price Glory 1924,S 6,14:3; 1924,S 21,VII,1:1;
1924,S 28,VII,1:1; 1929,Ap 28,IX,1:4;
1939,S 24,IX,1:1; 1949,Mr 3,33:2
What Shall We Tell Caroline? 1961,N 22,24:2
What the Butler Saw 1969,Mr 7,27:7; 1970,My 5,56:1
1970,My 17,II,1:1; 1970,O 14,38:1
What the Doctor Ordered 1927,Ag 19,20:2
What the Public Wants 1922,My 2,22:3
What Women Do? 1925,Jl 21,26:4
Whatever Goes Up 1935,N 26,28:2
Whatever Possessed Her 1934,Ja 26,21:2
What's in a Name? 1920,Mr 20,14:2

What's It to You? 1932,Mr 18,25:4
What's the Big Idea? 1926,Mr 24,20:3
What's the Use? 1926,S 7,19:1
What's Up 1943,N 12,24:6; 1943,N 21,II,1:1;
1953,O 28,37:2
What's Your Number? 1929,Ag 16,18:3
What's Your Wife Doing? 1923,O 2,10:3
Wheel, The 1921,My 8,VI,1:1; 1921,Ag 30,10:1
When Blue Hills Laughed 1927,O 9,VIII,2:1
When Chicago Was Young 1932,N 13,IX,3:8
When Crummles Played 1928,S 23,IX,2:2;
1928,O 2,34:3
When Did You Last See My Mother? 1967,Ja 5,27:5
When Differences Disappear 1941,Je 3,17:4
When Eve's Children Are Not Adam's
1932,Ap 23,11:2
When Father Smiles 1931,Mr 22,VIII,4:4
When Hell Froze 1930,O 5,IX,4:6
When I Was a Child 1960,D 9,38:1
When in Rome 1929,Je 16,VIII,2:1; 1934,F 28,22:6
When Ladies Meet 1932,Ag 14,IX,1:7; 1932,O 7,19:1;
1932,O 16,IX,1:1; 1933,Ap 27,15:4;
1933,My 14,IX,2:2
When the Bough Breaks 1932,F 17,19:2;
1950,My 9,25:5
When the Roll Is Called Up Yonder 1930,My 9,20:5
When We Are Married 1938,O 12,34:1;
1938,O 30,IX,1:2; 1939,N 21,19:5; 1939,D 10,X,5:6;
1939,D 26,22:3
When We Are Young 1920,N 23,11:1
When We Dead Awaken 1926,My 18,29:3;
1966,Ap 19,37:2
When You See Me You Know Me
1927,Ag 14,VII,1:7
When You Smile 1925,O 6,31:2
Where Angels Fear to Tread 1963,Je 8,14:6
Where Do We Go From Here? 1938,N 16,26:2
Where E'er We Go 1943,Je 15,16:1; 1943,Je 20,II,1:1
Where People Gather 1967,O 26,56:1
Where Stars Walk 1948,F 25,27:2
Where The Cross Is Made 1928,My 10,31:1
Where There's a Will 1939,Ja 18,16:6;
1953,Je 18,38:5
Where's Charley? 1948,O 12,33:2; 1948,O 24,II,1:1;
1949,Ap 3,II,2:3; 1950,Ag 20,II,1:1; 1951,Ja 30,21:7;
1958,Mr 16,II,3:1; 1966,My 26,57:1
Where's Daddy? 1966,Mr 3,27:1
Where's Your Husband? 1927,Ja 15,10:3
While Parents Sleep 1934,Je 5,28:2
While the Sun Shines 1944,S 20,21:3; 1944,S 24,II,1:1
Whim, The 1931,Ap 27,24:4
Whirl of New York, The 1921,Je 14,18:1
Whirlpool 1929,D 4,37:3
Whisky 1929,Ja 13,VIII,2:7
Whisper in God's Ear, A 1962,O 12,27:2
Whisper Into My Good Ear 1962,O 2,47:1
Whisper to Me 1960,N 22,38:6
Whispering Friends 1928,F 21,18:3
Whispering Gallery, The 1929,Ja 6,VIII,4:4;
1929,F 12,22:2; 1935,D 1,II,12:6
Whispering Well, The 1920,D 6,19:1
Whispering Wires 1922,Ag 8,26:2; 1928,Ja 8,VIII,2:3
Whispers on the Wind 1970,Je 4,50:1
Whistle in the Dark, A 1968,F 17,32:2;
1969,O 9,55:1; 1969,N 9,II,3:1
Whistler's Grandmother 1952,D 12,40:2
Whistling in the Dark 1932,Ja 20,16:6; 1932,N 4,25:2;
1933,D 6,29:3
Whistling Wizard and the Sultan of Tuffet
1970,F 1,70:1
White Assegai, The 1930,Ja 22,21:1
White Birds 1927,Je 26,VIII,1:3
White Blackbird, The 1925,N 15,VIII,2:1
White Cargo 1923,N 6,22:2; 1923,D 23,VII,1:1;
1924,My 25,VIII,1:8; 1925,O 25,30:3;
1925,N 22,VIII,1:8; 1941,My 14,24:3;
1960,D 30,12:1
White Christmas 1936,Jl 7,22:2
White Collars 1925,F 24,17:2
White Desert 1923,O 19,17:3
White Devil, The 1955,Mr 15,32:5; 1965,D 7,56:1;
1969,N 14,38:2
White Dress, The 1932,D 14,27:3
White Eagle, The 1927,N 27,IX,2:1; 1927,D 27,24:4
White Flame 1929,N 5,32:7
White Gold 1925,N 3,34:5
White Guard, The 1934,Ap 8,X,2:2; 1935,Mr 7,27:5;
1938,O 23,IX,3:1
White Haired Boy, The 1940,O 29,32:6
White-Headed Boy, The 1920,O 31,VI,1:4;
1921,S 16,20:1
White Hell 1935,Ag 13,20:3
White Horse Inn 1931,Ap 9,30:2; 1931,Ap 27,24:5;
1932,Ja 17,VIII,2:1; 1936,O 2,28:5
White House, The 1964,My 20,39:1
White House Happening 1967,Ag 27,II,4:8
White House Murder Case, The 1970,F 19,59:1;
1970,Mr 1,II,1:4; 1970,Mr 15,II,3:1
White Lies 1967,F 13,42:1; 1967,F 26,II,1:5;
1967,O 19,58:1
White Lights 1927,O 12,30:4
White Lilacs 1928,S 11,31:2
White Man 1936,O 19,22:4

White Peacock, The 1921,D 27,10:2;
1928,My 11,28:1; 1929,Ap 27,16:4
White Plume, The 1939,D 27,16:1
White Rose and the Red, The 1964,Mr 17,31:1
White Snake, The 1963,Ja 4,5:2; 1963,Ja 12,5:2
White Steed, The 1939,Ja 11,16:2; 1939,Ja 22,IX,1:1;
1939,Ag 16,21:3
White Villa, The 1921,F 15,7:1; 1921,F 20,VI,1:1
White Wings 1926,O 16,15:1; 1926,O 24,VIII,1:1
Whiteheaded Boy, The 1937,Ag 11,27:3
Whiteoaks 1936,Ap 15,25:2; 1936,My 17,IX,2:2;
1938,F 23,26:2; 1938,Mr 24,20:2;
1939,Ap 30,XI,2:2
Whiteshop, The 1968,Ag 24,24:2
Whitewashed 1924,Ap 24,22:2
Whitman Portrait, A 1966,O 12,37:1
Who Cares 1930,Jl 9,27:1
Who Fights This Battle? 1936,S 21,26:3
Who Goes Next? 1931,Mr 8,VIII,2:4
Who Is Leslie? 1941,My 20,15:5
Who Is Sylvia? 1950,O 25,45:7
Who Is Who? 1938,D 24,13:3
Who Was That Lady I Saw You With?
1958,Mr 4,33:2
Whole Town's Talking, The 1923,Ag 30,8:2;
1923,S 9,VII,1:1; 1926,S 8,19:3
Whole World Over, The 1947,Mr 28,28:2;
1947,Ap 6,II,1:1
Who'll Save the Plowboy? 1962,Ja 10,24:2;
1962,Ja 28,II,1:1
Whoop-Up 1958,O 23,2:7
Whoopee 1928,N 11,X,2:4; 1928,D 5,34:3;
1929,Ag 6,29:4
Whoops-A-Daisy 1968,D 13,61:1
Whores, Wars & Tin Pan Alley 1969,Je 17,37:1
Who's Afraid of Virginia Woolf? 1962,O 15,33:1;
1962,O 28,II,1:1; 1962,N 1,34:1; 1963,O 6,68:4;
1964,F 8,15:1; 1964,N 26,52:1; 1968,Jl 4,13:1
Who's Got His Own 1966,O 13,52:1; 1967,O 14,13:3
Who's Happy Now? 1969,N 18,39:1; 1970,F 15,II,1:1
Who's Taking Liberty 1939,D 17,IX,4:4
Who's Who 1924,Ap 18,19:2; 1934,S 21,28:4;
1938,Mr 2,16:2
Who's Who, Baby? 1968,Ja 30,36:1
Whose Turn Next? 1970,Ap 19,74:3
Why Do I Deserve This? 1966,Ja 19,31:2
Why Men Leave Home 1922,Jl 30,VI,1:3;
1922,S 13,18:2
Why Not? 1922,D 25,20:1; 1922,D 30,13:4;
1922,D 31,VII,1:1; 1923,Mr 11,VIII,1:3
Why We Misbehave 1935,Jl 25,14:8
Wicked Age, The 1927,O 2,VIII,4:6; 1927,N 5,16:6
Wicked Cooks, The 1967,Ja 24,42:1; 1967,F 5,II,1:1
Wicked Earl, The 1927,Mr 20,VIII,2:7
Widow in Green, A 1931,N 21,21:4
Widow Shannon, The 1923,Jl 15,VI,1:2
Widowers' Houses 1931,Ap 12,IX,2:1;
1952,S 21,II,1:1; 1959,Mr 3,39:2
Wie Werde Ich Reich und Gluecklich?
1930,Ag 31,VIII,2:1
Wieder Metropol 1926,D 5,VIII,8:7
Wiener Blut 1932,S 4,IX,2:2; 1964,S 12,14:1
Wife Insurance 1934,Ap 13,24:5
Wife of Bath's Tale, The 1969,F 4,34:1
Wife With a Smile, The 1921,N 29,20:1;
1921,D 4,VII,1:2
Wife's Away, The 1930,N 23,IX,3:5
Wild Birds 1925,Ap 10,16:1; 1925,Ap 26,VIII,1:1;
1929,Je 23,VIII,2:3
Wild December 1933,Je 25,IX,1:3
Wild Duck, The 1925,F 25,16:4; 1925,Mr 1,VII,1:1;
1928,F 19,VIII,2:1; 1928,N 19,17:1;
1938,Ap 16,16:5; 1951,D 27,17:1; 1956,Ja 8,II,3:1;
1967,Ja 12,49:1; 1967,Ja 22,II,1:1
Wild Justice 1935,Jl 9,24:3
Wild Man, The 1930,My 17,21:5
Wild Man of Borneo, The 1927,S 14,29:2;
1927,S 25,VIII,1:1
Wild Oats Lane 1922,Jl 23,VI,1:6; 1922,S 7,12:1
Wild Rose, The 1926,O 21,23:1
Wild Waves 1932,Ja 24,VIII,3:3; 1932,F 20,11:4
Wild Westcotts, The 1923,D 25,26:2
Wildcat 1960,D 17,20:2
Wildcat, The 1921,N 28,16:2
Wilde Evening with Shaw, A 1963,Mr 7,8:2
Wilderness Road 1955,Je 30,20:4
Wildflower 1923,F 8,17:2; 1923,F 9,10:1
Wilhelm Tell 1925,Mr 2,15:1; 1932,N 20,IX,3:5;
1933,Je 25,IX,1:2; 1964,Ja 19,II,5:1
Will, The 1930,My 6,33:1
Will and the Way, The 1957,D 3,46:5
Will Hill Be Pardoned 1930,Je 1,VIII,2:1
Will Morrissey's Folies Bergere Revue
1930,Ap 16,26:6
Will Morrissey's Newcomers 1923,Ag 9,16:2
Will O' the Wisp, The 1923,My 11,20:3
Will Shakespeare 1923,D 4,VII,1:3; 1923,Ja 2,14:1;
1923,Ja 21,VII,1:1
Will Success Spoil Rock Hunter? 1955,O 14,22:2
Will the Mail Train Run Tonight? 1964,Ja 10,18:1
Will You Kiss Me? 1920,D 5,VII,1:4
Will You Love Me Always? 1932,O 16,IX,3:7
William Had the Words! 1964,Mr 30,36:1

Willie Doesn't Live Here Anymore 1967,F 8,20:2
Willie the Weeper 1961,Ja 4,26:1
Willow and I, The 1942,D 11,32:2
Wilson in the Promise Land 1970,Ja 11,78:1;
  1970,My 27,41:1
Wind and the Rain, The 1933,N 5,IX,1:3;
  1934,F 2,20:6; 1935,Jl 11,24:2
Wind in the Sails 1940,Ag 1,24:6
Wind Is Ninety, The 1945,Je 22,12:2
Wind of Heaven, The 1945,Ap 22,II,2:3
Wind Remains, The 1943,Mr 31,16:6
Windfall 1934,F 27,17:8
Winding Journey, The 1934,My 8,28:6
Window Panes 1927,F 22,22:2
Window Shopping 1938,D 24,13:2
Windows 1922,My 21,VI,1:6; 1923,O 9,17:2;
  1923,O 14,VIII,1:1
Wine, Women and Song 1942,S 29,18:3
Wine of Choice 1937,D 14,32:3; 1938,F 22,18:4;
  1938,F 27,X,1:1
Winesburg, Ohio 1958,F 6,22:2
Winged Victory 1943,N 22,24:1; 1943,N 28,II,1:1
Wingless Victory, The 1936,N 25,17:5;
  1936,D 24,20:2; 1937,Ja 3,X,1:1
Wings of the Dove, The 1963,D 4,53:6
Wings Over Europe 1928,D 11,35:1;
  1928,D 23,VIII,1:1; 1932,My 15,VIII,1:8;
  1936,Mr 4,24:7
Winkelberg 1958,Ja 15,26:2
Winner, The 1954,F 18,34:1
Winner Loses, The 1925,N 8,VIII,2:1
Winners 1968,Jl 26,21:4
Winners and Losers 1947,F 27,27:2
Winnie the Pooh 1967,N 25,33:1; 1967,D 23,28:1;
  1968,Ap 15,41:1
Winslow Boy, The 1947,O 30,32:2; 1947,N 9,II,1:1
Winter Bound 1929,N 13,24:6
Winter Evening, A 1929,Ap 8,32:5
Winter Journey 1952,Ap 4,21:1; 1952,Ap 13,II,3:7;
  1968,Mr 13,39:1
Winter Soldiers 1942,N 30,19:2
Winter's Tale, A 1921,F 5,14:3
Winter's Tale, The 1921,F 13,VI,1:1; 1946,Ja 16,18:6;
  1946,Ja 20,II,1:1; 1958,Jl 21,17:4; 1958,Jl 23,34:3;
  1958,Jl 27,II,1:1; 1963,Je 29,13:1; 1963,Ag 16,14:1;
  1969,My 17,18:1; 1969,Je 1,II,4:5; 1969,S 1,13:1
Winterset 1935,S 26,19:2; 1935,O 6,XI,1:1;
  1936,Ap 5,IX,1:1; 1936,Je 2,35:2; 1946,O 27,II,2:4;
  1966,F 10,32:2; 1968,Jl 23,28:2
Wird Hill Amnestiert? 1930,Je 1,VIII,2:1
Wisdom Teeth 1936,Mr 3,25:2
Wisdom Tooth, The 1926,F 16,22:2;
  1926,F 28,VIII,1:1
Wise-Crackers, The 1925,D 17,26:1
Wise Fool, The 1938,O 10,15:3
Wise Girl 1932,Mr 20,VIII,2:5
Wise Have Not Spoken, The 1954,F 11,35:2
Wise Men of Chelm, The 1933,O 18,24:4
Wise Tomorrow 1937,F 18,19:1; 1937,O 5,29:2;
  1937,O 16,22:5
Wise Woman, The 1934,N 9,24:3
Wiser They Are, The 1931,Ap 7,31:1
Wish Me Luck! 1954,N 1,37:2
Wish You Were Here 1952,Je 26,26:6;
  1952,Ag 31,II,1:1; 1953,O 11,83:5; 1953,O 18,II,3:1
Wisteria Trees, The 1950,Mr 30,39:1;
  1950,Ap 9,II,1:1; 1955,F 3,20:2
Witch, The 1926,N 19,22:5; 1942,S 28,13:1;
  1962,F 16,35:2
Witch of Castile, The 1930,O 25,21:1
Witch of Edmonton, The 1936,D 9,34:1;
  1937,Ja 3,X,3:6; 1962,N 23,32:2
Witches' Sabbath 1962,Ap 20,22:2
Witchfinders, The 1956,My 11,22:6
With a Silk Thread 1950,Ap 13,34:3
With All My Heart 1935,Jl 30,17:1
With Open Eyes 1938,O 27,27:2
With Privileges 1930,S 16,30:2
Within Four Walls 1923,Ap 18,24:1
Within the Gates 1933,D 24,IX,2:2; 1934,F 8,14:4;
  1934,F 25,IX,3:7; 1934,O 23,23:1; 1934,O 28,IX,1:1;
  1934,N 25,IX,1:1
Within the Law 1928,Mr 6,20:1
Without Love 1942,Mr 5,20:7; 1942,Ap 28,17:4;
  1942,N 11,28:1; 1942,N 29,VIII,1:1
Without the Prince 1940,Ap 21,IX,1:6
Without the Walls 1920,Je 7,20:1; 1921,Mr 28,8:1;
  1922,Ap 17,17:1
Without Warning 1937,My 3,23:2
Without Witness 1933,D 28,25:1
Witness 1968,N 22,38:1
Witness for the Prosecution 1953,N 15,II,3:1;
  1954,D 17,35:2; 1954,D 26,II,1:1; 1957,Ja 9,27:4
Wittekind 1935,F 24,VIII,2:1
Wives, The 1965,My 18,35:4; 1965,Je 6,II,1:1
Wives of Henry VIII, The 1931,N 16,22:3
Wizard of Oz, The 1968,N 28,69:2
Woe to Wit 1936,S 13,X,1:1
Wolf! Wolf! 1925,O 30,21:1
Wolf's Cub, The 1927,Ag 30,21:2
Wolves 1924,D 28,VII,1:1; 1924,D 31,9:4;
  1932,Ja 7,26:3

Wolves of Tanner's Close, or the Crimes of Burke
  and Hare, The 1932,Ja 10,VIII,2:4
Woman, The 1929,O 6,IX,4:2; 1965,Ja 6,32:1;
  1965,O 21,56:1
Woman and Her Shadow, The 1923,Ag 12,III,19:1
Woman and the Blues, A 1966,Mr 29,35:2
Woman Bites Dog 1946,Ap 18,21:2
Woman Brown, The 1939,D 9,18:5
Woman Denied, A 1931,F 26,21:1
Woman Disputed, A 1926,S 29,23:2
Woman Hunter, The 1924,F 24,VII,2:5
Woman Is My Idea 1968,S 26,61:1
Woman Kind 1933,S 28,25:2
Woman of Bronze, The 1920,S 8,9:2; 1927,Je 16,25:4
Woman of Destiny, A 1936,Mr 3,25:2
Woman of the Earth, A 1927,F 1,24:6;
  1927,My 31,25:1; 1927,S 27,31:3
Woman of the Soil, A 1935,Mr 26,23:6
Woman on the Jury, The 1923,Ag 16,10:4;
  1923,Ag 26,VI,1:1
Woman to Woman 1921,S 10,12:3
Woman Who Laughed, The 1922,Ag 17,14:3
Woman's a Fool-To Be Clever, A 1938,O 19,18:6
Women, The 1928,S 16,IX,2:4; 1936,D 8,30:6;
  1936,D 28,13:1; 1938,N 5,14:1; 1939,Ap 21,21:2;
  1939,My 7,X,2:2
Women and Ladies 1925,My 10,VIII,4:4
Women Aren't Angels 1941,Ap 27,IX,1:6
Women at the Tomb, The 1961,Ap 25,41:1
Women Go on Forever 1927,S 8,25:1
Women Have Their Way, The 1930,Ja 28,28:1
Women in Politics 1933,O 22,IX,2:3
Women of New York 1931,Mr 23,24:3
Women of Property 1937,Jl 9,18:3; 1937,Ag 1,X,1:7
Women of Trachis 1960,Je 23,18:3
Women of Twilight 1952,Mr 4,22:2
Women's House, The 1930,Ap 27,IX,3:1
Wonder Bar, The 1930,D 7,31:3; 1931,Mr 6,26:6;
  1931,Mr 8,VIII,3:5; 1931,Mr 18,23:4
Wonder Boy 1931,O 24,20:1
Wonder World 1964,My 18,32:1
Wonderful Journey 1946,D 26,30:2
Wonderful Night, A 1929,N 1,23:3; 1937,Jl 14,17:1
Wonderful Thing, The 1920,F 18,9:1;
  1920,F 22,III,6:1
Wonderful Town 1953,F 26,22:3; 1953,Mr 8,II,1:1;
  1953,Ap 5,II,1:5; 1954,My 7,II,1:1; 1955,Mr 6,II,3:1;
  1955,My 17,33:4; 1955,N 13,II,3:1; 1958,Mr 6,32:4;
  1963,F 15,10:2; 1967,My 18,50:1
Wonderful Visit, The 1921,Ap 3,VII,1:3;
  1924,F 13,17:3; 1924,My 18,VII,1:1
Wonderful World of Burlesque, The 1965,Ap 29,38:1
Wonderful World of the Brothers Grimm, The
  1967,D 23,28:1
Wood Demon, The 1938,Ag 7,IX,1:5
Wooden Dish, The 1954,Jl 30,9:4; 1954,Ag 15,II,1:4;
  1955,O 7,20:1
Wooden Idol, The 1930,My 13,27:2
Wooden Kimono 1926,D 28,16:2
Wooden Slipper, The 1934,Ja 4,16:3
Wooden Soldier, The 1923,Je 23,28:4
Woof, Woof 1929,D 26,20:4
Wookey, The 1941,Ag 26,23:2; 1941,Ag 27,15:3;
  1941,S 11,20:5; 1941,S 21,IX,1:1; 1941,O 5,IX,1:1
Words and Music 1932,Ag 26,21:2; 1932,S 17,18:7;
  1932,O 9,IX,1:8
Words Upon the Window Pane, The 1930,N 19,19:5;
  1931,Ja 4,VIII,3:5; 1932,O 29,18:2
Work Is for Horses 1937,N 22,14:6
Workers 1932,D 11,IX,4:5
Workhouse Donkey, The 1963,Jl 9,26:1
Workhouse Ward, The 1937,F 15,13:2;
  1959,Ap 11,15:4
World Is a Stage, The 1962,N 5,37:4
World of Carl Sandburg, The 1959,O 13,44:6;
  1959,O 26,53:3; 1960,S 15,44:1; 1960,S 25,II,1:1
World of Charles Aznavour, The 1965,O 15,49:1
World of Cilli Wang, The 1957,O 15,38:4
World of Gunter Grass, The 1966,Ap 27,38:1
World of Illusion 1964,Je 25,26:2
World of Kurt Weill in Song, The 1964,My 13,53:1
World of Light, The 1931,Mr 31,25:6;
  1931,Ap 19,VIII,3:1; 1931,Ap 27,24:5
World of Lorraine Hansberry, The 1969,Ja 3,15:1
World of Mrs Solomon, The 1969,Je 4,37:1
World of My America, The 1966,O 4,53:1
World of Paul Slickey, The 1959,My 6,48:7
World of Ray Bradbury, The 1965,O 10,11:1
World of Sholom Aleichem, The 1953,S 12,13:2;
  1953,S 20,II,1:1; 1955,Ja 12,22:4
World of Suzie Wong, The 1958,O 15,47:1;
  1958,O 19,II,1:1; 1959,N 18,49:6
World Record, The 1932,Ap 17,VIII,3:8
World Trembles, The 1939,F 28,17:3
World Waits, The 1933,O 26,22:5; 1935,S 30,12:5
World War 2 1/2 1969,Mr 25,40:1
World We Live In, The 1922,N 1,16:1
World We Make, The 1939,N 21,19:1;
  1939,N 26,IX,1:3; 1939,D 3,IX,5:1
World's a Stage, The 1969,My 13,42:1
Worlds Apart 1941,Ja 23,19:3
World's Full of Girls, The 1943,D 7,31:2
World's My Onion, The 1935,Je 16,X,1:8

World's My Oyster, The 1956,Ag 10,10:4
Worlds of Oscar Brown Jr 1965,F 19,25:4
Worlds of Shakespeare, The 1963,D 5,58:1
Worm in Horseradish, A 1961,Mr 14,32:3
Worse Things Happen at Sea 1935,Ap 21,IX,2:2;
  1937,S 1,15:3
Would-Be Gentleman, The 1928,O 2,34:1;
  1930,Ap 30,29:2; 1936,Ag 4,15:1; 1946,Ja 10,29:2;
  1946,Ja 20,II,1:1
Would You Look At Them Smashing All the Lovely
  Windows! 1969,S 5,30:1
Wozzeck 1928,Ap 1,IX,2:4; 1966,Ap 6,34:1
Wrecker, The 1928,F 28,18:2
Wren, The 1921,S 25,VI,1:8; 1921,O 11,22:1;
  1921,O 16,VI,1:1
Wretched the Lionhearted 1962,S 13,31:2
Write Me a Murder 1961,O 27,28:2
Writing on the Wall, The 1923,Jl 3,25:2;
  1923,Jl 8,VI,1:1
Wrong Number 1934,Mr 14,23:6
Wrong Number, The 1921,Jl 17,VI,1:8
Wrong Way Light Bulb, The 1969,Mr 5,40:1
Wunder um Verdun 1930,F 9,IX,1:3
Wunderlichen Geschichten des Kapellmeister
  Kreisler, Die 1922,Ap 2,VI,1:2; 1922,Jl 23,VI,1:1
Wurzel-Flummery 1923,Ja 17,22:2
Wuthering Heights 1939,Ap 28,30:4
Wuziz! 1970,O 2,25:2

X

X Has No Value 1970,F 17,35:1
X Y Z 1929,Ap 7,X,4:4
Xmas in Las Vegas 1965,N 5,31:1

Y

Yahoo 1935,Jl 28,X,1:1
Yankee at the Court of King Arthur, A
  1929,O 27,IX,2:2
Yankee Doodle 1929,Ja 13,VIII,2:4
Yankee Doodle Boy 1939,D 19,29:5
Yankee Fable 1938,O 23,IX,3:5
Yankee Point 1942,N 24,28:2
Yankee Princess, The 1922,O 3,22:1
Yanqui and the Senorita, The 1952,Ag 8,8:7
Y'Avait un Prisonnier 1938,Ja 25,24:3
Yeah-Man 1932,My 27,27:3
Year Boston Won the Pennant, The 1969,My 23,38:1;
  1969,Je 8,II,1:7
Year of Pilar, The 1952,Ja 7,14:3
Year Round, The 1953,My 6,38:7
Yearling, The 1965,D 11,25:1
Years Ago 1946,D 4,44:2; 1946,D 15,II,3:1
Years Between, The 1931,Ap 23,28:5;
  1931,My 10,VIII,2:1; 1942,F 7,13:2
Years of the Locusts 1968,Ag 23,32:1
Yegor Bulevitch 1934,Ja 8,21:7
Yellow 1926,S 22,30:1
Yellow Jack 1934,Mr 7,22:6; 1934,Mr 18,IX,1:1;
  1944,Ap 7,23:3; 1944,Ap 16,II,1:1; 1947,F 28,26:2
Yellow Jacket, The 1921,Ja 5,11:1; 1923,F 9,10:6;
  1923,Ap 20,20:3; 1928,N 8,27:3; 1929,Ja 11,21:1;
  1934,F 25,IX,2:6
Yellow Sands 1926,N 21,VIII,4:1; 1927,S 12,29:3;
  1927,S 18,VII,1:1
Yellow Triangle, The 1929,My 10,32:2
Yeomen of the Guard, The 1933,My 2,20:4;
  1933,Ag 15,20:5; 1934,S 21,28:3; 1935,Jl 30,16:4;
  1936,S 15,37:2; 1939,Ja 24,17:1; 1939,Jl 16,30:4;
  1939,Jl 23,IX,2:1; 1941,D 19,34:3; 1944,Mr 5,34:3;
  1948,F 3,30:2; 1954,My 5,36:2; 1955,O 4,39:2;
  1957,My 22,28:3; 1961,Ap 28,23:1; 1962,Jl 11,28:1;
  1964,Mr 19,29:2; 1964,Ag 3,16:1; 1965,Ap 22,26:1;
  1965,Jl 8,34:1; 1968,My 9,53:1
Yerma 1952,F 8,18:4; 1966,D 9,60:1
Yershov Brothers, The 1959,Je 2,6:4
Yes 1928,F 19,VIII,4:4
Yes, M'Lord 1949,O 5,35:2
Yes, My Darling Daughter 1937,F 10,19:2;
  1937,F 28,XI,1:1; 1937,Je 4,26:2; 1938,Je 14,17:1;
  1938,Jl 13,19:2
Yes, Yes, No No 1969,Ja 1,16:1
Yes, Yes, Yvette 1927,O 4,32:3
Yes and No 1937,N 14,XI,3:1
Yes is for a Very Young Man 1949,Je 7,27:2;
  1963,Mr 6,7:5
Yesterday's Magic 1942,Ap 15,27:2
Yesterday's Orchids 1934,O 6,20:4
Yeux du Coeur, Les 1927,O 16,IX,4:7
Yip, Yip, Yaphank 1942,Jl 12,VIII,1:6
Yo Ho Hum 1927,My 7,15:1
Yoina Seeks a Bride 1936,O 20,31:1
Yokel Boy 1939,Jl 7,12:2
York Nativity Play, The 1956,D 5,49:2
Yosele the Nightingale 1949,O 21,30:4
Yoshe Kalb 1932,O 3,15:5; 1932,N 6,IX,2:1;
  1932,D 18,X,3:1; 1933,Ap 2,IX,6:6; 1933,D 29,27:2;
  1935,My 26,XI,2:2; 1935,Jl 31,20:5;
  1935,Ag 25,X,1:3; 1939,F 6,9:2
Yossel and His Wives 1937,S 19,II,8:3

You and I 1923,F 20,12:1; 1923,F 25,VII,1:1;
  1925,O 20,29:1
You Can't Beat a Woman 1925,Mr 24,26:5
You Can't Sleep Here 1941,My 11,I,42:6
You Can't Take It With You 1936,D 1,30:8;
  1936,D 6,XII,6:2; 1936,D 15,31:1; 1936,D 20,XI,3:1;
  1937,Ag 29,X,1:1; 1937,D 23,25:5; 1938,Ja 9,X,1:7;
  1938,Ja 16,X,1:6; 1945,Mr 27,23:7; 1951,Ap 7,8:6;
  1965,N 24,32:1; 1965,D 5,II,5:1
You Can't Win 1926,F 17,12:1
You Know I Can't Hear You When the Water's
  Running 1967,Mr 14,54:1; 1967,Mr 26,II,1:1;
  1968,Mr 29,33:1
You Need Luck 1938,My 18,16:5
You Never Can Tell 1923,Jl 13,18:4;
  1948,Mr 17,31:2; 1958,Je 17,25:1
You Never Know 1938,Mr 4,16:3; 1938,S 22,26:3
You Reach for Your Hat 1963,O 1,34:1
You Said It 1931,Ja 20,21:3
You Touched Me! 1943,O 17,II,2:4; 1945,S 26,27:2;
  1945,S 30,II,1:1
Youki 1932,O 16,IX,2:3
You'll Never Know 1921,Ap 21,9:2
You'll See Stars 1943,Ja 1,26:6
Young Abe Lincoln 1961,Ap 26,36:1
Young Alexander 1929,Mr 13,28:2
Young American, A 1946,Ja 18,14:5
Young Among Themselves, The 1970,Je 12,28:1
Young and Beautiful, The 1955,O 3,23:2;
  1956,Ag 16,30:6; 1959,My 29,13:1
Young and Fair, The 1948,N 23,35:2; 1949,Jl 1,14:3
Young Auchinleck 1962,Ag 23,24:4
Young Blood 1925,N 25,15:1; 1925,N 29,VIII,1:1
Young Couple Wanted 1940,Ja 25,16:2;
  1940,F 4,IX,1:1
Young Elizabeth, The 1952,Ap 3,45:1;
  1952,Ap 13,II,3:8
Young Go First, The 1935,My 29,16:2
Young Huntress, The 1933,F 19,IX,1:3
Young Idea, The 1923,F 11,VII,1:4
Young Imeson 1924,Mr 23,VIII,1:3
Young Love 1928,Ag 12,VII,1:2; 1928,S 30,IX,2:7;
  1928,O 31,28:1; 1929,Jl 4,8:4

Young Madame Conti 1936,N 20,26:4;
  1936,D 6,XII,7:6; 1937,Ap 1,18:4
Young Man's Fancy, A 1947,Ap 30,33:2
Young Marrieds Play Monopoly 1966,Mr 7,22:1
Young Master Dante, The 1968,D 31,19:1;
  1969,Ja 12,II,1:1
Young Mr Disraeli 1934,N 13,22:2; 1937,N 10,30:5
Young Provincials, The 1958,S 19,22:4
Young Sinners 1929,N 29,24:4; 1931,Ap 21,35:5;
  1933,Mr 7,20:4
Young Visitors, The 1920,N 30,14:1;
  1920,D 5,VII,1:1; 1920,D 26,VI,3:2;
  1928,Ja 29,VIII,2:6; 1968,D 26,48:1
Young Woodley 1925,O 11,VIII,2:6; 1925,N 3,34:1;
  1925,N 8,VIII,1:1; 1928,Mr 11,VIII,1:3
Youngest, The 1924,D 23,17:1
Youngest Verebezy Girl, The 1928,D 2,X,4:7
Your Loving Son 1941,Ap 5,13:2
Your Number's Up 1936,D 24,22:2
Yr Obedient Husband 1937,N 27,21:2;
  1938,Ja 11,26:5
Your Own Thing 1968,Ja 15,33:1; 1968,Ja 28,II,3:1;
  1969,F 8,23:2; 1969,Mr 29,39:1
Your Uncle Dudley 1929,N 19,26:4
Your Woman and Mine 1922,F 28,17:2
Your Young Men 1935,Ag 8,13:2
You're a Good Man, Charlie Brown 1967,Mr 8,51:1;
  1967,Ap 9,II,1:1; 1967,N 19,30:1; 1969,N 14,39:1
Yours, A Lincoln 1942,Jl 10,12:3
Yours Is My Heart 1946,S 6,16:5
Yours Truly 1927,Ja 26,16:5
Youth 1920,O 27,14:3
Youth at the Helm 1934,N 25,IX,3:1; 1935,F 21,22:1
Youth's the Season 1937,O 24,XI,3:3

Z

Zander the Great 1923,Ap 10,24:2;
  1923,Ap 15,VII,1:1
Zany Evening With Elsa Lanchester, A
  1960,N 5,27:2
Zapatera Prodigiosa, La 1964,S 3,23:2

Zaporogetz Za Dunayem 1937,My 9,II,5:3
Zar Laesst Sich Photographieren, Der
  1928,Ap 22,IX,6:7
Zarewitsch, Der 1927,Ap 3,VIII,2:1
Zelda 1969,Mr 6,38:1
Zenebona 1928,Ap 15,IX,4:1
Zeno 1923,Ja 21,VII,1:6; 1923,Ag 27,14:2
Zeppelin 1929,Ja 15,22:3
Zia Morta, La 1931,N 30,16:3; 1933,F 13,11:3
Ziegfeld Follies 1920,Je 23,14:1; 1921,Je 22,10:1;
  1922,Je 6,18:2; 1923,Ja 30,12:2; 1923,Je 5,24:3;
  1923,O 22,17:2; 1924,Mr 18,25:2; 1924,Je 25,26:1;
  1925,Je 28,VIII,1:1; 1927,Ag 17,27:3; 1931,Jl 2,30:5;
  1934,Ja 5,24:3; 1934,Ja 21,X,1:1; 1935,D 31,10:1;
  1936,Ja 5,IX,3:1; 1936,Ja 31,17:2; 1936,S 15,37:1;
  1943,Ap 2,16:2; 1943,Ap 11,II,1:1; 1957,Mr 2,19:2
Ziegfeld 9 o'clock Follies 1920,Mr 9,18:1
Ziegfeld's Midnight Frolic 1920,Mr 17,14:2;
  1929,F 19,22:4
Zizi 1964,N 23,51:1
Zizippe 1935,D 29,IX,2:1
Zombie 1932,F 11,17:2
Zoo 1964,F 15,15:3
Zoo, The 1927,O 9,VIII,1:3
Zoo, Zoo, Widdershins, Zoo 1969,S 5,30:1
Zoo Story, The 1959,S 29,45:1; 1960,Ja 15,37:2;
  1960,Ja 31,II,1:1; 1960,Ag 26,13:1; 1961,Jl 10,26:1;
  1963,My 29,39:6; 1963,Je 11,29:2; 1965,F 13,10:7;
  1965,Je 9,42:3; 1968,O 11,41:1
Zoom 1932,Ja 31,VIII,1:8
Zorba 1968,N 18,58:1; 1968,N 24,II,1:1
Zuider Zee 1928,D 19,24:4
Zuleika 1928,Mr 7,28:7; 1957,Ap 12,21:1
Zulu and the Zayda, The 1965,N 11,59:1
Zunguru 1938,Ag 3,14:5; 1938,Ag 7,IX,8:2;
  1940,Mr 21,30:5; 1940,Mr 24,IX,2:1
Zur Goldnen Liebe 1932,Ja 24,VIII,1:4
Zweimal Oliver 1926,N 7,VIII,4:3
Zwie Family, The 1934,Mr 2,22:8

Persons

NOTE: All persons mentioned in the theater reviews are listed here alphabetically, last name first. Their function in the plays is listed after the name in parentheses, such as director, producer, playwright, etc. In entries where no such qualifier appears, the person was a performer (actor, actress, singer). A person with multiple functions will have multiple entries; for example, an actor who later turned producer or director will have two listings. A person having two different functions in the same play will also have two listings; but if one person played several acting roles in the same play, his name will appear only once for all of those roles. Functions that are very uncommon or are given imprecisely in the reviews are designated miscellaneous (misc).

During the compilation of this index it was found that many names appeared in variant spellings and with different surnames, nicknames and middle initials. An intensive effort was undertaken to reconcile such differences and to assure that all names appear accurately and unambiguously.

Names beginning with Mc are alphabetized as though spelled Mac.

Entries under each name are by title of play, in chronological order.

For an explanation of the Index generally and of the citations, see page at the beginning of the Index section.

A

Aabel, Per
Accounting for Love 1954,D 2,37:6
Aaron, Jack
Journey of the Fifth Horse, The 1966,Ap 22,36:1
Nest, The 1970,Ap 10,46:1
Aaron, Joyce
Billygoat Eddie 1964,Ap 21,43:2
Up to Thursday 1965,F 11,45:1
Interview 1966,N 7,66:1
TV 1966,N 7,66:1
Party on Greenwich Avenue, The 1967,My 11,52:1
Aaron, Kenneth
Antigone 1967,Ja 14,18:1
Aaron, Paul (Director)
Salvation 1969,S 25,55:1
Paris Is Out! 1970,F 3,35:1
Dream Out of Time, A 1970,N 9,52:1
Aaron, Stephen (Director)
Doctor and the Devils, The 1959,Ja 21,27:8
Burning, The 1963,D 4,57:1
Aaron, Stephen (Miscellaneous)
Hand Is on the Gate, A 1966,S 22,54:1
Aaron Sisters
Vanities 1931,Ag 16,VIII,1:1
Aarons, Alex (Producer)
Hi-Ya Gentlemen 1940,D 4,34:2
Aarons, Alex A (Producer)
Oh, Kay! 1926,N 9,31:3
Funny Face 1927,N 23,28:2
Here's Howe! 1928,My 2,19:3
Hold Everything 1928,O 11,24:2
Treasure Girl 1928,N 9,22:1
Spring Is Here 1929,Mr 12,26:1
Heads Up! 1929,N 12,34:1
Girl Crazy 1930,O 15,27:1
Singin' the Blues 1931,Ap 12,IX,2:1
Singin' the Blues 1931,S 17,21:3
Adam Had Two Sons 1932,Ja 17,VIII,3:5
Pardon My English 1933,Ja 21,11:4
Aarons, Alfred A (Producer)
My Princess 1927,O 7,24:2
Aarons, Alfred E (Producer)
Headquarters 1929,D 5,32:4
Girl Outside, The 1932,O 25,24:3
$25 an Hour 1933,My 11,14:4
Aarons, Ruth Hughes (Lyricist)
Sleepy Hollow 1948,Je 4,26:3
Aaronson, Arthur (Scenic Designer)
Hello Charlie 1965,O 25,47:2
Aaronson, Celenthe
Logia a la Natividad de Nuestro Senor Jesucristo, El 1937,D 14,33:4
Aaronson, Fayre and Lane
Vaudeville (Palace) 1933,Ja 16,13:2
Aaronson, Irving
Vaudeville (Hollywood) 1932,Mr 22,17:5
Aaronson, Irving Commanders
Vaudeville (Hippodrome) 1926,Mr 16,22:2
Aaroon, Lynn
Stephen D 1966,Ag 5,17:1
Aarrah, Abd'Elkader (Scenic Designer)
Tempest, The 1963,Ap 3,43:1
Abadi, Moussa
Voyage de Monsieur Perrichon, Le 1937,N 2,32:3
Knock 1937,N 17,26:3
Roi Cerf, Le 1937,N 30,26:3
Jalousie du Barbouille, La 1937,D 28,28:7
Medecin Malgre Lui, Le 1937,D 28,28:7
Y'Avait un Prisonnier 1938,Ja 25,24:3
Fantasio 1938,F 8,17:2
Abady, Temple (Composer)
Savonarola Brown 1930,F 26,22:3
Abady, Temple (Lyricist)
Savonarola Brown 1930,F 26,22:3
Abamides, Angela
Let's Make an Opera 1950,D 14,50:2
Abarbanell, Judith
Jew Suss 1929,O 19,22:3
Roaming Stars 1930,Ja 25,12:2
Riverside Drive 1931,Ja 6,24:2
New Man, The 1932,Ap 22,23:2
Yoshe Kalb 1932,N 6,IX,2:1
Wise Men of Chelm, The 1933,O 18,24:4
Jacques Bergson 1936,O 31,24:6
Who Is Who? 1938,D 24,13:3
Abarbanell, Lina
Grand Duke, The 1921,N 2,20:1
Grand Duke, The 1921,N 27,VI,1:1
Happy-Go-Lucky 1926,O 1,27:2

Silver Swan, The 1929,N 28,34:5
Well of Romance, The 1930,N 8,21:2
Inspector General, The 1930,D 24,19:2
Theodora, the Queen 1934,F 1,15:3
Abarbanell, Lina (Director)
Chimes of Corneville, The 1934,Je 29,16:2
Abba, Marta
Diana e la Tuda 1927,Mr 13,II,9:3
Homme, la Bete et la Vertu, L'; Say It With Flowers 1931,D 13,VIII,2:2
Tovarich 1936,S 29,35:2
Tovarich 1936,O 16,31:4
Tovarich 1936,O 25,X,1:1
Abba, Marta (Translator)
Mountain Giants, The 1961,Ap 5,32:3
Abbad, Consuelo
Fuerza Ciega, La 1927,D 6,26:1
Amor 1937,Ap 22,18:6
Cuando Los Hijos De Eva No Son Los Hijos De Adan 1937,My 1,17:4
Tierra Baja 1937,My 8,22:4
Abbate, John A (Scenic Designer)
Merchant of Venice, The 1955,Ja 8,9:7
Abbe, Charles
Near Santa Barbara 1921,F 1,14:1
Intimate Strangers, The 1921,N 8,28:1
Alarm Clock, The 1923,D 25,26:2
Handy Man, The 1925,Mr 10,19:2
City Chap, The 1925,O 27,21:1
Puppy Love 1926,Ja 28,16:3
They All Want Something 1926,O 13,20:2
Heaven-Tappers, The 1927,Mr 9,28:3
Jimmie's Women 1927,S 27,30:3
Hotbed 1928,N 10,20:7
Zeppelin 1929,Ja 15,22:3
Church Mouse, A 1931,O 13,26:4
Abbey, Claire
Purple Canary, The 1963,Ap 23,31:1
Abbey, Edmund
Crooked Gamblers 1920,Ag 2,12:1
Abbey, Edna
Gay Divorce 1932,N 30,23:4
Abbey, Harold
Bitter Sweet 1934,My 8,28:4
Abbey, May
Anything Goes 1934,N 22,26:1
Red, Hot and Blue! 1936,O 30,26:3
Abbey Theatre
Ever the Twain 1929,O 20,III,3:5
Plough and the Stars, The 1937,O 8,26:5
Bugle in the Blood, The 1949,Mr 15,34:5
Abbey Theatre Irish Players (Producer)
Katie Roche 1937,O 4,17:4
Abbot, Bob (Pvt)
Swing Sister Wac Swing 1944,Ja 4,20:4
Abbot, Judy
Child of Manhattan 1932,Mr 2,15:1
Abbot, Prentice
Love in the Tropics 1927,O 19,24:3
Abbott, Annie
Moon Walk 1970,N 27,52:1
Abbott, Bob
Good Boy 1928,S 6,23:2
Abbott, Bud
Streets of Paris, The 1939,Je 25,IX,1:1
Abbott, Charles
Blood Red Roses 1970,Mr 23,48:1
Abbott, Charles (Playwright)
Singing Girl, The 1952,Je 4,31:8
Abbott, Edward
Mr Jiggins of Jigginstown 1936,D 18,30:2
Abbott, Eleanor Plaisted (Scenic Designer)
Emperor Jones, The 1945,Ja 17,18:4
Abbott, Eve
Key Largo 1939,N 28,30:2
Abbott, Evelyn
Romeo and Juliet 1935,D 24,10:2
Hamlet 1936,O 9,30:2
Star-Wagon, The 1937,S 30,18:5
Abbott, George
Broken Wing, The 1920,N 30,14:1
Zander the Great 1923,Ap 10,24:2
White Desert 1923,O 19,17:3
Hell-Bent Fer Heaven 1924,Ja 5,10:1
Lazybones 1924,Je 1,VII,4:3
Lazybones 1924,S 23,23:1
Processional 1925,Ja 13,17:1
Holy Terror, A 1925,S 29,31:2
Those We Love 1930,F 20,22:2
John Brown 1934,Ja 23,22:3
Skin of Our Teeth, The 1955,Je 29,25:3
Skin of Our Teeth, The 1955,Ag 18,16:1
Skin of Our Teeth, The 1955,Ag 28,II,1:1

Abbott, George (Director)
Love 'Em and Leave 'Em 1926,F 4,20:4
Broadway 1926,S 17,19:3
Chicago 1926,D 31,11:1
Spread Eagle 1927,Ap 5,30:2
Spread Eagle 1927,Ap 10,VIII,1:1
Four Walls 1927,S 20,33:1
Coquette 1927,N 9,23:1
Coquette 1927,N 13,IX,1:1
Bless You, Sister 1927,D 27,24:5
Coquette 1928,Jl 1,VIII,3:5
Gentlemen of the Press 1928,Ag 28,27:2
Ringside 1928,Ag 30,13:2
Poppa 1928,D 25,31:1
Those We Love 1930,F 20,22:2
Louder, Please! 1931,N 13,26:4
Lilly Turner 1932,S 20,26:1
Great Magoo, The 1932,D 3,20:7
20th Century 1932,D 30,15:1
Heat Lightning 1933,S 16,9:6
Drums Begin, The 1933,N 25,10:5
John Brown 1934,Ja 23,22:3
Kill That Story 1934,Ag 30,22:2
Small Miracle 1934,S 27,24:3
Ladies' Money 1934,N 2,26:6
Page Miss Glory 1934,N 28,24:2
Three Men on a Horse 1935,Ja 22,22:7
Three Men on a Horse 1935,Ja 31,22:3
Jumbo 1935,N 18,20:2
Jumbo 1935,N 24,IX,1:1
Boy Meets Girl 1935,N 19,27:2
Boy Meets Girl 1935,N 28,38:2
Boy Meets Girl 1935,D 15,XI,3:1
Sweet River 1936,O 29,30:2
Brother Rat 1936,D 17,34:5
Room Service 1937,My 20,16:1
Room Service 1937,My 30,X,1:1
Angel Island 1937,O 21,26:2
Brown Sugar 1937,D 3,29:2
All That Glitters 1938,Ja 20,18:2
What a Life 1938,Ap 14,26:2
You Never Know 1938,S 22,26:3
Boys From Syracuse, The 1938,N 24,36:1
Primrose Path, The 1939,Ja 16,16:3
Primrose Path, The 1939,Ja 16,11:2
Mrs O'Brien Entertains 1939,F 9,16:3
Too Many Girls 1939,O 19,26:2
Ring Two 1939,N 23,38:2
Unconquered, The 1940,F 14,25:2
Goodbye in the Night 1940,Mr 19,31:2
Pal Joey 1940,D 26,22:2
Best Foot Forward 1941,O 2,28:2
Beat the Band 1942,O 15,26:1
Sweet Charity 1942,D 29,26:4
Kiss and Tell 1943,Mr 18,22:1
Kiss and Tell 1943,Mr 28,II,1:1
Get Away Old Man 1943,N 25,40:2
Highland Fling, A 1944,Ap 29,13:2
Snafu 1944,O 26,19:5
On the Town 1944,D 29,11:4
Billion Dollar Baby 1945,D 22,17:2
Billion Dollar Baby 1945,D 30,II,1:1
It Takes Two 1947,F 4,33:4
Barefoot Boy With Cheek 1947,Ap 4,20:2
High Button Shoes 1947,O 10,32:2
Look, Ma, I'm Dancin' 1948,Ja 30,20:2
Mrs Gibsons' Boys 1949,My 5,35:2
Call Me Madam 1950,O 13,25:1
Out of This World 1950,D 22,17:3
Tree Grows in Brooklyn, A 1951,Ap 20,24:3
Number, The 1951,O 31,33:2
In Any Language 1952,O 9,40:2
Wonderful Town 1953,F 26,22:3
Me and Juliet 1953,My 29,17:1
Me and Juliet 1953,Je 7,II,1:1
Wonderful Town 1954,My 7,II,1:1
Pajama Game, The 1954,My 14,20:2
Pajama Game, The 1954,My 15,12:1
Pajama Game, The 1954,My 30,II,1:1
On Your Toes 1954,O 12,24:4
Damn Yankees 1955,My 6,17:1
New Girl in Town 1957,My 15,40:1
Drink to Me Only 1958,O 9,47:4
Once Upon a Mattress 1959,My 12,40:1
Once Upon a Mattress 1959,My 17,II,1:1
Fiorello! 1959,N 24,45:3
Fiorello! 1959,N 29,II,1:1
Tenderloin 1960,O 18,47:2
Call on Kuprin, A 1961,My 26,29:3
Take Her, She's Mine 1961,D 22,19:1
Funny Thing Happened on the Way to the Forum, A 1962,My 9,49:1

Abbott, George (Director)—Cont

Funny Thing Happened on the Way to the Forum,
  A 1962,My 20,II,1:1
Never Too Late 1962,N 28,42:1
Funny Thing Happened on the Way to the Forum,
  A 1963,Je 2,II,1:1
Never Too Late 1963,S 25,48:1
Fade Out--Fade In 1964,My 27,45:1
Fade Out--Fade In 1964,Je 21,II,1:1
Fade Out--Fade In 1965,F 16,40:2
Flora, the Red Menace 1965,My 12,41:2
Anya 1965,N 30,48:1
Help Stamp Out Marriage 1966,S 30,50:1
Agatha Sue, I Love You 1966,D 15,61:1
How Now, Dow Jones 1967,D 8,53:1
How Now, Dow Jones 1967,D 24,II,3:2
Education of H*Y*M*A*N K*A*P*L*A*N, The
  1968,Ap 5,57:1
Education of H*Y*M*A*N K*A*P*L*A*N, The
  1968,Ap 14,II,1:1
Fig Leaves Are Falling, The 1969,Ja 3,19:1
Three Men on a Horse 1969,O 17,35:1
Norman, Is That You? 1970,F 20,30:1
Not Now Darling 1970,O 30,33:1
Abbott, George (Miscellaneous)
On Your Toes 1954,O 12,24:4
Abbott, George (Original Author)
Boys From Syracuse, The 1938,N 24,36:1
Banjo Eyes 1941,N 8,10:6
Banjo Eyes 1941,D 26,20:2
On Your Toes 1954,O 12,24:4
Let It Ride 1961,O 13,27:4
Abbott, George (Playwright)
Fall Guy, The 1924,Jl 20,VII,1:7
Fall Guy, The 1925,Mr 11,19:1
Holy Terror, A 1925,S 29,31:2
Love 'Em and Leave 'Em 1926,F 4,20:4
Love 'Em and Leave 'Em 1926,F 14,VIII,1:1
Cowboy Crazy 1926,Ag 1,VII,4:1
Broadway 1926,S 17,19:3
Broadway 1926,S 26,VIII,1:1
Fall Guy, The 1926,O 10,VIII,2:1
Four Walls 1927,S 20,33:1
Four Walls 1927,O 2,VIII,1:1
Coquette 1927,N 9,23:1
Coquette 1927,N 13,IX,1:1
Broadway 1928,Mr 11,5:3
Ringside 1928,Ag 30,13:2
Those We Love 1930,F 20,22:2
Those We Love 1930,Mr 2,IX,1:1
Lilly Turner 1932,S 20,26:1
Heat Lightning 1933,S 16,9:6
Ladies' Money 1934,N 2,26:6
Three Men on a Horse 1935,Ja 22,22:7
Three Men on a Horse 1935,Ja 31,22:3
On Your Toes 1936,Mr 23,22:4
On Your Toes 1936,Ap 13,14:4
Sweet River 1936,O 29,30:2
You Never Know 1938,S 22,26:3
Boys From Syracuse, The 1938,N 13,IX,2:2
Best Foot Forward 1941,S 12,24:4
Three Men on a Horse 1942,O 10,10:2
Beat the Band 1942,O 15,26:1
Where's Charley? 1948,O 12,33:2
Where's Charley? 1950,Ag 20,II,1:1
Tree Grows in Brooklyn, A 1951,Ap 20,24:3
Tree Grows in Brooklyn, A 1951,Ap 29,II,1:1
Pajama Game, The 1954,My 14,20:2
Pajama Game, The 1954,My 15,12:1
Pajama Game, The 1954,My 30,II,1:1
Damn Yankees 1955,My 6,17:1
Best Foot Forward 1956,Mr 3,16:1
New Girl in Town 1957,My 15,40:1
Pajama Game, The 1957,My 16,27:1
New Girl in Town 1957,My 26,II,1:1
Pajama Game, The 1957,My 26,II,1:1
Where's Charley? 1958,Mr 16,II,3:1
Fiorello! 1959,N 24,45:3
Fiorello! 1959,N 29,II,1:1
Tenderloin 1960,O 18,47:2
Fiorello! 1962,Je 14,24:1
Boys From Syracuse, The 1963,Ap 16,31:1
Boys From Syracuse, The 1963,Je 2,II,1:1
Flora, the Red Menace 1965,My 12,41:2
Anya 1965,N 30,48:1
Where's Charley? 1966,My 26,57:1
Three Men on a Horse 1969,O 17,35:1
Abbott, George (Producer)
Lilly Turner 1932,S 20,26:1
20th Century 1932,D 30,15:1
Heat Lightning 1933,S 16,9:6
Drums Begin, The 1933,N 25,10:5
John Brown 1934,Ja 23,22:3
Kill That Story 1934,Ag 30,22:2
Boy Meets Girl 1935,N 19,27:2
Boy Meets Girl 1935,N 28,38:2
Sweet River 1936,O 29,30:2
Brother Rat 1936,D 8,30:6
Brother Rat 1936,D 17,34:5
Room Service 1937,My 20,16:1
Room Service 1937,My 30,X,1:1
Boy Meets Girl 1937,Jl 6,23:1
Angel Island 1937,O 21,26:2
Brown Sugar 1937,D 3,29:2

All That Glitters 1938,Ja 20,18:2
What a Life 1938,Ap 14,26:2
Boys From Syracuse, The 1938,N 24,36:1
Primrose Path, The 1939,Ja 5,16:3
Mrs O'Brien Entertains 1939,F 9,16:3
See My Lawyer 1939,S 28,29:1
Too Many Girls 1939,O 19,26:2
Too Many Girls 1939,O 29,IX,1:6
Ring Two 1939,N 14,20:3
Ring Two 1939,N 23,38:2
Unconquered, The 1940,F 14,25:2
Goodbye in the Night 1940,Mr 19,31:2
White Haired Boy, The 1940,O 29,32:6
Pal Joey 1940,D 26,22:2
Best Foot Forward 1941,S 12,24:4
Best Foot Forward 1941,O 2,28:2
Best Foot Forward 1941,O 26,IX,1:3
Jason 1942,Ja 22,12:2
Beat the Band 1942,O 15,26:1
Kiss and Tell 1943,Mr 18,22:1
Kiss and Tell 1943,Mr 28,II,1:1
Get Away Old Man 1943,N 25,40:2
Highland Fling, A 1944,Ap 29,13:2
Snafu 1944,O 26,19:5
Dancer, The 1946,Je 6,16:5
It Takes Two 1947,F 4,33:4
Barefoot Boy With Cheek 1947,Ap 4,20:2
Look, Ma, I'm Dancin' 1948,Ja 30,20:2
Mrs Gibsons' Boys 1949,My 5,35:2
Touch and Go 1949,O 14,34:2
Touch and Go 1949,O 30,II,1:1
Tree Grows in Brooklyn, A 1951,Ap 20,24:3
In Any Language 1952,O 9,40:2
In Any Language 1952,O 19,II,1:1
Abbott, George (Translator)
Ragged Edge, The 1927,F 13,VII,1:4
Abbott, Hal
Showboat Revue 1935,Ag 18,13:2
Abbott, Jack
Princess Ida 1925,Ap 14,27:2
Abbott, Jane
Miss Temple Is Willing 1936,Jl 21,13:1
Abbott, Jeremy
Bead-Tangle 1970,Jl 16,38:1
Abbott, Joan
George White's Scandals 1931,S 15,30:1
Keep Moving 1934,Ag 24,10:2
Abbott, John
Fall and Rise of Susan Lenox, The 1920,Je 11,11:2
Some Party 1922,Ap 17,22:1
He Who Gets Slapped 1946,Mr 21,31:4
He Who Gets Slapped 1946,Mr 31,II,1:1
Montserrat 1949,O 31,21:4
Waltz of the Toreadors, The 1957,Ja 18,17:2
Waltz of the Toreadors, The 1957,Ja 27,II,1:1
Abbott, Judith
Alice in Arms 1945,F 1,18:4
Abbott, Judith (Producer)
Agatha Sue, I Love You 1966,D 15,61:1
Abbott, L J (Composer)
Who's Who 1924,Ap 18,19:2
Not Now-Later 1928,Ap 14,25:1
Abbott, L J (Lyricist)
Who's Who 1924,Ap 18,19:2
Abbott, Margery
Gondoliers, The 1936,S 8,23:1
Yeomen of the Guard, The 1936,S 15,37:2
Princess Ida 1936,O 13,32:2
Trial by Jury 1939,Ja 6,25:1
Iolanthe 1939,Ja 13,16:3
Gondoliers, The 1939,Ja 20,14:2
Yeomen of the Guard, The 1939,Ja 24,17:1
Patience 1939,Ja 27,16:3
Abbott, Marion
Wren, The 1921,O 11,22:1
Mountain Man, The 1921,D 13,24:2
Dolly Jordan 1922,O 4,26:1
Exile, The 1923,Ap 10,24:2
For All of Us 1923,O 16,19:4
Slaves All 1926,D 7,24:4
Lombardi, Ltd 1927,Je 7,27:3
19th Hole, The 1927,O 12,30:3
Star of Bengal 1929,S 26,27:2
What a Question 1930,F 23,VIII,2:5
I Want My Wife 1930,Mr 21,30:7
Gold Braid 1930,My 14,31:2
Abbott, Martin
Her Man of Wax 1933,O 12,32:3
Abbott, Merriel (Choreographer)
Fine and Dandy 1930,S 24,26:1
Abbott, Michael
Traitor, The 1949,Ap 1,30:2
Abbott, Michael (Miscellaneous)
Very Special Baby, A 1956,N 15,43:2
Rashomon 1959,Ja 28,36:2
Abbott, Michael (Producer)
Late Love 1953,O 14,35:2
Abbott, O A
It's the Valet 1933,D 15,25:4
Abbott, Patsy
Borscht Capades 1951,S 18,38:3
Abbott, Philip
Harvest of Years 1948,Ja 13,29:2

Abbott, Philip—Cont

Home Is Tomorrow 1950,Je 2,27:2
Springtime Folly 1951,F 27,23:4
Angelic Doctor 1953,Ap 14,30:2
Square Root of Wonderful, The 1957,O 31,40:1
Five Posts in the Market Place 1961,Mr 6,30:1
Promises to Keep 1965,Jl 22,25:1
Abbott, Philip (Director)
Promises to Keep 1965,Jl 22,25:1
Abbott, Philip (Playwright)
Promises to Keep 1965,Jl 22,25:1
Abbott, Richard
Power of Darkness, The 1920,Ja 22,22:1
Hamlet 1920,Mr 17,14:2
Taming of the Shrew, The 1921,My 12,20:2
Merchant of Venice, The 1921,My 14,10:4
Masked Woman, The 1922,D 23,14:2
Little Clay Cart, The 1924,D 6,13:3
Polly 1925,O 12,19:1
Nica 1926,Ja 26,19:1
Abraham; Dulcitus; Callimachus 1926,Mr 29,24:2
Sam Abramovitch 1927,Ja 20,20:5
Jacob Slovak 1927,O 6,28:4
First Mortgage 1929,O 11,36:1
Winter Bound 1929,N 13,24:6
Last Mile, The 1930,F 14,21:2
Cloudy With Showers 1931,S 2,17:5
Dark Hours, The 1932,N 15,24:2
Sister Oakes 1949,Ap 25,19:4
Iceman Cometh, The 1956,My 8,38:1
Five Posts in the Market Place 1961,Mr 6,30:1
Abbott, Ron
Forensic and the Navigators 1970,Ap 2,43:1
Abbott, Ron (Miscellaneous)
Spiro Who? 1969,My 19,55:1
Abbott, Ruth
What the Doctor Ordered 1927,Ag 19,20:2
Middle Watch, The 1929,O 17,27:1
Melo 1931,Ap 17,26:6
Intimate Relations 1932,Mr 29,23:2
Too Many Boats 1934,S 12,26:3
Strip Girl 1935,O 21,22:6
Places, Please 1937,N 13,10:6
Journeyman 1938,Ja 31,14:2
Case History 1938,O 22,15:2
Abbott, Tommy
West Side Story 1957,S 27,14:4
Abbott, Tommy (Miscellaneous)
West Side Story 1964,Ap 9,24:2
Abbott, Victory
Brooklyn Biarritz 1941,F 28,16:2
Abbott and Costello
Streets of Paris, The 1939,Je 20,25:2
Abbott Dancers
George White's Scandals 1929,S 24,29:1
Abboud, Mona
Valmouth 1960,O 7,29:1
Cat and the Canary, The 1965,Ja 5,26:1
Abdallah's Arabs
Good Times 1920,Ag 10,10:1
Abdo, Eduardo
Mima 1928,D 13,24:2
Abdou, Ali (Oliver Jones) (Choreographer)
Slave Ship 1969,N 22,46:1
Abdul
Macbeth 1936,Ap 15,25:4
Abdullah, Achmed (Original Author)
Broadway Interlude 1934,Ap 20,16:3
Abdullah, Achmed (Playwright)
Toto 1921,Mr 22,15:2
Broadway Interlude 1934,Ap 20,16:3
Abe, Lisa Jo
King and I, The 1963,Je 13,30:2
Abel, Alan
Safari! 1955,My 12,32:6
Abel, Alan (Producer)
Safari! 1955,My 12,32:6
Abel, Alfred
Roulette 1932,Mr 27,VIII,3:1
Abel, Chele
Fly Blackbird 1962,F 6,26:2
Abel, Chele (Choreographer)
Jo 1964,F 13,25:1
Abel, Edmond
Little Dark Horse 1941,N 17,14:4
Harriet 1943,Mr 4,24:2
Abel, Joel
What a Killing 1961,Mr 28,41:1
Abel, Jonathan
Fashion 1959,Ja 21,27:1
Abel, Lionel (Playwright)
Death of Odysseus, The 1953,N 4,30:5
Absalom 1956,My 17,37:2
Pretender, The 1960,My 25,42:1
Wives, The 1965,My 18,35:4
Wives, The 1965,Je 6,II,1:1
Abel, Marietta
Fashion 1959,Ja 21,27:1
Abel, Rose Marie
Little Theatre Tournament; Yellow Triangle, The
  1929,My 10,32:2
Abel, Walter
Back to Methuselah (Part V: As Far as Thought
  Can Reach) 1922,Mr 14,11:2

Abel, Walter—Cont
Square Peg, A 1923,Ja 29,10:2
As You Like It 1923,Ap 24,24:1
Spook Sonata, The 1924,Ja 7,23:3
Fashion 1924,F 5,21:2
Crime in the Whistler Room, The 1924,O 10,22:2
S S Glencairn 1924,N 4,31:4
Desire Under the Elms 1924,N 12,20:7
Beyond 1925,Ja 27,14:1
Michel Auclair 1925,Mr 5,23:1
Love for Love 1925,Ap 1,21:2
Enemy, The 1925,O 21,20:1
Taming of the Shrew, The 1925,D 19,14:1
Hangman's House 1926,D 17,27:2
House of Women, The 1927,O 4,32:2
Skidding 1928,My 22,18:5
S S Glencairn 1929,Ja 10,24:5
Sea Gull, The 1929,Ap 10,32:2
First Mortgage 1929,O 11,36:1
At the Bottom 1930,Ja 10,24:3
Sea Gull, The 1930,F 26,22:2
I Love an Actress 1931,S 18,29:2
Mourning Becomes Electra 1932,F 21,VIII,2:6
Mourning Becomes Electra; Hunted, The 1932,My 10,25:2
Mourning Becomes Electra; Haunted, The 1932,My 10,25:2
Mourning Becomes Electra 1932,My 22,VIII,1:1
When Ladies Meet 1932,O 7,19:1
When Ladies Meet 1932,O 16,IX,1:1
Divine Drudge 1933,O 27,22:3
Drums Begin, The 1933,N 25,10:5
Wife Insurance 1934,Ap 13,24:5
Invitation to a Murder 1934,My 18,26:3
Merrily We Roll Along 1934,O 1,14:1
Merrily We Roll Along 1934,O 7,IX,1:1
Wingless Victory, The 1936,N 25,17:5
Wingless Victory, The 1936,D 24,20:2
What Every Woman Knows 1938,Ag 30,14:5
Mermaids Singing, The 1945,N 29,26:6
Parlor Story 1947,Mr 5,29:2
Biggest Thief in Town 1949,Mr 31,31:2
Wisteria Trees, The 1950,Mr 30,39:1
Wisteria Trees, The 1950,Ap 9,II,1:1
Long Watch, The 1952,Mr 21,19:5
Pleasure of His Company, The 1958,O 23,36:1
Pleasure of His Company, The 1958,N 2,II,1:1
Night Life 1962,O 24,44:1
Ninety Day Mistress, The 1967,N 7,49:1
Abele, Arta
Hair 1970,Ja 13,39:1
Abeles, Seymour
Empress of Destiny 1938,Mr 10,16:2
Abell, Kjell (Original Author)
Melody That Got Lost, The 1938,F 6,X,1:2
Abell, Kjell (Playwright)
Lost Melody, The 1936,Je 28,IX,1:6
Eve Serves a Term of Childhood 1937,Je 20,X,2:1
Abels, Gregory
Wars of the Roses, The (Part I) 1970,Jl 2,30:1
Wars of the Roses, The (Part II) 1970,Jl 3,15:1
Richard III 1970,Jl 4,11:1
Abels, Marcella
Girls in Uniform 1932,D 31,10:3
Lady Precious Stream 1936,Ja 28,15:2
Abelson, Hope (Miscellaneous)
Rainmaker, The 1954,O 29,28:1
Royal Hunt of the Sun, The 1965,O 27,36:2
Abelson, Hope (Producer)
Egghead, The 1957,O 10,39:1
Abensen, Marion
Hamlet 1937,Ag 24,24:4
Aber, Arline
Smiles 1930,N 19,19:2
Aber, Charline
Smiles 1930,N 19,19:2
Aber Twins
Strike Me Pink 1933,Mr 6,16:3
Abercrombie, Lascelles (Playwright)
Staircase, The 1923,Ja 29,11:2
Aberlin, Dora
Jeanne d'Arc 1922,Ap 22,9:3
Abernethy, T G (Miscellaneous)
Skits-Oh-Frantics 1967,Ap 3,39:2
Abert, Richard
Hook-Up, The 1935,My 9,24:6
Body Beautiful, The 1935,N 1,24:3
Hell Freezes Over 1935,D 30,14:2
Fields Beyond, The 1936,Mr 7,11:2
Ringside Seat 1938,N 23,24:5
Abilea, Maia
Flies, The; Mouches, Les 1947,Ap 18,26:3
Outside the Door 1949,Mr 2,33:2
Able, Will
Plain and Fancy 1955,Ja 28,14:2
Able, Will B
Bella 1961,N 17,40:1
All American 1962,Mr 20,44:1
Get Thee to Canterbury 1969,Ja 26,74:1
Coco 1969,D 19,66:1
Ableman, Paul (Playwright)
Blue Comedy 1968,O 23,36:1
Ablin, William
Captain Brassbound's Conversion 1950,D 28,21:1

Aborn, Milton (Director)
H M S Pinafore 1926,Ap 7,26:3
Sweethearts 1929,S 23,25:1
Mlle Modiste 1929,O 8,34:1
Naughty Marietta 1929,O 22,26:2
Robin Hood 1929,N 20,26:5
Merry Widow, The 1929,D 3,29:1
Babes in Toyland 1929,D 24,15:3
Prince of Pilsen, The 1930,Ja 14,24:3
Chocolate Soldier, The 1930,Ja 28,28:1
Count of Luxembourg, The 1930,F 18,28:2
Serenade, The 1930,Mr 5,26:7
Babes in Toyland 1930,D 22,17:1
Mikado, The; Town of Titipu, The 1931,My 5,33:2
H M S Pinafore 1931,My 19,25:2
Gondoliers, The 1931,Je 2,34:4
Patience 1931,Je 16,30:2
Pirates of Penzance, The; Slave of Duty, The 1931,Je 30,23:6
Iolanthe 1931,Jl 14,21:5
Trial by Jury 1931,Jl 28,17:6
H M S Pinafore 1931,Jl 28,17:6
Ruddigore 1931,Ag 11,28:3
Merry Widow, The 1931,S 8,39:1
Chocolate Soldier, The 1931,S 22,33:3
Geisha, The 1931,O 6,35:4
Chimes of Normandy, The 1931,N 3,31:3
Naughty Marietta 1931,N 17,31:2
Firefly, The 1931,D 1,23:2
Iolanthe 1932,Ja 5,20:2
Gondoliers, The 1932,Ja 12,29:1
Robin Hood 1932,Ja 28,25:4
Mikado, The 1933,Ap 18,13:4
Yeomen of the Guard, The 1933,My 2,20:4
H M S Pinafore 1933,My 9,20:3
Trial by Jury 1933,My 9,20:3
Patience 1933,My 23,22:6
Bohemian Girl, The 1933,Jl 28,18:5
Pirates of Penzance, The 1933,Ag 8,22:4
Yeomen of the Guard, The 1933,Ag 15,20:5
Aborn, Milton (Producer)
H M S Pinafore 1931,My 31,II,1:2
Mikado, The 1931,Ag 25,17:7
Merry Widow, The 1932,F 21,VIII,23:3
Mikado, The 1933,Ap 18,13:4
Yeomen of the Guard, The 1933,My 2,20:4
H M S Pinafore 1933,My 9,20:3
Trial by Jury 1933,My 9,20:3
Patience 1933,My 23,22:6
Bohemian Girl, The 1933,Jl 28,18:5
Pirates of Penzance, The 1933,Ag 8,22:4
Yeomen of the Guard, The 1933,Ag 15,20:5
Aborn, Sargent (Producer)
Broken Wing, The 1920,D 5,VII,1:1
Abouaf, Albert
He Who Gets Slapped 1956,F 2,18:1
Nobody's Child 1956,Ag 23,25:2
Abraham, F Murray
Man in the Glass Booth, The 1968,S 27,41:1
Tonight in Living Color; David Show, The 1969,Je 11,43:1
Abraham, Paul (Composer)
Zenebona 1928,Ap 15,IX,4:1
Youngest Verebezy Girl, The 1928,D 2,X,4:7
Victoria and Her Hussar 1930,S 21,IX,2:6
Flower of Hawaii; Blume von Hawaii, Die 1931,O 4,VIII,4:1
Ball at the Savoy 1933,F 19,IX,3:1
Ball at the Savoy 1933,S 9,9:7
Abraham, Paul (Musical Director)
Zenebona 1928,Ap 15,IX,4:1
Abraham, Saul (Producer)
Privilege Car 1931,Mr 4,33:1
Abrahams, Mason
Criminals, The 1941,D 22,24:3
Abrahamsen, Allen
H M S Pinafore 1960,Ja 29,14:1
Utopia, Limited 1960,Ap 8,27:2
Gondoliers, The 1961,D 8,44:1
Abramowitz, Bina
Green Fields 1920,Mr 26,11:2
Serving Folk 1920,Ap 22,11:3
Naomi 1920,My 7,12:2
Silent Forces 1920,Ag 30,12:1
One Life for Another 1920,D 18,11:2
Dybbuk, The 1921,S 2,9:2
Andersh; New Worlds 1922,S 26,18:2
Anathema 1923,F 9,10:2
Tenth Commandment, The 1926,N 18,27:1
Gold Diggers, The 1927,D 3,19:2
On Foreign Soil 1927,D 24,8:2
American Chasidim 1928,Mr 17,8:8
Stempenu, the Fiddler 1929,Mr 9,24:7
Angels on Earth 1929,D 11,34:7
Roaming Stars 1930,Ja 25,12:2
Once Upon a Time 1933,S 22,15:1
Organ Grinder, The 1934,Ja 1,28:3
Motel Peissi, The Contor's Kid 1934,N 29,33:3
Lost Paradise 1934,D 14,28:3
Abrams, Dave
Remote Control 1929,S 11,24:5
Abrams, Leon (Playwright)
Heat Lightning 1933,S 16,9:6

Abrams, Marnel
Liliom 1956,F 18,12:5
Abrams, Sally (Producer)
Mary and the Fairy 1956,Mr 24,15:2
Fortunato 1956,Mr 24,15:2
Abrams, William
We Bombed in New Haven 1967,D 7,58:1
Abramski, Joe
Waiting for Lefty 1967,D 19,58:2
Abramson, Charles H (Producer)
Veneer 1929,N 13,24:5
Web, The 1932,Je 28,24:4
All the King's Horses 1934,Ja 31,21:3
Orchids Preferred 1937,Ap 29,16:6
Orchids Preferred 1937,My 12,26:5
Abramson, George
Nautical but Nice 1931,Ap 19,31:6
Abramson, Mark (Miscellaneous)
Power of Darkness, The 1959,S 30,33:1
Abravanel, Maurice (Miscellaneous)
Seven Lively Arts 1944,D 8,26:6
Abravanel, Maurice (Musical Director)
Lady in the Dark 1941,S 3,26:6
Lady in the Dark 1943,Mr 1,14:2
One Touch of Venus 1943,O 8,14:1
Firebird of Florence 1945,Mr 23,13:4
Day Before Spring, The 1945,N 23,27:2
Street Scene 1947,Ja 10,17:2
Regina 1949,N 1,32:2
Abruzzo, Charles
Galileo 1967,Ap 14,31:1
Abruzzo, Rae
Alive and Kicking 1950,Ja 18,25:5
Abzug, Lionel
Way of the World, The 1950,Ap 9,73:5
Acaster, Donald (Lighting Director)
Heartbreak House 1968,Jl 6,9:1
Chemmy Circle, The 1968,Ag 10,17:2
Doctor's Dilemma, The 1969,Je 24,37:1
Accles, Bill (Director)
Macbeth 1969,D 23,25:1
Oedipus 1970,F 23,30:1
Accles, Bill (Miscellaneous)
Trumpets and Drums 1969,O 13,52:1
Acevedo, Myriam
Handful of Fire 1958,O 2,45:3
Achard, Marcel (Original Author)
Come Play With Me 1959,My 1,33:5
Achard, Marcel (Playwright)
Vie Est Belle, La 1928,Je 3,VIII,2:5
Jean de la Lune 1929,My 12,IX,5:3
Belle Mariniere, La 1929,D 8,X,2:2
Rendez-Vous, Le 1930,O 26,VIII,2:1
Domino 1932,F 28,VIII,1:1
Domino 1932,Ag 7,IX,1:1
Domino 1932,Ag 17,13:2
Femme en Blanc, La 1933,My 7,IX,2:5
Petrus 1933,D 31,IX,2:2
Noix de Coco 1936,Ja 12,IX,3:7
Jean de la Lune 1937,D 14,33:3
Petite Lili, La 1951,Mr 11,7:1
Idiote, L' 1960,S 16,39:4
Shot in the Dark, A 1961,O 19,40:1
Turlututu 1962,S 29,14:2
Achard, Marcel (Translator)
Harvey 1950,O 21,10:4
Harvey 1950,D 31,II,3:7
Acher, Frances
Flying Blind 1930,My 16,20:2
Acheson, Charlotte
Gabrielle 1941,Mr 26,26:2
New York Idea, The 1948,Ag 18,29:2
Doll's House, A 1956,My 8,29:2
Achez, Karl Ludwig (Director)
Wilhelm Tell 1933,Je 25,IX,1:2
Achmatova, Pauline
Clear All Wires! 1932,S 15,19:1
Achron, Joseph (Composer)
Tenth Commandment, The 1926,N 18,27:1
Stempenu, the Fiddler 1929,Mr 9,24:7
Witch of Castile, The 1930,O 25,21:1
Ackel, Albert
Right You Are (If You Think You Are) 1950,Je 29,37:2
Right You Are (If You Think You Are) 1957,Mr 5,37:1
Montserrat 1961,Ja 9,30:5
Acker, Mabel
Bluffing Bluffers 1924,D 23,17:2
Find Daddy 1926,Mr 9,21:3
Bye Bye Bonnie 1927,Ja 14,15:3
New York 1927,N 15,26:2
My Girl Friday! 1929,F 13,20:2
Late George Apley, The 1944,O 20,16:4
Late George Apley, The 1944,N 22,26:2
Acker, Sharon
Merry Wives of Windsor, The 1956,Je 21,34:4
Ackerley, J R (Playwright)
Prisoners of War 1935,Ja 29,24:1
Ackerman, Alfred
Half Moon Inn 1925,Mr 10,14:1
Ackerman, Bernice
Just Fancy! 1927,O 12,30:2

Ackerman, Bernice—Cont

Animal Crackers 1928,O 24,26:2
Ackerman, Bettye
Salvation on a String; No Count Boy, The
1954,Jl 7,23:1
Tartuffe 1957,O 9,39:1
Ackerman, Doreen (Costume Designer)
Bella 1961,N 17,40:1
View From the Bridge, A 1965,Ja 29,24:1
Ackerman, Dorothy
Dover Road, The 1924,D 20,18:2
Ackerman, Jean
Whoopee 1928,D 5,34:3
Smiles 1930,N 19,19:2
Ackerman, Leonard
Betty Behave 1927,Mr 9,28:4
Ackerman, Loni
George M! 1968,Ap 11,48:1
Ackerman, Michael (Playwright)
Glorious Ruler, The 1969,Jl 1,31:1
Ackerman, P Dodd (Scenic Designer)
Merry Merry 1925,S 25,24:3
Weak Woman, A 1926,Ja 27,16:3
Girl Friend, The 1926,Mr 18,26:5
What's the Big Idea? 1926,Mr 24,20:3
Climax, The 1926,My 18,29:3
Twinkle Twinkle 1926,N 17,22:2
Barker, The 1927,Ja 19,20:6
Trial Marriage 1927,F 1,24:3
Sinner 1927,F 8,20:2
Window Panes 1927,F 22,22:2
Crime 1927,F 23,27:3
Lost 1927,Mr 29,22:2
Half a Widow 1927,S 13,37:3
My Princess 1927,O 7,24:2
Springboard, The 1927,O 13,23:1
It Is to Laugh 1927,D 27,24:2
Excess Baggage 1927,D 27,24:2
Gringa, La 1928,F 2,17:1
Caravan 1928,Ag 30,13:3
Cross My Heart 1928,S 18,32:7
Just a Minute 1928,O 9,34:3
Hello, Yourself 1928,O 31,28:2
Freddy 1929,Jl 17,23:4
Murder on the Second Floor 1929,S 12,35:1
Mountain Fury 1929,S 26,27:2
Humbug, The 1929,N 28,34:5
Headquarters 1929,D 5,32:4
Phantoms 1930,Ja 14,24:3
Challenge of Youth 1930,Ja 21,28:5
Recapture 1930,Ja 30,16:4
Launcelot and Elaine 1930,Mr 10,24:3
I Want My Wife 1930,Mr 21,30:7
Dear Old England 1930,Mr 26,24:6
Courtesan 1930,Ap 30,29:3
9th Street Guest, The 1930,Ag 26,24:3
Long Road, The 1930,S 10,30:2
Farewell to Arms, A 1930,S 23,30:3
Frankie and Johnny 1930,S 26,16:5
Tyrant, The 1930,N 13,33:1
Five Star Final 1930,D 31,11:1
Nikki 1931,S 30,23:4
Divorce Me, Dear 1931,O 7,29:2
Steel 1931,N 19,26:5
Cold in Sables 1931,D 24,20:7
Devil Passes, The 1932,Ja 5,20:3
East of Broadway 1932,Ja 27,19:3
Inside Story, The 1932,F 23,23:2
Life Begins 1932,Mr 29,23:2
Budget, The 1932,S 21,26:4
Nona 1932,O 5,26:4
Girl Outside, The 1932,O 25,24:3
Marathon 1933,Ja 28,8:8
Strange Gods 1933,Ap 17,16:6
Sailor, Beware! 1933,S 29,24:4
Undesirable Lady, An 1933,O 10,24:4
Move on, Sister 1933,O 25,22:4
Divine Moment, A 1934,Ja 8,21:8
Hotel Alimony 1934,Ja 30,16:2
No Questions Asked 1934,F 6,24:3
Richard of Bordeaux 1934,F 15,16:2
Queer People 1934,F 16,16:2
Picnic 1934,My 3,15:2
Strangers at Home 1934,S 15,20:5
Red Cat, The 1934,S 20,21:1
Brittle Heaven 1934,N 14,22:5
Birthday 1934,D 27,24:2
Lady Detained, A 1935,Ja 10,23:3
Little Shot 1935,Ja 18,28:4
Touch of Brimstone, A 1935,S 23,20:1
Othello 1935,S 28,13:2
Macbeth 1935,O 8,26:4
Abide With Me 1935,N 22,19:2
How Beautiful With Shoes 1935,N 29,24:1
Stick-in-the-Mud 1935,D 2,18:2
Among Those Sailing 1936,F 12,24:4
In the Bag 1936,D 18,30:2
House in the Country, A 1937,Ja 12,18:3
Time and the Conways 1938,Ja 4,19:2
Happiest Days, The 1939,Ap 12,26:2
Ackerman, Robert
Ordinary Man, An 1968,S 10,39:1
Moby Dick 1970,Je 3,52:1

Ackerman, Sally
Never Live Over a Pretzel Factory 1964,Mr 30,37:1
Ackerman, Stanley
First Stop to Heaven 1941,Ja 6,10:7
Ackerman, Trude
Konzert, Das 1968,Mr 25,52:1
Jux Will Er Sich Machen, Einen 1968,Ap 3,41:1
Ackerman and Mensching, Inc (Scenic Designer)
Gasoline Gypsies 1931,Je 8,21:3
Acklan, Vern
Nobody's Child 1956,Ag 23,25:2
Ackland, Joss
Twelfth Night 1958,D 10,54:2
Hamlet 1958,D 17,2:7
Henry V 1958,D 26,2:7
Hotel in Amsterdam, The 1968,Jl 21,II,12:1
Come as You Are 1970,Ag 12,32:1
Ackland, Rodney
Ballerina 1933,O 29,IX,1:6
Ackland, Rodney (Playwright)
Dance With No Music 1930,Ag 24,VIII,2:7
Strange Orchestra 1932,O 23,IX,1:1
Ballerina 1933,O 11,26:3
Ballerina 1933,O 29,IX,1:6
Strange Orchestra 1933,N 29,23:2
White Guard, The 1934,Ap 8,X,2:2
Old Ladies, The 1935,Ap 4,21:2
Old Ladies, The 1935,Ap 28,X,2:3
Night in the House 1935,N 8,19:5
After October 1936,F 22,13:3
After October 1936,My 17,IX,2:2
Plot Twenty-One 1936,N 8,X,3:4
White Guard, The 1938,O 23,IX,3:1
Sixth Floor 1939,Je 11,IX,2:5
Dark River 1943,D 5,II,5:1
Crime and Punishment 1946,Jl 21,II,1:5
Crime and Punishment 1947,D 23,29:3
Crime and Punishment 1948,Ja 4,II,1:1
Diary of a Scoundrel 1956,N 5,41:1
Farewell, Farewell Eugene 1960,S 28,35:1
Ackland, Rodney (Producer)
Plot Twenty-One 1936,N 8,X,3:4
Ackles, Kenneth
Lulu; Earth Spirit 1970,Mr 28,32:1
Ackley, Gene
Cage, The 1970,Je 19,25:1
Ackley, Mary
Social Register, The 1931,N 10,28:2
Ackridge, William
Poet's Follies of 1955 1955,My 15,II,3:1
Ackroyd, David
'Tis Pity She's a Whore 1967,O 21,15:2
Henry IV 1968,F 7,40:1
Three Sisters, The 1968,Mr 18,56:1
Bacchae, The 1969,Mr 15,24:1
Rivals, The 1969,O 18,37:1
Metamorphoses 1969,D 12,69:1
Crimes and Crimes 1970,Ja 19,35:1
Don Juan 1970,My 26,32:1
Three Philip Roth Stories; Defender of the Faith
1970,Jl 31,14:1
Revenger's Tragedy, The 1970,D 2,58:1
Ackroyd, David (Director)
Cops and Horrors; Fly Paper 1970,Ag 11,27:1
Acly, Nancy
Moon in the Yellow River, The 1961,F 7,40:2
Merchant of Venice, The 1962,F 3,13:2
Living Room, The 1962,N 22,43:5
Month in the Country, A 1963,My 29,39:2
Portrait of a Queen 1968,F 29,29:1
Aco, Lucas
Around the World 1946,Je 1,9:5
Finian's Rainbow 1947,Ja 11,23:2
Acosta, Mercedes de (Playwright)
Jehanne d'Arc 1925,Je 13,10:1
Joan of Arc 1925,Je 21,VIII,1:2
Jehanne d'Arc 1925,Jl 12,VII,1:1
Acremant, Albert (Playwright)
Soir des Noces, Le 1930,N 30,IX,3:3
Acromaniacs
New Priorities of 1943 1942,S 16,28:2
Actman, Irving (Composer)
Hot Rhythm 1930,Ag 22,18:5
Illustrators' Show, The 1936,Ja 23,25:3
Maurice Chevalier 1947,Mr 11,37:2
Maurice Chevalier 1948,Mr 1,16:2
Actman, Irving (Lyricist)
Hot Rhythm 1930,Ag 22,18:5
Actman, Irving (Musical Director)
Sleepy Hollow 1948,Je 4,26:3
Guys and Dolls 1950,N 25,11:2
Girls Against the Boys, The 1959,N 3,26:1
Guys and Dolls 1965,Ap 29,39:1
Guys and Dolls 1966,Je 9,55:2
Wonderful Town 1967,My 18,50:1
Actman, John
Bertha 1962,F 12,27:1
Actman, John (Miscellaneous)
Mrs Dally Has a Lover 1962,O 2,47:1
Whisper Into My Good Ear 1962,O 2,47:1
Saving Grace, The 1963,Ap 19,28:1
Grand Music Hall of Israel, The 1968,F 7,42:1
Oh! Calcutta! 1969,Je 18,33:1

Acton, Wallace
Valley Forge 1934,D 11,28:3
As You Like It; Midsummer Night's Dream, A;
Comedy of Errors, The; Taming of the Shrew,
The 1939,My 9,28:4
As You Like It 1939,My 9,28:4
Pastoral 1939,N 2,26:2
Twelfth Night 1940,N 20,26:3
All the Comforts of Home 1942,My 26,24:5
Tempest, The 1945,N 13,24:6
Wonderful Journey 1946,D 26,30:2
Skipper Next to God 1948,Ja 5,14:5
Mr Pickwick 1952,S 18,36:3
Winesburg, Ohio 1958,F 6,22:2
Actor-Managers, Inc (Producer)
Ruth Draper 1928,D 26,14:5
Acuff, Edward
Heat Lightning 1933,S 16,9:6
Growing Pains 1933,N 24,24:2
John Brown 1934,Ja 23,22:3
Yellow Jack 1934,Mr 7,22:6
Hide and Seek 1934,Ag 7,20:2
Jayhawker 1934,N 6,34:2
Ada-May
Rio Rita 1927,F 3,18:3
Smiling Through 1932,Ja 3,VIII,3:1
Good Fairy, The 1932,N 18,22:3
Adachi, Yasuko
Majority of One, A 1959,F 17,28:2
Adair, Alan
Paul Bunyan 1941,My 6,25:1
Adair, Alma
Passing Show of 1922, The 1922,S 21,18:2
Adair, Janet
Passing Show of 1921, The 1920,D 30,16:2
Bombo 1921,O 7,20:2
Passing Show of 1922, The 1922,S 21,18:2
Grab Bag, The 1924,O 7,26:2
Adair, Jay
Adam Had Two Sons 1932,Ja 21,17:1
Adair, Jean
It's a Boy! 1922,S 20,18:3
Machinal 1928,S 8,10:3
That Ferguson Family 1928,D 24,10:7
Scarlet Pages 1929,S 10,26:3
Everything's Jake 1930,Ja 17,20:4
Rock Me, Julie 1931,F 4,21:1
Blessed Event 1932,F 13,23:2
Blessed Event 1932,F 21,VIII,1:1
Best Years 1932,S 8,16:2
Black Sheep 1932,O 14,22:6
Show-Off, The 1932,D 13,25:4
For Services Rendered 1933,Ap 13,15:5
Murder at the Vanities 1933,S 13,22:4
Broomsticks Amen! 1934,F 10,20:4
Picnic 1934,My 3,15:2
Ah, Wilderness! 1934,O 30,23:1
Mid-West 1936,Ja 2,21:2
Mid-West 1936,Ja 5,IX,3:1
Mid-West 1936,Ja 8,22:4
Middle Man 1936,S 8,23:1
Sun Kissed 1937,Mr 11,20:2
On Borrowed Time 1938,F 4,16:4
Morning's at Seven 1939,N 7,30:2
Morning's at Seven 1939,D 1,26:2
Goodbye in the Night 1940,Mr 19,31:2
Arsenic and Old Lace 1941,Ja 11,13:2
Arsenic and Old Lace 1941,F 23,IX,1:1
Star Spangled Family 1945,Ap 11,18:6
Next Half Hour, The 1945,O 30,14:6
Detective Story 1949,Mr 24,34:2
Bell, Book and Candle 1950,N 15,37:4
Bell, Book and Candle 1950,D 17,II,3:1
Crucible, The 1953,Ja 23,15:2
Adair, Jennet
Jay Walker, The 1926,F 9,23:1
Devils 1926,Mr 18,26:4
Adair, John
Caroline 1923,F 1,13:2
Artists and Models 1923,Ag 21,12:2
Katja 1926,O 19,27:3
On the Spot 1930,O 30,33:3
Best Sellers 1933,My 4,20:2
Keep Moving 1934,Ag 24,10:2
Chalk Dust 1936,Mr 5,24:5
It Can't Happen Here 1936,O 28,30:1
Cradle Will Rock, The 1937,D 6,19:4
Cradle Will Rock, The 1938,Ja 4,19:3
Knights of Song 1938,O 18,29:2
Ringside Seat 1938,N 23,24:5
Young Couple Wanted 1940,Ja 25,16:2
Russian Bank 1940,My 25,20:2
Popsy 1941,F 11,26:2
Sweet Charity 1942,D 29,26:4
Suds in Your Eye 1944,Ja 13,15:5
Adair, John Jr
Welcome Stranger 1920,S 14,12:1
Adair, Josephine
Clinging Vine, The 1922,D 25,20:2
Whoopee 1928,D 5,34:3
Adair, Laura (Miscellaneous)
Room in Red and White, A 1936,Ja 20,23:3

Adair, Laura (Playwright)
Rain Before Seven 1935,Ag 13,20:3
Adair, Marcia
Sun-Kist 1921,My 24,20:2
Adair, Robin
Giants, Sons of Giants 1962,Ja 8,26:2
Adair, Ronald
Tarzan of the Apes 1921,S 8,14:3
Right to Strike, The 1921,O 25,20:1
Adair, Ruth
Some Party 1922,Ap 17,22:1
Adair, Ted
Higher and Higher 1940,Ap 5,24:3
New Priorities of 1943 1942,S 16,28:2
Adair, Ted (Choreographer)
Borscht Capades 1951,S 18,38:3
Adair, Ted Dancers
Borscht Capades 1951,S 18,38:3
Adair, Tom (Lyricist)
Along Fifth Avenue 1949,Ja 14,28:2
Adair, Tom (Playwright)
California 1953,Je 18,38:5
Disney on Parade 1970,S 24,63:1
Adair, Yvonne
Lend an Ear 1948,D 17,38:2
Gentlemen Prefer Blondes 1949,D 9,35:3
Gentlemen Prefer Blondes 1949,D 18,II,3:1
Adaire, Rose
My Girl 1924,N 25,27:2
Adam, Angus
Hunky Dory 1922,S 5,21:2
Adam, James
Bassa Moona 1936,D 9,35:4
Adam, Noelle
No Strings 1962,Mr 16,24:1
Adam, Ronald
Wisdom Teeth 1936,Mr 3,25:2
Caesar and Cleopatra 1951,D 20,43:2
Antony and Cleopatra 1951,D 21,22:2
Adam, Ronald (Producer)
Murder Gang 1935,N 16,19:2
Adam, Ronald (Translator)
Melody That Got Lost, The 1938,F 6,X,1:2
Adam, Sylvia
Whoopee 1928,D 5,34:3
Adamov, Arthur (Playwright)
Ping-Pong 1959,Ap 17,22:1
Adamowska, Helenka
Sandro Botticelli 1923,Mr 27,24:2
Sweet Nell of Old Drury 1923,My 19,16:4
Pilgrimage, The; Pelerin, Le 1925,N 10,23:2
Half-Caste, The 1926,Mr 30,20:4
Adams, Abbott
Broadway Whirl, The 1921,Je 9,10:4
Straight Thru the Door 1928,O 5,17:2
Inspector Kennedy 1929,D 21,16:3
Adams, Ace
House in Berlin, A (Als der Kreig zu Ende War);
Als der Krieg zu Ende War (A House in Berlin)
1950,D 27,32:3
Pigeon, The 1957,My 17,19:2
Adams, Alfred R
Forever This Land 1951,Jl 29,II,1:1
Adams, Angus
Courting 1925,S 14,17:1
Adams, Annabelle
Pirates of Penzance, The 1961,S 7,41:1
Adams, Barbara
If This Be Treason 1935,S 24,28:2
Daughters of Atreus 1936,O 15,33:1
Adams, Barton
Right to Kill, The 1926,F 16,22:2
Cloudy With Showers 1931,S 2,17:5
Adams, Beatrice
Seven Mirrors 1945,O 26,17:2
Adams, Bil
Oh! Oh! Nurse 1925,D 8,28:4
Adams, Billy
Hellzapoppin 1938,S 23,34:2
New Hellzapoppin, The 1939,D 12,36:4
Adams, Bret
Enchantment 1953,Jl 1,24:3
Adams, Bret (Miscellaneous)
Ages of Man 1958,D 29,21:1
Adams, Bridges (Producer)
Tempest, The 1934,Ap 17,26:6
Adams, Bruce
Peter Rabbit 1928,D 27,26:4
Sinbad the Sailor 1929,S 27,26:5
Gold Braid 1930,My 14,31:2
Alchemist, The 1931,Je 5,27:1
Me and Harry 1942,Ap 3,24:6
Uncle Harry 1942,My 21,24:1
Cherry Orchard, The 1944,Ja 26,22:1
Adams, C H 3d
Tiger Smiles, The 1930,D 18,29:1
Adams, Carrie
Trial of Dr Beck, The 1937,Ag 10,22:2
Adams, Charles
Best People, The 1924,Ag 20,8:1
Sam Abramovitch 1927,Ja 20,20:5
Adams, Charles (Director)
Coming of Christ, The 1957,D 23,29:8

Adams, Charles (Producer)
Apple Cart, The 1956,O 19,23:1
Adams, Charles W
Skin Deep 1927,O 18,32:1
He 1931,S 22,33:1
Adams, Chase
Going Gay 1933,Ag 4,18:5
Patience 1935,S 3,24:4
Adams, Chester
Johnny 2X4 1942,Mr 17,24:6
Adams, Clifford
Tom Sawyer 1931,D 26,15:3
Adams, Dave
Jumbo 1935,N 18,20:2
Adams, David (Costume Designer)
Triumph of Robert Emmet, The 1969,My 8,54:1
Adams, David (Director)
Bad Place to Get Your Head, A 1970,Jl 16,38:1
Bead-Tangle 1970,Jl 16,38:1
Adams, David (Lighting Director)
Triumph of Robert Emmet, The 1969,My 8,54:1
Haunted Host, The 1969,O 28,43:1
Wuziz! 1970,O 2,25:2
Street Sounds 1970,O 23,32:1
Early Morning 1970,N 26,57:1
Adams, Diana
Trojan Women, The 1957,Mr 19,42:7
Adams, Don
Harold 1962,N 30,27:1
Adams, Don (Costume Designer)
Firebugs, The 1963,N 22,41:1
King Lear 1963,N 23,22:1
Adams, Donald
Iolanthe 1955,S 28,38:1
Mikado, The 1955,S 30,20:2
Yeomen of the Guard, The 1955,O 4,39:2
Pirates of Penzance, The 1955,O 7,21:1
Princess Ida 1955,O 14,22:3
H M S Pinafore 1955,O 18,48:1
Ruddigore 1955,O 21,32:2
Mikado, The 1962,N 14,43:1
Pirates of Penzance, The 1962,N 21,28:1
H M S Pinafore 1962,N 23,32:4
Iolanthe 1962,N 28,42:1
Iolanthe 1962,N 18,52:1
H M S Pinafore 1964,N 20,40:1
Pirates of Penzance, The 1964,N 27,43:1
Ruddigore 1964,D 4,44:1
Pirates of Penzance, The 1966,N 16,54:1
Mikado, The 1966,N 18,36:1
Ruddigore 1966,N 23,28:1
H M S Pinafore 1966,N 24,64:1
Patience 1966,N 30,58:1
H M S Pinafore 1968,O 30,35:1
Patience 1968,N 1,34:1
Mikado, The 1968,N 2,29:4
Pirates of Penzance, The 1968,N 7,54:1
Iolanthe 1968,N 9,37:3
Adams, Dorinda
Bootleggers, The 1922,N 28,24:1
Adams, Edith
Wonderful Town 1953,F 26,22:3
Wonderful Town 1953,Mr 8,II,1:1
Wonderful Town 1954,My 7,II,1:1
Li'l Abner 1956,N 16,24:2
Li'l Abner 1956,N 25,II,1:1
Adams, Elaine
Howdy Stranger 1937,Ja 15,17:5
Adams, Erich
Come Angel Band 1936,F 19,17:1
Adams, Frank R (Original Author)
Princess April 1924,D 2,23:2
Time, Place and the Girl, The 1942,O 22,24:3
Adams, Franklin P
Spring Tonic 1936,My 11,16:1
Adams, Franklin P (Miscellaneous)
Little Father of the Wilderness, The 1930,Je 3,27:1
Adams, Franklin P (Playwright)
49ers, The 1922,N 7,14:1
49ers, The 1922,N 12,VIII,1:1
Adams, Fritz
Johannes Kreisler 1922,D 25,20:3
Paid 1925,N 26,32:1
Adams, Gail
My Romance 1948,O 20,38:5
Adams, Gay
Hamlet 1936,N 11,54:2
Adams, Greg (Miscellaneous)
Chief Thing, The 1963,Ap 30,27:2
Adams, H Lee
Gang War 1928,Ag 21,27:2
Adams, Henrietta
What Women Do? 1925,Jl 21,26:4
Adams, Inge
Come Marching Home 1946,My 20,18:6
Blood Wedding 1949,F 7,16:2
Adams, Jack
Lulu 1935,S 30,24:1
Gay Life, The 1961,N 20,38:1
On the Necessity of Being Polygamous
1964,D 9,61:1
Adams, Jack (Miscellaneous)
Carnival! 1968,D 13,58:1

Adams, Jacqueline (Miscellaneous)
New Faces of 1956 1956,Je 15,32:1
Mask and Gown 1957,S 11,29:1
Miss Isobel 1957,D 27,22:1
Second String, A 1960,Ap 14,36:2
New Faces of 1962 1962,F 2,25:1
Adams, Jim
Galileo 1968,D 1,88:4
Adams, Joe
Jamaica 1957,N 1,32:2
Adams, John Quincy 3d
Night Is Black Bottles, The 1962,D 5,56:1
Adams, John T (Producer)
Heigh-Ho, Everybody 1932,My 26,31:2
Adams, Joseph
Truckline Cafe 1946,F 28,19:4
Adams, Julia (Composer)
Courageous One, The 1958,Ja 21,33:6
Adams, Julia (Miscellaneous)
Doll's House, A 1956,My 8,29:2
Adams, Kenny
Of Mice and Men 1958,D 5,38:1
Another Evening With Harry Stoones
1961,O 23,22:2
Adams, Kent
Danton's Death 1938,N 3,26:2
Eve of St Mark, The 1942,O 8,30:2
Adams, Laurel
Ringside 1928,Ag 30,13:2
Adams, Laurette
Boom Boom 1929,Ja 29,26:4
Adams, Lawrence
Most Immoral Lady, A 1928,N 27,36:1
Adams, Lee (Composer)
Littlest Revue, The 1956,My 23,37:2
Golden Boy 1964,N 1,II,1:1
Adams, Lee (Lyricist)
Littlest Revue, The 1956,My 23,37:2
Bye Bye Birdie 1960,Ap 15,13:4
All American 1962,Mr 20,44:1
Golden Boy 1964,O 21,56:1
Golden Boy 1964,N 1,II,1:1
It's a Bird . . . It's a Plane . . . It's Superman
1966,Mr 30,34:1
Applause 1970,Mr 31,35:1
Applause 1970,Ap 5,II,1:1
Adams, Lee (Playwright)
Shoestring '57 1956,N 6,31:1
Adams, Leroy
Pretender, The 1960,My 25,42:1
Adams, Leslie
Wild Westcotts, The 1923,D 25,26:2
Haunted House, The 1924,S 3,12:1
Beware of Widows 1925,D 2,22:3
Doctor X 1931,F 10,25:1
Carry Nation 1932,O 31,18:2
Goodbye Again 1932,D 29,16:4
As Thousands Cheer 1933,O 2,22:1
King's Messenger, The 1935,Ag 14,16:3
Life's Too Short 1935,S 21,18:5
Room in Red and White, A 1936,Ja 20,23:3
Adams, Lillian
Tin Top Valley 1947,Mr 1,11:2
Whisper in God's Ear, A 1962,O 12,27:2
Adams, Lionel
Wandering Jew, The 1921,O 27,22:1
Dorian Gray 1928,My 22,18:4
Launcelot and Elaine 1930,Mr 10,24:3
Spring Freshet 1934,O 5,28:3
Adams, Lowden
Prince and the Pauper, The 1920,N 2,15:1
Hamlet 1922,N 17,14:1
Merchants of Glory 1925,D 15,28:3
Right Age to Marry, The 1926,F 16,22:3
Great Adventure, The 1926,D 23,23:1
Cherry Orchard, The 1928,Mr 6,20:1
Adams, Margaret
Three Little Girls 1930,Ap 15,29:1
Student Prince, The 1931,Ja 30,18:1
Cat and the Fiddle, The 1931,O 16,26:4
Thumbs Up! 1934,D 28,24:1
Jubilee 1935,S 23,20:3
Jubilee 1935,O 14,20:1
American Jubilee 1940,My 13,20:5
Adams, Margot
Face the Music 1933,F 1,13:4
Adams, Marguerite
Top-Notchers 1942,My 30,8:5
Adams, Mark
Sam Abramovitch 1927,Ja 20,20:5
Pressing Business 1930,N 18,28:5
Adams, Marla
Visit, The 1958,My 6,40:1
Adams, Mary
Artists and Models 1930,Je 11,33:2
Hello Paris 1930,N 17,29:3
Professor Mamlock 1937,Ap 14,30:3
Medea 1949,My 3,31:2
Adams, Mason
Winter Soldiers 1942,N 30,19:2
Get Away Old Man 1943,N 25,40:2
Public Relations 1944,Ap 7,23:3
Career Angel 1944,My 24,23:7

Adams, Mason—Cont
Violet 1944,O 25,16:1
Shadow of My Enemy, A 1957,D 12,35:4
Tall Story 1959,Ja 30,33:2
Inquest 1970,Ap 24,38:1
Adams, Maude
Merchant of Venice, The 1931,N 4,31:1
Merchant of Venice, The 1931,N 9,22:2
Merchant of Venice, The 1932,Ja 10,II,6:4
Twelfth Night 1934,Jl 17,24:5
Twelfth Night 1934,Ag 21,12:4
Chantecler 1937,D 10,33:6
Adams, Maude (Director)
Twelfth Night 1934,Jl 17,24:5
Chantecler 1937,D 10,33:6
Adams, Minna
Carry Nation 1932,O 31,18:2
Adams, Mollie
Not So Long Ago 1920,My 5,14:1
Adams, Mountfort
Wall Street 1927,Ap 21,24:4
Adams, Nevile
Marie Vison, La 1970,Jl 15,29:1
Adams, Nicholas
Budget, The 1932,S 21,26:4
Dodsworth 1934,F 26,20:4
Adams, Paul
St Helena 1936,O 7,32:1
Cradle of Willow, A 1961,D 16,20:2
How to Succeed in Business Without Really Trying 1966,Ap 21,45:1
Show Boat 1966,Jl 20,48:1
Carousel 1966,D 16,56:2
Finian's Rainbow 1967,Ap 6,44:1
Wonderful Town 1967,My 18,50:1
Brigadoon 1967,D 14,59:2
Adams, Peter
Abraham Cochrane 1964,F 18,26:1
Adams, Phoebe
Canteen Show, The 1942,S 4,18:1
Adams, Phyllis
War and Peace 1942,My 22,26:3
Snark Was a Boojum, The 1943,S 2,14:4
Adams, Rachael
King Lear 1940,D 16,27:2
Adams, Ralph
Noose, The 1926,O 21,23:3
Racket, The 1927,N 23,28:3
Broken Chain, The 1929,F 21,30:4
Adams, Ray
Marie Antoinette 1921,N 23,16:1
Adams, Robert
Barnum Was Right 1923,Mr 13,19:3
Road Together, The 1924,Ja 18,21:2
Paths of Glory 1935,S 27,24:2
Shunned 1960,D 21,39:1
Adams, Robert J
Red Geranium, The 1922,My 9,22:3
Adams, Robert K
Richard II 1937,F 6,14:2
As You Like It 1937,N 1,25:2
First Stop to Heaven 1941,Ja 6,10:7
Adams, Robert K (Director)
Tattooed Countess, The 1961,My 4,40:2
Adams, Roger (Composer)
Hamlet 1945,D 14,25:2
Hamlet 1945,D 23,II,3:1
Adams, Roger (Miscellaneous)
Buttrio Square 1952,O 15,40:2
Pajama Game, The 1954,My 14,20:2
Happy Hunting 1956,D 7,30:1
New Girl in Town 1957,My 15,40:1
Pajama Game, The 1957,My 16,27:1
Redhead 1959,F 6,21:1
Once Upon a Mattress 1959,My 12,40:1
Ben Franklin in Paris 1964,O 28,52:1
Mame 1966,My 25,41:1
Illya Darling 1967,Ap 12,37:1
Adams, Roger (Musical Director)
Ankles Aweigh 1955,Ap 19,27:1
Damn Yankees 1955,My 6,17:1
Adams, Roland (Producer)
Battle Royal 1934,Ap 19,33:4
Adams, Ronald (Producer)
House of Borgia, The 1935,S 10,26:1
Adams, Roy
Twisting Road, The; Jewel of the South, The 1957,N 18,36:5
Twisting Road, The; One Tuesday Morning 1957,N 18,36:5
Ballad of Jazz Street, The 1959,N 12,28:1
Adams, Roy H
Goose, The 1960,Mr 16,44:1
Adams, Ruth
Bitter Sweet 1934,My 8,28:4
Adams, Sam
Variations of 1940 1940,Ja 29,12:1
Adams, Samuel Hopkins (Original Author)
Revelry 1927,S 13,37:1
Tenderloin 1960,O 18,47:2
Adams, Sancho
Smyth With a Y 1937,Je 30,19:5
Adams, Sandra
Song for a Certain Midnight 1959,S 17,49:1

Adams, Sonny
From Morn Till Midnight 1948,D 7,41:6
Finian's Rainbow 1953,Mr 7,13:2
Adams, Stanley (Composer)
Shady Lady 1933,Jl 6,26:3
Adams, Stanley (Lyricist)
Shady Lady 1933,Jl 6,26:3
Show Is On, The 1937,S 20,18:4
Lady Says Yes, A 1945,Ja 11,18:5
Adams, Sylvea
Keating 1927,D 26,26:6
Adams, Trude
Catch a Star! 1955,S 7,35:2
Leonard Bernstein's Theater Songs 1965,Je 29,27:2
Adams, Victor
Squealer, The 1928,N 13,36:3
Honor Code, The 1931,My 19,25:3
Adams, W
1776 1926,Ap 24,11:2
Adams, W Herbert (Miscellaneous)
Sinner 1927,F 8,20:2
Undesirable Lady, An 1933,O 10,24:4
Adams, W Herbert (Producer)
Port O' London 1926,F 10,20:2
What Do We Know 1927,D 24,8:1
Cyclone Lover, The 1928,Je 6,23:3
Adams, Wiley
Murder at the Vanities 1933,S 13,22:4
Adams, William
Merchant of Venice, The 1921,N 22,17:1
Honeymooning 1927,Mr 18,25:3
John 1927,N 5,16:4
Get Away Old Man 1943,N 25,40:2
Oedipus Rex 1945,D 17,16:7
Adams, William P
Macbeth 1924,Mr 17,18:1
Shelter 1926,Ja 26,18:2
Adams, William P (Director)
Jane-Our Stranger 1925,O 9,27:2
Primer for Lovers, A 1929,N 19,26:5
Adams, Wylie
Sex Fable, The 1931,O 21,26:1
Moon in the Yellow River, The 1932,Mr 1,19:3
Firebird 1932,N 22,25:2
Hotel Alimony 1934,Ja 30,16:2
Yellow Jack 1934,Mr 7,22:6
Red Cat, The 1934,S 20,21:1
Farmer Takes a Wife, The 1934,O 31,17:1
Ragged Edge, The 1935,N 26,28:3
Sweet River 1936,O 29,30:2
Miss Swan Expects 1939,F 21,15:2
Kind Lady 1940,S 4,28:3
Mr and Mrs North 1941,Ja 13,11:2
Adamson, H C (Composer)
Bulls and Belles 1931,Ap 18,17:2
Adamson, Harold (Composer)
Earl Carroll's Vanities 1931,Ag 28,18:7
Adamson, Harold (Lyricist)
Smiles 1930,N 19,19:2
Earl Carroll's Vanities 1931,Ag 28,18:7
Banjo Eyes 1941,D 26,20:2
As the Girls Go 1948,N 15,21:2
Around the World in 80 Days 1963,Je 24,22:1
Around the World in 80 Days 1964,Je 29,33:2
Adamy, John (Sgt)
Winged Victory 1943,N 22,24:1
Addams, Paul K
This Way Out 1929,Ap 28,24:4
Addinsell, Dick (Miscellaneous)
Earl Carroll's Vanities 1927,Ja 5,18:1
Addinsell, Richard (Composer)
Good Companions, The 1931,O 2,31:1
Alice in Wonderland 1932,D 12,18:3
Alice in Wonderland 1932,D 25,IX,1:1
Aiglon, L' 1934,N 5,22:2
Happy Hypocrite, The 1936,Ap 9,21:6
Happy Hypocrite, The 1936,My 10,X,1:1
Sigh No More 1945,Jl 12,8:4
Alice in Wonderland 1947,Ap 7,19:2
Alice in Wonderland 1947,Ap 13,II,1:1
Come of Age 1952,Ja 24,22:2
Joyce Grenfell Requests the Pleasure 1955,O 11,48:1
Joyce Grenfell 1958,Ap 8,32:1
Addinsell, Richard (Playwright)
Come of Age 1934,Ja 13,16:6
Addis, George
Tragical Historie of Doctor Faustus, The 1964,O 6,34:2
Pantagleize 1967,D 1,54:1
Addis, John
Oklahoma! 1951,My 30,15:2
Addis, Stephen (Composer)
Herne's Egg, The 1960,S 20,48:1
Addison, Bernard
Regina 1949,N 1,32:2
Addison, Dorothy
Broadway Whirl, The 1921,Je 9,10:4
Addison, Gordon
Until the Monkey Comes 1966,Je 21,38:1
Addison, Jerome N
Earth 1927,Mr 10,23:1

Addison, John (Composer)
Cranks 1956,My 14,23:1
Cranks 1956,N 27,32:1
Chairs, The 1958,Ja 10,20:3
Lesson, The 1958,Ja 10,20:3
Entertainer, The 1958,F 13,22:2
Luther 1963,S 26,41:1
St Joan of the Stockyards 1964,Je 12,45:1
Addison, John (Miscellaneous)
Lesson, The 1958,Ja 10,20:3
Chairs, The 1958,Ja 10,20:3
Addison, Thelma
Broadway Whirl, The 1921,Je 9,10:4
Addoms, Lee
Kitchen, The 1966,Je 14,50:1
Addy, Wesley
Panic 1935,Mr 16,18:4
How Beautiful With Shoes 1935,N 29,24:1
Hamlet 1936,N 11,54:2
Richard II 1937,S 16,28:2
Hamlet 1938,O 13,28:1
Henry IV, Part I 1939,Ja 31,17:2
Henry IV 1939,F 5,IX,1:1
Flight Into China 1939,S 12,28:1
Summer Night 1939,N 3,17:1
Romeo and Juliet 1940,My 10,27:1
Twelfth Night 1940,O 27,IX,1:5
Twelfth Night 1940,N 20,26:3
Battle of Angels 1941,Ja 5,IX,1:7
Somewhere in France 1941,Ap 29,16:8
Elizabeth the Queen 1941,O 17,27:2
Antigone 1946,F 19,21:3
Candida 1946,Ap 4,33:2
Candida 1946,Ap 14,II,1:1
Leading Lady 1948,O 19,33:1
Traitor, The 1949,Ap 1,30:2
Traitor, The 1949,Ap 10,II,1:1
Enchanted, The 1950,Ja 19,34:2
King Lear 1950,D 26,18:1
Evening With Will Shakespeare, An 1952,D 7,86:5
Strong Are Lonely, The 1953,S 30,38:3
First Gentleman, The 1957,Ap 26,22:2
For the Time Being 1957,D 18,42:7
South Pacific 1961,Ap 27,26:3
Month in the Country, A 1963,My 29,39:2
Candida 1970,Ap 7,41:1
Addy, William J (Producer)
Exhibition 1969,My 16,41:1
Ade, George (Playwright)
County Chairman, The 1936,My 26,26:5
Ade, Grace
Power of Darkness, The 1920,Ja 22,22:1
Shall We Join the Ladies? 1925,Ja 14,19:1
Hearts Are Trumps! 1927,Ap 8,21:1
Ade, William
Mister Roberts 1962,O 12,27:2
Madwoman of Chaillot, The 1970,Mr 23,48:3
Adedoyin, Adeola
Madmen and Specialists 1970,Ag 3,38:1
Adelaide, (Mlle)
Whirl of New York, The 1921,Je 14,18:1
Adelaide and Hughes
Vaudeville (Palace) 1923,Mr 13,19:2
Lace Petticoat 1927,Ja 5,18:2
Adelana, Femi
Madmen and Specialists 1970,Ag 3,38:1
Adelbert, Pierre (Producer)
Gualtier l'Oyseau 1926,D 5,VIII,6:1
Adelina (Monkey)
Romance 1926,N 4,VIII,4:7
Adelman, Chava
Dybbuk, The 1926,D 14,24:2
Eternal Jew, The 1926,D 21,21:2
Adelman, Howard
Solid Gold Cadillac, The 1953,N 6,24:2
Adelphi, Dorothy
Vaudeville (Palace) 1926,My 4,31:2
Vaudeville (Palace) 1926,Jl 13,19:4
Vaudeville (Palace) 1927,Mr 22,31:1
Adels, Marie
Solid Ivory 1925,N 17,29:3
Cyrano de Bergerac 1926,F 19,18:1
Immortal Thief, The 1926,O 4,21:1
Caponsacchi 1926,O 27,24:2
Enemy of the People, An 1927,O 4,32:5
Hamlet 1928,Ja 5,33:2
Henry V 1928,Mr 16,26:2
Mystery Square 1929,Ap 5,28:3
Bloody Laughter 1931,D 5,20:6
All Good Americans 1933,D 6,29:2
Twelfth Night 1934,Jl 17,24:5
Twelfth Night 1934,Ag 21,12:4
Retreat to Pleasure 1940,D 18,32:2
Adelugba, Dapo
Madmen and Specialists 1970,Ag 3,38:1
Aden, Lois (Costume Designer)
Shunned 1960,D 21,39:1
Purple Canary, The 1963,Ap 23,31:1
Adeney, Eric
As You Like It 1947,F 21,16:2
Merchant of Venice, The 1947,F 24,16:2
Hamlet 1947,F 27,27:2

Adeney, Eric (Scenic Designer)
Hamlet 1947,F 27,27:2
Aderer, Adolphe (Playwright)
Maitresse de Roi 1926,D 1,24:1
Ades, Daniel
Blood Wedding 1958,Ap 1,35:1
Witches' Sabbath 1962,Ap 20,22:2
Fun Couple, The 1962,O 27,15:2
Adiarte, Patrick
King and I, The 1956,Ap 19,35:4
Flower Drum Song 1958,D 2,44:1
Adler, Charles (Choreographer)
Jolly Orphan, The 1929,D 23,18:6
Adkins, Morton
Secret of Suzanne, The 1920,Ja 13,10:2
Adkins, Robert F (Playwright)
Slightly Delirious 1935,Ja 1,25:3
Adkins, Ted
On Your Toes 1954,O 12,24:4
Adkins, Tom
Merry Wives of Windsor, The 1954,F 17,27:1
Adler, Adolph
Wild Man, The 1930,My 17,21:5
Millions 1930,O 3,30:4
Adler, Bruce
It's a Funny World 1956,O 22,24:1
Kosher Widow, The 1959,N 2,40:2
My Son and I 1960,O 24,24:2
Go Fight City Hall 1961,N 3,28:5
Good Luck 1964,O 19,38:3
It's Never Too Late for Happiness 1968,O 21,59:3
Adler, Celia
Green Fields 1920,Mr 26,11:2
Mute, The 1920,Ap 9,11:4
Treasure, The 1920,O 5,13:1
Dybbuk, The 1921,S 2,9:2
Tenth Commandment, The 1926,N 18,27:1
God Man and Devil 1928,D 22,14:8
Othello 1929,F 4,21:2
Major Noah 1929,F 23,17:2
Stempenu, the Fiddler 1929,Mr 9,24:7
Millions 1930,O 3,30:4
Once Upon a Time 1933,S 22,15:1
Untitled-Revue 1935,S 23,20:2
Laugh Night 1936,S 14,25:1
Simple Woman, The 1937,Mr 29,14:1
'Round the Family Table 1938,O 8,10:3
Chaver, Nachman 1939,O 2,15:2
Life Marches On 1940,Ja 4,18:2
Flag Is Born, A 1946,S 7,10:6
Flag Is Born, A 1946,S 15,II,21:1
Sands of the Negev 1954,O 20,32:1
Devil's Game, A 1959,N 9,35:6
Worm in Horseradish, A 1961,Mr 14,32:3
Adler, Charles
Wild Man, The 1930,My 17,21:5
Millions 1930,O 3,30:4
Man From Cairo, The 1938,My 5,26:5
Johnny 2X4 1942,Mr 17,24:6
Adler, Charles (Choreographer)
His Wife's Lover 1929,O 21,30:6
Angels on Earth 1929,D 11,34:7
Adler, Charles J (Director)
How Come Lawd? 1937,O 1,18:5
Adler, David
Welcome Stranger 1920,S 14,12:1
Adler, Diane (Choreographer)
Sacco-Vanzetti 1969,F 9,78:1
Wars of the Roses, The (Part II) 1970,Jl 3,15:1
Adler, Emilie
Awake and Sing! 1938,D 23,16:6
Adler, Ernest (Miscellaneous)
Handful of Fire 1958,O 2,45:3
Look After Lulu 1959,Mr 4,35:1
First Impressions 1959,Mr 20,28:1
Destry Rides Again 1959,Ap 24,24:1
Gypsy 1959,My 22,31:6
Distant Bell, A 1960,Ja 14,29:1
Bye Bye Birdie 1960,Ap 15,13:4
Christine 1960,Ap 29,27:1
King and I, The 1960,My 12,40:1
Unsinkable Molly Brown, The 1960,N 4,28:1
Camelot 1960,D 5,42:1
All in Love 1961,N 11,15:2
Beauty Part, The 1962,D 28,5:2
Fade Out--Fade In 1964,My 27,45:1
Diary of Adam and Eve, The 1966,O 19,53:1
Lady or the Tiger?, The 1966,O 19,53:1
Passionella 1966,O 19,53:1
Golden Rainbow 1968,F 5,27:1
Plaza Suite; Visitor From Forest Hills
1968,F 15,49:1
Plaza Suite; Visitor From Hollywood
1968,F 15,49:1
Plaza Suite; Visitor From Mamaroneck
1968,F 15,49:1
Her First Roman 1968,O 21,53:3
Forty Carats 1968,D 27,45:1
1776 1969,Mr 17,46:2
Gantry 1970,F 16,44:1
Georgy 1970,F 27,26:1
Purlie 1970,Mr 16,53:1

Adler, Eva
Thousand and One Nights 1959,D 16,53:2
Mother's Sabbath Days 1960,N 21,33:2
Eleventh Inheritor, The 1962,N 22,43:5
Melody Lingers On, The 1969,N 17,55:1
Adler, Evelyn
Challenge of Youth 1930,Ja 21,28:5
Pirates of Penzance, The 1936,Ap 21,27:5
Adler, Fay
Vaudeville (Palace) 1929,O 7,22:4
Adler, Frances
Wild Man, The 1930,My 17,21:5
Millions 1930,O 3,30:4
Sarah Adler Testimonial 1939,Mr 15,18:2
Song of Dnieper 1946,O 26,10:5
Wandering Stars 1946,D 14,18:2
Flies, The; Mouches, Les 1947,Ap 18,26:3
Mrs Warren's Profession 1956,Je 7,35:2
Electra 1959,F 14,15:1
Harlequinade 1959,F 14,15:1
Adler, Frances (Producer)
Mrs Warren's Profession 1956,Je 7,35:2
Adler, Hans (Playwright)
Red Cat, The 1934,S 20,21:1
Tomorrow's a Holiday! 1935,D 31,10:2
Adler, Harry
Circle of Chalk, The 1950,D 2,8:3
Adler, Hyman
Broken Branches 1922,Mr 7,11:1
Drift 1925,N 25,15:3
Tales of Rigo 1927,My 31,25:3
57 Bowery 1928,Ja 27,14:3
There You Are! 1932,My 17,25:4
Adler, Hyman (Director)
Street Wolf, The 1929,Ja 1,61:1
Shatter'd Lamp, The 1934,Mr 22,26:3
Lady Luck 1936,Ap 16,21:2
Adler, Hyman (Original Author)
Tales of Rigo 1927,My 31,25:3
Adler, Hyman (Playwright)
Street Wolf, The 1929,Ja 1,61:1
Challenge of Youth 1930,Ja 21,28:5
Tomorrow's Harvest 1934,D 6,26:5
Lady Luck 1936,Ap 16,21:2
Adler, Hyman (Producer)
Skidding 1928,My 22,18:5
Street Wolf, The 1929,Ja 1,61:1
Challenge of Youth 1930,Ja 21,28:5
With Privileges 1930,S 16,30:2
There You Are! 1932,My 17,25:4
Shatter'd Lamp, The 1934,Mr 22,26:3
Adler, Irving
Wild Man, The 1930,My 17,21:5
Millions 1930,O 3,30:4
Adler, Jay
Man Bites Dog 1933,Ap 26,11:2
Blind Alley 1935,S 25,19:6
Prelude 1936,Ap 20,17:4
Bury the Dead 1936,Ap 20,17:4
Blind Alley 1940,O 16,28:2
Cafe Crown 1942,Ja 24,12:5
Adler, Jerry (Director)
Ofay Watcher, The 1969,S 16,40:1
Ofay Watcher, The 1969,S 21,II,1:2
Adler, Jerry (Miscellaneous)
My Fair Lady 1959,Ja 19,24:6
Jack Benny 1963,Mr 1,10:5
Oh What a Lovely War 1964,O 1,30:1
Grosse Valise, La 1965,D 15,52:1
Time for Singing, A 1966,My 23,48:2
Diary of Adam and Eve, The 1966,O 19,53:1
Lady or the Tiger?, The 1966,O 19,53:1
Passionella 1966,O 19,53:1
Little Murders 1967,Ap 26,38:1
Unknown Soldier and His Wife, The 1967,Jl 7,22:1
Halfway up the Tree 1967,N 8,52:1
Dear World 1969,F 7,33:1
Coco 1969,D 19,66:1
Home 1970,N 18,41:1
Adler, Jerry (Producer)
Moby Dick 1962,N 29,45:1
Drat! the Cat! 1965,O 11,54:2
Mark Twain Tonight! 1966,Mr 24,48:2
Black Comedy; White Lies 1967,F 13,42:1
Black Comedy 1967,F 13,42:1
Adler, Jerry Hilliard (Cpl)
Winged Victory 1943,N 22,24:1
Adler, Josef
Rhapsody, The 1930,S 16,30:3
Adler, Julia
Rosa Machree 1922,Ja 10,15:2
Merchant of Venice, The 1922,D 22,13:1
Wild Man, The 1930,My 17,21:5
Millions 1930,O 3,30:4
Little Giants 1933,D 2,9:5
Awake and Sing! 1939,Mr 8,18:2
Tovarich 1952,My 15,39:2
Adler, Julius
Wise Men of Chelm, The 1933,O 18,24:4
It Can't Happen Here 1936,O 28,30:1
Three Cities 1938,O 11,20:3
If I Were Rothschild 1940,Ja 1,28:7
Abi Gezunt 1949,O 10,19:4

Adler, Julius—Cont
Yosele the Nightingale 1949,O 21,30:4
Sadie Is a Lady 1950,Ja 28,9:2
It's a Funny World 1956,O 22,24:1
It Could Happen to You 1957,O 28,30:5
Nice People 1958,O 20,36:1
Kosher Widow, The 1959,N 2,40:2
My Son and I 1960,O 24,24:2
Go Fight City Hall 1961,N 3,28:5
Adler, Julius (Producer)
Stone for Danny Fisher, A 1954,O 22,24:2
It's a Funny World 1956,O 22,24:1
It Could Happen to You 1957,O 28,30:5
Nice People 1958,O 20,36:1
Kosher Widow, The 1959,N 2,40:2
Go Fight City Hall 1961,N 3,28:5
Adler, L
Aristocrats 1935,My 2,16:2
Adler, Larry
Smiles 1930,N 19,19:2
Flying Colors 1932,S 16,24:2
Keep Off the Grass 1940,My 5,X,1:6
Keep Off the Grass 1940,My 24,22:6
Adler, Lola
World We Live In, The 1922,N 1,16:1
Adler, Lutha
Red Rust 1929,D 18,31:1
Adler, Lutha J
Humoresque 1923,F 28,13:2
Adler, Luther
Monkey Talks, The 1925,D 29,20:1
Money Business 1926,Ja 21,18:1
We Americans 1926,O 13,20:4
Wild Man, The 1930,My 17,21:5
Millions 1930,O 3,30:4
Night Over Taos 1932,Mr 10,25:3
Success Story 1932,S 27,24:4
Success Story 1932,O 2,IX,1:1
Alien Corn 1933,F 14,19:5
Alien Corn 1933,F 21,17:2
Alien Corn 1933,F 26,IX,1:1
Men in White 1933,S 27,24:2
Men in White 1933,O 1,IX,1:1
Gold Eagle Guy 1934,N 29,33:4
Waiting for Lefty 1935,F 11,14:5
Awake and Sing! 1935,F 20,23:2
Paradise Lost 1935,D 10,31:5
Case of Clyde Griffiths 1936,Mr 14,10:4
Johnny Johnson 1936,N 20,26:3
Golden Boy 1937,N 5,18:5
Golden Boy 1938,Ja 23,XI,1:6
Golden Boy 1938,Je 22,27:5
Rocket to the Moon 1938,N 25,18:2
Awake and Sing! 1939,Mr 8,18:2
Sarah Adler Testimonial 1939,Mr 15,18:2
Awake and Sing! 1939,Mr 26,X,1:2
Thunder Rock 1939,N 15,18:1
Two on an Island 1940,Ja 23,17:2
Two on an Island 1940,Ja 28,IX,1:2
Two on an Island 1940,F 4,IX,1:1
Russian People, The 1942,D 16,21:3
Russian People, The 1942,D 30,17:2
Common Ground 1945,Ap 26,27:2
Common Ground 1945,My 6,II,1:1
Beggars Are Coming to Town 1945,O 29,16:2
Dunnigan's Daughter 1945,D 27,16:1
Dunnigan's Daughter 1946,Ja 6,II,1:1
Tovarich 1952,My 15,39:2
Merchant of Venice, The 1953,Mr 5,20:2
Month in the Country, A 1956,Ap 4,23:1
Month in the Country, A 1956,Ap 15,II,1:1
Very Special Baby, A 1956,N 15,43:2
Passion of Josef D, The 1964,F 12,29:1
Three Sisters, The 1964,Je 23,24:1
Three Sisters, The 1965,My 15,19:4
Adler, Luther (Director)
They Should Have Stood in Bed 1942,F 14,18:5
Flag Is Born, A 1946,S 7,10:6
Stone for Danny Fisher, A 1954,O 22,24:2
Adler, Mildred
Nautical but Nice 1931,Ap 19,31:6
Adler, Morris
Thousand and One Nights 1959,D 16,53:2
Mother's Sabbath Days 1960,N 21,33:2
Backlane Center 1961,N 23,51:1
Eleventh Inheritor, The 1962,N 22,43:5
Sage of Rottenburg, The 1963,N 20,48:1
Wandering Stars 1966,N 14,52:2
Bronx Express, 1968 1968,N 16,43:3
Melody Lingers On, The 1969,N 17,55:1
Brothers Ashkenazi, The 1970,N 17,53:2
Adler, Mr
Merchant of Venice, The 1921,Ap 2,14:2
Gold Eagle Guy 1934,D 9,X,1:1
Adler, Murray
Girl Who Came to Supper, The 1963,D 9,49:1
Adler, Nathan
Our Lan' 1947,S 29,16:5
Adler, Pearl
Millions 1930,O 3,30:4
Adler, Philip (Miscellaneous)
Weak Link, The 1940,Mr 5,19:2
Adler, Ralph
Imaginary Invalid, The 1922,Jl 26,26:2

Adler, Richard (Composer)
John Murray Anderson's Almanac 1953,D 11,42:2
Pajama Game, The 1954,My 14,20:2
Pajama Game, The 1954,My 15,12:1
Pajama Game, The 1954,My 30,II,1:1
Damn Yankees 1955,My 6,17:1
Pajama Game, The 1957,My 16,27:1
Pajama Game, The 1957,My 26,II,1:1
Kwamina 1961,O 24,42:1
Adler, Richard (Lyricist)
John Murray Anderson's Almanac 1953,D 11,42:2
Pajama Game, The 1954,My 14,20:2
Pajama Game, The 1954,My 15,12:1
Pajama Game, The 1954,My 30,II,1:1
Damn Yankees 1955,My 6,17:1
Pajama Game, The 1957,My 16,27:1
Kwamina 1961,O 24,42:1
Adler, Richard (Producer)
Sin of Pat Muldoon, The 1957,Mr 14,35:1
Adler, S L (Producer)
Winesburg, Ohio 1958,F 6,22:2
Adler, Sam
Serving Folk 1920,Ap 22,11:3
Adler, Sarah
Sarah Adler Testimonial 1939,Mr 15,18:2
Adler, Sarah (Mme)
Millions 1930,O 3,30:4
Adler, Stella
Big Lake 1927,Ap 9,17:2
Jew Suss 1929,O 19,22:3
Angels on Earth 1929,D 11,34:7
Roaming Stars 1930,Ja 25,12:2
Wild Man, The 1930,My 17,21:5
Witch of Castile, The 1930,O 25,21:1
Uncle Moses 1930,N 29,21:3
Riverside Drive 1931,Ja 6,24:2
Man With the Portfolio, The 1931,F 12,24:6
House of Connelly, The 1931,S 29,22:4
1931 1931,D 11,34:3
Night Over Taos 1932,Mr 10,25:3
Success Story 1932,S 27,24:4
Success Story 1932,O 2,IX,1:1
Big Night 1933,Ja 18,16:2
Hilda Cassidy 1933,My 5,18:3
Gentlewoman 1934,Mr 23,28:4
Gold Eagle Guy 1934,N 29,33:4
Gold Eagle Guy 1934,D 9,X,1:1
Awake and Sing! 1935,F 20,23:2
Paradise Lost 1935,D 10,31:5
Sarah Adler Testimonial 1939,Mr 15,18:2
Sons and Soldiers 1943,My 5,22:2
Pretty Little Parlor 1944,Ap 18,24:8
He Who Gets Slapped 1946,Mr 21,31:4
He Who Gets Slapped 1946,Mr 31,II,1:1
Oh Dad, Poor Dad, Mamma's Hung You in the
Closet and I'm Feelin' So Sad 1961,Jl 6,19:2
Adler, Stella (Director)
Morning Star 1940,Ap 17,26:4
Manhattan Nocturne 1943,O 27,26:2
Polonaise 1945,O 8,20:2
Sunday Breakfast 1952,My 30,12:2
Johnny Johnson 1956,O 22,24:1
Adler, Stella (Producer)
Johnny Johnson 1956,O 22,24:1
Adler, Weil and Herman
Vaudeville (Palace) 1926,Jl 20,17:4
Vaudeville (Palace) 1926,N 23,27:3
Adler, William
Red Rainbow, A 1953,S 15,37:4
Infernal Machine, The 1954,Mr 22,22:2
There Was a Little Girl 1960,Mr 1,28:1
Adler and Bradford
Earl Carroll's Vanities 1928,Ag 7,25:2
Admire, Jere
On the Town 1959,Ja 16,36:1
Cabaret 1966,N 21,62:1
Steambath 1970,Jl 1,49:1
Adolph, Gladys and Eddie
Vaudeville (Palace) 1930,F 10,20:3
Adolphe
My 3 Angels 1956,F 4,24:2
Adolphus, Theodore (Choreographer)
Sweethearts 1947,Ja 22,31:2
Adomian, Lan (Composer)
Johnny Doodle 1942,Mr 19,28:2
Peer Gynt 1951,Ja 29,15:2
Peer Gynt 1951,F 4,II,1:1
Adomian, Lan (Director)
Johnny Doodle 1942,Mr 19,28:2
Adomian, Lan (Musical Director)
Russian People, The 1942,D 30,17:2
Peer Gynt 1951,Ja 29,15:2
Adomowska, Helen
Money Lender, The 1924,N 23,VIII,2:4
Adoue, Tad (Producer)
Southern Exposure 1950,S 27,36:3
Adrian, Diane
Are You With It? 1945,N 12,17:3
Adrian, Henry
Antony and Cleopatra 1937,N 11,30:2
Adrian, Henry (Director)
Victory Belles 1943,O 27,26:3
Girl From Nantucket, The 1945,N 9,17:2

Adrian, Henry (Producer)
Victory Belles 1943,O 27,26:3
Girl From Nantucket, The 1945,N 9,17:2
Young Man's Fancy, A 1947,Ap 30,33:2
Adrian, Iris
Fabulous Invalid, The 1938,O 10,15:1
Adrian, Joan
Lady Precious Stream 1936,Ja 28,15:2
Hamlet 1936,N 11,54:2
Jeremiah 1939,F 4,11:2
Adrian, Louis (Musical Director)
Carousel 1953,My 6,38:1
Kismet 1953,D 4,2:4
Peter Pan 1954,O 21,30:2
Adrian, Max
First Episode 1934,S 18,18:1
Candide 1956,D 3,40:2
Candide 1956,D 9,II,5:1
Mary Stuart 1957,O 9,39:1
Mary Stuart 1957,O 20,II,1:1
Lesson, The 1958,Ja 10,20:3
Chairs, The; Lesson, The 1958,F 16,II,1:1
Deadly Game, The 1960,F 3,27:2
As You Like It 1961,Jl 5,30:1
Hollow Crown, The 1963,Ja 31,5:1
By George 1967,O 13,33:1
Adrian (Costume Designer)
Mrs January & Mr Ex 1944,Ap 1,10:2
Obsession 1946,O 2,39:2
Adriana and Charly
Laugh Time 1943,S 9,35:2
Adrienne
If the Shoe Fits 1946,D 6,29:4
Adu, Frank
Slave Ship 1969,N 22,46:1
Advincula, C Gilbert
Across the Board on Tomorrow Morning
1942,Ag 18,17:1
Aeberhard, Susi
Marriage of Mr Mississippi, The 1969,N 20,60:5
Firebugs, The 1969,N 27,52:1
Philipp Hotz 1969,N 27,52:1
Aeschylus (Miscellaneous)
Family Reunion, The 1958,O 26,II,1:1
Aeschylus (Playwright)
Persians, The 1927,F 27,VII,2:3
Agamemnon 1936,N 2,25:6
Prometheus Bound 1957,Ag 9,11:6
Eumenides 1961,S 27,32:4
Choephori 1961,S 27,32:4
Oresteia 1961,N 8,43:5
Oresteia 1966,Je 30,29:1
Prometheus Bound 1967,Je 11,II,1:1
House of Atreus, The 1968,D 18,55:1
Persians, The 1970,F 15,II,1:1
Persians, The 1970,Ap 26,II,1:3
Afford, Max (Playwright)
Lady in Danger 1945,Mr 30,18:6
Afin (Playwright)
Listen Professor! 1943,D 23,22:1
Afinogenov, Alexander (Original Author)
Listen Professor! 1943,D 23,22:1
Afinogenov, Alexander (Playwright)
Far Away 1936,O 11,X,1:4
Long Live Spain! 1937,Ja 10,X,3:3
Distant Point 1941,N 9,IX,3:6
Afton, Effie
Ritzy 1930,F 11,30:4
Sailor, Beware! 1933,S 29,24:4
Play, Genius, Play! 1935,O 31,17:2
My Sister Eileen 1940,D 27,23:2
Last Stop 1944,S 6,17:2
Topaze 1947,D 29,21:5
Courtin' Time 1951,Je 14,30:2
Red Rainbow, A 1953,S 15,37:4
Middle of the Night 1956,F 9,39:1
Agair, Laura
Merrily We Roll Along 1936,Je 30,15:1
Agar, Herbert (Playwright)
Healthy, Wealthy and Wise 1930,Mr 2,26:3
Healthy, Wealthy and Wise 1930,Mr 23,IX,2:3
Agar, Olive
Dear Brutus 1926,Jl 15,21:3
Agate, James (Playwright)
I Accuse 1937,O 26,19:1
Agate, May
Colonel Satan 1931,Ja 18,I,28:6
Mary Tudor 1935,D 13,30:6
Agee, James (Original Author)
All the Way Home 1960,D 1,42:1
All the Way Home 1960,D 18,II,3:1
Agee, John
Polly of Hollywood 1927,F 22,22:3
Agee's Horses
Vaudeville (Palace) 1929,F 18,29:1
Ageloff, Betty
Sandhog 1954,N 24,17:1
Agenoux, Soren (Miscellaneous)
Tonight We Improvise 1959,N 7,27:4
Ager, Milton (Composer)
Rain or Shine 1928,F 10,26:3
Murray Anderson's Almanac 1929,Ag 15,20:3

Agg, Howard (Playwright)
New School for Scandal 1937,My 5,28:2
Aghayan, Ray (Costume Designer)
Vintage '60 1960,S 13,41:1
Egg, The 1962,Ja 9,23:2
Eddie Fisher at the Winter Garden 1962,O 3,47:1
Applause 1970,Mr 31,35:1
Aghayan, Ray (Director)
Lady's Not for Burning, The 1957,F 22,26:2
Agin, Boyd
Main Street 1921,O 6,21:1
Mongolia 1927,D 27,24:5
Agin, Lambert J
Laugh It Off 1934,Ap 5,24:2
Agis (Playwright)
Strana Avventura, Una; Queer Adventure, A
1930,O 27,17:6
Agnes and Adelaide
Vaudeville (Palace) 1932,Ap 25,18:3
Agolia, Nguba
Madmen and Specialists 1970,Ag 3,38:1
Agran, Albert
Dole Brothers 1932,Mr 26,17:7
Agress, Ted
Dear World 1969,F 7,33:1
Agruss, Mitchell
At War With the Army 1949,Mr 9,32:2
King Lear 1950,D 26,18:1
Clandestine Marriage, The 1954,O 4,23:2
Clandestine Marriage, The 1954,O 17,II,1:1
White Devil, The 1955,Mr 15,32:5
Carefree Tree, The 1955,O 12,37:2
King John 1956,Je 28,33:5
Measure for Measure 1956,Je 29,16:1
Taming of the Shrew, The 1956,Ag 6,20:1
Measure for Measure 1957,Ja 23,24:1
Taming of the Shrew, The 1957,F 21,30:2
Duchess of Malfi, The 1957,Mr 20,33:1
Othello 1957,Je 24,19:2
Much Ado About Nothing 1957,Ag 8,15:2
Hamlet 1958,Je 21,11:1
Winter's Tale, The 1958,Jl 21,17:4
Aguglia, Argentina
Barbara 1929,N 18,24:5
Aguglia, Gigi
Barbara 1929,N 18,24:5
Signori, Il Figlio E' Nato 1935,Je 8,13:7
Aguglia, Mimi
Nemica, La 1926,S 7,24:6
Signori, Il Figlio E' Nato 1935,Je 8,13:7
Figlia Brutta, La; Ugly Daughter, The
1937,Ag 30,24:6
Aguilar, David
Shoemaker's Prodigious Wife, The 1962,S 2,44:4
Morning Sun 1963,O 7,36:2
Aguilar, Ramiro
Shoemaker's Prodigious Wife, The 1962,S 2,44:4
Aguilera, Manuel
Pluma en el Viento; Feather in the Wind
1932,Ap 2,13:4
Aguirre, Jose
Fuerza Ciega, La 1927,D 6,26:1
Aguirre, Sergio
Remolienda, La; Bawdy Party 1968,F 3,20:1
Ahearn, Charles
Vaudeville (Hippodrome) 1924,F 12,20:2
Vaudeville (Palace) 1931,Ap 6,24:3
Ahearn, Richard
Mr Jiggins of Jigginstown 1936,D 18,30:2
Empress of Destiny 1938,Mr 10,16:2
Ahearne, Tom
Guys and Dolls 1955,Ap 21,32:2
Good as Gold 1957,Mr 8,22:2
Rainy Day in Newark, A 1963,O 23,35:1
Hogan's Goat 1965,N 12,56:1
Displaced Person, The 1966,D 30,15:1
Ahern, Gladys
Vaudeville (Palace) 1926,Ap 13,28:3
Vaudeville (Palace) 1926,N 30,27:2
Sidewalks of New York 1927,O 4,33:1
Vaudeville (Palace) 1928,My 8,25:2
Vaudeville (Palace) 1929,My 20,22:8
Ahern, Pat
Get Me in the Movies 1928,My 22,18:3
Ahern, Townsend
Love Letter, The 1921,O 5,20:1
Ahern, Will
Vaudeville (Palace) 1926,Ap 13,28:3
Vaudeville (Palace) 1926,N 30,27:2
Sidewalks of New York 1927,O 4,33:1
Vaudeville (Palace) 1928,My 8,25:2
Vaudeville (Palace) 1928,Jl 10,17:3
Vaudeville (Palace) 1929,My 20,22:8
Simple Simon 1930,F 2,VIII,2:7
Simple Simon 1930,F 19,22:1
Aherne, Brian
Silver Cord, The 1927,O 2,VIII,1:3
She Stoops to Conquer 1928,S 2,VII,2:1
Barretts of Wimpole Street, The 1931,F 10,25:1
Barretts of Wimpole Street, The 1931,F 22,VIII,1:1
Lucrece 1932,N 30,22:8
Lucrece 1932,D 4,IX,3:3
Lucrece 1932,D 21,22:2

Aherne, Brian—Cont
Lucrece 1933,Ja 1,IX,1:1
Romeo and Juliet 1934,D 4,23:2
Romeo and Juliet 1934,D 21,30:3
Romeo and Juliet 1934,D 30,IX,1:1
Barretts of Wimpole Street, The 1935,F 26,16:2
Saint Joan 1936,Mr 10,27:4
Othello 1937,Ja 7,16:4
Barretts of Wimpole Street, The 1945,Mr 27,23:6
Barretts of Wimpole Street, The 1945,Ap 1,II,1:1
French Touch, The 1945,D 10,18:2
She Stoops to Conquer 1949,D 29,21:3
Constant Wife, The 1951,D 10,34:3
Constant Wife, The 1951,D 16,II,6:1
Escapade 1953,N 19,40:1
Escapade 1953,N 29,II,1:1
Qudrille 1954,N 4,39:2
Quadrille 1954,N 14,II,1:1
My Fair Lady 1957,Mr 26,33:4
Dear Liar 1960,Mr 18,19:2
Dear Liar 1960,Mr 27,II,1:1
Chinese Prime Minister, The 1965,My 21,21:1
Aherne, Richard
Bright Rebel 1938,D 28,24:2
Paint Your Wagon 1951,N 13,32:2
Ahi
East Wind 1931,O 28,19:1
Ahlers, Annie
Casanova 1928,N 4,IX,2:1
Victoria and Her Hussar 1930,S 21,IX,2:6
Lied der Liebe, Das 1932,F 7,VIII,1:3
Du Barry 1932,My 8,VIII,1:6
Ahlert, Fred E (Composer)
It Happens on Ice 1940,O 11,24:3
Ahrons, Mitchell
Lower North 1944,Ag 26,15:4
Ahy, Gus
Elsie Janis and Her Gang 1922,Ja 17,13:2
Ai, Tom
Paint Your Wagon 1951,N 13,32:2
Aicard, Jean (Playwright)
Silent Forces 1920,Ag 30,12:1
Aidman, Charles
Desire Under the Elms 1952,Ja 17,23:4
Boy With a Cart, The 1954,Ap 5,19:2
Cretan Woman, The 1954,Jl 8,18:2
Merchant of Venice, The 1955,F 23,23:2
Macbeth 1955,O 20,42:2
U S A 1956,D 19,41:4
Career 1957,My 1,42:6
Career 1957,My 19,II,1:1
Spoon River Anthology 1963,My 2,40:5
Spoon River Anthology 1963,S 30,23:2
King Lear 1964,Jl 28,18:2
Aidman, Charles (Director)
Spoon River Anthology 1963,My 2,40:5
Spoon River Anthology 1963,S 30,23:2
Aidman, Charles (Lyricist)
Spoon River Anthology 1963,S 30,23:2
Aidman, Charles (Miscellaneous)
Trial of Dmitri Karamazov, The 1958,Ja 28,30:1
Aidman, Charles (Playwright)
Spoon River Anthology 1963,My 2,40:5
Spoon River Anthology 1963,S 30,23:2
Spoon River Anthology 1964,F 15,14:7
Aiken, A L (Playwright)
Uncle Tom's Cabin 1933,My 30,13:4
Aiken, Alfred (Lyricist)
We're Civilized? 1962,N 9,30:1
Aiken, Alfred (Playwright)
We're Civilized? 1962,N 9,30:1
Aiken, Conrad (Original Author)
Coming Forth by Day of Osiris Jones, The; Kid,
The 1961,Mr 15,45:2
Aiken, David
Girl in Pink Tights, The 1954,Mr 6,13:2
Saint of Bleecker Street, The 1954,D 28,21:1
Hit the Deck 1960,Je 24,32:1
Aiken, Elaine
When Did You Last See My Mother?
1967,Ja 5,27:5
Aiken, Elaine (Producer)
Secret Concubine, The 1960,Mr 22,29:2
Aiken, William A 2d
Coriolanus 1927,Je 18,8:3
Aikens, Adolph
White Man 1936,O 19,22:4
Aikens, Vanoye
Carib Song 1945,S 28,17:2
Here's Josephine Premice 1966,Ap 26,54:4
Ailey, Alvin
House of Flowers 1954,D 31,11:2
Carefree Tree, The 1955,O 12,37:2
Jamaica 1957,N 1,32:2
Call Me by My Rightful Name 1961,F 1,31:1
Talking to You 1961,O 23,22:5
Tiger Tiger Burning Bright 1962,D 24,5:2
Ailey, Alvin (Choreographer)
Carmen Jones 1959,Ag 18,25:1
Strada, La 1969,D 15,63:1
Ailey, Alvin (Director)
Jericho-Jim Crow 1964,Ja 13,25:3
Aimagor, Dan (Playwright)
I'm Solomon 1968,Ap 24,51:1

Ainley, Henry
Oliver Cromwell 1923,F 25,VII,1:7
Oliver Cromwell 1923,My 30,10:5
Macbeth 1927,Ja 2,30:1
Macbeth 1927,Ja 16,VII,4:3
First Mrs Fraser, The 1929,Jl 21,VIII,1:4
Colonel Satan 1931,Ja 19,25:2
Anatomist, The 1931,O 25,VIII,2:6
Tobias and the Angel 1932,Ap 3,VIII,1:4
Ainley, Noel
Merchant of Venice, The 1930,D 3,29:2
Ainley, Richard
Rose and Glove 1934,S 9,35:5
Merchant of Venice, The 1938,My 15,X,1:5
Elisabeth of Austria 1938,N 20,IX,1:8
Foreigners 1939,D 6,30:2
Heart of a City 1942,F 13,24:6
Ainslee, Winifred
Brigadoon 1950,My 3,36:2
What's Up 1953,O 28,37:2
Arabian Nights 1954,Je 25,15:2
Auntie Mame 1958,Ag 12,33:2
Ainslie, Maude
Devil's Disciple, The 1923,Ap 24,24:1
Beau-Strings 1926,Ap 27,22:2
Only the Young 1932,S 22,25:2
Ainsworth, Fred
Dream Play 1960,N 23,22:1
Seagull, The 1964,Ap 6,36:1
Crucible, The 1964,Ap 7,30:2
Ainsworth, Frederick
Another City, Another Land 1968,O 9,42:1
Ainsworth, John
Nude With Violin 1957,N 15,36:1
Ainsworth, John (Director)
Pink String and Sealing Wax 1957,S 6,13:1
Aitken, Charles
Ebb Tide 1931,Je 9,33:6
Beauty and the Beast 1932,Ja 10,I,29:2
Aitwen, J Wright
Don't Tell 1920,S 29,12:1
Ajax
Wild Man of Borneo, The 1927,S 14,29:2
Virginia 1937,S 3,13:2
Liliom 1940,Mr 26,17:2
Ajayi, Afolabi
Trials of Brother Jero, The 1967,N 10,60:1
Strong Breed, The 1967,N 10,60:1
Kongi's Harvest 1968,Ap 15,49:1
Man Better Man 1969,Jl 3,22:1
Akokawe 1970,Je 5,21:1
Ajayi, Afolabi (Director)
Akokawe 1970,Je 5,21:1
Ajayi, Afolabi (Miscellaneous)
Strong Breed, The 1967,N 10,60:1
Trials of Brother Jero, The 1967,N 10,60:1
Ajello, Ann
Cocktails of 1934 1934,My 5,22:1
Ajello, Ann (Lyricist)
Cocktails of 1934 1934,My 5,22:1
Ajootian, David
Home Is Tomorrow 1950,Je 2,27:2
Everyman 1953,O 12,30:2
Ajoret, Daniele
Impromptu de Versailles, L' 1961,F 22,30:1
Britannicus 1961,Mr 3,17:1
Dindon, Le 1961,Mr 8,38:1
Akalaitis, JoAnne
Red Horse Animation, The 1970,N 20,32:1
Akar, John
Mister Johnson 1956,Mr 30,11:1
Akbar Kahn, Ali (Composer)
Goa 1968,F 23,46:1
Aked, Muriel
Love From a Stranger 1936,F 3,20:7
Love From a Stranger 1936,Ap 1,28:7
Love From a Stranger 1936,Ap 26,IX,2:2
Ship Comes Home, A 1937,My 18,27:1
Ship Comes Home, A 1937,Je 6,XI,1:3
Lace on Her Petticoat 1951,S 5,40:3
Akeisa, Daifmore
Innocent Voyage, The 1943,N 16,27:2
Akers, Andra
Brother to Dragons 1968,D 8,86:1
Charley's Aunt 1970,Jl 6,38:1
Aki, M
Congai 1928,N 28,24:3
Akimov, Nikolai (Director)
Hamlet 1932,Je 26,IX,1:3
Akimov, Nikolai (Producer)
Hamlet 1932,Je 26,IX,1:3
Akinlana, Babafemi
Kongi's Harvest 1968,Ap 15,49:1
Akokawe 1970,Je 5,21:1
Akins, Mary
Hansel and Gretel 1929,D 25,21:1
Akins, Zoe (Playwright)
Foot-Loose 1920,My 11,12:1
Foot-Loose 1920,Ag 15,VI,1:1
Daddy's Gone A-Hunting 1921,S 1,18:3
Daddy's Gone A-Hunting 1921,S 4,VI,1:1
Daddy's Gone A-Hunting 1921,S 25,VI,1:1
Daddy's Gone A-Hunting 1921,O 2,VII,1:1

Akins, Zoe (Playwright)—Cont
Varying Shore, The 1921,D 6,24:1
Varying Shore, The 1921,D 11,VI,1:1
Texas Nightingale, The 1922,N 21,15:2
Texas Nightingale, The 1922,D 3,VIII,1:1
Royal Fandango, A 1923,N 11,VIII,2:6
Royal Fandango, A 1923,N 13,25:1
Royal Fandango, A 1923,N 18,VIII,1:1
Moon-Flower, The 1924,Ja 27,VII,2:7
Moon-Flower, The 1924,F 26,15:1
Moon-Flower, The 1924,Mr 2,VIII,1:1
Pardon My Glove 1926,My 23,VIII,1:1
Crown Prince, The 1927,F 27,VII,4:6
Thou Desperate Pilot 1927,Mr 8,23:1
Crown Prince, The 1927,Mr 24,23:2
Furies, The 1928,Mr 8,23:1
Furies, The 1928,Mr 18,IX,1:1
Love Duel, The 1929,Ap 16,32:3
Greeks Had a Word for It, The 1930,S 26,16:5
Greeks Had a Word for It, The 1934,N 23,22:2
Old Maid, The 1935,Ja 8,26:1
Declassee 1935,Ag 6,20:3
O Evening Star 1935,D 26,20:1
O Evening Star 1936,Ja 9,24:6
Old Maid, The; Two Mothers, The 1937,F 24,19:3
I Am Different 1938,Ag 28,IX,2:5
Happy Days 1941,My 14,24:2
Mrs January & Mr Ex 1944,Ap 1,10:2
Old Maid, The 1949,Ja 27,20:6
Akos, Catherine
Saint of Bleecker Street, The 1954,D 28,21:1
Saint of Bleecker Street, The 1955,Ja 2,II,1:1
Akselrod, Marcel (Producer)
Gilbert Becaud Sings Love 1968,O 7,53:5
Hamlet 1969,My 2,38:1
Aksenov, Vasily (Playwright)
Colleagues, The 1962,Je 21,26:1
Akst, Harry (Composer)
Artists and Models 1927,N 16,28:2
Calling All Stars 1934,N 22,26:1
Calling All Stars 1934,D 14,28:2
Akutagawa, Hiroshi
Taming of the Shrew, The 1966,F 5,32:1
Akutagawa, Ryunosuke (Original Author)
Rashomon 1959,Ja 28,36:2
Rashomon 1959,F 8,II,1:1
al-Bayati, Saadoun
Mother Courage and Her Children 1964,My 12,32:2
Alaimo, Marc
Miracle in Brooklyn 1966,Je 24,30:2
Venus-Shot 1966,Je 24,30:2
Prince of Peasantmania 1970,F 22,88:1
Alaimo, Michael
Hamlet 1964,Je 17,49:1
Alaire, Berenice
Roberta 1933,N 20,18:4
Alamo, Nancy
Picture of Dorian Gray, The 1956,Ag 18,15:5
Alan, Charles (Director)
Eternal Road, The 1937,Ja 8,14:2
Alan, David
Demon Mirror, The 1968,Mr 13,42:1
Alan, Ephraim
Flies, The 1954,S 10,18:2
Alanova, Kyra
Awful Truth, The 1922,S 19,14:3
Nerves 1924,S 2,22:2
Little Clay Cart, The 1924,D 6,13:3
Alarie, Amanda
Ti-Coq 1951,F 10,10:2
Alba, Alney
Wanted 1928,Jl 3,19:2
Triplets 1932,S 22,25:2
Pigeons and People 1933,Ja 17,22:3
Order Please 1934,O 10,21:2
Few Are Chosen 1935,S 18,19:3
Bernardine 1952,O 17,33:4
Alba, Floriana
Cabalgata 1949,Jl 8,14:2
Albabaca, Elizabeth
Apocalypsis cum Figuris 1969,N 20,60:2
Albam, Manny (Miscellaneous)
Fig Leaves Are Falling, The 1969,Ja 3,19:1
Alban, Richard
Fedora 1924,Ja 24,14:2
Albanesi, Meggie
Skin Game, The 1920,My 23,VI,1:3
Charm School, The 1921,F 27,VI,1:6
Albani, Olga
New Moon, The 1928,S 20,33:1
Albani, Renato
Romanticismo 1933,My 1,10:5
Albano, Gene
Carousel 1966,D 16,56:2
Albaugh, J W Jr
Bulldog Drummond 1921,D 27,10:2
Albeck, Freddy
Lotte Goslar's Pantomime Circus-For Humans
Only 1957,D 17,45:1
Albee, Edward (Director)
American Dream, The 1968,O 3,55:1
Albee, Edward (Lyricist)
Bartleby 1961,Ja 25,28:1

Albee, Edward (Miscellaneous)
Happy Journey to Trenton and Camden, The 1966,S 7,53:1
Queens of France 1966,S 7,53:1
Long Christmas Dinner, The 1966,S 7,53:1
Butter and Egg Man, The 1966,O 18,49:1
Breakfast at Tiffany's 1966,D 15,60:1
Night of the Dunce 1966,D 29,21:1
Rimers of Eldritch, The 1967,F 21,53:1
Party on Greenwich Avenue, The 1967,My 11,52:1
Albee, Edward (Playwright)
Zoo Story, The 1959,S 29,45:1
Zoo Story, The 1960,Ja 15,37:2
Zoo Story, The 1960,Ja 31,II,1:1
Sandbox, The 1960,My 17,42:2
Zoo Story, The 1960,Ag 26,13:1
Fam and Yam 1960,O 26,44:1
American Dream, The 1961,Ja 25,28:1
Death of Bessie Smith, The 1961,Mr 2,19:1
Zoo Story, The 1961,Jl 10,26:1
American Dream, The; Death of Bessie Smith, The 1961,O 25,33:5
Who's Afraid of Virginia Woolf? 1962,O 15,33:1
Who's Afraid of Virginia Woolf? 1962,O 28,II,1:1
Who's Afraid of Virginia Woolf? 1962,N 1,34:1
Zoo Story, The 1963,My 29,39:6
American Dream, The 1963,My 29,39:6
Zoo Story, The 1963,Je 11,29:2
Death of Bessie Smith, The 1963,Je 11,29:2
Who's Afraid of Virginia Woolf? 1963,O 6,68:4
Ballad of the Sad Cafe, The 1963,O 31,27:1
Ballad of the Sad Cafe, The 1963,N 10,II,1:1
Who's Afraid of Virginia Woolf? 1964,F 8,15:1
Who's Afraid of Virginia Woolf? 1964,N 26,52:1
Tiny Alice 1964,D 30,14:2
Tiny Alice 1965,Ja 10,II,1:1
Zoo Story, The 1965,F 13,10:7
American Dream, The 1965,F 13,10:7
Zoo Story, The 1965,Je 9,42:3
Malcolm 1966,Ja 12,29:1
Delicate Balance, A 1966,S 23,44:1
Delicate Balance, A 1966,O 2,II,1:1
Delicate Balance, A 1967,O 28,35:2
Everything in the Garden 1967,N 30,60:1
Everything in the Garden 1967,D 10,II,5:1
Everything in the Garden 1968,Ja 25,32:4
Box-Mao-Box; Quotations From Chairman Mao Tse-Tung 1968,Mr 8,48:1
Box-Mao-Box; Box 1968,Mr 8,48:1
Box-Mao-Box 1968,Mr 17,II,1:6
Who's Afraid of Virginia Woolf? 1968,Jl 4,13:1
Box 1968,O 1,39:1
Quotations From Chairman Mao Tse-Tung 1968,O 1,39:1
Death of Bessie Smith, The 1968,O 3,55:1
American Dream, The 1968,O 3,55:1
Krapp's Last Tape 1968,O 11,41:1
Zoo Story, The 1968,O 11,41:1
Box 1968,O 13,II,5:1
Quotations From Chairman Mao Tse-Tung 1968,O 13,II,5:1
Tiny Alice 1969,S 30,42:1
Tiny Alice 1969,O 12,II,9:1
Tiny Alice 1970,Ja 17,24:1
Albee, Edward (Producer)
Corruption in the Palace of Justice 1963,O 9,49:2
Lover, The 1964,Ja 6,35:1
Play 1964,Ja 6,35:1
Funnyhouse of a Negro 1964,Ja 15,25:3
Play 1964,Mr 25,46:2
Dutchman 1964,Mr 25,46:2
Two Executioners, The 1964,Mr 25,46:2
Up to Thursday 1965,F 11,45:1
Balls 1965,F 11,45:1
Home Free! 1965,F 11,45:1
Conerico Was Here to Stay 1965,Mr 4,37:1
Pigeons 1965,Mr 4,37:1
Hunting the Jingo Birds 1965,Mr 26,27:1
Lovey 1965,Mr 26,27:1
Do Not Pass Go 1965,Ap 20,44:1
Happy Days 1965,S 14,45:2
Quotations From Chairman Mao Tse-Tung 1968,O 1,39:1
Box 1968,O 1,39:1
Death of Bessie Smith, The 1968,O 3,55:1
American Dream, The 1968,O 3,55:1
Krapp's Last Tape 1968,O 11,41:1
Zoo Story, The 1968,O 11,41:1
Happy Days 1968,O 14,54:1
Front Page, The 1969,My 12,54:2
Watercolor 1970,Ja 22,30:1
Criss-Crossing 1970,Ja 22,30:1
Alberg, Mildred Freed (Producer)
Little Moon of Alban 1960,D 2,34:1
Alberg, Somer
As We Forgive Our Debtors 1947,Mr 11,37:2
Set My People Free 1948,N 4,38:2
Devil's Disciple, The 1950,Ja 26,23:2
Shrike, The 1952,Ja 16,20:2
Shrike, The 1953,N 26,51:2
Alberghetti, Anna Maria
Carnival! 1961,Ap 14,22:2
Carnival! 1961,Ap 23,II,1:1

Albericci, Josephine (Director)
Devil Came From Dublin, The! 1955,Je 3,27:2
Albericci, Josephine (Producer)
Devil Came From Dublin, The! 1955,Je 3,27:2
Alberni, Luis
Checkerboard, The 1920,Ag 20,7:2
Outrageous Mrs Palmer, The 1920,O 13,18:1
Near Santa Barbara 1921,F 1,14:1
Smooth as Silk 1921,F 23,18:3
Dreams for Sale 1922,S 14,24:1
Rita Coventry 1923,F 20,12:2
Apache, The 1923,My 9,14:3
What Price Glory 1924,S 6,14:3
Deep River 1926,O 5,26:2
Lace Petticoat 1927,Ja 5,18:2
Lady Do 1927,Ap 19,24:2
My Princess 1927,O 7,24:2
Stairs, The 1927,N 8,32:7
Fallen Angels 1927,D 2,20:4
Silent House, The 1928,F 8,28:5
Albers, Hans
Verbrecher, Die 1928,D 23,VIII,4:1
What Price Glory 1929,Ap 28,IX,1:4
Albers, Hilde
Saint Joan 1936,Mr 10,27:4
Albert, Adele
Revolt of the Beavers, The 1937,My 21,19:2
Albert, Aleita
Priorities of 1942 1942,Mr 13,23:2
Albert, Don (Musical Director)
Vaudeville (Palace) 1949,My 20,32:4
Vaudeville (Palace) 1951,O 17,36:6
Albert, Eddie
O Evening Star 1936,Ja 9,24:6
Brother Rat 1936,D 17,34:5
Room Service 1937,My 20,16:1
Room Service 1937,My 30,X,1:1
Boys From Syracuse, The 1938,N 24,36:1
Miss Liberty 1949,Je 14,26:6
Miss Liberty 1949,Jl 16,6:5
Miss Liberty 1949,Jl 24,II,1:1
Miss Liberty 1949,Ag 7,II,6:4
Albert, Elizabeth
Republic, The 1970,Ap 28,49:1
Albert, Fred
Fedora 1924,Ja 24,14:2
Albert, James
More the Merrier, The 1941,S 16,19:3
Albert, Jeanne
Hamlet 1948,D 4,9:2
Albert, Jerry (Playwright)
In the Groove 1938,Ap 22,14:5
Albert, John
Say When 1934,N 9,24:2
Sun Kissed 1937,Mr 11,20:2
Albert, Katherine (Original Author)
Guest in the House 1942,F 25,25:2
Albert, Katherine (Playwright)
Loco 1946,O 17,29:2
Albert, Margot
Promenade 1969,Je 5,56:1
Only Jealousy of Emer, The 1970,Mr 25,36:4
Albert, Marvin H (Playwright)
Twist of Sand, A 1969,F 22,36:1
Albert, Mildred
Revolt of the Beavers, The 1937,My 21,19:2
Albert, Tony
Solitaire 1942,Ja 28,22:2
He Who Gets Slapped 1946,Mr 21,31:4
Country Girl, The 1950,N 11,10:6
Albert, Wil
Dinny and the Witches 1959,D 10,53:3
Top Secret 1960,S 6,40:1
Spitting Image 1969,Mr 3,28:1
Alberta, Laura
Miracle, The 1924,Ja 16,17:1
Park Avenue, Ltd 1932,Mr 4,17:1
Albertazzi, Giorgio
Hamlet 1964,Je 2,32:8
Alberti, Alberto
Miserabili I, 1934,O 1,14:2
Alberti, Mrs (Director)
Nevertheless 1920,D 28,9:1
Albertina Rasch ballet
George White's Scandals 1925,Je 23,24:2
Albertini, Ellen (Choreographer)
Tom Sawyer - Ballad of the Mississippi 1947,O 27,11:3
Alberts, Albert
Good Times 1920,Ag 10,10:1
Alberts, Paul
Paths of Glory 1935,S 27,24:2
Rugged Path, The 1945,N 12,17:2
He Who Gets Slapped 1946,Mr 21,31:4
Sappho 1960,Ja 12,22:1
Goose, The 1960,Mr 16,44:1
Albertson, Arthur
Gringo 1922,D 15,26:3
In the Next Room 1923,N 28,14:1
Fall of Eve, The 1925,S 1,18:1
Gypsy Fires 1925,D 8,28:3
Virgin, The 1926,F 23,26:1

Albertson, Carl
Cyrano de Bergerac 1953,N 13,24:3
No Time for Sergeants 1955,O 21,32:2
Albertson, Frank
Brother Rat 1936,D 8,30:6
Brother Rat 1936,D 17,34:5
More the Merrier, The 1941,S 16,19:3
Walrus and the Carpenter, The 1941,N 10,20:2
Mr Adam 1949,My 26,34:6
Seventeen 1951,Je 22,16:6
Late Love 1953,O 14,35:2
Albertson, Jack
Meet the People 1940,D 26,22:2
Allah Be Praised! 1944,Ap 21,14:2
Lady Says Yes, A 1945,Ja 11,18:5
Cradle Will Rock, The 1947,N 25,38:3
Cradle Will Rock, The 1947,D 27,11:2
Tickets, Please! 1950,Ap 28,25:2
Tickets, Please! 1950,My 7,II,1:1
Top Banana 1951,N 2,19:2
Subject Was Roses, The 1964,My 26,45:1
Subject Was Roses, The 1964,Je 7,II,1:1
Albertson, Kathryn
Lady in the Dark 1952,Mr 8,11:3
Albertson, Lillian
Six-Fifty, The 1921,O 25,20:1
Six-Fifty, The 1921,O 30,VI,1:1
Malvaloca 1922,O 3,22:1
Albertson, Mabel
Return of Ulysses, The 1943,Ja 28,22:2
Return of Ulysses, The 1943,F 7,II,1:6
Egg, The 1962,Ja 9,23:2
Xmas in Las Vegas 1965,N 5,31:1
Albertson, Mabel (Director)
Sam Ego's House 1947,N 1,11:3
Albertson, Merle
Singing Girl, The 1952,Je 4,31:8
Getting Married 1970,Ja 20,46:1
Albery, Bronson (Director)
Red Roses for Me 1946,Mr 10,II,2:1
Albery, Bronson (Miscellaneous)
Taming of the Shrew, The 1937,Ap 11,XI,2:1
French Without Tears 1937,S 29,19:1
Albery, Donald (Miscellaneous)
Taste of Honey, A 1960,O 5,46:1
Complaisant Lover, The 1961,N 2,43:2
Beyond the Fringe 1962,O 29,36:1
Semi-Detached 1963,O 8,49:1
Entertaining Mr Sloane 1965,O 13,41:1
Albery, Donald (Producer)
Living Room, The 1954,N 18,41:1
Oliver 1963,Ja 8,5:5
Severed Head, A 1964,O 29,40:1
Conduct Unbecoming 1970,O 13,50:1
Albery, Ian (Miscellaneous)
Oliver 1963,Ja 8,5:5
Albery, Ian B (Director)
Conduct Unbecoming 1970,O 13,50:1
Albion, Louis
Scrambled Wives 1920,Ag 6,16:1
Albra, Jerry
Clair de Lune 1921,Ap 19,15:1
Albrecht, Kurd (Scenic Designer)
Passion Play, The 1929,Ap 30,32:1
Albright, Clarence
Black Rhythm 1936,D 21,19:2
Albright, Hardie
Saturday Night 1926,O 26,25:1
Three Sisters, The 1926,O 27,24:1
Twelfth Night 1926,D 21,21:4
Cradle Song 1927,Ja 25,18:2
Such Is Life 1927,S 1,27:3
Merchant of Venice, The 1928,Ja 17,22:2
Gang War 1928,Ag 21,27:2
Hundred Years Old, A 1929,O 2,28:2
Greeks Had a Word for It, The 1930,S 26,16:5
Play, Genius, Play! 1935,O 31,17:2
Room Service 1935,N 17,II,7:7
Behind the Red Lights 1937,Ja 14,17:4
Albright, Hardie (Playwright)
All the Living 1938,Mr 25,14:4
Albrights, The
International Playgirls '64 1964,My 22,40:2
Albro, Arthur
Passing Show of 1922, The 1922,S 21,18:2
Hot Money 1931,N 9,22:2
Alburquerque, Jose
Road to Happiness, The 1927,My 3,24:1
Romantic Young Lady, The 1927,My 5,30:2
Girl and the Cat, The 1927,My 6,21:2
Albury, Robert W
Moon Vine, The 1943,F 12,22:2
Albus, Joanna
On Whitman Avenue 1946,My 9,28:2
Albus, Joanna (Director)
Streetcar Named Desire, A 1955,Mr 4,18:2
Albus, Joanna (Producer)
Red Roses for Me 1951,Ap 26,35:8
Albyn, G N (Playwright)
Moral Fabric 1932,N 22,25:3
Alcalde, Mario
Captain Brassbound's Conversion 1950,D 28,21:1
Billy the Kid 1951,Ag 21,23:2

Alcalde, Mario—Cont
Bullfight 1954,Ja 13,25:2
Flowering Peach, The 1954,D 29,19:2
Flowering Peach, The 1955,Ja 9,II,1:1
Lovers 1956,My 11,23:1
Diamond Orchid 1965,F 11,44:4
Alcarez, Jose (Director)
Emerald Slippers, The 1970,S 2,31:2
Alcarez, Jose (Playwright)
Emerald Slippers, The 1970,S 2,31:2
Alchevsky, Vasily
My Fair Lady 1964,D 29,22:1
Alcine, Arling
Craig's Wife 1925,O 13,21:2
Paradise 1927,D 26,26:4
Chrysalis 1932,N 16,15:2
Moor Born 1934,Ap 4,26:4
Moor Born 1934,Ap 8,X,2:7
Mother Lode 1934,D 24,16:5
Crime Marches on 1935,O 24,19:1
Tapestry in Gray 1935,D 28,10:2
Tell Me Pretty Maiden 1937,D 17,33:5
Come Across 1938,S 15,28:3
Glorious Morning 1938,N 28,10:3
Alcock, Muriel
Robin Hood 1929,N 20,26:5
Alcopra, Pete
Passenger to Bali, A 1940,Mr 15,26:2
Alcorn, John
Rapid Transit 1927,Ap 8,21:2
Alcorn, Olive Ann
Passing Show of 1922, The 1922,S 21,18:2
Untitled-Revue 1923,My 12,15:4
Passing Show of 1923, The 1923,Je 15,24:6
Alcott, Louisa May (Original Author)
Little Women 1931,D 8,36:2
Under the Lilacs 1934,N 19,13:3
Little Women 1944,D 13,29:2
Jo 1964,F 13,25:1
Alcova, Ina
Vaudeville (Palace) 1924,Ap 29,12:2
Alcover
Dompteur, Le, ou L'Anglais Tel Qu' On La Mange 1926,Ja 10,VII,1:3
Felix 1926,O 10,VIII,2:1
Mon Coeur au Ralenti 1927,Je 12,VII,2:1
Amis Comme Avant 1930,Ja 26,VIII,2:1
Tartuffe 1930,F 2,VIII,4:1
Ludo 1932,Je 12,X,1:3
Alda, Alan
Only in America 1959,N 20,35:1
Darwin's Theories 1960,O 19,53:2
Purlie Victorious 1961,S 29,29:1
Purlie Victorious 1961,O 8,II,1:1
Whisper in God's Ear, A 1962,O 12,27:2
Fair Game for Lovers 1964,F 11,43:2
Cafe Crown 1964,Ap 18,32:1
Owl and the Pussycat, The 1964,N 19,48:1
Diary of Adam and Eve, The 1966,O 19,53:1
Lady or the Tiger?, The 1966,O 19,53:1
Passionella 1966,O 19,53:1
Apple Tree, The 1966,O 30,II,1:1
Apple Tree, The 1967,O 12,56:1
Apple Tree, The 1967,N 10,61:1
Alda, Alan (Playwright)
Darwin's Theories 1960,O 19,53:2
Alda, Delyle
Ziegfeld Follies 1920,Je 23,14:1
Blue Eyes 1921,F 22,11:2
Snapshots of 1921 1921,Je 3,19:2
George White's Scandals 1923,Je 19,22:5
Alda, Frances (Madame)
Vaudeville (Palace) 1932,My 2,13:2
Alda, Robert
Guys and Dolls 1950,N 25,11:2
Guys and Dolls 1950,D 3,II,1:1
Guys and Dolls 1951,O 7,II,1:1
Harbor Lights 1956,O 5,20:1
What Makes Sammy Run? 1964,F 28,19:1
My Daughter, Your Son 1969,My 14,36:2
Aldcroft, Elena
Sport of Kings, The 1926,My 5,24:2
This Woman Business 1926,D 8,25:1
Aldebert, Pierre
Aiglon, L' 1924,O 21,21:1
Naked 1924,O 28,27:2
Madame Sans-Gene 1924,N 4,30:1
Alden, Betty
Anna Ascends 1920,S 23,14:1
Shore Leave 1922,Ag 9,20:2
Great Music 1924,O 6,24:1
Man in Evening Clothes, The 1924,D 6,13:4
Tangletoes 1925,F 18,17:1
Virgin Man, The 1927,Ja 19,20:4
Alden, Bonnie
Jenny Kissed Me 1948,D 24,12:2
Alden, Bonnie (Miscellaneous)
Late Love 1953,O 14,35:2
Alden, Clare
Show Boat 1948,S 9,33:2
Alden, H Lee Jr (Composer)
Best of Everything, The 1952,My 8,35:4
Alden, Hortense
Liliom 1921,Ap 21,18:1

Liliom 1921,My 1,VII,1:1
It's a Boy! 1922,S 20,18:3
As You Like It 1923,Ap 24,24:1
Locked Door, The 1924,Je 20,17:2
Firebrand, The 1924,O 16,33:1
Arabesque 1925,O 21,20:2
Ghosts 1926,Mr 17,28:2
Month in the Country, A 1930,Mr 18,30:5
Lysistrata 1930,Ap 29,30:5
Lysistrata 1930,Je 6,20:1
Grand Hotel 1930,N 14,30:4
Grand Hotel 1930,N 23,IX,1:1
Thunder on the Left 1933,N 1,25:2
But Not for Love 1934,N 27,26:2
Arms for Venus 1937,Mr 12,18:7
Here Come the Clowns 1938,D 8,36:2
Garden District; Suddenly Last Summer 1958,Ja 8,23:4
Garden District; Something Unspoken 1958,Ja 8,23:4
Garden District; Suddenly Last Summer 1958,Ja 19,II,1:1
Late Late Show, The 1968,N 4,57:3
Alden, Jane
Say When 1928,Je 27,29:3
Street Singer, The 1929,S 18,35:2
Green Grow the Lilacs 1931,Ja 27,21:2
Scandals 1931,Ag 11,28:4
George White's Scandals 1931,S 15,30:1
Sunday Nights at Nine 1934,Mr 5,18:5
Alden, Jerome (Miscellaneous)
Shakespeare Revisited 1962,Jl 19,19:2
Alden, Judith
Lady Has a Heart, The 1937,S 27,24:1
Merry Wives of Windsor, The 1938,Ap 15,22:3
Alden, Lester
Magda 1926,Ja 27,16:2
Grand Hotel 1930,N 14,30:4
American Dream; 1933 1933,F 22,24:5
Kultur 1933,S 27,24:3
Theodora, the Queen 1934,F 1,15:3
Roman Servant, A 1934,D 3,14:5
Ten Million Ghosts 1936,O 24,23:7
Land of Fame 1943,S 22,31:5
Alden, Lynn
Lady in the Dark 1943,Mr 1,14:2
Firebird of Florence 1945,Mr 23,13:4
Alden, Marian
Wonderful Night, A; Fledermaus, Die 1929,N 1,23:3
Alden, Phyllis
Czarina, The 1922,F 1,22:1
Aldene, Greta
Hi, Paisano 1961,O 2,36:2
Alder, Else
June Love 1921,Ap 26,20:1
Alderdice, Alfred
Clean Beds 1939,My 26,21:2
Alderman, Edwin J (Composer)
Flair-Flair the Idol of Paree 1935,Mr 13,16:1
Alderman, Edwin J (Lyricist)
Flair-Flair the Idol of Paree 1935,Mr 13,16:1
Alderman, Jacqueline
Singing Rabbi, The 1931,S 11,24:4
Alderman, James
Vogues of 1924 1924,Mr 28,14:3
Love Song, The 1925,Ja 14,19:4
Alderman, John
Cave Dwellers, The 1957,O 21,29:2
Look After Lulu 1959,Mr 4,35:1
Sign in Sidney Brustein's Window, The 1964,O 16,32:1
Alderman, Tom
Hasty Heart, The 1959,S 15,45:2
Alderson, Erville
Beyond the Horizon 1920,F 4,12:1
Alderson, William
Huui, Huui 1968,N 25,58:1
Aldini, Edmonda
Game of Heroes, The 1966,F 22,14:2
Aldis, Mary (Playwright)
Flying Blind 1930,My 16,20:2
Aldous, Lionel (William Jay) (Playwright)
Golden Wings 1941,D 9,46:6
Aldous, William
Marigold 1930,O 9,23:1
Aldredge, Theoni V (Costume Designer)
Augustus Does His Bit 1958,F 22,8:3
Androcles and the Lion 1958,F 22,8:3
Heloise 1958,S 25,28:4
Heloise 1958,O 5,II,1:1
Golden Six, The 1958,O 27,31:2
Saintliness of Margery Kempe, The 1959,F 3,35:6
Sweet Bird of Youth 1959,Mr 11,39:2
Geranium Hat, The 1959,Mr 18,45:1
Nervous Set, The 1959,My 13,43:1
Chic 1959,My 19,28:2
Flowering Cherry 1959,O 22,46:1
Silent Night, Lonely Night 1959,D 4,36:1
Distant Bell, A 1960,Ja 14,29:1
Best Man, The 1960,Ap 1,39:1
Measure for Measure 1960,Jl 27,33:1
Hedda Gabler 1960,N 10,61:1

Aldredge, Theoni V (Costume Designer)—Cont
Alligators, The 1960,N 15,47:1
Rosemary 1960,N 15,47:1
Romeo and Juliet 1961,F 24,24:1
Mary, Mary 1961,Mr 9,24:2
Devil's Advocate, The 1961,Mr 10,20:1
Under Milk Wood 1961,Mr 30,25:1
Smiling the Boy Fell Dead 1961,Ap 20,28:1
Much Ado About Nothing 1961,Jl 7,17:1
Midsummer Night's Dream, A 1961,Ag 3,13:1
Ghosts 1961,S 22,29:1
First Love 1961,D 26,20:2
I Can Get It for You Wholesale 1962,Mr 23,29:1
Rosmersholm 1962,Ap 12,42:1
Merchant of Venice, The 1962,Je 22,1:4
Tempest, The 1962,Jl 17,18:2
King Lear 1962,Ag 14,35:1
Mr President 1962,O 22,34:2
Tchin-Tchin 1962,O 26,26:2
Macbeth 1962,N 17,16:2
Strange Interlude 1963,Mr 13,5:2
Blue Boy in Black, The 1963,My 1,32:1
Antony and Cleopatra 1963,Je 21,33:1
As You Like It 1963,Jl 17,19:2
Winter's Tale, The 1963,Ag 16,14:1
Trojan Women, The 1963,D 24,7:6
Any Wednesday 1964,F 19,34:1
But for Whom Charlie 1964,Mr 13,42:2
Anyone Can Whistle 1964,Ap 6,36:1
Knack, The 1964,My 28,42:2
Hamlet 1964,Je 17,49:1
Three Sisters, The 1964,Je 23,24:1
Othello 1964,Jl 15,29:1
Electra 1964,Ag 12,42:1
Othello 1964,O 13,48:1
Luv 1964,N 12,43:1
Poor Richard 1964,D 3,59:1
Ready When You Are, C. B.! 1964,D 8,55:1
Love's Labour's Lost 1965,Je 16,46:1
Coriolanus 1965,Jl 15,23:1
Troilus and Cressida 1965,Ag 13,17:1
Skyscraper 1965,N 15,48:1
Playroom, The 1965,D 6,49:1
Cactus Flower 1965,D 9,60:2
Utbu 1966,Ja 5,24:1
First One Asleep, Whistle 1966,F 28,19:1
Serjeant Musgrave's Dance 1966,Mr 9,44:1
Happily Never After 1966,Mr 11,37:1
Time for Singing, A 1966,My 23,48:2
All's Well That Ends Well 1966,Je 17,39:1
Measure for Measure 1966,Jl 14,27:1
Richard III 1966,Ag 11,26:1
Delicate Balance, A 1966,S 23,44:1
You Know I Can't Hear You When the Water's Running; Footsteps of Doves, The 1967,Mr 14,54:1
You Know I Can't Hear You When the Water's Running; Shock of Recognition, The 1967,Mr 14,54:1
You Know I Can't Hear You When the Water's Running; I'll Be Home for Christmas 1967,Mr 14,54:1
You Know I Can't Hear You When the Water's Running; I'm Herbert 1967,Mr 14,54:1
That Summer-That Fall 1967,Mr 17,33:1
Illya Darling 1967,Ap 12,37:1
Little Murders 1967,Ap 26,38:1
Comedy of Errors, The 1967,Je 15,58:4
King John 1967,Jl 14,19:1
Titus Andronicus 1967,Ag 10,43:2
Daphne in Cottage D 1967,O 16,56:1
Hair 1967,O 30,55:1
Trial of Lee Harvey Oswald, The 1967,N 6,64:1
Hamlet 1967,D 27,45:1
Before You Go 1968,Ja 12,20:1
I Never Sang for My Father 1968,Ja 26,30:1
Portrait of a Queen 1968,F 29,29:1
Ergo 1968,Mr 4,29:1
Weekend 1968,Mr 14,50:2
Memorandum, The 1968,My 6,55:1
Only Game in Town, The 1968,My 21,42:1
Henry IV, Part I 1968,Je 30,54:7
Henry IV, Part II 1968,Jl 2,33:1
Hamlet 1968,Jl 4,15:1
Romeo and Juliet 1968,Ag 16,19:1
King Lear 1968,N 8,43:1
Huui, Huui 1968,N 25,58:1
Ballad for a Firing Squad 1968,D 12,64:2
Cities in Bezique; Owl Answers, The 1969,Ja 13,26:1
Cities in Bezique; Beast's Story, A 1969,Ja 13,26:1
Invitation to a Beheading 1969,Mr 18,36:1
Billy 1969,Mr 24,56:1
Gingham Dog, The 1969,Ap 24,41:1
Peer Gynt 1969,Jl 17,56:1
Electra 1969,Ag 8,14:1
Twelfth Night 1969,Ag 14,29:2
Wars of the Roses, The (Part I) 1970,Jl 2,30:1
Wars of the Roses, The (Part II) 1970,Jl 3,15:1
Richard III 1970,Jl 4,11:1
Happiness Cage, The 1970,O 5,56:4
Trelawny of the 'Wells' 1970,O 12,48:1
Colette 1970,O 15,58:1

Aldredge, Theoni V (Costume Designer)—Cont
Jack MacGowran in the Works of Samuel Beckett 1970,N 20,32:1
Aldredge, Theoni V (Miscellaneous)
P S I Love You 1964,N 20,40:1
Titus Andronicus 1967,Ag 10,43:2
Aldredge, Tom
Electra 1958,My 10,17:7
Nervous Set, The 1959,My 13,43:1
Tempest, The 1959,D 28,19:2
Between Two Thieves 1960,F 12,23:1
Henry V 1960,Je 30,23:1
Untitled-Revue 1961,Je 18,II,1:1
Premise, The 1962,Jl 27,15:5
Love's Labour's Lost 1965,Je 16,46:1
Troilus and Cressida 1965,Ag 13,17:1
Utbu 1966,Ja 5,24:1
Mutilated, The 1966,F 23,42:1
Measure for Measure 1966,Jl 14,27:1
Butter and Egg Man, The 1966,O 18,49:1
Midsummer Night's Dream, A 1967,Je 19,42:1
Antigone 1967,Je 19,43:1
Merchant of Venice, The 1967,Je 22,46:2
Macbeth 1967,Jl 31,21:1
Everything in the Garden 1967,N 30,60:1
Ergo 1968,Mr 4,29:1
Romeo and Juliet 1968,Ag 16,19:1
Twelfth Night 1969,Ag 14,29:2
Indians 1969,O 14,51:1
Engagement Baby, The 1970,My 22,40:1
Aldredge, Tom (Director)
Happiness Cage, The 1970,O 5,56:4
Aldrich, Arthur (Lighting Director)
Hamlet 1959,S 11,21:4
Aldrich, Charles T
Vaudeville (Palace) 1928,Ja 31,29:2
Aldrich, Maggie
Devil's Advocate, The 1961,Mr 10,20:1
Aldrich, Margaret (Miscellaneous)
How to Be a Jewish Mother 1967,D 29,18:1
Aldrich, Mariska
Miracle, The 1924,Ja 16,17:1
Miracle, The 1924,Ag 19,9:1
Miracle, The 1927,F 1,24:5
Aldrich, Meeka
Angela 1928,D 4,28:2
Aldrich, Richard (Director)
Doll's House, A 1937,Jl 18,II,6:8
Aldrich, Richard (Miscellaneous)
Be So Kindly 1937,F 9,19:4
Pygmalion 1945,D 27,16:1
Volpone 1948,Ja 9,24:6
John Bull's Other Island 1948,F 11,33:4
Old Lady Says No, The 1948,F 18,35:1
Where Stars Walk 1948,F 25,27:2
Goodbye My Fancy 1948,N 18,35:2
Caesar and Cleopatra 1949,D 22,28:2
Aldrich, Richard (Producer)
Three-Cornered Moon 1933,Mr 17,20:6
By Your Leave 1934,Ja 25,15:3
Pure in Heart, The 1934,Mr 21,24:3
Petticoat Fever 1935,Mr 5,22:2
Fresh Fields 1936,F 11,19:2
Aged 26 1936,D 22,32:1
Tide Rising 1937,Ja 26,17:2
Doll's House, A 1937,Jl 25,X,2:3
Ruy Blas 1938,Jl 24,IX,2:1
Lorelei 1938,N 30,21:7
Importance of Being Earnest, The 1939,Ja 13,16:2
Margin for Error 1939,O 15,48:7
Margin for Error 1939,N 4,11:3
My Dear Children 1940,F 1,16:2
Cue for Passion 1940,D 20,33:4
Plan M 1942,F 21,15:2
It Takes Two 1947,F 4,33:4
September Tide 1948,D 16,39:5
Western Wind 1949,Ag 9,20:6
Four Twelves Are 48 1951,Ja 18,30:2
Girl Can Tell, A 1953,O 30,28:2
Dear Charles 1954,S 16,37:2
Little Glass Clock, The 1956,Mr 27,40:2
Aldridge, Ed P (Miscellaneous)
Not While I'm Eating 1961,D 20,37:1
Aldridge, Harold E J (Playwright)
Forty-Ninth State, The 1947,My 27,30:4
Aldridge, Kay
Over Twenty-One 1944,Ja 4,20:2
Aldridge, Michael
Moon for the Misbegotten, A 1960,Ja 22,14:8
Antony and Cleopatra 1969,Ag 30,10:3
Aleichem, Sholem (Miscellaneous)
Untitled-Poetry Reading 1967,Jl 18,29:1
Aleichem, Sholem (Original Author)
Great Fortune, The 1922,D 9,11:1
Roaming Stars 1930,Ja 25,12:2
Motel Peissi, The Contor's Kid 1934,N 29,33:3
Tevye the Dairyman 1935,O 25,25:1
If I Were Rothschild 1940,Ja 1,28:7
Yosele the Nightingale 1949,O 21,30:4
World of Sholom Aleichem, The 1953,S 20,II,1:1
World of Sholom Aleichem, The 1955,Ja 12,22:4
Tevya and His Daughters 1957,S 17,38:2
Tevya and His Daughters 1957,S 29,II,1:1
Thousand and One Nights 1959,D 16,53:2

Going to America 1961,O 30,33:7
Fiddler on the Roof 1964,S 23,56:2
Fiddler on the Roof 1964,O 4,II,1:1
Fiddler on the Roof 1964,O 6,36:5
Fiddler on the Roof 1965,Je 9,40:1
Fiddler on the Roof 1965,Ag 15,II,2:5
Wandering Stars 1966,N 14,52:2
Fiddler on the Roof 1967,S 28,59:2
Fiddler on the Roof 1968,F 22,36:2
Fiddler on the Roof 1969,Ag 8,10:2
Fiddler on the Roof 1969,N 16,82:6
Fiddler on the Roof 1970,F 28,20:1
Fiddler on the Roof 1970,Jl 8,34:1
Aleichem, Sholem (Playwright)
Serving Folk 1920,Ap 22,11:3
Gold Diggers, The 1927,D 3,19:2
Stempenu, the Fiddler 1929,Mr 9,24:7
Tobias the Milkman 1930,Je 21,20:4
If I Were You 1931,S 24,21:1
Twice 100,000 1931,N 22,VIII,3:1
Twice 100,000 1934,N 23,22:6
Kapores 1936,S 28,14:3
200,000 1936,O 14,30:2
200,000 1936,N 29,XII,3:3
Mazal Tov 1938,My 23,21:3
Wandering Stars 1946,D 14,18:2
World of Sholom Aleichem, The 1953,S 20,II,1:1
Grass Is Always Greener, The 1955,F 16,25:2
When I Was a Child 1960,D 9,38:1
200,000 1966,F 15,33:5
Tevye the Milkman 1970,D 6,84:8
Alekin, B
Revisor; Inspector General, The 1935,F 18,19:6
Strange Child 1935,F 26,16:1
White Guard, The; Days of the Turbins 1935,Mr 7,27:5
Enemies 1935,Mr 19,24:7
Deluge, The 1935,Mr 26,23:7
Alekseyev, Nikolai
Three Sisters, The 1965,F 12,15:1
Kremlin Chimes 1965,F 25,23:1
Alene, Douglas
Ballyhoo 1930,D 23,24:1
Aleneff, M
Revue Russe, The 1922,O 6,28:1
Alenikoff, Frances
Dream Play 1960,N 23,22:1
Aleo, Anthony
Carousel 1949,Ja 26,28:2
Aleong, Aki
Teahouse of the August Moon, The 1956,N 9,33:2
Alessandro, Jose
Royal Fandango, A 1923,N 11,VIII,2:6
Royal Fandango, A 1923,N 13,25:1
Far Cry, The 1924,O 1,24:1
Passing Present, The 1931,D 8,36:2
Aleta
Buzzin' Around 1920,Jl 7,14:1
Rose Girl, The 1921,F 12,11:1
Aletter, Frank
These Are the Times 1950,My 11,37:2
Wish You Were Here 1952,Je 26,26:6
Time Limit! 1956,Ja 25,27:2
Bells Are Ringing 1956,N 29,43:4
Bells Are Ringing 1956,N 30,18:2
Gay Divorce 1960,Ap 4,37:1
Alevy, Maurice (Choreographer)
Difficult Woman, The 1962,Ap 26,22:7
Alevy, Maurice (Director)
Difficult Woman, The 1962,Ap 26,22:7
Alevy, Maurice (Playwright)
Difficult Woman, The 1962,Ap 26,22:7
Alex, Jimmy
Carnival in Flanders 1953,S 9,38:2
Boy Friend, The 1954,O 1,20:1
Alex, Sally
Coming Forth by Day of Osiris Jones, The; Kid, The 1961,Mr 15,45:2
Guns of Carrar, The 1968,D 10,53:1
Alexander, Alex
Merry Widow, The 1943,Ag 5,19:2
Merry Widow, The 1957,Ap 11,36:6
But Never Jam Today 1969,Ap 24,40:1
Alexander, Alice (Producer)
Right This Way 1938,Ja 6,22:3
Alexander, Amy
Merry Widow, The 1929,D 3,29:1
Alexander, Anna
Jeweled Tree, The 1926,O 8,26:2
Alexander, Arthur (Composer)
Lazarus Laughed 1928,Ap 10,33:1
Alexander, Barbara
Anya 1965,N 30,48:1
Alexander, Bill
Truce of the Bear 1957,O 24,39:1
Alexander, Bob
Quare Fellow, The 1958,N 28,34:1
Alexander, Brandy
Save It for Your Death Bed 1968,N 4,57:3
Alexander, Brooks (Musical Director)
Believers, The 1968,My 10,57:4
Alexander, C K
Flight Into Egypt 1952,Mr 19,33:2

Alexander, C K—Cont
Mr Pickwick 1952,S 18,36:3
Can-Can 1953,My 8,28:1
Oklahoma! 1955,Je 21,37:7
Merry Widow, The 1957,Ap 11,36:6
Dragon, The 1963,Ap 10,32:1
Corruption in the Palace of Justice 1963,O 9,49:2
Poor Bitos 1964,N 16,40:2
Alexander, C K (Miscellaneous)
Francesca da Rimini 1967,S 12,54:1
Alexander, Carlos
Once Over Lightly 1942,N 20,26:2
Alexander, Charles
Earl Carroll's Vanities 1924,S 11,23:6
Hidden Horizon 1946,S 20,42:2
Alexander, Cris
On the Town 1944,D 29,11:4
Present Laughter 1946,O 30,31:2
Wonderful Town 1953,F 26,22:3
Auntie Mame 1956,N 1,47:2
Wonderful Town 1958,Mr 6,32:4
Madness of Lady Bright, The 1966,Mr 23,42:1
Alexander, Cris (Miscellaneous)
Two by Two 1970,N 22,II,1:1
Alexander, D M
Espanola 1921,D 30,13:1
Alexander, Danny
Blackouts of 1949 1949,S 7,39:2
Alexander, David
Me and Harry 1942,Ap 3,24:6
Winter Soldiers 1942,N 30,19:2
Alexander, David (Director)
Petrified Forest, The 1943,N 2,30:6
There Is No End 1950,F 17,24:1
King of Friday's Men, The 1951,F 22,26:2
Pal Joey 1952,Ja 4,17:6
Pal Joey 1952,Ja 13,II,1:1
First Lady 1952,My 29,18:5
Hazel Flagg 1953,F 12,22:2
Vamp, The 1955,N 11,30:1
Livin' the Life 1957,Ap 29,20:1
Detour After Dark 1959,Je 9,11:4
Happiness Is Just a Little Thing Called a Rolls Royce 1968,My 13,54:5
Alexander, David   (Director)
Edwina Black 1950,N 22,20:5
Alexander, Denise
Children's Hour, The 1952,D 19,35:2
Alexander, Dorn
Career Angel 1944,My 24,23:7
Alexander, Doug
R U R 1942,D 4,30:2
Alexander, E
Rang Tang 1927,Jl 13,20:1
Alexander, Elizabeth
Innocent Idea, An 1920,My 26,9:4
Alexander, Ellen
Yeomen of the Guard, The 1968,My 9,53:1
Alexander, George
Nearly Married 1929,S 22,IX,4:1
Grand Hotel 1929,D 22,VIII,4:6
Rosse 1933,My 7,IX,2:5
Ti-Coq 1951,F 10,10:2
Richard III 1953,Jl 15,22:2
All's Well That Ends Well 1953,Jl 16,18:2
Alexander, Geraldine
Tip-Top 1920,O 6,13:2
George White's Scandals 1921,Jl 12,14:1
Alexander, Gordon
Show Boat 1948,S 9,33:2
Music in the Air 1951,O 9,32:2
Alexander, Guido
Old Bill, M P 1926,N 11,22:2
Pickwick 1927,S 6,35:2
Camels Are Coming, The 1931,O 3,20:4
Cradle Will Rock, The 1937,D 6,19:4
Cradle Will Rock, The 1938,Ja 4,19:3
Alexander, Gus
Great Way, The 1921,N 8,28:2
Virgin of Bethulia, The 1925,F 24,17:2
Angela 1928,D 4,28:2
Student Prince, The 1931,Ja 30,18:1
Alexander, H (Playwright)
Garrick Gaieties 1930,Je 5,29:2
Alexander, Helen
Kit Marlowe 1936,My 24,35:1
Arms and the Man 1937,Jl 20,19:3
Emperor Jones, The 1945,Ja 17,18:4
Boy With a Cart, The 1954,Ap 5,19:2
Noah 1954,O 11,32:2
Alexander, Helen (Costume Designer)
Boy With a Cart, The 1954,Ap 5,19:2
Noah 1954,O 11,32:2
In April Once 1955,Mr 14,29:3
Mandragola 1956,Mr 1,36:4
Alexander, Henry
Merchant of Venice, The 1930,N 16,VIII,3:1
Merchant of Venice, The 1930,D 3,29:2
Alexander, Hi (Playwright)
Illustrators' Show, The 1936,Ja 23,25:3
Alexander, Hugh
Unfair to Goliath 1970,Ja 26,27:1

Alexander, Inez
Logia a la Natividad de Nuestro Senor Jesucristo, El 1937,D 14,33:4
Alexander, Irena
There Was a Young Man 1940,F 27,17:4
Alexander, Irene (Playwright)
Greatest Show on Earth, The 1938,Ja 6,22:2
Alexander, Irinia
Romeo and Juliet 1940,Ap 16,28:4
Alexander, Jack
Dick Whittington and His Remarkable Cat 1950,N 25,10:5
Alexander, James
Innocent Voyage, The 1943,N 16,27:2
Earth Journey 1944,Ap 28,24:2
Men to the Sea 1944,O 4,25:2
Visit, The 1967,S 13,41:1
She Stoops to Conquer 1968,Ja 1,11:1
Twelfth Night 1968,Je 15,40:1
Serjeant Musgrave's Dance 1968,Je 16,52:4
Resistible Rise of Arturo Ui, The 1968,Ag 8,25:1
Merton of the Movies 1968,S 26,62:1
House of Atreus, The 1968,O 18,55:1
Resistible Rise of Arturo Ui, The 1968,D 23,44:1
Alexander, Jane
Great White Hope, The 1967,D 14,58:1
Great White Hope, The 1967,D 24,II,3:1
Iceman Cometh, The 1968,Ap 1,58:1
Great White Hope, The 1968,O 4,40:1
Great White Hope, The 1968,O 13,II,1:1
Alexander, Janet
Crucible, The 1953,Ja 23,15:2
Alexander, Jeff (Miscellaneous)
Ice Capades 1967,Je 2,33:1
Alexander, Joan
Poor Richard 1964,D 3,59:1
Alexander, John
Mirage, The 1920,O 1,14:1
Mary the 3d 1923,F 6,14:2
Cyrano de Bergerac 1923,N 2,14:1
Cyrano de Bergerac 1926,F 19,18:1
Jamboree 1932,N 25,18:4
Marathon 1933,Ja 28,8:8
Tragedy of the Ages, The 1933,Ap 7,22:7
Petrified Forest, The 1935,Ja 8,26:1
Nowhere Bound 1935,Ja 23,20:2
Mid-West 1936,Ja 8,22:4
Devil of Pei-Ling 1936,F 21,20:4
Swing Your Lady 1936,O 19,22:4
Red Harvest 1937,Mr 31,29:2
Greatest Show on Earth, The 1938,Ja 6,22:2
All the Living 1938,Mr 25,14:4
Kiss the Boys Goodbye 1938,S 29,30:2
Morning's at Seven 1939,N 7,30:2
Morning's at Seven 1939,D 1,26:2
Out From Under 1940,My 6,13:2
Arsenic and Old Lace 1941,Ja 11,13:2
Arsenic and Old Lace 1941,F 23,IX,1:1
Hilda Crane 1950,N 2,38:2
Ondine 1954,F 19,23:1
Ondine 1954,F 28,II,1:1
Teahouse of the August Moon, The 1956,N 9,33:2
Gondoliers, The 1961,Ja 26,33:2
Never Too Late 1962,N 28,42:1
Alexander, Joy
Aunt Caroline's Will 1954,Ag 11,21:1
Alexander, Katherine
Chains 1923,S 20,5:2
Leah Kleschna 1924,Ap 22,19:2
That Awful Mrs Eaton! 1924,S 30,27:1
Youngest, The 1924,D 23,17:1
Stork, The 1925,Ja 27,14:2
Ostriches 1925,Mr 31,16:1
It All Depends 1925,Ag 11,16:4
Call of Life, The 1925,O 10,10:1
Arms and the Man 1926,Ja 21,18:3
Gentle Grafters 1926,O 17,VIII,2:4
Gentle Grafters 1926,O 28,23:1
Hangman's House 1926,D 17,27:2
Queen's Husband, The 1928,Ja 26,17:2
Little Accident 1928,O 10,32:3
Boundry Line, The 1930,F 6,21:1
Hotel Universe 1930,Ap 15,29:1
Stepdaughters of War 1930,O 7,27:1
Left Bank, The 1931,O 6,35:3
Left Bank, The 1931,O 18,VIII,1:1
Best Years 1932,S 8,16:2
Honeymoon 1932,D 24,11:2
Party's Over, The 1933,Mr 28,23:3
Letters to Lucerne 1941,D 24,14:2
Little Brown Jug 1946,Mr 7,32:2
Time for Elizabeth 1948,S 28,32:3
Alexander, Ken
Duchess of Malfi, The 1962,Mr 5,27:1
Alexander, Kirkland B (Composer)
Take It Away 1936,D 15,30:5
Alexander, Kirkland B (Lyricist)
Take It Away 1936,D 15,30:5
Alexander, Kirkland B (Playwright)
What a Relief 1935,D 14,10:6
Alexander, Leon (Playwright)
Journeyman 1938,Ja 31,14:2

Alexander, Lewis
Salome 1923,My 8,22:2
Comedy of Errors, The 1923,My 16,22:5
Alexander, Manuel
Tin Pan Alley 1928,N 2,29:1
Alexander, Manuel A
Rollo's Wild Oat 1920,N 24,14:1
We've Got to Have Money 1923,Ag 21,12:1
Hurricane 1923,D 26,13:4
Dagger, The 1925,S 10,28:1
Alexander, Mara
Weep for the Virgins 1935,D 2,18:1
Who's Who 1938,Mr 2,16:2
Alexander, Maurine
Ramshackle Inn 1944,Ja 6,17:5
Alexander, Mimi
Hi, Paisano 1961,O 2,36:2
Alexander, Muriel
Indian Summer 1936,Ap 20,17:5
Alexander, Newton
George White's Scandals 1923,Je 19,22:5
Scandals 1924,Jl 1,16:1
Gay Paree 1925,Ag 19,14:3
Gay Paree 1926,N 10,24:2
Alexander, Ora
Abe Lincoln in Illinois 1938,O 17,12:2
Alexander, Paul
Little Theatre Tournament; Monkey's Paw, The 1929,My 10,32:2
Alexander, Peggy
Sunny River 1941,D 5,28:2
Alexander, Rod
Inside U S A 1948,Je 13,II,6:6
Great to Be Alive! 1950,Mr 24,28:2
Alexander, Rod (Choreographer)
Arabian Nights 1955,Je 24,16:1
Shinbone Alley 1957,Ap 15,23:2
Shinbone Alley 1957,Ap 28,II,1:1
13 Daughters 1961,Mr 3,17:2
Alexander, Rod (Director)
Merchant of Venice, The 1964,Jl 23,18:1
Alexander, Rolf
Green Table, The 1942,Ja 22,12:2
Prodigal Son, The 1942,F 18,22:2
Alexander, Ronald
Shakespeare's Merchant 1939 1939,Ja 10,16:3
Ghost for Sale 1941,S 30,27:4
Winter Soldiers 1942,N 30,19:2
Patriots, The 1943,Ja 30,11:2
Day Will Come, The 1944,S 8,17:2
Sophie 1944,D 26,22:7
Lady in Danger 1945,Mr 30,18:6
Little Brown Jug 1946,Mr 7,32:2
Christopher Blake 1946,D 2,33:2
Doctor Social 1948,F 12,29:5
Light Up the Sky 1948,N 19,34:2
Closing Door, The 1949,D 2,36:2
Alexander, Ronald (Playwright)
Time Out for Ginger 1952,N 27,50:4
Grand Prize, The 1955,Ja 27,17:1
Holiday for Lovers 1957,F 15,20:1
Nobody Loves an Albatross 1963,D 20,20:1
Nobody Loves an Albatross 1964,Ja 5,II,1:1
Alexander, Ross
Ladder, The 1926,O 23,15:1
Let Us Be Gay 1929,F 22,19:1
After Tomorrow 1930,Ag 10,VIII,2:3
That's Gratitude 1930,S 12,28:1
After Tomorrow 1931,Ag 27,22:4
Stork Is Dead, The 1932,S 24,18:2
Honeymoon 1932,D 24,11:2
Party's Over, The 1933,Mr 28,23:3
Under Glass 1933,O 31,24:3
Wooden Slipper, The 1934,Ja 4,16:3
No Questions Asked 1934,F 6,24:3
Gypsy Baron, The 1944,Je 15,17:3
Alexander, Ross (Translator)
Weathercock, The 1948,Ag 6,22:3
Alexander, Sally
On Strivers' Row 1946,Mr 1,17:2
Alexander, Vada
Manhattan Mary 1927,S 27,30:3
Alexander, Vincent
Sound of Music, The 1970,Jl 3,13:1
Alexander, Vincent (Choreographer)
Sound of Music, The 1970,Jl 3,13:1
Alexander Brothers and Evelyn
Vaudeville (Palace) 1929,S 16,30:4
Alexandre
Procureur Hallers, Le 1924,N 13,18:1
Alexandre, Alfred
Peer Gynt 1923,F 6,14:1
Alexandria, Eva
Antigone 1967,Ja 14,18:1
Alexandroff, Nikolai
Tsar Fyodor Ivanovitch 1923,Ja 9,26:1
Lower Depths, The 1923,Ja 16,16:1
Cherry Orchard, The 1923,Ja 23,18:1
Three Sisters, The 1923,Ja 30,12:2
Brothers Karamazov, The 1923,N 20,23:4
Ivanoff 1923,N 27,23:2
In the Claws of Life 1923,N 30,23:4

Alexandroff, Nikolai—Cont
Enough Stupidity in Every Wise Man 1923,D 6,23:1
Death of Pazukhin, The 1924,F 12,20:1
Alexandrova
Chauve-Souris 1929,Ja 23,20:2
Alexandrowa, Elisabeth
Dantons Tod 1927,D 21,28:3
Lebende Leichnam, Der, Der; Living Corpse, The 1928,Ja 24,26:2
Alexis
Street Sounds 1970,O 23,32:1
Alfard, Pauline
Nativity Play, The 1937,D 21,29:1
Alfasa, Joe
Streetcar Named Desire, A 1955,Mr 4,18:2
Capacity for Wings 1957,Ja 10,25:2
And the Wind Blows 1959,Ap 29,28:1
Zorba 1968,N 18,58:1
Penny Wars, The 1969,O 16,52:1
Alfaux, Bassine
Summer Wives 1936,Ap 14,18:1
Alfonso, Gerald (Musical Director)
Old Bucks and New Wings 1962,N 6,39:4
Alford, Bobby
Point of No Return 1957,Mr 23,17:2
Nude With Violin 1957,N 15,36:1
Alford, Edward
Henri Christophe 1945,Je 7,24:5
Alford, Frauline
Case of Philip Lawrence, The 1937,Je 9,31:1
Alford, Lamar
Caution: A Love Story 1969,Ap 4,45:1
Rat's Mass, A 1969,N 1,39:1
Moondreamers, The 1969,D 9,68:1
Arden of Faversham 1970,F 17,33:1
Ubu Roi 1970,F 17,33:1
Alford, Lamar (Composer)
Rat's Mass, A 1969,N 1,39:1
Ubu Roi 1970,F 17,33:1
Arden of Faversham 1970,F 17,33:1
Alford, Lamar (Musical Director)
Moondreamers, The 1969,D 9,68:1
Alford, R F
Front Page, The 1937,N 12,27:2
Alford, Rodger
Run, Little Chillun 1943,Ag 14,6:1
Green Pastures, The 1951,Mr 16,35:2
Alfred, Julian (Director)
Twinkle Twinkle 1926,N 17,22:2
Alfred, William (Lyricist)
Cry for Us All 1970,Ap 9,48:2
Alfred, William (Playwright)
Hogan's Goat 1965,N 12,56:1
Hogan's Goat 1965,N 21,II,1:2
Cry for Us All 1970,Ap 9,48:2
Algar, Robert
King Lear 1947,F 19,32:2
As You Like It 1947,F 21,16:2
Merchant of Venice, The 1947,F 24,16:2
Volpone 1947,F 25,32:2
Hamlet 1947,F 27,27:2
Hamlet 1958,D 17,2:7
Henry V 1958,D 26,2:7
Algeo, John S Jr
Fiesta 1933,D 16,12:2
Alger, Jim
Cranmer of Canterbury 1959,D 4,36:1
Alger, Joseph
It's Only Natural 1922,Ap 21,13:2
Alger, Joseph (Composer)
Wetward Ho 1921,Ap 22,13:2
It's Only Natural 1922,Ap 21,13:2
Alger, Joseph (Lyricist)
Wetward Ho 1921,Ap 22,13:2
It's Only Natural 1922,Ap 21,13:2
Who's Who 1924,Ap 18,19:2
1776 1926,Ap 24,11:2
Alger, Joseph (Playwright)
Wetward Ho 1921,Ap 22,13:2
Algonquins, The
Knickerbocker Holiday 1938,O 20,26:2
Algren, Nelson (Original Author)
Man With the Golden Arm, The 1956,My 22,28:1
Alhambra, Myrrha
What Never Dies 1926,D 29,24:2
Ali, George
White Wings 1926,O 16,15:1
Chee-Chee 1928,S 26,25:1
Ali, Muhammad (Cassius Clay)
Buck White 1969,D 3,63:1
Alia, Al Re
Sex 1926,Ap 27,22:4
Alice and Hannan
Grand Music Hall of Israel, The 1968,F 7,42:1
Alicoate, Jack (Playwright)
Extra 1923,Ja 24,22:3
When You Smile 1925,O 6,31:2
Aligier, Helene
Phedre 1969,Mr 1,20:1
Aliki
God Strikes Back 1943,F 27,11:2
Alin, Hans (Translator)
Pelican, The 1929,N 14,25:1

Alisberg, Nancy
Shunned 1960,D 21,39:1
Alisi, Art
Dial 'M' for Murder 1958,F 8,12:2
Alison, George
Dulcy 1921,Ag 15,14:1
Love Set, The 1923,Mr 20,24:2
Deep Tangled Wildwood, The 1923,N 6,22:1
Alarm Clock, The 1923,D 25,26:2
Lady Killer, The 1924,Mr 13,14:2
Butter and Egg Man, The 1925,S 24,28:1
Bless You, Sister 1927,D 27,24:5
Mrs Dane's Defense 1928,F 7,30:1
Sherlock Holmes 1928,F 21,18:4
Within the Law 1928,Mr 6,20:1
Kingdom of God, The 1928,D 21,30:2
Dinner at Eight 1932,O 24,18:2
Hat, a Coat, a Glove, A 1934,F 1,15:2
Too Much Party 1934,Mr 6,28:4
Merrily We Roll Along 1934,O 1,14:1
Aliwanag, Benito
Passenger to Bali, A 1940,Mr 15,26:2
Alix, Lucille
Proud Accent 1949,Ap 23,10:2
Alixandre (Miscellaneous)
Sail Away 1961,O 4,48:5
Aliza, Ben
Sign in Sidney Brustein's Window, The
1964,O 16,32:1
Alk, Howard
From the Second City 1961,S 27,32:1
Untitled-Revue; Second City 1962,Ja 12,30:2
Alk, Howard (Producer)
From the Second City 1961,S 27,32:1
Allain, Margot
Broadway Interlude 1934,Ap 20,16:3
Allair, John
Earthlight Theater 1970,N 4,38:2
Allaire, Edith
Romeo and Juliet 1934,D 21,30:3
Allais, Charles
Prunella; Love in a Garden 1926,Je 16,23:3
Juarez and Maximilian 1926,O 12,31:1
Window Panes 1927,F 22,22:2
Sonya's Search for the Christmas Star
1929,D 14,24:6
Allan, Betty
Up She Goes 1922,N 7,14:2
Allan, Carl
Romeo and Juliet 1935,D 24,10:2
Allan, Edgar
Great Waltz, The 1934,S 24,14:4
Allan, Edward
Three Cheers 1928,O 16,28:1
Allan, Floyd (Lighting Director)
Faith and Prudence 1952,O 15,40:2
Slightly Delinquent 1954,O 26,32:5
Bamboo Cross 1955,F 22,17:2
Song Out of Sorrow 1955,N 1,27:3
Age and Grace 1956,F 21,38:2
Comedian, The 1956,O 18,36:4
Parade at the Devil's Bridge 1957,F 19,35:7
Doctor Faustus 1957,F 19,35:7
Truce of the Bear 1957,O 24,39:1
Child of the Morning 1958,Ap 22,40:2
Listen to the Quiet 1958,O 28,40:2
Madre, La 1959,F 12,24:1
Allan, Floyd (Scenic Designer)
Restless Flame, The 1952,Ap 15,30:6
Faith and Prudence 1952,O 15,40:2
Late Arrival 1953,O 20,35:5
Slightly Delinquent 1954,O 26,32:5
Bamboo Cross 1955,F 22,17:2
Song Out of Sorrow 1955,N 1,27:3
Age and Grace 1956,F 21,38:2
Comedian, The 1956,O 18,36:4
Doctor Faustus 1957,F 19,35:7
Parade at the Devil's Bridge 1957,F 19,35:7
Truce of the Bear 1957,O 24,39:1
King's Standards, The 1958,F 14,19:1
Child of the Morning 1958,Ap 22,40:2
Listen to the Quiet 1958,O 28,40:2
Madre, La 1959,F 12,24:1
Allan, Gene (Composer)
Billy 1969,Mr 24,56:1
Allan, Gene (Lyricist)
Billy 1969,Mr 24,56:1
Allan, Jed
Viva Madison Avenue 1960,Ap 7,42:1
Paisley Convertible, The 1967,F 13,42:1
Allan, Joyce
Lovely Me 1946,D 26,30:4
Allan, Lane
Money Mad 1937,My 25,32:5
Allan, Leonora
Vaudeville (Palace) 1924,Ja 15,17:3
Allan, Lewis (Lyricist)
Of V We Sing 1942,F 16,20:3
It's Up to You 1943,Ap 1,19:1
Allan, Maude
Hindu, The 1922,Mr 22,13:3
Polly 1925,O 12,19:1
Arabian, The 1927,N 1,20:5

Midnight 1930,D 30,25:1
Another Language 1932,Ap 26,25:3
Another Language 1933,My 9,20:2
Allan, Nancy
We Americans 1926,O 13,20:4
Machinal 1928,S 8,10:3
Allan, Richard
Pins and Needles 1967,Je 9,51:2
Allan, Robert Lee
Padre, The 1926,D 28,16:3
Allan, Ted (Miscellaneous)
Oh What a Lovely War 1964,O 1,30:1
Allan, Valerie
Vaudeville (Palace) 1931,Ja 5,20:3
Alland, William
Julius Caesar 1937,N 12,26:6
Shoemaker's Holiday, The 1938,Ja 3,17:2
Danton's Death 1938,N 3,26:2
Allard, Bruce
Way of the World, The 1965,Je 2,40:1
Allard, Robert
Mes Amours 1940,My 3,16:5
Allardice, James B (Playwright)
At War With the Army 1949,Mr 9,32:2
At War With the Army 1949,Mr 20,II,1:1
Allardice, Peggy
Apology 1943,Mr 23,14:2
Listen Professor! 1943,D 23,22:1
Allarie, Irene
Burlesque 1946,D 26,30:3
Allbritton, Louise
Third Person 1955,D 30,13:4
Allee, John
Republic, The 1970,Ap 28,49:1
Allegretti, Ted
Insect Comedy, The 1948,Je 4,26:3
Allegri, A (Scenic Designer)
Maitresse de Roi 1926,D 1,24:1
Allegro, Alfred
American Holiday 1936,F 22,13:3
Sun and I, The 1937,F 27,9:5
Haiti 1938,Mr 3,16:1
Food for Midas 1942,Ja 31,12:7
Doodle Dandy of the U S A 1942,O 19,15:2
Allegro, Alfred (Director)
Food for Midas 1942,Ja 31,12:7
Allen, Adrianne
Private Lives 1930,O 12,VIII,1:8
Cynara 1931,N 3,31:1
Never Come Back 1932,O 29,18:6
Shining Hour, The 1934,F 14,22:6
Shining Hour, The 1934,F 25,IX,1:1
Shining Hour, The 1934,S 23,X,3:6
Pride and Prejudice 1935,O 23,19:2
Pride and Prejudice 1935,N 3,X,1:5
Pride and Prejudice 1935,N 6,32:4
Pride and Prejudice 1935,N 10,IX,2:5
Pride and Prejudice 1935,N 17,IX,1:1
Pride and Prejudice 1936,Ag 30,IX,1:1
Night of January 16 1936,S 30,29:3
Till the Cows Come Home 1936,O 28,30:6
Plan for a Hostess 1938,Mr 27,X,1:3
Flare Path 1942,Ag 23,VIII,1:6
Love for Love 1947,My 27,30:2
Reluctant Debutante, The 1956,O 11,50:1
Reluctant Debutante, The 1956,O 21,II,1:1
Allen, Albert
Romeo and Juliet 1935,D 24,10:2
To Quito and Back 1937,O 7,30:4
Knickerbocker Holiday 1938,O 20,26:2
Allen, Allan
She Loves Me Not 1933,N 21,22:4
Allen, Alvin
Career Angel 1944,My 24,23:7
Allen, Ambrose
Promis' Lan', De 1930,My 28,31:2
Allen, Amelia
Last Waltz, The 1921,My 11,20:3
Love Dreams 1921,O 11,22:2
Irving Berlin's New Music Box Revue
1922,O 24,18:1
Allen, Angie
Deep Channels 1929,O 19,22:3
Allen, Ann-Marie (Costume Designer)
Rat's Mass, A 1969,N 1,39:1
Allen, Ariane
Aries Is Rising 1939,N 22,16:5
Allen, Arthur
Mandarin, The 1920,N 10,18:2
Like a King 1921,O 4,10:1
Out of Step 1925,Ja 30,12:1
Field God, The 1927,Ap 22,18:2
County Chairman, The 1936,My 26,26:5
Our Town 1938,F 5,18:3
Horse Fever 1940,N 25,21:2
Our Town 1944,Ja 11,24:5
Don't, George! 1944,N 4,18:6
Allen, Arthur B
White Wings 1926,O 16,15:1
Allen, Arthur H
Friend Indeed 1926,Ap 27,22:3
Allen, Arthur H Jr
Spring Fever 1925,Ag 4,14:2

Allen, Austen (Playwright)
Pleasure Cruise 1932,My 15,VIII,1:1
Allen, Barbara
Secrets 1922,D 26,11:1
Farmer's Wife, The 1924,O 10,22:3
Bridge of Distances, The 1925,S 29,30:1
Ashes of Love 1926,Mr 23,24:3
Lady With a Lamp, The 1931,N 20,27:2
Lancashire Lass, The 1931,D 31,16:3
Allen, Barbara H
Nine Till Six 1936,Mr 14,10:3
Allen, Beatrice
Broken Branches 1922,Mr 7,11:1
Good Old Days, The 1923,Ag 15,21:2
Kosher Kitty Kelly 1925,Je 16,24:2
Sh! The Octopus 1928,F 22,19:2
Scorpion, The 1933,N 28,28:4
Allen, Ben
Biff, Bing, Bang 1921,My 10,20:1
Allen, Ben G (Composer)
Tall Story 1959,Ja 30,33:2
Allen, Betty
Great Temptations, The 1926,My 19,29:1
Katja 1926,O 19,27:3
Jubilee 1935,O 14,20:1
Red, Hot and Blue! 1936,O 30,26:3
Scandals 1939,Ag 29,17:2
Dream With Music 1944,My 19,15:2
Show Boat 1954,O 29,28:4
Allen, Betty Lou
Four Saints in Three Acts 1952,Ap 17,35:1
Allen, Billie
Mamba's Daughters 1953,Mr 21,12:6
Critic's Choice 1960,D 15,61:3
Black Monday 1962,Mr 7,29:1
Funnyhouse of a Negro 1964,Ja 15,25:3
Bohikee Creek 1966,Ap 29,39:1
This Bird of Dawning Singeth All Night Long
1968,D 31,19:1
Teaspoon Every Four Hours, A 1969,Je 16,57:1
Ofay Watcher, The 1969,S 16,40:1
Ofay Watcher, The 1969,S 21,II,1:2
Allen, Blanche (Composer)
Safari! 1955,My 12,32:6
Allen, Bobby
Buckaroo 1929,Mr 18,31:1
Allen, Bud
Harlem 1929,F 21,30:3
Allen, Buddy
Best Foot Forward 1941,O 2,28:2
Allen, Bunny
Hummin' Sam 1933,Ap 10,8:8
Allen, C Russell
On the Level 1937,Mr 26,24:4
Allen, Casey
Much Ado About Nothing 1955,Ag 20,20:4
Allen, Charles R
This Way Out 1929,Ap 28,24:4
Allen, Charme
Church Street 1948,F 10,27:2
Church Street 1948,F 15,II,1:3
Allen, Clark
World of Carl Sandburg, The 1959,O 26,53:3
World of Carl Sandburg, The 1960,S 15,44:1
World of Carl Sandburg, The 1960,S 25,II,1:1
Allen, Cliff
Fools Rush In 1934,D 26,19:2
New Faces of 1936 1936,My 20,24:5
Allen, D R
How to Steal an Election 1968,O 14,56:1
Allen, Dauna
Topaze 1930,F 13,25:3
Allen, Dawn
Love City, The 1926,Ja 26,18:2
Allen, Dion
Temporary Island, A 1948,Mr 15,27:3
Taming of the Shrew, The 1951,Ap 26,35:2
Saint Joan 1951,O 5,23:2
Under Milk Wood 1953,My 29,17:1
Strong Are Lonely, The 1953,S 30,38:3
Allen, Don
Alice in Wonderland 1947,Ap 7,19:2
Allen, Donald M (Translator)
Lesson, The 1956,O 3,29:2
Jack 1958,Je 4,39:2
Bald Soprano, The 1958,Je 4,39:2
Bald Soprano, The 1963,S 18,35:4
Lesson, The 1963,S 18,35:4
Allen, Edgar
Parade 1935,My 21,22:2
Allen, Edgar (Director)
Furnished Rooms 1934,My 30,14:6
Allen, Edgar (Producer)
Furnished Rooms 1934,My 30,14:6
Allen, Edward
Marjorie 1924,Ag 12,12:2
Annie Dear 1924,N 5,25:3
Judy 1927,F 8,20:2
Hit the Deck! 1927,Ap 26,32:1
Buckaroo 1929,Mr 18,31:1
Ripples 1930,F 12,26:1
Allen, Elizabeth
Dawn 1924,N 25,27:1

Allen, Elizabeth—Cont
Handy Man, The 1925,Mr 10,19:2
Holy Terror, A 1925,S 29,31:2
Revolt 1928,N 1,25:3
Lovers, Villains and Fools: A Shakespearean
  Variety Show 1956,O 24,44:7
Romanoff and Juliet 1957,O 11,24:1
Lend an Ear 1959,S 25,20:5
Gay Life, The 1961,N 20,38:1
Do I Hear a Waltz? 1965,Mr 19,28:1
Do I Hear a Waltz? 1965,Mr 28,II,1:1
Sherry! 1967,Mr 29,39:1
Sherry! 1967,Ap 9,II,1:1
Allen, Ellery
Sunday Nights at Nine 1934,Mr 5,18:5
Allen, Ernie
Cage, The 1970,Je 19,25:1
Allen, Ethel
Billie 1928,O 2,34:2
Hello, Daddy! 1928,D 27,26:5
Comedy of Women, A 1929,S 14,17:4
Allen, Eugene
Spring Production 1944,My 20,12:4
Allen, Evelyn
Sweet Mystery of Life 1935,O 12,13:3
Julius Caesar 1937,N 12,26:6
Allen, Floyd (Scenic Designer)
City of Kings 1949,F 18,27:2
Angelic Doctor 1953,Ap 14,30:2
Allen, Frank
Vaudeville (Palace) 1931,S 28,17:5
Allen, Frank (Playwright)
Deluge, The 1922,Ja 28,14:2
Allen, Franklin
Star Spangled Family 1945,Ap 11,18:6
Allen, Fred
Passing Show of 1922, The 1922,S 21,18:2
Vogues of 1924 1924,Mr 28,14:3
Vogues and Frolics 1924,Je 26,21:7
Rufus Le Maire's Affairs 1926,Jl 18,VII,1:7
Vaudeville (Palace) 1927,D 6,26:3
Polly 1929,Ja 9,28:3
Little Show, The 1929,My 1,28:5
Little Show, The 1929,My 12,IX,1:2
Three's a Crowd 1930,O 5,IX,4:6
Three's a Crowd 1930,O 16,28:3
Three's a Crowd 1930,O 26,VIII,1:1
Allen, Fred (Lyricist)
Ziegfeld Follies 1934,Ja 5,24:3
Allen, Fred (Miscellaneous)
Solid Gold Cadillac, The 1953,N 6,24:2
Allen, Fred (Playwright)
Ziegfeld Follies 1934,Ja 5,24:3
Allen, Gene
Wet Paint 1965,Ap 13,33:1
Allen, George
Virgin of Bethulia, The 1925,F 24,17:2
Red, White and Maddox 1969,Ja 27,27:1
Allen, George (Costume Designer)
Best Foot Forward 1956,Mr 3,16:1
Allen, Gracie
Vaudeville (Palace) 1926,Ag 24,19:3
Veils 1928,Mr 14,28:5
Vaudeville (Palace) 1930,Ag 11,13:3
Vaudeville (Palace) 1931,N 2,26:2
Friars Club Frolic 1933,My 15,16:4
Vaudeville (Palladium) 1949,Ag 17,19:3
Allen, Harry
Princess April 1924,D 2,23:2
Happy as Larry 1950,Ja 7,11:2
Peter Pan 1950,Ap 25,27:2
Allen, Harry E
Crucible 1933,S 5,22:4
Allen, Harry R
For Goodness Sake 1922,F 22,13:1
Her Temporary Husband 1922,S 1,16:2
Dust Heap, The 1924,Ap 25,20:2
Allen, Helen
Gay Divorce 1932,N 30,23:4
Allen, Howard
Julius Caesar 1931,N 18,26:3
Allen, J G
It's Only Natural 1922,Ap 21,13:2
Allen, Jane
Comedy of Women, A 1929,S 14,17:4
Little Orchard Annie 1930,Ap 22,33:1
Look Who's Here 1932,O 31,18:5
Allen, Jay (Playwright)
Prime of Miss Jean Brodie, The 1968,Ja 17,39:1
Prime of Miss Jean Brodie, The 1968,Ja 25,32:4
Prime of Miss Jean Brodie, The 1968,Ja 28,II,1:1
Forty Carats 1968,D 27,45:1
Forty Carats 1969,Ja 5,II,1:3
Allen, Joan
Red, Hot and Blue! 1936,O 30,26:3
Allen, Joanna
George White's Scandals 1931,S 15,30:1
Music Hall Varieties 1932,N 23,15:3
Allen, John
Drink to Me Only 1958,O 9,47:4
Call on Kuprin, A 1961,My 26,29:3
Allen, John (Costume Designer)
Cotton Club Revue of 1957 1957,Jl 10,23:4

Allen, John (Director)
Oh, Say Can You See L A 1968,F 9,50:1
Other Man, The 1968,F 9,50:1
But, Seriously... 1969,F 28,29:1
Allen, John (Miscellaneous)
Once Upon a Mattress 1959,My 12,40:1
Summer of Daisy Miller, The 1963,My 28,33:1
Fade Out--Fade In 1964,My 27,45:1
Flora, the Red Menace 1965,My 12,41:2
Anya 1965,N 30,48:1
Allen, John (Playwright)
Young Abe Lincoln 1961,Ap 26,36:1
Oh, Say Can You See L A 1968,F 9,50:1
Other Man, The 1968,F 9,50:1
Allen, Jonelle
Wisteria Trees, The 1955,F 3,20:2
Finian's Rainbow 1955,My 19,25:1
Small War on Murray Hill 1957,Ja 4,19:1
Hair 1967,O 30,55:1
George M! 1968,Ap 11,48:1
Someone's Comin' Hungry 1969,Ap 1,51:1
Moon on a Rainbow Shawl 1969,Ag 29,25:1
Old Judge Mose Is Dead 1969,Ag 29,25:1
Five on the Black Hand Side 1970,Ja 2,32:2
House of Leather, The 1970,Mr 19,56:1
Allen, Jonny
Seven Days of Mourning 1969,D 17,64:1
Allen, Joseph
Tavern, The 1921,My 24,20:1
Zander the Great 1923,Ap 10,24:2
Zander the Great 1923,Ap 15,VII,1:1
Dear Sir 1924,S 24,21:3
Patsy, The 1925,D 24,8:5
Heaven-Tappers, The 1927,Mr 9,28:3
Baby Cyclone, The 1927,S 13,37:4
Tavern, The 1930,My 20,32:1
Song and Dance Man, The 1930,Je 17,25:5
Reunion in Vienna 1931,N 17,31:1
Bulls, Bears and Asses 1932,My 7,11:3
Divine Drudge 1933,Jl 4,16:4
Whatever Possessed Her 1934,Ja 26,21:2
If a Body 1935,My 1,25:3
I'd Rather Be Right 1937,N 3,28:2
Village Green 1941,S 4,24:4
Allen, Joseph Jr
Men We Marry, The 1948,Ja 17,11:2
Allen, Juanita
Babes in Arms 1951,Mr 10,7:3
Allen, Judy
Carving a Statue 1968,My 1,43:1
Allen, June
Michael Todd's Peep Show 1950,Je 29,37:2
Allen, Katherine
Gentle People, The 1939,Ja 6,25:1
Night Music 1940,F 23,18:2
Criminals, The 1941,D 22,24:3
Allen, Kathy
Groove Tube 1969,O 12,88:3
Allen, Kirk
Sancho Panza 1923,N 27,23:1
Allen, Lee
Carmen Jones 1945,My 3,26:5
Marathon '33 1963,D 23,20:1
Allen, Leigh (Scenic Designer)
Mother Lode 1934,D 24,16:5
Allen, Lester
Scandals 1920,Je 8,9:1
George White's Scandals 1921,Jl 12,14:1
George White's Scandals 1922,Ag 29,10:1
George White's Scandals 1923,Je 19,22:5
Scandals 1924,Jl 1,16:1
Florida Girl 1925,N 3,34:1
LeMaire's Affairs 1927,Mr 29,22:4
Rufus Le Maire's Affairs 1927,Ap 10,VIII,1:1
Three Musketeers, The 1928,Mr 14,28:1
Top Speed 1929,N 17,IX,4:1
Top Speed 1929,D 26,20:1
Pajama Lady, The 1930,O 12,VIII,4:1
Dance of Death, The 1932,Ja 11,29:5
Vaudeville (Loew's State) 1932,Je 13,19:7
Shady Lady 1933,Jl 6,26:3
Allen, Lester (Composer)
Three Musketeers, The 1928,Mr 4,IX,2:3
Allen, Lester (Playwright)
Earl Carroll's Vanities 1925,Jl 7,24:1
Allen, Lester (Skeets)
Showboat Revue 1934,Je 6,24:2
Allen, Lewis (Director)
Laburnum Grove 1935,Ja 15,23:5
Amazing Dr. Clitterhouse, The 1937,Mr 3,26:4
I Have Been Here Before 1938,O 14,26:2
Ladies and Gentlemen 1939,O 18,30:2
Allen, Lewis (Miscellaneous)
Man in the Dog Suit, The 1958,O 31,34:2
Allen, Lewis (Producer)
Big Fish, Little Fish 1961,Mr 16,42:2
Ballad of the Sad Cafe, The 1963,O 31,27:1
Allen, Louise
Tickle Me 1920,Ag 18,9:1
Gingham Girl, The 1922,Ag 29,15:5
Four Flusher, The 1925,Ap 14,27:4
Allen, Mabel
Rosa Machree 1922,Ja 10,15:2

Allen, Marc 3d
South Pacific 1968,Je 30,54:2
Promenade 1969,Je 5,56:1
Look to the Lilies 1970,Mr 30,59:1
Allen, Marie
Floydada to Matador 1955,D 22,19:1
Opera Opera 1955,D 22,19:1
Allen, Marion
Ghosts 1922,F 7,12:1
Mister Pitt 1924,Ja 23,15:3
Leap, The 1924,My 23,16:5
Fake, The 1924,O 7,26:3
Morals 1925,D 1,22:2
Allen, Mark
Night Music 1951,Ap 9,29:6
Solid Gold Cadillac, The 1953,N 6,24:2
Ankles Aweigh 1955,Ap 19,27:1
Happiest Millionaire, The 1956,N 21,21:3
Body Beautiful, The 1958,Ja 24,15:2
Allen, Marsh
Skin Game, The 1920,O 21,11:1
Married Woman, The 1921,D 26,21:1
Madame Pierre 1922,F 16,11:1
Exciters, The 1922,S 23,10:4
Romantic Age, The 1922,N 15,22:1
Allen, Martha-Bryan
He Who Gets Slapped 1922,Ja 10,15:1
Back to Methuselah (Part IV: The Tragedy of an
  Elderly Gentleman); Tragedy of an Elderly
  Gentleman, The (Back to Methuselah, Part IV)
  1922,Mr 7,11:1
Back to Methuselah (Part V: As Far as Thought
  Can Reach); As Far as Thought Can Reach (Back
  to Methuselah, Part V) 1922,Mr 14,11:2
Devil's Disciple, The 1923,Ap 24,24:1
Devil's Disciple, The 1923,My 6,VII,1:1
Magnolia 1923,Ag 28,12:3
Gypsy Jim 1924,Ja 15,17:4
Lazybones 1924,S 23,23:1
O Nightingale 1925,Ap 16,25:2
Carolinian, The 1925,N 3,34:2
Monkey Talks, The 1925,D 29,20:1
Allen, Martin
Thieves' Carnival 1955,F 2,21:1
Allen, Martin (Director)
Gantry 1970,F 16,44:1
Allen, Martin (Miscellaneous)
Golden Rainbow 1968,F 5,27:1
1776 1969,Mr 17,46:2
Allen, Marty
I Had a Ball 1964,D 16,50:1
Allen, Maude
Thirsty Soil 1937,F 4,16:2
Allen, Michael K
Leonard Sillman's New Faces of 1968
  1968,My 3,43:1
Allen, Nina
Rosalinda; Fledermaus, Die 1942,O 29,26:5
Allen, Norman
Chips With Everything 1963,O 2,49:1
Half a Sixpence 1965,Ap 26,38:2
Rockefeller and the Red Indians 1968,O 25,37:1
Get Thee to Canterbury 1969,Ja 26,74:1
Borstal Boy 1970,Ap 1,38:1
Allen, Pat (Miss) (Producer)
Lady in Danger 1945,Mr 30,18:6
Allen, Patricia
Merrily We Roll Along 1934,O 1,14:1
Allen, Patrick
Cymbeline 1962,Jl 18,21:2
Allen, Paul Jr
Firebird 1932,N 22,25:2
Allen, Penelope
Plebeians Rehearse the Uprising, The
  1968,S 8,II,11:1
Criminals, The 1970,F 26,33:2
Jakey Fat Boy 1970,Ap 6,46:1
Allen, Phylicia Ayers
Moon on a Rainbow Shawl 1970,D 18,52:1
Allen, Rae
Pajama Game, The 1954,My 14,20:2
Damn Yankees 1955,My 6,17:1
I Knock at the Door 1956,Mr 19,27:5
Pictures in the Hallway 1956,My 28,23:1
Pictures in the Hallway 1956,S 17,23:2
Pictures in the Hallway 1956,S 23,II,1:1
U S A 1956,D 19,41:4
I Know at the Door 1957,S 30,27:2
Cock-A-Doodle Dandy 1958,N 13,39:2
Summer of the Seventeenth Doll 1959,O 14,52:1
Time to Go 1960,Mr 23,33:1
Tempest, The 1960,Je 20,35:1
Antony and Cleopatra 1960,Ag 1,19:1
Death of Bessie Smith, The 1961,Mr 2,19:1
Creditors 1962,Ja 26,19:1
King Lear 1964,Jl 28,18:2
Traveller Without Luggage 1964,S 18,26:2
I Knock at the Door 1964,N 26,53:2
Pictures in the Hallway 1964,D 17,51:1
Love's Labour's Lost 1965,Je 16,46:1
On a Clear Day You Can See Forever
  1965,O 18,44:1
Henry IV, Part II 1968,Jl 2,33:1

Allen, Rae—Cont

Henry IV, Part II 1968,Jl 14,II,1:1
Fiddler on the Roof 1969,Je 26,47:1
Allen, Rae (Producer)
I Knock at the Door 1956,Mr 19,27:5
Pictures in the Hallway 1956,My 28,23:1
Allen, Raymond
Yeomen of the Guard, The 1954,My 5,36:2
Utopia, Limited; Flowers of Progress, The
1957,F 27,21:1
Mikado, The 1957,Ap 24,28:2
H M S Pinafore 1957,My 1,42:6
Pirates of Penzance, The 1957,My 8,43:1
Yeomen of the Guard, The 1957,My 22,28:3
Gondoliers, The 1957,My 29,34:2
From Here to There; Otherwise Engaged
1958,Ap 24,37:3
From Here to There; Real Strange One, A
1958,Ap 24,37:3
H M S Pinafore 1960,Ja 29,14:1
Utopia, Limited 1960,Ap 8,27:2
Yeomen of the Guard, The 1961,Ap 28,23:1
Mikado, The 1961,My 5,23:1
Grand Duke, The 1961,My 12,24:1
Princess Ida 1961,My 19,23:1
Iolanthe 1961,My 26,29:6
H M S Pinafore 1961,Je 9,29:5
Student Prince, The 1961,Jl 14,14:1
Merry Widow, The 1961,O 27,28:2
Vagabond King, The 1961,N 24,36:1
Gondoliers, The 1961,D 8,44:1
Figuro in the Night 1962,O 31,33:1
Moon Shines on Kylenamoe, The 1962,O 31,33:1
H M S Pinafore 1964,Mr 21,13:4
My Fair Lady 1964,My 21,43:2
Hooray!! It's a Glorious Day. . .And All That
1966,Mr 10,28:1
H M S Pinafore 1968,Ap 29,47:2
Allen, Richard
Chinese Nightingale, The 1934,O 6,20:4
Let Freedom Ring 1935,N 7,26:2
This Our House 1935,D 12,33:3
Mimie Scheller 1936,O 1,28:4
200 Were Chosen 1936,N 21,21:1
Tide Rising 1937,Ja 26,17:2
Having Wonderful Time 1937,F 22,12:5
Rehearsal, The 1952,My 27,30:5
Groove Tube 1969,O 12,88:3
Allen, Rita
Teahouse of the August Moon, The
1956,Ap 20,22:1
Allen, Rita (Miscellaneous)
Grass Harp, The 1952,Mr 28,26:2
Allen, Rita (Producer)
My 3 Angels 1953,Mr 12,23:2
Teahouse of the August Moon, The 1956,My 7,31:8
Making of Moo, The 1958,Je 12,34:1
Harlequinade 1959,F 14,15:1
Electra 1959,F 14,15:1
Cut of the Axe 1960,F 2,38:2
Allen, Robert
Hamlet 1930,Mr 25,34:4
Macbeth 1930,Mr 26,24:6
Twelfth Night 1930,Mr 27,24:7
Merchant of Venice, The 1930,Mr 27,24:7
Taming of the Shrew, The 1930,Mr 28,22:8
Richard III 1930,Mr 31,24:1
King Lear 1930,Ap 1,34:6
As You Like It 1930,Ap 3,32:5
Julius Caesar 1930,Ap 4,22:3
Blessed Event 1932,F 13,23:2
Park Avenue, Ltd 1932,Mr 4,17:1
Few Wild Oats, A 1932,Mr 25,22:6
Carry Nation 1932,O 31,18:2
Sophisticrats, The 1933,F 14,19:5
Comic Artist, The 1933,Ap 20,20:3
Cat and the Canary, The 1935,Jl 9,24:4
Trelawney of the 'Wells' 1935,Jl 16,24:1
They Knew What They Wanted 1936,Jl 7,17:2
Octoroon, The 1936,S 1,24:2
As You Like It 1937,N 1,25:2
Escape This Night 1938,Ap 23,18:1
Three Sisters, The 1939,O 16,23:1
Man Who Came to Dinner, The 1940,F 10,19:5
Man Who Came to Dinner, The 1940,F 18,IX,3:6
Jeannie 1940,N 13,29:2
Popsy 1941,F 11,26:2
I Killed the Count 1942,S 4,18:1
Kiss Them for Me 1945,MR 21,27:2
Show Boat 1946,Ja 7,17:2
Auntie Mame 1956,N 1,47:2
Allen, Robert (Scenic Designer)
Live Like Pigs 1965,Je 8,48:2
Stop, You're Killing Me; Bad Bad Jo-Jo
1969,Mr 20,53:1
Stop, You're Killing Me; Laughs, Etc
1969,Mr 20,53:1
Stop, You're Killing Me; Terrible Jim Fitch
1969,Mr 20,53:1
Allen, Robert Lee
Champion, The 1921,Ja 4,11:1
Kempy 1922,My 16,14:2
Blossom Time 1923,Je 1,22:2
Blossom Time 1931,Mr 5,32:1

Music Hath Charms 1934,D 31,8:2
Allen, Roger
Ten Per Cent 1927,S 14,29:3
Allen, Ronald
Richard II 1956,O 24,44:1
Romeo and Juliet 1956,O 25,41:1
Troilus and Cressida 1956,D 27,21:1
Allen, Ross (Director)
Play of Risen Christ, The 1970,Mr 9,44:1
Allen, Roy
Walk Hard 1944,D 1,28:2
Henri Christophe 1945,Je 7,24:5
Power of Darkness, The 1948,O 11,28:2
Freight 1949,F 4,30:2
Lost in the Stars 1949,O 31,21:2
Allen, Ruth Collins (Director)
Playing With Love 1929,F 27,16:4
Allen, Sara
Sign of the Leopard 1928,D 12,34:4
Journey by Night, A 1935,Ap 17,26:3
Diamond Lil 1948,N 30,33:2
Allen, Sean
Half a Sixpence 1965,Ap 26,38:2
Allen, Seth
Viet Rock 1966,N 11,38:1
Futz 1968,Je 14,39:1
Candaules, Commissioner 1970,My 29,15:1
Allen, Seth (Director)
Rat's Mass, A 1969,N 1,39:1
Allen, Steve
Pink Elephant, The 1953,Ap 23,37:2
Allen, Steve (Composer)
Sophie 1963,Ap 16,32:1
Allen, Steve (Lyricist)
Sophie 1963,Ap 16,32:1
Allen, Sylvia
Song of Norway 1944,Ag 22,20:2
Allen, Tamzen
If Five Years Pass 1962,My 11,37:1
Allen, Tiny
Exile, The 1923,Ap 10,24:2
Allen, Tommy
Out West of Eighth 1951,S 21,20:3
Holiday on Ice 1965,S 2,38:4
Holiday on Ice 1966,S 1,30:1
Holiday on Ice 1967,Ag 31,29:2
Holiday on Ice 1968,Ag 29,44:1
Holiday on Ice 1969,Ag 28,44:1
Allen, Vera
Critic, The 1925,My 9,12:4
Grand Street Follies, The 1925,Je 19,24:1
Dybbuk, The 1925,D 16,22:2
Romantic Young Lady, The 1926,My 5,24:3
Slaves All 1926,D 7,24:4
Sinner 1927,F 8,20:2
Grand Street Follies, The 1928,My 29,16:2
Grand Street Follies, The 1928,Je 3,VIII,1:1
Hamlet 1930,Mr 25,34:4
Macbeth 1930,Mr 26,24:6
Twelfth Night 1930,Mr 27,24:7
Merchant of Venice, The 1930,Mr 27,24:7
Taming of the Shrew, The 1930,Mr 28,22:8
Richard III 1930,Mr 31,24:1
King Lear 1930,Ap 1,34:6
As You Like It 1930,Ap 3,32:5
Lean Harvest 1931,O 14,26:3
Money in the Air 1932,Mr 8,19:3
Strange Gods 1933,Ap 17,16:6
I Was Waiting for You 1933,N 14,23:3
At Home Abroad 1935,S 4,22:3
At Home Abroad 1935,S 20,17:4
Show Is On, The 1936,D 26,14:2
Susan and God 1937,Ap 11,II,12:3
Susan and God 1937,Ap 25,X,2:6
Lysistrata 1937,Jl 20,19:3
Susan and God 1937,O 8,26:4
Woman's a Fool-To Be Clever, A 1938,O 19,18:6
Glorious Morning 1938,N 28,10:3
Philadelphia Story, The 1939,Mr 29,21:1
Burning Deck, The 1940,Mr 2,9:2
Moon Vine, The 1943,F 12,22:2
Two Mrs Carrolls, The 1943,Ag 4,14:1
Strange Fruit 1945,N 30,18:6
Ladies of the Corridor, The 1953,O 22,33:5
Ladies of the Corridor, The 1953,N 1,II,1:1
Obbligato 1958,F 19,22:2
Allen, Virginia
Jubilee 1935,O 14,20:1
Camelot 1960,D 5,42:1
Allen, Vivienne
Stars on Ice 1942,Jl 3,12:2
Stars on Ice (2d Edition) 1943,Je 25,13:2
Allen, Walter
Clubs Are Trumps 1924,O 15,27:1
Tomorrow 1928,D 29,20:2
Country Girl, The 1966,S 30,55:1
Winter Journey 1968,Mr 13,39:1
Man in the Glass Booth, The 1968,S 27,41:1
Allen, William B (Producer)
In the Nick of Time 1967,Je 2,36:1
Allen, Woody
Play It Again, Sam 1969,F 13,52:3
Play It Again, Sam 1969,F 23,II,1:1

Allen, Woody—Cont

Play It Again, Sam 1969,Jl 13,II,1:1
Allen, Woody (Playwright)
From A to Z 1960,Ap 21,23:2
Don't Drink the Water 1966,N 18,37:1
Don't Drink the Water 1966,D 25,II,1:1
Play It Again, Sam 1969,F 13,52:3
Play It Again, Sam 1969,F 23,II,1:1
Play It Again, Sam 1970,F 7,25:2
Allenby, Frank
Man Who Pays the Piper, The 1931,Mr 1,VIII,2:4
Flat to Let 1931,D 20,VIII,3:6
Sweet Aloes 1934,N 1,24:1
Jealous God, The 1939,Mr 26,X,3:1
Winslow Boy, The 1947,O 30,32:2
Winslow Boy, The 1947,N 9,II,1:1
Allenby, Peggy
Two Strangers From Nowhere 1924,Ap 8,22:2
Schemers 1924,S 16,27:1
Sap, The 1924,D 16,28:3
Find Daddy 1926,Mr 9,21:3
Little Spitfire, The 1926,Ag 17,15:2
Synthetic Sin 1927,O 11,26:2
Within the Law 1928,Mr 6,20:1
Married-And How! 1928,Je 15,30:2
He Understood Women 1928,Ag 16,25:1
Conflict 1929,Mr 7,22:4
Among the Married 1929,O 4,24:3
Widow in Green, A 1931,N 21,21:4
Happy Journey to Trenton and Camden, The
1948,Mr 21,II,1:1
Blood Wedding 1949,F 7,16:2
Bruno and Sidney 1949,My 4,38:2
Death of a Salesman 1950,S 21,20:5
Idiot, The 1960,S 26,38:1
Allendorf, E Eugene (Mrs)
One Woman's Husband 1920,Mr 23,9:3
Alleneve, Korola
Aloma of the South Seas 1925,Ap 21,18:1
Allensworth, Carl
Streets of New York, The 1934,Jl 21,14:5
Oliver Twist 1934,Ag 11,16:5
Coquette 1935,Jl 10,24:1
Camille 1935,Jl 31,21:1
Late Christopher Bean, The 1935,Ag 28,13:1
Pursuit of Happiness, The 1936,Jl 15,14:1
Post Road 1936,Ag 5,15:4
Royal Family, The 1936,Ag 12,15:1
Whiteheaded Boy, The 1937,Ag 11,27:3
Ode to Liberty 1937,Ag 18,15:2
Elizabeth the Queen 1937,Ag 25,24:3
Animal Kingdom, The 1938,Jl 27,14:5
Arms and the Man 1938,Ag 10,14:1
What a Life 1939,Ag 2,17:5
Allensworth, Carl (Director)
Late Christopher Bean, The 1935,Ag 28,13:1
Kind Lady 1937,Jl 21,19:3
Candida 1937,Ag 4,14:5
Allensworth, Carl (Original Author)
Goodbye Again 1937,S 1,15:1
Allensworth, Carl (Playwright)
Party Line, The 1937,Ag 30,25:4
Village Green 1941,Je 17,24:7
Village Green 1941,Ag 27,15:3
Village Green 1941,S 4,24:4
Village Green 1941,S 14,IX,1:1
Allenton, Joseph
Piper, The 1920,Mr 20,14:2
Hail and Farewell 1923,F 20,12:1
Morals 1925,D 1,22:2
Lulu Belle 1926,F 10,20:1
Ladies Don't Lie 1929,O 11,36:3
Reunion in Vienna 1931,N 17,31:1
Best Sellers 1933,My 4,20:2
Pure in Heart, The 1934,Mr 21,24:3
Mr Jiggins of Jigginstown 1936,D 18,30:2
Allers, Franz (Musical Director)
Happy as Larry 1950,Ja 7,11:2
Paint Your Wagon 1951,N 13,32:2
My Darlin' Aida 1952,O 28,36:4
Plain and Fancy 1955,Ja 28,14:2
New Moon, The; Desert Song, The 1955,Jl 1,13:1
My Fair Lady 1956,Mr 16,20:2
Camelot 1960,O 3,35:1
Camelot 1960,D 5,42:1
My Fair Lady 1961,O 26,40:1
My Fair Lady 1962,S 7,34:1
To Broadway With Love 1964,Ap 30,28:6
King and I, The 1964,Jl 7,26:1
Merry Widow, The 1964,Ag 18,24:2
Kismet 1965,Je 23,45:1
Carousel 1965,Ag 11,39:1
Annie Get Your Gun 1966,Je 1,42:2
Show Boat 1966,Jl 20,48:1
Alley, Ben
Vaudeville (Loew's State) 1932,Jl 18,9:7
Allgood, Sara
Professor Tim 1927,Ap 17,VII,1:4
Plough and the Stars, The 1927,N 29,30:2
Plough and the Stars, The 1927,D 4,X,1:1
Juno and the Paycock 1927,D 20,32:2
Storm in a Teacup 1936,F 6,23:1
Storm Over Patsy 1937,Mr 2,16:4
Storm Over Patsy 1937,Mr 9,26:4

Allgood, Sara—Cont
Juno and the Paycock 1937,Ag 29,X,2:1
Shadow and Substance 1938,Ja 27,16:2
Juno and the Paycock 1940,Ja 17,24:2
Juno and the Paycock 1940,Ja 21,IX,1:2
Juno and the Paycock 1940,Ja 21,IX,1:1
To What Red Hell 1940,My 5,I,54:8
At the Stroke of Eight 1940,My 21,29:2
Lucky Finger, The 1948,Ja 21,30:5

Allinson, Michael
Importance of Being Earnest, The 1963,F 27,5:2
Major Barbara 1965,My 18,33:1
Hostile Witness 1966,F 18,26:1
Come Live With Me 1967,Ja 27,29:1
Coco 1969,D 19,66:1

Allio, Rene (Costume Designer)
George Dandin 1968,Je 28,36:1
Tartuffe 1968,Jl 3,28:2

Allio, Rene (Scenic Designer)
Cymbeline 1962,Jl 18,21:2
Three Musketeers, The 1968,Je 26,43:1
George Dandin 1968,Je 28,36:1
Tartuffe 1968,Jl 3,28:2
Beaux' Stratagem, The 1970,F 10,50:2

Alliot, Beatrice (Playwright)
Brooklyn Biarritz 1941,F 28,16:2

Allis, Ethel
Hassard Short's Ritz Revue 1924,S 18,19:1
Vaudeville (Palace) 1926,Ap 13,28:3

Allison, Bessie
Deep River 1926,O 5,26:2
Creoles 1927,S 23,33:3

Allison, Fred (Lighting Director)
God, Man & You, Baby! 1963,O 30,47:1
When We Dead Awaken 1966,Ap 19,37:2
Arms and the Man 1967,Je 23,44:2
Love and Let Love 1968,Ja 4,30:1
Three Men on a Horse 1969,O 17,35:1
Norman, Is That You? 1970,F 20,30:1

Allison, George
Montserrat 1954,My 26,34:2

Allison, Hughes (Playwright)
Trial of Dr Beck, The 1937,Ag 10,22:2

Allison, James
Sunny River 1941,D 5,28:2

Allison, Mildred
Green Pastures, The 1935,F 27,16:2

Allison, Nancy (Miscellaneous)
Nine Till Six 1936,Mr 14,10:3

Allison, Norman (Miscellaneous)
Cherry Orchard, The 1968,Mr 20,41:1

Allison, R H Jr
Coriolanus 1927,Je 18,8:3

Allison, Robert S Jr
Roof, The 1930,Je 14,9:2

Allison, Wana
Merry Widow, The 1943,Ag 5,19:2

Allister, Claud
Havoc 1924,S 2,22:2
Dark Angel, The 1925,F 11,19:2
Buccaneer, The 1925,O 3,10:2
School for Scandal, The 1925,O 24,19:1
Play's the Thing, The 1926,N 4,25:1
Red Peppers; Tonight at Eight 1940,Ag 6,15:3
Play's the Thing, The 1948,Ap 29,19:2
Play's the Thing, The 1948,My 9,II,1:1
Mighty Man Is He, A 1960,Ja 7,25:2

Allman, David
I'd Rather Be Right 1937,N 3,28:2

Allman, Jack
All-Star Jamboree 1921,Jl 14,18:1

Allmon, Clinton
Khaki Blue 1969,Mr 27,54:2

Alloway, Barbara
Child Buyer, The 1964,D 22,35:1

Alloway, Jacqueline
By Jupiter 1967,Ja 20,28:2
George M! 1968,Ap 11,48:1

Alloy, Al (Lighting Director)
Brights Lights of 1944 1943,S 17,27:4
Late George Apley, The 1944,N 22,26:2
Good as Gold 1957,My 8,22:2
Good Soup, The 1960,Mr 3,26:4

Allraum, Juana
Channel Road, The 1929,O 18,24:2

Alls, Roscoe
Jim Jam Jems 1920,O 5,13:2

Allsbrook, Bill
Applause 1970,Mr 31,35:1

Allshesky, Theola
Jazz a La Carte 1922,Je 3,8:3

Allsworth, Frank
No More Blondes 1920,Ja 8,22:1

Allvine, Glendon (Original Author)
Knights of Song 1938,O 18,29:2

Allvine, Glendon (Playwright)
Knights of Song 1938,O 18,29:2

Allwork, Ronald (Scenic Designer)
Fashion 1937,Mr 21,II,7:8

Allworth, Frank
Marry the Poor Girl 1920,S 27,18:3
Poppy God, The 1921,Ag 30,10:1
Pot-Luck 1921,S 30,10:1
Partners Again 1922,My 2,22:2

Chicken Feed 1923,S 25,10:2
Two Strangers From Nowhere 1924,Ap 8,22:2
Music Box Revue 1924,D 2,23:3
What the Doctor Ordered 1927,Ag 19,20:2
Lady for a Night, A 1928,Ap 17,26:4
Hold Everything 1928,O 11,24:2
Who Cares 1930,Jl 9,27:1
Riddle Me This! 1933,Mr 15,21:3
Queer People 1934,F 16,16:2
Potash and Perlmutter 1935,Ap 6,11:3

Allyn, Alan
Killers 1928,Mr 14,28:3
Big Fight, The 1928,S 19,33:1

Allyn, Alan (Director)
Decision 1929,My 28,37:3

Allyn, Harriett
Vaudeville (Palace) 1929,Ja 21,18:3
Undercurrent, The 1929,Ja 21,18:3

Allyn, Jane
Night Hostess 1928,S 13,31:2

Allyn, Mabel
Jarnegan 1928,S 25,29:2
Conflict 1929,Mr 7,22:4

Allyn, William
Flag Is Born, A 1946,S 7,10:6
Ring Around the Moon 1950,N 24,30:1

Allys, Ethel
Honeymoon Lane 1926,S 21,32:3

Allyson, June
Sing Out the News 1938,S 26,12:5
Best Foot Forward 1941,O 2,28:2
Forty Carats 1970,Ja 6,48:1

Alma, Lyda
Edith Piaf 1947,O 30,30:2

Almagor, Dan (Translator)
My Fair Lady 1964,F 20,24:4
Fiddler on the Roof 1965,Je 9,40:1

Almica, Princess
Savages Under the Skin 1927,Mr 25,25:2

Almoravids, Tchaka
Five on the Black Hand Side 1970,Ja 2,32:2

Almquist, Dean Lyman
Failures, The 1959,Ja 6,30:2
Dinny and the Witches 1959,D 10,53:3

Almy
Vaudeville (Palace) 1929,N 18,22:4

Alny, Sonia
Girofle-Girofla 1926,N 23,26:3
Perichole, La 1926,D 29,24:4
Trois Jeunes Filles Nues; Three Young Maids From
  the Folies Bergere 1929,Mr 5,28:2
Passionately; Passionately 1929,Mr 8,31:4
Comte Obligado 1929,Mr 12,26:2
Ta Bouche 1929,Mr 15,28:5
Bon Garcon, Un 1929,Mr 19,36:2
Pas Sur La Bouche; Not on the Lips
  1929,Mr 26,34:3

Alogna, Michael
Davy Jones's Locker 1966,D 25,48:5

Aloha Maids
Hellzapoppin 1938,S 23,34:2

Alomis, Sonia
Dybbuk, The 1924,Ja 29,17:7
Neveile, The 1924,F 9,16:2
Jealousy 1936,S 28,14:3
Kapores 1936,S 28,14:3

Alon, Meir
I'm Solomon 1968,Ap 24,51:1

Alonge, Frank
Gods of the Mountain, The 1950,My 25,36:2

Alonso, A G
Road to Happiness, The 1927,My 3,24:1
Girl and the Cat, The 1927,My 6,21:2
Blind Heart, The 1927,My 8,30:2

Alonso, Mariano
Pluma en el Viento; Feather in the Wind
  1932,Ap 2,13:4

Alonso, Odon (Miscellaneous)
Fiesta in Madrid 1969,My 29,49:1

Alpar, Gitta
Schoen ist die Welt 1931,Ja 11,VIII,1:8
Veilchen von Montmartre 1931,Mr 29,VIII,3:1
Du Barry 1931,S 20,VIII,2:7
Katharina 1932,O 2,IX,3:1
Ball at the Savoy 1933,F 19,IX,3:1
Home and Beauty 1937,F 3,26:2
Home and Beauty 1937,F 21,X,2:1

Alpe, James
Silver Tassie, The 1949,Jl 22,16:5
Cyanamide 1954,Mr 26,17:6
Lower Depths, The 1956,O 3,29:2
Enemy of the People, An 1958,F 26,24:2
Man Who Never Died, The 1958,N 22,27:2

Alper, Morty
Across the Board on Tomorrow Morning
  1942,Mr 21,13:5
Theatre of the Soul 1942,Mr 21,13:5

Alper, Murray
Spider, The 1927,Mr 23,29:1
Wild Man of Borneo, The 1927,S 14,29:2
Royal Family, The 1927,D 29,26:4
Room 349 1930,Ap 23,24:5
This Is New York 1930,N 29,21:1

Alper, Murray—Cont
Left Bank, The 1931,O 6,35:3
Broadway Boy 1932,My 4,23:5
Rendezvous 1932,O 13,22:3
Shooting Star 1933,Je 13,22:2
Sailor, Beware! 1933,S 29,24:4
Sky's the Limit, The 1934,D 18,25:5
Every Man for Himself 1940,D 10,32:3

Alpern, Morris Mark
Infantry, The 1966,N 15,51:1

Alpern, Susan
Joe Egg 1968,F 2,26:1

Alpert, Anita
Song of Norway 1959,Je 26,16:2
Kismet 1965,Je 23,45:1

Alpert, Herbert S (Producer)
Winter Journey 1968,Mr 13,39:1

Alpert, Hollis (Producer)
Evening With G B S, An; O'Flaherty, V C
  1957,F 19,35:7
An Evening With G B S; Press Cuttings
  1957,F 19,35:7

Alpert, Larry
Bagels and Yox 1951,S 13,38:2
Let It Ride 1961,O 13,27:4

Alpert, Millie (Lyricist)
Bagels and Yox 1951,S 13,38:2

Alpert, Mr
Tattle Tales 1930,Jl 20,VIII,2:1

Alpeter, Greta
Blossom Time 1931,Mr 5,32:1

Alphand, Claude
Wind Remains, The 1943,Mr 31,16:6

Alsberg, Arthur (Playwright)
Happiness Is Just a Little Thing Called a Rolls
  Royce 1968,My 13,54:5

Alsberg, Henry G (Playwright)
Dybbuk, The 1925,D 16,22:2
Princess Turandot 1926,N 13,14:2
Dybbuk, The 1926,D 17,27:2
Dybbuk, The 1954,O 27,33:6

Alsberg, Henry G (Producer)
Oedipus Rex 1945,D 17,16:7
Mayor of Zalamea, The 1946,Ja 28,15:5

Alsberg, Henry G (Translator)
Failures, The 1959,Ja 6,30:2

Alsberg (Playwright)
Konflikt 1933,Ap 16,IX,2:5

Alsop, Jean
Ice Capades 1960,S 1,30:1

Alsop, John
In the Days of the Turbins 1934,Mr 7,22:5

Alsop, John D
Whispering Gallery, The 1935,D 1,II,12:6
Wings Over Europe 1936,Mr 4,24:7

Alsop, Martin
Crooked Gamblers 1920,Ag 2,12:1

Alsop, Reese F
Watched Pot, The 1933,My 5,13:7

Alsop, Stewart J C
Wings Over Europe 1936,Mr 4,24:7

Alspach, Mary Jane
Culbin Sands 1935,Mr 23,10:3

Alssop, Stewart
In the Days of the Turbins 1934,Mr 7,22:5

Alstad, Lyn
Comedian, The 1956,O 18,36:4

Alstaetter, Antonia
Master of the Revels 1935,Ag 14,16:2

Alston, Andy
Teahouse of the August Moon, The
  1955,My 10,24:1

Alston, Barbara
Cabaret 1966,N 21,62:1

Alswang, Ralph (Costume Designer)
Beggars Are Comming to Town 1945,O 29,16:2
Whole World Over, The 1947,Mr 28,28:2
Last Dance, The 1948,Ja 28,27:2
Fair Game for Lovers 1964,F 11,43:2

Alswang, Ralph (Director)
Belafonte at the Palace 1959,D 16,55:1
Rugantino 1964,F 7,34:1
Comedy in Music, Opus 2 1964,N 10,54:1

Alswang, Ralph (Lighting Director)
Home of the Brave 1945,D 28,13:2
Swan Song 1946,My 16,29:2
Lysistrata 1946,O 18,27:5
Young Man's Fancy, A 1947,Ap 30,33:2
Our Lan' 1947,S 29,16:5
Gentleman From Athens, The 1947,D 10,42:4
Strange Bedfellows 1948,Ja 15,27:3
Play's the Thing, The 1948,Ap 29,19:2
Small Wonder 1948,S 16,33:5
Blood Wedding 1949,F 7,16:2
Me, The Sleeper 1949,My 16,18:6
Mikado, The 1949,O 5,35:2
Pirates of Penzance, The 1949,O 11,41:2
Trial by Jury 1949,O 18,34:2
H M S Pinafore 1949,O 18,34:2
How Long Till Summer 1949,D 28,30:3
Peter Pan 1950,Ap 25,27:2
Julius Caesar 1950,Je 21,30:1
Daphne Laureola 1950,S 19,38:6
Let's Make an Opera 1950,D 14,50:2

Alswang, Ralph (Lighting Director)—Cont

King Lear 1950,D 26,18:1
Courtin' Time 1951,Je 14,30:2
Out West of Eighth 1951,S 21,20:3
Conscience 1952,My 16,17:6
Two's Company 1952,D 16,43:5
Bat, The 1953,Ja 21,28:2
Pink Elephant, The 1953,Ap 23,37:2
Anna Russell and Her Little Show 1953,S 8,27:2
Ladies of the Corridor, The 1953,O 22,33:5
Sing Till Tomorrow 1953,D 29,17:2
Fragile Fox 1954,O 13,27:1
Rainmaker, The 1954,O 29,28:1
Troublemakers, The 1954,D 31,11:3
Southwest Corner, The 1955,F 4,18:2
Deadfall 1955,O 28,20:1
Time Limit! 1956,Ja 25,27:2
Hot Corner, The 1956,Ja 26,25:2
Affair of Honor 1956,Ap 7,12:3
Best House in Naples, The 1956,O 27,16:2
Uncle Willie 1956,D 21,17:1
Tunnel of Love, The 1957,F 14,31:4
Hide and Seek 1957,Ap 3,26:1
First Gentleman, The 1957,Ap 26,22:2
Sunrise at Campobello 1958,Ja 31,25:1
Epitaph for George Dillon 1958,N 5,44:1
Raisin in the Sun, A 1959,Mr 12,27:1
At the Drop of a Hat 1959,O 9,22:2
Girls Against the Boys, The 1959,N 3,26:1
Belafonte at the Palace 1959,D 16,55:1
Come Blow Your Horn 1961,F 23,31:3
Aqua Carnival 1962,Je 29,15:1
Beyond the Fringe 1962,O 29,36:1
School for Scandal, The 1963,Ja 26,5:2
Advocate, The 1963,O 15,46:7
Man and Boy 1963,N 13,34:1
Beyond the Fringe 1964 1964,Ja 10,18:1
Fair Game for Lovers 1964,F 11,43:2
Committee, The 1964,S 17,53:1
Comedy in Music, Opus 2 1964,N 10,54:1
World of Charles Aznavour, The 1965,O 15,49:1
Hostile Witness 1966,F 18,26:1
Gilbert Becaud on Broadway 1966,N 1,35:1
At Home at the Palace 1967,Ag 1,23:1
Halfway up the Tree 1967,N 8,52:1
Gilbert Becaud Sings Love 1968,O 7,53:5

Alswang, Ralph (Miscellaneous)

Julius Caesar 1950,Je 21,30:1

Alswang, Ralph (Producer)

Magic and the Loss, The 1954,Ap 10,10:3
First Gentleman, The 1957,Ap 26,22:2

Alswang, Ralph (Scenic Designer)

Comes the Revelation 1942,My 27,26:2
Home of the Brave 1945,D 28,13:2
I Like It Here 1946,Mr 23,8:6
Swan Song 1946,My 16,29:2
Lysistrata 1946,O 18,27:5
Whole World Over, The 1947,Mr 28,28:2
Young Man's Fancy, A 1947,Ap 30,33:2
Our Lan' 1947,S 29,16:5
Gentleman From Athens, The 1947,D 10,42:4
Strange Bedfellows 1948,Ja 15,27:3
Last Dance, The 1948,Ja 28,27:2
To Tell You the Truth 1948,Ap 19,28:6
Seeds in the Wind 1948,My 26,29:2
Small Wonder 1948,S 16,33:5
Story for Strangers, A 1948,S 22,39:2
Set My People Free 1948,N 4,38:2
Jenny Kissed Me 1948,D 24,12:2
Freight 1949,F 4,30:2
Riders to the Sea 1949,F 4,30:2
Blood Wedding 1949,F 7,16:2
Mikado, The 1949,O 5,35:2
Pirates of Penzance, The 1949,O 11,41:2
H M S Pinafore 1949,O 18,34:2
Trial by Jury 1949,O 18,34:2
How Long Till Summer 1949,D 28,30:3
Peter Pan 1950,Ap 25,27:2
Tickets, Please! 1950,Ap 28,25:2
Peter Pan 1950,Ap 30,II,1:1
Legend of Sarah 1950,O 12,42:4
Pride's Crossing 1950,N 21,37:5
Let's Make an Opera 1950,D 14,50:2
King Lear 1950,D 26,18:1
King Lear 1950,D 31,II,1:1
Courtin' Time 1951,Je 14,30:2
Out West of Eighth 1951,S 21,20:3
Love and Let Love 1951,O 20,11:2
Number, The 1951,O 31,33:2
Conscience 1952,My 16,17:6
Mikado, The 1952,O 21,35:2
Pirates of Penzance, The 1952,O 28,36:4
Trial by Jury 1952,N 4,32:2
H M S Pinafore 1952,N 4,32:2
Iolanthe 1952,N 11,26:3
Two's Company 1952,D 16,43:5
Two's Company 1952,D 21,II,3:1
Be Your Age 1953,Ja 15,24:2
Bat, The 1953,Ja 21,28:2
Pink Elephant, The 1953,Ap 23,37:2
Ladies of the Corridor, The 1953,O 22,33:5
Sing Till Tomorrow 1953,D 29,17:2
Magic and the Loss, The 1954,Ap 10,10:3
Fragile Fox 1954,O 13,27:1

Rainmaker, The 1954,O 29,28:1
Troublemakers, The 1954,D 31,11:3
Southwest Corner, The 1955,F 4,18:2
Catch a Star! 1955,S 7,35:2
Deadfall 1955,O 28,20:1
Time Limit! 1956,Ja 25,27:2
Hot Corner, The 1956,Ja 26,25:2
Time Limit! 1956,F 5,II,1:1
Affair of Honor 1956,Ap 7,12:3
Best House in Naples, The 1956,O 27,16:2
Uncle Willie 1956,D 21,17:1
Tunnel of Love, The 1957,F 14,31:4
Hide and Seek 1957,Ap 3,26:1
First Gentleman, The 1957,Ap 26,22:2
Sunrise at Campobello 1958,Ja 31,25:1
Love Me Little 1958,Ap 15,42:2
Epitaph for George Dillon 1958,N 5,44:1
Raisin in the Sun, A 1959,Mr 12,27:1
Detour After Dark 1959,Je 9,11:4
Girls Against the Boys, The 1959,N 3,26:1
Come Blow Your Horn 1961,F 23,31:3
Advocate, The 1963,O 15,46:7
Man and Boy 1963,N 13,34:1
Fair Game for Lovers 1964,F 11,43:2
Committee, The 1964,S 17,53:1
World of Charles Aznavour, The 1965,O 15,49:1
Hostile Witness 1966,F 18,26:1
Gilbert Becaud on Broadway 1966,N 1,35:1
At the Drop of Another Hat 1966,D 28,30:2
Sorrow of Frederick, The 1967,Jl 8,14:2
Halfway up the Tree 1967,N 8,52:1
Gilbert Becaud Sings Love 1968,O 7,53:5

Alter, Helene

Burning Bush, The 1949,D 17,15:5

Alter, Joe

Ten Nights in a Barroom 1928,Mr 28,31:2

Alter, Louis

Vaudeville (Palace) 1923,N 20,23:4

Alter, Louis (Composer)

A la Carte 1927,Ag 18,25:3
Ballyhoo 1930,D 14,IX,3:1
Ballyhoo 1930,D 23,24:1
Hold Your Horses 1933,S 26,26:4

Alter, Louis (Lyricist)

A la Carte 1927,Ag 18,25:3
Hold Your Horses 1933,S 26,26:4

Alter, Melba

White Lilacs 1928,S 11,31:2

Alter, Ronald

High Button Shoes 1955,Mr 12,10:6

Alter, Sidney

Kith and Kin 1930,My 14,31:1

Alters, Gerald (Choreographer)

Happiest Girl in the World, The 1961,Ap 4,42:1
Family Affair, A 1962,Ja 29,17:1

Alters, Gerald (Musical Director)

That Hat! 1964,S 24,45:1
Wet Paint 1965,Ap 13,33:1

Althoff, Charles

Free for All 1931,S 9,25:1
Yokel Boy 1939,Jl 7,12:2
Quare Fellow, The 1958,N 28,34:1
Our Town 1959,Mr 24,46:2

Alti, Sigh

Chinese O'Neill 1929,My 23,27:1

Altieri, John

Strictly Dishonorable 1929,S 19,37:1
Child of Manhattan 1932,Mr 2,15:1

Altman, Frieda

Carry Nation 1932,O 31,18:2
Hilda Cassidy 1933,My 5,18:3
I Was Waiting for You 1933,N 14,23:3
Picnic 1934,My 3,15:2
Spring Song 1934,O 2,18:2
Paradise Lost 1935,D 10,31:5
Timber 1936,Jl 29,11:5
Middle Man 1936,S 8,23:1
Timber House 1936,S 21,27:5
Days to Come 1936,D 16,35:1
Marching Song 1937,F 18,18:2
Yr Obedient Husband 1938,Ja 11,26:5
Pastoral 1939,N 2,26:2
Jeannie 1940,N 13,29:2
Gabrielle 1941,Mr 26,26:2
Guest in the House 1942,F 25,25:2
Counsellor-at-Law 1942,N 25,17:2
Naked Genius, The 1943,O 22,20:5
Hickory Stick 1944,My 9,15:6
Joy Forever, A 1946,Ja 8,20:2
Little Brown Jug 1946,Mr 7,32:2
Land's End 1946,D 12,37:5
Strange Bedfellows 1948,Ja 15,27:3
Young and Fair, The 1948,N 23,35:2
Southwest Corner, The 1955,F 4,18:2
Waltz of the Toreadors, The 1957,Ja 18,17:2
Visit, The 1958,My 6,40:1
Cheri 1959,O 13,44:1
Distant Bell, A 1960,Ja 14,29:1
Rendezvous at Senlis 1961,F 28,39:2
Shadow of Heroes 1961,D 6,59:1

Altman, Jane

Year Boston Won the Pennant, The
1969,My 23,38:1

Altman, John

Winter Soldiers 1942,N 30,19:2

Altman, Julian

Blue Butterfly, The 1929,F 17,29:3

Altman, Martin

Vegetable, The, or From President to Postman
1929,Ap 11,32:3

Altman, N (Scenic Designer)

Dybbuk, The 1948,My 3,26:3
Dybbuk, The 1964,F 4,30:2

Altman, Richard (Director)

Chic 1959,My 19,28:2
Mrs Dally Has a Lover 1962,O 2,47:1
Whisper Into My Good Ear 1962,O 2,47:1
Saving Grace 1963,Mr 19,28:1
Corruption in the Palace of Justice 1963,O 9,49:2
Child Buyer, The 1964,D 22,35:1
Party on Greenwich Avenue, The 1967,My 11,52:1
Fiddler on the Roof 1969,N 16,82:6
How Much, How Much? 1970,Ap 21,49:1

Altman, Ruth

Grand Duchess 1929,D 17,29:2
Gypsy Baron, The 1930,Ap 22,22:8
Luana 1930,S 18,28:1
H M S Pinafore 1931,My 19,25:2
Gondoliers, The 1931,Je 2,34:4
Merry Widow, The 1931,S 8,39:1
Gondoliers, The 1932,Ja 12,29:1
H M S Pinafore 1933,My 9,20:3
Trial by Jury 1933,My 9,20:3
Bohemian Girl, The 1933,Jl 28,18:5
Pirates of Penzance, The 1933,Ag 8,22:4
Yeomen of the Guard, The 1933,Ag 15,20:5
Wooden Slipper, The 1934,Ja 4,16:3
Clap Hands 1934,Ag 21,12:7
Sky's the Limit, The 1934,D 18,25:5
Boy Friend, The 1954,O 1,20:1
Boy Friend, The 1954,O 10,II,1:1

Altman, Thelma

Rosalinda; Fledermaus, Die 1942,O 29,26:5

Alto, Bobby

Lovers and Other Strangers 1968,S 19,63:1

Alton, Bill

Dynamite Tonight 1967,Mr 16,52:2

Alton, Kenneth

Liliom 1956,F 18,12:5

Alton, Maxine (Playwright)

Arrest That Woman 1936,S 19,20:4

Alton, Robert (Choreographer)

Hold Your Horses 1933,S 26,26:4
Ziegfeld Follies 1934,Ja 5,24:3
Life Begins at 8:40 1934,Ag 28,24:2
Anything Goes 1934,N 22,26:1
Parade 1935,My 21,22:2
Ziegfeld Follies 1936,Ja 31,17:2
Ziegfeld Follies 1936,S 15,37:1
White Horse Inn 1936,O 2,28:5
Show Is On, The 1936,D 26,14:2
Show Is On, The 1937,S 20,18:4
Hooray for What! 1937,D 2,32:5
Between the Devil 1937,D 23,24:5
Show Boat 1938,Je 30,21:1
You Never Know 1938,S 22,26:3
Leave It to Me! 1938,N 10,32:2
One for the Money 1939,F 6,9:2
Streets of Paris, The 1939,Je 20,25:2
Too Many Girls 1939,O 19,26:2
Du Barry Was a Lady 1939,D 7,34:2
Two for the Show 1940,F 18,IX,2:1
Higher and Higher 1940,Mr 17,X,2:5
Higher and Higher 1940,Ap 5,24:3
Panama Hattie 1940,O 31,28:2
Pal Joey 1940,D 26,22:2
Sons o' Fun 1941,D 2,28:2
By Jupiter 1942,Je 4,22:1
By Jupiter 1942,Ag 16,VIII,2:1
Count Me In 1942,O 9,24:2
Ziegfeld Follies 1943,Ap 2,16:2
Ziegfeld Follies 1943,Ap 11,II,1:1
Early to Bed 1943,Je 18,16:2
Laffing Room Only 1944,D 25,15:4
Pal Joey 1952,Ja 4,17:6
Pal Joey 1952,Ja 13,II,1:1
Pal Joey 1952,F 17,II,13:5
Hazel Flagg 1953,F 12,22:2
Me and Juliet 1953,My 29,17:1
Vamp, The 1955,N 11,30:1

Alton, Robert (Director)

Aquacade 1939,My 5,26:2
Me and Juliet 1953,Je 7,II,1:1
Judy Garland's New Variety Show 1956,S 27,43:2

Alton, Robert (Miscellaneous)

Pal Joey 1952,Ja 4,17:6
Vamp, The 1955,N 11,30:1

Alton, Royce

Canary Dutch 1925,S 9,22:1

Alton, Zohra

Venice Preserv'd 1955,D 13,54:4
Diary of a Scoundrel 1956,N 5,41:1

18

Altschuler, Modest (Musical Director)
Midsummer Night's Dream, A 1932,Jl 13,15:1
Altschuler, Robert (Miscellaneous)
Moon Walk 1970,N 27,52:1
Alvar, L (Translator)
Moment Difficile, Le 1926,D 26,VII,2:1
Alvarado, Arthur (Corp)
Swing Sister Wac Swing 1944,Ja 4,20:4
Alvarado, Arthur (Corp) (Costume Designer)
Swing Sister Wac Swing 1944,Ja 4,20:4
Alvarenga, Elton Anthony
Carmen Jones 1951,S 22,8:6
Alvarez, Anita
All in Fun 1940,D 28,11:2
Allah Be Praised! 1944,Ap 21,14:2
Finian's Rainbow 1947,Ja 11,23:2
Finian's Rainbow 1947,Ja 26,II,1:1
Gentlemen Prefer Blondes 1949,D 9,35:3
Finian's Rainbow 1955,My 19,25:1
Finian's Rainbow 1960,Ap 28,31:1
Alvarez, Carmen
Cyrano de Bergerac 1953,N 13,24:3
Li'l Abner 1956,N 16,24:2
To Broadway With Love 1964,Ap 30,28:6
That Hat! 1964,S 24,45:1
Decline and Fall of the Entire World As Seen
Through the Eyes of Cole Porter Revisited, The
1965,Mr 31,24:2
Yearling, The 1965,D 11,25:1
Passionella 1966,O 19,53:1
Lady or the Tiger?, The 1966,O 19,53:1
Apple Tree, The 1967,O 12,56:1
Zorba 1968,N 18,58:1
Look to the Lilies 1970,Mr 30,59:1
Alvarez, Fausto
Leyenda del Beso, La 1942,N 20,26:4
Alvarez, L
Road to Happiness, The 1927,My 3,24:1
Romantic Young Lady, The 1927,My 5,30:2
Girl and the Cat, The 1927,My 6,21:2
Blind Heart, The 1927,My 8,30:2
Cradle Song 1927,My 10,24:4
Pygmalion 1927,My 12,25:2
Alvarez, Marie
Provincetown Follies, The 1935,N 4,24:3
Alvers, Zinaida
Chauve-Souris of 1943 1943,Ag 13,13:2
Alves, Verne (Miscellaneous)
Judy Garland 1961,Ap 24,36:1
Alvin, Michael
Honor Code, The 1931,My 19,25:3
Alvin, Robert
Great Campaign, The 1947,Ap 1,33:2
Hope Is the Thing With Feathers 1948,Ap 12,24:2
Home Life of a Buffalo; Hope's the Thing
1948,My 12,34:6
Hope Is the Thing With Feathers; Hope's the
Thing 1948,My 12,34:6
Gone Tomorrow; Hope's the Thing
1948,My 12,34:6
Trial of Dmitri Karamazov, The 1958,Ja 28,30:1
Semi-Detached 1960,Mr 11,20:2
Alvo, Dick
Billy Budd 1959,F 28,13:3
Alwaise, Frances D (Father) (Playwright)
Simon's Wife 1945,Mr 9,16:4
Alwes, Betty Jane
Tall Kentuckian, The 1953,Je 17,30:1
Alworth, Alice
Field of Ermine 1935,F 9,10:4
Alycia, Marthe
Fil a la Paite, Un 1966,F 18,25:1
Alyn, Glen
Under the Counter 1947,O 4,10:2
Alyn, Kirk
Pie in the Sky 1941,D 23,26:5
Alzamara, Maria
Legend of Leonora, The 1926,My 1,10:1
Amac
Vaudeville (Palace) 1925,O 6,31:3
Vaudeville (Palace) 1926,Je 22,21:3
Aman, John
Now 1968,Je 6,53:1
Happy Hypocrite, The 1968,S 6,38:1
Of Thee I Sing 1969,Mr 8,19:1
Aman, John (Composer)
Now 1968,Je 6,53:1
Aman, Sara
Plain and Fancy 1955,F 6,II,6:6
Virtuous Island, The 1957,Ap 10,39:1
Amant, Saint
Plain and Fancy 1955,F 6,II,6:6
Amar
Gosseline 1921,Je 19,VI,1:8
Amateau, Rod (Director)
Venus at Large 1962,Ap 13,30:1
Amati, Patrice
Kingdom of God, The 1928,D 21,30:2
Amato, Albert
Jubilee 1935,O 14,20:1
Between the Devil 1937,D 23,24:5
Amato, Johnny
Arrow-Maker, The 1956,O 5,20:1

Amaya, Carmen
Laugh, Town, Laugh! 1942,Je 20,9:1
Laugh, Town, Laugh! 1942,Je 23,22:2
Laugh, Town, Laugh! 1942,Jl 23,15:3
Amazar, Tanya
Out of a Blue Sky 1930,F 10,20:6
Amazar, Tatiana
Hobo 1931,F 12,24:4
Ambandos, Demetrius (Director)
Corner of the Bed, A 1969,F 27,35:2
World of Mrs Solomon, The; Another Chance
1969,Je 4,37:1
World of Mrs Solomon, The; Second Mrs Aarons,
The 1969,Je 4,37:1
Ambigu, Nouvel (Producer)
Mademoiselle Josette Ma Femme 1924,Je 1,VII,1:7
Ambler, Frances
Flying Blind 1930,My 16,20:2
Ambler, Humphrey
Fratricide Punished 1925,Ap 21,19:1
Hamlet 1927,Ap 7,23:3
Ambler Brothers
Vaudeville (Palace) 1924,S 30,27:5
Ambos, Franklyn (Scenic Designer)
Mikado, The 1934,Ap 3,26:3
Pirates of Penzance, The 1934,Ap 10,26:5
Pirates of Penzance, The 1936,Ap 21,27:5
H M S Pinafore 1936,Ap 28,17:2
Trial by Jury 1936,Ap 28,17:2
Iolanthe 1936,My 5,26:2
Amboy, Milton
Billy Budd 1955,My 4,35:1
Ambrose, Amanda
Cities in Bezique; Beast's Story, A 1969,Ja 13,26:1
Ambrose, Helene
They All Want Something 1926,O 13,20:2
Life Line, The 1930,D 29,19:3
Life and Death of an American 1939,My 20,11:2
Meet a Body 1944,O 17,19:5
Ambrose, Martin
Joyful Noise, A 1966,D 16,57:1
How Now, Dow Jones 1967,D 8,53:1
Ambrose, Mary
Silks and Satins 1920,Jl 16,19:1
Ambrosio, Tom (Composer)
Nobody Hears A Broken Drum 1970,Mr 20,55:1
Amdur, Francine
Cave Dwellers, The 1957,O 21,29:2
Ame, Jerry
Hoofers, The 1969,Jl 30,23:4
Ameche, Don
Silk Stockings 1955,F 25,17:3
Silk Stockings 1955,Mr 27,II,1:1
Holiday for Lovers 1957,F 15,20:1
Goldilocks 1958,O 13,33:1
Goldilocks 1958,O 19,II,1:1
13 Daughters 1961,Mr 3,17:2
Henry, Sweet Henry 1967,O 24,51:2
Amend, Karle (Director)
I Must Love Someone 1939,F 8,18:7
Amend, Karle (Scenic Designer)
Allez-Opp! 1927,Ag 3,29:3
Town Boy 1929,O 5,22:4
Wooden Soldier, The 1931,Je 23,28:4
Devil's Host, The 1931,N 20,27:2
Few Wild Oats, A 1932,Mr 25,22:6
Border-Land 1932,Mr 30,15:5
Angeline Moves In 1932,Ap 20,27:5
Broadway Boy 1932,My 4,23:5
Shuffle Along of 1933 1932,D 27,11:3
Before Morning 1933,F 10,13:4
Under Glass 1933,O 31,24:3
No Mother to Guide Her 1933,D 26,18:5
Locked Room, The 1933,D 26,18:5
Too Much Party 1934,Mr 6,28:4
Broadway Interlude 1934,Ap 20,16:3
Her Majesty the Widow 1934,Je 19,24:5
Gypsy Blonde 1934,Je 26,22:5
Nowhere Bound 1935,Ja 23,20:2
Potash and Perlmutter 1935,Ap 6,11:3
Them's the Reporters 1935,My 30,21:4
Smile at Me 1935,Ag 24,18:4
One Good Year 1935,N 28,38:3
Sap Runs High, The 1936,F 5,15:3
Fresh Fields 1936,F 11,19:2
Devil of Pei-Ling 1936,F 21,20:4
Howdy Stranger 1937,Ja 15,17:5
Cross-Town 1937,Mr 18,21:5
When We Are Married 1939,D 26,22:3
Time, Place and the Girl, The 1942,O 22,24:3
Right Next to Broadway 1944,F 22,26:2
Amendolia, Don
Until the Monkey Comes 1966,Je 21,38:1
Amendt, Rudolf
Redemption: Lebende Leichnam, Der; Living
Corpse, The 1928,N 20,28:2
American Classic Players
Destruction 1932,Jl 1,19:5
American Negro Theatre
Anna Lucasta 1944,S 10,II,1:1
Amerique, Miss
Hello Paris 1930,N 17,29:3

Ames
Ragged Edge, The 1927,F 13,VII,1:4
Ames, Adrienne
Beggars Are Comming to Town 1945,O 29,16:2
Ames, April
Louisiana Purchase 1940,My 29,19:2
Ames, Barbara
Eastward in Eden 1947,N 19,33:2
Nineteenth Hole of Europe, The 1949,Mr 28,16:2
Three Sisters, The 1959,S 22,46:1
Three Sisters, The 1959,O 4,II,1:1
Five Posts in the Market Place 1961,Mr 6,30:1
Ames, Beatrice
Holiday 1928,N 27,36:1
Ames, Cindy
Hedda Gabler 1970,Ja 18,78:1
Ames, Delano L (Playwright)
No Sleep for the Wicked 1937,Jl 1,32:5
No Sleep for the Wicked 1937,Jl 18,X,1:5
Ames, Ed
One Flew Over the Cuckoo's Nest 1963,N 14,40:2
Ames, Florenz
Lady Butterfly 1923,Ja 23,18:1
Nifties of 1923 1923,S 26,10:1
Vaudeville (Palace) 1924,F 12,20:2
Madame Pompadour 1924,N 12,20:6
Sky High 1925,Mr 3,21:4
Great Temptations, The 1926,My 19,29:1
Angela 1928,D 4,28:2
Silver Swan, The 1929,N 28,34:5
Count of Luxembourg, The 1930,F 18,28:2
Who Cares 1930,Jl 9,27:1
Singing Rabbi, The 1931,S 11,24:4
Marching By 1931,N 15,VIII,4:2
Of Thee I Sing 1931,D 28,20:1
Church Mouse, A 1933,Je 27,13:7
Let 'Em Eat Cake 1933,O 23,18:1
First Lady 1935,N 27,17:4
I'd Rather Be Right 1937,N 3,28:2
Return of the Vagabond, The 1940,My 14,27:2
Snookie 1941,Je 4,26:2
Mr Big 1941,S 14,IX,2:5
Mr Big 1941,O 1,24:2
H M S Pinafore 1942,Ja 22,12:2
Mikado, The 1942,F 4,22:2
Pirates of Penzance, The 1942,F 18,22:2
Iolanthe 1942,F 24,26:4
Gondoliers, The 1942,Mr 4,22:3
Mikado, The 1944,F 12,11:3
Trial by Jury 1944,F 15,14:4
H M S Pinafore 1944,F 15,14:4
Cox and Box 1944,F 18,15:5
Pirates of Penzance, The 1944,F 18,15:5
Gondoliers, The 1944,F 22,26:3
Iolanthe 1944,F 23,17:1
Patience 1944,F 26,11:4
Ruddigore 1944,Mr 3,19:5
Yeomen of the Guard, The 1944,Mr 5,34:3
Arms and the Girl 1950,F 3,28:2
Of Thee I Sing 1952,My 6,34:2
Ames, Florenz (Choreographer)
Singing Rabbi, The 1931,S 11,24:4
Ames, Fred (Musical Director)
Bassa Moona 1936,D 9,35:4
Ames, Genevieve
New Yorkers, The 1927,Mr 11,24:3
Ames, Harriet (Miscellaneous)
Parisienne 1950,Jl 25,24:2
Hilda Crane 1950,N 2,38:2
Ames, Harriet (Producer)
Lady From the Sea, The 1950,Ag 8,23:2
Borned in Texas 1950,Ag 22,30:6
Ames, Jerry
Mrs Warren's Profession 1963,Ap 25,39:1
Ames, Joseph
Good Boy 1928,S 6,23:2
Ames, Kirk
Small Timers, The 1925,Ja 28,15:3
School for Scandal, The 1925,O 24,19:1
Most Immoral Lady, A 1928,N 27,36:1
Drunkard, The; Fallen Saved, The 1929,D 31,14:6
Long Road, The 1930,S 10,30:2
False Dreams, Farewell 1934,Ja 16,18:3
Ames, Leon
Bright Honor 1936,S 28,14:1
House in the Country, A 1937,Ja 12,18:3
Thirsty Soil 1937,F 4,16:2
Male Animal, The 1940,Ja 10,17:2
Male Animal, The 1940,Ja 21,IX,1:1
Land Is Bright, The 1941,O 21,28:5
Land Is Bright, The 1941,O 29,26:2
Guest in the House 1942,F 25,25:2
Little Darling 1942,O 28,26:2
Russian People, The 1942,D 16,21:3
Russian People, The 1942,D 30,17:2
Silk Hat Harry 1943,Ag 22,II,1:6
Slightly Married 1943,O 26,19:2
Winesburg, Ohio 1958,F 6,22:2
Howie 1958,S 18,35:2
Life With Father 1967,O 20,53:2
Ames, Lionel
Buttrio Square 1952,O 15,40:2
Time Limit! 1956,Ja 25,27:2

Ames, Lionel E
Cotton Stockings 1923,D 19,16:2
Ames, Louis B (Miscellaneous)
Maria Golovin 1958,N 6,43:1
Ames, Michael
Quiet, Please! 1940,N 9,20:3
My Sister Eileen 1940,D 27,23:2
Storm Operation 1944,Ja 12,28:2
Mrs Kimball Presents 1944,Mr 1,17:3
Public Relations 1944,Ap 7,23:3
That Old Devil 1944,Je 6,14:2
Ames, Nancy
Kiss Me, Kate 1965,My 13,31:1
Ames, Nell
Elsie 1923,Ap 3,26:1
Ames, Oscar
Light Wines and Beer 1930,N 11,28:6
Ames, Paul (Producer)
Guest in the House 1942,F 25,25:2
Ames, Percy
Peg o' My Heart 1921,F 15,7:1
Quarantine 1924,D 17,19:7
Proud Woman, A 1926,N 16,24:1
Thou Desperate Pilot 1927,Mr 8,23:1
Other Men's Wives 1929,N 13,24:4
Something Gay 1935,Ap 30,12:2
Alice Takat 1936,F 11,19:2
Ames, Robert
Pietro 1920,Ja 20,10:2
Nice People 1921,Mr 3,11:1
Hero, The 1921,Mr 15,14:1
Hero, The 1921,Mr 20,VI,1:1
Hero, The 1921,S 6,13:2
Hero, The 1921,S 11,VI,1:1
It's a Boy! 1922,Jl 23,VI,1:6
Lights Out 1922,Ag 18,8:4
It's a Boy! 1922,S 20,18:3
Ice-Bound 1923,F 12,16:2
We've Got to Have Money 1923,Ag 21,12:1
Kelly's Vacation 1924,Mr 16,VIII,2:1
Desert Flower, The 1924,N 19,18:2
Jack in the Pulpit 1925,Ja 7,33:1
Seed of the Brute 1926,N 2,34:3
Triumphant Bachelor, The 1927,S 16,21:1
Bless You, Sister 1927,D 27,24:5
Quicksand 1928,F 14,26:3
Ames, Rosemary
Matrimony, PFD 1936,N 6,28:4
Matrimony, PFD 1936,N 13,26:1
Wise Tomorrow 1937,O 16,22:5
Ames, Shirley
Temporary Island, A 1948,Mr 15,27:3
Ames, Stephen (Producer)
Guest in the House 1942,F 25,25:2
Ames, Winthrop
Beggar on Horseback 1924,F 17,VII,1:1
Ames, Winthrop (Director)
Minick 1924,S 25,20:1
Iolanthe 1926,Ap 20,24:2
Prunella; Love in a Garden 1926,Je 16,23:3
White Wings 1926,O 16,15:1
Mikado, The; Town of Titipu, The 1927,S 19,30:1
Escape 1927,O 27,33:1
Merchant of Venice, The 1928,Ja 17,22:2
Ames, Winthrop (Playwright)
Mr Samuel 1930,O 26,VIII,3:5
Mr Samuel 1930,N 11,28:4
Ames, Winthrop (Producer)
Beggar on Horseback 1924,F 13,17:2
Old Man Minick 1924,Ag 24,VII,1:8
Minick 1924,S 25,20:1
Old English 1924,D 24,11:2
Iolanthe 1926,Ap 20,24:2
Iolanthe 1926,Ap 25,VIII,1:1
White Wings 1926,O 16,15:1
Pirates of Penzance, The; Slave of Duty, The 1926,D 7,25:1
Pirates of Penzance, The 1926,D 12,VIII,3:1
Mikado, The 1927,S 25,VIII,1:1
Escape 1927,O 27,33:1
Escape 1927,N 6,IX,1:1
Iolanthe 1927,N 15,26:3
Keating 1927,D 26,26:6
Merchant of Venice, The 1928,Ja 10,38:6
Merchant of Venice, The 1928,Ja 17,22:2
Ames and Winthrop
Frivolities of 1920 1920,Ja 9,22:2
Amesbury, George
Tia Juana 1927,N 16,28:4
Ameta
Vaudeville (Palace) 1926,S 7,24:6
Amey, Frank
Master of the Revels 1935,Ag 14,16:2
Amherst, Frances
Death Takes a Holiday 1931,F 17,29:1
Young Mr Disraeli 1937,N 10,30:5
Amherst, Sybil (Hon) (Translator)
Via Crucis 1923,N 13,25:2
Amiard, Henriette
Peter Ibbetson 1931,Ap 9,30:3
Amic-Angelo, Andrew R
Unknown Soldier and His Wife, The 1967,Jl 7,22:1

Amidon, Laurie
New York Idea, The 1948,Ag 18,29:2
Peg o' My Heart 1948,Ag 25,29:2
Amidon, Priscilla
Lucky Sam McCarver 1950,Ap 15,10:6
Desire Under the Elms 1951,N 22,45:1
As You Like It 1955,O 29,12:2
Romeo and Juliet 1955,D 16,36:3
Amiel, Denys (Original Author)
Three and One 1933,O 26,22:6
Amiel, Denys (Playwright)
Smiling Madame Beudet 1921,My 1,VII,1:7
Wife With a Smile, The 1921,N 29,20:1
Image, L' 1928,Ja 1,VIII,2:3
Age du Fer, L' 1932,N 13,IX,2:5
Trois et Une 1933,Ja 1,IX,3:4
Homme, L' 1934,F 25,IX,2:3
Femme en Fleur, La 1936,F 23,X,2:3
Ma Liberte 1936,D 13,XI,5:1
Famille 1938,Je 12,X,2:3
Amin Brothers
Judy Garland's New Variety Show 1956,S 27,43:2
Amiot, Paul
Aiglon, L' 1924,O 21,21:1
Naked 1924,O 28,27:2
Madame Sans-Gene 1924,N 4,30:1
Amoureuse 1924,N 28,13:1
Amiran, Emanuel (Composer)
Each Had Six Wings 1964,Mr 12,39:1
Amiss, Jay
Devil and Daniel Webster, The 1939,My 19,26:1
Sunny River 1941,D 5,28:2
Amitai, Haim
David's Crown 1948,My 10,26:2
Oedipus Rex 1948,My 24,23:2
Dybbuk, The 1964,F 4,30:2
Each Had Six Wings 1964,Mr 12,39:1
Amlund, Dale (Scenic Designer)
Simple Life, A 1964,My 18,36:1
Amman, Max (Producer)
Change 1970,O 13,52:2
Ammann, Matthias
Censored 1938,F 28,18:2
Knickerbocker Holiday 1938,O 20,26:2
Ammirati, Frank A
Another City, Another Land 1968,O 9,42:1
Ammon, Clifford (Miscellaneous)
How to Steal an Election 1968,O 14,56:1
Corner of the Bed, A 1969,F 27,35:2
World of Mrs Solomon, The; Second Mrs Aarons, The 1969,Je 4,37:1
World of Mrs Solomon, The; Another Chance 1969,Je 4,37:1
Ammon, Clifford (Original Author)
Mattathias of Modin 1968,Ap 15,41:1
Ammon, Ernst von
Flying Blind 1930,My 16,20:2
Ammons & Johnson
Concert Varieties 1945,Je 2,10:7
Amoia, Angelo
Pigeon, The 1930,O 15,26:2
Amoit, Paul
Parisienne 1924,N 25,26:2
Caprice, Un 1924,N 25,26:2
Amonsin, Viraj
World of Suzie Wong, The 1958,O 15,47:1
Tenth of an Inch Makes the Difference, A 1962,N 13,44:1
Amorelli, Paul (Miscellaneous)
Second Time Around, The 1962,Ap 21,14:1
Amoroso, Jack
Lute Song 1946,F 7,29:2
Amory, Hobart
Journey by Night, A 1935,Ap 17,26:3
Amory, J J
Stags at Bay 1934,D 15,9:2
Amory, J S
It's Only Natural 1922,Ap 21,13:2
Amory, Jack
Plot Thickens, The 1922,S 6,16:1
Six Characters in Search of an Author 1922,O 31,11:2
Amory, John
Call the Doctor 1920,S 1,14:1
Amory, John R
Mask of Hamlet, The 1921,Ag 23,10:3
Amos, Ruth
Slightly Delirious 1935,Ja 1,25:3
Please, Mrs. Garibaldi 1939,Mr 17,24:3
Strange Bedfellows 1948,Ja 15,27:3
Tree Grows in Brooklyn, A 1951,Ap 20,24:3
Amoss, Jane
Fatal Lady, The 1936,Mr 19,23:7
Amouri, Ann
Beautiful Jailer, The 1957,My 17,19:2
Amram, David (Composer)
Hamlet 1951,Jl 20,13:6
Titus Andronicus 1956,D 3,40:2
Romeo and Juliet 1957,Je 28,30:2
Two Gentlemen of Verona 1957,Jl 23,21:5
Macbeth 1957,Ag 16,11:2
Richard III 1957,N 26,41:1
As You Like It 1958,Ja 21,33:6

Amram, David (Composer)—Cont
Edward II 1958,F 12,32:5
Sign of Winter 1958,My 8,35:1
Othello 1958,Jl 4,16:1
Twelfth Night 1958,Ag 7,21:4
Deathwatch 1958,O 10,34:2
Family Reunion, The 1958,O 21,39:1
Power and the Glory, The 1958,D 12,2:7
J B 1958,D 12,2:7
Antony and Cleopatra 1959,Ja 14,28:1
Rivalry, The 1959,F 9,24:2
Rivalry, The 1959,F 15,II,1:1
Beaux' Stratagem, The 1959,F 25,35:4
Kataki 1959,Ap 10,24:1
Romeo and Juliet 1959,Je 15,31:1
Julius Caesar 1959,Ag 4,30:1
Great God Brown, The 1959,O 7,48:1
Lysistrata 1959,N 25,19:4
Kataki 1959,D 16,55:1
Peer Gynt 1960,Ja 13,21:1
Peer Gynt 1960,Ja 24,II,1:1
Caligula 1960,F 17,31:1
Henry IV 1960,Mr 2,42:1
Henry IV 1960,Ap 19,41:1
Henry V 1960,Je 30,23:1
Measure for Measure 1960,Jl 27,33:1
Taming of the Shrew, The 1960,Ag 20,17:1
Romeo and Juliet 1961,F 24,24:1
Hamlet 1961,Mr 17,17:1
As You Like It 1961,Je 17,13:2
Macbeth 1961,Je 19,31:1
As You Like It 1961,Je 25,II,1:1
Much Ado About Nothing 1961,Jl 7,17:1
Midsummer Night's Dream, A 1961,Ag 3,13:1
Richard II 1961,Ag 30,25:1
Julius Caesar 1962,F 22,19:6
Merchant of Venice, The 1962,Je 22,1:4
Tempest, The 1962,Jl 17,18:2
King Lear 1962,Ag 14,35:1
Macbeth 1962,N 17,16:2
Antony and Cleopatra 1963,Je 21,33:1
Winter's Tale, The 1963,Ag 16,14:1
After the Fall 1964,Ja 24,18:1
Passion of Josef D, The 1964,F 12,29:1
But for Whom Charlie 1964,Mr 13,42:2
Hamlet 1964,Je 17,49:1
Midsummer Night's Dream, A 1964,Je 30,23:2
Othello 1964,Jl 15,29:1
Changeling, The 1964,O 30,32:2
Henry V 1965,Je 29,27:2
Coriolanus 1965,Jl 15,23:1
Troilus and Cressida 1965,Ag 13,17:1
All's Well That Ends Well 1966,Je 17,39:1
Measure for Measure 1966,Jl 14,27:1
That Summer-That Fall 1967,Mr 17,33:1
Volpone 1967,Je 30,29:1
King John 1967,Jl 14,19:1
Amram, David (Lyricist)
Romeo and Juliet 1957,Je 28,30:2
Macbeth 1957,Ag 16,11:2
Twelfth Night 1958,Ag 7,21:4
Beaux' Stratagem, The 1959,F 25,35:4
Henry IV 1960,Mr 2,42:1
Hamlet 1961,Mr 17,17:1
As You Like It 1961,Je 17,13:2
Tempest, The 1962,Jl 17,18:2
King Lear 1962,Ag 14,35:1
Winter's Tale, The 1963,Ag 16,14:1
Hamlet 1964,Je 17,49:1
Amster, James
Bursting the Barriers 1930,My 7,25:1
Amster, Morton
Mexican Mural; Moonlight Scene 1942,Ap 27,19:2
Amsterdam, Morey
Hilarities 1948,S 10,20:2
Elliott Murphy's Aquashow 1956,Je 20,26:2
Amsterdam, Morey (Miscellaneous)
Hilarities 1948,S 10,20:2
Amundsen, Monte
Juno 1959,Mr 10,41:1
Cafe Crown 1964,Ap 18,32:1
Amundsen, Oscar
Polly 1925,O 12,19:1
Amundson, Ethel V
Vagabond King, The 1935,N 29,22:7
Amy, Frank
Janie 1942,S 11,24:2
Amyx, Hurst
Mulatto 1935,Ag 8,13:2
Then Came the Dawn 1935,Ag 29,25:4
Mulatto 1935,O 25,25:2
Lady Luck 1936,Ap 16,21:2
Home Sweet Home 1936,Jl 1,29:2
Anabel, Elfrida
Pirates of Penzance, The 1936,Ap 21,27:5
Anania, Joan (Lyricist)
What a Killing 1961,Mr 28,41:1
Anania, John
Sweethearts 1947,Ja 22,31:2
Christine 1960,Ap 29,27:1
What a Killing 1961,Mr 28,41:1
Fly Blackbird 1962,Ap 29,II,1:1
Skyscraper 1965,N 15,48:1
Penny Wars, The 1969,O 16,52:1

Anania, John—Cont
Applause 1970,Mr 31,35:1
Anastasseva, Margarit
Kremlin Chimes 1965,F 25,23:1
Anatole Mayorov's Skating Bears
Moscow Circus on Ice 1970,D 9,63:1
Anatra, Charles
Trumpets and Drums 1969,O 13,52:1
Lady From Maxim's, The 1970,Je 1,41:1
Ancharoff, Alexander
Forbidden Melody 1936,N 3,33:1
Anchutina, Leda
Great Lady 1938,D 2,26:6
Ancker, Louis
Beyond Evil 1926,Je 8,23:2
Ancona, Tony
Darkness at Noon 1951,Ja 15,13:4
Anden, Mathew
Dreigroschenoper, Die 1965,Mr 12,24:1
Ander, Calvin
Enemy of the People, An 1958,F 26,24:2
Living Premise, The 1963,Je 14,34:1
Ander, Charlotte
Midsummer Night's Dream, A 1925,Mr 8,VII,2:1
Broadway 1928,Ap 15,IX,4:7
Blue Beard 1929,Jl 7,VIII,2:1
Anderman, Maureen
Othello 1970,Je 22,43:1
Devil's Disciple, The 1970,Je 30,48:1
Othello 1970,S 15,51:1
Anders, Glenn
Scrambled Wives 1920,Ag 6,16:1
Ghost Between, The 1921,Mr 23,11:2
Demi-Virgin, The 1921,O 19,22:1
Cold Feet 1923,My 22,14:2
Cold Feet 1923,My 22,14:3
What's Your Wife Doing? 1923,O 2,10:3
Hell-Bent Fer Heaven 1924,Ja 5,10:1
So This Is Politics 1924,Je 17,22:2
Bewitched 1924,O 2,26:3
They Knew What They Wanted 1924,N 25,27:1
Constant Nymph, The 1926,D 10,31:1
Constant Nymph, The 1926,D 19,VII,3:1
Constant Nymph, The 1927,Mr 6,VIII,1:4
Murray Hill 1927,S 30,29:1
Strange Interlude 1928,Ja 31,28:1
Strange Interlude 1928,F 5,VIII,1:1
Dynamo 1929,F 12,22:1
Hotel Universe 1930,Ap 15,29:1
Farewell to Arms, A 1930,S 23,30:3
In the Meantime 1930,D 7,IX,1:6
Midnight 1930,D 30,25:1
Lonely Way, The 1931,F 22,VIII,4:1
Another Language 1932,Ap 26,25:3
Another Language 1932,My 15,VIII,1:1
Another Language 1933,My 9,20:2
Love and Babies 1933,Ag 23,21:4
I Was Waiting for You 1933,N 14,23:3
False Dreams, Farewell 1934,Ja 16,18:3
Moor Born 1934,Ap 4,26:4
Moor Born 1934,Ap 8,X,2:7
Sleeping Clergyman, A 1934,O 9,16:1
On to Fortune 1935,Ja 15,23:2
On to Fortune 1935,F 5,22:2
If This Be Treason 1935,Jl 30,17:1
There's Wisdom in Women 1935,O 31,17:1
Call It a Day 1936,Ja 21,26:7
Call It a Day 1936,Ja 29,15:2
Call It a Day 1936,F 9,X,1:1
Masque of Kings, The 1937,Ja 31,XI,2:1
Masque of the Kings, The 1937,F 9,19:4
Three Waltzes 1937,D 27,10:2
I Am Different 1938,Ag 28,IX,2:5
Skylark 1939,O 12,32:2
Get Away Old Man 1943,N 25,40:2
Career Angel 1944,My 24,23:7
Soldier's Wife 1944,O 5,18:6
Soldier's Wife 1944,O 15,II,1:1
Light Up the Sky 1948,N 19,34:2
One Bright Day 1952,Mr 20,37:2
Remarkable Mr Pennypacker, The 1953,D 31,11:2
Time Remembered 1957,N 13,41:2
Time Remembered 1957,N 24,II,1:1
Visit, The 1960,Mr 9,38:3
Anders, Karen
Almost Crazy 1955,Je 21,37:1
Anders, Katie
Of Thee I Sing 1969,Mr 8,19:1
Anders, Margo
Fighting Cock, The 1959,D 9,57:3
Anders, Richard
Sunset 1966,My 13,34:1
Anders, Rudolph
Russian People, The 1942,D 30,17:2
Counterattack 1943,F 4,27:2
Andersen, Hans Christian (Original Author)
Chinese Nightingale, The 1934,O 6,20:4
Emperor's New Clothes, The 1941,D 27,15:5
Emperor's New Clothes, The 1950,Je 20,23:2
Andersen, Lillian
Vie Parisienne, La 1945,Ja 13,14:5
Anderson, Alan
Idiot's Delight 1937,Ag 10,22:7
Star-Wagon, The 1937,S 30,18:5

Anderson, Alan (Director)
Barefoot in Athens 1951,N 1,35:2
Anderson, Andy
She Loves Me Not 1933,N 21,22:4
On Borrowed Time 1938,F 4,16:4
Anderson, Andy (Miscellaneous)
Uncle Willie 1956,D 21,17:1
Merry Widow, The 1957,Ap 11,36:6
Anderson, Angela (Producer)
To Damascus 1961,F 15,40:2
Anderson, Ann
Go West, Young Man 1923,N 13,25:2
Launcelot and Elaine 1930,Mr 10,24:3
Anderson, Anne Renee
Lend an Ear 1948,D 17,38:2
Anderson, Arden
H M S Pinafore 1957,My 1,42:6
Utopia, Limited 1960,Ap 8,27:2
Yeomen of the Guard, The 1961,Ap 28,23:1
Mikado, The 1961,My 5,23:1
Grand Duke, The 1961,My 12,24:1
Princess Ida 1961,My 19,23:1
Iolanthe 1961,My 26,29:6
H M S Pinafore 1961,Je 9,29:5
Student Prince, The 1961,Jl 14,14:1
Anderson, Arlene
Bloomer Girl 1944,O 6,18:5
Anderson, Arthur
Second Hurricane 1937,Ap 22,18:4
Julius Caesar 1937,N 12,26:6
Shoemaker's Holiday, The 1938,Ja 3,17:2
Good Neighbor 1941,O 22,26:2
Doctor's Dilemma, The 1955,Ja 12,22:1
Last Love of Don Juan, The 1955,N 24,40:1
Lovers, Villains and Fools: A Shakespearean
  Variety Show 1956,O 24,44:7
Winkelberg 1958,Ja 15,26:2
Nekros 1960,O 26,44:1
Tiger Rag, The 1961,F 17,20:2
Anderson, Augustus
Wandering Jew, The 1921,O 27,22:1
Anderson, Barbara
Othello 1945,My 23,25:4
Anderson, Barbara (Playwright)
Tall Kentuckian, The 1953,Je 17,30:1
Anderson, Bette
Day Before Spring, The 1945,N 23,27:2
Anderson, Buck
Winterset 1966,F 10,32:2
Anderson, Burnes (Playwright)
One Is a Lonely Number 1964,Je 19,37:3
Anderson, Carl
Boubouroche 1921,N 29,20:1
Little Jessie James 1923,Ag 16,10:4
Anderson, Catherine
Sheppey 1944,Ap 19,27:2
Anderson, Charles
Commedia Dell' Arte 1957,Jl 5,13:2
Anderson, Chris F (Director)
Consul, The 1957,S 4,40:3
Anderson, Chris F (Producer)
Rosalie 1957,Je 26,28:2
Anderson, Claire
Pal Joey 1940,D 26,22:2
Mexican Hayride 1944,Ja 29,9:6
Anderson, Clarica
Hate Planters 1933,My 26,24:5
Anderson, Cletus (Costume Designer)
Simple Life, A 1964,My 18,36:1
Anderson, Clinton
Throng o' Scarlet 1947,D 2,37:2
Coast of Illyria, The 1949,Ap 13,39:2
Saint Joan 1950,Mr 4,10:6
Goodbye Charlie 1959,D 17,50:1
Fourth Avenue North 1961,S 28,50:2
Crucible, The 1964,Ap 7,30:2
Anderson, Dallas
Immortal Thief, The 1926,O 4,21:1
Caponsacchi 1926,O 27,24:2
Enemy of the People, An 1927,O 4,32:5
Hamlet 1928,Ja 5,33:2
Henry V 1928,Mr 16,26:2
Light of Asia, The 1928,O 10,32:2
Wild Duck, The 1928,N 19,17:1
Hedda Gabler 1929,F 4,20:3
Lady From the Sea, The 1929,Mr 19,36:1
Richelieu 1929,D 26,20:3
Richelieu 1934,My 22,28:1
Anderson, David
Portrait in Black 1947,My 15,30:2
Men We Marry, The 1948,Ja 17,11:2
Elizabeth the Queen 1966,N 4,30:1
Applause 1970,Mr 31,35:1
Anderson, David (Lighting Director)
Fun City 1968,Mr 7,53:2
Anderson, David-Rhys
Birds, The 1966,Jl 1,40:1
Anderson, Del
Paint Your Wagon 1951,N 13,32:2
Wonderful Town 1953,F 26,22:3
New Girl in Town 1957,My 15,40:1
Goldilocks 1958,O 13,33:1

Anderson, Dolores
Boys From Syracuse, The 1938,N 24,36:1
Anderson, Dorian
Medea 1920,Mr 23,12:2
Within Four Walls 1923,Ap 18,24:1
Anderson, Doris (Playwright)
Cold in Sables 1931,D 24,20:7
Anderson, Douglas
Seagull, The 1968,Jl 25,27:2
Measure for Measure 1969,Je 13,41:3
Anderson, E M
Espanola 1921,D 30,13:1
Anderson, Edmund (Miscellaneous)
Beauty Part, The 1962,D 28,5:2
Anderson, Edmund G
Fiesta 1933,D 16,12:2
Anderson, Edmund L (Producer)
Close Quarters 1939,Mr 7,19:2
Anderson, Elman
Colette 1970,O 15,58:1
Anderson, Elman (Miscellaneous)
Shoemaker's Holiday, The 1967,Mr 3,25:1
Anderson, Elman (Musical Director)
Shoemaker's Holiday, The 1967,Mr 3,25:1
Anderson, Ernest
Diamond Lil 1928,Ap 10,32:1
Rap, The 1931,Ap 7,31:2
Bloody Laughter 1931,D 5,20:6
Wolves 1932,Ja 7,26:3
Anderson, Esther
39 Steps 1938,Mr 12,13:1
Anderson, Eunice
Cock-A-Doodle-Doo 1949,F 28,16:5
Maids, The 1963,N 15,29:1
Anderson, Evelyn Norion (Costume Designer)
Jo 1964,F 13,25:1
Anderson, Everett
Hats Off to Ice 1944,Je 23,15:2
Anderson, Forbush (Costume Designer)
Hamlet 1928,Je 2,11:3
Anderson, Forbush (Scenic Designer)
Hamlet 1928,Je 2,11:3
Bourgeois Gentilhomme, Le 1929,Mr 17,30:4
Anderson, Frances
On the Stairs 1922,S 26,18:2
Trojan Women, The 1938,Ja 25,24:2
Shakespeare's Merchant 1939 1939,Ja 10,16:3
Anderson, Frank
Sun Showers 1923,F 6,14:2
Anderson, G
As You Like It 1923,Ap 24,24:1
Anderson, Garland (Playwright)
Appearances 1925,O 15,27:3
Appearances 1930,Mr 30,VIII,2:6
Anderson, George
Passing Show of 1922, The 1922,S 21,18:2
Gypsy Jim 1924,Ja 15,17:4
Vogues of 1924 1924,Mr 28,14:3
Strawberry Blonde, The 1927,F 8,20:3
Congratulations 1929,My 1,28:4
Nina Rosa 1930,My 31,19:3
Nina Rosa 1930,S 22,22:5
Melo 1931,Ap 17,26:6
Her Man of Wax 1933,O 12,32:3
Laburnum Grove 1935,Ja 15,23:5
Night of January 16 1935,S 17,26:4
Six Characters in Search of an Author
  1961,My 11,43:1
Two Executioners, The 1964,Mr 25,46:2
Anderson, George (Director)
Strawberry Blonde, The 1927,F 8,20:3
Anderson, Georgine
Measure for Measure 1967,F 15,37:1
Hamlet 1967,F 17,44:1
Romeo and Juliet 1967,F 22,18:1
Anderson, Gerald
Love Goes to Press 1947,Ja 2,22:2
Anderson, Gretta
Keep Shufflin' 1928,F 28,18:3
Anderson, Gwen
Janie 1942,S 11,24:2
Decision 1944,F 3,23:2
Decision 1944,F 13,II,1:1
Deep Mrs Sykes, The 1945,Mr 20,22:6
Much Ado About Nothing 1955,Ag 20,20:4
Anderson, Gwen D
Slave Ship 1969,N 22,46:1
Anderson, Hans Christian (Original Author)
Big Claus and Little Claus 1931,Mr 1,VIII,3:1
Anderson, Harold
City of Kings 1949,F 18,27:2
Finis for Oscar Wilde 1964,F 15,15:1
Anderson, Harold L (Playwright)
Smell the Sweet Savor 1940,F 3,8:4
War and Peace 1942,My 22,26:3
Anderson, Harry
Student Prince, The 1924,D 3,25:3
Holka Polka 1925,O 15,27:2
Forsaking All Others 1933,Mr 2,21:2
Anderson, Harry C
All Good Americans 1933,D 6,29:2
Anderson, Herbert
Caine Mutiny Court-Martial, The 1954,Ja 21,27:2

Anderson, Hilding (Composer)
Louisiana Lady 1947,Je 3,35:2
Anderson, Hilding (Musical Director)
Louisiana Lady 1947,Je 3,35:2
Anderson, Hugh A (Playwright)
Mystery Square 1929,Ap 5,28:3
Anderson, Ida
Pansy 1929,My 15,36:3
Paid Companions 1931,Je 23,28:4
Anderson, Jack (Lighting Director)
Family Portrait 1959,My 6,48:2
Anderson, Jack (Miscellaneous)
Tattooed Countess, The 1961,My 4,40:2
Anderson, James
In Times Square 1931,N 24,29:3
Anderson, Jane
Candida 1946,D 4,44:2
Othello 1946,D 4,44:2
Anderson, Jean
Family Portrait 1959,My 6,48:2
Anderson, Jeffrey
Macbeth 1955,O 8,12:6
Anderson, Jeremy
Sacco-Vanzetti 1969,F 9,78:1
Anderson, Jim
Brig, The 1963,My 16,40:1
Home Movies 1964,My 12,32:1
Anderson, Jim (Miscellaneous)
Frankenstein 1968,O 3,54:1
Anderson, Joan
Thurber Carnival, A 1960,S 13,41:1
Tiger Rag, The 1961,F 17,20:2
Anderson, John
Processional 1937,O 14,23:1
Emperor's Clothes, The 1953,F 10,24:2
High Button Shoes 1955,Mr 12,10:6
Last Love of Don Juan, The 1955,N 24,40:1
Thor, With Angels 1956,O 15,29:4
Tom Paine 1969,Mr 30,71:2
Anderson, John (Playwright)
Inspector General, The 1930,D 24,19:2
Collision 1932,F 17,19:2
Anderson, John G
Awhile to Work 1937,Mr 20,23:1
Anderson, John Murray (Director)
Greenwich Village Follies 1921,S 1,18:3
Greenwich Village Follies 1924,S 17,16:1
Music Box Revue 1924,D 2,23:3
Dearest Enemy 1925,S 19,9:2
Hello, Daddy! 1928,D 27,26:5
Ziegfeld Follies 1934,Ja 5,24:3
Life Begins at 8:40 1934,Ag 7,20:7
Life Begins at 8:40 1934,Ag 12,IX,1:1
Life Begins at 8:40 1934,Ag 28,24:2
Life Begins at 8:40 1934,S 2,IX,1:1
Thumbs Up! 1934,D 28,24:1
Jumbo 1935,N 18,20:2
Ziegfeld Follies 1936,Ja 5,IX,3:1
Ziegfeld Follies 1936,Ja 31,17:2
Ziegfeld Follies 1936,S 15,37:1
Home and Beauty 1937,F 3,26:2
Let's Play Fair 1938,Ja 19,26:4
One for the Money 1939,F 6,9:2
Two for the Show 1940,F 9,14:2
Two for the Show 1940,F 18,IX,1:1
New Aquacade Revue, The 1940,My 13,20:5
All in Fun 1940,D 28,11:2
Ziegfeld Follies 1943,Ap 2,16:2
Laffing Room Only 1944,D 25,15:4
Firebird of Florence 1945,Mr 23,13:4
Three to Make Ready 1946,Mr 8,16:2
Heaven on Earth 1948,S 17,29:2
New Faces of 1952 1952,My 17,23:2
New Faces of 1952 1952,My 25,II,1:1
Two's Company 1952,D 21,II,3:1
John Murray Anderson's Almanac 1953,D 11,42:2
Anderson, John Murray (Lighting Director)
One for the Money 1939,F 6,9:2
Two for the Show 1940,F 9,14:2
Heaven on Earth 1948,S 17,29:2
Anderson, John Murray (Lyricist)
Greenwich Village Follies 1920,Ag 31,7:3
Greenwich Village Follies 1922,S 13,18:2
Jack and Jill 1923,Mr 23,17:2
Greenwich Village Follies 1923,S 21,4:6
Greenwich Village Follies 1924,S 17,16:1
Murray Anderson's Almanac 1929,Ag 15,20:3
Anderson, John Murray (Miscellaneous)
Jumbo 1935,N 24,IX,1:1
One for the Money 1939,F 6,9:2
Two for the Show 1940,F 9,14:2
Sunny River 1941,D 5,28:2
Ziegfeld Follies 1943,Ap 2,16:2
Three to Make Ready 1946,Mr 8,16:2
Two's Company 1952,D 16,43:5
Anderson, John Murray (Musical Director)
Keep Moving 1934,Ag 24,10:2
Anderson, John Murray (Playwright)
Greenwich Village Follies 1920,Ag 31,7:3
Greenwich Village Follies 1921,S 1,18:3
Greenwich Village Follies 1924,S 17,16:1
Greenwich Village Follies 1924,S 21,VII,1:1

Fanfare 1932,Je 24,15:2
Anderson, John Murray (Producer)
What's in a Name? 1920,Mr 20,14:2
Murray Anderson's Almanac 1929,Ag 4,VIII,1:6
Murray Anderson's Almanac 1929,Ag 15,20:3
Almanac 1954,Ja 3,II,1:1
Anderson, Jonathan
Skin of Our Teeth, The 1955,Ag 18,16:1
Visit, The 1958,My 6,40:1
Anderson, Jonathan (Miscellaneous)
Annie Get Your Gun 1966,Je 1,42:2
Anderson, Jonathan (Musical Director)
Hang Down Your Head and Die 1964,O 19,38:1
Carousel 1966,D 16,56:2
Finian's Rainbow 1967,Ap 6,44:1
South Pacific 1967,Je 13,56:1
Brigadoon 1967,D 14,59:2
King and I, The 1968,My 24,39:1
Anderson, Judith
Peter Weston 1923,S 20,5:2
Peter Weston 1923,S 30,II,1:1
Cobra 1924,Ap 23,24:1
Cobra 1924,Ap 27,VIII,1:1
Dove, The 1925,F 12,17:3
Dove, The 1925,F 22,VIII,1:1
Dove, The 1925,Ag 25,12:2
Vaudeville (Palace) 1926,Je 8,23:1
Thieves 1926,Je 8,23:1
Behold the Bridegroom 1927,D 27,24:1
Behold the Bridegroom 1928,Ja 1,VIII,1:1
Anna 1928,My 17,25:2
As You Desire Me 1930,N 30,IX,3:6
As You Desire Me 1931,Ja 29,21:2
Mourning Becomes Electra 1932,F 21,VIII,2:6
Mourning Becomes Electra; Hunted, The
1932,My 10,25:2
Mourning Becomes Electra; Haunted, The
1932,My 10,25:2
Mourning Becomes Electra; Homecoming
1932,My 10,25:2
Mourning Becomes Electra 1932,My 22,VIII,1:1
Firebird 1932,N 22,25:2
Conquest 1933,F 20,11:3
Mask and the Face, The 1933,My 9,20:2
Drums Begin, The 1933,N 25,10:5
Come of Age 1934,Ja 13,16:6
Divided by Three 1934,S 28,26:3
Divided by Three 1934,O 3,24:2
Old Maid, The 1935,Ja 8,26:1
Hamlet 1936,O 1,28:3
Hamlet 1936,O 9,30:2
Macbeth 1937,N 27,21:3
Macbeth 1937,D 19,XI,3:7
Family Portrait 1939,Mr 9,18:4
Family Portrait 1939,Mr 19,XI,1:1
Macbeth 1941,N 12,30:2
Macbeth 1941,N 23,IX,1:1
Macbeth 1942,Je 3,26:4
Three Sisters, The 1942,D 22,31:2
Three Sisters, The 1942,D 27,VIII,1:1
Medea 1947,O 21,27:2
Medea 1947,O 26,II,1:1
Medea 1949,My 3,31:2
Tower Beyond Tragedy, The 1950,N 27,29:1
Tower Beyond Tragedy, The 1950,D 10,II,5:1
Medea 1951,S 14,22:5
Medea 1951,S 23,II,3:1
Come of Age 1952,Ja 24,22:2
John Brown's Body 1952,N 3,25:8
John Brown's Body 1952,D 16,43:5
John Brown's Body 1953,F 16,17:2
John Brown's Body 1953,F 22,II,1:1
In the Summer House 1953,D 30,17:1
In the Summer House 1954,Ja 10,II,1:1
Medea 1955,Je 16,35:4
Comes a Day 1958,N 7,22:1
Seagull, The 1960,Ag 24,33:2
Oresteia 1966,Je 30,29:1
Elizabeth the Queen 1966,N 4,30:1
Anderson, Judith (Producer)
Macbeth 1942,Je 3,26:4
Anderson, Katherine
Connecticut Yankee, A 1943,N 18,30:2
Deep Mrs Sykes, The 1945,Mr 20,22:6
Miracle in the Mountains 1947,Ap 26,10:2
Anybody Home 1949,F 26,10:5
Courtin' Time 1951,Je 14,30:2
Grey-Eyed People, The 1952,D 18,41:2
Anderson, Laura
Green Pastures, The 1935,F 27,16:2
Anderson, Lawrence
Berkeley Square 1926,O 24,VIII,2:1
Romeo and Juliet 1927,Ja 2,VII,2:5
Anderson, Leroy (Composer)
Naughty-Naught '00 1946,O 21,27:5
Goldilocks 1958,O 13,33:1
Goldilocks 1958,O 19,II,1:1
Anderson, Leroy (Miscellaneous)
Goldilocks 1958,O 13,33:1
Anderson, Leroy (Musical Director)
Naughty-Naught '00 1946,O 21,27:5

Anderson, Leslie G
Little Theatre Tournament; Sightseers
1929,My 8,34:4
Anderson, Lindsay (Director)
Home 1970,Je 20,23:1
Home 1970,Ag 17,32:1
Contractor, The 1970,Ag 17,32:1
Home 1970,N 18,41:1
Anderson, M J
Her Tin Soldier 1933,Ap 7,22:6
Anderson, Margaret
Party, A 1933,Ag 24,18:4
Old Maid, The 1935,Ja 8,26:1
And Now Goodbye 1937,F 3,26:4
Anderson, Marion
Pelleas and Melisande 1957,F 20,38:1
Anderson, Marjorie
Murder in the Cathedral 1938,F 17,16:2
Anderson, Mary
Guest in the House 1942,F 25,25:2
Lunatics and Lovers 1954,D 14,44:2
Love's Labour's Lost 1961,Je 23,19:1
Anderson, Maxwell (Lyricist)
Knickerbocker Holiday 1938,O 20,26:2
Whores, Wars & Tin Pan Alley 1969,Je 17,37:1
Anderson, Maxwell (Original Author)
Knickerbocker Holiday 1938,O 20,26:2
Anderson, Maxwell (Playwright)
White Desert 1923,O 19,17:3
What Price Glory 1924,S 6,14:3
What Price Glory 1924,S 21,VII,1:1
What Price Glory 1924,S 28,VII,1:1
Outside Looking In 1925,S 8,28:1
Outside Looking In 1925,S 13,VIII,1:1
First Flight 1925,S 18,26:2
Buccaneer, The 1925,S 20,VIII,2:4
First Flight 1925,S 27,VII,1:1
Buccaneer, The 1925,O 3,10:2
Saturday's Children 1927,Ja 27,13:1
Saturday's Children 1927,F 6,VII,1:1
Gods of the Lightning 1928,O 25,27:2
Gypsy 1929,Ja 15,22:2
Gypsy 1929,Ja 27,IX,1:1
What Price Glory 1929,Ap 28,IX,1:4
Outside Looking In 1929,Je 23,VIII,2:1
Marriage Recipe, The 1930,Ag 4,13:2
Elizabeth the Queen 1930,O 5,IX,4:6
Elizabeth the Queen 1930,N 4,37:1
Elizabeth the Queen 1930,N 9,IX,1:1
Gods of the Lightning 1931,F 19,21:4
Night Over Taos 1932,Mr 10,25:3
Both Your Houses 1933,Mr 7,20:3
Both Your Houses 1933,Mr 12,IX,1:1
Both Your Houses 1933,My 23,22:2
Mary of Scotland 1933,N 19,IX,2:5
Mary of Scotland 1933,N 28,28:3
Mary of Scotland 1933,D 3,IX,5:1
Valley Forge 1934,N 27,26:4
Valley Forge 1934,D 11,28:3
Valley Forge 1934,D 23,IX,1:1
Saturday's Children 1935,Jl 30,17:2
Winterset 1935,S 26,19:2
Winterset 1935,O 6,XI,1:1
Elizabeth and Essex 1935,N 9,18:8
Winterset 1936,Ap 5,IX,1:1
Winterset 1936,Je 2,35:2
Elizabeth the Queen 1936,Jl 28,23:4
Elizabeth the Queen 1936,Ag 4,15:2
Wingless Victory, The 1936,N 25,17:5
Wingless Victory, The 1936,D 24,20:2
High Tor 1936,D 31,20:3
Wingless Victory, The 1937,Ja 3,X,1:1
High Tor 1937,Ja 11,15:2
High Tor 1937,Ja 17,X,1:1
Masque of Kings, The 1937,Ja 19,28:3
Masque of Kings, The 1937,Ja 31,XI,2:1
Masque of the Kings, The 1937,F 9,19:4
Elizabeth the Queen 1937,Ag 25,24:3
Star-Wagon, The 1937,S 17,28:5
Star-Wagon, The 1937,S 30,18:5
Star-Wagon, The 1937,O 10,XI,1:1
Masque of Kings, The 1938,My 8,X,1:7
Knickerbocker Holiday 1938,O 2,IX,3:3
Knickerbocker Holiday 1938,N 20,IX,1:1
Key Largo 1939,O 31,26:6
Key Largo 1939,N 19,X,3:4
Key Largo 1939,N 28,30:2
Key Largo 1939,D 3,IX,5:3
Key Largo 1939,D 10,X,3:1
Journey to Jerusalem 1940,O 7,21:2
Candle in the Wind 1941,S 16,19:6
Elizabeth the Queen 1941,O 17,27:2
Candle in the Wind 1941,O 23,26:2
Candle in the Wind 1941,N 2,IX,1:1
Key Largo 1942,Je 21,VIII,1:8
Eve of St Mark, The 1942,O 8,30:2
Eve of St Mark, The 1942,O 18,VIII,1:1
Eve of St Mark, The 1943,Ja 10,VIII,3:5
Storm Operation 1944,Ja 12,28:2
Truckline Cafe 1946,F 28,19:4
Winterset 1946,O 27,II,2:4
Joan of Lorraine 1946,N 19,40:2
Joan of Lorraine 1946,N 24,II,1:1

Anderson, Maxwell (Playwright)—Cont

Joan of Lorraine 1947,N 14,29:1
Anne of the Thousand Days 1948,D 9,49:2
Anne of the Thousand Days 1948,D 19,II,3:1
What Price Glory 1949,Mr 3,33:2
Anne of the Thousand Days 1949,S 18,II,1:1
Lost in the Stars 1949,O 31,21:2
Lost in the Stars 1949,N 6,II,1:1
Barefoot in Athens 1951,N 1,35:2
Barefoot in Athens 1951,N 11,II,1:1
Bad Seed, The 1954,D 9,42:1
Bad Seed, The 1954,D 19,II,3:1
Joan of Lorraine 1955,Mr 26,12:2
Day the Money Stopped, The 1958,F 21,19:4
Golden Six, The 1958,My 2,31:5
Golden Six, The 1958,O 27,31:2
Winterset 1966,F 10,32:2
Elizabeth the Queen 1966,N 4,30:1
Winterset 1968,Jl 23,28:2

Anderson, Maxwell (Producer)

Abe Lincoln in Illinois 1938,O 17,12:2
Time Remembered 1957,N 13,41:2
Rope Dancers, The 1957,N 21,39:1

Anderson, May

Padre, The 1926,D 28,16:3

Anderson, Melville J

Wandering Jew, The 1921,O 27,22:1

Anderson, Mia

Tartuffe 1968,Je 12,39:1
Tartuffe 1968,Je 23,II,1:1
Five on the Black Hand Side 1970,Ja 2,32:2

Anderson, Milan (Costume Designer)

Full Moon in March, A 1960,S 20,48:1
Purgatory 1960,S 20,48:1

Anderson, Mildred

Dear Brutus 1926,Jl 15,21:3

Anderson, Mme

Chauve-Souris 1923,S 4,12:1

Anderson, Myrtle

Run, Little Chillun 1943,Ag 14,6:1

Anderson, Neva

Merry Duchess, The 1943,Je 24,25:1

Anderson, Ole

Anna Christie 1921,N 3,22:1

Anderson, Paul

Brigadoon 1947,Mr 14,28:2
Minnie and Mr Williams 1948,O 28,37:2
Uniform of Flesh 1949,Ja 31,15:2
She Stoops to Conquer 1949,D 29,21:3
Corn Is Green, The 1950,Ja 12,33:2
Devil's Disciple, The 1950,Ja 26,23:2
Heiress, The 1950,F 9,34:2
Pursuit of Happiness, The 1952,Mr 22,9:2

Anderson, Percy (Costume Designer)

Trial by Jury 1934,S 14,24:3
Yeomen of the Guard, The 1934,S 21,28:3
Ruddigore 1934,S 25,25:2
Princess Ida; Castle Adamant 1934,S 28,26:3
Yeomen of the Guard, The 1936,S 15,37:2
Princess Ida 1936,O 13,32:2

Anderson, Phyllis (Miscellaneous)

Come Back, Little Sheba 1950,F 16,28:5

Anderson, Presco

Great Lover, The 1932,O 12,27:3

Anderson, Quentin

Mary of Scotland 1933,N 28,28:3

Anderson, Richard

Royal Family, The 1936,Ag 12,15:1
Highest Tree, The 1959,N 5,41:1

Anderson, Richard (Costume Designer)

Soldiers 1968,My 2,58:1
Charley's Aunt 1970,Jl 6,38:1

Anderson, Robert

Theodora, the Queen 1934,F 1,15:3
Devil's Disciple, The 1950,Ja 26,23:2
Anna Christie 1952,Ja 10,33:1
Flies, The 1954,S 10,18:2

Anderson, Robert (Costume Designer)

Love Your Crooked Neighbor 1969,D 30,40:1

Anderson, Robert (Playwright)

Come Marching Home 1946,My 20,18:6
Dance Me a Song 1950,Ja 21,10:5
All Summer Long 1953,Ja 29,23:1
Tea and Sympathy 1953,O 1,35:1
Tea and Sympathy 1953,O 11,II,1:1
Tea and Sympathy 1954,Ag 15,II,1:1
All Summer Long 1954,S 24,26:2
All Summer Long 1954,O 3,II,1:1
Tea and Sympathy 1956,D 4,50:1
Tea and Sympathy 1957,Ap 26,22:5
Silent Night, Lonely Night 1959,D 4,36:1
Silent Night, Lonely Night 1959,D 13,II,3:1
Days Between, The 1965,Je 4,39:1
Days Between, The 1965,Je 27,II,1:1
You Know I Can't Hear You When the Water's
   Running; I'm Herbert 1967,Mr 14,54:1
You Know I Can't Hear You When the Water's
   Running; I'll Be Home for Christmas
   1967,Mr 14,54:1
You Know I Can't Hear You When the Water's
   Running; Shock of Recognition, The
   1967,Mr 14,54:1

You Know I Can't Hear You When the Water's
   Running; Footsteps of Doves, The
   1967,Mr 14,54:1
You Know I Can't Hear You When the Water's
   Running 1967,Mr 26,II,1:1
I Never Sang for My Father 1968,Ja 26,30:1
I Never Sang for My Father 1968,F 4,II,1:1
You Know I Can't Hear You When the Water's
   Running 1968,Mr 29,33:1

Anderson, Robert (Producer)

Time Remembered 1957,N 13,41:2
Rope Dancers, The 1957,N 21,39:1

Anderson, Roger

Young Go First, The 1935,My 29,16:2

Anderson, Ross

Infernal Machine, The 1954,Mr 22,22:2

Anderson, Russ

Sunny River 1941,D 5,28:2

Anderson, Ruth

Moon Vine, The 1943,F 12,22:2

Anderson, Sam

Porgy and Bess 1935,O 11,30:2

Anderson, Sara

Storm Operation 1944,Ja 12,28:2
Lower North 1944,Ag 26,15:4
Magic Touch, The 1947,S 4,30:1

Anderson, Sherwood (Original Author)

Winesburg, Ohio 1958,F 6,22:2

Anderson, Sherwood (Playwright)

Triumph of the Egg, The 1925,F 11,19:3

Anderson, Terence

Anne of the Thousand Days 1948,D 9,49:2

Anderson, Terry

Mystery of the Finding of the Cross, The
   1959,Ja 16,35:2

Anderson, Thomas

Macbeth 1936,Ap 15,25:4
Native Son 1942,O 24,10:6
Set My People Free 1948,N 4,38:2
Dodo Bird, The 1967,D 9,62:1
Peddler, The 1967,D 9,62:1

Anderson, Tom (Lighting Director)

World's My Oyster, The 1956,Ag 10,10:4

Anderson, Vienna

Cock-A-Doodle Dandy 1955,N 4,26:5

Anderson, Viola

Run, Little Chillun 1943,Ag 14,6:1

Anderson, Violet

Masked Woman, The 1922,D 23,14:2

Anderson, Walt (Playwright)

Me, Candido! 1956,O 16,36:2

Anderson, Warner

Medea 1920,Mr 23,12:2
Within Four Walls 1923,Ap 18,24:1
Criminals, The 1941,D 22,24:3
War and Peace 1942,My 22,26:3
Broken Journey 1942,Je 24,22:2
Remains to Be Seen 1951,O 4,37:1

Anderson, William

Three Sisters, The 1930,Ja 9,22:2
Antigone 1930,Ap 25,28:4

Anderson-Broeckling, Arden

Pirates of Penzance, The 1966,My 24,54:1
H M S Pinafore 1966,Je 8,41:2

Anderson-Ivantzoff, Elizabeth (Director)

Bridal Veil, The 1928,Ja 27,15:2
Boeuf sur le Toit, Le 1930,Ap 25,28:4

Anderton, Joseph G

Time of Their Lives 1937,O 26,19:1

Andes, Keith

Chocolate Soldier, The 1947,Mr 13,34:2
Maggie 1953,F 19,20:2
Wildcat 1960,D 17,20:2

Andes, Oliver

Love's Labour's Lost 1953,F 5,20:3

Andonian, Lucy

Kismet 1953,D 4,2:4

Andor, Paul

Private Life of the Master Race, The
   1945,Je 13,28:3
Tom Sawyer - Ballad of the Mississippi
   1947,D 27,11:3
Mid-Summer 1953,Ja 22,19:1
Oh, Men! Oh, Women! 1953,D 18,37:2
Iceman Cometh, The 1956,My 8,38:1
Brothers Karamazov, The 1957,D 9,39:4
Golem, The 1959,F 26,38:2
Country Scandal, A 1960,My 6,21:8
Seven at Dawn, The 1961,Ap 18,43:1
Cat and the Canary, The 1965,Ja 5,26:1
Dreigroschenoper, Die 1965,Mr 12,24:1

Andrada, David

Rose Girl, The 1921,F 12,11:1
Light Wines and Beer 1930,N 11,28:6
Jayhawker 1934,N 6,34:2

Andrade, Ruby

Born Yesterday 1958,Mr 22,12:6

Andral, Paule

Tu m'ePouseras 1927,Mr 13,VII,2:7

Andre, Andree

Vaudeville (Palace) 1952,Ap 14,23:2

Andre, Ann

Song of Norway 1944,Ag 22,20:2

Andre, Ann—Cont

Red Mill, The 1945,O 17,16:2

Andre, Anthony

Sancho Panza 1923,N 27,23:1
Love's Call 1925,S 11,20:1
Goat Song 1926,Ja 26,18:1
Immortal Thief, The 1926,O 4,21:1
Black Crook, The 1929,Mr 12,26:5

Andre, Bonnie

Vaudeville (Palace) 1952,Ap 14,23:2

Andre, Frank

Who's Who, Baby? 1968,Ja 30,36:1
Now 1968,Je 6,53:1
We Bombed in New Haven 1968,O 17,51:1

Andre, George

Russian Bank 1940,My 25,20:2
Candle in the Wind 1941,O 23,26:2
Winter Soldiers 1942,N 30,19:2

Andre, Jacqueline

Native Son 1941,Mr 25,26:5
Only the Heart 1942,D 7,22:3
Three's a Family 1943,N 19,24:3
Walk Hard 1944,D 1,28:2
On Strivers' Row 1946,Mr 1,17:2
Walk Hard 1946,Mr 28,34:2
Power of Darkness, The 1948,O 11,28:2
For Heaven's Sake Mother 1948,N 17,33:4
Crucible, The 1953,Ja 23,15:2
Crucible, The 1953,Jl 2,20:2

Andre, Jill

Madam Will You Walk 1953,D 2,2:4
Picnic 1957,F 21,32:1
Dark of the Moon 1958,F 27,22:2

Andre, Margot

Polly 1925,O 12,19:1

Andre, Margot (Director)

Sparkin' 1931,Mr 4,33:2
Psychological Moment, The 1931,Mr 4,33:2

Andre, Margot (Miscellaneous)

Divina Pastora, La 1931,Mr 4,33:2

Andre, Paul

Holiday on Ice 1967,Ag 31,29:2
Holiday on Ice 1968,Ag 29,44:1
Holiday on Ice 1969,Ag 28,44:1

Andre, Paul-Antoine (Playwright)

Chanson d'Asie 1937,My 16,X,2:6

Andre, Victor (Playwright)

Masque et Visage 1927,Ap 3,VIII,4:7

Andre (Miscellaneous)

Smiling Madame Beudet 1921,My 1,VII,1:7

Andrea, Saint (Playwright)

On Foreign Soil 1927,D 24,8:2

Andreas, Luke

Don't Drink the Water 1966,N 18,37:1

Andreas, Otto (Composer)

From Vienna 1939,Je 21,26:2

Andreassi, Maria

Consul, The 1950,Mr 16,41:1
Consul, The 1950,Mr 26,II,1:1

Andree, Edith

O Evening Star 1936,Ja 9,24:6

Andree, Jean

Du Barry 1932,N 23,15:2

Andreini Trio

Night in Spain, A 1927,My 4,28:2

Andreivich, Valentin (Scenic Designer)

Obratsov Russian Pupper Theater in an Unusual
   Concert 1963,O 3,28:1

Andrele, Jiri

Apparition Theater of Prague, The 1966,N 17,56:2

Andreopoulos, B

Oedipus Tyrannus 1952,N 25,35:2

Andreopoulos, V

Screwball, The 1957,My 25,24:7

Andres, Barbara

Boy Friend, The 1970,Ap 15,54:1

Andres, Dwight F

Fiesta 1933,D 16,12:2

Andress, Judith

Circle of Chalk, The 1950,D 2,8:3

Andretta, Gage (Miscellaneous)

Phaedra 1967,My 22,50:2
God Bless You, Harold Fineberg 1969,Mr 31,30:2

Andreu, Helene

H M S Pinafore 1960,Ja 29,14:1
Pirates of Penzance, The 1966,My 24,54:1
H M S Pinafore 1966,Je 8,41:2
Trial by Jury 1966,Je 8,41:2
Iolanthe 1967,O 18,40:1
Mikado, The 1967,O 25,42:2
H M S Pinafore 1967,N 1,40:1

Andreu, Mariano (Costume Designer)

Much Ado About Nothing 1959,S 18,25:2

Andreu, Mariano (Scenic Designer)

All's Well That Ends Well 1955,Je 7,37:4
Much Ado About Nothing 1959,S 18,25:2

Andreva, Stella

Yours Is My Heart 1946,S 6,16:5

Andrew, George

Julius Caesar 1930,Ap 4,22:3

Andrew, Lois

Scandals 1939,Ag 29,17:2

Andrew, Maud
Captain Applejack 1921,D 31,14:2
Shall We Join the Ladies? 1925,Ja 14,19:1
Tell Me More 1925,Ap 14,27:3
Andrew, Stella
Ring Around the Moon 1950,N 24,30:1
To Dorothy, A Son 1951,N 20,37:2
Deep Blue Sea, The 1952,N 6,38:3
Andrew, Thomas
Yeomen of the Guard, The 1964,Mr 19,29:2
Patience 1964,Mr 26,42:1
Andrews, A G
Tendresse, La 1922,S 26,18:1
Pasteur 1923,Mr 13,19:1
Casanova 1923,S 27,10:2
She Stoops to Conquer 1924,Je 10,24:3
Man With a Load of Mischief, The 1925,O 27,20:1
Fool's Bells 1925,D 24,8:3
Henry IV, Part I 1926,Je 1,29:1
Garden of Eden, The 1927,S 28,28:1
Revolt 1928,N 1,25:3
Play Without a Name, A 1928,N 26,30:5
Becky Sharp 1929,Je 4,29:1
Strong Man's House, A 1929,S 17,34:3
School for Scandal, The 1931,N 11,26:4
Richard of Bordeaux 1934,F 15,16:2
Laburnum Grove 1935,Ja 15,23:5
Alice Takat 1936,F 11,19:2
Richard II 1937,S 16,28:2
Lorelei 1938,N 30,21:2
Importance of Being Earnest, The 1939,Ja 13,16:2
Leave Her to Heaven 1940,F 28,16:2
Love for Love 1940,Je 4,19:5
Seventh Trumpet, The 1941,N 22,10:6
Cherry Orchard, The 1944,Ja 26,22:1
Cherry Orchard, The 1944,F 6,II,1:1
Andrews, Adora
Lollipop 1924,Ja 22,15:3
Money From Home 1927,Mr 1,30:2
19th Hole, The 1927,O 12,30:3
Smiling Faces 1932,Ag 31,12:3
False Dreams, Farewell 1934,Ja 16,18:3
Tovarich 1936,O 16,31:4
Andrews, Albert G
Marjolaine 1922,Ja 25,16:1
School for Scandal, The 1923,Je 5,24:3
What Never Dies 1926,D 29,24:2
Truth Game, The 1930,D 29,19:1
Andrews, Alex
Devil Came From Dublin, The! 1955,Je 3,27:2
Andrews, Ann
Hottentot, The 1920,Mr 2,9:1
Champion, The 1921,Ja 4,11:1
Champion, The 1921,Ja 9,VI,1:1
Her Temporary Husband 1922,S 1,16:2
Two Married Men 1925,Ja 14,19:1
Captive, The 1926,S 30,23:1
Dark, The 1927,F 2,22:5
Fanatics, The 1927,N 8,32:4
Royal Family, The 1927,D 29,26:4
Royal Family, The 1928,Ja 8,VIII,1:1
Biarritz 1929,Ag 11,VIII,2:1
Recapture 1930,Ja 19,VIII,2:6
Recapture 1930,Ja 30,16:4
Kiss of Importance, A 1930,D 2,31:3
Dinner at Eight 1932,O 24,18:2
Oliver Oliver 1934,Ja 6,18:5
Dark Victory 1934,N 10,18:2
De Luxe 1935,Mr 6,22:2
Reflected Glory 1936,S 18,19:5
Reflected Glory 1936,S 22,30:2
Three Waltzes 1937,D 27,10:2
Miss Swan Expects 1939,F 21,15:2
When We Are Married 1939,N 21,19:5
When We Are Married 1939,D 10,X,5:6
When We Are Married 1939,D 26,22:3
Spring Again 1941,O 28,28:3
Spring Again 1941,N 11,28:2
Public Relations 1944,Ap 7,23:3
Andrews, Avis
Parade 1935,My 21,22:2
Smile at Me 1935,Ag 24,18:4
Virginia 1937,S 3,13:2
Laughter Over Broadway 1939,Ja 16,10:3
Frank Fay's Vaudeville 1939,Mr 3,20:4
Susanna, Don't You Cry 1939,My 23,27:2
Andrews, Ben
Bacchae, The 1963,Ap 25,39:5
Andrews, Billy
Deep Harlem 1929,Ja 8,35:2
Harlem 1929,F 21,30:3
Pansy 1929,My 15,36:3
Bomboola 1929,Je 27,17:3
Sweet Chariot 1930,O 24,30:2
Andrews, Charlotte
Death Takes a Holiday 1931,F 17,29:1
Anybody's Game 1932,D 22,21:4
Mahogany Hall 1934,Ja 18,18:5
Andrews, Charlton (Original Author)
Good Night Ladies 1945,Ja 18,16:2
Ladies Night in a Turkish Bath 1961,Mr 22,38:1

Andrews, Charlton (Playwright)
Ladies' Night 1920,Ag 10,10:1
Bluebeard's Eighth Wife 1921,S 20,12:2
Sam Abramovitch 1927,Ja 20,20:5
Golden Age, The 1928,Ap 25,31:3
Get Me in the Movies 1928,My 22,18:3
Get Me in the Movies 1928,My 27,VIII,1:1
Fioretta 1929,F 6,30:3
Ladies' Night 1933,N 19,IX,3:7
Andrews, D H (Playwright)
Drifting 1922,Ja 3,20:3
Andrews, Dana
Captains and the Kings, The 1962,Ja 3,25:2
Andrews, David
Hidden Horizon 1946,S 20,42:2
Andrews, Dorothea
Stage Door 1936,O 23,26:3
Andrews, Edgar
Searching Wind, The 1944,Ap 13,25:2
Andrews, Edward
How Beautiful With Shoes 1935,N 29,24:1
So Proudly We Hail 1936,S 23,28:4
Behind the Red Lights 1937,Ja 14,17:4
Time of Your Life, The 1939,O 26,26:2
Time of Your Life, The 1949,S 24,27:2
They Knew What They Wanted 1949,F 17,28:2
Mrs Gibsons' Boys 1949,My 5,35:2
I Am a Camera 1951,N 29,39:6
Three by Thurber; Imperturbable Spirit, The 1955,Mr 8,23:2
Three by Thurber; Middle Years, The 1955,Mr 8,23:2
Three by Thurber; Mr Montoe Holds the Fort 1955,Mr 8,23:2
Gazebo, The 1958,D 13,2:7
Child Buyer, The 1962,My 14,35:1
Andrews, Ellen
Danton's Death 1938,N 3,26:2
Male Animal, The 1941,Jl 9,24:6
Holiday 1941,Jl 23,15:2
Drifting Apart: or, The Fisherman's Child 1941,Ag 20,16:6
Democratic Body, A 1942,F 13,24:7
Too Hot for Maneuvers 1945,My 3,26:5
Mayor of Zalamea, The 1946,Ja 28,15:5
Andrews, Frank
Red Geranium, The 1922,My 9,22:3
Listening In 1922,D 5,24:1
My Aunt From Ypsilanti 1923,My 2,22:6
Pickwick 1927,S 6,35:2
Quicksand 1928,F 14,26:3
Wanted 1928,Jl 3,19:2
Octoroon, The 1929,Mr 13,28:3
Torch Song 1930,Ag 28,23:1
Sing High, Sing Low 1931,N 13,26:4
Take My Tip 1932,Ap 12,25:2
Other One, The 1932,O 4,26:3
Arrest That Woman 1936,N 19,20:4
Boy Meets Girl 1937,Jl 6,23:1
Censored 1938,F 28,18:2
Abe Lincoln in Illinois 1938,O 17,12:2
Andrews, Grace
It All Depends 1925,Ag 11,16:4
Andrews, Harry
Detour, The 1921,Ag 24,12:2
First Man, The 1922,Mr 6,9:2
Hamlet 1936,O 9,30:2
Henry IV, Part I 1946,My 7,25:2
Henry IV, Part II 1946,My 8,33:4
Oedipus 1946,My 21,19:2
Richard II 1951,Mr 25,75:3
Caesar and Cleopatra 1951,D 20,43:2
Antony and Cleopatra 1951,D 21,22:2
Andrews, Herbert (Costume Designer)
My Heart's in the Highlands 1939,Ap 14,29:2
Swingin' the Dream 1939,N 30,24:2
Andrews, Herbert (Scenic Designer)
My Heart's in the Highlands 1939,Ap 14,29:2
Sing for Your Supper 1939,Ap 25,18:6
My Heart's in the Highlands 1939,My 7,X,1:1
Swingin' the Dream 1939,N 30,24:2
Cue for Passion 1940,D 20,33:4
Any Day Now 1941,Je 10,28:2
Porgy and Bess 1942,Ja 23,16:2
Mexican Mural; Moonlight Scene 1942,Ap 27,19:2
Mexican Mural; Miracle Painting 1942,Ap 27,19:2
Mexican Mural; Vera Cruz Interior 1942,Ap 27,19:2
Mexican Mural; Patio With Flamingo 1942,Ap 27,19:2
Let Freedom Sing 1942,O 6,18:2
Porgy and Bess 1943,S 14,26:2
Porgy and Bess 1944,F 8,13:2
Andrews, Ismay
Ol' Man Satan 1932,O 4,26:3
Natural Man 1941,My 8,20:4
Andrews, Jack
Kid Boots 1924,Ja 1,21:3
Andrews, Jack (Miscellaneous)
Golden Rainbow 1968,F 5,27:1
Jimmy 1969,O 24,38:1
Andrews, Jacqueline
Oklahoma! 1951,S 13,38:2

Andrews, Jane
Nine Till Six 1936,Mr 14,10:3
Andrews, Jerome
Hamlet 1931,N 6,28:4
Iron Flowers 1933,Je 13,22:2
Iron Flowers 1933,Je 18,VIII,5:2
Lady in the Dark 1941,Ja 24,14:2
Andrews, Jerome (Choreographer)
Iron Flowers 1933,Je 13,22:2
Iron Flowers 1933,Je 18,VIII,5:2
Straw Hat, The 1939,S 30,10:6
Andrews, Julie
Boy Friend, The 1954,O 1,20:1
Boy Friend, The 1954,O 10,II,1:1
My Fair Lady 1956,Mr 16,20:2
My Fair Lady 1956,Mr 25,II,1:1
My Fair Lady 1956,Je 3,II,1:1
My Fair Lady 1958,My 1,34:5
My Fair Lady 1958,My 4,II,3:1
Camelot 1960,O 3,35:1
Camelot 1960,D 5,42:1
Camelot 1960,D 11,II,5:1
Andrews, Linda
Look to the Lilies 1970,Mr 30,59:1
Andrews, Lyle D (Producer)
Merry Merry 1925,S 25,24:3
Peggy-Ann 1926,D 28,16:3
Connecticut Yankee, A 1927,N 4,24:2
Lady Fingers 1929,F 1,22:4
How's Your Health? 1929,N 27,30:3
Vanderbilt Revue, The 1930,N 6,22:6
Andrews, Maidie
Symphony in Two Flats 1930,S 17,30:4
Conversation Piece 1934,O 24,24:1
Full House 1935,Ag 22,20:3
Set to Music 1939,Ja 19,16:2
Andrews, Margaret
Cock-A-Doodle Dandy 1955,N 4,26:5
J B 1958,Ap 24,37:1
J B 1958,My 4,II,1:1
Egoists, The 1959,O 14,52:2
Stone Tower, The 1962,Ag 24,14:2
Andrews, Marie
Way of the World, The 1954,S 30,38:2
Thieves' Carnival 1955,F 2,21:1
Firstborn, The 1957,Ja 7,29:2
Blancs, Les 1970,N 16,48:4
Andrews, Martin
No for an Answer 1941,Ja 6,10:6
Andrews, Nancy
Hilarities 1948,S 10,20:2
Touch and Go 1949,O 14,34:2
Touch and Go 1949,O 30,II,1:1
Plain and Fancy 1955,Ja 28,14:2
Juno 1959,Mr 10,41:1
Christine 1960,Ap 29,27:1
Tiger Rag, The 1961,F 17,20:2
Madame Aphrodite 1961,D 30,13:1
Little Me 1962,N 19,41:3
Little Me 1962,D 2,II,1:1
Cradle Will Rock, The 1964,N 9,40:4
Say Nothing 1965,Ja 28,21:2
How Much, How Much? 1970,Ap 21,49:1
Andrews, Robert
Pelican, The 1925,S 22,23:2
City of Kings 1949,F 18,27:2
Andrews, Robert (Miscellaneous)
Power of Dreams, A 1958,Mr 11,33:1
Andrews, Stanley
Good Fellow, The 1926,O 6,22:1
Quicksand 1928,F 14,26:3
Andrews, Sydney
Blue and the Gray, The; War Is Hell Gray, The 1929,D 27,26:4
Boy Meets Girl 1937,Jl 6,23:1
Tell My Story 1939,Mr 16,26:6
Andrews, Tashamira
Iron Flowers 1933,Je 13,22:2
Andrews, Tige
Mister Roberts 1948,F 19,27:2
Stockade 1954,F 5,14:2
Threepenny Opera, The 1955,S 21,38:1
Threepenny Opera, The 1956,Mr 11,II,1:1
Andrews, Tod
Summer and Smoke 1947,Jl 9,18:5
Summer and Smoke 1947,Ag 10,II,1:1
Throng o' Scarlet 1947,D 2,37:2
Summer and Smoke 1948,O 7,33:2
Summer and Smoke 1948,O 17,II,1:1
Girl Can Tell, A 1953,O 30,28:2
Andrews, Violet
American Tragedy, An 1926,O 12,31:2
Andrews, Walter
Gondoliers, The 1935,Ag 6,20:5
Andrews, William
Bloodstream 1932,Mr 31,25:1
Roll Sweet Chariot 1934,O 3,24:3
Stage Door 1936,O 23,26:3
Cretan Woman, The 1954,Jl 8,18:2
Andrews, William L
Never No More 1932,Ja 8,27:1
Andrewski, Gene (Producer)
Valmouth 1960,O 7,29:1

Andrewski, Gene (Producer)—Cont
Anything Goes 1962,My 16,35:1
Andreyev, Leonid (Original Author)
Seven at Dawn, The 1961,Ap 18,43:1
Andreyev, Leonid (Playwright)
He Who Gets Slapped 1922,Ja 10,15:1
He Who Gets Slapped 1922,F 26,VI,1:6
Anathema 1923,F 9,10:2
Anathema 1923,Ap 11,16:2
Anathema 1923,Ap 15,VII,1:1
Life of Man, The 1923,Ap 17,26:1
He Who Gets Slapped 1927,N 27,IX,4:1
Waltz of the Dogs, The 1928,Ap 26,31:3
Katerina 1929,F 26,30:3
Betrayal 1931,Ja 25,VIII,2:7
He Who Gets Slapped 1946,Mr 31,II,1:1
He Who Gets Slapped 1956,F 2,18:1
Andreyev, Leonid (Translator)
He Who Gets Slapped 1946,Mr 21,31:4
Andriacopoulos, Thanos
Oedipus Tyrannus 1952,N 25,35:2
Andriessen, Louis (Composer)
Reconstruction 1969,Jl 8,36:1
Andriola, Howard
Trial by Jury 1949,O 18,34:2
Andrisano, Tom
Babu 1967,D 23,28:1
Andros, Dick (Choreographer)
What's Up 1953,O 28,37:2
Androsky, Carol
Critic, The 1965,Jl 26,15:2
Androyan, Alexander
Echmiadzin 1946,O 21,27:3
Andrsova, Jana
Laterna Magika 1964,Ag 4,21:1
Andrum, Morris
Buckaroo 1929,Mr 18,31:1
Andrus, Albert
Little Old New York 1920,S 9,9:2
Andrus, Eleanor
Penny Arcade 1930,Mr 11,24:5
School for Virtue 1931,Mr 11,23:4
Andrus, Kathleen
Young Visitors, The 1920,N 30,14:1
New Morality, The 1921,Ja 31,10:1
Andrus, Philip
Borak 1960,D 14,51:1
Andrushkevich, V
In the Heat of the Night 1969,F 6,12:3
Andruss, Albert
Nervous Wreck, The 1924,O 19,VIII,2:1
Applesauce 1925,S 29,31:2
Open House 1925,D 15,28:3
Order Please 1934,O 10,21:2
Andruss, Philip
Measure for Measure 1960,Jl 27,33:1
Andry, Stephen
Mystery of the Finding of the Cross, The
1959,Ja 16,35:2
Andrycz, Nina
Saint Joan 1956,D 15,20:3
Anello, Jerome
Prometheus Bound 1967,My 11,52:1
We Bombed in New Haven 1967,D 7,58:1
Don Juan 1970,My 26,32:1
Anet, Claude (Playwright)
Mademoiselle Bourrat 1923,F 4,VII,1:4
Mademoiselle Bourrat 1926,N 21,VIII,2:1
Mademoiselle Bourrat 1929,O 8,34:3
Anet, Claude (Translator)
Mademoiselle Bourrat 1929,O 8,34:3
Anfimoff, (Messr)
Chauve-Souris 1925,Ja 15,25:1
Angadi, Darien
Twelfth Night 1970,Ja 1,18:1
Angarola, Richard
Our Lan' 1947,S 29,16:5
Angel, Adrienne
Best Foot Forward 1956,Mr 3,16:1
Oklahoma! 1958,Mr 8,15:2
Promises, Promises 1968,D 2,59:3
Angel, Heather
London Wall 1931,My 24,VIII,1:6
Love of Women 1937,D 14,33:2
Wookey, The 1941,Ag 26,23:2
Wookey, The 1941,S 11,20:5
Angel, Lou
Hallelujah, Baby! 1967,Ap 27,51:1
Angel, Wilson
O'Flynn, The 1934,D 28,24:1
Angela, June
Teahouse of the August Moon, The
1955,My 10,24:1
South Pacific 1969,Jl 7,27:1
Lovely Ladies, Kind Gentlemen 1970,D 29,38:1
Angell, Albert
Red Rust 1929,D 18,31:1
Angelo, Charles
Passion Flower, The 1920,Ja 14,12:1
Three Musketeers, The 1921,My 20,18:5
Merry Widow, The 1921,S 6,13:1
Nancy Ann 1924,Ap 1,18:1
Wild Duck, The 1925,F 25,16:4
Sunny 1925,S 23,22:1

Napoleon 1928,Mr 9,21:1
Outsider, The 1928,Ap 10,32:2
Wanted 1928,Jl 3,19:2
New Yorkers, The 1930,D 9,31:1
Lingering Past, The 1932,Je 30,26:5
Du Barry 1932,N 23,15:2
All Good Americans 1933,D 6,29:2
Within the Gates 1934,O 23,23:1
Angelo, Dom
Alligators, The 1960,N 15,47:1
Pousse-Cafe 1966,Mr 19,19:2
Illya Darling 1967,Ap 12,37:1
Angelo, Waldo (Costume Designer)
Shuffle Along 1952,My 9,20:5
Angelus, Muriel
Boys From Syracuse, The 1938,N 24,36:1
Sunny River 1941,D 5,28:2
Early to Bed 1943,Je 18,16:2
Anger, Al
Wonderful World of Burlesque, The
1965,Ap 29,38:1
Angevine, Mildred
Post Road 1936,Ag 5,15:4
Royal Family, The 1936,Ag 12,15:1
Angevine, Robert
So Proudly We Hail 1936,S 23,28:4
Angle, Charles
Oh, Please! 1926,D 22,24:3
Student Prince, The 1931,Ja 30,18:1
Angleberger, Nancy
Mystery of the Finding of the Cross, The
1959,Ja 16,35:2
Way of the Cross, The 1959,Ja 16,35:2
Anglin, Anne
Midsummer Night's Dream, A 1968,Je 13,54:1
Hamlet 1969,Je 11,37:1
Alchemist, The 1969,Je 12,51:1
Measure for Measure 1969,Je 13,41:3
Hamlet 1969,Je 22,II,1:7
Alchemist, The 1969,Je 22,II,1:7
Anglin, Florence
Maya 1953,Je 10,35:1
Major Barbara 1954,Je 30,23:2
As You Like It 1955,O 29,12:2
Romeo and Juliet 1955,D 16,36:3
Machinal 1960,Ap 8,27:1
Anglin, Margaret
Woman of Bronze, The 1920,S 8,9:2
Trial of Joan of Arc, The 1921,Mr 28,8:2
Iphigenia in Aulis 1921,Ap 8,18:2
Iphigenia in Aulis 1921,Ap 17,VI,1:1
Trial of Joan of Arc, The 1921,Ap 17,VI,1:1
Open Fire, The 1921,Ag 21,VI,1:8
Sea Woman, The 1923,Ja 21,VII,1:6
Electra 1927,My 4,28:3
Electra 1927,My 15,VIII,1:1
Woman of Bronze, The 1927,Je 16,25:4
Gypsy April 1927,Jl 31,VII,1:7
Electra 1927,D 2,20:6
Diplomacy 1928,My 29,16:3
Diplomacy 1928,Je 3,VIII,1:1
Smarty's Party 1928,S 25,29:4
Vaudeville (Palace) 1928,S 25,29:4
Macbeth 1928,N 4,IX,1:3
Lady Dedlock 1929,Ja 1,61:2
Security 1929,Mr 10,X,4:5
Security 1929,Mr 29,20:1
Fresh Fields 1934,Jl 15,X,1:1
Fresh Fields 1935,Jl 24,20:4
Fresh Fields 1936,F 11,19:2
Fresh Fields 1936,Je 23,27:3
Fresh Fields 1936,Je 30,15:1
Retreat From Folly 1937,Je 29,18:3
Marriage Royal 1937,Jl 15,16:2
Anglin, Margaret (Director)
Lady Dedlock 1929,Ja 1,61:2
Retreat From Folly 1937,Je 29,18:3
Anglin, Margaret (Miscellaneous)
Retreat From Folly 1937,Je 29,18:3
Anglin, Margaret (Producer)
Electra 1927,My 4,28:3
Electra 1927,D 18,IX,6:1
Anglin, Winifred
Transplanting Jean 1921,Ja 4,11:2
Angoff, Charles (Playwright)
Moment Musical 1943,Je 1,18:1
Angold, Edith
Distant Shore, The 1935,F 22,26:2
Professor Mamlock 1937,Ap 14,30:3
Knickerbocker Holiday 1938,O 20,26:2
Barber Had Two Sons, The 1943,F 2,22:2
Tomorrow the World 1943,Ap 15,22:2
Angus, A Donald
Chief Thing, The 1926,Mr 23,24:2
Angus, Bernadine (Playwright)
Angel Island 1937,O 21,26:2
Brown Sugar 1937,D 3,29:2
Pie in the Sky 1941,D 23,26:5
Anhalt, Julian (Producer)
Petticoat Fever 1935,Jl 2,24:4
Anhalt, Lawrence (Producer)
Petticoat Fever 1935,Jl 2,24:4

Anhalt, Lawrence J (Producer)
Ruddigore 1927,My 21,25:2
Anisfeld, Boris (Costume Designer)
Turandot 1929,Ja 12,14:4
Anisfeld, Boris (Scenic Designer)
Schweiger 1926,Mr 24,20:4
Anisfeld, S
Aristocrats 1935,My 2,16:2
Hirsh Lekert 1936,Mr 11,23:2
Anisimova-Wolf, Irina (Producer)
Orpheus Descending 1961,Ag 28,21:2
Aniston, John
Little Mary Sunshine 1959,N 19,49:3
Little Mary Sunshine 1959,N 29,II,1:1
Ladies Night in a Turkish Bath 1961,Mr 22,38:1
Anker, Perryne
Song of Norway 1958,Je 23,19:2
Song of Norway 1959,Je 26,16:2
Anker, William
Great Way, The 1921,N 8,28:2
Ankers, Evelyn
Ladies in Retirement 1940,Mr 27,24:3
Ankers, Kathleen (Costume Designer)
Fancy Meeting You Again 1952,Ja 15,23:2
Ankers, Kathleen (Scenic Designer)
Mr Pickwick 1952,S 18,36:3
Mr Pickwick 1952,S 28,II,1:1
Anketell, Margaret
Othello 1962,S 28,27:1
Ankrum, Morris
Assumption of Hannele, The 1924,F 16,16:2
Blue Peter, The 1925,Mr 25,25:3
Fountain, The 1925,D 11,26:1
Glory Hallelujah 1926,Ap 7,26:2
Good Fellow, The 1926,O 6,22:1
Gods of the Lightning 1928,O 25,27:2
Within the Gates 1934,O 23,23:1
Ankrum, Morris (Playwright)
Mystery Man, The 1928,Ja 27,14:2
Ankrum, Morris (Producer)
Prologue to Glory 1938,Mr 18,22:2
Big Blow 1938,O 3,11:2
Pinocchio 1939,Ja 3,19:2
Ankrun, Morris
In the Next Room 1923,N 28,14:1
Annabella
As You Like It 1934,N 11,IX,3:6
Jacobowsky and the Colonel 1944,Mr 15,17:2
Jacobowsky and the Colonel 1944,Mr 19,II,1:1
No Exit 1946,N 27,21:1
Annals, Michael (Costume Designer)
Macbeth 1962,F 7,32:2
Royal Hunt of the Sun, The 1964,Jl 8,40:6
Royal Hunt of the Sun, The 1965,O 27,36:2
Those That Play the Clowns 1966,N 25,48:1
Prometheus Bound 1967,My 11,52:1
Iphigenia in Aulis 1967,N 22,40:2
Saint Joan 1968,Ja 5,42:1
Staircase 1968,Ja 11,41:2
Her First Roman 1968,O 21,53:3
Morning 1968,N 29,52:1
Noon 1968,N 29,52:1
Night 1968,N 29,52:1
Annals, Michael (Miscellaneous)
Hamlet 1969,My 2,38:1
Annals, Michael (Scenic Designer)
Macbeth 1962,F 7,32:2
Royal Hunt of the Sun, The 1964,Jl 8,40:6
Royal Hunt of the Sun, The 1965,O 27,36:2
Those That Play the Clowns 1966,N 25,48:1
Prometheus Bound 1967,My 11,52:1
Iphigenia in Aulis 1967,N 22,40:2
Staircase 1968,Ja 11,41:2
Her First Roman 1968,O 21,53:3
Noon 1968,N 29,52:1
Morning 1968,N 29,52:1
Night 1968,N 29,52:1
Beggar on Horseback 1970,My 15,47:2
Beggar on Horseback 1970,My 24,II,1:1
Anne, Julie
Zelda 1969,Mr 6,38:1
Anne, Miss
Political Party, A 1963,S 27,17:5
Anne, Miss (Costume Designer)
Political Party, A 1963,S 27,17:5
Anne, Philly
We'd Rather Switch 1969,D 20,35:1
Annegan, J B
Me and Juliet 1970,My 15,42:1
Annenkov, Youri (Scenic Designer)
Revisor; Inspector General, The 1935,F 18,19:6
Annis, Francesca
Hamlet 1969,My 2,38:1
Annis, Sidney (Miscellaneous)
Castro Complex, The 1970,N 19,40:1
Annunzio, Gabriele d' (Playwright)
Gioconda 1926,N 14,VIII,2:1
Francesca da Rimini 1927,D 3,19:1
Light Under the Bushel, The 1927,D 7,32:2
Citta Morta, La 1935,S 22,X,7:7
Annus, John (Scenic Designer)
Drums in the Night 1967,My 18,54:1

Ano, Bonnie (Miscellaneous)
Dames at Sea 1968,D 21,46:1
Anonymous (Playwright)
Arden of Faversham 1970,F 17,33:1
Anouilh, Jean (Director)
Ne Reveillez pas Madame 1970,O 24,29:5
Anouilh, Jean (Original Author)
Voyageur Sans Bagage, Le 1938,Ja 2,X,3:5
Antigone 1946,F 19,21:3
Fading Mansion 1949,S 1,25:4
Cry of the Peacock 1950,Ap 12,33:2
Anouilh, Jean (Playwright)
Hermine, L' 1932,My 29,VIII,1:7
Y'Avait un Prisonnier 1938,Ja 25,24:3
Sauvage, La 1938,Mr 27,X,2:1
Bal des Voleurs, Le 1938,N 29,26:4
Antigone 1946,Ja 10,28:2
Antigone 1946,F 24,II,1:1
Eurydice 1948,O 17,I,67:4
Ring Around the Moon 1950,Ja 27,29:2
Ring Around the Moon 1950,N 24,30:1
Point of Departure 1951,F 11,II,3:1
Colombe 1951,D 15,13:2
Legend of Lovers 1951,D 27,17:1
Repetition, La; Rehearsal, The 1952,N 28,22:2
Alouette, L' 1953,N 29,II,3:1
Mademoiselle Colombe 1954,Ja 7,26:1
Mademoiselle Colombe 1954,Ja 17,II,1:1
Thieves' Carnival 1955,F 2,21:1
Thieves' Carnival 1955,F 13,II,1:2
Time Remembered 1955,My 4,35:1
Lark, The 1955,My 13,21:2
Lark, The 1955,My 29,II,1:1
Lark, The 1955,N 18,20:1
Lark, The 1955,N 27,II,1:1
Lark, The 1956,Ja 8,II,3:1
Waltz of the Toreadors, The 1956,Mr 11,II,3:1
Antigone 1956,Ap 3,32:2
Waltz of the Toreadors, The 1956,D 22,14:8
Waltz of the Toreadors, The 1957,Ja 18,17:2
Waltz of the Toreadors, The 1957,Ja 27,II,1:1
Restless Heart 1957,My 9,37:4
Repetition, La 1957,S 3,23:2
Time Remembered 1957,N 13,41:2
Time Remembered 1957,N 24,II,1:1
Waltz of the Toreadors, The 1958,Mr 5,37:1
Ardele 1958,Ap 9,39:4
Antigone 1959,S 16,46:2
Legend of Lovers 1959,O 28,40:3
Fighting Cock, The 1959,D 9,57:3
Fighting Cock, The 1959,D 20,II,3:1
Jeannette 1960,Mr 25,20:2
Becket 1960,O 6,50:1
Becket 1960,O 16,II,1:1
Becket 1960,D 18,36:3
Rendezvous at Senlis 1961,F 28,39:2
Becket 1961,My 9,44:1
Becket 1961,Jl 12,35:6
Rehearsal, The 1963,S 24,45:2
Rehearsal, The 1963,O 20,II,1:1
Traveller Without Luggage 1964,S 18,26:2
Poor Bitos 1964,N 16,40:2
Colombe 1965,F 24,33:1
Medea 1966,D 21,42:1
Thieves' Carnival 1967,Je 5,52:1
Antigone 1967,Je 19,43:1
Ring Around the Moon 1968,N 2,28:1
Cher Antoine 1969,O 3,40:1
Romeo and Jeanette 1969,D 16,53:1
Poissons Rouges, Les 1970,F 3,39:1
Ne Reveillez pas Madame 1970,O 24,29:5
Anouilh, Jean (Translator)
Desire Under the Elms 1953,N 29,II,3:1
Ansah, Kwan (Director)
Adoption, The 1965,N 14,132:1
Ansah, Kwan (Playwright)
Adoption, The 1965,N 14,132:1
Ansah, Kwan (Producer)
Adoption, The 1965,N 14,132:1
Ansara, Alan
Private Life of the Master Race, The
1956,Ja 31,33:3
Absalom 1956,My 17,37:2
Lady From the Sea, The 1956,D 13,49:5
Judge, The 1958,My 14,36:2
Tonight We Improvise 1959,N 7,27:4
Breaking Wall, The 1960,Ja 26,27:5
Sudden End of Anne Cinquefoil, The
1961,Ja 11,25:2
Seven at Dawn, The 1961,Ap 18,43:1
Coriolanus 1965,Jl 15,23:1
Ansel, Alfred
Sherlock Holmes 1929,N 26,28:3
Anselmi, Rosina
Aria del Continente, L' 1927,O 5,30:2
Anshein, Carol
Midsummer Night's Dream, A 1967,Je 30,23:1
Ansimov, Georgi P (Director)
West Side Story 1965,S 25,37:2
Ansky, S (Playwright)
Dybbuk, The 1924,Ja 29,17:7
Dybbuk, The 1925,D 16,22:2
Dybbuk, The 1925,D 20,VII,3:1

Dybbuk, The 1926,Ja 6,16:2
Dybbuk, The 1926,Ja 17,VIII,1:1
Dybbuk, The 1926,N 21,VIII,1:3
Dybbuk, The 1926,D 14,24:2
Dybbuk, The 1926,D 17,27:2
Dybbuk, The 1926,D 26,VII,1:1
Dybbuk, The 1927,My 1,VIII,2:7
Dybbuk, The 1937,F 24,18:4
Dybbuk, The 1948,My 3,26:3
Dybbuk, The 1964,F 4,30:2
Ansley, Charles
I Must Love Someone 1939,F 8,18:7
There Shall Be No Night 1940,Ap 30,25:2
Anson, A E
Piper, The 1920,Mr 20,14:2
Romance 1921,Mr 1,18:2
Eileen 1922,Je 18,VI,1:6
Merchant of Venice, The 1922,D 22,13:1
As You Like It 1923,Ap 24,24:1
White Cargo 1923,N 6,22:2
Road Together, The 1924,Ja 18,21:2
Odd Man Out 1925,My 26,24:3
Furies, The 1928,Mr 8,23:1
Mima 1928,D 13,24:2
Young Alexander 1929,Mr 13,28:2
Soldiers and Women 1929,Ag 25,VIII,3:1
Soldiers and Women 1929,S 3,25:1
Soldiers and Women 1929,S 22,IX,1:1
That's the Woman 1930,S 4,27:2
Anson, A E (Director)
Just Beyond 1925,D 2,22:4
Anson, Barbara
Song for a Certain Midnight 1959,S 17,49:1
How to Steal an Election 1968,O 14,56:1
Ansorge, Joachim
Don Carlos 1964,N 25,40:1
Anspach, Elden
Master of the Revels 1935,Ag 14,16:2
Anspach, Susan
View From the Bridge, A 1965,Ja 29,24:1
And Things That Go Bump in the Night
1965,Ap 27,27:5
Journey of the Fifth Horse, The 1966,Ap 22,36:1
Journey of the Fifth Horse, The 1966,My 8,II,1:1
Midsummer Night's Dream, A 1967,Je 30,23:1
Anspacher, Louis K (Playwright)
Daddalums 1920,Jl 11,VI,1:6
That Day 1922,Jl 9,VI,1:4
That Day 1922,O 4,27:3
Dagmar 1923,Ja 23,18:2
Unchastened Woman, The 1926,F 17,12:1
Unchastened Woman, The 1926,F 21,VII,1:2
Rhapsody, The 1930,S 16,30:3
Anspecke, George
Dead End 1935,O 29,17:2
Ansteth, Robert
St Helena 1936,O 7,32:1
Anstey, F (Original Author)
One Touch of Venus 1943,O 8,14:1
Anstey, F (Playwright)
Would-Be Gentleman, The 1928,O 2,34:1
Would-Be Gentleman, The 1930,Ap 30,29:2
Anstruther, Harold
Young Visitors, The 1920,N 30,14:1
Ant, Janet
Mighty Nimrod, The 1931,My 13,23:1
Antarova, Irina Hicks
Chauve-Souris; Queen of Spades, The
1931,O 22,27:1
Antebi, Sidney S (Playwright)
Pigeon, The 1957,My 17,19:2
Antek, Samuel (Miscellaneous)
Bourgeois Gentilhomme, Le 1955,O 26,26:1
Antheil, George (Composer)
Oedipus Rex 1929,Mr 24,X,2:3
Fighting the Waves 1929,Ag 14,15:6
Fighting the Waves 1929,S 22,IX,4:1
Anthony, Adrian
Pal Joey 1940,D 26,22:2
Anthony, C L (Smith, Dodie) (Playwright)
Autumn Crocus 1931,Ap 26,VIII,2:4
Service 1932,N 13,IX,3:4
Autumn Crocus 1932,N 21,20:2
Touch Wood 1934,Jl 1,X,1:3
Call It a Day 1935,O 31,17:2
Bonnet Over the Windmill 1937,S 26,XI,2:5
Anthony, Carl
Poldekin 1920,S 10,12:1
Mongrel, The 1924,D 16,28:2
Rosmersholm 1925,My 6,27:2
Paid 1925,N 26,32:1
Ladder, The 1926,O 23,15:1
Hotbed 1928,N 10,20:7
Strictly Dishonorable 1929,S 19,37:1
Strictly Dishonorable 1929,S 29,IX,1:1
Anthony, Charles (Playwright)
Pagans 1921,Ja 5,11:1
Anthony, David
Othello 1955,S 8,27:2
Streetcar Named Desire, A 1956,F 16,24:1
Anthony, Don
In the Bag 1936,D 18,30:2

Anthony, Emmett
Liza 1922,N 28,24:1
Anthony, Jack
Hold Your Horses 1933,S 26,26:4
Anthony, Jill
Conversation Piece 1934,O 24,24:1
Anthony, Joe
Guimpes and Saddles 1967,O 11,36:3
Anthony, John
Prince and the Pauper, The 1920,N 2,15:1
Montmartre 1922,F 14,20:1
R U R 1922,O 10,16:1
Woman Disputed, A 1926,S 29,23:2
Golden Age, The 1928,Ap 25,31:3
Great Power, The 1928,S 12,25:1
Mrs Bumpstead-Leigh 1929,Ap 2,28:3
Anthony, John D
Jimmy 1969,O 24,38:1
Anthony, Joseph
Professor Mamlock 1937,Ap 14,30:3
Trojan Women, The 1938,Ja 25,24:2
On the Rocks 1938,Je 16,20:2
Skipper Next to God 1948,Ja 5,14:5
Afternoon Storm 1948,Ap 12,24:2
Peer Gynt 1951,Ja 29,15:2
Flight Into Egypt 1952,Mr 19,33:2
Flight Into Egypt 1952,Mr 30,II,1:1
Camino Real 1953,Mr 20,26:1
Camino Real 1953,Mr 29,II,1:1
Anastasia 1954,D 30,13:1
Anastasia 1955,Ja 16,II,1:1
Country Girl, The 1966,S 30,55:1
Anthony, Joseph (Director)
Celebration 1948,Ap 12,24:2
Fifth Horseman, The 1949,Je 14,26:6
Bullfight 1954,Ja 13,25:2
Rainmaker, The 1954,O 29,28:1
Rainmaker, The 1954,N 7,II,1:1
Once Upon a Tailor 1955,My 24,36:2
Lark, The 1955,N 18,20:1
Lark, The 1955,N 27,II,1:1
Most Happy Fella 1956,My 4,20:1
Most Happy Fella 1956,My 13,II,1:1
Clearing in the Woods, A 1957,Ja 11,20:2
Clearing in the Woods, A 1957,Ja 20,II,1:1
Winesburg, Ohio 1958,F 6,22:2
Marriage-Go-Round, The 1958,O 30,37:1
Marriage-Go-Round, The 1958,N 9,II,1:1
Best Man, The 1960,Ap 1,39:1
Best Man, The 1960,Ap 10,II,1:1
Under the Yum-Yum Tree 1960,N 17,45:1
Rhinoceros 1961,Ja 10,27:1
Rhinoceros 1961,Ja 22,II,1:1
Mary, Mary 1961,Mr 9,24:2
Captains and the Kings, The 1962,Ja 3,25:2
Romulus 1962,Ja 11,27:1
Dragon, The 1963,Ap 10,32:1
110 in the Shade 1963,O 25,37:1
Chinese Prime Minister, The 1964,Ja 3,14:1
Chinese Prime Minister, The 1964,Ja 12,II,1:1
Last Analysis, The 1964,O 2,30:1
Last Analysis, The 1964,O 11,II,1:1
Slow Dance on the Killing Ground 1964,D 1,50:1
Taming of the Shrew, The 1965,Je 24,32:2
Mrs Dally 1965,S 25,5:7
Playroom, The 1965,D 6,49:1
Happily Never After 1966,Mr 11,37:1
Falstaff 1966,Je 20,27:1
Weekend 1968,Mr 14,50:2
Weekend 1968,Mr 31,II,1:1
Jimmy 1969,O 24,38:1
Anthony, Joseph (Playwright)
Ship Comes in, A 1934,S 20,21:1
Anthony, Joseph (Scenic Designer)
Texas Town 1941,Ap 30,22:3
American Legend 1941,My 12,13:2
Out of My House 1942,Ja 8,28:6
Anthony, Leo
Pardon Our French 1950,O 6,22:4
Anthony, Mab
Elizabeth the Queen 1930,N 4,37:1
Anthony, Mary
Touch and Go 1949,O 14,34:2
Anthony, Mary (Choreographer)
Winter's Tale, The 1963,Ag 16,14:1
Anthony, Michael
Gertrude Stein's First Reader 1969,D 16,56:1
Anthony, Norman (Director)
Ballyhoo of 1932 1932,S 7,14:2
Anthony, Norman (Playwright)
Ballyhoo of 1932 1932,S 7,14:2
Brights Lights of 1944 1943,S 17,27:4
Anthony, Norman (Producer)
Ballyhoo of 1932 1932,S 7,14:2
Anthony, Robert
Man in the Glass Booth, The 1968,S 27,41:1
Anthony, Rock (Playwright)
Jackknife 1958,S 23,36:2
Courtyard 1960,Mr 1,28:1
Anthony, Sal (Costume Designer)
Buttrio Square 1952,O 15,40:2
Bad Seed, The 1954,D 9,42:1
Girls Against the Boys, The 1959,N 3,26:1

Anthony, Stephen (Miscellaneous)
Masks of Angels 1965,Ja 20,33:1
Anna Kleiber 1965,Ja 20,33:1
Anthony, Stuart (Playwright)
Come Angel Band 1936,F 19,17:1
Anthony, Thomas
Green Stick 1934,O 10,21:2
Anthony, Tony (Miscellaneous)
Follies of 1910, The 1960,Ja 15,37:3
Antiseri, Frank
Royal Fandango, A 1923,N 13,25:1
Antkies, Fred J (Miscellaneous)
Dinner at Eight 1966,S 28,38:1
Antle, Stephanie
Red White and Blue 1950,O 8,64:5
Antoine, Andre Paul (Original Author)
Fatal Woman, The 1930,Mr 2,IX,4:7
Antoine, Andre Paul (Playwright)
Crucifies, Les 1923,Ap 8,VIII,1:7
Crucifies, Les 1923,O 30,17:2
Suit Tragicue de Raspoutine 1924,Je 15,VII,1:4
Ennemie, L' 1929,Ap 28,IX,2:4
Love, Honor and Betray 1930,Mr 13,22:2
Prochaine, La 1932,My 1,VIII,2:6
Antoine, Robert
Song of Norway 1944,Ag 22,20:2
I Remember Mama 1944,O 20,16:2
Life With Mother 1948,O 21,32:2
Anton, Eleanor
Our Town 1944,Ja 11,24:5
Only the Heart 1944,Ap 5,17:2
Anton, Frank
Ten Nights in a Barroom 1932,Ja 21,17:1
Anton, Pauline
Familiar Pattern 1943,S 3,15:6
Anton, Robert (Costume Designer)
Arsenic and Old Lace 1970,N 5,59:1
Anton, Tony
Emerald Slippers, The 1970,S 2,31:2
Anton, Tony (Choreographer)
Emerald Slippers, The 1970,S 2,31:2
Anton, Virginia
Mandragola 1958,My 29,23:2
Antonacci, Greg
Coney Island Play 1970,O 31,34:2
Antonakes, Mike
Lower Depths, The 1956,O 3,29:2
Journey With Strangers, A 1958,N 27,53:1
Antonio
Perfectly Scandalous 1931,My 14,27:2
Antonio, James
Buffalo Skinner, The 1959,F 20,18:1
Billygoat Eddie 1964,Ap 21,43:2
Othello 1964,Jl 15,29:1
Othello 1964,O 13,48:1
Baal 1965,My 7,33:2
Coriolanus 1965,Jl 15,23:1
Nature of the Crime 1970,Mr 24,41:1
Antonio, Lou
Buffalo Skinner, The 1959,F 20,18:1
Power of Darkness, The 1959,S 30,33:1
Good Soup, The 1960,Mr 3,26:4
Cry of the Raindrop 1961,Mr 8,38:1
Garden of Sweets, The 1961,N 1,35:1
Andorra 1963,F 11,5:5
Lady of the Camellias, The 1963,Mr 22,7:1
Ballad of the Sad Cafe, The 1963,O 31,27:1
Ballad of the Sad Cafe, The 1963,N 10,II,1:1
Tragical Historie of Doctor Faustus, The
1964,O 6,34:2
Ready When You Are, C. B.! 1964,D 8,55:1
Antonoff, Serge
Clear All Wires! 1932,S 15,19:1
Antonutti, Omero
Venetian Twins, The 1968,My 29,23:1
Antony, Jacklyn
Picture of Dorian Gray, The 1956,Ag 18,15:5
Antoon, A J
Crimes and Crimes 1970,Ja 19,35:1
Antrim, Harry
30 Days Hath September 1938,O 1,10:5
Ringside Seat 1938,N 23,24:5
Miss Swan Expects 1939,F 21,15:2
Ladies and Gentlemen 1939,O 18,30:2
All in Favor 1942,Ja 21,20:6
Too Hot for Maneuvers 1945,My 3,26:5
Antrim, Henry
Silks and Satins 1920,Jl 16,19:1
In the Bag 1936,D 18,30:2
Behind the Red Lights 1937,Ja 14,17:4
Out of the Frying Pan 1941,F 12,24:2
Antrobus, John
Contractor, The 1970,Ag 17,32:1
Antwerp, John Van (Playwright)
Naughty-Naught '00 1937,Ja 25,23:2
Fireman's Flame, The 1937,O 11,26:2
Anunciacao, Jose Alves
Arena Conta Zumbi 1969,Ag 19,31:1
Anzell, Hy
Blood, Sweat & Stanley Poole 1961,O 6,31:1
Seidman and Son 1962,O 16,32:2
Pocket Watch, The 1966,Ja 6,18:1
God Bless You, Harold Fineberg 1969,Mr 31,30:2

Summertree 1969,D 10,60:1
How Much, How Much? 1970,Ap 21,49:1
Aoyama, Yoshio (Director)
Tale of Kasane, The 1969,F 25,36:1
Blueprints 1969,F 25,36:1
Gianni Schicci 1969,F 25,36:1
Aparicio, Manuel
Vida es Sueno, La 1964,Mr 18,49:1
Apel, Paul (Miscellaneous)
Beggar on Horseback 1924,F 13,17:2
Apfel, Kalman
Alt Heidelberg 1926,My 31,10:5
Apin, I F (Miscellaneous)
Three Sisters, The 1965,F 12,15:1
Apleton, Lewis
Stars on Ice (2d Edition) 1943,Je 25,13:2
Aplon, Boris
Show Boat 1954,My 6,44:1
Carousel 1954,Je 3,32:2
Candide 1956,D 3,40:2
Makropoulos Secret, The 1957,D 4,52:4
King of the Whole Damn World 1962,Ap 16,32:2
Anya 1965,N 30,48:1
Fiddler on the Roof 1970,F 28,20:1
Apolinar, Danny
Your Own Thing 1968,Ja 15,33:1
Apolinar, Danny (Composer)
Your Own Thing 1968,Ja 15,33:1
Your Own Thing 1968,Ja 28,II,3:1
Apolinar, Danny (Lyricist)
Your Own Thing 1968,Ja 15,33:1
Your Own Thing 1969,Mr 29,39:1
Apollo Quartette
George White's Scandals 1935,D 26,20:2
Apollon, Dave
Vaudeville (Palace) 1926,Ap 27,22:3
Vaudeville (Palace) 1926,Ag 17,21:2
Vaudeville (Palace) 1927,My 17,27:4
Vaudeville (Palace) 1927,D 20,33:4
Vaudeville (Palace) 1930,S 29,19:1
Vaudeville (Palace) 1932,Ap 25,18:3
Vaudeville (Palace) 1932,My 2,13:2
Vaudeville (Palace) 1932,My 9,19:3
Boys and Girls Together 1940,S 5,28:6
Boys and Girls Together 1940,O 2,19:2
Apollon, Dave Revue
Vaudeville (Hippodrome) 1925,D 8,28:6
Apopiantz, Lee (Miscellaneous)
Cocktails of 1934 1934,My 5,22:1
Aposhanski, Vladimir
Uncle Vanya 1960,F 13,13:4
Apostolides, J
Iphigenia 1931,Ja 6,24:1
Electra 1952,N 20,38:2
Oedipus Tyrannus 1952,N 25,35:2
Apostolides, Yannis
Electra 1930,D 27,16:1
Appel, Anna
Green Fields 1920,Mr 26,11:2
Naomi 1920,My 7,12:2
One Life for Another 1920,D 18,11:2
Dybbuk, The 1921,S 2,9:2
Andersh; New Worlds 1922,S 26,18:2
Tenth Commandment, The 1926,N 18,27:1
Gold Diggers, The 1927,D 3,19:2
Alexander Pushkin 1928,Ja 27,14:2
Poppa 1928,D 25,31:1
Jew Suss 1929,O 19,22:3
Angels on Earth 1929,D 11,34:7
Roaming Stars 1930,Ja 25,12:2
Uncle Moses 1930,N 29,21:3
Riverside Drive 1931,Ja 6,24:2
Man With the Portfolio, The 1931,F 12,24:6
Did I Say No? 1931,S 23,19:4
Armored Train No 1469 1931,N 28,20:3
Yoshe Kalb 1932,O 3,15:5
Yoshe Kalb 1932,N 6,IX,2:1
Chayim Lederer 1932,N 15,24:4
Motke Ganef 1932,D 30,15:2
Wise Men of Chelm, The 1933,O 18,24:4
In-Laws 1934,O 25,28:2
Treasure, The 1934,D 18,25:5
Saint and Sinners 1935,D 30,15:2
Jacques Bergson 1936,O 31,24:6
Jacques Bergson 1936,N 29,XII,3:3
Water Carrier, The 1936,D 25,20:2
Give Me Back My Heart 1937,O 4,17:6
Three Cities 1938,O 11,20:3
Yoshe Kalb 1939,F 6,9:2
Far-Away Corner, A 1939,F 15,15:2
Salvation 1939,S 29,19:2
If I Were Rothschild 1940,Ja 1,28:7
Worlds Apart 1941,Ja 23,19:3
Good Neighbor 1941,O 22,26:2
Oy, Is Dus a Leben!; Oh, What a Life!
1942,O 13,19:2
Song of Dnieper 1946,O 26,10:5
Wandering Stars 1946,D 14,18:2
Hershel, The Jester 1948,D 14,39:2
All You Need Is One Good Break 1950,F 10,20:3
Abie's Irish Rose 1954,N 19,19:1
Highway Robbery 1955,N 8,36:1
Me, Candido! 1956,O 16,36:2

Appel, Anna—Cont

Comic Strip 1958,My 15,26:2
Golem, The 1959,F 26,38:2
Appel, Bram (Producer)
Opening of a Window, The 1961,S 26,32:2
Appel, Charles (Playwright)
In the Nick of Time 1967,Je 2,36:1
Appel, Helen
Did I Say No? 1931,S 23,19:4
Verdict, The 1934,S 22,12:5
Parnosseh 1935,F 16,8:8
Motke Ganef 1935,Mr 18,15:2
Appelbe, David
Rain Before Seven 1935,Ag 13,20:3
Appell, Don
According to Law 1944,Je 2,20:3
Appell, Don (Director)
Career Angel 1944,My 24,23:7
This, Too, Shall Pass 1946,My 1,32:4
Doctor Social 1948,F 12,29:5
Girl Could Get Lucky, A 1964,S 21,36:1
Appell, Don (Playwright)
This, Too, Shall Pass 1946,My 1,32:4
Lullaby 1954,F 4,21:2
Milk and Honey 1961,O 11,52:1
Girl Could Get Lucky, A 1964,S 21,36:1
Apple, Betty
Lady Comes Across, The 1942,Ja 10,10:2
Applebaum, Gertrude H (Miscellaneous)
Roomful of Roses, A 1955,O 18,48:1
Applebaum, Louis (Composer)
Measure for Measure 1954,Je 30,23:1
Taming of the Shrew, The 1954,Jl 1,22:2
Henry V 1956,Je 20,27:2
Hamlet 1957,Jl 3,15:2
Two Gentlemen of Verona 1958,Mr 19,35:1
Much Ado About Nothing 1958,Je 26,22:1
Othello 1959,Jl 2,17:2
Romeo and Juliet 1960,Jl 1,14:1
Coriolanus 1961,Je 21,31:2
Henry VIII 1961,Je 22,22:1
Henry VIII 1961,Jl 2,II,1:1
Andorra 1963,F 11,5:5
Troilus and Cressida 1963,Je 19,40:2
Cyrano de Bergerac 1963,Je 20,30:1
King Lear 1964,Je 19,36:1
Julius Caesar 1965,Jl 2,18:1
Cherry Orchard, The 1965,Ag 2,17:2
Twelfth Night 1966,Je 10,51:2
Antony and Cleopatra 1967,Ag 2,25:1
Merry Wives of Windsor, The 1967,Ag 4,18:1
Antony and Cleopatra 1967,O 29,83:4
Romeo and Juliet 1968,Je 11,55:2
Hamlet 1969,Je 11,37:1
Applebaum, Louis (Miscellaneous)
H M S Pinafore 1960,S 8,41:1
Applebaum, Louis (Musical Director)
Tamburlaine the Great 1956,Ja 20,19:1
Pirates of Penzance, The 1961,S 7,41:1
Pirates of Penzance, The 1961,S 17,II,1:1
Gondoliers, The 1962,Jl 7,9:4
Yeomen of the Guard, The 1964,Ag 3,16:1
Applebaum, Mischa
Parisian Love 1927,Ja 28,15:5
Applebaum, Mischa (Director)
Parisian Love 1927,Ja 28,15:5
Applebee, James K
Sporting Thing to Do, The 1923,F 20,12:2
Deep Tangled Wildwood, The 1923,N 6,22:1
Across the Street 1924,Mr 25,24:1
Ruint 1925,Ap 8,24:2
Rope 1928,F 23,18:3
Appleby, Dorothy
Princess April 1924,D 2,23:2
Puzzles of 1925 1925,F 3,25:3
Square Crooks 1926,Mr 2,23:2
Young Sinners 1929,N 29,24:4
Young Sinners 1931,Ap 21,35:5
Young Sinners 1933,Mr 7,20:4
Springtime for Henry 1933,My 2,20:5
Appleby, Henrietta
Lingering Past, The 1932,Je 30,26:5
Appleby, Stephen Ker
Silent House, The 1932,N 9,28:3
Valley Forge 1934,D 11,28:3
Pride and Prejudice 1935,N 6,32:4
St Helena 1936,S 29,35:1
St Helena 1936,O 7,32:1
Country Wife, The 1936,D 2,34:1
Our Betters 1937,Jl 22,16:2
Mother, The 1939,Ap 26,26:2
Lady in Waiting 1940,Mr 28,19:1
Applegate, Cam
Stockade 1954,F 5,14:2
Applegate, Ray
Oh, Hector! 1929,Mr 6,33:2
Appleman, Chaim
Brothers Ashkenazi, The 1955,N 12,24:4
Appleman, Herbert (Director)
Unfair to Goliath 1970,Ja 26,27:1
Appleman, Herbert (Lyricist)
Unfair to Goliath 1970,Ja 26,27:1
Appleman, Herbert (Miscellaneous)
Unfair to Goliath 1970,Ja 26,27:1

Appleman, Mark J (Playwright)
Stockade 1954,F 5,14:2
Appler, Walter
Mr Sycamore 1942,N 14,13:2
Victory Belles 1943,O 27,26:3
Polonaise 1945,O 8,20:2
Appler, Walter F
Joy to the World 1948,Mr 19,28:2
Richard III 1949,F 9,33:2
Liar, The 1950,My 19,30:2
Billy the Kid 1951,Ag 21,23:2
Wild Duck, The 1951,D 27,17:1
Curious Savage, The 1956,Mr 17,12:3
Appleseed, John
Republic, The 1970,Ap 28,49:1
Appleton, Lewis
Polonaise 1945,O 8,20:2
Applewhite, Coy
Salome 1923,My 8,22:2
Comedy of Errors, The 1923,My 16,22:5
Applewhite, Herff (Director)
Galileo 1968,D 1,88:4
Applewhite, Herff (Producer)
Galileo 1968,D 1,88:4
Aprea, Andrew
Off Your Marx 1936,Ap 2,28:2
Life Begins in '40 1940,Ap 5,24:2
My Romance 1948,O 20,38:5
Arms and the Girl 1950,F 3,28:2
April
Right This Way 1938,Ja 6,22:3
Leave It to Me! 1938,N 10,32:2
Apstein, Theodore (Playwright)
Innkeepers, The 1956,F 3,19:1
Come Share My House 1960,F 19,20:2
Apter, Jeffrey
Peace 1969,Ja 28,49:1
Aptman, Arthur (Miscellaneous)
Trojan Women, The 1923,My 27,10:2
Aquabelles, The
Aquashow 1953,Je 24,29:2
Aquablades, The
Aquashow 1953,Je 24,29:2
Aquashow 1954,Je 23,20:4
Elliott Murphy's Aquashow 1955,Je 23,25:1
Aquadorables, The
Aquashow 1952,Je 25,25:1
Aquashow 1954,Je 23,20:4
Elliott Murphy's Aquashow 1955,Je 23,25:1
Aquamaniacs, The
Aquarama 1960 1960,Jl 1,14:6
Aquazanies, The
Aquashow 1952,Je 25,25:1
Aquashow 1953,Je 24,29:2
Aquashow 1954,Je 23,20:4
Elliott Murphy's Aquashow 1955,Je 23,25:1
Aquilera, Manuel
Cuando Los Hijos De Eva No Son Los Hijos De
Adan; When Eve's Children Are Not Adam's
1932,Ap 23,11:2
Aquilino, Umberto (Miscellaneous)
Festa Italiana 1966,S 30,55:1
Aquino, Florence
Bell for Adano, A 1944,D 7,21:2
Skipper Next to God 1948,Ja 5,14:5
Aquirre, Gene
Lend an Ear 1969,O 29,32:1
Arab, John
Gondoliers, The 1962,Jl 7,9:4
Arace, Thomas
Face the Music 1932,F 18,24:5
Arakis, The Tan
Vaudeville (Palace) 1926,Jl 27,15:4
Aramburu, Silva (Playwright)
Leyenda del Beso, La 1942,N 20,26:4
Aramini, Auguste
Rita Coventry 1923,F 20,12:2
Agent 666, L' 1923,My 30,10:5
Virgin, The 1926,F 23,26:1
Criss Cross 1926,O 13,20:2
Ada Beats the Drum 1930,My 9,20:4
Dancing Partner 1930,Ag 6,24:2
When Ladies Meet 1932,O 7,19:1
Tapestry in Gray 1935,D 28,10:2
Atout... Coeur 1936,Mr 27,25:4
Son Mari 1936,Ap 17,17:3
Dans Le Noir; In the Dark 1937,F 11,18:3
Christian 1937,F 25,18:6
Curtain Call 1937,Ap 23,24:7
Many Mansions 1937,O 28,28:6
Case of Youth, A 1940,Mr 25,10:3
Arams, Donald
Mikado, The 1964,N 27,43:1
Arana, Reinaldo
Golden Streets, The 1970,Ag 14,21:1
Aranha, Ray
Ododo 1970,N 25,26:1
Aranoff, Max (Scenic Designer)
Pigeon, The 1957,My 17,19:2
Arashi, Clifford
World of Suzie Wong, The 1958,O 15,47:1
Tenth of an Inch Makes the Difference, A
1962,N 13,44:1

Aratama, Michiyo
Othello 1960,S 11,II,7:1
Aratoli, Alfredo
Promessi Sposi I,; Betrothed, The 1934,O 22,13:2
Arbenina, Stella
Happy Husband, The 1927,Jl 10,VII,2:3
Arbenz, Mark
Mourning Becomes Electra; Hunted, The
1931,O 27,22:1
Arbenz, Mary
Autumn Violins 1929,F 10,IX,2:1
Hundred Years Old 1929,O 2,28:2
Stepdaughters of War 1930,O 7,27:1
In The Best of Families 1931,F 3,29:1
Mourning Becomes Electra; Homecoming
1931,O 27,22:1
Mourning Becomes Electra; Haunted, The
1931,O 27,22:1
Biography 1932,D 13,25:3
Arbetz, Mary
Mrs Moonlight 1936,Je 16,21:3
Arbolino, Jack G
Hit the Road 1941,Ap 4,18:3
Arbuckle, Ivan
Red Robe, The 1928,D 26,15:1
Count of Luxembourg, The 1930,F 18,28:2
Mother Lode 1934,D 24,16:5
Arbuckle, Maclyn
Daddy Dumplins 1920,N 23,11:1
Daddy Dumplins 1920,D 12,VI,1:3
In the Night Watch 1921,Ja 31,10:1
Wild Oats Lane 1922,Jl 23,VI,1:6
Wild Oats Lane 1922,S 7,12:1
Rivals, The 1923,My 9,14:2
She Stoops to Conquer 1924,Je 10,24:3
Poor Richard 1924,N 16,VIII,2:8
Arbuckle, Roscoe (Fatty)
Baby Mine 1927,Je 10,21:2
Vaudeville (Palace) 1932,My 23,18:7
Vaudeville (Loew's State) 1932,O 3,15:5
Arbury, Donald
Star Spangled 1936,Mr 11,23:1
Moroni 1936,Ag 19,19:1
Young Mr Disraeli 1937,N 10,30:5
On the Rocks 1938,Je 16,20:2
Hamlet 1938,O 13,28:1
Henry IV, Part I 1939,Ja 31,17:2
Good Neighbor 1941,O 22,26:2
Arbury, Guy
Winter's Tale, The 1946,Ja 16,18:6
Survivors, The 1948,Ja 20,27:2
King Lear 1950,D 26,18:1
Billy the Kid 1951,Ag 21,23:2
Touchstone 1953,F 4,33:2
Rehearsal, The 1963,S 24,45:2
Arbuzov, Aleksei (Playwright)
Deathless, The 1943,Jl 11,II,1:2
Irkutsk Story, An 1961,Ap 18,44:1
Promise, The 1967,N 15,38:1
Promise, The 1967,N 26,II,1:1
Arcaro, Flavia
Spice of 1922 1922,Jl 7,12:4
Patience 1924,D 30,15:1
Dearest Enemy 1925,S 19,9:2
Oh, Ernest! 1927,My 10,24:3
Sweethearts 1929,S 23,25:1
Mlle Modiste 1929,O 8,34:1
Inspector General, The 1930,D 24,19:2
Mr Papavert 1932,Ja 23,18:6
Hired Husband 1932,Je 4,9:5
Queer People 1934,F 16,16:2
Arceneaux, Michael (Costume Designer)
Fireworks; Fireworks for a Hot Fourth
1969,Je 12,51:1
Fireworks; Football 1969,Je 12,51:1
Fireworks; Report, The 1969,Je 12,51:1
Archangelsky, Alexei (Composer)
Chauve-Souris 1922,O 11,22:2
Chauve-Souris 1924,D 14,VIII,6:1
Chauve-Souris 1929,Ja 23,20:2
Chauve-Souris; Queen of Spades, The
1931,O 22,27:1
Archard, Marcel (Original Author)
I Know My Love 1949,N 3,36:1
I Know My Love 1949,N 20,II,1:1
Archdale, Alexander
Wind and the Rain, The 1934,F 2,20:6
Archdeacon, Sally
Oh, Herbert! 1945,Je 20,26:3
Archer, Charles (Translator)
Peer Gynt 1923,F 6,14:1
Archer, Cheryl
Love Life 1948,O 8,31:2
Archer, Claude E
Synthetic Sin 1927,O 11,26:2
Archer, Daniel (Playwright)
Mr Barry's Etchings 1950,F 1,26:2
Archer, Ethel
As You Like It 1936,Ap 24,18:4
Archer, Frances (Translator)
Wild Duck, The 1938,Ap 16,16:5
Archer, Frank
Red, Hot and Blue! 1936,O 30,26:3

Archer, Harry (Composer)
Little Jessie James 1923,Ag 16,10:4
Paradise Alley 1924,Ap 2,17:3
My Girl 1924,N 25,27:2
Merry Merry 1925,S 25,24:3
Twinkle Twinkle 1926,N 17,22:2
Just a Minute 1928,O 9,34:3
Keep It Clean 1929,Je 25,35:5
Lucky Break 1934,O 3,25:3
Lucky Break 1934,O 28,IX,3:4
Archer, Harry (Lyricist)
Keep It Clean 1929,Je 25,35:5
Archer, Herbert
Noye's Fludde 1959,Mr 17,41:2
Archer, Jane
Achilles Had a Heel 1935,O 14,20:2
Libel! 1935,D 21,10:5
Two Bouquets, The 1938,Je 1,19:2
Archer, Jeri
Million Dollar Baby 1945,D 22,17:2
Entertainer, The 1958,F 13,22:2
Magnificent Hugo, The 1961,Ap 8,12:2
Archer, Jerry
Tattle Tales 1933,Je 2,22:6
Archer, John
Odds on Mrs Oakley, The 1944,O 3,18:8
One-Man Show 1945,F 9,21:2
Place of Our Own, A 1945,Ap 3,23:7
Day Before Spring, The 1945,N 23,27:2
Day Before Spring, The 1945,D 2,II,1:1
This Time Tomorrow 1947,N 4,31:2
Strange Bedfellows 1948,Ja 15,27:3
Captain Brassbound's Conversion 1950,D 28,21:1
Archer, Laurie (Choreographer)
Happy as Larry 1961,Ap 26,36:1
Archer, Lynn
I'm Solomon 1968,Ap 24,51:1
Romeo and Jeanette 1969,D 16,53:1
Archer, Osceola
Between Two Worlds 1934,O 26,24:2
Panic 1935,Mr 16,18:4
Cat Screams, The 1942,Je 17,26:5
Hippolytus 1948,N 22,25:5
Riders to the Sea 1949,F 4,30:2
Hall of Healing 1952,My 8,35:6
Bedtime Story 1952,My 8,35:6
Debut 1956,F 23,32:1
Romeo and Juliet 1961,F 24,24:1
Crucible, The 1964,Ap 7,30:2
Guide, The 1968,Mr 7,50:1
Archer, Osceola (Director)
Sojourner Truth 1948,Ap 22,35:2
Archer, William (Playwright)
Green Goddess, The 1921,Ja 19,14:1
Green Goddess, The 1921,Ja 23,VI,1:1
Green Goddess, The 1921,Ja 30,VI,1:1
Green Goddess, The 1923,S 7,10:2
Ghosts 1927,Ja 11,36:3
Archer, William (Translator)
Peer Gynt 1923,F 6,14:1
Hedda Gabler 1926,Ja 27,16:5
Peer Gynt 1937,Mr 14,II,7:8
Master Builder Solness 1950,My 26,19:3
Archibald, Florence
Lost 1927,Mr 29,22:2
Archibald, Freddie
Green Pastures, The 1930,F 27,26:1
Green Pastures, The 1935,F 27,16:2
Archibald, H A (Playwright)
Coastwise 1931,D 1,23:1
Archibald, Jean (Playwright)
Call the Doctor 1920,S 1,14:1
Colette 1925,S 29,31:2
Marry the Man! 1929,Ap 23,26:3
Archibald, William
One for the Money 1939,F 6,9:2
Two for the Show 1940,F 9,14:2
Two for the Show 1940,F 18,IX,2:1
All in Fun 1940,D 28,11:2
Laffing Room Only 1944,D 25,15:4
Archibald, William (Choreographer)
Crystal Heart, The 1960,F 16,31:2
Archibald, William (Director)
Crystal Heart, The 1960,F 16,31:2
Cantilevered Terrace, The 1962,Ja 18,24:1
Willie Doesn't Live Here Anymore 1967,F 8,20:2
Archibald, William (Lyricist)
Carib Song 1945,S 28,17:2
Crystal Heart, The 1957,F 20,37:1
Crystal Heart, The 1960,F 16,31:2
Archibald, William (Miscellaneous)
Innocents, The 1959,Ap 21,41:2
Archibald, William (Playwright)
Carib Song 1945,S 28,17:2
Innocents, The 1950,F 2,30:2
Innocents, The 1950,F 12,II,1:1
Innocents, The 1952,Jl 4,9:7
Portrait of a Lady 1954,D 22,27:6
Crystal Heart, The 1957,F 20,37:1
Innocents, The 1959,Ap 21,41:2
Crystal Heart, The 1960,F 16,31:2
Cantilevered Terrace, The 1962,Ja 18,24:1
Cantilevered Terrace, The 1962,Ja 28,II,1:1

Archie, Dorothea
Roll Sweet Chariot 1934,O 3,24:3
Archie, Will
High Tor 1937,Ja 11,15:2
Arcidiacono, Rosario
Aria del Continente, L' 1927,O 5,30:2
Arcidiacono, Vittorina
Aria del Continente, L' 1927,O 5,30:2
Arco, Isaac
Song of Dnieper 1946,O 26,10:5
Arcoria, Tony
Gods of the Mountain, The 1950,My 25,36:2
Arcos, Pilar
Adam Had Two Sons 1932,Ja 21,17:1
Ard, Charles (Lighting Director)
Harold 1967,My 10,39:1
Sondra 1967,My 10,39:1
Ard, Charles (Scenic Designer)
Sondra 1967,My 10,39:1
Harold 1967,My 10,39:1
Ardath, Edwin
Armor of Light 1950,F 24,26:4
Ardath, Fred
Perfect Fool, The 1921,N 8,28:2
Chippies 1929,My 30,23:3
Show Boat 1948,S 9,33:2
Ardeeser, J Paul
Sun-Up 1930,My 10,25:1
Ardell, Franklyn
George White's Scandals 1922,Ag 29,10:1
Sweet Little Devil 1924,Ja 22,15:4
Cross My Heart 1928,S 18,32:7
She Got What She Wanted 1929,Mr 5,28:1
Ardell, Lillian
Field God, The 1927,Ap 22,18:2
Tobacco Road 1942,S 7,34:2
Tobacco Road 1943,S 6,21:3
Ardelle, Helen
Gypsy Baron, The 1930,Ap 22,22:8
Ardelle, Kathlyn
George White's Scandals 1922,Ag 29,10:1
Ardelli, Roberto
Deep River 1926,O 5,26:2
Arden, Christine
Please, Mrs. Garibaldi 1939,Mr 17,24:3
Arden, Dominique
Mariage de Figaro, Le 1964,F 26,41:2
Salut a Moliere 1964,Mr 4,33:2
Pieton de L'Air, Le 1964,Mr 4,33:2
Arden, Donn (Choreographer)
Hollywood Ice Revue 1955 1955,Ja 14,16:1
Hollywood Ice Revue 1956,Ja 13,17:1
Arden, Donn (Director)
Hollywood Ice Revue 1955 1955,Ja 14,16:1
Hollywood Ice Revue 1956,Ja 13,17:1
Holiday on Ice 1968,Ag 29,44:1
Holiday on Ice 1969,Ag 28,44:1
Arden, Donn (Lighting Director)
Hollywood Ice Revue 1955 1955,Ja 14,16:1
Hollywood Ice Revue 1956,Ja 13,17:1
Arden, Donn (Miscellaneous)
Holiday on Ice 1968,Ag 29,44:1
Arden, Donn (Playwright)
Holiday on Ice 1969,Ag 28,44:1
Arden, Elaine
Sketch Book 1935,Je 5,22:2
Arden, Eve
Ziegfeld Follies 1934,Ja 5,24:3
Parade 1935,My 21,22:2
Drums Professor, The 1935,Jl 30,17:2
Ziegfeld Follies 1936,Ja 5,IX,3:1
Ziegfeld Follies 1936,Ja 31,17:2
Very Warm for May 1939,N 18,23:2
Two for the Show 1940,F 9,14:2
Two for the Show 1940,F 18,IX,1:1
Let's Face It 1941,O 10,27:1
Let's Face It 1941,O 30,26:2
Arden, Florence
Ten Per Cent 1927,S 14,29:3
Trapped 1928,S 12,25:3
Arden, Helen
Revenge With Music 1934,N 29,33:5
Street Scene 1947,Ja 10,17:2
Arden, Helene
Houseboat on the Styx, The 1928,D 26,14:3
Gypsy Blonde 1934,Je 26,22:5
Gypsy Baron, The 1942,Je 20,8:5
Gypsy Baron, The 1942,Ag 7,12:4
Arden, Isabel
Uncle Harry 1942,My 21,24:1
Arden, John
Harold Muggins Is a Martyr 1968,Jl 14,II,4:5
Arden, John (Playwright)
Happy Haven, The 1963,My 10,40:6
Workhouse Donkey, The 1963,Jl 9,26:1
Live Like Pigs 1965,Je 8,48:2
Armstrong's Last Goodnight 1965,Jl 7,26:1
Serjeant Musgrave's Dance 1966,Mr 9,44:1
Serjeant Musgrave's Dance 1966,Mr 20,II,1:1
Serjeant Musgrave's Dance 1968,Je 16,52:4
Harold Muggins Is a Martyr 1968,Jl 14,II,4:5
Hero Rises Up, The 1968,N 9,26:2

Arden, Lynn
Grass Harp, The 1953,Ap 28,32:2
Arden, Mary
Ghost Writer, The 1933,Je 20,22:4
Arden, Michael (Playwright)
Dear Father 1924,D 21,VII,1:8
Arden, Victor
Lady Be Good 1924,D 2,23:4
Tip-Toes 1925,D 29,20:2
Treasure Girl 1928,N 9,22:1
Vaudeville (Palace) 1929,Ja 21,18:3
Spring Is Here 1929,Mr 12,26:1
Ardery, Ben
Fools Are Passing Through 1958,Ap 3,24:2
Ardery, Ben (Scenic Designer)
Lady From the Sea, The 1956,D 13,49:5
Ardine, Ottie
Honey Girl 1920,My 4,9:1
Ardizzone, Enrico
Venetian Twins, The 1968,My 29,23:1
Ardmore, Doris
Abie's Irish Rose 1937,My 13,30:2
Ardolino, Emile (Miscellaneous)
Oh! Calcutta! 1969,Je 18,33:1
Ardrey, Molly
Along Came a Spider 1963,My 28,33:1
Wayward Stork, The 1966,Ja 20,27:1
Ardrey, Robert (Playwright)
Star Spangled 1936,Mr 6,25:4
Star Spangled 1936,Mr 11,23:1
How to Get Tough About It 1938,F 9,16:2
Casey Jones 1938,F 21,14:2
Thunder Rock 1939,N 15,18:1
Thunder Rock 1939,N 19,X,3:6
Thunder Rock 1940,Jl 29,10:4
Thunder Rock 1940,Ag 11,IX,2:4
Jeb 1946,F 22,20:2
Jeb 1946,Mr 3,II,1:1
Sing Me No Lullaby 1954,O 15,17:2
Sing Me No Lullaby 1954,O 24,II,1:1
Thunder Rock 1956,F 27,18:1
Shadow of Heroes 1961,D 6,59:1
Arearo, Flavia
Humming Bird, The 1923,Ja 16,16:2
Arenal, Julie
This Side of Paradise 1962,F 22,19:6
Arenal, Julie (Choreographer)
Hair 1968,Ap 30,40:2
Hair 1969,S 13,30:1
Indians 1969,O 14,51:1
Hair 1970,Ja 13,39:1
Isabel's a Jezebel 1970,D 27,II,3:1
Arenal, Julie (Director)
Isabel's a Jezebel 1970,D 27,II,3:1
Arenal, P C
Family, The 1943,Mr 31,22:4
Arent, Arthur (Miscellaneous)
One-Third of a Nation 1938,Ja 18,27:2
Arent, Arthur (Playwright)
One-Third of a Nation 1937,Jl 31,6:4
Pins and Needles 1937,N 29,18:6
Pins and Needles 1939,Ap 21,26:2
It's Up to You 1943,Ap 1,19:1
Arenton, James
Armor of Light 1950,F 24,26:4
Master Builder Solness 1950,My 26,19:3
Daughters of the Late Colonel, The 1951,O 15,21:2
Richard III 1953,D 10,65:2
Nature's Way 1957,O 17,42:2
Andersonville Trial, The 1959,D 30,15:1
Arenzwari-Yushny, V
Blue Bird, The 1932,Ap 22,23:2
Ares, Albert
Galileo 1947,D 8,34:2
Arey, Wayne
Magnanimous Lover, The 1920,F 10,10:2
Girl in the Coffin, The 1920,F 10,10:2
Suppressed Desires 1920,F 10,10:2
Americans in France, The 1920,Ag 4,14:1
Professor Mamlock 1937,Ap 14,30:3
Arey, Wayne (Producer)
Magnanimous Lover, The 1920,F 10,10:2
Girl in the Coffin, The 1920,F 10,10:2
Suppressed Desires 1920,F 10,10:2
Argal, Else
Boudoir 1941,F 8,18:4
Argent, Maurice
Gift of Fury, A 1958,Mr 24,21:4
Argentina
Untitled-One Woman Show 1929,My 19,IX,2:1
International Revue 1930,F 26,22:2
Argentinita
International Revue 1930,F 9,VIII,4:2
Top-Notchers 1942,My 30,8:5
Argentinos, Los
Aquacircus 1958,Je 30,24:6
Argento, Dominick (Composer)
Saint Joan 1964,My 14,41:1
Volpone 1964,Jl 20,18:3
Shoemaker's Holiday, The 1967,Je 3,19:1
House of Atreus, The; Bringers of Offerings, The 1967,Jl 24,23:1
House of Atreus, The; Furies, The 1967,Jl 24,23:1

Argento, Dominick (Composer)—Cont
House of Atreus, The; Agamemnon 1967,Jl 24,23:1
House of Atreus, The 1968,D 18,55:1
Argento, Frank
Nights of Wrath; Nuits de la Colere, Les 1947,D 1,26:4
Arginteanu, Arthur
Nautical but Nice 1931,Ap 19,31:6
Arglic, Charles
Uniform of Flesh 1949,Ja 31,15:2
Argo, Gordon (Scenic Designer)
Fall 1957,N 22,19:1
Argus, Edwin
Beggar on Horseback 1924,F 13,17:2
Argyl, Christiane d'
Schoen und Schick 1928,Ag 26,II,1:2
Ari, Ben
Golem, The 1927,F 5,13:2
Ari, R Ben
War and Peace 1942,My 22,26:3
Winter Soldiers 1942,N 30,19:2
Arias, Adelardo Fernandez (Playwright)
Tragedia del Faro, La; Tragedy of the Lighthouse, The 1932,Je 3,23:2
Arim, Walter
Du Barry Was a Lady 1939,D 7,34:2
Ariosto, Ludovico (Original Author)
Orlando Furioso 1970,N 5,59:1
Aris, Ben
Hamlet 1969,My 2,38:1
Aristedes, John
New Girl in Town 1957,My 15,40:1
Foxy 1964,F 17,26:1
Man of La Mancha 1965,N 23,52:1
Aristocrats, The
Jerry Lewis' Variety Show 1957,F 8,18:5
Aristophanes (Original Author)
Paix, La 1933,Ja 15,IX,2:1
Lysistrata 1959,My 20,40:2
Lysistrata 1959,N 25,19:4
Happiest Girl in the World, The 1961,Ap 4,42:1
Peace 1969,Ja 28,49:1
Peace 1969,F 16,II,1:1
Aristophanes (Playwright)
Lysistrata 1925,Ja 11,VII,2:7
Lysistrata 1925,O 17,18:3
Lysistrata 1925,D 15,28:2
Birds, The 1928,F 19,VIII,4:4
Lysistrata 1930,Ap 29,30:5
Lysistrata 1930,Je 1,VIII,1:1
Lysistrata 1930,Je 6,20:1
Lysistrata 1930,D 14,IX,2:7
Birds, The 1935,Jl 21,II,3:2
Frogs, The 1941,N 14,25:3
Thesmophoriazusae, The; Goddesses of Athens, The 1955,D 14,52:4
Lysistrata 1959,D 6,II,5:1
Birds, The 1966,Jl 1,40:1
Frogs, The 1966,Jl 25,22:5
Birds, The 1967,My 7,67:1
Peace 1967,Ag 27,II,4:8
Peace 1968,N 10,87:1
Lysistrata 1968,N 15,42:1
Republic, The 1970,Ap 28,49:1
Peace 1970,S 2,30:2
Arkell, Reginald (Miscellaneous)
Paganini 1937,My 21,18:6
Arkell, Reginald (Playwright)
East of Broadway 1932,Ja 27,19:3
1066 and All That 1935,My 26,XI,2:5
Arker, Mabel
Land's End 1946,D 12,37:5
Arkin, Alan
Heloise 1958,S 25,28:4
From the Second City 1961,S 27,32:1
Untitled-Revue; Second City 1962,Ja 12,30:2
Man Out Loud, Girl Quiet 1962,Ap 4,38:1
Enter Laughing 1963,Mr 15,8:1
Enter Laughing 1963,Je 16,II,1:1
Luv 1964,N 12,43:1
Luv 1964,N 22,II,1:1
White House Murder Case, The 1970,Mr 1,II,1:4
White House Murder Case, The 1970,Mr 15,II,3:1
Arkin, Alan (Composer)
Man Out Loud, Girl Quiet 1962,Ap 4,38:1
Spanish Armada, The 1962,Ap 4,38:1
Arkin, Alan (Director)
Hail Scrawdyke! 1966,N 29,50:1
Little Murders 1969,Ja 6,38:1
Little Murders 1969,O 2,54:1
White House Murder Case, The 1970,F 19,59:1
White House Murder Case, The 1970,Mr 15,II,3:1
Arkin, David (Lighting Director)
Phedre 1966,F 11,36:1
Arkin, Juki
Overcoat, The 1960,S 7,45:1
Milk and Honey 1961,O 11,52:1
Arkin, Ted
Meet the People 1940,D 26,22:2
Arlaud, Rodolphe M (Playwright)
Matter of Days, A 1969,My 20,40:1
Arleaux, Sondra
Riddle Me This! 1933,Mr 15,21:3

Arledge, John
  American Primitive 1937,Ag 13,12:5
Arlen, Albert (Playwright)
  Son of the Grand Eunuch 1937,Ja 15,17:8
Arlen, Bob (Choreographer)
  Secret Life of Walter Mitty, The 1964,O 27,44:5
Arlen, Dee
  Tickets, Please! 1950,Ap 28,25:2
Arlen, Harold
  Vaudeville (Palace) 1931,Jl 20,20:3
  Vaudeville (Hollywood) 1932,F 16,24:3
Arlen, Harold (Composer)
  Nine Fifteen Revue, The 1930,F 12,26:2
  Earl Carroll's Vanities 1930,Jl 2,28:3
  You Said It 1931,Ja 20,21:3
  Vanities 1932,S 28,22:4
  Americana 1932,O 6,19:3
  Music Hall Varieties 1932,N 23,15:3
  Life Begins at 8:40 1934,Ag 28,24:2
  Hooray for What! 1937,D 2,32:5
  It's All Yours 1942,Mr 26,26:2
  Star and Garter 1942,Je 25,26:2
  Bloomer Girl 1944,O 6,18:5
  Bloomer Girl 1944,O 8,II,1:1
  St Louis Woman 1946,Ap 1,22:2
  House of Flowers 1954,D 31,11:2
  Jamaica 1957,N 1,32:2
  Jamaica 1957,N 10,II,1:1
  Saratoga 1959,D 8,59:4
  Free and Easy 1959,D 15,51:4
  Free and Easy 1959,D 20,II,3:2
  Harold Arlen Songbook, The 1967,Mr 1,48:1
  House of Flowers 1968,Ja 29,26:2
  Wizard of Oz, The 1968,N 28,69:2
Arlen, Harold (Lyricist)
  Nine Fifteen Revue, The 1930,F 12,26:2
  Earl Carroll's Vanities 1930,Jl 2,28:3
  Vanities 1932,S 28,22:4
  Music Hall Varieties 1932,N 23,15:3
  Show Is On, The 1937,S 20,18:4
  It's All Yours 1942,Mr 26,26:2
  Star and Garter 1942,Je 25,26:2
  House of Flowers 1954,D 31,11:2
  Harold Arlen Songbook, The 1967,Mr 1,48:1
Arlen, Harold (Miscellaneous)
  Bloomer Girl 1947,Ja 7,33:2
Arlen, Harold (Mrs) (Lyricist)
  House of Flowers 1968,Ja 29,26:2
Arlen, Jerry (Musical Director)
  House of Flowers 1954,D 31,11:2
  Saratoga 1959,D 8,59:4
Arlen, Michael (Original Author)
  Green Hat, The 1925,Ap 5,IX,2:4
Arlen, Michael (Playwright)
  Green Hat, The 1925,Ap 5,IX,2:4
  Green Hat, The 1925,S 16,23:2
  Green Hat, The 1925,S 20,VIII,1:1
  These Charming People 1925,O 7,31:2
  These Charming People 1925,O 11,VIII,1:1
  Zoo, The 1927,O 9,VIII,1:3
Arlen, Richard
  Too Hot for Maneuvers 1945,My 3,26:5
Arlen, Roxanne
  Who Was That Lady I Saw You With?
    1958,Mr 4,33:2
Arlen, Steve
  Cry for Us All 1970,Ap 9,48:2
Arletty
  Joies du Capitole, Les 1935,Ap 21,IX,2:1
  Streetcar Named Desire, A 1949,O 19,36:6
  Orpheus Descending 1959,Mr 18,44:6
  Etouffe Chretien, L' 1960,N 5,28:1
Arley, Jean
  Cradle Song 1955,D 2,32:2
  Wake Up, Darling 1956,My 3,34:2
  Bonds of Interest, The 1958,My 7,43:1
Arleys, The 3 1/2
  Vaudeville (Palace) 1926,S 21,32:5
Arling, Joyce
  Little Father of the Wilderness, The 1930,Je 3,27:1
  Kill That Story 1934,Ag 30,22:2
  Ladies' Money 1934,N 2,26:6
  Three Men on a Horse 1935,Ja 22,22:7
  Three Men on a Horse 1935,Ja 31,22:3
  Boy Meets Girl 1935,N 19,27:2
  Boy Meets Girl 1935,N 28,38:2
  Angel Island 1937,O 21,26:2
  What a Life 1938,Ap 14,26:2
  Miss Swan Expects 1939,F 21,15:2
Arlington, Florence
  Lady's Virtue, A 1925,N 24,28:2
  Fly by Night 1933,Je 3,16:2
  Her Man of Wax 1933,O 12,32:3
Arliss, Dimitra
  Indians 1969,O 14,51:1
Arliss, George
  Poldekin 1920,S 10,12:1
  Poldekin 1920,S 19,VI,1:1
  Green Goddess, The 1921,Ja 19,14:1
  Untitled-Benefit 1921,My 2,12:3
  Green Goddess, The 1923,S 7,10:2
  Old English 1924,D 24,11:2
  Old English 1924,D 28,VII,1:1

  Merchant of Venice, The 1928,Ja 10,38:6
  Merchant of Venice, The 1928,Ja 17,22:2
  Merchant of Venice, The 1929,Ja 27,IX,1:3
Arliss, Joen
  Spofford 1967,D 15,54:3
Arluck, Elliot (Lyricist)
  Meet Peter Grant 1961,My 11,41:4
Arluck, Elliot (Playwright)
  Meet Peter Grant 1961,My 11,41:4
Arm, Edith (Costume Designer)
  Utopia! 1963,My 7,47:4
Armant, Paul (Original Author)
  Purple Mask, The 1920,Ja 6,18:1
Armband, Abraham (Translator)
  Alexander Pushkin 1928,Ja 27,14:2
Armbruster, Richard
  Goldilocks 1958,O 13,33:1
  South Pacific 1965,Je 3,25:1
Armbruster, Robert (Composer)
  Bunk of 1926 1926,F 17,12:3
Armfield, Maxwell (Director)
  Winter's Tale, A 1921,F 5,14:3
Armfield, Maxwell (Mrs) (Director)
  Winter's Tale, A 1921,F 5,14:3
Armfield, Maxwell (Mrs) (Producer)
  Winter's Tale, The 1921,F 13,VI,1:1
Armfield, Maxwell (Producer)
  Winter's Tale, The 1921,F 13,VI,1:1
Armida
  Vaudeville (Palace) 1927,D 6,26:3
  Nina Rosa 1930,S 22,22:5
  Vaudeville (Palace) 1931,My 25,17:4
  Broadway Sho-Window 1936,Ap 13,14:5
Armijo, Lilian
  Miser, The 1950,Mr 27,19:5
  Difficult Woman, The 1962,Ap 26,22:7
Armin, Walter
  Anathema 1923,Ap 11,16:2
  Inspector General, The 1923,My 1,24:1
  Naughty Riquette 1926,S 14,25:2
  Greenwich Village Follies 1928,Ap 10,32:2
  Other Men's Wives 1929,N 13,24:4
  Unexpected Husband 1931,Je 3,29:4
  There You Are! 1932,My 17,25:4
  Red Planet 1932,D 19,19:2
  Evensong 1933,F 1,13:4
  Hold Your Horses 1933,S 26,26:4
  Caviar 1934,Je 8,19:2
  Revenge With Music 1934,N 29,33:5
  Play, Genius, Play! 1935,O 31,17:2
  Name Your Poison 1936,Ja 21,27:4
  Cross-Town 1937,Mr 18,21:5
  To Quito and Back 1937,O 7,30:4
  Tell Me Pretty Maiden 1937,D 17,33:5
  Schoolhouse on the Lot 1938,Mr 23,18:4
  Leave It to Me! 1938,N 10,32:2
  Nellie Bly 1946,Ja 22,32:2
Armini, Auguste
  Wonder Bar, The 1931,Mr 18,23:4
Armistead, Horace (Costume Designer)
  Medium, The 1947,My 2,28:2
  Telephone, The 1947,My 2,28:2
  Telephone, The 1948,D 8,41:6
  Medium, The 1948,D 8,41:6
Armistead, Horace (Scenic Designer)
  Fields Beyond, The 1936,Mr 7,11:2
  What Big Ears! 1942,Ap 21,18:5
  Medium, The 1947,My 2,28:2
  Telephone, The 1947,My 2,28:2
  Medium, The 1947,My 11,II,1:1
  Telephone, The 1948,D 8,41:6
  Medium, The 1948,D 8,41:6
  Regina 1949,N 1,32:2
  Regina 1949,N 13,II,1:1
  Arms and the Girl 1950,F 3,28:2
  Consul, The 1950,Mr 16,41:1
  Consul, The 1950,Mr 26,II,1:1
  Medium, The 1950,S 3,II,1:1
  Julius Caesar 1955,Jl 13,20:1
  Tempest, The 1955,Ag 2,18:2
  Tempest, The 1955,Ag 7,II,1:1
Armitage, Buford
  Mud Turtle, The 1925,Ag 21,8:2
  Move On 1926,Ja 19,30:1
  Eva the Fifth 1928,Ag 29,19:3
  Undertow 1929,N 10,X,4:8
  Claire Adams 1929,N 20,26:3
  School for Virtue 1931,Ap 22,29:2
  Louder, Please! 1931,N 13,26:4
  John Brown 1934,Ja 23,22:3
  Kill That Story 1934,Ag 30,22:2
  Schoolhouse on the Lot 1938,Mr 23,18:4
Armitage, Buford (Miscellaneous)
  What Every Woman Knows 1954,D 23,16:2
  Fourposter, The 1955,Ja 6,23:3
  Wisteria Trees, The 1955,F 3,20:2
  Young and Beautiful, The 1955,O 3,23:2
  Say Darling 1959,F 26,38:2
Armitage, Buford (Producer)
  Doctors Disagree 1943,D 29,15:2
Armitage, Pauline
  Cat-Bird, The 1920,F 17,18:1
  Wren, The 1921,O 11,22:1

Armitage, Pauline—Cont
  Virtue (?) 1922,N 17,14:1
  Nancy Ann 1924,Ap 1,18:1
  Easy Mark, The 1924,Ag 27,14:2
Armitage, Walter
  Melo 1931,O 20,29:3
Armitage, William (Miscellaneous)
  Enchanted, The 1958,Ap 23,41:1
  General Seeger 1962,Mr 1,26:2
  Seagull, The 1964,Ap 6,36:1
  Crucible, The 1964,Ap 7,30:2
  Imaginary Invalid, The 1967,My 2,53:1
  Touch of the Poet, 'A 1967,My 3,38:2
  Fumed Oak 1967,My 4,34:1
  Still Life 1967,My 4,34:1
  Ways and Means 1967,My 4,34:1
  John Brown's Body 1968,F 13,49:2
  Comedy of Errors, The 1968,F 28,40:2
  She Stoops to Conquer 1968,Ap 1,58:3
Armont, Paul (Original Author)
  Money Talks 1938,My 29,X,1:2
Armont, Paul (Playwright)
  French Doll, The 1922,F 21,20:2
  Hotel Mouse, The 1922,Mr 14,11:3
  Goldfish, The 1922,Ap 18,15:3
  Comedienne 1924,O 22,18:1
  Monsieur de Cleopatre, Le 1927,Ja 16,VII,2:1
  Enlevement, L' 1927,O 2,VIII,2:4
  Coiffeur Pour Dames 1928,Ja 1,VIII,2:3
  Excelsior 1928,S 30,IX,1:3
  Amoureuse Aventure, L' 1929,F 10,IX,4:6
  Fleurs de Luxe 1930,Mr 23,IX,2:1
Armor, Morris
  Half-Caste, The 1926,Mr 30,20:4
  Creeping Fire 1935,Ja 17,22:3
Armour, Rachel
  Dybbuk, The 1954,O 27,33:6
  Carefree Tree, The 1955,O 12,37:2
  Adding Machine, The 1956,F 10,17:1
  Golem, The 1959,F 26,38:2
  Macbeth 1962,N 17,16:2
Arms, Frances
  Scandals 1920,Je 8,9:1
  Sharlee 1923,N 23,20:1
Arms, Sara
  One Sunday Afternoon 1933,F 16,23:5
Armstrong, A
  Stags at Bay 1934,D 15,9:2
  What a Relief 1935,D 14,10:6
Armstrong, Aileen
  Rules of the Game, The 1960,D 20,44:1
Armstrong, Alexander
  What a Relief 1935,D 14,10:6
  Take It Away 1936,D 15,30:5
  Take It Away 1936,D 22,32:3
Armstrong, Anthony (Playwright)
  Ten Minute Alibi 1933,O 18,24:3
  Without Witness 1933,D 28,25:1
  Sitting on the Fence 1935,Mr 12,25:4
  Mile Away Murder 1937,Ap 3,17:2
  Mile Away Murder 1937,Ap 18,XI,1:4
Armstrong, Betty Coe (Costume Designer)
  Right You Are (If You Think You Are)
    1950,Je 29,37:2
  Johnny Johnson 1956,O 22,24:1
  Day the Money Stopped, The 1958,F 21,19:4
  God and Kate Murphy 1959,F 27,21:2
Armstrong, Betty Coe (Scenic Designer)
  Anvil, The 1962,O 31,33:3
Armstrong, Charlotte (Playwright)
  Happiest Days, The 1939,Ap 12,26:2
  Happiest Days, The 1939,Ap 16,X,1:2
  Ring Around Elizabeth 1941,N 18,32:2
Armstrong, Clyde
  It Pays to Sin 1933,N 4,18:6
Armstrong, Elizabeth (Playwright)
  Tulips Are Blooming, The 1935,D 4,27:6
Armstrong, Eunice Burton (Playwright)
  Technique 1931,My 15,21:1
Armstrong, Faye
  K Guy, The 1928,O 16,28:4
Armstrong, Frances
  Chameleon, The 1932,Jl 19,20:4
  Career 1957,My 1,42:6
Armstrong, Frank
  Elizabeth Sleeps Out 1936,Ap 21,27:6
Armstrong, George
  Opportunity 1920,Jl 31,5:1
Armstrong, Grattan
  Richard III 1957,N 26,41:1
Armstrong, Harry
  Friars Club Frolic 1933,My 15,16:4
Armstrong, James
  Susanna, Don't You Cry 1939,My 23,27:2
Armstrong, Jean
  Macbeth 1955,O 8,12:6
  Thesmophoriazusae, The; Goddesses of Athens,
    The 1955,D 14,52:4
  Bitch of Waverly Place, The 1965,Ap 2,26:1
Armstrong, Jean (Miscellaneous)
  Thesmophoriazusae, The; Goddesses of Athens,
    The 1955,D 14,52:4
Armstrong, John
  Man and Superman 1953,F 21,11:2

Armstrong, John—Cont

King and the Duke, The 1955,Je 2,25:2
Point of No Return 1957,Mr 23,17:2
Billy Budd 1959,F 28,13:3
Time of Vengeance 1959,D 11,39:1
Montserrat 1961,Ja 9,30:5

Armstrong, John (Costume Designer)

Tempest, The 1934,F 4,IX,3:4

Armstrong, John (Director)

Detective Story 1954,F 13,11:2

Armstrong, John (Scenic Designer)

Tempest, The 1934,F 4,IX,3:4

Armstrong, Louis

Swingin' the Dream 1939,N 30,24:2
Mardi Gras! 1966,Jl 11,32:2

Armstrong, Malcolm

Doctor's Dilemma, The 1969,Je 24,37:1

Armstrong, Margaret

That Awful Mrs Eaton! 1924,S 30,27:1
My Girl 1924,N 25,27:2
Celebrity 1927,D 27,24:3

Armstrong, Norman (Playwright)

Lifeline 1942,Jl 12,VIII,1:4
Lifeline 1942,D 1,20:3

Armstrong, Paul (Playwright)

Alias Jimmy Valentine 1921,D 9,20:3
Betty Lee 1924,D 26,18:2

Armstrong, R G

Cat on a Hot Tin Roof 1955,Mr 25,18:2
Cat on a Hot Tin Roof 1955,Ap 3,II,1:1
Orpheus Descending 1957,Mr 22,28:1
Orpheus Descending 1957,Mr 31,II,1:1
Long Dream, The 1960,F 18,36:2

Armstrong, Rena

Great Way, The 1921,N 8,28:2

Armstrong, Robert

Is Zat So? 1925,Ja 6,23:4
Is Zat So? 1925,F 1,VII,1:1
Lambs Gambol 1925,Ap 27,15:1
Sure Fire! 1926,O 21,23:1
Sleep No More 1944,S 1,11:5
What Price Glory 1949,Mr 3,33:2

Armstrong, Rod

Cicero 1961,F 9,37:2

Armstrong, Ron

Pirates of Penzance, The 1966,My 24,54:1
Trial by Jury 1966,Je 8,41:2
H M S Pinafore 1966,Je 8,41:2

Armstrong, Steven (Scenic Designer)

Great God Brown, The 1959,O 18,II,1:1
Androcles and the Lion 1968,Je 27,47:1

Armstrong, Thomas

Merry Duchess, The 1943,Je 24,25:1

Armstrong, Will Steven (Costume Designer)

Family Reunion, The 1958,O 21,39:1
Power and the Glory, The 1958,D 12,2:7
Beaux' Stratagem, The 1959,F 25,35:4
Great God Brown, The 1959,O 7,48:1
Lysistrata 1959,N 25,19:4
Peer Gynt 1960,Ja 13,21:1
Caligula 1960,F 17,31:1
Caligula 1960,F 28,II,1:1
Henry IV 1960,Mr 2,42:1
Henry IV 1960,Ap 19,41:1
King Lear 1963,Je 10,37:1
Comedy of Errors, The 1963,Je 13,28:1
Much Ado About Nothing 1964,Je 11,26:2
Richard III 1964,Je 12,44:2
Girl Could Get Lucky, A 1964,S 21,36:1
Coriolanus 1965,Je 21,36:1
King Lear 1965,Je 25,39:1
Lion in Winter, The 1966,Mr 4,23:1
Julius Caesar 1966,Je 24,29:2

Armstrong, Will Steven (Lighting Director)

Chaparral 1958,S 10,38:2
Ivanov 1958,O 8,42:1
Family Reunion, The 1958,O 21,39:1
Family Reunion, The 1958,O 26,II,1:1
Season of Choice 1959,Ap 14,40:1
Andersonville Trial, The 1959,D 30,15:1
Carnival! 1961,Ap 14,22:2
Cook for Mr General, A 1961,O 20,39:1
Kwamina 1961,O 24,42:1
Subways Are for Sleeping 1961,D 28,22:1
I Can Get It for You Wholesale 1962,Mr 23,29:1
Tchin-Tchin 1962,O 26,26:2
Dear Me, the Sky Is Falling 1963,Mr 4,9:1
Rattle of a Simple Man 1963,Ap 18,39:1
Semi-Detached 1963,O 8,49:1
One Flew Over the Cuckoo's Nest 1963,N 14,40:2
Nobody Loves an Albatross 1963,D 20,20:1
Passion of Josef D, The 1964,F 12,29:1
Benito Cereno 1964,N 2,62:2
My Kinsman, Major Molineux 1964,N 2,62:2
Ready When You Are, C. B.! 1964,D 8,55:1
I Had a Ball 1964,D 16,50:1
3 Bags Full 1966,Mr 7,22:1
Deer Park, The 1967,F 1,27:2
Something Different 1967,N 29,52:1
Zelda 1969,Mr 6,38:1

Armstrong, Will Steven (Miscellaneous)

Rehearsal, The 1963,S 24,45:2
I Had a Ball 1964,D 16,50:1

Armstrong, Will Steven (Scenic Designer)

Chaparral 1958,S 10,38:2
Ivanov 1958,O 8,42:1
Ivanov 1958,O 19,II,1:1
Power and the Glory, The 1958,D 12,2:7
Beaux' Stratagem, The 1959,F 25,35:4
Season of Choice 1959,Ap 14,40:1
Merry Wives of Windsor, The 1959,Jl 9,23:2
All's Well That Ends Well 1959,Ag 3,20:4
Great God Brown, The 1959,O 7,48:1
Lysistrata 1959,N 25,19:4
Andersonville Trial, The 1959,D 30,15:1
Peer Gynt 1960,Ja 13,21:1
Peer Gynt 1960,Ja 24,II,1:1
Caligula 1960,F 17,31:1
Caligula 1960,F 28,II,1:1
Henry IV 1960,Mr 2,42:1
Henry IV 1960,Ap 19,41:1
Carnival! 1961,Ap 14,22:2
Carnival! 1961,Ap 23,II,1:1
Cook for Mr General, A 1961,O 20,39:1
Kwamina 1961,O 24,42:1
Subways Are for Sleeping 1961,D 28,22:1
I Can Get It for You Wholesale 1962,Mr 23,29:1
Tchin-Tchin 1962,O 26,26:2
Dear Me, the Sky Is Falling 1963,Mr 4,9:1
King Lear 1963,Je 10,37:1
Comedy of Errors, The 1963,Je 13,28:1
One Flew Over the Cuckoo's Nest 1963,N 14,40:2
Nobody Loves an Albatross 1963,D 20,20:1
Passion of Josef D, The 1964,F 12,29:1
Much Ado About Nothing 1964,Je 11,26:2
Richard III 1964,Je 12,44:2
Three Sisters, The 1964,Je 23,24:1
Hamlet 1964,Jl 4,9:1
Benito Cereno 1964,N 2,62:2
My Kinsman, Major Molineux 1964,N 2,62:2
Ready When You Are, C. B.! 1964,D 8,55:1
Coriolanus 1965,Je 21,36:1
Romeo and Juliet 1965,Je 21,36:3
King Lear 1965,Je 25,39:1
Wayward Stork, The 1966,Ja 20,27:1
Lion in Winter, The 1966,Mr 4,23:1
3 Bags Full 1966,Mr 7,22:1
Pousse-Cafe 1966,Mr 19,19:2
Twelfth Night 1966,Je 23,28:1
Julius Caesar 1966,Je 24,29:2
Deer Park, The 1967,F 1,27:2
People Is the Thing That the World Is Fullest Of 1967,F 21,53:1
Imaginary Invalid, The 1967,My 2,53:1
Touch of the Poet, A 1967,My 3,38:2
Still Life 1967,My 4,34:1
Fumed Oak 1967,My 4,34:1
Ways and Means 1967,My 4,34:1
Something Different 1967,N 29,52:1
Love's Labour's Lost 1968,Je 28,36:1
Forty Carats 1968,D 27,45:1
Zelda 1969,Mr 6,38:1
Front Page, The 1969,My 12,54:2
Front Page, The 1969,N 2,86:1

Armstrong, William

National Anthem, The 1922,Ja 24,16:3

Armus, Sidney

Wish You Were Here 1952,Je 26,26:6
School for Scandal, The 1953,Je 24,29:2
Flowering Peach, The 1954,D 29,19:2
Johnny Johnson 1956,O 22,24:1
Cold Wind and the Warm, The 1958,D 9,55:1
Harold 1962,N 30,27:1
Never Live Over a Pretzel Factory 1964,Mr 30,37:1

Arnac, Beatrice

Untitled-Revue 1968,O 21,55:4
Cabaret Rive Gauche 1969,S 5,30:1

Arnall, Curtis

Red Rust 1929,D 18,31:1
Elizabeth the Queen 1930,N 4,37:1
Devil in the Mind 1931,My 2,23:2

Arnaud, Georges (Playwright)

Sweet Confession 1959,Ap 15,30:1

Arnaud, Jean-Claude

Avare, L', L'; Miser, The 1966,F 9,32:1
Reine Morte, La 1966,F 16,52:1
Fil a la Paite, Un 1966,F 18,25:1

Arnaud, Karin

Best Sellers 1933,My 4,20:2

Arnaud, Lucien

Lorenzaccio 1958,O 15,44:2
Marie Tudor 1958,O 22,39:1

Arnaud, Pierre (Producer)

Roman Servant, A 1934,D 3,14:5

Arnaud, Yvonne

And So to Bed 1927,N 10,23:1
Mischief 1928,Ag 5,VII,1:1
By Candle Light 1928,O 7,IX,2:7
Canaries Sometimes Sing 1929,N 10,X,2:1
Canaries Sometimes Sing 1930,O 21,34:2
Improper Duchess, The 1931,Ja 23,28:1
Improper Duchess, The 1931,F 8,VIII,3:3
Will You Love Me Always? 1932,O 16,IX,3:7
Henry V 1934,Ja 28,II,3:4
Worse Things Happen at Sea 1935,Ap 21,IX,2:2
Tread Softly 1935,N 8,19:6

Arnaud, Yvonne—Cont

Tread Softly 1935,D 8,X,5:1
Laughter in Court 1936,S 10,29:4
Laughter in Court 1936,S 27,X,3:5
Plan for a Hostess 1938,Mr 27,X,1:3
In Good King Charles's Golden Days 1939,Ag 13,28:1
Let Them Say 1939,Ag 27,IX,1:4
Nutmeg Tree 1941,O 19,IX,2:5
Jane 1947,Ja 30,19:6
Jane 1947,F 9,II,3:7
Colombe 1951,D 15,13:2
Dear Charles 1952,D 21,44:5
Dear Charles 1953,Ap 20,22:4

Arnaudy, Antoine

Maitre Bolbec et son Mari 1926,N 14,VIII,2:1
Topaze 1931,F 17,29:1

Arnaudy, Le Petit

Topaze 1931,F 17,29:1

Arnaut, Nellie

Vaudeville (Palace) 1932,Jl 4,14:5

Arnaut Brothers

Vaudeville (Palace) 1929,Ag 19,23:1
Untitled-Revue 1930,Ap 22,33:2
Vaudeville (Palace) 1931,My 11,15:5

Arnaz, Desi

Too Many Girls 1939,O 19,26:2

Arndt, Jurgen

Wozzeck 1966,Ap 6,34:1
Ratten, Die 1966,Ap 13,36:1

Arnell, France

Grosse Valise, La 1965,D 15,52:1

Arner, Gwen

Murderous Angels 1970,F 8,70:1

Arnes, Jane B

At Your Service 1937,Ag 17,23:1

Arnett, Ray

Banjo Eyes 1941,D 26,20:2

Arnheim, Gus and His Orchestra

Vaudeville (Palace) 1929,Je 24,27:4

Arnheim, Herman W

Oh, Hector! 1929,Mr 6,33:2

Arnheim, Norman

Betty Behave 1927,Mr 9,28:4
Upon My Soul 1927,Ap 22,19:1

Arniches, Carlos (Playwright)

Girl and the Cat, The 1927,My 6,21:2

Arno, Alfred

Tarzan of the Apes 1921,S 8,14:3

Arno, Owen G (Playwright)

Once for the Asking 1963,N 21,42:2

Arno, Peter (Original Author)

New Yorkers, The 1930,N 16,VIII,3:1

Arno, Peter (Playwright)

Murray Anderson's Almanac 1929,Ag 15,20:3
New Yorkers, The 1930,D 9,31:1
Here Goes the Bride 1931,N 4,31:2

Arno, Peter (Producer)

Here Goes the Bride 1931,N 4,31:2

Arno, Peter (Scenic Designer)

New Yorkers, The 1930,D 9,31:1
Here Goes the Bride 1931,N 4,31:2

Arno, Sig

Casanova 1928,N 4,IX,2:1
Three Musketeers 1929,O 13,IX,4:7
Im Weissen Roessel 1930,D 28,VIII,2:4
Song of Norway 1944,Ag 22,20:2
Lady From Paris, The 1950,S 27,36:1
Time Remembered 1957,N 13,41:2
Time Remembered 1957,N 24,II,1:1
Cold Wind and the Warm, The 1958,D 9,55:1
Song of Norway 1959,Je 26,16:2
Merry Widow, The 1964,Ag 18,24:2

Arnold, A (Director)

Moscow Circus on Ice 1970,D 9,63:1

Arnold, A (Playwright)

Moscow Circus on Ice 1970,D 9,63:1

Arnold, Ainsworth

Honest Liars 1926,Jl 20,17:2
Sam Abramovitch 1927,Ja 20,20:5
Pursuit of Happiness, The 1935,Jl 16,24:2
Merry Wives of Windsor, The 1938,Ap 15,22:3
Gloriana 1938,N 26,18:4
Importance of Being Earnest, The 1939,Ja 13,16:2
Time of Your Life, The 1939,O 26,26:2
Time of Your Life, The 1940,S 24,27:2
Sunny River 1941,D 5,28:2

Arnold, Barbara

Pie in the Sky 1941,D 23,26:5

Arnold, Barry (Lighting Director)

Curley McDimple 1967,N 23,59:2
In Circles 1968,Je 28,36:1
To Be Young Gifted and Black; World of Lorraine Hansberry, The 1969,Ja 3,15:1
Millionairess, The 1969,Mr 3,28:1
End of All Things Natural, The 1969,S 12,38:1
Love and Maple Syrup 1970,Ja 8,47:1

Arnold, Barry (Scenic Designer)

David Show, The 1968,N 1,34:2
End of All Things Natural, The 1969,S 12,38:1
President's Daughter, The 1970,N 4,41:2

Arnold, Carolyn

Charm School, The 1920,Ag 3,12:1

Arnold, David
Jubilee 1935,O 14,20:1
Arnold, Dick
Diamond Lil 1948,N 30,33:2
Diamond Lil 1949,F 7,16:2
Arnold, Edith
Jarnegan 1928,S 25,29:2
Censored 1938,F 28,18:2
Arnold, Edward
Beyond the Horizon 1920,F 4,12:1
Beyond the Horizon 1920,F 8,VIII,2:1
Mad Honeymoon, The 1923,Ag 8,10:1
Nervous Wreck, The 1923,O 10,16:1
Her Way Out 1924,Je 24,18:3
Easy Come, Easy Go 1925,O 27,20:2
Phantom Ship 1926,Je 27,VII,3:1
Julie 1927,My 10,24:4
Grey Fox, The 1928,O 23,32:3
Conflict 1929,Mr 7,22:4
Miracle at Verdun 1931,Mr 17,34:6
Third Little Show, The 1931,Je 2,34:3
Whistling in the Dark 1932,Ja 20,16:6
Arnold, Francis (Playwright)
Whole Town's Talking, The 1923,Ag 30,8:2
Arnold, Gaynor
Hamlet 1970,D 28,40:1
Arnold, Harry
American Tragedy, An 1926,O 12,31:2
Arnold, Helen
Music Hall Varieties 1932,N 23,15:3
Student Prince, The 1937,Jl 28,15:1
Roberta 1937,S 7,16:4
Arnold, Jack
Yoshe Kalb 1933,D 29,27:2
Shatter'd Lamp, The 1934,Mr 22,26:3
Young Go First, The 1935,My 29,16:2
But for the Grace of God 1937,Ja 13,21:4
Horse Fever 1940,N 25,21:2
Bell for Adano, A 1944,D 7,21:2
Front Page, The 1946,S 5,22:4
Arnold, James
Shuffle Along of 1933 1932,D 27,11:3
Troilus and Cressida 1965,Ag 13,17:1
Arnold, James Murray
Walk in Darkness 1963,O 29,30:2
Arnold, Jean
Threepenny Opera, The 1956,Mr 11,II,1:1
Arnold, Jeanne
Heartbreak House 1963,Je 8,14:2
Heartbreak House 1963,Je 28,24:1
Happy Time, The 1968,Ja 19,32:2
Coco 1969,D 19,66:1
Arnold, Kathleen
Seven Mirrors 1945,O 26,17:2
Arnold, Ken
Sweethearts 1947,Ja 22,31:2
Arnold, Laura
Virtue (?) 1922,N 17,14:1
Adrienne 1923,My 29,10:4
Arnold, Lois
It Is to Laugh 1927,D 27,24:2
Quicksand 1928,F 14,26:3
Conflict 1929,Mr 7,22:4
Overture 1930,N 25,31:2
Overture 1930,D 8,26:4
Arnold, Louise (Miscellaneous)
Moon Besieged, The 1962,D 6,54:1
Arnold, Lucille
Artists and Models 1927,N 16,28:2
Arnold, Madison
Picture of Dorian Gray, The 1963,Ag 29,37:4
Man in the Glass Booth, The 1968,S 27,41:1
Arnold, Marie
By the Way 1925,D 29,20:3
Arnold, Marjorie
New Yorkers, The 1930,D 9,31:1
Arnold, Maxine
On the Town 1944,D 29,11:4
Arnold, Monroe
Leave It to Jane 1959,My 26,30:2
Days and Nights of Beebee Fenstermaker, The
1962,S 18,33:1
Enter Laughing 1963,Mr 15,8:1
Arnold, Nancy
Patience 1928,Je 26,29:3
Arnold, Nicholas (Director)
Hamlet 1970,D 28,40:1
Arnold, Phil
Summer Wives 1936,Ap 14,18:1
Arnold, Richard
Make Mine Manhattan 1948,Ja 16,26:2
Sign of Jonah, The 1957,My 2,27:1
Everyman Today 1958,Ja 16,32:4
Cup of Trembling, The 1959,My 1,33:5
Arnold, Robert
Knickerbocker Holiday 1938,O 20,26:2
Arnold, Roberta
First Year, The 1920,O 21,11:2
First Year, The 1920,O 31,VI,1:1
Spite Corner 1921,Jl 17,VI,1:1
First Year, The 1921,N 27,VI,1:1
Chicken Feed 1923,S 25,10:2
Tantrum, The 1924,S 5,20:2

Downstream 1926,Ja 12,28:1
Sisters 1927,D 26,26:5
Adventure 1928,S 26,25:2
Arnold, Seth
Arabian Nightmare, The 1927,Ja 11,36:3
Quicksand 1928,F 14,26:3
Conflict 1929,Mr 7,22:4
Suspense 1930,Ag 13,22:3
Free for All 1931,S 9,25:1
Steel 1931,N 19,26:5
Mourning Becomes Electra; Homecoming
1932,My 10,25:2
Mourning Becomes Electra; Haunted, The
1932,My 10,25:2
Two Strange Women 1933,Ja 11,23:3
Unto the Third 1933,Ap 21,24:8
Tommy 1933,Ag 8,22:5
Pursuit of Happiness, The 1933,O 10,24:4
Symphony 1935,Ap 27,20:3
Pursuit of Happiness, The 1935,Jl 16,24:2
Ah, Wilderness! 1935,Ag 20,25:1
Lady Luck 1936,Ap 16,21:2
It Can't Happen Here 1936,O 28,30:1
Many Mansions 1937,O 28,28:6
Something for Nothing 1937,D 10,33:5
Escape Into Glory 1941,No 20,24:2
Village Green 1941,Je 17,24:7
Clash by Night 1941,D 29,20:2
Harriet 1943,Mr 4,24:2
Last Stop 1944,S 6,17:2
Place of Our Own, A 1945,Ap 3,23:7
Joy Forever, A 1946,Ja 8,20:2
I Like It Here 1946,Mr 23,8:6
Years Ago 1946,D 4,44:2
Arms and the Girl 1950,F 3,28:2
Arnold, Seth (Director)
Devil of Pei-Ling 1936,F 21,20:4
Arnold, Stanley (Composer)
Hilarities 1948,S 10,20:2
Arnold, Stanley (Lyricist)
Hilarities 1948,S 10,20:2
Arnold, Tom (Producer)
Affairs of State 1952,Ag 22,12:2
Arnold, Victor
Deputy, The 1964,F 27,26:1
Lovey 1965,Mr 26,27:1
Malcolm 1966,Ja 12,29:1
Fortune and Men's Eyes 1967,F 24,29:1
We Bombed in New Haven 1968,O 17,51:1
Time for Bed 1969,Je 14,24:1
Take Me to Bed 1969,Je 14,24:1
Arnold, Ward
Rainbow 1928,N 22,25:1
Face the Music 1932,F 18,24:5
Arnold (Original Author)
Rise and Shine 1936,My 8,21:4
Arnoldoff, Roman
Infinite Shoeblack, The 1930,F 18,28:1
His Majesty's Car 1930,O 24,30:1
Colonel Satan 1931,Ja 12,24:1
Wonder Bar, The 1931,Mr 18,23:4
Late One Evening 1933,Ja 10,27:3
Arnon, Charlotte
Jacques Bergson 1936,O 31,24:6
Arnou, Ely (Miscellaneous)
Mother's Sabbath Days 1960,N 21,33:2
Arnou, Fanny Anne
Picture of Dorian Gray, The 1956,Ag 18,15:5
Arnould, Georges (Playwright)
Palace aux Femmes 1926,O 10,VIII,2:1
Vrai Mistere de la Passion, Le 1937,S 5,X,5:3
Arnoux, Alexandre (Playwright)
Medecin de Son Honneur 1935,Mr 3,VIII,2:3
Arnovich, Nikola (Lighting Director)
Shakuntala 1959,S 10,41:2
Arnst, Bobbe
Greenwich Village Follies 1924,S 17,16:1
LeMaire's Affairs 1927,Mr 29,22:4
A la Carte 1927,Ag 18,25:3
Rosalie 1928,Ja 11,26:3
Simple Simon 1930,F 19,22:1
Fabulous Invalid, The 1938,O 10,15:1
Arnstein, Mark (Playwright)
Naomi 1920,My 7,12:2
Arnstein, Mark (Producer)
One Life for Another 1920,D 18,11:2
Arnt, Arthur (Miscellaneous)
1935 1936,My 13,28:2
Arnt, Arthur (Playwright)
Power 1937,F 24,18:5
Arnt, Charles
Idiot's Delight 1937,Ag 10,22:7
Knickerbocker Holiday 1938,O 20,26:2
Arnt, Charles E
Carry Nation 1932,O 31,18:2
Arnt, Charles E Jr
Hamlet 1927,Ap 7,23:3
Caesar and Cleopatra 1927,N 6,IX,2:1
Napoleon Passes 1927,D 21,29:2
Zuider Zee 1928,D 19,24:4
Torch Bearers, The 1929,Mr 22,30:4
Arnt, Charlie
Worse Things Happen at Sea 1937,S 1,15:3

Arnt, Charlie—Cont

Three Waltzes 1937,D 27,10:2
Arobbio, Inez
This Happy Breed 1952,Ap 4,23:2
Aron, Adele
Boy Friend, The 1958,Ja 27,24:4
Gay Divorce 1960,Ap 4,37:1
Arons, Frances
Diamond Lil 1948,N 30,33:2
Diamond Lil 1949,F 7,16:2
Aronson, Alvin
Grass Harp, The 1953,Ap 28,32:2
Aronson, Alvin (Director)
Nighthawks 1967,D 30,14:2
Aronson, Alvin (Playwright)
Pocket Watch, The 1966,Ja 6,18:1
Nighthawks 1967,D 30,14:2
Aronson, Arthur (Lighting Director)
Wayside 1957,Ap 18,34:1
Bei Mir Bistu Schoen 1961,O 23,22:2
Aronson, Arthur (Scenic Designer)
Rosmersholm 1946,N 23,11:5
Wayside 1957,Ap 18,34:1
'Tis Pity She's a Whore 1958,D 6,21:1
Alley of the Sunset 1959,D 31,11:1
Bei Mir Bistu Schoen 1961,O 23,22:2
Good Luck 1964,O 19,38:3
Aronson, Beatrice (Playwright)
This Is Today 1935,Jl 30,17:2
Aronson, Boris (Costume Designer)
Stempenu, the Fiddler 1929,Mr 9,24:7
Angels on Earth 1929,D 11,34:7
Heavenly Express 1940,Ap 19,24:2
Cabin in the Sky 1940,O 26,19:2
Cabin in the Sky 1940,N 3,IX,1:1
Price, The 1968,F 8,37:1
Aronson, Boris (Lighting Director)
Stranger, The 1945,F 13,21:2
Survivors, The 1948,Ja 20,27:2
Bird Cage, The 1950,F 23,32:2
Barefoot in Athens 1951,N 1,35:2
I Am a Camera 1951,N 29,39:6
Frogs of Spring, The 1953,O 21,36:2
Rope Dancers, The 1957,N 21,39:1
Aronson, Boris (Lyricist)
Season in the Sun 1950,S 29,31:2
Aronson, Boris (Miscellaneous)
Ladies' Money 1934,N 2,26:6
Fiddler on the Roof 1969,N 16,82:6
Company 1970,Ap 27,40:1
Aronson, Boris (Scenic Designer)
Stempenu, the Fiddler 1929,Mr 9,24:7
Jew Suss 1929,O 19,22:3
Angels on Earth 1929,D 11,34:7
Roaming Stars 1930,Ja 25,12:2
Jim Cooperkop 1930,O 18,23:1
Walk a Little Faster 1932,D 8,24:4
Small Miracle 1934,S 27,24:3
Battleship Gertie 1935,Ja 19,9:2
Three Men on a Horse 1935,Ja 31,22:3
Awake and Sing! 1935,F 20,23:2
Body Beautiful, The 1935,N 1,24:3
Weep for the Virgins 1935,D 2,18:1
Paradise Lost 1935,D 10,31:5
Western Waters 1937,O 29,17:1
Merchant of Yonkers, The 1938,D 29,14:2
Gentle People, The 1939,Ja 6,25:1
Awake and Sing! 1939,Mr 8,18:2
Ladies and Gentlemen 1939,O 18,30:2
Unconquered, The 1940,F 14,25:2
Heavenly Express 1940,Ap 19,24:2
Cabin in the Sky 1940,O 26,19:2
Cabin in the Sky 1940,N 3,IX,1:1
Night Before Christmas, The 1941,Ap 11,25:2
Clash by Night 1941,D 29,20:2
Clash by Night 1942,Ja 11,IX,1:1
Cafe Crown 1942,Ja 24,12:5
R U R 1942,D 4,30:2
Russian People, The 1942,D 30,17:2
Family, The 1943,Mr 31,22:4
What's Up 1943,N 12,24:6
South Pacific 1943,D 30,11:2
Sadie Thompson 1944,N 17,25:2
Stranger, The 1945,F 13,21:2
Assassin, The 1945,O 18,20:2
Desert Song, The 1946,Ja 9,20:2
Truckline Cafe 1946,F 28,19:4
Gypsy Lady 1946,S 18,25:6
Skipper Next to God 1948,Ja 5,14:5
Survivors, The 1948,Ja 20,27:2
Survivors, The 1948,Ja 25,II,1:1
Love Life 1948,O 8,31:2
Detective Story 1949,Mr 24,34:2
Detective Story 1949,Ap 3,II,1:1
Bird Cage, The 1950,F 23,32:2
Season in the Sun 1950,S 29,31:2
Season in the Sun 1950,O 8,II,1:1
Country Girl, The 1950,N 19,II,1:1
Rose Tattoo, The 1951,F 5,19:2
Rose Tattoo, The 1951,F 11,II,1:1
Barefoot in Athens 1951,N 1,35:2
Barefoot in Athens 1951,N 11,II,1:1
I Am a Camera 1951,N 29,39:6
I Am a Camera 1951,D 9,II,5:1

Aronson, Boris (Scenic Designer)—Cont
I've Got Sixpence 1952,D 3,44:2
I've Got Sixpence 1952,D 7,II,5:1
Crucible, The 1953,Ja 23,15:2
My 3 Angels 1953,Mr 12,23:2
Crucible, The 1953,Jl 2,20:2
Frogs of Spring, The 1953,O 21,36:2
Mademoiselle Colombe 1954,Ja 7,26:1
Mademoiselle Colombe 1954,Ja 17,II,1:1
Master Builder, The 1955,Mr 2,23:2
Bus Stop 1955,Mr 3,23:2
Bus Stop 1955,Mr 13,II,1:1
Master Builder, The 1955,Mr 20,II,1:1
Once Upon a Tailor 1955,My 24,36:2
Memory of Two Mondays, A 1955,S 30,21:1
View From the Bridge, A 1955,S 30,21:1
Diary of Anne Frank, The 1955,O 6,24:2
View From the Bridge, A 1955,O 9,II,1:1
Diary of Anne Frank, The 1955,O 16,II,1:1
Girls of Summer 1956,N 20,45:1
Small War on Murray Hill 1957,Ja 4,19:1
Small War on Murray Hill 1957,Ja 13,II,1:1
Hole in the Head, A 1957,Mr 1,15:1
Hole in the Head, A 1957,Mr 10,II,1:1
Orpheus Descending 1957,Mr 22,28:1
Orpheus Descending 1957,Mr 31,II,1:1
Rope Dancers, The 1957,N 21,39:1
Rope Dancers, The 1957,D 1,II,1:1
Firstborn, The 1958,My 1,35:1
Firstborn, The 1958,My 11,II,1:1
Firstborn, The 1958,Jl 4,16:3
Cold Wind and the Warm, The 1958,D 9,55:1
J B 1958,D 12,2:7
J B 1959,My 10,II,1:1
Flowering Cherry 1959,O 22,46:1
Loss of Roses, A 1959,N 30,27:1
Loss of Roses, A 1959,D 6,II,5:1
Semi-Detached 1960,Mr 11,20:2
Do Re Mi 1960,D 27,23:2
Do Re Mi 1961,Ja 8,II,1:1
Garden of Sweets, The 1961,N 1,35:1
Gift of Time, A 1962,F 23,34:1
Andorra 1963,F 11,5:5
Fiddler on the Roof 1964,S 23,56:2
Fiddler on the Roof 1964,O 4,II,1:1
Incident at Vichy 1964,D 4,44:1
Cabaret 1966,N 21,62:1
Cabaret 1966,D 4,II,5:1
Fiddler on the Roof 1967,S 7,50:1
Cabaret 1968,Ja 12,19:1
Price, The 1968,F 8,37:1
Price, The 1968,F 18,II,1:1
Zorba 1968,N 18,58:1
Zorba 1968,N 24,II,1:1
Cabaret 1969,F 2,74:2
Company 1970,Ap 27,40:1
Company 1970,My 3,II,1:4
Aronson, Boris (Scenic Designer) (Lighting Director)
Country Girl, The 1950,N 11,10:6
Aronson, Chaim
East Side Professor, The 1938,F 12,19:7
Aronson, Frances
Way of the World, The 1950,Ap 9,73:5
Aronson, Herbert (Producer)
Anatomist, The 1957,F 27,21:5
Aronson, Irene (Costume Designer)
Front Page, The 1946,S 5,22:4
Aronson, Jack
King Lear 1956,Ja 13,17:1
Lady's Not for Burning, The 1959,Ja 31,13:2
Aronson, John
Firstborn, The 1957,Ja 7,29:2
Doctor Faustus 1957,F 19,35:7
Cock-A-Doodle Dandy 1958,N 13,39:2
Aronson, Ruth Kanin (Costume Designer)
Born Yesterday 1946,F 5,18:2
Aronstein, Martin (Lighting Director)
Taming of the Shrew, The 1960,Ag 20,17:1
Romeo and Juliet 1961,F 24,24:1
Richard II 1961,Ag 30,25:1
Black Nativity 1961,D 12,54:2
Julius Caesar 1962,F 22,19:6
Electra 1962,Mr 22,42:1
Mister Roberts 1962,O 12,27:2
Winter's Tale, The 1963,Ag 16,14:1
Morning Sun 1963,O 7,36:2
Milk Train Doesn't Stop Here Anymore, The
  1964,Ja 2,33:1
White Rose and the Red, The 1964,Mr 17,31:1
Cindy 1964,Mr 20,24:1
Midsummer Night's Dream, A 1964,Je 30,23:2
Othello 1964,Jl 15,29:1
Electra 1964,Ag 12,42:1
Severed Head, A 1964,O 29,40:1
I Was Dancing 1964,N 9,40:4
Tiny Alice 1964,D 30,14:2
Love's Labour's Lost 1965,Je 16,46:1
Henry V 1965,Je 29,27:2
Coriolanus 1965,Jl 15,23:1
Troilus and Cressida 1965,Ag 13,17:1
Impossible Years, The 1965,O 14,55:1
Royal Hunt of the Sun, The 1965,O 27,36:2
Cactus Flower 1965,D 9,60:2
Condemned of Altona, The 1966,F 4,21:1

Mutilated, The 1966,F 23,42:1
Gnadiges Fraulein, The 1966,F 23,42:1
All's Well That Ends Well 1966,Je 17,39:1
Measure for Measure 1966,Jl 14,27:1
Richard III 1966,Ag 11,26:1
Investigation, The 1966,O 5,40:1
Those That Play the Clowns 1966,N 25,48:1
Persecution and Assassination of Marat As
  Performed by the Inmates of the Asylum of
  Charenton Under the Direction of the Marquis de
  Sade, The 1967,Ja 4,34:1
Astrakhan Coat, The 1967,Ja 13,18:1
East Wind, The 1967,F 10,30:1
Galileo 1967,Ap 14,31:1
Comedy of Errors, The 1967,Je 15,58:4
King John 1967,Jl 14,19:1
Titus Andronicus 1967,Ag 10,43:2
Song of the Grasshopper 1967,S 29,52:2
Hair 1967,O 30,55:1
How Now, Dow Jones 1967,D 8,53:1
Hamlet 1967,D 27,45:1
Guide, The 1968,Mr 7,50:1
Education of H*Y*M*A*N K*A*P*L*A*N, The
  1968,Ap 5,57:1
George M! 1968,Ap 11,48:1
I'm Solomon 1968,Ap 24,51:1
Memorandum, The 1968,My 6,55:1
Henry IV, Part I 1968,Je 30,54:7
Henry IV, Part II 1968,Jl 2,33:1
Romeo and Juliet 1968,Ag 16,19:1
Her First Roman 1968,O 21,53:3
Huui, Huui 1968,N 25,58:1
Night 1968,N 29,52:1
Morning 1968,N 29,52:1
Noon 1968,N 29,52:1
Promises, Promises 1968,D 2,59:3
Dames at Sea 1968,D 21,46:1
Forty Carats 1968,D 27,45:1
Cities in Bezique; Owl Answers, The
  1969,Ja 13,26:1
Cities in Bezique; Beast's Story, A 1969,Ja 13,26:1
Play It Again, Sam 1969,F 13,52:3
Dozens, The 1969,Mr 14,51:1
Invitation to a Beheading 1969,Mr 18,36:1
Billy 1969,Mr 24,56:1
Peer Gynt 1969,Jl 17,56:1
Twelfth Night 1969,Ag 14,29:2
Reckoning, The 1969,S 5,28:1
Penny Wars, The 1969,O 16,52:1
Buck White 1969,D 3,63:1
Strada, La 1969,D 15,63:1
Sambo 1969,D 22,42:1
Paris Is Out! 1970,F 3,35:1
Dr Fish 1970,Mr 11,42:2
Chinese, The 1970,Mr 11,42:2
Grin and Bare It 1970,Mr 17,36:1
Postcards 1970,Mr 17,36:1
Effect of Gamma Rays on Man-in-the-Moon
  Marigolds, The 1970,Ap 8,32:1
Park 1970,Ap 23,47:1
Mod Donna 1970,My 4,48:1
Wars of the Roses, The (Part I) 1970,Jl 2,30:1
Wars of the Roses, The (Part II) 1970,Jl 3,15:2
Richard III 1970,Jl 4,11:1
Happiness Cage, The 1970,O 5,56:4
Trelawny of the 'Wells' 1970,O 12,48:1
Jack MacGowran in the Works of Samuel Beckett
  1970,N 20,32:1
Gingerbread Lady, The 1970,D 14,58:3
Aronstein, Martin (Miscellaneous)
Much Ado About Nothing 1961,Jl 7,17:1
No Place to Be Somebody 1969,D 31,17:1
Arostegui, Diana
Romeo y Julieta 1965,Ag 28,13:3
Arquette, Michael
Automobile Graveyard, The 1961,N 14,46:2
Arquilliere
Potash and Perlmutter 1926,N 14,VIII,2:1
Assommoir, L' 1927,O 16,IX,4:7
Tombeau Sous l'Arc de Triomphe
  1929,Je 16,VIII,2:3
Arrabal, Fernando (Playwright)
Two Executioners, The 1960,My 17,42:2
Picnic on the Battlefield 1960,My 17,42:2
Automobile Graveyard, The 1961,N 14,46:2
Two Executioners, The 1964,Mr 25,46:2
Picnic on the Battlefield 1967,S 9,25:2
Labyrinth, The 1968,S 22,II,1:6
Guernica 1969,My 1,50:1
Pique-Nique en Campagne 1969,My 1,50:1
Jardin des Delices, Le 1969,N 4,54:1
Architect and the Emperor of Assyria, The
  1970,Jl 24,17:2
Architect and the Emperor of Assyria, The
  1970,Ag 9,II,1:5
Arren, Charlotte
Sketch Book 1935,Je 5,22:2
Jerry Lewis' Variety Show 1957,F 8,18:5
Arrick, Larry (Director)
Power of Dreams, A 1958,Mr 11,33:1
Sandbox, The 1960,My 17,42:2
Picnic on the Battlefield 1960,My 17,42:2
Chip, The 1960,My 17,42:2

Arrick, Larry (Director)—Cont
Two Executioners, The 1960,My 17,42:2
Death of Bessie Smith, The 1961,Mr 2,19:1
Heroine, The 1963,F 21,5:5
Journey of the Fifth Horse, The 1966,Ap 22,36:1
Carricknabauna 1967,Mr 31,30:1
Fragments 1967,O 3,56:1
Basement, The 1967,O 3,56:1
Fragments; Basement, The 1967,O 15,II,3:3
We Bombed in New Haven 1967,D 7,58:1
We Bombed in New Haven 1967,D 17,II,3:7
Three Sisters, The 1968,Mr 18,56:1
Coriolanus 1968,My 26,II,7:1
Empire Builders, The 1968,O 2,34:1
Witness 1968,N 22,38:1
Sweet Eros 1968,N 22,38:1
My Daughter, Your Son 1969,My 14,36:2
Metamorphoses 1969,D 12,69:1
Nest, The 1970,Ap 10,46:1
Three Philip Roth Stories; Conversion of the Jews
  1970,Jl 31,14:1
Three Philip Roth Stories; Defender of the Faith
  1970,Jl 31,14:1
Three Philip Roth Stories; Conversion of the Jews
  1970,Jl 31,14:1
Three Philip Roth Stories; Epstein 1970,Jl 31,14:1
Cops and Horrors; Dracula 1970,Ag 11,27:1
Cops and Horrors; Fly Paper 1970,Ag 11,27:1
Story Theater Repertory; Gimpel the Food
  1970,O 21,40:1
Story Theater Repertory; Saint Julian the
  Hospitaler 1970,O 21,40:1
Arrick, Larry (Playwright)
Three Philip Roth Stories; Epstein 1970,Jl 31,14:1
Three Philip Roth Stories; Defender of the Faith
  1970,Jl 31,14:1
Three Philip Roth Stories; Conversion of the Jews
  1970,Jl 31,14:1
Story Theater Repertory; Gimpel the Food
  1970,O 21,40:1
Arrick, Rose
Guitar 1959,N 11,42:5
Lady Akane, The 1960,N 16,51:4
Three Sisters, The 1968,Mr 18,56:1
Arrighi, Mel
Taming of the Shrew, The 1956,Ag 11,11:2
Sign of Jonah, The 1960,S 9,35:1
Sharon's Grave 1961,N 9,39:2
Arrighi, Mel (Playwright)
Ordinary Man, An 1968,S 10,39:1
Castro Complex, The 1970,N 19,40:1
Arrobio, Inez
Old Maid, The 1949,Ja 27,20:6
Post Road 1949,Ap 28,27:3
Arrol, Jane
Sweetheart Shop, The 1920,S 1,13:4
Clinging Vine, The 1922,D 25,20:2
Arrow, Jerry (Miscellaneous)
Jo 1964,F 13,25:1
Arrow, Margaret
Redemption: Lebende Leichnam, Der; Living
  Corpse, The 1928,N 20,28:2
Tomorrow 1928,D 29,20:2
See Naples and Die 1929,S 27,30:4
Unsophisticates, The 1929,D 31,14:5
Autumn Crocus 1932,N 21,20:2
Noah 1935,F 14,25:2
Arrowsmith, William (Translator)
Birds, The 1966,Jl 1,40:1
Arroyo, Felix
Concept, The 1968,My 7,51:1
Arroyo, Pilar
Leyenda del Beso, La 1942,N 20,26:4
Arshansky, Michael (Miscellaneous)
Mikado, The 1959,O 2,24:1
Artaud
Cenci, The 1935,Je 16,X,1:1
Artaud (Playwright)
Cenci, The 1935,Je 16,X,1:1
Artfield, Jules
Passing of the Third Floor Back, The
  1928,Ja 17,22:7
Passing of the Third Floor Back, The
  1928,F 21,18:2
Waltz of the Dogs, The 1928,Ap 26,31:3
Gods of the Lightning 1928,O 25,27:2
Uncle Vanya 1929,My 25,17:1
Arthur, Art (Original Author)
Hold It! 1948,My 6,31:5
Arthur, Beatrice
Adding Machine, The 1948,N 18,35:2
Yes is for a Very Young Man 1949,Je 7,27:2
Creditors 1949,N 22,36:5
Heartbreak House 1950,Mr 22,33:2
Threepenny Opera, The 1954,Mr 11,26:5
Threepenny Opera, The 1954,Mr 21,II,1:1
Shoestring Revue 1955,Mr 1,22:2
Seventh Heaven 1955,My 27,16:2
Threepenny Opera, The 1955,S 21,38:1
Threepenny Opera, The 1956,Mr 11,II,1:1
Hamlet 1957,Ja 29,27:1
Nature's Way 1957,O 17,42:2
Ulysses in Nighttown 1958,Je 6,30:1
Chic 1959,My 19,28:2

Arthur, Beatrice—Cont
Gay Divorce 1960,Ap 4,37:1
Fiddler on the Roof 1964,S 23,56:2
Mame 1966,My 25,41:1
Arthur, Carol
High Spirits 1964,Ap 8,34:1
Ben Bagley's New Cole Porter Revue 1965,D 23,20:1
Arthur, Dave
Ten Million Ghosts 1936,O 24,23:7
Arthur, Florence
Bunk of 1926 1926,F 17,12:3
Bunk of 1926 1926,Ap 23,25:2
Arthur, Frederick
Lady of the Lamp, The 1920,Ag 18,6:4
Arthur, Garrett
Way, The 1940,O 12,20:3
Arthur, George K
Vaudeville (Palace) 1929,O 21,31:2
Arthur, George K (Director)
E & O E 1935,Jl 12,15:3
Something More Important 1935,Jl 12,15:3
Old Women, The 1935,Jl 12,15:3
Arthur, George K (Playwright)
Provincetown Follies, The 1935,N 4,24:3
Arthur, George K (Producer)
E & O E 1935,Jl 12,15:3
Something More Important 1935,Jl 12,15:3
Old Women, The 1935,Jl 12,15:3
Arthur, Hartney (Director)
Legend of Lizzie, The 1959,F 10,39:1
Arthur, Hartney (Producer)
Legend of Lizzie, The 1959,F 10,39:1
Arthur, Helen
Grand Street Follies, The 1924,My 21,22:2
Grand Street Follies, The 1925,Je 19,24:1
Grand Street Follies, The 1926,Je 16,23:2
Arthur, Helen (Producer)
Night in the House 1935,N 8,19:5
Arthur, Helen Jean
Point of No Return 1957,Mr 23,17:2
Send Me No Flowers 1960,D 6,54:1
Arthur, Helene
Student Prince, The 1943,Je 9,16:2
Blossom Time 1943,S 6,21:2
Arthur, Henry
Right This Way 1938,Ja 6,22:3
Arthur, Hope
Song for a Certain Midnight 1959,S 17,49:1
Arthur, Howard
Trial of Dr Beck, The 1937,Ag 10,22:2
Arthur, Jack
Johnny 2X4 1942,Mr 17,24:6
Arthur, Jean
Foreign Affairs 1932,Ap 14,25:5
Man Who Reclaimed His Head 1932,S 9,17:3
$25 an Hour 1933,My 11,14:4
Curtain Rises, The 1933,O 20,15:2
Bride of Torozko, The 1934,Jl 10,24:7
Bride of Torozko, The 1934,S 14,24:2
Peter Pan 1950,Ap 25,27:2
Peter Pan 1950,Ap 30,II,1:1
Saint Joan 1954,S 18,12:1
Arthur, John
Elsie 1923,Ap 3,26:1
Time for Elizabeth 1948,S 28,32:3
Arthur, Julia
Macbeth 1921,F 18,16:1
Macbeth 1921,F 27,VI,1:1
Hamlet 1923,F 6,14:1
Arthur, Kathleen
Talking Parrot, The 1923,D 4,25:3
Arthur, Maureen
Something Different 1967,N 29,52:1
Arthur, Phil
Bell for Adano, A 1944,N 10,24:6
Bell for Adano, A 1944,D 7,21:2
Bathsheba 1947,Mr 27,40:2
With a Silk Thread 1950,Ap 13,34:3
Not for Children 1951,F 14,35:2
Point of No Return 1951,D 14,35:2
Mary Stuart 1956,Ap 28,10:2
Auntie Mame 1958,Ag 12,33:2
Arthur, Philip
Way, The 1940,O 12,20:3
Arthur, Raymond
Aiglon, L' 1927,D 27,24:3
Arthur, Roland
Wandering Jew, The 1927,F 2,22:4
Arthur, Sherwood (Director)
Apollo of Bellac, The 1957,Ap 10,39:1
Virtuous Island, The 1957,Ap 10,39:1
Song of Songs 1958,O 29,31:1
Maidens and Mistresses at Home at the Zoo 1958,O 29,31:1
Courtyard 1960,Mr 1,28:1
Magnificent Hugo, The 1961,Ap 8,12:2
Pocket Watch, The 1966,Ja 6,18:1
What Did We Do Wrong? 1967,O 23,56:1
What Did We Do Wrong? 1967,N 12,II,5:6
God Bless You, Harold Fineberg 1969,Mr 31,30:2
Arthur, T S (Original Author)
Ten Nights in a Barroom 1928,Mr 28,31:2
Ten Nights in a Barroom 1932,Ja 21,17:1

Arthur, Tom
New Faces of 1962 1962,F 2,25:1
Arthy, Judith
Arms and the Man 1970,Jl 10,18:1
Artic, Robert
X Has No Value 1970,F 17,35:1
Artist, Michael
Love's Old Sweet Song 1940,My 3,16:3
Blind Alley 1940,O 16,28:2
Brooklyn Biarritz 1941,F 28,16:2
Strings, My Lord, Are False, The 1942,My 20,24:2
Richard III 1943,Mr 27,8:3
Artley, Edith
Sweethearts 1929,S 23,25:1
Mlle Modiste 1929,O 8,34:1
Artmovsky, Simen (Composer)
Zaporogetz Za Dunayem 1937,My 9,II,5:3
Artmovsky, Simen (Playwright)
Zaporogetz Za Dunayem 1937,My 9,II,5:3
Artus, Louis (Playwright)
Homme d'Hier, L' 1929,My 19,IX,2:1
Artzibasheff, Michael (Original Author)
Lovers and Enemies 1927,S 21,27:1
Artzibasheff, Michael (Playwright)
War 1929,S 19,37:3
Jealousy 1930,D 20,31:4
Jealousy 1936,S 28,14:3
Aruda, Betty
Chief Thing, The 1963,Ap 30,27:2
Arundel, Frank
George Washington 1920,Mr 2,9:1
Lady Cristilinda, The 1922,D 26,11:2
King Lear 1923,Mr 10,9:4
As You Like It 1923,Ap 24,24:1
Wrecker, The 1928,F 28,18:2
Arundell, Dennis
Indian Summer 1936,Ap 20,17:5
Arvamo, Celia (Director)
Waltz of the Dogs, The 1928,Ap 26,31:3
Arvanitou, Phryne
Hippolytus 1968,N 20,38:3
Arville, Colette d'
Variations of 1940 1940,Ja 29,12:1
Arvold, Mason (Lighting Director)
Alive and Kicking 1950,Ja 18,25:5
Arzoomanian, Ralph (Director)
Moths, The 1970,My 12,46:1
Arzoomanian, Ralph (Playwright)
Coop, The 1966,Mr 2,48:1
Moths, The 1970,My 12,46:1
Asbury, Herbert (Miscellaneous)
Devil of Pei-Ling 1936,F 21,20:4
Ascarra, Maria
Spanish Love 1920,Ag 18,6:1
Ascencio, Ramon
King Lear 1968,Je 3,55:4
Asch, Jeanne
Worm in Horseradish, A 1961,Mr 14,32:3
Asch, Sholem (Original Author)
Kiddish Hashem 1928,S 30,IX,1:1
Uncle Moses 1930,N 29,21:3
Chayim Lederer 1932,N 15,24:4
Three Cities 1938,O 11,20:3
Salvation 1939,S 29,19:2
Asch, Sholem (Playwright)
God of Revenge, The 1921,N 4,15:2
God of Vengeance, The 1922,D 20,22:5
Night 1923,My 26,8:4
Chair, The 1930,O 4,15:4
Witch of Castile, The 1930,O 25,21:1
Motke Ganef 1932,D 30,15:2
Motke Ganef 1935,Mr 18,15:2
Asche, Oscar
Royal Visitor, The 1924,O 5,VIII,2:2
Merry Wives of Windsor, The: 1929 Version 1929,Jl 27,7:2
Julius Caesar 1932,F 28,VIII,2:4
Asche, Oscar (Director)
Julius Caesar 1932,F 28,VIII,2:4
Asche, Oscar (Playwright)
Mecca 1920,O 5,12:2
Merry Wives of Windsor, The: 1929 Version 1929,Jl 27,7:2
Eldorado 1930,S 4,26:3
Asche, Oscar (Producer)
Good Old Days, The 1925,N 1,VIII,1:3
Merry Wives of Windsor, The: 1929 Version 1929,Jl 27,7:2
Ascher, Anthony
Jane-Our Stranger 1925,O 9,27:2
Ascher, Anton
Just Married 1921,Ap 27,21:1
Spider, The 1927,Mr 23,29:1
Ash, A Montague
Hoboken Blues 1928,F 18,10:1
S S Glencairn 1929,Ja 10,24:5
Joy of Serpents 1930,Ap 4,22:4
Ash, A Montague (Director)
Joy of Serpents 1930,Ap 4,22:4
Ash, Annie
Holy Night 1941,D 22,23:3
Ash, Fred
Holy Night 1941,D 22,23:3

Ash, Gordon
Wonderful Thing, The 1920,F 18,9:1
Fanny Hawthorn 1922,My 12,22:2
Spring Cleaning 1923,N 10,16:3
Green Hat, The 1925,S 16,23:2
Garden of Eden, The 1927,S 28,28:1
Ash, Joyce
Pink String and Sealing Wax 1957,S 6,13:1
Ash, Luba
Dracula Sabbat 1970,O 2,28:2
Ash, Mony
Battle Hymn 1936,My 23,12:1
Ash, Russell
Wildcat, The 1921,N 28,16:2
Ash, Sam
Honeydew 1920,S 7,20:1
Wildcat, The 1921,N 28,16:2
Some Party 1922,Ap 17,22:1
Passing Show of 1922, The 1922,S 21,18:2
Lambs Gambol 1925,Ap 27,15:1
White Lights 1927,O 12,30:4
Houseboat on the Styx, The 1928,D 26,14:3
Singing Rabbi, The 1931,S 11,24:4
Ash, Walter Thompson (Lighting Director)
Belle of New York, The 1948,D 2,36:6
Ash, Walter Thompson (Miscellaneous)
Anna Lucasta 1944,Ag 31,15:1
Ash, Walter Thompson (Scenic Designer)
Belle of New York, The 1948,D 2,36:6
Ashburn, Carroll
Naked 1926,N 9,31:2
Out of the Night 1927,O 18,32:3
Tomorrow 1928,D 29,20:2
Earth Between, The 1929,Mr 6,33:1
Sea Gull, The 1929,Ap 10,32:2
Inspector Kennedy 1929,D 21,16:3
At the Bottom 1930,Ja 10,24:3
Sea Gull, The 1930,F 26,22:2
This One Man 1930,O 22,32:3
Life Line, The 1930,D 29,19:3
Jamboree 1932,N 25,18:4
We the People 1933,Ja 23,9:5
Move on, Sister 1933,O 25,22:4
They Shall Not Die 1934,F 22,24:4
Judgment Day 1934,S 13,26:4
Meet the Prince 1935,Jl 9,24:5
Dead End 1935,O 29,17:2
Ten Million Ghosts 1936,O 24,23:7
Brother Rat 1936,D 17,34:5
Angel Island 1937,O 21,26:2
Boys From Syracuse, The 1938,N 24,36:1
See My Lawyer 1939,S 28,29:1
World We Make, The 1939,N 21,19:1
Over Twenty-One 1944,Ja 4,20:2
Born Yesterday 1946,F 5,18:2
Ashby, Dorothy (Composer)
Game 1968,S 9,57:7
Ashby, Dorothy (Lyricist)
Game 1968,S 9,57:7
Ashby, Henry
New York 1927,N 15,26:2
Ashby, John (Director)
Game 1968,S 9,57:7
Ashby, John (Playwright)
Game 1968,S 9,57:7
Ashcraft, Edwin M (Composer)
Napoleon Passes 1927,D 21,29:2
Ashcraft, Edwin M (Lyricist)
Napoleon Passes 1927,D 21,29:2
Ashcroft, Earl
Vagabond King, The 1943,Je 30,24:2
Ashcroft, Edwin 3d
Fortuno 1925,D 23,22:1
Ashcroft, Peggy
Jew Suess 1929,O 6,IX,1:3
Othello 1930,My 20,33:1
Hassan 1931,Mr 8,VIII,2:6
Take Two From One 1931,O 4,VIII,2:6
Romeo and Juliet 1932,O 16,IX,3:7
Caesar and Cleopatra 1932,O 16,IX,3:7
Fraeulein Elsa 1932,D 18,X,5:8
Life That I Gave Him, The 1934,O 28,IX,3:4
Romeo and Juliet 1935,O 18,27:5
Romeo and Juliet 1935,N 17,IX,2:4
Romeo and Juliet 1935,D 29,IX,1:3
Seagull, The 1936,My 21,19:2
Seagull, The 1936,Je 21,IX,1:5
Seagull, The 1936,Ag 30,IX,1:1
High Tor 1936,D 31,20:3
High Tor 1937,Ja 11,15:2
High Tor 1937,Ja 17,X,1:1
Richard II 1937,S 7,16:3
Three Sisters, The 1938,F 13,X,3:3
Merchant of Venice, The 1938,My 15,X,1:5
White Guard, The 1938,O 23,IX,3:1
Twelfth Night 1938,D 18,IX,5:6
Importance of Being Earnest, The 1939,S 17,X,2:3
Cousin Muriel 1940,Mr 17,X,1:6
Dark River 1943,D 5,II,5:1
Midsummer Night's Dream, A 1945,Mr 25,II,2:4
Edward, My Son 1948,O 1,30:2
Edward My Son 1948,O 10,II,1:1
Heiress, The 1949,F 3,26:2

Ashcroft, Peggy—Cont

Heiress, The 1949,F 13,II,3:7
Twelfth Night 1950,D 3,II,3:1
Deep Blue Sea, The 1952,Mr 16,II,3:7
Deep Blue Sea, The 1952,D 7,II,7:2
Antony and Cleopatra 1953,My 10,II,1:1
Hedda Gabler 1954,O 24,II,3:3
Hedda Gabler 1954,D 12,II,5:1
Chalk Garden, The 1956,Ap 12,26:8
Chalk Garden, The 1956,My 13,II,3:1
Cymbeline 1957,Ag 25,II,1:5
Taming of the Shrew, The 1960,Je 22,29:1
Othello 1961,O 11,53:6
Cherry Orchard, The 1961,D 15,49:1
Flower of Cities All 1962,Jl 12,21:2
Wars of the Roses, The 1963,Jl 18,14:1
Landscape 1969,Jl 13,II,8:1
Henry VIII 1969,O 11,42:1

Ashe, Martin
Bathsheba 1947,Mr 27,40:2
Happiest Millionaire, The 1956,N 21,21:3
Alley of the Sunset 1959,D 31,11:1

Ashe, Oscar
Julius Caesar 1932,F 9,30:7

Ashe, Sam
Houseboat on the Styx, The 1928,D 16,IX,2:1

Ashe, Warren
Lady for a Night, A 1928,Ap 17,26:4
That's Gratitude 1932,Je 17,24:3
Show-Off, The 1932,D 13,25:4
Riddle Me This! 1933,Mr 15,21:3
Dangerous Corner 1933,Jl 18,20:4
Dead End 1936,S 20,IX,3:7
School for Brides 1944,Ag 2,19:4

Asher, Jane
Measure for Measure 1967,F 15,37:1
Romeo and Juliet 1967,F 22,18:1

Asherman, David (Scenic Designer)
Finian's Rainbow 1953,Mr 7,13:2
Eastward in Eden 1956,Ap 18,25:4

Asherson, Renee
Streetcar Named Desire, A 1949,O 13,33:6

Ashford, Daisy (Original Author)
Young Visitors, The 1920,N 30,14:1
Young Visitors, The 1920,D 5,VII,1:1
Young Visitors, The 1928,Ja 29,VIII,2:6
Young Visitors, The 1968,D 26,48:1

Ashford, Harry
Tragedy of Nan, The 1920,F 18,9:1
What the Public Wants 1922,My 2,22:3
Lucky One, The 1922,N 21,15:2
Tidings Brought to Mary, The 1922,D 25,20:1
Aren't We All? 1923,My 22,14:2

Ashford, Richard
Merton of the Movies 1968,S 26,62:1

Ashforth, Albert B Jr
Coriolanus 1927,Je 18,8:3

Ashforth, George
Sonya's Search for the Christmas Star 1929,D 14,24:6

Ashforth, George T
Coriolanus 1927,Je 18,8:3

Ashland, Camila
Day Will Come, The 1944,S 8,17:2
Hot Corner, The 1956,Ja 26,25:2
Case of Libel, A 1963,O 11,43:2
Black Comedy 1967,F 13,42:1
Black Comedy 1967,O 19,58:1
Darling of the Day 1968,Ja 29,26:2

Ashley, Alfonza
Legal Murder 1934,F 16,16:2

Ashley, Barbara
Canteen Show, The 1942,S 4,18:1
Liar, The 1950,My 19,30:2
Out of This World 1950,D 22,17:3

Ashley, C E
Potiphar's Wife 1928,D 24,10:7

Ashley, Carole
Mrs Patterson 1957,F 6,20:2

Ashley, Charles
Triumphant Bachelor, The 1927,S 16,21:1
Tyrant, The 1930,N 13,33:1
Murder at the Vanities 1933,S 13,22:4

Ashley, Clayton (Miscellaneous)
Lady Says Yes, A 1945,Ja 11,18:5

Ashley, Clayton (Original Author)
Lady Says Yes, A 1945,Ja 11,18:5

Ashley, Edward
Happy Days 1941,My 14,24:2

Ashley, Edward (Cpl)
Winged Victory 1943,N 22,24:1

Ashley, Elizabeth
Daphne Laureola 1950,S 19,38:6
Take Her, She's Mine 1961,D 22,19:1
Barefoot in the Park 1963,O 24,36:2

Ashley, Gene
Caviar 1934,Je 8,19:2

Ashley, Gischa (Playwright)
Third Party Risk 1939,My 28,X,2:5

Ashley, Joel
Sun Field, The 1942,D 10,33:2
War President 1944,Ap 25,17:3
Catherine Was Great 1944,Ag 3,16:1
As We Forgive Our Debtors 1947,Mr 11,37:2

Ashley, John
Dancers, The 1923,O 18,17:2

Ashley, John (Miscellaneous)
Tomorrow 1928,D 29,20:2

Ashley, Paul
Too Many Heroes 1937,N 16,26:2

Ashley, William (Miscellaneous)
Cockeyed Kite 1961,S 14,27:1

Ashlock, Jane
Anna Russell and Her Little Show 1953,S 8,27:2

Ashmore, Basil (Playwright)
Don Juan in the Russian Manner 1954,Ap 23,23:2

Ashmore, Basil (Translator)
I Only Want an Answer 1968,F 6,36:1

Ashmore, Peter (Director)
You Never Can Tell 1948,Mr 17,31:2
Edward, My Son 1948,O 1,30:2
Legend of Lovers 1951,D 27,17:1

Ashmore, Peter (Producer)
Ann Veronica 1949,My 21,9:2

Ashour
Boys and Girls Together 1940,S 5,28:6

Ashton, Charles
Hot Pan 1928,F 16,14:1

Ashton, D C
Little Theatre Tournament; Yellow Triangle, The 1929,My 10,32:2

Ashton, Don (Scenic Designer)
Photo Finish 1963,F 14,5:2

Ashton, Elizabeth
How the Other Half Loves 1970,Ag 7,23:1

Ashton, Frederick (Choreographer)
Midsummer Night's Dream, A 1954,S 22,33:1

Ashton, Herbert
Marie Antoinette 1921,N 23,16:1
Squaw Man, The 1921,O 27,10:3
Makers of Light 1922,My 24,22:3
Failures, The 1923,N 23,20:1
Saint Joan 1923,D 29,8:4
Passing Show of 1924, The 1924,S 4,13:4
Artists and Models 1925,Je 25,16:2
Slaves All 1926,D 7,24:4
Brothers Karamazov, The 1927,Ja 4,20:1
Weather Clear, Track Fast 1927,O 19,24:5
Napoleon 1928,Mr 9,21:1
Come-On Man, The 1929,Ap 23,26:2

Ashton, Herbert (Director)
Come-On Man, The 1929,Ap 23,26:2

Ashton, Herbert Jr
Come-On Man, The 1929,Ap 23,26:2
Mountain Fury 1929,S 26,27:2
Enemy Within 1931,O 6,35:3
Hired Husband 1932,Je 4,9:5

Ashton, Herbert Jr (Playwright)
Brothers 1928,D 26,14:3
Come-On Man, The 1929,Ap 23,26:2
Locked Room, The 1933,D 26,18:5

Ashton, Lillian
Lost Colony, The 1937,Jl 11,X,2:1

Ashton, Marcia
Alfie 1964,D 18,27:1

Ashton, Michael (Playwright)
Young Visitors, The 1968,D 26,48:1

Ashton, Millie
Window Panes 1927,F 22,22:2

Ashtons, The Seven
Jerry Lewis' Variety Show 1957,F 8,18:5

Ashwander, Donald
Hot Feet 1970,D 22,38:1

Ashwander, Donald (Composer)
Dandelion 1969,D 24,12:1
Hot Feet 1970,D 22,38:1

Ashwell, Lena (Miscellaneous)
Jotham Valley 1951,F 7,37:2

Ashwell, Lena (Playwright)
Crime and Punishment 1927,Mr 6,VIII,2:1
Dr Jeckyll and Mr Hyde 1927,Ap 24,VII,2:3

Ashwood, Michael (Playwright)
Policy Kings 1938,D 31,6:2

Ashwood, Michael (Producer)
Policy Kings 1938,D 31,6:2

Ashworth, Bradford (Scenic Designer)
Tight Britches 1934,S 12,26:2
Lost Horizons 1934,O 16,31:2
On Stage 1935,O 30,16:6
Whatever Goes Up 1935,N 26,28:2

Ashworth, E W
Processional 1937,O 14,23:1

Ashworth, Gale
Long Days, The 1951,Ap 21,10:5

Ashworth, Jean
Home Sweet Home 1936,Jl 1,29:2
Brooklyn Biarritz 1941,F 28,16:2

Ashworth, Mary
Naked Genius, The 1943,O 22,20:5

Ashworth, Tucker
Measure for Measure 1957,Ja 23,24:1
Taming of the Shrew, The 1957,F 21,30:2
Philoctetes 1959,Ja 14,28:1
School for Scandal, The 1962,Mr 19,36:1
Tavern, The 1962,Ap 5,29:1
All the King's Men 1963,Jl 12,12:1

Asia
Whoop-Up 1958,D 23,2:7
Lute Song 1959,Mr 13,24:1

Ask, Eli
Jackhammer, The 1962,F 6,26:2

Ask, Eli (Miscellaneous)
Jackhammer, The 1962,F 6,26:2
Ginger Man, The 1963,N 22,42:1
Knack, The 1964,My 28,42:2

Ask, Eli (Producer)
Biscuit 1966,My 17,51:2
Fitz 1966,My 17,51:2

Askam, Perry
Passing Show of 1921, The 1920,D 30,16:2
Blossom Time 1921,S 30,10:1

Askenas, Ruth
Psychological Moment, The 1931,Mr 4,33:2
Divina Pastora, La 1931,Mr 4,33:2
Sparkin' 1931,Mr 4,33:2
Old Maid, The 1949,Ja 27,20:6
Post Road 1949,Ap 28,27:3
This Happy Breed 1952,Ap 4,23:2
Mrs Moonlight 1952,N 21,21:1

Askew, Luke
Young Provincials, The 1958,S 19,22:4

Askew, Wilson
Blue Blood 1924,Ap 3,21:2

Askey, Darrell
Here's Where I Belong 1968,Mr 4,32:1

Askin, Harry (Producer)
Budget, The 1932,S 21,26:4

Askin, Leon
Faust 1947,N 29,9:2
Temporary Island, A 1948,Mr 15,27:3
Twentieth Century 1950,D 25,23:6

Askin, Leon (Director)
Faust 1947,N 29,9:2

Askowith, Bathsheba
Iphigenia in Aulis 1921,Ap 8,18:2

Askowith, Bathsheba (Producer)
Trojan Women, The 1923,My 27,10:2

Aslanian, Jean-Jacques (Director)
Ex-Napoleon 1960,D 29,16:3

Asner, Edward
Venice Preserv'd 1955,D 13,54:4
Romeo and Juliet 1959,Je 15,31:1
Merry Wives of Windsor, The 1959,Jl 9,23:2
All's Well That Ends Well 1959,Ag 3,20:4
Legend of Lovers 1959,O 28,40:3
Tempest, The 1959,D 28,19:2
Henry V 1960,Je 30,23:1
Face of a Hero 1960,O 21,29:5

Aspros, Basil (Playwright)
Cast of Characters 1959,Je 11,37:2

Asquith, Anthony
Flare Path 1942,Ag 23,VIII,1:6

Asquith, Ward
Boy With a Cart, The 1954,Ap 5,19:2

Asriel, Andre (Composer)
Peace 1970,S 2,30:2

Asro, Alexander
Dybbuk, The 1924,Ja 29,17:7
Neveile, The 1924,F 9,16:2
Should I Marry, or Shouldn't I? 1936,S 28,14:3
Jealousy 1936,S 28,14:3
Kapores 1936,S 28,14:3
Room Service 1937,My 20,16:1
Leave It to Me! 1938,N 10,32:2
Room Service 1953,Ap 7,34:1

Assaf, Najeeb
Savages Under the Skin 1927,Mr 25,25:2
Mima 1928,D 13,24:2

Asselin, Paul
Topaze 1931,F 17,29:1

Assen, Abdul
Kykunkor 1934,D 22,21:3
Zunguru 1938,Ag 3,14:5
Zunguru 1938,Ag 7,IX,8:2
Zunguru 1940,Mr 21,30:5

Assimakopoulou, Maria
Hippolytus 1968,N 20,38:3

Ast, Minna
Faraway Princess, The 1922,D 6,3:2

Astaire, Adele
Love Letter, The 1921,O 5,20:1
For Goodness Sake 1922,F 22,13:1
Bunch and Judy, The 1922,N 12,VIII,1:6
Bunch and Judy, The 1922,N 29,20:1
Flirting 1923,My 31,12:5
Lady Be Good 1924,D 2,23:4
Lady Be Good 1924,D 28,VII,1:1
Lady Be Good 1926,Ap 15,25:1
Funny Face 1927,N 23,28:2
Funny Face 1928,N 9,22:3
Smiles 1930,N 19,19:2
Band Wagon, The 1931,My 17,VIII,3:2
Band Wagon, The 1931,Je 4,31:3
Band Wagon, The 1931,Je 14,VIII,1:1
Flying Colors 1932,O 9,IX,1:1

Astaire, Fred
Love Letter, The 1921,O 5,20:1
For Goodness Sake 1922,F 22,13:1
Bunch and Judy, The 1922,N 12,VIII,1:6

Astaire, Fred—Cont
Bunch and Judy, The 1922,N 29,20:1
Flirting 1923,My 31,12:5
Lady Be Good 1924,D 2,23:4
Lady Be Good 1924,D 28,VII,1:1
Lambs Gambol 1925,Ap 27,15:1
Lady Be Good 1926,Ap 15,25:1
Funny Face 1927,N 23,28:2
Funny Face 1928,N 9,22:3
Smiles 1930,N 19,19:2
Band Wagon, The 1931,My 17,VIII,3:2
Band Wagon, The 1931,Je 4,31:3
Band Wagon, The 1931,Je 14,VIII,1:1
Flying Colors 1932,O 9,IX,1:1
Gay Divorce 1932,N 13,IX,1:7
Gay Divorce 1932,N 30,23:4
Gay Divorce 1933,N 19,IX,3:7

Astaire, Lilyan
Belmont Varieties 1932,S 29,17:2
Manhattan Varieties 1932,O 22,18:3

Astaires, The
Smiles 1930,N 2,VIII,1:3

Astar, Ben
Prescott Proposals, The 1953,D 27,II,3:1
On Your Toes 1954,O 12,24:4
Great Sebastians, The 1956,Ja 5,27:1
Compulsion 1957,O 25,21:1

Astbury, William (Director)
These Are My Loves 1960,Ap 19,41:2

Aste, Marcello
Venetian Twins, The 1968,My 29,23:1

Asther, Nils
Strong Are Lonely, The 1953,S 30,38:3

Astin, John
Threepenny Opera, The 1954,Mr 11,26:5
Threepenny Opera, The 1955,S 21,38:1
Threepenny Opera, The 1956,Mr 11,II,1:1
Major Barbara 1956,O 31,27:1
Ulysses in Nighttown 1958,Je 6,30:1
Tall Story 1959,Ja 30,33:2

Astin, John (Miscellaneous)
Ulysses in Nighttown 1958,Je 6,30:1

Astley, Joan
Courageous One, The 1958,Ja 21,33:6

Astley, John
Bill of Divorcement, A 1921,O 11,22:2
Caste 1927,D 24,8:1

Astor, Gina
Carmilla 1970,D 1,61:2

Astor, John
Dear Judas 1947,O 6,26:4

Astor, Lady
Lovely Ladies, Kind Gentlemen 1970,D 29,38:1

Astor, Mary
Among the Married 1929,D 8,X,2:7
Many Happy Returns 1945,Ja 6,15:5
Starcross Story, The 1954,Ja 14,25:2

Astor, Richard
Great Campaign, The 1947,Ap 1,33:2
Love's Labour's Lost 1953,F 5,20:3
Merchant of Venice, The 1953,Mr 5,20:2
Absalom 1956,My 17,37:2

Astor, Richard (Playwright)
Queen After Death 1956,Mr 13,33:2

Astor, Richard (Producer)
Queen After Death 1956,Mr 13,33:2

Astor, Suzanne
Leonard Sillman's New Faces of 1968
  1968,My 3,43:1

Astor, Vincent (Mrs)
Variations of 1940 1940,Ja 29,12:1

Astredo, Humbert Allen
Coriolanus 1965,Jl 15,23:1
Troilus and Cressida 1965,Ag 13,17:1
Arms and the Man 1967,Je 23,44:2
Fragments 1967,O 3,56:1
Blancs, Les 1970,N 16,48:4
Blancs, Les 1970,N 29,II,3:5
Blancs, Les 1970,N 29,II,3:1

Astrova, Marie
Ziegfeld Follies 1921,Je 22,10:1
Suzette 1921,N 25,18:3

Astwood, Norman
Policy Kings 1938,D 31,6:2

Asya
Bajour 1964,N 24,42:1

Ata, Te (Princess)
Art Antics of 1926 1926,Ap 19,24:2

Atcheley, Hooper
Across the Street 1924,Mr 25,24:1

Atchley, Hooper L
Jarnegan 1928,S 25,29:2

Aterridge, Howard (Lyricist)
Passing Show of 1922, The 1922,S 21,18:2

Aterridge, Howard (Playwright)
Passing Show of 1922, The 1922,S 21,18:2

Aterrier (Playwright)
Girofle-Girofla 1926,N 23,26:3

Ates, Nejla
Fanny 1954,N 5,16:1
Fanny 1954,N 21,II,1:1

Ates, Roscoe
Sea Legs 1937,My 19,26:5

Ates, Wendell
Good Night Ladies 1945,Ja 18,16:2

Atha, Steve (Miscellaneous)
Harvey 1970,F 25,41:1

Athans, James (Composer)
Madre, La 1959,F 12,24:1

Athas, Nick
Secret Life of Walter Mitty, The 1964,O 27,44:5
Illya Darling 1967,Ap 12,37:1

Atherton, Agnes
Title, The 1921,N 15,23:3
That Day 1922,O 4,27:3
Carolinian, The 1925,N 3,34:2

Atherton, Daisy
Torch Bearers, The 1922,Ag 30,10:2
Her Way Out 1924,Je 24,18:3
Appearances 1925,O 15,27:3
Her Friend the King 1929,O 8,34:5
Accent on Youth 1935,Jl 2,24:3
Jane's Legacy 1935,Ag 13,20:3
Service for Two 1935,Ag 20,25:1
Saturday's Children 1936,Jl 7,22:5
You Can't Take It With You 1945,Mr 27,23:7

Atherton, Gertrude (Original Author)
Alexander Hamilton 1949,Mr 30,29:2

Atherton, Margaret
Dew Drop Inn 1923,My 18,26:4

Atherton, Paul V
Sophie 1920,Mr 3,12:2

Atherton, U T
Cup of Trembling, The 1948,Ap 21,33:5

Atherton, Venie
Springtime of Youth 1922,O 27,15:1
Sweeney Todd 1924,Jl 19,10:4
Glass Slipper, The 1925,O 20,29:1
Hearts Are Trumps! 1927,Ap 8,21:1

Athey, Ted
Jazz Singer, The 1925,S 15,29:2
War Song, The 1928,S 25,29:3
Mendel, Inc 1929,N 26,28:5
Joseph 1930,F 13,25:3

Atienza, Edward
Romanoff and Juliet 1957,O 11,24:1
Becket 1960,O 6,50:1
Macbeth 1962,F 7,32:2
Romeo and Juliet 1962,F 14,39:1
Saint Joan 1962,F 21,57:4
Affair, The 1962,S 21,34:2
Andorra 1963,F 11,5:5
Ivanov 1966,My 4,50:1
Alchemist, The 1970,Ag 26,36:1

Atiyeh, Wadeeha
Forbidden Melody 1936,N 3,33:1
Ali Baba 1951,Mr 27,34:2

Atiyeh, Wadeeha (Playwright)
Ali Baba 1951,Mr 27,34:2

Atkin, Charles
Devil's Little Game, The 1932,Ag 2,20:4
Tell Me Pretty Maiden 1937,D 17,33:5
Knights of Song 1938,O 18,29:2
Bright Rebel 1938,D 28,24:2
Winter's Tale, The 1946,Ja 16,18:6

Atkin, Charles (Director)
South Pacific 1955,My 5,39:5

Atkin, Charles (Miscellaneous)
Christine 1960,Ap 29,27:1
Blood, Sweat & Stanley Poole 1961,O 6,31:1
Stephen D 1967,S 25,58:1

Atkin, Wendy
Electra 1932,Ja 9,21:4
Ghost Bereft 1933,F 1,13:5
Lake, The 1933,D 27,24:2
Post Road 1934,D 5,28:3
I Want a Policeman! 1936,Ja 15,15:5
Stranger, The 1945,F 13,21:2
Pygmalion 1945,D 27,16:1

Atkins, Al
I'd Rather Be Right 1937,N 3,28:2

Atkins, Alice
Chocolate Soldier, The 1932,F 9,30:3

Atkins, Charles
Lorelei 1938,N 30,21:2

Atkins, Charles (Miscellaneous)
No Strings 1962,Mr 16,24:1

Atkins, Dorothy
Jubilee 1935,O 14,20:1

Atkins, Eileen
Killing of Sister George, The 1965,Je 18,28:5
Killing of Sister George, The 1966,O 6,57:1
Promise, The 1967,N 15,38:1
Promise, The 1967,N 26,II,1:1
Vivat! Vivat Regina! 1970,My 24,80:1
Vivat! Vivat Regina! 1970,Jl 20,21:2

Atkins, Norman
Consul, The 1957,S 4,40:3
Most Happy Fella, The 1959,F 11,50:2
Paradise Island 1961,Je 24,11:1
Paradise Island 1962,Je 28,22:1
Most Happy Fella, The 1966,My 12,55:1
Arabian Nights 1967,Jl 3,12:1

Atkins, Robert
Rasputin 1929,My 12,IX,2:3
Napoleon: The Hundred Days 1932,Ap 19,25:2

Atkins, Robert—Cont
Napoleon: The Hundred Days 1932,My 8,VIII,1:3
Twelfth Night 1932,Ag 7,IX,1:6

Atkins, Robert (Director)
Napoleon: The Hundred Days 1932,Ap 19,25:2
Midsummer Night's Dream, A 1939,Jl 23,IX,1:3

Atkins, Robert (Producer)
Dybbuk, The 1927,My 1,VIII,2:7
Her Last Adventure 1936,Mr 31,17:1
Henry V 1936,N 30,24:6
Lysistrata 1938,Ag 7,IX,1:5
Taming of the Shrew, The 1941,Ag 17,IX,1:8

Atkins, Roland
Macbeth 1939,Je 4,IX,2:5

Atkins, T
Nobody Hears A Broken Drum 1970,Mr 20,55:1

Atkins, Tom
Keep It in the Family 1967,S 28,59:1
Whistle in the Dark, A 1968,F 17,32:2
Front Page, The 1969,My 12,54:2
Whistle in the Dark, A 1969,O 9,55:1
Whistle in the Dark, A 1969,N 9,II,3:1

Atkins, Tony
Month in the Country, A 1956,Ap 4,23:1
Under Milk Wood 1957,O 16,42:5
Body Beautiful, The 1958,Ja 24,15:2

Atkins, Van
Once Over Lightly 1942,N 20,26:2

Atkinson, Amy
Cross My Heart 1928,S 18,32:7
Firefly, The 1931,D 1,23:2
That's Gratitude 1932,Je 17,24:3

Atkinson, Arthur
Paradise Alley 1924,Ap 2,17:3

Atkinson, Betty
It Happens on Ice 1941,Ap 5,13:2

Atkinson, Beverly
And People All Around 1968,F 12,46:1

Atkinson, Catherine
Six Characters in Search of an Author
  1922,O 31,11:2

Atkinson, Clint
Shoemaker's Prodigious Wife, The 1949,Je 15,38:2
Burning, The 1963,D 4,57:1

Atkinson, Clint (Miscellaneous)
Burning, The 1963,D 4,57:1

Atkinson, Clinton
Man in the Glass Booth, The 1968,S 27,41:1

Atkinson, Clinton (Director)
Venus-Shot 1966,Je 24,30:2
Child and the Dragon, The 1966,Je 24,30:2
Miracle in Brooklyn 1966,Je 24,30:2
Pin Up 1966,Je 24,30:2
Getting Married 1970,Ja 20,46:1
Greenwillow 1970,D 8,60:1

Atkinson, David
Girl in Pink Tights, The 1954,Mr 6,13:2
Vamp, The 1955,N 11,30:1
Kiss Me, Kate 1956,My 10,27:2
Show Boat 1956,Je 22,16:1
Brigadoon 1957,Mr 28,37:1
Show Boat 1957,Je 28,30:2
Annie Get Your Gun 1958,F 20,29:2
Say Darling 1959,F 26,38:2
Can-Can 1959,Ag 26,25:4
All in Love 1961,N 11,15:2
Around the World in 80 Days 1964,Je 29,33:2
Mardi Gras! 1965,Je 28,33:2
Mardi Gras! 1966,Jl 11,32:2
Man of La Mancha 1967,N 24,61:1

Atkinson, Don
Happiest Girl in the World, The 1961,Ap 4,42:1

Atkinson, George (Costume Designer)
Days Without End 1934,Ap 24,26:7

Atkinson, George H (Playwright)
Survival of the Fittest 1921,Mr 15,14:1

Atkinson, Katherine
Don Juan 1921,S 8,14:2

Atkinson, Matthew
Greenwillow 1970,D 8,60:1

Atkinson, Olive
First in Heart, The 1947,N 14,29:2

Atkinson, Oriana (Original Author)
Julia, Jake, and Uncle Joe 1961,Ja 30,19:1

Atkinson, Rosalind
Macbeth 1962,F 7,32:2
Romeo and Juliet 1962,F 14,39:1

Atkinson, Sarah
Wait a Minim! 1966,Mr 8,43:1

Atlas, Allan (Miscellaneous)
Laughs and Other Events 1960,O 11,57:1

Atlas, Charles (Miscellaneous)
Peace 1969,Ja 28,49:1

Atlas, Leopold (Playwright)
Wednesday's Child 1934,Ja 17,23:2
Wednesday's Child 1934,Ja 28,IX,1:1
But for the Grace of God 1937,Ja 13,21:4

Atlas and LaMar
Heads Up! 1929,N 12,34:1

Atlee, Howard (Miscellaneous)
Mr Grossman 1964,My 6,43:1
Dark Corners 1964,My 6,43:1

Atlee, William
School for Virtue 1931,Ap 22,29:2

Atlee, William—Cont

Stage Door 1936,O 23,26:3
Attaway, Ruth
You Can't Take It With You 1936,D 15,31:1
Grass Harp, The 1953,Ap 28,32:2
Grass Harp, The 1953,My 24,II,1:1
Mrs Patterson 1954,D 2,37:1
Mister Johnson 1956,Mr 30,11:1
Egghead, The 1957,O 10,39:1
After the Fall 1964,Ja 24,18:1
Yerma 1966,D 9,60:1
Attenborough, Richard
Brighton Rock 1943,Ap 18,II,1:1
Atterbury, Malcolm
Black Eye, The 1938,Mr 8,22:4
One Flew Over the Cuckoo's Nest 1963,N 14,40:2
Atterbury, Malcolm (Director)
Don't Throw Glass Houses 1938,D 28,24:4
Atterbury, Malcolm (Producer)
Don't Throw Glass Houses 1938,D 28,24:4
Atteridge, Harold (Lyricist)
Cinderella on Broadway 1920,Je 25,18:1
Passing Show of 1921, The 1920,D 30,16:2
Mimic World of 1921, The 1921,Ag 18,9:2
Bombo 1921,O 7,20:2
Rose of Stamboul, The 1922,Mr 8,11:2
Make It Snappy 1922,Ap 14,20:2
Topics of 1923 1923,N 21,23:2
Innocent Eyes 1924,My 21,22:2
Marjorie 1924,Ag 12,12:2
Passing Show of 1924, The 1924,S 4,13:4
Pleasure Bound 1929,F 19,22:4
Atteridge, Harold (Playwright)
Cinderella on Broadway 1920,Je 25,18:1
Passing Show of 1921, The 1920,D 30,16:2
Last Waltz, The 1921,My 11,20:3
Mimic World of 1921, The 1921,Ag 18,9:2
Bombo 1921,O 7,20:2
Rose of Stamboul, The 1922,Mr 8,11:2
Make It Snappy 1922,Ap 14,20:2
Topics of 1923 1923,N 21,23:2
Innocent Eyes 1924,My 21,22:2
Marjorie 1924,Ag 12,12:2
Dream Girl, The 1924,Ag 21,12:2
Passing Show of 1924, The 1924,S 4,13:4
Big Boy 1925,Ja 8,28:2
Sky High 1925,Mr 3,21:4
Artists and Models 1925,Je 25,16:2
Gay Paree 1925,Ag 19,14:3
Night in Paris, A 1926,Ja 6,16:3
Great Temptations, The 1926,My 19,29:1
Night in Paris, A 1926,Jl 27,15:4
Gay Paree 1926,N 10,24:2
Night in Spain, A 1927,My 4,28:2
Ziegfeld Follies 1927,Ag 17,27:3
Greenwich Village Follies 1928,Ap 10,32:2
Pleasure Bound 1929,F 19,22:4
Everybody's Welcome 1931,S 20,VIII,3:2
Thumbs Up! 1934,D 28,24:1
Attianese, Dolph (Miscellaneous)
Nighthawks 1967,D 30,14:2
Attie, Paulette
Sensations 1970,O 26,48:2
Attle, John C
Fiddler on the Roof 1964,S 23,56:2
Jacques Brel Is Alive and Well and Living in Paris 1970,Ja 21,34:1
Attles, Joseph
John Henry 1940,Ja 11,18:2
Belle Helene, La 1941,Jl 8,14:1
Kwamina 1961,O 24,42:1
Tambourines to Glory 1963,N 4,47:1
Jericho-Jim Crow 1964,Ja 13,25:3
Cabin in the Sky 1964,Ja 22,32:1
Porgy and Bess 1965,Mr 6,17:1
Prodigal Son, The 1965,My 21,19:1
Exception and the Rule, The 1965,My 21,19:1
Reckoning, The 1969,S 5,28:1
Contributions; Shoes 1970,Mr 10,53:1
Atuka-Reid, Edith
Our Lan' 1947,Ap 19,11:2
Set My People Free 1948,N 4,38:2
Sister Oakes 1949,Ap 25,19:4
Atwater, Edith
Springtime for Henry 1933,My 2,20:5
Brittle Heaven 1934,N 14,22:5
This Our House 1935,D 12,33:3
Country Wife, The 1936,D 2,34:1
Susan and God 1937,Ap 25,X,2:6
Night of January 16 1937,Jl 20,19:3
Susan and God 1937,O 8,26:4
Man Who Came to Dinner, The 1939,O 1,IX,2:5
Man Who Came to Dinner, The 1939,O 17,31:1
Retreat to Pleasure 1940,D 18,32:2
Johnny on the Spot 1942,Ja 9,24:2
Broken Journey 1942,Je 24,22:2
R U R 1942,D 4,30:2
Parlor Story 1947,Mr 5,29:2
Gentleman From Athens, The 1947,N 30,I,78:2
Gentleman From Athens, The 1947,D 10,42:4
Metropole 1949,D 7,43:2
King Lear 1950,D 26,18:1
King Lear 1950,D 31,II,1:1
Flahooley 1951,My 15,39:1

Clerambard 1957,N 8,22:3
Clerambard 1957,N 17,II,1:1
Child Buyer, The 1962,My 14,35:1
Atwell, Allen
Teaser, The 1921,Jl 28,8:3
Bought and Paid For 1921,D 8,17:5
Drifting 1922,Ja 3,20:3
They Knew What They Wanted 1924,N 25,27:1
Love in the Tropics 1927,O 19,24:3
Quicksand 1928,F 14,26:3
This Is New York 1930,N 29,21:1
Atwell, Angela
After Tomorrow 1931,Ag 27,22:4
Atwell, George Jr (Mrs)
Variations of 1940 1940,Ja 29,12:1
Atwell, Grace
Machinal 1928,S 8,10:3
Atwell, Lester (Original Author)
Flora, the Red Menace 1965,My 12,41:2
Atwell, Meredith
Richard III 1930,Mr 31,24:1
Julius Caesar 1930,Ap 4,22:3
Atwell, Rick
Me and Juliet 1970,My 15,42:1
Atwell, Roy
Helen of Troy, New York 1923,Je 20,22:6
Americana 1926,Jl 27,15:3
Americana 1926,D 5,VIII,5:1
Murray Anderson's Almanac 1929,Ag 4,VIII,1:6
Murray Anderson's Almanac 1929,Ag 15,20:3
How's Your Health? 1929,N 27,30:3
Strike Me Pink 1933,Mr 6,16:3
Sunday Nights at Nine 1933,N 13,20:7
On to Fortune 1935,Ja 15,23:2
On to Fortune 1935,F 5,22:2
Atwill, Isabel
His Majesty's Car 1930,O 24,30:1
Atwill, Lionel
Deburau 1920,D 24,14:3
Deburau 1921,Ja 2,VI,3:1
Deburau 1921,Ja 30,VI,1:1
Grand Duke, The 1921,N 2,20:1
Grand Duke, The 1921,N 6,VI,1:1
Grand Duke, The 1921,N 27,VI,1:1
Comedian, The 1923,Mr 14,14:1
Comedian, The 1923,Mr 25,VIII,1:1
Comedian, The 1923,Ap 8,VIII,1:1
Heart of Cellini, The 1923,O 21,VIII,2:1
Outsider, The 1924,F 17,VII,2:8
Outsider, The 1924,Mr 4,16:4
Outsider, The 1924,Mr 9,VIII,1:1
Caesar and Cleopatra 1925,Ap 14,27:1
Beau Gallant 1926,Ap 6,26:3
Slaves All 1926,D 7,24:4
Thief, The 1927,Ap 23,15:2
Thief, The 1927,My 1,VIII,1:1
King Can Do No Wrong, The 1927,N 17,28:4
Napoleon 1928,Mr 9,21:1
Outsider, The 1928,Ap 10,32:2
Fioretta 1929,Ja 6,VIII,4:6
Fioretta 1929,F 6,30:3
Stripped 1929,Je 9,VIII,1:2
Stripped 1929,O 13,IX,5:1
Stripped 1929,O 22,26:1
Silent Witness, The 1931,F 22,VIII,4:4
Silent Witness, The 1931,Mr 24,31:5
Silent Witness, The 1931,My 10,VIII,3:5
Atwill, Lionel (Director)
Squall, The 1926,N 12,20:1
Lady Alone 1927,Ja 21,12:5
Thief, The 1927,Ap 23,15:2
Outsider, The 1928,Ap 10,32:2
Strong Man's House, A 1929,S 17,34:3
Stripped 1929,O 22,26:1
Seven 1929,D 28,10:5
Kiss of Importance, A 1930,D 2,31:3
Atwill, Lionel (Playwright)
Outsider, The 1928,Ap 10,32:2
Atwood, Bot (Choreographer)
13 Daughters 1961,Mr 3,17:2
Atwood, Donna
Ice Capades 1953,S 11,25:1
Ice Capades 1954,S 16,37:1
Ice Capades 1955,S 15,38:1
Atwood, Molly
Twelfth Night 1968,Je 15,40:1
Atwood, Persis (Mlle)
Girofle-Girofla 1926,N 23,26:3
Atwood, Robert (Miscellaneous)
Rumple 1957,N 7,42:2
Curley McDimple 1967,N 23,59:2
Atwood, Robert (Musical Director)
Curley McDimple 1967,N 23,59:2
Atwood, Ted
Captain Brassbound's Conversion 1950,D 28,21:1
Auberjonois, Rene
Once in a Lifetime 1962,O 30,30:1
Devils, The 1963,N 5,25:1
King Lear 1968,N 8,43:1
Cry of Players, A 1968,N 15,40:1
King Lear 1968,N 17,II,1:3
Fire! 1969,Ja 29,26:1

Auberjonois, Rene—Cont

Coco 1969,D 19,66:1
Coco 1969,D 28,II,1:1
Coco 1970,Ag 7,28:1
Aubert, Francis
Femmes Savantes, Les 1967,F 7,34:2
Aubert, Jane
Gay Paree 1926,N 10,24:2
Aubert, Jeanne
Prince Charming 1930,O 14,31:1
America's Sweetheart 1931,Ja 25,VIII,2:4
America's Sweetheart 1931,F 11,23:1
Laugh Parade, The 1931,N 3,31:2
Laugh Parade, The 1931,D 6,VIII,1:1
Vaudeville (Palace) 1932,My 30,16:7
Ballyhoo of 1932 1932,S 7,14:2
Melody 1933,F 15,17:4
Command Performance 1933,O 18,24:3
Aubert, Rowena
All Rights Reserved 1934,N 7,33:5
Aubray, Etienne
Misanthrope, Le 1960,Mr 9,38:3
Aubrey, Albert J
Hearts Are Trumps! 1927,Ap 8,21:1
Aubrey, J C
Good Companions, The 1931,O 2,31:1
Aubrey, James
Isle of Children 1962,Mr 17,16:2
Aubrey, John (Playwright)
Brief Lives 1967,D 19,60:4
Aubrey, Michael
Enemy of the People, An 1958,F 26,24:2
She Shall Have Music 1959,Ja 23,18:4
Aubrey, Michael (Choreographer)
Hello Charlie 1965,O 25,47:2
Aubrey, Monte (Musical Director)
Cats' Pajamas, The 1962,Je 1,16:2
Aubrey, Will
Vaudeville (Palace) 1931,Je 15,23:5
Aubrey, Wilson Trio
Vaudeville (Palace) 1925,O 6,31:3
Aubry, G Jean (Translator)
Moment Difficile, Le 1926,D 26,VII,2:1
Aubuchon, Jacques
Madwoman of Chaillot, The 1949,S 11,II,1:1
Madwoman of Chaillot, The 1950,Je 14,41:2
Mr Pickwick 1952,S 18,36:3
Mr Pickwick 1952,S 28,II,1:1
Cyrano de Bergerac 1953,N 13,24:3
Shrike, The 1953,N 26,51:2
Charley's Aunt 1953,D 23,22:2
In the Matter of J Robert Oppenheimer 1968,Je 7,31:1
In the Matter of J Robert Oppenheimer 1968,Je 9,II,1:1
Auburn, Denis
Richard III 1920,Mr 8,7:1
Sandro Botticelli 1923,Mr 27,24:2
Cymbeline 1923,O 3,12:1
Auburn, Jayne
Lady Be Good 1924,D 2,23:4
Auchincloss, J Douglas
In the Days of the Turbins 1934,Mr 7,22:5
Auchincloss, Louis
Whispering Gallery, The 1935,D 1,II,12:6
Auchincloss, Louis (Playwright)
Club Bedroom, The 1967,D 6,41:1
Auclair, Claude (Miscellaneous)
On Ne Badine Pas Avec l'Amour; No Trifling With Love 1968,Mr 5,35:1
Auclair, Michel
Tartuffe 1964,Mr 10,42:2
Tartuffe 1968,Jl 3,28:2
Auden, W H (Lyricist)
Pepper Mill 1937,Ja 6,19:4
No More Peace 1938,Ja 29,13:2
Auden, W H (Miscellaneous)
No More Peace 1937,F 27,9:1
Auden, W H (Original Author)
Paul Bunyan 1941,My 6,25:1
Auden, W H (Playwright)
Dance of Death, The 1935,O 2,26:2
Dog Beneath the Skin, The 1936,F 23,X,1:3
Dance of Death, The 1936,My 20,24:5
Pepper Mill 1937,Ja 6,19:4
Ascent of F 6, The 1937,Mr 28,XI,2:2
Duchess of Malfi, The 1946,O 16,35:2
For the Time Being 1957,D 18,42:7
Play of Daniel, The 1958,Ja 3,15:3
Play of Daniel, The 1958,Ja 26,II,1:1
Play of Daniel, The 1959,Ja 6,30:2
Play of Daniel, The 1960,D 27,23:6
Play of Daniel, The 1961,D 28,22:6
Audenrieth, Carl (Musical Director)
Everyman 1931,Jl 19,III,8:6
Audibert, Jacques (Playwright)
Brigitta, La 1962,S 25,30:1
Audier, Raoul (Producer)
Femme d'Amour, La 1927,Je 5,VII,2:1
Audley, Eleanor
Howdy King 1926,D 14,24:4
On Call 1928,N 10,20:7
Experience Unnecessary 1932,Mr 28,10:2
Pigeons and People 1933,Ja 17,22:3

Audley, Eleanor—Cont

Thunder on the Left 1933,N 1,25:2
Kill That Story 1934,Ag 30,22:2
Ladies' Money 1934,N 2,26:6
Susan and God 1937,O 8,26:4
Susan and God 1943,D 14,30:2
In Bed We Cry 1944,N 15,20:2

Audley, Lord (Playwright)
From This Hill 1963,Ap 2,54:2

Audley, Michael (Director)
Cry Havoc 1942,N 8,VIII,1:7

Audre (Costume Designer)
Three to Make Ready 1946,Mr 8,16:2
Topaze 1947,D 29,21:5
Arms and the Girl 1950,F 3,28:2
Electra 1959,F 14,15:1
Harlequinade 1959,F 14,15:1
Put It in Writing 1963,My 14,31:1
Country Girl, The 1966,S 30,55:1

Audree, Jeanne
Rosalie 1928,Ja 11,26:3

Audrey Sisters, The
Aquarama 1960 1960,Jl 1,14:6

Auensworth, Carl
Double Door 1935,Ag 21,22:2

Auer, Florence
Hail and Farewell 1923,F 20,12:1
Tell Me More 1925,Ap 14,27:3
Hot Water 1929,Ja 22,22:3
They Never Grow Up 1930,Ap 8,27:1
Up Pops the Devil 1930,S 2,19:1
Scrap Book 1932,Ag 2,20:3
American, Very Early 1934,Ja 31,21:2
Alice Takat 1936,F 11,19:2
One Flight Down 1937,D 14,32:4

Auer, Mischa
Morals 1925,D 1,22:2
Dope 1926,Ja 4,16:3
Lady Comes Across, The 1942,Ja 10,10:2
Lovely Me 1946,D 26,30:4
Tovarich 1953,N 29,II,3:1
Merry Widow, The 1964,Ag 18,24:2

Auerbach, Arnold (Miscellaneous)
Ziegfeld Follies 1957,Mr 2,19:2

Auerbach, Arnold (Playwright)
Call Me Mister 1946,Ap 19,26:2
Call Me Mister 1946,Ap 28,II,1:1
Inside U S A 1948,My 1,19:2
Inside U S A 1948,Ag 29,II,1:1
Bless You All 1950,D 15,42:2

Auerbach, Arnold M
Great Shakes 1931,Mr 12,22:2

Auerbach, Arnold M (Playwright)
How Revolting! 1932,Mr 11,14:6

Auerbach, Beverly
Mikado, The 1939,Mr 11,15:6

Auerbach, Boris
Oy, Is Dus a Leben!; Oh, What a Life!
1942,O 13,19:2
Song of Dnieper 1946,O 26,10:5
Wandering Stars 1946,D 14,18:2
Shylock and His Daughter 1947,S 30,22:2
Voice of Israel, The 1948,O 26,40:2
Hershel, The Jester 1948,D 14,39:2
Yosele the Nightingale 1949,O 21,30:4

Auerbach, George
Straw Hat, The 1926,O 15,20:2
Trumpet Shall Sound, The 1926,D 11,15:2

Auerbach, George (Director)
Big Lake 1927,Ap 9,17:2
Victim, The 1952,My 3,17:5

Auerbach, Helen
Dark Legend 1952,Mr 25,24:2

Auerbach, Leonard
Gentleman From Athens, The 1947,D 10,42:4

Auerbach, Leonard (Lighting Director)
Visit, The 1967,S 13,41:1
Tango 1968,Ja 1,11:1
Serjeant Musgrave's Dance 1968,Je 16,52:4
Master Builder, The 1968,Je 22,26:1
Merton of the Movies 1968,S 26,62:1

Auerbach, Leonard (Miscellaneous)
Hot Corner, The 1956,Ja 26,25:2
Holiday for Lovers 1957,F 15,20:1
Raisin in the Sun, A 1959,Mr 12,27:1
Semi-Detached 1960,Mr 11,20:2
Purlie Victorious 1961,S 29,29:1
Heroine, The 1963,F 21,5:5
Cafe Crown 1964,Ap 18,32:1
Owl and the Pussycat, The 1964,N 19,48:1
Nathan Weinstein, Mystic, Connecticut
1966,F 26,15:2
Ninety Day Mistress, The 1967,N 7,49:1
Resistible Rise of Arturo Ui, The 1968,Ag 8,25:1
Resistible Rise of Arturo Ui, The 1968,D 23,44:1
Does a Tiger Wear a Necktie? 1969,F 26,38:1
Purlie 1970,Mr 16,53:1

Aufricht, Mr (Director)
Italienische Nacht 1931,My 10,VIII,1:5

Auger, Germaine
As-tu du Coeur? 1926,O 31,VIII,2:4

Auger, Jacques
Ti-Coq 1951,F 10,10:2

Augier, Emile (Playwright)
Aventuriere, L' 1922,N 14,16:1
Aventuriere, L' 1926,D 17,27:3

Augsburger, O B
It's the Valet 1933,D 15,25:4
Fiesta 1933,D 16,12:2

August, Morris
Mother's Sabbath Days 1960,N 21,33:2

Augusta, Howard
Natural Man 1941,My 8,20:4
Three's a Family 1943,N 19,24:3
Walk Hard 1944,D 1,28:2
Walk Hard 1946,Mr 28,34:2
Rain 1948,F 2,15:2
Big Deal, The 1953,Mr 7,13:6
Juno and the Paycock 1955,F 24,20:4
Trouble in Mind 1955,N 5,23:2
Beaver Coat, The 1956,Mr 29,22:5

Augustin, William
Anna Christie 1921,N 3,22:1

Augustine, Basil
Galileo 1968,D 1,88:4

Augustine, Harold M
Vagabond King, The 1935,N 29,22:7

Augustine, Kermit
Trial of Dr Beck, The 1937,Ag 10,22:2

Augustine, Stephanie
Make Mine Manhattan 1948,Ja 16,26:2
Miss Liberty 1949,Jl 16,6:5
Peter Pan 1950,Ap 25,27:2

Augustine, William
He Understood Women 1928,Ag 16,25:1

Aul, Ronnie
Peter Pan 1950,Ap 25,27:2
Camino Real 1953,Mr 20,26:1

Auld, Georgie
Rat Race, The 1949,D 23,16:2

Auld, Vilma
Vintage '60 1960,S 13,41:1
Egg, The 1962,Ja 9,23:2

Auld, Vilma (Costume Designer)
Pajama Tops 1963,Je 1,15:1

Aulicino, Armand (Lyricist)
Shoemaker and the Peddler, The 1960,O 15,27:4
Sacco-Vanzetti 1969,F 9,78:1

Aulicino, Armand (Playwright)
Shoemaker and the Peddler, The 1960,O 15,27:4
Sacco-Vanzetti 1969,F 9,78:1

Aulisi, Joseph G (Costume Designer)
Ox Cart, The 1966,D 20,58:1
Wicked Cooks, The 1967,Ja 24,42:1
Saturday Night 1968,F 26,43:1
Man in the Glass Booth, The 1968,S 27,41:1
Someone's Comin' Hungry 1969,Ap 1,51:1
Transgressor Rides Again, The 1969,My 21,42:1
Pequod 1969,Je 30,33:1
American Hamburger League, The 1969,S 17,51:1
Passing Through From Exotic Places; Burial of
Esposito, The 1969,D 8,60:4
Passing Through From Exotic Places; Sunstroke
1969,D 8,60:4
Passing Through From Exotic Places; Son Who
Hunted Tigers in Jakarta, The 1969,D 8,60:4
Seven Days of Mourning 1969,D 17,64:1
Nobody Hears A Broken Drum 1970,Mr 20,55:1
Whispers on the Wind 1970,Je 4,50:1
Steambath 1970,Jl 1,49:1
Happy Birthday, Wanda June 1970,O 8,58:2
Dream Out of Time, A 1970,N 9,52:1
One Night Stands of a Noisy Passenger; Passage,
Un 1970,D 31,8:3
One Night Stands of a Noisy Passenger; Noisy
Passenger, The 1970,D 31,8:3
One Night Stands of a Noisy Passenger; Last
Stand 1970,D 31,8:3

Aull, Dorothy
Shinbone Alley 1957,Ap 15,23:2

Ault, Helen
Sweet Adeline 1929,S 4,33:1

Ault, Marie
Chauve-Souris; Queen of Spades, The
1931,O 22,27:1

Ault, Muriel
Under Milk Wood 1957,O 16,42:5

Aumen, Laurens (Lighting Director)
Romeo and Juliet 1962,Ap 3,42:1

Aumen, Laurens (Scenic Designer)
Romeo and Juliet 1962,Ap 3,42:1

Aumont, Jean Pierre
Rose Burke 1942,Ja 25,IX,2:5
My Name is Aquilon 1949,F 10,38:2
Heavenly Twins, The 1955,N 5,23:2
Second String, A 1960,Ap 14,36:2
Tovarich 1963,Ja 23,5:6
Tovarich 1963,Mr 20,5:1
Camino Real 1970,Ja 9,42:1
Camino Real 1970,Ja 18,II,1:1

Aumont, Jean Pierre (Translator)
My Name is Aquilon 1949,F 10,38:2

Aumont, Michel
Fourberies de Scapin, Les 1961,F 22,30:1
Impromptu de Versailles, L' 1961,F 22,30:1
Tartuffe 1961,Mr 1,28:1

Aumont, Michel—Cont
Dindon, Le 1961,Mr 8,38:1
Avare, L', L'; Miser, The 1966,F 9,32:1
Fil a la Paite, Un 1966,F 18,25:1

Auracher, Harry (Composer)
Frivolities of 1920 1920,Ja 9,22:2

Auracher, Harry (Lyricist)
Frivolities of 1920 1920,Ja 9,22:2

Aurelia, Vincent
Coriolanus 1965,Je 21,36:1

Aurelius, Mary
Happy Time, The 1950,Ja 25,24:1

Aurelius, Mary Elizabeth
Me, The Sleeper 1949,My 16,18:6

Auric, Georges (Composer)
Birds, The 1928,F 19,VIII,4:4
Roy de Malousie, Le 1928,Jl 1,VIII,1:8
Volpone 1928,D 9,X,2:7
Volpone 1957,F 5,27:2

Aurnou, Ely
Thousand and One Nights 1959,D 16,53:2
Eleventh Inheritor, The 1962,N 22,43:5
Enchanting Melody 1964,N 25,40:1
Wandering Stars 1966,N 14,52:2

Aurnov, Reuben
Brothers Ashkenazi, The 1970,N 17,53:2

Aurthur, Robert Alan (Playwright)
Very Special Baby, A 1956,N 15,43:2
Kwamina 1961,O 24,42:1
Carry Me Back to Morningside Heights
1968,F 28,41:1

Auslander, Joseph (Playwright)
Night in Spring, A 1935,Ag 7,22:2

Auspake, G W
Chicago 1926,D 31,11:1

Aussie and Czech
Vaudeville (Palace) 1927,My 31,25:1

Austen, Gerald
Hilarities 1948,S 10,20:2

Austen, Gladys
Doctor Faustus 1957,F 19,35:7

Austen, Jane (Original Author)
Pride and Prejudice 1935,O 23,19:2
Pride and Prejudice 1935,N 3,X,1:5
Pride and Prejudice 1935,N 6,32:4
Pride and Prejudice 1935,N 10,IX,2:5
Pride and Prejudice 1935,N 17,IX,1:1
Pride and Prejudice 1936,F 28,19:2
Pride and Prejudice 1936,Mr 29,IX,1:2
Pride and Prejudice 1936,Ag 30,IX,1:1
First Impressions 1959,Mr 29,II,1:1

Austen, Jerry
Barefoot Boy With Cheek 1947,Ap 4,20:2

Austen, Leslie
Cornered 1920,D 9,18:2
Voltaire 1922,Mr 21,17:1
Advertising of Kate, The 1922,My 9,22:2
Wasp, The 1923,Mr 28,14:3
Lass O' Laughter 1925,Ja 9,13:2
Wooden Kimono 1926,D 28,16:2
Midsummer Night's Dream, A 1932,Jl 13,15:1
Midsummer Night's Dream, A 1932,N 18,22:2
Twelfth Night 1932,N 19,20:5
Merchant of Venice, The 1932,N 24,34:5
Scorpion, The 1933,N 28,28:4
Murder With Pen and Ink 1935,Ag 20,25:1
Love From a Stranger 1936,S 30,28:1
Yr Obedient Husband 1938,Ja 11,26:5
Empress of Destiny 1938,Mr 10,16:2

Austen, Phyllis
Provincetown Follies, The 1935,N 4,24:3

Austin, Anna
Sunday Nights at Nine 1934,Mr 5,18:5

Austin, Burt (Miscellaneous)
Beautiful Jailer, The 1957,My 17,19:2

Austin, Clare
South 1955,My 2,17:4

Austin, Delores
Firebugs, The 1968,Jl 2,36:1

Austin, Doug
Ice Capades 1963,Ag 29,37:2

Austin, Ernest
Winkelberg 1958,Ja 15,26:2
Last Minstrel, The 1963,My 9,40:2

Austin, F F
Tiger Smiles, The 1930,D 18,29:1

Austin, Frederic (Composer)
Beggar's Opera, The 1941,Ag 12,14:6

Austin, George (Playwright)
Triumph 1935,O 15,18:5

Austin, Gerald
Private Life of the Master Race, The
1956,Ja 31,33:3

Austin, Henry
Let's Face It 1941,O 30,26:2

Austin, J W
Number 7 1926,S 9,21:3
Pygmalion 1926,N 16,24:1
Right You Are (If You Think You Are)
1927,F 24,27:1
Letter, The 1927,S 27,30:1
Launcelot and Elaine 1930,Mr 10,24:3
Puppet Show 1930,O 29,26:5
Doctor X 1931,F 10,25:1

Austin, J W—Cont
Miracle at Verdun 1931,Mr 17,34:6
Alchemist, The 1931,Je 5,27:1
Lady With a Lamp, The 1931,N 20,27:2
Singapore 1932,N 15,24:2
Peace Palace 1933,Je 6,30:2
Party, A 1933,Ag 24,18:4
Laughing Woman, The 1936,O 14,30:1
Storm Over Patsy 1937,Mr 9,26:4
Yr Obedient Husband 1938,Ja 11,26:5
Merry Wives of Windsor, The 1938,Ap 15,22:3
What Every Woman Knows 1938,Ag 30,14:5
Oscar Wilde 1938,O 11,20:2
Golden Wings 1941,D 9,46:6
Bird in Hand 1942,O 20,24:2
Austin, Jerry
Here Come the Clowns 1938,D 8,36:2
Me, Candido! 1956,O 16,36:2
Austin, Jesse
Horse Play 1937,Ag 28,8:3
Austin, John W
Come of Age 1934,Ja 13,16:6
Much Ado About Nothing 1952,My 2,20:1
Day by the Sea, A 1955,S 27,42:1
Austin, Kenneth (Lyricist)
Bureau-Crazy 1935,Ag 29,25:4
Austin, Kenneth (Playwright)
Bureau-Crazy 1935,Ag 29,25:4
Austin, Lee
Rose in the Wilderness 1949,Ja 5,21:2
Austin, Leonard
Silver Tassie, The 1929,O 25,26:1
Austin, Leslie
Old Lady Shows Her Medals, The 1932,Mr 8,19:3
Comedy of Errors, The 1932,N 22,25:3
Romeo and Juliet 1933,F 3,21:5
Orchids Preferred 1937,My 12,26:5
Austin, Lindsey
Laugh It Off 1925,Ap 25,18:4
Austin, Lois
Family Portrait 1939,Mr 9,18:4
Austin, Lyn (Miscellaneous)
In the Summer House 1953,D 30,17:1
Juno 1959,Mr 10,41:1
Best Man, The 1960,Ap 1,39:1
Alligators, The 1960,N 15,47:1
Rosemary 1960,N 15,47:1
Mary, Mary 1961,Mr 9,24:2
Far Country, A 1961,Ap 5,32:1
Blood, Sweat & Stanley Poole 1961,O 6,31:1
Romulus 1962,Ja 11,27:1
Calculated Risk 1962,N 1,35:1
Tiger Tiger Burning Bright 1962,D 24,5:2
Milk Train Doesn't Stop Here Anymore, The 1963,Ja 18,7:1
Children From Their Games 1963,Ap 12,33:1
Public Eye, The 1963,O 10,51:1
Private Ear, The 1963,O 10,51:1
Chinese Prime Minister, The 1964,Ja 3,14:1
In the Summer House 1964,Mr 26,43:1
Last Analysis, The 1964,O 2,30:1
Beekman Place 1964,O 8,50:1
Poor Richard 1964,D 3,59:1
Austin, Lyn (Producer)
Frogs of Spring, The 1953,O 21,36:2
Portrait of a Lady 1954,D 22,27:6
Joyce Grenfell Requests the Pleasure 1955,O 11,48:1
Terrible Swift Sword, The 1955,N 16,42:1
Adding Machine, The 1956,F 10,17:1
Copper and Brass 1957,O 18,19:2
Utbu 1966,Ja 5,24:1
Coop, The 1966,Mr 2,48:1
Stephen D 1967,S 25,58:1
Niggerlovers, The; Man and Dog 1967,O 2,54:2
Niggerlovers, The; Demonstration, The 1967,O 2,54:2
Exercise, The 1968,Ap 25,54:1
Collision Course; Camera Obscura 1968,My 9,55:2
Collision Course; Wandering 1968,My 9,55:2
Collision Course; Thoughts on the Instant of Greeting a Friend on the Street 1968,My 9,55:2
Collision Course; Jew! 1968,My 9,55:2
Collision Course; Stars and Stripes 1968,My 9,55:2
Collision Course; Rats 1968,My 9,55:2
Collision Course; Metaphors 1968,My 9,55:2
Collision Course; Skywriting 1968,My 9,55:2
Collision Course; Chuck 1968,My 9,55:2
Collision Course; Unexpurgated Memoirs of Bernard Mergendeiler, The 1968,My 9,55:2
Collision Course; Tour 1968,My 9,55:2
Adaptation 1969,F 11,27:1
Next 1969,F 11,27:1
Indians 1969,O 14,51:1
Alice in Wonderland 1970,O 9,43:1
Austin, Marguerite
Natja 1925,F 17,19:2
Austin, Marie
Johnny 2X4 1942,Mr 17,24:6
Austin, Mary
Victoria Regina 1935,D 27,15:2
Austin, Mary (Playwright)
Arrow-Maker, The 1956,O 5,20:1

Austin, Patty
Finian's Rainbow 1960,Ap 28,31:1
Austin, Paul John
Winterset 1966,F 10,32:2
Austin, Paul John (Director)
Glorious Ruler, The 1969,Jl 1,31:1
Austin, Paul John (Miscellaneous)
Deer Park, The 1967,F 1,27:2
Beard, The 1967,O 25,40:1
Guns of Carrar, The 1968,D 10,53:1
Cuba Si 1968,D 10,53:1
House of Leather, The 1970,Mr 19,56:1
Happy Birthday, Wanda June 1970,O 8,58:2
Austin, Phyllis
Oh, Ernest! 1927,My 10,24:3
Austin, Ralph
Cinderella on Broadway 1920,Je 25,18:1
Austin, Robert
Kiss Me, Kate 1954,Mr 27,13:2
Austin, Suzanne
Small Timers, The 1925,Ja 28,15:3
Austin, William
King Lear 1923,Mr 10,9:4
Pride 1923,My 3,22:3
Austrin, Lilija
Everyman 1953,O 12,30:2
Quick Years, The 1953,N 26,51:2
Queen After Death 1956,Mr 13,33:2
Mary and the Fairy 1956,Mr 24,15:2
Fortunato 1956,Mr 24,15:2
Autori, Fernando
Casanova 1932,Je 19,IX,2:1
Autran, Paulo
My Fair Lady 1962,Ag 23,24:6
Avakian, George (Miscellaneous)
Cradle Will Rock, The 1964,N 9,40:4
Avalos, Luis
Camino Real 1970,Ja 9,42:1
Good Woman of Setzuan, The 1970,N 6,51:1
Avant, Clarence (Miscellaneous)
Reckoning, The 1969,S 5,28:1
Avant, Lance
Judy Garland's New Variety Show 1956,S 27,43:2
Avchinnikova, Lydia
Uncle Vanya 1960,F 13,13:4
Ave, Evelyn
Beclch 1968,D 17,59:1
Avedon, Doe
Young and Fair, The 1948,N 23,35:2
My Name is Aquilon 1949,F 10,38:2
All the King's Men 1950,Jl 19,25:6
Avera, Tom
Insect Comedy, The 1948,Je 4,26:3
Sundown Beach 1948,S 8,37:1
Marathon '33 1963,D 23,20:1
Averill, Allen
Holy Night 1941,D 22,23:3
Averill, George
Some Party 1922,Ap 17,22:1
Hobo 1931,F 12,24:4
Nativity Play, The 1937,D 21,29:1
Aversano, Nicholas (Musical Director)
Wonderful World of Burlesque, The 1965,Ap 29,38:1
Avery, Arvil
Cross My Heart 1928,S 18,32:7
Avery, Brian
Time for Singing, A 1966,My 23,48:2
Avery, C R (Playwright)
Hervey House 1935,My 18,21:2
Avery, Charles
Ali Baba 1951,Mr 27,34:2
Avery, Emile
Man From Cairo, The 1938,My 5,26:5
Avery, Faith
Chalk Dust 1936,Mr 5,24:5
Path of Flowers, The 1936,S 18,19:3
Passing of the Third Floor Back, The 1937,Ag 3,20:6
Avery, Henry
Hamp 1967,Mr 10,32:1
Daniel Boone 1967,D 23,28:1
Avery, Phyllis
Orchids Preferred 1937,My 12,26:5
Charley's Aunt 1940,O 18,24:2
Letters to Lucerne 1941,D 9,47:6
Letters to Lucerne 1941,D 24,14:2
Little Darling 1942,O 28,26:2
Ask My Friend Sandy 1943,F 5,16:2
Winged Victory 1943,N 22,24:1
Brighten the Corner 1945,D 13,33:2
Avery, Rosalynd
To Dorothy, A Son 1951,N 20,37:2
Avery, Val
Nowhere to Go But Up 1962,N 12,36:2
Cafe Crown 1964,Ap 18,32:1
Front Page, The 1969,My 12,54:2
Front Page, The 1969,N 2,86:1
Avery, Virginia
Antigone 1923,My 4,18:4
Avey, West
Silks and Satins 1920,Jl 16,19:1

Avila, Doria
Medium, The 1950,S 3,II,1:1
Out of This World 1950,D 22,17:3
Avila, Tony
Passenger to Bali, A 1940,Mr 15,26:2
Aviv Dancers, The
Josephine Baker and Her Company 1964,F 5,30:1
Aviva
Peer Gynt 1951,Ja 29,15:2
Aviva (Composer)
Peer Gynt 1951,Ja 29,15:2
Avolons, The Five
Vaudeville (Palace) 1923,Ja 16,16:3
Avon Comedy Four
Vaudeville (Hippodrome) 1924,Mr 18,25:1
Vaudeville (Hippodrome) 1924,O 21,21:2
Earl Carroll's Vanities 1926,Ag 25,19:4
Vaudeville (Palace) 1928,D 17,23:3
Vaudeville (Palace) 1930,Jl 7,22:2
Avramo, Celia (Director)
Three 1928,D 4,28:2
Avrey
Chauve-Souris 1929,Ja 23,20:2
Avril, Arlene
Golden Six, The 1958,O 27,31:2
Avshaionov, Aaron (Composer)
Carefree Tree, The 1955,O 12,37:2
Awad, Jacqueline
Tale of Kasane, The 1969,F 25,36:1
Sganarelle 1970,Ja 13,41:1
Songs From Milk Wood 1970,Ja 13,41:1
Awan, Adrian (Director)
Red Mill, The 1945,O 17,16:2
Awan, Adrian (Lighting Director)
Red Mill, The 1945,O 17,16:2
Gypsy Lady 1946,S 18,25:6
Awan, Adrian (Miscellaneous)
Gypsy Lady 1946,S 18,25:6
Awe, James (Miscellaneous)
Potting Shed, The 1957,Ja 30,32:1
Axel, Tamma
Passing of Chow-Chow, The 1929,O 4,24:4
Axelrod, Carl
Half Moon Inn 1925,Mr 10,14:1
Betty Behave 1927,Mr 9,28:4
Axelrod, David (Composer)
Leonard Sillman's New Faces of 1968 1968,My 3,43:1
Axelrod, David (Lyricist)
Leonard Sillman's New Faces of 1968 1968,My 3,43:1
Axelrod, David (Miscellaneous)
Adding Machine, The 1970,D 5,40:1
Axelrod, David (Playwright)
Leonard Sillman's New Faces of 1968 1968,My 3,43:1
Axelrod, George (Director)
Will Success Spoil Rock Hunter? 1955,O 14,22:2
Once More With Feeling 1958,O 22,39:1
Goodbye Charlie 1959,D 17,50:1
Star-Spangled Girl, The 1966,D 22,38:1
Axelrod, George (Playwright)
Small Wonder 1948,S 16,33:5
Seven Year Itch, The 1952,N 21,21:2
Seven Year Itch, The 1952,N 30,II,1:1
Seven Year Itch, The 1953,My 18,26:8
Will Success Spoil Rock Hunter? 1955,O 14,22:2
Goodbye Charlie 1959,D 17,50:1
Axelrod, George (Producer)
Visit to a Small Planet 1957,F 8,18:1
Axelrod, Herman (Playwright)
You'll Never Know 1921,Ap 21,9:2
Axelrod, Jack
Macbeth 1969,D 23,25:1
Gandhi 1970,O 21,37:1
Axelson, Mary McDougal (Playwright)
Life Begins; Birth 1932,Mr 20,VIII,2:4
Life Begins 1932,Mr 29,23:2
Axenfeld, I (Original Author)
Recruits 1935,Ja 20,X,3:1
Axer, Erwin (Miscellaneous)
Tango 1969,Ja 20,33:1
Axler, George
Sign of Jonah, The 1960,S 9,35:1
Witches' Sabbath 1962,Ap 20,22:2
When We Dead Awaken 1966,Ap 19,37:2
Axman, Bela
Carry Nation 1932,O 31,18:2
Axtell, Hall (Composer)
Myself and I 1929,Ag 31,13:6
Axtell, Robert (Composer)
Myself and I 1929,Ag 31,13:6
Ayars, Ann
Medium, The 1949,N 7,32:4
Ayckbourn, Alan (Playwright)
How the Other Half Loves 1970,Ag 7,23:1
How the Other Half Loves 1970,S 11,33:2
Aydan, Sevda
Kiss Me, Kate 1964,F 16,29:1
Ayed, Ali ben
Othello 1964,Ag 3,16:6
Ayer, Eleanor
Susannah and the Elders 1959,O 19,37:3

Ayer, Ethan (Playwright)
Great Western Union, The 1965,F 10,45:1
Ayer, Frederick W (Producer)
Parnell 1935,N 12,24:2
Parnell 1936,My 5,26:2
Empress of Destiny 1938,Mr 10,16:2
Ayer, Jack
Biff, Bing, Bang 1921,My 10,20:1
Ayer, Nat
Vaudeville (Palace) 1926,Ag 31,15:3
Vaudeville (Palace) 1928,Ap 10,32:4
Ayers, Catherine
Porgy and Bess 1942,Ja 23,16:2
Porgy and Bess 1943,S 14,26:2
Long Way From Home, A 1948,F 9,25:2
Porgy and Bess 1953,Mr 10,25:5
Ayers, Edel
Little Theatre Tournament; End of the Dance, The
1929,My 11,22:2
Ayers, Elizabeth
From Morn Till Midnight 1948,D 7,41:6
Butter and Egg Man, The 1949,Ap 29,27:1
Ayers, Jackie
My Heart's in the Highlands 1939,Ap 14,29:2
Love's Old Sweet Song 1940,My 3,16:3
Macbeth 1941,N 12,30:2
Arsenic and Old Lace 1943,D 13,18:6
Take It As It Comes 1944,F 11,17:2
Ayers, Ken
Out of This World 1950,D 22,17:3
Wildcat 1960,D 17,20:2
Hello, Dolly! 1964,Ja 17,22:1
South Pacific 1965,Je 3,25:1
Skyscraper 1965,N 15,48:1
Joyful Noise, A 1966,D 16,57:1
Ayers, Lemuel (Costume Designer)
As You Like It 1941,O 21,29:2
Macbeth 1941,N 12,30:2
Angel Street 1941,D 6,15:2
St Louis Woman 1946,Ap 1,22:2
Cyrano de Bergerac 1946,O 9,33:2
Kiss Me, Kate 1948,D 31,10:3
Out of this World 1951,My 20,II,1:1
Kiss Me, Kate 1952,Ja 9,24:6
My Darlin' Aida 1952,O 28,36:4
See the Jaguar 1952,D 4,46:2
Merchant of Venice, The 1953,Mr 5,20:2
Kismet 1953,D 4,2:4
Pajama Game, The 1954,My 14,20:2
Pajama Game, The 1957,My 16,27:1
Ayers, Lemuel (Lighting Director)
Bloomer Girl 1944,O 6,18:5
Ayers, Lemuel (Miscellaneous)
Love's Labour's Lost 1953,F 5,20:3
Misalliance 1953,F 19,20:1
Ayers, Lemuel (Playwright)
Out of This World 1950,D 22,17:3
Ayers, Lemuel (Producer)
Kiss Me, Kate 1948,D 31,10:3
Kiss Me, Kate 1952,Ja 9,24:6
See the Jaguar 1952,D 4,46:2
Ayers, Lemuel (Scenic Designer)
Journey's End 1939,S 19,29:2
They Knew What They Wanted 1939,O 3,19:1
Eight O'Clock Tuesday 1941,Ja 7,18:2
They Walk Alone 1941,Mr 13,24:2
As You Like It 1941,O 21,29:2
Angel Street 1941,D 6,15:2
Plan M 1942,F 21,15:2
Autumn Hill 1942,Ap 14,17:4
Pirate, The 1942,N 26,39:2
Lifeline 1942,D 1,20:3
Willow and I, The 1942,D 11,32:2
Harriet 1943,Mr 4,24:2
Oklahoma! 1943,Ap 1,27:1
Peepshow 1944,F 4,12:2
Song of Norway 1944,Ag 22,20:2
Harriet 1944,S 28,26:1
Bloomer Girl 1944,O 6,18:5
Bloomer Girl 1944,O 8,II,1:1
St Louis Woman 1946,Ap 1,22:2
Cyrano de Bergerac 1946,O 9,33:2
Inside U S A 1948,My 1,19:2
Inside U S A 1948,My 23,II,1:1
Inside U S A 1948,Je 13,II,6:6
Kiss Me, Kate 1948,D 31,10:3
Out of This World 1950,D 22,17:3
Out of this World 1951,My 20,II,1:1
Oklahoma! 1951,My 30,15:2
Music in the Air 1951,O 9,32:2
Kiss Me, Kate 1952,Ja 9,24:6
My Darlin' Aida 1952,O 28,36:4
See the Jaguar 1952,D 4,46:2
Merchant of Venice, The 1953,Mr 5,20:2
Camino Real 1953,Mr 20,26:1
Camino Real 1953,Mr 29,II,1:1
Oklahoma! 1953,S 1,19:1
Kismet 1953,D 4,2:4
Pajama Game, The 1954,My 14,20:2
Pajama Game, The 1957,My 16,27:1
Pajama Game, The 1957,My 26,II,1:1
Oklahoma! 1958,Mr 20,32:3
Oklahoma! 1963,F 28,8:2

Oklahoma! 1963,My 16,40:1
Kismet 1965,Je 23,45:1
Oklahoma! 1965,D 16,62:1
Ayers, Lily
Poet's Follies of 1955 1955,My 15,II,3:1
Ayers, Lucien
Roll Sweet Chariot 1934,O 3,24:3
Ayers, Paula
Princess Ida 1925,Ap 14,27:2
Golden Dawn 1927,D 1,32:3
Ayers, Shirley (Producer)
Girl of the Golden West, The 1957,N 6,44:1
Ayers, Walter
Philadelphia 1929,S 17,34:5
Ayers, William
I Gotta Get Out 1947,S 26,27:2
Ayler, Ethel
Simply Heavenly 1957,My 22,28:2
Jamaica 1957,N 1,32:2
Carmen Jones 1959,Ag 18,25:1
Blacks, The 1961,My 5,23:1
Kwamina 1961,O 24,42:1
Ododo 1970,N 25,26:1
Aylesworth, Arthur
Go Easy Mabel 1922,My 9,22:2
Follow Thru 1929,Ja 10,24:3
Queen at Home 1930,D 30,25:2
Unexpected Husband 1931,Je 3,29:4
Amourette 1933,S 28,25:2
Ayliff, H K (Director)
Yellow Sands 1927,S 12,29:3
Taming of the Shrew, The 1927,O 26,26:4
Payment Deferred 1931,O 14,2:2
Black Eye, The 1935,O 12,13:5
Ayliff, H K (Playwright)
Comedy of Crooks, A 1936,Je 8,22:3
Ayliff, H K (Producer)
Taming of the Shrew, The 1928,My 27,VIII,1:8
Aylmer, Felix
Loyalties 1922,S 28,18:1
Last of Mrs Cheyney, The 1925,N 10,23:5
Garey Divorce Case, The 1929,My 12,IX,2:3
Cold Comfort Farm 1936,Mr 2,13:7
Yes and No 1937,N 14,XI,3:1
Power and Glory 1938,My 1,X,2:5
Flashing Stream, The 1938,S 2,21:4
Flashing Stream, The 1938,S 18,X,1:4
Flashing Stream, The 1939,Ap 11,19:2
Prescott Proposals, The 1953,D 17,53:1
Prescott Proposals, The 1953,D 27,II,3:1
Chalk Garden, The 1956,My 13,II,3:1
Aylsworth, Arthur
Come Seven 1920,Jl 20,10:1
Chicken Feed 1923,S 25,10:2
Haunted House, The 1924,S 3,12:1
Morning After, The 1925,Jl 28,24:2
Puppy Love 1926,Ja 28,16:3
Sisters 1927,D 26,26:5
Yankee Point 1942,N 24,28:2
Aylward, Tony
Gay Divorce 1960,Ap 4,37:1
Aylwin, Tracy
Little Theatre Tournament; Joint Owners in Spain
1929,My 7,28:1
Ayme, Marcel (Playwright)
Sorcieres de Salem, Les 1955,F 27,II,3:1
Clerambard 1957,N 8,22:3
Clerambard 1957,N 17,II,1:1
Moonbirds 1959,O 10,13:1
Louisiana 1961,O 8,II,3:4
Aynesworth, Allan
Transit of Venus, The 1927,My 22,VIII,2:1
High Road, The 1927,S 25,VIII,2:1
Counsel's Opinion 1931,S 13,IX,2:5
Tovarich 1935,Ap 25,19:8
Victoria Regina 1937,Jl 11,X,1:7
Ayre, Alfred
Last of Mrs Cheyney, The 1925,N 10,23:5
Interference 1927,O 19,24:3
Suspense 1930,Ag 13,22:3
Ayre, Jane
Allegro 1952,S 18,36:3
Ayre, Robert (Original Author)
Mr Sycamore 1942,N 14,13:2
Mr Sycamore 1942,N 29,VIII,1:1
Ayre, Tom
Wish You Were Here 1952,Je 26,26:6
Ayres, Ada
Brass Buttons 1927,D 6,26:3
Ayres, Catherine
Porgy and Bess 1935,O 11,30:2
Porgy and Bess 1944,F 8,13:2
Ayres, Charlotte
Mayflowers 1925,N 25,14:2
Sunny Days 1928,F 9,29:1
Vanderbilt Revue, The 1930,O 26,VIII,3:5
Vanderbilt Revue, The 1930,N 6,22:6
Ayres, Christine
Ziegfeld Follies 1943,Ap 2,16:2
Lady Says Yes, A 1945,Ja 11,18:5
Ayres, Gordon
Winners and Losers 1947,F 27,27:2

Ayres, Irish (Costume Designer)
Nat Turner 1960,N 7,46:3
Walk in Darkness 1963,O 29,30:2
Ayres, Jackie
Life With Father 1939,Ag 15,14:4
Tinker's Dam 1943,Ja 29,22:2
Ayres, James F
Partners Again 1922,My 2,22:2
Ayres, Matthew
Patriots, The 1943,D 21,22:5
Ayres, Mitchell (Musical Director)
Paradise Island 1962,Je 28,22:1
Around the World in 80 Days 1963,Je 24,22:1
Around the World in 80 Days 1964,Je 29,33:2
Mardi Gras! 1965,Je 28,33:2
Mardi Gras! 1966,Jl 11,32:2
Ayres, Robert (Composer)
Vogues and Frolics 1924,Je 26,21:7
Ayres, Walter
Farmer Takes a Wife, The 1934,O 31,17:1
Ayrez, Ann (Producer)
Housewarming 1932,Ap 8,25:1
Ayrtob, Robert
Lucky One, The 1922,N 21,15:2
Ayrton, Lulu
One 1920,S 15,12:2
Ayrton, Michael (Scenic Designer)
Macbeth 1942,Jl 26,VIII,1:7
Ayrton, Randal
One 1920,S 15,12:2
Hassan 1924,S 23,23:1
Ayrton, Robert
Champion, The 1921,Ja 4,11:1
Swifty 1922,O 17,14:1
Romeo and Juliet 1923,Ja 25,16:1
Antony and Cleopatra 1924,F 20,22:1
Azana, Manuel (Premier) (Playwright)
Corona, La 1932,Ap 13,23:3
Azara, Nancy (Costume Designer)
Orthee 1962,D 29,5:5
Antigone 1962,D 29,5:5
Azenberg, Emanuel (Miscellaneous)
Lion in Winter, The 1966,Mr 4,23:1
Azenberg, Emanuel (Producer)
Rendezvous at Senlis 1961,F 28,39:2
Mark Twain Tonight! 1966,Mr 24,48:2
Investigation, The 1966,O 5,40:1
Something Different 1967,N 29,52:1
Azertis, Lorenzo de (Playwright)
Casanova 1923,S 16,VII,2:8
Azikri, Nissim
Dybbuk, The 1964,F 4,30:2
Each Had Six Wings 1964,Mr 12,39:1
Aznavour, Charles (Composer)
World of Charles Aznavour, The 1965,O 15,49:1
Aznavour, Charles (Playwright)
World of Charles Aznavour, The 1965,O 15,49:1
Azorin (Playwright)
Old Spain 1927,My 8,VII,2:3
Azpiazu, Don
Vaudeville (Palace) 1931,Ap 13,17:2
Azuma, Haruyo
Azuma Kabuki Dancers and Musicians
1954,F 19,22:3
Azuma Kabuki Dancers and Musicians
1954,Mr 10,29:4
Azuma Kabuki Dancers and Musicians
1955,D 27,31:4
Azuma Kabuki Dancers and Musicians
1956,Ja 8,II,3:1
Azuma, Hideho
Evening of Rare Pleasures, An 1959,Je 4,26:2
Azuma, Tokuho
Azuma Kabuki Dancers and Musicians
1954,F 19,22:3
Azuma Kabuki Dancers and Musicians
1954,F 28,II,4:1
Azuma Kabuki Dancers and Musicians
1954,Mr 10,29:4
Azuma Kabuki Dancers and Musicians
1955,D 27,31:4
Azuma Kabuki Dancers and Musicians
1956,Ja 8,II,3:1
Azzara, Candy
Lovers and Other Strangers 1968,S 19,63:1
Engagement Baby, The 1970,My 22,40:1

B

Baade, Mabel
No Foolin' 1926,Je 25,25:1
Babab, E
Yegor Bulevitch 1934,Ja 8,21:7
Babad, A
Haunch, Paunch and Jowl 1935,D 27,22:4
Babb, Carroll and Surell
Vaudeville (Palace) 1924,Ja 22,15:6
Babb, Dorothy
Dream With Music 1944,My 19,15:2
Babbitt, James
Orchids Preferred 1937,My 12,26:5

Babbs, Dorothy
Lend an Ear 1948,D 17,38:2
Babcock, Barbara
Nature of the Crime 1970,Mr 24,41:1
Babcock, Burnside
Sun-Up 1923,My 25,28:1
Babcock, Celia
Hickory Stick 1944,My 9,15:6
Babcock, Donald
Student Gypsy, The; Prince of Liederkranz, The 1963,O 1,34:1
Babcock, Frank
I Remember Mama 1944,O 20,16:2
Babcock, Lucille (Miscellaneous)
H M S Pinafore 1960,Ja 29,14:1
Utopia, Limited 1960,Ap 8,27:2
Babcock, Robert
John Hawthorne 1921,Ja 24,16:1
Liliom 1921,Ap 21,18:1
Babcock, Theodore
One 1920,S 15,12:2
Two Strangers From Nowhere 1924,Ap 8,22:2
She Stoops to Conquer 1924,Je 10,24:3
Judy Drops In 1924,O 6,24:2
Yours Truly 1927,Ja 26,16:5
Top Speed 1929,D 26,20:1
Babcock, Thomas
Glamour Preferred 1940,N 16,13:2
Babe, Thomas
New York Idea, The 1963,Jl 13,12:2
Measure for Measure 1967,Ag 27,II,4:8
Babe, Thomas (Director)
Trojan Women, The 1967,Ag 27,II,4:8
Babel, Isaac (Playwright)
Sunset 1966,My 13,34:1
Babel, Sue
Fiddler on the Roof 1964,S 23,56:2
Baber, Alice (Scenic Designer)
Evening With G B S, An; O'Flaherty, V C 1957,F 19,35:7
An Evening With G B S; Press Cuttings 1957,F 19,35:7
Baber, James
All Wet 1925,Jl 7,24:1
Up and Up, The 1930,S 9,25:2
Good Companions, The 1931,O 2,31:1
Baber, Vivian
Ginger Snaps 1930,Ja 1,30:5
Sweet Chariot 1930,O 24,30:2
Savage Rhythm 1932,Ja 1,30:4
Baber, Vivienne
Make Me Know It 1929,N 5,32:5
Shuffle Along of 1933 1932,D 27,11:3
On Whitman Avenue 1946,My 9,28:2
Babochkin, Boris (Director)
Colleagues, The 1962,Je 21,26:1
Babson, Edith
Mr Moneypenny 1928,O 17,26:2
Babush, Beatrice
Mikado, The 1942,F 4,22:2
Pirates of Penzance, The 1942,F 18,22:2
Iolanthe 1942,F 24,26:4
Gondoliers, The 1942,Mr 4,22:3
Baca, Epy
Othello 1955,S 8,27:2
Bacall, Lauren
Johnny 2X4 1942,Mr 17,24:6
Goodbye Charlie 1959,D 17,50:1
Cactus Flower 1965,D 9,60:2
Applause 1970,Mr 31,35:1
Applause 1970,Ap 5,II,1:1
Bacarris, Gustavo (Costume Designer)
Evergreen 1930,D 21,VIII,1:6
Bacarris, Gustavo (Scenic Designer)
Evergreen 1930,D 21,VIII,1:6
Bacca, Jane (Producer)
Sold to the Movies; Life Size 1970,Je 18,54:2
Sold to the Movies; Crossing the Gap 1970,Je 18,54:2
Sold to the Movies; Type 424 Meet Type Oh-Oh, No! 1970,Je 18,54:2
Baccala, Donna
Impossible Years, The 1965,O 14,55:1
Bach
Rose of France 1933,O 29,II,3:3
Bach, Eileen
Child of Manhattan 1932,Mr 2,15:1
Bach, Ernest (Playwright)
Whole Town's Talking, The 1923,Ag 30,8:2
Bach, Johann Sebastian (Composer)
Dear Judas 1947,O 6,26:4
Bach, Reginald
Old English 1924,N 9,VIII,2:3
Double Dan 1927,Je 5,VII,2:1
Yellow Sands 1927,S 12,29:3
Taming of the Shrew, The 1927,O 26,26:4
Taming of the Shrew, The 1927,N 13,IX,1:1
Our Betters 1928,F 21,18:2
Queen's Husband, The 1931,N 15,VIII,2:1
Love on the Dole 1936,F 25,23:3
Love on the Dole 1936,Mr 8,IX,1:1
Green Waters 1936,N 5,34:4
Save Me the Waltz 1938,Mr 1,19:2

Knights of Song 1938,O 18,29:2
Mother, The 1939,Ap 26,26:2
Bach, Reginald (Director)
Our Betters 1928,F 21,18:2
Queen Who Kept Her Head, The 1934,F 21,23:4
Love on the Dole 1936,F 25,23:3
Green Waters 1936,N 5,34:4
Holmeses of Baker Street, The 1936,D 10,34:3
And Now Goodbye 1937,F 3,26:4
Antony and Cleopatra 1937,N 11,30:2
Foreigners 1939,D 6,30:2
Bach-Wilkens, Margaret
Fedora 1924,Ja 24,14:2
Bacharach, Burt (Composer)
Marlene Dietrich 1967,O 10,52:1
Marlene Dietrich 1968,O 4,36:1
Promises, Promises 1968,D 2,59:3
Promises, Promises 1968,D 15,II,3:1
Promises, Promises 1970,Ja 18,II,7:1
Bacharach, Burt (Musical Director)
Marlene Dietrich 1967,O 10,52:1
Bacharach, Burt (Playwright)
Promises, Promises 1969,O 4,26:4
Bacharach, Lester
Twelfth Night 1941,D 3,32:2
Bacharach, Richard (Producer)
Tenth of an Inch Makes the Difference, A 1962,N 13,44:1
Bache, Kenneth
Jack and the Beanstalk 1947,N 3,28:2
Bache, Theodore (Director)
Yours Is My Heart 1946,S 6,16:5
Bache, Violet
Vaudeville (Palace) 1926,O 26,24:2
Bachelors, The
Vaudeville (Palace) 1932,Jl 4,14:5
Bacher, John
Moondreamers, The 1969,D 9,68:1
Bacher, William (Producer)
Seventh Heaven 1955,My 27,16:2
Bachia, Guilo
Green Goddess, The 1921,Ja 19,14:1
Bachmann, Robert (Playwright)
Legal Grounds 1940,D 2,18:4
Bachwitz, Hans (Playwright)
Love City, The 1926,Ja 26,18:2
Joy of Living 1931,Ap 7,31:1
Baci
X Has No Value 1970,F 17,35:1
Street Sounds 1970,O 23,32:1
Backar, Sol
41 in a Sack 1960,Mr 26,15:2
Backe, Gloria Scott
Summer and Smoke 1952,Ap 25,19:5
American Gothic 1953,N 11,35:6
Iceman Cometh, The 1956,My 8,38:1
Backer, George (Playwright)
Honeymoon 1932,D 11,IX,5:1
Honeymoon 1932,D 24,11:2
Backer, George (Producer)
Great Music 1924,O 6,24:1
Backlin, Helen
Death of a Salesman 1963,Jl 20,11:2
Backo, John (Lighting Director)
Frugal Noon 1964,My 23,15:2
Acid Wine 1964,My 23,15:2
Backus, Carolyn
Play of Daniel, The 1960,D 27,23:6
Play of Daniel, The 1961,D 28,22:6
Backus, Frank
Drifting 1922,Ja 3,20:3
Backus, Frederick
Overture 1930,D 8,26:4
Backus, Georgia
Assumption of Hannele, The 1924,F 16,16:2
Complex, The 1925,Mr 4,17:2
One of the Family 1925,D 23,22:3
Backus, Ida
Peter Flies High 1931,N 10,28:3
Backus, James
Hitch Your Wagon! 1937,Ap 9,18:2
Too Many Heroes 1937,N 16,26:2
Baclanova, Olga
Lysistrata 1925,O 17,18:3
Lysistrata 1925,D 15,28:2
Vaudeville (Palace) 1929,My 20,22:8
$25 an Hour 1933,My 11,14:4
Murder at the Vanities 1933,S 13,22:4
Mahogany Hall 1934,Ja 18,18:5
Claudia 1941,F 13,24:2
Claudia 1942,My 25,11:3
Bacon, Catherine
Penny Wars, The 1969,O 16,52:1
Penny Wars, The 1969,O 26,II,1:1
Penny Wars, The 1970,F 15,II,1:1
Bacon, Ernst (Composer)
Tempest, The 1955,Ag 2,18:2
Bacon, Faith
Earl Carroll's Vanities 1930,Jl 2,28:3
Ziegfeld Follies 1931,Jl 2,30:5
Bacon, Frank
Untitled-Benefit 1921,My 2,12:3
Right of Possession 1930,My 9,20:5

Bacon, Frank (Playwright)
Lightnin' 1938,S 16,17:2
Bacon, Gaspar G Jr
Foemen of the Yard 1935,Ap 6,10:4
Lid's Off, The 1936,Ap 4,11:6
Bacon, Gaspar Jr (Playwright)
Come Across 1937,Ap 10,10:7
Bacon, Gerald F (Producer)
Betty, Be Careful 1931,My 5,33:3
Bacon, Glen (Composer)
Straw Hat, The 1939,S 30,10:6
All in Fun 1940,D 28,11:2
Bacon, Glen (Lyricist)
All in Fun 1940,D 28,11:2
Bacon, Richard
Changeling, The 1956,My 4,20:3
Bacon, Robert
Assorted Nuts 1940,Ap 7,I,44:6
One on the House 1941,Mr 30,I,47:3
Bacon, Robert (Lyricist)
Assorted Nuts 1940,Ap 7,I,44:6
Bacon, Roger
Getting Even 1929,Ag 20,31:1
Frankie and Johnny 1930,S 26,16:5
Jamboree 1932,N 25,18:4
Bacon, Roy
Titus Andronicus 1956,D 3,40:2
Trojan Women, The 1957,Mr 19,42:7
Bacon, Sam (Producer)
Charm 1929,N 29,24:5
Bacon, Winifred
Widowers' Houses 1959,Mr 3,39:2
Bacque, Andre
Aiglon, L' 1924,O 21,21:1
Naked 1924,O 28,27:2
Naked 1924,N 2,VII,1:1
Madame Sans-Gene 1924,N 4,30:1
Parisienne 1924,N 25,26:2
Badaloni, Dolores
They Knew What They Wanted 1939,O 3,19:1
They Knew What They Wanted 1949,F 17,28:2
Badaloni, Nera
Dice of the Gods, The 1923,Ap 6,20:2
Lady, The 1923,D 5,23:2
Masque of Venice, The 1926,Mr 3,27:3
Attore, L' 1929,Mr 11,29:5
Piacere Dell 'Onesta, Il 1929,Mr 25,33:1
Serata D'Inverno; Winter Evening, A 1929,Ap 8,32:5
Liane, Le (Ties That Bind); Ties That Bind (Le Liane) 1929,Ap 22,22:1
Assalto, L' 1929,My 20,23:2
Tutto Per Bene; All's Well That Ends Well 1929,Je 3,27:1
Romanticismo 1934,My 14,20:2
Miserabili I, 1934,S 24,15:1
Miserabili I, 1934,O 1,14:2
Vita Nuova; Life Begins Again 1935,F 26,16:2
Badaloni, Rodolfo
Dice of the Gods, The 1923,Ap 6,20:2
Lady, The 1923,D 5,23:2
Dancing Mothers 1924,Ag 12,12:2
Matinee Girl, The 1926,F 2,20:3
Potenza, La 1926,Je 29,21:3
Piggy 1927,Ja 12,22:2
Trial Marriage 1927,F 1,24:3
Merry Wives of Windsor, The 1928,Mr 20,20:1
Serata D'Inverno; Winter Evening, A 1929,Ap 8,32:5
Liane, Le (Ties That Bind); Ties That Bind (Le Liane) 1929,Ap 22,22:1
Assalto, L' 1929,My 20,23:2
Tutto Per Bene; All's Well That Ends Well 1929,Je 3,27:1
Nikki 1931,S 30,23:4
Experience Unnecessary 1931,D 31,16:2
Experience Unnecessary 1932,Mr 28,10:2
Baddeley, Angela
Hundred Years Old, A 1928,D 9,X,2:1
Rising Sun, The 1929,O 27,IX,2:2
School for Scandal, The 1929,D 15,X,4:2
Greeks Had a Word for It, The 1934,N 23,22:2
Night Must Fall 1936,S 29,34:1
Light of Heart, The 1940,Mr 3,X,3:4
Light of Heart, The 1941,Je 15,IX,2:5
Love's Labour's Lost 1949,O 24,18:3
Relative Values 1951,N 29,41:2
Day of the Prince 1963,My 15,33:4
Baddeley, Hermione
Forest, The 1924,Mr 16,VIII,1:7
Excelsior 1928,S 30,IX,1:3
Greeks Had a Word for It, The 1934,N 23,22:2
Floodlight 1937,Je 15,IX,2:6
Rise Above It 1941,Je 15,IX,2:6
Brighton Rock 1943,Ap 18,II,1:1
Taste of Honey, A 1961,My 17,43:1
Milk Train Doesn't Stop Here Anymore, The 1962,Jl 12,19:8
Milk Train Doesn't Stop Here Anymore, The 1963,Ja 18,7:1
I Only Want an Answer 1968,F 6,36:1
Canterbury Tales; Pilgrims, The 1969,F 4,34:1

Baddeley, Hermione—Cont
Canterbury Tales; Wife of Bath's Tale, The
1969,F 4,34:1
Bade, Annette
Cold Feet 1923,My 22,14:2
Vogues of 1924 1924,Mr 28,14:3
Bade, Tom
Perfect Match, The 1970,N 18,41:1
Badel, Alan
Measure for Measure 1950,Mr 10,33:5
Hamlet 1956,Ap 11,28:1
Rehearsal, The 1963,S 24,45:2
Rehearsal, The 1963,O 20,II,1:1
Badel, Sarah
Right Honourable Gentleman, The 1965,O 20,50:2
Heartbreak House 1967,Ag 27,II,1:1
Arms and the Man 1970,Ag 26,36:1
Bader, Gershon (Playwright)
Longing for Home 1933,S 22,15:1
Bader, S R Simcoff (Playwright)
Take It Easy 1950,D 25,23:6
Badet, Andre de (Playwright)
Vie Athenienne, La 1931,D 13,VIII,2:2
Badham, Frank
Harlem 1929,F 21,30:3
20th Century 1932,D 30,15:1
Badia, Leopold
Speakeasy 1927,S 27,30:1
Machinal 1928,S 8,10:3
School for Virtue 1931,Ap 22,29:2
American Holiday 1936,F 22,13:3
Siege 1937,D 9,31:4
Case of Youth, A 1940,Mr 25,10:3
Cyrano de Bergerac 1946,O 9,33:2
Cyrano de Bergerac 1947,Ja 17,27:2
Gentleman From Athens, The 1947,D 10,42:4
Cyrano de Bergerac 1953,N 13,24:3
Richard III 1953,D 10,65:2
Sixth Finger in a Five Finger Glove 1956,O 9,31:4
Worm in Horseradish, A 1961,Mr 14,32:3
Badii, Enjio
Night in Venice, A 1929,My 22,30:2
Badin, Max
Golden Ring, The 1930,F 1,14:7
Motke From Slobodke 1930,Ap 12,23:3
Hello Grandpa! 1931,Ja 2,25:3
Jolly World, A 1931,Ja 24,15:3
Kibitzer, The 1931,N 7,17:3
Mother's Son 1931,N 26,36:4
Under One Roof 1932,F 8,21:2
Two Hearts 1935,My 6,22:2
Badoch, Hadassah
Hut a Yid a Landele 1968,O 19,28:1
Badolati, Luigi
Sansone; Samson 1931,F 9,25:1
Sirena 1931,S 22,33:4
Cardinale, Il 1933,Ja 9,24:2
Istruttoria, L'; Judicial Inquiry, The 1933,F 13,11:3
Badolati, Mario
Ingeborg 1933,D 11,23:3
Conte di Monte Cristo, Il 1934,Ja 22,13:2
Padrone Delle Ferriere, Il 1934,Mr 19,13:5
Colonello Bridall, L' 1934,Ap 16,20:3
Romanticismo 1934,My 14,20:2
Miserabili I, 1934,S 24,15:1
Miserabili I, 1934,O 1,14:2
Signora Dalle Camelie, La; Camille 1934,O 22,13:2
Sparviero, Lo 1934,N 12,16:1
Processo dei Veleni, Il; Case of Poisons, The
1935,Ja 21,18:2
Vita Nuova; Life Begins Again 1935,F 26,16:2
Conte di Monte Cristo, Il 1935,Ap 1,17:6
Signo Della Croce, Il 1935,O 7,11:1
Adventurer, The 1935,N 11,21:1
Cardinale Giovanni de Medici, Il 1935,D 9,24:8
Three Guardsmen, The 1936,F 17,21:3
Bell for Adano, A 1944,D 7,21:2
Badolati, Mario (Director)
Vita Nuova; Life Begins Again 1935,F 26,16:2
Baechner, Louis (Playwright)
Daughters of the Late Colonel, The 1951,O 15,21:2
Baedecker, Harold
Seventeen 1926,My 1,10:1
Seven Keys to Baldpate 1930,Ja 8,25:2
Round Table, The 1930,F 28,20:5
Bael, Fred
Processional 1937,O 14,23:1
Baer, Abel
Vaudeville (Palace) 1926,Je 29,21:3
Baer, Abel (Composer)
Old Bill, M P 1926,N 11,22:2
Lady Do 1927,Ap 19,24:2
Baer, Arthur (Bugs)
Vaudeville (Hippodrome) 1926,F 23,26:2
No Foolin' 1926,Je 25,25:1
Baer, Arthur (Bugs) (Playwright)
Her Family Tree 1920,D 28,9:2
George White's Scandals 1921,Jl 12,14:1
Earl Carroll's Vanities 1925,Jl 7,24:1
New Americana 1928,N 30,32:4
Baer, Atra (Playwright)
Brandy Is My True Love's Name 1953,Je 18,38:5
Baer, Catherine
Beaux' Stratagem, The 1957,Jl 9,25:4

Man Who Never Died, The 1958,N 22,27:2
Baer, Cynthia (Director)
O Say Can You See! 1962,O 9,45:1
Baer, Cynthia (Producer)
Little Mary Sunshine 1959,N 19,49:3
Madame Aphrodite 1961,D 30,13:1
Crime and Crime 1963,D 17,51:2
Baer, Eddie
Black Rhythm 1936,D 21,19:2
Baer, Max
Hi-Ya Gentlemen 1940,D 4,34:2
Baer, Richard A
Volpone 1937,N 16,26:4
Fol-De-Rol 1937,D 11,22:4
Life and Death of Sir John Falstaff, The
1938,Mr 15,19:5
Danton's Death 1938,N 3,26:2
Baer, Richard A (Director)
Importance of Being Earnest, The 1936,O 22,31:2
Baer, Richard A (Playwright)
Life and Death of Sir John Falstaff, The
1938,Mr 15,19:5
Baer, William
County Chairman, The 1936,My 26,26:5
Baerwitz, Samuel (Producer)
Harry Delmar's Revels 1927,N 29,30:2
Baesing, Paul
Balls 1965,F 11,45:1
Baff, Reggie
Brownstone Urge, The 1969,D 18,63:1
Baffa, Emil (Musical Director)
Hollywood Ice Revue 1956,Ja 13,17:1
Baffrey, Stephen (Producer)
Critic, The 1965,Jl 26,15:2
Bafield, St Clair
We Moderns 1924,Mr 12,17:2
Bagby, George (Composer)
Fioretta 1929,F 6,30:3
Bagby, George (Lyricist)
Fioretta 1929,F 6,30:3
Bagdasarian, Ross
Time of Your Life, The 1939,O 26,26:2
Time of Your Life, The 1940,S 24,27:2
Bagdasarian, Ross (Director)
Son, The 1950,Ap 1,12:4
Bagely, Eleanore
Of V We Sing 1942,F 16,20:3
Baggett, Bruce
Carousel 1957,S 12,38:2
Baggetta, Vincent
Tragical Historie of Doctor Faustus, The
1964,O 6,34:2
Philosophy in the Boudoir 1969,My 22,55:2
Madwoman of Chaillot, The 1970,Mr 23,48:3
Bagley, Ben (Director)
Ben Bagley's New Cole Porter Revue
1965,D 23,20:1
Bagley, Ben (Miscellaneous)
Shoestring Revue 1955,Mr 1,22:2
Littlest Revue, The 1956,My 23,37:2
Shoestring '57 1956,N 6,31:1
Bagley, Ben (Playwright)
Littlest Revue, The 1956,My 23,37:2
Ben Bagley's New Cole Porter Revue
1965,D 23,20:1
Ben Bagley's Shoestring Revues 1970,O 24,22:1
Bagley, Ben (Producer)
Shoestring Revue 1955,Mr 1,22:2
Shoestring '57 1956,N 6,31:1
Decline and Fall of the Entire World As Seen
Through the Eyes of Cole Porter Revisited, The
1965,Mr 31,24:2
Bagley, Dolores
Pale Horse, Pale Rider 1957,O 30,26:1
Bagley, Eleanor
Make Mine Manhattan 1948,Ja 16,26:2
Baglin, Marjorie
Idiot's Delight 1936,Mr 25,25:2
Bagnell, Daniel
Scarlet Sister Mary 1930,N 26,19:2
Bagnell, William (Scenic Designer)
Round Table, The 1930,F 28,20:5
Bagnold, Enid (Playwright)
Lottie Dundass 1941,Ag 22,19:5
Lottie Dundass 1943,Ag 22,II,1:8
Gertie 1952,Ja 31,23:1
Chalk Garden, The 1955,O 27,29:1
Chalk Garden, The 1955,N 13,II,1:1
Chalk Garden, The 1956,Ap 12,26:8
Chalk Garden, The 1956,My 13,II,3:1
Chinese Prime Minister, The 1964,Ja 3,14:1
Chinese Prime Minister, The 1964,Ja 12,II,1:1
Chinese Prime Minister, The 1965,My 21,21:1
Bahn, Roma
Threepenny Opera, The 1928,D 2,X,4:4
Don Juan's Raincoat 1933,O 22,IX,2:3
Bahr, Hermann (Playwright)
Kinder 1924,Mr 2,VIII,2:1
Mongrel, The 1924,D 16,28:2
Josephine 1934,S 26,17:5
Josephine 1934,O 14,X,3:1
Konzert, Das 1968,Mr 25,52:1

Baierl, Helmut (Playwright)
Frau Flinz 1962,Jl 8,II,1:1
Baiko
Chushingura; Treasury of Loyal Retainers, The
1969,S 11,53:1
Kagami-Jishi; Mirror Lion Dance, The
1969,S 11,53:1
Momiji-Gari 1969,S 18,64:1
Bailey, Bill
Swingin' the Dream 1939,N 30,24:2
Bailey, Bob (Scenic Designer)
Servant of Two Masters, The 1958,F 11,35:2
Bailey, Buster
Regina 1949,N 1,32:2
Bailey, Cathie
Where Do We Go From Here? 1938,N 16,26:2
Time of Your Life, The 1939,O 26,26:2
Bailey, Charles (Lighting Director)
Ghosts 1961,S 22,29:1
Bailey, Charles (Scenic Designer)
Ghosts 1961,S 22,29:1
Rosmersholm 1962,Ap 12,42:1
Bailey, E Tomlin
His Majesty the Queen 1926,Mr 9,8:1
Bailey, Eve
Dead End 1936,S 20,IX,3:7
Bailey, Howard
Venetian, The 1931,N 2,26:1
Romeo and Juliet 1933,F 3,21:5
Bailey, James
Goodbye Again 1937,S 1,15:1
Bailey, James (Costume Designer)
As You Like It 1950,Ja 27,27:2
As You Like It 1950,F 19,II,1:1
Bailey, James (Scenic Designer)
As You Like It 1950,Ja 27,27:2
As You Like It 1950,F 19,II,1:1
Millionairess, The 1952,Je 28,12:2
Millionairess, The 1952,O 18,17:2
Way of the World, The 1953,Ap 10,17:1
Bailey, Jean
Jane Clegg 1920,F 25,14:1
Bailey, Jeff (Miscellaneous)
Lovely Me 1946,D 26,30:4
Bailey, Jim
Fly Blackbird 1962,F 6,26:2
Bailey, John Hammond
Stag at Bay, The 1935,Jl 30,17:1
Bailey, Leo
Goin' Home 1928,Ag 24,23:2
Make Me Know It 1929,N 5,32:5
Swing It 1937,Jl 23,17:2
Bailey, LeRoy
Dark Hours, The 1932,N 15,24:2
Bailey, LeRoy (Playwright)
Curtain Call 1937,Ap 23,24:7
Thanks for Tomorrow 1938,S 28,28:2
Bailey, Loretto Carroll
Job's Kinfolks 1929,N 24,31:1
Bailey, Loretto Carroll (Playwright)
Job's Kinfolks 1929,N 24,31:1
Bailey, Lynn
Starcross Story, The 1954,Ja 14,25:2
Bailey, Maureen
Girls Against the Boys, The 1959,N 3,26:1
Bailey, Maurice (Miscellaneous)
Best Foot Forward 1941,S 12,24:4
Bailey, Mildred
Variety Anthology 1932,Mr 21,19:4
Bailey, Oliver D (Director)
Crashing Through 1928,O 30,26:5
Great Barrington, The 1931,F 20,18:1
Bailey, Oliver D (Producer)
Crashing Through 1928,O 30,26:5
Great Barrington, The 1931,F 20,18:1
Bailey, Pearl
St Louis Woman 1946,Ap 1,22:2
Arms and the Girl 1950,F 3,28:2
Bless You All 1950,D 15,42:2
House of Flowers 1954,D 31,11:2
Hello, Dolly! 1967,N 13,61:1
Hello, Dolly! 1967,N 26,II,3:1
Bailey, Raymond
Last Stop 1944,S 6,17:2
Bat, The 1953,Ja 21,28:2
Sing Till Tomorrow 1953,D 29,17:2
Bailey, Robin
Cocktail Party, The 1950,My 7,II,2:5
My Fair Lady 1959,Ja 27,26:1
Jennie 1963,O 18,35:2
Severed Head, A 1964,O 29,40:1
Bailey, Russell
Curious Savage, The 1956,Mr 17,12:3
Crucible, The 1958,Mr 12,36:1
Legend of Lovers 1959,O 28,40:3
Donogoo 1961,Ja 19,25:3
Smiling the Boy Fell Dead 1961,Ap 20,28:1
Bailey, Ruth (Miscellaneous)
Butterflies Are Free 1969,O 22,30:1
Bailey, Stella
Red, Hot and Blue! 1936,O 30,26:3
Bailey, Stuart
Living Mask, The 1924,Ja 22,15:1

Bailey, T G
Cymbeline 1923,O 3,12:1
Twelfth Night 1923,O 23,17:1
Hamlet 1923,O 31,12:1
Merchant of Venice, The 1923,N 6,22:2
Bailey, William N
Up in the Clouds 1922,Ja 3,20:3
Bailey and Barnum
Greenwich Village Follies 1926,Mr 16,22:2
Bailin, Harriet (Composer)
Carricknabauna 1967,Mr 31,30:1
Bailio, David
Dance of Death, The 1967,O 20,50:1
Baillie, Luciele
Confederacy, The 1958,Jl 3,20:1
Baillie, Rai
Founders, The 1957,My 14,39:1
Confederacy, The 1958,Jl 3,20:1
Baily, William
Polly Preferred 1923,Ja 12,13:3
Bain, Charis
American Gothic 1953,N 11,35:6
Bain, Conrad
Jack and the Beanstalk 1947,N 3,28:2
Iceman Cometh, The 1956,My 8,38:1
Sixth Finger in a Five Finger Glove 1956,O 9,31:4
Makropoulos Secret, The 1957,D 4,52:4
Dark of the Moon 1958,F 27,22:2
Henry IV, Part I 1958,Je 25,23:3
Much Ado About Nothing 1958,Je 26,22:1
Winter's Tale, The 1958,Jl 23,34:3
Family Reunion, The 1958,O 21,39:1
Overruled 1959,My 27,32:2
Buoyant Billions 1959,My 27,32:2
Getting Married 1959,Je 5,18:2
Country Scandal, A 1960,My 6,21:8
Deuces Wild; It's All Yours 1962,Ap 25,31:1
Charlatans; Summer Ghost, A 1962,Ap 27,26:1
Hot Spot 1963,Ap 20,17:2
Firebugs, The 1963,N 22,41:1
King Lear 1963,N 23,22:1
Queen and the Rebels, The 1965,F 26,16:1
Square in the Eye 1965,My 20,54:1
Hogan's Goat 1965,N 12,56:1
Kitchen, The 1966,Je 14,50:1
Willie Doesn't Live Here Anymore 1967,F 8,20:2
Scuba Duba 1967,O 11,36:1
Cuban Thing, The 1968,S 25,36:2
Scuba Duba 1969,Ap 7,51:1
Nobody Hears A Broken Drum 1970,Mr 20,55:1
Steambath 1970,Jl 1,49:1
Steambath 1970,Jl 12,II,1:3
Bain, David
Burgomaster of Stilemonde, The 1923,N 16,15:3
Hamlet 1923,N 20,23:3
Bain, Donald
Our Town 1944,Ja 11,24:5
Importance of Being Earnest, The 1947,Mr 4,30:2
Love for Love 1947,My 27,30:2
Cocktail Party, The 1950,Ja 23,17:2
Out West of Eighth 1951,S 21,20:3
Bain, Donald (Miscellaneous)
They Walk Alone 1941,Mr 13,24:2
Bain, Emmett
King's Standards, The 1958,F 14,19:1
Bain, Paul
Great Campaign, The 1947,Ap 1,33:2
Bain, William
Americans in France, The 1920,Ag 4,14:1
Mirage, The 1920,O 1,14:1
Bainbridge, Barbara
Lady From the Sea, The 1935,D 14,11:3
Bainbridge, Constance (Playwright)
This Island Is Mine 1959,Jl 1,26:4
Bainbridge, Rolinda
Half-Naked Truth, The 1926,Je 8,23:1
Baine, Raymond
Panama Hattie 1940,O 31,28:2
Baines, Robert
Shakespeare's Merchant 1939 1939,Ja 10,16:3
Mister Roberts 1948,F 19,27:2
Detective Story 1954,F 13,11:2
Hamlet 1954,Ap 24,15:2
Twelfth Night 1954,N 10,42:2
Merchant of Venice, The 1955,F 23,23:2
Taming of the Shrew, The 1956,Ag 11,11:2
Girl of the Golden West, The 1957,N 6,44:1
Natural Affection 1963,F 2,5:2
Dark of the Moon 1970,Ap 4,21:2
Bainter, Fay
Pygmalion and Galatea 1920,Ap 28,9:3
Lady Cristilinda, The 1922,D 26,11:2
Other Rose, The 1923,D 16,IX,2:4
Other Rose, The 1923,D 21,15:2
Other Rose, The 1923,D 30,VII,1:1
Dream Girl, The 1924,Ag 21,12:2
Enemy, The 1925,O 21,20:1
Two Orphans, The 1926,Ap 6,26:2
Two Orphans, The 1926,Ap 11,VIII,1:1
Sour Grapes 1926,Jl 4,VII,3:2
First Love 1926,S 19,IX,1:3
First Love 1926,N 9,31:2
Vaudeville (Palace) 1927,Ap 26,33:1

Fallen Angels 1927,D 2,20:4
She Stoops to Conquer 1928,My 15,17:1
She Stoops to Conquer 1928,My 20,VIII,1:1
Beaux' Stratagem, The 1928,Je 5,20:1
Beaux' Stratagem, The 1928,Je 10,VIII,1:1
Jealousy 1928,O 23,32:2
Lysistrata 1930,Ap 29,30:5
Admirable Crichton, The 1931,Mr 10,23:2
Admirable Crichton, The 1931,Mr 29,VIII,1:1
Way of the World, The 1931,Je 2,34:3
Man Who Changed His Name, The 1932,My 3,25:3
Perfect Marriage, The 1932,N 17,23:2
For Services Rendered 1933,Ap 13,15:5
Uncle Tom's Cabin 1933,My 30,13:4
Move on, Sister 1933,O 25,22:4
Dodsworth 1934,F 26,20:4
Dodsworth 1934,Ag 21,12:3
Lambent Flame, The 1935,Jl 16,24:2
Next Half Hour, The 1945,O 30,14:6
Next Half Hour, The 1945,N 4,II,1:1
Gayden 1949,My 11,34:4
Bair, Sara
Patience 1931,Je 16,30:4
Merry Widow, The 1932,F 21,VIII,23:3
Baird, Anthony (Playwright)
Greater Love 1931,Mr 3,39:1
Baird, Audrey
Shore Leave 1922,Ag 9,20:2
Mr Moneypenny 1928,O 17,26:2
Baird, Beatrice
Tidings Brought to Mary, The 1922,D 25,20:1
Baird, Bil
Ziegfeld Follies 1943,Ap 2,16:2
Flahooley 1951,My 15,39:1
Davy Jones's Locker 1959,Mr 30,25:1
Davy Jones's Locker 1966,D 25,48:5
People Is the Thing That the World Is Fullest Of 1967,F 21,53:1
Wizard of Oz, The 1968,N 28,69:2
Whistling Wizard and the Sultan of Tuffet 1970,F 1,70:1
Baird, Bil (Composer)
Whistling Wizard and the Sultan of Tuffet 1970,F 1,70:1
Baird, Bil (Director)
Winnie the Pooh 1967,N 25,33:1
Winnie the Pooh 1967,D 23,28:1
Wizard of Oz, The 1968,N 28,69:2
Baird, Bil (Miscellaneous)
Davy Jones's Locker 1959,Mr 30,25:1
Davy Jones's Locker 1966,D 25,48:5
Winnie the Pooh 1968,Ap 15,41:1
Ali Baba and the Forty Thieves 1970,D 29,40:1
Baird, Bil (Original Author)
Davy Jones's Locker 1959,Mr 30,25:1
Davy Jones's Locker 1959,D 28,18:1
Baird, Bil (Playwright)
Bil and Cora Baird's Marionette Theater 1955,D 27,29:2
Bil and Cora Baird's Marionette Theater; Ali Baba and the Forty Thieves 1956,S 3,10:1
Bil and Cora Baird's Marionette Theater 1963,Ap 12,34:2
Davy Jones's Locker 1966,D 25,48:5
People Is the Thing That the World Is Fullest Of 1967,F 21,53:1
Wizard of Oz, The 1968,N 28,69:2
Baird, Bil Marionettes
Flahooley 1951,My 20,II,1:1
Vaudeville (Palace) 1953,O 15,42:1
Baker Street 1965,F 28,II,1:1
Winnie the Pooh 1967,N 25,33:1
Winnie the Pooh 1967,D 23,28:1
Baird, Bobbi
Annie Get Your Gun 1966,Je 1,42:2
Skits-Oh-Frantics 1967,Ap 3,39:2
South Pacific 1967,Je 13,56:1
Baird, Claribel
You Can't Take It With You 1965,N 24,32:1
Baird, Cora
Ziegfeld Follies 1943,Ap 2,16:2
Flahooley 1951,My 15,39:1
Davy Jones's Locker 1959,Mr 30,25:1
Davy Jones's Locker 1966,D 25,48:5
People Is the Thing That the World Is Fullest Of 1967,F 21,53:1
Baird, Ethel
Symphony in Two Flats 1930,S 17,30:4
Baird, Frances
Top Secret 1960,S 6,40:1
Baird, George
Davy Jones's Locker 1959,Mr 30,25:1
Baird, Henry
Variations of 1940 1940,Ja 29,12:1
Baird, Irene
Recruiting Officer, The 1958,F 8,12:2
Baird, John (Director)
Letters to Lucerne 1941,D 24,14:2
Baird, John (Miscellaneous)
Wayside 1957,Ap 18,34:1
Baird, Joseph
Zander the Great 1923,Ap 10,24:2
Fall Guy, The 1925,Mr 11,19:1

Baird, Joseph—Cont
If I Was Rich 1926,S 3,15:2
Virgin Man, The 1927,Ja 19,20:4
Mister Romeo 1927,S 6,35:3
Stairs, The 1927,N 8,32:7
Married-And How! 1928,Je 15,30:2
Possession 1928,O 3,35:1
Street Scene 1929,Ja 11,20:4
House Beautiful, The 1931,Mr 13,20:4
Baird, Raymond
Vaudeville (Palace) 1926,Ap 20,24:6
Baird, Robert
Out of This World 1950,D 22,17:3
Baird, Stewart
Cinderella on Broadway 1920,Je 25,18:1
Rose Girl, The 1921,F 12,11:1
Hotel Mouse, The 1922,Mr 14,11:3
Sancho Panza 1923,N 27,23:1
Loves of Lulu, The 1925,My 12,26:1
Mozart 1926,N 23,26:2
Baird, Stewart (Director)
Cape Cod Follies 1929,S 19,37:2
Baird, Stewart (Lyricist)
Cape Cod Follies 1929,S 19,37:2
Baird, Stewart (Playwright)
Cape Cod Follies 1929,S 19,37:2
Baird, Tom
Merry-Go-Round 1927,Je 1,25:4
Bairnsfather, Bruce
Vaudeville (Palace) 1927,Ja 25,18:3
Becky Sharp 1929,Je 4,29:1
Bairnsfather, Bruce (Playwright)
Old Bill, M P 1922,Ag 13,VI,1:8
Old Bill, M P 1926,N 11,22:2
Baisch, Jon (Director)
Will the Mail Train Run Tonight? 1964,Ja 10,18:1
Baisch, Jon (Producer)
Will the Mail Train Run Tonight? 1964,Ja 10,18:1
Baisho, Chieko
Scarlett 1970,Ja 3,19:1
Bajcar, Vera
Cradle of Willow, A 1961,D 16,20:2
Bajcar, Vera (Miscellaneous)
Christmas in the Market Place 1960,D 10,26:1
Bajor, Gizi
Chalk Circle, The 1928,Ja 15,VIII,2:1
Siberia 1928,Ap 15,IX,4:1
A Tabornok 1928,D 2,X,4:7
Bak, Samuel (Costume Designer)
200,000 1966,F 15,33:5
Bak, Samuel (Scenic Designer)
200,000 1966,F 15,33:5
Bakalyar, Beatrice
Country Scandal, A 1960,My 6,21:8
Country Scandal, A 1960,My 15,II,1:1
Bakanic, Bob
Seventeen 1951,Je 22,16:6
Bakarich, Nick
Honor Code, The 1931,My 19,25:3
Baker, Alice Ann
Cradle Snatchers 1932,N 17,23:2
Ragged Army 1934,F 27,16:5
Bitter Oleander 1935,F 12,24:3
Tide Rising 1937,Ja 26,17:2
Stop-Over 1938,Ja 12,16:5
Baker, Allen (Choreographer)
Hamlet of Stepney Green 1958,N 14,21:1
Baker, Anthony
Penal Law 2010 1930,Ap 19,14:2
Baker, Belle
Betsy 1926,D 29,24:3
Vaudeville (Palace) 1928,F 14,26:2
Vaudeville (Palace) 1928,N 19,16:3
Baker, Benny
You Said It 1931,Ja 20,21:3
Du Barry Was a Lady 1939,D 7,34:2
Let's Face It 1941,O 10,27:1
Let's Face It 1941,O 30,26:2
Jackpot 1944,Ja 14,15:2
Tempest, The 1945,N 13,24:6
Front Page, The 1946,S 5,22:4
My L A 1951,D 9,87:1
Baker, Betty
Rosalinda; Fledermaus, Die 1942,O 29,26:5
Baker, Buddy (Musical Director)
Disney on Parade 1970,S 24,63:1
Baker, Carroll
Escapade 1953,N 19,40:1
All Summer Long 1954,S 24,26:2
All Summer Long 1954,O 3,II,1:1
Come on Strong 1962,O 5,29:1
Baker, Charles
Shoemaker's Holiday, The 1938,Ja 3,17:2
Caukey 1944,F 18,15:4
Baker, Charles (Costume Designer)
Liliom 1956,F 18,12:5
Baker, Charles A
Great Necker, The 1928,Mr 7,28:2
Baker, Dan
Tip-Top 1920,O 6,13:2
Baker, David
Only in America 1959,N 20,35:1

Baker, David (Choreographer)
Do Re Mi 1960,D 27,23:2
Baker, David (Composer)
Phoenix '55 1955,Ap 25,20:2
Shoestring '57 1956,N 6,31:1
Copper and Brass 1957,O 18,19:2
Smiling the Boy Fell Dead 1961,Ap 20,28:1
Come Summer 1969,Mr 19,43:1
Baker, David (Miscellaneous)
Of Thee I Sing 1952,My 6,34:2
Flora, the Red Menace 1965,My 12,41:2
Yearling, The 1965,D 11,25:1
Cabaret 1966,N 21,62:1
Come Summer 1969,Mr 19,43:1
Baker, David Jr
Caution: A Love Story 1969,Ap 4,45:1
Baker, Doc
Vaudeville (Palace) 1928,My 29,17:4
Baker, Donald
Forty-Four Below 1935,Jl 23,24:3
Where There's a Will 1939,Ja 18,16:6
Baker, Dorothy (Original Author)
Trio 1944,D 30,13:4
Baker, Dorothy (Playwright)
Trio 1944,D 30,13:4
Baker, Earl
Trumpets of the Lord 1963,D 23,22:3
Trumpets of the Lord 1969,Ap 30,37:1
Baker, Edythe
Blushing Bride, The 1922,F 7,12:1
Dancing Girl, The 1923,Ja 25,16:2
Innocent Eyes 1924,My 21,22:2
Big Boy 1925,Ja 8,28:2
Big Boy 1925,Ag 25,12:2
Hello, Lola! 1926,Ja 13,30:1
Vaudeville (Palace) 1926,Mr 16,22:2
Baker, Elias B
This Mad Whirl 1937,Ja 10,II,4:8
Fifty-Fifty 1937,D 5,II,3:4
Baker, Elizabeth
Revolt of the Beavers, The 1937,My 21,19:2
Baker, Elliott (Playwright)
Penny Wars, The 1969,O 16,52:1
Penny Wars, The 1969,O 26,II,1:1
Baker, Ellis
Brook 1923,Ag 20,14:3
Arabian, The 1927,N 1,20:5
These Few Ashes 1928,O 31,28:1
Lady Windermere's Fan 1932,Ja 27,19:3
Constant Wife, The 1935,Jl 3,20:2
I Like It Here 1946,Mr 23,8:6
Baker, Fay
Danton's Death 1938,N 3,26:2
Audition of the Apprentice Theatre 1939,Je 2,26:2
Taming of the Shrew, The 1940,F 6,17:2
Journey to Jerusalem 1940,O 7,21:2
War and Peace 1942,My 22,26:3
Sun Field, The 1942,D 10,33:2
Another Love Story 1943,O 13,29:2
Violet 1944,O 25,16:1
Wonderful Journey 1946,D 26,30:2
Baker, Frank
Samarkand 1926,D 22,24:4
Napoleon Passes 1927,D 21,29:2
Baker, Fred
Bernardine 1952,O 17,33:4
Little Glass Clock, The 1956,Mr 27,40:2
Hotel Paradiso 1957,Ap 12,22:2
Baker, Gaylynn
Gay Divorce 1960,Ap 4,37:1
Baker, George
Restless Heart 1957,My 9,37:4
Look After Lulu 1959,Mr 4,35:1
Baker, George F Jr
Lid's Off, The 1936,Ap 4,11:6
Baker, George Pierce (Professor) (Director)
King's Coat, The 1933,Ja 12,21:4
Baker, Hazel
Priorities of 1942 1942,Mr 13,23:2
Baker, Henry
Kismet 1965,Je 23,45:1
Cities in Bezique; Owl Answers, The
1969,Ja 13,26:1
No Place to Be Somebody 1969,My 5,53:3
Sambo 1969,D 22,42:1
No Place to Be Somebody 1969,D 31,17:1
Baker, Herbert (Lyricist)
Helen Goes to Troy 1944,Ap 25,17:2
Jerry Lewis' Variety Show 1957,F 8,18:5
Baker, Howard (Costume Designer)
Babes in the Wood 1964,D 29,21:2
Baker, Howard (Playwright)
Trio 1944,D 30,13:4
Baker, Iris
House of Borgia, The 1935,S 10,26:1
House of Borgia, The 1935,O 6,XI,3:1
Baker, Jack
Let Freedom Sing 1942,O 6,18:2
What's Up 1943,N 12,24:6
Baker, James
Delightful Season, A 1960,S 29,30:1
Baker, Jennifer
Stop the World-I Want to Get Off 1962,O 4,45:4

Stop the World-I Want to Get Off 1962,O 14,II,1:1
Baker, Joe
John Brown's Body 1953,F 16,17:2
Baker, Joe Don
Blues for Mister Charlie 1964,Ap 24,24:1
Baker, John A 3d (Lighting Director)
Lend an Ear 1969,O 29,32:1
Baker, John A 3d (Scenic Designer)
Lend an Ear 1969,O 29,32:1
Baker, John P
Richelieu 1934,My 22,28:1
Richard III 1934,D 28,24:3
Baker, John William
Hamlet 1920,Mr 17,14:2
Baker, Josephine
Chocolate Dandies, The 1924,S 2,22:2
Untitled-Revue 1933,O 22,IX,2:2
Ziegfeld Follies 1935,D 31,10:1
Ziegfeld Follies 1936,Ja 5,IX,3:1
Ziegfeld Follies 1936,Ja 31,17:2
Josephine Baker and Her Company 1964,F 5,30:1
Baker, Josephine Turck (Playwright)
Apache, The 1923,My 9,14:3
Baker, Karin
George M! 1968,Ap 11,48:1
Baker, Keith
Love's Labour's Lost 1965,Je 16,46:1
Baker, Kenny
One Touch of Venus 1943,O 8,14:1
One Touch of Venus 1943,O 17,II,1:1
Baker, Lawrence Jr (Miscellaneous)
Young and Beautiful, The 1955,O 3,23:2
Baker, Lawrence Jr (Producer)
Best Foot Forward 1963,Ap 3,43:1
Baker, Lee
Daddy's Gone A-Hunting 1921,S 1,18:3
Love Child, The 1922,N 15,22:1
Garden of Weeds 1924,Ap 29,12:3
Ariadne 1925,F 24,17:1
Odd Man Out 1925,My 26,24:3
Glass Slipper, The 1925,O 20,29:1
Glass Slipper, The 1925,O 25,VIII,1:1
Merchants of Glory 1925,D 15,28:3
Merchants of Glory 1925,D 27,VII,1:1
Virgin, The 1926,F 23,26:1
Squall, The 1926,N 12,20:1
Command Performance, The 1928,O 4,27:1
Scarlet Pages 1929,S 10,26:3
Mourning Becomes Electra; Homecoming
1931,O 27,22:1
American Dream; 1650 1933,F 22,24:5
Undesirable Lady, An 1933,O 10,24:4
Ragged Army 1934,F 27,16:5
Judgment Day 1934,S 13,26:4
Paths of Glory 1935,S 19,29:1
Paths of Glory 1935,S 27,24:2
Hell Freezes Over 1935,D 30,14:2
Winterset 1936,Je 2,35:2
Ten Million Ghosts 1936,O 24,23:7
High Tor 1937,Ja 11,15:2
Richard II 1937,S 16,28:2
Glorious Morning 1938,N 28,10:3
Little Foxes, The 1939,F 16,16:2
Distant City, The 1941,S 23,27:5
Baker, Lenny
Conerico Was Here to Stay 1969,Mr 11,39:1
Paradise Gardens East 1969,Mr 11,39:1
Year Boston Won the Pennant, The
1969,My 23,38:1
Time of Your Life, The 1969,N 7,37:1
Time of Your Life, The 1969,N 16,II,1:4
Summertree 1969,D 10,60:1
Early Morning 1970,N 26,57:1
Baker, Lisa
Hamlet 1948,D 4,9:2
Wedding in Japan 1949,N 11,29:1
Peer Gynt 1951,Ja 29,15:2
Baker, Marilyn Cantor (Producer)
Lyle 1970,Mr 21,16:2
Baker, Melville (Playwright)
I Was Waiting for You 1933,N 14,23:3
Baker, Melville (Translator)
Swan, The 1923,O 24,15:3
Swan, The 1923,O 28,VIII,1:1
Carnaval 1924,D 30,15:1
Tale of the Wolf, The 1925,O 8,31:2
Tale of the Wolf, The 1925,O 18,IX,1:2
Baker, Mike
Hamlet 1970,D 28,40:1
Baker, Mildred
Park Avenue, Ltd 1932,Mr 4,17:1
Broadway Boy 1932,My 4,23:5
We the People 1933,Ja 23,9:5
Constant Wife, The 1935,Jl 3,20:2
Baker, Nancy
Jacob Slovak 1927,O 6,28:4
Carefree Tree, The 1955,O 12,37:2
Tall Story 1959,Ja 30,33:2
Baker, Nathan
Around the World 1946,Je 1,9:5
Baker, Nicky
Talent '54 1954,Ap 13,40:1

Baker, Paul (Director)
Hamlet 1956,My 8,28:5
Days Between, The 1965,Je 4,39:1
Latent Heterosexual, The 1968,Mr 22,52:1
Macbeth 1968,N 30,49:3
Baker, Paul (Miscellaneous)
Days Between, The 1965,Je 27,II,1:1
Baker, Phil
Music Box Revue 1923,S 24,5:3
Artists and Models 1925,Je 25,16:2
Night in Spain, A 1927,My 4,28:2
Night in Spain, A 1927,My 22,VIII,1:1
Night in Spain, A 1927,Jl 3,VII,1:1
Vaudeville (Palace) 1928,D 17,23:3
Vaudeville (Palace) 1928,D 24,10:8
Pleasure Bound 1929,F 10,IX,2:1
Pleasure Bound 1929,F 19,22:4
Vaudeville (Palace) 1930,F 10,20:3
Vaudeville (Palace) 1930,F 17,18:4
Artists and Models 1930,Je 11,33:2
Vaudeville (Palace) 1930,Ag 18,24:3
Vaudeville (Palace) 1931,Ja 26,21:5
Vaudeville (Palace) 1931,F 2,23:3
Vaudeville (Palace) 1931,Ap 6,24:3
Vaudeville (Palace) 1931,Ap 13,17:2
Vaudeville (Palace) 1931,Ap 20,16:2
Crazy Quilt 1931,My 20,28:4
Vaudeville (New Amsterdam Theatre)
1931,Je 22,17:3
Vaudeville (Palace) 1932,My 16,19:2
Calling All Stars 1934,N 22,26:1
Calling All Stars 1934,D 14,28:2
All in Fun 1940,N 22,26:2
Charley's Aunt 1941,Jl 31,12:4
Priorities of 1942 1942,Mr 13,23:2
Priorities of 1942 1942,Mr 29,VIII,1:1
Baker, Phil (Composer)
Song Writer, The 1928,Ag 14,15:2
Baker, Phil (Lyricist)
Song Writer, The 1928,Ag 14,15:2
Baker, Phil (Producer)
Cafe de Danse 1928,D 30,VIII,1:6
Cafe de Danse 1929,Ja 16,22:2
Geraniums in My Window 1934,O 27,20:6
Baker, Phyllis
You'll See Stars 1943,Ja 1,26:6
Baker, Robert (Producer)
Solitaire 1929,Mr 13,28:3
Baker, Russell
Jonah! 1967,S 22,52:2
Mike Downstairs 1968,Ap 19,35:1
Baker, Ruth
Persecution and Assassination of Marat As
Performed by the Inmates of the Asylum of
Charenton Under the Direction of the Marquis de
Sade, The 1965,D 28,35:1
Baker, Sam
Rip Van Wrinkle 1967,D 23,28:1
Baker, Stanley
Sleep of Prisoners, A 1951,O 17,36:2
Baker, Susan
Stop the World-I Want to Get Off 1962,O 4,45:4
Stop the World-I Want to Get Off 1962,O 14,II,1:1
Baker, Suzie
Nellie Bly 1946,Ja 22,32:2
Baker, Sybil
Idiot's Delight 1951,My 24,46:3
Scarecrow, The 1953,Je 17,31:1
Baker, Terri
South Pacific 1965,Je 3,25:1
Make Me Disappear 1969,My 14,34:1
Baker, Tom
Idiot, The 1970,Jl 30,39:1
Baker, Tommie
Journeyman 1938,Ja 31,14:2
Baker, Virginia
Tempest, The 1955,Ag 2,18:2
Baker, William
On Your Toes 1936,Ap 13,14:4
Baker, Word (Director)
Crucible, The 1958,Mr 12,36:1
Crucible, The 1958,Je 1,II,1:1
Fantasticks, The 1960,My 4,55:2
As You Like It 1961,Je 17,13:2
As You Like It 1961,Je 25,II,1:1
Fantasticks, The 1961,S 8,36:5
Tragical Historie of Doctor Faustus, The
1964,O 6,34:2
Room, The 1964,D 10,62:1
Slight Ache, A 1964,D 10,62:1
Now Is the Time for all Good Men 1967,S 27,42:1
Last Sweet Days of Isaac, The 1970,Ja 27,49:1
Last Sweet Days of Isaac, The 1970,F 8,II,1:6
Baker, Word (Producer)
Crucible, The 1958,Mr 12,36:1
Bakey, Ed
Walking Happy 1966,N 28,47:1
Bakis, Stanislaus
Scapegoat, The 1950,Ap 20,36:5
Baklanoff, George
Tales of Hoffmann 1932,Ja 10,VIII,1:6
Bakos, John
Tom Paine 1968,Mr 26,38:1

Bakos, John—Cont
Futz 1968,Je 14,39:1
Baksheieff, Peter
Tsar Fyodor Ivanovitch 1923,Ja 9,26:1
Lower Depths, The 1923,Ja 16,16:1
Death of Pazukhin, The 1924,F 12,20:1
Moscow Art Theatre 1924,My 13,25:2
Bakst, Andre (Scenic Designer)
Siegfried 1939,F 21,15:2
Bal, Jeanne
Call Me Madam 1950,O 13,25:1
Gay Life, The 1961,N 20,38:1
Balaban, Bob
You're a Good Man, Charlie Brown 1967,Mr 8,51:1
Plaza Suite; Visitor From Mamaroneck
  1968,F 15,49:1
Plaza Suite; Visitor From Forest Hills
  1968,F 15,49:1
Up Eden 1968,N 27,42:1
White House Murder Case, The 1970,F 19,59:1
Balaban, Emanuel (Composer)
Medium, The 1948,D 8,41:6
Telephone, The 1948,D 8,41:6
Balaban, Emanuel (Musical Director)
Medium, The 1947,My 2,28:2
Telephone, The 1947,My 2,28:2
Balachova, Tania (Director)
Huis Clos 1962,Ja 16,30:1
Balamos, John (Composer)
Mandragola 1958,My 29,23:2
Garden of Sweets, The 1961,N 1,35:1
Balanchine, George (Choreographer)
Ziegfeld Follies 1936,Ja 31,17:2
On Your Toes 1936,Ap 13,14:4
Babes in Arms 1937,Ap 15,18:4
I Married an Angel 1938,My 12,26:2
I Married an Angel 1938,My 22,XI,1:1
Boys From Syracuse, The 1938,N 13,IX,2:2
Boys From Syracuse, The 1938,N 24,36:1
Keep Off the Grass 1940,My 5,X,1:6
Keep Off the Grass 1940,My 24,22:6
Louisiana Purchase 1940,My 29,19:2
Cabin in the Sky 1940,N 10,IX,2:1
Lady Comes Across, The 1942,Ja 10,10:2
Rosalinda; Fledermaus, Die 1942,O 29,26:5
Merry Widow, The 1943,Ag 5,19:2
What's Up 1943,N 12,24:6
What's Up 1943,N 21,II,1:1
Dream With Music 1944,My 19,15:2
Song of Norway 1944,Ag 22,20:2
Song of Norway 1944,Ag 27,II,1:1
Merry Widow, The 1944,O 9,17:1
Chocolate Soldier, The 1947,Mr 13,34:2
Where's Charley? 1948,O 12,33:2
Romeo and Juliet 1951,Mr 12,21:2
Courtin' Time 1951,Je 14,30:2
On Your Toes 1954,O 12,24:4
Tempest, The 1955,Ag 2,18:2
Merry Widow, The 1957,Ap 11,36:6
Midsummer Night's Dream, A 1958,Je 23,19:1
Winter's Tale, The 1958,Jl 21,17:4
Romeo and Juliet 1959,Je 15,31:1
Merry Wives of Windsor, The 1959,Jl 9,23:2
Balanchine, George (Director)
Cabin in the Sky 1940,O 26,19:2
Cabin in the Sky 1940,N 10,IX,2:1
What's Up 1943,N 12,24:6
What's Up 1943,N 21,II,1:1
Balanchine, George (Miscellaneous)
Song of Norway 1944,Ag 22,20:2
Balash, Jerry (Lighting Director)
Juno and the Paycock 1955,F 24,20:4
2 for Fun; Switch in Time, A 1955,My 26,34:1
2 for Fun; Anniversary, The 1955,My 26,34:1
Balash, Jerry (Miscellaneous)
2 for Fun; Anniversary, The 1955,My 26,34:1
2 for Fun; Switch in Time, A 1955,My 26,34:1
Balasi Trio
Vaudeville (Palace) 1926,Je 8,23:1
Balaska, Mimika
Hippolytus 1968,N 20,38:3
Balavsky, M
Soul of a Woman, The 1930,F 22,13:1
Balazzi, M Charles
Bulls, Bears and Asses 1932,My 7,11:3
Balch, David Arnold (Director)
Jackson White 1935,Ap 22,14:6
Balch, David Arnold (Playwright)
Scarlet Lily, The 1927,Ja 31,12:3
Jackson White 1935,Ap 22,14:6
Balch, Jack (Director)
Arms and the Man 1956,O 2,39:4
Mrs Patterson 1957,F 6,20:2
Balch, Jack (Playwright)
Me, The Sleeper 1949,My 16,18:6
Balch, Jack (Producer)
Mrs Patterson 1957,F 6,20:2
Balchin, Nigel (Original Author)
Waiting For Gillian 1954,Ap 22,36:2
Balckton, Marion
Skylark 1921,Jl 26,10:6
Balcom, Harry
Penny Arcade 1930,Mr 11,24:5

Balcom, William (Composer)
Cyrano de Bergerac 1968,Ap 26,30:1
Instructions for the Running of Trains, etc on the
  Erie Railway to Go Into Effect January 1,1862
  1970,Ja 7,36:2
Baldauff, Patrick
Natural Look, The 1967,Mr 13,45:2
Winter Journey 1968,Mr 13,39:1
Dream of a Blacklisted Actor 1969,D 18,64:1
Criss-Crossing 1970,Ja 22,30:1
Baldauff, Patrick (Producer)
Bohikee Creek 1966,Ap 29,39:1
Balderston, John (Playwright)
Berkeley Square 1926,O 7,19:6
Berkeley Square 1926,O 24,VIII,2:1
Dracula 1927,O 6,29:1
Berkeley, Square 1929,Mr 24,X,4:5
Berkeley Square 1929,N 5,32:4
Berkeley Square 1929,D 1,X,1:1
Dracula 1931,Ap 14,33:3
Red Planet 1932,D 19,19:2
Berkeley Square 1935,Ag 20,25:1
Farewell Performance 1936,S 11,28:3
Farewell Performance 1936,O 4,IX,1:1
Baldi, Diana
Padrone Delle Ferriere, Il 1934,Mr 19,13:5
Signora Dalle Camelie, La; Camille 1934,O 22,13:2
Processo dei Veleni, Il; Case of Poisons, The
  1935,Ja 21,18:2
Romanzo di un Giovane Povero, Il 1935,F 25,12:3
Religione e Patria 1936,Mr 23,22:4
Due Orfanele, Le; Two Orphans, The
  1936,O 5,24:4
Tombola, La; Lottery, The 1936,N 9,23:4
Sansone; Samson 1936,N 30,25:2
Asino di Buridano, L' 1936,N 30,25:2
Feudalismo Oppure La Terra Bassa; Feudalism or
  the Lowland 1937,Mr 8,22:2
Sposa e la Cavalla, La 1937,Mr 22,26:5
Fantasmi 1937,Mr 22,26:5
Medico Delle Pazze, Il; Physician of Mad Woman,
  The 1937,S 27,24:2
Signora Dalle Camelie, La; Dame aux Camelias, La
  1937,O 9,16:3
Baldi, Hugo
O'Flynn, The 1934,D 28,24:1
Balding, Ivor David (Director)
Antigone 1959,S 16,46:2
Square in the Eye 1965,My 20,54:1
Young Marrieds Play Monopoly 1966,Mr 7,22:1
Princess Rebecca Birnbaum 1966,Mr 7,22:1
Make Like a Dog 1966,Mr 7,22:1
Suburban Tragedy 1966,Mr 7,22:1
Serjeant Musgrave's Dance 1966,Mr 9,44:1
Hand Is on the Gate, A 1966,S 22,54:1
Balding, Ivor David (Miscellaneous)
All the King's Men 1959,O 17,27:2
Balding, Ivor David (Producer)
Ginger Man, The 1963,N 22,42:1
Mad Show, The 1966,Ja 10,16:1
Serjeant Musgrave's Dance 1966,Mr 9,44:1
Kitchen, The 1966,Je 14,50:1
Hand Is on the Gate, A 1966,S 22,54:1
Scuba Duba 1967,O 11,36:1
Steambath 1970,Jl 1,49:1
Steambath 1970,Jl 12,II,1:3
Baldinger, Beatrice
Lord Byron's Love Letter 1955,Ja 19,23:2
Baldon, Robert
Firebird 1932,N 22,25:2
Baldridge, Harold (Lighting Director)
Blood Knot, The 1964,Mr 3,30:2
Slave, The 1964,D 17,51:1
Toilet, The 1964,D 17,51:1
Baldridge, Harold (Miscellaneous)
Slave, The 1964,D 17,51:1
Toilet, The 1964,D 17,51:1
Baldridge, Richard (Composer)
Macbeth 1959,Ag 1,9:2
Baldridge, Richard (Director)
Beggar's Opera, The 1957,Mr 14,35:1
Baldridge, Richard (Miscellaneous)
Love's Labour's Lost 1953,F 5,20:3
Merchant of Venice, The 1953,Mr 5,20:2
Baldridge, Richard (Playwright)
Beggar's Opera, The 1957,Mr 14,35:1
We Comrades Three 1962,O 12,26:1
We Comrades Three 1966,D 21,46:1
Baldwin, Carol
Crime 1927,F 23,27:3
Baldwin, Charles
Varying Shore, The 1921,D 6,24:1
Baldwin, David
Father Malachy's Miracle 1937,N 18,26:4
Blues for Mister Charlie 1964,Ap 24,24:1
Baldwin, Douglas
Front Page, The 1968,O 20,85:5
Baldwin, Duncan
Girl From Wyoming, The 1938,O 31,12:1
Sunday Breakfast 1952,My 30,12:2
Baldwin, Evan
Voice From the Minaret, The 1922,Ja 31,11:2

Baldwin, Faith (Original Author)
Broadway Interlude 1934,Ap 20,16:3
Baldwin, Franca
New Faces of 1956 1956,Je 15,32:1
Baldwin, Frank (Miscellaneous)
Waiting for Godot 1957,Ja 22,25:1
Baldwin, James (Playwright)
Blues for Mister Charlie 1964,Ap 24,24:1
Blues for Mister Charlie 1964,My 3,II,1:1
Amen Corner, The 1965,Ap 16,35:1
Amen Corner, The 1965,Ap 25,II,1:2
Blues for Mister Charlie 1965,My 5,52:1
Amen Corner, The 1965,My 13,82:4
Amen Corner, The 1965,Ag 9,19:5
Baldwin, Janet
Outside the Door 1949,Mr 2,33:2
Baldwin, Lyttleton M
Coriolanus 1927,Je 18,8:3
Baldwin, Raymond P
Clarence 1923,My 14,18:4
Baldwin, Robert
Oh, Please! 1926,D 22,24:3
Baldwin, Seth
Saint Joan 1923,D 29,8:4
Cherry Pie 1926,Ap 15,24:4
Baldwin, Walter
Changelings, The 1923,S 18,16:3
Nerves 1924,S 2,22:2
Good Fellow, The 1926,O 6,22:1
Front Page, The 1928,Ag 15,19:2
Grand Hotel 1930,N 14,30:4
Shooting Star 1933,Je 13,22:2
I Myself 1934,My 10,24:6
Jayhawker 1934,N 6,34:2
Battleship Gertie 1935,Ja 19,9:2
Mid-West 1936,Ja 8,22:4
Swing Your Lady 1936,O 19,22:4
Miss Quis 1937,Ap 8,20:5
Of Mice and Men 1937,N 24,20:5
Baldwin, Winnie
Mercenary Mary 1925,Ap 14,27:3
Vaudeville (Palace) 1926,Ap 13,28:3
Vaudeville (Hippodrome) 1926,Ap 27,22:3
Baldwin, Winnie (Playwright)
Divided Honors 1929,O 1,28:2
Bales, William (Choreographer)
Winter's Tale, The 1946,Ja 16,18:6
Balestro, Luigi
Sh! The Octopus 1928,F 22,19:2
Balf, Miriam (Playwright)
Sunday Breakfast 1952,My 30,12:2
Balfe, Michael W (Composer)
Bohemian Girl, The 1933,Jl 28,18:5
Balfe, Michael W (Original Author)
Gypsy Blonde 1934,Je 26,22:5
Balfior, Joe
Night Music 1951,Ap 9,29:6
Balfour, David
Winner, The 1954,F 18,34:1
Balfour, Eva
Love for Love 1925,Ap 1,21:2
Love for Love 1925,S 15,29:3
Half-Naked Truth, The 1926,Je 8,23:1
Balfour, Katharine
R U R 1942,D 4,30:2
Summer and Smoke 1947,Jl 9,18:5
Summer and Smoke 1947,Ag 10,II,1:1
Helen 1964,D 11,55:4
Balfour, Norah
Gooseberry Fool 1929,N 2,14:8
Nine Till Six 1930,S 29,17:2
Balfour, Val
Eleventh Hour, The 1956,Jl 10,26:7
Balfour, Val (Mrs)
Eleventh Hour, The 1956,Jl 10,26:7
Balfour, William
Survival of the Fittest 1921,Mr 15,14:1
Letty Pepper 1922,Ap 11,22:2
Anathema 1923,Ap 11,16:2
Road Together, The 1924,Ja 18,21:2
Complex, The 1925,Mr 4,17:2
Love Call, The 1927,O 25,33:1
Buckaroo 1929,Mr 18,31:1
Noble Rogue, A 1929,Ag 20,31:2
Charm 1929,N 29,24:5
Babes in Toyland 1929,D 24,15:3
Babes in Toyland 1930,D 22,17:1
American Tragedy, An 1931,F 21,15:5
Lost Boy 1932,Ja 6,24:4
Broadway Boy 1932,My 4,23:5
Whistling in the Dark 1932,N 4,25:2
Four O'Clock 1933,F 14,19:6
Murder at the Vanities 1933,S 13,22:4
Yesterday's Orchids 1934,O 6,20:4
O'Flynn, The 1934,D 28,24:1
Jackson White 1935,Ap 22,14:6
Ringside Seat 1938,N 23,24:5
Clean Beds 1939,My 26,21:2
Three Men on a Horse 1942,O 10,10:2
Balgi, Leon (Playwright)
Adam et Eve et Cie 1928,Je 17,VIII,1:4
Balieff, De Roze
Continental Varieties 1934,O 4,18:3

Balieff, Nikita
Chauve-Souris 1922,F 6,9:2
Chauve-Souris 1922,F 12,VI,1:1
Chauve-Souris 1925,Ja 15,25:1
Chauve-Souris 1927,O 23,VIII,1:1
Chauve-Souris 1929,Ja 23,20:2
1860: or, Aris; 1860, or an Interrupted Festival 1931,O 22,27:1
Continental Varieties 1934,O 4,18:3
Continental Varieties 1934,N 15,24:3
Balieff, Nikita (Miscellaneous)
Chauve-Souris 1922,Mr 26,VI,1:2
Balieff, Nikita (Mme) (Miscellaneous)
Chauve-Souris of 1943 1943,Ag 13,13:2
Balieff, Nikita (Playwright)
Chauve-Souris 1922,Je 6,17:4
Chauve-Souris 1922,O 11,22:2
Chauve-Souris 1929,Ja 23,20:2
Chauve-Souris; Romantic Adventure of an Italian Ballerina and a Marquis, A 1931,O 22,27:1
1860: or, Aris; 1860, or an Interrupted Festival 1931,O 22,27:1
Chauve-Souris; Queen of Spades, The 1931,O 22,27:1
Chauve-Souris of 1943 1943,Ag 13,13:2
Balieff, Nikita (Producer)
Chauve-Souris 1922,O 22,VIII,1:1
Chauve-Souris 1923,Ja 5,12:2
Chauve-Souris 1923,S 4,12:1
Chauve Souris 1924,O 2,26:4
Chauve-Souris 1924,O 12,VIII,1:6
Chauve-Souris 1924,D 14,VIII,6:1
Chauve-Souris 1925,Ja 25,VII,1:1
Untitled-Revue 1926,O 31,VIII,2:4
Chauve-Souris 1928,N 25,X,4:7
Balin, Edmund (Choreographer)
Babes in Arms 1951,Mr 10,7:3
Kaleidoscope 1957,Je 14,20:2
Balin, Edmund (Director)
By Hex 1956,Je 19,25:1
Balin, Ina
Compulsion 1957,O 25,21:1
Compulsion 1957,N 3,II,1:1
Majority of One, A 1959,F 17,28:2
Balin, Richard (Director)
Frere Jacques 1968,Je 8,23:2
Balistreri, Michael (Miscellaneous)
Yearling, The 1965,D 11,25:1
Balk, H Wesley (Director)
House of Leather, The 1970,Mr 19,56:1
Ball, Arthur
George White's Scandals 1925,Je 23,24:2
Ball, Constance
Mystery of the Finding of the Cross, The 1959,Ja 16,35:2
Cranmer of Canterbury 1959,D 4,36:1
Ball, Ernest R
Vaudeville (Palace) 1923,Ja 16,16:3
Vaudeville (Palace) 1926,Mr 30,20:4
Vaudeville (Palace) 1926,D 28,12:3
Ball, Jack
O Evening Star 1936,Ja 9,24:6
Never Say Horses 1951,D 7,34:4
Ball, Jane
Higher and Higher 1940,Ap 5,24:3
Let's Face It 1941,O 30,26:2
Ball, Jessica (Playwright)
Strange Gods 1933,Ap 17,16:6
Ball, John (Original Author)
In the Heat of the Night 1969,F 6,12:3
Ball, John (Playwright)
Never Say Horses 1951,D 7,34:4
Ball, Lucille
Wildcat 1960,D 17,20:2
Ball, Marion
Few Wild Oats, A 1932,Mr 25,22:6
Ball, Olive
Run, Little Chillun! 1933,Mr 2,21:3
Porgy and Bess 1935,O 11,30:2
Run, Little Chillun 1943,Ag 14,6:1
Ball, Patsy
Merry Malones, The 1927,S 27,30:2
Ball, Robert
Frankie and Johnny 1952,O 29,37:2
Ball, William
Misanthrope, The 1956,N 13,44:1
Hamlet 1957,Ja 29,27:1
Lady's Not for Burning, The 1957,F 22,26:2
Country Wife, The 1957,Je 27,22:1
Ball, William (Director)
Ivanov 1958,O 8,42:1
Month in the Country, A 1959,Mr 2,32:2
Tempest, The 1960,Je 20,35:1
Tempest, The 1960,Je 26,II,1:1
Under Milk Wood 1961,Mr 30,25:1
Under Milk Wood 1961,Ap 9,II,1:1
Porgy and Bess 1961,My 18,40:1
Six Characters in Search of an Author 1963,Mr 11,7:2
Homage to Shakespeare 1964,Mr 16,36:2
Yeomen of the Guard, The 1964,Ag 3,16:1
Tartuffe 1965,Ja 15,23:1
Hamlet 1968,Je 9,II,1:1

Hamlet 1968,Je 10,59:1
Three Sisters, The 1969,Ag 31,II,4:1
Tiny Alice 1969,S 30,42:1
Flea in Her Ear, A 1969,O 4,25:1
Three Sisters, The 1969,O 10,38:1
Tiny Alice 1969,O 12,II,9:1
Three Sisters, The 1969,O 19,II,3:1
Balla, Licci
Vienna at Night 1945,Ap 30,12:4
Ballance, Beatrice
Ordinary Man, An 1968,S 10,39:1
Ballantine, E J
Richard III 1920,Mr 8,7:1
Macbeth 1921,F 18,16:1
Macbeth 1921,F 27,VI,1:1
Gold 1921,Je 2,14:2
Claw, The 1921,O 18,20:1
Hamlet 1922,N 17,14:1
Scaramouche 1923,O 25,14:2
This Fine-Pretty World 1923,D 27,11:1
Ancient Mariner, The 1924,Ap 7,15:5
Crime in the Whistler Room, The 1924,O 10,22:2
S S Glencairn 1924,N 4,31:4
Love for Love 1925,Ap 1,21:2
Jest, The 1926,F 5,22:2
Final Balance, The 1928,O 31,28:3
S S Glencairn 1929,Ja 10,24:5
Sea Gull, The 1929,Ap 10,32:2
At the Bottom 1930,Ja 10,24:3
Sea Gull, The 1930,F 26,22:2
Passing Present, The 1931,D 8,36:2
Rendezvous 1932,O 13,22:3
Alien Corn 1933,F 21,17:2
Alien Corn 1933,F 26,IX,1:1
Paths of Glory 1935,S 27,24:2
Beautiful People, The 1941,Ap 22,27:2
Mr Big 1941,O 1,24:2
Moon Is Down, The 1942,Ap 8,22:2
King Lear 1950,D 26,18:1
Ballantine, E J (Director)
S S Glencairn 1929,Ja 10,24:5
Ballantine, Ian
Michel Auclair 1925,Mr 5,23:1
Ballantine, Lucille
Vaudeville (Palace) 1926,Ag 3,19:2
Ballantyne, Clare
Midsummer Night's Dream, A 1968,D 9,59:1
Ballantyne, Paul
Mrs O'Brien Entertains 1939,F 9,16:3
Brown Danube, The 1939,My 18,30:4
Man in Possession, The 1939,S 26,21:4
Unconquered, The 1940,F 14,25:2
Goodbye in the Night 1940,Mr 19,31:2
Susannah and the Elders 1940,O 13,47:7
Susannah and the Elders 1940,O 30,28:2
Saint Joan 1951,O 5,23:2
Love's Labour's Lost 1953,F 5,20:3
Love's Labour's Lost 1953,F 8,II,1:1
Strong Are Lonely, The 1953,S 30,38:3
Richard III 1953,D 10,65:2
27 Wagons Full of Cotton 1955,Ja 19,23:2
All That Fall 1957,O 8,41:2
Richard III 1957,N 26,41:1
Enchanted, The 1958,Ap 23,41:1
Hamlet 1963,My 9,41:1
Miser, The 1963,My 10,39:1
Death of a Salesman 1963,Jl 20,11:2
Henry V 1964,My 13,52:1
Saint Joan 1964,My 14,41:1
Way of the World, The 1965,Je 2,40:1
Richard III 1965,Je 3,26:1
Cherry Orchard, The 1965,Ag 2,17:2
Dance of Death, The 1966,Je 3,31:1
As You Like It 1966,Je 4,19:1
Thieves' Carnival 1967,Je 5,52:1
Harpers Ferry 1967,Je 6,52:2
Tango 1968,Ja 1,11:1
She Stoops to Conquer 1968,Ja 1,11:1
Twelfth Night 1968,Je 15,40:1
Serjeant Musgrave's Dance 1968,Je 16,52:4
Resistible Rise of Arturo Ui, The 1968,Ag 8,25:1
House of Atreus, The 1968,D 18,55:1
Resistible Rise of Arturo Ui, The 1968,D 23,44:1
Murderous Angels 1970,F 8,70:1
Ballantyne, William
Rivals, The 1969,O 18,37:1
Ballard, Beverly
Match-Play 1966,O 12,37:1
How to Steal an Election 1968,O 14,56:1
Ballard, Bob
Hats Off to Ice 1944,Je 23,15:2
Ballard, Dave
Jumbo 1935,N 18,20:2
Dream With Music 1944,My 19,15:2
Ballard, Francis Drake (Lyricist)
Joan of Arkansas 1925,Ap 5,16:1
Ballard, Fred (Playwright)
Rainy Day, The 1923,O 14,VIII,2:4
Out-A-Luck 1924,O 5,VIII,1:3
Henry's Harem 1926,S 14,25:2
Cyclone Lover, The 1928,Je 6,23:3
Ladies of the Jury 1929,O 6,IX,1:4
Ladies of the Jury 1929,O 22,26:2

Ballard, Fred (Playwright)—Cont
Sandy Hooker, The 1929,N 10,X,4:8
Ballard, Kaye
Talent '49 1949,Ap 13,39:4
Touch and Go 1950,My 20,9:2
Golden Apple, The 1954,Mr 12,15:2
Golden Apple, The 1954,Mr 21,II,1:1
Carnival! 1961,Ap 14,22:2
Wonderful Town 1963,F 15,10:2
Beast in Me, The 1963,My 17,29:1
Decline and Fall of the Entire World As Seen Through the Eyes of Cole Porter Revisited, The 1965,Mr 31,24:2
Ballard, Lucinda (Costume Designer)
As You Like It 1937,N 1,25:2
Great Lady 1938,D 2,26:6
Three Sisters, The 1939,O 16,23:1
Higher and Higher 1940,Ap 5,24:3
American Jubilee 1940,My 13,20:5
Stars on Ice 1942,Jl 3,12:2
Canteen Show, The 1942,S 4,18:1
Moon Vine, The 1943,F 12,22:2
Stars on Ice (2d Edition) 1943,Je 25,13:2
My Dear Public 1943,S 10,28:1
Listen Professor! 1943,D 23,22:1
Sing Out, Sweet Land! 1944,Ja 7,II,1:1
I Remember Mama 1944,O 20,16:2
Swing Out, Sweet Land! 1944,N 10,24:6
Sing Out, Sweet Land! 1944,D 28,24:2
Place of Our Own, A 1945,Ap 3,23:7
Memphis Bound 1945,My 25,23:2
Show Boat 1946,Ja 7,17:2
Show Boat 1946,Ja 13,II,1:1
Annie Get Your Gun 1946,My 17,14:2
Annie Get Your Gun 1946,My 26,II,1:1
Happy Birthday 1946,N 1,31:2
Another Part of the Forest 1946,N 21,42:2
Street Scene 1947,Ja 10,17:2
John Loves Mary 1947,F 5,29:2
Chocolate Soldier, The 1947,Mr 13,34:2
Allegro 1947,O 11,10:2
Streetcar Named Desire, A 1947,D 4,42:2
Show Boat 1948,S 9,33:2
Love Life 1948,O 8,31:2
Make Way for Lucia 1948,D 23,23:5
Rat Race, The 1949,D 23,16:2
Wisteria Trees, The 1950,Mr 30,39:1
Streetcar Named Desire, A 1950,My 24,36:1
Flahooley 1951,My 15,39:1
Fourposter, The 1951,O 25,34:2
Fourposter, The 1951,N 25,II,1:1
Mrs McThing 1952,F 21,22:1
Mrs McThing 1952,Mr 2,II,1:1
My 3 Angels 1953,Mr 12,23:2
Carnival in Flanders 1953,S 9,38:2
Fourposter, The 1955,Ja 6,23:3
Wisteria Trees, The 1955,F 3,20:2
Silk Stockings 1955,F 25,17:3
Cat on a Hot Tin Roof 1955,Mr 25,18:2
Clearing in the Woods, A 1957,Ja 11,20:2
Clearing in the Woods, A 1957,Ja 20,II,1:1
Orpheus Descending 1957,Mr 22,28:1
Dark at the Top of the Stairs, The 1957,D 6,38:1
Handful of Fire 1958,O 2,45:3
Girls in 509, The 1958,O 16,47:1
J B 1958,D 12,2:7
Sound of Music, The 1959,N 17,40:2
Loss of Roses, A 1959,N 30,27:1
Loss of Roses, A 1959,D 6,II,5:1
Invitation to a March 1960,O 31,27:2
Gay Life, The 1961,N 20,38:1
Romulus 1962,Ja 11,27:1
Lord Pengo 1962,N 20,41:2
Tiger Tiger Burning Bright 1962,D 24,5:2
Ballard, Lucinda (Scenic Designer)
Moon Vine, The 1943,F 12,22:2
Make Way for Lucia 1948,D 23,23:5
Ballard, Ronald
Street Sounds 1970,O 23,32:1
Ballard, Roy
Vie Parisienne, La 1945,Ja 13,14:5
Ballard, Shirley
Fair Game 1957,N 4,39:1
Ballards, The
Icetime 1946,Je 21,20:5
Aquashow 1954,Je 23,20:4
Ballas, Dianna
Miss Julie 1965,N 11,59:1
Stronger, The 1965,N 11,59:1
Ballas, John
Taming of the Shrew, The 1935,O 1,27:3
Ballauf, Charlotte
Holiday on Ice 1965,S 2,38:4
Holiday on Ice 1966,S 1,30:1
Ballen, Tony
Come Play With Me 1959,My 1,33:5
Ballenger, Bertha
Fanshastics 1924,Ja 17,13:2
Ballentine, Lucille
Broadway Whirl, The 1921,Je 9,10:4
Ballentine, Margaret
Fireman's Flame, The 1937,O 11,26:2
Ballester, Manuel Mendez (Playwright)
Crossroads 1969,Ag 7,28:1

Ballet Russe
  Song of Norway 1944,Ag 27,II,1:1
Ballew, Smith and His Orchestra
  Scrap Book 1932,Ag 2,20:3
Balley, Barbara
  Desert Song, The 1946,Ja 9,20:2
Ballif, Ariel (Costume Designer)
  Revenger's Tragedy, The 1970,D 2,58:1
Ballif, Ariel (Scenic Designer)
  Pin to See the Peepshow, A 1953,S 18,17:2
  All the King's Men 1963,Jl 12,12:1
Balliot, Lloyd
  Paradise Alley 1924,Ap 2,17:3
Ballou, David (Costume Designer)
  Machinal 1960,Ap 8,27:1
  Shoemaker and the Peddler, The 1960,O 15,27:4
Ballou, David (Lighting Director)
  Wake Up, Darling 1956,My 3,34:2
  Penny Change 1963,O 25,37:1
  Candyapple, The 1970,N 24,33:1
Ballou, David (Scenic Designer)
  Wake Up, Darling 1956,My 3,34:2
  Legend of Lizzie, The 1959,F 10,39:1
  Machinal 1960,Ap 8,27:1
  Machinal 1960,Ap 17,II,1:1
  Shoemaker and the Peddler, The 1960,O 15,27:4
  Madame Aphrodite 1961,D 30,13:1
  Cherry Orchard, The 1962,N 15,46:2
  Doll's House, A 1963,F 4,5:6
  Penny Change 1963,O 25,37:1
  Rose Tattoo, The 1966,O 21,36:2
  Candyapple, The 1970,N 24,33:1
Ballou, Joyce
  First Gentleman, The 1957,Ap 26,22:2
  Asmodee 1958,Mr 26,42:2
  Legend of Lizzie, The 1959,F 10,39:1
Ballou, Marion
  Home Fires 1923,Ag 21,12:1
  Beggar on Horseback 1924,F 13,17:2
  Man or Devil 1925,My 22,22:4
  Wisdom Tooth, The 1926,F 16,22:2
  Sandalwood 1926,S 23,23:1
  My Maryland 1927,S 13,37:2
  Through the Years 1932,Ja 29,13:3
Balmain, Pierre (Miscellaneous)
  Rape of the Belt, The 1960,N 7,46:1
Balmer, Clinton C
  Hamlet 1927,Ap 7,23:3
Balmer, John
  Dooley Cashes In 1935,Ag 17,18:6
  Taming of the Shrew, The 1935,O 1,27:3
  Glorious Morning 1938,N 28,10:3
  Shakespeare's Merchant 1939 1939,Ja 10,16:3
Balmer, Ray
  Holiday on Ice 1965,S 2,38:4
  Holiday on Ice 1966,S 1,30:1
  Holiday on Ice 1969,Ag 28,44:1
Balogh, Erno (Miscellaneous)
  $25 an Hour 1933,My 11,14:4
Balpetre
  Amour Magicien, L' 1926,D 26,VII,2:1
Balsam, Bernice L
  Blue Jeans 1933,Ap 9,31:5
Balsam, Clarice
  Patience 1929,D 16,34:5
Balsam, Lydia
  Tobias and the Angel 1937,Ap 29,16:5
Balsam, Martin
  Ghost for Sale 1941,S 30,27:4
  Fun With Music 1946,N 25,38:5
  Wanhope Building, The 1947,F 11,36:5
  Lamp at Midnight 1947,D 22,29:2
  Sundown Beach 1948,S 8,37:1
  Liar, The 1950,My 19,30:2
  Rose Tattoo, The 1951,F 5,19:2
  Camino Real 1953,Mr 20,26:1
  Middle of the Night 1956,F 9,39:1
  Middle of the Night 1956,F 19,II,1:1
  Nowhere to Go But Up 1962,O 9,46:6
  Nowhere to Go But Up 1962,N 12,36:2
  You Know I Can't Hear You When the Water's
    Running; Footsteps of Doves, The
    1967,Mr 14,54:1
  You Know I Can't Hear You When the Water's
    Running; Shock of Recognition, The
    1967,Mr 14,54:1
  You Know I Can't Hear You When the Water's
    Running; I'll Be Home for Christmas
    1967,Mr 14,54:1
  You Know I Can't Hear You When the Water's
    Running 1967,Mr 26,II,1:1
Balser, Evelyn
  Nathan the Wise 1962,Mr 7,29:1
  Before Sundown 1962,Mr 14,43:1
Balser, Ewald
  Gang zum Weiher, Der 1931,Ap 5,VIII,1:6
  Thomas Paine 1938,S 20,27:1
  Maria Stuart 1968,Mr 27,38:1
Baltus, Gerd
  Ides of March, The 1962,N 17,16:4
Balzac, Honore de (Playwright)
  Honor of the Family, The 1926,D 27,21:1
  Faiseur, Le 1936,Ja 12,IX,3:7

Faiseur, Le; Promoter, The 1938,D 27,12:3
Balzac, John
  Garden of Sweets, The 1961,N 1,35:1
Balzer, Elizabeth
  Musik um Susi 1933,Ja 1,IX,1:1
Balzer, George (Playwright)
  Are You With It? 1945,N 12,17:3
Bamberger, David (Lighting Director)
  Pirates of Penzance, The 1966,My 24,54:1
  Trial by Jury 1966,Je 8,41:2
  H M S Pinafore 1966,Je 8,41:2
Bamberger, David (Miscellaneous)
  That Hat! 1964,S 24,45:1
  Pirates of Penzance, The 1966,My 24,54:1
  H M S Pinafore 1966,Je 8,41:2
  Trial by Jury 1966,Je 8,41:2
  Experiment, The 1967,My 9,54:2
Bamberger, Muriel
  Bad Habits of 1925 1925,F 9,17:1
Bamberger, Theron (Producer)
  Man Bites Dog 1933,Ap 26,11:2
  Fly Away Home 1935,Ja 16,20:4
  Tomorrow the World 1943,Ap 15,22:2
  Wonderful Journey 1946,D 26,30:2
Bamboschek, Giuseppe (Musical Director)
  Nina Rosa 1930,My 31,19:3
  Student Prince, The 1936,Jl 12,II,5:2
  Rose Marie 1936,Jl 22,22:6
  Blossom Time 1936,Jl 29,23:1
  Countess Maritza 1936,Ag 19,18:2
  Bitter Sweet 1936,Ag 26,17:3
  Naughty Marietta 1936,S 2,19:5
  Roberta 1937,Je 27,II,6:1
  Maytime 1937,Jl 6,23:4
  Wonderful Night, A; Fledermaus, Die
    1937,Jl 14,17:1
  Gay Divorce 1937,Jl 20,19:4
  On Your Toes 1937,Ag 3,21:2
  Anything Goes 1937,Ag 17,23:4
  Nina Rosa 1937,Ag 26,24:3
  Circus Princess, The 1937,Ag 31,26:6
  Show Boat 1938,Je 30,21:1
Bambro, Frankie
  Swing Mikado, The 1939,Mr 2,18:2
Bamman, Catharine A (Producer)
  Sunday Nights at 9 1935,N 11,21:1
  Sunday Nights at Nine 1936,D 7,27:3
Bamman, George (Director)
  Prunella 1929,Ap 10,23:3
Bamman, George (Playwright)
  Mystery Square 1929,Ap 5,28:3
Bamman, Gerry
  Alice in Wonderland 1970,O 9,43:1
Bamshaw, Philip
  Caste 1927,D 24,8:1
Banach, Helen (Pvt)
  Swing Sister Wac Swing 1944,Ja 4,20:4
Banbury, Frith (Director)
  Deep Blue Sea, The 1952,N 6,38:3
  Deep Blue Sea, The 1953,Ap 4,8:6
  Flowering Cherry 1959,O 22,46:1
  Right Honourable Gentleman, The 1965,O 20,50:2
Banbury, Frith (Producer)
  Do Not Pass Go 1965,Ap 20,44:1
Banci, Lewis
  Macbeth 1955,O 8,12:6
Bancroft, Anne
  Two for the Seesaw 1958,Ja 17,15:1
  Two for the Seesaw 1958,Ja 26,II,1:1
  Miracle Worker, The 1959,O 20,44:1
  Miracle Worker, The 1959,N 1,II,1:1
  Miracle Worker, The 1959,D 20,II,5:1
  Mother Courage and Her Children 1963,Mr 30,5:5
  Devils, The 1965,N 17,51:2
  Devils, The 1965,N 28,II,1:1
  Little Foxes, The 1967,O 27,53:1
  Little Foxes, The 1967,N 5,II,1:1
  Cry of Players, A 1968,N 15,40:1
  Cry of Players, A 1968,N 24,II,9:4
Bancroft, Dorothea
  Petticoat Fever 1935,Jl 2,24:4
Bancroft, Duncan
  Summer and Smoke 1952,Ap 25,19:5
Bancroft, George
  Cinders 1923,Ap 4,22:1
  Rise of Rosie O'Reilly, The 1923,D 26,13:4
Bancroft, George E
  On the Rocks 1933,N 26,II,2:8
Bancroft, Jane
  There's Wisdom in Women 1935,Jl 16,24:1
  There's Wisdom in Women 1935,O 31,17:1
  Laughing Woman, The 1936,Jl 8,14:7
  Golden Journey, The 1936,S 16,28:6
  Now You've Done It 1937,Mr 6,10:4
  Damaged Goods 1937,My 18,27:2
  She Gave Him All She Had 1939,D 2,20:7
  Johnny Belinda 1940,S 19,26:2
Bancroft, Maude
  Nativity Play, The 1937,D 21,29:1
Bancroft, Millicent
  Houseboat on the Styx, The 1928,D 26,14:3
  Ripples 1930,F 12,26:1

Bancroft, Peggy
  Merrily We Roll Along 1934,O 1,14:1
Bancroft, Penny
  Seventeen 1951,Je 22,16:6
Banczak, Margaret
  Only Jealousy of Emer, The 1970,Mr 25,36:4
Bandes, Herman
  Belt, The 1927,O 20,33:1
  Centuries, The 1927,N 30,23:1
  Subway, The 1929,Ja 26,15:1
Bandler, Alan
  Valley Forge 1934,D 11,28:3
  Victoria Regina 1935,D 27,15:2
Bando, Kitsusaburo
  Azuma Kabuki Dancers and Musicians
    1954,F 19,22:3
  Azuma Kabuki Dancers and Musicians
    1954,Mr 10,29:4
Bando, Mitsuemon
  Azuma Kabuki Dancers and Musicians
    1955,D 27,31:4
  Azuma Kabuki Dancers and Musicians
    1956,Ja 8,II,3:1
Bando, Tsurunosuke
  Azuma Kabuki Dancers and Musicians
    1955,D 27,31:4
  Azuma Kabuki Dancers and Musicians
    1956,Ja 8,II,3:1
Bandole, Leo (Translator)
  Chief Thing, The 1926,Mr 23,24:2
Bandura, George
  Rose in the Wilderness 1949,Ja 5,21:2
  Ninth Month Midnight 1949,F 17,28:2
  When the Bough Breaks 1950,Mr 9,25:5
Bane, Paula
  Seven Lively Arts 1944,D 8,26:6
  Call Me Mister 1946,Ap 19,26:2
  Call Me Mister 1946,Ap 28,II,1:1
Banes, Warner P
  It's Only Natural 1922,Ap 21,13:2
Banfield, Beryle
  Horse Play 1937,Ag 28,8:3
Banfield, Frederick W
  Upon My Soul 1927,Ap 22,19:1
Banfield, Helen
  Medea 1960,Jl 26,25:2
Banfield, Wallace
  Merchant of Venice, The 1930,D 3,29:2
  Melo 1931,Ap 17,26:6
Bang, Charles
  Hook'n Ladder 1952,Ap 30,31:2
Banghart, Kenneth (Producer)
  Date With April, A 1953,Ap 16,36:2
Bangs, John Kendrick (Original Author)
  Houseboat on the Styx, The 1928,D 16,IX,2:1
Bangs, John Kendrick (Playwright)
  Houseboat on the Styx, The 1928,D 26,14:3
Bangs, William (Playwright)
  Menonite 1936,Mr 20,29:6
Banham, Sam
  Man's House, A 1943,Ap 3,10:4
  Othello 1943,O 20,18:1
  Sweet Genevieve 1945,Mr 21,27:3
Banics, Margaret
  Look, Ma, I'm Dancin' 1948,F 8,II,2:1
Banister, Harry C
  Passing Show of 1921, The 1920,D 30,16:2
Bank, Xenia
  Rosalinda; Fledermaus, Die 1942,O 29,26:5
  Merry Widow, The 1944,O 9,17:1
  Land's End 1946,D 12,37:5
  Evening With Beatrice Lillie, An 1952,O 3,17:2
  Evening With Beatrice Lillie, An 1952,O 12,II,1:1
Banke, Herbert
  South Pacific 1955,My 5,39:5
  Oklahoma! 1958,Mr 20,32:3
Banke, Richard
  Kismet 1965,Je 23,45:1
Banker, Adrienne
  Lonesome West, The 1936,Je 30,15:1
Banker, Frederick
  Battleship Gertie 1935,Ja 19,9:2
Bankhart, Nona
  Mandragola 1958,My 29,23:2
Bankhead, Tallulah
  Foot-Loose 1920,My 11,12:1
  Nice People 1921,Mr 3,11:1
  Everyday 1921,N 17,15:1
  Exciters, The 1922,S 23,10:4
  Dancers, The 1923,F 25,VII,1:7
  Gold Diggers, The 1926,D 19,VII,6:4
  Gold Diggers, The 1926,D 26,VII,4:3
  Garden of Eden, The 1927,Je 26,VIII,1:3
  Her Cardboard Lover 1928,S 9,IX,2:7
  He's Mine 1929,N 17,IX,2:4
  Lady of the Camellias, The 1930,Mr 6,16:4
  Lady of the Camellias, The 1930,Mr 23,IX,2:3
  Let Us Be Gay 1930,S 14,VIII,2:1
  Forsaking All Others 1933,Mr 2,21:2
  Dark Victory 1934,N 10,18:2
  Rain 1935,F 13,24:1
  Rain 1935,F 17,VIII,1:1
  Something Gay 1935,Ap 30,12:2

Bankhead, Tallulah—Cont

Reflected Glory 1936,Jl 22,23:1
Reflected Glory 1936,S 18,19:5
Reflected Glory 1936,S 22,30:2
Antony and Cleopatra 1937,O 14,23:2
Antony and Cleopatra 1937,N 11,30:2
Circle, The 1938,Ap 19,24:2
I Am Different 1938,Ag 28,IX,2:5
Little Foxes, The 1939,F 16,16:2
Little Foxes, The 1939,F 26,IX,1:1
Clash by Night 1941,D 29,20:2
Clash by Night 1942,Ja 11,IX,1:1
Skin of Our Teeth, The 1942,N 19,29:5
Skin of Our Teeth, The 1942,N 22,VIII,1:1
Foolish Notion 1945,Mr 14,23:2
Foolish Notion 1945,Mr 18,II,1:1
Eagle Has Two Heads, The 1947,Mr 20,39:2
Private Lives 1948,O 5,30:2
Private Lives 1948,N 7,II,1:1
Dear Charles 1954,S 16,37:2
Dear Charles 1954,S 26,II,1:1
Streetcar Named Desire, A 1956,F 16,24:1
Eugenia 1957,Ja 31,20:1
Midgie Purvis 1961,F 2,25:3
Midgie Purvis 1961,F 12,II,1:1
Milk Train Doesn't Stop Here Anymore, The
1964,Ja 2,33:1

Bankhead, Tallulah (Producer)
Reflected Glory 1936,S 18,19:5

Bankoff, Ivan
Greenwich Village Follies 1920,Ag 31,7:3

Banks, Aaron
Talking to You 1961,O 23,22:5
Across the Board on Tomorrow Morning
1961,O 23,22:5

Banks, Birleanna
Sweet River 1936,O 29,30:2

Banks, Bobby (Composer)
High John De Conquer 1969,Ap 23,39:1

Banks, Bobby (Miscellaneous)
Cabin in the Sky 1964,Ja 22,32:1

Banks, Charles
His Wife's Lover 1929,O 21,30:6

Banks, David
Picture of Dorian Gray, The 1956,Ag 18,15:5

Banks, Diana
Kismet 1965,Je 23,45:1
Annie Get Your Gun 1966,Je 1,42:2

Banks, Estar
Irving Berlin's New Music Box Revue
1922,O 24,18:1

Banks, Hugh
Big Boy 1925,Ja 8,28:2
Park Avenue, Ltd 1932,Mr 4,17:1

Banks, Joan
Snark Was a Boojum, The 1943,S 2,14:4

Banks, John
Mikado, The 1955,S 30,20:2
Yeomen of the Guard, The 1955,O 4,39:2
Princess Ida 1955,O 14,22:3
Trial by Jury 1955,O 18,48:1
Ruddigore 1955,O 21,32:2

Banks, Leslie
Peter Pan 1924,N 7,16:2
Asleep 1927,Je 12,VII,2:1
March Hares 1928,Ja 1,VIII,1:3
Emma Hamilton 1929,O 13,IX,4:1
Infinite Shoeblack, The 1930,F 18,28:1
Man in Possession, The 1930,O 12,VIII,4:1
Man in Possession, The 1930,N 3,19:1
Lean Harvest 1931,My 8,20:2
Lean Harvest 1931,O 4,VIII,2:2
Lean Harvest 1931,O 14,26:3
Springtime for Henry 1931,D 10,29:2
Springtime for Henry 1932,Ja 10,VIII,1:1
Way to the Stars, The 1932,O 2,IX,2:5
This Inconstancy 1933,Ap 16,IX,1:3
Clive of India 1934,F 18,IX,3:7
Man of Yesterday 1935,F 20,22:5
Man of Yesterday 1935,Mr 17,VIII,1:4
Two Mrs Carrolls, The 1935,Je 13,26:1
Two Mrs Carrolls, The 1935,Ag 4,IX,1:3
Till the Cows Come Home 1936,O 28,30:6
Till the Cows Come Home 1936,N 15,XI,3:2
Taming of the Shrew, The 1937,Ap 11,XI,2:1
To Quito and Back 1937,S 21,29:1
To Quito and Back 1937,S 26,XI,3:6
To Quito and Back 1937,O 7,30:4
Wine of Choice 1937,D 14,32:3
Wine of Choice 1938,F 22,18:4
Wine of Choice 1938,F 27,X,1:1
Sun Never Sets, The 1938,Je 26,IX,2:1
Man in Half Moon Street, The 1939,Ap 9,X,1:8
Cottage to Let 1941,My 18,IX,1:5
Duke in Darkness, The 1942,O 18,VIII,1:4
Midsummer Night's Dream, A 1945,Mr 25,II,2:4
Life With Father 1947,Je 6,27:3
Lost in the Stars 1949,O 31,21:2
Lost in the Stars 1949,N 6,II,1:1
Second Mrs Tanqueray, The 1950,O 8,II,3:7

Banks, Leslie (Director)
Infinite Shoeblack, The 1930,F 18,28:1
Lady With a Lamp, The 1931,N 20,27:2
Too True to Be Good 1932,Mr 1,19:2

Too True to Be Good 1932,Mr 6,VIII,1:1
Too True to Be Good 1932,Ap 5,27:5
Too True to Be Good 1932,Ap 10,VIII,1:1

Banks, Leslie (Scenic Designer)
Infinite Shoeblack, The 1930,F 18,28:1

Banks, Monty Jr
Hidden Horizon 1946,S 20,42:2

Banks, Nathaniel (Playwright)
Season of Choice 1959,Ap 14,40:1
Curate's Play, The 1961,D 18,41:3
Tableaux 1961,D 18,41:3

Banks, Norton (Scenic Designer)
Recruiting Officer, The 1958,F 8,12:2

Banks, Richard (Composer)
Doctor Faustus Lights the Lights 1951,D 3,23:4

Banks, Sadie
Honor Code, The 1931,My 19,25:3

Banky, Vilma
Cherries Are Ripe 1930,O 19,IX,3:4

Bann, Billy
Parisiana 1928,F 10,26:3

Bannard, Heath
Simple Life, A 1964,My 18,36:1

Bannen, Ian
Hamlet 1961,Ap 12,46:1
As You Like It 1961,Jl 5,30:1
Othello 1961,O 11,53:6
Touch of the Poet, A 1962,S 30,85:8

Banner, John
From Vienna 1939,Je 21,26:2
Pastoral 1939,N 2,26:2
Big Two, The 1947,Ja 9,21:2

Banner, Lucille
Volpone 1930,Mr 11,24:5

Bannerman, Celia
Come as You Are 1970,Ag 12,32:1

Bannerman, Guy
Alchemist, The 1969,Je 12,51:1

Bannerman, Lois
Talking to You 1942,Ag 18,17:1
Across the Board on Tomorrow Morning
1942,Ag 18,17:1

Bannerman, Margaret
Hen Upon a Steeple 1927,Ap 24,VII,2:3
Three Waltzes 1937,N 15,15:6
By Jupiter 1942,Je 4,22:1
Rebecca 1945,Ja 19,17:2
Deep Mrs Sykes, The 1945,Mr 20,22:6
Our Betters 1946,N 10,II,3:1
Getting Married 1951,My 14,28:5
Starcross Story, The 1954,Ja 14,25:2
Thor, With Angels 1956,O 15,29:4

Bannerman, Penryn
Conversation Piece 1934,O 24,24:1

Banning, Jack
Story Teller, The 1951,D 15,11:3
World of Sholom Aleichem, The 1953,S 12,13:2
Inherit the Wind 1955,Ap 22,20:2

Bannister, Albert
Plot Thickens, The 1922,S 6,16:1
Mud Turtle, The 1925,Ag 21,8:2

Bannister, Albert (Director)
Square Crooks 1926,Mr 2,23:2
Man From Toronto, The 1926,Je 18,27:2
Great Scott! 1929,S 3,25:1
Stepping Sisters 1930,Ap 23,24:2
Private Affair, A 1936,My 15,28:7
It's an Ill Wind 1957,Ap 24,28:1

Bannister, Albert (Playwright)
It's an Ill Wind 1957,Ap 24,28:1

Bannister, Albert (Producer)
Stepping Sisters 1930,Ap 23,24:2
Before Morning 1933,F 10,13:4
Are You Decent? 1934,Ap 20,16:2
Private Affair, A 1936,My 15,28:7
Sea Legs 1937,My 19,26:5

Bannister, Barbara
Forty-Four Below 1935,Jl 23,24:3
Artists and Models 1943,N 6,16:6

Bannister, Douglas (Scenic Designer)
Shall We Join the Ladies? 1929,Mr 17,30:4

Bannister, Frank (Lyricist)
Hello Paris 1930,N 17,29:3

Bannister, Georgiana
Chauve-Souris of 1943 1943,Ag 13,13:2

Bannister, Harry
Busybody, The 1924,S 30,27:5
Valley of Content, The 1925,Ja 14,19:2
Yellow 1926,S 22,30:1
Revelry 1927,S 13,37:1
Strange Interlude 1928,D 18,37:3
Good, The 1938,O 6,27:2
I Must Love Someone 1939,F 8,18:7
Strip for Action 1942,O 1,26:2
Polonaise 1945,O 8,20:2
John Loves Mary 1947,F 5,29:2
Forward the Heart 1949,Ja 29,9:2
Love Me Long 1949,N 8,34:5
Affairs of State 1950,S 26,37:2
Bat, The 1953,Ja 21,28:2
Mademoiselle Colombe 1954,Ja 7,26:1
Purple Dust 1956,D 28,15:1

Bannister, Harry (Director)
Murder in the Old Red Barn, The 1936,F 3,20:4
She Gave Him All She Had 1939,D 2,20:7

Bannister, Harry (Producer)
Late One Evening 1933,Ja 10,27:3
She Gave Him All She Had 1939,D 2,20:7

Bannister, Lemuel (Playwright)
Assorted Nuts 1940,Ap 7,I,44:6

Bannister, Leslie
Bitter Sweet 1929,N 6,30:2

Bannon, Edward
Play, A 1925,F 11,19:2

Banos, Theon
Caution: A Love Story 1969,Ap 4,45:1

Banow, Joel
Confederates, The 1959,S 29,45:1

Bantock, Granville (Composer)
Macbeth 1927,Ja 16,VII,4:3

Banton, Travis (Costume Designer)
Marie Antoinette in Pennsylvania 1949,My 12,26:2

Banyai, George (Miscellaneous)
Rope Dancers, The 1957,N 21,39:1
Look After Lulu 1959,Mr 4,35:1

Banyard, Beatrice
Dove, The 1925,F 12,17:3
Canary Dutch 1925,S 9,22:1
Vaudeville (Palace) 1926,S 21,32:5
Lily Sue 1926,N 17,22:2
Honor Be Damned! 1927,Ja 27,13:1
Scarlet Fox, The 1928,Mr 28,31:1

Bar, Jula
Zunguru 1940,Mr 21,30:5

Bar-Shavit, Shlomo
Dybbuk, The 1964,F 4,30:2
Each Had Six Wings 1964,Mr 12,39:1

Bara, Frank
Don Juan; Feast With the Statue, The
1956,Ja 4,21:4
America Hurrah; Interview; TV; Motel
1967,O 10,55:2
Ordinary Man, An 1968,S 10,39:1

Bara, Theda
Blue Flame, The 1920,Mr 16,18:1

Barab, Seymour (Composer)
Shadow of My Enemy, A 1957,D 12,35:4

Baraban, Juliet (Costume Designer)
Sign of Jonah, The 1957,My 2,27:1

Barabas, David (Scenic Designer)
Dracula Sabbat 1970,O 2,28:2

Baragrey, John
Right Next to Broadway 1944,F 22,26:2
Flag Is Born, A 1946,S 7,10:6
Western Wind 1949,Ag 9,20:6
Enchanted, The 1950,Ja 19,34:2
Pride's Crossing 1950,N 21,37:5
One Eye Closed 1954,N 25,45:2
Devils, The 1965,N 17,51:2
Elizabeth the Queen 1966,N 4,30:1

Baragwanath, John (Playwright)
All That Glitters 1938,Ja 20,18:2

Baraisho, Menachem (Playwright)
Girl From Warsaw, The 1931,S 14,15:5
One Woman 1931,D 14,16:4

Barakat, Lecla (Mme)
Homme Qui Assassina, L' 1924,N 11,20:1
Homme et Ses Fantomes, L' 1924,N 14,16:1

Baraks, Shifrah
Untitled-Recital 1931,Mr 23,24:3
Professor Mamlock 1937,Ap 14,30:3
Trojan Women, The 1941,Ap 9,32:5

Baran, Ria
Hollywood Ice Revue 1956,Ja 13,17:1

Baranga, Aurel (Playwright)
Prescription for Happiness 1957,My 19,34:1

Baranoff, Nicholas
Gods of the Lightning 1931,F 19,21:4
Devil in the Mind 1931,My 2,23:2

Baranski, Deborah
Melody Lingers On, The 1969,N 17,55:1

Barasch, Norman (Playwright)
Make a Million 1958,O 24,39:2
Send Me No Flowers 1960,D 6,54:1

Barat, Donna
Don Carlos 1962,F 28,27:5

Barat, Elayne
Moondreamers, The 1969,D 9,68:1

Baratoff, Ben-Zvi
Wolves 1924,D 31,9:4
Tenth Commandment, The 1926,N 18,27:1
Othello 1929,F 4,21:2
Major Noah 1929,F 23,17:2
Stempenu, the Fiddler 1929,Mr 9,24:7
Josephus 1933,D 1,22:5
Three Cities 1938,O 11,20:3
Yoshe Kalb 1939,F 6,9:2

Baratoff, Leonid
Lysistrata 1925,D 15,28:2

Baratoff, Marie
Call on Kuprin, A 1961,My 26,29:3

Baratov, Paul
He, She and the Ox 1934,F 21,22:7

Baratz, Abraham
Deluge, The 1927,Ja 11,36:2

Baratz, Abraham—Cont
Golem, The 1927,F 5,13:2
Dybbuk, The 1948,My 3,26:3
David's Crown 1948,My 10,26:2
Golem, The 1948,My 17,22:3
Baratz, David
Girl From Warsaw, The 1931,S 14,15:5
Baratz, Marty
Slaves of Luxury 1930,F 8,13:3
Sonitchka 1930,Mr 8,21:3
Little Bandit 1935,Ap 19,24:2
Little Tailor, The 1938,Mr 21,18:2
Baratz, Marty (Choreographer)
Sonitchka 1930,Mr 8,21:3
Barau, Franz
Friedens Tragoedie 1936,N 17,34:4
Baravelle, Victor (Musical Director)
Raquel Meller 1926,Ap 15,24:1
Barba, Roy
Too Late the Phalarope 1956,O 12,35:1
Barban, Zev (Director)
Highway Robbery 1955,N 8,36:1
Barbara, Joyce
Jonica 1930,Mr 30,VIII,2:7
Barbaris, Eileen
West Side Story 1968,Je 25,32:1
Barbee, Richard
Transplanting Jean 1921,Ja 4,11:2
Transplanting Jean 1921,Ja 9,VI,1:1
Wild Oats Lane 1922,S 7,12:1
Gringo 1922,D 15,26:3
Robert E Lee 1923,N 21,23:1
Beggar on Horseback 1924,F 13,17:2
Pomeroy's Past 1926,Ap 20,24:4
Saturday's Children 1927,Ja 27,13:1
Days Without End 1934,Ja 9,19:1
And Stars Remain 1936,O 13,32:2
Stars in Your Eyes 1939,F 10,18:2
Key Largo 1939,N 28,30:2
George Washington Slept Here 1940,O 19,20:3
Mr Big 1941,O 1,24:2
Guest in the House 1942,F 25,25:2
Another Love Story 1943,O 13,29:2
Small Hours, The 1951,F 16,22:1
Come of Age 1952,Ja 24,22:2
Barber, Albert
George White's Scandals 1922,Ag 29,10:1
Roseanne 1923,D 31,9:5
Barber, Cal
Antigone 1968,O 11,36:1
Barber, Dorothy
Betty Lee 1924,D 26,18:2
Gay Paree 1925,Ag 19,14:3
Girl Friend, The 1926,Mr 18,26:5
Luckee Girl 1928,S 17,28:6
Barber, Ellen
Mod Donna 1970,My 4,48:1
Barber, Elmer
Paul Bunyan 1941,My 6,25:1
Barber, Frank
Jazz a La Carte 1922,Je 3,8:3
Barber, Jack (Lighting Director)
Out of This World 1955,N 10,44:2
He Who Gets Slapped 1956,F 2,18:1
Barber, Jan Jazz Band
Vaudeville (Hippodrome) 1924,Ap 1,18:1
Barber, Julian
Merchant of Venice, The 1955,Ja 8,9:7
Barber, Martha
Son, The 1950,Ag 16,24:6
Barber, Maurice (Producer)
Love on the Dole 1936,F 25,23:3
Barber, Philip
American Dream; 1933 1933,F 22,24:5
Barber, Philip (Producer)
One-Third of a Nation 1938,Ja 18,27:2
Barber, Philip W (Director)
Don't Throw Glass Houses 1938,D 28,24:4
Barber, Philip W (Miscellaneous)
Androcles and the Lion 1938,D 17,10:5
Barber, Philip W (Producer)
Don't Throw Glass Houses 1938,D 28,24:4
Barbera, Philip
In Any Language 1952,O 9,40:2
Barbero, Christopher
Twilight Walk 1951,S 25,25:4
Barberova, Ann
Wake Up and Dream 1929,D 31,14:3
Barbet, Marga
Slight Case of Murder, A 1935,S 12,28:5
Barbette
Passing Show of 1924, The 1924,S 4,13:4
Vaudeville (Palace) 1927,F 8,20:3
Vaudeville (Palace) 1927,F 13,VII,1:1
Jumbo 1935,N 18,20:2
Barbi, Vincent
Buttrio Square 1952,O 15,40:2
Barbier, George
Beware of Dogs 1921,O 4,10:1
Brook 1923,Ag 20,14:3
Beggar on Horseback 1924,F 13,17:2
Lady's Virtue, A 1925,N 24,28:2
Loose Ankles 1926,Ag 17,15:1
Barker, The 1927,Ja 19,20:6

Box Seats 1928,Ap 20,27:2
Front Page, The 1928,Ag 15,19:2
Nice Women 1929,Je 11,27:4
Sweet Land of Liberty 1929,S 24,29:2
Cortez 1929,N 5,32:2
Your Uncle Dudley 1929,N 19,26:4
Penny Arcade 1930,Mr 11,24:5
Ada Beats the Drum 1930,My 9,20:4
That's Gratitude 1930,S 12,28:1
Barbier, Jean-Claude
Ecole des Femmes, L' 1961,Ap 28,23:1
Barbier, Peter
Cynara 1931,N 3,31:1
Barbier, Pierre (Playwright)
Roi Cerf, Le 1937,N 30,26:3
Barbier (Costume Designer)
Red Robe, The 1928,D 26,15:1
Barbieri, Gina
Carrosse du Saint-Sacrement, Le 1930,Mr 9,IX,2:7
Barbor, H M (Playwright)
Delilah 1930,O 12,VIII,1:8
Barbosa, James
Balls 1965,F 11,45:1
Motel 1966,N 7,66:1
TV 1966,N 7,66:1
Interview 1966,N 7,66:1
Terminal 1970,Ap 15,51:2
Endgame 1970,My 6,47:1
Serpent, The 1970,Je 2,35:1
Moon Walk 1970,N 27,52:1
Barbour, Ada Lytton
Catskill Dutch 1924,My 7,18:1
Big Mogul, The 1925,My 12,26:3
He Loved the Ladies 1927,My 11,29:2
Town Boy 1929,O 5,22:4
Barbour, James
White Lights 1927,O 12,30:4
Barbour, Joyce
Havoc 1924,S 2,22:2
Sky High 1925,Mr 3,21:4
Present Arms 1928,Ap 27,16:2
Spring Is Here 1929,Mr 12,26:1
Jonica 1930,Ap 8,27:1
Words and Music 1932,Ag 26,21:2
Indoor Fireworks 1934,Mr 30,26:6
George and Margaret 1937,F 26,25:2
Barbour, Oliver
Lone Valley 1933,Mr 11,18:6
Shooting Star 1933,Je 13,22:2
Drums Begin, The 1933,N 25,10:5
John Brown 1934,Ja 23,22:3
Kill That Story 1934,Ag 30,22:2
Dance With Your Gods 1934,O 8,14:3
Battleship Gertie 1935,Ja 19,9:2
Symphony 1935,Ap 27,20:3
Body Beautiful, The 1935,N 1,24:3
Ethan Frome 1936,Ja 22,15:2
Tide Rising 1937,Ja 26,17:2
Kind Lady 1937,Jl 6,23:1
Mamba's Daughters 1939,Ja 4,24:2
Barbour, Thomas
Jim Dandy 1941,N 8,10:5
Twelfth Night 1954,N 10,42:2
Twelfth Night 1954,D 12,II,3:1
Merchant of Venice, The 1955,F 23,23:2
Admirable Bashville, The 1956,F 21,38:1
Lady's Not for Burning, The 1957,F 22,26:2
Augustus Does His Bit 1958,F 22,8:3
Androcles and the Lion 1958,F 22,8:3
Enchanted, The 1958,Ap 23,41:1
Antony and Cleopatra 1959,Ja 14,28:1
Saintliness of Margery Kempe, The 1959,F 3,35:6
Dr Willy Nilly 1959,Je 5,18:2
Under the Sycamore Tree 1960,Mr 8,37:2
Epitaph for George Dillon 1960,D 29,17:1
Thracian Horses, The 1961,S 28,58:2
Curate's Play, The 1961,D 18,41:3
If Five Years Pass 1962,My 11,37:1
Antony and Cleopatra 1963,Je 21,33:1
Mr Simian 1963,O 22,44:1
My Kinsman, Major Molineux 1964,N 2,62:2
Serjeant Musgrave's Dance 1966,Mr 9,44:1
Portrait of a Queen 1968,F 29,29:1
Barbour, Thomas (Playwright)
Smokeweaver's Daughter, The 1959,Ap 15,30:1
Barbour, Thomas (Producer)
Smokeweaver's Daughter, The 1959,Ap 15,30:1
Barbour, Virginia
Naughty-Naught '00 1946,O 21,27:5
Barbour, William
Passing of the Third Floor Back, The 1928,Ja 17,22:7
Passing of the Third Floor Back, The 1928,F 21,18:2
Barby, Paul
Entertain a Ghost 1962,Ap 10,48:1
Barby, Paul (Miscellaneous)
Raisin' Hell in the Son 1962,Jl 3,13:2
Barcay, Eva
Mima 1928,D 13,24:2
Barcello, Rose
Audition of the Apprentice Theatre 1939,Je 2,26:2

Barcelo, Randy (Costume Designer)
Moondreamers, The 1969,D 9,68:1
Barcena, Catalina
Road to Happiness, The 1927,My 3,24:1
Romantic Young Lady, The 1927,My 5,30:2
Girl and the Cat, The 1927,My 6,21:2
Blind Heart, The 1927,My 8,30:2
Cradle Song 1927,My 10,24:4
Fragila Rosina 1927,My 10,24:4
Pygmalion 1927,My 12,25:2
Barcham, Bill
Macbeth 1957,Ag 16,11:2
Barcham, Cicely
Hamlet 1920,Mr 17,14:2
Barcinska, Eva
Jackpot 1944,Ja 14,15:2
Barclay, Bea
Johnny 2X4 1942,Mr 17,24:6
Barclay, Bruce
Jubilee 1935,O 14,20:1
Pirates of Penzance, The 1936,Ap 21,27:5
Forbidden Melody 1936,N 3,33:1
Barclay, Don
Vaudeville (Palace) 1923,Ja 23,18:2
Go-Go 1923,Mr 13,19:4
Greenwich Village Follies 1924,S 17,16:1
Oh! Oh! Nurse 1925,D 8,28:4
Merry-Go-Round 1927,Jl 5,19:4
Nina Rosa 1930,My 31,19:3
Nina Rosa 1930,S 22,22:5
Americana 1932,S 25,IX,1:6
Americana 1932,O 6,19:3
Barclay, Florence (Original Author)
Chatelaine de Shenstone, La 1930,Mr 23,IX,2:1
Barclay, Gretchen
If This Be Treason 1935,S 24,28:2
Barclay, Humphrey (Director)
Cambridge Circus 1964,O 7,53:1
Barclay, Jered
American Dream, The 1963,My 29,39:6
Zoo Story, The 1963,My 29,39:6
Next Time I'll Sing to You 1963,N 28,69:2
Persecution and Assassination of Marat As Performed by the Inmates of the Asylum of Charenton Under the Direction of the Marquis de Sade, The 1967,Ja 4,34:1
Patriot for Me, A 1969,O 6,58:1
Barclay, Jered (Director)
Tonight in Living Color; Golden Fleece, The 1969,Je 11,43:1
Tonight in Living Color; David Show, The 1969,Je 11,43:1
Barclay, John
Iolanthe 1926,Ap 20,24:2
Iolanthe 1926,Ap 25,VIII,1:1
Pirates of Penzance, The; Slave of Duty, The 1926,D 7,25:1
Pirates of Penzance, The 1926,D 12,VIII,3:1
Mikado, The; Town of Titipu, The 1927,S 19,30:1
Champagne, Sec 1933,O 16,20:2
Hamlet 1936,O 20,31:3
Hamlet 1936,N 11,54:2
Man in Dress Clothes, The 1937,Ag 24,24:4
Sea Gull, The 1938,Mr 29,19:2
Hamlet 1939,D 5,35:2
Richard II 1940,Ap 2,31:2
Barclay, Mary
Ti-Coq 1951,F 10,10:2
Witness for the Prosecution 1954,D 17,35:2
Barclay, Patricia
Blue Bird, The 1923,D 26,13:3
Fata Morgana 1924,Mr 4,16:3
Processional 1925,Ja 13,17:1
Wisdom Tooth, The 1926,F 16,22:2
Lally 1927,F 9,16:3
Immoral Isabella 1927,O 28,20:3
Mirrors 1928,Ja 19,17:1
Box Seats 1928,Ap 20,27:2
Little Accident 1928,O 10,32:3
Tonight at 12 1928,N 16,28:1
Remote Control 1929,S 11,24:5
I Want My Wife 1930,Mr 21,30:7
Absent Father 1932,O 18,23:5
Barclay, Remi
Macbeth 1969,N 21,51:1
Barcliff, Norman
Girl From Wyoming, The 1938,O 31,12:1
Barclift, Nelson
Lady in the Dark 1941,Ja 24,14:2
This Is the Army 1942,Jl 5,28:2
Marie Antoinette in Pennsylvania 1949,My 12,26:2
Barclift, Nelson (Choreographer)
Around the World 1946,Je 1,9:5
Marie Antoinette in Pennsylvania 1949,My 12,26:2
Barcone, Eugene (Miscellaneous)
Flea in Her Ear, A 1969,O 4,25:1
Three Sisters, The 1969,O 10,38:1
Barcroft, Judith
Mating Dance 1965,N 4,58:1
Dinner at Eight 1966,S 28,38:1
Barcy, Clara T
Red Poppy, The 1922,D 21,18:2

Barczy, Kato
Kek Roka; Blue Fox 1957,D 5,47:2
Egerfogo; Mousetrap, The 1958,Ja 30,18:6
Bard, Aza
Camino Real 1953,Mr 20,26:1
Metamorphosis 1957,F 20,38:1
Winkelberg 1958,Ja 15,26:2
Ulysses in Nighttown 1958,Je 6,30:1
Hard Travelin' 1965,Je 17,25:1
Lonesome Train, The 1965,Je 17,25:1
Bard, Ben
Dancing Girl, The 1923,Ja 25,16:2
Vaudeville (Palace) 1931,Ap 13,17:2
Bard, John
Sailor, Beware! 1933,S 29,24:4
Bard, Katharine
All the Living 1938,Mr 25,14:4
As You Like It 1939,My 9,28:4
Life With Father 1939,N 9,26:2
Ring Around Elizabeth 1941,N 18,32:2
Lily of the Valley 1942,Ja 27,25:2
Three's a Family 1943,My 6,24:2
Made in Heaven 1946,O 25,28:2
Hallams, The 1948,Mr 5,18:2
I Know My Love 1949,N 3,36:1
Pride's Crossing 1950,N 21,37:5
Long Days, The 1951,Ap 21,10:5
Bard, Maria
X Y Z 1929,Ap 7,X,4:4
What Price Glory 1929,Ap 28,IX,1:4
Road to Rome, The 1929,N 10,X,4:8
Napoleon Greift Ein 1930,Je 1,VIII,2:1
Jewel Robbery; Juwelenraub am Kurfurstendamm 1932,F 21,VIII,2:3
Twelfth Night 1932,O 23,IX,3:1
Bohemian Girl, The 1933,Jl 28,18:5
Lauter Luegen 1937,O 24,XI,3:1
Bard, Phil (Playwright)
Ninth Month Midnight 1949,F 17,28:2
Bard, Robert
New Faces of 1936 1936,My 20,24:5
Bard and Pearl
Topics of 1923 1923,N 21,23:2
Barde, Andre (Composer)
Untitled-Play 1925,D 27,VII,2:1
Barde, Andre (Lyricist)
Comte Obligado 1929,Mr 12,26:2
Pas Sur La Bouche; Not on the Lips 1929,Mr 26,34:3
Barde, Andre (Playwright)
Afgar 1920,N 9,13:2
Luckee Girl 1928,S 17,28:6
Comte Obligado 1929,Mr 12,26:2
Pas Sur La Bouche; Not on the Lips 1929,Mr 26,34:3
Arthur 1929,S 29,IX,4:7
Dame du Promenoir, La 1933,O 1,IX,1:3
Soeurs Hortensias, Les 1934,My 13,IX,2:2
Bardelang, Alfred
Sons o' Guns 1929,N 27,30:4
Bardella, Mario
Venetian Twins, The 1968,My 29,23:1
Barden, Lois
Cretan Woman, The 1954,My 21,17:2
Bardett, Trevor
At the Bottom 1930,Ja 10,24:3
Bardi, George
Processional 1937,O 14,23:1
Bardian, F G (Director)
Moscow Circus on Ice 1970,D 9,63:1
Bardoly, Louis S (Playwright)
Case History 1938,O 22,15:2
Magnificent Hugo, The 1961,Ap 8,12:2
Sunday Man, The 1964,My 14,41:3
Bardoly, Louis S (Producer)
Importance of Being Dressed, The 1963,N 3,87:3
Bardusk, Anthony
Entertain a Ghost 1962,Ap 10,48:1
Bardwell, Robert
Murder in the Cathedral 1935,D 21,11:3
Good Fairy, The 1939,Ag 30,15:5
Barefield, Eddie (Composer)
Time of Your Life, The 1955,Ja 20,34:1
Bareket, Itzchak
Dybbuk, The 1964,F 4,30:2
Each Had Six Wings 1964,Mr 12,39:1
Barend, Robert
Signs Along the Cynic Route 1961,D 15,49:5
On the Necessity of Being Polygamous 1964,D 9,61:1
Nathan Weinstein, Mystic, Connecticut 1966,F 26,15:2
Barer, Marshall (Composer)
Once Over Lightly 1955,Mr 16,39:1
New Faces of 1956 1956,Je 15,32:1
Ziegfeld Follies 1957,Mr 2,19:2
Barer, Marshall (Lyricist)
Once Over Lightly 1955,Mr 16,39:1
New Faces of 1956 1956,Je 15,32:1
Ziegfeld Follies 1957,Mr 2,19:2
Once Upon a Mattress 1959,My 12,40:1
Once Upon a Mattress 1959,My 17,II,1:1
Mad Show, The 1966,Ja 10,16:1

Pousse-Cafe 1966,Mr 19,19:2
Barer, Marshall (Playwright)
Once Upon a Mattress 1959,My 12,40:1
Once Upon a Mattress 1959,My 17,II,1:1
Bares, Joseph (Scenic Designer)
Peter and the Wolf 1969,N 30,85:5
Barfoot, Harry
Woman of Bronze, The 1920,S 8,9:2
Trial of Joan of Arc, The 1921,Mr 28,8:2
Iphigenia in Aulis 1921,Ap 8,18:2
Will Shakespeare 1923,Ja 2,14:1
Green Hat, The 1925,S 16,23:2
Woman of Bronze, The 1927,Je 16,25:4
Most Immoral Lady, A 1928,N 27,36:1
Good Earth, The 1932,O 18,23:4
Barger, Robert
Adding Machine, The 1970,D 5,40:1
Bargy, Jeanne (Composer)
Greenwich Village U S A 1960,S 29,30:5
Bargy, Jeanne (Lyricist)
Greenwich Village U S A 1960,S 29,30:5
Bargy, Jeanne (Miscellaneous)
Greenwich Village U S A 1960,S 29,30:5
Bari, George
Borak 1960,D 14,51:1
Bari, George (Miscellaneous)
Power of Dreams, A 1958,Mr 11,33:1
Bald Soprano, The 1958,Je 4,39:2
Jack 1958,Je 4,39:2
Sappho 1960,Ja 12,22:1
Blood Bugle, The 1961,Je 29,26:1
West of the Moon 1961,Je 29,26:1
Bari, Madelaine
Wisdom Tooth, The 1926,F 16,22:2
Barian, Joe (Lyricist)
Of V We Sing 1942,F 16,20:3
Bariello, Frances
Merry Widow, The 1929,D 3,29:1
Barillet, Pierre (Original Author)
Cactus Flower 1965,D 9,60:2
Forty Carats 1969,Ja 5,II,1:3
Barillet, Pierre (Playwright)
Four Pieces sur Jardin 1969,F 18,35:1
Baring, Isabel
Love in the Tropics 1927,O 19,24:3
Gambling 1929,Ag 27,31:2
Tavern, The 1930,My 20,32:1
Song and Dance Man, The 1930,Je 17,25:5
Just to Remind You 1931,S 8,39:1
Hat, a Coat, a Glove, A 1934,F 1,15:2
Baring, Mathilde
Tale of the Wolf, The 1925,O 8,31:2
Magda 1926,Ja 27,16:2
City Haul 1929,D 31,14:4
As Husbands Go 1931,Mr 6,26:5
Girls in Uniform 1932,D 31,10:3
As Husbands Go 1933,Ja 20,20:5
Shooting Star 1933,Je 13,22:2
Drums Begin, The 1933,N 25,10:5
Ragged Army 1934,F 27,16:5
Jefferson Davis 1936,F 19,17:2
Live Life Again 1945,O 1,14:7
Bariot, Audrey
Son Mari 1936,Ap 17,17:3
Barkan, Bernice (Producer)
Deep Are the Roots 1960,O 4,47:1
Barkan, Mark
Johnny Summit 1957,S 25,23:4
Barkdull, Les
Imaginary Invalid, The 1967,My 2,53:1
Touch of the Poet, A 1967,My 3,38:2
Still Life 1967,My 4,34:1
Ways and Means 1967,My 4,34:1
Barkentin, Marjorie (Miscellaneous)
Ulysses in Nighttown 1958,Je 6,30:1
Barkentin, Slater
Lady Precious Stream 1936,Ja 28,15:2
Barker, Albert W (Director)
Grandma's Diary 1948,S 23,36:2
Barker, Albert W (Playwright)
Buckaroo 1929,Mr 18,31:1
Man on Stilts, The 1931,S 10,23:2
Middletown 1934,Ap 23,24:6
American Holiday 1936,F 22,13:3
Memphis Bound 1945,My 25,23:2
Memphis Bound 1945,Je 10,II,1:1
Grandma's Diary 1948,S 23,36:2
Barker, Edith
Leah Kleschna 1924,Ap 22,19:2
Barker, Edward
Cherry Pie 1926,Ap 15,24:4
Barker, Edwin L (Playwright)
Buckaroo 1929,Mr 18,31:1
Man on Stilts, The 1931,S 10,23:2
Middletown 1934,Ap 23,24:6
American Holiday 1936,F 22,13:3
Barker, Granville (Playwright)
Deburau 1920,D 24,14:3
Deburau 1921,Ja 2,VI,3:1
Harlequinade 1921,My 11,20:3
Madras House, The 1921,O 30,VI,1:1
Madras House, The 1921,O 31,18:2
Madras House, The 1921,N 6,VI,1:1

Barker, Granville (Playwright)—Cont
Romantic Young Lady, The 1926,My 5,24:3
Prunella; Love in a Garden 1926,Je 16,23:3
Doctor Knock 1928,F 24,15:2
Prunella 1929,Ap 10,23:3
Barker, Granville (Producer)
Iphigenie in Tauris 1915,Je 1,15:5
Barker, Granville (Translator)
Kingdom of God, The 1928,D 21,30:2
Hundred Years Old, A 1929,Ap 19,27:5
Fortunato 1956,Mr 24,15:2
Barker, Harry
Sam Abramovitch 1927,Ja 20,20:5
Barker, Helen (Playwright)
Romantic Young Lady, The 1926,My 5,24:3
Barker, Helen (Translator)
Kingdom of God, The 1928,D 21,30:2
Hundred Years Old, A 1929,Ap 19,27:5
Barker, Howard (Costume Designer)
Little Mary Sunshine 1959,N 19,49:3
Barker, Howard (Producer)
Little Mary Sunshine 1959,N 19,49:3
Madame Aphrodite 1961,D 30,13:1
Barker, Howard (Scenic Designer)
Out of This World 1955,N 10,44:2
Little Mary Sunshine 1959,N 19,49:3
Little Mary Sunshine 1959,N 29,II,1:1
Who's Happy Now? 1969,N 18,39:1
Barker, Irving
Alternate Current 1939,D 23,8:3
Barker, Jack
Sally 1920,D 22,16:1
No, No, Nanette 1925,S 17,20:2
Cocoanuts, The 1925,D 9,30:1
Gang's All Here, The 1931,F 19,21:3
Barker, Jean
Cock-A-Doodle-Doo 1949,F 28,16:5
Three by Thurber; Imperturbable Spirit, The 1955,Mr 8,23:2
Three by Thurber; Middle Years, The 1955,Mr 8,23:2
Innkeepers, The 1956,F 3,19:1
Jack 1958,Je 4,39:2
French Way, The; Edward and Agrippina 1962,Mr 21,36:2
Tchin-Tchin 1962,O 26,26:2
Barker, Jess
Allure 1934,O 30,22:6
Ode to Liberty 1935,Jl 2,24:3
Ode to Liberty 1935,Jl 9,24:4
Ode to Liberty 1935,Ag 6,20:3
You Can't Take It With You 1936,D 6,XII,6:2
You Can't Take It With You 1936,D 15,31:1
White Cargo 1941,My 14,24:3
Flowers of Virtue, The 1942,F 6,22:2
Magic 1942,S 30,28:2
Barker, John
Love Call, The 1927,O 25,33:1
Follow Thru 1929,Ja 10,24:3
Pajama Lady, The 1930,O 12,VIII,4:1
Band Wagon, The 1931,Je 4,31:3
Face the Music 1933,F 1,13:4
Three Waltzes 1937,D 27,10:2
Barker, Julia
Wonderful Night, A; Fledermaus, Die 1929,N 1,23:3
Barker, Leonard
Wednesday's Child 1934,Ja 17,23:2
Post Road 1934,D 5,28:3
Barker, Lex
Merry Wives of Windsor, The 1938,Ap 15,22:3
Barker, Margaret
Age of Innocence, The 1928,N 28,24:2
Barretts of Wimpole Street, The 1931,F 10,25:1
Barretts of Wimpole Street, The 1931,F 22,VIII,1:1
House of Connelly, The 1931,S 29,22:4
Night Over Taos 1932,Mr 10,25:3
Success Story 1932,S 27,24:4
Black Diamond 1933,F 24,12:2
Hilda Cassidy 1933,My 5,18:3
Men in White 1933,S 27,24:2
Men in White 1933,O 1,IX,1:1
Gold Eagle Guy 1934,N 29,33:4
Gold Eagle Guy 1934,D 9,X,1:1
Till the Day I Die 1935,Mr 27,24:5
Weep for the Virgins 1935,D 2,18:1
Case of Clyde Griffiths 1936,Mr 14,10:4
Strings, My Lord, Are False, The 1942,My 20,24:2
Leading Lady 1948,O 19,33:1
Member of the Wedding, The 1950,Ja 6,26:6
Autumn Garden, The 1951,Mr 8,36:2
Autumn Garden, The 1951,Mr 18,II,1:1
See the Jaguar 1952,D 4,46:2
Ladies of the Corridor, The 1953,O 22,33:5
Ladies of the Corridor, The 1953,N 1,II,1:1
Master Builder, The 1955,Mr 2,23:2
Barker, Margaret (Director)
Cock-A-Doodle-Doo 1949,F 28,16:5
Barker, Margaret T (Miscellaneous)
Better Luck Next Time 1966,Ja 28,21:1
Walk in Dark Places, A 1966,Ja 28,21:1
Barker, Marian
Patience 1935,S 3,24:4

Barker, Mary
So Many Paths 1934,D 7,26:5
Barker, Nell
Hunky Dory 1922,S 5,21:2
Barker, Patricia
Oklahoma! 1951,My 30,15:2
Barker, Pete
In Clover 1937,O 14,23:1
Barker, Petronella
Dance of Death, The 1967,O 20,50:1
Love for Love 1967,O 21,17:1
Love for Love 1967,O 29,II,5:1
Love for Love 1967,O 30,59:1
Barker, Ronnie
Real Inspector Hound, The 1968,Je 19,38:2
Real Inspector Hound, The 1968,Jl 8,45:1
Barker, Sean
Gondoliers, The 1963,Je 5,33:2
Yeomen of the Guard, The 1964,Mr 19,29:2
Gondoliers, The 1964,Mr 28,14:1
Barkhausen, Henry
Whispering Gallery, The 1935,D 1,II,12:6
Barkley, Barbara
Make a Million 1958,O 24,39:2
Barklie, Lance (Playwright)
Bella 1961,N 17,40:1
Barklie, Lance (Producer)
Bella 1961,N 17,40:1
Barkow, Arthur A (Miscellaneous)
Wake Up, Darling 1956,My 3,34:2
Barksdale, Norman
Swing It 1937,Jl 23,17:2
Barksdale, Rebecca
I Feel Wonderful 1954,O 19,22:5
Barkworth, Peter
School for Scandal, The 1963,Ja 26,5:2
Barl, George (Miscellaneous)
Golem, The 1959,F 26,38:2
Barlach, Ernst (Playwright)
Blaue Boll, Der 1931,Ja 25,VIII,4:1
Barleon, Amelia
Panic 1935,Mr 16,18:4
Family Affair, A 1946,N 28,41:2
Barling, Kitty
Living Room, The 1962,N 22,43:5
Never Live Over a Pretzel Factory 1964,Mr 30,37:1
Barlo, Lesa
Tragicomedy of Don Cristobita and Dona Rosita,
The 1958,My 30,12:2
Barlog, Boleslaw (Director)
Don Carlos 1964,N 25,40:1
Captain of Koepenick, The 1964,D 2,60:1
Barlog, Boleslaw (Producer)
Diary of Anne Frank, The 1956,O 14,II,3:1
Barlow, Alan (Scenic Designer)
Murder in the Cathedral 1953,Ap 26,II,1:1
Shaughraun, The 1968,My 22,54:1
Barlow, Ann
Festival 1955,Ja 19,22:1
Barlow, Anna Marie (Director)
Cruising Speed 600 MPH 1970,Ja 6,48:3
Barlow, Anna Marie (Playwright)
Half-Past Wednesday 1962,Ap 7,16:2
Meeting, The 1967,D 13,55:1
Limb of Snow 1967,D 13,55:1
Cruising Speed 600 MPH 1970,Ja 6,48:3
Barlow, Audrey
Tapestry in Gray 1935,D 28,10:2
Barlow, Betty
Blue Kitten, The 1922,Ja 14,9:3
Skin Deep 1927,O 18,32:1
Vaudeville (Palace) 1928,S 25,29:4
Smarty's Party 1928,S 25,29:4
Barlow, Bruce
Much Ado About Nothing 1952,My 2,20:1
Barlow, Charles
New Faces of 1962 1962,F 2,25:1
Barlow, Graham (Costume Designer)
Measure for Measure 1967,F 15,37:1
Barlow, Graham (Scenic Designer)
Measure for Measure 1967,F 15,37:1
Hamlet 1967,F 17,44:1
Barlow, Harold (Composer)
Apothecary, The 1926,Mr 17,28:1
Barlow, Howard (Director)
Dybbuk, The 1925,D 16,22:2
Barlow, Howard (Miscellaneous)
Commedia Dell' Arte 1927,Ap 6,24:3
Barlow, Jane (Playwright)
Ghost Bereft 1933,F 1,13:5
Barlow, June
Ice Capades 1955,S 15,38:1
Barlow, Reginald
Big Game 1920,Ja 22,23:1
Big Game 1920,Ja 25,VIII,2:2
Piper, The 1920,Mr 20,14:2
Prince and the Pauper, The 1920,N 2,15:1
Six-Fifty, The 1921,O 25,20:1
Six-Fifty, The 1921,O 30,VI,1:1
Your Woman and Mine 1922,F 28,17:2
Drums of Jeopardy, The 1922,My 30,8:4
Breaking Point, The 1923,Ag 17,8:4
Go West, Young Man 1923,N 13,25:2

Blue Bird, The 1923,D 26,13:3
Outside Looking In 1925,S 8,28:1
Shelter 1926,Ja 26,18:2
Number 7 1926,S 9,21:3
Damn the Tears 1927,Ja 22,11:1
Heaven-Tappers, The 1927,Mr 9,28:3
Blood Money 1927,Ag 23,29:2
Out of the Sea 1927,D 6,26:2
Queen's Husband, The 1928,Ja 26,17:2
Silent Witness, The 1931,Mr 24,31:5
Blood on the Moon 1934,S 30,IX,3:1
Barlow, Reginald (Director)
Shelter 1926,Ja 26,18:2
Barlow, Richard (Miscellaneous)
Greenwich Village U S A 1960,S 29,30:5
Barlow, Robert (Musical Director)
Brass Butterfly, The 1970,Ja 31,34:1
Barlow, Samuel L M (Composer)
Amphitryon 38 1937,Je 24,30:2
Amphitryon 38 1937,N 2,32:2
Barlow, Samuel L M (Mrs)
Variations of 1940 1940,Ja 29,12:1
Barlow, Samuel L M (Musical Director)
Amphitryon 38 1937,N 2,32:2
Variations of 1940 1940,Ja 29,12:1
Barlow, Stuart
Taming of the Shrew, The 1935,O 1,27:3
Barnabe, Bruno
Much Ado About Nothing 1929,N 17,30:4
Escape Me Never! 1935,Ja 22,22:2
Barnaby, David
Embezzled Heaven 1944,N 1,20:2
Barnard, Charles (Playwright)
Forest Ring, The 1930,Ap 26,11:2
Barnard, Francis
Mikado, The 1954,Mr 24,31:1
Pirates of Penzance, The 1954,Mr 31,32:5
Gondoliers, The 1954,Ap 14,24:3
Ruddigore 1954,Ap 21,36:4
Yeomen of the Guard, The 1954,My 5,36:2
Beggar's Opera, The 1957,Mr 14,35:1
Pilgrim's Progress 1962,Mr 21,36:2
Barnard, Harold (Producer)
Doctor Social 1948,F 12,29:5
Barnard, Henry
First Million, The 1943,Ap 29,27:4
Othello 1943,O 20,18:1
Mrs January & Mr Ex 1944,Ap 1,10:2
Wind Is Ninety, The 1945,Je 22,12:2
Home of the Brave 1945,D 28,13:2
I Know My Love 1949,N 3,36:1
Barnard, Ivor
Bird in Hand 1929,Ap 5,28:2
Bird in Hand 1929,Ap 14,X,1:1
Monsieur Brotonneau 1930,O 5,IX,2:4
Grand Hotel 1931,S 27,VIII,1:4
Seagull, The 1936,Je 21,IX,1:5
Barnard, Julie
Small Timers, The 1925,Ja 28,15:3
Nirvana 1926,Mr 4,19:1
Barnard, Patricia
This Island Is Mine 1959,Jl 1,26:4
Barnart, Abner
Orange Blossoms 1922,S 20,18:1
Barnbaum, Louis
Sins of Mothers 1937,Mr 30,20:2
Barnbaum, Minnie
Sins of Mothers 1937,Mr 30,20:2
Barner, Stockman
Othello 1945,My 23,25:4
Barnes, Al
Son, The 1950,Ag 16,24:6
Barnes, Alexander
Doctored Wife, The 1950,Jl 12,33:2
Barnes, Barry
Vigil, The 1948,My 11,28:1
Barnes, Billy (Composer)
Billy Barnes Revue, The 1959,Je 10,42:2
Billy Barnes People, The 1961,Je 14,10:3
Barnes, Billy (Lyricist)
Billy Barnes Revue, The 1959,Je 10,42:2
Billy Barnes People, The 1961,Je 14,10:3
Barnes, Billy (Miscellaneous)
Billy Barnes Revue, The 1959,Je 10,42:2
Barnes, Billy (Musical Director)
Billy Barnes Revue, The 1959,Je 10,42:2
Barnes, Binnie
Red Peppers; Tonight at Eight 1940,Ag 6,15:3
Tonight at 8:30 1940,Ag 11,IX,11:2
Barnes, Carman (Original Author)
Schoolgirl 1930,N 2,VIII,3:5
Schoolgirl 1930,N 21,31:1
Barnes, Carman (Playwright)
Schoolgirl 1930,N 2,VIII,3:5
Schoolgirl 1930,N 21,31:1
Barnes, Charles
Babes in Toyland 1930,D 22,17:1
Barnes, Charles (Composer)
Priorities of 1942 1942,Mr 13,23:2
Barnes, Charles (Lyricist)
Priorities of 1942 1942,Mr 13,23:2
Barnes, Daniel
New Moon, The 1928,S 20,33:1

Barnes, Djuna
Tidings Brought to Mary, The 1922,D 25,20:1
Barnes, Djuna (Playwright)
Kurzy of the Sea 1920,Ap 4,VI,6:1
Little Theatre Tournament; Dove, The
1926,My 7,12:2
Barnes, Doug
Hair 1970,Ja 13,39:1
Barnes, Emily
Missouri Legend 1951,F 10,10:4
Barnes, Florence
Yellow Sands 1927,S 12,29:3
Barnes, Frank
Criminal Code, The 1929,O 3,28:2
Barnes, Gordon
Story of Mary Surratt, The 1947,F 10,25:2
Barnes, Helen
Innocent Idea, An 1920,My 26,9:4
Ladies' Night 1920,Ag 10,10:1
Barnes, Howard McKent (Playwright)
Her Unborn Child 1928,Mr 7,28:3
Barnes, Irving
Our Lan' 1947,S 29,16:5
Porgy and Bess 1953,Mr 10,25:5
Porgy and Bess 1961,My 18,40:1
Porgy and Bess 1964,My 7,32:1
Barnes, Jack
Wayside 1957,Ap 18,34:1
Barnes, Jacqueline
World's My Oyster, The 1956,Ag 10,10:4
Land Beyond the River, A 1957,Mr 29,15:7
Barnes, Johnny
Frank Fay's Vaudeville 1939,Mr 3,20:4
Du Barry Was a Lady 1939,D 7,34:2
More the Merrier, The 1941,S 16,19:3
Angel in the Wings 1947,D 12,36:4
Barnes, Kay
Imaginary Invalid, The 1922,Jl 26,26:2
My Aunt From Ypsilanti 1923,My 2,22:6
Deacon, The 1925,N 25,14:3
Porgy and Bess 1964,My 7,32:1
Barnes, Kempster
King Lear 1947,F 19,32:2
As You Like It 1947,F 21,16:2
Merchant of Venice, The 1947,F 24,16:2
Volpone 1947,F 25,32:2
Hamlet 1947,F 27,27:2
Barnes, Lois
Dream With Music 1944,My 19,15:2
Barnes, Lucille
Dream With Music 1944,My 19,15:2
Barnes, Mae
Rang Tang 1927,Jl 13,20:1
Hot Rhythm 1930,Ag 22,18:5
By the Beautiful Sea 1954,Ap 9,20:1
By the Beautiful Sea 1954,Ap 18,II,1:1
Barnes, Margaret (Playwright)
Age of Innocence, The 1928,N 28,24:2
Barnes, Margaret Ayer (Original Author)
Edna His Wife 1937,D 8,30:3
Barnes, Margaret Ayer (Playwright)
Jenny 1929,Je 2,VIII,1:2
Jenny 1929,O 9,34:4
Dishonored Lady 1930,Ja 26,VIII,2:1
Dishonored Lady 1930,F 5,27:1
Dishonored Lady 1930,My 25,IX,2:4
Barnes, Marian
Bitter Oleander 1935,F 12,24:3
Barnes, Mary
Haiti 1938,Mr 3,16:1
Barnes, Nell
Failures, The 1923,N 23,20:1
Barnes, Paul (Lighting Director)
Hotel Passionato 1965,O 23,16:1
Barnes, Paul (Scenic Designer)
Hotel Passionato 1965,O 23,16:1
Barnes, Peter (Playwright)
Ruling Class, The 1969,F 28,31:1
Barnes, Rob
Sambo 1969,D 22,42:1
Barnes, Rolf
Untitled-Revue 1965,Je 25,38:1
Barnes, Rolf (Miscellaneous)
Take It From the Top 1967,N 23,59:2
Barnes, Roy
Student Prince, The 1943,Je 9,16:2
Blossom Time 1943,S 6,21:2
Barnes, Spencer
Up Pops the Devil 1930,S 2,19:1
Everybody's Welcome 1931,O 14,26:3
American Dream; 1933 1933,F 22,24:5
Barnes, Theo
In Circles 1967,O 14,12:1
In Circles 1968,Je 28,36:1
Dracula Sabbat 1970,O 2,28:2
Barnes, Virginia
Strike Up the Band 1930,Ja 15,29:1
Polonaise 1945,O 8,20:2
Song of Norway 1959,Je 26,16:2
Barnett, Art
Annie Get Your Gun 1946,My 17,14:2
Pal Joey 1963,My 30,21:1

Barnett, Art—Cont
How to Succeed in Business Without Really Trying 1966,Ap 21,45:1
South Pacific 1969,Jl 7,27:1
Barnett, Arthur
Everywhere I Roam 1938,D 30,10:4
Anna Russell and Her Little Show 1953,S 8,27:2
Barnett, Ben W
Jealous Moon, The 1928,N 21,32:2
Barnett, Charles
Twelfth Night 1941,D 3,32:2
Barnett, David A (Composer)
His Majesty the Queen 1926,Mr 9,8:1
Barnett, Ella (Translator)
One Glorious Hour 1927,Ap 15,27:2
Barnett, Jack (Miscellaneous)
Toplitzky of Notre Dame 1946,D 27,13:4
Barnett, Joyce
Night Music 1951,Ap 9,29:6
Barnett, Jules D
Cocktails of 1934 1934,My 5,22:1
Barnett, Lee
Peter Pan 1950,Ap 25,27:2
Bless You All 1950,D 15,42:2
Barnett, Lincoln
How Revolting! 1932,Mr 11,14:6
Barnett, Mary
I'm Solomon 1968,Ap 24,51:1
Barnett, Nancy
Bitter Sweet 1929,N 6,30:2
Barnett, Spencer
No More Peace 1937,F 27,9:1
Barnett, Sylvia
Marching Song 1937,F 18,18:2
Barnett, Zoe
Jim Jam Jems 1920,O 5,13:2
Rose Girl, The 1921,F 12,11:1
Blossom Time 1921,S 30,10:1
Barney, Jay
Lamp at Midnight 1947,D 22,29:2
Blood Wedding 1949,F 7,16:2
Don't Go Away Mad 1949,My 10,28:2
Number, The 1951,O 31,33:2
Grass Harp, The 1952,Mr 28,26:2
Death of Odysseus, The 1953,N 4,30:5
Richard III 1953,D 10,65:2
Stockade 1954,F 5,14:2
Homeward Look, The 1954,Je 4,26:2
Joan of Lorraine 1955,Mr 26,12:2
Young and Beautiful, The 1955,O 3,23:2
Eugenia 1957,Ja 31,20:1
Sign of Winter 1958,My 8,35:1
Answered the Flute 1960,Mr 10,37:4
Anvil, The 1962,O 31,33:3
Route 1 1964,N 18,52:3
Parasite, The 1965,D 17,43:2
Beyond Desire 1967,O 11,36:1
Certain Young Man, A 1967,D 27,45:1
Goa 1968,F 23,46:1
David Show, The 1968,N 1,34:2
Fig Leaves Are Falling, The 1969,Ja 3,19:1
Barney, Marion
Woman of Bronze, The 1920,S 8,9:2
Trial of Joan of Arc, The 1921,Mr 28,8:2
Sancho Panza 1923,N 27,23:1
Right to Dream, The 1924,My 27,14:2
Habitual Husband, The 1924,D 25,27:3
Aloma of the South Seas 1925,Ap 21,18:1
Butter and Egg Man, The 1925,S 24,28:1
Woman of Bronze, The 1927,Je 16,25:4
Maggie, the Magnificent 1929,O 22,26:1
Philip Goes Forth 1931,Ja 4,VIII,2:2
Philip Goes Forth 1931,Ja 13,35:4
Far Away Horses 1933,Mr 22,21:6
Barney, Violet
Ten Per Cent 1927,S 14,29:3
Front Page, The 1928,Ag 15,19:2
Wild Waves 1932,F 20,11:4
Great Magoo, The 1932,D 3,20:7
Shooting Star 1933,Je 13,22:2
Furnished Rooms 1934,My 30,14:6
Small Miracle 1934,S 27,24:3
Barnhart, Abner
Sunny 1925,S 23,22:1
Barnhart, Robert (Scenic Designer)
Invitation to a Murder 1934,My 18,26:3
While Parents Sleep 1934,Je 5,28:2
Too Many Boats 1934,S 12,26:3
Petticoat Fever 1935,Mr 5,22:2
Two Bouquets, The 1938,Je 1,19:2
Good Morning, Corporal 1944,Ag 9,13:7
Barnicoat, Betty
Scrambled Wives 1920,Ag 6,16:1
Barnini, Pietro (Playwright)
Canto Della Vita, Il; Song of Life, The 1932,Ap 4,13:3
Barnitt, Roy
Three Plays of the Sea 1970,Ag 20,39:1
Barno, Peter
Antony and Cleopatra 1947,N 27,49:2
That Lady 1949,N 23,18:4
Barnolt, Louise
Wildcat, The 1921,N 28,16:2

Barnouw, Erick
Hamlet 1927,Ap 7,23:3
Barnowsky, Victor (Director)
Constant Nymph, The 1927,Ap 24,VII,2:1
Amphitryon 38 1931,Mr 15,IX,2:4
Faust 1932,Je 19,IX,1:3
Martyr Without Tears 1942,N 23,19:2
Iphigenie in Tauris 1949,Ap 9,8:1
Barnowsky, Victor (Producer)
Road to Rome, The 1929,N 10,X,4:8
Sturm im Wasserglas 1930,D 28,VIII,2:4
Royal Family, The 1931,Ap 12,IX,1:3
Braut von Torozko, Die 1932,Je 19,IX,1:6
Rosse 1933,My 7,IX,2:5
As You Like It 1934,N 11,IX,3:6
Barnstead, Margaret
Cyrano de Bergerac 1923,N 2,14:1
One Man's Woman 1926,My 26,25:1
Decision 1929,My 28,37:3
Silver Tassie, The 1929,O 25,26:1
Silver Tassie, The 1929,N 10,X,1:1
Barnum, Francis G Jr
Assorted Nuts 1940,Ap 7,I,44:6
Barnum, George W
Peter Weston 1923,S 20,5:2
Dust Heap, The 1924,Ap 25,20:2
Noose, The 1926,O 21,23:3
Barnum, Jo
Aquashow 1953,Je 24,29:2
Barnwell, Nancy
Schoolhouse on the Lot 1938,Mr 23,18:4
Baron, Al
Louie the 14th 1925,Mr 4,17:1
Desert Song, The 1926,D 1,24:2
Simple Simon 1931,Mr 10,23:2
Laugh Parade, The 1931,N 3,31:2
Alice Takat 1936,F 11,19:2
Hooray for What! 1937,D 2,32:5
Boys and Girls Together 1940,O 2,19:2
Baron, Charles
Just Fancy! 1927,O 12,30:2
Baron, Frank
Story Teller, The 1951,D 15,11:3
Baron, Helen
Awakening of Spring, The 1964,My 13,50:1
Baron, Henry (Playwright)
Tyranny of Love, The 1921,Mr 2,7:3
Rubicon, The 1922,F 22,13:1
My Aunt From Ypsilanti 1923,My 2,22:6
Strong, The 1924,F 27,15:3
Comedienne 1924,O 22,18:1
Bride Retires, The 1925,My 18,12:3
Baron, Henry (Producer)
Weak Woman, A 1926,Ja 27,16:3
Head or Tail 1926,N 10,24:1
Hearts Are Trumps! 1927,Ap 8,21:1
Silver Box, The 1928,Ja 18,23:1
Baron, Howard S
Thespis 1953,Ja 17,13:5
Baron, Julia
Jonica 1930,Ap 8,27:1
Baron, Milton (Miscellaneous)
Shrike, The 1952,Ja 16,20:2
Chase, The 1952,Ap 16,30:2
Baron, Milton (Producer)
Listen Professor! 1943,D 23,22:1
Thank You Svoboda 1944,Mr 2,13:2
Cloud 7 1958,F 15,15:2
Baron, Ray
Cabaret 1966,N 21,62:1
Baron, Samuel
New York Exchange 1926,D 31,11:2
Baron, Sandy
Tchin-Tchin 1962,O 26,26:2
Once in a Lifetime 1964,Ja 29,20:1
Generation 1965,O 8,5:6
Muzeeka 1968,Ap 29,47:2
Baron, Sheldon
Good Soldier Schweik, The 1963,Ap 9,57:1
Billygoat Eddie 1964,Ap 21,43:2
Experiment, The 1967,My 9,54:2
Baron, Shelly (Miscellaneous)
Fantasticks, The 1960,My 4,55:2
Baron, Sydney S (Producer)
Tambourines to Glory 1963,N 4,47:1
Baron, Wilbur
Best Foot Forward 1941,O 2,28:2
Baron, William
Best Foot Forward 1941,O 2,28:2
Lower Depths, The 1956,O 3,29:2
Barondess, Barbara
Crime 1927,F 23,27:3
Garden of Eden, The 1927,S 28,28:1
Barone, Caterina
Dice of the Gods, The 1923,Ap 6,20:2
Barone, Frank (Director)
Hasty Heart, The 1959,S 15,45:2
Barone, Frank (Miscellaneous)
Hasty Heart, The 1959,S 15,45:2
Barone, Frank (Producer)
Hasty Heart, The 1959,S 15,45:2
Baroni, Michelette
Enter Madame 1920,Ag 17,11:2

Baronne, Tisa
Once in a Lifetime 1964,Ja 29,20:1
Baronnet, Philippe
Matter of Days, A 1969,My 20,40:1
Baronova, Irina
Follow the Girls 1944,Ap 10,15:2
Dark Eyes 1948,Mr 25,34:4
Barons, Leon
Flame of Love 1924,Ap 22,19:2
Barova, Mario
Mr Strauss Goes to Boston 1945,S 7,20:2
Barovick, Fred (Composer)
Angel in the Wings 1947,D 12,36:4
Barr, Betty
Tenth Man, The 1929,Mr 21,29:2
Cape Cod Follies 1929,S 19,37:2
Forest Ring, The 1930,Ap 26,11:2
Little Princess, The 1931,F 7,11:3
Racketty Packetty House 1931,N 7,16:1
Barr, David
Road to Rio, The 1930,My 7,25:1
Barr, Edna
Harlem 1929,F 21,30:3
Louisiana 1933,F 28,15:5
Barr, Elinor
Road to Rio, The 1930,My 7,25:1
Barr, Geoffrey
Darkness at Noon 1951,Ja 15,13:4
Barr, George
Journey by Night, A 1935,Ap 17,26:3
Barr, Hazel
Aquashow 1954,Je 23,20:4
Barr, Herbert
Electra 1927,My 4,28:3
Electra 1927,D 2,20:6
Barr, Jeanne
Handful of Fire 1958,O 2,45:3
Sappho 1960,Ja 12,22:1
Barr, Joseph
Taming of the Shrew, The 1956,Ag 11,11:2
Taming of the Shrew, The 1956,Ag 26,II,1:1
Camille 1956,S 19,33:1
Children of Darkness 1958,Mr 1,11:4
Comes a Day 1958,N 7,22:1
Smokeweaver's Daughter, The 1959,Ap 15,30:1
Barr, Julia
Philanderer, The 1958,My 13,26:2
Barr, Kathy
Follies of 1910, The 1960,Ja 15,37:3
Barr, Kenn (Costume Designer)
Gabrielle 1941,Mr 26,26:2
What Big Ears! 1942,Ap 21,18:5
Sun Field, The 1942,D 10,33:2
Toplitzky of Notre Dame 1946,D 27,13:4
Southern Exposure 1950,S 27,36:3
Darkness at Noon 1951,Ja 15,13:4
Angels Kiss Me 1951,Ap 18,37:6
Climate of Eden, The 1952,N 7,20:2
Girls of Summer 1956,N 20,45:1
Warm Peninsula, The 1959,O 21,46:2
Barr, Madelaine
Mariners 1927,Mr 29,22:2
Little Accident 1928,O 10,32:3
Barr, Michael
Schoolgirl 1930,N 21,31:1
Intimate Relations 1932,Mr 29,23:2
Barr, Michael (Composer)
Who's Happy Now? 1969,N 18,39:1
Barr, Patrick
Young Madame Conti 1937,Ap 1,18:4
Barr, Richard (Director)
Volpone 1948,Ja 9,24:6
Angel Street 1948,Ja 23,26:6
On the Harmfulness of Tobacco 1948,F 6,29:2
Bear, The 1948,F 6,29:2
Tragedian in Spite of Himself, A 1948,F 6,29:2
Wedding, The 1948,F 6,29:2
Richard III 1949,F 9,33:2
Richard III 1949,F 13,II,1:1
Ivy Green, The 1949,Ap 6,37:2
Deirdre of the Sorrows 1949,D 15,51:2
Arms and the Man 1950,O 20,34:2
At Home With Ethel Waters 1953,S 23,36:1
Boy With a Cart, The 1954,Ap 5,19:2
Nekros 1960,O 26,44:1
Embers 1960,O 26,44:1
Fam and Yam 1960,O 26,44:1
Private Lives 1968,My 20,59:1
Krapp's Last Tape 1968,O 11,41:1
Zoo Story, The 1968,O 11,41:1
Barr, Richard (Lighting Director)
Richard III 1949,F 9,33:2
Richard III 1949,F 13,II,1:1
Barr, Richard (Miscellaneous)
Volpone 1948,Ja 9,24:6
Zoo Story, The 1960,Ja 15,37:2
Krapp's Last Tape 1960,Ja 15,37:2
Killer, The 1960,Mr 23,33:1
Happy Journey to Trenton and Camden, The 1966,S 7,53:1
Queens of France 1966,S 7,53:1
Long Christmas Dinner, The 1966,S 7,53:1
Delicate Balance, A 1966,S 23,44:1

Barr, Richard (Miscellaneous)—Cont
Match-Play 1966,O 12,37:1
Party for Divorce, A 1966,O 12,37:1
Butter and Egg Man, The 1966,O 18,49:1
Night of the Dunce 1966,D 29,21:1
Rimers of Eldritch, The 1967,F 21,53:1
Party on Greenwich Avenue, The 1967,My 11,52:1
Johnny No-Trump 1967,O 9,60:2
Everything in the Garden 1967,N 30,60:1
Barr, Richard (Producer)
At Home With Ethel Waters 1953,S 23,36:1
Ruth Draper 1954,Ja 26,21:2
All in One; Trouble in Tahiti 1955,Ap 20,40:3
All in One; 27 Wagons Full of Cotton
  1955,Ap 20,40:3
Fallen Angels 1956,Ja 18,27:1
Hotel Paradiso 1957,Ap 12,22:2
Season of Choice 1959,Ap 14,40:1
Sudden End of Anne Cinquefoil, The
  1961,Ja 11,25:2
American Dream, The 1961,Ja 25,28:1
Bartleby 1961,Ja 25,28:1
Death of Bessie Smith, The 1961,Mr 2,19:1
Gallows Humor 1961,Ap 19,35:1
Happy Days 1961,S 18,36:1
Bertha 1962,F 12,27:1
Endgame 1962,F 12,27:1
Mrs Dally Has a Lover 1962,O 2,47:1
Whisper Into My Good Ear 1962,O 2,47:1
Who's Afraid of Virginia Woolf? 1962,O 15,33:1
Who's Afraid of Virginia Woolf? 1962,N 1,34:1
Zoo Story, The 1963,My 29,39:6
American Dream, The 1963,My 29,39:6
Corruption in the Palace of Justice 1963,O 9,49:2
Play 1964,Ja 6,35:1
Lover, The 1964,Ja 6,35:1
Funnyhouse of a Negro 1964,Ja 15,25:3
Play 1964,Mr 25,46:2
Two Executioners, The 1964,Mr 25,46:2
Dutchman 1964,Mr 25,46:2
Giants' Dance, The 1964,N 17,48:2
Tiny Alice 1964,D 30,14:2
Up to Thursday 1965,F 11,45:1
Balls 1965,F 11,45:1
Home Free! 1965,F 11,45:1
Conerico Was Here to Stay 1965,Mr 4,37:1
Pigeons 1965,Mr 4,37:1
Lovey 1965,Mr 26,27:1
Hunting the Jingo Birds 1965,Mr 26,27:1
Do Not Pass Go 1965,Ap 20,44:1
That Thing at the Cherry Lane 1965,My 19,42:1
Happy Days 1965,S 14,45:2
Malcolm 1966,Ja 12,29:1
Boys in the Band, The 1968,Ap 15,48:1
Quotations From Chairman Mao Tse-Tung
  1968,O 1,39:1
Box 1968,O 1,39:1
American Dream, The 1968,O 3,55:1
Death of Bessie Smith, The 1968,O 3,55:1
Zoo Story, The 1968,O 11,41:1
Krapp's Last Tape 1968,O 11,41:1
Happy Days 1968,O 14,54:1
Front Page, The 1969,My 12,54:2
Watercolor 1970,Ja 22,30:1
Criss-Crossing 1970,Ja 22,30:1
Barr Twins, The
Frivolities of 1920 1920,Ja 9,22:2
Cinderella on Broadway 1920,Je 25,18:1
Barra, Vanda
Laughwind 1966,Mr 3,27:1
Barraclough, James
Hamlet 1970,D 28,40:1
Barrajanos, Daniel
Belafonte at the Palace 1959,D 16,55:1
House of Flowers 1968,Ja 29,26:2
But Never Jam Today 1969,Ap 24,40:1
Barrangon, Eloise (Original Author)
Spring Dance 1936,Ag 26,17:4
Barrangon, Eloise (Playwright)
Spring Dance 1936,Jl 7,22:2
Barras, Charles M (Playwright)
Black Crook, The 1929,Mr 12,26:5
Barrat, Maxine
One for the Money 1939,F 6,9:2
Very Warm for May 1939,N 18,23:2
All in Fun 1940,D 28,11:2
Barrat, Robert
Unwritten Chapter, The 1920,O 12,18:1
Breaking Point, The 1923,Ag 17,8:4
Kid Boots 1924,Ja 1,21:3
Chicago 1926,D 31,11:1
Marco Millions 1928,Ja 10,28:2
Lady for a Night, A 1928,Ap 17,26:4
Lady Lies, The 1928,N 27,36:2
Judas 1929,Ja 25,20:4
It's a Grand Life 1930,F 11,30:3
This Is New York 1930,N 29,21:1
Bulls, Bears and Asses 1932,My 7,11:3
Lilly Turner 1932,S 20,26:1
Barratt, Augustus (Composer)
Jack and Jill 1923,Mr 23,17:2
Barratt, Augustus (Lyricist)
Jack and Jill 1923,Mr 23,17:2

Barratt, Louise Bascom (Playwright)
Hot Water 1929,Ja 22,22:3
Barratt, Marty
Love and Politics 1929,O 21,30:7
Barratt, Watson (Costume Designer)
Rivals, The 1941,N 18,32:2
Rivals, The 1942,Ja 15,24:2
With a Silk Thread 1950,Ap 13,34:3
Barratt, Watson (Director)
Lady Has a Heart, The 1937,S 27,24:1
Brigadoon 1962,My 31,21:4
Barratt, Watson (Lighting Director)
With a Silk Thread 1950,Ap 13,34:3
Streetcar Named Desire, A 1956,F 16,24:1
Barratt, Watson (Miscellaneous)
Lady Has a Heart, The 1937,S 27,24:1
Most Happy Fella, The 1959,F 11,50:2
Lute Song 1959,Mr 13,24:1
Barratt, Watson (Producer)
Lady Has a Heart, The 1937,S 27,24:1
Lady Has a Heart, The 1937,O 3,XI,1:1
Wind in the Sails 1940,Ag 1,24:6
Barratt, Watson (Scenic Designer)
Farmer's Wife, The 1924,O 10,22:3
Student Prince, The 1924,D 3,25:3
Princess Flavia 1925,N 3,34:3
Lady's Virtue, A 1925,N 24,28:2
Mayflowers 1925,N 25,14:2
Night in Paris, A 1926,Ja 6,16:3
Great Temptations, The 1926,My 19,29:1
Night in Paris, A 1926,Jl 27,15:4
Countess Maritza 1926,S 20,21:1
Pearl of Great Price, The 1926,N 2,34:3
First Love 1926,N 9,31:2
Gay Paree 1926,N 10,24:2
Padre, The 1926,D 28,16:3
Nightingale, The 1927,Ja 4,20:4
Scarlet Lily, The 1927,Ja 31,12:3
Crown Prince, The 1927,Mr 24,23:2
Cherry Blossoms 1927,Mr 29,22:3
Circus Princess, The 1927,Ap 26,32:2
Mixed Doubles 1927,Ap 27,22:3
Night in Spain, A 1927,My 4,28:2
My Maryland 1927,S 13,37:2
Immoral Isabella 1927,O 28,20:3
Lovely Lady 1927,D 30,22:1
Silent House, The 1928,F 8,28:5
Sunny Days 1928,F 9,29:1
Greenwich Village Follies 1928,Ap 10,32:2
Luckee Girl 1928,S 17,28:6
Young Love 1928,O 31,28:1
Angela 1928,D 4,28:2
Kingdom of God, The 1928,D 21,30:2
Red Robe, The 1928,D 26,15:1
Boom Boom 1929,Ja 29,26:4
Pleasure Bound 1929,F 19,22:4
Music in May 1929,Ap 2,29:1
Love Duel, The 1929,Ap 16,32:3
Night in Venice, A 1929,My 22,30:2
Broadway Nights 1929,Jl 16,23:2
Street Singer, The 1929,S 18,35:2
Wonderful Night, A; Fledermaus, Die
  1929,N 1,23:3
Royal Virgin, The 1930,Mr 18,30:5
Three Little Girls 1930,Ap 15,29:1
Lost Sheep 1930,My 6,33:2
Nina Rosa 1930,My 31,19:3
Artists and Models 1930,Je 11,33:2
Nina Rosa 1930,S 22,22:5
Hello Paris 1930,N 17,29:3
Scarlet Sister Mary 1930,N 26,19:2
Meet My Sister 1930,D 31,11:1
As You Desire Me 1931,Ja 29,21:2
Blossom Time 1931,Mr 5,32:1
Wonder Bar, The 1931,Mr 18,23:4
Peter Ibbetson 1931,Ap 9,30:3
If I Were You 1931,S 24,21:1
Everybody's Welcome 1931,O 14,26:3
Cynara 1931,N 3,31:1
School for Scandal, The 1931,N 26,16:4
Experience Unnecessary 1931,D 31,16:2
Little Racketeer, The 1932,Ja 19,24:4
Smiling Faces 1932,Ag 31,12:3
Ten Minute Alibi 1933,O 18,24:3
Ziegfeld Follies 1934,Ja 5,24:3
No More Ladies 1934,Ja 24,20:3
Perfumed Lady, The 1934,Mr 13,27:2
Bitter Sweet 1934,My 8,28:4
Roman Servant, A 1934,D 3,14:5
So Many Paths 1934,D 7,26:5
Music Hath Charms 1934,D 31,8:2
Living Dangerously 1935,Ja 14,10:3
Laburnum Grove 1935,Ja 15,23:5
Knock on Wood 1935,My 29,16:2
Mid-West 1936,Ja 8,22:4
Lady Precious Stream 1936,Ja 28,15:2
Come Angel Band 1936,F 19,17:1
Case of Clyde Griffiths 1936,Mr 14,10:4
Student Prince, The 1936,Jl 12,II,5:2
Rose Marie 1936,Jl 22,22:6
Blossom Time 1936,Jl 29,23:1
My Maryland 1936,Ag 12,14:2
Florodora 1936,Ag 23,II,8:2

Barratt, Watson (Scenic Designer)—Cont
Bitter Sweet 1936,Ag 26,17:3
Blossom Time 1936,Ag 30,II,5:8
Naughty Marietta 1936,S 2,19:5
Golden Journey, The 1936,S 16,28:6
Laughing Woman, The 1936,O 14,30:1
Green Waters 1936,N 5,34:4
Black Limelight 1936,N 10,31:1
Frederika 1937,F 5,16:5
Hitch Your Wagon! 1937,Ap 9,18:2
Roberta 1937,Je 27,H,6:1
Student Prince, The 1937,Jl 28,15:1
On Your Toes 1937,Ag 3,21:2
Anything Goes 1937,Ag 17,23:4
Nina Rosa 1937,Ag 26,24:3
Anything Goes 1937,Ag 26,24:3
Wise Tomorrow 1937,O 16,22:5
Merely Murder 1937,D 4,21:4
Tell Me Pretty Maiden 1937,D 17,33:5
Three Waltzes 1937,D 27,10:2
Bachelor Born 1938,Ja 26,26:3
Three Waltzes 1938,Je 26,II,7:5
Show Boat 1938,Je 30,21:1
Sally, Irene and Mary 1938,Jl 5,13:4
Firefly, The 1938,Jl 12,15:4
Come Across 1938,S 15,28:3
You Never Know 1938,S 22,26:3
Madame Capet 1938,O 26,26:2
Outward Bound 1938,D 23,16:5
Blossom Time 1938,D 27,12:2
White Steed, The 1939,Ja 11,16:2
Importance of Being Earnest, The 1939,Ja 13,16:2
Close Quarters 1939,Mr 7,19:2
Clean Beds 1939,My 26,21:2
Time of Your Life, The 1939,O 26,26:2
Foreigners 1939,D 6,30:2
Billy Draws a Horse 1939,D 22,14:5
Leave Her to Heaven 1940,F 28,16:2
Love's Old Sweet Song 1940,My 3,16:3
Walk With Music 1940,Je 5,33:2
Time of Your Life, The 1940,S 24,27:2
Romantic Mr Dickens 1940,D 3,33:2
Night of Love 1941,Ja 8,14:2
My Fair Ladies 1941,Mr 24,12:7
Somewhere in France 1941,Ap 29,16:8
Ah, Wilderness! 1941,O 3,26:2
Rivals, The 1941,N 18,32:2
Hope for a Harvest 1941,N 27,28:2
Golden Wings 1941,D 9,46:6
Rivals, The 1942,Ja 15,24:2
Yesterday's Magic 1942,Ap 15,27:2
Magic 1942,S 30,28:2
Hello Out There 1942,S 30,28:2
Little Darling 1942,O 28,26:2
Ask My Friend Sandy 1943,F 5,16:2
This Rock 1943,F 19,23:2
Ziegfeld Follies 1943,Ap 2,16:2
Student Prince, The 1943,Je 9,16:2
Blossom Time 1943,S 6,21:2
Artists and Models 1943,N 6,16:6
Bright Boy 1944,Mr 3,19:5
Sheppey 1944,Ap 19,27:2
Pick-Up Girl 1944,My 4,25:2
Lady Says Yes, A 1945,Ja 11,18:5
Rebecca 1945,Ja 19,17:2
Happily Ever After 1945,Mr 16,21:2
January Thaw 1946,F 5,18:2
Flamingo Road 1946,Mr 20,18:2
Little A 1947,Ja 16,31:2
Heads or Tails 1947,My 3,10:6
Louisiana Lady 1947,Je 3,35:2
Ghosts 1948,F 17,31:2
My Romance 1948,O 20,38:5
With a Silk Thread 1950,Ap 13,34:3
Starcross Story, The 1954,Ja 14,25:2
Time of Your Life, The 1955,Ja 20,34:1
Time of Your Life, The 1955,Ja 30,II,1:1
Righteous Are Bold, The 1955,D 23,12:1
Streetcar Named Desire, A 1956,F 16,24:1
Kiss Me, Kate 1956,My 10,27:2
Beggar's Opera, The 1957,Mr 14,35:1
Barrau, Daniel (Lighting Director)
Diary of a Madman 1967,Mr 24,25:1
Barraud, George
Bulldog Drummond 1921,D 27,10:2
Awful Truth, The 1922,S 19,14:3
Fanatics, The 1927,N 8,32:4
Barrault, Jean-Louis
Numance 1937,Je 13,XI,2:1
Hamlet 1948,S 11,13:3
Baptiste 1952,N 13,34:2
Fausses Confidences, Les 1952,N 13,34:2
Proces, Le; Trial, The 1952,N 18,36:2
Fourberies de Scapin, Les 1952,N 21,21:2
Amphitryon 1952,N 21,21:2
Occupe-Toi d'Amelie; Keep Your Eyes on Amelie
  1952,N 25,35:2
Repetition, La; Rehearsal, The 1952,N 28,22:2
Hamlet 1952,D 2,39:1
Sleep of Prisoners, A 1955,Ja 15,10:5
Sleep of Prisoners, A 1955,F 27,II,3:1
Christophe Colomb 1957,Ja 31,20:5
Volpone 1957,F 5,27:2

Barrault, Jean-Louis—Cont

Misanthrope, Le 1957,F 8,19:1
Nuits de La Colere, Les; Nights of Fury
  1957,F 12,31:1
Intermezzo 1957,F 15,20:4
Adieux, Les 1957,F 19,36:1
Chien du Jardinier, Le; Gardener's Dog, The
  1957,F 19,36:1
Repetition, La 1957,S 3,23:2
Mariage de Figaro, Le 1964,F 26,41:2
Andromaque 1964,F 29,13:2
Salut a Moliere 1964,Mr 4,33:2
Pieton de L'Air, Le 1964,Mr 4,33:2
Vie Parisienne, La 1964,Mr 11,34:2
Happy Days 1965,S 14,45:2
Paravents, Les 1966,Ap 22,36:3
Rabelais 1968,D 20,63:1
Rabelais 1970,My 31,II,1:6
Barrault, Jean-Louis (Choreographer)
Baptiste 1952,N 13,34:2
Barrault, Jean-Louis (Director)
Fausses Confidences, Les 1952,N 13,34:2
Proces, Le; Trial, The 1952,N 18,36:2
Amphitryon 1952,N 21,21:2
Occupe-Toi d'Amelie; Keep Your Eyes on Amelie
  1952,N 25,35:2
Repetition, La; Rehearsal, The 1952,N 28,22:2
Hamlet 1952,D 2,39:1
Christophe Colomb 1957,Ja 31,20:5
Volpone 1957,F 5,27:2
Misanthrope, Le 1957,F 8,19:1
Feu la Mere de Madame; Dear Departed
  Mother-in-Law 1957,F 12,31:1
Nuits de La Colere, Les; Nights of Fury
  1957,F 12,31:1
Intermezzo 1957,F 15,20:4
Adieux, Les 1957,F 19,36:1
Chien du Jardinier, Le; Gardener's Dog, The
  1957,F 19,36:1
Mariage de Figaro, Le 1964,F 26,41:2
Andromaque 1964,F 29,13:2
Salut a Moliere 1964,Mr 4,33:2
Pieton de L'Air, Le 1964,Mr 4,33:2
Vie Parisienne, La 1964,Mr 11,34:2
Journees Entieres dans les Arbres, Des
  1965,D 4,20:1
Rabelais 1970,My 20,32:1
Barrault, Jean-Louis (Playwright)
Trial, The 1947,N 2,II,3:7
On Trial 1949,D 9,35:5
Proces, Le; Trial, The 1952,N 18,36:2
Rabelais 1970,My 20,32:1
Rabelais 1970,My 31,II,1:6
Barrault, Jean-Louis (Producer)
Numance 1937,Je 13,XI,2:1
Pour Lucrece 1953,N 29,II,3:1
Christopher Columbus 1953,N 29,II,3:1
Misanthrope, Le 1957,F 8,19:1
Salut a Moliere 1964,Mr 4,33:2
Paravents, Les 1966,Ap 22,36:3
Barreau
Madame Sans-Gene 1924,N 4,30:1
Barreau, Henriette
Phedre 1963,O 21,39:1
Barrera, Enrique
Cabalgata 1949,Jl 8,14:2
Barrera, Jose
Camino Real 1970,Ja 9,42:1
Barrere, C Francois
All Good Americans 1933,D 6,29:2
Barrere, Gaby
Atout... Coeur 1936,Mr 27,25:4
Martine 1936,N 26,38:2
Dejeuner d'Amoureax, Un; Lovers Breakfast, A
  1936,N 26,38:2
Bichon; Little Dear 1936,D 31,20:5
Sexe Fort, Le; Strong Sex, The 1937,Ja 14,17:4
Si Je Voulais; If I Wished to 1937,Ja 28,22:5
Dans Le Noir; In the Dark 1937,F 11,18:3
Christian 1937,F 25,18:6
Curtain Call 1937,Ap 23,24:7
Barrere, Georges
Clouds of the Sun 1922,My 6,11:2
Vaudeville (Carnegie Hall) 1931,Ap 12,I,30:4
Barrere, Jean
Too Many Heroes 1937,N 16,26:2
Barrere, Jean (Director)
Pajama Game, The 1957,My 16,27:1
Pajama Game, The 1957,My 26,II,1:1
Barrere, Jean (Miscellaneous)
Loud Red Patrick, The 1956,O 4,28:1
Copper and Brass 1957,O 18,19:2
Sunrise at Campobello 1958,Ja 31,25:1
Highest Tree, The 1959,N 5,41:1
Unsinkable Molly Brown, The 1960,N 4,28:1
Devil's Advocate, The 1961,Mr 10,20:1
Something About a Soldier 1962,Ja 5,36:2
Venus at Large 1962,Ap 13,30:1
Tovarich 1963,Mr 20,5:1
Rugantino 1964,F 7,34:1
Hamlet 1964,Ap 10,30:1
Comedy in Music, Opus 2 1964,N 10,54:1
Do I Hear a Waltz? 1965,Mr 19,28:1

Devils, The 1965,N 17,51:2
Barret, James
Good Old Days, The 1951,Jl 18,21:2
Barret, Leslie
Conditioned Reflex 1967,Ja 11,51:1
Barrett, Alan
Trial by Jury 1962,N 23,32:4
Barrett, Albert
Elton Case, The 1921,S 12,16:2
Last Warning, The 1922,O 25,23:1
Barrett, Alvin
Chrysalis 1932,N 16,15:2
Barrett, Bea
Threepenny Opera, The 1955,S 21,38:1
Barrett, E Blanche (Costume Designer)
Enemy of the People, An 1958,F 26,24:2
Barrett, Earl
Romeo and Juliet 1956,F 24,20:4
Barrett, Edith
Trelawney of the 'Wells' 1925,Je 2,16:2
Merchant of Venice, The 1925,D 28,12:1
Cyrano de Bergerac 1926,F 19,18:1
Immortal Thief, The 1926,O 4,21:1
Hamlet 1928,Ja 5,33:2
Caponsacchi 1928,Ja 25,20:3
Phantom Lover, The 1928,S 5,25:1
Becky Sharp 1929,Je 4,29:1
Michael and Mary 1929,D 14,23:3
Mrs Moonlight 1930,S 30,24:3
Troilus and Cressida 1932,Je 7,22:3
Perfect Marriage, The 1932,N 17,23:2
Strange Orchestra 1933,N 29,23:2
Moor Born 1934,Ap 4,26:4
Moor Born 1934,Ap 8,X,2:7
Allure 1934,O 30,22:6
Piper Paid 1934,D 26,19:1
Symphony 1935,Ap 27,20:3
Trelawney of the 'Wells' 1935,Jl 16,24:1
Parnell 1936,My 5,26:2
Wise Tomorrow 1937,O 5,29:2
Wise Tomorrow 1937,O 16,22:5
Shoemaker's Holiday, The 1938,Ja 3,17:2
Shoemaker's Holiday, The 1938,Ja 9,X,1:1
Wuthering Heights 1939,Ap 28,30:4
Barrett, Edwin
Servant in the House, The 1926,My 4,30:1
Barrett, Fenton
Du Barry 1932,N 23,15:2
Barrett, Florence
White Steed, The 1939,Ja 11,16:2
Barrett, Helen
Peter Ibbetson 1926,Mr 26,24:7
Barrett, Irving (Producer)
Birthright 1933,N 22,22:3
Barrett, J D Jr
Faun, The 1924,F 6,19:2
Faun, The 1924,Mr 28,17:2
Galloper, The 1924,D 19,26:2
Aiglon, L' 1925,O 31,20:3
Orestes 1926,Je 20,II,3:6
Barrett, James S
Zander the Great 1923,Ap 10,24:2
Clubs Are Trumps 1924,O 15,27:1
Betty Lee 1924,D 26,18:2
Florida Girl 1925,N 3,34:1
Pyramids 1926,Jl 20,17:2
House of Shadows, The 1927,Ap 22,18:4
White Lights 1927,O 12,30:4
Novice and the Duke, The 1929,D 11,37:2
Secret Garden, The 1931,N 8,31:4
Barrett, Jean
Broadway Whirl, The 1921,Je 9,10:4
Barrett, Jess
Wild Man of Borneo, The 1927,S 14,29:2
Barrett, Joe
Play, A 1925,F 11,19:2
Barrett, Joseph A
Diamond Lil 1928,Ap 10,32:1
Barrett, Katherine
Bernardine 1952,O 17,33:4
Barrett, Laura
Cyrano de Bergerac 1932,D 27,11:2
Cyrano de Bergerac 1936,Ap 28,17:1
Barrett, Laurinda
Merchant of Venice, The 1955,F 23,23:2
Othello 1955,S 8,27:2
Macbeth 1955,O 20,42:2
Midsummer Night's Dream, A 1956,Ja 14,12:2
Miss Julie 1956,F 22,23:2
Too Late the Phalarope 1956,O 12,35:1
Palm Tree in a Rose Garden, A 1957,N 27,26:2
Androcles and the Lion 1958,F 22,8:3
Girls in 509, The 1958,O 16,47:1
Prometheus Bound 1967,My 11,52:1
I Never Sang for My Father 1968,Ja 26,30:1
Fireworks; Football 1969,Je 12,51:1
Fireworks; Fireworks for a Hot Fourth
  1969,Je 12,51:1
Ah, Wilderness! 1969,N 9,86:1
Barrett, Lawrence
Jonah! 1967,S 22,52:2
Barrett, Leonard R
Hamlet 1927,Ap 7,23:3

Barrett, Leonard R—Cont

Caesar and Cleopatra 1927,N 6,IX,2:1
Barrett, Leslie
Sunup to Sundown 1938,F 2,14:3
There's Always a Breeze 1938,Mr 3,16:2
Primrose Path, The 1939,Ja 5,16:3
Primrose Path, The 1939,Ja 16,11:2
Horse Fever 1940,N 25,21:2
Good Neighbor 1941,O 22,26:2
All in Favor 1942,Ja 21,20:6
Counsellor-at-Law 1942,N 25,17:2
Deadfall 1955,O 28,20:1
Trial of Dmitri Karamazov, The 1958,Ja 28,30:1
Lady's Not for Burning, The 1959,Ja 31,13:2
Rhinoceros 1961,Ja 10,27:1
Dragon, The 1963,Ap 10,32:1
Investigation, The 1966,O 5,40:1
Hamp 1967,Mr 10,32:1
Barrett, Lillian (Playwright)
Dice of the Gods, The 1923,Ap 6,20:2
Barrett, Louise
Lovely Lady 1927,D 30,22:1
Remote Control 1929,S 11,24:5
Nine Fifteen Revue, The 1930,F 12,26:2
Barrett, Mace
Girls Against the Boys, The 1959,N 3,26:1
What Makes Sammy Run? 1964,F 28,19:1
Barrett, Malcolm
Richard III 1920,Mr 8,7:1
Jest, The 1926,F 5,22:2
Barrett, Marjorie
Flowering Peach, The 1954,D 29,19:2
Barrett, Mary Jane
Hook-Up, The 1935,My 9,24:6
Middle Man 1936,S 8,23:1
Frederika 1937,F 5,16:5
Barrett, Maurice
Hindu, The 1922,Mr 22,13:3
Straight Thru the Door 1928,O 5,17:2
Inspector Kennedy 1929,D 21,16:3
Old Rascal, The 1930,Mr 25,34:4
Heigh-Ho, Everybody 1932,My 26,31:2
Barrett, Maurice (Director)
Straight Thru the Door 1928,O 5,17:2
Old Rascal, The 1930,Mr 25,34:4
Traitor, The 1930,My 3,23:4
Barrett, Michael
Up the Rebels 1941,O 31,21:1
Johnny on the Spot 1942,Ja 9,24:2
Seven Lively Arts 1944,D 8,26:6
Marinka 1945,Jl 19,19:2
Barrett, Minnette
Lovely Lady 1925,O 15,27:1
Crime Marches on 1935,O 24,19:1
Bat, The 1937,Je 1,27:5
Desire Under the Elms 1952,Ja 17,23:4
Mrs McThing 1952,F 21,22:1
Barrett, Nancy
Telemachus Clay 1963,N 16,17:2
Tragical Historie of Doctor Faustus, The
  1964,O 6,34:2
Barrett, Pat S
Hurricane 1923,D 26,13:4
Up the Line 1926,N 23,26:1
Barrett, Paul
Surgeon, The 1932,O 28,23:1
Barrett, R J
Free Soul, A 1928,Ja 13,26:5
Barrett, Raina
Oh! Calcutta! 1969,Je 18,33:1
Barrett, Raymond
My Golden Girl 1920,F 3,18:2
Phantoms 1930,Ja 14,24:3
American Tragedy, An 1931,F 21,15:5
Barrett, Roger
Penny Change 1963,O 25,37:1
Barrett, Sheila
Experience Unnecessary 1931,D 31,16:2
Thumbs Up! 1934,D 28,24:1
One-Woman Show, A 1962,My 22,31:1
Barrett, Sheila (Playwright)
One-Woman Show, A 1962,My 22,31:1
Barrett, Sketch (Director)
Resounding Tinkle, The 1961,Ap 4,42:2
Barrett, Sketch (Miscellaneous)
Hole, The 1961,Ap 4,42:2
Barrett, Sondra
Pal Joey 1940,D 26,22:2
Let's Face It 1941,O 30,26:2
What's Up 1943,N 12,24:6
Barrett, Virginia
Pleasure Bound 1929,F 19,22:4
Laffing Room Only 1944,D 25,15:4
Barrett, William E (Original Author)
Look to the Lilies 1970,Mr 30,59:1
Barrett James S
Ledge, A 1929,N 19,26:3
Barretta, Louis
Rapid Transit 1927,Ap 8,21:2
Barri, Dario
Dark Is Light Enough, The 1955,F 24,20:1
Six Characters in Search of an Author
  1955,D 12,38:1
Idiot's Delight 1957,F 23,14:2

Mary Stuart 1957,O 9,39:1
Handful of Fire 1958,O 2,45:3
Barrian, Bill
Maggie Flynn 1968,O 24,52:1
Barrick, John
Idiot's Delight 1957,F 23,14:2
Barrie, Ann
Saluta 1934,Ag 29,13:4
Anything Goes 1937,Ag 17,23:4
Anything Goes 1937,Ag 26,24:3
Barrie, Anna Marie
Peter Ibbetson 1931,Ap 9,30:3
Barrie, Barbara
Wooden Dish, The 1955,O 7,20:1
Crucible, The 1958,Mr 12,36:1
Hamlet 1958,Je 21,11:1
Midsummer Night's Dream, A 1958,Je 23,19:1
Winter's Tale, The 1958,Jl 21,17:4
Beaux' Stratagem, The 1959,F 25,35:4
Merry Wives of Windsor, The 1959,Jl 9,23:2
All's Well That Ends Well 1959,Ag 3,20:4
Taming of the Shrew, The 1960,Ag 20,17:1
Miracle Worker, The 1961,Mr 10,22:4
Miracle Worker, The 1961,Ap 1,11:2
Miracle Worker, The 1961,My 1,35:3
Happily Never After 1966,Mr 11,37:1
All's Well That Ends Well 1966,Je 17,39:1
Horseman, Pass By 1969,Ja 16,46:4
Twelfth Night 1969,Ag 14,29:2
Company 1970,Ap 27,40:1
Company 1970,My 3,II,1:4
Barrie, Donald
Battle Hymn 1936,My 23,12:1
Barrie, Elaine
Katy Did So What? 1935,N 6,32:3
Return of Hannibal, The 1937,F 2,21:1
My Dear Children 1939,Mr 25,19:6
Barrie, Eleanor
Ebb Tide 1931,Je 9,33:6
Afternoon Storm 1948,Ap 12,24:2
Barrie, Eleanor A
Twelfth Night 1941,D 3;32:2
Barrie, Florence
Mister Pitt 1924,Ja 23,15:3
Barrie, Frank
Measure for Measure 1967,F 15,37:1
Hamlet 1967,F 17,44:1
Romeo and Juliet 1967,F 22,18:1
Barrie, Gracie
Strike Me Pink 1933,Mr 6,16:3
George White's Scandals 1935,D 26,20:2
Show Is On, The 1936,N 15,XI,2:1
Show Is On, The 1936,D 26,14:2
Crazy With the Heat 1940,D 26,22:1
Crazy With the Heat 1941,Ja 15,18:2
Crazy With the Heat 1941,Ja 31,15:2
Barrie, Hanna Marie
Midsummer Night's Dream, A 1932,N 18,22:2
Barrie, Jack
Caesar and Cleopatra 1925,Ap 14,27:1
Barrie, James M (Original Author)
Maggie 1953,F 19,20:2
Peter Pan 1954,Jl 20,15:3
Peter Pan 1954,O 31,II,1:1
Our Man Crichton 1964,D 23,21:1
Barrie, James M (Playwright)
Admirable Crichton, The 1920,F 29,V,5:3
Mary Rose 1920,My 16,VI,1:7
Mary Rose 1920,Ag 8,VI,1:1
Mary Rose 1920,D 23,9:2
Mary Rose 1920,D 26,VI,3:1
Twelve Pound Look, The 1921,Je 14,18:2
Shall We Join the Ladies? 1921,Je 26,VI,1:1
Shall We Join the Ladies? 1922,Mr 26,VI,1:2
Peter Pan 1924,N 7,16:2
Shall We Join the Ladies? 1925,Ja 14,19:1
Little Minister, The 1925,Mr 24,21:1
What Every Woman Knows 1926,Ap 14,20:2
What Every Woman Knows 1926,Ap 18,VIII,1:1
Legend of Leonora, The 1926,My 1,10:1
Little Theatre Tournament; Half an Hour 1926,My 7,12:2
Dear Brutus 1926,Jl 15,21:3
Old Lady Shows Her Medals, The 1926,O 31,VIII,2:4
Legend of Leonora, The 1927,Mr 30,22:4
Legend of Leonora, The 1927,Ap 3,VIII,1:1
Barbara's Wedding 1927,S 11,VIII,2:4
Vieille Maman, La 1927,N 6,IX,4:1
Peter Pan 1928,Ja 15,VIII,4:6
Little Theatre Tournament; Old Lady Shows Her Medals, The 1928,My 11,28:1
Peter Pan; Boy Who Would Not Grow Up, The 1928,N 27,36:3
What Every Woman Knows 1928,D 2,X,4:4
Shall We Join the Ladies? 1929,Mr 17,30:4
Little Theatre Tournament; Shall We Join the Ladies? 1929,My 9,34:3
Shall We Join the Ladies? 1929,My 12,28:3
Kiss for Cinderella, A 1930,F 1,14:6
Will, The 1930,My 6,33:1
Admirable Crichton, The 1931,Mr 10,23:2
Admirable Crichton, The 1931,Mr 29,VIII,1:1

Barbara's Wedding 1931,O 9,21:1
Alice Sit-By-The-Fire 1932,Mr 8,19:3
Old Lady Shows Her Medals, The 1932,Mr 8,19:3
Twelve Pound Look, The 1934,F 6,24:4
What Every Woman Knows 1936,Jl 21,13:1
Boy David, The 1936,N 22,VI,7:1
Boy David, The 1936,D 13,XI,5:3
Boy David, The 1936,D 15,30:6
What Every Woman Knows 1938,Ag 30,14:5
Boy David, The 1939,Ag 6,IX,2:1
Peter Pan 1941,D 31,22:3
Kiss for Cinderella, A 1942,Mr 11,22:2
Kiss for Cinderella, A 1942,Mr 15,VIII,1:1
What Every Woman Knows 1946,N 9,13:2
Peter Pan 1950,Ap 25,27:2
Peter Pan 1950,Ap 30,II,1:1
Dear Miss Phoebe 1950,O 14,13:8
Mary Rose 1951,Mr 5,25:2
Mary Rose 1951,Mr 11,II,1:1
What Every Woman Knows 1954,S 29,23:4
Peter Pan 1954,O 21,30:2
What Every Woman Knows 1954,D 23,16:2
Penny Friend, The 1966,D 27,46:1
Barrie, Joan
You'll See Stars 1943,Ja 1,26:6
Barrie, Johnne (Miss)
Damaged Goods 1937,My 18,27:2
Barrie, Johnnie
Iron Men 1936,O 20,30:6
Barrie, Lee
Of V We Sing 1942,F 16,20:3
Barrie, Leo
Bloomer Girl 1944,O 6,18:5
Barrie, Leslie
Paradise Alley 1924,Ap 2,17:3
Farmer's Wife, The 1924,O 10,22:3
Just Beyond 1925,D 2,22:4
At Mrs Beam's 1926,Ap 26,24:3
Enchantment 1927,Ap 28,27:3
Taming of the Shrew, The 1927,O 26,26:4
Love Duel, The 1929,Ap 16,32:3
Lady With a Lamp, The 1931,N 20,27:2
Anatomist, The 1932,O 25,24:3
Anything Goes 1934,N 22,26:1
Save Me the Waltz 1938,Mr 1,19:2
Doctor's Dilemma, The 1941,Mr 12,18:2
Strip for Action 1942,O 1,26:2
Climate of Eden, The 1952,N 7,20:2
Quare Fellow, The 1958,N 28,34:1
Barrie, Mona
Virginia 1937,S 3,13:2
Slightly Married 1943,O 26,19:2
Barrie, Richard
Play That on Your Old Piano 1965,O 15,49:1
Barrie, Virginia
Pied Piper of Hamelin, The 1950,Ap 3,19:2
Barrie, Wendy
Morning Star, The 1942,S 15,18:4
Morning Star, The 1942,S 20,VIII,1:1
Barried, Evealine
Glass Slipper, The 1925,O 20,29:1
Barrier, Edgar
Abraham; Dulcitus; Callimachus 1926,Mr 29,24:2
Last Torture, The 1927,Ja 13,28:4
Claw, The 1927,Ja 13,28:4
Butterflies 1927,F 2,22:4
Morgue, The 1927,F 2,22:4
We're All in the Gutter 1927,Mr 5,12:2
Maker of Images, The 1927,Mr 5,12:2
Broken Chain, The 1929,F 21,30:4
Alchemist, The 1931,Je 5,27:1
Lost Boy 1932,Ja 6,24:4
Border-Land 1932,Mr 30,15:5
Men Must Fight 1932,O 15,13:4
Mary of Scotland 1933,N 28,28:3
Twelfth Night 1934,Jl 24,21:1
Bitter Oleander 1935,F 12,24:3
This Is Today 1935,Jl 30,17:2
Paths of Glory 1935,S 27,24:2
Idiot's Delight 1936,Mr 25,25:2
Blow Ye Winds 1937,S 24,17:4
Danton's Death 1938,N 3,26:2
Magnificent Yankee, The 1946,Ja 2,23:6
Magnificent Yankee, The 1946,Ja 23,21:2
Eurydice 1948,O 17,I,67:4
My L A 1951,D 9,87:1
Barrier, Ernestine
On Whitman Avenue 1946,My 9,28:2
Barringer, Michael (Playwright)
Inquest 1931,Jl 19,VIII,1:8
Barringer, Robert
Fools Are Passing Through 1958,Ap 3,24:2
Barrington, Diana
Measure for Measure 1969,Je 13,41:3
Barrington, Douglas
Little Poor Man, The 1925,Ag 6,14:1
Bells, The 1926,Ap 14,20:3
Potiphar's Wife 1928,D 24,10:7
Barrington, Gail
Hate Planters 1933,My 26,24:5
Barrington, John
Good Hunting 1938,N 22,26:5

Barrington, Lewis
Adding Machine, The 1923,Mr 20,24:1
S S Glencairn 1924,N 4,31:4
Odd Man Out 1925,My 26,24:3
Barrington, Lowell (Christ, Louis B Jr) (Miscellaneous)
Ethan Frome 1936,Ja 22,15:2
Barrington, Michael
Portrait of a Queen 1968,F 29,29:1
Conduct Unbecoming 1970,O 13,50:1
Barrington, Victor
Infinite Shoeblack, The 1930,F 18,28:1
Barriscale, Bessie
Skirt, The 1921,N 8,28:1
Barrison, Philip
Girl With Carmine Lips, The 1920,Ag 11,6:1
Pigs 1924,S 2,22:5
Gossipy Sex, The 1927,Ap 20,28:3
Eva the Fifth 1928,Ag 29,19:3
Barron, Arthur
Mecca 1920,O 5,12:2
Barron, Arthur S (Producer)
Judge, The 1958,My 14,36:2
Barron, Bebe (Miscellaneous)
Visit to a Small Planet 1957,F 8,18:1
Barron, Charles
Treasure Girl 1928,N 9,22:1
Barron, Edwin
Much Ado About Nothing 1964,Jl 24,15:2
Measure for Measure 1964,Jl 27,22:3
Barron, Jon
Corner of the Bed, A 1969,F 27,35:2
Barron, Joseph
Confederacy, The 1958,Jl 3,20:1
Barron, Judith
Ziegfeld Follies 1934,Ja 5,24:3
Barron, Louis (Miscellaneous)
Visit to a Small Planet 1957,F 8,18:1
Barron, Patricia
Chief Thing, The 1926,Mr 23,24:2
Triple Crossed 1927,My 6,21:2
Stairs, The 1927,N 8,32:7
Barron, Richard
Heads or Tails 1947,My 3,10:6
Barron, S T
Reflected Glory 1936,S 18,19:5
Barror, Cecil
Devil Came From Dublin, The! 1955,Je 3,27:2
Barrow, Bernard
Hi Ho Figaro 1947,Jl 23,18:8
Barrow, Bernard (Director)
Spiro Who? 1969,My 19,55:1
Barrow, Bernard E
Play of Daniel, The 1958,Ja 3,15:3
Billy Budd 1959,F 28,13:3
Barrow, G Tracy
Bulldog Drummond 1921,D 27,10:2
Barrow, James
Lady With a Lamp, The 1931,N 20,27:2
Barrow, Janet
Black Chiffon 1950,S 28,39:2
Barrow, Margaret
Ice Capades 1958,S 4,33:2
Barrow, Richard
American Tragedy, An 1931,F 21,15:5
Barrow, Susan
Cave Dwellers, The 1961,O 16,34:2
Barrow, Tracy
Richard III 1920,Mr 8,7:1
Skin Game, The 1920,O 21,11:1
White Cargo 1923,N 6,22:2
Merry Wives of Windsor, The 1928,Mr 20,20:1
Dear Old England 1930,Mr 26,24:6
Barrows, Billy
On the Make 1932,My 24,23:2
Barrows, Evelyn
Aries Is Rising 1939,N 22,16:5
Barrows, John (Composer)
Brass Ring, The 1952,Ap 11,19:2
Hamlet 1957,Ja 29,27:1
Barrows, June
Strings, My Lord, Are False, The 1942,My 20,24:2
Barrows, Richard
Bat, The 1920,Ag 24,6:1
If Booth Had Missed 1932,F 5,24:2
Man Who Reclaimed His Head 1932,S 9,17:3
Come Angel Band 1936,F 19,17:1
Happy Valley, Limited 1936,Je 30,15:1
Marching Song 1937,F 18,18:2
Bat, The 1937,Je 1,27:5
Cat and the Canary, The 1937,Je 15,26:3
Barrows, Robert Guy (Director)
Bivouac at Lucca 1957,O 30,26:1
Barrows, Robert Guy (Playwright)
Bivouac at Lucca 1957,O 30,26:1
Barrows, William
Schemers 1924,S 16,27:1
Romeo and Juliet 1940,My 10,27:1
Barroy, Earl
Sally 1920,D 22,16:1
Barroy, Michel
Sancho Panza 1923,N 27,23:1
Homme Qui Assassina, L' 1924,N 11,20:1
Procureur Hallers, Le 1924,N 13,18:1

Barroy, Michel—Cont

Taming of the Shrew, The 1924,N 25,27:3
Grand Street Follies, The 1925,Je 19,24:1
Strange Prince, The 1926,D 8,24:2
Five O'Clock Girl, The 1927,O 11,26:3

Barrs, Norman

John Bull's Other Island 1948,F 11,33:4
Where Stars Walk 1948,F 25,27:2
Now I Lay Me Down to Sleep 1950,Mr 3,21:2
King of Friday's Men, The 1951,F 22,26:2
Little Glass Clock, The 1956,Mr 27,40:2
Apple Cart, The 1956,O 19,23:1
Buoyant Billions 1959,My 27,32:2
Getting Married 1959,Je 5,18:2
Little Moon of Alban 1960,D 2,34:1
Kwamina 1961,O 24,42:1
Poor Bitos 1964,N 16,40:2
Queen and the Rebels, The 1965,F 26,16:1
Zulu and the Zayda, The 1965,N 11,59:1
Hostile Witness 1966,F 18,26:1
Loot 1968,Mr 19,40:2
Little Boxes; Coffee Lace, The 1969,D 4,71:2
Little Boxes; Trevor 1969,D 4,71:2

Barrs, Norman (Director)

My 3 Angels 1956,F 4,24:2
Candida 1957,F 9,14:1

Barry, Ann

Show Boat 1954,My 6,44:1

Barry, Arthur

Cat-Bird, The 1920,F 17,18:1
Cave Girl, The 1920,Ag 19,12:2
Lady Cristilinda, The 1922,D 26,11:2
Little Miss Bluebeard 1923,Ag 29,12:1
Aloma of the South Seas 1925,Ap 21,18:1
Ghost Train, The 1926,Ag 26,17:2
Circus Princess, The 1927,Ap 26,32:2
Macbeth 1928,N 20,28:3
His Majesty's Car 1930,O 24,30:1

Barry, Bobby

He Who Gets Slapped 1946,Mr 21,31:4
Burlesque 1946,D 26,30:3

Barry, Clara

Vaudeville (Palace) 1926,Je 1,29:5
Vaudeville (Palace) 1928,Jl 31,13:5
Vaudeville (Palace) 1929,Ja 21,18:3
Vaudeville (Palace) 1930,S 29,19:1
Vaudeville (Palace) 1932,O 3,15:5

Barry, Dave

Borscht Capades 1951,S 18,38:3

Barry, Donna

Scent of Flowers, A 1969,O 21,42:1

Barry, Dudley

Elizabeth Sleeps Out 1936,Ap 21,27:6

Barry, Edward

Schoolhouse on the Lot 1938,Mr 23,18:4
Shakespeare's Merchant 1939 1939,Ja 10,16:3

Barry, Elaine

Up in Central Park 1945,Ja 29,17:2

Barry, Florence

Damaged Goods 1937,My 18,27:2

Barry, Fred

Up in Central Park 1945,Ja 29,17:2
Ti-Coq 1951,F 10,10:2

Barry, Fred (Miscellaneous)

Ti-Coq 1951,F 10,10:2

Barry, Gene

New Moon, The 1942,Ag 19,14:2
Rosalinda; Fledermaus, Die 1942,O 29,26:5
Merry Widow, The 1943,Ag 5,19:2
Catherine Was Great 1944,Ag 3,16:1
Would-Be Gentleman, The 1946,Ja 10,29:2
Happy as Larry 1950,Ja 7,11:2
Bless You All 1950,D 15,42:2
Perfect Setup, The 1962,O 25,47:1

Barry, George

Ivanov 1958,O 8,42:1
Seagull, The 1962,Mr 22,42:1

Barry, Harold (Playwright)

Return of Sherlock Holmes 1923,O 11,23:7

Barry, J J

From the Second City 1969,O 15,34:1
From the Second City 1969,O 26,III,31:5
White House Murder Case, The 1970,F 19,59:1

Barry, Jane

Cherry Pie 1926,Ap 15,24:4
Trumpet Shall Sound, The 1926,D 11,15:2
Belt, The 1927,O 20,33:1
Centuries, The 1927,N 30,23:1
International, The 1928,Ja 16,24:4
Hoboken Blues 1928,F 18,10:1
Box Seats 1928,Ap 20,27:2

Barry, Jean

Wake Up and Dream 1929,D 31,14:3
Wake Up and Dream 1930,Ja 12,9:1

Barry, Jeff (Composer)

Dirtiest Show in Town, The 1970,Je 29,43:2

Barry, Jimmie

Our Nell 1922,D 5,24:1
Poppy 1923,S 4,14:2
Vaudeville (Palace) 1926,My 4,31:2

Barry, Jimmie (Mr and Mrs)

Vaudeville (Palace) 1927,D 27,25:2

Barry, Jimmie (Mrs)

Our Nell 1922,D 5,24:1

Vaudeville (Palace) 1926,My 4,31:2

Barry, Joan

Gold Diggers, The 1926,D 26,VII,4:3
Mrs Moonlight 1928,D 23,VIII,4:7
Proscenium 1933,Je 15,21:2

Barry, Joanne

Jolly's Progress 1959,D 7,42:2

Barry, John

Simon Called Peter 1924,N 11,20:2
Secret Garden, The 1931,N 8,31:4
Life Begins in '40 1940,Ap 5,24:2

Barry, John D

Savonarola 1942,Ap 24,20:2
Seven Mirrors 1945,O 26,17:2

Barry, Judith

Be So Kindly 1937,F 9,19:4

Barry, Julian

Shinbone Alley 1957,Ap 15,23:2

Barry, Kenneth

Little Princess, The 1931,F 7,11:3

Barry, Lee

Silk Stockings 1955,F 25,17:3

Barry, Lelia

Bonds of Interest, The 1958,My 7,43:1
Tobacco Road 1960,My 11,44:2
Cherry Orchard, The 1962,N 15,46:2

Barry, Leonard

Fun With Music 1946,N 25,38:5
Night Music 1951,Ap 9,29:6

Barry, Leonard (Director)

Saturday Night Kid, The 1958,My 16,22:1

Barry, Leslie

Anything Goes 1937,Ag 26,24:3

Barry, Lloyd

Blind Alley 1935,S 25,19:6
Abe Lincoln in Illinois 1938,O 17,12:2

Barry, Michelle

It's a Bird . . . It's a Plane . . . It's Superman 1966,Mr 30,34:1

Barry, Norville

Passionate Pilgrim, The 1932,O 20,24:3
Before Morning 1933,F 10,13:4

Barry, Patricia

Pink Elephant, The 1953,Ap 23,37:2
Goodbye Again 1956,Ap 25,38:1

Barry, Paul

Burgomaster of Stilemonde, The 1923,N 16,15:3
Hamlet 1923,N 20,23:3
Romeo and Juliet 1961,F 24,24:1
Tiger Tiger Burning Bright 1962,D 24,5:2

Barry, Peter (Composer)

It's All Yours 1942,Mr 26,26:2

Barry, Peter (Lyricist)

It's All Yours 1942,Mr 26,26:2

Barry, Peter (Miscellaneous)

'Tis of Thee 1940,O 28,21:3

Barry, Peter (Playwright)

It's About Time 1942,Mr 31,28:3

Barry, Philip (Playwright)

You and I 1923,F 20,12:1
You and I 1923,F 25,VII,1:1
God Bless Our Home 1924,N 23,VIII,2:4
Youngest, The 1924,D 23,17:1
You and I 1925,O 20,29:1
In a Garden 1925,N 17,29:1
In a Garden 1925,N 22,VIII,1:1
White Wings 1926,O 16,15:1
White Wings 1926,O 24,VIII,1:1
John 1927,N 5,16:4
Paris Bound 1927,D 28,26:3
Paris Bound 1928,Ja 1,VIII,1:1
Cock Robin 1928,Ja 13,26:6
Paris Bound 1928,Ja 15,VIII,1:1
Paris Bound 1928,Jl 1,VIII,3:5
Holiday 1928,N 27,36:1
Holiday 1928,D 9,X,1:1
Paris Bound 1929,My 1,28:6
Paris Bound 1929,My 19,IX,1:8
Paris Bound 1929,Jl 20,8:3
Holiday 1930,F 6,21:2
Hotel Universe 1930,Ap 15,29:1
Hotel Universe 1930,Ap 20,VIII,1:1
Hotel Universe 1930,N 23,IX,1:3
Tomorrow and Tomorrow 1931,Ja 14,26:3
Tomorrow and Tomorrow 1931,Ja 25,VIII,1:1
Tomorrow and Tomorrow 1931,F 1,VIII,2:1
Animal Kingdom, The 1932,Ja 3,VIII,3:1
Animal Kingdom, The 1932,Ja 13,26:4
Animal Kingdom, The 1932,Ja 24,1:1
Joyous Season, The 1934,Ja 30,16:3
Joyous Season, The 1934,F 4,IX,1:1
Bright Star 1935,O 13,IX,1:6
Bright Star 1935,O 16,26:2
Joyous Season, The 1935,N 24,II,9:2
Spring Dance 1936,Jl 7,22:2
Spring Dance 1936,Ag 26,17:4
Animal Kingdom, The 1938,Jl 27,14:5
Here Come the Clowns 1938,D 8,36:2
Here Come the Clowns 1938,D 20,30:2
Philadelphia Story, The 1939,F 17,14:2
Philadelphia Story, The 1939,Mr 19,XI,2:6
Philadelphia Story, The 1939,Mr 29,21:1
Philadelphia Story, The 1939,Ap 2,X,1:1

Barry, Philip (Playwright)—Cont

Liberty Jones 1941,F 6,24:2
Holiday 1941,Jl 23,15:2
Without Love 1942,My 5,20:7
Without Love 1942,Ap 28,17:4
Without Love 1942,N 11,28:1
Without Love 1942,N 29,VIII,1:1
Foolish Notion 1945,Mr 14,23:2
Foolish Notion 1945,Mr 18,II,1:1
My Name is Aquilon 1949,F 10,38:2
Second Threshold 1951,Ja 3,23:2
Second Threshold 1951,Ja 14,II,1:1
Second Threshold 1952,S 25,38:8
Second Threshold 1952,O 12,II,3:7
Second Threshold 1952,N 9,II,3:2
Here Come the Clowns 1954,My 5,36:2
Here Come the Clowns 1960,S 20,48:1
Philadelphia Story, The 1967,Je 21,40:2
Philadelphia Story, The 1967,Je 22,46:4

Barry, Philip Jr (Miscellaneous)

Second Threshold 1951,Ja 3,23:2
Next Time I'll Sing to You 1963,N 28,69:2

Barry, Raymond

Terminal 1970,Ap 15,51:2
Serpent, The 1970,Je 2,35:1

Barry, Richard

Merry Malones, The 1927,S 27,30:2
Billie 1928,O 2,34:2

Barry, Richard (Playwright)

Barefoot 1925,O 20,29:2

Barry, Richard Jones

Measure for Measure 1967,F 15,37:1
Hamlet 1967,F 17,44:1
Romeo and Juliet 1967,F 22,18:1

Barry, Rita

Idiot's Delight 1951,My 24,46:3

Barry, Robert

Saint of Bleecker Street, The 1954,D 28,21:1
Brass Butterfly, The 1970,Ja 31,34:1

Barry, Rod

Leonard Sillman's New Faces of 1968 1968,My 3,43:1

Barry, Rodd

Yearling, The 1965,D 11,25:1

Barry, Roy

Yearling, The 1965,D 11,25:1

Barry, Sheila

Walk-Up 1961,F 24,24:1

Barry, Sylvia

Off Your Marx 1936,Ap 2,28:2

Barry, Thomas

Carousel 1965,Ag 11,39:1

Barry, Tom

Mexican Mural; Moonlight Scene 1942,Ap 27,19:2

Barry, Tom (Playwright)

Dawn 1924,O 19,VIII,2:6
Dawn 1924,N 25,27:1
Immortal Thief, The 1926,O 4,21:1
Courage 1928,O 9,34:2
Danger 1935,Ag 27,23:4

Barry, Vivian

Of Thee I Sing 1931,D 28,20:1
Let 'Em Eat Cake 1933,O 23,18:1

Barry, William

Simon Called Peter 1924,N 11,20:2
Free Soul, A 1928,Ja 13,26:5
Everything's Jake 1930,Ja 17,20:4
Anything Goes 1934,N 22,26:1
Little Inn, The 1935,Ag 20,25:1
Mr and Mrs North 1941,Ja 13,11:2

Barry, William E (Playwright)

Jade God, The 1929,My 14,28:3
Zoom 1932,Ja 31,VIII,I:8
Happy Landing 1932,Mr 28,10:5
Prodigal Father, The 1937,Ag 17,23:1

Barry, Winifred

Skull, The 1928,Ap 24,28:3
Elmer Gantry 1928,Ag 10,9:4
Mystery Moon 1930,Je 24,23:4

Barry, Zoe

Polly 1925,O 12,19:1

Barry and Ross

Harry Delmar's Revels 1927,N 29,30:2

Barry and Whitlege

Vaudeville (Palace) 1929,D 16,34:4
Vaudeville (Palace) 1930,S 29,19:1
Vaudeville (Palace) 1932,Ja 4,27:4

Barry Sisters

Borscht Capades 1951,S 18,38:3

Barrymore, Diana

Romantic Mr Dickens 1940,D 3,33:2
Happy Days 1941,My 14,24:2
Land Is Bright, The 1941,O 21,28:5
Land Is Bright, The 1941,O 29,26:2
Land Is Bright, The 1941,N 9,IX,1:1
Rebecca 1944,Ap 30,II,1:1
Rebecca 1945,Ja 19,17:2
Rebecca 1945,Ja 28,II,1:2
Hidden Horizon 1946,S 20,42:2
Ivory Branch, The 1956,My 25,27:1

Barrymore, Ethel

Clair de Lune 1921,Ap 19,15:1
Clair de Lune 1921,Ap 24,VI,1:1
Twelve Pound Look, The 1921,Je 14,18:2

Barrymore, Ethel—Cont
Vaudeville (Palace) 1921,Je 14,18:2
Rose Bernd 1922,S 27,17:1
Rose Bernd 1922,O 1,VII,1:1
Rose Bernd 1922,O 8,VI,1:2
Rose Bernd 1922,O 8,VI,1:1
Romeo and Juliet 1922,D 28,20:1
Laughing Lady, The 1923,F 13,25:1
Laughing Lady, The 1923,F 18,VII,1:1
School for Scandal, The 1923,Je 5,24:3
Royal Fandango, A 1923,N 11,VIII,2:6
Royal Fandango, A 1923,N 13,25:1
Royal Fandango, A 1923,N 18,VIII,1:1
Untitled-Recital 1923,D 29,8:2
Second Mrs Tanqueray, The 1924,S 28,VII,2:1
Second Mrs Tanqueray, The 1924,O 19,VIII,1:1
Second Mrs Tanqueray, The 1924,O 19,VIII,1:1
Second Mrs Tanqueray, The 1924,N 2,VII,1:1
Hamlet 1925,O 12,19:2
Merchant of Venice, The 1925,D 28,12:1
Hamlet; Merchant of Venice, The 1926,Ja 3,VII,1:1
Vaudeville (Palace) 1926,S 14,25:3
Constant Wife, The 1926,N 14,VIII,5:1
Constant Wife, The 1926,N 30,26:3
Constant Wife, The 1926,D 12,VIII,3:1
Vaudeville (Palace) 1926,D 28,12:3
Kingdom of God, The 1928,O 14,X,1:3
Kingdom of God, The 1928,D 21,30:2
Kingdom of God, The 1928,D 30,VIII,1:1
Love Duel, The 1929,Ap 16,32:3
Scarlet Sister Mary 1930,O 5,IX,4:6
Scarlet Sister Mary 1930,N 26,19:2
School for Scandal, The 1931,N 11,26:4
Twelve Pound Look, The 1934,F 6,24:4
Laura Garnett 1934,Jl 17,24:4
Aiglon, L' 1934,N 5,22:2
Constant Wife, The 1935,Jl 3,20:2
Silver Box, The 1935,Jl 16,24:2
Declassee 1935,Ag 6,20:3
Ghost of Yankee Doodle, The 1937,O 28,28:5
Ghost of Yankee Doodle, The 1937,N 7,XI,2:4
Ghost of Yankee Doodle, The 1937,N 23,26:3
Whiteoaks 1938,F 23,26:2
Whiteoaks 1938,Mr 24,20:2
Whiteoaks 1939,Ap 30,XI,2:2
Farm of Three Echoes 1939,N 29,18:3
Farm of Three Echoes 1939,D 3,IX,5:4
International Incident, An 1940,Mr 21,30:3
International Incident, An 1940,Ap 3,18:2
School for Scandal, The 1940,Je 18,29:5
School for Scandal, The 1940,Je 23,IX,1:1
Corn Is Green, The 1940,N 27,27:2
Corn Is Green, The 1940,D 1,X,1:1
Corn Is Green, The 1943,My 4,18:3
Corn Is Green, The 1943,My 9,II,1:1
Embezzled Heaven 1944,S 30,17:3
Embezzled Heaven 1944,N 1,20:2
Embezzled Heaven 1944,N 5,II,1:2
ANTA Album 1950,Ja 30,13:2
Barrymore, Ethel (Director)
Kingdom of God, The 1928,D 21,30:2
Love Duel, The 1929,Ap 16,32:3
Scarlet Sister Mary 1930,N 26,19:2
School for Scandal, The 1931,N 11,26:4
Barrymore, Ethel (Producer)
School for Scandal, The 1931,N 22,VIII,3:1
School for Scandal, The 1940,Je 23,IX,1:1
Barrymore, John
Jest, The 1920,F 1,VIII,2:2
Richard III 1920,Mr 8,7:1
Richard III 1920,Mr 21,VI,6:1
Clair de Lune 1921,Ap 19,15:1
Clair de Lune 1921,Ap 24,VI,1:1
Untitled-Benefit 1921,My 2,12:3
Hamlet 1922,N 17,14:1
Hamlet 1922,N 26,VIII,1:1
Hamlet 1922,D 17,VII,1:1
Hamlet 1923,Ja 14,VII,1:1
Hamlet 1923,Ap 22,VII,1:1
Hamlet 1923,N 27,23:6
Hamlet 1925,F 20,20:1
Hamlet 1925,Mr 29,VIII,1:1
My Dear Children 1939,Mr 25,19:6
My Dear Children 1939,My 3,26:4
My Dear Children 1939,S 10,IX,1:6
My Dear Children 1940,F 1,16:2
My Dear Children 1940,F 11,IX,1:1
Barrymore, John (Mrs)
Importance of Being Earnest, The 1925,Jl 28,24:2
Barrymore, John (Producer)
Hamlet 1923,N 25,VIII,1:1
Hamlet 1925,F 20,20:1
Barrymore, Lionel
Letter of the Law, The; Robe Rouge, La 1920,F 24,11:1
Letter of the Law, The 1920,F 29,V,5:1
Macbeth 1921,F 18,16:1
Macbeth 1921,F 20,VI,1:1
Macbeth 1921,F 27,VI,1:1
Claw, The 1921,O 2,VII,1:8
Claw, The 1921,O 18,20:1
Macbeth 1921,N 11,VII,1:1
Laugh, Clown, Laugh! 1923,O 28,VIII,2:1
Laugh, Clown, Laugh! 1923,N 29,30:1

Laugh, Clown, Laugh! 1923,D 9,IX,1:1
Piker, The 1925,Ja 16,14:1
Taps 1925,Ap 15,16:2
Man or Devil 1925,My 22,22:4
Barrys, The
Priorities of 1942 1942,Mr 13,23:2
Barsacq, Andre
Bal des Voleurs, Le 1938,N 29,26:4
Faiseur, Le; Promoter, The 1938,D 27,12:3
Chacun Sa Verite 1939,Ja 24,17:1
Enterrement, L' 1939,F 7,17:2
37 Sous de M Montaudoin, Les 1939,F 7,17:2
Siegfried 1939,F 21,15:2
Barsacq, Andre (Costume Designer)
Volpone 1957,F 5,27:2
Barsacq, Andre (Director)
Roi Cerf, Le 1937,N 30,26:3
Jean de la Lune 1937,D 14,33:3
Nationale 6 1938,Ja 11,26:6
Y'Avait un Prisonnier 1938,Ja 25,24:3
Caprice, Un 1938,F 8,17:2
Fantasio 1938,F 8,17:2
Bal des Voleurs, Le 1938,N 29,26:4
37 Sous de M Montaudoin, Les 1939,F 7,17:2
Enterrement, L' 1939,F 7,17:2
Siegfried 1939,F 21,15:2
Good Soup, The 1960,Mr 3,26:4
Berenice 1963,O 30,46:1
Piano Dans l'Herbe, Un 1970,S 17,56:1
Barsacq, Andre (Producer)
Jean de la Lune 1937,D 14,33:3
Barsacq, Andre (Scenic Designer)
Jalousie du Barbouille, La 1937,D 28,28:7
Chacun Sa Verite 1939,Ja 24,17:1
Enterrement, L' 1939,F 7,17:2
37 Sous de M Montaudoin, Les 1939,F 7,17:2
Volpone 1957,F 5,27:2
Barschi, Vivian
Audition of the Apprentice Theatre 1939,Je 2,26:2
Barse, Howard (Playwright)
All in Fun 1940,D 28,11:2
Barsha, Tony (Director)
Hawk, The 1968,Ap 18,54:1
Barsha, Tony (Playwright)
Hawk, The 1968,Ap 18,54:1
Barshay, Don
Twelfth Night 1968,Je 15,40:1
Serjeant Musgrave's Dance 1968,Je 16,52:4
Resistible Rise of Arturo Ui, The 1968,Ag 8,25:1
House of Atreus, The 1968,D 18,55:1
Resistible Rise of Arturo Ui, The 1968,D 23,44:1
Barshinger, H S
Don Quixote, Esquire 1920,My 7,12:6
Barsness, Larry
Venice Preserv'd 1955,D 13,54:4
Barso, Abe
Professor Mamlock 1937,Ap 14,30:3
Barsony, Rosy
Flower of Hawaii; Blume von Hawaii, Die 1931,O 4,VIII,4:1
Ball at the Savoy 1933,F 19,IX,3:1
Barstow, Edith (Choreographer)
Hell'z-A-Splashin' 1959,Je 25,22:2
Barstow, Edith (Director)
Hell'z-A-Splashin' 1959,Je 25,22:2
Barstow, Paul R
Merry Wives of Windsor, The 1954,F 17,27:1
New York Idea, The 1963,Jl 13,12:2
Barstow, Richard (Choreographer)
Barefoot Boy With Cheek 1947,Ap 4,20:2
Tonight at 8:30; Red Peppers 1948,F 21,8:2
Tonight at 8:30; Ways and Means 1948,F 21,8:2
Tomight at 8:30; Family Album 1948,F 21,8:2
Tonight at 8:30; Fumed Oak 1948,F 24,20:4
Tonight at 8:30; Hands Across the Sea 1948,F 24,20:4
Tonight at 8:30; Shadow Play 1948,F 24,20:4
Sally 1948,My 7,31:2
New Faces of 1952 1952,My 17,23:2
Judy Garland 1959,My 12,40:1
This Was Burlesque 1970,F 12,31:1
Barstow, Richard (Director)
Judy Garland 1959,My 12,40:1
Song of Norway 1959,Je 26,16:2
At Home at the Palace 1967,Ag 1,23:1
This Was Burlesque 1970,F 12,31:1
Barstow, William
Bon-bon 1920,Mr 1,16:2
Lenore 1920,Mr 1,16:3
Barstow, William (Playwright)
Lenore 1920,Mr 1,16:3
Bon-bon 1920,Mr 1,16:2
Barszczewska
Women's House, The 1930,Ap 27,IX,3:1
Bart, Harry
Folly Town 1920,My 18,9:2
Bart, Jean (Playwright)
Squall, The 1926,N 12,20:1
Squall, The 1927,D 4,X,1:3
Woman Denied, A 1931,F 26,21:1
Man Who Reclaimed His Head 1932,S 9,17:3
Bart, Lionel (Composer)
Blitz 1962,My 8,5:6

Bart, Lionel (Composer)—Cont
Strada, La 1969,D 15,63:1
Bart, Lionel (Lyricist)
Strada, La 1969,D 15,63:1
Bart, Lionel (Playwright)
Oliver 1962,S 27,32:3
Oliver 1963,Ja 8,5:5
Twang 1965,D 22,24:8
Bart and Mann
Dance of Death, The 1932,Ja 11,29:5
Barte, Leon
Gay Paree 1925,Ag 19,14:3
Barte, Louis
Machine Wreckers, The 1937,Ap 12,14:2
Bartel, Christina
Carnival! 1968,D 13,58:1
Bartel, Jean
Desert Song, The 1946,Ja 9,20:2
Bartel, Louis John (Playwright)
Show-Off, The 1924,Mr 16,VIII,1:1
Bartell, Richard
Evil Doers of Good, The 1923,Ja 17,22:2
Ragged Army 1934,F 27,16:5
Good Men and True 1935,O 26,12:4
Every Man for Himself 1940,D 10,32:3
Bartell, Victor
Don't Go Away Mad 1949,My 10,28:2
Bartels, Louis John
Show-Off, The 1924,F 6,16:2
Five O'Clock Girl, The 1927,O 11,26:3
Bartenieff, George
Whole World Over, The 1947,Mr 28,28:2
Tom Sawyer - Ballad of the Mississippi 1947,D 27,11:3
Montserrat 1949,O 31,21:4
When I Was a Child 1960,D 9,38:1
Brig, The 1963,My 16,40:1
Softly, and Consider the Nearness 1964,My 12,32:1
Home Movies 1964,My 12,32:1
Krapp's Last Tape 1965,Je 9,42:3
Zoo Story, The 1965,Je 9,42:3
All's Well That Ends Well 1966,Je 17,39:1
Walking to Waldheim 1967,N 11,25:2
Line of Least Existence, The 1968,Mr 25,53:1
Memorandum, The 1968,My 6,55:1
Quotations From Chairman Mao Tse-Tung 1968,O 1,39:1
Death of Bessie Smith, The 1968,O 3,55:1
Bacchae, The 1969,Mr 15,24:1
Home Fires 1969,Ap 8,42:1
Increased Difficulty of Concentration, The 1969,D 5,48:1
Room Service 1970,My 13,49:1
Room Service 1970,My 24,II,1:1
Trelawny of the 'Wells' 1970,O 12,48:1
Barter, George
Horse Eats Hat 1936,S 28,14:2
Barter, Theodore (Producer)
Lady Lies, The 1928,N 27,36:2
Bartfield, Carl (Original Author)
There You Are! 1932,My 17,25:4
Barth, Diana
Carefree Tree, The 1955,O 12,37:2
Barth, Gene (Costume Designer)
Tartuffe 1957,O 9,39:1
Miss Emily Adam 1960,Mr 30,43:1
Ronde, La 1960,My 10,44:2
Barth, Mr
Manhattan Mary 1927,S 27,30:3
Barthel, Otto
Devil's Little Game, The 1932,Ag 2,20:4
Barthelmess, Mary
Letters to Lucerne 1941,D 9,47:6
Letters to Lucerne 1941,D 24,14:2
Ramshackle Inn 1944,Ja 6,17:5
Barthelmess, Richard
Lambs Gambol 1925,Ap 27,15:1
Postman Always Rings Twice, The 1936,F 7,14:4
Postman Always Rings Twice, The 1936,F 26,17:2
Bartholomae, Philip (Director)
Tomorrow 1928,D 29,20:2
Bartholomae, Philip (Playwright)
Tangerine 1921,Ag 10,8:2
Personality 1921,Ag 29,14:3
Barnum Was Right 1923,Mr 13,19:3
Kitty's Kisses 1926,My 7,12:2
Bartholomew, Charles
Happy-Go-Lucky 1920,Ag 25,6:1
Bartholomew, Frank (Miscellaneous)
All by Myself 1964,Je 16,47:1
Bartholomew, Freddie
Red Peppers; Tonight at Eight 1940,Ag 6,15:3
Tonight at 8:30 1940,Ag 11,IX,11:2
Bartholomew, Mary Lou
Mikado, The 1942,F 4,22:2
Pirates of Penzance, The 1942,F 18,22:2
Iolanthe 1942,F 24,26:4
Gondoliers, The 1942,Mr 4,22:3
Bartholot, A L
Left Bank, The 1931,O 6,35:3
Bartik, Otokar (Director)
Pierrot the Prodigal; Enfant Prodigue, L' 1925,Mr 7,8:1

Bartis, John
I Feel Wonderful 1954,O 19,22:5
Shoestring '57 1956,N 6,31:1
Bartle, Barry
As You Like It 1963,Jl 17,19:2
Bartlett, Basil
Within the Gates 1934,F 8,14:4
Bartlett, Basil (Playwright)
Policeman's Holiday 1936,Ap 6,18:7
Bartlett, Basil (Translator)
Asmodee 1939,My 28,X,1:6
Bartlett, Bonnie
Natural Affection 1963,F 2,5:2
Telemachus Clay 1963,N 16,17:2
Lemon Sky 1970,My 18,40:1
Bartlett, Charles
Genius and the Crowd 1920,S 7,20:1
Bartlett, Dale S
House With the Twisty Windows, The
1930,My 8,32:5
Bartlett, E A
Man From Earth, The 1923,Ja 3,6:2
Bartlett, Elise
Scrambled Wives 1920,Ag 6,16:1
Adding Machine, The 1923,Mr 20,24:1
Houses of Sand 1925,F 18,17:1
Nirvana 1926,Mr 4,19:1
Pagan Lady 1930,O 21,34:2
Bulls, Bears and Asses 1932,My 7,11:3
Bartlett, Ellen
Centuries, The 1927,N 30,23:1
Bartlett, Geraldyne
Love's Call 1925,S 11,20:1
Bartlett, James
Half Moon Inn 1925,Mr 10,14:1
Samarkand 1926,D 22,24:4
Bartlett, Jud
Beautiful Dreamer 1960,D 28,22:1
Bartlett, Lawrence
House With the Twisty Windows, The
1930,My 8,32:5
Bartlett, Lois
Richard III 1920,Mr 8,7:1
Wake Up, Jonathan 1921,Ja 18,14:1
Bartlett, Martine
Devil's Disciple, The 1950,Ja 26,23:2
Square Root of Wonderful, The 1957,O 31,40:1
Sweet Bird of Youth 1959,Mr 11,39:2
Sweet Bird of Youth 1959,Mr 22,II,1:1
Garden of Sweets, The 1961,N 1,35:1
Bartlett, Michael
Through the Years 1932,Ja 29,13:3
School for Husbands, The 1933,O 17,26:5
Three Waltzes 1937,N 15,15:6
Three Waltzes 1937,D 27,10:2
Susanna, Don't You Cry 1939,My 23,27:2
Bartlett, Richard
Idiot's Delight 1937,Ag 10,22:7
Bartlett, William C
Spread Eagle 1935,N 5,33:6
Bartley, Betty
Across the Board on Tomorrow Morning
1942,Mr 21,13:5
Theatre of the Soul 1942,Mr 21,13:5
Twentieth Century 1950,D 25,23:6
Cyrano de Bergerac 1953,N 13,24:3
Time of Your Life, The 1955,Ja 20,34:1
Bartley, Thomas
Last Man In, The 1930,My 8,32:5
Barto, Betty Lou
As the Girls Go 1948,N 15,21:2
Barto, Britt
White Cargo 1960,D 30,12:1
Barto and Mann
Vaudeville (Palace) 1927,N 1,20:3
Earl Carroll's Vanities 1928,Ag 7,25:2
Vaudeville (Palace) 1929,Mr 11,22:5
New Hellzapoppin, The 1939,D 12,36:4
Bartoli, Yolanda
Pale Horse, Pale Rider 1957,O 30,26:1
Bartolot, A L
Patriarch, The 1929,N 26,28:5
Green Grow the Lilacs 1931,Ja 27,21:2
Bartolot, Al
Swing Your Lady 1936,O 19,22:4
Barton, Arthur (Director)
Man Bites Dog 1933,Ap 26,11:2
Barton, Arthur (Playwright)
Wonder Boy 1931,O 24,20:1
Man Bites Dog 1933,Ap 26,11:2
Sky's the Limit, The 1934,D 18,25:5
Barton, Barbara
Call Me Ziggy 1937,F 13,9:6
Up the Rebels 1941,O 31,21:1
Barton, Barton
Sunny River 1941,D 5,28:2
Barton, Donald
Design For A Stained Glass Window
1950,Ja 24,26:2
Goldilocks 1958,O 13,33:1
Where's Charley? 1966,My 26,57:1
Barton, Dora
Scrapped 1927,O 16,IX,2:7

Distaff Side, The 1933,S 24,X,1:6
Barton, Edward
Tarot 1970,D 12,19:1
Barton, Eileen
Angel in the Wings 1947,D 12,36:4
Barton, Fred
Bell for Adano, A 1944,D 7,21:2
Mister Roberts 1948,F 19,27:2
Barton, Frederick
Russet Mantle 1936,Ja 17,15:5
Barton, Gary
Unknown Soldier and His Wife, The 1967,Jl 7,22:1
Barton, Gertrude
Greatest Show on Earth, The 1938,Ja 6,22:2
Barton, Homer
Teaser, The 1921,Jl 28,8:3
Easy Terms 1925,S 23,22:2
Tragic 18 1926,O 11,18:2
19th Hole, The 1927,O 12,30:3
Good Earth, The 1932,O 18,23:4
Going Gay 1933,Ag 4,18:5
False Dreams, Farewell 1934,Ja 16,18:3
Barton, James
Last Waltz, The 1921,My 11,20:3
Friars Club Frolic 1921,Je 13,16:2
Rose of Stamboul, The 1922,My 8,11:2
Untitled-Benefit 1922,My 8,14:5
Dew Drop Inn 1923,My 18,26:4
Passing Show of 1924, The 1924,S 4,13:4
No Foolin' 1926,Je 25,25:1
Vaudeville (Palace) 1928,Mr 20,20:2
Vaudeville (Palace) 1928,Mr 27,30:5
Vaudeville (Palace) 1928,Ap 3,32:5
Vaudeville (Palace) 1928,Jl 31,13:5
Vaudeville (Palace) 1928,Ag 7,25:5
Vaudeville (Palace) 1928,Ag 14,15:5
Vaudeville (Palace) 1928,Ag 21,27:5
Vaudeville (Palace) 1929,F 18,29:1
Artists and Models 1930,S 28,VIII,2:5
Sweet and Low 1930,N 18,28:5
Vaudeville (Palace) 1931,My 18,21:1
Vaudeville (Palace) 1931,My 25,17:4
Vaudeville (Palace) 1931,O 19,28:5
Vaudeville (Palace) 1932,Ap 4,13:4
Tobacco Road 1934,Je 20,24:1
Tobacco Road 1940,D 5,32:3
Brights Lights of 1944 1943,S 17,27:4
Iceman Cometh, The 1946,O 10,31:3
Paint Your Wagon 1951,N 13,32:2
Paint Your Wagon 1951,N 18,II,1:1
Sin of Pat Muldoon, The 1957,Mr 14,35:1
Barton, John
Tobacco Road 1938,N 27,IX,3:4
Tobacco Road 1942,S 7,34:2
Tobacco Road 1943,S 6,21:3
Hollow Crown, The 1963,Ja 31,5:1
Barton, John (Director)
Taming of the Shrew, The 1960,Je 22,29:1
Hollow Crown, The 1963,Ja 31,5:1
Wars of the Roses, The; Henry VI; Richard III
1964,Ja 14,24:7
Troilus and Cressida 1968,Ag 9,30:5
Troilus and Cressida 1969,Jl 31,26:1
Barton, John (Miscellaneous)
Wars of the Roses, The 1963,Jl 18,14:1
King Lear 1964,My 19,43:2
Barton, John (Playwright)
Hollow Crown, The 1963,Ja 31,5:1
Twelfth Night 1969,S 1,13:1
Barton, John (Producer)
Measure for Measure 1970,Ap 5,71:1
Barton, Kathryn (Mrs James Barton)
Brights Lights of 1944 1943,S 17,27:4
Barton, Kit
Winners and Losers 1947,F 27,27:2
Barton, Larry
On Borrowed Time 1953,F 11,34:1
Caine Mutiny Court-Martial, The 1953,O 14,35:1
Barton, Margaret
Dear Ruth 1946,Mr 1,17:3
Barton, Michael
Moon on a Rainbow Shawl 1962,Ja 16,30:1
Bead-Tangle 1970,Jl 16,38:1
Barton, Mike
Long Voyage Home, The 1961,D 5,49:1
Barton, Ottilia
Rose of Stamboul, The 1922,Mr 8,11:2
Barton, Paul (Playwright)
Anybody's Game 1932,D 22,21:4
Barton, Reyner
Father, The 1931,O 9,21:1
Barton, Trumbull
Barchester Towers 1937,D 1,27:1
Barton, Virginia
Trojan Women, The 1941,Ap 9,32:5
Barton, Wilhelmina
Weep for the Virgins 1935,D 2,18:1
Barton, Willard
Cradle Snatchers 1925,S 8,28:2
Barton Brothers
Bagels and Yox 1951,S 13,38:2

Bartone, Jacqueline
Crime and Crime 1963,D 17,51:2
Bartour, William (Director)
Elizabeth the Queen 1941,O 17,27:2
Bartov, Hanoch (Playwright)
Each Had Six Wings 1964,Mr 12,39:1
Bartow, Art
Ben Franklin in Paris 1964,O 28,52:1
Bartow, Arthur
Sensations 1970,O 26,48:2
Bartram, Bert
Wild Duck, The 1951,D 27,17:1
Bartron, Robert
I Want a Policeman! 1936,Ja 15,15:5
Wuthering Heights 1939,Ap 28,30:4
Bartrop, Sybil
Grosse Valise, La 1965,D 15,52:1
Bartsch, Hans (Miscellaneous)
Chocolate Soldier, The 1947,Mr 13,34:2
Bartsch, Hans (Producer)
Chocolate Soldier, The 1942,Je 24,22:2
Merry Widow, The 1942,Jl 16,22:1
Barty, Ginia
Trois Jeunes Filles Nues; Three Young Maids From
the Folies Bergere 1929,Mr 5,28:2
Passionement; Passionately 1929,Mr 8,31:4
Comte Obligado 1929,Mr 12,26:2
Ta Bouche 1929,Mr 15,28:5
Bon Garcon, Un 1929,Mr 19,36:2
Pas Sur La Bouche; Not on the Lips
1929,Mr 26,34:3
Baruch, David
Each Had Six Wings 1964,Mr 12,39:1
Baruch, Donald E (Producer)
I Myself 1934,My 10,24:6
Little Shot 1935,Ja 18,28:4
Noble Prize, The 1935,Jl 9,24:3
She Cried for the Moon 1935,Jl 23,24:3
Abide With Me 1935,N 22,19:2
Hitch Your Wagon! 1937,Ap 9,18:2
Baruch, E DeMarnay (Playwright)
Judith of Israel 1928,F 17,24:2
Judith of Israel 1928,Mr 18,IX,4:8
Barwald, William
Antony and Cleopatra 1937,N 11,30:2
Barwald, William H
Poldekin 1920,S 10,12:1
Edgar Allan Poe 1925,O 6,31:1
Command Performance, The 1928,O 4,27:1
Sherlock Holmes 1929,N 26,28:3
Life Is Like That 1930,D 23,24:3
Judgment Day 1934,S 13,26:4
Barwald, William J
Head or Tail 1926,N 10,24:1
Barzel, Istar
If I Were You 1931,S 24,21:1
Barzel, Wolf
Relations 1928,Ag 21,27:3
Chair, The 1930,O 4,15:4
God's Thieves 1930,O 27,17:4
Salt and Pepper 1933,Ap 24,10:2
Back Streets 1933,My 18,17:4
In-Laws 1934,O 25,28:2
60,000 Heroes 1935,Ja 28,11:5
Parnosseh 1935,F 16,8:8
Motke Ganef 1935,Mr 18,15:2
Sappho 1935,Mr 22,26:4
Kibbetzers, Inc 1935,My 13,18:5
Having Wonderful Time 1937,F 22,12:5
In a Jewish Grocery 1939,O 2,15:2
Her Great Mistake 1940,F 5,12:6
Embezzled Heaven 1944,N 1,20:2
Place of Our Own, A 1945,Ap 3,23:7
Sky Drift 1945,N 14,25:2
He Who Gets Slapped 1946,Mr 21,31:4
He Who Gets Slapped 1946,Mr 31,II,1:1
Skipper Next to God 1948,Ja 5,14:5
Sing Till Tomorrow 1953,D 29,17:2
Stone for Danny Fisher, A 1954,O 22,24:2
Time of Your Life, The 1955,Ja 20,34:1
Highway Robbery 1955,N 8,36:1
Barzel, Wolf (Director)
We Live and Laugh 1936,My 9,10:3
Barzini, Luigi (Playwright)
Plot Thickens, The 1922,S 6,16:1
Barzman, Ben (Composer)
Meet the People 1940,D 26,22:2
Barzman, Ben (Lyricist)
Meet the People 1940,D 26,22:2
Barzman, Ben (Playwright)
Meet the People 1940,D 26,22:2
Barzman, Sol (Composer)
Meet the People 1940,D 26,22:2
Barzman, Sol (Lyricist)
Meet the People 1940,D 26,22:2
Barzman, Sol (Playwright)
Meet the People 1940,D 26,22:2
Barzun, Jacques Martin (Playwright)
Zuleika 1928,Mr 7,28:7
Bascetta, Alfred
In Any Language 1952,O 9,40:2
Bascetta, Joseph
Puppets of Passion 1927,F 25,24:4

Basch, Harry
Major Barbara 1954,Je 30,23:2
Automobile Graveyard, The 1961,N 14,46:2
Purple Canary, The 1963,Ap 23,31:1
Basch, Harry (Director)
Information Bureau, The 1962,Ja 31,21:1
Basch, Harry (Miscellaneous)
Lovers in the Metro, The 1962,Ja 31,21:1
Information Bureau, The 1962,Ja 31,21:1
Keyhole, The 1962,Ja 31,21:1
Basch, Pat
Creditors 1949,N 22,36:5
Basehart, Richard
Counterattack 1943,F 4,27:2
Land of Fame 1943,S 22,31:5
Take It As It Comes 1944,F 11,17:2
Hickory Stick 1944,My 9,15:6
Hasty Heart, The 1945,Ja 4,14:2
Hasty Heart, The 1945,Ja 14,II,1:1
Survivors, The 1948,Ja 20,27:2
Survivors, The 1948,Ja 25,II,1:1
Day the Money Stopped, The 1958,F 21,19:4
Richard II 1962,Je 18,20:2
Richard II 1962,Je 24,II,1:1
Uncle Vanya 1969,Ag 31,II,4:1
Baseleon, Michael
Tempest, The 1962,Jl 17,18:2
Dear Me, the Sky Is Falling 1963,Mr 4,9:1
Journey to the Day 1963,N 12,49:1
Electra 1964,Ag 12,42:1
Sondra 1967,My 10,39:1
Harold 1967,My 10,39:1
Ordinary Man, An 1968,S 10,39:1
Basenko, Ben
Untitled-Recital 1931,Mr 23,24:3
Jealousy 1934,D 20,31:4
60,000 Heroes 1935,Ja 28,11:5
Parnosseh 1935,F 16,8:8
Power That Builds, The 1935,Mr 9,18:4
Kibbetzers, Inc 1935,My 13,18:5
Untitled-Revue 1935,S 23,20:2
Jacques Bergson 1936,N 29,XII,3:3
Bash, Phyllis
Porgy and Bess 1965,Mr 6,17:1
Bashein, Henry
Sunup to Sundown 1938,F 2,14:3
Bashein, Nancy
Sunup to Sundown 1938,F 2,14:3
Bashevis, Isaac (Playwright)
Father Holds Court 1957,D 12,35:3
Basil, Elaine
Panic 1935,Mr 16,18:4
Basil, Nick
Hot-Cha! 1932,Mr 9,17:3
Basile, Charles
Pal Joey 1963,My 30,21:1
Basile, Jo (Miscellaneous)
International Soiree 1958,Mr 13,25:1
Basile, Jo (Musical Director)
Folies Bergere 1964,Je 3,36:1
Basile, Louis
Homo 1969,Ap 12,40:2
Basinger, John
Songs From Milk Wood 1970,Ja 13,41:1
Sganarelle 1970,Ja 13,41:1
Basinger, John (Composer)
Songs From Milk Wood 1970,Ja 13,41:1
Baskcomb, A W
Follow a Star 1930,S 18,28:2
Baskerville, Nancy
Rosalinda; Fledermaus, Die 1942,O 29,26:5
Baskett, Jimmy
Deep Harlem 1929,Ja 8,35:2
Basquette, Lina
Jack and Jill 1923,Mr 23,17:2
Nifties of 1923 1923,S 26,10:1
Follies 1925,Jl 7,24:3
Vaudeville (Hippodrome) 1926,Mr 23,24:3
Vaudeville (Hippodrome) 1926,Mr 30,20:4
LeMaire's Affairs 1927,Mr 29,22:4
Basquin, Peter (Miscellaneous)
Blitzstein! 1966,D 1,58:2
Bass, Alfie
World of Sholom Aleichem, The 1955,Ja 12,22:4
Bass, Emory
Kiss Me, Kate 1952,Ja 9,24:6
Chic 1959,My 19,28:2
Can-Can 1959,Ag 26,25:4
Susannah and the Elders 1959,O 19,37:3
Gay Divorce 1960,Ap 4,37:1
Bartleby 1961,Ja 25,28:1
Pal Joey 1961,Je 1,32:1
Pal Joey 1963,My 30,21:1
Where's Charley? 1966,My 26,57:1
By Jupiter 1967,Ja 20,28:2
Soap Opera 1968,My 10,54:7
1776 1969,Mr 17,46:2
Bass, James
Barber Had Two Sons, The 1943,F 2,22:2
Bass, Jules (Lyricist)
Month of Sundays 1968,S 17,50:1
Bass, Jules (Producer)
Month of Sundays 1968,S 17,50:1

Bass, Paul
My Magnolia 1926,Jl 13,19:2
Africana 1927,Jl 12,29:2
Bass, Robert
Mercy Street 1969,O 28,43:1
Bassae, Antony
Marie Vison, La 1970,Jl 15,29:1
Street Sounds 1970,O 23,32:1
Bassae, Antony (Costume Designer)
Marie Vison, La 1970,Jl 15,29:1
Street Sounds 1970,O 23,32:1
Bassage, Harold
Goodbye Again 1932,D 29,16:4
Wrong Number 1934,Mr 14,23:6
Bedrock 1934,N 18,II,6:3
Basse, Edward
Dream Girl, The 1924,Ag 21,12:2
Naughty Riquette 1926,S 14,25:2
Bassenko, Ben
Town Lunatics 1933,F 6,11:4
Salt and Pepper 1933,Ap 24,10:2
He, She and the Ox 1934,F 21,22:7
Basserman, Albert
Kean 1921,D 11,VI,1:4
Street Scene 1930,Mr 16,IX,4:1
Jemand; Somebody 1931,D 13,VIII,3:6
Embezzled Heaven 1944,S 30,17:3
Embezzled Heaven 1944,N 1,20:2
Embezzled Heaven 1944,N 5,II,1:2
Private Life of the Master Race, The
1945,Je 13,28:3
Private Life of the Master Race, The
1945,Je 17,II,1:1
Faust 1947,N 29,9:2
Rape of the Sabine Women, The 1949,F 5,10:5
Basserman, Else
Embezzled Heaven 1944,N 1,20:2
Private Life of the Master Race, The
1945,Je 13,28:3
Faust 1947,N 29,9:2
Rape of the Sabine Women, The 1949,F 5,10:5
Basset, William H
Lysistrata 1959,My 20,40:2
Bassett, Abe
Teahouse of the August Moon, The
1954,Ap 23,23:6
Bassett, Anthony
Mother Sings 1935,N 13,24:1
Bassett, T Reginald
Fiesta 1933,D 16,12:2
Bassett, William H
Lulu 1958,S 30,24:1
Moonbirds 1959,O 10,13:1
Hostage, The 1961,D 13,55:4
Step on a Crack 1962,O 18,48:1
Antony and Cleopatra 1963,Je 21,33:1
Journey of the Fifth Horse, The 1966,Ap 22,36:1
Basshe, Em Jo (Director)
Centuries, The 1927,N 30,23:1
Singing Jailbirds 1928,D 5,34:4
Roll Sweet Chariot 1934,O 3,24:3
Turpentine 1936,Je 27,21:6
Red Velvet Goat, The 1939,Ja 21,18:4
Coggerers, The 1939,Ja 21,18:4
Mr Banks of Birmingham 1939,Ja 21,18:4
Basshe, Em Jo (Playwright)
Adam Solitaire 1925,N 7,19:2
Adam Solitaire 1925,N 15,VIII,1:1
Earth 1927,Mr 10,23:1
Earth 1927,Mr 20,VIII,1:1
Centuries, The 1927,N 30,23:1
Bassie, Joan
Arms and the Man 1964,Ap 28,41:1
Imaginary Invalid, The 1967,My 2,53:1
Ways and Means 1967,My 4,34:1
Still Life 1967,My 4,34:1
Not Now Darling 1970,O 30,33:1
Bassler, Sidney
Winged Victory 1943,N 22,24:1
Volpone 1948,Ja 9,24:6
Bassman, Bruce (Lighting Director)
Nighthawks 1967,D 30,14:2
Bassman, George (Composer)
Nineteenth Hole of Europe, The 1949,Mr 28,16:2
Best House in Naples, The 1956,O 27,16:2
Bassman, George (Miscellaneous)
Alive and Kicking 1950,Ja 18,25:5
Guys and Dolls 1950,N 25,11:2
Bassman, George (Musical Director)
Guys and Dolls 1955,Ap 21,32:2
Bassoe, Henriette (Choreographer)
Love, Honor and Oh Baby 1940,Mr 29,25:2
Bastia, Jean (Playwright)
Odeon-Revue 1927,My 22,VIII,2:7
A l'Ombre de la Guillotine 1928,D 30,VIII,1:3
Bastian, Glenn
Celebration 1969,Ja 23,55:2
Bastiano, Anthony
Balls 1965,F 11,45:1
Bastiano, Anthony (Miscellaneous)
Glamour, Glory and Gold 1967,O 4,43:1

Bastida, Ramon (Composer)
Cabalgata 1949,Jl 8,14:2
Bastida, Ramon (Musical Director)
Cabalgata 1949,Jl 8,14:2
Bastin, Charles A
Winter Soldiers 1942,N 30,19:2
Bastug, Timur
Mother Courage and Her Children 1964,My 12,32:2
Bat-Ami
Eternal Jew, The 1926,D 21,21:2
Turandot 1929,Ja 12,14:4
Untitled-Recital 1931,Mr 23,24:3
Symphony 1935,Ap 27,20:3
Each Had Six Wings 1964,Mr 12,39:1
Bataille, Henri (Playwright)
Tendresse, La 1921,Ap 10,VI,1:1
Don Juan 1921,S 8,14:2
Homme a la Rose, L' 1921,S 11,VI,1:1
Tendresse, La 1922,S 26,18:1
Tendresse, La 1922,O 1,VII,1:1
Love Child, The 1922,N 15,22:1
Vierge Folle, La; Foolish Virgin, The
1924,Mr 22,12:2
Bataille, Nicholas (Director)
Cantatrice Chauve, La 1962,Ja 16,30:1
Laundry, The 1963,F 19,5:2
Batanides, Arthur
See the Jaguar 1952,D 4,46:2
Mandragola 1956,Mr 1,36:4
Batanides, Arthur (Producer)
Mandragola 1956,Mr 1,36:4
Batchelder, William H
Kiss Me, Kate 1965,My 13,31:1
Batcheller, Robin
Panic 1935,Mr 16,18:4
Batchelor, Walter (Producer)
Sentinels 1931,D 26,15:1
Batcholder, William (Miscellaneous)
Where's Charley? 1966,My 26,57:1
Bate, Anthony
Silence 1969,Jl 13,II,8:1
Bate, Dana
Tree Witch, The 1961,Je 5,39:4
Bate, Dorothy
Criss Cross 1926,O 13,20:2
Bate, Lorraine
Philadelphia Story, The 1939,Mr 29,21:1
Bate, Marden
Rosalinda; Fledermaus, Die 1942,O 29,26:5
Bate, Stanley (Composer)
Patriots, The 1943,Ja 30,11:2
Bate, Tom
Death Takes a Holiday 1929,D 27,26:4
Death Takes a Holiday 1931,F 17,29:1
Cynara 1931,N 3,31:1
Perfumed Lady, The 1934,Mr 13,27:2
Macbeth 1935,O 8,26:4
Co-Respondent Unknown 1936,F 12,24:4
And Now Goodbye 1937,F 3,26:4
Lady Has a Heart, The 1937,S 27,24:1
Wind in the Sails 1940,Ag 1,24:6
Romantic Mr Dickens 1940,D 3,33:2
My Romance 1948,O 20,38:5
Where's Charley? 1966,My 26,57:1
Bate, Tom (Director)
Wind in the Sails 1940,Ag 1,24:6
Bate, Tom (Miscellaneous)
Dark of the Moon 1958,F 27,22:2
Bateman, James
Five Little Peppers, The 1952,My 19,13:1
Bateman, Louise
His Majesty's Car 1930,O 24,30:1
Bateman, Phyliss
Red Mill, The 1945,O 17,16:2
Bateman, Werner
Victoria Regina 1937,S 26,XI,3:6
Victoria Regina 1938,O 4,20:2
Victoria Regina 1938,O 9,X,1:3
Bates, Add
Androcles and the Lion 1938,D 17,10:5
Bates, Alan
Look Back in Anger 1957,O 2,28:2
Look Back in Anger 1957,O 13,II,1:1
Caretaker, The 1961,O 5,42:3
Caretaker, The 1961,O 15,II,1:1
Poor Richard 1964,D 3,59:1
Richard III 1967,Je 14,43:1
Richard III 1967,Je 25,II,1:2
Merry Wives of Windsor, The 1967,Ag 4,18:1
Bates, Amy
One-Act Plays of the Sea; Long Voyage Home,
The 1937,O 30,23:2
Bates, Angeline
Clouds of the Sun 1922,My 6,11:2
Bates, Anna
Johannes Kreisler 1922,D 25,20:3
Bates, Blanche
Changelings, The 1923,S 18,16:3
Changelings, The 1923,S 30,II,1:1
Untitled-Recital 1923,D 29,8:2
Mrs Partridge Presents 1925,Ja 6,23:3
Lake, The 1933,D 19,26:3
Lake, The 1933,D 27,24:2

Bates, Blanche—Cont

Lake, The 1934,Ja 7,X,1:1

Bates, Brown

Roseanne 1923,D 31,9:5

Bates, Charles P

Eyvind of the Hills 1921,F 2,14:1
Nemesis 1921,Ap 5,24:3
Main Street 1921,O 6,21:1
It Is the Law 1922,N 30,28:2

Bates, Charlie

Aquarama 1960 1960,Jl 1,14:6

Bates, Edna

Honey Girl 1920,My 4,9:1

Bates, Esther Willard (Playwright)

Be Your Age 1929,F 5,27:1

Bates, Granville

Silence 1924,N 13,18:2
My Princess 1927,O 7,24:2
Stairs, The 1927,N 8,32:7
Gentlemen of the Press 1928,Ag 28,27:2
So Was Napoleon 1930,Ja 9,22:2
Once in a Lifetime 1930,S 25,22:3
Trick for Trick 1932,F 19,14:2
Lilly Turner 1932,S 20,26:1
20th Century 1932,D 30,15:1
Divine Drudge 1933,Jl 4,16:4
Double Door 1933,S 22,15:5
Come What May 1934,My 16,23:4
Merrily We Roll Along 1934,O 1,14:1
Rain 1935,F 13,24:1

Bates, H E (Playwright)

Carrie and Cleopatra 1939,My 14,XI,1:8
Day of Glory, The 1946,D 22,II,2:1

Bates, Harry

Pelican, The 1925,S 22,23:2
Houseboat on the Styx, The 1928,D 26,14:3

Bates, Jeanne

Now I Lay Me Down to Sleep 1949,Jl 23,7:3

Bates, Kenneth

New Faces 1934,Mr 16,24:5
Kind Lady 1937,Jl 21,19:3
Fly Away Home 1937,Jl 28,15:1
Candida 1937,Ag 4,14:5
Whiteheaded Boy, The 1937,Ag 11,27:3
Elizabeth the Queen 1937,Ag 25,24:3
Goodbye Again 1937,S 1,15:1
All That Glitters 1938,Ja 20,18:2
Yes, My Darling Daughter 1938,Jl 13,19:2
Animal Kingdom, The 1938,Jl 27,14:5
Biography 1938,Ag 3,14:7
Arms and the Man 1938,Ag 10,14:1
Bachelor Born 1938,Ag 17,23:1
Springtime for Henry 1938,Ag 31,12:5
Liliom 1940,Mr 26,17:2
Jeannie 1940,N 13,29:2
Letters to Lucerne 1941,D 24,14:2

Bates, Lawson

Simply Heavenly 1957,My 22,28:2

Bates, Lulu

Great to Be Alive! 1950,Mr 24,28:2
Flahooley 1951,My 15,39:1
New Girl in Town 1957,My 15,40:1
Family Affair, A 1962,Ja 29,17:1

Bates, Marie

Return of Peter Grimm, The 1921,S 22,12:2
Vaudeville (Palace) 1926,Jl 27,15:4

Bates, Michael

All's Well That Ends Well 1953,Jl 16,18:2
Cannibal Crackers 1969,N 25,52:1

Bates, Peg Leg

Vaudeville (Palace) 1929,N 18,22:4
Blackouts of 1949 1949,S 7,39:2

Bates, Peggy

Tea for Three 1935,Jl 9,24:4
Rain Before Seven 1935,Ag 13,20:3

Bates, R C

Successful Calamity, A 1921,Mr 19,11:2

Bates, Rawley

Stop the World—I Want to Get Off 1962,O 4,45:4

Bates, Ronald (Lighting Director)

Fishing for Wives 1966,Mr 16,50:1
General's Daughter, The 1966,Mr 16,50:1
Greengrocer's Daughter, The 1966,Mr 16,50:1

Bates, Ronald (Miscellaneous)

Chushingura; Treasury of Loyal Retainers, The 1969,S 11,53:1
Kagami-Jishi; Mirror Lion Dance, The 1969,S 11,53:1
Kumagai Jinya 1969,S 18,64:1
Momiji-Gari 1969,S 18,64:1

Bates, Ronald (Scenic Designer)

General's Daughter, The 1966,Mr 16,50:1
Fishing for Wives 1966,Mr 16,50:1
Greengrocer's Daughter, The 1966,Mr 16,50:1

Bates, Sally

American Tragedy, An 1926,O 12,31:2
Manhatters, The 1927,Jl 19,27:3
Manhatters, The 1927,Ag 4,25:4
Sweet Adeline 1929,S 4,33:1
Doctor X 1930,Jl 31,12:4
Up Pops the Devil 1930,S 2,19:1
Bulls, Bears and Asses 1932,My 7,11:3
Here Today 1932,S 7,14:2
Here Today 1932,S 18,IX,1:1

Goodbye Again 1932,D 29,16:4
Hello Again 1934,Je 14,28:4
Gather Ye Rosebuds 1934,N 29,33:2
Solitaire 1942,Ja 28,22:2

Bates, Scotty

Hello, Yourself 1928,O 31,28:2

Bates, Stephen (Director)

Here Come the Clowns 1954,My 5,36:2

Bates, Thorpe

Yankee Princess, The 1922,O 3,22:1

Bateson, Timothy

Caesar and Cleopatra 1951,D 20,43:2

Bathiat, Leonie (Arletty)

Etouffe Chretien, L' 1960,N 5,28:1

Batie, Franklyn

Bombo 1921,O 7,20:2
Big Boy 1925,Ja 8,28:2

Batisse, Andre

Mariage de Figaro, Le 1964,F 26,41:2

Batista, Germano

Arena Conta Zumbi 1969,Ag 19,31:1

Batiste, John

Winter Journey 1968,Mr 13,39:1

Batiste, John (Composer)

Winter Journey 1968,Mr 13,39:1

Batiste, John (Miscellaneous)

Big Man 1966,My 20,41:1
Duet for Three 1966,My 20,41:1

Batistio, Josef

Johannes Kreisler 1922,D 25,20:3

Batley, Dorothy

Rat, The 1924,Je 15,VII,1:4

Baton, Pierre

Cosmonaute Agricole, Le 1970,Ap 8,38:3

Batron, Harry

Here Come the Clowns 1954,My 5,36:2

Batson, Charner

Sweet Nell of Old Drury 1923,My 19,16:4

Batson, George (Playwright)

Treat Her Gently 1941,Mr 30,I,48:1
Ramshackle Inn 1944,Ja 6,17:5
Magnolia Alley 1949,Ap 19,29:2
Date With April, A 1953,Ap 16,36:2

Batson, Susan

Hair 1967,O 30,55:1
George M! 1968,Ap 11,48:1
Shoot Anything With Hair That Moves 1969,F 3,29:1
Adventures of the Black Girl in Her Search for God, The 1969,Mr 22,24:4

Batt, Boris

Diana 1929,D 10,37:1

Battan, Marcus

Burning Bush, The 1949,D 17,15:5

Batten, Edward

Conjur 1938,N 1,27:2

Batten, Tom

My Heart's in the Highlands 1950,F 18,8:4
Gantry 1970,F 16,44:1

Batterberry, Michael (Director)

Fourth Avenue North 1961,S 28,50:2

Batterberry, Michael (Producer)

Fourth Avenue North 1961,S 28,50:2

Batthyany, Julius (Count) (Scenic Designer)

Dream Queen 1930,F 23,III,7:2

Battis, Emery

Henry VIII 1946,N 7,42:2
Yellow Jack 1947,F 28,26:2
Misalliance 1961,S 26,32:2
Serjeant Musgrave's Dance 1968,Je 16,52:4
Resistible Rise of Arturo Ui, The 1968,Ag 8,25:1
Merton of the Movies 1968,S 26,62:1
House of Atreus, The 1968,D 18,55:1
Resistible Rise of Arturo Ui, The 1968,D 23,44:1

Battis, Peter

Does a Tiger Wear a Necktie? 1967,F 4,17:1

Battista, Joseph

Lazarus Laughed 1948,Ap 9,27:4

Battista, Lloyd

Those That Play the Clowns 1966,N 25,48:1
Miser, The 1969,My 9,35:1

Battista, Miriam

Short Cut, The 1930,Ja 28,28:2
Honor Code, The 1931,My 19,25:3
Hot-Cha! 1932,Mr 9,17:3
Saint Wench 1933,Ja 3,19:3
Our Wife 1933,Mr 3,13:2
Undesirable Lady, An 1933,O 10,24:4
No More Ladies 1934,Ja 24,20:3
Fools Rush In 1934,D 26,19:2
Tapestry in Gray 1935,D 28,10:2
Summer Wives 1936,Ap 14,18:1
Prelude to Exile 1936,N 17,34:6
Prelude to Exile 1936,N 22,XI,3:2
Prelude to Exile 1936,D 1,31:1
They Knew What They Wanted 1939,O 3,19:1

Battista, Miriam (Lyricist)

Sleepy Hollow 1948,Je 4,26:3

Battista, Miriam (Playwright)

Sleepy Hollow 1948,Je 4,26:3

Battistella, Antonio

Arlecchino, the Servant of Two Masters 1956,Ag 28,31:1

Battistini, Mario

Cardinale, Il; Cardinal, The 1931,Ja 12,24:2
Sansone; Samson 1931,F 9,25:1
Arzigogolo, L'; Whim, The 1931,Ap 27,24:4

Battle, George

Kilpatrick's Old-Time Minstrels 1930,Ap 21,20:2

Battle, John

Hot Pan 1928,F 16,14:1

Battle, John Tucker

First Flight 1925,S 18,26:2

Battle, John Tucker (Playwright)

Bottom of the Cup, The 1927,F 1,24:2

Battle, Joseph

Ten Nights in a Barroom 1927,Ja 16,VII,1:1
Bare Facts 1927,Je 30,35:1
Ten Nights in a Barroom 1928,Mr 28,31:2

Battle, Mr

Something Different 1967,N 29,52:1

Battles, George

Keep Shufflin' 1928,F 28,18:3

Battles, John

On the Town 1944,D 29,11:4
Allegro 1947,O 11,10:2
13 Daughters 1961,Mr 3,17:2

Battles, Margie

Bacchae, The 1963,Ap 25,39:5

Battles, Marjorie

Cactus Flower 1965,D 9,60:2

Battley, David

There'll Be Some Changes Made 1969,O 2,56:2

Batty, Archibald

Once Is Enough 1938,F 16,16:2

Batut, Pierre de la (Playwright)

Ville Sans Amour, Le 1928,D 16,IX,4:7

Baty, Gaston

Bifur 1932,F 28,VIII,1:1

Baty, Gaston (Costume Designer)

Faust 1937,Ag 29,X,1:3

Baty, Gaston (Director)

Amour Magicien, L' 1926,D 26,VII,2:1
Madame Bovary 1936,N 8,X,3:6
Arlequin Poli par l'Amour 1955,N 9,40:1

Baty, Gaston (Original Author)

Madame Bovary 1937,N 17,26:2

Baty, Gaston (Playwright)

Madame Bovary 1936,N 8,X,3:6
Madame Bovary 1937,O 6,28:4

Baty, Gaston (Producer)

Amour Magicien, L' 1926,D 26,VII,2:1
Dybbuk, The 1928,F 26,VIII,4:1
Cris des Coeurs 1928,Je 3,VIII,2:5
Departs 1928,D 23,VIII,2:1
Malade Imaginaire 1929,Ap 14,X,2:1
Karl und Anna 1929,My 5,IX,2:4
Feu du Ciel 1930,Mr 16,IX,4:3
Beau Danube Rouge 1931,My 17,VIII,1:5
Chambre d'Hotel 1932,Mr 20,VIII,2:2
Cyclone 1934,D 2,X,2:1
Voyage Circulaire 1934,D 2,X,2:1
Prosper 1935,Ja 13,IX,2:1
Hotel des Masques 1935,N 24,IX,3:7
Caprices de Marianne 1936,Ja 12,IX,3:7
Cris des Coeurs 1936,Ja 12,IX,3:7
Chandelier, Le 1939,Mr 19,XI,3:7

Baty, Gaston (Scenic Designer)

Faust 1937,Ag 29,X,1:3

Baublitz, Richard

Absalom 1956,My 17,37:2

Bauche, Henri (Playwright)

Laboratoire des Hallucinations, Le 1923,N 20,23:3

Bauder, Bob

Lucky Sam McCarver 1950,Ap 15,10:6
This Happy Breed 1952,Ap 4,23:2

Bauder, Harry (Costume Designer)

Rope Dancers, The 1959,Mr 14,26:1

Bauer, Alfred (Scenic Designer)

Few Are Chosen 1935,S 18,19:3

Bauer, Audrey

Grand Hotel 1930,N 14,30:4

Bauer, Charita

Thunder on the Left 1933,N 1,25:2
Remember the Day 1935,Jl 9,24:3
Remember the Day 1935,S 26,19:3
Women, The 1936,D 8,30:6
Women, The 1936,D 28,13:1
Madame Capet 1938,O 26,26:2
Your Loving Son 1941,Ap 5,13:2
Life of Reilly, The 1942,Ap 30,13:2
Good Morning, Corporal 1944,Ag 9,13:7
Family Portrait 1959,My 6,48:2

Bauer, David

Volpone 1957,Ja 8,27:1
Trial of Dmitri Karamazov, The 1958,Ja 28,30:1

Bauer, Franklyn

Ziegfeld Follies 1927,Ag 17,27:3

Bauer, George

Come of Age 1952,Ja 24,22:2

Bauer, George (Miscellaneous)

Joyce Grenfell 1958,Ap 8,32:1

Bauer, George (Musical Director)

Lend an Ear 1948,D 17,38:2
Joyce Grenfell Requests the Pleasure 1955,O 11,48:1

Bauer, George (Musical Director)—Cont
Lend an Ear 1959,S 25,20:5
Kukla, Burr and Ollie 1960,N 1,47:2
Bauer, Harold (Miscellaneous)
Neighborhood Playhouse Program 1930,F 21,23:1
Bauer, Ina
Ice Follies 1961,Ja 11,25:2
Ice Follies 1962,Ja 10,24:6
Ice Follies 1963,Ja 10,5:2
Ice Follies 1964,Ja 8,41:2
Ice Follies 1965,Ja 13,35:1
Ice Follies 1966,Ja 12,27:6
Ice Follies 1967,Ja 11,51:1
Bauer, Inez
Elsie Janis and Her Gang 1922,Ja 17,13:2
Bauer, Irv (Playwright)
Dream Out of Time, A 1970,N 9,52:1
Bauer, Jack
Just Fancy! 1927,O 12,30:2
Bauer, Katherine
Remember the Day 1935,S 26,19:3
Bauer, Morris K (Miscellaneous)
Be Your Age 1953,Ja 15,24:2
Bauer, Peggy
Ice Capades 1955,S 15,38:1
Bauer, Richard
Stephen D 1966,Ag 5,17:1
Great White Hope, The 1967,D 14,58:1
Iceman Cometh, The 1968,Ap 1,58:1
Indians 1969,My 27,43:1
Night Thoreau Spent in Jail, The 1970,N 2,66:1
Bauer, Rolland
Too Many Heroes 1937,N 16,26:2
Bauer, Rollin
Siege 1937,D 9,31:4
High Kickers 1941,N 1,21:2
Sweet Charity 1942,D 29,26:4
Joy Forever, A 1946,Ja 8,20:2
Bauer, Ted
Deirdre of the Sorrows 1949,D 15,51:2
Bauer, Vivian
Rape of Lucretia, The 1948,D 30,24:2
Bauer, William
Gypsy Lady 1946,S 18,25:6
Bauer, Wolfgang (Playwright)
Change 1970,O 13,52:2
Bauermeister, Mary (Translator)
Originale 1964,S 9,46:1
Bauers, Herbert
Last Enemy, The 1934,Jl 13,14:4
Bauersmith, Paula
Lean Harvest 1931,O 14,26:3
East of Broadway 1932,Ja 27,19:3
Warrior's Husband, The 1932,Mr 12,19:4
Anatomist, The 1932,O 25,24:3
Three-Cornered Moon 1933,Mr 17,20:6
All Good Americans 1933,D 6,29:2
Mahogany Hall 1934,Ja 18,18:5
Let Freedom Ring 1935,N 7,26:2
Bury the Dead 1936,Ap 20,17:4
Prelude 1936,Ap 20,17:4
200 Were Chosen 1936,N 21,21:1
Winter Soldiers 1942,N 30,19:2
Twentieth Century 1950,D 25,23:6
Fortunato 1956,Mr 24,15:2
Lesson, The 1956,O 3,29:2
Thor, With Angels 1956,O 15,29:4
Box of Watercolors, A 1957,F 18,22:2
Tobias and the Angel 1957,O 21,29:5
Lesson, The 1958,Ja 10,20:3
Marvellous History of Saint Bernard, The
1958,F 24,16:3
Potting Shed, The 1958,N 3,49:2
Sail Away 1961,O 4,48:5
John Brown's Body 1968,F 13,49:2
Comedy of Errors, The 1968,F 28,40:2
Baughman, Sara-Ann
Engaged! or Cheviot's Choice 1965,Ap 24,19:2
Baum, Charles
Peg o' My Dreams 1924,My 6,25:3
Criss Cross 1926,O 13,20:2
Baum, Greta (Costume Designer)
Few Are Chosen 1935,S 18,19:3
Baum, Harry (Lighting Director)
Sharon's Grave 1961,N 9,39:2
Fifth Commandment, The 1965,N 15,48:4
Baum, Harry (Producer)
Hop, Signor! 1962,My 8,45:2
Baum, Harry (Scenic Designer)
Lonesome Ship, The 1956,D 7,32:6
Father Holds Court 1957,D 12,35:3
Thousand and One Nights 1959,D 16,53:2
Breaking Wall, The 1960,Ja 26,27:5
Deep Are the Roots 1960,O 4,47:1
Hop, Signor! 1962,My 8,45:2
Fifth Commandment, The 1965,N 15,48:4
Bronx Express, 1968 1968,N 16,43:3
Melody Lingers On, The 1969,N 17,55:1
Brothers Ashkenazi, The 1970,N 17,53:2
Baum, L Frank (Playwright)
Wizard of Oz, The 1968,N 28,69:2
Baum, Martin
Outside the Door 1949,Mr 2,33:2

Baum, Vicki (Original Author)
Divine Drudge 1933,Jl 4,16:4
Divine Drudge 1933,O 27,22:3
At the Grand 1958,Ag 13,24:3
Baum, Vicki (Playwright)
Menschen im Hotel 1930,Mr 16,IX,4:1
Grand Hotel 1930,N 14,30:4
Grand Hotel 1930,N 23,IX,1:1
Pariser Platz 13 1931,Mr 1,VIII,1:3
Grand Hotel 1931,S 4,22:7
Divine Drudge 1933,Jl 4,16:4
Divine Drudge 1933,O 27,22:3
Summer Night 1939,N 3,17:1
Bauman, Henry
Paul Bunyan 1941,My 6,25:1
Bauman, Mordecai
Paul Bunyan 1941,My 6,25:1
Johnny Doodle 1942,Mr 19,28:2
Let Freedom Sing 1942,O 6,18:2
Sandhog 1954,N 24,17:1
Bauman, Richard
Tempest, The 1959,D 28,19:2
Coggerers, The 1960,Mr 23,33:1
Time to Go 1960,Mr 23,33:1
Baumann, Heinz
Nathan der Weise 1966,D 10,45:2
Baumann, Kathryn
Prime of Miss Jean Brodie, The 1968,Ja 17,39:1
Prime of Miss Jean Brodie, The 1968,Ja 28,II,1:1
Penny Wars, The 1969,O 16,52:1
Lemon Sky 1970,My 18,40:1
Baumbusch, Raymond
Little Theatre Tournament; White Peacock, The
1928,My 11,28:1
Baume, Lillian (Original Author)
Adventures of Marco Polo, The 1941,D 28,I,31:7
Baumer, Jacques
Felix 1926,O 10,VIII,2:1
Masque et Visage 1927,Ap 3,VIII,4:7
Vient de Paraitre 1927,D 11,IX,2:2
Vilaine Femme, Une 1933,Ja 1,IX,3:4
Baumer, Marie (Playwright)
Town Boy 1929,O 5,22:4
Penny Arcade 1930,Mr 11,24:5
House of Remsen 1934,Ap 3,26:4
Creeping Fire 1935,Ja 17,22:3
Seen But Not Heard 1936,Jl 22,23:4
Seen But Not Heard 1936,S 18,19:2
Little Brown Jug 1946,Mr 7,32:2
Baumgarten, Edward
Trial of Dr Beck, The 1937,Ag 10,22:2
Baumgartner, Bernard (Dr) (Musical Director)
Midsummer Night's Dream, A 1925,Mr 8,VII,2:1
Baur, Harry
Amants de Paris, Les 1927,N 6,IX,4:1
Trial of Mary Dugan, The 1929,F 24,IX,1:8
Autres, Les 1931,N 1,VIII,2:7
Fanny 1931,D 27,VIII,3:4
Voie Lactee, La 1933,F 26,IX,2:2
Mari Que J'ai Voulu, Le 1934,Ap 29,IX,2:2
Baur, Harry (Producer)
Trial of Mary Dugan, The 1929,F 24,IX,1:8
Baur, Jean
Madwoman of Chaillot, The 1970,Mr 23,48:3
Bauschulte, Friedrich W
Don Carlos 1964,N 25,40:1
Captain of Koepenick, The 1964,D 2,60:1
Bavaar, Tony
Paint Your Wagon 1951,N 13,32:2
Paint Your Wagon 1951,N 18,II,1:1
Bavan, Yolande
Midsummer Night's Dream, A 1964,Je 30,23:2
Jonah! 1966,F 16,52:1
House of Flowers 1968,Ja 29,26:2
Salvation 1969,S 25,55:1
Mira 1970,Je 3,51:1
Tarot 1970,D 12,19:1
Bavare, Zella
Neighbors 1966,N 15,51:4
March March, The 1966,N 15,51:4
Baverstock, Percy
Sweeney Todd 1924,Jl 19,10:4
White Gold 1925,N 3,34:5
Baviello, Frances
Sweethearts 1929,S 23,25:1
Mlle Modiste 1929,O 8,34:1
Naughty Marietta 1929,O 22,26:2
Babes in Toyland 1929,D 24,15:3
Prince of Pilsen, The 1930,Ja 14,24:3
Chocolate Soldier, The 1930,Ja 28,28:1
Count of Luxembourg, The 1930,F 18,28:2
Serenade, The 1930,Mr 5,26:7
Babes in Toyland 1930,D 22,17:1
Pirates of Penzance, The; Slave of Duty, The
1931,Je 30,23:6
Ruddigore 1931,Ag 11,28:3
Merry Widow, The 1931,S 8,39:1
Bohemian Girl, The 1933,Jl 28,18:5
Pirates of Penzance, The 1933,Ag 8,22:4
Pirates of Penzance, The 1934,Ap 10,26:5
Iolanthe 1934,My 1,26:4
Pirates of Penzance, The 1935,Jl 23,24:2
Gondoliers, The 1935,Ag 6,20:5

Baviello, Frances—Cont
Mikado, The 1936,Ap 11,18:4
Pirates of Penzance, The 1936,Ap 21,27:5
Iolanthe 1936,My 5,26:2
Bavier, Frances
Little Princess, The 1931,F 7,11:3
Racketty Packetty House 1931,N 7,16:1
Black Pit 1935,Mr 21,26:6
Mother, The 1935,N 20,26:3
Bitter Stream 1936,Mr 31,16:6
Marching Song 1937,F 18,18:2
Native Son 1941,Mr 25,26:5
Native Son 1942,O 24,10:6
Kiss and Tell 1943,Mr 18,22:1
Little A 1947,Ja 16,31:2
Jenny Kissed Me 1948,D 24,12:2
Magnolia Alley 1949,Ap 19,29:2
Point of No Return 1951,D 14,35:2
Bax, Clifford (Lyricist)
Trip to Scarborough, A 1929,Mr 18,31:2
Bax, Clifford (Playwright)
Socrates 1930,Ap 13,X,1:6
Venetian, The 1931,Mr 15,IX,4:3
Venetian, The 1931,O 11,VIII,4:5
Venetian, The 1931,N 2,26:1
Rose Without a Thorn 1932,Ap 3,VIII,1:5
House of Borgia, The 1935,S 10,26:1
House of Borgia, The 1935,O 6,XI,3:1
King and Mistress Shore, The 1936,N 6,28:5
King and Mistress Shore, The 1936,N 22,XI,1:3
Bax, Clifford (Translator)
Impresario From Smyrna 1935,D 24,10:3
Bax, Peter (Scenic Designer)
Venetian, The 1931,N 2,26:1
Baxandall, Lee (Translator)
Song of the Lusitanian Bogey, The 1968,Ja 3,52:1
Baxley, Barbara
Private Lives 1948,O 5,30:2
Private Lives 1948,N 7,II,1:1
Out West of Eighth 1951,S 21,20:3
Camino Real 1953,Mr 20,26:1
Camino Real 1953,Mr 29,II,1:1
Frogs of Spring, The 1953,O 21,36:2
Flowering Peach, The 1954,D 29,19:2
Flowering Peach, The 1955,Ja 9,II,1:1
Palm Tree in a Rose Garden, A 1957,N 27,26:2
Period of Adjustment 1960,N 11,34:1
Period of Adjustment 1960,N 20,II,1:1
She Loves Me 1963,Ap 24,39:1
She Loves Me 1963,My 5,II,1:1
Three Sisters, The 1964,Je 23,24:1
Measure for Measure 1966,Jl 14,27:1
Merchant of Venice, The 1967,Je 22,46:2
To Be Young Gifted and Black; World of Lorraine
Hansberry, The 1969,Ja 3,15:1
Oh, Pioneers 1969,N 12,41:1
Baxon, Don
Artists and Models 1943,N 6,16:6
Baxt, George
Theatre of the Soul 1942,Mr 21,13:5
Across the Board on Tomorrow Morning
1942,Mr 21,13:5
Baxt, George (Playwright)
Littlest Revue, The 1956,My 23,37:2
Baxter, Alan
Hamlet 1928,Je 2,11:3
Lone Valley 1933,Mr 11,18:6
Men in White 1933,S 27,24:2
Waiting for Lefty 1935,F 11,14:5
Black Pit 1935,Mr 21,26:6
Winged Victory 1943,N 22,24:1
Home of the Brave 1945,D 28,13:2
Home of the Brave 1946,Ja 6,II,1:1
Hallams, The 1948,Mr 5,18:2
Jenny Kissed Me 1948,D 24,12:2
South Pacific 1957,Ap 25,35:1
Baxter, Alan (Playwright)
Life Begins at 8:40 1934,Ag 28,24:2
Calling All Stars 1934,N 22,26:1
Calling All Stars 1934,D 14,28:2
Thumbs Up! 1934,D 28,24:1
Baxter, Anne
Seen But Not Heard 1936,Jl 22,23:4
Seen But Not Heard 1936,S 18,19:2
There's Always a Breeze 1938,Mr 3,16:2
Madame Capet 1938,O 26,26:2
Square Root of Wonderful, The 1957,O 31,40:1
Baxter, Barry
One Night in Rome 1920,Ap 30,1:2
Happy-Go-Lucky 1920,Ag 25,6:1
Bluebeard's Eighth Wife 1921,S 20,12:2
Baxter, Billy (Producer)
Mandingo 1961,My 23,43:6
Baxter, Cash
Great Scot! 1965,N 12,56:3
Baxter, Cash (Producer)
Candida 1970,Ap 7,41:1
Baxter, Charles
Everything in the Garden 1967,N 30,60:1
Baxter, Connie
Carousel 1945,Ap 20,24:2
Baxter, Connie (Costume Designer)
Eastward in Eden 1956,Ap 18,25:4

Baxter, David
Happy Ending 1936,Jl 15,14:3
Audition, The 1968,Jl 8,45:1
Baxter, Ernest (Lighting Director)
Day of Absence 1970,Mr 18,39:1
Brotherhood 1970,Mr 18,39:1
Akokawe 1970,Je 5,21:1
Ododo 1970,N 25,26:1
Baxter, Eugene
Last Pad, The 1970,D 8,61:1
Baxter, Frank
Catherine Was Great 1944,Ag 3,16:1
Baxter, George
Sweet Nell of Old Drury 1923,My 19,16:4
Windows 1923,O 9,17:2
Madre 1923,D 31,9:6
Milgrim's Progress 1924,D 23,17:1
Virgin of Bethulia, The 1925,F 24,17:2
Caesar and Cleopatra 1925,Ap 14,27:1
Glass Slipper, The 1925,O 20,29:1
Glass Slipper, The 1925,O 25,VIII,1:1
Night Duel, The 1926,F 16,22:3
No Foolin' 1926,Je 25,25:1
We Americans 1926,O 13,20:4
Rio Rita 1927,F 3,18:3
Headquarters 1929,D 5,32:4
Other One, The 1932,O 4,26:3
Perfect Marriage, The 1932,N 17,23:2
White Man 1936,O 19,22:4
Behind the Red Lights 1937,Ja 14,17:4
Three Waltzes 1937,D 27,10:2
Madame Capet 1938,O 26,26:2
George Washington Slept Here 1940,O 19,20:3
Mr Big 1941,O 1,24:2
Early to Bed 1943,Je 18,16:2
For Keeps 1944,Je 15,17:5
Rebecca 1945,Ja 19,17:2
Devils Galore 1945,S 13,27:2
Flag Is Born, A 1946,S 7,10:6
Louisiana Lady 1947,Je 3,35:2
Baxter, Ginny
Ice Capades 1952,S 12,18:1
Baxter, Gladys
Peg o' My Dreams 1924,My 6,25:3
Piggy 1927,Ja 12,22:2
Cherry Blossoms 1927,Mr 29,22:3
Music in May 1929,Ja 27,IX,1:3
Music in May 1929,Ap 2,29:1
Sweethearts 1929,S 23,25:1
Wonderful Night, A; Fledermaus, Die 1929,N 1,23:3
Prince Chu Chang 1930,O 12,VIII,4:1
Blossom Time 1931,Mr 5,32:1
Three Waltzes 1937,D 27,10:2
Baxter, Guy
Mourners' Bench, The 1950,S 22,35:7
Baxter, Helen
Get Me in the Movies 1928,My 22,18:3
Town's Woman, The 1929,Mr 12,26:2
Cortez 1929,N 5,32:2
Unsophisticates, The 1929,D 31,14:5
Baxter, James K (Playwright)
Spots of the Leopard, The 1963,S 25,38:1
Baxter, Jane
Importance of Being Earnest, The 1947,Ja 24,18:6
Importance of Being Earnest, The 1947,Mr 4,30:2
Importance of Being Earnest, The 1947,Mr 9,II,1:1
Young and Fair, The 1949,Jl 1,14:3
Baxter, Keith
Man for All Seasons, A 1961,N 23,51:1
Man for All Seasons, A 1961,D 3,II,1:1
Affair, The 1962,S 21,34:2
Where Angels Fear to Tread 1963,Je 8,14:6
Avanti 1968,F 1,29:1
Country Wife, The 1969,Ag 30,10:3
Antony and Cleopatra 1969,Ag 30,10:3
Sleuth 1970,N 13,25:1
Sleuth 1970,N 22,II,18:1
Baxter, Lee
Vigil, The 1948,My 22,8:6
Baxter, Lloyd
It Happens on Ice 1940,O 11,24:3
Baxter, Lora
Sex Fable, The 1931,O 21,26:1
Animal Kingdom, The 1932,Ja 13,26:4
Animal Kingdom, The 1932,Ja 24,1:1
Comic Artist, The 1933,Ap 20,20:3
Party, A 1933,Ag 24,18:4
Party, A 1933,S 3,IX,1:1
False Dreams, Farewell 1934,Ja 16,18:3
Rain Before Seven 1935,Ag 13,20:3
Laughing Woman, The 1936,O 14,30:1
Young Mr Disraeli 1937,N 10,30:5
Fledgling 1940,N 28,29:2
Baxter, Lora (Playwright)
Black Tower 1932,Ja 12,29:2
Baxter, Maisie
Pirates of Penzance, The; Slave of Duty, The 1934,S 7,24:3
Iolanthe 1934,S 11,24:3
Princess Ida; Castle Adamant 1934,S 28,26:3
Patience 1934,O 12,32:2

Baxter, Margaret
Alive and Kicking 1950,Ja 18,25:5
Baxter, Martha
Major Barbara 1951,F 24,10:2
Eastward in Eden 1956,Ap 18,25:4
Baxter, Roy (Miscellaneous)
Pets 1969,My 15,41:2
Baby With a Knife 1969,My 15,41:2
Silver Grey Toy Poodle 1969,My 15,41:2
Baxter, Skippy
It Happens on Ice 1941,Ap 5,13:2
It Happens on Ice 1941,Ag 31,IX,1:1
Stars on Ice 1942,Jl 3,12:2
Icetime 1947,My 29,28:2
Howdy Mr Ice 1948,Je 25,28:5
Howdy, Mr Ice of 1950 1949,My 27,24:2
Hollywood Ice Revue 1953,Ja 16,17:2
Hollywood Ice Revue 1954,Ja 15,16:2
Hollywood Ice Revue 1955 1955,Ja 14,16:1
Hollywood Ice Revue 1956,Ja 13,17:1
Baxter, Stanley
On the Brighter Side 1961,Je 25,II,3:5
Baxter, Stewart
Finian's Rainbow 1953,Mr 7,13:2
Baxter, Tommie
Sister Oakes 1949,Ap 25,19:4
Baxter, William
On the Level 1937,Mr 26,24:4
Bay
High Kickers 1941,N 1,21:2
Bay, Howard (Costume Designer)
Man of La Mancha 1965,N 23,52:1
Bay, Howard (Director)
As the Girls Go 1948,N 15,21:2
Bay, Howard (Lighting Director)
Chicken Every Sunday 1944,Ap 6,27:2
Follow the Girls 1944,Ap 10,15:2
Men to the Sea 1944,O 4,25:2
Up in Central Park 1945,Ja 29,17:2
Up in Central Park 1947,My 20,29:2
Magdalena 1948,S 21,31:2
Come Back, Little Sheba 1950,F 16,28:5
Autumn Garden, The 1951,Mr 8,36:2
Flahooley 1951,My 15,39:1
Two on the Aisle 1951,Jl 20,13:6
Grand Tour, The 1951,D 11,45:2
Shrike, The 1952,Ja 16,20:2
Mid-Summer 1953,Ja 22,19:1
Shrike, The 1953,N 26,51:2
Sandhog 1954,N 24,17:1
Desperate Hours, The 1955,F 11,20:2
Red Roses for Me 1955,D 29,15:2
Carmen Jones 1956,Je 1,28:2
Very Special Baby, A 1956,N 15,43:2
Night of the Auk 1956,D 4,50:2
Tevya and His Daughters 1957,S 17,38:2
Best of Burlesque 1957,S 30,27:2
Music Man, The 1957,D 20,31:1
Interlock 1958,F 7,18:1
Desert Incident, A 1959,Mr 25,40:1
Fighting Cock, The 1959,D 9,57:3
Cut of the Axe 1960,F 2,38:2
Cool World, The 1960,F 23,38:2
Toys in the Attic 1960,F 26,23:2
Finian's Rainbow 1960,Ap 28,31:1
Wall, The 1960,O 12,44:4
Show Boat 1961,Ap 13,32:1
Pal Joey 1961,Je 1,32:1
Milk and Honey 1961,O 11,52:1
Isle of Children 1962,Mr 17,16:2
My Mother, My Father and Me 1963,Mr 25,5:5
Bicycle Ride to Nevada 1963,S 25,38:1
Never Live Over a Pretzel Factory 1964,Mr 30,37:1
Music Man, The 1965,Je 17,26:4
Man of La Mancha 1965,N 23,52:1
Little Foxes, The 1967,O 27,53:1
Fire! 1969,Ja 29,26:1
Cry for Us All 1970,Ap 9,48:2
Bay, Howard (Miscellaneous)
Borned in Texas 1950,Ag 22,30:6
Look Back in Anger 1957,O 2,28:2
Romanoff and Juliet 1957,O 11,24:1
Bay, Howard (Scenic Designer)
Chalk Dust 1936,Mr 5,24:5
Battle Hymn 1936,My 23,12:1
Marching Song 1937,F 18,18:2
Power 1937,F 24,18:5
Native Ground 1937,Mr 24,28:4
One-Third of a Nation 1938,Ja 18,27:2
Sunup to Sundown 1938,F 2,14:3
Merry Wives of Windsor, The 1938,Ap 15,22:3
Little Foxes, The 1939,F 16,16:2
Life and Death of an American 1939,My 20,11:2
In a Jewish Grocery 1939,O 2,15:2
Fifth Column, The 1940,Mr 7,18:2
Morning Star 1940,Ap 17,26:4
Corn Is Green, The 1940,N 27,27:2
Beggar's Opera 1941,Ap 14,12:4:6
Man With Blonde Hair, The 1941,N 5,30:2
Brooklyn, U S A 1941,D 22,24:2
Brooklyn, U S A 1941,D 28,IX,1:1
Brooklyn, U S A 1942,Ja 11,IX,1:1
Johnny 2X4 1942,Mr 17,24:6

Bay, Howard (Scenic Designer)—Cont
Moon Is Down, The 1942,Ap 8,22:2
Strings, My Lord, Are False, The 1942,My 20,24:2
Uncle Harry 1942,My 21,24:1
Eve of St Mark, The 1942,O 8,30:2
Count Me In 1942,O 9,24:2
Great Big Doorstep, The 1942,N 27,26:2
Patriots, The 1943,Ja 30,11:2
Corn Is Green, The 1943,My 4,18:3
Merry Widow, The 1943,Ag 5,19:2
New Life, A 1943,S 16,26:6
One Touch of Venus 1943,O 8,14:1
Carmen Jones 1943,D 3,26:2
Listen Professor! 1943,D 23,22:1
Storm Operation 1944,Ja 12,28:2
Chicken Every Sunday 1944,Ap 6,27:2
Follow the Girls 1944,Ap 10,15:2
Searching Wind, The 1944,Ap 13,25:2
Ten Little Indians 1944,Je 28,21:2
Catherine Was Great 1944,Ag 3,16:1
Men to the Sea 1944,O 4,25:2
Merry Widow, The 1944,O 9,17:1
Visitor, The 1944,O 18,24:5
Violet 1944,O 25,16:1
Up in Central Park 1945,Ja 29,17:2
Carmen Jones 1945,My 3,26:5
Marinka 1945,Jl 19,19:2
Devils Galore 1945,S 13,27:2
Deep Are the Roots 1945,S 27,24:4
Polonaise 1945,O 8,20:2
Show Boat 1946,Ja 7,17:2
Would-Be Gentleman, The 1946,Ja 10,29:2
Show Boat 1946,Ja 13,II,1:1
Carmen Jones 1946,Ap 8,32:2
Woman Bites Dog 1946,Ap 18,21:2
Up in Central Park 1947,My 20,29:2
Magdalena 1948,Jl 28,27:2
Show Boat 1948,S 9,33:2
Magdalena 1948,S 21,31:2
As the Girls Go 1948,N 15,21:2
Big Knife, The 1949,F 25,27:5
Montserrat 1949,O 31,21:4
Come Back, Little Sheba 1950,F 16,28:5
Michael Todd's Peep Show 1950,Je 29,37:2
Parisienne 1950,Jl 25,24:2
Lady From the Sea, The 1950,Ag 8,23:2
Hilda Crane 1950,N 2,38:2
Autumn Garden, The 1951,Mr 8,36:2
Flahooley 1951,My 15,39:1
Flahooley 1951,My 20,II,1:1
Two on the Aisle 1951,Jl 20,13:6
Grand Tour, The 1951,D 11,45:2
Shrike, The 1952,Ja 16,20:2
Children's Hour, The 1952,D 19,35:2
Mid-Summer 1953,Ja 22,19:1
Shrike, The 1953,N 26,51:2
Show Boat 1954,My 6,44:1
Sandhog 1954,N 24,17:1
Desperate Hours, The 1955,F 11,20:2
Desperate Hours, The 1955,F 20,II,1:1
Finian's Rainbow 1955,My 19,25:1
Red Roses for Me 1955,D 29,15:2
Carmen Jones 1956,Je 1,28:2
Very Special Baby, A 1956,N 15,43:2
Night of the Auk 1956,D 4,50:2
Tevya and His Daughters 1957,S 17,38:2
Best of Burlesque 1957,S 30,27:2
Music Man, The 1957,D 20,31:1
Interlock 1958,F 7,18:1
Music Man, The 1958,S 28,II,1:1
Desert Incident, A 1959,Mr 25,40:1
Cut of the Axe 1960,F 2,38:2
Cool World, The 1960,F 23,38:2
Toys in the Attic 1960,F 26,23:2
Finian's Rainbow 1960,Ap 28,31:1
Wall, The 1960,O 12,44:4
Wall, The 1960,O 23,II,1:1
Show Boat 1961,Ap 13,32:1
Pal Joey 1961,Je 1,32:1
Milk and Honey 1961,O 11,52:1
Isle of Children 1962,Mr 17,16:2
My Mother, My Father and Me 1963,Mr 25,5:5
Pal Joey 1963,My 30,21:1
Bicycle Ride to Nevada 1963,S 25,38:1
Never Live Over a Pretzel Factory 1964,Mr 30,37:1
Music Man, The 1965,Je 17,26:4
Man of La Mancha 1965,N 23,52:1
Finian's Rainbow 1967,Ap 6,44:1
Little Foxes, The 1967,O 27,53:1
Fire! 1969,Ja 29,26:1
Cry for Us All 1970,Ap 9,48:2
Bay, Jane
Alcide Pepis 1923,O 30,17:2
Crucifies, Les 1923,O 30,17:2
Trois Masques, Les 1923,N 6,22:1
Sol Hyam's Brocanteur 1923,N 27,23:5
Petite Bonnie Serieuse 1923,N 27,23:5
Bay, Jeanne
Horrible Experience, L' 1923,O 23,16:1
Nounouche 1923,O 23,16:1
Laboratoire des Hallucinations, Le 1923,N 20,23:3
Bonheur, Le 1923,N 20,23:3
Bay, Louis de V Jr
Great Guns 1939,N 18,23:4

Bay, Richard (Scenic Designer)
Trojan Incident 1938,Ap 22,15:2
Bay, Robert
What's Up 1943,N 12,24:6
Toplitzky of Notre Dame 1946,D 27,13:4
Bayan, Adrienne
Hickory Stick 1944,My 9,15:6
Bayard, Beatrice
Kibitzer, The 1929,F 19,22:5
Bayer, Carole (Lyricist)
Georgy 1970,F 27,26:1
Bayer, Eleanor (Playwright)
Third Best Sport 1958,D 31,15:3
Bayer, Frank
Country Wife, The 1965,D 10,58:2
Alchemist, The 1966,O 14,48:1
Galileo 1967,Ap 14,31:1
Bayer, Frank (Miscellaneous)
Caretaker, The 1963,N 25,23:2
Miser, The 1969,My 9,35:1
Disintegration of James Cherry, The
1970,Ja 30,33:3
Landscape 1970,Ap 3,43:1
Silence 1970,Ap 3,43:1
Bayer, Leo (Playwright)
Third Best Sport 1958,D 31,15:3
Bayer, Rolf
Injury Sustained 1940,O 24,30:3
War and Peace 1942,My 22,26:3
Winter Soldiers 1942,N 30,19:2
Bayers, Margaret
Octoroon, The 1929,Mr 13,28:3
Bayes, Joanne
Picture of Dorian Gray, The 1956,Ag 18,15:5
Bayes, Nora
Her Family Tree 1920,D 28,9:2
Untitled-Benefit 1922,My 8,14:5
Queen O' Hearts 1922,O 11,22:1
Vaudeville (Palace) 1923,N 13,24:2
Vaudeville (Palace) 1923,N 20,23:4
Vaudeville (Loew's State) 1927,F 1,24:6
Bayes, Nora (Composer)
Round With Ring, A 1969,O 30,56:1
Bayes, Olive
Free for All 1931,S 9,25:1
Bayes, Sammy (Choreographer)
Fiddler on the Roof 1967,S 7,50:1
Canterbury Tales; Steward's Tale, The
1969,F 4,34:1
Canterbury Tales; Miller's Tale, The 1969,F 4,34:1
Canterbury Tales; Merchant's Tale, The
1969,F 4,34:1
Canterbury Tales; Pilgrims, The 1969,F 4,34:1
Canterbury Tales; Wife of Bath's Tale, The
1969,F 4,34:1
Bayes, Sammy (Director)
Fiddler on the Roof 1967,S 7,50:1
Bayfield, Al
Othello 1937,Ja 7,16:4
Bayfield, St Clair
Mob, The 1920,O 11,18:1
Deburau 1920,D 24,14:3
Bulldog Drummond 1921,D 27,10:2
Lady Cristilinda, The 1922,D 26,11:2
School for Scandal, The 1923,Mr 13,19:2
Lass O' Laughter 1925,Ja 9,13:2
Two by Two 1925,F 24,17:1
Bit o' Love, A 1925,My 13,24:2
Beaten Track, The 1926,F 9,23:2
Escape 1927,O 27,33:1
Lady Dedlock 1929,Ja 1,61:2
London Calling 1930,O 20,29:1
Lady With a Lamp, The 1931,N 20,27:2
Wild Waves 1932,F 20,11:4
Criminal at Large 1932,O 11,26:3
Peace Palace 1933,Je 6,30:2
They Shall Not Die 1934,F 22,24:4
Love on an Island 1934,Jl 24,20:5
Judgment Day 1934,S 13,26:4
Field of Ermine 1935,F 9,10:4
Mistress of the Inn, The 1937,Je 22,26:3
Princess Turandot 1937,Ag 3,20:5
Father Malachy's Miracle 1937,N 18,26:4
Father Malachy's Miracle 1937,D 5,XII,5:1
Glorious Morning 1938,N 28,10:3
Jeremiah 1939,F 4,11:2
Day in the Sun 1939,My 17,29:2
Old Foolishness, The 1940,D 21,20:2
Night Before Christmas, The 1941,Ap 11,25:2
Highland Fling, A 1944,Ap 29,13:2
Hand in Glove 1944,D 5,19:1
For Heaven's Sake Mother 1948,N 17,33:4
Bayh, Mary Alice
Fair Game 1957,N 4,39:1
Season of Choice 1959,Ap 14,40:1
Power of Darkness, The 1959,S 30,33:1
Viva Madison Avenue 1960,Ap 7,42:1
Mister Roberts 1962,O 12,27:2
Bayhl, Anna
Fruehlingsluft 1921,N 29,17:4
Bayless, Jean
Sound of Music, The 1961,My 19,22:6

Bayley, John W
Blue Monday 1932,Je 3,23:2
Bayley, William R
Grey Heir, The 1926,Ap 6,29:2
Baylies, Edmund
South Pacific 1961,Ap 27,26:3
Baylies, Edmund (Director)
Dear Charles 1954,S 16,37:2
Dear Charles 1954,S 26,II,1:1
Baylies, Edmund (Miscellaneous)
Fallen Angels 1956,Ja 18,27:1
Hotel Paradiso 1957,Ap 12,22:2
Interlock 1958,F 7,18:1
Dear Liar 1960,Mr 18,19:2
Midgie Purvis 1961,F 2,25:3
Fiddler on the Roof 1969,Je 26,47:1
Baylis, John
Crystal Heart, The 1960,F 16,31:2
Athenian Touch, The 1964,Ja 15,25:4
Bayliss, Gene (Choreographer)
Hit the Trail 1954,D 3,31:2
Half-Past Wednesday 1962,Ap 7,16:2
Carnival 1962,Je 6,37:1
Bayliss, Gene (Miscellaneous)
Carnival! 1961,Ap 14,22:2
Bayliss, Peter
Matchmaker, The 1955,D 6,45:6
Matchmaker, The 1955,D 18,II,3:1
How's the World Treating You? 1966,O 25,50:1
Rockefeller and the Red Indians 1968,O 25,37:1
Council of Love 1970,Ag 21,21:2
Council of Love 1970,S 12,32:2
Baylor, David
Surgeon, The 1932,O 28,23:1
Baylor, Ellen
Ol' Man Satan 1932,O 4,26:3
Bayne, Arthur
Hail and Farewell 1923,F 20,12:1
Bayne, Beverly
Vaudeville (Palace) 1926,N 9,30:3
From Eight to Twelve 1926,N 9,30:3
Escapade 1929,S 29,IX,5:1
Gala Night 1930,F 26,22:4
Only the Young 1932,S 22,25:2
Symphony 1935,Ap 27,20:3
I Like It Here 1946,Mr 23,8:6
Loco 1946,O 17,29:2
Cup of Trembling, The 1948,Ap 21,33:5
Bayne, Daphne
Hamlet 1936,N 11,54:2
Bayne, Mardi
Red Mill, The 1945,O 17,16:2
Wish You Were Here 1952,Je 26,26:6
Bazarini, John
Chief Thing, The 1963,Ap 30,27:2
Bazelon, Irwin (Composer)
Frankie and Johnny 1952,O 29,37:2
Taming of the Shrew, The 1956,Ag 6,20:1
Taming of the Shrew, The 1957,F 21,30:2
Merry Wives of Windsor, The 1959,Jl 9,23:2
Bazen, Lola
Adam Had Two Sons 1932,Ja 21,17:1
Bazzi, Maria
Rain 1925,S 27,28:6
Be Gar, Harry
Taming of the Shrew, The 1935,O 1,27:3
Taming of the Shrew, The 1940,F 6,17:2
Beaban, Charles (Original Author)
Society Girl 1931,D 31,16:1
Beaber, Jack
Coco 1969,D 19,66:1
Beaber, Jack (Director)
All in Love 1961,N 11,15:2
Beach, Albert A (Composer)
Mating Dance 1965,N 4,58:1
Beach, Beatrice
Streets of New York, The 1934,Jl 21,14:5
Whiteheaded Boy, The 1937,Ag 11,27:3
Beach, Beatrice (Director)
Coquette 1935,Jl 10,24:1
Camille 1935,Jl 31,21:1
Vinegar Tree, The 1935,Ag 14,16:1
Pursuit of Happiness, The 1936,Jl 15,14:1
Private Lives 1937,Jl 14,17:4
Fly Away Home 1937,Jl 28,15:1
Ode to Liberty 1937,Ag 18,15:2
Beach, Chisholm
Re-Echo 1934,Ja 12,28:4
Beach, Edward
Detective Story 1954,F 13,11:2
Beach, George
Blossom Time 1943,S 6,21:2
Beach, Gertrude
Janie 1942,S 11,24:2
Marriage Is for Single People 1945,N 22,38:2
Beach, Lewis (Director)
Merry Andrew 1929,Ja 22,22:2
Beach, Lewis (Playwright)
Square Peg, A 1923,Ja 29,10:2
Square Peg, A 1923,F 11,VII,1:1
Clod, The 1923,My 26,8:4
Goose Hangs High, The 1924,Ja 30,16:1
Goose Hangs High, The 1924,F 3,VII,1:1

Beach, Lewis (Playwright)—Cont
Merry Andrew 1929,Ja 13,VIII,2:4
Merry Andrew 1929,Ja 22,22:2
Ann Vroome 1930,Jl 27,VIII,2:3
Beach, Rex (Playwright)
Betty Lee 1924,D 26,18:2
Beach, Richard
Street Wolf, The 1929,Ja 1,61:1
Beach, Richard (Pvt)
Winged Victory 1943,N 22,24:1
Beach, Scott
Committee, The 1964,S 17,53:1
Beach, Stewart (Playwright)
Lend Me Your Ears! 1936,O 6,28:5
Beach, William
Sons and Soldiers 1943,My 5,22:2
Beachner, Louis
Moon Shines on Kylenamoe, The 1962,O 31,33:1
Figuro in the Night 1962,O 31,33:1
Georgy 1970,F 27,26:1
Beachner, Louis (Director)
Workhouse Ward, The 1959,Ap 11,15:4
Well of the Saints, The 1959,Ap 11,15:4
Beadle, Spofford
Third Best Sport 1958,D 31,15:3
Beadle, Spofford (Lighting Director)
Ah, Wilderness! 1953,F 7,10:6
Beadle, Spofford (Producer)
Major Barbara 1965,My 18,33:1
Beadling, Maybelle
Exceeding Small 1928,O 23,32:2
Beahan, Charles (Original Author)
Hold Your Horses 1933,S 26,26:4
Beahan, Charles (Playwright)
Jarnegan 1928,S 25,29:2
Buckaroo 1929,Mr 18,31:1
Little Orchard Annie 1930,Ap 22,33:1
Beahan, John
Madwoman of Chaillot, The 1950,Je 14,41:2
Beakel, Walter
Summer and Smoke 1952,Ap 25,19:5
Power of Dreams, A 1958,Mr 11,33:1
Beakel, Walter (Director)
Have You Heard This One 1953,N 9,23:4
Anna Christie 1955,N 22,41:1
Don Juan; Feast With the Statue, The
1956,Ja 4,21:4
Beakel, Walter (Miscellaneous)
Shadow of Heroes 1961,D 6,59:1
Beakey, Colin
Ice Follies 1963,Ja 10,5:2
Beakey, Molly
Ice Follies 1963,Ja 10,5:2
Beal, John
No More Frontier 1931,O 22,27:1
Wild Waves 1932,Ja 24,VIII,3:3
Wild Waves 1932,F 20,11:4
Another Language 1932,Ap 26,25:3
Another Language 1932,My 15,VIII,1:1
Another Language 1933,My 9,20:2
She Loves Me Not 1933,N 21,22:4
Russet Mantle 1936,Ja 17,15:5
Russet Mantle 1936,Ja 26,IX,1:1
Soliloquy 1938,N 29,26:4
Miss Swan Expects 1939,F 21,15:2
I Know What I Like 1939,N 25,13:5
Liberty Jones 1941,F 6,24:2
Eurydice 1948,O 17,I,67:4
Our Town 1959,Mr 24,46:2
Our Town 1959,Ap 5,II,1:1
Calculated Risk 1962,N 1,35:1
Queens of France 1966,S 7,53:1
Happy Journey to Trenton and Camden, The
1966,S 7,53:1
Long Christmas Dinner, The 1966,S 7,53:1
Our Town 1968,S 29,77:4
Front Page, The 1968,O 20,85:5
To Be Young Gifted and Black; World of Lorraine
Hansberry, The 1969,Ja 3,15:1
Billy 1969,Mr 24,56:1
Our Town 1969,N 28,50:1
Our Town 1969,D 7,II,7:1
Candyapple, The 1970,N 24,33:1
Beal, John (Director)
New Faces of 1952 1952,My 17,23:2
Beal, Kathleen
Babes Don't Cry Anymore 1968,F 21,55:1
Beal, Royal
Elizabeth the Queen 1930,N 4,37:1
Alley Cat 1934,S 18,18:1
Page Miss Glory 1934,N 28,24:2
Noah 1935,F 14,25:2
Achilles Had a Heel 1935,O 14,20:2
Boy Meets Girl 1935,N 19,27:2
Boy Meets Girl 1935,N 28,38:2
Lady Has a Heart, The 1937,S 27,24:1
All That Glitters 1938,Ja 20,18:2
Strangler Fig, The 1940,My 7,31:2
Susannah and the Elders 1940,O 30,28:2
Papa Is All 1942,Ja 7,22:2
Papa Is All 1942,Ja 18,IX,1:1
Without Love 1942,N 11,28:1
Woman Bites Dog 1946,Ap 18,21:2
Parlor Story 1947,Mr 5,29:2

Beal, Royal—Cont
Hallams, The 1948,Mr 5,18:2
Red Gloves 1948,D 6,28:2
Never Say Never 1951,N 21,21:2
No Time for Sergeants 1955,O 21,32:2
Drink to Me Only 1958,O 9,47:4
Kiss Me, Kate 1965,My 13,31:1

Beal, William
Sound of Hunting, A 1945,N 21,16:6

Beale, J H
Gentlemen, the Queen 1927,Ap 23,14:3

Beale, Joseph
Who's Who 1938,Mr 2,16:2
Good Hunting 1938,N 22,26:5

Bealin, Junior
Bright Honor 1936,S 28,14:1

Beall, Alex
Gloria and Esperanza 1969,Ap 5,30:1
Moondreamers, The 1969,D 9,68:1
Gloria and Esperanza 1970,F 5,32:1

Beall, Dickson
Tragical Historie of Doctor Faustus, The
 1964,O 6,34:2

Beals, Barbara
Back Fire 1932,Je 14,26:3
Children's Hour, The 1934,N 21,23:2

Beam, Alice
Song and Dance Man, The 1924,Ja 1,21:2

Beam, Alvin
Almost Crazy 1955,Je 21,37:1

Beam, Bob
Jackpot 1944,Ja 14,15:2

Beam, Jon
Little Boxes; Coffee Lace, The 1969,D 4,71:2

Beaman, Louise
Caesar and Cleopatra 1935,Ag 22,21:1

Beamer, Hazel
Mayflowers 1925,N 25,14:2

Beamer, Keola
13 Daughters 1961,Mr 3,17:2

Beamer, Nona (Miscellaneous)
13 Daughters 1961,Mr 3,17:2

Beamish, Dick (Translator)
Money! Money! 1931,Mr 15,IX,2:8

Beamish, Elsa
How Beautiful With Shoes 1935,N 29,24:1
Merrily We Roll Along 1936,Je 30,15:1

Bean, Adelaide
Late Christopher Bean, The 1932,N 1,24:3
Ah, Wilderness! 1933,O 3,28:2
Time to Go 1952,My 8,35:6

Bean, Adelaide (Playwright)
Bless the Child 1968,My 5,II,16:1

Bean, Alvin
Wonderful Town 1953,F 26,22:3

Bean, David
Peter Pan 1954,O 21,30:2
That Hat! 1964,S 24,45:1

Bean, Orson
Men of Distinction 1953,My 1,18:4
School for Scandal, The 1953,Je 24,29:2
John Murray Anderson's Almanac 1953,D 11,42:2
Almanac 1954,Ja 3,II,1:1
Will Success Spoil Rock Hunter? 1955,O 14,22:2
Mister Roberts 1956,D 6,46:2
Nature's Way 1957,O 17,42:2
Say Darling 1959,F 26,38:2
Subways Are for Sleeping 1961,D 28,22:1
Never Too Late 1962,N 28,42:1
I Was Dancing 1964,N 9,40:4
Illya Darling 1967,Ap 12,37:1
Illya Darling 1967,Ap 30,II,1:1
Round With Ring, A 1969,O 30,56:1

Bean, Reathel
Line of Least Existence, The 1968,Mr 25,53:1
Henry IV, Part II 1968,Jl 2,33:1
Peace 1968,N 10,87:1
Peace 1969,Ja 28,49:1

Beane, Fred
Virgin of Bethulia, The 1925,F 24,17:2

Beane, Frederick
Extra 1923,Ja 24,22:3

Beane, Reginald
Porgy and Bess 1935,O 11,30:2
Mamba's Daughters 1939,Ja 4,24:2
Time of Your Life, The 1939,O 26,26:2
Time of Your Life, The 1940,S 24,27:2
At Home With Ethel Waters 1953,S 23,36:1

Beane, Reginald (Miscellaneous)
Evening With Ethel Waters, An 1959,Ap 9,36:1
Oh, Kay! 1960,Ap 18,37:2

Bear, Chief
Russet Mantle 1936,Ja 17,15:5

Bear, Eddie
White Man 1936,O 19,22:4

Bear, Lone
Arrow-Maker, The 1956,O 5,20:1

Bear, The
Night in Venice, A 1929,My 22,30:2

Beard, Charles
Dark of the Moon 1970,Ap 4,21:2

Beard, Chuck
West Side Story 1968,Je 25,32:1

Beard, Des Moines
Tall Kentuckian, The 1953,Je 17,30:1

Beard, James
Henry V 1960,Je 30,23:1
Smiling the Boy Fell Dead 1961,Ap 20,28:1
Egg, The 1962,Ja 9,23:2
My Fair Lady 1968,Je 14,42:1

Beard, Joan
Public Relations 1944,Ap 7,23:3

Bearden, Romare (Scenic Designer)
Land Beyond the River, A 1957,Mr 29,15:7

Beardslee, Bethany
Play of Daniel, The 1959,D 28,17:6

Beardsley, Alice
Eastward in Eden 1956,Ap 18,25:4
Camino Real 1960,My 17,42:2
Boy on the Straight-Back Chair 1969,Mr 18,36:1

Bearson, Don
Ice Capades 1954,S 16,37:1
Ice Capades 1962,Ag 30,34:1

Beasley, Byron
Eyvind of the Hills 1921,F 2,14:1
Elton Case, The 1921,S 12,16:2
Your Woman and Mine 1922,F 28,17:2
Advertising of Kate, The 1922,My 9,22:2
Mike Angelo 1923,Ja 9,26:2
Alloy 1924,O 28,27:1
Night Hawk 1925,F 25,16:4
Barefoot 1925,O 20,29:2
Head First 1926,Ja 7,22:4
Sunshine 1926,Ag 18,15:2
Howdy King 1926,D 14,24:4

Beasley, Clarence
Virginia 1937,S 3,13:2

Beasley, Violet
Good Times 1920,Ag 10,10:1

Beaston, Frank
Judy Drops In 1924,O 6,24:2
Big Boy 1925,Ja 8,28:2
Gorilla, The 1925,Ap 29,24:2
She Couldn't Say No! 1926,S 1,27:3
Judy 1927,F 8,20:2
Wasp's Nest, The 1927,O 26,26:3
It Is to Laugh 1927,D 27,24:2

Beaton, Betzi
Ziegfeld Follies 1934,Ja 5,24:3
Only Girl, The 1934,My 22,28:2
Fools Rush In 1934,D 26,19:2

Beaton, Cecil
Lady Windermere's Fan 1946,O 15,29:2

Beaton, Cecil (Costume Designer)
Lady Windermere's Fan 1946,O 15,29:2
Second Mrs Tanqueray, The 1950,O 8,II,3:7
Gainsborough Girls, The 1951,Jl 17,31:5
Gainsborough Girls, The 1951,Ag 12,II,1:4
Grass Harp, The 1952,Mr 28,26:2
Quadrille 1952,S 13,10:7
Quadrille 1953,Ap 5,II,1:1
Qudrille 1954,N 4,39:2
Portrait of a Lady 1954,D 22,27:6
Chalk Garden, The 1955,O 27,29:1
My Fair Lady 1956,Mr 16,20:2
My Fair Lady 1956,Mr 25,II,1:1
Little Glass Clock, The 1956,Mr 27,40:2
My Fair Lady 1956,Ap 29,II,1:1
My Fair Lady 1958,Mr 9,II,1:1
Look After Lulu 1959,Mr 4,35:1
Saratoga 1959,D 8,59:4
Dear Liar 1960,Mr 18,19:2
Tenderloin 1960,O 18,47:2
School for Scandal, The 1962,My 18,34:2
My Fair Lady 1962,Je 14,24:1
My Fair Lady 1964,My 21,43:2
My Fair Lady 1968,Je 14,42:1
Coco 1969,D 19,66:1
Coco 1969,D 28,II,1:1

Beaton, Cecil (Lighting Director)
Lady Windermere's Fan 1946,O 15,29:2
Cry of the Peacock 1950,Ap 12,33:2

Beaton, Cecil (Miscellaneous)
Cry of the Peacock 1950,Ap 12,33:2

Beaton, Cecil (Playwright)
Gainsborough Girls, The 1951,Jl 17,31:5
Gainsborough Girls, The 1951,Ag 12,II,1:4

Beaton, Cecil (Scenic Designer)
Lady Windermere's Fan 1946,O 15,29:2
Second Mrs Tanqueray, The 1950,O 8,II,3:7
Gainsborough Girls, The 1951,Jl 17,31:5
Gainsborough Girls, The 1951,Ag 12,II,1:4
Grass Harp, The 1952,Mr 28,26:2
Grass Harp, The 1952,Ap 6,II,1:1
Quadrille 1952,S 13,10:7
Quadrille 1953,Ap 5,II,1:1
Qudrille 1954,N 4,39:2
Chalk Garden, The 1955,O 27,29:1
Little Glass Clock, The 1956,Mr 27,40:2
My Fair Lady 1958,My 1,34:5
Look After Lulu 1959,Mr 4,35:1
Saratoga 1959,D 8,59:4
Tenderloin 1960,O 18,47:2
School for Scandal, The 1962,My 18,34:2
Coco 1969,D 19,66:1

Beaton, Norman
Tempest, The 1970,Ag 29,14:1

Beatrice and Cappella
'Tis of Thee 1940,O 28,21:3

Beatrize, Audrey
Riders to the Sea 1949,F 4,30:2

Beattie, Aubrey
Bootleggers, The 1922,N 28,24:1
Exile, The 1923,Ap 10,24:2
Made for Each Other 1924,S 30,27:2
Playing the Game 1927,D 20,32:5
She Got What She Wanted 1929,Mr 5,28:1
If Booth Had Missed 1932,F 5,24:2

Beattie, Barbara Ann
Sound of Music, The 1970,Jl 3,13:1

Beattie, Brenton
Sketch Book 1935,Je 5,22:2

Beattie, Dorothy
Edward, My Son 1948,O 1,30:2

Beattie, Herbert
Mikado, The 1959,O 2,24:1
Pirates of Penzance, The 1960,O 7,29:1
Mikado, The 1961,Ja 18,26:1
Pirates of Penzance, The 1961,Ja 20,24:5
Yeomen of the Guard, The 1964,Mr 19,29:2
Mikado, The 1965,Ap 17,11:3
Pirates of Penzance, The 1965,Ap 21,50:6
Yeomen of the Guard, The 1965,Ap 22,26:1

Beattie, Richard Arnold
Sound of Music, The 1970,Jl 3,13:1

Beattie, Rosemary (Director)
Homecoming, The 1967,O 5,47:3

Beattle, Aubrey
Wooden Slipper, The 1934,Ja 4,16:3

Beatty, Babbette
Capacity for Wings 1957,Ja 10,25:2

Beatty, Babbette (Producer)
Capacity for Wings 1957,Ja 10,25:2

Beatty, Babs
Streetcar Named Desire, A 1955,Mr 4,18:2

Beatty, Bessie (Playwright)
Jamboree 1932,N 25,18:4

Beatty, Colin
Ice Follies 1959,Ja 14,30:1
Ice Follies 1961,Ja 11,25:2
Ice Follies 1962,Ja 10,24:6
Ice Follies 1966,Ja 12,27:6

Beatty, George
Vaudeville (Palace) 1929,N 25,22:4
Vaudeville (Palace) 1931,Je 22,17:2

Beatty, Juanita
Having Wonderful Time 1937,F 22,12:5

Beatty, Molly
Ice Follies 1959,Ja 14,30:1
Ice Follies 1961,Ja 11,25:2
Ice Follies 1962,Ja 10,24:6

Beatty, Ned
Devils, The 1963,N 5,25:1
Lonesome Train, The 1965,Je 17,25:1
Hard Travelin' 1965,Je 17,25:1
Great White Hope, The 1967,D 14,58:1
Iceman Cometh, The 1968,Ap 1,58:1
Night Thoreau Spent in Jail, The 1970,N 2,66:1

Beatty, Robert
Bell for Adano, A 1945,S 20,31:1

Beatty, Roberta
Good Morning, Dearie 1921,N 2,20:2
Bunch and Judy, The 1922,N 29,20:1
Cinders 1923,Ap 4,22:1
Aren't We All? 1923,My 22,14:2
Peg o' My Dreams 1924,My 6,25:3
Student Prince, The 1924,D 3,25:3
Thou Desperate Pilot 1927,Mr 8,23:1
Love Call, The 1927,O 25,33:1
Possession 1928,O 3,35:1
Sherlock Holmes 1929,N 26,28:3
Frankie and Johnny 1930,S 26,16:5
Broadway Boy 1932,My 4,23:5
Girls in Uniform 1932,D 31,10:3
Nine Pine Street 1933,Ap 28,15:5
Blue Widow, The 1933,Ag 31,20:2
Keeper of the Keys 1933,O 19,23:2
Roberta 1933,N 20,18:4
Lake, The 1933,D 27,24:2
Lady of Letters 1935,Mr 29,26:6

Beatty, Talley
Show Boat 1946,Ja 7,17:2

Beatty, Talley (Choreographer)
Apollo of Bellac, The 1957,Ap 10,39:1
Virtuous Island, The 1957,Ap 10,39:1
Fly Blackbird 1962,F 6,26:2
Ballad for Bimshire 1963,O 16,54:1
House of Flowers 1968,Ja 29,26:2
But Never Jam Today 1969,Ap 24,40:1
Bill Noname 1970,Mr 3,37:1
Don't Bother Me, I Can't Cope 1970,O 8,60:3

Beatty, Talley (Miscellaneous)
Blacks, The 1961,My 5,23:1

Beatty, Warren
Loss of Roses, A 1959,N 30,27:1
Loss of Roses, A 1959,D 6,II,5:1

Beattys, The
Ice Follies 1960,Ja 13,20:1

Beattys, The—Cont
Ice Follies 1965,Ja 13,35:1
Ice Follies 1969,My 23,38:1
Ice Follies 1970,My 23,27:1
Beauchamp
Baptiste 1952,N 13,34:2
Proces, Le; Trial, The 1952,N 18,36:2
Occupe-Toi d'Amelie; Keep Your Eyes on Amelie 1952,N 25,35:2
Hamlet 1952,D 2,39:1
Christophe Colomb 1957,Ja 31,20:5
Volpone 1957,F 5,27:2
Feu la Mere de Madame; Dear Departed Mother-in-Law 1957,F 12,31:1
Beauchamp, Guy (Playwright)
Come Across 1938,S 15,28:3
Beaudet, Louise
Nature's Nobleman 1921,N 15,23:2
White Lilacs 1928,S 11,31:2
Mother Lode 1934,D 24,16:5
Beaudouin, John D
Hit the Road 1941,Ap 4,18:3
Beaumar, Constance
Genius and the Crowd 1920,S 7,20:1
Tantrum, The 1924,S 5,20:2
Morning After, The 1925,Jl 28,24:2
Beaumarchais (Original Author)
Barbier de Seville, Le 1939,Mr 7,19:2
Once Over Lightly 1942,N 20,26:2
Mariage de Figaro, Le 1964,F 26,41:2
Beaumarchais (Playwright)
Barbier de Seville, Le 1955,N 9,40:1
Barbier de Seville, Le 1955,N 20,II,1:1
Beaumont, Bertie
June Love 1921,Ap 26,20:1
Bombo 1921,O 7,20:2
Gingham Girl, The 1922,Ag 29,15:5
Polly of Hollywood 1927,F 22,22:3
Beaumont, Diana
It Happened to Adam 1934,N 10,18:6
Good Fairy, The 1937,My 15,23:3
Beaumont, Francis (Playwright)
Knight of the Burning Pestle, The 1927,Ap 23,15:1
Knight of the Burning Pestle, The 1953,O 24,13:2
Beaumont, Gerald (Playwright)
Wild Oats Lane 1922,Jl 23,VI,1:6
Wild Oats Lane 1922,S 7,12:1
Dove, The 1925,F 12,17:3
Beaumont, John (Lighting Director)
Who's Who, Baby? 1968,Ja 30,36:1
Beaumont, John H (Producer)
Now 1968,Je 6,53:1
Beaumont, Lucy
Champion, The 1921,Ja 4,11:1
Wait Till We're Married 1921,S 27,14:1
Rosa Machree 1922,Ja 10,15:2
Berkeley Square 1929,N 5,32:4
John Ferguson 1933,Jl 11,15:7
Lake, The 1933,D 27,24:2
Bishop Misbehaves, The 1935,F 21,22:4
Beaumont, Maude
Mikado, The 1924,Jl 29,9:1
Beaumont, Paul de (Translator)
Streetcar Named Desire, A 1949,O 19,36:6
Desire Under the Elms 1953,N 29,II,3:1
Beaumont, Ralph (Choreographer)
Wonderful Town 1958,Mr 6,32:4
Saratoga 1959,D 8,59:4
Pal Joey 1961,Je 1,32:1
Wonderful Town 1963,F 15,10:2
Babes in the Wood 1964,D 29,21:2
Guys and Dolls 1965,Ap 29,39:1
Yearling, The 1965,D 11,25:1
Most Happy Fella, The 1966,My 12,55:1
Guys and Dolls 1966,Je 9,55:2
Wonderful Town 1967,My 18,50:1
Beaumont, Ralph (Director)
Most Happy Fella, The 1966,My 12,55:1
Beaumont, Robert
Caesar and Cleopatra 1951,D 20,43:2
Antony and Cleopatra 1951,D 21,22:2
Beaumont, Robert (Director)
King and I, The 1961,Mr 19,22:5
Beaumont, Sascha
Scandals 1920,Je 8,9:1
Demi-Virgin, The 1921,O 19,22:1
Merry Merry 1925,S 25,24:3
Oh, Kay! 1926,N 9,31:3
Bad Girl 1930,O 3,30:2
Trick for Trick 1932,F 19,14:2
Beaumont, Wilbert S
This Way Out 1929,Ap 28,24:4
Beauvais, Jeanne
Rosalinda; Fledermaus, Die 1942,O 29,26:5
Beggar's Opera, The 1957,Mr 14,35:1
Boy Friend, The 1970,Ap 26,II,5:7
Boy Friend, The 1970,Ap 26,II,5:7
Beauvais, Peter
Tortilla Flat 1938,Ja 13,16:2
Flowers of Virtue, The 1942,F 6,22:2
Talking to You 1942,Ag 18,17:1
Beaux, Ernesta (Playwright)
Thy People 1935,Ag 13,20:3

Beavers, Virgil (Scenic Designer)
Latent Heterosexual, The 1968,Mr 22,52:1
Beban, George Jr
Spring in Autumn 1937,Ag 17,23:1
Tell My Story 1939,Mr 16,26:6
Foreigners 1939,D 6,30:2
Bebout, Cynthia
Alchemist, The 1964,S 15,33:1
Billy Liar 1965,Mr 18,26:1
Becaud, Gilbert
Gilbert Becaud on Broadway 1966,N 1,35:1
Becaud, Gilbert (Miscellaneous)
Gilbert Becaud Sings Love 1968,O 7,53:5
Becaud, Gilbert (Musical Director)
Gilbert Becaud Sings Love 1968,O 7,53:5
Beche, Thomas (Costume Designer)
New Faces of 1952 1952,My 25,II,1:1
Becher, John
Henry VIII 1946,N 7,42:2
Androcles and the Lion 1946,D 20,29:2
Yellow Jack 1947,F 28,26:2
Alice in Wonderland 1947,Ap 7,19:2
Skipper Next to God 1948,Ja 5,14:5
Becher, John C
When the Bough Breaks 1950,Mr 9,25:5
Country Wife, The 1955,Ap 6,35:1
Brigadoon 1957,Mr 28,37:1
American Dream, The 1961,Ja 25,28:1
Happy Days 1961,S 18,36:1
Bertha 1962,F 12,27:1
Endgame 1962,F 12,27:1
Brigadoon 1962,My 31,21:4
Dumbwaiter, The 1962,N 27,44:1
Brigadoon 1963,F 1,6:2
Ballad of the Sad Cafe, The 1963,O 31,27:1
Child Buyer, The 1964,D 22,35:1
That Thing at the Cherry Lane 1965,My 19,42:1
Mame 1966,My 25,41:1
Harvey 1970,F 25,41:1
Becher, Thomas (Costume Designer)
Thumbs Up! 1934,D 28,24:1
New Faces of 1952 1952,My 17,23:2
John Murray Anderson's Almanac 1953,D 11,42:2
Almanac 1954,Ja 3,II,1:1
Catch a Star! 1955,S 7,35:2
New Faces of 1956 1956,Je 15,32:1
New Faces of 1962 1962,F 2,25:1
Family Way, The 1965,Ja 14,44:5
Bechet, Sidney
Hear That Trumpet 1946,O 8,19:2
Beck, Arthur (Miscellaneous)
Once Upon a Mattress 1959,My 12,40:1
Sophie 1963,Ap 16,32:1
Beck, Barbara
Henry, Sweet Henry 1967,O 24,51:2
Beck, Ed
Vaudeville (Palace) 1926,S 7,24:6
Beck, Emily H
Trojan Women, The 1941,Ap 9,32:5
Beck, Eve
Red Roses for Me 1955,D 29,15:2
Ulysses in Nighttown 1958,Je 6,30:1
Beck, Francis
Professor Mamlock 1937,Ap 14,30:3
Beck, Garrick
Many Loves 1959,Ja 14,28:1
Beck, Helen
New Hellzapoppin, The 1939,D 12,36:4
Priorities of 1942 1942,Mr 13,23:2
Beck, Hubert
Othello 1953,O 30,28:2
Prescott Proposals, The 1953,D 17,53:1
Beck, Jackson
Blue Jeans 1933,Ap 9,31:5
Beck, Janet
Jazz a La Carte 1922,Je 3,8:3
Beck, Joanne (Costume Designer)
Sharon's Grave 1961,N 9,39:2
Beck, John
Pepper Mill 1937,Ja 6,19:4
Beck, Julian
Tonight We Improvise 1959,N 7,27:4
Many Loves 1961,Je 16,29:1
Apple, The 1961,D 8,44:1
Antigone 1968,O 11,36:1
Beck, Julian (Director)
Many Loves 1959,Ja 14,28:1
Cave at Machpelah, The 1959,Jl 1,25:1
Tonight We Improvise 1959,N 7,27:4
Women of Trachis 1960,Je 23,18:3
Many Loves 1961,Je 16,29:1
Man Is Man 1962,S 19,31:1
Mysteries and Smaller Pieces 1966,F 26,14:1
Paradise Now 1968,Ag 22,47:4
Frankenstein 1968,O 3,54:1
Antigone 1968,O 11,36:1
Beck, Julian (Miscellaneous)
Mountain Giants, The 1961,Ap 5,32:3
Beck, Julian (Producer)
Many Loves 1961,Je 16,29:1
Paradise Now 1969,Je 10,52:3
Beck, Julian (Scenic Designer)
Doctor Faustus Lights the Lights 1951,D 3,23:4

Beck, Julian (Scenic Designer)—Cont
Many Loves 1959,Ja 14,28:1
Cave at Machpelah, The 1959,Jl 1,25:1
Connection, The 1959,Jl 16,30:2
Tonight We Improvise 1959,N 7,27:4
Women of Trachis 1960,Je 23,18:3
Marrying Maiden, The 1960,Je 23,18:3
In the Jungle of Cities 1960,D 21,39:1
Apple, The 1961,D 8,44:1
Man Is Man 1962,S 19,31:1
Brig, The 1963,My 16,40:1
Frankenstein 1968,O 3,54:1
Beck, Larry
Will Morrissey's Newcomers 1923,Ag 9,16:2
Merry Merry 1925,S 25,24:3
Jonica 1930,Ap 8,27:1
Polonaise 1945,O 8,20:2
Beck, Martin (Producer)
Madame Pompadour 1924,N 12,20:6
Vaudeville (Palace) 1932,My 16,19:2
Vaudeville (Palace) 1932,My 23,18:7
Chrysalis 1932,N 16,15:2
Beck, Max
Summer Wives 1936,Ap 14,18:1
When Differences Disappear 1941,Je 3,17:4
More the Merrier, The 1941,S 16,19:3
Beck, Morton
Vaudeville (Palace) 1926,S 7,24:6
Beck, Rolly
Front Page, The 1946,S 5,22:4
Beck, Sheila
Tall Kentuckian, The 1953,Je 17,30:1
Beck, Stanley
Mister Roberts 1956,D 6,46:2
Days and Nights of Beebee Fenstermaker, The 1962,S 18,33:1
After the Fall 1964,Ja 24,18:1
Marco Millions 1964,F 21,33:1
Changeling, The 1964,O 30,32:2
Incident at Vichy 1964,D 4,44:1
Caucasian Chalk Circle, The 1966,Mr 25,35:1
Beck, Sydney
Elizabethans, The 1962,Ja 22,19:1
Beck, Sydney (Composer)
Golden Age, The 1963,N 19,49:2
Beck, Sydney (Musical Director)
Elizabethans, The 1962,Ja 22,19:1
Golden Age, The 1963,N 19,49:2
Beck, Thomas
Mademoiselle 1932,O 19,22:4
Raw Meat 1933,Mr 23,13:2
Her Majesty the Widow 1934,Je 19,24:5
Temper the Wind 1946,D 28,10:2
Temper the Wind 1947,Ja 12,II,1:1
Beck, Vincent
Peter Pan 1950,Ap 25,27:2
Night Music 1951,Ap 9,29:6
World of Sholom Aleichem, The 1953,S 12,13:2
Merchant of Venice, The 1955,Ja 8,9:7
Almost Crazy 1955,Je 21,37:1
Moon Besieged, The 1962,D 6,54:1
Beck, Walter
Improvisations in June 1928,F 27,16:5
Would-Be Gentleman, The 1928,O 2,34:1
Invitation au Voyage, L' 1928,O 5,17:1
Cherry Orchard, The 1928,O 16,28:5
Peter Pan; Boy Who Would Not Grow Up, The 1928,N 27,36:3
On the High Road 1929,Ja 15,22:3
Katerina 1929,F 26,30:3
Sea Gull, The 1929,S 17,34:1
Living Corpse, The 1929,D 7,19:1
Women Have Their Way, The 1930,Ja 28,28:1
Romeo and Juliet 1930,Ap 22,33:1
Siegfried 1930,O 21,34:1
Alison's House 1930,D 2,31:2
Lady of the Camellias, The 1931,Ja 27,21:2
Liliom 1932,O 27,23:2
Camille 1932,O 28,23:2
Dear Jane 1932,N 15,24:3
Alice in Wonderland 1932,D 12,18:3
Alice in Wonderland 1932,D 25,IX,1:1
Cherry Orchard, The 1933,Mr 7,20:3
Aiglon, L' 1934,N 5,22:2
Rosmersholm 1935,D 3,32:5
Searching for the Sun 1936,F 20,22:6
Bitter Stream 1936,Mr 31,16:6
Othello 1937,Ja 7,16:4
Marching Song 1937,F 18,18:2
Fabulous Invalid, The 1938,O 10,15:1
Land Is Bright, The 1941,O 29,26:2
Guest in the House 1942,F 25,25:2
Doughgirls, The 1942,D 31,19:2
Beck, William
Valmouth 1960,O 7,29:1
Becker, Alan
Camille 1956,S 19,33:1
Becker, Barbara
Tartuffe 1957,O 9,39:1
Becker, Bruce
Cabaret 1966,N 21,62:1
Becker, Bruce (Producer)
Tonight in Samarkand 1955,F 17,22:2
Immoralist, The 1963,N 8,36:2

Becker, Bruce (Producer)—Cont

Untitled-Revue 1965,Je 25,38:1

Becker, Don

Fourth Pig, The 1965,Ja 27,24:6

Becker, Edward

Silk Stockings 1955,F 25,17:3
Body Beautiful, The 1958,Ja 24,15:2
Guys and Dolls 1965,Ap 29,39:1
Most Happy Fella, The 1966,My 12,55:1
Guys and Dolls 1966,Je 9,55:2
Illya Darling 1967,Ap 12,37:1
Jimmy 1969,O 24,38:1

Becker, George

Good Times 1920,Ag 10,10:1

Becker, George (Composer)

Riot Act, The 1963,Mr 9,5:2

Becker, Israel (Director)

Children of the Shadows 1964,F 27,26:1

Becker, Ivan (Playwright)

King's Darling, The 1951,Jl 25,17:2

Becker, Jack

Our Lan' 1947,S 29,16:5
Ali Baba 1951,Mr 27,34:2

Becker, John (Playwright)

If You Get It, Do You Want It? 1938,D 1,28:2

Becker, Lee

Once Over Lightly 1955,Mr 16,39:1
Livin' the Life 1957,Ap 29,20:1
West Side Story 1957,S 27,14:4
Tenderloin 1960,O 18,47:2

Becker, Lee (Choreographer)

Once Over Lightly 1955,Mr 16,39:1

Becker, Maria

Alcestiade 1957,Je 29,11:5
Captain of Koepenick, The 1964,D 2,60:1
Marriage of Mr Mississippi, The 1969,N 20,60:5
Firebugs, The 1969,N 27,52:1
Philipp Hotz 1969,N 27,52:1

Becker, Maria (Director)

Firebugs, The 1969,N 27,52:1

Becker, Marie

If I Were You 1938,Ja 9,II,3:2

Becker, Maximilian (Producer)

Oh, Herbert! 1945,Je 20,26:3
Bathsheba 1947,Mr 27,40:2

Becker, Ray

Choice, The 1930,My 9,20:5
Applause 1970,Mr 31,35:1

Becker, Raymond

Without the Walls 1921,Mr 28,8:1
Without the Walls 1922,Ap 17,17:1
Little Town of Bethlehem, The 1922,D 26,15:4

Becker, Robert

Servant of Two Masters, The 1958,F 11,35:2

Becker, Stanley

Where Do We Go From Here? 1938,N 16,26:2

Becker, Suzan

Dark of the Moon 1958,F 27,22:2

Becker, Terry (Miscellaneous)

Grass Is Always Greener, The 1955,F 16,25:2

Becker, William

Captain Brassbound's Conversion 1950,D 28,21:1

Becker, Z

Untitled-Revue 1935,N 11,21:2

Beckermann, Bernard (Dr) (Director)

Merry Wives of Windsor, The 1959,Mr 14,23:1

Becket, Roger

Junebug Graduates Tonight! 1967,F 27,35:1

Beckett, Hilary

Lion in Love, The 1963,Ap 26,28:3

Beckett, Margaret

Africana 1927,Jl 12,29:2

Beckett, Martha

Tree Grows in Brooklyn, A 1951,Ap 20,24:3

Beckett, Michael

Nathan Weinstein, Mystic, Connecticut
1966,F 26,15:2

Beckett, Samuel (Miscellaneous)

Oh! Calcutta! 1969,Je 18,33:1
Jack MacGowran in the Works of Samuel Beckett
1970,N 20,32:1

Beckett, Samuel (Original Author)

Beginning to End 1970,Ap 25,32:3

Beckett, Samuel (Playwright)

Waiting for Godot 1955,N 13,II,3:1
Waiting for Godot 1956,Ap 20,21:2
Waiting for Godot 1956,Ap 29,II,1:2
Waiting for Godot 1957,Ja 22,25:1
All That Fall 1957,O 8,41:2
Endgame 1958,Ja 29,32:4
Endgame 1958,F 16,II,1:1
Waiting for Godot 1958,Ag 6,22:1
Krapp's Last Tape 1960,Ja 15,37:2
Krapp's Last Tape 1960,Ja 31,II,1:1
Krapp's Last Tape 1960,Mr 29,47:6
Embers 1960,O 26,44:1
Old Tune, The 1961,Mr 24,37:1
Happy Days 1961,S 18,36:1
Happy Days 1961,O 1,II,1:1
Endgame 1962,F 12,27:1
Play 1964,Ja 6,35:1
Endgame 1964,F 21,32:1
Play 1964,Mr 25,46:2
Krapp's Last Tape 1965,Je 9,42:3

Happy Days 1965,S 14,45:2
Waiting for Godot 1968,Ap 23,38:1
Zoo Story, The 1968,O 11,41:1
Krapp's Last Tape 1968,O 11,41:1
Happy Days 1968,O 14,54:1
Oh! Calcutta! 1969,Je 29,II,1:7
Play 1969,O 19,II,12:1
Oh, Les Beaux Jours 1970,Ap 25,32:3
Endgame 1970,My 6,47:1
Beaux Jours, Les 1970,My 20,32:1

Beckett, Samuel (Translator)

Old Tune, The 1961,Mr 24,37:1

Beckett, Scotty

Slightly Married 1943,O 26,19:2

Beckhard, Arthur J (Director)

Another Language 1932,Ap 26,25:3
Another Language 1932,My 15,VIII,1:1
Goodbye Again 1932,D 29,16:4
Comic Artist, The 1933,Ap 20,20:3
Another Language 1933,My 9,20:2
I Was Waiting for You 1933,N 14,23:3
Broomsticks Amen! 1934,F 10,20:4
Wife Insurance 1934,Ap 13,24:5
Miles of Heaven, The 1937,Ag 31,27:4
Suspect 1940,Ap 10,30:4
Bright Boy 1944,Mr 3,19:5
And Be My Love 1945,F 22,30:4
Harvest of Years 1948,Ja 13,29:2

Beckhard, Arthur J (Producer)

Another Language 1932,Ap 26,25:3
Carry Nation 1932,O 31,18:2
Goodbye Again 1932,D 29,16:4
Comic Artist, The 1933,Ap 20,20:3
Another Language 1933,My 9,20:2
Spring in Autumn 1933,O 25,22:5
Picnic 1934,My 3,15:2
American Primitive 1937,Ag 13,12:5
Spring in Autumn 1937,Ag 17,23:1
Miles of Heaven, The 1937,Ag 31,27:4
Suspect 1940,Ap 10,30:4
Bright Boy 1944,Mr 3,19:5
And Be My Love 1945,F 22,30:4
Harvest of Years 1948,Ja 13,29:2

Beckhard, Richard

Miles of Heaven, The 1937,Ag 31,27:4
Male Animal, The 1940,Ja 10,17:2

Beckhard, Richard (Producer)

Madame Is Served 1949,F 15,28:1

Beckhardt, Fred

Cyanamide 1954,Mr 26,17:6

Beckhaus, Friedrich Georg

Faust, Part I; Play, The 1961,F 5,27:2

Beckley, Samuel

Wandering Stars 1946,D 14,18:2

Beckman, Al (Producer)

Bagels and Yox 1951,S 13,38:2

Beckman, Henry

Rumpelstiltskin 1948,Mr 15,27:3
Silver Tassie, The 1949,Jl 22,16:5
Silver Tassie, The 1949,S 4,II,1:1
Golden State, The 1950,N 27,29:3
Darkness at Noon 1951,Ja 15,13:4

Beckman, Suzanne

Another City, Another Land 1968,O 9,42:1
Trumpets and Drums 1969,O 13,52:1

Becknell, Howard (Lighting Director)

Bible Salesman, The 1961,F 21,40:1
Oldest Trick in the World, The 1961,F 21,40:1
Streets of New York, The 1963,O 30,47:1
Hamp 1967,Mr 10,32:1
Spiro Who? 1969,My 19,55:1

Becknell, Howard (Scenic Designer)

Bible Salesman, The 1960,F 22,12:2
Bride in the Morning, A 1960,My 26,38:2
Bible Salesman, The 1961,F 21,40:1
Oldest Trick in the World, The 1961,F 21,40:1
Streets of New York, The 1963,O 30,47:1

Beckwith, Geraldine

Swan, The 1923,O 24,15:3
Grand Duchess and the Waiter, The
1925,O 14,31:1

Beckwith, Marion

Floriani's Wife 1923,O 1,10:1
Wonderful Visit, The 1924,F 13,17:3

Beckwith, Randolph

Flame of Love 1924,Ap 22,19:2

Beckwith, Reginald (Playwright)

Boys in Brown 1940,Je 23,IX,2:5

Beckwith, William

Antigone 1967,Ja 14,18:1

Becque, Henri (Playwright)

Parisienne 1924,N 25,26:2
Parisienne, La 1929,N 21,X,4:6
Parisienne 1950,Jl 25,24:2

Becque, Lucy

Saint of Bleecker Street, The 1954,D 28,21:1

Beda (Lyricist)

Prosit Gypsy 1929,Je 2,VIII,2:6

Beda (Playwright)

Flower of Hawaii; Blume von Hawaii, Die
1931,O 4,VIII,4:1

Bedard, Hubert

Bourgeois Gentilhomme, Le 1964,Je 18,28:2

Beddoe, Don

Nigger Rich 1929,S 21,16:7
Penny Arcade 1930,Mr 11,24:5
Greeks Had a Word for It, The 1930,S 26,16:5
Sing High, Sing Low 1931,N 13,26:4
Warrior's Husband, The 1932,Mr 12,19:4
Man Bites Dog 1933,Ap 26,11:2
Blue Widow, The 1933,Ag 31,20:2
Birthright 1933,N 22,22:3
Nowhere Bound 1935,Ja 23,20:2
First Lady 1935,N 27,17:4
Father Malachy's Miracle 1937,N 18,26:4
Winged Victory 1943,N 22,24:1
Kismet 1965,Je 23,45:1

Bede, Claude

Midsummer Night's Dream, A 1960,Je 30,23:5
Cyrano de Bergerac 1962,Ag 1,21:1
Cyrano de Bergerac 1963,Je 20,30:1
Richard II 1964,Je 17,47:1
King Lear 1964,Je 19,36:1
Henry IV, Part I 1965,Je 30,42:1
Falstaff; Henry IV, Part II 1965,Jl 1,35:1
Julius Caesar 1965,Jl 2,18:1

Bedelia, Bonnie

Isle of Children 1962,Mr 17,16:2
Playroom, The 1965,D 6,49:1
My Sweet Charlie 1966,D 7,56:1

Bedessem, Nicholas

Oedipus Rex 1959,Ap 30,36:1

Bedford, Brian

Five Finger Exercise 1959,D 3,45:4
Five Finger Exercise 1959,D 13,II,3:1
Lord Pengo 1962,N 20,41:2
Private Ear, The 1963,O 10,51:1
Knack, The 1964,My 28,42:2
Knack, The 1964,Je 7,II,1:1
Astrakhan Coat, The 1967,Ja 13,18:1
Unknown Soldier and His Wife, The 1967,Jl 7,22:1
Seven Descents of Myrtle, The 1968,Mr 28,54:1
Seven Descents of Myrtle, The 1968,Ap 7,II,1:5
Cocktail Party, The 1968,O 8,42:1
Misanthrope, The 1968,O 10,59:1
Misanthrope, The 1968,O 20,II,1:1
Cocktail Party, The 1968,O 20,II,1:1
Hamlet 1969,Je 30,33:1
Hamlet 1969,Jl 6,II,1:1
Three Sisters, The 1969,Ag 4,29:1
Three Sisters, The 1969,Ag 10,II,3:1
Private Lives 1969,D 5,52:1
Private Lives 1969,D 14,II,3:3

Bedford, Eleanore

Lolly 1929,O 17,26:2
Everything's Jake 1930,Ja 17,20:4
Oh, Promise Me 1930,N 25,31:1
Divorce Me, Dear 1931,O 7,29:2

Bedford, James

Victoria Regina 1935,D 27,15:2
Victoria Regina 1938,O 4,20:2

Bedford, Patrick

Philadelphia, Here I Come! 1966,F 17,28:1
Mundy Scheme, The 1969,D 12,75:1

Bedford, Ronnie

Thurber Carnival, A 1960,F 27,13:2

Bedford, Virginia

Half-Caste, The 1926,Mr 30,20:4

Bedient, Kenny (Scenic Designer)

Shadow and Substance 1956,Mr 14,38:1

Bedient, Kent (Scenic Designer)

No Exit 1956,Ag 15,23:1

Bedini, Jean

Vaudeville (Palace) 1928,O 9,35:2

Bedsow, Len (Miscellaneous)

Night Circus, The 1958,D 3,44:1

Bedsow, Len (Producer)

Sophie 1963,Ap 16,32:1

Beebe, Harold (Miscellaneous)

O, Oysters! 1961,Ja 23,31:1

Beebe, Harold (Musical Director)

O, Oysters! 1961,Ja 31,23:1
I Want You 1961,S 15,29:1

Beebe, Irving

Betty, Be Good 1920,My 5,14:2
Afgar 1920,N 9,13:2
Marjolaine 1922,Ja 25,16:1
Sweet Little Devil 1924,Ja 22,15:4
Florida Girl 1925,N 3,34:1
Dark Hours, The 1932,N 15,24:2

Beebe, Stuart

Pigeon, The 1930,O 15,26:2
Ghosts 1933,My 24,24:5
Mulatto 1935,Ag 8,13:2
Then Came the Dawn 1935,Ag 29,25:4
Mulatto 1935,O 25,25:2

Beebe, Stuart (Director)

Pigeon, The 1930,O 15,26:2
Devil's Little Game, The 1932,Ag 2,20:4

Beech, Barbara

Abie's Irish Rose 1937,My 13,30:2
Retreat to Pleasure 1940,D 18,32:2

Beech, Ralph

Peace Palace 1933,Je 6,30:2

Beeche, Philip

Sea Dogs 1939,N 7,30:3

Beecher, Georgia (Costume Designer)
Crucible, The 1958,Mr 17,21:1
Beecher, Janet
Cat-Bird, The 1920,F 17,18:1
Call the Doctor 1920,S 1,14:1
Bill of Divorcement, A 1921,O 11,22:2
Bill of Divorcement, A 1921,O 16,VI,1:1
Love Child, The 1922,N 15,22:1
Vaudeville (Palace) 1924,Ap 1,18:1
Steam Roller, The 1924,O 26,VIII,2:1
Steam Roller, The 1924,N 11,20:2
Ostriches 1925,Mr 31,16:1
Kiss in a Taxi, The 1925,Ag 26,14:1
Vaudeville (Palace) 1927,My 3,25:2
Courage 1928,O 9,34:2
Olivia Bows to Mrs Grundy 1932,Ap 3,VIII,2:5
When Ladies Meet 1932,Ag 14,IX,1:7
Men Must Fight 1932,O 15,13:4
Slightly Scandalous 1944,Je 14,16:2
Late George Apley, The 1944,O 20,16:4
Late George Apley, The 1944,N 22,26:2
Late George Apley, The 1944,D 3,II,1:1
Beecher, Marjorie
What's Up 1943,N 12,24:6
Beecher, Robert W (Producer)
Crucible, The 1958,Mr 17,21:1
Beecher, Sylvia
Seventh Heart, The 1927,My 3,24:4
Beecroft, Eleanor
Heartbreak House 1968,Jl 6,9:1
Beecroft, Victor
Right to Strike, The 1921,O 25,20:1
Last Warning, The 1922,O 25,23:1
Undercurrent, The 1925,F 4,18:2
Scarlet Fox, The 1928,Mr 28,31:1
Bridal Wise 1932,My 31,15:5
Peace Palace 1933,Je 6,30:2
World Waits, The 1933,O 26,22:5
Amazing Dr. Clitterhouse, The 1937,Mr 3,26:4
At Mrs Beam's 1937,Jl 27,24:2
Father Malachy's Miracle 1937,N 18,26:4
Knights of Song 1938,O 18,29:2
Journey's End 1939,S 19,29:2
Passenger to Bali, A 1940,Mr 15,26:2
Wookey, The 1941,S 11,20:5
Heart of a City 1942,F 13,24:6
Lifeline 1942,D 1,20:3
This Rock 1943,F 19,23:2
Sheppey 1944,Ap 19,27:2
Hand in Glove 1944,D 5,19:1
Winter's Tale, The 1946,Ja 16,18:6
S S Glencairn; Long Voyage Home, The
    1948,My 21,21:2
Beege and Qupee
Vaudeville (Palace) 1924,O 21,21:2
Beekman, Jack (Producer)
Baby With a Knife 1969,My 15,41:2
Silver Grey Toy Poodle 1969,My 15,41:2
Pets 1969,My 15,41:2
Beekman, Jackie
Will Morrissey's Folies Bergere Revue
    1930,Ap 16,26:6
Beeler, Virginia
Medium, The 1947,My 2,28:2
Medium, The 1948,D 8,41:6
Beems, Patti
Hear! Hear! 1955,S 28,38:1
Beene, Geoffrey (Miscellaneous)
Avanti 1968,F 1,29:1
Beenk, Rosemarie (Director)
Aucassin and Nicolette 1947,Ap 28,26:2
Beer, Keith
Hamlet 1931,Ap 24,26:4
Beer, Rudolph (Miscellaneous)
Miracle at Verdun 1932,O 9,IX,3:8
Beer, Thomas (Playwright)
Plot Thickens, The 1922,S 6,16:1
Beer (Playwright)
Farmer General, The 1931,Mr 31,24:8
Bauerngeneral, Der 1931,Ap 19,VIII,2:4
Beer-Hoffman, Richard (Playwright)
Jacob's Dream 1926,N 21,VIII,1:3
Jacob's Dream 1927,Ja 4,20:2
Beer-Hofmann, Gabriel (Director)
Anatol 1931,Ja 17,23:3
Greater Love 1931,Mr 3,39:1
Beerbohm, Claude
Bonehead, The 1920,Ap 13,12:1
Bonehead, The 1920,Ap 18,VI,2:4
Beerbohm, Claude (Producer)
Bonehead, The 1920,Ap 18,VI,2:4
Beerbohm, Max (Original Author)
Happy Hypocrite, The 1936,Ap 9,21:6
Happy Hypocrite, The 1936,My 10,X,1:1
Zuleika 1957,Ap 12,21:1
Happy Hypocrite, The 1968,S 6,38:1
Beerbohm, Max (Playwright)
Savonarola Brown 1930,F 26,22:3
Beers, Francine
King of the Whole Damn World 1962,Ap 16,32:2
Cafe Crown 1964,Ap 18,32:1
Kiss Mama 1964,O 2,30:1
Princess Rebecca Birnbaum 1966,Mr 7,22:1

Beers, Jesse (Scenic Designer)
King Midas and the Golden Touch 1948,O 25,28:3
Indian Captive, The 1949,Ja 31,15:2
Shadow Years, The 1957,My 9,26:2
Chairs, The 1958,Ja 10,20:3
Lesson, The 1958,Ja 10,20:3
Beers, Leo
Century Revue and the Midnight Rounders, The
    1920,Jl 13,9:1
Century Review, The 1920,Jl 22,9:5
Vaudeville (Palace) 1924,O 21,21:2
Honeymoon Lane 1926,S 21,32:3
Party, A 1933,Ag 24,18:4
Beery, Frank (Miscellaneous)
Champagne Complex 1955,Ap 13,33:1
Beery, Lee
Oklahoma! 1969,Je 24,37:1
Oklahoma! 1969,Jl 6,II,1:1
Beery, Noah
Up in Central Park 1945,Ja 29,17:2
Bees, Albert
Children of Darkness 1930,Ja 8,25:1
Beeson, Nora (Playwright)
Five Evenings 1963,My 10,37:3
Beethoven, Ludwig von (Composer)
Mum's the Word 1940,D 6,28:5
Begelman, David (Producer)
Judy Garland 1961,Ap 24,36:1
Begg, Jeannie
Verge, The 1921,N 15,23:2
Blonde Beast, The 1923,Mr 3,9:3
Sweeney Todd 1924,Jl 19,10:4
S S Glencairn 1924,N 4,31:4
Triumph of the Egg, The 1925,F 11,19:3
Ruint 1925,Ap 8,24:2
Beggs, James
Long and the Short and the Tall, The
    1962,Mr 30,28:2
Beggs, Lee
Stork, The 1925,Ja 27,14:2
Virgin of Bethulia, The 1925,F 24,17:2
Pearl of Great Price, The 1926,N 2,34:3
Lawyers' Dilemma, The 1928,Jl 10,17:2
Red Robe, The 1928,D 26,15:1
Student Prince, The 1931,Ja 30,18:1
Take a Chance 1932,N 28,11:2
Woman of Destiny, A 1936,Mr 3,25:2
Beggs, Madeline
What's Your Number? 1929,Ag 16,18:3
Beggs, Malcolm Lee
What's Your Number? 1929,Ag 16,18:3
Bitter Stream 1936,Mr 31,16:6
Devils Galore 1945,S 13,27:2
Up in Central Park 1947,My 20,29:2
Seventh Heaven 1955,My 27,16:2
Vamp, The 1955,N 11,30:1
Mr Wonderful 1956,Mr 23,23:2
Beggs, Malcolm Lee (Director)
What's Your Number? 1929,Ag 16,18:3
Begleiter, David
Wooden Soldier, The 1931,Je 23,28:4
Begley, Bill
Ballad of John Ogilvie, The 1968,O 9,42:4
Begley, Ed
Land of Fame 1943,S 22,31:5
Get Away Old Man 1943,N 25,40:2
Pretty Little Parlor 1944,Ap 18,24:8
All My Sons 1947,Ja 30,21:2
All My Sons 1947,F 9,II,1:1
All Summer Long 1954,S 24,26:2
All Summer Long 1954,O 3,II,1:1
Inherit the Wind 1955,Ap 22,20:2
Inherit the Wind 1955,S 25,II,1:1
Shadow of My Enemy, A 1957,D 12,35:4
Look Homeward, Angel 1958,Ag 31,II,1:1
Semi-Detached 1960,Mr 11,20:2
Advise and Consent 1960,N 18,25:1
Zelda 1969,Mr 6,38:1
Our Town 1969,N 28,50:1
Our Town 1969,D 7,II,7:1
Begley, Edward
Eyvind of the Hills 1921,F 2,14:1
Begovic, Miliam (Original Author)
Saint Wench 1933,Ja 3,19:3
Behan, Brendan (Original Author)
Borstal Boy 1967,O 11,39:2
Borstal Boy 1967,O 12,55:2
Borstal Boy 1970,Ap 1,38:1
Behan, Brendan (Playwright)
Quare Fellow, The 1956,Jl 25,24:1
Quare Fellow, The 1958,N 28,34:1
Hostage, The 1960,S 21,42:1
Hostage, The 1960,O 2,II,1:1
Hostage, The 1960,O 30,II,1:1
Hostage, The 1961,D 13,55:4
Behar, Samuel
Beyond Desire 1967,O 11,36:1
Behn, Noel (Producer)
Purple Dust 1956,D 28,15:1
Endgame 1958,Ja 29,32:4
Gay Divorce 1960,Ap 4,37:1
Ernest in Love 1960,My 5,39:4
Elsa Lanchester-Herself 1961,F 6,28:1

Behn, Susan (Playwright)
Improvisations in June 1928,F 27,16:5
Behnee, Harriet
Beggar Student, The 1921,Ja 8,9:3
Trumpeter of Sakkingen 1921,Ja 15,11:3
Behning, Evelyn
Blue Butterfly, The 1929,F 17,29:3
Behr, Beatrice
Ladies' Money 1934,N 2,26:6
Behrendt, Rachel
Caste 1929,F 24,IX,4:3
Behrens, Arthur
Ashes 1924,O 21,21:2
That's the Woman 1930,S 4,27:2
Behrens, Bernard
King John 1960,Je 29,26:2
Coriolanus 1961,Je 21,31:2
Henry VIII 1961,Je 22,22:1
Coriolanus 1961,Jl 5,30:1
Taming of the Shrew, The 1962,Je 21,25:1
Tempest, The 1962,Je 22,14:1
Henry V 1966,Je 8,38:1
Henry VI 1966,Je 9,55:2
Richard III 1967,Je 14,43:1
Antony and Cleopatra 1967,Ag 2,25:1
Merry Wives of Windsor, The 1967,Ag 4,18:1
Government Inspector, The 1967,O 28,34:1
Romeo and Juliet 1968,Je 11,55:2
Midsummer Night's Dream, A 1968,Je 13,54:1
Midsummer Night's Dream, A 1968,Je 23,II,1:1
Hamlet 1969,Je 11,37:1
Alchemist, The 1969,Je 12,51:1
Measure for Measure 1969,Je 13,41:3
Alchemist, The 1969,Je 22,II,1:7
Merchant of Venice, The 1970,Je 10,39:1
School for Scandal, The 1970,Je 11,51:1
Behrens, Elsie
No Foolin' 1926,Je 25,25:1
Behrens, Olive
Window Panes 1927,F 22,22:2
Ten Nights in a Barroom 1928,Mr 28,31:2
Behrman, David
Originale 1964,S 9,46:1
Behrman, David (Translator)
Originale 1964,S 9,46:1
Behrman, S N (Original Author)
Serena Blandish 1929,Ja 24,30:3
Cold Wind and the Warm, The 1958,D 9,55:1
Lord Pengo 1962,N 20,41:2
Behrman, S N (Playwright)
Second Man, The 1927,Ap 12,24:3
Love Is Like That 1927,Ap 19,24:1
Second Man, The 1927,Ap 24,VII,1:1
Second Man, The 1928,F 12,VIII,2:1
Serena Blandish 1929,Ja 13,VIII,2:4
Serena Blandish 1929,Ja 24,30:3
Serena Blandish 1929,F 3,VIII,1:1
Meteor 1929,D 8,X,2:1
Meteor 1929,D 24,15:1
Second Man, The 1930,My 25,IX,2:3
Brief Moment 1931,O 25,VIII,2:1
Brief Moment 1931,N 10,28:2
Brief Moment 1932,F 28,VIII,1:1
Biography 1932,D 13,25:3
Biography 1933,Ja 22,IX,1:1
Biography 1934,F 6,24:4
Biography 1934,My 20,IX,2:4
Rain From Heaven 1934,D 11,26:5
Rain From Heaven 1934,D 16,XI,2:1
Rain From Heaven 1934,D 25,28:4
Rain From Heaven 1935,Ja 6,IX,3:1
End of Summer 1936,Ja 31,17:1
End of Summer 1936,F 9,X,2:3
End of Summer 1936,F 18,26:4
End of Summer 1936,Mr 1,IX,1:1
Biography 1937,Ap 11,II,12:8
Amphitryon 38 1937,Je 24,30:2
Amphitryon 38 1937,N 7,XI,1:1
Wine of Choice 1937,D 14,32:3
Wine of Choice 1938,F 22,18:4
Wine of Choice 1938,F 27,X,1:1
Biography 1938,Ag 3,14:7
No Time for Comedy 1939,Mr 31,18:4
No Time for Comedy 1939,Ap 18,26:4
No Time for Comedy 1939,Ap 30,XI,1:1
Talley Method, The 1941,F 25,26:3
Talley Method, The 1941,Mr 2,IX,1:1
Pirate, The 1942,S 15,18:6
Pirate, The 1942,N 26,39:2
Pirate, The 1942,D 6,VIII,1:1
Jacobowsky and the Colonel 1944,Mr 15,17:2
Jacobowsky and the Colonel 1944,Mr 19,II,1:1
Jacobowsky and the Colonel 1944,My 21,II,1:1
Jacobowsky and the Colonel 1945,Je 24,II,1:3
Dunnigan's Daughter 1945,D 27,16:1
Dunnigan's Daughter 1946,Ja 6,II,1:1
Jane 1947,Ja 30,19:6
Jane 1947,F 9,II,3:7
I Know My Love 1949,F 24,29:2
I Know My Love 1949,Ap 23,10:2
I Know My Love 1949,N 3,36:1
I Know My Love 1949,N 20,II,1:1
Jane 1952,F 2,10:2

Behrman, S N (Playwright)—Cont
Jane 1952,F 10,II,1:1
Fanny 1954,N 5,16:1
Fanny 1954,N 21,II,1:1
Cold Wind and the Warm, The 1958,D 9,55:1
Cold Wind and the Warm, The 1959,Ja 18,II,1:1
Lord Pengo 1962,N 20,41:2
But for Whom Charlie 1964,Mr 13,42:2
Behrman, S N (Producer)
Abe Lincoln in Illinois 1938,O 17,12:2
Behrman, S N (Translator)
Amphitryon 38 1937,N 2,32:2
Beich, Albert (Playwright)
Man in the Dog Suit, The 1958,O 31,34:2
Bein, Albert (Director)
Land of Fame 1943,S 22,31:5
Bein, Albert (Original Author)
Land of Fame 1943,S 22,31:5
Bein, Albert (Playwright)
Little Ol' Boy 1933,Ap 25,15:5
Let Freedom Ring 1935,N 7,26:2
Little Ol' Boy 1936,My 11,16:1
Heavenly Express 1940,Ap 19,24:2
Heavenly Express 1940,Ap 28,IX,1:1
Land of Fame 1943,S 22,31:5
Bein, Albert (Producer)
Let Freedom Ring 1935,N 7,26:2
Land of Fame 1943,S 22,31:5
Bein, Mary (Playwright)
Land of Fame 1943,S 22,31:5
Beir, Fred
Men in White 1955,F 26,13:2
Terrible Swift Sword, The 1955,N 16,42:1
Beirne, Deborah (Playwright)
Park Avenue, Ltd 1932,Mr 4,17:1
Beirne, Deborah (Producer)
Park Avenue, Ltd 1932,Mr 4,17:1
Beirne, Michael
Anvil, The 1962,O 31,33:3
Score 1970,O 29,57:4
Beirne, Roger
Russian People, The 1942,D 30,17:2
Beissier, Fernand (Playwright)
Bird Cage, The 1925,Je 3,26:2
Beistel, John
Rapid Transit 1927,Ap 8,21:2
Beith, Ian Hay (Major) (Director)
Sport of Kings, The 1926,My 5,24:2
Beith, Ian Hay (Major) (Playwright)
Sport of Kings, The 1926,My 5,24:2
Bekassy, Stephen
Whole World Over, The 1947,Mr 28,28:2
Whole World Over, The 1947,Ap 6,II,1:1
Bekefi Ballet, The
A la Carte 1927,Ag 18,25:3
Bel Geddes, Barbara
Out of the Frying Pan 1941,F 12,24:2
Little Darling 1942,O 28,26:2
Nine Girls 1943,Ja 14,26:2
Mrs January & Mr Ex 1944,Ap 1,10:2
Deep Are the Roots 1945,S 27,24:4
Deep Are the Roots 1945,O 7,II,1:1
Burning Bright 1950,O 19,40:2
Burning Bright 1950,O 29,II,1:1
Moon Is Blue, The 1951,Mr 9,29:2
Living Room, The 1954,N 18,41:1
Living Room, The 1954,N 28,II,1:1
Cat on a Hot Tin Roof 1955,Mr 25,18:2
Cat on a Hot Tin Roof 1955,Ap 3,II,1:1
Sleeping Prince, The 1956,N 2,31:1
Silent Night, Lonely Night 1959,D 4,36:1
Silent Night, Lonely Night 1959,D 13,II,3:1
Mary, Mary 1961,Mr 9,24:2
Everything in the Garden 1967,N 30,60:1
Everything in the Garden 1967,D 10,II,5:1
Bel Geddes, Edith Lutyens (Costume Designer)
Do You Know the Milky Way? 1961,O 17,45:1
Giants, Sons of Giants 1962,Ja 8,26:2
Gift of Time, A 1962,F 23,34:1
Dear Me, the Sky Is Falling 1963,Mr 4,9:1
Too True to Be Good 1963,Mr 14,8:2
Bicycle Ride to Nevada 1963,S 25,38:1
Deputy, The 1964,F 27,26:1
Life With Father 1967,O 20,53:2
Bel Geddes, Norman (Costume Designer)
Miracle, The 1924,Ja 16,17:1
Miracle, The 1924,F 17,4:3
Miracle, The 1924,Ag 19,9:1
Joan of Arc 1925,Je 21,VIII,1:2
Lysistrata 1930,Je 6,20:1
Hamlet 1931,N 6,28:4
Eternal Road, The 1937,Ja 8,14:2
It Happens on Ice 1940,O 11,24:3
Bel Geddes, Norman (Director)
Jehanne d'Arc 1925,Je 13,10:1
Joan of Arc 1925,Je 21,VIII,1:2
Jehanne d'Arc 1925,Jl 12,VII,1:1
Arabesque 1925,O 21,20:2
Lysistrata 1930,Ap 29,30:5
Lysistrata 1930,Je 6,20:1
Hamlet 1931,O 25,VIII,2:2
Hamlet 1931,N 6,28:4
Hamlet 1931,N 22,VIII,8:3
Iron Men 1936,O 20,30:6

Bel Geddes, Norman (Lighting Director)
Joan of Arc 1925,Je 21,VIII,1:2
Jehanne d'Arc 1925,Jl 12,VII,1:1
Hamlet 1931,N 6,28:4
Flying Colors 1932,S 16,24:2
Flying Colors 1932,O 9,IX,1:1
Eternal Road, The 1937,Ja 8,14:2
It Happens on Ice 1940,O 11,24:3
Bel Geddes, Norman (Miscellaneous)
Hamlet 1931,N 6,28:4
Siege 1937,D 9,31:4
Bel Geddes, Norman (Producer)
Arabesque 1925,O 21,20:2
Hamlet 1931,N 15,VIII,1:1
Hamlet 1931,N 22,VIII,8:3
Dead End 1935,O 29,17:2
Dead End 1936,S 20,IX,3:7
Iron Men 1936,O 20,30:6
Sons and Soldiers 1943,My 5,22:2
Bel Geddes, Norman (Scenic Designer)
Miracle, The 1924,Ja 16,17:1
Miracle, The 1924,Ja 20,VII,1:1
Miracle, The 1924,F 17,4:3
Miracle, The 1924,Ag 19,9:1
Poor Richard 1924,N 16,VIII,2:8
Lady Be Good 1924,D 2,23:4
Quarantine 1924,D 17,19:7
Lady Be Good 1924,D 28,VII,1:1
Follies 1925,Mr 11,19:2
Follies 1925,Jl 7,24:3
Arabesque 1925,O 21,20:2
Devil in the Cheese, The 1926,D 30,22:4
Damn the Tears 1927,Ja 22,11:1
Spread Eagle 1927,Ap 5,30:2
Spread Eagle 1927,Ap 10,VIII,1:1
Julius Caesar 1927,Je 7,27:2
Creoles 1927,S 23,33:3
Five O'Clock Girl, The 1927,O 11,26:3
John 1927,N 5,16:4
Patriot, The 1928,Ja 20,15:1
Patriot, The 1928,Ja 29,VIII,1:1
Fifty Million Frenchmen 1929,N 28,34:4
Lysistrata 1930,Je 1,VIII,1:1
Lysistrata 1930,Je 6,20:1
Hamlet 1931,N 6,28:4
Flying Colors 1932,S 16,24:2
Flying Colors 1932,O 9,IX,1:1
Dead End 1935,O 29,17:2
Dead End 1935,N 3,X,1:1
Iron Men 1936,O 20,30:6
Eternal Road, The 1937,Ja 8,14:2
Eternal Road, The 1937,Ap 25,X,1:6
Siege 1937,D 9,31:4
It Happens on Ice 1940,O 11,24:3
It Happens on Ice 1941,Ag 31,IX,1:1
Sons and Soldiers 1943,My 5,22:2
Seven Lively Arts 1944,D 8,26:6
Bel Monte, Herman
Trojan Women, The 1941,Ap 9,32:5
Bela, Nicholas
Nowhere Bound 1935,Ja 23,20:2
Bela, Nicholas (Miscellaneous)
Sleepy Hollow 1948,Je 4,26:3
Bela, Nicholas (Playwright)
Fire-Weed 1950,Mr 30,38:2
Bela, Sreemati
Ramayana 1931,Ja 13,35:4
Belack, Doris
Comedian, The 1956,O 18,36:4
Firstborn, The 1957,Ja 7,29:2
Semi-Detached 1960,Mr 11,20:2
PS 193 1962,O 31,33:1
Heroine, The 1963,F 21,5:5
Nathan Weinstein, Mystic, Connecticut 1966,F 26,15:2
Ninety Day Mistress, The 1967,N 7,49:1
Belafonte, Harry
Sojourner Truth 1948,Ap 22,35:2
John Murray Anderson's Almanac 1953,D 11,42:2
Almanac 1954,Ja 3,II,1:1
3 for Tonight 1955,Ap 7,23:2
3 for Tonight 1955,Ap 17,II,1:1
Belafonte at the Palace 1959,D 16,55:1
Belafonte, Harry (Miscellaneous)
Moonbirds 1959,O 10,13:1
Belafonte, Harry (Producer)
Belafonte at the Palace 1959,D 16,55:1
To Be Young Gifted and Black; World of Lorraine Hansberry, The 1969,Ja 3,15:1
Belafsky, Morris
Josephus 1933,D 1,22:5
Wandering Stars 1946,D 14,18:2
Belagorsky, Jacob
Mother's Sabbath Days 1960,N 21,33:2
Beland, Millie
Merchant of Venice, The 1920,D 30,16:2
Drifting 1922,Ja 3,20:3
Belanger, Guy
King John 1960,Je 29,26:2
Belanger, Terry (Playwright)
Dear Nobody 1968,Jl 31,33:1
Belasco, David
Vaudeville (Palace) 1925,Ap 7,16:3

Belasco, David (Director)
Harem, The 1924,D 3,24:1
Ladies of the Evening 1924,D 24,11:2
Canary Dutch 1925,S 9,22:1
Accused 1925,S 30,20:1
Lulu Belle 1926,F 10,20:1
Fanny 1926,S 22,30:1
Lily Sue 1926,N 17,22:2
Hidden 1927,O 5,30:4
Bachelor Father, The 1928,F 29,28:2
Big Fight, The 1928,Ag 31,23:1
Big Fight, The 1928,S 19,33:1
Mima 1928,D 13,24:2
Passion Play, The 1929,Ap 30,32:1
Passion Play, The 1929,My 5,IX,1:1
It's a Wise Child 1929,Ag 7,29:1
Dancing Partner 1930,Ag 6,24:2
Tonight or Never 1930,N 19,19:3
Belasco, David (Playwright)
Return of Peter Grimm, The 1921,S 22,12:2
Kiki 1921,N 30,13:1
Comedian, The 1923,Mr 14,14:1
Laugh, Clown, Laugh! 1923,O 28,VIII,2:1
Laugh, Clown, Laugh! 1923,N 29,30:1
Fanny 1926,S 22,30:1
Mima 1928,D 13,24:2
Girl of the Golden West, The 1957,N 6,44:1
Belasco, David (Producer)
Deburau 1921,Ja 2,VI,3:1
Easiest Way, The 1921,S 11,VI,1:1
Grand Duke, The 1921,N 6,VI,1:1
Man in Dress Clothes, The 1922,Ap 30,VII,1:8
Merchant of Venice, The 1923,Ja 7,VII,1:1
Merchant of Venice, The 1923,Ja 21,VII,1:1
Comedian, The 1923,Mr 25,VIII,1:1
Comedian, The 1923,Ap 8,VIII,1:1
Mary, Mary, Quite Contrary 1923,S 2,VI,2:6
Mary, Mary, Quite Contrary 1923,S 16,VII,1:1
Laugh, Clown, Laugh! 1923,O 28,VIII,2:1
Laugh, Clown, Laugh! 1923,D 9,IX,1:1
Other Rose, The 1923,D 16,IX,2:4
Other Rose, The 1923,D 30,VII,1:1
Tiger Cats 1924,O 19,VIII,2:6
Tiger Cats 1924,O 22,18:1
Harem, The 1924,N 16,VIII,2:8
Harem, The 1924,D 3,24:1
Ladies of the Evening 1924,D 24,11:2
Dove, The 1925,Ag 25,12:2
Canary Dutch 1925,S 9,22:1
Accused 1925,S 20,VIII,2:4
Colette 1925,S 29,31:2
Accused 1925,S 30,20:1
Lulu Belle 1926,F 10,20:1
Lulu Belle 1926,F 14,VIII,1:1
All the Way From Texas 1926,Ag 8,VII,3:1
Fanny 1926,S 22,30:1
Lily Sue 1926,N 17,22:2
Lily Sue 1926,N 28,VIII,1:1
What Never Dies 1926,D 29,24:2
Hidden 1927,S 25,VIII,4:8
Hidden 1927,O 5,30:4
Bachelor Father, The 1928,F 29,28:2
Mima 1928,D 13,24:2
Mima 1928,D 23,VIII,1:1
It's a Wise Child 1929,Jl 28,VIII,1:6
It's a Wise Child 1929,Ag 7,29:1
It's a Wise Child 1929,Ag 25,VIII,1:1
Dancing Partner 1930,Jl 27,VIII,2:3
Dancing Partner 1930,Ag 6,24:2
Tonight or Never 1930,N 9,IX,3:2
Tonight or Never 1930,N 19,19:3
Dinner at Eight 1933,Ap 9,IX,1:7
Belasco, Dolaro (Costume Designer)
Cure for Matrimony 1939,O 26,26:3
Belasco, Genevieve
Money Lender, The 1928,Ag 28,27:3
Woman Denied, A 1931,F 26,21:1
Near to the Stars 1932,F 23,23:2
Wrong Number 1934,Mr 14,23:6
Bride of Torozko, The 1934,S 14,24:2
Bitter Oleander 1935,F 12,24:3
One Good Year 1935,N 28,38:3
Belasco, Jaques (Composer)
Girl From Nantucket, The 1945,N 9,17:2
Belasco, Leon
Vaudeville (Palace) 1932,Je 6,18:2
Flowers of Virtue, The 1942,F 6,22:2
Silk Stockings 1955,F 25,17:3
Happy Hunting 1956,D 7,30:1
Once More With Feeling 1958,O 22,39:1
Belasco, Muriel
Young Sinners 1929,N 29,24:4
Belavsky, Miriom
His Wife's Lover 1929,O 21,30:6
Belavsky, Morris
His Wife's Lover 1929,O 21,30:6
Yoshe Kalb 1933,D 29,27:2
Jealousy 1934,D 20,31:4
60,000 Heroes 1935,Ja 28,11:5
Parnosseh 1935,F 16,8:8
Belavsky, Moyshe
Song of Dnieper 1946,O 26,10:5

Belbridge, David
Great Way, The 1921,N 8,28:2
Blushing Bride, The 1922,F 7,12:1
School for Scandal, The 1925,O 24,19:1
Maker of Images, The 1927,Mr 5,12:2
Rapid Transit 1927,Ap 8,21:2
Belcourt, Emile
Kiss Me, Kate 1970,D 26,10:4
Belden, Eileen
I Have Been Here Before 1938,O 14,26:2
In Good King Charles's Golden Days
1939,Ag 13,28:1
Belden, Valerie
Blind Angel, The 1965,Ap 2,26:1
Beldner, Sarah (Producer)
Love Your Crooked Neighbor 1969,D 30,40:1
Beldon, Bernice
Loose Ends 1926,N 2,34:2
Beldon, Eileen
Yellow Sands 1927,S 12,29:3
Fanatics, The 1927,N 8,32:4
Fallen Angels 1927,D 2,20:4
Runaways, The 1928,D 2,X,4:1
Apple Cart, The 1929,Ag 20,30:2
Caravan 1932,My 1,VIII,2:2
Belew, Pat (Scenic Designer)
Gondoliers, The 1963,Je 5,33:2
Belfance, Robert (Miscellaneous)
Dr Willy Nilly 1959,Je 5,18:2
Belfast Repertory Players
Workers 1932,D 11,IX,4:5
Belfiore, Giovanna
'Il Tesoro D'Isacco; Treasure of Isaac, The
1928,Ja 26,17:1
Belford, Cora Louise
Son, The 1950,Ag 16,24:6
Belford, Esther
Man Who Ate the Popomack, The 1924,Mr 25,24:1
Way of the World, The 1924,N 18,23:4
Belfrage, Bruce
Lord of the Manor, The 1928,O 14,X,2:1
Belgrave, Cynthia
And the Wind Blows 1959,Ap 29,28:1
Blacks, The 1961,My 5,23:1
Alcestis Comes Back 1962,Ap 24,33:1
Kumquat in the Persimmon Tree, The
1962,Je 19,27:2
Funnyhouse of a Negro 1964,Ja 15,25:3
Mr Grossman 1964,My 6,43:1
Lovey 1965,Mr 26,27:1
Amen Corner, The 1965,Ap 16,35:1
Junebug Graduates Tonight! 1967,F 27,35:1
Trials of Brother Jero, The 1967,N 10,60:1
Cities in Bezique; Owl Answers, The
1969,Ja 13,26:1
Belgrave, Cynthia (Director)
Strong Breed, The 1967,N 10,60:1
Trials of Brother Jero, The 1967,N 10,60:1
Belgrave, Jack
Egotist, The 1922,D 27,12:1
Belian, Erni
Bajadere, Die 1925,O 2,26:2
Anneliese von Dessau 1926,F 26,24:3
Belin, Charles
Music in the Air 1932,N 9,28:2
Beline, Martin
Good Morning 1937,D 4,20:7
Belink, Susan
Another Evening With Harry Stoones
1961,O 23,22:2
Belita
Ulysses in Nighttown 1958,Je 6,30:1
Beliveau, Juliette
Ti-Coq 1951,F 10,10:2
Belk, Diana
Oklahoma! 1958,Mr 8,15:2
Belkin, Beatrice
Laugh Parade, The 1931,S 20,VIII,3:1
Belkin, Jeanna
Dragon, The 1963,Ap 10,32:1
Bell, Al Jr (Miscellaneous)
Reckoning, The 1969,S 5,28:1
Bell, Alexander C
Fiesta 1933,D 16,12:2
Bell, Alice
China Rose 1925,Ja 20,18:1
Bell, Ann
Help Stamp Out Marriage 1966,S 30,50:1
Bell, Aron
Compulsion 1957,O 25,21:1
Bell, Arthur
All in the Family 1935,Jl 24,20:4
Bell, Barbara Terry
Tableaux 1961,D 18,41:3
Bell, Charles
Flowers of Virtue, The 1942,F 6,22:2
Men in White 1955,F 26,13:2
Bell, Charles W (Playwright)
Elsie 1923,Ap 3,26:1
Paradise Alley 1924,Ap 2,17:3
Bell, Cornelia
Tapestry in Gray 1935,D 28,10:2

Bell, Daphne
Nine Till Six 1936,Mr 14,10:3
Bell, David
Home Is the Hero 1945,Ja 20,16:4
Bell, Dorothy
Murder in the Cathedral 1935,D 21,11:3
Bell, Edith
Remains to Be Seen 1951,O 4,37:1
Oh, Kay! 1960,Ap 18,37:2
Bell, Elizabeth
Uncle Vanya 1970,Mr 15,II,7:3
Bell, Enid (Scenic Designer)
Country Wife, The 1931,Ap 19,31:5
Bell, Eric
Porgy and Bess 1935,O 11,30:2
Bell, Esther
Young Woodley 1925,N 3,34:1
Bell, Eugene
Days of Our Youth, The 1941,N 29,15:2
Criminals, The 1941,D 22,24:3
Bell, F Gatenby
If Winter Comes 1923,Ap 3,26:1
Aren't We All? 1923,My 22,14:2
Bell, F Gatenby (Director)
Her Friend the King 1929,O 8,34:5
Bell, Francesca
Oh, Kay! 1960,Ap 18,37:2
Bell, Francis
Grab Bag, The 1924,O 7,26:2
Bell, Frederick
Her Majesty the Widow 1934,Je 19,24:5
Straw Hat, The 1937,D 31,8:2
Bell, Gail (Director)
End of All Things Natural, The 1969,S 12,38:1
Bell, Gail (Miscellaneous)
Who's Who, Baby? 1968,Ja 30,36:1
David Show, The 1968,N 1,34:2
Colette 1970,O 15,58:1
Bell, Galt (Producer)
Drunkard, The 1936,S 20,IX,3:4
Bell, Gary
Hamlet 1970,O 27,54:2
Bell, George
Music in the Air 1932,N 9,28:2
Flair-Flair the Idol of Paree 1935,Mr 13,16:1
Bell, Gladys
Cynara 1931,N 3,31:1
Bell, Gordon Knox Jr
Variations of 1940 1940,Ja 29,12:1
Bell, Hugo
Scarlet Coat, The 1924,D 24,11:1
Samarkand 1926,D 22,24:4
Bell, Ian
Letter to the Times, A 1966,D 5,63:1
Bell, Ian (Director)
Letter to the Times, A 1966,D 5,63:1
Bell, James
Sweet Nell of Old Drury 1923,My 19,16:4
Lucky Sam McCarver 1925,O 22,22:1
Buckaroo 1929,Mr 18,31:1
Your Uncle Dudley 1929,N 19,26:4
Last Mile, The 1930,F 14,21:2
House Beautiful, The 1931,Mr 13,20:4
House Beautiful, The 1931,Mr 22,VIII,1:1
Lilly Turner 1932,S 20,26:1
Thunder on the Left 1933,N 1,25:2
Pure in Heart, The 1934,Mr 21,24:3
Kill That Story 1934,Ag 30,22:2
Order Please 1934,O 10,21:2
Tobacco Road 1934,D 4,22:5
Most of the Game 1935,O 2,27:4
Sap Runs High, The 1936,F 1,9:4
Sap Runs High, The 1936,F 5,15:3
But for the Grace of God 1937,Ja 13,21:4
Too Many Heroes 1937,N 16,26:2
Goodbye in the Night 1940,Mr 19,31:2
First Stop to Heaven 1941,Ja 6,10:7
Bell, James H
Bad Man, The 1920,Ag 31,7:1
Humoresque 1923,F 28,13:2
Jarnegan 1928,S 25,29:2
Bell, James T
Free Soul, A 1928,Ja 13,26:5
Bell, Jean
Garden of Weeds 1924,Ap 29,12:3
Bell, John
Merry-Go-Round 1932,Ap 23,11:2
Great White Hope, The 1967,D 14,58:1
Bell, John S
Once Over Lightly 1938,D 10,13:4
Bell, Joseph
What's Your Wife Doing? 1923,O 2,10:3
Chivalry 1925,D 16,22:3
Love 'Em and Leave 'Em 1926,F 4,20:4
Carry On 1928,Ja 24,26:1
Bell, Leonard
Bees and the Flowers, The 1946,S 27,19:3
Fragile Fox 1954,O 13,27:1
Bell, Margaret
Private Life of the Master Race, The
1945,Je 13,28:3
Bell, Marie
Roi Dagobert, Le 1926,N 14,VIII,2:1

Bell, Marie—Cont
Belle Mariniere, La 1929,D 8,X,2:2
Phedre 1963,O 21,39:1
Berenice 1963,O 30,46:1
Bell, Marion
Swing Sister Wac Swing 1944,Ja 4,20:4
Brigadoon 1947,Mr 14,28:2
Bell, Mark
Galileo 1968,D 1,88:4
Bell, Mary
Volpone 1928,Ap 10,32:1
Three Little Girls 1930,Ap 15,29:1
Unto Such Glory 1937,My 7,28:2
Devil's Disciple, The 1950,Ja 26,23:2
High Ground, The 1951,F 21,31:2
Shrike, The 1952,Ja 16,20:2
Scarecrow, The 1953,Je 17,31:1
Shrike, The 1953,N 26,51:2
Cloud 7 1958,F 15,15:2
Diamond Orchid 1965,F 11,44:4
Beyond Desire 1967,O 11,36:1
Bell, Mary Hayley
Billy Draws a Horse 1939,D 22,14:5
Bell, Mary Hayley (Playwright)
Men in Shadow 1942,S 27,VIII,2:1
Men in Shadow 1943,Mr 11,16:2
Duet for Two Hands 1947,O 8,28:3
Bell, Mary Kay
Life Begins 1932,Mr 29,23:2
Bell, Mary Whitis
Doodle Dandy of the U S A 1942,O 19,15:2
Bell, Pershing
Contrast, The 1940,Mr 26,17:2
Bell, Philip (Producer)
Time for Bed 1969,Je 14,24:1
Take Me to Bed 1969,Je 14,24:1
Bell, Ralph
What a Life 1938,Ap 14,26:2
Stop Press 1939,Mr 20,13:2
See My Lawyer 1939,S 28,29:1
Any Day Now 1941,Je 10,28:2
Native Son 1942,O 24,10:6
Great Big Doorstep, The 1942,N 27,26:2
Crucible, The 1953,Jl 2,20:2
Memory of Two Mondays, A 1955,S 30,21:1
View From the Bridge, A 1955,S 30,21:1
Maybe Tuesday 1958,Ja 30,18:3
Fair Game for Lovers 1964,F 11,43:2
Veronica 1965,N 19,31:1
Bananas 1968,D 5,60:1
In the Matter of J Robert Oppenheimer
1969,Mr 7,28:1
Time of Your Life, The 1969,N 7,37:1
Camino Real 1970,Ja 9,42:1
Bell, Robert
Trial of Joan of Arc, The 1921,Mr 28,8:2
Mr Faust 1922,Ja 31,11:2
Bird Cage, The 1925,Je 3,26:2
Bell, Robert (Director)
Hangman's Whip 1933,F 25,20:2
London Assurance 1937,F 19,14:5
Bell, Ronald
Hamlet 1954,Ap 24,15:2
Bell, Sally
Pirates of Penzance, The 1942,F 20,20:2
Bell, Service
Run, Little Chillun! 1933,Mr 2,21:3
Macbeth 1936,Ag 15,25:4
One-Act Plays of the Sea; Moon of the Caribbees
1937,O 30,23:2
Run, Little Chillun 1943,Ag 14,6:1
Our Lan' 1947,Ap 19,11:2
Our Lan' 1947,S 29,16:5
Power of Darkness, The 1948,O 11,28:2
Bell, Stanley
Doctor's Dilemma, The 1941,Mr 12,18:2
Candida 1942,Ap 28,24:4
Candida 1942,My 3,VIII,1:1
Three Sisters, The 1942,D 22,31:2
Love on Leave 1944,Je 21,23:4
While the Sun Shines 1944,S 20,21:3
While the Sun Shines 1944,S 24,II,1:1
Stranger, The 1945,F 13,21:2
Lady Windermere's Fan 1946,O 15,29:2
Affair of Honor 1956,Ap 7,12:3
Measure for Measure 1956,Je 29,16:1
Taming of the Shrew, The 1956,Ag 6,20:1
Othello 1957,Je 24,19:2
Merchant of Venice, The 1957,Jl 11,19:5
Much Ado About Nothing 1957,Ag 8,15:2
Bell, Stanley (Director)
Heat Wave 1931,F 18,14:6
Bell, Stanley (Producer)
St Moritz 1937,Jl 16,22:5
Bell, Stanley (Scenic Designer)
Stepdaughters of War 1930,O 7,27:1
Company's Coming! 1931,Ap 21,35:5
Bell, Thomas
Peter Pan 1924,N 7,16:2
Criss Cross 1926,O 13,20:2
Bell, Thomas (Original Author)
World's Full of Girls, The 1943,D 7,31:2
Bell, Tommy
Tip-Top 1920,O 6,13:2

Bell, W S
Lulu Belle 1926,F 10,20:1
Bell Brothers
Better Times 1922,S 4,14:2
Bella, Joseph F (Costume Designer)
Philosophy in the Boudoir 1969,My 22,55:2
Bellacosa, Mary
Veronica's Veil 1950,F 12,II,1:5
Bellacosa, Victor
Veronica's Veil 1950,F 12,II,1:5
Bellah, Robert G
Vagabond King, The 1935,N 29,22:7
Bellair, Clarence
Pietro 1920,Ja 20,10:2
Beau Gallant 1926,Ap 6,26:3
Behold the Bridegroom 1927,D 27,24:1
Oh, Promise Me 1930,N 25,31:1
Cloudy With Showers 1931,S 2,17:5
Heigh-Ho, Everybody 1932,My 26,31:2
I Was Waiting for You 1933,N 14,23:3
Wooden Slipper, The 1934,Ja 4,16:3
Bellair, Myrta
Launcelot and Elaine 1930,Mr 10,24:3
Spook House 1930,Je 4,33:3
Bellairs, Elizabeth
Squaw Man, The 1921,D 27,10:3
Gift, The 1924,Ja 23,15:4
Bellak, George (Director)
Play With a Tiger 1964,D 31,14:2
Bellak, George (Playwright)
Edge of the Sword, The 1949,N 10,40:3
Troublemakers, The 1952,N 9,II,3:2
Troublemakers, The 1954,D 31,11:3
Bellak, George (Producer)
Play With a Tiger 1964,D 31,14:2
Bellamy, Francis R (Playwright)
Buy, Buy Baby 1926,O 8,26:2
Bellamy, Frank
Gentle Rain 1936,S 20,IX,1:4
Bellamy, H Franklyn
Bulldog Drummond 1921,D 27,10:2
Bellamy, Ralph
Town Boy 1929,O 5,22:4
Roadside 1930,S 27,21:1
Tomorrow the World 1943,Ap 15,22:2
Tomorrow the World 1943,Ap 25,II,1:1
State of the Union 1945,N 7,21:3
State of the Union 1945,N 15,25:2
State of the Union 1945,N 25,II,1:1
State of the Union 1946,S 8,II,1:1
Detective Story 1949,Mr 24,34:2
Detective Story 1949,Ap 3,II,1:1
Sunrise at Campobello 1958,Ja 31,25:1
Sunrise at Campobello 1958,F 9,II,1:1
Bellamy, Ralph (Director)
Pretty Little Parlor 1944,Ap 18,24:8
Bellamy, Ralph (Producer)
Pretty Little Parlor 1944,Ap 18,24:8
Bellarina, Bella
King Saul 1925,S 18,26:3
He, She and the Ox 1934,F 21,22:7
Bellaver, Harry
1931 1931,D 11,34:3
Night Over Taos 1932,Mr 10,25:3
Merry-Go-Round 1932,Ap 23,11:2
Carry Nation 1932,O 31,18:2
We the People 1933,Ja 23,9:5
Threepenny Opera, The 1933,Ap 14,22:4
Sellout, The 1933,S 7,17:2
She Loves Me Not 1933,N 21,22:4
Page Miss Glory 1934,N 28,24:2
Noah 1935,F 14,25:2
How Beautiful With Shoes 1935,N 29,24:1
Russet Mantle 1936,Ja 17,15:5
Russet Mantle 1936,Ja 26,IX,1:1
St Helena 1936,O 7,32:1
Chalked Out 1937,Mr 26,24:2
To Quito and Back 1937,O 7,30:4
Tortilla Flat 1938,Ja 13,16:2
Tell My Story 1939,Mr 16,26:6
Johnny 2X4 1942,Mr 17,24:6
Yours, A Lincoln 1942,Jl 10,12:3
Mr Sycamore 1942,N 14,13:2
World's Full of Girls, The 1943,D 7,31:2
Annie Get Your Gun 1946,My 17,14:2
Annie Get Your Gun 1946,My 26,II,1:1
Annie Get Your Gun 1946,S 29,II,1:1
Annie Get Your Gun 1958,F 20,29:2
Annie Get Your Gun 1966,Je 1,42:2
Belle, Gwendolyn
Carmen Jones 1956,Je 1,28:2
Belle, Marjorie
Dark of the Moon 1945,Mr 15,27:2
Bellec, Anne
Phedre 1969,Mr 1,20:1
Belledna, Alex (Playwright)
Pansy 1929,My 15,36:3
Bellenden-Clarke, E
Victoria Regina 1935,D 27,15:2
Beller, Mary Linn
Leaf and Bough 1949,Ja 22,10:2
Have I Got a Girl for You! 1963,D 3,53:2

Belleran, Lisa
Strada, La 1969,D 15,63:1
Bellesi, Joseph
Gondoliers, The 1969,My 10,35:1
Bellett and Lamb
Vaudeville (Palace) 1932,My 30,16:7
Bellew, Cosmo
Havoc 1924,S 2,22:2
Lass O' Laughter 1925,Ja 9,13:2
Carolinian, The 1925,N 3,34:2
Bellew, Kyrle
Risk, The; Caducee, Le 1922,Jl 30,VI,1:7
Bride of the Lamb 1934,Mr 29,26:1
Bellin, Charles
Richard of Bordeaux 1934,F 15,16:2
Field of Ermine 1935,F 9,10:4
Achilles Had a Heel 1935,O 14,20:2
Dead End 1935,O 29,17:2
Dame Nature 1938,S 27,24:3
One Eye Closed 1954,N 25,45:2
Bellin, Charles (Miscellaneous)
Bourgeois Gentilhomme, Le 1955,O 26,26:1
Bellin, Junior
Cross-Town 1937,Mr 18,21:5
Bellin, Olga
Port-Royal 1960,Ap 26,41:1
Man for All Seasons, A 1961,N 23,51:1
Man for All Seasons, A 1961,D 3,II,1:1
Bellin, Thomas
Great God Brown, The 1959,O 7,48:1
Henry IV 1960,Mr 2,42:1
Henry IV 1960,Ap 19,41:1
Belling, Andrew (Composer)
Huckleberry 1962,Je 3,43:1
Belling, Andrew (Playwright)
Huckleberry 1962,Je 3,43:1
Bellinger, Roberta
It All Depends 1925,Ag 11,16:4
Americana 1926,Jl 27,15:3
House of Women, The 1927,O 4,32:2
Getting Even 1929,Ag 20,31:1
Brass Ankle 1931,Ap 24,26:4
Hill Between, The 1938,Mr 12,12:5
Two on an Island 1940,Ja 23,17:2
Bellinger, Walter
Masked Woman, The 1922,D 23,14:2
Bellini, Cal
Shakuntala 1959,S 10,41:2
Cut of the Axe 1960,F 2,38:2
Across the Board on Tomorrow Morning
1961,O 23,22:5
Talking to You 1961,O 23,22:5
Ross 1961,D 27,20:2
Immoralist, The 1963,N 8,36:2
Royal Hunt of the Sun, The 1965,O 27,36:2
Goa 1968,F 23,46:1
Her First Roman 1968,O 21,53:3
Bellis, Bob
Yeomen of the Guard, The 1965,Jl 8,34:1
Bellis, W Messenger
Ghost Between, The 1921,Mr 23,11:2
Fair Circassian, The 1921,D 7,22:3
Antonia 1925,O 21,20:1
Golden Dawn 1927,D 1,32:3
Let and Sub-Let 1930,My 20,32:2
Long Road, The 1930,S 10,30:2
Alchemist, The 1931,Je 5,27:1
Devil's Little Game, The 1932,Ag 2,20:4
Cyrano de Bergerac 1932,D 27,11:2
Bello, Teodorina
Ox Cart, The 1966,D 20,58:1
Bellomo, Joan
Another City, Another Land 1968,O 9,42:1
Bellomo, Joe
South Pacific 1965,Je 3,25:1
Bellon, Stephen (Director)
Narrow Road to the Deep North 1970,F 11,39:2
Bellou, A
Electra 1952,N 20,38:2
Bellow, Saul (Original Author)
Victim, The 1952,My 3,17:5
Bellow, Saul (Playwright)
Last Analysis, The 1964,O 2,30:1
Last Analysis, The 1964,O 11,II,1:1
Bellow Plays, The; Out From Under; Orange
Souffle; Wen, The 1966,Je 8,42:2
Orange Souffle; Wen, The; Out From Under
1966,Jl 16,14:6
Under the Weather 1966,O 28,35:1
Under the Weather 1966,D 25,II,1:1
Bellows, Charles
Foemen of the Yard 1935,Ap 6,10:4
Bellows, Jean
Kai Khosru 1925,Ap 27,14:2
Scarlet Letter, The 1926,Ja 8,16:5
Small Miracle 1934,S 27,24:3
New Faces of 1936 1936,My 20,24:5
Kind Lady 1937,Jl 6,23:1
I Am My Youth 1938,Mr 8,22:4
Three's a Family 1943,My 6,24:2
Hand in Glove 1944,D 5,19:1
Happy Birthday 1946,N 1,31:2

Bellridge, David
Pasteur 1923,Mr 13,19:1
Bellson, Louis (Composer)
Portofino 1958,F 22,8:3
Bellwood, Peter (Playwright)
Gantry 1970,F 16,44:1
Bellwood, Peter L (Miscellaneous)
Serjeant Musgrave's Dance 1966,Mr 9,44:1
Belmont, August (Mrs) (Playwright)
In the Next Room 1923,O 3,15:3
Belmont, Bessie
Paris Bound 1929,Jl 20,8:3
Criminal Code, The 1929,O 3,28:2
Belmont, Ralf
Casanova 1923,S 27,10:2
Rust 1924,F 1,12:1
Izzy 1924,S 17,16:2
Divine Drudge 1933,O 27,22:3
Belmonte, Herman
New Moon, The 1928,S 20,33:1
Belmonte, Nena (Playwright)
Spring in Autumn 1933,O 25,22:5
Belmore, Bertha
Sporting Thing to Do, The 1923,F 20,12:2
Grounds for Divorce 1924,S 24,20:1
Whispering Gallery, The 1929,F 12,22:2
Warrior's Husband, The 1932,Mr 12,19:4
Reunion in Vienna 1934,Ja 4,17:1
Big Business 1937,F 19,15:3
Virginia 1937,S 3,13:2
Johnny Belinda 1940,S 19,26:2
Heart of a City 1942,F 13,24:6
By Jupiter 1942,Je 4,22:1
By Jupiter 1942,Ag 16,VIII,2:1
By Jupiter 1942,Ag 30,VIII,1:1
Naked Genius, The 1943,O 22,20:5
Rhapsody 1944,N 23,37:2
Antigone 1946,F 19,21:3
Harlequinade 1949,O 13,32:2
Caesar and Cleopatra 1949,D 22,28:2
Gigi 1951,N 26,20:4
Belmore, Daisy
One 1920,S 15,12:2
Marjolaine 1922,Ja 25,16:1
Faithful Heart, The 1922,O 11,22:1
Romantic Age, The 1922,N 15,22:1
Dancers, The 1923,O 18,17:2
American Born 1925,S 27,VII,2:1
American Born 1925,O 6,31:3
At Mrs Beam's 1926,Ap 26,24:3
Royal Box, The 1928,N 21,32:3
Sakura 1928,D 26,14:4
Carry Nation 1932,O 31,18:2
Late One Evening 1933,Ja 10,27:3
Spring in Autumn 1933,O 25,22:5
Mahogany Hall 1934,Ja 18,18:5
Love on an Island 1934,Jl 24,20:5
Prisoners of War 1935,Ja 29,24:1
Miles of Heaven, The 1937,Ag 31,27:4
Soliloquy 1938,N 29,26:4
Woman Brown, The 1939,D 9,18:5
Love for Love 1940,Je 4,19:5
Last Stop 1944,S 6,17:2
Rose Tattoo, The 1951,F 5,19:2
Belmore, Herbert
Faithful Heart, The 1922,O 11,22:1
Scaramouche 1923,O 25,14:2
Great Music 1924,O 6,24:1
Happy-Go-Lucky 1926,O 1,27:2
Old Bill, M P 1926,N 11,22:2
Heavy Traffic 1928,S 6,23:3
Bellamy Trial, The 1931,Ap 23,28:6
Adam Had Two Sons 1932,Ja 21,17:1
Midsummer Night's Dream, A 1932,Jl 13,15:1
Romeo and Juliet 1933,F 3,21:5
Belmore, Ruth
Merry Wives of Windsor, The 1938,Ap 15,22:3
Belmore-Cliffe, Alice
Rain From Heaven 1934,D 25,28:4
Madame Bovary 1937,N 17,26:2
Belogorsky, Jacob
Eleventh Inheritor, The 1962,N 22,43:5
Enchanting Melody 1964,N 25,40:1
Beloin, Edmund (Playwright)
In Any Language 1952,O 9,40:2
In Any Language 1952,O 19,II,1:1
Belokurov, Vladimir
Dead Souls 1965,F 5,34:1
Three Sisters, The 1965,F 12,15:1
Kremlin Chimes 1965,F 25,23:1
Belong, Nik
Delightful Season, A 1960,S 29,30:1
Belostozky, Boris
Miss Swan Expects 1939,F 21,15:2
Russian People, The 1942,D 30,17:2
Belson, Edmund
Secret Life of Walter Mitty, The 1964,O 27,44:5
Belt, Madeline
Hot Chocolates 1929,Je 21,17:4
Hummin' Sam 1933,Ap 10,8:8
Beltram, Anita
Doctor Cupid 1952,Ag 14,19:6

eltz, Donald
Hansel and Gretel 1929,D 25,21:1
Orpheus in Hades 1930,D 16,30:1
eltzer, Lee (Miscellaneous)
Lovers and Other Strangers 1968,S 19,63:1
Spiro Who? 1969,My 19,55:1
elvawney, Miss
George Barnwell; London Merchant, The 1928,O 2,34:3
elwin, Alma
Unwritten Chapter, The 1920,O 12,18:1
Hero, The 1921,S 6,13:2
emach, Benjamin (Choreographer)
Outlaw, The 1937,O 6,28:1
emberg, George (Playwright)
Someone to Talk To 1956,Jl 19,30:2
emelmans, Ludwig (Costume Designer)
Noah 1935,F 14,25:2
emelmans, Ludwig (Miscellaneous)
Noah 1935,F 14,25:2
emelmans, Ludwig (Original Author)
Now I Lay Me Down to Sleep 1949,Jl 23,7:3
Now I Lay Me Down to Sleep 1950,Mr 3,21:2
Now I Lay Me Down to Sleep 1950,Mr 19,II,1:1
emelmans, Ludwig (Scenic Designer)
Noah 1935,F 14,25:2
ement, Barbara
Technique 1931,My 15,21:1
emis, Fred
Front Page, The 1946,S 5,22:4
emis and Brown
Vaudeville (Palace) 1928,O 2,35:1
en Ali, Robert
Ghost of Elsinore, The 1949,Ap 16,10:2
en-Ami, Arnold
Journey to Jerusalem 1940,O 7,21:2
en-Ami, Jacob
Green Fields 1920,Mr 26,11:2
Mute, The 1920,Ap 9,11:4
Serving Folk 1920,Ap 22,11:3
Naomi 1920,My 7,12:2
Samson and Delilah 1920,N 18,18:1
Samson and Delilah 1920,N 28,VI,1:1
Samson and Delilah 1920,D 5,VII,1:1
Samson and Delilah 1920,D 12,VI,1:3
Samson and Delilah 1920,D 26,VI,3:2
Idle Inn, The 1921,D 21,26:2
Idle Inn, The 1922,Ja 22,VI,1:1
Johannes Kreisler 1922,D 25,20:3
Johannes Kreisler 1923,Ja 21,VII,1:1
Failures, The 1923,N 23,20:1
Failures, The 1923,D 2,VIII,1:1
Race With the Shadow, The 1924,Ja 21,20:5
Welded 1924,Mr 18,24:1
Welded 1924,Mr 23,VIII,1:1
Man and the Masses 1924,Ap 15,25:1
Masse Mensch; Man and the Masses 1924,Ap 20,VIII,1:1
Schweiger 1926,Mr 24,20:4
John 1927,N 5,16:4
Diplomacy 1928,My 29,16:3
Diplomacy 1928,Je 3,VIII,1:1
Sea Gull, The 1929,S 17,34:1
Living Corpse, The 1929,D 7,19:1
Romeo and Juliet 1930,Ap 22,33:1
Sea Gull, The 1930,My 4,XI,1:1
Green Cockatoo, The 1930,O 10,20:5
Siegfried 1930,O 21,34:1
Lady of the Camellias, The 1931,Ja 27,21:2
Evensong 1933,F 1,13:4
Ship Comes in, A 1934,S 20,21:1
Three Cities 1938,O 11,20:3
Who Is Who? 1938,D 24,13:3
Yosne Kalb 1939,F 6,9:2
Far-Away Corner, A 1939,F 15,15:2
Chaver, Nachman 1939,O 2,15:2
Life Marches On 1940,Ja 4,18:2
Day of Judgement, The 1941,O 9,27:3
Sea Gull, The 1956,O 23,38:1
Infernal Machine, The 1958,F 4,33:1
Tenth Man, The 1959,N 6,24:2
Tenth Man, The 1959,N 15,II,1:1
Dybbuk, The 1964,F 4,30:2
Happiness 1967,N 11,25:2
Walking to Waldheim 1967,N 11,25:2
Ben-Ami, Jacob (Director)
Goat Song 1926,Ja 26,18:1
Goat Song 1926,F 7,VII,1:1
Schweiger 1926,Mr 24,20:4
Living Corpse, The 1929,D 7,19:1
Bitter Stream 1936,Mr 31,16:6
Chaver, Nachman 1939,O 2,15:2
Ben-Ami, Jacob (Translator)
Living Corpse, The 1929,D 7,19:1
Ben-Ari
Untitled-Revue 1939,Ja 16,11:3
Ben-Ari, Raikin
Dybbuk, The 1926,D 14,24:2
Eternal Jew, The 1926,D 21,21:2
Deluge, The 1927,Ja 11,36:2
Burning Bush, The 1949,D 17,15:5
Ben-Ari, Raikin (Director)
East Side Professor, The 1938,F 12,19:7

Ben-Artoff, Jacob
60,000 Heroes 1935,Ja 28,11:5
Ben-Astar, Mr
Othello 1949,My 16,17:4
ben Avram, Rachmael (Director)
Murder in the Cathedral 1958,Mr 22,12:4
Ben Bernie's Orchestra
Here's Howe! 1928,My 2,19:3
Ben-Chaim
Dybbuk, The 1926,D 14,24:2
Ben-Haim, Zvi
Dybbuk, The 1948,My 3,26:3
David's Crown 1948,My 10,26:2
Golem, The 1948,My 17,22:3
Oedipus Rex 1948,My 24,23:2
Ben Joseph, Abraham
My Fair Lady 1964,F 20,24:4
Ben-Yano (Scenic Designer)
Third Parade, The 1933,O 23,18:2
Ben Yost's Variety Eight
Ziegfeld Follies 1936,S 15,37:1
Ben-Zissi, Fordhaus (Musical Director)
Dybbuk, The 1948,My 3,26:3
David's Crown 1948,My 10,26:2
Golem, The 1948,My 17,22:3
Benary, Barbara (Composer)
Only Jealousy of Emer, The 1970,Mr 25,36:4
Renard 1970,Mr 25,36:4
Only Jealousy of Emer, The 1970,Ap 26,II,1:3
Benassi, Memo
Donna Del Mare, La; Lady From the Sea, The 1923,O 30,17:1
Spretti; Ghosts 1923,N 7,14:1
Cosi Sia; Thy Will be Done 1923,N 14,29:2
Porta Chiusa, La; Closed Door, The 1923,N 21,23:1
Citta Morta, La 1935,S 22,X,7:7
Benassi, Mento
Citta Morta, La; Dead City, The 1923,N 28,14:1
Benatzky, Ralph (Composer)
Casanova 1928,N 4,IX,2:1
Three Musketeers 1929,O 13,IX,4:7
Meet My Sister 1930,D 31,11:1
Im Weissen Roessel 1931,Ja 4,VIII,3:5
Cocktail 1931,F 15,VIII,3:2
Zur Goldnen Liebe 1932,Ja 24,VIII,1:4
Circus Aimee 1932,My 22,VII,2:2
Bezauberndes Fraeulein 1933,N 19,IX,3:1
Flying Trapeze, The 1935,Je 2,IX,2:3
White Horse Inn 1936,O 2,28:5
Benatzky, Ralph (Lyricist)
Meet My Sister 1930,D 31,11:1
Benatzky, Ralph (Playwright)
Bezauberndes Fraeulein 1933,N 19,IX,3:1
Benavente, Jacinto (Original Author)
Esta Noche... Teatro 1968,O 15,40:1
Benavente, Jacinto (Playwright)
Passion Flower, The 1920,Ja 14,12:1
Evil Doers of Good, The 1923,Ja 17,22:2
Saturday Night 1926,O 26,25:1
Saturday Night 1926,N 7,VIII,1:1
Mariposa que Volo Sobre el Mar, La 1926,D 24,19:1
Mariposa Que Volo Sobre el Mar, La 1927,My 8,VII,2:3
Princess, The 1929,Mr 10,X,4:6
Bonds of Interest, The 1929,O 15,34:2
Suprise for the Countess, A 1930,Mr 25,34:6
Cuando Los Hijos De Eva No Son Los Hijos De Adan; When Eve's Children Are Not Adam's 1932,Ap 23,11:2
De Muy Buena Familia; Of Very Good Family 1932,Ap 29,13:3
Field of Ermine 1935,F 9,10:4
Cuando Los Hijos De Eva No Son Los Hijos De Adan 1937,My 1,17:4
Bonds of Interest, The 1951,D 1,7:2
Bonds of Interest, The 1958,My 7,43:1
Bench, Judi
Twelfth Night 1958,Ag 27,32:1
Benchley, Nathan G
Come Across 1937,Ap 10,10:7
Benchley, Nathaniel (Playwright)
So Proudly We Hail 1938,Mr 30,18:5
So Proudly We Hail 1938,Ap 9,11:1
Frogs of Spring, The 1953,O 21,36:2
Benchley, Robert
Nantucket Follies 1927,Jl 30,13:2
Untitled-Revue 1928,N 19,16:2
Benchley, Robert (Playwright)
49ers, The 1922,N 7,14:1
49ers, The 1922,N 12,VIII,1:1
Bencsath, Henrik (Scenic Designer)
Kek Roka; Blue Fox 1957,D 5,47:2
Egerfogo; Mousetrap, The 1958,Ja 30,18:6
Benczak, Margaret
Only Jealousy of Emer, The 1970,Ap 26,II,1:3
Gertrude 1970,N 13,29:1
Carmilla 1970,D 1,61:2
Benda, G K (Costume Designer)
Silent Knight, The 1937,D 5,XII,5:8
Benda, G K (Miscellaneous)
French Without Tears 1937,S 29,19:1

Benda, G K (Scenic Designer)
Old Music 1937,S 5,X,2:1
Silent Knight, The 1937,D 5,XII,5:8
Benda, Marion
Home Fires 1923,Ag 21,12:1
Rio Rita 1927,F 3,18:3
Bender, Bill
Elmer the Great 1928,S 25,29:1
Bender, Charles
New Yorkers, The 1927,Mr 11,24:3
Bender, Dave
Just a Minute 1928,O 9,34:3
Bender, E H
Party, A 1933,Ag 24,18:4
Aristocrats 1935,My 2,16:2
Bender, Josephene
If You Get It, Do You Want It? 1938,D 1,28:2
Bender, Leslie
Roberta 1937,Je 27,II,6:1
Bender, M H
Wooden Slipper, The 1934,Ja 4,16:3
Bender, Peter
Sweet Adeline 1929,S 4,33:1
Bender, Richard
Regular Guy, A; Man's Man, A 1931,Je 5,27:1
Merrily We Roll Along 1936,Je 30,15:1
Bender, Richard (Miscellaneous)
Reluctant Debutante, The 1956,O 11,50:1
Golden Fleecing 1959,O 16,24:5
Bender, Theodora
Life of Reilly, The 1942,Ap 30,13:2
Boy Meets Girl 1943,Je 23,15:5
Bender, Wesley
Frederika 1937,F 5,16:5
You Never Know 1938,S 22,26:3
Bender, William
Bloomer Girl 1944,O 6,18:5
Bendersky, Laura
Volpone 1967,Je 30,29:1
Bendile, Vinah
Sponono 1964,Ap 3,28:1
Bendix, Ernst (Miscellaneous)
Electra 1958,My 10,17:7
Bendix, Max (Musical Director)
Girofle-Girofla 1926,N 24,26:2
Bendix, William
Trial of Dr Beck, The 1937,Ag 10,22:2
One Thing After Another 1937,D 29,17:2
Run Sheep Run 1938,N 4,26:2
Miss Swan Expects 1939,F 21,15:2
Time of Your Life, The 1939,O 26,26:2
Time of Your Life, The 1940,S 24,27:2
Bendow, Wilhelm
Von Mund zu Mund 1926,D 5,VIII,8:7
Blue Beard 1929,Jl 7,VIII,2:1
Bendtsen, France
Sonya 1921,Ag 16,18:3
Twelfth Night 1921,N 1,17:1
Merchant of Venice, The 1921,N 22,17:1
Dice of the Gods, The 1923,Ap 6,20:2
Sun-Up 1923,My 25,28:1
Cymbeline 1923,O 3,12:1
Twelfth Night 1923,O 23,17:1
Hamlet 1923,O 31,12:1
Accused 1925,S 30,20:1
What Never Dies 1926,D 29,24:2
Merry Wives of Windsor, The 1928,Mr 20,20:1
Gala Night 1930,F 26,22:4
Mr Samuel 1930,N 11,28:4
Merchant of Venice, The 1931,N 17,31:1
Julius Caesar 1931,N 18,26:3
Hamlet 1931,N 19,26:6
It Happened Tomorrow 1933,My 6,11:5
Fly by Night 1933,Je 3,16:2
Another Love 1934,Mr 20,26:3
As Husbands Go 1935,Jl 2,23:1
Cat and the Canary, The 1935,Jl 9,24:4
Trelawney of the 'Wells' 1935,Jl 16,24:1
All This While 1935,Jl 30,17:2
Declassee 1935,Ag 6,20:3
Accent on Youth 1935,Ag 13,20:3
Bury the Dead 1936,Ap 20,17:4
Prelude 1936,Ap 20,17:4
Horse Eats Hat 1936,S 28,14:2
Waltz in Goose Step 1938,N 2,26:2
Bendtsen, Franz
Little Orchard Annie 1930,Ap 22,33:1
Child of Manhattan 1932,Mr 2,15:1
As You Like It 1939,My 9,28:4
As You Like It; Midsummer Night's Dream, A; Comedy of Errors, The; Taming of the Shrew, The 1939,My 9,28:4
Richard II 1940,Ap 2,31:2
Vagabond King, The 1943,Je 30,24:2
Hamlet 1945,D 14,25:2
Bendyk, Betty
Time of Storm 1954,F 26,14:2
Courageous One, The 1958,Ja 21,33:6
Judge, The 1958,My 14,36:2
Comedy of Errors, The 1963,Je 13,28:1
Henry V 1963,Je 14,37:1
Benedet, Jose
Sirena Varada, La 1937,O 23,15:3

Benedet, Julian
Tragedia del Faro, La; Tragedy of the Lighthouse, The 1932,Je 3,23:2
Benedetti, Lino
Rugantino 1964,F 7,34:1
Benedetto, Angelo
Career Angel 1943,N 19,24:2
Benedetto, Frank
Man Who Washed His Hands, The 1967,F 16,33:1
Benedict, Barbara
S S Glencairn 1924,N 4,31:4
Dream Play 1926,Ja 21,18:2
East Lynne 1926,Mr 11,18:4
S S Glencairn 1929,Ja 10,24:5
Sea Gull, The 1929,Ap 10,32:2
Pelican, The 1929,N 14,25:1
Drunkard, The; Fallen Saved, The 1929,D 31,14:6
Devil in the Mind 1931,My 2,23:2
Amateur Hour 1936,Jl 21,13:1
Benedict, Jean
It Pays to Sin 1933,N 4,18:6
Benedict, Joan
Doctor Faustus 1957,F 19,35:7
Benedict, Lawrence
Romeo and Juliet 1968,Je 11,55:2
Hamlet 1969,Je 11,37:1
Alchemist, The 1969,Je 12,51:1
Benedict, Leon
Girl From Samos, The 1954,N 24,17:1
Liliom 1956,F 18,12:5
Mary and the Fairy 1956,Mr 24,15:2
Fortunato 1956,Mr 24,15:2
Brothers Karamazov, The 1957,D 9,39:4
Utopia! 1963,My 7,47:4
Benedict, Paul
Live Like Pigs 1965,Je 8,48:2
Infantry, The 1966,N 15,51:1
Little Murders 1969,Ja 6,38:1
Local Stigmatic, The 1969,N 4,55:2
Local Stigmatic, The; That's All 1969,N 4,55:2
Local Stigmatic, The; Trouble in the Works 1969,N 4,55:2
Local Stigmatic, The; That's Your Trouble 1969,N 4,55:2
Local Stigmatic, The; Last to Go 1969,N 4,55:2
Local Stigmatic, The; Request Stop 1969,N 4,55:2
Local Stigmatic, The; Interview 1969,N 4,55:2
White House Murder Case, The 1970,F 19,59:1
Benedict, Richard
Tell My Story 1939,Mr 16,26:6
Proud Accent 1949,Ap 23,10:2
Benedict, Robert
Henry V 1963,Je 14,37:1
Much Ado About Nothing 1964,Je 11,26:2
Richard III 1964,Je 12,44:2
Coriolanus 1965,Je 21,36:1
Romeo and Juliet 1965,Je 21,36:3
Coriolanus 1965,Je 21,36:1
Taming of the Shrew, The 1965,Je 24,32:2
King Lear 1965,Je 25,39:1
Benedict, Ruth (Director)
Keating 1927,D 26,26:6
Benedictus, David (Original Author)
Fourth of June, The 1964,F 1,12:1
Benedictus, David (Playwright)
Fourth of June, The 1964,F 1,12:1
Benedito, Adolfo
Pluma en el Viento; Feather in the Wind 1932,Ap 2,13:4
Tambor y Cascabel; Drum and Bell 1932,Ap 21,25:4
Cuando Los Hijos De Eva No Son Los Hijos De Adan; When Eve's Children Are Not Adam's 1932,Ap 23,11:2
De Muy Buena Familia; Of Very Good Family 1932,Ap 29,13:3
Beneker, Julius Maria (Playwright)
Peace Ship, The 1927,F 6,8:2
Benell, Julie
To My Husband 1936,Je 2,35:2
Benelli, Sandro (Musical Director)
Passion Play 1937,Mr 22,26:6
Benelli, Sem (Playwright)
Jest, The 1926,F 5,22:2
Jest, The 1926,F 14,VIII,1:1
Cena Delle Beffe, La; Jest, The 1930,N 24,26:4
Arzigogolo, L'; Whim, The 1931,Ap 27,24:4
Benenson, Sanford
Thespis 1953,Ja 17,13:5
Benesch, Isaac (Scenic Designer)
Patience 1928,Je 26,29:3
Merry-Go-Round 1932,Ap 23,11:2
Sophisticrats, The 1933,F 14,19:5
Benet, Stephen Vincent (Original Author)
John Brown's Body 1952,N 3,25:8
John Brown's Body 1952,D 16,43:5
John Brown's Body 1953,F 16,17:2
John Brown's Body 1953,F 22,II,1:1
Benet, Stephen Vincent (Playwright)
Awful Mrs Eaton, The 1924,Jl 20,VII,1:7
Nerves 1924,S 2,22:2
That Awful Mrs Eaton! 1924,S 30,27:1
Headless Horseman, The 1937,Mr 6,10:4

Devil and Daniel Webster, The 1939,My 19,26:1
Devil and Daniel Webster, The 1939,My 21,X,1:1
John Brown's Body 1960,Je 22,31:1
John Brown's Body 1964,Je 29,33:1
John Brown's Body 1968,F 13,49:2
Benetti, Carlo
Golden Dawn 1927,D 1,32:3
Beneveds, Bob
Family Portrait 1959,My 6,48:2
Benezet, Carol
Bewitched 1924,O 2,26:3
Benfield, Bette
Abe Lincoln in Illinois 1938,O 17,12:2
Legal Grounds 1940,D 2,18:4
Bengal, Ben (Playwright)
Plant in the Sun 1937,D 13,22:8
Plant in the Sun 1938,Ja 31,14:2
Bengali, Richard
Adventure 1928,S 26,25:2
Farewell to Arms, A 1930,S 23,30:3
Hobo 1931,F 12,24:4
Enemy Within 1931,O 6,35:3
Her Man of Wax 1933,O 12,32:3
Censored 1938,F 28,18:2
Tell My Story 1939,Mr 16,26:6
Mexican Hayride 1944,Ja 29,9:6
French Touch, The 1945,D 10,18:2
Prescott Proposals, The 1953,D 17,53:1
Deputy, The 1964,F 27,26:1
Bengis, Robert
Twelfth Night 1954,N 10,42:2
Benglia, Habib
Emperor Jones, The 1923,N 1,24:1
Emperor Jones, The 1923,N 18,VIII,2:8
Bengston, Paul (Director)
Exhibition 1969,My 16,41:1
Bengston, Paul (Miscellaneous)
Trumpets and Drums 1969,O 13,52:1
Benham, Earle
Ed Wynn's Carnival 1920,Ap 6,18:2
Right Girl, The 1921,Mr 16,12:1
Benham, Joan
Midsummer Night's Dream, A 1954,S 22,33:1
Benham, Suzanne
Stephen D 1966,Ag 5,17:1
Benhight
Spring Production 1944,My 20,12:4
Beni, Jimi
Music in the Air 1951,O 9,32:2
Where There's a Will 1953,Je 18,38:5
Brandy Is My True Love's Name 1953,Je 18,38:5
California 1953,Je 18,38:5
Hopalong--Freud 1953,Je 18,38:5
Beniades, Ted
Wonderful Town 1953,F 26,22:3
Wonderful Town 1954,My 7,II,1:1
Wonderful Town 1958,Mr 6,32:4
King and I, The 1960,My 12,40:1
Garden of Sweets, The 1961,N 1,35:1
Fortuna 1962,Ja 4,26:1
Wonderful Town 1963,F 15,10:2
Golden Boy 1964,O 21,56:1
King and I, The 1968,My 24,39:1
Oklahoma! 1969,Je 24,37:1
Oklahoma! 1969,Jl 6,II,1:1
Benisch, Natalie
Petrified Forest, The 1943,N 2,30:6
Temporary Island, A 1948,Mr 15,27:3
Benjamin, Charles
Four O'Clock 1933,F 14,19:6
Dead End 1935,O 29,17:2
You Can't Take It With You 1945,Mr 27,23:7
Benjamin, Clelia
Back to Methuselah (Part V: As Far as Thought Can Reach) 1922,Mr 14,11:2
Dice of the Gods, The 1923,Ap 6,20:2
Kreutzer Sonata, The 1924,My 15,22:3
Benjamin, Edward
Topaze 1947,D 29,21:5
Peter Pan 1950,Ap 25,27:2
Benjamin, Elsie
Garden of Time 1945,Mr 10,13:7
Carib Song 1945,S 28,17:2
Benjamin, Faiga
Othello 1929,F 4,21:2
Benjamin, James
Joy 1970,Ja 28,50:1
Benjamin, Joe
Look to the Lilies 1970,Mr 30,59:1
Benjamin, John
Riot 1968,D 20,64:1
Benjamin, John W
Betty Behave 1927,Mr 9,28:4
Benjamin, Joseph (Playwright)
Riverwind 1962,D 14,5:5
Benjamin, Julian
Embezzled Heaven 1944,N 1,20:2
Benjamin, Mary
Julius Caesar 1923,F 9,10:4
Benjamin, Park (Mrs)
Vaudeville (Hippodrome) 1926,My 4,31:2

Benjamin, Paul
Hamlet 1967,D 27,45:1
Hamlet 1968,Jl 4,15:1
Cities in Bezique; Owl Answers, The 1969,Ja 13,26:1
No Place to Be Somebody 1969,My 5,53:3
No Place to Be Somebody 1969,My 18,II,22:1
Year Boston Won the Pennant, The 1969,My 23,38:1
Camino Real 1970,Ja 9,42:1
Operation Sidewinder 1970,Mr 13,33:1
Benjamin, Rene (Playwright)
Paris 1932,F 14,VIII,2:5
Girouette 1935,My 5,IX,2:4
Benjamin, Richard
As You Like It 1963,Jl 17,19:2
Star-Spangled Girl, The 1966,D 22,38:1
Benjamin, Richard (Director)
Great Airplane Snatch, The 1969,My 28,36:1
Arf 1969,My 28,36:1
Benjamin, Romeyn
Fashion 1924,F 5,21:2
Crime in the Whistler Room, The 1924,O 10,22:2
Desire Under the Elms 1924,N 12,20:7
Benjamin, Zelda
House of Bernarda Alba, The 1951,Ja 8,14:6
Benko, J Anthony (Costume Designer)
To Damascus 1961,F 15,40:2
Benkoil, Maury (Miscellaneous)
Dream Out of Time, A 1970,N 9,52:1
Benlian, Arden
Love's Call 1925,S 11,20:1
Gang War 1928,Ag 21,27:2
Benlell, Julie
One More Genius 1936,Ag 11,24:6
Benner, Bill
Red, Hot and Blue! 1936,O 30,26:3
Hill Between, The 1938,Mr 12,12:5
Everywhere I Roam 1938,D 30,10:4
Bennet, Eloise
Lovely Lady 1927,D 30,22:1
Bennet, George (Scenic Designer)
Arms and the Man 1938,Ag 10,14:1
Bennet, Seldon
Broken Chain, The 1929,F 21,30:4
Bennethum, John
Come What May 1934,My 16,23:4
Bennett, Alan
Beyond the Fringe 1961,Je 25,II,3:5
Beyond the Fringe 1962,O 29,36:1
Beyond the Fringe 1964 1964,Ja 10,18:1
40 Years On 1969,Jl 26,14:1
Bennett, Alan (Playwright)
Beyond the Fringe 1962,O 29,36:1
40 Years On 1968,N 5,53:3
40 Years On 1969,Jl 26,14:1
Forty Years On 1970,Ag 30,II,1:1
Bennett, Arnold (Original Author)
Riceyman Steps 1926,D 12,VIII,4:7
Darling of the Day 1968,F 11,II,3:1
Bennett, Arnold (Playwright)
Sacred and Profane Love 1920,F 24,11:1
Sacred and Profane Love 1920,F 29,V,5:2
Great Adventure, The 1921,F 26,9:2
Title, The 1921,N 15,23:3
What the Public Wants 1922,My 2,22:3
Body and Soul 1922,O 8,VI,1:7
Great Adventure, The 1926,D 23,23:1
Mr Prohack 1927,D 4,X,1:3
Mr Prohack 1928,Ja 1,VIII,1:3
Return Journey, The 1928,S 9,III,3:5
Return Journey, The 1928,S 23,IX,1:3
Milestones 1930,Je 3,27:1
Flora 1935,O 30,17:4
Darling of the Day 1968,Ja 29,26:2
Bennett, Barbara
Dancers, The 1923,O 18,17:2
Stork, The 1925,Ja 27,14:2
Vaudeville (Palace) 1928,Jl 17,15:5
Victory Belles 1943,O 27,26:3
Bennett, Belle
Wandering Jew, The 1921,O 27,22:1
Bennett, Billy
Laughter Over London 1936,D 8,31:3
Bennett, Brenda
Pirates of Penzance, The 1936,S 1,24:4
Gondoliers, The 1936,S 8,23:1
Iolanthe 1936,S 22,30:3
Patience 1936,O 6,28:6
Ruddigore 1936,O 23,26:4
Bennett, Caesar
Porgy and Bess 1935,O 11,30:2
Bennett, Carlyle
Satellite 1935,N 21,27:5
Bennett, Charles
Candida 1926,O 24,VIII,2:1
Bennett, Charles (Playwright)
Last Hour, The 1929,Ja 6,VIII,1:4
Page From a Diary 1936,Ja 17,14:6
Page From a Diary 1936,F 9,X,3:1
Bennett, Chester
Five O'Clock Girl, The 1927,O 11,26:3

Bennett, Christine
Henry VIII 1961,Je 22,22:1
Troilus and Cressida 1963,Je 19,40:2
Cyrano de Bergerac 1963,Je 20,30:1
Comedy of Errors, The 1963,Je 21,35:3
Hedda Gabler 1970,Je 12,28:1
Bennett, Christopher
Jeb 1946,F 22,20:2
Daddy Come Home 1963,Ap 17,33:1
Bennett, Constance
Easy Virtue 1939,D 31,18:4
We Were Dancing; Tonight at Eight 1940,Ag 6,15:3
Tonight at 8:30 1940,Ag 11,IX,11:2
Date With April, A 1953,Ap 16,36:2
Bennett, Dave (Choreographer)
Criss Cross 1926,O 13,20:2
Oh, Please! 1926,D 22,24:3
Earl Carroll's Vanities 1927,Ja 5,18:1
Lucky 1927,Mr 23,28:3
Golden Dawn 1927,D 1,32:3
Lovely Lady 1927,D 30,22:1
Three Cheers 1928,O 16,28:1
Bennett, Dave (Director)
Manhatters, The 1927,Ag 4,25:4
My Princess 1927,O 7,24:2
Bennett, David
Iolanthe 1965,My 19,42:1
Yeomen of the Guard, The 1965,Jl 8,34:1
Bennett, Dorothy (Playwright)
Best Sellers 1933,My 4,20:2
Fly Away Home 1935,Ja 16,20:4
Fly Away Home 1936,Jl 21,13:1
Fly Away Home 1937,Jl 27,24:3
Fly Away Home 1937,Jl 28,15:1
Woman's a Fool-To Be Clever, A 1938,O 19,18:6
Bennett, Edna
Champion, The 1925,Ap 24,16:4
Tia Juana 1927,N 16,28:4
Big Fight, The 1928,S 19,33:1
Cynara 1931,N 3,31:1
Billy Draws a Horse 1939,D 22,14:5
Bennett, Eloise
Will Morrissey's Folies Bergere Revue 1930,Ap 16,26:6
Women, The 1936,D 28,13:1
Bennett, Evelyn
Merry-Go-Round 1927,Je 1,25:4
Allez-Opp! 1927,Ag 3,29:3
Good Boy 1928,S 6,23:2
Bennett, Fletcher
Shunned 1960,D 21,39:1
Bennett, Fran
Me, Candido! 1956,O 16,36:2
Land Beyond the River, A 1957,Mr 29,15:7
Goose, The 1960,Mr 16,44:1
Mandingo 1961,My 23,43:6
Cantilevered Terrace, The 1962,Ja 18,24:1
Ballad for Bimshire 1963,O 16,54:1
House of Atreus, The 1968,D 18,55:1
Bennett, Fran (Miscellaneous)
Land Beyond the River, A 1957,Mr 29,15:7
Bennett, Frank (Composer)
'Tis Pity She's a Whore 1967,O 21,15:2
Bennett, Frank (Miscellaneous)
'Tis Pity She's a Whore 1967,O 21,15:2
Bennett, Gage
Merchant of Venice, The 1921,Ap 2,14:2
Caponsacchi 1928,Ja 25,20:3
Henry V 1928,Mr 16,26:2
Light of Asia, The 1928,O 10,32:2
Richelieu 1929,D 26,20:3
Bennett, George (Scenic Designer)
Yes, My Darling Daughter 1938,Jl 13,19:2
Bachelor Born 1938,Ag 17,23:1
Springtime for Henry 1938,Ag 31,12:5
Bennett, Gordon
Marion Show, The 1923,My 8,22:3
Bennett, Harry Gordon (Scenic Designer)
Mother Sings 1935,N 13,24:1
All the Comforts of Home 1942,My 26,24:5
Oy, Is Dus a Leben!; Oh, What a Life! 1942,O 13,19:2
Strange Play, A 1944,Je 2,20:3
According to Law 1944,Je 2,20:3
Eternal Cage 1945,Mr 22,19:7
You Can't Take It With You 1945,Mr 27,23:7
Lady in Danger 1945,Mr 30,18:6
Duchess of Malfi, The 1946,O 16,35:2
Bennett, Helen
By Jupiter 1942,Je 4,22:1
Early to Bed 1943,Je 18,16:2
Allah Be Praised! 1944,Ap 21,14:2
Dream Girl 1945,D 15,13:2
Bennett, Henry
Nantucket Follies 1927,Jl 30,13:2
Bennett, High (Producer)
Lady Behave 1943,N 17,30:1
Bennett, Holland
Evensong 1933,F 1,13:4
Bennett, Howard (Miscellaneous)
Postmark Zero 1965,N 2,28:1
Bennett, Hugh
Take the Air 1927,N 23,28:2

Bennett, Ida
Malinda 1929,D 4,37:2
Bennett, J Moy
Schemers 1924,S 16,27:1
Spring 3100 1928,F 16,14:2
Scarlet Pages 1929,S 10,26:3
Bennett, Jack
Two Fellows and a Girl 1923,Jl 20,8:2
Silence 1924,N 13,18:2
Kept 1926,S 18,13:3
Conflict 1929,Mr 7,22:4
It Never Rains 1929,N 20,26:4
Humbug, The 1929,N 28,34:5
They Never Grow Up 1930,Ap 8,27:1
Greeks Had a Word for It, The 1930,S 26,16:5
It Never Rains 1931,D 25,29:3
Merry-Go-Round 1932,Ap 23,11:2
Bennett, James (Composer)
Thanks for Tomorrow 1938,S 28,28:2
Bennett, Jill
Night of The Ball, The 1955,Ja 13,31:8
Lily of Little India, A 1966,Ja 22,17:2
Time Present 1968,My 25,38:1
Time Present 1968,Je 2,II,3:6
Time Present 1968,Jl 5,20:1
Three Months Gone 1970,S 10,59:1
Bennett, Joan
Jarnegan 1928,S 25,29:2
Pirate, The 1929,Ap 21,IX,1:4
Love Me Little 1958,Ap 15,42:2
Never Too Late 1963,S 25,48:1
Bennett, Joe
West Side Story 1964,Ap 9,24:2
Bennett, John
Precedent 1931,Ap 15,24:5
Bennett, John A
On Location 1937,S 28,19:1
Bennett, Jules
Easy Come, Easy Go 1925,O 27,20:2
We Americans 1926,O 13,20:4
If Love Were All 1931,N 14,14:5
American Landscape 1938,D 5,19:2
Bennett, Jules J
Welcome Stranger 1920,S 14,12:1
Bennett, Laura
Song and Dance Man, The 1924,Ja 1,21:2
Bennett, Leila
First Year, The 1920,O 21,11:2
First Year, The 1920,O 31,VI,1:1
Wheel, The 1921,Ag 30,10:1
Chicken Feed 1923,S 25,10:2
Holy Terror, A 1925,S 29,31:2
It's a Wise Child 1929,Ag 7,29:1
It's a Wise Child 1929,Ag 25,VIII,1:1
Company's Coming! 1931,Ap 21,35:5
Bennett, Libby
Too Many Girls 1939,O 19,26:2
Bennett, Lillian
Trojan Women, The 1941,Ap 9,32:5
Rosalinda; Fledermaus, Die 1942,O 29,26:5
Bennett, Linda
Brigadoon 1964,D 24,9:1
Wonderful Town 1967,My 18,50:1
Arabian Nights 1967,Jl 3,12:1
Bennett, Lois
Iolanthe 1926,Ap 20,24:2
Mikado, The; Town of Titipu, The 1927,S 19,30:1
Bennett, Magda
Judy 1927,F 8,20:2
Bennett, Margot
Irregular Verb to Love, The 1963,S 19,22:2
Bennett, Mary
Tattle Tales 1933,Je 2,22:6
Bennett, Michael (Choreographer)
Joyful Noise, A 1966,D 16,57:1
Henry, Sweet Henry 1967,O 24,51:2
Promises, Promises 1968,D 15,II,3:1
Coco 1969,D 28,II,1:1
Company 1970,My 3,II,1:4
Bennett, Michael (Director)
Promises, Promises 1968,D 2,59:3
Company 1970,Ap 27,40:1
Bennett, Michael (Miscellaneous)
Coco 1969,D 19,66:1
Bennett, Monroe
Cortez 1929,N 5,32:2
Bennett, Murray
Cat Comes Back, The 1923,Ja 29,11:2
Hail and Farewell 1923,F 20,12:1
Roseanne 1923,D 31,9:5
Main Line, The 1924,Mr 26,19:4
Comedienne 1924,O 22,18:1
Carolinian, The 1925,N 3,34:2
Dope 1926,Ja 4,16:3
Nirvana 1926,Mr 4,19:1
Criminal Code, The 1929,O 3,28:2
Behind the Red Lights 1937,Ja 14,17:4
Kind Lady 1938,Jl 11,14:2
Bennett, Paul
Oedipus 1970,F 23,30:1

Bennett, Peter
Love Goes to Press 1947,Ja 2,22:2
Bennett, Richard
Beyond the Horizon 1920,F 4,12:1
Beyond the Horizon 1920,F 8,VIII,2:1
Merchant of Venice, The 1921,Ap 2,14:2
Hero, The 1921,S 6,13:2
Hero, The 1921,S 11,VI,1:1
He Who Gets Slapped 1922,Ja 10,15:1
Dancers, The 1923,O 18,17:2
They Knew What They Wanted 1924,N 25,27:1
Oh, Please! 1926,D 22,24:3
Jarnegan 1928,S 25,29:2
Vaudeville (Palace) 1929,D 23,19:1
In Command 1930,Mr 9,IX,4:3
Solid South 1930,My 11,IX,2:6
Solid South 1930,O 15,27:1
Winterset 1935,S 26,19:2
Bennett, Robert
Creaking Chair, The 1926,F 23,26:1
Libel! 1935,D 21,10:5
Bennett, Robert Russell (Composer)
Macbeth 1921,F 18,16:1
Firebrand, The 1924,O 16,33:1
Music in the Air 1932,O 23,IX,3:3
Hold Your Horses 1933,Ag 31,20:4
Hold Your Horses 1933,S 26,26:4
Carmen Jones 1946,Ap 8,32:2
Happy Birthday 1946,N 1,31:2
If the Shoe Fits 1946,D 6,29:4
Sweethearts 1947,Ja 22,31:2
Heaven on Earth 1948,S 17,29:2
Kiss Me, Kate 1948,D 31,10:3
Texas Li'l Darlin' 1949,N 26,10:5
Great to Be Alive! 1950,Mr 24,28:2
On a Clear Day You Can See Forever 1965,O 18,44:1
Bennett, Robert Russell (Lyricist)
Hold Your Horses 1933,S 26,26:4
Rhapsody 1944,N 23,37:2
Bennett, Robert Russell (Miscellaneous)
Revenge With Music 1934,N 29,33:5
Jubilee 1935,O 14,20:1
George White's Scandals 1935,D 26,20:2
Count Me In 1942,O 9,24:2
Oklahoma! 1943,Ap 11,II,1:1
Bloomer Girl 1944,O 6,18:5
Finian's Rainbow 1947,Ja 11,23:2
Allegro 1947,O 11,10:2
Dance Me a Song 1950,Ja 21,10:5
Out of This World 1950,D 22,17:3
King and I, The 1951,Mr 30,26:2
King and I, The 1951,Ap 8,II,1:1
Tree Grows in Brooklyn, A 1951,Ap 20,24:3
Oklahoma! 1951,My 30,15:2
Music in the Air 1951,O 9,32:2
Kiss Me, Kate 1952,Ja 9,24:6
Paris '90 1952,Mr 5,33:2
Three Wishes for Jamie 1952,Mr 22,9:2
King and I, The 1952,O 5,II,1:1
Oklahoma! 1953,S 1,19:1
My Fair Lady 1956,Mr 16,20:2
King and I, The 1956,Ap 19,35:4
Show Boat 1956,Je 22,16:1
Bells Are Ringing 1956,N 29,43:4
Bells Are Ringing 1956,N 30,18:2
Ziegfeld Follies 1957,Mr 2,19:2
New Girl in Town 1957,My 15,40:1
Show Boat 1957,Je 28,30:2
Flower Drum Song 1958,D 2,44:1
Redhead 1959,F 6,21:1
Juno 1959,Mr 10,41:1
Sound of Music, The 1959,N 17,40:2
Finian's Rainbow 1960,Ap 28,31:1
King and I, The 1960,My 12,40:1
King and I, The 1960,My 22,II,1:1
Camelot 1960,D 5,42:1
13 Daughters 1961,Mr 3,17:2
Happiest Girl in the World, The 1961,Ap 4,42:1
King and I, The 1963,Je 13,30:2
Jennie 1963,O 18,35:2
Girl Who Came to Supper, The 1963,D 9,49:1
My Fair Lady 1964,My 21,43:2
King and I, The 1964,Jl 7,26:1
Annie Get Your Gun 1966,Je 1,42:2
Show Boat 1966,Jl 20,48:1
South Pacific 1967,Je 13,56:1
King and I, The 1968,My 24,39:1
My Fair Lady 1968,Je 14,42:1
South Pacific 1968,Je 30,54:2
Oklahoma! 1969,Je 24,37:1
South Pacific 1969,Jl 7,27:1
Bennett, Robert Russell (Musical Director)
Carmen Jones 1943,O 20,17:2
Carmen Jones 1943,D 3,26:2
Carmen Jones 1943,D 12,II,3:1
Carmen Jones 1943,D 19,II,9:1
Bloomer Girl 1944,O 8,II,1:1
Carmen Jones 1945,My 3,26:5
Louisiana Lady 1947,Je 3,35:2
Inside U S A 1948,My 1,19:2
Sally 1948,My 7,31:2
Inside U S A 1948,My 23,II,1:1

Bennett, Robert Russell (Musical Director)—Cont
Show Boat 1948,S 9,33:2
South Pacific 1949,Ap 8,30:2
By the Beautiful Sea 1954,Ap 9,20:1
South Pacific 1955,My 5,39:5
Finian's Rainbow 1955,My 19,25:1
Pipe Dream 1955,D 1,44:1
Sound of Music, The 1970,Jl 3,13:1
Bennett, Robert Russell (Playwright)
Rhapsody 1944,N 23,37:2
Carmen Jones 1956,Je 1,28:2
Carmen Jones 1959,Ag 18,25:1
Bennett, Ronald
Possessed, The 1939,O 25,26:2
Twelfth Night 1941,D 3,32:2
Bennett, Ross
Sin of Pat Muldoon, The 1957,Mr 14,35:1
Bennett, Rudolph (Miscellaneous)
Oklahoma! 1963,My 16,40:1
Pal Joey 1963,My 30,21:1
Bennett, Sam
Wooden Soldier, The 1931,Je 23,28:4
Bennett, Seldon
World We Live In, The 1922,N 1,16:1
Enchanted Cottage, The 1923,Ap 2,22:3
Tale of the Wolf, The 1925,O 8,31:2
Tip-Toes 1925,D 29,20:2
Taming of the Shrew, The 1927,O 26,26:4
Jonesy 1929,Ap 10,32:2
Channel Road, The 1929,O 18,24:2
Joseph 1930,F 13,25:3
Very Warm for May 1939,N 18,23:2
Weak Link, The 1940,Mr 5,19:2
Horse Fever 1940,N 25,21:2
Show Boat 1946,Ja 7,17:2
Show Boat 1948,S 9,33:2
Bennett, Stanley (Miscellaneous)
Change Your Luck 1930,Je 7,10:2
Bennett, Stellar
Our Town 1969,N 28,50:1
Bennett, Suzanne
Rat, The 1925,F 11,19:3
Port O' London 1926,F 10,20:2
Nic-Nax of 1926 1926,Ag 5,19:1
What Do We Know 1927,D 24,8:1
Cyclone Lover, The 1928,Je 6,23:3
Guns 1928,Ag 7,25:2
Bennett, Tom
Crucible 1933,S 5,22:4
Mikado, The 1944,F 12,11:3
Bennett, Tom (Composer)
Othello 1943,O 20,18:1
Streets Are Guarded, The 1944,N 21,19:7
Othello 1945,My 23,25:4
Bennett, Tony
Untitled-Judy Garland 1967,D 26,45:1
Bennett, Vivienne
Peer Gynt 1935,S 24,28:2
Agamemnon 1936,N 2,25:6
Bennett, Wilda
Irving Berlin's Music Box Revue 1921,S 23,18:2
Lady in Ermine, The 1922,O 3,22:2
Madame Pompadour 1924,N 12,20:6
Vaudeville (Palace) 1927,Mr 29,22:6
Benning, Achim
Professor Bernhardi 1968,Mr 20,38:1
Maria Stuart 1968,Mr 27,38:1
Bennion, Peggy
Hall of Healing 1952,My 8,35:6
As You Like It 1955,O 29,12:2
Romeo and Juliet 1955,D 16,36:3
Titus Andronicus 1956,D 3,40:2
Two Gentlemen of Verona 1957,Jl 23,21:5
Macbeth 1957,Ag 16,11:2
Twelfth Night 1958,Ag 7,21:4
Bennison, Louis
Heaven 1920,Je 13,VI,1:8
Personality 1921,Ag 29,14:3
Nobody's Business 1923,O 23,17:1
Vagabond, The 1923,D 28,13:4
Dust Heap, The 1924,F 24,VII,2:5
Dust Heap, The 1924,Ap 25,20:2
Badges 1924,D 4,25:1
All Dressed Up 1925,S 10,28:1
Virgin, The 1926,F 23,26:1
Heaven-Tappers, The 1927,Mr 9,28:3
Bennison, Louis (Playwright)
Virgin, The 1926,F 23,26:1
Benno, Cesar
Fanny 1955,D 17,19:6
Bennthum, John
Happy Valley, Limited 1936,Je 30,15:1
Benny, Ben
Molly Darling 1922,S 2,10:2
Paradise Alley 1924,Ap 2,17:3
Benny, Jack
Great Temptations, The 1926,My 19,29:1
Vaudeville (Palace) 1927,S 20,33:3
Vaudeville (Palace) 1928,N 12,18:7
Vaudeville (Palace) 1928,N 19,16:3
Vaudeville (Palace) 1929,D 30,16:3
Earl Carroll's Vanities 1930,Jl 2,28:3
Vaudeville (Palace) 1931,My 25,17:4

Vaudeville (New Amsterdam Theatre) 1931,Je 22,17:3
Vaudeville (Palace) 1931,S 7,19:2
Vaudeville (Hollywood) 1932,Ap 19,25:5
Friars Club Frolic 1933,My 15,16:4
Bring on the Girls 1934,O 23,23:2
Jack Benny 1963,Mr 1,10:5
Untitled-Revue 1965,Je 25,38:1
Benny and Western
Vaudeville (Palace) 1928,N 6,35:2
Benois, Alexandre (Scenic Designer)
Imperatrice aux Rochers, L' 1927,Mr 20,VIII,2:4
Benois, M
Revue Russe, The 1922,O 6,28:1
Benois, Nicolas (Costume Designer)
Chauve-Souris 1924,D 14,VIII,6:1
Benois, Nicolas (Scenic Designer)
Chauve-Souris 1924,D 14,VIII,6:1
Benoit, Denise
Mariage de Figaro, Le 1964,F 26,41:2
Vie Parisienne, La 1964,Mr 11,34:2
Benoit, Joan
New Moon, The 1942,Ag 19,14:2
Benoit, Patricia
Glad Tidings 1951,O 12,33:2
Brass Ring, The 1952,Ap 11,19:2
Time Limit! 1956,Ja 25,27:2
Have I Got a Girl for You! 1963,D 3,53:2
Benoit, Pierre (Original Author)
Lac Sale, Le 1926,S 5,II,6:5
Lac Sale, Le 1926,O 3,VIII,2:1
Benoit, Victor
Casanova 1923,S 27,10:2
Benrath, Martin
Mitschuldigen, Die 1966,Ap 6,34:1
Ratten, Die 1966,Ap 13,36:1
Benrimo, J Harry (Director)
Yellow Jacket, The 1928,N 8,27:3
Well of Romance, The 1930,N 8,21:2
Right of Happiness 1931,Ap 3,34:2
Benrimo, J Harry (Original Author)
Cherry Blossoms 1927,Mr 29,22:3
Benrimo, J Harry (Playwright)
Yellow Jacket, The 1928,N 8,27:3
Bensal, Mark
Hamlet 1970,O 27,54:2
Rosencrantz and Guildenstern Are Dead 1970,N 19,39:3
Bensen, Carl
Catherine Was Great 1944,Ag 3,16:1
Galileo 1968,D 1,88:4
Benskin, Sammy
Time of Your Life, The 1955,Ja 20,34:1
Here's Josephine Premice 1966,Ap 26,54:4
Benskin, Sammy (Composer)
Bill Noname 1970,Mr 3,37:1
Benskin, Sammy (Miscellaneous)
Cindy 1964,Mr 20,24:1
Bill Noname 1970,Mr 3,37:1
Benskin, Sammy (Musical Director)
Ballad for Bimshire 1963,O 16,54:1
Bill Noname 1970,Mr 3,37:1
Benson, Alice Merton
Happiness Cage, The 1970,O 5,56:4
Benson, Betty
John Brown's Body 1953,F 16,17:2
3 for Tonight 1955,Ap 7,23:2
3 for Tonight 1955,Ap 17,II,1:1
Benson, Carl
Pony Cart, The 1954,S 15,39:2
Benson, Court
Ross 1961,D 27,20:2
Benson, E F (Original Author)
Make Way for Lucia 1948,D 23,23:5
Benson, Esther
Sweeney Todd 1957,Ag 28,21:4
Journey With Strangers, A 1958,N 27,53:1
Poppa Is Home 1961,D 20,37:1
Living Room, The 1962,N 22,43:5
Wild Duck, The 1967,Ja 12,49:1
Rate of Exchange 1968,Ap 2,50:1
Benson, George
Two Bouquets, The 1936,S 13,X,1:5
Winslow Boy, The 1947,O 30,32:2
Love's Labour's Lost 1949,O 24,18:3
Tempest, The 1970,Ag 29,14:1
Benson, Harry
New Yorkers, The 1927,Mr 11,24:3
Benson, Islay
Hand in Glove 1944,D 5,19:1
Benson, John
Heaven-Tappers, The 1927,Mr 9,28:3
Long Voyage Home, The 1961,D 5,49:1
Nature of the Crime 1970,Mr 24,41:1
Happiness Cage, The 1970,O 5,56:4
Benson, John (Miscellaneous)
Diff'rent 1961,O 18,52:1
Long Voyage Home, The 1961,D 5,49:1
Creditors 1962,Ja 26,19:1
Benson, Leslie R
Right to Strike, The 1921,O 25,20:1
Benson, Lucille
Good Night Ladies 1945,Ja 18,16:2

Benson, Lucille—Cont
Day Before Spring, The 1945,N 23,27:2
Hotel Paradiso 1957,Ap 12,22:2
Orpheus Descending 1959,O 6,45:2
Seven Scenes for Yeni 1963,My 13,36:2
Billygoat Eddie 1964,Ap 21,43:2
Walking Happy 1966,N 28,47:1
Benson, Maggie
Caution: A Love Story 1969,Ap 4,45:1
Benson, Ralph
Flight to the West 1940,D 31,19:1
Benson, Richard
Sweethearts 1947,Ja 22,31:2
Benson, Rita
Cure for Matrimony 1939,O 26,26:3
Benson, Robby
Zelda 1969,Mr 6,38:1
Rothschilds, The 1970,O 20,40:1
Benson, Robert
Milk Train Doesn't Stop Here Anymore, The 1965,Jl 27,25:1
Midsummer Night's Dream, A 1967,Je 30,23:1
Cyrano de Bergerac 1968,Ap 26,30:1
Benson, Robert L (Lighting Director)
Behind the Wall 1960,N 1,47:1
Rate of Exchange 1968,Ap 2,50:1
Benson, Roy
Manhattan Varieties 1932,O 22,18:3
Benson, Roy (Miscellaneous)
Carnival! 1961,Ap 14,22:2
Benson, Sally (Original Author)
Junior Miss 1941,N 19,28:2
Junior Miss 1941,N 30,IX,1:1
Benson, Sally (Playwright)
Memphis Bound 1945,My 25,23:2
Memphis Bound 1945,Je 10,II,1:1
Seventeen 1951,Je 22,16:6
Seventeen 1951,Jl 1,II,1:1
Young and Beautiful, The 1955,O 3,23:2
Young and Beautiful, The 1956,Ag 16,30:6
Young and Beautiful, The 1959,My 29,13:1
Benson, T F
War Song, The 1928,S 25,29:3
Benson and Massimo
Vaudeville (Palace) 1924,Ap 29,12:2
Benstock, Melvin
Happy Valley, Limited 1936,Je 30,15:1
Timber House 1936,S 21,27:5
Bent, Marion
Love Birds 1921,Mr 16,12:1
Vaudeville (Palace) 1923,F 13,25:1
Vaudeville (Palace) 1926,Mr 30,20:4
Vaudeville (Palace) 1926,Je 29,21:3
Vaudeville (Palace) 1929,O 7,22:4
Bentell and Gould
Vaudeville (Palace) 1926,S 7,24:6
Benter, Richard
Sharon's Grave 1961,N 9,39:2
Benter, Richard (Miscellaneous)
Sharon's Grave 1961,N 9,39:2
Benthall, Michael (Director)
Caesar and Cleopatra 1951,My 11,32:8
Caesar and Cleopatra 1951,D 20,43:2
Antony and Cleopatra 1951,D 21,22:2
Caesar and Cleopatra 1951,D 30,II,1:1
Antony and Cleopatra 1951,D 30,II,1:1
Millionairess, The 1952,O 18,17:2
Millionairess, The 1952,O 26,II,1:1
Hamlet 1953,Ag 25,18:6
Midsummer Night's Dream, A 1954,S 1,31:3
Macbeth 1954,S 5,II,3:7
Midsummer Night's Dream, A 1954,S 22,33:1
Romeo and Juliet 1956,S 19,34:6
Richard II 1956,O 24,44:1
Macbeth 1956,O 30,42:2
Twelfth Night 1958,D 10,54:2
Hamlet 1958,D 17,2:7
Henry V 1958,D 26,2:7
Double Dealer, The 1959,Ag 25,36:2
Macbeth 1961,Ja 10,28:1
Doctor Faustus 1961,Ag 22,23:1
Macbeth 1962,F 7,32:2
Macbeth 1962,F 25,II,1:1
Man and Boy 1963,N 13,34:1
I'm Solomon 1968,Ap 24,51:1
Coco 1969,D 19,66:1
Coco 1969,D 28,II,1:1
Benthall, Michael (Miscellaneous)
I'm Solomon 1968,Ap 24,51:1
Benthall, Michael (Producer)
Hamlet 1948,My 9,II,2:5
As You Like It 1950,F 19,II,1:1
Millionairess, The 1952,Je 28,12:2
Macbeth 1956,My 24,27:1
Richard II 1956,Jl 4,15:1
Twelfth Night 1958,Ag 27,32:1
Bentham, Josephine (Playwright)
Janie 1942,S 11,24:2
Bentivegna, Warner
Servant of Two Masters, The 1960,F 24,42:2
Bentley, Anna
Deacon, The 1925,N 25,14:3
Bentley, Benjamin Conkling
Myself and I 1929,Ag 31,13:6

Bentley, Beverly
Heroine, The 1963,F 21,5:5
Heroine, The 1963,Je 16,II,1:1
Deer Park, The 1967,F 1,27:2
Bentley, Carlton H
No for an Answer 1941,Ja 6,10:6
Bentley, Eric (Director)
International Set, The 1953,Je 12,19:3
Good Woman of Setzuan, The 1956,D 19,41:2
Bentley, Eric (Miscellaneous)
Vida es Sueno, La 1964,Mr 18,49:1
Life Is a Dream 1964,Mr 20,24:1
Bentley, Eric (Playwright)
Private Life of the Master Race, The
1945,Je 17,II,1:1
Ronde, La 1955,Je 28,24:2
Private Life of the Master Race, The
1956,Ja 31,33:3
Good Woman of Setzuan, The 1956,D 19,41:2
Right You Are (If You Think You Are)
1957,Mr 5,37:1
Jewish Wife 1961,N 15,52:2
Man's a Man, A 1962,S 20,30:2
Mother Courage and Her Children 1963,Mr 30,5:5
Mother Courage and Her Children 1964,My 12,32:2
Baal 1965,My 7,33:2
Exception and the Rule, The 1965,My 21,19:1
Caucasian Chalk Circle, The 1966,Mr 25,35:1
Right You Are (If You Think You Are)
1966,N 23,34:2
Henry IV 1968,F 7,40:1
Bentley, Eric (Translator)
Private Life of the Master Race, The
1945,Je 13,28:3
Good Woman of Setzuan, The 1956,D 30,II,1:1
Right You Are (If You Think You Are)
1964,Mr 5,37:1
Bentley, Herschel
Two on an Island 1940,Ja 23,17:2
Craig's Wife 1947,F 13,35:2
For Heaven's Sake Mother 1948,N 17,33:4
Bentley, Jordan
Tree Grows in Brooklyn, A 1951,Ap 20,24:3
Wonderful Town 1953,F 26,22:3
Wonderful Town 1958,Mr 6,32:4
Bentley, Lorrie
Capacity for Wings 1957,Ja 10,25:2
Bentley, Miriam
Gondoliers, The 1940,O 1,29:2
Bentley, Muriel
Call Me Madam 1950,O 13,25:1
Bentley, Peter
Black Velvet 1927,S 28,28:1
Bentley, Robert
Wooden Kimono 1926,D 28,16:2
Wicked Age, The 1927,N 5,16:6
Napoleon 1928,Mr 9,21:1
Forbidden Roads 1928,Ap 17,26:4
Married-And How! 1928,Je 15,30:2
Squealer, The 1928,N 13,36:3
My Girl Friday! 1929,F 13,20:2
Strike Up the Band 1930,Ja 15,29:1
Russet Mantle 1936,Ag 18,15:2
Eternal Road, The 1937,Ja 8,14:2
Bentley, Savannah
Little Eyolf 1964,Mr 17,31:1
Bentley, Spencer
Annie Dear 1924,N 5,25:3
Mama Loves Papa 1926,F 23,26:2
Home Towners, The 1926,Ag 24,19:3
Lady Alone 1927,Ja 21,12:5
So Was Napoleon 1930,Ja 9,22:2
Little Orchard Annie 1930,Ap 22,33:1
Crucible 1933,S 5,22:4
Furnished Rooms 1934,My 30,14:6
Bentley, Wendell
Lower Depths, The 1956,O 3,29:2
Capacity for Wings 1957,Ja 10,25:2
Bentley, Wilmer
Sweetheart Time 1926,Ja 20,23:2
Benton, Audrey
Cure for Matrimony 1939,O 26,26:3
Benton, Blanche
Congratulations 1929,My 1,28:4
Benton, Charles
Henri Christophe 1945,Je 7,24:5
Benton, Eva
Great Way, The 1921,N 8,28:2
Lulu Belle 1926,F 10,20:1
Bottom of the Cup, The 1927,F 1,24:2
Aiglon, L' 1927,D 27,24:3
Benton, Howard
Mirage, The 1920,O 1,14:1
Extra 1923,Ja 24,22:3
Peter Pan 1924,N 7,16:2
Precious 1929,Ja 15,22:5
Security 1929,Mr 29,20:1
Benton, James
Miss Gulliver Travels 1931,N 26,36:4
Benton, Jean
Broadway Whirl, The 1921,Je 9,10:4
Benton, John
On the Level 1937,Mr 26,24:4

Pal Joey 1940,D 26,22:2
Benton, Marguerite
Let's Face It 1941,O 30,26:2
Benton, Nicholas (Producer)
Salad Days 1958,N 11,24:1
Benton, Perce
Fall and Rise of Susan Lenox, The 1920,Je 11,11:2
Texas Nightingale, The 1922,N 21,15:2
Dawn 1924,N 25,27:1
Gypsy Fires 1925,D 8,28:3
Boy Meets Girl 1937,Jl 6,23:1
Censored 1938,F 28,18:2
Eye on the Sparrow 1938,My 4,26:3
Benton, Robert (Miscellaneous)
Oh! Calcutta! 1969,Je 18,33:1
Benton, Robert (Playwright)
It's a Bird . . . It's a Plane . . . It's Superman
1966,Mr 30,34:1
Benton, Roderick
Her Man of Wax 1933,O 12,32:3
Bentulan, Rossal
Passenger to Bali, A 1940,Mr 15,26:2
Bentz, Cecil (Composer)
Infernal Machine, The 1954,Mr 22,22:2
Merchant of Venice, The 1955,Ja 8,9:7
Commedia Dell' Arte 1957,Jl 5,13:2
Bentzen, Robert
She Loves Me Not 1933,N 21,22:4
Petticoat Fever 1935,Mr 5,22:2
Benusan, Inez
Matriarch, The 1930,Mr 19,24:5
Benware, Rex K
Living Mask, The 1924,Ja 22,15:1
Benwell, Jack
Richard of Bordeaux 1934,F 15,16:2
Love for Love 1940,Je 4,19:5
Benyamini, Menachem
Dybbuk, The 1948,My 3,26:3
David's Crown 1948,My 10,26:2
Oedipus Rex 1948,My 24,23:2
Benz, Barbara (Costume Designer)
Much Ado About Nothing 1963,Jl 15,25:2
Benz, Hamilton
New Moon, The 1944,My 18,16:2
Benzel, Herman (Miscellaneous)
Cocktails of 1934 1934,My 5,22:1
Benzell, Mimi
It's About Time 1942,Mr 31,28:3
Nightingale, The 1947,Jl 17,16:4
Rosalie 1957,Je 26,28:2
Milk and Honey 1961,O 11,52:1
Benzies, Ralph
Last Night of Don Juan, The 1925,N 10,23:2
Fountain, The 1925,D 11,26:1
Benzoni, Peter
Italian Straw Hat, The 1957,O 1,37:2
Julius Caesar 1959,Ag 4,30:1
Beppo
Treat 'Em Rough 1926,O 5,26:2
Beranger, Clara (Playwright)
His Chinese Wife 1920,My 18,9:3
Beranger, Lynn
Passing Present, The 1931,D 8,36:2
American, Very Early 1934,Ja 31,21:2
Spring Freshet 1934,O 5,28:3
Berard, Christian (Costume Designer)
Madwoman of Chaillot, The 1949,Ja 9,II,1:1
Ecole des Femmes, L'; School for Wives
1951,Mr 19,22:1
Amphitryon 1952,N 21,21:2
Fourberies de Scapin, Les 1952,N 21,21:2
Berard, Christian (Scenic Designer)
Madwoman of Chaillot, The 1949,Ja 9,II,1:1
Ecole des Femmes, L'; School for Wives
1951,Mr 19,22:1
Amphitryon 1952,N 21,21:2
Fourberies de Scapin, Les 1952,N 21,21:2
Berard, Roxanne
Doctor in Spite of Himself, The 1957,F 28,18:4
Berchman, Leonard
This Is the Army 1942,Jl 5,28:2
Bercler, Gerald
Mikado, The 1944,F 12,11:3
Berco, Jean-Claude
Annonce Faite a Marie, L' 1965,Ap 6,33:2
Bercovici, Leonardo (Playwright)
Substitute for Murder 1935,O 23,18:6
Holmeses of Baker Street, The 1936,D 10,34:3
Gabrielle 1941,Mr 26,26:2
Bercowitz, Anna (Translator)
Dole Brothers 1932,Mr 26,17:7
Bercowitz, Larry
Che! 1969,Mr 24,56:1
Berdeen, Robert
Dream of Swallows, A 1964,Ap 15,46:1
Royal Hunt of the Sun, The 1965,O 27,36:2
Me and Juliet 1970,My 15,42:1
Berdeshevsky, Margo Ann
Yerma 1966,D 9,60:1
Basement, The 1968,O 16,40:1
Berenda, Lisa
Hipper's Holiday 1934,O 19,26:2

Berendt, Charles
Othello 1970,Je 22,43:1
Berendt, Rachel
Aventuriere, L' 1922,N 14,16:1
Duel, Le 1922,N 16,22:2
Megere Apprivoisee, La 1922,N 20,21:2
Misanthrope, Le 1922,N 22,18:2
Amours 1929,Ja 13,VIII,2:7
Judith 1931,N 29,VIII,3:1
Jeanne de Pantin 1933,D 17,IX,5:8
Chaud et Froid 1935,Ja 6,IX,2:1
Berens, Beatrice
Revenge With Music 1934,N 29,33:5
Berens, Susan
Ice Follies 1969,My 23,38:1
Ice Follies 1970,My 23,27:1
Berens, William
Slightly Scandalous 1944,Je 14,16:2
Berenson, Beatrice
Bitter Sweet 1934,My 8,28:4
Berenson, Meyer
Sancho Panza 1923,N 27,23:1
Recapture 1930,Ja 19,VIII,2:6
Recapture 1930,Ja 30,16:4
Achilles Had a Heel 1935,O 14,20:2
Iron Men 1936,O 20,30:6
Beresford, Douglas
Allez-Opp! 1927,Ag 3,29:3
Beresford, Edmond
Marigold 1930,O 9,23:1
Beresford, Evelyn
Miss Gulliver Travels 1931,N 26,36:4
Firebird 1932,N 22,25:2
Threepenny Opera, The 1933,Ap 14,22:4
Beresford, Florence
Live Life Again 1945,O 1,14:7
Cellar and the Well, The 1950,D 11,30:2
Beresford, Harry
Shavings 1920,F 17,18:1
Shavings 1920,F 22,III,6:1
Old Soak, The 1922,Ag 23,14:5
She Stoops to Conquer 1924,Je 10,24:3
Out-A-Luck 1924,O 5,VIII,1:3
Undercurrent, The 1925,F 4,18:2
Stolen Fruit 1925,O 8,31:4
Perfect Alibi, The 1928,N 28,24:2
Michael and Mary 1929,D 14,23:3
Beresford, Helen
Beyond Evil 1926,Je 8,23:2
Berest, Fredric
As You Like It 1936,Ap 24,18:4
Face, The 1941,N 29,15:3
Berg, Albert
Honor of the Family, The 1926,D 27,21:1
Killers 1928,Mr 14,28:3
Married-And How! 1928,Je 15,30:2
Hot Money 1931,N 9,22:2
Broadway Boy 1932,My 4,23:5
Dark Hours, The 1932,N 15,24:2
Fly by Night 1933,Je 3,16:2
Berg, Armuta
Gardener's Dog, The 1927,O 21,27:1
Berg, Dale
Love Your Crooked Neighbor 1969,D 30,40:1
Berg, Don
Streetcar Named Desire, A 1955,Mr 4,18:2
Berg, Earl
Cranmer of Canterbury 1959,D 4,36:1
Berg, Einar
All's Well That Ends Well 1966,Je 17,39:1
Berg, Gene
It Happens on Ice 1940,O 11,24:3
It Happens on Ice 1941,Ap 5,13:2
Berg, Gertrude
Me and Molly 1948,F 27,27:2
Me and Molly 1948,Mr 7,II,1:1
Majority of One, A 1959,F 17,28:2
Majority of One, A 1959,F 22,II,1:1
Dear Me, the Sky Is Falling 1963,Mr 4,9:1
Berg, Gertrude (Playwright)
Me and Molly 1948,F 27,27:2
Me and Molly 1948,Mr 7,II,1:1
Dear Me, the Sky Is Falling 1963,Mr 4,9:1
Berg, H A (Producer)
Errant Lady 1934,S 18,18:2
Berg, Harold K (Producer)
Piper Paid 1934,D 26,19:1
Smile at Me 1935,Ag 24,18:4
Berg, Jimmy (Composer)
From Vienna 1939,Je 21,26:2
Berg, Julia
Arsenic and Old Lace 1942,My 11,18:6
Berg, Nancy
Mister Roberts 1956,D 6,46:2
Too Much Johnson 1964,Ja 16,29:1
Berg, Oliver
Protective Custody 1956,D 29,8:7
Shoemaker and the Peddler, The 1960,O 15,27:4
Berg, Rima
Merchant of Venice, The 1955,Ja 8,9:7
Berg, Rivka (Costume Designer)
Birthday Party, The 1961,My 15,34:6

Bergdorf Goodman (Miscellaneous)
Hilda Crane 1950,N 2,38:2
Berge, Alphonse
Blackouts of 1949 1949,S 7,39:2
Bergelson, David (Playwright)
Prince Reuvaini 1967,N 19,83:1
Bergema, Pieter
Secret Concubine, The 1960,Mr 22,29:2
Dream Play 1960,N 23,22:1
Bergen, Edgar
Vaudeville (Palace) 1926,Je 29,21:3
Bergen, Jerry
Russell Patterson's Sketch-Book 1960,F 8,35:1
Bergen, Mabel D
Dark Hammock 1944,D 12,27:8
Bergen, Polly
John Murray Anderson's Almanac 1953,D 11,42:2
Champagne Complex 1955,Ap 13,33:1
First Impressions 1959,Mr 20,28:1
First Impressions 1959,Mr 29,II,1:1
Bergen, Thurlow
Pietro 1920,Ja 20,10:2
Virgin of Bethulia, The 1925,F 24,17:2
Taps 1925,Ap 15,16:2
Man or Devil 1925,My 22,22:4
Silent Witness, The 1931,Mr 24,31:5
If Booth Had Missed 1932,F 5,24:2
Bergenthal, Hugo
Alt Heidelberg 1926,My 31,10:5
Bergeon, Rosemarie (Miscellaneous)
Recruiting Officer, The 1958,F 8,12:2
Berger
Topaze 1931,F 17,29:1
Berger, Anna
Silver Tassie, The 1949,Jl 22,16:5
Silver Tassie, The 1949,S 4,II,1:1
Twilight Walk 1951,S 25,25:4
Berger, Anna Vita
Tevya and His Daughters 1957,S 17,38:2
Berger, Bill
Misalliance 1955,F 12,10:6
Look After Lulu 1959,Mr 4,35:1
Silent Night, Lonely Night 1959,D 4,36:1
Cherry Orchard, The 1960,Je 4,17:2
Who's Afraid of Virginia Woolf? 1962,N 1,34:1
Berger, Bob
Nobody's Child 1956,Ag 23,25:2
Dr Cook's Garden 1967,S 26,52:1
Another City, Another Land 1968,O 9,42:1
Berger, Burt
Viva Madison Avenue 1960,Ap 7,42:1
Berger, Elizabeth
Venus-Shot 1966,Je 24,30:2
Miracle in Brooklyn 1966,Je 24,30:2
Berger, George B Jr
Coriolanus 1927,Je 18,8:3
Berger, Gustave
Song of Dnieper 1946,O 26,10:5
Wandering Stars 1946,D 14,18:2
Shylock and His Daughter 1947,S 30,22:2
Voice of Israel, The 1948,O 26,40:2
Hershel, the Jester 1948,D 14,39:2
Yosele the Nightingale 1949,O 21,30:4
Shepherd King, The 1955,O 13,36:2
Brothers Ashkenazi, The 1955,N 12,24:4
Father and Son 1956,O 20,17:4
Berger, Harris
Achilles Had a Heel 1935,O 14,20:2
Sunup to Sundown 1938,F 2,14:3
Berger, Henning (Playwright)
Deluge, The 1922,Ja 28,14:2
Deluge, The 1927,Ja 11,36:2
Deluge, The 1935,Mr 26,23:7
Berger, Henry
Patriot, The 1928,Ja 20,15:1
Berger, Herbert L (Miscellaneous)
Arabian Nights 1954,Je 25,15:2
Arabian Nights 1955,Je 24,16:1
Berger, Herbert L (Producer)
Let's Make an Opera 1950,D 14,50:2
Berger, Ion
Deputy, The 1964,F 27,26:1
Berger, Julius
Mirele Efros 1967,O 20,55:1
Mother Courage 1967,N 17,55:1
Berger, Lauree
Now 1968,Je 6,53:1
Berger, Marie-Louise
Maitresse de Roi 1926,D 1,24:1
Dame aux Camelias, La 1926,D 7,24:2
Misanthrope, Le 1926,D 10,31:2
Berger, Mel
Becket 1960,O 6,50:1
Becket 1961,My 9,44:1
Berger, Milton
Cocktails of 1934 1934,My 5,22:1
Berger, Molly
Kith and Kin 1930,My 14,31:1
Berger, Richard H (Playwright)
Tom Sawyer 1958,Jl 15,21:8
Berger, Robert
Homecoming 1942,N 17,28:5
Hamlet 1945,D 14,25:2

Trouble in July 1949,D 2,36:2
Berger, Ted (Lyricist)
Shoemaker's Holiday, The 1967,Mr 3,25:1
Berger, Ted (Playwright)
Shoemaker's Holiday, The 1967,Mr 3,25:1
Berger, William (Producer)
Wonderful World of Burlesque, The
1965,Ap 29,38:1
Berger, Zachary
Story of Mary Surratt, The 1947,F 10,25:2
Bergere, Lee
Lady in the Dark 1943,Mr 1,14:2
Right Next to Broadway 1944,F 22,26:2
Lady in the Dark 1952,Mr 8,11:3
Happiness Is Just a Little Thing Called a Rolls
Royce 1968,My 13,54:5
Bergere, Valerie
Vaudeville (Palace) 1926,D 21,20:5
Congai 1928,N 28,24:3
Inspector Kennedy 1929,D 21,16:3
Penny Arcade 1930,Mr 11,24:5
Hobo 1931,F 12,24:4
Lady Beyond the Moon 1931,Ap 1,36:5
Honor Code, The 1931,My 19,25:3
Scrap Book 1932,Ag 2,20:3
Melody 1933,F 15,17:4
Locked Room, The 1933,D 26,18:5
Tomorrow's Harvest 1934,D 6,26:5
Moon Over Mulberry Street 1935,S 5,24:6
Bergere, Yvonne
Circle, The 1939,Jl 12,17:2
What a Life 1939,Ag 2,17:5
White Steed, The 1939,Ag 16,21:3
Blind Alley 1939,Ag 23,18:8
Good Fairy, The 1939,Ag 30,15:5
Bergeron, Hugh
Confederacy, The 1958,Jl 3,20:1
Bergersen, Baldwin (Composer)
Who's Who 1938,Mr 2,16:2
All in Fun 1940,D 28,11:2
Allah Be Praised! 1944,Ap 21,14:2
Carib Song 1945,S 28,17:2
Small Wonder 1948,S 16,33:5
Crystal Heart, The 1957,F 20,37:1
Crystal Heart, The 1960,F 16,31:2
Bergersen, Baldwin (Lyricist)
All in Fun 1940,D 28,11:2
Bergersen, Baldwin (Miscellaneous)
Ziegfeld Follies 1943,Ap 2,16:2
Crystal Heart, The 1960,F 16,31:2
Bergersen, Baldwin (Musical Director)
American Legend 1941,My 12,13:2
Crystal Heart, The 1960,F 16,31:2
Double Dublin 1963,D 27,16:2
Bergersen, Beau (Composer)
Of V We Sing 1942,F 16,20:3
Bergey, Carol
Song of Norway 1958,Je 23,19:2
Mikado, The 1968,My 2,59:1
Bergfeld, Elliot
Twelfth Disciple, The 1930,My 17,21:4
Bergh, Albert
Jig Saw 1934,My 1,26:3
All Editions 1936,D 23,17:2
Enemy of the People, An 1937,F 16,19:1
Penny Wise 1937,Ap 20,28:6
In Clover 1937,O 14,23:1
Escape This Night 1938,Ap 23,18:1
Brown Danube, The 1939,My 18,30:4
Flight Into China 1939,S 12,28:1
Cue for Passion 1940,D 20,33:4
Mr Sycamore 1942,N 14,13:2
Sons and Soldiers 1943,My 5,22:2
Try and Get It 1943,Ag 3,13:2
Secret Room, The 1945,N 8,16:2
Long Watch, The 1952,Mr 21,19:5
Bergh, Arthur (Composer)
Love's Call 1925,S 11,20:1
Rhapsody, The 1930,S 16,30:3
Bergh, Billie
Man in the Making, The 1921,S 21,16:2
Bergh, Caroline
Heart of a City 1942,F 13,24:6
Bergh and Moore
Hellzapoppin 1938,S 23,34:2
New Hellzapoppin, The 1939,D 12,36:4
Berghof, Herbert
King Lear 1940,D 16,27:2
Criminals, The 1941,D 22,24:3
Nathan the Wise 1942,Mr 12,25:4
Nathan the Wise 1942,Ap 4,18:4
Winter Soldiers 1942,N 30,19:2
Russian People, The 1942,D 30,17:2
Innocent Voyage, The 1943,N 16,27:2
Nathan the Wise 1944,F 22,26:3
Man Who Had All the Luck, The 1944,N 24,18:5
Little Women 1944,D 13,29:2
Beggars Are Comming to Town 1945,O 29,16:2
Mayor of Zalamea, The 1946,Ja 28,15:5
Temper the Wind 1946,D 28,10:2
Profile 1947,Ag 12,26:1
Ghosts 1948,F 17,31:2
Hedda Gabler 1948,F 25,27:2

Berghof, Herbert—Cont
Iphigenie in Tauris 1949,Ap 9,8:1
Miss Liberty 1949,Jl 16,6:5
Lady From the Sea, The 1950,Ag 8,23:2
Tovarich 1952,My 15,39:2
Deep Blue Sea, The 1952,N 6,38:3
Andersonville Trial, The 1959,D 30,15:1
Andersonville Trial, The 1960,Ja 10,II,1:1
In the Matter of J Robert Oppenheimer
1969,Mr 7,28:1
In the Matter of J Robert Oppenheimer
1969,Mr 16,II,1:3·
Berghof, Herbert (Director)
From Vienna 1939,Je 21,26:2
Reunion in New York 1940,F 22,28:4
Rip Van Winkle 1947,Jl 16,28:2
Waiting for Godot 1956,Ap 20,21:2
Waiting for Godot 1956,Ap 29,II,1:2
Protective Custody 1956,D 29,8:7
Waiting for Godot 1957,Ja 22,25:1
Infernal Machine, The 1958,F 4,33:1
Twelfth Night 1959,Jl 11,10:2
Port-Royal 1960,Ap 26,41:1
Do You Know the Milky Way? 1961,O 17,45:1
This Side of Paradise 1962,F 22,19:6
Berghof, Herbert (Playwright)
Rip Van Winkle 1947,Jl 16,28:2
Bergine, Vera
Danse de Minuit, La 1924,Mr 23,VIII,1:3
Bergling, Ella
Bird Cage, The 1925,Je 3,26:2
Bergman, Alan (Lyricist)
Something More! 1964,N 11,36:1
Bergman, Caryl
Show Girl 1929,Jl 3,19:3
Sweet Adeline 1929,S 4,33:1
Through the Years 1932,Ja 29,13:3
Bergman, Harry
Nights of Wrath; Nuits de la Colere, Les
1947,D 1,26:4
Billy the Kid 1951,Ag 21,23:2
See the Jaguar 1952,D 4,46:2
Lovers 1956,My 11,23:1
Month in the Country, A 1959,Mr 2,32:2
Clandestine on the Morning Line 1959,D 5,18:2
Caucasian Chalk Circle, The 1961,N 1,35:1
Once in a Lifetime 1962,O 30,30:1
Devils, The 1963,N 5,25:1
Bergman, Henry
Vaudeville (Palace) 1930,Mr 10,24:4
I Loved You Wednesday 1932,O 12,27:1
Friars Club Frolic 1933,My 15,16:4
Bergman, Herbert T
Belt, The 1927,O 20,33:1
Centuries, The 1927,N 30,23:1
International, The 1928,Ja 26,24:4
Hoboken Blues 1928,F 18,10:1
Singing Jailbirds 1928,D 5,34:4
Airways, Inc 1929,F 21,30:5
Bergman, Hjalmar (Playwright)
Markurells in Wadkoeping 1930,N 2,VIII,3:2
Swedenhielms 1931,My 1,VIII,3:1
His Excellency's Last Will and Testament
1931,O 11,VIII,4:5
Joe et Cie; Patrasket 1932,Je 12,X,1:2
Noble Prize, The 1933,Jl 4,16:4
Noble Prize, The 1935,Jl 9,24:3
Bergman, Ingmar (Director)
Seagull, The 1961,Ja 8,84:5
Hedda Gabler 1968,Je 5,39:1
Dream Play 1970,Ap 17,45:1
Hedda Gabler 1970,Jl 18,12:1
Bergman, Ingmar (Playwright)
Frenzy 1948,Ap 22,35:2
Bergman, Ingmar (Producer)
Who's Afraid of Virginia Woolf? 1963,O 6,68:4
Bergman, Ingrid
Liliom 1940,Mr 26,17:2
Liliom 1940,Mr 31,IX,1:1
Anna Christie 1941,Ag 10,IX,1:8
Joan of Lorraine 1946,N 19,40:2
Joan of Lorraine 1946,N 24,II,1:1
Joan At The Stake 1954,Je 25,15:3
Tea and Sympathy 1956,D 4,50:1
Hedda Gabler 1962,D 13,8:5
More Stately Mansions 1967,S 14,54:1
More Stately Mansions 1967,N 1,40:1
More Stately Mansions 1967,N 12,II,1:1
Bergman, Joy (Miscellaneous)
No Exit 1956,Ag 15,23:1
Bible Salesman, The 1960,F 22,12:2
Bergman, Lee (Producer)
Meet Peter Grant 1961,My 11,41:4
Bergman, Leonard (Producer)
Peter Flies High 1931,N 10,28:3
Bergman, Marilyn (Lyricist)
Something More! 1964,N 11,36:1
Bergman, Rilla (Miscellaneous)
Let Them Down, Gently; Our Man in Madras
1968,Ja 31,28:2
Let Them Down, Gently; On Vacation
1968,Ja 31,28:2
Songs From Milk Wood 1970,Ja 13,41:1

Bergman, Sallie
Deburau 1920,D 24,14:3
Bergman, Teddy
Double Dummy 1936,N 12,30:1
House in the Country, A 1937,Ja 12,18:3
Bergmann, Alan
Montserrat 1954,My 26,34:2
Venice Preserv'd 1955,D 13,54:4
Purple Dust 1956,D 28,15:1
Here Come the Clowns 1960,S 20,48:1
Gideon 1961,N 10,38:1
Night Life 1962,O 24,44:1
Danton's Death 1965,O 22,46:1
Jumping Fool, The 1970,F 10,53:1
Bergner, Elisabeth
Saint Joan 1924,N 9,VII,2:3
Constant Nymph, The 1927,Ap 24,VII,2:1
Merchant of Venice, The 1928,Ap 1,IX,2:4
Romeo and Juliette 1928,D 2,X,4:4
Amphitryon 38 1931,Mr 15,IX,2:4
Gabriel Schillings Flucht 1932,D 4,IX,1:6
Escape Me Not 1933,D 9,18:6
Escape Me Never! 1934,Ja 7,X,3:5
Escape Me Never! 1935,Ja 22,22:2
Escape Me Never! 1935,F 10,VIII,1:1
Boy David, The 1936,N 22,VI,7:1
Boy David, The 1936,D 13,XI,5:3
Boy David, The 1936,D 15,30:6
Two Mrs Carrolls, The 1943,Ag 4,14:1
Two Mrs Carrolls, The 1943,Ag 8,II,1:1
Duchess of Malfi, The 1946,O 16,35:2
Cup of Trembling, The 1948,Ap 21,33:5
Iphigenie in Tauris 1949,Ap 9,8:1
Gay Invalid, The 1951,F 11,II,3:1
Dear Liar 1959,O 6,44:6
Bergner, Elisabeth (Director)
Overtons, The 1945,F 7,16:6
Bergner, Ludwig (Director)
Heilige aus U.S.A, Die; Saint From USA, The
1931,D 13,VIII,3:5
Bergner, Yossel (Miscellaneous)
Each Had Six Wings 1964,Mr 12,39:1
Bergold, Annette
Logia a la Natividad de Nuestro Senor Jesucristo,
El 1937,D 14,33:4
Bergovey, Helen
Bit o' Love, A 1925,My 13,24:2
Bergquist, Eleanor
Walking Happy 1966,N 28,47:1
Bergreen, Jacob
Town Lunatics 1933,F 6,11:4
Kibbetzers, Inc 1935,My 13,18:5
It Can't Happen Here 1936,O 28,30:1
Bergstrom, Lorraine
All in Love 1961,N 11,15:2
Beri, Ben
Sons o' Fun 1941,D 2,28:2
Beri, Beth
Jack and Jill 1923,Mr 23,17:2
Kid Boots 1924,Ja 1,21:3
No Foolin' 1926,Je 25,25:1
LeMaire's Affairs 1927,Mr 29,22:4
Beringer, Esme
Ugly Duchess, The 1930,Je 1,VIII,2:8
Beringer, Vera (Playwright)
Ugly Duchess, The 1930,Je 1,VIII,2:8
Beringola, Juan
Pluma en el Viento; Feather in the Wind
1932,Ap 2,13:4
Tambor y Cascabel; Drum and Bell
1932,Ap 21,25:4
Cuando Los Hijos De Eva No Son Los Hijos De
Adan; When Eve's Children Are Not Adam's
1932,Ap 23,11:2
De Muy Buena Familia; Of Very Good Family
1932,Ap 29,13:3
Berini, Mario
Gypsy Baron, The 1942,Ag 7,12:4
Flag Is Born, A 1946,S 7,10:6
Berinoff and Eulalie
International Revue 1930,F 26,22:2
Berjer, Barbara
Tempest, The 1959,D 28,19:2
Best Man, The 1960,Ap 1,39:1
Dylan 1964,Ja 20,18:1
Berk, Fred (Choreographer)
Merry-Go-Rounders, The 1956,N 22,50:1
Berk, Max
Hilda Cassidy 1933,My 5,18:3
Berk, Roy D
John Brown's Body 1953,F 16,17:2
Berka, Herma
Diable 1926,O 31,VIII,2:4
Berke, Maxine
Mistress of the House, The 1950,Ja 31,19:1
Berke, Norma
Commedia Dell' Arte 1957,Jl 5,13:2
Master Builder, The 1957,D 18,42:7
Berke, Norma (Scenic Designer)
Master Builder, The 1957,D 18,42:7
Berke, Sandra (Miscellaneous)
Nuns, The 1970,Je 2,35:1

Berkeley, Ballard
Under the Counter 1947,O 4,10:2
Berkeley, Busby
Present Arms 1928,Ap 27,16:2
Berkeley, Busby (Choreographer)
Wild Rose, The 1926,O 21,23:1
Connecticut Yankee, A 1927,N 4,24:2
White Eagle, The 1927,D 27,24:4
Present Arms 1928,Ap 27,16:2
Present Arms 1928,Jl 22,VII,6:1
Earl Carroll's Vanities 1928,Ag 7,25:2
Good Boy 1928,S 6,23:2
Rainbow 1928,N 22,25:1
Pleasure Bound 1929,F 19,22:4
Broadway Nights 1929,Jl 16,23:2
International Revue 1930,F 26,22:2
Sweet and Low 1930,N 18,28:5
Berkeley, Busby (Director)
Night in Venice, A 1929,My 22,30:2
Street Singer, The 1929,S 18,35:2
Nine Fifteen Revue, The 1930,F 12,26:2
Berkeley, Busby (Musical Director)
Hello, Daddy! 1928,D 27,26:5
Berkeley, Busby (Producer)
Street Singer, The 1929,S 18,35:2
Berkeley, George
Lovers 1956,My 11,23:1
Berkeley, Lennox (Composer)
Tiger at the Gates 1955,O 4,40:1
Berkeley, Martin
Starlight 1925,Mr 4,17:2
Lady's Virtue, A 1925,N 24,28:2
Lucky 1927,Mr 23,28:3
Grey Fox, The 1928,O 23,32:3
Meteor 1929,D 24,15:1
Berkeley, Martin (Playwright)
Seen But Not Heard 1936,Jl 22,23:4
Seen But Not Heard 1936,S 18,19:2
Roosty 1938,F 15,21:2
Berkeley, Mary
Late Arrival 1953,O 20,35:5
Berkeley, Regina (Producer)
Machines 1930,N 7,32:1
Berkeley, Reginald (Playwright)
French Leave 1920,N 9,13:1
Lady With a Lamp, The 1929,Ja 27,IX,2:1
Machines 1930,N 23,IX,2:4
O H M S 1931,Mr 29,VIII,2:1
Lady With a Lamp, The 1931,N 20,27:2
Tiger, The 1936,S 15,36:5
Tiger, The 1936,O 4,IX,3:7
Berkeley, Rosemary (Producer)
Pink String and Sealing Wax 1957,S 6,13:1
Berkeley-Boone, Forrest
No More Frontier 1931,O 22,27:1
Berkes, Johnnie
Vaudeville (Palace) 1927,N 15,27:2
Berkett, Viva
Death Takes a Holiday 1929,D 27,26:4
Berkey, Ralph (Playwright)
Time Limit! 1956,Ja 25,27:2
Time Limit! 1956,F 5,II,1:1
Berkman, Alexander (Translator)
Prisoner, The 1927,D 30,22:2
Berkman, John (Choreographer)
Jimmy 1969,O 24,38:1
Berkman, John (Miscellaneous)
Come Summer 1969,Mr 19,43:1
Berkman, John (Musical Director)
Minnie's Boys 1970,Mr 27,27:1
Berkman, Lee
Naughty-Naught '00 1937,Ja 25,23:2
Liliom 1940,Mr 26,17:2
Berko, Alex
Wedding, The 1948,F 6,29:2
Tragedian in Spite of Himself, A 1948,F 6,29:2
On the Harmfulness of Tobacco 1948,F 6,29:2
Bear, The 1948,F 6,29:2
Boy With a Cart, The 1954,Ap 5,19:2
Berko, Otto
Cocktails of 1934 1934,My 5,22:1
Berkoff, Freda
Vaudeville (Palace) 1928,Ag 21,27:5
Berkoff, Louis
Vaudeville (Palace) 1928,Ag 21,27:5
Berkowitz, Frieda
Yellow Jacket, The 1923,Ap 20,20:3
Berkowitz, I D (Playwright)
Gold Diggers, The 1927,D 3,19:2
Berkowitz, Judith (Costume Designer)
Home Movies 1964,My 12,32:1
Berkowitz, Sol (Composer)
Miss Emily Adam 1960,Mr 30,43:1
Nowhere to Go But Up 1962,N 12,36:2
Berkowitz, Sol (Miscellaneous)
Unsinkable Molly Brown, The 1960,N 4,28:1
Morning Sun 1963,O 7,36:2
Ice Capades 1966,Je 2,50:2
Berkowitz, Tamara (Playwright)
If I Were You 1931,S 24,21:1
Berkson, Michael
Hang Down Your Head and Die 1964,O 19,38:1
Billy Liar 1965,Mr 18,26:1

Berkson, Michael—Cont
Walking Happy 1966,N 28,47:1
Show Me Where the Good Times Are
1970,Mr 6,32:1
Berkson, Muriel
Ah, Wilderness! 1953,F 7,10:6
In the Summer House 1953,D 30,17:1
Master Builder, The 1955,Mr 2,23:2
Berl, Kathe (Costume Designer)
Port-Royal 1960,Ap 26,41:1
Berlad, Sol
Kith and Kin 1930,My 14,31:1
Berland, Howard
Career Angel 1943,N 19,24:2
Earth Journey 1944,Ap 28,24:2
Berland, Mae
God of Vengeance, The 1922,D 20,22:5
Berland, Rae
Mongrel, The 1924,D 16,28:2
Berle, Milton
Vaudeville (Palace) 1932,My 23,18:7
Vanities 1932,S 18,IX,2:1
Vanities 1932,S 28,22:4
Saluta 1934,Ag 29,13:4
Lost Paradise 1934,D 14,28:3
See My Lawyer 1939,S 28,29:1
Ziegfeld Follies 1943,Ap 2,16:2
Ziegfeld Follies 1943,Ap 11,II,1:1
Goodbye People, The 1968,D 4,52:1
Goodbye People, The 1968,D 15,II,3:1
Berle, Milton (Lyricist)
Saluta 1934,Ag 29,13:4
Berle, Milton (Producer)
I'll Take the High Road 1943,N 10,28:3
Seventeen 1951,Je 22,16:6
Berlein, Annie Mack
Wasp, The 1923,Mr 28,14:3
Canary Dutch 1925,S 9,22:1
Square Crooks 1926,Mr 2,23:2
Berley, Andre
Eunuque, L' 1927,Ap 3,VIII,4:7
Berley, Denise
Bal des Voleurs, Le 1938,N 29,26:4
Precieuses Ridicules, Les 1938,D 13,30:3
Fourberies de Scapin, Les 1938,D 13,30:3
Faiseur, Le; Promoter, The 1938,D 27,12:3
Paquebot Tenacity, Le 1939,Ja 10,16:4
Occasion, L' 1939,Ja 10,16:4
Chacun Sa Verite 1939,Ja 24,17:1
Enterrement, L' 1939,F 7,17:2
37 Sous de M Montaudoin, Les 1939,F 7,17:2
Siegfried 1939,F 21,15:2
Berliant, Elsie
Is Zat So? 1925,Ap 25,18:2
Berlin, Alexandra
Ronde, La 1960,My 10,44:2
Knack, The 1964,My 28,42:2
Knack, The 1964,Je 7,II,1:1
All in Good Time 1965,F 19,25:1
Love's Labour's Lost 1965,Je 16,46:1
Eh? 1966,O 17,47:1
Birthday Party, The 1967,O 4,40:2
Happiness Is Just a Little Thing Called a Rolls
Royce 1968,My 13,54:5
Berlin, Irving
Friars Club Frolic 1921,Je 13,16:2
Irving Berlin's Music Box Revue 1921,S 23,18:2
Lambs Gambol 1925,Ap 27,15:1
Berlin, Irving (Composer)
Ziegfeld Follies 1920,Je 23,14:1
Irving Berlin's Music Box Revue 1921,S 23,18:2
Irving Berlin's New Music Box Revue
1922,O 24,18:1
Music Box Revue 1923,My 20,VII,1:3
Music Box Revue 1924,D 2,23:3
Cocoanuts, The 1925,D 9,30:1
Cocoanuts, The 1925,D 13,IX,3:1
Cocoanuts, The 1926,Ap 18,VIII,1:1
Cocoanuts, The 1926,Je 11,25:2
Follies 1927,Ag 7,VII,1:8
Ziegfeld Follies 1927,Ag 17,27:3
Follies 1927,Ag 28,VII,1:1
Face the Music 1932,F 4,25:4
Face the Music 1932,F 18,24:5
As Thousands Cheer 1933,S 10,II,5:3
As Thousands Cheer 1933,O 15,IX,1:1
Louisiana Purchase 1940,My 29,19:2
This Is the Army 1942,Jl 5,28:2
This Is the Army 1942,Jl 12,VII,6:1
This Is the Army 1942,Ag 16,VIII,1:1
This Is the Army 1943,N 11,30:3
Annie Get Your Gun 1946,Mr 29,18:2
Annie Get Your Gun 1946,My 17,14:2
Annie Get Your Gun 1946,My 26,II,1:1
Annie Get Your Gun 1946,S 29,II,1:1
Miss Liberty 1949,Je 14,26:6
Miss Liberty 1949,Jl 16,6:5
Miss Liberty 1949,Jl 24,II,1:1
Call Me Madam 1950,O 13,25:1
Call Me Madam 1950,O 22,II,1:1
Call Me Madam 1952,Mr 16,84:3
Annie Get Your Gun 1957,F 28,18:6
Annie Get Your Gun 1957,Ag 31,18:2
Annie Get Your Gun 1958,F 20,29:2

Berlin, Irving (Composer)—Cont
Mr President 1962,Ag 29,18:4
Mr President 1962,S 26,36:1
Mr President 1962,O 14,II,1:7
Mr President 1962,O 22,34:2
Annie Get Your Gun 1966,Je 1,42:2
Berlin, Irving (Lyricist)
Ziegfeld Follies 1920,Je 23,14:1
Irving Berlin's Music Box Revue 1921,S 23,18:2
Irving Berlin's New Music Box Revue
   1922,O 24,18:1
Music Box Revue 1924,D 2,23:3
Cocoanuts, The 1925,D 9,30:1
Ziegfeld Follies 1927,Ag 17,27:3
As Thousands Cheer 1933,O 15,IX,1:1
Louisiana Purchase 1940,My 29,19:2
This Is the Army 1942,Jl 5,28:2
This Is the Army 1942,Jl 12,VII,6:1
This Is the Army 1942,Ag 16,VIII,1:1
Annie Get Your Gun 1946,My 17,14:2
Annie Get Your Gun 1946,My 26,II,1:1
Miss Liberty 1949,Jl 16,6:5
Miss Liberty 1949,Jl 24,II,1:1
Annie Get Your Gun 1957,Mr 9,15:5
Annie Get Your Gun 1958,F 20,29:2
Mr President 1962,O 14,II,1:7
Mr President 1962,O 22,34:2
Annie Get Your Gun 1966,Je 1,42:2
Berlin, Irving (Playwright)
Ziegfeld Follies 1920,Je 23,14:1
Broadway Brevities, 1920 1920,S 30,12:2
Face the Music 1933,F 1,13:4
As Thousands Cheer 1933,O 2,22:1
This Is the Army 1942,Ag 16,VIII,1:1
Berlin, Irving (Producer)
Miss Liberty 1949,Jl 16,6:5
Berlin, Linda
Cyrano de Bergerac 1953,N 13,24:3
Time of Your Life, The 1955,Ja 20,34:1
Wisteria Trees, The 1955,F 3,20:2
Berlin, Oscar
Hat, a Coat, a Glove, A 1934,F 1,15:2
Berlin, Zeke (Director)
Safari! 1955,My 12,32:6
Born Yesterday 1958,Mr 22,12:6
Rendezvous at Senlis 1961,F 28,39:2
Berliner, Martin
Big Two, The 1947,Ja 9,21:2
Tenth Man, The 1962,O 3,46:1
Berliner, Vera
Woman of Bronze, The 1920,S 8,9:2
Humoresque 1923,F 28,13:2
Berlinger, Warren
Bernardine 1952,O 17,33:4
Anniversary Waltz 1954,Ap 8,34:1
Roomful of Roses, A 1955,O 18,48:1
Blue Denim 1958,F 28,17:1
Blue Denim 1958,Ap 20,II,1:1
Come Blow Your Horn 1961,F 23,31:3
Berlo Sisters
Good Times 1920,Ag 10,10:1
Better Times 1922,S 4,14:2
Berlow, George
Sun Showers 1923,F 6,14:2
Berlow, Reginald
Shore Leave 1922,Ag 9,20:2
Bermain, George
When the Bough Breaks 1950,Mr 9,25:5
Bermal, Albert (Translator)
Sganarelle 1970,Ja 13,41:1
Berman, A L (Producer)
All for All 1943,S 30,25:2
Berman, David (Lighting Director)
My Heart's in the Highlands 1950,F 18,8:4
Berman, David (Scenic Designer)
Ninth Month Midnight 1949,F 17,28:2
Silver Tassie, The 1949,Jl 22,16:5
Berman, Florence
Recruiting Officer, The 1958,F 8,12:2
Berman, Howard A
Blossom Time 1921,S 30,10:1
Berman, June
X Has No Value 1970,F 17,35:1
Berman, Mark
As You Like It 1966,Je 4,19:1
Berman, Martin
Tiny Alice 1969,S 30,42:1
Berman, Otto
Little Theatre Tournament; Shall We Join the
   Ladies? 1929,My 9,34:3
Shall We Join the Ladies? 1929,My 12,28:3
Berman, S
Front Page, The 1937,N 12,27:2
Berman, Sam
Nautical but Nice 1931,Ap 19,31:6
Berman, Shelley
Slightly Delinquent 1954,O 26,32:5
Girls Against the Boys, The 1959,N 3,26:1
Girls Against the Boys, The 1959,N 8,II,1:1
Family Affair, A 1962,Ja 29,17:1
Berman, William
Mikado, The 1942,F 4,22:2
Pirates of Penzance, The 1942,F 18,22:2
Iolanthe 1942,F 24,26:4

Gondoliers, The 1942,Mr 4,22:3
Bermel, Albert (Playwright)
Infernal Machine, The 1958,F 4,33:1
Bermingham, John A
Martyr Without Tears 1942,N 23,19:2
Bermudez, John
Passenger to Bali, A 1940,Mr 15,26:2
Bern, David
I Myself 1934,My 10,24:6
Rain Before Seven 1935,Ag 13,20:3
Immoral Support 1935,S 3,24:3
Bern, Mina
Untitled-Revue 1966,O 3,62:5
Let's Sing Yiddish 1966,N 10,63:1
Sing Israel Sing 1967,My 12,50:1
Hut a Yid a Landele 1968,O 19,28:1
Light, Lively and Yiddish 1970,O 28,58:1
Bern, Mina (Director)
Let's Sing Yiddish 1966,N 10,63:1
Sing Israel Sing 1967,My 12,50:1
Light, Lively and Yiddish 1970,O 28,58:1
Bern, Mina (Playwright)
Light, Lively and Yiddish 1970,O 28,58:1
Bern, Mini
Father and Son 1956,O 20,17:4
Bernac, Jean (Playwright)
Sol Hyam's Brocanteur 1923,N 27,23:5
Bernading, C P (Father) (Playwright)
Veronica's Veil 1931,F 23,36:2
Bernard
Little Theatre Tournament; Rhythm of the City,
   The 1929,My 7,28:1
Bernard, Andre
Captain Brassbound's Conversion 1950,D 28,21:1
Bernard, Anthony (Composer)
Winter's Tale, The 1946,Ja 16,18:6
Bernard, Barney
Two Blocks Away 1921,Ag 31,8:3
Partners Again 1922,My 2,22:2
Untitled-Benefit 1922,My 8,14:5
Partners Again 1922,My 14,VII,1:1
Bernard, Ben
Squealer, The 1928,N 13,36:3
Bernard, Ben (Director)
Blackberries of 1932 1932,Ap 5,27:5
Bernard, Bern (Miscellaneous)
Native Son 1941,Mr 25,26:5
Bernard, Bern (Producer)
Brooklyn, U S A 1941,D 22,24:2
Bernard, Bob
Fiorello! 1959,N 24,45:3
Bernard, Dorothy
Personality 1921,Ag 29,14:3
Little Inn, The 1935,Ag 20,25:1
Ragged Edge, The 1935,N 26,28:3
Two Time Mary 1937,Ag 3,20:5
Prodigal Father, The 1937,Ag 17,23:1
Love in My Fashion 1937,D 4,21:4
Life With Father 1939,N 9,26:2
Life With Mother 1948,O 21,32:2
Bernard, Ed
Five on the Black Hand Side 1970,Ja 2,32:2
Bernard, Fields
Across the Board on Tomorrow Morning
   1942,Mr 21,13:5
Theatre of the Soul 1942,Mr 21,13:5
Bernard, Frank
Bombo 1921,O 7,20:2
Passing Show of 1923, The 1923,Je 15,24:6
Bernard, Fred
Vaudeville (Palace) 1923,O 30,16:1
Bernard, Henry (Playwright)
Miss Smith 1936,Jl 5,IX,1:8
Bernard, Ian (Director)
Chocolates 1967,Ap 11,51:1
Bernard, Ian (Playwright)
Chocolates 1967,Ap 11,51:1
Bernard, James
Hotel Paradiso 1957,Ap 12,22:2
Bernard, Jean-Jacques (Original Author)
Ame en Peine, L'; Unquiet Spirit, The
   1937,N 14,XI,3:1
Bernard, Jean-Jacques (Playwright)
Ame en Peine, L' 1928,F 12,VIII,2:1
Martine 1928,Ap 5,19:3
Roy de Malouise, Le 1928,Jl 1,VIII,1:8
Invitation au Voyage, L' 1928,O 5,17:1
Feu Qui Reprend Mal, Le 1929,N 10,X,4:1
Invitation au Voyage, L' 1930,Ja 26,VIII,1:8
Soeurs Guedonee, Les 1931,D 13,VIII,2:2
Jeanne de Pantin 1933,D 17,IX,5:8
Nationale 6 1935,N 24,IX,3:7
Martine 1936,N 26,38:2
Nationale 6 1938,Ja 11,26:6
Ame en Peine, L' 1950,My 31,25:2
Bernard, Jean-Pierre
Three Musketeers, The 1968,Je 26,43:1
Bernard, Jim
Simpleton of the Unexpected Isles, The
   1954,Ja 12,19:1
Bernard, Joe
Winter Soldiers 1942,N 30,19:2
Skipper Next to God 1948,Ja 5,14:5

Bernard, Joe—Cont
Mister Roberts 1948,F 19,27:2
Golden Boy 1952,Mr 13,24:3
Stone for Danny Fisher, A 1954,O 22,24:2
Guys and Dolls 1955,Ap 21,32:2
Lark, The 1955,N 18,20:1
Bernard, Joseph
Candide 1956,D 3,40:2
Look Homeward, Angel 1957,N 29,33:1
Rhinoceros 1961,Ja 10,27:1
Bernard, Joseph (Producer)
Marathon 1933,Ja 28,8:8
Bernard, Joseph E
Rat Race, The 1949,D 23,16:2
Bernard, Josephine
Young Visitors, The 1920,N 30,14:1
Bernard, Kenneth (Playwright)
Moke Eaters, The 1968,O 28,55:3
Bernard, Leon
Turcaret 1928,Mr 4,IX,4:5
Moloch 1929,Ja 27,IX,2:8
Bernard, Lester
Good Boy 1928,S 6,23:2
Booster, The 1929,O 25,26:2
Bernard, Lucien (Playwright)
Homme Qui N'est Plus de ce Nonde
   1924,Mr 23,VIII,1:3
Bernard, Lydia
Jane's Legacy 1935,Ag 13,20:3
Bernard, Lygia
Champion, The 1921,Ja 4,11:1
Bernard, Manuel
Prelude to Exile 1936,D 1,31:1
Empress of Destiny 1938,Mr 10,16:2
Bernard, Maurice
Mongrel, The 1924,D 16,28:2
Bernard, Milbridge
Moon Is a Gong, The 1926,Mr 13,21:3
Bernard, Miss
Love and Politics 1929,O 21,30:7
Bernard, Nan
Jehovah Joe 1929,Ag 25,VIII,3:1
Bernard, Nicolette
Henry IV, Part II 1946,My 8,33:4
Oedipus; Critic, The 1946,My 21,19:2
Oedipus 1946,My 21,19:2
Bernard, Paul
Petit Peche 1926,O 24,VIII,2:1
Viens Avec Nous Petit! 1927,F 20,VII,2:1
Vingt ans, Madame 1928,Ap 8,VIII,4:1
Bernard, Raymond (Musical Director)
Gilbert Becaud on Broadway 1966,N 1,35:1
Gilbert Becaud Sings Love 1968,O 7,53:5
Bernard, Robert
I Must Love Someone 1939,F 8,18:7
She Gave Him All She Had 1939,D 2,20:7
Arsenic and Old Lace 1944,Jl 3,7:3
Song of Norway 1944,Ag 22,20:2
Man With the Golden Arm, The 1956,My 22,28:1
It's an Ill Wind 1957,Ap 24,28:1
Zorba 1968,N 18,58:1
Bernard, Rosalind
Piggy 1927,Ja 12,22:2
Bernard, Sam
As You Were 1920,Ja 28,22:3
Irving Berlin's Music Box Revue 1921,S 23,18:2
Vaudeville (Palace) 1926,Mr 23,24:3
Vaudeville (Hippodrome) 1926,Ap 13,28:2
Piggy 1927,Ja 12,22:2
Bernard, Sam 2d
Light Wines and Beer 1930,N 11,28:6
Bernard, Sam 2d (Composer)
Belmont Varieties 1932,S 29,17:2
Bernard, Sam 2d (Director)
Belmont Varieties 1932,S 29,17:2
Bernard, Sam 2d (Lyricist)
Belmont Varieties 1932,S 29,17:2
Bernard, Sam 2d (Playwright)
Belmont Varieties 1932,S 29,17:2
Bernard, Suzanne
New Faces of 1956 1956,Je 15,32:1
Bernard, Tristan (Playwright)
Triplepatte 1926,N 14,VIII,2:1
Sexe Fort, Le 1927,F 13,VII,4:1
Odeon-Revue 1927,My 22,VIII,2:7
Danseur Inconnu, Le 1928,S 23,IX,2:1
Jules, Juliette et Julien, ou L'Ecole du Sentiment
   1929,Je 9,VIII,2:4
Ecole des Charlatans, L' 1930,Ap 27,IX,2:1
Langrevin Pere et Fils 1930,Je 8,IX,2:4
Ami d'Argentine, Un 1930,N 30,IX,3:3
Bloch de Chicago 1933,O 1,IX,1:3
Bloch de Chicago 1933,O 15,IX,1:8
Sexe Fort, Le; Strong Sex, The 1937,Ja 14,17:4
Bernard, Verna
Pirates of Penzance, The 1938,Je 3,16:2
Bernard-Luc, Jean (Playwright)
Faithfully Yours 1951,O 19,22:5
Bernardi, Cynthia (Scenic Designer)
Blitzstein! 1966,D 1,58:2
Bernardi, Helen
Sappho 1935,Mr 22,26:4
Bernardi, Herschel
Jacques Bergson 1936,O 31,24:6

ernardi, Herschel—Cont
Bajour 1964,N 24,42:1
Fiddler on the Roof 1967,S 28,59:2
Zorba 1968,N 18,58:1
Zorba 1968,N 24,II,1:1

ernardi, Herschel (Producer)
Nathan Weinstein, Mystic, Connecticut
 1966,F 26,15:2

ernardi, Roberto
Viva O'Brien 1941,O 10,27:2

ernardini, Lina
Nemica, La 1926,S 7,24:6

ernardt, Melvin (Director)
Father Uxbridge Wants to Marry 1967,O 30,57:1

ernardy, Michel
Fourberies de Scapin, Les 1961,F 22,30:1
Impromptu de Versailles, L' 1961,F 22,30:1
Tartuffe 1961,Mr 1,28:1
Britannicus 1961,Mr 3,17:1
Dindon, Le 1961,Mr 8,38:1

ernath, Sander (Costume Designer)
Sonya's Search for the Christmas Star
 1929,D 14,24:6

ernau, Alfred (Director)
Victoria Regina 1938,Ap 17,X,2:1

ernau, Christopher
Boys in the Band, The 1970,Ap 18,34:1

ernauer, Rudolph (Lyricist)
Chocolate Soldier, The 1921,D 13,24:2
Chocolate Soldier, The 1930,Ja 28,28:1

ernauer, Rudolph (Miscellaneous)
Chocolate Soldier, The 1947,Mr 13,34:2

ernauer, Rudolph (Playwright)
Johannes Kreisler 1922,D 25,20:3
Garden of Eden, The 1927,S 28,28:1
Mikado, The 1927,O 30,IX,4:6
Konto X 1930,N 2,VIII,3:1
Chocolate Soldier, The 1931,S 22,33:3
Chocolate Soldier, The 1934,My 3,15:3
Chocolate Soldier, The 1942,Je 24,22:2

ernay, Lynn
Harry, Noon and Night 1965,My 6,44:1

ernays, Robert
Night of January 16 1936,S 30,29:3

ernbach, Cynthia
Dance of Death, The 1969,My 26,53:1

ernbach, Doyle Dane (Miscellaneous)
Orlando Furioso 1970,N 5,59:1

ernd, Bert
Everyman 1941,My 9,19:2

ernd, Milton J
Iphigenia in Aulis 1921,Ap 8,18:2
Wild Duck, The 1925,F 25,16:4
Dream Play 1926,Ja 21,18:2

erne, Ben (Producer)
Cafe de Danse 1928,D 30,VIII,1:6

erne, Eric
Inherit the Wind 1955,Ap 22,20:2
Mother Courage and Her Children 1964,My 12,32:2

erneis, Peter (Director)
Many Happy Returns 1945,Ja 6,15:5

erners, Lord (Composer)
Cochran's 1930 Revue 1930,Ap 13,X,1:6

ernette, Sheila
Time Gentlemen Please! 1961,N 9,40:4

erney, Paul (Producer)
Commuting Distance 1936,Je 30,15:1
Miss Temple Is Willing 1936,Jl 21,13:1
Suddenly a Stranger 1936,Ag 4,15:2
Bough Breaks, The 1937,N 20,21:4

erney, William (Miscellaneous)
Sally 1948,My 7,31:2

erney, William (Playwright)
Dark of the Moon 1945,Mr 15,27:2
Dark of the Moon 1945,Mr 25,II,1:1
Design For A Stained Glass Window
 1950,Ja 24,26:2
Protective Custody 1956,D 29,8:7
Dark of the Moon 1958,F 27,22:2
Dark of the Moon 1970,Ap 4,21:2

ernhard, Emil (Playwright)
Prisoner, The 1927,D 30,22:2

ernhard, Samuel
Rich Man, Poor Man 1950,F 13,15:4

ernhard, Thomas (Playwright)
Fest Fuer Boris, Ein 1970,O 13,52:2

ernhardt, Colin
Merchant of Venice, The 1970,Je 10,39:1

ernhardt, Melvin (Director)
Conerico Was Here to Stay 1965,Mr 4,37:1
Pigeons 1965,Mr 4,37:1
Muzeeka 1968,Ap 29,47:2
Honor and Offer 1968,D 1,II,3:1
Home Fires 1969,Ap 8,42:1
Cop-Out 1969,Ap 8,42:1
Effect of Gamma Rays on Man-in-the-Moon
 Marigolds, The 1970,Ap 8,32:1
Early Morning 1970,N 26,57:1

ernhardt, Sarah
Gloire, La 1921,O 23,22:2

ernheim, Edward
Front Page, The 1968,O 20,85:5

Bernice and Emily
George White's Scandals 1928,Jl 3,19:1

International Revue 1930,F 26,22:2
Vaudeville (Palace) 1931,S 28,17:5
Vaudeville (Palace) 1932,F 15,13:3

Bernie, Al
Calling All Stars 1934,N 22,26:1
Calling All Stars 1934,D 14,28:2

Bernie, Ben
Vaudeville (Palace) 1924,Ap 29,12:2
Gay Paree 1927,Mr 22,31:1
Here's Howe! 1928,My 2,19:3
Vaudeville (Palace) 1930,Mr 7,21:2
Vaudeville (Palace) 1932,Je 13,19:7

Bernie, Ben (Producer)
Cafe de Danse 1929,Ja 16,22:2

Bernie, Ben and His Orchestra
Vaudeville (Palace) 1923,Ap 3,26:4
Vaudeville (Palace) 1927,Ja 18,23:2
Vaudeville (Palace) 1927,Mr 1,31:2
Vaudeville (Palace) 1929,F 18,29:1
Vaudeville (Palace) 1929,Ap 8,32:7

Bernie, Dick
Heaven on Earth 1948,S 17,29:2
Along Fifth Avenue 1949,Ja 14,28:2
Whistler's Grandmother 1952,D 12,40:2
This Was Burlesque 1965,Mr 17,55:3

Bernie, Murray
Earl Carroll's Vanities 1930,Jl 2,28:3

Bernier, Buddy (Composer)
Hear! Hear! 1955,S 28,38:1

Bernier, Buddy (Playwright)
Hear! Hear! 1955,S 28,38:1

Bernier, Daisy
Sing Out the News 1938,S 26,12:5

Bernier, Estelle
Singin' the Blues 1931,S 17,21:3

Bernier, Paul
Au Rat Mort, Cabinet No 6 1923,O 16,18:1
Horrible Experience, L' 1923,O 23,16:1
Crucifies, Les 1923,O 30,17:2
Catherine Goulden 1923,N 6,22:1
Trois Masques, Les 1923,N 6,22:1
Laboratoire des Hallucinations, Le 1923,N 20,23:3
Griffe, La 1923,N 27,23:5
Sol Hyam's Brocanteur 1923,N 27,23:5

Bernier, Peggy
Me for You 1929,S 22,IX,2:6
You Said It 1931,Ja 20,21:3

Bernini, Mario
Gypsy Baron, The 1942,Je 20,8:5

Bernius, June
Comedian, The 1956,O 18,36:4

Bernnard, Ilse
Late Arrival 1953,O 20,35:5

Berno, Marie
Within Four Walls 1923,Ap 18,24:1

Berns, Julie (Director)
For Heaven's Sake Mother 1948,N 17,33:4

Berns, Julie (Playwright)
For Heaven's Sake Mother 1948,N 17,33:4
Uncle Willie 1956,D 21,17:1

Bernsohn, Sophie
Dybbuk, The 1925,D 16,22:2
Burmese Pwe, A 1926,Mr 17,28:1
Commedia Dell' Arte 1927,Ap 6,24:3

Bernstein, Alice (Costume Designer)
Alison's House 1930,D 2,31:2

Bernstein, Alice (Scenic Designer)
Alison's House 1930,D 2,31:2

Bernstein, Aline
Grand Street Follies, The 1927,My 20,22:3
To Quito and Back 1937,S 26,XI,3:6

Bernstein, Aline (Costume Designer)
Little Clay Cart, The 1924,D 6,13:3
Grand Street Follies, The 1925,Je 19,24:1
Hamlet 1925,N 10,23:1
Dybbuk, The 1925,D 16,22:2
Apothecary, The 1926,Mr 17,28:1
Romantic Young Lady, The 1926,My 5,24:3
Grand Street Follies, The 1926,Je 16,23:2
Dybbuk, The 1926,D 17,27:2
Tone Pictures and the White Peacock
 1927,Ap 6,24:3
Grand Street Follies, The 1927,My 20,22:3
If 1927,O 30,IX,1:1
Hedda Gabler 1928,Mr 27,30:2
Grand Street Follies, The 1928,My 29,16:2
Grand Street Follies, The 1928,Je 3,VIII,1:1
Katerina 1929,F 26,30:3
Grand Street Follies, The 1929,My 2,20:4
Grand Street Follies, The 1929,My 12,IX,1:2
Sea Gull, The 1929,S 17,34:1
Mademoiselle Bourrat 1929,O 8,34:3
Game of Love and Death, The 1929,N 26,28:4
Living Corpse, The 1929,D 7,19:1
Open Door, The 1930,Ja 28,28:1
Romeo and Juliet 1930,Ap 22,33:1
Siegfried 1930,O 21,34:1
Lady of the Camellias, The 1931,Ja 27,21:2
Camille 1932,O 28,23:2
Dear Jane 1932,N 15,24:3
Cherry Orchard, The 1933,Mr 7,20:3
Judgment Day 1934,S 13,26:4
Aiglon, L' 1934,N 5,22:2

Bernstein, Aline (Costume Designer)—Cont
Night in the House 1935,N 8,19:5
To Quito and Back 1937,O 7,30:4
American Landscape 1938,D 5,19:2
Little Foxes, The 1939,F 16,16:2
Willow and I, The 1942,D 11,32:2
Harriet 1943,Mr 4,24:2
Innocent Voyage, The 1943,N 16,27:2
Feathers in a Gale 1943,D 22,26:2
Searching Wind, The 1944,Ap 13,25:2
Harriet 1944,S 28,26:1
Eagle Has Two Heads, The 1947,Mr 20,39:2
Regina 1949,N 1,32:2
Regina 1949,N 13,II,1:1
Happy Time, The 1950,Ja 25,24:1
Burning Bright 1950,O 19,40:2
Let's Make an Opera 1950,D 14,50:2
Enemy of the People, An 1950,D 29,14:1
Mary Rose 1951,Mr 5,25:2
World of Sholom Aleichem, The 1953,S 12,13:2
World of Sholom Aleichem, The 1953,S 20,II,1:1

Bernstein, Aline (Scenic Designer)
Little Clay Cart, The 1924,D 6,13:3
Dybbuk, The 1925,D 16,22:2
Apothecary, The 1926,Mr 17,28:1
Romantic Young Lady, The 1926,My 5,24:3
Grand Street Follies, The 1926,Je 16,23:2
Ned McCobb's Daughter 1926,N 30,26:2
Dybbuk, The 1926,D 17,27:2
Tone Pictures and the White Peacock
 1927,Ap 6,24:3
Grand Street Follies, The 1927,My 20,22:3
If 1927,O 26,26:2
If 1927,O 30,IX,1:1
Love Nest, The 1927,D 23,17:1
First Stone, The 1928,Ja 14,12:2
Maya 1928,F 22,19:1
Improvisations in June 1928,F 27,16:5
Hedda Gabler 1928,Mr 27,30:2
Grand Street Follies, The 1928,My 29,16:2
Grand Street Follies, The 1928,Je 3,VIII,1:1
Invitation au Voyage, L' 1928,O 5,17:1
Cherry Orchard, The 1928,O 16,28:5
Caprice 1929,Ja 1,61:1
Katerina 1929,F 26,30:3
Grand Street Follies, The 1929,My 2,20:4
Grand Street Follies, The 1929,My 12,IX,1:2
Sea Gull, The 1929,S 17,34:1
Mademoiselle Bourrat 1929,O 8,34:3
Game of Love and Death, The 1929,N 26,28:4
Living Corpse, The 1929,D 7,19:1
Open Door, The 1930,Ja 28,28:1
Grand Hotel 1930,N 14,30:4
Grand Hotel 1930,N 23,IX,1:1
Tomorrow and Tomorrow 1931,Ja 14,26:3
Lady of the Camellias, The 1931,Ja 27,21:2
Getting Married 1931,Mr 31,25:5
He 1931,S 22,33:1
Reunion in Vienna 1931,N 17,31:1
Animal Kingdom, The 1932,Ja 13,26:4
Jewel Robbery 1932,Ja 14,17:2
Lenin's Dowry 1932,My 13,17:3
Clear All Wires! 1932,S 15,19:1
Liliom 1932,O 27,23:2
Camille 1932,O 28,23:2
Late Christopher Bean, The 1932,N 1,24:3
Dear Jane 1932,N 15,24:3
Firebird 1932,N 22,25:2
Good Woman, Poor Thing, A 1933,Ja 10,27:3
We the People 1933,Ja 23,9:5
Cherry Orchard, The 1933,Mr 7,20:3
Thunder on the Left 1933,N 1,25:2
Mackerel Skies 1934,Ja 24,20:4
Hat, a Coat, a Glove, A 1934,F 1,15:2
Judgment Day 1934,S 13,26:4
Between Two Worlds 1934,O 26,24:2
Aiglon, L' 1934,N 5,22:2
Children's Hour, The 1934,N 21,23:2
Night in the House 1935,N 8,19:5
And Stars Remain 1936,O 13,32:2
Days to Come 1936,D 16,35:1
Storm Over Patsy 1937,Mr 2,16:4
Storm Over Patsy 1937,Mr 9,26:4
To Quito and Back 1937,O 7,30:4
American Landscape 1938,D 5,19:2
Male Animal, The 1940,Ja 10,17:2
Happy Time, The 1950,Ja 25,24:1
Enemy of the People, An 1950,D 29,14:1

Bernstein, Dorothy (Playwright)
Bridge, The 1930,My 6,33:1

Bernstein, Elmer (Composer)
John Brown 1950,My 4,32:7
Peter Pan 1954,O 21,30:2
How Now, Dow Jones 1967,D 8,53:1

Bernstein, Helen
Flies, The; Mouches, Les 1947,Ap 18,26:3

Bernstein, Henri (Playwright)
Claw, The 1921,O 2,VII,1:8
Claw, The 1921,O 18,20:1
Judith 1922,O 13,14:2
Judith 1924,Mr 2,VIII,2:7
Galerie des Glaces, La 1924,N 16,III,7:4

Bernstein, Henri (Playwright)—Cont
Virgin of Bethulia, The 1925,F 24,17:2
Felix 1926,O 10,VIII,2:1
Thief, The 1927,Ap 23,15:2
Thief, The 1927,My 1,VIII,1:1
Secret, Le 1928,Mr 25,IX,4:6
Melo 1929,Ap 7,X,1:3
Melo 1929,Ap 14,X,2:1
Assalto, L' 1929,My 20,23:2
Melo 1931,Ap 17,26:6
Melo 1931,O 20,29:3
Ladro, Il; Thief, The 1932,F 22,23:4
Bonheur 1933,My 14,IX,1:4
Messager, Le 1933,D 31,IX,2:2
Espoir 1935,Ja 6,IX,2:1
Espoir 1935,F 3,VIII,3:3
Coeur, Le 1936,Mr 8,IX,3:7
Promise 1936,Mr 22,XI,1:7
Coeur, Le 1936,O 4,IX,1:1
Voyage, Le 1937,F 28,XI,2:1
Cap des Tempetes 1937,N 14,XI,2:1
Elvire 1940,F 11,IX,2:5
Rose Burke 1942,Ja 25,IX,2:5
Secret 1946,O 10,33:2
Soif, La 1949,F 9,33:2
Evangeline 1952,O 3,17:1
Bernstein, Henri (Original Author)
Promise 1936,D 31,20:4
Bernstein, Henri (Producer)
Secret, Le 1928,Mr 25,IX,4:6
Double 1929,Ja 13,VIII,2:7
Espoir 1935,F 3,VIII,3:3
Born Yesterday 1948,Ap 9,26:3
Soif, La 1949,F 9,33:2
Bernstein, Herman (Playwright)
Mandarin, The 1920,N 10,18:2
Right to Kill, The 1926,F 16,22:2
Command to Love, The 1927,S 21,27:1
Anna 1928,My 17,25:2
First Law, The 1929,My 7,28:4
Ladies Don't Lie 1929,O 11,36:3
Noble Prize, The 1935,Jl 9,24:3
Bernstein, Herman (Producer)
Love Goes to Press 1947,Ja 2,22:2
Bernstein, Herman (Translator)
Anathema 1923,Ap 11,16:2
Chief Thing, The 1926,Mr 23,24:2
Waltz of the Dogs, The 1928,Ap 26,31:3
Phantom Lover, The 1928,S 5,25:1
Katerina 1929,F 26,30:3
Chief Thing, The 1963,Ap 30,27:2
Bernstein, Ira (Miscellaneous)
Major Barbara 1956,O 31,27:1
Georgy 1970,F 27,26:1
Bernstein, Ira (Producer)
Golden Rainbow 1968,F 5,27:1
Bernstein, Jay
Eternal Sabbath 1963,O 19,17:2
Bernstein, Joe
Big Fight, The 1928,S 19,33:1
Bernstein, Joseph M
Orestes 1926,Je 20,II,3:6
Coriolanus 1927,Je 18,8:3
Bernstein, Leonard
Cradle Will Rock, The 1947,N 25,38:3
Cradle Will Rock, The 1947,D 27,11:2
Bernstein, Leonard (Composer)
On the Town 1944,D 29,11:4
On the Town 1945,Ja 7,II,1:1
On the Town 1945,F 4,II,5:1
Peter Pan 1950,Ap 25,27:2
Peter Pan 1950,Ap 30,II,1:1
Wonderful Town 1953,F 26,22:3
Wonderful Town 1953,Mr 8,II,1:1
Wonderful Town 1953,Ap 5,II,1:5
Wonderful Town 1954,My 7,II,1:1
All in One 1955,Ap 24,II,1:1
Wonderful Town 1955,My 17,33:4
Lark, The 1955,N 18,20:1
Candide 1956,D 3,40:2
Candide 1956,D 9,II,5:1
West Side Story 1957,S 27,14:4
West Side Story 1957,O 6,II,1:1
West Side Story 1957,O 13,II,9:1
Wonderful Town 1958,Mr 6,32:4
Firstborn, The 1958,My 1,35:1
Party With Betty Comden and Adolph Green, A
  1958,D 24,2:7
On the Town 1959,Ja 16,36:1
On the Town 1959,Ja 25,II,1:1
On the Town 1959,F 14,15:1
Candide 1959,My 1,35:4
West Side Story 1960,Ap 28,31:1
West Side Story 1960,My 8,II,1:1
West Side Story 1961,Mr 31,22:3
Wonderful Town 1963,F 15,10:2
On the Town 1963,My 31,30:7
West Side Story 1964,Ap 9,24:2
West Side Story 1965,Je 25,37:2
Leonard Bernstein's Theater Songs 1965,Je 29,27:2
Wonderful Town 1967,My 18,50:1
West Side Story 1968,Je 25,32:1
West Side Story 1968,S 1,II,20:4

Bernstein, Leonard (Lyricist)
On the Town 1944,D 29,11:4
On the Town 1945,F 4,II,5:1
Peter Pan 1950,Ap 25,27:2
Leonard Bernstein's Theater Songs 1965,Je 29,27:2
Bernstein, Leonard (Miscellaneous)
Cradle Will Rock, The 1947,D 27,11:2
Candide 1956,D 3,40:2
West Side Story 1957,S 27,14:4
West Side Story 1960,Ap 28,31:1
Cradle Will Rock, The 1964,N 9,40:4
West Side Story 1968,Je 25,32:1
Bernstein, Leonard (Musical Director)
Cradle Will Rock, The 1947,N 25,38:3
Bernstein, Leonard (Playwright)
All in One; Trouble in Tahiti 1955,Ap 20,40:3
Bernstein, Mary
When Differences Disappear 1941,Je 3,17:4
Bernstein, Melville (Scenic Designer)
Cure for Matrimony 1939,O 26,26:3
Steel 1939,D 20,30:2
Bernstein, Pearl
Off the Record; Mayor Answers the Newspapers!
  Wow! 1935,Je 19,23:3
Bernstein, Richard (Lighting Director)
Now I Lay Me Down to Sleep 1950,Mr 3,21:2
Bernstein, Richard (Scenic Designer)
Virginia Reel 1947,Ap 15,28:2
Sojourner Truth 1948,Ap 22,35:2
Bernstein, Richard N (Playwright)
Young Abe Lincoln 1961,Ap 26,36:1
Bernstein, Robert A (Playwright)
Almost Crazy 1955,Je 21,37:1
Bernstein, Robert Allen (Director)
Way of the World, The 1950,Ap 9,73:5
Bernstein, Shirley (Miscellaneous)
My Darlin' Aida 1952,O 28,36:4
Mademoiselle Colombe 1954,Ja 7,26:1
Isle of Children 1962,Mr 17,16:2
Bernstein, Sid (Miscellaneous)
Joyful Noise, A 1966,D 16,57:1
Bernstein, Sid (Producer)
World of Charles Aznavour, The 1965,O 15,49:1
Bernstein, Sidney (Producer)
Year Round, The 1953,My 6,38:7
Volpone 1957,Ja 8,27:1
John Turner Davis 1958,Jl 2,25:1
Midnight Caller, The 1958,Jl 2,25:1
Summer of the Seventeenth Doll 1959,O 14,52:1
Blacks, The 1961,My 5,23:1
Firebugs, The 1963,F 13,7:2
Blood Knot, The 1964,Mr 3,30:2
Bernstein, Walter (Playwright)
All in Favor 1942,Ja 21,20:6
Beroza, Janet (Miscellaneous)
World War 2 1/2 1969,Mr 25,40:1
Little Boxes; Coffee Lace, The 1969,D 4,71:2
Little Boxes; Trevor 1969,D 4,71:2
Berr, Georges (Playwright)
Maitre Bolbec et son Mari 1926,N 14,VIII,2:1
Mademoiselle Flute 1927,Je 12,VII,2:1
Lady-in-Law, The 1927,O 23,VIII,4:1
Passage de Venus, Le 1928,Mr 18,IX,2:1
Ma Soeur et Moi 1928,Ap 29,IX,2:3
Guignol 1930,Mr 30,VIII,2:4
Miss France 1930,Ap 13,X,2:7
Meet My Sister 1930,D 31,11:1
Autres, Les 1931,N 1,VIII,2:7
Avril 1932,O 16,IX,2:2
Ecole des Contribuables, L' 1934,Ap 29,IX,2:2
Homme au Foulard Bleu, L' 1935,My 26,XI,2:2
Fontaines Lumineuses, Les 1935,D 29,IX,2:1
Berre, Charles
New York Exchange 1926,D 31,11:2
Lost Boy 1932,Ja 6,24:4
Diff'rent 1937,N 21,II,10:7
Pygmalion 1938,Ja 27,16:3
Captain Jinks of the Horse Marines 1938,Ja 28,16:2
No More Peace 1938,Ja 29,13:2
Coriolanus 1938,F 2,14:5
As You Like It 1939,My 9,28:4
Berri, Antonio
Farewell to Arms, A 1930,S 23,30:3
Berrian, William
My Romance 1948,O 20,38:5
Auntie Mame 1958,Ag 12,33:2
Berriau, Simone (Director)
Jardin des Delices, Le 1969,N 4,54:1
Berrier, Edgar
This Is Edwin Booth 1958,Ag 27,32:7
Berrigan, Daniel (S J) (Playwright)
Trial of the Catonsville Nine, The 1970,Ag 16,II,1:7
Berry, Aline
Fata Morgana 1924,Mr 4,16:3
Paolo and Francesca 1924,D 3,24:2
Berry, Aninias
Untitled-One Man Show 1930,Mr 31,24:1
Berry, Audrey
Yours Truly 1927,Ja 26,16:5
Take the Air 1927,N 23,28:2
Remote Control 1929,S 11,24:5
Berry, Betty
Vagabond King, The 1943,Je 30,24:2

Berry, Charles
Low Bridge 1933,F 10,13:4
Berry, Dorothy
Black Eye, The 1938,Mr 8,22:4
Berry, Eddie
Howdy, Mr Ice of 1950 1949,My 27,24:2
Berry, Eric
Boy Friend, The 1954,O 1,20:1
Two Gentlemen of Verona 1958,Mr 19,35:1
Broken Jug, The 1958,Ap 2,36:1
Family Reunion, The 1958,O 21,39:1
Power and the Glory, The 1958,D 12,2:7
Beaux' Stratagem, The 1959,F 25,35:4
Great God Brown, The 1959,O 7,48:1
Pictures in the Hallway 1959,D 28,19:1
Peer Gynt 1960,Ja 13,21:1
Henry IV 1960,Mr 2,42:1
Henry IV 1960,Mr 13,II,1:1
Henry IV 1960,Ap 19,41:1
Henry IV, Part II 1960,Ap 24,II,1:1
Gideon 1961,N 10,38:1
Henry IV, Part I 1962,Je 18,20:4
Henry IV, Part I 1962,Je 24,II,1:1
White House, The 1964,My 20,39:1
Tiny Alice 1964,D 30,14:2
Tiny Alice 1965,Ja 10,II,1:1
White Devil, The 1965,D 7,56:1
Charley's Aunt 1970,Jl 6,38:1
Berry, George
Mask of Hamlet, The 1921,Ag 23,10:3
Berry, Jack
'Tis of Thee 1940,O 28,21:3
Berry, John
Hymn to the Rising Sun 1937,My 7,28:2
Shoemaker's Holiday, The 1938,Ja 3,17:2
Danton's Death 1938,N 3,26:2
Native Son 1941,Mr 25,26:5
Native Son 1942,O 24,10:6
All You Need Is One Good Break 1950,F 10,20:3
Berry, John (Director)
All You Need Is One Good Break 1950,F 10,20:3
Blood Knot, The 1964,Mr 3,30:2
First One Asleep, Whistle 1966,F 28,19:1
Boesman and Lena 1970,Je 23,35:1
Blancs, Les 1970,N 16,48:4
Blancs, Les 1970,N 29,II,3:5
Berry, John (Miscellaneous)
Boesman and Lena 1970,Je 23,35:1
Berry, Jules
Baccara 1927,Ap 3,VIII,4:7
Livree de M le Comte, La 1927,N 20,IX,4:4
Untitled-Play 1928,F 5,VIII,2:1
Homme de Joie, L' 1929,Mr 17,X,2:7
Aube, le Jour Et la Nuit, L' 1929,Je 9,VIII,2:4
Lui 1929,N 24,X,2:1
Guignol 1930,Mr 30,VIII,2:4
Quick 1930,N 23,IX,1:1
Deodat 1931,Ap 19,VIII,2:8
Bluff 1932,Ja 3,VIII,2:4
Cabrioles 1932,N 20,IX,2:1
Berry, Jules (Producer)
Vie Est Belle, La 1928,Je 3,VIII,2:5
Berry, Kelly-Marie
Moon on a Rainbow Shawl 1962,Ja 16,30:1
Son, Come Home, A 1968,Mr 9,23:2
Clara's Ole Man 1968,Mr 9,23:2
Berry, Ken
Billy Barnes Revue, The 1959,Je 10,42:2
Billy Barnes People, The 1961,Je 14,10:3
Berry, Kenneth
Carry Nation 1932,O 31,18:2
I Was Waiting for You 1933,N 14,23:3
Berry, Leonard
May Wine 1935,D 6,30:3
Berry, Lynn
Daffy Dill 1922,Ag 23,14:5
Little Poor Man, The 1925,Ag 6,14:1
Up the Line 1926,N 23,26:1
Berry, Mady
Petit Peche 1926,O 24,VIII,2:1
Berry, Marilyn
Simply Heavenly 1957,My 22,28:2
Berry, Marion
Verge, The 1921,N 15,23:2
Chains of Dew 1922,Ap 28,20:2
Berry, Mimi
Connecticut Yankee, A 1943,N 18,30:2
Berry, Neal
Hamlet 1936,O 9,30:2
Richard II 1937,S 16,28:2
Family Portrait 1939,Mr 9,18:4
Berry, Peter
Nobody's Child 1956,Ag 23,25:2
Mountain Giants, The 1961,Ap 5,32:3
Berry, Peter (Musical Director)
Coach With the Six Insides, The 1967,My 12,50:1
Berry, Stanley
Fountain, The 1925,D 11,26:1
Berry, Virginia
Red Rust 1929,D 18,31:1
Berry, W H
Helen 1932,Ja 31,I,5:2

Berry, Warren
Goose, The 1960,Mr 16,44:1
Moon on a Rainbow Shawl 1962,Ja 16,30:1
Berry Brothers
Lew Leslie's Blackbirds of 1930 1930,O 23,34:5
Vaudeville (Palace) 1931,F 16,16:3
Rhapsody in Black 1931,My 5,33:2
Show Time 1942,S 17,20:2
Star Time 1944,S 13,16:2
Star Time 1944,S 17,II,1:1
Berryhill, Elizabeth (Playwright)
Cup of Trembling, The 1959,My 1,33:5
Berse, Ellen
Noye's Fludde 1959,Mr 17,41:2
Milk and Honey 1961,O 11,52:1
Bersen, Harry Jr (Producer)
Laterna Magika 1964,Ag 4,21:1
Berson, Beulah
George White's Scandals 1923,Je 19,22:5
Berstein, Albert B
You'll Never Know 1921,Ap 21,9:2
Berstl, Julius (Playwright)
Dover-Calais 1927,My 1,VIII,1:3
Scribby's Suppen Sind die Besten
1929,D 22,VIII,4:6
Napi 1931,Mr 12,22:5
Bert, Flo
Cinderella on Broadway 1920,Je 25,18:1
Vaudeville (Palace) 1926,Mr 16,22:2
Bert, Guy (Miscellaneous)
Salut a Moliere 1964,Mr 4,33:2
Pieton de L'Air, Le 1964,Mr 4,33:2
Bert, Lee
Seven Against One 1930,My 7,25:1
Bert, Mabel
His Chinese Wife 1920,My 18,9:3
Accused 1925,S 30,20:1
Bert, Monique
Rose of France 1933,O 29,II,3:3
Bert, Paul (Costume Designer)
Femmes Savantes, Les 1967,F 7,34:2
Bertacca, Uberto (Scenic Designer)
Orlando Furioso 1970,N 5,59:1
Bertay, Michel
Mariage de Figaro, Le 1964,F 26,41:2
Salut a Moliere 1964,Mr 4,33:2
Pieton de L'Air, Le 1964,Mr 4,33:2
Vie Parisienne, La 1964,Mr 11,34:2
Berte, Emile (Composer)
Music in May 1929,Ap 2,29:1
Berte, H (Composer)
Blossom Time 1921,S 30,10:1
Blossom Time 1931,Mr 5,32:1
Blossom Time 1943,S 6,21:2
Bertelson, Paul
In the Summer House 1953,D 30,17:1
Bertelson, Paul (Lighting Director)
French Way, The; Grand Vizier, The
1962,Mr 21,36:2
French Way, The; Deceased, The 1962,Mr 21,36:2
French Way, The; Edward and Agrippina
1962,Mr 21,36:2
Major Barbara 1965,My 18,33:1
Bertelson, Paul (Scenic Designer)
Old Maid, The 1949,Ja 27,20:6
Lady in the Dark 1952,Mr 8,11:3
French Way, The; Grand Vizier, The
1962,Mr 21,36:2
French Way, The; Deceased, The 1962,Mr 21,36:2
French Way, The; Edward and Agrippina
1962,Mr 21,36:2
Major Barbara 1965,My 18,33:1
Bertens, Rosa
Constant Wife, The 1928,My 20,VIII,2:1
Berthelson, Larry (Miscellaneous)
Geranium Hat, The 1959,Mr 18,45:1
Berthez, Armand (Producer)
Miroir Qui Fait Rire, Le 1927,My 1,VIII,2:4
Berthier
Felix 1926,O 10,VIII,2:1
Berti, Dehl
Manhattan Nocturne 1943,O 27,26:2
Thank You Svoboda 1944,Mr 2,13:2
Hickory Stick 1944,My 9,15:6
Fifth Horseman, The 1949,Je 14,26:6
Strong Are Lonely, The 1953,S 30,38:3
Richard III 1953,D 10,65:2
Bertil, Guy
Grosse Valise, La 1965,D 15,52:1
Bertin, John C
Bronx Express 1922,Ap 27,12:2
Bertin, John G
Dream Child 1934,S 28,26:2
Abie's Irish Rose 1937,My 13,30:2
Bertin, Pierre
Fausses Confidences, Les 1952,N 13,34:2
Proces, Le; Trial, The 1952,N 18,36:2
Fourberies de Scapin, Les 1952,N 21,21:2
Repetition, La; Rehearsal, The 1952,N 28,22:2
Hamlet 1952,D 2,39:1
Christophe Colomb 1957,Ja 31,20:5
Volpone 1957,F 5,27:2
Misanthrope, Le 1957,F 8,19:1

Feu la Mere de Madame; Dear Departed
Mother-in-Law 1957,F 12,31:1
Intermezzo 1957,F 15,20:4
Chien du Jardinier, Le; Gardener's Dog, The
1957,F 19,36:1
Adieux, Les 1957,F 19,36:1
Mariage de Figaro, Le 1964,F 26,41:2
Vie Parisienne, La 1964,Mr 11,34:2
Bertin, Roland
Grand Vizir, Le 1970,Ap 8,38:3
Cosmonaute Agricole, Le 1970,Ap 8,38:3
Bertini, Renato
Tragedy of the Ages, The 1933,Ap 7,22:7
Bertino, Al (Playwright)
Disney on Parade 1970,S 24,63:1
Bertolini, Michael
Cock-A-Doodle Dandy 1955,N 4,26:5
Bertolini, Vincenzo
T'Amo E Sarai Mia; I Love You and You'll Be
Mine 1932,Mr 21,19:4
Berton, Eugene (Playwright)
Louisiana Lady 1947,Je 3,35:2
Marie Antoinette in Pennsylvania 1949,My 12,26:2
Berton, Eugene L (Composer)
Cherry Pie 1926,Ap 15,24:4
Loud Speaker 1927,Mr 3,27:2
Berton, Pierre
Tenth Man, The 1929,Mr 21,29:2
Berton, Ralph
Cherry Pie 1926,Ap 15,24:4
Bertonoff, B
Deluge, The 1927,Ja 11,36:2
Golem, The 1927,F 5,13:2
Bertonoff, Debora
Oedipus Rex 1948,My 24,23:2
Bertonov, Joshua
Dybbuk, The 1948,My 3,26:3
David's Crown 1948,My 10,26:2
Golem, The 1948,My 17,22:3
Oedipus Rex 1948,My 24,23:2
Bertonow, E
Jacob's Dream 1927,Ja 4,20:2
Bertonow, J
Dybbuk, The 1926,D 14,24:2
Bertram, Bert
Bat, The 1953,Ja 21,28:2
Streetcar Named Desire, A 1956,F 16,24:1
Child of Fortune 1956,N 14,41:1
Tea Party 1968,O 16,40:1
Bertram, Helen
Robin Hood 1932,Ja 28,25:4
Bertram, Herman H
Once Over Lightly 1938,D 10,13:4
Bertrand, Jacqueline
Ruy Blas 1957,D 14,16:3
Geranium Hat, The 1959,Mr 18,45:1
Ronde, La 1960,My 10,44:2
Child and the Dragon, The 1966,Je 24,30:2
Miracle in Brooklyn 1966,Je 24,30:2
Bertrand, Rosemary
Good Night Ladies 1945,Ja 18,16:2
Bertuch, Max (Playwright)
Liebling Adieu 1931,N 29,VIII,4:2
Madonna Wo Bist Du? 1932,Jl 17,IX,1:3
Glueckliche Reise 1933,Ja 1,IX,1:1
Beruh, Joseph
Threepenny Opera, The 1954,Mr 11,26:5
Beruh, Joseph (Director)
Sound of Hunting, A 1954,Ap 7,41:1
Seven at Dawn, The 1961,Ap 18,43:1
Beruh, Joseph (Miscellaneous)
Look to the Lilies 1970,Mr 30,59:1
Engagement Baby, The 1970,My 22,40:1
Beruh, Joseph (Producer)
Leave It to Jane 1959,My 26,30:2
Kittiwake Island 1960,O 13,43:1
Promenade 1969,Je 5,56:1
Instructions for the Running of Trains, etc on the
Erie Railway to Go Into Effect January 1,1862
1970,Ja 7,36:2
Berval, Chabert (Mrs)
Fanny 1931,D 27,VIII,3:4
Berwick, Arthur
Henry V 1965,Je 29,27:2
Francesca da Rimini 1967,S 12,54:1
Comedy of Errors, The 1968,F 28,40:2
She Stoops to Conquer 1968,Ap 1,58:3
Beryl, Edwin
Passion Flower, The 1920,Ja 14,12:1
Bes-Arlene
Skits-Oh-Frantics 1967,Ap 3,39:2
Besch, Anthony (Director)
Yeomen of the Guard, The 1962,Jl 11,28:1
Mikado, The 1964,N 27,43:1
Besch, Betty Ann (Producer)
Muzeeka 1968,Ap 29,47:2
Red Cross 1968,Ap 29,47:2
Besenko, Ben
Jacques Bergson 1936,O 31,24:6
Besier, Rudolf (Playwright)
Secrets 1922,O 8,VI,1:7
Secrets 1922,D 26,11:1
Secrets 1922,D 31,VII,1:1

Besier, Rudolf (Playwright)—Cont
Captain Briquet 1923,S 16,VII,2:8
Lesson in Love, A 1923,S 25,10:1
Lesson in Love, A 1923,S 30,II,1:1
Barretts of Wimpole Street, The 1930,Ag 21,13:4
Barretts of Wimpole Street, The 1930,S 7,IX,2:1
Barretts of Wimpole Street, The 1931,F 1,VIII,3:5
Barretts of Wimpole Street, The 1931,F 10,25:1
Barretts of Wimpole Street, The 1931,F 22,VIII,1:1
Famiglia Barrett, La 1933,N 19,IX,1:3
Miss Ba; Barretts of Wimpole Street, The
1934,N 11,IX,3:6
Barretts of Wimpole Street, The 1935,F 26,16:2
Barretts of Wimpole Street, The 1944,S 17,II,1:3
Barretts of Wimpole Street, The 1945,Mr 27,23:6
Barretts of Wimpole Street, The 1945,Ap 1,II,1:1
Besnard, Lucien (Playwright)
Coeur Partage, Le 1927,Ja 9,VII,2:5
Dans l'Ombre du Harem 1927,My 29,VII,2:7
Besoyan, Rick (Composer)
Little Mary Sunshine 1959,N 19,49:3
Little Mary Sunshine 1959,N 29,II,1:1
Student Gypsy, The; Prince of Liederkranz, The
1963,O 1,34:1
Besoyan, Rick (Director)
Out of This World 1955,O 13,35:2
Out of This World 1955,N 10,44:2
Student Gypsy, The; Prince of Liederkranz, The
1963,O 1,34:1
Babes in the Wood 1964,D 29,21:2
Besoyan, Rick (Lyricist)
Little Mary Sunshine 1959,N 19,49:3
Little Mary Sunshine 1959,N 29,II,1:1
Student Gypsy, The; Prince of Liederkranz, The
1963,O 1,34:1
Besoyan, Rick (Miscellaneous)
Out of This World 1955,N 10,44:2
Besoyan, Rick (Playwright)
Little Mary Sunshine 1959,N 19,49:3
Little Mary Sunshine 1959,N 29,II,1:1
Little Mary Sunshine 1962,My 18,35:8
Student Gypsy, The; Prince of Liederkranz, The
1963,O 1,34:1
Babes in the Wood 1964,D 29,21:2
Bessel, Ehmi
Faust, Part I; Play, The 1961,F 5,27:2
Bessell, Frank (Producer)
Crimes of Passion; Ruffian on the Stair, The
1969,O 27,54:1
Crimes of Passion; Erpingham Camp, The
1969,O 27,54:1
Besser, Joe
Sons o' Fun 1941,D 2,28:2
If the Shoe Fits 1946,D 6,29:4
Besser, Joel (Lighting Director)
Frugal Noon 1964,My 23,15:2
Acid Wine 1964,My 23,15:2
Bessie, Alvah C
Loud Speaker 1927,Mr 3,27:2
Besson, Benno (Director)
Peace 1970,S 2,30:2
Besson, Cassia
Tarot 1970,D 12,19:1
Besson, Rene
Ecole des Femmes, L'; School for Wives
1951,Mr 19,22:1
Besson, Violet
School for Scandal, The 1923,Mr 13,19:2
Dear Old England 1930,Mr 26,24:6
Distant Shore, The 1935,F 22,26:2
Saturday's Children 1936,Jl 7,22:5
Country Wife, The 1936,D 2,34:1
Bessou, Claude (Costume Designer)
Femmes Savantes, Les 1967,F 7,34:2
Bessou, Claude (Scenic Designer)
Femmes Savantes, Les 1967,F 7,34:2
Best, Charles (Playwright)
Gordon Reilly 1952,N 26,20:5
Best, Constance
Easy Virtue 1925,D 8,28:2
Best, Edna
Polly With a Past 1921,Mr 3,13:6
Elopement, The 1923,S 2,VI,1:7
These Charming People 1925,O 7,31:2
Constant Nymph, The 1926,O 3,VIII,2:1
Come With Me 1928,My 20,VIII,2:3
High Road, The 1928,S 11,31:1
Paris Bound 1929,My 19,IX,1:8
Michael and Mary 1930,F 2,5:1
Michael and Mary 1930,F 23,VIII,2:1
Swan, The 1930,Jl 27,VIII,1:8
Melo 1931,Ap 17,26:6
There's Always Juliet 1931,O 13,26:5
There's Always Juliet 1932,F 16,24:2
There's Always Juliet 1932,F 28,VIII,1:1
Another Language 1932,D 25,IX,1:1
Dark Tower, The 1934,Je 10,IX,1:1
Murder at Mayfair 1934,S 6,23:5
Murder in Mayfair 1934,S 23,X,3:6
Promise 1936,Mr 22,XI,1:7
Follow Your Saint 1936,S 25,20:3
Follow Your Saint 1936,O 11,X,3:1
Sun Never Sets, The 1938,Je 26,IX,2:1
Can We Tell? 1938,O 9,X,3:2

Best, Edna—Cont
Delicate Story 1940,D 5,32:2
Yankee Point 1942,N 24,28:2
Browning Version, The 1949,O 13,32:2
Harlequinade 1949,O 13,32:2
Browning Version, The 1949,O 23,II,1:1
Heiress, The 1950,F 9,34:2
Captain Brassbound's Conversion 1950,D 28,21:1
Jane 1952,F 2,10:2
Jane 1952,F 10,II,1:1
First Lady 1952,My 29,18:5
International Set, The 1953,Je 12,19:3
Ladies of the Corridor, The 1953,O 22,33:5
Ladies of the Corridor, The 1953,N 1,II,1:1
Mademoiselle Colombe 1954,Ja 7,26:1
Mademoiselle Colombe 1954,Ja 17,II,1:1
Qudrille 1954,N 4,39:2
Quadrille 1954,N 14,II,1:1
Best, Edna (Costume Designer)
Red White and Blue 1950,O 8,64:5
Best, Jack (Musical Director)
Hear! Hear! 1955,S 28,38:1
Best, Larry
Hello Solly! 1967,Ap 6,44:3
Best, Mary
School for Brides 1944,Ag 2,19:4
Star Spangled Family 1945,Ap 11,18:6
Angels Kiss Me 1951,Ap 18,37:6
Best, Paul
Vie Parisienne, La 1941,N 6,20:3
Firebird of Florence 1945,Mr 23,13:4
Day Before Spring, The 1945,N 23,27:2
Sweethearts 1947,Ja 22,31:2
Silk Stockings 1955,F 25,17:3
Best, Richard
Pirates of Penzance, The 1966,My 24,54:1
Best, Robert B (Miscellaneous)
Enchanting Melody 1964,N 25,40:1
Best, Wade
Lysistrata 1968,N 15,42:1
Betbeze, Yolande (Producer)
Macbeth 1955,O 8,12:6
Last Love of Don Juan, The 1955,N 24,40:1
Thesmophoriazusae, The; Goddesses of Athens,
The 1955,D 14,52:4
Beth, Lise
Sometime Jam Today 1967,F 13,41:1
Bethe, David
Ol' Man Satan 1932,O 4,26:3
Bethea, Dale Ellen
Miracle Worker, The 1959,O 20,44:1
Bethea, David
Pirate, The 1942,N 26,39:2
Early to Bed 1943,Je 18,16:2
Bethea, Juanita
Miracle Worker, The 1959,O 20,44:1
Emperor Jones, The 1964,Ag 6,20:4
Bethel, Anna (Director)
Mikado, The 1947,D 30,18:2
Bethel, Tom
Kilpatrick's Old-Time Minstrels 1930,Ap 21,20:2
Bethel, Virginia
Wonderful Night, A; Fledermaus, Die
1929,N 1,23:3
Bethell, Anna (Director)
Trial by Jury 1948,Ja 6,27:2
Pirates of Penzance, The 1948,Ja 6,27:2
Iolanthe 1948,Ja 13,29:3
H M S Pinafore 1948,Ja 20,26:2
Cox and Box 1948,Ja 20,26:2
Gondoliers, The 1948,Ja 27,31:2
Yeomen of the Guard, The 1948,F 3,30:2
Patience 1948,F 10,27:2
Bethencourt, Francis
Much Ado About Nothing 1955,Ag 20,20:4
Six Characters in Search of an Author
1955,D 12,38:1
Six Characters in Search of an Author
1955,D 25,II,3:1
Visit to a Small Planet 1957,F 8,18:1
Ross 1961,D 27,20:2
Right Honourable Gentleman, The 1965,O 20,50:2
Hamp 1967,Mr 10,32:1
Borstal Boy 1970,Ap 1,38:1
Bethune, Donald
Varying Shore, The 1921,D 6,24:1
Red Geranium, The 1922,My 9,22:3
Bethune, Ivy
Girl From Samos, The 1954,N 24,17:1
Amedee: or, How to Disentangle Yourself
1955,N 1,27:3
Bethune, Patton
Tenth Man, The 1929,Mr 21,29:2
Bethune, Zina
Most Happy Fella, The 1956,My 4,20:1
Betinis, N
Oedipus Tyrannus 1952,N 25,35:2
Betke, Lotte
Richard III 1937,My 30,X,2:2
Betove (Michel Levy) (Composer)
Pom' Pom' ! 1928,Ap 1,IX,4:7
Betten, Mary
Cindy 1964,S 25,33:1

Bettenbender, John (Director)
There Is a Play Tonight 1961,F 16,24:2
Bettenbender, John (Playwright)
There Is a Play Tonight 1961,F 16,24:2
Bettger, Lyle
Dance Night 1938,O 15,20:5
Flying Gerardos, The 1940,D 30,21:4
Moon Is Down, The 1942,Ap 8,22:2
All for All 1943,S 30,25:2
Oh, Herbert! 1945,Je 20,26:3
John Loves Mary 1947,F 5,29:2
Betti, Henri (Composer)
Folies Bergere 1964,Je 3,36:1
Betti, Ugo (Original Author)
Gambler, The 1952,O 14,40:1
Betti, Ugo (Playwright)
Island of Goats 1955,O 5,40:1
Queen and the Rebels, The 1956,F 5,II,3:1
Time of Vengeance 1959,D 11,39:1
Time of Vengeance 1959,D 27,II,1:1
Corruption in the Palace of Justice 1963,O 9,49:2
Queen and the Rebels, The 1965,F 26,16:1
Troubled Waters 1965,Je 4,40:2
Bettis, Charles
Long Moment, The 1950,My 22,16:6
Trouble in Mind 1955,N 5,23:2
Bettis, Valerie
Inside U S A 1948,My 1,19:2
Inside U S A 1948,My 23,II,1:1
Inside U S A 1948,Je 13,II,6:6
Inside U S A 1948,Ag 29,II,1:1
Great to Be Alive! 1950,Mr 24,28:2
Bless You All 1950,D 15,42:2
Back to Methuselah 1958,Mr 27,41:5
Back to Methuselah 1958,Ap 6,II,1:1
Bettis, Valerie (Choreographer)
Beggar's Holiday 1946,D 27,13:3
Peer Gynt 1951,Ja 29,15:2
Peer Gynt 1951,F 4,II,1:1
Ulysses in Nighttown 1958,Je 15,II,1:1
Pousse-Cafe 1966,Mr 19,19:2
Bettis, Valerie (Director)
Ulysses in Nighttown 1958,Je 6,30:1
If Five Years Pass 1962,My 11,37:1
Betts, Dorothy
Opportunity 1920,Jl 31,5:1
Betts, Jack
Country Wife, The 1955,Ap 6,35:1
Firstborn, The 1958,My 1,35:1
Cock-A-Doodle Dandy 1958,N 13,39:2
Death of Cuchulain, The 1959,Ap 13,34:4
On Baile's Strand 1959,Ap 13,34:4
Greenwich Village U S A 1960,S 29,30:5
Banquet for the Moon, A 1961,Ja 20,24:2
Betts, Roberts
Orpheus in Hades 1930,D 16,30:1
Betts, William
Polly Preferred 1923,Ja 12,13:3
Bettymae
Hellzapoppin 1938,S 23,34:2
Betz, Carl
Long Watch, The 1952,Mr 21,19:5
Beudukov, Anatol (Director)
Marriage of Cana, The 1932,F 3,22:4
Beuerman, Eugene
Little Theatre Tournament; Thirst 1929,My 10,32:2
Beuerman, Gus
Eyvind of the Hills 1921,F 2,14:1
Beuhler, Buddy
Woman Brown, The 1939,D 9,18:5
Beutelle, Leona
It's a Grand Life 1930,F 11,30:3
Beuvell and Miss Tova
Tattle Tales 1933,Je 2,22:6
Bevan, Donald (Playwright)
Stalag 17 1951,My 9,41:2
Stalag 17 1953,Ap 6,24:2
Bevan, Frank (Costume Designer)
Greatest Show on Earth, The 1938,Ja 6,22:2
Knickerbocker Holiday 1938,O 20,26:2
Rhapsody 1944,N 23,37:2
Bevan, Fred (Costume Designer)
King's Coat, The 1933,Ja 12,21:4
Bevan, Isla
Bitter Sweet 1929,N 6,30:2
Bevan, Pamela
Trumpets and Drums 1969,O 13,52:1
Oedipus 1970,F 23,30:1
Bevan, Yolande
Tarot 1970,D 12,19:1
Bevans, Lawrence
Ivory Door, The 1927,O 19,24:5
Bevans, Lionel
Cock o' the Roost 1924,O 14,23:1
Revelry 1927,S 13,37:1
Napoleon 1928,Mr 9,21:1
Wings Over Europe 1928,D 11,35:1
Bevans, Lionel (Director)
Absent Father 1932,O 18,23:5
Good Fairy, The 1932,N 18,22:3
Best People, The 1933,Mr 16,21:5
Bevans, Philippa
Stepdaughters of War 1930,O 7,27:1

Bevans, Philippa—Cont
Bellamy Trial, The 1931,Ap 23,28:6
Alchemist, The 1931,Je 5,27:1
Caesar and Cleopatra 1935,Ag 22,21:1
Millionairess, The 1952,Ag 16,22:5
Stop Press 1939,Mr 20,13:2
Man in Possession, The 1939,S 26,21:4
Ah, Wilderness! 1941,O 3,26:2
Harriet 1943,Mr 4,24:2
Harriet 1944,S 28,26:1
Dream Girl 1945,D 15,13:2
Harvest of Years 1948,Ja 13,29:2
Temporary Island, A 1948,Mr 15,27:3
Afternoon Storm 1948,Ap 12,24:2
S S Glencairn; Long Voyage Home, The
1948,My 21,21:2
Madame Is Served 1949,F 15,28:1
Relapse, The 1950,N 23,54:2
Buy Me Blue Ribbons 1951,O 18,33:2
Mr Pickwick 1952,S 18,36:3
Starcross Story, The 1954,Ja 14,25:2
My Fair Lady 1956,Mr 16,20:2
Look After Lulu 1959,Mr 4,35:1
Ignorants Abroad, The 1960,My 24,43:2
Valmouth 1960,O 7,29:1
Moon in the Yellow River, The 1961,F 7,40:2
Arms and the Man 1964,Ap 28,41:1
Major Barbara 1965,My 18,33:1
What Did We Do Wrong? 1967,O 23,56:1
Beveridge, Glen
Crucible 1933,S 5,22:4
Beveridge, Philip
Half Gods 1929,D 23,18:5
Beverley, Gaile
Present Arms 1928,Ap 27,16:2
Beverley, Trazana
Instructions for the Running of Trains, etc on the
Erie Railway to Go Into Effect January 1,1862
1970,Ja 7,36:2
Beverley Sisters
Look Who's Here 1932,O 31,18:5
Beverly, Gaile
Will Morrissey's Newcomers 1923,Ag 9,16:2
Mayflowers 1925,N 25,14:2
Queen High 1926,S 9,21:2
Beverly, Helen
Clean Beds 1939,My 26,21:2
Uriel Acosta 1939,D 31,18:3
Beverly, Mildred
Channel Road, The 1929,O 18,24:2
Bevill, Nancy
Cyrano de Bergerac 1926,F 19,18:1
Three Sisters, The 1926,O 27,24:1
When Crummles Played 1928,O 2,34:3
Bewley, Lois
First Impressions 1959,Mr 20,28:1
Bey, James Hawthorne
Shrike, The 1952,Ja 16,20:2
Bey, LaRocque (Choreographer)
Hajj Malik, El 1970,O 4,II,5:1
Bey, Michael
Catherine Was Great 1944,Ag 3,16:1
Duchess of Malfi, The 1946,O 16,35:2
Bey, Rahman
Untitled-Magic Show 1926,My 24,24:2
Beydts, Louis (Composer)
S A D M P, La 1937,N 14,XI,7:5
Barbier de Seville, Le 1955,N 9,40:1
Beye, Holly (Playwright)
Deuces Wild; Thus 1962,Ap 25,31:1
Deuces Wild; It's All Yours 1962,Ap 25,31:1
Beyea, Basil (Playwright)
Cat Screams, The 1942,Je 17,26:5
Beyer, Abigail
Lysistrata 1968,N 15,42:1
Beyer, Edward (Miscellaneous)
Night of the Iguana, The 1961,D 29,10:1
Beyer, Gregory
Blancs, Les 1970,N 16,48:4
Beyer, Margery
Bolls of Cotton 1925,D 22,18:3
Beyer, William
Critic, The 1925,My 9,12:4
Beyerlein, Franz Adam (Playwright)
Taps 1925,Ap 15,16:2
Beyers, Robert
Buckaroo 1929,Mr 18,31:1
Young Sinners 1929,N 29,24:4
Beymer, Richard
Country Girl, The 1966,S 30,55:1
Beyo, Mascha (Translator)
Awakening of Spring, The 1964,My 13,50:1
Bezar, Fran
Lion in Love, The 1963,Ap 26,28:3
Bezazian and White
Vaudeville (Hippodrome) 1926,My 11,25:3
Bhaduri, Biswanath
Ramayana 1931,Ja 13,35:4
Bhaduri, Sisir Kumar
Ramayana 1931,Ja 13,35:4
Bhaduri, Tarakumar
Ramayana 1931,Ja 13,35:4
Bhaskar
Christine 1960,Ap 29,27:1

Bhaskar—Cont
King of the Dark Chamber 1961,F 10,21:1
King of the Dark Chamber 1961,Ap 9,II,1:1
We're Civilized? 1962,N 9,30:1
Bhaskar (Choreographer)
King of the Dark Chamber 1961,F 10,21:1
We're Civilized? 1962,N 9,30:1
Bhattacharyya, Manoranjan
Ramayana 1931,Ja 13,35:4
Bhumibol, Prince Chakrband (King of Thailand) /(Composer)
Michael Todd's Peep Show 1950,Je 29,37:2
Bhumibol, Prince Chakrband (King of Thailand) /(Lyricist)
Michael Todd's Peep Show 1950,Je 29,37:2
Biala, Sarah
Broken Chain, The 1929,F 21,30:4
Biales, Rosetta
House on Grand Street, A 1953,O 10,12:6
Hole in the Head, A 1958,N 26,25:2
Bialik, Chaim (Playwright)
Light, Lively and Yiddish 1970,O 28,58:1
Bialik, Chaim (Translator)
Dybbuk, The 1948,My 3,26:3
Dybbuk, The 1964,F 4,30:2
Bialis, Rosetta
Motke Ganef 1932,D 30,15:2
Wise Men of Chelm, The 1933,O 18,24:4
Stranger, The 1935,N 7,26:2
Saint and Sinners 1935,D 30,15:2
Voice of Israel, The 1948,O 26,40:2
Hershel, The Jester 1948,D 14,39:2
Shepherd King, The 1955,O 13,36:2
Bialkin, Morris
Blue Butterfly, The 1929,F 17,29:3
Bianca, June
Edge of the Sword, The 1949,N 10,40:3
Deirdre of the Sorrows 1949,D 15,51:2
Aria Da Capo 1950,My 25,36:2
Biancardo, Pascal (Director)
Paradise 1931,My 12,29:2
Biancardo, Pascal (Playwright)
Paradise 1931,My 12,29:2
Bianchi, Lois (Producer)
Country Scandal, A 1960,My 6,21:8
Buskers, The 1961,O 31,28:1
Call It Virtue 1963,Mr 28,8:2
Bianchi, Richard (Lighting Director)
Buskers, The 1961,O 31,28:1
Call It Virtue 1963,Mr 28,8:2
Bianchi, Richard (Scenic Designer)
Judge, The 1958,My 14,36:2
Enemy of the People, An 1959,F 5,24:4
Country Scandal, A 1960,My 6,21:8
Behind the Wall 1960,N 1,47:1
Buskers, The 1961,O 31,28:1
Call It Virtue 1963,Mr 28,8:2
Winterset 1966,F 10,32:2
Bianchini, Mlle
Affaires Son les Affaires, Les 1924,Mr 11,17:1
Monsieur Brotonneau 1924,Mr 13,14:1
Blanchette 1924,Mr 19,19:4
Bianco, Pierre
Three Musketeers, The 1968,Je 26,43:1
Biancoli, Oreste (Playwright)
Casa di Tutti, La; Everybody's Home 1932,D 5,21:4
Biasco, John (Miscellaneous)
Don Juan in Hell 1960,O 4,47:3
Bibb, Leon
Flight Into Egypt 1952,Mr 19,33:2
Talent '54 1954,Ap 13,40:1
Sandhog 1954,N 24,17:1
Hand Is on the Gate, A 1966,S 22,54:1
Carnival! 1968,D 13,58:1
Biberman, Abner
Sailors of Cattaro 1934,D 11,28:4
Panic 1935,Mr 16,18:4
Waiting for Lefty 1935,Mr 27,24:5
Till the Day I Die 1935,Mr 27,24:5
Winterset 1935,S 26,19:2
Siege 1937,D 9,31:4
Roosty 1938,F 15,21:2
Biberman, Herbert J
Somebody's Lion 1921,Ap 13,20:1
Patriarch, The 1926,D 11,15:1
Faust 1928,O 9,34:1
Karl and Anna 1929,O 8,34:1
Red Rust 1929,D 18,31:1
Biberman, Herbert J (Director)
Red Rust 1929,D 18,31:1
Roar China! 1930,O 28,23:1
Green Grow the Lilacs 1931,Ja 27,21:2
Miracle at Verdun 1931,Mr 17,34:6
Man Who Reclaimed His Head 1932,S 9,17:3
Peace Palace 1933,Je 6,30:2
Iron Flowers 1933,Je 13,22:2
Valley Forge 1934,D 11,28:3
Woman, The 1965,O 21,56:1
Biberman, Herbert J (Producer)
Peace Palace 1933,Je 6,30:2
Iron Flowers 1933,Je 13,22:2
Iron Flowers 1933,Je 18,VIII,5:2

Bibesco, Antoine (Prince) (Original Author)
Ladies All 1930,Jl 20,VIII,2:1
Bibesco, Antoine (Prince) (Playwright)
Laquelle 1927,O 16,IX,4:7
Laquelle 1927,N 20,IX,4:4
Quatuor 1928,N 11,X,2:7
Ladies All 1930,Jl 29,25:2
Mon Heritier 1930,O 26,VIII,2:1
Bibo, Guenther (Playwright)
Valliere, La 1933,Ap 16,IX,2:5
Bibo, Irving (Lyricist)
Letty Pepper 1922,Ap 11,22:2
Bicat, Andre (Scenic Designer)
Murder in the Cathedral 1938,F 17,16:2
Bick, Kitty
Toto 1921,Mr 22,15:2
Bickart, Sanford
Paths of Glory 1935,S 27,24:2
Double Dummy 1936,N 12,30:1
Call Me Ziggy 1937,F 13,9:6
Ringside Seat 1938,N 23,24:5
Steps Leading Up 1941,Ap 19,20:6
Johnny on the Spot 1942,Ja 9,24:2
Boy Meets Girl 1943,Je 23,15:5
Bickel, Frederick
Deburau 1920,D 24,14:3
Lawbreaker, The 1922,F 7,12:1
Zeno 1923,Ag 27,14:2
Bickel, George
Scandals 1920,Je 8,9:1
George White's Scandals 1921,Jl 12,14:1
Good Old Days, The 1923,Ag 15,21:2
Good Old Days, The 1923,Ag 19,VI,1:1
Paradise Alley 1924,Ap 2,17:3
Circus Princess, The 1927,Ap 26,32:2
Bickel, Margaret
Mikado, The; Town of Titipu, The 1931,My 5,33:2
Bickerton, Joseph P Jr (Miscellaneous)
Easy Virtue 1925,D 8,28:2
Bickerton, Joseph P Jr (Producer)
Jacob Slovak 1927,O 6,28:4
Lilly Turner 1932,S 20,26:1
Men Must Fight 1932,O 15,13:4
Bickford, Charles
Houses of Sand 1925,F 18,17:1
Something to Brag About 1925,Ag 14,14:3
Outside Looking In 1925,S 8,28:1
Outside Looking In 1925,S 13,VIII,1:1
Glory Hallelujah 1926,Ap 7,26:2
No More Women 1926,Ag 4,17:2
Chicago 1926,D 31,11:1
Bless You, Sister 1927,D 27,24:5
Gods of the Lightning 1928,O 25,27:2
Casey Jones 1938,F 21,14:2
Bickford, Charles (Playwright)
Cyclone Lover, The 1928,Je 6,23:3
Sandy Hooker, The 1929,N 10,X,4:8
Bickle, Bill
Ice Follies 1961,Ja 11,25:2
Bickley, Felton
Ten Million Ghosts 1936,O 24,23:7
Arms for Venus 1937,Mr 12,18:7
Bickley, Tony
Days of Our Youth, The 1941,N 29,15:2
Without Love 1942,N 11,28:1
Made in Heaven 1946,O 25,28:2
Man and Superman 1947,O 9,31:2
Grey-Eyed People, The 1952,D 18,41:2
Best Man, The 1960,Ap 1,39:1
Bidart, Gay Darlene
Cruce de Vias 1969,N 2,86:5
Biddeau, Geffrey
Mister Johnson 1956,Mr 30,11:1
Biddell, Sidney M (Miscellaneous)
9th Street Guest, The 1930,Ag 26,24:3
Biddell, Sidney M (Producer)
Divorce Me, Dear 1931,O 7,29:2
Biddle, Cordelia Drexel (Original Author)
Happiest Millionaire, The 1956,N 21,21:3
Happiest Millionaire, The 1956,D 2,II,1:1
Biddle, Dorothea
Disenchanted, The 1958,D 4,53:4
Biddle, Temple
Sonya's Search for the Christmas Star 1929,D 14,24:6
Biddle, Vernon
After Such Pleasures 1934,F 8,15:2
Biddy and Baddy
Ice Follies 1970,My 23,27:1
Bideau, Jean (Playwright)
Last Torture, The 1927,Ja 13,28:4
Bidgood, James (Costume Designer)
Hi, Paisano 1961,O 2,36:2
Love Nest, The 1963,Ja 28,7:6
Of Thee I Sing 1969,Mr 8,19:1
Bidsted, Erik
My Fair Lady 1962,S 7,34:1
Bidwell, Martin (Playwright)
Lower North 1944,Ag 26,15:4
Bieber, Ethel (Lyricist)
Hooray!! It's a Glorious Day. . .And All That 1966,Mr 10,28:1

Bieber, Kurt
Absalom 1956,My 17,37:2
Biegen, Anthony Sr
Veronica's Veil 1950,F 12,II,1:5
Biegler, Othmar
Midsummer Night's Dream, A 1927,N 18,21:1
Jedermann 1927,D 8,33:2
Dantons Tod 1927,D 21,28:3
Peripherie 1928,Ja 3,29:1
Diener Zweier Herren; Servant of Two Masters, The 1928,Ja 10,28:3
Kabale und Liebe 1928,Ja 17,22:3
Lebende Leichnam, Der, Der; Living Corpse, The 1928,Ja 24,39:2
Redemption: Lebende Leichnam, Der; Living Corpse, The 1928,N 20,28:2
Ghosts; Gespenster 1929,F 6,30:3
Biel, Nicholas (Playwright)
Winners and Losers 1947,F 27,27:2
Bielavsky, Morris
Shylock and His Daughter 1947,S 30,22:2
Voice of Israel, The 1948,O 26,40:2
Hershel, The Jester 1948,D 14,39:2
Yosele the Nightingale 1949,O 21,30:4
Bielinska, Olga
Carefree Tree, The 1955,O 12,37:2
Month in the Country, A 1956,Ap 4,23:1
Month in the Country, A 1956,Ap 15,II,1:1
Protective Custody 1956,D 29,8:7
Bienbryer, Eddie (Composer)
Tattle Tales 1933,Je 2,22:6
Bienbryer, Eddie (Lyricist)
Tattle Tales 1933,Je 2,22:6
Bier, Burt
Scrapbooks 1953,N 6,24:2
Detective Story 1954,F 13,11:2
Skyscraper 1965,N 15,48:1
Bier, Marianne
Storm Operation 1944,Ja 12,28:2
Bier, Stanton
Wednesday's Child 1934,Ja 17,23:2
Come What May 1934,My 16,23:4
Bieri, Ramon
Duchess of Malfi, The 1962,Mr 5,27:1
Macbeth 1962,N 17,16:2
Antony and Cleopatra 1963,Je 21,33:1
Winter's Tale, The 1963,Ag 16,14:1
Mr Simian 1963,O 22,44:1
Passion of Josef D, The 1964,F 12,29:1
View From the Bridge, A 1965,Ja 29,24:1
Bierman, Mary Ruth
Sparkin' 1931,Mr 4,33:2
Psychological Moment, The 1931,Mr 4,33:2
Divina Pastora, La 1931,Mr 4,33:2
Biever, Curtis (Composer)
Salvation on a String; Supper for the Dead 1954,Jl 7,23:1
Salvation on a String; No Count Boy, The 1954,Jl 7,23:1
Salvation on a String; Chair Endowed 1954,Jl 7,23:1
Big Rosie
Jumbo 1935,N 18,20:2
Bigbee, North (Playwright)
Farewell Summer 1937,Mr 30,20:2
Bigby, Dorothy
Star and Garter 1942,S 13,VIII,1:1
Bigelow, A S
Gentlemen, the Queen 1927,Ap 23,14:3
Bigelow, Dorothie
Oh, Please! 1926,D 22,24:3
Skyrocket, The 1929,Ja 12,14:7
Truth Game, The 1930,D 29,19:1
Bigelow, Dudley
In Fondo Al Cuore; Depths of the Heart, The 1930,D 8,27:1
Cardinale, Il; Cardinal, The 1931,Ja 12,24:2
Delitto e Castigo; Crime and Punishment 1931,Ja 26,20:5
Sansone; Samson 1931,F 9,25:1
Arzigogolo, L'; Whim, The 1931,Ap 27,24:4
Giuochi di Prestigio 1931,N 2,26:1
Signo Della Croce, Il 1935,O 7,11:1
Religione e Patria 1936,Mr 23,22:4
Bigelow, Edward
Rosalinda; Fledermaus, Die 1942,O 29,26:5
Bigelow, H
Gentlemen, the Queen 1927,Ap 23,14:3
Bigelow, Hugh
Parnell 1936,My 5,26:2
Bigelow, Jesse
Lion in Love, The 1963,Ap 26,28:3
Bigelow, Joe (Playwright)
Duchess Misbehaves, The 1946,F 14,32:2
Bigelow, Louise
Prunella 1929,Ap 10,23:3
Sonya's Search for the Christmas Star 1929,D 14,24:6
Bigelow, Otis
Noah 1954,O 11,32:2
Bigelow, Otis (Choreographer)
Noah 1954,O 11,32:2
Bigelow, Otis (Miscellaneous)
To Dorothy, A Son 1951,N 20,37:2

Bigelow, Otis (Miscellaneous)—Cont
Sweet Eros 1968,N 22,38:1
Witness 1968,N 22,38:1
Who's Happy Now? 1969,N 18,39:1
Bigelow, Otis (Playwright)
Giants' Dance, The 1964,N 17,48:2
Bigelow, Samuel
In the Days of the Turbins 1934,Mr 7,22:5
Bigelow, Walter
Girl Friend, The 1926,Mr 18,26:5
Bigger, Henry (Miscellaneous)
Now Is the Time for all Good Men 1967,S 27,42:1
Bigger, Stuart (Miscellaneous)
To Be Young Gifted and Black; World of Lorraine
Hansberry, The 1969,Ja 3,15:1
Biggers, Earl Derr (Original Author)
Keeper of the Keys 1933,O 19,23:2
Seven Keys to Baldpate 1935,My 28,30:2
Biggers, Earl Derr (Playwright)
Three's a Crowd 1923,F 4,VII,1:4
Seven Keys to Baldpate 1930,Ja 8,25:2
Bigley, Isabel
Guys and Dolls 1950,N 25,11:2
Guys and Dolls 1950,D 3,II,1:1
Guys and Dolls 1951,O 7,II,1:1
Me and Juliet 1953,My 29,17:1
Me and Juliet 1953,Je 7,II,1:1
Bigtree, Norma
Curley McDimple 1967,N 23,59:2
Bigus, Harriette
Flies, The 1954,S 10,18:2
Bijou, Victor (Costume Designer)
Dirtiest Show in Town, The 1970,Je 29,43:2
Bikel, Theodore
Tonight in Samarkand 1955,F 17,22:2
Lark, The 1955,N 18,20:1
Lark, The 1955,N 27,II,1:1
Rope Dancers, The 1957,N 21,39:1
Rope Dancers, The 1957,D 1,II,1:1
Sound of Music, The 1959,N 17,40:2
Cafe Crown 1964,Ap 18,32:1
Pousse-Cafe 1966,Mr 19,19:2
Bilbrooke, Lydia
If Winter Comes 1923,Ap 3,26:1
Bildt, Paul
Robbers, The 1926,N 21,VIII,1:3
Lulu 1927,Ja 30,VII,4:3
Outside Looking In 1929,Je 23,VIII,2:1
Love in the Country 1930,S 28,VIII,4:4
Brest-Litovsk 1930,N 30,IX,2:1
Heilige Crispin, Der 1933,Je 25,IX,1:2
Bildt, Paul (Director)
What Every Woman Knows 1928,D 2,X,4:4
Kreuzabnahme 1929,My 26,IX,2:3
Bilencova, Elizabeth
Prologue to Glory 1938,Mr 18,22:2
Bilibine, Jean (Costume Designer)
Glass of Water, A 1930,Mr 6,16:3
Bilibine, Jean (Scenic Designer)
Glass of Water, A 1930,Mr 6,16:3
Bilis, Teddy
Bourgeois Gentilhomme, Le 1955,O 26,26:1
Barbier de Seville, Le 1955,N 9,40:1
Bill, Edward
Libel! 1935,D 21,10:5
Bill, Leo
Night in Paris, A 1926,Ja 6,16:3
Billam, George (Playwright)
Spring Tide 1936,Ag 9,IX,1:5
Billetdoux, Francois (Original Author)
Tchin-Tchin 1962,O 9,37:3
Tchin-Tchin 1962,O 26,26:2
Billetdoux, Francois (Playwright)
Tchin-Tchin 1962,N 25,II,1:1
Billett, Don
My Mother, My Father and Me 1963,Mr 25,5:5
Bridal Night, The 1966,N 8,45:1
Eternal Triangle 1966,N 8,45:1
We Bombed in New Haven 1968,O 17,51:1
Rooming House, The 1970,Ja 23,25:1
Borstal Boy 1970,Ap 1,38:1
Billig, Bob
Dames at Sea 1970,Ja 5,46:3
Billiken, Billie
Silks and Satins 1920,Jl 16,19:1
Billing, Noel Pemberton (Playwright)
High Treason 1928,N 9,52:2
Billinger, Richard (Playwright)
Rauhnacht 1932,F 21,VIII,2:1
Rosse 1933,My 7,IX,2:5
Billings, Andrew (Producer)
Career Angel 1944,My 24,23:7
Billings, Betty
Rosalinda; Fledermaus, Die 1942,O 29,26:5
Billings, Clarke
Blue Peter, The 1925,Mr 25,25:3
Man's Man, A 1925,O 14,31:2
Billings, Fanny
What Next 1920,Ja 27,7:2
Billings, James
June Love 1921,Ap 26,20:1
Billington, Ken (Lighting Director)
Fortune and Men's Eyes 1969,O 23,55:1

Billington, Lee
But, Seriously... 1969,F 28,29:1
Billman, Larry
Vintage '60 1960,S 13,41:1
Bills, Leo
Vaudeville (Palace) 1926,Ap 27,22:3
Bilodeau, Thomas H
On the Level 1937,Mr 26,24:4
Bilotti, Quina
O Evening Star 1936,Ja 9,24:6
Postman Always Rings Twice, The 1936,F 26,17:2
Bilowit, Ira J (Lyricist)
Of Mice and Men 1958,D 5,38:1
Bilowit, Ira J (Playwright)
Of Mice and Men 1958,D 5,38:1
Bilowit, Ira J (Producer)
Of Mice and Men 1958,D 5,38:1
Secret Concubine, The 1960,Mr 22,29:2
Biltmorettes, The
Sons o' Fun 1941,D 2,28:2
Bilton, Le Verria
Porgy and Bess 1935,O 11,30:2
Bimko, F (Playwright)
Thieves 1920,Ap 9,11:4
Father and Son 1956,O 20,17:4
Binder, Sybille
Menschen im Hotel 1930,Mr 16,IX,4:1
Sturm im Wasserglas 1930,D 28,VIII,2:4
Bines, David (Director)
Danny Kaye's International Show 1953,Ja 19,20:2
Liberace's Variety Bill 1957,Ap 22,29:5
Bines, David (Lighting Director)
Danny Kaye's International Show 1953,Ja 19,20:2
Jerry Lewis' Variety Show 1957,F 8,18:5
Liberace's Variety Bill 1957,Ap 22,29:5
Bines, David (Miscellaneous)
Difficult Woman, The 1962,Ap 26,22:7
Binet (Playwright)
Horrible Experience, L' 1923,O 23,16:1
Bing, Herman
Laughter Over Broadway 1939,Ja 16,10:3
Bing, Julius
Beggars Are Comming to Town 1945,O 29,16:2
Ist Geraldine ein Engel? 1946,N 4,33:4
It Takes Two 1947,F 4,33:4
Bing, Mack
Master Builder, The 1955,Mr 2,23:2
Bingham, Amelia
Mamma's Affair 1920,Ja 20,10:1
Ostriches 1925,Mr 31,16:1
Trelawney of the 'Wells' 1925,Je 2,16:2
Pearl of Great Price, The 1926,N 2,34:3
Bingham, C T
Galloper, The 1924,D 19,26:2
Orestes 1926,Je 20,II,3:6
Coriolanus 1927,Je 18,8:3
Bingham, John
Home Fires 1923,Ag 21,12:1
Easy Come, Easy Go 1925,O 27,20:2
Bingham, Joseph
Bewitched 1924,O 2,26:3
Man in Evening Clothes, The 1924,D 6,13:4
Bingham, Kitty
Dear Old England 1930,Mr 26,24:6
Bingham, Le Roy
Comedy of Errors, The 1923,My 16,22:5
Bingham, Leslie
So That's That 1925,D 15,28:3
Spook House 1930,Je 4,33:3
Of Thee I Sing 1931,D 28,20:1
Merrily We Roll Along 1934,O 1,14:1
Flowers of the Forest 1935,Ap 9,25:2
Triumph 1935,O 15,18:5
First Lady 1935,N 27,17:4
Hedda Gabler 1936,N 17,34:4
Too Many Heroes 1937,N 16,26:2
White Steed, The 1939,Ja 11,16:2
Johnny Belinda 1940,S 19,26:2
Seventh Trumpet, The 1941,N 22,10:6
Patriots, The 1943,Ja 30,11:2
Patriots, The 1943,D 21,22:5
Bingham, Mary Alice
Firebird of Florence 1945,Mr 23,13:4
Three to Make Ready 1946,Mr 8,16:2
Bingham, Oliver H
Little Miss Charity 1920,S 3,6:3
Bingham, Paul
Emperor Jones, The 1936,Ag 11,24:6
Bingham, Susan Hulsman (Composer)
Mod Donna 1970,My 4,48:1
Mod Donna 1970,My 10,II,1:1
Bingo (Dog)
Valley Forge 1934,D 11,28:3
Binney, Constance
Sweet Little Devil 1924,Ja 22,15:4
Binney, Faire
He and She 1920,F 13,16:3
Teaser, The 1921,Jl 28,8:3
Binns, Edward
Command Decision 1947,O 2,30:2
Sundown Beach 1948,S 8,37:1
Detective Story 1949,Mr 24,34:2
Peer Gynt 1951,Ja 29,15:2

Binns, Edward—Cont
Caligula 1960,F 17,31:1
Caligula 1960,F 28,II,1:1
Harpers Ferry 1967,Je 6,52:2
House of Atreus, The; Agamemnon 1967,Jl 24,23:1
Visit, The 1967,S 13,41:1
Binyon, Laurence (Playwright)
Arthur 1923,Mr 18,VII,1:1
Binyon, S K
Sing High, Sing Low 1931,N 13,26:4
Binyon, Spencer
That Ferguson Family 1928,D 24,10:7
Birabeau, Andre (Playwright)
Petit Peche 1926,O 24,VIII,2:1
Eunuque, L' 1927,Ap 3,VIII,4:7
Mauvais Ange, Le 1927,Je 5,VII,2:1
Untitled-Play 1928,Je 17,VIII,1:4
Untitled-Play 1928,N 11,X,2:7
Dejeuner d'Amoureux 1929,My 5,IX,2:4
Folle de son Corps 1932,My 1,VIII,2:6
Ma Soeur de Luxe 1933,Je 4,IX,1:6
Dejeuner d'Amoureax, Un; Lovers Breakfast, A
1936,N 26,38:2
Chaleur du Sein, La 1938,Je 12,X,2:3
Dame Nature 1938,S 27,24:3
Little Dark Horse 1941,N 17,14:4
Souviens-Toi, Mon Amour 1954,N 28,II,3:1
Birbeck, Olga
Death Takes a Holiday 1929,D 27,26:4
Little Father of the Wilderness, The 1930,Je 3,27:1
Death Takes a Holiday 1931,F 17,29:1
Birch, Pat
West Side Story 1960,Ap 28,31:1
Fortuna 1962,Ja 4,26:1
Birch, Patricia (Director)
Up Eden 1968,N 27,42:1
Me Nobody Knows, The 1970,My 19,42:1
Me Nobody Knows, The 1970,My 31,II,1:6
Birch, Patricia (Miscellaneous)
You're a Good Man, Charlie Brown 1967,Mr 8,51:1
Fireworks; Football 1969,Je 12,51:1
Fireworks; Fireworks for a Hot Fourth
1969,Je 12,51:1
Fireworks; Report, The 1969,Je 12,51:1
Birch, Paul
Caine Mutiny Court-Martial, The 1953,O 14,35:1
Caine Mutiny Court-Martial, The 1954,Ja 21,27:2
Birch, Peter
New Moon, The 1942,Ag 19,14:2
Vagabond King, The 1943,Je 30,24:2
Dream With Music 1944,My 19,15:2
Carousel 1945,Ap 20,24:2
Gentlemen Prefer Blondes 1949,D 9,35:3
Birch, Reginald
Little Father of the Wilderness, The 1930,Je 3,27:1
Birch, Wyrley
Laff That Off 1925,N 3,34:2
Menace 1927,Mr 15,28:2
Silent House, The 1928,F 8,28:5
In Times Square 1931,N 24,29:3
Another Language 1932,Ap 26,25:3
Another Language 1933,My 9,20:2
Spring in Autumn 1933,O 25,22:5
Wednesday's Child 1934,Ja 17,23:2
Kill That Story 1934,Ag 30,22:2
Small Miracle 1934,S 27,24:3
Masque of the Kings, The 1937,F 9,19:4
Whiteoaks 1938,Mr 24,20:2
Arsenic and Old Lace 1941,Ja 11,13:2
All for All 1943,S 30,25:2
Chicken Every Sunday 1944,Ap 6,27:2
How I Wonder 1947,O 1,34:2
Desperate Hours, The 1955,F 11,20:2
Sixth Finger in a Five Finger Glove 1956,O 9,31:4
Birchby, Rosamund
Play's the Thing, The 1935,Jl 24,20:4
Birckhead, Sally
H M S Pinafore 1960,Ja 29,14:1
Utopia, Limited 1960,Ap 8,27:2
Yeomen of the Guard, The 1961,Ap 28,23:1
Mikado, The 1961,My 5,23:1
Grand Duke, The 1961,My 12,24:1
Princess Ida 1961,My 19,23:1
Iolanthe 1961,My 26,29:6
H M S Pinafore 1961,Je 9,29:5
Student Prince, The 1961,Jl 14,14:1
Merry Widow, The 1961,O 27,28:2
Gondoliers, The 1961,D 8,44:1
Bird, Charles E
Katy Did 1927,My 10,24:3
Sons o' Guns 1929,N 27,30:4
Bird, David
Lark, The 1955,My 13,21:2
Bird, Dorothy
Around the World 1946,Je 1,9:5
Park Avenue 1946,N 5,31:2
Sleepy Hollow 1948,Je 4,26:3
Bird, Edward
Babes in Toyland 1930,D 22,17:1
Mikado, The 1944,F 12,11:3
Bird, Howard
Chinese Nightingale, The 1934,O 6,20:4
Cradle Will Rock, The 1937,D 6,19:4
Cradle Will Rock, The 1938,Ja 4,19:3

Bird, John (Playwright)
Council of Love 1970,Ag 21,21:2
Council of Love 1970,S 12,32:2
Bird, Joseph
Skin of Our Teeth, The 1960,O 14,24:1
Moon in the Yellow River, The 1961,F 7,40:2
Go Show Me a Dragon 1961,O 28,18:1
Electra 1962,Mr 22,42:1
Right You Are (If You Think You Are)
1964,Mr 5,37:1
Tavern, The 1964,Mr 6,39:2
Scapin 1964,Mr 10,43:1
Lower Depths, The 1964,Mr 31,30:1
Man and Superman 1964,D 7,45:2
War and Peace 1965,Ja 12,32:1
Judith 1965,Mr 25,42:2
You Can't Take It With You 1965,N 24,32:1
School for Scandal, The 1966,N 22,33:2
Right You Are (If You Think You Are)
1966,N 23,34:2
Wild Duck, The 1967,Ja 12,49:1
War and Peace 1967,Mr 22,42:1
Pantagleize 1967,D 1,54:1
Show-Off, The 1967,D 6,40:2
Misanthrope, The 1968,O 10,59:1
Cock-A-Doodle Dandy 1969,Ja 21,40:1
Bird, Margaret
Martinique 1920,Ap 27,18:2
Bird, Norman
Time Remembered 1955,My 4,35:1
Bird, Richard
Havoc 1924,S 2,22:2
Havoc 1924,S 7,VII,1:1
Candida 1924,D 13,12:3
Candida 1924,D 21,VII,1:1
Fanatics, The 1927,N 8,32:4
Diversion 1928,Ja 6,26:3
Diversion 1928,Ja 12,25:1
March Hares 1928,Ap 3,32:6
Journey's End 1930,Ag 5,26:4
Journey's End 1930,Ag 24,VIII,1:1
Purity 1930,D 26,18:2
Frailties 1931,Ja 30,18:3
Dangerous Corner 1932,My 11,15:3
Whistling in the Dark 1933,D 6,29:3
It Happened to Adam 1934,N 10,18:6
Composite Man, The 1936,S 27,X,3:5
Love in a Mist 1941,N 30,IX,3:1
Bird, Richard (Director)
Women Aren't Angels 1941,Ap 27,IX,1:6
Bird, Richard (Playwright)
Marriage By Instalments 1923,Ap 8,VIII,1:7
Bird, Richard (Producer)
Wish You Were Here 1953,O 11,83:5
Bird, Robert Montgomery (Playwright)
Man Without Money, A 1929,N 3,27:4
Birdie Sisters (Costume Designer)
Gloria and Esperanza 1970,F 5,32:1
Birdwood, Judy (Costume Designer)
Cambridge Circus 1964,O 7,53:1
Birell, Tala
Order Please 1934,O 10,21:2
My Dear Children 1939,Mr 25,19:6
My Dear Children 1940,F 1,16:2
Birenbaum, Ada (Musical Director)
Thespis 1953,Ja 17,13:5
Birge, Walter
Hades, the Ladies 1934,Mr 29,25:3
Foemen of the Yard 1935,Ap 6,10:4
Birgel, John
Flair-Flair the Idol of Paree 1935,Mr 13,16:1
Birimisa, George
Sunset 1966,My 13,34:1
Birinski, Leo (Playwright)
Nowhere Bound 1935,Ja 23,20:2
Day Will Come, The 1944,S 8,17:2
Birkhead, Muriel
Most Happy Fella, The 1959,F 11,50:2
Birkmayer, Toni
Wake Up and Dream 1929,D 31,14:3
Wake Up and Dream 1930,Ja 12,9:1
Birman, Len
Tempest, The 1962,Je 22,14:1
Troilus and Cressida 1963,Je 19,40:2
Cyrano de Bergerac 1963,Je 20,30:1
Timon of Athens 1963,Jl 31,19:2
Richard II 1964,Je 17,47:1
King Lear 1964,Je 19,36:1
Birmingham, Alan
Will Shakespeare 1923,Ja 2,14:1
Sun-Up 1923,My 25,28:1
New Englander, The 1924,F 8,22:2
Saturday Night 1926,O 26,25:1
Three Sisters, The 1926,O 27,24:1
Locandiera, La; Mistress of the Inn, The
1926,N 23,26:1
Twelfth Night 1926,D 21,21:4
Inheritors 1927,Mr 8,23:1
Synthetic Sin 1927,O 11,26:2
Forbidden Roads 1928,Ap 17,26:4
Great Power, The 1928,S 12,25:1
Birmingham, George (Playwright)
Send for Dr O'Grady 1923,Jl 29,VI,1:6

General John Regan 1930,Ja 30,16:5
Birmingham, Michael (Director)
Far Away Horses 1933,Mr 22,21:6
Birmingham, Michael (Original Author)
Far Away Horses 1933,Mr 22,21:6
Birmingham, Virginia
Broadway Whirl, The 1921,Je 9,10:4
Birmingham Four
Deep Harlem 1929,Ja 8,35:2
Birnbaum, Bernard
Lady of the Lamp, The 1920,Ag 18,6:4
Birnbaum, Louis
Little Bandit 1935,Ap 19,24:2
Birnbaum, Martin
Untitled-Poetry Reading 1967,Jl 18,29:1
Birnbaum, Martin (Miscellaneous)
Untitled-Poetry Reading 1967,Jl 18,29:1
Birnbaum, Max
Once Over Lightly 1942,N 20,26:2
Birnbaum (Miscellaneous)
Who Fights This Battle? 1936,S 21,26:3
Birney, David
Comedy of Errors, The 1967,Je 15,58:4
King John 1967,Jl 14,19:1
Titus Andronicus 1967,Ag 10,43:2
Ceremony of Innocence, The 1968,Ja 2,33:1
Summertree 1968,Mr 4,29:1
Miser, The 1969,My 9,35:1
Crimes of Passion; Ruffian on the Stair, The
1969,O 27,54:1
Crimes of Passion; Erpingham Camp, The
1969,O 27,54:1
Crimes of Passion; Erpingham Camp, The; Ruffian
on the Stair, The 1969,N 9,II,1:1
Good Woman of Setzuan, The 1970,N 6,51:1
Good Woman of Setzuan, The 1970,N 15,II,1:5
Birney, Estelle
Magic Ring, The 1923,O 2,10:1
Birney, John (Mrs)
Untitled-Passion Play 1926,Mr 30,20:2
Birnkrant, Arthur (Playwright)
Davy Jones's Locker 1966,D 25,48:5
Birnkrant, Samuel (Playwright)
Whisper in God's Ear, A 1962,O 12,27:2
Biro, Barnet
Antony and Cleopatra 1947,N 27,49:2
Stockade 1954,F 5,14:2
My 3 Angels 1956,F 4,24:2
Biro, F
Aristocrats 1935,My 2,16:2
Biro, Lajos (Original Author)
Moon-Flower, The 1924,Mr 2,VIII,1:1
Biro, Lajos (Playwright)
Czarina, The 1922,F 1,22:1
Moon-Flower, The 1924,F 26,15:1
School For Slavery 1942,Mr 29,VIII,2:2
Biro, Lynn
New York Idea, The 1948,Ag 18,29:2
Birris, Paul
Searching for the Sun 1936,F 20,22:6
Birse, Dara
Any Day Now 1941,Je 10,28:2
Birse, Mme
Chauve-Souris 1922,Je 6,17:4
Chauve-Souris 1925,Ja 15,25:1
Chauve-Souris 1929,Ja 23,20:2
Birsky, Socrates (Choreographer)
Curtains Up! 1959,N 3,26:3
Bisch, Louis E (Playwright)
Complex, The 1925,Mr 4,17:2
Killers 1928,Mr 14,28:3
Bischoff, Edgar (Composer)
Overcoat, The 1960,S 7,45:1
Bisco, Diana
Six Characters in Search of an Author
1963,Mr 11,7:2
Biscot
Rejouissance, La 1929,F 24,IX,1:8
Bishop, Adelaide
Blossom Time 1943,S 6,21:2
Girl From Nantucket, The 1945,N 9,17:2
Old Maid and the Thief, The 1949,N 7,32:4
Fledermaus, Die 1954,My 20,38:5
Bishop, Andrew
Deep Harlem 1929,Ja 8,35:2
Bishop, Anne
South 1955,My 2,17:4
Bishop, Carole
Promises, Promises 1968,D 2,59:3
Bishop, D M
Paolo and Francesca 1929,Ap 2,28:2
Bishop, David (Director)
And People All Around 1968,F 12,46:1
Bishop, David (Miscellaneous)
Tiger Rag, The 1961,F 17,20:2
All Kinds of Giants 1961,D 19,40:1
Richard II 1962,Je 18,20:2
Henry IV, Part I 1962,Je 18,20:4
Shakespeare Revisited 1962,Jl 19,19:2
King Lear 1963,Je 10,37:1
Comedy of Errors, The 1963,Je 13,28:1
Henry V 1963,Je 14,37:1
Coriolanus 1965,Jl 15,23:1

Bishop, Don
My House Is Your House 1970,O 16,53:2
Bishop, Edward
Little Mary Sunshine 1962,My 18,35:8
Rehearsal, The 1963,S 24,45:2
Bishop, Gordon (Playwright)
Purple Canary, The 1963,Ap 23,31:1
Bishop, Isabel
Live Life Again 1945,O 1,14:7
O'Daniel 1947,F 25,32:2
Bishop, Jeff (Miscellaneous)
Goose, The 1960,Mr 16,44:1
Bishop, Jock
Wind in the Sails 1940,Ag 1,24:6
Bishop, Joe
Happiest Millionaire, The 1956,N 21,21:3
Bishop, John (Director)
Jo 1964,F 13,25:1
H M S Pinafore 1965,Ap 15,39:1
Up Eden 1968,N 27,42:1
Bishop, John (Miscellaneous)
Seven at Dawn, The 1961,Ap 18,43:1
Bishop, Kenyon
Spanish Love 1920,Ag 18,6:1
Bronx Express 1922,Ap 27,12:2
Bishop, Linda
Michael Todd's Peep Show 1950,Je 29,37:2
Bishop, Philip
Skirt, The 1921,N 8,28:1
Quarantine 1924,D 17,19:7
What's the Big Idea? 1926,Mr 24,20:3
Maid of All Work 1927,Ja 13,28:4
Last Torture, The 1927,Ja 13,28:4
Butterflies 1927,F 2,22:4
Mima 1928,D 13,24:2
Within the Gates 1934,O 23,23:1
Puritan, The 1936,Ja 24,14:3
Bishop, Raymond
Savage Rhythm 1932,Ja 1,30:4
Bridal Wise 1932,My 31,15:5
Bishop, Richard
Missouri Legend 1938,S 20,27:2
Key Largo 1939,N 28,30:2
Wind in the Sails 1940,Ag 1,24:6
I Remember Mama 1944,O 20,16:2
Happiest Years, The 1949,Ap 26,29:8
Music in the Air 1951,O 9,32:2
Damn Yankees 1955,My 6,17:1
Bishop, Richard S
One Good Year 1935,N 28,38:3
Farewell Summer 1937,Mr 30,20:2
One Thing After Another 1937,D 29,17:2
Where Do We Go From Here? 1938,N 16,26:2
International Incident, An 1940,Ap 3,18:2
Bishop, Ronald
Othello 1943,O 20,18:1
Othello 1945,My 23,25:4
Julius Caesar 1957,O 24,39:1
Playboy of the Western World, The 1958,My 9,19:2
King Lear 1959,Ja 3,11:2
Visit, The 1960,Mr 9,38:3
Donogoo 1961,Ja 19,25:3
Man and Superman 1964,D 7,45:2
War and Peace 1965,Ja 12,32:1
Judith 1965,Mr 25,42:2
Saint Joan 1968,Ja 5,42:1
Honor and Offer 1968,D 1,II,3:1
Tempest, The 1970,F 15,67:1
Bishop, Rummy
Susan Slept Here 1961,Jl 12,35:2
Bishop, Stuart (Director)
Candyapple, The 1970,N 24,33:1
Bishop, Stuart (Playwright)
She Shall Have Music 1959,Ja 23,18:4
Sweet Miani 1962,S 26,33:2
Bishop, Stuart (Producer)
She Shall Have Music 1959,Ja 23,18:4
Bishop, Stuart (Scenic Designer)
'Toinette 1961,N 21,46:1
Bishop, Ward
Design for Living 1933,Ja 3,19:5
Design for Living 1933,Ja 25,13:2
Bishop, William
Victoria Regina 1938,O 4,20:2
Bisland, Eddie
Peek-A-Boo 1921,My 17,20:3
Bisoglio, Val
Kiss Mama 1964,O 2,30:1
Wait Until Dark 1966,F 3,21:1
Bisoglio, Val (Director)
Bench, The 1968,Mr 5,35:2
Bispham, William
Mighty Nimrod, The 1931,My 13,23:1
Bissainthe, Toto
Bonnes, Les 1963,S 4,34:3
Bissel, Richard (Original Author)
Pajama Game, The 1954,My 14,20:2
Bissell, Gene P (Composer)
Leonard Sillman's New Faces of 1968
1968,My 3,43:1
Bissell, Gene P (Lyricist)
Leonard Sillman's New Faces of 1968
1968,My 3,43:1

Bissell, Lea
Rivals, The 1969,O 18,37:1
Bissell, Marian (Original Author)
Say Darling 1958,Ap 4,17:1
Bissell, Marian (Playwright)
Say Darling 1959,F 26,38:2
Bissell, Richard (Mrs) (Playwright)
Say Darling 1958,Ap 13,II,1:1
Bissell, Richard (Original Author)
Pajama Game, The 1954,My 15,12:1
Pajama Game, The 1954,My 30,II,1:1
Pajama Game, The 1957,My 16,27:1
Pajama Game, The 1957,My 26,II,1:1
Say Darling 1958,Ap 13,II,1:1
Say Darling 1959,F 26,38:2
Bissell, Richard (Playwright)
Pajama Game, The 1954,My 14,20:2
Pajama Game, The 1954,My 15,12:1
Pajama Game, The 1957,My 16,27:1
Pajama Game, The 1957,My 26,II,1:1
Say Darling 1958,Ap 4,17:1
Say Darling 1958,Ap 13,II,1:1
Say Darling 1959,F 26,38:2
Bissell, Tallman
Any Moment Now 1939,N 25,13:6
Bissell, Tallman (Composer)
Once Over Lightly 1938,D 10,13:4
Bissell, Tallman (Lyricist)
Once Over Lightly 1938,D 10,13:4
Bissell, Tommi
Marching Song 1937,F 18,18:2
To Quito and Back 1937,O 7,30:4
Bissell, Whitner
Alice in Wonderland 1932,D 12,18:3
Wrong Number 1934,Mr 14,23:6
American Holiday 1936,F 22,13:3
Shining Hour, The 1936,Ag 12,15:3
Octoroon, The 1936,S 1,24:2
Hamlet 1936,O 9,30:2
Star-Wagon, The 1937,S 30,18:5
As You Like It 1937,N 1,25:2
American Way, The 1939,Ja 23,9:2
Two on an Island 1940,Ja 23,17:2
Cue for Passion 1940,D 20,33:4
Gabrielle 1941,Mr 26,26:2
Cafe Crown 1942,Ja 24,12:5
Sweet Charity 1942,D 29,26:4
Winged Victory 1943,N 22,24:1
Yellow Jack 1944,Ap 7,23:3
Bissinger, Tom (Director)
Young Master Dante, The 1968,D 31,19:1
Acquisition, The 1968,D 31,19:1
Bisson
Bourgeois Gentilhomme, Le 1955,O 26,26:1
Bisson, Alexandre (Original Author)
Night Boat, The 1920,F 3,18:1
Madame X 1927,Jl 7,29:3
Bitar, Virginia
Yeomen of the Guard, The 1964,Mr 19,29:2
Patience 1964,Mr 26,42:1
Pirates of Penzance, The 1965,Ap 21,50:6
Bitoaff, George
Hairy Ape, The 1929,S 23,27:2
Bitter, Marietto
If 1927,O 26,26:2
Bitters, Adeline
Career 1943,O 29,22:6
Bittner, Jack
King Lear 1940,D 16,27:2
Days of Our Youth, The 1941,N 29,15:2
Criminals, The 1941,D 22,24:3
Nathan the Wise 1942,Ap 4,18:4
War and Peace 1942,My 22,26:3
Land of Fame 1943,S 22,31:5
Petrified Forest, The 1943,N 2,30:6
Nathan the Wise 1944,F 22,26:3
Bobino 1944,Ap 7,23:4
Rip Van Winkle 1947,Jl 16,28:2
All the King's Men 1950,Jl 19,25:6
Room Service 1953,Ap 7,34:1
Troilus and Cressida 1953,Ag 19,25:2
Coriolanus 1953,Ag 21,9:2
Richard III 1953,D 10,65:2
Witness for the Prosecution 1954,D 17,35:2
Witness for the Prosecution 1954,D 26,II,1:1
Tiger at the Gates 1955,O 4,40:1
Hidden River, The 1957,Ja 24,32:1
Othello 1957,Je 24,19:2
Merchant of Venice, The 1957,Jl 11,19:5
Much Ado About Nothing 1957,Ag 8,15:2
Hamlet 1958,Je 21,11:1
Midsummer Night's Dream, A 1958,Je 23,19:1
Winter's Tale, The 1958,Jl 21,17:4
Ivanov 1958,O 8,42:1
Ivanov 1958,O 19,II,1:1
Rashomon 1959,Ja 28,36:2
Romeo and Juliet 1959,Je 15,31:1
Romeo and Juliet 1959,Je 21,II,1:1
Merry Wives of Windsor, The 1959,Jl 9,23:2
All's Well That Ends Well 1959,Ag 3,20:4
Sap of Life, The 1961,O 3,44:1
First Love 1961,D 26,20:2
Venus at Large 1962,Ap 13,30:1

Abe Lincoln in Illinois 1963,Ja 23,5:2
Nobody Loves an Albatross 1963,D 20,20:1
Nobody Loves an Albatross 1964,Ja 5,II,1:1
Yeomen of the Guard, The 1964,Ag 3,16:1
Porgy and Bess 1965,Mr 6,17:1
Pirates of Penzance, The 1968,Ap 26,32:1
Yeomen of the Guard, The 1968,My 9,53:1
Bittner, Julius (Composer)
Walzer aus Wien 1930,N 25,30:3
Bixby, Bill
Under the Yum-Yum Tree 1964,My 29,18:1
Paisley Convertible, The 1967,F 13,42:1
Bixby, Carl
Little Theatre Tournament; Prison Bars
1928,My 10,31:1
Bixby, Carl (Playwright)
Little Theatre Tournament; Prison Bars
1928,My 10,31:1
Bixby, Frank
Respect for Riches, The 1920,My 12,9:1
Bad Man, The 1920,Ag 31,7:1
Bizet, Georges (Composer)
Carmen Jones 1943,D 3,26:2
Carmen Jones 1943,D 12,II,3:1
Carmen Jones 1943,D 19,II,9:1
Carmen Jones 1945,My 3,26:5
Carmen Jones 1946,Ap 8,32:2
Carmen Jones 1951,S 22,8:6
Carmen Jones 1956,Je 1,28:2
Carmen Jones 1959,Ag 18,25:1
Bjorkman, Edwin (Translator)
Spook Sonata, The 1924,Ja 7,23:3
Dream Play 1926,Ja 21,18:2
Bridal Crown, The 1938,F 7,11:2
Bjornson (Playwright)
Mary Stuart in Scotland 1960,S 1,31:1
Bjoze, Judy
Cyanamide 1954,Mr 26,17:6
Blacam, Aodh de (Translator)
Saint in a Hurry, A 1935,D 29,IX,2:1
Black, Arnold (Composer)
Ulysses in Nighttown 1958,Je 6,30:1
Thracian Horses, The 1961,S 28,58:2
French Way, The; Deceased, The 1962,Mr 21,36:2
French Way, The; Edward and Agrippina
1962,Mr 21,36:2
French Way, The; Grand Vizier, The
1962,Mr 21,36:2
Black, Arnold (Musical Director)
Exception and the Rule, The 1965,My 21,19:1
Black, Betty
Right You Are (If You Think You Are)
1950,Je 29,37:2
Black, Clarence
Petticoat Fever 1935,Je 25,14:5
Black, David (Miscellaneous)
Look: We've Come Through 1961,O 26,40:1
Knack, The 1964,My 28,42:2
Until the Monkey Comes 1966,Je 21,38:1
Black, David (Producer)
Aspern Papers, The 1962,F 8,26:1
Semi-Detached 1963,O 8,49:1
Cambridge Circus 1964,O 7,53:1
Ready When You Are, C. B.! 1964,D 8,55:1
Impossible Years, The 1965,O 14,55:1
Those That Play the Clowns 1966,N 25,48:1
Natural Look, The 1967,Mr 13,45:2
To Clothe the Naked 1967,Ap 28,30:1
George M! 1968,Ap 11,48:1
Fire! 1969,Ja 29,26:1
Salvation 1969,S 25,55:1
Paris Is Out! 1970,F 3,35:1
Black, Donald
Nightingale, The 1927,Ja 4,20:4
Sunny Days 1928,F 9,29:1
Falstaff 1928,D 26,14:2
Near to the Stars 1932,F 23,23:2
Peace on Earth 1933,N 30,39:2
Knock on Wood 1935,My 29,16:2
Jumbo 1935,N 18,20:2
Ghost of Yankee Doodle, The 1937,N 23,26:3
Escape This Night 1938,Ap 23,18:1
Knickerbocker Holiday 1938,O 20,26:2
Black, Doris
Garden of Time 1945,Mr 10,13:7
Black, Dorothy
Brontes, The 1933,My 7,IX,1:4
Black, Edward (Musical Director)
Treasure Island 1938,My 15,II,2:3
Black, Frank (Dr) (Composer)
Duchess Misbehaves, The 1946,F 14,32:2
Black, George (Producer)
Vaudeville (Palladium) 1931,My 12,28:4
Black, Gerry
Hamlet 1967,D 27,45:1
Hamlet 1968,Jl 4,15:1
King Lear 1968,N 8,43:1
Cry of Players, A 1968,N 15,40:1
Five on the Black Hand Side 1970,Ja 2,32:2
Black, Jack (Original Author)
Jamboree 1932,N 25,18:4
Black, Jack (Playwright)
Jamboree 1932,N 25,18:4

Black, Jay
Pygmalion 1945,D 27,16:1
Black, Jean Ferguson (Playwright)
Thunder on the Left 1933,N 1,25:2
Penny Wise 1935,Jl 2,24:2
Penny Wise 1937,Ap 20,28:6
Black, Jimmy Clark
Absolutely Freeee 1967,My 25,58:1
Black, John
Last Days of Lincoln, The 1961,O 19,39:7
Black, Jonathan (Director)
To Clothe the Naked 1967,Ap 28,30:1
Black, Karen
We're Civilized? 1962,N 9,30:1
Uncommon Denominator, The 1963,My 8,35:2
Twelfth Night 1963,O 9,47:1
Playroom, The 1965,D 6,49:1
Happily Never After 1966,Mr 11,37:1
Keep It in the Family 1967,S 28,59:1
Black, Karen (Composer)
Uncommon Denominator, The 1963,My 8,35:2
Black, Kitty (Playwright)
Legend of Lovers 1951,D 27,17:1
Rehearsal, The 1963,S 24,45:2
Rehearsal, The 1963,O 20,II,1:1
Black, Kitty (Translator)
Legend of Lovers 1959,O 28,40:3
Black, Leonard A
Injury Sustained 1940,O 24,30:3
When Differences Disappear 1941,Je 3,17:4
Black, Leonard A (Director)
When Differences Disappear 1941,Je 3,17:4
Black, Leonard A (Playwright)
When Differences Disappear 1941,Je 3,17:4
Black, Leonard A (Producer)
When Differences Disappear 1941,Je 3,17:4
Black, Malcolm (Director)
Thracian Horses, The 1961,S 28,58:2
Curate's Play, The 1961,D 18,41:3
Pimpernel! 1964,Ja 7,26:6
Black, Malcolm (Miscellaneous)
Salad Days 1958,N 11,24:1
Black, Mary
Unto Such Glory 1937,My 7,28:2
Black, Maurice
Hitchy-Koo, 1920 1920,O 20,11:3
Black, Phil
Old Bucks and New Wings 1962,N 6,39:4
Black, Robert
Wilson in the Promise Land 1970,Ja 11,78:1
Wilson in the Promise Land 1970,My 27,41:1
Black, Sadie
Rainbow 1928,N 22,25:1
Black, Sandy (Miscellaneous)
Comedy of Errors, The 1964,My 21,43:1
Black, Sol
I'd Rather Be Right 1937,N 3,28:2
Black, Stuart
Macbeth 1921,F 18,16:1
Black, Terence
Hair 1970,Ja 13,39:1
Black, Valerie
Big White Fog 1940,O 23,26:2
Our Lan' 1947,Ap 19,11:2
Our Lan' 1947,S 29,16:5
Black, Walter
Command Decision 1947,O 2,30:2
Buttrio Square 1952,O 15,40:2
Black, William
Company's Coming! 1931,Ap 21,35:5
Black Rhythm Swingsters
Black Rhythm 1936,D 21,19:2
Blackburn, Arline
Seventeen 1924,Ap 12,18:2
Close Harmony 1924,D 2,23:1
Bride of the Lamb 1926,Mr 31,20:3
Bride of the Lamb 1926,Ap 4,VIII,1:1
Ballyhoo 1927,Ja 5,18:1
Blackburn, Audrey
Simpleton of the Unexpected Isles, The
1954,Ja 12,19:1
Blackburn, Clarice
Great Big Doorstep, The 1950,Mr 18,8:6
Grass Harp, The 1953,Ap 28,32:2
Grass Harp, The 1953,My 24,II,1:1
American Gothic 1953,N 11,35:6
Desk Set, The 1955,O 25,36:7
Infernal Machine, The 1958,F 4,33:1
Juno 1959,Mr 10,41:1
Juno 1959,Mr 15,II,1:1
Miracle Worker, The 1961,F 7,40:2
Queen and the Rebels, The 1965,F 26,16:1
Good Day 1965,O 19,51:1
Blackburn, Dorothy
New Brooms 1924,N 18,23:5
Sweet Land of Liberty 1929,S 24,29:2
Spook House 1930,Je 4,33:3
Damn Deborah 1937,Ag 17,23:1
Pick-Up Girl 1944,My 4,25:2
High Named Today 1954,D 11,11:2
Desk Set, The 1955,O 25,36:7
Auntie Mame 1956,N 1,47:2
Desert Incident, A 1959,Mr 25,40:1

Blackburn, Dorothy—Cont
Passage to India, A 1962,F 1,23:1
Loves of Cass McGuire, The 1966,O 7,36:1
Harvey 1970,F 25,41:1
Blackburn, Fayne
Villa of Madame Vidac, The 1959,O 1,40:1
Once for the Asking 1963,N 21,42:2
Persecution and Assassination of Marat As
   Performed by the Inmates of the Asylum of
   Charenton Under the Direction of the Marquis de
   Sade, The 1967,Ja 4,34:1
Bench, The 1968,Mr 5,35:2
Blackburn, Freddie (Miscellaneous)
Shunned 1960,D 21,39:1
Blackburn, Harrison
Kilpatrick's Old-Time Minstrels 1930,Ap 21,20:2
Sweet Chariot 1930,O 24,30:2
Sugar Hill 1931,D 26,15:2
Blackburn, Maurice (Composer)
Ti-Coq 1951,F 10,10:2
Blackburn, Ramon
200 Were Chosen 1936,N 21,21:1
As You Like It 1937,N 1,25:2
Stop-Over 1938,Ja 12,16:5
Blackburn, Robert
King Lear 1956,Ja 13,17:1
Misanthrope, The 1956,N 13,44:1
Volpone 1957,Ja 8,27:1
Romeo and Juliet 1957,Je 28,30:2
Two Gentlemen of Verona 1957,Jl 23,21:5
Richard III 1957,N 26,41:1
As You Like It 1958,Ja 21,33:6
King Lear 1959,Ja 3,11:2
Beaux' Stratagem, The 1959,F 25,35:4
Henry IV 1960,Mr 2,42:1
Henry IV 1960,Ap 19,41:1
She Stoops to Conquer 1960,N 2,42:5
Plough and the Stars, The 1960,D 7,56:2
Octoroon, The 1961,Ja 28,13:1
Hamlet 1961,Mr 17,17:1
Black Monday 1962,Mr 7,29:1
All the King's Men 1963,Jl 12,12:1
Blackburn, Robert (Director)
All the King's Men 1963,Jl 12,12:1
Blackburn, Royce
200 Were Chosen 1936,N 21,21:1
As You Like It 1937,N 1,25:2
Everywhere I Roam 1938,D 30,10:4
Blackburn, Ruby
One Heluva Night 1924,Je 5,18:1
Decision 1929,My 28,37:3
Blackburn, Tom
Post Road 1949,Ap 28,27:3
Blackburn Twins
Sons o' Fun 1941,D 2,28:2
Blackburne, Jean (Costume Designer)
Ledge, A 1929,N 19,26:3
Blackburne, Luise
Vaudeville (Palace) 1926,O 26,24:2
Blackey, Donald
Consul, The 1950,Mr 16,41:1
Carousel 1954,Je 3,32:2
Blackman, Beatrice (Playwright)
Terrible Turk, The 1934,F 25,IX,1:6
Blackman, George
Assorted Nuts 1940,Ap 7,I,44:6
One on the House 1941,Mr 30,I,47:3
Blackman, Honor
Twist of Sand, A 1969,F 22,36:1
Blackman, Jack (Lighting Director)
If Five Years Pass 1962,My 11,37:1
One-Woman Show, A 1962,My 22,31:1
Strong Breed, The 1967,N 10,60:1
Trials of Brother Jero, The 1967,N 10,60:1
Another City, Another Land 1968,O 9,42:1
Just for Love 1968,O 18,40:1
Spitting Image 1969,Mr 3,28:1
Lyle 1970,Mr 21,16:2
Blackman, Jack (Scenic Designer)
Kataki 1959,D 16,55:1
If Five Years Pass 1962,My 11,37:1
Sign in Sidney Brustein's Window, The
   1964,O 16,32:1
Postmark Zero 1965,N 2,28:1
Strong Breed, The 1967,N 10,60:1
Trials of Brother Jero, The 1967,N 10,60:1
Another City, Another Land 1968,O 9,42:1
Just for Love 1968,O 18,40:1
Lyle 1970,Mr 21,16:2
Blackman, Martha
Play of Daniel, The 1960,D 27,23:6
Elizabethans, The 1962,Ja 22,19:1
Blackmar, Beatrice (Playwright)
Man's Estate 1929,Ap 2,28:2
Blackmarr, Richard
Good Woman of Setzuan, The 1956,D 19,41:2
Blackmer, Sidney
Trimmed in Scarlet 1920,F 3,18:1
Not So Long Ago 1920,My 5,14:1
Not So Long Ago 1920,Ag 29,VI,1:3
Robbery, The 1921,Mr 1,18:1
Mountain Man, The 1921,D 13,24:2
Love Child, The 1922,N 15,22:1
Rivals, The 1923,My 9,14:2

Scaramouche 1923,O 25,14:2
Moon-Flower, The 1924,Ja 27,VII,2:7
Moon-Flower, The 1924,F 26,15:1
Moon-Flower, The 1924,Mr 2,VIII,1:1
Blue Bandanna, The 1924,Je 24,18:4
Quarantine 1924,N 23,VIII,2:4
Quarantine 1924,D 17,19:7
Carolinian, The 1925,N 3,34:2
Love in a Mist 1926,Ap 13,28:3
Springboard, The 1927,O 13,23:1
Vaudeville (Palace) 1928,My 8,25:2
Mima 1928,D 13,24:2
Social Register, The 1931,O 4,VIII,2:3
Social Register, The 1931,N 10,28:2
Stop-Over 1938,Ja 12,16:5
Pretty Little Parlor 1944,Ap 18,24:8
Round Trip 1945,My 30,16:4
Wonderful Journey 1946,D 26,30:2
Portrait in Black 1947,My 15,30:2
Come Back, Little Sheba 1950,F 16,28:5
Come Back, Little Sheba 1950,F 26,II,1:1
Come Back, Little Sheba 1950,My 14,II,1:1
Brass Ring, The 1952,Ap 11,19:2
Sweet Bird of Youth 1959,Mr 11,39:2
Sweet Bird of Youth 1959,Mr 22,II,1:1
Case of Libel, A 1963,O 11,43:2
Blackstone, Ann
Russell Patterson's Sketch-Book 1960,F 8,35:1
Blackstone, Marvin
Double Dummy 1936,N 12,30:1
Blackstone, Milton (Producer)
Eddie Fisher at the Winter Garden 1962,O 3,47:1
Blackstone, Nan
Nine Fifteen Revue, The 1930,F 12,26:2
Garrick Gaieties 1930,Je 5,29:2
Blackton, Jack
Put It in Writing 1963,My 14,31:1
Blackton, Jay (Composer)
Chocolate Soldier, The 1947,Mr 13,34:2
Blackton, Jay (Miscellaneous)
Redhead 1959,F 6,21:1
Blackton, Jay (Musical Director)
Annie Get Your Gun 1946,My 17,14:2
Chocolate Soldier, The 1947,Mr 13,34:2
Promised Valley 1947,Jl 23,18:3
Inside U S A 1948,My 1,19:2
Miss Liberty 1949,Je 14,26:6
Miss Liberty 1949,Jl 16,6:5
Call Me Madam 1950,O 13,25:1
Tree Grows in Brooklyn, A 1951,Ap 20,24:3
Wish You Were Here 1952,Je 26,26:6
By the Beautiful Sea 1954,Ap 9,20:1
New Faces of 1956 1956,Je 15,32:1
Happy Hunting 1956,D 7,30:1
Oh Captain! 1958,F 5,21:2
Redhead 1959,F 6,21:1
Christine 1960,Ap 29,27:1
Pal Joey 1961,Je 1,32:1
Let It Ride 1961,O 13,27:4
Fiorello! 1962,Je 14,24:1
Mr President 1962,O 22,34:2
Girl Who Came to Supper, The 1963,D 9,49:1
Hello, Dolly! 1965,O 10,3:3
Time for Singing, A 1966,My 23,48:2
Sherry! 1967,Mr 29,39:1
George M! 1968,Ap 11,48:1
Oklahoma! 1969,Je 24,37:1
Two by Two 1970,N 11,37:1
Blackton, C Thomas
Incident at Vichy 1964,D 4,44:1
Blackwell, Carlyle
Play's the Thing, The 1935,Jl 24,20:4
Hairpin Harmony 1943,O 2,18:5
Blackwell, Charles
Fanny 1954,N 21,II,1:1
Blackwell, Charles (Miscellaneous)
Carnival! 1961,Ap 14,22:2
Clandestine on the Morning Line 1961,O 31,28:1
Rattle of a Simple Man 1963,Ap 18,39:1
How Now, Dow Jones 1967,D 8,53:1
Seven Descents of Myrtle, The 1968,Mr 28,54:1
Promises, Promises 1968,D 2,59:3
Blackwell, Donald
Meet the Prince 1929,F 26,30:5
Ghost Parade, The 1929,O 31,28:4
Infinite Shoeblack, The 1930,F 18,28:1
Puppet Show 1930,O 29,26:5
First Night 1930,N 27,32:3
If Love Were All 1931,N 14,14:5
Society Girl 1931,D 31,16:1
Blackwell, Donald (Director)
Going Gay 1933,Ag 4,18:5
Night in the House 1935,N 8,19:5
Our Betters 1937,Jl 22,16:2
Run Sheep Run 1938,N 4,26:2
Willow and I, The 1942,D 11,32:2
Blackwell, Donald (Original Author)
Nine Pine Street 1933,Ap 28,15:5
Blackwell, Donald (Playwright)
Going Gay 1933,Ag 4,18:5
Distant Shore, The 1935,F 22,26:2
All This While 1935,Jl 30,17:2
Illustrators' Show, The 1936,Ja 23,25:3

Blackwell, Donald (Producer)
Run Sheep Run 1938,N 4,26:2
Little Dark Horse 1941,N 17,14:4
Willow and I, The 1942,D 11,32:2
Blackwell, Earl (Playwright)
Aries Is Rising 1939,N 22,16:5
Blackwell, George
Guys and Dolls 1959,Jl 22,22:2
Happy Town 1959,O 8,49:2
Bye Bye Birdie 1960,Ap 15,13:4
Her First Roman 1968,O 21,53:3
Blackwell, Vera (Translator)
Memorandum, The 1968,My 6,55:1
Increased Difficulty of Concentration, The
   1969,D 5,48:1
Blackwood, George
Glory Hallelujah 1926,Ap 7,26:2
Witch, The 1926,N 19,22:5
Doctor X 1931,F 10,25:1
So Many Paths 1934,D 7,26:5
Reprise 1935,My 2,16:2
Royal Family, The 1935,Je 25,14:5
Front Page, The 1935,Jl 9,24:4
Patsy, The 1935,Jl 16,24:1
Post Road 1935,Jl 23,24:3
Caste 1935,Ag 13,20:3
Elizabeth Sleeps Out 1935,Ag 27,23:4
Personal Appearance 1936,Je 16,23:4
Personal Appearance 1936,Je 23,27:3
Eternal Cage 1945,Mr 22,19:7
Blackwood, Pat
Poupees de Paris, Les 1962,D 13,8:2
Poupees de Paris, Les 1964,My 16,11:1
Bladd, Marilyn
Show Boat 1954,My 6,44:1
Carousel 1954,Je 3,32:2
Blades, Edwina
It Happens on Ice 1940,O 11,24:3
It Happens on Ice 1941,Ap 5,13:2
It Happens on Ice 1941,Ag 31,IX,1:1
Blagden, Frances M
Variations of 1940 1940,Ja 29,12:1
Blagden, Minnie
White Assegai, The 1930,Ja 22,21:1
Ugly Duchess, The 1930,Je 1,VIII,2:8
Blain, Gerard
Shock Troops 1969,F 22,36:1
Blaine, Bruce
Front Page, The 1968,O 20,85:5
Front Page, The 1969,My 12,54:2
Charley's Aunt 1970,Jl 6,38:1
Blaine, Bruce (Miscellaneous)
Beg, Borrow or Steal 1960,F 11,39:4
Blaine, Edward
Mimie Scheller 1936,O 1,28:4
Blaine, Howard
Louisiana Lady 1947,Je 3,35:2
Cradle Will Rock, The 1947,D 27,11:2
Blaine, Joan
Mystery Square 1929,Ap 5,28:3
Ghost Parade, The 1929,O 31,28:4
Blaine, Laine
Bye Bye Bonnie 1927,Ja 14,15:3
Blaine, Mart O'Brien
Embezzled Heaven 1944,N 1,20:2
Blaine, Martin
Summer Night 1939,N 3,17:1
Man Who Killed Lincoln, The 1940,Ja 18,26:4
Morning Star 1940,Ap 17,26:4
Listen Professor! 1943,D 23,22:1
Blaine, Martin (Producer)
It's About Time 1942,Mr 31,28:3
Blaine, Richard
Bare Facts 1927,Ag 17,27:5
Blaine, Terry
Sitting Pretty 1924,Ap 9,24:2
Blaine, Vivian
Guys and Dolls 1950,N 25,11:2
Guys and Dolls 1950,D 3,II,1:1
Guys and Dolls 1953,My 29,17:5
Guys and Dolls 1953,Je 7,II,1:3
Say Darling 1958,Ap 4,17:1
Say Darling 1958,Ap 13,II,1:1
Enter Laughing 1963,Mr 15,8:1
Enter Laughing 1963,Je 16,II,1:1
Guys and Dolls 1966,Je 9,55:2
Blair, Anthony
Rope 1928,F 23,18:3
Up and Up, The 1930,S 9,25:2
Mr Papavert 1932,Ja 23,18:6
Threepenny Opera, The 1933,Ap 14,22:4
Ghost Writer, The 1933,Je 20,22:4
Locked Room, The 1933,D 26,18:5
Mahogany Hall 1934,Ja 18,18:5
If a Body 1935,My 1,25:3
Winterset 1935,S 26,19:2
Seen But Not Heard 1936,S 18,19:2
Eternal Road, The 1937,Ja 8,14:2
Father Malachy's Miracle 1937,N 18,26:4
Christmas Eve 1939,D 28,17:2
Barber Had Two Sons, The 1943,F 2,22:2
Early to Bed 1943,Je 18,16:2
Place of Our Own, A 1945,Ap 3,23:7

Blair, Barbara
Vaudeville (Palace) 1929,Je 10,22:6
Vaudeville (Palace) 1931,Ja 19,25:3
Scandals 1931,Ag 11,28:4
Scandals 1931,Ag 16,VIII,1:1
George White's Scandals 1931,S 15,30:1
Blair, Betsy
Beautiful People, The 1941,Ap 22,27:2
Richard II 1951,Ja 25,21:2
Face of a Hero 1960,O 21,29:5
Blair, Don
Priest in the Cellar, The 1969,F 19,39:1
Blair, Doris
Maya 1953,Je 10,35:1
Blair, Eugenie
Poor Little Ritz Girl 1920,Jl 29,7:1
Outrageous Mrs Palmer, The 1920,O 13,18:1
True to Form 1921,S 13,12:1
Anna Christie 1921,N 3,22:1
Anna Christie 1922,Ja 15,III,3:1
Blair, Gertrude
Phoebe of Quality Street 1921,My 10,20:1
Blair, Helen
Martinique 1920,Ap 27,18:2
What Do We Know 1927,D 24,8:1
Wild Waves 1932,F 20,11:4
Blair, Irene
Now-A-Days 1929,Ag 6,29:3
Breadwinner, The 1931,S 23,19:4
Blair, Jack
New Faces of 1936 1936,My 20,24:5
Who's Who 1938,Mr 2,16:2
Night of Love 1941,Ja 8,14:2
Show Boat 1954,O 29,28:4
Blair, Janet
South Pacific 1950,Ap 26,36:5
Girl Can Tell, A 1953,O 30,28:2
Bells Are Ringing 1957,N 15,37:1
Blair, Jimmy
It's About Time 1942,Mr 31,28:3
Blair, Joan
Playing the Game 1927,D 20,32:5
57 Bowery 1928,Ja 27,14:3
Flight 1929,F 19,22:3
Made in France 1930,N 12,21:1
Gods We Make, The 1934,Ja 4,16:4
Escape Me Never! 1935,Ja 22,22:2
Soliloquy 1938,N 29,26:4
Blair, John
He Who Gets Slapped 1922,Ja 10,15:1
Outsider, The 1924,Mr 4,16:4
Divine Drudge 1933,O 27,22:3
Three Wise Fools 1936,Mr 2,12:2
Blair, June
New Faces of 1936 1936,My 20,24:5
Who's Who 1938,Mr 2,16:2
Blair, Marjorie
Window Shopping 1938,D 24,13:2
Blair, Mary
Power of Darkness, The 1920,Ja 22,22:1
Diff'rent 1920,D 29,8:1
Hairy Ape, The 1922,Mr 10,18:2
Shoot 1922,Je 8,14:2
Manhattan 1922,Ag 16,7:5
World We Live In, The 1922,N 1,16:1
Dragon, The 1922,D 27,12:1
Spook Sonata, The 1924,Ja 7,23:3
Fashion 1924,F 5,21:2
All God's Chillun Got Wings 1924,My 16,22:3
All God's Chillun Got Wings 1924,Ag 19,9:1
All God's Chillun Got Wings 1924,Ag 24,VII,1:1
Crime in the Whistler Room, The 1924,O 10,22:2
Patience 1924,D 30,15:1
Diff'rent 1925,F 11,19:3
Diff'rent 1925,Mr 1,VII,1:1
Dope 1926,Ja 4,16:3
East Lynne 1926,Mr 11,18:4
Beyond Evil 1926,Je 8,23:2
Claw, The 1927,Ja 13,28:4
Florentine Tragedy, A 1927,F 2,22:4
Maker of Images, The 1927,Mr 5,12:2
Casualties 1927,Mr 5,12:2
Marco Millions 1928,Ja 10,28:2
Before Breakfast 1929,Mr 6,33:1
Lysistrata 1930,Ap 29,30:5
Lysistrata 1930,Je 1,VIII,1:1
American Dream; 1933 1933,F 22,24:5
Blair, Maud
Excess Baggage 1927,D 27,24:2
Blair, Michael
Earth Journey 1944,Ap 28,24:2
Lute Song 1946,F 7,29:2
Blair, O'Donnell
Laffing Room Only 1944,D 25,15:4
Blair, Pauline
Gay Paree 1925,Ag 19,14:3
Bunk of 1926 1926,F 17,12:3
Bunk of 1926 1926,Ap 23,25:2
Blair, Richard
Make a Million 1958,O 24,39:2
Dr Willy Nilly 1959,Je 5,18:2
Blair, Tony
Pardon My English 1933,Ja 21,11:4

Blair, Virginia
Pirates of Penzance, The 1942,F 20,20:2
Blair, William W (Director)
Short Cut, The 1930,Ja 28,28:2
Blaire, Laine
Sweetheart Time 1926,Ja 20,23:2
Merry World, The 1926,Je 9,18:3
Silver Swan, The 1929,N 28,34:5
Top Speed 1929,D 26,20:1
Well of Romance, The 1930,N 8,21:2
Simple Simon 1931,Mr 10,23:2
Blaisdell, Frances (Miscellaneous)
I Know at the Door 1957,S 30,27:2
Blaisdell, Nesbitt
Metamorphosis 1957,F 20,38:1
Blaisdell, William
Drifting 1922,Ja 3,20:3
Blake, Alma
Big Mogul, The 1925,My 12,26:3
Jay Walker, The 1926,F 9,23:1
Blake, Arthur
Measure for Measure 1967,F 15,37:1
Hamlet 1967,F 17,44:1
Romeo and Juliet 1967,F 22,18:1
Blake, Barry
Mid-Summer 1953,Ja 22,19:1
Blake, Beulah
Bitter Sweet 1934,My 8,28:4
Forbidden Melody 1936,N 3,33:1
Blake, Bobby
Hollywood Ice Revue 1954,Ja 15,16:2
Hollywood Ice Revue 1955 1955,Ja 14,16:1
Blake, Carter
Page Miss Glory 1934,N 28,24:2
Schoolhouse on the Lot 1938,Mr 23,18:4
Mr and Mrs North 1941,Ja 13,11:2
Blake, Charles
Tom Sawyer - Ballad of the Mississippi
1947,D 27,11:3
Blake, Cynthia
Prisoner, The 1927,D 30,22:2
Killers 1928,Mr 14,28:3
Merchant of Venice, The 1931,N 9,22:2
He Who Gets Slapped 1946,Mr 21,31:4
Blake, Doris
Helen Goes to Troy 1944,Ap 25,17:2
Firebird of Florence 1945,Mr 23,13:4
Blake, Eubie
Chocolate Dandies, The 1924,S 2,22:2
Will Morrissey's Folies Bergere Revue
1930,Ap 16,26:6
Shuffle Along of 1933 1932,D 27,11:3
Shuffle Along 1952,My 9,20:5
Blake, Eubie (Composer)
Shuffle Along 1921,My 23,16:2
Chocolate Dandies, The 1924,S 2,22:2
Will Morrissey's Folies Bergere Revue
1930,Ap 16,26:6
Lew Leslie's Blackbirds of 1930 1930,O 23,34:5
Shuffle Along of 1933 1932,D 27,11:3
Shuffle Along 1952,My 9,20:5
Blake, Eubie (Lyricist)
Chocolate Dandies, The 1924,S 2,22:2
Lew Leslie's Blackbirds of 1930 1930,O 23,34:5
Blake, Eubie (Miscellaneous)
In Bamville 1924,Mr 16,VIII,2:1
Blake, Eubie (Playwright)
Shuffle Along 1921,My 23,16:2
Swing It 1937,Jl 23,17:2
Blake, Eubie and His Orchestra
Lew Leslie's Blackbirds of 1930 1930,O 23,34:5
Singin' the Blues 1931,S 17,21:3
Blake, Eugene
Elmer Gantry 1928,Ag 10,9:4
Blake, George (Lyricist)
Russell Patterson's Sketch-Book 1960,F 8,35:1
Blake, Grey
Cocktail Party, The 1950,Ja 23,17:2
Blake, Guy
Lady Windermere's Fan 1946,O 15,29:2
Blake, Henry
Green Pastures, The 1935,F 27,16:2
Blake, Jamo
Three Sisters, The 1959,S 22,46:1
Blake, Judy
Ghost for Sale 1941,S 30,27:4
Blithe Spirit 1946,Je 5,17:3
Blake, Katharine
Caesar and Cleopatra 1951,D 20,43:2
Antony and Cleopatra 1951,D 21,22:2
Blake, Kenneth
Sweet Bird of Youth 1959,Mr 11,39:2
Blake, Leslie
Priest in the Cellar, The 1969,F 19,39:1
Blake, Margaret
Pipe in the Fields, The 1931,Mr 14,23:4
Blake, Marie
But for the Grace of God 1937,Ja 13,21:4
Blake, Mervyn
Hamlet 1957,Jl 3,15:2
Twelfth Night 1957,Jl 4,16:4
Henry IV, Part I 1958,Je 25,23:3
Much Ado About Nothing 1958,Je 26,22:1

Blake, Mervyn—Cont
Winter's Tale, The 1958,Jl 23,34:3
As You Like It 1959,Jl 1,27:1
Othello 1959,Jl 2,17:2
Romeo and Juliet 1960,Jl 1,14:1
Romeo and Juliet 1960,Jl 1,14:1
Henry VIII 1961,Je 22,22:1
Love's Labour's Lost 1961,Je 23,19:1
Love's Labour's Lost 1961,Jl 2,II,1:1
Taming of the Shrew, The 1962,Je 21,25:1
Cyrano de Bergerac 1962,Ag 1,21:1
Cyrano de Bergerac 1963,Je 20,30:1
Comedy of Errors, The 1963,Je 21,35:3
Timon of Athens 1963,Jl 31,19:2
Richard II 1964,Je 17,47:1
Bourgeois Gentilhomme, Le 1964,Je 18,28:2
King Lear 1964,Je 19,36:1
Henry IV, Part I 1965,Je 30,42:1
Falstaff; Henry IV, Part II 1965,Jl 1,35:1
Cherry Orchard, The 1965,Ag 2,17:2
Henry V 1966,Je 8,38:1
Henry VI 1966,Je 9,55:2
Government Inspector, The 1967,Je 15,55:1
Merry Wives of Windsor, The 1967,Ag 4,18:1
Government Inspector, The 1967,O 28,34:1
Romeo and Juliet 1968,Je 11,55:2
Tartuffe 1968,Je 12,39:1
Seagull, The 1968,Jl 25,27:2
Hamlet 1969,Je 11,37:1
Alchemist, The 1969,Je 12,51:1
Measure for Measure 1969,Je 13,41:3
School for Scandal, The 1970,Je 11,51:1
Blake, Michael (Director)
Endgame 1964,F 21,32:1
Blake, Mitzie
Member of the Wedding, The 1950,Ja 6,26:6
Blake, Nigel
Angel Island 1937,O 21,26:2
Blake, Oliver
Mr Adam 1949,My 26,34:6
Blake, Paul
Tour De Four 1963,Je 19,41:1
Blake, Peggy
Rio Rita 1927,F 3,18:3
Blake, Phyllis
Red Falcon, The 1924,O 8,22:1
Kingdom of God, The 1928,D 21,30:2
Mikado, The 1942,F 4,22:2
Pirates of Penzance, The 1942,F 18,22:2
Iolanthe 1942,F 24,26:4
Gondoliers, The 1942,Mr 4,22:3
Blake, Robert
57 Bowery 1928,Ja 27,14:3
Street Wolf, The 1929,Ja 1,61:1
War 1929,S 19,37:3
Harry, Noon and Night 1965,My 6,44:1
Blake, Robert (Producer)
Public Relations 1944,Ap 7,23:3
Blake, Susan
Kingdom of God, The 1928,D 21,30:2
Blake, T R
Pirates of Penzance, The 1942,F 20,20:2
Blake, Thomas
Black Tower 1932,Ja 12,29:2
Blake, Tom
Elmer the Great 1928,S 25,29:1
Crooks' Convention, The 1929,S 19,37:4
Blake, Valle (Scenic Designer)
Dance of Death, The 1969,My 26,53:1
Blake, Virginia
It's About Time 1942,Mr 31,28:3
Blake, William D (Director)
Pelican, The 1929,N 14,25:1
Drunkard, The; Fallen Saved, The 1929,D 31,14:6
Blake, William E
Honor Code, The 1931,My 19,25:3
Hot Money 1931,N 9,22:2
I Was Waiting for You 1933,N 14,23:3
Blakeley, Louise
Good Boy 1928,S 6,23:2
Blakeley, Wendy
Earthlight Theater 1970,N 4,38:2
Blakelock, Denys
Silver Cord, The 1927,O 2,VIII,1:3
Blakely, Bidda
Patience 1935,S 3,24:4
Sing for Your Supper 1939,Ap 25,18:6
Blakely, Colin
As You Like It 1961,Jl 5,30:1
Royal Hunt of the Sun, The 1964,Jl 8,40:6
Crucible, The 1965,Ja 20,35:1
Oedipus 1968,Mr 31,II,5:1
Uncle Vanya 1970,Mr 15,II,7:3
Blakely, Don
Great White Hope, The 1967,D 14,58:1
Great White Hope, The 1967,D 24,II,3:1
Blakely, Gene
Brighten the Corner 1945,D 13,33:2
Traitor, The 1949,Ap 1,30:2
Mr Barry's Etchings 1950,F 1,26:2
Mighty Man Is He, A 1960,Ja 7,25:2
Calculated Risk 1962,N 1,35:1
Weekend 1968,Mr 14,50:2

Blakemore, Harry
For Value Received 1923,My 8,22:3
Nancy Ann 1924,Ap 1,18:1
Outside Looking In 1925,S 8,28:1
Breaks, The 1928,Ap 17,26:3

Blakemore, Michael (Director)
Joe Egg 1968,F 2,26:1
Resistible Rise of Arturo Ui, The 1968,Ag 30,22:2
Resistible Rise of Arturo Ui, The 1969,Ag 18,28:1
National Health 1969,O 19,75:1

Blakeney, Olive
Gay Divorce 1933,N 19,IX,3:7
On Your Toes 1937,F 6,15:2
Harlequinade 1949,O 13,32:2
Royal Family, The 1951,Ja 11,28:2

Blakey, Leila
Tall Kentuckian, The 1953,Je 17,30:1

Blakiston, Clarence
Unknown, The 1920,Ag 29,VI,1:4

Blanc, Betty
Cherry Lane Follies, The 1930,Je 30,22:4

Blanc, Maire Lys
Zizi 1964,N 23,51:1

Blanc, Murray
Chicago 70 1970,My 26,33:1

Blanc, Shirley
White Rose and the Red, The 1964,Mr 17,31:1

Blanc, Whitney Lee (Scenic Designer)
Ceremonies in Dark Old Men 1969,F 6,33:1

Blanch, Dorothy
Dance of Death, The 1960,S 14,51:1
Dream Play 1960,N 23,22:1

Blanch (Costume Designer)
Feast of Panthers 1961,Mr 21,32:1

Blanchan, Pierre
Possessed, The 1959,Ja 31,13:7

Blanchar
Melo 1929,Ap 7,X,1:3

Blanchar, Dominique
Ecole des Femmes, L'; School for Wives 1951,Mr 19,22:1

Blanchard, B E
Boundry Line, The 1930,F 6,21:1

Blanchard, Barbara
H M S Pinafore 1968,Ap 29,47:2

Blanchard, Donald
Joan of Arc 1927,Ap 15,26:2

Blanchard, George (Miscellaneous)
Moon for the Misbegotten, A 1968,Je 13,55:2
Arf 1969,My 28,36:1
Great Airplane Snatch, The 1969,My 28,36:1
Five on the Black Hand Side 1970,Ja 2,32:2
Two Times One; Duet for Solo Voice 1970,Ap 5,76:4
Two Times One; Last Straw, The 1970,Ap 5,76:4

Blanchard, Jerri
Burlesque 1946,D 26,30:3

Blanchard, John
Everyman Today 1958,Ja 16,32:4

Blanchard, Scott
South Pacific 1965,Je 3,25:1

Blanchard, Susan
Me and Juliet 1970,My 15,42:1

Blanche, Francis
Etouffe Chretien, L' 1960,N 5,28:1

Blanche, William
Ballyhoo 1930,D 23,24:1

Blancke, Kate
Girl With Carmine Lips, The 1920,Ag 11,6:1

Blanco, Domingo (Miscellaneous)
Don Juan Tenorio 1953,N 20,18:5
El Alcalde De Zalamea 1953,N 23,32:5

Blanco, Gerardo
Fuerza Ciega, La 1927,D 6,26:1

Bland, A Trevor
Caesar and Cleopatra 1925,Ap 14,27:1
Seventh Heart, The 1927,My 3,24:4
Ivory Door, The 1927,O 19,24:5
General John Regan 1930,Ja 30,16:5
Affair of State, An 1930,N 20,30:3
Devil's Host, The 1931,N 20,27:2

Bland, Alan (Translator)
Comedian, The 1956,O 18,36:4

Bland, Hubert
Firebird of Florence 1945,Mr 23,13:4
King and I, The 1956,Ap 19,35:4

Bland, Joyce
Crime at Blossoms, The 1931,Je 7,VIII,2:1
Maedchen in Uniform 1932,N 6,IX,1:3
Before Sunset 1933,O 15,IX,1:6
Present From Margate, The 1933,D 15,28:1
Spring, 1600 1934,F 1,14:1
Spring, 1600 1934,Mr 4,IX,3:8
Moon Is Red, The 1934,D 5,29:1
Mary Tudor 1935,D 13,30:6
Mary Tudor 1936,Ja 12,IX,1:5

Bland, Margaret (Playwright)
Little Theatre Tournament; Pink and Patches 1928,My 11,28:1

Blandick, Clara
Enchanted Cottage, The 1923,Ap 2,22:3
Enchanted Cottage, The 1923,Ap 8,VIII,1:1
Hell-Bent Fer Heaven 1924,Ja 5,10:1

Applesauce 1925,S 29,31:2
Good Fellow, The 1926,O 6,22:1
Fog-Bound 1927,Ap 2,21:2
Ink 1927,N 2,24:2
Gringa, La 1928,F 2,17:1
Buzzard, The 1928,Mr 15,29:1
Skidding 1928,My 22,18:5
Skyrocket, The 1929,Ja 12,14:7

Blane, Ralph
New Faces of 1936 1936,My 20,24:5
Louisiana Purchase 1940,My 29,19:2

Blane, Ralph (Composer)
Best Foot Forward 1941,O 2,28:2
Best Foot Forward 1941,O 26,IX,1:3
Three Wishes for Jamie 1952,Mr 22,9:2
Best Foot Forward 1956,Mr 3,16:1

Blane, Ralph (Lyricist)
Best Foot Forward 1941,O 2,28:2
Best Foot Forward 1941,O 26,IX,1:3
Best Foot Forward 1956,Mr 3,16:1

Blane, Ralph (Playwright)
Best Foot Forward 1963,Ap 3,43:1

Blaney, H Clay (Producer)
Lady Refuses, The 1933,Mr 8,18:6
House in Paris, The 1944,Mr 21,17:1
Meet a Body 1944,O 17,19:5
Laura 1947,Je 27,16:1
Portrait of a Queen 1968,F 29,29:1

Blaney, Norah
Louie the 14th 1925,N 17,29:3
Vaudeville (Palace) 1925,D 29,21:2

Blaney and Farrar
Vaudeville (Palace) 1925,D 8,28:6

Blank, Benjamin (Musical Director)
My Little Girl 1931,F 2,22:4

Blank, Edel
Lenz 1926,Ap 29,20:4
Dantons Tod 1927,D 21,28:3
Armseligen Besenbinder, Die 1928,N 19,16:2

Blank, Jacob
Parnosseh 1939,F 20,12:5

Blank, L Daniel (Producer)
What Big Ears! 1942,Ap 21,18:5
R U R 1942,D 4,30:2

Blank, Leon
Village Wedding, A 1930,S 24,26:2
My Little Girl 1931,F 2,22:4
Night in the Woods, A 1931,Mr 2,19:3
Lucky Night, The 1931,S 14,15:5
Great Miracle, The 1931,D 12,23:5
Rich Paupers 1932,Mr 14,13:4
Big Surprise, The 1932,O 17,18:3
Love for Sale 1932,D 5,21:4
Untitled-Benefit 1933,Ja 25,13:3
Honeymoon for Three, A 1933,Ja 30,9:6
Jewish Melody, The 1933,Mr 27,12:4

Blank, Leon (Producer)
My Little Girl 1931,F 2,22:4

Blankenchip, John (Costume Designer)
Hippolytus 1948,N 22,25:5
Angel in the Pawnshop 1951,Ja 19,20:3
Long Watch, The 1952,Mr 21,19:5
Moon in Capricorn 1953,O 28,37:2
High Named Today 1954,D 11,11:2
Country Wife, The 1955,Ap 6,35:1

Blankenchip, John (Director)
Emperor's New Clothes, The 1950,Je 20,23:2

Blankenchip, John (Lighting Director)
Angel in the Pawnshop 1951,Ja 19,20:3
Long Watch, The 1952,Mr 21,19:5
High Named Today 1954,D 11,11:2
Country Wife, The 1955,Ap 6,35:1

Blankenchip, John (Scenic Designer)
Hippolytus 1948,N 22,25:5
Angel in the Pawnshop 1951,Ja 19,20:3
Long Watch, The 1952,Mr 21,19:5
Moon in Capricorn 1953,O 28,37:2
High Named Today 1954,D 11,11:2
Country Wife, The 1955,Ap 6,35:1

Blankenship, Roger
Let Freedom Ring 1935,N 7,26:2
Searching for the Sun 1936,F 20,22:6
Country Wife, The 1936,D 2,34:1

Blankenship, Vicki
My Beginning 1962,Ja 31,21:1
Conerico Was Here to Stay 1965,Mr 4,37:1
Long Christmas Dinner, The 1966,S 7,53:1
Butter and Egg Man, The 1966,O 18,49:1

Blankfort, Dorothy (Playwright)
Monique 1957,O 23,38:1

Blankfort, Henry (Composer)
Meet the People 1940,D 26,22:2

Blankfort, Henry (Lyricist)
Meet the People 1940,D 26,22:2

Blankfort, Henry (Playwright)
Meet the People 1940,D 26,22:2

Blankfort, Michael (Director)
Peace on Earth 1933,N 30,39:2
Stevedore 1934,Ap 19,33:2
Stevedore 1934,O 2,18:2

Blankfort, Michael (Playwright)
Sailors of Cattaro 1934,D 11,28:4
Crime, The 1936,Mr 2,12:3

Blankfort, Michael (Playwright)—Cont
Battle Hymn 1936,My 23,12:1
Brave and the Blind, The 1937,Mr 22,26:5
Monique 1957,O 23,38:1

Blankfort, Michael (Producer)
Merry-Go-Round 1932,Ap 23,11:2

Blankman, Howard (Composer)
By Hex 1956,Je 19,25:1

Blankman, Howard (Lyricist)
By Hex 1956,Je 19,25:1

Blanshard, Joby
King's Darling, The 1951,Jl 25,17:2

Blanshard, Lynn
Ali Baba 1951,Mr 27,34:2

Blanton, Joseph
Journey to Jerusalem 1940,O 7,21:2

Blare, Irene
Judge's Husband, The 1926,S 28,31:1

Blase, Pearl
Kiss for Cinderella, A 1930,F 1,14:6

Blaszka, Felix
Zizi 1964,N 23,51:1

Blatchley, John (Director)
Measure for Measure 1962,Ap 11,47:4

Blatt, Edward A (Producer)
Harlem 1929,F 21,30:3
Subway Express 1929,S 25,34:3
Up and Up, The 1930,S 9,25:2

Blatt, Jack
Devils, The 1963,N 5,25:1

Blatt, Jerry (Composer)
Have I Got One for You 1968,Ja 8,32:1

Blatt, Jerry (Lyricist)
Have I Got One for You 1968,Ja 8,32:1

Blatt, Jerry (Playwright)
Have I Got One for You 1968,Ja 8,32:1

Blatt, Leslie Alan
Festival 1955,Ja 19,22:1

Blatt, William (Playwright)
All in the Family 1935,Jl 24,20:4

Blatter, Johanna
Consul, The 1951,S 8,9:3

Blau, Bela
Goat Song 1926,Ja 26,18:1

Blau, Bela (Director)
Mad Hopes, The 1932,D 2,26:3
Shooting Star 1933,Je 13,22:2
First Apple, The 1933,D 28,25:1
Man in Possession, The 1939,S 26,21:4

Blau, Bela (Miscellaneous)
Two Bouquets, The 1938,Je 1,19:2

Blau, Bela (Producer)
Overture 1930,N 25,31:2
Mad Hopes, The 1932,D 2,26:3
Everywhere I Roam 1938,D 30,10:4

Blau, Eric (Lyricist)
O, Oysters! 1961,Ja 31,23:1
Jacques Brel Is Alive and Well and Living in Paris 1968,Ja 23,25:2

Blau, Eric (Miscellaneous)
Jacques Brel Is Alive and Well and Living in Paris 1968,Ja 23,25:2
Jacques Brel Is Alive and Well and Living in Paris 1970,Ja 21,34:1

Blau, Eric (Playwright)
O, Oysters! 1961,Ja 31,23:1

Blau, Eric (Producer)
O, Oysters! 1961,Ja 31,23:1

Blau, Herbert (Director)
Gift of Fury, A 1958,Mr 24,21:4
Waiting for Godot 1958,Ag 6,22:1
Touch of the Poet, A 1961,My 15,34:6
King Lear 1961,My 15,34:6
Galileo 1963,Ja 5,5:2
Caretaker, The 1963,N 25,23:2
House of Bernarda Alba, The 1963,N 25,23:2
Danton's Death 1965,O 22,46:1
Condemned of Altona, The 1966,F 4,21:1
Condemned of Altona, The 1966,F 13,II,1:1
Yerma 1966,D 9,60:1

Blau, Herbert (Playwright)
Gift of Fury, A 1958,Mr 24,21:4

Blau, Herbert (Producer)
Danton's Death 1965,O 31,II,1:1

Blau, Marion
Frankie and Johnny 1930,S 26,16:5

Blau, Mr
Man Without Money, A 1929,N 3,27:4

Blausen, Whitney (Costume Designer)
Day of Absence 1965,N 16,56:1
Happy Ending 1965,N 16,56:1
Shoemaker's Holiday, The 1967,Mr 3,25:1
Country People 1970,Ja 19,35:1
How Much, How Much? 1970,Ap 21,49:1

Blausen, Whitney (Scenic Designer)
Moths, The 1970,My 12,46:1

Blauvelt, Elaine
Hook-Up, The 1935,My 9,24:6
Strip Girl 1935,O 21,22:6

Blauvelt, Larry
Death of the Well-Loved Boy, The 1967,My 16,48:1

Blaxill, Peter
Littlest Circus, The 1959,D 26,5:6

Blaxill, Peter—Cont
Persecution and Assassination of Marat As
  Performed by the Inmates of the Asylum of
  Charenton Under the Direction of the Marquis de
  Sade, The 1967,Ja 4,34:1
Blay, Helen
Jealousy 1934,D 20,31:4
Motke Ganef 1935,Mr 18,15:2
World of Mrs Solomon, The; Another Chance
  1969,Je 4,37:1
Trees Die Standing, The 1969,O 13,52:1
Mirele Efros 1969,D 26,41:1
Blay, John S (Playwright)
Take It Away 1936,D 15,30:5
Blay, Roger
Architect and the Emperor of Assyria, The
  1970,Jl 24,17:2
Architect and the Emperor of Assyria, The
  1970,Ag 9,II,1:5
Bleasdale, George
Tapestry in Gray 1935,D 28,10:2
Love on the Dole 1936,F 25,23:3
Corn Is Green, The 1940,N 27,27:2
Corn Is Green, The 1943,My 4,18:3
Corn Is Green, The 1950,Ja 12,33:2
Blech, Leo (Musical Director)
Tales of Hoffmann 1932,Ja 10,VIII,1:6
Blechman, Burt (Original Author)
My Mother, My Father and Me 1963,Mr 25,5:5
Blechman, Marcus
School for Husbands, The 1933,O 17,26:5
Bleck, Robert
I'd Rather Be Right 1937,N 3,28:2
Bleckner, Jeff
Henry IV 1968,F 7,40:1
Bleckner, Jeff (Director)
Coriolanus 1968,My 26,II,7:1
Unseen Hand, The 1970,Ap 2,43:1
Forensic and the Navigators 1970,Ap 2,43:1
Bledsoe, Gil
Dumbbell People in a Barbell World 1962,F 15,25:1
Bledsoe, Gil (Miscellaneous)
Dumbbell People in a Barbell World 1962,F 15,25:1
Bledsoe, Gilbert (Producer)
Play That on Your Old Piano 1965,O 15,49:1
Bledsoe, H
Under the Gaslight 1929,Ap 3,27:1
Bledsoe, Jules
Deep River 1926,S 26,VIII,2:7
Deep River 1926,O 5,26:2
In Abraham's Bosom 1926,D 31,10:2
Show Boat 1927,D 28,26:1
Show Boat 1928,Ja 8,VIII,1:1
Vaudeville (Palace) 1929,Jl 1,31:4
Vaudeville (Palace) 1930,Mr 31,24:2
Blees, William
Ring Two 1939,N 23,38:2
Unconquered, The 1940,F 14,25:2
Ramshackle Inn 1944,Ja 6,17:5
Bleezarde, Gloria
Never Live Over a Pretzel Factory 1964,Mr 30,37:1
That Thing at the Cherry Lane 1965,My 19,42:1
Leonard Sillman's New Faces of 1968
  1968,My 3,43:1
Three Men on a Horse 1969,O 17,35:1
Blegler, Othmar
Er Ist an Allem Schuld; He Is to Blame for
  Everything 1928,Ja 10,28:3
Bleh, Betty
Gypsy Baron, The 1944,Je 15,17:3
Bleibtreu, Hedwig
Everyman 1931,Jl 19,III,8:6
Bleich, Judah
God's Thieves 1930,O 27,17:4
Armored Train No 1469 1931,N 28,20:3
All God's Chillum Got Shoes 1932,Ap 23,11:3
Town Lunatics 1933,F 6,11:4
Salt and Pepper 1933,Ap 24,10:2
Back Streets 1933,My 18,17:4
Once Upon a Time 1933,S 22,15:1
Germany Aflame 1933,O 28,20:5
Little Giants 1933,D 2,9:5
Happy Days 1934,Ap 2,12:5
Verdict, The 1934,S 22,12:5
In-Laws 1934,O 25,28:2
Jealousy 1934,D 20,31:4
60,000 Heroes 1935,Ja 28,11:5
Sappho 1935,Mr 22,26:4
Kibbetzers, Inc 1935,My 13,18:5
Laugh Night 1936,S 14,25:1
All the Living 1938,Mr 25,14:4
'Round the Family Table 1938,O 8,10:3
In a Jewish Grocery 1939,O 2,15:2
Her Great Mistake 1940,F 5,12:6
Wish Me Luck! 1954,N 1,37:2
Bleich, Judah (Director)
We Live and Laugh 1936,My 9,10:3
Wish Me Luck! 1954,N 1,37:2
Bleich, Judah (Miscellaneous)
Highway Robbery 1955,N 8,36:1
Bleifer, Jacob
Dybbuk, The 1924,Ja 29,17:7
Berlin 1931,D 31,16:1

Bleifer, John Melvin
Clear All Wires! 1932,S 15,19:1
Blendick, James
Richard III 1967,Je 14,43:1
Antony and Cleopatra 1967,Ag 2,25:1
Government Inspector, The 1967,O 28,34:1
Midsummer Night's Dream, A 1968,Je 13,54:1
Midsummer Night's Dream, A 1968,Je 23,II,1:1
Three Musketeers, The 1968,Jl 24,49:2
Hamlet 1969,Je 11,37:1
Alchemist, The 1969,Je 12,51:1
Alchemist, The 1969,Je 22,II,1:7
Merchant of Venice, The 1970,Je 10,39:1
School for Scandal, The 1970,Je 11,51:1
Blenk, William Jr
Climate of Eden, The 1953,N 21,11:2
Bless, Sybil
Dreaming Dust, The 1955,D 8,46:5
Blessington, Edward
Journey With Strangers, A 1958,N 27,53:1
Blessington, Steve
Hard Travelin' 1965,Je 17,25:1
Blessum, Ben (Playwright)
In the Land of the Midnight Sun 1930,Ja 7,27:4
Blett, William
Kid Boots 1924,Ja 1,21:3
Blevins, Sheryl
When Did You Last See My Mother?
  1967,Ja 5,27:5
Bley, Helen
60,000 Heroes 1935,Ja 28,11:5
Power That Builds, The 1935,Mr 9,18:4
Bleyer, Archie (Miscellaneous)
Beat the Band 1942,O 15,26:1
Bleyer, Ella
Vienna at Night 1945,Ap 30,12:4
Blick, Newton
Confidential Clerk, The 1954,F 12,22:1
Blickinberg, Georg
Green Pastures, The 1932,O 30,IX,2:4
Bliedung, J Alexander
Hoot Mon, or Clans Across the Sea 1927,My 8,29:4
Blin, Roger (Director)
Happy Days 1965,S 14,45:2
Paravents, Les 1966,Ap 22,36:3
Oh, Les Beaux Jours 1970,Ap 25,32:3
Blinn, Beatrice
Adorable Liar, The 1926,Ag 31,15:2
Romancing 'Round 1927,O 4,32:4
Song Writer, The 1928,Ag 14,15:2
Napi 1931,Mr 12,22:5
Dark Tower, The 1933,N 27,20:3
Merrily We Roll Along 1934,O 1,14:1
Stage Door 1936,O 23,26:3
Blinn, Holbrook
Famous Mrs Fair, The 1920,Ap 24,20:4
Bad Man, The 1920,Ag 31,7:1
Dove, The 1925,F 12,17:3
Dove, The 1925,F 22,VIII,1:1
Dove, The 1925,Ag 25,12:2
Play's the Thing, The 1926,N 4,25:1
Blinn, Holbrook (Director)
Play's the Thing, The 1926,N 4,25:1
Blinnikov, Sergei
Kremlin Chimes 1965,F 25,23:1
Bliss, Albert (Scenic Designer)
Unchastened Woman, The 1926,F 17,12:1
One Day More 1926,Mr 19,24:3
Easter 1926,Mr 19,24:3
Kept 1926,S 18,13:3
Ink 1927,N 2,24:2
Meek Mose 1928,F 7,30:1
Bliss, E F
Processional 1925,Ja 13,17:1
Bliss, Helen
Wrong Number 1934,Mr 14,23:6
Bliss, Helena
Let's Face It 1941,O 30,26:2
Song of Norway 1944,Ag 22,20:2
Gypsy Lady 1946,S 18,25:6
Romany Love 1947,Mr 10,25:1
Show Boat 1954,My 6,44:1
Show Boat 1956,Je 22,16:1
Show Boat 1957,Je 28,30:2
Bliss, Herbert
Rosalinda; Fledermaus, Die 1942,O 29,26:5
Bliss, Imogene
Persecution and Assassination of Marat As
  Performed by the Inmates of the Asylum of
  Charenton Under the Direction of the Marquis de
  Sade, The 1967,Ja 4,34:1
Your Own Thing 1968,Ja 15,33:1
Bliss, James
That Awful Mrs Eaton! 1924,S 30,27:1
Bliss, Leila
Time for Elizabeth 1948,S 28,32:3
Bliss, Leila (Miscellaneous)
Thirsty Soil 1937,F 4,16:2
Bliss, Lela
Rose Marie 1924,S 3,12:2
Bliss, Tamara (Miscellaneous)
Enchanting Melody 1964,N 25,40:1

Blitz, Edouard
Way of the World, The 1965,Je 2,40:1
Blitzer, Morris A (Playwright)
Bad Habits of 1925 1925,F 9,17:1
Blitzstein, Marc
Cradle Will Rock, The 1937,D 6,19:4
Cradle Will Rock, The 1938,Ja 4,19:3
Blitzstein, Marc (Composer)
Garrick Gaieties 1930,Je 5,29:2
Julius Caesar 1937,N 12,26:6
Cradle Will Rock, The 1937,D 6,19:4
Danton's Death 1938,N 3,26:2
Danton's Death 1938,N 13,IX,1:1
Another Part of the Forest 1946,N 21,42:2
Androcles and the Lion 1946,D 20,29:2
Cradle Will Rock, The 1947,N 25,38:3
Regina 1949,N 1,32:2
Regina 1949,N 13,II,1:1
King Lear 1950,D 26,18:1
King Lear 1956,Ja 13,17:1
Midsummer Night's Dream, A 1958,Je 23,19:1
Winter's Tale, The 1958,Jl 21,17:4
Juno 1959,Mr 10,41:1
Juno 1959,Mr 15,II,1:1
Blitzstein, Marc (Lyricist)
Let's Make an Opera 1950,D 14,50:2
Blitzstein, Marc (Lyricist)
Cradle Will Rock, The 1937,D 6,19:4
Regina 1949,N 1,32:2
King Lear 1950,D 26,18:1
Threepenny Opera, The 1954,Mr 11,26:5
Threepenny Opera, The 1954,Mr 21,II,1:1
Threepenny Opera, The 1955,S 21,38:1
Midsummer Night's Dream, A 1958,Je 23,19:1
Juno 1959,Mr 10,41:1
Juno 1959,Mr 15,II,1:1
Blitzstein, Marc (Miscellaneous)
Let Freedom Sing 1942,O 6,18:2
Threepenny Opera, The 1956,D 30,II,1:1
Juno 1959,Mr 10,41:1
Blitzstein, Marc (Original Author)
Cradle Will Rock, The 1937,D 6,19:4
Blitzstein, Marc (Playwright)
Pins and Needles 1937,N 29,18:6
Cradle Will Rock, The 1938,Ja 4,19:3
No for an Answer 1941,Ja 6,10:6
Cradle Will Rock, The 1947,N 25,38:3
Cradle Will Rock, The 1947,D 27,11:2
Regina 1952,Je 2,25:4
Threepenny Opera, The 1954,Mr 11,26:5
Threepenny Opera, The 1954,Mr 21,II,1:1
Threepenny Opera, The 1955,S 21,38:1
Cradle Will Rock, The 1964,N 9,40:4
Threepenny Opera, The 1966,O 28,33:1
Whores, Wars & Tin Pan Alley 1969,Je 17,37:1
Blitzstein, Marc (Translator)
Threepenny Opera, The 1954,Ap 4,II,7:1
Bliven, Harry
Gods of the Lightning 1928,O 25,27:2
Blivers, Gary
Lady in Danger 1945,Mr 30,18:6
Bloch, Anne
Iolanthe 1965,My 19,42:1
Bloch, Augustyn (Composer)
Book, The 1965,Ja 6,32:1
Jacob and the Angel 1965,Ja 6,32:1
Kernel and the Shell, The 1965,Ja 6,32:1
Post Office, The 1965,Ja 6,32:1
Labyrinth, The 1965,Ja 6,32:1
Jaselka 1965,Ja 6,32:1
Nightmare, The 1965,Ja 6,32:1
Woman, The 1965,Ja 6,32:1
Bloch, Bertram (Playwright)
Glory Hallelujah 1926,Ap 7,26:2
Glory Hallelujah 1926,Ap 11,VIII,1:1
Even in Egypt 1930,Ja 19,VIII,2:6
Joseph 1930,F 13,25:3
Jewel Robbery 1932,Ja 14,17:2
Dark Victory 1934,N 10,18:2
Spring Again 1941,O 28,28:3
Spring Again 1941,N 11,28:2
Bloch, Freda (Translator)
White Guard, The 1934,Ap 8,X,2:2
Bloch, Jean-Richard (Playwright)
Dernier Empereur, Le 1926,D 19,VIII,3:3
Bloch, Pedro (Playwright)
Conscience 1952,My 16,17:6
Enemies Don't Send Flowers 1957,F 20,38:1
Bloch, Stella (Director)
Kai Khosru 1925,Ap 27,14:2
Bloch, Suzanne (Miscellaneous)
House of Breath, The 1957,Ap 15,23:2
Blocher, Walter Jr
Tiger Rag, The 1961,F 17,20:2
Pilgrim's Progress 1962,Mr 21,36:2
Block, Anita Rowe (Playwright)
Love and Kisses 1963,D 19,39:1
Block, Carolyn
Fifth Season, The 1953,Ja 24,13:2
Block, Chad
Do Re Mi 1960,D 27,23:2
Come on Strong 1962,O 5,29:1
Walking Happy 1966,N 28,47:1

Block, Chad—Cont
Hallelujah, Baby! 1967,Ap 27,51:1
Coco 1969,D 19,66:1

Block, Doris
Strange Fruit 1945,N 30,18:6
Rain 1948,F 2,15:2
Long Way From Home, A 1948,F 9,25:2

Block, Edward E
Lady in the Dark 1952,Mr 8,11:3

Block, Fritzi (Playwright)
Bet Your Life 1937,Ap 6,20:2

Block, Hal (Playwright)
Sons o' Fun 1941,D 2,28:2

Block, Herman
Bloody Laughter 1931,D 5,20:6

Block, Hudey
Having Wonderful Time 1937,F 22,12:5

Block, Jerry (Composer)
Rothschilds, The 1970,N 1,II,1:1

Block, Jesse
Vaudeville (Palace) 1930,Ag 4,13:2
Vaudeville (Palace) 1930,O 20,29:1

Block, Maxine (Playwright)
Eyes 1930,My 10,25:1

Block, Mildred
Little Cantor, The 1930,S 24,26:2

Block, Rae
Broken Engagement, The 1921,My 12,20:2

Block, Richard (Miscellaneous)
Ghosts 1961,S 22,29:1

Block, Stella (Choreographer)
Garrick Gaieties 1930,Je 5,29:2

Block, Vivien
Second Hurricane 1937,Ap 22,18:4
'Tis of Thee 1940,O 28,21:3

Block and Sully
Dance of Death, The 1932,Ja 11,29:5
Lost Paradise 1934,D 14,28:3

Blocki, Fritz (Original Author)
Money Mad 1937,My 25,32:5

Blocki, Fritz (Playwright)
Yoshe Kalb 1933,D 29,27:2
Money Mad 1937,My 25,32:5

Blodget, Alden S (Director)
Paris '90 1952,Mr 5,33:2

Blodget, Alden S (Producer)
Paris '90 1952,Mr 5,33:2

Bloecher, Ted
Shoemaker and the Peddler, The 1960,O 15,27:4
Eccentricities of Davy Crockett, The 1961,Ja 4,26:1

Bloede, Ilse
Skin Deep 1927,O 18,32:1

Bloedel, Lawrence (Mrs)
Bourgeois Gentilhomme, Le 1929,Mr 17,30:4

Bloedoorn, Peter
As You Like It 1966,Je 4,19:1

Blofson, Richard
Finian's Rainbow 1955,My 19,25:1

Blofson, Richard (Miscellaneous)
Carefree Tree, The 1955,O 12,37:2
Great God Brown, The 1959,O 7,48:1
Lysistrata 1959,N 25,19:4
Pictures in the Hallway 1959,D 28,19:1
Peer Gynt 1960,Ja 13,21:1
Henry IV 1960,Mr 2,42:1
Henry IV 1960,Ap 19,41:1
Garden of Sweets, The 1961,N 1,35:1
I Can Get It for You Wholesale 1962,Mr 23,29:1
Tambourines to Glory 1963,N 4,47:1
Baby Want a Kiss 1964,Ap 20,32:1
Hughie 1964,D 23,21:2

Blohm, Beatrice (Lyricist)
Bless the Child 1968,My 5,II,16:1

Blohm, Beatrice (Playwright)
Bless the Child 1968,My 5,II,16:1

Blok, Alexander (Playwright)
Show Booth, The 1923,Ap 4,22:2
Show Booth, The 1923,Ap 8,VIII,1:1

Blondell, Gloria
Iron Men 1936,O 20,30:6

Blondell, Joan
Maggie, the Magnificent 1929,O 22,26:1
Penny Arcade 1930,Mr 11,24:5
Good-Bye to Love 1940,Je 8,18:1
Naked Genius, The 1943,O 31,II,1:1
Naked Genius, The 1943,N 7,II,1:6
Rope Dancers, The 1957,N 21,39:1
Rope Dancers, The 1957,D 1,II,1:1

Blondo, Albert
Antigone 1946,F 19,21:3

Blood, Bourn
Hamlet 1936,N 11,54:2

Blood, Denis Jeffrey (Composer)
Donogoo 1961,Ja 19,25:3

Bloodgood, Alice
Squaring the Circle 1936,Ag 12,15:3

Bloodgood, Margaret
Jay Walker, The 1926,F 9,23:1

Bloom, Claire
Ring Around the Moon 1950,Ja 27,29:2
Romeo and Juliet 1952,S 17,34:6
Romeo and Juliet 1952,O 12,II,3:8
Hamlet 1953,Ag 25,18:6
King Lear 1955,Jl 28,19:2

Romeo and Juliet 1956,Je 13,45:8
Romeo and Juliet 1956,S 19,34:6
Richard II 1956,O 24,44:1
Romeo and Juliet 1956,O 25,41:1
Rashomon 1959,Ja 28,36:2
Rashomon 1959,F 8,II,1:1

Bloom, Harold (Producer)
Spots of the Leopard, The 1963,S 25,38:1

Bloom, Harry (Playwright)
King Kong 1961,F 24,24:1

Bloom, J Michael
Gantry 1970,F 16,44:1

Bloom, Leo
Titus Andronicus 1956,D 3,40:2
Two Gentlemen of Verona 1957,Jl 23,21:5
Macbeth 1957,Ag 16,11:2
Mis-Guided Tour 1959,O 13,44:7
I Want You 1961,S 15,29:1
Drat! the Cat! 1965,O 11,54:2

Bloom, Lillian
Little Giants 1933,D 2,9:5

Bloom, Paul
John Brown's Body 1953,F 16,17:2

Bloom, Rube (Composer)
Lew Leslie's Blackbirds of 1939 1939,F 13,12:2

Bloom, Verna
Persecution and Assassination of Marat As
Performed by the Inmates of the Asylum of
Charenton Under the Direction of the Marquis de
Sade, The 1967,Ja 4,34:1

Bloomberg, Larry
Doctored Wife, The 1950,Jl 12,33:2

Bloomberg, Sol
Will, The 1930,My 6,33:1

Bloomenfeld, L (Translator)
Wolves 1924,D 31,9:4

Bloomer, Charles
Meet the Wife 1923,N 27,23:4
Man Who Died Twice, The 1925,D 14,19:1

Bloomer, Raymond
Richard III 1920,Mr 8,7:1
Macbeth 1921,F 18,16:1
Swords 1921,S 2,9:3

Bloomfield, Charles
Mr Jiggins of Jigginstown 1936,D 18,30:2

Bloomfield, Ernest
Green Pastures, The 1951,Mr 16,35:2

Bloomfield, Harry (Miscellaneous)
Polonaise 1945,O 8,20:2

Bloomfield, Harry (Producer)
Many Happy Returns 1945,Ja 6,15:5

Bloomfield, Henry
Carnaval 1924,D 30,15:1

Bloomgarden, Kermit (Miscellaneous)
Another Part of the Forest 1946,N 21,42:2
Next Time I'll Sing to You 1963,N 28,69:2

Bloomgarden, Kermit (Producer)
Heavenly Express 1940,Ap 19,24:2
Deep Are the Roots 1945,S 27,24:4
Deep Are the Roots 1945,O 7,II,1:1
Woman Bites Dog 1946,Ap 18,21:2
Command Decision 1947,O 2,30:2
Command Decision 1947,O 12,II,1:1
Death of a Salesman 1949,F 11,27:2
Montserrat 1949,O 31,21:4
Man, The 1950,Ja 20,28:2
Legend of Sarah 1950,O 12,42:4
Autumn Garden, The 1951,Mr 8,36:2
Children's Hour, The 1952,D 19,35:2
Crucible, The 1953,Ja 23,15:2
Crucible, The 1953,Jl 2,20:2
Wedding Breakfast 1954,N 22,29:2
View From the Bridge, A 1955,S 30,21:1
Memory of Two Mondays, A 1955,S 30,21:1
Diary of Anne Frank, The 1955,O 6,24:2
Lark, The 1955,N 18,20:1
Most Happy Fella, The 1956,My 4,20:1
Night of the Auk 1956,D 4,50:2
Look Homeward, Angel 1957,N 29,33:1
Music Man, The 1957,D 20,31:1
Gang's All Here, The 1959,O 2,23:1
Toys in the Attic 1960,F 26,23:2
Wall, The 1960,O 12,44:4
Gay Life, The 1961,N 20,38:1
Moon on a Rainbow Shawl 1962,Ja 16,30:1
Moon on a Rainbow Shawl 1962,Ja 28,II,1:1
Nowhere to Go But Up 1962,O 9,46:6
Nowhere to Go But Up 1962,N 12,36:2
My Mother, My Father and Me 1963,Mr 25,5:5
Anyone Can Whistle 1964,Ap 6,36:1
Playroom, The 1965,D 6,49:1
Illya Darling 1967,Ap 12,37:1
Hello and Goodbye 1969,S 19,54:1

Bloomingdale, Alfred (Miscellaneous)
Your Loving Son 1941,Ap 5,13:2
Early to Bed 1943,Je 18,16:2
Assassin, The 1945,O 18,20:2

Bloomingdale, Alfred (Producer)
High Kickers 1941,N 1,21:2
Ring Around Elizabeth 1941,N 18,32:2
Sweet Charity 1942,D 29,26:4
Ziegfeld Follies 1943,Ap 2,16:2
Allah Be Praised! 1944,Ap 21,14:2

Bloomstein, Henry (Playwright)
Calling in Crazy 1969,O 7,42:2

Blore, Eric
Little Miss Bluebeard 1923,Ag 29,12:1
Ghost Train, The 1926,Ag 26,17:2
Mixed Doubles 1927,Ap 27,22:3
Just Fancy! 1927,O 12,30:2
Here's Howe! 1928,My 2,19:3
Angela 1928,D 4,28:2
Meet the Prince 1929,F 26,30:5
Meet the Prince 1929,Mr 10,X,1:1
Paris Bound 1929,Jl 20,8:3
Roar China! 1930,O 28,23:1
Give Me Yesterday 1931,Mr 5,32:1
Here Goes the Bride 1931,N 4,31:2
Gay Divorce 1932,N 30,23:4

Blossom, Henry (Lyricist)
Mlle Modiste 1929,O 8,34:1
Red Mill, The 1945,O 17,16:2

Blossom, Henry (Playwright)
Mlle Modiste 1929,O 8,34:1
Only Girl, The 1934,My 22,28:2
Red Mill, The 1945,O 17,16:2

Blossom, Henry (Producer)
Honey Girl 1920,My 4,9:1

Blossom, June
Flying Colors 1932,S 16,24:2
Wind and the Rain, The 1934,F 2,20:6
All Paris Knows 1934,Jl 24,20:1
Danger 1935,Ag 27,23:4
Immoral Support 1935,S 3,24:3

Blossom, Roberts
Evening With Shaw, An; Village Wooing
1955,Ag 13,6:6
Escurial 1956,O 3,29:2
Infernal Machine, The 1958,F 4,33:1
Making of Moo, The 1958,Je 12,34:1
Ivanov 1958,O 8,42:1
Ivanov 1958,O 19,II,1:1
Victims of Duty 1960,Ja 20,26:1
Henry V 1960,Je 30,23:1
Bartleby 1961,Ja 25,28:1
Death of Bessie Smith, The 1961,Mr 2,19:1
Cook for Mr General, A 1961,O 20,39:1
Whisper Into My Good Ear 1962,O 2,47:1
Ballad of the Sad Cafe, The 1963,O 31,27:1
Physicists, The 1964,O 14,52:1
Do Not Pass Go 1965,Ap 20,44:1
Sunset 1966,My 13,34:1
Operation Sidewinder 1970,Mr 13,33:1

Blosson, Richard (Miscellaneous)
In the Counting House 1962,D 15,5:5
Strange Interlude 1963,Mr 13,5:2

Blount, Clementine
Zunguru 1938,Ag 3,14:5
Zunguru 1938,Ag 7,IX,8:2
Zunguru 1940,Mr 21,30:5

Blount, Helon
Fly Blackbird 1962,F 6,26:2
Fly Blackbird 1962,Ap 29,II,1:1
Riverwind 1962,D 14,5:5
Do I Hear a Waltz? 1965,Mr 19,28:1
My Wife and I 1966,O 11,53:2
Curley McDimple 1967,N 23,59:2
Fig Leaves Are Falling, The 1969,Ja 3,19:1

Blount, Ken
Utopia, Limited 1960,Ap 8,27:2

Blow, Sidney (Playwright)
His Wild Oat 1926,D 1,24:1
Fritzi 1935,D 21,10:3

Blue, Andy (Producer)
Fitz 1966,My 17,51:2
Biscuit 1966,My 17,51:2

Blue, Ben
Vaudeville (Palace) 1929,F 4,21:4
Vaudeville (Palace) 1929,Jl 1,31:4
Vaudeville (Palace) 1930,Ap 21,20:7
Vaudeville (Palace) 1931,Ja 5,20:3
Vaudeville (Palace) 1931,Mr 9,25:7
Vaudeville (Palace) 1931,Ap 6,24:3
Scandals 1939,Ag 20,IX,2:1
Scandals 1939,Ag 29,17:2
Scandals 1939,S 3,IX,1:1
Vaudeville (Palace) 1952,F 27,22:2

Blue, Clarissa
Lulu Belle 1926,F 10,20:1

Blue, Dan (Playwright)
Dumbbell People in a Barbell World 1962,F 15,25:1
Play That on Your Old Piano 1965,O 15,49:1

Blue, Samuel Jr
Volpone 1967,Je 30,29:1
John Brown's Body 1968,F 13,49:2
Comedy of Errors, The 1968,F 28,40:2
She Stoops to Conquer 1968,Ap 1,58:3
Ceremonies in Dark Old Men 1969,F 6,33:1
Malcochon 1969,Ap 2,37:1
Man Better Man 1969,Jl 3,22:1
Man Better Man 1969,Jl 13,II,1:1

Blue, Toney
X Has No Value 1970,F 17,35:1

Blum, Abraham (Original Author)
Long Live America 1939,Ja 2,28:3

Blum, Abraham (Playwright)
Meet My Sister 1930,D 31,11:1
Great Miracle, The 1931,D 12,23:5
Big Surprise, The 1932,O 17,18:3
Jewish Melody, The 1933,Mr 27,12:4
Brownsville Grandfather, The 1935,Ap 19,24:6
Holiday in Town, A 1935,S 30,12:3
Blum, Abraham (Translator)
Queen Mother 1938,D 26,29:4
Blum, Alla (Composer)
Taming of the Shrew, The 1956,Ag 11,11:2
Blum, Daniel (Producer)
Country Wife, The 1957,N 28,56:1
Blum, Doris (Miscellaneous)
Man With the Golden Arm, The 1956,My 22,28:1
Blum, Edwin Harvey (Playwright)
Kick Back, The 1936,Je 23,27:3
I Am My Youth 1938,Mr 8,22:4
Saving Grace, The 1963,Ap 19,28:1
Blum, Elnora
Pastoral 1939,N 2,26:2
Blum, Gustav (Director)
Little Stone House, The 1923,My 11,20:3
Little Stone House, The 1923,My 13,16:2
Caught 1925,O 6,31:2
Beaten Track, The 1926,F 9,23:2
Henry-Behave 1926,Ag 24,19:4
Gertie 1926,N 16,24:2
Mystery Ship, The 1927,Mr 15,28:2
Her First Affaire 1927,Ag 23,29:2
Spring Song 1927,D 22,26:3
Mystery Man, The 1928,Ja 27,14:2
Phantom Lover, The 1928,S 5,25:1
That Ferguson Family 1928,D 24,10:7
Love Expert, The 1929,S 24,29:1
Truly Valiant 1936,Ja 10,17:3
Don't Look Now! 1936,N 4,41:3
Walk Hard 1946,Mr 28,34:2
Blum, Gustav (Producer)
Caught 1925,O 6,31:2
Beaten Track, The 1926,F 9,23:2
Henry-Behave 1926,Ag 24,19:4
Gertie 1926,N 16,24:2
Mystery Ship, The 1927,Mr 15,28:2
Her First Affaire 1927,Ag 23,29:2
Spring Song 1927,D 22,26:3
Mystery Man, The 1928,Ja 27,14:2
Phantom Lover, The 1928,S 5,25:1
That Ferguson Family 1928,D 24,10:7
Love Expert, The 1929,S 24,29:1
Truly Valiant 1936,Ja 10,17:3
Don't Look Now! 1936,N 4,41:3
Walk Hard 1946,Mr 28,34:2
Blum, Lilyan
Shoemaker's Prodigious Wife, The 1949,Je 15,38:2
Blum, Samuel
Parisian Love 1927,Ja 28,15:5
Blumberg, Sylvia
Bridal Crown, The 1938,F 7,11:2
Blumenfeld, Anna
Jazz a La Carte 1922,Je 3,8:3
Blumenfeld, Diana
House on Grand Street, A 1953,O 10,12:6
Blumenfeld, Norman (Lighting Director)
Simply Heavenly 1957,My 22,28:2
Twisting Road, The; One Tuesday Morning 1957,N 18,36:5
Twisting Road, The; Housekeeper, The 1957,N 18,36:5
Twisting Road, The; Jewel of the South, The 1957,N 18,36:5
Courageous One, The 1958,Ja 21,33:6
Long Gallery, The 1958,Mr 7,17:2
Blumenfeld, Robert
All's Well That Ends Well 1970,Je 16,53:1
Othello 1970,Je 22,43:1
Othello 1970,S 15,51:1
Blumenstein, Harry
Birds, The 1967,My 7,67:1
Blumenthal, A C (Producer)
Eight Bells 1933,O 30,14:2
Blumenthal, Milton
Wookey, The 1941,S 11,20:5
Blumenthal (Original Author)
Im Weissen Roessel 1931,Ja 4,VIII,3:5
Blumlein, Michael
Bacchae, The 1969,Mr 15,24:1
Blumstein, Bessie Samose
Me and Molly 1948,F 27,27:2
Blumstein, Sam (Composer)
In-Laws 1960,O 17,32:4
Blumstein, Sam (Miscellaneous)
Both Kooney Lemels 1964,O 12,37:2
Blumstein, Sam (Musical Director)
Going to America 1961,O 30,33:7
World Is a Stage, The 1962,N 5,37:4
Blunkall, E J
Dust Heap, The 1924,Ap 25,20:2
Shooting Shadows 1924,Je 27,16:5
Made in America 1925,O 15,27:2
Love in the Tropics 1927,O 19,24:3
Brain Sweat 1934,Ap 5,24:4
Abie's Irish Rose 1937,My 13,30:2

Return of the Vagabond, The 1940,My 14,27:2
Banjo Eyes 1941,D 26,20:2
Blunkall, E J (Director)
Scarlet Lily, The 1927,Ja 31,12:3
Scalawag, The 1927,Mr 30,22:3
Mountain Fury 1929,S 26,27:2
Bluthal, John
Kiss Me, Kate 1970,D 26,10:4
Bly, Dan
Gnadiges Fraulein, The 1966,F 23,42:1
Mutilated, The 1966,F 23,42:1
School for Scandal, The 1966,N 22,33:2
Wild Duck, The 1967,Ja 12,49:1
Pantagleize 1967,D 1,54:1
Bly, Ron
Man and Superman 1964,D 7,45:2
Blyden, Huron L
Lily Sue 1926,N 17,22:2
Honor Be Damned! 1927,Ja 27,13:1
Blyden, Larry
Miser, The 1950,Mr 27,19:5
Wish You Were Here 1952,Je 26,26:6
Oh, Men! Oh, Women! 1953,D 18,37:2
Italian Straw Hat, The 1957,O 1,37:2
Flower Drum Song 1958,D 2,44:1
Flower Drum Song 1958,D 7,II,5:1
Foxy 1962,Jl 4,12:2
Foxy 1964,F 17,26:1
Passionella 1966,O 19,53:1
Lady or the Tiger?, The 1966,O 19,53:1
Diary of Adam and Eve, The 1966,O 19,53:1
Apple Tree, The 1966,O 30,II,1:1
Apple Tree, The 1966,O 12,56:1
Christmas Carol, A 1967,D 23,28:1
You Know I Can't Hear You When the Water's Running 1968,Mr 29,33:1
Mother Lover, The 1969,F 3,28:1
Blyden, Larry (Director)
Harold 1962,N 30,27:1
Mother Lover, The 1969,F 3,28:1
Blyth, Anne
Watch on the Rhine 1941,Ap 2,26:2
Blyth, Gordon
Pigeon, The 1922,F 3,13:1
Blyth, Paul (Miscellaneous)
Hi, Paisano 1961,O 2,36:2
Blythe, Betty
Vaudeville (Palace) 1926,Ag 24,19:3
House Afire 1930,Ap 1,34:7
Paging Danger 1931,F 27,19:2
Man Who Came to Dinner, The 1940,F 18,IX,3:6
Public Relations 1944,Ap 7,23:3
Blythe, E M (Ethel Barrymore) (Director)
Kingdom of God, The 1928,D 21,30:2
Love Duel, The 1929,Ap 16,32:3
Scarlet Sister Mary 1930,N 26,19:2
School for Scandal, The 1931,N 11,26:4
Blythe, Frances
Gay Paree 1926,N 10,24:2
Blythe, Harry
Three Times the Hour 1931,Ag 26,15:5
Blythe, Larry
Gondoliers, The 1957,My 29,34:2
Blythe, Peter
King Lear 1964,My 19,43:2
Comedy of Errors, The 1964,My 21,43:1
Creeper, The 1965,Jl 15,21:1
Blythe, Richard
King Lear 1947,F 19,32:2
As You Like It 1947,F 21,16:2
Merchant of Venice, The 1947,F 24,16:2
Volpone 1947,F 25,32:2
Hamlet 1947,F 27,27:2
Blythe, Susan
Miss Emily Adam 1960,Mr 30,43:1
Blythe, Violet
Afgar 1920,N 9,13:2
Farmer's Wife, The 1924,O 10,22:3
Boag, Gil (Producer)
Murray Anderson's Almanac 1929,Ag 15,20:3
City Haul 1929,D 31,14:4
Boag, William
Return of Peter Grimm, The 1921,S 22,12:2
Tiger Cats 1924,O 22,18:1
Canary Dutch 1925,S 9,22:1
Lulu Belle 1926,F 10,20:1
Mima 1928,D 13,24:2
Social Register, The 1931,N 10,28:2
Boal, Augusto (Director)
Arena Conta Zumbi 1969,Ag 19,31:1
Arena Conte Bolivar 1970,Mr 31,33:1
Boal, Augusto (Playwright)
Arena Conta Zumbi 1969,Ag 19,31:1
Arena Conte Bolivar 1970,Mr 31,33:1
Boal, Augusto (Producer)
Arena Conte Bolivar 1970,Mr 31,33:1
Boal, William S (Producer)
Thracian Horses, The 1961,S 28,58:2
Board, Brewster
If 1927,O 26,26:2
Love Nest, The 1927,D 23,17:1
Curtain Call 1937,Ap 23,24:7

Board, Bruce
Abraham; Dulcitus; Callimachus 1926,Mr 29,24:2
Boardley, Fred
Singing Jailbirds 1928,D 5,34:4
Boardley, Harold
Hoboken Blues 1928,F 18,10:1
Boardman, Don
Lady From the Sea, The 1935,D 14,11:3
Boardman, Emerson (Scenic Designer)
Doll's House, A 1954,N 15,32:2
Boardman, True
Gang War 1928,Ag 21,27:2
Boardman, Virginia True
Carnival 1929,Ap 25,32:5
Boarmann, Marshall I
Martyr Without Tears 1942,N 23,19:2
Boasberg, Al (Miscellaneous)
Vaudeville (Palace) 1932,My 30,16:7
Boasberg, Al (Playwright)
Vaudeville (Palace) 1932,Mr 7,13:4
Boase, Alexander
Fatal Lady, The 1936,Mr 19,23:7
Boatner, Adelaide
Jamaica 1957,N 1,32:2
Boatsman, J S
Night Hostess 1928,S 13,31:2
Buckaroo 1929,Mr 18,31:1
Boatwright, Helen
Elizabethans, The 1962,Ja 22,19:1
Boaz, Charles
Joy Forever, A 1946,Ja 8,20:2
Big Two, The 1947,Ja 9,21:2
Gramercy Ghost 1951,Ap 27,20:2
Male Animal, The 1952,My 1,35:1
Black-Eyed Susan 1954,D 24,7:5
Skin of Our Teeth, The 1955,Ag 18,16:1
Last Analysis, The 1964,O 2,30:1
Boaz and Nechemia
Grand Music Hall of Israel, The 1968,F 7,42:1
Bob and Ray
Bob and Ray-The Two and Only 1970,O 4,II,3:1
Bobley, Edward
Dole Brothers 1932,Mr 26,17:7
Bobri (Costume Designer)
Othello 1929,F 4,21:2
Bobri (Scenic Designer)
Othello 1929,F 4,21:2
Bobrick, Sam (Playwright)
Norman, Is That You? 1970,F 20,30:1
Bobrowska, Lilliana
Jaselka 1965,Ja 6,32:1
Woman, The 1965,Ja 6,32:1
Labyrinth, The 1965,Ja 6,32:1
Nightmare, The 1965,Ja 6,32:1
Kernel and the Shell, The 1965,Ja 6,32:1
Book, The 1965,Ja 6,32:1
Jacob and the Angel 1965,Ja 6,32:1
Post Office, The 1965,Ja 6,32:1
Boccaccio (Original Author)
Decameron, The 1961,Ap 13,32:1
Boccalini, Clement
Nautical but Nice 1931,Ap 19,31:6
Boccio, Michael
White Devil, The 1965,D 7,56:1
Bocher, Main (Costume Designer)
Call Me Madam 1950,O 22,II,1:1
Not for Children 1951,F 14,35:2
Point of No Return 1951,D 14,35:2
Point of No Return 1951,D 23,II,3:1
Wonderful Town 1953,F 26,22:3
Kind Sir 1953,S 28,21:2
Kind Sir 1953,N 5,41:2
Kind Sir 1953,N 15,II,1:1
Prescott Proposals, The 1953,D 17,53:1
Prescott Proposals, The 1953,D 27,II,3:1
Great Sebastians, The 1956,Ja 5,27:1
Bocher, Main (Miscellaneous)
Call Me Madam 1950,O 13,25:1
Bochner, Lloyd
Richard III 1953,Jl 15,22:2
All's Well That Ends Well 1953,Jl 16,18:2
Measure for Measure 1954,Je 30,23:1
Taming of the Shrew, The 1954,Jl 1,22:2
Julius Caesar 1955,Je 29,23:3
Merchant of Venice, The 1955,Jl 1,13:1
Tamburlaine the Great 1956,Ja 20,19:1
Henry V 1956,Je 20,27:2
Merry Wives of Windsor, The 1956,Je 21,34:4
Hamlet 1957,Jl 3,15:2
Twelfth Night 1957,Jl 4,16:4
Two Gentlemen of Verona 1958,Mr 19,35:1
Bock, Jerry (Choreographer)
Never Too Late 1962,N 28,42:1
Bock, Jerry (Composer)
Mr Wonderful 1956,Mr 23,23:2
Body Beautiful, The 1958,Ja 24,15:2
Fiorello! 1959,N 24,45:3
Fiorello! 1959,N 29,II,1:1
Tenderloin 1960,O 18,47:2
Fiorello! 1962,Je 14,24:1
Bil and Cora Baird's Marionette Theater 1963,Ap 12,34:2

Bock, Jerry (Composer)—Cont
She Loves Me 1963,Ap 24,39:1
She Loves Me 1963,My 5,II,1:1
Fiddler on the Roof 1964,S 23,56:2
Fiddler on the Roof 1964,O 4,II,1:1
Passionella 1966,O 19,53:1
Diary of Adam and Eve, The 1966,O 19,53:1
Lady or the Tiger?, The 1966,O 19,53:1
Apple Tree, The 1966,O 30,II,1:1
Fiddler on the Roof 1967,S 28,59:2
Fiddler on the Roof 1969,Je 26,47:1
Fiddler on the Roof 1969,N 16,82:6
Fiddler on the Roof 1970,F 28,20:1
Oh, Johnny: or, Jonny Spielt Auf 1970,Mr 15,88:4
Rothschilds, The 1970,O 20,40:1

Bock, Jerry (Lyricist)
Mr Wonderful 1956,Mr 23,23:2
Fiddler on the Roof 1964,O 4,II,1:1
Oh, Johnny: or, Jonny Spielt Auf 1970,Mr 15,88:4

Bock, Jerry (Playwright)
To Broadway With Love 1964,Ap 30,28:6
Passionella 1966,O 19,53:1
Lady or the Tiger?, The 1966,O 19,53:1
Diary of Adam and Eve, The 1966,O 19,53:1

Bock, William
Miss Swan Expects 1939,F 21,15:2
Steps Leading Up 1941,Ap 19,20:6
Seven Mirrors 1945,O 26,17:2

Bockman, George
Lady in the Dark 1941,Ja 24,14:2
Lady in the Dark 1941,S 3,26:6
Alive and Kicking 1950,Ja 18,25:5

Bockman, George (Costume Designer)
Chase, The 1952,Ap 16,30:2

Bockmiller, Vashti
Montmartre 1922,F 14,20:1

Bockner, Sey
Bridal Crown, The 1938,F 7,11:2
Case of Youth, A 1940,Mr 25,10:3

Bockoven, Elizabeth
Song of Norway 1944,Ag 22,20:2

Boda (Playwright)
Victoria and Her Hussar 1930,S 21,IX,2:6

Bodanzky, Robert (Playwright)
Count of Luxembourg, The 1930,F 18,28:2

Boddington, Diana (Miscellaneous)
Dance of Death, The 1967,O 20,50:1
Love for Love 1967,O 21,17:1
Flea in Her Ear, A 1967,O 30,59:1

Bodeen, DeWitt (Playwright)
Harvest of Years 1948,Ja 13,29:2

Bodel, Burman
Maid in the Ozarks 1946,Jl 16,20:3

Bodenheim, Maxwell
Across the Board on Tomorrow Morning 1942,Ag 18,17:1

Bodenstein, Arthur (Mrs)
Bad Habits of 1925 1925,F 9,17:1

Bodiford, Edgar
Thorntons, The 1956,F 15,26:1
Ivory Branch, The 1956,My 25,27:1

Bodin, Duane
Fiddler on the Roof 1964,S 23,56:2
1776 1969,Mr 17,46:2

Bodin, Harry
Catherine Was Great 1944,Ag 3,16:1

Bodine, Eleanor
Lady From the Sea, The 1935,D 14,11:3
Fuente Ovejuna; Sheep Well, The 1936,My 3,II,4:1

Bodine, Eleanor (Miscellaneous)
Nine Till Six 1936,Mr 14,10:3

Bodkin, Billi
Cradle Will Rock, The 1938,Ja 4,19:3

Bodkin, Ernest
Wandering Jew, The 1927,F 2,22:4

Bodkin, Prunella
Launcelot and Elaine 1930,Mr 10,24:3

Bodkins, Billy
Cradle Will Rock, The 1937,D 6,19:4

Bodroghy, Adele
Polonaise 1945,O 8,20:2

Bodry, Penelope
Exchange 1970,F 9,47:2

Boeche, Donald
Possessed, The 1939,O 25,26:2
Texas Town 1941,Ap 30,22:3
Out of My House 1942,Ja 8,28:6

Boeckler, Charles W
Sale and a Sailor, A, or Glory! What Price! 1926,Ap 25,30:4

Boegner, Richard
Green Stick 1934,O 10,21:2

Boehm, Andreas
Porgy and Bess 1950,N 26,II,7:8

Boehm, David (Playwright)
Sing High, Sing Low 1931,N 13,26:4
It Happened to Adam 1934,N 10,18:6
It Happened to Adam 1934,N 25,IX,3:1

Boehm, Marjery
Boutique Fantasque, La 1929,D 28,10:6

Boehn, John
Now-A-Days 1929,Ag 6,29:3

Boehnel, William (Playwright)
Flood Tide 1938,Mr 24,20:8

Boen, Earl
Way of the World, The 1965,Je 2,40:1
Richard III 1965,Je 3,26:1
Skin of Our Teeth, The 1966,Je 2,51:1
As You Like It 1966,Je 4,19:1
Shoemaker's Holiday, The 1967,Je 3,19:1
Harpers Ferry 1967,Je 6,52:2
Visit, The 1967,S 13,41:1

Boesch, Beatrice
Quo Vadis 1932,O 17,18:2

Boesen, William H
Ballad of John Ogilvie, The 1968,O 9,42:4

Boesing, Martha
Jack Jack 1968,Je 23,74:5

Boesing, Paul
Balls 1965,F 11,45:1
Blind Angel, The 1965,Ap 2,26:1

Boesing, Paul (Composer)
Jack Jack 1968,Je 23,74:5

Boettcher, Eva
Rhinoceros 1959,N 2,41:1
Nathan the Wise 1962,Mr 7,29:1
Before Sundown 1962,Mr 14,43:1

Boettcher, Henry
Beware of the Bull 1933,My 30,13:7
Orphee 1935,Mr 23,10:3

Boettcher, Henry (Miscellaneous)
Antigone 1956,Ap 3,32:2

Boettcher, Henry (Producer)
River Line, The 1957,Ja 3,29:2

Boffinger, Hazel
George White's Scandals 1931,S 15,30:1
Music Hall Varieties 1932,N 23,15:3

Bogaert, Lucienne
Carrosse du Saint-Sacrement, Le 1926,O 3,VIII,2:1
Amphitryon 38 1929,D 1,X,4:1
Eau Fraiche, L' 1931,Je 7,VIII,3:5
Taciturne, Un 1931,N 22,VIII,1:6
Margrave, La 1932,D 18,X,3:6
Miss Ba; Barretts of Wimpole Street, The 1934,N 11,IX,3:6

Bogard, Travis (Miscellaneous)
Angel Comes to Babylon, An 1962,S 29,15:2

Bogart, David
Mikado, The 1944,F 12,11:3
Ruddigore 1944,Mr 3,19:5

Bogart, H D
Drifting 1922,Ja 3,20:3

Bogart, Humphrey
Swifty 1922,O 17,14:1
Meet the Wife 1923,N 27,23:4
Nerves 1924,S 2,22:2
Hell's Bells! 1925,Ja 27,14:2
Cradle Snatchers 1925,S 8,28:2
Baby Mine 1927,Je 10,21:2
Skyrocket, The 1929,Ja 12,14:7
It's a Wise Child 1929,Ag 7,29:1
After All 1931,D 4,28:4
Mad Hopes, The 1932,My 29,VIII,2:2
I Loved You Wednesday 1932,O 12,27:1
Chrysalis 1932,N 16,15:2
Our Wife 1933,Mr 3,13:2
Mask and the Face, The 1933,My 9,20:2
Invitation to a Murder 1934,My 18,26:3
Petrified Forest, The 1934,D 21,31:6
Petrified Forest, The 1935,Ja 8,26:1
Stag at Bay, The 1935,Jl 30,17:1
Rain 1935,Ag 27,23:4

Bogathy, Mihaly
Egerfogo; Mousetrap, The 1958,Ja 30,18:6

Bogdanoff, Rose
Americana 1928,O 14,X,1:6

Bogdanoff, Rose (Costume Designer)
Cream in the Well, The 1941,Ja 21,19:2
Circle of Chalk, The 1941,Mr 27,28:4
Nathan the Wise 1942,Ap 4,18:4
War and Peace 1942,My 22,26:3
Patriots, The 1943,Ja 30,11:2
New Life, A 1943,S 16,26:6
Storm Operation 1944,Ja 12,28:2
Chicken Every Sunday 1944,Ap 6,27:2
Last Stop 1944,S 6,17:2
Sophie 1944,D 26,22:7
Stranger, The 1945,F 13,21:2
It's A Gift 1945,Mr 13,18:7
Lysistrata 1946,O 18,27:5
Great Campaign, The 1947,Ap 1,33:2
Survivors, The 1948,Ja 20,27:2
Kathleen 1948,F 4,26:2
Long Way From Home, A 1948,F 9,25:2
Me and Molly 1948,F 27,22:2
Summer and Smoke 1948,O 7,33:2
Bravo! 1948,N 12,31:2
Peer Gynt 1951,Ja 29,15:2
Rose Tattoo, The 1951,F 5,19:2
Trip to Bountiful, The 1953,N 4,30:3

Bogdanov, A
Revisor; Inspector General, The 1935,F 18,19:6
Poverty Is No Crime 1935,F 21,22:5
Strange Child 1935,F 26,16:1
White Guard, The; Days of the Turbins 1935,Mr 7,27:5
Enemies 1935,Mr 19,24:7

Bogdanovich, Peter
Othello 1958,Jl 4,16:1
Twelfth Night 1958,Ag 7,21:4

Bogdanovich, Peter (Director)
Big Knife, The 1959,N 13,25:1
Once in a Lifetime 1964,Ja 29,20:1

Bogdanovich, Peter (Producer)
Big Knife, The 1959,N 13,25:1
Once in a Lifetime 1964,Ja 29,20:1

Bogen, Steve
Recruiting Officer, The 1958,F 8,12:2

Bogert, William
Country Wife, The 1957,Je 27,22:1
Port-Royal 1960,Ap 26,41:1
Man for All Seasons, A 1964,Ja 28,24:2
Love's Labour's Lost 1965,Je 16,46:1
Sudden and Accidental Re-education of Horse Johnson, The 1968,D 19,63:1

Boggia, Norma
Ora di Diana, L' 1937,My 17,22:3

Boggiano, Norma
Ora di Diana, L' 1937,My 17,22:3

Bogin, Abba (Miscellaneous)
Another Evening With Harry Stoones 1961,O 23,22:2
Riverwind 1962,D 14,5:5
That Thing at the Cherry Lane 1965,My 19,42:1
Guys and Dolls 1966,Je 9,55:2
By Jupiter 1967,Ja 20,28:2

Bogin, Abba (Musical Director)
Mrs Patterson 1954,D 2,37:1
Most Happy Fella, The 1959,F 11,50:2
Greenwillow 1960,Mr 9,38:1
Another Evening With Harry Stoones 1961,O 23,22:2
New Faces of 1962 1962,F 2,25:1
Most Happy Fella, The 1966,My 12,55:1
Fig Leaves Are Falling, The 1969,Ja 3,19:1
Megilla of Itzik Manger, The 1969,Ap 21,55:1
Blood Red Roses 1970,Mr 23,48:1

Bogin, Bernard
Summer and Smoke 1952,Ap 25,19:5
Grass Harp, The 1953,Ap 28,32:2
Threepenny Opera, The 1954,Mr 11,26:5

Bogiotopoulos, St
Oedipus Tyrannus 1952,N 25,35:2

Bogue, Galen (Producer)
Queer People 1934,F 16,16:2

Boguslav, Raphael
Belafonte at the Palace 1959,D 16,55:1

Bohan, Dennis
Mr Peebles and Mr Hooker 1946,O 11,29:2
Open House 1947,Je 4,33:4

Bohan, James C
That's That 1924,Ap 30,19:2
Joan of Arkansas 1925,Ap 5,16:1

Bohanna, Bob
Earthlight Theater 1970,N 4,38:2

Bohdanetzky, Thomas (Miscellaneous)
Staircase 1968,Ja 11,41:2
Romeo and Juliet 1968,Je 11,55:2
Tartuffe 1968,Je 12,39:1
Midsummer Night's Dream, A 1968,Je 13,54:1

Boheme, Hans (Original Author)
Saturday It Rained 1932,D 14,27:3

Bohlman, Edgar (Scenic Designer)
Ledge, A 1929,N 19,26:3
Novice and the Duke, The 1929,D 11,37:2
Everything's Jake 1930,Ja 17,20:4
They Never Grow Up 1930,Ap 8,27:1
Venetian Glass Nephew, The 1931,F 24,26:3

Bohn, Jack
Miss Lulu Bett 1920,D 28,9:1
Three Times the Hour 1931,Ag 26,15:5

Bohn, John
Dreams for Sale 1922,S 14,24:1
Great Man, The 1931,Ap 8,20:6
Web, The 1932,Je 28,24:4
Ceiling Zero 1935,Ap 11,26:2
Paths of Glory 1935,S 27,24:2

Bohn, Peanuts
Keep Off the Grass 1940,My 24,22:6

Bohne, Fred (Lighting Director)
One Is a Lonely Number 1964,Je 19,37:3

Bohnen, Michael
Casanova 1928,N 4,IX,2:1
Marietta 1929,D 8,X,4:4
Toni aus Wien, Die 1931,Ag 30,VIII,2:2

Bohnen, Roman
As Husbands Go 1931,Mr 6,26:5
Bulls, Bears and Asses 1932,My 7,11:3
Big Night 1933,Ja 18,16:2
Best Sellers 1933,My 4,20:2
Divine Drudge 1933,Jl 4,16:4
Divine Drudge 1933,O 27,22:3
Gentlewoman 1934,Mr 23,28:4
Lady From the Sea, The 1934,My 2,25:2
Gold Eagle Guy 1934,N 29,33:4
Waiting for Lefty 1935,F 11,14:5
Awake and Sing! 1935,F 20,23:2
Till the Day I Die 1935,Mr 27,24:5
Waiting for Lefty 1935,Mr 27,24:5
White Hell 1935,Ag 13,20:3

Bohnen, Roman—Cont
Paradise Lost 1935,D 10,31:5
Case of Clyde Griffiths 1936,Mr 14,10:4
Johnny Johnson 1936,N 20,26:3
Golden Boy 1937,N 5,18:5
Gentle People, The 1939,Ja 6,25:1
Thunder Rock 1939,N 15,18:1
Night Music 1940,F 23,18:2
Five Alarm Waltz 1941,Mr 14,16:2
Bohnen, Roman (Playwright)
Incubator 1932,N 2,23:3
Bohnert, Bill (Scenic Designer)
Dumbbell People in a Barbell World 1962,F 15,25:1
Boice, Betty
That's the Woman 1930,S 4,27:2
Boileau, Dwight
Jotham Valley 1951,F 7,37:2
Boileau, Emily
Magda 1926,Ja 27,16:2
Salvation 1928,F 1,31:1
Boileau, La Grange (Playwright)
Troupe Du Roi, La 1970,F 4,38:1
Boileau, Pierre (Original Author)
Monique 1957,O 23,38:1
Bois, Curt
Von Mund zu Mund 1926,D 5,VIII,8:7
Escape 1928,My 20,VIII,2:1
Scribby's Suppen Sind die Besten
1929,D 22,VIII,4:6
Phaea 1930,Ag 31,VIII,2:1
Weaker Sex, The 1931,Mr 1,VIII,1:3
Tomorrow's a Holiday! 1935,D 31,10:2
Help Yourself! 1936,Jl 15,15:1
Polonaise 1945,O 8,20:2
Boissiere, Carl
Prayer Meeting: or, The First Militant Minister
1969,Ap 27,92:1
Great Goodness of Life (A Coon Show)
1969,Ap 27,92:1
Gentleman Caller, The 1969,Ap 27,92:1
Black Quartet, A; Prayer Meeting or The First
Militant Minister 1969,Jl 31,28:1
Black Quartet, A; Great Goodness of Life (A Coon
Show) 1969,Jl 31,28:1
Black Quartet, A; Gentleman Caller, The
1969,Jl 31,28:1
Boizon, Blanche
Red Poppy, The 1922,D 21,18:2
Bojanowicz, Elzbieta
Jacob and the Angel 1965,Ja 6,32:1
Post Office, The 1965,Ja 6,32:1
Kernel and the Shell, The 1965,Ja 6,32:1
Book, The 1965,Ja 6,32:1
Nightmare, The 1965,Ja 6,32:1
Labyrinth, The 1965,Ja 6,32:1
Jaselka 1965,Ja 6,32:1
Woman, The 1965,Ja 6,32:1
Bojar, Alvin (Miscellaneous)
Folies Bergere 1964,Je 3,36:1
Bokee, Mary
Patience 1928,Je 26,29:3
Boker, George Henry (Playwright)
Francesca da Rimini 1967,S 12,54:1
Boker, Rita
What Next 1920,Ja 27,7:2
Bokor, Margit
Gypsy Baron, The 1942,Je 20,8:5
Gypsy Baron, The 1942,Ag 7,12:4
Beggar Student, The 1942,S 26,11:4
Vienna at Night 1945,Ap 30,12:4
Bokwe, John Knox (Miscellaneous)
Sponono 1964,Ap 3,28:1
Bolam, James
How's the World Treating You? 1966,O 25,50:1
Bolan, Alexis
Russian Bank 1940,My 25,20:2
Bolan, Jeanne
I Am a Camera 1961,Jl 10,26:1
Miss Julie 1961,Jl 10,26:1
Boland, Bridget (Playwright)
Time Out of Mind 1970,Jl 15,29:1
Boland, Clay A (Composer)
Sale and a Sailor, A, or Glory! What Price!
1926,Ap 25,30:4
Hoot Mon, or Clans Across the Sea 1927,My 8,29:4
Red Rhumba 1936,Ap 14,18:1
This Mad Whirl 1937,Ja 10,II,4:8
Fifty-Fifty 1937,N 20,21:1
Fifty-Fifty 1937,D 5,II,3:4
Great Guns 1939,N 18,23:4
Boland, Clay A (Lyricist)
Red Rhumba 1936,Ap 14,18:1
Great Guns 1939,N 18,23:4
Boland, Clay A (Original Author)
This Mad Whirl 1937,Ja 10,II,4:8
Boland, Joseph
Conflict 1929,Mr 7,22:4
Goodbye My Fancy 1948,N 18,35:2
Borned in Texas 1950,Ag 22,30:6
Greatest Man Alive!, The 1957,My 9,37:2
Rope Dancers, The 1957,N 21,39:1
Third Best Sport 1958,D 31,15:3
Jolly's Progress 1959,D 7,42:2
Have I Got a Girl for You! 1963,D 3,53:2

Philadelphia, Here I Come! 1966,F 17,28:1
Spofford 1967,D 15,54:3
Boland, Mary
Alias Jimmy Valentine 1921,D 9,20:3
Advertising of Kate, The 1922,My 9,22:2
Torch Bearers, The 1922,Ag 30,10:2
Meet the Wife 1923,N 27,23:4
Meet the Wife 1923,D 16,IX,1:1
Cradle Snatchers 1925,S 8,28:2
Women Go on Forever 1927,S 8,25:1
Heavy Traffic 1928,S 6,23:3
Meet the Wife 1928,D 3,30:6
Vaudeville (Palace) 1928,D 3,30:6
Ada Beats the Drum 1930,My 9,20:4
Vinegar Tree, The 1930,N 20,30:3
Vinegar Tree, The 1930,D 7,IX,1:1
Face the Music 1932,F 4,25:4
Face the Music 1932,F 18,24:5
Face the Music 1932,Mr 20,VIII,1:1
Face the Music 1933,F 1,13:4
Jubilee 1935,S 23,20:3
Jubilee 1935,S 29,X,1:1
Jubilee 1935,O 14,20:1
Jubilee 1935,O 27,IX,1:1
Rivals, The 1941,N 18,32:2
Rivals, The 1942,Ja 15,24:2
Open House 1947,Je 4,33:4
ANTA Album 1951,My 7,22:7
Lullaby 1954,F 4,21:2
Boland, Peggy
Mrs Jimmie Thompson 1920,Mr 30,9:1
Buckaroo 1929,Mr 18,31:1
Bolasni, Saul (Costume Designer)
Courtin' Time 1951,Je 14,30:2
Threepenny Opera, The 1954,Ap 4,II,7:1
Rainmaker, The 1954,O 29,28:1
Duchess of Malfi, The 1957,Mr 20,33:1
Of Love Remembered 1967,F 20,46:5
Minor Adjustment, A 1967,O 7,33:3
Bolce, Phylis
Mr Jiggins of Jigginstown 1936,D 18,30:2
Bolcom, William (Composer)
Red Eye of Love 1961,Je 13,28:1
Three Times Three; Twenty-Five Cent White Cap,
The 1962,Mr 2,24:1
Dynamite Tonight 1964,Mr 16,36:2
Dynamite Tonight 1967,Mr 16,52:2
Miser, The 1969,My 9,35:1
Bold, Richard
Love Birds 1921,Mr 16,12:1
George White's Scandals 1922,Ag 29,10:1
George White's Scandals 1923,Je 19,22:5
Scandals 1924,Jl 1,16:1
Gay Paree 1925,Ag 19,14:3
Gay Paree 1926,N 10,24:2
Optimists, The 1928,Ja 31,28:2
Earl Carroll's Vanities 1928,Ag 7,25:2
Bolden, Harry
Run, Little Chillun! 1933,Mr 2,21:3
Stevedore 1934,Ap 19,33:2
Porgy and Bess 1935,O 11,30:2
Sweet River 1936,O 29,30:2
Jeb 1946,F 22,20:2
Long Way From Home, A 1948,F 9,25:2
Set My People Free 1948,N 4,38:2
Member of the Wedding, The 1950,Ja 6,26:6
Bolek, Allen
House of Breath, The 1957,Ap 15,23:2
Bolek, Bernice
Simpleton of the Unexpected Isles, The
1954,Ja 12,19:1
Bolen, Samuel
Lulu Belle 1926,F 10,20:1
Bolen, Virginia
Sing for Your Supper 1939,Ap 25,18:6
Heart of a City 1942,F 13,24:6
It's All Yours 1942,Mr 26,26:2
Bolen, Virginia (Miscellaneous)
Emperor's Clothes, The 1953,F 10,24:2
Bolender, Charles
Beggar's Opera, The 1957,Mr 14,35:1
Take Me Along 1959,O 23,22:2
Killer, The 1960,Mr 23,33:1
Bolender, Todd
Rosalinda; Fledermaus, Die 1942,O 29,26:5
Bolender, Todd (Choreographer)
Love's Labour's Lost 1953,F 25,20:3
Merchant of Venice, The 1953,Mr 5,20:2
Love Doctor, The 1959,O 14,52:4
Cry for Us All 1970,Ap 9,48:2
Fiddler on the Roof 1970,Jl 8,34:1
Bolender, Todd (Miscellaneous)
Killer, The 1960,Mr 23,33:1
Boles, Glen
Coquette 1935,My 22,23:4
Ragged Edge, The 1935,N 26,28:3
Boles, Jim
Goodbye Again 1943,N 10,28:4
Victors, The 1948,D 27,17:2
All That Fall 1957,O 8,41:2
Boles, John
Mercenary Mary 1925,Ap 14,27:3
Love Spell, The 1925,N 25,14:2

Boles, John—Cont
Kitty's Kisses 1926,My 7,12:2
One Touch of Venus 1943,O 8,14:1
Boles, Viola
Flossie 1924,Je 4,25:2
Boleslavsky, Natasha
They All Come to Moscow 1933,My 12,20:6
False Dreams, Farewell 1934,Ja 16,18:3
Star Spangled 1936,Mr 11,23:1
Russian Bank 1940,My 25,20:2
Boleslavsky, Richard (Choreographer)
Falstaff 1928,D 26,14:2
Boleslavsky, Richard (Costume Designer)
Judas 1929,Ja 25,20:4
Boleslavsky, Richard (Director)
Lady From the Provinces, The 1923,F 27,14:2
Player Queen, The 1923,O 17,14:2
Shewing-Up of Blanco Posnet, The 1923,O 17,14:2
Miracle, The 1924,Ag 19,9:1
Saint, The 1924,O 13,20:3
Twelfth Night 1925,O 25,VIII,1:1
Taming of the Shrew, The 1925,D 19,14:1
Taming of the Shrew, The 1925,D 27,VII,1:1
Ballyhoo 1927,Ja 5,18:1
Granite 1927,F 12,13:1
Much Ado About Nothing 1927,N 19,14:6
At the Gate of the Kingdom 1927,D 9,28:5
White Eagle, The 1927,D 27,24:4
Doctor Knock 1928,F 24,15:2
Three Musketeers, The 1928,Mr 14,28:1
Martine 1928,Ap 5,19:3
Mr Moneypenny 1928,O 17,26:2
Falstaff 1928,D 26,14:2
Judas 1929,Ja 25,20:4
Boley, Ann
Peer Gynt 1951,Ja 29,15:2
Boley, Joseph
Career Angel 1943,N 19,24:2
Simon's Wife 1945,Mr 9,16:4
If in the Green Wood 1947,Ja 17,27:6
City of Kings 1949,F 18,27:2
Too Late the Phalarope 1956,O 12,35:1
Idiot's Delight 1957,F 23,14:2
Tartuffe 1957,O 9,39:1
Electra 1958,My 10,17:7
Jackknife 1958,S 23,36:2
And the Wind Blows 1959,Ap 29,28:1
Five Posts in the Market Place 1961,Mr 6,30:1
Dock Brief, The 1961,N 22,24:2
What Shall We Tell Caroline? 1961,N 22,24:2
Book of Job, The 1962,F 10,13:1
Boley, May
Rose Girl, The 1921,F 12,11:1
Go-Go 1923,Mr 13,19:4
Vogues of 1924 1924,Mr 28,14:3
Princess April 1924,D 2,23:2
Oh! Nurse 1925,D 8,28:4
Jubilee 1935,S 23,20:3
Jubilee 1935,O 14,20:1
Boleyn, Eleanor
Early to Bed 1943,Je 18,16:2
Happy Birthday 1946,N 1,31:2
Touch and Go 1949,O 14,34:2
Pal Joey 1952,Ja 4,17:6
Bolger, Frank
Hasty Heart, The 1959,S 15,45:2
Bolger, Gail
Pride and Prejudice 1935,N 6,32:4
Bolger, Ray
Merry World, The 1926,Je 9,18:3
Night in Paris, A 1926,Jl 27,15:4
Vaudeville (Palace) 1927,D 6,26:3
Me for You 1929,S 22,IX,2:6
Heads Up! 1929,N 12,34:1
Scandals 1931,Ag 11,28:4
Scandals 1931,Ag 16,VIII,1:1
George White's Scandals 1931,S 15,30:1
Life Begins at 8:40 1934,Ag 7,20:7
Life Begins at 8:40 1934,Ag 28,24:2
Life Begins at 8:40 1934,S 2,IX,1:1
On Your Toes 1936,Ap 13,14:4
Keep Off the Grass 1940,My 5,X,1:6
Keep Off the Grass 1940,My 24,22:6
By Jupiter 1942,Je 4,22:1
By Jupiter 1942,Ag 16,VIII,2:1
By Jupiter 1942,Ag 30,VIII,1:1
Three to Make Ready 1946,Mr 8,16:2
Three to Make Ready 1946,Mr 17,II,1:1
Where's Charley? 1948,O 12,33:2
Where's Charley? 1948,O 24,II,1:1
Where's Charley? 1949,Ap 3,II,2:3
Where's Charley? 1950,Ag 20,II,1:1
Where's Charley? 1951,Ja 30,21:7
All American 1962,Mr 20,44:1
All American 1962,Ap 8,II,1:2
Come Summer 1969,Mr 19,43:1
Bolger, Robert
Cup of Trembling, The 1948,Ap 21,33:5
Bolin, Shannon
Damn Yankees 1955,My 6,17:1
Only in America 1959,N 20,35:1
Student Gypsy, The; Prince of Liederkranz, The
1963,O 1,34:1
Xmas in Las Vegas 1965,N 5,31:1

Bolin, Shannon—Cont
Promenade 1969,Je 5,56:1
Promenade 1969,Je 15,II,1:1
Bolitho, Hector (Playwright)
Grey Farm 1940,My 4,12:7
Bolitho, William (Playwright)
Overture 1930,N 25,31:2
Overture 1930,D 8,26:4
Overture 1930,D 14,IX,1:1
Bolke, Bradley
Jonah! 1967,S 22,52:2
Bolling, Gary
Toilet, The 1964,D 17,51:1
Son, Come Home, A 1968,Mr 9,23:2
Clara's Ole Man 1968,Mr 9,23:2
Bollinger, John (Miscellaneous)
Moon Walk 1970,N 27,52:1
Bollinger, Percy
So That's That 1925,D 15,28:3
Bollmer, George
Overture 1930,D 8,26:4
Bolo, Jean
Annonce Faite a Marie, L' 1965,Ap 6,33:2
Bolo, Pierre
Femmes Savantes, Les 1967,F 7,34:2
Bologna, Joseph (Playwright)
Lovers and Other Strangers 1968,S 19,63:1
Lovers and Other Strangers 1968,S 29,II,1:1
Bolotine, Leonid
Elizabethans, The 1962,Ja 22,19:1
Golden Age, The 1963,N 19,49:2
Bolster, Anita
Where There's a Will 1939,Ja 18,16:6
Lady in Waiting 1940,Mr 28,19:1
Pygmalion 1945,D 27,16:1
Kathleen 1948,F 4,26:2
Bolster, Stephen
Education of H*Y*M*A*N K*A*P*L*A*N, The
1968,Ap 5,57:1
Lovely Ladies, Kind Gentlemen 1970,D 29,38:1
Bolt, David
Antony and Cleopatra 1967,Ag 2,25:1
Bolt, Jonathan
Don't Drink the Water 1966,N 18,37:1
United States vs Julius and Ethel Rosenberg, The
1969,Ap 20,II,3:1
Bolt, Robert (Playwright)
Flowering Cherry 1959,O 22,46:1
Tiger and the Horse, The 1960,Ag 25,26:5
Man for All Seasons, A 1961,N 23,51:1
Man for All Seasons, A 1961,D 3,II,1:1
Man for All Seasons, A 1962,S 23,II,1:1
Man for All Seasons, A 1963,My 11,15:1
Gentle Jack 1963,N 29,50:7
Man for All Seasons, A 1964,Ja 28,24:2
Vivat! Vivat Regina! 1970,My 24,80:1
Vivat! Vivat Regina! 1970,Jl 20,21:2
Boltom, Lois
Mrs Gibsons' Boys 1949,My 5,35:2
Bolton, Guy (Lyricist)
Leave It to Jane 1959,My 26,30:2
Bolton, Guy (Miscellaneous)
Song of Sixpence, A 1930,Ap 6,IX,2:1
Bolton, Guy (Original Author)
Anything Goes 1934,N 18,IX,1:7
Anything Goes 1937,Ag 26,24:3
Hold On to Your Hats 1940,S 12,30:3
Chocolate Soldier, The 1947,Mr 13,34:2
Sally 1948,My 7,31:2
Anya 1965,N 30,48:1
Bolton, Guy (Playwright)
Light of the World, The 1920,Ja 7,17:1
Cave Girl, The 1920,Ag 19,12:2
Sally 1920,D 22,16:1
Tangerine 1921,Ag 10,8:2
Nightcap, The 1921,Ag 16,18:3
Hotel Mouse, The 1922,Mr 14,11:3
Daffy Dill 1922,Ag 23,14:5
Polly Preferred 1923,Ja 12,13:3
Chicken Feed 1923,S 25,10:2
Nobody's Business 1923,O 23,17:1
Nobody's Business 1923,O 28,VIII,1:1
Grounds for Divorce 1924,Mr 2,VIII,2:7
Sitting Pretty 1924,Mr 30,VIII,2:7
Sitting Pretty 1924,Ap 9,24:2
Polly Preferred 1924,Ap 13,VIII,1:3
Grounds for Divorce 1924,S 24,20:1
Lady Be Good 1924,D 2,23:4
Tip-Toes 1925,D 29,20:2
Tree of Aphrodite, The 1926,Jl 18,VII,1:7
Ramblers, The 1926,S 21,32:2
Oh, Kay! 1926,N 9,31:3
Nightingale, The 1927,Ja 4,20:4
Rio Rita 1927,F 3,18:3
Five O'Clock Girl, The 1927,O 11,26:3
She's My Baby 1928,Ja 4,22:2
Rosalie 1928,Ja 11,26:3
Polly 1929,Ja 9,28:3
Red and Black 1929,F 10,IX,2:1
Top Speed 1929,N 17,IX,4:1
Top Speed 1929,D 26,20:1
Simple Simon 1930,F 2,VIII,2:7
Girl Crazy 1930,O 5,IX,4:6

Girl Crazy 1930,O 15,27:1
Simple Simon 1931,Mr 10,23:2
Who's Who 1934,S 21,28:4
Anything Goes 1934,N 22,26:1
Seeing Stars 1935,N 1,25:5
At the Silver Swan 1936,F 20,22:2
Going Places 1936,O 9,30:5
Three After Three 1939,N 25,13:5
Walk With Music 1940,Je 5,33:2
Theatre 1941,O 26,IX,2:3
Theatre 1941,N 13,34:2
Golden Wings 1941,N 25,33:3
Golden Wings 1941,D 9,46:6
Jackpot 1944,Ja 14,15:2
Follow the Girls 1944,Ap 10,15:2
Follow the Girls 1944,Ap 16,II,1:2
Larger Than Life 1950,F 8,33:2
Larger Than Life 1950,Mr 12,II,3:7
Adorable Julia 1954,N 28,II,3:1
Anastasia 1955,Ja 16,II,1:1
Ankles Aweigh 1955,Ap 19,27:1
Ankles Aweigh 1955,Ap 24,II,1:1
Child of Fortune 1956,N 14,41:1
Rosalie 1957,Je 26,28:2
Leave It to Jane 1959,My 26,30:2
Oh, Kay! 1960,Ap 18,37:2
Anything Goes 1962,My 16,35:1
Anya 1965,N 30,48:1
Bolton, Guy (Stephen Powys) (Original Author)
Walk With Music 1940,Je 5,33:2
Bolton, Guy (Translator)
Anastasia 1954,D 30,13:1
Bolton, Harold
Jerry for Short 1929,Ag 13,23:4
City Haul 1929,D 31,14:4
Midnight 1930,D 30,25:1
Happy Landing 1932,Mr 28,10:5
Foolscap 1933,Ja 12,21:2
Church Mouse, A 1933,Je 27,13:7
Summer Night 1939,N 3,17:1
Bolton, Harold (Director)
Professor Mamlock 1937,Ap 14,30:3
Trojan Incident 1938,Ap 22,15:2
Bolton, Helen
My Golden Girl 1920,F 3,18:2
Pitter Patter 1920,S 29,12:2
Up She Goes 1922,N 7,14:2
My Girl 1924,N 25,27:2
Bolton, Kathleen
Anne of the Thousand Days 1948,D 9,49:2
Cellar and the Well, The 1950,D 11,30:2
Small Hours, The 1951,F 16,22:1
Bolton, Larry
Pure in Heart, The 1934,Mr 21,24:3
I Myself 1934,My 10,24:6
Lorelei 1938,N 30,21:2
Susanna, Don't You Cry 1939,My 23,27:2
Across the Board on Tomorrow Morning
1942,Ag 18,17:1
On the Town 1944,D 29,11:4
Wise Have Not Spoken, The 1954,F 11,35:2
Comic Strip 1958,My 15,26:2
Bolton, Lawrence
Belt, The 1927,O 20,33:1
Centuries, The 1927,N 30,23:1
International, The 1928,Ja 16,24:4
Hoboken Blues 1928,F 18,10:1
Him 1928,Ap 19,23:3
After Dark: or, Neither Maid, Wife nor Widow
1929,F 10,IX,1:1
Houseparty 1929,S 10,26:5
City Haul 1929,D 31,14:4
Trick for Trick 1932,F 19,14:2
Bolton, Lawrence (Director)
Pleased to Meet You 1928,O 30,27:2
Royal Virgin, The 1930,Mr 18,30:5
Old Man Murphy 1931,My 19,25:2
Trick for Trick 1932,F 19,14:2
Bolton, Lois
Billeted 1922,My 10,22:4
American Holiday 1936,F 22,13:3
Let's Face It 1941,O 30,26:2
Mexican Hayride 1944,Ja 29,9:6
Joy Forever, A 1946,Ja 8,20:2
As the Girls Go 1948,N 15,21:2
Bolton, M W (Mrs) (Playwright)
Strange Rhythm 1937,Ap 20,29:2
Bolton, Richard
Day Will Come, The 1944,S 8,17:2
Bolton, Richard (Miscellaneous)
Mr Winkle's Holliday 1946,Je 24,27:6
Bolton, Richard (Scenic Designer)
Anna Lucasta 1944,Je 17,10:1
Bolton, Ruth (Playwright)
Simple Simon 1930,F 19,22:1
Bolton-Carter, Joy
Green Table, The 1942,Ja 22,12:2
Prodigal Son, The 1942,F 18,22:2
Bolyard, Lewis
Pal Joey 1952,Ja 4,17:6
Bomgardner, Harold E
Student Prince, The 1931,Ja 30,18:1

Bomhard, Moritz (Musical Director)
Tall Kentuckian, The 1953,Je 17,30:1
Bommart, Jean (Original Author)
Man of Yesterday 1935,F 20,22:5
Bonaccorso, D Rusty (Miscellaneous)
Baker Street 1965,F 17,36:1
Zorba 1968,N 18,58:1
Boy Friend, The 1970,Ap 15,54:1
Bonal, Denise
Femmes Savantes, Les 1967,F 7,34:2
Bonanni, Luciano
Rugantino 1964,F 7,34:1
Bonanova, Fortunio
Dishonored Lady 1930,Ja 26,VIII,2:1
Dishonored Lady 1930,F 5,27:1
Silent Witness, The 1931,Mr 24,31:5
Bonati, Narcisa
Servant of Two Masters, The 1960,F 24,42:2
Bonaventura, Robert (Miscellaneous)
Tiny Alice 1969,S 30,42:1
Bonay, Armand
Body Beautiful, The 1958,Ja 24,15:2
Bonazzi, Elaine
Yeomen of the Guard, The 1965,Ap 22,26:1
Bond, Bianca
If This Be Treason 1935,S 24,28:2
Bond, Brenda
Spread Eagle 1927,Ap 5,30:2
Yes, Yes, Yvette 1927,O 4,32:3
Just a Minute 1928,O 9,34:3
Bond, Edward (Playwright)
Early Morning 1968,Ap 9,58:1
Narrow Road to the Deep North 1968,Je 27,49:2
Narrow Road to the Deep North 1969,D 2,64:1
Narrow Road to the Deep North 1970,F 11,39:2
Saved 1970,O 29,57:1
Saved 1970,N 1,II,10:1
Early Morning 1970,N 26,57:1
Bond, Francine
In Any Language 1952,O 9,40:2
Me and Juliet 1953,My 29,17:1
Bond, Frank G
Monkey Talks, The 1925,D 29,20:1
Treasure Girl 1928,N 9,22:1
Carnival 1929,Ap 25,32:5
Chinese O'Neill 1929,My 23,27:1
Bond, Frank G (Director)
He Understood Women 1928,Ag 16,25:1
Bond, Gary
Chips With Everything 1963,O 2,49:1
Bond, George
Dead End 1935,O 29,17:2
Bond, Gertrude
Kiki 1921,N 30,13:1
Bond, Lillian
Stepping Out 1929,My 21,29:1
Luana 1930,S 18,28:1
Free for All 1931,S 9,25:1
Three and One 1933,O 26,22:6
Little Shot 1935,Ja 18,28:4
All Men Are Alike 1941,O 7,27:2
Bond, Nancy
Milk Train Doesn't Stop Here Anymore, The
1965,Jl 27,25:1
Bond, Raleigh
Donogoo 1961,Ja 19,25:3
On the High Road 1961,Ap 21,26:2
Bond, Raymond
Thirsty Soil 1937,F 4,16:2
Bond, Raymond (Playwright)
Thirsty Soil 1937,F 4,16:2
Bond, Richard
Too Many Boats 1934,S 12,26:3
Abie's Irish Rose 1937,My 13,30:2
Bond, Ridge
Oklahoma! 1951,My 30,15:2
Oklahoma! 1951,S 13,38:2
Oklahoma! 1953,S 1,19:1
Bond, Rudy
O'Daniel 1947,F 25,32:2
Streetcar Named Desire, A 1947,D 4,42:2
Bird Cage, The 1950,F 23,32:2
Romeo and Juliet 1951,Mr 12,21:2
Glad Tidings 1951,O 12,33:2
Golden Boy 1952,Mr 13,24:3
Streetcar Named Desire, A 1956,F 16,24:1
Big Man 1966,My 20,41:1
Match-Play 1966,O 12,37:1
Illya Darling 1967,Ap 12,37:1
Papp 1969,My 6,39:1
Bond, Ruth
Red, Hot and Blue! 1936,O 30,26:3
One Touch of Venus 1943,O 8,14:1
Bond, Sally
Let's Face It 1941,O 30,26:2
Bond, Sheila
Allah Be Praised! 1944,Ap 21,14:2
Street Scene 1947,Ja 10,17:2
Make Mine Manhattan 1948,Ja 16,26:2
Live Wire, The 1950,Ag 18,16:2
Wish You Were Here 1952,Je 26,26:6
Lunatics and Lovers 1954,D 14,44:2
Deadfall 1955,O 28,20:1

Bond, Sheila—Cont

Pal Joey 1961,Je 1,32:1
Bond, Sudie
Slice It Thin 1945,My 11,22:5
From Morn Till Midnight 1948,D 7,41:6
Doctor Faustus Lights the Lights 1951,D 3,23:4
Tovarich 1952,My 15,39:2
Waltz of the Toreadors, The 1957,Ja 18,17:2
Waltz of the Toreadors, The 1957,Ja 27,II,1:1
Auntie Mame 1958,Ag 12,33:2
Sandbox, The 1960,My 17,42:2
Shepherd's Chameleon, The 1960,N 30,41:1
American Dream, The 1961,Ja 25,28:1
Egg, The 1962,Ja 9,23:2
Endgame 1962,F 12,27:1
Bertha 1962,F 12,27:1
Harold 1962,N 30,27:1
My Mother, My Father and Me 1963,Mr 25,5:5
American Dream, The 1963,My 29,39:6
Home Movies 1964,My 12,32:1
Softly, and Consider the Nearness 1964,My 12,32:1
Great Western Union, The 1965,F 10,45:1
Impossible Years, The 1965,O 14,55:1
Keep It in the Family 1967,S 28,59:1
Memorandum, The 1968,My 6,55:1
Quotations From Chairman Mao Tse-Tung
    1968,O 1,39:1
American Dream, The 1968,O 3,55:1
Local Stigmatic, The; Request Stop 1969,N 4,55:2
Local Stigmatic, The; That's All 1969,N 4,55:2
Local Stigmatic, The; Applicant 1969,N 4,55:2
Local Stigmatic, The; That's Your Trouble
    1969,N 4,55:2
Hay Fever 1970,N 10,55:1
Bond, Sudie (Choreographer)
From Morn Till Midnight 1948,D 7,41:6
Bond, Ward
What Price Glory 1949,Mr 3,33:2
Bond, Willard
Exception and the Rule, The 1965,My 21,19:1
Bond, Willard (Miscellaneous)
Javelin 1966,N 10,63:1
Bonda, Leonora
Church Mouse, A 1931,My 3,VIII,2:1
Bondhill, Gertrude
Mulatto 1935,O 25,25:2
Bondi, Alexander (Playwright)
Obratsov Russian Pupper Theater in an Unusual
    Concert 1963,O 3,28:1
Bondi, Beulah
One of the Family 1925,D 23,22:3
Saturday's Children 1927,Ja 27,13:1
Mariners 1927,Mr 29,22:2
Cock Robin 1928,Ja 13,26:6
Street Scene 1929,Ja 11,20:4
Milestones 1930,Je 3,27:1
Distant Drums 1932,Ja 19,24:3
Distant Drums 1932,Ja 31,VIII,1:1
Late Christopher Bean, The 1932,N 1,24:3
Mother Lode 1934,D 24,16:5
Hilda Crane 1950,N 2,38:2
On Borrowed Time 1953,Ja 1,19:1
On Borrowed Time 1953,F 11,34:1
Bondirieff, Alexei
Tsar Fyodor Ivanovitch 1923,Ja 9,26:1
Lower Depths, The 1923,Ja 16,16:1
Cherry Orchard, The 1923,Ja 23,18:1
Brothers Karamazov, The 1923,N 20,23:4
Ivanoff 1923,N 27,23:2
In the Claws of Life 1923,N 30,23:4
Death of Pazukhin, The 1924,F 12,20:1
Bondon, Mona
New York Exchange 1926,D 31,11:2
Bonds, Margaret
U S A 1956,D 19,41:4
Shakespeare in Harlem 1959,O 28,40:7
Bonds, Margaret (Composer)
Shakespeare in Harlem 1960,F 21,II,1:1
Clandestine on the Morning Line 1961,O 31,28:1
Bonds, Robert
Picnic on the Battlefield 1967,S 9,25:2
Bone, Gene (Composer)
Americana Pastoral 1968,D 11,51:1
Bonefein, Evelyn
Would-Be Gentleman, The 1930,Ap 30,29:2
Bonelle, Dick
Lyle 1970,Mr 21,16:2
Bonelli, Richard
Merry Widow, The 1933,Ag 13,IX,1:3
Bonelli, William
Pietro 1920,Ja 20,10:2
Big Boy 1925,Ja 8,28:2
Romancing 'Round 1927,O 4,32:4
First Night 1930,N 27,32:3
Precedent 1931,Ap 15,24:5
Tree, The 1932,Ap 13,23:5
Wrong Number 1934,Mr 14,23:6
I Myself 1934,My 10,24:6
Bonerz, Peter
White House Murder Case, The 1970,F 19,59:1
Story Theater 1970,O 27,54:1
Bonestell, Mary
R U R 1922,O 10,16:1

Bonetti, Margaret
From Morn Till Midnight 1948,D 7,41:6
Bonetti, Silvio
Colonello Bridall, L' 1934,Ap 16,20:3
Processo dei Veleni, Il; Case of Poisons, The
    1935,Ja 21,18:2
Bonfils, Helen
Topaze 1947,D 29,21:5
Fundamental George, The 1949,Ag 17,19:4
Bonfils, Helen (Producer)
Sun Kissed 1937,Mr 11,20:2
Greatest Show on Earth, The 1938,Ja 6,22:2
Brown Danube, The 1939,My 18,30:4
Pastoral 1939,N 2,26:2
Come Play With Me 1959,My 1,33:5
Thurber Carnival, A 1960,F 27,13:2
Chips With Everything 1963,O 2,49:1
White House, The 1964,My 20,39:1
P S I Love You 1964,N 20,40:1
Killing of Sister George, The 1966,O 6,57:1
Come Live With Me 1967,Ja 27,29:1
Promise, The 1967,N 15,38:1
Lovers; Losers 1968,Jl 26,21:4
Lovers; Winners 1968,Jl 26,21:4
We Bombed in New Haven 1968,O 17,51:1
Mundy Scheme, The 1969,D 12,75:1
Sleuth 1970,N 13,25:1
Bongini, Raffaello
Barbara 1929,N 18,24:5
Tristi Amori; Unhappy Loves 1930,O 27,17:6
Piacere Del'Onesta, Il; Happiness of Probity, The
    1930,N 10,16:4
Cena Delle Beffe, La; Jest, The 1930,N 24,26:4
In Fondo Al Cuore; Depths of the Heart, The
    1930,D 8,27:1
Gli Spettri 1930,D 22,16:4
Cardinale, Il; Cardinal, The 1931,Ja 12,24:2
Sansone; Samson 1931,F 9,25:1
Marchese di Priola, Il 1931,Mr 2,19:3
Cantico dei Cantici, Il; Song of Songs
    1931,Ap 13,17:3
My Wife Is Different 1931,Ap 27,24:4
Cantico dei Cantici, Il; Song of Songs
    1931,My 18,21:4
Alba, Il Gioro, La Notte, L'; Dawn, the Day, the
    Night, The 1931,My 18,21:4
Zia Morta, La; Dead Aunt, The 1931,N 30,16:3
Piccolo Santo, Il; Little Saint, The 1931,D 14,16:4
Civil Death, The 1932,Ja 25,20:3
Canto Della Vita, Il; Song of Life, The
    1932,Ap 4,13:3
Casa di Tutti, La; Everybody's Home 1932,D 5,21:4
Cardinale, Il 1933,Ja 9,24:2
Zia Morta, La; Dead Aunt, The 1933,F 13,11:3
Istruttoria, L'; Judicial Inquiry, The 1933,F 13,11:3
Curioso Accidente, Un 1933,Mr 6,16:3
Romanticismo 1933,My 1,10:5
Ingeborg 1933,D 11,23:3
Conte di Monte Cristo, Il 1934,Ja 22,13:2
Padrone Delle Ferriere, Il 1934,Mr 19,13:5
Colonello Bridall, L' 1934,Ap 16,20:3
Romanticismo 1934,My 14,20:2
Miserabili I, 1934,S 24,15:1
Miserabili I, 1934,O 1,14:2
Signora Dalle Camelie, La; Camille 1934,O 22,13:2
Processo dei Veleni, Il; Case of Poisons, The
    1935,Ja 21,18:2
Romanzo di un Giovane Povero, Il 1935,F 25,12:3
Vita Nuova; Life Begins Again 1935,F 26,16:2
Conte di Monte Cristo, Il 1935,Ap 1,17:6
Signo Della Croce, Il 1935,O 7,11:1
Cardinale Giovanni de Medici, Il 1935,D 9,24:8
Testamento della Zia d'America, Il; American
    Aunt's Will, The 1936,Mr 23,22:4
Religione e Patria 1936,Mr 23,22:4
Due Orfanelle, Le; Two Orphans, The
    1936,O 5,24:4
Tombola, La; Lottery, The 1936,N 9,23:4
Sansone; Samson 1936,N 30,25:2
Feudalismo Oppure La Terra Bassa; Feudalism or
    the Lowland 1937,Mr 8,22:2
Ora di Diana, L' 1937,My 17,22:3
Medico Delle Pazze, Il; Physician of Mad Woman,
    The 1937,S 27,24:2
Signora Dalle Camelie, La; Dame aux Camelias, La
    1937,O 9,16:3
BonGiovanni, Gaetano
Picnic on the Battlefield 1967,S 9,25:2
Bonham, Eugene
Paul Bunyan 1941,My 6,25:1
Bonhoff, Don
Dark Hours, The 1932,N 15,24:2
Late One Evening 1933,Ja 10,27:3
Boni, Daniela
All Summer Long 1954,S 24,26:2
All Summer Long 1954,O 3,II,1:1
Boni, John A
Most Happy Fella, The 1966,My 12,55:1
Bonilia, Jose M
Conerico Was Here to Stay 1965,Mr 4,37:1
Bonime, Abby
Kiss for Cinderella, A 1942,Mr 11,22:2
Strings, My Lord, Are False, The 1942,My 20,24:2

Bonime, Abby—Cont

Innocent Voyage, The 1943,N 16,27:2
Seeds in the Wind 1948,Ap 26,27:2
Seeds in the Wind 1948,My 26,29:2
Bonini, Peggy
Yanqui and the Senorita, The 1952,Ag 8,8:7
Bonitz, John Jr (Lighting Director)
Wilderness Road 1955,Je 30,20:4
Bonn, Carl (Scenic Designer)
Skin of Our Teeth, The 1945,N 18,II,2:5
Abdication 1948,S 28,32:5
Bonn, Theodor
At Home Abroad 1935,S 20,17:4
Bonn, Walter
We Are No Longer Children 1932,Ap 1,17:2
Bonnard, Andre (Translator)
Antigone 1960,D 14,52:1
Bonnard, Robert (Director)
Watch-Pit 1969,Ja 30,39:1
Bonnard, Robert Andrew
York Nativity Play, The 1956,D 5,49:2
Bonnelii, William
Pleasure Bound 1929,F 19,22:4
Bonnell, Jay
Stone Tower, The 1962,Ag 24,14:2
Ben Bagley's Shoestring Revues 1970,O 24,22:1
Bonnell, Marian
Five O'Clock Girl, The 1927,O 11,26:3
Bonnell, Sam
Final Balance, The 1928,O 31,28:3
Street Scene 1929,Ja 11,20:4
Counsellor-at-Law 1931,N 7,17:2
Between Two Worlds 1934,O 26,24:2
Revolt of the Beavers, The 1937,My 21,19:2
Counsellor-at-Law 1942,N 25,17:2
One Touch of Venus 1943,O 8,14:1
Woman Bites Dog 1946,Ap 18,21:2
Joy to the World 1948,Mr 19,28:2
Grand Tour, The 1951,D 11,45:2
Bonnelli, William
Marilyn's Affairs 1933,Mr 16,21:5
Bonner, Barry
Awakening of Spring, The 1964,My 13,50:1
Bonner, Eugene (Composer)
Young Alexander 1929,Mr 13,28:2
Bonner, Eugene (Musical Director)
Venetian Glass Nephew, The 1931,F 24,26:3
Bonner, Isabel
Let Freedom Ring 1935,N 7,26:2
Processional 1937,O 14,23:1
Trojan Incident 1938,Ap 22,15:2
Medicine Show 1940,Ap 13,20:6
Front Page, The 1946,S 5,22:4
Me, The Sleeper 1949,My 16,18:6
Shrike, The 1952,Ja 16,20:2
Shrike, The 1953,N 26,51:2
Bonner, Lota
This Is New York 1930,N 29,21:1
Bonner, Paul (Producer)
Acropolis 1933,N 24,25:8
Bonner, Paul Hyde
Passing of the Third Floor Back, The 1924,F 8,19:4
Bonner, Rudolph (Playwright)
Wait Till We're Married 1921,S 27,14:1
Bonnet, James
Sunrise at Campobello 1958,Ja 31,25:1
Bonnett, Walter
Deirdre of the Sorrows 1959,O 15,46:1
Bonney, Aurora
Bridal Crown, The 1938,F 7,11:2
Bonney, John
Henry V 1958,D 26,2:7
Bonnington, Keith
Trial by Jury 1964,N 20,40:1
Bonny, Fred
Louisiana 1933,F 28,15:5
Bono, Steve (Producer)
Salvage 1957,Ap 10,39:2
Bonomo, Joe
Vaudeville (Palace) 1930,F 17,18:4
Bonsall, Marie
Apache, The 1923,My 9,14:3
Bonsilau, Emilio A
Tia Juana 1927,N 16,28:4
Bonstelle, Helen
Dumbbell People in a Barbell World 1962,F 15,25:1
Bonstelle, Jessie (Director)
Heaven 1920,Je 13,VI,1:8
Leah Kleschna 1924,Ap 22,19:2
Awful Mrs Eaton, The 1924,Jl 20,VII,1:7
That Awful Mrs Eaton! 1924,S 30,27:1
Now-A-Days 1929,Ag 6,29:3
Bontecou, Lee
Untitled-Nativity Play 1941,D 25,28:5
Bontemps, Arna (Miscellaneous)
Free and Easy 1959,D 15,51:4
Bontemps, Arna (Original Author)
St Louis Woman 1946,Ap 1,22:2
Bontemps, Mimi
Journey by Night, A 1935,Ap 17,26:3
Bonton, Elaine
Don Juan 1921,S 8,14:2
Bonura, Aldo
Hedda Gabler 1970,Ja 18,78:1

Bonus, Ben
Father and Son 1956,O 20,17:4
Let's Sing Yiddish 1966,N 10,63:1
Sing Israel Sing 1967,My 12,50:1
Light, Lively and Yiddish 1970,O 28,58:1
Bonus, Ben (Playwright)
Light, Lively and Yiddish 1970,O 28,58:1
Bonus, Ben (Producer)
Let's Sing Yiddish 1966,N 10,63:1
Sing Israel Sing 1967,My 12,50:1
Bonville, Nace
Florodora 1920,Ap 6,18:1
Excess Baggage 1927,D 27,24:2
Second Mate, The 1930,Mr 25,34:5
Bonwit, Elise
Poor Little Ritz Girl 1920,Jl 29,7:1
Round the Town 1924,My 22,14:3
Bad Habits of 1926 1926,My 1,11:1
Twinkle Twinkle 1926,N 17,22:2
Bonynge, Leta
Strange Bedfellows 1948,Ja 15,27:3
Ivy Green, The 1949,Ap 6,37:2
Lady in the Dark 1952,Mr 8,11:3
My Fair Lady 1968,Je 14,42:1
Inner Journey, The 1969,Mr 21,42:1
Miser, The 1969,My 9,35:1
Time of Your Life, The 1969,N 7,37:1
Camino Real 1970,Ja 9,42:1
Boockvor, Steven
Cabaret 1966,N 21,62:1
Billy 1969,Mr 24,56:1
Boodkin, Celia
Souls for Sale 1936,S 21,27:6
Book, Harold P
Great Shakes 1931,Mr 12,22:2
Booke, Sorrell
White Devil, The 1955,Mr 15,32:5
Moby Dick 1955,Ap 26,25:3
Carefree Tree, The 1955,O 12,37:2
King Lear 1956,Ja 13,17:1
Month in the Country, A 1956,Ap 4,23:1
Henry V 1956,Jl 7,11:2
Sleeping Prince, The 1956,N 2,31:1
Nature's Way 1957,O 17,42:2
Winkelberg 1958,Ja 15,26:2
Heartbreak House 1959,O 19,37:1
Caligula 1960,F 17,31:1
Jeannette 1960,Mr 25,20:2
Finian's Rainbow 1960,Ap 28,31:1
Wedding, The 1961,Ap 21,26:2
On the High Road 1961,Ap 21,26:2
Anniversary, The 1961,Ap 21,26:2
Purlie Victorious 1961,S 29,29:1
Purlie Victorious 1961,O 8,II,1:1
Fiorello! 1962,Je 14,24:1
White House, The 1964,My 20,39:1
Jonah! 1966,F 16,52:1
Come Live With Me 1967,Ja 27,29:1
Noon 1968,N 29,52:1
Night 1968,N 29,52:1
Morning 1968,N 29,52:1
Booker, George
Swing It 1937,Jl 23,17:2
Booker, Leonard
Three Musketeers, The 1921,My 20,18:5
Sweet Nell of Old Drury 1923,My 19,16:4
American Born 1925,O 6,31:3
First Love 1926,N 9,31:2
Bookins, Fred (Miscellaneous)
Summer and Smoke 1950,O 29,II,3:7
Bookwalter, DeVeren
Romeo and Juliet 1965,Je 21,36:3
Coriolanus 1965,Je 21,36:1
King Lear 1965,Je 25,39:1
As You Like It 1968,Je 24,42:3
Philosophy in the Boudoir 1969,My 22,55:2
Boomer, Eastman (Producer)
Anna Russell and Her Little Show 1953,S 8,27:2
Boone, Frank (Producer)
Bohikee Creek 1966,Ap 29,39:1
Boone, John
Lancashire Lass, The 1931,D 31,16:3
Boone, P
Gentlemen, the Queen 1927,Ap 23,14:3
Boone, Richard
Medea 1947,O 21,27:2
Man, The 1950,Ja 20,28:2
Rivalry, The 1959,F 9,24:2
Rivalry, The 1959,F 15,II,1:1
Boonio, S
Processional 1937,O 14,23:1
Booraem, Hendrik
Reunion in Vienna 1931,N 17,31:1
Black Diamond 1933,F 24,12:2
Valley Forge 1934,D 11,28:3
Booraem, Hendrik (Playwright)
Sky's the Limit, The 1934,D 18,25:5
Boot, Gladys
Yes, M'Lord 1949,O 5,35:2
Cocktail Party, The 1950,My 7,II,2:5
Booth, Anita
New Poor, The 1924,Ja 8,26:1
Out of Step 1925,Ja 30,12:1

Booth, Anne
Virginia 1937,S 3,13:2
Booth, Carol
Beekman Place 1964,O 8,50:1
Alfie 1964,D 18,27:1
Booth, Constance
Winter's Tale, The 1963,Je 29,13:1
Midsummer Night's Dream, A 1963,Jl 1,19:2
Booth, Hilliard (Playwright)
Breakfast in Bed 1920,F 4,12:1
Booth, James
Alchemist, The 1970,Ag 26,36:1
Booth, Jim
Would-Be Gentleman, The 1930,Ap 30,29:2
Booth, John (Costume Designer)
Houseboat on the Styx, The 1928,D 26,14:3
All the King's Horses 1934,Ja 31,21:3
Saluta 1934,Ag 29,13:4
Viva O'Brien 1941,O 10,27:2
Booth, John Hunter (Playwright)
Like a King 1921,O 4,10:1
Fever of Youth, The 1926,Ag 8,VII,3:1
No Trespassing! 1926,S 8,19:1
Talk About Girls 1927,Je 15,31:3
Brass Buttons 1927,D 6,26:3
Booth, Joyce
Edgar Allan Poe 1925,O 6,31:1
Allez-Opp! 1927,Ag 3,29:3
Booth, Lillian
Caught 1925,O 6,31:2
Right Age to Marry, The 1926,F 16,22:3
Booth, Marie
Piper, The 1920,Mr 20,14:2
Booth, Marjorie
Suzette 1921,N 25,18:3
Shore Leave 1922,Ag 9,20:2
Booth, Mildred
Deep Tangled Wildwood, The 1923,N 6,22:1
Trouper, The 1926,Mr 9,21:1
Booth, Philip
Murder in the Cathedral 1935,D 21,11:3
Booth, Shirley
Hell's Bells! 1925,Ja 27,14:2
Laff That Off 1925,N 3,34:2
Buy, Buy Baby 1926,O 8,26:2
High Gear 1927,O 7,24:3
War Song, The 1928,S 25,29:3
School for Virtue 1931,Ap 22,29:2
Camels Are Coming, The 1931,O 3,20:4
Coastwise 1931,D 1,23:1
Mask and the Face, The 1933,My 9,20:2
After Such Pleasures 1934,Ja 6,18:6
After Such Pleasures 1934,F 8,15:2
Sunday Nights at Nine 1934,Mr 5,18:5
Dream Child 1934,Jl 31,20:2
Nude in Washington Square, The 1934,Ag 7,20:1
Sunday Nights at Nine 1934,N 19,12:1
Three Men on a Horse 1935,Ja 22,22:7
Three Men on a Horse 1935,Ja 31,22:3
Sunday Nights at 9 1935,N 11,21:1
Excursion 1937,Ap 10,11:4
Too Many Heroes 1937,N 16,26:2
Philadelphia Story, The 1939,Mr 29,21:1
My Sister Eileen 1940,D 27,23:2
Tomorrow the World 1943,Ap 15,22:2
Tomorrow the World 1943,Ap 25,II,1:1
Hollywood Pinafore 1945,Je 1,20:1
Land's End 1946,D 12,37:5
Cradle Will Rock, The 1947,N 25,38:3
Men We Marry, The 1948,Ja 17,11:2
Goodbye My Fancy 1948,N 18,35:2
Goodbye My Fancy 1948,N 28,II,1:1
Love Me Long 1949,N 8,34:5
Come Back, Little Sheba 1950,F 16,28:5
Come Back, Little Sheba 1950,F 26,II,1:1
Come Back, Little Sheba 1950,My 14,II,1:1
Tree Grows in Brooklyn, A 1951,Ap 20,23:1
Tree Grows in Brooklyn, A 1951,Ap 29,II,1:1
ANTA Album 1951,My 7,22:7
Tree Grows in Brooklyn, A 1951,My 20,II,1:1
Time of the Cuckoo, The 1952,O 16,37:4
Time of the Cuckoo, The 1952,N 2,II,1:1
Time of the Cuckoo, The 1953,Ja 4,II,1:1
By the Beautiful Sea 1954,Ap 9,20:1
By the Beautiful Sea 1954,Ap 18,II,1:1
Desk Set, The 1955,O 25,36:7
Miss Isobel 1957,D 27,22:1
Juno 1959,Mr 10,41:1
Juno 1959,Mr 15,II,1:1
Second String, A 1960,Ap 14,36:2
Look to the Lilies 1970,Mr 30,59:1
Look to the Lilies 1970,Ap 12,II,3:7
Hay Fever 1970,N 10,55:1
Hay Fever 1970,N 22,II,18:6
Booth, Sydney
Checkerboard, The 1920,Ag 20,7:2
Minick 1924,S 25,20:1
Joker, The 1925,N 17,29:1
Seed of the Brute 1926,N 2,34:3
Merchant of Venice, The 1928,Ja 17,22:2
Most Immoral Lady, A 1928,N 27,36:1
Top O' the Hill 1929,N 27,30:4
Five Star Final 1930,D 31,11:1

Booth, Sydney—Cont
Slight Case of Murder, A 1935,S 12,28:5
Three Wise Fools 1936,Mr 2,12:2
Booth, Thelma
Claire Adams 1929,N 20,26:3
Booth, Walter
Scarlet Coat, The 1924,D 24,11:1
Fortuno 1925,D 23,22:1
Boothe, Clare (Original Author)
Women, The 1938,N 5,14:1
Boothe, Clare (Playwright)
Abide With Me 1935,N 22,19:2
Women, The 1936,D 8,30:6
Women, The 1936,D 28,13:1
Kiss the Boys Goodbye 1938,S 29,30:2
Women, The 1939,Ap 21,21:2
Women, The 1939,My 7,X,2:1
Margin for Error 1939,O 15,48:7
Margin for Error 1939,N 4,11:3
Margin for Error 1939,N 12,IX,1:1
Margin for Error 1940,Ag 11,IX,2:4
Boothe, Clare Luce
Candida 1945,Ag 7,25:3
Boothe, Clare Luce (Playwright)
Child of the Morning 1951,N 17,9:7
Child of the Morning 1958,Ap 22,40:2
Boothe, Earle (Director)
Jonesy 1929,Ap 10,32:2
Apron Strings 1930,F 18,28:2
Betty, Be Careful 1931,My 5,33:3
Uncle Tom's Cabin 1933,My 30,13:4
Boothe, Earle (Producer)
Shannons of Broadway, The 1927,S 27,30:4
Jonesy 1929,Ap 10,32:2
Boothe, Wade
Sally 1920,D 22,16:1
Vaudeville (Palace) 1928,Ap 17,26:2
Boots, Antoinette
Topsy and Eva 1924,D 24,11:1
Boots, George
Rivals, The 1942,Ja 15,24:2
Lifeline 1942,D 1,20:3
Booty, Jill (Translator)
Knight From Olmedo, The 1962,N 26,36:2
Boralle, Edward
Elmer Gantry 1928,Ag 10,9:4
Boras, George
Buoyant Billions 1959,My 27,32:2
Getting Married 1959,Je 5,18:2
Shewing-Up of Blanco Posnet, The 1959,S 19,26:7
Borass, Feriake
Kreutzer Sonata, The 1924,My 15,22:3
Borbus, Alice
Merry Widow, The 1944,O 9,17:1
Borchardt, Ann (Translator)
Square, The 1961,Mr 24,37:1
Borchert, Wolfgang (Playwright)
Outside the Door 1949,Mr 2,33:2
Bordages, Asa (Playwright)
Brooklyn, U S A 1941,D 22,24:2
Brooklyn, U S A 1941,D 28,IX,1:1
Brooklyn, U S A 1942,Ja 11,IX,1:1
Borde, Albert (Miscellaneous)
Follow the Girls 1944,Ap 10,15:2
Borde, Percival
Mister Johnson 1956,Mr 30,11:1
Borde, Percival (Choreographer)
Man Better Man 1969,Jl 3,22:1
Harangues, The 1970,Ja 14,42:1
Akokawe 1970,Je 5,21:1
Borde, Percival (Composer)
Man Better Man 1969,Jl 13,II,3:6
Bordeau, Francine
Star Time 1944,S 13,16:2
Borden, Anna
Cross Roads 1929,N 12,34:2
Borden, Eddie
Vaudeville (Palace) 1928,S 25,29:4
Borden, Essie
Peace 1969,Ja 28,49:1
Borden, Ethel
Ziegfeld Follies 1931,Jl 2,30:5
Design for Living 1933,Ja 3,19:5
Design for Living 1933,Ja 25,13:2
Borden, Ethel (Playwright)
Anne of England 1941,O 8,26:2
Borden, Ethel (Translator)
Hedda Gabler 1942,Ja 30,22:2
Borden, Eugene
French Doll, The 1922,F 21,20:2
Borden, Flora
Bad Habits of 1926 1926,My 1,11:1
Borden, Geoffrey
Anne of England 1941,O 8,26:2
Borden, Johnny
Bye Bye Birdie 1960,Ap 15,13:4
Borden, Joyce
Barefoot 1925,O 20,29:2
Borden, Marshall
Cherry Orchard, The 1970,My 7,63:2
Borden, Mary (Playwright)
Jane-Our Stranger 1925,O 9,27:2
Borden, Norris
Only in America 1959,N 20,35:1

Borden, Norris—Cont
Deep Are the Roots 1960,O 4,47:1
White Cargo 1960,D 30,12:1
Borden, Rod
Christmas in the Market Place 1960,D 10,26:1
Borden, William H
What a Relief 1935,D 14,10:6
Take It Away 1936,D 15,30:5
Borden, William H (Composer)
What a Relief 1935,D 14,10:6
What a Relief 1935,D 19,34:4
Take It Away 1936,D 22,32:3
Borden, William H (Lyricist)
What a Relief 1935,D 14,10:6
What a Relief 1935,D 19,34:4
Take It Away 1936,D 22,32:3
Bordner and Boyer
Vaudeville (Palace) 1926,Ap 13,28:3
Bordo, Ed
Last Analysis, The 1964,O 2,30:1
Inquest 1970,Ap 24,38:1
Bordoni, Glendinning
Untitled-Benefit 1922,My 8,14:5
Bordoni, Irene
As You Were 1920,Ja 28,22:3
French Doll, The 1922,F 21,20:2
Untitled-Benefit 1922,My 8,14:5
Little Miss Bluebeard 1923,Ag 29,12:1
Little Miss Bluebeard 1923,S 2,VI,1:1
Naughty Cinderella 1925,O 4,IX,2:1
Naughty Cinderella 1925,N 10,23:6
Mozart 1926,N 23,26:2
Vaudeville (Palace) 1927,My 3,25:2
Vaudeville (Palace) 1927,My 10,25:3
Vaudeville (Palace) 1927,N 29,30:4
Paris 1928,O 9,34:3
Vaudeville (Palace) 1930,S 8,17:3
Great Lady 1938,D 2,26:6
Louisiana Purchase 1940,My 29,19:2
Lady From Paris, The 1950,S 27,36:1
Bordoni, Robert
Reflected Glory 1936,S 18,19:5
Reflected Glory 1936,S 22,30:2
Bored, Emile
Merry World, The 1926,Je 13,VII,1:1
Fifth Column, The 1940,Mr 17,X,1:1
Borell, Louis
Heart's Content 1936,D 24,22:2
Candle in the Wind 1941,O 23,26:2
Made in Heaven 1946,O 25,28:2
My Name is Aquilon 1949,F 10,38:2
Idiot's Delight 1951,My 24,46:3
Boren, William
Ivory Door, The 1927,O 19,24:5
Queen's Husband, The 1928,Ja 26,17:2
Congai 1928,N 28,24:3
Overture 1930,D 8,26:4
Company's Coming! 1931,Ap 21,35:5
Boreo, Emile
Chauve-Souris 1922,Je 6,17:4
Merry World, The 1926,Je 9,18:3
Passions of 1926 1926,Ag 3,19:4
Vaudeville (Palace) 1927,N 1,20:3
Vaudeville (Palace) 1930,O 20,29:1
Fifth Column, The 1940,Mr 7,18:2
Boretz, Allen (Lyricist)
Garrick Gaieties 1930,Je 5,29:2
Boretz, Allen (Playwright)
Room Service 1935,N 17,II,7:7
Room Service 1937,My 20,16:1
Room Service 1937,My 30,X,1:1
Room Service 1937,D 16,35:4
Flying Ginzburgs, The 1938,N 13,IX,2:2
Off to Buffalo! 1939,F 22,18:2
Room Service 1953,Ap 7,34:1
Hot Corner, The 1956,Ja 26,25:2
Room Service 1970,My 13,49:1
Room Service 1970,Jl 5,II,1:2
Boretz, Allen (Producer)
Ring Around Elizabeth 1941,N 18,32:2
Borge, Victor
Comedy in Music 1953,O 3,15:2
Comedy in Music, Opus 2 1964,N 10,54:1
Comedy in Music 1964,N 22,II,1:1
Borgeaud, Nelly
Tartuffe 1968,Jl 3,28:2
Borgen, Grete
Holiday on Ice 1967,Ag 31,29:2
Holiday on Ice 1968,Ag 29,44:1
Holiday on Ice 1969,Ag 28,44:1
Borgen, Johan (Playwright)
Mens Vi Venter 1939,Ap 9,X,2:3
Borgen, Richard (Lighting Director)
She Stoops to Conquer 1968,Ja 1,11:1
Resistible Rise of Arturo Ui, The 1968,Ag 8,25:1
Borger, Bob
Good News 1927,S 7,35:4
Orchids Preferred 1937,My 12,26:5
Borger, Harriett
Merry Widow, The 1942,Jl 16,22:1
Borgese, Giovanna
Hedda Gabler 1934,Je 5,28:3
Borgia, Philippe
Manhattan Varieties 1932,O 22,18:3

Borgman, Frank
Finian's Rainbow 1953,Mr 7,13:2
Finian's Rainbow 1955,My 19,25:1
Last Love of Don Juan, The 1955,N 24,40:1
Thesmophoriazusae, The; Goddesses of Athens,
The 1955,D 14,52:4
Music Shop, The 1962,F 16,35:2
Vagrant, The 1962,F 16,35:2
Night Is Black Bottles, The 1962,D 5,56:1
Impromptu, L' 1965,Mr 8,34:1
Foursome 1965,Mr 8,34:1
Leader, The 1965,Mr 8,34:1
Oh, Pioneers 1969,N 12,41:1
Immaculate Misconception, The 1970,O 28,63:3
Borgnine, Ernest
Mrs McThing 1952,F 21,22:1
Borgus, Jerry (Costume Designer)
Pursuit of Happiness, The 1952,Mr 22,9:2
Bori, Diana
We Are No Longer Children 1932,Ap 1,17:2
Foolscap 1933,Ja 12,21:2
Borice, Andre
Noble Rogue, A 1929,Ag 20,31:2
Borio, Giuseppina
Piccolo Santo, Il; Little Saint, The 1931,D 14,16:4
Boris, Ruthanna
Blue Butterfly, The 1929,F 17,29:3
Hooray for What! 1937,D 2,32:5
Straw Hat, The 1939,S 30,10:6
Annie Get Your Gun 1958,F 20,29:2
Boris, Ruthanna (Choreographer)
Student Prince, The 1943,Je 9,16:2
Two on the Aisle 1951,Jl 20,13:6
Borisov, B
Untitled-Revue 1935,S 23,20:2
Bork, Geraldine
Pirates of Penzance, The 1936,Ap 21,27:5
Bork, Hanne
Come Live With Me 1967,Ja 27,29:1
Halfway up the Tree 1967,N 8,52:1
Borkh, Inge
Consul, The 1951,S 8,9:3
Borland, Barlowe
Romeo and Juliet 1922,D 28,20:1
Lass O' Laughter 1925,Ja 9,13:2
Little Minister, The 1925,Mr 24,21:1
Saturday Night 1926,O 26,25:1
Locandiera, La; Mistress of the Inn, The
1926,N 23,26:1
Twelfth Night 1926,D 21,21:4
Cradle Song 1927,Ja 25,18:2
Baby Cyclone, The 1927,S 13,37:4
Lancashire Lass, The 1931,D 31,16:3
Anatomist, The 1932,O 25,24:3
Borland, Jim (Miscellaneous)
Time for the Gentle People, A 1967,My 26,50:1
Borland, Leslie (Miscellaneous)
Time for the Gentle People, A 1967,My 26,50:1
Borland, Leslie Jane
Time for the Gentle People, A 1967,My 26,50:1
Born, John
Betty Behave 1927,Mr 9,28:4
Born, Walter
Music in the Air 1951,O 9,32:2
Kiss Me, Kate 1954,Mr 27,13:2
Borne, Hal (Composer)
Alive and Kicking 1950,Ja 18,25:5
Bornwasser, Mitzi
Tall Kentuckian, The 1953,Je 17,30:1
Borod, Robert (Miscellaneous)
Fly Blackbird 1962,F 6,26:2
Journey to the Day 1963,N 12,49:1
Borodin, Alexander (Miscellaneous)
Kismet 1953,D 4,2:4
Kismet 1965,Je 23,45:1
Borodkin, Michael
Othello 1937,Ja 7,16:4
Boroff, George (Producer)
Once Upon a Tailor 1955,My 24,36:2
Boroff, John
Happy Valley, Limited 1936,Je 30,15:1
Borofsky, Richard
Much Ado About Nothing 1963,Jl 15,25:2
Boros, Elmer (Playwright)
World Record, The 1932,Ap 17,VIII,3:8
Boros, Feriki
Chicago 1926,D 31,11:1
Borough, Margaret
Hospitality 1922,N 14,16:1
Hell-Bent Fer Heaven 1924,Ja 5,10:1
Interference 1928,My 8,25:4
Borough, Marguerite
Tales of Rigo 1927,My 31,25:3
Ledge, A 1929,N 19,26:3
Lone Valley 1933,Mr 11,18:6
Borowska, Olga
Clair de Lune 1921,Ap 19,15:1
Borowsky, Serge
Russian Isba 1920,F 17,19:2
Borowsky, Serge (Musical Director)
Russian Isba 1920,F 17,19:2
Borowsky, Serge (Producer)
Russian Isba 1920,F 17,19:2

Borrale, Edward
Master of the Inn, The 1925,D 23,22:2
Borras, Tomas (Playwright)
El Alcalde De Zalamea 1953,N 23,32:5
Borroughs, Don
Scarlet Man, The 1921,Ag 23,10:3
Borroughs, Margarita
Othello 1953,O 30,28:2
Borrow, Ernest
Geneva 1940,Ja 31,15:2
Borrup, Doan
Sophisticrats, The 1933,F 14,19:5
Borsche, Dieter
Stellvertreter, Der 1963,F 23,7:8
Borsella, Walter (Miscellaneous)
Liberace's Variety Bill 1957,Ap 22,29:5
Borske, Haal
Wuziz! 1970,O 2,25:2
Borsody, Emil
Time Remembered 1957,N 13,41:2
Borst, Stephen
Macbeth 1969,N 21,51:1
Borstler, Robert (Miscellaneous)
Pictures in the Hallway 1956,My 28,23:1
Borsuk, Alice
Madame Aphrodite 1961,D 30,13:1
This Side of Paradise 1962,F 22,19:6
Bortolussi, Dick
House of Leather, The 1970,Mr 19,56:1
Boruff, John
Roof, The 1930,Je 14,9:2
Racket, The 1930,N 20,30:6
Peace on Earth 1933,N 30,39:2
Sailors of Cattaro 1934,D 11,28:4
Ceiling Zero 1935,Ap 2,24:3
Ceiling Zero 1935,Ap 11,26:2
Mother, The 1935,N 20,26:3
Bitter Stream 1936,Mr 31,16:6
They Knew What They Wanted 1936,Jl 8,14:2
Daughters of Atreus 1936,O 15,33:1
Waltz in Goose Step 1938,N 2,26:2
Three Sisters, The 1939,O 16,23:1
Male Animal, The 1940,Ja 10,17:2
When the Bough Breaks 1950,Mr 9,25:5
49th Cousin, The 1960,O 28,22:1
Bicycle Ride to Nevada 1963,S 25,38:1
Boruff, John (Playwright)
Timber 1936,Jl 29,11:5
Timber House 1936,S 21,27:5
Washington Jitters 1938,My 3,19:1
Bright Boy 1944,Mr 3,19:5
Loud Red Patrick, The 1956,O 4,28:1
Borup, Anette
County Chairman, The 1936,My 26,26:5
Borup, Doan
Henry IV, Part I 1926,Je 1,29:1
Junk 1927,Ja 6,25:1
Julius Caesar 1927,Je 7,27:2
Judas 1929,Ja 25,20:4
Young Alexander 1929,Mr 13,28:2
Becky Sharp 1929,Je 4,29:1
Star of Bengal 1929,S 26,27:2
City Haul 1929,D 31,14:4
Little Father of the Wilderness, The 1930,Je 3,27:1
If Booth Had Missed 1932,F 5,24:2
Merry-Go-Round 1932,Ap 23,11:2
Rendezvous 1932,O 13,22:3
Tight Britches 1934,S 12,26:2
American Holiday 1936,F 22,13:3
Help Yourself! 1936,Jl 15,15:1
On the Rocks 1938,Je 16,20:2
Bosan, Alonzo
Hummin' Sam 1933,Ap 10,8:8
Walk Together Chillun 1936,F 5,15:2
Turpentine 1936,Je 27,21:6
Androcles and the Lion 1938,D 17,10:5
Dark Hammock 1944,D 12,27:8
Strange Fruit 1945,N 30,18:6
Long Way From Home, A 1948,F 9,25:2
Set My People Free 1948,N 4,38:2
Two Blind Mice 1949,Mr 3,32:2
Wisteria Trees, The 1950,Mr 30,39:1
Green Pastures, The 1951,Mr 16,35:2
Green Pastures, The 1951,Ap 1,II,1:1
Seventeen 1951,Je 22,16:6
My Darlin' Aida 1952,O 28,36:4
Wisteria Trees, The 1955,F 3,20:2
Boscana, Lucy
Ox Cart, The 1966,D 20,58:1
Bosch, John Valentine
This Mad Whirl 1937,Ja 10,II,4:8
Bosche, Peter
Mary Stuart 1956,Ap 28,10:2
Sappho 1960,Ja 12,22:1
Magnificent Hugo, The 1961,Ap 8,12:2
Falstaff 1966,Je 20,27:1
Murder in the Cathedral 1966,Je 21,38:1
Julius Caesar 1966,Je 24,29:2
Hamp 1967,Mr 10,32:1
Ceremony of Innocence, The 1968,Ja 2,33:1
Awake and Sing! 1970,My 28,35:1
Arsenic and Old Lace 1970,N 5,59:1

Boschini, Augusta
Alba, Il Gioro, La Notte, L'; Dawn, the Day, the Night, The 1931,My 18,21:4
Bosco, Philip
Auntie Mame 1958,Ag 12,33:2
Month in the Country, A 1959,Mr 2,32:2
Clandestine on the Morning Line 1959,D 5,18:2
Measure for Measure 1960,Jl 27,33:1
Rape of the Belt, The 1960,N 7,46:1
Donnybrook! 1961,My 19,23:1
Donnybrook! 1961,My 28,II,1:1
Ticket-of-Leave Man, The 1961,D 23,15:1
Richard II 1962,Je 18,20:2
Henry IV, Part I 1962,Je 18,20:4
Henry IV, Part I 1962,Je 24,II,1:1
Richard II 1962,Je 24,II,1:1
King Lear 1963,Je 10,37:1
Comedy of Errors, The 1963,Je 13,28:1
Henry V 1963,Je 14,37:1
Caesar and Cleopatra 1963,Ag 1,18:2
Much Ado About Nothing 1964,Je 11,26:2
Richard III 1964,Je 12,44:2
Hamlet 1964,Jl 4,9:1
Coriolanus 1965,Je 21,36:1
Richard III 1966,Ag 11,26:1
Alchemist, The 1966,O 14,48:1
Alchemist, The 1966,O 30,II,1:1
East Wind, The 1967,F 10,30:1
Galileo 1967,Ap 14,31:1
Saint Joan 1968,Ja 5,42:1
Tiger at the Gates 1968,Mr 1,30:1
Tiger at the Gates 1968,Mr 10,II,1:1
Cyrano de Bergerac 1968,Ap 26,30:1
King Lear 1968,N 8,43:1
King Lear 1968,N 17,II,1:3
Great Career, A 1968,D 30,25:1
Evening for Merlin Finch, An 1969,Ja 26,II,1:1
In the Matter of J Robert Oppenheimer 1969,Mr 7,28:1
Miser, The 1969,My 9,35:1
Time of Your Life, The 1969,N 7,37:1
Time of Your Life, The 1969,N 16,II,1:4
Camino Real 1970,Ja 9,42:1
Operation Sidewinder 1970,Mr 13,33:1
Amphitryon 1970,My 29,13:1
Good Woman of Setzuan, The 1970,N 6,51:1
Good Woman of Setzuan, The 1970,N 15,II,1:5
Bose, Rrabinda
Ramayana 1931,Ja 13,35:4
Boselli, Emy
Cave at Machpelah, The 1959,Jl 1,25:1
Boshell, Ada
Letter of the Law, The; Robe Rouge, La 1920,F 24,11:1
Boshell, James A
Bulldog Drummond 1921,D 27,10:2
Right to Kill, The 1926,F 16,22:2
Just Life 1926,S 15,33:3
Wasp's Nest, The 1927,O 26,26:3
Bosler, Virginia
Brigadoon 1947,Mr 14,28:2
Out of This World 1950,D 22,17:3
New Faces of 1952 1952,My 17,23:2
Red Roses for Me 1955,D 29,15:2
Brigadoon 1957,Mr 28,37:1
If Five Years Pass 1962,My 11,37:1
Brigadoon 1963,F 1,6:2
Bosley, Tom
Thieves' Carnival 1955,F 2,21:1
Morning's at Seven 1955,Je 23,25:1
Curious Savage, The 1956,Mr 17,12:3
Sea Gull, The 1956,O 23,38:1
Apollo of Bellac, The 1958,Mr 7,17:2
Browning Version, The 1958,Mr 7,17:2
Beaux' Stratagem, The 1959,F 25,35:4
Fiorello! 1959,N 24,45:3
Fiorello! 1959,N 29,II,1:1
Nowhere to Go But Up 1962,O 9,46:6
Nowhere to Go But Up 1962,N 12,36:2
Natural Affection 1963,F 2,5:2
Murderer Among Us, A 1964,Mr 26,43:1
Catch Me if You Can 1965,Mr 10,50:1
Education of H*Y*M*A*N K*A*P*L*A*N, The 1968,Ap 5,57:1
Education of H*Y*M*A*N K*A*P*L*A*N, The 1968,Ap 14,II,1:1
Bosnell, James
Spook House 1930,Je 4,33:3
Mourning Becomes Electra; Hunted, The 1931,O 27,22:1
Bosner, Phillip
Dust Heap, The 1924,Ap 25,20:2
Bosotina, James
Shoemaker and the Peddler, The 1960,O 15,27:4
Boss, Charles (Scenic Designer)
Carry Nation 1932,O 31,18:2
Boss, Roberto (Translator)
Crossroads 1969,Ag 7,28:1
Bossac, Serge
Berenice 1963,O 30,46:1
Bosseau, Jason
Macbeth 1969,N 21,51:1

Bosshardt, Sonja
Dream Play 1960,N 23,22:1
Bossifer, Stingy
Growing Pains 1933,N 24,24:2
Bossis, Helena
Streetcar Named Desire, A 1949,O 19,36:6
Bost, Pierre (Playwright)
Imbecile 1923,N 1,24:1
Deux Paires d'Amis 1926,O 3,VIII,2:1
Power and the Glory, The 1958,D 12,2:7
Bostain, James
Caucasian Chalk Circle, The 1961,N 1,35:1
Bostick, Irene
Prince Charming 1930,O 14,31:1
Bostick, Jack
Right Next to Broadway 1944,F 22,26:2
Tempest, The 1945,Ja 26,17:2
Cock-A-Doodle-Doo 1949,F 28,16:5
Saint Joan 1950,Mr 4,10:6
Bostock, Homan
Dark Hours, The 1932,N 15,24:2
Bostock, Kenneth
School for Husbands, The 1933,O 17,26:5
Walk With Music 1940,Je 5,33:2
Bostock and Dudley
Three After Three 1939,N 25,13:5
Bostock Riding School
Vaudeville (Hippodrome) 1925,S 1,18:3
Boston, T L (Miscellaneous)
Dames at Sea 1968,D 21,46:1
Last Sweet Days of Isaac, The 1970,Ja 27,49:1
Bostwick, Barry
Cock-A-Doodle Dandy 1969,Ja 21,40:1
Hamlet 1969,Mr 4,34:1
House of Leather, The 1970,Mr 19,56:1
Colette 1970,My 7,60:1
Bostwick, E F
Meanest Man in the World, The 1920,O 13,18:2
Back Pay 1921,Ag 31,8:2
Barnum Was Right 1923,Mr 13,19:3
Woman on the Jury, The 1923,Ag 16,10:4
Business Widow, The 1923,D 11,27:1
Desert Flower, The 1924,N 19,18:2
Devil Within, The 1925,Mr 17,19:4
Crime 1927,F 23,27:3
Bostwick, E F (Director)
Dear Old England 1930,Mr 26,24:6
Bostwick, Harold
Burlesque 1946,D 26,30:3
Bostwick, Herbert
Little Jessie James 1923,Ag 16,10:4
Bostwick, Jack (Director)
Great Magician, The 1951,N 22,45:1
Boswell, John
Sun Showers 1923,F 6,14:2
Boswell Sisters
Vaudeville (Palace) 1931,O 19,28:5
Vaudeville (Hollywood) 1932,F 16,24:3
Bosworth, Francis (Playwright)
Fields Beyond, The 1933,F 14,19:5
Fields Beyond, The 1936,Mr 7,11:2
Bosworth, Hallam
Eyvind of the Hills 1921,F 2,14:1
Letty Pepper 1922,Ap 11,22:2
Lights Out 1922,Ag 18,8:4
Roger Bloomer 1923,Mr 2,18:3
Damn the Tears 1927,Ja 22,11:1
Bottled 1928,Ap 11,25:1
Exceeding Small 1928,O 23,32:2
That Ferguson Family 1928,D 24,10:7
Congratulations 1929,My 1,28:4
Love Expert, The 1929,S 24,29:1
Whirlpool 1929,D 4,37:3
Dora Mobridge 1930,Ap 21,20:2
Trick for Trick 1932,F 19,14:2
Peace on Earth 1933,N 30,39:2
This Our House 1935,D 12,33:3
Devil of Pei-Ling 1936,F 21,20:4
It Can't Happen Here 1936,O 28,30:1
Sun and I, The 1937,F 27,9:5
Scene of the Crime, The 1940,Mr 29,24:1
Not in Our Stars 1941,Ap 26,20:5
Bosworth, Hobart
Vaudeville (Palace) 1932,Jl 18,9:7
Bosworth, Patricia
Small War on Murray Hill 1957,Ja 4,19:1
Small War on Murray Hill 1957,Ja 13,II,1:1
Sin of Pat Muldoon, The 1957,Mr 14,35:1
Howie 1958,S 18,35:2
Jeannette 1960,Mr 25,20:2
Moon Is Blue, The 1961,Ag 9,29:1
Bosworth, Stanley (Translator)
Eagle Has Two Heads, The 1956,D 14,37:2
Botelho, Candido
All in Fun 1940,D 28,11:2
Botemy, Sophia
Mes Amours 1940,My 3,16:5
Both, Richard J
Assorted Nuts 1940,Ap 7,I,44:6
Bothwell, Mary
Happy-Go-Lucky 1926,O 1,27:2
Botrot, Jean (Playwright)
Terre d'Israel 1930,O 12,VIII,4:2

Bottega, Omino
Jazz a La Carte 1922,Je 3,8:3
Bottino, Mariano
'Il Tesoro D'Isacco; Treasure of Isaac, The 1928,Ja 26,17:1
Botto, Louis (Playwright)
New Faces of 1956 1956,Je 15,32:1
Bottomley, Gordon (Playwright)
Acts of St Peter 1934,Ap 22,IX,1:6
Culbin Sands 1935,Mr 23,10:3
Bottomley, Rita (Costume Designer)
Salad of the Mad Cafe, The 1964,Ap 1,43:1
Bottomley, Roland
Lassie 1920,Ap 7,9:2
Nemesis 1921,Ap 5,24:3
Yankee Princess, The 1922,O 3,22:1
Julius Caesar 1927,Je 7,27:2
Death Takes a Holiday 1929,D 27,26:4
Death Takes a Holiday 1931,F 17,29:1
Gay Divorce 1932,N 30,23:4
Hotel Alimony 1934,Ja 30,16:2
Mother Lode 1934,D 24,16:5
Othello 1935,S 28,13:2
Macbeth 1935,O 8,26:4
They Knew What They Wanted 1936,Jl 7,17:2
Laughing Woman, The 1936,O 14,30:1
Cross-Town 1937,Mr 18,21:5
White Steed, The 1939,Ja 11,16:2
Wind in the Sails 1940,Ag 1,24:6
Wookey, The 1941,S 11,20:5
Kiss for Cinderella, A 1942,Mr 11,22:2
Bottomley, Roland (Playwright)
Olivia Bows to Mrs Grundy 1932,Ap 3,VIII,2:5
Slightly Scandalous 1944,Je 14,16:2
Bottoms, John
Young Master Dante, The 1968,D 31,19:1
Botwinik, Norman I
Wings Over Europe 1936,Mr 4,24:7
Boucari, Ali Taieb
Chinese O'Neill 1929,My 23,27:1
Insult 1930,S 16,30:2
Boucet
Untitled-Revue 1930,N 30,IX,3:3
Bouchard, Patricia
Young and Fair, The 1948,N 23,35:2
Bouchateau, Simone
Lorenzaccio 1958,O 15,44:2
Cid, Le 1958,O 31,35:2
Bouche, Don
Pied Piper of Hamelin, The 1950,Ap 3,19:2
Ali Baba 1951,Mr 27,34:2
Bouche, Michel (Producer)
All the King's Men 1959,O 17,27:2
Bouchene, Dimitri (Costume Designer)
Prodigal Son, The 1942,F 18,22:2
Boucher, Jean (Playwright)
Day of Surprises, A 1921,My 1,VII,1:7
Boucher, Victor
Vient de Paraitre 1927,D 11,IX,2:2
Trou Dans le Mur, Le 1929,F 24,IX,1:8
Banque Nemo, La 1931,D 13,VIII,2:2
Tour au Paradis, Un 1933,D 3,IX,7:7
Fric Frac 1936,N 29,XII,2:4
Boucher, Victor (Miscellaneous)
Temps Difficiles, Le 1934,Mr 11,X,2:4
Boucher, Victor (Producer)
Do, Mi, Sol, Do 1935,F 3,VIII,3:3
Boucicault, Dion
Shall We Join the Ladies? 1921,Je 26,VI,1:1
Truth About Blayds, The 1922,Ja 15,VI,1:7
Eileen 1922,Je 18,VI,1:6
Belinda 1922,Jl 30,VI,1:7
Boucicault, Dion (Original Author)
Banker's Daughter, The 1962,Ja 23,37:1
Boucicault, Dion (Playwright)
After Dark 1928,D 11,35:2
After Dark: or, Neither Maid, Wife nor Widow 1929,F 10,IX,1:1
Octoroon, The 1929,Mr 13,28:3
Streets of New York, The 1931,O 7,29:1
London Assurance 1932,Ag 28,IX,1:1
Streets of New York, The 1934,Jl 21,14:5
Octoroon, The 1936,S 1,24:2
London Assurance 1937,F 19,14:5
Octoroon, The 1961,Ja 28,13:1
Streets of New York, The 1963,O 30,47:1
Shaughraun, The 1968,My 22,54:1
Corsican Brothers, The 1970,Mr 20,56:2
London Assurance 1970,Je 25,55:2
London Assurance 1970,Ag 7,26:1
Boucicault, Ruth Holt
Electra 1927,My 4,28:3
Electra 1927,My 15,VIII,1:1
Boucree, Gladys
Swing Mikado, The 1939,Mr 2,18:2
Boudet, Micheline
Bourgeois Gentilhomme, Le 1955,O 26,26:1
Bourgeois Gentilhomme, Le 1955,O 30,II,1:1
Barbier de Seville, Le 1955,N 9,40:1
Arlequin Poli par l'Amour 1955,N 9,40:1
Jeu de l'Amour et du Hasard, Le 1955,N 16,42:4
Fourberies de Scapin, Les 1961,F 22,30:1
Impromptu de Versailles, L' 1961,F 22,30:1

Boudet, Micheline—Cont
Tartuffe 1961,Mr 1,28:1
Dindon, Le 1961,Mr 8,38:1
Boudon, Jorge
Remolienda, La; Bawdy Party 1968,F 3,20:1
Boudrot, Mel
Francesca da Rimini 1967,S 12,54:1
Boudwin, Barbara
Song of Norway 1944,Ag 22,20:2
Boughs, Tristam
As You Like It 1936,Ap 24,18:4
Boughton, Rutland (Composer)
Lily Maid, The 1937,Ja 13,20:4
Boughton, Rutland (Playwright)
Lily Maid, The 1937,Ja 13,20:4
Bouhelier, Saint-Georges de (Playwright)
Carnaval des Enfants, Le 1923,Mr 18,VII,1:1
Imperatrice aux Rochers, L' 1927,Mr 20,VIII,2:4
Flambeaux de la Noce, Les 1927,Ap 17,VII,2:3
Celebre Histoire, La 1928,My 13,IX,2:2
Sang de Danton, Le 1931,Je 28,VIII,1:8
Bouie, John
Henri Christophe 1945,Je 7,24:5
Set My People Free 1948,N 4,38:2
City of Kings 1949,F 18,27:2
Tobacco Road 1950,Mr 7,23:2
Green Pastures, The 1951,Mr 16,35:2
Remains to Be Seen 1951,O 4,37:1
Mamba's Daughters 1953,Mr 21,12:6
Finian's Rainbow 1955,My 19,25:1
Carmen Jones 1956,Je 1,28:2
Simply Heavenly 1957,My 22,28:2
Annie Get Your Gun 1958,F 20,29:2
Bouillaud, Jean-Claude
Femmes Savantes, Les 1967,F 7,34:2
Bouise, Jean
Three Musketeers, The 1968,Je 26,43:1
George Dandin 1968,Je 28,36:1
Tartuffe 1968,Jl 3,28:2
Boulais, Adele
My Golden Girl 1920,F 3,18:2
Bould, Beckett
Geneva 1940,Ja 31,15:2
Bould, James (Costume Designer)
Gallant Cassian 1934,N 14,22:2
School for Wives 1934,N 14,22:2
Bould, James (Scenic Designer)
School for Wives 1934,N 14,22:2
Boulden, Alice
Gay Paree 1925,Ag 19,14:3
Gay Paree 1926,N 10,24:2
Hold Everything 1928,O 11,24:2
Heads Up! 1929,N 12,34:1
Fine and Dandy 1930,S 7,IX,2:4
Fine and Dandy 1930,S 24,26:1
Boulden, Howard
Genius and the Crowd 1920,S 7,20:1
Meanest Man in the World, The 1920,O 13,18:2
Wandering Jew, The 1921,O 27,22:1
Betty Lee 1924,D 26,18:2
Boulden, Ron
Dance of Death, The 1966,Je 3,31:1
As You Like It 1966,Je 4,19:1
Harpers Ferry 1967,Je 6,52:2
Visit, The 1967,S 13,41:1
Bouldin, Eloise
World We Make, The 1939,N 21,19:1
Boulet, Bill
Trumpets and Drums 1969,O 13,52:1
Bouley, Frank
Yearling, The 1965,D 11,25:1
Cabaret 1966,N 21,62:1
Boulez, Pierre (Composer)
Adieux, Les 1957,F 19,36:1
Chien du Jardinier, Le; Gardener's Dog, The 1957,F 19,36:1
Boulez, Pierre (Miscellaneous)
Intermezzo 1957,F 15,20:4
Boulez, Pierre (Musical Director)
Amphitryon 1952,N 21,21:2
Christophe Colomb 1957,Ja 31,20:5
Boulia, William
Crime 1927,F 23,27:3
Excess Baggage 1927,D 27,24:2
Guns 1928,Ag 7,25:2
Boulle, Pierre (Original Author)
Face of a Hero 1960,O 21,29:5
Boulter, Lewis
Little Poor Man, The 1925,Ag 6,14:1
Boulter, Rosalyn
George and Margaret 1937,S 23,32:2
Boulting, John (Miscellaneous)
All in Good Time 1965,F 19,25:1
Boulting, Roy (Miscellaneous)
All in Good Time 1965,F 19,25:1
Boulton, Guy Pelham
Time and the Conways 1938,Ja 4,19:2
Boulton, Lawrence
Bad Girl 1930,O 3,30:2
Boulton, Matthew
Good Companions, The 1931,O 2,31:1
Night Must Fall 1936,S 29,34:1
Aged 26 1936,D 22,32:1

Boulton, Matthew (Playwright)
Little Theatre Tournament; Brass Door Knob, The 1926,My 8,21:2
Boulton, Milo
No Questions Asked 1934,F 6,24:3
Petrified Forest, The 1935,Ja 8,26:1
Paths of Glory 1935,S 27,24:2
Cyrano de Bergerac 1936,Ap 28,17:1
Rumple 1957,N 7,42:2
Cut of the Axe 1960,F 2,38:2
Call Me by My Rightful Name 1961,F 1,31:1
My Mother, My Father and Me 1963,Mr 25,5:5
Rainy Day in Newark, A 1963,O 23,35:1
Music Man, The 1965,Je 17,26:4
Henry, Sweet Henry 1967,O 24,51:2
Our Town 1969,N 28,50:1
My House Is Your House 1970,O 16,53:2
Bouquet, Romain
Suzanne 1929,F 17,IX,4:2
Bour, Armand (Director)
Dernier Empereur, Le 1926,D 19,VIII,3:3
Bourbon, Diana
Loyalties 1922,S 28,18:1
Tancred 1923,Jl 17,14:4
Bourbon, Ray
Catherine Was Great 1944,Ag 3,16:1
Diamond Lil 1948,N 30,33:2
Bourchier, Arthur
Risk, The; Caducee, Le 1922,Jl 30,VI,1:7
Bourdelle, Jean
Damn the Tears 1927,Ja 22,11:1
Bourdelle, Joan
Very Wise Virgin, A 1927,Je 3,25:3
Congratulations 1929,My 1,28:4
Bourdelle, John
Shanghai Gesture, The 1926,F 2,20:2
Bourdet, Edouard (Director)
Ecole des Maris, L' 1939,Mr 19,XI,3:1
Bourdet, Edouard (Original Author)
Sex Fable, The 1931,O 21,26:1
Best Sellers 1933,My 4,20:2
Bourdet, Edouard (Playwright)
Rubicon, The 1922,F 22,13:1
Other Rose, The 1923,D 16,IX,2:4
Other Rose, The 1923,D 21,15:2
Other Rose, The 1923,D 30,VII,1:1
Captive, The 1926,S 30,23:1
Rubicon, Le 1926,O 3,VIII,2:1
Captive, The 1926,O 10,VIII,1:1
Captive, The 1926,O 24,VIII,2:1
Vient de Paraitre 1927,D 11,IX,2:2
Prisonniere, La 1928,Ja 1,VIII,1:3
Vient de Paraitre 1928,S 23,IX,2:1
Sexe Faible, La 1929,D 29,VIII,2:6
Weaker Sex, The 1931,Mr 1,VIII,1:3
Fleur des Pois, La 1932,O 30,IX,3:7
Temps Difficiles, Le 1934,Mr 11,X,2:4
Times Have Changed 1935,F 19,28:2
Times Have Changed 1935,F 26,16:1
Heure du Berger, L'; Propitious Moment, The 1936,N 12,30:1
Fric Frac 1936,N 29,XII,2:4
Bourdin, Roger
Rose of France 1933,O 29,II,3:3
Bourdon, Renee
Christian 1937,F 25,18:6
Bourgeois, Maurice (Translator)
Emperor Jones, The 1923,N 1,24:1
Hairy Ape, The 1929,S 23,27:2
Hairy Ape, The 1929,S 29,IX,4:7
Bourget, Diane
Going Gay 1933,Ag 4,18:5
Bourget, Paul (Original Author)
Chatiment, Un 1929,My 5,IX,2:4
Bourgoyne, Ollie
Promis' Lan', De 1930,My 28,31:2
Bourillon, Henri (Pierre Hamp) (Playwright)
Deraillement du T P 33 1927,F 13,VII,4:1
Bourjaily, Vance (Playwright)
Quick Years, The 1953,N 26,51:2
Bourjaily, Betty
Lady of Letters 1935,Mr 29,26:6
Othello 1935,S 28,13:2
Macbeth 1935,O 8,26:4
Bourke, Fan
Chivalry 1925,D 16,22:3
Chrysalis 1932,N 16,15:2
Bourlas, George
Prometheus Bound 1957,Ag 9,11:6
Bourman, Anatole (Choreographer)
Cafe de Danse 1929,Ja 16,22:2
Bourne, Charles
Vaudeville (Palace) 1926,S 28,30:4
Bourne, Dorothy
Saturday's Children 1936,Jl 7,22:5
Bourne, Helen
Orpheus in Hades 1930,D 16,30:1
Bourne, Melvin (Lighting Director)
Seagulls Over Sorrento 1952,S 12,18:4
Bourne, Melvin (Scenic Designer)
Male Animal, The 1952,My 1,35:1
Seagulls Over Sorrento 1952,S 12,18:4
End as a Man 1953,S 16,39:1

Bourne, Nettie
Cornered 1920,D 9,18:2
Bourne, Timothy
Three Philip Roth Stories; Conversion of the Jews 1970,Jl 31,14:1
Cops and Horrors; Fly Paper 1970,Ag 11,27:1
Cops and Horrors; Dracula 1970,Ag 11,27:1
Bourne, Whitney
Firebird 1932,N 22,25:2
John Brown 1934,Ja 23,22:3
O Evening Star 1936,Ja 9,24:6
Case of Clyde Griffiths 1936,Mr 14,10:4
Bourneuf, Philip
Night Remembers, The 1934,N 28,24:3
Beggarman, Thief 1935,Jl 16,24:1
Dead End 1935,O 29,17:2
Ten Million Ghosts 1936,O 24,23:7
Fireman's Flame, The 1937,O 11,26:2
On the Rocks 1938,Je 16,20:2
One for the Money 1939,F 6,9:2
Taming of the Shrew, The 1940,F 6,17:2
Medicine Show 1940,Ap 13,20:6
Native Son 1941,Mr 25,26:5
As You Like It 1941,O 21,29:2
Rivals, The 1941,N 18,32:2
Rivals, The 1942,Ja 15,24:2
Strings, My Lord, Are False, The 1942,My 20,24:2
Moon Vine, The 1943,F 12,22:2
Richard III 1943,Mr 27,8:3
Winged Victory 1943,N 22,24:1
Yellow Jack 1944,Ap 7,23:3
Flamingo Road 1946,Mr 20,18:2
Henry VIII 1946,N 7,42:2
What Every Woman Knows 1946,N 9,13:2
Androcles and the Lion 1946,D 20,29:2
Pound on Demand 1946,D 20,29:3
Yellow Jack 1947,F 28,26:2
Alice in Wonderland 1947,Ap 7,19:2
Rip Van Winkle 1947,Jl 16,28:2
Last Dance, The 1948,Ja 28,27:2
Temporary Island, A 1948,Mr 15,27:3
Richard III 1949,F 9,33:2
Richard III 1949,F 13,II,1:1
Miss Liberty 1949,Jl 16,6:5
ANTA Album 1950,Ja 30,13:2
Faithfully Yours 1951,O 19,22:5
Love's Labour's Lost 1953,F 5,20:3
Love's Labour's Lost 1953,F 8,II,1:1
Merchant of Venice, The 1953,Mr 5,20:2
International Set, The 1953,Je 12,19:3
Strong Are Lonely, The 1953,S 30,38:3
What Every Woman Knows 1954,D 23,16:2
Doctor's Dilemma, The 1955,Ja 12,22:1
Doctor's Dilemma, The 1955,Ja 23,II,1:1
Infernal Machine, The 1958,F 4,33:1
Lute Song 1959,Mr 13,24:1
Caligula 1960,F 17,31:1
Port-Royal 1960,Ap 26,41:1
Touch of the Poet, A 1961,My 15,34:6
Case of Libel, A 1963,O 11,43:2
Bourseiller, Antoine (Director)
Don Juan 1970,F 7,24:2
Bourseiller, Antoine (Playwright)
Foudroye 1963,Je 6,40:6
Bousard, Joe (Musical Director)
Plot Against the Chase Manhattan Bank, The 1963,N 27,29:1
Bousquet, Jacques (Composer)
Mannequins 1925,D 27,VII,2:1
Bousquet, Jacques (Playwright)
Comedienne 1924,O 22,18:1
Joies du Capitole, Les 1935,Ap 21,IX,2:1
Boutelle, Leona
Family Affairs 1929,D 11,34:6
Boutet, Frederic (Playwright)
Au Coin Joli 1923,O 23,16:1
Bouton, Howard
Bachelor Father, The 1928,F 29,28:2
Bouvellet, Jehan
Au Clair de la Lune 1929,N 10,X,4:1
Bouvier, Lee
Philadelphia Story, The 1967,Je 21,40:2
Philadelphia Story, The 1967,Je 22,46:4
Bouvier, Yvonne and Gilbert, Gloria
Streets of Paris, The 1939,Je 20,25:2
Bova, Joseph
On the Town 1959,Ja 16,36:1
Once Upon a Mattress 1959,My 12,40:1
Taming of the Shrew, The 1960,Ag 20,17:1
Rape of the Belt, The 1960,N 7,46:1
Hot Spot 1963,Ap 20,17:2
Cradle Will Rock, The 1964,N 9,40:4
Love's Labour's Lost 1965,Je 16,46:1
Troilus and Cressida 1965,Ag 13,17:1
Richard III 1966,Ag 11,26:1
Comedy of Errors, The 1967,Je 15,58:4
Romeo and Juliet 1968,Ag 16,19:1
Invitation to a Beheading 1969,Mr 18,36:1
Invitation to a Beheading 1969,Mr 30,II,1:1
Chinese, The 1970,Mr 11,42:2
Chinese, The 1970,Mr 22,II,3:1
Bovasso, Bernard X (Scenic Designer)
Moondreamers, The 1969,D 9,68:1

Bovasso, Julie
Naked 1950,S 7,39:2
Typewriter, The 1955,Jl 29,8:3
Amedee: or, How to Disentangle Yourself
  1955,N 1,27:3
Lesson, The 1956,O 3,29:2
Monique 1957,O 23,38:1
Dinny and the Witches 1959,D 10,53:3
Victims of Duty 1960,Ja 20,26:1
Gallows Humor 1961,Ap 19,35:1
Henry IV, Part I 1962,Je 18,20:4
Gloria and Esperanza 1970,F 5,32:1
Gloria and Esperanza 1970,F 15,II,7:5
Bovasso, Julie (Director)
Escurial 1956,O 3,29:2
Gloria and Esperanza 1969,Ap 5,30:1
Moondreamers, The 1969,D 9,68:1
Moondreamers, The 1969,D 21,II,3:1
Gloria and Esperanza 1970,F 5,32:1
Gloria and Esperanza 1970,F 15,II,7:5
Bovasso, Julie (Playwright)
Gloria and Esperanza 1969,Ap 5,30:1
Moondreamers, The 1969,D 9,68:1
Moondreamers, The 1969,D 21,II,3:1
Gloria and Esperanza 1970,F 5,32:1
Gloria and Esperanza 1970,F 15,II,7:5
Bovasso, Julie (Producer)
Typewriter, The 1955,Jl 29,8:3
Escurial 1956,O 3,29:2
Lesson, The 1956,O 3,29:2
Gloria and Esperanza 1970,F 15,II,7:5
Bove, Claude
Don Juan in the Russian Manner 1954,Ap 23,23:2
Bove, Laura
Don Juan Tenorio 1953,N 20,18:5
Bove, Linda
Gianni Schicci 1969,F 25,36:1
Songs From Milk Wood 1970,Ja 13,41:1
Sganarelle 1970,Ja 13,41:1
Boverio, Auguste
Don Juan 1934,F 27,16:5
Bovy, Berthe
Vieille Maman, La 1927,N 6,IX,4:1
Turcaret 1928,Mr 4,IX,4:5
Moloch 1929,Ja 27,IX,2:8
Voix Humaine, La 1930,Mr 9,IX,2:7
Bow, Dorothy
Cross My Heart 1928,S 18,32:7
Bowab, John (Miscellaneous)
Sweet Charity 1966,Ja 31,22:1
Mame 1966,My 25,41:1
Bowab, John (Producer)
Maggie Flynn 1968,O 24,52:1
Fig Leaves Are Falling, The 1969,Ja 3,19:1
Bowan, Sibyl
Sketch Book 1935,Je 5,22:2
Visit to a Small Planet 1957,F 8,18:1
Visit to a Small Planet 1957,F 24,II,1:1
First Impressions 1959,Mr 20,28:1
Donnybrook! 1961,My 19,23:1
Music Man, The 1965,Je 17,26:4
Maggie Flynn 1968,O 24,52:1
Jimmy 1969,O 24,38:1
Bowden, Charles
Ten Million Ghosts 1936,O 24,23:7
Antony and Cleopatra 1937,N 11,30:2
Hamlet 1938,O 13,28:1
Henry IV, Part I 1939,Ja 31,17:2
Taming of the Shrew, The 1940,F 6,17:2
I Know My Love 1949,N 3,36:1
Bowden, Charles (Director)
Seagulls Over Sorrento 1952,S 12,18:4
Fallen Angels 1956,Ja 18,27:1
Auntie Mame 1958,Ag 12,33:2
Season of Choice 1959,Ap 14,40:1
Song of the Grasshopper 1967,S 29,52:2
Bowden, Charles (Producer)
Seagulls Over Sorrento 1952,S 12,18:4
At Home With Ethel Waters 1953,S 23,36:1
Ruth Draper 1954,Ja 26,21:2
All in One; Trouble in Tahiti 1955,Ap 20,40:3
All in One; 27 Wagons Full of Cotton
  1955,Ap 20,40:3
Fallen Angels 1956,Ja 18,27:1
Hotel Paradiso 1957,Ap 12,22:2
Season of Choice 1959,Ap 14,40:1
Caligula 1960,F 17,31:1
Night of the Iguana, The 1961,D 29,10:1
Mutilated, The 1966,F 23,42:1
Gnadiges Fraulein, The 1966,F 23,42:1
Bowdin, Rae
Sweet Little Devil 1924,Ja 22,15:4
Bowditch, Vincent Y
You Can't Take It With You 1951,Ap 7,8:6
Bowe, Morton
H M S Pinafore 1942,Ja 22,12:2
Mikado, The 1942,F 4,22:2
Pirates of Penzance, The 1942,F 18,22:2
Iolanthe 1942,F 24,26:4
Gondoliers, The 1942,Mr 4,22:3
Mikado, The 1949,O 5,35:2
Pirates of Penzance, The 1949,O 11,41:2
H M S Pinafore 1949,O 18,34:2

Trial by Jury 1949,O 18,34:2
Bowen, Bill (Miscellaneous)
Hi, Paisano 1961,O 2,36:2
Bowen, Burton
Othello 1937,Ja 7,16:4
Infernal Machine, The 1937,D 13,22:7
Comedy of Good and Evil, A 1938,Ap 8,16:3
Bowen, Burton (Miscellaneous)
Comedy of Good and Evil, A 1938,Ap 8,16:3
Bowen, David
Henry IV, Part I 1955,S 22,34:2
Venice Preserv'd 1955,D 13,54:4
Bowen, Edmund
Rose Bernd 1922,S 27,17:1
Bowen, Elizabeth (Original Author)
House in Paris, The 1944,Mr 21,17:1
Bowen, Idwa
Deputy, The 1964,F 27,26:1
Bowen, J David
Macbeth 1955,O 8,12:6
Shadow Years, The 1957,Ja 9,26:2
Bowen, J David (Miscellaneous)
Private Life of the Master Race, The
  1956,Ja 31,33:3
Shadow Years, The 1957,Ja 9,26:2
Bowen, J David (Producer)
Shadow Years, The 1957,Ja 9,26:2
Bowen, John
On the Level 1937,Mr 26,24:4
Bowen, John (Playwright)
After the Rain 1966,S 3,13:5
After the Rain 1967,O 10,54:1
Little Boxes; Coffee Lace, The; Trevor
  1968,Jl 5,20:1
Little Boxes; Trevor 1969,D 4,71:2
Little Boxes; Coffee Lace, The 1969,D 4,71:2
Little Boxes 1969,D 14,II,3:3
Corsican Brothers, The 1970,Mr 20,56:2
Bowen, Kenneth (Miscellaneous)
Ruddigore 1965,Ag 27,16:1
Pirates of Penzance, The 1966,My 24,54:1
Trial by Jury 1966,Je 8,41:2
H M S Pinafore 1966,Je 8,41:2
Bowen, Marjorie (George Preedy) (Playwright)
Court Cards 1934,N 9,24:3
Bowen, Robert
Star of Bengal 1929,S 26,27:2
I Love an Actress 1931,S 18,29:2
Bowen, William (Miscellaneous)
Emerald Slippers, The 1970,S 2,31:2
Bower, Arthur
Young Sinners 1933,Mr 7,20:4
Bower, Ellen (Composer)
Twelfth Night 1954,N 10,42:2
Merchant of Venice, The 1955,F 23,23:2
Midsummer Night's Dream, A 1956,Ja 14,12:2
Bower, Jay (Miscellaneous)
New Faces of 1962 1962,F 2,25:1
Bower, Joan
Nineteenth Hole of Europe, The 1949,Mr 28,16:2
Bower, Marian (Playwright)
Quince Bush, The 1932,Ag 21,IX,1:1
Bower, Virginia
Mikado, The 1954,Mr 24,31:1
Gondoliers, The 1954,Ap 14,24:3
Aunt Caroline's Will 1954,Ag 11,21:1
Bower, William
Desert Song, The 1946,Ja 9,20:2
Bower Sisters
I'll Say She Is 1924,My 20,15:1
Bowers, Charles (Cookie)
Vaudeville (Palace) 1933,Ja 16,13:2
Show Is On, The 1937,S 20,18:4
Bowers, Faubion (Translator)
Chushingura; Treasury of Loyal Retainers, The
  1969,S 11,53:1
Kagami-Jishi; Mirror Lion Dance, The
  1969,S 11,53:1
Momiji-Gari 1969,S 18,64:1
Kumagai Jinya 1969,S 18,64:1
Bowers, Ian
Dark Hours, The 1932,N 15,24:2
Bowers, Jordan
Sophie 1963,Ap 16,32:1
Bowers, Kenny
Best Foot Forward 1941,O 2,28:2
Annie Get Your Gun 1946,My 17,14:2
Annie Get Your Gun 1946,My 26,II,1:1
Bowers, Lally
Killing of Sister George, The 1965,Je 18,28:5
Killing of Sister George, The 1966,O 6,57:1
Council of Love 1970,S 12,32:2
Bowers, Lucette
Show Boat 1956,Je 22,16:1
Show Boat 1957,Je 28,30:2
Bowers, Robert
Bring Me a Warm Body 1962,Ap 17,29:3
Bowers, Robert (Composer)
Digging for Apples 1962,S 28,29:4
Bowers, Robert (Director)
Digging for Apples 1962,S 28,29:4
Bowers, Robert (Playwright)
Digging for Apples 1962,S 28,29:4

Bowers, Robert Hood (Composer)
Oh, Ernest! 1927,My 10,24:3
Bowers, William
Porgy and Bess 1942,Ja 23,16:2
Bowers, William (Playwright)
Where Do We Go From Here? 1938,N 16,26:2
Bowes, Sherry
Stephen D 1966,Ag 5,17:1
Bowhan, Gustav
Toto 1921,Mr 22,15:2
Egotist, The 1922,D 27,12:1
Great Lover, The 1932,O 12,27:3
Bowhan, Gustav (Director)
Great Lover, The 1932,O 12,27:3
Whistling in the Dark 1932,N 4,25:2
Bowhan, Sibylla
Rose of Stamboul, The 1922,Mr 8,11:2
Ginger 1923,O 17,14:1
Who Cares 1930,Jl 9,27:1
Bowie, Buster
Hot Rhythm 1930,Ag 22,18:5
Bowie, John (Playwright)
Just Life 1926,S 15,33:3
Bowie, W R (Lyricist)
Assorted Nuts 1940,Ap 7,I,44:6
Bowker, Aldrich
Nirvana 1926,Mr 4,19:1
Meet the Prince 1935,Jl 9,24:5
Let Freedom Ring 1935,N 7,26:2
Bury the Dead 1936,Ap 20,17:4
Prelude 1936,Ap 20,17:4
Laughing Woman, The 1936,Jl 8,14:7
Golden Journey, The 1936,S 16,28:6
200 Were Chosen 1936,N 21,21:1
Bowker, Alice
Riff-Raff 1926,F 9,18:6
Bowlby, Charles
Bright Boy 1944,Mr 3,19:5
Bowlen, Bert
Some Party 1922,Ap 17,22:1
Bowler, Diane
Johnny Doodle 1942,Mr 19,28:2
Bowler, Norman
Caretaker, The 1964,Ja 31,16:1
Bowler, Richard
Romeo and Juliet 1923,Ja 25,16:1
Antony and Cleopatra 1924,F 20,22:1
Carnaval 1924,D 30,15:1
Starlight 1925,Mr 4,17:2
Dagger, The 1925,S 10,28:1
Weak Woman, A 1926,Ja 27,16:3
Spellbound 1927,F 16,17:2
Menace 1927,Mr 15,28:2
Spellbound 1927,N 15,26:2
Divided Honors 1929,O 1,28:2
Man Who Reclaimed His Head 1932,S 9,17:3
Hamlet 1934,D 26,19:3
Richard III 1934,D 28,24:3
Cyrano de Bergerac 1936,Ap 28,17:1
Enemy of the People, An 1937,F 16,19:1
Lady Has a Heart, The 1937,S 27,24:1
Porgy and Bess 1943,S 14,26:2
Porgy and Bess 1944,F 8,13:2
Arsenic and Old Lace 1944,Jl 3,7:3
Morning's at Seven 1955,Je 23,25:1
Iceman Cometh, The 1956,My 8,38:1
Seven at Dawn 1961,Ap 18,43:1
Seagull, The 1964,Ap 6,36:1
Crucible, The 1964,Ap 7,30:2
Bowles, Anthony (Composer)
Dance of Death, The 1967,O 20,50:1
Bowles, Anthony (Musical Director)
Cranks 1956,N 27,32:1
Bowles, F H
Betty Behave 1927,Mr 9,28:4
Bowles, Jane (Original Author)
In the Summer House 1964,Mr 26,43:1
Bowles, Jane (Playwright)
In the Summer House 1953,D 30,17:1
In the Summer House 1954,Ja 10,II,1:1
Bowles, Kenneth
Live Life Again 1945,O 1,14:7
Bowles, Paul (Composer)
Who Fights This Battle? 1936,S 21,26:3
Horse Eats Hat 1936,S 28,14:2
Doctor Faustus 1937,Ja 9,21:2
My Heart's in the Highlands 1939,Ap 14,29:2
My Heart's in the Highlands 1939,My 7,X,1:1
Love's Old Sweet Song 1940,My 3,16:3
Twelfth Night 1940,N 20,26:3
Liberty Jones 1941,F 6,24:2
Watch on the Rhine 1941,Ap 2,26:2
Wind Remains, The 1943,Mr 31,16:6
Jacobowsky and the Colonel 1944,Mr 15,17:2
Glass Menagerie, The 1945,Ap 2,15:5
On Whitman Avenue 1946,My 9,28:2
Dancer, The 1946,Je 6,16:5
Cyrano de Bergerac 1946,O 9,33:2
Land's End 1946,D 12,37:5
Summer and Smoke 1948,O 7,33:2
Cyrano de Bergerac 1953,N 13,24:3
In the Summer House 1953,D 30,17:1
Glass Menagerie, The 1956,N 22,50:1

Bowles, Paul (Composer)—Cont
Orpheus Descending 1957,Mr 22,28:1
Edwin Booth 1958,N 25,37:1
Sweet Bird of Youth 1959,Mr 11,39:2
Sweet Bird of Youth 1959,Mr 22,II,1:1
Milk Train Doesn't Stop Here Anymore, The 1963,Ja 18,7:1
Glass Menagerie, The 1965,My 5,53:2
Bowles, Paul (Playwright)
No Exit 1967,O 31,38:2
Bowles, Paul (Translator)
No Exit 1946,N 27,21:1
Bowles, Peter
Romeo and Juliet 1956,O 25,41:1
Bowley, Paul
Home Is Tomorrow 1950,Je 2,27:2
Bowman, Brooks
Fiesta 1933,D 16,12:2
Stags at Bay 1934,D 15,9:2
What a Relief 1935,D 14,10:6
Spring Dance 1936,Ag 26,17:4
Bowman, Brooks (Composer)
What a Relief 1935,D 14,10:6
What a Relief 1935,D 19,34:4
Bowman, Brooks (Lyricist)
What a Relief 1935,D 14,10:6
What a Relief 1935,D 19,34:4
Bowman, Cicely Paget
Girl's Best Friend, A 1929,N 10,X,2:1
Bowman, Diana
Brown Danube, The 1939,My 18,30:4
Bowman, Dolores
Barrier, The 1950,N 3,32:2
Bowman, Ford
Hill Between, The 1938,Mr 12,12:5
Bowman, G
Plain Dealer, The 1929,My 23,27:1
Bowman, Genevieve
Just to Remind You 1931,S 8,39:1
Bowman, George
Wrecker, The 1928,F 28,18:2
Bowman, Grace
Night in Spain, A 1927,My 4,28:2
Ned Wayburn's Gambols 1929,Ja 16,22:3
Bowman, Hazel
Earl Carroll's Vanities 1926,Ag 25,19:4
Bowman, Jack A (Director)
Movie Man 1959,O 28,40:4
Bowman, James
First Flight 1925,S 18,26:2
Barefoot 1925,O 20,29:2
Bowman, Jeremy
Come of Age 1934,Ja 13,16:6
Bowman, Jerry
Marry the Man! 1929,Ap 23,26:3
Twelfth Night 1930,O 16,28:2
Twelfth Night 1930,O 19,IX,4:5
Bowman, Joan
Seventeen 1951,Je 22,16:6
Bowman, John
Shoestring Revue 1955,Mr 1,22:2
Bowman, John A (Director)
Dance of Death, The 1960,S 14,51:1
Dream Play 1960,N 23,22:1
Feast of Panthers 1961,Mr 21,32:1
Bowman, John A (Playwright)
Dance of Death, The 1960,S 14,51:1
Dream Play 1960,N 23,22:1
Bowman, John A (Producer)
Dance of Death, The 1960,S 14,51:1
Dream Play 1960,N 23,22:1
Feast of Panthers 1961,Mr 21,32:1
Bowman, Judith
Audition of the Apprentice Theatre 1939,Je 2,26:2
Bowman, Laura
Chip Woman's Fortune, The 1923,My 8,22:2
Salome 1923,My 8,22:2
Comedy of Errors, The 1923,My 16,22:5
Meek Mose 1928,F 7,30:1
Sentinels 1931,D 26,15:1
Tree, The 1932,Ap 13,23:5
Louisiana 1933,F 28,15:5
Jezebel 1933,D 20,26:3
Yesterday's Orchids 1934,O 6,20:4
Plumes in the Dust 1936,N 7,14:2
Conjur 1938,N 1,27:2
Please, Mrs. Garibaldi 1939,Mr 17,24:3
Jeb 1946,F 22,20:2
Bowman, Lee
Magic and the Loss, The 1954,Ap 10,10:3
Bowman, Patricia
Ziegfeld Follies 1934,Ja 5,24:3
Calling All Stars 1934,N 22,26:1
Calling All Stars 1934,D 14,28:2
Virginia 1937,S 3,13:2
Rhapsody 1944,N 23,37:2
Lady From Paris, The 1950,S 27,36:1
Bowman, Polly
Her Family Tree 1920,D 28,9:2
Bowman, Ross (Miscellaneous)
Best House in Naples, The 1956,O 27,16:2
Shadow of My Enemy, A 1957,D 12,35:4
Advise and Consent 1960,N 18,25:1
Ross 1961,D 27,20:2

Oliver 1963,Ja 8,5:5
Ready When You Are, C. B.! 1964,D 8,55:1
Don't Drink the Water 1966,N 18,37:1
Bowman, Thomas
Show Boat 1946,Ja 7,17:2
Bowman, Willard
Cat-Bird, The 1920,F 17,18:1
Liliom 1921,Ap 21,18:1
Wife With a Smile, The 1921,N 29,20:1
Boubouroche 1921,N 29,20:1
Rockbound 1929,Ap 20,23:2
Bowman, William
Rust 1924,F 1,12:1
Bowmer, Angus L
Merchant of Venice, The 1964,Jl 23,18:1
Bowmer, Angus L (Director)
King Lear 1964,Jl 23,18:1
Bowne, Mary
What of It? 1929,Mr 9,24:2
Bowyer, Arthur
Skin Game, The 1920,O 21,11:1
Rubicon, The 1922,F 22,13:1
Sandro Botticelli 1923,Mr 27,24:2
Living Mask, The 1924,Ja 22,15:1
Harem, The 1924,D 3,24:1
Kiss in a Taxi, The 1925,Ag 26,14:1
Jeweled Tree, The 1926,O 8,26:2
Padre, The 1926,D 28,16:3
Crown Prince, The 1927,Mr 24,23:2
Young Sinners 1929,N 29,24:4
Young Sinners 1931,Ap 21,35:5
Miss Gulliver Travels 1931,N 26,36:4
Warrior's Husband, The 1932,Mr 12,19:4
Silent House, The 1932,N 9,28:3
Foolscap 1933,Ja 12,21:2
One Wife or Another 1933,F 7,23:6
Box, Mr (Playwright)
Cathedral, The 1930,D 28,VIII,2:6
Boxer, John
Escape Me Never! 1935,Ja 22,22:2
Boxer, John (Costume Designer)
Very Special Baby, A 1956,N 15,43:2
Compulsion 1957,O 25,21:1
Advise and Consent 1960,N 18,25:1
Boxhorn, Jerry (Costume Designer)
Slice It Thin 1945,My 11,22:5
Hook'n Ladder 1952,Ap 30,31:2
Best House in Naples, The 1956,O 27,16:2
Follies of 1910, The 1960,Ja 15,37:3
Boxhorn, Jerry (Scenic Designer)
Slice It Thin 1945,My 11,22:5
Boxill, Patrick
Richard II 1964,Je 17,47:1
King Lear 1964,Je 19,36:1
Heartbreak House 1968,Jl 6,9:1
Chemmy Circle, The 1968,Ag 10,17:2
Doctor's Dilemma, The 1969,Je 24,37:1
Boxill, Roger Evan
Macbeth 1955,O 8,12:6
Golden Six, The 1958,O 27,31:2
Boxwill, James
Run, Little Chillun! 1933,Mr 2,21:3
Blackbirds 1933,D 4,22:3
Swing It 1937,Jl 23,17:2
Boy, Rad
Tempest, The 1955,S 3,8:6
Boyajian, Hajop
Roof, The 1931,O 31,22:4
Boyajian, Zabelle C (Original Author)
Echmiadzin 1946,O 21,27:3
Boyar, Ben A (Playwright)
As You Like It 1941,O 21,29:2
Boyar, Ben A (Producer)
They Walk Alone 1941,Mr 13,24:2
Boyar, Jerry
Sophie 1944,D 26,22:7
Boyar, Monica
Summer and Smoke 1948,O 7,33:2
13 Daughters 1961,Mr 3,17:2
Boyarsky, A
Inspector General, The 1923,My 1,24:1
Boyce, Betty
Banjo Eyes 1941,D 26,20:2
Boyce, Burke
Manhatters, The 1927,Jl 19,27:3
Manhatters, The 1927,Ag 4,25:4
Boyce, Gladys Wilson
Choice, The 1930,My 9,20:5
Boyce, Trevor
Blue Blood 1924,Ap 3,21:2
Boyd, Barbara
Bellamy Trial, The 1928,Ag 20,21:1
Boyd, Dallas
Story of Mary Surratt, The 1947,F 10,25:2
Boyd, Eric Forbes (Playwright)
Knight Errant 1928,S 2,VII,2:1
Boyd, Ernest (Playwright)
Weak Woman, A 1926,Ja 27,16:3
Puppets of Passion 1927,F 25,24:4
Invitation au Voyage, L' 1928,O 5,17:1
Boyd, Ernest (Translator)
What Never Dies 1926,D 29,24:2
2 + 2 = 5 1927,N 29,30:3

Boyd, Ernest (Translator)—Cont
Maya 1928,F 22,19:1
Invitation au Voyage, L' 1930,Ja 26,VIII,1:8
Boyd, Frank
Hamlet 1922,N 17,14:1
Boyd, Howard
Jotham Valley 1951,F 7,37:2
Boyd, Hutcheson (Playwright)
Wait Till We're Married 1921,S 27,14:1
Talking Parrot, The 1923,D 4,25:3
Naked Man, The 1923,D 16,IX,2:4
Naked Man, The 1925,N 8,VIII,2:1
Lady for a Night, A 1928,Ap 17,26:4
Perfectly Scandalous 1931,My 14,27:2
Boyd, Jennifer
Lady From Maxim's, The 1970,Je 1,41:1
Boyd, John
Hamlet 1923,N 27,23:6
Undesirable Lady, An 1933,O 10,24:4
Hipper's Holiday 1934,O 19,26:2
Mulatto 1935,O 25,25:2
Patriots, The 1943,D 21,22:5
Meet a Body 1944,O 17,19:5
Detective Story 1949,Mr 24,34:2
Confederates, The 1959,S 29,45:1
Boyd, Lawrence (Producer)
Before You're 25 1929,Ap 17,30:2
Boyd, Lester
Adam Solitaire 1925,N 7,19:2
Boyd, Malcolm (Rev) (Playwright)
Boy; Job, The; Study in Color 1964,Ag 1,13:1
Boyd, Mel
Scarlet Lullaby 1968,Mr 11,48:1
Boyd, Rex
Kibitzer, The 1929,F 19,22:5
Boyd, Ruth
Jezebel 1933,D 20,26:3
Point Valaine 1935,Ja 17,22:2
Boyd, Sydney
Are You With It? 1945,N 12,17:3
Land's End 1946,D 12,37:5
Boyd, Thomas
Utopia, Limited; Flowers of Progress, The 1957,F 27,21:1
From Here to There; Real Strange One, A 1958,Ap 24,37:3
From Here to There; Otherwise Engaged 1958,Ap 24,37:3
Great Scot! 1965,N 12,56:3
Walking Happy 1966,N 28,47:1
Boyd, Wayne
Brigadoon 1964,D 24,9:1
Zorba 1968,N 18,58:1
Boyd, William
Sporting Thing to Do, The 1923,F 20,12:2
What Price Glory 1924,S 6,14:3
Tenth Avenue 1927,Ag 16,31:1
Lady Lies, The 1928,N 11,X,2:4
Lady Lies, The 1928,N 27,36:2
Boyd and Wailin
Vaudeville (Palace) 1926,Je 8,23:1
Vaudeville (Palace) 1929,S 30,22:3
Boyd Triplets, The
Duchess Misbehaves, The 1946,F 14,32:2
Boyden, Carl
Sea Dogs 1939,N 7,30:3
Boyden, Merryl
Victoria Regina 1938,O 4,20:2
Boyer
Melo 1929,Ap 7,X,1:3
Boyer, Arthur
Four in Hand 1923,S 7,10:2
Boyer, Carol
Bitter Sweet 1934,My 8,28:4
Boyer, Charles
Bonheur 1933,My 14,IX,1:4
Red Gloves 1948,D 6,28:2
Red Gloves; Mains Sales, Les 1948,D 12,II,3:1
Don Juan in Hell 1951,O 23,34:4
Don Juan in Hell 1951,N 4,II,1:1
Kind Sir 1953,S 28,21:2
Kind Sir 1953,N 5,41:2
Kind Sir 1953,N 15,II,1:1
Marriage-Go-Round, The 1958,O 30,37:1
Marriage-Go-Round, The 1958,N 9,II,1:1
Lord Pengo 1962,N 20,41:2
Man and Boy 1963,S 5,28:1
Man and Boy 1963,N 13,34:1
Man and Boy 1963,D 1,II,1:1
Boyer, Josephine
Tidbits of 1946 1946,Jl 9,17:2
Boyer, Ken
Oscar Wilde 1957,Ap 20,21:3
Marvellous History of Saint Bernard, The 1958,F 24,16:3
Boyer, Lucien
Ice Follies 1970,My 23,27:1
Boyer, Lucienne
Continental Varieties 1934,O 4,18:3
Continental Varieties 1934,N 15,24:3
Continental Varieties 1935,D 27,15:3
Boyer, M J (Miscellaneous)
Absence of a Cello 1964,S 22,45:1
Iolanthe 1965,My 19,42:1

•yer, M J (Miscellaneous)—Cont
Yeomen of the Guard, The 1965,Jl 8,34:1
Ruddigore 1965,Ag 27,16:1
•yer, Martha
Bitter Sweet 1934,My 8,28:4
•yer, Patricia
My Romance 1948,O 20,38:5
•yer, Rika
Ice Follies 1970,My 23,27:1
•yer, William (Lighting Director)
Old Maid, The 1949,Ja 27,20:6
•yers, The
Ice Follies 1969,My 23,38:1
•ykin, Ralph
Paradise 1931,My 12,29:2
•ykins, Smalls
Carmen Jones 1951,S 22,8:6
•ylan, Arthur
Artists and Models 1923,Ag 21,12:2
•ylan, Mary
Dance Night 1938,O 15,20:5
Audition of the Apprentice Theatre 1939,Je 2,26:2
Susannah and the Elders 1940,O 30,28:2
Walrus and the Carpenter, The 1941,N 10,20:2
Our Town 1944,Ja 11,24:5
Live Life Again 1945,O 1,14:7
Full Moon in March, A 1960,S 20,48:1
Billygoat Eddie 1964,Ap 21,43:2
To Bury a Cousin 1967,My 17,38:3
Young Among Themselves, The 1970,Je 12,28:1
•ylan, Mary (Composer)
Curley McDimple 1967,N 23,59:2
•ylan, Mary (Playwright)
Curley McDimple 1967,N 23,59:2
Curley McDimple 1969,N 25,53:1
•ylan, Peter
Topaze 1930,F 13,25:3
•ylan, R D (Translator)
Don Carlos 1962,F 28,27:5
•ylan, Rose
Artists and Models 1923,Ag 21,12:2
Boyland, Malcolm Stuart (Playwright)
Difficult Woman, The 1962,Ap 26,22:7
Boyle, Bill
Canterbury Tales 1968,S 7,23:3
Boyle, Jack
Meet the People 1940,D 26,22:2
Boyle, John
Shoot the Works! 1931,Jl 22,19:5
Shoot the Works! 1931,Jl 26,VIII,2:1
Boyle, John (Choreographer)
No Foolin' 1926,Je 25,25:1
Castles in the Air 1926,S 7,19:2
Broadway 1926,S 17,19:3
Piggy 1927,Ja 12,22:2
Padlocks of 1927 1927,Jl 6,23:4
Excess Baggage 1927,D 27,24:2
Boom Boom 1929,Ja 29,26:4
Top Speed 1929,D 26,20:1
Shoot the Works! 1931,Jl 22,19:5
Shoot the Works! 1931,Jl 26,VIII,2:1
Americana 1932,O 6,19:3
Boyle, John (Director)
Shoot the Works! 1931,Jl 26,VIII,2:1
Pudding on the Ritz 1932,Ap 9,18:3
Boyle, Marte
Rendezvous at Senlis 1961,F 28,39:2
Boyle, Peter
Third Ear, The 1964,My 29,16:1
Boyle, Ray
Great Campaign, The 1947,Ap 1,33:2
Mary Rose 1951,Mr 5,25:2
Mary Rose 1951,Mr 11,II,1:1
Southwest Corner, The 1955,F 4,18:2
Tobias and the Angel 1957,O 21,29:5
Boyle, Ray (Director)
Macbeth 1955,O 8,12:6
Last Love of Don Juan, The 1955,N 24,40:1
Boyle, Ray (Miscellaneous)
Coriolanus 1954,Ja 20,34:2
Boyle, Ray (Producer)
Macbeth 1955,O 8,12:6
Last Love of Don Juan, The 1955,N 24,40:1
Thesmophoriazusae, The; Goddesses of Athens,
The 1955,D 14,52:4
Boyle, Roger (Director)
Best of Everything, The 1952,My 8,35:4
Boyle, Roger (Miscellaneous)
Common Glory, The 1947,Jl 19,11:2
Common Glory, The 1947,Jl 27,II,1:1
Boyle, Walden
Her Man of Wax 1933,O 12,32:3
Shatter'd Lamp, The 1934,Mr 22,26:3
Boyle, William (Playwright)
Building Fund, The 1928,Je 6,23:4
Boyle and Bennett
Vaudeville (Hippodrome) 1924,F 12,20:2
Boylen, Alfred
Twelfth Night 1941,D 3,32:2
Boylen, Margaret
Twelfth Night 1941,D 3,32:2
Boyll, Lawrence
Anya 1965,N 30,48:1

Boylston, Augusta E
Hot Water 1929,Ja 22,22:3
Boyman, William (Director)
Theatre of the Soul 1942,Mr 21,13:5
Boyne, Eva Leonard
Wonderful Thing, The 1920,F 18,9:1
Fan, The 1921,O 4,10:1
Shanghai Gesture, The 1926,F 2,20:2
Sacred Flame, The 1928,N 20,28:2
Security 1929,Mr 29,20:1
Time of Your Life, The 1939,O 26,26:2
Time of Your Life, The 1940,S 24,27:2
Pin to See the Peepshow, A 1953,S 18,17:2
Boyne, Peter
Golden Wings 1941,N 25,33:3
Golden Wings 1941,D 9,46:6
Heart of a City 1942,F 13,24:6
Second Best Bed 1946,Je 4,20:2
Boynton, Edmund (Costume Designer)
Fratricide Punished 1925,Ap 21,19:1
Romio and Julietta 1925,Ap 21,19:1
Boynton, Louise
Nine Till Six 1936,Mr 14,10:3
Boynton-Devinney (Composer)
Stop, You're Killing Me; Terrible Jim Fitch
1969,Mr 20,53:1
Stop, You're Killing Me; Bad Bad Jo-Jo
1969,Mr 20,53:1
Stop, You're Killing Me; Laughs, Etc
1969,Mr 20,53:1
Boyt, John (Costume Designer)
Flag Is Born, A 1946,S 7,10:6
Playboy of the Western World, The 1946,O 28,18:3
Years Ago 1946,D 4,44:2
Antony and Cleopatra 1947,N 27,49:2
Antony and Cleopatra 1947,D 7,II,5:1
Infernal Machine, The 1954,Mr 22,22:2
Show Boat 1954,My 6,44:1
Fledermaus, Die 1954,My 20,38:5
Carousel 1954,Je 3,32:2
Wooden Dish, The 1955,O 7,20:1
Lovers 1956,My 11,23:1
Boyt, John (Lighting Director)
Girl of the Golden West, The 1957,N 6,44:1
Queen and the Rebels, The 1965,F 26,16:1
Boyt, John (Scenic Designer)
Playboy of the Western World, The 1946,O 28,18:3
Misalliance 1953,F 19,20:1
Infernal Machine, The 1954,Mr 22,22:2
Debut 1956,F 23,32:1
Exiles 1957,Mr 13,27:1
Girl of the Golden West, The 1957,N 6,44:1
Queen and the Rebels, The 1965,F 26,16:1
Boytel, Leona
Camille 1932,N 2,23:3
Bozardt, Victor
Artists and Models 1923,Ag 21,12:2
Nightingale, The 1927,Ja 4,20:4
Boze, Billy
Artists and Models 1943,N 6,16:6
Boze, Wynne
Vickie 1942,S 23,28:1
Bozeman, Anya
Emperor's New Clothes, The 1950,Je 20,23:2
Bozeman, Beverlee
Peer Gynt 1951,Ja 29,15:2
Littlest Revue, The 1956,My 23,37:2
Bozickovic-Popovic, Vera (Costume Designer)
Victor, or The Children Take Over 1968,Jl 10,22:4
Bozyk, Max
Abi Gezunt 1949,O 10,19:4
Sadie Is a Lady 1950,Ja 28,9:2
Father and Son 1956,O 20,17:4
Devil's Game, A 1959,N 9,35:6
Going to America 1961,O 30,33:7
Honeymoon in Israel, A 1962,O 15,33:5
Don't Worry Brother! 1963,O 14,35:2
Both Kooney Lemels 1964,O 12,37:2
Let's Sing Yiddish 1966,N 10,63:1
Sing Israel Sing 1967,My 12,50:1
Bozyk, Max (Director)
Both Kooney Lemels 1964,O 12,37:2
Bozyk, Max (Producer)
Devil's Game, A 1959,N 9,35:6
Both Kooney Lemels 1964,O 12,37:2
Bozyk, Reizl
Abi Gezunt 1949,O 10,19:4
Sadie Is a Lady 1950,Ja 28,9:2
Father and Son 1956,O 20,17:4
Devil's Game, A 1959,N 9,35:6
Going to America 1961,O 30,33:7
Honeymoon in Israel, A 1962,O 15,33:5
Don't Worry Brother! 1963,O 14,35:2
Both Kooney Lemels 1964,O 12,37:2
Untitled-Revue 1966,O 3,62:5
Let's Sing Yiddish 1966,N 10,63:1
Sing Israel Sing 1967,My 12,50:1
Mirele Efros 1969,D 26,41:1
Light, Lively and Yiddish 1970,O 28,58:1
Bozzini, Aldo
Bivouac at Lucca 1957,O 30,26:1
Braban, Harvey
Oedipus Rex 1923,O 26,14:1

Braban, Harvey—Cont
Via Crucis 1923,N 13,25:2
Hamlet 1923,N 20,23:3
Geneva 1940,Ja 31,15:2
Brabham, David
Concept, The 1968,My 7,51:1
Braca, Elia
Dreaming Dust, The 1955,D 8,46:5
Picture of Dorian Gray, The 1956,Ag 18,15:5
Fall 1957,N 22,19:1
Women at the Tomb, The 1961,Ap 25,41:1
Bracchitta, John
Building Blocks 1954,My 8,14:4
Bracciante, Joseph
Marvellous History of Saint Bernard, The
1958,F 24,16:3
Bracco, Roberto (Playwright)
Piccolo Santo, Il; Little Saint, The 1931,D 14,16:4
Brace, Charles C
Hippolytus 1935,Je 15,20:4
Brace, Clement
Whispering Gallery, The 1935,D 1,II,12:6
Across the Board on Tomorrow Morning
1942,Mr 21,13:5
Theatre of the Soul 1942,Mr 21,13:5
R U R 1942,D 4,30:2
Wind Remains, The 1943,Mr 31,16:6
Land's End 1946,D 12,37:5
Afternoon Storm 1948,Ap 12,24:2
Ladies of the Corridor, The 1953,O 22,33:5
Good as Gold 1957,Mr 8,22:2
Bracey, Clara T
Passion Flower, The 1920,Ja 14,12:1
Brachita, John
Dark of the Moon 1958,F 27,22:2
Brack, Paul
Rain or Shine 1928,F 10,26:3
Fine and Dandy 1930,S 24,26:1
Brackebusch, Lotte
Faust, Part I; Play, The 1961,F 5,27:2
Bracken, Ann
Lady in the Dark 1941,Ja 24,14:2
Bracken, Dick
Once Over Lightly 1942,N 20,26:2
Bracken, Eddie
So Proudly We Hail 1936,S 23,28:4
What a Life 1938,Ap 14,26:2
Too Many Girls 1939,O 19,26:2
Shinbone Alley 1957,Ap 15,23:2
Shinbone Alley 1957,Ap 28,II,1:1
Beg, Borrow or Steal 1960,F 11,39:4
Bracken, Eddie (Director)
How to Make a Man 1961,F 3,16:1
Bracken, Eddie (Producer)
Beg, Borrow or Steal 1960,F 11,39:4
Bracken, Edward
Would-Be Gentleman, The 1930,Ap 30,29:2
Lady Refuses, The 1933,Mr 8,18:6
Life's Too Short 1935,S 21,18:5
Iron Men 1936,O 20,30:6
Bracken, Larry (Miscellaneous)
Liberace's Variety Bill 1957,Ap 22,29:5
Bracken, Mona
It Is to Laugh 1927,D 27,24:2
Brackett, Dorothy
Let Freedom Ring 1935,N 7,26:2
Prelude 1936,Ap 20,17:4
Bury the Dead 1936,Ap 20,17:4
200 Were Chosen 1936,N 21,21:1
Excursion 1937,Ap 10,11:4
Journeyman 1938,Ja 31,14:2
Washington Jitters 1938,My 3,19:1
Brackett, Kristin (Choreographer)
Much Ado About Nothing 1963,Jl 15,25:2
Bracy, Clara T
Blood and Sand 1921,S 21,16:2
Bradbury, Fred
Storm Center 1927,D 1,33:2
Bradbury, James
Shavings 1920,F 17,18:1
Whole Town's Talking, The 1923,Ag 30,8:2
Two Strangers From Nowhere 1924,Ap 8,22:2
Lady Be Good 1924,D 2,23:4
Bradbury, James Jr
Wild Oats Lane 1922,S 7,12:1
Magnolia 1923,Ag 28,12:3
Bully, The 1924,D 26,18:1
Bradbury, Lane
J B 1958,D 12,2:7
Gypsy 1959,My 22,31:6
Night of the Iguana, The 1961,D 29,10:1
Marathon '33 1963,D 23,20:1
Bradbury, Mary
Exceeding Small 1928,O 23,32:2
Bradbury, Monica (Costume Designer)
'Tis Pity She's a Whore 1958,D 6,21:1
Bradbury, Ray (Playwright)
World of Ray Bradbury, The; Pedestrian, The;
Veldt, The; To the Chicago Abyss 1965,O 10,11:1
Bradby, E J (Playwright)
Au Clair de la Lune 1929,N 10,X,4:1
Braddell, Maurice
In The Best of Families 1931,F 3,29:1
It's You I Want 1933,Mr 19,IX,2:2

Braddell, Maurice (Playwright)—Cont
It's You I Want 1935,F 6,23:3
In the Best of Families 1937,Jl 1,32:5
Braddell, Michael
Loose Ends 1926,N 2,34:2
Braddock, Lisette
Sweethearts 1929,S 23,25:1
Merry Widow, The 1929,D 3,29:1
Braden, Bernard
Man, The 1953,Ja 25,II,3:1
Anniversary Waltz 1955,D 2,31:3
Period of Adjustment 1962,Je 4,24:2
Spoon River Anthology 1964,F 15,14:7
Braden, John
Passion, Poison and Petrifaction 1959,Ag 21,13:1
Purification, The 1959,D 9,57:5
Crime and Crime 1963,D 17,51:2
Saint Joan 1968,Ja 5,42:1
Tiger at the Gates 1968,Mr 1,30:1
Cyrano de Bergerac 1968,Ap 26,30:1
Braden, John (Costume Designer)
Yes, Yes, No No 1969,Ja 1,16:1
Braden, John (Lighting Director)
Meet Peter Grant 1961,My 11,41:4
Yes, Yes, No No 1969,Ja 1,16:1
Braden, John (Miscellaneous)
Golden Streets, The 1970,Ag 14,21:1
Braden, John (Scenic Designer)
Single Man at a Party 1959,Ap 22,30:4
Meet Peter Grant 1961,My 11,41:4
Carving a Statue 1968,My 1,43:1
Winterset 1968,Jl 23,28:2
Yes, Yes, No No 1969,Ja 1,16:1
Candida 1970,Ap 7,41:1
Golden Streets, The 1970,Ag 14,21:1
Bradford, Alex
Don't Bother Me, I Can't Cope 1970,O 8,60:3
Bradford, Alex (Miscellaneous)
But Never Jam Today 1969,Ap 24,40:1
Don't Bother Me, I Can't Cope 1970,O 8,60:3
Bradford, Alex and Singers
Black Nativity 1961,D 12,54:2
Bradford, Billy
Billie 1928,O 2,34:2
Bradford, Bruce
Magnificent Yankee, The 1946,Ja 23,21:2
Bradford, Catherine
Moment Musical 1943,Je 1,18:1
Bradford, Charles Sr
Shannons of Broadway, The 1927,O 9,VIII,1:1
Bradford, Dick
Blues for Mister Charlie 1964,Ap 24,24:1
Bradford, Elaine
Temporary Island, A 1948,Mr 15,27:3
Young and Fair, The 1948,N 23,35:2
Bradford, Ethelynn
Killers 1928,Mr 14,28:3
Married-And How! 1928,Je 15,30:2
Bradford, George
King Lear 1947,F 19,32:2
As You Like It 1947,F 21,16:2
Merchant of Venice, The 1947,F 24,16:2
Volpone 1947,F 25,32:2
Hamlet 1947,F 27,27:2
Bradford, John
Hamlet 1927,Ap 7,23:3
Bradford, John (Miscellaneous)
Caesar and Cleopatra 1927,N 6,IX,2:1
Bradford, Marshall
Chee-Chee 1928,S 26,25:1
Unconquered, The 1940,F 14,25:2
Another Sun 1940,F 24,8:6
Return of the Vagabond, The 1940,My 14,27:2
Romantic Mr Dickens 1940,D 3,33:2
Night Before Christmas, The 1941,Ap 11,25:2
Bradford, Michael
Dark of the Moon 1958,F 27,22:2
Great Day in the Morning 1962,Mr 29,29:1
Bradford, Perry (Composer)
Put and Take 1921,Ag 24,12:3
Bradford, Perry (Lyricist)
Messin' Around 1929,Ap 23,26:3
Bradford, Phil S
Little Theatre Tournament; Trifles 1928,My 11,28:1
Bradford, Roark (Lyricist)
John Henry 1940,Ja 11,18:2
Bradford, Roark (Miscellaneous)
Green Pastures, The 1930,F 27,26:1
Bradford, Roark (Original Author)
Green Pastures, The 1932,O 11,26:6
Green Pastures, The 1935,F 27,16:2
John Henry 1940,Ja 11,18:2
Green Pastures, The 1951,Ap 1,II,1:1
Bradford, Roark (Playwright)
John Henry 1939,D 12,36:4
John Henry 1939,D 17,IX,5:6
John Henry 1940,Ja 11,18:2
Bradford, Roy (Playwright)
Chameleon, The 1949,F 7,16:2
Bradford, Teddy
Vaudeville (Palace) 1929,O 7,22:4
Bradford and Hamilton
A la Carte 1927,Ag 18,25:3

Bradford Singers, The
Don't Bother Me, I Can't Cope 1970,O 8,60:3
Bradlee, Frederick
Dame Nature 1938,S 27,24:3
Fledgling 1940,N 28,29:2
Happy Days 1941,My 14,24:2
Theatre 1941,N 13,34:2
Harlequinade 1949,O 13,32:2
Browning Version, The 1949,O 13,32:2
Second Threshold 1951,Ja 3,23:2
Second Threshold 1951,Ja 14,II,1:1
Arms and the Man 1964,Ap 28,41:1
Bradlee, J T
It's Only Natural 1922,Ap 21,13:2
Bradler, Howard
Familiar Pattern 1943,S 3,15:6
Bradley, Adele
Paolo and Francesca 1924,D 3,24:2
Bradley, Adelle
Climate of Eden, The 1953,N 21,11:2
Bradley, Beatrice
Not so Fast 1923,My 23,18:4
Bradley, Bill
Allegro 1947,O 11,10:2
Talent '49 1949,Ap 13,39:4
Miss Liberty 1949,Jl 16,6:5
Bradley, Carla
Mlle Modiste 1937,My 5,28:5
Bradley, Charles
King Lear 1923,Mr 10,9:4
Bradley, Edwin T
Caesar and Cleopatra 1927,N 6,IX,2:1
Bradley, Francis B (Producer)
Beau-Strings 1926,Ap 27,22:2
Bradley, Frank
Goodbye Again 1943,N 10,28:4
Lower North 1944,Ag 26,15:4
Bradley, Gertrude
Doctor's Dilemma, The 1969,Je 24,37:1
Bradley, Harry C
Back Pay 1921,Ag 31,8:2
Abie's Irish Rose 1922,My 24,22:4
Luana 1930,S 18,28:1
Bradley, Jean
Carnival in Flanders 1953,S 9,38:2
Bradley, Jeanette
Jubilee 1935,O 14,20:1
Red, Hot and Blue! 1936,O 30,26:3
Bradley, John
I'll Take the High Road 1943,N 10,28:3
Bradley, John (pseud) (Playwright)
Kopf in der Schlinge; Head in the Noose 1931,D 27,VIII,2:6
Bradley, June
Whole Town's Talking, The 1923,Ag 30,8:2
Bradley, Lillian Trimble (Director)
Elton Case, The 1921,Jl 5,15:1
Red Falcon, The 1924,O 8,22:1
Bradley, Lillian Trimble (Playwright)
Wonderful Thing, The 1920,F 18,9:1
Wonderful Thing, The 1920,F 22,III,6:1
Red Hawk, The 1923,D 2,VIII,2:1
Izzy 1924,S 17,16:2
Red Falcon, The 1924,O 8,22:1
Out Goes She 1928,D 30,VIII,4:1
Bradley, Louise
S S Glencairn 1924,N 4,31:4
Weak Woman, A 1926,Ja 27,16:3
S S Glencairn 1929,Ja 10,24:5
Bradley, Maria
This Was Burlesque 1965,Mr 17,55:3
Bradley, Marion
My Romance 1948,O 20,38:5
Bradley, Preston
Slave Ship 1969,N 22,46:1
Bradley, Thomas
Queen O' Hearts 1922,O 11,22:1
Bradley, Virginia
Sing Till Tomorrow 1953,D 29,17:2
Bradley, Wilbert (Choreographer)
Tempest, The 1970,F 15,67:1
Bradley, Willis E
Nativity Play, The 1937,D 21,29:1
Bradley, Wilson
Mamba's Daughters 1940,Mr 25,10:4
Cabin in the Sky 1940,O 26,19:2
Bradna, Mme
Vaudeville (Palace) 1924,Mr 18,25:1
Bradshaw, Alison
Mirage, The 1920,O 1,14:1
Don Juan 1921,S 8,14:2
Dancing Mothers 1924,Ag 12,12:2
Undercurrent, The 1925,F 4,18:2
Just Beyond 1925,D 2,22:4
Sport of Kings, The 1926,My 5,24:2
Loose Ends 1926,N 2,34:2
Enchantment 1927,Ap 28,27:3
Hotbed 1928,N 10,20:7
Bradshaw, Booker T Jr
And People All Around 1968,F 12,46:1
Bradshaw, Booker T Jr (Composer)
And People All Around 1968,F 12,46:1

Bradshaw, Booker T Jr (Lyricist)
And People All Around 1968,F 12,46:1
Bradshaw, Booker T Jr (Miscellaneous)
And People All Around 1968,F 12,46:1
Bradshaw, Dawn
Trial by Jury 1962,N 23,32:4
Bradshaw, Fannie (Playwright)
White Rose and the Red, The 1964,Mr 17,31:1
Bradshaw, Fannie (Producer)
White Rose and the Red, The 1964,Mr 17,31:1
Bradshaw, George (Composer)
Napoleon Passes 1927,D 21,29:2
Bradshaw, George (Lyricist)
Napoleon Passes 1927,D 21,29:2
Bradshaw, George (Playwright)
Napoleon Passes 1927,D 21,29:2
Under Glass 1933,O 31,24:3
It's You I Want 1935,F 6,23:3
Bradshaw, Kenneth
Rap, The 1931,Ap 7,31:2
Bradshaw, Michael
Portrait of a Queen 1968,F 29,29:1
Conduct Unbecoming 1970,O 13,50:1
Bradshaw, Richard
Woman Disputed, A 1926,S 29,23:2
Brady, Agnes
Becky Sharp 1929,Je 4,29:1
Little Father of the Wilderness, The 1930,Je 3,27:1
Brady, Alice
Anna Ascends 1920,S 23,14:1
Love Letter, The 1921,O 5,20:1
Drifting 1922,Ja 3,20:3
Zander the Great 1923,Ap 10,24:2
Zander the Great 1923,Ap 15,VII,1:1
Dew Drop Inn 1923,My 18,26:4
Oh! Mama 1925,Ag 20,22:2
Oh! Mama 1925,Ag 30,VII,1:1
Bride of the Lamb 1926,Mr 31,20:3
Bride of the Lamb 1926,Ap 4,VIII,1:1
Sour Grapes 1926,S 7,19:1
Sour Grapes 1926,S 12,VIII,1:1
Witch, The 1926,N 19,22:5
Lady Alone 1927,Ja 16,VII,2:4
Lady Alone 1927,Ja 21,12:5
Thief, The 1927,Ap 23,15:2
Thief, The 1927,My 1,VIII,1:1
Bless You, Sister 1927,D 27,24:5
Vaudeville (Palace) 1928,Ap 17,26:2
Most Immoral Lady, A 1928,N 11,X,2:4
Most Immoral Lady, A 1928,N 27,36:1
Karl and Anna 1929,O 8,34:1
Game of Love and Death, The 1929,N 26,28:4
Fatal Woman, The 1930,Mr 2,IX,4:7
Love, Honor and Betray 1930,Mr 13,22:2
Brass Ankle 1931,Ap 24,26:4
Mourning Becomes Electra; Homecoming 1931,O 27,22:1
Mourning Becomes Electra; Haunted, The 1931,O 27,22:1
Mourning Becomes Electra; Hunted, The 1931,O 27,22:1
Mourning Becomes Electra 1931,N 1,VIII,1:1
Mourning Becomes Electra 1932,Ap 10,VIII,1:1
Mademoiselle 1932,O 9,IX,3:6
Mademoiselle 1932,O 19,22:4
Brady, Arthur
Threepenny Opera, The 1933,Ap 14,22:4
Brady, Barbara
Velvet Glove, The 1949,D 27,26:2
Brady, Bob
Hole, The 1961,Ap 4,42:2
Brady, Fay
Vaudeville (Palace) 1931,F 2,23:3
Brady, Florence
Her Family Tree 1920,D 28,9:2
Earl Carroll's Vanities 1926,Ag 25,19:4
Vaudeville (Palace) 1930,Mr 24,24:5
Brady, Frank (Costume Designer)
Great Magician, The 1951,N 22,45:1
Time of Storm 1954,F 26,14:2
Brady, Helen
Blind Mice 1930,O 16,28:2
Brady, Irving
Crossroads 1969,Ag 7,28:1
Brady, James
Book of Charm, The 1925,S 4,26:3
Brady, Jasper Ewing (Playwright)
Personality 1921,Ag 29,14:3
Brady, June
Alive and Kicking 1950,Ja 18,25:5
Brady, Leo (Director)
Front Page, The 1968,O 20,85:5
Brady, Leo (Playwright)
Yankee Doodle Boy 1939,D 19,29:5
Count Me In 1942,O 9,24:2
Oedipus Rex 1959,Ap 30,36:1
Brady, Marie
Sweetheart Shop, The 1920,S 1,13:4
Brady, Olive
LeMaire's Affairs 1927,Mr 29,22:4
Whoopee 1928,D 5,34:3
Girl Crazy 1930,O 5,IX,4:6
Girl Crazy 1930,O 15,27:1

Brady, Patti
Highland Fling, A 1944,Ap 29,13:2
Song of Norway 1944,Ag 22,20:2
Brady, Ruth
By Jupiter 1942,Je 4,22:1
Brady, Scott
Destry Rides Again 1959,Ap 24,24:1
Brady, Veronica
Sunshine Sisters 1933,N 26,IX,3:6
Brady, W K
Hold Your Horses 1933,S 26,26:4
Brady, William
Woman of Destiny, A 1936,Mr 3,25:2
Brady, William A
Friars Club Frolic 1921,Je 13,16:2
Brady, William A (Director)
While Parents Sleep 1934,Je 5,28:2
Brady, William A (Miscellaneous)
Come Across 1938,S 15,28:3
Kind Lady 1940,S 4,28:3
Brady, William A (Mrs) (Grace George) (Translator)
Domino 1932,Ag 17,13:2
Brady, William A (Playwright)
Little Women 1931,D 8,36:2
Brady, William A (Producer)
Leah Kleschna 1924,Ap 22,19:2
Leah Kleschna 1924,Ap 27,VIII,1:1
Awful Mrs Eaton, The 1924,Jl 20,VII,1:7
That Awful Mrs Eaton! 1924,S 30,27:1
Simon Called Peter 1924,N 11,20:2
She Had to Know 1925,F 3,25:3
Great Gatsby, The 1926,F 3,22:1
What Every Woman Knows 1926,Ap 14,20:2
Kitty's Kisses 1926,My 7,12:2
Slaves All 1926,D 7,24:4
Dark, The 1927,F 2,22:5
Legend of Leonora, The 1927,Mr 30,22:4
Thief, The 1927,Ap 23,15:2
Free Soul, A 1928,Ja 13,26:5
Back Here 1928,N 27,36:3
Now-A-Days 1929,Ag 6,29:3
First Mrs Fraser, The 1929,D 30,16:2
Golden Cinderella, A 1931,O 4,VIII,2:2
Adams' Wife 1931,D 29,27:1
Alice Sit-By-The-Fire 1932,Mr 8,19:3
Old Lady Shows Her Medals, The 1932,Mr 8,19:3
Domino 1932,Ag 7,IX,1:1
Domino 1932,Ag 17,13:2
Mademoiselle 1932,O 9,IX,3:6
Mademoiselle 1932,O 19,22:4
Bad Manners 1933,Ja 31,15:5
Saturday Night 1933,Mr 1,13:2
Her Tin Soldier 1933,Ap 7,22:6
Party, A 1933,Ag 24,18:4
While Parents Sleep 1934,Je 5,28:2
Fools Rush In 1934,D 26,19:2
Matrimony, PFD 1936,N 13,26:3
Circle, The 1938,Ap 19,24:2
Outward Bound 1938,D 23,16:5
Billy Draws a Horse 1939,D 22,14:5
Brady, William A Jr (Director)
Two Orphans, The 1926,Ap 6,26:2
Hangman's House 1926,D 17,27:2
Grey Fox, The 1928,O 23,32:3
Little Women 1931,D 8,36:2
We Are No Longer Children 1932,Ap 1,17:2
Bad Manners 1933,Ja 31,15:5
Too Many Boats 1934,S 12,26:3
Brady, William A Jr (Miscellaneous)
Two Orphans, The 1926,Ap 6,26:2
Hangman's Whip 1933,F 25,20:2
Brady, William A Jr (Producer)
Lucky Sam McCarver 1925,O 22,22:1
Little Eyolf 1926,F 3,22:1
Masque of Venice, The 1926,Mr 3,27:3
Devils 1926,Mr 18,26:4
Seed of the Brute 1926,N 2,34:3
Hangman's House 1926,D 17,27:2
Road to Rome, The 1927,F 1,24:2
House of Shadows, The 1927,Ap 22,18:4
Women Go on Forever 1927,S 8,25:1
Command to Love, The 1927,S 21,27:1
Queen's Husband, The 1928,Ja 26,17:2
Grey Fox, The 1928,O 23,32:3
Jealous Moon, The 1928,N 21,32:2
Most Immoral Lady, A 1928,N 27,36:1
Judas 1929,Ja 25,20:4
Paolo and Francesca 1929,Ap 2,28:2
Little Show, The 1929,My 1,28:5
Jenny 1929,O 9,34:4
Second Little Show, The 1930,S 3,36:1
We Are No Longer Children 1932,Ap 1,17:2
Too Many Boats 1934,S 12,26:3
Jane Brady-Editor 1935,Jl 2,24:3
Noble Prize, The 1935,Jl 9,24:3
She Cried for the Moon 1935,Jl 23,24:3
Brady, William J
Man of the People, A 1920,S 8,9:2
Nobody's Money 1921,Ag 18,9:3
Easy Mark, The 1924,Ag 27,14:2
Baby Mine 1927,Je 10,21:2
Brady, William S (Lyricist)
Silver Swan, The 1929,N 28,34:5

Brady, William S (Playwright)
Silver Swan, The 1929,N 28,34:5
Brady and Wells
Vaudeville (Palace) 1929,F 18,29:1
Brae, Barbara
Wind Remains, The 1943,Mr 31,16:6
Brae, Bonnie
Seventeen 1951,Je 22,16:6
Brae, Rupert
Trigger 1927,D 7,32:1
Braen, Robert
Drifting Apart: or, The Fisherman's Child
1941,Ag 20,16:6
Braff, Ruby
Pipe Dream 1955,D 1,44:1
Bragdon, Claude (Scenic Designer)
Othello 1925,Ja 12,11:1
Hamlet 1925,O 12,19:2
Merchant of Venice, The 1925,D 28,12:1
Immortal Thief, The 1926,O 4,21:1
Enemy of the People, An 1927,O 4,32:5
Hamlet 1928,Ja 5,33:2
Henry V 1928,Mr 16,26:2
Light of Asia, The 1928,O 10,32:2
Bonds of Interest, The 1929,O 15,34:2
Richelieu 1929,D 26,20:3
Cyrano de Bergerac 1932,D 27,11:2
Richelieu 1934,My 22,28:1
Hamlet 1934,D 26,19:3
Richard III 1934,D 28,24:3
Achilles Had a Heel 1935,O 14,20:2
Cyrano de Bergerac 1936,Ap 28,17:1
Enemy of the People, An 1937,F 16,19:1
Bragdon, Guy (Director)
Crucible 1933,S 5,22:4
Bragg, Bernard
Gianni Schicci 1969,F 25,36:1
Critic, The 1969,Mr 9,76:5
Sganarelle 1970,Ja 13,41:1
Songs From Milk Wood 1970,Ja 13,41:1
Bragg, Bernard (Playwright)
Songs From Milk Wood 1970,Ja 13,41:1
Bragg, John
Lady Fingers 1929,F 1,22:4
Braggiotti, Frances
Untitled-Revue 1928,N 19,16:2
Braggiotti, Francesca
Three Times the Hour 1931,Ag 26,15:5
Braggiotti, Herbert
Woman Denied, A 1931,F 26,21:1
Braggiotti, Mario
Vaudeville (Carnegie Hall) 1931,Ap 12,I,30:4
Maurice Chevalier 1932,F 10,26:6
Braggiotti, Mario (Composer)
Vanderbilt Revue, The 1930,N 6,22:6
Braggiotti, S Herbert
Red Robe, The 1928,D 26,15:1
Braggiotti, Stiano
Ten Minute Alibi 1933,O 18,24:3
Closed Room, The 1934,Jl 24,20:2
Aiglon, L' 1934,N 5,22:2
Retreat From Folly 1937,Je 29,18:3
At the Theatre 1937,Ag 4,14:1
Merely Murder 1937,D 4,21:4
Empress of Destiny 1938,Mr 10,16:2
Eye on the Sparrow 1938,My 4,26:3
My Dear Children 1939,Mr 25,19:6
My Dear Children 1940,F 1,16:2
Kind Lady 1940,S 4,28:3
Candle in the Wind 1941,S 16,19:6
Lady Comes Across, The 1942,Ja 10,10:2
Two Mrs Carrolls, The 1943,Ag 4,14:1
Two Mrs Carrolls, The 1943,Ag 8,II,1:1
For Heaven's Sake Mother 1948,N 17,33:4
Idiot's Delight 1951,My 24,46:3
Antigone 1956,Ap 3,32:2
Bragglia, Carolina
Malia 1921,S 10,12:3
Bragia, Giancarlo
Long Day's Journey Into Night 1956,O 17,40:1
Bragin, David (Scenic Designer)
Acid Wine 1964,My 23,15:2
Frugal Noon 1964,My 23,15:2
Braham, Horace
Voltaire 1922,Mr 21,17:1
Merchant of Venice, The 1922,D 22,13:1
Casanova 1923,S 27,10:2
Cheaper to Marry 1924,Ap 16,26:1
Mask and the Face, The 1924,S 11,27:3
Rat, The 1925,F 11,19:3
Made in America 1925,O 15,27:2
Taming of the Shrew, The 1925,D 19,14:1
Find Daddy 1926,Mr 9,21:3
Bells, The 1926,Ap 14,20:3
Squall, The 1926,N 12,20:1
Midsummer Night's Dream, A 1927,Je 27,25:1
Caste 1927,D 24,8:1
Mrs Dane's Defense 1928,F 7,30:1
Sherlock Holmes 1928,F 21,18:4
She Stoops to Conquer 1928,My 15,17:1
Relations 1928,Ag 21,27:3
Gods of the Lightning 1928,O 25,27:2
Street Scene 1929,Ja 11,20:4

Braham, Horace—Cont
Scarlet Sister Mary 1930,N 26,19:2
Left Bank, The 1931,O 6,35:3
Girl Outside, The 1932,O 25,24:3
Church Mouse, A 1933,Je 27,13:7
Yoshe Kalb 1933,D 29,27:2
Theodora, the Queen 1934,F 1,15:3
Shatter'd Lamp, The 1934,Mr 22,26:3
Musical Chairs 1934,Jl 31,20:7
Too Many Boats 1934,S 12,26:3
Aiglon, L' 1934,N 5,22:2
Journey to Jerusalem 1940,O 7,21:2
R U R 1942,D 4,30:2
Antigone 1946,F 19,21:3
Bathsheba 1947,Mr 27,40:2
Hippolytus 1948,N 22,25:5
Julius Caesar 1950,Je 21,30:1
Witness for the Prosecution 1954,D 17,35:2
Witness for the Prosecution 1954,D 26,II,1:1
Braham, Lionel
Mecca 1920,O 5,12:2
Miracle, The 1924,Ja 16,17:1
Miracle, The 1924,Ag 19,9:1
Miracle, The 1926,D 28,16:2
Miracle, The 1927,F 1,24:5
Mima 1928,D 13,24:2
Jewel Robbery 1932,Ja 14,17:2
Man Who Reclaimed His Head 1932,S 9,17:3
Brahlton, T Berry Jr
Any Moment Now 1939,N 25,13:6
Braidon, Thomas A
Peg o' My Heart 1921,F 15,7:1
On the Stairs 1922,S 26,18:2
Vortex, The 1925,S 17,20:1
Constant Wife, The 1926,N 30,26:3
Wings Over Europe 1928,D 11,35:1
Apple Cart, The 1930,F 25,30:1
Miracle at Verdun 1931,Mr 17,34:6
Good Fairy, The 1932,N 18,22:3
Best People, The 1933,Mr 16,21:5
Braidwood, Margaret
Tamburlaine the Great 1956,Ja 20,19:1
Shewing-Up of Blanco Posnet, The 1959,S 19,26:7
Loss of Roses, A 1959,N 30,27:1
Duel of Angels 1960,Ap 20,42:2
Magnificent Hugo, The 1961,Ap 8,12:2
Passage to India, A 1962,F 1,23:1
Dylan 1964,Ja 20,18:1
Traveller Without Luggage 1964,S 18,26:2
Saved 1970,O 29,57:1
Saved 1970,N 1,II,10:1
Brainard, Edward M
Empress of Destiny 1938,Mr 10,16:2
Brainard, Jack
Johnny on the Spot 1942,Ja 9,24:2
Brainard, Ralph
Genius and the Crowd 1920,S 7,20:1
Be Yourself! 1924,S 4,13:3
Count of Luxembourg, The 1930,F 18,28:2
Braine, Robertson
Skin Game, The 1920,O 21,11:1
Brainerd, Joan
From Here to There; Otherwise Engaged
1958,Ap 24,37:3
From Here to There; Slow Dusk 1958,Ap 24,37:3
Brainerd, William
Kosher Kitty Kelly 1925,Je 16,24:2
Brainin, Jerome (Composer)
Star and Garter 1942,Je 25,26:2
Brainin, Jerome (Lyricist)
Star and Garter 1942,Je 25,26:2
Braithwaite, Lilian
Vortex, The 1925,S 17,20:1
Silver Cord, The 1927,O 2,VIII,1:3
Truth Game, The 1928,O 21,IX,1:3
Savonarola Brown 1930,F 26,22:3
Symphony in Two Flats 1930,S 17,30:4
Flat to Let 1931,D 20,VIII,3:6
Party, A 1932,Jl 10,IX,1:2
Fresh Fields 1933,F 5,IX,3:5
All's Over, Then? 1934,Je 10,IX,1:1
Family Affairs 1934,Ag 23,13:3
Family Affairs 1934,S 16,X,2:1
Full House 1935,Ag 22,20:3
Full House 1935,S 22,X,3:3
Bats in the Belfry 1937,Mr 12,19:4
Bats in the Belfry 1937,Ap 4,X,2:4
Comedienne 1938,Jl 3,IX,2:1
House in the Square 1940,Ap 14,IX,1:6
Ducks and Drakes 1941,D 14,IX,4:3
Arsenic and Old Lace 1943,Ja 1,26:5
Arsenic And Old Lace 1943,Ja 10,VIII,1:6
Brakeley, George Archibald Jr
This Mad Whirl 1937,Ja 10,II,4:8
Bramall, John
No More Ladies 1934,Ja 24,20:3
Living Dangerously 1935,Ja 14,10:3
Braman, G D Jr (Lighting Director)
Caesar and Cleopatra 1927,N 6,IX,2:1
Braman, John
Thunder in the Air 1929,N 12,34:3
Braman, Jonathan
Rich Full Life, The 1945,N 10,9:2

Braman, Lawrence
Scarlet Coat, The 1924,D 24,11:1
Brambell, Wilfred
Kelly 1965,F 8,28:2
Canterbury Tales 1968,S 7,23:3
Bramhall, John
Young Sinners 1933,Mr 7,20:4
June Moon 1933,My 16,15:5
Bramhall, Mark
Our Town 1968,S 29,77:4
Bramlett, Robert
Harlem 1929,F 21,30:3
Bramlette, Sallie
Eccentricities of Davy Crockett, The 1961,Ja 4,26:1
I Want You 1961,S 15,29:1
Bramlette, William
Legend of Lovers 1959,O 28,40:3
Emperor, The 1963,Ap 17,30:1
Bramley, Jane
Washington Heights 1931,S 30,23:4
Fatal Alibi, The 1932,F 10,26:6
Silent House, The 1932,N 9,28:3
Shatter'd Lamp, The 1934,Mr 22,26:3
While Parents Sleep 1934,Je 5,28:2
Bramley, Raymond
Not Herbert 1926,Ja 27,16:2
Barker, The 1927,Ja 19,20:6
House Unguarded 1929,Ja 16,22:2
This Is New York 1930,N 29,21:1
Man on Stilts, The 1931,S 10,23:2
East Wind 1931,O 28,19:1
Black Tower 1932,Ja 12,29:2
Keeping Expenses Down 1932,O 21,25:2
Her Man of Wax 1933,O 12,32:3
Three and One 1933,O 26,22:6
Theodora, the Queen 1934,F 1,15:3
Judgment Day 1934,S 13,26:4
Cross Ruff 1935,F 20,23:3
Remember the Day 1935,Jl 9,24:3
Stag at Bay, The 1935,Jl 30,17:1
Little Inn, The 1935,Ag 20,25:1
Rain 1935,Ag 27,23:4
Whatever Goes Up 1935,N 26,28:2
Tomorrow's a Holiday! 1935,D 31,10:2
Golden Journey, The 1936,S 16,28:6
Holmeses of Baker Street, The 1936,D 10,34:3
Sleep No More 1944,S 1,11:5
Hear That Trumpet 1946,O 8,19:2
Young Man's Fancy, A 1947,Ap 30,33:2
Two Blind Mice 1949,Mr 3,32:2
One Bright Day 1952,Mr 20,37:2
Tovarich 1952,My 15,39:2
Crucible, The 1953,Ja 23,15:2
Wake Up, Darling 1956,My 3,34:2
Apple Cart, The 1956,O 19,23:1
Tenderloin 1960,O 18,47:2
Bramley, William
Age and Grace 1956,F 21,38:2
Lovers 1956,My 11,23:1
Capacity for Wings 1957,Ja 10,25:2
West Side Story 1957,S 27,14:4
Brammar, Julius (Original Author)
Circus Princess, The 1937,Ag 31,26:6
Brammer, Dieter
Nathan der Weise 1966,D 10,45:2
Minna von Barnhelm 1968,N 13,37:1
Schloss, Das 1968,N 20,35:3
Amphitryon 1970,N 18,40:1
Kleinburgerhochzeit, Die 1970,N 25,25:1
Kurve, Die 1970,N 25,25:1
Brammer, Julius (Lyricist)
Countess Maritza 1926,S 20,21:1
Circus Princess, The 1927,Ap 26,32:2
Brammer, Julius (Playwright)
Yankee Princess, The 1922,O 3,22:1
Countess Maritza 1926,Mr 30,20:3
Countess Maritza 1926,S 20,21:1
Countess Maritza 1927,Ja 30,VII,4:3
Circus Princess, The 1927,Ap 26,32:2
Herzogin von Chicago, Die 1929,F 17,IX,2:3
Farmer General, The 1931,Mr 31,24:8
Bauerngeneral, Der 1931,Ap 19,VIII,2:4
Bramson, David (Miscellaneous)
Big Two, The 1947,Ja 9,21:2
Bramson, Karen (Playwright)
Strong, The 1924,F 27,15:3
Professor Klenow 1924,Mr 2,VII,2:1
Tiger Cats 1924,O 22,18:1
Godless, The 1926,Ja 10,VII,1:3
Professeur Klenow, Le 1933,Je 4,IX,1:6
Bramwell, John
No More Ladies 1934,S 4,23:2
Bramwell, Raymond
Love on an Island 1934,Jl 24,20:5
Brancati, John (Composer)
Love Your Crooked Neighbor 1969,D 30,40:1
Brancato, Rosemarie
Rhapsody 1944,N 23,37:2
Branch, Billy
Streets of Paris, The 1939,Je 20,25:2
Branch, James
Lady of Mexico 1962,O 20,13:2

Branch, Phyllis
Year Round, The 1953,My 6,38:7
Branch, William (Playwright)
Medal for Willie, A 1951,O 16,35:2
In Splendid Error 1954,O 27,33:6
Branche, Gretchen
Blackbirds 1933,D 4,22:3
Brand, Georgiana
Chalk Dust 1936,Mr 5,24:5
Native Ground 1937,Mr 24,28:4
Pinocchio 1939,Ja 3,19:2
Unconquered, The 1940,F 14,25:2
Days of Our Youth, The 1941,N 29,15:2
Brand, Hans
Professor Bernhardi 1968,Mr 20,38:1
Maria Stuart 1968,Mr 27,38:1
Brand, Max (Original Author)
Destry Rides Again 1959,Ap 24,24:1
Brand, Millen (Original Author)
World We Make, The 1939,N 21,19:1
World We Make, The 1939,N 26,IX,1:3
World We Make, The 1939,D 3,IX,5:1
Brand, Motele
Wedding Chains 1932,Mr 28,10:5
Brand, Neville
Night Life 1962,O 2,45:2
Night Life 1962,O 24,44:1
Brand, Oscar (Composer)
Joyful Noise, A 1966,D 16,57:1
Education of H*Y*M*A*N K*A*P*L*A*N, The 1968,Ap 5,57:1
How to Steal an Election 1968,O 14,56:1
Brand, Oscar (Lyricist)
Joyful Noise, A 1966,D 16,57:1
Education of H*Y*M*A*N K*A*P*L*A*N, The 1968,Ap 5,57:1
How to Steal an Election 1968,O 14,56:1
Brand, Oscar (Musical Director)
In White America 1963,N 1,26:1
Brand, Phoebe
Little Poor Man, The 1925,Ag 6,14:1
Elizabeth the Queen 1930,N 4,37:1
1931 1931,D 11,34:3
Night Over Taos 1932,Mr 10,25:3
Big Night 1933,Ja 18,16:2
Men in White 1933,S 27,24:2
Waiting for Lefty 1935,F 11,14:5
Awake and Sing! 1935,F 20,23:2
Weep for the Virgins 1935,D 2,18:1
Case of Clyde Griffiths 1936,Mr 14,10:4
Johnny Johnson 1936,N 20,26:3
Golden Boy 1937,N 5,18:5
Awake and Sing! 1939,Mr 8,18:2
World of Sholom Aleichem, The 1953,S 12,13:2
Brand, Phoebe (Director)
Portrait of the Artist as a Young Man, A 1962,My 29,21:1
Barroom Monks, The 1962,My 29,21:1
Shoemaker's Prodigious Wife, The 1962,S 2,44:4
Bungler, The 1968,Ag 2,24:1
Que Vida de Perro 1968,Ag 2,24:1
Brand, Phoebe (Playwright)
Portrait of the Artist as a Young Man, A 1962,My 29,21:1
Bungler, The 1968,Ag 2,24:1
Brand, Robert (Lighting Director)
Oklahoma! 1958,Mr 8,15:2
'Tis Pity She's a Whore 1958,D 6,21:1
Lady's Not for Burning, The 1959,Ja 31,13:2
Mr Simian 1963,O 22,44:1
Immoralist, The 1963,N 8,36:2
MacBird! 1967,F 23,38:1
Branda, Richard
Tragical Historie of Doctor Faustus, The 1964,O 6,34:2
Brandeaux, Pal (Choreographer)
Jonica 1930,Ap 8,27:1
Artists and Models 1930,Je 11,33:2
Hello Paris 1930,N 17,29:3
Nikki 1931,S 30,23:4
This Was Burlesque 1962,Mr 7,29:1
Brandeaux, Pal (Costume Designer)
This Was Burlesque 1962,Mr 7,29:1
Brandeis, E John (Producer)
Thirsty Soil 1937,F 4,16:2
Brandeis, Ruth
Nighthawks 1967,D 30,14:2
Branden, Ethel
Blossom Time 1921,S 30,10:1
Brander, Arthur
Seventh Heart, The 1927,My 3,24:4
Brander, Margot
Sons o' Fun 1941,D 2,28:2
Brandes, Hildegart (Costume Designer)
Earth Journey 1944,Ap 28,24:2
Brandler, Annette
Oklahoma! 1958,Mr 8,15:2
Athenian Touch, The 1964,Ja 15,25:4
Brandlon, Richard
Gentlemen Prefer Blondes 1926,S 29,23:1
Penal Law 2010 1930,Ap 19,14:2
Brando, Jocelyn
First Crocus, The 1942,Ja 3,14:6

Brando, Jocelyn—Cont
Mister Roberts 1948,F 19,27:2
Golden State, The 1950,N 27,29:3
Desire Under the Elms 1952,Ja 17,23:4
Brando, Marlon
I Remember Mama 1944,O 20,16:2
Truckline Cafe 1946,F 28,19:4
Candida 1946,Ap 4,33:2
Candida 1946,Ap 14,II,1:1
Flag Is Born, A 1946,S 7,10:6
Streetcar Named Desire, A 1947,D 4,42:2
Streetcar Named Desire, A 1947,D 14,II,3:1
Brandon, Bill
George M! 1968,Ap 11,48:1
Brandon, Charles (Costume Designer)
Of Mice and Men 1958,D 5,38:1
White Cargo 1960,D 30,12:1
Brandon, Charles (Lighting Director)
In Good King Charles's Golden Days 1957,Ja 25,16:1
House Remembered, A 1957,F 7,20:2
Salvage 1957,Ap 10,39:2
Boy Friend, The 1958,Ja 27,24:4
Of Mice and Men 1958,D 5,38:1
Brandon, Charles (Scenic Designer)
Best Foot Forward 1956,Mr 3,16:1
In Good King Charles's Golden Days 1957,Ja 25,16:1
House Remembered, A 1957,F 7,20:2
Annie Get Your Gun 1957,Mr 9,15:5
Salvage 1957,Ap 10,39:2
Simply Heavenly 1957,My 22,28:2
Courageous One, The 1958,Ja 21,33:6
Boy Friend, The 1958,Ja 27,24:4
Blood Wedding 1958,Ap 1,35:1
Of Mice and Men 1958,D 5,38:1
Smokeweaver's Daughter, The 1959,Ap 15,30:1
White Cargo 1960,D 30,12:1
Not While I'm Eating 1961,D 20,37:1
Heroine, The 1963,F 21,5:5
Honest-to-God Schnozzola, The 1969,Ap 22,40:2
Leader, The 1969,Ap 22,40:2
Brandon, Dorothy (Playwright)
Outsider, The 1923,Je 10,VII,1:4
Outsider, The 1924,Mr 4,16:4
Outsider, The 1928,Ap 10,32:2
Black Ace, The 1929,Je 2,VIII,2:7
Brandon, Eunice
Friday Night; River, The 1965,F 9,42:5
Brandon, Henry
Spring in Autumn 1937,Ag 17,23:1
Boudoir 1941,F 8,18:4
Macbeth 1941,N 12,30:2
Medea 1949,My 3,31:2
Twelfth Night 1949,O 4,33:2
Lucky Sam McCarver 1950,Ap 15,10:6
Lady's Not for Burning, The 1957,F 22,26:2
Brandon, John
Born Yesterday 1958,Mr 22,12:6
'Tis Pity She's a Whore 1958,D 6,21:1
Brandon, John G (Playwright)
Silent House, The 1927,Jl 3,VII,1:4
Silent House, The 1928,F 8,28:5
Silent House, The 1932,N 9,28:3
Brandon, Johnny (Composer)
Cindy 1964,Mr 20,24:1
Who's Who, Baby? 1968,Ja 30,36:1
Bill Noname 1970,Mr 3,37:1
Brandon, Johnny (Lyricist)
Cindy 1964,Mr 20,24:1
Who's Who, Baby? 1968,Ja 30,36:1
Bill Noname 1970,Mr 3,37:1
Brandon, Mary
Welcome Stranger 1920,S 14,12:1
Nature's Nobleman 1921,N 15,23:2
Up the Ladder 1922,Mr 7,11:2
Brandon, Michael
Does a Tiger Wear a Necktie? 1969,F 26,38:1
Brandon, Nancy
Nine Till Six 1936,Mr 14,10:3
Brandon, Peter
Cry of the Peacock 1950,Ap 12,33:2
Come of Age 1952,Ja 24,22:2
Tovarich 1952,My 15,39:2
Cyrano de Bergerac 1953,N 13,24:3
Ondine 1954,F 19,23:1
Young and Beautiful, The 1955,O 3,23:2
Hidden River, The 1957,Ja 24,32:1
Infernal Machine, The 1958,F 4,33:1
Man for All Seasons, A 1961,N 23,51:1
Man for All Seasons, A 1962,S 23,II,1:1
Investigation, The 1966,O 5,40:1
Brandon, Phil
In Heaven and Earth 1936,Mr 27,24:8
Brandon, Philip
Ugly Duchess, The 1930,Je 1,VIII,2:8
Brandon, Theodore
Saint of Bleecker Street, The 1954,D 28,21:1
Brandon, Thomas H
Kilpatrick's Old-Time Minstrels 1930,Ap 21,20:2
Brandston, Howard (Lighting Director)
Corn Is Green, The 1954,F 27,10:2
Brandt, C Edwin
Fast Life 1928,S 27,35:2

Brandt, C Edwin—Cont
Romeo and Juliet 1933,F 3,21:5
When in Rome 1934,F 28,22:6
Brandt, Eddie (Composer)
Woof, Woof 1929,D 26,20:4
Brandt, Eddie (Lyricist)
Woof, Woof 1929,D 26,20:4
Brandt, Edwin
Romeo and Juliet 1922,D 28,20:1
Roar China! 1930,O 28,23:1
Brandt, Frances
She Loves Me Not 1933,N 21,22:4
Pride and Prejudice 1935,N 6,32:4
First Stop to Heaven 1941,Ja 6,10:7
Silver Whistle, The 1948,N 25,49:2
Loves of Cass McGuire, The 1966,O 7,36:1
Brandt, Frances E
Once in a Lifetime 1930,S 25,22:3
Brandt, George
Good Hunting 1938,N 22,26:5
Brandt, George (Producer)
Native Son 1942,O 24,10:6
Manhattan Nocturne 1943,O 27,26:2
Springtime for Henry 1951,Mr 15,36:2
Diamond Lil 1951,S 15,8:2
Detour After Dark 1959,Je 9,11:4
Brandt, Harry (Miscellaneous)
Father, The 1949,N 17,36:2
Brandt, Harry (Producer)
Doctor X 1931,F 10,25:1
Brandt, Helga
Hats Off to Ice 1944,Je 23,15:2
Brandt, Inge
Hats Off to Ice 1944,Je 23,15:2
Brandt, Ivan
Rope's End 1929,S 20,34:5
Brandt, Jennie
Anathema 1923,Ap 11,16:2
Brandt, Joseph L
Surgeon, The 1932,O 28,23:1
Brandt, Louis
Professor Mamlock 1937,Ap 14,30:3
Awake and Sing! 1938,D 23,16:6
Brandt, Louis (Producer)
Native Son 1942,O 24,10:6
Brandt, Martin
Men in Shadow 1943,Mr 11,16:2
Temper the Wind 1946,D 28,10:2
Uniform of Flesh 1949,Ja 31,15:2
Billy Budd 1951,F 12,18:3
Sherlock Holmes 1953,O 31,11:2
Great Sebastians, The 1956,Ja 5,27:1
Billy Budd 1959,F 28,13:3
Marching Song 1959,D 29,20:1
Brandt, Mike
Exchange 1970,F 9,47:2
Brandt, Mike (Composer)
Exchange 1970,F 9,47:2
Brandt, Mike (Lyricist)
Exchange 1970,F 9,47:2
Brandt, Mike (Miscellaneous)
Exchange 1970,F 9,47:2
Brandt, Rudolf
Don Carlos 1964,N 25,40:1
Brandt, Sverre (Playwright)
Sonya's Search for the Christmas Star
1929,D 14,24:6
Brandt, Volker
Faust, Part I; Prologue in Heaven 1961,F 5,27:2
Brandt, William (Producer)
Doctor X 1931,F 10,25:1
Society Girl 1931,D 31,16:1
Brandt, Yanna (Miscellaneous)
Exception and the Rule, The 1965,My 21,19:1
Prodigal Son, The 1965,My 21,19:1
Brandt Sisters
Stars on Ice 1942,Jl 3,12:2
Icetime 1946,Je 21,20:5
Icetime 1947,My 29,28:2
Brandy
Teahouse of the August Moon, The 1956,N 9,33:2
Branhall, Mark
New York Idea, The 1963,Jl 13,12:2
Branner, H C (Playwright)
Judge, The 1958,My 14,36:2
Brannigan, Robert (Lighting Director)
Egg, The 1962,Ja 9,23:2
Last Minstrel, The 1963,My 9,40:2
Save Me a Place at Forest Lawn 1963,My 9,40:2
Brannon, H G
Night at an Inn, A 1930,My 10,25:1
Brannum, Lumpy
Hear! Hear! 1955,S 28,38:1
Brannum, Lumpy (Composer)
Hear! Hear! 1955,S 28,38:1
Brannum, Lumpy (Playwright)
Hear! Hear! 1955,S 28,38:1
Brannum, Tom
Time of Your Life, The 1955,Ja 20,34:1
Liliom 1956,F 18,12:5
Once There Was a Russian 1961,F 20,32:2
Take Her, She's Mine 1961,D 22,19:1
Devils, The 1963,N 5,25:1
We Bombed in New Haven 1968,O 17,51:1

Room Service 1970,My 13,49:1
Branon, John
Guide, The 1968,Mr 7,50:1
Glorious Ruler, The 1969,Jl 1,31:1
Branon, John Saunders (Miscellaneous)
Hamlet 1968,Jl 4,15:1
Bransford, Bradley
Man and Superman 1953,F 21,11:2
Bransky, Harry (Translator)
Gardener's Dog, The 1927,O 21,27:1
Brant, Harry (Composer)
Lysistrata 1946,O 18,27:5
Brantley, Marion
Swing It 1937,Jl 23,17:2
Branz, Cecilia
Gondoliers, The 1931,Je 2,34:4
Branz, Celia
Earl Carroll's Vanities 1925,Jl 7,24:1
Braschi, Valentina
Onda e lo Scoglio, L'; Wave and the Rock, The
1931,Ap 13,17:3
Arzigogolo, L'; Whim, The 1931,Ap 27,24:4
Alba, Il Gioro, La Notte, L'; Dawn, the Day, the
Night, The 1931,My 18,21:4
Incendio Doloso, L'; False Flame, The
1931,N 16,22:4
Profumo di Mia Moglie, Il; My Wife's Perfume
1932,Ja 11,29:5
Trio 1932,F 8,21:1
Ladro, Il; Thief, The 1932,F 22,23:4
T'Amo E Sarai Mia; I Love You and You'll Be
Mine 1932,Mr 21,19:4
Canto Della Vita, Il; Song of Life, The
1932,Ap 4,13:3
Promessi Sposi I,; Betrothed, The 1934,O 22,13:2
Due Orfanelle, Le; Two Orphans, The
1936,O 5,24:4
Morte Civile, La; Civic Death 1936,N 9,23:4
Sansone; Samson 1936,N 30,25:2
Brascia, John
Hazel Flagg 1953,F 12,22:2
Brash, Arthur F (Playwright)
Now-A-Days 1929,Ag 6,29:3
Brash, Marion
Courtyard 1960,Mr 1,28:1
Hidden Stranger 1963,Ja 10,5:5
Dreigroschenoper, Die 1965,Mr 12,24:1
Brasington, Alan
Cock-A-Doodle Dandy 1969,Ja 21,40:1
Hamlet 1969,Mr 4,34:1
Patriot for Me, A 1969,O 6,58:1
Brasno, George
Variety Anthology 1932,Mr 21,19:4
Hop, Signor! 1962,My 8,45:2
Brasno, Olive
Variety Anthology 1932,Mr 21,19:4
Brassard, Fran (Costume Designer)
Butterfly Dream, The 1966,My 20,41:1
Hamp 1967,Mr 10,32:1
Brasseur, Claude
Three Musketeers, The 1968,Je 26,43:1
Tartuffe 1968,Jl 3,28:2
Brasseur, Pierre
Trouble, Le 1928,Ap 29,IX,2:3
Roi, Le 1931,Ap 5,VIII,3:1
Grisou 1935,Je 30,X,1:4
Diable et le Bon Dieu, Le 1951,Je 8,32:6
Diable et le Bon Dieu, Le 1951,Ag 19,II,1:6
Brasseur, Pierre (Playwright)
Coeur a Gauche 1929,F 3,VIII,2:3
Grisou 1935,Je 30,X,1:4
Brasseurl, Claude
Shock Troops 1969,F 22,36:1
Brassfield, Jay
Sun Field, The 1942,D 10,33:2
Othello 1945,My 23,25:4
Brassler, Muriel
Tapestry in Gray 1935,D 28,10:2
Greatness Comes to the Maronies 1937,Ag 18,15:2
Julius Caesar 1937,N 12,26:6
Brastoff, Sascha (S/Sgt)
Winged Victory 1943,N 22,24:1
Braswell, Charles
Heel, The 1954,My 27,33:2
Purification, The 1954,My 29,12:1
Apollo of Bellac, The 1954,My 29,12:1
Season of the Beast 1958,Mr 14,29:2
Thurber Carnival, A 1960,F 27,13:2
Wildcat 1960,D 17,20:2
Sail Away 1961,O 4,48:5
Hot Spot 1963,Ap 20,17:2
Me and Thee 1965,D 8,58:4
Mame 1966,My 25,41:1
Company 1970,Ap 27,40:1
Company 1970,My 3,II,1:4
Braswell, John
Renard 1970,Mr 25,36:4
Carmilla 1970,D 1,61:2
Braswell, John (Director)
Renard 1970,Mr 25,36:4
Only Jealousy of Emer, The 1970,Mr 25,36:4
Only Jealousy of Emer, The 1970,Ap 26,II,1:3

Braswell, Joseph (Costume Designer)
Aunt Caroline's Will 1954,Ag 11,21:1
Braswell, Joseph (Scenic Designer)
Doctor Cupid 1952,Ag 14,19:6
Aunt Caroline's Will 1954,Ag 11,21:1
Bratsburg, Harry
Virginian, The 1937,Ag 10,22:7
Golden Boy 1937,N 5,18:5
Gentle People, The 1939,Ja 6,25:1
My Heart's in the Highlands 1939,Ap 14,29:2
Thunder Rock 1939,N 15,18:1
Night Music 1940,F 23,18:2
Heavenly Express 1940,Ap 19,24:2
Heavenly Express 1940,Ap 28,IX,1:1
Cream in the Well, The 1941,Ja 21,19:2
Night Before Christmas, The 1941,Ap 11,25:2
Hello Out There 1941,S 11,20:6
Bratt, George
Little Clay Cart, The 1924,D 6,13:3
Wild Duck, The 1925,F 25,16:4
Dybbuk, The 1925,D 16,22:2
Humble, The 1926,O 14,22:2
Dybbuk, The 1926,D 17,27:2
Pinwheel 1927,F 4,16:4
Hoboken Blues 1928,F 18,10:1
Grand Street Follies, The 1928,My 29,16:2
Wild Duck, The 1928,N 19,17:1
Broken Chain, The 1929,F 21,30:4
Troika 1930,Ap 2,32:6
Bratt, Max
Beggar Student, The 1921,Ja 8,9:3
Fruehlingsluft 1921,N 29,17:4
Tanzgraefin, Die 1925,S 18,26:3
Bratton, S T
Reflected Glory 1936,S 22,30:2
Brattsburt, H H
At Mrs Beam's 1937,Jl 27,24:2
Brauer, Kenneth
Sound of Hunting, A 1945,N 21,16:6
Brauer, Theodore R (Producer)
Under the Weather 1966,O 28,35:1
Braun, Alfred
Friedens Tragoedie 1936,N 17,34:4
Braun, Carin
Wozzeck 1966,Ap 6,34:1
Ratten, Die 1966,Ap 13,36:1
Braun, Dorothy
Merry-Go-Round 1932,Ap 23,11:2
Braun, Elsa
Sandro Botticelli 1923,Mr 27,24:2
Braun, Eugene (Lighting Director)
Stars on Ice (2d Edition) 1943,Je 25,13:2
Hats Off to Ice 1944,Je 23,15:2
Icetime 1946,Je 21,20:5
Icetime 1947,My 29,28:2
Howdy, Mr Ice of 1950 1949,My 27,24:2
Arabian Nights 1955,Je 24,16:1
Braun, Gertrude
Legend of Leonora, The 1926,My 1,10:1
Braun, Judith
Tiger at the Gates 1955,O 4,40:1
Braun, Justine
Fall and Rise of Susan Lenox, The 1920,Je 11,11:2
Braun, Roger
George M! 1968,Ap 11,48:1
Braun, Victor
Gondoliers, The 1962,Jl 7,9:4
Braun, Wilbur
Marry the Poor Girl 1920,S 27,18:3
Braunschlagerova, Jana
Laterna Magika 1964,Ag 4,21:1
Braunstein, Breine
His Wife's Lover 1929,O 21,30:6
Braunstein, Lawrence
Mighty Nimrod, The 1931,My 13,23:1
Braunstein, Ora (Choreographer)
Sands of the Negev 1954,O 20,32:1
Brause, B B
Here's Howe 1923,Ap 26,19:3
Brausewetter, Hans
Trial of Mary Dugan, The 1928,Je 24,VIII,1:4
Journey's End 1929,S 22,IX,4:1
Street Scene 1930,Mr 16,IX,4:1
Strictly Dishonorable 1931,Ap 12,IX,1:3
Journalisten, Die 1932,Jl 17,IX,1:1
Bravassa, Miss
George Barnwell; London Merchant, The
1928,O 2,34:3
Braveman, Sarah
Red Eye of Love 1961,Je 13,28:1
Brawn, John P
Easiest Way, The 1921,S 7,14:1
American, Very Early 1934,Ja 31,21:2
Brawner, Hilda
Cherry Orchard, The 1955,O 19,38:1
Sweet Bird of Youth 1959,Mr 11,39:2
Rape of the Belt, The 1960,N 7,46:1
Lover, The 1964,Ja 6,35:1
Braxleton, Thomas B Jr
Fol-De-Rol 1937,D 11,22:4
Braxton, Elizabeth
Roseanne 1923,D 31,9:5

Bray, Barbara (Translator)
Place Without Doors, A 1970,D 1,60:1
Bray, Florence
Evening With Beatrice Lillie, An 1952,O 3,17:2
Evening With Beatrice Lillie, An 1952,O 12,II,1:1
Brayford, Frank
Biff, Bing, Bang 1921,My 10,20:1
Brayton, Lillie
You and I 1925,O 20,29:1
Field God, The 1927,Ap 22,18:2
Julius Caesar 1932,F 9,30:7
Brazelton, T Berry
Once Over Lightly 1938,D 10,13:4
Brazwell, Damon W
Man Better Man 1969,Jl 3,22:1
Man Better Man 1969,Jl 13,II,3:6
Man Better Man 1969,Jl 13,II,1:1
Harangues, The 1970,Ja 14,42:1
Breakstone, Herbert
Professor Mamlock 1937,Ap 14,30:3
Gypsy Baron, The 1944,Je 15,17:3
Breasted, James
Tiger Smiles, The 1930,D 18,29:1
Breathnach, Michael (Director)
Silver Tassie, The 1929,O 25,26:1
Playboy of the Western World, The 1930,Ja 3,20:4
Breaux, Marc
Kiss Me, Kate 1948,D 31,10:3
Kiss Me, Kate 1949,Ja 30,II,6:5
Barrier, The 1950,N 3,32:2
Catch a Star! 1955,S 7,35:2
Li'l Abner 1956,N 16,24:2
Destry Rides Again 1959,Ap 24,24:1
Breaux, Marc (Choreographer)
Do Re Mi 1960,D 27,23:2
Breaux, Marc (Director)
Minnie's Boys 1970,Mr 27,27:1
Minnie's Boys 1970,Ap 5,II,3:1
Lovely Ladies, Kind Gentlemen 1970,D 29,38:1
Breaux, Marc (Miscellaneous)
Subways Are for Sleeping 1961,D 28,22:1
Breazeale, Burt
Founders, The 1957,My 14,39:1
Brecher, Egon
Dr David's Dad 1924,Ag 14,10:3
Versunkene Glocke, Die 1924,N 3,21:2
Alt Heidelberg 1924,D 8,23:2
Wilhelm Tell 1925,Mr 2,15:1
Taps 1925,Ap 15,16:2
Man or Devil 1925,My 22,22:4
What Women Do? 1925,Jl 21,26:4
Call of Life, The 1925,O 10,10:1
Master Builder, The 1925,N 11,27:1
Master Builder, The 1925,N 15,VIII,1:1
Fountain, The 1925,D 11,26:1
John Gabriel Borkman 1926,Ja 30,13:1
Saturday Night 1926,O 26,25:1
Three Sisters, The 1926,O 27,24:1
Locandiera, La; Mistress of the Inn, The
1926,N 23,26:1
Twelfth Night 1926,D 21,21:4
Cradle Song 1927,Ja 25,18:2
Inheritors 1927,Mr 8,23:1
Good Hope, The 1927,O 19,24:2
2 + 2 = 5 1927,N 29,30:3
First Stone, The 1928,Ja 14,12:2
Improvisations in June 1928,F 27,16:5
Would-Be Gentleman, The 1928,O 2,34:1
Peter Pan; Boy Who Would Not Grow Up, The
1928,N 27,36:3
On the High Road 1929,Ja 15,22:3
Sea Gull, The 1929,S 17,34:1
Mademoiselle Bourrat 1929,O 8,34:3
Living Corpse, The 1929,D 7,19:1
Women Have Their Way, The 1930,Ja 28,28:1
Green Cockatoo, The 1930,O 10,20:5
Siegfried 1930,O 21,34:1
Steel 1931,N 19,26:5
Moon in the Yellow River, The 1932,F 21,VIII,2:1
Moon in the Yellow River, The 1932,Mr 1,19:3
Clear All Wires! 1932,S 15,19:1
Brecher, Egon (Director)
Goat Alley 1927,Ap 21,24:3
2 + 2 = 5 1927,N 29,30:3
Two Seconds 1931,O 10,20:6
Two Strange Women 1933,Ja 11,23:3
Brecher, Gustav (Producer)
Zar Laesst Sich Photographieren, Der
1928,Ap 22,IX,6:7
Brecher, Irving (Playwright)
Sweet Charity 1942,D 29,26:4
Brecht, Bertolt (Director)
Happy End 1929,O 27,IX,4:1
Brecht, Bertolt (Lyricist)
Threepenny Opera, The 1954,Ap 4,II,7:1
Dreigroschenoper, Die 1965,Mr 12,24:1
Baal 1965,My 7,33:2
Threepenny Opera, The 1966,O 28,33:1
Whores, Wars & Tin Pan Alley 1969,Je 17,37:1
Brecht, Bertolt (Miscellaneous)
Threepenny Opera, The 1954,Mr 11,26:5
Brecht, Bertolt (Original Author)
Brecht on Brecht 1962,Ja 14,II,1:1

Brecht, Bertolt (Playwright)
Mann Ist Mann 1928,Ap 15,IX,4:7
Threepenny Opera, The 1928,D 2,X,4:4
Happy End 1929,O 27,IX,4:1
Threepenny Opera, The 1933,Ap 14,22:4
Mother, The 1935,N 20,26:3
Private Life of the Master Race, The
1945,Je 13,28:3
Private Life of the Master Race, The
1945,Je 17,II,1:1
Galileo 1947,Ag 1,21:4
Galileo 1947,D 8,34:2
Threepenny Opera, The 1954,Mr 21,II,1:1
Threepenny Opera, The 1954,Ap 4,II,7:1
Threepenny Opera, The 1955,S 21,38:1
Private Life of the Master Race, The
1956,Ja 31,33:3
Threepenny Opera, The 1956,F 12,83:1
Threepenny Opera, The 1956,Mr 11,II,1:1
Threepenny Opera, The 1956,Ap 8,II,3:1
Days of the Commune, The 1956,N 20,44:4
Good Woman of Setzuan, The 1956,D 19,41:2
Good Woman of Setzuan, The 1956,D 30,II,1:1
Puntila 1959,My 15,26:2
Schweik in the Second World War 1959,My 23,18:3
Resistible Rise of Arturo Ui, The 1960,N 16,51:2
In the Jungle of Cities 1960,D 21,39:1
Resistable Ascension of Arturo Ui, The
1960,D 25,II,5:1
Good Woman of Setzuan, The 1960,D 25,II,5:1
In the Jungle of Cities 1961,Ja 15,II,1:1
Caucasian Chalk Circle, The 1961,N 1,35:1
Jewish Wife 1961,N 15,52:2
Brecht on Brecht 1962,Ja 4,26:1
Caucasian Chalk Circle, The 1962,Mr 30,28:1
Man Is Man 1962,S 19,31:1
Man's a Man, A 1962,S 20,30:2
Galileo 1963,Ja 5,5:2
Hofmeister, Der 1963,Ag 10,9:1
Arturo Ui 1963,N 12,49:1
Arturo Ui 1963,N 24,II,1:1
Mother Courage and Her Children 1964,My 12,32:2
St Joan of the Stockyards 1964,Je 12,45:1
Master Puntila and His Valet, Matti 1964,N 21,34:1
Dreigroschenoper, Die 1965,Mr 21,II,13:1
Baal 1965,My 7,33:2
Exception and the Rule, The 1965,My 21,19:1
Baal 1965,Je 6,II,1:1
Exception and the Rule, The 1965,Je 6,II,1:1
Caucasian Chalk Circle, The 1966,Mr 25,35:1
Caucasian Chalk Circle, The 1966,Ap 10,II,1:1
Galileo 1967,Ap 14,31:1
Galileo 1967,Ap 23,II,1:1
Drums in the Night 1967,My 18,54:1
Schweik in the Second World War
1967,N 12,II,17:1
Mother Courage 1967,N 17,55:1
Edward II 1968,My 2,58:4
Resistible Rise of Arturo Ui, The 1968,Ag 8,25:1
Resistible Rise of Arturo Ui, The 1968,Ag 30,22:2
Resistible Rise of Arturo Ui, The 1968,S 2,14:2
Antigone 1968,O 11,36:1
Galileo 1968,D 1,88:4
Guns of Carrar, The 1968,D 10,53:1
Resistible Rise of Arturo Ui, The 1968,D 23,44:1
Lesson in Consent, A 1969,My 26,55:2
Flight of Lindbergh, The 1969,My 26,55:2
Resistible Rise of Arturo Ui, The 1969,Ag 18,28:1
Trumpets and Drums 1969,O 13,52:1
Jungle of Cities 1970,Mr 1,75:2
Mahagonny 1970,Ap 29,51:1
Mahagonny 1970,My 10,II,1:1
Good Woman of Setzuan, The 1970,N 6,51:1
Good Woman of Setzuan, The 1970,N 15,II,1:5
Kleinburgerhochzeit, Die 1970,N 25,25:1
Brecht, Mary (Costume Designer)
Bluebeard 1970,My 5,58:1
Breck, Peter
Man of Destiny, The 1957,Ap 1,21:2
Breckenridge, Betty
Blind Mice 1930,O 16,28:2
Spring Again 1941,O 28,28:3
Spring Again 1941,N 11,28:2
Janie 1942,S 11,24:2
Breckinridge, Elinor
Kiss for Cinderella, A 1942,Mr 11,22:2
Breckinridge, Robert
Watched Pot, The 1933,My 5,13:7
Hades, the Ladies 1934,Mr 29,25:3
Bredi, James (Composer)
Happy Hypocrite, The 1968,S 6,38:1
Bree, Chester
Connecticut Yankee, A 1927,N 4,24:2
Rainbow 1928,N 22,25:1
Anything Goes 1934,N 22,26:1
Liliom 1940,Mr 26,17:2
Breecher, Lawrence
When the Bough Breaks 1950,Mr 9,25:5
Gods of the Mountain, The 1950,My 25,36:2
Breed, William (Lighting Director)
Dr Faustus 1926,O 27,25:5
Breeden, John
Doctor X 1930,Jl 31,12:4

Breeden, John—Cont
Greater Love 1931,Mr 3,39:1
Breeden, Marshall
Widowers' Houses 1959,Mr 3,39:2
Man and Superman 1960,Ag 17,35:3
Tender Trap, The 1961,Ag 26,15:1
Breeding, Guinevare
Queens of France 1966,S 7,53:1
Long Christmas Dinner, The 1966,S 7,53:1
Breen, Bernice (Playwright)
Little Theatre Tournament; Sightseers
1929,My 8,34:4
Breen, Bobby
Safari! 1955,My 12,32:6
Breen, David
Simple Simon 1931,Mr 10,23:2
Whatever Goes Up 1935,N 26,28:2
Breen, Edwin
Sojourner Truth 1948,Ap 22,35:2
Breen, George
Out of My House 1942,Ja 8,28:6
Breen, Margaret
George White's Scandals 1923,Je 19,22:5
Princess Flavia 1925,N 3,34:3
Merry World, The 1926,Je 9,18:3
Peggy-Ann 1926,D 28,16:3
Simple Simon 1931,Mr 10,23:2
Breen, Nellie
Passing Show of 1922, The 1922,S 21,18:2
Mercenary Mary 1925,Ap 14,27:3
Florida Girl 1925,N 3,34:1
Desert Song, The 1926,D 1,24:2
Breen, Robert
Gloriana 1938,N 26,18:4
Speak of the Devil! 1939,O 7,21:7
Steps Leading Up 1941,Ap 19,20:6
Male Animal, The 1941,Jl 9,24:6
Holiday 1941,Jl 23,15:2
Breen, Robert (Director)
Speak of the Devil! 1939,O 7,21:7
ANTA Album 1950,Ja 30,13:2
House of Bernarda Alba, The 1951,Ja 8,14:6
Mary Rose 1951,Mr 5,25:2
Ecole des Femmes, L'; School for Wives
1951,Mr 19,22:1
Night Music 1951,Ap 9,29:6
Porgy and Bess 1953,Mr 10,25:5
Porgy and Bess 1953,Mr 15,II,1:1
Porgy and Bess 1954,Jl 15,24:2
Porgy and Bess 1954,S 23,42:6
Porgy and Bess 1955,Ap 22,20:6
Porgy and Bess 1956,Ja 11,36:1
Porgy and Bess 1956,Ja 15,II,3:1
Free and Easy 1959,D 20,II,3:2
Breen, Robert (Miscellaneous)
Cellar and the Well, The 1950,D 11,30:2
Breen, Robert (Producer)
Hamlet 1949,Je 18,9:6
Porgy and Bess 1952,Ag 6,17:7
Porgy and Bess 1953,F 17,21:1
Porgy and Bess 1953,Mr 10,25:5
Porgy and Bess 1954,Jl 15,24:2
Porgy and Bess 1954,D 17,36:7
Porgy and Bess 1955,F 8,23:4
Porgy and Bess 1955,D 27,29:1
Breen, Taylor
Hamlet 1921,Je 21,20:2
Breen, Tom
Jumbo 1935,N 18,20:2
Breen Brothers, The
George White's Scandals 1923,Je 19,22:5
Breens, The
Nifties of 1923 1923,S 26,10:1
Breer, Robert
Originale 1964,S 9,46:1
Breese, Edmund
Welcome Stranger 1920,S 14,12:1
Bluebeard's Eighth Wife 1921,S 20,12:2
So This Is London 1922,Ag 31,18:2
Chivalry 1925,D 16,22:3
Vaudeville (Palace) 1926,Mr 30,20:4
Night of January 16 1935,S 10,26:1
Night of January 16 1935,S 17,26:4
Breffort, Alexandre
Irma la Douce 1960,S 30,31:2
Breffort, Alexandre (Playwright)
Irma la Douce 1960,S 30,31:2
Bregis, Danielle
Rose of France 1933,O 29,II,3:3
Bregman, Buddy (Composer)
Jerry Lewis' Variety Show 1957,F 8,18:5
Brehm, June
Twelfth Night 1940,N 20,26:3
Breil, Joseph Carl (Composer)
Climax, The 1926,My 18,29:3
Breines, Jennie
Our Lan' 1947,Ap 19,11:2
G-II 1948,My 28,27:3
Breisach, Paul (Composer)
Rape of Lucretia, The 1948,D 30,24:2
Breisach, Paul (Musical Director)
Rape of Lucretia, The 1948,D 30,24:2

reiseth, Tilman (Playwright)
As We Forgive Our Debtors 1936,Ag 11,24:6
As We Forgive Our Debtors 1947,Mr 11,37:2

reit, Harvey (Playwright)
Disenchanted, The 1958,D 4,53:4
Disenchanted, The 1959,Ja 11,II,1:1
Guide, The 1968,Mr 7,50:1

reit, Jeremy
Macbeth 1956,O 30,42:2

Breitbart
Vaudeville (Hippodrome) 1923,D 18,16:1
Vaudeville (Hippodrome) 1924,Ja 1,21:1
Vaudeville (Hippodrome) 1924,Ja 22,15:6

Breiter, John Stuart
You'll See Stars 1943,Ja 1,26:6
You Can't Take It With You 1951,Ap 7,8:6

Breitman, Donahl
Priest in the Cellar, The 1969,F 19,39:1

Breitman, George (Miscellaneous)
Hajj Malik, El 1970,O 4,II,5:1

Breitsamter, Melchior
Untitled-Passion Play 1950,My 19,29:6

Breivogel, George
Will, The 1930,My 6,33:1

Breker's Bears
Vaudeville (Hippodrome) 1924,Ja 22,15:6

Brel, Jacques
Man of La Mancha 1968,D 12,61:1

Brel, Jacques (Composer)
Jacques Brel Is Alive and Well and Living in Paris 1968,Ja 23,25:2
Jacques Brel Is Alive and Well and Living in Paris 1970,Ja 21,34:1

Brel, Jacques (Lyricist)
Jacques Brel Is Alive and Well and Living in Paris 1970,Ja 21,34:1

Brel, Jacques (Miscellaneous)
O, Oysters! 1961,Ja 31,23:1

Brel, Jacques (Translator)
Man of La Mancha 1968,D 12,61:1

Bremers, Beverly Ann
Me Nobody Knows, The 1970,My 19,42:1

Brendel, El
Cinderella on Broadway 1920,Je 25,18:1
Vaudeville (Palace) 1926,Mr 16,22:2

Brendel and Bert
Mimic World of 1921, The 1921,Ag 18,9:2
Vaudeville (Palace) 1927,S 27,31:3
Vaudeville (Palace) 1929,Mr 18,30:5

Brender, Margot
Laffing Room Only 1944,D 25,15:4

Brenes, Maria
Macbeth 1966,Ag 29,23:4

Brenlin, George
Master Builder, The 1955,Mr 2,23:2
I Knock at the Door 1956,Mr 19,27:5
Pictures in the Hallway 1956,My 28,23:1
Pictures in the Hallway 1956,S 17,23:2
Pictures in the Hallway 1956,S 23,II,1:1
I Know at the Door 1957,S 30,27:2
Drums Under the Windows 1960,O 14,26:1

Brenn, Jani
Mod Donna 1970,My 4,48:1

Brennan, Allison
Bacchae, The 1969,Mr 15,24:1

Brennan, Buddy
Show Boat 1957,Je 28,30:2

Brennan, Dan
Red Pepper 1922,My 30,8:3

Brennan, Denis
John Bull's Other Island 1948,F 11,33:4
Where Stars Walk 1948,F 25,27:2

Brennan, Eileen
Little Mary Sunshine 1959,N 19,49:3
Little Mary Sunshine 1959,N 29,II,1:1
King and I, The 1963,Je 13,30:2
Student Gypsy, The; Prince of Liederkranz, The 1963,O 1,34:1
Hello, Dolly! 1964,Ja 17,22:1

Brennan, Frederick
Up the Ladder 1922,Mr 7,11:2

Brennan, Frederick Hazlitt (Playwright)
Battleship Gertie 1935,Ja 19,9:2
Stick-in-the-Mud 1935,D 2,18:2
Wookey, The 1941,Ag 26,23:2
Wookey, The 1941,Ag 27,15:3
Wookey, The 1941,S 11,20:5
Wookey, The 1941,S 21,IX,1:1
Wookey, The 1941,O 5,IX,1:1
Magdalena 1948,Jl 28,27:2
Magdalena 1948,S 21,31:2
Magdalena 1948,S 26,II,1:1

Brennan, George H (Director)
Ghosts 1933,My 24,24:5

Brennan, George H (Producer)
Mongolia 1927,D 27,24:5
Ghosts 1933,My 24,24:5

Brennan, J Keirn (Lyricist)
Artists and Models 1927,N 16,28:2
Boom Boom 1929,Ja 29,26:4
Music in May 1929,Ap 2,29:1
Night in Venice, A 1929,My 22,30:2
Luana 1930,S 18,28:1

Brennan, Jack
Quick Years, The 1953,N 26,51:2

Brennan, Jay
Vaudeville (Palace) 1924,Ap 1,18:1
Hassard Short's Ritz Revue 1924,S 18,19:1
Fioretta 1929,Ja 6,VIII,4:6
Fioretta 1929,F 6,30:3
Vaudeville (Hollywood) 1932,F 16,24:3

Brennan, Joseph
Return of Peter Grimm, The 1921,S 22,12:2
Nervous Wreck, The 1923,O 10,16:1
Sandalwood 1926,S 23,23:1
Banshee, The 1927,D 6,26:2

Brennan, Patty
County Chairman, The 1936,My 26,26:5

Brennan, Robert (Playwright)
Bystander 1931,F 1,VIII,3:4
Bystander 1937,S 15,27:1

Brennan, Suzanne
Nautical but Nice 1931,Ap 19,31:6

Brennan, Tom
In the Shadow of the Glen 1957,Mr 7,24:1
Between Two Thieves 1960,F 12,23:1
Pullman Car Hiawatha 1962,D 4,46:2
Color of Darkness: An Evening in the World of James Purdy; Don't Call Me By My Right Name 1963,O 1,34:1
Color of Darkness: An Evening in the World of James Purdy; Encore 1963,O 1,34:1

Brennan, Tom (Director)
Sweet Confession 1959,Ap 15,30:1
I Rise in Flame, Cried the Phoenix 1959,Ap 15,30:1
Glory in the Flower 1959,D 9,57:5
Purification, The 1959,D 9,57:5
Crime and Crime 1963,D 17,51:2

Brennan, Tom (Miscellaneous)
All in Love 1961,N 11,15:2

Brennan, Walter
Red Robe, The 1928,D 26,15:1

Brennan, William
Little Theatre Tournament; House With the Twisty Windows, The 1929,My 8,34:4

Brennan and Rogers
Artists and Models 1925,Je 25,16:2
Night in Spain, A 1927,My 4,28:2
Night in Spain, A 1927,My 22,VIII,1:1
Vaudeville (Palace) 1927,Je 7,27:3
Vaudeville (Palace) 1927,O 25,33:2
Vaudeville (Palace) 1928,Mr 27,30:5

Brennard, Lillian
Foot-Loose 1920,My 11,12:1
Skin Game, The 1920,O 21,11:1
Bill of Divorcement, A 1921,O 11,22:2
Secrets 1922,D 26,11:1
Way Things Happen, The 1924,Ja 29,17:5
Steam Roller, The 1924,N 11,20:2

Brenner, Carolyn
Come Blow Your Horn 1961,F 23,31:3

Brenner, Lynn
Adding Machine, The 1970,D 5,40:1

Brenner, Maggie
In White America 1965,F 9,42:5

Brenner, Maurice
Bees and the Flowers, The 1946,S 27,19:3
Madwoman of Chaillot, The 1950,Je 14,41:2
Sing Till Tomorrow 1953,D 29,17:2
Lunatics and Lovers 1954,D 14,44:2
Highway Robbery 1955,N 8,36:1
Worm in Horseradish, A 1961,Mr 14,32:3
Beauty Part, The 1962,D 28,5:2
Once for the Asking 1963,N 21,42:2
How Much, How Much? 1970,Ap 21,49:1

Brenner, Paul
Sun-Up 1930,My 10,25:1

Brenner, Ruth (Scenic Designer)
Starlight 1925,Mr 4,17:2

Brenon, Juliet
Patience 1924,D 30,15:1
Wise-Crackers, The 1925,D 17,26:1
Rapid Transit 1927,Ap 8,21:2

Brenska, Betty
Dove, The 1925,F 12,17:3
What Never Dies 1926,D 29,24:2
Scarlet Fox, The 1928,Mr 28,31:1
Mr Moneypenny 1928,O 17,26:2

Brent, Chuck (Miscellaneous)
Americana Pastoral 1968,D 11,51:1

Brent, Doris
It's A Gift 1945,Mr 13,18:7

Brent, Eleanor
Slight Case of Murder, A 1935,S 12,28:5
Bough Breaks, The 1937,N 20,21:4

Brent, George
Seven Year Love 1929,O 27,IX,2:1
Fatal Woman, The 1930,Mr 2,IX,4:7
Love, Honor and Betray 1930,Mr 13,22:2

Brent, Gerry
Every Man for Himself 1940,D 10,32:3

Brent, Henry
Hat, a Coat, a Glove, A 1934,F 1,15:2

Brent, Max
Fedora 1922,F 11,18:1
Henry IV, Part II 1946,My 8,33:4

Brent, Max—Cont
Oedipus; Critic, The 1946,My 21,19:2

Brent, Mona
Wurzel-Flummery 1923,Ja 17,22:2

Brent, Olga
Man's Man, A 1925,O 14,31:2

Brent, Plumath
World's My Oyster, The 1956,Ag 10,10:4

Brent, Romney
Lucky One, The 1922,N 21,15:2
Tidings Brought to Mary, The 1922,D 25,20:1
Peer Gynt 1923,F 6,14:1
Flame of Love 1924,Ap 22,19:2
Garrick Gaieties 1925,My 18,12:2
Androcles and the Lion 1925,N 24,28:1
Chief Thing, The 1926,Mr 23,24:2
Garrick Gaieties 1926,My 11,25:2
Squall, The 1926,N 12,20:1
Loud Speaker 1927,Mr 3,27:2
Katy Did 1927,My 10,24:3
Merchant of Venice, The 1928,Ja 17,22:2
Phantom Lover, The 1928,S 5,25:1
Be Your Age 1929,F 5,27:1
Little Show, The 1929,My 1,28:5
Little Show, The 1929,My 12,IX,1:2
Inspector General, The 1930,D 24,19:2
Getting Married 1931,Mr 31,25:5
Streets of New York, The 1931,O 7,29:1
Pillars of Society, The 1931,O 15,19:1
Warrior's Husband, The 1932,Mr 12,19:4
Words and Music 1932,Ag 26,21:2
Words and Music 1932,S 17,18:7
Simpleton of the Unexpected Isles, The 1935,F 19,27:5
Simpleton of the Unexpected Isles, The 1935,F 24,VIII,1:1
Three Men on a Horse 1936,F 19,16:2
Three Men on a Horse 1936,Mr 15,X,2:1
Love for Love 1936,Je 4,19:5
Bird in Hand 1942,O 20,24:2
Deep Mrs Sykes, The 1945,Mr 20,22:6
Winter's Tale, The 1946,Ja 16,18:6
Winter's Tale, The 1946,Ja 20,II,1:1
Joan of Lorraine 1946,N 19,40:2
Parisienne 1950,Jl 25,24:2
Tovarich 1952,My 15,39:2
International Set, The 1953,Je 12,19:3

Brent, Romney (Director)
Night Before Christmas, The 1941,Ap 11,25:2
Lady Comes Across, The 1942,Ja 10,10:2
Winter's Tale, The 1946,Ja 16,18:6
One Eye Closed 1954,N 25,45:2
Teahouse of the August Moon, The 1956,Ap 20,22:1

Brent, Romney (Playwright)
Mad Hopes, The 1932,My 29,VIII,2:2
Mad Hopes, The 1932,D 2,26:3
Nymph Errant 1933,O 7,18:2
Tomorrow's a Holiday! 1935,D 31,10:2
Winter's Tale, The 1946,Ja 16,18:6

Brent, Sheila
Tobacco Road 1942,S 7,34:2

Brent, Terry
Ice Capades 1955,S 15,38:1

Brentano, Felix (Director)
Man Who Killed Lincoln, The 1940,Ja 18,26:4
Merry Widow, The 1942,Jl 16,22:1
Rosalinda; Fledermaus, Die 1942,O 29,26:5
Merry Widow, The 1943,Ag 5,19:2
Merry Widow, The 1943,S 26,II,1:5
Merry Widow, The 1944,O 9,17:1
Mr Strauss Goes to Boston 1945,S 7,20:2
Chocolate Soldier, The 1947,Mr 13,34:2
Merry Widow, The 1957,Ap 11,36:6
Rosalie 1957,Je 26,28:2

Brentano, Felix (Miscellaneous)
Vie Parisienne, La 1941,N 6,20:3
Festival 1955,Ja 19,22:1

Brentano, Felix (Playwright)
Vie Parisienne, La 1945,Ja 13,14:5

Brentano, Felix (Producer)
Mr Strauss Goes to Boston 1945,S 7,20:2

Brentano, Lily
Winner, The 1954,F 18,34:1

Brentano, Lowell (Playwright)
Spider, The 1927,F 13,VII,1:4
Spider, The 1927,Mr 23,29:1
Spider, The 1927,Mr 27,VII,1:1
Zeppelin 1929,Ja 15,22:3
Family Affairs 1929,D 11,34:6
Danger-Men Working 1936,F 7,14:4
Great Lady 1938,D 2,26:6

Brente, Gerard
Henry, Sweet Henry 1967,O 24,51:2

Brently, Marion
Fireworks on the James 1940,My 15,30:2

Brenton, William
Scarlet Coat, The 1924,D 24,11:1
Fratricide Punished 1925,Ap 21,19:1
Romio and Julietta 1925,Ap 21,19:1
Fortuno 1925,D 23,22:1
Candida 1926,Mr 17,28:3
Dover Road, The 1926,Ap 29,20:3
Dr Faustus 1926,O 27,25:5

Brenton, William—Cont
Samarkand 1926,D 22,24:4
Hamlet 1927,Ap 7,23:3
Candida 1927,Ag 31,19:4
Brenton, William (Playwright)
Samarkand 1926,D 22,24:4
Brents, Frank (Composer)
Egg and I, The 1958,S 11,43:4
Brents, Frank (Miscellaneous)
Egg and I, The 1958,S 11,43:4
Brenzell, Martin (Director)
Mira 1970,Je 3,51:1
Breon, Edmond
On Approval 1927,My 15,VIII,2:6
Fast Service 1931,N 18,26:3
Tread Softly 1935,D 8,X,5:1
Laughter in Court 1936,S 27,X,3:5
Corn Is Green, The 1940,N 27,27:2
Brereton, D (Composer)
Zuider Zee 1928,D 19,24:4
Brereton, D (Lyricist)
Zuider Zee 1928,D 19,24:4
Bresch, Thomas
Everyman Today 1958,Ja 16,32:4
Breschitz, Frank
Paradise 1931,My 12,29:2
Breskin, Sally (Composer)
Ivanov 1958,O 8,42:1
Breslaw, Bobbie
Little Jessie James 1923,Ag 16,10:4
Sweet Little Devil 1924,Ja 22,15:4
Criss Cross 1926,O 13,20:2
Breslin, Pat
Wayward Saint, The 1955,F 18,17:1
Wayward Saint, The 1955,F 27,II,1:1
Breslin, Tommy
Who's Who, Baby? 1968,Ja 30,36:1
Moon Walk 1970,N 27,52:1
Bressart, Felix
Konto X 1930,N 2,VIII,3:1
Cocktail 1931,F 15,VIII,3:2
Royal Family, The 1931,Ap 12,IX,1:3
Journalisten, Die 1932,Jl 17,IX,1:1
Auslandreise 1932,N 20,IX,3:5
Big Two, The 1947,Ja 9,21:2
Bressel, Claribel
Crime Marches on 1935,O 24,19:1
County Chairman, The 1936,My 26,26:5
Bresslaw, Bernard
Day of the Prince 1963,My 15,33:4
Bressler, Charles
Shadow of My Enemy, A 1957,D 12,35:4
Play of Daniel, The 1958,Ja 3,15:3
Play of Daniel, The 1959,Ja 6,30:2
Play of Daniel, The 1959,D 28,17:6
Play of Daniel, The 1960,D 27,23:6
Play of Daniel, The 1961,D 28,22:6
Bressoud, Paul
Mother Said No 1951,Ap 17,34:2
Bressoud, Paul (Producer)
Mother Said No 1951,Ap 17,34:2
Brethwaite, S H Jr
Tiger Smiles, The 1930,D 18,29:1
Bretnall, Marjorie
Antigone 1930,Ap 25,28:4
Breton, Elise
Art and Mrs Bottle 1930,N 19,19:3
Breton, Robert
Guest in the House 1942,F 25,25:2
Lower North 1944,Ag 26,15:4
Laffing Room Only 1944,D 25,15:4
Breton, Tomas (Composer)
Fiesta in Madrid 1969,My 29,49:1
Bretschneider, Carl (Playwright)
Love Song, The 1925,Ja 14,19:4
Brett, George
This Fine-Pretty World 1923,D 27,11:1
Brett, Jeremy
Richard II 1956,O 24,44:1
Romeo and Juliet 1956,O 25,41:1
Troilus and Cressida 1956,D 27,21:1
Variations on a Theme 1958,My 9,16:5
Deputy, The 1964,F 27,26:1
As You Like It 1968,Jl 6,9:1
Hedda Gabler 1970,Jl 18,12:1
Merchant of Venice, The 1970,Jl 30,39:1
Brett, Leonard
Candida 1926,O 24,VIII,2:1
Brett, Margaret
Prunella 1929,Ap 10,23:3
Sonya's Search for the Christmas Star 1929,D 14,24:6
Bretton, Elise (Composer)
Wuziz! 1970,O 2,25:2
Bretton, Elise (Lyricist)
Wuziz! 1970,O 2,25:2
Bretty, Beatrice
Bourgeois Gentilhomme, Le 1955,O 26,26:1
Bretz, Ruth
House With the Twisty Windows, The 1930,My 8,32:5
Bretzfelder, Helen
Mr Pim Passes By 1935,Ag 7,22:2

Breuer, Bessie (Playwright)
Sundown Beach 1948,S 8,37:1
Sundown Beach 1948,S 12,II,1:1
Breuer, Gustav
Winners and Losers 1947,F 27,27:2
Breuer, Kurt (Playwright)
Music in May 1929,Ap 2,29:1
Breuer, Lee (Director)
House of Bernarda Alba, The 1963,N 25,23:2
Red Horse Animation, The 1970,N 20,32:1
Breuer, Lee (Playwright)
Red Horse Animation, The 1970,N 20,32:1
Breuer, Ruth
House of Bernarda Alba, The 1963,N 25,23:2
Dutchman; Slave, The 1965,N 17,53:7
Breustedt, Pauline
Wild Oats Lane 1922,S 7,12:1
Breustein, Robert
Tempest, The 1955,S 3,8:6
Brew, Elizabeth
One-Man Show 1945,F 9,21:2
Make Yourself at Home 1945,S 14,21:2
Brewer, Alice Hope
Tall Kentuckian, The 1953,Je 17,30:1
Brewer, Betty
Barretts of Wimpole Street, The 1945,Mr 27,23:6
Brewer, Conde
Love's Call 1925,S 11,20:1
Sex 1926,Ap 27,22:4
Brewer, George
Master of the Revels 1935,Ag 14,16:2
Brewer, George Jr (Playwright)
Dark Victory 1934,N 10,18:2
Tide Rising 1937,Ja 26,17:2
Brewer, George Jr (Producer)
Big Blow 1938,O 3,11:2
Brewer, J H
Happy-Go-Lucky 1920,Ag 25,6:1
Right to Strike, The 1921,O 25,20:1
Fair Circassian, The 1921,D 7,22:3
Red Poppy, The 1922,D 21,18:2
Cinders 1923,Ap 4,22:1
Little Angel, The 1924,S 29,10:3
Dark Angel, The 1925,F 11,19:2
Bit o' Love, A 1925,My 13,24:2
School for Scandal, The 1925,O 24,19:1
Bells, The 1926,Ap 14,20:3
Constant Nymph, The 1926,D 10,31:1
Murray Hill 1927,S 30,29:1
Mrs Dane's Defense 1928,F 7,30:1
Sherlock Holmes 1928,F 21,18:4
Within the Law 1928,Mr 6,20:1
This Thing Called Love 1928,S 18,32:7
Stripped 1929,O 22,26:1
Unsophisticates, The 1929,D 31,14:5
Ritzy 1930,F 11,30:4
Aiglon, L' 1934,N 5,22:2
Brewer, Johnnie
One, Two, Three! 1930,S 30,24:2
Violet, The 1930,S 30,24:2
Kiss of Importance, A 1930,D 2,31:3
In The Best of Families 1931,F 3,29:1
Widow in Green, A 1931,N 21,21:4
Good Woman, Poor Thing, A 1933,Ja 10,27:3
Brewer, Sherri Peaches
Hello, Dolly! 1967,N 13,61:1
Brewster
Way of the World, The 1953,Ap 10,17:1
Brewster, Ellen
Woman of the Soil, A 1935,Mr 26,23:6
Brewster, Henrietta
Peg o' My Dreams 1924,My 6,25:3
Brewster, Jean
Way, The 1940,O 12,20:3
Brewster, John
Wild Duck, The 1925,F 25,16:4
Window Panes 1927,F 22,22:2
Woman of Bronze, The 1927,Je 16,25:4
Madame X 1927,Jl 7,29:3
Mystery Square 1929,Ap 5,28:3
Jerry for Short 1929,Ag 13,23:4
Lolly 1929,O 17,26:2
Plutocrat, The 1930,F 21,23:3
Brewster, Jonathan
Remains to Be Seen 1951,O 4,37:1
Brewster, Margaret
Dark Lady of the Sonnets, The 1959,Ag 21,13:1
Shewing-Up of Blanco Posnet, The 1959,S 19,26:7
Coggerers, The 1960,Mr 23,33:1
Time to Go 1960,Mr 23,33:1
Red Roses for Me 1961,N 28,41:1
Moon Shines on Kylenamoe, The 1962,O 31,33:1
Figuro in the Night 1962,O 31,33:1
Major Barbara 1965,My 18,33:1
End of All Things Natural, The 1969,S 12,38:1
Brewster, Pat
Laffing Room Only 1944,D 25,15:4
Brewster, Walter Rice
Henry IV 1920,Je 20,II,9:2
Breyer, Elizabeth
Little Inn, The 1935,Ag 20,25:1
Brez, Melvin
Tonight We Improvise 1959,N 7,27:4

Brez, Melvin—Cont
Sign of Jonah, The 1960,S 9,35:1
Brialy, Jean Claude
Shock Troops 1969,F 22,36:1
Brian, Antony
Conversation Piece 1934,O 24,24:1
Brian, Donald
Chocolate Soldier, The 1921,D 13,24:2
Up She Goes 1922,N 7,14:2
Barnum Was Right 1923,Mr 13,19:3
Vaudeville (Palace) 1924,S 16,26:5
Vaudeville (Palace) 1928,Mr 6,20:5
Becky Sharp 1929,Je 4,29:1
How's Your Health? 1929,N 27,30:3
Joy of Living 1931,Ap 7,31:1
Merry Widow, The 1931,S 8,39:1
Merry Widow, The 1932,F 21,VIII,23:3
Merry Widow, The 1932,N 27,IX,1:2
Very Warm for May 1939,N 18,23:2
Brian, Donald (Producer)
Chocolate Soldier, The 1934,My 3,15:3
Brian, Edward
Grey-Eyed People, The 1952,D 18,41:2
Brian, Mary
Vaudeville (Palace) 1932,Ap 4,13:4
Three After Three 1939,N 25,13:5
Off the Record 1940,D 1,63:5
Brian, Ruth
Hidden Stranger 1963,Ja 10,5:5
Brianchon, Maurice (Costume Designer)
Fausses Confidences, Les 1952,N 13,34:2
Intermezzo 1957,F 15,20:4
Brianchon, Maurice (Scenic Designer)
Fausses Confidences, Les 1952,N 13,34:2
Intermezzo 1957,F 15,20:4
Briand, Dominique
Henry VI 1966,Je 9,55:2
Briant, Roger
Cabaret 1966,N 21,62:1
West Side Story 1968,Je 25,32:1
Briant, Roy (Playwright)
Four in Hand 1923,S 7,10:2
Imaginative Girl, The 1926,Ag 8,VII,3:1
Adorable Liar, The 1926,Ag 31,15:2
Briants, The
Vaudeville (Palace) 1925,D 29,21:2
Hooray for What! 1937,D 2,32:5
Briault, Denies
Icetime 1946,Je 21,20:5
Brice, Carol
Saratoga 1959,D 8,59:4
Finian's Rainbow 1960,Ap 28,31:1
Show Boat 1961,Ap 13,32:1
Porgy and Bess 1961,My 18,40:1
Porgy and Bess 1964,My 7,32:1
Porgy and Bess 1965,Mr 6,17:1
Finian's Rainbow 1967,Ap 6,44:1
Brice, Culver
Girl With Carmine Lips, The 1920,Ag 11,6:1
Brice, Elizabeth
Buzzin' Around 1920,Jl 7,14:1
Vaudeville (Palace) 1927,S 13,36:3
Brice, Eugene
Porgy and Bess 1965,Mr 6,17:1
Brice, Fannie
Ziegfeld 9 o'clock Follies 1920,Mr 9,18:1
Ziegfeld Midnight Frolic 1920,Mr 17,14:2
Ziegfeld Follies 1920,Je 23,14:1
Ziegfeld Follies 1921,Je 22,10:1
Ziegfeld Follies 1923,O 22,17:2
Music Box Revue 1924,D 2,23:3
Fanny 1926,S 22,30:1
Vaudeville (Palace) 1927,N 22,33:2
Vaudeville (Palace) 1927,N 29,30:4
Vaudeville (Palace) 1927,D 6,26:3
Vaudeville (Palace) 1928,My 1,33:2
Vaudeville (Palace) 1928,O 30,27:3
Vaudeville (Palace) 1928,N 6,35:2
Fioretta 1929,Ja 6,VIII,4:6
Fioretta 1929,F 6,30:3
Vaudeville (Palace) 1930,F 10,20:3
Sweet and Low 1930,N 18,28:5
Crazy Quilt 1931,My 20,28:4
Follies 1933,N 19,IX,2:5
Ziegfeld Follies 1934,Ja 5,24:3
Ziegfeld Follies 1934,Ja 21,X,1:1
Ziegfeld Follies 1935,D 31,10:1
Ziegfeld Follies 1936,Ja 5,IX,3:1
Ziegfeld Follies 1936,Ja 31,17:2
Ziegfeld Follies 1936,S 15,37:1
Brice, Fannie (Costume Designer)
Crazy Quilt 1931,My 20,28:4
Brice, Hope
Beau Brummell 1924,Ap 4,19:2
Brice, Jonathan
Susanna, Don't You Cry 1939,My 23,27:2
Brice, Lew
All-Star Jamboree 1921,Jl 14,18:1
Americana 1926,Jl 27,15:3
Americana 1926,D 5,VIII,5:1
Crazy Quilt 1931,My 20,28:4
Brice, Percy
Trumpets of the Lord 1969,Ap 30,37:1

iceno, Alcides
Innocent Voyage, The 1943,N 16,27:2
ick, James
We Bombed in New Haven 1967,D 7,58:1
Rivals, The 1969,O 18,37:1
Metamorphoses 1969,D 12,69:1
Three Philip Roth Stories; Epstein 1970,Jl 31,14:1
Three Philip Roth Stories; Defender of the Faith 1970,Jl 31,14:1
Three Philip Roth Stories; Conversion of the Jews 1970,Jl 31,14:1
Cops and Horrors; Dracula 1970,Ag 11,27:1
Cops and Horrors; Fly Paper 1970,Ag 11,27:1
Story Theater Repertory; Saint Julian the Hospitaler 1970,O 21,40:1
Story Theater Repertory; Gimpel the Food 1970,O 21,40:1
Revenger's Tragedy, The 1970,D 2,58:1
icker, Alice
Guest of Honor, The 1920,S 21,12:1
ickert, Carlton
Uptown West 1923,Ap 4,22:2
Pyramids 1926,Jl 20,17:2
Daisy Mayme 1926,O 26,24:2
What Do We Know 1927,D 24,8:1
ricklayers, The
Keep 'Em Laughing 1942,Ap 25,9:2
Top-Notchers 1942,My 30,8:5
New Priorities of 1943 1942,S 16,28:2
Laugh Time 1943,S 9,35:2
rickman, William W (Prof) (Playwright)
Uncle Sam in Israel 1952,D 8,38:5
ricusse, Leslie (Composer)
Stop the World-I Want to Get Off 1962,O 4,45:4
Stop the World-I Want to Get Off 1962,O 14,II,1:1
Pickwick 1965,O 6,5:3
ricusse, Leslie (Lyricist)
Stop the World-I Want to Get Off 1962,O 4,45:4
Stop the World-I Want to Get Off 1962,O 14,II,1:1
Pickwick 1963,Jl 5,13:2
Pickwick 1965,O 6,5:3
ricusse, Leslie (Playwright)
Stop the World-I Want to Get Off 1962,O 4,45:4
Stop the World-I Want to Get Off 1962,O 14,II,1:1
Roar of the Greasepaint-the Smell of the Crowd 1965,My 17,46:2
Bridewell, Carrie
Storm Over Patsy 1937,Mr 9,26:4
Merry Wives of Windsor, The 1938,Ap 15,22:3
Bridge, Betsy
Saint of Bleecker Street, The 1954,D 28,21:1
Bridge, Dwight
Play Without a Name, A 1928,N 26,30:5
Bridge, Peter (Miscellaneous)
Calculated Risk 1962,N 1,35:1
Stephen D 1966,Ag 5,17:1
Help Stamp Out Marriage 1966,S 30,50:1
Stephen D 1967,S 25,58:1
Man in the Glass Booth, The 1968,S 27,41:1
Bridge, Peter (Producer)
Promise, The 1967,N 15,38:1
Bridgeman, Betty Gale
Com Zaa 1945,Ja 10,28:2
Bridgeman, Betty Gale (Choreographer)
Com Zaa 1945,Ja 10,28:2
Bridgeman, Kenneth (Scenic Designer)
Semi-Detached 1963,O 8,49:1
Bridgers, Ann
Clouds of the Sun 1922,My 6,11:2
Bridgers, Ann Preston (Playwright)
Coquette 1927,N 9,23:1
Coquette 1927,N 13,IX,1:1
Coquette 1928,Jl 1,VIII,3:5
Bridges, Beau
Where's Daddy? 1966,Mr 3,27:1
Bridges, Kenneth
Gantry 1970,F 16,44:1
Bridges, Lloyd
Othello 1937,Ja 7,16:4
Infernal Machine, The 1937,D 13,22:7
Comedy of Good and Evil, A 1938,Ap 8,16:3
Audition of the Apprentice Theatre 1939,Je 2,26:2
Susannah and the Elders 1940,O 30,28:2
Dead Pigeon 1953,D 24,10:2
Guys and Dolls 1959,Jl 22,22:2
Cactus Flower 1967,D 16,48:1
Bridges, Lorraine
Saint of Bleecker Street, The 1954,D 28,21:1
Bridges, Neill
Crime 1927,F 23,27:3
Bridges, Robert (Playwright)
Humours of the Court, The 1930,Ja 26,VIII,1:8
Bridgewater, Leslie (Composer)
Escape Me Never! 1935,Ja 22,22:2
Lady Windermere's Fan 1946,O 15,29:2
Importance of Being Earnest, The 1947,Mr 4,30:2
Time Remembered 1955,My 4,35:1
Much Ado About Nothing 1959,S 18,25:2
School for Scandal, The 1963,Ja 26,5:2
Bridie, James (Miscellaneous)
Storm Over Patsy 1937,Mr 9,26:4
Bridie, James (Playwright)
Anatomist, The 1931,O 25,VIII,2:6

Tobias and the Angel 1932,Ap 3,VIII,1:4
Anatomist, The 1932,O 25,24:3
Jonah and the Whale 1933,Ja 8,IX,3:3
Sleeping Clergyman, A 1933,S 21,24:2
Sleeping Clergyman, A 1933,O 8,X,2:4
Marriage Is No Joke 1934,F 7,16:2
Sleeping Clergyman, A 1934,O 9,16:1
Mary Read 1934,N 22,26:7
Mary Read 1934,D 16,XI,3:4
Black Eye, The 1935,O 12,13:5
Black Eye, The 1935,N 10,IX,3:1
Storm in a Teacup 1936,F 6,23:1
Storm Over Patsy 1937,Mr 2,16:4
What It Is to Be Young 1937,Ap 27,18:6
Tobias and the Angel 1937,Ap 29,16:5
Susannah and the Elders 1937,N 21,XI,3:6
Black Eye, The 1938,Mr 8,22:4
King of Nowhere, The 1938,Ap 3,XI,1:8
Last Trump, The 1938,Ag 6,7:1
Last Trump, The 1938,Ag 14,IX,2:1
Let Them Say 1939,Ag 27,IX,1:4
Jonah and the Whale 1940,My 5,II,8:4
Mr Bolfry 1943,Ag 22,II,1:8
Forrigan Reel, The 1945,N 11,II,2:6
Mr Gillie 1950,Mr 10,31:2
Tobias and the Angel 1950,Ap 26,36:3
Queen's Comedy, The 1950,S 10,II,3:1
Daphne Laureola 1950,S 19,38:6
Daphne Laureola 1950,S 24,II,1:1
Tobias and the Angel 1957,O 21,29:5
Susannah and the Elders 1959,O 19,37:3
Bridou, Lucienne
Mime and Me, The 1960,Ap 8,27:3
Funny Thing Happened on the Way to the Forum, A 1962,My 9,49:1
Bridson, John
Mikado, The 1954,Mr 24,31:1
Iolanthe 1954,Ap 28,36:8
Yeomen of the Guard, The 1954,My 5,36:2
Sorcerer, The 1954,My 26,34:3
Utopia, Limited; Flowers of Progress, The 1957,F 27,21:1
Mikado, The 1957,Ap 24,28:2
H M S Pinafore 1957,My 1,42:6
Pirates of Penzance, The 1957,My 8,43:1
Yeomen of the Guard, The 1957,My 22,28:3
Gondoliers, The 1957,My 29,34:2
H M S Pinafore 1960,Ja 29,14:1
Utopia, Limited 1960,Ap 8,27:2
Yeomen of the Guard, The 1961,Ap 28,23:1
Mikado, The 1961,My 5,23:1
Grand Duke, The 1961,My 12,24:1
Princess Ida 1961,My 19,23:1
Gondoliers, The 1961,D 8,44:1
Iolanthe 1962,Ag 8,34:2
Gondoliers, The 1963,Je 5,33:2
Briel, Joseph Carl (Composer)
Climax, The 1933,Je 14,22:2
Brien, Louise
Return of Hannibal, The 1937,F 2,21:1
Briere, Claire
Girofle-Girofla 1926,N 23,26:3
Cloches de Cornville, Les; Chimes of Normandy, The 1926,D 14,24:4
Perichole, La 1926,D 29,24:4
Brierley, David (Miscellaneous)
King Lear 1964,My 19,43:2
Brierre, Maurice
Try It With Alice 1924,Je 24,18:4
Briers, Richard
Real Inspector Hound, The 1968,Je 19,38:2
Real Inspector Hound, The 1968,Jl 8,45:1
Two of Us, The 1970,Ag 1,13:2
Two of Us, The 1970,S 11,33:2
Briess, Fred
Yours Is My Heart 1946,S 6,16:5
Brieux, Eugene (Playwright)
Americans Chez Nous, Les 1920,F 15,VIII,2:1
Letter of the Law, The; Robe Rouge, La 1920,F 24,11:1
Letter of the Law, The 1920,F 29,V,5:1
Americans Chez Nous, Les 1920,Mr 7,V,6:1
Americans in France, The 1920,Ag 4,14:1
Robe Rouge, La 1922,F 5,VI,1:7
Madame Pierre 1922,F 16,11:1
Madame Pierre 1922,F 19,VI,1:1
Blanchette 1924,Mr 19,19:4
Accused 1925,S 20,VIII,2:4
Accused 1925,S 30,20:1
Accused 1925,O 11,VIII,1:1
Famille Lavolette, La 1926,O 10,VIII,2:1
Puisque Je T'Aime 1929,My 26,IX,4:1
Brieux, Eugene (Translator)
Damaged Goods 1937,My 18,27:2
Briey, Jeanne
Exaltation, L' 1929,Mr 10,X,1:8
Briggs, Bunny
Are You With It? 1945,N 12,17:3
Briggs, Charles (Miscellaneous)
Shoot Anything With Hair That Moves 1969,F 3,29:1
Briggs, Clare
Untitled-Revue 1923,My 12,15:4

Briggs, Cynthia
Tarot 1970,D 12,19:1
Briggs, Don
Never Say Never 1951,N 21,21:2
Julia, Jake, and Uncle Joe 1961,Ja 30,19:1
Briggs, Harlan
Up the Line 1926,N 23,26:1
Garden of Eden, The 1927,S 28,28:1
Big Pond, The 1928,Ag 22,25:1
Tired Business Man, The 1929,Je 5,32:5
It's a Wise Child 1929,Ag 7,29:1
It's a Wise Child 1929,Ag 25,VIII,1:1
Nona 1932,O 5,26:4
Forsaking All Others 1933,Mr 2,21:2
It's a Wise Child 1933,My 17,15:2
Tommy 1933,Ag 8,22:5
Give Us This Day 1933,O 28,20:6
Dodsworth 1934,F 26,20:4
Dodsworth 1934,Ag 21,12:3
Flying Gerardos, The 1940,D 30,21:4
Sweet Charity 1942,D 29,26:4
First Million, The 1943,Ap 29,27:4
Ramshackle Inn 1944,Ja 6,17:5
Story of Mary Surratt, The 1947,F 10,25:2
Time for Elizabeth 1948,S 28,32:3
Briggs, Harlan (Director)
It's a Wise Child 1933,My 17,15:2
Briggs, Jean
I Loved You Wednesday 1932,O 12,27:1
New Faces 1934,Mr 16,24:5
Dream Child 1934,S 28,26:2
Fields Beyond, The 1936,Mr 7,11:2
Briggs, Leslie
Sign of the Leopard 1928,D 12,34:4
Briggs, Matt
Brothers 1928,D 26,14:3
Wonder Boy 1931,O 24,20:1
Blessed Event 1932,F 13,23:2
20th Century 1932,D 30,15:1
Kill That Story 1934,Ag 30,22:2
So Many Paths 1934,D 7,26:5
Nowhere Bound 1935,Ja 23,20:2
Sweet River 1936,O 29,30:2
Off to Buffalo! 1939,F 22,18:2
Day in the Sun 1939,My 17,29:2
Male Animal, The 1940,Ja 10,17:2
Male Animal, The 1940,Ja 21,IX,1:1
Village Green 1941,S 4,24:4
Junior Miss 1941,N 19,28:2
That Old Devil 1944,Je 6,14:2
Bloomer Girl 1944,O 6,18:5
Bloomer Girl 1947,Ja 7,33:2
Hallams, The 1948,Mr 5,18:2
Good Housekeeping 1949,Ag 17,19:3
Male Animal, The 1952,My 1,35:1
Male Animal, The 1952,My 18,II,1:1
Briggs, Oceana
Spofford 1967,D 15,54:3
Briggs, Warren
Any Day Now 1941,Je 10,28:2
Briggs-Hall, Austin
Garden of Time 1945,Mr 10,13:7
Henri Christophe 1945,Je 7,24:5
On Strivers' Row 1946,Mr 1,17:2
Hamlet 1951,Jl 20,13:6
Brigham, Constance
Land Is Bright, The 1941,O 29,26:2
Would-Be Gentleman, The 1946,Ja 10,29:2
All in One; Trouble in Tahiti 1955,Ap 20,40:3
Beggar's Opera, The 1957,Mr 14,35:1
Guitar 1959,N 11,42:5
Brigham, Mary H
Marshall 1930,My 10,25:1
Brighouse, Harold (Playwright)
Walking Happy 1966,N 28,47:1
Bright, Betty
Tenth of an Inch Makes the Difference, A 1962,N 13,44:1
Route 1 1964,N 18,52:3
Bright, Chester
H M S Pinafore 1926,Ap 7,26:3
Bright, Douglas
Pot-Luck 1921,S 30,10:1
Bright, Iona
Murder in the Cathedral 1936,Mr 21,13:5
Bright, Ione
Spanish Love 1920,Ag 18,6:1
Bright, John (Playwright)
Brooklyn, U S A 1941,D 22,24:2
Brooklyn, U S A 1941,D 28,IX,1:1
Brooklyn, U S A 1942,Ja 11,IX,1:1
Bright, Joseph C Jr
William Had the Words! 1964,Mr 30,36:1
Bright, Patricia
You'll See Stars 1943,Ja 1,26:6
Tickets, Please! 1950,Ap 28,25:2
Tickets, Please! 1950,My 7,II,1:1
Bright, Richard
Beard, The 1967,O 25,40:1
Bright, Sylvester
Midsummer Night's Dream, A 1958,Je 23,19:1
Brighton, Bruce
Othello 1943,O 20,18:1

Brighton, Bruce—Cont
Affair of Honor 1956,Ap 7,12:3
Send Me No Flowers 1960,D 6,54:1
Brigitte
Ice Capades 1962,Ag 30,34:1
Ice Capades 1963,Ag 29,37:2
Ice Capades 1964,Ag 27,27:2
Brignold, Raymond
Ruy Blas 1957,D 14,16:3
Brilant, Arthur M (Playwright)
Menace 1927,Mr 15,28:2
Brilhante, Patricia
Meet the People 1940,D 26,22:2
Brill, Charles
Peter Pan 1950,Ap 25,27:2
Brill, Dudley
Bursting the Barriers 1930,My 7,25:1
Brill, Fran
Red, White and Maddox 1969,Ja 27,27:1
Brill, Hubert
Cocktails of 1934 1934,My 5,22:1
Brill, King
Show Boat 1948,S 9,33:2
Brill, Klaus
Reunion in New York 1940,F 22,28:4
Brill, Leighton K (Lyricist)
Ballyhoo 1930,D 14,IX,3:1
Ballyhoo 1930,D 23,24:1
Brill, Leighton K (Miscellaneous)
Oh, Kay! 1960,Ap 18,37:2
Brill, Leighton K (Playwright)
Ballyhoo 1930,D 14,IX,3:1
Ballyhoo 1930,D 23,24:1
Brill, Marty (Lyricist)
Cafe Crown 1964,Ap 18,32:1
Brill, Michael (Director)
H M S Pinafore 1969,D 8,61:2
Patience 1970,My 10,72:4
Brill, Robert
20th Century 1932,D 30,15:1
Brilliant, Lord
Gypsy Fires 1925,D 8,28:3
Brilliantine, Lance (Costume Designer)
Man and Superman 1970,F 24,48:1
Brimm, Tom 2d
Kongi's Harvest 1968,Ap 15,49:1
Beclch 1968,D 17,59:1
Brin, Charles
Dybbuk, The 1954,O 27,33:6
Three Sisters, The 1955,F 26,13:2
Inherit the Wind 1955,Ap 22,20:2
Brinckerhoff, Burt
Blue Denim 1958,F 28,17:1
Blue Denim 1958,Ap 20,II,1:1
Answered the Flute 1960,Mr 10,37:4
Cactus Flower 1965,D 9,60:2
Keep It in the Family 1967,S 28,59:1
Brinckerhoff, Burt (Director)
Saturday Night 1968,F 26,43:1
Someone's Comin' Hungry 1969,Ap 1,51:1
Pequod 1969,Je 30,33:1
Whispers on the Wind 1970,Je 4,50:1
Brink, Frank (Playwright)
Cry of the Wild Ram 1960,Jl 16,10:8
Brink, Leo
Ice Capades 1956,S 13,41:2
Brink, Robert
Dream With Music 1944,My 19,15:2
Pirates of Penzance, The 1966,My 24,54:1
H M S Pinafore 1966,Je 8,41:2
Trial by Jury 1966,Je 8,41:2
Narrow Road to the Deep North 1969,D 2,64:1
Nuns, The 1970,Je 2,35:1
Brink, Roscoe W (Playwright)
Catskill Dutch 1924,My 4,VIII,2:1
Catskill Dutch 1924,My 7,18:1
Catskill Dutch 1924,My 11,VIII,1:1
Brinker, Lynn
Commedia Dell' Arte 1957,Jl 5,13:2
Greenwillow 1960,Mr 9,38:1
Brinkley, Grace
Greenwich Village Follies 1928,Ap 10,32:2
White Lilacs 1928,S 11,31:2
Pleasure Bound 1929,F 19,22:4
Flying High 1930,F 9,VIII,4:2
Flying High 1930,Mr 4,24:4
Here Goes the Bride 1931,N 4,31:2
Of Thee I Sing 1931,D 28,20:1
Brinkley, John
Hamlet 1954,Ap 24,15:2
Eastward in Eden 1956,Ap 18,25:4
Brinkman, Edward (Miscellaneous)
Merry Widow, The 1957,Ap 11,36:6
Brinkmann, Ruth
Spoon River Anthology 1964,Je 27,15:2
Brinn, Isis
Mahogany Hall 1934,Ja 18,18:5
First Lady 1935,N 27,17:4
Brinsfield, Dortha
Summer Night 1939,N 3,17:1
Brinson, Philip
Green Pastures, The 1951,Mr 16,35:2
Brinton, C R (Composer)
Kid Himself, The 1925,D 25,23:2

Brinton, Florence
Little Accident 1928,O 10,32:3
Brinton, Robert
Blood and Sand 1921,S 21,16:2
Brioni (Miscellaneous)
Wonder World 1964,My 18,32:1
Briquet, Paul (Playwright)
Vogue 1921,O 23,22:2
Paris-Boulevards 1926,N 21,VIII,2:1
Brisbane, William
Reflected Glory 1936,S 18,19:5
Reflected Glory 1936,S 22,30:2
Briscoe, Donald
Tavern, The 1964,Mr 6,39:2
Impromptu at Versailles 1964,Mr 10,43:1
Briscoe, Murray
Wine, Women and Song 1942,S 29,18:3
Briscoe, Olive
Order Please 1934,O 10,21:2
Brisgal, Earl
Sunup to Sundown 1938,F 2,14:3
30 Days Hath September 1938,O 1,10:5
Briski, Gladys
Jazz a La Carte 1922,Je 3,8:3
Briskin, Arthur V (Producer)
To Be or Not to Be-What Kind of a Question Is
That? 1970,O 20,39:1
Brislin, Lauretta
Chocolate Soldier, The 1934,My 3,15:3
Brisman, C
Dostigayev 1935,Ja 14,10:5
Chains 1937,Ja 22,25:1
Outlaw, The 1937,O 6,28:1
Brisson, Alexandre (Playwright)
Madame X 1927,Ap 3,VIII,1:4
Brisson, Carl
Forbidden Melody 1936,O 13,30:3
Forbidden Melody 1936,N 3,33:1
Brisson, Frederick (Producer)
Pajama Game, The 1954,My 14,20:2
Damn Yankees 1955,My 6,17:1
New Girl in Town 1957,My 15,40:1
Pleasure of His Company, The 1958,O 23,36:1
Gazebo, The 1958,D 13,2:7
Five Finger Exercise 1959,D 3,45:4
Under the Yum-Yum Tree 1960,N 17,45:1
Caretaker, The 1961,O 5,42:3
First Love 1961,D 26,20:2
Alfie 1964,D 18,27:1
Flip Side, The 1968,O 11,36:1
Coco 1969,D 19,66:1
Bristed, Grace
What Next 1920,Ja 27,7:2
Brister, Robert
Poppy God, The 1921,Ag 30,10:1
Dagger, The 1925,S 10,28:1
Blood Money 1927,Ag 23,29:2
Storm Center 1927,D 1,33:2
57 Bowery 1928,Ja 27,14:3
Gods of the Lightning 1928,O 25,27:2
House of Doom, The 1932,Ja 26,20:4
Angeline Moves In 1932,Ap 20,27:5
Bristol, W D (Playwright)
Reprise 1935,My 2,16:2
Bristow, Charles (Lighting Director)
Kiss Me, Kate 1970,D 26,10:4
Bristow, Frank (Pfc)
Swing Sister Wac Swing 1944,Ja 4,20:4
Bristow, Gwen (Original Author)
9th Street Guest, The 1930,Ag 26,24:3
Bristow, Ninita
Marry the Poor Girl 1920,S 27,18:3
Brit-Neva, Maria
Streetcar Named Desire, A 1955,Mr 4,18:2
Brito, Elida
Legend of Lovers 1959,O 28,40:3
Britt, Irene
Elizabeth Sleeps Out 1936,Ap 21,27:6
Britt, Jacqueline
Minnie's Boys 1970,Mr 27,27:1
Britt, Leo
Day by the Sea, A 1955,S 27,42:1
Brittain, Gladys
Hansel and Gretel 1929,D 25,21:1
Brittain, Mary
Dreams for Sale 1922,S 14,24:1
Brittain, R (Miscellaneous)
Chips With Everything 1963,O 2,49:1
Britten, Benjamin (Composer)
They Walk Alone 1941,Mr 13,24:2
Paul Bunyan 1941,My 6,25:1
Duchess of Malfi, The 1946,O 16,35:2
Rape of Lucretia, The 1948,D 30,24:2
Let's Make an Opera 1950,D 14,50:2
Noye's Fludde 1959,Mr 17,41:2
This Way to the Tomb 1961,D 9,21:1
Britten, Bill
Don Juan in the Russian Manner 1954,Ap 23,23:2
Britten, Dolly
Little Theatre Tournament; Edna 1929,My 11,22:2
Britten, Dorothy
Sketch Book 1929,Jl 2,33:5

Brittenum, Hattie
Tall Kentuckian, The 1953,Je 17,30:1
Brittingham, J W
Tiger Smiles, The 1930,D 18,29:1
Britton, Al
Red Light Annie 1923,Ag 22,10:3
Britton, Barbara
Getting Married 1951,My 14,28:5
Wake Up, Darling 1956,My 3,34:2
How to Make a Man 1961,F 3,16:1
Me and Thee 1965,D 8,58:4
Spofford 1967,D 15,54:3
Britton, David
Timon of Athens 1963,Jl 31,19:2
Britton, Don
Happiest Millionaire, The 1956,N 21,21:3
Britton, Donald R (Director)
Cherry Orchard, The 1970,My 7,63:2
Britton, Dorothy
Earl Carroll's Vanities 1930,Jl 2,28:3
Britton, Ethel
Strike Up the Band 1930,Ja 15,29:1
Du Barry 1932,N 23,15:2
Is This a Zither? 1935,Je 11,24:3
Accent on Youth 1935,Jl 9,24:5
Drums Professor, The 1935,Jl 30,17:2
Meet the Prince 1935,Ag 6,20:4
Bishop Misbehaves, The 1935,Ag 27,23:4
Britton, Florence
Lake, The 1933,D 27,24:2
Sleeping Clergyman, A 1934,O 9,16:1
Kind Lady 1935,Ap 24,24:5
Private Affair, A 1936,My 15,28:7
All That Glitters 1938,Ja 20,18:2
Set to Music 1939,Ja 19,16:2
Britton, Frank
Vaudeville (Palace) 1930,D 22,16:5
Vaudeville (Palace) 1930,D 29,19:3
Ziegfeld Follies 1931,Jl 2,30:5
Vaudeville (Palace) 1932,Ap 4,13:4
Britton, Gary
Awakening of Spring, The 1964,My 13,50:1
Hamp 1967,Mr 10,32:1
Britton, George
Great Shakes 1931,Mr 12,22:2
How Revolting! 1932,Mr 11,14:6
Gypsy Lady 1946,S 18,25:6
Britton, Huton
Wandering Jew, The 1927,F 2,22:4
Britton, Jacqueline
White Devil, The 1965,D 7,56:1
Britton, Jeff (Director)
Pirates of Penzance, The 1966,My 24,54:1
H M S Pinafore 1966,Je 8,41:2
Trial by Jury 1966,Je 8,41:2
Britton, Jeff (Miscellaneous)
King of the Whole Damn World 1962,Ap 16,32:2
Britton, Jeff (Producer)
Iolanthe 1962,Ag 8,34:2
Emperor, The 1963,Ap 17,30:1
Gondoliers, The 1963,Je 5,33:2
Lovely Light, A 1964,Ja 21,24:2
Murderer Among Us, A 1964,Mr 26,43:1
Absence of a Cello 1964,S 22,45:1
Iolanthe 1965,My 19,42:1
Yeomen of the Guard, The 1965,Jl 8,34:1
Ruddigore 1965,Ag 27,16:1
Hooray!! It's a Glorious Day. . .And All That
1966,Mr 10,28:1
Warm Body, A 1967,Ap 17,44:2
Perfect Party, The 1969,Mr 21,42:1
Me Nobody Knows, The 1970,My 19,42:1
Castro Complex, The 1970,N 19,40:1
Britton, Jocelyn
Midsummer Night's Dream, A 1954,S 22,33:1
Britton, John
Country Wife, The 1931,Ap 19,31:5
Britton, Kenneth Phillips (Playwright)
Houseparty 1929,S 10,26:5
Sophisticrats, The 1933,F 14,19:5
Britton, Leonhard
Jar, The 1969,Ap 23,42:1
Britton, Margery
Sunup to Sundown 1938,F 2,14:3
Britton, Milt
Vaudeville (Palace) 1930,D 22,16:5
Vaudeville (Palace) 1930,D 29,19:3
Ziegfeld Follies 1931,Jl 2,30:5
Vaudeville (Palace) 1932,Ap 4,13:4
Britton, Mozelle
Alley Cat 1934,S 18,18:1
Seperate Rooms 1940,Mr 25,10:3
Britton, Pamela
Brigadoon 1947,Mr 14,28:2
Brigadoon 1947,Mr 23,II,1:1
Britton, Sherry
Peer Gynt 1951,Ja 29,15:2
Best of Burlesque 1957,S 30,27:2
Drink to Me Only 1958,O 9,47:4
Britton, Tony
Boston Story, A 1968,S 21,26:2
Lady Frederick 1970,S 17,57:1

Brivic, Robert
Tom Sawyer - Ballad of the Mississippi 1947,D 27,11:3
Brixey, Alan
Fly Away Home 1937,Ap 27,18:1
Mother, The 1939,Ap 26,26:2
My Sister Eileen 1940,D 27,23:2
Brizard, Leo
Nuit au Bouge, Une 1923,O 16,18:1
Au Coin Joli 1923,O 23,16:1
Horrible Experience, L' 1923,O 23,16:1
Crucifies, Les 1923,O 30,17:2
Sur la Dalle 1923,O 30,17:2
Peu de Musique, Un 1923,N 6,22:1
Trois Masques, Les 1923,N 6,22:1
Broad, Bertha
Power of Darkness, The 1920,Ja 22,22:1
Peer Gynt 1923,F 6,14:1
Right to Dream, The 1924,My 27,14:2
Broad, Jay (Director)
Witches' Sabbath 1962,Ap 20,22:2
Life Is a Dream 1964,Mr 20,24:1
Lee Harvey Oswald: A Far Mean Streak of Independence Brought on by Negleck 1968,Ap 19,35:1
Red, White and Maddox 1968,N 3,87:1
Red, White and Maddox 1969,Ja 27,27:1
Broad, Jay (Playwright)
Red, White and Maddox 1968,O 5,71:4
Red, White and Maddox 1969,Ja 27,27:1
Broad, Jay (Producer)
Witches' Sabbath 1962,Ap 20,22:2
Vida es Sueno, La 1964,Mr 18,49:1
Life Is a Dream 1964,Mr 20,24:1
Broad, Lois
Red, White and Maddox 1969,Ja 27,27:1
Broadbent, Aida (Choreographer)
Red Mill, The 1945,O 17,16:2
Desert Song, The 1946,Ja 9,20:2
Gypsy Lady 1946,S 18,25:6
Broadbent, Lynne
Oklahoma! 1953,S 1,19:1
Broadhurst, Cecil
Jotham Valley 1951,F 7,37:2
Broadhurst, Cecil (Composer)
Jotham Valley 1951,F 7,37:2
Broadhurst, Cecil (Lyricist)
Jotham Valley 1951,F 7,37:2
Broadhurst, Cecil (Playwright)
Jotham Valley 1951,F 7,37:2
Broadhurst, George (Playwright)
Tarzan of the Apes 1921,S 8,14:3
Bought and Paid For 1921,D 8,17:5
Wild Oats Lane 1922,Jl 23,VI,1:6
Wild Oats Lane 1922,S 7,12:1
Red Hawk, The 1923,D 2,VIII,2:1
Izzy 1924,S 17,16:2
Red Falcon, The 1924,O 8,22:1
Broadhurst, George (Producer)
Elton Case, The 1921,Jl 5,15:1
Red Falcon, The 1924,O 8,22:1
Broadhurst, Joan
Broadway Whirl, The 1921,Je 9,10:4
Broadhurst, Kent
Fourth Wall, The 1968,S 5,53:1
Broadhurst, Kent (Director)
Dark of the Moon 1970,Ap 4,21:2
Broadhurst, Kent (Scenic Designer)
Fourth Wall, The 1968,S 5,53:1
Dark of the Moon 1970,Ap 4,21:2
Broadhurst, Thomas W (Playwright)
Butterflies 1927,F 2,22:4
Broadley, Edward
Romeo and Juliet 1923,Ja 25,16:1
Moon-Flower, The 1924,F 26,15:1
Milgrim's Progress 1924,D 23,17:1
Lady Screams, The 1927,My 3,24:2
Spellbound 1927,N 15,26:2
Salvation 1928,F 1,31:1
Father, The 1928,My 12,9:4
Caravan 1928,Ag 30,13:3
Girl Trouble 1928,O 26,22:3
Be Your Age 1929,F 5,27:1
Before You're 25 1929,Ap 17,30:2
Nice Women 1929,Je 11,27:4
Claire Adams 1929,N 20,26:3
Lost Sheep 1930,My 6,33:2
Venetian, The 1931,N 2,26:1
New York to Cherbourg 1932,F 20,11:4
Masks and Faces 1933,Mr 20,18:5
Unto the Third 1933,Ap 21,24:8
Party, A 1933,Ag 24,18:4
Lake, The 1933,D 27,24:2
Alley Cat 1934,S 18,18:1
Within the Gates 1934,O 23,23:1
On to Fortune 1935,F 5,22:2
Lady of Letters 1935,Mr 29,26:6
Othello 1935,S 28,13:2
Macbeth 1935,O 8,26:4
Seen But Not Heard 1936,S 18,19:2
Masque of the Kings, The 1937,F 9,19:4
Soliloquy 1938,N 29,26:4
Mother, The 1939,Ap 26,26:2

I Know What I Like 1939,N 25,13:5
Sarah Simple 1940,N 18,22:5
Peepshow 1944,F 4,12:2
Broadley, Edward (Director)
Lady Screams, The 1927,My 3,24:2
Broadley, Prudy
Cradle Song 1955,D 2,32:2
Broadnax, Edward
Porgy and Bess 1935,O 11,30:2
Broadribb, Donald
Mystery of the Finding of the Cross, The 1959,Ja 16,35:2
Broadwater, Henry (Playwright)
Hurricane 1934,D 23,IX,1:8
Broadway, Bob
Purple Canary, The 1963,Ap 23,31:1
God, Man & You, Baby! 1963,O 30,47:1
House of Flowers 1968,Ja 29,26:2
Broadway Jones
Will Morrissey's Folies Bergere Revue 1930,Ap 16,26:6
Brocco, Peter
Centuries, The 1927,N 30,23:1
Merry Wives of Windsor, The 1938,Ap 15,22:3
Brochu, James
Unfair to Goliath 1970,Ja 26,27:1
To Be or Not to Be-What Kind of a Question Is That? 1970,O 20,39:1
Greenwillow 1970,D 8,60:1
Brock, Alan
Last Stop 1944,S 6,17:2
Brock, Alma
Moral Fabric 1932,N 22,25:3
Brock, Carl (Miscellaneous)
Faust, Part I; Prelude in the Theater 1961,F 5,27:2
Faust, Part I; Prologue in Heaven 1961,F 5,27:2
Faust, Part I; Play, The 1961,F 5,27:2
Brock, Frances
Hot Mikado, The 1939,Mr 24,26:2
Brock, Gertha (Costume Designer)
Firebugs, The 1963,F 13,7:2
Summer of the Seventeenth Doll 1968,F 21,59:1
Daddy Goodness 1968,Je 5,37:1
Ceremonies in Dark Old Men 1969,F 6,33:1
Contribution 1969,Ap 2,37:1
String 1969,Ap 2,37:1
Malcochon 1969,Ap 2,37:1
Reckoning, The 1969,S 5,28:1
Who's Happy Now? 1969,N 18,39:1
Five on the Black Hand Side 1970,Ja 2,32:2
Harangues, The 1970,Ja 14,42:1
Brotherhood 1970,Mr 18,39:1
Day of Absence 1970,Mr 18,39:1
Brock, Heinie
Ice Follies 1937,D 22,29:1
Ice Follies 1941,D 2,32:2
Brock, Karl
Dear Judas 1947,O 6,26:4
Brockbank, Harrison
Last Waltz, The 1921,My 11,20:3
Caroline 1923,F 1,13:2
Love Song, The 1925,Ja 14,19:4
Lambs Gambol 1925,Ap 27,15:1
Three Musketeers, The 1928,Mr 14,28:1
Mystery Moon 1930,Je 24,23:4
Melody 1933,F 15,17:4
Eight Bells 1933,O 30,14:2
Hotel Alimony 1934,Ja 30,16:2
Brockman, Arnold M (Producer)
All the King's Men 1959,O 17,27:2
Brockman, Suzanne
Love Nest, The 1963,Ja 28,7:6
Brockmeier, Marlene (Miscellaneous)
Beclch 1968,D 17,59:1
Brockmeyer, John
Bluebeard 1970,My 5,58:1
Brockway, Howard
Great Campaign, The 1947,Ap 1,33:2
Brod, Max (Playwright)
Adventures of the Worthy Soldier Schwejk, The 1928,Mr 4,IX,2:1
Schloss, Das 1968,N 20,35:3
Broder, Edith
First Night 1930,N 27,32:3
Heigh-Ho, Everybody 1932,My 26,31:2
Broder, Jane (Miscellaneous)
Command Decision 1947,O 2,30:2
Broder, Martin
Blood and Sand 1921,S 21,16:2
Broderick, Helen
Nifties of 1923 1923,S 26,10:1
Wild Westcotts, The 1923,D 25,26:2
Mama Loves Papa 1926,F 23,26:2
Oh, Please! 1926,D 22,24:3
Vaudeville (Palace) 1928,N 19,16:3
Fifty Million Frenchmen 1929,N 28,34:4
Band Wagon, The 1931,My 17,VIII,3:2
Band Wagon, The 1931,Je 4,31:3
Band Wagon, The 1931,Je 14,VIII,1:1
Band Wagon, The 1931,S 27,VIII,3:7
Vanities 1932,S 18,IX,2:1
Vanities 1932,S 28,22:4
As Thousands Cheer 1933,S 10,II,5:3

Broderick, Helen—Cont
As Thousands Cheer 1933,O 2,22:1
As Thousands Cheer 1933,O 15,IX,1:1
Broderick, James
Maggie 1953,F 19,20:2
Johnny Johnson 1956,O 22,24:1
Glass Menagerie, The 1961,Mr 6,30:1
Glass Menagerie, The 1961,Ap 21,29:1
Glass Menagerie, The 1961,My 1,35:3
Glass Menagerie, The 1961,Je 16,27:3
Across the Board on Tomorrow Morning 1961,O 23,22:5
Talking to You 1961,O 23,22:5
Beyond the Horizon 1962,O 26,27:2
Firebugs, The 1963,F 13,7:2
Walk in Dark Places, A 1966,Ja 28,21:1
Better Luck Next Time 1966,Ja 28,21:1
Johnny No-Trump 1967,O 9,60:2
Time of Your Life, The 1969,N 7,37:1
Time of Your Life, The 1969,N 16,II,1:4
Broderick, Johnny
Sketch Book 1935,Je 5,22:2
Jerry Lewis' Variety Show 1957,F 8,18:5
Broderick, Lillian
Ziegfeld Follies 1920,Je 23,14:1
Vaudeville (Palace) 1924,F 12,20:2
Broderick, M Adrien
Oh, Hector! 1929,Mr 6,33:2
Broderick, Paul
Red Poppy, The 1922,D 21,18:2
Broderick, William
Puzzles of 1925 1925,F 3,25:3
Polly 1925,O 12,19:1
Broderson, Margaret
Song of Norway 1958,Je 23,19:2
Brodhage, Clarence
King Lear 1964,Je 19,36:1
Brodhead, James E
Dream Play 1960,N 23,22:1
Brodie, Franklyn
Half Moon Inn 1923,Mr 21,19:2
Brodkin, Herbert (Director)
Volpone 1948,Ja 9,24:6
Brodkin, Herbert (Lighting Director)
O'Daniel 1947,F 25,32:2
As We Forgive Our Debtors 1947,Mr 11,37:2
Virginia Reel 1947,Ap 15,28:2
Volpone 1948,Ja 9,24:6
Angel Street 1948,Ja 23,26:6
Tragedian in Spite of Himself, A 1948,F 6,29:2
On the Harmfulness of Tobacco 1948,F 6,29:2
Bear, The 1948,F 6,29:2
Wedding, The 1948,F 6,29:2
Alchemist, The 1948,My 7,31:4
S S Glencairn; Long Voyage Home, The 1948,My 21,21:2
S S Glencairn; Moon of the Caribbees 1948,My 21,21:2
S S Glencairn; In the Zone 1948,My 21,21:2
S S Glencairn; Bound East for Cardiff 1948,My 21,21:2
Insect Comedy, The 1948,Je 4,26:3
Silver Whistle, The 1948,N 25,49:2
Brodkin, Herbert (Miscellaneous)
Something About a Soldier 1962,Ja 5,36:2
Brodkin, Herbert (Scenic Designer)
O'Daniel 1947,F 25,32:2
This Time Tomorrow 1947,N 4,31:2
Angel Street 1948,Ja 23,26:6
Tragedian in Spite of Himself, A 1948,F 6,29:2
Bear, The 1948,F 6,29:2
On the Harmfulness of Tobacco 1948,F 6,29:2
Wedding, The 1948,F 6,29:2
Alchemist, The 1948,My 7,31:4
S S Glencairn; Moon of the Caribbees 1948,My 21,21:2
S S Glencairn; In the Zone 1948,My 21,21:2
S S Glencairn; Long Voyage Home, The 1948,My 21,21:2
S S Glencairn; Bound East for Cardiff 1948,My 21,21:2
Insect Comedy, The 1948,Je 4,26:3
Silver Whistle, The 1948,N 25,49:2
Brodley, Rita
King's Darling, The 1951,Jl 25,17:2
Brandy Is My True Love's Name 1953,Je 18,38:5
Hopalong--Freud 1953,Je 18,38:5
Where There's a Will 1953,Je 18,38:5
California 1953,Je 18,38:5
Enchantment 1953,Jl 1,24:3
Brodrick, Malcolm
Frogs of Spring, The 1953,O 21,36:2
Desperate Hours, The 1955,F 11,20:2
Brodsky, Charles
Once Upon a Time 1939,D 21,28:2
Brodsky, Nikolaus (Composer)
Home and Beauty 1937,F 3,26:2
Brodsky, Vera
Spring Tonic 1936,My 11,16:1
Brody, Ann
Having Wonderful Time 1937,F 22,12:5
Time of Your Life, The 1940,S 24,27:2
Brody, Anne
Antonia 1925,O 21,20:1

Brody, Bonnie
Stop the World-I Want to Get Off 1962,O 4,45:4
Brody, Lee
Shoot the Works! 1931,Jl 22,19:5
Straw Hat, The 1939,S 30,10:6
Brody, Lee (Playwright)
Streets of Paris, The 1939,Je 20,25:2
Brody, Leo (Miscellaneous)
Romeo and Juliet 1955,D 16,36:3
Brody, Leonore
Prince of Pilsen, The 1930,Ja 14,24:3
Brody, Stuart
Feathers in a Gale 1943,D 22,26:2
Hippolytus 1948,N 22,25:5
Brody, Thomas
Sister Oakes 1949,Ap 25,19:4
Brody (Composer)
Jewish Heart, The 1939,Ja 25,16:6
Brody (Lyricist)
Jewish Heart, The 1939,Ja 25,16:6
Brodzinska, Claudia
Don Carlos 1964,N 25,40:1
Broe, Catherine
Femmes Savantes, Les 1967,F 7,34:2
On Ne Badine Pas Avec l'Amour; No Trifling With
Love 1968,Mr 5,35:1
Broekman, David (Composer)
Gambler, The 1952,O 14,40:1
Brogan, Donald
So Proudly We Hail 1936,S 23,28:4
Brogan, Harry
Juno and the Paycock 1964,My 6,41:1
Brogan, Patricia
Double Dublin 1963,D 27,16:2
Brogan, Ron
In the Matter of J Robert Oppenheimer
1968,Je 7,31:1
Brogan, Ronald
American Holiday 1936,F 22,13:3
Sun and I, The 1937,F 27,9:5
Chalked Out 1937,Mr 26,24:2
Places, Please 1937,N 13,10:6
Escape This Night 1938,Ap 23,18:1
Brogden, Dorothy
Adding Machine, The 1970,D 5,40:1
Brogden, Dorothy (Costume Designer)
Adding Machine, The 1970,D 5,40:1
Broghan, Harry
Marks and Mabel 1945,S 9,II,1:4
Brogsdale, Walter
Just a Minute 1928,O 9,34:3
Messin' Around 1929,Ap 23,26:3
Brown Buddies 1930,O 8,29:1
Yeah-Man 1932,My 27,27:3
Conjur' Man Dies 1936,Mr 12,18:5
Brohn, Bill (Musical Director)
Sensations 1970,O 26,48:2
Brokate, Charles
Shannons of Broadway, The 1927,S 27,30:4
Brokaw, Charles
White Peacock, The 1921,D 27,10:2
Antony and Cleopatra 1924,F 20,22:1
Depths, The 1925,Ja 28,15:3
Road to Rome, The 1927,F 1,24:2
Jenny 1929,O 9,34:4
Elizabeth the Queen 1930,N 4,37:1
Decoy, The 1932,Ap 2,13:4
Troilus and Cressida 1932,Je 7,22:3
Great Waltz, The 1934,S 24,14:4
Jubilee 1935,O 14,20:1
Elizabeth the Queen 1941,O 17,27:2
Brokaw, George T (Mrs)
Passing of the Third Floor Back, The 1924,F 8,19:4
Brokaw, Irving
In the Land of the Midnight Sun 1930,Ja 7,27:4
Brokaw, Olive
Holiday 1930,F 6,21:2
Brombacher, Gardy
Nathan der Weise 1966,D 10,45:2
Bromberg, Conrad
Tevya and His Daughters 1957,S 17,38:2
PS 193 1962,O 31,33:1
Love Nest, The 1963,Ja 28,7:6
Bromberg, Conrad (Playwright)
Dream of a Blacklisted Actor 1969,D 18,64:1
Rooming House, The 1970,Ja 23,25:1
Dr Galley 1970,Ja 23,25:1
Transfers 1970,Ja 23,25:1
Transfers 1970,F 1,II,7:2
Bromberg, Dave
Tragicomedy of Don Cristobita and Dona Rosita,
The 1958,My 30,12:2
Bromberg, Edgar
Half Moon Inn 1925,Mr 10,14:1
His Majesty the Queen 1926,Mr 9,8:1
Bromberg, J Edward
Princess Turandot 1926,N 13,14:2
Inheritors 1927,Mr 8,23:1
Good Hope, The 1927,O 19,24:2
2 + 2 = 5 1927,N 29,30:3
Improvisations in June 1928,F 27,16:5
Would-Be Gentleman, The 1928,O 2,34:1
Cherry Orchard, The 1928,O 16,28:5

Peter Pan; Boy Who Would Not Grow Up, The
1928,N 27,36:3
On the High Road 1929,Ja 15,22:3
Lady From Alfaqueque, The; Consulesa, La
1929,Ja 15,22:3
Katerina 1929,F 26,30:3
Living Corpse, The 1929,D 7,19:1
Women Have Their Way, The 1930,Ja 28,28:1
Romeo and Juliet 1930,Ap 22,33:1
Siegfried 1930,O 21,34:1
Inspector General, The 1930,D 24,19:2
House of Connelly, The 1931,S 29,22:4
1931 1931,D 11,34:3
Night Over Taos 1932,Mr 10,25:3
Foreign Affairs 1932,Ap 14,25:5
Big Night 1933,Ja 18,16:2
Both Your Houses 1933,Mr 7,20:3
Both Your Houses 1933,My 23,22:2
Men in White 1933,S 27,24:2
Men in White 1933,O 1,IX,1:1
Gold Eagle Guy 1934,N 18,IX,1:7
Gold Eagle Guy 1934,N 29,33:4
Gold Eagle Guy 1934,D 9,X,1:1
Waiting for Lefty 1935,F 11,14:5
Awake and Sing! 1935,F 20,23:2
Weep for the Virgins 1935,D 2,18:1
Awake and Sing! 1939,Mr 8,18:2
Anna Christie 1941,Ag 10,IX,1:8
Jacobowsky and the Colonel 1944,Mr 15,17:2
Jacobowsky and the Colonel 1944,Mr 19,II,1:1
Toplitzky of Notre Dame 1946,D 27,13:4
Big Knife, The 1949,F 25,27:5
Big Knife, The 1949,Mr 6,II,1:1
All You Need Is One Good Break 1950,F 10,20:3
Royal Family, The 1951,Ja 11,28:2
Not for Children 1951,F 14,35:2
Bromberg, J Edward (Director)
All You Need Is One Good Break 1950,F 10,20:3
Bromberg, J Edward (Playwright)
Group Theatre Sketches 1935,F 11,14:5
Bromberg, Louis (Director)
Blue Monday 1932,Je 3,23:2
Bromberg, Louis (Scenic Designer)
Noble Experiment, The 1930,O 28,21:4
Intimate Relations 1932,Mr 29,23:2
Hipper's Holiday 1934,O 19,26:2
Truly Valiant 1936,Ja 10,17:3
Thirsty Soil 1937,F 4,16:2
Russian Bank 1940,My 25,20:2
Bromberger, Anne (Translator)
Professor Mamlock 1937,Ap 14,30:3
Brombers, Conrad
Mother Courage and Her Children 1963,Mr 30,5:5
Bromfield, Louis
Here Today, Gone Tomorrow 1940,D 5,32:6
Bromfield, Louis (Original Author)
House of Women, The 1927,S 11,VIII,1:3
House of Women, The 1927,O 4,32:2
House of Women, The 1927,O 9,VIII,1:1
Bromfield, Louis (Playwright)
House of Women, The 1927,S 11,VIII,1:3
House of Women, The 1927,O 4,32:2
House of Women, The 1927,O 9,VIII,1:1
Times Have Changed 1935,F 19,28:2
De Luxe 1935,F 20,22:1
De Luxe 1935,F 24,VIII,3:4
Times Have Changed 1935,F 26,16:1
De Luxe 1935,Mr 6,22:2
Here Today, Gone Tomorrow 1940,D 5,32:6
Bromfield, William
Twelfth Night 1949,O 4,33:2
Brominski, Eugene
Troika 1930,Ap 2,32:6
Bromley, Harald
Me and Harry 1942,Ap 3,24:6
Bromley, Harald (Director)
Springtime for Henry 1951,Mr 15,36:2
Dead Pigeon 1953,D 24,10:2
Bromley, Harald (Producer)
Life of Reilly, The 1942,Ap 30,13:2
Seeds in the Wind 1948,My 26,29:2
Springtime for Henry 1951,Mr 15,36:2
Glad Tidings 1951,O 12,33:2
Dead Pigeon 1953,D 24,10:2
Bromley, Lou (Scenic Designer)
Don't Look Now! 1936,N 4,41:3
Bromley, Sheila
Eternal Cage 1945,Mr 22,19:7
Time for Elizabeth 1948,S 28,32:3
Bromley-Davenport, Mr
Elizabeth of England 1931,O 18,VIII,1:3
Broms, Martin
Sunset 1966,My 13,34:1
Bronaugh, Anne
Bedfellows 1929,Jl 3,19:2
Bronaugh, Elinor
Riff-Raff 1926,F 9,18:6
Brone, Johne
Cafe Crown 1942,Ja 24,12:5
Bronesky, Leon J (Producer)
How Long Till Summer 1949,D 28,30:3
Bronetsky, Sam
With Open Eyes 1938,O 27,27:2

Bronlee, Lark
Spring, The 1921,F 6,VI,1:2
Bronn, Helen
Vaudeville (Palace) 1930,D 8,27:2
Bronner, Cleveland
Passing Show of 1921, The 1920,D 30,16:2
Blue Bird, The 1923,D 26,13:3
Vaudeville (Hippodrome) 1924,Ap 29,12:2
Bronner, Edwin M (Playwright)
Young American, A 1946,Ja 18,14:5
Bronner, Eyolf
Nautical but Nice 1931,Ap 19,31:6
Bronowicz, Yvonne (Costume Designer)
Tonight in Living Color; David Show, The
1969,Je 11,43:1
Tonight in Living Color; Golden Fleece, The
1969,Je 11,43:1
Ofay Watcher, The 1969,S 16,40:1
Bronson, Earl (Composer)
Marion Show, The 1923,My 8,22:3
Bronson, James
Come of Age 1952,Ja 24,22:2
Bronson, James (Miscellaneous)
Company 1970,Ap 27,40:1
Bronson, Lillian
Five Star Final 1930,D 31,11:1
Lean Harvest 1931,O 14,26:3
Tiara, The 1932,D 12,18:3
Druid Circle, The 1947,O 23,29:5
Bronson, Michael
Maidens and Mistresses at Home at the Zoo
1958,O 29,31:1
Bronson, Virginia
Hamlet 1920,D 28,9:3
Merchant of Venice, The 1920,D 30,16:2
Hamlet 1930,Mr 25,34:4
Macbeth 1930,Mr 26,24:6
Twelfth Night 1930,Mr 27,24:7
Merchant of Venice, The 1930,Mr 27,24:7
Taming of the Shrew, The 1930,Mr 28,22:8
Richard III 1930,Mr 31,24:1
King Lear 1930,Ap 1,34:6
As You Like It 1930,Ap 3,32:5
Julius Caesar 1930,Ap 4,22:3
King Lear 1930,D 26,18:2
Bronson, Yank
Change Your Luck 1930,Je 7,10:2
Bronstein, Samuel (Miscellaneous)
Cuban Thing, The 1968,S 25,36:2
Angela 1969,O 31,33:1
Bronstein, Samuel (Producer)
Who's Happy Now? 1969,N 18,39:1
Bronston, Samuel (Producer)
Peepshow 1944,F 4,12:2
Bronte, Charlotte (Original Author)
Jane Eyre 1936,F 28,19:2
Jane Eyre 1936,O 14,31:3
Jane Eyre 1936,N 8,X,3:4
Jane Eyre 1937,Ja 3,X,2:1
Jane Eyre 1937,F 7,X,1:1
Jane Eyre 1958,My 2,31:1
Bronte, Emily (Original Author)
Wuthering Heights 1939,Ap 28,30:4
Bronte, Peter (Miscellaneous)
Kean 1961,N 3,28:2
King and I, The 1964,Jl 7,26:1
Bronti, John
Susannah and the Elders 1959,O 19,37:3
Brook, Clive
Gioconda Smile, The 1948,Je 20,II,2:3
Second Threshold 1951,Ja 3,23:2
Second Threshold 1951,Ja 14,II,1:1
Second Threshold 1952,S 25,38:8
Second Threshold 1952,O 12,II,3:7
Second Threshold 1952,N 9,II,3:2
One Bright Day 1956,Ap 8,II,3:1
Brook, Diane
Anna 1928,My 17,25:2
Brook, Faith
Letters to Lucerne 1941,D 9,47:6
Letters to Lucerne 1941,D 24,14:2
You Never Can Tell 1948,Mr 17,31:2
Kidders, The 1957,N 13,40:6
Brook, Harold Ten
Luana 1930,S 18,28:1
Brook, Katherine
Sacred and Profane Love 1920,F 24,11:1
Madras House, The 1921,O 31,18:2
Gentlemen Prefer Blondes 1926,S 29,23:1
Brook, Lyndon
Antony and Cleopatra 1951,D 21,22:2
South 1955,My 2,17:4
Kidders, The 1957,N 13,40:6
Brook, Pamela
School for Scandal, The 1970,Je 11,51:1
Brook, Peter (Director)
Dark of the Moon 1949,Ap 3,II,3:1
Colombe 1951,D 15,13:2
Little Hut, The 1953,O 8,37:2
House of Flowers 1954,D 31,11:2
Lark, The 1955,My 13,21:2
Power and the Glory, The 1956,Ap 6,14:3
View From the Bridge, A 1956,O 12,35:3

Brook, Peter (Director)—Cont

Tempest, The 1957,Ag 14,21:1
Visit, The 1958,My 6,40:1
Visit, The 1958,My 18,II,1:1
Visit, The 1958,S 7,II,1:1
Visit, The 1958,N 16,II,1:1
Fighting Cock, The 1959,D 9,57:3
Visit, The 1960,Mr 9,38:3
Irma la Douce 1960,S 30,31:2
King Lear 1962,N 7,49:3
Tempest, The 1963,Ap 3,43:1
King Lear 1964,My 19,43:2
King Lear 1964,My 31,II,1:1
Physicists, The 1964,O 14,52:1
Physicists, The 1964,O 25,II,1:1
Persecution and Assassination of Marat As
  Performed by the Inmates of the Asylum of
  Charenton Under the Direction of the Marquis de
  Sade, The 1965,D 28,35:1
Persecution and Assassination of Marat As
  Performed by the Inmates of the Asylum of
  Charenton Under the Direction of the Marquis de
  Sade, The 1966,Ja 9,II,1:1
US 1966,O 15,32:1
US 1966,N 6,II,1:5
Oedipus 1968,Mr 31,II,5:1
Oedipus 1968,Ap 2,54:1
Midsummer Night's Dream, A 1970,Ag 28,15:1
Midsummer Night's Dream, A 1970,S 13,II,7:1

Brook, Peter (Producer)

Romeo and Juliet 1947,Ap 7,18:5
Measure for Measure 1950,Mr 10,33:5
Hamlet 1955,N 24,40:7
Family Reunion, The 1956,Je 9,13:6
Oedipus 1968,Jl 31,29:1

Brook, Peter (Scenic Designer)

King Lear 1964,My 19,43:2
King Lear 1964,My 31,II,1:1
Oedipus 1968,Jl 31,29:1

Brook, S

Dybbuk, The 1926,D 14,24:2
Golem, The 1927,F 5,13:2

Brook, Sara (Costume Designer)

Whitman Portrait, A 1966,O 12,37:1
Just for Love 1968,O 18,40:1
Big Time Buck White 1968,D 9,58:1
Home Away From, A 1969,Ap 29,40:3
Front Page, The 1969,My 12,54:2
Child's Play 1970,F 18,39:1
Chinese, The 1970,Mr 11,42:2
Dr Fish 1970,Mr 11,42:2
Nature of the Crime 1970,Mr 24,41:1
Inquest 1970,Ap 24,38:1
Candyapple, The 1970,N 24,33:1

Brook, Sebastian

Queen After Death 1956,Mr 13,33:2

Brook, Shlomo

Dybbuk, The 1964,F 4,30:2
Children of the Shadows 1964,F 27,26:1

Brook, Sidney

Queen O' Hearts 1922,O 11,22:1

Brooke, Bobby

These Are the Times 1950,My 11,37:2

Brooke, Catherine

Rain 1922,N 8,18:2

Brooke, Clifford

Lady Detained, A 1935,Ja 10,23:3
As Husbands Go 1935,Jl 10,24:1
Where There's a Will 1939,Ja 18,16:6

Brooke, Clifford (Director)

Passing of the Third Floor Back, The 1924,F 8,19:4
Werewolf, The 1924,Ag 26,6:1
Dawn 1924,N 25,27:1
Two Married Men 1925,Ja 14,19:1
Puppy Love 1926,Ja 28,16:3
Howdy King 1926,D 14,24:4
Sam Abramovitch 1927,Ja 20,20:5
Mulberry Bush, The 1927,O 27,33:1
Carry On 1928,Ja 24,26:1
Mrs Dane's Defense 1928,F 7,30:1
Sherlock Holmes 1928,F 21,18:4
Within the Law 1928,Mr 6,20:1
Command Performance, The 1928,O 4,27:1
These Few Ashes 1928,O 31,28:1
Fioretta 1929,F 6,30:3
House Afire 1930,Ap 1,34:7
Mr Samuel 1930,N 11,28:4
Art and Mrs Bottle 1930,N 19,19:3
Man Who Changed His Name, The 1932,My 3,25:3
Caviar 1934,Je 8,19:2
Allure 1934,O 30,22:6
Piper Paid 1934,D 26,19:1
Lady Detained, A 1935,Ja 10,23:3

Brooke, Cynthia

Skin Game, The 1920,O 21,11:1

Brooke, Eleanor (Playwright)

King of Hearts 1954,Ap 2,23:1
King of Hearts 1954,Ap 11,II,1:1

Brooke, Harrison

Courageous One, The 1958,Ja 21,33:6

Brooke, Holly

Portrait of a Queen 1968,F 29,29:1

Brooke, Hugh

Lady, The 1923,D 5,23:2

Dancing Mothers 1924,Ag 12,12:2

Brooke, Irene

Oliver Cromwell 1923,F 25,VII,1:7

Brooke, J Clifford (Director)

Hearts Are Trumps! 1927,Ap 8,21:1

Brooke, John

Nikki 1931,S 30,23:4

Brooke, Louise

Fuente Ovejuna; Sheep Well, The 1936,My 3,II,4:1

Brooke, Mills

Sunup to Sundown 1938,F 2,14:3

Brooke, Myra

I Was Waiting for You 1933,N 14,23:3

Brooke, Ralph

All in Favor 1942,Ja 21,20:6
Sound of Hunting, A 1945,N 21,16:6
Tenting Tonight 1947,Ap 3,32:2

Brooke, Tyler

Hitchy-Koo, 1920 1920,O 20,11:3

Brooke, Walter

Romeo and Juliet 1940,My 10,27:1
Barber Had Two Sons, The 1943,F 2,22:2
Two Blind Mice 1949,Mr 3,32:2
Twilight Walk 1951,S 25,25:4
Seagulls Over Sorrento 1952,S 12,18:4
Hide and Seek 1957,Ap 3,26:1

Brooke Johns's All-American Collegians

Piggy 1927,Ja 12,22:2

Brooke-Taylor, Tim

Cambridge Circus 1964,O 7,53:1
New Cambridge Circus, The 1965,Ja 15,22:2

Brookes, Jacqueline

Othello 1953,O 30,28:2
Cretan Woman, The 1954,Jl 8,18:2
Cretan Woman, The 1954,S 5,II,1:1
Clandestine Marriage, The 1954,O 4,23:2
Clandestine Marriage, The 1954,O 17,II,1:1
White Devil, The 1955,Mr 15,32:5
Tiger at the Gates 1955,O 4,40:1
King John 1956,Je 28,33:5
Measure for Measure 1956,Je 29,16:1
Misanthrope, The 1956,N 13,44:1
Measure for Measure 1957,Ja 23,24:1
Duchess of Malfi, The 1957,Mr 20,33:1
Othello 1957,Je 24,19:2
Othello 1957,Je 30,II,1:1
Much Ado About Nothing 1957,Ag 8,15:2
Ivanov 1958,O 8,42:1
Ivanov 1958,O 19,II,1:1
Six Characters in Search of an Author
  1963,Mr 11,7:2
Winter's Tale, The 1963,Je 29,13:1
Midsummer Night's Dream, A 1963,Jl 1,19:2
Much Ado About Nothing 1964,Je 11,26:2
Richard III 1964,Je 12,44:2
Evening's Frost, An 1965,O 12,56:1
Oresteia 1966,Ja 30,29:1
Come Slowly, Eden 1966,D 7,56:1
Increased Difficulty of Concentration, The
  1969,D 5,48:1
Watercolor 1970,Ja 22,30:1
Persians, The 1970,Ap 16,53:1
Persians, The 1970,Ap 26,II,1:3
Sunday Dinner 1970,N 3,28:1

Brookings, Harriet

Return of Ulysses, The 1943,F 7,II,1:6

Brookins, Fred

Show Boat 1948,S 9,33:2

Brookins, Harriet

Return of Ulysses, The 1943,Ja 28,22:2

Brookman, Jerome (Playwright)

Press Time 1938,N 28,10:4

Brookmeyer, Bob

Next President, The 1958,Ap 10,34:3

Brookmire, S Kennard

If Booth Had Missed 1931,My 14,27:1

Brooks, Alan

Merchants of Venus 1920,S 28,14:2
Because of Helen 1920,N 14,VI,1:4
Expressing Willie 1924,Ap 17,22:1
Piker, The 1925,Ja 16,14:1
Los Angeles 1927,D 20,32:3
She Got What She Wanted 1929,Mr 5,28:1
Gone Hollywood 1930,D 28,VIII,2:1
Broadway Boy 1932,My 4,23:5

Brooks, Alan (Playwright)

Merchants of Venus 1920,S 28,14:2
Because of Helen 1920,N 14,VI,1:4

Brooks, Alan (Producer)

Because of Helen 1920,N 14,VI,1:4

Brooks, Alfred (Composer)

Of Mice and Men 1958,D 5,38:1

Brooks, Alfred Pope

In the Days of the Turbins 1934,Mr 7,22:5

Brooks, Alice

Black Pit 1935,Mr 21,26:6
Marching Song 1937,F 18,18:2

Brooks, Arthur

George White's Scandals 1922,Ag 29,10:1

Brooks, Barbara

Bathsheba 1947,Mr 27,40:2

Brooks, Beatrice

View From the Bridge, A 1965,Ja 29,24:1

Brooks, Beatrice—Cont

Persecution and Assassination of Marat As
  Performed by the Inmates of the Asylum of
  Charenton Under the Direction of the Marquis
  de Sade, The 1967,Ja 4,34:1

Brooks, Bernard (Scenic Designer)

Moral Fabric 1932,N 22,25:3
One Wife or Another 1933,F 7,23:6

Brooks, Catherine

Shuffle Along of 1933 1932,D 27,11:3

Brooks, Charles

Thomas Paine 1930,Mr 21,30:7

Brooks, David

Bloomer Girl 1944,O 6,18:5
Brigadoon 1947,Mr 14,28:2
Sandhog 1954,N 24,17:1
New Moon, The; Desert Song, The 1955,Jl 1,13:1
Rosalie 1957,Je 26,28:2
Mr President 1962,O 22,34:2
Sunday Man, The 1964,My 14,41:3
Park 1970,Ap 23,47:1

Brooks, David (Director)

All in One; Trouble in Tahiti 1955,Ap 20,40:3
Jack 1958,Je 4,39:2
Bald Soprano, The 1958,Je 4,39:2
Geranium Hat, The 1959,Mr 18,45:1
Shepherd's Chameleon, The 1960,N 30,41:1
Banker's Daughter, The 1962,Ja 23,37:1

Brooks, David (Miscellaneous)

Endgame 1958,Ja 29,32:4

Brooks, Donald (Costume Designer)

No Strings 1962,Mr 16,24:1
Barefoot in the Park 1963,O 24,36:2
Amorous Flea, The 1964,F 18,26:1
Fade Out--Fade In 1964,My 27,45:1
Beekman Place 1964,O 8,50:1
Poor Bitos 1964,N 16,40:2
Diamond Orchid 1965,F 11,44:4
Flora, the Red Menace 1965,My 12,41:2
Promises, Promises 1968,D 2,59:3
Last of the Red Hot Lovers 1969,D 29,37:1
Minnie's Boys 1970,Mr 27,27:1

Brooks, Donald L

Beclch 1968,D 17,59:1

Brooks, Doris

Here Come the Clowns 1954,My 5,36:2

Brooks, Eda

Sweet Shadow 1935,Ag 7,22:2

Brooks, Edward

Antony and Cleopatra 1924,F 20,22:1
Dancing Mothers 1924,Ag 12,12:2

Brooks, Elaine

Boo Hoo! East Lynne 1959,S 9,50:4

Brooks, Eleanor

Artists and Models 1927,N 16,28:2
Vaudeville (Palace) 1929,D 16,34:4
Vaudeville (Palace) 1929,D 23,19:1

Brooks, Eleanor Stimson (Translator)

Game of Love and Death, The 1929,N 26,28:4

Brooks, Esther (Composer)

Benito Cereno 1964,N 2,62:2
My Kinsman, Major Molineux 1964,N 2,62:2

Brooks, Evelyn

Top-Notchers 1942,My 30,8:5
Beat the Band 1942,O 15,26:1

Brooks, Flo

George White's Scandals 1926,Je 15,23:2

Brooks, Frank

House of Doom, The 1932,Ja 26,20:4

Brooks, George S (Playwright)

Spread Eagle 1927,Ap 5,30:2
Spread Eagle 1927,Ap 10,VIII,1:1
Spread Eagle 1928,Jl 22,VII,1:3
Spread Eagle 1929,N 10,X,4:8
Spread Eagle 1935,N 5,33:6

Brooks, Geraldine

Time of the Cuckoo, The 1952,O 16,37:4
Brightower 1970,Ja 29,32:1

Brooks, Gwendolyn (Original Author)

We Real Cool 1965,Jl 3,10:5

Brooks, H A (Playwright)

Stags at Bay 1934,D 15,9:2

Brooks, Hamilton

Three Times the Hour 1931,Ag 26,15:5
Christopher Comes Across 1932,Je 1,19:2

Brooks, Harry

Tobias and the Angel 1937,Ap 29,16:5

Brooks, Harry (Composer)

Hot Chocolates 1929,Je 21,17:4

Brooks, Helen

Most Immoral Lady, A 1928,N 27,36:1
Jonesy 1929,Ap 10,32:2
Jenny 1929,O 9,34:4
Long Road, The 1930,S 10,30:2
Vinegar Tree, The 1930,N 20,30:3
Life Begins 1932,Mr 29,23:2
Black Sheep 1932,O 14,22:6
Sophisticrats, The 1933,F 14,19:5
I Was Waiting for You 1933,N 14,23:3
Oliver Oliver 1934,Ja 6,18:5
Perfumed Lady, The 1934,Mr 13,27:2
But Not for Love 1934,N 27,26:2
Cross Ruff 1935,F 20,23:3
As Husbands Go 1935,Jl 2,24:3

Brooks, Helen—Cont

Cat and the Canary, The 1935,Jl 9,24:4
Trelawney of the 'Wells' 1935,Jl 16,24:1
Declassee 1935,Ag 6,20:3
Accent on Youth 1935,Ag 13,20:3
Berkeley Square 1935,Ag 20,25:1
In Old Kentucky 1935,Ag 27,23:4
Jumbo 1935,N 18,20:2
First Lady 1935,N 27,17:4
Shining Hour, The 1936,Ag 12,15:3
Octoroon, The 1936,S 1,24:2
Many Mansions 1937,Ag 3,20:5
Lightnin' 1938,S 16,17:2
Bicentennial 1939,Ag 29,18:2
Arsenic and Old Lace 1941,Ja 11,13:2

Brooks, Henni

Sunny River 1941,D 5,28:2

Brooks, Henry

In The Best of Families 1931,F 3,29:1
Crime Marches on 1935,O 24,19:1

Brooks, Hildy

Happiness Is Just a Little Thing Called a Rolls
Royce 1968,My 13,54:5
Inquest 1970,Ap 24,38:1

Brooks, Irving

Skirt, The 1921,N 8,28:1

Brooks, Jack (Composer)

Winnie the Pooh 1967,N 25,33:1
Winnie the Pooh 1967,D 23,28:1

Brooks, James

Blind Alley 1935,S 25,19:6

Brooks, Jan

Jane Eyre 1958,My 2,31:1

Brooks, Jay

Our Lan' 1947,Ap 19,11:2
Our Lan' 1947,S 29,16:5

Brooks, Jeremy

Triumph of Robert Emmet, The 1969,My 8,54:1

Brooks, Jimmy

Judy Garland's New Variety Show 1956,S 27,43:2

Brooks, Joan

Fuente Ovejuna; Sheep Well, The 1936,My 3,II,4:1

Brooks, Joy

Canteen Show, The 1942,S 4,18:1

Brooks, Ken

Tobacco Road 1960,My 11,44:2
Tender Trap, The 1961,Ag 26,15:1

Brooks, Ken (Miscellaneous)

Burning Bright 1959,O 17,27:2
Tobacco Road 1960,My 11,44:2
Intimate Relations 1962,N 2,27:1

Brooks, Laird

These Are the Times 1950,My 11,37:2

Brooks, Lawrence

Song of Norway 1944,Ag 22,20:2
Song of Norway 1944,Ag 27,II,1:1
My Romance 1948,O 20,38:5
Buttrio Square 1952,O 15,40:2
Riverwind 1962,D 14,5:5
Anya 1965,N 30,48:1

Brooks, Lewis

Heimkehr aus der Fremde, Die; Stranger, The
1949,S 2,14:1
Merry Widow, The 1957,Ap 11,36:6

Brooks, Marcia

Light, Lively and Yiddish 1970,O 28,58:1

Brooks, Mari-Anne

Guitar 1959,N 11,42:5

Brooks, Marjorie

Charlot's Revue 1924,Ja 10,18:1

Brooks, Martin

Burning Bright 1950,O 19,40:2
Enemy of the People, An 1950,D 29,14:1
I Am a Camera 1951,N 29,39:6
I Am a Camera 1951,D 9,II,5:1
Grass Is Always Greener, The 1955,F 16,25:2
Miser, The 1955,Mr 18,34:2
Night of the Auk 1956,D 4,50:2
Saturday Night Kid, The 1958,My 16,22:1
Advocate, The 1963,O 15,46:7

Brooks, Mary

Everybody's Welcome 1931,O 14,26:3

Brooks, Matt (Original Author)

Hold On to Your Hats 1940,S 12,30:3
Hold It! 1948,My 6,31:5

Brooks, Matt (Playwright)

Scandals 1939,Ag 29,17:2

Brooks, Maude

Power of Darkness, The 1920,Ja 22,22:1
Wife With a Smile, The 1921,N 29,20:1
Sam Abramovitch 1927,Ja 20,20:5
Spring 3100 1928,F 16,14:2
Chippies 1929,My 30,23:3
Mystery Moon 1930,Je 24,23:4

Brooks, Mel

New Faces of 1952 1952,My 25,II,1:1

Brooks, Mel (Playwright)

New Faces of 1952 1952,My 17,23:2
Once Over Lightly 1955,Mr 16,39:1
Shinbone Alley 1957,Ap 15,23:2
Shinbone Alley 1957,Ap 28,II,1:1
All American 1962,Mr 20,44:1

Brooks, Myra

Dagmar 1923,Ja 23,18:2

Kreutzer Sonata, The 1924,My 15,22:3

Brooks, Norman

Golden Boy 1952,Mr 13,24:3

Brooks, Norman A (Playwright)

Fragile Fox 1954,O 13,27:1

Brooks, Pat (Choreographer)

Yerma 1952,F 8,18:4

Brooks, Patricia

Grass Harp, The 1953,Ap 28,32:2
King and the Duke, The 1955,Je 2,25:2
Iceman Cometh, The 1956,My 8,38:1

Brooks, Peter (Director)

Titus Andronicus 1957,Jl 2,33:8

Brooks, Phyllis

Stage Door 1936,S 29,35:1
Stage Door 1936,O 4,IX,2:1
Stage Door 1936,O 23,26:3
Panama Hattie 1940,O 4,28:4
Panama Hattie 1940,O 31,28:2
Night Before Christmas, The 1941,Mr 30,I,48:2
Night Before Christmas, The 1941,Ap 11,25:2
Round Trip 1945,My 30,16:4

Brooks, Polly

What Next 1920,Ja 27,7:2

Brooks, R Boland

Upon My Soul 1927,Ap 22,19:1

Brooks, Randall (Miscellaneous)

Daughter of Silence 1961,D 1,28:1
Lord Pengo 1962,N 20,41:2
Jennie 1963,O 18,35:2
Royal Hunt of the Sun, The 1965,O 27,36:2
Hail Scrawdyke! 1966,N 29,50:1
Black Comedy; White Lies 1967,F 13,42:1
Black Comedy 1967,F 13,42:1
Night 1968,N 29,52:1
Morning 1968,N 29,52:1
Noon 1968,N 29,52:1

Brooks, Randolph (Miscellaneous)

Avanti 1968,F 1,29:1

Brooks, Robert

Doctor and the Devils, The 1959,Ja 21,27:8
Greenwillow 1970,D 8,60:1

Brooks, Rudulf

Ship Comes in, A 1934,S 20,21:1
Menagerie 1935,Jl 2,24:3
Howdy Stranger 1937,Ja 15,17:5

Brooks, Sara (Costume Designer)

Month of Sundays 1968,S 17,50:1
Effect of Gamma Rays on Man-in-the-Moon
Marigolds, The 1970,Ap 8,32:1

Brooks, Sebastian

Trilby 1958,Ja 9,40:3

Brooks, Shelton

Plantation Revue, The 1922,Jl 18,18:4
Dixie to Broadway 1924,O 30,22:1
Brown Buddies 1930,O 8,29:1
Blackouts of 1949 1949,S 7,39:2

Brooks, Shelton (Composer)

Brown Buddies 1930,O 8,29:1

Brooks, Sinclair

Black Rhythm 1936,D 21,19:2

Brooks, Sydney (Costume Designer)

Romeo and Jeanette 1969,D 16,53:1
Ben Bagley's Shoestring Revues 1970,O 24,22:1

Brooks, Teresa

Wanted 1928,Jl 3,19:2

Brooks, Tyler

All-Star Jamboree 1921,Jl 14,18:1

Brooks, Vernon (Playwright)

House in Berlin, A (Als der Kreig zu Ende War);
Als der Krieg zu Ende War (A House in Berlin)
1950,D 27,32:3

Brooks, Walter (Choreographer)

White Lights 1927,O 12,30:4

Brooks, Walter (Director)

Oh! Oh! Nurse 1925,D 8,28:4
Happy 1927,D 6,26:3
Shuffle Along of 1933 1932,D 27,11:3
Thanks for Tomorrow 1938,S 28,28:2

Brooks, Walter (Producer)

Thanks for Tomorrow 1938,S 28,28:2

Brooks, Walter (Composer)

Dream Girl 1951,My 10,39:1

Brooks, William (Miscellaneous)

Tovarich 1952,My 15,39:2
Love's Labour's Lost 1953,F 5,20:3

Brooks, William (Musical Director)

Merchant of Venice, The 1953,Mr 5,20:2

Brooks, Wilson

Simon's Wife 1945,Mr 9,16:4
Slice It Thin 1945,My 11,22:5
Farther Off From Heaven 1947,Je 4,33:3
Summer and Smoke 1947,Jl 9,18:5
Throng o' Scarlet 1947,D 2,37:2
Coast of Illyria, The 1949,Ap 5,37:4
Come Back, Little Sheba 1950,F 16,28:5

Brooks (Costume Designer)

Aquashow 1952,Je 25,25:1

Broome, John (Director)

And People All Around 1968,F 12,46:1

Broomfield, Martin

Hamlet 1969,Je 30,33:1
Henry V 1969,N 11,43:1

Broones, Martin

Vaudeville (Palace) 1926,My 4,31:2

Broones, Martin (Composer)

LeMaire's Affairs 1927,Mr 29,22:4
Seeing Stars 1935,N 1,25:5

Brophy, Daniel F (Miscellaneous)

Hero of Santa Maria, The 1926,My 1,10:1
Man of Destiny, The 1926,My 1,10:1

Brophy, Edmund (Producer)

Sweet Miani 1962,S 26,33:2

Brophy, Fred

What Price Glory 1924,S 6,14:3

Brophy, John

As the Girls Go 1948,N 15,21:2

Brophy, Sallie

Peter Pan 1954,O 21,30:2

Brose, Marianna

Flies, The 1954,S 10,18:2
Trial, The 1955,Je 15,35:2
Spring's Awakening 1955,O 10,30:2

Brosnan, Alma (Playwright)

Scrapped 1927,O 16,IX,2:7

Brosnan, Charles (Playwright)

Dark Isle 1930,Ja 26,VIII,4:3

Brosset, Colette

Plume de Ma Tante, La 1958,N 12,42:1
Plume de Ma Tante, La 1959,S 13,II,1:1

Brosset, Colette (Choreographer)

Plume de Ma Tante, La 1958,N 12,42:1
Grosse Valise, La 1965,D 15,52:1

Brother, Mitchell

Marie Antoinette in Pennsylvania 1949,My 12,26:2

Brothers, Edna

Play, A 1925,F 11,19:2

Brothers Byrne, The

Good Times 1920,Ag 10,10:1

Brotherson, Eric

Between the Devil 1937,D 23,24:5
Lady in the Dark 1941,S 3,26:6
Lady in the Dark 1943,Mr 1,14:2
My Dear Public 1943,S 10,28:1
Gentlemen Prefer Blondes 1949,D 9,35:3
Room Service 1953,Ap 7,34:1
Hot Corner, The 1956,Ja 26,25:2
King and I, The 1964,Jl 7,26:1

Brotherton, Jane

Knickerbocker Holiday 1938,O 20,26:2

Brotherton, Thomas J R (Producer)

Our Wife 1933,Mr 3,13:2

Brott, Robert

Young Visitors, The 1920,N 30,14:1

Broudy, Jerrold

Hello Out There 1955,D 22,19:1
Floydada to Matador 1955,D 22,19:1

Brough, Mary

Plunder 1928,Jl 22,VII,1:3

Brougham, Nancy

Ah, Wilderness! 1953,F 7,10:6

Broughton, James (Producer)

Poet's Follies of 1955 1955,My 15,II,3:1

Broughton, L Schuyler

Betty Behave 1927,Mr 9,28:4

Broughton, Lewis

Charlatan, The 1922,Ap 25,14:2
Spring Cleaning 1923,N 10,16:3

Broughton, Lewis (Director)

Last of Mrs Cheyney, The 1925,N 10,23:5

Broughton, Philip (Composer)

Nine Fifteen Revue, The 1930,F 12,26:2

Broughton, Philip (Lyricist)

Nine Fifteen Revue, The 1930,F 12,26:2

Broughton, Philip F

County Chairman, The 1936,My 26,26:5

Broughton, Shirley

Shoemaker's Prodigious Wife, The 1949,Je 15,38:2

Broun, Daniel S (Miscellaneous)

Harbor Lights 1956,O 5,20:1
Girl of the Golden West, The 1957,N 6,44:1
Thurber Carnival, A 1960,F 27,13:2
Soldiers 1968,My 2,58:1

Broun, Daniel S (Producer)

Exiles 1957,Mr 13,27:1

Broun, Helen (Playwright)

Clouds 1925,S 3,32:1

Broun, Heywood Hale

Round the Town 1924,My 22,14:3
Shoot the Works! 1931,Jl 22,19:5
Love Me Long 1949,N 8,34:5
Bird Cage, The 1950,F 23,32:2
Live Wire, The 1950,Ag 18,16:2
Point of No Return 1951,D 14,35:2
Pink Elephant, The 1953,Ap 23,37:2
His and Hers 1954,Ja 8,18:2
Send Me No Flowers 1960,D 6,54:1
Take Her, She's Mine 1961,D 22,19:1
My Mother, My Father and Me 1963,Mr 25,5:5
My Kinsman, Major Molineux 1964,N 2,62:2
Little Murders 1967,Ap 26,38:1

Broun, Heywood Hale (Original Author)

Sun Field, The 1942,D 10,33:2

Broun, Heywood Hale (Playwright)

49ers, The 1922,N 7,14:1
49ers, The 1922,N 12,VIII,1:1

roun, Heywood Hale (Playwright)—Cont
Small Hours, The 1951,F 16,22:1
Xmas in Las Vegas 1965,N 5,31:1
roun, Heywood Hale (Producer)
Shoot the Works! 1931,Jl 22,19:5
Shoot the Works! 1931,Jl 26,VIII,2:1
Shoot the Works! 1931,Ag 21,20:2
roussard, Mary
Merry Widow, The 1944,O 9,17:1
roussard, William
Skyrocket, The 1929,Ja 12,14:7
routa, Julio (Playwright)
Pygmalion 1927,My 12,25:2
rouwer, Aart
Lotte Goslar's Pantomime Circus-For Humans Only 1957,D 17,45:1
rowder, William
Othello 1945,My 23,25:4
rowe, Margie (Costume Designer)
Red Horse Animation, The 1970,N 20,32:1
rower, Alfred
Girl From Wyoming, The 1938,O 31,12:1
rower, Jay (Miscellaneous)
On the Town 1959,Ja 16,36:1
rower, Jay (Musical Director)
Delightful Season, A 1960,S 29,30:1
rower, Joan
Mikado, The 1954,Mr 24,31:1
Pirates of Penzance, The 1954,Mr 31,32:5
Gondoliers, The 1954,Ap 14,24:3
Iolanthe 1954,Ap 28,36:8
Yeomen of the Guard, The 1954,My 5,36:2
rower, Kay
Gay Divorce 1960,Ap 4,37:1
Delightful Season, A 1960,S 29,30:1
rower, Millicent
Madwoman of Chaillot, The 1950,Je 14,41:2
rower, Walter
Cinderella on Broadway 1920,Je 25,18:1
rower, William
Lamp at Midnight 1947,D 22,29:2
Church Street 1948,F 10,27:2
Happy Journey to Trenton and Camden, The 1948,Mr 21,II,1:1
Brown, A K
Here's Howe 1923,Ap 26,19:3
Brown, A O
Lambs Gambol 1925,Ap 27,15:1
Brown, A Seymour (Director)
New Americana 1928,N 30,32:4
Brown, A Seymour (Lyricist)
Adrienne 1923,My 29,10:4
Brown, A Seymour (Playwright)
Adrienne 1923,My 29,10:4
Brown, Ada
Brown Buddies 1930,O 8,29:1
Memphis Bound 1945,My 25,23:2
Brown, Albert
Toto 1921,Mr 22,15:2
Brown, Alfred
Tip-Top 1920,O 6,13:2
Final Balance, The 1928,O 31,28:3
They Shall Not Die 1934,F 22,24:4
Brown, Alice (Playwright)
Little Theatre Tournament; Joint Owners in Spain 1929,My 7,28:1
Brown, Aline
Diversions 1958,N 8,14:4
Brown, Allen
Abortion 1959,O 28,40:4
Brown, Anne
Porgy and Bess 1935,O 1,27:2
Porgy and Bess 1935,O 11,30:2
Mamba's Daughters 1939,Ja 4,24:2
Mamba's Daughters 1939,Ja 15,IX,1:1
Pins and Needles 1939,Ap 21,26:2
Belle Helene, La 1941,Jl 8,14:1
Porgy and Bess 1942,Ja 23,16:2
Brown, Anthony
American Tragedy, An 1926,O 12,31:2
Brown, Anthony (Director)
Tobacco Road 1933,D 5,31:2
First Legion, The 1934,O 2,18:2
Eldest, The 1935,F 12,24:3
How Beautiful With Shoes 1935,N 29,24:1
Bright Honor 1936,S 28,14:1
Marching Song 1937,F 18,18:2
Work Is for Horses 1937,N 22,14:6
John Henry 1940,Ja 11,18:2
Johnny 2X4 1942,Mr 17,24:6
Tobacco Road 1942,S 7,34:2
Tobacco Road 1943,S 6,21:3
Take It As It Comes 1944,F 11,17:2
Sound of Hunting, A 1945,N 21,16:6
Brown, Anthony (Playwright)
How Beautiful With Shoes 1935,N 29,24:1
Brown, Anthony (Producer)
Tobacco Road 1933,D 5,31:2
Work Is for Horses 1937,N 22,14:6
Brown, Anthony (Scenic Designer)
Tobacco Road 1938,N 27,IX,3:4
Brown, Arnold
Hit the Deck! 1927,Ap 26,32:1

Brown, Arthur
Dearest Enemy 1925,S 19,9:2
Brown, Arvin (Director)
Whistle in the Dark, A 1968,F 17,32:2
Whistle in the Dark, A 1969,O 9,55:1
Country People 1970,Ja 19,35:1
Hay Fever 1970,N 10,55:1
Hay Fever 1970,N 22,II,18:6
Place Without Doors, A 1970,D 1,60:1
Brown, Barbara
Relations 1928,Ag 21,27:3
Play, Genius, Play! 1935,O 31,17:2
Spread Eagle 1935,N 5,33:6
Personal Appearance 1935,D 8,X,5:8
Personal Appearance 1936,Je 16,23:4
Personal Appearance 1936,Je 23,27:3
Sun Kissed 1937,Mr 11,20:2
Springtime for Henry 1940,F 27,16:3
Happy as Larry 1961,Ap 26,36:1
Brown, Beth (Original Author)
Behind the Red Lights 1937,Ja 14,17:4
Brown, Beth (Playwright)
Behind the Red Lights 1937,Ja 14,17:4
Brown, Bill
Captain Jinks 1925,S 9,22:1
Happy 1927,D 6,26:3
Brown, Billings (Lyricist)
Small Wonder 1948,S 16,33:5
Small Wonder 1948,S 26,II,1:1
Brown, Billy
Tip-Top 1920,O 6,13:2
Brown, Blair
School for Scandal, The 1970,Je 11,51:1
Brown, Burton
Little Miss Bluebeard 1923,Ag 29,12:1
Vaudeville (Palace) 1928,O 30,27:3
Brown, Calvin (Playwright)
Say When 1928,Je 27,29:3
Brown, Carol Curtis
Billy Draws a Horse 1939,D 22,14:5
Brown, Carrie
Dragon, The 1963,Ap 10,32:1
Brown, Chamberlain (Playwright)
Scrap Book 1932,Ag 2,20:3
Brown, Chamberlain (Producer)
Kept 1926,S 18,13:3
Immoral Isabella 1927,O 28,20:3
Mrs Dane's Defense 1928,F 7,30:1
Sherlock Holmes 1928,F 21,18:4
Within the Law 1928,Mr 6,20:1
Great Necker, The 1928,Mr 7,28:2
Lady for a Night, A 1928,Ap 17,26:4
Mouthpiece, The 1929,Je 16,VIII,2:1
Sporting Blood 1929,Jl 28,VIII,1:6
Forcing Bed, The 1929,Ag 4,VIII,1:6
Biarritz 1929,Ag 11,VIII,2:1
Third Day, The 1929,Ag 13,23:4
Jehovah Joe 1929,Ag 25,VIII,3:1
Parade 1929,S 1,VIII,1:1
Prima Donna 1929,S 22,IX,2:6
Tabloid 1929,S 29,IX,5:1
Church Mouse, A 1933,Je 27,13:7
Taken From Life 1938,Ja 29,34:4
Brown, Charles
Broadway Whirl, The 1921,Je 9,10:4
Red Pepper 1922,My 30,8:3
Vogues of 1924 1924,Mr 28,14:3
Top Hole 1924,S 2,22:3
His Queen 1925,My 12,26:1
All Wet 1925,Jl 7,24:1
Noose, The 1926,O 21,23:3
Murder on the Second Floor 1929,S 12,35:1
Three Little Girls 1930,Ap 15,29:1
Christopher Comes Across 1932,Je 1,19:2
Conquest 1933,F 20,11:3
Diamond Lil 1951,S 15,8:2
Kumquat in the Persimmon Tree, The 1962,Je 19,27:2
Brown, Charles D
Gold 1921,Je 2,14:2
Puppets 1925,Mr 10,19:1
Book of Charm, The 1925,S 4,26:3
Book of Charm, The 1925,S 13,VIII,1:1
Two Orphans, The 1926,Ap 6,26:2
Loose Ankles 1926,Ag 17,15:1
Loose Ankles 1926,Ag 29,VII,1:1
Say It With Flowers 1926,D 6,29:1
Spread Eagle 1927,Ap 5,30:2
Burlesque 1927,S 2,15:3
Blow the Man Down 1929,Ag 25,VIII,3:1
Commodore Marries, The 1929,S 5,26:3
Commodore Marries, The 1929,S 15,IX,1:1
Top O' the Hill 1929,N 27,30:4
Blessed Event 1932,F 13,23:2
Blessed Event 1932,F 21,VIII,1:1
Here Today 1932,S 7,14:2
Here Today 1932,S 18,IX,1:1
Alien Corn 1933,F 14,19:5
Alien Corn 1933,F 21,17:2
Alien Corn 1933,F 26,IX,1:1
She Loves Me Not 1933,N 21,22:4
Page Miss Glory 1934,N 28,24:2
Parade 1935,My 21,22:2

Brown, Charles D—Cont
Crime Marches on 1935,O 24,19:1
Dear Old Darling 1936,Mr 3,25:1
Double Dummy 1936,N 12,30:1
High Tor 1937,Ja 11,15:2
High Tor 1937,Ja 17,X,1:1
Brown, Charles H (Playwright)
Traitor, The 1930,My 3,23:4
Brown, Charles H (Producer)
Traitor, The 1930,My 3,23:4
Brown, Charles Hubert
Child of Manhattan 1932,Mr 2,15:1
Brown, Charles S
Foolscap 1933,Ja 12,21:2
Brown, Clarence
Case of Philip Lawrence, The 1937,Je 9,31:1
Brown, Constance
Broadway 1926,S 17,19:3
Brown, David (Producer)
Athenian Touch, The 1964,Ja 15,25:4
Brown, Dewey
Dance With Your Gods 1934,O 8,14:3
Brown, Dolores
Tomorrow's a Holiday! 1935,D 31,10:2
They Knew What They Wanted 1949,F 17,28:2
Brown, Donald
Say When 1934,N 9,24:2
Jubilee 1935,O 14,20:1
County Chairman, The 1936,My 26,26:5
Stork Mad 1936,O 1,28:4
Schoolhouse on the Lot 1938,Mr 23,18:4
Brown, Doris
Carmen Jones 1951,S 22,8:6
Brown, Dorothy
Hassard Short's Ritz Revue 1924,S 18,19:1
Polly 1925,O 12,19:1
Squealer, The 1928,N 13,36:3
Seven Mirrors 1945,O 26,17:2
Brown, Dulcie Cooper
Abe Lincoln in Illinois 1963,Ja 23,5:2
Brown, Eddy
Vaudeville (Palace) 1926,Jl 20,17:4
Brown, Edgar
Brown Buddies 1930,O 8,29:1
Brown, Edith H
Carnaval 1924,D 30,15:1
Brown, Edward Sargent (Director)
Intruder, The 1928,Jl 26,25:4
Ladies Don't Lie 1929,O 11,36:3
Gray Shadow 1931,Mr 11,23:4
Weather Permitting 1935,My 24,24:5
Brown, Edward Sargent (Miscellaneous)
Ladies Don't Lie 1929,O 11,36:3
Brown, Edward Sargent (Playwright)
Weather Permitting 1935,My 24,24:5
Brown, Edward Sargent (Producer)
Intruder, The 1928,Jl 26,25:4
Gray Shadow 1931,Mr 11,23:4
Weather Permitting 1935,My 24,24:5
Brown, Edwin A
Devil to Pay, The 1925,D 4,26:2
One Day More 1926,Mr 19,24:3
Brown, Elaine (Musical Director)
Noye's Fludde 1959,Mr 17,41:2
Brown, Elizabeth
Trumpets of the Lord 1963,D 23,22:3
Dark of the Moon 1970,Ap 4,21:2
Brown, Elliott C Jr
Othello 1937,Ja 7,16:4
Brown, Elmer
Tendresse, La 1922,S 26,18:1
Pasteur 1923,Mr 13,19:1
Changelings, The 1923,S 18,16:3
Hassard Short's Ritz Revue 1924,S 18,19:1
Man in Evening Clothes, The 1924,D 6,13:4
Sunny 1925,S 23,22:1
Grand Duchess and the Waiter, The 1925,O 14,31:1
Embers 1926,F 2,20:3
Counsellor-at-Law 1931,N 7,17:2
Between Two Worlds 1934,O 26,24:2
Fly Away Home 1935,Ja 16,20:4
House in the Country, A 1937,Ja 12,18:3
Counsellor-at-Law 1942,N 25,17:2
Affairs of State 1950,S 26,37:2
Brown, Elmer H (Director)
House of Fear, The 1929,O 8,34:2
Brown, Ernest
Kiss Me, Kate 1952,Ja 9,24:6
Kiss Me, Kate 1965,My 13,31:1
Brown, Erni (Miscellaneous)
Miss Emily Adam 1960,Mr 30,43:1
Brown, Erni (Producer)
Opening Night 1963,O 3,28:2
Matter of Like Life and Death, A 1963,O 3,28:2
Brown, Evelyn
Babes in Toyland 1929,D 24,15:3
Brown, Felix
Victoria Regina 1935,D 27,15:2
Victoria Regina 1938,O 4,20:2
Brown, Florence
Hummin' Sam 1933,Ap 10,8:8
Come Marching Home 1946,My 20,18:6

Brown, Fodi
Night in Venice, A 1929,My 22,30:2
Brown, Forman (Composer)
Sunday Nights at 9 1935,N 11,21:1
It's a Small World 1938,N 7,22:4
Pie-Eyed Piper, The 1942,Je 14,VIII,2:1
No Strings 1942,Je 14,VIII,2:1
Brown, Forman (Lyricist)
Pie-Eyed Piper, The 1942,Je 14,VIII,2:1
No Strings 1942,Je 14,VIII,2:1
Red Mill, The 1945,O 17,16:2
Music in My Heart 1947,O 3,30:2
Merry Widow, The 1964,Ag 18,24:2
Brown, Forman (Playwright)
Mister Noah 1933,Ja 18,16:2
Elsa Lanchester-Herself 1961,F 6,28:1
Brown, Frank
I Know What I Like 1939,N 25,13:5
Brown, Frank Emmons (Director)
Wonderful Journey 1946,D 26,30:2
Brown, Frankie
Blues for Mister Charlie 1964,Ap 24,24:1
Brown, Fred
Tip-Top 1920,O 6,13:2
Brown, G Edward
Porgy 1927,O 11,26:2
Brown, Gabriel
Macbeth 1936,Ap 15,25:4
Horse Play 1937,Ag 28,8:3
Brown, Garfield
Paradise Alley 1924,Ap 2,17:3
Brown, Gena
Stevedore 1934,Ap 19,33:2
Brown, Geoffrey (Miscellaneous)
Legend of Lovers 1959,O 28,40:3
Fantasticks, The 1960,My 4,55:2
Smiling the Boy Fell Dead 1961,Ap 20,28:1
School for Scandal, The 1962,Mr 19,36:1
Tavern, The 1962,Ap 5,29:1
We Comrades Three 1962,O 12,26:1
Brown, George
Fashion 1924,F 5,21:2
Princess Turandot 1926,N 13,14:2
Manhatters, The 1927,Ag 4,25:4
Green Pastures, The 1935,F 27,16:2
Brown, George Carleton (Playwright)
School for Brides 1944,Ag 2,19:4
Brown, George L
His Chinese Wife 1920,My 18,9:3
Brown, George Stanford
All's Well That Ends Well 1966,Je 17,39:1
Murderous Angels 1970,F 8,70:1
Brown, Georgia
Oliver 1963,Ja 8,5:5
Brown, Georgie
Queen O' Hearts 1922,O 11,22:1
Brown, Geraldine
It's a Wise Child 1933,My 17,15:2
Post Road 1934,D 5,28:3
Brown, Geryl
Mr Papavert 1932,Ja 23,18:6
Brown, Gilmor
Lazarus Laughed 1928,Ap 10,33:1
Brown, Gilmor (Director)
Lazarus Laughed 1928,Ap 10,33:1
Brown, Gilmor (Producer)
Return of Ulysses, The 1943,F 7,II,1:6
Ghost of Elsinore, The 1949,Ap 16,10:2
Serpent in the Orchard, The 1949,Ap 24,II,1:1
Brown, Graham
Hamlet 1963,My 9,41:1
Henry V 1964,My 13,52:1
Saint Joan 1964,My 14,41:1
Way of the World, The 1965,Je 2,40:1
Richard III 1965,Je 3,26:1
Weekend 1968,Mr 14,50:2
Man in the Glass Booth, The 1968,S 27,41:1
God Is a (Guess What?) 1968,D 18,56:1
Neighbors 1969,Ja 15,38:2
Malcochon 1969,Ap 2,37:1
Man Better Man 1969,Jl 3,22:1
Man Better Man 1969,Jl 13,II,1:1
Brown, H
It's Only Natural 1922,Ap 21,13:2
Brown, Halbert
Marry the Poor Girl 1920,S 27,18:3
Nightcap, The 1921,Ag 16,18:3
Jefferson Davis 1936,F 19,17:2
Brown, Harold
Fledermaus, Die 1954,My 20,38:5
Brown, Harris
Galileo 1947,D 8,34:2
Joy to the World 1948,Mr 19,28:2
Brown, Harry
Tip-Top 1920,O 6,13:2
Brown, Harry (Playwright)
Sound of Hunting, A 1945,N 21,16:6
Sound of Hunting, A 1945,D 2,II,1:1
Sound of Hunting, A 1954,Ap 7,41:1
Brown, Harry Joe (Director)
What Price Glory 1949,Mr 3,33:2
Brown, Harry Joe (Miscellaneous)
But Not Goodbye 1944,Ap 12,19:2

Brown, Harry Joe Jr (Director)
Antigone 1959,S 16,46:2
Brown, Harry Joe Jr (Miscellaneous)
Krapp's Last Tape 1960,Ja 15,37:2
Zoo Story, The 1960,Ja 15,37:2
Brown, Harry Joe Jr (Producer)
Antigone 1959,S 16,46:2
Moon on a Rainbow Shawl 1962,Ja 16,30:1
Brown, Harvey
That Girl at the Bijou 1956,N 10,15:4
That Girl at the Bijou 1956,N 18,II,11:2
Brown, Haskell (Composer)
Little Racketeer, The 1932,Ja 19,24:4
Brown, Helen
Ziegfeld Follies 1927,Ag 17,27:3
Vaudeville (Palace) 1928,D 17,23:3
R U R 1930,F 18,28:1
Brown, Henriette
Roll Sweet Chariot 1934,O 3,24:3
Brown, Henry
Merchant of Venice, The 1922,D 22,13:1
Wall Street 1927,Ap 21,24:4
Hill Between, The 1938,Mr 12,12:5
Brown, Hirsh
Shylock and His Daughter 1947,S 30,22:2
Brown, Honey
Keep Shufflin' 1928,F 28,18:3
Brown, Hubert
Sweet Chariot 1930,O 24,30:2
Constant Sinner, The 1931,S 15,30:1
Hangman's Whip 1933,F 25,20:2
Let Freedom Ring 1935,N 7,26:2
Censored 1938,F 28,18:2
Abe Lincoln in Illinois 1938,O 17,12:2
Brown, Ian
Streets of New York, The 1963,O 30,47:1
Brown, Ida
Shuffle Along of 1933 1932,D 27,11:3
Jezebel 1933,D 20,26:3
Brown, Isabelle
Wine, Women and Song 1942,S 29,18:3
Brown, J K
East of Broadway 1932,Ja 27,19:3
Brown, J Mardo
Take a Brace 1923,Ap 20,20:3
Chocolate Dandies, The 1924,S 2,22:2
Kilpatrick's Old-Time Minstrels 1930,Ap 21,20:2
Ballyhoo 1930,D 23,24:1
Hummin' Sam 1933,Ap 10,8:8
St Louis Woman 1946,Ap 1,22:2
Born Yesterday 1954,Ja 1,16:6
Brown, J Terry Jr (Miscellaneous)
Red Roses for Me 1961,N 28,41:1
Brown, J Terry Jr (Producer)
All in Love 1961,N 11,15:2
Brown, Jack
Geneva 1940,Ja 31,15:2
Brown, Jack (Lighting Director)
Natural Affection 1963,F 2,5:2
Dylan 1964,Ja 20,18:1
Beekman Place 1964,O 8,50:1
Ben Franklin in Paris 1964,O 28,52:1
Slow Dance on the Killing Ground 1964,D 1,50:1
Stephen D 1967,S 25,58:1
Niggerlovers, The; Demonstration, The 1967,O 2,54:2
Niggerlovers, The; Man and Dog 1967,O 2,54:2
Persians, The 1970,Ap 16,53:1
Brown, Jack (Miscellaneous)
Persians, The 1970,Ap 16,53:1
Brown, Jack (Scenic Designer)
Stephen D 1967,S 25,58:1
Niggerlovers, The; Demonstration, The 1967,O 2,54:2
Niggerlovers, The; Man and Dog 1967,O 2,54:2
Bill Noname 1970,Mr 3,37:1
Persians, The 1970,Ap 16,53:1
Brown, James
Damn Your Honor 1929,D 31,14:3
Brown, James A
Pirates of Penzance, The 1938,Je 3,16:2
Brown, James Ambrose (Playwright)
Babu 1967,D 23,28:1
Brown, Jane
Caroline 1923,F 1,13:2
Pageant of the Nativity of Christ 1948,D 25,6:7
Brown, Jean
Sally, Irene and Mary 1922,S 5,21:2
Brown, Jeff
Othello 1943,O 20,18:1
Bright Boy 1944,Mr 3,19:5
Hickory Stick 1944,My 9,15:6
Brown, Jerry
It's About Time 1942,Mr 31,28:3
Brown, Jessica
Girl From Home, The 1920,My 4,9:2
Cinderella on Broadway 1920,Je 25,18:1
Century Revue and the Midnight Rounders, The 1920,Jl 13,9:1
Brown, Joan
American Tragedy, An 1926,O 12,31:2
Mirrors 1928,Ja 19,17:1

Brown, Joanna
Shadow Years, The 1957,Ja 9,26:2
Cue for Passion 1958,N 26,25:2
Brown, Joe E
Jim Jam Jems 1920,O 5,13:2
Greenwich Village Follies 1923,S 21,4:6
Vaudeville (Palace) 1923,O 23,18:2
Betty Lee 1924,D 26,18:2
Captain Jinks 1925,S 9,22:1
Twinkle Twinkle 1926,N 17,22:2
Elmer the Great 1940,N 1,32:2
Courtin' Time 1951,Je 14,30:2
Courtin' Time 1951,Jl 1,II,1:1
Show Boat 1961,Ap 13,32:1
Brown, Joe Jr
Remember the Day 1935,Jl 9,24:3
Remember the Day 1935,S 26,19:3
Sap Runs High, The 1936,F 5,15:3
But for the Grace of God 1937,Ja 13,21:4
Something for Nothing 1937,D 10,33:5
Schoolhouse on the Lot 1938,Mr 23,18:4
Brown, John
Six Characters in Search of an Author 1931,Ap 16,29:2
Peace on Earth 1933,N 30,39:2
Milky Way, The 1934,My 9,23:2
Pirate, The 1942,N 26,39:2
Brown, John H
Kith and Kin 1930,My 14,31:1
Brown, Johnny
Golden Boy 1964,O 21,56:1
Carry Me Back to Morningside Heights 1968,F 28,41:1
Brown, Joie Jr
Wednesday's Child 1934,Ja 17,23:2
Between Two Worlds 1934,O 26,24:2
Brown, Joseph
Hot Rhythm 1930,Ag 22,18:5
Brown, Josephine
Passing Present, The 1931,D 8,36:2
Bachelor Born 1938,Ja 26,26:3
I Remember Mama 1944,O 20,16:2
Man and Superman 1947,O 9,31:2
Man and Superman 1949,My 17,28:6
Arms and the Man 1950,O 20,34:2
Gigi 1951,N 26,20:4
Diary of a Scoundrel 1956,N 5,41:1
Brown, Joyce (Musical Director)
Ballad for a Firing Squad 1968,D 12,64:2
Purlie 1970,Mr 16,53:1
Brown, Judy
Untitled-Nativity Play 1950,D 25,15:2
Brown, Julio
Birthright 1933,N 22,22:3
Sea Shells 1935,Jl 16,24:2
Love in My Fashion 1937,D 4,21:4
Brown, June
Hamlet 1939,D 5,35:2
Brown, Katharine (Producer)
Suds in Your Eye 1944,Ja 13,15:5
Brown, Katherine S (Director)
Tom Sawyer 1931,D 26,15:3
Brown, Kathryn
Spring Fever 1925,Ag 4,14:2
Brown, Kay
Conquering Hero, The 1961,Ja 17,40:2
Brown, Kelly
Rosalie 1957,Je 26,28:2
Goldilocks 1958,O 13,33:1
Chic 1959,My 19,28:2
From A to Z 1960,Ap 21,23:2
To Broadway With Love 1964,Ap 30,28:6
Kiss Me, Kate 1965,My 13,31:1
Brown, Kenneth H (Playwright)
Brig, The 1963,My 16,40:1
Brown, Kermit
Death of the Well-Loved Boy, The 1967,My 16,48:1
Pantagleize 1967,D 1,54:1
Cherry Orchard, The 1968,Mr 20,41:1
Millionairess, The 1969,Mr 3,28:1
Brown, Kernit
Winterset 1966,F 10,32:2
Brown, Kirk
Lady Alone 1927,Ja 21,12:5
Room 349 1930,Ap 23,24:5
Precedent 1931,Ap 15,24:5
Man on Stilts, The 1931,S 10,23:2
Park Avenue, Ltd 1932,Mr 4,17:1
Decoy, The 1932,Ap 2,13:4
Triplets 1932,S 22,25:2
Mrs O'Brien Entertains 1939,F 9,16:3
Me and Harry 1942,Ap 3,24:6
For Love or Money 1947,N 5,36:2
Gramercy Ghost 1951,Ap 27,20:2
Remains to Be Seen 1951,O 4,37:1
Brown, L Slade (Miscellaneous)
Bye Bye Birdie 1960,Ap 15,13:2
All American 1962,Mr 20,44:1
Brown, Laurence
Stevedore 1935,My 7,26:2
Brown, Lawrence R (Playwright)
Comic, The 1927,Ap 20,28:2

Brown, Le Roy
He 1931,S 22,33:1
Brown, Leon
Starlight 1925,Mr 4,17:2
Brown, Lew (Composer)
Manhattan Mary 1927,S 27,30:3
George White's Scandals 1928,Jl 3,19:1
Follow Thru 1929,Ja 10,24:3
George White's Scandals 1931,S 15,30:1
Hot-Cha! 1932,F 21,VIII,2:1
Hot-Cha! 1932,Mr 9,17:3
Forward March 1932,O 23,IX,3:5
Strike Me Pink 1933,Mr 6,16:3
Yokel Boy 1939,Jl 7,12:2
Brown, Lew (Director)
Calling All Stars 1934,D 14,28:2
Yokel Boy 1939,Jl 7,12:2
Crazy With the Heat 1941,Ja 31,15:2
Brown, Lew (Lyricist)
George White's Scandals 1925,Je 23,24:2
George White's Scandals 1926,Je 15,23:2
Piggy 1927,Ja 12,22:2
Good News 1927,S 7,35:4
Manhattan Mary 1927,S 27,30:3
George White's Scandals 1928,Jl 3,19:1
Follow Thru 1929,Ja 10,24:3
Flying High 1930,Mr 4,24:4
Hot-Cha! 1932,Mr 9,17:3
Calling All Stars 1934,D 14,28:2
Brown, Lew (Original Author)
Hot-Cha! 1932,Mr 9,17:3
Yokel Boy 1939,Jl 7,12:2
Brown, Lew (Playwright)
Manhattan Mary 1927,S 27,30:3
Flying High 1930,F 9,VIII,4:2
Flying High 1930,Mr 4,24:4
George White's Scandals 1931,S 15,30:1
Strike Me Pink 1933,Mr 6,16:3
Calling All Stars 1934,D 14,28:2
George White's Scandals 1935,D 26,20:2
Crazy With the Heat 1941,Ja 31,15:2
Brown, Lew (Producer)
Forward March 1932,O 23,IX,3:5
Strike Me Pink 1933,Mr 6,16:3
Calling All Stars 1934,N 22,26:1
Calling All Stars 1934,D 14,28:2
Yokel Boy 1939,Jl 7,12:2
Brown, Lewis (Costume Designer)
Richard II 1961,Ag 30,25:1
Persecution and Assassination of Marat As
    Performed by the Inmates of the Asylum of
    Charenton Under the Direction of the Marquis de
    Sade, The 1967,Ja 4,34:1
Jimmy Shine 1968,D 6,52:1
Fire! 1969,Ja 29,26:1
Flea in Her Ear, A 1969,O 4,25:1
Murderous Angels 1970,F 8,70:1
Brown, Lewis (Scenic Designer)
Henry V 1964,My 13,52:1
Glass Menagerie, The 1964,Jl 20,18:3
Richard III 1965,Je 3,26:1
Dance of Death, The 1966,Je 3,31:1
Harpers Ferry 1967,Je 6,52:2
Brown, Lillian
Queen at Home 1930,D 30,25:2
Baby Pompadour 1934,D 28,24:2
Brown, Lillyn
Regina 1949,N 1,32:2
Kiss Me, Kate 1952,Ja 9,24:6
Mamba's Daughters 1953,Mr 21,12:6
Brown, Lionel (Playwright)
Prince of Wisdom, The 1932,Jl 10,IX,1:4
There's Always Tomorrow 1934,My 13,IX,2:6
Constant Sinner 1937,Ap 6,21:2
To Have and to Hold 1937,Je 9,31:2
To Have and to Hold 1937,Je 27,X,1:3
Brown, Lois
Cloudy With Showers 1931,S 2,17:5
Brown, Louis (Miscellaneous)
Jerry Lewis' Variety Show 1957,F 8,18:5
Brown, Louise
Captain Jinks 1925,S 9,22:1
Love Spell, The 1925,N 25,14:2
No Foolin' 1926,Je 25,25:1
Rainbow 1928,N 22,25:1
Lady Fingers 1929,Ja 13,VIII,2:4
Lady Fingers 1929,F 1,22:4
Woof, Woof 1929,D 26,20:4
Brown, Marie
Streets of New York, The 1934,Jl 21,14:5
Oliver Twist 1934,Ag 11,16:5
Coquette 1935,Jl 10,24:1
Hay Fever 1935,Jl 24,20:4
Camille 1935,Jl 31,21:1
Mr Pim Passes By 1935,Ag 7,22:2
Vinegar Tree, The 1935,Ag 14,16:1
Double Door 1935,Ag 21,22:2
Late Christopher Bean, The 1935,Ag 28,13:1
How Beautiful With Shoes 1935,N 29,24:1
Mrs O'Brien Entertains 1939,F 9,16:3
Brown, Marjorie
American Tragedy, An 1931,F 21,15:5
Class of '29 1936,My 16,10:3

Hero Is Born, A 1937,O 2,18:6
Brown, Marlyn
Adam Solitaire 1925,N 7,19:2
Wise-Crackers, The 1925,D 17,26:1
Saturday Night 1926,O 26,25:1
Three Sisters, The 1926,O 27,24:1
Twelfth Night 1926,D 21,21:4
Brown, Martha
Merrily We Roll Along 1934,O 1,14:1
Brown, Martin (Playwright)
Innocent Idea, An 1920,My 26,9:4
Exciters, The 1922,S 23,10:4
Love Child, The 1922,N 15,22:1
Lady, The 1923,D 5,23:2
Lady, The 1923,D 16,IX,1:1
Cobra 1924,Ap 6,VIII,2:1
Cobra 1924,Ap 23,24:1
Cobra 1924,Ap 27,VIII,1:1
Great Music 1924,O 6,24:1
Great Music 1924,O 12,VIII,1:1
Dark, The 1925,Ag 9,VII,1:8
Praying Curve 1927,Ja 16,VII,2:4
Praying Curve 1927,Ja 25,18:2
Dark, The 1927,F 2,22:5
Strawberry Blonde, The 1927,F 8,20:3
Paris 1928,O 9,34:3
Roamin' Gentleman, A 1930,F 23,VIII,2:5
Delusion 1935,Mr 29,26:4
Brown, Mathew
Dover Road, The 1924,D 20,18:2
Brown, Maurice
Yeomen of the Guard, The 1964,Ag 3,16:1
Brown, Max (Miscellaneous)
Destry Rides Again 1959,Ap 24,24:1
Brown, Max J (Producer)
Butterflies Are Free 1969,O 22,30:1
Minnie's Boys 1970,Mr 27,27:1
Look to the Lilies 1970,Mr 30,59:1
Brown, Maxine
Sue, Dear 1922,Jl 11,16:2
Moonlight 1924,Ja 31,13:7
Brown, Michael (Composer)
New Faces of 1952 1952,My 17,23:2
Littlest Revue, The 1956,My 23,37:2
New Faces of 1956 1956,Je 15,32:1
Brown, Michael (Lyricist)
New Faces of 1952 1952,My 17,23:2
Littlest Revue, The 1956,My 23,37:2
New Faces of 1956 1956,Je 15,32:1
Brown, Mildred
Sweet Little Devil 1924,Ja 22,15:4
Flossie 1924,Je 4,25:2
Stork, The 1925,Ja 27,14:2
No More Women 1926,Ag 4,17:2
Brown, Minnie
Lulu Belle 1926,F 10,20:1
Brown, Morris L
Laugh It Off 1925,Ap 25,18:4
Brown, Morton
Scarlet Letter, The 1926,Ja 8,16:5
Straw Hat, The 1926,O 15,20:2
Brown, Myrtle
Great Power, The 1928,S 12,25:1
Brown, Nacio Herb (Composer)
Take a Chance 1932,N 28,11:2
Brown, Nancy
Bitter Sweet 1929,N 6,30:2
Gay Masquerade 1935,My 15,26:1
Brown, Ned (Producer)
One More Honeymoon 1934,Ap 2,13:5
Brown, Norma
It's Up to You 1921,Mr 29,20:1
Banjo Eyes 1941,D 26,20:2
Brown, Norman
Playboy of Newark, The 1943,Mr 20,11:2
Brown, Oscar Jr
Worlds of Oscar Brown Jr 1965,F 19,25:4
Joy 1970,Ja 28,50:1
Brown, Oscar Jr (Composer)
Worlds of Oscar Brown Jr 1965,F 19,25:4
Buck White 1969,D 3,63:1
Big Time Buck White 1969,D 7,II,5:1
Brown, Oscar Jr (Director)
Buck White 1969,D 3,63:1
Brown, Oscar Jr (Lyricist)
Worlds of Oscar Brown Jr 1965,F 19,25:4
Buck White 1969,D 3,63:1
Brown, Oscar Jr (Playwright)
Buck White 1969,D 3,63:1
Joy 1970,Ja 28,50:1
Brown, Pamela
Claudia 1942,S 27,VIII,2:2
Claudia 1942,O 4,VIII,2:1
King Lear 1946,O 13,II,2:3
Importance of Being Earnest, The 1947,Ja 24,18:6
Importance of Being Earnest, The 1947,Mr 4,30:2
Importance of Being Earnest, The 1947,Mr 9,II,1:1
Love for Love 1947,My 27,30:2
Gioconda Smile, The 1948,Je 20,II,2:3
Lady's Not for Burning, The 1950,N 9,42:2
Lady's Not for Burning, The 1950,N 26,II,1:1
Way of the World, The 1953,Ap 10,17:1
Country Wife, The 1957,N 28,56:1

Brown, Pamela—Cont
Heartbreak House 1959,O 19,37:1
Heartbreak House 1959,O 25,II,1:1
Brown, Patrika (Lighting Director)
Gertrude Stein's First Reader 1969,D 16,56:1
Brown, Paul
All the King's Men 1948,Ja 19,19:2
Brown, Peggie
Mimic World of 1921, The 1921,Ag 18,9:2
Brown, Phil
My Heart's in the Highlands 1939,Ap 14,29:2
Thunder Rock 1939,N 15,18:1
Night Music 1940,F 23,18:2
Heavenly Express 1940,Ap 19,24:2
Days of Our Youth, The 1941,N 29,15:2
Streets Are Guarded, The 1944,N 21,19:7
Brown, Phil (Director)
Kidders, The 1957,N 13,40:6
Brown, Pickering
Ledge, A 1929,N 19,26:3
Brown, R G
Time of Storm 1954,F 26,14:2
Major Barbara 1954,Je 30,23:2
Land Beyond the River, A 1957,Mr 29,15:7
New Faces of 1962 1962,F 2,25:1
Great Career, A 1968,D 30,25:1
Whispers on the Wind 1970,Je 4,50:1
Brown, R G (Playwright)
New Faces of 1962 1962,F 2,25:1
Brown, R Victor
Here Come the Clowns 1960,S 20,48:1
Much Ado About Nothing 1963,Jl 15,25:2
Brown, Ralph
Lew Leslie's Blackbirds of 1939 1939,F 13,12:2
Brown, Ralph (Miscellaneous)
Song of Bernadette 1946,Mr 27,22:2
Brown, Ray
Jamboree 1932,N 25,18:4
Sweeney Todd 1957,Ag 28,21:4
Brown, Ray (Miscellaneous)
Ballad of Jazz Street, The 1959,N 12,28:1
Brown, Reed
Nerves 1924,S 2,22:2
Devil Within, The 1925,Mr 17,19:4
Jay Walker, The 1926,F 9,23:1
Devils 1926,Mr 18,26:4
Brown, Reed Jr
Big Pond, The 1928,Ag 22,25:1
Merry Andrew 1929,Ja 22,22:2
He Walked in Her Sleep 1929,Ap 5,28:2
Broken Dishes 1929,N 6,28:3
Torch Song 1930,Ag 28,23:1
House Beautiful, The 1931,Mr 13,20:4
World Waits, The 1933,O 26,22:5
Jezebel 1933,D 20,26:3
Touch of Brimstone, A 1935,S 23,20:1
Fields Beyond, The 1936,Mr 7,11:2
Doughgirls, The 1942,D 31,19:2
Secret Room, The 1945,N 8,16:2
I Gotta Get Out 1947,S 26,27:2
Town House 1948,S 24,31:2
Metropole 1949,D 7,43:2
Blood, Sweat & Stanley Poole 1961,O 6,31:1
Brown, Regina
Common Sin, The 1928,O 16,28:2
Brown, Richard
Richard III 1957,N 26,41:1
Brown, Richard (Lighting Director)
Dance of Death, The 1969,My 26,53:1
Brown, Richard (Miscellaneous)
Sojourner Truth 1948,Ap 22,35:2
Power of Darkness, The 1948,O 11,28:2
Brown, Richard (Scenic Designer)
Almost Faithful 1948,Je 5,9:2
Brown, Robert
Hamlet 1951,Jl 20,13:6
Barefoot in Athens 1951,N 1,35:2
Come of Age 1952,Ja 24,22:2
Fortunato 1956,Mr 24,15:2
Mary and the Fairy 1956,Mr 24,15:2
Ulysses in Nighttown 1958,Je 6,30:1
Portrait of the Artist as a Young Man, A
    1962,My 29,21:1
Dark of the Moon 1970,Ap 4,21:2
Brown, Robert Delford
Originale 1964,S 9,46:1
Brown, Robert F
Hoot Mon, or Clans Across the Sea 1927,My 8,29:4
Brown, Roberta
And So to Bed 1927,N 10,23:1
Brown, Roger
Guys and Dolls 1966,Je 9,55:2
South Pacific 1967,Je 13,56:1
Brown, Rosa
Hot Mikado, The 1939,Mr 24,26:2
Brown, Rose
My Dear Public 1943,S 10,28:1
Brown, Rowland (Playwright)
Johnny 2X4 1942,Mr 17,24:6
Brown, Rowland (Producer)
Johnny 2X4 1942,Mr 17,24:6
Brown, Rudy
Hair 1970,Ja 13,39:1

Brown, Russ
Vaudeville (Palace) 1926,Je 15,23:3
Ups-A-Daisy 1928,O 9,34:2
Flying High 1930,F 9,VIII,4:2
Flying High 1930,Mr 4,24:4
Vaudeville (Palace) 1932,Mr 7,13:4
One Good Year 1935,N 28,38:3
Howdy Stranger 1937,Ja 15,17:5
Hold On to Your Hats 1940,S 12,30:3
Viva O'Brien 1941,O 10,27:2
Hollywood Pinafore 1945,Je 1,20:1
Up in Central Park 1947,My 20,29:2
Biggest Thief in Town 1949,Mr 31,31:2
Damn Yankees 1955,My 6,17:1
Brown, Sadie
Garden of Time 1945,Mr 10,13:7
Brown, Sally
High Button Shoes 1955,Mr 12,10:6
Brown, Samuel
To Quito and Back 1937,O 7,30:4
Set My People Free 1948,N 4,38:2
Brown, Sarah
Wonderful Night, A; Fledermaus, Die 1929,N 1,23:3
Brown, Sarah Emily
Streets of New York, The 1934,Jl 21,14:5
Post Road 1936,Ag 5,15:4
Fly Away Home 1937,Jl 28,15:1
Goodbye Again 1937,S 1,15:1
Brown, Sarah Emily (Costume Designer)
Orphee 1935,Mr 23,10:3
Camille 1935,Jl 31,21:1
Mr Pim Passes By 1935,Ag 7,22:2
Double Door 1935,Ag 21,22:2
Late Christopher Bean, The 1935,Ag 28,13:1
Brown, Sarah Emily (Scenic Designer)
Vinegar Tree, The 1935,Ag 14,16:1
Pursuit of Happiness, The 1936,Jl 15,14:1
Royal Family, The 1936,Ag 12,15:1
Kind Lady 1937,Jl 21,19:3
Candida 1937,Ag 4,14:5
Ode to Liberty 1937,Ag 18,15:2
Elizabeth the Queen 1937,Ag 25,24:3
Brown, Shirley
Beggar's Opera, The 1941,Ag 12,14:6
Brown, Slade (Producer)
Entertaining Mr Sloane 1965,O 13,41:1
Hotel Passionato 1965,O 23,16:1
Until the Monkey Comes 1966,Je 21,38:1
Joyful Noise, A 1966,D 16,57:1
Brown, Sonia Gordon (Translator)
Crime and Punishment 1935,Ja 23,20:3
Brown, Stuart
Wisdom Tooth, The 1926,F 16,22:2
Wild Waves 1932,F 20,11:4
Brown, Susan
Escape Me Never! 1935,Ja 22,22:2
High Named Today 1954,D 11,11:2
Dandy Dick 1956,Ja 11,37:2
Cut of the Axe 1960,F 2,38:2
Death of Satan, The 1960,Ap 6,49:1
Girl in the Freudian Slip, The 1967,My 19,34:3
Brown, Susaye
Singin' the Blues 1931,S 17,21:3
Blackberries of 1932 1932,Ap 5,27:5
Brown, Suzanne
Four Walls 1927,S 20,33:1
Brown, Tally
Jackass, The 1960,Mr 24,39:2
Brown, Ted
Under the Yum-Yum Tree 1964,My 29,18:1
Brown, Teddie
Vaudeville (Palladium) 1931,My 12,28:4
Brown, Thatcher M Jr
Coriolanus 1927,Je 18,8:3
Brown, Thomas
Delicate Story 1940,D 5,32:2
Brown, Tom
Black and White Revue, The 1923,O 28,VIII,2:1
Neighbors 1923,D 27,11:1
Is Zat So? 1925,Ja 6,23:4
Is Zat So? 1925,Ap 25,18:2
Vaudeville (Hippodrome) 1926,Mr 23,24:3
Paradise 1927,D 26,26:4
Atlas and Eva 1928,F 7,30:2
Many a Slip 1930,F 4,29:2
Brown, Tom (Choreographer)
Taming of the Shrew, The 1954,Jl 1,22:2
Two Gentlemen of Verona 1958,Mr 19,35:1
Much Ado About Nothing 1958,Je 26,22:1
Brown, Tom (Director)
Merry Wives of Windsor, The 1956,Je 21,34:4
Brown, Tom (Miscellaneous)
Candide 1956,D 3,40:2
Brown, Tommy
God Is Back, Black and Singing Gospel at the Fortune Theater 1969,N 19,48:1
Brown, Troy
Swingin' the Dream 1939,N 30,24:2
Brown, Tyrone (Miscellaneous)
No Exit 1967,O 31,38:2
Little Private World of Arthur Morton Fenwick, The 1967,O 31,38:2

Brown, Vanessa
Seven Year Itch, The 1952,N 21,21:2
Seven Year Itch, The 1952,N 30,II,1:1
Brown, Verne
Tip-Top 1920,O 6,13:2
Brown, Vernon
His Chinese Wife 1920,My 18,9:3
Brown, Virginia
Bystander 1937,S 15,27:1
Brown, Vivian
Sweeney Todd 1957,Ag 28,21:4
Brown, Walter
Ghost Between, The 1921,Mr 23,11:2
Humoresque 1923,F 28,13:2
Gentle Grafters 1926,O 28,23:1
High Flyers 1927,Je 26,VIII,1:1
Colombe 1965,F 24,33:1
Brown, Walter P
Show Boat 1954,O 29,28:4
Finian's Rainbow 1955,My 19,25:1
Carmen Jones 1956,Je 1,28:2
Carmen Jones 1959,Ag 18,25:1
South Pacific 1965,Je 3,25:1
Skyscraper 1965,N 15,48:1
Hello, Dolly! 1967,N 13,61:1
Brown, Warren
South Pacific 1955,My 5,39:5
Pipe Dream 1955,D 1,44:1
Brown, Warwick (Costume Designer)
American Gothic 1953,N 11,35:6
Brown, Warwick (Lighting Director)
American Gothic 1953,N 11,35:6
Brown, Warwick (Scenic Designer)
American Gothic 1953,N 11,35:6
Once Over Lightly 1955,Mr 16,39:1
Lend an Ear 1959,S 25,20:5
Epitaph for George Dillon 1960,D 29,17:1
Banquet for the Moon, A 1961,Ja 20,24:2
Brown, Wayne (Lighting Director)
Pink String and Sealing Wax 1957,S 6,13:1
Trip to Bountiful, The 1959,F 27,20:4
Brown, Wayne (Miscellaneous)
Pink String and Sealing Wax 1957,S 6,13:1
Brown, William
Conjur' Man Dies 1936,Mr 12,18:5
Case of Philip Lawrence, The 1937,Je 9,31:1
Brown, William F (Miscellaneous)
Leonard Sillman's New Faces of 1968 1968,My 3,43:1
Brown, William F (Playwright)
Girl in the Freudian Slip, The 1967,My 19,34:3
Leonard Sillman's New Faces of 1968 1968,My 3,43:1
How to Steal an Election 1968,O 14,56:1
Brown and Lahart
Vaudeville (Palace) 1927,O 11,27:2
Brown and O'Donnell
Vaudeville (Palace) 1921,Jl 5,15:1
Brown and Whittaker
Vaudeville (Palace) 1927,Je 7,27:3
Brown Brothers, The Six
Bunch and Judy, The 1922,N 29,20:1
Black and White Revue, The 1923,O 28,VIII,2:1
Browne, Alfred A
Incubator 1932,N 2,23:3
Browne, Benjamin
Porgy and Bess 1935,O 11,30:2
Browne, Catherine (Costume Designer)
Romeo and Juliet 1967,F 22,18:1
Browne, Catherine (Scenic Designer)
Romeo and Juliet 1967,F 22,18:1
Browne, Cicely
Grass Is Always Greener, The 1955,F 16,25:2
Browne, Coral
Basalik 1935,Ap 8,22:5
Tamburlaine the Great 1956,Ja 20,19:1
Tamburlaine the Great 1956,Ja 29,II,1:1
Macbeth 1956,My 24,27:1
Macbeth 1956,O 30,42:2
Troilus and Cressida 1956,D 27,21:1
Rehearsal, The 1963,S 24,45:2
Right Honourable Gentleman, The 1965,O 20,50:2
Browne, E Martin
Murder in the Cathedral 1938,F 17,16:2
Mystery of the Finding of the Cross, The 1959,Ja 16,35:2
Browne, E Martin (Director)
Murder in the Cathedral 1938,F 17,16:2
Cocktail Party, The 1950,Ja 23,17:2
Cocktail Party, The 1950,Ja 29,II,1:1
Confidential Clerk, The 1954,F 12,22:1
Confidential Clerk, The 1954,F 21,II,1:1
York Nativity Play, The 1956,D 5,49:2
Firstborn, The 1957,Ja 7,29:2
Elder Statesman, The 1958,Ag 26,35:1
Elder Statesman, The 1958,Ag 31,II,3:1
Mystery of the Finding of the Cross, The 1959,Ja 16,35:2
Way of the Cross, The 1959,Ja 16,35:2
Cranmer of Canterbury 1959,D 4,36:1
Family Reunion, The 1960,D 10,26:1
Planctus Mariae 1968,Ap 29,49:1
Visitatio Sepulchri; Peregrinus 1968,Ap 29,49:1

Browne, E Martin (Mrs) (Henzie Raeburn)
/(Miscellaneous)
Cranmer of Canterbury 1959,D 4,36:1
Browne, E Martin (Playwright)
York Nativity Play, The 1956,D 5,49:2
This Way to the Tomb 1961,D 9,21:1
Browne, E Martin (Producer)
Cocktail Party, The 1949,Ag 23,28:6
Browne, Earle
Alias Jimmy Valentine 1921,D 9,20:3
Browne, Earle (Director)
Earth 1927,Mr 10,23:1
Browne, Earle (Miscellaneous)
Maids, The 1963,N 15,29:1
Browne, Edward
Lady in the Dark 1943,Mr 1,14:2
Browne, Florence
Spice of 1922 1922,Jl 7,12:4
Browne, Gore (Playwright)
Cynara 1930,Jl 13,VIII,1:3
King, Queen, Knave 1932,F 18,24:4
Browne, Graham
Good Gracious, Annabelle 1923,F 15,23:2
Marquise, The 1927,Mr 20,VIII,2:7
Browne, Harry C
Only 38 1921,S 14,22:2
Some Party 1922,Ap 17,22:1
Vaudeville (Palace) 1924,Ap 1,18:1
Backslapper, The 1925,Ap 13,25:2
Candida 1925,N 10,23:4
Browne, Irene
Zoo, The 1927,O 9,VIII,1:3
Happy Husband, The 1928,My 8,25:2
Happy Husband, The 1928,My 27,VIII,1:1
Security 1929,Mr 29,20:1
Sunshine Sisters 1933,N 26,IX,3:6
Conversation Piece 1934,O 24,24:1
Country Wife, The 1936,D 2,34:1
Promise 1936,D 31,20:4
George and Margaret 1937,S 23,32:2
Jane 1947,Ja 30,19:6
Jane 1947,F 9,II,3:7
Jane 1952,F 2,10:2
Jane 1952,F 10,II,1:1
After The Ball 1954,Je 11,19:3
Girl Who Came to Supper, The 1963,D 9,49:1
Browne, Laurett
Chivalry 1925,D 16,22:3
Browne, Lewis Allen (Playwright)
Princess April 1924,D 2,23:2
Browne, Lillian W
Little Theatre Tournament; Aristocrat, The 1929,My 8,34:4
Browne, Lori
It's a Bird . . . It's a Plane . . . It's Superman 1966,Mr 30,34:1
Browne, Louise
Jill Darling 1934,D 20,29:8
Swing Along 1936,S 20,IX,1:4
Browne, Lynette
Public Relations 1944,Ap 7,23:3
Browne, Mallory
Hamlet 1927,Ap 7,23:3
Browne, Maurice
Mr Faust 1922,Ja 31,11:2
Candida 1922,Mr 23,11:1
Unknown Warrior, The 1928,Mr 4,IX,4:7
Brass Paperweight, The 1928,N 4,IX,2:1
Othello 1930,My 20,33:1
Unknown Warrior, The 1931,O 23,28:4
Browne, Maurice (Director)
Iphigenia in Aulis 1921,Ap 17,VI,1:1
Browne, Maurice (Miscellaneous)
Journey's End 1929,Mr 23,23:1
Journey's End 1930,Ag 5,26:4
Punchinello 1932,Mr 27,VIII,2:1
Browne, Maurice (Playwright)
Wings Over Europe 1928,D 11,35:1
Wings Over Europe 1928,D 23,VIII,1:1
Journey's End 1929,Ja 23,20:3
Wings Over Europe 1932,My 15,VIII,1:8
Browne, Maurice (Producer)
New Gossoon, The 1931,Ap 27,24:5
Venetian, The 1931,O 11,VIII,4:5
Venetian, The 1931,N 2,26:1
Viceroy Sarah 1935,F 13,27:4
Browne, Porter Emerson (Playwright)
Bad Man, The 1920,Ag 31,7:1
Bad Man, The 1921,O 2,VII,1:3
Bad Man, The 1923,F 25,VII,1:7
Bad Man, The 1923,Mr 11,VIII,2:4
Browne, Roscoe Lee
Titus Andronicus 1956,D 3,40:2
Romeo and Juliet 1957,Je 28,30:2
Aria Da Capo 1958,Je 27,18:5
Antigone 1959,S 16,46:2
Cool World, The 1960,F 23,38:2
Pretender, The 1960,My 25,42:1
Blacks, The 1961,My 5,23:1
General Seeger 1962,Mr 1,26:2
King Lear 1962,Ag 14,35:1
Tiger Tiger Burning Bright 1962,D 24,5:2
Winter's Tale, The 1963,Ag 16,14:1

Browne, Roscoe Lee—Cont
Ballad of the Sad Cafe, The 1963,O 31,27:1
Benito Cereno 1964,N 2,62:2
Troilus and Cressida 1965,Ag 13,17:1
Danton's Death 1965,O 22,46:1
Hand Is on the Gate, A 1966,S 22,54:1
Volpone 1967,Je 30,29:1
Tartuffe 1967,S 18,60:1
Browne, Roscoe Lee (Director)
Hand Is on the Gate, A 1966,S 22,54:1
Browne, Roscoe Lee (Miscellaneous)
Hand Is on the Gate, A 1966,S 22,54:1
Browne, Theodore
Ponder Heart, The 1956,F 17,14:2
Browne, Theodore (Playwright)
Natural Man 1941,My 8,20:4
Browne, Thomas (Playwright)
Man Who Had Nothing, The 1937,Je 8,30:1
Plan for a Hostess 1938,Mr 27,X,1:3
Browne, W Graham
Serpent's Tooth, A 1922,Ag 25,8:5
Vinegar Tree, The 1932,Je 9,27:7
Browne, W Graham (Director)
Colonel Satan 1931,Ja 18,I,28:6
Browne, William H
Sancho Panza 1923,N 27,23:1
Browne, William J
Rainbow's End 1928,D 26,14:6
Browne, Wynyard (Playwright)
Holly and the Ivy, The 1950,My 21,II,3:2
Question of Fact, A 1954,Ja 17,II,4:4
Brownell, Atherton (Playwright)
Sakura 1928,D 26,14:4
Brownell, Barbara
Play It Again, Sam 1969,F 13,52:3
Brownell, Benned
Post Road 1949,Ap 28,27:3
Devil's Disciple, The 1950,Ja 26,23:2
Brownell, John Charles
Cyclone Lover, The 1928,Je 6,23:3
Dream Child 1934,S 28,26:2
Brownell, John Charles (Playwright)
Nut Farm, The 1929,O 15,34:3
Brain Sweat 1934,Ap 5,24:4
Her Majesty the Widow 1934,Je 19,24:5
Woman of the Soil, A 1935,Mr 26,23:6
Brownell, Lalive
Malvaloca 1922,O 3,22:1
Romeo and Juliet 1923,Ja 25,16:1
Getting Even 1929,Ag 20,31:1
Chrysalis 1932,N 16,15:2
Ragged Army 1934,F 27,16:5
Tell Me Pretty Maiden 1937,D 17,33:5
Case of Youth, A 1940,Mr 25,10:3
Brownell, Mabel (Director)
Immoral Isabella 1927,O 28,20:3
Brownell, Nyan
Still Waters 1926,Mr 2,23:1
Brownfoot, Andrew (Costume Designer)
Boy Friend, The 1970,Ap 15,54:1
Brownfoot, Andrew (Scenic Designer)
Boy Friend, The 1970,Ap 15,54:1
Brownfoot, Margaret (Costume Designer)
Boy Friend, The 1970,Ap 15,54:1
Brownfoot, Margaret (Scenic Designer)
Boy Friend, The 1970,Ap 15,54:1
Browning, Ethel
Gentleman From Athens, The 1947,D 10,42:4
Browning, Fred
All's Well That Ends Well 1966,Je 17,39:1
Browning, Joe
Vaudeville (Palace) 1927,Ja 25,18:3
Vaudeville (Palace) 1928,Ag 28,27:3
Browning, Marjorie (Costume Designer)
John Gabriel Borkman 1959,N 26,57:4
Browning, Mortimer
Gala Night 1930,F 26,22:4
Browning, Mortimer (Composer)
Gala Night 1930,F 26,22:4
Browning, Natalie
Prunella; Love in a Garden 1926,Je 16,23:3
Marco Millions 1928,Ja 10,28:2
Give Me Yesterday 1931,Mr 5,32:1
If I Were You 1931,S 24,21:1
$25 an Hour 1933,My 11,14:4
Browning, Pam
Night Hawk 1926,D 27,21:3
Browning, Robert
Candida 1970,Ap 7,41:1
Browning, Robert (Original Author)
Caponsacchi 1926,O 27,24:2
Caponsacchi 1927,F 20,VII,1:1
Caponsacchi 1928,Ja 25,20:3
Pied Piper of Hamelin, The 1950,Ap 3,19:2
Browning, Rod
Richard III 1966,Ag 11,26:1
Browning, Susan
Love and Kisses 1963,D 19,39:1
Jo 1964,F 13,25:1
Collision Course; Wandering 1968,My 9,55:2
Collision Course; Chuck 1968,My 9,55:2
Collision Course; Stars and Stripes 1968,My 9,55:2
Collision Course; Camera Obscura 1968,My 9,55:2
Collision Course; Jew! 1968,My 9,55:2

Company 1970,Ap 27,40:1
Company 1970,My 3,II,1:4
Company 1970,Jl 29,31:1
Browning, William E
Ramblers, The 1926,S 21,32:2
Brownlaw, J Taylor
Frankie and Johnny 1930,S 26,16:5
Brownlee, Cathy
Ice Follies 1969,My 23,38:1
Brownlee, Deli
Finian's Rainbow 1953,Mr 7,13:2
Brownlee, John
Vagabond King, The 1943,Je 30,24:2
Tempest, The 1955,S 3,8:6
Hamlet 1970,O 27,54:2
Brownstone, Joseph (Miscellaneous)
Touch of the Poet, A 1958,O 3,23:2
Visit, The 1960,Mr 9,38:3
Evening With Mike Nichols and Elaine May, An 1960,O 10,37:1
Tchin-Tchin 1962,O 26,26:2
Bicycle Ride to Nevada 1963,S 25,38:1
Murderer Among Us, A 1964,Mr 26,43:1
Brox Sisters
Untitled-Benefit 1922,My 8,14:5
Music Box Revue 1923,S 24,5:3
Music Box Revue 1924,D 2,23:3
Cocoanuts, The 1926,Je 11,25:2
Ziegfeld Follies 1927,Ag 17,27:3
Vaudeville (Palace) 1930,N 17,21:2
Brubaker, Joe
You Can't Take It With You 1951,Ap 7,8:6
Bruce, Alan
Drunkard, The; Fallen Saved, The 1959,Je 24,37:2
Emmanuel 1960,D 5,42:2
Bruce, Allan
Great Scot! 1965,N 12,56:3
Bruce, Almon
Hand in Glove 1944,D 5,19:1
Bruce, Arthur
Stevedore 1934,Ap 19,33:2
But for the Grace of God 1937,Ja 13,21:4
Bruce, Barbara
Silver Cord, The 1926,D 21,21:1
Lady With a Lamp, The 1931,N 20,27:2
Bruce, Betty
Boys From Syracuse, The 1938,N 24,36:1
Keep Off the Grass 1940,My 5,X,1:6
Keep Off the Grass 1940,My 24,22:6
Untitled-Revue 1941,My 18,IX,1:1
High Kickers 1941,N 1,21:2
Something for the Boys 1943,Ja 17,VIII,1:1
Up in Central Park 1945,Ja 29,17:2
Up in Central Park 1947,My 20,29:2
Bruce, Beverly
Detective Story 1954,F 13,11:2
Miss Julie 1956,F 22,23:2
Bruce, Brenda
Gioconda Smile, The 1948,Je 20,II,2:3
Gently Does It 1953,O 29,43:4
Gently Does It 1953,N 8,II,1:1
Village Wooing 1956,S 5,22:6
Twelfth Night 1969,S 1,13:1
Hamlet 1970,Ag 3,37:3
Bruce, Carol
Louisiana Purchase 1940,My 29,19:2
New Priorities of 1943 1942,S 16,28:2
Show Boat 1946,Ja 7,17:2
Show Boat 1946,Ja 13,II,1:1
Show Boat 1948,S 9,33:2
Along Fifth Avenue 1949,Ja 14,28:2
Pal Joey 1954,Ap 1,40:5
Pal Joey 1954,Ap 11,II,2:1
Pal Joey 1961,Je 1,32:1
Do I Hear a Waltz? 1965,Mr 19,28:1
Do I Hear a Waltz? 1965,Mr 28,II,1:1
Henry, Sweet Henry 1967,O 24,51:2
Bruce, Carolyn
Concept, The 1968,My 7,51:1
Bruce, David K E (Mrs)
Variations of 1940 1940,Ja 29,12:1
Bruce, Donald
Eight Bells 1933,O 30,14:2
Bruce, Dorothy
Dancing Girl, The 1923,Ja 25,16:2
Bruce, Eddie
Vaudeville (Palace) 1930,F 17,18:4
Smile at Me 1935,Ag 24,18:4
Finian's Rainbow 1947,Ja 11,23:2
Finian's Rainbow 1955,My 19,25:1
Finian's Rainbow 1960,Ap 28,31:1
Bruce, Edwin
Arsenic and Old Lace 1943,D 13,18:6
Rip Van Winkle 1947,Jl 16,28:2
Survivors, The 1948,Ja 20,27:2
Cafe Crown 1964,Ap 18,32:1
Bruce, Elizabeth
Little Accident 1928,O 10,32:3
Honeymoon 1932,D 24,11:2
By Your Leave 1934,Ja 25,15:3
Bruce, Eve
After the Angels 1961,F 11,27:5

Bruce, George Ritner
Oh Captain! 1958,F 5,21:2
Bruce, H Langdon
Trial of Joan of Arc, The 1921,Mr 28,8:2
Billeted 1922,My 10,22:4
Dancers, The 1923,O 18,17:2
Me 1925,N 24,28:1
Perfect Alibi, The 1928,N 28,24:2
Lady With a Lamp, The 1931,N 20,27:2
Late One Evening 1933,Ja 10,27:3
Bruce, Herbert
Thumbs Down 1923,Ag 7,20:1
Bruce, Hilda
Street Scene 1929,Ja 11,20:4
All Good Americans 1933,D 6,29:2
Run Sheep Run 1938,N 4,26:2
Fifth Column, The 1940,Mr 7,18:2
Fifth Column, The 1940,Mr 17,X,1:1
Bruce, James
Man on Stilts, The 1931,S 10,23:2
Bruce, Judith
Kiss Me, Kate 1970,D 26,10:4
Bruce, Katherine
Rimers of Eldritch, The 1967,F 21,53:1
Bruce, Kenneth F
Marshall 1930,My 10,25:1
Bruce, Langdon
Woman of Bronze, The 1920,S 8,9:2
Shanghai Gesture, The 1926,F 2,20:2
Bruce, Lydia
Twelfth Night 1957,Ja 5,12:2
Call on Kuprin, A 1961,My 26,29:3
Call on Kuprin, A 1961,Je 4,II,1:1
Night Is Black Bottles, The 1962,D 5,56:1
Rate of Exchange 1968,Ap 2,50:1
Bruce, Marie
Samson and Delilah 1920,N 18,18:1
Claw, The 1921,O 18,20:1
Close Harmony 1924,D 2,23:1
In a Garden 1925,N 17,29:1
Paris Bound 1927,D 28,26:3
These Days 1928,N 13,36:2
Channel Road, The 1929,O 18,24:2
Tomorrow and Tomorrow 1931,Ja 14,26:3
Strangers at Home 1934,S 15,20:5
Spring Dance 1936,Jl 7,22:2
Spring Dance 1936,Ag 26,17:4
Bruce, Mariel
Many Waters 1929,S 26,27:1
Bruce, Nigel
This Was a Man 1926,N 24,27:1
Letter, The 1927,Mr 27,VII,2:6
Dishonored Lady 1930,My 25,IX,2:4
Colonel Satan 1931,Ja 18,I,28:6
Lean Harvest 1931,O 14,26:3
Springtime for Henry 1931,D 10,29:2
Springtime for Henry 1932,Ja 10,VIII,1:1
This Inconstancy 1933,Ap 16,IX,1:3
Virginia 1937,S 3,13:2
Virginia 1937,O 5,29:1
Knights of Song 1938,O 18,29:2
We Were Dancing; Tonight at Eight 1940,Ag 6,15:3
Tonight at 8:30 1940,Ag 11,IX,11:2
Bruce, Norman (Playwright)
All for All 1943,S 30,25:2
Bruce, Richard (Lyricist)
Girl in the Spotlight, The 1920,Jl 13,9:3
Bruce, Richard (Playwright)
Girl in the Spotlight, The 1920,Jl 13,9:3
Bruce, Robert
Murder in the Cathedral 1936,Mr 21,13:5
Elizabeth Sleeps Out 1936,Ap 21,27:6
Class of '29 1936,My 16,10:3
It Can't Happen Here 1936,O 28,30:1
Hero Is Born, A 1937,O 2,18:6
Enemy of the People, An 1958,F 26,24:2
Bruce, Solomon
Salome 1923,My 8,22:2
Chip Woman's Fortune, The 1923,My 8,22:2
Comedy of Errors, The 1923,My 16,22:5
Bruce, Thomas
Fantasticks, The 1960,My 4,55:2
Bruce, Virginia
America's Sweetheart 1931,F 11,23:1
Bruce, William
Bells, The 1926,Ap 14,20:3
Bruce Johnson's Washboard Serenaders
Singin' the Blues 1931,S 17,21:3
Brucken, Hugo
Wonder Bar, The 1931,Mr 18,23:4
Bruckmans, The (Costume Designer)
Grand Duchess 1929,D 17,29:2
Bruckner, Ferdinand (Original Author)
Elizabeth of England 1931,O 18,VIII,1:3
Bruckner, Ferdinand (Playwright)
Verbrecher, Die 1928,D 23,VIII,4:1
Criminals 1929,D 29,VIII,2:6
Timon 1932,Mr 6,VIII,2:1
Gloriana 1938,N 26,18:4
Criminals, The 1941,D 22,24:3
Nathan the Wise 1942,Mr 12,25:4
Nathan the Wise 1942,Ap 4,18:4
Nathan the Wise 1944,F 22,26:3

Bruckner, Ferdinand (Theodor Tagger) (Playwright)
Kreatur, Die 1930,My 25,IX,1:8
Elisabeth von England 1930,D 14,IX,4:1
Bruder, Patricia
Sap of Life, The 1961,O 3,44:1
Bruder, Patsy
Lace on Her Petticoat 1951,S 5,40:3
King and the Duke, The 1955,Je 2,25:2
Livin' the Life 1957,Ap 29,20:1
Brudern, Gerd
Ratten, Die 1966,Ap 13,36:1
Brudick, William (Choreographer)
Romeo and Juliet 1965,Je 21,36:3
Bruenberg, Jacques
Tidings Brought to Mary, The 1922,D 25,20:1
Bruening, Muriel
Sweethearts 1947,Ja 22,31:2
Bruhl, George (Playwright)
Ride a Cock Horse 1937,Ap 4,II,9:7
Bruises, The
It Happens on Ice 1940,O 11,24:3
It Happens on Ice 1941,Ag 31,IX,1:1
Icetime 1946,Je 21,20:5
Icetime 1947,My 29,28:2
Howdy, Mr Ice of 1950 1949,My 27,24:2
Hollywood Ice Revue 1954,Ja 15,16:2
Hollywood Ice Revue 1955 1955,Ja 14,16:1
Hollywood Ice Revue 1956,Ja 13,17:1
Bruk, Shimon
Dybbuk, The 1948,My 3,26:3
Bruk, Shlomo
Dybbuk, The 1948,My 3,26:3
David's Crown 1948,My 10,26:2
Golem, The 1948,My 17,22:3
Oedipus Rex 1948,My 24,23:2
Bruland, Ragnhilde (Playwright)
Furnished Rooms 1934,My 30,14:6
Brule, Andre
Notre Amour 1926,O 31,VIII,2:4
Amants 1928,Mr 4,IX,4:5
Danseur Inconnu, Le 1928,S 23,IX,2:1
IIIe Chambre, La 1929,N 24,X,2:1
Untitled-Play 1932,Ja 31,VIII,3:1
Avril 1932,O 16,IX,2:2
Brumaire, Marcel (Playwright)
Untitled-Play 1935,O 27,IX,2:1
Brummer, Andrew
Blue Butterfly, The 1929,F 17,29:3
Brummer, Delford (Lighting Director)
Now I Lay Me Down to Sleep 1949,Jl 23,7:3
Brummit, Houston (Producer)
Raisin' Hell in the Son 1962,Jl 3,13:2
Bruncati, Ron (Miscellaneous)
Mister Roberts 1962,O 12,27:2
Cradle Will Rock, The 1964,N 9,40:4
Master Builder, The 1968,Je 22,26:1
Merton of the Movies 1968,S 26,62:1
Brundin, Bo
Infantry, The 1966,N 15,51:1
Brune, Gabrielle
Two Bouquets, The 1938,Je 1,19:2
Brune, Phoebe
Song of the Flame 1925,D 31,10:2
Bruner, Jerome
Her Family Tree 1920,D 28,9:2
Bruner, Julia
House of Remsen 1934,Ap 3,26:4
Brunet, Andrew
City of Kings 1949,F 18,27:2
Brunetti, Arturo
In Fondo Al Cuore; Depths of the Heart, The
1930,D 8,27:1
Brunetti, Primo
Barbara 1929,N 18,24:5
Gli Spettri 1930,D 22,16:4
Cardinale, Il; Cardinal, The 1931,Ja 12,24:2
Delitto e Castigo; Crime and Punishment
1931,Ja 26,20:5
Bruni, Peter
Littlest Circus, The 1959,D 26,5:6
Bruning, Albert
Wandering Jew, The 1921,O 27,22:1
Back to Methuselah (Part II: The Gospel of the
Brothers Barnabas); Gospel of the Brothers
Barnabas, The (Back to Methuselah, Part II)
1922,F 28,17:2
Back to Methuselah (Part IV: The Tragedy of an
Elderly Gentleman); Tragedy of an Elderly
Gentleman, The (Back to Methuselah, Part IV)
1922,Mr 7,11:1
Merchant of Venice, The 1922,D 22,13:1
Pasteur 1923,Mr 13,19:1
School for Scandal, The 1923,Je 5,24:3
Launzi 1923,O 11,16:3
Saint Joan 1923,D 29,8:4
Saint Joan 1924,Ja 6,VII,1:1
Red Falcon, The 1924,O 8,22:1
Don't Bother Mother 1925,F 4,18:2
Caesar and Cleopatra 1925,Ap 14,27:1
Hamlet 1925,O 12,19:2
Hamlet 1925,N 22,VIII,1:1
Goat Song 1926,Ja 26,18:1
Goat Song 1926,F 7,VII,1:1

Climax, The 1926,My 18,29:3
Juarez and Maximilian 1926,O 12,31:1
Ladder, The 1927,O 7,24:2
Caste 1927,D 24,8:1
Napoleon 1928,Mr 9,21:1
Outsider, The 1928,Ap 10,32:2
Crashing Through 1928,O 30,26:5
Bruning, Alfred
Regina 1949,N 1,32:2
Bruning, Francesca
One Sunday Afternoon 1933,F 16,23:5
One Sunday Afternoon 1933,Mr 19,IX,1:1
Amourette 1933,S 28,25:2
House of Remsen 1934,Ap 3,26:4
Spring Freshet 1934,O 5,28:3
Cat and the Canary, The 1935,Jl 9,24:4
Berkeley Square 1935,Ag 20,25:1
Remember the Day 1935,S 26,19:3
Remember the Day 1935,O 13,IX,1:1
Sun Kissed 1937,Mr 11,20:2
Escape This Night 1938,Ap 23,18:1
Bright Rebel 1938,D 28,24:2
Junior Miss 1941,N 19,28:2
Brunius, Pauline
Henry VIII 1930,Jl 13,VIII,2:1
Dear Octopus 1939,N 12,IX,2:5
Brunjes, Hank
West Side Story 1957,S 27,14:4
Mutilated, The 1966,F 23,42:1
Brunn, Francis
Liberace's Variety Bill 1957,Ap 22,29:5
At Home at the Palace 1967,Ag 1,23:1
Brunner, Cecil
Tell Me More 1925,Ap 14,27:3
Brunner, Willis
Make Mine Manhattan 1948,Ja 16,26:2
Bruno, George
New Moon, The 1944,My 18,16:2
Bruno, Jean
Mother Said No 1951,Ap 17,34:2
Beg, Borrow or Steal 1960,F 11,39:4
Midgie Purvis 1961,F 2,25:3
Minnie's Boys 1970,Mr 27,27:1
Trelawny of the 'Wells' 1970,O 12,48:1
Trelawney of the 'Wells' 1970,O 25,II,16:1
Bruno, Luis
Evensong 1933,F 1,13:4
Bruno, Pierrette
Marius 1956,F 6,27:4
Bruno, Stella
Mother Martyr 1935,Ja 28,10:3
Brunot
Roi Dagobert, Le 1926,N 14,VIII,2:1
Belle Mariniere, La 1929,D 8,X,2:2
Brunoy, Blanchette
Nationale 6 1935,N 24,IX,3:7
Bruns, Jack
Hit the Deck! 1927,Ap 26,32:1
Rosalie 1928,Ja 11,26:3
Flying High 1930,Mr 4,24:4
Gang's All Here, The 1931,F 19,21:3
Bruns, John B
Little Theatre Tournament; Shall We Join the
Ladies? 1929,My 9,34:3
Shall We Join the Ladies? 1929,My 12,28:3
Rogues and Vagabonds 1930,My 8,32:5
Bruns, Julia
Beware of Dogs 1921,O 4,10:1
Bruns, Loran (Lighting Director)
Hamlet 1970,O 19,51:1
Bruns, Mona
Praying Curve 1927,Ja 25,18:2
Wednesday's Child 1934,Ja 17,23:2
Born Yesterday 1946,F 5,18:2
Bruns, Philip
Merry Wives of Windsor, The 1954,F 17,27:1
Cock-A-Doodle Dandy 1955,N 4,26:5
Servant of Two Masters, The 1958,F 11,35:2
Jack 1958,Je 4,39:2
Bald Soprano, The 1958,Je 4,39:2
Come Play With Me 1959,My 1,33:5
Dr Willy Nilly 1959,Je 5,18:2
Shepherd's Chameleon, The 1960,N 30,41:1
Mr Simian 1963,O 22,44:1
Deputy, The 1964,F 27,26:1
Square in the Eye 1965,My 20,54:1
Butter and Egg Man, The 1966,O 18,49:1
Spitting Image 1969,Mr 3,28:1
Henry V 1969,N 11,43:1
Blood Red Roses 1970,Mr 23,48:1
Moths, The 1970,My 12,46:1
Dream Out of Time, A 1970,N 9,52:1
Brunsma, Donna (Musical Director)
John Brown's Body 1964,Je 29,33:1
Brunswick, Charles
Othello 1937,Ja 7,16:4
Brush, Albert (Lyricist)
Galileo 1947,D 8,34:2
Brush, C E III
It's the Valet 1933,D 15,25:4
Brush, C E III (Scenic Designer)
It's the Valet 1933,D 15,25:4

Brush, Helen (Director)
Nine Till Six 1936,Mr 14,10:3
Brusher, Betty
Magdalena 1948,S 21,31:2
Brusiloff, Nat
Vaudeville (Palace) 1932,Ag 1,11:5
Bruskin, Perry
Young Go First, The 1935,My 29,16:2
Revolt of the Beavers, The 1937,My 21,19:2
Dance Night 1938,O 15,20:5
Medicine Show 1940,Ap 13,20:6
Of V We Sing 1942,F 16,20:3
Make Mine Manhattan 1948,Ja 16,26:2
Grand Prize, The 1955,Ja 27,17:1
Bruskin, Perry (Director)
Hostage, The 1961,D 13,55:4
Billy Liar 1965,Mr 18,26:1
Me and Thee 1965,D 8,58:4
Perfect Party, The 1969,Mr 21,42:1
Little Boxes; Trevor 1969,D 4,71:2
Little Boxes; Coffee Lace, The 1969,D 4,71:2
Bruskin, Perry (Miscellaneous)
Warm Peninsula, The 1959,O 21,46:2
Hostage, The 1960,S 21,42:1
Beauty Part, The 1962,D 28,5:2
Foxy 1964,F 17,26:1
Paisley Convertible, The 1967,F 13,42:1
Brussing, Louis
Naked Man, The 1935,Jl 2,24:3
Brustein, Robert
Shoemaker's Prodigious Wife, The 1949,Je 15,38:2
Brustein, Robert (Director)
Don Juan 1970,My 26,32:1
Story Theater Repertory; Gimpel the Food
1970,O 21,40:1
Story Theater Repertory; Saint Julian the
Hospitaler 1970,O 21,40:1
Revenger's Tragedy, The 1970,D 2,58:1
Revenger's Tragedy, The 1970,D 6,II,5:1
Brustein, Robert (Producer)
Don Juan 1970,My 31,II,1:6
Bruyez, Rene (Playwright)
Puissance des Mots, La 1928,F 12,VIII,1:3
Bruzovna, Halina
Mandarin, The 1920,N 10,18:2
Bruzzichelli, Aldo (Director)
Maids, The 1963,N 15,29:1
Sunset 1966,My 13,34:1
Bry, Richard J
Watched Pot, The 1933,My 5,13:7
Bry, Sydelle
Devil's Little Game, The 1932,Ag 2,20:4
Bryan, Al (Lyricist)
Century Revue and the Midnight Rounders, The
1920,Jl 13,9:1
Night in Spain, A 1927,My 4,28:2
Bryan, Baron
Goat Alley 1927,Ap 21,24:3
Bryan, Bill
Let's Laugh Again 1937,Ag 24,24:5
Bryan, Buddy
Kismet 1965,Je 23,45:1
Bryan, C D B (Composer)
Political Party, A 1963,S 27,17:5
Bryan, C D B (Lyricist)
Political Party, A 1963,S 27,17:5
Bryan, C D B (Playwright)
Political Party, A 1963,S 27,17:5
Bryan, Dora
They Don't Grow on Trees 1968,D 7,63:1
Alchemist, The 1970,Ag 26,36:1
Bryan, Douglas
Biography 1938,Ag 3,14:7
Bachelor Born 1938,Ag 17,23:1
Bryan, Frances
Best Foot Forward 1941,O 2,28:2
Bryan, Frederic A
Damn the Tears 1927,Ja 22,11:1
Wall Street 1927,Ap 21,24:4
Bryan, Gertrude
Sitting Pretty 1924,Ap 9,24:2
Way of the World, The 1924,N 18,23:4
Flight 1929,F 19,22:3
Queen Bee 1929,N 13,25:1
Bryan, Jack
Finian's Rainbow 1955,My 19,25:1
Bryan, James Orr
Sun-Up 1929,F 19,22:6
Bryan, John
Merchant of Venice, The 1930,N 23,IX,1:3
Merchant of Venice, The 1931,N 17,31:1
Julius Caesar 1931,N 18,26:3
Hamlet 1931,N 19,26:6
Passionate Pilgrim, The 1932,O 20,24:3
Bryan, Joseph 3d (Lyricist)
Samarkand 1926,D 22,24:4
Bryan, Kathleen
Laugh Parade, The 1931,N 3,31:2
Bryan, Tom
Her Family Tree 1920,D 28,9:2
Vaudeville (Palace) 1924,F 12,20:2
Bryan, Virginia
Meet the People 1940,D 26,22:2

Bryan, Warren
  Lilly Turner 1932,S 20,26:1
  Little Ol' Boy 1933,Ap 25,15:5
  Good, The 1938,O 6,27:2
Bryan, Winsor
  According to Law 1944,Je 2,20:3
Bryant, Ben
  Hang Down Your Head and Die 1964,O 19,38:1
  Cradle Will Rock, The 1964,N 9,40:4
  Pousse-Cafe 1966,Mr 19,19:2
Bryant, Betty
  Ten Nights in a Barroom 1932,Ja 21,17:1
Bryant, Billy
  Ten Nights in a Barroom 1932,Ja 21,17:1
Bryant, Billy (Producer)
  Hamlet 1932,N 13,IX,3:8
Bryant, Charles
  Dagmar 1923,Ja 23,18:2
  And So to Bed 1927,N 10,23:1
  Dark Hours, The 1932,N 15,24:2
  Lady Refuses, The 1933,Mr 8,18:6
  Richard of Bordeaux 1934,F 15,16:2
  Distaff Side, The 1934,S 26,17:2
  If This Be Treason 1935,Jl 30,17:1
  If This Be Treason 1935,S 24,28:2
  Forbidden Melody 1936,N 3,33:1
  Yes, My Darling Daughter 1937,F 10,19:2
Bryant, Charles (Director)
  Right to Kill, The 1926,F 16,22:2
Bryant, Charles (Producer)
  Right to Kill, The 1926,F 16,22:2
Bryant, Doris
  Very Wise Virgin, A 1927,Je 3,25:3
Bryant, Frances
  He and She 1920,F 13,16:3
Bryant, Frances (Playwright)
  Adrienne 1923,My 29,10:4
Bryant, Geoffrey
  Bedfellows 1929,Jl 3,19:2
  Wiser They Are, The 1931,Ap 7,31:1
  Caught Wet 1931,N 5,29:1
  Here Today 1932,S 7,14:2
  Here Today 1932,S 18,IX,1:1
  Party's Over, The 1933,Mr 28,23:3
  Ceiling Zero 1935,Ap 11,26:2
  Stick-in-the-Mud 1935,D 2,18:2
  Auntie Mame 1956,N 1,47:2
  Visit, The 1960,Mr 9,38:3
  Conquering Hero, The 1961,Ja 17,40:2
Bryant, George (Playwright)
  Second Comin', The 1931,D 9,32:4
  Inside Story, The 1932,F 23,23:2
  Granite Fires 1936,Jl 22,22:4
Bryant, Glenn
  Carmen Jones 1943,D 3,26:2
  Carmen Jones 1945,My 3,26:5
  Carmen Jones 1946,Ap 8,32:2
Bryant, Hugh
  Cranks 1956,My 14,23:1
  Cranks 1956,N 27,32:1
Bryant, Jean
  It Is to Laugh 1927,D 27,24:2
Bryant, John
  Hamlet 1945,D 14,25:2
Bryant, Josephine
  Ten Nights in a Barroom 1932,Ja 21,17:1
Bryant, Joshua
  And People All Around 1968,F 12,46:1
Bryant, Joyce
  Porgy and Bess 1965,Mr 6,17:1
Bryant, Leona
  Medea 1960,Jl 26,25:2
Bryant, Mardi
  I Like It Here 1946,Mr 23,8:6
Bryant, Marie
  Beggar's Holiday 1946,D 27,13:3
  Beggar's Holiday 1947,Ja 26,II,1:1
  Hello, Dolly! 1967,N 13,61:1
Bryant, Mary
  Song of Songs 1958,O 29,31:1
Bryant, Michael
  Five Finger Exercise 1959,D 3,45:4
  Five Finger Exercise 1959,D 13,II,3:1
  Duel, The 1968,Ap 18,56:1
  This Story of Yours 1968,D 14,60:4
Bryant, Mildred
  Gospel Glow 1962,O 28,87:5
Bryant, Nana
  Firebrand, The 1924,O 16,33:1
  No More Women 1926,Ag 4,17:2
  Wild Rose, The 1926,O 21,23:1
  Padre, The 1926,D 28,16:3
  Connecticut Yankee, A 1927,N 4,24:2
  Heigh-Ho, Everybody 1932,My 26,31:2
  Stork Is Dead, The 1932,S 24,18:2
  Du Barry 1932,N 23,15:2
  First Apple, The 1933,D 28,25:1
  Ship Comes in, A 1934,S 20,21:1
  Baby Pompadour 1934,D 28,24:2
  Marriage Is for Single People 1945,N 22,38:2
Bryant, Sam
  Ten Nights in a Barroom 1932,Ja 21,17:1

Bryant, Sybil
  Lulu Belle 1926,F 10,20:1
Bryant, Theodore
  Doughgirls, The 1942,D 31,19:2
Bryant, Willie
  Mamba's Daughters 1939,Ja 4,24:2
  Mamba's Daughters 1939,Ja 15,IX,1:1
  Mamba's Daughters 1940,Mr 25,10:4
  Blue Holiday 1945,My 22,13:3
Bryar, Marie
  Ruined Lady, The 1920,Ja 21,10:2
  Deburau 1920,D 24,14:3
Bryard, John
  King Lear 1940,D 16,27:2
Bryce, Ed
  Fair Game 1957,N 4,39:1
Bryce, Edward S
  Cradle Will Rock, The 1947,D 27,11:2
Bryce, Josephine
  My Girl 1924,N 25,27:2
Bryden, Eugene S (Director)
  As You Like It 1941,O 21,29:2
  Love on Leave 1944,Je 21,23:4
  Pirates of Penzance, The 1946,My 17,14:6
  If the Shoe Fits 1946,D 6,29:4
Bryden, Eugene S (Producer)
  As You Like It 1941,O 21,29:2
Brydon, W B
  Long and the Short and the Tall, The
    1962,Mr 30,28:2
  Serjeant Musgrave's Dance 1966,Mr 9,44:1
  Unknown Soldier and His Wife, The 1967,Jl 7,22:1
  Moon for the Misbegotten, A 1968,Je 13,55:2
Bryggman, Larry
  Charlatans; Summer Ghost, A 1962,Ap 27,26:1
  Stop, You're Killing Me; Terrible Jim Fitch
    1969,Mr 20,53:1
  Mod Donna 1970,My 4,48:1
Brymer (Costume Designer)
  Murder at the Vanities 1933,S 13,22:4
Brymn, Tim
  Tobias and the Angel 1937,Ap 29,16:5
Brymn, Tim (Composer)
  Put and Take 1921,Ag 24,12:3
Brymn, Tim (Director)
  Bomboola 1929,Je 27,17:3
Bryne, Barbara
  Henry VI 1966,Je 9,55:2
  Twelfth Night 1966,Je 10,51:2
  Richard III 1967,Je 14,43:1
  Government Inspector, The 1967,Je 15,55:1
  Government Inspector, The 1967,O 28,34:1
  Tartuffe 1968,Je 12,39:1
  Midsummer Night's Dream, A 1968,Je 13,54:1
  Tartuffe 1968,Je 23,II,1:1
Brynner, Roc
  Opium 1970,O 6,58:1
Brynner, Roc (Playwright)
  Opium 1970,O 6,58:1
Brynner, Vera
  Consul, The 1950,Mr 16,41:1
Brynner, Yul
  Twelfth Night 1941,D 3,32:2
  Annonce Faite a Marie, L'; Tidings Brought to
    Mary, The 1942,My 21,24:1
  Lute Song 1946,F 7,29:2
  Lute Song 1948,O 12,32:3
  King and I, The 1951,Mr 30,26:2
  King and I, The 1951,Ap 8,II,1:1
  King and I, The 1952,Ap 14,23:1
  King and I, The 1952,O 5,II,1:1
Bryon, Jeanette (Costume Designer)
  Critic, The 1965,Jl 26,15:2
Bryon, Lisa
  Trumpets and Drums 1969,O 13,52:1
  Macbeth 1969,D 23,25:1
Brysak, Peter (Director)
  God Is Back, Black and Singing Gospel at the
    Fortune Theater 1969,N 19,48:1
Bryson, Arthur
  Florida Girl 1925,N 3,34:1
  Woof, Woof 1929,D 26,20:4
  Hot Rhythm 1930,Ag 22,18:5
Bryson, Claibourne
  Earl Carroll's Vanities 1930,Jl 2,28:3
  Madwoman of Chaillot, The 1950,Je 14,41:2
Bryson, Fern
  Orpheus in Hades 1930,D 16,30:1
Bryson, Frances
  Legend of Leonora, The 1926,My 1,10:1
Bryson, Kendall
  Oh, Herbert! 1945,Je 20,26:3
Bryson, Ralph
  Runnin' Wild 1923,O 30,17:3
Bryson, Sidney
  Daughters of Atreus 1936,O 15,33:1
Bryson, Tom (Miscellaneous)
  Three to Make Ready 1946,Mr 8,16:2
Bryson and Jones
  Vaudeville (Palace) 1926,O 26,24:2
Brzozowski, Stanislaw
  Kernel and the Shell, The 1965,Ja 6,32:1
  Post Office, The 1965,Ja 6,32:1

Brzozowski, Stanislaw—Cont
  Jacob and the Angel 1965,Ja 6,32:1
  Book, The 1965,Ja 6,32:1
  Nightmare, The 1965,Ja 6,32:1
  Jaselka 1965,Ja 6,32:1
  Labyrinth, The 1965,Ja 6,32:1
  Woman, The 1965,Ja 6,32:1
Bua, Gus
  Paradise 1931,My 12,29:2
Bubbles, Jim
  Weather Clear, Track Fast 1927,O 19,24:5
Bubbles, John
  Porgy and Bess 1935,O 1,27:2
  Porgy and Bess 1935,O 11,30:2
  Virginia 1937,S 3,13:2
  Carmen Jones 1945,My 3,26:5
  Carmen Jones 1946,Ap 8,32:2
  Judy Garland 1959,My 12,40:1
  At Home at the Palace 1967,Ag 1,23:1
Buccaneers, The
  It Happens on Ice 1940,O 11,24:3
Bucci, Mark (Composer)
  New Faces of 1962 1962,F 2,25:1
Bucci, Mark (Lyricist)
  New Faces of 1962 1962,F 2,25:1
Bucci, Mark (Miscellaneous)
  New Faces of 1962 1962,F 2,25:1
  Thistle in My Bed 1963,N 20,48:1
Buccolo, Robert (Producer)
  Clandestine on the Morning Line 1961,O 31,28:1
  Thistle in My Bed 1963,N 20,48:1
  Caretaker, The 1964,Ja 31,16:1
Buch, Rene (Director)
  Pericas, Las 1969,N 2,86:5
Buchan, John (Miscellaneous)
  Savonarola Brown 1930,F 26,22:3
Buchan, Peter
  Cyrano de Bergerac 1953,N 13,24:3
Buchan, Peter Kerr (Lighting Director)
  Enemies Don't Send Flowers 1957,F 20,38:1
  God Slept Here, A 1957,F 20,38:1
Buchan, Peter Kerr (Scenic Designer)
  God Slept Here, A 1957,F 20,38:1
  Enemies Don't Send Flowers 1957,F 20,38:1
Buchanan, Aleen
  Great to Be Alive! 1950,Mr 24,28:2
Buchanan, Alice
  Anathema 1923,Ap 11,16:2
  Co-Respondent Unknown 1936,F 12,24:4
Buchanan, Bonnie (Miscellaneous)
  How to Steal an Election 1968,O 14,56:1
Buchanan, Charles (Playwright)
  As Good as new 1930,O 19,IX,3:4
Buchanan, Frank A (Producer)
  Foolscap 1933,Ja 12,21:2
Buchanan, Harry
  Skirt, The 1921,N 8,28:1
  Spooks 1925,Je 2,16:4
Buchanan, Howard
  At the Gate of the Kingdom 1927,D 9,28:5
Buchanan, Jack
  Charlot's Revue 1924,Ja 10,18:1
  Charlot's Revue 1924,Ap 6,VIII,1:1
  Toni 1924,My 18,VII,2:8
  Charlot's Revue 1925,N 11,27:1
  Charlot's Revue 1925,N 15,VIII,1:1
  Charlot's's Revue 1925,D 27,VII,1:1
  Wake Up and Dream 1929,D 31,14:3
  Wake Up and Dream 1930,Ja 12,VIII,1:1
  Wake Up and Dream 1930,Ja 12,9:1
  Pardon My English 1932,D 11,IX,5:2
  Mr Whittington 1934,F 2,21:4
  Flying Trapeze, The 1935,Je 2,IX,2:3
  Between the Devil 1937,O 15,19:1
  Between the Devil 1937,O 24,XI,2:1
  Between the Devil 1937,D 23,24:5
  Don't Listen, Ladies 1948,D 29,16:2
Buchanan, Jack (Choreographer)
  Wake Up and Dream 1929,D 31,14:3
Buchanan, Jack (Producer)
  Flowers of the Forest 1934,N 21,23:2
  Don't Listen, Ladies 1948,D 29,16:2
Buchanan, Jane
  Once in a Lifetime 1930,S 25,22:3
  Louder, Please! 1931,N 13,26:4
  She Loves Me Not 1933,N 21,22:4
  Times Have Changed 1935,F 26,15:1
  Journey by Night, A 1935,Ap 17,26:3
  Stage Door 1936,S 29,35:1
  Stage Door 1936,O 23,26:3
  Star-Wagon, The 1937,S 30,18:5
  Star-Wagon, The 1937,O 10,XI,1:1
  Shrike, The 1953,N 26,51:2
  Winner, The 1954,F 18,34:1
  Journey of the Fifth Horse, The 1966,Ap 22,36:1
Buchanan, Larry
  Dear Judas 1947,O 6,26:4
Buchanan, Malcolm (Mrs)
  Importance of Being Earnest, The 1936,O 22,31:2
Buchanan, Pat
  Paradise 1931,My 12,29:2
Buchanan, Thompson (Director)
  Port O' London 1926,F 10,20:2

Buchanan, Thompson (Playwright)
Sporting Thing to Do, The 1923,F 20,12:2
Sporting Thing to Do, The 1923,F 25,VII,1:1
Pride 1923,My 3,22:3
Civilian Clothes 1923,Jl 26,13:2
Bluffing Bluffers 1924,D 23,17:2
Sinner 1927,F 8,20:2
Star of Bengal 1929,S 26,27:2
As Good As New 1930,N 4,37:3
Buchauer, Georg
Passion Play 1932,My 2,13:1
Büchel, Brian
Evensong 1933,F 1,13:4
Buchholz, Horst
Cheri 1959,O 13,44:1
Andorra 1963,F 11,5:5
Buchman, Harold (Playwright)
Snafu 1944,O 26,19:5
Buchman, Irving (Miscellaneous)
Girls of Summer 1956,N 20,45:1
Sin of Pat Muldoon, The 1957,Mr 14,35:1
Shadow of a Gunman, The 1958,N 21,26:1
Rivalry, The 1959,F 9,24:2
Buchman, Nachum
Oedipus Rex 1948,My 24,23:2
Dybbuk, The 1964,F 4,30:2
Each Had Six Wings 1964,Mr 12,39:1
Buchman, Sidney R (Playwright)
This One Man 1930,O 22,32:3
Storm Song 1931,Ja 4,VIII,2:2
This One Man 1933,Ap 23,X,1:3
Buchner, Georg (Playwright)
Dantons Tod 1927,D 21,28:3
Danton's Death 1928,Ja 1,VIII,1:1
Wozzeck 1928,Ap 1,IX,2:4
Death of Danton, The 1928,O 28,IX,2:1
Danton's Death 1938,N 3,26:2
Danton's Death 1938,N 13,IX,1:1
Danton's Death 1965,O 22,46:1
Danton's Death 1965,O 31,II,1:1
Wozzeck 1966,Ap 6,34:1
Buchsbaum, Molly
Professor Mamlock 1937,Ap 14,30:3
Buchter, Barry (Scenic Designer)
Thorntons, The 1956,F 15,26:1
Ivory Branch, The 1956,My 25,27:1
Buchwald, Art (Original Author)
Art of Living, The 1960,Ag 20,16:4
Buchwald, Art (Playwright)
Sheep on the Runway 1970,F 2,28:3
Sheep on the Runway 1970,F 8,II,5:5
Buchwald, Charlotte
Singing Jailbirds 1928,D 5,34:4
Buchwald, Marshall L
Bright Honor 1936,S 28,14:1
Buck, Ashley
Gold 1921,Je 2,14:2
Six Characters in Search of an Author 1922,O 31,11:2
Buck, Clara
Bridge, The 1930,My 6,33:1
Buck, Ford
Carmen Jones 1945,My 3,26:5
Carmen Jones 1946,Ap 8,32:2
Buck, Ford L
Porgy and Bess 1935,O 11,30:2
Virginia 1937,S 3,13:2
Buck, Gene
Follies 1925,Mr 11,19:2
Buck, Gene (Composer)
Ziegfeld Follies 1920,Je 23,14:1
Ziegfeld Follies 1931,Jl 2,30:5
Buck, Gene (Director)
Yours Truly 1927,Ja 26,16:5
Buck, Gene (Lyricist)
Ziegfeld Follies 1920,Je 23,14:1
Ziegfeld Follies 1921,Je 22,10:1
Ziegfeld Follies 1922,Je 6,18:2
Ziegfeld Follies 1924,Je 25,26:1
Lambs Gambol 1925,Ap 27,15:1
Follies 1925,Jl 7,24:3
No Foolin' 1926,Je 25,25:1
Take the Air 1927,N 23,28:2
Buck, Gene (Miscellaneous)
Ziegfeld Follies 1931,Jl 2,30:5
Buck, Gene (Playwright)
Ziegfeld Follies 1920,Je 23,14:1
No Foolin' 1926,Je 25,25:1
Take the Air 1927,N 23,28:2
Ziegfeld Follies 1931,Jl 2,30:5
Buck, Gene (Producer)
Yours Truly 1927,Ja 26,16:5
Take the Air 1927,N 23,28:2
Ringside 1928,Ag 30,13:2
Buck, Helen
She Loves Me Not 1933,N 21,22:4
Hide and Seek 1934,Ag 7,20:2
Say When 1934,N 9,24:2
Buck, Herb
Immaculate Misconception, The 1970,O 28,63:3
Buck, Joe
Weather Clear, Track Fast 1927,O 19,24:5

Buck, John Jr
Oresteia 1966,Je 30,29:1
Buck, Pearl S (Lyricist)
Christine 1960,Ap 29,27:1
Buck, Pearl S (Original Author)
Good Earth, The 1932,S 25,IX,1:6
Good Earth, The 1932,O 18,23:4
Good Earth, The 1932,O 23,IX,1:1
Buck, Pearl S (Playwright)
Flight Into China 1939,S 12,28:1
First Wife, The 1945,N 28,21:5
Desert Incident, A 1959,Mr 25,40:1
Christine 1960,Ap 29,27:1
Buck, Richard
If Five Years Pass 1962,My 11,37:1
Cyrano de Bergerac 1968,Ap 26,30:1
Brightower 1970,Ja 29,32:1
Buck and Bubbles
Vaudeville (Palace) 1928,S 18,34:6
Vaudeville (Palace) 1928,S 25,29:4
Vaudeville (Palace) 1929,D 2,28:6
Lew Leslie's Blackbirds of 1930 1930,O 23,34:5
Dance of Death, The 1932,Ja 11,29:5
Vaudeville (Loew's State) 1932,Jl 18,9:7
Laugh Time 1943,S 9,35:2
Carmen Jones 1946,Ap 14,II,1:2
Buckar, Elsie
Veronica's Veil 1930,Mr 10,14:3
Buckhantz, Allan A (Director)
Happy Town 1959,O 8,49:2
Buckhantz, Allan A (Producer)
Happy Town 1959,O 8,49:2
Bucklee, Roy
Taming of the Shrew, The 1921,My 12,20:2
Merchant of Venice, The 1921,My 14,10:4
Abraham; Dulcitus; Callimachus 1926,Mr 29,24:2
My Country 1926,Ag 10,19:1
Decision 1929,My 28,37:3
Buckler, Henry
Imaginary Invalid, The 1922,Jl 26,26:2
Man Who Died Twice, The 1925,D 14,19:1
Dream Play 1926,Ja 21,18:2
Bells, The 1926,Ap 14,20:3
Witch, The 1926,N 19,22:5
Master of the Revels 1935,Ag 14,16:2
This Our House 1935,D 12,33:3
American Holiday 1936,F 22,13:3
Moroni 1936,Ag 19,19:1
Prologue to Glory 1938,Mr 18,22:2
Buckler, Hugh
Lesson in Love, A 1923,S 25,10:1
Schweiger 1926,Mr 24,20:4
Two Orphans, The 1926,Ap 6,26:2
Ladder, The 1926,O 23,15:1
Say It With Flowers 1926,D 6,29:1
Strange Prince, The 1926,D 8,24:2
Revolt 1928,N 1,25:3
Wings Over Europe 1928,D 11,35:1
Chinese O'Neill 1929,My 23,27:1
Arms and the Man 1929,Ag 13,23:4
Elizabeth and Essex 1930,Mr 2,IX,4:7
Royal Virgin, The 1930,Mr 18,30:5
Lost Sheep 1930,My 6,33:2
Merchant of Venice, The 1930,D 3,29:2
Heat Wave 1931,F 18,14:6
Getting Married 1931,Mr 31,25:5
If Love Were All 1931,N 14,14:5
Money in the Air 1932,Mr 8,19:3
Late One Evening 1933,Ja 10,27:3
Before Morning 1933,F 10,13:4
Conquest 1933,F 20,11:3
Richard of Bordeaux 1934,F 15,16:2
Aiglon, L' 1934,N 5,22:2
Hedda Gabler 1934,D 4,22:5
Rosmersholm 1935,D 3,32:5
Buckler, John
Green Hat, The 1925,S 16,23:2
John Gabriel Borkman 1926,Ja 30,13:1
Very Wise Virgin, A 1927,Je 3,25:3
Letter, The 1927,S 27,30:1
Play Without a Name, A 1928,N 26,30:5
Chinese O'Neill 1929,My 23,27:1
Comedy of Women, A 1929,S 14,17:4
Barretts of Wimpole Street, The 1931,F 10,25:1
Electra 1932,Ja 9,21:4
Late One Evening 1933,Ja 10,27:3
Iron Flowers 1933,Je 13,22:2
Eight Bells 1933,O 30,14:2
Eight Bells 1933,N 5,IX,1:1
Richard of Bordeaux 1934,F 15,16:2
Shatter'd Lamp, The 1934,Mr 22,26:3
Buckler, Marion
Golden Days 1921,N 2,20:1
Buckles, Ann
Mrs McThing 1952,F 21,22:1
Mr Wonderful 1956,Mr 23,23:2
Pajama Game, The 1957,My 16,27:1
Buckley, Anna
George White's Scandals 1922,Ag 29,10:1
Buckley, Arthur
Lambs Gambol 1925,Ap 27,15:1
Buckley, Betty
1776 1969,Mr 17,46:2

Buckley, Betty—Cont
1776 1969,Mr 23,II,1:1
Buckley, Dorothy
Scandals 1920,Je 8,9:1
Buckley, Edwin
Ponder Heart, The 1956,F 17,14:2
Buckley, Emerson (Musical Director)
Off Your Marx 1936,Ap 2,28:2
Buckley, Floyd
No Time for Sergeants 1955,O 21,32:2
Buckley, Gerald
Shadow and Substance 1938,Ja 27,16:2
Fiddler's House, The 1941,Mr 28,27:5
Tinker's Dam 1943,Ja 29,22:2
Derryowen 1946,O 29,34:2
Faith and Prudence 1952,O 15,40:2
Buckley, Guy
Mary Rose 1920,D 23,9:2
Buckley, Hal
Not While I'm Eating 1961,D 20,37:1
Cradle Will Rock, The 1964,N 9,40:4
Love in E Flat 1967,F 14,38:1
Buckley, James
X Has No Value 1970,F 17,35:1
Buckley, Jean
Path of Flowers, The 1936,S 18,19:3
Buckley, Joseph
Blue Flame, The 1920,Mr 16,18:1
Buckley, Kay
Naked Genius, The 1943,O 22,20:5
Burlesque 1946,D 26,30:3
Sally 1948,My 7,31:2
Buckley, Lawrence J
Comforter, The 1964,O 22,42:1
Go, Go, Go, God is Dead! 1966,O 12,37:1
Buckley, Louise
Leaf and Bough 1949,Ja 22,10:2
Someone Waiting 1956,F 15,26:1
Buckley, Mabel
Last of Mrs Cheyney, The 1925,N 10,23:5
Man in Possession, The 1930,N 3,19:1
Buckley, Mary
Katja 1926,O 19,27:3
Buckley, May
Pigs 1924,S 2,22:5
These Days 1928,N 13,36:2
Tell Me Pretty Maiden 1937,D 17,33:5
Buckley, Neil
Cloudy With Showers 1931,S 2,17:5
Round-Up, The 1932,Mr 8,19:4
Buckley, Robert
If Five Years Pass 1962,My 11,37:1
Buckley, Thomas
What Price Glory 1924,S 6,14:3'
Buckley, Tom
Harlequinade 1959,F 14,15:1
Electra 1959,F 14,15:1
Buckman, Edward
Belt, The 1927,O 20,33:1
Buckman, Robert
Midsummer Night's Dream, A 1968,D 9,59:1
Buckmaster, Henry (Scenic Designer)
World's My Oyster, The 1956,Ag 10,10:4
Buckmaster, John
Call It a Day 1936,Ja 21,26:7
Call It a Day 1936,Ja 29,15:2
Call It a Day 1936,F 9,X,1:1
Oscar Wilde 1938,O 11,20:2
Lady Windermere's Fan 1946,O 15,29:2
Inspector Calls, An 1947,O 22,38:2
Caesar and Cleopatra 1949,D 22,28:2
Getting Married 1950,Je 14,41:2
Getting Married 1951,My 14,28:5
Saint Joan 1951,O 5,23:2
Saint Joan 1951,O 14,II,1:1
Bucknall, Nina
Escape Me Never! 1935,Ja 22,22:2
Buckner, Mary
Tom Sawyer 1931,D 26,15:3
Buckner, Robert
Grey Fox, The 1928,O 23,32:3
Buckner, Robert L (Playwright)
Affair of State, An 1930,N 20,30:3
Then Came the Dawn 1935,Ag 29,25:4
Primrose Path, The 1939,Ja 5,16:3
Primrose Path, The 1939,Ja 16,11:2
Buckner, Ruth
Sonya's Search for the Christmas Star 1929,D 14,24:6
Bucko, Ilona
King's Coat, The 1933,Ja 12,21:4
Buckridge, Kenneth
Flair-Flair the Idol of Paree 1935,Mr 13,16:1
Buckstone, Rowland
Deburau 1920,D 24,14:3
Twelfth Night 1921,N 1,17:1
Merchant of Venice, The 1921,N 22,17:1
Buckstone, Sally
Thespis 1953,Ja 17,13:5
Buckwalter, John
Land of Fame 1943,S 22,31:5
Angels of Anadarko 1962,O 11,47:1
Buckwalter, John (Director)
Butter and Egg Man, The 1949,Ap 29,27:1

Buckwalter, John (Miscellaneous)
From Morn Till Midnight 1948,D 7,41:6
Buckwitz, Harry (Director)
Schweik in the Second World War 1959,My 23,18:3
Bucsko, Edward
Twilight Walk 1951,S 25,25:4
Budaloni, R
Piacere Dell 'Onesta, Il 1929,Mr 25,33:1
Budberg, Moura (Translator)
Three Sisters, The 1970,F 12,30:1
Budd, Norman
As You Like It 1937,N 1,25:2
They Should Have Stood in Bed 1942,F 14,18:5
Me and Harry 1942,Ap 3,24:6
Tobacco Road 1942,S 7,34:2
Merry Widow, The 1944,O 9,17:1
As You Like It 1945,Jl 4,10:4
O'Daniel 1947,F 25,32:2
Fortunato 1956,Mr 24,15:2
Mary and the Fairy 1956,Mr 24,15:2
Merry Widow, The 1957,Ap 11,36:6
Winkelberg 1958,Ja 15,26:2
Mandragola 1958,My 29,23:2
Beyond Desire 1967,O 11,36:1
Budd, Ruth
Midnight Frolic 1920,Ag 4,7:1
Vaudeville (Palace) 1926,Jl 6,19:3
Buddecke, Minette
Leap, The 1924,My 23,16:5
Two by Two 1925,F 24,17:1
Budkin, Celia
One Woman 1931,D 14,16:4
In a Tenement House 1932,Ja 25,20:4
Pioneers 1932,F 26,22:5
Wedding Chains 1932,Mr 28,10:5
Saint and Sinners 1935,D 30,15:2
Stepsisters 1936,O 13,32:3
Of One Mother 1937,Ja 18,21:3
Parnosseh 1939,F 20,12:5
Budley, Bide (Lyricist)
Matinee Girl, The 1926,F 2,20:3
Budley, Bide (Playwright)
Matinee Girl, The 1926,F 2,20:3
Budnitsky, Gennady
Moscow Circus on Ice 1970,D 9,63:1
Buechi, Ella
Faust, Part I; Play, The 1961,F 5,27:2
Buechner, Robert
Espanola 1921,D 30,13:1
Buehler, Betty
Hippolytus 1948,N 22,25:5
Buehler, Buddy
Achilles Had a Heel 1935,O 14,20:2
Victoria Regina 1935,D 27,15:2
Merry Wives of Windsor, The 1938,Ap 15,22:3
Counsellor-at-Law 1942,N 25,17:2
Buehler, Elaine
Allegro 1952,S 18,36:3
Buell, Juliet
Ruddigore 1927,My 21,25:2
Buell, Lois
Racketty Packetty House 1931,N 7,16:1
Buell, Mabel A (Scenic Designer)
Cradle Snatchers 1932,N 17,23:2
Blackbirds 1933,D 4,22:3
Summer Wives 1936,Ap 14,18:1
Sea Legs 1937,My 19,26:5
Lew Leslie's Blackbirds of 1939 1939,F 13,12:2
Buell, Tait (Producer)
Long Days, The 1951,Ap 21,10:5
Buelow, Eda von
Song and Dance Man, The 1930,Je 17,25:5
Everyman 1941,My 9,19:2
Buetens, Stanley
Taming of the Shrew, The 1963,Mr 8,9:1
Buetens, Stanley (Composer)
Taming of the Shrew, The 1963,Mr 8,9:1
Buetens, Stanley (Miscellaneous)
Tristram 1962,O 29,36:1
Bufano, Remo
Puppets 1925,Mr 10,19:1
Retablo de Maese Pedro, El 1925,D 30,10:1
Untitled-Puppet Show 1929,Mr 4,20:4
Skin of Our Teeth, The 1942,N 19,29:5
On the Town 1944,D 29,11:4
Bufano, Remo (Costume Designer)
Alice in Wonderland 1947,Ap 13,II,1:1
Bufano, Remo (Director)
Oliver Twist 1937,F 21,II,4:4
Bufano, Remo (Miscellaneous)
Damn the Tears 1927,Ja 22,11:1
Little King; Untitled-Puppet Show 1932,My 25,23:4
Noah 1935,F 14,25:2
Androcles and the Lion 1946,D 20,29:2
Alice in Wonderland 1947,Ap 7,19:2
Rip Van Winkle 1947,Jl 16,28:2
Bufano, Remo Puppets
Cinderella; Julius Caesar's Circus 1928,D 27,26:4
Bufano, Rene
Fantastic Fricassee, A 1922,S 12,24:1
Bufano, Rocco
Happiest Millionaire, The 1956,N 21,21:3

Bufano, Rocco (Director)
Horseman, Pass By 1969,Ja 16,46:4
Bufano, Rocco (Playwright)
Horseman, Pass By 1969,Ja 16,46:4
Buffalino, Frances
Show Boat 1966,Jl 20,48:1
Buffalo, Bills
Music Man, The 1958,S 28,II,1:1
Buffett, Kenneth
Best Foot Forward 1941,O 2,28:2
What's Up 1943,N 12,24:6
Buffett, Kenny
Laffing Room Only 1944,D 25,15:4
Hold It! 1948,My 6,31:5
Buffham, Elmer
Piper, The 1920,Mr 20,14:2
Buffler, Esther
Trelawny of the 'Wells' 1970,O 12,48:1
Buffy, John (Musical Director)
As You Like It 1968,Je 24,42:3
Bufman, Zev (Miscellaneous)
Fair Game for Lovers 1964,F 11,43:2
Bufman, Zev (Producer)
Vintage '60 1960,S 13,41:1
Egg, The 1962,Ja 9,23:2
Pajama Tops 1963,Je 1,15:1
Persecution and Assassination of Marat As
    Performed by the Inmates of the Asylum of
    Charenton Under the Direction of the Marquis de
    Sade, The 1967,Ja 4,34:1
Spofford 1967,D 15,54:3
Your Own Thing 1968,Ja 15,33:1
Mike Downstairs 1968,Ap 19,35:1
Soldiers 1968,My 2,58:1
Jimmy Shine 1968,D 6,52:1
Big Time Buck White 1968,D 9,58:1
Spitting Image 1969,Mr 3,28:1
Buck White 1969,D 3,63:1
Story Theater 1970,O 27,54:1
Bugbee, Geneva
Once in a Lifetime 1962,O 30,30:1
Taming of the Shrew, The 1965,Je 24,32:2
Bugeaud, Maurice (Scenic Designer)
Evening With Shaw, An; Excerpts From Shaw
    1955,Ag 13,6:6
Evening With Shaw, An; Village Wooing
    1955,Ag 13,6:6
Fortunato 1956,Mr 24,15:2
Mary and the Fairy 1956,Mr 24,15:2
Bugge, Stein (Playwright)
Too Famous for Words 1936,My 21,19:4
Bugge, Stein (Producer)
Catiline 1936,Ja 28,14:6
Bugler, Gertrude
Tess of the d'Urbervilles 1929,Ag 18,VIII,1:3
Buh, Ronald (Musical Director)
Iolanthe 1962,Ag 8,34:2
Buhler, C H
Parson's Bride, The 1929,Ja 22,22:3
Buhler, Neal Vernon
Bright Honor 1936,S 28,14:1
Buhr, Arturo Garcia
Amor 1937,Ap 22,18:6
Todo un Hombre 1937,Ap 28,19:2
Cuando Los Hijos De Eva No Son Los Hijos De
    Adan 1937,My 1,17:4
Tierra Baja 1937,My 8,22:4
Buhrman, Bob
Power of Dreams, A 1958,Mr 11,33:1
Buka, Donald
Taming of the Shrew, The 1940,F 6,17:2
Steps Leading Up 1941,Ap 19,20:6
Bright Boy 1944,Mr 3,19:5
Helen Goes to Troy 1944,Ap 25,17:2
Sophie 1944,D 26,22:7
Live Life Again 1945,O 1,14:7
Hippolytus 1948,N 22,25:5
Adding Machine, The 1956,F 10,17:1
Firstborn, The 1957,Ja 7,29:2
Hamlet 1957,Ja 29,27:1
Buka, Donald (Miscellaneous)
Tenth Man, The 1967,N 9,54:1
Bulak, Cindi
Celebration 1969,Ja 23,55:2
Bulcock, Marjorie
Blue Butterfly, The 1929,F 17,29:3
Bulgakoff, Ivan
Lower Depths, The 1923,Ja 16,16:1
Bulgakoff, Lyoff
Cherry Orchard, The 1923,Ja 23,18:1
Three Sisters, The 1923,Ja 30,12:2
Lady From the Provinces, The 1923,F 27,14:2
Brothers Karamazov, The 1923,N 20,23:4
Ivanoff 1923,N 27,23:2
In the Claws of Life 1923,N 30,23:4
Enemy of the People, An 1923,D 4,25:1
Enough Stupidity in Every Wise Man
    1923,D 6,23:1
Uncle Vanya 1924,Ja 29,16:2
Brothers Karamazov, The 1924,My 6,25:2
Moscow Art Theatre 1924,My 13,25:2
Bulgakov, Alexander
Night Remembers, The 1934,N 28,24:3

Bulgakov, Barbara
Cricket on the Hearth, The 1925,My 29,20:2
Princess Turandot 1926,N 13,14:2
Love Is Like That 1927,Ap 19,24:1
Hot Pan 1928,F 16,14:1
Goin' Home 1928,Ag 24,23:2
Sea Gull, The 1929,Ap 10,32:2
At the Bottom 1930,Ja 10,24:3
Sea Gull, The 1930,F 26,22:2
Devil in the Mind 1931,My 2,23:2
Wonder Boy 1931,O 24,20:1
Lovely Me 1946,D 26,30:4
Bulgakov, Barbara (Director)
Escape Into Glory 1941,Mr 20,24:2
Uncle Vanya 1960,F 13,13:4
Bulgakov, Leo
Cricket on the Hearth, The 1925,My 29,20:2
Lovers and Enemies 1927,S 21,27:1
Spring Song 1927,D 22,26:3
Gods of the Lightning 1928,O 25,27:2
Street Scene 1929,Ja 11,20:4
Devil in the Mind 1931,My 2,23:2
Billy Draws a Horse 1939,D 22,14:5
Another Sun 1940,F 24,8:6
Hope for the Best 1945,F 8,14:4
Bulgakov, Leo (Director)
Princess Turandot 1926,N 13,14:2
Cherry Orchard, The 1928,N 8,26:8
Sea Gull, The 1929,Ap 10,32:2
At the Bottom 1930,Ja 10,24:3
Courtesan 1930,Ap 30,29:3
This One Man 1930,O 22,32:3
Life Line, The 1930,D 29,19:3
Devil in the Mind 1931,My 2,23:2
One Sunday Afternoon 1933,F 16,23:5
One Sunday Afternoon 1933,Mr 19,IX,1:1
Amourette 1933,S 28,25:2
Come What May 1934,My 16,23:4
Night Remembers, The 1934,N 28,24:3
Lend Me Your Ears! 1936,O 6,28:5
Prologue to Glory 1938,Mr 18,22:2
Close Quarters 1939,Mr 7,19:2
Bulgakov, Leo (Producer)
Life Line, The 1930,D 29,19:3
One Sunday Afternoon 1933,F 16,23:5
One Sunday Afternoon 1933,S 17,X,2:4
Amourette 1933,S 28,25:2
Night Remembers, The 1934,N 28,24:3
Lend Me Your Ears! 1936,O 6,28:5
Bulgakov, Michael (Playwright)
Days of the Turbins 1926,N 7,20:1
Bagrovyostrov 1928,D 16,III,3:5
Dark Red Island 1928,D 23,III,3:8
In the Days of the Turbins 1934,Mr 7,22:5
White Guard, The 1934,Ap 8,X,2:2
White Guard, The; Days of the Turbins
    1935,Mr 7,27:5
Dead Souls 1936,S 27,X,1:1
White Guard, The 1938,O 23,IX,3:1
Dead Souls 1965,F 5,34:1
Bulgakova, Varvara
Lower Depths, The 1923,Ja 16,16:1
Cherry Orchard, The 1923,Ja 23,18:1
Three Sisters, The 1923,Ja 30,12:2
Mistress of the Inn, The; Locandiera, La
    1923,N 22,16:1
In the Claws of Life 1923,N 30,23:4
Death of Pazukhin, The 1924,F 12,20:1
Bulger, Bozeman (Playwright)
Earl Carroll's Vanities 1925,Jl 7,24:1
Bulger, Harry Jr
Noose, The 1926,O 21,23:3
Bulifant, Joyce
Tall Story 1959,Ja 30,33:2
Whisper to Me 1960,N 22,38:6
There Is a Play Tonight 1961,F 16,24:2
Paisley Convertible, The 1967,F 13,42:1
Bulk, Neville (Costume Designer)
Fuente Ovejuna; Sheep Well, The 1936,My 3,II,4:1
Bull, Mildred
Sonya's Search for the Christmas Star
    1929,D 14,24:6
Bull, Peter
Escape Me Never! 1935,Ja 22,22:2
Lady's Not for Burning, The 1950,N 9,42:2
Lady's Not for Burning, The 1950,N 26,II,1:1
Luther 1963,S 26,41:1
Pickwick 1965,O 6,5:3
Black Comedy 1967,F 13,42:1
Bull, Richard
Scapegoat, The 1950,Ap 20,36:5
Bull, Roland
Measure for Measure 1954,Je 30,23:1
Taming of the Shrew, The 1954,Jl 1,22:2
Merchant of Venice, The 1955,Jl 1,13:1
Bullard, Dex
X Has No Value 1970,F 17,35:1
Bullard, R P
Take a Brace 1923,Ap 20,20:3
Bullard, Renee
Land of Smiles 1931,My 9,15:2
Buller, H G (Director)
New York to Cherbourg 1932,F 20,11:4

Buller, H G (Playwright)
New York to Cherbourg 1932,F 20,11:4
Bullett, Gerald (Playwright)
Scandal in Assyria 1939,My 28,X,2:5
Bulling, Erich (Composer)
Trumpets and Drums 1969,O 13,52:1
Bullins, Ed (Playwright)
Electronic Nigger, The 1968,Mr 9,23:2
Son, Come Home, A 1968,Mr 9,23:2
Clara's Ole Man 1968,Mr 9,23:2
How Do You Do? 1968,My 21,42:1
In the Wine Time 1968,D 22,II,7:1
Gentleman Caller, The 1969,Ap 13,II,3:3
How Do You Do? 1969,Ap 13,II,3:3
Gentleman Caller, The 1969,Ap 27,92:1
Gentleman Caller, The 1969,My 4,II,1:5
Black Quartet, A; Gentleman Caller, The
1969,Jl 31,28:1
Gentleman Caller, The 1969,Ag 3,II,1:4
Black Quartet, A 1969,S 22,36:1
Pig Pen, The 1970,My 21,47:1
Pig Pen, The 1970,My 31,II,1:6
Street Sounds 1970,O 23,32:1
Bullivant, Laurette
Congratulations 1929,My 1,28:4
Her Majesty the Widow 1934,Je 19,24:5
Bullman, Gertie
Mazel Tov, Rabbi 1938,N 28,10:4
Bullock, H Ridgely Jr (Miscellaneous)
Fallen Angels 1956,Ja 18,27:1
Bullock, H Ridgely Jr (Producer)
Hotel Paradiso 1957,Ap 12,22:2
Season of Choice 1959,Ap 14,40:1
Caligula 1960,F 17,31:1
On an Open Roof 1963,Ja 30,7:3
Bullock, Turner (Director)
Path of Flowers, The 1936,S 18,19:3
Bullock, Turner (Playwright)
Lady of Letters 1935,Mr 29,26:6
Sing for Your Supper 1939,Ap 25,18:6
Bullock, Walter (Lyricist)
Great to Be Alive! 1950,Mr 24,28:2
Bullock, Walter (Playwright)
Mr Barry's Etchings 1950,F 1,26:2
Great to Be Alive! 1950,Mr 24,28:2
Bullock, Wynne
Music Box Revue 1924,D 2,23:3
Bulman, Gertrude
Radio Girl, The 1929,O 19,22:4
Jolly Orphan, The 1929,D 23,18:6
Little Clown, The 1930,Mr 15,23:3
Mother's Son 1931,N 26,36:4
Under One Roof 1932,F 8,21:2
Wedding Chains 1932,Mr 28,10:5
Here Runs the Bride 1934,S 20,21:3
One in a Million 1934,N 17,13:2
Motel Peissi, The Contor's Kid 1934,N 29,33:3
What Girls Do 1935,Ja 14,10:4
Heaven on Earth 1935,O 8,26:2
Tevye the Dairyman 1935,O 25,25:1
Oh, You Girls! 1935,D 2,19:5
My Malkele 1937,S 20,18:6
Jewish Heart, The 1939,Ja 25,16:6
Three Men and a Girl 1939,F 6,9:3
Buloff, Joseph
Tenth Commandment, The 1926,N 18,27:1
Witch of Castile, The 1930,O 25,21:1
Uncle Moses 1930,N 29,21:3
Riverside Drive 1931,Ja 6,24:2
Man With the Portfolio, The 1931,F 12,24:6
Kibitzer, The 1931,N 7,17:3
Pleasure 1931,D 28,20:2
Under One Roof 1932,F 8,21:2
All God's Chillum Got Shoes 1932,Ap 23,11:3
Back Streets 1933,My 18,17:4
Once Upon a Time 1933,S 22,15:1
Germany Aflame 1933,O 28,20:5
He, She and the Ox 1934,F 21,22:7
Verdict, The 1934,S 22,12:5
In-Laws 1934,O 25,28:2
Jealousy 1934,D 20,31:4
60,000 Heroes 1935,Ja 28,11:5
Parnosseh 1935,F 16,8:8
Power That Builds, The 1935,Mr 9,18:4
Motke Ganef 1935,Mr 18,15:2
Kibbetzers, Inc 1935,My 13,18:5
Don't Look Now! 1936,N 4,41:3
Call Me Ziggy 1937,F 13,9:6
To Quito and Back 1937,S 21,29:1
To Quito and Back 1937,S 26,XI,3:6
To Quito and Back 1937,O 7,30:4
Man From Cairo, The 1938,My 5,26:5
Untitled-Revue 1939,Ja 16,11:3
One Sabbath Afternoon 1939,Ja 17,27:5
Topsy-Turvy 1939,F 13,12:3
Parnosseh 1939,F 20,12:5
Morning Star 1940,Ap 17,26:4
Spring Again 1941,O 28,28:3
Spring Again 1941,N 11,28:2
Oklahoma! 1943,Ap 1,27:1
Oklahoma! 1943,Ap 11,II,1:1
Whole World Over, The 1947,Mr 28,28:2
Whole World Over, The 1947,Ap 6,II,1:1

Oklahoma! 1953,S 6,II,1:1
Fifth Season, The 1954,F 25,24:5
Moonbirds 1959,O 10,13:1
Wall, The 1960,O 12,44:4
Wall, The 1960,O 23,II,1:1
Music Shop, The 1962,F 16,35:2
Vagrant, The 1962,F 16,35:2
Witch, The 1962,F 16,35:2
Indians 1969,My 27,43:1
Brothers Ashkenazi, The 1970,N 17,53:2
Buloff, Joseph (Director)
Kibitzer, The 1931,N 7,17:3
Verdict, The 1934,S 22,12:5
Jealousy 1934,D 20,31:4
60,000 Heroes 1935,Ja 28,11:5
Chains 1937,Ja 22,25:1
Mrs McThing 1952,F 21,22:1
Mrs McThing 1952,Mr 2,II,1:1
Brothers Ashkenazi, The 1970,N 17,53:2
Bultitude, Henry F
Riff-Raff 1926,F 9,18:6
Bulwer-Lytton, Edward (Sir) (Original Author)
Richelieu 1934,My 22,28:1
Bulzomi, Michael
Saint of Bleecker Street, The 1954,D 28,21:1
Bumgardner, Jim
Caine Mutiny Court-Martial, The 1953,O 14,35:1
Bumpas, Martha
Heel, The 1954,My 27,33:2
Bumstead
Adding Machine, The 1970,D 5,40:1
Bunce, Alan
First Man, The 1922,Mr 6,9:2
Roger Bloomer 1923,Mr 2,18:3
Home Fires 1923,Ag 21,12:1
Pigs 1924,S 2,22:5
Laff That Off 1925,N 3,34:2
Tommy 1927,Ja 11,36:4
Perfect Alibi, The 1928,N 28,24:2
Privilege Car 1931,Mr 4,33:1
Unexpected Husband 1931,Je 3,29:4
Life Begins 1932,Mr 29,23:2
Lambs Gambol 1932,Ap 25,18:2
Fly by Night 1933,Je 3,16:2
Tommy 1933,Ag 8,22:5
Birthright 1933,N 22,22:3
Big Hearted Herbert 1934,Ja 2,17:3
Dream Child 1934,Jl 31,20:2
Dream Child 1934,S 28,26:2
Valley Forge 1934,D 11,28:3
De Luxe 1935,Mr 6,22:2
Kind Lady 1935,Ap 24,24:5
Long Frontier, The 1935,Jl 23,24:4
Mr Shaddy 1936,Jl 15,14:4
Golden Journey, The 1936,S 16,28:6
Tell Me Pretty Maiden 1937,D 17,33:5
Run Sheep Run 1938,N 4,26:2
Copper and Brass 1957,O 18,19:2
Sunrise at Campobello 1958,Ja 31,25:1
Sunrise at Campobello 1958,F 9,II,1:1
Cook for Mr General, A 1961,O 20,39:1
Child Buyer, The 1964,D 22,35:1
Bunce, Alan (Director)
Tommy 1933,Ag 8,22:5
Bunch, T H
Humble, The 1926,O 14,22:2
Bunda, Oka
Rain 1922,N 8,18:2
Bunde, Irene
Papers 1968,D 3,54:1
Harangues, The 1970,Ja 14,42:1
Candyapple, The 1970,N 24,33:1
Bundoon, M
Such Is Life 1927,S 1,27:3
Bundsmann, Anton
Blue Peter, The 1925,Mr 25,25:3
Uncle Vanya 1929,My 25,17:1
Streets of New York, The 1931,O 7,29:1
Bride the Sun Shines On, The 1931,D 28,20:2
Bundsmann, Anton (Director)
Thunder on the Left 1933,N 1,25:2
New Faces of 1936 1936,My 20,24:5
So Proudly We Hail 1936,S 23,28:4
Big Blow 1938,O 3,11:2
Bundy, Stephen (Costume Designer)
Gondoliers, The 1962,N 16,25:2
Bundy, Stephen (Scenic Designer)
Gondoliers, The 1962,N 16,25:2
Bunim, Shmuel (Director)
Megilla of Itzik Manger, The 1968,O 10,60:1
Megilla of Itzik Manger, The 1969,Ap 21,55:1
Bunim, Shmuel (Playwright)
Megilla of Itzik Manger, The 1968,O 10,60:1
Megilla of Itzik Manger, The 1969,Ap 21,55:1
Bunin, Elinor (Miscellaneous)
In the Matter of J Robert Oppenheimer
1968,Je 7,31:1
In the Matter of J Robert Oppenheimer
1969,Mr 7,28:1
Bunin Puppets
Vaudeville (Palace) 1952,Mr 12,31:2
Vaudeville (Palace) 1952,Mr 16,II,1:1

Bunker, Eleanor
New Faces of 1936 1936,My 20,24:5
Bunker, Jennifer
Years Ago 1946,D 4,44:2
Bunker, Kenneth L
Hit the Road 1941,Ap 4,18:3
Bunker, Ralph
Minick 1924,S 25,20:1
Paolo and Francesca 1924,D 3,24:2
Move On 1926,Ja 19,30:1
Blonde Sinner, The 1926,Jl 15,21:2
Pickwick 1927,S 6,35:2
Three Waltzes 1937,D 27,10:2
Here Come the Clowns 1938,D 8,36:2
Jeannie 1940,N 13,29:2
What Big Ears! 1942,Ap 21,18:5
Beat the Band 1942,O 15,26:1
Early to Bed 1943,Je 18,16:2
Dream With Music 1944,My 19,15:2
Goodbye My Fancy 1948,N 18,35:2
Twentieth Century 1950,D 25,23:6
Paint Your Wagon 1951,N 13,32:2
Men of Distinction 1953,My 1,18:4
Reclining Figure 1954,O 8,26:5
Lady's Not for Burning, The 1957,F 22,26:2
Once More With Feeling 1958,O 22,39:1
Bunn, Alfred (Playwright)
Bohemian Girl, The 1933,Jl 28,18:5
Bunn, John T L
Sweet River 1936,O 29,30:2
Brown Sugar 1937,D 3,29:2
Conjur 1938,N 1,27:2
Bunnage, Avis
Hostage, The 1960,S 21,42:1
Bunnell, Charles
Faust 1927,Ja 4,20:1
Babbling Brookes 1927,F 26,13:2
Octoroon, The 1929,Mr 13,28:3
Bunster, Carmen
Remolienda, La; Bawdy Party 1968,F 3,20:1
Bunston, Herbert
Enchanted Cottage, The 1923,Ap 2,22:3
That Awful Mrs Eaton! 1924,S 30,27:1
Simon Called Peter 1924,N 11,20:2
Young Woodley 1925,N 3,34:1
Dracula 1927,O 6,29:1
Bunt, George
It's a Bird . . . It's a Plane . . . It's Superman
1966,Mr 30,34:1
My Fair Lady 1968,Je 14,42:1
Minnie's Boys 1970,Mr 27,27:1
Bunt, George (Choreographer)
Me and Juliet 1970,My 15,42:1
Bunting, Emma
London Calling 1930,O 20,29:1
No Questions Asked 1934,F 6,24:3
As Husbands Go 1935,Jl 2,24:3
You Can't Take It With You 1945,Mr 27,23:7
Bunyan, John (Original Author)
Pilgrim's Progress 1948,Jl 20,27:5
Bunyea, Mabel
Street Wolf, The 1929,Ja 1,61:1
Bunyea, Ninon
Silver Swan, The 1929,N 28,34:5
Stork Is Dead, The 1932,S 24,18:2
Buono, Victor
Amazing Grace 1967,D 10,82:1
Camino Real 1970,Ja 9,42:1
Buquo, Dorothy
Home Is the Hero 1945,Ja 20,16:4
Burack, Rowena
Taming of the Shrew, The 1956,Ag 11,11:2
Trojan Women, The 1957,Mr 19,42:7
Pale Horse, Pale Rider 1957,O 30,26:1
Burand, Micheiette
Far Cry, The 1924,O 1,24:1
Burani, Claude
All Good Americans 1933,D 6,29:2
Burani, Michelette
Vierge Folle, La; Foolish Virgin, The
1924,Mr 22,12:2
Pierrot the Prodigal; Enfant Prodigue, L'
1925,Mr 7,8:1
Puppets 1925,Mr 10,19:1
Trial of Mary Dugan, The 1927,S 20,33:1
Colonel Satan 1931,Ja 12,24:1
Our Wife 1933,Mr 3,13:2
All Good Americans 1933,D 6,29:2
Ode to Liberty 1935,Jl 2,24:3
Ode to Liberty 1935,Ag 6,20:3
Atout... Coeur 1936,Mr 27,25:4
Son Mari 1936,Ap 17,17:3
Heure du Berger, L'; Propitious Moment, The
1936,N 12,30:1
Martine 1936,N 26,38:2
Dejeuner d'Amoureax, Un; Lovers Breakfast, A
1936,N 26,38:2
Homme Que J'Ai Tue, L'; Man Whom I Have
Killed, The 1936,D 10,34:3
Bichon; Little Dear 1936,D 31,20:5
Curtain Call 1937,Ap 23,24:7
Time of Your Life, The 1939,O 26,26:2
Lady in Waiting 1940,Mr 28,19:1

Burani, Michelette—Cont
Candle in the Wind 1941,O 23,26:2
Men in Shadow 1943,Mr 11,16:2
Two Mrs Carrolls, The 1943,Ag 4,14:1
Duchess of Malfi, The 1946,O 16,35:2
Detective Story 1949,Mr 24,34:2
Burbage, Clarence
Cock-A-Doodle Dandy 1955,N 4,26:5
Burbage, Edward (Playwright)
Years Between, The 1942,F 7,13:2
Burbage, Henry
Lady Cristilinda, The 1922,D 26,11:2
Burbage, Madge
Yellow Sands 1927,S 12,29:3
Burbank, Daniel E
On the Level 1937,Mr 26,24:4
Burbank, Monroe (Lighting Director)
Saint's Parade 1930,N 1,23:4
Burbeck, Frank
Wheel, The 1921,Ag 30,10:1
Nest, The 1922,F 2,20:1
For All of Us 1923,O 16,19:4
Night Duel, The 1926,F 16,22:3
Yellow 1926,S 22,30:1
Burbie, Janne
Earth Between, The 1929,Mr 6,33:1
Burbridge, Douglas
Hassan 1924,S 23,23:1
Miss Julie 1927,O 30,IX,2:1
Burbridge, Edward (Scenic Designer)
Misalliance 1961,S 26,32:2
Persecution and Assassination of Marat As
Performed by the Inmates of the Asylum of
Charenton Under the Direction of the Marquis de
Sade, The 1967,Ja 4,34:1
Song of the Lusitanian Bogey, The 1968,Ja 3,52:1
Summer of the Seventeenth Doll 1968,F 21,59:1
Kongi's Harvest 1968,Ap 15,49:1
Mike Downstairs 1968,Ap 19,35:1
Daddy Goodness 1968,Je 5,37:1
Jimmy Shine 1968,D 6,52:1
Big Time Buck White 1968,D 9,58:1
God Is a (Guess What?) 1968,D 18,56:1
Does a Tiger Wear a Necktie? 1969,F 26,38:1
Spitting Image 1969,Mr 3,28:1
Does a Tiger Wear a Necktie? 1969,Mr 16,II,4:5
Malcochon 1969,Ap 2,37:1
Contribution 1969,Ap 2,37:1
String 1969,Ap 2,37:1
Man Better Man 1969,Jl 3,22:1
Reckoning, The 1969,S 5,28:1
Our Town 1969,N 28,50:1
Buck White 1969,D 3,63:1
Five on the Black Hand Side 1970,Ja 2,32:2
Steal the Old Man's Bundle 1970,My 16,30:1
Shepherd of Avenue B, The 1970,My 16,30:1
Ododo 1970,N 25,26:1
Burbridge, William
Native Ground 1937,Mr 24,28:4
Burby, Gordon
Medea 1920,Mr 23,12:2
Champion, The 1921,Ja 4,11:1
First Man, The 1922,Mr 6,9:2
Romeo and Juliet 1923,Ja 25,16:1
Pelleas and Melisande 1923,D 5,23:2
Antony and Cleopatra 1924,F 20,22:1
Depths, The 1925,Ja 28,15:3
Sex 1926,Ap 27,22:4
Connecticut Yankee, A 1927,N 4,24:2
Twelfth Night 1930,O 16,28:2
Merchant of Venice, The 1931,N 17,31:1
Julius Caesar 1931,N 18,26:3
Hamlet 1931,N 19,26:6
Parnell 1935,N 12,24:2
Parnell 1936,My 5,26:2
No More Peace 1938,Ja 29,13:2
Coriolanus 1938,F 2,14:5
Burby, Jane
Ruint 1925,Ap 8,24:2
Just Life 1926,S 15,33:3
Burce, Betty
High Kickers 1941,N 1,21:2
Burcell, Gertrude
March Hares 1921,Ag 12,8:3
Burch, Helen
Brother Elks 1925,S 15,29:2
Burch, John
Fast Life 1928,S 27,35:2
Burch, Pat (Choreographer)
Carefree Tree, The 1955,O 12,37:2
Burch, Ramsey (Director)
Old Maid, The 1949,Ja 27,20:6
Post Road 1949,Ap 28,27:3
Angels Kiss Me 1951,Ap 18,37:6
Season of the Beast 1958,Mr 14,29:2
Burch, Thayer (Producer)
Nest, The 1970,Ap 10,46:1
Burckhalter, Clark
Boy on the Straight-Back Chair 1969,Mr 18,36:1
Burckley, Arthur
Bye Bye, Barbara 1924,Ag 26,6:3
Mlle Modiste 1929,O 8,34:1
Burden, Hugh (Playwright)
To My Love 1956,Je 7,35:3

Burden, Laverne
Hooray!! It's a Glorious Day. . .And All That
1966,Mr 10,28:1
Burden, Nannie
Tobias and the Angel 1937,Ap 29,16:5
Burdett, Florence
Young Visitors, The 1920,N 30,14:1
Burdette, Glenn
Handy Man, The 1925,Mr 10,19:2
Burdette, Richard
Daughters of Atreus 1936,O 15,33:1
Burdick, Hal
Last Love of Don Juan, The 1955,N 24,40:1
Ivory Branch, The 1956,My 25,27:1
Friends and Lovers; Proposal, The 1961,My 11,43:1
Friends and Lovers; In the Zone; Bound East for
Cardiff 1961,My 11,43:1
Billygoat Eddie 1964,Ap 21,43:2
Burdick, Rose
Dreams for Sale 1922,S 14,24:1
It Is the Law 1922,N 30,28:2
Elmer Gantry 1928,Ag 10,9:4
Camel Through the Needle's Eye, The
1929,Ap 16,32:2
Birthright 1933,N 22,22:3
Between Two Worlds 1934,O 26,24:2
Burdick, William (Choreographer)
Much Ado About Nothing 1964,Je 11,26:2
As You Like It 1968,Je 24,42:3
Much Ado About Nothing 1969,Je 16,57:1
All's Well That Ends Well 1970,Je 16,53:1
Burdon, Albert
Evergreen 1930,D 21,VIII,1:6
Burdzhaloff, Giorgi
Tsar Fyodor Ivanovitch 1923,Ja 9,26:1
Lower Depths, The 1923,Ja 16,16:1
Brothers Karamazov, The 1923,N 20,23:4
Mistress of the Inn, The; Locandiera, La
1923,N 22,16:1
Ivanoff 1923,N 27,23:2
In the Claws of Life 1923,N 30,23:4
Burford, Roger (Playwright)
Jam Today 1942,Mr 1,VIII,1:3
Burge, James
Grin and Bare It 1970,Mr 17,36:1
Burge, Stuart
Venus Observed 1952,F 14,24:2
Burge, Stuart (Director)
Richard II 1964,Je 17,47:1
Henry IV, Part I 1965,Je 30,42:1
Falstaff; Henry IV, Part II 1965,Jl 1,35:1
Serjeant Musgrave's Dance 1966,Mr 9,44:1
Serjeant Musgrave's Dance 1966,Mr 20,II,1:1
Burge, Stuart (Producer)
Workhouse Donkey, The 1963,Jl 9,26:1
Ruling Class, The 1969,F 28,31:1
Burge, William H (Director)
Icetime 1946,Je 21,20:5
Burger, Eric (Playwright)
Best Man, The 1960,O 5,44:6
Fire to the Sea 1961,N 15,20:5
Burger, Eric (Translator)
Tenth Man, The 1962,O 3,46:1
Burgess, Christopher
Measure for Measure 1967,F 15,37:1
Hamlet 1967,F 17,44:1
Romeo and Juliet 1967,F 22,18:1
Burgess, Dorothy
Imaginative Girl, The 1926,Ag 8,VII,3:1
Adorable Liar, The 1926,Ag 31,15:2
Bye Bye Bonnie 1927,Ja 14,15:3
Synthetic Sin 1927,O 11,26:2
She Cried for the Moon 1935,Jl 23,24:3
Burgess, Elizabeth
All in Love 1961,N 11,15:2
Burgess, Everett (Scenic Designer)
Quiet, Please! 1940,N 9,20:3
Burgess, Gladys
If Winter Comes 1923,Ap 3,26:1
Mary, Mary, Quite Contrary 1923,S 12,14:1
Grounds for Divorce 1924,S 24,20:1
Burgess, Grace
Crooked Square, The 1923,S 11,10:2
Dancing Mothers 1924,Ag 12,12:2
Gentlemen Prefer Blondes 1926,S 29,23:1
Burgess, Grover
Roseanne 1923,D 31,9:5
Big Lake 1927,Ap 9,17:2
Much Ado About Nothing 1927,N 19,14:6
At the Gate of the Kingdom 1927,D 9,28:5
Mr Moneypenny 1928,O 17,26:2
Singing Jailbirds 1928,D 5,34:4
Earth Between, The 1929,Mr 6,33:1
War 1929,S 19,37:3
Joy of Serpents 1930,Ap 4,22:4
People on the Hill 1931,S 26,25:5
1931 1931,D 11,34:3
Night Over Taos 1932,Mr 10,25:3
Big Night 1933,Ja 18,16:2
Men in White 1933,S 27,24:2
Valley Forge 1934,D 11,28:3
Paradise Lost 1935,D 10,31:5
Case of Clyde Griffiths 1936,Mr 14,10:4

Burgess, Grover—Cont
Battle Hymn 1936,My 23,12:1
Johnny Johnson 1936,N 20,26:3
Marching Song 1937,F 18,18:2
Julius Caesar 1937,N 12,26:6
Gentle People, The 1939,Ja 6,25:1
Time of Your Life, The 1939,O 26,26:2
Time of Your Life, The 1940,S 24,27:2
Land Is Bright, The 1941,O 29,26:2
Comes the Revelation 1942,My 27,26:2
Eve of St Mark, The 1942,O 8,30:2
Petrified Forest, The 1943,N 2,30:6
Take It As It Comes 1944,F 11,17:2
For Keeps 1944,Je 15,17:5
Man Who Had All the Luck, The 1944,N 24,18:5
Jeb 1946,F 22,20:2
Mr Peebles and Mr Hooker 1946,O 11,29:2
For Love or Money 1947,N 5,36:2
Burgess, Hazele
Tantrum, The 1924,S 5,20:2
Judy Drops In 1924,O 6,24:2
Appearances 1925,O 15,27:3
Flamingo Road 1946,Mr 20,18:2
Burgess, Joan
Gay Divorce 1932,N 30,23:4
Burgess, John
As You Like It 1945,Jl 4,10:4
Burgess, John (Miscellaneous)
As You Like It 1945,Jl 4,10:4
Burgess, John (Playwright)
Chicago/Conspiracy 1970,Ag 26,35:1
Burgess, John (Producer)
As You Like It 1945,Jl 4,10:4
Burgess, Lee
Overture 1930,D 8,26:4
Venetian Glass Nephew, The 1931,F 24,26:3
Burgess, Mary
Yeomen of the Guard, The 1964,Mr 19,29:2
Mikado, The 1965,Ap 17,11:3
Pirates of Penzance, The 1965,Ap 21,50:6
Yeomen of the Guard, The 1965,Ap 22,26:1
Mikado, The 1968,My 2,59:1
Yeomen of the Guard, The 1968,My 9,53:1
Patience 1968,My 16,52:1
Burgess, Maynard
Gods of the Lightning 1928,O 25,27:2
One Way Street 1928,D 25,31:2
Sea Gull, The 1929,Ap 10,32:2
Penal Law 2010 1930,Ap 19,14:2
Forest Ring, The 1930,Ap 26,11:2
Burgess, Neil
Creoles 1927,S 23,33:3
Burgess, Paul
Age and Grace 1956,F 21,38:2
Burgess, Robert
Love's Labour's Lost 1965,Je 16,46:1
Burgess, Stephen
York Nativity Play, The 1956,D 5,49:2
Burgess, Victor
Valley Forge 1934,N 27,26:4
Burgess, Walter
Salad Days 1958,N 11,24:1
Burgess, William
Mikado, The 1942,F 4,22:2
Pirates of Penzance, The 1942,F 18,22:2
Iolanthe 1942,F 24,26:4
Gondoliers, The 1942,Mr 4,22:3
Burgette, Gladys
49ers, The 1922,N 7,14:1
Jack and Jill 1923,Mr 23,17:2
Burghardt, Arthur
Universal Nigger, The 1970,Mr 21,18:1
Burgher, Fairfax
Fashions for Men 1922,D 6,22:1
Heart of Frances, The 1923,Ja 29,11:2
March Hares 1923,Mr 13,19:5
Steam Roller, The 1924,N 11,20:2
Caught 1925,O 6,31:2
House of Ussher, The 1926,Ja 14,18:4
Strange Prince, The 1926,D 8,24:2
Road to Rome, The 1927,F 1,24:2
Plutocrat, The 1930,F 21,23:3
Mr Samuel 1930,N 11,28:4
Moroni 1936,Ag 19,19:1
Barber Had Two Sons, The 1943,F 2,22:2
Lunatics and Lovers 1954,D 14,44:2
Burghoff, Gary
You're a Good Man, Charlie Brown 1967,Mr 8,51:1
Burgi, Richard T
Oedipus Tyrannus 1941,My 10,13:8
Burgie, Irving (Composer)
Ballad for Bimshire 1963,O 16,54:1
Burgie, Irving (Lyricist)
Ballad for Bimshire 1963,O 16,54:1
Burgie, Irving (Playwright)
Ballad for Bimshire 1963,O 16,54:1
Burgin, Jon (Producer)
Once for the Asking 1963,N 21,42:2
Burgos, Edilberto G
To Quito and Back 1937,O 7,30:4
Burgos, Robert
Golden Streets, The 1970,Ag 14,21:1
Burgos, Robert (Miscellaneous)
Open 24 Hours 1969,F 12,31:1

Burgos, Robert (Miscellaneous)—Cont
Satisfaction Guaranteed 1969,F 12,31:1
Candyapple, The 1970,N 24,33:1
Burgos, Santiago
And the Wind Blows 1959,Ap 29,28:1
Burgoyne, Olga
Run, Little Chillun! 1933,Mr 2,21:3
Places, Please 1937,N 13,10:6
Burgoyne, Olive
Lady Lies, The 1928,N 27,36:2
Solitaire 1929,Mr 13,28:3
Budget, The 1932,S 21,26:4
Dance With Your Gods 1934,O 8,14:3
Burgoyne, Ollie
Lulu Belle 1926,F 10,20:1
Tired Business Man, The 1929,Je 5,32:5
Make Me Know It 1929,N 5,32:5
Constant Sinner, The 1931,S 15,30:1
Blessed Event 1932,F 13,23:2
Perfumed Lady, The 1934,Mr 13,27:2
All Rights Reserved 1934,N 7,33:5
Horse Play 1937,Ag 28,8:3
Kiss the Boys Goodbye 1938,S 29,30:2
Burian, Jarka
Doctored Wife, The 1950,Jl 12,33:2
Son, The 1950,Ag 16,24:6
Burk, Francis
Kitty's Kisses 1926,My 7,12:2
Trumpet Shall Sound, The 1926,D 11,15:2
Much Ado About Nothing 1927,N 19,14:6
Doctor Knock 1928,F 24,15:2
These Days 1928,N 13,36:2
Burk, Frank
Big Lake 1927,Ap 9,17:2
Burk, Robert
Wonderful Night, A; Fledermaus, Die
1929,N 1,23:3
Burk, Robert (Composer)
Belmont Varieties 1932,S 29,17:2
Burk, Robert (Lyricist)
Belmont Varieties 1932,S 29,17:2
Burka, Petra
Holiday on Ice 1966,S 1,30:1
Burkan, May
Respectfully Yours 1947,My 14,29:4
Burke, Alexander
Calvary 1960,Jl 22,13:1
Burke, Alexander (Producer)
Devil's Little Game, The 1932,Ag 2,20:4
Burke, Amy
Borstal Boy 1970,Ap 1,38:1
Burke, Billie
Intimate Strangers, The 1921,N 8,28:1
Annie 1924,O 12,VIII,2:1
Annie Dear 1924,N 5,25:3
Pardon My Glove 1926,My 23,VIII,1:1
Marquise, The 1927,N 15,26:4
Happy Husband, The 1928,My 8,25:2
Happy Husband, The 1928,My 27,VIII,1:1
Family Affairs 1929,D 1,X,4:7
Family Affairs 1929,D 11,34:6
Truth Game, The 1930,D 29,19:1
Mad Hopes, The 1932,My 29,VIII,2:2
This Rock 1943,F 19,23:2
Mrs January & Mr Ex 1944,Ap 1,10:2
Burke, Billie (Miscellaneous)
Ziegfeld Follies 1934,Ja 5,24:3
Burke, Brendan
Happy as Larry 1961,Ap 26,36:1
Sharon's Grave 1961,N 9,39:2
Electra 1962,Mr 22,42:1
Burke, Brendan (Composer)
Happy as Larry 1961,Ap 26,36:1
Burke, C L
Born Yesterday 1946,F 5,18:2
Burke, Charles R M
Coriolanus 1927,Je 18,8:3
Burke, David
Topaze 1947,D 29,21:5
Me and Molly 1948,F 27,27:2
Seeds in the Wind 1948,Ap 26,27:2
Seeds in the Wind 1948,My 26,29:2
Hotel in Amsterdam, The 1968,Jl 21,II,12:1
Burke, Dorothy (Choreographer)
Du Barry 1932,N 23,15:2
Burke, Earl
Sweet River 1936,O 29,30:2
Burke, Edmund
Song of the Flame 1925,D 11,26:4
Song of the Flame 1925,D 20,VII,4:1
Burke, Edwin
Vaudeville (Palace) 1928,Mr 13,23:2
Burke, Edwin (Playwright)
From Eight to Twelve 1926,N 9,30:3
This Thing Called Love 1928,S 18,32:7
This Thing Called Love 1935,Jl 2,24:4
Burke, Eileen
Mr Gilhooley 1930,O 1,26:1
Burke, Elizabeth
Charlatans; On Circe's Island 1962,Ap 27,26:1
Burke, Fred J
Big Blow 1938,O 3,11:2
Burke, Georgia
Mamba's Daughters 1939,Ja 4,24:2

Mamba's Daughters 1940,Mr 25,10:4
Cabin in the Sky 1940,O 26,19:2
Sun Field, The 1942,D 10,33:2
Decision 1944,F 3,23:2
Decision 1944,My 21,II,1:1
Anna Lucasta 1944,Ag 31,15:1
Wisteria Trees, The 1950,Mr 30,39:1
Grass Harp, The 1952,Mr 28,26:2
Grass Harp, The 1952,Ap 6,II,1:1
Porgy and Bess 1953,Mr 10,25:5
Interlock 1958,F 7,18:1
Killer, The 1960,Mr 23,33:1
Mandingo 1961,My 23,43:6
Bohikee Creek 1966,Ap 29,39:1
Burke, Gerard A (Miscellaneous)
Delightful Season, A 1960,S 29,30:1
Burke, Harriette
Americana 1926,Jl 27,15:3
Burke, Hilda
Yeomen of the Guard, The 1939,Jl 16,30:4
Yeomen of the Guard, The 1939,Jl 23,IX,2:1
Burke, Jack
Catherine Was Great 1944,Ag 3,16:1
Burke, Joe (Composer)
Howdy Stranger 1937,Ja 15,17:5
Burke, John
Minute's Wait, A 1920,Je 22,9:1
Merchant of Venice, The 1920,D 30,16:2
Hamlet 1930,Mr 25,34:4
Macbeth 1930,Mr 26,24:6
Merchant of Venice, The 1930,Mr 27,24:7
Twelfth Night 1930,Mr 27,24:7
Taming of the Shrew, The 1930,Mr 28,22:8
Richard III 1930,Mr 31,24:1
King Lear 1930,Ap 1,34:6
As You Like It 1930,Ap 3,32:5
Julius Caesar 1930,Ap 4,22:3
King Lear 1930,D 26,18:2
Merchant of Venice, The 1931,N 17,31:1
Julius Caesar 1931,N 18,26:3
Hamlet 1931,N 19,26:6
If Booth Had Missed 1932,F 5,24:2
Saint Wench 1933,Ja 3,19:3
Tragedy of the Ages, The 1933,Ap 7,22:7
Mountain, The 1933,S 12,28:6
Yoshe Kalb 1933,D 29,27:2
Rip Van Winkle 1935,Ag 7,22:2
Master of the Revels 1935,Ag 14,16:2
Moroni 1936,Ag 19,19:1
Burke, Johnny
Vaudeville (Palace) 1923,Ja 30,12:2
Vaudeville (Hippodrome) 1926,Mr 16,22:2
New Priorities of 1943 1942,S 16,28:2
Burke, Johnny (Composer)
Donnybrook! 1961,My 19,23:1
Donnybrook! 1961,My 28,II,1:1
Burke, Johnny (Lyricist)
Nellie Bly 1946,Ja 22,32:2
Nellie Bly 1946,Ja 27,II,1:1
Carnival in Flanders 1953,S 9,38:2
Donnybrook! 1961,My 19,23:1
Donnybrook! 1961,My 28,II,1:1
Burke, Johnny (Producer)
Carnival in Flanders 1953,S 9,38:2
Burke, Joseph
Immoral Isabella 1927,O 28,20:3
Burke, Katherine
No Foolin' 1926,Je 25,25:1
Rio Rita 1927,F 3,18:3
Rosalie 1928,Ja 11,26:3
Whoopee 1928,D 5,34:3
Smiles 1930,N 19,19:2
Burke, Lee
Fireman's Flame, The 1937,O 11,26:2
Burke, Lynn
Mermaid's Holiday 1961,Jl 1,8:1
Burke, Mabel
Yellow Jacket, The 1923,Ap 20,20:3
Beau Brummell 1924,Ap 4,19:2
Burke, Malcolm K
Hippolytus 1935,Je 15,20:4
Burke, Marie
One 1920,S 15,12:2
Make It Snappy 1922,Ap 14,20:2
Lady in Ermine, The 1922,O 3,22:2
Nancy Ann 1924,Ap 1,18:1
American Tragedy, An 1931,F 21,15:5
Port Said 1931,N 22,VIII,2:1
Great Waltz, The 1934,S 24,14:4
Great Waltz, The 1935,Ag 6,20:5
Dead End 1935,O 29,17:2
Burke, Marion
Top Banana 1951,N 2,19:2
Burke, Maurice
Congai 1928,N 28,24:3
Inspector Kennedy 1929,D 21,16:3
Room of Dreams 1930,N 6,22:4
Times Have Changed 1935,F 26,16:1
Kick Back, The 1936,Je 23,27:3
It Can't Happen Here 1936,O 28,30:1
But for the Grace of God 1937,Ja 13,21:4
Chalked Out 1937,Mr 26,24:2
Everyman 1941,My 9,19:2

Burke, Maurice—Cont
In Time to Come 1941,D 29,20:2
Doughgirls, The 1942,D 31,19:2
No Way Out 1944,O 31,23:1
Up in Central Park 1945,Ja 29,17:2
Small Hours, The 1951,F 16,22:1
Burke, Melville (Director)
Her Unborn Child 1928,Mr 7,28:3
Buzzard, The 1928,Mr 15,29:1
K Guy, The 1928,O 16,28:4
Tonight at 12 1928,N 18,26:1
Precious 1929,Ja 15,22:5
Privilege Car 1931,Mr 4,33:1
Just to Remind You 1931,S 8,39:1
Church Mouse, A 1931,O 13,26:4
Adam Had Two Sons 1932,Ja 21,17:1
Collision 1932,F 17,19:2
Bulls, Bears and Asses 1932,My 7,11:3
Perfect Marriage, The 1932,N 17,23:2
Saturday Night 1933,Mr 1,13:2
Queer People 1934,F 16,16:2
All Rights Reserved 1934,N 7,33:5
Remember the Day 1935,Jl 9,24:3
Stag at Bay, The 1935,Jl 30,17:1
Little Inn, The 1935,Ag 20,25:1
Remember the Day 1935,S 26,19:3
Remember the Day 1935,O 13,IX,1:1
Room Service 1935,N 17,II,7:7
Mid-West 1936,Ja 2,21:2
Mid-West 1936,Ja 5,IX,3:1
Mid-West 1936,Ja 8,22:4
Come Angel Band 1936,F 19,17:1
Feather in the Breeze 1936,Jl 14,22:2
White Man 1936,O 19,22:4
House in the Country, A 1937,Ja 12,18:3
Two Time Mary 1937,Ag 3,20:5
Prodigal Father, The 1937,Ag 17,23:1
Love in My Fashion 1937,D 4,21:4
Off to Buffalo! 1939,F 22,18:2
Life With Father 1939,Ag 15,14:4
Sea Dogs 1939,N 7,30:3
Little Dark Horse 1941,N 17,14:4
Barber Had Two Sons, The 1943,F 2,22:2
Slightly Married 1943,O 26,19:2
Little A 1947,Ja 16,31:2
Burke, Melville (Playwright)
Her Unborn Child 1928,Mr 7,28:3
Burke, Melville (Producer)
Slightly Married 1943,O 26,19:2
Burke, Michele
Three Wishes for Jamie 1952,Mr 22,9:2
Wonderful Town 1953,F 26,22:3
Copper and Brass 1957,O 18,19:2
Boy Friend, The 1958,Ja 27,24:4
President's Daughter, The 1970,N 4,41:2
Burke, Mildred
Pirates of Penzance, The 1936,Ap 21,27:5
Burke, Orrin
World We Live In, The 1922,N 1,16:1
Padre, The 1926,D 28,16:3
Wild Duck, The 1928,N 19,17:1
Crooks' Convention, The 1929,S 19,37:4
Cross Roads 1929,N 12,34:2
Sentinels 1931,D 26,15:1
If Booth Had Missed 1932,F 5,24:2
We the People 1933,Ja 23,9:5
Mother Lode 1934,D 24,16:5
Burke, Patricia
Taming of the Shrew, The 1947,D 7,II,7:1
Burke, Patrick
Arden of Faversham 1970,F 17,33:1
Ubu Roi 1970,F 17,33:1
Burke, Patty
Wisteria Trees, The 1955,F 3,20:2
Burke, Peggy
Great Day in the Morning 1962,Mr 29,29:1
Burke, Peter
Carmen Jones 1956,Je 1,28:2
Burke, Randolph S
Laugh It Off 1925,Ap 25,18:4
Burke, Sheila
Pleasure Bound 1929,F 19,22:4
Burke, Sonny (Composer)
Alive and Kicking 1950,Ja 18,25:5
Burke, Sonny (Lyricist)
Alive and Kicking 1950,Ja 18,25:5
Burke, T Patrick (Playwright)
After the Angels 1961,F 11,27:5
Burke, Tom
Dancing Girl, The 1923,Ja 25,16:2
Vaudeville (Palace) 1923,O 23,18:2
Hassard Short's Ritz Revue 1924,S 18,19:1
Mikado, The 1925,Ap 13,25:1
Holka Polka 1925,O 15,27:2
H M S Pinafore 1926,Ap 7,26:3
Lace Petticoat 1927,Ap 5,18:2
Gay Masquerade 1935,My 15,26:1
Burke, Ulick (Playwright)
Bride, The 1931,F 22,VIII,3:5
Burke, Virginia
????? 1939,Ja 2,28:2
'Tis of Thee 1940,O 28,21:3
Burke, Wailliam H (Miscellaneous)
Stars on Ice (2d Edition) 1943,Je 25,13:2

Burke, Walter
Padlocks of 1927 1927,Jl 6,23:4
Help Yourself! 1936,Jl 15,15:1
Sun and I, The 1937,F 27,9:5
Red Harvest 1937,Mr 31,29:2
Old Foolishness, The 1940,D 21,20:2
Not in Our Stars 1941,Ap 26,20:5
World's Full of Girls, The 1943,D 7,31:2
Sadie Thompson 1944,N 17,25:2
Up in Central Park 1945,Ja 29,17:2
Up in Central Park 1947,My 20,29:2
Billy Budd 1951,F 12,18:3
Three Wishes for Jamie 1952,Mr 22,9:2
Major Barbara 1956,O 31,27:1
Burke, William
Polly 1925,O 12,19:1
Peter Pan 1954,O 21,30:2
Burke, William H (Director)
Hats Off to Ice 1944,Je 23,15:2
Howdy Mr Ice 1948,Je 25,28:5
Burke, William H (Miscellaneous)
Icetime 1947,My 29,28:2
Hollywood Ice Revue 1953,Ja 16,17:2
Hollywood Ice Revue 1954,Ja 15,16:2
Hollywood Ice Revue 1955 1955,Ja 14,16:1
Hollywood Ice Revue 1956,Ja 13,17:1
Burke, William H (Producer)
Stars on Ice 1942,Jl 3,12:2
Burke-Hennessy, Cecily
Escape Into Glory 1941,Mr 20,24:2
Burkell, John
Rose Bernd 1922,S 27,17:1
Spider, The 1927,Mr 23,29:1
Under the Gaslight 1929,Ap 3,27:1
Crooks' Convention, The 1929,S 19,37:4
Inside Story, The 1932,F 23,23:2
Burkhardt, Bob
Gentlemen Prefer Blondes 1949,D 9,35:3
Burkhardt, Harry
Kiki 1921,N 30,13:1
Honor of the Family, The 1926,D 27,21:1
Burkhart, Jack
Flies, The; Mouches, Les 1947,Ap 18,26:3
Nights of Wrath; Nuits de la Colere, Les
1947,D 1,26:4
Hamlet 1948,D 4,9:2
Iphigenie in Tauris 1949,O 22,11:2
Burko, Billie
Rose Briar 1922,D 26,11:3
Burks, Charles
Great Scot! 1965,N 12,56:3
Tiger at the Gates 1968,Mr 1,30:1
Burks, Donnie
Hair 1968,Ap 30,40:2
Hair 1969,F 5,36:1
Bill Noname 1970,Mr 3,37:1
Burks, Edgar
Green Pastures, The 1930,F 27,26:1
Burks, Hattie
Jimmie 1920,N 18,15:3
Burlar, Cora
Noah 1935,F 14,25:2
Doctor Faustus 1937,Ja 9,21:2
Burleigh, Alston
Meek Mose 1928,F 7,30:1
Run, Little Chillun! 1933,Mr 2,21:3
Jezebel 1933,D 20,26:3
Too Many Boats 1934,S 12,26:3
Burleigh, Alston (Composer)
Jezebel 1933,D 20,26:3
Dance With Your Gods 1934,O 8,14:3
Burleigh, Alston (Director)
Meek Mose 1928,F 7,30:1
Mrs Partridge Presents 1936,F 29,10:1
Burleigh, Frederick
Beware of the Bull 1933,My 30,13:7
Burleigh, Jack
Hold Your Horses 1933,S 26,26:4
Burlen, Robert
Good Fellow, The 1926,O 6,22:1
Burleson, Jim
Mother Courage and Her Children 1964,My 12,32:2
In the Matter of J Robert Oppenheimer
1968,Je 7,31:1
Burley, Douglas
Americana 1928,O 31,28:2
New Americana 1928,N 30,32:4
Burley, Jack
Fine and Dandy 1930,S 24,26:1
Storm Over Patsy 1937,Mr 9,26:4
Burling Triplets
Ice Capades 1956,S 13,41:2
Burlingame, Lloyd (Costume Designer)
Caesar and Cleopatra 1963,Ag 1,18:2
Alchemist, The 1964,S 15,33:1
Great Western Union, The 1965,F 10,45:1
Astrakhan Coat, The 1967,Ja 13,18:1
Arms and the Man 1967,Je 23,44:2
Love Is a Time of Day 1969,D 23,21:3
Burlingame, Lloyd (Lighting Director)
Collection, The 1962,N 27,44:1
Dumbwaiter, The 1962,N 27,44:1
Lady of the Camellias, The 1963,Mr 22,7:1

Blue Boy in Black, The 1963,My 1,32:1
Pimpernel! 1964,Ja 7,26:6
Secret Life of Walter Mitty, The 1964,O 27,44:5
Boeing-Boeing 1965,F 3,30:1
Right Honourable Gentleman, The 1965,O 20,50:2
Inadmissible Evidence 1965,D 1,52:1
Persecution and Assassination of Marat As
Performed by the Inmates of the Asylum of
Charenton Under the Direction of the Marquis de
Sade, First One Asleep, Whistle 1966,F 28,19:1
Help Stamp Out Marriage 1966,S 30,50:1
There's a Girl in My Soup 1967,O 19,58:1
Brief Lives 1967,D 19,60:4
Joe Egg 1968,F 2,26:1
Flip Side, The 1968,O 11,36:1
Rockefeller and the Red Indians 1968,O 25,37:1
Hadrian VII 1969,Ja 9,22:1
Love Is a Time of Day 1969,D 23,21:3
Opium 1970,O 6,58:1
Burlingame, Lloyd (Miscellaneous)
Lady of the Camellias, The 1963,Mr 22,7:1
Physicists, The 1964,O 14,52:1
Burlingame, Lloyd (Scenic Designer)
Leave It to Jane 1959,My 26,30:2
Answered the Flute 1960,Mr 10,37:4
Cockeyed Kite 1961,S 14,27:1
Moon on a Rainbow Shawl 1962,Ja 16,30:1
School for Scandal, The 1962,Mr 19,36:1
Seagull, The 1962,Mr 22,42:1
Tavern, The 1962,Ap 5,29:1
Half-Past Wednesday 1962,Ap 7,16:2
Blue Boy in Black, The 1963,My 1,32:1
Caesar and Cleopatra 1963,Ag 1,18:2
Pimpernel! 1964,Ja 7,26:6
Tavern, The 1964,Mr 6,39:2
Alchemist, The 1964,S 15,33:1
That 5 A.M. Jazz 1964,O 20,42:2
Secret Life of Walter Mitty, The 1964,O 27,44:5
Alfie 1964,D 18,27:1
Great Western Union, The 1965,F 10,45:1
Persecution and Assassination of Marat As
Performed by the Inmates of the Asylum of
Charenton Under the Direction of the Marquis de
Sade, The 1965,D 28,35:1
Philadelphia, Here I Come! 1966,F 17,28:1
First One Asleep, Whistle 1966,F 28,19:1
Loves of Cass McGuire, The 1966,O 7,36:1
Astrakhan Coat, The 1967,Ja 13,18:1
Arms and the Man 1967,Je 23,44:2
Keep It in the Family 1967,S 28,59:1
Joe Egg 1968,F 2,26:1
Woman Is My Idea 1968,S 26,61:1
Love Is a Time of Day 1969,D 23,21:3
Not Now Darling 1970,O 30,33:1
Burman, Howard (Playwright)
Happily Ever After 1945,Mr 16,21:2
Burman, Paul
Lower Depths, The 1956,O 3,29:2
Burmeister, V (Choreographer)
Moscow Circus on Ice 1970,D 9,63:1
Burmeister, Warren
Richard III 1949,F 9,33:2
Post Road 1949,Ap 28,27:3
Burmester, Agusta
Right to Dream, The 1924,My 27,14:2
Burn, Jonathan
Persecution and Assassination of Marat As
Performed by the Inmates of the Asylum of
Charenton Under the Direction of the Marquis de
Sade, The 1965,D 28,35:1
Burn, Michael (Playwright)
Night of The Ball, The 1955,Ja 13,31:8
Night of The Ball, The 1955,F 13,II,3:1
Burn, Roy F
Parson's Bride, The 1929,Ja 22,22:3
Burnam, Nan
Thesmophoriazusae, The; Goddesses of Athens,
The 1955,D 14,52:4
Burnand, F C (Lyricist)
Cox and Box 1939,Ja 17,27:5
Burnand, F C (Playwright)
Cox and Box 1934,S 7,24:3
Cox and Box 1936,S 29,34:2
Cox and Box 1942,F 20,20:2
Cox and Box 1948,Ja 20,26:2
Cox and Box 1951,F 20,21:2
Burnand, Lylia
Deburau 1920,D 24,14:3
Burne, Gaylea
Man of La Mancha 1970,Ja 25,70:6
Burnell, Buster
Wine, Women and Song 1942,S 29,18:3
Burnell, Buster (Choreographer)
Old Bucks and New Wings 1962,N 6,39:4
Burnell, Francis
Winter's Tale, The 1946,Ja 16,18:6
Burnell, Lotta
Up and Up, The 1930,S 9,25:2
Threepenny Opera, The 1933,Ap 14,22:4
Burnell, Peter
Henry IV, Part I 1968,Je 30,54:7
Henry IV, Part II 1968,Jl 2,33:1

Burnell, Sylvia
Three Times Three; Not Enough Rope
1962,Mr 2,24:1
Burnell, W A
Opportunity 1920,Jl 31,5:1
Censored 1938,F 28,18:2
Burnes, Maud
Father Malachy's Miracle 1937,N 18,26:4
Burnet, Dana (Director)
Boundry Line, The 1930,F 6,21:1
Burnet, Dana (Playwright)
Habitual Husband, The 1924,D 25,27:3
Four Walls 1927,S 20,33:1
Four Walls 1927,O 2,VIII,1:1
Little Theatre Tournament; Rain 1929,My 11,22:2
Boundry Line, The 1930,F 6,21:1
Bad Manners 1933,Ja 31,15:5
Burnet, Susan
Flowering Cherry 1959,O 22,46:1
Oh Dad, Poor Dad, Mamma's Hung You in the
Closet and I'm Feelin' So Sad 1961,Jl 6,19:2
Burnett, Brevard
Goin' Home 1928,Ag 24,23:2
Bomboola 1929,Je 27,17:3
Make Me Know It 1929,N 5,32:5
Burnett, Carol
Once Upon a Mattress 1959,My 12,40:1
Once Upon a Mattress 1959,My 17,II,1:1
Fade Out--Fade In 1964,My 27,45:1
Fade Out--Fade In 1964,Je 21,II,1:1
Fade Out--Fade In 1965,F 16,40:2
Burnett, Connie
West Side Story 1968,Je 25,32:1
Zorba 1968,N 18,58:1
Burnett, Edyth
Adding Machine, The 1923,Mr 20,24:1
Burnett, Frances Hodgson (Original Author)
Racketty Packetty House 1931,N 7,16:1
Secret Garden, The 1931,N 8,31:4
Burnett, Frances Hodgson (Playwright)
Little Princess, The 1931,F 7,11:3
Burnett, Harry
Pursuit of Happiness, The 1936,Jl 15,14:1
Royal Family, The 1936,Ag 12,15:1
Fly Away Home 1937,Jl 28,15:1
No Strings 1942,Je 14,VIII,2:1
Burnett, Harry (Director)
Mister Noah 1933,Ja 18,16:2
Burnett, Marge
Hostage, The 1961,D 13,55:4
Burnett, Martha
Scandals 1939,Ag 29,17:2
By Jupiter 1942,Je 4,22:1
Up in Central Park 1945,Ja 29,17:2
Burnett, Murray (Playwright)
Hickory Stick 1944,My 9,15:6
Burnett, Robert
Prince Charlie and Flora 1931,Ag 29,16:5
Burnett, Varda (Miss)
Phoebe of Quality Street 1921,My 10,20:1
Burnett, William
Dope 1926,Ja 4,16:3
Out of the Sea 1927,D 6,26:2
Scarlet Pages 1929,S 10,26:3
Burney, Fanny (Original Author)
Dear Nobody 1968,Jl 31,33:1
Burnham, Barbara (Playwright)
Maedchen in Uniform 1932,N 6,IX,1:3
Burnham, Barbara (Translator)
Girls in Uniform 1932,D 31,10:3
Burnham, Charles
Nativity Play, The 1937,D 21,29:1
Burnham, David (Composer)
Napoleon Passes 1927,D 21,29:2
Burnham, David (Lyricist)
Napoleon Passes 1927,D 21,29:2
Burnham, David (Playwright)
Napoleon Passes 1927,D 21,29:2
Burnham, Edward (Producer)
Under Milk Wood 1956,Ag 22,25:3
Burnham, Lucille
Gondoliers, The 1954,Ap 14,24:3
Burnham, Lucille (Composer)
H M S Pinafore 1949,Jl 29,13:2
Burnham, Lucille (Musical Director)
Mikado, The 1954,Mr 24,31:1
Patience 1967,O 13,32:1
Iolanthe 1967,O 18,40:1
Mikado, The 1967,O 25,42:2
Gondoliers, The 1967,O 29,83:1
H M S Pinafore 1967,N 1,40:1
Burnham, Richard
Coming Forth by Day of Osiris Jones, The; Kid,
The 1961,Mr 15,45:2
Burns, Art
Hamlet 1970,O 19,51:1
Burns, Arthur (Playwright)
Davy Jones's Locker 1959,Mr 30,25:1
Davy Jones's Locker 1959,D 28,18:1
Bil and Cora Baird's Marionette Theater
1963,Ap 12,34:2
Burns, Artie
When Differences Disappear 1941,Je 3,17:4

Burns, Barry
West Side Story 1960,Ap 28,31:1
Burns, Bart
Barefoot in Athens 1951,N 1,35:2
One Bright Day 1952,Mr 20,37:2
Burns, Bernard K (Playwright)
Woman on the Jury, The 1923,Ag 16,10:4
Burns, Bill
After the Rain 1967,O 10,54:1
Burns, Carolyn
Aunt Caroline's Will 1954,Ag 11,21:1
Burns, Catherine
Prime of Miss Jean Brodie, The 1968,Ja 17,39:1
Prime of Miss Jean Brodie, The 1968,Ja 28,II,1:1
Dream of a Blacklisted Actor 1969,D 18,64:1
Disintegration of James Cherry, The
   1970,Ja 30,33:3
Operation Sidewinder 1970,Mr 13,33:1
Dear Janet Rosenberg, Dear Mr Kooning
   1970,Ap 6,46:1
Dear Janet Rosenberg, Dear Mr Kooning
   1970,Ap 26,II,5:7
Burns, Clara
Paid 1925,N 26,32:1
Burns, David
Polly Preferred 1923,Ja 12,13:3
Face the Music 1932,F 18,24:5
Dinner at Eight 1933,Ja 7,11:5
Nymph Errant 1933,O 7,18:2
Them's the Reporters 1935,My 30,21:4
They Came by Night 1937,Jl 25,X,1:3
Man Who Came to Dinner, The 1939,O 17,31:1
Lunchtime Follies, The 1942,Je 23,22:3
My Dear Public 1943,S 10,28:1
Oklahoma! 1943,N 14,II,1:1
Million Dollar Baby 1945,D 22,17:2
Billion Dollar Baby 1945,D 30,II,1:1
I Gotta Get Out 1947,S 26,27:2
Make Mine Manhattan 1948,Ja 16,26:2
Heaven on Earth 1948,S 17,29:2
Alive and Kicking 1950,Ja 18,25:5
Out of This World 1950,D 22,17:3
Two's Company 1952,D 16,43:5
Two's Company 1952,D 21,II,3:1
Men of Distinction 1953,My 1,18:4
Catch a Star! 1955,S 7,35:2
Hole in the Head, A 1957,Mr 1,15:1
Hole in the Head, A 1957,Mr 10,II,1:1
Music Man, The 1957,D 20,31:1
Music Man, The 1958,S 28,II,1:1
Do Re Mi 1960,D 27,23:2
Do Re Mi 1961,Ja 8,II,1:1
Funny Thing Happened on the Way to the Forum,
   A 1962,My 9,49:1
Funny Thing Happened on the Way to the Forum,
   A 1962,My 20,II,1:1
Funny Thing Happened on the Way to the Forum,
   A 1962,Jl 6,22:5
Hello, Dolly! 1964,Ja 17,22:1
Hello, Dolly! 1964,Ja 26,II,1:1
Hello, Dolly! 1965,Ag 10,17:2
Price, The 1968,O 30,39:1
Sheep on the Runway 1970,F 2,28:3
Sheep on the Runway 1970,F 8,II,5:5
Lovely Ladies, Kind Gentlemen 1970,D 29,38:1
Burns, Eileen
General John Regan 1930,Ja 30,16:5
Daughters of Atreus 1936,O 15,33:1
Women, The 1936,D 28,13:1
Native Son 1941,Mr 25,26:5
Native Son 1942,O 24,10:6
Small Hours, The 1951,F 16,22:1
Burns, George
Vaudeville (Palace) 1926,Ag 24,19:3
Vaudeville (Palace) 1930,Ag 11,13:3
Vaudeville (Palace) 1931,Ja 5,20:3
Vaudeville (Palace) 1931,N 2,26:2
Friars Club Frolic 1933,My 15,16:4
Vaudeville (Palladium) 1949,Ag 17,19:3
Untitled-Revue 1962,Je 7,31:1
Burns, George E (Producer)
Hobo 1961,Ap 11,41:2
Burns, Harry
Earl Carroll's Vanities 1923,Jl 6,8:2
Vaudeville (Palace) 1927,Ja 18,23:2
Vaudeville (Palace) 1927,Ja 23,VII,1:1
Vaudeville (Palace) 1928,N 12,18:7
Vaudeville (Palace) 1931,Ap 13,17:2
Laffing Room Only 1944,D 25,15:4
Burns, Helen
Merchant of Venice, The 1955,Jl 1,13:1
Merry Wives of Windsor, The 1956,Je 21,34:4
First Gentleman, The 1957,Ap 26,22:2
Broken Jug, The 1958,Ap 2,36:1
Salad Days 1958,N 11,24:1
King John 1960,Je 29,26:2
Midsummer Night's Dream, A 1960,Je 30,23:5
Bourgeois Gentilhomme, Le 1964,Je 18,28:2
Country Wife, The 1964,Ag 3,16:1
Burns, Jack
Helen 1964,D 11,55:4

Burns, Janie
When the Roll Is Called Up Yonder
   1930,My 9,20:5
Burns, John J
Arabian, The 1927,N 1,20:5
Strange Interlude 1928,Ja 31,28:1
Burns, Julie
Dark of the Moon 1958,F 27,22:2
Burns, Leo
Vaudeville (Hippodrome) 1926,My 4,31:2
Burns, Marion
They Don't Mean Any Harm 1932,F 24,25:2
Intimate Relations 1932,Mr 29,23:2
Burns, Maryann
Cabaret 1966,N 21,62:1
Burns, Maud
Man on Stilts, The 1931,S 10,23:2
Burns, Maurice
Beautiful Dreamer 1960,D 28,22:1
Burns, Mickey J Jr (Lighting Director)
Shout From the Rooftops 1964,O 29,40:1
Burns, Nat
Them's the Reporters 1935,My 30,21:4
Robin Hood 1935,Jl 15,20:6
Straw Hat, The 1937,D 31,8:2
30 Days Hath September 1938,O 1,10:5
Clean Beds 1939,My 26,21:2
Great Big Doorstep, The 1942,N 27,26:2
My Romance 1948,O 20,38:5
Kiss Me, Kate 1952,Ja 9,24:6
Much Ado About Nothing 1952,My 2,20:1
Master Builder, The 1955,Mr 2,23:2
Miser, The 1955,Mr 18,34:2
Song of Norway 1958,Je 23,19:2
Foenix in Choir 1958,O 28,40:2
Jolly's Progress 1959,D 7,42:2
Becket 1961,My 9,44:1
Thracian Horses, The 1961,S 28,58:2
Burns, Nat (Director)
Straw Hat, The 1937,D 31,8:2
Burns, Nat (Producer)
Straw Hat, The 1937,D 31,8:2
Burns, Paul
Letty Pepper 1922,Ap 11,22:2
Go-Go 1923,Mr 13,19:4
Music Hath Charms 1934,D 31,8:2
Slight Case of Murder, A 1935,S 12,28:5
Burns, Ralph (Director)
Illya Darling 1967,Ap 12,37:1
Burns, Ralph (Miscellaneous)
Copper and Brass 1957,O 18,19:2
No Strings 1962,Mr 16,24:1
Little Me 1962,N 19,41:3
Hot Spot 1963,Ap 20,17:2
Funny Girl 1964,Mr 27,15:1
Fade Out--Fade In 1964,My 27,45:1
Golden Boy 1964,O 21,56:1
Something More! 1964,N 11,36:1
Do I Hear a Waltz? 1965,Mr 19,28:1
Sweet Charity 1966,Ja 31,22:1
Darling of the Day 1968,Ja 29,26:2
Burns, Ralph (Musical Director)
Phoenix '55 1955,Ap 25,20:2
Breakfast at Tiffany's 1966,D 15,60:1
Minnie's Boys 1970,Mr 27,27:1
Burns, Reese
Beautiful Dreamer 1960,D 28,22:1
How to Succeed in Business Without Really Trying
   1966,Ap 21,45:1
Burns, Richard
Lady Windermere's Fan 1946,O 15,29:2
Burns, Richard (Lighting Director)
Night Music 1951,Ap 9,29:6
Knight of the Burning Pestle, The 1953,O 24,13:2
Lady's Not for Burning, The 1957,F 22,26:2
Burns, Richard (Scenic Designer)
Night Music 1951,Ap 9,29:6
Knight of the Burning Pestle, The 1953,O 24,13:2
Lady's Not for Burning, The 1957,F 22,26:2
Villa of Madame Vidac, The 1959,O 1,40:1
Burns, Robert
Jubilee 1935,O 14,20:1
Captain Brassbound's Conversion 1950,D 28,21:1
Burns, Robert D
Three Musketeers, The 1928,Mr 14,28:1
Burns, Robert Glenn
Legal Grounds 1940,D 2,18:4
Burns, Walter (Director)
De Sade Illustrated 1969,My 13,42:4
Burns and Allen
Vaudeville (Palace) 1930,Ag 11,13:3
Vaudeville (Palace) 1930,D 29,19:3
Vaudeville (Palace) 1931,Ap 6,24:3
Burnside, Kathryne
Criss Cross 1926,O 13,20:2
Just Fancy! 1927,O 12,30:2
Burnside, Molly
Bad Habits of 1926 1926,My 1,11:1
Burnside, Nell
Thesmophoriazusae, The; Goddesses of Athens,
   The 1955,D 14,52:4
Burnside, R H
Lambs Gambol 1925,Ap 27,15:1

Burnside, R H (Director)
Madame Pompadour 1924,N 12,20:6
City Chap, The 1925,O 27,21:1
Criss Cross 1926,O 13,20:2
Three Cheers 1928,O 16,28:1
How's Your Health? 1929,N 27,30:3
Smiling Faces 1932,Ag 31,12:3
Hold Your Horses 1933,S 26,26:4
Only Girl, The 1934,My 22,28:2
Mikado, The 1935,Jl 16,24:4
Pirates of Penzance, The 1935,Jl 23,24:2
Yeomen of the Guard, The 1935,Jl 30,16:4
Gondoliers, The 1935,Ag 6,20:5
Trial by Jury 1935,Ag 13,20:6
H M S Pinafore 1935,Ag 13,20:6
Walk With Music 1940,Je 5,33:2
H M S Pinafore 1942,Ja 22,12:2
Mikado, The 1942,F 4,22:2
Pirates of Penzance, The 1942,F 18,22:2
Iolanthe 1942,F 24,26:4
Gondoliers, The 1942,Mr 4,22:3
H M S Pinafore 1944,F 15,14:4
Trial by Jury 1944,F 15,14:4
Pirates of Penzance, The 1944,F 18,15:5
Cox and Box 1944,F 18,15:5
Gondoliers, The 1944,F 22,26:3
Iolanthe 1944,F 23,17:1
Patience 1944,F 26,11:4
Robin Hood 1944,N 8,28:2
Burnside, R H (Lyricist)
Tip-Top 1920,O 6,13:2
Burnside, R H (Playwright)
Good Times 1920,Ag 10,10:1
Tip-Top 1920,O 6,13:2
Some Party 1922,Ap 17,22:1
Better Times 1922,S 4,14:2
Stepping Stones 1923,N 7,14:3
Three Cheers 1928,O 16,28:1
Burnside, R H (Producer)
How's Your Health? 1929,N 27,30:3
Mikado, The 1944,F 12,11:3
Ruddigore 1944,Mr 3,19:5
Yeomen of the Guard, The 1944,Mr 5,34:3
Robin Hood 1944,N 8,28:2
Burnson, George
Desert Song, The 1946,Ja 9,20:2
Burnstein, Mike
Megilla of Itzik Manger, The 1968,O 10,60:1
Buron, Jacques
Troupe Du Roi, La 1970,F 4,38:1
Amphitryon 1970,F 4,38:1
Don Juan 1970,F 7,24:2
Femmes Savaantes, Les 1970,F 14,12:1
Malade Imaginaire, Le 1970,F 18,40:2
Burr, Anne
Native Son 1941,Mr 25,26:5
Native Son 1941,Ap 6,IX,1:1
Plan M 1942,F 21,15:2
Native Son 1942,O 24,10:6
Lovers and Friends 1943,N 30,23:2
While the Sun Shines 1944,S 20,21:3
While the Sun Shines 1944,S 24,II,1:1
Hasty Heart, The 1945,Ja 4,14:2
Hasty Heart, The 1945,Ja 14,II,1:1
O'Daniel 1947,F 25,32:2
Gambler, The 1952,O 14,40:1
Burr, Anne (Playwright)
Huui, Huui 1968,N 25,58:1
Huui, Huui 1968,D 8,II,5:4
Burr, Charles H
Jim Dandy 1941,N 8,10:5
Burr, Courtney (Producer)
Walk a Little Faster 1932,D 8,24:4
Sailor, Beware! 1933,S 29,24:4
All Good Americans 1933,D 6,29:2
Small Miracle 1934,S 27,24:3
Ladies' Money 1934,N 2,26:6
Battleship Gertie 1935,Ja 19,9:2
Happiest Days, The 1939,Ap 12,26:2
Case of Youth, A 1940,Mr 25,10:3
Night Before Christmas, The 1941,Mr 30,I,48:2
Night Before Christmas, The 1941,Ap 11,25:2
Little Brown Jug 1946,Mr 7,32:2
Inspector Calls, An 1947,O 22,38:2
Season in the Sun 1950,S 29,31:2
Out West of Eighth 1951,S 21,20:3
Seven Year Itch, The 1952,N 21,21:2
Wayward Saint, The 1955,F 18,17:1
Speaking of Murder 1956,D 20,37:1
Genius and the Goddess, The 1957,D 11,41:1
Jane Eyre 1958,My 2,31:1
Golden Fleecing 1959,O 16,24:5
Send Me No Flowers 1960,D 6,54:1
Burr, Courtney Jr
Wanhope Building, The 1947,F 11,36:5
Burr, Donald
Marching By 1931,N 15,VIII,4:2
Marching By 1932,Mr 4,17:1
Walk a Little Faster 1932,D 8,24:4
Twelfth Night 1940,O 27,IX,1:5
Twelfth Night 1940,N 20,26:3
Rivals, The 1941,N 18,32:2
Rivals, The 1942,Ja 15,24:2

Burr, Donald—Cont
Would-Be Gentleman, The 1946,Ja 10,29:2
Annie Get Your Gun 1957,Ag 31,18:2
Skyscraper 1965,N 15,48:1
Sherry! 1967,Mr 29,39:1
Burr, Donald (Director)
Annie Get Your Gun 1958,F 20,29:2
Burr, Fritzi
Family Way, The 1965,Ja 14,44:5
Burr, John
Great Adventure, The 1921,F 26,9:2
It Is the Law 1922,N 30,28:2
Hamlet 1925,N 10,23:1
Burr, Maida (Costume Designer)
Merry-Go-Rounders, The 1956,N 22,50:1
Burr, Mary
Paint Your Wagon 1951,N 13,32:2
Paint Your Wagon 1951,N 18,II,1:1
Burr, Otho
And People All Around 1968,F 12,46:1
Burr, Raymond
Duke in Darkness, The 1944,Ja 25,15:2
Burr, Robert
King Lear 1956,Ja 13,17:1
Lovers 1956,My 11,23:1
Beggar's Opera, The 1957,Mr 14,35:1
Who Was That Lady I Saw You With?
 1958,Mr 4,33:2
King Lear 1959,Ja 3,11:2
Andersonville Trial, The 1959,D 30,15:1
Luther 1963,S 26,41:1
Hamlet 1964,Je 18,28:1
Bajour 1964,N 24,42:1
Coriolanus 1965,Jl 15,23:1
White Devil, The 1965,D 7,56:1
Dinner at Eight 1966,S 28,38:1
Dinner at Eight 1966,O 9,II,1:1
King John 1967,Jl 14,19:1
Wars of the Roses, The (Part I) 1970,Jl 2,30:1
Burr, William Alfred
This Mad Whirl 1937,Ja 10,II,4:8
Burrage, Alice
Kiss of Importance, A 1930,D 2,31:3
America's Sweetheart 1931,F 11,23:1
Keeping Expenses Down 1932,O 21,25:2
Before Morning 1933,F 10,13:4
Let 'Em Eat Cake 1933,O 23,18:1
Burrage, William S Jr
Watched Pot, The 1933,My 5,13:7
Burrascano, Giovanni
Sansone; Samson 1931,F 9,25:1
Marchese di Priola, Il 1931,Mr 2,19:3
Arzigogolo, L'; Whim, The 1931,Ap 27,24:4
Piccolo Santo, Il; Little Saint, The 1931,D 14,16:4
Casa di Tutti, La; Everybody's Home 1932,D 5,21:4
Cardinale, Il 1933,Ja 9,24:2
Romanticismo 1933,My 1,10:5
Romanticismo 1934,My 14,20:2
Burrell, Edward
Chips With Everything 1963,O 2,49:1
Burrell, Fred
Illya Darling 1967,Ap 12,37:1
Memorandum, The 1968,My 6,55:1
Burrell, James L A (Playwright)
Comic, The 1927,Ap 20,28:2
Fata Morgana 1931,D 26,15:3
Chinese Nightingale, The 1934,O 6,20:4
Burrell, James L A (Translator)
Fata Morgana 1924,Mr 4,16:3
Room of Dreams 1930,N 6,22:4
Burrell, John (Director)
Henry IV, Part I 1946,My 7,25:2
Henry IV, Part II 1946,My 8,33:4
Uncle Vanya 1946,My 14,18:2
Peter Pan 1950,Ap 25,27:2
Peter Pan 1950,Ap 30,II,1:1
Mr Pickwick 1952,S 18,36:3
Mr Pickwick 1952,S 28,II,1:1
Much Ado About Nothing 1955,Ag 20,20:4
Burrell, John (Miscellaneous)
King of Friday's Men, The 1951,F 22,26:2
Burrell, Michael
King Lear 1964,My 19,43:2
Comedy of Errors, The 1964,My 21,43:1
Burrell, Pamela
Arms and the Man 1967,Je 23,44:2
Burrell, Randal C (Playwright)
Makropoulos Secret, The 1926,Ja 22,12:4
Burrell, Sheila
Abdication 1948,S 28,32:5
Severed Head, A 1964,O 29,40:1
Burres, Helen
Two Gentlemen of Verona 1958,Mr 19,35:1
Burress, William
Girl From Home, The 1920,My 4,9:2
Burrill, Ena
Worse Things Happen at Sea 1935,Ap 21,IX,2:2
Coincidence 1935,D 1,XI,5:3
Private Company 1936,F 11,19:3
People in Love 1937,My 28,17:5
Uncle Harry 1944,Ap 30,II,1:4
Henry IV, Part I 1946,My 7,25:2
Henry IV, Part II 1946,My 8,33:4
Uncle Vanya 1946,My 14,18:2

Oedipus 1946,My 21,19:2
Burris, Barbara
Man Out Loud, Girl Quiet 1962,Ap 4,38:1
Spanish Armada, The 1962,Ap 4,38:1
Burris, Glenn
Liar, The 1950,My 19,30:2
Burritt, Lance
Twelve Miles Out 1925,N 17,29:2
Stairs, The 1927,N 8,32:7
Silver Box, The 1928,Ja 18,23:1
Burrough, Marguerite
Beau Gallant 1926,Ap 6,26:3
Burrough, Marion
Merry Duchess, The 1943,Je 24,25:1
Burroughs, Cindy
Hajj Malik, El 1970,O 4,II,5:1
Burroughs, Don
Jimmie 1920,N 18,15:3
Everyday 1921,N 17,15:1
French Doll, The 1922,F 21,20:2
Burroughs, Edgar Rice (Original Author)
Tarzan of the Apes 1921,S 8,14:3
Burroughs, Eric
Macbeth 1936,Ap 15,25:4
Brown Sugar 1937,D 3,29:2
Long Way From Home, A 1948,F 9,25:2
Set My People Free 1948,N 4,38:2
Burroughs, Gwen
One Heluva Night 1924,Je 5,18:1
Burroughs, Gwen Day
Last Enemy, The 1930,O 31,21:1
Truth Game, The 1930,D 29,19:1
Devil Passes, The 1932,Ja 5,20:3
Good Woman, Poor Thing, A 1933,Ja 10,27:3
Unto the Third 1933,Ap 21,24:8
Burroughs, Jackie
Richard II 1964,Je 17,47:1
Bourgeois Gentilhomme, Le 1964,Je 18,28:2
Burroughs, Judyth
Along Fifth Avenue 1949,Ja 14,28:2
Burroughs, Neal
Caesar and Cleopatra 1935,Ag 22,21:1
Burroughs, William
Chicago/Conspiracy 1970,Ag 26,35:1
Burrow, David
Up Eden 1968,N 27,42:1
Burrows, Abe (Director)
Two on the Aisle 1951,Jl 20,13:6
Three Wishes for Jamie 1952,Mr 22,9:2
Can-Can 1953,My 8,28:1
Can-Can 1953,My 17,II,1:1
Reclining Figure 1954,O 8,26:5
Happy Hunting 1956,D 7,30:1
Say Darling 1958,Ap 4,17:1
Say Darling 1958,Ap 13,II,1:1
First Impressions 1959,Mr 20,28:1
Golden Fleecing 1959,O 16,24:5
How to Succeed in Business Without Really Trying
 1961,O 16,34:1
What Makes Sammy Run? 1964,F 28,19:1
Foxy 1964,Mr 20,30:1
Cactus Flower 1965,D 9,60:2
Forty Carats 1968,D 27,45:1
Forty Carats 1969,Ja 5,II,1:3
Forty Carats 1970,Ja 6,48:1
Burrows, Abe (Playwright)
Guys and Dolls 1950,N 25,11:2
Guys and Dolls 1950,D 3,II,1:1
Guys and Dolls 1951,O 7,II,1:1
Three Wishes for Jamie 1952,Mr 22,9:2
Can-Can 1953,My 8,28:1
Can-Can 1953,My 17,II,1:1
Can-Can 1954,O 24,II,3:1
Silk Stockings 1955,F 25,17:3
Silk Stockings 1955,Mr 27,II,1:1
Guys and Dolls 1955,Ap 21,32:2
Say Darling 1958,Ap 4,17:1
Say Darling 1958,Ap 13,II,1:1
Say Darling 1959,F 26,38:2
First Impressions 1959,Mr 20,28:1
Guys and Dolls 1959,Jl 22,22:2
Can-Can 1959,Ag 26,25:4
How to Succeed in Business Without Really Trying
 1961,O 16,34:1
Can-Can 1962,My 17,32:2
Guys and Dolls 1965,Ap 29,39:1
Cactus Flower 1965,D 9,60:2
How to Succeed in Business Without Really Trying
 1966,Ap 21,45:1
Guys and Dolls 1966,Je 9,55:2
Breakfast at Tiffany's 1966,D 15,60:1
Cactus Flower 1967,D 16,48:1
Burrows, Arthur
Play of Daniel, The 1960,D 27,23:6
Play of Daniel, The 1966,Ja 2,64:4
Burrows, Charles
Face the Music 1932,F 18,24:5
American Holiday 1936,F 22,13:3
Help Yourself! 1936,Jl 15,15:1
January Thaw 1946,F 5,18:2
Burrows, Charles R
Johannes Kreisler 1922,D 25,20:3
Minick 1924,S 25,20:1

Burrows, Charles R—Cont
Squall, The 1926,N 12,20:1
Birthright 1933,N 22,22:3
Burrows, Charles W
Wandering Jew, The 1921,O 27,22:1
Burrows, E G
Front Page, The 1937,N 12,27:2
Burrows, Gwen
In Heaven and Earth 1936,Mr 27,24:8
Burrows, James (Director)
Castro Complex, The 1970,N 19,40:1
Burrows, James (Miscellaneous)
Forty Carats 1968,D 27,45:1
Burrows, Joe (Playwright)
Will Morrissey's Newcomers 1923,Ag 9,16:2
Burrows, Jonathan (Miscellaneous)
Fire! 1969,Ja 29,26:1
Hello and Goodbye 1969,S 19,54:1
Burrows, Jonathan (Producer)
Contributions; Plantation 1970,Mr 10,53:1
Contributions; Contribution 1970,Mr 10,53:1
Contributions; Shoes 1970,Mr 10,53:1
Burrows, Robert
As You Like It 1959,Jl 1,27:1
Burrows, Thomas (Miscellaneous)
Balcony, The 1960,Mr 4,21:1
Marcus in the High Grass 1960,N 22,38:6
Serjeant Musgrave's Dance 1966,Mr 9,44:1
Burrows, Vinie
City of Kings 1949,F 18,27:2
Wisteria Trees, The 1950,Mr 30,39:1
Green Pastures, The 1951,Mr 16,35:2
Mrs Patterson 1954,D 2,37:1
Skin of Our Teeth, The 1955,Ag 18,16:1
Ponder Heart, The 1956,F 17,14:2
Come Share My House 1960,F 19,20:2
Nat Turner 1960,N 7,46:3
Mandingo 1961,My 23,43:6
Worlds of Shakespeare, The 1963,D 5,58:1
Walk Together Children 1968,N 12,54:1
Burrus, Ron
Brownstone Urge, The 1969,D 18,63:1
Burry, Allan
Sign of Jonah, The 1957,My 2,27:1
Burry, Solen
Having Wonderful Time 1937,F 22,12:5
World We Make, The 1939,N 21,19:1
Cafe Crown 1942,Ja 24,12:5
Brights Lights of 1944 1943,S 17,27:4
Devils Galore 1945,S 13,27:2
Barefoot Boy With Cheek 1947,Ap 4,20:2
Mrs McThing 1952,F 21,22:1
Burse, Mme
Chauve-Souris 1923,S 4,12:1
Bursk, Sybil
My Girl 1924,N 25,27:2
Burson, Letha
Great Day! 1929,O 18,24:3
Bursor, George
Will, The 1930,My 6,33:1
Burstain, Paul
Love Thief, The 1931,Ja 19,24:5
Burstein, Alexandra (Playwright)
Uncle Tom's Cabin 1949,Ap 18,13:3
Burstein, Lonnie (Lyricist)
Have I Got One for You 1968,Ja 8,32:1
Burstein, Lonnie (Playwright)
Have I Got One for You 1968,Ja 8,32:1
Burstein, Mike
Megilla of Itzik Manger, The 1969,Ap 21,55:1
Burstein, Paul
His Jewish Girl 1936,D 9,34:1
Burstein, Pesach
Megilla of Itzik Manger, The 1968,O 10,60:1
Megilla of Itzik Manger, The 1969,Ap 21,55:1
Burstin, Joe (Miscellaneous)
From Israel With Laughter 1969,O 17,34:1
Burston, Buddy (Miscellaneous)
Ziegfeld Follies 1943,Ap 2,16:2
Burston, Saul (Miscellaneous)
Stick-in-the-Mud 1935,D 2,18:2
Burt, Benjamin Hapgood (Lyricist)
Florida Girl 1925,N 3,34:1
Burt, Benjamin Hapgood (Playwright)
Lambs Gambol 1925,Ap 27,15:1
Florida Girl 1925,N 3,34:1
Burt, Cass
Bottom of the Cup, The 1927,F 1,24:2
Burt, David (Composer)
Assorted Nuts 1940,Ap 7,I,44:6
Burt, David S
Assorted Nuts 1940,Ap 7,I,44:6
Burt, Elizabeth
Slightly Scandalous 1944,Je 14,16:2
Burt, Frederic
Pagans 1921,Ja 5,11:1
Triumph of X, The 1921,Ag 25,8:2
First Man, The 1922,Mr 6,9:2
Malvaloca 1922,O 3,22:1
Elsie 1923,Ap 3,26:1
Catskill Dutch 1924,My 7,18:1
Minick 1924,S 25,20:1
Kongo 1926,Mr 31,20:5
Set a Thief 1927,F 22,22:1

Burt, Frederic—Cont
Tia Juana 1927,N 16,28:4
Mongolia 1927,D 27,24:5
Breaks, The 1928,Ap 17,26:3
Burt, Harry
Play, A 1925,F 11,19:2
Burt, Laura
School for Scandal, The 1923,Mr 13,19:2
Sweet Nell of Old Drury 1923,My 19,16:4
Strange Prince, The 1926,D 8,24:2
Julius Caesar 1927,Je 7,27:2
Burt, Nellie
Toto 1921,Mr 22,15:2
Face Value 1921,D 27,10:2
Night Call, The 1922,Ap 27,12:2
Casanova 1923,S 27,10:2
Right to Love, The 1925,Je 9,16:4
Goodbye Again 1932,D 29,16:4
On Location 1937,S 28,19:1
Tell Me Pretty Maiden 1937,D 17,33:5
Life With Father 1939,N 9,26:2
Boy Who Lived Twice, A 1945,S 12,31:2
Girls of Summer 1956,N 20,45:1
Burt, Sadie
Vaudeville (Palace) 1927,Ap 26,33:1
Burtin, John G
Dream Child 1934,Jl 31,20:2
Burtis, Eric
Now You've Done It 1937,Mr 6,10:4
Burtis, James
Clubs Are Trumps 1924,O 15,27:1
Solid Ivory 1925,N 17,29:3
Burtis, Janet Maria
Devil's Disciple, The 1950,Ja 26,23:2
Burtis, Junior Eric
Swing Your Lady 1936,O 19,22:4
Greatest Show on Earth, The 1938,Ja 6,22:2
Burtis, Thomson (Playwright)
Town's Woman, The 1929,Mr 12,26:2
Sisters of the Chorus 1930,My 18,VIII,3:1
Sisters of the Chorus 1930,O 21,34:3
Burtis, Thomson (Producer)
Town's Woman, The 1929,Mr 12,26:2
Burton, Alberta
Tavern, The 1920,S 28,14:1
Burton, Alice
George White's Scandals 1922,Ag 29,10:1
Burton, Barbara
Our Town 1944,Ja 11,24:5
Burton, Bob
Great Day! 1929,O 18,24:3
Burton, Christine
Commedia Dell' Arte 1927,Ap 6,24:3
Burton, Clara
Fall and Rise of Susan Lenox, The 1920,Je 11,11:2
Afgar 1920,N 9,13:2
Burton, Clyde
Midsummer Night's Dream, A 1964,Je 30,23:2
Royal Hunt of the Sun, The 1965,O 27,36:2
Alchemist, The 1969,Je 12,51:1
Burton, David (Director)
Swan, The 1923,O 28,VIII,1:1
Seventeen 1924,Ap 12,18:2
Dear Sir 1924,S 24,21:3
Firebrand, The 1924,O 16,33:1
New Gallantry, The 1925,S 25,24:2
Black Boy 1926,O 7,30:2
Puppets of Passion 1927,F 25,24:4
Triumphant Bachelor, The 1927,S 16,21:1
Marquise, The 1927,N 15,26:4
Royal Family, The 1927,D 29,26:4
Royal Family, The 1928,Ja 8,VIII,1:1
Lady Lies, The 1928,N 27,36:2
Peepshow 1944,F 4,12:2
Lower North 1944,Ag 26,15:4
Burton, Dorothy
Humoresque 1923,F 28,13:2
Burton, Frank
First Mortgage 1929,O 11,36:1
Burton, Frederick
Roger Bloomer 1923,Mr 2,18:3
Neighbors 1923,D 27,11:1
Her Way Out 1924,Je 24,18:3
Close Harmony 1924,D 2,23:1
White Collars 1925,F 24,17:2
Lambs Gambol 1925,Ap 27,15:1
Hush Money 1926,Mr 16,22:3
My Country 1926,Ag 10,19:1
Deep River 1926,O 5,26:2
Wall Street 1927,Ap 21,24:4
Revelry 1927,S 13,37:1
Coquette 1927,N 9,23:1
Roadside 1930,S 27,21:1
Burton, G Marian
Little Theatre Tournament; Shall We Join the Ladies? 1929,My 9,34:3
Shall We Join the Ladies? 1929,My 12,28:3
Burton, G Marion (Playwright)
Houses of Sand 1925,F 18,17:1
Burton, George
Blackouts of 1949 1949,S 7,39:2
Burton, George (Director)
Incubator 1932,N 2,23:3

Burton, George (Producer)
Incubator 1932,N 2,23:3
Burton, Herschell
Buck White 1969,D 3,63:1
Burton, Irving
Dandelion 1969,D 24,12:1
Hot Feet 1970,D 22,38:1
Burton, Irving (Director)
Hot Feet 1970,D 22,38:1
Burton, Jean
Oh! Mama 1925,Ag 20,22:2
Burton, Jean (Playwright)
Left Turn 1936,Jl 7,22:3
Burton, Joseph
Bootleggers, The 1922,N 28,24:1
Best People, The 1924,Ag 20,8:1
Crooked Friday, The 1925,O 9,27:3
Joker, The 1925,N 17,29:1
Virgin, The 1926,F 23,26:1
Woman Disputed, A 1926,S 29,23:2
Scalawag, The 1927,Mr 30,22:3
Burlesque 1927,S 2,15:3
Crooks' Convention, The 1929,S 19,37:4
Decoy, The 1932,Ap 2,13:4
On the Make 1932,My 24,23:2
Best People, The 1933,Mr 16,21:5
Queer People 1934,F 16,16:2
Young Madame Conti 1937,Ap 1,18:4
Too Many Heroes 1937,N 16,26:2
Burton, Julian
Comedian, The 1956,O 18,36:4
Burton, Kenneth
Head First 1926,Ja 7,22:4
Cape Cod Follies 1929,S 19,37:2
Frankie and Johnny 1930,S 26,16:5
Burton, Langhorne
Dolly Jordan 1922,O 4,26:1
Burton, Martin
Night Hawk 1926,D 27,21:3
Playing the Game 1927,D 20,32:5
Cafe de Danse 1929,Ja 16,22:2
Love Duel, The 1929,Ap 16,32:3
Death Takes a Holiday 1929,D 27,26:4
Merchant of Venice, The 1931,N 9,22:2
It Pays to Sin 1933,N 4,18:6
Burton, Martin (Producer)
Broken Journey 1942,Je 24,22:2
Feathers in a Gale 1943,D 22,26:2
Burton, Miriam
Run, Little Chillun 1943,Ag 14,6:1
House of Flowers 1954,D 31,11:2
Ballad for Bimshire 1963,O 16,54:1
Burton, Neil
Blue Bonnet 1920,Ag 30,12:1
Burton, Norman
Sound of Hunting, A 1954,Ap 7,41:1
Anna Christie 1955,N 22,41:1
Quare Fellow, The 1958,N 28,34:1
Burton, Perry
Once Upon a Time 1939,D 21,28:2
Burton, Philip (Director)
Purple Dust 1956,D 28,15:1
Purple Dust 1957,Ja 6,II,1:1
Interlock 1958,F 7,18:1
Cock-A-Doodle Dandy 1958,N 13,39:2
Harlequinade 1959,F 14,15:1
Electra 1959,F 14,15:1
Overruled 1959,My 27,32:2
Buoyant Billions 1959,My 27,32:2
Getting Married 1959,Je 5,18:2
Dark Lady of the Sonnets, The 1959,Ag 21,13:1
Overruled 1959,Ag 21,13:1
Passion, Poison and Petrifaction 1959,Ag 21,13:1
Untitled-Poetry Reading 1964,Je 22,23:4
Burton, Richard
Lady's Not for Burning, The 1950,N 9,42:2
Henry V 1951,Ag 12,II,1:4
Legend of Lovers 1951,D 27,17:1
Montserrat 1952,My 11,II,3:8
Hamlet 1953,Ag 25,18:6
Hamlet 1953,Ag 30,II,2:1
Othello 1956,Mr 11,II,3:1
Time Remembered 1957,N 13,41:2
Time Remembered 1957,N 24,II,1:1
Camelot 1960,O 3,35:1
Camelot 1960,D 5,42:1
Camelot 1960,D 11,II,5:1
Hamlet 1964,F 28,17:5
Hamlet 1964,Ap 10,30:1
Hamlet 1964,Ap 19,II,1:1
Untitled-Poetry Reading 1964,Je 22,23:4
Dr Faustus 1966,F 16,49:1
Burton, Robert
Salt Water 1929,N 27,30:3
Joseph 1930,F 13,25:3
Riddle Me This! 1932,F 26,22:5
Divine Drudge 1933,Jl 4,16:4
Invitation to a Murder 1934,My 18,26:3
Fools Rush In 1934,D 26,19:2
Touch of Brimstone, A 1935,S 23,20:1
Tomorrow's a Holiday! 1935,D 31,10:2
Three Wise Fools 1936,Mr 2,12:2
New Faces of 1936 1936,My 20,24:5

Burton, Robert—Cont
Straw Hat, The 1939,S 30,10:6
Skylark 1939,O 12,32:2
Theatre 1941,N 13,34:2
Three's a Family 1943,My 6,24:2
Happy Birthday 1946,N 1,31:2
Burton, Robert (Director)
Savage Rhythm 1932,Ja 1,30:4
That's Gratitude 1932,Je 17,24:3
As Husbands Go 1933,Ja 20,20:5
Riddle Me This! 1933,Mr 15,21:3
Susan and God 1943,D 14,30:2
Burton, Ruth
Lightnin' 1938,S 16,17:2
Burton, Sam A
Charley's Aunt 1925,Je 2,16:2
Burton, Sarah
Horse Eats Hat 1936,S 28,14:2
Set to Music 1939,Ja 19,16:2
Kiss for Cinderella, A 1942,Mr 11,22:2
Made in Heaven 1946,O 25,28:2
Tonight at 8:30; Ways and Means 1948,F 21,8:2
Tonight at 8:30; Family Album 1948,F 21,8:2
Tonight at 8:30; Shadow Play 1948,F 24,20:4
Tonight at 8:30; Hands Across the Sea 1948,F 24,20:4
Julius Caesar 1950,Je 21,30:1
Conversation Piece 1957,N 19,38:2
Julius Caesar 1959,Ag 4,30:1
Man for All Seasons, A 1961,N 23,51:1
Man for All Seasons, A 1964,Ja 28,24:2
Burton, Tom
Potters, The 1923,D 10,21:4
Americana 1926,Jl 27,15:3
Americana 1926,O 31,28:2
First Night 1930,N 27,32:3
Social Register, The 1931,N 10,28:2
Burton, Walter
Horse Eats Hat 1936,S 28,14:2
Burton, Warren
Hair 1967,O 30,55:1
Patriot for Me, A 1969,O 6,58:1
Burton-Mercur, Paul (Director)
Love Is No Heaven 1943,Mr 16,15:3
Burton-Mercur, Paul (Playwright)
Love Is No Heaven 1943,Mr 16,15:3
Burton-Mercur, Paul (Producer)
Love Is No Heaven 1943,Mr 16,15:3
Burtonya, Clee
Electra 1969,Ag 8,14:1
Burtt, Robert
False Dreams, Farewell 1934,Ja 16,18:3
Burwell, Basil
Infernal Machine, The 1937,D 13,22:7
Burwell, Basil (Playwright)
Carricknabauna 1967,Mr 31,30:1
Burwell, Evelyn (Director)
Green Pastures, The 1935,F 27,16:2
Burwell, Faith
Trial, The 1955,Je 15,35:2
Bury, Anne
Dark Eyes 1943,Ja 15,20:2
Bury, John (Costume Designer)
Physicists, The 1964,O 14,52:1
Rothschilds, The 1970,O 20,40:1
Bury, John (Lighting Director)
Oh What a Lovely War 1964,O 1,30:1
Physicists, The 1964,O 14,52:1
Bury, John (Scenic Designer)
Macbeth 1962,Je 6,35:2
Wars of the Roses, The 1963,Jl 18,14:1
Blood Knot, The 1964,Mr 3,30:2
Afore Night Come 1964,Je 26,34:1
Oh What a Lovely War 1964,O 1,30:1
Physicists, The 1964,O 14,52:1
Homecoming, The 1967,Ja 6,29:1
Indians 1968,Jl 9,30:2
Landscape; Silence 1969,Jl 25,34:1
Rothschilds, The 1970,O 20,40:1
Bury, Margaret (Costume Designer)
Hostage, The 1960,S 21,42:1
Hostage, The 1961,D 13,55:4
Burzhardt, Betty
Our Lan' 1947,S 29,16:5
Bus-Fekete, Ladislaus (Original Author)
Lady's Gentleman, A 1937,D 24,20:5
Ladies and Gentlemen 1939,S 24,IX,2:5
Ladies and Gentlemen 1939,O 18,30:2
Ladies and Gentlemen 1939,O 29,IX,1:3
Bus-Fekete, Ladislaus (Playwright)
Twin Stars 1928,Ja 15,VIII,2:1
Lady Has a Heart, The 1937,O 3,XI,1:1
Embezzled Heaven 1944,N 1,20:2
Embezzled Heaven 1944,N 5,II,1:2
Alice in Arms 1945,F 1,18:4
Big Two, The 1947,Ja 9,21:2
Faithfully Yours 1951,O 19,22:5
Bus-Fekete, Ladislaus (Translator)
Lady Has a Heart, The 1937,S 27,24:1
Busanovsky, Nicholas
Clear All Wires! 1932,S 15,19:1
Busby, Nate
Blue Ghost, The 1930,Mr 11,24:5

Busch, Berthold
Johannes Kreisler 1922,D 25,20:3
Busch, Betty Ann
Sweethearts 1947,Ja 22,31:2
Busch, Bobby
Crazy With the Heat 1941,Ja 15,18:2
Volpone 1948,Ja 9,24:6
Wedding, The 1948,F 6,29:2
On the Harmfulness of Tobacco 1948,F 6,29:2
Bear, The 1948,F 6,29:2
Tragedian in Spite of Himself, A 1948,F 6,29:2
Insect Comedy, The 1948,Je 4,26:3
Busch, Ernst
Ich Tanze um die Welt mit Dir 1930,Ag 31,VIII,2:1
Busch, Gundi
Hollywood Ice Revue 1955 1955,Ja 14,16:1
Hollywood Ice Revue 1956,Ja 13,17:1
Busch, Lou (Miscellaneous)
Amorous Flea, The 1964,F 18,26:1
Busch, Mack
Insect Comedy, The 1948,Je 4,26:3
Busch, Robert
Once Upon a Time 1939,D 21,28:2
Romeo and Juliet 1940,My 10,27:1
Buse, Frederick
David Garrick 1929,Ag 2,17:5
Buser, Mel A
Merton of the Movies 1922,N 14,16:2
Cafe de Danse 1929,Ja 16,22:2
Busey, Alice
Roseanne 1923,D 31,9:5
Bush, A M
Johannes Kreisler 1922,D 25,20:3
Rust 1924,F 1,12:1
Bush, Alan (Composer)
Macbeth 1948,Ap 1,30:2
Bush, Anita
Swing It 1937,Jl 23,17:2
Bush, Beverly
As You Like It 1945,Jl 4,10:4
Bush, Beverly (Director)
As You Like It 1945,Jl 4,10:4
Bush, Beverly (Producer)
As You Like It 1945,Jl 4,10:4
Bush, Donald (Musical Director)
Grand Duke, The 1961,My 12,24:1
Bush, Gilmore
Romeo and Juliet 1934,D 21,30:3
Barretts of Wimpole Street, The 1935,F 26,16:2
Caesar and Cleopatra 1935,Ag 22,21:1
Taming of the Shrew, The 1935,O 1,27:3
Idiot's Delight 1936,Mr 25,25:2
Taming of the Shrew, The 1940,F 6,17:2
Joan of Lorraine 1946,N 19,40:2
Bush, Helene
Tapestry in Gray 1935,D 28,10:2
Bush, Jonathan
Johnny Johnson 1956,O 22,24:1
Oklahoma! 1958,Mr 8,15:2
Bush, Josef (Playwright)
De Sade Illustrated 1969,My 13,42:4
Bush, Josef (Scenic Designer)
De Sade Illustrated 1969,My 13,42:4
Bush, Josef (Translator)
De Sade Illustrated 1969,My 13,42:4
Bush, Norman
Goose, The 1960,Mr 16,44:1
Funnyhouse of a Negro 1964,Ja 15,25:3
Toilet, The 1964,D 17,51:1
Servant of Two Masters, The 1966,Je 28,51:1
Summer of the Seventeenth Doll 1968,F 21,59:1
Summer of the Seventeenth Doll 1968,Mr 3,II,3:1
Kongi's Harvest 1968,Ap 15,49:1
Daddy Goodness 1968,Je 5,37:1
God Is a (Guess What?) 1968,D 18,56:1
Malcochon 1969,Ap 2,37:1
Man Better Man 1969,Jl 3,22:1
Day of Absence 1970,Mr 18,39:1
Akokawe 1970,Je 5,21:1
Bush, Phil (Producer)
Married-And How! 1928,Je 15,30:2
Bush, Ronald
H M S Pinafore 1949,Jl 29,13:2
Mikado, The 1954,Mr 24,31:1
Gondoliers, The 1954,Ap 14,24:3
Ruddigore 1954,Ap 21,36:4
Iolanthe 1954,Ap 28,36:8
Yeomen of the Guard, The 1954,My 5,36:2
H M S Pinafore 1954,My 19,36:8
Mikado, The 1957,Ap 24,28:2
H M S Pinafore 1957,My 1,42:6
Pirates of Penzance, The 1957,My 8,43:1
Yeomen of the Guard, The 1957,My 22,28:3
Gondoliers, The 1957,My 29,34:2
H M S Pinafore 1960,Ja 29,14:1
Utopia, Limited 1960,Ap 8,27:2
Burn Me to Ashes 1963,N 20,48:1
Red, White and Maddox 1969,Ja 27,27:1
Bush, Ronald (Composer)
H M S Pinafore 1960,Ja 29,14:1
Bush, Ronald (Miscellaneous)
From Here to There; Otherwise Engaged 1958,Ap 24,37:3

From Here to There; Real Strange One, A 1958,Ap 24,37:3
From Here to There; Slow Dusk 1958,Ap 24,37:3
Iolanthe 1965,My 19,42:1
Yeomen of the Guard, The 1965,Jl 8,34:1
Ruddigore 1965,Ag 27,16:1
Bush, Ronald (Musical Director)
Utopia, Limited; Flowers of Progress, The 1957,F 27,21:1
Mikado, The 1957,Ap 24,28:2
H M S Pinafore 1957,My 1,42:6
Pirates of Penzance, The 1957,My 8,43:1
Yeomen of the Guard, The 1957,My 22,28:3
Gondoliers, The 1957,My 29,34:2
From Here to There; Real Strange One, A 1958,Ap 24,37:3
From Here to There; Slow Dusk 1958,Ap 24,37:3
From Here to There; Otherwise Engaged 1958,Ap 24,37:3
Gondoliers, The 1960,F 7,II,1:1
Utopia, Limited 1960,Ap 8,27:2
Yeomen of the Guard, The 1961,Ap 28,23:1
Mikado, The 1961,My 5,23:1
Princess Ida 1961,My 19,23:1
Iolanthe 1961,My 26,29:6
H M S Pinafore 1961,Je 9,29:5
Student Prince, The 1961,Jl 14,14:1
Merry Widow, The 1961,O 27,28:2
Vagabond King, The 1961,N 24,36:1
Gondoliers, The 1961,D 8,44:1
Gondoliers, The 1963,Je 5,33:2
Ruddigore 1965,Ag 27,16:1
Bush, Thommie
Hair 1967,O 30,55:1
Bill Noname 1970,Mr 3,37:1
Bush, William
Lucky Sam McCarver 1950,Ap 15,10:6
Captain Brassbound's Conversion 1950,D 28,21:1
Barefoot in Athens 1951,N 1,35:2
Shrike, The 1952,Ja 16,20:2
Shrike, The 1953,N 26,51:2
Girls in 509, The 1958,O 16,47:1
Queen and the Rebels, The 1965,F 26,16:1
Bushar, George (Producer)
Mackerel Skies 1934,Ja 24,20:4
Moor Born 1934,Ap 8,X,2:7
Order Please 1934,O 10,21:2
Within the Gates 1934,O 23,23:1
Mother Lode 1934,D 24,16:5
Dominant Sex, The 1935,Ap 2,24:5
Crime Marches on 1935,O 24,19:1
Black Limelight 1936,N 10,31:1
Tell Me Pretty Maiden 1937,D 17,33:5
Come Across 1938,S 15,28:3
Bushee, Al
Song and Dance Man, The 1924,Ja 1,21:2
Bushee, Marion
Howdy King 1926,D 14,24:4
Bushell, Anthony
Sacred Flame, The 1928,N 20,28:2
Bushelle, John
Teahouse of the August Moon, The 1954,My 2,II,3:1
Busher, George (Producer)
Moor Born 1934,Ap 4,26:4
Busher, Leverne
Ice Follies 1939,D 5,38:2
Bushkin, Joe
Rat Race, The 1949,D 23,16:2
Bushman, Edward
Live Life Again 1945,O 1,14:7
Bushnell, Adelyn (Director)
Case History 1938,O 22,15:2
Bushnell, Adelyn (Playwright)
I Myself 1934,My 10,24:6
Buska, Rosa
Bruder Straubinger 1921,N 16,22:3
Fruehlingsluft 1921,N 29,17:4
Buskin, Joseph
Galileo 1968,D 1,88:4
Busley, Jessie
Daisy Mayme 1926,O 26,24:2
Tomorrow 1928,D 29,20:2
Paris Bound 1929,Jl 20,8:3
Affair of State, An 1930,N 20,30:3
Streets of New York, The 1931,O 7,29:1
Pillars of Society, The 1931,O 15,19:1
Bride the Sun Shines On, The 1931,D 28,20:2
Alien Corn 1933,F 21,17:2
Alien Corn 1933,F 26,IX,1:1
Great Waltz, The 1934,S 24,14:4
First Lady 1935,N 27,17:4
Women, The 1936,D 28,13:1
Over Twenty-One 1944,Ja 4,20:2
Rich Full Life, The 1945,N 10,9:2
Happiest Years, The 1949,Ap 26,29:8
Busley, Margalo
Women, The 1936,D 8,30:6
Buss, Helena
Song of Norway 1944,Ag 27,II,1:1
Show Boat 1954,O 29,28:4
Busse, Edith
Versunkene Glocke, Die 1936,N 20,26:3

Busse, Henry and Orchestra
Say When 1928,Je 27,29:3
Bussey, George
Ice Capades 1962,Ag 30,34:1
Ice Capades 1963,Ag 29,37:2
Ice Capades 1964,Ag 27,27:2
Bussey, James R Jr
What a Relief 1935,D 14,10:6
Bussey, Raymond
Moondreamers, The 1969,D 9,68:1
Bussey, Raymond (Choreographer)
Moondreamers, The 1969,D 9,68:1
Gloria and Esperanza 1970,F 5,32:1
Bussey, Raymond (Director)
Gloria and Esperanza 1970,F 5,32:1
Bussey, Raymond (Miscellaneous)
Moondreamers, The 1969,D 9,68:1
Bussiere, Tadema (Playwright)
Find Daddy 1926,Mr 9,21:3
Gertie 1926,N 16,24:2
Bussinger, Elena
Zaporogetz Za Dunayem 1937,My 9,II,5:3
Bussmann, Christian (Scenic Designer)
Amphitryon 1970,N 18,40:1
Busten, Mike
Inquest 1970,Ap 24,38:1
Buting, Emma
As Husbands Go 1935,Jl 10,24:1
Butkovic, Milutin
Progress of Bora, The Tailor, The 1968,Je 27,49:2
Ubu Roi 1968,Je 29,20:1
Victor, or The Children Take Over 1968,Jl 10,22:4
Butler, Ann
Keep Kool 1924,My 23,16:4
Vaudeville (Palace) 1928,Ja 10,28:5
One More Honeymoon 1934,Ap 2,13:5
War and Peace 1942,My 22,26:3
Butler, Belle
Little Theatre Tournament; Rachel Cowan 1929,My 9,34:3
Butler, Bill
Hamlet 1948,D 4,9:2
Cyrano de Bergerac 1953,N 13,24:3
Richard III 1953,D 10,65:2
Candida 1957,Mr 29,18:5
Butler, Bill (Director)
Never Say Horses 1951,D 7,34:4
Third Person 1955,D 30,13:4
Adding Machine, The 1956,F 10,17:1
Crystal Heart, The 1957,F 20,37:1
Delightful Season, A 1960,S 29,30:1
Butler, Bill (Miscellaneous)
Saint of Bleecker Street, The 1954,D 28,21:1
Butler, Billy (Musical Director)
Blue Holiday 1945,My 22,13:3
Butler, Buddy
Daddy Goodness 1968,Je 5,37:1
Butler, Buddy (Lighting Director)
Man Better Man 1969,Jl 3,22:1
Harangues, The 1970,Ja 14,42:1
Butler, Buddy (Miscellaneous)
String 1969,Ap 2,37:1
Contribution 1969,Ap 2,37:1
Malcochon 1969,Ap 2,37:1
Ododo 1970,N 25,26:1
Butler, Calvin
Chicago 70 1970,My 26,33:1
Chicago 70 1970,Je 7,II,3:1
Butler, Clark
Othello 1937,Ja 7,16:4
Butler, Edward
In the Next Room 1923,N 28,14:1
Dope 1926,Ja 4,16:3
Great Gatsby, The 1926,F 3,22:1
Glory Hallelujah 1926,Ap 7,26:2
Honor of the Family, The 1926,D 27,21:1
Synthetic Sin 1927,O 11,26:2
It Is to Laugh 1927,D 27,24:2
Fata Morgana 1931,D 26,15:3
Bulls, Bears and Asses 1932,My 7,11:3
Sweet Mystery of Life 1935,O 12,13:3
Western Union 1937,Ag 10,22:7
Ghost of Yankee Doodle, The 1937,N 23,26:3
Escape This Night 1938,Ap 23,18:1
Day in the Sun 1939,My 17,29:2
Cue for Passion 1940,D 20,33:4
Butler, Ethel
Mascaiada 1929,D 28,10:6
Butler, Evelyn
Mascaiada 1929,D 28,10:6
Butler, F Cecil
Mountebank, The 1923,My 8,22:2
Escape 1927,O 27,33:1
Before You're 25 1929,Ap 17,30:2
Butler, Frank
Wild Man of Borneo, The 1927,S 14,29:2
Lamp at Midnight 1947,D 22,29:2
Church Street 1948,F 10,27:2
Butler, Frank (Playwright)
Hangman's Whip 1933,F 25,20:2
Butler, George
Wandering Jew, The 1927,F 2,22:4

Butler, George—Cont

Dick Whittington and His Remarkable Cat 1950,N 25,10:5

Butler, Hal
Vaudeville (Palace) 1928,D 17,23:3

Butler, Harry (Director)
Joy of Living 1931,Ap 7,31:1

Butler, J Fred (Director)
Great Necker, The 1928,Mr 7,28:2

Butler, James E (Director)
Digging for Apples 1962,S 28,29:4

Butler, James E (Lyricist)
Digging for Apples 1962,S 28,29:4

Butler, James E (Playwright)
Digging for Apples 1962,S 28,29:4

Butler, John
Just Married 1921,Ap 27,21:1
Little Accident 1928,O 10,32:3
Boundry Line, The 1930,F 6,21:1
In Times Square 1931,N 24,29:3
Happy Landing 1932,Mr 28,10:5
Great Magoo, The 1932,D 3,20:7
Both Your Houses 1933,Mr 7,20:3
Ah, Wilderness! 1933,O 3,28:2

Butler, John (Choreographer)
Consul, The 1950,Mr 16,41:1
Ice Capades 1952,S 12,18:1
Livin' the Life 1957,Ap 29,20:1
Much Ado About Nothing 1957,Ag 8,15:2
Willie the Weeper 1961,Ja 4,26:1
Family Affair, A 1962,Ja 29,17:1
Beast in Me, The 1963,My 17,29:1

Butler, John A
Butter and Egg Man, The 1925,S 24,28:1
Tenth Avenue 1927,Ag 16,31:1
Congratulations 1929,My 1,28:4
Nigger Rich 1929,S 21,16:7
Mr Gilhooley 1930,O 1,26:1

Butler, Joseph
Blue Blood 1924,Ap 3,21:2

Butler, Joseph (Playwright)
Blue Blood 1924,Ap 3,21:2

Butler, Joseph Campbell
Hair 1969,F 5,36:1

Butler, Lilian
Second Comin', The 1931,D 9,32:4

Butler, Lilliam
Broken Engagement, The 1921,My 12,20:2

Butler, Michael (Producer)
Hair 1968,Ap 30,40:2
Hair 1970,Ja 13,39:1

Butler, Miriam
Miracle Worker, The 1959,O 20,44:1

Butler, Mossette
Journeyman 1938,Ja 31,14:2

Butler, Nan
Meet a Body 1944,O 17,19:5
Many Happy Returns 1945,Ja 6,15:5

Butler, Norman
Hajj Malik, El 1970,O 4,II,5:1

Butler, Paul
Tenth Man, The 1929,Mr 21,29:2

Butler, Paul (Producer)
Stockade 1954,F 5,14:2

Butler, Rachel Barton (Playwright)
Mamma's Affair 1920,Ja 20,10:1
Mama's Affair 1920,Ja 25,VIII,2:1
Alice in Wonderland 1920,Ap 13,12:1

Butler, Sally
Sonya's Search for the Christmas Star 1929,D 14,24:6

Butler, Shirley (Director)
Poor Bitos 1964,N 16,40:2

Butler, Ted
Land Beyond the River, A 1957,Mr 29,15:7
Journey With Strangers, A 1958,N 27,53:1
Shakespeare in Harlem 1959,O 28,40:7
God's Trombones 1960,F 10,43:4
Shakespeare in Harlem 1960,F 10,43:4
God's Trombones 1960,F 10,43:4
Black Monday 1962,Mr 7,29:1

Butler, Terence (Playwright)
Apricot Season, The 1962,O 4,43:8

Butler, Todd
My Fair Lady 1968,Je 14,42:1

Butler, Virginia
Man Who Married a Dumb Wife, The 1930,My 9,20:5

Butleroff, Helen
Light, Lively and Yiddish 1970,O 28,58:1

Butleroff, Helen (Choreographer)
Oh What a Wedding! 1969,O 20,60:1

Butman, P W
It's Only Natural 1922,Ap 21,13:2

Buton, Richard
Richard II 1951,Mr 25,75:3

Butt, Alfred (Sir)
Rainbow, The 1923,Ap 8,VIII,1:7

Butt, Dan (Lighting Director)
Women at the Tomb, The 1961,Ap 25,41:1
Philoktetes 1961,Ap 25,41:1
Coach With the Six Insides, The 1962,N 27,44:1

Butt, Dan (Scenic Designer)
Women at the Tomb, The 1961,Ap 25,41:1

Philoktetes 1961,Ap 25,41:1
Coach With the Six Insides, The 1967,My 12,50:1

Butterfield, Everett
Main Street 1921,O 6,21:1
Ghosts 1922,F 7,12:1
Go West, Young Man 1923,N 13,25:2

Butterfield, Herbert
Blue Peter, The 1925,Mr 25,25:3

Butterfield, Millie
Don Juan 1921,S 8,14:2
Green Ring, The 1922,Ap 5,22:1
Johannes Kreisler 1922,D 25,20:3
Main Line, The 1924,Mr 26,19:4
Pearl of Great Price, The 1926,N 2,34:3

Butterfield, Walton
Liliom 1921,Ap 21,18:1
Cloister, The 1921,Je 6,16:3
Jitta's Atonement 1923,Ja 18,16:3
Saint Joan 1923,D 29,8:4
Book of Charm, The 1925,S 4,26:3
Book of Charm, The 1925,S 13,VIII,1:1
Trouper, The 1926,Mr 9,21:1
Henry-Behave 1926,Ag 24,19:4
One for All 1927,My 14,25:5
Golden Age, The 1928,Ap 25,31:3
One Way Street 1928,D 25,31:2
Big Knife, The 1959,N 13,25:1

Butters, Mary (Costume Designer)
Three Plays of the Sea 1970,Ag 20,39:1

Butterworth, Bette
Places, Please 1937,N 13,10:6
Many Moons 1947,D 15,35:2
Rumpelstiltskin 1948,Mr 15,27:3
King Midas and the Golden Touch 1948,O 25,28:3
Pied Piper of Hamelin, The 1950,Ap 3,19:2

Butterworth, Bette (Costume Designer)
Jack and the Beanstalk 1947,N 3,28:2
Many Moons 1947,D 15,35:2
Little Red Riding Hood 1948,Ja 12,15:3
Rumpelstiltskin 1948,Mr 15,27:3
King Midas and the Golden Touch 1948,O 25,28:3
Indian Captive, The 1949,Ja 31,15:2
Ali Baba 1951,Mr 27,34:2

Butterworth, Bette (Playwright)
Pied Piper of Hamelin, The 1950,Ap 3,19:2

Butterworth, Charles
Americana 1926,Jl 27,15:3
Americana 1926,D 5,VIII,5:1
Allez-Opp! 1927,Ag 3,29:3
Good Boy 1928,S 6,23:2
Sweet Adeline 1929,Ag 25,VIII,3:1
Sweet Adeline 1929,S 4,33:1
Flying Colors 1932,S 16,24:2
Flying Colors 1932,O 9,IX,1:1
Count Me In 1942,O 9,24:2
Brighten the Corner 1945,D 13,33:2

Butterworth, Mabel
Blackouts of 1949 1949,S 7,39:2

Butterworth, Paul
Simple Simon 1931,Mr 10,23:2

Butterworth, Walter
Sleepy Hollow 1948,Je 4,26:3

Buttigol, Val
Louisiana Lady 1947,Je 3,35:2

Buttoff, David
Jazz a La Carte 1922,Je 3,8:3

Button, Dick
Ice Capades 1952,S 12,18:1
Mister Roberts 1956,D 6,46:2
South Pacific 1957,Ap 25,35:1

Button, Dick (Producer)
Do You Know the Milky Way? 1961,O 17,45:1

Button, Jeanne (Costume Designer)
Ah, Wilderness! 1953,F 7,10:6
Scrapbooks 1953,N 6,24:2
Misalliance 1955,F 12,10:6
Macbeth 1955,O 8,12:6
Last Love of Don Juan, The 1955,N 24,40:1
MacBird! 1967,F 23,38:1
Now Is the Time for all Good Men 1967,S 27,42:1
Niggerlovers, The; Demonstration, The 1967,O 2,54:2
Niggerlovers, The; Man and Dog 1967,O 2,54:2
Bench, The 1968,Mr 5,35:2
Four Seasons, The 1968,Mr 15,32:1
Kongi's Harvest 1968,Ap 15,49:1
Get Thee to Canterbury 1969,Ja 26,74:1
Watering Place, The 1969,Mr 13,51:1
World War 2 1/2 1969,Mr 25,40:1
Henry V 1969,Je 9,57:1
Henry V 1969,N 11,43:1
Sensations 1970,O 26,48:2
Carpenters, The 1970,D 22,40:1

Button, Jeanne (Director)
Thesmophoriazusae, The; Goddesses of Athens, The 1955,D 14,52:4

Buttons, Red
Vickie 1942,S 23,28:1
Winged Victory 1943,N 22,24:1
Barefoot Boy With Cheek 1947,Ap 4,20:2
Hold It! 1948,My 6,31:5
Midsummer Night's Dream, A 1956,Jl 20,9:5

Butts, Dorothy
Man Who Never Died, The 1958,N 22,27:2

Butz, Fritz (Costume Designer)
Why Do I Deserve This? 1966,Ja 19,31:2

Buwen, John
Hit the Deck 1960,Je 24,32:1

Buxton, Lewis
Merton of the Movies 1922,N 14,16:2

Buxton, Reb
Connelly vs Connelly 1961,F 18,11:3
Lady of Mexico 1962,O 20,13:2
Philoctetes 1964,Ag 19,29:1
Patrick--The First 1965,F 19,25:1
Man Who Washed His Hands, The 1967,F 16,33:1
Ballad of John Ogilvie, The 1968,O 9,42:4

Buyle, Evelyne
Piano Dans l'Herbe, Un 1970,S 17,56:1

Buzante, George
Chinese O'Neill 1929,My 23,27:1
Dead End 1935,O 29,17:2

Buzgan, Chewel
Tevye the Milkman 1970,D 6,84:8

Buzzel, Robert
Ali Baba 1951,Mr 27,34:2

Buzzell, Eddie
Gingham Girl, The 1922,Ag 29,15:5
No Other Girl 1924,Ag 14,10:4
Sweetheart Time 1926,Ja 20,23:2
Desert Song, The 1926,D 1,24:2
Good Boy 1928,S 6,23:2
Lady Fingers 1929,F 1,22:4

Buzzell, Eddie (Playwright)
Lady Fingers 1929,Ja 13,VIII,2:4
Lady Fingers 1929,F 1,22:4

Buzzell, Robert (Miscellaneous)
Donogoo 1961,Ja 19,25:3
Red Roses for Me 1961,N 28,41:1
Riverwind 1962,D 14,5:5
Carricknabauna 1967,Mr 31,30:1
Other Man, The 1968,F 9,50:1
Oh, Say Can You See L A 1968,F 9,50:1
Make Me Disappear 1969,My 14,34:1

Buzzell, Robert C (Miscellaneous)
Route 1 1964,N 18,52:3

Buzzi, Ruth
Mis-Guided Tour 1959,O 13,44:7
Man's a Man, A 1962,S 20,30:2
Babes in the Wood 1964,D 29,21:2
Sweet Charity 1966,Ja 31,22:1

Byall, Franklin
At Mrs Beam's 1923,Mr 11,VIII,2:4

Byam, John
Century Revue and the Midnight Rounders, The 1920,Jl 13,9:1
Make It Snappy 1922,Ap 14,20:2
Annie Dear 1924,N 5,25:3
Bye Bye Bonnie 1927,Ja 14,15:3
Night in Venice, A 1929,My 22,30:2
Vaudeville (Palace) 1930,Mr 24,24:5

Byam-Shaw, Glen
And So to Bed 1927,N 10,23:1

Byatt, Irene
H M S Pinafore 1960,S 8,41:1
Pirates of Penzance, The 1961,S 7,41:1
By Jupiter 1967,Ja 20,28:2
South Pacific 1967,Je 13,56:1

Bybell, Patricia
Allegro 1947,O 11,10:2
Alive and Kicking 1950,Ja 18,25:5
Singing Girl, The 1952,Je 4,31:8

Byck, Lehman
Manhatters, The 1927,Jl 19,27:3

Byer, Marta (Director)
To Damascus 1961,F 15,40:2

Byer, Marta (Miscellaneous)
To Damascus 1961,F 15,40:2

Byers, Bill (Miscellaneous)
Beast in Me, The 1963,My 17,29:1

Byers, Billy
Evening With Yves Montand, An 1959,S 23,45:1

Byers, Eugenia
Garrick Gaieties 1926,My 11,25:2

Byers, Jim
Tarot 1970,D 12,19:1

Byers, Margaret
Her Unborn Child 1928,Mr 7,28:3
Babes in Toyland 1929,D 24,15:3
Babes in Toyland 1930,D 22,17:1

Byers, Trudy
Priorities of 1942 1942,Mr 13,23:2

Bygraves, Max
Vaudeville (Palace) 1951,O 17,36:6

Byington, Homer M Jr
Coriolanus 1927,Je 18,8:3

Byington, Spring
Beggar on Horseback 1924,F 13,17:2
Weak Sisters 1925,O 14,31:3
Puppy Love 1926,Ja 28,16:3
Great Adventure, The 1926,D 23,23:1
Skin Deep 1927,O 18,32:1
Merchant of Venice, The 1928,Ja 17,22:2
Tonight at 12 1928,N 16,28:1
Be Your Age 1929,F 5,27:1

Byington, Spring—Cont
Jonesy 1929,Ap 10,32:2
Ladies Don't Lie 1929,O 11,36:3
What a Question 1930,F 23,VIII,2:5
I Want My Wife 1930,Mr 21,30:7
Once in a Lifetime 1930,S 25,22:3
Once in a Lifetime 1930,D 7,IX,1:1
Ladies of Creation 1931,S 9,25:1
We Are No Longer Children 1932,Ap 1,17:2
When Ladies Meet 1932,O 7,19:1
When Ladies Meet 1932,O 16,IX,1:1
First Apple, The 1933,D 28,25:1
No Questions Asked 1934,F 6,24:3
Jig Saw 1934,My 1,26:3
Piper Paid 1934,D 26,19:1

Bynder, Jerry
Me, The Sleeper 1949,My 16,18:6

Byng, Douglas
Hotel Paradiso 1957,Ap 12,22:2
Hotel Paradiso 1957,Ap 21,II,1:1

Byram, Gene
Brothers 1928,D 26,14:3

Byram, John (Producer)
Wayward Saint, The 1955,F 18,17:1

Byrd, Ackie
Here Be Dragons 1970,D 21,52:1

Byrd, Anne Gee
Hamlet 1964,Jl 4,9:1

Byrd, Anne Gee (Costume Designer)
Diff'rent 1961,O 18,52:1

Byrd, Carl W (Miscellaneous)
Ballad for Bimshire 1963,O 16,54:1

Byrd, Charlie (Composer)
Clandestine on the Morning Line 1959,D 5,18:2

Byrd, David
Duchess of Malfi, The 1962,Mr 5,27:1
Henry V 1963,Je 14,37:1
Caesar and Cleopatra 1963,Ag 1,18:2
Much Ado About Nothing 1964,Je 11,26:2
Richard III 1964,Je 12,44:2
Hamlet 1964,Jl 4,9:1

Byrd, Dorothy
Lady in the Dark 1941,Ja 24,14:2

Byrd, Evelyn
Merchant of Venice, The 1932,N 24,34:5
Devil Takes a Bride, The 1938,O 8,10:3

Byrd, James (Lighting Director)
Confederacy, The 1958,Jl 3,20:1

Byrd, Joe
Lucky Sambo 1925,Je 8,19:4
Lucky Sambo 1926,My 26,24:2
Singin' the Blues 1931,S 17,21:3
Black Rhythm 1936,D 21,19:2
Lew Leslie's Blackbirds of 1939 1939,F 13,12:2
Harlem Cavalcade 1942,My 2,11:2

Byrd, John
Hamlet 1936,N 11,54:2
Bloomer Girl 1944,O 6,18:5

Byrd, Josephine
Green Pastures, The 1930,F 27,26:1

Byrd, Sam
Incubator 1932,N 2,23:3
We the People 1933,Ja 23,9:5
Lambs Gambol 1933,Ap 24,10:1
Tobacco Road 1933,D 5,31:2
White Man 1936,O 19,22:4
Of Mice and Men 1937,N 24,20:5
Man Who Killed Lincoln, The 1939,D 30,9:1
Man Who Killed Lincoln, The 1940,Ja 18,26:4
Good Neighbor 1941,O 22,26:2
Chase, The 1952,Ap 16,30:2

Byrd, Sam (Producer)
White Man 1936,O 19,22:4
Journeyman 1938,Ja 31,14:2
John Henry 1940,Ja 11,18:2
Good Neighbor 1941,O 22,26:2

Byrn, Robert
Connecticut Yankee, A 1943,N 18,30:2
Carousel 1945,Ap 20,24:2
Allegro 1947,O 11,10:2
Love Life 1948,O 8,31:2

Byrne, Beatrice
What Next 1920,Ja 27,7:2

Byrne, Cecily
High Road, The 1927,S 25,VIII,2:1
Without Witness 1933,D 28,25:1

Byrne, David
Mid-West 1936,Ja 8,22:4
Susan and God 1937,O 8,26:4

Byrne, Dolly (Playwright)
Enter Madame 1920,Ag 17,11:2

Byrne, Donn (Original Author)
Hangman's House 1926,D 17,27:2

Byrne, Francis
Man in the Making, The 1921,S 21,16:2
Banco 1922,S 21,18:1
Jitta's Atonement 1923,Ja 18,16:3

Byrne, Gaylea
All in Love 1961,N 11,15:2
Music Man, The 1965,Je 17,26:4

Byrne, Gypsy
Just a Minute 1928,O 9,34:3

Byrne, J Edmund (Producer)
Sea Legs 1937,My 19,26:5

Byrne, Jack
Street Wolf, The 1929,Ja 1,61:1
Tired Business Man, The 1929,Je 5,32:5
Commodore Marries, The 1929,S 5,26:3
Roadside 1930,S 27,21:1
Mourning Becomes Electra; Haunted, The 1931,O 27,22:1
Mourning Becomes Electra; Homecoming 1931,O 27,22:1
She Loves Me Not 1933,N 21,22:4
Swing Your Lady 1936,O 19,22:4
Storm Over Patsy 1937,Mr 9,26:4
Room Service 1937,My 20,16:1
What a Life 1938,Ap 14,26:2

Byrne, John
Mr Papavert 1932,Ja 23,18:6

Byrne, John (Playwright)
Painted Days, The 1961,Ap 7,24:1

Byrne, M St Clare (Playwright)
Busman's Honeymoon, A 1936,D 17,35:2
Busman's Honeymoon, A 1937,Ja 10,X,1:8

Byrne, Patsy
Caucasian Chalk Circle, The 1962,Mr 30,28:1
Jew of Malta, The 1965,Ap 17,9:1

Byrne, Sheila
What Next 1920,Ja 27,7:2

Byrnes, Ann
Rubicon, The 1922,F 22,13:1

Byrnes, Dolly
Some Party 1922,Ap 17,22:1

Byrnes, Helen
Little Accident 1928,O 10,32:3

Byrnes, Maureen
Grosse Valise, La 1965,D 15,52:1

Byrnes, Patsy
As You Like It 1961,Jl 5,30:1

Byrnes, Raphael
Outside Looking In 1925,S 8,28:1

Byrns, Harold (Miscellaneous)
Day Before Spring, The 1945,N 23,27:2

Byrns, Renee
Decameron, The 1961,Ap 13,32:1

Byron, Arthur
Transplanting Jean 1921,Ja 4,11:2
Transplanting Jean 1921,Ja 9,VI,1:1
Ghost Between, The 1921,Mr 23,11:2
Lady Cristilinda, The 1922,D 26,11:2
But for the Grace of God 1923,S 9,VII,2:4
Spring Cleaning 1923,N 10,16:3
Spring Cleaning 1923,N 18,VIII,1:1
Kiss in a Taxi, The 1925,Ag 26,14:1
Kiss in a Taxi, The 1925,Ag 30,VII,1:1
Not Herbert 1926,Ja 27,16:2
Shelf, The 1926,S 28,31:1
Lace Petticoat 1927,Ja 5,18:2
Lady Do 1927,Ap 19,24:2
Padlocks of 1927 1927,Jl 6,23:4
Black Velvet 1927,S 28,28:1
Marquise, The 1927,N 15,26:4
Killers 1928,Mr 14,28:3
Vaudeville (Palace) 1928,Mr 20,20:2
Criminal Code, The 1929,O 3,28:2
Criminal Code, The 1929,O 13,IX,1:1
One, Two, Three! 1930,S 30,24:2
Five Star Final 1930,D 31,11:1
Devil Passes, The 1932,Ja 5,20:3
Devil Passes, The 1932,Ja 10,VIII,1:1
Saint Joan 1936,Mr 10,27:4
Saint Joan 1936,Mr 15,X,1:1
Hamlet 1936,O 1,28:3
Hamlet 1936,O 9,30:2
Prodigal Father, The 1937,Ag 17,23:1
Stop-Over 1938,Ja 12,16:5
Jeremiah 1939,F 4,11:2

Byron, Betty
Babes in Toyland 1929,D 24,15:3
Babes in Toyland 1930,D 22,17:1

Byron, Brooke
Leading Lady 1948,O 19,33:1
Someone Waiting 1956,F 15,26:1
Speaking of Murder 1956,D 20,37:1

Byron, Delma
Up in Central Park 1945,Ja 29,17:2

Byron, Edward A (Director)
Distant City, The 1941,S 23,27:5

Byron, Eileen
Serena Blandish 1929,Ja 24,30:3
One, Two, Three! 1930,S 30,24:2
Tomorrow and Tomorrow 1931,Ja 14,26:3
Peter Ibbetson 1931,Ap 9,30:3
Little Inn, The 1935,Ag 20,25:1

Byron, Franklyn
Dancing Girl, The 1923,Ja 25,16:2

Byron, Freddie
Vaudeville (Palace) 1928,Jl 31,13:5

Byron, G D
If I Was Rich 1926,S 3,15:2

Byron, Gene
Gasoline Gypsies 1931,Je 8,21:3

Byron, George
New Faces of 1936 1936,My 20,24:5

Byron, Henry J (Playwright)
Lancashire Lass, The 1931,D 31,16:3

Byron, John
Henry V 1966,Je 8,38:1
Henry VI 1966,Je 9,55:2

Byron, Kate
Black Velvet 1927,S 28,28:1
Sherlock Holmes 1929,N 26,28:3
Mr Samuel 1930,N 11,28:4
She Means Business 1931,Ja 27,21:2
Six Characters in Search of an Author 1931,Ap 16,29:2

Byron, Lorna
Red Mill, The 1945,O 17,16:2

Byron, Marcia
Lights Out 1922,Ag 18,8:4
Extra 1923,Ja 24,22:3
Out of Step 1925,Ja 30,12:1
Spooks 1925,Je 2,16:4
Nirvana 1926,Mr 4,19:1

Byron, Marinos
Deburau 1920,D 24,14:3

Byron, Michael (Producer)
Brightower 1970,Ja 29,32:1

Byron, Mildred
Caravan 1928,Ag 30,13:3
Jefferson Davis 1936,F 19,17:2

Byron, Paul
Zeno 1923,Ag 27,14:2
Jazz Singer, The 1925,S 15,29:2
So Was Napoleon 1930,Ja 9,22:2
Lady Refuses, The 1933,Mr 8,18:6
Prologue to Glory 1938,Mr 18,22:2
Devils Galore 1945,S 13,27:2
Madwoman of Chaillot, The 1950,Je 14,41:2

Byron, Roy
Mouthpiece, The 1929,Je 16,VIII,2:1

Byron, Virginia
Chameleon, The 1932,Jl 19,20:4

Byrs, Henri (Miscellaneous)
Charles Aznavour 1970,F 5,32:4

Byrs, Henri (Musical Director)
Charles Aznavour 1970,F 5,32:4

Byrs, Henry (Musical Director)
World of Charles Aznavour, The 1965,O 15,49:1

Byrt, Bertha
Mendel, Inc 1929,N 26,28:5

C

Caan, Jimmy
Ronde, La 1960,My 10.44:2

Cabal, Alan
Happy Journey to Trenton and Camden, The 1966,S 7,53:1
Queens of France 1966,S 7,53:1
Galileo 1967,Ap 14,31:1

Caballero, Angel
But Never Jam Today 1969,Ap 24,40:1

Cabanila, Don
Passenger to Bali, A 1940,Mr 15,26:2

Cabanne, Martha (Martha Kayser) (Original Author)
Way, The 1940,O 12,20:3

Cabanne, Martha (Martha Kayser) (Playwright)
Way, The 1940,O 12,20:3

Cabanne, Mimi
Arms and the Girl 1950,F 3,28:2

Cabell, James Branch (Playwright)
Little Theatre Tournament; Simon's Hour 1926,My 6,23:3

Cabellero, Ramon
King and I, The 1963,Je 13,30:2
West Side Story 1968,Je 25,32:1

Cabellero, Shirley
Great Scot! 1965,N 12,56:3

Cabes, Eleanor A
South Pacific 1965,Je 3,25:1

Cable, Christopher
Drunkard, The 1970,Ap 14,54:1

Cabor, Susan
Intimate Relations 1962,N 2,27:1

Cabot, Bruce
Off the Record 1940,D 1,63:5

Cabot, Eliot
Six Characters in Search of an Author 1922,O 31,11:2
Cat Comes Back, The 1923,Ja 29,11:2
Sylvia 1923,Ap 26,22:1
Sun-Up 1923,My 25,28:1
In His Arms 1924,O 14,23:1
Mrs Partridge Presents 1925,Ja 6,23:3
All Dressed Up 1925,S 10,28:1
Great Gatsby, The 1926,F 3,22:1
Silver Cord, The 1926,D 21,21:1
Coquette 1927,N 9,23:1
Coquette 1927,N 13,IX,1:1
Major Barbara 1928,N 20,28:4
Major Barbara 1928,D 2,X,1:1
Camel Through the Needle's Eye, The 1929,Ap 16,32:2
Camel Through the Needle's Eye, The 1929,Ap 28,IX,1:1
Month in the Country, A 1930,Mr 18,30:5
Way of the World, The 1931,Je 2,34:3

Cabot, Eliot—Cont
Troilus and Cressida 1932,Je 7,22:3
Jig Saw 1934,My 1,26:3
Good Men and True 1935,O 26,12:4
Season Changes, The 1935,D 24,10:2
Ghost of Yankee Doodle, The 1937,O 28,28:5
Ghost of Yankee Doodle, The 1937,N 23,26:3
Cabot, Louisa
Love of Two Hours, The 1962,O 27,16:2
Dylan 1964,Ja 20,18:1
Cabot, Sebastian
Love for Love 1947,My 27,30:2
Cabot, Susan
Stone for Danny Fisher, A 1954,O 22,24:2
Cabot, Tony (Musical Director)
Dance Me a Song 1950,Ja 21,10:5
Caccia, Roger
Plume de Ma Tante, La 1958,N 12,42:1
Plume de Ma Tante, La 1959,S 13,II,1:1
Cacoyannis, Michael (Choreographer)
Trojan Women, The 1963,D 24,7:6
Cacoyannis, Michael (Director)
Trojan Women, The 1963,D 24,7:6
Trojan Women, The 1965,Mr 18,25:1
And Things That Go Bump in the Night
1965,Ap 27,27:5
Devils, The 1965,N 17,51:2
Iphigenia in Aulis 1967,N 22,40:2
Iphigenia in Aulis 1967,D 3,II,1:1
Iphigenia in Aulis 1968,Ap 6,43:1
Caddon, Carr
All Rights Reserved 1934,N 7,33:5
Cade, Jim
Hobo 1961,Ap 11,41:2
Cadell, Jean
Enchanted Cottage, The 1922,Mr 2,21:4
At Mrs Beam's 1923,Mr 11,VIII,2:4
At Mrs Beam's 1926,Ap 26,24:3
At Mrs Beam's 1926,My 2,VIII,1:1
Devil, The 1930,F 2,VIII,2:4
Evergreen 1930,D 21,VIII,1:6
Hollywood Holiday 1931,N 8,VIII,4:1
Black Eye, The 1935,O 12,13:5
Black Eye, The 1935,N 10,IX,3:1
Boy David, The 1936,N 22,VI,7:1
Spring Meeting 1938,D 9,30:4
Importance of Being Earnest, The 1947,Mr 4,30:2
Importance of Being Earnest, The 1947,Mr 9,II,1:1
Caden, Joe
Man of Destiny, The 1956,Ap 26,38:1
Cadenhead, Ian
Cock-A-Doodle Dandy 1955,N 4,26:5
J B 1958,Ap 24,37:1
Antigone 1959,S 16,46:2
Twelfth Night 1963,O 9,47:1
Cadenhead, Ian (Lighting Director)
Decameron, The 1961,Ap 13,32:1
Cadenhead, Ian (Miscellaneous)
Decameron, The 1961,Ap 13,32:1
Basement, The 1968,O 16,40:1
Tea Party 1968,O 16,40:1
Cadet, Anne
Streetcar Named Desire, A 1955,Mr 4,18:2
Cadle, Shirley
Arabian Nights 1955,Je 24,16:1
Cadou, Andre (Composer)
Arlequin Poli par l'Amour 1955,N 9,40:1
Cadou, Andre (Musical Director)
Athalie 1939,My 14,XI,6:5
Bourgeois Gentilhomme, Le 1955,O 26,26:1
Barbier de Seville, Le 1955,N 9,40:1
Cadoza, Dorothy
How Come Lawd? 1937,O 1,18:5
Cadwallader, Fran
Don Juan; Feast With the Statue, The
1956,Ja 4,21:4
Cady, James
Rivals, The 1969,O 18,37:1
Caesar, Adolph
Falstaff 1966,Je 20,27:1
Murder in the Cathedral 1966,Je 21,38:1
Twelfth Night 1966,Je 23,28:1
Julius Caesar 1966,Je 24,29:2
Harpers Ferry 1967,Je 6,52:2
Visit, The 1967,S 13,41:1
Caesar, Arthur (Playwright)
Out of the Seven Seas 1923,N 4,VIII,2:7
Out of the Seven Seas 1923,N 20,23:3
Napoleon's Barber 1927,F 2,22:4
Off Key 1927,F 9,16:2
Maker of Images, The 1927,Mr 5,12:2
Caesar, Dina
Jack in the Box 1960,My 19,43:3
Caesar, Irving (Composer)
Polly 1929,Ja 9,28:3
Nine Fifteen Revue, The 1930,F 12,26:2
Music Hall Varieties 1932,N 23,15:3
My Dear Public 1943,S 10,28:1
Caesar, Irving (Lyricist)
Pins and Needles 1922,F 2,20:1
Greenwich Village Follies 1922,S 13,18:2
Greenwich Village Follies 1923,S 21,4:6
Greenwich Village Follies 1924,S 17,16:1
Betty Lee 1924,D 26,18:2

No, No, Nanette 1925,S 17,20:2
Sweetheart Time 1926,Ja 20,23:2
No Foolin' 1926,Je 25,25:1
Talk About Girls 1927,Je 15,31:3
Yes, Yes, Yvette 1927,O 4,32:3
Here's Howe! 1928,My 2,19:3
Americana 1928,O 31,28:2
New Americana 1928,N 30,32:4
Polly 1929,Ja 9,28:3
George White's Scandals 1929,S 24,29:1
Nina Rosa 1929,O 27,IX,2:1
Ripples 1930,F 2,VIII,2:7
Nine Fifteen Revue, The 1930,F 12,26:2
Ripples 1930,F 12,26:1
Nina Rosa 1930,My 31,19:3
Nina Rosa 1930,S 22,22:5
Wonder Bar, The 1931,Mr 18,23:4
Melody 1933,F 15,17:4
White Horse Inn 1936,O 2,28:5
Russian Bank 1940,My 25,20:2
Hit the Deck 1960,Je 24,32:1
Caesar, Irving (Playwright)
No Foolin' 1926,Je 25,25:1
Betsy 1926,D 29,24:3
Wonder Bar, The 1931,Mr 18,23:4
George White's Scandals 1931,S 15,30:1
Shady Lady 1933,Jl 6,26:3
My Dear Public 1943,S 10,28:1
Caesar, Irving (Producer)
My Dear Public 1943,S 10,28:1
Caesar, J (Playwright)
Broadway Brevities, 1920 1920,S 30,12:2
Caesar, James
Hats Off to Ice 1944,Je 23,15:2
Icetime 1946,Je 21,20:5
Icetime 1947,My 29,28:2
Elliott Murphy's Aquashow 1955,Je 23,25:1
Caesar, Robert
By Hex 1956,Je 19,25:1
Caesar, Sid
Make Mine Manhattan 1948,Ja 16,26:2
Little Me 1962,O 10,58:2
Little Me 1962,N 19,41:3
Little Me 1962,D 2,II,1:1
Cafarella, Donald
Life and Death of an American 1939,My 20,11:2
Caffin, John
Pequod 1969,Je 30,33:1
Caffrey, Julann
Your Loving Son 1941,Ap 5,13:2
Manhattan Nocturne 1943,O 27,26:2
Caesar and Cleopatra 1949,D 22,28:2
Caffrey, Paul (Miscellaneous)
Digging for Apples 1962,S 28,29:4
Caffy, Gregory K
Macbeth 1968,N 30,49:3
Cage, John (Composer)
Marrying Maiden, The 1960,Je 23,18:3
Orestes 1968,F 17,32:5
Cagney, James
Outside Looking In 1925,S 8,28:1
Outside Looking In 1925,S 13,VIII,1:1
Women Go on Forever 1927,S 8,25:1
Grand Street Follies, The 1928,My 29,16:2
Grand Street Follies, The 1929,My 2,20:4
Maggie, the Magnificent 1929,O 22,26:1
Penny Arcade 1930,Mr 11,24:5
Cagney, James (Choreographer)
Grand Street Follies, The 1928,My 29,16:2
Cagney, Jeanne
I'll Take the High Road 1943,N 10,28:3
Streets Are Guarded, The 1944,N 21,19:7
Place of Our Own, A 1945,Ap 3,23:7
Iceman Cometh, The 1946,O 10,31:3
Cahan, Paddy
Love and Politics 1929,O 21,30:7
Cahen, Helen
Nautical but Nice 1931,Ap 19,31:6
Cahill, Bernard
General John Regan 1930,Ja 30,16:5
Pipe in the Fields, The 1931,Mr 14,23:4
Cahill, James
Taming of the Shrew, The 1957,F 21,30:2
Blood Bugle, The 1961,Je 29,26:1
Hostage, The 1961,D 13,55:4
Figuro in the Night 1962,O 31,33:1
Alchemist, The 1964,S 15,33:1
Foursome 1965,Mr 8,34:1
Leader, The 1965,Mr 8,34:1
Bedlam Galore, for Two or More 1965,Mr 8,34:1
Impromptu, L' 1965,Mr 8,34:1
Persecution and Assassination of Marat As
Performed by the Inmates of the Asylum of
Charenton Under the Direction of the Marquis de
Sade, The 1967,Ja 4,34:1
Evening for Merlin Finch, An 1968,D 30,25:1
Crimes of Passion; Erpingham Camp, The
1969,O 27,54:1
Disintegration of James Cherry, The
1970,Ja 30,33:3
Cahill, John
Half Moon Inn 1923,Mr 21,19:2

Cahill, Lily
Purple Mask, The 1920,Ja 6,18:1
Opportunity 1920,Jl 31,5:1
So This Is London 1922,Ag 31,18:2
Lovely Lady 1925,O 15,27:1
Caprice 1929,Ja 1,61:1
Tyrant, The 1930,N 13,33:1
As Husbands Go 1931,Mr 6,26:5
Chrysalis 1932,N 16,15:2
Alien Corn 1933,F 21,17:2
Alien Corn 1933,F 26,IX,1:1
Woman Kind 1933,S 28,25:2
And Be My Love 1934,Ja 19,25:2
Rain From Heaven 1934,D 25,28:4
First Lady 1935,N 27,17:4
Cahill, Marie
Vaudeville (Palace) 1924,F 19,12:1
Vaudeville (Palace) 1925,Ap 21,18:1
Vaudeville (Palace) 1925,O 20,29:2
Vaudeville (Palace) 1926,O 26,24:2
Vaudeville (Palace) 1926,N 2,35:2
Merry-Go-Round 1927,Je 1,25:4
Caprice 1929,Je 23,VIII,1:3
New Yorkers, The 1930,N 16,VIII,3:1
New Yorkers, The 1930,D 9,31:1
Cahill, Michael
Borstal Boy 1970,Ap 1,38:1
Cahill, Paul
Curley McDimple 1967,N 23,59:2
Cahill, Richard
Cure for Matrimony 1939,O 26,26:3
Steel 1939,D 20,30:2
Cahill, T M
Deep Tangled Wildwood, The 1923,N 6,22:1
Cahill, Thomas
Lend an Ear 1959,S 25,20:5
Cahn, Alan
Captain Brassbound's Conversion 1950,D 28,21:1
Cahn, Gregory
Scapegoat, The 1950,Ap 20,36:5
Cahn, Sammy (Composer)
High Button Shoes 1947,O 10,32:2
High Button Shoes 1948,D 23,23:7
High Button Shoes 1955,Mr 12,10:6
Eddie Fisher at the Winter Garden 1962,O 3,47:1
Cahn, Sammy (Lyricist)
High Button Shoes 1947,O 10,32:2
High Button Shoes 1948,D 23,23:7
Two's Company 1952,D 16,43:5
High Button Shoes 1955,Mr 12,10:6
Eddie Fisher at the Winter Garden 1962,O 3,47:1
Poupees de Paris, Les 1964,My 16,11:1
Skyscraper 1965,N 15,48:1
Walking Happy 1966,N 28,47:1
Look to the Lilies 1970,Mr 30,59:1
Cahn, William (Producer)
Devils Galore 1945,S 13,27:2
I Like It Here 1946,Mr 23,8:6
Toplitzky of Notre Dame 1946,D 27,13:4
Cahoon, Wyn
It Happened Tomorrow 1933,My 6,11:5
Jubilee 1935,O 14,20:1
Brother Rat 1936,D 17,34:5
Caiano, Vincenzo
Sansone; Samson 1936,N 30,25:2
Caicedo, Franklin
Remolienda, La; Bawdy Party 1968,F 3,20:1
Caicedo, George (Scenic Designer)
John Brown's Body 1964,Je 29,33:1
Caillabet, Pierre
Avare, L'; Miser, The 1924,Mr 12,17:3
Monsieur Brotonneau 1924,Mr 13,14:1
Blanchette 1924,Mr 19,19:4
Caillavet, Gaston de (Playwright)
Transplanting Jean 1921,Ja 4,11:2
Transplanting Jean 1921,Ja 9,VI,1:1
Monsieur Brotonneau 1923,Ap 8,VIII,1:7
Habit Vert, L' 1927,Ja 16,VII,2:1
Caille, Robert
Elizabeth the Queen 1930,N 4,37:1
Stevedore 1934,Ap 19,33:2
Cain, Alfred (Miscellaneous)
Amen Corner, The 1965,Ap 16,35:1
Cain, James M (Original Author)
Postman Always Rings Twice, The 1936,F 7,14:4
Postman Always Rings Twice, The 1936,F 26,17:2
Cain, James M (Playwright)
Postman Always Rings Twice, The 1936,F 7,14:4
Postman Always Rings Twice, The 1936,F 26,17:2
Cain, Jess
Stalag 17 1951,My 9,41:2
Cain, Robert
Jarnegan 1928,S 25,29:2
Cain, Sibol
Carmen Jones 1943,D 3,26:2
Carmen Jones 1945,My 3,26:5
Carmen Jones 1946,Ap 8,32:2
Carmen Jones 1951,S 22,8:6
Cain, William
Jericho-Jim Crow 1964,Ja 13,25:3
Brother to Dragons 1968,D 8,86:1
Wilson in the Promise Land 1970,Ja 11,78:1
Wilson in the Promise Land 1970,My 27,41:1

Caine, Betty
Point of No Return 1957,Mr 23,17:2
Caine, Gary
Point of No Return 1957,Mr 23,17:2
Caine, Georgia
Mary 1920,O 19,12:1
O'Brien Girl, The 1921,O 4,10:2
Little Nellie Kelly 1922,N 14,16:1
Be Yourself! 1924,S 4,13:3
Home Towners, The 1926,Ag 24,19:3
Baby Cyclone, The 1927,S 13,37:4
Cafe 1930,Ag 29,11:1
Smiles 1930,N 19,19:2
Dinner at Eight 1933,Ap 9,IX,1:7
Slight Case of Murder, A 1935,S 12,28:5
Caine, Howard
School for Scandal, The 1953,Je 24,29:2
Inherit the Wind 1955,Ap 22,20:2
Tiger at the Gates 1955,O 4,40:1
Annie Get Your Gun 1957,Mr 9,15:5
Caine, John-Ellen
Hotel Paradiso 1957,Ap 12,22:2
Caine, Richard
Ben Bagley's Shoestring Revues 1970,O 24,22:1
Cairney, John
Young Auchinleck 1962,Ag 23,24:4
Cairns, Angus
Othello 1945,My 23,25:4
Henry VIII 1946,N 7,42:2
Androcles and the Lion 1946,D 20,29:2
Yellow Jack 1947,F 28,26:2
Alice in Wonderland 1947,Ap 7,19:2
Brigadoon 1950,My 3,36:2
Engagement Baby, The 1970,My 22,40:1
Cairns, Hugh Jr
As You Desire Me 1931,Ja 29,21:2
Caites Brothers
Artists and Models 1925,Je 25,16:2
Caits, Joseph
Ups-A-Daisy 1928,O 9,34:2
Caits, Louis
Ups-A-Daisy 1928,O 9,34:2
Cakes, Betty
She Shall Have Music 1959,Ja 23,18:4
Calabrese, Dick
Wedding in Japan 1957,Mr 12,37:7
Calabrese, Teresa (Miscellaneous)
Portofino 1958,F 22,8:3
Calabrese, Tony (Director)
Baby With a Knife 1969,My 15,41:2
Pets 1969,My 15,41:2
Silver Grey Toy Poodle 1969,My 15,41:2
Calahan, Gene (Scenic Designer)
Pursuit of Happiness, The 1952,Mr 22,9:2
Calahan, Helene
Yesterday's Orchids 1934,O 6,20:4
Calbes, Eleanor
South Pacific 1967,Je 13,56:1
King and I, The 1968,My 24,39:1
Lovely Ladies, Kind Gentlemen 1970,D 29,38:1
Calbi, Luigi Salvatore
And So to Bed 1927,N 10,23:1
Calde, Carlos
Cup, The 1923,N 13,25:1
Calder, Alexander (Miscellaneous)
Happy as Larry 1950,Ja 7,11:2
Calder, Crane (Miscellaneous)
Seventeen 1951,Je 22,16:6
Plain and Fancy 1955,Ja 28,14:2
Calder, Crane (Musical Director)
Seventh Heaven 1955,My 27,16:2
Calder, Gilchrist (Director)
Alfie 1964,D 18,27:1
Calder, King
Poppy God, The 1921,Ag 30,10:1
Tightwad, The 1927,Ap 18,18:2
Humbug, The 1929,N 28,34:5
Blue Ghost, The 1930,Mr 11,24:5
Cafe 1930,Ag 29,11:1
Five Star Final 1930,D 31,11:1
Bidding High 1932,S 29,17:2
Best People, The 1933,Mr 16,21:5
Errant Lady 1934,S 18,18:2
All Rights Reserved 1934,N 7,33:5
Tomorrow's a Holiday! 1935,D 31,10:2
Black Widow 1936,F 13,24:3
To My Husband 1936,Je 2,35:2
Scene of the Crime, The 1940,Mr 29,24:1
Doughgirls, The 1942,D 31,19:2
Bravo! 1948,N 12,31:2
Season in the Sun 1950,S 29,31:2
Season in the Sun 1950,O 8,II,1:1
Seventeen 1951,Je 22,16:6
Calder, Stephen
Priest in the Cellar, The 1969,F 19,39:1
Calder-Marshall, Anna
Uncle Vanya 1970,Mr 15,II,7:3
Calderisi, David (Playwright)
Experiment, The 1967,My 9,54:2
Calderon, George (Playwright)
Little Stone House, The 1923,My 11,20:3
Little Stone House, The 1923,My 13,16:2

Calderon, George (Translator)
Cherry Orchard, The 1928,Mr 6,20:1
Calderon de la Barca, Pedro (Original Author)
Grosses Welttheater 1933,Ap 16,IX,2:5
Constant Prince, The 1969,O 26,II,1:1
Calderon de la Barca, Pedro (Playwright)
Medecin de Son Honneur 1935,Mr 3,VIII,2:3
Mayor of Zalamea, The 1946,Ja 28,15:5
David's Crown 1948,My 10,26:2
El Alcalde De Zalamea 1953,N 23,32:5
Vida es Sueno, La 1964,Mr 18,49:1
Life Is a Dream 1964,Mr 20,24:1
Caldon, Walter (Composer)
Man Is Man 1962,S 19,31:1
Caldwell, Anne (Lyricist)
Night Boat, The 1920,F 3,18:1
Sweetheart Shop, The 1920,S 1,13:4
Tip-Top 1920,O 6,13:2
Hitchy-Koo, 1920 1920,O 20,11:3
Good Morning, Dearie 1921,N 2,20:2
Bunch and Judy, The 1922,N 29,20:1
Stepping Stones 1923,N 7,14:3
Peg o' My Dreams 1924,My 6,25:3
Magnolia Lady, The 1924,N 26,17:2
City Chap, The 1925,O 27,21:1
Yours Truly 1927,Ja 26,16:5
Take the Air 1927,N 23,28:2
Three Cheers 1928,O 16,28:1
Caldwell, Anne (Playwright)
Night Boat, The 1920,F 3,18:1
Sweetheart Shop, The 1920,S 1,13:4
Tip-Top 1920,O 6,13:2
Good Morning, Dearie 1921,N 2,20:2
Bunch and Judy, The 1922,N 12,VIII,1:6
Bunch and Judy, The 1922,N 29,20:1
Stepping Stones 1923,N 7,14:3
Magnolia Lady, The 1924,N 26,17:2
Criss Cross 1926,O 13,20:2
Oh, Please! 1926,D 22,24:3
Take the Air 1927,N 23,28:2
Three Cheers 1928,O 16,28:1
Never Trouble Trouble 1937,Ag 18,15:2
Caldwell, Ben (Playwright)
Prayer Meeting: or, The First Militant Minister
1969,Ap 27,92:1
Black Quartet, A; Prayer Meeting or The First
Militant Minister 1969,Jl 31,28:1
Prayer Meeting: or, The First Militant Minister
1969,Ag 3,II,1:4
Black Quartet, A 1969,S 22,36:1
Caldwell, Edwin
Bewitched 1924,O 2,26:3
Caldwell, Elizabeth (Miscellaneous)
Canterbury Tales; Steward's Tale, The
1969,F 4,34:1
Canterbury Tales; Wife of Bath's Tale, The
1969,F 4,34:1
Canterbury Tales; Merchant's Tale, The
1969,F 4,34:1
Canterbury Tales; Miller's Tale, The 1969,F 4,34:1
Canterbury Tales; Pilgrims, The 1969,F 4,34:1
Butterflies Are Free 1969,O 22,30:1
Caldwell, Emma Jane
Bubble Along 1930,Je 3,27:3
Caldwell, Erskine (Director)
Journeyman 1938,Ja 31,14:2
Caldwell, Erskine (Original Author)
Tobacco Road 1933,D 5,31:2
Journeyman 1938,Ja 31,14:2
Tobacco Road 1938,N 27,IX,3:4
Tobacco Road 1940,D 5,32:3
Tobacco Road 1942,S 7,34:2
Tobacco Road 1943,S 6,21:3
Tobacco Road 1949,Ag 11,27:5
Trouble in July 1949,D 2,36:2
Tobacco Road 1950,Mr 7,23:2
Tobacco Road 1960,My 11,44:2
Caldwell, Frank
No Mother to Guide Her 1933,D 26,18:5
Caldwell, Gladys
Iolanthe 1920,Ja 6,13:3
H M S Pinafore 1920,Ja 13,10:2
Ruddigore 1920,Ja 20,11:2
Ruddigore 1920,F 1,VIII,2:2
Girl From Home, The 1920,My 4,9:2
Tip-Top 1920,O 6,13:2
Bombo 1921,O 7,20:2
Caldwell, H H (Original Author)
Little Stranger 1938,Jl 14,16:2
Caldwell, H H (Playwright)
Little Stranger 1938,Jl 31,IX,1:3
Caldwell, Herbert
Mlle Modiste 1937,My 5,28:5
Caldwell, Irma
Roseanne 1923,D 31,9:5
Caldwell, Joseph (Playwright)
Cockeyed Kite 1961,S 14,27:1
Caldwell, Nathan Jr (Miscellaneous)
Cindy 1964,Mr 20,24:1
Midsummer Night's Dream, A 1964,Je 30,23:2
Caldwell, Neal
Man Who Ate the Popomack, The 1924,Mr 25,24:1

Caldwell, Orville
Mecca 1920,O 5,12:2
Miracle, The 1924,Ja 16,17:1
Androcles and the Lion 1925,N 24,28:1
Miracle, The 1927,F 1,24:5
Caldwell, Paul
Rendezvous 1932,O 13,22:3
Caldwell, Robert
Wonderful Journey 1946,D 26,30:2
Caldwell, Zoe
All's Well That Ends Well 1959,Ap 22,30:3
Love's Labour's Lost 1961,Je 23,19:1
Love's Labour's Lost 1961,Jl 2,II,1:1
Miser, The 1963,My 10,39:1
Miser, The 1963,My 19,II,1:1
Three Sisters, The 1963,Jl 22,19:2
Way of the World, The 1965,Je 2,40:1
Gnadiges Fraulein, The 1966,F 23,42:1
Richard III 1967,Je 14,43:1
Antony and Cleopatra 1967,Ag 2,25:1
Merry Wives of Windsor, The 1967,Ag 4,18:1
Antony and Cleopatra 1967,S 17,II,1:1
Antony and Cleopatra 1967,O 29,83:4
Prime of Miss Jean Brodie, The 1968,Ja 17,39:1
Prime of Miss Jean Brodie, The 1968,Ja 25,32:4
Prime of Miss Jean Brodie, The 1968,Ja 28,II,1:1
Colette 1970,My 7,60:1
Colette 1970,My 17,II,1:1
Bequest to the Nation, A 1970,S 25,36:1
Cale, Katherine
Othello 1935,S 28,13:2
Macbeth 1935,O 8,26:4
Lost Colony, The 1937,Jl 11,X,2:1
Calee, Katherine
Noah 1954,O 11,32:2
Caley, Dorothy
It Happens on Ice 1940,O 11,24:3
It Happens on Ice 1941,Ap 5,13:2
Stars on Ice 1942,Jl 3,12:2
Hats Off to Ice 1944,Je 23,15:2
Caley, Hazel
It Happens on Ice 1940,O 11,24:3
It Happens on Ice 1941,Ap 5,13:2
Hats Off to Ice 1944,Je 23,15:2
Calfa, Don
Mating Dance 1965,N 4,58:1
Calfee, R
Plain Dealer, The 1929,My 23,27:1
Calgarys, The
Hilarities 1948,S 10,20:2
Calhern, Louis
Roger Bloomer 1923,Mr 2,18:3
Song and Dance Man, The 1924,Ja 1,21:2
Cobra 1924,Ap 23,24:1
Cobra 1924,Ap 27,VIII,1:1
Dark, The 1925,Ag 9,VII,1:8
In a Garden 1925,N 17,29:1
Hedda Gabler 1926,Ja 27,16:5
Hedda Gabler 1926,F 21,VII,1:2
Pardon My Glove 1926,My 23,VIII,1:1
Woman Disputed, A 1926,S 29,23:2
Up the Line 1926,N 23,26:1
Dark, The 1927,F 2,22:5
Savages Under the Skin 1927,Mr 25,25:2
Distant Drum, A 1928,Ja 21,13:1
Love Duel, The 1929,Ap 16,32:3
Rhapsody, The 1930,S 16,30:3
Tyrant, The 1930,N 13,33:1
Give Me Yesterday 1931,Mr 5,32:1
Brief Moment 1931,N 10,28:2
Inside Story, The 1932,F 23,23:2
Dinner at Eight 1933,Ap 9,IX,1:7
Birthday 1934,D 27,24:2
Hell Freezes Over 1935,D 30,14:2
Robin Landing 1937,N 19,26:4
Summer Night 1939,N 3,17:1
Royal Family, The 1940,Ag 13,15:3
Great Big Doorstep, The 1942,N 27,26:2
Jacobowsky and the Colonel 1944,Mr 15,17:2
Jacobowsky and the Colonel 1944,Mr 19,II,1:1
Magnificent Yankee, The 1946,Ja 2,23:6
Magnificent Yankee, The 1946,Ja 23,21:2
Magnificent Yankee, The 1946,F 3,II,1:2
Survivors, The 1948,Ja 20,27:2
Survivors, The 1948,Ja 25,II,1:1
Play's the Thing, The 1948,Ap 29,19:2
Play's the Thing, The 1948,My 9,II,1:1
King Lear 1950,D 26,18:1
King Lear 1950,D 31,II,1:1
Wooden Dish, The 1955,O 7,20:1
Calhern, Louis (Director)
Wooden Dish, The 1955,O 7,20:1
Calhern, Louis (Playwright)
Royal Family, The 1940,Ag 13,15:3
Calhoun, Robert (Miscellaneous)
Seagull, The 1964,Ap 6,36:1
Crucible, The 1964,Ap 7,30:2
Calhoun, Virginia
Mother Said No 1951,Ap 17,34:2
Calhoun, Walt
Show Boat 1956,Je 22,16:1
Calhoun, William B
Killers 1928,Mr 14,28:3

Calhoun, William B—Cont
Mendel, Inc 1929,N 26,28:5
Cali, Joseph (Director)
Slow Memories 1970,N 18,41:1
California Collegians
Vaudeville (Palace) 1928,Ap 24,29:2
Vaudeville (Palace) 1929,Je 3,27:4
Three's a Crowd 1930,O 16,28:3
Vaudeville (Palace) 1931,Je 22,17:2
Roberta 1933,N 20,18:4
California Four
Tangerine 1921,Ag 10,8:2
California Ramblers, The
Vaudeville (Palace) 1923,Mr 6,26:1
Caligary, Andre
Vaudeville (Palace) 1931,Jl 13,13:4
Calin, Mickey
West Side Story 1957,S 27,14:4
Calkins, Cora
Opportunity 1920,Jl 31,5:1
Calkins, Florence (Playwright)
Hey, Nonny, Nonny! 1932,Je 7,22:3
Calkins, Thomas
Here Comes Santa Claus 1962,My 18,34:1
Call, Anthony
Tonight in Living Color; David Show, The
1969,Je 11,43:1
Call, Donald
Martinique 1920,Ap 27,18:2
Her Salary Man 1921,N 29,20:1
Dagmar 1923,Ja 23,18:2
Call, Edward Payson (Director)
As You Like It 1966,Je 4,19:1
Tango 1968,Ja 1,11:1
Resistible Rise of Arturo Ui, The 1968,Ag 8,25:1
Resistible Rise of Arturo Ui, The 1968,D 23,44:1
Call, Edward Payson (Miscellaneous)
Our Town 1959,Mr 24,46:2
One Way Pendulum 1961,S 19,38:2
Golden Age, The 1963,N 19,49:2
Call, John
So Proudly We Hail 1936,S 23,28:4
But for the Grace of God 1937,Ja 13,21:4
Be So Kindly 1937,F 9,19:4
Bet Your Life 1937,Ap 6,20:2
Father Malachy's Miracle 1937,N 18,26:4
Merchant of Yonkers, The 1938,D 29,14:2
Flying Gerardos, The 1940,D 30,21:4
As You Like It 1941,O 21,29:2
They Should Have Stood in Bed 1942,F 14,18:5
Life of Reilly, The 1942,Ap 30,13:2
Bloomer Girl 1944,O 6,18:5
Bloomer Girl 1947,Ja 7,33:2
Three by Thurber; Imperturbable Spirit, The
1955,Mr 8,23:2
Three by Thurber; Middle Years, The
1955,Mr 8,23:2
Pipe Dream 1955,D 1,44:1
Touch of the Poet, A 1958,O 3,23:2
Henry V 1960,Je 30,23:1
Measure for Measure 1960,Jl 27,33:1
Taming of the Shrew, The 1960,Ag 20,17:1
Farewell, Farewell Eugene 1960,S 28,35:1
Much Ado About Nothing 1961,Jl 7,17:1
Midsummer Night's Dream, A 1961,Ag 3,13:1
Sharon's Grave 1961,N 9,39:2
Giants, Sons of Giants 1962,Ja 8,26:2
Merchant of Venice, The 1962,Je 22,1:4
Oliver 1963,Ja 8,5:5
Time for Singing, A 1966,My 23,48:2
Comedy of Errors, The 1967,Je 15,58:4
Hamlet 1967,D 27,45:1
Romeo and Juliet 1968,Ag 16,19:1
Call, Mildred
Deburau 1920,D 24,14:3
Call, William
Double Dummy 1936,N 12,30:1
Callabot, Pierre
Affaires Son les Affaires, Les 1924,Mr 11,17:1
Callaghan, Tim
Tenth Man, The 1959,N 6,24:2
Callahan, Bill
Mexican Hayride 1944,Ja 29,9:6
Call Me Mister 1946,Ap 19,26:2
As the Girls Go 1948,N 15,21:2
Two's Company 1952,D 16,43:5
Callahan, Florine
Boys From Syracuse, The 1938,N 24,36:1
Callahan, Frank
Big Fight, The 1928,S 19,33:1
Callahan, Fred
Ever Green Lady, The 1922,O 12,25:2
Callahan, George (Miscellaneous)
Love and Let Love 1968,Ja 4,30:1
Callahan, George W
Meanest Man in the World, The 1920,O 13,18:2
Play, A 1925,F 11,19:2
Up Pops the Devil 1930,S 2,19:1
Mourning Becomes Electra; Hunted, The
1932,My 10,25:2
Mourning Becomes Electra; Haunted, The
1932,My 10,25:2
Five Little Peppers, The 1952,My 19,13:1

Callahan, Kristina
Burning, The 1963,D 4,57:1
Henry V 1964,My 13,52:1
Volpone 1964,Jl 20,18:3
Way of the World, The 1965,Je 2,40:1
Cherry Orchard, The 1965,Ag 2,17:2
Fireworks; Fireworks for a Hot Fourth
1969,Je 12,51:1
Callahan, Margaret
Clap Hands 1934,Ag 21,12:7
Spring Freshet 1934,O 5,28:3
Ladies' Money 1934,N 2,26:6
Scene of the Crime, The 1940,Mr 29,24:1
Two Story House 1941,S 2,20:3
Cuckoos on the Hearth 1941,S 17,26:2
Callahan, Marie
Good Morning, Dearie 1921,N 2,20:2
Ziegfeld Follies 1923,O 22,17:2
Kid Boots 1924,Ja 1,21:3
New Moon, The 1928,S 20,33:1
Callahan, Nellie
Forbidden 1923,O 2,10:2
Bottled 1928,Ap 11,25:1
Callahan, Patricia
Devil's Disciple, The 1970,Je 30,48:1
Callahan Boys
Earl Carroll's Vanities 1923,Jl 6,8:2
Callam, Alexander
Student Prince, The 1931,Ja 30,18:1
Callan, Bill (Miscellaneous)
Inquest 1970,Ap 24,38:1
Callan, J Paul
Enchanted Isle 1927,S 20,33:2
Callan, Josephine McGarry (Dr) (Director)
Oedipus Rex 1959,Ap 30,36:1
Callan, William
Anastasia 1954,D 30,13:1
Many Loves 1959,Ja 14,28:1
Visit, The 1960,Mr 9,38:3
Midgie Purvis 1961,F 2,25:3
Man for All Seasons, A 1964,Ja 28,24:2
Malcolm 1966,Ja 12,29:1
Callas, May (Scenic Designer)
Lady From the Sea, The 1950,Ag 8,23:2
Borned in Texas 1950,Ag 22,30:6
Callaway, Joe A
As You Like It; Midsummer Night's Dream, A;
Comedy of Errors, The; Taming of the Shrew,
The 1939,My 9,28:4
As You Like It 1939,My 9,28:4
I Am a Camera 1956,O 10,47:2
Man Who Never Died, The 1958,N 22,27:2
Calleia, Joseph
All My Sons 1948,My 12,33:3
Callejo, Cecilia
Cat Screams, The 1942,Je 17,26:5
Callender, George
Lulu Belle 1926,F 10,20:1
Callender, Romaine
Sacred and Profane Love 1920,F 24,11:1
Blood and Sand 1921,S 21,16:2
Merton of the Movies 1922,N 14,16:2
School for Scandal, The 1925,D 7,18:2
Racket, The 1927,N 23,28:3
Racket, The 1927,D 18,IX,1:1
Mima 1928,D 13,24:2
Grand Hotel 1930,N 14,30:4
Man Who Reclaimed His Head 1932,S 9,17:3
Keeper of the Keys 1933,O 19,23:2
Another Love 1934,Mr 20,26:3
Judgment Day 1934,S 13,26:4
Post Road 1934,D 5,28:3
Calley, Robert
Lady in Ermine, The 1922,O 3,22:2
Student Prince, The 1924,D 3,25:3
Calligan, Walter
Home Towners, The 1926,Ag 24,19:3
Callis, David M
Bonehead, The 1920,Ap 13,12:1
Callister, Herbert (Costume Designer)
Arms for Venus 1937,Mr 12,18:7
Calloway, Cab
Vaudeville (Palace) 1931,Je 15,23:5
Vaudeville (Loew's State) 1932,Je 13,19:7
Porgy and Bess 1952,Ag 6,17:7
Porgy and Bess 1952,S 8,18:2
Porgy and Bess 1952,S 18,36:5
Porgy and Bess 1952,O 10,21:4
Porgy and Bess 1953,Mr 10,25:5
Porgy and Bess 1953,Mr 15,II,1:1
Cotton Club Revue of 1957 1957,Jl 10,23:4
Hello, Dolly! 1967,N 13,61:1
Hello, Dolly! 1967,N 26,II,3:1
Calloway, Cab Troupe
Vaudeville (Palace) 1930,O 13,31:3
Calloway, Chris
Hello, Dolly! 1967,N 13,61:1
Calloway, Northern
Saint Joan 1968,Ja 5,42:1
Tiger at the Gates 1968,Mr 1,30:1
Cyrano de Bergerac 1968,Ap 26,30:1
Me Nobody Knows, The 1970,My 19,42:1

Calsi, Rose L
Sparkin' 1931,Mr 4,33:2
Divina Pastora, La 1931,Mr 4,33:2
Psychological Moment, The 1931,Mr 4,33:2
Caltabiano, Frank
March March, The 1966,N 15,51:4
X Has No Value 1970,F 17,35:1
Calthrop, Dion (Playwright)
Harlequinade 1921,My 11,20:3
Calthrop, Donald
Double-Or Quit 1922,O 8,VI,1:7
Merry World, The 1926,Je 9,18:3
Merry World, The 1926,Je 13,VII,1:1
Calthrop, Donald (Playwright)
Kate 1924,Mr 2,VIII,2:7
Calthrop, Gladys E (Costume Designer)
Cradle Song 1927,Ja 25,18:2
Bitter Sweet 1929,N 6,30:2
Conversation Piece 1934,Mr 11,X,3:6
Conversation Piece 1934,O 24,24:1
Conversation Piece 1934,N 18,IX,1:1
Set to Music 1939,Ja 19,16:2
Calthrop, Gladys E (Miscellaneous)
Autumn Crocus 1932,N 21,20:2
Dear Octopus 1939,Ja 12,22:2
Set to Music 1939,Ja 19,16:2
Calthrop, Gladys E (Scenic Designer)
Cradle Song 1927,Ja 25,18:2
Bitter Sweet 1929,N 6,30:2
Private Lives 1931,Ja 28,24:1
Design for Living 1933,Ja 3,19:5
Design for Living 1933,Ja 25,13:2
Conversation Piece 1934,Mr 11,X,3:6
Conversation Piece 1934,O 24,24:1
Conversation Piece 1934,N 18,IX,1:1
Point Valaine 1935,Ja 17,22:2
Tonight at 8:30; Hands Across the Sea; Astonished
Heart, The; Red Peppers 1936,O 27,30:7
Red Peppers 1936,N 25,17:2
Hands Across the Sea 1936,N 25,17:2
Astonished Heart, The 1936,N 25,17:2
Shadow Play 1936,N 28,13:1
Fumed Oak 1936,N 28,13:1
We Were Dancing 1936,N 28,13:1
Still Life 1936,D 1,31:1
Family Album 1936,D 1,31:1
Ways and Means 1936,D 1,31:1
Excursion 1937,Ap 10,11:4
Calvan, Joe
Tree Grows in Brooklyn, A 1951,Ap 20,24:3
Calvan, Joe (Miscellaneous)
West Side Story 1960,Ap 28,31:1
Wonder World 1964,My 18,32:1
Dozens, The 1969,Mr 14,51:1
Calvani, Ciro
Donna Del Mare, La; Lady From the Sea, The
1923,O 30,17:1
Calve, Emma
Vaudeville (Palace) 1927,N 8,33:3
Calve, Jean-Francois
Baptiste 1952,N 13,34:2
Fausses Confidences, Les 1952,N 13,34:2
Proces, Le; Trial, The 1952,N 18,36:2
Amphitryon 1952,N 21,21:2
Fourberies de Scapin, Les 1952,N 21,21:2
Occupe-Toi d'Amelie; Keep Your Eyes on Amelie
1952,N 25,35:2
Repetition, La; Rehearsal, The 1952,N 28,22:2
Hamlet 1952,D 2,39:1
Huis Clos 1962,Ja 16,30:1
Berenice 1963,O 30,46:1
Calvert, Carey
Ame en Peine, L' 1950,My 31,25:2
Calvert, Catherine
Blood and Sand 1921,S 21,16:2
Calvert, George
Burning Deck, The 1940,Mr 2,9:2
Doughgirls, The 1942,D 31,19:2
Happily Ever After 1945,Mr 16,21:2
Calvert, Henry
Miss Julie 1954,Mr 29,24:3
Hamlet 1959,S 11,21:4
Interview 1966,N 7,66:1
TV 1966,N 7,66:1
Spiro Who? 1969,My 19,55:1
Ah, Wilderness! 1969,N 9,86:1
Calvert, Henry (Director)
Miss Julie 1954,Mr 29,24:3
When We Dead Awaken 1966,Ap 19,37:2
Calvert, Henry (Producer)
Hamlet 1959,S 11,21:4
Calvert, Louis
Daddalums 1920,Jl 11,VI,1:6
Blood and Sand 1921,S 21,16:2
He Who Gets Slapped 1922,Ja 10,15:1
What the Public Wants 1922,My 2,22:3
R U R 1922,O 10,16:1
R U R 1922,O 15,VIII,1:1
Adding Machine, The 1923,Mr 20,24:1
You Never Can Tell 1923,Jl 13,18:4

Calvert, Louis (Director)
Julius Caesar 1923,F 9,10:4
Calvert, Mary (Costume Designer)
Hamlet 1959,S 11,21:4
Calvert, Mary (Director)
Miss Julie 1954,Mr 29,24:3
Calvert, Maxine
Forbidden Roads 1928,Ap 17,26:4
Calvert, Patricia
You Never Can Tell 1923,Jl 13,18:4
Meet the Wife 1923,N 27,23:4
Stronger Than Love 1925,D 29,20:2
Ten Per Cent 1927,S 14,29:3
Bellamy Trial, The 1928,Ag 20,21:1
Whispering Gallery, The 1929,F 12,22:2
Lost Sheep 1930,My 6,33:2
Lean Harvest 1931,O 14,26:3
After All 1931,D 4,28:4
Experience Unnecessary 1931,D 31,16:2
They Don't Mean Any Harm 1932,F 24,25:2
Christopher Comes Across 1932,Je 1,19:2
Nona 1932,O 5,26:4
Autumn Crocus 1932,N 21,20:2
Strange Orchestra 1933,N 29,23:2
Lord Blesses the Bishop, The 1934,N 28,24:5
Simpleton of the Unexpected Isles, The
1935,F 19,27:5
Coward, The 1935,Jl 16,24:1
May Wine 1935,D 6,30:3
Three Sisters, The 1942,D 22,31:2
Duchess of Malfi, The 1946,O 16,35:2
Calvert, Phyllis
Flare Path 1942,Ag 23,VIII,1:6
Complaisant Lover, The 1959,Je 19,28:3
Blithe Spirit 1970,S 17,57:1
Calvert, William
Injury Sustained 1940,O 24,30:3
Calvi, Gabrielle
Maitresse de Roi 1926,D 1,24:1
Dame aux Camelias, La 1926,D 7,24:2
Misanthrope, Le 1926,D 10,31:2
Calvi, Gerard (Composer)
Plume de Ma Tante, La 1958,N 12,42:1
Grosse Valise, La 1965,D 15,52:1
Calvi, Gerard (Miscellaneous)
Plume de Ma Tante, La 1958,N 12,42:1
Calvin, David (Sgt)
Winged Victory 1943,N 22,24:1
Calvin, Harold
Topaze 1947,D 29,21:5
Calvin, Henry
Chocolate Soldier, The 1947,Mr 13,34:2
Sally 1948,My 7,31:2
Happy as Larry 1950,Ja 7,11:2
Kismet 1953,D 4,2:4
Kismet 1965,Je 23,45:1
Calvo, Alberto
Farewell to Arms, A 1930,S 23,30:3
Calvo, Mireille
Three Musketeers, The 1968,Je 26,43:1
Calvo, Ofelia
Spanish Love 1920,Ag 18,6:1
Calvo, Pilar
Cabalgata 1949,Jl 8,14:2
Calvo, Rafael
Don Juan Tenorio 1953,N 20,18:5
El Alcalde De Zalamea 1953,N 23,32:5
Calvo, Ricardo
Farewell to Arms, A 1930,S 23,30:3
Calzada, Manuel
Don Juan Tenorio 1953,N 20,18:5
El Alcalde De Zalamea 1953,N 23,32:5
Camacho, Francisco
Don Juan Tenorio 1953,N 20,18:5
El Alcalde De Zalamea 1953,N 23,32:5
Camara, Ladii
Blancs, Les 1970,N 16,48:4
Camargo, Ralph
Lamp at Midnight 1947,D 22,29:2
To Tell You the Truth 1948,Ap 19,28:6
Cambeilh, Paul
No Strings 1962,Mr 16,24:1
Camber, Susan
Education of H*Y*M*A*N K*A*P*L*A*N, The
1968,Ap 5,57:1
Cambridge, Ed
Clandestine on the Morning Line 1961,O 31,28:1
Cambridge, Ed (Director)
Egg and I, The 1958,S 11,43:4
Ballad for Bimshire 1963,O 16,54:1
Cambridge, Ed (Miscellaneous)
Blood Knot, The 1964,Mr 3,30:2
Slave, The 1964,D 17,51:1
Toilet, The 1964,D 17,51:1
Sunset 1966,My 13,34:1
Song of the Lusitanian Bogey, The 1968,Ja 3,52:1
Cambridge, Edmund
Our Lan' 1947,Ap 19,11:2
Our Lan' 1947,S 29,16:5
Cambridge, Edmund (Director)
Summer of the Seventeenth Doll 1968,F 21,59:1
Ceremonies in Dark Old Men 1969,F 6,33:1
Malcochon 1969,Ap 2,37:1

String 1969,Ap 2,37:1
String 1969,Ap 13,II,1:1
Ceremonies in Dark Old Men 1969,O 11,42:1
Cambridge, Edmund (Miscellaneous)
God Is a (Guess What?) 1968,D 18,56:1
Man Better Man 1969,Jl 3,22:1
Cambridge, Edward (Miscellaneous)
Kongi's Harvest 1968,Ap 15,49:1
Cambridge, Godfrey
Take a Giant Step 1956,S 26,30:1
Nature's Way 1957,O 17,42:2
Androcles and the Lion 1958,F 22,8:3
Shakespeare in Harlem 1959,O 28,40:7
Blacks, The 1961,My 5,23:1
Purlie Victorious 1961,S 29,29:1
Purlie Victorious 1961,O 8,II,1:1
Living Premise, The 1963,Je 14,34:1
How to Be a Jewish Mother 1967,D 29,18:1
Cambridge, John
Back Here 1928,N 27,36:3
Between Two Worlds 1934,O 26,24:2
Cameron, Audrey
If Winter Comes 1923,Ap 3,26:1
Mary, Mary, Quite Contrary 1923,S 12,14:1
Nine Till Six 1930,S 29,17:2
Cameron, Cecil
Happy-Go-Lucky 1920,Ag 25,6:1
Cameron, Constance
Friend Indeed 1926,Ap 27,22:3
You Can't Take It With You 1951,Ap 7,8:6
Cameron, Donald
Wake Up, Jonathan 1921,Ja 18,14:1
Dreams for Sale 1922,S 14,24:1
Dice of the Gods, The 1923,Ap 6,20:2
Brook 1923,Ag 20,14:3
Queen Victoria 1923,N 16,15:1
Bride, The 1924,My 6,25:1
Good Bad Woman, A 1925,F 10,21:1
Dunce Boy, The 1925,Ap 4,20:2
Good Hope, The 1927,O 19,24:2
First Stone, The 1928,Ja 14,12:2
Improvisations in June 1928,F 27,16:5
Hedda Gabler 1928,Mr 27,30:2
Vaudeville (Palace) 1928,Je 26,29:4
Open Door, The 1928,Je 26,29:4
Vaudeville (Palace) 1928,Jl 3,19:2
Would-Be Gentleman, The 1928,O 2,34:1
Invitation au Voyage, L' 1928,O 5,17:1
Cherry Orchard, The 1928,O 16,28:5
Peter Pan; Boy Who Would Not Grow Up, The
1928,N 27,36:3
Lady From Alfaqueque, The; Consulesa, La
1929,Ja 15,22:3
Katerina 1929,F 26,30:3
Living Corpse, The 1929,D 7,19:1
Open Door, The 1930,Ja 28,28:1
Women Have Their Way, The 1930,Ja 28,28:1
Romeo and Juliet 1930,Ap 22,33:1
Siegfried 1930,O 21,34:1
Alison's House 1930,D 2,31:2
Lady of the Camellias, The 1931,Ja 27,21:2
Liliom 1932,O 27,23:2
Camille 1932,O 28,23:2
Dear Jane 1932,N 15,24:3
Alice in Wonderland 1932,D 12,18:3
Cherry Orchard, The 1933,Mr 7,20:3
Laura Garnett 1934,Jl 17,24:4
Aiglon, L' 1934,N 5,22:2
Hedda Gabler 1934,D 4,22:5
Rosmersholm 1935,D 3,32:5
Love for Love 1936,Je 30,15:4
Timber 1936,Jl 29,11:5
Timber House 1936,S 21,27:5
Mistress of the Inn, The 1937,Je 22,26:3
Stop-Over 1938,Ja 12,16:5
Escape This Night 1938,Ap 23,18:1
Hamlet 1938,O 13,28:1
Henry IV, Part I 1939,Ja 31,17:2
Hamlet 1939,D 5,35:2
Richard II 1940,Ap 2,31:2
Counterattack 1943,F 4,27:2
Jacobowsky and the Colonel 1944,Mr 15,17:2
Cameron, Donna
Garden District; Suddenly Last Summer
1958,Ja 8,23:4
Garden District; Suddenly Last Summer
1958,Ja 19,II,1:1
Cameron, Frances
Afgar 1920,N 9,13:2
Cameron, Frank
New York Idea, The 1948,Ag 18,29:2
Cameron, Hope
All My Sons 1947,Ja 30,21:2
Death of a Salesman 1949,F 11,27:2
Cameron, Hugh
As You Were 1920,Ja 28,22:3
Meanest Man in the World, The 1920,O 13,18:2
Princess Virtue 1921,My 5,20:2
Irving Berlin's Music Box Revue 1921,S 23,18:2
Music Box Revue 1923,S 24,5:3
Lambs Gambol 1925,Ap 27,15:1
Song of the Flame 1925,D 11,26:4
Song of the Flame 1925,D 31,10:2

Cameron, Hugh—Cont
Harry Delmar's Revels 1927,N 29,30:2
Vaudeville (Palace) 1928,N 6,35:2
Back Seat Drivers 1928,D 26,14:4
Simple Simon 1930,F 19,22:1
Unexpected Husband 1931,Je 3,29:4
Papavert 1931,D 30,25:1
Mr Papavert 1932,Ja 23,18:6
Ballyhoo of 1932 1932,S 7,14:2
It's a Wise Child 1933,My 17,15:2
Caviar 1934,Je 8,19:2
Thumbs Up! 1934,D 28,24:1
Ziegfeld Follies 1936,S 15,37:1
American Way, The 1939,Ja 23,9:2
Du Barry Was a Lady 1939,D 7,34:2
Cameron, Ian
Hamlet 1964,Je 17,49:1
Cameron, Jack
Babes in Toyland 1930,D 22,17:1
Cameron, James (Miscellaneous)
Madame Aphrodite 1961,D 30,13:1
Cameron, Jean
High Ground, The 1951,F 21,31:2
Lace on Her Petticoat 1951,S 5,40:3
Three Love Affairs; Still Life 1958,Mr 11,33:1
Three Love Affairs; Bedtime Story 1958,Mr 11,33:1
Importance of Being Earnest, The 1963,F 27,5:2
Astrakhan Coat, The 1967,Ja 13,18:1
Not Now Darling 1970,O 30,33:1
Cameron, John
Joseph 1930,F 13,25:3
Penny Arcade 1930,Mr 11,24:5
Gold Braid 1930,My 14,31:2
Yeomen of the Guard, The 1962,Jl 11,28:1
Cameron, John (Composer)
Beaux' Stratagem, The 1970,F 10,50:2
Cameron, John (Director)
Gods We Make, The 1934,Ja 4,16:4
Creeping Fire 1935,Ja 17,22:3
Woman of the Soil, A 1935,Mr 26,23:6
Satellite 1935,N 21,27:5
Cameron, John (Producer)
Gods We Make, The 1934,Ja 4,16:4
Creeping Fire 1935,Ja 17,22:3
Woman of the Soil, A 1935,Mr 26,23:6
Satellite 1935,N 21,27:5
Cameron, Kathryn
Comes the Revelation 1942,My 27,26:2
Dark of the Moon 1945,Mr 15,27:2
Sally 1948,My 7,31:2
Cameron, Kay
Jubilee 1935,O 14,20:1
Between the Devil 1937,D 23,24:5
Cameron, Kenneth (Playwright)
Papp 1969,My 6,39:1
Papp 1969,Je 8,II,1:7
Cameron, Lew
Great Temptations, The 1926,My 19,29:1
Cameron, Madeline
Betty Lee 1924,D 26,18:2
Happy-Go-Lucky 1926,O 1,27:2
Betsy 1926,D 29,24:3
Hit the Deck! 1927,Ap 26,32:1
Follow Thru 1929,Ja 10,24:3
Cameron, Madge
Pousse-Cafe 1966,Mr 19,19:2
Cameron, Marjorie
All in the Family 1935,Jl 24,20:4
Cameron, Marlene
Annie Get Your Gun 1946,My 17,14:2
As the Girls Go 1948,N 15,21:2
Happy Time, The 1950,Ja 25,24:1
Love Me Little 1958,Ap 15,42:2
Cameron, Phyllis
Revels of 1936 1935,S 30,12:4
Illustrators' Show, The 1936,Ja 23,25:3
Tickets, Please! 1950,Ap 28,25:2
Cameron, Richard
Hamlet 1936,N 11,54:2
Cameron, Rudolph
Sitting Pretty 1924,Ap 9,24:2
Her Way Out 1924,Je 24,18:3
First Flight 1925,S 18,26:2
Bye Bye Bonnie 1927,Ja 14,15:3
Cameron, William
Girl in the Spotlight, The 1920,Jl 13,9:3
Elsie 1923,Ap 3,26:1
Bringing Up Father 1925,Mr 31,16:1
Cameron, Yukona
Vaudeville (Palace) 1929,D 30,16:3
Second Little Show, The 1930,Ag 17,VIII,2:2
Second Little Show, The 1930,S 3,36:1
Vaudeville (Palladium) 1931,My 12,28:4
Vaudeville (Palace) 1931,Je 8,21:2
Variety Anthology 1932,Mr 21,19:4
Camerons, Four, The
Vaudeville (Palace) 1923,Ja 16,16:3
Camia, William
Twilight Walk 1951,S 25,25:4
Camier, Regina
40 CV du Roi, La 1927,O 23,VIII,2:2
Lady Hamilton 1929,N 17,IX,2:6
Mariee Eperdue, La 1935,My 26,XI,2:2

Camilla, John (Director)
Silhouettes 1969,S 9,41:1
Camille, Velerie
Alive and Kicking 1950,Ja 18,25:5
Camillo, Marvin
But Never Jam Today 1969,Ap 24,40:1
Moon on a Rainbow Shawl 1970,D 18,52:1
Camilo, Joseph
Lute Song 1946,F 7,29:2
Camin, Alfonso (Original Author)
Picara Molinera, La 1929,Ja 3,25:2
Caminiti, Filippo
Barbara 1929,N 18,24:5
Camm, Walter (Composer)
Lady Refuses, The 1933,Mr 8,18:6
Cammarotta, Bill (Miscellaneous)
After the Angels 1961,F 11,27:5
Cammerlohr, Franz (Playwright)
Tiefstapler, Der 1932,S 4,IX,2:1
Bargold Lacht 1932,N 6,IX,3:2
Camoin, Rene
Fourberies de Scapin, Les 1961,F 22,30:1
Impromptu de Versailles, L' 1961,F 22,30:1
Dindon, Le 1961,Mr 8,38:1
Camoletti, Marc (Playwright)
Boeing-Boeing 1961,Ja 3,35:2
Boeing-Boeing 1965,F 3,30:1
Camp, Duane (Lighting Director)
Take It From the Top 1967,N 23,59:2
Camp, Duane (Miscellaneous)
Come Play With Me 1959,My 1,33:5
All American 1962,Mr 20,44:1
Student Gypsy, The; Prince of Liederkranz, The
1963,O 1,34:1
Camp, Duane (Scenic Designer)
Take It From the Top 1967,N 23,59:2
Camp, Florenzo (Composer)
Servant of Two Masters, The 1960,F 29,31:5
Camp, Frank
Inside Story, The 1932,F 23,23:2
Pursuit of Happiness, The 1934,Je 24,IX,1:4
Tight Britches 1934,S 12,26:2
Mother Lode 1934,D 24,16:5
Three Men on a Horse 1935,Ja 31,22:3
Off to Buffalo! 1939,F 22,18:2
Camp, Hamilton
Committee, The 1964,S 17,53:1
Committee, The 1964,S 27,II,1:1
Kelly 1965,F 8,28:2
On a Clear Day You Can See Forever
1965,O 18,44:1
Story Theater 1970,O 27,54:1
Camp, Helen Page
Sudden End of Anne Cinquefoil, The
1961,Ja 11,25:2
Death of Bessie Smith, The 1961,Mr 2,19:1
Camp, Helen Page (Miscellaneous)
Nekros 1960,O 26,44:1
Embers 1960,O 26,44:1
Fam and Yam 1960,O 26,44:1
Sudden End of Anne Cinquefoil, The
1961,Ja 11,25:2
Camp, Ray
Mahagonny 1970,Ap 29,51:1
Camp, Richard
Men to the Sea 1944,O 4,25:2
Little Women 1945,D 24,18:2
Bernardine 1952,O 17,33:4
Camp, Sarah
Light Wines and Beer 1930,N 11,28:6
Camp, Shep
Rose Girl, The 1921,F 12,11:1
What's Your Wife Doing? 1923,O 2,10:3
Flossie 1924,Je 4,25:2
Love Call, The 1927,O 25,33:1
Camp, Shep (Composer)
Half a Widow 1927,S 13,37:3
Camp, Wadsworth (Original Author)
Last Warning, The 1922,O 25,23:1
Prowling Death 1923,Ja 21,VII,1:3
Campagna, Angelo
Aria del Continente, L' 1927,O 5,30:2
Campagna, Cecchina
Aria del Continente, L' 1927,O 5,30:2
Campan, Zanie
Don Juan 1958,O 29,29:1
Campanella, Frank
Volpone 1948,Ja 9,24:6
Tragedian in Spite of Himself, A 1948,F 6,29:2
On the Harmfulness of Tobacco 1948,F 6,29:2
Bear, The 1948,F 6,29:2
Wedding, The 1948,F 6,29:2
Stalag 17 1951,My 9,41:2
Remains to Be Seen 1951,O 4,37:1
Sixth Finger in a Five Finger Glove 1956,O 9,31:4
Mister Roberts 1956,D 6,46:2
Deadly Game, The 1960,F 3,27:2
Nowhere to Go But Up 1962,N 12,36:2
Nobody Loves an Albatross 1963,D 20,20:1
Nobody Loves an Albatross 1964,Ja 5,II,1:1
Guys and Dolls 1965,Ap 29,39:1
Guys and Dolls 1966,Je 9,55:2

Campanella, Joseph
Captains and the Kings, The 1962,Ja 3,25:2
Gift of Time, A 1962,F 23,34:1
Hot Spot 1963,Ap 20,17:2
Campanella, Philip
Lady From Maxim's, The 1970,Je 1,41:1
Hamlet 1970,O 19,51:1
Campanella, Philip (Composer)
Hamlet 1970,O 19,51:1
Campanile, Festa (Playwright)
Rugantino 1964,F 7,34:1
Campbel, Douglas
Oedipus Rex 1954,Jl 17,6:6
Campbell, Alan
Good Hope, The 1927,O 19,24:2
Show Boat 1927,D 28,26:1
Furies, The 1928,Mr 8,23:1
Congai 1928,N 28,24:3
Damn Your Honor 1929,D 31,14:3
Scarlet Sister Mary 1930,N 26,19:2
Way of the World, The 1931,Je 2,34:3
Warrior's Husband, The 1932,Mr 12,19:4
Border-Land 1932,Mr 30,15:5
Show Boat 1932,My 20,22:2
Troilus and Cressida 1932,Je 7,22:3
Design for Living 1933,Ja 3,19:5
Design for Living 1933,Ja 25,13:2
Joyous Season, The 1934,Ja 30,16:3
Campbell, Alexander
Coastwise 1931,D 1,23:1
Child of Manhattan 1932,Mr 2,15:1
Her Majesty the Widow 1934,Je 19,24:5
Porgy and Bess 1935,O 11,30:2
There's Always a Breeze 1938,Mr 3,16:2
Feathers in a Gale 1943,D 22,26:2
Campbell, Alice
Back Fire 1932,Je 14,26:3
Campbell, Alice (Playwright)
Two Share a Dwelling 1935,O 9,26:3
Two Share a Dwelling 1935,N 3,X,1:7
Campbell, Argyle (Director)
What's the Use? 1926,S 7,19:1
Campbell, Argyle (Playwright)
Spring 3100 1928,F 16,14:2
Campbell, Arthur
What Price Glory 1924,S 6,14:3
Deep River 1926,O 5,26:2
Mystery Moon 1930,Je 24,23:4
Campbell, Benedict
Falstaff; Henry IV, Part II 1965,Jl 1,35:1
Campbell, Bill (Costume Designer)
Poupees de Paris, Les 1962,D 13,8:2
Poupees de Paris, Les 1964,My 16,11:1
Ice Capades 1969,Ja 8,42:1
Ice Capades 1970,Ja 7,35:1
Campbell, Bruce
H M S Pinafore 1967,N 1,40:1
Campbell, Camelia
Dawn 1924,N 25,27:1
Arabian, The 1927,N 1,20:5
Murder in the Cathedral 1936,Mr 21,13:5
Help Yourself! 1936,Jl 15,15:1
It Can't Happen Here 1936,O 28,30:1
Goodbye Again 1943,N 10,28:4
Campbell, Carolee
Fashion 1959,Ja 21,27:1
Campbell, Catherine
Earth Journey 1944,Ap 28,24:2
Campbell, Charles
Lady Dedlock 1929,Ja 1,61:2
Ladies of Creation 1931,S 9,25:1
Church Mouse, A 1931,O 13,26:4
Peacock 1932,O 12,27:1
Mask and the Face, The 1933,My 9,20:2
Wind and the Rain, The 1934,F 2,20:6
Distaff Side, The 1934,S 26,17:2
Naked Man, The 1935,Ja 2,24:3
Murder With Pen and Ink 1935,Ag 20,25:1
Private Affair, A 1936,My 15,28:7
Othello 1937,Ja 7,16:4
Merely Murder 1937,D 4,21:4
Clutterbuck 1949,D 5,29:2
Wild Duck, The 1951,D 27,17:1
Rehearsal, The 1952,My 27,30:5
Sixth Finger in a Five Finger Glove 1956,O 9,31:4
Single Man at a Party 1959,Ap 22,30:4
Blacks, The 1961,My 5,23:1
Campbell, Claudia
Tree Grows in Brooklyn, A 1951,Ap 20,24:3
Campbell, Clyne
Don't Tell 1920,S 29,12:1
Campbell, Colin
Marjolaine 1922,Ja 25,16:1
Yankee Princess, The 1922,O 3,22:1
My Aunt From Ypsilanti 1923,My 2,22:6
9 O'Clock Revue 1923,O 5,22:1
Bye Bye, Barbara 1924,Ag 26,6:3
Big Boy 1925,Ja 8,28:2
Potiphar's Wife 1928,D 24,10:7
O'Flynn, The 1934,D 28,24:1
Good-Bye to Love 1940,Je 8,18:1
Campbell, Constance
Ah! Wah! 1932,My 11,15:2

Campbell, Constance (Director)
Ah! Wah! 1932,My 11,15:2
Campbell, Constance (Lyricist)
Ah! Wah! 1932,My 11,15:2
Campbell, Craig
Ruddigore 1920,F 1,VIII,2:2
Vaudeville (Hippodrome) 1924,Ja 22,15:6
Vaudeville (Hippodrome) 1926,My 11,25:3
Vaudeville (Palace) 1926,N 30,27:2
Ruddigore 1927,My 21,25:2
Ruddigore 1931,Ag 11,28:3
Campbell, Danny
Jack Jack 1968,Je 23,74:5
Campbell, Dean
Look, Ma, I'm Dancin' 1948,Ja 30,20:2
Top Banana 1951,N 2,19:2
Campbell, Diana
Most of the Game 1935,O 2,27:4
Campbell, Dick
Brain Sweat 1934,Ap 5,24:4
Cabin in the Sky 1940,O 26,19:2
Campbell, Dirk
Winter's Tale, The 1958,Jl 23,34:3
Campbell, Donald
Fool's Bells 1925,D 24,8:3
Pyramids 1926,Jl 20,17:2
Madame X 1927,Jl 7,29:3
Speakeasy 1927,S 27,30:1
Happy 1927,D 6,26:3
Mr Moneypenny 1928,O 17,26:2
Come-On Man, The 1929,Ap 23,26:2
Sherlock Holmes 1929,N 26,28:3
Meet My Sister 1930,D 31,11:1
Undesirable Lady, An 1933,O 10,24:4
Sleeping Clergyman, A 1934,O 9,16:1
Glorious Morning 1938,N 28,10:3
Steel 1939,D 20,30:2
Campbell, Douglas
Diff'rent 1938,Ja 26,26:4
Pygmalion 1938,Ja 27,16:3
Captain Jinks of the Horse Marines 1938,Ja 28,16:2
No More Peace 1938,Ja 29,13:2
Coriolanus 1938,F 2,14:5
Richard III 1953,Jl 15,22:2
All's Well That Ends Well 1953,Jl 16,18:2
Measure for Measure 1954,Je 30,23:1
Taming of the Shrew, The 1954,Jl 1,22:2
Taming of the Shrew, The 1954,Jl 4,II,1:1
Measure for Measure 1954,Jl 4,II,1:1
Julius Caesar 1955,Je 29,23:3
Henry V 1956,Je 20,27:2
Merry Wives of Windsor, The 1956,Je 21,34:4
Henry V 1956,Je 24,II,1:1
Oedipus Rex 1956,S 4,32:6
Hamlet 1957,Jl 3,15:2
Twelfth Night 1957,Jl 4,16:4
Twelfth Night 1957,Jl 7,II,1:1
Mary Stuart 1957,O 9,39:1
Mary Stuart 1957,O 20,II,1:1
Two Gentlemen of Verona 1958,Mr 19,35:1
Broken Jug, The 1958,Ap 2,36:1
Henry IV, Part I 1958,Je 25,23:3
As You Like It 1959,Jl 1,27:1
Othello 1959,Jl 2,17:2
Othello 1959,Jl 5,II,1:1
As You Like It 1959,Jl 5,II,1:1
H M S Pinafore 1960,S 8,41:1
Coriolanus 1961,Je 21,31:2
Henry VIII 1961,Je 22,22:1
Henry VIII 1961,Jl 2,II,1:1
Gideon 1961,N 10,38:1
Gideon 1961,N 19,II,1:1
Elizabethans, The 1962,Ja 22,19:1
Gondoliers, The 1962,Jl 7,9:4
Golden Age, The 1963,N 19,49:2
Saint Joan 1964,My 14,41:1
Volpone 1964,Jl 20,18:3
Henry IV, Part I 1965,Je 30,42:1
Cherry Orchard, The 1965,Ag 2,17:2
Shoemaker's Holiday, The 1967,Je 3,19:1
House of Atreus, The; Bringers of Offerings, The
1967,Jl 24,23:1
House of Atreus, The; Furies, The 1967,Jl 24,23:1
House of Atreus, The; Agamemnon 1967,Jl 24,23:1
House of Atreus, The 1968,D 18,55:1
Adventures of the Black Girl in Her Search for
God, The 1969,Mr 22,24:4
Tempest, The 1970,F 15,67:1
Vatzlav 1970,Ag 23,II,1:6
Campbell, Douglas (Choreographer)
H M S Pinafore 1960,S 8,41:1
Pirates of Penzance, The 1961,S 7,41:1
Campbell, Douglas (Director)
Soldier's Tale, A 1955,Jl 13,21:2
Winter's Tale, The 1958,Jl 23,34:3
Winter's Tale, The 1958,Jl 27,II,1:1
Midsummer Night's Dream, A 1960,Je 30,23:5
Elizabethans, The 1962,Ja 22,19:1
Moby Dick 1962,N 29,45:1
Miser, The 1963,My 10,39:1
Miser, The 1963,My 19,II,1:1
Death of a Salesman 1963,Jl 20,11:2
Golden Age, The 1963,N 19,49:2

Campbell, Douglas (Director)—Cont
Saint Joan 1964,My 14,41:1
Way of the World, The 1965,Je 2,40:1
Julius Caesar 1965,Jl 2,18:1
Skin of Our Teeth, The 1966,Je 2,51:1
Dance of Death, The 1966,Je 3,31:1
Shoemaker's Holiday, The 1967,Je 3,19:1
She Stoops to Conquer 1968,Ja 1,11:1
Romeo and Juliet 1968,Je 11,55:2
Campbell, Douglas (Miscellaneous)
Richard III 1965,Je 3,26:1
Campbell, Edith
Vaudeville (Palace) 1927,My 17,27:4
Follow Thru 1929,Ja 10,24:3
Hamlet 1931,N 19,26:6
Merry Wives of Windsor, The 1938,Ap 15,22:3
Campbell, Emerin
Holy Terror, A 1925,S 29,31:2
Journeyman 1938,Ja 31,14:2
Mrs O'Brien Entertains 1939,F 9,16:3
Campbell, Flo
Vaudeville (Palace) 1926,N 9,30:3
Vaudeville (Palace) 1930,My 26,25:2
Campbell, Flora
Whatever Possessed Her 1934,Ja 26,21:2
Laughing Woman, The 1936,Jl 8,14:7
Country Wife, The 1936,D 2,34:1
Excursion 1937,Ap 10,11:4
Many Mansions 1937,Ag 3,20:5
Many Mansions 1937,O 28,28:6
Glamour Preferred 1940,N 16,13:2
Land Is Bright, The 1941,O 29,26:2
All for All 1943,S 30,25:2
Foxhole in the Parlor 1945,My 24,15:4
Curious Savage, The 1950,O 25,44:3
Only in America 1959,N 20,35:1
Angels of Anadarko 1962,O 11,47:1
Journey to the Day 1963,N 12,49:1
Campbell, Frances Ross
Hunky Dory 1922,S 5,21:2
Infinite Shoeblack, The 1930,F 18,28:1
Campbell, Frederick
Texas Town 1941,Ap 30,22:3
Campbell, Gary
Deer Park, The 1967,F 1,27:2
Campbell, George (Playwright)
Poor Little Ritz Girl 1920,Jl 29,7:1
Campbell, Gerald
Slightly Delinquent 1954,O 26,32:5
Campbell, Graeme
Macbeth 1956,O 30,42:2
Campbell, Gurney (Mrs) (Director)
J B 1964,N 11,38:6
Campbell, Gurney (Playwright)
Gandhi 1970,O 21,37:1
Campbell, Ian
Watched Pot, The 1947,O 29,31:4
Campbell, Jerry
Best Foot Forward 1956,Mr 3,16:1
Campbell, Jim
Slightly Delinquent 1954,O 26,32:5
Last Days of Lincoln, The 1961,O 19,39:7
Campbell, Joan
Electra 1959,F 14,15:1
Campbell, John
H M S Pinafore 1920,Ja 13,10:2
Ruddigore 1920,Ja 20,11:2
Don't Tell 1920,S 29,12:1
Shewing-Up of Blanco Posnet, The 1923,O 17,14:2
Finta Giardiniera, La 1927,Ja 19,20:5
Lady Screams, The 1927,My 3,24:2
Years Between, The 1942,F 7,13:2
Hasty Heart, The 1945,Ja 4,14:2
Mister Roberts 1948,F 19,27:2
Iolanthe 1965,My 19,42:1
Yeomen of the Guard, The 1965,Jl 8,34:1
Ruddigore 1965,Ag 27,16:1
All's Well That Ends Well 1966,Je 17,39:1
Richard III 1966,Ag 11,26:1
Campbell, Judy
Present Laughter 1943,My 9,II,1:1
This Happy Breed 1943,My 9,II,1:1
Royal Highness 1949,Ap 14,29:3
Campbell, Kane (Original Author)
Enchanted April, The 1925,Ag 25,12:3
Campbell, Ken
Enchantment 1953,Jl 1,24:3
Campbell, Kenneth
All's Well That Ends Well 1970,Je 16,53:1
Campbell, Kippy
Square Root of Wonderful, The 1957,O 31,40:1
Campbell, Lackland
Romantic Mr Dickens 1940,D 3,33:2
Popsy 1941,F 11,26:2
Trojan Women, The 1941,Ap 9,32:5
Campbell, Lawton (Playwright)
Immoral Isabella 1927,O 28,20:3
Solid South 1930,My 11,IX,2:6
Solid South 1930,O 15,27:1
Campbell, Louise
Ah, Wilderness! 1935,Ag 20,25:1
Julie the Great 1936,Ja 15,15:3
White Man 1936,O 19,22:4
House in the Country, A 1937,Ja 12,18:3

Guest in the House 1942,F 25,25:2
Campbell, Marci
Shunned 1960,D 21,39:1
Campbell, Margaret
Way of the World, The 1924,N 18,23:4
Campbell, Maris (Director)
Legend of Leonora, The 1926,My 1,10:1
Campbell, Muriel
Princess Turandot 1926,N 13,14:2
Devil in the Mind 1931,My 2,23:2
Adam Had Two Sons 1932,Ja 21,17:1
Great Magoo, The 1932,D 3,20:7
Bring on the Girls 1934,O 23,23:2
Having Wonderful Time 1937,F 22,12:5
Night Before Christmas, The 1941,Ap 11,25:2
Campbell, Naomi
Dear Octopus 1939,Ja 12,22:2
Campbell, Norman (Composer)
Anne 1965,Ag 22,82:2
Campbell, Norman (Director)
Pirates of Penzance, The 1961,S 7,41:1
Campbell, Norman (Lyricist)
Anne 1965,Ag 22,82:2
Campbell, Norman (Playwright)
Anne of Green Gables 1969,Ap 18,39:1
Anne of Green Gables 1969,Ag 25,41:1
Campbell, Oscar (Dr) (Translator)
Weathercock, The 1948,Ag 6,22:3
Campbell, Pat (Costume Designer)
All in One; Trouble in Tahiti 1955,Ap 20,40:3
All in One; 27 Wagons Full of Cotton
1955,Ap 20,40:3
Campbell, Pat (Lighting Director)
Grand Prize, The 1955,Ja 27,17:1
Campbell, Pat (Scenic Designer)
Grand Prize, The 1955,Ja 27,17:1
Campbell, Patrick (Mrs)
What Might Happen 1926,Je 20,VII,1:1
Adventurous Age, The 1927,F 8,20:1
Tents of Israel; Matriarch, The 1929,My 26,IX,1:3
Sex Fable, The 1931,O 21,26:1
Electra 1932,Ja 9,21:4
Party, A 1933,Ag 24,18:4
Party, A 1933,S 3,IX,1:1
Campbell, Patrick (Mrs) (Miscellaneous)
Dear Liar 1960,Mr 18,19:2
Dear Liar 1962,Mr 19,36:1
Campbell, Patton (Costume Designer)
Fallen Angels 1956,Ja 18,27:1
Hole in the Head, A 1957,Mr 1,15:1
Makropoulos Secret, The 1957,D 4,52:4
Howie 1958,S 18,35:2
Mikado, The 1959,O 2,24:1
There Was a Little Girl 1960,Mr 1,28:1
Ignorants Abroad, The 1960,My 24,43:2
Pirates of Penzance, The 1960,O 7,29:1
Conquering Hero, The 1961,Ja 17,40:2
Mikado, The 1961,Ja 18,26:1
H M S Pinafore 1961,F 2,26:6
All American 1962,Mr 20,44:1
Month in the Country, A 1963,My 29,39:2
H M S Pinafore 1964,Mr 21,13:4
H M S Pinafore 1965,Ap 15,39:1
Glass Menagerie, The 1965,My 5,53:2
Great Scot! 1965,N 12,56:3
Man of La Mancha 1965,N 23,52:1
Wait a Minim! 1966,Mr 8,43:1
Agatha Sue, I Love You 1966,D 15,61:1
Come Live With Me 1967,Ja 27,29:1
Natural Look, The 1967,Mr 13,45:2
Loot 1968,Mr 19,40:2
Pirates of Penzance, The 1968,Ap 26,32:1
H M S Pinafore 1968,Ap 29,47:2
Mikado, The 1968,My 2,59:1
Campbell, Patton (Lighting Director)
Ignorants Abroad, The 1960,My 24,43:2
Campbell, Patton (Scenic Designer)
Ignorants Abroad, The 1960,My 24,43:2
H M S Pinafore 1961,F 2,26:6
H M S Pinafore 1964,Mr 21,13:4
H M S Pinafore 1965,Ap 15,39:1
H M S Pinafore 1968,Ap 29,47:2
Campbell, Paul
Marinka 1945,Jl 19,19:2
Campbell, Peggy
Bloomer Girl 1947,Ja 7,33:2
Campbell, Percy
Biff, Bing, Bang 1921,My 10,20:1
Campbell, Phillip
Brother Elks 1925,S 15,29:2
Campbell, Phyllis
Safari! 1955,My 12,32:6
Campbell, Phyllis Rene
Harriet 1944,S 28,26:1
Campbell, Raymond
Bottomland 1927,Je 28,29:3
Campbell, Roy (Translator)
Life Is a Dream 1964,Mr 20,24:1
Campbell, Sande (Musical Director)
Man With a Load of Mischief, The 1966,N 7,65:1
Campbell, Sandy
Rugged Path, The 1945,N 12,17:2
I Know My Love 1949,N 3,36:1

Campbell, Sandy—Cont
Cyrano de Bergerac 1953,N 13,24:3
Richard III 1953,D 10,65:2
Spring's Awakening 1955,O 10,30:2
Streetcar Named Desire, A 1956,F 16,24:1
Quare Fellow, The 1958,N 28,34:1
Susannah and the Elders 1959,O 19,37:3
Campbell, Shawn
Joyful Noise, A 1966,D 16,57:1
Campbell, Stella
Hunky Dory 1922,S 5,21:2
Campbell, Susan
South Pacific 1967,Je 13,56:1
Ben Bagley's Shoestring Revues 1970,O 24,22:1
Campbell, Ted
Sing Till Tomorrow 1953,D 29,17:2
Campbell, Violet
This Was a Man 1926,N 24,27:1
Campbell, Virginia
Your Young Men 1935,Ag 8,13:2
Farewell Summer 1937,Mr 30,20:2
Black Eye, The 1938,Mr 8,22:4
Run Sheep Run 1938,N 4,26:2
Family Portrait 1939,Mr 9,18:4
Pastoral 1939,N 2,26:2
Medicine Show 1940,Ap 13,20:6
Cream in the Well, The 1941,Ja 21,19:2
Cherry Orchard, The 1944,Ja 26,22:1
Campbell, Walter (Director)
Yeah-Man 1932,My 27,27:3
Campbell, Walter (Producer)
Brother Elks 1925,S 15,29:2
My Magnolia 1926,Jl 13,19:2
Yeah-Man 1932,My 27,27:3
Campbell, Winifred
Conversation Piece 1934,O 24,24:1
Campbell-Walker, Edith
Cinders 1923,Ap 4,22:1
Campion, Charles
Legend 1930,My 7,25:1
Campion, Cyril (Playwright)
Lash, The 1926,N 4,VIII,4:7
Asleep 1927,Je 12,VII,2:1
Ladies-in-Waiting 1934,Je 10,IX,1:1
Campion, Joyce
Romeo and Juliet 1968,Je 11,55:2
Hamlet 1969,Je 11,37:1
Alchemist, The 1969,Je 12,51:1
Measure for Measure 1969,Je 13,41:3
Campisi, Frank
Aquashow 1953,Je 24,29:2
Aquashow 1954,Je 23,20:4
Campo, Julius
Meet My Sister 1930,D 31,11:1
Campos, Roberto (Translator)
On the Necessity of Being Polygamous
1964,D 9,61:1
Campton, David (Playwright)
Mixed Doubles 1969,Ap 12,43:2
Camus, Albert (Director)
Possessed, The 1959,Ja 31,13:7
Camus, Albert (Playwright)
Caligula 1949,Ap 23,10:2
Caligula 1950,D 31,II,3:7
Possessed, The 1959,Ja 31,13:7
Caligula 1960,F 17,31:1
Caligula 1960,F 28,II,1:1
Camus, Albert (Translator)
Requiem for a Nun 1956,S 24,23:6
Camuti, Louis
School for Wives 1957,Je 20,23:4
Camuti, Louis J Jr
Billygoat Eddie 1964,Ap 21,43:2
Cana (Playwright)
Werewolf, The 1922,Jl 23,VI,1:1
Canada, Jan
Annie Get Your Gun 1958,F 20,29:2
West Side Story 1961,Mr 31,22:3
Canaday, Harper
Little Theatre Tournament; Shall We Join the
Ladies? 1929,My 9,34:3
Shall We Join the Ladies? 1929,My 12,28:3
Canali, Maria
Piccolo Santo, Il; Little Saint, The 1931,D 14,16:4
Canarie, Doris
Merry Wives of Windsor, The 1954,F 17,27:1
Canary, David
Kittiwake Island 1960,O 13,43:1
Happiest Girl in the World, The 1961,Ap 4,42:1
Hi, Paisano 1961,O 2,36:2
Great Day in the Morning 1962,Mr 29,29:1
Canby, Linda
Power of Darkness, The 1959,S 30,33:1
Opening of a Window, The 1961,S 26,32:2
Cancilla, Elaine
Flora, the Red Menace 1965,My 12,41:2
Sweet Charity 1966,Ja 31,22:1
Cry for Us All 1970,Ap 9,48:2
Candeau, Alberto
Barranca Abajo 1963,Je 1,16:2
Candee, Edward D
What a Relief 1935,D 14,10:6
Candese
Megere Apprivoisee, La 1922,N 20,21:2

141

Candese—Cont

Avare, L'; Miser, The 1924,Mr 12,17:3
Candidus, Edward
Dover Road, The 1924,D 20,18:2
Candip, Rhoda
Carmilla 1970,D 1,61:2
Cane, C E
Somebody's Lion 1921,Ap 13,20:1
Here's Howe 1923,Ap 26,19:3
Canemaker, John
Pimpernel! 1964,Ja 7,26:6
Route 1 1964,N 18,52:3
Papers 1968,D 3,54:1
Canepa, Maria
Remolienda, La; Bawdy Party 1968,F 3,20:1
Canetti, Jacques (Miscellaneous)
Evening With Yves Montand, An 1959,S 23,45:1
Evening With Yves Montand, An 1961,O 25,30:1
Canfield, Curtis (Director)
J B 1958,Ap 24,37:1
J B 1958,My 4,II,1:1
John Brown's Body 1960,Je 22,31:1
Here Comes Santa Claus 1962,My 18,34:1
Simple Life, A 1964,My 18,36:1
Canfield, F O
Bulls and Belles 1931,Ap 18,17:2
Canfield, Mary Cass (Playwright)
Anne of England 1941,O 8,26:2
Canfield, Mary Cass (Translator)
Hedda Gabler 1942,Ja 30,22:2
Canfield, Mary Grace
Grey-Eyed People, The 1952,D 18,41:2
Frogs of Spring, The 1953,O 21,36:2
Immortal Husband, The 1955,F 15,32:2
Waltz of the Toreadors, The 1957,Ja 18,17:2
Waltz of the Toreadors, The 1957,Ja 27,II,1:1
Waltz of the Toreadors, The 1958,Mr 5,37:1
Jack 1958,Je 4,39:2
Bald Soprano, The 1958,Je 4,39:2
In the Summer House 1964,Mr 26,43:1
Beekman Place 1964,O 8,50:1
Canfield, William F
Trial of Joan of Arc, The 1921,Mr 28,8:2
To the Ladies! 1922,F 21,20:1
Processional 1925,Ja 13,17:1
Cangdon, Fritz
Great Big Doorstep, The 1950,Mr 18,8:6
Cannan, Denis (Playwright)
Colombe 1951,D 15,13:2
Power and the Glory, The 1958,D 12,2:7
Colombe 1965,F 24,33:1
Cannefax, Charles
Artists and Models 1924,O 16,33:3
Canning, Horace
Little Theatre Tournament; Prison Bars
1928,My 10,31:1
Cannon, Alice
Man With a Load of Mischief, The 1966,N 7,65:1
Cannon, Alice (Playwright)
Great Day in the Morning 1962,Mr 29,29:1
Cannon, Anthony
Camino Real 1960,My 17,42:2
Cannon, Dyan
Fun Couple, The 1962,O 27,15:2
Ninety Day Mistress, The 1967,N 7,49:1
Cannon, George
Valley Forge 1934,D 11,28:3
Cannon, Glenn
House Remembered, A 1957,F 7,20:2
Moon for the Misbegotten, A 1957,My 3,21:2
Jackknife 1958,S 23,36:2
Critic, The 1965,Jl 26,15:2
Cannon, J D
Year of Pilar, The 1952,Ja 7,14:3
Julius Caesar 1955,Jl 13,20:1
As You Like It 1955,O 29,12:2
Romeo and Juliet 1955,D 16,36:3
Changeling, The 1956,My 4,20:3
Taming of the Shrew, The 1956,Ag 11,11:2
Taming of the Shrew ' 1956,Ag 26,II,1:1
Duchess of Malfi, The ' Mr 20,33:1
Romeo and Juliet 1957,J 30:2
Two Gentlemen of Vero '7,Jl 23,21:5
Macbeth 1957,Ag 16,11:.
Richard III 1957,N 26,41:1
As You Like It 1958,Ja 21,33:6
Children of Darkness 1958,Mr 1,11:4
Power and the Glory, The 1958,D 12,2:7
Masquerade 1959,Mr 17,42:1
Great God Brown, The 1959,O 7,48:1
Pictures in the Hallway 1959,D 28,19:1
Peer Gynt 1960,Ja 13,21:1
Henry IV 1960,Mr 2,42:1
Henry IV 1960,Mr 13,II,1:1
Henry IV 1960,Ap 19,41:1
Taming of the Shrew, The 1960,Ag 20,17:1
Much Ado About Nothing 1961,Jl 7,17:1
Richard II 1961,Ag 30,25:1
Great Day in the Morning 1962,Mr 29,29:1
Blood Knot, The 1964,Mr 3,30:2
Umbrella, The 1965,My 27,31:1
Mating Dance 1965,N 4,58:1
All's Well That Ends Well 1966,Je 17,39:1

Cannon, Matt
Everyman 1953,O 12,30:2
Cannon, Maureen
Best Foot Forward 1941,S 12,24:4
Best Foot Forward 1941,O 2,28:2
Best Foot Forward 1941,O 26,IX,1:3
Hairpin Harmony 1943,O 2,18:5
Up in Central Park 1945,Ja 29,17:2
Up in Central Park 1947,My 20,29:2
Cannon, Nat
Aquashow 1954,Je 23,20:4
Elliott Murphy's Aquashow 1955,Je 23,25:1
Cannon, Norman
Old English 1924,D 24,11:2
Carolinian, The 1925,N 3,34:2
Cannon, Norman (Playwright)
He Walked in Her Sleep 1929,F 3,VIII,2:1
He Walked in Her Sleep 1929,Ap 5,28:2
Canon, Lillian
Song of the Bridge 1942,Ap 7,27:5
Canova, Ann
Calling All Stars 1934,D 14,28:2
Yokel Boy 1939,Jl 7,12:2
Canova, Judy
Calling All Stars 1934,N 22,26:1
Calling All Stars 1934,D 14,28:2
Ziegfeld Follies 1935,D 31,10:1
Ziegfeld Follies 1936,Ja 5,IX,3:1
Ziegfeld Follies 1936,Ja 31,17:2
Yokel Boy 1939,Jl 7,12:2
Canova, Leon
Oh, Please! 1926,D 22,24:3
Canova, Les
Edith Piaf 1947,O 30,30:2
Canova, Pete
Calling All Stars 1934,D 14,28:2
Canova, Zeke
Calling All Stars 1934,D 14,28:2
Yokel Boy 1939,Jl 7,12:2
Cansino, Carmina
Aries Is Rising 1939,N 22,16:5
Cansino, Eduardo
Girl From Home, The 1920,My 4,9:2
Cansino, Elisa
Girl From Home, The 1920,My 4,9:2
Canter, Harry (Composer)
Hot Rhythm 1930,Ag 22,18:5
Canter, Harry (Lyricist)
Hot Rhythm 1930,Ag 22,18:5
Canter, Lynn
Vaudeville (Palace) 1927,Ap 19,24:3
Vaudeville (Palace) 1928,Ap 10,32:4
Vaudeville (Palace) 1929,My 13,26:3
Canterbury Choral Society
Coming of Christ, The 1957,D 23,29:8
Canto-Janis, George
Topaze 1930,F 13,25:3
Cantor, Arthur (Director)
Trigon, The 1965,O 11,62:2
Tenth Man, The 1967,N 9,54:1
Wizard of Oz, The 1968,N 28,69:2
Cantor, Arthur (Miscellaneous)
All the Way Home 1960,D 1,42:1
Grosse Valise, La 1965,D 15,52:1
Cantor, Arthur (Playwright)
Wizard of Oz, The 1968,N 28,69:2
Cantor, Arthur (Producer)
Davy Jones's Locker 1959,Mr 30,25:1
Tenth Man, The 1959,N 6,24:2
Gideon 1961,N 10,38:1
Elizabethans, The 1962,Ja 22,19:1
Thousand Clowns, A 1962,Ap 6,31:2
Put It in Writing 1963,My 14,31:1
Golden Age, The 1963,N 19,49:2
Passion of Josef D, The 1964,F 12,29:1
Committee, The 1964,S 17,53:1
World of Gunter Grass, The 1966,Ap 27,38:1
Of Love Remembered 1967,F 20,46:5
People Is the Thing That the World Is Fullest Of
1967,F 21,53:1
By George 1967,O 13,33:1
Concept, The 1968,My 7,51:1
Venetian Twins, The 1968,My 29,23:1
Wizard of Oz, The 1968,N 28,69:2
Tango 1969,Ja 20,33:1
Whistling Wizard and the Sultan of Tuffet
1970,F 1,70:1
Ali Baba and the Forty Thieves 1970,D 29,40:1
Cantor, Eddie
Ziegfeld Follies 1920,Je 23,14:1
Broadway Brevities, 1920 1920,S 30,12:2
Friars Club Frolic 1921,Je 13,16:2
Make It Snappy 1922,Ap 14,20:2
Friar's Club Frolic 1922,Je 5,16:1
Ziegfeld Follies 1923,Je 5,24:3
Follies 1923,Je 26,14:5
Kid Boots 1923,D 16,IX,2:4
Kid Boots 1924,Ja 1,21:3
Follies 1927,Ag 7,VII,1:8
Ziegfeld Follies 1927,Ag 17,27:3
Follies 1927,Ag 28,VII,1:1
Vaudeville (Palace) 1927,N 22,33:2
Whoopee 1928,N 11,X,2:4

Cantor, Eddie—Cont

Whoopee 1928,D 5,34:3
Whoopee 1929,Ag 6,29:4
Vaudeville (Palace) 1930,D 29,19:3
Vaudeville (Palace) 1931,Ja 5,20:3
Vaudeville (Palace) 1931,N 2,26:2
Banjo Eyes 1941,N 8,10:6
Banjo Eyes 1941,D 26,20:2
Actors Fund Fete 1942,F 23,24:5
My Forty Years in Show Business 1950,Mr 22,33:2
Forty Years in Show Business 1950,O 2,19:5
Cantor, Eddie (Playwright)
Ziegfeld Follies 1927,Ag 17,27:3
Sketch Book 1929,Jl 2,33:5
Nine Fifteen Revue, The 1930,F 12,26:2
Cantor, Eddie (Producer)
Nellie Bly 1946,Ja 22,32:2
Cantor, Gloria (Miscellaneous)
Belafonte at the Palace 1959,D 16,55:1
Cantor, Laurence
Moby Dick 1970,Je 3,52:1
Cantor, Lew (Director)
Mendel, Inc 1929,N 26,28:5
Cantor, Lew (Producer)
Skull, The 1928,Ap 24,28:3
Courage 1928,O 9,34:2
All the King's Men 1929,F 5,27:1
Lovebound 1929,My 19,IX,2:1
Soldiers and Women 1929,S 3,25:1
Mendel, Inc 1929,N 26,28:5
Many a Slip 1930,F 4,29:2
Great Man, The 1931,Ap 8,20:6
Play, Genius, Play! 1935,O 31,17:2
Cantor, Nat
Off to Buffalo! 1939,F 22,18:2
Lunatics and Lovers 1954,D 14,44:2
Cantor, Selma
Here Runs the Bride 1934,S 20,21:3
Cantreau, Beth
Tell My Story 1939,Mr 16,26:6
Circle of Chalk, The 1941,Mr 27,28:4
Cantrell, Nick
Camino Real 1970,Ja 9,42:1
Cantril, Ken
By Hex 1956,Je 19,25:1
Cantwell, John
Three Doors 1925,Ap 24,16:4
Cantwell, John (Playwright)
Who Cares 1930,Jl 9,27:1
Canty, Marietta
Co-Respondent Unknown 1936,F 12,24:4
Ring Two 1939,N 23,38:2
Horse Fever 1940,N 25,21:2
Canty, Patricia John
Out West of Eighth 1951,S 21,20:3
Cantzen, Conrad
Sandro Botticelli 1923,Mr 27,24:2
Green Beetle, The 1924,S 3,12:3
Arabesque 1925,O 21,20:2
Shanghai Gesture, The 1926,F 2,20:2
Breaks, The 1928,Ap 17,26:3
Solitaire 1929,Mr 13,28:3
Six Characters in Search of an Author
1931,Ap 16,29:2
Good Earth, The 1932,O 18,23:4
Mimie Scheller 1936,O 1,28:4
Enemy of the People, An 1937,F 16,19:1
Canudo, Eugene R
Off the Record; Mayor Answers the Newspapers!
Wow! 1935,Je 19,23:3
Canzoneri, Tony
They Should Have Stood in Bed 1942,F 14,18:5
Capaccio, Augie
Merry Wives of Windsor, The 1954,F 17,27:1
Hour Glass, The 1955,O 17,33:1
Thor, With Angels 1956,O 15,29:4
Capalbo, Carmen (Director)
Threepenny Opera, The 1954,Mr 11,26:5
Threepenny Opera, The 1954,Ap 4,II,7:1
Threepenny Opera, The 1955,S 21,38:1
Threepenny Opera, The 1956,Mr 11,II,1:1
Threepenny Opera, The 1956,D 30,II,1:1
Potting Shed, The 1957,Ja 30,32:1
Potting Shed, The 1957,F 10,II,1:1
Moon for the Misbegotten, A 1957,My 3,21:2
Cave Dwellers, The 1957,O 21,29:2
Cave Dwellers, The 1957,O 27,II,1:1
Threepenny Opera, The 1960,S 15,44:3
Seidman and Son 1962,O 16,32:2
Mahagonny 1970,Ap 29,51:1
Capalbo, Carmen (Miscellaneous)
Mahagonny 1970,Ap 29,51:1
Capalbo, Carmen (Producer)
Threepenny Opera, The 1954,Mr 11,26:5
Threepenny Opera, The 1955,S 21,38:1
Threepenny Opera, The 1956,Mr 11,II,1:1
Potting Shed, The 1957,Ja 30,32:1
Moon for the Misbegotten, A 1957,My 3,21:2
Moon for the Misbegotten, A 1957,My 12,II,1:1
Cave Dwellers, The 1957,O 21,29:2
Mahagonny 1970,Ap 29,51:1
Mahagonny 1970,My 10,II,1:1
Mahagonny 1970,My 10,II,15:1

Cape, Raymond
Popsy 1941,F 11,26:2
Cape, Vandy
Sunday Nights at Nine 1933,N 13,20:7
Fools Rush In 1934,D 26,19:2
Sunday Nights at 9 1935,N 11,21:1
Sunday Nights at Nine 1936,D 7,27:3
Capek, Josef (Playwright)
World We Live In, The 1922,N 1,16:1
Insect Comedy, The 1948,Je 4,26:3
Capek, Karel (Original Author)
Power and Glory 1938,My 1,X,2:5
Mother, The 1939,Mr 19,XI,3:3
Mother, The 1939,Ap 26,26:2
Capek, Karel (Playwright)
R U R 1922,O 10,16:1
R U R 1922,O 15,VIII,1:1
R U R 1922,O 22,VIII,1:1
World We Live In, The 1922,N 1,16:1
Insect Comedy, The 1922,N 5,VIII,1:1
R U R 1922,D 24,VII,1:1
Makropoulos Secret, The 1926,Ja 22,12:4
R U R 1930,F 18,28:1
R U R 1942,D 4,30:2
Insect Comedy, The 1948,Je 4,26:3
R U R 1950,My 7,IV,13:6
Makropoulos Secret, The 1957,D 4,52:4
Capek Brothers (Playwright)
Insect Play, The 1923,My 13,VIII,3:5
Insect Play, The 1936,Jl 26,IX,1:3
Capel, Josephine
Corn Is Green, The 1943,My 4,18:3
Capell, Peter
Lamp at Midnight 1947,D 22,29:2
Blood Wedding 1949,F 7,16:2
Sun and I, The 1949,Mr 21,18:4
How Long Till Summer 1949,D 28,30:3
Sands of the Negev 1954,O 20,32:1
Capellari, A
Electra 1952,N 20,38:2
Capers, Virginia
Saratoga 1959,D 8,59:4
Caperton, Henriette
After Such Pleasures 1934,F 8,15:2
Capes, Edith May
Broadway Whirl, The 1921,Je 9,10:4
Capilla, Jose
Tambor y Cascabel; Drum and Bell
1932,Ap 21,25:4
Cuando Los Hijos De Eva No Son Los Hijos De
Adan; When Eve's Children Are Not Adam's
1932,Ap 23,11:2
Capillupo, Rinaldo (Director)
Hobo 1961,Ap 11,41:2
Capitsines, C
Electra 1952,N 20,38:2
Caplan, Arthur (Playwright)
Life's Too Short 1935,S 21,18:5
Caplan, Joan
H M S Pinafore 1968,Ap 29,47:2
Sound of Music, The 1970,Jl 3,13:1
Caplan, Lillie
Josephus 1933,D 1,22:5
Caplan, Phillip
Abe Lincoln in Illinois 1938,O 17,12:2
Caples, Martha (Composer)
New Faces 1934,Mr 16,24:5
Caplin, Gertrude (Producer)
Sixth Finger in a Five Finger Glove 1956,O 9,31:4
Capo, Bobby Jr
West Side Story 1968,Je 25,32:1
Capobianco, Tito (Director)
Fiesta in Madrid 1969,My 29,49:1
Capobianco, Tito (Playwright)
Fiesta in Madrid 1969,My 29,49:1
Capodice, John
Rosencrantz and Guildenstern Are Dead
1970,N 19,39:3
Capodilupo, Tony
Royal Hunt of the Sun, The 1965,O 27,36:2
MacBird! 1967,F 23,38:1
To Clothe the Naked 1967,Ap 28,30:1
Carving a Statue 1968,My 1,43:1
Man With the Flower in His Mouth, The
1969,Ap 23,42:1
Jar, The 1969,Ap 23,42:1
License, The 1969,Ap 23,42:1
Capone, Clifford (Costume Designer)
Lady From the Sea, The 1956,D 13,49:5
Riders to the Sea 1957,Mr 7,24:1
Tinker's Wedding, The 1957,Mr 7,24:1
In the Shadow of the Glen 1957,Mr 7,24:1
Blood Wedding 1958,Ap 1,35:1
Confederates, The 1959,S 29,45:1
Shadow and Substance 1959,N 4,42:1
After the Angels 1961,F 11,27:5
Route 1 1964,N 18,52:3
Medea 1965,N 29,46:1
Capone, Joseph
Volpone 1967,Je 30,29:1
Don Juan 1970,My 26,32:1
Capote, Truman (Lyricist)
House of Flowers 1954,D 31,11:2

Harold Arlen Songbook, The 1967,Mr 1,48:1
House of Flowers 1968,Ja 29,26:2
Capote, Truman (Original Author)
Grass Harp, The 1953,Ap 28,32:2
House of Flowers 1954,D 31,11:2
Breakfast at Tiffany's 1966,D 15,60:1
Capote, Truman (Playwright)
Grass Harp, The 1952,Mr 28,26:2
Grass Harp, The 1952,Ap 6,II,1:1
Grass Harp, The 1953,Ap 28,32:2
Grass Harp, The 1953,My 24,II,1:1
Capp, Al (Miscellaneous)
Li'l Abner 1956,N 25,II,1:1
Capp, Al (Playwright)
Li'l Abner 1956,N 16,24:2
Capp, Madeline (Miscellaneous)
Razzle Dazzle 1951,F 20,21:1
Cappa, V E
Assalto, L' 1929,My 20,23:2
Cappelletti, John
Way of the World, The 1965,Je 2,40:1
Richard III 1965,Je 3,26:1
Cappo Brothers and Pastor, The
Vaudeville (Hippodrome) 1926,Mr 30,20:4
Capps, Kendall
Boom Boom 1929,Ja 29,26:4
You Said It 1931,Ja 20,21:3
Cappy, Ted (Choreographer)
Ring Around the Moon 1950,N 24,30:1
Idiot's Delight 1951,My 24,46:3
Three Wishes for Jamie 1952,Mr 22,9:2
Dinny and the Witches 1959,D 10,53:3
Hit the Deck 1960,Je 24,32:1
Cappy, Ted (Miscellaneous)
Two on the Aisle 1951,Jl 20,13:6
To Broadway With Love 1964,Ap 30,28:6
Capron, Robert
Chimes of Normandy, The 1931,N 3,31:3
Naughty Marietta 1931,N 17,31:2
Firefly, The 1931,D 1,23:2
There You Are! 1932,My 17,25:4
Crucible 1933,S 5,22:4
Capuana, Luigi (Playwright)
Malia 1921,S 10,12:3
Capurro, Carmelo
'Il Tesoro D'Isacco; Treasure of Isaac, The
1928,Ja 26,17:1
Capus, Albert (Playwright)
Adventurer, The 1935,N 11,21:1
Caputi, Linda
Midsummer Night's Dream, A 1967,Je 19,42:1
Cara, Irene
Me Nobody Knows, The 1970,My 19,42:1
Carabella, Angela
Louisiana Lady 1947,Je 3,35:2
Caradimas, Lana
Shoemaker's Holiday, The 1967,Mr 3,25:1
Gondoliers, The 1967,O 29,83:1
Carafa, Richard
Time of the Cuckoo, The 1958,O 28,40:2
Caramounte (Costume Designer)
No Exit 1956,Ag 15,23:1
Carb, David (Playwright)
Immodest Violet 1920,Ag 25,6:2
Immodest Violet 1920,Ag 29,VI,1:1
Queen Victoria 1923,N 16,15:1
Queen Victoria 1923,N 25,VIII,1:1
Carberry, Albert
Red Light Annie 1923,Ag 22,10:3
Carberry, James (Director)
Oh, Johnny: or, Jonny Spielt Auf 1970,Mr 15,88:4
Carberry, James (Playwright)
Oh, Johnny: or, Jonny Spielt Auf 1970,Mr 15,88:4
Carberry, Jeanne
Time for the Gentle People, A 1967,My 26,50:1
Carbone, Anthony
Edward II 1958,F 12,32:5
Carbone, Antony (Director)
Man of Destiny, The 1956,Ap 26,38:1
On the Harmfulness of Tobacco 1956,Ap 26,38:1
Carboneri, Emile
Rapid Transit 1927,Ap 8,21:2
Carbonetto, Linda
Ice Capades 1970,Ja 7,35:1
Carby, Fanny
Oh What a Lovely War 1964,O 1,30:1
Carco, Francis (Original Author)
Deux Amis, Les 1927,Je 12,VII,2:1
Prisons de Femmes 1931,O 4,VIII,2:4
Card, Kathryn
Room of Dreams 1930,N 6,22:4
Card, Margery
Distant Drum, A 1928,Ja 21,13:1
Card, Virginia (Producer)
From Here to There; Real Strange One, A
1958,Ap 24,37:3
From Here to There; Otherwise Engaged
1958,Ap 24,37:3
From Here to There; Slow Dusk 1958,Ap 24,37:3
Carde, Howard
Seven Against One 1930,My 7,25:1
Cardell, Tony
Million Dollar Baby 1945,D 22,17:2

Cardell Twins
LeMaire's Affairs 1927,Mr 29,22:4
Cardelli, Giovanni (Producer)
Rape of Lucretia, The 1948,D 30,24:2
Carden, Charles
Brothers Karamazov, The 1927,Ja 4,20:1
Wings Over Europe 1928,D 11,35:1
Carden, Frances
Dance Night 1938,O 15,20:5
Carden, George
Call Me Madam 1952,Mr 16,84:3
Cardenas, Rudy
Vaudeville (Palace) 1952,Mr 12,31:2
Vaudeville (Palace) 1952,Mr 16,II,1:1
Carder, Floyd
Oh, Please! 1926,D 22,24:3
Cardew, Colin
Barbara's Wedding 1931,O 9,21:1
Cardew, Valerie
Pin to See the Peepshow, A 1953,S 18,17:2
Cardin, Pierre (Costume Designer)
Misanthrope, Le 1960,Mr 9,38:3
Huis Clos 1962,Ja 16,30:1
Lady of the Camellias, The 1963,Mr 22,7:1
Cardinal, Arthur
Cinderella on Broadway 1920,Je 25,18:1
Ballyhoo 1930,D 23,24:1
Cardini, John
Vaudeville (Palace) 1930,O 13,31:3
Vaudeville (Palace) 1932,Ja 4,27:4
O'Flynn, The 1934,D 28,24:1
Pirates of Penzance, The 1936,Ap 21,27:5
Cardino, Jerome
Run, Thief, Run 1957,My 2,27:1
Cardino, Jerome (Miscellaneous)
Run, Thief, Run 1957,My 2,27:1
Cardon, Charles
Tyrants 1924,Mr 5,14:1
American Born 1925,O 6,31:3
If 1927,O 26,26:2
Silver Box, The 1928,Ja 18,23:1
Roar China! 1930,O 28,23:1
Cardon, Jean
Zizi 1964,N 23,51:1
Cardoso, Sergio
Hughie 1959,O 15,48:1
Cardoza, Betty
Crucible 1933,S 5,22:4
Carduner, J (Producer)
Hedda Gabler 1970,Ja 18,78:1
Cardwell, Carolyn Y
No Exit 1967,O 31,38:2
Clara's Ole Man 1968,Mr 9,23:2
Carell, Karlheinz
Blaue Boll, Der 1931,Ja 25,VIII,4:1
Carelli, Cara (Playwright)
Go West, Young Man 1923,N 13,25:2
Carelman, Jacques (Costume Designer)
Diary of a Madman 1967,Mr 24,25:1
Carelman, Jacques (Scenic Designer)
Diary of a Madman 1967,Mr 24,25:1
Careno, Odali
Vaudeville (Palace) 1926,S 21,32:5
Vaudeville (Palace) 1927,S 20,33:3
Vaudeville (Palace) 1928,Mr 27,30:5
Carerre, Anne
Proces, Le; Trial, The 1952,N 18,36:2
Carew, Beryl
Meet the People 1940,D 26,22:2
Carew, Daniel
Holy Terror, A 1925,S 29,31:2
Near to the Stars 1932,F 23,23:2
Hat, a Coat, a Glove, A 1934,F 1,15:2
Carew, Edith
Victoria Regina 1938,O 4,20:2
Carew, Frank
Lady With a Lamp, The 1931,N 20,27:2
Carew, Helen
Kempy 1922,My 16,14:2
Roger Bloomer 1923,Mr 2,18:3
Rising Son, The 1924,O 28,27:2
Human Nature 1925,S 25,24:3
Trouper, The 1926,Mr 9,21:1
Wooden Kimono 1926,D 28,16:2
Breaks, The 1928,Ap 17,26:3
Lonely Way, The 1931,F 22,VIII,4:1
Family Upstairs, The 1933,O 28,20:6
Dream Child 1934,Jl 31,20:2
Dream Child 1934,S 28,26:2
Ah, Wilderness! 1935,Ag 20,25:1
Our Town 1938,Ja 23,II,10:6
Our Town 1938,Ja 26,27:4
Our Town 1938,F 5,18:3
Our Town 1938,F 13,X,1:1
Village Green 1941,Je 17,24:7
Hope for a Harvest 1941,N 27,28:2
Broken Journey 1942,Je 24,22:2
Harriet 1943,Mr 4,24:2
Mrs January & Mr Ex 1944,Ap 1,10:2
Place of Our Own, A 1945,Ap 3,23:7
January Thaw 1946,F 5,18:2
Traveling Lady 1954,O 28,45:2

Carew, James
Apple Cart, The 1929,Ag 20,30:2
Carew, Peter
Purple Canary, The 1963,Ap 23,31:1
Carewe, Edwin (Director)
Heaven-Tappers, The 1927,Mr 9,28:3
Carewe, Edwin (Miscellaneous)
Heaven-Tappers, The 1927,Mr 9,28:3
Carewe, Joseph
Merry-Go-Round 1932,Ap 23,11:2
Carewe, Richard
Immortal Thief, The 1926,O 4,21:1
Hamlet 1934,D 26,19:3
Carey, Addison
Chocolate Dandies, The 1924,S 2,22:2
Carey, Addison (Director)
Brown Buddies 1930,O 8,29:1
Carey, Alex
Dancers, The 1923,O 18,17:2
Carey, Ann
Ruddigore 1931,Ag 11,28:3
Chocolate Soldier, The 1931,S 22,33:3
Geisha, The 1931,O 6,35:4
Naughty Marietta 1931,N 17,31:2
Carey, Bob
Kittiwake Island 1960,O 13,43:1
Carey, Catherine
Ethan Frome 1936,Ja 22,15:2
Carey, Cecile
Red, Hot and Blue! 1936,O 30,26:3
Carey, Charles
Gala Night 1930,F 26,22:4
Devil Came From Dublin, The! 1955,Je 3,27:2
Carey, Claude
Tapestry in Gray 1935,D 28,10:2
Carey, Dan
Elmer the Great 1928,S 25,29:1
Gambling 1929,Ag 27,31:2
Tavern, The 1930,My 20,32:1
Merry-Go-Round 1932,Ap 23,11:2
Man Bites Dog 1933,Ap 26,11:2
Crucible 1933,S 5,22:4
Dear Old Darling 1936,Mr 3,25:1
Carey, David
Light, Lively and Yiddish 1970,O 28,58:1
Carey, Denis
Parnell of Avondale 1934,O 3,24:4
Murder in the Cathedral 1938,F 17,16:2
Spring Meeting 1938,D 9,30:4
Carey, Denis (Director)
Julius Caesar 1955,Jl 13,20:1
Julius Caesar 1955,Jl 17,II,1:1
Tempest, The 1955,Ag 2,18:2
Tempest, The 1955,Ag 7,II,1:1
Romanoff and Juliet 1956,My 19,12:5
Man of Distinction 1957,Ag 27,33:7
Carey, Ellen
Ah, Wilderness! 1940,Ag 20,23:2
Carey, Frank
Great Goodness of Life (A Coon Show) 1969,Ap 27,92:1
Gentleman Caller, The 1969,Ap 27,92:1
Black Quartet, A; Gentleman Caller, The 1969,Jl 31,28:1
Black Quartet, A; Great Goodness of Life (A Coon Show) 1969,Jl 31,28:1
Carey, Grace
Bitter Oleander 1935,F 12,24:3
Carey, Harry
Heavenly Express 1940,Ap 19,24:2
Heavenly Express 1940,Ap 28,IX,1:1
Ah, Wilderness! 1940,Ag 20,23:2
Ah, Wilderness! 1941,O 3,26:2
Ah, Wilderness! 1941,O 12,IX,1:1
But Not Goodbye 1944,Ap 12,19:2
Carey, Harry Jr
What Price Glory 1949,Mr 3,33:2
Carey, Helen
Skin of Our Teeth, The 1966,Je 2,51:1
Dance of Death, The 1966,Je 3,31:1
As You Like It 1966,Je 4,19:1
Shoemaker's Holiday, The 1967,Je 3,19:1
Thieves' Carnival 1967,Je 5,52:1
Tango 1968,Ja 1,11:1
Twelfth Night 1968,Je 15,40:1
Master Builder, The 1968,Je 22,26:1
Merchant of Venice, The 1970,Je 10,39:1
School for Scandal, The 1970,Je 11,51:1
Carey, Joseph
Ziegfeld Follies 1934,Ja 5,24:3
Carey, Joyce
Easy Virtue 1925,D 8,28:2
Road to Rome, The 1927,F 1,24:2
Jealous Moon, The 1928,N 21,32:2
Paolo and Francesca 1929,Ap 2,28:2
Jenny 1929,O 9,34:4
Twelfth Night 1930,O 16,28:2
Twelfth Night 1930,N 2,VIII,1:1
Art and Mrs Bottle 1930,N 19,19:3
Barretts of Wimpole Street, The 1931,F 10,25:1
Electra 1932,Ja 9,21:4
Lucrece 1932,N 30,22:8
Lucrece 1932,D 21,22:2

Lucrece 1933,Ja 1,IX,1:1
Barretts of Wimpole Street, The 1935,F 26,16:2
Sweet Aloes 1936,F 25,23:5
Sweet Aloes 1936,Mr 5,24:5
Tonight at 8:30; Hands Across the Sea; Astonished Heart, The; Red Peppers 1936,O 27,30:7
Red Peppers 1936,N 25,17:2
Astonished Heart, The 1936,N 25,17:2
Hands Across the Sea 1936,N 25,17:2
Shadow Play 1936,N 28,13:1
Fumed Oak 1936,N 28,13:1
We Were Dancing 1936,N 28,13:1
Ways and Means 1936,D 1,31:1
Family Album 1936,D 1,31:1
Still Life 1936,D 1,31:1
Nude With Violin 1957,N 15,36:1
Carey, Leighton
Home Sweet Home 1936,Jl 1,29:2
Carey, Leonard
Shewing-Up of Blanco Posnet, The 1923,O 17,14:2
Tyrants 1924,Mr 5,14:1
Farmer's Wife, The 1924,O 10,22:3
Eve's Leaves 1925,Mr 27,22:2
Affair of State, An 1930,N 20,30:3
Many Happy Returns 1945,Ja 6,15:5
Carey, Macdonald
Lady in the Dark 1941,Ja 5,IX,1:7
Lady in the Dark 1941,Ja 24,14:2
Anniversary Waltz 1954,Ap 8,34:1
Music Man, The 1963,Ag 15,24:1
Carey, Mary
Earl Carroll's Vanities 1924,S 11,23:6
Carey, Richard
Late One Evening 1933,Ja 10,27:3
Carey, Ron
Lovers and Other Strangers 1968,S 19,63:1
Carey, Sarah
Under the Gaslight 1929,Ap 3,27:1
Carey, Stephen
Ah, Wilderness! 1940,Ag 20,23:2
Carey, Thomas
Daddy Dumplins 1920,N 23,11:1
Carey, Thomas F (Rev) (Miscellaneous)
Angelic Doctor 1953,Ap 14,30:2
Carey, Tom
Carmen Jones 1959,Ag 18,25:1
Carey, William
My Girl Friday! 1929,F 13,20:2
Queen at Home 1930,D 30,25:2
Happy Landing 1932,Mr 28,10:5
Carfax, Bruce
At the Silver Swan 1936,F 20,22:2
Carfrae, Elizabeth
Forest Ring, The 1930,Ap 26,11:2
Cargill, Judith
Pillar to Post 1943,D 11,11:2
Years Ago 1946,D 4,44:2
Cargill, Patrick (Producer)
Play on Love 1970,Ja 16,31:1
Carhartt, Peter
Escape This Night 1938,Ap 23,18:1
Caridi, Carmine
View From the Bridge, A 1965,Ja 29,24:1
Carnival! 1968,D 13,58:1
Caridi, Tony
Let's Face It 1941,O 30,26:2
Carillo, Alberto
Laugh It Off 1925,Ap 25,18:4
Crashing Through 1928,O 30,26:5
Carillo, Leo
Mike Angelo 1923,Ja 9,26:2
Gypsy Jim 1924,Ja 6,VII,1:1
Gypsy Jim 1924,Ja 20,VII,1:1
Saint, The 1924,O 13,20:3
Lambs Gambol 1932,Ap 25,18:2
Caringi, Loreto
Avanti 1968,F 1,29:1
Caringi, Rudy
End of All Things Natural, The 1969,S 12,38:1
Cariou, Len
Troilus and Cressida 1963,Je 19,40:2
Richard II 1964,Je 17,47:1
Bourgeois Gentilhomme, Le 1964,Je 18,28:2
Skin of Our Teeth, The 1966,Je 2,51:1
As You Like It 1966,Je 4,19:1
Shoemaker's Holiday, The 1967,Je 3,19:1
Harpers Ferry 1967,Je 6,52:2
House of Atreus, The; Bringers of Offerings, The 1967,Jl 24,23:1
House of Atreus, The; Furies, The 1967,Jl 24,23:1
Visit, The 1967,S 13,41:1
Twelfth Night 1968,Je 15,40:1
Serjeant Musgrave's Dance 1968,Je 16,52:4
House of Atreus, The 1968,D 18,55:1
Henry V 1969,Je 9,57:1
Henry V 1969,Je 15,II,3:1
Much Ado About Nothing 1969,Je 16,57:1
Three Sisters, The 1969,Ag 4,29:1
Three Sisters, The 1969,Ag 10,II,3:1
Henry V 1969,N 11,43:1
Applause 1970,Mr 31,35:1
Applause 1970,Ap 5,II,1:1

Carisi, John (Miscellaneous)
Birds, The 1966,Jl 1,40:1
Carl, Ruth
Meek Mose 1928,F 7,30:1
Carle, John
Princess Ida 1967,Ap 17,46:2
Patience 1967,O 13,32:1
Iolanthe 1967,O 18,40:1
Mikado, The 1967,O 25,42:2
Gondoliers, The 1967,O 29,83:1
H M S Pinafore 1967,N 1,40:1
Carle, Richard
Broadway Whirl, The 1921,Je 9,10:4
Friars Club Frolic 1921,Je 13,16:2
Adrienne 1923,My 29,10:4
New Yorkers, The 1930,N 16,VIII,3:1
New Yorkers, The 1930,D 9,31:1
Carleen, Ellen
Street Scene 1947,Ja 10,17:2
Carleton, Alice
George White's Scandals 1935,D 26,20:2
Carleton, Claire
Blue Monday 1932,Je 3,23:2
Great Magoo, The 1932,D 3,20:7
Come Easy 1933,Ag 30,22:5
Kill That Story 1934,Ag 30,22:2
Long Frontier, The 1935,Jl 23,24:4
Bet Your Life 1937,Ap 6,20:2
Without Warning 1937,My 3,23:2
Love in My Fashion 1937,D 4,21:4
I Must Love Someone 1939,F 8,18:7
Clutterbuck 1949,D 5,29:2
Carleton, George
Broomsticks Amen! 1934,F 10,20:4
Every Thursday 1934,My 11,25:5
Kill That Story 1934,Ag 30,22:2
Porgy and Bess 1935,O 11,30:2
Where Do We Go From Here? 1938,N 16,26:2
Aries Is Rising 1939,N 22,16:5
Carleton, Graeme (Director)
Pilgrim's Progress 1962,Mr 21,36:2
Carleton, Jane
Anna Ascends 1920,S 23,14:1
Carleton, Lloyd
Brothers 1928,D 26,14:3
Carleton, Randolph
Henry V 1928,Mr 16,26:2
Carleton, Robert
Make Yourself at Home 1945,S 14,21:2
Carleton, Verna
Little Theatre Tournament; Aristocrat, The 1929,My 8,34:4
Carleton, William
Lord Byron's Cain 1925,Ap 9,20:3
Love Call, The 1927,O 25,33:1
Macbeth 1928,N 20,28:3
Star of Bengal 1929,S 26,27:2
Carley, Marion
Regina 1949,N 1,32:2
Carlin, Cynthia
He Who Gets Slapped 1946,Mr 21,31:4
Carlin, Kay
Caroline 1923,F 1,13:2
Queer People 1934,F 16,16:2
Carlin, Thomas
Thieves' Carnival 1955,F 2,21:1
Time Limit! 1956,Ja 25,27:2
Holiday for Lovers 1957,F 15,20:1
Man in the Dog Suit, The 1958,O 31,34:2
Geranium Hat, The 1959,Mr 18,45:1
Cook for Mr General, A 1961,O 20,39:1
Great Day in the Morning 1962,Mr 29,29:1
Carlin, Walter
Miss Julie 1956,F 22,23:2
Carling, Lisa
Revenger's Tragedy, The 1970,D 2,58:1
Carling, Mary
Veronica's Veil 1931,F 23,36:2
Carlino, Lewis John (Playwright)
Cages; Snowangel; Epiphany 1963,Je 14,36:1
Telemachus Clay 1963,N 16,17:2
Sarah and the Sax 1964,My 5,53:1
Dirty Old Man, The 1964,My 5,53:1
Exercise, The 1968,Ap 25,54:1
Exercise, The 1968,My 12,II,1:1
Carlisle, Alexandra
Tragedy of Nan, The 1920,F 18,9:1
Tragedy of Nan, The 1920,F 22,III,6:1
Respect for Riches 1920,My 12,9:1
Truth About Blayds, The 1922,Mr 15,22:1
Fools Errant 1922,Ag 22,12:3
Criminal at Large 1932,O 11,26:3
Oliver Oliver 1934,Ag 6,18:5
Fresh Fields 1934,Jl 15,X,1:1
Othello 1935,S 13,19:2
Othello 1935,S 28,13:2
Macbeth 1935,O 8,26:4
Woman of Destiny, A 1936,Mr 3,25:2
Carlisle, Kevin (Choreographer)
Fiorello! 1962,Je 14,24:1
Hallelujah, Baby! 1967,Ap 27,51:1
Hallelujah, Baby! 1967,My 7,II,1:1

Carlisle, Kevin (Miscellaneous)
Happy Time, The 1968,Ja 19,32:2
Carlisle, Kitty
Champagne, Sec 1933,O 16,20:2
White Horse Inn 1936,O 2,28:5
Three Waltzes 1937,D 27,10:2
Walk With Music 1940,Je 5,33:2
Rape of Lucretia, The 1948,D 30,24:2
Anniversary Waltz 1954,Ap 8,34:1
Kiss Me, Kate 1956,My 10,27:2
Carlisle, Margaret
Nina Rosa 1930,My 31,19:3
Carlisle, Margaret (Composer)
Adventures of Marco Polo, The 1941,D 28,I,31:7
Carlisle, Marion
Bitter Sweet 1934,My 8,28:4
Carlisle, Patricia
Sweeney Todd 1957,Ag 28,21:4
Carlisle, Sidney
Children's Tragedy, The 1921,O 12,18:2
Anathema 1923,Ap 11,16:2
Carlisle, Sybil
Pelican, The 1925,S 22,23:2
Magda 1926,Ja 27,16:2
Carlisle, Una Mae
Harlem Cavalcade 1942,My 2,11:2
Carlo
Betty Lee 1924,D 26,18:2
Carlo, Michael
Red Harvest 1937,Mr 31,29:2
Carlo, Monte (Composer)
Louisiana Lady 1947,Je 3,35:2
Carlo, Monte (Lyricist)
Louisiana Lady 1947,Je 3,35:2
Carlo (Composer)
Oh! Oh! Nurse 1925,D 8,28:4
Carlo (Lyricist)
Oh! Oh! Nurse 1925,D 8,28:4
Carlo and Sanders (Composer)
Tangerine 1921,Ag 10,8:2
Houseboat on the Styx, The 1928,D 26,14:3
Mystery Moon 1930,Je 24,23:4
Carlo and Sanders (Lyricist)
Houseboat on the Styx, The 1928,D 26,14:3
Mystery Moon 1930,Je 24,23:4
Carlon, Fran
Lucky Sam McCarver 1950,Ap 15,10:6
Men of Distinction 1953,My 1,18:4
Carlon, Frances
Play, Genius, Play! 1935,O 31,17:2
Carlon, Linda
Broadway Shadows 1930,Ap 1,34:6
Three Times the Hour 1931,Ag 26,15:5
Carlos and Inez
Make It Snappy 1922,Ap 14,20:2
Magic Ring, The 1923,O 2,10:1
Carlos and Valeria
Greenwich Village Follies 1928,Ap 10,32:2
Carlow, George
Paradise 1931,My 12,29:2
Carlozzi, Richard (Costume Designer)
Enemies Don't Send Flowers 1957,F 20,38:1
God Slept Here, A 1957,F 20,38:1
Carlsen, Carla
Lauf ins Glueck 1935,My 19,IX,2:5
Carlson, Charles
Trojan Women, The 1957,Mr 19,42:7
Cut of the Axe 1960,F 2,38:2
Carlson, Curtis
Dracula Sabbat 1970,O 2,28:2
Carlson, Donna (Original Author)
Demon Mirror, The 1968,Mr 13,42:1
Carlson, Donna (Scenic Designer)
Now You See It 1967,N 20,59:1
Carlson, Eric
Trumpets and Drums 1969,O 13,52:1
Carlson, Harry
Here Come the Clowns 1960,S 20,48:1
Carlson, Jon
Candida 1969,F 3,29:1
Carlson, Judith
Peter and the Wolf 1969,N 30,85:5
Carlson, Julia
Corn Is Green, The 1943,My 4,18:3
Carlson, Linda
Harangues, The 1970,Ja 14,42:1
Carlson, Natalie
What's Up 1953,O 28,37:2
Carlson, Nione (Scenic Designer)
Streetcar Named Desire, A 1955,Mr 4,18:2
Carlson, Philip
Until the Monkey Comes 1966,Je 21,38:1
Carlson, Richard
Now You've Done It 1937,Mr 6,10:4
Ghost of Yankee Doodle, The 1937,N 23,26:3
Whiteoaks 1938,Mr 24,20:2
Stars in Your Eyes 1939,F 10,18:2
Carlson, Richardson (Director)
Western Waters 1937,D 29,17:1
Carlson, Richardson (Playwright)
Western Waters 1937,D 29,17:1
Carlson, Robert Eric
Finian's Rainbow 1947,Ja 11,23:2

Carlson, Stanley
Alchemist, The 1948,My 7,31:4
Insect Comedy, The 1948,Je 4,26:3
Liar, The 1950,My 19,30:2
Flahooley 1951,My 15,39:1
My Darlin' Aida 1952,O 28,36:4
Cyrano de Bergerac 1953,N 13,24:3
Richard III 1953,D 10,65:2
Fledermaus, Die 1954,My 20,38:5
Carousel 1954,Je 3,32:2
Oh Captain! 1958,F 5,21:2
Carlson, Terry
Woman of Destiny, A 1936,Mr 3,25:2
Carlson, Vicki
Joy to the World 1948,Mr 19,28:2
Young and Fair, The 1948,N 23,35:2
Carlson, Violet
Student Prince, The 1924,D 3,25:3
Nightingale, The 1927,Ja 4,20:4
Love Call, The 1927,O 25,33:1
Red Robe, The 1928,D 26,15:1
Sweet Adeline 1929,S 4,33:1
Vaudeville (Palace) 1932,Je 6,18:2
Caviar 1934,Je 8,19:2
Carlsson, Elsa
Father, The 1962,My 15,49:1
Carlstedt
Big Hearted Herbert 1934,Ja 2,17:3
Carlsten, Rune
Henry VIII 1930,Jl 13,VIII,2:1
Carlstrom, Gustav (Scenic Designer)
Autumn Manoeuvers 1938,N 27,IX,3:6
Carlton, Carl H
Ten Nights in a Barroom 1932,Ja 21,17:1
Carlton, Carle (Composer)
Paradise Alley 1924,Ap 2,17:3
Lace Petticoat 1927,Ja 5,18:2
Carlton, Carle (Director)
Lace Petticoat 1927,Ja 5,18:2
Carlton, Carle (Producer)
Lace Petticoat 1927,Ja 5,18:2
Carlton, Claire
Body Beautiful, The 1935,N 1,24:3
Carlton, Elizabeth
Little Theatre Tournament; Sightseers
1929,My 8,34:4
Carlton, Florence
Mlle Modiste 1937,My 5,28:5
Carlton, Henry Fisk (Playwright)
Shooting Shadows 1924,Je 27,16:5
Up the Line 1926,N 23,26:1
Carlton, Jack
Candle-Light 1929,O 1,28:2
Carlton, John (Playwright)
King's Leisure, The 1936,My 31,II,6:8
Carlton, Louise
Lancelot and Elaine 1921,S 13,12:1
Carlton, Reed
Four O'Clock 1933,F 14,19:6
Carlton, Rex (Producer)
Open House 1947,Je 4,33:4
Carlton, Thelma
Her Family Tree 1920,D 28,9:2
Carlucci, Giovanni
Miserabili I, 1934,O 1,14:2
Signora Dalle Camelie, La; Camille 1934,O 22,13:2
Processo dei Veleni, Il; Case of Poisons, The
1935,Ja 21,18:2
Romanzo di un Giovane Povero, Il 1935,F 25,12:3
Feudalismo Oppure La Terra Bassa; Feudalism or
the Lowland 1937,Mr 8,22:2
Carlucci, Giuseppe
Colonello Bridall, L' 1934,Ap 16,20:3
Romanticismo 1934,My 14,20:2
Signora Dalle Camelie, La; Dame aux Camelias, La
1937,O 9,16:3
Carluccio, Iolanda
Piccolo Santo, Il; Little Saint, The 1931,D 14,16:4
Carluccio, Rose
Blue Butterfly, The 1929,F 17,29:3
Carlyle, Aileen
No Strings 1942,Je 14,VIII,2:1
Carlyle, Grace
Her Salary Man 1921,N 29,20:1
Love Song, The 1925,Ja 14,19:4
White Gold 1925,N 3,34:5
Carlyle, John C
Just Beyond 1925,D 2,22:4
What Do We Know 1927,D 24,8:1
Carlyle, Louise
Of Thee I Sing 1952,My 6,34:2
Carlyle, Meta
Keep Moving 1934,Ag 24,10:2
Carlyle, Richard
Seventh Heaven 1922,O 31,11:1
Dawn 1924,N 25,27:1
Holy Terror, A 1925,S 29,31:2
Mrs Gibsons' Boys 1949,My 5,35:2
Mr Barry's Etchings 1950,F 1,26:2
Out West of Eighth 1951,S 21,20:3
Fragile Fox 1954,O 13,27:1
Desperate Hours, The 1955,My 1,II,3:1

Carlyle, Rita
Brothers 1928,D 26,14:3
Carlyle, Robert
Dorian Gray 1936,Jl 21,13:3
Carlyle, Sidney
Humoresque 1923,F 28,13:2
Carlyle, Wanda
Tavern, The 1920,S 28,14:1
Carlysle, Lynn
P S I Love You 1964,N 20,40:1
Carman, John
Silence 1924,N 13,18:2
Carmel, Evelyn
Lady Comes Across, The 1942,Ja 10,10:2
Carmel, Roger C
Plough and the Stars, The 1956,Ap 6,14:1
Picture of Dorian Gray, The 1956,Ag 18,15:5
Hamlet 1956,O 29,34:1
All the King's Men 1959,O 17,27:2
Death of Satan, The 1960,Ap 6,49:1
Henry V 1960,Je 30,23:1
Measure for Measure 1960,Jl 27,33:1
Taming of the Shrew, The 1960,Ag 20,17:1
Once There Was a Russian 1961,F 20,32:2
Hole, The 1961,Ap 4,42:2
Purlie Victorious 1961,S 29,29:1
Irregular Verb to Love, The 1963,S 19,22:2
Carmela
Penny Change 1963,O 25,37:1
Carmelim, The
Grand Music Hall of Israel, The 1968,F 7,42:1
Carmen, Karl
Montmartre 1922,F 14,20:1
Carmen, Lillian
Sketch Book 1935,Je 5,22:2
Carmen, May
As You Were 1920,Ja 28,22:3
Carmen, Rita
Canteen Show, The 1942,S 4,18:1
Carmi, Maria (Princess Marchiabelli)
Miracle, The 1924,Ja 26,10:1
Carmichael, Coralie
Anna Christie 1930,My 4,XI,3:1
Ascendancy 1935,Ja 31,22:3
Magic 1935,Mr 14,19:2
Hamlet 1957,O 29,34:2
Carmichael, Hoagy (Composer)
Three After Three 1939,N 25,13:5
Walk With Music 1940,Je 5,33:2
It's All Yours 1942,Mr 26,26:2
Carmichael, Hoagy (Lyricist)
Show Is On, The 1937,S 20,18:4
Three After Three 1939,N 25,13:5
It's All Yours 1942,Mr 26,26:2
Carmichael, Ian
Tunnel of Love, The 1957,D 5,47:2
Love Doctor, The 1959,O 14,52:4
Critic's Choice 1961,D 7,53:2
Boeing-Boeing 1965,F 3,30:1
Carmichael, James (Musical Director)
Amen Corner, The 1965,Ap 16,35:1
Carmichael, Patricia (Director)
Death of the Well-Loved Boy, The
1967,My 16,48:1
One Night Stands of a Noisy Passenger; Passage,
Un 1970,D 31,8:3
One Night Stands of a Noisy Passenger; Noisy
Passenger, The 1970,D 31,8:3
One Night Stands of a Noisy Passenger; Last
Stand 1970,D 31,8:3
Carminati, Tullio
Strictly Dishonorable 1929,S 19,37:1
Strictly Dishonorable 1929,S 29,IX,1:1
Christopher Comes Across 1932,Je 1,19:2
Music in the Air 1932,N 9,28:2
Music in the Air 1932,N 20,IX,1:1
Great Lady 1938,D 2,26:6
Carmine
Bead-Tangle 1970,Jl 16,38:1
Carmines, Al
Way of the Cross, The 1959,Ja 16,35:2
Mystery of the Finding of the Cross, The
1959,Ja 16,35:2
Cup of Trembling, The 1959,My 1,33:5
Cranmer of Canterbury 1959,D 4,36:1
Family Reunion 1960,D 10,26:1
Home Movies 1964,My 12,32:1
In Circles 1967,O 14,12:1
In Circles 1968,Je 28,36:1
Peace 1969,Ja 28,49:1
Peace 1969,F 16,II,1:1
Carmines, Al (Composer)
Softly, and Consider the Nearness 1964,My 12,32:1
Home Movies 1964,My 12,32:1
Gorilla Queen 1967,Ap 25,36:1
In Circles 1967,O 14,12:1
In Circles 1967,N 5,II,1:7
Line of Least Existence, The 1968,Mr 25,53:1
In Circles 1968,Je 28,36:1
Peace 1968,N 10,87:1
Peace 1969,Ja 28,49:1
Peace 1969,F 16,II,1:1
Promenade 1969,Je 5,56:1

Carmines, Al (Composer)—Cont
Promenade 1969,Je 15,II,1:1
Much Ado About Nothing 1969,Je 16,57:1
Carmines, Al (Lyricist)
Gorilla Queen 1967,Ap 25,36:1
Carmines, Al (Miscellaneous)
Peace 1969,Ja 28,49:1
Carmines, Al (Musical Director)
Promenade 1969,Je 5,56:1
Carmita
Continental Varieties 1934,O 4,18:3
Carmody, David B
Great Shakes 1931,Mr 12,22:2
Carmody, Eileen
Nightingale, The 1927,Ja 4,20:4
Carmody, John
Ladies of the Evening 1924,D 24,11:2
God Loves Us 1926,O 20,22:2
He Loved the Ladies 1927,My 11,29:2
Uninvited Guest, The 1927,S 28,28:2
How's Your Health? 1929,N 27,30:3
It's a Wise Child 1933,My 17,15:2
Mrs O'Brien Entertains 1939,F 9,16:3
Goodbye in the Night 1940,Mr 19,31:2
Carmole, Louis
Career 1943,O 29,22:6
Carn, Anthony
Uniform of Flesh 1949,Ja 31,15:2
Carnahan, Peter M (Director)
Dreaming Dust, The 1955,D 8,46:5
Carnahan, Thomas
One Way Street 1928,D 25,31:2
Tired Business Man, The 1929,Je 5,32:5
Gold Braid 1930,My 14,31:2
Jefferson Davis 1936,F 19,17:2
Carnduff, Thomas (Playwright)
Workers 1932,D 11,IX,4:5
Castlereagh 1935,F 20,22:4
Carne, Judy
Boy Friend, The 1970,Ap 15,54:1
Boy Friend, The 1970,Ap 26,II,5:7
Carnegie, Hall
New Moon, The 1944,My 18,16:2
Carnegie, Hattie (Costume Designer)
Lady in the Dark 1941,Ja 24,14:2
Lady in the Dark 1941,S 3,26:6
Lady in the Dark 1943,Mr 1,14:2
Overtons, The 1945,F 7,16:6
Tonight at 8:30; Family Album 1948,F 21,8:2
Tonight at 8:30; Red Peppers 1948,F 21,8:2
Tonight at 8:30; Ways and Means 1948,F 21,8:2
Tonight at 8:30; Shadow Play 1948,F 24,20:4
Tonight at 8:30; Hands Across the Sea 1948,F 24,20:4
Tonight at 8:30; Fumed Oak 1948,F 24,20:4
Goodbye My Fancy 1948,N 18,35:2
Carney, Alan
Whistler's Grandmother 1952,D 12,40:2
Fanny 1954,N 5,16:1
Carney, Art
Rope Dancers, The 1957,N 21,39:1
Rope Dancers, The 1957,D 1,II,1:1
Take Her, She's Mine 1961,D 22,19:1
Odd Couple, The 1965,Mr 11,36:1
Odd Couple, The 1965,Mr 21,II,1:1
Flora, the Red Menace 1965,My 12,41:2
Lovers; Winners 1968,Jl 26,21:4
Lovers; Losers 1968,Jl 26,21:4
Carney, Frank (Playwright)
Righteous Are Bold, The 1946,O 27,II,1:3
Righteous Are Bold, The 1955,D 23,12:1
Carney, Frederick
Hamlet 1938,O 13,28:1
Henry IV, Part I 1939,Ja 31,17:2
Hamlet 1939,D 5,35:2
Elizabeth the Queen 1941,O 17,27:2
Carney, George
Good Companions, The 1931,O 2,31:1
Good Companions, The 1931,O 11,VIII,1:1
Egg in Your Beer 1945,My 13,II,1:3
Carney, Grace
Family Portrait 1959,My 6,48:2
Donnybrook! 1961,My 19,23:1
Billygoat Eddie 1964,Ap 21,43:2
Carney, John J
Aqua Carnival 1962,Je 29,15:1
Hamlet 1969,My 2,38:1
Carney, Kay
Viet Rock 1966,N 11,38:1
Calling in Crazy 1969,O 7,42:2
Universal Nigger, The 1970,Mr 21,18:1
Carney, Lee
Pygmalion 1938,Ja 27,16:3
Captain Jinks of the Horse Marines 1938,Ja 28,16:2
Young Man's Fancy, A 1947,Ap 30,33:2
Carney, Len
Aquashow 1953,Je 24,29:2
Aquashow 1954,Je 23,20:4
Carney, Mary
Rainbow 1928,N 22,25:1
Carney, Milton
Pygmalion 1952,F 9,11:2
Maya 1953,Je 10,35:1
Scarecrow, The 1953,Je 17,31:1

School for Scandal, The 1953,Je 24,29:2
Little Clay Cart, The 1953,Jl 1,25:1
View From the Bridge, A 1955,S 30,21:1
Doctor in Spite of Himself, The 1957,F 28,18:4
Carney, Thom
Flies, The; Mouches, Les 1947,Ap 18,26:3
All the King's Men 1948,Ja 19,19:2
Carney, Thom (Director)
Missouri Legend 1951,F 10,10:4
Carnovsky, Morris
God of Vengeance, The 1922,D 20,22:5
Failures, The 1923,N 23,20:1
Saint Joan 1923,D 29,8:4
Juarez and Maximilian 1926,O 12,31:1
Ned McCobb's Daughter 1926,N 30,26:2
Brothers Karamazov, The 1927,Ja 4,20:1
Right You Are (If You Think You Are) 1927,F 24,27:1
Doctor's Dilemma, The 1927,N 22,33:1
Marco Millions 1928,Ja 10,28:2
Volpone 1928,Ap 10,32:1
Camel Through the Needle's Eye, The 1929,Ap 16,32:2
Uncle Vanya 1929,My 25,17:1
Apple Cart, The 1930,F 25,30:1
Hotel Universe 1930,Ap 15,29:1
Elizabeth the Queen 1930,N 4,37:1
House of Connelly, The 1931,S 29,22:4
1931 1931,D 11,34:3
Night Over Taos 1932,Mr 10,25:3
Success Story 1932,S 27,24:4
Both Your Houses 1933,Mr 7,20:3
Men in White 1933,S 27,24:2
Men in White 1933,O 1,IX,1:1
Gentlewoman 1934,Mr 23,28:4
Gold Eagle Guy 1934,N 29,33:4
Gold Eagle Guy 1934,D 9,X,1:1
Waiting for Lefty 1935,F 11,14:5
Awake and Sing! 1935,F 20,23:2
Paradise Lost 1935,D 10,31:5
Case of Clyde Griffiths 1936,Mr 14,10:4
Johnny Johnson 1936,N 19,XII,1:1
Johnny Johnson 1936,N 20,26:3
Golden Boy 1937,N 5,18:5
Golden Boy 1938,Ja 23,XI,1:6
Rocket to the Moon 1938,N 25,18:2
Rocket to the Moon 1938,D 4,X,5:1
Awake and Sing! 1939,Mr 8,18:2
Sarah Adler Testimonial 1939,Mr 15,18:2
Awake and Sing! 1939,Mr 26,X,1:2
Thunder Rock 1939,N 15,18:1
Night Music 1940,F 23,18:2
Night Music 1940,Mr 3,X,1:1
Susannah and the Elders 1940,O 13,47:7
Susannah and the Elders 1940,O 30,28:2
My Sister Eileen 1940,D 27,23:2
Cafe Crown 1942,Ja 24,12:5
Counterattack 1943,F 4,27:2
Counterattack 1943,F 14,II,1:1
Joy to the World 1948,Mr 19,28:2
Enemy of the People, An 1950,D 29,14:1
Enemy of the People, An 1951,Ja 7,II,1:1
World of Sholom Aleichem, The 1953,S 12,13:2
World of Sholom Aleichem, The 1953,S 20,II,1:1
Three Sisters, The 1955,F 26,13:2
Three Sisters, The 1955,Mr 20,II,1:1
Moby Dick 1955,Ap 26,25:3
Tiger at the Gates 1955,O 4,40:1
Lovers 1956,My 11,23:1
King John 1956,Je 28,33:5
Measure for Measure 1956,Je 29,16:1
Taming of the Shrew, The 1956,Ag 6,20:1
Measure for Measure 1957,Ja 23,24:1
Taming of the Shrew, The 1957,F 21,30:2
Merchant of Venice, The 1957,Jl 11,19:5
Much Ado About Nothing 1957,Ag 8,15:2
Merchant of Venice, The 1957,Ag 18,II,1:1
Nude With Violin 1957,N 15,36:1
Hamlet 1958,Je 21,11:1
Midsummer Night's Dream, A 1958,Je 23,19:1
Cold Wind and the Warm, The 1958,D 9,55:1
Romeo and Juliet 1959,Je 15,31:1
Romeo and Juliet 1959,Je 21,II,1:1
Merry Wives of Windsor, The 1959,Jl 9,23:2
Twelfth Night 1960,Je 9,29:4
Tempest, The 1960,Je 20,35:1
Tempest, The 1960,Je 26,II,1:1
Antony and Cleopatra 1960,Ag 1,19:1
Rhinoceros 1961,Ja 10,27:1
Rhinoceros 1961,Ja 22,II,1:1
Family Affair, A 1962,Ja 29,17:1
King Lear 1963,Je 10,37:1
King Lear 1964,Jl 28,18:2
King Lear 1965,Je 25,39:1
Antigone 1967,Je 19,43:1
Merchant of Venice, The 1967,Je 22,46:2
Schweik in the Second World War 1967,N 12,II,17:1
Hamlet 1969,Je 30,33:1
Hamlet 1969,Jl 6,II,1:1
Three Sisters, The 1969,Ag 4,29:1
Three Sisters, The 1969,Ag 10,II,3:1

Carnovsky, Morris (Playwright)
Group Theatre Sketches 1935,F 11,14:5
Caro, Warren (Miscellaneous)
Summer of the Seventeenth Doll 1958,Ja 23,23:2
Glass Menagerie, The 1961,Je 16,27:3
Carol, Cecil
Noble Rogue, A 1929,Ag 20,31:2
Carol, Charles
Make Yourself at Home 1945,S 14,21:2
Carol, John
Oscar Wilde 1938,O 11,20:2
Carol, Patsy
Wisteria Trees, The 1950,Mr 30,39:1
Carol, Sylvia
June Days 1925,Ag 7,12:5
Carola, Edith
All for Love 1938,Ap 5,19:4
Carolan, P J
Things That Are Caesar's, The 1932,O 18,23:4
Far-Off Hills, The 1932,O 19,22:4
Juno and the Paycock 1932,O 20,24:3
Playboy of the Western World, The 1932,O 21,25:1
New Gossoon, The 1932,O 22,18:2
Words Upon the Window Pane, The 1932,O 29,18:2
Shadow of a Gunman, The 1932,O 31,18:1
Cathleen ni Houlihan 1932,O 31,18:1
Birthright 1932,N 4,25:1
Crabbed Youth and Age 1932,N 4,25:1
Autumn Fire 1932,D 29,16:3
Big House, The 1933,Ja 5,19:3
King Oedipus 1933,Ja 16,12:4
Plough and the Stars, The 1934,N 13,22:2
Drama at Inish 1934,N 15,24:2
Look at the Heffernans 1934,N 17,13:2
Church Street 1934,N 20,24:5
Resurrection 1934,N 20,24:5
Coiner, The 1934,N 22,26:2
Well of the Saints, The 1934,N 22,26:2
Plough and the Stars, The 1937,O 8,26:5
Far-Off Hills, The 1937,O 12,30:4
In the Train 1937,N 22,14:5
Playboy of the Western World, The 1937,N 22,14:5
New Gossoon, The 1937,N 30,26:2
Juno and the Paycock 1937,D 7,32:5
Drama at Inish 1937,D 14,33:2
Carole, Joseph (Playwright)
Seperate Rooms 1940,Mr 25,10:3
Caron, Andree
Girls in Uniform 1932,D 31,10:3
Caron, Charles
Drunkard, The; Fallen Saved, The 1959,Je 24,37:2
Machinal 1960,Ap 8,27:1
Idiot, The 1960,S 26,38:1
Man and Superman 1960,N 7,46:2
Emmanuel 1960,D 5,42:2
Caron, Harriet
But for the Grace of God 1937,Ja 13,21:4
Caron, Leslie
Gigi 1956,My 24,27:1
Caron, Sandra
Return of Second City in "20,000 Frozen Grenadiers," The 1966,Ap 22,36:1
Love and Maple Syrup 1970,Ja 8,47:1
Carot, W A (Playwright)
Anteroom, The 1936,Ag 15,6:7
Anteroom, The 1936,S 6,IX,1:1
Carotenuto, Mario
My Fair Lady 1963,N 16,16:1
Carow, Joe
Dark of the Moon 1958,F 27,22:2
Carow, Joey
Finian's Rainbow 1967,Ap 6,44:1
Carpell, Adele
Ebb Tide 1931,Je 9,33:6
Carpen, Remy
Daisy 1921,O 23,22:2
Plot Thickens, The 1922,S 6,16:1
Carpenger, Anne
Beggar on Horseback 1924,F 13,17:2
Happy Landing 1932,Mr 28,10:5
Carpens, Ben
Paul Bunyan 1941,My 6,25:1
Carpenter, Carleton
Bright Boy 1944,Mr 3,19:5
Career Angel 1944,My 24,23:7
Three to Make Ready 1946,Mr 8,16:2
Magic Touch, The 1947,S 4,30:1
John Murray Anderson's Almanac 1953,D 11,42:2
Box of Watercolors, A 1957,F 18,22:2
Hotel Paradiso 1957,Ap 12,22:2
Hotel Paradiso 1957,Ap 21,II,1:1
Stage Affair, A 1962,Ja 17,30:2
Carpenter, Carol
Father Uxbridge Wants to Marry 1967,O 30,57:1
Carpenter, Clifford
Eve of St Mark, The 1942,O 8,30:2
Caesar and Cleopatra 1949,D 22,28:2
Borned in Texas 1950,Ag 22,30:6
Time to Go 1952,My 8,35:6
Sunrise at Campobello 1958,Ja 31,25:1
Carpenter, Constance
Oh, Kay! 1926,N 9,31:3

Carpenter, Constance—Cont
Connecticut Yankee, A 1927,N 4,24:2
Third Little Show, The 1931,My 10,VIII,2:4
Third Little Show, The 1931,Je 2,34:3
Music Hath Charms 1934,D 31,8:2
King and I, The 1952,O 5,II,1:1
Valmouth 1960,O 7,29:1
Carpenter, Dennis
Gondoliers, The 1967,O 29,83:1
Carpenter, Doris
White Peacock, The 1921,D 27,10:2
Carpenter, Edward Childs (Director)
Scotch Mist 1926,S 21,32:3
Order Please 1934,O 10,21:2
Public Relations 1944,Ap 7,23:3
Carpenter, Edward Childs (Original Author)
Mes Amours 1940,My 3,16:5
Carpenter, Edward Childs (Playwright)
Bab 1920,O 19,12:1
Pot-Luck 1921,S 30,10:1
Connie Goes Home 1923,Jl 1,VI,1:4
Connie Goes Home 1923,S 7,10:1
Bachelor Father, The 1928,F 29,28:2
Bachelor Father, The 1929,O 20,IX,1:4
Whistling in the Dark 1932,Ja 20,16:6
Whistling in the Dark 1932,N 4,25:2
Melody 1933,F 15,17:4
Order Please 1934,O 10,21:2
Carpenter, Edward Childs (Producer)
Whistling in the Dark 1932,N 4,25:2
Carpenter, Francis
Shoemaker's Holiday, The 1938,Ja 3,17:2
King Lear 1956,Ja 13,17:1
King Lear 1956,Ja 22,II,1:1
Carpenter, Ike
Ice Capades 1956,S 13,41:2
Carpenter, Imogene
New Priorities of 1943 1942,S 16,28:2
Ziegfeld Follies 1943,Ap 2,16:2
Carpenter, Irving
Night Boat, The 1920,F 3,18:1
Carpenter, John
Coriolanus 1965,Je 21,36:1
Romeo and Juliet 1965,Je 21,36:3
Taming of the Shrew, The 1965,Je 24,32:2
King Lear 1965,Je 25,39:1
Dinner at Eight 1966,S 28,38:1
Galileo 1967,Ap 14,31:1
After the Rain 1967,O 10,54:1
South Pacific 1968,Je 30,54:2
Ordinary Man, An 1968,S 10,39:1
Corner of the Bed, A 1969,F 27,35:2
Carpenter, Karen
Midsummer Night's Dream, A 1959,Jl 29,34:1
Carpenter, Kevin
Tall Story 1959,Ja 30,33:2
Carpenter, Laura
Mystery Square 1929,Ap 5,28:3
Carpenter, Lorayne
Arabian, The 1927,N 1,20:5
Carpenter, Louise (Producer)
Sentinels 1931,D 26,15:1
Carpenter, Natalie
Whatever Goes Up 1935,N 26,28:2
Carpenter, Peter
Man in Evening Clothes, The 1924,D 6,13:4
Easy Virtue 1925,D 8,28:2
Carpenter, Russell
Racketty Packetty House 1931,N 7,16:1
Carpenter, Thelma
Memphis Bound 1945,My 25,23:2
Inside U S A 1948,My 1,19:2
Shuffle Along 1952,My 9,20:5
Ankles Aweigh 1955,Ap 19,27:1
Carpenter, Tyler
This Time Tomorrow 1947,N 4,31:2
Set My People Free 1948,N 4,38:2
Carpenter, Wes
Sound of Hunting, A 1954,Ap 7,41:1
Carpenter, William
This Is New York 1930,N 29,21:1
Accent on Youth 1934,D 26,19:1
Carpentier, Christiane
Andromaque 1964,F 29,13:2
Salut a Moliere 1964,Mr 4,33:2
Pieton de L'Air, Le 1964,Mr 4,33:2
Carpentier, Georges
Lac Sale, Le 1926,S 5,II,6:5
Lac Sale, Le 1926,O 3,VIII,2:1
Carpentier, Petra
Nine Till Six 1930,S 29,17:2
Carpentier, Rosamund
Oh, Promise Me 1930,N 25,31:1
Carpi, Florenzo (Composer)
Servant of Two Masters, The 1960,F 24,42:2
Carples, Adele
Seed of the Brute 1926,N 2,34:3
Carr, Alexander
Partners Again 1922,My 2,22:2
Partners Again 1922,My 14,VII,1:1
Vaudeville (Palace) 1927,S 13,36:3
Guinea Pig, The 1929,Ja 8,35:1
Mendel, Inc 1929,N 26,28:5

Wooden Soldier, The 1931,Je 23,28:4
Carr, Alexander (Playwright)
Wooden Soldier, The 1931,Je 23,28:4
Carr, Andrew
Everybody's Welcome 1931,O 14,26:3
Take a Chance 1932,N 28,11:2
Carr, Betty
What of It? 1929,Mr 9,24:2
Mask and Gown 1957,S 11,29:1
Carr, Caddie
Puppets of Passion 1927,F 25,24:4
Carr, Carl
Without Warning 1937,My 3,23:2
Carr, Catherine Ann
Midsummer Night's Dream, A 1932,N 18,22:2
Carr, Clark (Miscellaneous)
Critic, The 1965,Jl 26,15:2
Carr, Cora Gay (Producer)
Sudden and Accidental Re-education of Horse
  Johnson, The 1968,D 19,63:1
Corner of the Bed, A 1969,F 27,35:2
Carr, Eddie
Fables 1922,F 7,12:2
Carr, George
Letter, The 1927,Mr 27,VII,2:6
These Few Ashes 1929,My 5,IX,1:3
Middle Watch, The 1929,O 17,27:1
Hamlet 1931,N 6,28:4
Country Wife, The 1936,D 2,34:1
Carr, Gerry
Vickie 1942,S 23,28:1
Carr, Ginna
Guys and Dolls 1965,Ap 29,39:1
Carr, Gladys
Don Juan 1921,S 8,14:2
Carr, Helen
Camille 1935,Jl 31,21:1
Carr, Jack
Run, Little Chillun! 1933,Mr 2,21:3
Yellow Jack 1934,Mr 7,22:6
Porgy and Bess 1935,O 11,30:2
Paradise Lost 1935,D 10,31:5
Iron Men 1936,O 20,30:6
Days to Come 1936,D 16,35:1
Porgy and Bess 1942,Ja 23,16:2
Carmen Jones 1943,D 3,26:2
Carmen Jones 1945,My 3,26:5
Carmen Jones 1946,Ap 8,32:2
Carr, James
Airways, Inc 1929,F 21,30:5
Little Theatre Tournament; Man Who Died at
  Twelve O'Clock, The 1929,My 11,22:2
Carr, Jane
Her Last Adventure 1936,Mr 31,17:1
Carr, Jimmy Silver
Keep It Clean 1929,Je 25,35:5
Noble Rogue, A 1929,Ag 20,31:2
Vaudeville (Palace) 1930,Mr 31,24:2
Carr, Joan
Violet, The 1930,S 30,24:2
One, Two, Three! 1930,S 30,24:2
Domino 1932,Ag 7,IX,1:1
Domino 1932,Ag 17,13:2
Heat Lightning 1933,S 16,9:6
School for Husbands, The 1933,O 17,26:5
Carr, John
Chalk Dust 1936,Mr 5,24:5
Carr, June
Girl Crazy 1930,O 5,IX,4:6
Carr, Kenneth
Impossible Years, The 1965,O 14,55:1
West Side Story 1968,Je 25,32:1
Parents and Children 1969,Ja 13,26:6
Sambo 1969,D 22,42:1
Carr, Lawrence
Henry IV, Part I 1946,My 7,25:2
Carr, Lawrence (Producer)
By the Beautiful Sea 1954,Ap 9,20:1
Desk Set, The 1955,O 25,36:7
Shangri-La 1956,Je 14,40:1
Auntie Mame 1956,N 1,47:2
Redhead 1959,F 6,21:1
There Was a Little Girl 1960,Mr 1,28:1
Advise and Consent 1960,N 18,25:1
Passage to India, A 1962,F 1,23:1
Hot Spot 1963,Ap 20,17:2
Sweet Charity 1966,Ja 31,22:1
Mame 1966,My 25,41:1
Fig Leaves Are Falling, The 1969,Ja 3,19:1
Carr, Leon (Composer)
Secret Life of Walter Mitty, The 1964,O 27,44:5
Carr, Lester
Me and Molly 1948,F 27,27:2
Carr, Louise
Take a Chance 1932,N 28,11:2
Carr, Lynda
Distant Bell, A 1960,Ja 14,29:1
Carr, Marian
Seidman and Son 1962,O 16,32:2
Immoralist, The 1963,N 8,36:2
Carr, Martin (Producer)
Saturday Night Kid, The 1958,My 16,22:1

Carr, Michael
Power of Darkness, The 1920,Ja 22,22:1
Carr, Paul
Virtuous Island, The 1957,Ap 10,39:1
Carr, Percy
Three Musketeers, The 1921,My 20,18:5
Persons Unknown 1922,O 26,12:1
Hurricane 1923,D 26,13:4
Carr, Philip (Translator)
Siegfried 1930,O 21,34:1
Carr, Robert Fryer-Lawrence (Producer)
Auntie Mame 1958,Ag 12,33:2
Carr, Ruth
Earth 1927,Mr 10,23:1
Carr, Susan
Seagull, The 1964,Ap 6,36:1
Crucible, The 1964,Ap 7,30:2
Midsummer Night's Dream, A 1964,Je 30,23:2
Boeing-Boeing 1965,F 3,30:1
Carra, Lawrence
Great Magician, The 1951,N 22,45:1
Carra, Lawrence (Director)
Leave It to Jane 1959,My 26,30:2
Kittiwake Island 1960,O 13,43:1
Carra, Lawrence (Playwright)
Candida 1970,Ap 7,41:1
Carra, Lawrence (Producer)
Kittiwake Island 1960,O 13,43:1
Carradine, David
Royal Hunt of the Sun, The 1965,O 27,36:2
Royal Hunt of the Sun, The 1965,N 14,II,1:1
Transgressor Rides Again, The 1969,My 21,42:1
Carradine, John
Duchess of Malfi, The 1946,O 16,35:2
Galileo 1947,D 8,34:2
Volpone 1948,Ja 9,24:6
Tragedian in Spite of Himself, A 1948,F 6,29:2
Wedding, The 1948,F 6,29:2
Bear, The 1948,F 6,29:2
On the Harmfulness of Tobacco 1948,F 6,29:2
Cup of Trembling, The 1948,Ap 21,33:5
Leading Lady 1948,O 19,33:1
Madwoman of Chaillot, The 1949,Ja 9,II,1:1
Madwoman of Chaillot, The 1949,S 11,II,1:1
Madwoman of Chaillot, The 1950,Je 14,41:2
Time of Your Life, The 1955,Ja 20,34:1
Time of Your Life, The 1955,Ja 30,II,1:1
Funny Thing Happened on the Way to the Forum,
  A 1962,My 9,49:1
Funny Thing Happened on the Way to the Forum,
  A 1962,My 20,II,1:1
Carrara, Matilde
Aria del Continente, L' 1927,O 5,30:2
Carrara, Pietro
Aria del Continente, L' 1927,O 5,30:2
Carrara, Saffo
Aria del Continente, L' 1927,O 5,30:2
Carrara, Toto
Aria del Continente, L' 1927,O 5,30:2
Carras, Nicholas (Miscellaneous)
Happy Town 1959,O 8,49:2
Carrasco, Gustavo
Belmont Varieties 1932,S 29,17:2
Carraway, Robert
Golden Fleecing 1959,O 16,24:5
Carre, Michel (Playwright)
Afgar 1920,N 9,13:2
Pierrot the Prodigal; Enfant Prodigue, L'
  1925,Mr 7,8:1
Carrel, Judd
Black Diamond 1933,F 24,12:2
Come of Age 1934,Ja 13,16:6
Carrera, Liane
Gentle Grafters 1926,O 28,23:1
Lady in Love, A 1927,F 22,22:1
Carrera, Valentino (Playwright)
Alexander Pushkin 1928,Ja 27,14:2
Carreras, C
Assalto, L' 1929,My 20,23:2
Tutto Per Bene; All's Well That Ends Well
  1929,Je 3,27:1
Carrere, Anne
Baptiste 1952,N 13,34:2
Fourberies de Scapin, Les 1952,N 21,21:2
Amphitryon 1952,N 21,21:2
Occupe-Toi d'Amelie; Keep Your Eyes on Amelie
  1952,N 25,35:2
Hamlet 1952,D 2,39:1
Carrere, Fernando (Scenic Designer)
Ice Follies 1959,Ja 14,30:1
Carrette, Florence
Oh, Henry! 1920,My 6,14:2
Captain Jinks of the Horse Marines 1938,Ja 28,16:2
Carrey, David
Oh What a Wedding! 1969,O 20,60:1
Carrey, Mitchell
Henry IV, Part II 1968,Jl 2,33:1
Carricart, Robert
Antony and Cleopatra 1947,N 27,49:2
Richard III 1949,F 9,33:2
Scapegoat, The 1950,Ap 20,36:5
Captain Brassbound's Conversion 1950,D 28,21:1
Rose Tattoo, The 1951,F 5,19:2

Carricart, Robert—Cont
Detective Story 1954,F 13,11:2
Carrick, Christopher
All's Well That Ends Well 1966,Je 17,39:1
Carrier, Irma Hart (Director)
Is It Murder? 1951,Je 3,54:5
Carrier, Irma Hart (Producer)
Is It Murder? 1951,Je 3,54:5
Corrigan, Thomas
Mongolia 1927,D 27,24:5
Carriger, Ruth
Mikado, The 1942,F 4,22:2
Pirates of Penzance, The 1942,F 18,22:2
Iolanthe 1942,F 24,26:4
Gondoliers, The 1942,Mr 4,22:3
Carrillo, Alberto
Lolly 1929,O 17,26:2
Carrillo, Leo
Love Chef, The 1921,Je 12,VI,1:6
Magnolia 1923,Je 24,VII,1:4
Magnolia 1923,Ag 28,12:3
Magnolia 1923,S 2,VI,1:1
Gypsy Jim 1924,Ja 15,17:4
Vaudeville (Palace) 1926,Mr 16,22:2
Rough Diamond, A 1926,D 19,VII,6:1
Padre, The 1926,D 28,16:3
Lombardi, Ltd 1927,Je 7,27:3
Carrimore, Francine
Storm Song 1931,Ja 4,VIII,2:2
Carringer, Walter (Miscellaneous)
Bonds of Interest, The 1958,My 7,43:1
Carrington, Bruce
Here Goes the Bride 1931,N 4,31:2
Carrington, Elaine Sterne (Playwright)
Nightstick 1927,N 11,20:4
Carrington, Evelyn Carter
Madras House, The 1921,O 31,18:2
Madame Pierre 1922,F 16,11:1
Shore Leave 1922,Ag 9,20:2
Catskill Dutch 1924,My 7,18:1
Lombardi, Ltd 1927,Je 7,27:3
Get Me in the Movies 1928,My 22,18:3
Carrington, Frank
Abraham; Dulcitus; Callimachus 1926,Mr 29,24:2
Carrington, Frank (Director)
Shadow Play 1939,Ag 15,14:5
Jeannie 1940,N 13,29:2
Papa Is All 1942,Ja 7,22:2
I Killed the Count 1942,S 4,18:1
Carrington, Frank (Producer)
I Killed the Count 1942,S 4,18:1
Carrington, Helen
Plain Jane 1924,My 13,24:2
Dear Sir 1924,S 24,21:3
Jack in the Pulpit 1925,Ja 7,33:1
Spring Fever 1925,Ag 4,14:2
Queen High 1926,S 9,21:2
Here's Howe! 1928,My 2,19:3
Band Wagon, The 1931,Je 4,31:3
Flying Colors 1932,S 16,24:2
Carrington, Katherine
Little Accident 1928,O 10,32:3
Face the Music 1932,F 18,24:5
Music in the Air 1932,O 23,IX,3:3
Music in the Air 1932,N 9,28:2
Music in the Air 1932,N 20,IX,1:1
Eternal Road, The 1937,Ja 8,14:2
Carrington, Mickey
Ice Capades 1953,S 11,25:1
Carrington, Nell
Make It Snappy 1922,Ap 14,20:2
Carrington, Phyllis
Dover Road, The 1921,D 24,7:2
Carrington, Reginald
Dolly Jordan 1922,O 4,26:1
This Fine-Pretty World 1923,D 27,11:1
Flame of Love 1924,Ap 22,19:2
Prisoner, The 1927,D 30,22:2
Patriot, The 1928,Ja 20,15:1
Skull, The 1928,Ap 24,28:3
Mima 1928,D 13,24:2
Dear Old England 1930,Mr 26,24:6
Evensong 1933,F 1,13:4
Party, A 1933,Ag 24,18:4
Lake, The 1933,D 27,24:2
Living Dangerously 1935,Ja 14,10:3
Touch of Brimstone, A 1935,S 23,20:1
Carrington, Robert (Miscellaneous)
Night of the Auk 1956,D 4,50:2
Carrion, Fred (Miscellaneous)
Kill the One-Eyed Man 1965,O 21,56:1
Carrithers, Bruce
Iolanthe 1961,My 26,29:6
H M S Pinafore 1961,Je 9,29:5
Student Prince, The 1961,Jl 14,14:1
Merry Widow, The 1961,O 27,28:2
Vagabond King, The 1961,N 24,36:1
Gondoliers, The 1961,D 8,44:1
Carrm, Helen
Coquette 1935,Jl 10,24:1
Hay Fever 1935,Jl 24,20:4
Mr Pim Passes By 1935,Ag 7,22:2
Vinegar Tree, The 1935,Ag 14,16:1
Double Door 1935,Ag 21,22:2

Late Christopher Bean, The 1935,Ag 28,13:1
Carro, Conchita
Fuente Ovejuna; Sheep Well, The 1936,My 3,II,4:1
Carroit, Anita
Love Is No Heaven 1943,Mr 16,15:3
Carrol, Judy
Send Me No Flowers 1960,D 6,54:1
Carroll, Albert
Mob, The 1920,O 11,18:1
Great Adventure, The 1921,F 26,9:2
Harlequinade 1921,My 11,20:3
Madras House, The 1921,O 31,18:2
Green Ring, The 1922,Ap 5,22:1
Makers of Light 1922,My 24,22:3
49ers, The 1922,N 7,14:1
Dragon, The 1922,D 27,12:1
Peer Gynt 1923,F 6,14:1
Shewing-Up of Blanco Posnet, The 1923,O 17,14:2
This Fine-Pretty World 1923,D 27,11:1
Time Is a Dream 1924,Ap 23,24:2
Little Clay Cart, The 1924,D 6,13:3
Grand Street Follies, The 1925,Je 19,24:1
Grand Street Follies, The 1925,Je 28,VIII,1:1
Dybbuk, The 1925,D 16,22:2
Apothecary, The 1926,Mr 17,28:1
Romantic Young Lady, The 1926,My 5,24:3
Grand Street Follies, The 1926,Je 16,23:2
Lion Tamer, The 1926,O 8,26:1
Lion Tamer, The 1926,O 17,VIII,1:1
Dybbuk, The 1926,D 17,27:2
Pinwheel 1927,F 4,16:4
Commedia Dell' Arte 1927,Ap 6,24:3
Grand Street Follies, The 1927,My 20,22:3
Grand Street Follies, The 1927,Je 1,24:2
Grand Street Follies, The 1927,Jl 3,VII,1:1
Lovers and Enemies 1927,S 21,27:1
If 1927,O 26,26:2
Love Nest, The 1927,D 23,17:1
Grand Street Follies, The 1928,My 29,16:2
Grand Street Follies, The 1928,Je 3,VIII,1:1
Grand Street Follies, The 1929,My 2,20:4
Grand Street Follies, The 1929,My 12,IX,1:2
Grand Street Follies, The 1929,Je 19,34:3
Magic and Mimicry 1929,D 23,18:6
Garrick Gaieties 1930,Je 5,29:2
Ziegfeld Follies 1931,Jl 2,30:5
Americana 1932,S 25,IX,1:6
Americana 1932,O 6,19:3
Good Girl, The 1934,Je 26,22:5
Nine O'Clock Revue 1936,Jl 8,14:3
Hamlet 1936,N 11,54:2
Merry Wives of Windsor, The 1938,Ap 15,22:3
Savonarola 1942,Ap 24,20:2
Inside Story 1942,O 30,22:2
Man's House, A 1943,Ap 3,10:4
Duke in Darkness, The 1944,Ja 25,15:2
Seven Lively Arts 1944,D 8,26:6
Carroll, Allace
Peace on Earth 1933,N 30,39:2
Carroll, Art
Touch and Go 1949,O 14,34:2
Tree Grows in Brooklyn, A 1951,Ap 20,24:3
Carroll, Barbara
Me and Juliet 1953,My 29,17:1
Carroll, Beeson
Coriolanus 1965,Jl 15,23:1
Unseen Hand, The 1970,Ap 2,43:1
Carroll, Bob
To Broadway With Love 1964,Ap 30,28:6
Carroll, Brandon
Crucible, The 1958,Mr 17,21:1
Carroll, C A
Puppet Show 1930,O 29,26:5
Carroll, Carleen (Choreographer)
After the Angels 1961,F 11,27:5
Carroll, Carroll (Lyricist)
Cherry Pie 1926,Ap 15,24:4
Carroll, Carroll (Playwright)
Garrick Gaieties 1930,Je 5,29:2
Carroll, Christina
Gypsy Baron, The 1942,Je 20,8:5
Gypsy Baron, The 1942,Ag 7,12:4
Carroll, Christopher
Lend an Ear 1969,O 29,32:1
Carroll, Clare
Buzzin' Around 1920,Jl 7,14:1
Some Party 1922,Ap 17,22:1
Carroll, Clay
Oh, Henry! 1920,My 6,14:2
Carroll, Danny
Music Man, The 1957,D 20,31:1
Boys From Syracuse, The 1963,Ap 16,31:1
Boys From Syracuse, The 1963,Je 2,II,1:1
Babes in the Wood 1964,D 29,21:2
Flora, the Red Menace 1965,My 12,41:2
George M! 1968,Ap 11,48:1
Billy 1969,Mr 24,56:1
Carroll, David (Producer)
Cage, The 1970,Je 19,25:1
Carroll, Diahann
House of Flowers 1954,D 31,11:2
No Strings 1962,Mr 16,24:1
No Strings 1962,Mr 25,II,1:1

Carroll, E J (Miscellaneous)
Wrecker, The 1928,F 28,18:2
Carroll, Earl (Director)
Earl Carroll's Vanities 1926,Ag 25,19:4
Earl Carroll's Vanities 1927,Ja 5,18:1
Nine Fifteen Revue, The 1930,F 12,26:2
Vanities 1932,S 28,22:4
Murder at the Vanities 1933,S 13,22:4
Sketch Book 1935,Je 5,22:2
Carroll, Earl (Playwright)
Lady of the Lamp, The 1920,Ag 18,6:4
Daddy Dumplins 1920,N 23,11:1
Bavu 1922,F 27,16:1
Earl Carroll's Vanities 1923,Jl 6,8:2
Earl Carroll's Vanities 1924,S 11,23:6
Fioretta 1929,F 6,30:3
Murder at the Vanities 1933,S 13,22:4
Carroll, Earl (Producer)
Florida Girl 1925,N 3,34:1
Laff That Off 1925,N 3,34:2
Vanities 1926,Ja 10,VII,1:1
Earl Carroll's Vanities 1926,Ag 25,19:4
Number 7 1926,S 9,21:3
Earl Carroll's Vanities 1927,Ja 5,18:1
What Ann Brought Home 1927,F 22,22:2
Vanities 1927,F 22,19:1
Earl Carroll's Vanities 1928,Ag 7,25:2
Fioretta 1929,Ja 6,VIII,4:6
Fioretta 1929,F 6,30:3
Sketch Book 1929,Jl 2,33:5
Earl Carroll's Vanities 1930,Jl 2,28:3
Vanities 1931,Ag 11,28:4
Vanities 1931,Ag 16,VIII,1:1
Earl Carroll's Vanities 1931,Ag 28,18:7
Vanities 1931,S 6,VIII,1:1
Vanities 1932,S 18,IX,2:1
Vanities 1932,S 28,22:4
Murder at the Vanities 1933,Ag 31,20:1
Murder at the Vanities 1933,S 13,22:4
Sketch Book 1935,Je 5,22:2
Earl Carroll's Vanities 1940,Ja 15,11:2
Carroll, Edward
Master of the Revels 1935,Ag 14,16:2
Carroll, Frank
Juno 1959,Mr 10,41:1
Ice Follies 1961,Ja 11,25:2
Ice Follies 1963,Ja 10,5:2
Carroll, Georgia
Louisiana Purchase 1940,My 29,19:2
Carroll, Gladys Hasty (Playwright)
As the Earth Turns 1938,Ag 7,IX,2:1
Carroll, Grace
Song of Norway 1944,Ag 22,20:2
Carroll, Harry
Vaudeville (Palace) 1922,F 14,21:1
Vaudeville (Palace) 1923,Mr 13,19:2
Vaudeville (Palace) 1923,O 23,18:2
Vaudeville (Hippodrome) 1924,Mr 18,25:1
Vaudeville (Palace) 1927,Ja 18,23:2
Vaudeville (Palace) 1928,Ag 21,27:5
Vaudeville (Palace) 1929,Je 3,27:4
Vaudeville (Palace) 1930,D 1,19:1
Carroll, Harry (Composer)
Midnight Frolic 1920,Ag 4,7:1
Carroll, Harry (Miscellaneous)
Vaudeville (Palace) 1928,Ap 24,29:2
Carroll, Harry Revue
Vaudeville (Palace) 1930,F 17,18:4
Carroll, Helen
Virginia 1937,S 3,13:2
Knickerbocker Holiday 1938,O 20,26:2
Key Largo 1939,N 28,30:2
Carroll, Helena
Wise Have Not Spoken, The 1954,F 11,35:2
Shadow and Substance 1956,Mr 14,38:1
Separate Tables 1956,O 26,33:1
Playboy of the Western World, The 1958,My 9,19:2
Shadow and Substance 1959,N 4,42:1
Little Moon of Alban 1960,D 2,34:1
Happy as Larry 1961,Ap 26,36:1
Sharon's Grave 1961,N 9,39:2
Oliver 1963,Ja 8,5:5
Bridal Night, The 1966,N 8,45:1
Eternal Triangle 1966,N 8,45:1
Frying Pan, The 1966,N 8,45:1
Something Different 1967,N 29,52:1
Georgy 1970,F 27,26:1
Carroll, Helena (Director)
Shadow and Substance 1956,Mr 14,38:1
Carroll, Irene
Mr Winkle's Holliday 1946,Je 24,27:6
Carroll, Irv (Musical Director)
Bagels and Yox 1951,S 13,38:2
Carroll, James C
One Kiss 1923,N 28,14:2
Port O' London 1926,F 10,20:2
Black Sheep 1932,O 14,22:6
Carroll, Jane
Ziegfeld Follies 1920,Je 23,14:1
Love Letter, The 1921,O 5,20:1
Blushing Bride, The 1922,F 7,12:1
Yankee Princess, The 1922,O 3,22:1
No Other Girl 1924,Ag 14,10:4

Carroll, Jane—Cont

Artists and Models 1925,Je 25,16:2
Vagabond King, The 1925,S 22,23:3
Carroll, Jean
Dew Drop Inn 1923,My 18,26:4
Eastwood Ho 1936,Jl 8,14:2
Vaudeville (Palace) 1952,F 27,22:2
Carroll, Jennifer (Scenic Designer)
One Is a Lonely Number 1964,Je 19,37:3
Carroll, Jimmy
Aquacircus 1958,Je 30,24:6
Carroll, Joan
Panama Hattie 1940,O 4,28:4
Panama Hattie 1940,O 31,28:2
Panama Hattie 1940,N 10,IX,1:1
Carroll, Joe
Say When 1934,N 9,24:2
Carroll, John
So's Your Old Manhattan 1927,My 5,30:5
Carroll, John (Director)
Untitled-Recital 1970,S 3,36:1
Carroll, Joseph (Playwright)
Barroom Monks, The 1962,My 29,21:1
Carroll, Joyce
Street Scene 1947,Ja 10,17:2
Trial by Jury 1949,O 18,34:2
Carroll, June
New Faces of 1952 1952,My 17,23:2
New Faces of 1952 1952,My 25,II,1:1
Family Portrait 1959,My 6,48:2
Carroll, June (Composer)
New Faces of 1952 1952,My 17,23:2
New Faces of 1956 1956,Je 15,32:1
Mask and Gown 1957,S 11,29:1
New Faces of 1962 1962,F 2,25:1
Cats' Pajamas, The 1962,Je 1,16:2
Leonard Sillman's New Faces of 1968
  1968,My 3,43:1
Carroll, June (Lyricist)
If the Shoe Fits 1946,D 6,29:4
New Faces of 1952 1952,My 17,23:2
New Faces of 1952 1952,My 25,II,1:1
New Faces of 1956 1956,Je 15,32:1
Mask and Gown 1957,S 11,29:1
Hi, Paisano 1961,O 2,36:2
New Faces of 1962 1962,F 2,25:1
Cats' Pajamas, The 1962,Je 1,16:2
Leonard Sillman's New Faces of 1968
  1968,My 3,43:1
Carroll, June (Miscellaneous)
New Faces of 1943 1942,D 23,22:2
Carroll, June (Playwright)
If the Shoe Fits 1946,D 6,29:4
Carroll, Ken
Great to Be Alive! 1950,Mr 24,28:2
Carroll, Lambert (Playwright)
Everybody's Welcome 1931,O 14,26:3
Carroll, Leatham
Richard III 1967,Je 14,43:1
Merry Wives of Windsor, The 1967,Ag 4,18:1
Carroll, Lee
Ice Follies 1961,Ja 11,25:2
Ice Follies 1962,Ja 10,24:6
Ice Follies 1963,Ja 10,5:2
Ice Follies 1965,Ja 13,35:1
Ice Follies 1966,Ja 12,27:6
Carroll, Leo G
Havoc 1924,S 2,22:2
Carnaval 1924,D 30,15:1
Vortex, The 1925,S 17,20:1
Constant Nymph, The 1926,D 10,31:1
Speakeasy 1927,S 27,30:1
Diversion 1928,Ja 12,25:1
Heavy Traffic 1928,S 6,23:3
Perfect Alibi, The 1928,N 28,24:2
Novice and the Duke, The 1929,D 11,37:2
Mrs Moonlight 1930,S 30,24:3
Too True to Be Good 1932,Mr 1,19:2
Too True to Be Good 1932,Mr 6,VIII,1:1
Too True to Be Good 1932,Ap 5,27:5
Troilus and Cressida 1932,Je 7,22:3
For Services Rendered 1933,Ap 13,15:5
Mask and the Face, The 1933,My 9,20:2
Green Bay Tree, The 1933,O 21,11:5
Green Bay Tree, The 1933,O 29,IX,1:1
Petticoat Fever 1935,Mr 5,22:2
May Wine 1935,D 6,30:3
Mainly for Lovers 1936,F 11,19:5
Mainly for Lovers 1936,F 22,13:2
Queen's Husband, The 1936,Je 2,33:2
Prelude to Exile 1936,N 22,XI,3:2
Prelude to Exile 1936,D 1,31:1
Masque of Kings, The 1937,Ja 31,XI,2:1
Masque of the Kings, The 1937,F 9,19:4
Storm Over Patsy 1937,Mr 9,26:4
Between the Devil 1937,O 15,19:1
Love of Women 1937,D 14,33:2
Save Me the Waltz 1938,Mr 1,19:2
Two Bouquets, The 1938,Je 1,19:2
Love for Love 1940,Je 4,19:5
Anne of England 1941,O 8,26:2
Angel Street 1941,D 6,15:2
Late George Apley, The 1944,O 20,16:4
Late George Apley, The 1944,N 22,26:2

Late George Apley, The 1944,D 3,II,1:1
Druid Circle, The 1947,O 23,29:5
Druid Circle, The 1947,N 16,II,1:1
You Never Can Tell 1948,Mr 17,31:2
Jenny Kissed Me 1948,D 24,12:2
Once an Actor 1950,Ag 1,19:8
Mary Rose 1951,Mr 5,25:2
Mary Rose 1951,Mr 11,II,1:1
Lo and Behold! 1951,D 13,45:2
On Borrowed Time 1953,Ja 1,19:1
On Borrowed Time 1953,F 11,34:1
Someone Waiting 1956,F 15,26:1
Carroll, Leo G (Director)
Love of Women 1937,D 14,33:2
Carroll, Lewis (Original Author)
Alice in Wonderland 1932,D 12,18:3
Alice in Wonderland 1932,D 25,IX,1:1
Alice in Wonderland 1933,F 2,21:2
Alice in Wonderland 1935,N 10,43:5
Alice in Wonderland 1947,Ap 7,19:2
Alice in Wonderland 1947,Ap 13,II,1:1
Alice in Wonderland 1967,Mr 20,27:1
But Never Jam Today 1969,Ap 24,40:1
Alice in Wonderland 1970,O 9,43:1
Alice in Wonderland 1970,O 18,II,3:1
Carroll, Lewis (Playwright)
Chicago 70 1970,My 26,33:1
Carroll, Lida
Leap, The 1924,My 23,16:5
Carroll, Lisa
Tender Trap, The 1961,Ag 26,15:1
Carroll, Lorna
Jerry for Short 1929,Ag 13,23:4
Carroll, Lorreto (Playwright)
Little Theatre Tournament; Roads and Rain
  1926,My 6,23:3
Carroll, Lucia
School for Brides 1944,Ag 2,19:4
Carroll, Lyn (Costume Designer)
King of the Dark Chamber 1961,F 10,21:1
Carroll, Lynn
Annie Get Your Gun 1966,Je 1,42:2
Carroll, Madeleine
Dance With No Music 1930,Ag 24,VIII,2:7
Toy Cart, The 1930,D 7,IX,2:7
Little Catherine 1931,N 19,27:2
Little Catherine 1931,D 6,VIII,2:7
Duet in Floodlight 1935,Je 5,22:1
Goodbye My Fancy 1948,N 18,35:2
Goodbye My Fancy 1948,N 28,II,1:1
Carroll, Marie
My Golden Girl 1920,F 3,18:2
Charm School, The 1920,Ag 3,12:1
Two Blocks Away 1921,Ag 31,8:3
Love Dreams 1921,O 11,22:2
Abie's Irish Rose 1922,My 24,22:4
So This Is London 1922,Ag 31,18:2
Schemers 1924,S 16,27:1
Tightwad, The 1927,Ap 18,18:2
Such Is Life 1927,S 1,27:3
She Stoops to Conquer 1928,My 15,17:1
She Stoops to Conquer 1928,My 20,VIII,1:1
Third Day, The 1929,Ag 13,23:4
Hamlet 1930,Mr 25,34:4
Macbeth 1930,Mr 26,24:6
Merchant of Venice, The 1930,Mr 27,24:7
Taming of the Shrew, The 1930,Mr 28,22:8
Richard III 1930,Mr 31,24:1
King Lear 1930,Ap 1,34:6
As You Like It 1930,Ap 3,32:5
Julius Caesar 1930,Ap 4,22:3
Show Is On, The 1936,D 26,14:2
Sun Kissed 1937,Mr 11,20:2
Caucasian Chalk Circle, The 1961,N 1,35:1
Carroll, Marjorie L
Madre, La 1959,F 12,24:1
Madame Lafayette 1960,Mr 4,21:1
Carroll, Mary
Mob, The 1920,O 11,18:1
Cradle Song 1921,Mr 1,18:2
Brook 1923,Ag 20,14:3
Potters, The 1923,D 10,21:4
Dunce Boy, The 1925,Ap 4,20:2
Creaking Chair, The 1926,F 23,26:1
Rope 1928,F 23,18:3
Rope 1928,Mr 4,IX,1:1
Guinea Pig, The 1929,Ja 8,35:1
Carroll, Mary (Miscellaneous)
King Lear 1959,Ja 3,11:2
Carroll, Mickey
Young Man's Fancy, A 1947,Ap 30,33:2
Carroll, Mollie
Minute's Wait, A 1920,Je 22,9:1
O'Flaherty, V C 1920,Je 22,9:1
Carroll, Moon
Cradle Snatchers 1925,S 8,28:2
Loose Ankles 1926,Ag 17,15:1
And So to Bed 1927,N 10,23:1
Carroll, Nancy
Mayflowers 1925,N 25,14:2
Undesirable Lady, An 1933,O 10,24:4
For Heaven's Sake Mother 1948,N 17,33:4
Cindy 1964,S 25,33:1

Carroll, Pat
Catch a Star! 1955,S 7,35:2
On the Town 1959,Ja 16,36:1
On the Town 1959,Ja 25,II,1:1
Carroll, Patricia
Work Is for Horses 1937,N 22,14:6
Carroll, Paul Vincent (Playwright)
Things That Are Caesar's, The 1932,S 18,IX,1:6
Things That Are Caesar's, The 1932,O 18,23:4
Things That Are Caesar's, The 1933,Ja 29,IX,1:3
Shadow and Substance 1938,Ja 23,XI,1:6
Shadow and Substance 1938,Ja 27,16:2
Shadow and Substance 1938,F 6,X,1:1
White Steed, The 1939,Ja 11,16:2
Coggerers, The 1939,Ja 21,18:4
White Steed, The 1939,Ja 22,IX,1:1
White Steed, The 1939,Ag 16,21:3
Kindred 1939,O 8,IX,3:5
Kindred 1939,D 27,17:2
Kindred 1940,Ja 7,IX,1:1
Old Foolishness, The 1940,D 21,20:2
Strings, My Lord, Are False, The 1942,Mr 18,29:3
Strings, My Lord, Are False, The 1942,My 20,24:2
Wise Have Not Spoken, The 1954,F 11,35:2
Wayward Saint, The 1955,F 18,17:1
Wayward Saint, The 1955,F 27,II,1:1
Devil Came From Dublin, The! 1955,Je 3,27:2
Shadow and Substance 1956,Mr 14,38:1
Shadow and Substance 1959,N 4,42:1
Coggerers, The 1960,Mr 23,33:1
Carroll, Peggy
Let's Face It 1941,O 30,26:2
Carroll, Phyllis
Hold Your Horses 1933,S 26,26:4
Carroll, R F (Lyricist)
Bringing Up Father 1925,Mr 31,16:1
Carroll, Renee
Brights Lights of 1944 1943,S 17,27:4
Carroll, Rhoda B
Recruiting Officer, The 1958,F 8,12:2
Square, The 1961,Mr 24,37:1
Carroll, Robert
Mary of Magdala 1946,Mr 26,24:5
Cyrano de Bergerac 1946,O 9,33:2
Cyrano de Bergerac 1947,Ja 17,27:2
Music in My Heart 1947,O 3,30:2
Wedding, The 1948,F 6,29:2
On the Harmfulness of Tobacco 1948,F 6,29:2
Bear, The 1948,F 6,29:2
Tragedian in Spite of Himself, A 1948,F 6,29:2
Alchemist, The 1948,My 7,31:4
S S Glencairn; Moon of the Caribbees
  1948,My 21,21:2
S S Glencairn; Bound East for Cardiff
  1948,My 21,21:2
S S Glencairn; In the Zone 1948,My 21,21:2
S S Glencairn; Long Voyage Home, The; Moon of
  the Caribbees; In the Zone; Bound East for
  Cardiff 1948,My 30,II,1:1
Insect Comedy, The 1948,Je 4,26:3
Silver Whistle, The 1948,N 25,49:2
Twentieth Century 1950,D 25,23:6
My 3 Angels 1953,Mr 12,23:2
Little Glass Clock, The 1956,Mr 27,40:2
Villa of Madame Vidac, The 1959,O 1,40:1
Andersonville Trial, The 1959,D 30,15:1
Carroll, Ronn
Annie Get Your Gun 1966,Je 1,42:2
Finian's Rainbow 1967,Ap 6,44:1
Wonderful Town 1967,My 18,50:1
Carroll, Sidney (Miscellaneous)
Mask and Gown 1957,S 11,29:1
Carroll, Sidney
Madwoman of Chaillot, The 1970,Mr 23,48:3
Carroll, Sydney (Producer)
Family Affairs 1934,Ag 23,13:3
Mask of Virtue, The 1935,My 16,20:1
Carroll, Sydney W (Miscellaneous)
After All 1931,D 4,28:4
Carroll, Sydney W (Producer)
Henry IV, Part I 1935,Mr 1,16:1
Carroll, Terry
America's Sweetheart 1931,F 11,23:1
Wiser They Are, The 1931,Ap 7,31:1
Hired Husband 1932,Je 4,9:5
Scrap Book 1932,Ag 2,20:3
Carroll, Theresa
Riders to the Sea 1957,Mr 7,24:1
Carroll, Vinnette
Outside the Door 1949,Mr 2,33:2
Streetcar Named Desire, A 1956,F 16,24:1
Small War on Murray Hill 1957,Ja 4,19:1
Crucible, The 1958,Mr 12,36:1
Jolly's Progress 1959,D 7,42:2
Octoroon, The 1961,Ja 28,13:1
Moon on a Rainbow Shawl 1962,Ja 16,30:1
Carroll, Vinnette (Director)
Black Nativity 1961,D 12,54:2
Prodigal Son, The 1965,My 21,19:1
But Never Jam Today 1969,Ap 24,40:1
Old Judge Mose Is Dead 1969,Ag 29,25:1
Moon on a Rainbow Shawl 1969,Ag 29,25:1
Don't Bother Me, I Can't Cope 1970,O 8,60:3

Carroll, Vinnette (Director)—Cont
Moon on a Rainbow Shawl 1970,D 18,52:1
Carroll, Vinnette (Playwright)
Trumpets of the Lord 1963,D 23,22:3
But Never Jam Today 1969,Ap 24,40:1
Trumpets of the Lord 1969,Ap 30,37:1
Don't Bother Me, I Can't Cope 1970,O 8,60:3
Carroll, Virginia Ann
Pirates of Penzance, The 1954,Mr 31,32:5
Yeomen of the Guard, The 1954,My 5,36:2
Point of No Return 1957,Mr 23,17:2
Bed Time 1958,Ap 11,20:2
Carroll, Walter
Tin Top Valley 1947,Mr 1,11:2
Carroll, Walter (Playwright)
Tin Top Valley 1947,Mr 1,11:2
Long Way From Home, A 1948,F 9,25:2
Carroll, William
Song of Norway 1944,Ag 22,20:2
Carron, Elizabeth
Saint of Bleecker Street, The 1954,D 28,21:1
Carruth, Burr
Little Women 1931,D 8,36:2
Carruthers, Jim
Under the Sycamore Tree 1960,Mr 8,37:2
Carruthers, Mabel
Partners Again 1922,My 2,22:2
Carruthers, Reina
Bluffing Bluffers 1924,D 23,17:2
Carsdale, Betty
Clair de Lune 1921,Ap 19,15:1
Carshon, Charles
Billy Budd 1951,F 12,18:3
Carson, Alexander (Producer)
Vamp, The 1955,N 11,30:1
Carson, Bernard (Producer)
Freight 1950,Ap 27,36:2
Phoenix Too Frequent, A 1950,Ap 27,36:2
Carson, Charles
Scrapped 1927,O 16,IX,2:7
Master Builder, The 1928,O 21,IX,1:3
Lad, The 1929,Ja 13,VIII,4:5
Apple Cart, The 1929,Ag 20,30:2
Nelson Touch, The 1931,S 20,VIII,2:6
On the Rocks 1933,N 26,II,2:8
Six of Calais, The 1934,Ag 12,IX,1:3
Apple Cart, The 1956,O 19,23:1
Carson, Chuck (Lighting Director)
Three...With Women in Mind; How a Nice Girl
Named Janet Contracted Syphilis 1970,N 28,22:1
Three...With Women in Mind; I Hear It Kissing Me
Ladies 1970,N 28,22:1
Three...With Women in Mind; Jeff Chandler
1970,N 28,22:1
Carson, Doris
Americana 1928,O 31,28:2
Show Girl 1929,Jl 3,19:3
Strike Up the Band 1930,Ja 15,29:1
Luana 1930,S 18,28:1
Cat and the Fiddle, The 1931,O 16,26:4
On Your Toes 1936,Ap 13,14:4
On Your Toes 1937,Ag 3,21:2
Carson, E N
Take a Brace 1923,Ap 20,20:3
Who's Who 1924,Ap 18,19:2
Carson, Edward
Three Men and a Woman 1932,Ja 12,29:2
Carson, Eugenie
Hill Between, The 1938,Mr 12,12:5
Carson, Frances
Hottentot, The 1920,Mr 2,9:1
Bad Man, The 1920,Ag 31,7:1
Scarlet Man, The 1921,Ag 23,10:3
Blue Lagoon, The 1921,S 15,16:1
Havoc 1924,Ja 27,VII,2:4
Two Married Men 1925,Ja 14,19:1
Potiphar's Wife 1928,D 24,10:7
First Law, The 1929,My 7,28:4
Mulberry Bush, The 1930,My 18,VIII,2:6
Slightly Scandalous 1944,Je 14,16:2
Visitor, The 1944,O 18,24:5
Carson, Henry (Producer)
Continental Varieties 1935,D 27,15:3
Carson, Irwin (Composer)
No Hard Feelings 1965,Ap 5,33:8
Carson, Jack
Of Thee I Sing 1952,My 6,34:2
Of Thee I Sing 1952,My 11,II,1:1
Carson, James B
Girl in the Spotlight, The 1920,Jl 13,9:3
Little Jessie James 1923,Ag 16,10:4
Magic Ring, The 1923,O 2,10:1
Great Necker, The 1928,Mr 7,28:2
Gone Hollywood 1930,D 28,VIII,2:1
Carson, Janice
Seidman and Son 1962,O 16,32:2
Carson, Jean
Bravo! 1948,N 12,31:2
Metropole 1949,D 7,43:2
Bird Cage, The 1950,F 23,32:2
Men of Distinction 1953,My 1,18:4
Anniversary Waltz 1954,Ap 8,34:1
Carson, Jeannie
Finian's Rainbow 1960,Ap 28,31:1

Blood Red Roses 1970,Mr 23,48:1
Carson, John
Joe Egg 1968,F 2,26:1
Joe Egg 1968,F 11,II,1:1
Carson, Kid
Hair 1970,Ja 13,39:1
Carson, Mark
Merry Wives of Windsor, The 1959,Jl 9,23:2
Carson, Maxine
Sunny Days 1928,F 9,29:1
Carson, Mindy
South Pacific 1957,Ap 25,35:1
Body Beautiful, The 1958,Ja 24,15:2
Say Darling 1959,F 26,38:2
Ronde, La 1960,My 10,44:2
Voice of the Turtle, The 1961,Je 28,41:1
Dinner at Eight 1966,S 28,38:1
Carson, Neil
Richard III 1953,Jl 15,22:2
Measure for Measure 1954,Je 30,23:1
Carson, Pat
And People All Around 1968,F 12,46:1
Carson, Sally (Playwright)
Crooked Cross 1937,Ja 14,16:4
Crooked Cross 1937,F 7,X,3:5
Carson, Stanley
Gypsy Baron, The 1944,N 15,20:3
Carson, Trudy
Leonard Sillman's New Faces of 1968
1968,My 3,43:1
Carson, Wayne
Desk Set, The 1955,O 25,36:7
Far Country, A 1961,Ap 5,32:1
Carson, Wayne (Miscellaneous)
Villa of Madame Vidac, The 1959,O 1,40:1
Exercise, The 1968,Ap 25,54:1
Carstarphen, Frank E (Playwright)
Bellamy Trial, The 1928,Ag 20,21:1
Bellamy Trial, The 1931,Ap 23,28:6
Carswell, Ben
Hit the Deck! 1927,Ap 26,32:1
Carten, Audrey
Dancers, The 1923,F 25,VII,1:7
Carten, Audrey (Playwright)
Fame 1929,Mr 10,X,4:6
Late One Evening 1933,Ja 10,27:3
Mademoiselle 1936,O 4,IX,3:7
Destination Unknown 1937,Jl 6,23:4
Carten, Kenneth
Red Peppers 1936,N 25,17:2
Hands Across the Sea 1936,N 25,17:2
We Were Dancing 1936,N 28,13:1
Shadow Play 1936,N 28,13:1
Ways and Means 1936,D 1,31:1
Still Life 1936,D 1,31:1
Family Album 1936,D 1,31:1
Set to Music 1939,Ja 19,16:2
Carten, Waveney (Playwright)
Fame 1929,Mr 10,X,4:6
Late One Evening 1933,Ja 10,27:3
Destination Unknown 1937,Jl 6,23:4
Carter, Arthur (Playwright)
Number, The 1951,O 31,33:2
Carter, Barrington
Goat Alley 1921,Je 21,20:2
Magnolia 1923,Ag 28,12:3
My Magnolia 1926,Jl 13,19:2
Carter, Benjamin (Composer)
Believers, The 1968,My 10,57:4
Carter, Benjamin (Lyricist)
Believers, The 1968,My 10,57:4
Carter, Betty Lee
Bedfellows 1929,Jl 3,19:2
Carter, Beulah
Mill Shadows 1932,F 29,20:7
Carter, Bill
First Impressions 1959,Mr 20,28:1
Carter, Carvel
Carnival! 1961,Ap 14,22:2
Carter, Catherine
Egotist, The 1922,D 27,12:1
Carter, David
Beaux' Stratagem, The 1957,Jl 9,25:4
Carter, David W (Miscellaneous)
I Want You 1961,S 15,29:1
Carter, Denise
Across the Board on Tomorrow Morning
1942,Mr 21,13:5
Theatre of the Soul 1942,Mr 21,13:5
Carter, Desmond (Lyricist)
Great Waltz, The 1934,S 24,14:4
Carter, Desmond (Miscellaneous)
Wake Up and Dream 1929,D 31,14:3
Carter, Desmond (Original Author)
Great Waltz, The 1934,S 24,14:4
Carter, Desmond (Playwright)
Jill Darling 1934,D 20,29:8
Rise and Shine 1936,My 8,21:4
Carter, Desmond (Translator)
Du Barry 1932,N 23,15:2
Carter, Dixie
Winter's Tale, The 1963,Ag 16,14:1
Carousel 1965,Ag 11,39:1

Carter, Donald
Betty Behave 1927,Mr 9,28:4
Carter, Dorothy
Strange Fruit 1945,N 30,18:6
On Strivers' Row 1946,Mr 1,17:2
Walk Hard 1946,Mr 28,34:2
Take a Giant Step 1953,O 4,II,1:1
Carter, Douglas
Tightwad, The 1927,Ap 18,18:2
Mr Moneypenny 1928,O 17,26:2
Carter, E Ryland
Rogues and Vagabonds 1930,My 8,32:5
Carter, Edith (Playwright)
Lass O' Laughter 1922,My 21,VI,1:6
Lass O' Laughter 1925,Ja 9,13:2
Carter, Elaine
It's A Gift 1945,Mr 13,18:7
Carter, Francis
Foolscap 1933,Ja 12,21:2
Carter, Fred
Walk Hard 1944,D 1,28:2
Henri Christophe 1945,Je 7,24:5
On Strivers' Row 1946,Mr 1,17:2
Walk Hard 1946,Mr 28,34:2
Tin Top Valley 1947,Mr 1,11:2
Almost Faithful 1948,Je 5,9:2
Carter, Gaile
Thesmophoriazusae, The; Goddesses of Athens,
The 1955,D 14,52:4
Carter, Garfield (Playwright)
Double Exposure 1937,Ag 18,15:2
Carter, George
Antony and Cleopatra 1924,F 20,22:1
Carter, Harry
Cradle Will Rock, The 1938,Ja 4,19:3
Carter, Harry W
Wicked Age, The 1927,N 5,16:6
Carter, Helen
Processional 1937,O 14,23:1
Cradle Will Rock, The 1937,D 6,19:4
Journeyman 1938,Ja 31,14:2
Good Neighbor 1941,O 22,26:2
Carter, Hubert
Oedipus Rex 1923,O 26,14:1
Marriage by Purchase 1931,Je 21,VIII,1:3
Carter, Irving
Big Boy 1925,Ja 8,28:2
Carter, J Patrick
Show Boat 1961,Ap 13,32:1
Carter, Jack
Goat Alley 1927,Ap 21,24:3
Porgy 1929,S 14,17:3
Singin' the Blues 1931,Ap 12,IX,2:1
Singin' the Blues 1931,S 17,21:3
Stevedore 1934,Ap 19,33:2
Stevedore 1934,O 2,18:2
Macbeth 1936,Ap 15,25:4
Doctor Faustus 1937,Ja 9,21:2
Aquashow 1952,Je 25,25:1
Mr Wonderful 1956,Mr 23,23:2
Carter, James
Middle Watch, The 1929,O 17,27:1
Icetime 1947,My 29,28:2
Carter, Jean
Strip for Action 1942,O 1,26:2
Strip for Action 1942,O 11,VIII,1:1
Carter, Joan Mann
Harbor Lights 1956,O 5,20:1
Carter, Joey
New Faces of 1962 1962,F 2,25:1
Carter, Joey (Playwright)
New Faces of 1962 1962,F 2,25:1
Carter, John
Sandhog 1954,N 24,17:1
What a Killing 1961,Mr 28,41:1
Carter, John (Producer)
Candida 1970,Ap 7,41:1
Carter, Kenneth
Emperor Jones, The 1945,Ja 17,18:4
Carter, Lavada
Shuffle Along of 1933 1932,D 27,11:3
Carter, Leslie (Mrs)
Circle, The 1921,S 13,12:1
Circle, The 1921,S 18,VI,1:1
Stella Dallas 1924,Ja 20,VII,2:8
Shanghai Gesture, The 1925,D 20,VII,4:1
She Stoops to Conquer 1928,My 15,17:1
She Stoops to Conquer 1928,My 20,VIII,1:1
Carter, Lon
Move On 1926,Ja 19,30:1
Intruder, The 1928,Jl 26,25:4
Getting Even 1929,Ag 20,31:1
Town Boy 1929,O 5,22:4
Gray Shadow 1931,Mr 11,23:4
Carter, Louise
Clouds 1925,S 3,32:1
Ballyhoo 1927,Ja 5,18:1
He Loved the Ladies 1927,My 11,29:2
So Am I 1928,Ja 28,9:1
Scarlet Fox, The 1928,Mr 28,31:1
Skidding 1928,My 22,18:5
Dora Mobridge 1930,Ap 21,20:2

Carter, Louise (Playwright)
Bedfellows 1929,Jl 3,19:2
Joy of Living 1931,Ap 7,31:1
Carter, Lucius Jr
Roll Sweet Chariot 1934,O 3,24:3
Carter, Lynne
Legal Grounds 1940,D 2,18:4
Vickie 1942,S 23,28:1
Hear That Trumpet 1946,O 8,19:2
Fun City 1968,Mr 7,53:2
Carter, M Lloyd (Producer)
Squat Betty 1964,F 25,24:1
Sponge Room, The 1964,F 25,24:1
Carter, Mabel
Swing Mikado, The 1939,Mr 2,18:2
Carter, Marian T (Producer)
Hipper's Holiday 1934,O 19,26:2
Carter, Marilyn
Bacchae, The 1969,Mr 15,24:1
Carter, Marion
Vie Parisienne, La 1945,Ja 13,14:5
Carter, Mary
Hamlet 1934,D 26,19:3
Murder in the Cathedral 1966,Je 21,38:1
Glorious Ruler, The 1969,Jl 1,31:1
Carter, Maryce
Moon on a Rainbow Shawl 1969,Ag 29,25:1
Moon on a Rainbow Shawl 1970,D 18,52:1
Carter, Michael
Winter Soldiers 1942,N 30,19:2
Carter, Myra
Major Barbara 1956,O 31,27:1
Maybe Tuesday 1958,Ja 30,18:3
Secret Concubine, The 1960,Mr 22,29:2
Helen 1964,D 11,55:4
Carter, Nell
When Crummles Played 1928,O 2,34:3
Carter, Oscar M (Playwright)
Three Little Business Men, The 1923,S 4,12:1
Money Business 1926,Ja 21,18:1
Carter, Patrick
Beaux' Stratagem, The 1970,F 10,50:2
Three Sisters, The 1970,F 12,30:1
Three Sisters, The 1970,F 12,30:1
Carter, Paul
Let's Make an Opera 1950,D 14,50:2
Carter, Phil
All You Need Is One Good Break 1950,F 10,20:3
Carter, Philip
Roll Sweet Chariot 1934,O 3,24:3
Carter, Pola
Three Little Business Men, The 1923,S 4,12:1
Jolly Tailors, The 1923,N 3,13:3
Money Business 1926,Ja 21,18:1
My Country 1926,Ag 10,19:1
Carter, Ralph
Nancy Ann 1924,Ap 1,18:1
Carter, Randolph (Director)
Gabrielle 1941,Mr 26,26:2
Late Late Show, The 1968,N 4,57:3
Save It for Your Death Bed 1968,N 4,57:3
I Saw a Monkey 1968,N 4,57:3
Carter, Randolph (Playwright)
Arms for Venus 1937,Mr 12,18:7
Wuthering Heights 1939,Ap 28,30:4
Eugenia 1957,Ja 31,20:1
I Saw a Monkey 1968,N 4,57:3
Save It for Your Death Bed 1968,N 4,57:3
Late Late Show, The 1968,N 4,57:3
Carter, Rex
Last Waltz, The 1921,My 11,20:3
Carter, Roderick
Murder in the Cathedral 1958,Mr 22,12:4
Carter, Rosalind
Bridal Crown, The 1938,F 7,11:2
Carter, Rosanna
Hamhocks 1968,Ag 24,24:2
Carter, Samuel (Composer)
Samarkand 1926,D 22,24:4
Carter, Samuel (Lyricist)
Samarkand 1926,D 22,24:4
Carter, Samuel (Playwright)
Samarkand 1926,D 22,24:4
Carter, Samuel 3d
Fortuno 1925,D 23,22:1
Carter, Samuel 3d (Lyricist)
Fortuno 1925,D 23,22:1
Carter, Samuel 3d (Playwright)
Fortuno 1925,D 23,22:1
Carter, Sara
Little Theatre Tournament; Pink and Patches
1928,My 11,28:1
Carter, Shirley
Death of Cuchulain, The 1959,Ap 13,34:4
Carter, Sidney (Playwright)
For Charity 1937,Ag 25,24:3
Carter, Steve (Scenic Designer)
Raisin' Hell in the Son 1962,Jl 3,13:2
Carter, Steven
Horse Eats Hat 1936,S 28,14:2
Carter, Terry
Mrs Patterson 1954,D 2,37:1
Finian's Rainbow 1955,My 19,25:1

Kwamina 1961,O 24,42:1
Carter, Wendy
Hasty Heart, The 1959,S 15,45:2
Carter, Winifred
Mystery Square 1929,Ap 5,28:3
Carter, Winifred (Playwright)
Queen Who Kept Her Head, The 1934,F 21,23:4
Carter and Bowie
Sons o' Fun 1941,D 2,28:2
Carter-Waddell, Joan
Piggy 1927,Ja 12,22:2
Little Show, The 1929,My 1,28:5
Venetian Glass Nephew, The 1931,F 24,26:3
Hey, Nonny, Nonny! 1932,Je 7,22:3
Carteret, Doris
Enchanted April, The 1925,Ag 25,12:3
Carthage, Sally
Flamingo Road 1946,Mr 20,18:2
Carthay, Dan
Keep Moving 1934,Ag 24,10:2
Carthay (Choreographer)
Blossom Time 1943,S 6,21:2
Cartier, Deidre (Costume Designer)
Iceman Cometh, The 1956,My 8,38:1
Comedian, The 1956,O 18,36:4
Shadow of Heroes 1961,D 6,59:1
Witches' Sabbath 1962,Ap 20,22:2
Condemned of Altona, The 1966,F 4,21:1
Collision Course; Wandering 1968,My 9,55:2
Collision Course; Chuck 1968,My 9,55:2
Collision Course; Unexpurgated Memoirs of
Bernard Mergendeiler, The 1968,My 9,55:2
Collision Course; Camera Obscura 1968,My 9,55:2
Collision Course; Jew! 1968,My 9,55:2
Collision Course; Thoughts on the Instant of
Greeting a Friend on the Street 1968,My 9,55:2
Collision Course; Tour 1968,My 9,55:2
Collision Course; Rats 1968,My 9,55:2
Collision Course; Stars and Stripes 1968,My 9,55:2
Collision Course; Skywriting 1968,My 9,55:2
Collision Course; Metaphors 1968,My 9,55:2
Happy Hypocrite, The 1968,S 6,38:1
Tea Party 1968,O 16,40:1
Basement, The 1968,O 16,40:1
Exhibition 1969,My 16,41:1
Scent of Flowers, A 1969,O 21,42:1
Blood Red Roses 1970,Mr 23,48:1
Lulu; Earth Spirit 1970,Mr 28,32:1
Cartier, Deidre (Miscellaneous)
Country Wife, The 1965,D 10,58:2
Cartier, Jacques
Manhatters, The 1927,Jl 19,27:3
Manhatters, The 1927,Ag 4,25:4
Golden Dawn 1927,D 1,32:3
Ziegfeld Follies 1934,Ja 5,24:3
Cartier, Jacques (Director)
Firebugs, The 1968,Jl 2,36:1
Cartier, John
Gondoliers, The 1962,N 16,25:2
Cartier, Ken
Wanted 1928,Jl 3,19:2
Cartier, Mamie
Savage Rhythm 1932,Ja 1,30:4
Cartier, Renee
Colonel Satan 1931,Ja 12,24:1
Paging Danger 1931,F 27,19:2
All Good Americans 1933,D 6,29:2
Atout... Coeur 1936,Mr 27,25:4
Son Mari 1936,Ap 17,17:3
Cartier, Robert
Girofle-Girofla 1926,N 23,26:3
Girofle-Girofla 1926,N 24,26:2
Cartland, Barbara (Playwright)
Blood Money 1925,N 1,VIII,1:3
Cartland, Gilbert
Big Mogul, The 1925,My 12,26:3
Cartmell, Van Henry
Prunella 1929,Ap 10,23:3
Sonya's Search for the Christmas Star
1929,D 14,24:6
Cartmell, Van Henry Jr (Playwright)
Why Not? 1922,D 30,13:4
Carton, Harold
Via Crucis 1923,N 13,25:2
Hamlet 1923,N 20,23:3
Carton, Waveney (Playwright)
Mademoiselle 1936,O 4,IX,3:7
Cartright, Walter
American Tragedy, An 1931,F 21,15:5
Cartwright, Bruce
Around the World 1946,Je 1,9:5
Cartwright, Burt
Legal Murder 1934,F 16,16:2
Cartwright, John
Heimkehr aus der Fremde, Die; Stranger, The
1949,S 2,14:1
Cartwright, Levering
Fratricide Punished 1925,Ap 21,19:1
Cartwright, Marguerite
Roll Sweet Chariot 1934,O 3,24:3
Cartwright, Peggy
Americana 1932,S 25,IX,1:6

Cartwright, Peggy—Cont
Americana 1932,O 6,19:3
Cartwright, Walter
Ladies Don't Lie 1929,O 11,36:3
Oh, Professor 1930,My 2,19:6
Show-Off, The 1950,Je 1,24:5
Carty, Jim
George White's Scandals 1926,Je 15,23:2
George White's Scandals 1929,S 24,29:1
Caru, Ernestine
Vaudeville (Palace) 1921,Jl 5,15:1
Caru, Eva Perez (Choreographer)
Mexicana 1939,My 7,X,3:1
Caruba, Gloria
Mary Stuart 1956,Ap 28,10:2
Carubbi, Luigi
Venetian Twins, The 1968,My 29,23:1
Caruso, Audrey
39 Steps 1938,Mr 12,13:1
Caruso, Barbara
Picture of Dorian Gray, The 1963,Ag 29,37:4
And People All Around 1968,F 12,46:1
Millionairess, The 1969,Mr 3,28:1
Wars of the Roses, The (Part I) 1970,Jl 2,30:1
Wars of the Roses, The (Part II) 1970,Jl 3,15:1
Richard III 1970,Jl 4,11:1
Henry VI, Parts I, II, III 1970,Jl 5,II,3:1
Caruso, Joseph
Arms and the Girl 1950,F 3,28:2
Caruso, Rosanne
Jack in the Box 1960,My 19,43:3
Caruso, Sal
Troubled Waters 1965,Je 4,40:2
Caruth, Ann
East of Broadway 1932,Ja 27,19:3
Singapore 1932,N 15,24:2
Caruth, Burr
Purple Mask, The 1920,Ja 6,18:1
Johannes Kreisler 1922,D 25,20:3
Brother Elks 1925,S 15,29:2
Mongolia 1927,D 27,24:5
Skidding 1928,My 22,18:5
Criminal Code, The 1929,O 3,28:2
Tyrant, The 1930,N 13,33:1
Zombie 1932,F 11,17:2
We the People 1933,Ja 23,9:5
Carvalho, Claire (Playwright)
Paging Danger 1931,F 27,19:2
Carvel, Gene
Buccaneer, The 1925,O 3,10:2
Carvel, Joan
Gossipy Sex, The 1927,Ap 20,28:3
Kingdom of God, The 1928,D 21,30:2
Carvelle, Marjorie
Mimic World of 1921, The 1921,Ag 18,9:2
Carver, Ada Jack (Playwright)
Little Theatre Tournament; Cajun, The
1926,My 6,23:3
Carver, Charles
Vagabond King, The 1925,S 22,23:3
Red Robe, The 1928,D 26,15:1
Count of Luxembourg, The 1930,F 18,28:2
Carver, Edgar (Composer)
Life Begins in '40 1940,Ap 5,24:2
Hit the Road 1941,Ap 4,18:3
Carver, Jack
Pardon My English 1933,Ja 21,11:4
Carver, Jody
Hayride 1954,S 14,24:2
Carver, John
Brigadoon 1963,F 1,6:2
Oklahoma! 1963,F 28,8:2
Carver, Keith
John Brown's Body 1953,F 16,17:2
Carver, Mary
Out West of Eighth 1951,S 21,20:3
Pursuit of Happiness, The 1952,Mr 22,9:2
Talent '54 1954,Ap 13,40:1
Carver, Phyllis
Texas Town 1941,Ap 30,22:3
Out of My House 1942,Ja 8,28:6
Carver, Ronny
You'll See Stars 1943,Ja 1,26:6
Carver, Rosemary
Danton's Death 1938,N 3,26:2
Susannah and the Elders 1940,O 30,28:2
Carver, Tina
Good Old Days, The 1951,Jl 18,21:2
Carvill, Henry
Fair Circassian, The 1921,D 7,22:3
Loyalties 1922,S 28,18:1
Tiger Cats 1924,O 22,18:1
Wild Duck, The 1925,F 25,16:4
Old Bill, M P 1926,N 11,22:2
Patriot, The 1928,Ja 20,15:1
Man With Red Hair, A 1928,N 9,22:2
Peter Ibbetson 1931,Ap 9,30:3
Carwin, James
Fortune Teller, The 1929,N 5,32:3
Cary, Allan
Faith and Prudence 1952,O 15,40:2
Cary, Christopher
Harlequinade 1959,F 14,15:1
Painted Days, The 1961,Ap 7,24:1

Cary, Claiborne
On the Town 1959,F 14,15:1
Beg, Borrow or Steal 1960,F 11,39:4
Kukla, Burr and Ollie 1960,N 1,47:2
Smiling the Boy Fell Dead 1961,Ap 20,28:1
All Kinds of Giants 1961,D 19,40:1
Cary, Edward
Long Moment, The 1950,My 22,16:6
Sing Till Tomorrow 1953,D 29,17:2
Adding Machine, The 1956,F 10,17:1
Cary, Hope
Merchant of Venice, The 1928,Ja 17,22:2
Cary, Joyce (Original Author)
Mister Johnson 1956,Mr 30,11:1
Cary, Leonard
Drifting 1922,Ja 3,20:3
Cary, Ned
Black Monday 1962,Mr 7,29:1
All the King's Men 1963,Jl 12,12:1
Cary, Tristram (Composer)
Macbeth 1962,F 7,32:2
Cary, Tristram (Miscellaneous)
Macbeth 1962,F 7,32:2
Cary, Willard
First Stop to Heaven 1941,Ja 6,10:7
Caryl, Bernice
Money Mad 1937,My 25,32:5
Caryl, William (Director)
Take My Advice 1927,N 2,24:3
Woof, Woof 1929,D 26,20:4
Little Racketeer, The 1932,Ja 19,24:4
Caryl, William (Producer)
Gypsy Fires 1925,D 8,28:3
Take My Advice 1927,N 2,24:3
Perfect Marriage, The 1932,N 17,23:2
Caryle, Jack
Unknown Lady, The 1923,N 6,22:1
Caryll, Ivan (Composer)
Tip-Top 1920,O 6,13:2
Kissing Time 1920,O 12,18:2
Hotel Mouse, The 1922,Mr 14,11:3
Caryll, Primrose
Kissing Time 1920,O 12,18:2
Some Party 1922,Ap 17,22:1
Criss Cross 1926,O 13,20:2
Casaday, James Lewis (Costume Designer)
Hamlet 1928,Je 2,11:3
Bourgeois Gentilhomme, Le 1929,Mr 17,30:4
Casaday, James Lewis (Director)
Bourgeois Gentilhomme, Le 1929,Mr 17,30:4
Casaday, James Lewis (Scenic Designer)
Hamlet 1928,Je 2,11:3
Casadesus, Robert
Ma Tante d' Honfleur 1920,Ja 27,18:3
Foot-Loose 1920,My 11,12:1
Casady, Barnard
Wurzel-Flummery 1923,Ja 17,22:2
Casalis, Jeanne de
Colonel Satan 1931,Ja 18,I,28:6
Casals, Don Enrique (Musical Director)
Dama Boba, La; Villano En Su Rincon, El;
Fuenteovejuna 1935,S 22,X,2:5
Casamo, William
High Tor 1937,Ja 11,15:2
Casanova, Eve
Lady of the Lamp, The 1920,Ag 18,6:4
Caught 1925,O 6,31:2
Love City, The 1926,Ja 26,18:2
Lally 1927,F 9,16:3
Menace 1927,Mr 15,28:2
Gods We Make, The 1934,Ja 4,16:4
Way, The 1940,O 12,20:3
Casanova, Jimmy
Night in Venice, A 1952,Je 27,18:6
Night in Venice, A 1952,Jl 13,II,1:1
Casares, Maria
Diable et le Bon Dieu, Le 1951,Je 8,32:6
Triomphe de l'Amour, Le 1958,O 17,32:1
Marie Tudor 1958,O 22,39:1
Cid, Le 1958,O 31,35:2
Enchaines; Welded 1965,Mr 13,17:1
Paravents, Les 1966,Ap 22,36:3
Casartelli, Gabrielle
Invitation au Voyage, L' 1930,Ja 26,VIII,1:8
Casas, Myrna
Soles Truncos, Los; House on Cristo Street, The
1959,Ag 31,15:2
Casavant, Louis
Saint, The 1924,O 13,20:3
Louie the 14th 1925,Mr 4,17:1
My Maryland 1927,S 13,37:2
Woof, Woof 1929,D 26,20:4
Colonel Satan 1931,Ja 12,24:1
Her Man of Wax 1933,O 12,32:3
Cascio, Gigi
Engagement Baby, The 1970,My 22,40:1
Cascio, Gigi (Director)
Goose, The 1960,Mr 16,44:1
Time of the Key, A 1963,S 12,33:3
Cascio, Gigi (Lighting Director)
Cats' Pajamas, The 1962,Je 1,16:2
Cascio, Gigi (Miscellaneous)
Seven at Dawn, The 1961,Ap 18,43:1

Moon on a Rainbow Shawl 1962,Ja 16,30:1
Cats' Pajamas, The 1962,Je 1,16:2
Riverwind 1962,D 14,5:5
Time of the Key, A 1963,S 12,33:3
Ginger Man, The 1963,N 22,42:1
Sing to Me Through Open Windows
1965,Mr 16,45:1
Day the Whores Came Out to Play Tennis, The
1965,Mr 16,45:1
First One Asleep, Whistle 1966,F 28,19:1
Fragments 1967,O 3,56:1
Basement, The 1967,O 3,56:1
Woman Is My Idea 1968,S 26,61:1
To Be Young Gifted and Black; World of Lorraine
Hansberry, The 1969,Ja 3,15:1
Jar, The 1969,Ap 23,42:1
License, The 1969,Ap 23,42:1
Man With the Flower in His Mouth, The
1969,Ap 23,42:1
Fortune and Men's Eyes 1969,O 23,55:1
Engagement Baby, The 1970,My 22,40:1
Case, Allen
South Pacific 1957,Ap 25,35:1
Once Upon a Mattress 1959,My 12,40:1
Hallelujah, Baby! 1967,Ap 27,51:1
Case, Anita
Night in Venice, A 1929,My 22,30:2
Case, Anna
Vaudeville (Hippodrome) 1926,Mr 16,22:2
Vaudeville (Hippodrome) 1926,Ap 27,22:3
Vaudeville (Palace) 1926,O 26,24:2
Case, David
Medea 1920,Mr 23,12:2
Case, Edith True
By the Beautiful Sea 1954,Ap 9,20:1
Case, Evelyn
Time, Place and the Girl, The 1942,O 22,24:3
Case, Gloria (Producer)
Out of This World 1955,O 13,35:2
Case, Helen
Topsy and Eva 1924,D 24,11:1
Case, John Carol
Yeomen of the Guard, The 1962,Jl 11,28:1
Case, John P (Miscellaneous)
Guitar 1959,N 11,42:5
Case, Michael
Coming of Christ, The 1957,D 23,29:8
Case, Richard
My Heart's in the Highlands 1950,F 18,8:4
Music in the Air 1951,O 9,32:2
Mr Pickwick 1952,S 18,36:3
Emperor's Clothes, The 1953,F 10,24:2
Case, Russ (Miscellaneous)
Russell Patterson's Sketch-Book 1960,F 8,35:1
Case, Russ (Musical Director)
Pilgrim's Progress 1962,Mr 21,36:2
Case, Virginia
Good Boy 1928,S 6,23:2
Casella, Alberto (Original Author)
Death Takes a Holiday 1929,N 24,X,4:5
Death Takes a Holiday 1931,F 17,29:1
Casella, Alberto (Playwright)
Death Takes a Holiday 1929,D 27,26:4
Caselle, Florence
Mlle Modiste 1929,O 8,34:1
Caselle, Jean
Afgar 1920,N 9,13:2
Caselle, Jeanne
Bright Rebel 1938,D 28,24:2
Casey, Edward (Producer)
School for Virtue 1931,Ap 22,29:2
Casey, Ethel
Bedtime Story 1957,Ap 1,21:2
Portrait of a Madonna 1957,Ap 1,21:2
Apollo of Bellac, The 1958,Mr 7,17:2
Browning Version, The 1958,Mr 7,17:2
Skin of Our Teeth, The 1960,O 14,24:1
Casey, Evelyn
Yellow Jacket, The 1923,Ap 20,20:3
Casey, Francis M
Made for Each Other 1924,S 30,27:2
Casey, James P
Little Theatre Tournament; Rhythm of the City,
The 1929,My 7,28:1
Casey, Judy
Ice Follies 1969,My 23,38:1
Casey, Kenneth
Lady in the Dark 1941,Ja 24,14:2
Casey, Kittye
Hello, Lola! 1926,Ja 13,30:1
Casey, Leslie (Producer)
These Two 1934,My 8,28:3
Fresh Fields 1934,Jl 15,X,1:1
Casey, Michael (Director)
Sweeney Todd 1957,Ag 28,21:4
Casey, Richard
Savonarola 1942,Ap 24,20:2
Casey, Richard (Director)
Bedlam Galore, for Two or More 1965,Mr 8,34:1
Impromptu, L' 1965,Mr 8,34:1
Leader, The 1965,Mr 8,34:1
Foursome 1965,Mr 8,34:1

Casey, Rosemary (Playwright)
Agatha Calling 1935,O 1,27:5
Mary Goes to See 1938,Mr 6,XI,3:6
Velvet Glove, The 1949,D 27,26:2
Once an Actor 1950,Ag 1,19:8
Late Love 1953,O 14,35:2
Casey, Stuart
Ghost Parade, The 1929,O 31,28:4
Recapture 1930,Ja 19,VIII,2:6
Recapture 1930,Ja 30,16:4
Lady Clara 1930,Ap 18,28:7
Wonder Bar 1931,Mr 18,23:4
Lady With a Lamp, The 1931,N 20,27:2
Jewel Robbery 1932,Ja 14,17:2
Man Who Reclaimed His Head 1932,S 9,17:3
Dream of Sganarelle, The 1933,O 17,26:5
School for Husbands, The 1933,O 17,26:5
Holmeses of Baker Street, The 1936,D 10,34:3
Plan M 1942,F 21,15:2
Richard III 1943,Mr 27,8:3
Connecticut Yankee, A 1943,N 18,30:2
Casey, Taggard
Cradle Will Rock, The 1947,D 27,11:2
Casey, Trudy
Ice Follies 1969,My 23,38:1
Casey, William J (Miscellaneous)
Firebugs, The 1963,F 13,7:2
Cash, Nat
Harlem 1929,F 21,30:3
Cash, Nat (Choreographer)
Will Morrissey's Folies Bergere Revue
1930,Ap 16,26:6
Cash, Nat (Director)
Hot Rhythm 1930,Ag 22,18:5
Cash, Nat (Miscellaneous)
Pansy 1929,My 15,36:3
Cash, Roberta
Kongi's Harvest 1968,Ap 15,49:1
Cash, Rosalind
Wayward Stork, The 1966,Ja 20,27:1
Junebug Graduates Tonight! 1967,F 27,35:1
To Bury a Cousin 1967,My 17,38:3
Song of the Lusitanian Bogey, The 1968,Ja 3,52:1
Kongi's Harvest 1968,Ap 15,49:1
Daddy Goodness 1968,Je 5,37:1
God Is a (Guess What?) 1968,D 18,56:1
Ceremonies in Dark Old Men 1969,F 6,33:1
Ceremonies in Dark Old Men 1969,F 23,II,5:1
Malcochon 1969,Ap 2,37:1
Man Better Man 1969,Jl 3,22:1
Harangues, The 1970,Ja 14,42:1
Day of Absence 1970,Mr 18,39:1
Casher, Jenny
Song of Dnieper 1946,O 26,10:5
Shylock and His Daughter 1947,S 30,22:2
Yosele the Nightingale 1949,O 21,30:4
Cashier, Isidore
Wolves 1924,D 31,9:4
Shakespeare and Company 1925,O 22,22:5
Dybbuk, The 1926,Ja 6,16:2
Tenth Commandment, The 1926,N 18,27:1
Jew Suss 1929,O 19,22:3
Angels on Earth 1929,D 11,34:7
Chains 1930,F 23,29:2
One Woman 1931,D 14,16:4
In a Tenement House 1932,Ja 25,20:4
Pioneers 1932,F 26,22:5
Wedding Chains 1932,Mr 28,10:5
Yoshe Kalb 1932,O 3,15:5
Yoshe Kalb 1932,N 6,IX,2:1
Bread 1932,D 14,27:3
Revolt 1933,Ja 12,21:3
Wise Men of Chelm, The 1933,O 18,24:4
Josephus 1933,D 1,22:5
Brothers Ashkenazi, The 1937,S 21,28:6
Three Cities 1938,O 11,20:3
Who Is Who? 1938,D 24,13:3
Yoshe Kalb 1939,F 6,9:2
Far-Away Corner, A 1939,F 15,15:2
Salvation 1939,S 29,19:2
Worlds Apart 1941,Ja 23,19:3
Oy, Is Dus a Leben!; Oh, What a Life!
1942,O 13,19:2
Family Carnovsky, The 1943,O 19,16:7
Doctor Herzl 1945,D 21,25:4
Song of Dnieper 1946,O 26,10:5
Shylock and His Daughter 1947,S 30,22:2
Cashier, Isidore (Producer)
Soul of a Woman, The 1930,F 22,13:1
Cashman, Edward (Composer)
Ticket-of-Leave Man, The 1961,D 23,15:1
Casile, Genevieve
Avare, L', L'; Miser, The 1966,F 9,32:1
Cid, Le 1966,F 12,17:1
Reine Morte, La 1966,F 16,52:1
Fil a la Paite, Un 1966,F 18,25:1
Amphitryon 1970,F 4,38:1
Troupe Du Roi, La 1970,F 4,38:1
Don Juan 1970,F 7,24:2
Femmes Savaantes, Les 1970,F 14,12:1
Casimir, Golda
Teahouse of the August Moon, The
1955,My 10,24:1

Caskey, Bill
Athenian Touch, The 1964,Ja 15,25:4
Caskey, William
Androcles and the Lion 1958,F 22,8:3
Casler, Richard (Costume Designer)
J B 1958,Ap 24,37:1
Cranmer of Canterbury 1959,D 4,36:1
Family Reunion, The 1960,D 10,26:1
This Way to the Tomb 1961,D 9,21:1
House of Flowers 1968,Ja 29,26:2
Casler, Richard (Lighting Director)
Everyman Today 1958,Ja 16,32:4
Cranmer of Canterbury 1959,D 4,36:1
Crystal Heart, The 1960,F 16,31:2
Family Reunion, The 1960,D 10,26:1
This Way to the Tomb 1961,D 9,21:1
Saving Grace, The 1963,Ap 19,28:1
Thistle in My Bed 1963,N 20,48:1
Anya 1965,N 30,48:1
Red, White and Maddox 1969,Ja 27,27:1
Casler, Richard (Miscellaneous)
Red, White and Maddox 1969,Ja 27,27:1
Casler, Richard (Scenic Designer)
Everyman Today 1958,Ja 16,32:4
Cup of Trembling, The 1959,My 1,33:5
Cranmer of Canterbury 1959,D 4,36:1
Crystal Heart, The 1960,F 16,31:2
Snow Maiden, The 1960,Ap 5,43:3
Family Reunion, The 1960,D 10,26:1
Magnificent Hugo, The 1961,Ap 8,12:2
This Way to the Tomb 1961,D 9,21:1
Saving Grace, The 1963,Ap 19,28:1
Thistle in My Bed 1963,N 20,48:1
Casman, Nellie
Little Cantor, The 1930,S 24,26:2
Casmore, Vic
Tickle Me 1920,Ag 18,9:1
Lady Butterfly 1923,Ja 23,18:1
Yours Truly 1927,Ja 26,16:5
Casmore, Victor
Nina Rosa 1930,My 31,19:3
Nina Rosa 1930,S 22,22:5
Marching By 1932,Mr 4,17:1
Bitter Sweet 1934,My 8,28:4
May Wine 1935,D 6,30:3
Pygmalion 1938,Ja 27,16:3
Captain Jinks of the Horse Marines 1938,Ja 28,16:2
Coriolanus 1938,F 2,14:5
Casner, Dolly
Broadway Whirl, The 1921,Je 9,10:4
Cason, Barbara
Persecution and Assassination of Marat As Performed by the Inmates of the Asylum of Charenton Under the Direction of the Marquis de Sade, The 1967,Ja 4,34:1
Death of the Well-Loved Boy, The 1967,My 16,48:1
Firebugs, The 1968,Jl 2,36:1
Jimmy Shine 1968,D 6,52:1
Spitting Image 1969,Mr 3,28:1
Casona, Alejandro (Playwright)
Sirena Varada, La 1937,O 23,15:3
Trees Die Standing, The 1969,O 13,52:1
"Caspar"
Variations of 1940 1940,Ja 29,12:1
Caspary, Vera (Original Author)
Laura 1947,Je 27,16:1
Caspary, Vera (Playwright)
Blind Mice 1930,S 7,IX,2:4
Blind Mice 1930,O 16,28:2
Geraniums in My Window 1934,O 27,20:6
Laura 1947,Je 27,16:1
Casper, Colonel
Ripples 1930,F 12,26:1
Casper, Robert
Oscar Wilde 1957,Ap 20,21:3
Casrillo (Costume Designer)
My Name is Aquilon 1949,F 10,38:2
Cass, Bradley
Americana 1928,O 31,28:2
After Dark 1928,D 11,35:2
After Dark: or, Neither Maid, Wife nor Widow 1929,F 10,IX,1:1
Holiday 1930,F 6,21:2
No More Ladies 1934,Ja 24,20:3
No More Ladies 1934,S 4,23:2
Cass, Byrle (Director)
Hit the Trail 1954,D 3,31:2
Cass, Deborah
Tamburlaine the Great 1956,Ja 20,19:1
Midsummer Night's Dream, A 1960,Je 30,23:5
Cass, Gil
Louisiana Lady 1947,Je 3,35:2
Cass, Henry (Director)
Antony and Cleopatra 1934,S 18,18:2
Cass, Lee
New Moon, The; Desert Song, The 1955,Jl 1,13:1
Most Happy Fella, The 1956,My 4,20:1
Most Happy Fella, The 1959,F 11,50:2
Greenwillow 1960,Mr 9,38:1
Greenwillow 1960,Mr 20,II,1:1
All in Love 1961,N 11,15:2
H M S Pinafore 1964,Mr 21,13:4

H M S Pinafore 1965,Ap 15,39:1
Hotel Passionato 1965,O 23,16:1
Most Happy Fella, The 1966,My 12,55:1
Arabian Nights 1967,Jl 3,12:1
Sound of Music, The 1970,Jl 3,13:1
Cass, Leslie
Doctor Faustus 1961,Ap 26,36:1
Night Thoreau Spent in Jail, The 1970,N 2,66:1
Cass, Mary
Burning, The 1963,D 4,57:1
Cass, Maurice
Merchant of Venice, The 1921,Ap 2,14:2
Caesar and Cleopatra 1925,Ap 14,27:1
Man Who Died Twice, The 1925,D 14,19:1
Taming of the Shrew, The 1927,O 26,26:4
Broken Chain, The 1929,F 21,30:4
Novice and the Duke, The 1929,D 11,37:2
One Chaste Man 1930,Je 11,33:5
One, Two, Three! 1930,S 30,24:2
Overture 1930,N 25,31:2
Overture 1930,D 8,26:4
Country Wife, The 1931,Ap 19,31:5
Alchemist, The 1931,Je 5,27:1
Wild Waves 1932,F 20,11:4
Broadway Boy 1932,My 4,23:5
Sky's the Limit, The 1934,D 18,25:5
Cass, Maurice (Playwright)
Strange Prince, The 1926,D 8,24:2
Cass, Peggy
Touch and Go 1949,O 14,34:2
Live Wire, The 1950,Ag 18,16:2
Bernardine 1952,O 17,33:4
Othello 1955,S 8,27:2
Henry IV, Part I 1955,S 22,34:2
Auntie Mame 1956,N 1,47:2
Auntie Mame 1956,N 11,II,1:1
Thurber Carnival, A 1960,F 27,13:2
Thurber Carnival, A 1960,Mr 6,II,1:1
Children From Their Games 1963,Ap 12,33:1
Front Page, The 1969,My 12,54:2
Front Page, The 1969,My 25,II,1:1
Front Page, The 1969,N 2,86:1
Plaza Suite 1970,Mr 22,90:3
Cass, Robert
Twelfth Night 1954,N 10,42:2
Twelfth Night 1954,D 12,II,3:1
Merchant of Venice, The 1955,F 23,23:2
Midsummer Night's Dream, A 1956,Ja 14,12:2
Twelfth Night 1957,Ja 5,12:2
Cass, Sheila
Hit the Deck 1960,Je 24,32:1
Cass-Owen and Topsy
Earl Carroll's Vanities 1940,Ja 15,11:2
Cassanova, Eve
Yellow 1926,S 22,30:1
Gala Night 1930,F 26,22:4
Cassard, Frances
On the Town 1944,D 29,11:4
Cassavant, Louis
Fables 1922,F 7,12:2
Cassavou, V
Electra 1952,N 20,38:2
Cassedy, A B
Who's Who 1924,Ap 18,19:2
Cassel, Arthur
Me and Molly 1948,F 27,27:2
Cassel, Jean-Pierre
Idiote, L' 1960,S 16,39:4
Cassel, Milton (Producer)
Making of Moo, The 1958,Je 12,34:1
Electra 1959,F 14,15:1
Harlequinade 1959,F 14,15:1
Cassel, Sid
Fifth Column, The 1940,Mr 7,18:2
Hold On to Your Hats 1940,S 12,30:3
Church Street 1948,F 10,27:2
Summer and Smoke 1948,O 7,33:2
Summer and Smoke 1948,O 17,II,1:1
What Every Woman Knows 1954,D 23,16:2
Cassel, Walter
All in Fun 1940,D 28,11:2
Beggar's Opera, The 1941,Ag 12,14:6
Desert Song, The 1946,Ja 9,20:2
New Moon, The; Desert Song, The 1955,Jl 1,13:1
Casselberry, Horace
Merry-Go-Round 1932,Ap 23,11:2
Hat, a Coat, a Glove, A 1934,F 1,15:2
Late Wisdom 1934,Ap 24,27:4
Judgment Day 1934,S 13,26:4
Battle Hymn 1936,My 23,12:1
Cassell, Milton (Producer)
Cut of the Axe 1960,F 2,38:2
Cassell, Richard
Saint of Bleecker Street, The 1954,D 28,21:1
Cassellberry, George
Salvation 1928,F 1,31:1
Troika 1930,Ap 2,32:6
Casselle, Jeanne
Distant Shore, The 1935,F 22,26:2
Cassen, Jackie (Miscellaneous)
Reincarnation of Christ Show, The 1966,D 4,II,5:1
Cassey, Chuck (Composer)
Holiday on Ice 1965,S 2,38:4

Cassey, Chuck (Miscellaneous)
Holiday on Ice 1966,S 1,30:1
Holiday on Ice 1967,Ag 31,29:2
Holiday on Ice 1968,Ag 29,44:1
Cassidy, David
Fig Leaves Are Falling, The 1969,Ja 3,19:1
Cassidy, Frank (Miscellaneous)
Shadow and Substance 1959,N 4,42:1
Live Like Pigs 1965,Je 8,48:2
Stop, You're Killing Me; Terrible Jim Fitch 1969,Mr 20,53:1
Stop, You're Killing Me; Laughs, Etc 1969,Mr 20,53:1
Stop, You're Killing Me; Bad Bad Jo-Jo 1969,Mr 20,53:1
Cassidy, Jack
Small Wonder 1948,S 16,33:5
Alive and Kicking 1950,Ja 18,25:5
Wish You Were Here 1952,Je 26,26:6
Sandhog 1954,N 24,17:1
Oklahoma! 1955,Je 21,37:7
Oklahoma! 1955,Jl 11,19:7
Shangri-La 1956,Je 14,40:1
Beggar's Opera, The 1957,Mr 14,35:1
She Loves Me 1963,Ap 24,39:1
She Loves Me 1963,My 5,II,1:1
Fade Out--Fade In 1964,My 27,45:1
Fade Out--Fade In 1964,Je 21,II,1:1
It's a Bird . . . It's a Plane . . . It's Superman 1966,Mr 30,34:1
Maggie Flynn 1968,O 24,52:1
Maggie Flynn 1968,N 3,II,1:1
Mundy Scheme, The 1969,D 12,75:1
Cassidy, John
Firebird of Florence 1945,Mr 23,13:4
Cassidy, Martin J
Red Roses for Me 1961,N 28,41:1
Barroom Monks, The 1962,My 29,21:1
Portrait of the Artist as a Young Man, A 1962,My 29,21:1
Cassidy, Martin T
Riverwind 1962,D 14,5:5
Cassidy, Maureen
Ah, Wilderness! 1954,Ag 21,20:4
Cassilly, Richard
Saint of Bleecker Street, The 1954,D 28,21:1
Cassini, Oleg (Costume Designer)
As the Girls Go 1948,N 15,21:2
His and Hers 1954,Ja 8,18:2
Critic's Choice 1960,D 15,61:3
Come on Strong 1962,O 5,29:1
Cassive
Monsieur Qui Se Regrette, Un 1928,D 9,X,2:7
Casson, Ann
Roof, The 1929,N 6,30:4
Roof, The 1929,N 24,X,1:6
Babes in the Zoo 1930,F 26,22:3
Boy David, The 1939,Ag 6,IX,2:1
Jacob 1942,Je 14,VIII,1:7
King John 1960,Je 29,26:2
Romeo and Juliet 1960,Jl 1,14:1
Gondoliers, The 1962,Jl 7,9:4
Tango 1968,Ja 1,11:1
She Stoops to Conquer 1968,Ja 1,11:1
Tempest, The 1970,F 15,67:1
Casson, Christopher
Ding and Company 1934,N 20,24:2
Murder in the Cathedral 1938,F 17,16:2
Lady of the Sea 1945,S 9,II,1:5
Hamlet 1957,O 29,34:2
Casson, Hugh F S
Evensong 1933,F 1,13:4
Casson, Jane
Government Inspector, The 1967,O 28,34:1
Tartuffe 1968,Je 12,39:1
Midsummer Night's Dream, A 1968,Je 13,54:1
Hamlet 1969,Je 11,37:1
Alchemist, The 1969,Je 12,51:1
Merchant of Venice, The 1970,Je 10,39:1
School for Scandal, The 1970,Je 11,51:1
Casson, Lewis
Judith of Israel 1928,Mr 18,IX,4:8
Mariners 1929,My 19,IX,1:8
Exiled 1929,Jl 7,VIII,1:3
Socrates 1930,Ap 13,X,1:6
Bluestone Quarry 1931,N 29,VIII,2:2
Ballerina 1933,O 11,26:3
Ballerina 1933,O 29,IX,1:6
Men in White 1934,Je 29,16:3
Victoria Regina 1935,D 27,15:2
King Lear 1940,Ap 28,IX,1:7
Medea 1941,Ag 3,IX,2:2
Jacob 1942,Je 14,VIII,1:7
Moon Is Down, The 1943,Jl 11,II,1:5
Potting Shed, The 1957,Ja 30,32:1
Potting Shed, The 1957,F 10,II,1:1
Uncle Vanya 1962,Jl 17,18:4
Casson, Lewis (Director)
Medea 1941,Ag 3,IX,2:2
Casson, Lewis (Sir)
Linden Tree, The 1947,S 14,II,3:7
Douglas Once 1950,S 10,II,3:1
Day by the Sea, A 1953,N 27,22:3

Casson, Lewis (Sir)—Cont
Day by the Sea, A 1953,D 20,II,4:2
Family Reunion, The 1956,Je 9,13:6
Untitled-Reading 1957,Ap 17,35:1
Waiting in the Wings 1960,Ag 9,31:4
Casson, Mary
Peter Pan 1928,Ja 15,VIII,4:6
Castaldo, Erne
West Side Story 1957,S 27,14:4
Castaldo, James
Concept, The 1968,My 7,51:1
Castang, Veronica
Trigon, The 1965,O 11,62:2
Castano, Helen
We're All in the Gutter 1927,Mr 5,12:2
Castano, Tony
White Cargo 1960,D 30,12:1
Castanos, Luz
Eternal Sabbath 1963,O 19,17:2
Castanos, Luz (Director)
Cruce de Vias 1969,N 2,86:5
Difunta, La 1969,N 2,86:5
Castel, Nico
Patience 1968,My 16,52:1
Fiesta in Madrid 1969,My 29,49:1
Castella, Bob
Evening With Yves Montand, An 1959,S 23,45:1
Castella, Bob (Miscellaneous)
Evening With Yves Montand, An 1961,O 25,30:1
Castellano, Richard
View From the Bridge, A 1965,Ja 29,24:1
Investigation, The 1966,O 5,40:1
That Summer-That Fall 1967,Mr 17,33:1
Antigone 1967,Je 19,43:1
Macbeth 1967,Jl 31,21:1
Mike Downstairs 1968,Ap 19,35:1
Lovers and Other Strangers 1968,S 19,63:1
Sheep on the Runway 1970,F 2,28:3
Sheep on the Runway 1970,F 8,II,5:5
Castellanos, Julio (Scenic Designer)
Mexicana 1939,Ap 22,14:4
Castelli, Bertrand (Director)
Hair 1969,S 13,30:1
Castelli, Bertrand (Playwright)
Umbrella, The 1965,My 27,31:1
Castelli, Bertrand (Producer)
Hair 1968,Ap 30,40:2
Hair 1970,Ja 13,39:1
Castelli, Victor
Peter and the Wolf 1969,N 30,85:5
Castellini, John (Musical Director)
Dawn's Early Light 1950,O 25,44:3
Castello, Almeda M (Mrs) (Playwright)
One Woman's Husband 1920,Mr 23,9:3
Castello, John
Kiss Me, Kate 1948,D 31,10:3
Kiss Me, Kate 1949,Ja 30,II,6:5
Finian's Rainbow 1953,Mr 7,13:2
Castillo (Costume Designer)
Medea 1947,O 21,27:2
Play's the Thing, The 1948,Ap 29,19:2
Inside U S A 1948,My 1,19:2
Bravo! 1948,N 12,31:2
Ring Around the Moon 1950,N 24,30:1
Tower Beyond Tragedy, The 1950,N 27,29:1
Goldilocks 1958,O 19,II,1:1
Castillo (Miscellaneous)
Present Laughter 1946,O 30,31:2
Castle, Dorene
Mandragola 1958,My 29,23:2
Castle, Gene
Legitimate Steal, The 1958,Ap 1,35:1
Best Foot Forward 1963,Ap 3,43:1
High Spirits 1964,Ap 8,34:1
George M! 1968,Ap 11,48:1
George M! 1968,Ap 21,II,1:5
Castle, Hancey
And Be My Love 1934,Ja 19,25:2
Divided by Three 1934,O 3,24:2
Rain From Heaven 1934,D 25,28:4
Noble Prize, The 1935,Jl 9,24:3
Curse You, Jack Dalton 1935,Jl 16,24:1
All Bow Down 1935,Ag 6,20:4
Touch of Brimstone, A 1935,S 23,20:1
Her Week-End 1936,Mr 20,28:5
Castle, Hubert
Circus-Madison Square Garden 1939,Ap 6,23:5
Castle, Irene
Shadow Play 1939,Ag 15,14:5
Castle, Joann
Collision 1932,F 17,19:2
Castle, John
Georgy 1970,F 15,II,1:1
Georgy 1970,F 27,26:1
Castle, Mae
Bright Star 1935,O 16,26:2
Castle, Nancy
Jane Brady-Editor 1935,Jl 2,24:3
Castle, Nick (Choreographer)
Heaven on Earth 1948,S 17,29:2
Castle, Nick (Director)
Jerry Lewis' Variety Show 1957,F 8,18:5
Castle, Nick (Lyricist)
Heaven on Earth 1948,S 17,29:2

Castle, Paul
Stars on Ice 1942,Jl 3,12:2
Stars on Ice (2d Edition) 1943,Je 25,13:2
Hats Off to Ice 1944,Je 23,15:2
Icetime 1946,Je 21,20:5
Icetime 1947,My 29,28:2
Howdy Mr Ice 1948,Je 25,28:5
Howdy, Mr Ice of 1950 1949,My 27,24:2
Ice Capades 1952,S 12,18:1
Ice Capades 1953,S 11,25:1
Ice Capades 1958,S 4,33:2
Castle, Richard
Dinosaur Wharf 1951,N 9,23:2
Castle, Richard (Director)
Nobody's Child 1956,Ag 23,25:2
Castle, Richard (Producer)
Nobody's Child 1956,Ag 23,25:2
Castle, Roy
Pickwick 1965,O 6,5:3
Castle, William
Torch Bearers, The 1922,Ag 30,10:2
Ebb Tide 1931,Je 9,33:6
No More Frontier 1931,O 22,27:1
Walk With Music 1940,Je 5,33:2
Castle, William (Director)
Meet a Body 1944,O 17,19:5
Star Spangled Family 1945,Ap 11,18:6
Castle, William (Scenic Designer)
Captive, The 1926,S 30,23:1
Squall, The 1926,N 12,20:1
Castle, Yvonne
Happy Valley, Limited 1936,Je 30,15:1
They Knew What They Wanted 1936,Jl 8,14:2
Audition of the Apprentice Theatre 1939,Je 2,26:2
Castleton, Maxine
Student Prince, The 1936,Jl 12,II,5:2
Blossom Time 1936,Jl 29,23:1
Countess Maritza 1936,Ag 19,18:2
Blossom Time 1936,Ag 30,II,5:8
Wonderful Night, A; Fledermaus, Die 1937,Jl 14,17:1
Firefly, The 1937,Ag 4,14:1
Castleton and Mack
Topics of 1923 1923,N 21,23:2
Vaudeville (Palace) 1926,My 11,25:3
Castner, Alan
West Side Story 1968,Je 25,32:1
Foreplay 1970,D 11,58:2
Casto, Jean
All That Glitters 1938,Ja 20,18:2
I Must Love Someone 1939,F 8,18:7
Pal Joey 1940,D 26,22:2
Three Men on a Horse 1942,O 10,10:2
Decision 1944,F 3,23:2
No Way Out 1944,O 31,23:1
Carousel 1945,Ap 20,24:2
Carousel 1945,Ap 29,II,1:1
Small Hours, The 1951,F 16,22:1
Pink Elephant, The 1953,Ap 23,37:2
Castro, Belgian
Remolienda, La; Bawdy Party 1968,F 3,20:1
Castro, Johnny (Miscellaneous)
Walk Down Mah Street! 1968,Je 13,54:1
Castro, Sebastian
Cabalgata 1949,Jl 8,14:2
Castro-Lopez, Albert (Scenic Designer)
Step a Little Closer 1948,My 28,26:6
Catal, Frank
Let's Make an Opera 1950,D 14,50:2
Catal, Henrietta
Enchanted, The 1950,Ja 19,34:2
Catalini
Vaudeville (Palace) 1928,Ja 10,28:5
Cataly, Ralph
Roof, The 1931,O 31,22:4
Catania, Fred
Fifth Column, The 1940,Mr 7,18:2
Johnny 2X4 1942,Mr 17,24:6
Lady Says Yes, A 1945,Ja 11,18:5
Diamond Lil 1948,N 30,33:2
Cates, Barney
Heartbreak House 1950,Mr 22,33:2
Cates, Gilbert (Producer)
You Know I Can't Hear You When the Water's Running; I'll Be Home for Christmas 1967,Mr 14,54:1
You Know I Can't Hear You When the Water's Running; Footsteps of Doves, The 1967,Mr 14,54:1
You Know I Can't Hear You When the Water's Running; I'm Herbert 1967,Mr 14,54:1
You Know I Can't Hear You When the Water's Running; Shock of Recognition, The 1967,Mr 14,54:1
I Never Sang for My Father 1968,Ja 26,30:1
Dr Fish 1970,Mr 11,42:2
Chinese, The 1970,Mr 11,42:2
Cates, John M Jr
Hippolytus 1935,Je 15,20:4
Cates, Joseph (Producer)
Spoon River Anthology 1963,S 30,23:2
What Makes Sammy Run? 1964,F 28,19:1
Joe Egg 1968,F 2,26:1

Cates, Joseph (Producer)—Cont
Her First Roman 1968,O 21,53:3
Gantry 1970,F 16,44:1
Cates, Madlyn
Sunset 1966,My 13,34:1
Kitchen, The 1966,Je 14,50:1
Persecution and Assassination of Marat As Performed by the Inmates of the Asylum of Charenton Under the Direction of the Marquis de Sade, The 1967,Ja 4,34:1
Patriot for Me, A 1969,O 6,58:1
Cates, Norma
Big Knife, The 1959,N 13,25:1
Cathcart, Countess
Ashes of Love 1926,Mr 16,23:1
Ashes of Love 1926,Mr 23,24:3
Cathcart, Countess (Playwright)
Ashes of Love 1926,Mr 16,23:1
Ashes of Love 1926,Mr 23,24:3
Cathcart, Jack (Miscellaneous)
Judy Garland's New Variety Show 1956,S 27,43:2
Cathie, Philip (Composer)
Wandering Jew, The 1927,F 2,22:4
Cathren, Cliff
Devil's Disciple, The 1950,Ja 26,23:2
Cathrey, George
What Every Woman Knows 1954,D 23,16:2
Catlett, Mary Jo
Along Came a Spider 1963,My 28,33:1
Hello, Dolly! 1964,Ja 17,22:1
Canterbury Tales; Wife of Bath's Tale, The 1969,F 4,34:1
Greenwillow 1970,D 8,60:1
Catlett, Sid
Concert Varieties 1945,Je 2,10:7
Catlett, Walter
Sally 1920,D 22,16:1
Dear Sir 1924,S 24,21:3
Lady Be Good 1924,D 2,23:4
Lady Be Good 1924,D 28,VII,1:1
Lambs Gambol 1925,Ap 27,15:1
Lucky 1927,Mr 23,28:3
Treasure Girl 1928,N 9,22:1
Catlett, Walter (Playwright)
Irving Berlin's New Music Box Revue 1922,O 24,18:1
Catlin, Don
Sweethearts 1929,S 23,25:1
Babes in Toyland 1929,D 24,15:3
Catlin, Paul
Merry Widow, The 1929,D 3,29:1
Catlin, Shirley
King Lear 1950,Ag 30,26:2
Cato, Bob (Miscellaneous)
Gertrude Stein's First Reader 1969,D 16,56:1
Cato, Minto
Lew Leslie's Blackbirds of 1930 1930,O 23,34:5
John Henry 1939,D 17,IX,5:6
John Henry 1940,Ja 11,18:2
Caton, Edward (Choreographer)
Sadie Thompson 1944,N 17,25:2
Nellie Bly 1946,Ja 22,32:2
Dybbuk, The 1954,O 27,33:6
Caton, Ray (Lighting Director)
Solo 1962,Ap 27,26:1
Catron, Arthur
Babes in Arms 1951,Mr 10,7:3
Catron, Stanley
Babes in Arms !951,Mr 10,7:3
Catsileros, E
Oedipus Tyrannus 1952,N 25,35:2
Cattand, Gabriel
Proces, Le; Trial, The 1952,N 18,36:2
Fourberies de Scapin, Les 1952,N 21,21:2
Occupe-Toi d'Amelie; Keep Your Eyes on Amelie 1952,N 25,35:2
Hamlet 1952,D 2,39:1
Volpone 1957,F 5,27:2
Misanthrope, Le 1957,F 8,19:1
Nuits de La Colere, Les; Nights of Fury 1957,F 12,31:1
Chien du Jardinier, Le; Gardener's Dog, The 1957,F 19,36:1
Adieux, Les 1957,F 19,36:1
Cattell, Irene
Fast Life 1928,S 27,35:2
Wild Waves 1932,F 20,11:4
Another Language 1932,Ap 26,25:3
Hipper's Holiday 1934,O 19,26:2
Loose Moments 1935,F 5,22:3
Whatever Goes Up 1935,N 26,28:2
Tide Rising 1937,Ja 26,17:2
Excursion 1937,Ap 10,11:4
Escape This Night 1938,Ap 23,18:1
Catto, Max (Playwright)
Green Waters 1936,N 5,34:4
They Walk Alone 1939,F 5,IX,3:2
Punch Without Judy 1939,D 17,IX,4:3
They Walk Alone 1941,Mr 13,24:2
Catusi, James
Mother Courage and Her Children 1963,Mr 30,5:5
Cuba Si 1968,D 10,53:1
Catusi, James (Miscellaneous)
Hay Fever 1970,N 10,55:1

Catusi, Larry (Miscellaneous)
Bench, The 1968,Mr 5,35:2
Caubaye, Suzanne
Easy Terms 1925,S 23,22:2
Squall, The 1926,N 12,20:1
Ringside 1928,Ag 30,13:2
Seven 1929,D 28,10:5
Plutocrat, The 1930,F 21,23:3
Dancing Partner 1930,Jl 27,VIII,2:3
Dancing Partner 1930,Ag 6,24:2
Great Barrington, The 1931,F 20,18:1
Angeline Moves In 1932,Ap 20,27:5
Singapore 1932,N 15,24:2
Monster, The 1933,F 11,11:5
Another Love 1934,Mr 20,26:3
Broadway Interlude 1934,Ap 20,16:3
Symphony 1935,Ap 27,20:3
American Holiday 1936,F 22,13:3
Sun and I, The 1937,F 27,9:5
It's A Gift 1945,Mr 13,18:7
Mid-Summer 1953,Ja 22,19:1
Caubisens, Henri (Miscellaneous)
Most Happy Fella, The 1956,My 4,20:1
Music Man, The 1957,D 20,31:1
Happiest Girl in the World, The 1961,Ap 4,42:1
Case of Libel, A 1963,O 11,43:2
Pousse-Cafe 1966,Mr 19,19:2
Cauble, Rebekah
Tangerine 1921,Ag 10,8:2
Oh! Oh! Nurse 1925,D 8,28:4
Caudy, Douglas
Rosalinda; Fledermaus, Die 1942,O 29,26:5
Cauldwell, Brendan
Devil Came From Dublin, The! 1955,Je 3,27:2
Cauley, Harry (Playwright)
Paisley Convertible, The 1967,F 13,42:1
Caulfield, Betty
Tenting Tonight 1947,Ap 3,32:2
I Know My Love 1949,F 24,29:2
I Know My Love 1949,N 3,36:1
Caulfield, Edward (Playwright)
There's Always a Breeze 1938,Mr 3,16:2
And Be My Love 1945,F 22,30:4
Bruno and Sidney 1949,My 4,38:2
Caulfield, Joan
Beat the Band 1942,O 15,26:1
Kiss and Tell 1943,Mr 18,22:1
Kiss and Tell 1943,Mr 28,II,1:1
Caulkins, Ogaenia
Throng o' Scarlet 1950,F 6,20:5
Caulkins, Thomas V
Little Theatre Tournament; Sightseers 1929,My 8,34:4
Caully, Zachary
Nina Rosa 1930,S 22,22:5
Down to Miami 1944,S 12,23:5
Caunter, Tony
Chips With Everything 1963,O 2,49:1
Caupolican, Chief
Whoopee 1928,D 5,34:3
Causey, Alan
Macbeth 1967,Jl 31,21:1
Causey, Elwin
Long Gallery, The 1958,Mr 7,17:2
Man Who Never Died, The 1958,N 22,27:2
Orpheus Descending 1959,O 6,45:2
Causland, Chauncey
Squaw Man, The 1921,D 27,10:3
Puppets of Passion 1927,F 25,24:4
Caute, David (Playwright)
Demonstration, The 1969,N 20,60:1
Cauthen, Dona
Point of No Return 1957,Mr 23,17:2
Cautna, Bertha
No Mother to Guide Her 1933,D 26,18:5
Cautna, Leila
No Mother to Guide Her 1933,D 26,18:5
Cavallaro, Gaylord
Teahouse of the August Moon, The 1955,My 10,24:1
Cavallaro, Joe Jr (Producer)
Salvage 1957,Ap 10,39:2
Cavallaro, Michael
Can-Can 1953,My 8,28:1
Cavalli, Katherine
Drift 1925,N 25,15:3
Cavalli, Rina
Sweeney Todd 1924,Jl 19,10:4
Cavallo, Robert M (Producer)
Burning Bright 1959,O 17,27:2
Ignorants Abroad, The 1960,My 24,43:2
Cavallotti, Felice (Playwright)
Cantico dei Cantici, Il; Song of Songs 1931,Ap 13,17:3
Cantico dei Cantici, Il; Song of Songs 1931,My 18,21:4
Cavanagh, Edward
Birds, The 1967,My 7,67:1
Cavanagh, Maura (Producer)
Poker Session, The 1967,S 20,42:2
Cavanagh, Paul
Scotland Yard 1929,S 28,16:6

King's Leisure, The 1936,My 31,II,6:8
Cavanaugh, Alice
Lilies of the Field 1921,O 5,20:1
Sue, Dear 1922,Jl 11,16:2
Flossie 1924,Je 4,25:2
On the Make 1932,My 24,23:2
Woman of Destiny, A 1936,Mr 3,25:2
Cavanaugh, Bernard
Bye Bye Bonnie 1927,Ja 14,15:3
Cavanaugh, Evelyn
My Golden Girl 1920,F 3,18:2
Love Birds 1921,Mr 16,12:1
Wildflower 1923,F 8,17:2
Dew Drop Inn 1923,My 18,26:4
Girl Friend, The 1926,Mr 18,26:5
Cavanaugh, Hobart
Nervous Wreck, The 1923,O 10,16:1
Her Way Out 1924,Je 24,18:3
Sunshine 1926,Ag 18,15:2
Kibitzer, The 1929,F 19,22:5
Remote Control 1929,S 11,24:5
Remote Control 1929,S 22,IX,1:1
Made in France 1930,N 12,21:1
Man on Stilts, The 1931,S 10,23:2
Hot Money 1931,N 9,22:2
Bulls, Bears and Asses 1932,My 7,11:3
Tell Her the Truth 1932,O 29,18:2
Sweet Mystery of Life 1935,O 12,13:3
As the Girls Go 1948,N 15,21:2
Cavanaugh, Jeff
Lower Depths, The 1956,O 3,29:2
Cavanaugh, Jerry
Blue and the Gray, The; War Is Hell Gray, The 1929,D 27,26:4
Cavanaugh, John J
What Price Glory 1924,S 6,14:3
Cavanaugh, Ruth
Let Freedom Sing 1942,O 6,18:2
Cavanaugh, Slim
Buckaroo 1929,Mr 18,31:1
Cavander, Kenneth (Lyricist)
Story Theater Repertory; Saint Julian the Hospitaler 1970,O 21,40:1
Cavander, Kenneth (Playwright)
Metamorphoses 1969,D 12,69:1
Don Juan 1970,My 26,32:1
Cops and Horrors; Fly Paper 1970,Ag 11,27:1
Cops and Horrors; Dracula 1970,Ag 11,27:1
Story Theater Repertory; Saint Julian the Hospitaler 1970,O 21,40:1
Cavander, Kenneth (Scenic Designer)
Bacchae, The 1969,Mr 23,II,11:1
Cavander, Kenneth (Translator)
Bacchae, The 1969,Mr 15,24:1
Don Juan 1970,My 31,II,1:6
Alice in Wonderland 1970,O 9,43:1
Cave, Ted
Gay Blades 1937,N 12,26:6
Gay Blades 1937,N 16,27:1
Cavell, Butch
My Heart's in the Highlands 1949,N 22,36:7
My Heart's in the Highlands 1950,F 18,8:4
Cavell, Dallas
Chips With Everything 1963,O 2,49:1
Cavell, Gerald
Natural Affection 1963,F 2,5:2
Cavell, Maurice
Duchess of Malfi, The 1946,O 16,35:2
Cavell, Miriam
Countess Maritza 1936,Ag 19,18:2
Cavell, Rudolph
Oedipus 1946,My 21,19:2
Fundamental George, The 1949,Ag 17,19:4
Cavell, Sonny
Topaze 1947,D 29,21:5
City of Kings 1949,F 18,27:2
My Heart's in the Highlands 1950,F 18,8:4
Caveness, Pamela
Show Boat 1948,S 9,33:2
Cavens, Albert
Cyrano de Bergerac 1968,Ap 26,30:1
Cavens, Albert (Miscellaneous)
Cyrano de Bergerac 1968,Ap 26,30:1
Caverly, Carol
Ice Follies 1959,Ja 14,30:1
Ice Follies 1960,Ja 13,20:1
Ice Follies 1961,Ja 11,25:2
Ice Follies 1962,Ja 10,24:6
Cavett, Frank Morgan (Playwright)
Forsaking All Others 1933,Mr 2,21:2
Cavey, George
Shoemaker's Holiday, The 1967,Mr 3,25:1
Ben Bagley's Shoestring Revues 1970,O 24,22:1
Cavey, George (Miscellaneous)
Bohikee Creek 1966,Ap 29,39:1
My Wife and I 1966,O 11,53:2
Cavic, Dejan
Ubu Roi 1968,Je 29,20:1
Cawley, Agnes
Patience 1929,D 16,34:5
Cawthorn, Joseph
Half-Moon, The 1920,N 2,15:2

Cawthorn, Joseph—Cont
Blue Kitten, The 1922,Ja 14,9:3
Bunch and Judy, The 1922,N 12,VIII,1:6
Sunny 1925,S 23,22:1
Cawthorne, Herbert
Lambs Gambol 1925,Ap 27,15:1
Cawthorne, Wilfrid
Young Visitors, The 1920,N 30,14:1
Cayley, George
Everyman 1953,O 12,30:2
Caylor, Rose (Playwright)
Man-Eating Tiger, The 1927,S 25,VIII,4:8
Uncle Vanya 1930,Ap 16,26:5
Uncle Vanya 1930,My 4,XI,1:1
Caymmi, Dorival (Composer)
Star and Garter 1942,Je 25,26:2
Caymmi, Dorival (Lyricist)
Star and Garter 1942,Je 25,26:2
Cayroi, Soiago (Mme)
Taming of the Shrew, The 1924,N 25,27:3
Cayrol, Solange (Mme)
Homme Qui Assassina, L' 1924,N 11,20:1
Homme et Ses Fantomes, L' 1924,N 14,16:1
Merchant of Venice, The 1924,N 18,23:2
Cazale, John
Indian Wants the Bronx, The 1968,Ja 18,47:2
Country People 1970,Ja 19,35:1
Cazalet, Joseph
Volpone 1967,Je 30,29:1
Cazelle, Florence
Sweethearts 1929,S 23,25:1
Ce, Camille (Playwright)
Boucheur N'Est Pas de ce Monde, Le 1926,D 26,VII,2:1
Ceballos, Larry (Choreographer)
Merry World, The 1926,Je 9,18:3
Ceballos, Larry (Miscellaneous)
Fifty Million Frenchmen 1929,N 28,34:4
Cebron, Jean
Lotte Goslar's Pantomime Circus-For Humans Only 1957,D 17,45:1
Cebron-Norbens (Mme)
Ca. . . C'Est Paris 1927,F 6,VII,4:1
Cecala, Dominick
Matty and the Moron and Madonna 1965,Mr 30,53:1
Cecchini, A
Tristi Amori; Unhappy Loves 1930,O 27,17:6
Cena Delle Beffe, La; Jest, The 1930,N 24,26:4
Cecchini, Gustavo
Signori, Il Figlio E' Nato 1935,Je 8,13:7
Cecil, Ernest (Playwright)
As a Matter of Fact 1921,My 29,VI,1:7
Cecil, Henry (Playwright)
Settled Out of Court 1960,O 20,44:4
Cecil, Lawrence
Macbeth 1921,F 18,16:1
Hamlet 1922,N 17,14:1
King Lear 1923,Mr 10,9:4
March Hares 1923,Mr 13,19:5
Devil's Disciple, The 1923,Ap 24,24:1
Hamlet 1923,N 27,23:6
Macbeth 1924,Mr 17,18:1
S S Glencairn 1924,N 4,31:4
Caesar and Cleopatra 1925,Ap 14,27:1
Grand Duchess and the Waiter, The 1925,O 14,31:1
Henry IV, Part I 1926,Je 1,29:1
Julius Caesar 1927,Je 7,27:2
Blood Money 1927,Ag 23,29:2
Merry Wives of Windsor, The 1928,Mr 20,20:1
Falstaff 1928,D 26,14:2
Freddy 1929,Jl 17,23:4
Julius Caesar 1929,N 19,26:5
Hamlet 1930,Mr 25,34:4
Macbeth 1930,Mr 26,24:6
Twelfth Night 1930,Mr 27,24:7
Merchant of Venice, The 1930,Mr 27,24:7
Taming of the Shrew, The 1930,Mr 28,22:8
Richard III 1930,Mr 31,24:1
King Lear 1930,Ap 1,34:6
As You Like It 1930,Ap 3,32:5
Julius Caesar 1930,Ap 4,22:3
King Lear 1930,D 26,18:2
Fatal Alibi, The 1932,F 10,26:6
Cecil, Lawrence (Director)
Legend of Leonora, The 1926,My 1,10:1
Knight of the Burning Pestle, The 1927,Ap 23,15:1
King Lear 1930,D 26,18:2
Cecil, Mary
Rubicon, The 1922,F 22,13:1
Scaramouche 1923,O 25,14:2
Maggie, the Magnificent 1929,O 22,26:1
Women, The 1936,D 28,13:1
Man Who Came to Dinner, The 1940,F 10,19:5
Cecil, Ron
Almost Crazy 1955,Je 21,37:1
Vamp, The 1955,N 11,30:1
Cecil, Sylvia
Mikado, The 1936,Ag 21,13:2
Gondoliers, The 1936,S 8,23:1
Yeomen of the Guard, The 1936,S 15,37:2
H M S Pinafore 1936,S 29,34:2
Patience 1936,O 6,28:6

Cecil, Sylvia—Cont
Princess Ida 1936,O 13,32:2
Cecil and Kaye
Will Morrissey's Newcomers 1923,Ag 9,16:2
Topics of 1923 1923,N 21,23:2
Cecil Mack's Choir
Rhapsody in Black 1931,My 5,33:2
Blackbirds 1933,D 4,22:3
Ceeley, Leonard
Lollipop 1924,Ja 22,15:3
My Princess 1927,O 7,24:2
Cafe de Danse 1929,Ja 16,22:2
Great Day! 1929,O 18,24:3
Nina Rosa 1929,O 27,IX,2:1
Nina Rosa 1930,My 31,19:3
Nina Rosa 1930,S 22,22:5
Marching By 1931,N 15,VIII,4:2
Marching By 1932,Mr 4,17:1
Beau Brummell 1933,Ag 9,20:6
Bitter Sweet 1934,My 8,28:4
Celada, Raul
Look, Ma, I'm Dancin' 1948,Ja 30,20:2
Look, Ma, I'm Dancin' 1948,F 8,II,2:1
Celeste, Mona
Greenwich Village Follies 1920,Ag 31,7:3
Celestin, Jack (Original Author)
Silent Witness, The 1931,My 10,VIII,3:5
Celestin, Jack (Playwright)
Silent Witness, The 1931,F 22,VIII,4:4
Silent Witness, The 1931,Mr 24,31:5
Line Engaged 1934,O 25,28:5
Cellier, Albert (Composer)
Mountebanks, The 1955,D 2,32:3
Cellier, Antoinette
Firebird 1932,S 25,IX,1:3
Bellairs 1933,Ap 23,X,1:3
Birthday 1934,D 27,24:2
Fight's On, The; Uneasy Virtue; Pardon My Back
  1937,Ag 4,14:1
Cellier, Frank
Mozart 1926,N 23,26:2
Marquise, The 1927,Mr 20,VIII,2:7
Good Morning, Bill! 1927,D 25,VIII,1:4
Fourth Wall, The 1928,Mr 25,IX,1:3
Lord of the Manor, The 1928,O 14,X,2:1
Rising Sun, The 1929,O 27,IX,2:2
School for Scandal, The 1929,D 15,X,4:2
Bellairs 1933,Ap 23,X,1:3
Inside the Room 1934,D 23,15:3
Mask of Virtue, The 1935,My 16,20:1
Mask of Virtue, The 1935,Je 9,IX,1:1
Espionage 1935,N 10,IX,3:1
Cellier, Frank (Producer)
School for Scandal, The 1929,D 15,X,4:2
Cellier, Marguerite
Marigold 1930,O 9,23:1
Cellier, Peter
Lark, The 1955,My 13,21:2
Twelfth Night 1958,D 10,54:2
Hamlet 1958,D 17,2:7
Henry V 1958,D 26,2:7
Cellini, Enrico
Horse Eats Hat 1936,S 28,14:2
Celtic Players
Deirdre of the Sorrows 1920,S 26,VI,1:4
Center, Susan
Volpone 1948,Ja 9,24:6
On the Harmfulness of Tobacco 1948,F 6,29:2
Tragedian in Spite of Himself, A 1948,F 6,29:2
Bear, The 1948,F 6,29:2
Wedding, The 1948,F 6,29:2
Centurier, Albert (Playwright)
Ecole des Charlatans, L' 1930,Ap 27,IX,2:1
Ceough, Richard
Candida 1925,D 19,14:2
Dear Brutus 1926,Jl 15,21:3
Ship, The 1929,N 21,24:7
Magic 1929,D 17,28:5
Seven Keys to Baldpate 1930,Ja 8,25:2
Cephas, Willanna (Costume Designer)
Sojourner Truth 1948,Ap 22,35:2
Cerdan, Esteban
Noble Rogue, A 1929,Ag 20,31:2
Cerf, Bettina
Leave Her to Heaven 1940,F 28,16:2
Susannah and the Elders 1940,O 30,28:2
Nathan the Wise 1942,Mr 12,25:4
Nathan the Wise 1942,Ap 4,18:4
Embezzled Heaven 1944,N 1,20:2
Cerf, Elizabeth
Richard of Bordeaux 1934,F 15,16:2
Cerf, Kurt
Too Late the Phalarope 1956,O 12,35:1
Cerf, Kurt (Director)
All by Myself 1964,Je 16,47:1
Cern, Jules
Penny Arcade 1930,Mr 11,24:5
Cernik, Lud (Producer)
Magistrate, The 1959,My 14,30:6
Cernovich, Nicola (Director)
Bertha 1962,F 12,27:1
Cernovich, Nicola (Lighting Director)
Bald Soprano, The 1958,Je 4,39:2

Jack 1958,Je 4,39:2
Ulysses in Nighttown 1958,Je 6,30:1
Many Loves 1959,Ja 14,28:1
Saintliness of Margery Kempe, The 1959,F 3,35:6
Royal Gambit 1959,Mr 5,34:2
Geranium Hat, The 1959,Mr 18,45:1
Cave at Machpelah, The 1959,Jl 1,25:1
Connection, The 1959,Jl 16,30:2
Tonight We Improvise 1959,N 7,27:4
Ronde, La 1960,My 10,44:2
Women of Trachis 1960,Je 23,18:3
Marrying Maiden, The 1960,Je 23,18:3
Herne's Egg, The 1960,S 20,48:1
Purgatory 1960,S 20,48:1
Full Moon in March, A 1960,S 20,48:1
In the Jungle of Cities 1960,D 21,39:1
Red Eye of Love 1961,Je 13,28:1
Apple, The 1961,D 8,44:1
Don Carlos 1962,F 28,27:5
Man Is Man 1962,S 19,31:1
Firebugs, The 1963,F 13,7:2
Brig, The 1963,My 16,40:1
Trumpets of the Lord 1963,D 23,22:3
Home Movies 1964,My 12,32:1
Softly, and Consider the Nearness 1964,My 12,32:1
Cerro, Enrique
Don Juan Tenorio 1953,N 20,18:5
Cervantes, Miguel de (Original Author)
Sancho Panza 1923,D 2,VIII,1:1
Sancho's Master 1927,Ap 10,VIII,4:7
Man of La Mancha 1966,O 5,42:5
Cervantes, Miguel de (Playwright)
Cave of Salamanca, The 1930,Mr 25,34:6
Numance 1937,Je 13,XI,2:1
Siege of Numancia 1966,O 5,42:5
Cesaire, Aime (Playwright)
Saison au Congo, Une 1967,D 3,II,10:6
Cessna, Bob
Beyond the Fringe, '65 1964,D 16,49:2
Let Them Down, Gently; On Vacation
  1968,Ja 31,28:2
Cetrulo, Dean
Cyrano de Bergerac 1953,N 13,24:3
Chabannes, Jacques (Playwright)
Pelerin Sentimental, Le 1930,N 23,IX,1:1
Voyage Circulaire 1934,D 2,X,2:1
Chabot, Roland
Paradise 1931,My 12,29:2
Chabrier, Marcel
Homme Qui Assassina, L' 1924,N 11,20:1
Procureur Hallers, Le 1924,N 13,18:1
Merchant of Venice, The 1924,N 18,23:2
Bourgeois Gentilhomme, Le 1924,N 20,21:2
Odeon-Revue 1927,My 22,VIII,2:7
Chabrol, Jean Pierre (Original Author)
Shock Troops 1969,F 22,36:1
Chace, Dorothy
Three Men on a Horse 1969,O 17,35:1
Chace, John (Director)
Neighbors 1969,Ja 15,38:2
Chace, Pierre
Masque of the Kings, The 1937,F 9,19:4
Chadbourn, Alfred (Miscellaneous)
Hamlet 1957,Ja 29,27:1
Chadler, Miss
Constant Nymph, The 1926,D 19,VII,3:1
Chadman, Christopher
Billy 1969,Mr 24,56:1
Rothschilds, The 1970,O 20,40:1
Chadwell, Wallace
That Lady 1949,N 23,18:4
Chadwick, Cyril
Three Live Ghosts 1920,S 30,12:1
Richard of Bordeaux 1934,F 15,16:2
Geraniums in My Window 1934,O 27,20:6
Music Hath Charms 1934,D 31,8:2
Chadwick, Gordon (Playwright)
Take It Away 1936,D 15,30:5
Take It Away 1936,D 22,32:3
Chadwick, Gordon (Scenic Designer)
What a Relief 1935,D 14,10:6
Take It Away 1936,D 15,30:5
Take It Away 1936,D 22,32:3
Chadwick, Ida May
Vaudeville (Palace) 1923,O 23,18:2
Paradise Alley 1924,Ap 2,17:3
Vaudeville (Palace) 1926,Ag 24,19:3
Chadwick, Thomas
Sweet Adeline 1929,S 4,33:1
East Wind 1931,O 28,19:1
Chadziskos, Nikolaos
Medea 1964,S 1,31:1
Electra 1964,S 8,33:1
Chaffee, George
Helen Goes to Troy 1944,Ap 25,17:2
Chaffee, Louise
Crab Apple 1936,Jl 8,14:2
Stage Door 1936,O 23,26:3
Chaffee, W H
Tiger Smiles, The 1930,D 18,29:1
Chaffey, Don (Director)
Twist of Sand, A 1969,F 22,36:1

Chaffin, Edward
Blue Blood 1924,Ap 3,21:2
Chaffin, H Lawson
Bronx Express 1922,Ap 27,12:2
Chagnon, Pierre (Composer)
Ca. . . C'Est Paris 1927,F 6,VII,4:1
Chagrin, Claude (Choreographer)
Royal Hunt of the Sun, The 1964,Jl 8,40:6
Chagrin, Claude (Miscellaneous)
Royal Hunt of the Sun, The 1965,O 27,36:2
Chaifetz, Vladimir (Costume Designer)
Wandering Stars 1966,N 14,52:2
Chaiken, Fay
Persecution and Assassination of Marat As
  Performed by the Inmates of the Asylum of
  Charenton Under the Direction of the Marquis de
  Sade, The 1967,Ja 4,34:1
Chaikin, Joseph
Dark of the Moon 1958,F 27,22:2
Cave at Machpelah, The 1959,Jl 1,25:1
Tonight We Improvise 1959,N 7,27:4
Escurial 1960,Jl 22,13:1
Santa Claus 1960,Jl 22,13:1
Calvary 1960,Jl 22,13:1
Mountain Giants, The 1961,Ap 5,32:3
Man Is Man 1962,S 19,31:1
New Tenant, The 1964,My 28,40:2
Victims of Duty 1964,My 28,40:2
Sing to Me Through Open Windows
  1965,Mr 16,45:1
Exception and the Rule, The 1965,My 21,19:1
Exception and the Rule, The 1965,Je 6,II,1:1
Endgame 1970,My 6,47:1
Chaikin, Joseph (Director)
Motel 1966,N 7,66:1
TV 1966,N 7,66:1
Interview 1966,N 7,66:1
America Hurrah; Interview; TV; Motel
  1967,Ag 13,II,3:6
America Hurrah; Interview; TV; Motel
  1967,O 10,55:2
Terminal 1970,Ap 15,51:2
Terminal 1970,My 24,II,3:1
Serpent, The 1970,Je 2,35:1
Chaikin, Joseph (Playwright)
Serpent, The 1969,F 9,II,1:4
Chaikin, Shami
Viet Rock 1966,N 11,38:1
America Hurrah; Interview; TV; Motel
  1967,O 10,55:2
Terminal 1970,Ap 15,51:2
Serpent, The 1970,Je 2,35:1
Chailee, J T
Pietro 1920,Ja 20,10:2
Chain, Del
Sun-Kist 1921,My 24,20:2
Vaudeville (Palace) 1923,Ja 23,18:2
Chain and Archer
Vaudeville (Palace) 1927,O 18,32:4
Chaine, Pierre (Playwright)
Au Rat Mort, Cabinet No 6 1923,O 16,18:1
Padre, The 1926,D 28,16:3
Heure H, L' 1936,My 31,X,2:1
Chakraband (Lyricist)
Peep Show 1950,Je 7,34:5
Chakrin, Jack
Trojan Horse, The 1940,O 31,28:3
Chalazzi, Gino (Playwright)
Canto Della Vita, Il; Song of Life, The
  1932,Ap 4,13:3
Chalez, Leo
Time of Your Life, The 1940,S 24,27:2
Chalfant, Lucille
All-Star Jamboree 1921,Jl 14,18:1
Greenwich Village Follies 1922,S 13,18:2
Chalfen, Morris (Producer)
Holiday on Ice 1965,S 2,38:4
Holiday on Ice 1966,S 1,30:1
Holiday on Ice 1967,Ag 31,29:2
Holiday on Ice 1968,Ag 29,44:1
Holiday on Ice 1969,Ag 28,44:1
Moscow Circus on Ice 1970,D 9,63:1
Chaliapin, Feodor
Gentleman From Athens, The 1947,D 10,42:4
Now I Lay Me Down to Sleep 1949,Jl 23,7:3
Chaliapin, Lydia
Continental Varieties 1934,O 4,18:3
Chalif, Louis H (Choreographer)
Midsummer Night's Dream, A 1932,Jl 13,15:1
O'Flynn, The 1934,D 28,24:1
Chalkley, Ann
King Lear 1947,F 19,32:2
As You Like It 1947,F 21,16:2
Challee, William
Moon Is a Gong, The 1926,Mr 13,21:3
Rapid Transit 1927,Ap 8,21:2
Prisoner, The 1927,D 30,22:2
Hot Pan 1928,F 16,14:1
Faust 1928,O 9,34:1
Three 1928,D 4,28:2
Judas 1929,Ja 25,20:4
Earth Between, The 1929,Mr 6,33:1
Sea Gull, The 1929,Ap 10,32:2

Challee, William—Cont

Red Rust 1929,D 18,31:1
Inspector General, The 1930,D 24,19:2
House of Connelly, The 1931,S 29,22:4
Wonder Boy 1931,O 24,20:1
1931 1931,D 11,34:3
Night Over Taos 1932,Mr 10,25:3
Success Story 1932,S 27,24:4
Men in White 1933,S 27,24:2
Waiting for Lefty 1935,F 11,14:5
Panic 1935,Mr 16,18:4
Till the Day I Die 1935,Mr 27,24:5
Waiting for Lefty 1935,Mr 27,24:5
Paradise Lost 1935,D 10,31:5
Case of Clyde Griffiths 1936,Mr 14,10:4
Wild Duck, The 1938,Ap 16,16:5
Rocket to the Moon 1938,N 25,18:2
Awake and Sing! 1939,Mr 8,18:2
Key Largo 1939,N 28,30:2
First Stop to Heaven 1941,Ja 6,10:7
Across the Board on Tomorrow Morning 1942,Ag 18,17:1

Challee, William (Director)
One-Act Plays of the Sea; Bound East for Cardiff 1937,O 30,23:2
One-Act Plays of the Sea; In the Zone 1937,O 30,23:2
One-Act Plays of the Sea; Long Voyage Home, The 1937,O 30,23:2
One-Act Plays of the Sea; Moon of the Caribbees 1937,O 30,23:2

Challenger, Rudy
Tiger Tiger Burning Bright 1962,D 24,5:2
Along Came a Spider 1963,My 28,33:1

Challenor, Bromley
Three's a Crowd 1923,F 4,VII,1:4

Challis, Bennett
Aiglon, L' 1934,N 5,22:2
Eternal Road, The 1937,Ja 8,14:2

Challis, Stan
Joan of Lorraine 1955,Mr 26,12:2

Chalmers, Arthur H (Playwright)
Taken From Life 1938,Ja 29,34:4

Chalmers, Brian
Around the World in 80 Days 1964,Je 29,33:2

Chalmers, Keith
Bachelor Born 1938,Ag 17,23:1

Chalmers, Lionel
Yankee Princess, The 1922,O 3,22:1
Sweet Nell of Old Drury 1923,My 19,16:4

Chalmers, Nancy
Veils 1928,Mr 14,28:5

Chalmers, Thomas
Living Mask, The 1924,Ja 22,15:1
Wild Duck, The 1925,F 25,16:4
Bit o' Love, A 1925,My 13,24:2
Call of Life, The 1925,O 10,10:1
Morals 1925,D 1,22:2
Love 'Em and Leave 'Em 1926,F 4,20:4
Henry IV, Part I 1926,Je 1,29:1
Humble, The 1926,O 14,22:2
Beyond the Horizon 1926,D 1,24:2
Heaven-Tappers, The 1927,Mr 9,28:3
Julius Caesar 1927,Je 7,27:2
Mourning Becomes Electra; Homecoming 1931,O 27,22:1
Mourning Becomes Electra; Hunted, The 1931,O 27,22:1
Far Away Horses 1933,Mr 22,21:6
Uncle Tom's Cabin 1933,My 30,13:4
Oliver Oliver 1934,Ja 6,18:5
Ragged Army 1934,F 27,16:5
Mother Lode 1934,D 24,16:5
Kind Lady 1935,Ap 24,24:5
If This Be Treason 1935,S 24,28:2
Eternal Road, The 1937,Ja 8,14:2
Antony and Cleopatra 1937,N 11,30:2
Western Waters 1937,D 29,17:1
Outward Bound 1938,D 23,16:5
Morning's at Seven 1939,N 7,30:2
Morning's at Seven 1939,D 1,26:2
Love for Love 1940,Je 4,19:5
Visitor, The 1944,O 18,24:5
Live Life Again 1945,O 1,14:7
Hamlet 1945,D 14,25:2
Hamlet 1945,D 23,II,3:1
Bathsheba 1947,Mr 27,40:2
Death of a Salesman 1949,F 11,27:2
Remarkable Mr Pennypacker, The 1953,D 31,11:2
Bad Seed, The 1954,D 9,42:1
All the Way Home 1960,D 1,42:1

Chalzel, Leo
Jubilee 1935,O 14,20:1
Forbidden Melody 1936,N 3,33:1
Othello 1937,Ja 7,16:4
Idiot's Delight 1937,Ag 10,22:7
Hooray for What! 1937,D 2,32:5
Waltz in Goose Step 1938,N 2,26:2
Here Come the Clowns 1938,D 8,36:2
Close Quarters 1939,Mr 7,19:2
My Dear Children 1939,Mr 25,19:6
My Dear Children 1940,F 1,16:2
I'll Take the High Road 1943,N 10,28:3
Iceman Cometh, The 1946,O 10,31:3

Chamarat, Georges
Bourgeois Gentilhomme, Le 1955,O 26,26:1
Bourgeois Gentilhomme, Le 1955,O 30,II,1:1
Barbier de Seville, Le 1955,N 9,40:1
Troupe Du Roi, La 1970,F 4,38:1
Don Juan 1970,F 7,24:2
Femmes Savaantes, Les 1970,F 14,12:1
Malade Imaginaire, Le 1970,F 18,40:2

Chamber, Robert
Little Mary Sunshine 1959,N 29,II,1:1

Chamberlain, Bert
Waiting for Godot 1957,Ja 22,25:1

Chamberlain, Frank
Devil and Daniel Webster, The 1939,My 19,26:1
Susanna, Don't You Cry 1939,My 23,27:2

Chamberlain, George Agnew (Playwright)
Lost 1927,Mr 29,22:2

Chamberlain, Howland
Achilles Had a Heel 1935,Ap 28,X,1:1
Achilles Had a Heel 1935,O 14,20:2
Courageous One, The 1958,Ja 21,33:6
Julius Caesar 1959,Ag 4,30:1
Hop, Signor! 1962,My 8,45:2

Chamberlain, Ida Hoyt (Composer)
Enchanted Isle 1927,S 20,33:2

Chamberlain, Ida Hoyt (Lyricist)
Enchanted Isle 1927,S 20,33:2

Chamberlain, Ida Hoyt (Playwright)
Enchanted Isle 1927,S 20,33:2

Chamberlain, Mike (Costume Designer)
Burning Bush, The 1949,D 17,15:5

Chamberlain, Peggy
Vaudeville (Palace) 1928,F 21,19:2
Here's Howe! 1928,My 2,19:3
Off to Buffalo! 1939,F 22,18:2

Chamberlain, Ralph
Fashion 1937,Mr 21,II,7:8

Chamberlain, Ralph (Director)
Fashion 1937,Mr 21,II,7:8

Chamberlain, Richard
Breakfast at Tiffany's 1966,D 15,60:1
Hamlet 1969,Mr 14,51:1

Chamberlain, Robert
Watch-Pit 1969,Ja 30,39:1

Chamberlain, Sally
Twelfth Night 1949,O 4,33:2
Julius Caesar 1959,Ag 4,30:1

Chamberlain, Themis
Bonds of Interest, The 1958,My 7,43:1

Chamberlain and Hines
Ziegfeld Follies 1927,Ag 17,27:3
Vaudeville (Palace) 1928,F 28,18:7
Vaudeville (Palace) 1928,Jl 3,19:2

Chamberlayne, Pye
Founders, The 1957,My 14,39:1

Chamberlin, Dorothy
Finta Giardiniera, La 1927,Ja 19,20:5

Chamberlin, Lee
Slave Ship 1969,N 22,46:1

Chambers, Ernest (Playwright)
Show Girl 1961,Ja 13,37:1
Hi, Paisano 1961,O 2,36:2

Chambers, Everett
There Is No End 1950,F 17,27:4

Chambers, Gertie
Change Your Luck 1930,Je 7,10:2

Chambers, Haddon (Playwright)
Card Players, The 1922,Ap 27,17:4
Card Players, The 1922,My 21,VI,1:6
Thief, The 1927,Ap 23,15:2

Chambers, Jane
Single Man at a Party 1959,Ap 22,30:4

Chambers, Jeff (Miscellaneous)
Penny Wars, The 1969,O 16,52:1

Chambers, Joan
Middle of the Night 1956,F 9,39:1
Come Share My House 1960,F 19,20:2

Chambers, Lyster
First Year, The 1920,O 21,11:2
That's the Woman 1930,S 4,27:2
Uncle Tom's Cabin 1933,My 30,13:4
Lost Horizons 1934,O 16,31:2
Triumph 1935,O 15,18:5
County Chairman, The 1936,My 26,26:5
On the Rocks 1938,Je 16,20:2
Signature 1945,F 15,25:2

Chambers, Madelaine
Alive and Kicking 1950,Ja 18,25:5

Chambers, Marie
Scrambled Wives 1920,Ag 6,16:1
Smooth as Silk 1921,F 23,18:3
Saturday Night 1924,F 11,18:1
Is Zat So? 1925,Ja 6,23:4
Scarlet Fox, The 1928,Mr 28,31:1
Launcelot and Elaine 1930,Mr 10,24:3

Chambers, Marion
Poppy 1923,S 4,14:2
Sons o' Guns 1929,N 27,30:4

Chambers, Michael (Costume Designer)
Huui, Huui 1968,N 25,58:1

Chambers, Michael (Miscellaneous)
Twelfth Night 1969,Ag 14,29:2

Chambers, Norma
Let Freedom Ring 1935,N 7,26:2
Bury the Dead 1936,Ap 20,17:4
Prelude 1936,Ap 20,17:4
200 Were Chosen 1936,N 21,21:1
Stop-Over 1938,Ja 12,16:5
Washington Jitters 1938,My 3,19:1
Fledgling 1940,N 28,29:2
Mexican Mural; Miracle Painting 1942,Ap 27,19:2
Mexican Mural; Patio With Flamingo 1942,Ap 27,19:2
Richard III 1943,Mr 27,8:3
Sleep, My Pretty One 1944,N 3,26:8
Street Scene 1947,Ja 10,17:2
Afternoon Storm 1948,Ap 12,24:2

Chambers, Pauline
Ziegfeld Midnight Frolic 1920,Mr 17,14:2

Chambers, Peter
Band Wagon, The 1931,Je 4,31:3
Cat and the Fiddle, The 1931,O 16,26:4
Susanna, Don't You Cry 1939,My 23,27:2

Chambers, Ralph
Lost Boy 1932,Ja 6,24:4
Decoy, The 1932,Ap 2,13:4
Now You've Done It 1937,Mr 6,10:4
Antony and Cleopatra 1937,N 11,30:2
Brooklyn Biarritz 1941,F 28,16:2
Steps Leading Up 1941,Ap 19,20:6
More the Merrier, The 1941,S 16,19:3
Clash by Night 1941,D 29,20:2
Johnny 2X4 1942,Mr 17,24:6
Snafu 1944,O 26,19:5
Show Boat 1946,Ja 7,17:2
John Loves Mary 1947,F 5,29:2
Diamond Lil 1948,N 30,33:2
Call Me Madam 1950,O 13,25:1
Pajama Game, The 1954,My 14,20:2
Pajama Game, The 1957,My 16,27:1
Gazebo, The 1958,D 3,2:7

Chambers, Robert
Little Mary Sunshine 1959,N 19,49:3

Chambers, Robert (Composer)
Smokeweaver's Daughter, The 1959,Ap 15,30:1
Susannah and the Elders 1959,O 19,37:3

Chambers, Robert (Miscellaneous)
O Say Can You See! 1962,O 9,45:1

Chambers, Robert (Producer)
Little Mary Sunshine 1959,N 19,49:3
Madame Aphrodite 1961,D 30,13:1

Chambers, Vernon
Caukey 1944,F 18,15:4

Chambers, William
200 Were Chosen 1936,N 21,21:1
Excursion 1937,Ap 10,11:4
Tell My Story 1939,Mr 16,26:6
Billy Draws a Horse 1939,D 22,14:5
Johnny Belinda 1940,S 19,26:2
One on the House 1941,Mr 30,I,47:3
Sky Drift 1945,N 14,25:2

Chambers, William (Miscellaneous)
Girls in 509, The 1958,O 16,47:1
Tumbler, The 1960,F 25,32:2
Period of Adjustment 1960,N 11,34:1

Chambliss, Erika
Possessed, The 1939,O 25,26:2

Chambliss, Woodrow
Possessed, The 1939,O 25,26:2

Chambord, Jacqueline
Henry V 1960,Je 30,23:1

Chambrun, Jacques (Producer)
Boudoir 1941,F 8,18:4
Sheppey 1944,Ap 19,27:2

Chamorro, Kathy
Vida es Sueno, La 1964,Mr 18,49:1

Champagne
Make Me Disappear 1969,My 14,34:1

Champell, Germain
Famille Lavolette, La 1926,O 10,VIII,2:1

Champion, Gower
Lady Comes Across, The 1942,Ja 10,10:2
3 for Tonight 1955,Ap 7,23:2
3 for Tonight 1955,Ap 17,II,1:1

Champion, Gower (Choreographer)
Small Wonder 1948,S 16,33:5
Small Wonder 1948,S 26,II,1:1
Lend an Ear 1948,D 17,38:2
Make a Wish 1951,Ap 19,38:1
Make a Wish 1951,My 20,II,1:1
Bye Bye Birdie 1960,Ap 15,13:4
Carnival! 1961,Ap 14,22:2
Hello, Dolly! 1964,Ja 17,22:1
Hello, Dolly! 1964,Ja 26,II,1:1
Hello, Dolly! 1965,D 3,43:1
Hello, Dolly! 1967,N 13,61:1
Happy Time, The 1968,Ja 19,32:2
Carnival! 1968,D 13,58:1

Champion, Gower (Director)
Lend an Ear 1948,D 17,38:2
3 for Tonight 1955,Ap 7,23:2
3 for Tonight 1955,Ap 17,II,1:1
Bye Bye Birdie 1960,Ap 15,13:4
Carnival! 1961,Ap 14,22:2
Carnival! 1961,Ap 23,II,1:1

My Mother, My Father and Me 1963,Mr 25,5:5
Hello, Dolly! 1964,Ja 17,22:1
Hello, Dolly! 1965,D 3,43:1
3 Bags Full 1966,Mr 7,22:1
I Do! I Do! 1966,D 6,58:1
I Do! I Do! 1966,D 18,II,3:1
Hello, Dolly! 1967,Je 14,38:1
Hello, Dolly! 1967,N 13,61:1
Hello, Dolly! 1967,N 26,II,3:1
I Do! I Do! 1967,N 28,54:1
Happy Time, The 1968,Ja 19,32:2
Happy Time, The 1968,Ja 28,II,3:1
Carnival! 1968,D 13,58:1
Flea in Her Ear, A 1969,O 4,25:1
Flea in Her Ear, A 1969,O 12,II,9:1
Champion, Gower (Miscellaneous)
Happy Time, The 1968,Ja 19,32:2
Champion, Janet
Ice Follies 1957,Ja 16,36:1
Ice Follies 1958,Ja 15,26:2
Ice Follies 1959,Ja 14,30:1
Ice Follies 1960,Ja 13,20:1
Ice Follies 1961,Ja 11,25:2
Ice Follies 1962,Ja 10,24:6
Ice Follies 1963,Ja 10,5:2
Champion, Marge
3 for Tonight 1955,Ap 7,23:2
3 for Tonight 1955,Ap 17,II,1:1
Champion, Marge (Director)
Hello, Dolly! 1970,Mr 30,52:1
Champlain, Robert
Romeo and Juliet 1934,D 21,30:3
Barretts of Wimpole Street, The 1935,F 26,16:2
Romeo and Juliet 1935,D 24,10:2
Saint Joan 1936,Mr 10,27:4
Crime at Blossoms, The 1937,Jl 17,12:8
Champlin, Charles K
House of Doom, The 1932,Ja 26,20:4
Champlin, Charles K (Playwright)
House of Doom, The 1932,Ja 26,20:4
Champlin, Stephen (Playwright)
One Shot Fired 1927,N 8,32:5
Kidding Kidders 1928,Ap 24,28:3
Chan, Alice
First Wife, The 1945,N 28,21:5
Chan, Donald (Musical Director)
Salad of the Mad Cafe, The 1964,Ap 1,43:1
Chan, Peter
Diamond Lil 1949,F 7,16:2
Flower Drum Song 1958,D 2,44:1
Chancerel, Leon (Playwright)
Veritable Histoire de Mignon, La 1927,F 20,VII,2:1
Chandler, Anna
Mendel, Inc 1929,N 26,28:5
Chandler, Colin (Director)
Yes, M'Lord 1949,O 5,35:2
Chandler, Douglas
Hasty Heart, The 1945,Ja 4,14:2
Hold It! 1948,My 6,31:5
Live Wire, The 1950,Ag 18,16:2
Captain Brassbound's Conversion 1950,D 28,21:1
Chandler, Eugene (Director)
Promis' Lan', De 1930,My 28,31:2
Chandler, Evelyn
International Ice Frolics, The 1938,My 7,18:3
Ice Follies 1939,D 5,38:2
Ice Follies 1941,D 2,32:2
Aquashow 1953,Je 24,29:2
Chandler, Helen
Light of the World, The 1920,Ja 7,17:1
Richard III 1920,Mr 8,7:1
Daddy Dumplins 1920,N 23,11:1
Macbeth 1921,F 18,16:1
Steam Roller, The 1924,N 11,20:2
Wild Duck, The 1925,F 25,16:4
Servant in the House, The 1925,Ap 8,24:2
First Flight 1925,S 18,26:2
Hamlet 1925,N 10,23:1
Moon is a Gong, The 1926,Mr 13,21:3
Pomeroy's Past 1926,Ap 20,24:4
Pomeroy's Past 1926,My 2,VIII,1:1
Constant Nymph, The 1926,D 10,31:1
Mr Pim Passes By 1927,Ap 19,24:1
Creoles 1927,S 23,33:3
Ivory Door, The 1927,O 19,24:5
Silent House, The 1928,F 8,28:5
Faust 1928,O 9,34:1
Faust 1928,N 4,IX,4:1
Marriage Bed, The 1929,Ja 8,35:1
Springtime for Henry 1931,D 10,29:2
These Two 1934,My 8,28:3
It's You I Want 1935,F 6,23:3
Dominant Sex, The 1935,Ap 2,24:5
Pride and Prejudice 1935,O 23,19:2
Pride and Prejudice 1935,N 3,X,1:5
Pride and Prejudice 1935,N 6,32:4
Pride and Prejudice 1935,N 10,IX,2:5
Pride and Prejudice 1935,N 17,IX,1:1
Lady Precious Stream 1936,Ja 28,15:2
Lady Precious Stream 1936,F 23,X,1:1
Boy Meets Girl 1936,My 28,18:8
Boy Meets Girl 1936,Je 28,IX,1:8
Holmeses of Baker Street, The 1936,D 10,34:3

Man From Cairo, The 1938,My 5,26:5
Ruy Blas 1938,Jl 24,IX,2:1
Outward Bound 1938,D 23,16:5
Outward Bound 1939,Ja 1,IX,1:1
Chandler, Hope
Abie's Irish Rose 1937,My 13,30:2
Chandler, Jeff
People vs Ranchman, The 1968,O 28,56:1
Chandler, Joan
Late George Apley, The 1944,O 20,16:4
Late George Apley, The 1944,N 22,26:2
Late George Apley, The 1944,D 3,II,1:1
Lady From the Sea, The 1950,Ag 8,23:2
My 3 Angels 1953,Mr 12,23:2
Tempest, The 1955,Ag 2,18:2
Tempest, The 1955,Ag 7,II,1:1
Chandler, Joe (Producer)
Mrs Kimball Presents 1944,Mr 1,17:3
Chandler, Julia
Free for All 1931,S 9,25:1
Chandler, Julia (Playwright)
Gift, The 1924,Ja 23,15:4
Chandler, Julie
Mister Romeo 1927,S 6,35:3
Marathon 1933,Ja 28,8:8
Chandler, Leland
All Soul's Eve 1920,My 13,9:1
Daddy Dumplins 1920,N 23,11:1
Starlight 1925,Mr 4,17:2
Straight Thru the Door 1928,O 5,17:2
Chandler, Mary
Pleasure Bound 1929,F 19,22:4
Chandler, Mildred
Mrs McThing 1952,F 21,22:1
Six Characters in Search of an Author 1955,D 12,38:1
Roman Candle 1960,F 4,34:2
Goa 1968,F 23,46:1
Chandler, Pat (Miscellaneous)
Visit to a Small Planet 1957,F 8,18:1
Josephine Baker and Her Company 1964,F 5,30:1
Wiener Blut 1964,S 12,14:1
Chandler, Penelope
As You Like It 1947,F 21,16:2
Chandler, Perdita
Firebird of Florence 1945,Mr 23,13:4
Chandler, Richard (Producer)
Sweet Enemy, The 1965,F 16,39:1
Celebration 1969,Ja 23,55:2
Chandler, Richard R (Miscellaneous)
Sarah and the Sax 1964,My 5,53:1
Dirty Old Man, The 1964,My 5,53:1
Chandler, Ruth
Rat, The 1925,F 11,19:3
Chandler, Thelma (Miscellaneous)
Morning Sun 1963,O 7,36:2
Chandler, William
New Faces of 1936 1936,My 20,24:5
Chandra Kaly Dancers
Vaudeville (Palace) 1952,F 27,22:2
Chandrasakara, Fred K
Heat Wave 1931,F 18,14:6
Chaney, Frances
Assassin, The 1945,O 18,20:2
Three Sisters, The 1955,F 26,13:2
Lovers 1956,My 11,23:1
Winkelberg 1958,Ja 15,26:2
Julia, Jake, and Uncle Joe 1961,Ja 30,19:1
Seidman and Son 1962,O 16,32:2
Chaney, Jan
Portofino 1958,F 22,8:3
O Say Can You See! 1962,O 9,45:1
Chaney, Lon
Hoofers, The 1969,Jl 30,23:4
Chaney, Stewart (Costume Designer)
Old Maid, The 1935,Ja 8,26:1
Parnell 1935,N 12,24:2
Parnell 1936,My 5,26:2
New Faces of 1936 1936,My 20,24:5
Hamlet 1936,N 11,54:2
Aged 26 1936,D 22,32:1
Life With Father 1939,N 9,26:2
Twelfth Night 1940,O 27,IX,1:5
Susannah and the Elders 1940,O 30,28:2
Twelfth Night 1940,N 20,26:3
Lady Comes Across, The 1942,Ja 10,10:2
Duke in Darkness, The 1944,Ja 25,15:2
Late George Apley, The 1944,N 22,26:2
Winter's Tale, The 1946,Ja 16,18:6
Bathsheba 1947,Mr 27,40:2
Inspector Calls, An 1947,O 22,38:2
You Never Can Tell 1948,Mr 17,31:2
Ivy Green, The 1949,Ap 6,37:2
I Know My Love 1949,N 3,36:1
Design For A Stained Glass Window 1950,Ja 24,26:2
Great to Be Alive! 1950,Mr 24,28:2
House of Bernarda Alba, The 1951,Ja 8,14:6
King of Friday's Men, The 1951,F 22,26:2
Lo and Behold! 1951,D 13,45:2
Much Ado About Nothing 1952,My 2,20:1
Sherlock Holmes 1953,O 31,11:2
Severed Head, A 1964,O 29,40:1

Chaney, Stewart (Director)
Wuthering Heights 1939,Ap 28,30:4
Belle Helene, La 1941,Jl 8,14:1
Morning Star, The 1942,S 15,18:4
Chaney, Stewart (Lighting Director)
Hamlet 1936,O 25,X,1:5
Down to Miami 1944,S 12,23:5
Obsession 1946,O 2,39:2
Bathsheba 1947,Mr 27,40:2
Inspector Calls, An 1947,O 22,38:2
Druid Circle, The 1947,O 23,29:5
Doctor Social 1948,F 12,29:5
I Know My Love 1949,N 3,36:1
Design For A Stained Glass Window 1950,Ja 24,26:2
Great to Be Alive! 1950,Mr 24,28:2
King of Friday's Men, The 1951,F 22,26:2
Moon Is Blue, The 1951,Mr 9,29:2
Lo and Behold! 1951,D 13,45:2
Much Ado About Nothing 1952,My 2,20:1
Late Love 1953,O 14,35:2
Hidden River, The 1957,Ja 24,32:1
49th Cousin, The 1960,O 28,22:1
Chaney, Stewart (Producer)
Belle Helene, La 1941,Jl 8,14:1
House of Bernarda Alba, The 1951,Ja 8,14:6
Summer of Daisy Miller, The 1963,My 28,33:1
Chaney, Stewart (Scenic Designer)
Kill That Story 1934,Ag 30,22:2
Bride of Torozko, The 1934,S 14,24:2
Dream Child 1934,S 28,26:2
Old Maid, The 1935,Ja 8,26:1
On to Fortune 1935,F 5,22:2
Times Have Changed 1935,F 26,16:1
Parnell 1935,N 12,24:2
Ghosts 1935,D 13,30:6
O Evening Star 1935,D 26,20:1
O Evening Star 1936,Ja 9,24:6
Parnell 1936,My 5,26:2
New Faces of 1936 1936,My 20,24:5
Spring Dance 1936,Ag 26,17:4
Hamlet 1936,O 20,31:3
Hedda Gabler 1936,O 25,X,1:5
Hamlet 1936,N 11,54:2
Hedda Gabler 1936,N 17,34:4
Aged 26 1936,D 22,32:1
But for the Grace of God 1937,Ja 13,21:4
Having Wonderful Time 1937,F 22,12:5
Wuthering Heights 1939,Ap 28,30:4
Life With Father 1939,N 9,26:2
International Incident, An 1940,Ap 3,18:2
Twelfth Night 1940,O 27,IX,1:5
Susannah and the Elders 1940,O 30,28:2
Twelfth Night 1940,N 20,26:3
Belle Helene, La 1941,Jl 8,14:1
More the Merrier, The 1941,S 16,19:3
Blithe Spirit 1941,N 6,26:2
Sunny River 1941,D 5,28:2
Lady Comes Across, The 1942,Ja 10,10:2
Dark Eyes 1943,Ja 15,20:2
Three's a Family 1943,My 6,24:2
Innocent Voyage, The 1943,N 16,27:2
World's Full of Girls, The 1943,D 7,31:2
Voice of the Turtle 1943,D 9,30:3
Voice of the Turtle, The 1943,D 19,II,3:1
Duke in Darkness, The 1944,Ja 25,15:2
Jacobowsky and the Colonel 1944,Mr 15,17:2
House in Paris, The 1944,Mr 21,17:1
Public Relations 1944,Ap 7,23:3
Pretty Little Parlor 1944,Ap 18,24:8
Dream With Music 1944,My 19,15:2
Down to Miami 1944,S 12,23:5
Embezzled Heaven 1944,N 1,20:2
Embezzled Heaven 1944,N 5,II,1:2
Late George Apley, The 1944,N 22,26:2
Late George Apley, The 1944,D 3,II,1:1
Laffing Room Only 1944,D 25,15:4
Trio 1944,D 30,13:4
Many Happy Returns 1945,Ja 6,15:5
One-Man Show 1945,F 9,21:2
Signature 1945,F 15,25:2
Dunnigan's Daughter 1945,D 27,16:1
Joy Forever, A 1946,Ja 8,20:2
Winter's Tale, The 1946,Ja 16,18:6
Obsession 1946,O 2,39:2
Craig's Wife 1947,F 13,35:2
Bathsheba 1947,Mr 27,40:2
Laura 1947,Je 27,16:1
Inspector Calls, An 1947,O 22,38:2
Druid Circle, The 1947,O 23,29:5
Doctor Social 1948,F 12,29:5
You Never Can Tell 1948,Mr 17,31:2
Sally 1948,My 7,31:2
Life With Mother 1948,Je 9,36:3
Life With Mother 1948,O 21,32:2
Red Gloves 1948,D 6,28:2
My Name is Aquilon 1949,F 10,38:2
Ivy Green, The 1949,Ap 6,37:2
I Know My Love 1949,N 3,36:1
Design For A Stained Glass Window 1950,Ja 24,26:2
Great to Be Alive! 1950,Mr 24,28:2
House of Bernarda Alba, The 1951,Ja 8,14:6

Chaney, Stewart (Scenic Designer)—Cont
King of Friday's Men, The 1951,F 22,26:2
Moon Is Blue, The 1951,Mr 9,29:2
Seventeen 1951,Je 22,16:6
Lo and Behold! 1951,D 13,45:2
Much Ado About Nothing 1952,My 2,20:1
Late Love 1953,O 14,35:2
Girl Can Tell, A 1953,O 30,28:2
Sherlock Holmes 1953,O 31,11:2
Into Thin Air 1955,My 25,39:1
Hidden River, The 1957,Ja 24,32:1
49th Cousin, The 1960,O 28,22:1
Summer of Daisy Miller, The 1963,My 28,33:1
Squat Betty 1964,F 25,24:1
Sponge Room, The 1964,F 25,24:1
Severed Head, A 1964,O 29,40:1
Life With Father 1967,O 20,53:2
I Only Want an Answer 1968,F 6,36:1
Chang, Marian
First Wife, The 1945,N 28,21:5
Chang, Tisa
Lovely Ladies, Kind Gentlemen 1970,D 29,38:1
Chang, Virginia
Evening in Cathay, An 1939,F 2,16:2
Chanin, John Morris (Producer)
Comes the Revelation 1942,My 27,26:2
Magic Touch, The 1947,S 4,30:1
Channing, Carol
No for an Answer 1941,Ja 6,10:6
Proof Thro' the Night 1942,D 26,14:2
Lend an Ear 1948,D 17,38:2
Gentlemen Prefer Blondes 1949,D 9,35:3
Gentlemen Prefer Blondes 1949,D 18,II,3:1
Wonderful Town 1954,My 7,II,1:1
Vamp, The 1955,N 11,30:1
Show Girl 1961,Ja 13,37:1
Show Girl 1961,Ja 29,II,1:1
Untitled-Revue 1962,Je 7,31:1
Hello, Dolly! 1964,Ja 17,22:1
Hello, Dolly! 1964,Ja 26,II,1:1
Channing, Stockard
Arsenic and Old Lace 1970,N 5,59:1
Chanot, A
Mozart 1926,D 28,16:1
Illusioniste, L' 1927,Ja 11,36:5
Chanslor, Roy (Playwright)
Tabloid 1929,S 29,IX,5:1
Chanson, Les Compagnons de la
Edith Piaf 1947,O 30,30:2
Chantavoine, Jean (Translator)
Rosenkavalier, Der 1927,Mr 6,VII,4:4
Chanteuses, Les Huit
Pardon Our French 1950,O 6,22:4
Chantler, Everett (Playwright)
Lady Screams, The 1927,My 3,24:2
Ch'ao-li
Time Limit! 1956,Ja 25,27:2
Chapel, Billy
Ice Capades 1967,Je 2,33:1
Ice Capades 1969,Ja 8,42:1
Ice Capades 1970,Ja 7,35:1
Chapell, Wallace
Much Ado About Nothing 1963,Jl 15,25:2
Chapelle, Alyce
Blossom Time 1938,D 27,12:2
Chapelle, Chappy
Sugar Hill 1931,D 26,15:2
Chapelle, Sara
Melody Man, The 1924,My 14,14:2
Chaperau, Albert N (Producer)
Make Yourself at Home 1945,S 14,21:2
Chapier, Harold J (Playwright)
Love Your Crooked Neighbor 1969,D 30,40:1
Chapin, Alice
Meanest Man in the World, The 1920,O 13,18:2
Trojan Women, The 1923,N 8,17:6
Michel Auclair 1925,Mr 5,23:1
Adam Solitaire 1925,N 7,19:2
Chapin, Alice (Producer)
Trojan Women, The 1923,N 8,17:6
Chapin, Anne Morrison (Playwright)
No Questions Asked 1934,F 6,24:3
Chapin, Billy
Three Wishes for Jamie 1952,Mr 22,9:2
Chapin, Brian
Jennie 1963,O 18,35:2
Child Buyer, The 1964,D 22,35:1
Chapin, Carl
Sing for Your Supper 1939,Ap 25,18:6
Chapin, Doug
Physicists, The 1964,O 14,52:1
Chapin, Harold (Playwright)
New Morality, The 1921,Ja 31,10:1
Chapin, Jacques
Voice From the Minaret, The 1922,Ja 31,11:2
Chapin, Jane
Valley of Content, The 1925,Ja 14,19:2
Made in America 1925,O 15,27:2
Chapin, Katherine Garrison (Playwright)
Sojourner Truth 1948,Ap 22,35:2
Chapin, Ken
House Remembered, A 1957,F 7,20:2
Chapin, Robert (Miscellaneous)
Great American Family, The 1939,D 10,X,5:6

Chapin, Thomas C
Coriolanus 1927,Je 18,8:3
Chapin, Victor
Kiss for Cinderella, A 1942,Mr 11,22:2
Hasty Heart, The 1945,Ja 4,14:2
Chaplin, Charles Jr
Now I Lay Me Down to Sleep 1950,Mr 3,21:2
Chaplin, Charlie
Vaudeville (Palace) 1923,Mr 13,19:2
Chaplin, Geraldine
Little Foxes, The 1968,Ja 6,24:4
Chaplin, Lita Grey
Vaudeville (Palace) 1931,Mr 9,25:7
Chaplin, Saul (Composer)
Party With Betty Comden and Adolph Green, A 1958,D 24,2:7
Chaplin, Sydney
Son, The 1950,Ap 1,12:4
Bells Are Ringing 1956,N 29,43:4
Bells Are Ringing 1956,N 30,18:2
Goodbye Charlie 1959,D 17,50:1
Subways Are for Sleeping 1961,D 28,22:1
In the Counting House 1962,D 15,5:5
Funny Girl 1964,Mr 27,15:1
Chaplin, Victor
Ah, Wilderness! 1941,O 3,26:2
Chapman, Albert
Bitter Sweet 1929,N 6,30:2
Chapman, Barbara
Hay Fever 1935,Jl 24,20:4
Camille 1935,Jl 31,21:1
Chapman, Bert
Last Warning, The 1922,O 25,23:1
Kreutzer Sonata, The 1924,My 15,22:3
Solid Ivory 1925,N 17,29:3
Show Boat 1927,D 28,26:1
Chapman, Blanche
Golden Days 1921,N 2,20:1
Deep Tangled Wildwood, The 1923,N 6,22:1
Schemers 1924,S 16,27:1
Chapman, Bret
Strawberry Blonde, The 1927,F 8,20:3
Chapman, Byrony
Henry IV, Part II 1946,My 8,33:4
Uncle Vanya 1946,My 14,18:2
Chapman, Carl
Quiet, Please! 1940,N 9,20:3
Chapman, Catherine
George White's Scandals 1926,Je 15,23:2
Chapman, Christopher (Miscellaneous)
Happy Time, The 1968,Ja 19,32:2
Chapman, David (Costume Designer)
Red, White and Maddox 1969,Ja 27,27:1
Chapman, David (Lighting Director)
Lulu; Earth Spirit 1970,Mr 28,32:1
Chapman, David (Scenic Designer)
Red, White and Maddox 1969,Ja 27,27:1
Lulu; Earth Spirit 1970,Mr 28,32:1
Chapman, Dewey
Tom Paine 1969,Mr 30,71:2
Tempest, The 1970,F 15,67:1
Chapman, Donald
Trial by Jury 1966,Je 8,41:2
Chapman, Edward
Good Companions, The 1931,My 15,20:8
Good Companions, The 1931,My 31,VIII,2:6
How D'you Do? 1933,Ap 26,13:4
Napoleon 1934,S 4,23:2
It Happened to Adam 1934,N 10,18:6
Charlotte Corday 1936,O 27,31:1
Chapman, F M
They Never Come Back 1920,D 19,I,22:3
Man From Earth, The 1923,Ja 3,6:2
Chapman, Frank
Variations of 1940 1940,Ja 29,12:1
Chapman, Grace
Twelfth Night 1957,Ja 5,12:2
Midsummer Night's Dream, A 1957,Je 27,21:3
Royal Gambit 1959,Mr 5,34:2
Drunkard, The; Fallen Saved, The 1959,Je 24,37:2
Sign of Jonah, The 1960,S 9,35:1
Man and Superman 1960,N 7,46:2
Nathan the Wise 1962,Mr 23,29:1
Chapman, Graham
Cambridge Circus 1964,O 7,53:1
Chapman, James W
Technique 1931,My 15,21:1
Chapman, Joe
Meek Mose 1928,F 7,30:1
Chapman, John (Playwright)
Not Now Darling 1970,O 30,33:1
Chapman, Kathy
Season in the Sun 1950,S 29,31:2
Chapman, Lonny
Come Back, Little Sheba 1950,F 16,28:5
Missouri Legend 1951,F 10,10:4
Chase, The 1952,Ap 16,30:2
Whistler's Grandmother 1952,D 12,40:2
Ladies of the Corridor, The 1953,O 22,33:5
Ladies of the Corridor, The 1953,N 1,II,1:1
Traveling Lady 1954,O 28,45:2
Time of Your Life, The 1955,Ja 20,34:1
Time of Your Life, The 1955,Ja 30,II,1:1

Chapman, Lonny—Cont
Glass Menagerie, The 1956,N 22,50:1
Glass Menagerie, The 1956,D 2,II,1:1
General Seeger 1962,Mr 1,26:2
Marathon '33 1963,D 23,20:1
Chapman, Lonny (Director)
Buffalo Skinner, The 1959,F 20,18:1
Nature of the Crime 1970,Mr 24,41:1
Chapman, Lonny (Playwright)
Buffalo Skinner, The 1959,F 20,18:1
Cry of the Raindrop 1961,Mr 8,38:1
Chapman, Nolia
Bride in the Morning, A 1960,My 26,38:2
Chapman, Penny
New York Idea, The 1948,Ag 18,29:2
Chapman, Robert (Playwright)
Uniform of Flesh 1949,Ja 31,15:2
Billy Budd 1951,F 12,18:3
Billy Budd 1951,F 18,II,1:1
Billy Budd 1951,Ap 15,II,1:1
Billy Budd 1951,My 6,II,1:1
Billy Budd 1955,My 4,35:1
Billy Budd 1959,F 28,13:3
Chapman, Robert (Producer)
New York Idea, The 1963,Jl 13,12:2
Chapman, Robert H
Life and Death of Sir John Falstaff, The 1938,Mr 15,19:5
Hamlet 1938,N 8,26:1
Once Over Lightly 1938,D 10,13:4
Romeo and Juliet 1940,Ap 16,28:4
Many a Slip 1940,N 16,12:7
Chapman, Robert H (Playwright)
Many a Slip 1940,N 16,12:7
Chapman, Ruth
Days of Our Youth, The 1941,N 29,15:2
Chapman, T S
It's the Valet 1933,D 15,25:4
Chapman, Ted
Rope Dancers, The 1959,Mr 14,26:1
What a Killing 1961,Mr 28,41:1
Red Roses for Me 1961,N 28,41:1
Gogo Loves You 1964,O 10,19:2
Chapman, Tomes
May Wine 1935,D 6,30:3
Forbidden Melody 1936,N 3,33:1
Chapman, Virginia
Our Lan' 1947,S 29,16:5
Chapman, William
Arabian Nights 1954,Je 25,15:2
Arabian Nights 1955,Je 24,16:1
Candide 1956,D 3,40:2
Maria Golovin 1958,N 6,43:1
Greenwillow 1960,Mr 9,38:1
Greenwillow 1960,Mr 20,II,1:1
Pirates of Penzance, The 1960,O 7,29:1
Pirates of Penzance, The 1961,Ja 20,24:5
H M S Pinafore 1961,F 2,26:6
South Pacific 1961,Ap 27,26:3
Milk Train Doesn't Stop Here Anymore, The 1962,Jl 12,19:8
H M S Pinafore 1964,Mr 21,13:4
Patience 1964,Mr 26,42:1
H M S Pinafore 1965,Ap 15,39:1
Patience 1965,Ap 16,34:1
Pirates of Penzance, The 1965,Ap 21,50:6
Pirates of Penzance, The 1968,Ap 26,32:1
Patience 1968,My 16,52:1
Chapman, Y S
It's the Valet 1933,D 15,25:4
Chapman (Playwright)
Conspiracy and Tragedy of the Duke of Byron, The 1929,Ag 18,VIII,1:3
Chappel, Clementine
Would-Be Gentleman, The 1930,Ap 30,29:2
Chappel, Edward
Make Mine Manhattan 1948,Ja 16,26:2
Allegro 1952,S 18,36:3
Chappel, Wallace
In the Matter of J Robert Oppenheimer 1968,Je 7,31:1
Chappell, C Haviland
Macbeth 1921,F 18,16:1
Lady Cristilinda, The 1922,D 26,11:2
Anything Might Happen 1923,F 21,22:3
Spring Cleaning 1923,N 10,16:3
Mrs Partridge Presents 1925,Ja 6,23:3
Shanghai Gesture, The 1926,F 2,20:2
Sign of the Leopard 1928,D 12,34:4
Scotland Yard 1929,S 28,16:6
Chappell, Delos (Miscellaneous)
Camille 1932,N 2,23:3
Chappell, Delos (Producer)
Camille 1932,N 2,23:3
Come of Age 1934,Ja 13,16:6
Cross Ruff 1935,F 20,23:3
Daughters of Atreus 1936,O 15,33:1
Father Malachy's Miracle 1937,N 18,26:4
Chappell, Fred
Red, White and Maddox 1969,Ja 27,27:1
Chappell, William (Director)
Time Remembered 1955,My 4,35:1
Chappelle, Chappie
Deep Harlem 1929,Ja 8,35:2

Chappelle, Frederic (Composer)
Pins and Needles 1922,F 2,20:1
Chappelle and Carlton
Vaudeville (Palace) 1926,Ag 31,15:3
Chappelle and Stinette
Plantation Revue, The 1922,Jl 18,18:4
Chaqueneau, Julien St Charles (Producer)
Waltz in Goose Step 1938,N 2,26:2
Charadieff, Igor (Original Author)
Simple Woman, The 1937,Mr 29,14:1
Charash, Jack (Translator)
Schweiger 1926,Mr 24,20:4
Charba, Mari-Claire
Birdbath 1966,Ap 12,43:1
This Is the Rill Speaking 1966,Ap 12,43:1
Chicago 1966,Ap 13,36:1
War 1966,Ap 13,36:1
Recluse, The 1966,Ap 13,36:1
Tom Paine 1968,Mr 26,38:1
Futz 1968,Je 14,39:1
Chard, Beatrice
Prunella 1929,Ap 10,23:3
Chard, Dorothea
Garrick Gaieties 1926,My 11,25:2
Merry-Go-Round 1927,Je 1,25:4
Manhatters, The 1927,Ag 4,25:4
Wasp's Nest, The 1927,O 26,26:3
Mirrors 1928,Ja 19,17:1
Atlas and Eva 1928,F 7,30:2
On Call 1928,N 10,20:7
Cortez 1929,N 5,32:2
Let and Sub-Let 1930,My 20,32:2
Cinderelative 1930,S 19,18:4
Sisters of the Chorus 1930,O 21,34:3
Chard, Evelyn
Transplanting Jean 1921,Ja 4,11:2
Liliom 1921,Ap 21,18:1
Chard, Marjorie
Mountebank, The 1923,My 8,22:2
Love Scandal, A 1923,N 7,14:1
Evensong 1933,F 1,13:4
Chardet, Anthony (Miscellaneous)
School for Scandal, The 1963,Ja 26,5:2
Chardieno, Rajah
Cabin in the Sky 1940,O 26,19:2
Charell, Erik (Director)
Mikado, The 1927,O 30,IX,4:6
White Horse Inn 1936,O 2,28:5
Swingin' the Dream 1939,N 30,24:2
Charell, Erik (Playwright)
White Horse Inn 1931,Ap 27,24:5
Swingin' the Dream 1939,N 30,24:2
Charell, Erik (Producer)
Von Mund zu Mund 1926,D 5,VIII,8:7
Casanova 1928,N 4,IX,2:1
Merry Widow, The 1929,F 17,IX,2:3
Three Musketeers 1929,O 13,IX,4:7
Im Weissen Roessel 1930,D 28,VIII,2:4
White Horse Inn 1931,Ap 9,30:2
Casanova 1932,Je 19,IX,2:1
Alt Heidelberg; Student Prince, The
1932,N 20,IX,3:3
White Horse Inn 1936,O 2,28:5
Charell, Erik (Scenic Designer)
Flying Trapeze, The 1935,Je 2,IX,2:3
Charig, Phil (Composer)
Americana 1926,Jl 27,15:3
Allez-Opp! 1927,Ag 3,29:3
Yes, Yes, Yvette 1927,O 4,32:3
Just Fancy! 1927,O 12,30:2
Polly 1929,Ja 9,28:3
Nikki 1931,S 30,23:4
Artists and Models 1943,N 6,16:6
Follow the Girls 1944,Ap 10,15:2
Follow the Girls 1944,Ap 16,II,1:2
Catch a Star! 1955,S 7,35:2
Charig, Phil (Lyricist)
Polly 1929,Ja 9,28:3
Pajama Lady, The 1930,O 12,VIII,4:1
Artists and Models 1943,N 6,16:6
Follow the Girls 1944,Ap 10,15:2
Charin, Martin (Director)
Ballad for a Firing Squad 1968,D 12,64:2
Charioteers
Hellzapoppin 1938,S 23,34:2
New Hellzapoppin, The 1939,D 12,36:4
Charise, Andre
At Home Abroad 1935,O 27,IX,8:1
Very Warm for May 1939,N 18,23:2
Lady in the Dark 1941,Ja 24,14:2
Charisse, Rita
Grosse Valise, La 1965,D 15,52:1
Charissi, Calliope
Vaudeville (Hippodrome) 1923,D 18,16:1
Vaudeville (Hippodrome) 1924,Ja 1,21:1
Charland, Hectar
Untitled-Passion Play 1925,Ag 17,8:1
Charlap, Mark (Composer)
Peter Pan 1954,Jl 20,15:3
Peter Pan 1954,O 21,30:2
Charlap, Moose (Composer)
Shoestring '57 1956,N 6,31:1
Whoop-Up 1958,D 23,2:7

Conquering Hero, The 1961,Ja 17,40:2
Kelly 1965,F 8,28:2
Charles, Allen
Green Pastures, The 1935,F 27,16:2
Charles, C C
Drums Begin, The 1933,N 25,10:5
Charles, Cyril
Gala Night 1930,F 26,22.4
Charles, Edgar
Invitation to a Murder 1934,My 18,26:3
Bet Your Life 1937,Ap 6,20:2
Charles, Edward (Costume Designer)
Tour De Four 1963,Je 19,41:1
Charles, Ellis
Winners and Losers 1947,F 27,27:2
Deputy of Paris, The 1947,Mr 22,9:5
Sister Oakes 1949,Ap 25,19:4
Charles, Ernest
George White's Scandals 1929,S 24,29:1
Story Teller, The 1951,D 15,11:3
Charles, Frances
School for Brides 1944,Ag 2,19:4
Brigadoon 1947,Mr 14,28:2
Charles, George (Producer)
And the Wind Blows 1959,Ap 29,28:1
Charles, Irwin
Three to Make Ready 1946,Mr 8,16:2
Charles, John
Back Pay 1921,Ag 31,8:2
Green Pastures, The 1935,F 27,16:2
Charles, Keith
Death of the Well-Loved Boy, The
1967,My 16,48:1
Celebration 1969,Ja 23,55:2
Oh, Pioneers 1969,N 12,41:1
Happy Birthday, Wanda June 1970,O 8,58:2
Happy Birthday, Wanda June 1970,O 18,II,1:1
Charles, Lee
Livin' the Life 1957,Ap 29,20:1
Charles, Leon
Star Spangled Family 1945,Ap 11,18:6
Charles, Lewis
Summer Night 1939,N 3,17:1
Good Neighbor 1941,O 22,26:2
What Big Ears! 1942,Ap 21,18:5
Talking to You 1942,Ag 18,17:1
Across the Board on Tomorrow Morning
1942,Ag 18,17:1
Sun Field, The 1942,D 10,33:2
Apology 1943,Mr 23,14:2
Milky Way, The 1943,Je 10,17:2
Boy Meets Girl 1943,Je 23,15:5
Naked Genius, The 1943,O 22,20:5
Streets Are Guarded, The 1944,N 21,19:7
Star Spangled Family 1945,Ap 11,18:6
Charles, Lucile
Life Begins 1932,Mr 29,23:2
Charles, Mary
Playing the Game 1927,D 20,32:5
Charles, Paul
Best Foot Forward 1963,Ap 3,43:1
Joyful Noise, A 1966,D 16,57:1
Strada, La 1969,D 15,63:1
Charles, Richard
Desert Song, The 1946,Ja 9,20:2
Charles, Robert
Our Town 1959,Mr 24,46:2
Daddy Come Home 1963,Ap 17,33:1
Charles, Robert (Costume Designer)
Five Star Saint 1970,F 11,41:2
Charles, Robert (Lighting Director)
Babes Don't Cry Anymore 1968,F 21,55:1
Charles, Robert (Playwright)
Enchantment 1953,Jl 1,24:3
Charles, Robert (Scenic Designer)
Guimpes and Saddles 1967,O 11,36:3
Babes Don't Cry Anymore 1968,F 21,55:1
Charles, Theodore (Playwright)
Jealous Moon, The 1928,N 21,32:2
Charles, Vicki
Sunny River 1941,D 5,28:2
Charles, Zachary A
Criminals, The 1941,D 22,24:3
One Touch of Venus 1943,O 8,14:1
Pick-Up Girl 1944,My 4,25:2
Live Life Again 1945,O 1,14:7
Sky Drift 1945,N 14,25:2
Top Banana 1951,N 2,19:2
Annie Get Your Gun 1957,Ag 31,18:2
Charles-Dean, B (Producer)
Mainly for Lovers 1936,F 22,13:2
Charles Weidman and his dancers
As Thousands Cheer 1933,O 2,22:1
Charleston, Helen
Vaudeville (Palace) 1929,D 9,33:2
Vaudeville (Palace) 1930,N 3,19:2
Summer Wives 1936,Ap 14,18:1
Charleston, Milton
Vaudeville (Palace) 1929,D 9,33:2
Vaudeville (Palace) 1930,N 3,19:2
Sketch Book 1935,Je 5,22:2
Sons o' Fun 1941,D 2,28:2
Blackouts of 1949 1949,S 7,39:2

Charlesworth, Tom
Kismet 1953,D 4,2:4
Charlet, Alan (Miscellaneous)
Americana Pastoral 1968,D 11,51:1
Charley I of Albuquerque (Dog)
Love Is a Time of Day 1969,D 23,21:3
Charlie (Seal)
Vaudeville (Palace) 1930,Ag 18,24:3
Charlier, Dan
Wild Waves 1932,F 20,11:4
Charlip, Remy
Doctor Faustus Lights the Lights 1951,D 3,23:4
Charlip, Remy (Choreographer)
Doctor Faustus Lights the Lights 1951,D 3,23:4
Jonah! 1966,F 16,52:1
Charlip, Remy (Costume Designer)
Bertha 1962,F 12,27:1
Jonah! 1966,F 16,52:1
Charlip, Remy (Scenic Designer)
Bertha 1962,F 12,27:1
Jonah! 1966,F 16,52:1
Charlot, Andre (Playwright)
London Calling 1923,S 2,VI,1:7
Charlot, Andre (Producer)
Charlot's Revue 1924,Ap 6,VIII,1:1
Charlot's Revue 1924,Ap 15,25:2
Charlot's Masquerade 1930,S 5,30:7
How D'you Do? 1933,Ap 26,13:4
Day I Forgot, The 1933,My 13,16:6
Please 1933,N 17,22:2
Please 1933,D 3,IX,7:6
Char-A-Bang 1935,My 5,IX,1:7
Charlot, Mark
Midsummer Night's Dream, A 1967,Je 30,23:1
Charlotte-Clasis, Mme
Get Together 1921,S 5,12:2
Merchant of Venice, The 1924,N 18,23:2
Bourgeois Gentilhomme, Le 1924,N 20,21:2
Taming of the Shrew, The 1924,N 25,27:3
Vaudeville (Hippodrome) 1925,D 29,21:2
Charlson, Natalie (Miscellaneous)
Smiling the Boy Fell Dead 1961,Ap 20,28:1
Charlson, Natalie (Musical Director)
Boy Friend, The 1958,Ja 27,24:4
Tour De Four 1963,Je 19,41:1
Babes in the Wood 1964,D 29,21:2
That Thing at the Cherry Lane 1965,My 19,42:1
Charlton, Chris
Vaudeville (Palace) 1930,Mr 31,24:2
Charlton, Everett
Sun and I, The 1937,F 27,9:5
Abe Lincoln in Illinois 1938,O 17,12:2
Charlton, Frank
Little Old New York 1920,S 9,9:2
Claire Adams 1929,N 20,26:3
Ada Beats the Drum 1930,My 9,20:4
Charlton, Richard
Oscar Wilde 1938,O 11,20:2
Charlton, Richard (Producer)
Cranks 1956,N 27,32:1
Charlys, Robert
Topaze 1931,F 17,29:1
Charmette, Jules
It Pays to Sin 1933,N 4,18:6
Charmoli, Tony
Dear Judas 1947,O 6,26:4
Make Mine Manhattan 1948,Ja 16,26:2
Charmoli, Tony (Choreographer)
Ankles Aweigh 1955,Ap 19,27:1
Eddie Fisher at the Winter Garden 1962,O 3,47:1
Charmoli, Tony (Director)
Laughs and Other Events 1960,O 11,57:1
Charnay, Lynne
Way of the World, The 1950,Ap 9,73:5
Julia, Jake, and Uncle Joe 1961,Ja 30,19:1
Charney, Elizabeth
Everyman 1941,My 9,19:2
Charney, Jordan
Song of Songs 1958,O 29,31:1
Telemachus Clay 1963,N 16,17:2
Place for Chance, The 1964,My 15,44:2
Hang Down Your Head and Die 1964,O 19,38:1
Harry, Noon and Night 1965,My 6,44:1
Mutilated, The 1966,F 23,42:1
Viet Rock 1966,N 11,38:1
Glorious Ruler, The 1969,Jl 1,31:1
Slow Memories 1970,N 18,41:1
Charney, Jordan (Producer)
Viet Rock 1966,N 11,38:1
Charney, Libbey
Yoshe Kalb 1933,D 29,27:2
Charnin, Martin
West Side Story 1957,S 27,14:4
West Side Story 1960,Ap 28,31:1
Charnin, Martin (Composer)
Fallout 1959,My 21,36:2
Charnin, Martin (Lyricist)
Fallout 1959,My 21,36:2
Hot Spot 1963,Ap 20,17:2
Ballad for a Firing Squad 1968,D 12,64:2
Two by Two 1970,N 11,37:1
Charnin, Martin (Miscellaneous)
Fallout 1959,My 21,36:2

Charnin, Martin (Playwright)
Fallout 1959,My 21,36:2
Charnoff, M (Playwright)
Shakespeare and Company 1925,O 22,22:5
Charon, Jacques
Bourgeois Gentilhomme, Le 1955,O 26,26:1
Bourgeois Gentilhomme, Le 1955,O 30,II,1:1
Arlequin Poli par l'Amour 1955,N 9,40:1
Jeu de l'Amour et du Hasard, Le 1955,N 16,42:4
Impromptu de Versailles, L' 1961,F 22,30:1
Fourberies de Scapin, Les 1961,F 22,30:1
Tartuffe 1961,Mr 1,28:1
Dindon, Le 1961,Mr 8,38:1
File a la Patte, Il 1962,Jl 8,II,1:1
Fil a la Paite, Un 1966,F 18,25:1
Troupe Du Roi, La 1970,F 4,38:1
Don Juan 1970,F 7,24:2
Femmes Savaantes, Les 1970,F 14,12:1
Malade Imaginaire, Le 1970,F 18,40:2
Charon, Jacques (Director)
Arlequin Poli par l'Amour 1955,N 9,40:1
Impromptu de Versailles, L' 1961,F 22,30:1
Fourberies de Scapin, Les 1961,F 22,30:1
File a la Patte, Il 1962,Jl 8,II,1:1
Fil a la Paite, Un 1966,F 18,25:1
Dance of Death 1967,O 29,II,5:1
Flea in Her Ear, A 1967,O 30,59:1
Charpentier, Gabriel (Composer)
Comedy of Errors, The 1963,Je 21,35:3
Bourgeois Gentilhomme, Le 1964,Je 18,28:2
Tartuffe 1968,Je 12,39:1
Alchemist, The 1969,Je 12,51:1
Merchant of Venice, The 1970,Je 10,39:1
Charpentier, Marc Antoine (Composer)
Troupe Du Roi, La 1970,F 4,38:1
Charpentier, Raymond (Composer)
Roi Dagobert, Le 1926,N 14,VIII,2:1
Charpin, Fernand
Aventuriere, L' 1922,N 14,16:1
Charr (Scenic Designer)
Mary Stuart 1956,Ap 28,10:2
Charras, Charles (Miscellaneous)
Midsummer Night's Dream, A 1965,N 21,123:1
Charters, Spencer
Oh, Henry! 1920,My 6,14:2
Tavern, The 1920,S 28,14:1
Dew Drop Inn 1923,My 18,26:4
Annie Dear 1924,N 5,25:3
Four Flusher, The 1925,Ap 14,27:4
Fanny 1926,S 22,30:1
Talk About Girls 1927,Je 15,31:3
Wild Man of Borneo, The 1927,S 14,29:2
Out of the Night 1927,O 18,32:3
Whoopee 1928,D 5,34:3
Charters, Ted
Biff, Bing, Bang 1921,My 10,20:1
Chartock, S M (Director)
Mikado, The 1949,O 5,35:2
Pirates of Penzance, The 1949,O 11,41:2
H M S Pinafore 1949,O 18,34:2
Trial by Jury 1949,O 18,34:2
Mikado, The 1952,O 21,35:2
Pirates of Penzance, The 1952,O 28,36:4
Trial by Jury 1952,N 4,32:2
H M S Pinafore 1952,N 4,32:2
Iolanthe 1952,N 11,26:3
Chartock, S M (Miscellaneous)
Pirates of Penzance, The 1936,Ap 21,27:5
Trial by Jury 1936,Ap 28,17:2
H M S Pinafore 1936,Ap 28,17:2
Iolanthe 1936,My 5,26:2
Pirates of Penzance, The 1949,O 11,41:2
H M S Pinafore 1949,O 18,34:2
Trial by Jury 1949,O 18,34:2
Chartock, S M (Producer)
Mikado, The 1934,Ap 3,26:3
Pirates of Penzance, The 1934,Ap 10,26:5
Trial by Jury 1934,Ap 17,27:2
H M S Pinafore 1934,Ap 17,27:2
Mikado, The 1934,Ap 24,27:5
Iolanthe 1934,My 1,26:4
Mikado, The 1934,My 22,28:2
Mikado, The 1936,My 11,18:4
Mikado, The 1949,O 5,35:2
Mikado, The 1952,O 21,35:2
Pirates of Penzance, The 1952,O 28,36:4
Trial by Jury 1952,N 4,32:2
H M S Pinafore 1952,N 4,32:2
Iolanthe 1952,N 11,26:3
Chartrand, James
Devil and Daniel Webster, The 1939,My 19,26:1
Charvay, Robert (Playwright)
Mademoiselle Josette Ma Femme 1924,Je 1,VII,1:7
Chasch, Dave
Earl Carroll's Vanities 1925,Jl 7,24:1
Chase, Adelaide M
Drift 1925,N 25,15:3
Chase, Alden
Wooden Kimono 1926,D 28,16:2
Zeppelin 1929,Ja 15,22:3
Live and Learn 1930,Ap 10,24:6
People on the Hill 1931,S 26,25:5
Reflected Glory 1936,S 18,19:5

Reflected Glory 1936,S 22,30:2
Chase, Ann
On Call 1928,N 10,20:7
Chase, Billy
Greenwich Village Follies 1924,S 17,16:1
Chase, Carol
Peter Pan 1924,N 7,16:2
Bit o' Love, A 1925,My 13,24:2
Jeweled Tree, The 1926,O 8,26:2
Chase, Chaz
Follies 1925,Jl 7,24:3
Vaudeville (Palace) 1926,Je 29,21:3
Ballyhoo 1930,D 23,24:1
Saluta 1934,Ag 29,13:4
Laughter Over Broadway 1939,Ja 16,10:3
High Kickers 1941,N 1,21:2
Chase, Chevy
Groove Tube 1969,O 12,88:3
Chase, Clarence
Last Mile, The 1930,F 14,21:2
Hobo 1931,F 12,24:4
Steel 1931,N 19,26:5
Fields Beyond, The 1936,Mr 7,11:2
Cross-Town 1937,Mr 18,21:5
Chase, Diana
Luana 1930,S 18,28:1
Chase, Dorothy
Romance 1921,Mr 1,18:2
Chase, Elizabeth
Sweet Aloes 1936,Mr 5,24:5
Chase, Erma
Lace Petticoat 1927,Ja 5,18:2
Chase, Frank
Semi-Detached 1960,Mr 11,20:2
Chase, Harold R
Clubs Are Trumps 1924,O 15,27:1
Creaking Chair, The 1926,F 23,26:1
Synthetic Sin 1927,O 11,26:2
Killers 1928,Mr 14,28:3
Wanted 1928,Jl 3,19:2
Chase, Ilka
Red Falcon, The 1924,O 8,22:1
Shall We Join the Ladies? 1925,Ja 14,19:1
Antonia 1925,O 21,20:1
Embers 1926,F 2,20:3
Happy Husband, The 1928,My 8,25:2
Animal Kingdom, The 1932,Ja 13,26:4
Forsaking All Others 1933,Mr 2,21:2
Days Without End 1934,Ja 9,19:1
Wife Insurance 1934,Ap 13,24:5
While Parents Sleep 1934,Je 5,28:2
Small Miracle 1934,S 27,24:3
Revenge With Music 1934,N 29,33:5
On to Fortune 1935,Ja 15,23:2
On to Fortune 1935,F 5,22:2
Co-Respondent Unknown 1936,F 12,24:4
Women, The 1936,D 8,30:6
Women, The 1936,D 28,13:1
Keep Off the Grass 1940,My 5,X,1:6
Keep Off the Grass 1940,My 24,22:6
Beverly Hills 1940,N 8,24:2
In Bed We Cry 1944,N 15,20:2
Chase, Ilka (Original Author)
In Bed We Cry 1944,N 15,20:2
Chase, Ilka (Playwright)
In Bed We Cry 1944,N 15,20:2
Chase, Ilka (Translator)
We Are No Longer Children 1932,Ap 1,17:2
Chase, Jay (Producer)
Angels of Anadarko 1962,O 11,47:1
Matty and the Moron and Madonna
1965,Mr 30,53:1
Chase, Jo Flores
Rose Tattoo, The 1966,O 21,36:2
Beyond Desire 1967,O 11,36:1
Chase, Justine
Button, Button 1929,O 24,26:1
Kind Lady 1935,Ap 24,24:5
Chase, Kathleen
Lucrece 1932,D 21,22:2
One Wife or Another 1933,F 7,23:6
After Such Pleasures 1934,Ja 6,18:6
After Such Pleasures 1934,F 8,15:2
Chase, Marjorie (Playwright)
Man's Name, The 1921,N 16,22:1
Chase, Mary (Playwright)
Harvey 1944,N 2,23:2
Harvey 1944,N 12,II,1:1
Harvey 1945,My 8,16:1
Next Half Hour, The 1945,O 30,14:6
Next Half Hour, The 1945,N 4,II,1:1
Harvey 1949,Ja 6,29:2
Harvey 1949,F 13,II,3:7
Harvey 1949,Mr 24,34:1
Harvey 1950,O 21,10:4
Harvey 1950,D 31,II,3:7
Mrs McThing 1952,F 21,22:1
Mrs McThing 1952,Mr 2,II,1:1
Bernardine 1952,O 17,33:4
Bernardine 1952,N 9,II,1:1
Midgie Purvis 1961,F 2,25:3
Midgie Purvis 1961,F 12,II,1:1
Harvey 1970,F 25,41:1

Chase, Mary (Playwright)—Cont
Harvey 1970,Mr 8,II,1:1
Chase, Mary Coyle (Playwright)
Now You've Done It 1937,Mr 6,10:4
Chase, Mary Ellen (Original Author)
Land's End 1946,D 12,37:5
Chase, Miss
Man Without Money, A 1929,N 3,27:4
Chase, Sara
Contrast, The 1926,O 1,26:2
Chase, Stanley (Producer)
Threepenny Opera, The 1954,Mr 11,26:5
Threepenny Opera, The 1955,S 21,38:1
Potting Shed, The 1957,Ja 30,32:1
Moon for the Misbegotten, A 1957,My 3,21:2
Cave Dwellers, The 1957,O 21,29:2
Free and Easy 1959,D 15,51:4
Free and Easy 1959,D 20,II,3:2
Chase, Stephen
Uncle Harry 1942,My 21,24:1
Strange Fruit 1945,N 30,18:6
Allegro 1947,O 11,10:2
Caine Mutiny Court-Martial, The 1954,Ja 21,27:2
Captains and the Kings, The 1962,Ja 3,25:2
Chase, Susan
Groove Tube 1969,O 12,88:3
Chasen, Dave
Earl Carroll's Vanities 1924,S 11,23:6
Rain or Shine 1928,F 10,26:3
Rain or Shine 1928,F 19,VIII,1:1
Fine and Dandy 1930,S 7,IX,2:4
Fine and Dandy 1930,S 24,26:1
Hold Your Horses 1933,S 26,26:4
Chasen, David (Producer)
Mating Season, The 1927,Jl 19,27:6
Chasen, Heather
Severed Head, A 1964,O 29,40:1
Chasier, Isidor
Roaming Stars 1930,Ja 25,12:2
Chasman, Tanya (Producer)
World of Kurt Weill in Song, The 1964,My 13,53:1
Entertaining Mr Sloane 1965,O 13,41:1
Chason, Cornelia
Marching By 1932,Mr 4,17:1
Chasseing, Michel
Femmes Savantes, Les 1967,F 7,34:2
Chastain, Don
No Strings 1962,Mr 16,24:1
It's a Bird . . . It's a Plane . . . It's Superman
1966,Mr 30,34:1
Chateauneuf, Robert
Tidings Brought to Mary, The 1922,D 25,20:1
Chatham, Myra
Without the Walls 1920,Je 7,20:1
Little Town of Bethlehem, The 1920,D 27,11:1
Without the Walls 1921,Mr 28,8:1
Without the Walls 1922,Ap 17,17:1
Chatrain, Erckmann MM (Playwright)
Bells, The 1926,Ap 14,20:3
Chatterjee, Monimohon
Ramayana 1931,Ja 13,35:4
Chatterjee, Ramendu
Ramayana 1931,Ja 13,35:4
Chatterjee, Sris
Ramayana 1931,Ja 13,35:4
Chatterly, E J
Merton of the Movies 1922,N 14,16:2
Chatterton, Arthur
Divided by Three 1934,O 3,24:2
Romeo and Juliet 1934,D 21,30:3
Flowers of the Forest 1935,Ap 9,25:2
Romeo and Juliet 1935,D 24,10:2
Saint Joan 1936,Mr 10,27:4
Wingless Victory, The 1936,N 25,17:5
Wingless Victory, The 1936,D 24,20:2
Save Me the Waltz 1938,Mr 1,19:2
Three Sisters, The 1942,D 22,31:2
Three Sisters, The 1942,D 27,VIII,1:1
Chatterton, Ruth
Maker of Dreams, The 1920,Ap 28,9:3
Mary Rose 1920,D 23,9:2
Tendresse, La 1922,S 26,18:1
Tendresse, La 1922,O 1,VII,1:1
Changelings, The 1923,Ag 26,VI,2:1
Changelings, The 1923,S 18,16:3
Changelings, The 1923,S 30,II,1:1
Untitled-Recital 1923,D 29,8:2
Magnolia Lady, The 1924,N 26,17:2
Little Minister, The 1925,Mr 24,21:1
Women and Ladies 1925,My 10,VIII,4:4
Man With a Load of Mischief, The 1925,O 27,20:1
Man With a Load of Mischief, The
1925,N 1,VIII,1:1
Let Us Divorce; Counsel's Opinion
1932,Ap 17,VIII,2:6
Constant Wife, The 1937,Je 6,XI,1:5
Leave Her to Heaven 1940,F 28,16:2
Treat Her Gently 1941,Mr 30,I,48:1
Second Best Bed 1946,Je 4,20:2
Idiot's Delight 1951,My 24,46:3
Chatterton, Ruth (Director)
Second Best Bed 1946,Je 4,20:2
Chatterton, Ruth (Miscellaneous)
Second Best Bed 1946,Je 4,20:2

Chatterton, Ruth (Playwright)
Monsieur Brotonneau 1930,O 5,IX,2:4
Chatterton, Ruth (Translator)
Man in Evening Clothes, The 1924,D 6,13:4
Chatterton, Will T
House of Ussher, The 1926,Ja 14,18:4
Frankie and Johnny 1930,S 26,16:5
Chaucer, Geoffrey (Original Author)
Canterbury Tales 1968,S 7,23:3
Get Thee to Canterbury 1969,Ja 26,74:1
Canterbury Tales 1969,F 16,II,1:1
Chaucer, Geoffrey (Playwright)
Canterbury Tales; Merchant's Tale, The
1969,F 4,34:1
Canterbury Tales; Wife of Bath's Tale, The
1969,F 4,34:1
Canterbury Tales; Pilgrims, The 1969,F 4,34:1
Canterbury Tales; Miller's Tale, The 1969,F 4,34:1
Canterbury Tales; Steward's Tale, The
1969,F 4,34:1
Chaumette, Francois
Fourberies de Scapin, Les 1961,F 22,30:1
Tartuffe 1961,Mr 1,28:1
Britannicus 1961,Mr 3,17:1
Dindon, Le 1961,Mr 8,38:1
Avare, L', L'; Miser, The 1966,F 9,32:1
Cid, Le 1966,F 12,17:1
Reine Morte, La 1966,F 16,52:1
Chaumette, Monique
Triomphe de l'Amour, Le 1958,O 17,32:1
Marie Tudor 1958,O 22,39:1
Don Juan 1958,O 29,29:1
Cid, Le 1958,O 31,35:2
Enchaines; Welded 1965,Mr 13,17:1
Chauvel, Denise
Ecole des Femmes, L' 1961,Ap 28,23:1
Chauvenet, Virginia
Royal Fandango, A 1923,N 13,25:1
Mrs Partridge Presents 1925,Ja 6,23:3
Woman of Bronze, The 1927,Je 16,25:4
Lady of the Orchids, The 1928,D 14,37:3
Reunion in Vienna 1931,N 17,31:1
Escape This Night 1938,Ap 23,18:1
I Know What I Like 1939,N 25,13:5
Chavales de Espana, Los
Vaudeville (Palace) 1953,O 15,42:1
Chavance (Miscellaneous)
Quand Je Voudrais 1924,Je 29,VII,1:8
Chavassieux, Gilles
Three Musketeers, The 1968,Je 26,43:1
Chavez, Alfonso
To Quito and Back 1937,O 7,30:4
Chayefsky, Paddy (Director)
Passion of Josef D, The 1964,F 12,29:1
Chayefsky, Paddy (Playwright)
Middle of the Night 1956,F 9,39:1
Middle of the Night 1956,F 19,II,1:1
Tenth Man, The 1959,N 6,24:2
Tenth Man, The 1959,N 15,II,1:1
Tenth Man, The 1961,Ap 14,23:4
Gideon 1961,N 10,38:1
Gideon 1961,N 19,II,1:1
Tenth Man, The 1962,O 3,46:1
Passion of Josef D, The 1964,F 12,29:1
Passion of Josef D, The 1964,F 23,II,1:1
10th Man, The 1966,Ap 23,15:6
Tenth Man, The 1967,N 9,54:1
Latent Heterosexual, The 1968,Mr 22,52:1
Latent Heterosexual, The 1968,Mr 31,II,3:1
Chayres, Nestor
Concert Varieties 1945,Je 2,10:7
Chazal, Mireille
Grosse Valise, La 1965,D 15,52:1
Cheatham, Adolphus
Pirate, The 1942,N 26,39:2
Cheatham, Jack
Diamond Lil 1928,Ap 10,32:1
Straight Thru the Door 1928,O 5,17:2
Cheatle, Syd (Playwright)
Straight Up 1970,S 2,30:2
Checco, Al
Lend an Ear 1948,D 17,38:2
Buttrio Square 1952,O 15,40:2
Leave It to Jane 1959,My 26,30:2
Lend an Ear 1959,S 25,20:5
Chechik-Efroti
Eternal Jew, The 1926,D 21,21:2
Checkov, Mme
Tsar Fyodor Ivanovitch 1923,My 22,14:3
Chedister, America
Jack and Jill 1923,Mr 23,17:2
Chee, Grace
Roar China! 1930,O 28,23:1
Cheetah
Little Hut, The 1961,Jl 26,34:2
Cheetham, Everett
Green Grow the Lilacs 1931,Ja 27,21:2
Cheever, John (Original Author)
Town House 1948,S 24,31:2
Cheffer, Ch (Playwright)
Light, Lively and Yiddish 1970,O 28,58:1
Cheffey, Mary
Time of Your Life, The 1939,O 26,26:2

Chehov
Hamlet 1925,Ja 11,VII,2:7
Cheirel, Jeanne
Bapteme, Le 1928,Mr 11,VIII,2:7
Ascension de Virginie, L' 1929,N 3,IX,4:2
Chekhov, Anton (Miscellaneous)
Wisteria Trees, The 1950,Ap 9,II,1:1
Chekhov, Anton (Original Author)
Cherry Orchard, The 1933,Mr 7,20:3
Country Scandal, A 1960,My 15,II,1:1
Witch, The 1962,F 16,35:2
Vagrant, The 1962,F 16,35:2
Music Shop, The 1962,F 16,35:2
Seagull, The 1964,Ap 6,36:1
Three Sisters, The 1964,Je 23,24:1
Cherry Orchard, The 1965,Ag 2,17:2
Duel, The 1968,Ap 18,56:1
Que Vida de Perro 1968,Ag 2,24:1
Chekhov, Anton (Playwright)
Cherry Orchard, The 1923,Ja 23,18:1
Cherry Orchard, The 1923,Ja 28,VII,1:1
Three Sisters, The 1923,Ja 30,12:2
Cherry Orchard, The; Three Sisters, The
1923,F 4,VII,1:1
Ivanoff 1923,N 27,23:2
Uncle Vanya 1924,Ja 29,16:2
Cherry Orchard, The 1926,O 17,VIII,2:1
Three Sisters, The 1926,O 27,24:1
Three Sisters, The 1926,N 7,VIII,1:1
Three Sisters, The 1927,Mr 13,VII,2:4
Cherry Orchard, The 1928,Mr 6,20:1
Cherry Orchard, The 1928,O 16,28:5
Cherry Orchard, The 1928,N 8,26:8
Cherry Orchard, The 1928,N 18,IX,1:2
On the High Road 1929,Ja 15,22:3
Three Sisters 1929,F 17,IX,4:2
Man Platonof, The 1929,Mr 3,VIII,3:1
Sea Gull, The 1929,Ap 10,32:2
Uncle Vanya 1929,My 25,17:1
Cherry Orchard, The 1929,Je 2,VIII,1:1
Sea Gull, The 1929,S 17,34:1
Three Sisters, The 1930,Ja 9,22:2
Sea Gull, The 1930,F 23,III,7:2
Sea Gull, The 1930,F 26,22:2
Uncle Vanya 1930,Ap 16,26:5
Uncle Vanya 1930,Ap 20,VIII,1:1
Sea Gull, The 1930,My 4,XI,1:1
Uncle Vanya 1930,My 4,XI,1:1
Uncle Vanya 1930,S 23,30:3
I Forgot 1935,Mr 12,24:8
Seagull, The 1936,My 21,19:2
Seagull, The 1936,Je 21,IX,1:5
Seagull, The 1936,Ag 30,IX,1:1
Three Sisters, The 1938,F 13,X,3:3
Sea Gull, The 1938,Mr 17,16:5
Sea Gull, The 1938,Mr 29,19:2
Sea Gull, The 1938,Ap 3,XI,1:1
Wood Demon, The 1938,Ag 7,IX,1:5
Three Sisters, The 1939,O 16,23:1
Fireworks on the James 1940,My 15,30:2
Cherry Orchard, The 1941,S 7,IX,2:5
I Forgot 1942,S 28,13:1
Happy Ending 1942,S 28,13:1
Witch, The 1942,S 28,13:1
After the Theatre 1942,S 28,13:1
Story of Miss N N, The 1942,S 28,13:1
Three Sisters, The 1942,D 22,31:2
Cherry Orchard, The 1944,Ja 26,22:1
Cherry Orchard, The 1944,F 6,II,1:1
Uncle Vanya 1946,My 14,18:2
Uncle Vanya 1946,My 19,II,1:1
Wedding, The 1948,F 6,29:2
Bear, The 1948,F 6,29:2
On the Harmfulness of Tobacco 1948,F 6,29:2
Tragedian in Spite of Himself, A 1948,F 6,29:2
Sea Gull, The 1949,Ap 23,10:2
Swan Song 1951,O 16,35:2
Don Juan in the Russian Manner 1954,Ap 23,23:2
Sea Gull, The 1954,My 12,38:1
Sea Gull, The 1954,My 23,II,1:1
Sea Gull, The 1954,Jl 7,22:1
Wisteria Trees, The 1955,F 3,20:2
Three Sisters, The 1955,F 26,13:2
Three Sisters, The 1955,Mr 20,II,1:1
2 for Fun; Anniversary, The 1955,My 26,34:1
Cherry Orchard, The 1955,O 19,38:1
Uncle Vanya 1956,F 1,25:2
Uncle Vanya 1956,F 12,II,1:1
Uncle Vanya 1956,Mr 4,II,1:1
On the Harmfulness of Tobacco 1956,Ap 26,38:1
Sea Gull, The 1956,O 23,38:1
Cherry Orchard, The 1958,My 16,22:2
Ivanov 1958,O 8,42:1
Ivanov 1958,O 19,II,1:1
On the Harmful Effects of Tobacco
1959,Ap 16,28:1
On the Harmful Effects of Tobacco
1959,Ap 26,II,1:1
Three Sisters, The 1959,S 22,46:1
Three Sisters, The 1959,O 4,II,1:1
Uncle Vanya 1960,F 13,13:4
Uncle Vanya 1960,F 14,19:1
Country Scandal, A 1960,My 6,21:8

Chekhov, Anton (Playwright)—Cont
Seagull, The 1960,Je 2,26:4
Cherry Orchard, The 1960,Je 4,17:2
Seagull, The 1960,Ag 24,33:2
Seagull, The 1961,Ja 8,84:5
Wedding, The 1961,Ap 21,26:2
On the High Road 1961,Ap 21,26:2
Anniversary, The 1961,Ap 21,26:2
Friends and Lovers; Proposal, The 1961,My 11,43:1
Cherry Orchard, The 1961,D 15,49:1
Seagull, The 1962,Mr 22,42:1
Seagull, The 1962,Ap 1,II,1:1
Uncle Vanya 1962,Jl 17,18:4
Cherry Orchard, The 1962,N 15,46:2
Three Sisters, The 1963,Je 20,30:7
Uncle Vanya 1963,Jl 2,16:2
Three Sisters, The 1963,Jl 22,19:2
Cherry Orchard, The 1964,Je 18,29:5
Three Sisters, The 1964,Jl 5,II,1:1
Three Sisters, The 1964,Jl 28,26:7
Cherry Orchard, The 1965,F 10,46:1
Three Sisters, The 1965,F 12,15:1
Three Sisters, The 1965,My 15,19:4
Ivanov 1966,My 4,50:1
Ivanov 1966,My 15,II,1:1
Marriage Proposal, The 1966,Je 28,51:1
Victims, The; On the Hazards of Smoking Tobacco
1968,Mr 6,34:1
Three Sisters, The 1968,Mr 18,56:1
Cherry Orchard, The 1968,Mr 20,41:1
Cherry Orchard, The 1968,Ap 7,II,3:7
Seagull, The 1968,Jl 25,27:2
On the Harmfulness of Tobacco 1969,Mr 9,76:5
Three Sisters, The 1969,Ag 4,29:1
Three Sisters, The 1969,Ag 10,II,3:1
Three Sisters, The 1969,Ag 31,II,4:1
Uncle Vanya 1969,Ag 31,II,4:1
Three Sisters, The 1969,O 10,38:1
Three Sisters, The 1969,O 19,II,3:1
Three Sisters, The 1970,F 12,30:1
Three Sisters, The 1970,F 22,II,1:1
Uncle Vanya 1970,Mr 15,II,7:3
Cherry Orchard, The 1970,My 7,63:2
Proposal, The 1970,Ag 26,36:1
Chekhov, Michael
Revisor; Inspector General, The 1935,F 18,19:6
Inspector General, The 1935,F 24,VIII,3:1
I Forgot 1935,Mr 12,24:8
Deluge, The 1935,Mr 26,23:7
I Forgot 1942,S 28,13:1
Witch, The 1942,S 28,13:1
Chekhov, Michael (Director)
Revisor; Inspector General, The 1935,F 18,19:6
Inspector General, The 1935,F 24,VIII,3:1
Possessed, The 1939,O 25,26:2
Twelfth Night 1941,D 3,32:2
I Forgot 1942,S 28,13:1
Happy Ending 1942,S 28,13:1
Witch, The 1942,S 28,13:1
Story of Miss N N, The 1942,S 28,13:1
After the Theatre 1942,S 28,13:1
Chekhov, Michael (Producer)
Twelfth Night 1941,D 3,32:2
Chello, Aleck (Miscellaneous)
Dance of Death, The 1960,S 14,51:1
Chello, Xander
Dance of Death, The 1960,S 14,51:1
Utopia! 1963,My 7,47:4
Chelquist, Norman
Trial of Dr Beck, The 1937,Ag 10,22:2
Medea 1960,Jl 26,25:2
Chelquist, Norman (Director)
Medea 1960,Jl 26,25:2
Chelsi, Lawrence
Golden Apple, The 1954,Mr 12,15:2
She Shall Have Music 1959,Ja 23,18:4
Cheltenham, Charles
He Who Gets Slapped 1922,Ja 10,15:1
Lady Cristilinda, The 1922,D 26,11:2
Fata Morgana 1924,Mr 4,16:3
Caesar and Cleopatra 1925,Ap 14,27:1
Chelton, Tsilla
Chaises, Les 1970,My 6,49:1
Chemodurov, E G (Scenic Designer)
Moscow Circus on Ice 1970,D 9,63:1
Chen-tsu, Wang (Producer)
Peh Shuh Tchuwan; White Snake, The 1963,Ja 4,5:2
Chenault, Lawrence
Ol' Man Satan 1932,O 4,26:3
Macbeth 1936,Ap 15,25:4
Chenaval, Mildred
Leave It to Me! 1938,N 10,32:2
Chenery, Howard (Playwright)
That Ferguson Family 1928,D 24,10:7
Devil of Pei-Ling 1936,F 21,20:4
Cheney, Bushnell
Trip to Scarborough, A 1929,Mr 18,31:2
Dragon, The 1929,Mr 26,34:2
Cheney, Eddie
Laugh Parade, The 1931,N 3,31:2
Cheney, Frances
Audition of the Apprentice Theatre 1939,Je 2,26:2
Cheney, Genevieve
Virginian, The 1937,Ag 10,22:7

Cheng, Chun-tao
Paint Your Wagon 1951,N 13,32:2
Cheng, Stephen
Who Was That Lady I Saw You With?
  1958,Mr 4,33:2
World of Suzie Wong, The 1958,O 15,47:1
Harold 1962,N 30,27:1
Chenkin, Victor
Motel Peissi, The Contor's Kid 1934,N 29,33:3
Cherardi, Piero (Costume Designer)
White Devil, The 1969,N 14,38:2
Cherenko, Fanya
Marching Song 1937,F 18,18:2
Cherer-Bekefi, Marie
Miracle, The 1927,F 1,24:5
Cherif, Cipriano Rivas (Director)
Dama Boba, La; Villano En Su Rincon, El;
  Fuenteovejuna 1935,S 22,X,2:5
Cherin, Robert (Producer)
By Jupiter 1967,Ja 20,28:2
Cherkasov, G K (Musical Director)
West Side Story 1965,Je 25,37:2
Chermak, Cy
Seeds in the Wind 1948,Ap 26,27:2
Chernak, Steve (Director)
Square, The 1961,Mr 24,37:1
Old Tune, The 1961,Mr 24,37:1
Dock Brief, The 1961,N 22,24:2
What Shall We Tell Caroline? 1961,N 22,24:2
Cherneff, J Robert (Composer)
Life Begins in '40 1940,Ap 5,24:2
Cherniavsky, Joseph (Composer)
Three Little Business Men, The 1923,S 4,12:1
Jolly Tailors, The 1923,N 3,13:3
Cherniavsky, Joseph (Musical Director)
Parisian Love 1927,Ja 28,15:5
Chernichovsky, S (Translator)
As You Like It 1930,S 19,18:5
Oedipus Rex 1948,My 24,23:2
Chernin, Leah
Enchanted, The 1950,Ja 19,34:2
Chernis, Jay (Composer)
Date With April, A 1953,Ap 16,36:2
Stockade 1954,F 5,14:2
Chernov, Pyotr
Three Sisters, The 1965,F 12,15:1
Kremlin Chimes 1965,F 25,23:1
Chernowsky, Joseph (Playwright)
Morris, the Fiddler 1920,Ap 9,11:4
Chernuck, Dorothy (Director)
Kilgo Run, The 1953,D 13,105:1
Rate of Exchange 1968,Ap 2,50:1
Cherpak, Larisa
Moscow Circus on Ice 1970,D 9,63:1
Cherrie, John
Robin Hood 1929,N 20,26:5
Cherry, Catherine
Choice, The 1930,My 9,20:5
Cherry, Charles
Tyranny of Love, The 1921,My 3,20:2
Tyranny of Love, The 1921,My 8,VI,1:1
Dover Road, The 1921,D 24,7:2
Success 1923,Jl 8,VI,1:1
Camel's Back, The 1923,N 4,19:2
Camel's Back, The 1923,N 18,VIII,1:1
Vaudeville (Palace) 1924,Ja 15,17:3
Cherry, Ewing
Minstrel Boy, The 1948,O 15,28:2
Moon Shines on Kylenamoe, The 1962,O 31,33:1
Chief Thing, The 1963,Ap 30,27:2
Cherry, Frances H
Holka Polka 1925,O 15,27:2
Cherry, Harold
Caesar and Cleopatra 1963,Ag 1,18:2
This Here Nice Place 1966,N 2,35:2
Cherry, James
Hell's Bells! 1925,Ja 27,14:2
Appearances 1925,O 15,27:3
Cherry, Joetta
Here's Where I Belong 1968,Mr 4,32:1
X Has No Value 1970,F 17,35:1
Cherry, Joetta (Choreographer)
X Has No Value 1970,F 17,35:1
Cherry, John
Suzette 1921,N 25,18:3
Glory 1922,D 26,10:1
Talking Parrot, The 1923,D 4,25:3
Nic-Nax of 1926 1926,Ag 5,19:1
Gossipy Sex, The 1927,Ap 20,28:3
Serenade, The 1930,Mr 5,26:7
Robin Hood 1932,Ja 28,25:4
Lambs Gambol 1932,Ap 25,18:2
School for Husbands, The 1933,O 17,26:5
Mikado, The 1934,Ap 3,26:3
Pirates of Penzance, The 1934,Ap 10,26:5
Trial by Jury 1934,Ap 17,27:2
H M S Pinafore 1934,Ap 17,27:2
Mikado, The 1934,Ap 24,27:5
Robin Hood 1935,Jl 15,20:6
Excursion 1937,Ap 10,11:4
Of Thee I Sing 1937,Ag 10,22:3
Of Thee I Sing 1937,Ag 18,14:4
I'd Rather Be Right 1937,N 3,28:2

Foreigners 1939,D 6,30:2
Return of the Vagabond, The 1940,My 14,27:2
Viva O'Brien 1941,O 10,27:2
Merry Widow, The 1942,Jl 16,22:1
Connecticut Yankee, A 1943,N 18,30:2
Violet 1944,O 25,16:1
Rhapsody 1944,N 23,37:2
Cherry, Malcolm
Old House, The 1920,Jl 11,VI,1:6
Cherry, Margaret
Johnny Belinda 1940,S 19,26:2
Cherry, Paul (Lyricist)
Park 1970,Ap 23,47:1
Cherry, Paul (Playwright)
Park 1970,Ap 23,47:1
Cherryman, Rex
Topsy and Eva 1924,D 24,11:1
Valley of Content, The 1925,Ja 14,19:2
Downstream 1926,Ja 12,28:1
Noose, The 1926,O 21,23:3
Madame X 1927,Jl 7,29:3
Trial of Mary Dugan, The 1927,S 20,33:1
Chertoff, Alex (Scenic Designer)
Wolves 1924,D 31,9:4
Major Noah 1929,F 23,17:2
His Wife's Lover 1929,O 21,30:6
If the Rabbi Wants 1929,D 23,18:5
Witch of Castile, The 1930,O 25,21:1
Yoshe Kalb 1932,N 6,IX,2:1
Longing for Home 1933,S 22,15:1
Wise Men of Chelm, The 1933,O 18,24:4
Yoshe Kalb 1933,D 29,27:2
Verdict, The 1934,S 22,12:5
Madame Pagliacci 1935,S 30,12:3
If I Were Rothschild 1940,Ja 1,28:7
Esterke 1940,O 18,24:2
Wandering Stars 1946,D 14,18:2
Chertok, Kenneth
Silk Stockings 1955,F 25,17:3
Chertov, Morris
Dead End 1935,O 29,17:2
Chertov, Robert (Scenic Designer)
Path of Flowers, The 1936,S 18,19:3
Hymn to the Rising Sun 1937,My 7,28:2
Unto Such Glory 1937,My 7,28:2
Chesleigh, Irene
Vaudeville (Palace) 1929,S 23,24:6
Chesley, Castleman De Tolley
Red Rhumba 1936,Ap 14,18:1
This Mad Whirl 1937,Ja 10,II,4:8
Chesley, Jo
Mikado, The 1961,My 5,23:1
Iolanthe 1962,Ag 8,34:2
Chesmond, Dorothy
Tobias and the Angel 1937,Ap 29,16:5
Chesney, Charles
Music in May 1929,Ap 2,29:1
Wonderful Night, A; Fledermaus, Die
  1929,N 1,23:3
Student Prince, The 1931,Ja 30,18:1
Student Prince, The 1943,Je 9,16:2
Chesney, Jayne
Sitting Pretty 1924,Ap 9,24:2
Chesney, Nancy
Master Builder, The 1957,D 18,42:7
Chessid, Herman (Composer)
All's Well That Ends Well 1959,Ag 3,20:4
Twelfth Night 1960,Je 9,29:4
Troilus and Cressida 1961,Jl 24,15:1
Henry IV, Part I 1962,Je 18,20:4
Comedy of Errors, The 1963,Je 13,28:1
Henry V 1963,Je 14,37:1
Caesar and Cleopatra 1963,Ag 1,18:2
Birds, The 1966,Jl 1,40:1
Chessid, Herman (Lyricist)
Twelfth Night 1960,Je 9,29:4
Henry IV, Part I 1962,Je 18,20:4
Chester, Albert
Malinda 1929,D 4,37:2
Sugar Hill 1931,D 26,15:2
Chester, Alfred
Pansy 1929,My 15,36:3
Chester, Alma
Plain Jane 1924,My 13,24:2
Chester, Arthur
Taming of the Shrew, The 1935,O 1,27:3
Chester, Charva
There Shall Be No Night 1940,Ap 30,25:2
Chester, Eddie
Artists and Models 1927,N 16,28:2
Chester, Elizabeth
Paris 1928,O 9,34:3
Chester, Ford
Tarzan of the Apes 1921,S 8,14:3
I Will IF You Will 1922,Ag 30,10:4
Chester, George Randolph (Original Author)
Izzy 1924,S 17,16:2
Chester, Lillian (Original Author)
Izzy 1924,S 17,16:2
Chester, R F (Playwright)
Little Theatre Tournament; Edna 1929,My 11,22:2
Chester, Shirley
Beggar's Opera, The 1957,Mr 14,35:1

Chesterfields, The Two
Hummin' Sam 1933,Ap 10,8:8
Chesterton, Gilbert Keith (Playwright)
Magic 1929,D 17,28:5
Judgment of Dr Johnson, The 1932,F 7,VIII,2:4
Magic 1935,Mr 14,19:2
Magic 1942,S 30,28:2
Cheston, Dorothy
Medea 1920,Mr 23,12:2
Byron 1929,F 10,IX,4:7
Cheston, Laura
Lightnin' 1938,S 16,17:2
Cheswick, Diana
Gay Apprentice, The 1960,F 3,27:2
Chetham-Strode (Playwright)
Man Proposes 1933,D 24,IX,2:2
Chetwyn, Robert (Director)
There's a Girl in My Soup 1967,O 19,58:1
Importance of Being Earnest, The 1968,Jl 6,9:1
Country Wife, The 1969,Ag 30,10:3
Chetwynd, Ross
Few Wild Oats, A 1932,Mr 25,22:6
O Evening Star 1936,Ja 9,24:6
Love on the Dole 1936,F 25,23:3
Amazing Dr. Clitterhouse, The 1937,Mr 3,26:4
Woman Brown, The 1939,D 9,18:5
Walking Gentleman, The 1942,My 8,26:2
Land's End 1946,D 12,37:5
Carousel 1949,Ja 26,28:2
Chevalier, Kay
Cicero 1961,F 9,37:2
Trojan Women, The 1963,D 24,7:6
Chevalier, Marie Aude
Intermezzo 1957,F 15,20:4
Chevalier, Maurice
White Birds 1927,Je 26,VIII,1:3
Untitled-Revue 1928,Ja 15,VIII,2:3
Untitled-Revue 1928,Mr 11,VIII,2:7
Ziegfeld's Midnight Frolic 1929,F 19,22:4
Untitled-One Man Show 1930,Mr 31,24:1
Untitled-One Man Show 1930,D 2,31:2
Vaudeville (Carnegie Hall) 1931,Ap 12,I,30:4
Vaudeville (New Amsterdam Theatre)
  1931,Je 22,17:3
Untitled-One Man Show 1952,O 31,30:6
Songs and Impressions 1955,S 29,38:2
Maurice Chevalier 1963,Ja 30,7:2
Maurice Chevalier at 77 1965,Ap 2,26:1
Untitled-One Man Show 1967,N 20,61:1
Chevalier Brothers, The
Puzzles of 1925 1925,F 3,25:3
Vaudeville (Palace) 1929,Je 10,22:6
Vaudeville (Palace) 1929,D 23,19:1
Cheveley, Roger (Scenic Designer)
Opium 1970,O 6,58:1
Chevers, Osbert
Twelfth Night 1940,N 20,26:3
Cheval, Jane
Trial of Mary Dugan, The 1929,F 24,IX,1:8
Chevrel, Jeanne
Homme Qui Jouait du Banjo, L' 1926,O 24,VIII,2:1
Eunuque, L' 1927,Ap 3,VIII,4:7
Robe de Perles, La 1928,Ja 15,VIII,2:3
Chevrier, Jean
Enchaines; Welded 1965,Mr 13,17:1
Chew, Frank
Beverly Hills 1940,N 8,24:2
Chew, King Lan
Continental Varieties 1935,D 27,15:3
Chew, Virgilia
All This While 1935,Jl 30,17:2
Ethan Frome 1936,Ja 22,15:2
Women, The 1936,D 28,13:1
Orpheus Descending 1957,Mr 22,28:1
Sotoba Komachi 1961,F 1,15:1
Damask Drum, The 1961,F 4,15:1
Dumbbell People in a Barbell World 1962,F 15,25:1
Winterset 1966,F 10,32:2
Yerma 1966,D 9,60:1
Cheyette, Irving
Madre 1923,D 31,9:6
Chi, Norman
First Lady 1952,My 29,18:5
Chi, Shun-hain Chang (Scenic Designer)
First Wife, The 1945,N 28,21:5
Chianese, Dominic
Winterset 1966,F 10,32:2
Ballad for a Firing Squad 1968,D 12,64:2
Paradise Gardens East 1969,Mr 11,39:1
Conerico Was Here to Stay 1969,Mr 11,39:1
Chiarelli, Luigi (Original Author)
Mask and the Face, The 1933,My 9,20:2
Chiarelli, Luigi (Playwright)
Mask and the Face, The 1924,S 11,27:3
Masque et Visage 1927,Ap 3,VIII,4:7
Money! Money! 1931,Mr 15,IX,2:8
Chiari, Walter
Gay Life, The 1961,N 20,38:1
Chiarmello, Giancarlo (Composer)
Venetian Twins, The 1968,My 29,23:1
Chiaro, Edward
Enemy of the People, An 1959,F 5,24:4

Chiaro, Edward—Cont
Buskers, The 1961,O 31,28:1
Chick and Andy
Here Goes the Bride 1931,N 4,31:2
Chidgey, Norman
Murder in the Cathedral 1938,F 17,16:2
Chiesa, Ivo (Director)
Venetian Twins, The 1968,My 29,23:1
Chika, Inger
Most Immoral Lady, A 1928,N 27,36:1
Chilcott, Barbara
Measure for Measure 1954,Je 30,23:1
Taming of the Shrew, The 1954,Jl 1,22:2
Tamburlaine the Great 1956,Ja 20,19:1
Glass Cage, The 1957,Mr 11,21:2
Child, Alan (Playwright)
Pursuit of Happiness, The 1933,O 10,24:4
Champagne, Sec 1933,O 16,20:2
Child, Edwin
Pillars of Society, The 1931,O 15,19:1
Child, Edwin (Miscellaneous)
Butter and Egg Man, The 1949,Ap 29,27:1
Child, Edwin (Producer)
From Morn Till Midnight 1948,D 7,41:6
Child, Marilyn
Leonard Sillman's New Faces of 1968
 1968,My 3,43:1
New Faces of 1968 1968,My 12,II,7:1
Child, Nellise (Playwright)
Weep for the Virgins 1935,D 2,18:1
Sister Oakes 1949,Ap 25,19:4
Child, Thurston (Director)
Way of the Cross, The 1959,Ja 16,35:2
Child, Thurston (Miscellaneous)
Mystery of the Finding of the Cross, The
 1959,Ja 16,35:2
Childers, Michael (Miscellaneous)
Oh! Calcutta! 1969,Je 18,33:1
Children's Players
Racketty Packetty House 1931,N 7,16:1
Childress, Alice
Natural Man 1941,My 8,20:4
Anna Lucasta 1944,Je 17,10:1
Anna Lucasta 1944,Ag 31,15:1
Anna Lucasta 1944,S 10,II,1:1
Rain 1948,F 2,15:2
Almost Faithful 1948,Je 5,9:2
Emperor's Clothes, The 1953,O 23,19:7
Cool World, The 1960,F 23,38:2
Childress, Alice (Director)
Trouble in Mind 1955,N 5,23:2
Childress, Alice (Playwright)
Trouble in Mind 1955,N 5,23:2
String 1969,Ap 2,37:1
String 1969,Ap 13,II,1:1
Childress, Alvin
Savage Rhythm 1932,Ja 1,30:4
Brown Sugar 1937,D 3,29:2
Haiti 1938,Mr 3,16:1
Natural Man 1941,My 8,20:4
Anna Lucasta 1944,Je 17,10:1
Anna Lucasta 1944,Ag 31,15:1
Rain 1948,F 2,15:2
Childress, Florence
Tall Kentuckian, The 1953,Je 17,30:1
Childress, Yolanda
Troubled Waters 1965,Je 4,40:2
Childs, Araby
If You Get It, Do You Want It? 1938,D 1,28:2
Childs, Eddie
By the Way 1925,D 29,20:3
Childs, Hannah Lee
Everywhere I Roam 1938,D 30,10:4
Childs, Lee
May Wine 1935,D 6,30:3
Childs, Michael
Purification, The 1959,D 9,57:5
Childs, Michael (Choreographer)
Purification, The 1959,D 9,57:5
Childs, Michael (Composer)
Purification, The 1959,D 9,57:5
Childs, Monroe
Dancers, The 1923,O 18,17:2
Stork, The 1925,Ja 27,14:2
Machinal 1928,S 8,10:3
Childs, Polly
There Is a Play Tonight 1961,F 16,24:2
Child... iss
Mast... ...lder, The 1955,Mr 2,23:2
Childs, Su...en (Lighting Director)
Bacchae, The 1969,Mr 15,24:1
Bacchae, The 1969,Mr 23,II,11:1
Chilson, Bea
Girl From Samos, The 1954,N 24,17:1
Chilton, Charles (Composer)
Portrait of a Queen 1968,F 29,29:1
Chilton, Charles (Playwright)
Oh What a Lovely War 1964,O 1,30:1
Chilton, Dorothy
New Faces of 1936 1936,My 20,24:5
Chilton, Eleanor (Playwright)
Healthy, Wealthy and Wise 1930,Mr 2,26:3
Healthy, Wealthy and Wise 1930,Mr 23,IX,2:3

Chilton, Eleanor Carroll (Original Author)
Fledgling 1940,N 28,29:2
Chilton, Eleanor Carroll (Playwright)
Fledgling 1940,N 28,29:2
Chilton, Frederick
Caesar and Cleopatra 1925,Ap 14,27:1
Androcles and the Lion 1925,N 24,28:1
Chilton, H S
Night at an Inn, A 1930,My 10,25:1
Chilton, Marling
Man and the Masses 1924,Ap 15,25:1
Chilton, Nola
Skipper Next to God 1948,Ja 5,14:5
Chilton, Nola (Director)
Banquet for the Moon, A 1961,Ja 20,24:2
Chilton, Nola (Producer)
Once Over Lightly 1955,Mr 16,39:1
Chilton, Robert
Audition of the Apprentice Theatre 1939,Je 2,26:2
Chilvers, Chat
It's About Time 1942,Mr 31,28:3
Chilvers, Hugh
Bootleggers, The 1922,N 28,24:1
Poppy 1923,S 4,14:2
Great Music 1924,O 6,24:1
Edgar Allan Poe 1925,O 6,31:1
Countess Maritza 1926,S 20,21:1
Red Robe, The 1928,D 26,15:1
Great Day! 1929,O 18,24:3
Chilvers, Natalie
Woman Brown, The 1939,D 9,18:5
Chin, Allen
Carefree Tree, The 1955,O 12,37:2
Chin, Ching-Ming
Bamboo Cross 1955,F 22,17:2
Chin, Chueck Ming
Suds in Your Eye 1944,Ja 13,15:5
Chin, Clark
First Wife, The 1945,N 28,21:5
Chin, Tanya
Bamboo Cross 1955,F 22,17:2
Chinese Cultural Mission
Evening in Cathay, An 1939,F 2,16:2
Chinese Whoopee Revue
Vaudeville (Palace) 1930,Mr 10,24:4
Ching, Grace
Bamboo Cross 1955,F 22,17:2
Ching, William
Allegro 1947,O 11,10:2
Chinitz, Samuel
Processional 1925,Ja 13,17:1
Chinley, Jeannette
Pride and Prejudice 1935,N 6,32:4
Cat and the Canary, The 1937,Je 15,26:3
Devil Takes a Bride, The 1938,O 8,10:3
Journey to Jerusalem 1940,O 7,21:2
Susan and God 1943,D 14,30:2
Right Next to Broadway 1944,F 22,26:2
Chinn, Lori
Lovely Ladies, Kind Gentlemen 1970,D 29,38:1
Chinnery, Dennis
Time Remembered 1955,My 4,35:1
Chippendale, Affie
Dancers, The 1923,O 18,17:2
Chippendale, Lenore
Twelfth Night 1921,N 1,17:1
Merchant of Venice, The 1921,N 22,17:1
Romeo and Juliet 1922,D 28,20:1
Cymbeline 1923,O 3,12:1
Twelfth Night 1923,O 23,17:1
Hamlet 1923,O 31,12:1
Kingdom of God, The 1928,D 21,30:2
Chinese O'Neill 1929,My 23,27:1
Lady Clara 1930,Ap 18,28:7
Nine Till Six 1930,S 29,17:2
Happy Landing 1932,Mr 28,10:5
Fresh Fields 1934,Jl 15,X,1:1
Field of Ermine 1935,F 9,10:4
Whiteoaks 1938,Mr 24,20:2
Lady in Waiting 1940,Mr 28,19:1
Chippendale, Mary
Sex Fable, The 1931,O 21,26:1
Chiquita & Johnson
Jerry Lewis' Variety Show 1957,F 8,18:5
Chisholm, Ann
Cyrano de Bergerac 1953,N 13,24:3
Chisholm, Doris
Cornered 1920,D 9,18:2
Chisholm, Eric (Playwright)
Dark Sonnet 1958,Mr 12,36:1
Chisholm, Hazel (Composer)
Life Is Like That 1930,D 23,24:3
Chisholm, Hugh J Jr
Wings Over Europe 1936,Mr 4,24:7
Chisholm, Robert
Vaudeville (Palace) 1926,N 2,35:2
Golden Dawn 1927,O 2,VIII,4:6
Golden Dawn 1927,D 1,32:3
Vaudeville (Palace) 1928,My 15,17:1
Sweet Adeline 1929,S 4,33:1
Luana 1930,S 18,28:1
Threepenny Opera, The 1933,Ap 14,22:4
Frederika 1937,Jl 28,15:2

Chisholm, Robert—Cont
Nina Rosa 1937,Ag 26,24:3
Circus Princess, The 1937,Ag 31,26:6
Two Bouquets, The 1938,Je 1,19:2
Knights of Song 1938,O 18,29:2
Susanna, Don't You Cry 1939,My 23,27:2
Higher and Higher 1940,Ap 5,24:3
Night of Love 1941,Ja 8,14:2
Without Love 1942,N 11,28:1
Blossom Time 1943,S 6,21:2
Connecticut Yankee, A 1943,N 18,30:2
On the Town 1944,D 29,11:4
Million Dollar Baby 1945,D 22,17:2
Billion Dollar Baby 1945,D 30,II,1:1
Park Avenue 1946,N 5,31:2
Cradle Will Rock, The 1947,N 25,38:3
Topaze 1947,D 29,21:5
Bless You All 1950,D 15,42:2
Chisolm, Helen
Carolinian, The 1925,N 3,34:2
Chitos, Richard
Body Beautiful, The 1958,Ja 24,15:2
Chiu, Liang Shih (Producer)
Hamlet 1942,D 18,1:6
Chiusano, Michael
Princess Ida 1967,Ap 17,46:2
Chlumberg, Hans (Playwright)
Blaue vom Himmel, Das 1930,Ap 20,VIII,2:1
Wunder um Verdun 1930,D 7,IX,1:3
Miracle at Verdun 1931,Mr 17,34:6
Miracle at Verdun 1932,O 9,IX,3:8
Miracle at Verdun 1932,O 16,IX,3:7
Chlumberg, Hans (Translator)
Out of a Blue Sky 1930,F 10,20:6
Chmara, G
Revisor; Inspector General, The 1935,F 18,19:6
Poverty Is No Crime 1935,F 21,22:5
Enemies 1935,Mr 19,24:7
Deluge, The 1935,Mr 26,23:7
Chmara, G (Director)
Enemies 1935,Mr 19,24:7
Choate, Edward (Lighting Director)
Common Ground 1945,Ap 26,27:2
Choate, Edward (Producer)
I Was Waiting for You 1933,N 14,23:3
Kindred 1939,D 27,17:2
Juno and the Paycock 1940,Ja 17,24:2
Flying Gerardos, The 1940,D 30,21:4
Strings, My Lord, Are False, The 1942,My 20,24:2
Yankee Point 1942,N 24,28:2
Decision 1944,F 3,23:2
Alice in Arms 1945,F 1,18:4
Common Ground 1945,Ap 26,27:2
Gently Does It 1953,O 29,43:4
Choate, Edward (Scenic Designer)
Common Ground 1945,Ap 26,27:2
Chobanian, Haig
Shoemaker and the Peddler, The 1960,O 15,27:4
Tenth Man, The 1967,N 9,54:1
Mattathias of Modin 1968,Ap 15,41:1
Fireworks; Football 1969,Je 12,51:1
Fireworks; Fireworks for a Hot Fourth
 1969,Je 12,51:1
Chobrier, Marcel
Taming of the Shrew, The 1924,N 25,27:3
Chochom, Koren
Untitled-Revue 1939,Ja 16,11:3
Chocolateers, The
Blue Holiday 1945,My 22,13:3
Choder, Jill
Best Foot Forward 1963,Ap 3,43:1
Chodorov, Edward
Sam Abramovitch 1927,Ja 20,20:5
Chodorov, Edward (Director)
Those Endearing Young Charms 1943,Je 17,16:3
Decision 1944,F 3,23:2
Common Ground 1945,Ap 26,27:2
Oh, Men! Oh, Women! 1953,D 18,37:2
Chodorov, Edward (Playwright)
Wonder Boy 1931,O 24,20:1
Kind Lady 1935,Ap 24,24:5
Kind Lady 1935,Ap 28,X,1:1
Kind Lady 1935,Jl 23,24:4
Kind Lady 1935,N 19,27:3
Kind Lady 1936,Je 12,19:3
Kind Lady 1937,Jl 6,23:1
Kind Lady 1937,Jl 21,19:3
Kind Lady 1938,Jl 11,14:2
Kind Lady 1940,S 4,28:3
Cue for Passion 1940,D 20,33:4
Those Endearing Young Charms 1943,Je 17,16:3
Decision 1944,F 3,23:2
Decision 1944,F 13,II,1:1
Decision 1944,My 21,II,1:1
Common Ground 1945,Ap 26,27:2
Common Ground 1945,My 6,II,1:1
Director Riggs' Crime; Decision 1949,O 18,34:4
Oh, Men! Oh, Women! 1953,D 18,37:2
Chodorov, Jerome (Director)
Wonderful Town 1958,Mr 6,32:4
Make a Million 1958,O 24,39:2
Gazebo, The 1958,D 13,2:7
Blood, Sweat & Stanley Poole 1961,O 6,31:1

Chodorov, Jerome (Miscellaneous)
Alive and Kicking 1950,Ja 18,25:5
Chodorov, Jerome (Original Author)
Wonderful Town 1953,F 26,22:3
Chodorov, Jerome (Playwright)
Schoolhouse on the Lot 1938,Mr 23,18:4
My Sister Eileen 1940,D 27,23:2
My Sister Eileen 1941,Ja 5,IX,1:1
Junior Miss 1941,N 19,28:2
Junior Miss 1941,N 30,IX,1:1
French Touch, The 1945,D 10,18:2
Wonderful Town 1953,F 26,22:3
Wonderful Town 1953,Mr 8,II,1:1
Girl in Pink Tights, The 1954,Mr 6,13:2
Anniversary Waltz 1954,Ap 8,34:1
Anniversary Waltz 1954,Ap 25,II,1:1
Wonderful Town 1954,My 7,II,1:1
Anniversary Waltz 1955,D 2,31:3
Anniversary Waltz 1955,D 11,II,7:1
Ponder Heart, The 1956,F 17,14:2
Ponder Heart, The 1956,F 26,II,1:1
Wonderful Town 1958,Mr 6,32:4
Wonderful Town 1963,F 15,10:2
I Had a Ball 1964,D 16,50:1
3 Bags Full 1966,Mr 7,22:1
Wonderful Town 1967,My 18,50:1
Chodosh, Richard (Composer)
Legend of Lovers 1959,O 28,40:3
Streets of New York, The 1963,O 30,47:1
Cholet, Blanche
Othello 1953,O 30,28:2
Cretan Woman, The 1954,Jl 8,18:2
Clandestine Marriage, The 1954,O 4,23:2
Chomsky, Marvin (Lighting Director)
Montserrat 1954,My 26,34:2
Chomsky, Marvin (Scenic Designer)
Montserrat 1954,My 26,34:2
Rendezvous at Senlis 1961,F 28,39:2
Chong, Ah
Hit the Deck! 1927,Ap 26,32:1
Chong, Leilani
Bamboo Cross 1955,F 22,17:2
Chong, Peter Goo
Fast Life 1928,S 27,35:2
These Few Ashes 1928,O 31,28:1
House Unguarded 1929,Ja 16,22:2
Inspector Kennedy 1929,D 21,16:3
As You Desire Me 1931,Ja 29,21:2
Border-Land 1932,Mr 30,15:5
Jamboree 1932,N 25,18:4
Hotel Alimony 1934,Ja 30,16:2
Petticoat Fever 1935,Mr 5,22:2
Run Sheep Run 1938,N 4,26:2
They Knew What They Wanted 1939,O 3,19:1
Beverly Hills 1940,N 8,24:2
Little Darling 1942,O 28,26:2
Choos, George
Vaudeville (Palace) 1929,O 14,20:4
Choos, George (Producer)
Busybody, The 1924,S 30,27:5
Hello, Yourself 1928,O 31,28:2
Lost Sheep 1930,My 6,33:2
Choos, George (Scenic Designer)
Cradle Call 1930,N 23,IX,1:3
Chopin, Frederic (Composer)
Mum's the Word 1940,D 6,28:5
Polonaise 1945,O 8,20:2
Polonaise 1945,O 14,II,1:1
Choppa, Larry
Anthony on Overtime 1961,O 21,13:2
Choraleers, The
Funzapoppin 1949,Jl 1,16:2
Chords, The
Vaudeville (Palace) 1949,My 20,32:4
Chorpenning, Charlotte (Director)
Jack and the Beanstalk 1947,N 3,28:2
Many Moons 1947,D 15,35:2
Chorpenning, Charlotte (Playwright)
Jack and the Beanstalk 1947,N 3,28:2
Many Moons 1947,D 15,35:2
Little Red Riding Hood 1948,Ja 12,15:3
Rumpelstiltskin 1948,Mr 15,27:3
King Midas and the Golden Touch 1948,O 25,28:3
Indian Captive, The 1949,Ja 31,15:2
Marco Polo and the Drum of Ahmad 1950,D 18,34:2
Chorpenning, Miss (Lyricist)
Garrick Gaieties 1930,Je 5,29:2
Chorpenning, Ruth
Jolly Roger, The 1923,Ag 31,10:4
Cyrano de Bergerac 1923,N 2,14:1
Charley's Aunt 1925,Je 2,16:2
Cyrano de Bergerac 1926,F 19,18:1
Sam Abramovitch 1927,Ja 20,20:5
International, The 1928,Ja 16,24:4
Hot Pan 1928,F 16,14:1
Dorian Gray 1928,My 22,18:4
Fiesta 1929,S 18,35:1
Red Rust 1929,D 18,31:1
Garrick Gaieties 1930,Je 5,29:2
Green Grow the Lilacs 1931,Ja 27,21:2
Lost Boy 1932,Ja 6,24:4
Jamboree 1932,N 25,18:4

Marathon 1933,Ja 28,8:8
Ah, Wilderness! 1933,O 3,28:2
Puritan, The 1936,Ja 24,14:3
As We Forgive Our Debtors 1936,Ag 11,24:6
Swing Your Lady 1936,O 19,22:4
Sun Kissed 1937,Mr 11,20:2
Love in My Fashion 1937,D 4,21:4
Family Portrait 1939,Mr 9,18:4
Ring Around Elizabeth 1941,N 18,32:2
Chorpenning, Ruth (Playwright)
Garrick Gaieties 1930,Je 5,29:2
Chosnyk, William
Green Grow the Lilacs 1931,Ja 27,21:2
Chotzinoff, Samuel (Miscellaneous)
Maria Golovin 1958,N 6,43:1
Chotzinoff, Samuel (Playwright)
Honeymoon 1932,D 11,IX,5:1
Honeymoon 1932,D 24,11:2
Choumansky, Olga (Playwright)
Revisor 1927,My 1,VIII,2:4
Chow, Caryn
King and I, The 1968,My 24,39:1
Chowdhury, Jogesh
Ramayana 1931,Ja 13,35:4
Chowdhury, Soilen
Ramayana 1931,Ja 13,35:4
Chown, Avril
Hair 1970,Ja 13,39:1
Chris, Marilyn
In the Jungle of Cities 1960,D 21,39:1
Apple, The 1961,D 8,44:1
Man Is Man 1962,S 19,31:1
Good Soldier Schweik, The 1963,Ap 9,57:1
Junebug Graduates Tonight! 1967,F 27,35:1
Nobody Hears A Broken Drum 1970,Mr 20,55:1
Chrisholm, Milton
Pal Joey 1940,D 26,22:2
Chrisman, Carolyn
Greenwillow 1970,D 8,60:1
Chrisman, Patricia (Miscellaneous)
Tempest, The 1970,F 15,67:1
Christ, John
Mother Courage and Her Children 1964,My 12,32:2
Christ, Louis B Jr (Barrington, Lowell) (Miscellaneous)
Ethan Frome 1936,Ja 22,15:2
Christal, William
Pillar to Post 1943,D 11,11:2
Christenberry, C W Jr (Director)
Salvation on a String; Chair Endowed 1954,Jl 7,23:1
Salvation on a String; No Count Boy, The 1954,Jl 7,23:1
Salvation on a String; Supper for the Dead 1954,Jl 7,23:1
Hit the Trail 1954,D 3,31:2
Christenberry, C W Jr (Producer)
Salvation on a String; No Count Boy, The 1954,Jl 7,23:1
Salvation on a String; Supper for the Dead 1954,Jl 7,23:1
Salvation on a String; Chair Endowed 1954,Jl 7,23:1
Christenberry, Robert K (Miscellaneous)
Pink Elephant, The 1953,Ap 23,37:2
Christensen, Charles
Dodsworth 1934,F 26,20:4
Christensen, Don
Tartuffe 1957,O 9,39:1
Christensen, Lew (Choreographer)
Liberty Jones 1941,F 6,24:2
Christenson, Irma
Father, The 1962,My 15,49:1
Miss Julie 1962,My 17,31:1
Christi, Elena
Rose Tattoo, The 1966,O 21,36:2
Christi, Vito
Hickory Stick 1944,My 9,15:6
Tempest, The 1945,Ja 26,17:2
Rugged Path, The 1945,N 12,17:2
Streetcar Named Desire, A 1947,D 4,42:2
Christian, Anita
Eternal Sabbath 1963,O 19,17:2
Christian, Arthur
Golden Days 1921,N 2,20:1
Move On 1926,Ja 19,30:1
Christian, Claude
Porgy and Bess 1935,O 11,30:2
Christian, Jean
It's an Ill Wind 1957,Ap 24,28:1
Christian, Mady
Hamlet 1938,O 30,IX,1:1
Christian, Pat
Caucasian Chalk Circle, The 1961,N 1,35:1
Christian, Robert
Fortune and Men's Eyes 1967,F 24,29:1
We Bombed in New Haven 1968,O 17,51:1
Does a Tiger Wear a Necktie? 1969,F 26,38:1
Boys in the Band, The 1970,Ap 18,34:1
Christian, Victor
Brooklyn, U S A 1941,D 22,24:2
Christian, William C (Original Author)
Mulatto 1967,N 16,61:4
Christian-Danus, Richard
Comforter, The 1964,O 22,42:1

Christiana, Elouise
Hats Off to Ice 1944,Je 23,15:2
Christiani
Pinocchio 1939,Ja 3,19:2
Christiani, Rita
Horse Play 1937,Ag 28,8:3
Show Boat 1948,S 9,33:2
Christiani Troupe
Artists and Models 1943,N 6,16:6
Christians, Mady
Midsummer Night's Dream, A 1925,Mr 8,VII,2:1
Cocktail 1931,F 15,VIII,3:2
Toni aus Wien, Die 1931,Ag 30,VIII,2:1
Marching By 1931,N 15,VIII,4:2
Story of the Wolf 1932,N 6,IX,3:4
Divine Drudge 1933,Je 16,16:4
Divine Drudge 1933,O 27,22:3
Light Behind the Shadow, The 1936,Ja 21,26:6
Alice Takat 1936,F 11,19:2
Save Me the Waltz 1938,Mr 1,19:2
Heartbreak House 1938,Ap 30,18:2
Hamlet 1938,O 13,28:1
Henry IV, Part I 1939,Ja 31,17:2
Henry IV 1939,F 5,IX,1:1
Viceroy Sarah 1939,Ag 15,14:4
Hamlet 1939,D 5,35:2
Return Engagement 1940,N 2,19:2
Lady Who Came to Stay, The 1941,Ja 3,13:2
Watch on the Rhine 1941,Mr 25,26:7
Watch on the Rhine 1941,Ap 2,26:2
Watch on the Rhine 1941,Ap 13,IX,1:1
Watch on the Rhine 1941,Ag 24,IX,1:1
Elizabeth the Queen 1941,O 17,27:2
I Remember Mama 1944,O 20,16:2
I Remember Mama 1944,O 29,II,1:1
Message for Margaret 1947,Ap 17,34:2
Father, The 1949,N 17,36:2
Father, The 1949,N 27,II,1:1
Getting Married 1950,Je 14,41:2
Christians, Margarethe
Anatol 1922,F 5,VI,1:7
Christians, Margarethe (Mady)
Potasch und Perlmutter 1921,Je 5,VI,1:3
Christiansen, Sigurd (Playwright)
Journey in the Night, A; Reise I Natten, En 1932,Ja 31,VIII,2:1
Christianson, Chris
Moondreamers, The 1969,D 9,68:1
Christie, Agatha (Original Author)
Fatal Alibi, The 1932,F 10,26:6
Signor Bracoli 1932,O 2,IX,2:3
Love From a Stranger 1936,F 3,20:7
Love From a Stranger 1936,Ap 1,28:7
Love From a Stranger 1936,Ap 26,IX,2:2
Love From a Stranger 1936,S 22,31:5
Love From a Stranger 1936,S 30,28:1
Ten Little Indians 1944,Je 28,21:2
Hidden Horizon 1946,S 20,42:2
Untitled-Play 1950,Ja 8,II,3:7
Christie, Agatha (Playwright)
Ten Little Indians 1944,Je 28,21:2
Murder on the Nile 1946,Mr 21,32:2
Hidden Horizon 1946,S 20,42:2
Mousetrap, The 1952,D 7,II,7:1
Witness for the Prosecution 1953,N 15,II,3:1
Spider's Web, The 1954,D 15,41:1
Witness for the Prosecution 1954,D 17,35:2
Witness for the Prosecution 1954,D 26,II,1:1
Spider's Web, The 1955,Ja 9,II,3:1
Witness for the Prosecution 1955,Ja 9,27:4
Verdict, The 1958,My 24,19:8
Go Back for Murder 1960,Mr 24,40:2
Mousetrap, The 1960,N 7,46:1
Christie, Alfred (Director)
Right You Are (If You Think You Are) 1957,Mr 5,37:1
Mr and Mrs Lyman 1968,Mr 6,35:1
Christie, Audrey
Shady Lady 1933,Jl 6,26:3
Sailor, Beware! 1933,S 29,24:4
Alley Cat 1934,S 18,18:1
Geraniums in My Window 1934,O 27,20:6
Women, The 1936,D 28,13:1
I Married an Angel 1938,My 12,26:2
I Married an Angel 1938,My 22,XI,1:1
Return Engagement 1940,N 2,19:2
Banjo Eyes 1941,N 8,10:6
Banjo Eyes 1941,D 26,20:2
Without Love 1942,N 11,28:1
Voice of the Turtle 1943,D 9,30:3
Voice of the Turtle, The 1943,D 19,II,3:1
Voice of the Turtle, The 1944,D 19,27:2
Duchess Misbehaves, The 1946,F 14,32:2
Light Up the Sky 1948,N 19,34:2
Light Up the Sky 1948,D 5,II,5:1
Buy Me Blue Ribbons 1951,O 18,33:2
Holiday for Lovers 1957,F 15,20:1
Nature's Way 1957,O 17,42:2
Mame 1968,Ap 20,25:1
Christie, Bob
All Around the Town 1952,Mr 26,33:2
Christie, Charles
Marching By 1932,Mr 4,17:1

Christie, Dinah
Henry VIII 1961,Je 22,22:1
Tempest, The 1962,Je 22,14:1
Cyrano de Bergerac 1962,Ag 1,21:1
Christie, Dorothy
Follow Thru 1929,Ja 10,24:3
Christie, Edwin
Me and Harry 1942,Ap 3,24:6
Captain Brassbound's Conversion 1950,D 28,21:1
Billy the Kid 1951,Ag 21,23:2
Christie, George
Your Woman and Mine 1922,F 28,17:2
Greenwich Village Follies 1922,S 13,18:2
Greenwich Village Follies 1924,S 17,16:1
Free Soul, A 1928,Ja 13,26:5
Launcelot and Elaine 1930,Mr 10,24:3
New York to Cherbourg 1932,F 20,11:4
Take My Tip 1932,Ap 12,25:2
We the People 1933,Ja 23,9:5
Uncle Tom's Cabin 1933,My 30,13:4
They Shall Not Die 1934,F 22,24:4
Seven Keys to Baldpate 1935,My 28,30:2
Slight Case of Murder, A 1935,S 12,28:5
County Chairman, The 1936,My 26,26:5
Abe Lincoln in Illinois 1938,O 17,12:2
Christie, Helen
Ivanov 1966,My 4,50:1
Christie, John
Family Reunion, The 1947,N 29,9:2
Christie, Julie
Comedy of Errors, The 1964,My 21,43:1
Christie, Ken (Costume Designer)
American Jubilee 1940,My 13,20:5
Christie, Madeleine
Love and Libel 1960,D 8,44:1
Christie, Margot
Glass Cage, The 1957,Mr 11,21:2
Christie, Marice
Blossom Time 1931,Mr 5,32:1
Christie, Robert
Richard III 1953,Jl 15,22:2
Measure for Measure 1954,Je 30,23:1
Taming of the Shrew, The 1954,Jl 1,22:2
Julius Caesar 1955,Je 29,23:3
Merchant of Venice, The 1955,Jl 1,13:1
Tamburlaine the Great 1956,Ja 20,19:1
Henry V 1956,Je 20,27:2
Merry Wives of Windsor, The 1956,Je 21,34:4
Love and Libel 1960,D 8,44:1
Christie, Timothy
Dance of Death, The 1966,Je 3,31:1
As You Like It 1966,Je 4,19:1
Christie and Nelson
Vaudeville (Palace) 1930,My 5,27:5
Christine, Bobette
Roberta 1933,N 20,18:4
Christine, Henri (Composer)
J'Aime 1927,Ja 23,VII,2:1
Arthur 1929,S 29,IX,4:7
Dame du Promenoir, La 1933,O 1,IX,1:3
Christine, Lilly
Michael Todd's Peep Show 1950,Je 29,37:2
Christine & Moll
Michael Todd's Peep Show 1950,Je 29,37:2
Christman, Dan
Emperor Jones, The 1945,Ja 17,18:4
Christmann, Theo
Alt Heidelberg 1924,D 8,23:2
Armseligen Besenbinder, Die 1928,N 19,16:2
Christmas, David
Butter and Egg Man, The 1966,O 18,49:1
Dames at Sea 1968,D 21,46:1
Dames at Sea 1970,Ja 5,46:3
Grin and Bare It 1970,Mr 17,36:1
Christmas, Eric
Hamlet 1957,Jl 3,15:2
Two Gentlemen of Verona 1958,Mr 19,35:1
Broken Jug, The 1958,Ap 2,36:1
Much Ado About Nothing 1958,Je 26,22:1
Winter's Tale, The 1958,Jl 23,34:3
Salad Days 1958,N 11,24:1
Look After Lulu 1959,Mr 4,35:1
As You Like It 1959,Jl 1,27:1
King John 1960,Je 29,26:2
Little Moon of Alban 1960,D 2,34:1
Once There Was a Russian 1961,F 20,32:2
Coriolanus 1961,Je 21,31:2
Henry VIII 1961,Je 22,22:1
Love's Labour's Lost 1961,Je 23,19:1
Love's Labour's Lost 1961,Jl 2,II,1:1
Taming of the Shrew, The 1962,Je 21,25:1
Cyrano de Bergerac 1962,Ag 1,21:1
Troilus and Cressida 1963,Je 19,40:2
Cyrano de Bergerac 1963,Je 20,30:1
Comedy of Errors, The 1963,Je 21,35:3
Bourgeois Gentilhomme, Le 1964,Je 18,28:2
King Lear 1964,Je 19,36:1
Henry IV, Part I 1965,Je 30,42:1
Falstaff; Henry IV, Part II 1965,Jl 1,35:1
Julius Caesar 1965,Jl 2,18:1
Henry V 1966,Je 8,38:1
Twelfth Night 1966,Je 10,51:2
Antony and Cleopatra 1967,Ag 2,25:1

Merry Wives of Windsor, The 1967,Ag 4,18:1
Christofferson, Nancy (Costume Designer)
Peace 1969,Ja 28,49:1
Christophe, Francoise
Et l'Enfer, Isabelle 1963,S 21,13:3
Piano Dans l'Herbe, Un 1970,S 17,56:1
Christopher, Blanche
Our Lan' 1947,S 29,16:5
Christopher, Don (Lyricist)
Love and Let Love 1968,Ja 4,30:1
Christopher, Edward
Carmen Jones 1943,D 3,26:2
Carmen Jones 1945,My 3,26:5
Carmen Jones 1946,Ap 8,32:2
Carmen Jones 1951,S 22,8:6
Christopher, Ellen
Tiger at the Gates 1955,O 4,40:1
Christopher, John (Miscellaneous)
Lovely Light, A 1960,F 9,27:4
Christopher, Jordan
White Lies 1967,O 19,58:1
Black Comedy 1967,O 19,58:1
Christopher, Milbourne
Now You See It 1954,Ap 20,35:2
Christopher's Wonders 1960,S 27,41:1
Christopher, Patrick
Hamlet 1969,Je 11,37:1
Alchemist, The 1969,Je 12,51:1
Christopoulos, Christos
Iphigenia in Aulis 1968,N 13,40:1
Hippolytus 1968,N 20,38:3
Christy, Eileen
Carousel 1965,Ag 11,39:1
Christy, Gloria
Gay Paree 1926,N 10,24:2
Christy, Hamilton
Respect for Riches, The 1920,My 12,9:1
Dora Mobridge 1930,Ap 21,20:2
Christy, Harlan P
Rainbow's End 1928,D 26,14:6
Christy, Julie
Lady in the Dark 1952,Mr 8,11:3
Christy, Lew
Florodora 1920,Ap 6,18:1
Plain Jane 1924,My 13,24:2
No Foolin' 1926,Je 25,25:1
Half a Widow 1927,S 13,37:3
Christy, Madge
Airways, Inc 1929,F 21,30:5
Christy, Orrin E Jr (Miscellaneous)
Irregular Verb to Love, The 1963,S 19,22:2
Christy, Orrin Jr (Producer)
Glass Menagerie, The 1965,My 5,53:2
Chromchak, Rudy (Miscellaneous)
Man and Superman 1960,Ag 17,35:3
Chrow, Lawrence B
Liliom 1921,Ap 21,18:1
Chryll, Primrose
Stepping Stones 1923,N 7,14:3
Chrysler, Walter P Jr (Miscellaneous)
Camino Real 1953,Mr 20,26:1
Chrysler, Walter P Jr (Producer)
Strong Are Lonely, The 1953,S 30,38:3
Chu, Marilyn
Kiss for Cinderella, A 1942,Mr 11,22:2
Chu, Moana
Battleship Gertie 1935,Ja 19,9:2
Chuan
Carefree Tree, The 1955,O 12,37:2
Chugg, Gail
Antony and Cleopatra 1963,S 14,12:4
King Lear 1964,Jl 23,18:1
Chuma, K (Scenic Designer)
Coney Island Play 1970,O 31,34:2
Chun-ling, Tsao (Director)
Tio Ch'an; Beautiful Bait, The 1962,N 13,44:1
Church, Corrynne
Stars on Ice (2d Edition) 1943,Je 25,13:2
Church, Esme
Matchmaker, The 1955,D 6,45:6
Matchmaker, The 1955,D 18,II,3:1
Church, George
Ziegfeld Follies 1936,Ja 31,17:2
Boys From Syracuse, The 1938,N 24,36:1
Hold On to Your Hats 1940,S 12,30:3
What Big Ears! 1942,Ap 21,18:5
Oklahoma! 1943,Ap 1,27:1
Oklahoma! 1943,My 9,II,6:4
On Your Toes 1954,O 12,24:4
Pal Joey 1963,My 30,21:1
110 in the Shade 1963,O 25,37:1
Church, Harden (Composer)
Caviar 1934,Je 8,19:2
Church, Harvey
Vintage '60 1960,S 13,41:1
Church, James
Blood and Sand 1921,S 21,16:2
Church, John
King Lear 1964,My 19,43:2
Comedy of Errors, The 1964,My 21,43:1
Royal Hunt of the Sun, The 1965,O 27,36:2
Imaginary Invalid, The 1967,My 2,53:1
Ways and Means 1967,My 4,34:1

Church, John—Cont
Still Life 1967,My 4,34:1
Church, Sandra
Holiday for Lovers 1957,F 15,20:1
Winesburg, Ohio 1958,F 6,22:2
Gypsy 1959,My 22,31:6
Gypsy 1959,My 31,II,1:1
Under the Yum-Yum Tree 1960,N 17,45:1
Church, Stanley
Ballad for a Firing Squad 1968,D 12,64:2
Church, Tony
Cymbeline 1962,Jl 18,21:1
King Lear 1964,My 19,43:2
Comedy of Errors, The 1964,My 21,43:1
Hamlet 1965,Ag 20,18:2
Soldiers 1968,My 2,58:1
Churchill, Berton
Six-Cylinder Love 1921,Ag 26,8:2
In Love With Love 1923,Ag 7,20:1
Connie Goes Home 1923,S 7,10:1
Robert E Lee 1923,N 21,23:1
Fanshastics 1924,Ja 17,13:2
Cheaper to Marry 1924,Ap 16,26:1
Carnaval 1924,D 30,15:1
Deacon, The 1925,N 25,14:3
Revelry 1927,S 13,37:1
Carry On 1928,Ja 24,26:1
Final Fling, The 1928,O 7,IX,2:3
9th Street Guest, The 1930,Ag 26,24:3
Five Star Final 1930,D 31,11:1
George Washington Slept Here 1940,S 24,27:3
Churchill, Beverly
Frankie and Johnny 1952,O 29,37:2
Churchill, Diana
Composite Man, The 1936,S 27,X,3:5
Yes and No 1937,N 14,XI,3:1
Vigil, The 1948,My 11,28:1
Love's Labour's Lost 1949,O 24,18:3
She Stoops to Conquer 1950,Je 18,34:4
Under the Sycamore Tree 1952,My 11,II,3:7
Desperate Hours, The 1955,My 1,II,3:1
Churchill, Elizabeth (Director)
Blue Butterfly, The 1929,My 4,17:2
Churchill, Elizabeth (Playwright)
Blue Butterfly, The 1929,F 17,29:3
Blue Butterfly, The 1929,My 4,17:2
Churchill, Jane
Noah 1935,F 14,25:2
Churchill, Joan
In the Bag 1936,D 18,30:2
Churchill, Kathryn Fisk (Director)
Blue Butterfly, The 1929,My 4,17:2
Churchill, Lois
Youth 1920,O 27,14:3
Churchill, Marguerite
Why Not? 1922,D 25,20:1
Prunella; Love in a Garden 1926,Je 16,23:3
House of Shadows, The 1927,Ap 22,18:4
Wild Man of Borneo, The 1927,S 14,29:2
Skidding 1928,My 22,18:5
Inside Story, The 1932,F 23,23:2
Dinner at Eight 1932,O 24,18:2
And Now Goodbye 1937,F 3,26:4
Churchill, Marie
Restless Women 1927,D 27,24:1
Churchill, Mary Hand (Mrs)
Variations of 1940 1940,Ja 29,12:1
Churchill, Sarah
Follow the Sun 1935,D 24,10:3
Philadelphia Story, The 1949,Je 28,32:4
Gramercy Ghost 1951,Ap 27,20:2
From This Hill 1963,Ap 2,54:2
Chute, B J (Original Author)
Greenwillow 1960,Mr 9,38:1
Greenwillow 1960,Mr 20,II,1:1
Greenwillow 1970,D 8,60:1
Chute, Joy (Producer)
Sweet Genevieve 1945,Mr 21,27:3
Chute, Marchette (Playwright)
Sweet Genevieve 1945,Mr 21,27:3
Worlds of Shakespeare, The 1963,D 5,58:1
Chute, Marchette (Producer)
Sweet Genevieve 1945,Mr 21,27:3
Ciampa, John
Pardon Our French 1950,O 6,22:4
Ciampi, Yves (Director)
Matter of Days, A 1969,My 20,40:1
Ciampi, Yves (Original Author)
Matter of Days, A 1969,My 20,40:1
Ciampi, Yves (Playwright)
Matter of Days, A 1969,My 20,40:1
Ciampi, Yves (Producer)
Matter of Days, A 1969,My 20,40:1
Ciampolini, Felix
Cardinale, Il; Cardinal, The 1931,Ja 12,24:2
Cianacaglini, Elena
Miserabili I, 1934,S 24,15:1
Morte Civile, La; Civic Death 1936,N 9,23:4
Feudalismo Oppure La Terra Bassa; Feudalism or
the Lowland 1937,Mr 8,22:2
Ciannelli, Eduardo
Rose Marie 1924,S 3,12:2
Puppets of Passion 1927,F 25,24:4
Front Page, The 1928,Ag 15,19:2

Ciannelli, Eduardo—Cont
Sari 1930,Ja 29,27:1
This Man's Town 1930,Mr 11,24:4
Uncle Vanya 1930,Ap 16,26:5
Uncle Vanya 1930,S 23,30:3
Inspector General, The 1930,D 24,19:2
Wiser They Are, The 1931,Ap 7,31:1
Reunion in Vienna 1931,N 17,31:1
Foolscap 1933,Ja 12,21:2
Mahogany Hall 1934,Ja 18,18:5
Yellow Jack 1934,Mr 7,22:6
Gather Ye Rosebuds 1934,N 29,33:2
Journey by Night 1935,Ap 7,IX,2:1
Journey by Night, A 1935,Ap 17,26:3
Mad Morning 1935,Je 25,14:1
Winterset 1935,S 26,19:2
Saint Joan 1936,Mr 10,27:4
Devil's Advocate, The 1961,Mr 10,20:1
Devil's Advocate, The 1961,Mr 19,II,1:1
Ciannelli, Eduardo (Director)
Mahogany Hall 1934,Ja 18,18:5
Ciannelli, Eduardo (Playwright)
Puppets of Passion 1927,F 25,24:4
Foolscap 1933,Ja 12,21:2
Cibelli, Alfred
Oklahoma! 1943,N 14,II,1:1
Cibelli, Alfred Jr
Oklahoma! 1953,S 1,19:1
Cibelli, Renato
Happy Hunting 1956,D 7,30:1
Man of La Mancha 1965,N 23,52:1
Ciccarelli, Chic
Brig, The 1963,My 16,40:1
Ciceri, Leo
Tiger at the Gates 1955,O 4,40:1
Tiger at the Gates 1955,O 23,II,1:1
Midsummer Night's Dream, A 1960,Je 30,23:5
Romeo and Juliet 1960,Jl 1,14:1
Henry VIII 1961,Je 22,22:1
Love's Labour's Lost 1961,Je 23,19:1
Tempest, The 1962,Je 22,14:1
Troilus and Cressida 1963,Je 19,40:2
Cyrano de Bergerac 1963,Je 20,30:1
Timon of Athens 1963,Jl 31,19:2
Richard II 1964,Je 17,47:1
Bourgeois Gentilhomme, Le 1964,Je 18,28:2
King Lear 1964,Je 19,36:1
Henry IV, Part I 1965,Je 30,42:1
Falstaff; Henry IV, Part II 1965,Jl 1,35:1
Julius Caesar 1965,Jl 2,18:1
Henry VI 1966,Je 9,55:2
Twelfth Night 1966,Je 10,51:2
Richard III 1967,Je 14,43:1
Government Inspector, The 1967,Je 15,55:1
Antony and Cleopatra 1967,Ag 2,25:1
Government Inspector, The 1967,O 28,34:1
Whistle in the Dark, A 1968,F 17,32:2
Romeo and Juliet 1968,Je 11,55:2
Tartuffe 1968,Je 12,39:1
Tartuffe 1968,Je 23,II,1:1
Three Musketeers, The 1968,Jl 24,49:2
Measure for Measure 1969,Je 13,41:3
Hamlet 1969,Je 22,II,1:7
Merchant of Venice, The 1970,Je 10,39:1
Hedda Gabler 1970,Je 12,28:1
Cymbeline 1970,Jl 24,17:2
Cicil, Mary
Jack in the Pulpit 1925,Ja 7,33:1
Cierc, Julien
Hair 1969,S 13,30:1
Cieslak, Ryszard
Constant Prince, The 1969,O 18,36:1
Constant Prince, The 1969,O 26,II,1:1
Acropolis 1969,N 5,40:1
Apocalypsis cum Figuris 1969,N 20,60:2
Cieslak, Ryszard (Miscellaneous)
Apocalypsis cum Figuris 1969,N 20,60:2
Cilento, Diane
Tiger at the Gates 1955,Je 3,27:1
Tiger at the Gates 1955,O 4,40:1
Tiger at the Gates 1955,O 23,II,1:1
Heartbreak House 1959,O 19,37:1
Good Soup, The 1960,Mr 3,26:4
Idiot, The 1970,Jl 17,18:1
Idiot, The 1970,Jl 30,39:1
Cimara, Luigi
Famiglia Barrett, La 1933,N 19,IX,1:3
Cimber, Alphonse
Mister Johnson 1956,Mr 30,11:1
Cimber, Matt
Walk-Up 1961,F 24,24:1
Cimber, Matt (Director)
Young and Beautiful, The 1959,My 29,13:1
Burning Bright 1959,O 17,27:2
Ignorants Abroad, The 1960,My 24,43:2
Walk-Up 1961,F 24,24:1
Voice of the Turtle, The 1961,Je 28,41:1
Susan Slept Here 1961,Jl 12,35:2
Little Hut, The 1961,Jl 26,34:2
Moon Is Blue, The 1961,Ag 9,29:1
Tender Trap, The 1961,Ag 26,15:1
Intimate Relations 1962,N 2,27:1
Antigone 1962,D 29,5:5
Orthee 1962,D 29,5:5

Cimber, Matt (Miscellaneous)
Voice of the Turtle, The 1961,Je 28,41:1
Cimberg, Jessie
When Differences Disappear 1941,Je 3,17:4
Student Prince, The 1943,Je 9,16:2
Cimino, Leonardo
Middle Man 1936,S 8,23:1
Mayor of Zalamea, The 1946,Ja 28,15:5
Cyrano de Bergerac 1946,O 9,33:2
Cyrano de Bergerac 1947,Ja 17,27:2
Bear, The 1948,F 6,29:2
Wedding, The 1948,F 6,29:2
On the Harmfulness of Tobacco 1948,F 6,29:2
Tragedian in Spite of Himself, A 1948,F 6,29:2
Alchemist, The 1948,My 7,31:4
S S Glencairn; Bound East for Cardiff
    1948,My 21,21:2
Insect Comedy, The 1948,Je 4,26:3
Wild Duck, The 1951,D 27,17:1
Three Sisters, The 1955,F 26,13:2
Three Sisters, The 1955,Mr 20,II,1:1
Cherry Orchard, The 1955,O 19,38:1
Brothers Karamazov, The 1957,D 9,39:4
Brothers Karamazov, The 1957,D 22,II,3:1
Handful of Fire 1958,O 2,45:3
Power and the Glory, The 1958,D 12,2:7
Vincent 1959,O 1,40:1
Vincent 1959,O 11,II,1:1
Henry V 1960,Je 30,23:1
Montserrat 1961,Ja 9,30:5
Passage to India, A 1962,F 1,23:1
Night Life 1962,O 24,44:1
Firebugs, The 1963,F 13,7:2
Corruption in the Palace of Justice 1963,O 9,49:2
Caretaker, The 1964,Ja 31,16:1
Diamond Orchid 1965,F 11,44:4
Matty and the Moron and Madonna
    1965,Mr 30,53:1
Dodo Bird, The 1967,D 9,62:1
Mike Downstairs 1968,Ap 19,35:1
Tempest, The 1970,F 15,67:1
Cioffi, Charles
Three Sisters, The 1963,Jl 22,19:2
Henry V 1964,My 13,52:1
Whistle in the Dark, A 1968,F 17,32:2
Richard II 1968,Je 24,42:3
As You Like It 1968,Je 24,42:3
Androcles and the Lion 1968,Je 27,47:1
Richard II 1968,Jl 7,II,1:1
King Lear 1968,N 8,43:1
In the Matter of J Robert Oppenheimer
    1969,Mr 7,28:1
Much Ado About Nothing 1969,Je 16,57:1
Hamlet 1969,Je 30,33:1
Three Sisters, The 1969,Ag 10,II,3:1
Whistle in the Dark, A 1969,O 9,55:1
Whistle in the Dark, A 1969,N 9,II,3:1
Cioffi, William F (Producer)
Giants, Sons of Giants 1962,Ja 8,26:2
Ciolko, William
Fuente Ovejuna; Sheep Well, The 1936,My 3,II,4:1
Ciolli, Augusta
In Fondo Al Cuore; Depths of the Heart, The
    1930,D 8,27:1
Gli Spettri 1930,D 22,16:4
Delitto e Castigo; Crime and Punishment
    1931,Ja 26,20:5
Sansone; Samson 1931,F 9,25:1
Marchese di Priola, Il 1931,Mr 2,19:3
Kiss Mama 1964,O 2,30:1
Ciotti, Charles
Saint Joan 1964,My 14,41:1
Cipin, John
Untitled-Passion Play 1927,Jl 31,VII,1:6
Cipriani, Anita
Take a Giant Step 1956,S 26,30:1
Circeri, Leo
Hamlet 1969,Je 11,37:1
Cirillino
Vaudeville (Hippodrome) 1924,Mr 18,25:1
Cirker, Ira
Winged Victory 1943,N 22,24:1
Sundown Beach 1948,S 8,37:1
Cirker, Ira (Director)
Take a Giant Step 1956,S 26,30:1
Clerambard 1957,N 8,22:3
Clerambard 1957,N 17,II,1:1
Entertain a Ghost 1962,Ap 10,48:1
Whisper in God's Ear, A 1962,O 12,27:2
Cirker, Ira (Miscellaneous)
Master Builder, The 1955,Mr 2,23:2
Take a Giant Step 1956,S 26,30:1
Cirker, Ira (Producer)
Entertain a Ghost 1962,Ap 10,48:1
Cirker (Scenic Designer)
Woman Denied, A 1931,F 26,21:1
Great Man, The 1931,Ap 8,20:6
Lightnin' 1938,S 16,17:2
Cirker & Robbins (Scenic Designer)
She Lived Next to the Firehouse 1931,F 11,23:1
Blow Ye Winds 1937,S 24,17:4
Goodbye in the Night 1940,Mr 19,31:2

Ciron, Jacques
Misanthrope, Le 1960,Mr 9,38:3
Cisiphe, Jean-Paul
Lacune, La 1970,My 6,49:1
Chaises, Les 1970,My 6,49:1
Cisney, Marcella (Director)
Whisper to Me 1960,N 22,38:6
Skin of Our Teeth, The 1961,My 31,28:1
Evening's Frost, An 1965,O 12,56:1
Amazing Grace 1967,D 10,82:1
Cisney, Michael
Battle Hymn 1936,My 23,12:1
Native Ground 1937,Mr 24,28:4
Trojan Incident 1938,Ap 22,15:2
Citro, Michael
Galileo 1947,D 8,34:2
Seeds in the Wind 1948,Ap 26,27:2
Seeds in the Wind 1948,My 26,29:2
Citron, Samuel J (Director)
Rich Man, Poor Man 1950,F 13,15:4
Citron, Samuel J (Playwright)
Rich Man, Poor Man 1950,F 13,15:4
Ciulla, Lou
Chiaroscuro; Judges, The 1963,Je 6,40:8
Ciulla, Lou (Miscellaneous)
Chiaroscuro; Kitty, I Hardly Knew You
    1963,Je 6,40:8
Chiaroscuro; Judges, The 1963,Je 6,40:8
Chiaroscuro; Maggie French Understands
    1963,Je 6,40:8
Clair, Al
Rio Rita 1927,F 3,18:3
Clair, Clairette
Bruder Straubinger 1921,N 16,22:3
Fruehlingsluft 1921,N 29,17:4
Clair, Irwin (Miscellaneous)
Bed Time 1958,Ap 11,20:2
Clair, Nina
Farewell, Farewell Eugene 1960,S 28,35:1
Clair, Rene (Director)
French Touch, The 1945,D 10,18:2
Clair, Rene (Translator)
Born Yesterday 1948,Ap 9,26:3
Clair, Richard
Sextet 1958,N 27,53:1
Clair, Richard (Miscellaneous)
Sextet 1958,N 27,53:1
Claire, Bernice
Vaudeville (Palace) 1928,My 29,17:4
Vaudeville (Palace) 1930,N 17,21:2
Chocolate Soldier, The 1934,My 3,15:3
Salute to Spring 1937,Jl 14,16:2
Claire, Dorothy
Face the Music 1932,F 18,24:5
Jimmy 1969,O 24,38:1
Claire, Erji
Seven Mirrors 1945,O 26,17:2
Claire, Frances
Guns 1928,Ag 7,25:2
Claire, Helen
Michael and Mary 1929,D 14,23:3
Schoolgirl 1930,N 21,31:1
Girls in Uniform 1932,D 31,10:3
Jezebel 1933,D 20,26:3
Queer People 1934,F 16,16:2
Eldest, The 1935,F 12,24:3
Fields Beyond, The 1936,Mr 7,11:2
Cat and the Canary, The 1937,Je 15,26:3
Kiss the Boys Goodbye 1938,S 29,30:2
I Know What I Like 1939,N 25,13:5
Beverly Hills 1940,N 8,24:2
Sunny River 1941,D 5,28:2
Violet 1944,O 25,16:1
Lady in Danger 1945,Mr 30,18:6
Claire, Ina
Bluebeard's Eighth Wife 1921,S 20,12:2
Awful Truth, The 1922,S 19,14:3
Grounds for Divorce 1924,Mr 2,VIII,2:7
Grounds for Divorce 1924,S 24,20:1
Last of Mrs Cheyney, The 1925,N 1,VIII,2:4
Last of Mrs Cheyney, The 1925,N 10,23:5
Our Betters 1928,F 21,18:2
Our Betters 1928,Mr 4,IX,1:1
Biography 1932,D 13,25:3
Biography 1933,Ja 22,IX,1:1
Biography 1934,F 6,24:4
Biography 1934,My 20,IX,2:4
Ode to Liberty 1934,D 11,28:2
Ode to Liberty 1934,D 22,20:2
Ode to Liberty 1935,Jl 2,24:3
Ode to Liberty 1935,Jl 9,24:4
Love Is Not So Simple 1935,N 5,33:1
Love Is Not So Simple 1935,N 10,IX,1:6
End of Summer 1936,Ja 31,17:1
End of Summer 1936,F 9,X,2:3
End of Summer 1936,F 18,26:4
Barchester Towers 1937,N 19,26:6
Barchester Towers 1937,D 1,27:1
Once Is Enough 1938,Ja 28,17:2
Once Is Enough 1938,F 16,16:2
Yankee Fable 1938,O 23,IX,3:5
Talley Method, The 1941,F 25,26:3
Talley Method, The 1941,Mr 2,IX,1:1

Claire, Ina—Cont

Fatal Witness, The 1946,N 20,43:2
Confidential Clerk, The 1954,F 12,22:1
Confidential Clerk, The 1954,F 21,II,1:1

Claire, Irene (Choreographer)
Fiddler on the Roof 1969,N 16,82:6

Claire, Joan
If I Were You 1931,S 24,21:1

Claire, Ludi
Tower Beyond Tragedy, The 1950,N 27,29:1
Small Hours, The 1951,F 16,22:1
Legend of Lovers 1951,D 27,17:1
Silk Stockings 1955,F 25,17:3
Someone Waiting 1956,F 15,26:1
First Gentleman, The 1957,Ap 26,22:2
Country Wife, The 1957,N 28,56:1
Duel of Angels 1960,Ap 20,42:2
Lady of the Camellias, The 1963,Mr 22,7:1

Claire, Marion
Great Waltz, The 1934,S 24,14:4

Claire, Mavis
Father of Lies 1935,Ja 27,VIII,3:1

Claire, Rosalie
Greenwich Village Follies 1924,S 17,16:1
White Lights 1927,O 12,30:4
Sunny Days 1928,F 9,29:1

Claire, Shelley
Room 349 1930,Ap 23,24:5

Claire, Stella
Boy Friend, The 1954,O 1,20:1

Claire, Teddy
Artists and Models 1925,Je 25,16:2

Claire, Will
Kansas City Kitty 1929,S 26,27:4
Singing Rabbi, The 1931,S 11,24:4
Lady Precious Stream 1936,Ja 28,15:2

Claire, Willis
Hitch Your Wagon! 1937,Ap 9,18:2
30 Days Hath September 1938,O 1,10:5

Claire, Wills
They All Want Something 1926,O 13,20:2
By Request 1928,S 28,30:2

Clairem, Simone
Topaze 1931,F 17,29:1

Clairon, Laura
His Chinese Wife 1920,My 18,9:3
Show Boat 1927,D 28,26:1
Fine and Dandy 1930,S 24,26:1
Show Boat 1932,My 20,22:2

Clairton, James
Rendezvous 1932,O 13,22:3
Blow Ye Winds 1937,S 24,17:4

Clairville (Playwright)
Cloches de Cornville, Les; Chimes of Normandy, The 1926,D 14,24:4

Clairy, Claire
Blaue Hemd von Ithaka, Das 1931,Mr 15,IX,2:4

Claman, Dolores (Composer)
Cast of Characters 1959,Je 11,37:2

Clancy, Charles
Lower North 1944,Ag 26,15:4

Clancy, Deidre (Costume Designer)
Landscape 1970,Ap 3,43:1
Silence 1970,Ap 3,43:1

Clancy, Deirdre (Scenic Designer)
Hedda Gabler 1970,Je 12,28:1

Clancy, Harry
Wednesday's Child 1934,Ja 17,23:2
Come What May 1934,My 16,23:4

Clancy, James H (Director)
Much Ado About Nothing 1963,Jl 15,25:2

Clancy, Liam
All That Fall 1957,O 8,41:2
Guests of the Nation 1958,My 21,40:1
Guests of the Nation 1958,Je 27,18:5
Aria Da Capo 1958,Je 27,18:5
Quare Fellow, The 1958,N 28,34:1
On Baile's Strand 1959,Ap 13,34:4
This Island Is Mine 1959,Jl 1,26:4
Shadow and Substance 1959,N 4,42:1
Little Moon of Alban 1960,D 2,34:1

Clancy, Patrick
Wise Have Not Spoken, The 1954,F 11,35:2
Guests of the Nation 1958,My 21,40:1
Guests of the Nation 1958,Je 27,18:5

Clancy, Thaddeus
Holiday 1928,N 27,36:1
Half Gods 1929,D 23,18:5
This Is New York 1930,N 29,21:1
Passing Present, The 1931,D 8,36:2
Valley Forge 1934,D 11,28:3
Brigadoon 1950,My 3,36:2

Clancy, Tom
Wise Have Not Spoken, The 1954,F 11,35:2
Sound of Hunting, A 1954,Ap 7,41:1
Macbeth 1955,O 8,12:6
King Lear 1956,Ja 13,17:1
Shadow and Substance 1956,Mr 14,38:1
Plough and the Stars, The 1956,Ap 6,14:1
Hamlet 1957,Ja 29,27:1
Under Milk Wood 1957,O 16,42:5
Winkelberg 1958,Ja 15,26:2
Guests of the Nation 1958,My 21,40:1
Ulysses in Nighttown 1958,Je 6,30:1

Guests of the Nation 1958,Je 27,18:5
Touch of the Poet, A 1958,O 3,23:2
Juno 1959,Mr 10,41:1

Clancy, Tom (Miscellaneous)
Plough and the Stars, The 1956,Ap 6,14:1

Claney, Howard
Liliom 1921,Ap 21,18:1
Don Juan 1921,S 8,14:2
Steamship Tenacity 1922,Ja 3,20:2
Voltaire 1922,Mr 21,17:1
Macbeth 1924,Mr 17,18:1
Little Poor Man, The 1925,Ag 6,14:1
Immortal Thief, The 1926,O 4,21:1
Hamlet 1928,Ja 5,33:2
Henry V 1928,Mr 16,26:2
Lolly 1929,O 17,26:2
Evening With G B S, An; O'Flaherty, V C 1957,F 19,35:7
Romeo and Juliet 1962,Ap 3,42:1
Figuro in the Night 1962,O 31,33:1

Claney, Hugh (Playwright)
Rainbow's End 1928,D 26,14:6

Clanton, Hampton
Toilet, The 1964,D 17,51:1

Clanton, Ralph
Macbeth 1941,N 12,30:2
God Strikes Back 1943,F 27,11:2
Richard III 1943,Mr 27,8:3
Victory Belles 1943,O 27,26:3
Strange Play, A 1944,Je 2,20:3
Othello 1945,My 23,25:4
Lute Song 1946,F 7,29:2
Cyrano de Bergerac 1946,O 9,33:2
Cyrano de Bergerac 1947,Ja 17,27:2
Antony and Cleopatra 1947,N 27,49:2
Design For A Stained Glass Window 1950,Ja 24,26:2
Taming of the Shrew, The 1951,Ap 26,35:2
Cyrano de Bergerac 1953,N 13,24:3
Burning Glass, The 1954,Mr 5,15:2
Ceremony of Innocence, The 1968,Ja 2,33:1
Endecott and the Red Cross 1968,My 7,50:1

Clapp, Dorothy
What Next 1920,Ja 27,7:2

Clapp, Gordon
Early Morning 1970,N 26,57:1

Clapp, Thaddeus (Costume Designer)
Hamlet 1928,Je 2,11:3

Clapp, Thaddeus (Scenic Designer)
Hamlet 1928,Je 2,11:3

Clapper, Theodore
Plan M 1942,F 21,15:2

Clapsaddle, Robert
Junebug Graduates Tonight! 1967,F 27,35:1

Clara and Sana
Laughter Over Broadway 1939,Ja 16,10:3

Clarance, Mlle
Avare, L'; Miser, The 1924,Mr 12,17:3
Blanchette 1924,Mr 19,19:4

Clare, Edwin
Centuries, The 1927,N 30,23:1
Mighty Nimrod, The 1931,My 13,23:1
Sailors of Cattaro 1934,D 11,28:4

Clare, Ennis
Silver Tassie, The 1929,O 25,26:1

Clare, Gloria
Red, Hot and Blue! 1936,O 30,26:3

Clare, Mary
Skin Game, The 1920,My 23,VI,1:3
Squall, The 1927,D 4,X,1:3
Return of the Soldier, The 1928,Jl 8,VIII,1:7
Cheri 1930,N 16,VIII,4:1
Cavalcade 1931,N 1,VIII,2:1
Battle Royal 1934,Ap 19,33:4
Wise Woman, The 1934,N 9,24:3
After October 1936,F 22,13:3
Ship Comes Home, A 1937,My 18,27:1
Ship Comes Home, A 1937,Je 6,XI,1:3
Heaven and Charing Cross 1939,Ap 16,X,2:4
Heaven and Charing Cross 1939,Ap 16,X,2:3
Ladies in Retirement 1939,D 24,IX,1:7
Ladies in Retirement 1941,Ag 17,IX,1:8
Accounting for Love 1954,D 2,37:6

Clare, Norah Wyn
Good Companions, The 1931,O 2,31:1

Clare, Paul
Adam Solitaire 1925,N 7,19:2
Virgin Man, The 1927,Ja 19,20:4
Gentlemen of the Press 1928,Ag 28,27:2
Young Sinners 1933,Mr 7,20:4
Eldest, The 1935,F 12,24:3
Rain 1935,Ag 27,23:4
Johnny 2X4 1942,Mr 17,24:6

Clare, Wyn
Wake Up and Dream 1929,D 31,14:3
Nine Till Six 1930,S 29,17:2

Claremont, Arthur
Yellow Sands 1927,S 12,29:3

Clarence, O B
Pietro 1920,Ja 20,10:2
Mary Rose 1920,D 23,9:2
Murder on the Second Floor 1929,S 12,35:1
Last Enemy, The 1930,Ja 5,VIII,2:2

Clarence, O B—Cont

Ugly Duchess, The 1930,Je 1,VIII,2:8
Last Enemy, The 1930,O 31,21:1
Cherry Orchard, The 1941,S 7,IX,2:5

Clarendon, Hal
Wicked Age, The 1927,N 5,16:6
Phantoms 1930,Ja 14,24:3
Paid Companions 1931,Je 23,28:4
Angels Don't Kiss 1932,Ap 6,22:5
Way, The 1940,O 12,20:3

Clarendon, Jean
Dunce Boy, The 1925,Ap 4,20:2
Fast Life 1928,S 27,35:2
One Way Street 1928,D 25,31:2
Merry-Go-Round 1932,Ap 23,11:2
Raw Meat 1933,Mr 23,13:2

Clarens, Harry
Two by Two 1925,F 24,17:1
Heaven-Tappers, The 1927,Mr 9,28:3
Killers 1928,Mr 14,28:3

Clariond, Aime
Ludo 1932,Je 12,X,1:3
Miss Ba; Barretts of Wimpole Street, The 1934,N 11,IX,3:6

Clarissa
Desert Song, The 1946,Ja 9,20:2

Clark
Continental Varieties 1934,N 15,24:3

Clark, Alexander
Erminie 1921,Ja 4,11:1
Golden Days 1921,N 2,20:1
Merton of the Movies 1922,N 14,16:2
Comedienne 1924,O 22,18:1
Jack in the Pulpit 1925,Ja 7,33:1
Natja 1925,F 17,19:2
Rainbow Rose 1926,Mr 17,28:2
Judge's Husband, The 1926,S 28,31:1
Fog 1927,F 8,20:1
Tightwad, The 1927,Ap 18,18:2
Julie 1927,My 10,24:4
Ruddigore 1927,My 21,25:2
Too True to Be Good 1932,Mr 1,19:2
Too True to Be Good 1932,Ap 5,27:5
Biography 1932,D 13,25:3
Lambs Gambol 1933,Ap 24,10:1
American, Very Early 1934,Ja 31,21:2
Spring Freshet 1934,O 5,28:3
Octoroon, The 1936,S 1,24:2
Naughty-Naught 'OO 1937,Ja 25,23:2
Merchant of Venice, The 1938,Ja 15,18:8
Victoria Regina 1938,O 4,20:2
In Time to Come 1941,D 29,20:2
Native Son 1942,O 24,10:6
Counsellor-at-Law 1942,N 25,17:2
Listen Professor! 1943,D 23,22:1
Sheppey 1944,Ap 19,27:2
Fundamental George, The 1949,Ag 17,19:4
Not for Children 1951,F 14,35:2
Legend of Lovers 1951,D 27,17:1
Say Darling 1959,F 26,38:2
Shewing-Up of Blanco Posnet, The 1959,S 19,26:7
Julia, Jake, and Uncle Joe 1961,Ja 30,19:1
Pal Joey 1961,Je 1,32:1
Captains and the Kings, The 1962,Ja 3,25:2
Brigadoon 1962,My 31,21:4
Calculated Risk 1962,N 1,35:1
Case of Libel, A 1963,O 11,43:2
Brigadoon 1964,D 24,9:1
Kiss Me, Kate 1965,My 13,31:1
Falstaff 1966,Je 20,27:1
Murder in the Cathedral 1966,Je 21,38:1
Carousel 1966,D 16,56:2
Life With Father 1967,O 20,53:2
Brigadoon 1967,D 14,59:2

Clark, Ann
Crimes and Crimes 1970,Ja 19,35:1

Clark, Anna
Many Mansions 1937,O 28,28:6

Clark, Austin
Good Boy 1928,S 6,23:2

Clark, B Wallis
Light of the World, The 1920,Ja 7,17:1

Clark, Barbara J (Miscellaneous)
Lower Depths, The 1956,O 3,29:2

Clark, Barrett H (Translator)
Wolves 1932,Ja 7,26:3

Clark, Barry
Aquashow 1953,Je 24,29:2

Clark, Bayard
Assorted Nuts 1940,Ap 7,I,44:6

Clark, Bayard (Lyricist)
Assorted Nuts 1940,Ap 7,I,44:6

Clark, Bert
Vaudeville (Forty-Fourth Street Theatre) 1921,S 20,12:2

Clark, Betty Jean
Ice Follies 1961,Ja 11,25:2
Ice Follies 1963,Ja 10,5:2

Clark, Bobby
Peek-A-Boo 1921,My 17,20:3
Untitled-Revue 1922,Jl 9,VI,1:1
Ramblers, The 1926,S 21,32:2
Ramblers, The 1926,N 28,VIII,1:1
Strike Up the Band 1930,Ja 15,29:1

Clark, Bobby—Cont
Vaudeville (Pavilion) 1931,Mr 20,29:3
Here Goes the Bride 1931,N 4,31:2
Vaudeville (Hollywood) 1932,F 16,24:3
Thumbs Up! 1934,D 28,24:1
Ziegfeld Follies 1936,S 15,37:1
Streets of Paris, The 1939,Je 20,25:2
Streets of Paris, The 1939,Je 25,IX,1:1
Love for Love 1940,Je 4,19:5
All Men Are Alike 1941,O 7,27:2
Rivals, The 1941,N 18,32:2
Rivals, The 1942,Ja 15,24:2
Rivals, The 1942,Ja 25,IX,1:1
Star and Garter 1942,Je 25,26:2
Star and Garter 1942,S 13,VIII,1:1
Mexican Hayride 1944,Ja 29,9:6
Mexican Hayride 1944,F 6,II,1:1
Would-Be Gentleman, The 1946,Ja 10,29:2
Would-Be Gentleman, The 1946,Ja 20,II,1:1
Sweethearts 1947,Ja 22,31:2
Sweethearts 1947,F 2,II,1:1
As the Girls Go 1948,N 15,21:2
ANTA Album 1950,Ja 30,13:2
Peep Show 1950,Jl 9,II,1:1
Jollyanna; Flahooley 1952,Ag 13,17:7
Clark, Bobby (Director)
Michael Todd's Peep Show 1950,Je 29,37:2
Clark, Bobby (Playwright)
Would-Be Gentleman, The 1946,Ja 10,29:2
Would-Be Gentleman, The 1946,Ja 20,II,1:1
Michael Todd's Peep Show 1950,Je 29,37:2
Clark, Bonnie
Unto Such Glory 1937,My 7,28:2
Clark, Buddy
Brights Lights of 1944 1943,S 17,27:4
Clark, C M
Gentlemen, the Queen 1927,Ap 23,14:3
Clark, Calvin (Playwright)
Bully, The 1924,D 26,18:1
Clark, Carl
Summer of the Seventeenth Doll 1959,O 14,52:1
Clark, Carl (Miscellaneous)
Sponge Room, The 1964,F 25,24:1
Squat Betty 1964,F 25,24:1
Clark, Carroll
Porgy and Bess 1935,O 11,30:2
Skin of Our Teeth, The 1942,N 19,29:5
Clark, Charles Dow
Shavings 1920,F 17,18:1
Give and Take 1923,Ja 19,13:1
Rainy Day, The 1923,O 14,VIII,2:4
Lucky Break 1925,Ag 12,16:2
If I Was Rich 1926,S 3,15:2
Fog 1927,F 8,20:1
Petrified Forest, The 1934,D 21,31:6
Petrified Forest, The 1935,Ja 8,26:1
For Valor 1935,N 19,27:5
Miss Quis 1937,Ap 8,20:5
Clark, Clifford (Miscellaneous)
Ginger Man, The 1963,N 22,42:1
Clark, Connie
Merry Widow, The 1944,O 9,17:1
Clark, Dane
Number, The 1951,O 31,33:2
Fragile Fox 1954,O 13,27:1
Brecht on Brecht 1962,Ja 4,26:1
Brecht on Brecht 1962,Ja 14,II,1:1
Mike Downstairs 1968,Ap 19,35:1
Clark, Dorothy
Good Times 1920,Ag 10,10:1
Sonny 1921,Ag 17,12:2
Clark, Dort
Years Between, The 1942,F 7,13:2
Sweet Charity 1942,Je 29,26:4
Tinker's Dam 1943,Ja 29,22:2
First Million, The 1943,Ap 29,27:4
Lower North 1944,Ag 26,15:4
Snafu 1944,O 26,19:5
Happy Birthday 1946,N 1,31:2
Mr Barry's Etchings 1950,F 1,26:2
Wonderful Town 1953,F 26,22:3
Bells Are Ringing 1956,N 29,43:4
Bells Are Ringing 1956,N 30,18:2
South Pacific 1961,Ap 27,26:3
Let It Ride 1961,O 13,27:4
Fiorello! 1962,Je 14,24:1
Harvey 1970,F 25,41:1
Clark, E F (Playwright)
Not Now-Later 1928,Ap 14,25:1
Clark, Edward
Relations 1928,Ag 21,27:3
Time for Elizabeth 1948,S 28,32:3
Clark, Edward (Director)
Relations 1928,Ag 21,27:3
Clark, Edward (Lyricist)
Little Miss Charity 1920,S 3,6:3
Cinders 1923,Ap 4,22:1
1776 1926,Ap 24,11:2
Clark, Edward (Playwright)
Little Miss Charity 1920,S 3,6:3
Blushing Bride, The 1922,F 7,12:1
Cinders 1923,Ap 4,22:1
Paradise Alley 1924,Ap 2,17:3
Gentlemen, the Queen 1927,Ap 23,14:3

Relations 1928,Ag 21,27:3
Clark, Edward W (Producer)
Once Over Lightly 1938,D 10,13:4
Clark, Enid
Hamlet 1931,Ap 24,26:4
Clark, Ernest
Cocktail Party, The 1950,Ja 23,17:2
Escapade 1953,Ap 8,37:2
Witness for the Prosecution 1954,D 17,35:2
Witness for the Prosecution 1954,D 26,II,1:1
Clark, Ernest J
Horse Play 1937,Ag 28,8:3
Clark, Ethel
Mikado, The; Town of Titipu, The 1931,My 5,33:2
H M S Pinafore 1931,My 19,25:2
H M S Pinafore 1931,Jl 28,17:6
Ruddigore 1931,Ag 11,28:3
Mikado, The 1931,Ag 25,17:7
Geisha, The 1931,O 6,35:4
Mikado, The 1933,Ap 18,13:4
Clark, Eva
Sun-Kist 1921,My 24,20:2
Our Nell 1922,D 5,24:1
Mary Jane McKane 1923,D 26,13:2
Madame Pompadour 1924,N 12,20:6
Vaudeville (Palace) 1926,Je 22,21:3
Clark, Everett (Director)
Soles Truncos, Los; House on Cristo Street, The
1959,Ag 31,15:2
Clark, Florence
Anything Might Happen 1923,F 21,22:3
Vaudeville (Palace) 1927,D 13,33:5
Clark, Frances
Bronx Express 1922,Ap 27,12:2
Farmer's Wife, The 1924,O 10,22:3
Clark, Francis
Imaginary Invalid, The 1922,Jl 26,26:2
Ruddigore 1931,Ag 11,28:3
Clark, Frank
Robin Hood 1932,Ja 28,25:4
Clark, Fred
Mister Roberts 1956,D 6,46:2
Romanoff and Juliet 1957,O 11,24:1
Viva Madison Avenue 1960,Ap 7,42:1
Never Too Late 1963,S 25,48:1
Absence of a Cello 1964,S 22,45:1
Clark, Frederic
Schoolhouse on the Lot 1938,Mr 23,18:4
Ringside Seat 1938,N 23,24:5
Clark, Frederick (Director)
Let's Go 1924,My 20,15:1
Clark, Frederick (Playwright)
Let's Go 1924,My 20,15:1
Clark, G Davison
Gift, The 1924,Ja 23,15:4
Mercenary Mary 1925,Ap 14,27:3
Hush Money 1926,Mr 16,22:3
Howdy King 1926,D 14,24:4
Los Angeles 1927,D 20,32:3
Great Power, The 1928,S 12,25:1
Fioretta 1929,F 6,30:3
Clark, George
Vaudeville (Palace) 1929,S 16,30:4
Paid Companions 1931,Je 23,28:4
Clark, Georgette
To Tell You the Truth 1948,Ap 19,28:6
Clark, Gordon
Here Goes the Bride 1931,N 4,31:2
Sing for Your Supper 1939,Ap 25,18:6
Clark, Hannam
Servant in the House, The 1921,My 3,20:1
Taming of the Shrew, The 1921,My 12,20:2
Merchant of Venice, The 1921,My 14,10:4
Merry Wives of Windsor, The 1928,Mr 20,20:1
Waterloo Bridge 1930,Ja 7,29:2
Little Father of the Wilderness, The 1930,Je 3,27:1
Bellamy Trial, The 1931,Ap 23,28:6
Cynara 1931,N 3,31:1
Richelieu 1934,My 22,28:1
Hamlet 1934,D 26,19:3
Richard III 1934,D 28,24:3
Othello 1935,S 28,13:2
Macbeth 1935,O 8,26:4
Cyrano de Bergerac 1936,Ap 28,17:1
Enemy of the People, An 1937,F 16,19:1
Jeremiah 1939,F 4,11:2
Clark, Harriet
Crazy With the Heat 1941,Ja 15,18:2
Clark, Henry
Half-Caste, The 1926,Mr 30,20:4
Big Fight, The 1928,S 19,33:1
Excursion 1937,Ap 10,11:4
Clark, Herbert
Will Shakespeare 1923,Ja 2,14:1
My Son 1924,S 18,18:2
Patsy, The 1925,D 24,8:5
We All Do 1927,Mr 1,30:3
Excess Baggage 1927,D 27,24:2
Money Lender, The 1928,Ag 28,27:3
Clark, Herma (Playwright)
When Chicago Was Young 1932,N 13,IX,3:8
Clark, Holman
Send for Dr O'Grady 1923,Jl 29,VI,1:6

Clark, Howard
Father Malachy's Miracle 1937,N 18,26:4
Clark, Inez
Mlle Modiste 1937,My 5,28:5
Clark, Irene
Meet Peter Grant 1961,My 11,41:4
Let Them Down, Gently; On Vacation
1968,Ja 31,28:2
Clark, Jackie
Hilda Cassidy 1933,My 5,18:3
Clark, Jacqueline
Delicate Story 1940,D 5,32:2
Blithe Spirit 1941,N 6,26:2
Blithe Spirit 1941,N 16,IX,1:1
Clark, James
Shrike, The 1953,N 26,51:2
Clark, James N
Admirable Bashville, The 1956,F 21,38:1
Marching Song 1959,D 29,20:1
Clark, James Nisbet (Director)
Bald Soprano, The 1963,S 18,35:4
Lesson, The 1963,S 18,35:4
Where People Gather 1967,O 26,56:1
Clark, James Nisbet (Lighting Director)
Bald Soprano, The 1963,S 18,35:4
Lesson, The 1963,S 18,35:4
All Women Are One 1965,Ja 8,21:1
Peddler, The 1967,D 9,62:1
Dodo Bird, The 1967,D 9,62:1
Jacques Brel Is Alive and Well and Living in Paris
1968,Ja 23,25:2
Clark, James Nisbet (Miscellaneous)
Smokeweaver's Daughter, The 1959,Ap 15,30:1
Opening of a Window, The 1961,S 26,32:2
Clark, James Nisbet (Scenic Designer)
Bald Soprano, The 1963,S 18,35:4
Lesson, The 1963,S 18,35:4
All Women Are One 1965,Ja 8,21:1
Where People Gather 1967,O 26,56:1
Clark, Jane
Would-Be Gentleman, The 1930,Ap 30,29:2
Clark, Jeanne
Bonds of Interest, The 1929,O 15,34:2
Clark, Jim
2 for Fun; Switch in Time, A 1955,My 26,34:1
2 for Fun; Anniversary, The 1955,My 26,34:1
Clark, Jinx
Howdy Mr Ice 1948,Je 25,28:5
Howdy, Mr Ice of 1950 1949,My 27,24:2
Clark, Joe
Hair 1970,Ja 13,39:1
Clark, Joseph
Sally, Irene and Mary 1922,S 5,21:2
Clark, Keith
Vanities 1932,S 18,IX,2:1
Clark, Kendall
End of Summer 1936,F 18,26:4
Storm Over Patsy 1937,Mr 9,26:4
Retreat From Folly 1937,Je 29,18:3
At Mrs Beam's 1937,Jl 27,24:2
Washington Jitters 1938,My 3,19:1
Big Blow 1938,O 3,11:2
Life and Death of an American 1939,My 20,11:2
Fifth Column, The 1940,Mr 7,18:2
George Washington Slept Here 1940,O 19,20:3
Home of the Brave 1945,D 28,13:2
Eagle Has Two Heads, The 1947,Mr 20,39:2
First Mrs Fraser, The 1947,N 6,36:2
Saint Joan 1951,O 5,23:2
Shrike, The 1952,Ja 16,20:2
Shrike, The 1953,N 26,51:2
Richard III 1953,D 10,65:2
Desperate Hours, The 1955,F 11,20:2
King John 1956,Je 28,33:5
Taming of the Shrew, The 1956,Ag 6,20:1
Taming of the Shrew, The 1957,F 21,30:2
Othello 1957,Je 24,19:2
Merchant of Venice, The 1957,Jl 11,19:5
Much Ado About Nothing 1957,Ag 8,15:2
Dr Willy Nilly 1959,Je 5,18:2
Shadow and Substance 1959,N 4,42:1
Caucasian Chalk Circle, The 1961,N 1,35:1
Burning of the Lepers, The 1962,Ap 5,29:1
Clark, Kitty
Booster, The 1929,O 25,26:2
Clark, Larry
Rendezvous 1932,O 13,22:3
Clark, Les
Tattle Tales 1933,Je 2,22:6
Clark, Lillion
Forbidden Melody 1936,N 3,33:1
Clark, Lon
Church Street 1948,F 10,27:2
Roman Candle 1960,F 4,34:2
Dumbbell People in a Barbell World 1962,F 15,25:1
Seven Scenes for Yeni 1963,My 13,36:2
Clark, Lyle
On the Town 1944,D 29,11:4
Clark, M G
Tiger Smiles, The 1930,D 18,29:1
Clark, Mae
Noose, The 1926,O 21,23:3
Manhattan Mary 1927,S 27,30:3

Clark, Marilyn
Seven Year Itch, The 1952,N 21,21:2
Dinner at Eight 1966,S 28,38:1
Clark, Marlene
Baby With a Knife 1969,My 15,41:2
Clark, Maurice (Director)
Button, Button 1929,O 24,26:1
Haiti 1938,Mr 3,16:1
Clark, Maurice (Playwright)
Tragic 18 1926,O 11,18:2
Button, Button 1929,O 24,26:1
Clark, Most
Vaudeville (Palace) 1926,Ap 20,24:6
Clark, Myrtle
That's Gratitude 1930,S 12,28:1
That's Gratitude 1930,S 21,IX,1:1
Clark, Nancy
Johnny 2X4 1942,Mr 17,24:6
Clark, Nevin
Right to Strike, The 1921,O 25,20:1
Bronx Express 1922,Ap 27,12:2
Imaginary Invalid, The 1922,Jl 26,26:2
Clark, Norma Lee
Rehearsal, The 1952,My 27,30:5
Man and Superman 1953,F 21,11:2
Clark, Norman (Playwright)
I Take Care of My Friends 1936,Jl 21,13:2
Window Shopping 1938,D 24,13:2
Clark, Oliver
Ben Franklin in Paris 1964,O 28,52:1
Caucasian Chalk Circle, The 1966,Mr 25,35:1
Don't Drink the Water 1966,N 18,37:1
Spiro Who? 1969,My 19,55:1
Spiro Who? 1969,Je 15,II,3:6
Passing Through From Exotic Places; Sunstroke 1969,D 8,60:4
Passing Through From Exotic Places 1969,D 21,II,3:1
Two Times One; Last Straw, The 1970,Ap 5,76:4
Clark, Patrice
Two Little Girls in Blue 1921,My 4,10:3
Good Morning, Dearie 1921,N 2,20:2
Bunch and Judy, The 1922,N 29,20:1
One Kiss 1923,N 28,14:2
Clark, Peggy (Costume Designer)
Girl From Wyoming, The 1938,O 31,12:1
Uncle Harry 1942,My 21,24:1
Ramshackle Inn 1944,Ja 6,17:5
Dark of the Moon 1945,Mr 15,27:2
Devils Galore 1945,S 13,27:2
High Ground, The 1951,F 21,31:2
Clark, Peggy (Lighting Director)
High Button Shoes 1947,O 10,32:2
Medea 1947,O 21,27:2
Topaze 1947,D 29,21:5
Love Life 1948,O 8,31:2
Rape of Lucretia, The 1948,D 30,24:2
Touch and Go 1949,O 14,34:2
Gentlemen Prefer Blondes 1949,D 9,35:3
All You Need Is One Good Break 1950,F 10,20:3
Cry of the Peacock 1950,Ap 12,33:2
Brigadoon 1950,My 3,36:2
Bless You All 1950,D 15,42:2
High Ground, The 1951,F 21,31:2
Paint Your Wagon 1951,N 13,32:2
Pal Joey 1952,Ja 4,17:6
Of Thee I Sing 1952,My 6,34:2
Maggie 1953,F 19,20:2
Wonderful Town 1953,F 26,22:3
Trip to Bountiful, The 1953,N 4,30:3
Kismet 1953,D 4,2:4
In the Summer House 1953,D 30,17:1
On Your Toes 1954,O 12,24:4
Peter Pan 1954,O 21,30:2
Plain and Fancy 1955,Ja 28,14:2
Immortal Husband, The 1955,F 15,32:2
Threepenny Opera, The 1955,S 21,38:1
No Time for Sergeants 1955,O 21,32:2
Righteous Are Bold, The 1955,D 23,12:1
Threepenny Opera, The 1956,Mr 11,II,1:1
Mr Wonderful 1956,Mr 23,23:2
New Faces of 1956 1956,Je 15,32:1
Auntie Mame 1956,N 1,47:2
Glass Menagerie, The 1956,N 22,50:1
Bells Are Ringing 1956,N 30,18:2
Potting Shed, The 1957,Ja 30,32:1
Eugenia 1957,Ja 31,20:1
Brigadoon 1957,Mr 28,37:1
Merry Widow, The 1957,Ap 11,36:6
South Pacific 1957,Ap 25,35:1
Pajama Game, The 1957,My 16,27:1
Carousel 1957,S 12,38:2
Nude With Violin 1957,N 15,36:1
Annie Get Your Gun 1958,F 20,29:2
Wonderful Town 1958,Mr 6,32:4
Oklahoma! 1958,Mr 20,32:3
Say Darling 1958,Ap 4,17:1
Auntie Mame 1958,Ag 12,33:2
Flower Drum Song 1958,D 2,44:1
Say Darling 1959,F 26,38:2
Juno 1959,Mr 10,41:1
Billy Barnes Revue, The 1959,Je 10,42:2
Cheri 1959,O 13,44:1

Goodbye Charlie 1959,D 17,50:1
Distant Bell, A 1960,Ja 14,29:1
Bye Bye Birdie 1960,Ap 15,13:4
Unsinkable Molly Brown, The 1960,N 4,28:1
Under the Yum-Yum Tree 1960,N 17,45:1
Show Girl 1961,Ja 13,37:1
Mary, Mary 1961,Mr 9,24:2
Paradise Island 1961,Je 24,11:1
Sail Away 1961,O 4,48:5
Romulus 1962,Ja 11,27:1
Paradise Island 1962,Je 28,22:1
Eddie Fisher at the Winter Garden 1962,O 3,47:1
Brigadoon 1963,F 1,6:2
Wonderful Town 1963,F 15,10:2
Oklahoma! 1963,F 28,8:2
Oklahoma! 1963,My 16,40:1
Pal Joey 1963,My 30,21:1
King and I, The 1963,Je 13,30:2
Around the World in 80 Days 1963,Je 24,22:1
Girl Who Came to Supper, The 1963,D 9,49:1
Around the World in 80 Days 1964,Je 29,33:2
Bajour 1964,N 24,42:1
Poor Richard 1964,D 3,59:1
Brigadoon 1964,D 24,9:1
Guys and Dolls 1965,Ap 29,39:1
Kiss Me, Kate 1965,My 13,31:1
South Pacific 1965,Je 3,25:1
Oklahoma! 1965,D 16,62:1
Best Laid Plans, The 1966,Mr 26,15:2
How to Succeed in Business Without Really Trying 1966,Ap 21,45:1
Most Happy Fella, The 1966,My 12,55:1
Where's Charley? 1966,My 26,57:1
Guys and Dolls 1966,Je 9,55:2
Rose Tattoo, The 1966,O 21,36:2
Finian's Rainbow 1967,Ap 6,44:1
Sound of Music, The 1967,Ap 27,52:1
Wonderful Town 1967,My 18,50:1
Arabian Nights 1967,Jl 3,12:1
Brigadoon 1967,D 14,59:2
Darling of the Day 1968,Ja 29,26:2
South Pacific 1968,Je 30,54:2
South Pacific 1969,Jl 7,27:1
Jimmy 1969,O 24,38:1
Last of the Red Hot Lovers 1969,D 29,37:1
Sound of Music, The 1970,Jl 3,13:1
Clark, Peggy (Miscellaneous)
It's All Yours 1942,Mr 26,26:2
Clark, Peggy (Scenic Designer)
Flight Into China 1939,S 12,28:1
Man in Possession, The 1939,S 26,21:4
Gabrielle 1941,Mr 26,26:2
Attack 1942,S 8,13:4
High Ground, The 1951,F 21,31:2
Glass Menagerie, The 1956,N 22,50:1
Where's Charley? 1966,My 26,57:1
Clark, Peter
Porgy 1927,O 11,26:2
Zombie 1932,F 11,17:2
Clark, Phillip
We Have Always Lived in the Castle 1966,O 20,53:1
Clark, Phillip (Miscellaneous)
We Have Always Lived in the Castle 1966,O 20,53:1
Clark, Preston (Director)
Elizabeth Sleeps Out 1936,Ap 21,27:6
Clark, Rachel May
Desert Song, The 1926,D 1,24:2
Clark, Richard
Opportunity 1920,Jl 31,5:1
Mendel, Inc 1929,N 26,28:5
Bloody Laughter 1931,D 5,20:6
Wolves 1932,Ja 7,26:3
Dead End 1935,O 29,17:2
Brother Rat 1936,D 17,34:5
Susanna, Don't You Cry 1939,My 23,27:2
Young Couple Wanted 1940,Ja 25,16:2
Medicine Show 1940,Ap 13,20:6
Susannah and the Elders 1940,O 30,28:2
Woman Bites Dog 1946,Ap 18,21:2
Tenting Tonight 1947,Ap 3,32:2
Saint Joan 1968,Ja 5,42:1
Tiger at the Gates 1968,Mr 1,30:1
Cyrano de Bergerac 1968,Ap 26,30:1
Conduct Unbecoming 1970,O 13,50:1
Clark, Robert
Desert Flower, The 1924,N 19,18:2
Tale of the Wolf, The 1925,O 8,31:2
Cradle Will Rock, The 1937,D 6,19:4
Cradle Will Rock, The 1938,Ja 4,19:3
Susanna, Don't You Cry 1939,My 23,27:2
Carmen Jones 1943,D 3,26:2
Carmen Jones 1945,My 3,26:5
Carmen Jones 1946,Ap 8,32:2
Carmen Jones 1951,S 22,8:6
Clark, Roger
Alice in Arms 1945,F 1,18:4
Front Page, The 1946,S 5,22:4
Anybody Home 1949,F 26,10:5
Clark, Roger (Director)
Collector's Item 1952,F 9,11:2

Clark, Roger (Miscellaneous)
Sleep, My Pretty One 1944,N 3,26:8
Clark, Roger (Producer)
Gramercy Ghost 1951,Ap 27,20:2
Collector's Item 1952,F 9,11:2
Clark, Ron (Playwright)
Norman, Is That You? 1970,F 20,30:1
Clark, Rupert
Gray Shadow 1931,Mr 11,23:4
Any Woman 1934,Ag 28,24:4
Clark, Ruth G
Main Street 1921,O 6,21:1
Clark, Sam
York Nativity Play, The 1956,D 5,49:2
Clark, Saville (Musical Director)
Tonight We Improvise 1959,N 7,27:4
Clark, Siena
Cicero 1961,F 9,37:2
Clark, Stephen
Deep Channels 1929,O 19,22:3
Blue Ghost, The 1930,Mr 11,24:5
Clark, Stephen (Director)
Blue Ghost, The 1930,Mr 11,24:5
Clark, Sterling
Half a Sixpence 1965,Ap 26,38:2
Clark, Sylvia
Greenwich Village Follies 1920,Ag 31,7:3
Vaudeville (Palace) 1926,Ap 20,24:6
Vaudeville (Palace) 1927,Jl 12,29:3
Vaudeville (Palace) 1928,Ap 17,26:2
Vaudeville (Palace) 1929,D 23,19:1
Clark, Terry
Lovers, Villains and Fools: A Shakespearean Variety Show 1956,O 24,44:7
Clark, Thomas B (Miscellaneous)
Life Begins in '40 1940,Ap 5,24:2
Clark, Tony
Sacco-Vanzetti 1969,F 9,78:1
Clark, Virginia
Jim Jam Jems 1920,O 5,13:2
Clinging Vine, The 1922,D 25,20:2
Clark, W R
Piper, The 1920,Mr 20,14:2
Don Quixote, Esquire 1920,My 7,12:6
Somebody's Lion 1921,Ap 13,20:1
Here's Howe 1923,Ap 26,19:3
Mongrel, The 1924,D 16,28:2
Clark, Wallis
Dulcy 1921,Ag 15,14:1
Exile, The 1923,Ap 10,24:2
Tweedles 1923,Ag 14,10:1
Out of the Seven Seas 1923,N 20,23:3
Dorian Gray 1928,My 22,18:4
These Few Ashes 1928,O 31,28:1
Zeppelin 1929,Ja 15,22:3
Sherlock Holmes 1929,N 26,28:3
Mr Samuel 1930,N 11,28:4
She Means Business 1931,Ja 27,21:2
Napi 1931,Mr 12,22:5
Peter Ibbetson 1931,Ap 9,30:3
Suspect 1940,Ap 10,30:4
To What Red Hell 1940,My 5,I,54:8
At the Stroke of Eight 1940,My 21,29:2
Little A 1947,Ja 16,31:2
Clark, William T
Main Street 1921,O 6,21:1
Dice of the Gods, The 1923,Ap 6,20:2
Honor of the Family, The 1926,D 27,21:1
Clark, Wister
Man Who Killed Lincoln, The 1940,Ja 18,26:4
Clark, Wynne
Duet for Two Hands 1947,O 8,28:3
Romeo and Juliet 1956,S 19,34:6
Romeo and Juliet 1956,O 25,41:1
Macbeth 1956,O 30,42:2
Clark and Bergman
Vaudeville (Palace) 1927,N 29,30:4
Clark and McCullough
Chuckles of 1922 1922,My 2,22:2
Irving Berlin's New Music Box Revue 1922,O 24,18:1
Vaudeville (Palace) 1924,Ap 29,12:2
Vaudeville (Hippodrome) 1924,S 30,27:5
Music Box Revue 1924,D 2,23:3
Lambs Gambol 1925,Ap 27,15:1
Vaudeville (Palace) 1928,Mr 6,20:5
Strike Up the Band 1929,D 29,VIII,4:3
Music in the Air 1932,N 20,IX,1:1
Walk a Little Faster 1932,D 8,24:4
Clark Brothers
Funzapoppin 1949,Jl 1,16:2
Clarke, Agnes (Costume Designer)
Young Alexander 1929,Mr 13,28:2
Clarke, Betty Ross
Red Poppy, The 1922,D 21,18:2
Clarke, Boyd
Tarzan of the Apes 1921,S 8,14:3
If Winter Comes 1923,Ap 3,26:1
Hamlet 1923,N 27,23:6
Caught 1925,O 6,31:2
Clarke, Burke
Light of the World, The 1920,Ja 7,17:1
Nobody's Business 1923,O 23,17:1

Clarke, Burke—Cont

Hell-Bent Fer Heaven 1924,Ja 5,10:1
Octoroon, The 1929,Mr 13,28:3
Scarlet Sister Mary 1930,N 26,19:2
Peter Flies High 1931,N 10,28:3
Sentinels 1931,D 26,15:1
Trick for Trick 1932,F 19,14:2
Petticoat Fever 1935,Jl 2,24:4
As Husbands Go 1935,Jl 10,24:1
How Beautiful With Shoes 1935,N 29,24:1
Come Angel Band 1936,F 19,17:1
Possessed, The 1939,O 25,26:2
Distant City, The 1941,S 23,27:5

Clarke, Carolyn
Noose, The 1926,O 21,23:3
Long Road, The 1930,Jl 20,VIII,2:1

Clarke, Cecil (Director)
Measure for Measure 1954,Je 30,23:1
Measure for Measure 1954,Jl 4,II,1:1

Clarke, Constance
Kitchen, The 1966,Je 14,50:1

Clarke, David
200 Were Chosen 1936,N 21,21:1
Journeyman 1938,Ja 31,14:2
Washington Jitters 1938,My 3,19:1
Abe Lincoln in Illinois 1938,O 17,12:2
Audition of the Apprentice Theatre 1939,Je 2,26:2
See the Jaguar 1952,D 4,46:2
Emperor's Clothes, The 1953,F 10,24:2
Madam Will You Walk 1953,D 2,2:4
Memory of Two Mondays, A 1955,S 30,21:1
View From the Bridge, A 1955,S 30,21:1
Orpheus Descending 1957,Mr 22,28:1
Visit, The 1958,My 6,40:1
Visit, The 1960,Mr 9,38:3
Last Days of Lincoln, The 1961,O 19,39:7
Ballad of the Sad Cafe, The 1963,O 31,27:1
Kitchen, The 1966,Je 14,50:1
Displaced Person, The 1966,D 30,15:1
Rose 1969,O 29,30:1
Inquest 1970,Ap 24,38:1

Clarke, Donald
Sunny River 1941,D 5,28:2
Regina 1949,N 1,32:2

Clarke, Douglas
Sophie 1963,Ap 16,32:1

Clarke, G T (Director)
Slightly Delirious 1935,Ja 1,25:3

Clarke, Gage
Ledge, A 1929,N 19,26:3
Venetian Glass Nephew, The 1931,F 24,26:3
Country Wife, The 1931,Ap 19,31:5
Devil in the Mind 1931,My 2,23:2
Inside Story, The 1932,F 23,23:2
Jezebel 1933,D 20,26:3
Lost Horizons 1934,O 16,31:2
Parnell 1936,My 5,26:2
Many Mansions 1937,O 28,28:6
Escape This Night 1938,Ap 23,18:1
Great Lady 1938,D 2,26:6
Summer Night 1939,N 3,17:1
I Know What I Like 1939,N 25,13:5
Happy Time, The 1950,Ja 25,24:1

Clarke, Georgia
Getting Even 1929,Ag 20,31:1

Clarke, Gordon B
Arms and the Man 1956,O 2,39:4
Say Darling 1958,Ap 4,17:1
Say Darling 1959,F 26,38:2
Best Man, The 1960,Ap 1,39:1
Dylan 1964,Ja 20,18:1
Cradle Will Rock, The 1964,N 9,40:4
Yearling, The 1965,D 11,25:1
Investigation, The 1966,O 5,40:1

Clarke, Grant (Lyricist)
Dixie to Broadway 1924,O 30,22:1

Clarke, Grant (Playwright)
Ed Wynn's Carnival 1920,Ap 6,18:2

Clarke, Harold
Long Road, The 1930,S 10,30:2

Clarke, Harold A (Playwright)
Chalk Dust 1936,Mr 5,24:5

Clarke, Harry
Dew Drop Inn 1923,My 18,26:4
Princess April 1924,D 2,23:2
China Rose 1925,Ja 20,18:1
Amorous Antic, The 1929,D 3,29:2
Night Remembers, The 1934,N 28,24:3
Pins and Needles 1939,Ap 21,26:2
New Pins and Needles 1939,N 21,19:2
Skin of Our Teeth, The 1942,N 19,29:5
One Touch of Venus 1943,O 8,14:1
Kiss Me, Kate 1948,D 31,10:3
Wish You Were Here 1952,Je 26,26:6
Will Success Spoil Rock Hunter? 1955,O 14,22:2

Clarke, Harry (Lyricist)
It's Up to You 1921,Mr 29,20:1
Who Cares 1930,Jl 9,27:1

Clarke, Harry (Playwright)
Little Racketeer, The 1931,O 11,VIII,4:7
Little Racketeer, The 1932,Ja 19,24:4
Smiling Faces 1932,Ag 31,12:3

Clarke, Harry (Translator)
Marching By 1932,Mr 4,17:1

Clarke, Harry Corson
Blushing Bride, The 1922,F 7,12:1
Rotters, The 1922,My 23,12:4

Clarke, Helen
All the King's Men 1948,Ja 19,19:2

Clarke, Henry
Oklahoma! 1951,My 30,15:2

Clarke, Hope
House of Flowers 1968,Ja 29,26:2

Clarke, Hughie
You Said It 1931,Ja 20,21:3

Clarke, John
Ziegfeld Follies 1921,Je 22,10:1
Hamlet 1922,N 17,14:1
Dream Girl, The 1924,Ag 21,12:2
Princess Flavia 1925,N 3,34:3
Three Musketeers, The 1928,Mr 4,IX,2:3
Three Musketeers, The 1928,Mr 14,28:1
Du Barry 1932,N 23,15:2
Music Hath Charms 1934,D 31,8:2
Boy Meets Girl 1935,N 28,38:2
Bet Your Life 1937,Ap 6,20:2
Money Mad 1937,My 25,32:5
Boys From Syracuse, The 1938,N 24,36:1
Man in Possession, The 1939,S 26,21:4
Woman Brown, The 1939,D 9,18:5
Pal Joey 1940,D 26,22:2
Beat the Band 1942,O 15,26:1
Silver Tassie, The 1949,Jl 22,16:5
Top Secret 1960,S 6,40:1
Lion in Love, The 1963,Ap 26,28:3
Hostile Witness 1966,F 18,26:1
MacBird! 1967,F 23,38:1

Clarke, John S Jr
Big Lake 1927,Ap 9,17:2

Clarke, Kenneth
Corn Is Green, The 1940,N 27,27:2
Corn Is Green, The 1943,My 4,18:3

Clarke, Lawrence
Professor Mamlock 1937,Ap 14,30:3

Clarke, Lawrence (Playwright)
All the King's Horses 1934,Ja 31,21:3

Clarke, Lulu Belle
Animal Kingdom, The 1938,Jl 27,14:5
Legal Grounds 1940,D 2,18:4
Heads or Tails 1947,My 3,10:6
Arms and the Girl 1950,F 3,28:2
Miser, The 1955,Mr 18,34:2

Clarke, Lynne
Sh! The Octopus 1928,F 22,19:2

Clarke, Marian Marcus
Great Way, The 1921,N 8,28:2

Clarke, Marjorie
Angels Don't Kiss 1932,Ap 6,22:5
Any Woman 1934,Ag 28,24:4
Katy Did So What? 1935,N 6,32:3

Clarke, Marty
Athenian Touch, The 1964,Ja 15,25:4

Clarke, Nell
Pin to See the Peepshow, A 1953,S 18,17:2

Clarke, Patricia
Lady Be Good 1924,D 2,23:4
Du Barry 1932,N 23,15:2

Clarke, Paul
Mrs Moonlight 1952,N 21,21:1
Adding Machine, The 1956,F 10,17:1
Queen After Death 1956,Mr 13,33:2

Clarke, Philip
On Whitman Avenue 1946,My 9,28:2

Clarke, Polly
Remote Control 1929,S 11,24:5

Clarke, Ray
Yokel Boy 1939,Jl 7,12:2

Clarke, Redfield
Man of the People, A 1920,S 8,9:2
Processional 1925,Ja 13,17:1
Edgar Allan Poe 1925,O 6,31:1
Man Who Died Twice, The 1925,D 14,19:1

Clarke, Victor
Love Life 1948,O 8,31:2

Clarke, Warren
Return Engagement 1940,N 2,19:2
Untitled-Nativity Play 1946,D 25,46:1
Home 1970,Ag 17,32:1

Clarke, Wilfred
Girl With Carmine Lips, The 1920,Ag 11,6:1
Hello, Daddy! 1928,D 27,26:5
Company's Coming! 1931,Ap 21,35:5
Social Register, The 1931,N 10,28:2
Saint Wench 1933,Ja 3,19:3
Woman of Destiny, A 1936,Mr 3,25:2

Clarke-Laurence, Michael
Ulysses in Nighttown 1958,Je 6,30:1
Gazebo, The 1958,D 13,2:7
Camelot 1960,D 5,42:1

Clarke-Laurence, Michael (Director)
Happy as Larry 1961,Ap 26,36:1

Clarke-Laurence, Michael (Scenic Designer)
Happy as Larry 1961,Ap 26,36:1
Sharon's Grave 1961,N 9,39:2

Clarke-Smith, C
Max and Mr Max 1932,Ja 24,VIII,3:5

Clarke-Smith, D A
These Few Ashes 1929,My 5,IX,1:3
Savonarola Brown 1930,F 26,22:3
Insult 1930,S 16,30:2
Chastity, My Brother 1936,My 9,27:3
Edward, My Son 1948,O 1,30:2

Clarke-Smith, D A (Director)
Insult 1930,S 16,30:2

Clarkson, George
Killers 1928,Mr 14,28:3

Clarkson, Joan
Sunshine Sisters 1933,N 26,IX,3:6

Clarkson, Lucy
Wolf! Wolf! 1925,O 30,21:1
Technique 1931,My 15,21:1

Clarkson, Max (Producer)
Foursome 1965,Mr 8,34:1
Bedlam Galore, for Two or More 1965,Mr 8,34:1
Leader, The 1965,Mr 8,34:1
Impromptu, L' 1965,Mr 8,34:1

Clarkson, Nicholas
Mikado, The 1924,Jl 29,9:1

Clarkson, Olivia
Wolf! Wolf! 1925,O 30,21:1

Clary, Pat
Big Mogul, The 1925,My 12,26:3

Clary, Robert
New Faces of 1952 1952,My 17,23:2
Seventh Heaven 1955,My 27,16:2
Around the World in 80 Days 1963,Je 24,22:1
Around the World in 80 Days 1964,Je 29,33:2

Clary, Roy
Love and Let Love 1968,Ja 4,30:1

Clary, Wells
Grand Duchess 1929,D 17,29:2
Orpheus in Hades 1930,D 16,30:1
Chocolate Soldier, The 1932,F 9,30:3
Fledermaus, Die 1933,My 14,II,3:8
Yeomen of the Guard, The 1941,D 19,34:3
Pirates of Penzance, The 1942,F 20,20:2
Cox and Box 1942,F 20,20:2

Clary, Wilton
Desert Song, The 1946,Ja 9,20:2
Barrier, The 1950,N 3,32:2
ANTA Album 1951,My 7,22:7
Three Wishes for Jamie 1952,Mr 22,9:2

Clasis, Charlotte (Mme)
Homme et Ses Fantomes, L' 1924,N 14,16:1

Clasper, Edith
Vaudeville (Palace) 1923,Ap 3,26:4

Classon, Jack
Girl Crazy 1930,O 15,27:1

Clatworthy, David
Amahl and the Night Visitors 1970,D 24,10:2

Claude, Ferna
George Dandin 1968,Je 28,36:1

Claude, Sarah
Wise-Crackers, The 1925,D 17,26:1

Claude and Marion
Vaudeville (Palace) 1923,Mr 6,26:1

Claude Hopkins All-Stars
Woman and the Blues, A 1966,Mr 29,35:2

Claudel, Paul (Original Author)
Noontide 1961,Je 2,37:1

Claudel, Paul (Playwright)
Tidings Brought to Mary, The 1922,D 25,20:1
Tidings Brought to Mary, The 1922,D 31,VII,1:1
Woman and Her Shadow, The 1923,Ag 12,III,19:1
Annonce Faite A Marie, L' 1927,N 6,IX,4:1
Tidings Brought to Mary, The 1929,Ap 7,X,2:7
Annonce Faite a Marie, L'; Tidings Brought to Mary, The 1942,My 21,24:1
Partage De Midi, Le; Pain' Dur, Le 1949,My 1,II,3:1
Christopher Columbus 1953,N 29,II,3:1
Joan At The Stake 1954,Je 25,15:3
Christophe Colomb 1957,Ja 31,20:5
Otage, L' 1959,O 27,42:1
Hostage, The; Crusts 1962,N 30,28:1

Claudel, Pierre
Annonce Faite a Marie, L'; Tidings Brought to Mary, The 1942,My 21,24:1

Claudel, Pierre (Mme) (Costume Designer)
Annonce Faite a Marie, L'; Tidings Brought to Mary, The 1942,My 21,24:1

Claudet, Frances
Gay Blades 1937,N 12,26:6
Gay Blades 1937,N 16,27:1
Ice Follies 1941,D 2,32:2

Claudet, Frances (Choreographer)
Ice Follies 1958,Ja 15,26:2
Ice Follies 1959,Ja 14,30:1
Ice Follies 1960,Ja 13,20:1
Ice Follies 1964,Ja 8,41:2
Ice Follies 1965,Ja 13,35:1
Ice Follies 1966,Ja 12,27:6
Ice Follies 1967,Ja 11,51:1
Ice Follies 1969,My 23,38:1
Ice Follies 1970,My 23,27:1

Claudet, Frances (Director)
Ice Follies 1957,Ja 16,36:1
Ice Follies 1961,Ja 11,25:2
Ice Follies 1962,Ja 10,24:6

Claudio, Joseph
Desert Song, The 1946,Ja 9,20:2
Claudius, Marieluise
Lauter Luegen 1937,O 24,XI,3:1
Claudius and Scarlet
Better Times 1922,S 4,14:2
Claughton, Susan
Old House, The 1920,Jl 11,VI,1:6
Claus, Hugo (Director)
Reconstruction 1969,Jl 8,36:1
Claus, Hugo (Playwright)
Bride in the Morning, A 1960,My 26,38:2
Reconstruction 1969,Jl 8,36:1
Clausen, Claus
Richard III 1937,My 30,X,2:2
Clausen, Constance
Gambler, The 1952,O 14,40:1
Clausen, Harold
Contrast, The 1926,O 1,26:2
Man Without Money, A 1929,N 3,27:4
Clauss, Elsie
Watched Pot, The 1947,O 29,31:4
Claussen, Joy
Happiest Girl in the World, The 1961,Ap 4,42:1
Moths, The 1970,My 12,46:1
Clauyel, Dominique (Playwright)
Amedee: or, How to Disentangle Yourself
1955,N 1,27:3
Clavert, Patricia
Barretts of Wimpole Street, The 1945,Mr 27,23:6
Clawson Triplets
Hairpin Harmony 1943,O 2,18:5
Clay, Cassius (Muhammad Ali)
Buck White 1969,D 3,63:1
Big Time Buck White 1969,D 7,II,5:1
Clay, Dorothy
Genius and the Crowd 1920,S 7,20:1
Clay, Eddie
Carmen Jones 1951,S 22,8:6
Clay, Edwin
Everyman 1941,My 9,19:2
Oklahoma! 1943,Ap 1,27:1
Kiss Me, Kate 1948,D 31,10:3
Clay, Frances
Straw Hat, The 1937,D 31,8:2
Clay, Jack
Rehearsal, The 1952,My 27,30:5
Clay, James
Forever This Land 1951,Jl 29,II,1:1
Clay, Louise
Persecution and Assassination of Marat As
Performed by the Inmates of the Asylum of
Charenton Under the Direction of the Marquis de
Sade, The 1967,Ja 4,34:1
Rondelay 1969,N 6,55:1
Clay, Melvin
Many Loves 1959,Ja 14,28:1
Clay, Melvin (Miscellaneous)
Many Loves 1959,Ja 14,28:1
Clayborne, H (Harry Clay Blaney) (Producer)
Lady Refuses, The 1933,Mr 8,18:6
Clayburgh, Jill
Sudden and Accidental Re-education of Horse
Johnson, The 1968,D 19,63:1
Calling in Crazy 1969,O 7,42:2
Nest, The 1970,Ap 10,46:1
Rothschilds, The 1970,O 20,40:1
Rothschilds, The 1970,N 1,II,1:1
Claypoole, Mabel
Little Theatre Tournament; Shall We Join the
Ladies? 1929,My 9,34:3
Shall We Join the Ladies? 1929,My 12,28:3
Claypoole, Walter
Little Theatre Tournament; Shall We Join the
Ladies? 1929,My 9,34:3
Shall We Join the Ladies? 1929,My 12,28:3
Rogues and Vagabonds 1930,My 8,32:5
Clayton, Clay
From Morn Till Midnight 1948,D 7,41:6
Butter and Egg Man, The 1949,Ap 29,27:1
Clayton, Don Allan (Playwright)
Delightful Season, A 1960,S 29,30:1
Clayton, Evelyn
Old Bill, M P 1926,N 11,22:2
Clayton, Frederic
My Son 1924,S 18,18:2
Clayton, Frederic (Producer)
Decoy, The 1932,Ap 2,13:4
Clayton, Frederick
Body Beautiful, The 1935,N 1,24:3
Clayton, Ginger
Ice Follies 1960,Ja 13,20:1
Clayton, Herbert (Playwright)
Dear Love 1930,My 18,VIII,3:1
Clayton, J M
Far Away Horses 1933,Mr 22,21:6
Clayton, Jackson and Durante
Vaudeville (Palace) 1928,Ap 17,26:2
Vaudeville (Palace) 1928,Je 5,21:3
Show Girl 1929,Ag 25,VIII,1:1
Vaudeville (Palace) 1929,N 11,20:5
New Yorkers, The 1930,N 16,VIII,3:1
Vaudeville (Palace) 1931,My 18,21:1

Clayton, Jan
Carousel 1945,Ap 20,24:2
Carousel 1945,Ap 29,II,1:1
Show Boat 1946,Ja 7,17:2
Show Boat 1946,Ja 13,II,1:1
Carousel 1953,My 6,38:1
King and I, The 1956,Ap 19,35:4
Clayton, Joseph
Show-Off, The 1924,F 6,16:2
Happy 1927,D 6,26:3
Fine and Dandy 1930,S 24,26:1
Clayton, Lou
Show Girl 1929,Jl 3,19:3
New Yorkers, The 1930,D 9,31:1
New Yorkers, The 1930,D 28,VIII,1:1
Vaudeville (Palace) 1931,My 11,15:5
Clayton, Marion
Jotham Valley 1951,F 7,37:2
Clayton, Merle
Arrest That Woman 1936,S 19,20:4
Clayton, Pat
Madcap, The 1928,F 1,31:2
Sari 1930,Ja 29,27:1
Clayton, Richard
Miss Temple Is Willing 1936,Jl 21,13:1
Hamlet 1936,N 11,54:2
Dance Night 1938,O 15,20:5
Pardon Our French 1950,O 6,22:4
Clayton, Ruth
Viva O'Brien 1941,O 10,27:2
Clayton and Lennie
Vaudeville (Palace) 1926,S 21,32:5
Clayworth, June
Torch Song 1930,Ag 28,23:1
Page Pygmalion 1932,Ag 4,17:5
Cleamandh, Julien
Cloches de Cornville, Les; Chimes of Normandy,
The 1926,D 14,24:4
Clear, Robert
Command Performance, The 1928,O 4,27:1
Clearman, John
General John Regan 1930,Ja 30,16:5
Lysistrata 1930,Je 6,20:1
Cleary, Karen
Cradle Will Rock, The 1964,N 9,40:4
Cleary, Michael H (Composer)
Hey, Nonny, Nonny! 1932,Je 7,22:3
Illustrators' Show, The 1936,Ja 23,25:3
Sea Legs 1937,My 19,26:5
Cleary, Michael H (Lyricist)
Hey, Nonny, Nonny! 1932,Je 7,22:3
Cleary, Peggy (Producer)
Bough Breaks, The 1937,N 20,21:4
Cleary, William
Tempest, The 1970,F 15,67:1
Cleator, Carl
Iron Men 1936,O 20,30:6
Cleaver, Hylton (Playwright)
Lady's Gentleman, A 1937,D 24,20:5
His Wife's Castle 1939,O 1,IX,2:2
Cleaver, Walter
Aquashow 1953,Je 24,29:2
Elliott Murphy's Aquashow 1955,Je 23,25:1
Cleaves, Ardelle
Poor Little Ritz Girl 1920,Jl 29,7:1
Cleaves, Catherine
Midsummer Night's Dream, A 1967,Je 30,23:1
Cleaves, Edwin (Composer)
Bare Facts of Today 1930,Ap 17,24:4
Cleaves, Edwin (Lyricist)
Bare Facts of Today 1930,Ap 17,24:4
Cleese, John
Cambridge Circus 1964,O 7,53:1
New Cambridge Circus, The 1965,Ja 15,22:2
Half a Sixpence 1965,Ap 26,38:2
Cleese, John (Playwright)
New Cambridge Circus, The 1965,Ja 15,22:2
Cleff, Michael (Miscellaneous)
Sold to the Movies; Life Size 1970,Je 18,54:2
Sold to the Movies; Type 424 Meet Type Oh-Oh,
No! 1970,Je 18,54:2
Sold to the Movies; Crossing the Gap
1970,Je 18,54:2
Clefs, Gospel
God Is Back, Black and Singing Gospel at the
Fortune Theater 1969,N 19,48:1
Clegg, Darryl (Scenic Designer)
Pullman Car Hiawatha 1962,D 4,46:2
Clegg, Fred
To Quito and Back 1937,O 7,30:4
Clegg, Jane (Miscellaneous)
How Much, How Much? 1970,Ap 21,49:1
Cleghorne, Rodney
Street Sounds 1970,O 23,32:1
Clein, Ed
Cannibals, The 1968,N 4,60:1
Clein, John (Producer)
Swan Song 1946,My 16,29:2
Clemandh, Julien
Girofle-Girofla 1926,N 23,26:3
Perichole, La 1926,D 29,24:4
Clemens, Cameron
Partners Again 1922,My 2,22:2

Clemens, Cameron—Cont
Mystery Man, The 1928,Ja 27,14:2
Phantom Lover, The 1928,S 5,25:1
Holiday 1928,N 27,36:1
Clemens, Clara
Joan of Arc 1926,Ap 24,21:2
Joan of Arc 1927,Ap 15,26:2
Clemens, Gertrude
Lilies of the Field 1921,O 5,20:1
My Girl 1924,N 25,27:2
Oh, Please! 1926,D 22,24:3
Wasp's Nest, The 1927,O 26,26:3
Escape This Night 1938,Ap 23,18:1
Clemens, Joy
Pirates of Penzance, The 1960,O 7,29:1
Clemens, Le Roy (Playwright)
Blue Eyes 1921,F 22,11:2
Poppy God, The 1921,Ag 30,10:1
Aloma of the South Seas 1925,Ap 21,18:1
Deacon, The 1925,N 25,14:3
Cortez 1929,N 5,32:2
Clemens, Nina
Quiet, Please! 1940,N 9,20:3
Clemens, Richard
Girl From Nantucket, The 1945,N 9,17:2
Clemens, Samuel (Original Author)
Joan of Arc 1926,Ap 24,21:2
Clemens, William
Highway Robbery 1955,N 8,36:1
Deirdre of the Sorrows 1959,O 15,46:1
Clement, Claiborne E
Pageant of the Nativity of Christ 1948,D 25,6:7
Clement, Clay
Shipwrecked 1924,N 13,18:1
Savages Under the Skin 1927,Mr 25,25:2
Matrimonial Bed, The 1927,O 13,23:2
Rosalie 1928,Ja 11,26:3
House of Fear, The 1929,O 8,34:2
Nina Rosa 1930,S 22,22:5
Washington Heights 1931,S 30,23:4
Reflected Glory 1936,S 18,19:5
Reflected Glory 1936,S 22,30:2
Cue for Passion 1940,D 20,33:4
Lily of the Valley 1942,Ja 27,25:2
Walking Gentleman, The 1942,My 8,26:2
Great Big Doorstep, The 1942,N 27,26:2
Apology 1943,Mr 23,14:2
Assassin, The 1945,O 18,20:2
Rugged Path, The 1945,N 12,17:2
High Button Shoes 1947,O 10,32:2
Joy to the World 1948,Mr 19,28:2
Gayden 1949,My 11,34:4
Captain Brassbound's Conversion 1950,D 28,21:1
Clement, Dale (Costume Designer)
Little Clay Cart, The 1953,Jl 1,25:1
Clement, Dora
Harvey 1944,N 2,23:2
Clement, Dudley
Her Salary Man 1921,N 29,20:1
Clement, Elsa
Sinbad the Sailor 1929,D 27,26:5
Clement, Henry
Failures, The 1923,N 23,20:1
Clement, Joan
Don Juan 1921,S 8,14:2
He Who Gets Slapped 1922,Ja 10,15:1
Tidings Brought to Mary, The 1922,D 25,20:1
Helen of Troy, New York 1923,Je 20,22:6
Sunny 1925,S 23,22:1
She's My Baby 1928,Ja 4,22:2
Three's a Crowd 1930,O 16,28:3
Clement, John (Producer)
Arms and the Man 1970,Jl 10,18:1
Clement, Lyle
Lady Killer, The 1924,Mr 13,14:2
Clement, Wilhelmina (Miscellaneous)
God's Trombones 1960,F 10,43:4
Shakespeare in Harlem 1960,F 10,43:4
Clements, Colin (Playwright)
Glamour Preferred 1940,N 16,13:2
Harriet 1943,Ja 22,22:1
Harriet 1943,Mr 4,24:2
Harriet 1943,Mr 14,V,1:1
Harriet 1944,S 28,26:1
Strange Bedfellows 1948,Ja 15,27:3
Clements, Dolly
Poor Little Ritz Girl 1920,Jl 29,7:1
Clements, Dudley
Shavings 1920,F 17,18:1
Haunted House, The 1924,S 3,12:1
Wooden Kimono 1926,D 28,16:2
Night in Venice, A 1929,My 22,30:2
Strike Up the Band 1930,Ja 15,29:1
Hobo 1931,F 12,24:4
Here Goes the Bride 1931,N 4,31:2
Of Thee I Sing 1931,D 28,20:1
Let 'Em Eat Cake 1933,O 23,18:1
Caviar 1934,Je 8,19:2
Hide and Seek 1934,Ag 7,20:2
Saluta 1934,Ag 29,13:4
Stick-in-the-Mud 1935,D 2,18:2
Postman Always Rings Twice, The 1936,F 26,17:2
Double Dummy 1936,N 12,30:1
In the Bag 1936,D 18,30:2

Clements, Dudley—Cont

Off to Buffalo! 1939,F 22,18:2
Man Who Came to Dinner, The 1939,O 17,31:1
Sunny River 1941,D 5,28:2
Song of Norway 1944,Ag 22,20:2

Clements, Hazel
O'Brien Girl, The 1921,O 4,10:2

Clements, John
Mrs Jimmie Thompson 1920,Mr 30,9:1
White Villa, The 1921,F 15,7:1
Wheel, The 1921,Ag 30,10:1
Serpent's Tooth, A 1922,Ag 25,8:5
Seventh Heaven 1922,O 31,11:1
They Came to a City 1943,Je 6,II,1:6
Happy Marriage, The 1952,Ag 8,9:2
Rivals, The 1956,Mr 11,II,3:1
Macbeth 1962,F 7,32:2
Saint Joan 1962,F 21,57:4
Tulip Tree, The 1962,N 30,25:5
Masters, The 1963,Je 1,16:8
Heartbreak House 1967,Ag 27,II,1:1
Antony and Cleopatra 1969,Ag 30,10:3

Clements, John (Director)
Heartbreak House 1967,Ag 27,II,1:1
Arms and the Man 1970,Ag 26,36:1

Clements, John (Playwright)
Sweet Seventeen 1924,Mr 18,24:2
Made for Each Other 1924,S 30,27:2
Happy Marriage, The 1952,Ag 8,9:2

Clements, John (Producer)
Rivals, The 1956,Mr 11,II,3:1

Clements, John (Sir) (Miscellaneous)
Country Wife, The 1969,Ag 30,10:3
Antony and Cleopatra 1969,Ag 30,10:3

Clements, Joy
King and I, The 1960,My 12,40:1
King and I, The 1960,My 22,II,1:1
Pirates of Penzance, The 1961,Ja 20,24:5
Gondoliers, The 1962,Ap 19,34:2
Paradise Island 1962,Je 28,22:1
King and I, The 1963,Je 13,30:2
Patience 1968,My 16,52:1

Clements, Kathleen
House With the Twisty Windows, The
1930,My 8,32:5

Clements, L D
Yeomen of the Guard, The 1961,Ap 28,23:1
Mikado, The 1961,My 5,23:1
Grand Duke, The 1961,My 12,24:1
Princess Ida 1961,My 19,23:1
Iolanthe 1961,My 26,29:6
H M S Pinafore 1961,Je 9,29:5
Student Prince, The 1961,Jl 14,14:1
Gondoliers, The 1961,D 8,44:1
King and I, The 1963,Je 13,30:2

Clements, Marjorie
Demi-Virgin, The 1921,O 19,22:1

Clements, Mary Will
Faith of Our Fathers 1950,Ag 6,72:2

Clements, Steve
Trumpets and Drums 1969,O 13,52:1

Clemmer, Richard (Director)
Noah 1954,O 11,32:2

Clemons, Cameron
Young Blood 1925,N 25,15:1

Clemons, James
Greenwich Village Follies 1920,Ag 31,7:3
Greenwich Village Follies 1924,S 17,16:1
Untitled-Revue 1926,O 26,18:3

Clemons, Vivian
I Want You 1961,S 15,29:1

Clemson, John Osborne
Bye Bye Bonnie 1927,Ja 14,15:3
Houseboat on the Styx, The 1928,D 26,14:3

Clemson, John Osborne (Producer)
Borrowed Love 1929,Je 18,29:2

Clennon, David
Titus Andronicus 1967,Ag 10,43:2
Henry IV 1968,F 7,40:1
Unseen Hand, The 1970,Ap 2,43:1
Forensic and the Navigators 1970,Ap 2,43:1

Clerc, Henri (Playwright)
Beau Metier, Le 1930,Ja 12,VIII,4:1

Clerc, Norma
Delicate Story 1940,D 5,32:2
Counsellor-at-Law 1942,N 25,17:2
For Keeps 1944,Je 15,17:5

Clermont, Rene
Piano Dans l'Herbe, Un 1970,S 17,56:1

Clermont, Robert
Robe de Perles, La 1928,Ja 15,VIII,2:3
Bapteme, Le 1928,Mr 11,VIII,2:7
Lelia 1928,D 2,X,2:1

Cless, Downing
Does a Tiger Wear a Necktie? 1967,F 4,17:1

Clether, Brenda
Conversation Piece 1934,O 24,24:1

Cleugh, Dennis
Madras House, The 1921,O 31,18:2
Goldfish, The 1922,Ap 18,15:3
Shewing-Up of Blanco Posnet, The 1923,O 17,14:2
Player Queen, The 1923,O 17,14:2
Tyrants 1924,Mr 5,14:1
Man Who Ate the Popomack, The 1924,Mr 25,24:1

What Every Woman Knows 1926,Ap 14,20:2
Crown Prince, The 1927,Mr 24,23:2
Very Wise Virgin, A 1927,Je 3,25:3
Pleased to Meet You 1928,O 30,27:2

Cleveland, Anna
Leap, The 1924,My 23,16:5

Cleveland, De Lancy
Crime 1927,F 23,27:3

Cleveland, Del
Prunella; Love in a Garden 1926,Je 16,23:3
Gods of the Lightning 1928,O 25,27:2
Buckaroo 1929,Mr 18,31:1
Seven 1929,D 28,10:5
Three Times the Hour 1931,Ag 26,15:5
Forsaking All Others 1933,Mr 2,21:2
She Loves Me Not 1933,N 21,22:4
Thanks for Tomorrow 1938,S 28,28:2
Dance Night 1938,O 15,20:5

Cleveland, Francis
Night Remembers, The 1934,N 28,24:3
Beggarman, Thief 1935,Jl 16,24:1
Dead End 1935,O 29,17:2
Co-Respondent Unknown 1936,Ag 19,18:5
Tide Rising 1937,Ja 26,17:2
Our Town 1938,F 5,18:3
Brown Danube, The 1939,My 18,30:4

Cleveland, George
Made in America 1925,O 15,27:2
Honor Be Damned! 1927,Ja 27,13:1

Cleveland, Georgine
Right of Happiness 1931,Ap 3,34:2
Paid Companions 1931,Je 23,28:4

Cleveland, Jean
My Fair Ladies 1941,Mr 24,12:7
Mexican Hayride 1944,Ja 29,9:6
Devils Galore 1945,S 13,27:2
On Whitman Avenue 1946,My 9,28:2

Cleveland, Patience
Apple Cart, The 1956,O 19,23:1

Cleveland, Phyllis
Annie Dear 1924,N 5,25:3
Tell Me More 1925,Ap 14,27:3
City Chap, The 1925,O 27,21:1

Cleveland Orchestra
Neighborhood Playhouse Program 1930,F 21,23:1

Clevenger, Helen
Little Theatre Tournament; Shall We Join the
Ladies? 1929,My 9,34:3
Shall We Join the Ladies? 1929,My 12,28:3

Cleverdon, Douglas (Director)
Under Milk Wood 1957,O 16,42:5

Cleverdon, Douglas (Producer)
Under Milk Wood 1956,Ag 22,25:3

Cleverie, Ann
Girl From Wyoming, The 1938,O 31,12:1

Clewely, Maida
Gala Night 1930,F 26,22:4

Clewes, Lorraine
House in Paris, The 1944,Mr 21,17:1
Women of Twilight 1952,Mr 4,22:2

Clewis, Cullen
Lace Petticoat 1927,Ja 5,18:2

Clide, Frank
Move on, Sister 1933,O 25,22:4

Cliff, Alice Belmore
Androcles and the Lion 1925,N 24,28:1

Cliff, Cooper
American Born 1925,S 27,VII,2:1

Cliff, Jeanette
G-II 1948,My 28,27:3
Phoenix Too Frequent, A 1958,Mr 16,II,1:1

Cliff, Laddie
Over She Goes 1936,S 24,28:7

Cliff, Oliver
Antigone 1946,F 19,21:3
Candida 1946,Ap 4,33:2
Antony and Cleopatra 1947,N 27,49:2
Bravo! 1948,N 12,31:2
Ivy Green, The 1949,Ap 6,37:2
That Lady 1949,N 23,18:4
Happy Time, The 1950,Ja 25,24:1

Cliffe, Alice Belmore
No More Blondes 1920,Ja 8,22:1
Paddy the Next Best Thing 1920,Ag 28,5:5
Fanny Hawthorn 1922,My 12,22:2
Windows 1923,O 9,17:2
Failures, The 1923,N 23,20:1
Mongrel, The 1924,D 16,28:2
Hay Fever 1925,O 5,25:1
Chief Thing, The 1926,Mr 23,24:2
Meet the Prince 1929,F 26,30:5
Michael and Mary 1929,D 14,23:3
Stepdaughters of War 1930,O 7,27:1
I Love an Actress 1931,S 18,29:2
Hay Fever 1931,D 30,25:1
Wooden Slipper, The 1934,Ja 4,16:3
Dream Child 1934,Jl 31,20:2
Dream Child 1934,S 28,26:2
Flowers of the Forest 1935,Ap 9,25:2
Taming of the Shrew, The 1935,O 1,27:3
Greatest Show on Earth, The 1938,Ja 6,22:2
Dear Octopus 1939,Ja 12,22:2
Doctor's Dilemma, The 1941,Mr 12,18:2

Cliffe, Alice Belmore—Cont

Three Sisters, The 1942,D 22,31:2
Three Sisters, The 1942,D 27,VIII,1:1

Cliffe, Alice Cooper
Major Barbara 1928,N 20,28:4
Major Barbara 1928,D 2,X,1:1

Cliffe, H Cooper
Genius and the Crowd 1920,S 7,20:1
Squaw Man, The 1921,D 27,10:3
Comedian, The 1923,Mr 14,14:1
Silence 1924,N 13,18:2
American Born 1925,O 6,31:3
Aged 26 1936,D 22,32:1

Clifford, Billy
Go-Go 1923,Mr 13,19:4

Clifford, C P
Laugh It Off 1925,Ap 25,18:4

Clifford, Charles L (Original Author)
Too Many Boats 1934,S 12,26:3

Clifford, Edith
Vaudeville (Palace) 1927,My 31,25:1

Clifford, Ethel
Frankie and Johnny 1930,S 26,16:5

Clifford, George
Jimmie 1920,N 18,15:3
Music Box Revue 1924,D 2,23:3
Piggy 1927,Ja 12,22:2

Clifford, Jack
Glory 1922,D 26,10:1
Racket, The 1927,N 23,28:3
Elmer the Great 1928,S 25,29:1
Frankie and Johnny 1930,S 26,16:5
First Night 1930,N 27,32:3
Angels Don't Kiss 1932,Ap 6,22:5
Rendezvous 1932,O 13,22:3
Jamboree 1932,N 25,18:4
Tragedy of the Ages, The 1933,Ap 7,22:7
Orchids Preferred 1937,My 12,26:5

Clifford, Jack Rube
Vaudeville (Palace) 1926,Ag 3,19:2

Clifford, Joseph E
Wings Over Europe 1936,Mr 4,24:7

Clifford, Margaret
Fledgling 1940,N 28,29:2

Clifford, Nelson
Vaudeville (Palace) 1932,Jl 4,14:5
White Horse Inn 1936,O 2,28:5

Clifford, Pamela
Let's Face It 1941,O 30,26:2

Clifford, Ray
Headquarters 1929,D 5,32:4
Short Cut, The 1930,Ja 28,28:2
One Wife or Another 1933,F 7,23:6

Clifford, Willard
Great Gatsby, The 1926,F 3,22:1

Clifford, William
Tale of the Wolf, The 1925,O 8,31:2
Legal Murder 1934,F 16,16:2
Wild Justice 1935,Jl 9,24:3
Taming of the Shrew, The 1935,O 1,27:3

Clifford, Yvonne
Arms and the Man 1956,O 2,39:4

Clifford and Marion
Vaudeville (Palace) 1928,My 29,17:4
Vaudeville (Palace) 1929,Jl 8,17:6
Vaudeville (Palace) 1930,Mr 3,18:5
Vaudeville (Palace) 1931,Jl 13,13:4

Cliffton, Vala
Macbeth 1966,Ag 29,23:4

Clift, Alice
Happy Town 1959,O 8,49:2

Clift, Denison (Playwright)
Woman Disputed, A 1926,S 29,23:2
Scotland Yard 1929,S 28,16:6
Moon Is Red, The 1934,D 5,29:1
Moon Is Red, The 1934,D 23,IX,1:8
Gentle Rain 1936,S 2,18:2
Gentle Rain 1936,S 20,IX,1:4

Clift, E P (Miscellaneous)
Reluctant Debutante, The 1956,O 11,50:1

Clift, Jeanette
Three Love Affairs; Phoenix Too Frequent, A
1958,Mr 11,33:1
Three Love Affairs; Bedtime Story 1958,Mr 11,33:1
Three Love Affairs; Still Life 1958,Mr 11,33:1
Jackass, The 1960,Mr 24,39:2
Romeo and Juliet 1961,F 24,24:1
Galileo 1968,D 1,88:4

Clift, Montgomery
Fly Away Home 1935,Ja 16,20:4
Jubilee 1935,O 14,20:1
Yr Obedient Husband 1938,Ja 11,26:5
Eye on the Sparrow 1938,My 4,26:3
Dame Nature 1938,S 27,24:3
Mother, The 1939,Ap 26,26:2
There Shall Be No Night 1940,Ap 30,25:2
Mexican Mural; Vera Cruz Interior 1942,Ap 27,19:2
Skin of Our Teeth, The 1942,N 19,29:5
Skin of Our Teeth, The 1942,N 22,VIII,1:1
Our Town 1944,Ja 11,24:5
Searching Wind, The 1944,Ap 13,25:2
Searching Wind, The 1944,Ap 23,II,1:1
Foxhole in the Parlor 1945,My 24,15:4
You Touched Me! 1945,S 26,27:2

Clift, Montgomery—Cont

You Touched Me! 1945,S 30,II,1:1
Sea Gull, The 1954,My 12,38:1
Sea Gull, The 1954,My 23,II,1:1
Clift, Montgomery (Playwright)
Sea Gull, The 1954,My 12,38:1
Clifton, Burt (Playwright)
Good-Bye Please 1934,O 25,26:6
Clifton, Eileen
Conversation Piece 1934,O 24,24:1
Clifton, Ethel (Playwright)
For Value Received 1923,My 8,22:3
Clifton, Evelyn (Costume Designer)
Earth 1927,Mr 10,23:1
Final Balance, The 1928,O 31,28:3
Clifton, Harry
Pygmalion 1938,Ja 27,16:3
Captain Jinks of the Horse Marines 1938,Ja 28,16:2
No More Peace 1938,Ja 29,13:2
Clifton, Herbert
Vaudeville (Palace) 1923,Ja 23,18:2
Clifton, John (Composer)
Man With a Load of Mischief, The 1966,N 7,65:1
Clifton, John (Lyricist)
Man With a Load of Mischief, The 1966,N 7,65:1
Clifton, John (Miscellaneous)
Man With a Load of Mischief, The 1966,N 7,65:1
Clifton, Margie
Vaudeville (Palace) 1923,O 30,16:1
Clifton, Marguerite
Highland Fling, A 1944,Ap 29,13:2
Men to the Sea 1944,O 4,25:2
Sophie 1944,D 26,22:7
Cline, Carroll (Scenic Designer)
Jackknife 1958,S 23,36:2
Cline, Charles H
Steadfast 1923,O 31,12:1
Incubator 1932,N 2,23:3
Cline, Duane A (Costume Designer)
Shout From the Rooftops 1964,O 29,40:1
Cline, Duane A (Scenic Designer)
Shout From the Rooftops 1964,O 29,40:1
Cline, Edward (Director)
Laffing Room Only 1944,D 25,15:4
Heads or Tails 1947,My 3,10:6
Cline, Fred
Streets of New York, The 1963,O 30,47:1
Half a Sixpence 1965,Ap 26,38:2
Cline, Hattie
Unto Such Glory 1937,My 7,28:2
Cline, Louis (Director)
American Tragedy, An 1931,F 21,15:5
Cline, Robert (Miscellaneous)
Not a Way of Life 1967,Mr 23,28:1
Clingerman, J W
Tiger Smiles, The 1930,D 18,29:1
Clinton, Draynard
On Strivers' Row 1946,Mr 1,17:2
Clinton, Edith
Food for Midas 1942,Ja 31,12:7
Clinton, Francis Wright
One Woman's Husband 1920,Mr 23,9:3
Clinton, Katherine
Wife With a Smile, The 1921,N 29,20:1
Boubouroche 1921,N 29,20:1
Caravan 1928,Ag 30,13:3
Clinton, Mildred
Qudrille 1954,N 4,39:2
Wrong Way Light Bulb, The 1969,Mr 5,40:1
Clinton, William
Little Theatre Tournament; White Peacock, The 1928,My 11,28:1
Clinton-Braddeley, V C (Playwright)
Jolly Roger 1933,Mr 26,IX,1:1
Clintons, The
Vaudeville (Lexington) 1921,O 18,20:2
Clive, Colin
Journey's End 1929,Jl 14,IX,5:1
Forty-Seven 1930,F 4,29:1
Swan, The 1930,Jl 27,VIII,1:8
Overture 1930,N 25,31:2
Overture 1930,D 8,26:4
Crime at Blossoms, The 1931,Je 7,VIII,2:1
Eight Bells 1933,O 30,14:2
Eight Bells 1933,N 5,IX,1:1
Lake, The 1933,D 19,26:3
Lake, The 1933,D 27,24:2
Lake, The 1934,Ja 7,X,1:1
Libel! 1935,D 3,32:8
Libel! 1935,D 8,X,5:8
Libel! 1935,D 21,10:5
Clive, David
Tragedian in Spite of Himself, A 1948,F 6,29:2
Wedding, The 1948,F 6,29:2
On the Harmfulness of Tobacco 1948,F 6,29:2
Bear, The 1948,F 6,29:2
Richard III 1949,F 9,33:2
Trip to Bountiful, The 1953,N 4,30:3
Clive, David (Director)
Say Darling 1959,F 26,38:2
Clive, David (Producer)
Third Person 1955,D 30,13:4
Clive, E E
Creaking Chair, The 1926,F 23,26:1

Clive, E E (Director)
Creaking Chair, The 1926,F 23,26:1
Whispering Gallery, The 1929,F 12,22:2
Bellamy Trial, The 1928,Ag 20,21:1
Bellamy Trial, The 1931,Ap 23,28:6
Clive, E E (Director)
Creaking Chair, The 1926,F 23,26:1
Whispering Gallery, The 1929,F 12,22:2
Bellamy Trial, The 1931,Ap 23,28:6
Clive, E E (Miscellaneous)
Creaking Chair, The 1926,F 23,26:1
Sport of Kings, The 1926,My 5,24:2
Clive, E E (Producer)
Whispering Gallery, The 1929,Ja 6,VIII,4:4
Whispering Gallery, The 1929,F 12,22:2
Clive, Helen C
Rio Rita 1927,F 3,18:3
Clive, Joan
Angels Don't Kiss 1932,Ap 6,22:5
Come Easy 1933,Ag 30,22:5
Clive, Madeleine
To My Husband 1936,Je 2,35:2
Strangler Fig, The 1940,My 7,31:2
Day After Tomorrow 1950,O 27,25:2
Angels Kiss Me 1951,Ap 18,37:6
Point of No Return 1951,D 14,35:2
Qudrille 1954,N 4,39:2
Happy Hunting 1956,D 7,30:1
Clock, William
Little Theatre Tournament; White Peacock, The 1928,My 11,28:1
Cloffi, Charles
Three Sisters, The 1969,Ag 4,29:1
Cloffi, Janice
Sweethearts 1947,Ja 22,31:2
Cloire, Helen
Nine Pine Street 1933,Ap 28,15:5
Cloninger, Margaret
Aiglon, L' 1934,N 5,22:2
Cloninger, Ralph
Pierre of the Plains 1929,Ja 6,VIII,4:4
Clonis, C (Scenic Designer)
Electra 1952,N 20,38:2
Oedipus Tyrannus 1952,N 25,35:2
Cloquemin, P (Playwright)
Gardiens de Phare 1923,N 13,24:2
Clork, Harry (Playwright)
Milky Way, The 1934,My 9,23:2
Milky Way, The 1934,My 20,IX,1:1
See My Lawyer 1939,S 28,29:1
Milky Way, The 1943,Je 10,17:2
Close, Del
9 by Six: A Cry of Players 1956,D 5,49:2
Nervous Set, The 1959,My 13,43:1
Close, Hugh W Jr
Great Guns 1939,N 18,23:4
Close, Jack
Life Begins in '40 1940,Ap 5,24:2
Closser, Myla Jo (Playwright)
Raw Meat 1933,Mr 23,13:2
Clotz, Florence (Costume Designer)
On an Open Roof 1963,Ja 30,7:3
Cloud, Kate
Big Blow 1938,O 3,11:2
Clough, George M
Blue Monday 1932,Je 3,23:2
Clough, Inez
Chocolate Dandies, The 1924,S 2,22:2
Earth 1927,Mr 10,23:1
Wanted 1928,Jl 3,19:2
Harlem 1929,F 21,30:3
Wade in de Water 1929,S 14,17:2
Promis' Lan', De 1930,My 28,31:2
Savage Rhythm 1932,Ja 1,30:4
Clovelly, Cecil
Richard III 1920,Mr 8,7:1
Hamlet 1922,N 17,14:1
Love for Love 1925,Ap 1,21:2
Buccaneer, The 1925,O 3,10:2
In a Garden 1925,N 17,29:1
Jest, The 1926,F 5,22:2
Dybbuk, The 1926,D 17,27:2
Hearts Are Trumps! 1927,Ap 8,21:1
Wild Duck, The 1928,N 19,17:1
Cape Cod Follies 1929,S 19,37:2
Family Affairs 1929,D 11,34:6
Topaze 1930,F 13,25:3
Forest Ring, The 1930,Ap 26,11:2
They All Come to Moscow 1933,My 12,20:6
Anne of the Thousand Days 1948,D 9,49:2
Clovelly, Cecil (Director)
Lady From the Sea, The 1929,Mr 19,36:1
You Can't Take It With You 1951,Ap 7,8:6
Clovis, Hall
Grand Duchess 1929,D 17,29:2
Orpheus in Hades 1930,D 16,30:1
Chocolate Soldier, The 1932,F 9,30:3
Clow, Steve (Playwright)
Bare Facts of Today 1930,Ap 17,24:4
Cloy, Robert C
Half a Widow 1927,S 13,37:3
Clubley, John
Town Boy 1929,O 5,22:4
Goose for the Gander, A 1945,Ja 24,16:4
You Can't Take It With You 1945,Mr 27,23:7

Cluchey, Rick
Cage, The 1970,Je 19,25:1
Cluchey, Rick (Playwright)
Cage, The 1970,Je 19,25:1
Cludet, Frances (Choreographer)
Ice Follies 1963,Ja 10,5:2
Clugston, Glenn (Choreographer)
Athenian Touch, The 1964,Ja 15,25:4
Clugston, Glenn (Director)
Athenian Touch, The 1964,Ja 15,25:4
Clugston, Katharine (Playwright)
These Days 1928,N 4,IX,1:3
These Days 1928,N 13,36:2
Clugston, Katherine T
Patriarch, The 1926,D 11,15:1
Clukey, James
Tartuffe 1957,O 9,39:1
Clulow, Jeremy
Anatomist, The 1957,F 27,21:5
Clunes, Alec
Othello 1946,D 4,44:2
Candida 1946,D 4,44:2
Twelfth Night 1950,D 3,II,3:1
Henry V 1951,F 11,II,3:1
Firstborn, The 1952,Ja 30,22:5
Firstborn, The 1952,F 10,II,2:1
Clunes, Alec (Director)
Awake and Sing! 1942,My 31,VIII,2:3
Clurman, Harold
Caesar and Cleopatra 1925,Ap 14,27:1
Goat Song 1926,Ja 26,18:1
Chief Thing, The 1926,Mr 23,24:2
Juarez and Maximilian 1926,O 12,31:1
Sarah Adler Testimonial 1939,Mr 15,18:2
Clurman, Harold (Director)
Awake and Sing! 1935,F 20,23:2
Paradise Lost 1935,D 10,31:5
Golden Boy 1937,N 5,18:5
Golden Boy 1938,Ja 23,XI,1:6
Rocket to the Moon 1938,N 25,18:2
Gentle People, The 1939,Ja 6,25:1
Awake and Sing! 1939,Mr 8,18:2
Night Music 1940,F 23,18:2
Retreat to Pleasure 1940,D 18,32:2
Russian People, The 1942,D 30,17:2
Beggars Are Coming to Town 1945,O 29,16:2
Truckline Cafe 1946,F 28,19:4
Whole World Over, The 1947,Mr 28,28:2
Young and Fair, The 1948,N 23,35:2
Member of the Wedding, The 1950,Ja 6,26:6
Member of the Wedding, The 1950,Ja 15,II,1:1
Bird Cage, The 1950,F 23,32:2
Member of the Wedding, The 1950,S 17,II,1:1
Autumn Garden, The 1951,Mr 8,36:2
Autumn Garden, The 1951,Mr 18,II,1:1
Desire Under the Elms 1952,Ja 17,23:4
Desire Under the Elms 1952,Ja 20,II,1:1
Time of the Cuckoo, The 1952,O 16,37:4
Time of the Cuckoo, The 1952,N 2,II,1:1
Emperor's Clothes, The 1953,F 10,24:2
Ladies of the Corridor, The 1953,O 22,33:5
Ladies of the Corridor, The 1953,N 1,II,1:1
Mademoiselle Colombe 1954,Ja 7,26:1
Mademoiselle Colombe 1954,Ja 17,II,1:1
Saint Joan 1954,S 18,12:1
Bus Stop 1955,Mr 3,23:2
Bus Stop 1955,Mr 13,II,1:1
Tiger at the Gates 1955,Mr 3,27:1
Tiger at the Gates 1955,Je 12,II,1:1
Tiger at the Gates 1955,O 4,40:1
Tiger at the Gates 1955,O 23,II,1:1
Pipe Dream 1955,D 1,44:1
Waltz of the Toreadors, The 1956,D 22,14:8
Waltz of the Toreadors, The 1957,Ja 18,17:2
Waltz of the Toreadors, The 1957,Ja 27,II,1:1
Orpheus Descending 1957,Mr 22,28:1
Orpheus Descending 1957,Mr 31,II,1:1
Day the Money Stopped, The 1958,F 21,19:4
Waltz of the Toreadors, The 1958,Mr 5,37:1
Touch of the Poet, A 1958,O 3,23:2
Touch of the Poet, A 1958,O 12,II,1:1
Cold Wind and the Warm, The 1958,D 9,55:1
Cold Wind and the Warm, The 1959,Ja 18,II,1:1
Heartbreak House 1959,O 19,37:1
Heartbreak House 1959,O 25,II,1:1
Jeannette 1960,Mr 25,20:2
Shot in the Dark, A 1961,O 19,40:1
Judith 1962,Je 21,25:4
Incident at Vichy 1964,D 4,44:1
Incident at Vichy 1964,D 20,II,3:1
Where's Daddy? 1966,Mr 3,27:1
Uncle Vanya 1969,Ag 31,II,4:1
Clurman, Harold (Producer)
Truckline Cafe 1946,F 28,19:4
All My Sons 1947,Ja 30,21:2
Clute, Chester
She Couldn't Say No! 1926,S 1,27:3
New Yorkers, The 1927,Mr 11,24:3
Oh, Promise Me 1930,N 25,31:1
Triplets 1932,S 22,25:2
Page Miss Glory 1934,N 28,24:2
Ceiling Zero 1935,Ap 11,26:2
Forty-Four Below 1935,Jl 23,24:3

Clyde, David
Adventurous Age, The 1927,F 8,20:1
Bellamy Trial, The 1928,Ag 20,21:1
Clyde, Jean
Courting 1925,S 14,17:1
Courting 1925,S 20,VIII,1:1
Marigold 1930,O 9,23:1
Clyde, Jeremy
Conduct Unbecoming 1969,Jl 26,14:1
Conduct Unbecoming 1970,O 13,50:1
Clyde, June
Lucky Break 1934,O 3,25:3
Flying Trapeze, The 1935,Je 2,IX,2:3
Hooray for What! 1937,D 2,32:5
Little Stranger 1938,Jl 14,16:2
Banjo Eyes 1941,D 26,20:2
Clyde, Sylvia
Yeomen of the Guard, The 1941,D 19,34:3
Clymas, Sari
Rumple 1957,N 7,42:2
Clymer, John
Raw Meat 1933,Mr 23,13:2
Clymer, Warren (Scenic Designer)
Write Me a Murder 1961,O 27,28:2
Coady, C D
1776 1926,Ap 24,11:2
Coakley, Marion
Genius and the Crowd 1920,S 7,20:1
Meanest Man in the World, The 1920,O 13,18:2
Wait Till We're Married 1921,S 27,14:1
Drums of Jeopardy, The 1922,My 30,8:4
Wild Oats Lane 1922,S 7,12:1
Barnum Was Right 1923,Mr 13,19:3
Alarm Clock, The 1923,D 25,26:2
Werewolf, The 1924,Ag 26,6:1
Jack in the Pulpit 1925,Ja 7,33:1
Spring Fever 1925,Ag 4,14:2
Service for Two 1926,Ag 31,15:1
Arabian Nightmare, The 1927,Ja 11,36:3
Mixed Doubles 1927,Ap.27,22:3
Julius Caesar 1927,Je 7,27:2
Racket, The 1927,N 23,28:3
Coakley, Sally (Mlle)
Girofle-Girofla 1926,N 23,26:3
Coale, Virginia
If Love Were All 1931,N 14,14:5
Coan, Cricket Cannon
Universal Nigger, The 1970,Mr 21,18:1
Coast, John
Student Prince, The 1924,D 3,25:3
Coate, Richard
As You Like It 1958,Ja 21,33:6
Arms and the Man 1965,Je 24,32:5
Coate, Richard (Miscellaneous)
Titus Andronicus 1956,D 3,40:2
Coates, Alan
Henry IV, Part I 1955,S 22,34:2
I Am a Camera 1956,O 10,47:2
Sweeney Todd 1957,Ag 28,21:4
Apollo of Bellac, The 1958,Mr 7,17:2
Browning Version, The 1958,Mr 7,17:2
Month in the Country, A 1959,Mr 2,32:2
Coates, Carolyn
Trouble in July 1949,D 2,36:2
American Mime Theatre 1958,S 25,28:4
Trojan Women, The 1963,D 24,7:6
Country Wife, The 1965,D 10,58:2
Condemned of Altona, The 1966,F 4,21:1
Condemned of Altona, The 1966,F 13,II,1:1
Whitman Portrait, A 1966,O 12,37:1
Party on Greenwich Avenue, The 1967,My 11,52:1
Club Bedroom, The 1967,D 6,41:1
American Dream, The 1968,O 3,55:1
Death of Bessie Smith, The 1968,O 3,55:1
Fire! 1969,Ja 29,26:1
Scent of Flowers, A 1969,O 21,42:1
Disintegration of James Cherry, The 1970,Ja 30,33:3
Coates, Eleanor
Red Geranium, The 1922,My 9,22:3
Coates, Harold
Aquashow 1953,Je 24,29:2
Elliott Murphy's Aquashow 1955,Je 23,25:1
Coates, Jefferson
Russian People, The 1942,D 30,17:2
Second Best Bed 1946,Je 4,20:2
Flag Is Born, A 1946,S 7,10:6
Coates, Margaret
Bobino 1944,Ap 7,23:4
Coates, Patricia
Texas Town 1941,Ap 30,22:3
Out of My House 1942,Ja 8,28:6
Coats, James
Time Remembered 1955,My 4,35:1
Cobb, Bruce
Twelfth Night 1969,Ag 14,29:2
Cobb, Buff (Miscellaneous)
Let It Ride 1961,O 13,27:4
Cobb, Buff (Producer)
Too True to Be Good 1963,Mr 14,8:2
Never Live Over a Pretzel Factory 1964,Mr 30,37:1
Cobb, Daniel
Sadie Thompson 1944,N 17,25:2

Cobb, Eliwell
After Such Pleasures 1934,Ja 6,18:6
Cobb, Elizabeth (Playwright)
Men We Marry, The 1948,Ja 17,11:2
Cobb, Elwell
On Borrowed Time 1938,F 4,16:4
Cobb, Emily
Skin of Our Teeth, The 1955,Ag 18,16:1
Cobb, Humphrey (Original Author)
Paths of Glory 1935,S 19,29:1
Paths of Glory 1935,S 27,24:2
Cobb, Ira (Lyricist)
Yours Is My Heart 1946,S 6,16:5
Cobb, Ira (Original Author)
Yours Is My Heart 1946,S 6,16:5
Cobb, Jean
Heads or Tails 1947,My 3,10:6
Cobb, Jean Arden
Swan, The 1954,Ag 17,16:6
Cobb, John S (Producer)
Almost Crazy 1955,Je 21,37:1
Cobb, Julia
Sylvia 1923,Ap 26,22:1
Long Road, The 1930,S 10,30:2
Cobb, Julie
Nancy's Private Affair 1930,Ja 14,24:3
Cobb, Lee J
Crime and Punishment 1935,Ja 23,20:3
Waiting for Lefty 1935,Mr 27,24:5
Till the Day I Die 1935,Mr 27,24:5
Mother, The 1935,N 20,26:3
Bitter Stream 1936,Mr 31,16:6
Happy Valley, Limited 1936,Je 30,15:1
Johnny Johnson 1936,N 20,26:3
Golden Boy 1937,N 5,18:5
Gentle People, The 1939,Ja 6,25:1
Thunder Rock 1939,N 15,18:1
Fifth Column, The 1940,Ja 27,9:1
Fifth Column, The 1940,F 4,IX,1:6
Fifth Column, The 1940,Mr 7,18:2
Fifth Column, The 1940,Mr 17,X,1:1
Clash by Night 1941,D 29,20:2
Clash by Night 1942,Ja 11,IX,1:1
Winged Victory 1943,N 22,24:1
Death of a Salesman 1949,F 11,27:2
Death of a Salesman 1949,F 20,II,1:1
Golden Boy 1952,Mr 13,24:3
Golden Boy 1952,Mr 23,II,1:1
Emperor's Clothes, The 1953,F 10,24:2
King Lear 1968,N 8,43:1
King Lear 1968,N 17,II,1:3
Cobb, Mary Alice
Fiesta 1928,D 13,25:2
Cobb, R C
Where People Gather 1967,O 26,56:1
Certain Young Man, A 1967,D 27,45:1
Cobb, Vincent
Our Town 1968,D 14,62:1
Cobden-Smith, R
Witness for the Prosecution 1954,D 17,35:2
Coben, Marion
Ever Since Paradise 1957,Jl 12,18:4
Coben, Marion (Miscellaneous)
Oklahoma! 1958,Mr 8,15:2
Cobert, Gerry
Flies, The; Mouches, Les 1947,Ap 18,26:3
Cobert, Robert (Composer)
U S A 1959,O 29,38:1
God's Trombones 1960,F 10,43:4
Time to Go 1960,Mr 23,33:1
Cobert, Robert (Musical Director)
God's Trombones 1960,F 10,43:4
Shakespeare in Harlem 1960,F 10,43:4
Time to Go 1960,Mr 23,33:1
Cobey, Herbert (Playwright)
Stranger in the Hills 1949,O 10,19:2
Cobey, Todd (Playwright)
No Hard Feelings 1965,Ap 5,33:8
Cobian, Carlos Orchestra
Vaudeville (Palace) 1926,Je 15,23:3
Coble, Harry
House in Berlin, A (Als der Kreig zu Ende War);
Als der Krieg zu Ende War (A House in Berlin)
1950,D 27,32:3
Coble, Tom
Time for the Gentle People, A 1967,My 26,50:1
Gandhi 1970,O 21,37:1
Coble, Tom (Director)
Time for the Gentle People, A 1967,My 26,50:1
Coble, Tom (Playwright)
Time for the Gentle People, A 1967,My 26,50:1
Coble, Vic
Aquarama 1960 1960,Jl 1,14:6
Cobleigh, Stanley (Producer)
Billy the Kid 1951,Ag 21,23:2
Cobner, John
King Lear 1964,My 19,43:2
Coburn, (Mrs) (Producer)
Yellow Jacket, The 1928,N 8,27:3
Coburn, Barbara
Goodbye Again 1943,N 10,28:4
Coburn, Charles
French Leave 1920,N 9,13:1

Coburn, Charles—Cont
Bronx Express 1922,Ap 27,12:2
Imaginary Invalid, The 1922,Jl 26,26:2
Farmer's Wife, The 1924,O 10,22:3
Trelawney of the 'Wells' 1925,Je 2,16:2
Right Age to Marry, The 1926,F 16,22:3
Old Bill, M P 1926,N 11,22:2
Better 'Ole, The 1927,Ag 23,29:3
Diplomacy 1928,My 29,16:3
Diplomacy 1928,Je 3,VIII,1:1
Yellow Jacket, The 1928,N 8,27:3
Falstaff 1928,D 26,14:2
Yellow Jacket, The 1929,Ja 11,21:1
Peter Ibbetson 1931,Ap 9,30:3
Troilus and Cressida 1932,Je 7,22:3
Kultur 1933,S 27,24:3
Sunday Nights at Nine 1933,N 13,20:7
Yellow Jacket, The 1934,F 25,IX,2:6
First Legion, The 1934,O 2,18:2
Rip Van Winkle 1935,Ag 7,22:2
Master of the Revels 1935,Ag 14,16:2
Three Wise Fools 1936,Ja 14,25:2
Three Wise Fools 1936,Mr 2,12:2
County Chairman, The 1936,My 26,26:5
Macbeth 1936,Jl 22,17:5
Around the Corner 1936,D 29,17:2
Sun Kissed 1937,Mr 11,20:2
Coburn, Charles (Director)
Farmer's Wife, The 1924,O 10,22:3
Right Age to Marry, The 1926,F 16,22:3
Junk 1927,Ja 6,25:1
Plutocrat, The 1930,F 21,23:3
Kultur 1933,S 27,24:3
Moroni 1936,Ag 19,19:1
Coburn, Charles (Miscellaneous)
Master of the Revels 1935,Ag 14,16:2
Coburn, Charles (Mrs)
French Leave 1920,N 9,13:1
Bronx Express 1922,Ap 27,12:2
Imaginary Invalid, The 1922,Jl 26,26:2
Farmer's Wife, The 1924,O 10,22:3
Right Age to Marry, The 1926,F 16,22:3
Better 'Ole, The 1927,Ag 23,29:3
Yellow Jacket, The 1928,N 8,27:3
Falstaff 1928,D 26,14:2
Yellow Jacket, The 1929,Ja 11,21:1
Sunday Nights at Nine 1933,N 13,20:7
Yellow Jacket, The 1934,F 25,IX,2:6
Rip Van Winkle 1935,Ag 7,22:2
Master of the Revels 1935,Ag 14,16:2
Macbeth 1936,Jl 22,17:5
Coburn, Charles (Mrs) (Playwright)
Imaginary Invalid, The 1922,Jl 26,26:2
Coburn, Charles (Playwright)
Imaginary Invalid, The 1922,Jl 26,26:2
Coburn, Charles (Producer)
Old Bill, M P 1926,N 11,22:2
Ghosts 1927,Ja 11,36:3
Yellow Jacket, The 1928,N 8,27:3
Falstaff 1928,D 26,14:2
Plutocrat, The 1930,F 21,23:3
Long Watch, The 1952,Mr 21,19:5
Coburn, Gladys
Up in the Clouds 1922,Ja 3,20:3
Ziegfeld Follies 1923,O 22,17:2
Lucky Sam McCarver 1925,O 22,22:1
Coburn, Helen
Scarlet Letter, The 1926,Ja 8,16:5
Trumpet Shall Sound, The 1926,D 11,15:2
Big Lake 1927,Ap 9,17:2
People on the Hill 1931,S 26,25:5
Coburn, Ivah
Plutocrat, The 1930,F 21,23:3
Troilus and Cressida 1932,Je 7,22:3
Coburn, Joan
I Feel Wonderful 1954,O 19,22:5
Threepenny Opera, The 1955,S 21,38:1
Coburn, Mary
Champion, The 1925,Ap 24,16:4
Coburn, Sydney
American Tragedy, An 1926,O 12,31:2
Coburns, The
Right Age to Marry, The 1926,F 7,VII,2:3
Coby, Donald E
Coriolanus 1927,Je 18,8:3
Coca, Imogene
Vaudeville (Palace) 1928,Ag 28,27:3
Garrick Gaieties 1930,O 17,21:2
Shoot the Works! 1931,Jl 22,19:5
Flying Colors 1932,S 16,24:2
New Faces 1934,Mr 16,24:5
Fools Rush In 1934,D 26,19:2
New Faces of 1936 1936,My 20,24:5
Spring Dance 1936,Jl 7,22:2
Who's Who 1938,Mr 2,16:2
Straw Hat, The 1939,S 30,10:6
All in Fun 1940,N 22,26:2
All in Fun 1940,D 28,11:2
Concert Varieties 1945,Je 2,10:7
Janus 1956,Je 12,39:6
Girls in 509, The 1958,O 16,47:1

Cocea, Alice
On Ne Roule pas Antoinette 1927,Ap 10,VIII,2:7
Enlevement, L' 1927,O 2,VIII,2:4
Je T'Attendais 1929,Ja 20,VIII,1:8
Coucou 1930,Je 1,VIII,2:1
Petite Catherine, La 1930,N 2,VIII,2:1
Voie Lactee, La 1933,F 26,IX,2:2
Mari Que J'ai Voulu, Le 1934,Ap 29,IX,2:2
Jeune Fille a Reve, Une 1935,My 5,IX,2:4
Pacifique 1937,N 14,XI,2:1
Coch, Robert (Miscellaneous)
Joy 1970,Ja 28,50:1
Cochet, Jean-Laurent
Boys in the Band, The 1969,S 20,21:2
Cochet, Jean-Laurent (Director)
Boys in the Band, The 1969,S 20,21:2
Malade Imaginaire, Le 1970,F 18,40:2
Cochran, Alice
Happy 1927,D 6,26:3
Who Cares 1930,Jl 9,27:1
Cochran, Ann
Happy 1927,D 6,26:3
Who Cares 1930,Jl 9,27:1
Cochran, C B (Mrs) (Playwright)
Nine to Six 1930,Ja 31,24:3
Cochran, C B (Mrs) (Producer)
Nine to Six 1930,Ja 31,24:3
Cochran, C B (Producer)
Traite d'Auteuil, Le 1921,Jl 17,VI,1:8
Cochran, Charles B (Miscellaneous)
Silver Tassie, The 1929,O 25,26:1
Bitter Sweet 1929,N 6,30:2
Conversation Piece 1934,O 24,24:1
Escape Me Never! 1935,Ja 22,22:2
Paganini 1937,Je 6,XI,1:2
Cochran, Charles B (Playwright)
Home and Beauty 1937,F 21,X,2:1
Paganini 1937,My 21,18:6
Cochran, Charles B (Producer)
One Night in Rome 1920,Ap 30,1:2
Man in Dress Clothes, The 1922,Ap 30,VII,1:8
Music Box Revue 1923,My 20,VII,1:3
Little Nellie Kelly 1923,Jl 3,25:2
Little Nellie Kelly 1923,S 30,II,1:6
On With the Dance 1925,My 1,22:4
Six Characters in Search of an Author
   1925,Je 16,26:4
Blackbirds 1926,S 25,21:5
Wake Up and Dream 1929,Ap 14,X,1:8
Many Waters 1929,S 26,27:1
Middle Watch, The 1929,O 17,27:1
Silver Tassie, The 1929,N 10,X,1:1
Wake Up and Dream 1929,D 31,14:3
Wake Up and Dream 1930,Ja 12,9:1
Cochran's 1930 Revue 1930,Ap 13,X,1:6
Private Lives 1930,O 12,VIII,1:8
Evergreen 1930,O 14,31:2
Evergreen 1930,D 4,30:4
Evergreen 1930,D 21,VIII,1:6
Vaudeville (Palace Theatre London) 1931,Ja 6,24:6
Private Lives 1931,Ja 28,24:1
Vaudeville (Pavilion) 1931,Mr 20,29:3
Cavalcade 1931,O 14,26:4
Helen 1932,Ja 31,I,5:2
Miracle, The 1932,Ap 10,I,18:1
Miracle, The 1932,My 8,VIII,2:2
Words and Music 1932,Ag 26,21:2
Words and Music 1932,S 17,18:7
Words and Music 1932,O 9,IX,1:8
Dinner at Eight 1933,Ja 7,11:5
Dinner at Eight 1933,Ja 29,IX,1:3
Mother of Pearl 1933,F 26,IX,3:1
Music in the Air 1933,My 20,11:3
Wild December 1933,Je 25,IX,1:3
Nymph Errant 1933,O 7,18:2
Nymph Errant 1933,O 29,IX,1:6
Escape Me Not 1933,D 9,18:6
Escape Me Never! 1934,Ja 7,X,3:5
Conversation Piece 1934,F 17,20:5
Magnolia Street 1934,Mr 9,22:6
Magnolia Street 1934,Ap 1,X,1:7
Streamline 1934,S 29,13:1
Streamline 1934,O 21,IX,1:3
Black Eye, The 1935,O 12,13:5
Follow the Sun 1935,D 24,10:3
Follow the Sun 1936,F 5,15:8
Blackbirds 1936,Jl 10,15:1
Laughter in Court 1936,S 27,X,3:5
Boy David, The 1936,N 22,VI,7:1
Home and Beauty 1937,F 3,26:2
Home and Beauty 1937,F 21,X,2:1
Happy Returns 1938,My 20,16:6
Lights Up 1940,F 18,IX,2:5
Big Top 1942,My 17,VIII,1:3
Big Ben 1946,Ag 4,II,1:4
Bless the Bride 1947,My 5,31:2
Bless the Bride 1947,My 11,II,3:7
Tough at the Top 1949,Jl 17,58:5
Tough at the Top 1949,Ag 7,II,1:4
Cochran, Dorcas (Lyricist)
Earl Carroll's Vanities 1940,Ja 15,11:2
Cochran, Dorcas (Playwright)
Earl Carroll's Vanities 1940,Ja 15,11:2

Cochran, Gifford (Playwright)
Threepenny Opera, The 1933,Ap 14,22:4
Cochran, Gifford (Producer)
Threepenny Opera, The 1933,Ap 14,22:4
Cochran, James (Costume Designer)
Haiti 1938,Mr 3,16:1
Cochran, Mabel
American Gothic 1953,N 11,35:6
Cradle Song 1955,D 2,32:2
Exiles 1957,Mr 13,27:1
Conversation Piece 1957,N 19,38:2
Season of the Beast 1958,Mr 14,29:2
Distant Bell, A 1960,Ja 14,29:1
Cochran, Mickey
I Gotta Get Out 1947,S 26,27:2
Cochran, Roy
Fair Circassian, The 1921,D 7,22:3
Window Panes 1927,F 22,22:2
Cochran, Steve
Hickory Stick 1944,My 9,15:6
Broken Hearts of Broadway 1944,Je 13,16:2
Diamond Lil 1948,N 30,33:2
Diamond Lil 1949,F 7,16:2
Cochran, Vera
Purple Canary, The 1963,Ap 23,31:1
Cochran, Vera (Producer)
Empire Builders, The 1968,O 2,34:1
Cochrane, James (Costume Designer)
Pinocchio 1939,Ja 3,19:2
Cochrane, Jeannetta (Costume Designer)
Love for Love 1947,My 27,30:2
Cochrane, June
Garrick Gaieties 1925,My 18,12:2
Girl Friend, The 1926,Mr 18,26:5
Connecticut Yankee, A 1927,N 4,24:2
Cochrane, Mabel
Sport of Kings, The 1926,My 5,24:2
Cochrane, Roy
Clair de Lune 1921,Ap 19,15:1
Plot Thickens, The 1922,S 6,16:1
Lady Cristilina 1922,D 26,11:2
Dice of the Gods, The 1923,Ap 6,20:2
Forbidden 1923,O 2,10:2
Best People, The 1924,Ag 20,8:1
Little Minister, The 1925,Mr 24,21:1
Bit o' Love, A 1925,My 13,24:2
Accused 1925,S 30,20:1
Old Bill, M P 1926,N 11,22:2
Mixed Doubles 1927,Ap 27,22:3
19th Hole, The 1927,O 12,30:3
Cockerill, Betty
Tall Kentuckian, The 1953,Je 17,30:1
Cockram, Joan
Dancing Mothers 1924,Ag 12,12:2
Cocks, John
New Freedom, The 1930,My 15,32:4
New Freedom, The 1930,My 17,21:4
Cocktails, The
Vaudeville (Palace) 1928,O 23,32:5
Coco, Carlos
Vanderbilt Revue, The 1930,O 26,VIII,3:5
Coco, James
Salome 1956,F 14,24:4
Hotel Paradiso 1957,Ap 12,22:2
Darwin's Theories 1960,O 19,53:2
Moon in the Yellow River, The 1961,F 7,40:2
Everybody Loves Opal 1961,O 12,40:2
Passage to India, A 1962,F 1,23:1
Squat Betty 1964,F 25,24:1
Sponge Room, The 1964,F 25,24:1
That 5 A.M. Jazz 1964,O 20,42:2
Lovey 1965,Mr 26,27:1
Devils, The 1965,N 17,51:2
Astrakhan Coat, The 1967,Ja 13,18:1
Basement, The 1967,O 3,56:1
Fragments 1967,O 3,56:1
Fragments; Basement, The 1967,O 15,II,3:3
Here's Where I Belong 1968,Mr 4,32:1
Witness 1968,N 22,38:1
Next 1969,F 11,27:1
Next 1969,F 23,II,1:1
Last of the Red Hot Lovers 1969,D 29,37:1
Last of the Red Hot Lovers 1970,Ja 4,II,1:1
Cocteau, Jean (Playwright)
Voix Humaine, La 1930,Mr 9,IX,2:7
Antigone 1930,Ap 25,28:4
Boeuf sur le Toit, Le 1930,Ap 25,28:4
Machine Infernale, La 1934,My 13,IX,2:2
Orphee 1935,Mr 23,10:3
Machine Infernale, La 1935,Ap 21,IX,2:2
Chevaliers de la Table Ronde 1938,Je 12,X,2:3
Azrael; Eagle Has Two Heads, The 1946,S 16,9:7
Streetcar Named Desire, A 1949,O 19,36:6
Infernal Machine, The 1954,Mr 22,22:2
Typewriter, The 1955,Jl 29,8:3
Eagle Has Two Heads, The 1956,D 14,37:2
Infernal Machine, The 1958,F 4,33:1
Intimate Relations 1962,N 2,27:1
Intimate Relations 1962,N 25,II,1:1
Opium 1970,O 6,58:1
Cocteau, Jean (Translator)
Infernal Machine, The 1937,D 13,22:7
Eagle Has Two Heads, The 1947,Mr 20,39:2

Cod, Jack
Gay Divorce 1937,Jl 20,19:4
Coda, Alfred
Lady of Mexico 1962,O 20,13:2
Coda, Frank
Oh What a Lovely War 1964,O 1,30:1
Coddington, Jack (Miscellaneous)
Carmilla 1970,D 1,61:2
Code, Grant
Too Late the Phalarope 1956,O 12,35:1
Legend of Lizzie, The 1959,F 10,39:1
Coggerers, The 1960,Mr 23,33:1
Time to Go 1960,Mr 23,33:1
In the Jungle of Cities 1960,D 21,39:1
Moon Shines on Kylenamoe, The 1962,O 31,33:1
Dylan 1964,Ja 20,18:1
Trelawny of the 'Wells' 1970,O 12,48:1
Codee, Ann
Vaudeville (Palace) 1926,O 19,27:5
Vaudeville (Palace) 1930,D 1,19:1
Coder, Richard
Son, The 1950,Ag 16,24:6
Codina, Jose Feliu y (Playwright)
Spanish Love 1920,Ag 18,6:1
Codori, Joe (Costume Designer)
On the Town 1959,Ja 16,36:1
On the Town 1959,Ja 25,II,1:1
Legend of Lovers 1959,O 28,40:3
There Is a Play Tonight 1961,F 16,24:2
Codori, Joseph (Miscellaneous)
Fiorello! 1962,Je 14,24:1
Codron, Michael (Miscellaneous)
Rattle of a Simple Man 1963,Ap 18,39:1
Play 1964,Ja 6,35:1
Lover, The 1964,Ja 6,35:1
Hang Down Your Head and Die 1964,O 19,38:1
Poor Bitos 1964,N 16,40:2
Entertaining Mr Sloane 1965,O 13,41:1
Killing of Sister George, The 1966,O 6,57:1
Hail Scrawdyke! 1966,N 29,50:1
Flip Side, The 1968,O 11,36:1
Not Now Darling 1970,O 30,33:1
Codron, Michael (Producer)
There's a Girl in My Soup 1967,O 19,58:1
Cody, Clay
Sweet Chariot 1930,O 24,30:2
Black Tower 1932,Ja 12,29:2
Jefferson Davis 1936,F 19,17:2
Help Yourself! 1936,Jl 15,15:1
Cody, Ethel
Plain and Fancy 1955,Ja 28,14:2
Auntie Mame 1956,N 1,47:2
Cody, Katherine
Journey to Jerusalem 1940,O 7,21:2
Cody, Lew
Vaudeville (Palace) 1927,O 4,34:3
Coe, Fred (Director)
Thousand Clowns, A 1962,Ap 6,31:2
Thousand Clowns, A 1962,Ap 15,II,1:1
Xmas in Las Vegas 1965,N 5,31:1
Coe, Fred (Miscellaneous)
Journey to the Day 1963,N 12,49:1
Coe, Fred (Producer)
Trip to Bountiful, The 1953,N 4,30:3
Two for the Seesaw 1958,Ja 17,15:1
Miracle Worker, The 1959,O 20,44:1
All the Way Home 1960,D 1,42:1
Gideon 1961,N 10,38:1
Thousand Clowns, A 1962,Ap 6,31:2
Xmas in Las Vegas 1965,N 5,31:1
Wait Until Dark 1966,F 3,21:1
Georgy 1970,F 27,26:1
Coe, Frederick
Day Will Come, The 1944,S 8,17:2
Coe, George
Telemachus Clay 1963,N 16,17:2
What Makes Sammy Run? 1964,F 28,19:1
Shout From the Rooftops 1964,O 29,40:1
Mame 1966,My 25,41:1
Company 1970,Ap 27,40:1
Company 1970,My 3,II,1:4
Coe, John
Oedipus Rex 1960,Ap 30,15:2
Marrying Maiden, The 1960,Je 23,18:3
In the Jungle of Cities 1960,D 21,39:1
Mountain Giants, The 1961,Ap 5,32:3
Apple, The 1961,D 8,44:1
Thistle in My Bed 1963,N 20,48:1
Passion of Josef D, The 1964,F 12,29:1
Jonah! 1966,F 16,52:1
Wicked Cooks, The 1967,Ja 24,42:1
Junebug Graduates Tonight! 1967,F 27,35:1
Father Uxbridge Wants to Marry 1967,O 30,57:1
Man in the Glass Booth, The 1968,S 27,41:1
Strada, La 1969,D 15,63:1
Nobody Hears A Broken Drum 1970,Mr 20,55:1
Coe, Peter (Director)
Macbeth 1962,Je 20,41:1
Oliver 1963,Ja 8,5:5
Pickwick 1963,Jl 5,13:2
Rehearsal, The 1963,S 24,45:2
Rehearsal, The 1963,O 20,II,1:1
Next Time I'll Sing to You 1963,N 28,69:2

Coe, Peter (Director)—Cont
Pickwick 1965,O 6,5:3
King's Mare, The 1966,Jl 21,23:1
Skin of Our Teeth, The 1968,S 12,55:1
Coe, Peter (Producer)
Kiss Me, Kate 1970,D 26,10:4
Coelos, Roger Manuel
This Mad Whirl 1937,Ja 10,II,4:8
Coerver, Michael
Mime Theatre of Etienne Decroux, The
1959,D 24,15:1
Calvary 1960,Jl 22,13:1
Coffee, Lenore (Playwright)
Family Portrait 1939,Mr 19,XI,1:1
Family Portrait; Familie, Eine 1946,N 11,44:1
Family Portrait 1959,My 6,48:2
Coffeen, Peter
Millionairess, The 1969,Mr 3,28:1
Coffey, Al
Aquarama 1960 1960,Jl 1,14:6
Aqua Carnival 1962,Je 29,15:1
Coffey, Bud (Miscellaneous)
Wicked Cooks, The 1967,Ja 24,42:1
Shoemaker's Holiday, The 1967,Mr 3,25:1
Spitting Image 1969,Mr 3,28:1
Philosophy in the Boudoir 1969,My 22,55:2
American Hamburger League, The 1969,S 17,51:1
Effect of Gamma Rays on Man-in-the-Moon
Marigolds, The 1970,Ap 8,32:1
Coffield, Peter
Cock-A-Doodle Dandy 1969,Ja 21,40:1
Hamlet 1969,Mr 4,34:1
Coffin, Gene (Costume Designer)
Dear Charles 1954,S 16,37:2
Someone Waiting 1956,F 15,26:1
Affair of Honor 1956,Ap 7,12:3
Jolly's Progress 1959,D 7,42:2
49th Cousin, The 1960,O 28,22:1
Rendezvous at Senlis 1961,F 28,39:2
Coffin, Haskell
Glamour Preferred 1940,N 16,13:2
Wanhope Building, The 1947,F 11,36:5
Lucky Sam McCarver 1950,Ap 15,10:6
Mrs Warren's Profession 1950,O 26,39:2
Here Come the Clowns 1954,My 5,36:2
Coffin, Hayden
School for Scandal, The 1929,D 15,X,4:2
Coffin, Lois
Sonya's Search for the Christmas Star
1929,D 14,24:6
Coffin, Ruth
Bedrock 1934,N 18,II,6:3
Coffin, William Haskell Jr
Julius Caesar 1923,F 9,10:4
Coffman, Robert
Lady of Mexico 1962,O 20,13:2
Cofino, I
Electra 1952,N 20,38:2
Cogan, B C
Take a Brace 1923,Ap 20,20:3
Cogan, David J (Producer)
Raisin in the Sun, A 1959,Mr 12,27:1
In the Counting House 1962,D 15,5:5
Cogan, Eugene
Caesar and Cleopatra 1935,Ag 22,21:1
Cogan, Sheridan (Choreographer)
Thesmophoriazusae, The; Goddesses of Athens,
The 1955,D 14,52:4
Cogan, Susan
Man's a Man, A 1962,S 20,30:2
Guys and Dolls 1966,Je 9,55:2
Cogen, Eugene (Producer)
Judge, The 1958,My 14,36:2
Cogert, Jed
Crucible 1933,S 5,22:4
Cogert, Joe
Squealer, The 1928,N 13,36:3
Street Scene 1929,Ja 11,20:4
Coggin, Barbara
Go, Go, Go, God is Dead! 1966,O 12,37:1
Coggio, Roger
Lorenzaccio 1958,O 15,44:2
Diary of a Madman 1967,Mr 24,25:1
Coggio, Roger (Director)
Diary of a Madman 1967,Mr 24,25:1
Coggio, Roger (Playwright)
Diary of a Madman 1964,Ap 17,29:2
Diary of a Madman 1967,Mr 24,25:1
Coghill, Nevill (Lyricist)
Canterbury Tales 1968,S 7,23:3
Canterbury Tales; Miller's Tale, The 1969,F 4,34:1
Canterbury Tales; Pilgrims, The 1969,F 4,34:1
Canterbury Tales; Steward's Tale, The
1969,F 4,34:1
Canterbury Tales; Wife of Bath's Tale, The
1969,F 4,34:1
Canterbury Tales; Merchant's Tale, The
1969,F 4,34:1
Coghill, Nevill (Playwright)
Canterbury Tales 1968,S 7,23:3
Canterbury Tales; Wife of Bath's Tale, The
1969,F 4,34:1
Canterbury Tales; Steward's Tale, The
1969,F 4,34:1

Canterbury Tales; Merchant's Tale, The
1969,F 4,34:1
Canterbury Tales; Pilgrims, The 1969,F 4,34:1
Canterbury Tales; Miller's Tale, The 1969,F 4,34:1
Coghill, Nevill (Translator)
Canterbury Tales; Steward's Tale, The
1969,F 4,34:1
Canterbury Tales; Merchant's Tale, The
1969,F 4,34:1
Canterbury Tales; Pilgrims, The 1969,F 4,34:1
Canterbury Tales; Wife of Bath's Tale, The
1969,F 4,34:1
Canterbury Tales; Miller's Tale, The 1969,F 4,34:1
Coghill, Neville (Director)
Midsummer Night's Dream, A 1945,Mr 25,II,2:4
Coghlan, Austin
Heigh-Ho, Everybody 1932,My 26,31:2
As You Like It 1939,My 9,28:4
Chicken Every Sunday 1944,Ap 6,27:2
Coghlan, Charles
Letter of the Law, The; Robe Rouge, La
1920,F 24,11:1
Coghlan, Charles (Playwright)
Royal Box, The 1928,N 21,32:3
Coghlan, Gertrude
Sweet Stranger 1930,O 22,23:3
Home Sweet Home 1936,Jl 1,29:2
Plumes in the Dust 1936,N 7,14:2
Coghlan, Rose
Deburau 1921,Ja 2,VI,3:1
Untitled-Benefit 1921,My 2,12:3
Cogut, Jed
Fast Service 1931,N 18,26:3
Cafe Crown 1942,Ja 24,12:5
Cogut, Judah
Steps Leading Up 1941,Ap 19,20:6
Cohan, Charles
Radio Girl, The 1929,O 19,22:4
Jolly Orphan, The 1929,D 23,18:6
Little Clown, The 1930,Mr 15,23:3
Love Thief, The 1931,Ja 19,24:5
Kibitzer, The 1931,N 7,17:3
Pleasure 1931,D 28,20:2
Under One Roof 1932,F 8,21:2
Freidel Becomes a Bride 1936,F 10,14:3
In a Jewish Grocery 1939,O 2,15:2
Oy, Is Dus a Leben!; Oh, What a Life!
1942,O 13,19:2
Right Next to Broadway 1944,F 22,26:2
Song of Dnieper 1946,O 26,10:5
Shylock and His Daughter 1947,S 30,22:2
Voice of Israel, The 1948,O 26,40:2
Hershel, The Jester 1948,D 14,39:2
Abi Gezunt 1949,O 10,19:4
Sadie Is a Lady 1950,Ja 28,9:2
Second Marriage 1953,O 12,30:1
Cohan, George
Revolt of the Beavers, The 1937,My 21,19:2
Pinocchio 1939,Ja 3,19:2
Cohan, George M
Meanest Man in the World, The 1920,O 8,14:4
Meanest Man in the World, The 1920,O 13,18:2
Meanest Man in the World, The 1920,O 24,VI,1:1
Tavern, The 1921,My 24,20:1
Friars Club Frolic 1921,Je 13,16:2
Friar's Club Frolic 1922,Je 5,16:1
Song and Dance Man, The 1924,Ja 1,21:2
American Born 1925,S 27,VII,2:1
American Born 1925,O 6,31:3
Merry Malones, The 1927,S 11,VIII,1:3
Merry Malones, The 1927,S 27,30:2
Merry Malones, The 1927,N 20,IX,1:1
Gambling 1929,Ag 27,31:2
Gambling 1929,S 22,IX,1:1
Tavern, The 1930,My 20,32:1
Song and Dance Man, The 1930,Je 17,25:5
Friendship 1931,My 10,VIII,2:5
Vaudeville (New Amsterdam Theatre)
1931,Je 22,17:3
Friendship 1931,S 1,30:2
Friendship 1931,S 13,IX,1:1
Confidential Service 1932,Ap 3,VIII,2:5
Pigeons and People 1933,Ja 1,IX,2:5
Pigeons and People 1933,Ja 17,22:3
Ah, Wilderness! 1933,S 26,26:3
Ah, Wilderness! 1933,O 3,28:2
Ah, Wilderness! 1934,O 30,23:1
Seven Keys to Baldpate 1935,My 28,30:2
Dear Old Darling 1935,D 31,10:1
Dear Old Darling 1936,F 2,IX,1:3
Dear Old Darling 1936,Mr 3,25:1
Fulton of Oak Falls 1937,Ja 2,15:3
Fulton of Oak Falls 1937,F 11,18:2
I'd Rather Be Right 1937,O 12,27:6
I'd Rather Be Right 1937,O 17,XI,2:1
I'd Rather Be Right 1937,O 26,18:2
I'd Rather Be Right 1937,N 3,28:2
I'd Rather Be Right 1937,N 14,XI,1:1
I'd Rather Be Right 1938,Ja 23,XI,1:6
Madam Will You Walk 1939,N 14,20:3
Return of the Vagabond, The 1940,Ap 21,IX,1:8
Return of the Vagabond, The 1940,My 14,27:2

Cohan, George M (Composer)
Little Nellie Kelly 1922,Ag 6,VI,1:7
Little Nellie Kelly 1922,N 14,16:1
Merry Malones, The 1927,S 27,30:2
George M! 1968,Ap 11,48:1
Cohan, George M (Director)
American Born 1925,O 6,31:3
Cohan, George M (Lyricist)
Little Nellie Kelly 1922,Ag 6,VI,1:7
Little Nellie Kelly 1922,N 14,16:1
Merry Malones, The 1927,S 27,30:2
George M! 1968,Ap 11,48:1
Cohan, George M (Miscellaneous)
Elmer the Great 1928,S 30,IX,1:1
Cohan, George M (Playwright)
Meanest Man in the World, The 1920,O 8,14:4
Tavern, The 1920,O 10,VI,1:1
Tavern, The 1921,My 24,20:1
All-Star Jamboree 1921,Jl 14,18:1
Madeleine and the Movies 1922,Mr 7,11:1
Little Nellie Kelly 1922,Ag 6,VI,1:7
Little Nellie Kelly 1922,N 14,16:1
So This Is London 1923,Ap 12,22:1
Little Nellie Kelly 1923,Jl 3,25:2
Little Nellie Kelly 1923,Jl 8,VI,1:1
Rise of Rosie O'Reilly, The 1923,D 26,13:4
Song and Dance Man, The 1924,Ja 1,21:2
American Born 1925,S 27,VII,2:1
American Born 1925,O 6,31:3
Home Towners, The 1926,My 16,VIII,2:2
Home Towners, The 1926,Ag 24,19:3
Home Towners, The 1926,Ag 29,VII,1:1
Home Towners, The 1926,S 5,VII,1:1
Baby Cyclone, The 1927,Ag 14,VII,2:1
Merry Malones, The 1927,S 11,VIII,1:3
Baby Cyclone, The 1927,S 13,37:4
Merry Malones, The 1927,S 27,30:2
Merry Malones, The 1927,N 20,IX,1:1
Whispering Friends 1928,F 21,18:3
Baby Cyclone, The 1928,Ap 11,25:1
Billie 1928,O 2,34:2
Gambling 1929,My 19,IX,2:1
Gambling 1929,Ag 27,31:2
Seven Keys to Baldpate 1930,Ja 8,25:2
Song and Dance Man, The 1930,Je 17,25:5
Friendship 1931,My 10,VIII,2:5
Friendship 1931,S 1,30:2
Friendship 1931,S 13,IX,1:1
Confidential Service 1932,Ap 3,VIII,2:5
Pigeons and People 1933,Ja 1,IX,2:5
Seven Keys to Baldpate 1935,My 28,30:2
Dear Old Darling 1935,D 31,10:1
Dear Old Darling 1936,F 2,IX,1:3
Dear Old Darling 1936,Mr 3,25:1
Fulton of Oak Falls 1937,F 11,18:2
Return of the Vagabond, The 1940,Ap 13,20:1
Return of the Vagabond, The 1940,My 14,27:2
Tavern, The 1962,Ap 5,29:1
Tavern, The 1964,Mr 6,39:2
Cohan, George M (Producer)
Meanest Man in the World, The 1920,O 8,14:4
Tavern, The 1920,O 10,VI,1:1
Mary 1920,O 19,12:1
Meanest Man in the World, The 1920,O 24,VI,1:1
Tavern, The 1921,My 24,20:1
Little Nellie Kelly 1922,Ag 6,VI,1:7
Song and Dance Man, The 1924,Ja 1,21:2
American Born 1925,O 6,31:3
Home Towners, The 1926,Ag 24,19:3
Yellow 1926,S 22,30:1
Baby Cyclone, The 1927,Ag 14,VII,2:1
Baby Cyclone, The 1927,S 13,37:4
Merry Malones, The 1927,S 27,30:2
Merry Malones, The 1927,N 20,IX,1:1
Los Angeles 1927,D 20,32:3
Whispering Friends 1928,F 21,18:3
Elmer the Great 1928,S 25,29:1
By Request 1928,S 28,30:2
Billie 1928,O 2,34:2
Vermont 1929,Ja 9,28:1
Gambling 1929,Ag 27,31:2
Tavern, The 1930,My 20,32:1
Song and Dance Man, The 1930,Je 17,25:5
Rhapsody, The 1930,S 16,30:3
Friendship 1931,S 1,30:2
Confidential Service 1932,Ap 3,VIII,2:5
Pigeons and People 1933,Ja 17,22:3
Dear Old Darling 1936,F 2,IX,1:3
Dear Old Darling 1936,Mr 3,25:1
Fulton of Oak Falls 1937,Ja 2,15:3
Fulton of Oak Falls 1937,F 11,18:2
Return of the Vagabond, The 1940,My 14,27:2
Cohan, George M Jr
Vaudeville (New Amsterdam Theatre)
1931,Je 22,17:3
Cohan, Georgette
Vaudeville (Palace) 1921,Ja 25,14:2
Madeleine and the Movies 1922,Mr 7,11:1
Diplomacy 1928,My 29,16:3
Diplomacy 1928,Je 3,VIII,1:1
Girl Trouble 1928,O 7,IX,2:3
Rivals, The 1930,Mr 14,24:4

Cohan, Helen F
Friendship 1931,My 10,VIII,2:5
Friendship 1931,S 1,30:2
Cohan, Mary (Miscellaneous)
George M! 1968,Ap 11,48:1
Cohan, Mary Anne
Can-Can 1953,My 8,28:1
Cohan, Robert
Shangri-La 1956,Je 14,40:1
Cohen, Al
Get Thee to Canterbury 1969,Ja 26,74:1
Billy 1969,Mr 24,56:1
Cohen, Alexander H (Director)
Beyond the Fringe 1962,O 29,36:1
Beyond the Fringe 1964 1964,Ja 10,18:1
Cohen, Alexander H (Miscellaneous)
Angel Street 1941,D 6,15:2
They Should Have Stood in Bed 1942,F 14,18:5
Of V We Sing 1942,F 16,20:3
Courtin' Time 1951,Je 14,30:2
Evening With Yves Montand, An 1961,O 25,30:1
Cohen, Alexander H (Playwright)
King Lear 1950,D 26,18:1
Cohen, Alexander H (Producer)
Ghost for Sale 1941,S 30,27:4
Brights Lights of 1944 1943,S 17,27:4
Duke in Darkness, The 1944,Ja 25,15:2
Jenny Kissed Me 1948,D 24,12:2
Make a Wish 1951,Ap 19,38:1
Be Your Age 1953,Ja 15,24:2
Magic and the Loss, The 1954,Ap 10,10:3
First Gentleman, The 1957,Ap 26,22:2
Love Me Little 1958,Ap 15,42:2
At the Drop of a Hat 1959,O 9,22:2
Littlest Circus, The 1959,D 26,5:6
Evening With Mike Nichols and Elaine May, An
1960,O 10,37:1
Beyond the Fringe 1962,O 29,36:1
School for Scandal, The 1963,Ja 26,5:2
Maurice Chevalier 1963,Ja 30,7:2
Lorenzo 1963,F 16,5:2
Ages of Man 1963,Ap 15,36:1
Man and Boy 1963,N 13,34:1
Beyond the Fringe 1964 1964,Ja 10,18:1
Rugantino 1964,F 2,II,1:4
Rugantino 1964,F 7,34:1
Hamlet 1964,Ap 10,30:1
Comedy in Music, Opus 2 1964,N 10,54:1
Beyond the Fringe, '65 1964,D 16,49:2
Baker Street 1965,F 17,36:1
Maurice Chevalier at 77 1965,Ap 2,26:1
Devils, The 1965,N 17,51:2
Ivanov 1966,My 4,50:1
Time for Singing, A 1966,My 23,48:2
At the Drop of Another Hat 1966,D 28,30:2
Homecoming, The 1967,Ja 6,29:1
Black Comedy; White Lies 1967,F 13,42:1
Black Comedy 1967,F 13,42:1
Little Murders 1967,Ap 26,38:1
Unknown Soldier and His Wife, The 1967,Jl 7,22:1
Marlene Dietrich 1967,O 10,52:1
Halfway up the Tree 1967,N 8,52:1
Dear World 1969,F 7,33:1
Home 1970,N 18,41:1
Cohen, Alvin (Director)
Culbin Sands 1935,Mr 23,10:3
Cohen, Arthur
Around the World 1946,Je 1,9:5
Scapegoat, The 1950,Ap 20,36:5
Home Is Tomorrow 1950,Je 2,27:2
Cohen, Beckie
Love and Politics 1929,O 21,30:7
Cohen, Charon Lee (Choreographer)
Trumpets and Drums 1969,O 13,52:1
Cohen, Edward E (Producer)
Stop-Over 1938,Ja 12,16:5
Cohen, Frederic (Composer)
Green Table, The 1942,Ja 22,12:2
Prodigal Son, The 1942,F 18,22:2
Cohen, Frederic (Director)
Noye's Fludde 1959,Mr 17,41:2
Cohen, Frederic (Playwright)
Green Table, The 1942,Ja 22,12:2
Cohen, Harold D (Producer)
Norman, Is That You? 1970,F 20,30:1
Cohen, Harriet
Hair 1970,Ja 13,39:1
Cohen, Harry I (Miscellaneous)
Wrecker, The 1928,F 28,18:2
Cohen, Herb (Producer)
Absolutely Freeee 1967,My 25,58:1
Cohen, Jacob
Tenth Commandment, The 1926,N 18,27:1
Cohen, James Adrian
Winterset 1966,F 10,32:2
Cohen, Jane (Miscellaneous)
Sound of Silence, A 1965,Mr 9,30:1
Something Different 1967,N 29,52:1
Cohen, Jay J (Producer)
Exercise, The 1968,Ap 25,54:1
Cohen, Joel (Composer)
William Had the Words! 1964,Mr 30,36:1

Cohen, Julian (Miscellaneous)
Journey to the Day 1963,N 12,49:1
Cohen, Kip (Miscellaneous)
Golden Age, The 1963,N 19,49:2
Committee, The 1964,S 17,53:1
Cohen, Larry (Playwright)
Nature of the Crime 1970,Mr 24,41:1
Cohen, Laurence (Miscellaneous)
Slave Ship 1969,N 22,46:1
Cohen, Leo K (Scenic Designer)
Emerald Slippers, The 1970,S 2,31:2
Cohen, Lester (Playwright)
Web and the Rock, The 1950,Ag 20,II,1:1
Cohen, Martin B (Director)
We're Civilized? 1962,N 9,30:1
International Playgirls '64 1964,My 22,40:2
Cohen, Martin B (Producer)
Vamp, The 1955,N 11,30:1
Christine 1960,Ap 29,27:1
Cohen, Michael (Composer)
Leonard Sillman's New Faces of 1968
1968,My 3,43:1
Cohen, Michael (Lyricist)
Leonard Sillman's New Faces of 1968
1968,My 3,43:1
Cohen, Mortimer (Playwright)
In the Groove 1938,Ap 22,14:5
Cohen, Moss
This Side of Paradise 1962,F 22,19:6
Cohen, Octavus Roy (Playwright)
Come Seven 1920,Jl 20,10:1
Cohen, Peggy
Early Morning 1970,N 26,57:1
Cohen, Reuben
Jubilee 1935,O 14,20:1
Cohen, Robert P (Miscellaneous)
Macbeth 1969,N 21,51:1
Cohen, Rose
Mascaiada 1929,D 28,10:6
Cohen, Sam
Deputy of Paris, The 1947,Mr 22,9:5
Me, Candido! 1956,O 16,36:2
Cohen, Sammy
Vaudeville (Palace) 1932,My 30,16:7
Cohen, Samuel H (Original Author)
Of One Mother 1937,Ja 18,21:3
Cohen, Sheila Rachel
Earthlight Theater 1970,N 4,38:2
Cohen, Susan
Homo 1969,Ap 12,40:2
Cohen, Sy
Anna Kleiber 1965,Ja 20,33:1
Frere Jacques 1968,Je 8,23:2
Cohen, Theodore
Sailors of Cattaro 1934,D 11,28:4
Cohen, Walter (Miscellaneous)
Christine 1960,Ap 29,27:1
Cohen, Wilbur Jr
Green Pastures, The 1935,F 27,16:2
Cohen, Zeleva (Choreographer)
Mod Donna 1970,My 4,48:1
Cohn, Abe (Producer)
So Many Paths 1934,D 7,26:5
Cohn, Al (Composer)
Sarah and the Sax 1964,My 5,53:1
Dirty Old Man, The 1964,My 5,53:1
Cohn, G
Seven Against One 1930,My 7,25:1
Cohn, Julia
Seventeen 1926,My 1,10:1
Sam Abramovitch 1927,Ja 20,20:5
Cohn, Sam (Producer)
Saturday Night Kid, The 1958,My 16,22:1
Saintliness of Margery Kempe, The 1959,F 3,35:6
Red Eye of Love 1961,Je 13,28:1
Fortuna 1962,Ja 4,26:1
Three Times Three; George Washington Crossing
the Delaware 1962,Mr 2,24:1
Three Times Three; Twenty-Five Cent White Cap,
The 1962,Mr 2,24:1
Three Times Three; Not Enough Rope
1962,Mr 2,24:1
Coiby, Barbara
Devils, The 1965,N 17,51:2
Coil, Cleo
Young Alexander 1929,Mr 13,28:2
Coit, (Miss) (Miscellaneous)
Kai Khosru 1925,Ap 27,14:2
Coit, Dorothy (Director)
Aucassin and Nicolette 1937,F 14,II,3:6
Coit, Sam
Jack in the Pulpit 1925,Ja 7,33:1
Stork, The 1925,Ja 27,14:2
Captain Jinks 1925,S 9,22:1
Gods of the Lightning 1928,O 25,27:2
Nut Farm, The 1929,O 15,34:3
Coizeau (M)
Berlioz 1927,F 20,VII,2:1
Coke, Peter
Faithful, The 1935,Ja 20,X,3:8
Coker, Norman
Bassa Moona 1936,D 9,35:4

Coker, Norman (Playwright)
Bassa Moona 1936,D 9,35:4
Cola-Pinto, William
Three Plays of the Sea 1970,Ag 20,39:1
Colacino, Richard
On the Town 1959,F 14,15:1
Boys From Syracuse, The 1963,Ap 16,31:1
Colaer, Zena
Midnight 1930,D 30,25:1
Colaizzi, Dominick (Playwright)
Arabian Nightmare, The 1927,Ja 11,36:3
Colamor, Jerome
Hamlet 1920,Mr 17,14:2
Colan, George
Salvation 1928,F 1,31:1
Subway Express 1929,S 25,34:3
Steel 1931,N 19,26:5
Lost Boy 1932,Ja 6,24:4
How Beautiful With Shoes 1935,N 29,24:1
Colasanto, Nicholas
Across the Board on Tomorrow Morning
1961,O 23,22:5
Colavitti, Luigi
Cosi Sia; Thy Will be Done 1923,N 14,29:2
Colberg, Michele
Eisrevue 1969,O 23,55:1
Colbert, Claudette
Wild Westcotts, The 1923,D 25,26:2
Kiss in a Taxi, The 1925,Ag 26,14:1
Ghost Train, The 1926,Ag 26,17:2
Pearl of Great Price, The 1926,N 2,34:3
Barker, The 1927,Ja 19,20:6
Barker, The 1927,Ja 23,VII,1:1
Mulberry Bush, The 1927,O 27,33:1
Gringa, La 1928,F 2,17:1
Within the Law 1928,Mr 6,20:1
Barker, The 1928,Je 10,VIII,1:3
Fast Life 1928,S 27,35:2
Tin Pan Alley 1928,N 2,29:1
Dynamo 1929,F 12,22:1
See Naples and Die 1929,S 27,30:4
Marriage-Go-Round, The 1958,O 30,37:1
Marriage-Go-Round, The 1958,N 9,II,1:1
Julia, Jake, and Uncle Joe 1961,Ja 30,19:1
Irregular Verb to Love, The 1963,S 19,22:2
Irregular Verb to Love, The 1963,S 29,II,1:1
Colbert, Helen
Porgy and Bess 1952,S 18,36:5
Porgy and Bess 1953,Mr 10,25:5
Colbert, Jean
Penal Law 2010 1930,Ap 19,14:2
Creeping Fire 1935,Ja 17,22:3
Colbin, Rod
King John 1956,Je 28,33:5
Measure for Measure 1956,Je 29,16:1
Taming of the Shrew, The 1957,F 21,30:2
Legend of Lizzie, The 1959,F 10,39:1
Machinal 1960,Ap 8,27:1
Madame Aphrodite 1961,D 30,13:1
Physicists, The 1964,O 14,52:1
Colbin, Rod (Choreographer)
Macbeth 1967,Jl 31,21:1
Colbin, Rod (Director)
Hamlet 1969,Mr 4,34:1
Colbin, Rod (Miscellaneous)
Macbeth 1955,O 8,12:6
King John 1956,Je 28,33:5
King Lear 1959,Ja 3,11:2
Colbourn, Harv
Adding Machine, The 1970,D 5,40:1
Colbourne, Maurice
Saint Joan 1923,D 29,8:4
Mongrel, The 1924,D 16,28:2
Merchant of Venice, The 1925,D 28,12:1
Cyrano de Bergerac 1926,F 19,18:1
Queen's Husband, The 1931,N 15,VIII,2:1
And Be My Love 1934,Ja 19,25:2
Charles the King 1936,O 10,20:6
Geneva 1940,Ja 31,15:2
There Shall Be No Night 1940,Ap 30,25:2
Colbourne, Maurice (Director)
And Be My Love 1934,Ja 19,25:2
Geneva 1940,Ja 31,15:2
To My Love 1956,Je 7,35:3
Colbourne, Maurice (Miscellaneous)
Geneva 1940,Ja 31,15:2
Colbourne, Maurice (Playwright)
Charles the King 1936,O 10,20:6
Colbourne, Maurice (Producer)
Queen's Husband, The 1931,N 15,VIII,2:1
Woman Kind 1933,S 28,25:2
And Be My Love 1934,Ja 19,25:2
Colburn, Anna Mae
Firefly, The 1931,D 1,23:2
Colby, Barbara
Murder in the Cathedral 1966,Je 21,38:1
Julius Caesar 1966,Je 24,29:2
Murderous Angels 1970,F 8,70:1
Murderous Angels 1970,Mr 15,II,1:4
Colby, Betty
Almost Crazy 1955,Je 21,37:1
Sophie 1963,Ap 16,32:1

Colby, Charles
And Be My Love 1945,F 22,30:4
For Heaven's Sake Mother 1948,N 17,33:4
Listen to the Quiet 1958,O 28,40:2
Colby, Jack
Ballyhoo 1930,D 23,24:1
Colby, James
Enemy of the People, An 1958,F 26,24:2
Colby, John
Catherine Was Great 1944,Ag 3,16:1
Colby, Marion
Meet the People 1940,D 26,22:2
Toplitzky of Notre Dame 1946,D 27,13:4
Pajama Game, The 1954,My 14,20:2
Colby, Robert (Composer)
Half-Past Wednesday 1962,Ap 7,16:2
Colby, Robert (Lyricist)
Half-Past Wednesday 1962,Ap 7,16:2
Colby, Ronald
Dream Play 1960,N 23,22:1
Spots of the Leopard, The 1963,S 25,38:1
Colby, Ronald (Miscellaneous)
Dream Play 1960,N 23,22:1
What a Killing 1961,Mr 28,41:1
Colby and Murry
Vaudeville (Palace) 1932,Mr 7,13:4
Colcord, Mabel
Woman on the Jury, The 1923,Ag 16,10:4
Antonia 1925,O 21,20:1
Buy, Buy Baby 1926,O 8,26:2
Uninvited Guest, The 1927,S 28,28:2
Tia Juana 1927,N 16,28:4
Gasoline Gypsies 1931,Je 8,21:3
Distant Drums 1932,Ja 19,24:3
Story to Be Whispered 1937,Ag 20,21:4
Colcord, Ray
Mary of Magdala 1946,Mr 26,24:5
If in the Green Wood 1947,Ja 17,27:6
Cole, Ardelle
Ice Follies 1966,Ja 12,27:6
Cole, Arthur
Fanshastics 1924,Ja 17,13:2
Angela 1928,D 4,28:2
City Haul 1929,D 31,14:4
Cole, Austin
Pansy 1929,My 15,36:3
Cole, Barbara
Will the Mail Train Run Tonight? 1964,Ja 10,18:1
Cole, Barbara (Choreographer)
Faith of Our Fathers 1950,Ag 6,72:2
Cole, Beatrice
How Beautiful With Shoes 1935,N 29,24:1
Case of Clyde Griffiths 1936,Mr 14,10:4
Women, The 1936,D 28,13:1
Kiss for Cinderella, A 1942,Mr 11,22:2
Cole, Beatrice (Playwright)
Lovely Me 1946,D 26,30:4
Cole, Betty
Let's Laugh Again 1937,Ag 24,24:5
Cole, Bill
Twelfth Night 1957,Jl 4,16:4
Two Gentlemen of Verona 1958,Mr 19,35:1
Broken Jug, The 1958,Ap 2,36:1
Cole, Bobby (Musical Director)
At Home at the Palace 1967,Ag 1,23:1
Cole, Bonnie (Playwright)
Fair Game 1957,N 4,39:1
Cole, Carl
Murder in the Cathedral 1958,Mr 22,12:4
Cole, Carol
Seventeen 1951,Je 22,16:6
Weekend 1968,Mr 14,50:2
Weekend 1968,Mr 31,II,1:1
Cole, Catriona
Clarence 1923,My 14,18:4
Cole, Cosy
Carmen Jones 1943,D 12,II,3:1
Carmen Jones 1946,Ap 14,II,1:2
Cole, Cozy
Carmen Jones 1943,D 3,26:2
Carmen Jones 1945,My 3,26:5
Holiday on Broadway 1948,Ap 28,33:3
Carmen Jones 1956,Je 1,28:2
Cole, David
Innocents, The 1950,F 2,30:2
Innocents, The 1950,F 12,II,1:1
Reluctant Debutante, The 1956,O 11,50:1
Cole, Debra (Costume Designer)
Here Comes Santa Claus 1962,My 18,34:1
Cole, Deen
Synthetic Sin 1927,O 11,26:2
Cole, Dennis
Brigadoon 1964,D 24,9:1
Carousel 1966,D 16,56:2
Brigadoon 1967,D 14,59:2
Cole, Dennis (Director)
Brigadoon 1967,D 14,59:2
Cole, Dora
All God's Chillun Got Wings 1924,My 16,22:3
All God's Chillun Got Wings 1924,Ag 19,9:1
All God's Chillun Got Wings 1924,Ag 24,VII,1:1
Cole, Doris (Producer)
Blue Holiday 1945,My 22,13:3

Cole, E B
Bulls and Belles 1931,Ap 18,17:2
Pudding on the Ritz 1932,Ap 9,18:3
Cole, Edward C (Miscellaneous)
Doctor X 1930,Jl 31,12:4
Cole, Elizabeth
Highest Tree, The 1959,N 5,41:1
Cole, Helen
Jubilee 1935,O 14,20:1
Cole, Jack
Caviar 1934,Je 8,19:2
Thumbs Up! 1934,D 28,24:1
May Wine 1935,D 6,30:3
Keep 'Em Laughing 1942,My 10,VIII,8:3
Ziegfeld Follies 1943,Ap 2,16:2
Cole, Jack (Choreographer)
Allah Be Praised! 1944,Ap 21,14:2
Magdalena 1948,Jl 28,27:2
Magdalena 1948,S 21,31:2
Magdalena 1948,N 7,II,6:5
Alive and Kicking 1950,Ja 18,25:5
Kismet 1953,D 4,2:4
Jamaica 1957,N 1,32:2
Donnybrook! 1961,My 19,23:1
Kean 1961,N 3,28:2
Funny Thing Happened on the Way to the Forum,
    A 1962,My 9,49:1
Foxy 1964,F 17,26:1
Kismet 1965,Je 23,45:1
Man of La Mancha 1965,N 23,52:1
Cole, Jack (Director)
Donnybrook! 1961,My 19,23:1
Donnybrook! 1961,My 28,II,1:1
Kean 1961,N 3,28:2
Cole, Jack and his Dancers
Keep 'Em Laughing 1942,Ap 25,9:2
Alive and Kicking 1950,Ja 18,25:5
Cole, Jan
Galileo 1968,D 1,88:4
Cole, Judson
Vaudeville (Palace) 1926,Jl 27,15:4
Cole, Kay
Best Foot Forward 1963,Ap 3,43:1
Cole, Lester
Peggy-Ann 1926,D 28,16:3
Room of Dreams 1930,N 6,22:4
Vaudeville (Palace) 1932,Je 13,19:7
Cole, Louis
Bottomland 1927,Je 28,29:3
Cole, Marie
Crime 1927,F 23,27:3
Cole, Mina (Director)
Sweet Genevieve 1945,Mr 21,27:3
Cole, Mina (Producer)
Sweet Genevieve 1945,Mr 21,27:3
Cole, Muriel
Johnny 2X4 1942,Mr 17,24:6
Cole, Nancy
Much Ado About Nothing 1963,Jl 15,25:2
Cole, Nat (Mrs) (Producer)
Amen Corner, The 1965,Ap 16,35:1
Cole, Olivia
Skin of Our Teeth, The 1966,Je 2,51:1
As You Like It 1966,Je 4,19:1
School for Scandal, The 1966,N 22,33:2
War and Peace 1967,Mr 22,42:1
Electra 1969,Ag 8,14:1
Cole, Rachel
Crucible, The 1958,Mr 17,21:1
Cole, Robert H (Miscellaneous)
Sextet 1958,N 27,53:1
Cole, Stephan
Clash by Night 1941,D 29,20:2
Skin of Our Teeth, The 1942,N 19,29:5
Cole, Stephen
Much Ado About Nothing 1963,Jl 15,25:2
Cole, Susan (Lighting Director)
Puntila 1959,My 15,26:2
Cole, Susan (Miscellaneous)
Machinal 1960,Ap 8,27:1
Cole, Ted
417 1961,Mr 6,30:1
Cole, Tom
Pansy 1929,My 15,36:3
Cole, Vera Bayles
Bombo 1921,O 7,20:2
Cole, Veronica
Day by the Sea, A 1955,S 27,42:1
Cole, Virginia
Forbidden Melody 1936,N 3,33:1
Firefly, The 1938,Jl 12,15:4
Cole, Wendell (Scenic Designer)
Now I Lay Me Down to Sleep 1949,Jl 23,7:3
Critic, The 1965,Jl 26,15:2
Cole, Willard
Parson's Bride, The 1929,Ja 22,22:3
Colebrook, Edward
Love Child, The 1922,N 15,22:1
Right to Dream, The 1924,My 27,14:2
Fog 1927,F 8,20:1
Mating Season, The 1927,Jl 19,27:6
Arabian, The 1927,N 1,20:5
Phantoms 1930,Ja 14,24:3

Colebrook, Edward—Cont
They Never Grow Up 1930,Ap 8,27:1
Find the Fox 1930,Je 21,20:4
Enemy Within 1931,O 6,35:3
Mr Papavert 1932,Ja 23,18:6
Anybody's Game 1932,D 22,21:4
Page Miss Glory 1934,N 28,24:2
Colebrook, Edward T
Noble Experiment, The 1930,O 28,21:4
Man Who Reclaimed His Head 1932,S 9,17:3
Colebrook, Victor
Wanted for Murder 1937,Ag 26,25:3
Colebrooke, Marie
Henrietta the Eighth 1935,Je 25,15:4
Colecord, Fred
Trojan Horse, The 1940,O 31,28:3
Coleman, Anne
Men in White 1955,F 26,13:2
Coleman, Basil (Director)
Dark Lady of the Sonnets, The 1959,Ag 21,13:1
Overruled 1959,Ag 21,13:1
Passion, Poison and Petrifaction 1959,Ag 21,13:1
Coleman, Carole
High Button Shoes 1947,O 10,32:2
Coleman, Charles
Face the Music 1932,F 18,24:5
Amourette 1933,S 28,25:2
Four Saints in Three Acts 1952,Ap 17,35:1
Coleman, Claudia
Vaudeville (Palace) 1928,Jl 17,15:5
Coleman, Cy (Composer)
John Murray Anderson's Almanac 1953,D 11,42:2
Compulsion 1957,O 25,21:1
Wildcat 1960,D 17,20:2
Little Me 1962,N 19,41:3
Little Me 1962,D 2,II,1:1
Sweet Charity 1966,Ja 31,22:1
Sweet Charity 1967,Jl 1,13:1
Coleman, Cy (Lyricist)
John Murray Anderson's Almanac 1953,D 11,42:2
Coleman, Cy (Musical Director)
Compulsion 1957,O 25,21:1
Coleman, E H (Composer)
Kid Himself, The 1925,D 25,23:2
Coleman, Emil
Laugh, Town, Laugh! 1942,Je 23,22:2
Coleman, Emil (Miscellaneous)
Deadly Game, The 1960,F 3,27:2
Coleman, Fletcher
J B 1958,Ap 24,37:1
Coleman, Frank
Kismet 1965,Je 23,45:1
Sacco-Vanzetti 1969,F 9,78:1
Coleman, Frank 4th
Ah, Wilderness! 1969,N 9,86:1
Coleman, George
Beclch 1968,D 17,59:1
Coleman, Harry
Kissing Time 1920,O 12,18:2
Coleman, Herbert
St Louis Woman 1946,Ap 1,22:2
City of Kings 1949,F 18,27:2
Lost in the Stars 1949,O 31,21:2
Taming of the Shrew, The 1951,Ap 26,35:2
Much Ado About Nothing 1952,My 2,20:1
Coleman, Janet (Producer)
Coop, The 1966,Mr 2,48:1
Coleman, John
Chivalry 1925,D 16,22:3
Not Herbert 1926,Ja 27,16:2
Sound of Hunting, A 1954,Ap 7,41:1
Coleman, Kia
House of Leather, The 1970,Mr 19,56:1
Coleman, Kitty
Katja 1926,O 19,27:3
Rainbow 1928,N 22,25:1
Great Day! 1929,O 18,24:3
Coleman, Leo
Medium, The 1947,My 2,28:2
Medium, The 1947,My 11,II,1:1
Medium, The 1948,D 8,41:6
Medium, The 1949,N 7,32:4
Medium, The 1950,Jl 20,22:5
Coleman, Lonnie (Original Author)
Jolly's Progress 1959,D 7,42:2
Coleman, Lonnie (Playwright)
Jolly's Progress 1959,D 7,42:2
Warm Body, A 1967,Ap 17,44:2
Place for Polly, A 1970,Ap 20,45:1
Coleman, Marilyn B
Tartuffe 1967,S 18,60:1
Five on the Black Hand Side 1970,Ja 2,32:2
Ododo 1970,N 25,26:1
Coleman, Millicent
Dark of the Moon 1945,Mr 15,27:2
Coleman, Nancy
Liberty Jones 1941,F 6,24:2
Sacred Flame, The 1952,O 8,35:2
Desperate Hours, The 1955,F 11,20:2
Desperate Hours, The 1955,F 20,II,1:1
Glass Menagerie, The 1961,Mr 6,30:1
Glass Menagerie, The 1961,My 1,35:3
Glass Menagerie, The 1961,Je 16,27:3
Black Monday 1962,Mr 7,29:1

Coleman, Nancy—Cont

Lemonade 1968,D 14,60:1

Coleman, Oliver

Carmen Jones 1946,Ap 8,32:2
Carmen Jones 1946,Ap 14,II,1:2

Coleman, Patricia

Caesar and Cleopatra 1935,Ag 22,21:1
Emperor Jones, The 1936,Ag 11,24:6

Coleman, Patricia (Playwright)

Moon Vine, The 1943,F 12,22:2

Coleman, Ralf

Roll Sweet Chariot 1934,O 3,24:3

Coleman, Robert H

Assorted Nuts 1940,Ap 7,I,44:6
One on the House 1941,Mr 30,I,47:3

Coleman, Robert H (Miscellaneous)

One on the House 1941,Mr 30,I,47:3

Coleman, Shepard (Musical Director)

Student Gypsy, The; Prince of Liederkranz, The
1963,O 1,34:1
Hello, Dolly! 1964,Ja 17,22:1
Oh What a Lovely War 1964,O 1,30:1
Henry, Sweet Henry 1967,O 24,51:2

Coleman, Stephen

King John 1967,Jl 14,19:1

Coleman, Stephen (Miscellaneous)

Firebugs, The 1968,Jl 2,36:1

Coleman, Val (Playwright)

Jackhammer, The 1962,F 6,26:2

Coleman, Vincent

Martinique 1920,Ap 27,18:2

Coleman, Warren

Roll Sweet Chariot 1934,O 3,24:3
Roll Sweet Chariot 1934,O 14,X,1:1
Porgy and Bess 1935,O 1,27:2
Porgy and Bess 1935,O 11,30:2
Porgy and Bess 1942,Ja 23,16:2
Porgy and Bess 1943,S 14,26:2
Porgy and Bess 1944,F 8,13:2
Lost in the Stars 1949,O 31,21:2
Lost in the Stars 1949,N 6,II,1:1

Coleman, Yvonne

St Louis Woman 1946,Ap 1,22:2

Colenback, John

Man for All Seasons, A 1961,N 23,51:1
Twelfth Night 1963,O 9,47:1
After the Rain 1967,O 10,54:1
Scent of Flowers, A 1969,O 21,42:1

Coleridge, Samuel Taylor (Original Author)

Ancient Mariner, The 1924,Ap 7,15:5
Ancient Mariner, The 1924,Ap 13,VIII,1:1

Coleridge, Sylvia

Big Ben 1939,S 10,IX,2:2

Coles, Joyce

Vaudeville (Palace) 1928,Je 26,29:4
Broadway Nights 1929,Jl 16,23:2
Strike Up the Band 1930,Ja 15,29:1
Du Barry 1932,N 23,15:2
Paese dei Campanelli, Il; Land of Bells, The
1935,My 10,25:4

Coles, Stanley

Merchant of Venice, The 1970,Je 10,39:1

Coles, Stedman (Playwright)

Press Time 1938,N 28,10:4

Coles, Zaida

Weekend 1968,Mr 14,50:2
Zelda 1969,Mr 6,38:1
Life and Times of J Walter Smintheus, The
1970,D 10,59:1

Coles and Atkins

Gentlemen Prefer Blondes 1949,D 9,35:3

Colette (Original Author)

Cheri 1921,D 25,VI,1:8
Gigi 1951,N 26,20:4
Cheri 1959,O 13,44:1
Colette 1970,O 15,58:1

Colette (Playwright)

Cheri 1921,D 25,VI,1:8

Coletti, Frank

Farewell to Arms, A 1930,S 23,30:3
Smiles 1930,N 19,19:2
Hotel Alimony 1934,Ja 30,16:2
Caviar 1934,Je 8,19:2
Night Remembers, The 1934,N 28,24:3
For Valor 1935,N 19,27:5

Coletti, Frank (Director)

Strangler Fig, The 1940,My 7,31:2

Coletti, Frank (Miscellaneous)

Donnybrook! 1961,My 19,23:1

Coley, Hylah

Schoolhouse on the Lot 1938,Mr 23,18:4

Coley, Thomas

Taming of the Shrew, The 1935,O 1,27:3
Our Town 1938,F 5,18:3
Swingin' the Dream 1939,N 30,24:2
Return Engagement 1940,N 2,19:2
Cue for Passion 1940,D 20,33:4
My Fair Ladies 1941,Mr 24,12:7
Mr Peebles and Mr Hooker 1946,O 11,29:2
Great Campaign, The 1947,Ap 1,33:2
Portrait in Black 1947,My 15,30:2
Front Page, The 1968,O 20,85:5
Our Town 1969,N 28,50:1
Passage to E M Forster, A 1970,O 28,62:1

Coley, Thomas (Playwright)

Happiest Years, The 1949,Ap 26,29:8
Passage to E M Forster, A 1970,O 28,62:1

Colgan, Joe

Stairs, The 1927,N 8,32:7

Colgate, Patricia

Hit the Deck 1960,Je 24,32:1

Colicchio, Michael (Composer)

Mary Stuart 1957,O 9,39:1

Colicos, John

King Lear 1956,Ja 13,17:1
King Lear 1956,Ja 22,II,1:1
Othello 1957,Je 24,19:2
Merchant of Venice, The 1957,Jl 11,19:5
Much Ado About Nothing 1957,Ag 8,15:2
Mary Stuart 1957,O 9,39:1
Mary Stuart 1957,O 20,II,1:1
Hamlet 1958,Je 21,11:1
Midsummer Night's Dream, A 1958,Je 23,19:1
Winter's Tale, The 1958,Jl 21,17:4
Winter's Tale, The 1958,Jl 27,II,1:1
Death of Cuchulain, The 1959,Ap 13,34:4
On Baile's Strand 1959,Ap 13,34:4
Coriolanus 1961,Je 21,31:2
Love's Labour's Lost 1961,Je 23,19:1
Love's Labour's Lost 1961,Je 2,II,1:1
Taming of the Shrew, The 1962,Je 21,25:1
Tempest, The 1962,Je 22,14:1
Cyrano de Bergerac 1962,Ag 1,21:1
Troilus and Cressida 1963,Je 19,40:2
Cyrano de Bergerac 1963,Je 20,30:1
Timon of Athens 1963,Jl 31,19:2
King Lear 1964,Je 19,36:1
Country Wife, The 1964,Ag 3,16:1
Devils, The 1965,N 17,51:2
Serjeant Musgrave's Dance 1966,Mr 9,44:1
Serjeant Musgrave's Dance 1966,Mr 20,II,1:1
Macbeth 1967,Jl 31,21:1
Soldiers 1968,Mr 3,88:2
Soldiers 1968,Mr 10,II,1:1
Soldiers 1968,My 2,58:1
Soldiers 1968,My 12,II,3:1
Soldiers 1969,Ja 5,II,3:1

Coliette, Estelle

Silks and Satins 1920,Jl 16,19:1

Colin, Julia

Blind Mice 1930,O 16,28:2
Peace on Earth 1933,N 30,39:2
Theodora, the Queen 1934,F 1,15:3

Colin, Saul (Producer)

Once Over Lightly 1942,N 20,26:2

Colitti, Rick

Montserrat 1961,Ja 9,30:5
Mister Roberts 1962,O 12,27:2
Purple Canary, The 1963,Ap 23,31:1
Queen and the Rebels, The 1965,F 26,16:1

Colitti, Rik

Gandhi 1970,O 21,37:1

Colker, Leon

Processional 1937,O 14,23:1

Coll, Owen

New Yorkers, The 1930,D 9,31:1
Man on Stilts, The 1931,S 10,23:2
Double Dummy 1936,N 12,30:1
Philadelphia Story, The 1939,Mr 29,21:1
Our Town 1944,Ja 11,24:5
Public Relations 1944,Ap 7,23:3
Catherine Was Great 1944,Ag 3,16:1
Swan Song 1946,My 16,29:2
Another Part of the Forest 1946,N 21,42:2
Call Me Madam 1950,O 13,25:1

Colla-Negri, Adelyn

Danton's Death 1938,N 3,26:2

Collada, Benito (Director)

Cuando Los Hijos De Eva No Son Los Hijos De
Adan; When Eve's Children Are Not Adam's
1932,Ap 23,11:2
De Muy Buena Familia; Of Very Good Family
1932,Ap 29,13:3

Collada, Benjamin (Miscellaneous)

Pluma en el Viento; Feather in the Wind
1932,Ap 2,13:4
Tambor y Cascabel; Drum and Bell
1932,Ap 21,25:4

Collado, M

Road to Happiness, The 1927,My 3,24:1
Girl and the Cat, The 1927,My 6,21:2
Blind Heart, The 1927,My 8,30:2
Cradle Song 1927,My 10,24:4

Collado, Manuel

Romantic Young Lady, The 1927,My 5,30:2
Fragila Rosina 1927,My 10,24:4
Pygmalion 1927,My 12,25:2

Collamore, James (Director)

Rockbound 1929,Ap 20,23:2

Collamore, Jerome

Twelfth Night 1921,N 1,17:1
Merchant of Venice, The 1921,N 22,17:1
Jacob Slovak 1927,O 6,28:4
Red Dust 1928,Ja 3,29:2
Potiphar's Wife 1928,D 24,10:7
Borrowed Love 1929,Je 18,29:2
I Want My Wife 1930,Mr 21,30:7

Collamore, Jerome—Cont

Iphigenie in Tauris 1949,O 22,11:2
Cheri 1959,O 13,44:1
Moon Shines on Kylenamoe, The 1962,O 31,33:1
Figuro in the Night 1962,O 31,33:1
Desire Under the Elms 1963,Ja 11,5:6
Saving Grace, The 1963,Ap 19,28:1
Abraham Cochrane 1964,F 18,26:1
That Hat! 1964,S 24,45:1

Collande, Volker von

Lauter Luegen 1937,O 24,XI,3:1

Collard, Avalon (Director)

Knights of Song 1938,O 18,29:2

Colleano, Bonar

Streetcar Named Desire, A 1949,O 13,33:6

Colleano, Bonar Jr

Bell for Adano, A 1945,S 20,31:1

Colleano, Con

Vaudeville (Hippodrome) 1924,O 21,21:2
Vaudeville (Palace) 1926,D 7,24:3
Vaudeville (Palace) 1930,N 10,17:1
Show Time 1942,S 17,20:2
Show Time 1942,O 4,VIII,1:1

Colleano, Maurice

Dance of Death, The 1932,Ja 11,29:5
Vaudeville (Palace) 1932,My 23,18:7

Colleano Family, The

Vaudeville (Palace) 1929,N 4,29:1
Vaudeville (Palace) 1931,Jl 6,24:6

Collenette, Beatrice

Lady Billy 1920,D 15,18:2

Collenette, Joan

Polonaise 1945,O 8,20:2

Collens, Gina

Rose Tattoo, The 1966,O 21,36:2
Saturday Night 1968,F 26,43:1

Collens, Linda

Bedrock 1934,N 18,II,6:3
Lady From the Sea, The 1935,D 14,11:3

Collett, Irene

Johnny 2X4 1942,Mr 17,24:6

Collett, Richard

South Pacific 1955,My 5,39:5

Collette

Rio Rita 1927,F 3,18:3

Collette, Augustus

Polly Preferred 1923,Ja 12,13:3

Collette, Estelle

Vaudeville (Palace) 1932,My 9,19:3

Collette, Janet

Little Princess, The 1931,F 7,11:3

Collette (Original Author)

Cheri 1930,N 16,VIII,4:1

Collette Sisters

Earl Carroll's Vanities 1930,Jl 2,28:3

Colletti, Frank

Cyrano de Bergerac 1926,F 19,18:1

Colletti, Frank (Miscellaneous)

Show Girl 1961,Ja 13,37:1

Collier, Constance

Hamlet 1925,F 20,20:1
Meet the Wife 1927,Jl 3,VII,1:4
John 1927,N 5,16:4
Spot on the Sun, The 1927,D 25,VIII,2:3
Our Betters 1928,F 21,18:2
Our Betters 1928,Mr 4,IX,1:1
Serena Blandish 1929,Ja 13,VIII,2:4
Serena Blandish 1929,Ja 24,30:3
Serena Blandish 1929,F 3,VIII,1:1
Matriarch, The 1930,Ja 26,VIII,2:1
Matriarch, The 1930,Mr 19,24:5
Hay Fever 1931,D 6,VIII,2:8
Hay Fever 1931,D 30,25:1
Dinner at Eight 1932,O 24,18:2
Aries Is Rising 1939,N 22,16:5

Collier, Constance (Director)

Lady of the Camellias, The 1931,Ja 27,21:2
Peter Ibbetson 1931,Ap 9,30:3
Camille 1932,O 28,23:2

Collier, Constance (Playwright)

Rat, The 1924,Je 15,VII,1:4
Rat, The 1924,Je 29,VII,1:8
Peter Ibbetson 1931,Ap 9,30:3

Collier, Frank

Double-Or Quit 1922,O 8,VI,1:7

Collier, Ian

Hamlet 1969,My 2,38:1

Collier, John

Life of Man, The 1923,Ap 17,26:1
Beranger 1923,Ap 20,20:3
Heartbreak House 1950,Mr 22,33:2

Collier, John C

What a Relief 1935,D 14,10:6

Collier, Kathryn

Macbeth 1930,Mr 26,24:6
Twelfth Night 1930,Mr 27,24:7
Taming of the Shrew, The 1930,Mr 28,22:8
Richard III 1930,Mr 31,24:1
As You Like It 1930,Ap 3,32:5
Julius Caesar 1930,Ap 4,22:3
Mrs Moonlight 1930,S 30,24:3
Within the Gates 1934,O 23,23:1
Dominant Sex, The 1935,Ap 2,24:5
And Now Goodbye 1937,F 3,26:4

Collier, Patience
Hostage, The 1960,S 21,42:1
Hostage, The 1960,O 2,II,1:1
Collier, Philip
Jacobowsky and the Colonel 1944,Mr 15,17:2
Collier, S F
Laugh It Off 1925,Ap 25,18:4
Collier, Samuel C
In the Days of the Turbins 1934,Mr 7,22:5
Collier, William
Hottentot, The 1920,Mr 2,9:1
Friars Club Frolic 1921,Je 13,16:2
All-Star Jamboree 1921,Jl 14,18:1
Irving Berlin's Music Box Revue 1921,S 23,18:2
Friar's Club Frolic 1922,Je 5,16:1
Wild Rose, The 1926,O 21,23:1
Vaudeville (Palace) 1927,O 11,27:2
Collier, William (Director)
Tickle Me 1920,Ag 18,9:1
All-Star Jamboree 1921,Jl 14,18:1
Collier, William (Original Author)
Pitter Patter 1920,S 29,12:2
Collier, William (Playwright)
Hottentot, The 1920,Mr 2,9:1
Irving Berlin's Music Box Revue 1921,S 23,18:2
Collier, William Jr (Buster)
Vaudeville (Palace) 1927,O 11,27:2
Colligan, J
Whirl of New York, The 1921,Je 14,18:1
Colligan, James (Producer)
Cry of the Peacock 1950,Ap 12,33:2
Colligan, Walter
Dark, The 1927,F 2,22:5
Command to Love, The 1927,S 21,27:1
Criminal Code, The 1929,O 3,28:2
Vinegar Tree, The 1930,N 20,30:3
Collignon, George
Headquarters 1929,D 5,32:4
Colling, E S
Skylark 1921,Jl 26,10:6
Colling, E S (Composer)
Pleased to Meet You 1928,O 30,27:2
Collinge, Patricia
Just Suppose 1920,N 2,15:1
Rivals, The 1922,Je 6,18:2
Dark Angel, The 1925,F 11,19:2
Hedda Gabler 1926,Ja 27,16:5
Hedda Gabler 1926,F 21,VII,1:2
Importance of Being Earnest, The 1926,My 4,30:1
Comic, The 1927,Ap 20,28:2
Venus 1927,D 26,26:5
She Stoops to Conquer 1928,My 15,17:1
She Stoops to Conquer 1928,My 20,VIII,1:1
Becky Sharp 1929,Je 4,29:1
Anatol 1931,Ja 17,23:3
Men Must Fight 1931,Ap 12,IX,2:1
Lady With a Lamp, The 1931,N 20,27:2
Autumn Crocus 1932,N 21,20:2
To See Ourselves 1935,My 1,25:2
Little Foxes, The 1939,F 16,16:2
Little Foxes, The 1939,F 26,IX,1:1
Heiress, The 1947,S 30,22:2
Heiress, The 1947,O 5,II,1:1
Mary Rose 1951,Mr 5,25:2
Mary Rose 1951,Mr 11,II,1:1
I've Got Sixpence 1952,D 3,44:2
I've Got Sixpence 1952,D 7,II,5:1
Collinge, Roberta
Live Like Pigs 1965,Je 8,48:2
Collings, Patricia (Translator)
Dame Nature 1938,S 27,24:3
Collins, Allen
Jane 1952,F 2,10:2
Under Milk Wood 1953,My 29,17:1
Collins, Allen F (Lighting Director)
Firstborn, The 1957,Ja 7,29:2
Collins, Ann
Gondoliers, The 1963,Je 5,33:2
Macbeth 1966,Ag 29,23:4
Collins, Anne (Playwright)
Bottled 1928,Ap 11,25:1
Collins, Arthur
Mourners' Bench, The 1950,S 22,35:7
Collins, Arthur (Producer)
Good Luck 1923,O 7,IX,2:2
Collins, Arthur Greville (Director)
Cold in Sables 1931,D 24,20:7
Collins, Arthur Greville (Producer)
Cold in Sables 1931,D 24,20:7
Collins, Beryl
Bootleggers, The 1922,N 28,24:1
Collins, Bill
Gondoliers, The 1967,O 29,83:1
Collins, Blanche
Song of the Flame 1925,D 31,10:2
Rapid Transit 1927,Ap 8,21:2
Lido Girl, The 1928,Ag 24,23:2
Congai 1928,N 28,24:3
Subway Express 1929,S 25,34:3
Scarlet Sister Mary 1930,N 26,19:2
Doctor Faustus 1937,Ja 9,21:2
Cradle Will Rock, The 1937,D 6,19:4
Cradle Will Rock, The 1938,Ja 4,19:3

Life and Death of an American 1939,My 20,11:2
Hamlet 1945,D 14,25:2
Single Man at a Party 1959,Ap 22,30:4
Sharon's Grave 1961,N 9,39:2
On a Clear Day You Can See Forever
1965,O 18,44:1
My Fair Lady 1968,Je 14,42:1
Collins, Catherine
Blue Bird, The 1923,D 26,13:3
Welded 1924,Mr 18,24:1
Sky's the Limit, The 1934,D 18,25:5
Loose Moments 1935,F 5,22:3
Collins, Charles
Ripples 1930,F 12,26:1
Vaudeville (Palace) 1931,S 28,17:5
Smiling Faces 1932,Ag 31,12:3
Say When 1934,N 9,24:2
Macbeth 1936,Ap 15,25:4
Fly Away Home 1936,Jl 21,13:1
Sea Legs 1937,My 19,26:5
Gay Divorce 1937,Jl 20,19:4
Gay Divorce 1937,Ag 11,27:2
You Can't Take It With You 1945,Mr 27,23:7
Red Mill, The 1945,O 17,16:2
Here Come the Clowns 1954,My 5,36:2
Collins, Daniel
Play of Risen Christ, The 1970,Mr 9,44:1
Collins, Diane
Devil's Advocate, The 1961,Mr 10,20:1
Collins, Douglas
Sandhog 1954,N 24,17:1
Collins, Eddie
Ice Follies 1960,Ja 13,20:1
Collins, Emmett
You and I 1925,O 20,29:1
Collins, Frank
Trapped 1928,S 12,25:3
Cafe de Danse 1929,Ja 16,22:2
Incubator 1932,N 2,23:3
Collins, Frank (Director)
This Year of Grace 1928,N 8,27:1
Wake Up and Dream 1929,D 31,14:3
Collins, Frank J (Playwright)
Mouthpiece, The 1929,Je 16,VIII,2:1
Seven 1929,D 28,10:5
Collins, G Pat
Easy Mark, The 1924,Ag 27,14:2
New Gallantry, The 1925,S 25,24:2
Trial Marriage 1927,F 1,24:3
Mister Romeo 1927,S 6,35:3
Racket, The 1927,N 23,28:3
Lady From the Sea, The 1929,Mr 19,36:1
Free for All 1931,S 9,25:1
Air-Minded 1932,F 11,17:3
Case History 1938,O 22,15:2
Ringside Seat 1938,N 23,24:5
Collins, Gene
Happy 1927,D 6,26:3
Collins, George E (Composer)
Octoroon, The 1929,Mr 13,28:3
Collins, George P
Bootleggers, The 1922,N 28,24:1
Collins, Georgia (Costume Designer)
Clandestine on the Morning Line 1961,O 31,28:1
Collins, Gina
Mandragola 1956,Mr 1,36:4
Collins, Gladys
Seven Mirrors 1945,O 26,17:2
Collins, Grace
Wookey, The 1941,S 11,20:5
Collins, Grenville (Producer)
Sun-Up 1925,Ag 14,13:4
Collins, Guy
Afgar 1920,N 9,13:2
Tidings Brought to Mary, The 1922,D 25,20:1
Collins, Ira
Audition of the Apprentice Theatre 1939,Je 2,26:2
Collins, J Palmer
Rollo's Wild Oat 1920,N 24,14:1
Collins, Jack
Counsellor-at-Law 1931,N 7,17:2
Take Me Along 1959,O 23,22:2
Jimmy 1969,O 24,38:1
Collins, Jack (Producer)
What a Killing 1961,Mr 28,41:1
Collins, James
Bringing Up Father 1925,Mr 31,16:1
Sisters of the Chorus 1930,O 21,34:3
Collins, Janet
Out of This World 1950,D 22,17:3
Collins, Jaycee
Bella 1961,N 17,40:1
Collins, John
Merchant of Venice, The 1955,Ja 8,9:7
Tom Paine 1969,Mr 30,71:2
Collins, Jose
Catherine 1923,S 30,II,1:6
Frasquita 1925,My 3,VIII,2:1
White Birds 1927,Je 26,VIII,1:3
Destination Unknown 1937,Jl 6,23:4
Collins, Joseph
Thomas Paine 1930,Mr 21,30:7

Collins, Judy
Peer Gynt 1969,Jl 17,56:1
Collins, K W (Translator)
He Who Gets Slapped 1956,F 2,18:1
Collins, Kitty
Banshee, The 1927,D 6,26:2
Silver Tassie, The 1929,O 25,26:1
Collins, Madeline
Vaudeville (Palace) 1923,Ja 30,12:2
Natja 1925,F 17,19:2
Collins, Mary Alice
Tangerine 1921,Ag 10,8:2
Buckaroo 1929,Mr 18,31:1
Blind Mice 1930,N 6,28:2
Smiles 1930,N 19,19:2
I Loved You Wednesday 1932,O 12,27:1
Shooting Star 1933,Je 13,22:2
Women, The 1939,Ap 21,21:2
Collins, May
Outrageous Mrs Palmer, The 1920,O 13,18:1
Clubs Are Trumps 1924,O 15,27:1
School for Scandal, The 1925,D 7,18:2
House Afire 1930,Ap 1,34:7
Ladies All 1930,Jl 29,25:2
Abe Lincoln in Illinois 1938,O 17,12:2
Collins, Melville (Playwright)
Livree de M le Comte, La 1927,N 20,IX,4:4
Collins, Milt
New Yorkers, The 1927,Mr 11,24:3
Collins, Miriam
Lassie 1920,Ap 7,9:2
Collins, Monty (Director)
It Pays to Sin 1933,N 4,18:6
Collins, Pat
Double Dummy 1936,N 12,30:1
Collins, Patricia (Lighting Director)
Golem, The 1959,F 26,38:2
Breaking Wall, The 1960,Ja 26,27:5
Camino Real 1960,My 17,42:2
Camino Real 1960,My 29,II,1:1
That Hat! 1964,S 24,45:1
Collins, Paul
Say Nothing 1965,Ja 28,21:2
Royal Hunt of the Sun, The 1965,O 27,36:2
Minor Adjustment, A 1967,O 7,33:3
Comedy of Errors, The 1968,F 28,40:2
She Stoops to Conquer 1968,Ap 1,58:3
Collins, Peter
Night Circus, The 1958,D 3,44:1
Spiro Who? 1969,My 19,55:1
Collins, Radley
May Wine 1935,D 6,30:3
Now You've Done It 1937,Mr 6,10:4
Collins, Ray
Blue Bandanna, The 1924,Je 24,18:4
Conscience 1924,S 12,19:3
Eve's Leaves 1925,Mr 27,22:2
Bridge of Distances, The 1925,S 29,30:1
Half-Naked Truth, The 1926,Je 8,23:1
Donovan Affair, The 1926,Ag 31,15:2
On Call 1928,N 10,20:7
Strong Man's House, A 1929,S 17,34:3
Paging Danger 1931,F 27,19:2
Native Son 1941,Mr 25,26:5
Absolutely Freeee 1967,My 25,58:1
Collins, Richard
Immodest Violet 1920,Ag 25,6:2
Doctor Cupid 1952,Ag 14,19:6
Collins, Rita
One Sunday Afternoon 1933,F 16,23:5
Collins, Robert
Knights of Song 1938,O 18,29:2
Everywhere I Roam 1938,D 30,10:4
Collins, Rufus
Brig, The 1963,My 16,40:1
Antigone 1968,O 11,36:1
Collins, Russell
Success Story 1932,S 27,24:4
Big Night 1933,Ja 18,16:2
Both Your Houses 1933,Mr 7,20:3
Men in White 1933,S 27,24:2
Gentlewoman 1934,Mr 23,28:4
Gold Eagle Guy 1934,N 29,33:4
Waiting for Lefty 1935,F 11,14:5
Panic 1935,Mr 16,18:4
Waiting for Lefty 1935,Mr 27,24:5
Till the Day I Die 1935,Mr 27,24:5
Paradise Lost 1935,D 10,31:5
Johnny Johnson 1936,N 19,XII,1:1
Johnny Johnson 1936,N 20,26:3
Star-Wagon, The 1937,S 30,18:5
Star-Wagon, The 1937,O 10,XI,1:1
Missouri Legend 1938,S 20,27:2
Here Come the Clowns 1938,D 8,36:2
Happiest Days, The 1939,Je 12,26:2
Morning's at Seven 1939,N 7,30:2
Morning's at Seven 1939,D 1,26:2
Morning's at Seven 1939,D 17,IX,3:1
Heavenly Express 1940,Ap 19,24:2
Heavenly Express 1940,Ap 28,IX,1:1
In Time to Come 1941,D 29,20:2
Moon Is Down, The 1942,Ap 8,22:2
Mr Sycamore 1942,N 14,13:2

Collins, Russell—Cont
Playboy of Newark, The 1943,Mr 20,11:2
First Million, The 1943,Ap 29,27:4
War President 1944,Ap 25,17:3
Carousel 1945,Ap 20,24:2
Carousel 1945,Ap 29,II,1:1
He Who Gets Slapped 1946,Mr 21,31:4
Iceman Cometh, The 1946,O 10,31:3
Survivors, The 1948,Ja 20,27:2
Enchanted, The 1950,Ja 19,34:2
Liar, The 1950,My 19,30:2
Mister Roberts 1950,Jl 23,II,1:6
Grass Harp, The 1952,Mr 28,26:2
Grass Harp, The 1952,Ap 6,II,1:1
Sabrina Fair 1953,N 12,37:1
Sabrina Fair 1953,N 22,II,1:1
View From the Bridge, A 1955,S 30,21:1
Memory of Two Mondays, A 1955,S 30,21:1
Greatest Man Alive!, The 1957,My 9,37:2
Face of a Hero 1960,O 21,29:5
Romulus 1962,Ja 11,27:1
Child Buyer, The 1962,My 14,35:1
Calculated Risk 1962,N 1,35:1
Collins, Sewell (Playwright)
Anne-One Hundred 1927,Je 26,VIII,1:3
Collins, Shelley
Adding Machine, The 1948,N 18,35:2
Collins, Sherod
Dark of the Moon 1945,Mr 15,27:2
Collins, Shirley
Crucible, The 1958,Mr 17,21:1
Collins, Sonny
Trigger 1927,D 7,32:1
Collins, Stephen
Twelfth Night 1969,Ag 14,29:2
Collins, Thomas
Promise 1936,D 31,20:4
Collins, Tom
Naughty Marietta 1931,N 17,31:2
Pirates of Penzance, The 1938,Je 3,16:2
Collins, Ulric
Opportunity 1920,Jl 31,5:1
Leah Kleschna 1924,Ap 22,19:2
That Awful Mrs Eaton! 1924,S 30,27:1
Mountain, The 1933,S 12,28:6
Collins, Una (Costume Designer)
Oh What a Lovely War 1964,O 1,30:1
Collins, Verne
Cymbeline 1923,O 3,12:1
Collins, Walter
Junior Miss 1941,N 19,28:2
Collins, Willard
Bewitched 1924,O 2,26:3
Collins and Hart
Greenwich Village Follies 1920,Ag 31,7:3
Vaudeville (Palace) 1923,Ja 23,18:2
Vaudeville (Palace) 1926,Ag 31,15:3
Collison, Barbara
Legend of Leonora, The 1926,My 1,10:1
Collison, Michele
Arden of Faversham 1970,F 17,33:1
Ubu Roi 1970,F 17,33:1
Collison, Wilson (Playwright)
Girl With Carmine Lips, The 1920,Ag 11,6:1
Getting Gertie's Garter 1921,Ag 2,16:2
Bachelor's Night, A 1921,O 18,20:1
Desert Sands 1922,F 14,20:1
Vagabond, The 1923,D 28,13:4
Red Dust 1928,Ja 3,29:2
Collodi, C (Original Author)
Pinocchio 1939,Ja 3,19:2
Collomb, Jean (Director)
Ex-Napoleon 1960,D 29,16:3
Colly, Peter
Patriot for Me, A 1969,O 6,58:1
Collyer, Clayton
Life Begins 1932,Mr 29,23:2
Fields Beyond, The 1936,Mr 7,11:2
Angel Island 1937,O 21,26:2
Collyer, David
Allegro 1947,O 11,10:2
Liar, The 1950,My 19,30:2
Pardon Our French 1950,O 6,22:4
Can-Can 1953,My 8,28:1
Seventh Heaven 1955,My 27,16:2
Fiorello! 1959,N 24,45:3
Collyer, Eve
Right Honourable Gentleman, The 1965,O 20,50:2
Comedy of Errors, The 1967,Je 15,58:4
Collyer, Robert
Processional 1925,Ja 13,17:1
Black Boy 1926,O 7,30:2
Lally 1927,F 9,16:3
Colman, Booth
Assassin, The 1945,O 18,20:2
Hamlet 1945,D 14,25:2
Tonight at 8:30; Family Album 1948,F 21,8:2
Tonight at 8:30; Ways and Means 1948,F 21,8:2
Tonight at 8:30; Red Peppers 1948,F 21,8:2
Tonight at 8:30; Hands Across the Sea 1948,F 24,20:4
Tonight at 8:30; Shadow Play 1948,F 24,20:4
Now I Lay Me Down to Sleep 1950,Mr 3,21:2

Colman, Charles
Porgy and Bess 1943,S 14,26:2
Porgy and Bess 1944,F 8,13:2
Colman, Charles (Miscellaneous)
Belafonte at the Palace 1959,D 16,55:1
Colman, George (Playwright)
Jealous Wife, The 1930,N 16,VIII,4:1
Clandestine Marriage, The 1954,O 17,II,1:1
Colman, John
All in One; Paul Draper Dance Program 1955,Ap 20,40:3
Colman, Ronald
Nightcap, The 1921,Ag 16,18:3
Tendresse, La 1922,S 26,18:1
Colman, Wilson
Yellow Sands 1927,S 12,29:3
Boy David, The 1936,N 22,VI,7:1
Colmant, Jean-Louis (Director)
Dallas, Nov 22, 1963 1966,N 13,80:1
Colmar, Andrew
Javelin 1966,N 10,63:1
Colmore, Henry
Fratricide Punished 1925,Ap 21,19:1
Coloma, Juan Nadal de Stata
Tragedia del Faro, La; Tragedy of the Lighthouse, The 1932,Je 3,23:2
Coloma (Father) (Original Author)
Hoy 1929,Ja 3,25:2
Colombini, Willy
Rugantino 1964,F 7,34:1
Colombo, Lindoro
Aria del Continente, L' 1927,O 5,30:2
Colon, Alex
Golden Streets, The 1970,Ag 14,21:1
Gingerbread Lady, The 1970,D 14,58:3
Colon, Miriam
In the Summer House 1953,D 30,17:1
Highway Robbery 1955,N 8,36:1
Innkeepers, The 1956,F 3,19:1
Me, Candido! 1956,O 16,36:2
Retabilillo de Don Cristobal, El; Puppet Theater of Don Cristobal, The; Zapatera Prodigiosa, La; Shoemaker's Prodigious Wife, The 1964,S 3,23:2
Matty and the Moron and Madonna 1965,Mr 30,53:1
Ox Cart, The 1966,D 20,58:1
Winterset 1968,Jl 23,28:2
Wrong Way Light Bulb, The 1969,Mr 5,40:1
Colon, Miriam (Director)
Golden Streets, The 1970,Ag 14,21:1
Colonel
Storm Over Patsy 1937,Mr 9,26:4
Colonna, Bob
Winter's Tale, The 1963,Je 29,13:1
Midsummer Night's Dream, A 1963,Jl 1,19:2
Colonna, Robert J
Ah, Wilderness! 1967,Mr 19,II,7:1
Brother to Dragons 1968,D 8,86:1
Wilson in the Promise Land 1970,Ja 11,78:1
Wilson in the Promise Land 1970,My 27,41:1
Colony, Beatrice
House Afire 1930,Ap 1,34:7
Greatness Comes to the Maronies 1937,Ag 18,15:2
Colorado, Hortensia
Kitchen, The 1966,Je 14,50:1
Colquhoun, Elizabeth
Hedda Gabler 1960,N 10,61:1
Colson, C David
Last Sweet Days of Isaac, The 1970,Ja 27,49:1
Last Sweet Days of Isaac, The 1970,F 8,II,1:6
Purlie 1970,Mr 16,53:1
Colson, David
Measure for Measure 1956,Je 29,16:1
Colson, Elsie
Mr Sampson 1927,My 8,30:1
Colson, Osborne
Ice Follies 1937,D 22,29:1
Ice Follies 1939,D 5,38:2
Ice Follies 1941,D 2,32:2
Colson, Robert
Awakening of Spring, The 1964,My 13,50:1
Colson, Robert (Miscellaneous)
Rope Dancers, The 1959,My 14,26:1
Importance of Being Earnest, The 1963,F 27,5:2
Awakening of Spring, The 1964,My 13,50:1
Colston, Percy
My Magnolia 1926,Jl 13,19:2
Colston, Warren
Hot Pan 1928,F 16,14:1
Ringside 1928,Ag 30,13:2
Earth Between, The 1929,Mr 6,33:1
Fiesta 1929,S 18,35:1
Winter Bound 1929,N 13,24:6
Colt, Alvin (Costume Designer)
On the Town 1944,D 29,11:4
Around the World 1946,Je 1,9:5
Barefoot Boy With Cheek 1947,Ap 4,20:2
Music in My Heart 1947,O 3,30:2
Clutterbuck 1949,D 5,29:2
Guys and Dolls 1950,N 25,11:2
Guys and Dolls 1950,D 3,II,1:1
Top Banana 1951,N 2,19:2
Tall Kentuckian, The 1953,Je 17,30:1

Colt, Alvin (Costume Designer)—Cont
Frogs of Spring, The 1953,O 21,36:2
Madam Will You Walk 1953,D 2,2:4
Coriolanus 1954,Ja 20,34:2
Coriolanus 1954,Ja 24,II,1:1
Golden Apple, The 1954,Mr 12,15:2
Golden Apple, The 1954,Mr 21,II,1:1
Sea Gull, The 1954,My 12,38:1
Sing Me No Lullaby 1954,O 15,17:2
Fanny 1954,N 5,16:1
Fanny 1954,N 21,II,1:1
Doctor's Dilemma, The 1955,Ja 12,22:1
Master Builder, The 1955,Mr 2,23:2
Guys and Dolls 1955,Ap 21,32:2
Phoenix '55 1955,Ap 25,20:2
Finian's Rainbow 1955,My 19,25:1
Carefree Tree, The 1955,O 12,37:2
Lark, The 1955,N 18,20:1
Pipe Dream 1955,D 1,44:1
Six Characters in Search of an Author 1955,D 12,38:1
Six Characters in Search of an Author 1955,D 25,II,3:1
Miss Julie 1956,F 22,23:2
Stronger, The 1956,F 22,23:2
Month in the Country, A 1956,Ap 4,23:1
Month in the Country, A 1956,Ap 15,II,1:1
Kiss Me, Kate 1956,My 10,27:2
Littlest Revue, The 1956,My 23,37:2
Sleeping Prince, The 1956,N 2,31:1
Diary of a Scoundrel 1956,N 5,41:1
Li'l Abner 1956,N 16,24:2
Li'l Abner 1956,N 25,II,1:1
Livin' the Life 1957,Ap 29,20:1
Mary Stuart 1957,O 9,39:1
Copper and Brass 1957,O 18,19:2
Rumple 1957,N 7,42:2
Infernal Machine, The 1958,F 4,33:1
Blue Denim 1958,F 28,17:1
Say Darling 1958,Ap 4,17:1
Hamlet 1958,Je 21,11:1
Say Darling 1959,F 26,38:2
First Impressions 1959,Mr 20,28:1
Destry Rides Again 1959,Ap 24,24:1
Destry Rides Again 1959,My 3,II,1:1
Greenwillow 1960,Mr 9,38:1
Christine 1960,Ap 29,27:1
Wildcat 1960,D 17,20:2
13 Daughters 1961,Mr 3,17:2
Aspern Papers, The 1962,F 8,26:1
Beauty Part, The 1962,D 28,5:2
Abe Lincoln in Illinois 1963,Ja 23,5:2
Here's Love 1963,O 4,28:1
Yeomen of the Guard, The 1964,Mr 19,29:2
Seagull, The 1964,Ap 6,36:1
Crucible, The 1964,Ap 7,30:2
Wonder World 1964,My 18,32:1
Paisley Convertible, The 1967,F 13,42:1
Imaginary Invalid, The 1967,My 2,53:1
Touch of the Poet, A 1967,My 3,38:2
Fumed Oak 1967,My 4,34:1
Ways and Means 1967,My 4,34:1
Still Life 1967,My 4,34:1
Henry, Sweet Henry 1967,O 24,51:2
Golden Rainbow 1968,F 5,27:1
John Brown's Body 1968,F 13,49:2
She Stoops to Conquer 1968,Ap 1,58:3
Yeomen of the Guard, The 1968,My 9,53:1
Goodbye People, The 1968,D 4,52:1
Colt, Alvin (Scenic Designer)
Music in My Heart 1947,O 3,30:2
Tall Kentuckian, The 1953,Je 17,30:1
Colt, Dorothy (Director)
Aucassin and Nicolette 1947,Ap 28,26:2
Colt, Ethel Barrymore
Scarlet Sister Mary 1930,O 5,IX,4:6
Scarlet Sister Mary 1930,N 26,19:2
Scandals 1931,Ag 11,28:4
Scandals 1931,Ag 16,VIII,1:1
George White's Scandals 1931,S 15,30:1
Under Glass 1933,O 31,24:3
Laura Garnett 1934,Jl 17,24:4
Aiglon, L' 1934,N 5,22:2
London Assurance 1937,F 19,14:5
Orchids Preferred 1937,Ap 29,16:6
Whiteoaks 1938,Mr 24,20:2
Come of Age 1952,Ja 24,22:2
Curtains Up! 1959,N 3,26:3
Take It From the Top 1967,N 23,59:2
Madrigal of Shakespeare, A 1968,F 14,56:2
Colt, Ethel Barrymore (Lyricist)
London Assurance 1937,F 19,14:5
Colt, Ethel Barrymore (Miscellaneous)
London Assurance 1937,F 19,14:5
Colt, John Drew
School for Scandal, The 1931,N 11,26:4
Saint Wench 1933,Ja 3,19:3
Little Ol' Boy 1933,Ap 25,15:5
Church Mouse, A 1933,Je 27,13:7
Laura Garnett 1934,Jl 17,24:4
Ceiling Zero 1935,Ap 11,26:2
High Tor 1937,Ja 11,15:2
Live Wire, The 1950,Ag 18,16:2

Colt, Phyllis
Boys and Girls Together 1940,O 2,19:2
Colt, Sam
Spite Corner 1922,S 26,18:1
Wooden Kimono 1926,D 28,16:2
Colt, Samuel (Barrymore)
Aiglon, L' 1934,N 5,22:2
Colt, Warren
Chippies 1929,My 30,23:3
Coltellacci, Giulio (Costume Designer)
Rugantino 1964,F 7,34:1
Coltellacci, Giulio (Scenic Designer)
Rugantino 1964,F 7,34:1
Colter, John
Ice Capades 1957,S 5,33:2
Coltoff, Harry
War 1929,S 19,37:3
Colton, Arabella
Dracula Sabbat 1970,O 2,28:2
Colton, Chevi
Insect Comedy, The 1948,Je 4,26:3
Time of Storm 1954,F 26,14:2
O Marry Me 1961,O 28,13:1
Penny Change 1963,O 25,37:1
Colton, Jacque Lynn
This Is the Rill Speaking 1966,Ap 12,43:1
Thank You, Miss Victoria 1966,Ap 12,43:1
Recluse, The 1966,Ap 13,36:1
Chicago 1966,Ap 13,36:1
In Circles 1967,O 14,12:1
In Circles 1968,Je 28,36:1
Huui, Huui 1968,N 25,58:1
Boy on the Straight-Back Chair 1969,Mr 18,36:1
Disintegration of James Cherry, The
1970,Ja 30,33:3
Knack With Horses, A 1970,D 21,52:1
Colton, John (Playwright)
Drifting 1922,Ja 3,20:3
Rain 1922,O 15,VIII,1:8
Rain 1922,N 8,18:2
Shanghai Gesture, The 1925,D 20,VII,4:1
Shanghai Gesture, The 1926,F 2,20:2
Rain 1926,O 12,27:1
Shanghai Gesture, The 1929,Je 2,VIII,2:7
Saint Wench 1933,Ja 3,19:3
Nine Pine Street 1933,Ap 28,15:5
Rain 1935,F 13,24:1
Rain 1935,F 17,VIII,1:1
Sadie Thompson 1944,N 17,25:2
Rain 1948,F 2,15:2
Colton, Rita
High Named Today 1954,D 11,11:2
Colton, Scott
I Must Love Someone 1939,F 8,18:7
Colton, Steve
Ghost for Sale 1941,S 30,27:4
Colton, Tommy
Good Times 1920,Ag 10,10:1
Monkey Talks, The 1925,D 29,20:1
Colton, Victor
Tomorrow's a Holiday! 1935,D 31,10:2
Wingless Victory, The 1936,D 24,20:2
Colum, Padraic (Playwright)
Betrayal, The 1928,Je 6,23:4
Mogul of the Desert 1932,F 7,VIII,3:2
Fiddler's House, The 1941,Mr 28,27:5
Balloon 1946,Ag 13,30:3
Ulysses in Nighttown 1958,Je 6,30:1
Carricknabauna 1967,Mr 31,30:1
Columbara, Signora Medea
Wonder Bar, The 1931,Mr 18,23:4
Columbo, Russ
Radio Carnival 1932,Mr 14,13:3
Variety Anthology 1932,Mr 21,19:4
Vaudeville (Palace) 1932,Jl 18,9:7
Columbus, Charles
Music Box Revue 1923,S 24,5:3
Oh, Please! 1926,D 22,24:3
Fioretta 1929,F 6,30:3
Hello Paris 1930,N 17,29:3
Vaudeville (Palace) 1931,S 7,19:2
Columbus, George
Frederika 1937,F 5,16:5
Colvan, Zeke (Director)
Show Boat 1927,D 28,26:1
Company's Coming! 1931,Ap 21,35:5
Threepenny Opera, The 1933,Ap 14,22:4
Colvig, Helen (Costume Designer)
Ice Follies 1969,My 23,38:1
Ice Follies 1970,My 23,27:1
Colville, Edwina
Candida 1925,D 19,14:2
Dear Brutus 1926,Jl 15,21:3
As You Like It 1936,Ap 24,18:4
Colvin, Donald A
What a Relief 1935,D 14,10:6
Colvin, John
Drums of Jeopardy, The 1922,My 30,8:4
Colyer, Austin
Darwin's Theories 1960,O 19,53:2
How to Succeed in Business Without Really Trying
1966,Ap 21,45:1
Where's Charley? 1966,My 26,57:1

Finian's Rainbow 1967,Ap 6,44:1
Wonderful Town 1967,My 18,50:1
Maggie Flynn 1968,O 24,52:1
Colyer, Carlton
Smokeweaver's Daughter, The 1959,Ap 15,30:1
Face of a Hero 1960,O 21,29:5
Tiger Rag, The 1961,F 17,20:2
Comacho, Leu
House of Flowers 1954,D 31,11:2
Comadore, Joe
Shrike, The 1952,Ja 16,20:2
Coman, John J (Playwright)
Help Yourself! 1936,Jl 15,15:1
Coman, Morgan
Cornered 1920,D 9,18:2
Comathiere, A B
Goat Alley 1927,Ap 21,24:3
Porgy 1927,O 11,26:2
Make Me Know It 1929,N 5,32:5
Second Comin', The 1931,D 9,32:4
Ol' Man Satan 1932,O 4,26:3
Louisiana 1933,F 28,15:5
Brain Sweat 1934,Ap 5,24:4
Too Many Boats 1934,S 12,26:3
Comber, Robert
Bourgeois Gentilhomme, Le 1964,Je 18,28:2
Combes, Barbara
Straw Hat, The 1937,D 31,8:2
Combine, The
Stomp 1969,N 23,II,1:1
Combs, Frederick
Taste of Honey, A 1961,My 17,43:1
Great Western Union, The 1965,F 10,45:1
Boys in the Band, The 1968,Ap 15,48:1
Boys in the Band, The 1968,Ap 28,II,1:6
Combs, Roger
Chalked Out 1937,Mr 26,24:2
Comden, Betty
On the Town 1944,D 29,11:4
Party With Betty Comden and Adolph Green, A
1958,D 24,2:7
Comden, Betty (Composer)
Say Darling 1958,Ap 4,17:1
Say Darling 1958,Ap 13,II,1:1
Say Darling 1959,F 26,38:2
Comden, Betty (Lyricist)
On the Town 1944,D 29,11:4
Million Dollar Baby 1945,D 22,17:2
Two on the Aisle 1951,Jl 20,13:6
Wonderful Town 1953,F 26,22:3
Wonderful Town 1953,Mr 8,II,1:1
Wonderful Town 1953,Ap 5,II,1:5
Peter Pan 1954,O 21,30:2
Bells Are Ringing 1956,N 29,43:4
Bells Are Ringing 1956,N 30,18:2
Wonderful Town 1958,Mr 6,32:4
Say Darling 1958,Ap 13,II,1:1
On the Town 1959,Ja 16,36:1
On the Town 1959,Ja 25,II,1;1
On the Town 1959,F 14,15:1
Do Re Mi 1960,D 27,23:2
Do Re Mi 1961,Ja 8,II,1:1
Subways Are for Sleeping 1961,D 28,22:1
Wonderful Town 1963,F 15,10:2
On the Town 1963,My 31,30:7
Fade Out--Fade In 1964,My 27,45:1
Leonard Bernstein's Theater Songs 1965,Je 29,27:2
Hallelujah, Baby! 1967,Ap 27,51:1
Hallelujah, Baby! 1967,My 7,II,1:1
Wonderful Town 1967,My 18,50:1
Comden, Betty (Playwright)
On the Town 1944,D 29,11:4
On the Town 1945,Ja 7,II,1:1
Million Dollar Baby 1945,D 22,17:2
Billion Dollar Baby 1945,D 30,II,1:1
Two on the Aisle 1951,Jl 20,13:6
Two on the Aisle 1951,Jl 29,II,1:1
Bells Are Ringing 1956,N 29,43:4
Bells Are Ringing 1956,N 30,18:2
On the Town 1959,Ja 16,36:1
On the Town 1959,Ja 25,II,1:1
On the Town 1959,F 14,15:1
Subways Are for Sleeping 1961,D 28,22:1
On the Town 1963,My 31,30:7
Fade Out--Fade In 1964,My 27,45:1
Applause 1970,Mr 31,35:1
Applause 1970,Ap 5,II,1:1
Comedie Francaise
Bourgeois Gentilhomme, Le 1954,Ap 14,26:7
Comegys, Gretchen
All the Living 1938,Mr 25,14:4
Comegys, Kathleen
Man in the Making, The 1921,S 21,16:2
Roseanne 1923,D 31,9:5
Loose Ankles 1926,Ag 17,15:1
Chrysalis 1932,N 16,15:2
Tight Britches 1934,S 12,26:2
Lost Horizons 1934,O 16,31:2
Country Wife, The 1935,Jl 2,24:2
Coward, The 1935,Jl 16,24:1
If This Be Treason 1935,Jl 30,17:1
If This Be Treason 1935,S 24,28:2
Russet Mantle 1936,Ag 18,15:2

Comegys, Kathleen—Cont
At Mrs Beam's 1937,Jl 27,24:2
Ghost of Yankee Doodle, The 1937,N 23,26:3
Craig's Wife 1947,F 13,35:2
Craig's Wife 1947,Mr 30,II,1:1
Silver Whistle, The 1948,N 25,49:2
Traveling Lady 1954,O 28,45:2
Portrait of a Lady 1954,D 22,27:6
Man in the Dog Suit, The 1958,O 31,34:2
Miracle Worker, The 1959,O 20,44:1
Comellas, Josine
Cosmonaute Agricole, Le 1970,Ap 8,38:3
Comer, Bruce
Wicked Cooks, The 1967,Ja 24,42:1
Comer, Henry (Playwright)
Just for Love 1968,O 18,40:1
Comer, Natalie
Take It Easy 1950,D 25,23:6
Comer, Sybil
Nina Rosa 1930,My 31,19:3
Comer, Virginia Lee (Director)
Blind Alley 1939,Ag 23,18:8
Comerford, Gladys
Good Times 1920,Ag 10,10:1
Comerford, Mariel
Patience 1929,D 16,34:5
Comes, Robert (Director)
One-Woman Show, A 1962,My 22,31:1
Comfort, Vaughan
Vaudeville (Palace) 1923,F 13,25:1
Comingore, Dorothy
Beggars Are Comming to Town 1945,O 29,16:2
Commanders, The
Puzzles of 1925 1925,F 3,25:3
Commerlink (Playwright)
Kindischen Verlieben, Die 1924,Mr 2,VIII,2:1
Commons, Milt (Miscellaneous)
Rendezvous at Senlis 1961,F 28,39:2
Witches' Sabbath 1962,Ap 20,22:2
Vida es Sueno, La 1964,Mr 18,49:1
Life Is a Dream 1964,Mr 20,24:1
She Stoops to Conquer 1968,Ja 1,11:1
Twelfth Night 1968,Je 15,40:1
Comor, Henry
Just for Love 1968,O 18,40:1
Comor, Henry (Director)
Just for Love 1968,O 18,40:1
Comoroda, Charles
Knock on Wood 1935,My 29,16:2
Comorthoon, James (Playwright)
Every Other Evil 1961,Ja 23,20:2
Compagnie des Quinze, La
Bataille de la Marne 1932,F 21,VIII,1:8
Compagnons de la Chanson, Les
Untitled-Revue 1947,N 23,II,1:1
Vaudeville (Palace) 1952,F 27,22:2
Compano, Janet
Yearling, The 1965,D 11,25:1
Comper, Edward
Operette 1938,F 18,22:3
Competello, Tom (Director)
Kill the One-Eyed Man 1965,O 21,56:1
Compton, Betty
Vogues of 1924 1924,Mr 28,14:3
City Chap, The 1925,O 27,21:1
Americana 1926,Jl 27,15:3
Oh, Kay! 1926,N 9,31:3
Funny Face 1927,N 23,28:2
Hold Everything 1928,O 11,24:2
Fifty Million Frenchmen 1929,N 28,34:4
Simpleton of the Unexpected Isles, The
1954,Ja 12,19:1
Compton, Charles
Whispering Well, The 1920,D 6,19:1
Compton, Christine
Launzi 1923,O 11,16:3
Edgar Allan Poe 1925,O 6,31:1
Stripped 1929,O 22,26:1
Compton, Dean (Miscellaneous)
Trelawny of the 'Wells' 1970,O 12,48:1
Compton, Dorothy
Between the Devil 1937,D 23,24:5
Compton, Fay
Mary Rose 1920,My 16,VI,1:7
Mary Rose 1920,Ag 8,VI,1:1
Hamlet 1925,F 20,20:1
Liliom 1927,Ja 2,30:1
Liliom 1927,Ja 9,VII,2:1
Constant Wife, The 1927,My 1,VIII,2:7
Olympia 1928,O 17,26:1
Dishonored Lady 1930,My 25,IX,2:4
Hamlet 1931,Mr 22,VIII,2:1
Autumn Crocus 1931,Ap 26,VIII,2:4
Once a Husband 1932,N 20,IX,3:6
Proscenium 1933,Je 15,21:2
Indoor Fireworks 1934,Mr 30,26:6
Murder at Mayfair 1934,S 6,23:5
Murder in Mayfair 1934,S 23,X,3:6
Hervey House 1935,My 18,21:2
Call It a Day 1935,O 31,17:2
Call It a Day 1935,N 24,IX,1:2
Hamlet 1939,Jl 7,12:2
Hamlet 1939,Jl 16,IX,2:1
King Lear 1940,Ap 28,IX,1:7

Compton, Fay—Cont

Blithe Spirit 1941,Jl 13,IX,1:4
Little Foxes, The 1942,N 1,VIII,2:1
No Medals 1944,N 19,II,2:4
Othello 1946,D 4,44:2
Candida 1946,D 4,44:2
Family Portrait 1948,Mr 14,II,2:5
Bonaventure 1950,Ja 8,II,3:7
Red Letter Day, The 1952,F 22,14:4
Red Letter Day 1952,Mr 16,II,3:7
Hamlet 1953,Ag 25,18:6
God and Kate Murphy 1959,F 27,21:2

Compton, Forrest

Othello 1953,O 30,28:2

Compton, Francis

March Hares 1928,Ap 3,32:6
K Guy, The 1928,O 16,28:4
Lady Dedlock 1929,Ja 1,61:2
Silent Witness, The 1931,Mr 24,31:5
Yellow Jack 1934,Mr 7,22:6
Between Two Worlds 1934,O 26,24:2
Prisoners of War 1935,Ja 29,24:1
Distant Shore, The 1935,F 22,26:2
Kind Lady 1935,Ap 24,24:5
Caesar and Cleopatra 1935,Ag 22,21:1
Idiot's Delight 1936,Mr 25,25:2
To Quito and Back 1937,O 7,30:4
Bachelor Born 1938,Ja 26,26:3
Wuthering Heights 1939,Ap 28,30:4
Taming of the Shrew, The 1940,F 6,17:2
Leave Her to Heaven 1940,F 28,16:2
Theatre 1941,N 13,34:2
Willow and I, The 1942,D 11,32:2
Patriots, The 1943,Ja 30,11:2
Snark Was a Boojum, The 1943,S 2,14:4
Susan and God 1943,D 14,30:2
Thank You Svoboda 1944,Mr 2,13:2
Othello 1945,My 23,25:4
Next Half Hour, The 1945,O 30,14:6
Song of Bernadette 1946,Mr 27,22:2
Cyrano de Bergerac 1946,O 9,33:2
Cyrano de Bergerac 1947,Ja 17,27:2
Play's the Thing, The 1948,Ap 29,19:2
Play's the Thing, The 1948,My 9,II,1:1
Red Gloves 1948,D 6,28:2
Mrs Gibsons' Boys 1949,My 5,35:2
Montserrat 1949,O 31,21:4
Ring Around the Moon 1950,N 24,30:1
Green Bay Tree, The 1951,F 2,18:2
Gigi 1951,N 26,20:4
International Set, The 1953,Je 12,19:3
Small War on Murray Hill 1957,Ja 4,19:1
Small War on Murray Hill 1957,Ja 13,II,1:1
Under Milk Wood 1957,O 16,42:5
Jane Eyre 1958,My 2,31:1
Romulus 1962,Ja 11,27:1
Affair, The 1962,S 21,34:2
Lady of the Camellias, The 1963,Mr 22,7:1

Compton, Gardner (Miscellaneous)

Oh! Calcutta 1969,Je 18,33:1

Compton, Jane

Little Red Riding Hood 1948,Ja 12,15:3

Compton, John

Ryan Girl, The 1945,S 25,28:2
You Can't Take It With You 1951,Ap 7,8:6

Compton, Juleen

Cherry Orchard, The 1955,O 19,38:1
Good as Gold 1957,Mr 8,22:2
Lysistrata 1959,My 20,40:2
Jeannette 1960,Mr 25,20:2

Compton, June

Sherry! 1967,Mr 29,39:1
Your Own Thing 1969,Mr 29,39:1

Compton, Linda

Hair 1967,O 30,55:1

Compton, Madge

Winslow Boy, The 1947,O 30,32:2

Compton, Ranney

Paths of Glory 1935,S 27,24:2

Compton, Ranulf

Choice, The 1930,My 9,20:5

Compton, William C (Scenic Designer)

Once Over Lightly 1938,D 10,13:4

Compton-Burnett, Ivy (Original Author)

Heritage and Its History, A 1965,My 19,42:1

Comstock, Alzada P (Playwright)

Mount Holyoke Milestones 1933,Ap 9,II,3:4

Comstock, F Ray (Producer)

Lysistrata 1925,D 15,28:2

Comstock, Frances

Bitter Sweet 1934,My 8,28:4
One for the Money 1939,F 6,9:2
Two for the Show 1940,F 9,14:2
Chocolate Soldier, The 1942,Je 24,22:2
Magic Touch, The 1947,S 4,30:1

Comstock, Howard Warren (Playwright)

Stepping Sisters 1930,Ap 23,24:2
Doctor X 1930,Jl 31,12:4
Doctor X 1931,F 10,25:1

Comstock, Nannette

Up the Ladder 1922,Mr 7,11:2

Comstock, Ruthie

Stepsisters 1936,O 13,32:3

Comtois, George

West Side Story 1968,Je 25,32:1

Conant, Isabel Fiske (Playwright)

Clouds of the Sun 1922,My 6,11:2

Conaree, Doris Michael

Witchfinders, The 1956,My 11,22:6

Conaree, Michael

Tinker's Wedding, The 1957,Mr 7,24:1
Riders to the Sea 1957,Mr 7,24:1
Riders to the Sea 1957,Mr 17,II,1:1

Conaway, Charles (Miscellaneous)

Pousse-Cafe 1966,Mr 19,19:2

Conaway, Charles (Producer)

Ziegfeld Follies 1957,Mr 2,19:2

Conaway, Charles Jr

Follow the Girls 1944,Ap 10,15:2

Conche, Robert

International Revue 1930,F 26,22:2

Conchita

Panama Hattie 1940,O 31,28:2

Concklin, Eric

Triumph of Robert Emmet, The 1969,My 8,54:1

Concklin, Eric (Director)

Haunted Host, The 1969,O 28,43:1

Condell, H A (Costume Designer)

Nathan the Wise 1942,Mr 12,25:4
Yours Is My Heart 1946,S 6,16:5

Condell, H A (Scenic Designer)

Criminals, The 1941,D 22,24:3
Nathan the Wise 1942,Mr 12,25:4
War and Peace 1942,My 22,26:3
Winter Soldiers 1942,N 30,19:2
Nathan the Wise 1944,F 22,26:3
Doctor Herzl 1945,D 21,25:4
Pirates of Penzance, The 1946,My 17,14:6
Yours Is My Heart 1946,S 6,16:5
Outside the Door 1949,Mr 2,33:2
Burning Bush, The 1949,D 17,15:5
Rich Man, Poor Man 1950,F 13,15:4
Barrier, The 1950,N 3,32:2
House in Berlin, A (Als der Kreig zu Ende War);
  Als der Krieg zu Ende War (A House in Berlin)
  1950,D 27,32:3
Springtime for Henry 1951,Mr 15,36:2
Pirates of Penzance, The 1960,O 7,29:1

Condit, W B

Front Page, The 1937,N 12,27:2

Condon, Eva

Oh, Henry! 1920,My 6,14:2
Detour, The 1921,Ag 24,12:2
First Man, The 1922,Mr 6,9:2
Makers of Light 1922,My 24,22:3
Spite Corner 1922,S 26,18:1
Ice-Bound 1923,F 12,16:2
Best People, The 1924,Ag 20,8:1
Move On 1926,Ja 19,30:1
Girl Friend, The 1926,Mr 18,26:5
Sandalwood 1926,S 23,23:1
Gossipy Sex, The 1927,Ap 20,28:3
What the Doctor Ordered 1927,Ag 19,20:2
Lovers and Enemies 1927,S 21,27:1
Gringa, La 1928,F 2,17:1
Gods of the Lightning 1928,O 25,27:2
Roar China! 1930,O 28,23:1
Collision 1932,F 17,19:2
Give Us This Day 1933,O 28,20:6
Small Miracle 1934,S 27,24:3
Hook-Up, The 1935,My 9,24:6
Higher and Higher 1940,Ap 5,24:3
Popsy 1941,F 11,26:2
World's Full of Girls, The 1943,D 7,31:2
Calico Wedding 1945,Mr 8,18:6
Oh, Herbert! 1945,Je 20,26:3
Closing Door, The 1949,D 2,36:2
Dark Is Light Enough, The 1955,F 24,20:1

Condon, Max

Stars on Ice (2d Edition) 1943,Je 25,13:2

Condon, Richard (Miscellaneous)

Stalag 17 1951,My 9,41:2

Condon, Richard (Playwright)

Men of Distinction 1953,My 1,18:4

Condos, Dimo

Cannibals, The 1968,N 4,60:1
Guns of Carrar, The 1968,D 10,53:1
Moths, The 1970,My 12,46:1

Condos, Frank

Earl Carroll's Vanities 1930,Jl 2,28:3

Condos, Harry

Earl Carroll's Vanities 1930,Jl 2,28:3

Condos, Steve

Heaven on Earth 1948,S 17,29:2

Condou, P

Electra 1952,N 20,38:2

Condre, Michelle

Springtime Folly 1951,F 27,23:4

Cone, Irving (Miscellaneous)

Inquest 1970,Ap 24,38:1

Cone, Jacob

Witch of Castile, The 1930,O 25,21:1

Cone, Rhett (Producer)

Eastward in Eden 1956,Ap 18,25:4
Palm Tree in a Rose Garden, A 1957,N 27,26:2
Ardele 1958,Ap 9,39:4

Cone, Rhett (Producer)—Cont

Hamlet of Stepney Green 1958,N 14,21:1
Redemptor, The 1959,My 5,40:1
What Did You Say "What" For? 1959,My 5,40:1
Montserrat 1961,Ja 9,30:5
Five Posts in the Market Place 1961,Mr 6,30:1

Conescu, Arthur (Miscellaneous)

I Am a Camera 1956,O 10,47:2

Conescu, Arthur (Producer)

Harry, Noon and Night 1965,My 6,44:1

Conforti, Donna

Annie Get Your Gun 1966,Je 1,42:2

Conforti, Gino

She Loves Me 1963,Ap 24,39:1
Never Live Over a Pretzel Factory 1964,Mr 30,37:1
Fiddler on the Roof 1964,S 23,56:2
Poor Bitos 1964,N 16,40:2
Man of La Mancha 1965,N 23,52:1

Congdon, David

Huui, Huui 1968,N 25,58:1

Congdon, James

Loud Red Patrick, The 1956,O 4,28:1
Miracle Worker, The 1959,O 20,44:1
Moon Besieged, The 1962,D 6,54:1
Wait Until Dark 1966,F 3,21:1
How Now, Dow Jones 1967,D 8,53:1

Congedo, Joseph M (Rev) (Original Author)

Tragedy of the Ages, The 1933,Ap 7,22:7

Congreve, William (Playwright)

Way of the World, The 1924,N 18,23:4
Love for Love 1925,Ap 1,21:2
Love for Love 1925,Ap 5,IX,1:2
Love for Love 1925,S 15,29:3
Way of the World, The 1931,Je 2,34:3
Love for Love 1936,Je 30,15:4
Love for Love 1940,Je 4,19:5
Love for Love 1944,N 19,II,2:4
Love for Love 1947,My 27,30:2
Love for Love 1947,Je 1,II,1:1
Way of the World, The 1948,N 7,II,3:1
Way of the World, The 1950,Ap 9,73:5
Way of the World, The 1953,Ap 10,17:1
Way of the World, The 1954,S 30,38:2
Way of the World, The 1954,O 17,II,1:1
Double Dealer, The 1959,Ag 25,36:2
Way of the World, The 1965,Je 2,40:1
Love for Love 1967,O 21,17:1
Love for Love 1967,O 29,II,5:1
Love for Love 1967,O 30,59:1
Way of the World, The 1969,Ag 7,29:1
Double Dealer, The 1969,Ag 7,29:1

Conibear, Betty

Corn Is Green, The 1943,My 4,18:3

Conkey, Aida

Face the Music 1932,F 18,24:5

Conkey, Thomas

Our Nell 1922,D 5,24:1
Lambs Gambol 1925,Ap 27,15:1

Conkle, E P (Playwright)

Sparkin' 1931,Mr 4,33:2
200 Were Chosen 1936,N 21,21:1
200 Were Chosen 1936,N 29,XII,1:1
Prologue to Glory 1938,Mr 18,22:2
Prologue to Glory 1938,Mr 27,X,1:1
One-Act Variety Theatre; What D' You Call It?
  1940,Mr 20,36:2
Afternoon Storm 1948,Ap 12,24:2

Conklin, Bill (Lyricist)

O Say Can You See! 1962,O 9,45:1

Conklin, Bill (Playwright)

O Say Can You See! 1962,O 9,45:1

Conklin, Cathy

Oklahoma! 1953,S 1,19:1

Conklin, Charles

Let 'Em Eat Cake 1933,O 23,18:1

Conklin, Harold

Blue Widow, The 1933,Ag 31,20:2
If a Body 1935,My 1,25:3
Julie the Great 1936,Ja 15,15:3
Daughters of Atreus 1936,O 15,33:1
She Gave Him All She Had 1939,D 2,20:7
Wonderful Journey 1946,D 26,30:2
Our Lan' 1947,Ap 19,11:2
Our Lan' 1947,S 29,16:5

Conklin, John (Costume Designer)

Sap of Life, The 1961,O 3,44:1
Tambourines to Glory 1963,N 4,47:1
Phaedra 1967,My 22,50:2
Have I Got One for You 1968,Ja 8,32:1

Conklin, John (Scenic Designer)

Decameron, The 1961,Ap 13,32:1
Sap of Life, The 1961,O 3,44:1
Tambourines to Glory 1963,N 4,47:1
Have I Got One for You 1968,Ja 8,32:1
Firebugs, The 1968,Jl 2,36:1
Place Without Doors, A 1970,D 1,60:1

Conklin, Peggy

His Majesty's Car 1930,O 24,30:1
Purity 1930,D 26,18:2
Old Man Murphy 1931,My 19,25:2
Hot Money 1931,N 9,22:2
Mademoiselle 1932,O 19,22:4
Party's Over, The 1933,Mr 28,23:3

Conklin, Peggy—Cont

Ghost Writer, The 1933,Je 20,22:4
Pursuit of Happiness, The 1933,O 10,24:4
Pursuit of Happiness, The 1934,Je 24,IX,1:4
Petrified Forest, The 1934,D 21,31:6
Petrified Forest, The 1935,Ja 8,26:1
Petrified Forest, The 1935,Ja 13,IX,1:1
Co-Respondent Unknown 1936,F 12,24:4
Yes, My Darling Daughter 1937,F 10,19:2
Yes, My Darling Daughter 1937,F 28,XI,1:1
Casey Jones 1938,F 21,14:2
Miss Swan Expects 1939,F 21,15:2
Madam Will You Walk 1939,N 14,20:3
Mr and Mrs North 1941,Ja 13,11:2
Mr and Mrs North 1941,F 23,IX,1:1
Feathers in a Gale 1943,D 22,26:2
Alice in Arms 1945,F 1,18:4
Wisteria Trees, The 1950,Mr 30,39:1
Wisteria Trees, The 1950,Ap 9,II,1:1
Picnic 1953,F 20,14:7
Picnic 1953,Mr 1,II,1:1
Howie 1958,S 18,35:2

Conky, Thomas
Rose Marie 1925,D 4,26:1

Conlan, Francis
Backslapper, The 1925,Ap 13,25:2
Seven Keys to Baldpate 1935,My 28,30:2

Conlan, Frank
Front Page, The 1928,Ag 15,19:2
June Moon 1929,Ag 4,VIII,1:6
June Moon 1929,O 10,34:5
Inspector General, The 1930,D 24,19:2
Streets of New York, The 1931,O 7,29:1
Pillars of Society, The 1931,O 15,19:1
Bride the Sun Shines On, The 1931,D 28,20:2
Housewarming 1932,Ap 8,25:1
Foolscap 1933,Ja 12,21:2
Strike Me Pink 1933,Mr 6,16:3
Hide and Seek 1934,Ag 7,20:2
Caesar and Cleopatra 1935,Ag 22,21:1
Rag Picker of Paris, The: or, Modest Modiste
  1935,N 12,23:7
Come Angel Band 1936,F 19,17:1
Bitter Stream 1936,Mr 31,16:6
You Can't Take It With You 1936,D 15,31:1
You Can't Take It With You 1936,D 20,XI,3:1
You Can't Take It With You 1937,Ag 29,X,1:1
Ladies and Gentlemen 1939,O 18,30:2
All in Favor 1942,Ja 21,20:6
Vickie 1942,S 23,28:1

Conlan, Frank (Playwright)
Our Little Wife 1927,My 10,25:3

Conlan, James S (Rev) (Playwright)
Priest in the Cellar, The 1969,F 19,39:1

Conland, Frank
Dr Knock 1936,Jl 14,22:1

Conley, Corinne
Love and Libel 1960,D 8,44:1

Conley, Harry
Vaudeville (Palace) 1925,S 29,31:2
Vaudeville (Palace) 1928,Ag 14,15:5
Vaudeville (Palace) 1929,F 4,21:4
Broadway Nights 1929,Je 23,VIII,2:4
Broadway Nights 1929,Jl 16,23:2
This Was Burlesque 1970,F 12,31:1

Conley, Hi Wilberforce
Michael Todd's Peep Show 1950,Je 29,37:2
Peep Show 1950,Jl 9,II,1:1

Conley, Jay
Bitter Sweet 1934,My 8,28:4

Conley, Matt
Drunkard, The; Fallen Saved, The 1959,Je 24,37:2
Vincent 1959,O 1,40:1
I Got Shoes 1963,Ja 25,12:2
Does a Tiger Wear a Necktie? 1967,F 4,17:1
Fire! 1968,My 12,II,7:1
Bungler, The 1968,Ag 2,24:1

Conley, Matt (Director)
Man and Superman 1960,N 7,46:2
Emmanuel 1960,D 5,42:2

Conley, Matt (Miscellaneous)
Hamlet of Stepney Green 1958,N 14,21:1

Conley, Robert (Scenic Designer)
Bedtime Story 1957,Ap 1,21:2
Portrait of a Madonna 1957,Ap 1,21:2
Man of Destiny, The 1957,Ap 1,21:2
Autumn's Here 1966,O 26,40:1
Shoemaker's Holiday, The 1967,Mr 3,25:1

Conley, Ruth
No Other Girl 1924,Ag 14,10:4
Merry Merry 1925,S 25,24:3
Holiday 1930,F 6,21:2
Up and Up, The 1930,S 9,25:2
Scrap Book 1932,Ag 2,20:3
Marathon 1933,Ja 28,8:8
Sailor, Beware! 1933,S 29,24:4
Jackson White 1935,Ap 22,14:6
Alice Takat 1936,F 11,19:2
Tell Me Pretty Maiden 1937,D 17,33:5
Window Shopping 1938,D 24,13:2
Brooklyn Biarritz 1941,F 28,16:2
Proof Thro' the Night 1942,D 26,14:2

Conley, Will
Mikado, The 1924,Jl 29,9:1

Conliffe, Jeanette
Medal for Willie, A 1951,O 16,35:2

Conlon, Noel
Candyapple, The 1970,N 24,33:1

Conlow, Peter
Razzle Dazzle 1951,F 20,21:1
Courtin' Time 1951,Je 14,30:2
Three Wishes for Jamie 1952,Mr 22,9:2
Shoestring Revue 1955,Mr 1,22:2
Copper and Brass 1957,O 18,19:2
Boy Friend, The 1958,Ja 27,24:4
Take Me Along 1959,O 23,22:2

Conlow, Peter (Choreographer)
Guys and Dolls 1959,Jl 22,22:2
Tiger Rag, The 1961,F 17,20:2

Conlow, Peter (Director)
All Kinds of Giants 1961,D 19,40:1

Conlow, Peter (Miscellaneous)
New Faces of 1956 1956,Je 15,32:1
Finian's Rainbow 1960,Ap 28,31:1

Conly, Paul (Composer)
Unseen Hand, The 1970,Ap 2,43:1
Forensic and the Navigators 1970,Ap 2,43:1

Conmes, Marie
Devil Came From Dublin, The! 1955,Je 3,27:2

Conn, Richard
Vaudeville (Palace) 1924,Ap 29,12:2

Conn, William
Man of Destiny, The 1957,Ap 1,21:2
Portrait of a Madonna 1957,Ap 1,21:2
Ruy Blas 1957,D 14,16:3

Connaire, Joseph
Tree Witch, The 1961,Je 5,39:4

Connard, Phyllis
At Mrs Beam's 1926,Ap 26,24:3
Pygmalion 1926,N 16,24:1
Brothers Karamazov, The 1927,Ja 4,20:1
Right You Are (If You Think You Are)
  1927,F 24,27:1
Doctor's Dilemma, The 1927,N 22,33:1
Major Barbara 1928,N 20,28:4
Admirable Crichton, The 1931,Mr 10,23:2
Reunion in Vienna 1931,N 17,31:1
Design for Living 1933,Ja 3,19:5
Design for Living 1933,Ja 25,13:2
Point Valaine 1935,Ja 17,22:2
Parnell 1935,N 12,24:2
Parnell 1936,My 5,26:2
Qudrille 1954,N 4,39:2

Connaught, Brian
Candle in the Wind 1941,O 23,26:2
Beat the Band 1942,O 15,26:1

Connaughton, William (Lighting Director)
West of the Moon 1961,Ag 29,26:1
Blood Bugle, The 1961,Je 29,26:1

Connell, Gertrude
Little Theatre Tournament; Tale Retold, A
  1928,My 10,31:1

Connell, Gordon
Subways Are for Sleeping 1961,D 28,22:1
Hello, Dolly! 1964,Ja 17,22:1

Connell, Gordon (Musical Director)
Put It in Writing 1963,My 14,31:1

Connell, Grace
Flesh 1925,My 8,22:3
Weak Sisters 1925,O 14,31:3

Connell, Jane
Threepenny Opera, The 1955,S 21,38:1
New Faces of 1956 1956,Je 15,32:1
Once Upon a Mattress 1960,S 21,43:4
Oldest Trick in the World, The 1961,F 21,40:1
Fortuna 1962,Ja 4,26:1
Golden Apple, The 1962,F 13,38:2
Put It in Writing 1963,My 14,31:1
Drat! the Cat! 1965,O 11,54:2
Mame 1966,My 25,41:1
Dear World 1969,F 7,33:1
Dear World 1969,F 16,II,1:1

Connell, John
Time Limit! 1956,Ja 25,27:2
Uncle Willie 1956,D 21,17:1

Connell, Leigh (Miscellaneous)
Iceman Cometh, The 1956,My 8,38:1
Camino Real 1960,My 17,42:2

Connell, Leigh (Producer)
Cradle Song 1955,D 2,32:2
Long Day's Journey Into Night 1956,N 8,47:2
House of Breath, The 1957,Ap 15,23:2
Children of Darkness 1958,Mr 1,11:4
Quare Fellow, The 1958,N 28,34:1
Our Town 1959,Mr 24,46:2

Connell, Louise Fox (Playwright)
Queen Bee 1929,N 13,25:1

Connell, Tom (Lyricist)
There You Are! 1932,My 17,25:4

Connell, Vivian (Playwright)
Throng o' Scarlet 1947,D 2,37:2
Nineteenth Hole of Europe, The 1949,Mr 28,16:2
Throng o' Scarlet 1950,F 6,20:5

Connelly, Albert R
Coriolanus 1927,Je 18,8:3

Connelly, Bobby (Director)
Flying High 1930,Mr 4,24:4

Connelly, Bobby (Director)—Cont
Prince Charming 1930,O 14,31:1

Connelly, Bobby (Miscellaneous)
Follow Thru 1929,Ja 10,24:3

Connelly, Bobby (Musical Director)
Melody 1933,F 15,17:4

Connelly, D Hubert (Playwright)
Crucible 1933,S 5,22:4

Connelly, D Hubert (Producer)
Crucible 1933,S 5,22:4

Connelly, Eddie
Brothers 1928,D 26,14:3

Connelly, Jack C
Lancashire Lass, The 1931,D 31,16:3

Connelly, Kathleen
Beau Brummell 1924,Ap 4,19:2

Connelly, Marc
Our Town 1944,Ja 11,24:5
Our Town 1944,Ja 16,II,1:1
Our Town 1946,My 2,27:3
Tall Story 1959,Ja 30,33:2

Connelly, Marc (Director)
Wild Man of Borneo, The 1927,S 14,29:2
Green Pastures, The 1930,F 27,26:1
Overture 1930,N 25,31:2
Anatol 1931,Ja 17,23:3
Acropolis 1933,N 24,25:8
Acropolis 1933,D 10,X,3:6
Farmer Takes a Wife, The 1934,O 31,17:1
Green Pastures, The 1935,F 27,16:2
Having Wonderful Time 1937,F 22,12:5
Having Wonderful Time 1937,F 28,XI,1:1
Two Bouquets, The 1938,Je 1,19:2
Everywhere I Roam 1938,D 30,10:4
Happiest Days, The 1939,Ap 12,26:2
Flowers of Virtue, The 1942,F 6,22:2
Hope for the Best 1945,F 8,14:4
Story for Strangers, A 1948,S 22,39:2
Green Pastures, The 1951,Mr 16,35:2

Connelly, Marc (Miscellaneous)
Solid Gold Cadillac, The 1953,N 6,24:2

Connelly, Marc (Playwright)
Erminie 1921,Ja 4,11:1
Dulcy 1921,Ag 15,14:1
Dulcy 1921,Ag 21,VI,1:1
To the Ladies! 1922,F 21,20:1
To the Ladies! 1922,Mr 12,VI,1:1
49ers, The 1922,N 7,14:1
49ers, The 1922,N 12,VIII,1:1
Merton of the Movies 1922,N 14,16:2
Helen of Troy, New York 1923,Je 20,22:6
Deep Tangled Wildwood, The 1923,N 6,22:1
Beggar on Horseback 1924,F 13,17:2
Beggar on Horseback 1924,F 17,VII,1:1
Be Yourself! 1924,Ag 24,VII,1:8
Be Yourself! 1924,S 4,13:3
Wisdom Tooth, The 1926,F 16,22:2
Wisdom Tooth, The 1926,F 28,VIII,1:1
Wild Man of Borneo, The 1927,S 14,29:2
Wild Man of Borneo, The 1927,S 25,VIII,1:1
Keating 1927,D 26,26:6
Green Pastures, The 1930,F 27,26:1
Green Pastures, The 1930,Mr 2,IX,1:1
Green Pastures, The 1930,Mr 9,IX,1:1
Green Pastures, The 1931,Mr 1,VIII,1:1
Green Pastures, The 1932,O 11,26:6
Green Pastures, The 1932,O 30,IX,2:4
Green Pastures, The 1933,O 5,24:5
Green Pastures, The 1933,O 22,IX,1:6
Farmer Takes a Wife, The 1934,O 9,17:2
Farmer Takes a Wife, The 1934,O 28,IX,3:1
Farmer Takes a Wife, The 1934,O 31,17:1
Farmer Takes a Wife, The 1934,N 11,IX,1:1
Green Pastures, The 1935,F 27,16:2
Green Pastures, The 1935,Mr 24,VIII,1:1
Everywhere I Roam 1938,D 30,10:4
Everywhere I Roam 1939,Ja 8,IX,1:1
Flowers of Virtue, The 1942,F 6,22:2
Story for Strangers, A 1948,S 22,39:2
Green Pastures, The 1951,Mr 16,35:2
Hunter's Moon 1958,Mr 16,II,3:1
Merton of the Movies 1968,S 26,62:1
Beggar on Horseback 1970,My 15,47:2
Beggar on Horseback 1970,My 24,II,1:1

Connelly, Marc (Producer)
Having Wonderful Time 1937,F 22,12:5
Two Bouquets, The 1938,Je 1,19:2
Everywhere I Roam 1938,D 30,10:4
Hope for the Best 1945,F 8,14:4

Connelly, Walter
Midsummer Night's Dream, A 1934,S 19,15:1

Conner, Rosemary
Thesmophoriazusae, The; Goddesses of Athens,
  The 1955,D 14,52:4

Conners, Barry (Playwright)
Mad Honeymoon, The 1923,Ag 8,10:1
So This Is Politics 1924,Je 17,22:2
Applesauce 1924,O 12,VIII,2:1
Hell's Bells! 1925,Ja 27,14:2
Applesauce 1925,S 29,31:2
Patsy, The 1925,D 24,8:5
Girl Trouble 1928,O 7,IX,2:3
Girl Trouble 1928,O 26,22:3
Patsy, The 1930,My 11,IX,3:1

Conners, Barry (Playwright)—Cont
Unexpected Husband 1931,Je 3,29:4
Patsy, The 1935,Jl 16,24:1
Connery, John
Hamlet 1923,N 27,23:6
Macbeth 1924,Mr 17,18:1
Machinal 1928,S 8,10:3
Mighty Conlon 1933,F 21,17:3
Connes, Keith
Thespis 1953,Ja 17,13:5
Mardi Gras! 1965,Je 28,33:2
Conness, Luke
Brothers 1928,D 26,14:3
Conness, Robert
Bootleggers, The 1922,N 28,24:1
Steadfast 1923,O 31,12:1
Right to Kill, The 1926,F 16,22:2
Uninvited Guest, The 1927,S 28,28:2
Courage 1928,O 9,34:2
Elizabeth the Queen 1930,N 4,37:1
Unto the Third 1933,Ap 21,24:8
Sellout, The 1933,S 7,17:2
Woman of Destiny, A 1936,Mr 3,25:2
Connett, Ewel (Director)
Hatfields & McCoys 1970,Je 23,34:1
Connick, Louis Jr
Hay-Foot, Straw-Foot 1942,O 24,11:6
Conning, Brace
Faust 1927,Ja 4,20:1
Babbling Brookes 1927,F 26,13:2
Babbling Brookes 1927,F 26,13:2
Danger 1935,Ag 27,23:4
Witness for the Prosecution 1954,D 17,35:2
Conning, Brace (Director)
Immoral Support 1935,S 3,24:3
One More Genius 1936,Ag 11,24:6
Corn Is Green, The 1954,F 27,10:2
Conning, Brace (Miscellaneous)
Rain Before Seven 1935,Ag 13,20:3
In Gold We Trust 1936,S 1,24:1
Conning, Brace (Mrs) (Original Author)
Tea for Three 1935,Jl 9,24:4
Conning, Katharine S (Composer)
Ballad of John Ogilvie, The 1968,O 9,42:4
Connolly, Babs
Sonya's Search for the Christmas Star
1929,D 14,24:6
Connolly, Bobby (Choreographer)
Kitty's Kisses 1926,My 7,12:2
Honeymoon Lane 1926,S 21,32:3
Samarkand 1926,D 22,24:4
Judy 1927,F 8,20:2
Funny Face 1927,N 23,28:2
New Moon, The 1928,S 20,33:1
Treasure Girl 1928,N 9,22:1
Spring Is Here 1929,Mr 12,26:1
Show Girl 1929,Jl 3,19:3
Ziegfeld Follies 1931,Jl 2,30:5
Free for All 1931,S 9,25:1
East Wind 1931,O 28,19:1
East Wind 1931,D 11,VIII,4:3
Hot-Cha! 1932,Mr 9,17:3
Ballyhoo of 1932 1932,S 7,14:2
Connolly, Bobby (Director)
Good News 1927,S 7,35:4
Sons o' Guns 1929,N 27,30:4
America's Sweetheart 1931,F 11,23:1
Ballyhoo of 1932 1932,S 7,14:2
Look Who's Here 1932,O 31,18:5
Take a Chance 1932,N 28,11:2
Ziegfeld Follies 1934,Ja 5,24:3
Casino Varieties 1934,Ap 3,26:4
Connolly, Bobby (Miscellaneous)
Zuider Zee 1928,D 19,24:4
Connolly, Bobby (Producer)
Sons o' Guns 1929,N 27,30:4
Prince Charming 1930,O 14,31:1
Ballyhoo of 1932 1932,S 7,14:2
Follies 1933,N 19,IX,2:5
Connolly, Daniel
Star of Bengal 1929,S 26,27:2
Connolly, Dolly
Right Girl, The 1921,Mr 16,12:1
Connolly, Don
Caviar 1934,Je 8,19:2
Connolly, Eliza
Cyrano de Bergerac 1936,Ap 28,17:1
Connolly, Frank (Mrs)
Prunella 1929,Ap 10,23:3
Connolly, George
Up Eden 1968,N 27,42:1
Borstal Boy 1970,Ap 1,38:1
Connolly, Jack C
Straight Thru the Door 1928,O 5,17:2
Veneer 1929,N 13,24:5
Triplets 1932,S 22,25:2
Connolly, John
Threepenny Opera, The 1933,Ap 14,22:4
Connolly, June
Children's Hour, The 1952,D 19,35:2
Connolly, Marc (Miscellaneous)
Sleepy Hollow 1948,Je 4,26:3
Connolly, Marc (Playwright)
Green Pastures, The 1951,Ap 1,II,1:1

Connolly, Mickie
Solid Ivory 1925,N 17,29:3
Connolly, Robert (Director)
Desert Song, The 1926,D 1,24:2
Connolly, Thomas
Moon in the Yellow River, The 1961,F 7,40:2
Riot Act, The 1963,Mr 9,5:2
Philadelphia, Here I Come! 1966,F 17,28:1
Connolly, Walter
Woman of Bronze, The 1920,S 8,9:2
Talking Parrot, The 1923,D 4,25:3
Applesauce 1925,S 29,31:2
Treat 'Em Rough 1926,O 5,26:2
Praying Curve 1927,Ja 25,18:2
Springboard, The 1927,O 13,23:1
Trigger 1927,D 7,32:1
Behavior of Mrs Crane, The 1928,Mr 21,30:1
Happy Husband, The 1928,My 8,25:2
Behavior of Mrs Crane, The 1928,My 27,VIII,1:1
Happy Husband, The 1928,My 27,VIII,1:1
Possession 1928,O 3,35:1
Vaudeville (Palace) 1928,D 3,30:6
Meet the Wife 1928,D 3,30:6
Merry Andrew 1929,Ja 13,VIII,2:4
Merry Andrew 1929,Ja 22,22:2
Stepping Out 1929,My 21,29:1
Paris Bound 1929,Jl 20,8:3
Ladies Leave 1929,O 2,28:3
Your Uncle Dudley 1929,N 19,26:4
Uncle Vanya 1930,Ap 16,26:5
Uncle Vanya 1930,My 4,XI,1:1
Uncle Vanya 1930,S 23,30:3
Anatol 1931,Ja 17,23:3
Six Characters in Search of an Author
1931,Ap 16,29:2
Good Fairy, The 1931,N 25,17:1
Late Christopher Bean, The 1932,N 1,24:3
Gather Ye Rosebuds 1934,N 29,33:2
Gather Ye Rosebuds 1934,D 2,X,1:1
Bishop Misbehaves, The 1935,F 21,22:4
Connor, Allen
Let and Sub-Let 1930,My 20,32:2
Lady Beyond the Moon 1931,Ap 1,36:5
Connor, Frank
His Chinese Wife 1920,My 18,9:3
Montmartre 1922,F 14,20:1
Connor, George
Wanted 1928,Jl 3,19:2
Connor, Kaye
Gypsy Lady 1946,S 18,25:6
Allegro 1952,S 18,36:3
Carousel 1953,My 6,38:1
Connor, T C
Jamboree 1932,N 25,18:4
One Sunday Afternoon 1933,F 16,23:5
Connor, Tim (Miscellaneous)
Thunder Rock 1956,F 27,18:1
Connor, Whitfield
Hamlet 1946,Je 4,18:4
Duchess of Malfi, The 1946,O 16,35:2
Kathleen 1948,F 4,26:2
Winner, The 1954,F 18,34:1
Six Characters in Search of an Author
1955,D 12,38:1
Six Characters in Search of an Author
1955,D 25,II,3:1
Ever Since Paradise 1957,Jl 12,18:4
Makropoulos Secret, The 1957,D 4,52:4
Disenchanted, The 1958,D 4,53:4
Disenchanted, The 1959,Ja 11,II,1:1
There Was a Little Girl 1960,Mr 1,28:1
Everything in the Garden 1967,N 30,60:1
In the Matter of J Robert Oppenheimer
1969,Mr 7,28:1
Connor, William J
Career Angel 1943,N 19,24:2
Connor Twins
Ziegfeld Follies 1922,Je 6,18:2
No Foolin' 1926,Je 25,25:1
Connors, Barry (Playwright)
Applesauce 1924,S 7,VII,1:4
Connors, Frank
Don Q Jr 1926,Ja 28,16:3
Connors, Jack (Choreographer)
Nic-Nax of 1926 1926,Ag 5,19:1
Connors, Jack (Producer)
Roman Servant, A 1934,D 3,14:5
Connors, Noel
Silence 1924,N 13,18:2
Connors, Thomas
Too Many Heroes 1937,N 16,26:2
Connorty, Lyn
Boy Friend, The 1954,O 1,20:1
Connoughton, John
Richard III 1953,D 10,65:2
Conod, Agnes
Veronica's Veil 1950,F 12,II,1:5
Conolle, Jean (Playwright)
King's Mare, The 1966,Jl 21,23:1
Conolly, Patricia
You Can't Take It With You 1965,N 24,32:1
Right You Are (If You Think You Are)
1966,N 23,34:2

Conolly, Patricia—Cont
We Comrades Three 1966,D 21,46:1
Pantagleize 1967,D 1,54:1
Exit the King 1968,Ja 10,48:1
Exit the King 1968,Ja 21,II,1:2
Cherry Orchard, The 1968,Mr 20,41:1
Cocktail Party, The 1968,O 8,42:1
Misanthrope, The 1968,O 10,59:1
Cocktail Party, The 1968,O 20,II,1:1
Cock-A-Doodle Dandy 1969,Ja 21,40:1
Conoly, Marybeth
Sari 1930,Ja 29,27:1
Three's a Crowd 1930,O 16,28:3
Conova, Dorothy (Choreographer)
Aquacircus 1958,Je 30,24:6
Conover, Gordon
Big Fight, The 1928,S 19,33:1
Chinese O'Neill 1929,My 23,27:1
Conover, Grandin (Playwright)
Party on Greenwich Avenue, The 1967,My 11,52:1
Conover, Theresa Maxwell
Don Juan 1921,S 8,14:2
Why Men Leave Home 1922,S 13,18:2
School for Scandal, The 1923,Mr 13,19:2
Peacocks 1924,Mr 2,VIII,2:7
Parasites 1924,N 20,21:1
Trelawney of the 'Wells' 1925,Je 2,16:2
New Gallantry 1925,S 25,24:2
Little Spitfire, The 1926,Ag 17,15:2
Comedy of Women, A 1929,S 14,17:4
Stepping Sisters 1930,Ap 23,24:2
Lady Windermere's Fan 1932,Ja 27,19:3
Play, Genius, Play! 1935,O 31,17:2
Dear Old Darling 1936,Mr 3,25:1
Conquest, Avril
Cocktail Party, The 1950,Ja 23,17:2
Conrad, Barbara
Yerma 1966,D 9,60:1
Conrad, Barnaby (Original Author)
Bicycle Ride to Nevada 1963,S 25,38:1
Conrad, Catherine
Lady in the Dark 1941,Ja 24,14:2
Conrad, Con (Composer)
Greenwich Village Follies 1923,S 21,4:6
Moonlight 1924,Ja 31,13:7
Betty Lee 1924,D 26,18:2
Mercenary Mary 1925,Ap 14,27:3
Kitty's Kisses 1926,My 7,12:2
Americana 1926,Jl 27,15:3
Conrad, Con (Lyricist)
Mercenary Mary 1925,Ap 14,27:3
Conrad, Constance
Foenix in Choir 1958,O 28,40:2
Conrad, Donald
Anne of the Thousand Days 1948,D 9,49:2
Conrad, Eddie
Hassard Short's Ritz Revue 1924,S 18,19:1
Gay Paree 1925,Ag 19,14:3
Vaudeville (Palace) 1926,Jl 13,19:4
Piggy 1927,Ja 12,22:2
Vaudeville (Palace) 1928,Ja 17,23:3
Cross My Heart 1928,S 18,32:7
Vaudeville (Palace) 1931,O 26,22:3
Conrad, Eugene (Lyricist)
Broadway Sho-Window 1936,Ap 13,14:5
Conrad, Eugene (Playwright)
Top Hole 1924,S 2,22:3
Woof, Woof 1929,D 26,20:4
Earl Carroll's Vanities 1930,Jl 2,28:3
Murder at the Vanities 1933,S 13,22:4
Saluta 1934,Ag 29,13:4
Sketch Book 1935,Je 5,22:2
Broadway Sho-Window 1936,Ap 13,14:5
Horse Fever 1940,N 25,21:2
Laffing Room Only 1944,D 25,15:4
Conrad, Genie
Familiar Pattern 1943,S 3,15:6
Career 1943,O 29,22:6
Spring Production 1944,My 20,12:4
Conrad, John
Quick Years, The 1953,N 26,51:2
Noah 1954,O 11,32:2
As You Like It 1955,O 29,12:2
Romeo and Juliet 1955,D 16,36:3
This Island Is Mine 1959,Jl 1,26:4
Conrad, Joseph (Playwright)
One Day More 1926,Mr 19,24:3
One Day More 1933,F 1,13:5
Conrad, Karen
Hairpin Harmony 1943,O 2,18:5
Conrad, Lucille
Lend Me Your Ears! 1936,O 6,28:5
Conrad, Marion
Folies Bergere 1964,Je 3,36:1
Conrad, Michael
Antigone 1956,Ap 3,32:2
Mrs Warren's Profession 1958,Je 26,22:1
Man's a Man, A 1962,S 20,30:2
Conrad, Mona
Having Wonderful Time 1937,F 22,12:5
Conrad, Sid
Trial, The 1955,Je 15,35:2
Conrad Janis and His Tail Gate 5 (Composer)
Marathon '33 1963,D 23,20:1

Conradi, Guy
Petrified Forest, The 1935,Ja 8,26:1
Conradt, Mark (Playwright)
Great Scot! 1965,N 12,56:3
Conray, Allen
New Faces of 1952 1952,My 17,23:2
Conreid, Alice
Noble Prize, The 1935,Jl 9,24:3
Curse You, Jack Dalton 1935,Jl 16,24:1
Conrey, Robert
Mrs O'Brien Entertains 1939,F 9,16:3
Conried, Hans
Can-Can 1953,My 8,28:1
Can-Can 1953,My 17,II,1:1
Tall Story 1959,Ja 30,33:2
Conrow, Emma
Silver Tassie, The 1929,O 25,26:1
Conroy, Audrey
Twelfth Night 1957,Jl 4,16:4
Conroy, Carroll
Tevya and His Daughters 1957,S 17,38:2
All That Fall 1957,O 8,41:2
Cock-A-Doodle Dandy 1958,N 13,39:2
Conroy, Frances
Legend of Lovers 1959,O 28,40:3
Conroy, Frank
Bad Man, The 1920,Ag 31,7:1
Daddy's Gone A-Hunting 1921,S 1,18:3
Daddy's Gone A-Hunting 1921,O 2,VII,1:1
Rose Briar 1922,D 26,11:3
Nobody's Business 1923,O 23,17:1
Fake, The 1924,O 7,26:3
Piker, The 1925,Ja 16,14:1
Sapphire Ring, The 1925,Ap 16,25:2
Human Nature 1925,S 25,24:3
In a Garden 1925,N 17,29:1
Hedda Gabler 1926,Ja 27,16:5
Hedda Gabler 1926,F 21,VII,1:2
Sour Grapes 1926,S 7,19:1
Constant Wife, The 1926,N 30,26:3
Wings Over Europe 1928,D 11,35:1
Karl and Anna 1929,O 8,34:1
Game of Love and Death, The 1929,N 26,28:4
Man Who Changed His Name, The 1932,My 3,25:3
Anatomist, The 1932,O 25,24:3
O Evening Star 1935,D 26,20:1
O Evening Star 1936,Ja 9,24:6
Ghost of Yankee Doodle, The 1937,O 28,28:5
Ghost of Yankee Doodle, The 1937,N 23,26:3
On Borrowed Time 1938,F 4,16:4
Little Foxes, The 1939,F 16,16:2
Little Foxes, The 1939,F 26,IX,1:1
For Keeps 1944,Je 15,17:5
One-Man Show 1945,F 9,21:2
One-Man Show 1945,F 18,II,1:1
Hear That Trumpet 1946,O 8,19:2
Bravo! 1948,N 12,31:2
Point of No Return 1951,O 31,32:2
Point of No Return 1951,D 14,35:2
Point of No Return 1951,D 23,II,3:1
Kind Sir 1953,S 28,21:2
Kind Sir 1953,N 5,41:2
Potting Shed, The 1957,Ja 30,32:1
Potting Shed, The 1957,F 10,II,1:1
Face of a Hero 1960,O 21,29:5
Calculated Risk 1962,N 1,35:1
Conroy, Frank (Producer)
Anatomist, The 1932,O 25,24:3
Conroy, Padraic
Nobody Hears A Broken Drum 1970,Mr 20,55:1
Nobody Hears A Broken Drum 1970,Mr 20,55:1
Conroy, Pamela
Skin of Our Teeth, The 1945,Mr 20,22:8
Conroy, Suzanne
Heigh-Ho, Everybody 1932,My 26,31:2
Conroy, Thom
Johnny 2X4 1942,Mr 17,24:6
Considine, Stephen
John Brown's Body 1953,F 16,17:2
Consorte, Renato
Arena Conta Zumbi 1969,Ag 19,31:1
Constable, Isham
House in Paris, The 1944,Mr 21,17:1
Constance, Beatrice
Lady Billy 1920,D 15,18:2
Constanduros, Mabel (Playwright)
Cold Comfort Farm 1936,Mr 2,13:7
Constant, Connie
Jackpot 1944,Ja 14,15:2
Constant, Lucille
Silver Swan, The 1929,N 28,34:5
Constant, Yvonne
Gay Life, The 1961,N 20,38:1
Come Live With Me 1967,Ja 27,29:1
Constant-Remy
Vocation, La 1926,D 19,VII,3:3
Constanten, Tom
Tarot 1970,D 12,19:1
Constanten, Tom (Composer)
Tarot 1970,D 12,19:1
Constantin, Normand
Mima 1928,D 13,24:2

Constantine, Michael
Cyanamide 1954,Mr 26,17:6
Compulsion 1957,O 25,21:1
Compulsion 1957,N 3,II,1:1
Comic Strip 1958,My 15,26:2
Twelfth Night 1959,Jl 11,10:2
Miracle Worker, The 1959,O 20,44:1
Egg, The 1962,Ja 9,23:2
Arturo Ui 1963,N 12,49:1
Constantinowitz, N (Playwright)
Simple Woman, The 1937,Mr 29,14:1
Conte, Carlo
Jack and Jill 1923,Mr 23,17:2
Night in Paris, A 1926,Ja 6,16:3
Triumph 1935,O 15,18:5
May Wine 1935,D 6,30:3
Bitter Stream 1936,Mr 31,16:6
Conte, Jerry
Long Gallery, The 1958,Mr 7,17:2
Conte, John
Allegro 1947,O 11,10:2
Arms and the Girl 1950,F 3,28:2
Carousel 1954,Je 3,32:2
International Playgirls '64 1964,My 22,40:2
Conte, Louise
Cardinal of Spain, The 1960,D 22,16:6
Conte, Nicholas
My Heart's in the Highlands 1939,Ap 14,29:2
Night Music 1940,F 23,18:2
Heavenly Express 1940,Ap 19,24:2
Walk Into My Parlor 1941,N 20,38:2
Jason 1942,Ja 22,12:2
Family, The 1943,Mr 31,22:4
Conti, Giulia (Playwright)
Enter Madame 1920,Ag 17,11:2
Continentals, The
Show Is On, The 1937,S 20,18:4
Continer, Anthony (Scenic Designer)
Decision 1929,My 28,37:3
Great Scott! 1929,S 3,25:1
Contini, Anita
Man and Superman 1970,F 24,48:1
Moby Dick 1970,Je 3,52:1
Contreras, Bruna (Costume Designer)
Remolienda, La; Bawdy Party 1968,F 3,20:1
Contreras, Bruna (Scenic Designer)
Remolienda, La; Bawdy Party 1968,F 3,20:1
Conty, Fay
Shuffle Along of 1933 1932,D 27,11:3
Converse, Converse
Servant of Two Masters, The 1958,F 11,35:2
Converse, Frank
Henry V 1963,Je 14,37:1
Caesar and Cleopatra 1963,Ag 1,18:2
Much Ado About Nothing 1964,Je 11,26:2
Richard III 1964,Je 12,44:2
Hamlet 1964,Jl 4,9:1
First One Asleep, Whistle 1966,F 28,19:1
Converse, Harry (Composer)
Keep It Clean 1929,Je 25,35:5
Converse, Harry (Lyricist)
Keep It Clean 1929,Je 25,35:5
Converse, Leighton
Old Bill, M P 1926,N 11,22:2
Faust 1927,Ja 4,20:1
Converse, Nan
Exceeding Small 1928,O 23,32:2
Converse, Nell
Young Madame Conti 1937,Ap 1,18:4
Converse, Peggy
Miss Quis 1937,Ap 8,20:5
Infernal Machine, The 1937,D 13,22:7
Comedy of Good and Evil, A 1938,Ap 8,16:3
Wuthering Heights 1939,Ap 28,30:4
Convey, Johnny
Variety Anthology 1932,Mr 21,19:4
Conville, David (Miscellaneous)
Midsummer Night's Dream, A 1962,Jl 2,22:2
Conville, Frank
Ankles Aweigh 1955,Ap 19,27:1
Convy, Bert
Billy Barnes Revue, The 1959,Je 10,42:2
Vintage '60 1960,S 13,41:1
Nowhere to Go But Up 1962,N 12,36:2
Beast in Me, The 1963,My 17,29:1
Morning Sun 1963,O 7,36:2
Love and Kisses 1963,D 19,39:1
Fiddler on the Roof 1964,S 23,56:2
Impossible Years, The 1965,O 14,55:1
Cabaret 1966,N 21,62:1
Cabaret 1966,D 4,II,5:1
Shoot Anything With Hair That Moves
1969,F 3,29:1
Front Page, The 1969,My 12,54:2
Front Page, The 1969,My 25,II,1:1
Front Page, The 1969,N 2,86:1
Conway, Bert
Golden Boy 1937,N 5,18:5
Dance Night 1938,O 15,20:5
Night Music 1940,F 23,18:2
Cue for Passion 1940,D 20,33:4
No for an Answer 1941,Ja 6,10:6
Golden Boy 1952,Mr 13,24:3

Conway, Bert—Cont
Lovers 1956,My 11,23:1
J B 1958,D 12,2:7
As You Like It 1963,Jl 17,19:2
Last Analysis, The 1964,O 2,30:1
Conway, Bert (Director)
Deep Are the Roots 1960,O 4,47:1
Conway, Blade Stanhope
Roof, The 1931,O 31,22:4
Roof, The 1931,N 8,VIII,1:1
Conway, Curt
Midsummer Night's Dream, A 1932,N 18,22:2
Young Go First, The 1935,My 29,16:2
Crime, The 1936,Mr 2,12:3
Marching Song 1937,F 18,18:2
Casey Jones 1938,F 21,14:2
Time of Your Life, The 1939,O 26,26:2
Heavenly Express 1940,Ap 19,24:2
No for an Answer 1941,Ja 6,10:6
Five Alarm Waltz 1941,Mr 14,16:2
Man With Blonde Hair, The 1941,N 5,30:2
Days of Our Youth, The 1941,N 29,15:2
Of V We Sing 1942,F 16,20:3
Troublemakers, The 1954,D 31,11:3
View From the Bridge, A 1955,S 30,21:1
Memory of Two Mondays, A 1955,S 30,21:1
Touch of the Poet, A 1958,O 3,23:2
Conway, Curt (Director)
'Toinette 1961,N 21,46:1
Conway, Dianne
Hello, Dolly! 1967,N 13,61:1
Conway, Edward Charles
Hush Money 1926,Mr 16,22:3
Conway, Fawn
Pirates of Penzance, The 1938,Je 3,16:2
Conway, James
Winter's Tale, The 1958,Jl 21,17:4
Conway, Janet
Hamlet 1954,Ap 24,15:2
Conway, John
Man Who Came to Dinner, The 1940,F 10,19:5
World's Full of Girls, The 1943,D 7,31:2
But Not Goodbye 1944,Ap 12,19:2
Love on Leave 1944,Je 21,23:4
Lower North 1944,Ag 26,15:4
Late George Apley, The 1944,O 20,16:4
Late George Apley, The 1944,N 22,26:2
Story of Mary Surratt, The 1947,F 10,25:2
I Gotta Get Out 1947,S 26,27:2
Conway, Joseph
They Knew What They Wanted 1939,O 3,19:1
Conway, Kate
Tom Sawyer 1931,D 26,15:3
Conway, Kevin
Muzeeka 1968,Ap 29,47:2
Saved 1970,O 29,57:1
Conway, Leo
Earl Carroll's Vanities 1924,S 11,23:6
Conway, Morgan
If a Body 1935,My 1,25:3
Summer Wives 1936,Ap 14,18:1
Mimie Scheller 1936,O 1,28:4
In the Bag 1936,D 18,30:2
Angel Island 1937,O 21,26:2
Conway, Patricia
Mira 1970,Je 3,51:1
Conway, Peggy
They Knew What They Wanted 1924,N 25,27:1
Garrick Gaieties 1925,My 18,12:2
Chief Thing, The 1926,Mr 23,24:2
Hit the Deck! 1927,Ap 26,32:1
Adventure 1928,S 26,25:2
Channel Road, The 1929,O 18,24:2
Conway, Robert C
Strange Orchestra 1933,N 29,23:2
Conway, Russ
Stop Press 1939,Mr 20,13:2
Land Is Bright, The 1941,O 29,26:2
Johnny 2X4 1942,Mr 17,24:6
Roomful of Roses, A 1955,O 18,48:1
Conway, Shane
Little Theatre Tournament; Rachel Cowan
1929,My 9,34:3
Conway, Shane (Playwright)
Little Theatre Tournament; Rachel Cowan
1929,My 9,34:3
Conway, Shirl
Plain and Fancy 1955,Ja 28,14:2
Plain and Fancy 1955,F 6,II,1:1
Plain and Fancy 1956,F 5,II,3:1
Conway, William (Lighting Director)
Importance of Being Earnest, The 1947,Mr 4,30:2
Love for Love 1947,My 27,30:2
Conwell, John
From Morn Till Midnight 1948,D 7,41:6
Earth Spirit 1950,Je 7,33:4
Conwell, Virginia
Talent '49 1949,Ap 13,39:4
Miss Liberty 1949,Jl 16,6:5
Conyngham, Richard
Lazarus Laughed 1948,Ap 9,27:4
Conzona, Federico
Before You're 25 1929,Ap 17,30:2

Coogan, Bob
Mamba's Daughters 1939,Ja 4,24:2
Coogan, Jackie
Vaudeville (Palace) 1929,My 13,26:3
Vaudeville (Palace) 1929,My 13,26:3
Coogan, Richard
Alice in Arms 1945,F 1,18:4
Skipper Next to God 1948,Ja 5,14:5
S S Glencairn; In the Zone 1948,My 21,21:2
S S Glencairn; Bound East for Cardiff
  1948,My 21,21:2
S S Glencairn; Moon of the Caribbees
  1948,My 21,21:2
S S Glencairn; Long Voyage Home, The; Moon of
  the Caribbees; In the Zone; Bound East for
  Cardiff 1948,My 30,II,1:1
Diamond Lil 1948,N 30,33:2
Diamond Lil 1949,F 7,16:2
Rainmaker, The 1954,O 29,28:1
Rainmaker, The 1954,N 7,II,1:1
Coogan and Casey
Vaudeville (Palace) 1926,Ag 17,21:2
Cook, Aileen
Vaudeville (Palace) 1932,Mr 7,13:4
Cook, Barbara
Flahooley 1951,My 15,39:1
Oklahoma! 1953,S 1,19:1
Carousel 1954,Je 3,32:2
Plain and Fancy 1955,Ja 28,14:2
Plain and Fancy 1955,F 6,II,6:6
Candide 1956,D 3,40:2
Candide 1956,D 9,II,5:1
Carousel 1957,S 12,38:2
Music Man, The 1957,D 20,31:1
Music Man, The 1958,S 28,II,1:1
King and I, The 1960,My 12,40:1
King and I, The 1960,My 22,II,1:1
Gay Life, The 1961,N 20,38:1
She Loves Me 1963,Ap 24,39:1
She Loves Me 1963,My 5,II,1:1
Something More! 1964,N 11,36:1
Show Boat 1966,Jl 20,48:1
Little Murders 1967,Ap 26,38:1
Cook, Charles
Kiss Me, Kate 1952,Ja 9,24:6
Kiss Me, Kate 1965,My 13,31:1
Cook, Charles (Miscellaneous)
Happy as Larry 1950,Ja 7,11:2
Cook, Clyde
Vaudeville (Hippodrome) 1924,Ja 1,21:1
Vaudeville (Hippodrome) 1924,Ja 22,15:6
Vaudeville (Palace) 1924,F 12,20:2
Ziegfeld Follies 1924,Mr 18,25:2
Vaudeville (Hippodrome) 1925,D 8,28:6
Vaudeville (Palace) 1930,S 29,19:1
Story of Mary Surratt, The 1947,F 10,25:2
Cook, David
Little Boxes; Coffee Lace, The; Trevor
  1968,Jl 5,20:1
Corsican Brothers, The 1970,Mr 20,56:2
Cook, Donald
Let Us Be Gay 1937,Je 29,18:3
Pride and Prejudice 1937,Ag 3,20:5
Wine of Choice 1938,F 22,18:4
American Landscape 1938,D 5,19:2
Skylark 1939,O 12,32:2
Claudia 1941,F 13,24:2
Claudia 1942,My 25,11:3
Foolish Notion 1945,Mr 14,23:2
Foolish Notion 1945,Mr 18,II,1:1
Made in Heaven 1946,O 25,28:2
Portrait in Black 1947,My 15,30:2
Private Lives 1948,O 5,30:2
Private Lives 1948,N 7,II,1:1
Moon Is Blue, The 1951,Mr 9,29:2
King of Hearts 1954,Ap 2,23:1
King of Hearts 1954,Ap 11,II,1:1
Champagne Complex 1955,Ap 13,33:1
Goodbye Again 1956,Ap 25,38:1
Love Me Little 1958,Ap 15,42:2
Masquerade 1959,Mr 17,42:1
Moon Is Blue, The 1961,Ag 9,29:1
Cook, Donn
Seed of the Brute 1926,N 2,34:3
New York Exchange 1926,D 31,11:2
Spellbound 1927,N 15,26:2
Paris Bound 1927,D 28,26:3
Paris Bound 1928,Ja 15,VIII,1:1
Gypsy 1929,Ja 15,22:2
Half Gods 1929,D 23,18:5
Cook, Donna
Rebound 1930,F 4,29:1
Cook, Elisha
Crooked Friday, The 1925,O 9,27:3
Hello, Lola! 1926,Ja 13,30:1
Henry-Behave 1926,Ag 24,19:4
Gertie 1926,N 16,24:2
Her Unborn Child 1928,Mr 7,28:3
Kingdom of God, The 1928,D 21,30:2
Many a Slip 1930,F 4,29:2
Privilege Car 1931,Mr 4,33:1
Lost Boy 1932,Ja 6,24:4
Merry-Go-Round 1932,Ap 23,11:2

Chrysalis 1932,N 16,15:2
Three-Cornered Moon 1933,Mr 17,20:6
Ah, Wilderness! 1933,S 26,26:3
Ah, Wilderness! 1933,O 3,28:2
Ah, Wilderness! 1934,O 30,23:1
Crime Marches on 1935,O 24,19:1
Come Angel Band 1936,F 19,17:1
Arturo Ui 1963,N 12,49:1
Cook, Fielder (Director)
Cook for Mr General, A 1961,O 20,39:1
Cook, Frank
When the Bough Breaks 1950,Mr 9,25:5
Cook, G Whitfield (Playwright)
Saint's Parade 1930,N 1,23:4
Cook, George
Trial by Jury 1955,O 18,48:1
H M S Pinafore 1955,O 18,48:1
Mikado, The 1962,N 14,43:1
Pirates of Penzance, The 1962,N 21,28:1
H M S Pinafore 1962,N 23,32:4
Trial by Jury 1962,N 23,32:4
Trial by Jury 1964,N 20,40:1
H M S Pinafore 1964,N 20,40:1
Pirates of Penzance, The 1964,N 27,43:1
Mikado, The 1964,N 27,43:1
Ruddigore 1964,D 4,44:1
Pirates of Penzance, The 1966,N 16,54:1
Mikado, The 1966,N 18,36:1
Ruddigore 1966,N 23,28:1
H M S Pinafore 1966,N 24,64:1
H M S Pinafore 1968,O 30,35:1
Mikado, The 1968,N 2,29:4
Pirates of Penzance, The 1968,N 7,54:1
Cook, George Cram (Playwright)
Spring, The 1921,F 6,VI,1:2
Cook, Gerald
Blues, Ballads and Sin-Songs 1954,O 5,23:4
Cook, Gerald (Composer)
Darker Flower, A 1963,Mr 11,7:2
Cook, Gloria
Revels of 1936 1935,S 30,12:4
Summer Wives 1936,Ap 14,18:1
Cook, Gordon
Tenderloin 1960,O 18,47:2
Brigadoon 1967,D 14,59:2
I'm Solomon 1968,Ap 24,51:1
Cook, Jack
Duchess of Malfi, The 1946,O 16,35:2
Cook, James
Ol' Man Satan 1932,O 4,26:3
Goa 1968,F 23,46:1
Miser, The 1969,My 9,35:1
Good Woman of Setzuan, The 1970,N 6,51:1
Cook, Joe
Earl Carroll's Vanities 1923,Jl 6,8:2
Earl Carroll's Vanities 1924,S 11,23:6
Earl Carroll's Vanities 1925,D 29,20:3
Vanities 1926,Ja 10,VII,1:1
Rain or Shine 1928,F 10,26:3
Rain or Shine 1928,F 19,VIII,1:1
Rain or Shine 1929,Ja 6,VIII,4:4
Fine and Dandy 1930,S 7,IX,2:4
Fine and Dandy 1930,S 24,26:1
Fine and Dandy 1930,O 5,IX,1:1
Fanfare 1932,Je 24,15:2
Hold Your Horses 1933,Ag 31,20:4
Hold Your Horses 1933,S 26,26:4
Hold Your Horses 1933,O 15,IX,1:1
Off to Buffalo! 1939,F 22,18:2
It Happens on Ice 1940,O 11,24:3
Cook, Joe Jr
This Is the Army 1942,Jl 5,28:2
This Is the Army 1942,Ag 16,VIII,1:1
Cook, Joel (Lighting Director)
Billygoat Eddie 1964,Ap 21,43:2
Cook, Joel (Scenic Designer)
Billygoat Eddie 1964,Ap 21,43:2
Cook, John (Composer)
Merry Wives of Windsor, The 1956,Je 21,34:4
Twelfth Night 1957,Jl 4,16:4
Henry IV, Part I 1958,Je 25,23:3
Winter's Tale, The 1958,Jl 23,34:3
As You Like It 1959,Jl 1,27:1
King John 1960,Je 29,26:2
Love's Labour's Lost 1961,Je 23,19:1
Love's Labour's Lost 1961,Jl 2,II,1:1
Taming of the Shrew, The 1962,Je 21,25:1
Tempest, The 1962,Je 22,14:1
Richard II 1964,Je 17,47:1
Henry IV, Part I 1965,Je 30,42:1
Falstaff; Henry IV, Part II 1965,Jl 1,35:1
Henry V 1966,Je 8,38:1
Henry VI 1966,Je 9,55:2
Prime of Miss Jean Brodie, The 1968,Ja 17,39:1
Cook, John (Miscellaneous)
Henry V 1956,Je 20,27:2
Cook, Junior
Jimmie's Women 1927,S 27,30:3
Cook, Karle
Nativity Play, The 1937,D 21,29:1
Cook, Lawrence
Volpone 1967,Je 30,29:1
Wrong Way Light Bulb, The 1969,Mr 5,40:1

Cook, Louise
Hot Chocolates 1929,Je 21,17:4
Hummin' Sam 1933,Ap 10,8:8
Cook, Lucius Moore (Director)
Class of '29 1936,My 16,10:3
Help Yourself! 1936,Jl 15,15:1
Cook, Mildred
Great Magician, The 1951,N 22,45:1
American Gothic 1953,N 11,35:6
Conversation Piece 1957,N 19,38:2
Cook, Muriel
Big White Fog 1940,O 23,26:2
Cook, Natalie
What Next 1920,Ja 27,7:2
Cook, Nila Cram
Song of Daphnis, The 1938,Je 23,26:5
Cook, Nila Cram (Choreographer)
Song of Daphnis, The 1938,Je 23,26:5
Cook, Nila Cram (Costume Designer)
Song of Daphnis, The 1938,Je 23,26:5
Cook, Olga
Blossom Time 1921,S 30,10:1
Blossom Time 1921,O 9,VI,1:1
Passing Show of 1924, The 1924,S 4,13:4
Cook, Patrick
Dark of the Moon 1970,Ap 4,21:2
Early Morning 1970,N 26,57:1
Cook, Patsy
Ice Follies 1965,Ja 13,35:1
Ice Follies 1966,Ja 12,27:6
Ice Follies 1967,Ja 11,51:1
Cook, Peter
Beyond the Fringe 1961,Je 25,II,3:5
Beyond the Fringe 1962,O 29,36:1
Beyond the Fringe 1964 1964,Ja 10,18:1
Cook, Peter (Director)
Square in the Eye 1965,My 20,54:1
Princess Rebecca Birnbaum 1966,Mr 7,22:1
Make Like a Dog 1966,Mr 7,22:1
Young Marrieds Play Monopoly 1966,Mr 7,22:1
Suburban Tragedy 1966,Mr 7,22:1
Serjeant Musgrave's Dance 1966,Mr 9,44:1
Hand Is on the Gate, A 1966,S 22,54:1
Cook, Peter (Playwright)
Beyond the Fringe 1962,O 29,36:1
Cook, Phil (Lyricist)
Molly Darling 1922,S 2,10:2
Plain Jane 1924,My 13,24:2
When You Smile 1925,O 6,31:2
Cook, Phil (Playwright)
Plain Jane 1924,My 13,24:2
Cook, Philip
Oklahoma! 1951,My 30,15:2
Oklahoma! 1951,S 13,38:2
Cook, Ray
Great Magician, The 1951,N 22,45:1
Show Boat 1957,Je 28,30:2
Cook, Richard (Miscellaneous)
Innkeepers, The 1956,F 3,19:1
Wake Up, Darling 1956,My 3,34:2
Cook, Robert
They Knew What They Wanted 1924,N 25,27:1
Loose Ankles 1926,Ag 17,15:1
S S Glencairn 1929,Ja 10,24:5
Week-end 1929,O 23,26:4
Cook, Roderick
Kean 1961,N 3,28:2
Girl Who Came to Supper, The 1963,D 9,49:1
Roar Like a Dove 1964,My 22,40:2
Scent of Flowers, A 1969,O 21,42:1
Cook, Roderick (Miscellaneous)
Noel Coward's Sweet Potato 1968,S 30,59:1
Cook, Rodger
Galileo 1968,D 1,88:4
Cook, Vergel
Cave Dwellers, The 1957,O 21,29:2
Cook, Wayne Arey
Mr Jiggins of Jigginstown 1936,D 18,30:2
Cook, Whitfield
Tide Rising 1937,Ja 26,17:2
Cook, Whitfield (Director)
Violet 1944,O 25,16:1
Cook, Whitfield (Original Author)
Violet 1944,O 25,16:1
Cook, Whitfield (Playwright)
Violet 1944,O 25,16:1
Cook, William
Liza 1922,N 28,24:1
Talk About Girls 1927,Je 15,31:3
Cook and Brown
Vaudeville (Palace) 1949,My 20,32:4
Cook Family
Holiday on Ice 1969,Ag 28,44:1
Cooke, Alan
King Lear 1950,Ag 30,26:2
Cooke, Alan (Director)
Queen After Death 1956,Mr 13,33:2
Diary of a Scoundrel 1956,N 5,41:1
Cooke, Alistair (Director)
Hades, the Ladies 1934,Mr 29,25:3
Cooke, Beach
Toto 1921,Mr 22,15:2
Pride 1923,My 3,22:3

Cooke, Beach—Cont
Poor Nut, The 1925,Ap 28,18:1
Cooke, C
Bulls and Belles 1931,Ap 18,17:2
Cooke, Charles (Musical Director)
Boy Friend, The 1970,Ap 15,54:1
Cooke, Charles E (Miscellaneous)
Shuffle Along 1952,My 9,20:5
Cooke, Charles L (Miscellaneous)
Hot Mikado, The 1939,Mr 24,26:2
Cooke, Charles L (Musical Director)
Boy Friend, The 1954,O 1,20:1
Cooke, F O (Composer)
Zuider Zee 1928,D 19,24:4
Cooke, F O (Lyricist)
Zuider Zee 1928,D 19,24:4
Cooke, Geraldine
Clean Beds 1939,My 26,21:2
Cooke, Harry M
Holy Terror, A 1925,S 29,31:2
Strange Prince, The 1926,D 8,24:2
Spread Eagle 1927,Ap 5,30:2
Celebrity 1927,D 27,24:3
Ringside 1928,Ag 30,13:2
Button, Button 1929,O 24,26:1
Red Rust 1929,D 18,31:1
Roar China! 1930,O 28,23:1
Good Earth, The 1932,O 18,23:4
Drums Begin, The 1933,N 25,10:5
John Brown 1934,Ja 23,22:3
I Myself 1934,My 10,24:6
Bride of Torozko, The 1934,Jl 10,24:7
Bride of Torozko, The 1934,S 14,24:2
Stop-Over 1938,Ja 12,16:5
Dance Night 1938,O 15,20:5
Night Music 1940,F 23,18:2
Mr Big 1941,O 1,24:2
Beggars Are Comming to Town 1945,O 29,16:2
Cooke, J Allen
Spring Fever 1925,Ag 4,14:2
Cooke, Jean
Mr Pickwick 1952,S 18,36:3
Ah, Wilderness! 1953,F 7,10:6
Cooke, John (Miscellaneous)
Richard II 1951,Ja 25,21:2
Cooke, John Starr
King Lear 1940,D 16,27:2
Cooke, Martin
Polonaise 1945,O 8,20:2
Cooke, Stephen
Long Christmas Dinner, The 1966,S 7,53:1
Cooke, Thomas Coffin
Loves of Lulu, The 1925,My 12,26:1
Constant Nymph, The 1926,D 10,31:1
Out of the Sea 1927,D 6,26:2
She Stoops to Conquer 1928,My 15,17:1
Sweet Land of Liberty 1929,S 24,29:2
Mr Samuel 1930,N 11,28:4
Rock Me, Julie 1931,F 4,21:1
Black Souls 1932,Mr 31,25:1
Page Pygmalion 1932,Ag 4,17:5
Peace on Earth 1933,N 30,39:2
Hide and Seek 1934,Ag 7,20:2
Stevedore 1934,O 2,18:2
Crime and Punishment 1935,Ja 23,20:3
Bitter Oleander 1935,F 12,24:3
For Valor 1935,N 19,27:5
Daughters of Atreus 1936,O 15,33:1
All the Living 1938,Mr 25,14:4
Dame Nature 1938,S 27,24:3
Cooke, Thomas Coffin (Director)
Judge's Husband, The 1926,S 28,31:1
Cooke, Wanda
All in Love 1961,N 11,15:2
Cooks, Martin
Polonaise 1945,O 8,20:2
Cooksey, Curtis
Thy Name Is Woman 1920,N 16,19:1
Welded 1924,Mr 18,24:1
Play, A 1925,F 11,19:2
Arabesque 1925,O 21,20:2
Fountain, The 1925,D 11,26:1
Jay Walker, The 1926,F 9,23:1
One Man's Woman 1926,My 26,25:1
Man From Toronto, The 1926,Je 18,27:2
Lily Sue 1926,N 17,22:2
Fog-Bound 1927,Ap 2,21:2
House of Women, The 1927,O 4,32:2
Red Dust 1928,Ja 3,29:2
Diamond Lil 1928,Ap 10,32:1
Midsummer Night's Dream, A 1932,N 18,22:2
Twelfth Night 1932,N 19,20:5
Comedy of Errors, The 1932,N 22,25:3
Merchant of Venice, The 1932,N 24,34:5
Romeo and Juliet 1933,F 3,21:5
Chinese Nightingale, The 1934,O 6,20:4
Rip Van Winkle 1935,Ag 7,22:2
Master of the Revels 1935,Ag 14,16:2
Mid-West 1936,Ja 2,21:2
Mid-West 1936,Ja 5,IX,3:1
Mid-West 1936,Ja 8,22:4
Come Angel Band 1936,F 19,17:1
Family Man, A 1936,Jl 8,14:2
Moroni 1936,Ag 19,19:1

There's Always a Breeze 1938,Mr 3,16:2
Boudoir 1941,F 8,18:4
Beautiful People, The 1941,Ap 22,27:2
Vagabond King, The 1943,Je 30,24:2
Our Town 1944,Ja 11,24:5
Take It As It Comes 1944,F 11,17:2
Ryan Girl, The 1945,S 25,28:2
Open House 1947,Je 4,33:4
Cooksey, Curtis (Director)
Bough Breaks, The 1937,N 20,21:4
Cookson, Georgina
Love Goes to Press 1947,Ja 2,22:2
Ring Around the Moon 1950,N 24,30:1
Cookson, Peter
Let's Laugh Again 1937,Ag 24,24:5
Message for Margaret 1947,Ap 17,34:2
Heiress, The 1947,S 30,22:2
Little Blue Light, The 1951,Ap 30,17:2
Can-Can 1953,My 8,28:1
Can-Can 1953,My 17,II,1:1
River Line, The 1957,Ja 3,29:2
Four Winds 1957,S 26,21:2
Girl of the Golden West, The 1957,N 6,44:1
Wonderful Town 1958,Mr 6,32:4
Cookson, Peter (Miscellaneous)
Little Blue Light, The 1951,Ap 30,17:2
Seagulls Over Sorrento 1952,S 12,18:4
Rashomon 1959,Ja 28,36:2
Cookson, Peter (Producer)
Innocents, The 1950,F 2,30:2
Right Honourable Gentleman, The 1965,O 20,50:2
Cool, Janet
Left Bank, The 1931,O 6,35:3
Cool, Walter (Director)
Lady of Mexico 1962,O 20,13:2
Daddy Come Home 1963,Ap 17,33:1
Eternal Sabbath 1963,O 19,17:2
Comforter, The 1964,O 22,42:1
Patrick--The First 1965,F 19,25:1
Go, Go, Go, God is Dead! 1966,O 12,37:1
Man Who Washed His Hands, The 1967,F 16,33:1
Happy Faculty, The 1967,Ap 19,50:1
Guimpes and Saddles 1967,O 11,36:3
Babes Don't Cry Anymore 1968,F 21,55:1
Ballad of John Ogilvie, The 1968,O 9,42:4
Priest in the Cellar, The 1969,F 19,39:1
Reunion of Sorts 1969,O 15,40:1
Five Star Saint 1970,F 11,41:2
Cooley, Isabelle
Long Dream, The 1960,F 18,36:2
Cooley, Leslie
Small Timers, The 1925,Ja 28,15:3
House of Shadows, The 1927,Ap 22,18:4
Cherry Orchard, The 1928,O 16,28:5
Cooley, Scott
Homecoming 1942,N 17,28:5
Coolidge, Joseph
So Proudly We Hail 1938,Mr 30,18:5
So Proudly We Hail 1938,Ap 9,11:1
Coolidge, Philip
Our Town 1938,F 5,18:3
Merchant of Yonkers, The 1938,D 29,14:2
Family Portrait 1939,Mr 9,18:4
Margin for Error 1939,N 4,11:3
Susannah and the Elders 1940,O 30,28:2
In Time to Come 1941,D 29,20:2
Jacobowsky and the Colonel 1944,Mr 15,17:2
Sing Out, Sweet Land! 1944,D 28,24:2
Barefoot Boy With Cheek 1947,Ap 4,20:2
Traitor, The 1949,Ap 1,30:2
Liar, The 1950,My 19,30:2
Legend of Sarah 1950,O 12,42:4
Darkness at Noon 1951,Ja 15,13:4
Barefoot in Athens 1951,N 1,35:2
Gambler, The 1952,O 14,40:1
Crucible, The 1953,Ja 23,15:2
Crucible, The 1953,Jl 2,20:2
Kismet 1953,D 4,2:4
Visit to a Small Planet 1957,F 8,18:1
Visit to a Small Planet 1957,F 24,II,1:1
Rhinoceros 1961,Ja 10,27:1
Hamlet 1964,Ap 10,30:1
Coolidge, Richard
He Who Gets Slapped 1922,Ja 10,15:1
Set a Thief 1927,F 22,22:1
Round Table, The 1930,F 28,20:5
Coolus, Romain (Playwright)
Alarm Clock, The 1923,D 25,26:2
Vacances de Paques, Les 1927,Ja 2,VII,2:1
Guepe, La 1928,O 21,IX,5:6
Antoinette Sabrier 1929,Je 16,VIII,2:3
Pardon, Madame 1930,F 9,VIII,2:6
Coombs, John Marshall (Scenic Designer)
No More Frontier 1931,O 22,27:1
Coon Creek Girls
Hayride 1954,S 14,24:2
Coonan, Sheila
Cyanamide 1954,Mr 26,17:6
Candida 1957,F 9,14:1
Prime of Miss Jean Brodie, The 1968,Ja 17,39:1
Coonen, Paula
Meet Peter Grant 1961,My 11,41:4

Cooney, Dennis
Whisper to Me 1960,N 22,38:6
Every Other Evil 1961,Ja 23,20:2
Ross 1961,D 27,20:2
Love and Kisses 1963,D 19,39:1
In the Summer House 1964,Mr 26,43:1
Midsummer Night's Dream, A 1964,Je 30,23:2
Major Barbara 1965,My 18,33:1
Lion in Winter, The 1966,Mr 4,23:1
Tiger at the Gates 1968,Mr 1,30:1
Cyrano de Bergerac 1968,Ap 26,30:1
Cooney, Edward
Low Bridge 1933,F 10,13:4
Cooney, Edwin
Broken Hearts of Broadway 1944,Je 13,16:2
Cooney, Ray (Playwright)
Not Now Darling 1970,O 30,33:1
Coons, John D
Bright Honor 1936,S 28,14:1
Cooper, Alexander
Earth Journey 1944,Ap 28,24:2
Cooper, Anita
Burning Bush, The 1949,D 17,15:5
Gertie 1952,Ja 31,23:1
Once Upon a Tailor 1955,My 24,36:2
Highway Robbery 1955,N 8,36:1
Beggar's Opera, The 1957,Mr 14,35:1
Cooper, Anthony Kemble
Lass O' Laughter 1925,Ja 9,13:2
School for Scandal, The 1925,D 7,18:2
Thief, The 1927,Ap 23,15:2
Command to Love, The 1927,S 21,27:1
Silent Witness, The 1931,Mr 24,31:5
Aged 26 1936,D 22,32:1
Gloriana 1938,N 26,18:4
Quiet, Please! 1940,O 20,IX,2:3
Quiet, Please! 1940,N 9,20:3
Anne of England 1941,O 8,26:2
Richard III 1943,Mr 27,8:3
Ten Little Indians 1944,Je 28,21:2
Mr Pickwick 1952,S 18,36:3
Foxy 1964,F 17,26:1
Hostile Witness 1966,F 18,26:1
Cooper, Ashley
Topsy and Eva 1924,D 24,11:1
Joker, The 1925,N 17,29:1
Friend Indeed 1926,Ap 27,22:3
Vaudeville (Palace) 1927,Ap 26,33:1
Ringside 1928,Ag 30,13:2
Brothers 1928,D 26,14:3
Let and Sub-Let 1930,My 20,32:2
Singin' the Blues 1931,S 17,21:3
Bulls, Bears and Asses 1932,My 7,11:3
It Happened Tomorrow 1933,My 6,11:5
Tobacco Road 1933,D 5,31:2
New York Idea, The 1948,Ag 18,29:2
Cooper, Bernarr
Across the Board on Tomorrow Morning
  1942,Mr 21,13:5
Theatre of the Soul 1942,Mr 21,13:5
War and Peace 1942,My 22,26:3
Cooper, Bernarr (Director)
Theatre of the Soul 1942,Mr 21,13:5
Cooper, Bryan (Major) (Playwright)
Let the Credit Go 1930,O 26,VIII,4:6
Cooper, Catherine
Joseph 1930,F 13,25:3
Cooper, Charles
All You Need Is One Good Break 1950,F 10,20:3
Winner, The 1954,F 18,34:1
Cooper, Charles (Miscellaneous)
Time to Go 1952,My 8,35:6
Hall of Healing 1952,My 8,35:6
Bedtime Story 1952,My 8,35:6
Cooper, Charlotte
President's Daughter, The 1970,N 4,41:2
Cooper, Chester
Squaring the Circle 1936,Ag 12,15:3
Cooper, Christine
S S Glencairn 1929,Ja 10,24:5
Dark of the Moon 1970,Ap 4,21:2
Cooper, Clancy
Casey Jones 1938,F 21,14:2
Stop Press 1939,Mr 20,13:2
Summer Night 1939,N 3,17:1
Night Music 1940,F 23,18:2
Horse Fever 1940,N 25,21:2
Eight O'Clock Tuesday 1941,Ja 7,18:2
Cooper, Claude
Hottentot, The 1920,Mr 2,9:1
Detour, The 1921,Ag 24,12:2
Steamship Tenacity 1922,Ja 3,20:2
Up the Ladder 1922,Mr 7,11:2
Malvaloca 1922,O 3,22:1
Hospitality 1922,N 14,16:1
Shame Woman, The 1923,O 17,14:1
My Son 1924,S 18,18:2
My Son 1924,S 28,VII,1:1
Mud Turtle, The 1925,Ag 21,8:2
Mud Turtle, The 1925,S 6,VII,1:1
Move On 1926,Ja 19,30:1
You Can't Win 1926,F 17,12:1
Juno and the Paycock 1926,Mr 16,22:1

Cooper, Claude—Cont

Juno and the Paycock 1926,Mr 21,VIII,1:1
Seed of the Brute 1926,N 2,34:3
Crime 1927,F 23,27:3
Celebrity 1927,D 27,24:3
Breaks, The 1928,Ap 17,26:3
Front Page, The 1928,Ag 15,19:2
Front Page, The 1928,Ag 26,VII,1:1
Salt Water 1929,N 27,30:3
They Never Grow Up 1930,Ap 8,27:1
Long Road, The 1930,Jl 20,VIII,2:1
Long Road, The 1930,S 10,30:2
Inspector General, The 1930,D 24,19:2
Gray Shadow 1931,Mr 11,23:4

Cooper, Colleen

Queer People 1934,F 16,16:2

Cooper, Dick

Ice Follies 1966,Ja 12,27:6

Cooper, Doris

Venice Preserv'd 1955,D 13,54:4

Cooper, Dulcie

Clutching Claw, The 1928,F 15,20:1
Married-And How! 1928,Je 15,30:2
Courage 1928,O 9,34:2
Peter Flies High 1931,N 10,28:3
Biography 1937,Ap 11,II,12:8
Fly Away Home 1937,Ap 27,18:1
Happily Ever After 1945,Mr 16,21:2
Brighten the Corner 1945,D 13,33:2
Open House 1947,Je 4,33:4

Cooper, Edward

Legend of Leonora, The 1927,Mr 30,22:4
Lady Dedlock 1929,Ja 1,61:2
Lost Sheep 1930,My 6,33:2
Roar China! 1930,O 28,23:1
Hay Fever 1931,D 30,25:1
Saint Joan 1950,Mr 4,10:6

Cooper, Edwin

Twelfth Night 1926,D 21,21:4
Ship Comes in, A 1934,S 20,21:1
Let Freedom Ring 1935,N 7,26:2
Bury the Dead 1936,Ap 20,17:4
Prelude 1936,Ap 20,17:4
It Can't Happen Here 1936,O 28,30:1
Miss Quis 1937,Ap 8,20:5
Stop-Over 1938,Ja 12,16:5
Washington Jitters 1938,My 3,19:1
Dame Nature 1938,S 27,24:3
Big Blow 1938,O 3,11:2
Ring Around Elizabeth 1941,N 18,32:2
War and Peace 1942,My 22,26:3
Eve of St Mark, The 1942,O 8,30:2
Snafu 1944,O 26,19:5
Gang's All Here, The 1959,O 2,23:1
Deep are the Roots 1960,O 4,47:1
Best Foot Forward 1963,Ap 3,43:1
Displaced Person, The 1966,D 30,15:1
To Bury a Cousin 1967,My 17,38:3

Cooper, Enid

Parnell 1936,My 5,26:2
Empress of Destiny 1938,Mr 10,16:2
Escape This Night 1938,Ap 23,18:1

Cooper, Florence (Playwright)

Group Theatre Sketches 1935,F 11,14:5

Cooper, Fred

Illustrators' Show, The 1936,Ja 23,25:3

Cooper, Fred G (Playwright)

Murray Anderson's Almanac 1929,Ag 15,20:3

Cooper, George

Henry IV, Part I 1946,My 7,25:2
Oedipus; Critic, The 1946,My 21,19:2

Cooper, George W

Blackbirds 1928,My 10,31:3

Cooper, Gerald

Marie Vison, La 1970,Jl 15,29:1

Cooper, Giles (Original Author)

Everything in the Garden 1967,D 10,II,5:1
Everything in the Garden 1968,Ja 25,32:4

Cooper, Giles (Playwright)

Lady of the Camellias, The 1963,Mr 22,7:1
Everything in the Garden 1967,N 30,60:1

Cooper, Gladys

Second Mrs Tanqueray, The 1922,Jl 9,VI,1:1
Diplomacy 1924,Mr 16,VIII,1:7
Letter, The 1927,Mr 27,VII,2:6
Excelsior 1928,S 30,IX,1:3
Sacred Flame, The 1929,Mr 3,VIII,2:5
Cynara 1930,Jl 13,VIII,1:3
Painted Veil, The 1931,O 11,VIII,2:4
King, Queen, Knave 1932,F 18,24:4
King, Queen, Knave 1932,Mr 6,VIII,2:4
Dr Pygmalion 1932,Ap 24,VIII,1:1
Firebird 1932,S 25,IX,1:3
Rats of Norway, The 1933,Ap 30,IX,1:7
Acropolis 1933,N 24,25:8
Acropolis 1933,D 10,X,3:6
Shining Hour, The 1934,F 14,22:6
Shining Hour, The 1934,F 25,IX,1:1
Shining Hour, The 1934,S 5,25:4
Shining Hour, The 1934,S 23,X,3:6
Untitled-Benefit 1935,Je 23,IX,1:3
Othello 1935,S 13,19:2
Macbeth 1935,S 17,26:3
Othello 1935,S 22,X,2:5

Othello 1935,S 28,13:2
Macbeth 1935,O 8,26:4
Call It a Day 1936,Ja 21,26:7
Call It a Day 1936,Ja 29,15:2
Call It a Day 1936,F 9,X,1:1
White Christmas 1936,Jl 7,22:2
Close Quarters 1938,II,3:5
Good-Bye to Yesterday 1937,N 21,XI,3:6
Dodsworth 1938,F 23,26:2
Dodsworth 1938,Mr 13,XI,3:1
Lysistrata 1938,Ag 7,IX,1:5
Spring Meeting 1938,D 9,30:4
Astonished Heart, The; Tonight at Eight
  1940,Ag 6,15:3
Tonight at 8:30 1940,Ag 11,IX,11:2
Morning Star, The 1942,S 15,18:4
Morning Star, The 1942,S 20,VIII,1:1
Indifferent Shepherd, The 1948,Mr 14,II,2:4
Relative Values 1951,N 29,41:2
Relative Values 1951,D 9,II,7:7
Question of Fact, A 1954,Ja 17,II,4:4
Night of The Ball, The 1955,Ja 13,31:8
Night of The Ball, The 1955,F 13,II,3:1
Chalk Garden, The 1955,O 27,29:1
Chalk Garden, The 1955,N 13,II,1:1
Crystal Heart, The 1957,F 20,37:1
Bird of Time 1961,Je 25,II,3:5
Passage to India, A 1962,F 1,23:1
Passage to India, A 1962,F 11,II,1:1

Cooper, Gladys (Director)

Astonished Heart, The; Tonight at Eight
  1940,Ag 6,15:3

Cooper, Gladys (Producer)

Spring Meeting 1938,D 9,30:4

Cooper, Greta Kemble

Peg o' My Heart 1921,F 15,7:1
Tarzan of the Apes 1921,S 8,14:3
National Anthem, The 1922,Ja 24,16:3
Manhattan 1922,Ag 16,7:5
Dagmar 1923,Ja 23,18:2
Furies, The 1928,Mr 8,23:1

Cooper, Guy

Mr Papavert 1932,Ja 23,18:6

Cooper, Hal

First Lady 1952,My 29,18:5

Cooper, Harry

All the King's Men 1963,Jl 12,12:1

Cooper, Hazel

Howdy King 1926,D 14,24:4

Cooper, Helen (Playwright)

Have I Got a Girl for You! 1963,D 3,53:2

Cooper, Helmar

Hajj Malik, El 1970,O 4,II,5:1

Cooper, Hi (Playwright)

Girl From Nantucket, The 1945,N 9,17:2

Cooper, Horace

Champion, The 1921,Ja 4,11:1
Secrets 1922,D 26,11:1
Merry Wives of Windsor, The 1928,Mr 20,20:1
See Naples and Die 1929,S 27,30:4
Unconquered, The 1940,F 14,25:2
Mr and Mrs North 1941,Ja 13,11:2
Duke in Darkness, The 1944,Ja 25,15:2
Sheppey 1944,Ap 19,27:2
Sleep No More 1944,S 1,11:5
Million Dollar Baby 1945,D 22,17:2
Land's End 1946,D 12,37:5
Where's Charley? 1948,O 12,33:2
Where's Charley? 1951,Ja 30,21:7
Room Service 1953,Ap 7,34:1
Hot Corner, The 1956,Ja 26,25:2
Hotel Paradiso 1957,Ap 12,22:2
Killer, The 1960,Mr 23,33:1

Cooper, Irving (Miscellaneous)

Does a Tiger Wear a Necktie? 1969,F 26,38:1

Cooper, Irving (Playwright)

Have I Got a Girl for You! 1963,D 3,53:2

Cooper, Irving (Producer)

Bomboola 1929,Je 27,17:3
There's Always a Breeze 1938,Mr 3,16:2
Grey Farm 1940,My 4,12:7
Number, The 1951,O 31,33:2

Cooper, Jackie

Magnolia Alley 1949,Ap 19,29:2
Mister Roberts 1950,Jl 20,22:4
Mister Roberts 1951,Jl 23,II,1:6
Remains to Be Seen 1951,O 4,37:1
King of Hearts 1954,Ap 2,23:1
King of Hearts 1954,Ap 11,II,1:1

Cooper, James Wayne

Aiglon, L' 1925,O 31,20:3

Cooper, Jane

Light of the World, The 1920,Ja 7,17:1
Clair de Lune 1921,Ap 19,15:1
George White's Scandals 1935,D 26,20:2

Cooper, Jerry

Revels of 1936 1935,S 30,12:4
Boys and Girls Together 1940,O 2,19:2

Cooper, Jimmie (Playwright)

Fata Morgana 1931,D 26,15:3

Cooper, Jimmie (Producer)

Zeppelin 1929,Ja 15,22:3
Seven 1929,D 28,10:5

Cooper, Jimmie (Producer)—Cont

Blue Ghost, The 1930,Mr 11,24:5
Woman Denied, A 1931,F 26,21:1

Cooper, John D (Playwright)

Ruy Blas 1957,D 14,16:3

Cooper, John D (Translator)

Ruy Blas 1957,D 14,16:3

Cooper, John W

Kilpatrick's Old-Time Minstrels 1930,Ap 21,20:2

Cooper, Josephine

Power of Darkness, The 1948,O 11,28:2

Cooper, Judith (Costume Designer)

House of Leather, The 1970,Mr 19,56:1

Cooper, June

Help! Help! the Globolinks 1970,D 24,10:2

Cooper, Laura

Electra 1969,Ag 8,14:1

Cooper, Lew (Producer)

Run, Little Chillun 1943,Ag 14,6:1

Cooper, Lillian Kemble

Night Boat, The 1920,F 3,18:1
New Morality, The 1921,Ja 31,10:1
National Anthem, The 1922,Ja 24,16:3
Mountebank, The 1923,My 8,22:2
New Poor, The 1924,Ja 8,26:1
Our Betters 1928,F 21,18:2
Twelfth Night 1932,N 19,20:5
For Services Rendered 1933,Ap 13,15:5
Roman Servant, A 1934,D 3,14:5
Astonished Heart, The; Tonight at Eight
  1940,Ag 6,15:3

Cooper, Lou (Composer)

Of V We Sing 1942,F 16,20:3

Cooper, Lou (Miscellaneous)

Let Freedom Sing 1942,O 6,18:2

Cooper, Mae

Bobino 1944,Ap 7,23:4

Cooper, Marilyn

Annie Get Your Gun 1957,Mr 9,15:5
West Side Story 1957,S 27,14:4
Gypsy 1959,My 22,31:6
I Can Get It for You Wholesale 1962,Mr 23,29:1
West Side Story 1964,Ap 9,24:2
Hallelujah, Baby! 1967,Ap 27,51:1
Golden Rainbow 1968,F 5,27:1
Teaspoon Every Four Hours, A 1969,Je 16,57:1
Two by Two 1970,N 11,37:1

Cooper, Mary

Doughgirls, The 1942,D 31,19:2
Winged Victory 1943,N 22,24:1
French Touch, The 1945,D 10,18:2
Cloud 7 1958,F 15,15:2
What Shall We Tell Caroline? 1961,N 22,24:2

Cooper, Maurice

Swing Mikado, The 1939,Mr 2,18:2

Cooper, Maury

Othello 1964,Jl 15,29:1
Othello 1964,O 13,48:1
Baal 1965,My 7,33:2
Coriolanus 1965,Jl 15,23:1
All's Well That Ends Well 1966,Je 17,39:1
Gloria and Esperanza 1970,F 5,32:1
Good Woman of Setzuan, The 1970,N 6,51:1

Cooper, Melville

Journey's End 1929,Jl 14,IX,5:1
Laburnum Grove 1935,Ja 15,23:5
Laburnum Grove 1935,Ja 20,X,1:1
Jubilee 1935,S 23,20:3
Jubilee 1935,S 29,X,1:1
Jubilee 1935,O 14,20:1
Tovarich 1937,Ap 25,X,2:4
Merry Widow, The 1943,Ag 5,19:2
Merry Widow, The 1943,Ag 22,II,5:1
Merry Widow, The 1943,S 26,II,1:5
While the Sun Shines 1944,S 20,21:3
While the Sun Shines 1944,S 24,II,1:1
Firebird of Florence 1945,Mr 23,13:4
Pygmalion 1945,D 27,16:1
Pygmalion 1946,Ja 6,II,1:1
Gypsy Lady 1946,S 18,25:6
Haven, The 1946,N 14,39:4
Inspector Calls, An 1947,O 22,38:2
Eurydice 1948,O 17,I,67:4
Liar, The 1950,My 19,30:2
Day After Tomorrow 1950,O 27,25:2
Make a Wish 1951,Ap 19,38:1
Much Ado About Nothing 1952,My 2,20:1
Escapade 1953,N 19,40:1
Escapade 1953,N 29,II,1:1
Merry Widow, The 1957,Ap 11,36:6
Importance of Being Earnest, The 1963,F 27,5:2
Hostile Witness 1966,F 18,26:1
Charley's Aunt 1970,Jl 6,38:1

Cooper, Melville (Director)

Helen Goes to Troy 1944,Ap 25,17:2

Cooper, Miriam

Joy of Serpents 1930,Ap 4,22:4

Cooper, Norton (Playwright)

Ballad of Jazz Street, The 1959,N 12,28:1

Cooper, Olive

Girl With Carmine Lips, The 1920,Ag 11,6:1

Cooper, Pat

Jimmy Roselli Show, The 1969,My 3,39:1

Cooper, Patricia (Miscellaneous)
Serpent, The 1970,Je 2,35:1
Cooper, Peggy
Zorba 1968,N 18,58:1
Strada, La 1969,D 15,63:1
Rothschilds, The 1970,O 20,40:1
Cooper, Ralph
Vaudeville (Palace) 1932,My 23,18:7
Cooper, Reni
Miss Emily Adam 1960,Mr 30,43:1
Cooper, Rex
By the Beautiful Sea 1954,Ap 9,20:1
Cooper, Rex (Choreographer)
Seventeen 1951,Jl 1,II,9:5
Cooper, Richmond
Dooley Cashes In 1935,Ag 17,18:6
Cooper, Robert
Gentlemen Prefer Blondes 1949,D 9,35:3
Cooper, Roy
Prime of Miss Jean Brodie, The 1968,Ja 17,39:1
Prime of Miss Jean Brodie, The 1968,Ja 28,II,1:1
Canterbury Tales; Miller's Tale, The 1969,F 4,34:1
Canterbury Tales; Merchant's Tale, The
  1969,F 4,34:1
Canterbury Tales; Pilgrims, The 1969,F 4,34:1
Canterbury Tales; Steward's Tale, The
  1969,F 4,34:1
Cooper, Sally
Lady Windermere's Fan 1946,O 15,29:2
Cooper, Saralou
Greenwillow 1960,Mr 9,38:1
Greenwich Village U S A 1960,S 29,30:5
Cooper, Scott
Gold 1921,Je 2,14:2
World We Live In, The 1922,N 1,16:1
Cooper, Tamar
Cyrano de Bergerac 1953,N 13,24:3
Cooper, Terence
Fantasticks, The 1961,S 8,36:5
Cooper, Tex
Tickle Me 1920,Ag 18,9:1
Green Grow the Lilacs 1931,Ja 27,21:2
Round-Up, The 1932,Mr 8,19:4
Cooper, Theodore (Lighting Director)
Texas Li'l Darlin' 1949,N 26,10:5
Cooper, Theodore (Scenic Designer)
Texas Li'l Darlin' 1949,N 26,10:5
Story for a Sunday Evening, A 1950,N 18,10:5
King Lear 1956,Ja 13,17:1
Cooper, Violet Kemble
Clair de Lune 1921,Ap 19,15:1
Clair de Lune 1921,Ap 24,VI,1:1
Silver Fox, The 1921,S 6,13:1
Laughing Lady, The 1923,F 13,25:1
Camel's Back, The 1923,N 4,19:2
Camel's Back, The 1923,N 18,VIII,1:1
Vaudeville (Palace) 1924,Ap 1,18:1
Hassan 1924,S 23,23:1
Servant in the House, The 1925,Ap 8,24:2
Last Night of Don Juan, The 1925,N 10,23:2
Unchastened Woman, The 1926,F 21,VII,1:2
On Approval 1926,O 19,27:1
Command to Love, The 1927,S 21,27:1
Apple Cart, The 1930,F 25,30:1
Lysistrata 1930,Je 1,VIII,1:1
Lysistrata 1930,Je 6,20:1
Lonely Way, The 1931,F 22,VIII,4:1
He 1931,S 22,33:1
Mad Hopes, The 1932,D 2,26:3
Cooper, Winifred
Polly 1923,Ap 8,VIII,1:7
Cooper, Wyatt
Picnic 1957,F 21,32:1
Cooper and Redello
Vanities 1927,F 22,19:1
Cooper-Cliffe, H
Tendresse, La 1922,S 26,18:1
Scaramouche 1923,O 25,14:2
Miss Gulliver Travels 1931,N 26,36:4
O'Flynn, The 1934,D 28,24:1
Cooperman, Doris
John Brown 1950,My 4,32:7
Coopersmith, Jerome (Miscellaneous)
Lady or the Tiger?, The 1966,O 19,53:1
Passionella 1966,O 19,53:1
Diary of Adam and Eve, The 1966,O 19,53:1
Coopersmith, Jerome (Playwright)
Baker Street 1965,F 17,36:1
Ballad for a Firing Squad 1968,D 12,64:2
Cooperstein, Nancy (Producer)
Viet Rock 1966,N 11,38:1
Cooray, William
Hindu, The 1922,Mr 22,13:3
Heat Wave 1931,F 18,14:6
Coote, Robert
Love of Four Colonels, The 1953,Ja 16,17:2
Dear Charles 1954,S 16,37:2
Dear Charles 1954,S 26,II,1:1
My Fair Lady 1956,Mr 16,20:2
My Fair Lady 1956,Mr 25,II,1:1
My Fair Lady 1956,Je 3,II,1:1
Camelot 1960,D 5,42:1

Coots, Clayton
Rumple 1957,N 7,42:2
Coots, Clayton (Miscellaneous)
Tall Story 1959,Ja 30,33:2
Coots, J Fred
Vaudeville (Palace) 1931,Je 15,23:5
Chalked Out 1937,Mr 26,24:2
Cuckoos on the Hearth 1941,S 17,26:2
Coots, J Fred (Composer)
Spice of 1922 1922,Jl 7,12:4
Sally, Irene and Mary 1922,S 5,21:2
Artists and Models 1924,O 16,33:3
Artists and Models 1925,Je 25,16:2
June Days 1925,Ag 7,12:5
Gay Paree 1925,Ag 19,14:3
Night in Paris, A 1926,Ja 6,16:3
Merry World, The 1926,Je 9,18:3
Night in Paris, A 1926,Jl 27,15:4
White Lights 1927,O 12,30:4
Carry On 1929,N 3,IX,1:7
Sons o' Guns 1929,N 27,30:4
Coots, J Fred (Lyricist)
Sons o' Guns 1929,N 27,30:4
Coover, Rex
Smiling Faces 1932,Ag 31,12:3
Copani, Peter
Courtyard 1960,Mr 1,28:1
Copani, Peter (Playwright)
Where People Gather 1967,O 26,56:1
Cope, John
Cave Girl, The 1920,Ag 19,12:2
Two Blocks Away 1921,Ag 31,8:3
Abie's Irish Rose 1922,My 24,22:4
Cope, Norman
King Lear 1923,Mr 10,9:4
Sylvia 1923,Ap 26,22:1
Copeau, Jacques
Locandiera, La 1923,N 1,24:1
Imbecile 1923,N 1,24:1
As You Like It 1934,N 11,IX,3:6
Napoleon Unique 1936,N 13,27:3
Copeau, Jacques (Director)
Paquebot Tenacity, Le 1920,Ag 15,VI,1:1
Brothers Karamazov, The 1927,Ja 4,20:1
Brothers Karamazov, The 1927,Ja 9,VII,1:1
Napoleon Unique 1936,N 13,27:3
As You Like It 1938,Jl 31,IX,6:8
Copeau, Jacques (Playwright)
Brothers Karamazov, The 1927,Ja 4,20:1
Illusion, L' 1928,D 16,IX,2:1
As You Like It 1934,N 11,IX,3:6
Copelan, Sheila
Miser, The 1955,Mr 18,34:2
Song of Songs 1958,O 29,31:1
Another Evening With Harry Stoones
  1961,O 23,22:2
Copeland, Aaron (Musical Director)
Miracle at Verdun 1931,Mr 17,34:6
Copeland, Andrew
Sugar Hill 1931,D 26,15:2
Copeland, Bill
Mahagonny 1970,Ap 29,51:1
Copeland, George
Untitled-Recital 1923,D 29,8:2
Copeland, George (Composer)
Assumption of Hannele, The 1924,F 16,16:2
Copeland, George (Miscellaneous)
Pierrot the Prodigal; Enfant Prodigue, L'
  1925,Mr 7,8:1
Pierrot the Prodigal 1925,Mr 15,VIII,1:1
Copeland, James
These Are the Times 1950,My 11,37:2
Master Builder, The 1957,D 18,42:7
Copeland, Jane
Tree Grows in Brooklyn, A 1951,Ap 20,24:3
Copeland, Joan
Sundown Beach 1948,S 8,37:1
Detective Story 1949,Mr 24,34:2
Not for Children 1951,F 14,35:2
Grass Is Always Greener, The 1955,F 16,25:2
Miser, The 1955,Mr 18,34:2
Conversation Piece 1957,N 19,38:2
Handful of Fire 1958,O 2,45:3
Delightful Season, A 1960,S 29,30:1
Something More! 1964,N 11,36:1
Two by Two 1970,N 11,37:1
Two by Two 1970,N 22,II,1:1
Copeland, John
Romeo and Jeanette 1969,D 16,53:1
Copeland, Kayo
Nine Girls 1943,Ja 14,26:2
Copeland, Martha
Woof, Woof 1929,D 26,20:4
Copeland, Mary Jean
Men to the Sea 1944,O 4,25:2
Copeland, Maurice
Tempest, The 1970,F 15,67:1
Copeland, Nick
Tattle Tales 1933,Je 2,22:6
Copeland, Nick (Playwright)
Tattle Tales 1933,Je 2,22:6

Copeland, Norval
Guests of the Nation 1958,Je 27,18:5
Copeland, Vincent
Missouri Legend 1938,S 20,27:2
Mamba's Daughters 1940,Mr 25,10:4
Copeland, Virginia
Lightnin' 1938,S 16,17:2
Saint of Bleecker Street, The 1954,D 28,21:1
Saint of Bleecker Street, The 1955,Ja 2,II,1:1
Copeland, William
Pirates of Penzance, The 1966,My 24,54:1
H M S Pinafore 1966,Je 8,41:2
Copelin, David
Bacchae, The 1969,Mr 15,24:1
Copenhaver, Charles (Producer)
Kumquat in the Persimmon Tree, The
  1962,Je 19,27:2
Copenhaver, Charles (Scenic Designer)
Kumquat in the Persimmon Tree, The
  1962,Je 19,27:2
Copes, Juan Carlos
New Faces of 1962 1962,F 2,25:1
Copland, Aaron (Composer)
Garrick Gaieties 1930,Je 5,29:2
Pepper Mill 1937,Ja 6,19:4
Second Hurricane 1937,Ap 22,18:4
Copley, Peter
Henry IV, Part I 1946,My 7,25:2
Henry IV, Part II 1946,My 8,33:4
Oedipus; Critic, The 1946,My 21,19:2
Copley, Peter (Miscellaneous)
Henry IV, Part I 1946,My 7,25:2
Oedipus; Critic, The 1946,My 21,19:2
Copp, Marian
House of Bernarda Alba, The 1951,Ja 8,14:6
Coppage, Keith
Bitter Tulips 1936,Mr 5,24:6
Coppel, Alec (Mrs) (Original Author)
Gazebo, The 1958,D 13,2:7
Coppel, Alec (Original Author)
Gazebo, The 1958,D 13,2:7
Coppel, Alec (Playwright)
I Killed the Count 1937,D 11,23:4
I Killed the Count 1942,S 4,18:1
Genius and the Goddess, The 1957,D 11,41:1
Gazebo, The 1958,D 13,2:7
Coppicus, F C (Producer)
Mei Lan-Fang 1930,F 17,18:2
Pepper Mill 1937,Ja 6,19:4
Coppin, Grace
Fireman's Flame, The 1937,O 11,26:2
All the Living 1938,Mr 25,14:4
As You Like It 1939,My 9,28:4
As You Like It; Midsummer Night's Dream, A;
  Comedy of Errors, The; Taming of the Shrew,
  The 1939,My 9,28:4
Flight Into China 1939,S 12,28:1
Taming of the Shrew, The 1940,F 6,17:2
Medicine Show 1940,Ap 13,20:6
Gabrielle 1941,Mr 26,26:2
Trojan Women, The 1941,Ap 9,32:5
Moon Vine, The 1943,F 12,22:2
Secret Room, The 1945,N 8,16:2
Rip Van Winkle 1947,Jl 16,28:2
Tragedian in Spite of Himself, A 1948,F 6,29:2
On the Harmfulness of Tobacco 1948,F 6,29:2
Wedding, The 1948,F 6,29:2
Bear, The 1948,F 6,29:2
Richard III 1949,F 9,33:2
Richard III 1949,F 13,II,1:1
Coppola, Anton (Miscellaneous)
New Faces of 1952 1952,My 17,23:2
Coppola, Anton (Musical Director)
Livin' the Life 1957,Ap 29,20:1
Bravo Giovanni 1962,My 21,41:2
Rugantino 1964,F 7,34:1
My Fair Lady 1964,My 21,43:2
South Pacific 1965,Je 3,25:1
How to Succeed in Business Without Really Trying
  1966,Ap 21,45:1
My Fair Lady 1968,Je 14,42:1
Coppola, William
Show Boat 1961,Ap 13,32:1
Porgy and Bess 1961,My 18,40:1
Lend an Ear 1969,O 29,32:1
Coquatrix, Bruno (Miscellaneous)
Grand Music Hall of Israel, The 1968,F 7,42:1
Coquelin, Jean
Cyrano de Bergerac 1926,Ja 24,II,8:5
Cora Youngblood Corson's Band
He Loved the Ladies 1927,My 11,29:2
Coral, Cecile
Pirates of Penzance, The 1942,F 20,20:2
Coral, Tito
Night in Spain, A 1927,My 4,28:2
Hot-Cha! 1932,Mr 9,17:3
Mexicana 1939,Ap 22,14:4
My Romance 1948,O 20,38:5
Coram, Ralph
Night in Paris, A 1926,Ja 6,16:3
Vaudeville (Palace) 1928,Ja 24,26:4
Vaudeville (Palace) 1928,Jl 10,17:3

Coray, Ann
Joan of Lorraine 1946,N 19,40:2
Coray, Jerome
Blue and the Gray, The; War Is Hell Gray, The 1929,D 27,26:4
Corbeau, Abbe
Rust 1924,F 1,12:1
Corbet, Gerald
Laughing Woman, The 1936,O 14,30:1
Corbet, James (Playwright)
Chinese Bungalow, The 1929,F 3,VIII,2:1
Corbeth, Jimmie
Shakespeare in Harlem 1959,O 28,40:7
Corbett, Alastair
Hands Across the Sea 1936,N 25,17:2
Corbett, Dee
'Toinette 1961,N 21,46:1
Corbett, Dee (Miscellaneous)
'Toinette 1961,N 21,46:1
Corbett, Don
Piggy 1927,Ja 12,22:2
Corbett, Frank
They Never Come Back 1920,D 19,I,22:3
Espanola 1921,D 30,13:1
I'll Say She Is 1924,My 20,15:1
Forest Ring, The 1930,Ap 26,11:2
Corbett, Frank T (Composer)
They Never Come Back 1920,D 19,I,22:3
Espanola 1921,D 30,13:1
Man From Earth, The 1923,Ja 3,6:2
Corbett, George
Mr Jiggins of Jigginstown 1936,D 18,30:2
Corbett, Gretchen
After the Rain 1967,O 10,54:1
Bench, The 1968,Mr 5,35:2
Forty Carats 1968,D 27,45:1
Forty Carats 1969,Ja 5,II,1:3
Wars of the Roses, The (Part I) 1970,Jl 2,30:1
Henry VI, Parts I, II, III 1970,Jl 5,II,3:1
Corbett, Hilary (Costume Designer)
Heartbreak House 1968,Jl 6,9:1
Chemmy Circle, The 1968,Ag 10,17:2
Doctor's Dilemma, The 1969,Je 24,37:1
Corbett, James
Circle, The 1938,Ap 19,24:2
Woman Brown, The 1939,D 9,18:5
Corbett, James J
Friars Club Frolic 1921,Je 13,16:2
All-Star Jamboree 1921,Jl 14,18:1
Vaudeville (Hippodrome) 1926,F 23,26:2
Vaudeville (New Amsterdam Theatre) 1931,Je 22,17:3
Corbett, Jim
Connection, The 1959,Jl 16,30:2
New Faces of 1962 1962,F 2,25:1
Corbett, Leonora
Business With America 1933,Ja 1,IX,1:3
Inside the Room 1934,D 23,15:3
Dusty Ermine 1936,Mr 7,11:6
Sarah Simple 1937,My 23,X,2:1
Blithe Spirit 1941,N 6,26:2
Blithe Spirit 1941,N 16,IX,1:1
Park Avenue 1946,N 5,31:2
Corbett, Tony (Composer)
William Had the Words! 1964,Mr 30,36:1
Corbett, Tony (Lighting Director)
Twelfth Night 1970,Ja 1,18:1
Corbett, William
Wasp, The 1923,Mr 28,14:3
Robert E Lee 1923,N 21,23:1
Thoroughbreds 1924,S 9,12:1
Milgrim's Progress 1924,D 23,17:1
Not Herbert 1926,Ja 27,16:2
Her Unborn Child 1928,Mr 7,28:3
Under the Gaslight 1929,Ap 3,27:1
Privilege Car 1931,Mr 4,33:1
Cradle Snatchers 1932,N 17,23:2
John Brown 1934,Ja 23,22:3
Corbie, Francis
Cape Smoke 1925,F 17,19:1
Corbin, Albert
Wayward Saint, The 1955,F 18,17:1
White Devil, The 1955,Mr 15,32:5
Henry IV, Part I 1955,S 22,34:2
Carefree Tree, The 1955,O 12,37:2
Venice Preserv'd 1955,D 13,54:4
School for Wives 1957,Je 20,23:4
Edward II 1958,F 12,32:5
Bonds of Interest, The 1958,My 7,43:1
Fashion 1959,Ja 21,27:1
Duchess of Malfi, The 1962,Mr 5,27:1
Devils, The 1963,N 5,25:1
Colombe 1965,F 24,33:1
White Devil, The 1965,D 7,56:1
Stephen D 1966,Ag 5,17:1
Tiger at the Gates 1968,Mr 1,30:1
Prince of Peasantmania 1970,F 22,88:1
Corbin, Barry
Richard II 1968,Je 24,42:3
Love's Labour's Lost 1968,Je 28,36:1
Hamlet 1969,Je 30,33:1
Henry V 1969,N 11,43:1

Corbin, Clayton
Moby Dick 1955,Ap 26,25:3
Ivory Branch, The 1956,My 25,27:1
Land Beyond the River, A 1957,Mr 29,15:7
Raisin' Hell in the Son 1962,Jl 3,13:2
Seven Scenes for Yeni 1963,My 13,36:2
Telemachus Clay 1963,N 16,17:2
Benito Cereno 1964,N 2,62:2
My Kinsman, Major Molineux 1964,N 2,62:2
Prodigal Son, The 1965,My 21,19:1
Royal Hunt of the Sun, The 1965,O 27,36:2
Prometheus Bound 1967,My 11,52:1
Titus Andronicus 1967,Ag 10,43:2
Tempest, The 1970,F 15,67:1
Corbin, Dick
Love Is No Heaven 1943,Mr 16,15:3
Corbin, Dick (Scenic Designer)
Love Is No Heaven 1943,Mr 16,15:3
Corbin, W H (Miscellaneous)
It's the Valet 1933,D 15,25:4
Corbit Twins
Variety Anthology 1932,Mr 21,19:4
Corby, Don
South Pacific 1961,Ap 27,26:3
Corby, Ellen
Child Buyer, The 1962,My 14,35:1
Corby, Joseph
Illya Darling 1967,Ap 12,37:1
Ballad for a Firing Squad 1968,D 12,64:2
Corby, Richard
Home Is the Hero 1945,Ja 20,16:4
Corciade
Bourgeoise, La 1927,O 2,VIII,2:4
Corcoran, Catherine
Kit Marlowe 1936,My 24,35:1
Corcoran, Gladys
Trojan Women, The 1923,My 27,10:2
Corcoran, Jane
Drifting 1922,Ja 3,20:3
World We Live In, The 1922,N 1,16:1
Kitty's Kisses 1926,My 7,12:2
Street Scene 1929,Ja 11,20:4
Little Orchard Annie 1930,Ap 22,33:1
Little Women 1931,D 8,36:2
Old Lady Shows Her Medals, The 1932,Mr 8,19:3
Alice Sit-By-The-Fire 1932,Mr 8,19:3
Saturday Night 1933,Mr 1,13:2
Party, A 1933,Ag 24,18:4
While Parents Sleep 1934,Je 5,28:2
Corda, Michael (Composer)
Safari! 1955,My 12,32:6
Corday, Audree
Ever Green Lady, The 1922,O 12,25:2
Barefoot 1925,O 20,29:2
Woman Disputed, A 1926,S 29,23:2
Henry V 1928,Mr 16,26:2
Guinea Pig, The 1929,Ja 8,35:1
Scotland Yard 1929,S 28,16:6
Modern Virgin, A 1931,My 21,33:4
Divorce Me, Dear 1931,O 7,29:2
Fatal Alibi, The 1932,F 10,26:6
Firebird 1932,N 22,25:2
Nine Pine Street 1933,Ap 28,15:5
Private Affair, A 1936,My 15,28:7
Corday, Clyde
Shadow Years, The 1957,Ja 9,26:2
Corday, Denise
Sacred and Profane Love 1920,F 24,11:1
Dolly Jordan 1922,O 4,26:1
Royal Fandango, A 1923,N 13,25:1
Corday, Diana
Merry Widow, The 1942,Jl 16,22:1
Rosalinda; Fledermaus, Die 1942,O 29,26:5
Hollywood Pinafore 1945,Je 1,20:1
Corday, Mary
Blue Bird, The 1923,D 26,13:3
Peter Pan 1924,N 7,16:2
Corday, Ottilie
Sharlee 1923,N 23,20:1
Corday, Peggy
Helen Goes to Troy 1944,Ap 25,17:2
Corday, Theodore
Marching Song 1937,F 18,18:2
I Must Love Someone 1939,F 8,18:7
Cordell, Cathleen
Inside the Room 1934,D 23,15:3
Never Trouble Trouble 1937,Ag 18,15:2
Love of Women 1937,D 14,33:2
Romantic Mr Dickens 1940,D 3,33:2
Golden Wings 1941,D 9,46:6
Yesterday's Magic 1942,Ap 15,27:2
Sheppey 1944,Ap 19,27:2
While the Sun Shines 1944,S 20,21:3
While the Sun Shines 1944,S 24,II,1:1
Linden Tree, The 1948,Mr 3,28:2
Cordell, Sandyl
Vamp, The 1955,N 11,30:1
Cordello, Cosmo
Home Is Tomorrow 1950,Je 2,27:2
Cordery, Clara
Great Campaign, The 1947,Ap 1,33:2
Dear Judas 1947,O 6,26:4

Cordes, Helen
Trip to Bountiful, The 1953,N 4,30:3
Cordes, James J
Everyman 1953,O 12,30:2
Cordes, Joan
Ghosts 1933,My 24,24:5
Cordes, Ruth (Costume Designer)
Christmas in the Market Place 1960,D 10,26:1
Cordier, Reina (Translator)
Escurial 1956,O 3,29:2
Cordier, Robert (Director)
Ping-Pong 1959,Ap 17,22:1
Grand Vizier, The 1961,D 13,55:5
Cayenne Pepper 1961,D 13,55:5
Cordier, Robert (Translator)
Escurial 1956,O 3,29:2
Ping-Pong 1959,Ap 17,22:1
Cordner, Blaine
Roseanne 1923,D 31,9:5
First Flight 1925,S 18,26:2
Dream Play 1926,Ja 21,18:2
Ramblers, The 1926,S 21,32:2
Hello, Yourself 1928,O 31,28:2
Grand Street Follies, The 1929,My 2,20:4
Show Girl 1929,Jl 3,19:3
We the People 1933,Ja 23,9:5
World Waits, The 1933,O 26,22:5
False Dreams, Farewell 1934,Ja 16,18:3
Bridal Quilt 1934,O 11,28:5
Greater Lust, The 1936,Jl 14,22:4
Curtain Call 1937,Ap 23,24:7
Blow Ye Winds 1937,S 24,17:4
Canteen Show, The 1942,S 4,18:1
New Life, A 1943,S 16,26:6
Bloomer Girl 1944,O 6,18:5
Set My People Free 1948,N 4,38:2
Cordoba, Daniel (Choreographer)
Cabalgata 1949,Jl 8,14:2
Cordoba, Daniel (Director)
Cabalgata 1949,Jl 8,14:2
Cordoba, Daniel (Producer)
Night in Spain, A 1949,Ag 28,II,1:1
Cordon, Norman
Street Scene 1947,Ja 10,17:2
Cordova, Victoria
Viva O'Brien 1941,O 10,27:2
Around the World 1946,Je 1,9:5
Louisiana Lady 1947,Je 3,35:2
Cordrey, Peggy
Early to Bed 1943,Je 18,16:2
Core, Natalie
Broken Hearts of Broadway 1944,Je 13,16:2
Sister Oakes 1949,Ap 25,19:4
Not for Children 1951,F 14,35:2
Saratoga 1959,D 8,59:4
Corell, Zoe
Romeo and Juliet 1957,Je 28,30:2
Macbeth 1957,Ag 16,11:2
Corelli, Alan (Miscellaneous)
Broken Hearts of Broadway 1944,Je 13,16:2
Corelli, Carlo
Music in the Air 1951,O 9,32:2
Corelli, Sadonia
Monkey Talks, The 1925,D 29,20:1
Coren, Robert
Henri Christophe 1945,Je 7,24:5
Corenne, Marcelle
Vaudeville (Palace) 1926,N 23,27:3
Vaudeville (Palace) 1929,Mr 25,33:2
Corey, Arthur
Up in the Clouds 1922,Ja 3,20:3
Corey, Bryn
Alive and Kicking 1950,Ja 18,25:5
Corey, Chappell Jr
Roseanne 1923,D 31,9:5
Corey, Charles
Gianni Schicci 1969,F 25,36:1
Corey, George H (Playwright)
Not in Our Stars 1941,Ap 26,20:5
Corey, Gertrude
Texas Town 1941,Ap 30,22:3
Out of My House 1942,Ja 8,28:6
Church Street 1948,F 10,27:2
Ardele 1958,Ap 9,39:4
Overruled 1959,Ag 21,13:1
French Way, The; Deceased, The 1962,Mr 21,36:2
French Way, The; Grand Vizier, The 1962,Mr 21,36:2
Corey, Gertrude (Playwright)
French Way, The; Grand Vizier, The 1962,Mr 21,36:2
French Way, The; Deceased, The 1962,Mr 21,36:2
French Way, The; Edward and Agrippina 1962,Mr 21,36:2
Corey, Herb (Lyricist)
Greenwich Village U S A 1960,S 29,30:5
Corey, Irene (Scenic Designer)
Book of Job, The 1962,F 10,13:1
Corey, Irwin
Emperor's New Clothes, The 1941,D 27,15:5
New Faces of 1943 1942,D 23,22:2
Heaven on Earth 1948,S 17,29:2
Happy as Larry 1950,Ja 7,11:2

Corey, Irwin—Cont

Flahooley 1951,My 15,39:1
Flahooley 1951,My 20,II,1:1
Mrs McThing 1952,F 21,22:1
Good Soldier Schweik, The 1963,Ap 9,57:1
Seven Scenes for Yeni 1963,My 13,36:2

Corey, Jeff

In the Matter of J Robert Oppenheimer
1968,Je 7,31:1

Corey, Lillian

Wind in the Sails 1940,Ag 1,24:6

Corey, Orlon (Director)

Book of Job, The 1962,F 10,13:1

Corey, Orlon (Playwright)

Book of Job, The 1962,F 10,13:1

Corey, Wendell

Texas Town 1941,Ap 30,22:3
Comes the Revelation 1942,My 27,26:2
First Million, The 1943,Ap 29,27:4
Manhattan Nocturne 1943,O 27,26:2
Jackpot 1944,Ja 14,15:2
But Not Goodbye 1944,Ap 12,19:2
Wind Is Ninety, The 1945,Je 22,12:2
Dream Girl 1945,D 15,13:2
Dream Girl 1945,D 23,II,3:1
Night of the Auk 1956,D 4,50:2
Jolly's Progress 1959,D 7,42:2

Corigliano, John (Composer)

Helen 1964,D 11,55:4
Wars of the Roses, The (Part I) 1970,Jl 2,30:1
Wars of the Roses, The (Part II) 1970,Jl 3,15:1
Richard III 1970,Jl 4,11:1

Corio, Ann

White Cargo 1941,My 14,24:3
This Was Burlesque 1965,Mr 17,55:3
This Was Burlesque 1970,F 12,31:1

Corio, Ann (Director)

This Was Burlesque 1962,Mr 7,29:1
This Was Burlesque 1965,Mr 17,55:3
This Was Burlesque 1970,F 12,31:1

Corio, Ann (Miscellaneous)

This Was Burlesque 1962,Mr 7,29:1
This Was Burlesque 1970,F 12,31:1

Corio, Ann (Playwright)

This Was Burlesque 1970,F 12,31:1

Corio, Rafael

Sex Fable, The 1931,O 21,26:1
Pie in the Sky 1941,D 23,26:5
I Killed the Count 1942,S 4,18:1

Corio, William

View From the Bridge, A 1965,Ja 29,24:1

Corish, M Fintan

Devil Came From Dublin, The! 1955,Je 3,27:2

Corke, Jimmy

Banjo Eyes 1941,D 26,20:2

Corkill, Cathy

Company 1970,Ap 27,40:1

Corle, Edwin

Othello 1934,Jl 22,23:4

Corle, Edwin (Original Author)

Solitaire 1942,Ja 28,22:2
Solitaire 1942,F 8,IX,1:1
Man in the Dog Suit, The 1958,O 31,34:2

Corlett, Irene

Glamour Preferred 1940,N 16,13:2
By Jupiter 1942,Je 4,22:1
Hairpin Harmony 1943,O 2,18:5

Corley, Pat

Breaking Wall, The 1960,Ja 26,27:5
Blues for Mister Charlie 1964,Ap 24,24:1

Cormack, Bartlett (Playwright)

Racket, The 1927,N 23,28:3
Racket, The 1927,D 18,IX,1:1
Racket, The 1930,N 20,30:6
Painted Veil, The 1931,O 11,VIII,2:4
Hey Diddle Diddle 1937,Ja 22,24:2

Cormack, Beale (Playwright)

Aaron Slick From Punkin Crick 1935,Ap 6,11:4

Corman, Robert (Miscellaneous)

Belafonte at the Palace 1959,D 16,55:1

Cormon, Eugene (Playwright)

Two Orphans, The 1926,Ap 6,26:2

Corn, Alfred

Peter Pan; Boy Who Would Not Grow Up, The
1928,N 27,36:3
East of Broadway 1932,Ja 27,19:3
Another Love 1934,Mr 20,26:3
Come What May 1934,My 16,23:4

Corn, Belmont Jr (Scenic Designer)

Laugh It Off 1934,Ap 5,24:2

Corn, Olive

Growing Pains 1933,N 24,24:2
Picnic 1934,My 3,15:2

Cornberg, Sol (Lighting Director)

Growing Pains 1933,N 24,24:2

Corne, Martin

Journey by Night, A 1935,Ap 17,26:3

Corneille, Pierre (Playwright)

Cid, Le 1958,O 31,35:2
Cid, Le 1963,N 8,36:2
Cid, Le 1966,F 9,32:1

Cornejo, Rudolfo

Midsummer Night's Dream, A 1954,S 22,33:1
Pipe Dream 1955,D 1,44:1

Cornelis, Marcel

International Soiree 1958,Mr 13,25:1

Cornell, Clarice

Achilles Had a Heel 1935,O 14,20:2
Come Angel Band 1936,F 19,17:1

Cornell, Elmer

Cornered 1920,D 9,18:2
Tantrum, The 1924,S 5,20:2
Harvest 1925,S 21,16:2
Hamlet 1925,N 10,23:1
Love 'Em and Leave 'Em 1926,F 4,20:4
God Loves Us 1926,O 20,22:2
Damn the Tears 1927,Ja 22,11:1
Salvation 1928,F 1,31:1
Gentlemen of the Press 1928,Ag 28,27:2
Scarlet Pages 1929,S 10,26:3
Man on Stilts, The 1931,S 10,23:2

Cornell, F Griffith

Betty Behave 1927,Mr 9,28:4

Cornell, Frederic

Let's Laugh Again 1937,Ag 24,24:5
Petrified Forest, The 1943,N 2,30:6
Wanhope Building, The 1947,F 11,36:5

Cornell, Gerald

Robert E Lee 1923,N 21,23:1
Me 1925,N 24,28:1
Bride of the Lamb 1926,Mr 31,20:3
Sam Abramovitch 1927,Ja 20,20:5
Tonight at 12 1928,N 16,28:1
Abraham Lincoln 1929,O 22,26:3
Lord Blesses the Bishop, The 1934,N 28,24:5
Field of Ermine 1935,F 9,10:4
Schoolhouse on the Lot 1938,Mr 23,18:4
Little Darling 1942,O 28,26:2

Cornell, Grace

Gentlemen Prefer Blondes 1926,S 29,23:1

Cornell, John

Romeo and Juliet 1935,D 24,10:2
Mamba's Daughters 1939,Ja 4,24:2

Cornell, John (Miscellaneous)

Carmen Jones 1956,Je 1,28:2
Summer of the Seventeenth Doll 1958,Ja 23,23:2
Requiem for a Nun 1959,Ja 31,13:2
In the Summer House 1964,Mr 26,43:1

Cornell, John (Scenic Designer)

Morning's at Seven 1955,Je 23,25:1

Cornell, Katharine

Nice People 1921,Mr 3,11:1
Bill of Divorcement, A 1921,O 11,22:2
Bill of Divorcement, A 1921,O 16,VI,1:1
Will Shakespeare 1923,Ja 2,14:1
Enchanted Cottage, The 1923,Ap 2,22:3
Enchanted Cottage, The 1923,Ap 8,VIII,1:1
Casanova 1923,S 16,VII,2:8
Casanova 1923,S 27,10:2
Casanova 1923,O 2,10:3
Way Things Happen, The 1923,D 30,VII,2:1
Way Things Happen, The 1924,Ja 29,17:5
Way Things Happen, The 1924,F 3,VII,1:1
Outsider, The 1924,Mr 4,16:4
Outsider, The 1924,Mr 9,VIII,1:1
Tiger Cats 1924,O 19,VIII,2:6
Tiger Cats 1924,O 22,18:1
Candida 1924,D 13,12:3
Candida 1924,D 21,VII,1:1
Candida 1925,Ja 11,VII,1:2
Green Hat, The 1925,Ap 5,IX,2:4
Candida 1925,Ap 26,VIII,1:1
Green Hat, The 1925,S 16,23:2
Green Hat, The 1925,S 20,VIII,1:1
Letter, The 1927,S 27,30:1
Letter, The 1927,O 2,VIII,1:1
Age of Innocence, The 1928,N 18,IX,2:6
Age of Innocence, The 1928,N 28,24:2
Dishonored Lady 1930,Ja 26,VIII,2:1
Dishonored Lady 1930,F 5,27:1
Barretts of Wimpole Street, The 1931,F 1,VIII,3:5
Barretts of Wimpole Street, The 1931,F 10,25:1
Barretts of Wimpole Street, The 1931,F 15,VIII,1:8
Barretts of Wimpole Street, The 1931,F 22,VIII,1:1
Lucrece 1932,N 30,22:8
Lucrece 1932,D 4,IX,3:3
Lucrece 1932,D 21,22:2
Lucrece 1933,Ja 1,IX,1:1
Alien Corn 1933,F 14,19:5
Alien Corn 1933,F 21,17:2
Alien Corn 1933,F 26,IX,1:1
Romeo and Juliet 1933,N 30,38:5
Romeo and Juliet 1934,D 4,23:2
Romeo and Juliet 1934,D 21,30:3
Romeo and Juliet 1934,D 30,IX,1:1
Barretts of Wimpole Street, The 1935,F 26,16:2
Flowers of the Forest 1935,Ap 5,21:6
Flowers of the Forest 1935,Ap 9,25:2
Romeo and Juliet 1935,D 24,10:2
Saint Joan 1936,Mr 10,27:4
Saint Joan 1936,Mr 15,X,1:1
Wingless Victory, The 1936,N 25,17:5
Wingless Victory, The 1936,D 24,20:2
Wingless Victory, The 1937,Ja 3,X,1:1
Candida 1937,Mr 11,20:2
Candida 1937,Mr 21,XI,1:1
Herod and Mariamne 1938,O 27,27:2

Cornell, Katharine—Cont

No Time for Comedy 1939,Mr 31,18:4
No Time for Comedy 1939,Ap 18,26:4
No Time for Comedy 1939,Ap 30,XI,1:1
Doctor's Dilemma, The 1941,F 18,26:6
Doctor's Dilemma, The 1941,Mr 12,18:2
Doctor's Dilemma, The 1941,Mr 30,IX,1:1
Rose Burke 1942,Ja 25,IX,2:5
Candida 1942,Ap 28,24:4
Candida 1942,My 3,VIII,1:1
Three Sisters, The 1942,D 22,31:2
Three Sisters, The 1942,D 27,VIII,1:1
Lovers and Friends 1943,N 30,23:2
Lovers and Friends 1943,D 5,II,5:1
Barretts of Wimpole Street, The 1944,S 17,II,1:3
Barretts of Wimpole Street, The 1945,Mr 27,23:6
Barretts of Wimpole Street, The 1945,Ap 1,II,1:1
Antigone 1946,Ja 10,28:2
Antigone 1946,F 19,21:3
Antigone 1946,F 24,II,1:1
Candida 1946,Ap 4,33:2
Candida 1946,Ap 14,II,1:1
Antony and Cleopatra 1947,N 27,49:2
Antony and Cleopatra 1947,D 7,II,5:1
That Lady 1949,O 20,38:8
That Lady 1949,N 23,18:4
That Lady 1949,D 4,II,5:1
Constant Wife, The 1951,D 10,34:3
Constant Wife, The 1951,D 16,II,6:1
Prescott Proposals, The 1953,D 17,53:1
Prescott Proposals, The 1953,D 27,II,3:1
Dark Is Light Enough, The 1955,F 24,20:1
Dark Is Light Enough, The 1955,Mr 6,II,1:1
Firstborn, The 1958,My 1,35:1
Firstborn, The 1958,My 11,II,1:1
Firstborn, The 1958,Jl 4,16:3
Dear Liar 1960,Mr 18,19:2
Dear Liar 1960,Mr 27,II,1:1

Cornell, Katharine (Miscellaneous)

Romeo and Juliet 1934,D 21,30:3
Saint Joan 1936,Mr 10,27:4
Barretts of Wimpole Street, The 1945,Mr 27,23:6
Candida 1946,Ap 4,33:2

Cornell, Katharine (Producer)

Barretts of Wimpole Street, The 1931,F 10,25:1
Barretts of Wimpole Street, The 1931,F 15,VIII,1:8
Lucrece 1932,D 21,22:2
Alien Corn 1933,F 21,17:2
Romeo and Juliet 1934,D 4,23:2
Romeo and Juliet 1934,D 21,30:3
Romeo and Juliet 1934,D 30,IX,1:1
Barretts of Wimpole Street, The 1935,F 26,16:2
Flowers of the Forest 1935,Ap 9,25:2
Flowers of the Forest 1935,Ap 14,IX,1:1
Romeo and Juliet 1935,D 24,10:2
Saint Joan 1936,Mr 15,X,1:1
Wingless Victory, The 1936,D 24,20:2
Candida 1937,Mr 11,20:2
Doctor's Dilemma, The 1941,F 18,26:6
Doctor's Dilemma, The 1941,Mr 12,18:2
Rose Burke 1942,Ja 25,IX,2:5
Three Sisters, The 1942,D 22,31:2
Three Sisters, The 1942,D 27,VIII,1:1
Lovers and Friends 1943,N 30,23:2
Lovers and Friends 1943,D 5,II,5:1
Antigone 1946,F 19,21:3
Antigone 1946,F 24,II,1:1
Candida 1946,Ap 14,II,1:1
Antony and Cleopatra 1947,N 27,49:2
That Lady 1949,N 23,18:4
That Lady 1949,D 4,II,5:1
Constant Wife, The 1951,D 10,34:3
Dark Is Light Enough, The 1955,F 24,20:1
Firstborn, The 1958,My 1,35:1
Firstborn, The 1958,Jl 4,16:3

Cornell, Neil

Improvisations in June 1928,F 27,16:5

Cornell, Nord

Blossom Time 1943,S 6,21:2

Cornell, Olive

Ziegfeld Follies 1920,Je 23,14:1

Cornell, P Steven

Mr Winkle's Holliday 1946,Je 24,27:6

Cornell, Peggy

Sunny Days 1928,F 9,29:1
Angela 1928,D 4,28:2
Broadway Nights 1929,Jl 16,23:2
Street Singer, The 1929,S 18,35:2
Vaudeville (Palace) 1932,Je 6,18:2
As Thousands Cheer 1933,O 2,22:1

Cornell, Phyllis

Censored 1938,F 28,18:2
Escape This Night 1938,Ap 23,18:1

Cornell, Ted (Director)

No Place to Be Somebody 1969,My 5,53:3
No Place to Be Somebody 1969,My 18,II,22:1
No Place to Be Somebody 1969,My 18,II,1:1
No Place to Be Somebody 1969,D 31,17:1

Cornell, Ted (Miscellaneous)

Hamlet 1967,D 27,45:1

Corner, James

What a Life 1938,Ap 14,26:2
Run Sheep Run 1938,N 4,26:2
Ring Two 1939,N 23,38:2

Corner, James—Cont

Out From Under 1940,My 6,13:2
Cornett, Barbara
Young Abe Lincoln 1961,Ap 26,36:1
Cornett, Ewel
Meet Peter Grant 1961,My 11,41:4
Corney, Camille (Director)
Carrosse du Saint-Sacrement, Le 1930,Mr 9,IX,2:7
Cornish, Roger (Playwright)
Satisfaction Guaranteed 1969,F 12,31:1
Open 24 Hours 1969,F 12,31:1
Cornwall, Donald
Years Between, The 1942,F 7,13:2
Cornwell, Jack H (Costume Designer)
Go Show Me a Dragon 1961,O 28,18:1
Kiss Mama 1964,O 2,30:1
Friday Night; Mary Agnes Is Thirty-Five
1965,F 9,42:5
Friday Night; River, The 1965,F 9,42:5
Friday Night; Passport 1965,F 9,42:5
Cornwell, Jack H (Scenic Designer)
Billy Budd 1959,F 28,13:3
Ballad of Jazz Street, The 1959,N 12,28:1
Jackass, The 1960,Mr 24,39:2
Marcus in the High Grass 1960,N 22,38:6
Cicero 1961,F 9,37:2
Go Show Me a Dragon 1961,O 28,18:1
King of the Whole Damn World 1962,Ap 16,32:2
Witches' Sabbath 1962,Ap 20,22:2
O Say Can You See! 1962,O 9,45:1
We're Civilized? 1962,N 9,30:1
Kiss Mama 1964,O 2,30:1
Friday Night; River, The 1965,F 9,42:5
Friday Night; Mary Agnes Is Thirty-Five
1965,F 9,42:5
Friday Night; Passport 1965,F 9,42:5
Saturday Night 1968,F 26,43:1
Corona, Isabella
Amphitryon 38 1939,Jl 16,IX,1:1
Coronado, Edgar
West Side Story 1968,Je 25,32:1
Corp, Joan
Mrs Kimball Presents 1944,Mr 1,17:3
Corpell, Katharine (Producer)
No Time for Comedy 1939,Ap 18,26:4
Corpora, James
Hamlet 1959,S 11,21:4
Corr, Daryle Ann (Miscellaneous)
God, Man & You, Baby! 1963,O 30,47:1
Corr, J P
Possessed, The 1939,O 25,26:2
Corredor, Evaristo (Producer)
Leyenda del Beso, La 1942,N 20,26:4
Correia, Guilherme
Hughie 1959,O 15,48:1
Correll, Mady
Young Sinners 1933,Mr 7,20:4
Springtime for Henry 1933,My 2,20:5
June Moon 1933,My 16,15:5
Too Much Party 1934,Mr 6,28:4
Sweet Mystery of Life 1935,O 12,13:3
Dead End 1936,S 20,IX,3:7
Corrett, William
Stepping Sisters 1930,Ap 23,24:2
Corri, Adrienne
Jane 1952,F 2,10:2
Rehearsal, The 1963,S 24,45:2
Corrie, Bill
Enemy of the People, An 1958,F 26,24:2
Corrigan, Emmett
Martinique 1920,Ap 27,18:2
Nemesis 1921,Ap 5,24:3
Alias Jimmy Valentine 1921,D 9,20:3
Bully, The 1924,D 26,18:1
Corrigan, Lloyd
Man of Wax, The 1933,Ag 6,X,1:6
Her Man of Wax 1933,O 12,32:3
Corrigan, Mary Ann
Foxy 1964,F 17,26:1
Corrin, George (Lighting Director)
Major Barbara 1954,Je 30,23:2
In Splendid Error 1954,O 27,33:6
Antigone 1956,Ap 3,32:2
Leave It to Jane 1959,My 26,30:2
Goose, The 1960,Mr 16,44:1
Kittiwake Island 1960,O 13,43:1
Cockeyed Kite 1961,S 14,27:1
Corrin, George (Scenic Designer)
Major Barbara 1954,Je 30,23:2
In Splendid Error 1954,O 27,33:6
Corrinth, Kurt (Playwright)
Trojaner 1929,My 26,IX,2:3
Corroll, Clay
Within Four Walls 1923,Ap 18,24:1
Corry, Pittman
Allah Be Praised! 1944,Ap 21,14:2
Lady Says Yes, A 1945,Ja 11,18:5
Corry, Will
All the King's Men 1959,O 17,27:2
Corsaro, Ben (Director)
Hatful of Rain, A 1955,D 4,II,1:1
Corsaro, Frank
Bourgeois Gentleman, The 1949,Ag 31,27:2
Merchant of Venice, The 1953,Mr 5,20:2

Corsaro, Frank (Director)
Family Reunion, The 1947,N 29,9:2
Creditors 1949,N 22,36:5
Heartbreak House 1950,Mr 22,33:2
Naked 1950,S 7,39:2
Scarecrow, The 1953,Je 17,31:1
Honeys, The 1955,Ap 29,26:1
Hatful of Rain, A 1955,N 10,44:1
Making of Moo, The 1958,Je 12,34:1
Night Circus, The 1958,D 3,44:1
Oh Dad, Poor Dad, Mamma's Hung You in the
Closet and I'm Feelin' So Sad 1961,Jl 6,19:2
Night of the Iguana, The 1961,D 29,10:1
Night of the Iguana, The 1962,Ja 7,II,1:1
Baby Want a Kiss 1964,Ap 20,32:1
Sweet Enemy, The 1965,F 16,39:1
Fitz 1966,My 17,51:2
Biscuit 1966,My 17,51:2
Corsaro, Frank (Miscellaneous)
Twelfth Night 1958,Ag 7,21:4
Corsaro, Frank (Playwright)
Creditors 1949,N 22,36:5
Corsaro, Frank (Translator)
Naked 1950,S 7,39:2
Corsbie, Flora
Girl in the Spotlight, The 1920,Jl 13,9:3
Corsell, Henry
Good Boy 1928,S 6,23:2
Corson, Chuck (Playwright)
Disney on Parade 1970,S 24,63:1
Corson, Emilie
Arabian Nightmare, The 1927,Ja 11,36:3
Cort, A Jr
Tiger Smiles, The 1930,D 18,29:1
Cort, Alex
Bacchants, The 1967,F 25,14:1
To Clothe the Naked 1967,Ap 28,30:1
Cort, Harry L (Playwright)
Jim Jam Jems 1920,O 5,13:2
Go-Go 1923,Mr 13,19:4
Sharlee 1923,N 23,20:1
China Rose 1925,Ja 20,18:1
Cort, Harry L (Producer)
Polly of Hollywood 1927,F 22,22:3
Veneer 1929,N 13,24:5
All the King's Horses 1934,Ja 31,21:3
Cort, Harvey (Producer)
Innocents, The 1959,Ap 21,41:2
Cort, Irene
Policy Kings 1938,D 31,6:2
Cort, John
Love on the Dole 1936,F 25,23:3
Bright Honor 1936,S 28,14:1
Cort, John (Producer)
New Gallantry, The 1925,S 25,24:2
Cort, Paul
Paradise 1931,My 12,29:2
Cort, Suzanne
Few Are Chosen 1935,S 18,19:3
Cort, William
Great Power, The 1928,S 12,25:1
Cortelyou, Winthrop (Composer)
Kiss Me! 1927,Jl 22,17:1
Cortes, Jose
Cabalgata 1949,Jl 8,14:2
Cortez
Boom Boom 1929,Ja 29,26:4
Cortez, Armand
Mima 1928,D 13,24:2
Other Men's Wives 1929,N 13,24:4
Seven 1929,D 28,10:5
Plutocrat, The 1930,F 21,23:3
Farewell to Arms, A 1930,S 23,30:3
Overture 1930,N 25,31:2
Overture 1930,D 8,26:4
Wonder Bar, The 1931,Mr 18,23:4
First Lady 1935,N 27,17:4
Star Time 1944,S 13,16:2
Cortez, Aurora
Great Way, The 1921,N 8,28:2
Cortez, Billie
Bomboola 1929,Je 27,17:3
Cortez, Don
Street Singer, The 1929,S 18,35:2
Louisiana Purchase 1940,My 29,19:2
Girl From Nantucket, The 1945,N 9,17:2
Cortez, Esteben
Nina Rosa 1930,My 31,19:3
Cortez, John
Pardon My English 1933,Ja 21,11:4
Cortez, Patti
Tweedles 1923,Ag 14,10:1
Cortez, Stephen
Bombo 1921,O 7,20:2
Nina Rosa 1930,S 22,22:5
Cortez, Tamm
Vagabond King, The 1925,S 22,23:3
Cortez & Peggy
Nifties of 1923 1923,S 26,10:1
Cortez and Peggy
Passing Show of 1921, The 1920,D 30,16:2
Vaudeville (Hippodrome) 1924,O 21,21:2
Puzzles of 1925 1925,F 3,25:3

Cortez and Peggy—Cont

Night in Spain, A 1927,My 4,28:2
Corthay, Sylvain
Phedre 1969,Mr 1,20:1
Corthell, Herbert
Untitled-Benefit 1921,My 2,12:3
All-Star Idlers of 1921, The 1921,Jl 16,5:2
Fables 1922,F 7,12:2
Topics of 1923 1923,N 21,23:2
Lambs Gambol 1925,Ap 27,15:1
Trelawney of the 'Wells' 1925,Je 2,16:2
Artists and Models 1925,Je 25,16:2
Vagabond King, The 1925,S 22,23:3
My Princess 1927,O 7,24:2
Octoroon, The 1929,Mr 13,28:3
Stepping Out 1929,My 21,29:1
How's Your Health? 1929,N 27,30:3
Papavert 1931,D 30,25:1
Mr Papavert 1932,Ja 23,18:6
Round-Up, The 1932,Mr 8,19:4
Story to Be Whispered 1937,Ag 20,21:4
Pie in the Sky 1941,D 23,26:5
Corti, Angelo
Servant of Two Masters, The 1960,F 24,42:2
Corti, Mario
Giuochi di Prestigio 1931,N 2,26:1
Cortini
Vaudeville (Palace) 1928,F 14,26:2
Cortis, (Mme)
1860: or, Aris; 1860, or an Interrupted Festival
1931,O 22,27:1
Cortis, Ernest (Director)
One for All 1927,My 14,25:5
Cortis, Ernest (Playwright)
One for All 1927,My 14,25:5
Cortis, Louise (Playwright)
One for All 1927,My 14,25:5
Cortlandt, Charlyne
Young Visitors, The 1920,N 30,14:1
Corto, Diana
13 Daughters 1961,Mr 3,17:2
Stop the World-I Want to Get Off 1962,O 4,45:4
Her First Roman 1968,O 21,53:3
Corum, Paul
All's Well That Ends Well 1970,Je 16,53:1
Othello 1970,Je 22,43:1
Othello 1970,S 15,51:1
Corvera, Lucita
Artists and Models 1924,O 16,33:3
Merry World, The 1926,Je 9,18:3
Corvette, Rikki
Poet's Follies of 1955 1955,My 15,II,3:1
Corvino, Alfredo
Green Table, The 1942,Ja 22,12:2
Prodigal Son, The 1942,F 18,22:2
Corvino, Ernesta
Midsummer Night's Dream, A 1964,Je 30,23:2
Corvo, Baron (Fr Rolfe) (Playwright)
Hadrian VII 1969,Ja 9,22:1
Corvo, Baron (Frederick Rolfe) (Original Author)
Hadrian VII 1968,Jl 4,14:1
Corwey, Ferry
Good Times 1920,Ag 10,10:1
Get Together 1921,S 5,12:2
Vaudeville (Palace) 1926,Ag 17,21:2
Corwin, Arlene
Nervous Set, The 1959,My 13,43:1
Corwin, Clinton
Six Characters in Search of an Author
1931,Ap 16,29:2
Corwin, Lorri
Magistrate, The 1959,My 14,30:6
Corwin, Norman (Director)
Rivalry, The 1959,F 9,24:2
World of Carl Sandburg, The 1959,O 13,44:6
World of Carl Sandburg, The 1959,O 26,53:3
World of Carl Sandburg, The 1960,S 15,44:1
World of Carl Sandburg, The 1960,S 25,II,1:1
Corwin, Norman (Playwright)
Mary and the Fairy 1956,Mr 24,15:2
Rivalry, The 1959,F 9,24:2
Rivalry, The 1959,F 15,II,1:1
World of Carl Sandburg, The 1959,O 13,44:6
World of Carl Sandburg, The 1959,O 26,53:3
World of Carl Sandburg, The 1960,S 15,44:1
Cory, Chappell Jr
Beggar on Horseback 1924,F 13,17:2
Cory, George
Kiss Them for Me 1945,Mr 21,27:2
He Who Gets Slapped 1946,Mr 21,31:4
Coryell, Eleanor (Director)
Will O' the Wisp, The 1923,My 11,20:3
Coryell, Esther Jane
On the Town 1959,Ja 16,36:1
On the Town 1959,Ja 25,II,1:1
Witches' Sabbath 1962,Ap 20,22:2
Mating Dance 1965,N 4,58:1
Corzatte, Clayton
Henry IV, Part I 1955,S 22,34:2
Midsummer Night's Dream, A 1957,Je 27,21:3
Apollo of Bellac, The 1958,Mr 7,17:2
Lady's Not for Burning, The 1959,Ja 31,13:2
Twelfth Night 1960,Je 9,29:4
Tempest, The 1960,Je 20,35:1

Corzatte, Clayton—Cont

School for Scandal, The 1962,Mr 19,36:1
Seagull, The 1962,Mr 22,42:1
Portrait of the Artist as a Young Man, A
  1962,My 29,21:1
Barroom Monks, The 1962,My 29,21:1
We Comrades Three 1962,O 12,26:1
Hamlet 1963,My 9,41:1
Miser, The 1963,My 10,39:1
Three Sisters, The 1963,Jl 22,19:2
Tavern, The 1964,Mr 6,39:2
Scapin 1964,Mr 10,43:1
Lower Depths, The 1964,Mr 31,30:1
Man and Superman 1964,D 7,45:2
War and Peace 1965,Ja 12,32:1
Judith 1965,Mr 25,42:2
You Can't Take It With You 1965,N 24,32:1
You Can't Take It With You 1965,D 5,II,5:1
School for Scandal, The 1966,Ja 22,33:2
School for Scandal, The 1966,D 11,II,3:1
Wild Duck, The 1967,Ja 12,49:1
Wild Duck, The 1967,Ja 22,II,1:1
War and Peace 1967,Mr 22,42:1
Show-Off, The 1967,D 6,40:2
Show-Off, The 1967,D 17,II,3:7
Exit the King 1968,Ja 10,48:1
Exit the King 1968,Ja 21,II,1:2
Cherry Orchard, The 1968,Mr 20,41:1
Cherry Orchard, The 1968,Ap 7,II,3:7

Cosby, John
Merrily We Roll Along 1934,O 1,14:1
Mikado, The 1935,Jl 16,24:4
Yeomen of the Guard, The 1935,Jl 30,16:4
Gondoliers, The 1935,Ag 6,20:5
H M S Pinafore 1935,Ag 13,20:6

Cosby, Lawrence
Sea Dogs 1939,N 7,30:3

Cosby, Vivian (Playwright)
Queen at Home 1930,N 2,VIII,3:5
Queen at Home 1930,D 30,25:2
Trick for Trick 1932,F 19,14:2

Cosden, Robert
Mr Winkle's Holliday 1946,Je 24,27:6
Athenian Touch, The 1964,Ja 15,25:4

Cosens, Monica (Playwright)
Cautious Campbell 1927,Ag 14,VII,1:7
Madame Plays Nap 1929,D 18,31:2

Cosentino, Nicholas (Playwright)
Moon Over Mulberry Street 1935,S 5,24:6

Cosgriff, Kittie
Prologue to Glory 1938,Mr 18,22:2
Scene of the Crime, The 1940,Mr 29,24:1

Cosgrove, Douglas
Fall and Rise of Susan Lenox, The 1920,Je 11,11:2
Sue, Dear 1922,Jl 11,16:2
Blue Ghost, The 1930,Mr 11,24:5

Cosic, Illeana (Translator)
Who's Afraid of Virginia Woolf? 1968,Jl 4,13:1

Cosio, Rosita
Sky Drift 1945,N 14,25:2

Coslow, Jacqueline
Arms and the Man 1967,Je 23,44:2

Coslow, Sam
Vaudeville (Palace) 1926,Ag 31,15:3

Coslow, Sam (Lyricist)
Artists and Models 1924,O 16,33:3

Cosmopolitan Trio
Vaudeville (Palace) 1924,F 19,12:1

Cosor, Louis
Scapegoat, The 1950,Ap 20,36:5

Cossart, Ernest
Skin Game, The 1920,O 21,11:1
Title, The 1921,N 15,23:3
He Who Gets Slapped 1922,Ja 10,15:1
Six Characters in Search of an Author
  1922,O 31,11:2
Love Habit, The 1923,Mr 15,17:1
Casanova 1923,S 27,10:2
Saint Joan 1923,D 29,8:4
Steam Roller, The 1924,N 11,20:2
Candida 1924,D 13,12:3
Arms and the Man 1925,S 15,28:1
Arms and the Man 1925,O 4,IX,1:1
Taming of the Shrew, The 1925,D 19,14:1
Taming of the Shrew, The 1925,D 27,VII,1:1
Chief Thing, The 1926,Mr 23,24:2
What Never Dies 1926,D 29,24:2
Doctor's Dilemma, The 1927,N 22,33:1
Marco Millions 1928,Ja 10,28:2
Volpone 1928,Ap 10,32:1
Volpone 1928,Ap 22,IX,1:1
Caprice 1929,Ja 1,61:1
Becky Sharp 1929,Je 4,29:1
Apple Cart, The 1930,F 25,30:1
Milestones 1930,Je 3,27:1
Getting Married 1931,Mr 31,25:5
Way of the World, The 1931,Je 2,34:3
Roof, The 1931,O 31,22:4
Roof, The 1931,N 8,VIII,1:1
Devil Passes, The 1932,Ja 5,20:3
Devil Passes, The 1932,Ja 10,VIII,1:1
Too True to Be Good 1932,Mr 1,19:2
Too True to Be Good 1932,Mr 6,VIII,1:1
Too True to Be Good 1932,Ap 5,27:5

Mask and the Face, The 1933,My 9,20:2
Mary of Scotland 1933,N 28,28:3
Great Waltz, The 1934,S 24,14:4
Accent on Youth 1934,D 26,19:1
Madame Bovary 1937,O 6,28:4
Madame Bovary 1937,N 17,26:2
Tonight at 8:30 1940,Ag 11,IX,11:2
Devils Galore 1945,S 13,27:2
Play's the Thing, The 1948,Ap 29,19:2
Play's the Thing, The 1948,My 9,II,1:1
Ivy Green, The 1949,Ap 6,37:2

Cossart, Valerie
Lost Sheep 1930,My 6,33:2
Miracle at Verdun 1931,Mr 17,34:6
Hay Fever 1931,D 30,25:1
Strange Orchestra 1933,N 29,23:2
Point Valaine 1935,Ja 17,22:2
Call It a Day 1936,Ja 29,15:2
Storm Over Patsy 1937,Mr 9,26:4
Retreat From Folly 1937,Je 29,18:3
At Mrs Beam's 1937,Jl 27,24:2
Madame Bovary 1937,N 17,26:2
Shadow and Substance 1938,Ja 27,16:2
Case of Youth, A 1940,Mr 25,10:3
To What Red Hell 1940,My 5,I,54:8
At the Stroke of Eight 1940,My 21,29:2
Golden Wings 1941,D 9,46:6
Haven, The 1946,N 14,39:4
Tonight at 8:30; Ways and Means 1948,F 21,8:2
Tonight at 8:30; Family Album 1948,F 21,8:2
Tonight at 8:30; Shadow Play 1948,F 24,20:4
Tonight at 8:30; Fumed Oak 1948,F 24,20:4
Tonight at 8:30; Hands Across the Sea
  1948,F 24,20:4
Day After Tomorrow 1950,O 27,25:2

Cossette, Pierre (Producer)
Egg, The 1962,Ja 9,23:2

Cossins, James
Portrait of a Queen 1968,F 29,29:1

Costa, Bill (Miscellaneous)
Greenwich Village U S A 1960,S 29,30:5

Costa, Hilda
Sunday Nights at Nine 1933,N 13,20:7

Costa, Mary
Candide 1959,My 1,35:4

Costa, P Mario (Composer)
Bird Cage, The 1925,Je 3,26:2

Costa-Gavras (Director)
Shock Troops 1969,F 22,36:1

Costa-Gavras (Playwright)
Shock Troops 1969,F 22,36:1

Costantino, Raffaele
Due Orfanelle, Le; Two Orphans, The
  1936,O 5,24:4
Medico Delle Pazze, Il; Physician of Mad Woman,
  The 1937,S 27,24:2
Signora Dalle Camelie, La; Dame aux Camelias, La
  1937,O 9,16:3

Costanza, Peter
My Fair Lady 1968,Je 14,42:1

Coste, Georges
Mariage de Figaro, Le 1964,F 26,41:2
Pieton de L'Air, Le 1964,Mr 4,33:2
Salut a Moliere 1964,Mr 4,33:2

Costello, Alfredo
Sunny River 1941,D 5,28:2

Costello, Amby
Murder at the Vanities 1933,S 13,22:4

Costello, Ann
Lower Depths, The 1956,O 3,29:2

Costello, Anthony
Riot Act, The 1963,Mr 9,5:2

Costello, Audrey
Lady in the Dark 1941,Ja 24,14:2

Costello, Diosa
Too Many Girls 1939,O 19,26:2
Crazy With the Heat 1941,Ja 31,15:2
South Pacific 1950,Ap 26,36:5
South Pacific 1951,Jl 10,30:5

Costello, Dolores
George White's Scandals 1922,Ag 29,10:1

Costello, Don
Jerry for Short 1929,Ag 13,23:4
Last Mile, The 1930,F 14,21:2
Paid Companions 1931,Je 23,28:4
Crucible 1933,S 5,22:4
Bride of Torozko, The 1934,S 14,24:2
Ghost of Yankee Doodle, The 1937,N 23,26:3
Censored 1938,F 28,18:2
Come Across 1938,S 15,28:3
Weak Link, The 1940,Mr 5,19:2

Costello, Helene
Octoroon, The 1936,S 1,24:2

Costello, J M (Playwright)
Bulls and Belles 1931,Ap 18,17:2

Costello, John
Schemers 1924,S 16,27:1
Scarlet Pages 1929,S 10,26:3

Costello, Julian
Walk Together Chillun 1936,F 5,15:2
Conjur' Man Dies 1936,Mr 12,18:5
Horse Play 1937,Ag 28,8:3
Androcles and the Lion 1938,D 17,10:5

Costello, Katie
Three Philip Roth Stories; Epstein 1970,Jl 31,14:1
Cops and Horrors; Dracula 1970,Ag 11,27:1

Costello, Lou
Streets of Paris, The 1939,Je 25,IX,1:1

Costello, Mariclare
After the Fall 1964,Ja 24,18:1
But for Whom Charlie 1964,Mr 13,42:2
Changeling, The 1964,O 30,32:2
Tartuffe 1965,Ja 15,23:1
Lovers and Other Strangers 1968,S 19,63:1
Patriot for Me, A 1969,O 6,58:1
Harvey 1970,F 25,41:1

Costello, Maurice
Little Theatre Tournament; Yellow Triangle, The
  1929,My 10,32:2

Costello, Robert (Producer)
Elsa Lanchester-Herself 1961,F 6,28:1

Costello, Tom
Alice in Wonderland 1970,O 9,43:1

Costello, Ward
Father, The 1949,Ag 21,II,1:1
Prescott Proposals, The 1953,D 17,53:1
Moby Dick 1955,Ap 26,25:3
Lark, The 1955,N 18,20:1
Enemy of the People, An 1959,F 5,24:4
Investigation, The 1966,O 5,40:1

Coster, Nicholas
Browning Version, The 1958,Mr 7,17:2
Apollo of Bellac, The 1958,Mr 7,17:2
Month in the Country, A 1959,Mr 2,32:2
Thracian Horses, The 1961,S 28,58:2
O Say Can You See! 1962,O 9,45:1
Hamlet 1963,My 9,41:1
Death of a Salesman 1963,Jl 20,11:2
Three Sisters, The 1963,Jl 22,19:2
Ninety Day Mistress, The 1967,N 7,49:1
Hello and Goodbye 1968,N 13,36:2
But, Seriously... 1969,F 28,29:1
Happy Birthday, Wanda June 1970,O 8,58:2
Happy Birthday, Wanda June 1970,O 18,II,1:1

Costi, Carmen
Johnny 2X4 1942,Mr 17,24:6
Wonderful Journey 1946,D 26,30:2
Skipper Next to God 1948,Ja 5,14:5
Come Out, Carlo! 1962,My 4,27:2
In the Penal Colony 1962,My 4,27:2

Costigan, Charles
What Price Glory 1924,S 6,14:3

Costigan, James
Beast in Me, The 1963,My 17,29:1
Baby Want a Kiss 1964,Ap 20,32:1

Costigan, James (Lyricist)
Beast in Me, The 1963,My 17,29:1

Costigan, James (Playwright)
Little Moon of Alban 1960,D 2,34:1
Beast in Me, The 1963,My 17,29:1
Baby Want a Kiss 1964,Ap 20,32:1

Costigan, Ken (Director)
Shoemaker's Holiday, The 1967,Mr 3,25:1

Costigan, Ken (Producer)
Shoemaker's Holiday, The 1967,Mr 3,25:1

Costigan, Kenneth (Miscellaneous)
O, Oysters! 1961,Ja 31,23:1
Hostage, The 1961,D 13,55:4

Costin, Bill
Ankles Aweigh 1955,Ap 19,27:1

Costin, William G Jr (Miscellaneous)
Number, The 1951,O 31,33:2
On Borrowed Time 1953,F 11,34:1

Costley, Grace A
Burning Bush, The 1949,D 17,15:5

Coston, Rex
Cradle Will Rock, The 1947,D 27,11:2

Cota, Keith
Happy Hypocrite, The 1968,S 6,38:1

Cote, Emil
Sidewalks of New York 1927,O 4,33:1

Cotes, Peter (Director)
Pin to See the Peepshow, A 1953,S 18,17:2
Hidden Stranger 1963,Ja 10,5:5

Cothran, Robert (Scenic Designer)
Clandestine on the Morning Line 1961,O 31,28:1

Cothren, Clifford
One Flew Over the Cuckoo's Nest 1963,N 14,40:.

Cotler, Gordon (Playwright)
Step a Little Closer 1948,My 28,26:6

Cotlow, Marilyn
Telephone, The 1947,My 2,28:2
Telephone, The 1947,My 11,II,1:1

Cotner, Robyn
Cock-A-Doodle Dandy 1955,N 4,26:5
Servant of Two Masters, The 1958,F 11,35:2

Cotopouli, Marika
Shadow, The 1930,N 17,21:2
Electra 1930,D 27,16:1
Iphigenia 1931,Ja 6,24:1

Cotopouli, Marika (Producer)
Electra 1930,D 27,16:1

Cotsopoulos, Thanos
Electra 1952,N 20,38:2
Oedipus Tyrannus 1952,N 25,35:2

Cotsworth, Staats
First Episode 1934,S 18,18:1
Othello 1935,S 28,13:2
Macbeth 1935,O 8,26:4
Damaged Goods 1937,My 18,27:2
Our Betters 1937,Jl 22,16:2
As You Like It 1937,N 1,25:2
Stop-Over 1938,Ja 12,16:5
Madame Capet 1938,O 26,26:2
Boudoir 1941,F 8,18:4
Macbeth 1941,N 12,30:2
She Stoops to Conquer 1949,D 29,21:3
Evening With Will Shakespeare, An 1952,D 7,86:5
Richard III 1953,D 10,65:2
Inherit the Wind 1955,Ap 22,20:2
I Knock at the Door 1956,Mr 19,27:5
Pictures in the Hallway 1956,My 28,23:1
Pictures in the Hallway 1956,S 17,23:2
Pictures in the Hallway 1956,S 23,II,1:1
Apollo of Bellac, The 1957,Ap 10,39:1
Virtuous Island, The 1957,Ap 10,39:1
I Know at the Door 1957,S 30,27:2
Julius Caesar 1959,Ag 4,30:1
Julius Caesar 1959,Ag 16,II,1:1
Advise and Consent 1960,N 18,25:1
Ghosts 1961,S 22,29:1
Tristram 1962,O 29,36:1
White Rose and the Red, The 1964,Mr 17,31:1
Hamlet 1964,Je 17,49:1
Hamlet 1964,Je 18,28:1
I Knock at the Door 1964,N 26,53:2
Pictures in the Hallway 1964,D 17,51:1
Coriolanus 1965,Jl 15,23:1
Right Honourable Gentleman, The 1965,O 20,50:2
All's Well That Ends Well 1966,Je 17,39:1
King John 1967,Jl 14,19:1
Weekend 1968,Mr 14,50:2
Patriot for Me, A 1969,O 6,58:1
Madwoman of Chaillot, The 1970,Mr 23,48:3
Cott, Alvin (Costume Designer)
Something More! 1964,N 11,36:1
Cottell, Mildred
Good Companions, The 1931,O 2,31:1
Cotten, Joseph
Absent Father 1932,O 18,23:5
Jezebel 1933,D 20,26:3
Loose Moments 1935,F 5,22:3
Postman Always Rings Twice, The 1936,F 26,17:2
Please Do Not Disturb 1936,Je 23,27:1
Horse Eats Hat 1936,S 28,14:2
Triple Play 1937,Ag 24,24:4
Julius Caesar 1937,N 12,26:6
Shoemaker's Holiday, The 1938,Ja 3,17:2
Danton's Death 1938,N 3,26:2
Philadelphia Story, The 1939,Mr 29,21:1
Sabrina Fair 1953,N 12,37:1
Sabrina Fair 1953,N 22,II,1:1
Once More With Feeling 1958,O 22,39:1
Calculated Risk 1962,O 17,33:3
Calculated Risk 1962,N 1,35:1
Cotter, Donald (Scenic Designer)
Scarlet Lullaby 1968,Mr 11,48:1
Cotter, Jayne
Spring Again 1941,O 28,28:3
Spring Again 1941,N 11,28:2
Another Love Story 1943,O 13,29:2
Many Happy Returns 1945,Ja 6,15:5
Kiss Them for Me 1945,Mr 21,27:2
Cottman, Catherine B
Tableaux 1961,D 18,41:3
Cotton, Fred
Brown Danube, The 1939,My 18,30:4
Winged Victory 1943,N 22,24:1
Yellow Jack 1944,Ap 7,23:3
State of the Union 1945,N 15,25:2
Anne of the Thousand Days 1948,D 9,49:2
Cotton, George
Marco Millions 1928,Ja 10,28:2
R U R 1930,F 18,28:1
Lysistrata 1930,Je 6,20:1
Hamlet 1931,N 6,28:4
Dead End 1935,O 29,17:2
Gloriana 1938,N 26,18:4
Three Sisters, The 1939,O 16,23:1
Unconquered, The 1940,F 14,25:2
My Sister Eileen 1940,D 27,23:2
First Million, The 1943,Ap 29,27:4
Naked Genius, The 1943,O 22,20:5
Story for Strangers, A 1948,S 22,39:2
Bravo! 1948,N 12,31:2
Bruno and Sidney 1949,My 4,38:2
Metropole 1949,D 7,43:2
Kiss Me, Kate 1954,Mr 27,13:2
Lysistrata 1959,My 20,40:2
Not a Way of Life 1967,Mr 23,28:1
Inherit the Wind 1967,Je 23,50:1
Cotton, Joe
Second Hurricane 1937,Ap 22,18:4
Cotton, Robert
Digging for Apples 1962,S 28,29:4
Cotton, Robert (Choreographer)
Digging for Apples 1962,S 28,29:4

Cotton, Robert (Lighting Director)
Digging for Apples 1962,S 28,29:4
Cotton, Will (Playwright)
Bride the Sun Shines On, The 1931,D 28,20:2
Bride the Sun Shines On, The 1936,Jl 1,29:2
Cotton, Zelda
Prelude 1936,Ap 20,17:4
Cottrell, Richard
Taming of the Shrew, The 1957,F 21,30:2
Serjeant Musgrave's Dance 1968,Je 16,52:4
Resistible Rise of Arturo Ui, The 1968,Ag 8,25:1
House of Atreus, The 1968,D 18,55:1
Resistible Rise of Arturo Ui, The 1968,D 23,44:1
Cottrell, Richard (Director)
Midsummer Night's Dream, A 1968,D 9,59:1
Richard II 1969,S 4,50:1
Cottrell, William
Six Characters in Search of an Author
  1955,D 12,38:1
King John 1956,Je 28,33:5
Measure for Measure 1956,Je 29,16:1
Measure for Measure 1957,Ja 23,24:1
Taming of the Shrew, The 1957,F 21,30:2
Duchess of Malfi, The 1957,Mr 20,33:1
Othello 1957,Je 24,19:2
Merchant of Venice, The 1957,Jl 11,19:5
Much Ado About Nothing 1957,Ag 8,15:2
Ticket-of-Leave Man, The 1961,D 23,15:1
Traveller Without Luggage 1964,S 18,26:2
Come Summer 1969,Mr 19,43:1
Cottrelly, Mathilde
Abie's Irish Rose 1922,My 24,22:4
Good Old Days, The 1923,Ag 15,21:2
Good Old Days, The 1923,Ag 19,VI,1:1
Potash and Perlmutter, Detectives; Poisoned by
  Pictures 1926,S 1,27:3
Cotts, Campbell
Millionairess, The 1952,O 18,17:2
Cotts, Rudy
Breaking Wall, The 1960,Ja 26,27:5
Cottsworth, Statts
Rain From Heaven 1934,D 25,28:4
Cotureau, Jacques
Labyrinth, The 1968,S 22,II,1:6
Couch, Ellen (Miscellaneous)
Hamlet 1970,O 27,54:2
Rosencrantz and Guildenstern Are Dead
  1970,N 19,39:3
Couche, Carole
Apollo of Bellac, The 1957,Ap 10,39:1
Palm Tree in a Rose Garden, A 1957,N 27,26:2
Rope Dancers, The 1959,Mr 14,26:1
Time of Vengeance 1959,D 11,39:1
Couchman, Brent
Master Builder, The 1957,D 18,42:7
Couderc
Avare, L'; Miser, The 1924,Mr 12,17:3
Monsieur Brotonneau 1924,Mr 13,14:1
Blanchette 1924,Mr 19,19:4
Coudray, Peggy
Demi-Virgin, The 1921,O 19,22:1
Relations 1928,Ag 21,27:3
Cradle Will Rock, The 1937,D 6,19:4
Cradle Will Rock, The 1938,Ja 4,19:3
Run Sheep Run 1938,N 4,26:2
Sing for Your Supper 1939,Ap 25,18:6
Coudy, George (Choreographer)
Hollywood Pinafore 1945,Je 1,20:1
Coughlin, James
Murder at the Vanities 1933,S 13,22:4
Coughlin, Kevin
Frogs of Spring, The 1953,O 21,36:2
King and I, The 1956,Ap 19,35:4
Square Root of Wonderful, The 1957,O 31,40:1
Coughlin, Rose
Deburau 1920,D 24,14:3
Smyth With a Y 1937,Je 30,19:5
Coule, Helen
Danton's Death 1938,N 3,26:2
Coulidge, Richard
R U R 1922,O 10,16:1
Couloumbis, Akila
Kitchen, The 1966,Je 14,50:1
Coulouris, George
Novice and the Duke, The 1929,D 11,37:2
Late Christopher Bean, The 1932,N 1,24:3
Best Sellers 1933,My 4,20:2
Mary of Scotland 1933,N 28,28:3
Valley Forge 1934,D 11,28:3
Coward, The 1935,Jl 16,24:1
If This Be Treason 1935,Jl 30,17:1
Blind Alley 1935,S 25,19:6
Saint Joan 1936,Mr 10,27:4
Ten Million Ghosts 1936,O 24,23:7
Julius Caesar 1937,N 12,26:6
Shoemaker's Holiday, The 1938,Ja 3,17:2
Heartbreak House 1938,Ap 30,18:2
Madame Capet 1938,O 26,26:2
White Steed, The 1939,Ja 11,16:2
White Steed, The 1939,Ja 22,IX,1:1
Cue for Passion 1940,D 20,33:4
Watch on the Rhine 1941,Ap 2,26:2
Watch on the Rhine 1941,Ap 13,IX,1:1

Coulouris, George—Cont
Watch on the Rhine 1941,Ag 24,IX,1:1
Richard III 1943,Mr 27,8:3
Alchemist, The 1948,My 7,31:4
S S Glencairn; Moon of the Caribbees
  1948,My 21,21:2
Insect Comedy, The 1948,Je 4,26:3
Beekman Place 1964,O 8,50:1
Condemned of Altona, The 1966,F 4,21:1
Condemned of Altona, The 1966,F 13,II,1:1
Sorrow of Frederick, The 1967,Jl 8,14:2
Coulouris, George (Director)
Richard III 1943,Mr 27,8:3
Coult, Carol
Sing for Your Supper 1939,Ap 25,18:6
Coulter, Claire
Richard II 1964,Je 17,47:1
Coulter, Frazer
Man in the Making, The 1921,S 21,16:2
Lawful Larceny 1922,Ja 3,20:2
Secrets 1922,D 26,11:1
She Stoops to Conquer 1924,Je 10,24:3
Cape Smoke 1925,F 17,19:1
Henry IV, Part I 1926,Je 1,29:1
Julius Caesar 1927,Je 7,27:2
Age of Innocence, The 1928,N 28,24:2
Becky Sharp 1929,Je 4,29:1
Little Father of the Wilderness, The 1930,Je 3,27:1
Oh, Promise Me 1930,N 25,31:1
Coulter, Glenn
Trial of Joan of Arc, The 1921,Mr 28,8:2
Street Scene 1929,Ja 11,20:4
Mackerel Skies 1934,Ja 24,20:4
Tell Me Pretty Maiden 1937,D 17,33:5
Abe Lincoln in Illinois 1938,O 17,12:2
Coulter, J Hamilton
Roof, The 1930,Je 14,9:2
Coulter, Kay
Banjo Eyes 1941,D 26,20:2
Dear Ruth 1944,D 14,29:2
On Your Toes 1954,O 12,24:4
Coultoff, Harry
Three Sisters, The 1930,Ja 9,22:2
Coulton, S D
Tiger Smiles, The 1930,D 18,29:1
Council, Elizabeth
Scarlet Pages 1929,S 10,26:3
Council, Jim (Miscellaneous)
Servant of Two Masters, The 1958,F 11,35:2
Countryman, William
Troubled Waters 1965,Je 4,40:2
Billy 1969,Mr 24,56:1
Counts, Elinor
Catherine Was Great 1944,Ag 3,16:1
Coupe, Diana
Grosse Valise, La 1965,D 15,52:1
Mame 1966,My 25,41:1
Couper, Barbara
Innocent as Hell 1960,Je 30,2:6
Couper, M A
Little Theatre Tournament; White Peacock, The
  1928,My 11,28:1
Courday, Peggy
Ladies' Night 1920,Ag 10,10:1
Cournos, John (Translator)
Fireworks on the James 1940,My 15,30:2
Court, Caralyn
Marvellous History of Saint Bernard, The
  1958,F 24,16:3
Court, Lilyan
Marvellous History of Saint Bernard, The
  1958,F 24,16:3
Courteline, Georges (Playwright)
Boubouroche 1921,N 29,20:1
Client Serieux, Un 1927,Mr 27,VII,4:8
Article 330, L' 1930,N 23,IX,1:1
Hortense, to Bed With You 1949,Jl 9,9:2
Courtenay, Fay
Pearls 1921,Je 14,15:2
Squaring the Triangle 1921,Je 14,15:2
Advertising of Kate, The 1922,My 9,22:2
Saturday Night 1924,F 11,18:1
She Couldn't Say No! 1926,S 1,27:3
It Never Rains 1929,N 20,26:4
Off to Buffalo! 1939,F 22,18:2
Courtenay, Margaret
Romeo and Juliet 1956,O 25,41:1
Macbeth 1956,O 30,42:2
Troilus and Cressida 1956,D 27,21:1
Hamlet 1958,D 17,2:7
Henry V 1958,D 26,2:7
Alfie 1964,D 18,27:1
Arms and the Man 1970,Ag 26,36:1
Courtenay, Shiela
Title, The 1921,N 15,23:3
Courtenay, Tom
Hamlet 1968,Ag 21,40:2
She Stoops to Conquer 1969,Ag 18,28:1
Peer Gynt 1970,D 23,12:5
Courtenay, William
Honors Are Even 1921,Ag 11,8:2
Lawbreaker, The 1922,F 7,12:1
Her Temporary Husband 1922,S 1,16:2
Harem, The 1924,N 16,VIII,2:8

Courtenay, William—Cont
Harem, The 1924,D 3,24:1
Inside Story, The 1932,F 23,23:2
Courteol, Ouida
Midsummer Night's Dream, A 1931,Ag 19,19:3
Courtines, Jacques (Director)
Cosmonaute Agricole, Le 1970,Ap 8,38:3
Grand Vizir, Le 1970,Ap 8,38:3
Jeune Fille a Marier, La 1970,My 6,49:1
Chaises, Les 1970,My 6,49:1
Lacune, La 1970,My 6,49:1
Courtines, Jacques (Miscellaneous)
Pique-Nique en Campagne 1969,My 1,50:1
Guernica 1969,My 1,50:1
Courtines, Jacques (Producer)
Femmes Savantes, Les 1967,F 7,34:2
Diary of a Madman 1967,Mr 24,25:1
Courtland, Charlyne
Henry-Behave 1926,Ag 24,19:4
Courtland, Jerome
Flahooley 1951,My 15,39:1
Courtleigh, Robert
Saturday Night 1933,Mr 1,13:2
Courtleigh, Stephen
Napi 1931,Mr 12,22:5
School for Virtue 1931,Ap 22,29:2
Birthright 1933,N 22,22:3
Murder in the Cathedral 1936,Mr 21,13:5
Help Yourself! 1936,Jl 15,15:1
St Helena 1936,O 7,32:1
Richard II 1937,F 6,14:2
Prologue to Glory 1938,Mr 18,22:2
Prologue to Glory 1938,Mr 27,X,1:1
Fabulous Invalid, The 1938,O 10,15:1
Courtleigh, William
Some Party 1922,Ap 17,22:1
Drums of Jeopardy, The 1922,My 30,8:4
Last Warning, The 1922,O 25,23:1
Helena's Boys 1924,Ap 8,22:2
So This Is Politics 1924,Je 17,22:2
Episode 1925,F 5,23:2
Trelawney of the 'Wells' 1925,Je 2,16:2
Henry IV, Part I 1926,Je 1,29:1
Lily Sue 1926,N 17,22:2
Honor Be Damned! 1927,Ja 27,13:1
Electra 1927,My 4,28:3
Julius Caesar 1927,Je 7,27:2
Weather Clear, Track Fast 1927,O 19,24:5
Aiglon, L' 1927,D 27,24:3
Beaux' Stratagem, The 1928,Je 5,20:1
Judas 1929,Ja 25,20:4
Patriarch, The 1929,N 26,28:5
Hamlet 1930,Mr 25,34:4
Macbeth 1930,Mr 26,24:6
Julius Caesar 1930,Ap 4,22:3
9th Street Guest, The 1930,Ag 26,24:3
Courtleigh, William (Mrs)
Jefferson Davis 1936,F 19,17:2
Courtleigh, William Jr
Growing Pains 1933,N 24,24:2
Courtnay, Alex
Twelfth Night 1940,N 20,26:3
Macbeth 1941,N 12,30:2
Courtnay, Margaret
Midsummer Night's Dream, A 1954,S 22,33:1
Courtneidge, Charles
By the Way 1925,D 29,20:3
By the Way 1926,Ap 16,20:3
Pygmalion 1926,N 16,24:1
Brothers Karamazov, The 1927,Ja 4,20:1
Spellbound 1927,N 15,26:2
Cherry Orchard, The 1928,Mr 6,20:1
Major Barbara 1928,N 20,28:4
Major Barbara 1928,D 2,X,1:1
Courtneidge, Cicely
By the Way 1925,D 29,20:3
By the Way 1926,Ap 4,VIII,1:1
By the Way 1926,Ap 16,20:3
Full Swing 1942,My 3,VIII,1:7
Under the Counter 1947,O 4,10:2
High Spirits 1964,N 4,46:4
Courtney, Alex
Stage Door 1936,O 23,26:3
Taming of the Shrew, The 1940,F 6,17:2
Courtney, Alexander
Rosencrantz and Guildenstern Are Dead 1967,O 17,53:1
Courtney, C C
Salvation 1969,S 25,55:1
Courtney, C C (Composer)
Salvation 1969,Mr 13,53:1
Salvation 1969,S 25,55:1
Courtney, C C (Lyricist)
Salvation 1969,S 25,55:1
Courtney, C C (Playwright)
Salvation 1969,Mr 13,53:1
Salvation 1969,S 25,55:1
Salvation 1969,O 5,II,1:1
Courtney, Hubert
Spread Eagle 1927,Ap 5,30:2
Royal Family, The 1927,D 29,26:4
Steel 1931,N 19,26:5
Courtney, Inez
Wild Rose, The 1926,O 21,23:1

Good News 1927,Ag 14,VII,2:1
Good News 1927,S 7,35:4
Polly 1929,Ja 9,28:3
Spring Is Here 1929,Mr 12,26:1
America's Sweetheart 1931,Ja 25,VIII,2:4
America's Sweetheart 1931,F 11,23:1
Dinner at Eight 1933,Ap 9,IX,1:7
Hold Your Horses 1933,Ag 31,20:4
Hold Your Horses 1933,S 26,26:4
Courtney, James
Diamond Lil 1951,S 15,8:2
Courtney, Marguerite (Playwright)
Jennie 1963,O 18,35:2
Courtney, Marianna
Mummers and Men 1962,Mr 27,41:6
Courtney, Marianna (Miscellaneous)
Run, Thief, Run 1957,My 2,27:1
Courtney, Marion
George White's Scandals 1922,Ag 29,10:1
Courtney, Nan
Follies of 1910, The 1960,Ja 15,37:3
Valmouth 1960,O 7,29:1
Courtney, Perqueta
Eve's Leaves 1925,Mr 27,22:2
Merry Merry 1925,S 25,24:3
Twinkle Twinkle 1926,N 17,22:2
Courtney, Richard
Mad Morning 1935,Je 25,14:1
Caesar and Cleopatra 1935,Ag 22,21:1
Slight Case of Murder, A 1935,S 12,28:5
Courtney, Robert (Playwright)
Clock, The 1923,My 10,22:3
Courtney, W L (Playwright)
Oedipus Rex 1923,O 26,14:1
Courtney-James, Geene
Skits-Oh-Frantics 1967,Ap 3,39:2
Courtright, Eugenie (Playwright)
Eldest, The 1935,F 12,24:3
Cousin, Catherine
Intermezzo 1957,F 15,20:4
Cousins, Derek (Scenic Designer)
Canterbury Tales; Merchant's Tale, The 1969,F 4,34:1
Canterbury Tales; Pilgrims, The 1969,F 4,34:1
Canterbury Tales; Wife of Bath's Tale, The 1969,F 4,34:1
Canterbury Tales; Steward's Tale, The 1969,F 4,34:1
Canterbury Tales; Miller's Tale, The 1969,F 4,34:1
Coussonneau
Don Juan 1958,O 29,29:1
Coutand, Lucien (Costume Designer)
Birds, The 1928,F 19,VIII,4:4
Coutant, Harold
Fuente Ovejuna; Sheep Well, The 1936,My 3,II,4:1
Coutant, Roger
Saison d'Amour 1926,O 31,VIII,2:4
Coutaud, Lucien (Costume Designer)
As You Like It 1938,Jl 31,IX,6:8
Couvelaire, Emile (Producer)
Dans l'Ombre du Harem 1927,My 29,VII,2:7
Couvreur, George (Composer)
Androcles and the Lion 1938,D 17,10:5
Cov, Johnny
Along Fifth Avenue 1949,Ja 14,28:2
Covan, Jenny (Costume Designer)
General John Regan 1930,Ja 30,16:5
Covan, Jenny (Playwright)
Uncle Vanya 1929,My 25,17:1
Covan, Jenny (Translator)
Tsar Fyodor Ivanovitch 1923,Ja 9,26:1
Lower Depths, The 1923,Ja 16,16:1
Lower Depths, The 1923,Ja 21,VII,1:1
Cherry Orchard, The 1923,Ja 23,18:1
Covan and Ruffin
Tell Me More 1925,Ap 14,27:3
Vaudeville (Palace) 1926,Jl 6,19:3
Covanna, Elise
Morals 1925,D 1,22:2
Covarrubias, Miguel (Costume Designer)
Androcles and the Lion 1925,N 24,28:1
Androcles and the Lion 1925,N 29,VIII,1:1
Covarrubias, Miguel (Scenic Designer)
Garrick Gaieties 1925,Je 8,VIII,2:1
Androcles and the Lion 1925,N 24,28:1
Androcles and the Lion 1925,N 29,VIII,1:1
Coveney, Michael
Midsummer Night's Dream, A 1968,D 9,59:1
Cover, Franklin
Julius Caesar 1959,Ag 4,30:1
Henry IV 1960,Mr 2,42:1
Henry IV 1960,Ap 19,41:1
Henry IV, Part II 1960,Ap 24,II,1:1
She Stoops to Conquer 1960,N 2,42:5
Plough and the Stars, The 1960,D 7,56:2
Octoroon, The 1961,Ja 28,13:1
Hamlet 1961,Mr 17,17:1
Giants, Sons of Giants 1962,Ja 8,26:2
Abraham Cochrane 1964,F 18,26:1
Investigation, The 1966,O 5,40:1
Warm Body, A 1967,Ap 17,44:2
Forty Carats 1968,D 27,45:1

Cover, Mildred
Coquette 1935,My 22,23:4
Cover, Thomas
Conduct Unbecoming 1970,O 13,50:1
Covert, Bruce
Red, Hot and Blue! 1936,O 30,26:3
Covert, Don
Top Banana 1951,N 2,19:2
Covert, Doris
Virtue's Bed 1930,Ap 16,26:5
Life Is Like That 1930,D 23,24:3
Covette, Peter
Bacchae, The 1969,Mr 15,24:1
Revenger's Tragedy, The 1970,D 2,58:1
Covington, Julie
Midsummer Night's Dream, A 1968,D 9,59:1
Cowan, Curtiss (Scenic Designer)
Clandestine on the Morning Line 1959,D 5,18:2
Nathan the Wise 1962,Mr 23,29:1
Cowan, Gilbert
Small Timers, The 1925,Ja 28,15:3
Cowan, Helen
Count of Luxembourg, The 1930,F 18,28:2
Cowan, Irene
Out West of Eighth 1951,S 21,20:3
Third Best Sport 1958,D 31,15:3
Cowan, Jerome
We've Got to Have Money 1923,Ag 21,12:1
Frankie and Johnny 1930,S 26,16:5
Just to Remind You 1931,S 8,39:1
Rendezvous 1932,O 13,22:3
Little Black Book, The 1932,D 27,11:2
Marathon 1933,Ja 28,8:8
Both Your Houses 1933,Mr 7,20:3
As Thousands Cheer 1933,O 2,22:1
Ladies' Money 1934,N 2,26:6
Paths of Glory 1935,S 19,29:1
Paths of Glory 1935,S 27,24:2
Boy Meets Girl 1935,N 19,27:2
Boy Meets Girl 1935,N 28,38:2
My 3 Angels 1953,Mr 12,23:2
Rumple 1957,N 7,42:2
Say Darling 1958,Ap 4,17:1
Say Darling 1958,Ap 13,II,1:1
Cowan, Lillian
Porgy and Bess 1935,O 11,30:2
Porgy and Bess 1942,Ja 23,16:2
Cowan, Marianne
Murder in the Old Red Barn, The 1936,F 3,20:4
Cowan, Mitchell
Forbidden Melody 1936,N 3,33:1
Cowan, Pascal
Beggar on Horseback 1924,F 13,17:2
Man on Stilts, The 1931,S 10,23:2
Cowan, Royal
El Cristo 1926,My 9,II,1:4
Cowan, Tom
Nic-Nax of 1926 1926,Ag 5,19:1
Cowan, William
Man Bites Dog 1933,Ap 26,11:2
Coward, Father (Playwright)
Veronica's Veil 1935,Mr 11,14:2
Coward, Noel
Young Idea, The 1923,F 11,VII,1:4
Vortex, The 1925,S 8,21:5
Vortex, The 1925,S 17,20:1
Vortex, The 1925,S 27,VII,1:1
Constant Nymph, The 1926,O 3,VIII,2:1
Second Man, The 1928,F 12,VIII,2:1
This Year of Grace 1928,N 8,27:1
Private Lives 1930,S 25,14:2
Private Lives 1930,O 12,VIII,1:8
Private Lives 1931,Ja 28,24:1
Design for Living 1933,Ja 3,19:5
Design for Living 1933,Ja 8,IX,3:2
Design for Living 1933,Ja 25,13:2
Design for Living 1933,Ja 29,IX,1:1
Conversation Piece 1934,F 17,20:5
Conversation Piece 1934,Mr 11,X,3:6
Tonight at Seven-Thirty; We Were Dancing; Astonished Heart, The; Red Peppers 1935,O 17,28:3
Tonight at Seven-Thirty; Hands Across the Sea; Fumed Oak; Shadow Play 1935,O 22,16:5
Family Album 1936,Ja 10,16:1
Tonight at 8:30 1936,Ja 10,16:1
Red Peppers 1936,Ja 10,16:1
Astonished Heart, The 1936,Ja 10,16:1
Tonight at ,:O/ 1936,Ja 11,9:4
Hands Across the Sea 1936,Ja 14,25:1
Shadow Play 1936,Ja 14,25:1
Fumed Oak 1936,Ja 14,25:1
Astonished Heart, The 1936,F 2,IX,3:4
Hands Across the Sea 1936,F 16,IX,3:1
Tonight at 8:30; Hands Across the Sea; Astonished Heart, The; Red Peppers 1936,O 27,30:7
Astonished Heart, The 1936,N 25,17:2
Red Peppers 1936,N 25,17:2
Hands Across the Sea 1936,N 25,17:2
We Were Dancing 1936,N 28,13:1
Shadow Play 1936,N 28,13:1

Coward, Noel—Cont

Fumed Oak 1936,N 28,13:1
Still Life 1936,D 1,31:1
Ways and Means 1936,D 1,31:1
Family Album 1936,D 1,31:1
Tonight at 8:30; Astonished Heart, The; Hands
 Across the Sea; Red Peppers; We Were Dancing;
 Fumed Oak; Shadow Play 1936,D 6,XII,5:1
Apple Cart, The 1953,My 8,29:3
Nude With Violin 1957,N 15,36:1
Song at Twilight, A 1966,Ap 17,86:5
Shadows of the Evening; Come Into the Garden,
 Maud 1966,Ap 27,38:1

Coward, Noel (Composer)

On With the Dance 1925,My 1,22:4
This Year of Grace 1928,Mr 23,14:2
This Year of Grace 1928,N 8,27:1
Bitter Sweet 1929,Jl 19,14:2
Bitter Sweet 1929,O 27,IX,2:1
Bitter Sweet 1929,D 29,VIII,4:1
Words and Music 1932,Ag 26,21:2
Words and Music 1932,O 9,IX,1:8
Conversation Piece 1934,F 17,20:5
Conversation Piece 1934,Mr 11,X,3:6
Bitter Sweet 1934,My 8,28:4
Bitter Sweet 1936,Ag 26,17:3
Hands Across the Sea 1936,N 25,17:2
Red Peppers 1936,N 25,17:2
Astonished Heart, The 1936,N 25,17:2
Operette 1938,F 18,22:3
Operette 1938,Mr 17,17:4
Sigh No More 1945,Jl 12,8:4
Sigh No More 1945,S 2,II,1:2
Pacific 1860 1946,D 20,30:4
Pacific 1860 1947,Ja 12,II,3:6
Ace of Clubs 1950,Jl 8,7:2
After The Ball 1954,Je 11,19:3
Sail Away 1961,Ag 10,17:7
Sail Away 1961,O 4,48:5
Girl Who Came to Supper, The 1963,D 9,49:1

Coward, Noel (Costume Designer)

Operette 1938,Mr 17,17:4

Coward, Noel (Director)

Hay Fever 1925,O 5,25:1
Bitter Sweet 1929,N 6,30:2
Private Lives 1931,Ja 28,24:1
Design for Living 1933,Ja 25,13:2
Biography 1934,My 20,IX,2:4
Conversation Piece 1934,O 24,24:1
Theatre Royal 1934,N 11,IX,1:1
Point Valaine 1935,Ja 17,22:2
Red Peppers 1936,N 25,17:2
Hands Across the Sea 1936,N 25,17:2
Astonished Heart, The 1936,N 25,17:2
Fumed Oak 1936,N 28,13:1
We Were Dancing 1936,N 28,13:1
Shadow Play 1936,N 28,13:1
Ways and Means 1936,D 1,31:1
Still Life 1936,D 1,31:1
Family Album 1936,D 1,31:1
Set to Music 1939,Ja 19,16:2
Blithe Spirit 1941,N 16,IX,1:1
Tonight at 8:30; Family Album 1948,F 21,8:2
Tonight at 8:30; Red Peppers 1948,F 21,8:2
Tonight at 8:30; Ways and Means 1948,F 21,8:2
Tonight at 8:30; Shadow Play 1948,F 24,20:4
Tonight at 8:30; Fumed Oak 1948,F 24,20:4
Tonight at 8:30; Hands Across the Sea
 1948,F 24,20:4
Nude With Violin 1957,N 15,36:1
Sail Away 1961,O 4,48:5
High Spirits 1964,Ap 8,34:1

Coward, Noel (Lyricist)

On With the Dance 1925,My 1,22:4
This Year of Grace 1928,Mr 23,14:2
This Year of Grace 1928,N 8,27:1
Bitter Sweet 1929,O 27,IX,2:1
Words and Music 1932,Ag 26,21:2
Bitter Sweet 1934,My 8,28:4
Operette 1938,F 18,22:3
Sigh No More 1945,S 2,II,1:2
Ace of Clubs 1950,Jl 8,7:2
After The Ball 1954,Je 11,19:3
Sail Away 1961,Ag 10,17:7
Sail Away 1961,O 4,48:5
Girl Who Came to Supper, The 1963,D 9,49:1

Coward, Noel (Miscellaneous)

George and Margaret 1937,S 23,32:2

Coward, Noel (Original Author)

High Spirits 1964,Ap 8,34:1
High Spirits 1964,N 4,46:4
Noel Coward's Sweet Potato 1968,S 30,59:1

Coward, Noel (Playwright)

Young Idea, The 1923,F 11,VII,1:4
Vortex, The 1924,N 30,VIII,2:1
On With the Dance 1925,My 1,22:4
Fallen Angels 1925,My 10,VIII,1:3
Vortex, The 1925,S 8,21:5
Vortex, The 1925,S 17,20:1
Vortex, The 1925,S 27,VII,1:1
Hay Fever 1925,O 5,25:1
Easy Virtue 1925,D 8,28:2
Vortex, The 1926,Ja 3,VII,1:1
Easy Virtue 1926,Je 10,29:2

Rat Trap, A 1926,N 7,VIII,1:3
This Was a Man 1926,N 24,27:1
This Was a Man 1926,N 28,VIII,1:1
Marquise, The 1927,Mr 20,VIII,2:7
Home Chat 1927,N 13,IX,2:1
Marquise, The 1927,N 15,26:4
Sirocco 1927,N 25,24:4
Fallen Angels 1927,D 2,20:4
Sirocco 1927,D 18,IX,4:1
This Year of Grace 1928,Mr 23,14:2
This Was a Man 1928,My 20,VIII,2:1
Hay Fever 1928,O 7,IX,5:3
This Year of Grace 1928,N 8,27:1
This Year of Grace 1928,N 25,X,1:1
Murray Anderson's Almanac 1929,Ag 15,20:3
Bitter Sweet 1929,O 27,IX,2:1
Bitter Sweet 1929,N 6,30:2
Private Lives 1930,S 25,14:2
Private Lives 1930,O 12,VIII,1:8
Bitter Sweet 1930,N 4,37:3
Private Lives 1931,Ja 28,24:1
Post Mortem 1931,Ap 28,31:6
Private Lives 1931,My 12,29:3
Cavalcade 1931,O 14,26:4
Cavalcade 1931,N 1,VIII,2:1
Hay Fever 1931,D 6,VIII,2:8
Hay Fever 1931,D 30,25:1
Home Chat 1932,F 7,VIII,3:1
Words and Music 1932,Ag 26,21:2
Words and Music 1932,S 17,18:7
Words and Music 1932,O 9,IX,1:8
Design for Living 1933,Ja 3,19:5
Design for Living 1933,Ja 8,IX,3:2
Design for Living 1933,Ja 25,13:2
Design for Living 1933,Ja 29,IX,1:1
Design for Living 1933,N 19,IX,2:5
Conversation Piece 1934,F 17,20:5
Conversation Piece 1934,Mr 11,X,3:6
Bitter Sweet 1934,My 8,28:4
Conversation Piece 1934,O 24,24:1
Conversation Piece 1934,N 18,IX,1:1
Point Valaine 1934,D 26,19:3
Point Valaine 1934,D 30,IX,1:6
Point Valaine 1935,Ja 17,22:2
Point Valaine 1935,F 3,VIII,1:1
Private Lives 1935,Ap 21,IX,2:1
Design for Living 1935,Ap 21,IX,2:1
Private Lives 1935,Je 26,18:3
Hay Fever 1935,Jl 24,20:4
Hay Fever 1935,Ag 6,20:3
Tonight at Seven-Thirty; We Were Dancing;
 Astonished Heart, The; Red Peppers
 1935,O 17,28:3
Tonight at Seven-Thirty; Hands Across the Sea;
 Fumed Oak; Shadow Play 1935,O 22,16:5
Astonished Heart, The 1936,Ja 10,16:1
Tonight at 8:30 1936,Ja 10,16:1
Family Album 1936,Ja 10,16:1
Red Peppers 1936,Ja 10,16:1
Tonight at ,:O/ 1936,Ja 11,9:4
Hands Across the Sea 1936,Ja 14,25:1
Fumed Oak 1936,Ja 14,25:1
Shadow Play 1936,Ja 14,25:1
Red Peppers 1936,F 2,IX,3:4
Family Album 1936,F 2,IX,3:4
Astonished Heart, The 1936,F 2,IX,3:4
Fumed Oak 1936,F 16,IX,3:1
Shadow Play 1936,F 16,IX,3:1
Hands Across the Sea 1936,F 16,IX,3:1
Bitter Sweet 1936,Ag 26,17:3
Tonight at 8:30; Hands Across the Sea; Astonished
 Heart, The; Red Peppers 1936,O 27,30:7
Red Peppers 1936,N 25,17:2
Hands Across the Sea 1936,N 25,17:2
Astonished Heart, The 1936,N 25,17:2
Fumed Oak 1936,N 28,13:1
Shadow Play 1936,N 28,13:1
We Were Dancing 1936,N 28,13:1
Still Life 1936,D 1,31:1
Family Album 1936,D 1,31:1
Ways and Means 1936,D 1,31:1
Tonight at 8:30; Astonished Heart, The; Hands
 Across the Sea; Red Peppers; We Were Dancing;
 Fumed Oak; Shadow Play 1936,D 6,XII,5:1
Private Lives 1937,Jl 14,17:4
Hands Across the Sea 1937,Ag 24,24:5
Fumed Oak 1937,Ag 24,24:5
Still Life 1937,Ag 24,24:5
Operette 1938,F 18,22:3
Operette 1938,Mr 17,17:4
Post Mortem 1938,Ap 3,II,3:7
Operette 1938,Ap 3,XI,1:8
Set to Music 1939,Ja 19,16:2
Shadow Play 1939,Ag 15,14:5
Tonight at 8:30 1939,Ag 15,14:5
Easy Virtue 1939,D 31,18:4
Blithe Spirit 1941,Jl 3,13:1
Blithe Spirit 1941,Jl 13,IX,1:4
Blithe Spirit 1941,N 6,26:2
Blithe Spirit 1941,N 16,IX,1:1
Present Laughter 1943,My 9,II,1:1
This Happy Breed 1943,My 9,II,1:1
Present Laughter 1943,My 23,II,1:7

Coward, Noel (Playwright)—Cont

Blithe Spirit 1943,S 12,II,1:1
Sigh No More 1945,Jl 12,8:4
Sigh No More 1945,Ag 24,15:1
Sigh No More 1945,S 2,II,1:2
Blithe Spirit 1946,Je 5,17:3
Present Laughter 1946,O 30,31:2
Pacific 1860 1947,Ja 12,II,3:6
Peace in Our Time 1947,Jl 23,18:5
Peace in Our Time 1947,Ag 24,II,1:6
Tonight at 8:30; Ways and Means 1948,F 21,8:2
Tonight at 8:30; Red Peppers 1948,F 21,8:2
Tonight at 8:30; Family Album 1948,F 21,8:2
Tonight at 8:30; Hands Across the Sea
 1948,F 24,20:4
Tonight at 8:30; Shadow Play 1948,F 24,20:4
Tonight at 8:30; Fumed Oak 1948,F 24,20:4
Private Lives 1948,O 5,30:2
Private Lives 1948,N 7,II,1:1
Ace of Clubs 1950,Jl 8,7:2
Ace of Clubs 1950,Ag 13,II,1:5
Relative Values 1951,N 29,41:2
Relative Values 1951,D 9,II,7:7
Blithe Spirit 1952,F 23,7:5
This Happy Breed 1952,Ap 4,23:2
Quadrille 1952,Jl 17,20:4
Quadrille 1952,S 13,10:7
Quadrille 1952,O 12,II,3:7
Quadrille 1953,Ap 5,II,1:1
After The Ball 1954,Jl 18,II,1:6
Qudrille 1954,N 4,39:2
Quadrille 1954,N 14,II,1:1
Fallen Angels 1956,Ja 18,27:1
South Sea Bubble 1956,Ap 26,37:6
South Sea Bubble 1956,My 13,II,3:1
Nude With Violin 1956,S 25,30:1
Nude With Violin 1956,D 2,II,3:1
Nude With Violin 1957,N 15,36:1
Conversation Piece 1957,N 19,38:2
Three Love Affairs; Still Life 1958,Mr 11,33:1
Still Life 1958,Mr 16,II,1:1
Look After Lulu 1959,Mr 4,35:1
Look After Lulu 1959,Jl 30,20:1
Waiting in the Wings 1960,Ag 9,31:4
Waiting in the Wings 1960,S 8,40:3
Sail Away 1961,Ag 10,17:7
Sail Away 1961,O 4,48:5
Sail Away 1962,Je 23,14:3
Private Lives 1963,Jl 4,8:5
Ways and Means 1967,My 4,34:1
Fumed Oak 1967,My 4,34:1
Still Life 1967,My 4,34:1
Private Lives 1968,My 20,59:1
Private Lives 1969,D 5,52:1
Private Lives 1969,D 14,II,3:3
Blithe Spirit 1970,S 17,57:1
Hay Fever 1970,N 10,55:1
Hay Fever 1970,N 22,II,18:6

Coward, Noel (Producer)

Bitter Sweet 1929,O 27,IX,2:1
Cavalcade 1931,N 1,VIII,2:1
Words and Music 1932,O 9,IX,1:8
Theatre Royal; Royal Family, The 1934,O 24,24:2
Point Valaine 1935,Ja 17,22:2
We Were Dancing; Tonight at Eight 1940,Ag 6,15:3
Astonished Heart, The; Tonight at Eight
 1940,Ag 6,15:3
Red Peppers; Tonight at Eight 1940,Ag 6,15:3
Tonight at 8:30 1940,Ag 11,IX,11:2
Pacific 1860 1946,D 20,30:4

Cowden, Madge

Gypsy Baron, The 1930,Ap 22,22:8

Cowdery, Richard

What a Relief 1935,D 14,10:6
What a Relief 1935,D 19,34:4
Take It Away 1936,D 15,30:5
Take It Away 1936,D 22,32:3
Fol-De-Rol 1937,D 11,22:4
Knickerbocker Holiday 1938,O 20,26:2
Key Largo 1939,N 28,30:2
Charley's Aunt 1940,O 18,24:2
Cyrano de Bergerac 1953,N 13,24:3
Richard III 1953,D 10,65:2
Charley's Aunt 1953,D 23,22:2

Cowell, George

Chicago 1926,D 31,11:1
Solitaire 1929,Mr 13,28:3
Shooting Star 1933,Je 13,22:2

Cowell, Henry (Composer)

King Lear 1940,D 16,27:2

Cowell, John W

Fall and Rise of Susan Lenox, The 1920,Je 11,11:2

Cowels, Chandler (Producer)

Leper, The 1970,Ap 24,40:1

Cowen, Frederick (Sir) (Composer)

Enchanted Cottage, The 1922,Mr 2,21:4

Cowen, Lawrence (Playwright)

Biddy 1927,D 7,32:1

Cowen, Lenore Coffee (Original Author)

Family Portrait 1939,Mr 9,18:4

Cowen, Marion

Polly 1925,O 12,19:1

Cowen, Ron (Playwright)

Summertree 1968,Mr 4,29:1

Cowen, Ron (Playwright)—Cont
Summertree 1968,Mr 17,II,1:6
Summertree 1969,D 10,60:1
Cowen, William B Jr (Director)
Conjur 1938,N 1,27:2
Cowen, William Joyce (Original Author)
Family Portrait 1939,Mr 9,18:4
Cowen, William Joyce (Playwright)
Family Portrait 1939,Mr 19,XI,1:1
Family Portrait; Familie, Eine 1946,N 11,44:1
Family Portrait 1959,My 6,48:2
Cowens, Herbert
Pirate, The 1942,N 26,39:2
Cowger, John
Emmanuel 1960,D 5,42:2
Cowgill, Dick
Billy Budd 1959,F 28,13:3
Cowie, Laura
Enchanted Cottage, The 1922,Mr 2,21:4
Punchinello 1932,Mr 27,VIII,2:1
Strange Orchestra 1932,O 23,IX,1:1
Dinner at Eight 1933,Ja 7,11:5
Queen Who Kept Her Head, The 1934,F 21,23:4
Apple a Day, An 1936,My 25,23:5
Ride a Cock Horse 1937,Ap 4,II,9:7
Ship Comes Home, A 1937,My 18,27:1
Mourning Becomes Electra 1937,D 12,XI,3:8
Cowie, Margaaret (Miscellaneous)
Three Plays of the Sea 1970,Ag 20,39:1
Cowie, Margaret
Three Plays of the Sea 1970,Ag 20,39:1
Cowl, Jane
Smilin' Through 1920,Ja 4,IX,2:1
Untitled-Benefit 1921,My 2,12:3
Untitled-Benefit 1922,My 8,14:5
Malvaloca 1922,O 3,22:1
Romeo and Juliet 1923,Ja 25,16:1
Romeo and Juliet 1923,F 4,VII,1:1
Romeo and Juliet 1923,Ap 22,VII,1:1
Pelleas and Melisande 1923,D 5,23:2
Pelleas and Melisande 1923,D 16,IX,1:1
Antony and Cleopatra 1924,F 20,22:1
Antony and Cleopatra 1924,F 24,VII,1:1
Antony and Cleopatra 1924,Mr 2,VIII,1:1
Antony and Cleopatra 1924,Mr 9,VIII,1:1
Depths, The 1925,Ja 28,15:3
Depths, The 1925,F 8,VII,1:1
One Trip of the Silver Star 1925,Jl 12,VII,1:8
Easy Virtue 1925,D 8,28:2
Easy Virtue 1926,Je 10,29:2
Vaudeville (Palace) 1926,N 30,27:2
Road to Rome, The 1927,F 1,24:2
Jealous Moon, The 1928,O 21,IX,2:1
Jealous Moon, The 1928,N 21,32:2
Paolo and Francesca 1929,Ap 2,28:2
Jenny 1929,Je 2,VIII,1:2
Jenny 1929,O 9,34:4
Twelfth Night 1930,S 14,VIII,2:8
When Hell Froze 1930,O 5,IX,4:6
Twelfth Night 1930,O 16,28:2
Twelfth Night 1930,O 19,IX,4:5
Twelfth Night 1930,N 2,VIII,1:1
Art and Mrs Bottle 1930,N 19,19:3
Thousand Summers, A 1932,My 25,23:4
Rain From Heaven 1934,D 11,26:5
Rain From Heaven 1934,D 16,XI,2:1
Rain From Heaven 1934,D 25,28:4
Rain From Heaven 1935,Ja 6,IX,1:1
Romance 1935,Ag 27,23:4
First Lady 1935,N 11,21:3
First Lady 1935,N 27,17:4
First Lady 1935,D 8,X,3:1
First Lady 1936,O 11,X,3:1
Merchant of Yonkers, The 1938,D 13,30:1
Merchant of Yonkers, The 1938,D 18,IX,3:2
Merchant of Yonkers, The 1938,D 29,14:2
Old Acquaintance 1940,D 10,33:5
Old Acquaintance 1940,D 24,18:3
Ring Around Elizabeth 1941,N 18,32:2
First Mrs Fraser, The 1947,N 6,36:2
Cowl, Jane (Director)
Diversion 1928,Ja 6,26:3
Diversion 1928,Ja 12,25:1
Cowl, Jane (Playwright)
Depths, The 1925,F 8,VII,1:1
Jealous Moon, The 1928,O 21,IX,2:1
Jealous Moon, The 1928,N 21,32:2
Hervey House 1935,My 18,21:2
Cowle, Laura
Hamlet 1934,N 15,25:1
Hamlet 1934,D 2,X,3:6
Cowles, Albert
To the Ladies! 1922,F 21,20:1
Merton of the Movies 1922,N 14,16:2
Cowles, Albert (Playwright)
Lady Do 1927,Ap 19,24:2
Cowles, Chandler
Cradle Will Rock, The 1947,N 25,38:3
Cradle Will Rock, The 1947,D 27,11:2
Small Wonder 1948,S 16,33:5
Men of Distinction 1953,My 1,18:4
Cowles, Chandler (Director)
Consul, The 1957,S 4,40:3

Cowles, Chandler (Miscellaneous)
Medium, The 1948,D 8,41:6
Telephone, The 1948,D 8,41:6
Telephone, The 1950,Jl 20,22:5
Medium, The 1950,Jl 20,22:5
Cowles, Chandler (Producer)
Telephone, The 1947,My 2,28:2
Medium, The 1947,My 2,28:2
Consul, The 1950,Mr 16,41:1
Billy Budd 1951,F 12,18:3
Fancy Meeting You Again 1952,Ja 15,23:2
Of Thee I Sing 1952,My 6,34:2
Men of Distinction 1953,My 1,18:4
Saint of Bleecker Street, The 1954,D 28,21:1
Julius Caesar 1955,Jl 13,20:1
Tempest, The 1955,Ag 2,18:2
Caligula 1960,F 17,31:1
Cowles, Frances
Burmese Pwe, A 1926,Mr 17,28:1
Cowles, Jeanine B
Lady in the Dark 1952,Mr 8,11:3
Cowles, Matthew
Malcolm 1966,Ja 12,29:1
King John 1967,Jl 14,19:1
Indian Wants the Bronx, The 1968,Ja 18,47:2
I Saw a Monkey 1968,N 4,57:3
Stop, You're Killing Me; Bad Bad Jo-Jo 1969,Mr 20,53:1
Time of Your Life, The 1969,N 7,37:1
Cowles, Virginia (Playwright)
Love Goes to Press 1946,Je 19,16:2
Love Goes to Press 1947,Ja 2,22:2
Cowley, Eric
Happy Husband, The 1927,Jl 10,VII,2:3
Petticoat Influence 1930,D 16,34:6
Breadwinner, The 1931,S 23,19:4
Hay Fever 1931,D 6,VIII,2:8
Hay Fever 1931,D 30,25:1
Once Is Enough 1938,F 16,16:2
Cowley, Frederick Kitson (Director)
Twelfth Disciple, The 1930,My 17,21:4
Cowley, Harry
Bootleggers, The 1922,N 28,24:1
Deep Tangled Wildwood, The 1923,N 6,22:1
Goose Hangs High, The 1924,Ja 30,16:1
Cowley, William (Miscellaneous)
H M S Pinafore 1968,O 30,35:1
Mikado, The 1968,N 2,29:4
Pirates of Penzance, The 1968,N 7,54:1
Iolanthe 1968,N 9,37:3
Cowman, Herbert
Ice Capades 1955,S 15,38:1
Ice Capades 1956,S 13,41:2
Ice Capades 1957,S 5,33:2
Ice Capades 1959,S 4,12:1
Ice Capades 1960,S 1,30:1
Ice Capades 1962,Ag 30,34:1
Cox, Ainslee (Miscellaneous)
Penny Friend, The 1966,D 27,46:1
Cox, Andrew
Idiot, The 1960,S 26,38:1
Emmanuel 1960,D 5,42:2
Cox, Baby
Hot Chocolates 1929,Je 21,17:4
Cox, Bill
Town's Woman, The 1929,Mr 12,26:2
Cox, Constance (Playwright)
Vanity Fair 1946,N 10,II,3:1
Two Cities 1969,Mr 1,22:1
Cox, Constance (Producer)
Vanity Fair 1946,N 3,I,54:6
Cox, Dorothy Murdock
Buzzard, The 1928,Mr 15,29:1
Cox, Edwin R Jr
That's That 1924,Ap 30,19:2
Joan of Arkansas 1925,Ap 5,16:1
Cox, Eleanor
Rollo's Wild Oat 1920,N 24,14:1
Cox, Gertrude (Baby)
Hummin' Sam 1933,Ap 10,8:8
Cox, Hazel L
Black Crook, The 1929,Mr 12,26:5
Cox, India
Prince of Pilsen, The 1930,Ja 14,24:3
Cox, June
Counsellor-at-Law 1931,N 7,17:2
Growing Pains 1933,N 24,24:2
Cox, Lawrence
Between Two Thieves 1960,F 12,23:1
Cox, Michael Graham
Saint Joan 1962,F 21,57:4
Cox, Orange
Sweet River 1936,O 29,30:2
Cox, Richard
We Bombed in New Haven 1967,D 7,58:1
Saved 1970,O 29,57:1
Cox, Ronny
Hard Travelin' 1965,Je 17,25:1
Iceman Cometh, The 1968,Ap 1,58:1
Indians 1969,My 27,43:1
Wars of the Roses, The (Part I) 1970,Jl 2,30:1
Happiness Cage, The 1970,O 5,56:4

Cox, Ronny (Composer)
Happiness Cage, The 1970,O 5,56:4
Cox, Rosanna
Family Portrait 1959,My 6,48:2
Cox, Shirley
Antigone 1962,D 29,5:5
Orthee 1962,D 29,5:5
Cox, Thomas
Wild Duck, The 1928,N 19,17:1
Cox, Vita
Hall of Healing 1952,My 8,35:6
Cox, Wally
Dance Me a Song 1950,Ja 21,10:5
Moonbirds 1959,O 10,13:1
Cox, Wally (Playwright)
Dance Me a Song 1950,Ja 21,10:5
Cox, Wilbur
Three Showers 1920,Ap 6,18:1
Six-Fifty, The 1921,O 25,20:1
Six-Fifty, The 1921,O 30,VI,1:1
Play, A 1925,F 11,19:2
Scarlet Sister Mary 1930,N 26,19:2
Passionate Pilgrim, The 1932,O 20,24:3
Cox, William
Four Walls 1927,S 20,33:1
All's Well That Ends Well 1966,Je 17,39:1
Richard III 1966,Ag 11,26:1
Cox, Wilma
Hey, Nonny, Nonny! 1932,Je 7,22:3
Strike Me Pink 1933,Mr 6,16:3
Coxe, Daniel
Lolly 1929,O 17,26:2
Coxe, Daniel (Playwright)
Room of Dreams 1930,N 6,22:4
Coxe, Louis O (Playwright)
Uniform of Flesh 1949,Ja 31,15:2
Billy Budd 1951,F 12,18:3
Billy Budd 1951,F 18,II,1:1
Billy Budd 1951,Ap 15,II,1:1
Billy Budd 1951,My 6,II,1:1
Billy Budd 1955,My 4,35:1
Witchfinders, The 1956,My 11,22:6
Billy Budd 1959,F 28,13:3
Coxe, Maria
Marching Song 1937,F 18,18:2
Coxe, William James
This Mad Whirl 1937,Ja 10,II,4:8
Coxe (Playwright)
Kit Marlowe 1936,My 24,35:1
Coxhead, Hope
Charley's Aunt 1925,Je 2,16:2
Coxwell, David
Anvil, The 1962,O 31,33:3
Coy, Judith
Red Roses for Me 1955,D 29,15:2
Metamorphosis 1957,F 20,38:1
Coy, Stephen
Here Comes Santa Claus 1962,My 18,34:1
Coy, Walter
R U R 1930,F 18,28:1
Marco Millions 1930,Mr 4,24:4
Lonely Way, The 1931,F 22,VIII,4:1
House of Connelly, The 1931,S 29,22:4
1931 1931,D 11,34:3
Night Over Taos 1932,Mr 10,25:3
Men in White 1933,S 27,24:2
Gold Eagle Guy 1934,N 29,33:4
Waiting for Lefty 1935,F 11,14:5
Panic 1935,Mr 16,18:4
Till the Day I Die 1935,Mr 27,24:5
Waiting for Lefty 1935,Mr 27,24:5
Paradise Lost 1935,D 10,31:5
Case of Clyde Griffiths 1936,Mr 14,10:4
Many Mansions 1937,O 28,28:6
Escape This Night 1938,Ap 23,18:1
Night Music 1940,F 23,18:2
Fledgling 1940,N 28,29:2
Lady in the Dark 1941,S 3,26:6
Hamlet 1945,D 14,25:2
Hamlet 1945,D 23,II,3:1
Land's End 1946,D 12,37:5
O'Daniel 1947,F 25,32:2
Volpone 1948,Ja 9,24:6
Coy, Walter (Playwright)
Group Theatre Sketches 1935,F 11,14:5
Coyle, Elizabeth
Good Times 1920,Ag 10,10:1
Coyle, J J (Playwright)
Ninety Day Mistress, The 1967,N 7,49:1
Coyle, Jack
Mating Season, The 1927,Jl 19,27:6
Footlights 1927,Ag 20,8:2
Coyle, James
Madame X 1927,Jl 7,29:3
Mr Moneypenny 1928,O 17,26:2
Tree, The 1932,Ap 13,23:5
Man Who Reclaimed His Head 1932,S 9,17:3
Battle Hymn 1936,My 23,12:1
Little Darling 1942,O 28,26:2
Live Life Again 1945,O 1,14:7
Coyle, John
Noah 1954,O 11,32:2
In April Once 1955,Mr 14,29:3

Coyle, John (Miscellaneous)
Cocktails of 1934 1934,My 5,22:1
Coyle, Tom
Journey by Night, A 1935,Ap 17,26:3
Coyle, Wally
Good News 1927,S 7,35:4
Up in Central Park 1947,My 20,29:2
Coyne, Arthur V
Feast of Panthers 1961,Mr 21,32:1
Coyne, Joseph
Katinka 1923,Ag 31,15:4
Katinka 1923,S 2,VI,1:7
Coyne, Kathleen
Getting Married 1970,Ja 20,46:1
Coyne, Phoebe
Jitta's Atonement 1923,Ja 18,16:3
Venetian, The 1931,N 2,26:1
Coyne, Thomas J
Great Way, The 1921,N 8,28:2
Cozine, W C
Night at an Inn, A 1930,My 10,25:1
Cozza, Paul
Seven Scenes for Yeni 1963,My 13,36:2
Cozzens, Catherine
Sylvia 1923,Ap 26,22:1
Cozzens, Ethel
He and She 1920,F 13,16:3
Crabbe, Buster
New Aquacade Revue, The 1940,My 13,20:5
Aquarama 1960 1960,Jl 1,14:6
Crabtree, Don
Destry Rides Again 1959,Ap 24,24:1
Happiest Girl in the World, The 1961,Ap 4,42:1
Sophie 1963,Ap 16,32:1
110 in the Shade 1963,O 25,37:1
Golden Boy 1964,O 21,56:1
Pousse-Cafe 1966,Mr 19,19:2
Mahagonny 1970,Ap 29,51:1
Crabtree, Paul
Men to the Sea 1944,O 4,25:2
Streets Are Guarded, The 1944,N 21,19:7
Sky Drift 1945,N 14,25:2
Iceman Cometh, The 1946,O 10,31:3
Story for a Sunday Evening, A 1950,N 18,10:5
Lo and Behold! 1951,D 13,45:2
Crabtree, Paul (Director)
O'Daniel 1947,F 25,32:2
This Time Tomorrow 1947,N 4,31:2
Silver Whistle, The 1948,N 25,49:2
Texas Li'l Darlin' 1949,N 26,10:5
Story for a Sunday Evening, A 1950,N 18,10:5
Mid-Summer 1953,Ja 22,19:1
Stage Affair, A 1962,Ja 17,30:2
Crabtree, Paul (Playwright)
Story for a Sunday Evening, A 1950,N 18,10:5
Stage Affair, A 1962,Ja 17,30:2
Crabtree, Paul (Producer)
Mid-Summer 1953,Ja 22,19:1
Cracraft, Tom Adrian (Scenic Designer)
Second Mate, The 1930,Mr 25,34:5
Goodbye Again 1932,D 29,16:4
Hilda Cassidy 1933,My 5,18:3
They All Come to Moscow 1933,My 12,20:6
Shady Lady 1933,Jl 6,26:3
Love and Babies 1933,Ag 23,21:4
Kultur 1933,S 27,24:3
Wednesday's Child 1934,Ja 17,23:2
Broomsticks Amen! 1934,F 10,20:4
I Myself 1934,My 10,24:6
Alley Cat 1934,S 18,18:1
Roll Sweet Chariot 1934,O 3,24:3
All Rights Reserved 1934,N 7,33:5
Black Pit 1935,Mr 21,26:6
Symphony 1935,Ap 27,20:3
Country Wife, The 1935,Jl 2,24:2
Coward, The 1935,Jl 16,24:1
If This Be Treason 1935,Jl 30,17:1
American Holiday 1936,F 22,13:3
Murder in the Cathedral 1936,Mr 21,13:5
Class of '29 1936,My 16,10:3
Help Yourself! 1936,Jl 15,15:1
It Can't Happen Here 1936,O 28,30:1
Sun and I, The 1937,F 27,9:5
Hero Is Born, A 1937,O 2,18:6
Hill Between, The 1938,Mr 12,12:5
Window Shopping 1938,D 24,13:2
Popsy 1941,F 11,26:2
Craddock, Earle
No Other Girl 1924,Ag 14,10:4
In the Near Future 1925,Mr 11,19:1
Don Q Jr 1926,Ja 28,16:3
Friend Indeed 1926,Ap 27,22:3
Good Fellow, The 1926,O 6,22:1
Craddock, Louis
Kilpatrick's Old-Time Minstrels 1930,Ap 21,20:2
Craddock and Shadney
Bottomland 1927,Je 28,29:3
Crafa, Art (Sgt)
Swing Sister Wac Swing 1944,Ja 4,20:4
Crafa, Art (Sgt) (Director)
Swing Sister Wac Swing 1944,Ja 4,20:4
Craft, Ethel
Harriet 1944,S 28,26:1

All Summer Long 1953,Ja 29,23:1
Craft, Marcela
Secret of Suzanne, The 1920,Ja 13,10:2
Craft, Thomas
Dark of the Moon 1970,Ap 4,21:2
Crafts, Charles
Round the Town 1924,My 22,14:3
Crafts, Griffin
Happy Landing 1932,Mr 28,10:5
Bulls, Bears and Asses 1932,My 7,11:3
Ghost Writer, The 1933,Je 20,22:4
Crafts and Haley
Vaudeville (Palace) 1924,F 19,12:1
Cragin, William
Streets of New York, The 1934,Jl 21,14:5
Russet Mantle 1936,Ag 18,15:2
Laughing Woman, The 1936,O 14,30:1
Wind in the Sails 1940,Ag 1,24:6
Craib, Brian
As You Like It 1959,Jl 1,27:1
Craig, Alice
Boys From Syracuse, The 1938,N 24,36:1
Pal Joey 1940,D 26,22:2
Craig, Bob
Burning Bush, The 1949,D 17,15:5
Craig, Charles G (Mrs)
Passion Flower, The 1920,Ja 14,12:1
Beware of Dogs 1921,O 4,10:1
On the Stairs 1922,S 26,18:2
Craig, Colin
King Lear 1940,D 16,27:2
Days of Our Youth, The 1941,N 29,15:2
Johnny Doodle 1942,Mr 19,28:2
Family Portrait 1959,My 6,48:2
Jonah! 1967,S 22,52:2
Craig, Collin
King Lear 1940,D 16,27:2
Craig, David
Pal Joey 1949,Mr 7,17:2
Craig, David (Lyricist)
Phoenix '55 1955,Ap 25,20:2
Copper and Brass 1957,O 18,19:2
Craig, David (Miscellaneous)
Of Thee I Sing 1952,My 6,34:2
Craig, David (Playwright)
Copper and Brass 1957,O 18,19:2
Craig, Dick
Howdy Mr Ice 1948,Je 25,28:5
Howdy, Mr Ice of 1950 1949,My 27,24:2
Craig, E F (Composer)
1776 1926,Ap 24,11:2
Not Now-Later 1928,Ap 14,25:1
Craig, E F (Lyricist)
Not Now-Later 1928,Ap 14,25:1
Craig, Edith
Life With Father 1939,Ag 15,14:4
Craig, Edward
Johnny Belinda 1940,S 19,26:2
Craig, George
Blushing Bride, The 1922,F 7,12:1
Craig, Gordon (Scenic Designer)
Macbeth 1928,N 4,IX,1:3
Macbeth 1928,N 20,28:3
Craig, Helen
Russet Mantle 1936,Ja 17,15:5
New Faces of 1936 1936,My 20,24:5
American Primitive 1937,Ag 13,12:5
Soliloquy 1938,N 29,26:4
Unconquered, The 1940,F 14,25:2
Johnny Belinda 1940,S 19,26:2
As You Like It 1941,O 21,29:2
Lute Song 1946,F 7,29:2
Land's End 1946,D 12,37:5
House of Bernarda Alba, The 1951,Ja 8,14:6
Maya 1953,Je 10,35:1
Diamond Orchid 1965,F 11,44:4
Medea 1965,N 29,46:1
To Clothe the Naked 1967,Ap 28,30:1
More Stately Mansions 1967,N 1,40:1
Craig, Jack (Miscellaneous)
Hello, Dolly! 1967,N 13,61:1
Craig, James
Missouri Legend 1938,S 20,27:2
Craig, Jane
Awhile to Work 1937,Mr 20,23:1
Craig, Jerry
Gentlemen Prefer Blondes 1949,D 9,35:3
Craig, Jessica (Costume Designer)
Song Out of Sorrow 1955,N 1,27:3
Age and Grace 1956,F 21,38:2
Craig, John
Nemesis 1921,Ap 5,24:3
Nemesis 1921,Ap 10,VI,1:1
Ambush 1921,O 11,22:1
Rivals, The 1922,Je 6,18:2
Jitta's Atonement 1923,Ja 18,16:3
As You Like It 1923,Ap 24,24:1
Rivals, The 1923,My 9,14:2
School for Scandal, The 1923,Je 5,24:3
Woman on the Jury, The 1923,Ag 16,10:4
Morals 1925,D 1,22:2
Diana 1929,D 10,37:1
Rivals, The 1930,Mr 14,24:4

Craig, John (Director)
Julius Caesar 1927,Je 7,27:2
Craig, John 2d (Producer)
Storm Child 1936,Ap 18,18:4
At Your Service 1937,Ag 17,23:1
Craig, Louise
All You Need Is One Good Break 1950,F 10,20:3
Craig, Lucretia
Honey Girl 1920,My 4,9:1
Honey Girl 1920,My 4,9:1
Snapshots of 1921 1921,Je 3,19:2
Up She Goes 1922,N 7,14:2
Craig, May
Words Upon the Window Pane, The
1931,Ja 4,VIII,3:5
Things That Are Caesar's, The 1932,O 18,23:4
Far-Off Hills, The 1932,O 19,22:4
Juno and the Paycock 1932,O 20,24:3
Playboy of the Western World, The 1932,O 21,25:1
New Gossoon, The 1932,O 22,18:2
Words Upon the Window Pane, The
1932,O 29,18:2
Shadow of a Gunman, The 1932,O 31,18:1
Cathleen ni Houlihan 1932,O 31,18:1
Autumn Fire 1932,D 29,16:3
Big House, The 1933,Ja 5,19:3
King Oedipus 1933,Ja 16,12:4
Church Street 1934,My 23,15:5
Plough and the Stars, The 1934,N 13,22:2
Drama at Inish 1934,N 15,24:2
Look at the Heffernans 1934,N 17,13:2
Church Street 1934,N 20,24:5
Well of the Saints, The 1934,N 22,26:2
Plough and the Stars, The 1937,O 8,26:5
Far-Off Hills, The 1937,O 12,30:4
In the Train 1937,N 22,14:5
Playboy of the Western World, The 1937,N 22,14:5
New Gossoon, The 1937,N 30,26:2
Juno and the Paycock 1937,D 7,32:5
Juno and the Paycock 1966,Ag 3,40:1
Craig, Michael
Homecoming, The 1967,Ja 6,29:1
Craig, Miriam
Slice It Thin 1945,My 11,22:5
Time of Storm 1954,F 26,14:2
Juno and the Paycock 1955,F 24,20:4
Doll's House, A 1956,My 8,29:2
Craig, Noel
Rosencrantz and Guildenstern Are Dead
1967,O 17,53:1
Patriot for Me, A 1969,O 6,58:1
Conduct Unbecoming 1970,O 13,50:1
Craig, Peter
Tom Paine 1968,Mr 26,38:1
Futz 1968,Je 14,39:1
Craig, Phyllis
Borstal Boy 1970,Ap 1,38:1
Craig, Polly
Failures, The 1923,N 23,20:1
Shadow, The 1923,D 15,16:2
Bridge of Distances, The 1925,S 29,30:1
Dream Play 1926,Ja 21,18:2
Craig, Richard
Sons o' Fun 1941,D 2,28:2
Icetime 1946,Je 21,20:5
Icetime 1947,My 29,28:2
Craig, Richy Jr
Dear Sir 1924,S 24,21:3
Ramblers, The 1926,S 21,32:2
Vaudeville (Palace) 1931,S 28,17:5
Hey, Nonny, Nonny! 1932,Je 7,22:3
Vaudeville (Palace) 1932,Jl 11,11:6
Craig, Richy Jr (Playwright)
Hey, Nonny, Nonny! 1932,Je 7,22:3
Craig, Robert
Two Blocks Away 1921,Ag 31,8:3
Give and Take 1923,Ja 19,13:1
White Collars 1925,F 24,17:2
Lucky Sam McCarver 1925,O 22,22:1
Great Gatsby, The 1926,F 3,22:1
Possession 1928,O 3,35:1
Strong Man's House, A 1929,S 17,34:3
School for Virtue 1931,Ap 22,29:2
Hot Money 1931,N 9,22:2
Trick for Trick 1932,F 19,14:2
Tragedy of the Ages, The 1933,Ap 7,22:7
Move on, Sister 1933,O 25,22:4
Craig, Virginia
Hot Spot 1963,Ap 20,17:2
Look to the Lilies 1970,Mr 30,59:1
Craig, W Gordon
Mima 1928,D 13,24:2
Craig, Walter
Ah, Wilderness! 1941,O 3,26:2
Three Sisters, The 1942,D 22,31:2
Wanhope Building, The 1947,F 11,36:5
Craig, Walter (Director)
One Thing After Another 1937,D 29,17:2
Craig, Walter (Producer)
One Thing After Another 1937,D 29,17:2
Craig, Wendy
Epitaph for George Dillon 1958,N 5,44:1

Craig, William C (Director)
Everyman Today 1958,Ja 16,32:4
Craik, Robert
Roseanne 1923,D 31,9:5
Vagabond King, The 1925,S 22,23:3
Crain, Alan (Lighting Director)
Land Beyond the River, A 1957,Mr 29,15:7
Crain, Jon
Gondoliers, The 1962,Ap 19,34:2
Cramer, Gail
Salvage 1957,Ap 10,39:2
Johnny Summit 1957,S 25,23:4
Cramer, Richard
Sancho Panza 1923,N 27,23:1
Cramer and Johnson (Composer)
A la Carte 1927,Ag 18,25:3
Cramer and Johnson (Lyricist)
A la Carte 1927,Ag 18,25:3
Crampton-Smith, Howard (Miscellaneous)
Brownstone Urge, The 1969,D 18,63:1
Nobody Hears A Broken Drum 1970,Mr 20,55:1
Crandall, Burr
Knights of Song 1938,O 18,29:2
Crandall, Carlin
Agent 666, L' 1923,My 30,10:5
Rust 1924,F 1,12:1
Great Music 1924,O 6,24:1
Jane-Our Stranger 1925,O 9,27:2
Naked 1926,N 9,31:2
Caste 1927,D 24,8:1
Crandall, Catherine
Allez-Opp! 1927,Ag 3,29:3
Crandall, Edward
Merchant of Venice, The 1922,D 22,13:1
Ostriches 1925,Mr 31,16:1
Loves of Lulu, The 1925,My 12,26:1
Young Woodley 1925,N 3,34:1
Play's the Thing, The 1926,N 4,25:1
Venus 1927,D 26,26:5
Our Betters 1928,F 21,18:2
Heavy Traffic 1928,S 6,23:3
Lady of the Orchids, The 1928,D 14,37:3
His Majesty's Car 1930,O 24,30:1
Give Me Yesterday 1931,Mr 5,32:1
Fatal Alibi, The 1932,F 10,26:6
Absent Father 1932,O 18,23:5
Party, A 1933,Ag 24,18:4
Small Miracle 1934,S 27,24:3
Kiss Them for Me 1945,MR 21,27:2
Crandall, Elizabeth
Hello, Daddy! 1928,D 27,26:5
Count of Luxembourg, The 1930,F 18,28:2
Serenade, The 1930,Mr 5,26:7
Bitter Sweet 1934,My 8,28:4
Music Hath Charms 1934,D 31,8:2
Crandall, Patti
Ice Follies 1959,Ja 14,30:1
Crandall, Victoria (Producer)
Jo 1964,F 13,25:1
Crandall, W W (Producer)
Caesar and Cleopatra 1927,N 6,IX,2:1
Crane, Alan
Ups-A-Daisy 1928,O 9,34:2
Partition 1948,O 29,31:2
Crane, Bart
Bloodstream 1932,Mr 31,25:1
Crane, Bettymae
New Hellzapoppin, The 1939,D 12,36:4
Crane, Beverly
Hellzapoppin 1938,S 23,34:2
New Hellzapoppin, The 1939,D 12,36:4
Crane, Cliff
Keep Moving 1934,Ag 24,10:2
Crane, Dean
Lute Song 1959,Mr 13,24:1
Carnival! 1961,Ap 14,22:2
Carnival! 1968,D 13,58:1
Crane, Dorothy M (Director)
God Innis 1937,Ag 25,24:3
Crane, Hal
Leah Kleschna 1924,Ap 22,19:2
Crane, Harold
New Sin, The 1923,My 28,18:3
Dearest Enemy 1925,S 19,9:2
Pleasure Bound 1929,F 19,22:4
Du Barry 1932,N 23,15:2
In Bed We Cry 1944,N 15,20:2
Qudrille 1954,N 4,39:2
Crane, Helen
Firebird 1932,N 22,25:2
Shooting Star 1933,Je 13,22:2
Crane, Henry
Billy Budd 1955,My 4,35:1
Crane, J Monte
Boubouroche 1921,N 29,20:1
Inspector General, The 1923,My 1,24:1
Crane, James
Opportunity 1920,Jl 31,5:1
Varying Shore, The 1921,D 6,24:1
On the Stairs 1922,S 26,18:2
House Divided, The 1923,N 12,14:1
Odd Man Out 1925,My 26,24:3
All Dressed Up 1925,S 10,28:1

Black Cockatoo, The 1926,D 31,11:1
Lost 1927,Mr 29,22:2
Revelry 1927,S 13,37:1
Crane, James L Jr
Fiesta 1933,D 16,12:2
Crane, Lor (Composer)
Whispers on the Wind 1970,Je 4,50:1
Crane, Mary
Daddy Dumplins 1920,N 23,11:1
Crane, Ned
Confederacy, The 1958,Jl 3,20:1
Crane, Ned (Scenic Designer)
Triplets 1932,S 22,25:2
Crane, Norma
Career 1957,My 1,42:6
Career 1957,My 19,II,1:1
Isle of Children 1962,Mr 17,16:2
Crane, P V
Laugh It Off 1925,Ap 25,18:4
Crane, Payson
Once in a Lifetime 1930,S 25,22:3
Crane, Raymond
Merry Widow, The 1921,S 6,13:1
Clinging Vine, The 1922,D 25,20:2
Crane, Robert
In Clover 1937,O 14,23:1
Crane, Stephen
Paths of Glory 1935,S 27,24:2
Crane, Ted
Brothers Ashkenazi, The 1970,N 17,53:2
Crane, Thurston
Red, Hot and Blue! 1936,O 30,26:3
Crane, Tom
Hogan's Goat 1965,N 12,56:1
Crane, Vernon
Searching for the Sun 1936,F 20,22:6
So Proudly We Hail 1936,S 23,28:4
Richard II 1937,S 16,28:2
Crane, Walter
Piper Paid 1934,D 26,19:1
Crane, Warren (Lighting Director)
Darwin's Theories 1960,O 19,53:2
Crane, Warren (Miscellaneous)
Hollow Crown, The 1963,Ja 31,5:1
Beast in Me, The 1963,My 17,29:1
White House, The 1964,My 20,39:1
P S I Love You 1964,N 20,40:1
Come Live With Me 1967,Ja 27,29:1
Promise, The 1967,N 15,38:1
Loot 1968,Mr 19,40:2
Lovers; Winners 1968,Jl 26,21:4
Lovers; Losers 1968,Jl 26,21:4
We Bombed in New Haven 1968,O 17,51:1
Mundy Scheme, The 1969,D 12,75:1
Sleuth 1970,N 13,25:1
Crane, William
Washington Heights 1931,S 30,23:4
Craney, Bernard
Whirlpool 1929,D 4,37:3
Air-Minded 1932,F 11,17:3
Cranger, John
Little Hut, The 1953,O 8,37:2
Cranham, Kenneth
Loot 1968,Mr 19,40:2
Cranko, John (Director)
Cranks 1956,My 14,23:1
Cranks 1956,N 27,32:1
Cranko, John (Lyricist)
Cranks 1956,My 14,23:1
Cranko, John (Playwright)
Cranks 1956,N 27,32:1
Crankshaw, Edward (Translator)
No More Peace 1938,Ja 29,13:2
Crankshaw (Translator)
Miracle in America 1934,O 2,18:4
Cranney, Jon
Harpers Ferry 1967,Je 6,52:2
She Stoops to Conquer 1968,Ja 1,11:1
Resistible Rise of Arturo Ui, The 1968,Ag 8,25:1
House of Atreus, The 1968,D 18,55:1
Resistible Rise of Arturo Ui, The 1968,D 23,44:1
Crans, Tec (Director)
Sunset 1966,My 13,34:1
Cranton, Hal (Original Author)
Buttrio Square 1952,O 15,40:2
Cranzano, Joe (Miscellaneous)
Diary of Adam and Eve, The 1966,O 19,53:1
Lady or the Tiger?, The 1966,O 19,53:1
Passionella 1966,O 19,53:1
Crapa, Mary Morley (Playwright)
Bedrock 1934,N 18,II,6:3
Crask, Lamar
Tall Kentuckian, The 1953,Je 17,30:1
Crauer, Sylvia Decker
Little Theatre Tournament; White Peacock, The 1928,My 11,28:1
Crause, Gertrude
Soul of a Woman, The 1930,F 22,13:1
Cravat, Noel
Eternal Road, The 1937,Ja 8,14:2
Between the Devil 1937,D 23,24:5
????? 1939,Ja 2,28:2

Cravath, Martin
If I Were You 1931,S 24,21:1
Gay Divorce 1932,N 30,23:4
Yoshe Kalb 1933,D 29,27:2
Cravath, Martin (Composer)
Bloody Laughter 1931,D 5,20:6
Craven, David
Midsummer Night's Dream, A 1967,Je 30,23:1
Craven, Doris Hawes
Gypsy Baron, The 1930,Ap 22,22:8
Craven, Edward
Little Ol' Boy 1933,Ap 25,15:5
Sailor, Beware! 1933,S 29,24:4
Ragged Edge, The 1935,N 26,28:3
Star Spangled 1936,Mr 11,23:1
Fulton of Oak Falls 1937,Ja 2,15:3
Fulton of Oak Falls 1937,F 11,18:2
Without Warning 1937,My 3,23:2
Tortilla Flat 1938,Ja 13,16:2
Great Lady 1938,D 2,26:6
Craven, Frank
Girl From Home, The 1920,My 4,9:2
First Year, The 1920,O 21,11:2
First Year, The 1920,O 31,VI,1:1
Fall Guy, The 1924,Jl 20,VII,1:7
Money From Home 1927,Mr 1,30:2
19th Hole, The 1927,O 12,30:3
Nineteenth Hole, The 1929,Ja 6,VIII,4:4
Salt Water 1929,N 27,30:3
That's Gratitude 1930,S 12,28:1
Riddle Me This! 1932,F 26,22:5
For Valor 1935,N 12,24:4
For Valor 1935,N 19,27:5
Our Town 1938,Ja 23,II,10:6
Our Town 1938,Ja 26,27:4
Our Town 1938,Ja 30,X,3:1
Our Town 1938,F 5,18:3
Our Town 1938,F 13,X,1:1
Village Green 1941,Je 17,24:7
Village Green 1941,Ag 27,15:3
Village Green 1941,S 4,24:4
Village Green 1941,S 14,IX,1:1
Flowers of Virtue, The 1942,F 6,22:2
Mrs January & Mr Ex 1944,Ap 1,10:2
Craven, Frank (Director)
Pigs 1924,Je 8,VII,1:8
New Brooms 1924,N 18,23:5
Twinkle Twinkle 1926,N 17,22:2
Money From Home 1927,Mr 1,30:2
That's Gratitude 1930,S 12,28:1
Whistling in the Dark 1932,Ja 20,16:6
Riddle Me This! 1932,F 26,22:5
Bridal Wise 1932,My 31,15:5
Touch of Brimstone, A 1935,S 23,20:1
For Valor 1935,N 19,27:5
Craven, Frank (Playwright)
Girl From Home, The 1920,My 4,9:2
First Year, The 1920,O 21,11:2
First Year, The 1920,O 31,VI,1:1
Spite Corner 1921,Jl 17,VI,1:1
First Year, The 1921,N 27,VI,1:1
Spite Corner 1922,S 26,18:1
Up She Goes 1922,N 7,14:2
New Brooms 1924,N 18,23:5
First Year, The 1926,D 19,VII,6:4
Money From Home 1927,Mr 1,30:2
19th Hole, The 1927,O 2,VIII,4:6
19th Hole, The 1927,O 12,30:3
Nineteenth Hole, The 1929,Ja 6,VIII,4:4
That's Gratitude 1930,S 12,28:1
That's Gratitude 1930,S 21,IX,1:1
That's Gratitude 1932,Je 17,24:3
Craven, Frank (Producer)
New Brooms 1924,N 18,23:5
Craven, Harry
Laugh, Clown, Laugh! 1923,N 29,30:1
Craven, James
Ross 1961,D 27,20:2
Craven, John
Our Town 1938,Ja 23,II,10:6
Our Town 1938,Ja 26,27:4
Our Town 1938,Ja 30,X,3:1
Our Town 1938,F 5,18:3
Happiest Days, The 1939,Ap 12,26:2
Happiest Days, The 1939,Ap 16,X,1:2
Aries Is Rising 1939,N 22,16:5
Two on an Island 1940,Ja 16,18:4
Two on an Island 1940,Ja 23,17:2
Two on an Island 1940,Ja 28,IX,1:2
Two on an Island 1940,F 4,IX,1:1
Delicate Story 1940,D 5,32:2
Village Green 1941,Je 17,24:7
Village Green 1941,S 4,24:4
Village Green 1941,S 14,IX,1:1
Spring Again 1941,O 28,28:3
Spring Again 1941,N 11,28:2
They Knew What They Wanted 1949,F 17,28:2
Craven, Margaret
Romeo and Juliet 1934,D 21,30:3
Panic 1935,Mr 16,18:4
Craven, Peggy
Having Wonderful Time 1937,F 22,12:5

Craven, Robert
Dear Octopus 1939,Ja 12,22:2
Foreigners 1939,D 6,30:2
Glamour Preferred 1940,N 16,13:2
Craven, Robin
Hand in Glove 1944,D 5,19:1
Present Laughter 1946,O 30,31:2
Strange Bedfellows 1948,Ja 15,27:3
Corn Is Green, The 1950,Ja 12,33:2
King and I, The 1951,Mr 30,26:2
Witness for the Prosecution 1954,D 17,35:2
Witness for the Prosecution 1954,D 26,II,1:1
My Fair Lady 1958,Mr 9,II,1:1
Passage to India, A 1962,F 1,23:1
Craven, Ruby
Adding Machine, The 1923,Mr 20,24:1
Craven, Sally
Boys and Girls Together 1940,O 2,19:2
Cravens, Kathryn
Twelfth Disciple, The 1930,My 17,21:4
Cravet, Noel
Night of Love 1941,Ja 8,14:2
Crawford, Alice
Carmen Jones 1951,S 22,8:6
Crawford, Alice (Playwright)
Berlin 1931,D 31,16:1
Crawford, Ann
Fatal Wedding, The 1924,Je 3,22:3
Crawford, Anne
Green Bay Tree, The 1951,F 2,18:2
Crawford, Antoinette
Passing of the Third Floor Back, The
1928,F 21,18:2
Waltz of the Dogs, The 1928,Ap 26,31:3
Crawford, Archer
Class of '29 1936,My 16,10:3
Crawford, Bobby (Producer)
Seperate Rooms 1940,Mr 25,10:3
Crawford, Boyd
Ladies' Money 1934,N 2,26:6
Battleship Gertie 1935,Ja 19,9:2
Prodigal Father, The 1935,Jl 2,24:2
Traveler's Track 1936,Jl 21,13:5
Around the Corner 1936,D 29,17:2
Yes, My Darling Daughter 1937,F 10,19:2
Gloriana 1938,N 26,18:4
Summer Night 1939,N 3,17:1
Swingin' the Dream 1939,N 30,24:2
Druid Circle, The 1947,O 23,29:5
Crawford, Broderick
Point Valaine 1935,Ja 17,22:2
Sweet Mystery of Life 1935,O 12,13:3
Of Mice and Men 1937,N 24,20:5
Of Mice and Men 1937,D 12,XI,3:1
Crawford, Carl
Black Souls 1932,Mr 31,25:1
Macbeth 1936,Ap 15,25:4
Second Hurricane 1937,Ap 22,18:4
Big White Fog 1940,O 23,26:2
Crawford, Cheryl
Juarez and Maximilian 1926,O 12,31:1
Crawford, Cheryl (Director)
House of Connelly, The 1931,S 29,22:4
Big Night 1933,Ja 18,16:2
Till the Day I Die 1935,Mr 27,24:5
Weep for the Virgins 1935,D 2,18:1
House of Bernarda Alba, The 1951,Ja 8,14:6
Mary Rose 1951,Mr 5,25:2
Ecole des Femmes, L'; School for Wives
1951,Mr 19,22:1
Night Music 1951,Ap 9,29:6
Crawford, Cheryl (Miscellaneous)
Porgy and Bess 1944,F 8,13:2
Skipper Next to God 1948,Ja 5,14:5
Cellar and the Well, The 1950,D 11,30:2
Paint Your Wagon 1951,N 13,32:2
Crawford, Cheryl (Producer)
All the Living 1938,Mr 25,14:4
Family Portrait 1939,Mr 9,18:4
Another Sun 1940,F 24,8:6
Theatre of the Piccoli 1940,Mr 22,22:2
Porgy and Bess 1942,Ja 23,16:2
Porgy and Bess 1942,F 1,IX,1:1
Flowers of Virtue, The 1942,F 6,22:2
Kiss for Cinderella, A 1942,Mr 11,22:2
Porgy and Bess 1943,S 14,26:2
One Touch of Venus 1943,O 8,14:1
One Touch of Venus 1943,O 17,II,1:1
Perfect Marriage, The 1944,O 27,17:6
Tempest, The 1945,Ja 26,17:2
Tempest, The 1945,F 4,II,1:1
Brigadoon 1947,Mr 14,28:2
Temporary Island, A 1948,Mr 15,27:3
Love Life 1948,O 8,31:2
Regina 1949,N 1,32:2
Closing Door, The 1949,D 2,36:2
Brigadoon 1950,My 3,36:2
Peer Gynt 1951,Ja 29,15:2
Rose Tattoo, The 1951,F 5,19:2
Flahooley 1951,My 15,39:1
Camino Real 1953,Mr 20,26:1
Oh, Men! Oh, Women! 1953,D 18,37:2
Honeys, The 1955,Ap 29,26:1

Mister Johnson 1956,Mr 30,11:1
Girls of Summer 1956,N 20,45:1
Good as Gold 1957,Mr 8,22:2
Comes a Day 1958,N 7,22:1
Shadow of a Gunman, The 1958,N 21,26:1
Rivalry, The 1959,F 9,24:2
Sweet Bird of Youth 1959,Mr 11,39:2
Kukla, Burr and Ollie 1960,N 1,47:2
Period of Adjustment 1960,N 11,34:1
Brecht on Brecht 1962,Ja 4,26:1
Andorra 1963,F 11,5:5
Mother Courage and Her Children 1963,Mr 30,5:5
Jennie 1963,O 18,35:2
Sarah and the Sax 1964,My 5,53:1
Dirty Old Man, The 1964,My 5,53:1
Celebration 1969,Ja 23,55:2
Colette 1970,O 15,58:1
Crawford, Clarisse
Regina 1949,N 1,32:2
Regina 1952,Je 2,25:4
Crawford, Claudia
Rope Dancers, The 1959,Mr 14,26:1
Crawford, Collette
You Can't Take It With You 1951,Ap 7,8:6
Crawford, Don (Costume Designer)
Way of the World, The 1954,S 30,38:2
Morning's at Seven 1955,Je 23,25:1
Dragon's Mouth 1955,N 17,45:1
Dandy Dick 1956,Ja 11,37:2
Crawford, Don (Scenic Designer)
Way of the World, The 1954,S 30,38:2
Way of the World, The 1954,O 17,II,1:1
Thieves' Carnival 1955,F 2,21:1
Dandy Dick 1956,Ja 11,37:2
Crawford, Dorothy
Dorothy Crawford - Recital 1939,Mr 13,12:1
Crawford, Dorothy (Playwright)
Dorothy Crawford - Recital 1939,Mr 13,12:1
Crawford, Douglas S (Producer)
On the Town 1959,Ja 16,36:1
Crawford, Edna Archer
Innocent Idea, An 1920,My 26,9:4
Paging Danger 1931,F 27,19:2
Singing Rabbi, The 1931,S 11,24:4
Devil's Host, The 1931,N 20,27:2
Hotel Alimony 1934,Ja 30,16:2
Crawford, Elizabeth
Roof, The 1930,Je 14,9:2
Crawford, J R
As You Like It 1963,Jl 17,19:2
Electra 1964,Ag 12,42:1
Crawford, Jean
What of It? 1929,Mr 9,24:2
Crawford, John
This Fine-Pretty World 1923,D 27,11:1
Crawford, Joseph
Porgy and Bess 1935,O 11,30:2
Porgy and Bess 1953,Mr 10,25:5
Christine 1960,Ap 29,27:1
Crawford, Kathryn
New Yorkers, The 1930,D 9,31:1
Crawford, Lester
Vaudeville (Palace) 1926,Ap 20,24:6
Fifty Million Frenchmen 1929,N 28,34:4
Vanities 1932,S 28,22:4
Crawford, Lew (Choreographer)
Blackberries of 1932 1932,Ap 5,27:5
Crawford, Mary
Have I Got One for You 1968,Ja 8,32:1
Crawford, Mary Ann
Lady Comes Across, The 1942,Ja 10,10:2
Crawford, Michael
Black Comedy; White Lies 1967,F 13,42:1
Black Comedy 1967,F 13,42:1
White Lies 1967,F 26,II,1:5
Black Comedy 1967,F 26,II,1:5
Crawford, Miriam Lipps
Dust Heap, The 1924,Ap 25,20:2
Crawford, Mona
Skits-Oh-Frantics 1967,Ap 3,39:2
Crawford, Nan
Marjorie 1924,Ag 12,12:2
Crawford, Oliver
Gentleman From Athens, The 1947,D 10,42:4
Crawford, Oliver (Miscellaneous)
Hot Corner, The 1956,Ja 26,25:2
Crawford, Oliver (Playwright)
Proud Accent 1949,Ap 23,10:2
Crawford, Pat
Bamboo Cross 1955,F 22,17:2
Run, Thief, Run 1957,My 2,27:1
Enemy of the People, An 1958,F 26,24:2
Crawford, Prof (Translator)
Menaechmi 1925,Je 9,16:2
Crawford, Robert M
Scarlet Coat, The 1924,D 24,11:1
Crawford, Robert M (Composer)
Man From Earth, The 1923,Ja 3,6:2
Drake's Drum 1923,D 26,17:7
Scarlet Coat, The 1924,D 24,11:1
Crawford, Robert M (Musical Director)
Samarkand 1926,D 22,24:4

Crawford, Rosetta
Lew Leslie's Blackbirds of 1939 1939,F 13,12:2
Crawford, Terry (Miscellaneous)
Harold Arlen Songbook, The 1967,Mr 1,48:1
Crawford, Traverse
Memphis Bound 1945,My 25,23:2
Crawford and Broderick
Puzzles of 1925 1925,F 3,25:3
Crawford, Cheryl (Producer)
Long Dream, The 1960,F 18,36:2
Crawley, Edward
Evening With G B S, An; O'Flaherty, V C
1957,F 19,35:7
Crawley, Eilene
First in Heart, The 1947,N 14,29:2
Crawley, Eric
Hop, Signor! 1962,My 8,45:2
Crawley, Jack
Hasty Heart, The 1954,Mr 13,10:1
Crawley, John
Romeo and Juliet 1923,Ja 25,16:1
Crawley, Robert
Great Big Doorstep, The 1942,N 27,26:2
Moon Vine, The 1943,F 12,22:2
Harvest of Years 1948,Ja 13,29:2
Montserrat 1949,O 31,21:4
Ondine 1954,F 19,23:1
Elizabeth the Queen 1966,N 4,30:1
Crawley, Robert (Lighting Director)
Emlyn Williams as Charles Dickens 1970,N 4,41:1
Crawley, Robert (Miscellaneous)
Emlyn Williams as Charles Dickens 1970,N 4,41:1
Crawley, Sayre
Macbeth 1921,F 18,16:1
Merchant of Venice, The 1921,Ap 2,14:2
Pelleas and Melisande 1923,D 5,23:2
Antony and Cleopatra 1924,F 20,22:1
John Gabriel Borkman 1926,Ja 30,13:1
Saturday Night 1926,O 26,25:1
Three Sisters, The 1926,O 27,24:1
Locandiera, La; Mistress of the Inn, The
1926,N 23,26:1
Twelfth Night 1926,D 21,21:4
Inheritors 1927,Mr 8,23:1
Good Hope, The 1927,O 19,24:2
2 + 2 = 5 1927,N 29,30:3
Improvisations in June 1928,F 27,16:5
Hedda Gabler 1928,Mr 27,30:2
Would-Be Gentleman, The 1928,O 2,34:1
Cherry Orchard, The 1928,O 16,28:5
Peter Pan; Boy Who Would Not Grow Up, The
1928,N 27,36:3
On the High Road 1929,Ja 15,22:3
Living Corpse, The 1929,D 7,19:1
Women Have Their Way, The 1930,Ja 28,28:1
Romeo and Juliet 1930,Ap 22,33:1
Sentinels 1931,D 26,15:1
Troilus and Cressida 1932,Je 7,22:3
Liliom 1932,O 27,23:2
Alice in Wonderland 1932,D 12,18:3
Alice in Wonderland 1932,D 25,IX,1:1
Cherry Orchard, The 1933,Mr 7,20:3
Aiglon, L' 1934,N 5,22:2
Love of Women 1937,D 14,33:2
Gloriana 1938,N 26,18:4
Corn Is Green, The 1940,N 27,27:2
Late George Apley, The 1944,O 20,16:4
Late George Apley, The 1944,N 22,26:2
Crawley, Tom
Twelfth Night 1969,Ag 14,29:2
Macbeth 1969,N 21,51:1
Persians, The 1970,Ap 16,53:1
Cray, Michael
Madre, La 1959,F 12,24:1
Crayhon, Joseph (Composer)
I Want You 1961,S 15,29:1
Crayhon, Joseph (Lyricist)
I Want You 1961,S 15,29:1
Crayhon, Joseph (Producer)
I Want You 1961,S 15,29:1
Crayon (Scenic Designer)
Hilarities 1948,S 10,20:2
Crazy Gang
Joker Wild 1955,My 20,19:4
Untitled-Revue 1957,Ja 20,II,3:7
Creamer, Henry (Director)
Deep Harlem 1929,Ja 8,35:2
Creamer, Henry (Lyricist)
Keep Shufflin' 1928,F 28,18:3
Deep Harlem 1929,Ja 8,35:2
Creamer, Marianne
Man and Superman 1970,F 24,48:1
Creamer (Playwright)
Strut Miss Lizzie 1922,Je 20,22:6
Crean, Patrick
Geneva 1940,Ja 31,15:2
Richard II 1964,Je 17,47:1
King Lear 1964,Je 19,36:1
Henry IV, Part I 1965,Je 30,42:1
Falstaff; Henry IV, Part II 1965,Jl 1,35:1
Julius Caesar 1965,Jl 2,18:1
Henry VI 1966,Je 9,55:2
Government Inspector, The 1967,O 28,34:1

Crean, Patrick—Cont
Hamlet 1969,Je 11,37:1
Alchemist, The 1969,Je 12,51:1
Crean, Patrick (Miscellaneous)
Macbeth 1962,Je 20,41:1
Cyrano de Bergerac 1962,Ag 1,21:1
Richard II 1964,Je 17,47:1
King Lear 1964,Je 19,36:1
Henry IV, Part I 1965,Je 30,42:1
Julius Caesar 1965,Jl 2,18:1
Hamlet 1967,F 17,44:1
Three Musketeers, The 1968,Jl 24,49:2
Crean, Robert (Playwright)
Time to Laugh, A 1962,Ap 25,31:4
Creasap, C D
Seven Days of Mourning 1969,D 17,64:1
Creasap, Charles
Pullman Car Hiawatha 1962,D 4,46:2
Desire Under the Elms 1963,Ja 11,5:6
Drums in the Night 1967,My 18,54:1
Creash, Robert
P S I Love You 1964,N 20,40:1
Creatore, Luigi (Composer)
Maggie Flynn 1968,O 24,52:1
Maggie Flynn 1968,N 3,II,1:1
Creatore, Luigi (Lyricist)
Maggie Flynn 1968,O 24,52:1
Creatore, Luigi (Playwright)
Maggie Flynn 1968,O 24,52:1
Cree, Walter Mitchell
H M S Pinafore 1960,Ja 29,14:1
Utopia, Limited 1960,Ap 8,27:2
Cree, Walter Mitchell (Miscellaneous)
Merry Widow, The 1961,O 27,28:2
Vagabond King, The 1961,N 24,36:1
Gondoliers, The 1961,D 8,44:1
Creech, Sudie
When the Roll Is Called Up Yonder
1930,My 9,20:5
Creed, Barbara
Lend an Ear 1959,S 25,20:5
Creed, Kay
Fiesta in Madrid 1969,My 29,49:1
Creekmore, Charles
Confederacy, The 1958,Jl 3,20:1
Creel, Frances
Jezebel 1933,D 20,26:3
Red Harvest 1937,Mr 31,29:2
Crefcouer, Martine
Diary of Anne Frank, The 1956,N 29,43:1
Cregan, David (Playwright)
Houses by the Green, The 1968,O 4,42:3
Comedy of the Changing Years, A 1969,Mr 4,37:5
Cregan, N R
One for All 1927,My 14,25:5
Hawk Island 1929,S 17,34:7
Overture 1930,D 8,26:4
Crehan, Joseph
Ringside 1928,Ag 30,13:2
Merry Andrew 1929,Ja 22,22:2
Sweet Land of Liberty 1929,S 24,29:2
Those We Love 1930,F 20,22:2
Angels Don't Kiss 1932,Ap 6,22:5
Lilly Turner 1932,S 20,26:1
20th Century 1932,D 30,15:1
Creighton, Anthony (Miscellaneous)
Epitaph for George Dillon 1958,N 16,II,1:1
Creighton, Anthony (Playwright)
Epitaph for George Dillon 1958,F 12,33:8
Epitaph for George Dillon 1958,N 5,44:1
Tomorrow With Pictures 1960,Je 3,26:3
Epitaph for George Dillon 1960,D 29,17:1
Creighton, Bertha
Bronx Express 1922,Ap 27,12:2
Imaginary Invalid, The 1922,Jl 26,26:2
Creighton, Georgia
Anyone Can Whistle 1964,Ap 6,36:1
Skyscraper 1965,N 15,48:1
Penny Friend, The 1966,D 27,46:1
Creighton, Robert
Big White Fog 1940,O 23,26:2
Creley, Jack
Burning Bush, The 1949,D 17,15:5
Circle of Chalk, The 1950,D 2,8:3
Rehearsal, The 1952,My 27,30:5
Salad Days 1958,N 11,24:1
King John 1960,Je 29,26:2
Romeo and Juliet 1960,Jl 1,14:1
Coriolanus 1961,Je 21,31:2
Henry VIII 1961,Je 22,22:1
Love's Labour's Lost 1961,Je 23,19:1
Henry VIII 1961,Jl 2,II,1:1
Love's Labour's Lost 1961,Jl 2,II,1:1
Man for All Seasons, A 1961,N 23,51:1
Gondoliers, The 1962,Jl 7,9:4
Chemmy Circle, The 1968,Ag 10,17:2
Cremer, Bruno
Shock Troops 1969,F 22,36:1
Cremers, Paul Joseph (Playwright)
Marneschlacht, Die 1933,Mr 19,IX,2:2
Cremesini, Marino (Musical Director)
Clizia 1939,Jl 23,IX,6:3
Cremieux, Benjamin (Translator)
Naked 1924,O 28,27:2

Chacun Sa Verite 1939,Ja 24,17:1
Cremieux, Carol
Homme Qui Jouait du Banjo, L' 1926,O 24,VIII,2:1
Cremieux, Henri
Homme Qui Jouait du Banjo, L' 1926,O 24,VIII,2:1
Cremin, William A
It's the Valet 1933,D 15,25:4
Fiesta 1933,D 16,12:2
Cremonesi, P
Piacere Dell 'Onesta, Il 1929,Mr 25,33:1
Cena Delle Beffe, La; Jest, The 1930,N 24,26:4
Cremonesi, Paul
Farewell to Arms, A 1930,S 23,30:3
Crespi, Lee
In Circles 1967,O 14,12:1
In Circles 1968,Je 28,36:1
Peace 1969,Ja 28,49:1
Crespo, Jose
Vida es Sueno, La 1964,Mr 18,49:1
Crespo, Jose (Director)
Vida es Sueno, La 1964,Mr 18,49:1
Crespo, Jose (Producer)
Vida es Sueno, La 1964,Mr 18,49:1
Life Is a Dream 1964,Mr 20,24:1
Cresson, James
Take Me Along 1959,O 23,22:2
Hi, Paisano 1961,O 2,36:2
Hot Spot 1963,Ap 20,17:2
Flora, the Red Menace 1965,My 12,41:2
Creston, Louise
Iron Flowers 1933,Je 13,22:2
Creston, Paul (Composer)
Iron Flowers 1933,Je 13,22:2
Creswell, Peter (Director)
Flashing Stream, The 1939,Ap 11,19:2
Creswell, Saylor
Carving a Statue 1968,My 1,43:1
Creswell, Saylor (Miscellaneous)
Antigone 1962,D 29,5:5
Orthee 1962,D 29,5:5
Crews, Jerry
Sunrise at Campobello 1958,Ja 31,25:1
Crews, Laura Hope
Mr Pim Passes By 1921,Mr 1,18:1
Mr Pim Passes By 1921,Mr 6,VI,1:2
Changelings, The 1923,S 18,16:3
Changelings, The 1923,S 30,II,1:1
Fanshastics 1924,Ja 17,13:2
Merry Wives of Gotham 1924,Ja 27,VII,1:1
Werewolf, The 1924,Ag 26,6:1
Ariadne 1925,F 24,17:1
Hay Fever 1925,O 5,25:1
Embers 1926,F 2,20:3
Pomeroy's Past 1926,Ap 20,24:4
Pomeroy's Past 1926,My 2,VIII,1:1
Buy, Buy Baby 1926,O 8,26:2
Silver Cord, The 1926,D 21,21:1
Right You Are (If You Think You Are)
1927,F 24,27:1
Mr Pim Passes By 1927,Ap 19,24:1
Mr Pim Passes By 1927,My 22,VIII,1:1
Silver Cord, The 1928,F 19,VIII,2:1
Olympia 1928,O 17,26:1
Her Master's Voice 1933,O 24,24:3
Her Master's Voice 1933,D 10,X,3:1
Save Me the Waltz 1938,Mr 1,19:2
Arsenic and Old Lace 1941,Mr 25,26:7
Crews, Laura Hope (Director)
Hay Fever 1925,O 5,25:1
Crews, Laurie
No Place to Be Somebody 1969,My 5,53:3
No Place to Be Somebody 1969,D 31,17:1
Crews, Lyndon
Student Prince, The 1943,Je 9,16:2
Criado, Tarsila
Pluma en el Viento; Feather in the Wind
1932,Ap 2,13:4
Cuando Los Hijos De Eva No Son Los Hijos De
Adan; When Eve's Children Are Not Adam's
1932,Ap 23,11:2
De Muy Buena Familia; Of Very Good Family
1932,Ap 29,13:3
Cribari, Wolfango
Little Theatre Tournament; Little Italy
1928,My 10,31:1
Crichton, Don
Fade Out--Fade In 1964,My 27,45:1
Crichton, Kyle (Lyricist)
Parade 1935,My 21,22:2
Crichton, Kyle (Original Author)
Happiest Millionaire, The 1956,N 21,21:3
Happiest Millionaire, The 1956,D 2,II,1:1
Crichton, Kyle (Playwright)
Happiest Millionaire, The 1956,N 21,21:3
Happiest Millionaire, The 1956,D 2,II,1:1
Happiest Millionaire, The 1957,N 16,16:5
Crilley, Eileen
Riders to the Sea 1957,Mr 7,24:1
Crilley, Jack
Riders to the Sea 1957,Mr 7,24:1
Crimans, William
Scaramouche 1923,O 25,14:2
Nancy Ann 1924,Ap 1,18:1

Crimans, William—Cont
Jack in the Pulpit 1925,Ja 7,33:1
One Day More 1926,Mr 19,24:3
Lady Alone 1927,Ja 21,12:5
Cyclone Lover, The 1928,Je 6,23:3
One Way Street 1928,D 25,31:2
Company's Coming! 1931,Ap 21,35:5
Sweet River 1936,O 29,30:2
Hill Between, The 1938,Mr 12,12:5
30 Days Hath September 1938,O 1,10:5
Criner, J Lawrence
Meek Mose 1928,F 7,30:1
Power of Darkness, The 1948,O 11,28:2
Stevedore 1949,F 23,30:2
Cripps, Harvey
If 1927,O 26,26:2
Cripps, Kernan
Jack in the Pulpit 1925,Ja 7,33:1
Crisa, Tino
Folies Bergere 1939,D 25,28:2
Criscuolo, Louis
Matty and the Moron and Madonna
1965,Mr 30,53:1
Hooray!! It's a Glorious Day. . .And All That
1966,Mr 10,28:1
Crisham, Wally
Captain Jinks 1925,S 9,22:1
Sweet Adeline 1929,S 4,33:1
Nine Fifteen Revue, The 1930,F 12,26:2
Crisp, Charles
Golden Boy 1937,N 5,18:5
Crispin, Jeanine
Femme en Fleur, La 1936,F 23,X,2:3
Criss, Louis
Silver Tassie, The 1949,Jl 22,16:5
Ladies of the Corridor, The 1953,O 22,33:5
Passion of Gross, The 1955,Ja 24,20:2
Tiger at the Gates 1955,O 4,40:1
Criss, Louis (Director)
Narrow Road to the Deep North 1969,D 2,64:1
Jungle of Cities 1970,Mr 1,75:2
In 3 Zones 1970,N 3,28:1
Criss, Louis (Miscellaneous)
Major Barbara 1956,O 31,27:1
Galileo 1968,D 1,88:4
Criss, Nicholas
What a Relief 1935,D 14,10:6
Cristan, Don Diago
Marcel Marceau 1970,Ap 8,38:3
Criswell, Jeron (Playwright)
Dorian Gray 1936,Jl 21,13:3
Critcherson, Sam
Bombo 1921,O 7,20:2
Top Speed 1929,D 26,20:1
Crittenden, Marie
Song of Norway 1958,Je 23,19:2
Crittendon, Ritta
Bolls of Cotton 1925,D 22,18:3
Croce, Johnny
Hickory Stick 1944,My 9,15:6
Crocker, Donald
My Romance 1948,O 20,38:5
Crocker, Earle (Composer)
Illustrators' Show, The 1936,Ja 23,25:3
Crocker, Earle (Lyricist)
Happy 1927,D 6,26:3
Crocker, Emerson
Orphee 1935,Mr 23,10:3
Crocker, Emerson (Miscellaneous)
King Lear 1956,Ja 13,17:1
Crockett, A D
Tiger Smiles, The 1930,D 18,29:1
Crockett, Keene
Dream Girl 1945,D 15,13:2
O'Daniel 1947,F 25,32:2
Not for Children 1951,F 14,35:2
Crofoot, Alan
Mahagonny 1970,Ap 29,51:1
Mahagonny 1970,My 10,II,15:1
Croft, Kenneth (Director)
Hate Planters 1933,My 26,24:5
Croft, Michael (Producer)
Apprentices, The 1968,Ag 21,40:5
Croft, Paddy
Hostage, The 1961,D 13,55:4
Man and Superman 1964,D 7,45:2
Billy Liar 1965,Mr 18,26:1
Croft, Peter
King of Rome, The 1935,My 15,26:1
Croisille, Nicole
Overcoat, The 1960,S 7,45:1
Folies Bergere 1964,Je 3,36:1
Croissant, Dorothy (Costume Designer)
Lamp at Midnight 1947,D 22,29:2
Church Street 1948,F 10,27:2
Respectful Prostitute, The 1948,F 10,27:2
Blood Wedding 1949,F 7,16:2
Major Barbara 1954,Je 30,23:2
In Splendid Error 1954,O 27,33:6
Juno and the Paycock 1955,F 24,20:4
Croisset, Francis de (Playwright)
Ciboulette 1926,O 31,VIII,2:4
Diable a Paris, Le 1927,N 13,IX,4:2
Livree de M le Comte, La 1927,N 20,IX,4:4

Croisset, Francis de (Playwright)—Cont
Pierre ou Jack? 1931,Ap 19,VIII,2:7
Sparviero, Lo 1934,N 12,16:1
Croix, Joan
Ringside Seat 1938,N 23,24:5
Croker-King, Charles
Bulldog Drummond 1921,D 27,10:2
Little Angel, The 1924,S 29,10:3
Rat, The 1925,F 11,19:3
Hearts Are Trumps! 1927,Ap 8,21:1
Midsummer Night's Dream, A 1927,Je 27,25:1
Taming of the Shrew, The 1927,O 26,26:4
Twelve Thousand 1928,Mr 13,23:1
White Lilacs 1928,S 11,31:2
His Majesty's Car 1930,O 24,30:1
School for Scandal, The 1931,N 11,26:4
Autumn Crocus 1932,N 21,20:2
Twelfth Night 1934,Jl 17,24:5
Roman Servant, A 1934,D 3,14:5
Nowhere Bound 1935,Ja 23,20:2
Crolius, Gladys
Shannons of Broadway, The 1927,S 27,30:4
Crombie, Laura
Gondoliers, The 1948,Ja 27,31:2
Cromer, Allan
Old Bill, M P 1926,N 11,22:2
Cromer, Charles
Faust 1927,Ja 4,20:1
Lady Lies, The 1928,N 27,36:2
Lady Dedlock 1929,Ja 1,61:2
Houseparty 1929,S 10,26:5
Child of Manhattan 1932,Mr 2,15:1
Cromer, Harold
Du Barry Was a Lady 1939,D 7,34:2
Early to Bed 1943,Je 18,16:2
Crommelynck, Fernand (Playwright)
Carine, ou la Jeune Fille Folle de son Ame
  1930,Ja 19,VIII,4:1
Femme Qu'a le Coeur Trop Petit, Une
  1934,F 11,IX,3:2
Chaud et Froid 1935,Ja 6,IX,2:1
Crommette, Jessie
Kempy 1922,My 16,14:2
Dumb-Bell 1923,N 27,23:2
Neighbors 1923,D 27,11:1
Applesauce 1925,S 29,31:2
Judge's Husband, The 1926,S 28,31:1
Front Page, The 1928,Ag 15,19:2
Queen at Home 1930,D 30,25:2
Crompton, Charles
Venetian, The 1931,N 2,26:1
Crompton, Nanci
John Murray Anderson's Almanac 1953,D 11,42:2
Crompton, Richmal (Original Author)
Up the Garden Path 1937,Jl 7,26:2
Cromwell, Carolyn
Johnny 2X4 1942,Mr 17,24:6
Cromwell, Helen
Anna Ascends 1920,S 23,14:1
Main Street 1921,O 6,21:1
Nest, The 1922,F 2,20:1
Anything Might Happen 1923,F 21,22:3
Devils 1926,Mr 18,26:4
Queen's Husband, The 1928,Ja 26,17:2
Cromwell, James
All's Well That Ends Well 1970,Je 16,53:1
Othello 1970,Je 22,43:1
Devil's Disciple, The 1970,Je 30,48:1
Othello 1970,S 15,51:1
Cromwell, John
Immodest Violet 1920,Ag 25,6:2
Teaser, The 1921,Jl 28,8:3
Personality 1921,Ag 29,14:3
Marie Antoinette 1921,N 23,16:1
Lawbreaker, The 1922,F 7,12:1
Oh! Mama 1925,Ag 20,22:2
Lucky Sam McCarver 1925,O 22,22:1
Lucky Sam McCarver 1925,N 1,VIII,1:1
Little Eyolf 1926,F 3,22:1
Devils 1926,Mr 18,26:4
Fanny 1926,S 22,30:1
Racket, The 1927,N 23,28:3
Racket, The 1927,D 18,IX,1:1
Gentlemen of the Press 1928,Ag 28,27:2
Gentlemen of the Press 1928,S 2,VII,1:1
Old Maid, The 1935,Ja 8,26:1
Romeo and Juliet 1935,D 24,10:2
Saint Joan 1936,Mr 10,27:4
Hamlet 1936,O 9,30:2
Macbeth 1937,O 11,26:3
Bright Rebel 1938,D 28,24:2
Grey Farm 1940,My 4,12:7
Gabrielle 1941,Mr 26,26:2
Yankee Point 1942,N 24,28:2
Pygmalion 1945,D 27,16:1
Naughty-Naught '00 1946,O 21,27:5
Point of No Return 1951,O 31,32:2
Point of No Return 1951,D 14,35:2
Point of No Return 1951,D 23,II,3:1
Climate of Eden, The 1952,N 7,20:2
Climate of Eden, The 1952,N 16,II,1:1
Sabrina Fair 1953,N 12,37:1
Sabrina Fair 1953,N 22,II,1:1
What Every Woman Knows 1954,D 23,16:2

Mary, Mary 1961,Mr 9,24:2
Hamlet 1963,My 9,41:1
Miser, The 1963,My 10,39:1
Hamlet 1963,My 19,II,1:1
Death of a Salesman 1963,Jl 20,11:2
Henry V 1964,My 13,52:1
Saint Joan 1964,My 14,41:1
Richard III 1965,Je 3,26:1
Country People 1970,Ja 19,35:1
Don Juan 1970,My 26,32:1
Don Juan 1970,My 31,II,1:6
Cromwell, John (Director)
Bewitched 1924,O 2,26:3
She Had to Know 1925,F 3,25:3
Devils 1926,Mr 18,26:4
Kitty's Kisses 1926,My 7,12:2
Silver Cord, The 1926,D 21,21:1
What the Doctor Ordered 1927,Ag 19,20:2
Women Go on Forever 1927,S 8,25:1
Queen's Husband, The 1928,Ja 26,17:2
Ghost of Yankee Doodle, The 1937,N 23,26:3
Yr Obedient Husband 1937,N 27,21:2
Yr Obedient Husband 1938,Ja 11,26:5
Yankee Point 1942,N 24,28:2
Moon Vine, The 1943,F 12,22:2
Cromwell, John (Miscellaneous)
Lucky Sam McCarver 1925,O 22,22:1
Women Go on Forever 1927,S 8,25:1
Cromwell, John (Playwright)
Banquet for the Moon, A 1961,Ja 20,24:2
Matter of Like Life and Death, A 1963,O 3,28:2
Opening Night 1963,O 3,28:2
Cromwell, John (Producer)
Bewitched 1924,O 2,26:3
Ghost of Yankee Doodle, The 1937,N 23,26:3
Yr Obedient Husband 1938,Ja 11,26:5
Cromwell, Richard
So Proudly We Hail 1936,S 23,28:4
Crone, John
Piggy 1927,Ja 12,22:2
Speakeasy 1927,S 27,30:1
Crone, Kitty Don (Costume Designer)
John Brown's Body 1960,Je 22,31:1
Crone, Otto
Friedens Tragoedie 1936,N 17,34:4
Peace Tragedy 1937,Ja 3,X,3:1
Cronier, Gaston (Playwright)
Peu de Musique, Un 1923,N 6,22:1
Cronin, A J (Dr) (Playwright)
Jupiter Laughs 1940,S 10,27:1
Jupiter Laughs 1941,N 9,IX,3:5
Cronin, Harry
Henry V 1964,My 13,52:1
Cronin, Jack
Sancho Panza 1923,N 27,23:1
Cronin, Jackie
Lady or the Tiger?, The 1966,O 19,53:1
Passionella 1966,O 19,53:1
Cronin, James (Lighting Director)
School for Wives 1957,Je 20,23:4
Cronin, Jane
Bald Soprano, The 1963,S 18,35:4
Postmark Zero 1965,N 2,28:1
Cronin, Joe
Best Foot Forward 1956,Mr 3,16:1
Pale Horse, Pale Rider 1957,O 30,26:1
Cronin, John
Piggy 1927,Ja 12,22:2
Cronin, Joseph
Love Me Little 1958,Ap 15,42:2
Cronk, Harry
Gentlemen of the Press 1928,Ag 28,27:2
Cronyn, Hume
Hipper's Holiday 1934,O 19,26:2
High Tor 1937,Ja 11,15:2
There's Always a Breeze 1938,Mr 3,16:2
Escape This Night 1938,Ap 23,18:1
Flying Ginzburgs, The 1938,N 13,IX,2:2
Off to Buffalo! 1939,F 22,18:2
Three Sisters, The 1939,O 16,23:1
Weak Link, The 1940,Mr 5,19:2
Retreat to Pleasure 1940,D 18,32:2
Mr Big 1941,S 7,I,51:3
Mr Big 1941,S 14,IX,2:5
Mr Big 1941,O 1,24:2
It's All Yours 1942,Mr 26,26:2
Survivors, The 1948,Ja 20,27:2
Survivors, The 1948,Ja 25,II,1:1
Fourposter, The 1951,O 25,34:2
Fourposter, The 1951,N 25,II,1:1
Madam Will You Walk 1953,D 2,2:4
Madam Will You Walk 1953,D 20,II,3:1
Fourposter, The 1955,Ja 6,23:3
Honeys, The 1955,Ap 29,26:1
Day by the Sea, A 1955,S 27,42:1
Day by the Sea, A 1955,O 2,II,1:1
Man in the Dog Suit, The 1958,O 31,34:2
On the Harmful Effects of Tobacco
  1959,Ap 16,28:1
Bedtime Story 1959,Ap 16,28:1
Pound on Demand, A 1959,Ap 16,28:1
Portrait of a Madonna 1959,Ap 16,28:1

Cronyn, Hume—Cont
On the Harmful Effects of Tobacco
  1959,Ap 26,II,1:1
Triple Play 1959,Ap 26,II,1:1
Big Fish, Little Fish 1961,Mr 16,42:2
Big Fish, Little Fish 1961,Mr 26,II,1:1
Miser, The 1963,My 10,39:1
Miser, The 1963,My 19,II,1:1
Death of a Salesman 1963,Jl 20,11:2
Three Sisters, The 1963,Jl 22,19:2
Hamlet 1964,F 28,17:5
Hamlet 1964,Ap 10,30:1
Hamlet 1964,Ap 19,II,1:1
Physicists, The 1964,O 14,52:1
Physicists, The 1964,O 25,II,1:1
Richard III 1965,Je 3,26:1
Cherry Orchard, The 1965,Ag 2,17:2
Delicate Balance, A 1966,S 23,44:1
Delicate Balance, A 1966,O 2,II,1:1
Cronyn, Hume (Director)
Now I Lay Me Down to Sleep 1949,Jl 23,7:3
Now I Lay Me Down to Sleep 1950,Mr 3,21:2
Now I Lay Me Down to Sleep 1950,Mr 19,II,1:1
Hilda Crane 1950,N 2,38:2
Madam Will You Walk 1953,D 2,2:4
Madam Will You Walk 1953,D 20,II,3:1
Egghead, The 1957,O 10,39:1
Bedtime Story 1959,Ap 16,28:1
On the Harmful Effects of Tobacco
  1959,Ap 16,28:1
Portrait of a Madonna 1959,Ap 16,28:1
Pound on Demand, A 1959,Ap 16,28:1
Pound on Demand, A 1959,Ap 26,II,1:1
Bedtime Story 1959,Ap 26,II,1:1
Cronyn, Hume (Miscellaneous)
It's All Yours 1942,Mr 26,26:2
Little Blue Light, The 1951,Ap 30,17:2
Cronyn, Hume (Producer)
Now I Lay Me Down to Sleep 1949,Jl 23,7:3
Slow Dance on the Killing Ground 1964,D 1,50:1
Cronyn, Tandy
Good Woman of Setzuan, The 1970,N 6,51:1
Crook, John (Composer)
Peter Pan; Boy Who Would Not Grow Up, The
  1928,N 27,36:3
Crooke, Frederick (Costume Designer)
Troilus and Cressida 1956,D 27,21:1
Crooke, Frederick (Scenic Designer)
Troilus and Cressida 1956,D 27,21:1
Crooker, Earle (Lyricist)
Thumbs Up! 1934,D 28,24:1
Great Lady 1938,D 2,26:6
Crooker, Earle (Playwright)
Zeppelin 1929,Ja 15,22:3
Family Affairs 1929,D 11,34:6
Intimate Relations 1932,Mr 29,23:2
Salute to Spring 1937,Jl 14,16:2
Great Lady 1938,D 2,26:6
Cropper, Anna
Little Boxes; Coffee Lace, The; Trevor
  1968,Jl 5,20:1
Cropper, Elsie
Rogues and Vagabonds 1930,My 8,32:5
Cropper, Herschel
Tyrant, The 1930,N 13,33:1
Paths of Glory 1935,S 27,24:2
This Our House 1935,D 12,33:3
Chalk Dust 1936,Mr 5,24:5
Too Many Heroes 1937,N 16,26:2
All the Living 1938,Mr 25,14:4
Glorious Morning 1938,N 28,10:3
Cropper, Herschel (Director)
Cinderelative 1930,S 19,18:4
Cropper, Roy
Blossom Time 1921,S 30,10:1
Blossom Time 1922,O 24,18:2
Ziegfeld Follies 1923,O 22,17:2
Ziegfeld Follies 1924,Mr 18,25:2
LeMaire's Affairs 1927,Mr 29,22:4
Naughty Marietta 1929,O 22,26:2
Fortune Teller, The 1929,N 5,32:3
Robin Hood 1929,N 20,26:5
Merry Widow, The 1929,D 3,29:1
Prince of Pilsen, The 1930,Ja 14,24:3
Chocolate Soldier, The 1930,Ja 28,28:1
Count of Luxembourg, The 1930,F 18,28:2
Serenade, The 1930,Mr 5,26:7
Vaudeville (Palace) 1930,Mr 24,24:5
Merry Widow, The 1931,S 8,39:1
Chocolate Soldier, The 1931,S 22,33:3
Geisha, The 1931,O 6,35:4
Chimes of Normandy, The 1931,N 3,31:3
Naughty Marietta 1931,N 17,31:2
Firefly, The 1931,D 1,23:2
Merry Widow, The 1932,F 21,VIII,23:3
There You Are! 1932,My 17,25:4
Mikado, The 1933,Ap 18,13:4
Yeomen of the Guard, The 1933,My 2,20:4
H M S Pinafore 1933,My 9,20:3
Trial by Jury 1933,My 9,20:3
Patience 1933,My 23,22:6
Bohemian Girl, The 1933,Jl 28,18:5
Pirates of Penzance, The 1933,Ag 8,22:4
Yeomen of the Guard, The 1933,Ag 15,20:5

Cropper, Roy—Cont
Mikado, The 1934,Ap 3,26:3
Pirates of Penzance, The 1934,Ap 10,26:5
H M S Pinafore 1934,Ap 17,27:2
Trial by Jury 1934,Ap 17,27:2
Iolanthe 1934,My 1,26:4
Mikado, The 1936,Ap 11,18:4
Pirates of Penzance, The 1936,Ap 21,27:5
H M S Pinafore 1936,Ap 28,17:2
Trial by Jury 1936,Ap 28,17:2
Iolanthe 1936,My 5,26:2
Rose Marie 1936,Jl 22,22:6
Wonderful Night, A; Fledermaus, Die
  1937,Jl 14,17:1
Show Is On, The 1937,S 20,18:4
Blossom Time 1938,D 27,12:2
Blossom Time 1943,S 6,21:2

Crosby, Henry
Great Adventure, The 1921,F 26,9:2
Failures, The 1923,N 23,20:1
That Awful Mrs Eaton! 1924,S 30,27:1
Simon Called Peter 1924,N 11,20:2
Veils 1928,Mr 14,28:5
Sisters of the Chorus 1930,My 18,VIII,3:1
Sisters of the Chorus 1930,O 21,34:3
Wonder Bar, The 1931,Mr 18,23:4
Peter Flies High 1931,N 10,28:3

Crosby, Joe (Costume Designer)
Boy Friend, The 1958,Ja 27,24:4
Oklahoma! 1958,Mr 8,15:2
Beautiful Dreamer 1960,D 28,22:1
Will the Mail Train Run Tonight? 1964,Ja 10,18:1

Crosby, Juliette
Martinique 1920,Ap 27,18:2
Nest, The 1922,F 2,20:1
Love Child, The 1922,N 15,22:1
Home Fires 1923,Ag 21,12:1
Show-Off, The 1924,F 6,16:2
Nirvana 1926,Mr 4,19:1
Chicago 1926,D 31,11:1

Crosby, Michael
Another City, Another Land 1968,O 9,42:1
Getting Married 1970,Ja 20,46:1

Crosby, Mirian
Lovely Lady 1927,D 30,22:1

Crosby, Patrick Henry
Dreams for Sale 1922,S 14,24:1

Crosby, Phoebe
Magic Ring, The 1923,O 2,10:1

Crosby, Thomas M
Hippolytus 1935,Je 15,20:4

Crosby Sisters
Aquashow 1953,Je 24,29:2

Crosier, Emmet (Playwright)
Ned Wayburn's Gambols 1929,Ja 16,22:3

Crosley, Chase
Midsummer Night's Dream, A 1957,Je 27,21:3
Troilus and Cressida 1965,Ag 13,17:1

Crosley, Harry (Choreographer)
International Revue 1930,F 26,22:2

Crosman, Henrietta
Children of the Moon 1923,Ag 18,10:3
Children of the Moon 1923,Ag 26,VI,1:1
Children of the Moon 1923,S 9,VII,1:1
Children of the Moon 1923,S 16,VII,1:1
Vaudeville (Palace) 1924,F 12,20:2
Sweet Peggy Clive 1924,F 12,20:2
School for Scandal, The 1925,D 7,18:2
School for Scandal, The 1925,D 13,IX,3:1
Two Orphans, The 1926,Ap 6,26:2
Two Orphans, The 1926,Ap 11,VIII,1:1
Trelawney of the 'Wells' 1927,F 1,24:4
Trelawney of the 'Wells' 1927,F 6,VII,1:1
Merry Wives of Windsor, The 1928,Mr 20,20:1
Beaux' Stratagem, The 1928,Je 5,20:1
Beaux' Stratagem, The 1928,Je 10,VIII,1:1
Crashing Through 1928,O 30,26:5
Thunder in the Air 1929,N 12,34:3
Bad Penny, A 1931,Ag 23,VIII,2:4
In Clover 1937,S 21,29:1

Cross, Abe
Hello Grandpa! 1931,Ja 2,25:3

Cross, Alan
Take a Bow 1944,Je 16,15:3

Cross, Albert
Divorce a la Carte 1928,Mr 27,30:3

Cross, Alexander
Adam Had Two Sons 1932,Ja 21,17:1
Tree, The 1932,Ap 13,23:5
Man Who Reclaimed His Head 1932,S 9,17:3

Cross, Alfred
Babies a La Carte 1927,Ag 16,31:1
We Never Learn 1928,Ja 24,26:1

Cross, Allan
Vaudeville (Palace) 1923,O 30,16:1

Cross, Beverly (Playwright)
One More River 1960,Mr 19,12:2
Boeing-Boeing 1965,F 3,30:1
Half a Sixpence 1965,Ap 26,38:2

Cross, George
Matriarch, The 1930,Mr 19,24:5
Flashing Stream, The 1939,Ap 11,19:2

Cross, Helen
Little Theatre Tournament; Severed Cord, The
  1929,My 9,34:3

Cross, Hugh
Hamlet 1947,F 27,27:2

Cross, James A
This Is the Army 1942,Ag 16,VIII,1:1

Cross, Jules
Mayflowers 1925,N 25,14:2

Cross, Milton (Miscellaneous)
Ice Capades 1960,S 1,30:1

Cross, Rhoda
Guinea Pig, The 1929,Ja 8,35:1

Cross, Richard
Maria Golovin 1958,N 6,43:1

Cross, Sam
Change Your Luck 1930,Je 7,10:2

Cross, Walter
Vagabond King, The 1925,S 22,23:3
White Eagle, The 1927,D 27,24:4

Cross, Wellington
All-Star Idlers of 1921, The 1921,Jl 16,5:2
No, No, Nanette 1925,S 17,20:2

Crossen, Henry
House Unguarded 1929,Ja 16,22:2
Criminal Code, The 1929,O 3,28:2

Crossland, Gordon
Ice Follies 1958,Ja 15,26:2
Ice Follies 1959,Ja 14,30:1

Crossland, Marjorie
Is Zat So? 1925,Ja 6,23:4
Annie Get Your Gun 1946,My 17,14:2

Crossley, John
Richard III 1930,Mr 31,24:1

Crosson, Cornelius
Roll Sweet Chariot 1934,O 3,24:3

Crosson, Joanna
Most Happy Fella, The 1966,My 12,55:1

Crosswell, Rudolph (Composer)
Glorious Ruler, The 1969,Jl 1,31:1

Crosswell, Rudolph (Miscellaneous)
Glorious Ruler, The 1969,Jl 1,31:1

Crossy, Franceys
So Was Napoleon 1930,Ja 9,22:2

Croswell, Anne (Lyricist)
Ernest in Love 1960,My 5,39:4
Tovarich 1963,Mr 20,5:1
I'm Solomon 1968,Ap 24,51:1

Croswell, Anne (Miscellaneous)
Tovarich 1963,Ja 23,5:6

Croswell, Anne (Playwright)
Ernest in Love 1960,My 5,39:4
I'm Solomon 1968,Ap 24,51:1

Crothers, Joel
Remarkable Mr Pennypacker, The 1953,D 31,11:2
Easter 1957,Ja 17,35:2
Case of Libel, A 1963,O 11,43:2

Crothers, Rachel
He and She 1920,F 13,16:3
He and She 1920,F 22,III,6:2

Crothers, Rachel (Director)
Expressing Willie 1924,My 4,VIII,1:1
Book of Charm, The 1925,S 4,26:3
Lady's Virtue, A 1925,N 24,28:2
Thou Desperate Pilot 1927,Mr 8,23:1
Venus 1927,D 26,26:5
Exceeding Small 1928,O 23,32:2
Let Us Be Gay 1929,F 22,19:1
When in Rome 1929,Je 16,VIII,2:1
As Husbands Go 1931,Mr 6,26:5
Caught Wet 1931,N 5,29:1
When Ladies Meet 1932,O 7,19:1
Susan and God 1937,Ap 11,II,12:3
Susan and God 1937,O 8,26:4
Old Foolishness, The 1940,D 21,20:2

Crothers, Rachel (Miscellaneous)
Old Foolishness, The 1940,D 21,20:2

Crothers, Rachel (Playwright)
He and She 1920,F 13,16:3
He and She 1920,F 22,III,6:2
Nice People 1921,Mr 3,11:1
Nice People 1921,Mr 6,VI,1:2
Everyday 1921,N 17,15:1
Mary the 3d 1923,F 6,14:2
Mary the 3d 1923,F 11,VII,1:1
Expressing Willie 1924,Ap 17,22:1
Expressing Willie 1924,Ap 27,VIII,1:1
Expressing Willie 1924,My 4,VIII,1:1
Lady's Virtue, A 1925,N 24,28:2
Lady's Virtue, A 1925,D 16,VIII,5:1
Venus 1927,D 26,26:5
Let Us Be Gay 1929,F 22,19:1
Bon Voyage 1929,D 29,VIII,4:3
Let Us Be Gay 1930,S 14,VIII,2:1
As Husbands Go 1931,Mr 6,26:5
As Husbands Go 1931,Mr 15,IX,1:1
Caught Wet 1931,N 5,29:1
When Ladies Meet 1932,Ag 14,IX,1:7
When Ladies Meet 1932,O 7,19:1
When Ladies Meet 1932,O 16,IX,1:1
As Husbands Go 1933,Ja 20,20:5
When Ladies Meet 1933,Ap 27,15:4
When Ladies Meet 1933,My 14,IX,2:2

Crothers, Rachel (Playwright)—Cont
As Husbands Go 1935,Jl 2,24:3
As Husbands Go 1935,Jl 10,24:1
Susan and God 1937,Ap 11,II,12:3
Susan and God 1937,Ap 25,X,2:6
Let Us Be Gay 1937,Je 29,18:3
Susan and God 1937,O 8,26:4
Susan and God 1937,O 17,XI,1:1
Susan and God 1943,D 14,30:2

Crothers, Rachel (Producer)
Expressing Willie 1924,Ap 27,VIII,1:1
Book of Charm, The 1925,S 4,26:3
Thou Desperate Pilot 1927,Mr 8,23:1
When Ladies Meet 1933,My 14,IX,2:2

Crouch, Charles (Playwright)
Thunder in the Air 1929,N 12,34:3

Croue
Roi Dagobert, Le 1926,N 14,VIII,2:1
Turcaret 1928,Mr 4,IX,4:5

Croue, Jean (Playwright)
Brothers Karamazov, The 1927,Ja 4,20:1

Crouse, Lindsay Ann
Moon Walk 1970,N 27,52:1

Crouse, Russel
Gentlemen of the Press 1928,Ag 28,27:2

Crouse, Russel (Musical Director)
Gang's All Here, The 1931,F 19,21:3

Crouse, Russel (Original Author)
Hooray for What! 1937,D 2,32:5

Crouse, Russel (Playwright)
Hold Your Horses 1933,Ag 31,20:4
Hold Your Horses 1933,S 26,26:4
Anything Goes 1934,N 18,IX,1:7
Anything Goes 1934,N 22,26:1
Anything Goes 1935,S 15,IX,1:1
Red, Hot and Blue! 1936,O 8,26:1
Red, Hot and Blue! 1936,O 11,X,3:1
Red, Hot and Blue! 1936,O 30,26:3
Anything Goes 1937,Ag 26,24:3
Hooray for What! 1937,N 7,XI,2:4
Life With Father 1939,Ag 15,14:4
Life With Father 1939,N 9,26:2
Life With Father 1939,N 19,X,1:1
Life With Father 1940,Mr 3,X,2:5
Life With Father 1940,Ag 18,IX,1:1
Arsenic and Old Lace 1941,Mr 25,26:7
Strip for Action 1942,O 1,26:2
Strip for Action 1942,O 11,VIII,1:1
State of the Union 1945,N 7,21:3
State of the Union 1945,N 15,25:2
State of the Union 1945,N 25,II,1:1
State of the Union 1946,S 8,II,1:1
State of the Union 1947,Jl 15,26:2
Life With Mother 1948,Je 9,36:3
Life With Mother 1948,O 21,32:2
Life With Mother 1948,O 31,II,1:1
Life With Mother 1949,Mr 27,II,1:1
Call Me Madam 1950,O 13,25:1
Call Me Madam 1950,O 22,II,1:1
Remains to Be Seen 1951,O 4,37:1
Call Me Madam 1952,Mr 16,84:3
Remains to Be Seen 1952,D 17,44:4
Remains to Be Seen 1953,Ja 25,II,3:1
Prescott Proposals, The 1953,D 17,53:1
Prescott Proposals, The 1953,D 27,II,3:1
Great Sebastians, The 1956,Ja 5,27:1
Great Sebastians, The 1956,Ja 15,II,1:1
Happy Hunting 1956,D 7,30:1
Happy Hunting 1956,D 16,II,3:1
Tall Story 1959,Ja 30,33:2
Sound of Music, The 1959,N 17,40:2
Anything Goes 1962,My 16,35:1
Mr President 1962,Ag 29,18:4
Mr President 1962,S 26,36:1
Mr President 1962,O 14,II,1:7
Mr President 1962,O 22,34:2
Sound of Music, The 1967,My 27,52:1
Life With Father 1967,O 20,53:2
Sound of Music, The 1970,Jl 3,13:1

Crouse, Russel (Producer)
Arsenic and Old Lace 1941,Ja 11,13:2
Arsenic and Old Lace 1942,My 11,18:6
Strip for Action 1942,O 1,26:2
Hasty Heart, The 1945,Ja 4,14:2
Hasty Heart, The 1945,Ja 14,II,1:1
Detective Story 1949,Mr 24,34:2
One Bright Day 1952,Mr 20,37:2
Great Sebastians, The 1956,Ja 5,27:1

Crouzet, Roger
Marius 1956,F 6,27:4

Crow, Albert
Founders, The 1957,My 14,39:1

Crow, Carl
Tour De Four 1963,Je 19,41:1

Crow, Gene
Last Love of Don Juan, The 1955,N 24,40:1
Shadow Years, The 1957,Ja 9,26:2

Crowden, Graham
Flea in Her Ear, A 1967,O 30,59:1
Love for Love 1967,O 30,59:1
Tempest, The 1970,Ag 29,14:1

Crowder, Jack
Fly Blackbird 1962,F 6,26:2
Hello, Dolly! 1967,N 13,61:1

205

Crowder, Jack—Cont
Hello, Dolly! 1967,N 26,II,3:1
Crowe, Brian
Becket 1961,My 9,44:1
Crowe, Eileen
Trifles 1927,F 13,VII,4:6
Far-Off Hills, The 1932,O 19,22:4
Juno and the Paycock 1932,O 20,24:3
Playboy of the Western World, The 1932,O 21,25:1
New Gossoon, The 1932,O 22,18:2
Shadow of a Gunman, The 1932,O 31,18:1
Cathleen ni Houlihan 1932,O 31,18:1
Shadow of the Glen, The 1932,N 4,25:1
Crabbed Youth and Age 1932,N 4,25:1
Autumn Fire 1932,D 29,16:3
Big House, The 1933,Ja 5,19:3
King Oedipus 1933,Ja 16,12:4
Days Without End 1934,Ap 24,26:7
Church Street 1934,My 23,15:5
On the Rocks 1934,Jl 11,20:4
Plough and the Stars, The 1934,N 13,22:2
Drama at Inish 1934,N 15,24:2
Look at the Heffernans 1934,N 17,13:2
Church Street 1934,N 20,24:5
Candida 1935,O 27,IX,2:5
Katie Roche 1937,O 4,17:4
Far-Off Hills, The 1937,O 12,30:4
In the Train 1937,N 22,14:5
New Gossoon, The 1937,N 30,26:2
Juno and the Paycock 1937,D 7,32:5
Drama at Inish 1937,D 14,33:2
Kindred 1939,O 8,IX,3:5
Marks and Mabel 1945,S 9,II,1:4
Bugle in the Blood, The 1949,Mr 15,34:5
Red Roses for Me 1955,D 29,15:2
Red Roses for Me 1956,Ja 8,II,1:1
Crowe, Gillian (Producer)
Bohikee Creek 1966,Ap 29,39:1
Crowe, Gordon (Miscellaneous)
Scuba Duba 1967,O 11,36:1
Lovers and Other Strangers 1968,S 19,63:1
Oh! Calcutta! 1969,Je 18,33:1
Crowe, Lee
Out of a Blue Sky 1930,F 10,20:6
Little Women 1931,D 8,36:2
Few Wild Oats, A 1932,Mr 25,22:6
Crowe, Richard
Arrow-Maker, The 1956,O 5,20:1
Crowell, Arlo
Stevedore 1949,F 23,30:2
Crowell, Connie
Idiot's Delight 1936,Mr 25,25:2
Idiot's Delight 1937,Ag 10,22:7
Father Malachy's Miracle 1937,N 18,26:4
Crowell, David
Mr Big 1941,O 1,24:2
Crowell, William
Tidings Brought to Mary, The 1922,D 25,20:1
Crowley, Ann
Seventeen 1951,Je 22,16:6
Seventeen 1951,Jl 1,II,1:1
Crowley, Daniel
Building Fund, The 1928,Je 6,23:4
Crowley, Dick (Choreographer)
Buskers, The 1961,O 31,28:1
Crowley, Edward
Admirable Bashville, The 1956,F 21,38:1
Dark Lady of the Sonnets, The 1956,F 21,38:1
Dark Lady of the Sonnets, The 1956,Mr 4,II,1:1
Once Around the Block 1956,O 29,34:1
Make a Million 1958,O 24,39:2
Little Hut, The 1961,Jl 26,34:2
I Want You 1961,S 15,29:1
Lion in Love, The 1963,Ap 26,28:3
Family Way, The 1965,Ja 14,44:5
Hair 1967,O 30,55:1
How to Steal an Election 1968,O 14,56:1
Evening for Merlin Finch, An 1968,D 30,25:1
Crowley, Florence
Brother Elks 1925,S 15,29:2
Crowley, John
Book of Job, The 1936,Mr 5,24:6
Importance of Being Earnest, The 1936,O 22,31:2
Crowley, Mart (Playwright)
Boys in the Band, The 1968,Ap 15,48:1
Boys in the Band, The 1968,Ap 28,II,1:6
Boys in the Band, The 1969,F 13,52:2
Boys in the Band, The 1969,F 18,36:1
Boys in the Band, The 1969,S 20,21:2
Boys in the Band, The 1970,Ap 18,34:1
Remote Asylum 1970,D 13,II,3:1
Crowley, Matt
Eve of St Mark, The 1942,O 8,30:2
Decision 1944,F 3,23:2
Decision 1944,F 13,II,1:1
I Never Sang for My Father 1968,Ja 26,30:1
Crowley, Matthew
Front Page, The 1928,Ag 15,19:2
Crowley, Pat
Southern Exposure 1950,S 27,36:3
Four Twelves Are 48 1951,Ja 18,30:2
Tovarich 1952,My 15,39:2
Crown, Alfred (Producer)
Deputy, The 1964,F 27,26:1

Crowne, Marion
Boeuf sur le Toit, Le 1930,Ap 25,28:4
Crownstine, J J
Rose, The 1922,D 30,13:4
Crowther, John
Midsummer Night Scream, A 1960,D 16,45:1
Something About a Soldier 1962,Ja 5,36:2
Seidman and Son 1962,O 16,32:2
Crowthers, Dorothy (Playwright)
Jazz a La Carte 1922,Je 3,8:3
Croxton, Darryl
Volpone 1967,Je 30,29:1
Croy, Homer (Original Author)
So This Is Paris 1930,Ap 27,IX,2:3
They Had to See Paris 1930,Ap 27,IX,2:3
Hello Paris 1930,N 17,29:3
Croydon, Joan
Coriolanus 1937,O 10,VI,4:7
Pygmalion 1938,Ja 27,16:3
Coriolanus 1938,F 2,14:5
First Crocus, The 1942,Ja 3,14:6
Moment Musical 1943,Je 1,18:1
Heel, The 1954,My 27,33:2
Apollo of Bellac, The 1954,My 29,12:1
Purification, The 1954,My 29,12:1
Bad Seed, The 1954,D 9,42:1
Potting Shed, The 1957,Ja 30,32:1
Compulsion 1957,O 25,21:1
Jeannette 1960,Mr 25,20:2
Rosmersholm 1962,Ap 12,42:1
Rosmersholm 1962,Ap 22,II,1:1
Six Characters in Search of an Author
1963,Mr 11,7:2
Croye, Diana
On the Make 1932,My 24,23:2
This Thing Called Love 1935,Jl 2,24:4
Sweet Shadow 1935,Ag 7,22:2
Croyle, Dorothy
Earl Carroll's Vanities 1927,Ja 5,18:1
Hello, Daddy! 1928,D 27,26:5
Crozier, Eric (Lyricist)
Let's Make an Opera 1950,D 14,50:2
Crozier, Eric (Playwright)
Let's Make an Opera 1950,D 14,50:2
Christmas in the Market Place 1960,D 10,26:1
Crozier, Jim (Composer)
Touch 1970,N 9,52:1
Crozier, Robert
Restless Women 1927,D 27,24:1
Jonesy 1929,Ap 10,32:2
Unto the Third 1933,Ap 21,24:8
Darkness at Noon 1951,Ja 15,13:4
Crozier, Robert Jr
Merry-Go-Round 1932,Ap 23,11:2
Crozier, Wilson
Sign of the Leopard 1928,D 12,34:4
Cruddas, Audrey (Costume Designer)
Caesar and Cleopatra 1951,D 20,43:2
Antony and Cleopatra 1951,D 21,22:2
Caesar and Cleopatra 1951,D 30,II,1:1
Antony and Cleopatra 1951,D 30,II,1:1
Macbeth 1956,O 30,42:2
Hamlet 1958,D 17,2:7
Henry V 1958,D 26,2:7
Cruddas, Audrey (Scenic Designer)
Henry IV 1955,My 15,II,1:1
Macbeth 1956,O 30,42:2
Hamlet 1958,D 17,2:7
Henry V 1958,D 26,2:7
Cruger, Louis
Glass Slipper, The 1925,O 20,29:1
Once in a Lifetime 1930,S 25,22:3
Merrily We Roll Along 1934,O 1,14:1
Sun and I, The 1937,F 27,9:5
Sleep No More 1944,S 1,11:5
Miracle in the Mountains 1947,Ap 26,10:2
Cruikshank, Andrew
Richard of Bordeaux 1934,F 15,16:2
Karl and Anna 1935,O 13,IX,3:1
Saint Joan 1951,O 5,23:2
Cruise, Chris
Never Say Horses 1951,D 7,34:4
Crumbley, W
Pansy 1929,My 15,36:3
Crumbley, Walter
If 1927,O 26,26:2
Swing It 1937,Jl 23,17:2
Crume, Camilla
Dear Me 1921,Ja 18,14:1
Hell's Bells! 1925,Ja 27,14:2
Jane-Our Stranger 1925,O 9,27:2
Chivalry 1925,D 16,22:3
Love 'Em and Leave 'Em 1926,F 4,20:4
They All Want Something 1926,O 13,20:2
Scalawag, The 1927,Mr 30,22:3
Skull, The 1928,Ap 24,28:3
Virtue's Bed 1930,Ap 16,26:5
Crumit, Frank
Betty, Be Good 1920,My 5,14:2
Tangerine 1921,Ag 10,8:2
Nifties of 1923 1923,S 26,10:1
Vaudeville (Palace) 1923,N 13,24:2
Vaudeville (Palace) 1923,N 20,23:4

Crumit, Frank—Cont
Vaudeville (Palace) 1924,F 12,20:2
Vaudeville (Palace) 1929,F 4,21:4
Lambs Gambol 1933,Ap 24,10:1
Crumit, Frank (Miscellaneous)
Great Lady 1938,D 2,26:6
Crumit, Frank (Playwright)
Lambs Gambol 1932,Ap 25,18:2
Crummles, Master
George Barnwell; London Merchant, The
1928,O 2,34:3
Crummles, Ninetta (Miss)
George Barnwell; London Merchant, The
1928,O 2,34:3
Crummles, Vincent
George Barnwell; London Merchant, The
1928,O 2,34:3
Crummles, Vincent (Mrs)
George Barnwell; London Merchant, The
1928,O 2,34:3
Crump, Florence
Nine Till Six 1936,Mr 14,10:3
Crump, Frederick
Vaudeville (Palace) 1931,S 28,17:5
Crump, John
Street Scene 1929,Ja 11,20:4
Crump, John (Playwright)
Hipper's Holiday 1934,O 19,26:2
Don't Look Now! 1936,N 4,41:3
Crump, Owen (Playwright)
Southern Exposure 1950,S 27,36:3
Crump, Owen (Producer)
Red White and Blue 1950,O 8,64:5
Crump, Roland (Director)
Disney on Parade 1970,S 24,63:1
Crumpton, Charles
Light of the World, The 1920,Ja 7,17:1
Crumpton, Ruth
Carmen Jones 1943,D 3,26:2
Carmen Jones 1945,My 3,26:5
Carmen Jones 1946,Ap 8,32:2
Carmen Jones 1951,S 22,8:6
Crusellas, Ramon (Director)
Stranger in the Hills 1949,O 10,19:2
Crutchley, Rosalie
Crucible, The 1956,Ap 11,28:3
Cruz, Miriam
And the Wind Blows 1959,Ap 29,28:1
Pericas, Las 1969,N 2,86:5
Cruz, Nils L (Director)
Abortion 1959,O 28,40:4
Cruz, Nils L (Miscellaneous)
Sniper, The 1959,O 28,40:4
Abortion 1959,O 28,40:4
Movie Man 1959,O 28,40:4
Dance of Death, The 1960,S 14,51:1
Cruz, Nils L (Producer)
Every Other Evil 1961,Ja 23,20:2
Cryer, David
Streets of New York, The 1963,O 30,47:1
Now Is the Time for all Good Men 1967,S 27,42:1
Come Summer 1969,Mr 19,43:1
Whispers on the Wind 1970,Je 4,50:1
Cryer, David (Miscellaneous)
Futz 1968,Je 14,39:1
Cryer, David (Producer)
Now Is the Time for all Good Men 1967,S 27,42:1
Cryer, Gretchen (Lyricist)
Now Is the Time for all Good Men 1967,S 27,42:1
Last Sweet Days of Isaac, The 1970,Ja 27,49:1
Cryer, Gretchen (Miscellaneous)
Now Is the Time for All Good Men 1967,O 27,49:
Cryer, Gretchen (Playwright)
Now Is the Time for all Good Men 1967,S 27,42:1
Last Sweet Days of Isaac, The 1970,Ja 27,49:1
Last Sweet Days of Isaac, The 1970,F 8,II,1:6
Crystal, Bill
Arden of Faversham 1970,F 17,33:1
Ubu Roi 1970,F 17,33:1
Crystal, Diane
Merry-Go-Round 1932,Ap 23,11:2
Crystal, Ida
Nineteenth Hole of Europe, The 1949,Mr 28,16:2
Crystal Twins
Sons o' Fun 1941,D 2,28:2
Csatho, Kalman (Original Author)
Go on Smoking Ladany! 1927,Mr 20,VIII,4:3
Csatho, Kalman (Playwright)
Go on Smoking Ladany! 1927,Mr 20,VIII,4:3
Lilla 1928,Mr 4,IX,2:7
Cselenyi, Joseph (Scenic Designer)
Chemmy Circle, The 1968,Ag 10,17:2
Csortos
Siberia 1928,Ap 15,IX,4:1
Hairy Ape, The 1928,Je 10,VIII,2:8
A Tabornok 1928,D 2,X,4:7
Cuaranta, Giuseppe
Sansone; Samson 1936,N 30,25:2
Cuates Castilla, The
Mexicana 1939,Ap 22,14:4
Cubana Trio
Caribbean Carnival 1947,D 6,12:2
Cubanola, Havana Rumba Band
Artists and Models 1930,Je 11,33:2

ubit, Lizzie
Bitter Stream 1936,Mr 31,16:6
ubitt, Clara
What Never Dies 1926,D 29,24:2
Merry Wives of Windsor, The 1938,Ap 15,22:3
ubitt, Elizabeth
Strings, My Lord, Are False, The 1942,My 20,24:2
ubitt, Lizzie
Night Remembers, The 1934,N 28,24:3
ubitt, Richard
Weather Clear, Track Fast 1927,O 19,24:5
Distant Drums 1932,Ja 19,24:3
uby and Smith
Vaudeville (Palace) 1926,Ag 3,19:2
ucaneili, Peter
Horse Fever 1940,N 25,21:2
ucci, Frank (Playwright)
Ofay Watcher, The 1969,S 16,40:1
Ofay Watcher, The 1969,S 21,II,1:2
ucci, John
Blood Wedding 1949,F 7,16:2
uchman, Edwin
Signature 1945,F 15,25:2
uckovic, Maja
Ubu Roi 1968,Je 29,20:1
uddy, Margaret
My Fair Lady 1964,My 21,43:2
ude, Marianne
Best Foot Forward 1941,O 2,28:2
uenod, Hugh
Bitter Sweet 1929,N 6,30:2
uerden, Keith (Costume Designer)
Grass Harp, The 1953,Ap 28,32:2
Girl on the Via Flaminia, The 1954,F 10,37:1
Infancy 1962,Ja 12,28:1
Someone From Assisi 1962,Ja 12,28:1
Childhood 1962,Ja 12,28:1
Plays for Bleecker Street 1962,Ja 12,28:1
uerden, Keith (Scenic Designer)
Summer and Smoke 1952,Ap 25,19:5
Summer and Smoke 1952,My 4,II,1:1
Grass Harp, The 1953,Ap 28,32:2
Grass Harp, The 1953,My 24,II,1:1
Girl on the Via Flaminia, The 1954,F 10,37:1
King and the Duke, The 1955,Je 2,25:2
Moon for the Misbegotten, A 1958,Je 7,10:6
Camino Real 1960,My 17,42:2
Camino Real 1960,My 29,II,1:1
ui, Cesar (Composer)
Untitled-Marionettes 1923,S 11,10:2
uitino, Vincente Martinez (Playwright)
Fuerza Ciega, La 1927,D 6,26:1
uka, Frances
Taste of Honey, A 1961,My 17,43:1
Silence 1969,Jl 13,II,8:1
Silver Tassle, The 1969,S 12,35:2
uker, Elliot
Utopia! 1963,My 7,47:4
Harangues, The 1970,Ja 14,42:1
ukor, George (Director)
Antonia 1925,O 21,20:1
Great Gatsby, The 1926,F 3,22:1
Dark, The 1927,F 2,22:5
Trigger 1927,D 7,32:1
Free Soul, A 1928,Ja 13,26:5
Furies, The 1928,Mr 8,23:1
Young Love 1928,O 31,28:1
Gypsy 1929,Ja 15,22:2
Astonished Heart, The; Tonight at Eight
1940,Ag 6,15:3
ulbertson, Caroline
Kumquat in the Persimmon Tree, The
1962,Je 19,27:2
ulbertson, Ernest Howard (Playwright)
Goat Alley 1921,Je 21,20:2
Goat Alley 1927,Ap 21,24:3
ulbertson, John
First American Dictator 1939,Mr 15,18:2
ulbertson, Sandy
Ice Capades 1958,S 4,33:2
Ice Capades 1960,S 1,30:1
Ice Capades 1961,Ag 31,24:4
uljak, John
White Devil, The 1965,D 7,56:1
ulkin, Philip (Composer)
Marjorie 1924,Ag 12,12:2
ulkin, Philip R
Front Page Stuff 1926,D 29,24:4
ulkin, Terry
Shakuntala 1959,S 10,41:2
Physicists, The 1964,O 14,52:1
ull, Howard
Sport of Kings, The 1926,My 5,24:2
Dorian Gray 1928,My 22,18:4
ull, James
Chemmy Circle, The 1968,Ag 10,17:2
ullan, Campbell (Director)
Sign of the Leopard 1928,D 12,34:4
ullen, Countee (Miscellaneous)
Free and Easy 1959,D 15,51:4
ullen, Countee (Original Author)
St Louis Woman 1946,Ap 1,22:2

Cullen, Countee (Playwright)
One Way to Heaven 1936,S 29,35:1
Cullen, Donald
Beyond the Fringe, '65 1964,D 16,49:2
Cullen, Edward
Malvaloca 1922,O 3,22:1
Brigadoon 1947,Mr 14,28:2
Cullen, Eileen
LeMaire's Affairs 1927,Mr 29,22:4
Cullen, Malan
Red Harvest 1937,Mr 31,29:2
Cullen, Myra
Scandals 1920,Je 8,9:1
George White's Scandals 1921,Jl 12,14:1
George White's Scandals 1922,Ag 29,10:1
George White's Scandals 1923,Je 19,22:5
Cullen, Raymond
Madame Pompadour 1924,N 12,20:6
Cullen, William
Straight Thru the Door 1928,O 5,17:2
Inspector Kennedy 1929,D 21,16:3
Cullens, Bryan
Castlereagh 1935,F 20,22:4
Culley, Fred (Musical Director)
Hear! Hear! 1955,S 28,38:1
Culliford, James
Twelfth Night 1958,D 10,54:2
Henry V 1958,D 26,2:7
Cullimore, Gwyneth
Trial by Jury 1948,Ja 6,27:2
Iolanthe 1948,Ja 13,29:3
Gondoliers, The 1948,Ja 27,31:2
Yeomen of the Guard, The 1948,F 3,30:2
Patience 1948,F 10,27:2
Cullinan, Mary
Tom Sawyer 1931,D 26,15:3
Cullinan, Raloward, Norah
Innocent Voyage, The 1943,N 16,27:2
Cullinan, Ralph
Juno and the Paycock 1926,Mr 16,22:1
Hangman's House 1926,D 17,27:2
Lady Screams, The 1927,My 3,24:2
John Ferguson 1928,Ja 18,23:1
Goin' Home 1928,Ag 24,23:2
Goin' Home 1928,S 2,VII,1:1
Silver Tassie, The 1929,O 25,26:1
Mr Gilhooley 1930,O 1,26:1
Anatomist, The 1932,O 25,24:3
Crucible 1933,S 5,22:4
Is Life Worth Living? 1933,N 10,24:6
Within the Gates 1934,O 23,23:1
Dominant Sex, The 1935,Ap 2,24:5
Green Waters 1936,N 5,34:4
Father Malachy's Miracle 1937,N 18,26:4
White Steed, The 1939,Ja 11,16:2
Johnny Belinda 1940,S 19,26:2
Strings, My Lord, Are False, The 1942,My 20,24:2
Skin of Our Teeth, The 1942,N 19,29:5
Rugged Path, The 1945,N 12,17:2
Second Best Bed 1946,Ja 4,20:2
Gone Tomorrow; Hope's the Thing
1948,My 12,34:6
Home Life of a Buffalo; Hope's the Thing
1948,My 12,34:6
Hope Is the Thing With Feathers; Hope's the
Thing 1948,My 12,34:6
Cullinan, Ralph (Playwright)
Loggerheads 1925,F 10,21:1
You Can't Win 1926,F 17,12:1
Banshee, The 1927,D 6,26:2
Caravan 1928,Ag 30,13:3
Cullingham, Mark (Director)
Two of Us, The 1970,S 11,33:2
Cullison, Barry
Tom Paine 1969,Mr 30,71:2
Cullitan, Daniel
Othello 1945,My 23,25:4
Cullman, Joan
King Midas and the Golden Touch 1948,O 25,28:3
Culloo, Billy
Circus Princess, The 1927,Ap 26,32:2
New Yorkers, The 1930,D 9,31:1
Culloo, William
Battleship Gertie 1935,Ja 19,9:2
Cullum, John
Julius Caesar 1957,O 24,39:1
Jackass, The 1960,Mr 24,39:2
Measure for Measure 1960,Jl 27,33:1
Camelot 1960,D 5,42:1
King Lear 1962,Ag 14,35:1
Saving Grace, The 1963,Ap 19,28:1
Thistle in My Bed 1963,N 20,48:1
Hamlet 1964,Ap 10,30:1
On a Clear Day You Can See Forever
1965,O 18,44:1
Bridal Night, The 1966,N 8,45:1
Eternal Triangle 1966,N 8,45:1
Frying Pan, The 1966,N 8,45:1
Cullum, John (Miscellaneous)
King Lear 1959,Ja 3,11:2
Cully, Mr (Musical Director)
Aquashow 1952,Je 25,25:1

Culp, Robert
Prescott Proposals, The 1953,D 17,53:1
He Who Gets Slapped 1956,F 2,18:1
Diary of a Scoundrel 1956,N 5,41:1
Clearing in the Woods, A 1957,Ja 11,20:2
Culpepper, Bill
Point of No Return 1957,Mr 23,17:2
Culshaw, Bernard (Scenic Designer)
Hamlet 1970,D 28,40:1
Culshaw, Eileen
Cafe de Danse 1929,Ja 16,22:2
Culver, Carol
Boy Friend, The 1970,Ap 15,54:1
Culver, Michael
Henry V 1958,D 26,2:7
Culver, Roland
Deep Blue Sea, The 1953,Ap 4,8:6
Little Hut, The 1953,O 8,37:2
Five Finger Exercise 1959,D 3,45:4
Five Finger Exercise 1959,D 13,II,3:1
Ivanov 1966,My 4,50:1
Culvert, Grace
Love Dreams 1921,O 11,22:2
Cumberbatch, Billy
Anna Lucasta 1944,Je 17,10:1
Cumberbatch, William
Macbeth 1936,Ap 15,25:4
One-Act Plays of the Sea; Bound East for Cardiff
1937,O 30,23:2
One-Act Plays of the Sea; In the Zone
1937,O 30,23:2
One-Act Plays of the Sea; Long Voyage Home,
The 1937,O 30,23:2
Cumberland, A
Fedora 1924,Ja 24,14:2
Cumberland, Alan
Dance of Death, The 1967,O 20,50:1
Love for Love 1967,O 21,17:1
Cumberland, David
South Pacific 1968,Je 30,54:2
Cumberland, John
Ladies' Night 1920,Ag 10,10:1
Scarlet Man, The 1921,Ag 23,10:3
Lady Bug 1922,Ap 18,15:3
Trelawney of the 'Wells' 1925,Je 2,16:2
Henry IV, Part I 1926,Je 1,29:1
Henry-Behave 1926,Ag 24,19:4
Pickwick 1927,F 16,17:4
Mr Pickwick 1927,F 20,VII,2:6
Pickwick 1927,Mr 13,VII,1:1
Pickwick 1927,S 6,35:2
Pickwick 1927,S 11,VIII,1:1
Furies, The 1928,Mr 8,23:1
Precious 1929,Ja 15,22:5
Cumberland, Marten (Playwright)
Inside the Room 1934,D 23,15:3
Climbing 1937,Ja 20,18:2
Cumby, Billy
Green Pastures, The 1930,F 27,26:1
Green Pastures, The 1935,F 27,16:2
Policy Kings 1938,D 31,6:2
Cumings, Thayer
Laugh It Off 1925,Ap 25,18:4
Cumming, Dorothy
Judas 1929,Ja 25,20:4
Cumming, Jean
Lady in the Dark 1941,Ja 24,14:2
Cumming, Richard (Composer)
Bonds of Interest, The 1958,My 7,43:1
Policemen, The 1961,N 22,24:2
Duchess of Malfi, The 1962,Mr 5,27:1
Brother to Dragons 1968,D 8,86:1
Wilson in the Promise Land 1970,Ja 11,78:1
Wilson in the Promise Land 1970,My 27,41:1
Cumming, Richard (Miscellaneous)
Wilson in the Promise Land 1970,Ja 11,78:1
Cumming, Richard (Musical Director)
Shoemaker and the Peddler, The 1960,O 15,27:4
Cumming, Robert (Producer)
H M S Pinafore 1960,Ja 29,14:1
Cummingham, Leon
Only 38 1921,S 14,22:2
Cummings, Bob
Wayward Stork, The 1966,Ja 20,27:1
Cummings, Cecile
Drift 1925,N 25,15:3
Cummings, Constance
Accent on Youth 1934,D 26,19:1
Young Madame Conti 1936,N 20,26:4
Young Madame Conti 1936,D 6,XII,7:6
Young Madame Conti 1937,Ap 1,18:4
Three Set Out 1937,Je 23,29:3
Madame Bovary 1937,O 6,28:4
Madame Bovary 1937,N 17,26:2
If I Were You 1938,Ja 9,II,3:2
If I Were You 1938,Ja 25,24:2
Jealous God, The 1939,Mr 26,X,3:1
Skylark 1942,Ap 12,VIII,1:6
Petrified Forest, The 1943,Ja 10,VIII,1:6

Cummings, Constance—Cont
One-Man Show 1945,F 9,21:2
One-Man Show 1945,F 18,II,1:1
Return to Tyassi 1950,D 1,31:4
Rape of the Belt, The 1960,N 7,46:1
Hamlet 1969,My 2,38:1
Cummings, David (Miscellaneous)
Me and Molly 1948,F 27,27:2
Cummings, Don
Vaudeville (Palace) 1929,My 13,26:3
Tattle Tales 1933,Je 2,22:6
Crazy With the Heat 1941,Ja 15,18:2
Crazy With the Heat 1941,Ja 31,15:2
Cummings, E E (Playwright)
Him 1928,Ap 19,23:3
Him 1928,Ap 29,IX,1:1
Santa Claus 1957,D 18,42:7
Santa Claus 1960,Jl 22,13:1
Cummings, Forrest
Dope 1926,Ja 4,16:3
Cummings, Gretel
Home Movies 1964,My 12,32:1
Only a Countess May Dance When She's Crazy
(An Almost Historical Camp) 1968,Mr 19,41:1
Last Triangle, The (An Embroidered Camp)
1968,Mr 19,41:1
Cummings, Hamilton
American Born 1925,O 6,31:3
Cummings, Marie
Genius and the Crowd 1920,S 7,20:1
Cummings, Patrick (Choreographer)
Gantry 1970,F 16,44:1
Cummings, Ralph
Rope 1928,F 23,18:3
Cummings, Ralph Waldo
Finian's Rainbow 1947,Ja 11,23:2
Cummings, Robert
Nemesis 1921,Ap 5,24:3
Fables 1922,F 7,12:2
Fools Errant 1922,Ag 22,12:3
Fool, The 1922,O 24,18:1
Song and Dance Man, The 1924,Ja 1,21:2
Desert Flower, The 1924,N 19,18:2
Piker, The 1925,Ja 16,14:1
Something to Brag About 1925,Ag 14,14:3
Downstream 1926,Ja 12,28:1
Still Waters 1926,Mr 2,23:1
Woman Disputed, A 1926,S 29,23:2
Trial of Mary Dugan, The 1927,S 20,33:1
Congratulations 1929,My 1,28:4
She Means Business 1931,Ja 27,21:2
Man on Stilts, The 1931,S 10,23:2
Murder at the Vanities 1933,S 13,22:4
Lady From the Sea, The 1935,D 14,11:3
American Primitive 1937,Ag 13,12:5
Faithfully Yours 1951,O 19,22:5
Cummings, Robert (Director)
Gondoliers, The 1969,My 10,35:1
Cummings, Roy
Passing Show of 1923, The 1923,Je 15,24:6
Topics of 1923 1923,N 21,23:2
Vaudeville (Palace) 1929,My 13,26:3
Cummings, Sanford
Remember the Day 1935,Jl 9,24:3
Cummings, T (Lyricist)
1776 1926,Ap 24,11:2
Cummings, Vicki
Furnished Rooms 1934,My 30,14:6
Orchids Preferred 1937,Ap 29,16:6
Orchids Preferred 1937,My 12,26:5
Time, Place and the Girl, The 1942,O 22,24:3
Mrs Kimball Presents 1944,Mr 1,17:3
Lady in Danger 1945,Mr 30,18:6
For Love or Money 1947,N 5,36:2
Oh, Mr Meadowbrook! 1948,D 27,17:2
Mr Barry's Etchings 1950,F 1,26:2
Phoenix Too Frequent, A 1950,Ap 27,36:2
Buy Me Blue Ribbons 1951,O 18,33:2
Hook'n Ladder 1952,Ap 30,31:2
I've Got Sixpence 1952,D 3,44:2
I've Got Sixpence 1952,D 7,II,5:1
Mid-Summer 1953,Ja 22,19:1
Homeward Look, The 1954,Je 4,26:2
Lunatics and Lovers 1954,D 14,44:2
Hot Corner, The 1956,Ja 26,25:2
Palm Tree in a Rose Garden, A 1957,N 27,26:2
How to Make a Man 1961,F 3,16:1
Butter and Egg Man, The 1966,O 18,49:1
Cummings, Victoria
Here Goes the Bride 1931,N 4,31:2
Cummins, Bernie and His Biltmore Hotel Orchestra
Vaudeville (Palace) 1929,F 4,21:4
Cummins, Ina
Under Milk Wood 1957,O 16,42:5
Look After Lulu 1959,Mr 4,35:1
Cummins, Peggy
Junior Miss 1943,Ap 18,II,1:1
Cummins, Ronn
Harbor Lights 1956,O 5,20:1
Cunard, Lance
You Can't Take It With You 1945,Mr 27,23:7
Trial, The 1955,Je 15,35:2
Spring's Awakening 1955,O 10,30:2
Volpone 1957,Ja 8,27:1
Volpone 1957,Ja 13,II,10:1
Richard III 1957,N 26,41:1

As You Like It 1958,Ja 21,33:6
Sign of Winter 1958,My 8,35:1
Legend of Lizzie, The 1959,F 10,39:1
Visit, The 1960,Mr 9,38:3
Rules of the Game, The 1960,D 20,44:1
Orthee 1962,D 29,5:5
Corruption in the Palace of Justice 1963,O 9,49:2
Midsummer Night's Dream, A 1964,Je 30,23:2
Colombe 1965,F 24,33:1
Henry V 1965,Je 29,27:2
Taming of the Shrew, The 1965,Jl 3,10:5
Deadly Game, The 1966,F 14,34:1
Cuneo, Ernest
Betty Behave 1927,Mr 9,28:4
Cunerty, Joseph
Trial of Dr Beck, The 1937,Ag 10,22:2
Cunliffe, Jerry
Tom Paine 1968,Mr 26,38:1
Futz 1968,Je 14,39:1
Cunliffe, Owen
Antigone 1959,S 16,46:2
Cunliffe, Tom
Anna Kleiber 1965,Ja 20,33:1
Cunneff, Joseph
Girl From Nantucket, The 1945,N 9,17:2
Cunnigham, Ronnie
Marinka 1945,Jl 19,19:2
Cunningham, Al
Petrified Forest, The 1935,Ja 8,26:1
Postman Always Rings Twice, The 1936,F 26,17:2
Cunningham, Arthur
Hitchy-Koo, 1920 1920,O 20,11:3
My Maryland 1927,S 13,37:2
Ripples 1930,F 12,26:1
Cunningham, Beatrice (Miscellaneous)
To Broadway With Love 1964,Ap 30,28:6
Cunningham, Beckie (Miscellaneous)
Interview 1966,N 7,66:1
Motel 1966,N 7,66:1
TV 1966,N 7,66:1
Cunningham, Bill
Time of Your Life, The 1969,N 7,37:1
Cunningham, Cecil
Vaudeville (Palace) 1924,S 30,27:5
Vaudeville (Palace) 1927,Mr 29,22:6
Cyanamide 1954,Mr 26,17:6
Take a Giant Step 1956,S 26,30:1
Cunningham, Cliff
Patience 1967,O 13,32:1
Cunningham, Dan
Caesar and Cleopatra 1951,D 20,43:2
Antony and Cleopatra 1951,D 21,22:2
Cunningham, Davis
Lady in the Dark 1941,Ja 24,14:2
Saint of Bleecker Street, The 1954,D 28,21:1
Cunningham, Ethel
Stairs, The 1927,N 8,32:7
Master Builder, The 1955,Mr 2,23:2
Cunningham, George
Tall Kentuckian, The 1953,Je 17,30:1
Cunningham, Guy
Macbeth 1921,F 18,16:1
Out of the Sea 1927,D 6,26:2
Diplomacy 1928,My 29,16:3
Cunningham, Helen
Demi-Virgin, The 1921,O 19,22:1
Cunningham, Henry
Two Orphans, The 1926,Ap 6,26:2
Cunningham, Joan
Don Carlos 1962,F 28,27:5
Cunningham, Joan (Miscellaneous)
Don Carlos 1962,F 28,27:5
Cunningham, Joe
Friars Club Frolic 1933,My 15,16:4
Cunningham, Joe (Miscellaneous)
Antigone 1959,S 16,46:2
Cunningham, John
Purification, The 1959,D 9,57:5
Pimpernel! 1964,Ja 7,26:6
Coriolanus 1965,Je 21,36:1
Romeo and Juliet 1965,Je 21,36:3
Taming of the Shrew, The 1965,Je 24,32:2
King Lear 1965,Je 25,39:1
Play of Daniel, The 1966,Ja 2,64:4
Falstaff 1966,Je 20,27:1
Murder in the Cathedral 1966,Je 21,38:1
Twelfth Night 1966,Je 23,28:1
Midsummer Night's Dream, A 1967,Je 19,42:1
Merchant of Venice, The 1967,Je 22,46:2
Macbeth 1967,Jl 31,21:1
Love and Let Love 1968,Ja 4,30:1
Zorba 1968,N 18,58:1
Zorba 1968,N 24,II,1:1
Company 1970,Ap 27,40:1
Company 1970,My 3,II,1:4
Cunningham, Leon
Vagabond King, The 1925,S 22,23:3
White Eagle, The 1927,D 27,24:4
Cunningham, Leon (Playwright)
Hospitality 1922,N 14,16:1
Hospitality 1922,D 3,VIII,1:1
Neighbors 1923,D 27,11:1

Cunningham, M
O'Brien Girl, The 1921,O 4,10:2
Cunningham, Margo
Dance of Death, The 1967,O 20,50:1
Love for Love 1967,O 21,17:1
Love for Love 1967,O 30,59:1
Cunningham, Merce
Variations of 1940 1940,Ja 29,12:1
Wind Remains, The 1943,Mr 31,16:6
Cunningham, Merce (Choreographer)
Wind Remains, The 1943,Mr 31,16:6
Cave at Machpelah, The 1959,Jl 1,25:1
Cunningham, Michael
Poor Little Ritz Girl 1920,Jl 29,7:1
Cunningham, Nikola
Artists and Models 1923,Ag 21,12:2
Cunningham, Olma (Costume Designer)
Miracle, The 1960,D 5,42:3
Cunningham, Owen
Right to Love, The 1925,Je 9,16:4
Casualties 1927,Mr 5,12:2
Love Expert, The 1929,S 24,29:1
Wolves 1932,Ja 7,26:3
Cunningham, Patti
Ice Follies 1966,Ja 12,27:6
Cunningham, Philip Jr
Wandering Jew, The 1927,F 2,22:4
Cunningham, Robert
Come Back, Little Sheba 1950,F 16,28:5
Cunningham, Robert G
Black Cockatoo, The 1926,D 31,11:1
Cunningham, Ronnie
Banjo Eyes 1941,D 26,20:2
Doctor in Spite of Himself, The 1957,F 28,18:4
By Jupiter 1967,Ja 20,28:2
Cunningham, Sarah
Church Street 1948,F 10,27:2
Blood Wedding 1949,F 7,16:2
House of Bernarda Alba, The 1951,Ja 8,14:6
World of Sholom Aleichem, The 1953,S 12,13:2
World of Sholom Aleichem, The 1953,S 20,II,1:1
Fair Game 1957,N 4,39:1
Barroom Monks, The 1962,My 29,21:1
Portrait of the Artist as a Young Man, A
1962,My 29,21:1
Zulu and the Zayda, The 1965,N 11,59:1
My Sweet Charlie 1966,D 7,56:1
Oh, Pioneers 1969,N 12,41:1
Cunningham, Scott
Pretender, The 1960,My 25,42:1
After the Fall 1964,Ja 24,18:1
Marco Millions 1964,F 21,33:1
Changeling, The 1964,O 30,32:2
Cunningham, Sean S (Miscellaneous)
Tonight in Living Color; Golden Fleece, The
1969,Je 11,43:1
Tonight in Living Color; David Show, The
1969,Je 11,43:1
Cunningham, Zamah
Tragedy of the Ages, The 1933,Ap 7,22:7
Give Us This Day 1933,O 28,20:6
Gentlewoman 1934,Mr 23,28:4
Are You Decent? 1934,Ap 20,16:2
Reprise 1935,My 2,16:2
Trelawney of the 'Wells' 1935,Jl 16,24:1
Triumph 1935,O 15,18:5
Season Changes, The 1935,D 24,10:2
Hallowe'en 1936,F 21,20:3
Around the Corner 1936,D 29,17:2
In Clover 1937,O 14,23:1
Siege 1937,D 9,31:4
Roosty 1938,F 15,21:2
Run Sheep Run 1938,N 4,26:2
Young Couple Wanted 1940,Ja 25,16:2
Medicine Show 1940,Ap 13,20:6
Horse Fever 1940,N 25,21:2
Tanyard Street 1941,F 5,16:2
Trojan Women, The 1941,Ap 9,32:5
Days of Our Youth, The 1941,N 29,15:2
Feathers in a Gale 1943,D 22,26:2
Robin Hood 1944,N 8,28:2
Beggar's Opera, The 1957,Mr 14,35:1
Shadow of a Gunman, The 1958,N 21,26:1
Shadow of a Gunman, The 1958,N 30,II,1:1
Cuny, Alain
Phedre 1963,O 21,39:1
Cuomo, James
Carmilla 1970,D 1,61:2
Cuomo, James (Miscellaneous)
Carmilla 1970,D 1,61:2
Cuomo, James (Musical Director)
Gertrude 1970,N 13,29:1
Carmilla 1970,D 1,61:2
Cuozzo, Alberta
Jar, The 1969,Ap 23,42:1
Curby, J E
Tiger Smiles, The 1930,D 18,29:1
Curci, Elvira
Sirena 1931,S 22,33:4
Curci, Gennaro Mario (Original Author)
Woman Denied, A 1931,F 26,21:1
Curci, Gennaro Mario (Playwright)
Barbara 1929,N 18,24:5

...ci, Gennaro Mario (Playwright)—Cont
...oolscap 1933,Ja 12,21:2
...ci, Vanda
...adies of the Jury 1929,O 22,26:2
...ci (Mme)
...ly Wife Is Different 1931,Ap 27,24:4
...ci-Caccia, Elvira
...arbara 1929,N 18,24:5
...rcio, Armando (Playwright)
...ortuna 1962,Ja 4,26:1
...rel, Francois de (Playwright)
...iveuse et le Moribond, La 1926,F 14,III,11:1
...Orage Mystique 1927,D 18,IX,4:4
...Dark Saint, The; Envers d'une Sainte, L'
   1932,F 21,VIII,1:6
...relop, Shepard
...Naughty-Naught '00 1946,O 21,27:5
...ri, Robert
...Mikado, The 1942,F 4,22:2
...Pirates of Penzance, The 1942,F 18,22:2
...Iolanthe 1942,F 24,26:4
...Gondoliers, The 1942,Mr 4,22:3
...riale, Charles
...Purple Canary, The 1963,Ap 23,31:1
...rk, Kay
...Pirates of Penzance, The 1936,Ap 21,27:5
...rley, George
...Fantasticks, The 1960,My 4,55:2
...rley, H T (Miscellaneous)
...Ghost Parade, The 1929,O 31,28:4
...rley, Leo
...Skirt, The 1921,N 8,28:1
...Schemers 1924,S 16,27:1
...Red Dust 1928,Ja 3,29:2
...Criminal Code, The 1929,O 3,28:2
...Distant Drums 1932,Ja 19,24:3
...Little Ol' Boy 1933,Ap 25,15:5
...Jezebel 1933,D 20,26:3
...They Shall Not Die 1934,F 22,24:4
...Petticoat Fever 1935,Mr 5,22:2
...If This Be Treason 1935,Jl 30,17:1
...If This Be Treason 1935,S 24,28:2
...Ragged Edge, The 1935,N 26,28:3
...Alice Takat 1936,F 11,19:2
...rley, Tom
...Jubilee 1935,O 14,20:1
...rley, Virginia
...Budget, The 1932,S 21,26:4
...Peacock 1932,O 12,27:1
...House of Remsen 1934,Ap 3,26:4
...Personal Appearance 1936,Jl 9,17:4
...rley, Wilma
...West Side Story 1957,S 27,14:4
...West Side Story 1964,Ap 9,24:2
...rling, Kate
...Things That Are Caesar's, The 1932,O 18,23:4
...Far-Off Hills, The 1932,O 19,22:4
...Juno and the Paycock 1932,O 20,24:3
...Playboy of the Western World, The 1932,O 21,25:1
...New Gossoon, The 1932,O 22,18:2
...Words Upon the Window Pane, The
   1932,O 29,18:2
...Crabbed Youth and Age 1932,N 4,25:1
...Autumn Fire 1932,D 29,16:3
...rnock, Richard
...Oh What a Lovely War 1964,O 1,30:1
...Stephen D 1966,Ag 5,17:1
...Cherry Orchard, The 1970,My 7,63:2
...rrah, Brian (Scenic Designer)
...Caretaker, The 1961,O 5,42:3
...After the Rain 1967,O 10,54:1
...rran, Eileen
...Birthright, The 1920,My 25,14:2
...Kathleen ni Houlihan 1920,Je 29,9:2
...Private Life of the Master Race, The
   1956,Ja 31,33:3
...rran, Florence
...Treasure, The 1920,O 5,13:1
...rran, Frank
...Trojan Incident 1938,Ap 22,15:2
...rran, Homer (Miscellaneous)
...Reflected Glory 1936,S 22,30:2
...Obsession 1946,O 2,39:2
...Lady Windermere's Fan 1946,O 15,29:2
...Tonight at 8:30; Red Peppers 1948,F 21,8:2
...Tonight at 8:30; Ways and Means 1948,F 21,8:2
...Tonight at 8:30; Family Album 1948,F 21,8:2
...Tonight at 8:30; Hands Across the Sea
   1948,F 24,20:4
...Tonight at 8:30; Shadow Play 1948,F 24,20:4
...Tonight at 8:30; Fumed Oak 1948,F 24,20:4
...Curran, Homer (Original Author)
...Song of Norway 1944,Ag 22,20:2
...Song of Norway 1958,Je 23,19:2
...Song of Norway 1959,Je 26,16:2
...Curran, Homer (Playwright)
...Magdalena 1948,Jl 28,27:2
...Magdalena 1948,S 21,31:2
...Curran, Homer (Producer)
...Tovarich 1937,Ap 25,X,2:4
...Magdalena 1948,S 21,31:2
...Curran, James
...Lady Fingers 1929,F 1,22:4

Curran, Maggie
Great Big Doorstep, The 1950,Mr 18,8:6
Curran, Maggie (Miscellaneous)
Trial of Dmitri Karamazov, The 1958,Ja 28,30:1
Curran, Pamela
Who Was That Lady I Saw You With?
   1958,Mr 4,33:2
Curran, Paul
Beaux' Stratagem, The 1970,F 10,50:2
Three Sisters, The 1970,F 12,30:1
Curran, Sharon
Taming of the Shrew, The 1940,F 6,17:2
Curran, William
Veronica's Veil 1931,F 23,36:2
Curran (Producer)
Dinner at Eight 1933,Ap 9,IX,1:7
Currie, Clive
Double Dan 1927,Je 5,VII,2:1
Baa, Baa, Black Sheep 1929,My 12,IX,2:3
Currie, Don
Royal Box, The 1928,N 21,32:3
Sakura 1928,D 26,14:4
Currie, Donald (Miscellaneous)
Legitimate Steal, The 1958,Ap 1,35:1
Sweet Miani 1962,S 26,33:2
Currie, Earl J
If Booth Had Missed 1931,My 14,27:1
Currie, Finlay
Not for Children 1935,N 25,23:8
Not for Children 1935,D 22,IX,3:3
Too Late the Phalarope 1956,O 12,35:1
Diamond Orchid 1965,F 11,44:4
Currie, Jack
Jotham Valley 1951,F 7,37:2
Currie, Janet
Once in a Lifetime 1930,S 25,22:3
Currie, Kipp
Red Roses for Me 1961,N 28,41:1
Currie, Michael
Love and Kisses 1963,D 19,39:1
Currie, Robert D (Miscellaneous)
Corruption in the Palace of Justice 1963,O 9,49:2
Lover, The 1964,Ja 6,35:1
Play 1964,Ja 6,35:1
Two Executioners, The 1964,Mr 25,46:2
Dutchman 1964,Mr 25,46:2
Play 1964,Mr 25,46:2
Currier, B W
It's Only Natural 1922,Ap 21,13:2
Currier, Esma
Vagabond King, The 1935,N 29,22:7
Currier, George
Flies, The 1954,S 10,18:2
Currier, H E
Tinker's Dam 1943,Ja 29,22:2
Currier, Hal
Night Music 1951,Ap 9,29:6
Currier, Lucy
Crime in the Whistler Room, The 1924,O 10,22:2
Currimbhoy, Asif (Playwright)
Goa 1968,F 23,46:1
Currin, Brenda
Ah, Wilderness! 1969,N 9,86:1
Curro, Mary Frances
Founders, The 1957,My 14,39:1
Curruth, Burr
Drifting 1922,Ja 3,20:3
Curry, Ada
Noble Prize, The 1935,Jl 9,24:3
Curry, Edward A
Playing the Game 1927,D 20,32:5
Curry, Frank
Rendezvous 1932,O 13,22:3
Curry, Hazel
All Good Americans 1933,D 6,29:2
Curry, Helen
Blue Flame, The 1920,Mr 16,18:1
Curry, Jack
Hymn to the Rising Sun 1937,My 7,28:2
Curry, Julia
Triumph of Robert Emmet, The 1969,My 8,54:1
Curry, Kenneth
Florida Girl 1925,N 3,34:1
Curry, Mason
Ramshackle Inn 1944,Ja 6,17:5
Magnificent Yankee, The 1946,Ja 23,21:2
Curry, Richard
Devil's Disciple, The 1950,Ja 26,23:2
Out of This World 1950,D 22,17:3
Curry, Roberta
White Eagle, The 1927,D 27,24:4
Curry, Sarah (Miscellaneous)
Mr Whistler 1931,D 6,VIII,2:6
Curry, Steve
Christine 1960,Ap 29,27:1
West Side Story 1964,Ap 9,24:2
Hair 1968,Ap 30,40:2
Curry, Virgil
Another Evening With Harry Stoones
   1961,O 23,22:2
Sweet Miani 1962,S 26,33:2
Curson, Anne
Lady Windermere's Fan 1946,O 15,29:2

Curtin, Harry
Good Old Days, The 1923,Ag 15,21:2
Curtin, Joseph
Merchant of Venice, The 1931,N 9,22:2
Searching for the Sun 1936,F 20,22:6
Curtin, Paul
Cretan Woman, The 1954,My 21,17:2
Curtin, Phyllis
Susannah 1955,F 25,18:4
Curtis, Barbara
Wonderful World of Burlesque, The
   1965,Ap 29,38:1
Curtis, Beatrice
Vaudeville (Palace) 1926,Je 29,21:3
Vaudeville (Palace) 1926,D 21,20:5
Vaudeville (Palace) 1927,O 11,27:2
Vaudeville (Palace) 1928,N 26,31:2
Curtis, Billy
Anything Goes 1934,N 22,26:1
Every Man for Himself 1940,D 10,32:3
Curtis, Donald
Anybody Home 1949,F 26,10:5
Curtis, Donna
Merry Widow, The 1961,O 27,28:2
Vagabond King, The 1961,N 24,36:1
H M S Pinafore 1966,Je 8,41:2
Now Is the Time for all Good Men 1967,S 27,42:1
Lend an Ear 1969,O 29,32:1
Curtis, Florence
Bursting the Barriers 1930,My 7,25:1
Curtis, Floyd
Sunrise at Campobello 1958,Ja 31,25:1
Curtis, Francis (Producer)
Give Us This Day 1933,O 28,20:6
I Want a Policeman! 1936,Ja 15,15:5
Curtis, Francis I
Sale and a Sailor, A, or Glory! What Price!
   1926,Ap 25,30:4
Hoot Mon, or Clans Across the Sea 1927,My 8,29:4
Curtis, Greely
Moon Is a Gong, The 1926,Mr 13,21:3
Much Ado About Nothing 1927,N 19,14:6
At the Gate of the Kingdom 1927,D 9,28:5
Curtis, Harry (Costume Designer)
Carnival! 1968,D 13,58:1
Curtis, Jack
Torch Bearers, The 1922,Ag 30,10:2
Zeno 1923,Ag 27,14:2
Craig's Wife 1925,O 13,21:2
Tenth Avenue 1927,Ag 16,31:1
Relations 1928,Ag 21,27:3
Curtis, Jack (Producer)
Stick-in-the-Mud 1935,D 2,18:2
Postman Always Rings Twice, The 1936,F 7,14:4
Postman Always Rings Twice, The 1936,F 26,17:2
Behind the Red Lights 1937,Ja 14,17:4
Places, Please 1937,N 13,10:6
Curtis, Jackie
Glamour, Glory and Gold 1967,O 4,43:1
Curtis, Jackie (Playwright)
Glamour, Glory and Gold 1967,O 4,43:1
Curtis, Jean (Translator)
Richard II 1962,Ag 8,36:1
Curtis, Jewell
Family Affair, A 1946,N 28,41:2
Curtis, Joe
Revolt of the Beavers, The 1937,My 21,19:2
Nativity Play, The 1937,D 21,29:1
Curtis, Joseph
Simple Life, A 1964,My 18,36:1
Curtis, Josephine
Gondoliers, The 1934,S 4,23:1
Gondoliers, The 1936,S 8,23:1
Curtis, Julia (Producer)
MacBird! 1967,F 23,38:1
Curtis, June
Schoolhouse on the Lot 1938,Mr 23,18:4
Dance Night 1938,O 15,20:5
Curtis, Keene
Right You Are (If You Think You Are)
   1964,Mr 5,37:1
Tavern, The 1964,Mr 6,39:2
Scapin 1964,Mr 10,43:1
Impromptu at Versailles 1964,Mr 10,43:1
Lower Depths, The 1964,Mr 31,30:1
Man and Superman 1964,D 7,45:2
War and Peace 1965,Ja 12,32:1
Judith 1965,Mr 25,42:2
You Can't Take It With You 1965,N 24,32:1
School for Scandal, The 1966,N 22,33:2
Right You Are (If You Think You Are)
   1966,N 23,34:2
War and Peace 1967,Mr 22,42:1
Pantagleize 1967,D 1,54:1
Cherry Orchard, The 1968,Mr 20,41:1
Cocktail Party, The 1968,O 8,42:1
Misanthrope, The 1968,O 10,59:1
Cock-A-Doodle Dandy 1969,Ja 21,40:1
Hamlet 1969,Mr 4,34:1
Patriot for Me, A 1969,O 6,58:1
Colette 1970,My 7,60:1
Rothschilds, The 1970,O 20,40:1
Rothschilds, The 1970,N 1,II,1:1

Curtis, Keene (Miscellaneous)
Four Winds 1957,S 26,21:2
Firstborn, The 1958,My 1,35:1
Look After Lulu 1959,Mr 4,35:1
Silent Night, Lonely Night 1959,D 4,36:1
Curtis, Kenneth
Great Necker, The 1928,Mr 7,28:2
Curtis, King (Miscellaneous)
Much Ado About Nothing 1959,S 18,25:2
Curtis, Margaret
Point Valaine 1935,Ja 17,22:2
Yes, My Darling Daughter 1937,F 10,19:2
Father Malachy's Miracle 1937,N 18,26:4
Strangler Fig, The 1940,My 7,31:2
King Lear 1940,D 16,27:2
Doctor's Dilemma, The 1941,Mr 12,18:2
Highland Fling, A 1944,Ap 29,13:2
Curtis, Margaret (Playwright)
Highland Fling, A 1944,Ap 29,13:2
Curtis, Marie
Time 1923,N 27,23:3
Nerves 1924,S 2,22:2
Rising Son, The 1924,O 28,27:2
Close Harmony 1924,D 2,23:1
Kept 1926,S 18,13:3
Big Pond, The 1928,Ag 22,25:1
Little Women 1931,D 8,36:2
Mimie Scheller 1936,O 1,28:4
Curtain Call 1937,Ap 23,24:7
Damaged Goods 1937,My 18,27:2
She Gave Him All She Had 1939,D 2,20:7
Curtis, Mary B (Director)
Trojan Women, The 1923,My 27,10:2
Curtis, Miriam
Jubilee 1935,O 14,20:1
Curtis, Norman
Treasure Girl 1928,N 9,22:1
Curtis, Norman (Composer)
Walk Down Mah Street! 1968,Je 13,54:1
Curtis, Norman (Miscellaneous)
Walk Down Mah Street! 1968,Je 13,54:1
Curtis, Patricia Taylor (Director)
Walk Down Mah Street! 1968,Je 13,54:1
Curtis, Patricia Taylor (Lyricist)
Walk Down Mah Street! 1968,Je 13,54:1
Curtis, Patricia Taylor (Playwright)
Walk Down Mah Street! 1968,Je 13,54:1
Curtis, Paul
Beaux' Stratagem, The 1928,Je 5,20:1
Pirates of Penzance, The 1936,Ap 21,27:5
All the King's Men 1948,Ja 19,19:2
American Mime Theatre 1958,S 25,28:4
Curtis, Paul (Director)
American Mime Theatre 1958,S 25,28:4
Curtis, Ralph
Mary of Magdala 1946,Mr 26,24:5
Curtis, Raymond (Composer)
Thanks for Tomorrow 1938,S 28,28:2
Curtis, Raymond (Producer)
Run Sheep Run 1938,N 4,26:2
Little Dark Horse 1941,N 17,14:4
Willow and I, The 1942,D 11,32:2
Curtis, Richard
Damn Your Honor 1929,D 31,14:3
Live and Learn 1930,Ap 10,24:6
Curtis, Virginia
Great to Be Alive! 1950,Mr 24,28:2
Curtis, William C (Playwright)
Kumquat in the Persimmon Tree, The
1962,Je 19,27:2
Curtis-Brown, Carol
Lady in Waiting 1940,Mr 28,19:1
Curtiss, Archie
Alias Jimmy Valentine 1921,D 9,20:3
Curtright, Jorja
Streetcar Named Desire, A 1950,My 24,36:1
Curtsinger, Gene
Magdalena 1948,S 21,31:2
Curvin, Jack
Traffic Signals 1937,Ag 7,7:4
Curwen, Patric
Flashing Stream, The 1939,Ap 11,19:2
Curwood, James Oliver (Original Author)
River's End, The 1924,Mr 16,VIII,2:1
Curzon, George
Home Chat 1927,N 13,IX,2:1
Moving Finger, The 1928,S 16,IX,1:4
Healthy, Wealthy and Wise 1930,Mr 23,IX,2:3
Punchinello 1932,Mr 27,VIII,2:1
Parnell 1935,N 12,24:2
Black Limelight 1936,N 10,31:1
Hitch Your Wagon! 1937,Ap 9,18:2
Yes, M'Lord 1949,O 5,35:2
Little Glass Clock, The 1956,Mr 27,40:2
Cusack, Cyril
Candida 1935,O 27,IX,2:5
Bishop's Bonfire, The 1955,Mr 1,22:8
Bishop's Bonfire, The 1955,Mr 6,II,3:1
Moon for the Misbegotten, A 1957,My 3,21:2
Moon for the Misbegotten, A 1957,My 12,II,1:1
Hamlet 1957,O 29,34:2
Goodwill Ambassador 1959,Mr 3,39:2
Shaughraun, The 1968,My 22,54:1

Cusack, Cyril (Producer)
Bishop's Bonfire, The 1955,Mr 6,II,3:1
Cusack, Margaret
Bully, The 1924,D 26,18:1
Handy Man, The 1925,Mr 10,19:2
Cusack, Philip
3 Bags Full 1966,Mr 7,22:1
Cusack, Ronald
Twilight Walk 1951,S 25,25:4
Cusanelli, Peter
Summer Night 1939,N 3,17:1
Night Before Christmas, The 1941,Ap 11,25:2
As You Like It 1941,O 21,29:2
Cusenza, Salvatore
Tia Juana 1927,N 16,28:4
Cushan, J G
Who's Who 1924,Ap 18,19:2
Cushing, Catherine Chisholm (Lyricist)
Lassie 1920,Ap 7,9:2
Cushing, Catherine Chisholm (Playwright)
Lassie 1920,Ap 7,9:2
Marjolaine 1922,Ja 25,16:1
Topsy and Eva 1924,D 24,11:1
Edgar Allan Poe 1925,O 6,31:1
Edgar Allan Poe 1925,O 11,VIII,1:1
Master of the Inn, The 1925,D 23,22:2
Sari 1930,Ja 29,27:1
Cushing, Peter
Seventh Trumpet, The 1941,N 22,10:6
Cushing, R (Scenic Designer)
House of Bernarda Alba, The 1963,N 25,23:2
Cushing, T M (Director)
Patience 1928,Je 26,29:3
Fatal Lady, The 1936,Mr 19,23:7
Cushing, Tom (Playwright)
Blood and Sand 1921,S 21,16:2
Thank You 1921,O 4,10:2
Thank You 1921,O 16,VI,1:1
Laugh, Clown, Laugh! 1923,O 28,VIII,2:1
Laugh, Clown, Laugh! 1923,N 29,30:1
Out o' Luck 1925,D 19,15:1
Devil in the Cheese, The 1926,D 30,22:4
Gringa, La 1928,F 2,17:1
Grin and Bare It 1970,Mr 17,36:1
Cushing, Winnifred
Wanhope Building, The 1947,F 11,36:5
Diamond Lil 1948,N 30,33:2
Death of a Salesman 1949,F 11,27:2
Climate of Eden, The 1952,N 7,20:2
Pin to See the Peepshow, A 1953,S 18,17:2
Cushman, Dan (Original Author)
Whoop-Up 1958,D 23,2:7
Cushman, Dan (Playwright)
Whoop-Up 1958,D 23,2:7
Cushman, Edwin
Taming of the Shrew, The 1921,My 12,20:2
Merchant of Venice, The 1921,My 14,10:4
Servant in the House, The 1926,My 4,30:1
Caponsacchi 1926,O 27,24:2
Hamlet 1928,Ja 5,33:2
Henry V 1928,Mr 16,26:2
Light of Asia, The 1928,O 10,32:2
Richelieu 1929,D 26,20:3
First Night 1930,N 27,23:2
Richelieu 1934,My 22,28:1
Hamlet 1934,D 26,19:3
Richard III 1934,D 28,24:3
Achilles Had a Heel 1935,O 14,20:2
Plumes in the Dust 1936,N 7,14:2
Around the Corner 1936,D 29,17:2
Gloriana 1938,N 26,18:4
Feathers in a Gale 1943,D 22,26:2
Jeb 1946,F 22,20:2
Cushman, James
Dearest Enemy 1925,S 19,9:2
Ballyhoo 1930,D 23,24:1
Cushman, John
Junior Miss 1941,N 19,28:2
Bright Boy 1944,Mr 3,19:5
Cushman, Nancy
White Man 1936,O 19,22:4
Gloriana 1938,N 26,18:4
Janie 1942,S 11,24:2
Be Your Age 1953,Ja 15,24:2
Man in the Dog Suit, The 1958,O 31,34:2
Mighty Man Is He, A 1960,Ja 7,25:2
American Dream, The 1961,Ja 25,28:1
Little Me 1962,N 19,41:3
Child Buyer, The 1964,D 22,35:1
Skyscraper 1965,N 15,48:1
Harold 1967,My 10,39:1
Cushman, Rose
Trojan Women, The 1923,My 27,10:2
Cushman, Wilbur
Topsy and Eva 1924,D 24,11:1
Cusick, Peter (Miscellaneous)
Reclining Figure 1954,O 8,26:5
Cusin, Georges
Christophe Colomb 1957,Ja 31,20:5
Volpone 1957,F 5,27:2
Nuits de La Colere, Les; Nights of Fury
1957,F 12,31:1
Adieux, Les 1957,F 19,36:1

Cusin, Georges—Cont
Chien du Jardinier, Le; Gardener's Dog, The
1957,F 19,36:1
Custier, Robert C (Producer)
Alice Adams 1947,Ag 5,26:1
Cutava, Tanzi
Pile ou Face 1936,Jl 5,IX,1:8
Cutell, Lou
Point of No Return 1957,Mr 23,17:2
Young Abe Lincoln 1961,Ap 26,36:1
Madame Aphrodite 1961,D 30,13:1
How to Succeed in Business Without Really Try[ing]
1966,Ap 21,45:1
Cutler, Ben
Eternal Road, The 1937,Ja 8,14:2
Fireman's Flame, The 1937,O 11,26:2
Cutler, Benjamin C
Orestes 1926,Je 20,II,3:6
Cutler, Bunty
Quiet, Please! 1940,N 9,20:3
Cutler, Edward
Just Fancy! 1927,O 12,30:2
Gods of the Lightning 1928,O 25,27:2
Devil's Host, The 1931,N 20,27:2
Cutler, Leslie (Miscellaneous)
Man Who Never Died, The 1958,N 22,27:2
These Are My Loves 1960,Ap 19,41:2
Cutler, Lester (Producer)
Magnolia Alley 1949,Ap 19,29:2
Cutler, Miriam
Great Adventure, The 1926,D 23,23:1
Cutler, Robert F (Miscellaneous)
One for the Money 1939,F 6,9:2
Cutler, Robert F (Producer)
Emperor Jones, The 1936,Ag 11,24:6
Middle Man 1936,S 8,23:1
Let Us Be Gay 1937,Je 29,18:3
Idiot's Delight 1937,Ag 10,22:7
Fumed Oak 1937,Ag 24,24:5
Hands Across the Sea 1937,Ag 24,24:5
Still Life 1937,Ag 24,24:5
Worse Things Happen at Sea 1937,S 1,15:3
Cutler, Robert P
Once Over Lightly 1938,D 10,13:4
Cutler, Sonia
Roaming Stars 1930,Ja 25,12:2
Cutlerova, Alla
Clear All Wires! 1932,S 15,19:1
Cutrufello, Martha
Lysistrata 1959,N 25,19:4
Cutter, Royal
It's Up to You 1921,Mr 29,20:1
Marjolaine 1922,Ja 25,16:1
Sancho Panza 1923,N 27,23:1
White Eagle, The 1927,D 27,24:4
Day in the Sun 1939,My 17,29:2
Cutting, Blair
Possessed, The 1939,O 25,26:2
Wanhope Building, The 1947,F 11,36:5
Madame Is Served 1949,F 15,28:1
Cuttler, Byron
Carib Song 1945,S 28,17:2
Cutts, John
Measure for Measure 1969,Je 13,41:3
Cutts, Patricia
Twelfth Night 1959,Jl 11,10:2
Kean 1961,N 3,28:2
Cuvillier, Charles (Composer)
Afgar 1920,N 9,13:2
Cuyle, Ann
Robert E Lee 1923,N 21,23:1
Cynkutis, Zbigniew
Constant Prince, The 1969,O 18,36:1
Acropolis 1969,N 5,40:1
Apocalypsis cum Figuris 1969,N 20,60:2
Cypher, Jon
Disenchanted, The 1958,D 4,53:4
Great Western Union, The 1965,F 10,45:1
Wives, The 1965,My 18,35:4
Man of La Mancha 1965,N 23,52:1
Sherry! 1967,Mr 29,39:1
Great White Hope, The 1968,O 4,40:1
Coco 1969,D 19,66:1
Cypkin, Deborah
Melody Lingers On, The 1969,N 17,55:1
Cypkin, Diane
Wandering Stars 1966,N 14,52:2
Prince Reuvaini 1967,N 19,83:1
It's Never Too Late for Happiness 1968,O 21,59:3
Light, Lively and Yiddish 1970,O 28,58:1
Cyrus, Kenneth
When the Bough Breaks 1950,Mr 9,25:5
Gods of the Mountain, The 1950,My 25,36:2
Czaja, C Sager
Farewell to Arms, A 1930,S 23,30:3
Smiles 1930,N 19,19:2
Czajkowski, Michael (Composer)
King Lear 1968,Je 3,55:4
Czarnota, Leszek
Labyrinth, The 1965,Ja 6,32:1
Woman, The 1965,Ja 6,32:1
Jaselka 1965,Ja 6,32:1
Nightmare, The 1965,Ja 6,32:1
Post Office, The 1965,Ja 6,32:1

zarnota, Leszek—Cont
Kernel and the Shell, The 1965,Ja 6,32:1
Jacob and the Angel 1965,Ja 6,32:1
Book, The 1965,Ja 6,32:1
zathe, Coloman (Playwright)
Mary Wants to Go on the Stage 1930,Mr 9,IX,8:5
zechoslovakian National Band
Vaudeville (Hippodrome) 1924,F 19,12:1
zekalska, Ewa
Post Office, The 1965,Ja 6,32:1
Jacob and the Angel 1965,Ja 6,32:1
Kernel and the Shell, The 1965,Ja 6,32:1
Nightmare, The 1965,Ja 6,32:1
Jaselka 1965,Ja 6,32:1
Labyrinth, The 1965,Ja 6,32:1
Woman, The 1965,Ja 6,32:1
Book, The 1965,Ja 6,32:1
zepa, Frau
Love Is Not So Simple 1935,N 20,26:7
zernicki, Gene (Scenic Designer)
Will the Mail Train Run Tonight? 1964,Ja 10,18:1
zettel, Ladislas (Costume Designer)
Fair Helen 1931,Ag 30,VIII,2:1
Rosalinda; Fledermaus, Die 1942,O 29,26:5
Helen Goes to Troy 1944,Ap 25,17:2
Helen Goes to Troy 1944,Ap 30,II,1:1
zinner, Paul (Director)
Cup of Trembling, The 1948,Ap 21,33:5
zinner, Paul (Miscellaneous)
Duchess of Malfi, The 1946,O 16,35:2
zinner, Paul (Producer)
Overtons, The 1945,F 7,16:6
Cup of Trembling, The 1948,Ap 21,33:5
zobor
Abie's Irish Rose 1928,Je 10,VIII,2:8

D

a Costa, Morton
Skin of Our Teeth, The 1942,N 19,29:5
War President 1944,Ap 25,17:3
It's A Gift 1945,Mr 13,18:7
Hamlet 1945,D 14,25:2
Man and Superman 1949,My 17,28:6
a Costa, Morton (Director)
Alchemist, The 1948,My 7,31:4
Captain Brassbound's Conversion 1950,D 28,21:1
Dream Girl 1951,My 10,39:1
Wild Duck, The 1951,D 27,17:1
Dark Legend 1952,Mr 25,24:2
Grey-Eyed People, The 1952,D 18,41:2
Plain and Fancy 1955,Ja 28,14:2
Plain and Fancy 1955,F 6,II,1:1
No Time for Sergeants 1955,O 21,32:2
No Time for Sergeants 1955,N 6,II,1:1
Auntie Mame 1956,N 1,47:2
Auntie Mame 1956,N 11,II,1:1
Music Man, The 1957,D 20,31:1
Music Man, The 1958,S 28,II,1:1
Saratoga 1959,D 8,59:4
Wall, The 1960,O 12,44:4
To Broadway With Love 1964,Ap 30,28:6
Maggie Flynn 1968,O 24,52:1
Maggie Flynn 1968,N 3,II,1:1
Show Me Where the Good Times Are
    1970,Mr 6,32:1
a Costa, Morton (Miscellaneous)
Auntie Mame 1958,Ag 12,33:2
a Costa, Morton (Original Author)
Wall, The 1960,O 23,II,1:1
a Costa, Morton (Playwright)
To Broadway With Love 1964,Ap 30,28:6
Maggie Flynn 1968,O 24,52:1
a Silva, Daniel
Half a Widow 1927,S 13,37:3
a Silva, Howard
Romeo and Juliet 1930,Ap 22,33:1
Siegfried 1930,O 21,34:1
Alison's House 1930,D 2,31:2
Liliom 1932,O 27,23:2
Dear Jane 1932,N 15,24:3
Alice in Wonderland 1932,D 12,18:3
Cherry Orchard, The 1933,Mr 7,20:3
Sailors of Cattaro 1934,D 11,28:4
Black Pit 1935,Mr 21,26:6
Golden Boy 1937,N 5,18:5
Cradle Will Rock, The 1937,D 6,19:4
Cradle Will Rock, The 1938,Ja 4,19:3
Casey Jones 1938,F 21,14:2
Abe Lincoln in Illinois 1938,O 17,12:2
Summer Night 1939,N 3,17:1
Two on an Island 1940,Ja 23,17:2
Oklahoma! 1943,Ap 1,27:1
Oklahoma! 1943,Ap 11,II,1:1
Cradle Will Rock, The 1947,N 25,38:3
Burning Bright 1950,O 19,40:2
World of Sholom Aleichem, The 1953,S 12,13:2
World of Sholom Aleichem, The 1953,S 20,II,1:1
Adding Machine, The 1956,F 10,17:1
Diary of a Scoundrel 1956,N 5,41:1
Volpone 1957,Ja 8,27:1
Volpone 1957,Ja 13,II,10:1
Compulsion 1957,O 25,21:1

Compulsion 1957,N 3,II,1:1
Dr Willy Nilly 1959,Je 5,18:2
Fiorello! 1959,N 24,45:3
Fiorello! 1959,N 29,II,1:1
Romulus 1962,Ja 11,27:1
In the Counting House 1962,D 15,5:5
Dear Me, the Sky Is Falling 1963,Mr 4,9:1
Hamlet 1964,Je 17,49:1
Unknown Soldier and His Wife, The 1967,Jl 7,22:1
1776 1969,Mr 17,46:2
1776 1969,Mr 23,II,1:1
Da Silva, Howard (Director)
Cradle Will Rock, The 1947,D 27,11:2
Proud Accent 1949,Ap 23,10:2
World of Sholom Aleichem, The 1953,S 12,13:2
Sandhog 1954,N 24,17:1
Tevya and His Daughters 1957,S 17,38:2
Purlie Victorious 1961,S 29,29:1
Purlie Victorious 1961,O 8,II,1:1
Cages; Snowangel; Epiphany 1963,Je 14,36:1
Advocate, The 1963,O 15,46:7
Thistle in My Bed 1963,N 20,48:1
Cradle Will Rock, The 1964,N 9,40:4
My Sweet Charlie 1966,D 7,56:1
Da Silva, Howard (Miscellaneous)
Sandhog 1954,N 24,17:1
Tevya and His Daughters 1957,S 17,38:2
Da Silva, Howard (Playwright)
Zulu and the Zayda, The 1965,N 11,59:1
Da Silva, Howard (Producer)
World of Sholom Aleichem, The 1953,S 12,13:2
Best of Burlesque 1957,S 30,27:2
All That Fall 1957,O 8,41:2
Dr Willy Nilly 1959,Je 5,18:2
da Zara, Nini
Tristi Amori; Unhappy Loves 1930,O 27,17:6
Piacere Del'Onesta, Il; Happiness of Probity, The
    1930,N 10,16:4
Daab, Frederick F (Musical Director)
Vaudeville (Forty-Fourth Street Theatre)
    1921,S 20,12:2
Daab, Hyatt (Playwright)
Ringside 1928,Ag 30,13:2
Dabdoub, Jack
What's Up 1953,O 28,37:2
Arabian Nights 1954,Je 25,15:2
Arabian Nights 1955,Je 24,16:1
Camelot 1960,D 5,42:1
Hot Spot 1963,Ap 20,17:2
Anya 1965,N 30,48:1
Annie Get Your Gun 1966,Je 1,42:2
Time for the Gentle People, A 1967,My 26,50:1
Her First Roman 1968,O 21,53:3
Man of La Mancha 1969,My 3,38:4
Coco 1969,D 19,66:1
Dabney, Ardelle
Harlem 1929,F 21,30:3
Dabney, Augusta
Abe Lincoln in Illinois 1938,O 17,12:2
Return Engagement 1940,N 2,19:2
Lady Who Came to Stay, The 1941,Ja 3,13:2
Sweet Charity 1942,D 29,26:4
Another Love Story 1943,O 13,29:2
Playroom, The 1965,D 6,49:1
Everything in the Garden 1967,N 30,60:1
Dabney, Ford (Composer)
Rang Tang 1927,Jl 13,20:1
Dabney, Kathleen
Androcles and the Lion 1968,Je 27,47:1
Love's Labour's Lost 1968,Je 28,36:1
Dabney, Malvina
Harlem 1929,F 21,30:3
Dabney, Marian
Greenwich Village Follies 1923,S 21,4:6
Dack, Etha
Broken Dishes 1929,N 6,28:3
Dacqmine, Jacques
Hamlet 1948,S 11,13:3
Proces, Le; Trial, The 1952,N 18,36:2
Amphitryon 1952,N 21,21:2
Occupe-Toi d'Amelie; Keep Your Eyes on Amelie
    1952,N 25,35:2
Repetition, La; Rehearsal, The 1952,N 28,22:2
Hamlet 1952,D 2,39:1
Repetition, La 1957,S 3,23:2
Hedda Gabler 1962,D 13,8:5
Dade, Frances
Collision 1932,F 17,19:2
Dade, Valerie
They All Want Something 1926,O 13,20:2
Buzzard, The 1928,Mr 15,29:1
Virtue's Bed 1930,Ap 16,26:5
Dade and Jesse
Will Morrissey's Folies Bergere Revue
    1930,Ap 16,26:6
Dae, Frank
Nobody's Business 1923,O 23,17:1
So That's That 1925,D 15,28:3
Spread Eagle 1927,Ap 5,30:2
Ten Per Cent 1927,S 14,29:3
Coquette 1927,N 9,23:1
So Was Napoleon 1930,Ja 9,22:2
Troika 1930,Ap 2,32:6

Dae, Frank—Cont
Up and Up, The 1930,S 9,25:2
Five Star Final 1930,D 31,11:1
Merry-Go-Round 1932,Ap 23,11:2
Jamboree 1932,N 25,18:4
Sellout, The 1933,S 7,17:2
Night Remembers, The 1934,N 28,24:3
If This Be Treason 1935,Jl 30,17:1
If This Be Treason 1935,S 24,28:2
First Lady 1935,N 27,17:4
All Editions 1936,D 23,17:2
Daffi
Moondreamers, The 1969,D 9,68:1
Gloria and Esperanza 1970,F 5,32:1
Daffydills Droll
Vaudeville (Broadway) 1932,D 27,11:4
Dafora, Asadata
Kykunkor 1934,D 22,21:3
Zunguru 1938,Ag 3,14:5
Zunguru 1938,Ag 7,IX,8:2
Zunguru 1940,Mr 21,30:5
Dafora, Asadata (Choreographer)
Kykunkor 1934,D 22,21:3
Zunguru 1940,Mr 21,30:5
Zunguru 1940,Mr 24,IX,2:1
Dafora, Asadata (Director)
Kykunkor 1934,D 22,21:3
Zunguru 1938,Ag 3,14:5
Zunguru 1938,Ag 7,IX,8:2
Zunguru 1940,Mr 21,30:5
Zunguru 1940,Mr 24,IX,2:1
Dafora, Asadata (Playwright)
Kykunkor 1934,D 22,21:3
Zunguru 1938,Ag 3,14:5
Zunguru 1938,Ag 7,IX,8:2
Daggett, J L
Hoot Mon, or Clans Across the Sea 1927,My 8,29:4
Daggett, Robert
Strange Fruit 1945,N 30,18:6
Daggett, Robert T
Little Poor Man, The 1925,Ag 6,14:1
Dagmar, Doris
Beware of Widows 1925,D 2,22:3
Maggie, the Magnificent 1929,O 22,26:1
Dagnell, William E (Scenic Designer)
Seven Keys to Baldpate 1930,Ja 8,25:2
Dagnie, Sigrid
Higher and Higher 1940,Ap 5,24:3
Dagny, Robert
King of the Dark Chamber 1961,F 10,21:1
D'Agostino, Gaetano
This Happy Breed 1952,Ap 4,23:2
Mrs Moonlight 1952,N 21,21:1
D'Agostino, Inez
Mrs Moonlight 1952,N 21,21:1
Dagover, Lil
Amphitryon 38 1931,Mr 15,IX,2:4
Don Juan's Raincoat 1933,O 22,IX,2:3
Dahdah, Robert (Composer)
Curley McDimple 1967,N 23,59:2
Curley McDimple 1969,N 25,53:1
Dahdah, Robert (Director)
Spots of the Leopard, The 1963,S 25,38:1
Curley McDimple 1967,N 23,59:2
Curley McDimple 1969,N 25,53:1
Dahdah, Robert (Lyricist)
Curley McDimple 1969,N 25,53:1
Dahdah, Robert (Playwright)
Curley McDimple 1967,N 23,59:2
Curley McDimple 1969,N 25,53:1
Dahdah, Robert (Scenic Designer)
Spots of the Leopard, The 1963,S 25,38:1
Dahiman, Lou
You'll See Stars 1943,Ja 1,26:6
Dahl, Arlene
Mr Strauss Goes to Boston 1945,S 7,20:2
Cyrano de Bergerac 1953,N 13,24:3
Dahl, Carolyn
Frere Jacques 1968,Je 8,23:2
Dahl, Roald (Playwright)
Honeys, The 1955,Ap 29,26:1
Dahl, Sven
Hot Pan 1928,F 16,14:1
Dahlberg, Gilda (Miscellaneous)
Rebecca 1945,Ja 19,17:2
Never Say Never 1951,N 21,21:2
Dahlen, Brenda
Dishonored Lady 1930,F 5,27:1
9th Street Guest, The 1930,Ag 26,24:3
Greater Love 1931,Mr 3,39:1
Laura Garnett 1934,Jl 17,24:4
Lost Horizons 1934,O 16,31:2
Beggarman, Thief 1935,Jl 16,24:1
Room in Red and White, A 1936,Ja 20,23:3
Dahlia, Richard
Trumpets and Drums 1969,O 13,52:1
Daigeau, Sara
Porgy and Bess 1935,O 11,30:2
Daigneau, Kenneth
Love Set, The 1923,Mr 20,24:2
When in Rome 1934,F 28,22:6
One Thing After Another 1937,D 29,17:2
Dail, Calvin
Romio and Julietta 1925,Ap 21,19:1

Dailey, Allan
All Rights Reserved 1934,N 7,33:5
Pygmalion 1938,Ja 27,16:3
Captain Jinks of the Horse Marines 1938,Ja 28,16:2
Coriolanus 1938,F 2,14:5
Dailey, Dan
Stars in Your Eyes 1939,F 10,18:2
Catch Me if You Can 1965,Mr 10,50:1
Dailey, Irene
Canteen Show, The 1942,S 4,18:1
Nine Girls 1943,Ja 14,26:2
Truckline Cafe 1946,F 28,19:4
Springtime Folly 1951,F 27,23:4
Idiot's Delight 1951,My 24,46:3
Good Woman of Setzuan, The 1956,D 19,41:2
Idiot's Delight 1957,F 23,14:2
Miss Lonelyhearts 1957,O 4,26:2
Tomorrow With Pictures 1960,Je 3,26:3
Andorra 1963,F 11,5:5
Subject Was Roses, The 1964,My 26,45:1
Subject Was Roses, The 1964,Je 7,II,1:1
Better Luck Next Time 1966,Ja 28,21:1
Walk in Dark Places, A 1966,Ja 28,21:1
You Know I Can't Hear You When the Water's
 Running 1968,Mr 29,33:1
Dailey, J Hammond
Roger Bloomer 1923,Mr 2,18:3
Thumbs Down 1923,Ag 7,20:1
Flame of Love 1924,Ap 22,19:2
Gentlemen of the Press 1928,Ag 28,27:2
Merry Andrew 1929,Ja 22,22:2
Subway Express 1929,S 25,34:3
Privilege Car 1931,Mr 4,33:1
Counsellor-at-Law 1931,N 7,17:2
Counsellor-at-Law 1932,S 13,17:2
Remember the Day 1935,Jl 9,24:3
Little Inn, The 1935,Ag 20,25:1
Remember the Day 1935,S 26,19:3
Come Angel Band 1936,F 19,17:1
Feather in the Breeze 1936,Jl 14,22:2
Excursion 1937,Ap 10,11:4
Two Time Mary 1937,Ag 3,20:5
Siege 1937,D 9,31:4
Dailey, Jack B
John Brown's Body 1953,F 16,17:2
Dailey, Jerome
Hit the Deck! 1927,Ap 26,32:1
Dailey, Joseph
Easy Mark, The 1924,Ag 27,14:2
Poor Nut, The 1925,Ap 28,18:1
She Couldn't Say No! 1926,S 1,27:3
Daily, Willis
Porgy and Bess 1953,Mr 10,25:5
Dain, Jeremy (Miscellaneous)
Hamlet 1970,D 28,40:1
Dainard, Neil
Henry VI 1966,Je 9,55:2
Twelfth Night 1966,Je 10,51:2
Government Inspector, The 1967,Je 15,55:1
Antony and Cleopatra 1967,Ag 2,25:1
Government Inspector, The 1967,O 28,34:1
Romeo and Juliet 1968,Je 11,55:2
Midsummer Night's Dream, A 1968,Je 13,54:1
Midsummer Night's Dream, A 1968,Je 23,II,1:1
Seagull, The 1968,Jl 25,27:2
Hamlet 1969,Je 11,37:1
Alchemist, The 1969,Je 12,51:1
Measure for Measure 1969,Je 13,41:3
Hamlet 1969,Je 22,II,1:7
Daine, Lois
Inadmissible Evidence 1965,D 1,52:1
Dair, Betty
Pleasure Bound 1929,F 19,22:4
Marching By 1932,Mr 4,17:1
Daish, Sidney
Imaginary Invalid, The 1922,Jl 26,26:2
Dakin, Philip
Merry Wives of Windsor, The 1938,Ap 15,22:3
Happy Birthday 1946,N 1,31:2
Dal Porto, Lita
That Lady 1949,N 23,18:4
Come of Age 1952,Ja 24,22:2
Dalamatoff, Michael
Chauve-Souris of 1943 1943,Ag 13,13:2
Dalba, Marie
Everything's Jake 1930,Ja 17,20:4
Dalberg, Camilla
Pride 1923,My 3,22:3
Hurricane 1923,D 26,13:4
Drift 1925,N 25,15:3
Money From Home 1927,Mr 1,30:2
Garden of Eden, The 1927,S 28,28:1
These Modern Women 1928,F 14,26:2
D'Albert, Suzanne
School for Wives 1957,Je 20,23:4
Dalbey, Cynthia
Play It Again, Sam 1969,F 13,52:3
D'Albrew, Peppy
Queer People 1934,F 16,16:2
Dalby, Edmund
Her Friend the King 1929,O 8,34:5
Old Rascal, The 1930,Mr 25,34:4
It Pays to Sin 1933,N 4,18:6

Dalby, Helen
Romeo and Juliet 1968,Ag 16,19:1
Dale, Alan
Susan Slept Here 1961,Jl 12,35:2
Dale, Ann
Just Because 1922,Mr 23,11:1
Dale, Audray
Apron Strings 1930,F 18,28:2
One, Two, Three! 1930,S 30,24:2
This Is New York 1930,N 29,21:1
Dale, Barbara
Fireworks on the James 1940,My 15,30:2
Dale, Bobby
Padlocks of 1927 1927,Jl 6,23:4
Dale, Charles
Whirl of New York, The 1921,Je 14,18:1
Sidewalks of New York 1927,O 4,33:1
Vaudeville (Palace) 1929,Jl 8,17:6
Mendel, Inc 1929,S 1,VIII,1:1
Mendel, Inc 1929,N 26,28:5
Vaudeville (Palace) 1930,Jl 7,22:2
Sky's the Limit, The 1934,D 18,25:5
Summer Wives 1936,Ap 14,18:1
Laugh, Town, Laugh! 1942,Je 20,9:1
Laugh, Town, Laugh! 1942,Je 23,22:2
Brights Lights of 1944 1943,S 17,27:4
Dale, Dana
Bright Rebel 1938,D 28,24:2
Dale, Esther
Carry Nation 1932,O 31,18:2
Another Language 1933,My 9,20:2
Spring in Autumn 1933,O 25,22:5
By Your Leave 1934,Ja 25,15:3
Picnic 1934,My 3,15:2
Spring Freshet 1934,O 5,28:3
Spring in Autumn 1937,Ag 17,23:1
And Be My Love 1945,F 22,30:4
Harvest of Years 1948,Ja 13,29:2
Dale, Frances
Los Angeles 1927,D 20,32:3
Eternal Cage 1945,Mr 22,19:7
Dale, Gene
Yes is for a Very Young Man 1963,Mr 6,7:5
Dale, Gladys
Fall and Rise of Susan Lenox, The 1920,Je 11,11:2
Dale, Glen
Moonlight 1924,Ja 31,13:7
Desert Song, The 1926,D 1,24:2
Harry Delmar's Revels 1927,N 29,30:2
Dale, Glenn
Love Life 1948,O 8,31:2
Dale, Gordon
Dope 1926,Ja 4,16:3
Dale, Grover
West Side Story 1957,S 27,14:4
Fallout 1959,My 21,36:2
Greenwillow 1960,Mr 9,38:1
Sail Away 1961,O 4,48:5
Too Much Johnson 1964,Ja 16,29:1
Half a Sixpence 1965,Ap 26,38:2
Dale, Grover (Choreographer)
Steambath 1970,Jl 1,49:1
Dale, Grover (Director)
Billy 1969,Mr 24,56:1
Dale, James
Loyalties 1922,S 28,18:1
We Moderns 1924,Mr 12,17:2
Hassan 1924,S 23,23:1
Two Married Men 1925,Ja 14,19:1
School for Scandal, The 1925,D 7,18:2
Silver Box, The 1928,Ja 18,23:1
Death Takes a Holiday 1929,N 24,X,4:5
Death Takes a Holiday 1929,D 27,26:4
Green Bay Tree, The 1933,O 21,11:5
Green Bay Tree, The 1933,O 29,IX,1:1
Murder Gang 1935,N 16,19:2
Dale, James (Playwright)
Wild Justice 1935,Jl 9,24:3
Dale, Jean
Audition of the Apprentice Theatre 1939,Je 2,26:2
Our Town 1944,Ja 11,24:5
Dale, Jim
Merchant of Venice, The 1970,Jl 30,39:1
Dale, John
Perfect Fool, The 1921,N 8,28:2
Sky's the Limit, The 1934,D 18,25:5
Dale, Johnny
Rat Race, The 1949,D 23,16:2
Dale, Loretta
Nativity Play, The 1937,D 21,29:1
Dale, Louise
Silks and Satins 1920,Jl 16,19:1
Dale, Margaret
Charm School, The 1920,Ag 3,12:1
In the Night Watch 1921,Ja 31,10:1
Tyranny of Love, The 1921,Mr 2,7:3
Married Woman, The 1921,D 26,21:1
Charlatan, The 1922,Ap 25,14:2
Charlatan, The 1922,Ap 30,VII,1:1
On the Stairs 1922,S 26,18:2
Cinders 1923,Ap 4,22:1
Best People, The 1924,Ag 20,8:1
Cradle Snatchers 1925,S 8,28:2

Dale, Margaret—Cont
Rosalie 1928,Ja 11,26:3
Sex Fable, The 1931,O 21,26:1
Dinner at Eight 1932,O 24,18:2
Dark Tower, The 1933,N 27,20:3
Gather Ye Rosebuds 1934,N 29,33:2
Old Maid, The 1935,Ja 8,26:1
Tovarich 1936,O 16,31:4
Dear Octopus 1939,Ja 12,22:2
Lady in the Dark 1941,Ja 5,IX,1:7
Lady in the Dark 1941,Ja 24,14:2
Lady in the Dark 1941,S 3,26:6
Lady in the Dark 1943,Mr 1,14:2
Late George Apley, The 1944,O 20,16:4
Late George Apley, The 1944,N 22,26:2
Town House 1948,S 24,31:2
Dale, Maryon
Americana 1926,Jl 27,15:3
Merry-Go-Round 1927,Je 1,25:4
Belmont Varieties 1932,S 29,17:2
Dale, Nonie
Caviar 1934,Je 8,19:2
Dale, Norman
Sun-Up 1923,My 25,28:1
Dale, Robert
Silks and Satins 1920,Jl 16,19:1
Dale, Serena
Breaks, The 1928,Ap 17,26:3
Dale, Sunny
Top Speed 1929,D 26,20:1
Dale, Teresa
Come-On Man, The 1929,Ap 23,26:2
Mr Samuel 1930,N 11,28:4
Strange Interlude 1931,F 22,VIII,1:3
Primrose Path, The 1939,Ja 5,16:3
Sleep, My Pretty One 1944,N 3,26:8
Dale, Teresa (Director)
Wild Justice 1935,Jl 9,24:3
Dale, Thomas
New Moon, The 1928,S 20,33:1
Dale, Ursula
Silks and Satins 1920,Jl 16,19:1
Dale, Violet
Humming Bird, The 1923,Ja 16,16:2
Dale, Virginia
Final Balance, The 1928,O 31,28:3
Dale, William
Admirable Crichton, The 1931,Mr 10,23:2
Dalecki, Seweryn
Mother Courage 1967,N 17,55:1
d'Alessandro, Aldo
Paese dei Campanelli, Il; Land of Bells, The
 1935,My 10,25:4
D'Alessio, Vincent
Macbeth 1969,D 23,25:1
Daley, Cass
Ziegfeld Follies 1936,S 15,37:1
Daley, D F
1776 1926,Ap 24,11:2
Daley, Frank
Great Day! 1929,O 18,24:3
Daley, Jack
Noose, The 1926,O 21,23:3
Show Boat 1927,D 28,26:1
Hot-Cha! 1932,Mr 9,17:3
Show Boat 1932,My 20,22:2
Stevedore 1934,Ap 19,33:2
Show Boat 1946,Ja 7,17:2
Daley, Jerome
Wild Rose, The 1926,O 21,23:1
House Unguarded 1929,Ja 16,22:2
On the Make 1932,My 24,23:2
Melody 1933,F 15,17:4
Daley, John
Girl Crazy 1930,O 15,27:1
Daley, Mary
Nautical but Nice 1931,Ap 19,31:6
Daley, Olga
Kiss for Cinderella, A 1942,Mr 11,22:2
Daley, Stephen
Fashion 1959,Ja 21,27:1
Cherry Orchard, The 1960,Je 4,17:2
Daley, Timothy
Cinderella on Broadway 1920,Je 25,18:1
Lady in Ermine, The 1922,O 3,22:2
D'Algy, Helena
Sex Fable, The 1931,O 21,26:1
Dall, Evelyn
Parade 1935,My 21,22:2
Dall, John
Dear Ruth 1944,D 14,29:2
Dear Ruth 1944,D 31,II,1:1
Red Gloves 1948,D 6,28:2
Red Gloves; Mains Sales, Les 1948,D 12,II,3:1
Heiress, The 1950,F 9,34:2
Champagne Complex 1955,Ap 13,33:1
Dallansky, Bruno
Rendezvous in Wien 1956,S 5,23:1
Nathan der Weise 1966,D 10,45:2
Dallas, Lorna
Sound of Music, The 1970,Jl 3,13:1
Dallas, Meredith
Twelfth Night 1958,Ag 7,21:4
Family Reunion, The 1958,O 21,39:1

Dallas, Meredith—Cont
Power and the Glory, The 1958,D 12,2:7
Beaux' Stratagem, The 1959,F 25,35:4
This Island Is Mine 1959,Jl 1,26:4
Dallas, Meredith (Director)
Pericles 1953,Ag 21,9:2
Dallett, Liza
Fountain, The 1925,D 11,26:1
Dalley, J Hammond
American Landscape 1938,D 5,19:2
Dally, Orlando
Royal Family, The 1928,Ja 8,VIII,1:1
Dalmain, Jean (Director)
Mariage Force, Le; Forced Wedding, The
    1958,My 7,43:1
Sganarelle; Imaginary Cuckold, The 1958,My 7,43:1
Jalousie du Barbouille, La; Jealousy of the
    Barbouille, The 1958,My 7,43:1
Dalmatoff
Chauve-Souris 1922,Je 6,17:4
Chauve-Souris 1925,Ja 15,25:1
Chauve-Souris 1929,Ja 23,20:2
Dalmatoff, Michael
Miracle, The 1927,F 1,24:5
Wonder Bar, The 1931,Mr 18,23:4
Melody 1933,F 15,17:4
Swan Song 1946,My 16,29:2
d'Almeida, Louis
Oscar Wilde 1957,Ap 20,21:3
d'Almeida, Louis (Miscellaneous)
Masquerade 1959,Mr 17,42:1
Dalmes, Mony
Caprice, Un 1955,N 16,42:4
Jeu de l'Amour et du Hasard, Le 1955,N 16,42:4
Unsinkable Molly Brown, The 1960,N 4,28:1
Dalrymple, Alfred
Caesar and Cleopatra 1927,N 6,IX,2:1
Golden Dog, The 1929,D 25,21:2
Tiger Smiles, The 1930,D 18,29:1
Carry Nation 1932,O 31,18:2
Goodbye Again 1932,D 29,16:4
Wednesday's Child 1934,Ja 17,23:2
Dalrymple, Jean
Teahouse of the August Moon, The
    1956,Ap 20,22:1
Dalrymple, Jean (Miscellaneous)
Burlesque 1946,D 26,30:3
Red Gloves 1948,D 6,28:2
Cyrano de Bergerac 1953,N 13,24:3
Shrike, The 1953,N 26,51:2
Richard III 1953,D 10,65:2
Charley's Aunt 1953,D 23,22:2
Dalrymple, Jean (Producer)
Hope for the Best 1945,F 8,14:4
Brighten the Corner 1945,D 13,33:2
ANTA Album 1951,My 7,22:7
What Every Woman Knows 1954,D 23,16:2
Fourposter, The 1955,Ja 6,23:3
Time of Your Life, The 1955,Ja 20,34:1
Wisteria Trees, The 1955,F 3,20:2
Othello 1955,S 8,27:2
Henry IV, Part I 1955,S 22,34:2
King Lear 1956,Ja 13,17:1
Marcel Marceau 1956,F 2,18:1
Streetcar Named Desire, A 1956,F 16,24:1
Teahouse of the August Moon, The 1956,My 7,31:8
Teahouse of the August Moon, The 1956,N 9,33:2
Glass Menagerie, The 1956,N 22,50:1
Mister Roberts 1956,D 6,46:2
Beggar's Opera, The 1957,Mr 14,35:1
Brigadoon 1957,Mr 28,37:1
Merry Widow, The 1957,Ap 11,36:6
South Pacific 1957,Ap 25,35:1
Pajama Game, The 1957,My 16.27:1
Carousel 1957,S 12,38:2
Annie Get Your Gun 1958,F 20,29:2
Wonderful Town 1958,Mr 6,32:4
Oklahoma! 1958,Mr 20,32:3
Most Happy Fella, The 1959,F 11,50:2
Say Darling 1959,F 26,38:2
Lute Song 1959,Mr 13,24:1
Carmen Jones 1959,Ag 18,25:1
Can-Can 1959,Ag 26,25:4
Finian's Rainbow 1960,Ap 28,31:1
King and I, The 1960,My 12,40:1
Overcoat, The 1960,S 7,45:1
Show Boat 1961,Ap 13,32:1
South Pacific 1961,Ap 27,26:3
Porgy and Bess 1961,My 18,40:1
Pal Joey 1961,Je 1,32:1
Can-Can 1962,My 17,32:2
Brigadoon 1962,My 31,21:4
Fiorello! 1962,Je 14,24:1
Marcel Marceau 1963,Ja 3,5:7
Brigadoon 1963,F 1,6:2
Wonderful Town 1963,F 15,10:2
Oklahoma! 1963,F 28,8:2
Oklahoma! 1963,My 16,40:1
Pal Joey 1963,My 30,21:1
King and I, The 1963,Je 13,30:2
West Side Story 1964,Ap 9,24:2
Porgy and Bess 1964,My 7,32:1
My Fair Lady 1964,My 21,43:2
Brigadoon 1964,D 24,9:1

Guys and Dolls 1965,Ap 29,39:1
Kiss Me, Kate 1965,My 13,31:1
South Pacific 1965,Je 3,25:1
Music Man, The 1965,Je 17,26:4
Marcel Marceau 1965,N 18,56:1
Oklahoma! 1965,D 16,62:1
How to Succeed in Business Without Really Trying
    1966,Ap 21,45:1
Most Happy Fella, The 1966,My 12,55:1
Where's Charley? 1966,My 26,57:1
Guys and Dolls 1966,Je 9,55:2
Country Girl, The 1966,S 30,55:1
Rose Tattoo 1966,O 21,36:2
Elizabeth the Queen 1966,N 4,30:1
Carousel 1966,D 16,56:2
Finian's Rainbow 1967,Ap 6,44:1
Wonderful Town 1967,My 18,50:1
Beyond Desire 1967,O 11,36:1
Life With Father 1967,O 20,53:2
Tenth Man, The 1967,N 9,54:1
Postcards 1967,D 6,41:1
Brigadoon 1967,D 14,59:2
My Fair Lady 1968,Je 14,42:1
Carnival! 1968,D 13,58:1
Tiny Alice 1969,S 30,42:1
Flea in Her Ear, A 1969,O 4,25:1
Three Sisters, The 1969,O 10,38:1
Henry V 1969,N 11,43:1
Our Town 1969,N 28,50:1
No Place to Be Somebody 1969,D 31,17:1
Songs From Milk Wood 1970,Ja 13,41:1
Watercolor 1970,Ja 22,30:1
Criss-Crossing 1970,Ja 22,30:1
Harvey 1970,F 25,41:1
Cherry Orchard, The 1970,My 7,63:2
Wilson in the Promise Land 1970,My 27,41:1
Dalrymple, Leona (Playwright)
Fool's Bells 1925,D 24,8:3
Dalska, Betty
Magnolia Street 1934,Mr 9,22:6
Dalsky, M Russian Choir
Vanderbilt Revue, The 1930,N 6,22:6
Dalsky, Michael
They All Come to Moscow 1933,My 12,20:6
Dalton, Alice
Electra 1932,Ja 9,21:4
Dalton, Charles
Three Live Ghosts 1920,S 30,12:1
Wake Up, Jonathan 1921,Ja 18,14:1
What the Public Wants 1922,My 2,22:3
Guilty One, The 1923,Mr 21,19:1
Meet the Wife 1923,N 27,23:4
Enemy, The 1925,O 21,20:1
Window Panes 1927,F 22,22:2
Electra 1927,My 4,28:3
Electra 1927,My 15,VIII,1:1
Interference 1927,O 19,24:3
Excess Baggage 1927,D 27,24:2
Young Alexander 1929,Mr 13,28:2
Hundred Years Old, A 1929,O 2,28:2
Children of Darkness 1930,Ja 8,25:1
Suspense 1930,Ag 13,22:3
Great Barrington, The 1931,F 20,18:1
Wolves 1932,Ja 7,26:3
Alice Sit-By-The-Fire 1932,Mr 8,19:3
Party, A 1933,Ag 24,18:4
Mary of Scotland 1933,N 28,28:3
Romeo and Juliet 1935,D 24,10:2
Saint Joan 1936,Mr 10,27:4
Richard II 1937,F 6,14:2
Richard II 1937,S 16,28:2
Henry IV, Part I 1939,Ja 31,17:2
Richard II 1940,Ap 2,31:2
Dalton, Claire
Icetime 1946,Je 21,20:5
Icetime 1947,My 29,28:2
Dalton, Doris
Country Wife, The 1931,Ap 19,31:5
Petticoat Fever 1935,Mr 5,22:2
Life's Too Short 1935,S 21,18:5
Tomorrow's a Holiday! 1935,D 31,10:2
Sweet Aloes 1936,Mr 5,24:5
Green Waters 1936,N 5,34:4
Blow Ye Winds 1937,S 8,20:5
Blow Ye Winds 1937,S 24,17:4
Fabulous Invalid, The 1938,O 10,15:1
I Killed the Count 1942,S 4,18:1
Another Love Story 1943,O 13,29:2
Ryan Girl, The 1945,S 25,28:2
Present Laughter 1946,O 30,31:2
Men We Marry, The 1948,Ja 17,11:2
Pal Joey 1949,Mr 7,17:2
Fundamental George, The 1949,Ag 17,19:4
Seventeen 1951,Je 22,16:6
Dalton, Doris (Costume Designer)
Present Laughter 1946,O 30,31:2
Dalton, F D
Blood and Sand 1921,S 21,16:2
Dalton, Fred
Rio Rita 1927,F 3,18:3
Dalton, Kathie
Cabaret 1966,N 21,62:1

Dalton, Lassie
Little Poor Man, The 1925,Ag 6,14:1
D'Alton, Louis (Playwright)
Tanyard Street 1941,F 5,16:2
Dalton, Marjorie
Paid 1925,N 26,32:1
Bless You, Sister 1927,D 27,24:5
Mystery Man, The 1928,Ja 27,14:2
Uncle Vanya 1929,My 25,17:1
Stepping Sisters 1930,Ap 23,24:2
Friendship 1931,My 10,VIII,2:5
Friendship 1931,S 1,30:2
Passing Present, The 1931,D 8,36:2
Man Who Reclaimed His Head 1932,S 9,17:3
They All Come to Moscow 1933,My 12,20:6
Weather Permitting 1935,My 24,24:5
Class of '29 1936,My 16,10:3
Waltz in Goose Step 1938,N 2,26:2
Miracle in the Mountains 1947,Ap 26,10:2
Dalton, Nancy
West Side Story 1968,Je 25,32:1
Dalton, Peter
Oh What a Lovely War 1964,O 1,30:1
Dalton, Richard
Arsenic and Old Lace 1943,D 13,18:6
Our Town 1944,Ja 11,24:5
Dalton, Test (Playwright)
Adam's Apple 1929,Je 11,27:5
Daltrey, Roger
Tommy 1969,O 26,82:1
Daltry, Joseph S (Playwright)
Gondoliers, The 1940,O 1,29:2
Daly, Arnold
Tavern, The 1920,S 28,14:1
Tavern, The 1920,O 10,VI,1:1
Van Dyck, The 1921,O 12,18:2
Boubouroche 1921,N 29,20:1
Wife With a Smile, The 1921,N 29,20:1
Wife With a Smile, The; Boubouroche
    1921,D 4,VII,1:2
Voltaire 1922,Mr 21,17:1
On the Stairs 1922,S 26,18:2
Fashions of 1924 1923,Jl 19,18:2
Race With the Shadow, The 1924,Ja 21,20:5
Leah Kleschna 1924,Ap 22,19:2
How He Lied to Her Husband 1924,S 30,27:5
Vaudeville (Palace) 1924,S 30,27:5
Masque of Venice, The 1926,Mr 3,27:3
Masque of Venice, The 1926,Mr 7,VIII,1:2
Juarez and Maximilian 1926,O 12,31:1
Juarez and Maximilian 1926,O 17,VIII,1:1
Phantoms 1930,Ja 14,24:3
Dracula 1931,Ap 14,33:3
Daly, Arnold (Producer)
Children's Tragedy, The 1921,O 16,VI,1:1
Daly, Augustin (Playwright)
Under the Gaslight 1929,Ap 3,27:1
Daly, Blyth
Charm School, The 1920,Ag 3,12:1
Happy-Go-Lucky 1920,Ag 25,6:1
Varying Shore, The 1921,D 6,24:1
Spring Cleaning 1923,N 10,16:3
New Brooms 1924,N 18,23:5
Outside Looking In 1925,S 8,28:1
Most Immoral Lady, A 1928,N 27,36:1
Ladies Leave 1929,O 2,28:3
Two Seconds 1931,O 10,20:6
Riddle Me This! 1932,F 26,22:5
Bridal Wise 1932,My 31,15:5
Daly, Carroll
Wicked Age, The 1927,N 5,16:6
Daly, Evelyn
It's A Gift 1945,Mr 13,18:7
Daly, Frank
Pygmalion 1937,Jl 7,26:3
Diff'rent 1937,N 21,II,10:7
Diff'rent 1938,Ja 26,26:4
Pygmalion 1938,Ja 27,16:3
Captain Jinks of the Horse Marines 1938,Ja 28,16:2
No More Peace 1938,Ja 29,13:2
Coriolanus 1938,F 2,14:5
King Lear 1940,D 16,27:2
Sudden End of Anne Cinquefoil, The
    1961,Ja 11,25:2
In the Penal Colony 1962,My 4,27:2
Physicists, The 1964,O 14,52:1
Daly, James
Virginia Reel 1947,Ap 15,28:2
Man and Superman 1949,My 17,28:6
Billy Budd 1951,F 12,18:3
Mary Rose 1951,Mr 5,25:2
Mary Rose 1951,Mr 11,II,1:1
Saint Joan 1951,O 5,23:2
Dark Legend 1952,Mr 25,24:2
Merchant of Venice, The 1953,Mr 5,20:2
Miss Julie 1956,F 22,23:2
Miss Julie 1956,Mr 4,II,1:1
Glass Menagerie, The 1956,N 22,50:1
Glass Menagerie, The 1956,D 2,II,1:1
Handful of Fire 1958,O 2,45:3
Period of Adjustment 1960,N 11,34:1
Period of Adjustment 1960,N 20,II,1:1
Advocate, The 1963,O 15,46:7

Daly, James—Cont

Advocate, The 1963,O 27,II,1:1
White House, The 1964,My 20,39:1
Trial of the Catonsville Nine, The 1970,Ag 16,II,1:7

Daly, Jerome

Polly of Hollywood 1927,F 22,22:3
Caravan 1928,Ag 30,13:3
She Loves Me Not 1933,N 21,22:4

Daly, Joseph

Dance of Death, The 1960,S 14,51:1
Figuro in the Night 1962,O 31,33:1
Viet Rock 1966,N 11,38:1
Dark of the Moon 1970,Ap 4,21:2
Early Morning 1970,N 26,57:1

Daly, Lee

Sweethearts 1929,S 23,25:1
Mlle Modiste 1929,O 8,34:1

Daly, Lee (Director)

Mikado, The 1934,Ap 3,26:3
Pirates of Penzance, The 1934,Ap 10,26:5
Trial by Jury 1934,Ap 17,27:2
H M S Pinafore 1934,Ap 17,27:2
Iolanthe 1934,My 1,26:4

Daly, Mary T

Patience 1929,D 16,34:5

Daly, Orlando

Purple Mask, The 1920,Ja 6,18:1
Toto 1921,Mr 22,15:2
Face Value 1921,D 27,10:2
Secrets 1922,D 26,11:1
Mary, Mary, Quite Contrary 1923,S 12,14:1
Fata Morgana 1924,Mr 4,16:3
Fake, The 1924,O 7,26:3
Ariadne 1925,F 24,17:1
Dagger, The 1925,S 10,28:1
Naughty Cinderella 1925,N 10,23:6
First Love 1926,N 9,31:2
We All Do 1927,Mr 1,30:3
Thief, The 1927,Ap 23,15:2
Royal Family, The 1927,D 29,26:4

Daly, Phil

Good Boy 1928,S 6,23:2

Daly, Thomas

First American Dictator 1939,Mr 15,18:2

Daly, Thy

Betty, Be Good 1920,My 5,14:2

Daly, Timothy

Last Waltz, The 1921,My 11,20:3

Daly, Tom

Naked Genius, The 1943,O 22,20:5
Right Next to Broadway 1944,F 22,26:2
Story of Mary Surratt, The 1947,F 10,25:2

Daly, Tomy

What Big Ears! 1942,Ap 21,18:5

Daly, Tyne

Butter and Egg Man, The 1966,O 18,49:1
That Summer-That Fall 1967,Mr 17,33:1

Daly, Virginia

Revolt of the Beavers, The 1937,My 21,19:2
Between the Devil 1937,D 23,24:5
Audition of the Apprentice Theatre 1939,Je 2,26:2

Daly, William

Constant Sinner, The 1931,S 15,30:1
Let 'Em Eat Cake 1933,O 3,26:5

Daly, William (Composer)

For Goodness Sake 1922,F 22,13:1
Our Nell 1922,D 5,24:1

Dalya, Jacqueline

French Touch, The 1945,D 10,18:2
Now I Lay Me Down to Sleep 1950,Mr 3,21:2

Dalzell, Allan Cameron (Producer)

Angels Don't Kiss 1932,Ap 6,22:5

Dalzell, Duval

Great Way, The 1921,N 8,28:2

Dalzell, R D

Front Page, The 1937,N 12,27:2

Dalzell, Shirley

Sweet Miani 1962,S 26,33:2

Damashek, Barbara

'Tis Pity She's a Whore 1967,O 21,15:2
Three Sisters, The 1968,Mr 18,56:1
Rivals, The 1969,O 18,37:1
Crimes and Crimes 1970,Ja 19,35:1
Don Juan 1970,My 26,32:1
Three Philip Roth Stories; Epstein 1970,Jl 31,14:1
Cops and Horrors; Fly Paper 1970,Ag 11,27:1
Cops and Horrors; Dracula 1970,Ag 11,27:1
Story Theater Repertory; Gimpel the Food 1970,O 21,40:1

Damashek, Barbara (Composer)

Metamorphoses 1969,D 12,69:1
Story Theater Repertory; Saint Julian the Hospitaler 1970,O 21,40:1
Story Theater Repertory; Gimpel the Food 1970,O 21,40:1

Damashek, Barbara (Lyricist)

Story Theater Repertory; Gimpel the Food 1970,O 21,40:1

D'Amato, Ernest

Laffing Room Only 1944,D 25,15:4

D'Amboise, Jacques

Shinbone Alley 1957,Ap 15,23:2
Shinbone Alley 1957,Ap 28,II,1:1

D'Amboise, Jacques (Director)

Rondelay 1969,N 6,55:1

D'Ambra, Lucio (Playwright)

Incendio Doloso, L'; False Flame, The 1931,N 16,22:4

D'Ambricourt, Adrienne

French Doll, The 1922,F 21,20:2

D'Ambroise, Erik Retsin (Miscellaneous)

Architruc 1970,Ap 16,55:1
Lettre Morte 1970,Ap 16,55:1

D'Ambrosia, Angela

Guide, The 1968,Mr 7,50:1

Dame, Beverly

Medium, The 1947,My 2,28:2

Dame, Donald

Beggar Student, The 1942,S 26,11:4

Damia (Mme)

Untitled-One Woman Show 1926,S 25,21:3
Procureur Hallers, Le 1927,F 13,VII,4:1

Damier, J A Francis

Hate Planters 1933,My 26,24:5

Damita, Lily

Carry On 1929,N 3,IX,1:7
Sons o' Guns 1929,N 27,30:4
Sons o' Guns 1930,Ja 12,VIII,1:1
Music Hall Varieties 1932,N 23,15:3
Here's How 1934,F 23,22:4

Damkoehler, William

Brother to Dragons 1968,D 8,86:1
Wilson in the Promise Land 1970,Ja 11,78:1
Wilson in the Promise Land 1970,My 27,41:1

Damon, Bruno

Streetcar Named Desire, A 1956,F 16,24:1

Damon, Cathryn

Vamp, The 1955,N 11,30:1
Best Foot Forward 1956,Mr 3,16:1
Shinbone Alley 1957,Ap 15,23:2
Family Affair, A 1962,Ja 29,17:1
Boys From Syracuse, The 1963,Ap 16,31:1
Funny Thing Happened on the Way to the Forum, A 1963,Je 2,II,1:1
Foxy 1964,F 17,26:1
Secret Life of Walter Mitty, The 1964,O 27,44:5
Flora, the Red Menace 1965,My 12,41:2
Utbu 1966,Ja 5,24:1
Come Summer 1969,Mr 19,43:1
Criss-Crossing 1970,Ja 22,30:1
Show Me Where the Good Times Are 1970,Mr 6,32:1
Place for Polly, A 1970,Ap 20,45:1

Damon, Les

Girls in 509, The 1958,O 16,47:1

Damon, Lester

Eye on the Sparrow 1938,My 4,26:3

Damon, Nell Jane

Side-Show 1931,My 16,13:1

Damon, Peter

Men in White 1955,F 26,13:2

Damon, Stuart

From A to Z 1960,Ap 21,23:2
Irma la Douce 1960,S 30,31:2
Entertain a Ghost 1962,O 10,48:1
Boys From Syracuse, The 1963,Ap 16,31:1
Boys From Syracuse, The 1963,Je 2,II,1:1
Do I Hear a Waltz? 1965,Mr 19,28:1
Do I Hear a Waltz? 1965,Mr 28,II,1:1

Damon, William

Hamlet 1954,Ap 24,15:2

Damrosch, Anita

She Had to Know 1925,F 3,25:3
Lady Lies, The 1928,N 27,36:2

Damrosch, Gretchen (Playwright)

Life Line, The 1930,D 29,19:3
Passing Present, The 1931,N 29,VIII,2:2
Passing Present, The 1931,D 8,36:2

Damrosch, Leopoldine

Rita Coventry 1923,F 20,12:2

Damrosch, Leopoldine (Playwright)

Garrick Gaieties 1930,Je 5,29:2

Damrosch, Walter (Composer)

Iphigenia in Aulis 1921,Ap 8,18:2

Damroth, George

All in the Family 1935,Jl 24,20:4

Damroth, George (Director)

Storm Child 1935,Jl 16,24:1
All in the Family 1935,Jl 24,20:4

Damur, Hene

Symphony 1935,Ap 27,20:3
Man in Dress Clothes, The 1937,Ag 24,24:4
I Married an Angel 1938,My 12,26:2

Damy, Arnold

Leah Kleschna 1924,Ap 27,VIII,1:1

Dan, Yoel

New Music Hall of Israel, The 1969,O 3,40:1

Dana, Barbara

Clearing in the Woods, A 1959,F 13,32:1
Worm in Horseradish, A 1961,Mr 14,32:3
Angels of Anadarko 1962,O 11,47:1
Enter Laughing 1963,Mr 15,8:1
Enter Laughing 1963,Je 16,II,1:1
Where's Daddy? 1966,Mr 3,27:1
Room Service 1970,My 13,49:1

Dana, Dick

As the Girls Go 1948,N 15,21:2
Michael Todd's Peep Show 1950,Je 29,37:2

Dana, F Mitchell (Lighting Director)

Dynamite Tonight 1967,Mr 16,52:2
Calling in Crazy 1969,O 7,42:2
Joy 1970,Ja 28,50:1
Nuns, The 1970,Je 2,35:1
Charley's Aunt 1970,Jl 6,38:1

Dana, Frank

Take a Giant Step 1956,S 26,30:1

Dana, Jack

John Brown 1950,My 4,32:7

Dana, Kenneth

Pride 1923,My 3,22:3
Book of Charm, The 1925,S 4,26:3
Book of Charm, The 1925,S 13,VIII,1:1
Rope 1928,F 23,18:3
Exceeding Small 1928,O 23,32:2
Exceeding Small 1928,N 4,IX,1:1
Charm 1929,N 29,24:5
Five Star Final 1930,D 31,11:1
Fast Service 1931,N 18,26:3
Blessed Event 1932,F 13,23:2
War and Peace 1942,My 22,26:3
War President 1944,Ap 25,17:3
Adding Machine, The 1956,F 10,17:1

Dana, Leora

Madwoman of Chaillot, The 1949,Ja 9,II,1:1
Madwoman of Chaillot, The 1949,S 11,II,1:1
Happy Time, The 1950,Ja 25,24:1
Point of No Return 1951,O 31,32:2
Point of No Return 1951,N 14,35:2
Point of No Return 1951,D 23,II,3:1
Julius Caesar 1955,Jl 13,20:1
Tempest, The 1955,Ag 2,18:2
Best Man, The 1960,Ap 1,39:1
In the Summer House 1964,Mr 26,43:1
Beekman Place 1964,O 8,50:1
Long Christmas Dinner, The 1966,S 7,53:1
Collision Course; Stars and Stripes 1968,My 9,55:2
Collision Course; Camera Obscura 1968,My 9,55:2
Collision Course; Skywriting 1968,My 9,55:2
Collision Course; Tour 1968,My 9,55:2
This Bird of Dawning Singeth All Night Long 1968,D 31,19:1
This Bird of Dawning Singeth All Night Long 1969,Ja 12,II,1:1
Increased Difficulty of Concentration, The 1969,D 5,48:1

Dana, Marie Louise

Honeymooning 1927,Mr 18,25:3
Jerry for Short 1929,Ag 13,23:4
I'd Rather Be Right 1937,N 3,28:2
Return of the Vagabond, The 1940,My 14,27:2
R U R 1942,D 4,30:2
Naked Genius, The 1943,O 22,20:5

Dana, Marshall

Tiger Smiles, The 1930,D 18,29:1

Dana, Mildred

Katy Did So What? 1935,N 6,32:3

Dana, Natasha

Between the Devil 1937,D 23,24:5

Dana, Nicholas

Gods of the Mountain, The 1950,My 25,36:2
Almost Crazy 1955,Je 21,37:1
Mary Stuart 1956,Ap 28,10:2

Danaroff, Alexander

Clear All Wires! 1932,S 15,19:1
Nowhere Bound 1935,Ja 23,20:2

Dance, Bill

Cry for Us All 1970,Ap 9,48:2

Dancer, Earl (Director)

Black Rhythm 1936,D 21,19:2

Dancer, Earl (Producer)

Africana 1927,Jl 12,29:2
Black Rhythm 1936,D 21,19:2

d'Ancona, Miranda

Master Builder Solness 1950,My 26,19:3

d'Ancona, Miranda (Director)

Master Builder Solness 1950,My 26,19:3
Moon in Capricorn 1953,O 28,37:2

d'Ancona, Miranda (Producer)

Knight of the Burning Pestle, The 1953,O 24,13:2
Moon in Capricorn 1953,O 28,37:2
Song of the Grasshopper 1967,S 29,52:2

Dancourt, Julia

Three Musketeers, The 1968,Je 26,43:1
George Dandin 1968,Je 28,36:1

Dancy, Jacques Ch

Roof, The 1931,O 31,22:4

Dancy, Virginia (Lighting Director)

Kicking the Castle Down 1967,Ja 19,43:1
Whistle in the Dark, A 1968,F 17,32:2

Dancy, Virginia (Scenic Designer)

Kicking the Castle Down 1967,Ja 19,43:1
Whistle in the Dark, A 1968,F 17,32:2
Country People 1970,Ja 19,35:1

Dandes, Berman

Vegetable, The, or From President to Postman 1929,Ap 11,32:3

Dandies, The Four Chocolate

Vaudeville (Palace) 1926,Mr 23,24:3

D'Andrea, Ann
Go, Go, Go, God is Dead! 1966,O 12,37:1
Man Who Washed His Hands, The 1967,F 16,33:1
D'Andrea, Carole
West Side Story 1957,S 27,14:4
d'Andrea, Cecile
Spice of 1922 1922,Jl 7,12:4
I'll Say She Is 1924,My 20,15:1
Dandridge, Dorothy
Swingin' the Dream 1939,N 30,24:2
Dandridge, Etta
Swingin' the Dream 1939,N 30,24:2
Dandridge, Putney
Brown Buddies 1930,O 8,29:1
Dandridge, Vivian
Swingin' the Dream 1939,N 30,24:2
Dandry, Evelyne
How to Succeed in Business Without Really Trying;
 Comment Reussir Dans les Affaires Sans
 Vraiment Se Fatiguer 1964,F 12,30:1
Dandy, Jess
Just Married 1921,Ap 27,21:1
Dane, Clemence (Director)
Come of Age 1934,Ja 13,16:6
Moonlight Is Silver 1934,S 20,21:1
Dane, Clemence (Playwright)
Bill of Divorcement, A 1921,O 11,22:2
Bill of Divorcement, A 1921,O 16,VI,1:1
Will Shakespeare 1921,D 4,VII,1:3
Will Shakespeare 1923,Ja 2,14:1
Will Shakespeare 1923,Ja 21,VII,1:1
Way Things Happen, The 1923,D 30,VII,2:1
Way Things Happen, The 1924,Ja 29,17:5
Way Things Happen, The 1924,F 3,VII,1:1
Bill of Divorcement, A 1924,S 7,VII,1:1
Granite 1926,Je 20,VII,1:1
Granite 1927,F 12,13:1
Mariners 1927,Mr 29,22:2
Mariners 1927,Ap 3,VIII,1:1
Mariners 1929,My 19,IX,1:8
Gooseberry Fool 1929,N 2,14:8
Wild December 1933,Je 25,IX,1:3
Come of Age 1934,Ja 13,16:6
Here Lies Truth 1934,Ag 28,24:6
Moonlight Is Silver 1934,S 20,21:1
Moonlight Is Silver 1934,O 7,IX,3:7
Aiglon, L' 1934,N 5,22:2
Granite 1936,Ja 14,24:6
Happy Hypocrite, The 1936,Ap 9,21:6
Happy Hypocrite, The 1936,My 10,X,1:1
Herod and Mariamne 1938,O 27,27:2
Cousin Muriel 1940,Mr 17,X,1:6
Call Home the Heart 1947,Ap 13,I,54:2
Come of Age 1952,Ja 24,22:2
Dane, Conrad
Heartbreak House 1950,Mr 22,33:2
Dane, Essex
Beau-Strings 1926,Ap 27,22:2
Infinite Shoeblack, The 1930,F 18,28:1
Lady Windermere's Fan 1932,Ja 27,19:3
Make Way for Lucia 1948,D 23,23:5
Dane, Ethel
Fair Circassian, The 1921,D 7,22:3
Dane, Faith
Gypsy 1959,My 22,31:6
Dane, Paul
Old Bill, M P 1926,N 11,22:2
Spring in Autumn 1933,O 25,22:5
Daneborg, Anton
Redemption: Lebende Leichnam, Der; Living
 Corpse, The 1928,N 20,28:2
Daneel, Sylvia
Girl on the Via Flaminia, The 1954,F 10,37:1
Girl on the Via Flaminia, The 1954,Ap 6,35:5
Tunnel of Love, The 1957,F 14,31:4
Romanoff and Juliet 1957,O 11,24:1
Desert Incident, A 1959,Mr 25,40:1
Danehey, James
Achilles Had a Heel 1935,O 14,20:2
Daneman, Paul
Henry IV 1955,My 15,II,1:1
Henry VI (Part III) 1957,O 18,19:5
Doctor Faustus 1961,Ag 22,23:1
Danesi, Alfredo (Miscellaneous)
Festa Italiana 1966,S 30,55:1
Danesi, Natalia
Revenge With Music 1934,N 29,33:5
To Quito and Back 1937,O 7,30:4
Spring Thaw 1938,Mr 22,18:1
Danforth, William
Iolanthe 1920,Ja 6,13:3
H M S Pinafore 1920,Ja 13,10:2
Ruddigore 1920,F 1,VIII,2:2
Blossom Time 1921,S 30,10:1
Blossom Time 1921,O 9,VI,1:1
Mikado, The 1925,Ap 13,25:1
Princess Flavia 1925,N 3,34:3
H M S Pinafore 1926,Ap 7,26:3
Ruddigore 1927,My 21,25:2
Houseboat on the Styx, The 1928,D 16,IX,2:1
Houseboat on the Styx, The 1928,D 26,14:3
Robin Hood 1929,N 20,26:5
Mikado, The; Town of Titipu, The 1931,My 5,33:2

H M S Pinafore 1931,My 19,25:2
Gondoliers, The 1931,Je 2,34:4
Patience 1931,Je 16,30:4
Pirates of Penzance, The; Slave of Duty, The
 1931,Je 30,23:6
H M S Pinafore 1931,Jl 28,17:6
Trial by Jury 1931,Jl 28,17:6
Ruddigore 1931,Ag 11,28:3
Mikado, The 1931,Ag 25,17:7
Gondoliers, The 1932,Ja 12,29:1
Robin Hood 1932,Ja 28,25:4
Mikado, The 1933,Ap 18,13:4
Yeomen of the Guard, The 1933,My 2,20:4
H M S Pinafore 1933,My 9,20:3
Trial by Jury 1933,My 9,20:3
Patience 1933,My 23,22:6
Pirates of Penzance, The 1933,Ag 8,22:4
Yeomen of the Guard, The 1933,Ag 15,20:5
Mikado, The 1934,Ap 3,26:3
Pirates of Penzance, The 1934,Ap 10,26:5
Trial by Jury 1934,Ap 17,27:2
H M S Pinafore 1934,Ap 17,27:2
Mikado, The 1934,Ap 24,27:5
Iolanthe 1934,My 1,26:4
Mikado, The 1935,Jl 16,24:4
Pirates of Penzance, The 1935,Jl 23,24:2
Yeomen of the Guard, The 1935,Jl 30,16:4
Gondoliers, The 1935,Ag 6,20:5
H M S Pinafore 1935,Ag 13,20:6
Trial by Jury 1935,Ag 13,20:6
Mikado, The 1936,Ap 11,18:4
Pirates of Penzance, The 1936,Ap 21,27:5
Trial by Jury 1936,Ap 28,17:2
H M S Pinafore 1936,Ap 28,17:2
D'Angelo, Mark
Night Thoreau Spent in Jail, The 1970,N 2,66:1
D'Angelo, R M
We've Got to Have Money 1923,Ag 21,12:1
Dangler, Anita
Affair of Honor 1956,Ap 7,12:3
Hostage, The 1960,S 21,42:1
Angels of Anadarko 1962,O 11,47:1
Coach With the Six Insides, The 1962,N 27,44:1
Right You Are (If You Think You Are)
 1966,N 23,34:2
Coach With the Six Insides, The 1967,My 12,50:1
Hamlet 1967,D 27,45:1
Hamlet 1968,Jl 4,15:1
Danhelova, Milada
Apparition Theater of Prague, The 1966,N 17,56:2
Daniaud, Jacques
Femmes Savantes, Les 1967,F 7,34:2
Daniaud, Jacques (Miscellaneous)
Femmes Savantes, Les 1967,F 7,34:2
Daniderff, Lee (Composer)
Follies 1925,Jl 7,24:3
Daniel, Billie Lynn
Porgy and Bess 1961,My 18,40:1
Daniel, Billy
Let's Face It 1941,O 30,26:2
Daniel, Chuck
You Can't Take It With You 1965,N 24,32:1
Daniel, Flora
Brother Elks 1925,S 15,29:2
Daniel, James
King John 1967,Jl 14,19:1
Love's Labour's Lost 1968,Je 28,36:1
Daniel, Leslie
Coco 1969,D 19,66:1
Daniel, Mary
Deep Tangled Wildwood, The 1923,N 6,22:1
Right to Love, The 1925,Je 9,16:4
Jay Walker, The 1926,F 9,23:1
One Shot Fired 1927,N 8,32:5
Daniel, Saul
Summer Wives 1936,Ap 14,18:1
Daniel, Tamara
Grass Is Always Greener, The 1955,F 16,25:2
Birds, The 1966,Jl 1,40:1
Daniele, Graciela
What Makes Sammy Run? 1964,F 28,19:1
Here's Where I Belong 1968,Mr 4,32:1
Coco 1969,D 19,66:1
Danielewski, Tad (Director)
Desert Incident, A 1959,Mr 25,40:1
Brouhaha 1960,Ap 27,31:2
Miss Julie 1961,Jl 10,26:1
Danielewski, Tad (Producer)
Desert Incident, A 1959,Mr 25,40:1
Daniell, E S
Laugh It Off 1925,Ap 25,18:4
Daniell, Eric (Director)
Bring Me a Warm Body 1962,Ap 17,29:3
Daniell, Henry
Clair de Lune 1921,Ap 19,15:1
Woman on the Jury, The 1923,Ag 16,10:4
Second Mrs Tanqueray, The 1924,O 28,27:1
Play's the Thing, The 1928,D 23,VIII,4:7
Serena Blandish 1929,Ja 24,30:3
Serena Blandish 1929,F 3,VIII,1:1
Heat Wave 1931,F 18,14:6
For Services Rendered 1933,Ap 13,15:5
Kind Lady 1935,Ap 24,24:5

Daniell, Henry—Cont
Kind Lady 1935,Ap 28,X,1:1
With All My Heart 1935,Jl 30,17:1
Rag Picker of Paris, The: or, Modest Modiste
 1935,N 12,23:7
Kind Lady 1935,N 19,27:3
Hedda Gabler 1942,Ja 30,22:2
Murder Without Crime 1943,Ag 19,24:6
Lovers and Friends 1943,N 30,23:2
Lovers and Friends 1943,D 5,II,5:1
Winter's Tale, The 1946,Ja 16,18:6
Winter's Tale, The 1946,Ja 20,II,1:1
Lady Windermere's Fan 1946,O 15,29:2
First Mrs Fraser, The 1947,N 6,36:2
That Lady 1949,O 20,38:8
That Lady 1949,N 23,18:4
That Lady 1949,D 4,II,5:1
My 3 Angels 1953,Mr 12,23:2
Lord Pengo 1962,N 20,41:2
Danielle, Martha
Show Boat 1966,Jl 20,48:1
Danielli, Fred (Choreographer)
Where's Charley? 1948,O 12,33:2
Daniels, Beaulah
Goat Alley 1921,Je 21,20:2
Daniels, Bebe
Scandals 1931,S 27,VIII,3:7
Panama Hattie 1943,D 5,II,5:1
Daniels, Billy
Memphis Bound 1945,My 25,23:2
Seagulls Over Sorrento 1952,S 12,18:4
Golden Boy 1964,O 21,56:1
Daniels, Carolan
Telemachus Clay 1963,N 16,17:2
Slow Dance on the Killing Ground 1964,D 1,50:1
Me and Thee 1965,D 8,58:4
Young Marrieds Play Monopoly 1966,Mr 7,22:1
Princess Rebecca Birnbaum 1966,Mr 7,22:1
Make Like a Dog 1966,Mr 7,22:1
Daniels, Danny
Best Foot Forward 1941,O 2,28:2
Million Dollar Baby 1945,D 22,17:2
Billion Dollar Baby 1945,D 30,II,1:1
Street Scene 1947,Ja 10,17:2
Make Mine Manhattan 1948,Ja 16,26:2
Daniels, Danny (Choreographer)
Shoestring '57 1956,N 6,31:1
All American 1962,Mr 20,44:1
Best Foot Forward 1963,Ap 3,43:1
High Spirits 1964,Ap 8,34:1
Ciao, Rudy 1966,Ja 11,19:6
Annie Get Your Gun 1966,Je 1,42:2
Walking Happy 1966,N 28,47:1
Daniels, Danny (Director)
Best Foot Forward 1963,Ap 3,43:1
Daniels, David
Plain and Fancy 1955,Ja 28,14:2
Oh, Kay! 1960,Ap 18,37:2
Banker's Daughter, The 1962,Ja 23,37:1
Pimpernel! 1964,Ja 7,26:6
Daniels, Douglas
At Home Abroad 1935,S 20,17:4
Daniels, Edgar
New Girl in Town 1957,My 15,40:1
She Shall Have Music 1959,Ja 23,18:4
Caligula 1960,F 17,31:1
Finian's Rainbow 1960,Ap 28,31:1
Shadow of Heroes 1961,D 6,59:1
Alcestis Comes Back 1962,Ap 24,33:1
At Sea 1962,Ap 24,33:1
Affair, The 1962,S 21,34:2
Man for All Seasons, A 1964,Ja 28,24:2
Hostile Witness 1966,F 18,26:1
Galileo 1967,Ap 14,31:1
Tiger at the Gates 1968,Mr 1,30:1
Cyrano de Bergerac 1968,Ap 26,30:1
Daniels, Eleanor
Ashes 1924,O 21,21:2
Beaten Track, The 1926,F 9,23:2
Juno and the Paycock 1926,Mr 16,22:1
Lady Screams, The 1927,My 3,24:2
Diversion 1928,Ja 12,25:1
Far Away Horses 1933,Mr 22,21:6
Daniels, Elizabeth
Tree Witch, The 1961,Je 5,39:4
Daniels, Ellis
Tragedian in Spite of Himself, A 1948,F 6,29:2
Bear, The 1948,F 6,29:2
Wedding, The 1948,F 6,29:2
On the Harmfulness of Tobacco 1948,F 6,29:2
Daniels, Ernest A
Failures, The 1923,N 23,20:1
Daniels, J B (Director)
Blind Alley 1940,O 16,28:2
Brooklyn Biarritz 1941,F 28,16:2
Hickory Stick 1944,My 9,15:6
Down to Miami 1944,S 12,23:5
Daniels, J B (Miscellaneous)
Land of Fame 1943,S 22,31:5
Daniels, J Brainard
Bride of Torozko, The 1934,Jl 10,24:7
Daniels, Jack
Backslapper, The 1925,Ap 13,25:2
Exceeding Small 1928,O 23,32:2

Daniels, Jack—Cont
Wild Duck, The 1928,N 19,17:1
Man on Stilts, The 1931,S 10,23:2
Good Earth, The 1932,O 18,23:4
Living Dangerously 1935,Ja 14,10:3
Paths of Glory 1935,S 27,24:2
Daniels, Jack (Director)
Alice in Arms 1945,F 1,18:4
Daniels, Jack (Lighting Director)
Dark Hammock 1944,D 12,27:8
Daniels, James
Savage Rhythm 1932,Ja 1,30:4
Daniels, Jimmy
Dishonored Lady 1930,F 5,27:1
Daniels, Joe
It's All Yours 1942,Mr 26,26:2
Daniels, Joy
Firebugs, The 1963,N 22,41:1
Daniels, Leon
Buttrio Square 1952,O 15,40:2
Daniels, Leonard
Via Crucis 1923,N 13,25:2
Burgomaster of Stilemonde, The 1923,N 16,15:3
Hamlet 1923,N 20,23:3
Daniels, Leslie
Oklahoma! 1958,Mr 8,15:2
Daniels, Lew
Sky's the Limit, The 1934,D 18,25:5
Daniels, Lisa
Under Milk Wood 1957,O 16,42:5
Daniels, Marc
Dead End 1935,O 29,17:2
Yeomen of the Guard, The 1939,Jl 16,30:4
Winged Victory 1943,N 22,24:1
Daniels, Marc (Director)
Phoenix '55 1955,Ap 25,20:2
Copper and Brass 1957,O 18,19:2
Girl in the Freudian Slip, The 1967,My 19,34:3
Daniels, Marc (Miscellaneous)
Reunion in New York 1940,F 22,28:4
Mr Winkle's Holliday 1946,Je 24,27:6
Daniels, Marguerite
Her Family Tree 1920,D 28,9:2
Daniels, Maurice (Director)
Taming of the Shrew, The 1962,Ap 24,33:3
Daniels, Mickey
Vaudeville (Palace) 1927,Ap 12,25:4
Daniels, Ted
Show Boat 1927,D 28,26:1
Panama Hattie 1940,O 31,28:2
Daniels, Walker
Stephen D 1967,S 25,58:1
Hair 1967,O 30,55:1
Hair 1967,N 14,50:1
Get Thee to Canterbury 1969,Ja 26,74:1
Daniels, Wilbur
At Home Abroad 1935,S 20,17:4
Daniels, William
Legend of Lizzie, The 1959,F 10,39:1
Twelfth Night 1959,Jl 11,10:2
Zoo Story, The 1960,Ja 15,37:2
Zoo Story, The 1960,Ja 31,II,1:1
Alligators, The 1960,N 15,47:1
Rosemary 1960,N 15,47:1
I Am a Camera 1961,Jl 10,26:1
Zoo Story, The 1961,Jl 10,26:1
Thousand Clowns, A 1962,Ap 6,31:2
Thousand Clowns, A 1962,Ap 15,II,1:1
Dear Me, the Sky Is Falling 1963,Mr 4,9:1
One Flew Over the Cuckoo's Nest 1963,N 14,40:2
On a Clear Day You Can See Forever 1965,O 18,44:1
Daphne in Cottage D 1967,O 16,56:1
Daphne in Cottage D 1967,N 5,II,3:1
1776 1969,Mr 17,46:2
1776 1969,Mr 23,II,1:1
Daniels, William Lopez
Natural Man 1941,My 8,20:4
Daniels (Translator)
Finta Giardiniera, La 1927,F 6,VII,1:1
Danies, Irwin
Oklahoma! 1958,Mr 8,15:2
Danilova, Alexandra
Great Waltz, The 1934,S 24,14:4
Song of Norway 1944,Ag 22,20:2
Song of Norway 1944,Ag 27,II,1:1
Oh Captain! 1958,F 5,21:2
Danilovic-Cincar, Ljiljana
Progress of Bora, The Tailor, The 1968,Je 27,49:2
d'Aniou, Richard (Miscellaneous)
Happy Days 1965,S 14,45:2
Danis, Lew
Tapestry in Gray 1935,D 28,10:2
Danjou, Jean
Flossie 1924,Je 4,25:2
Dank, David
Little Cantor, The 1930,S 24,26:2
Life Is a Dream 1962,Ja 15,22:3
Country Boy, The 1963,O 28,20:1
Dann, Bette
Cock-A-Doodle Dandy 1955,N 4,26:5
Dann, Elonzo
Anatomist, The 1957,F 27,21:5

Dann, Larry
Oh What a Lovely War 1964,O 1,30:1
Danne, Margot
Ice Capades 1969,Ja 8,42:1
Dannenborg, George
Ouija Board, The 1920,Mr 30,9:1
Danner, Blythe
Infantry, The 1966,N 15,51:1
Summertree 1968,Mr 4,29:1
Up Eden 1968,N 27,42:1
Someone's Comin' Hungry 1969,Ap 1,51:1
Miser, The 1969,My 9,35:1
Butterflies Are Free 1969,O 22,30:1
Butterflies Are Free 1969,N 2,II,1:1
Danner, Harry
Bajour 1964,N 24,42:1
Danner, Joseph
Passion Play, The 1929,Ap 30,32:1
d'Annunzio, Gabriele (Playwright)
Citta Morta, La; Dead City, The 1923,N 28,14:1
Daughter of Iorio 1927,S 12,6:4
Fiaccola Sotto il Moggio, La 1927,D 25,VIII,4:3
D'Annunzio, Lola
Summer and Smoke 1952,Ap 25,19:5
Grass Harp, The 1953,Ap 28,32:2
Girl on the Via Flaminia, The 1954,F 10,37:1
Girl on the Via Flaminia, The 1954,Ap 6,35:5
Cradle Song 1955,D 2,32:2
Danny, William (Composer)
Antony and Cleopatra 1963,S 14,12:4
Danny, William (Musical Director)
Antony and Cleopatra 1963,S 14,12:4
Dano, Edward
Up She Goes 1922,N 7,14:2
Dano, Paul (Miscellaneous)
Deuces Wild; It's All Yours 1962,Ap 25,31:1
Deuces Wild; Thus 1962,Ap 25,31:1
Charlatans; On Circe's Island 1962,Ap 27,26:1
Charlatans; Summer Ghost, A 1962,Ap 27,26:1
Dano, Royal
Finian's Rainbow 1947,Ja 11,23:2
Mrs Gibsons' Boys 1949,My 5,35:2
Metropole 1949,D 7,43:2
She Stoops to Conquer 1949,D 29,21:3
Four Twelves Are 48 1951,Ja 18,30:2
Three Wishes for Jamie 1952,Mr 22,9:2
Tall Kentuckian, The 1953,Je 17,30:1
Dans, Joseph (Producer)
Sweet Shadow 1935,Ag 7,22:2
Danscha, Billie
Afgar 1920,N 9,13:2
Dansker, William
Professor Mamlock 1937,Ap 14,30:3
Dantchenko, Nemirovitch (Director)
Lysistrata 1925,O 17,18:3
Dante, Bea
Aquacircus 1958,Je 30,24:6
Dante, Jeanne
Brass Ankle 1931,Ap 24,26:4
Thunder on the Left 1933,N 1,25:2
Birthday 1934,D 27,24:2
Sea Shells 1935,Jl 16,24:2
News Item 1935,Ag 6,20:3
Call It a Day 1936,Ja 21,26:7
Call It a Day 1936,Ja 29,15:2
Call It a Day 1936,F 9,X,1:1
Glorious Morning 1938,N 28,10:3
Dante, Lionel
Four Walls 1927,S 20,33:1
Kingdom of God, The 1928,D 21,30:2
Camels Are Coming, The 1931,O 3,20:4
Judgment Day 1934,S 13,26:4
Dante, Ron (Composer)
Billy 1969,Mr 24,56:1
Dante, Ron (Lyricist)
Billy 1969,Mr 24,56:1
Dante (Harry A Jansen)
Sim Sala Bim 1940,S 10,27:1
Sim Sala Bim 1940,S 15,IX,1:1
Dantes, Suzanne
Onzieme Commandement 1932,My 15,VIII,2:2
Dantine, Helmut
Eagle Has Two Heads, The 1947,Mr 20,39:2
Parisienne 1950,Jl 25,24:2
Lady From Paris, The 1950,S 27,36:1
Danton, Arlette
Blind Angel, The 1965,Ap 2,26:1
D'Antonakis, Fleury
Do I Hear a Waltz? 1965,Mr 19,28:1
Do I Hear a Waltz? 1965,Mr 28,II,1:1
Danus, Ed
John Gabriel Borkman 1959,N 26,57:4
Danvers-Walker, Aubrey (Playwright)
Heaven and Charing Cross 1939,Ap 16,X,2:3
Heaven and Charing Cross 1939,Ap 16,X,2:4
Danzer, Emmerich
Eisrevue 1969,O 23,55:1
Danzi, Michael
Threepenny Opera, The 1955,S 21,38:1
Danzig, Samuel
St Helena 1936,O 7,32:1
Danzing, Helen
Bursting the Barriers 1930,My 7,25:1

Dapoigny, Jacques
Aventuriere, L' 1922,N 14,16:1
Megere Apprivoisee, La 1922,N 20,21:2
Madame Sans-Gene 1924,N 4,30:1
Maitresse de Roi 1926,D 1,24:1
Dame aux Camelias, La 1926,D 7,24:2
Misanthrope, Le 1926,D 10,31:2
Aventuriere, L' 1926,D 17,27:3
Dapoigny, Jacques (Playwright)
Comment l'Esprit Vient aux Garcons 1929,O 6,IX,2:2
Daprato, William
Burning, The 1963,D 4,57:1
Mike Downstairs 1968,Ap 19,35:1
dar Boggia, P E
Ora di Diana, L' 1937,My 17,22:3
dar Boggia, P E (Miscellaneous)
Ora di Diana, L' 1937,My 17,22:3
dar Boggia, P E (Playwright)
Ora di Diana, L' 1937,My 17,22:3
Darbee, Henry (Scenic Designer)
Wings Over Europe 1936,Mr 4,24:7
Darbritz, Arno (Composer)
Americans on the Rhine 1934,O 11,28:4
Darbritz, Arno (Lyricist)
Americans on the Rhine 1934,O 11,28:4
Darby, J B
Drake's Drum 1923,D 26,17:7
Darby, Joe
Sambo 1970,Jl 23,24:1
Darby, Myrna
Whoopee 1928,D 5,34:3
Darby, Phillip
I'll Say She Is 1924,My 20,15:1
Darby, Susan
Birthday Party, The 1961,My 15,34:6
Galileo 1963,Ja 5,5:2
House of Bernarda Alba, The 1963,N 25,23:2
Darcel, Denise
Pardon Our French 1950,O 6,22:4
Little Hut, The 1961,Jl 26,34:2
Darcey, Mr
Trois Jeunes Filles Nues; Three Young Maids From the Folies Bergere 1929,Mr 5,28:2
D'Arclay, Louis
Guest of Honor, The 1920,S 21,12:1
I Will IF You Will 1922,Ag 30,10:4
Rose Briar 1922,D 26,11:3
Cold Feet 1923,My 22,14:2
Synthetic Sin 1927,O 11,26:2
Our Betters 1928,F 21,18:2
d'Arcy, Alexander
Yours Is My Heart 1946,S 6,16:5
D'Arcy, Belle
Air-Minded 1932,F 11,17:3
d'Arcy, David
Polly 1925,O 12,19:1
Darcy, Don
Town's Woman, The 1929,Mr 12,26:2
Three Men on a Horse 1942,O 10,10:2
Porgy and Bess 1943,S 14,26:2
Porgy and Bess 1944,F 8,13:2
Odds on Mrs Oakley, The 1944,O 3,18:8
Darcy, Gloria
Poppy 1924,D 21,VII,1:8
D'Arcy, M
Light of Asia, The 1928,O 10,32:2
d'Arcy, Margaretta
Harold Muggins Is a Martyr 1968,Jl 14,II,4:5
d'Arcy, Margaretta (Playwright)
Harold Muggins Is a Martyr 1968,Jl 14,II,4:5
Darcy, Maurice
Orange Blossoms 1922,S 20,18:1
Breaking Point, The 1923,Ag 17,8:4
D'Arcy, Mike
Five Star Final 1930,D 31,11:1
D'Arcy, Murray
Squaw Man, The 1921,D 27,10:3
Jolly Roger, The 1923,Ag 31,10:4
Othello 1925,Ja 12,11:1
Henry V 1928,Mr 16,26:2
Bonds of Interest, The 1929,O 15,34:2
Hamlet 1934,D 26,19:3
Cyrano de Bergerac 1936,Ap 28,17:1
Enemy of the People, An 1937,F 16,19:1
D'Arcy, Richard
On the Town 1944,D 29,11:4
All for Love 1949,Ja 24,16:5
D'Arcy, Richard (Director)
Show Girl 1961,Ja 13,37:1
D'Arcy, Roy
Vaudeville (Palace) 1929,Je 24,27:4
Room 349 1930,Ap 23,24:5
D'Arcy, Scotti (Miscellaneous)
Single Man at a Party 1959,Ap 22,30:4
Darden, Norma
Weekend 1968,Mr 14,50:2
Street Sounds 1970,O 23,32:1
Darden, Severn
Hamlet 1958,Je 21,11:1
Midsummer Night's Dream, A 1958,Je 23,19:1
Winter's Tale, The 1958,Jl 21,17:4
Romeo and Juliet 1959,Je 15,31:1

Darden, Severn—Cont

Merry Wives of Windsor, The 1959,Jl 9,23:2
All's Well That Ends Well 1959,Ag 3,20:4
From the Second City 1961,S 27,32:1
Untitled-Revue; Second City 1962,Ja 12,30:2
PS 193 1962,O 31,33:1
Open Season at Second City 1964,Ja 23,25:1
Murderer Among Us, A 1964,Mr 26,43:1

Dare, Daniel M (Producer)
Sentinels 1931,D 26,15:1

Dare, Danny
Dew Drop Inn 1923,My 18,26:4
Vaudeville (Hippodrome) 1926,Mr 16,22:2
Five O'Clock Girl, The 1927,O 11,26:3

Dare, Danny (Choreographer)
Little Show, The 1929,My 1,28:5
Sweet Adeline 1929,S 4,33:1
Sweet and Low 1930,N 18,28:5
You Said It 1931,Ja 20,21:3

Dare, Danny (Composer)
Meet the People 1940,D 26,22:2

Dare, Danny (Director)
Meet the People 1940,D 26,22:2

Dare, Danny (Lyricist)
Meet the People 1940,D 26,22:2

Dare, Danny (Miscellaneous)
Tattle Tales 1933,Je 2,22:6

Dare, Danny (Playwright)
Meet the People 1940,D 26,22:2

Dare, Danny (Producer)
New Meet the People, The 1943,Ag 22,II,1:6

Dare, Debby
Summer Wives 1936,Ap 14,18:1

Dare, Deborah
Failures, The 1959,Ja 6,30:2
Magnificent Hugo, The 1961,Ap 8,12:2

Dare, Dorothy
America's Sweetheart 1931,F 11,23:1
Here Goes the Bride 1931,N 4,31:2
Strike Me Pink 1933,Mr 6,16:3
Only Girl, The 1934,My 22,28:2

Dare, Jeanne
Rat, The 1925,F 11,19:3

Dare, Joan
Priorities of 1942 1942,Mr 13,23:2

Dare, Madeleine
It's Up to You 1921,Mr 29,20:1

Dare, Mary
Unto Such Glory 1937,My 7,28:2

Dare, Thelma
Kismet 1953,D 4,2:4

Dare, Zena
Second Man, The 1928,F 12,VIII,2:1
Proscenium 1933,Je 15,21:2
My Fair Lady 1958,My 1,34:5

Dare and Wahl
Earl Carroll's Vanities 1924,S 11,23:6
Vaudeville (Palace) 1926,Mr 30,20:4
Vaudeville (Hippodrome) 1926,Ap 27,22:3

Darewski, Herman (Composer)
As You Were 1920,Ja 28,22:3

Darfler, Gene
Out West of Eighth 1951,S 21,20:3

Darge, James
Ballad of John Ogilvie, The 1968,O 9,42:4

Darian, Anita
King and I, The 1960,My 12,40:1
King and I, The 1960,My 22,II,1:1
Shoemaker and the Peddler, The 1960,O 15,27:4
Show Boat 1961,Ap 13,32:1
King and I, The 1963,Je 13,30:2
Saint of Bleecker Street, The 1965,Mr 19,28:1
King and I, The 1968,My 24,39:1

Darias (Miscellaneous)
Liberace's Variety Bill 1957,Ap 22,29:5

Darion, Joe
You Can't Sleep Here 1941,My 11,I,42:6

Darion, Joe (Lyricist)
Bil and Cora Baird's Marionette Theater
1955,D 27,29:2
Bil and Cora Baird's Marionette Theater; Ali Baba
and the Forty Thieves 1956,S 3,10:1
Shinbone Alley 1957,Ap 15,23:2
Man of La Mancha 1965,N 23,52:1
Illya Darling 1967,Ap 12,37:1

Darion, Joe (Miscellaneous)
These Are the Times 1950,My 11,37:2
Megilla of Itzik Manger, The 1968,O 10,60:1
Megilla of Itzik Manger, The 1969,Ap 21,55:1
Ali Baba and the Forty Thieves 1970,D 29,40:1

Darion, Joe (Playwright)
Shinbone Alley 1957,Ap 15,23:2
Shinbone Alley 1957,Ap 28,II,1:1

Darius, Adam
Jack in the Box 1960,My 19,43:3

Darius, Adam (Choreographer)
Jack in the Box 1960,My 19,43:3

Darius, Adam (Playwright)
Jack in the Box 1960,My 19,43:3

Dark, John
Lovers in the Metro, The 1962,Ja 31,21:1

Darke, Rebecca
Peer Gynt 1951,Ja 29,15:2
Maya 1953,Je 10,35:1

Little Clay Cart, The 1953,Jl 1,25:1
Once Upon a Tailor 1955,My 24,36:2
Midnight Caller, The 1958,Jl 2,25:1
John Turner Davis 1958,Jl 2,25:1
Sweet Confession 1959,Ap 15,30:1
Who'll Save the Plowboy? 1962,Ja 10,24:2
Undercover Man 1966,Je 3,30:2
Party for Divorce, A 1966,O 12,37:1

D'Arle, Yvonne
Countess Maritza 1926,Mr 30,20:3
Countess Maritza 1926,S 20,21:1
Three Musketeers, The 1928,Mr 4,IX,2:3
Three Musketeers, The 1928,Mr 14,28:1
Three Musketeers, The 1928,Mr 25,IX,1:1

Darley, J B
Man From Earth, The 1923,Ja 3,6:2

Darling, Beatrice
Rose Girl, The 1921,F 12,11:1

Darling, Candy
Glamour, Glory and Gold 1967,O 4,43:1

Darling, Clifton
Babes in Arms 1937,Ap 15,18:4

Darling, Dorothy
Two on an Island 1940,Ja 23,17:2
New Life, A 1943,S 16,26:6

Darling, Elizabeth
Rose Girl, The 1921,F 12,11:1

Darling, Harriet
Peter Pan 1924,N 7,16:2

Darling, Hattie
Tick-Tack-Toe 1920,F 24,11:2

Darling, Jean
Carousel 1945,Ap 20,24:2
Pal Joey 1949,Mr 7,17:2

Darling, Jennifer
MacBird! 1967,F 23,38:1
How Now, Dow Jones 1967,D 8,53:1
Maggie Flynn 1968,O 24,52:1
Fire! 1969,Ja 29,26:1
Twelfth Night 1969,Ag 14,29:2

Darling, Joan
Untitled-Revue 1961,Je 18,II,1:1
Premise, The 1962,Jl 27,15:5
Squat Betty 1964,F 25,24:1
Sponge Room, The 1964,F 25,24:1
Murder in the Cathedral 1966,Je 21,38:1
Twelfth Night 1966,Je 23,28:1
Julius Caesar 1966,Je 24,29:2
Minor Adjustment, A 1967,O 7,33:3

Darling, Joan (Director)
Living Premise, The 1963,Je 14,34:1

Darling, Robert (Costume Designer)
Six Characters in Search of an Author
1963,Mr 11,7:2

Darling, Robert (Lighting Director)
Another Evening With Harry Stoones
1961,O 23,22:2
Cambridge Circus 1964,O 7,53:1
Helen 1964,D 11,55:4

Darling, Robert (Scenic Designer)
Another Evening With Harry Stoones
1961,O 23,22:2
Six Characters in Search of an Author
1963,Mr 11,7:2
All by Myself 1964,Je 16,47:1
Helen 1964,D 11,55:4
Baal 1965,My 7,33:2

Darling, Sandra
Pirates of Penzance, The 1966,My 24,54:1
Trial by Jury 1966,Je 8,41:2
Patience 1967,O 13,32:1
Iolanthe 1967,O 18,40:1
Gondoliers, The 1967,O 29,83:1
H M S Pinafore 1967,N 1,40:1

Darling, Sylvia
Peter Pan 1924,N 7,16:2

Darling Twins
Ziegfeld Follies 1921,Je 22,10:1
Good Morning, Dearie 1921,N 2,20:2

Darlington, W Y A (Playwright)
Carpet Slippers 1931,Ja 18,VIII,2:6

D'Armond, Frank (Composer)
Saluta 1934,Ag 29,13:4

D'Arms, Ted
On an Open Roof 1963,Ja 30,7:3
Hard Travelin' 1965,Je 17,25:1
Lonesome Train, The 1965,Je 17,25:1
Saint Joan 1968,Ja 5,42:1
Tiger at the Gates 1968,Mr 1,30:1
Cyrano de Bergerac 1968,Ap 26,30:1

Darnault, Marc
Maitresse de Roi 1926,D 1,24:1
Dame aux Camelias, La 1926,D 7,24:2
Misanthrope, Le 1926,D 10,31:2
Aventurier, L' 1926,D 17,27:3

Darnay, Dearon
Reunion 1938,Ap 12,26:4
Escape This Night 1938,Ap 23,18:1
Abe Lincoln in Illinois 1938,O 17,12:2
Steps Leading Up 1941,Ap 19,20:6
Johnny 2X4 1942,Mr 17,24:6

Darnay, Toni
When the Bough Breaks 1950,Mr 9,25:5

Darnay, Toni—Cont

Affair of Honor 1956,Ap 7,12:3
Life With Father 1967,O 20,53:2
Possibilities 1968,D 5,60:1

Darnell, Belle
Frivolities of 1920 1920,Ja 9,22:2

Darnell, Bob
On the Town 1959,Ja 16,36:1

Darnell, Caroline Worth
Secret Life of Walter Mitty, The 1964,O 27,44:5

Darnell, Deede
Minnie's Boys 1970,Mr 27,27:1

Darnell, Linda
Harbor Lights 1956,O 5,20:1

D'Arnell, Nydia
Topsy and Eva 1924,D 24,11:1
Mayflowers 1925,N 25,14:2
H M S Pinafore 1926,Ap 7,26:3
Happy-Go-Lucky 1926,O 1,27:2
Golden Dawn 1927,D 1,32:3

Darnell, Robert
Young Abe Lincoln 1961,Ap 26,36:1
Gingham Dog, The 1968,O 13,II,18:6
Who's Happy Now? 1969,N 18,39:1

Darnell, Robert (Miscellaneous)
Spoon River Anthology 1963,S 30,23:2

Darnell, Robert (Scenic Designer)
Tempest, The 1959,D 28,19:2

Darner, Phena
First Gentleman, The 1957,Ap 26,22:2

Daroy, Jacques
Heure du Berger, L'; Propitious Moment, The
1936,N 12,30:1
Homme Que J'Ai Tue, L'; Man Whom I Have
Killed, The 1936,D 10,34:3
Sexe Fort, Le; Strong Sex, The 1937,Ja 14,17:4

Darr, Sefton
Anastasia 1954,D 30,13:1
Bedtime Story 1957,Ap 1,21:2
Man of Destiny, The 1957,Ap 1,21:2

Darras, Jean-Pierre
Lorenzaccio 1958,O 15,44:2
Triomphe de l'Amour, Le 1958,O 17,32:1
Marie Tudor 1958,O 22,39:1
Don Juan 1958,O 29,29:1

Darras Brothers
Vaudeville (Palace) 1926,My 11,25:3

Darras Sisters
Vaudeville (Palace) 1929,N 11,20:5

Darrell, James
Barber Had Two Sons, The 1943,F 2,22:2

Darrell, Maisie
Scrapped 1927,O 16,IX,2:7
Many Waters 1929,S 26,27:1
Many Waters 1929,O 6,IX,1:1
Father, The 1931,O 9,21:1

Darrell, Robert
Babes in Toyland 1930,D 22,17:1

Darrell, Rupert
Babes in Toyland 1929,D 24,15:3
Four O'Clock 1933,F 14,19:6

Darrell, Rupert (Director)
Four O'Clock 1933,F 14,19:6

Darrell, Rupert (Playwright)
Four O'Clock 1933,F 14,19:6

Darrid, William
Dinosaur Wharf 1951,N 9,23:2
Inherit the Wind 1955,Ap 22,20:2

Darrid, William (Producer)
Disenchanted, The 1958,D 4,53:4
Andersonville Trial, The 1959,D 30,15:1
Cook for Mr General, A 1961,O 20,39:1

Darrieux, Danielle
Untitled-Play 1937,Ja 24,X,2:1
Evangeline 1952,O 3,17:1
Coco 1970,Ag 7,28:1

Darrow, Richard
I Dreamt I Dwelt in Bloomingdale's 1970,F 13,26:1

d'Arte, Teatro (Playwright)
Sansone; Samson 1931,F 9,25:1
Cantico dei Cantici, Il; Song of Songs
1931,My 18,21:4

d'Arte, Teatro (Producer)
Cardinale, Il; Cardinal, The 1931,Ja 12,24:2
Delitto e Castigo; Crime and Punishment
1931,Ja 26,20:5
Marchese di Priola, Il 1931,Mr 2,19:3
Arzigogolo, L'; Whim, The 1931,Ap 27,24:4

D'Artois, Arthur
Sable Brush, The 1956,N 28,41:1

Darvas, Lili
Everyman 1926,Ag 9,1:1
Midsummer Night's Dream, A 1927,N 18,21:1
Midsummer Night's Dream, A 1927,D 4,X,6:1
Jedermann 1927,D 8,33:2
Jedermann 1927,D 18,IX,6:1
Dantons Tod 1927,D 21,28:3
Diener Zweier Herren; Servant of Two Masters,
The 1928,Ja 10,28:3
Kabale und Liebe 1928,Ja 17,22:3
Lebende Leichnam, Der, Der; Living Corpse, The
1928,Ja 24,26:2
Journey to Pressburg, The 1931,Mr 8,VIII,2:7
Kabale und Liebe 1931,N 1,VIII,4:2

Darvas, Lili—Cont

Jemand; Somebody 1931,D 13,VIII,3:6
Kiss Before the Mirror, The 1932,N 13,IX,3:7
Great Love, The 1935,D 24,11:5
Criminals, The 1941,D 22,24:3
Soldier's Wife 1944,O 5,18:6
Hamlet 1945,D 14,25:2
Hamlet 1946,Je 4,18:4
Ist Geraldine ein Engel? 1946,N 4,33:4
Bravo! 1948,N 12,31:2
Cry of the Peacock 1950,Ap 12,33:2
Horses in Midstream 1953,Ap 3,18:7
Hidden River, The 1957,Ja 24,32:1
Waltz of the Toreadors, The 1958,Mr 5,37:1
Cheri 1959,O 13,44:1
Far Country, A 1961,Ap 5,32:1
First Love 1961,D 26,20:2
My Mother, My Father and Me 1963,Mr 25,5:5
Happiness 1967,N 11,25:2
Miser, The 1969,My 9,35:1
Blancs, Les 1970,N 16,48:4
Blancs, Les 1970,N 29,II,3:1
Blancs, Les 1970,N 29,II,3:5
Darvas and Julia
Danny Kaye's International Show 1953,Ja 19,20:2
Darveris, George (Miscellaneous)
Cocktail Party, The 1968,O 8,42:1
Cock-A-Doodle Dandy 1969,Ja 21,40:1
Hamlet 1969,Mr 4,34:1
D'Arville, Colette
Here's Howe! 1928,My 2,19:3
Darville, Evelyn
Orange Blossoms 1922,S 20,18:1
My Princess 1927,O 7,24:2
Darwell, Jane
Merchants of Venus 1920,S 28,14:2
Swords 1921,S 2,9:3
Suds in Your Eye 1944,Ja 13,15:5
Darzens, Rodolphe (Producer)
Lac Sale, Le 1926,O 3,VIII,2:1
Jazz 1927,Ja 23,VII,2:1
Great Catherine, The 1927,Ap 3,VIII,4:7
Das, Gurcharan (Playwright)
Mira 1970,Je 3,51:1
Daschbach, Leo
Hot Money 1931,N 9,22:2
Dascomb, E Brooks
Subway, The 1929,Ja 26,15:1
Dash, Calvin
Green Pastures, The 1951,Mr 16,35:2
Four Saints in Three Acts 1952,Ap 17,35:1
Dashiell, Willard
Apache, The 1923,My 9,14:3
American Tragedy, An 1926,O 12,31:2
Happy 1927,D 6,26:3
Mystery Man, The 1928,Ja 27,14:2
Gods of the Lightning 1928,O 25,27:2
Whirlpool 1929,D 4,37:3
Hot Money 1931,N 9,22:2
Papavert 1931,D 30,25:1
House of Doom, The 1932,Ja 26,20:4
Decoy, The 1932,Ap 2,13:4
Evensong 1933,F 1,13:4
All Good Americans 1933,D 6,29:2
Queer People 1934,F 16,16:2
Potash and Perlmutter 1935,Ap 6,11:3
Sea Shells 1935,Jl 16,24:2
News Item 1935,Ag 6,20:3
Jumbo 1935,N 18,20:2
She Gave Him All She Had 1939,D 2,20:7
Dassie Brothers, The
Vaudeville (Palace) 1952,Ap 14,23:2
Dassin, Jules
Hate Planters 1933,My 26,24:5
Revolt of the Beavers, The 1937,My 21,19:2
Clinton Street 1939,O 13,27:2
Dassin, Jules (Director)
Medicine Show 1940,Ap 13,20:6
Joy to the World 1948,Mr 19,28:2
Magdalena 1948,Jl 28,27:2
Magdalena 1948,S 21,31:2
Two's Company 1952,D 16,43:5
Isle of Children 1962,Mr 17,16:2
Illya Darling 1967,Ap 12,37:1
Illya Darling 1967,Ap 30,II,1:1
Illya Darling 1967,N 2,58:1
Dassin, Jules (Original Author)
Illya Darling 1967,N 2,58:1
Dassin, Jules (Playwright)
Illya Darling 1967,Ap 12,37:1
Illya Darling 1967,Ap 30,II,1:1
Illya Darling 1967,N 2,58:1
Daste, Jean
Voyage de Monsieur Perrichon, Le 1937,N 2,32:3
Knock 1937,N 17,26:3
Roi Cerf, Le 1937,N 30,26:3
Jean de la Lune 1937,D 14,33:3
Nationale 6 1938,Ja 11,26:6
Y'Avait un Prisonnier 1938,Ja 25,24:3
Fantasio 1938,F 8,17:2
Caprice, Un 1938,F 8,17:2
Bal des Voleurs, Le 1938,N 29,26:4
Faiseur, Le; Promoter, The 1938,D 27,12:3
Paquebot Tenacity, Le 1939,Ja 10,16:4

Chacun Sa Verite 1939,Ja 24,17:1
37 Sous de M Montaudoin, Les 1939,F 7,17:2
Enterrement, L' 1939,F 7,17:2
37 Sous de M Montaudoin, Les 1939,F 7,17:2
Siegfried 1939,F 21,15:2
Barbier de Seville, Le 1939,Mr 7,19:2
Daste, M M (Director)
Fantasio 1938,F 8,17:2
Caprice, Un 1938,F 8,17:2
Daste, Marie
Hamlet 1948,S 11,13:3
Daste, Marie-Helene
Don Juan 1934,F 27,16:5
Fausses Confidences, Les 1952,N 13,34:2
Proces, Le; Trial, The 1952,N 18,36:2
Fourberies de Scapin, Les 1952,N 21,21:2
Hamlet 1952,D 2,39:1
Christophe Colomb 1957,Ja 31,20:5
Pieton de L'Air, Le 1964,Mr 4,33:2
Salut a Moliere 1964,Mr 4,33:2
Vie Parisienne, La 1964,Mr 11,34:2
Daste, Marie-Helene (Costume Designer)
Oedipus 1946,My 21,19:2
Annonce Faite a Marie, L' 1965,Ap 6,33:2
Daste, Marie-Helene (Miscellaneous)
Christophe Colomb 1957,Ja 31,20:5
Daste, Mr
Precieuses Ridicules, Les 1938,D 13,30:3
Fourberies de Scapin, Les 1938,D 13,30:3
Daste, Mr (Director)
Medecin Malgre Lui, Le 1937,D 28,28:7
D'Ath, Cyril
Vaudeville (Palace) 1926,My 11,25:3
Vaudeville (Palace) 1926,N 30,27:2
D'Ath, Virginia
Vaudeville (Palace) 1926,My 11,25:3
Vaudeville (Palace) 1926,N 30,27:2
D'Attili, Maria
Medium, The 1948,D 8,41:6
Telephone, The 1948,D 8,41:6
Tough at the Top 1949,Jl 17,58:5
Dattore, Luba
Marie Vison, La 1970,Jl 15,29:1
Datz, Philippe P (Playwright)
Avons-Nous Tuee?, L' 1927,F 13,VII,4:1
Daube, Harda
Prince and the Pauper, The 1920,N 2,15:1
Marie Antoinette 1921,N 23,16:1
Tyrants 1924,Mr 5,14:1
O Nightingale 1925,Ap 16,25:2
Daubek, Jarmila
Cyrano de Bergerac 1953,N 13,24:3
Wisteria Trees, The 1955,F 3,20:2
Daubenas, Joseph
Lute Song 1959,Mr 13,24:1
Balcony, The 1960,Mr 4,21:1
Dream Play 1960,N 23,22:1
Daubeny, Peter (Producer)
Aspern Papers, The 1959,Ag 13,21:5
D'Auburn, Denis
Miracle, The 1924,Ag 19,9:1
Daudet, Alphonse (Original Author)
Sappho 1960,Ja 12,22:1
Daudet, Lucien (Playwright)
Paradis Perdu, Le 1923,D 12,VIII,3:4
Daufy, Jose
Trois Jeunes Filles Nues; Three Young Maids From the Folies Bergere 1929,Mr 5,28:2
Passionement; Passionately 1929,Mr 8,31:4
Comte Obligado 1929,Mr 12,26:2
Bon Garcon, Un 1929,Mr 19,36:2
Pas Sur La Bouche; Not on the Lips 1929,Mr 26,34:3
Daugherty, Dennis (Scenic Designer)
Horseman, Pass By 1969,Ja 16,46:4
Daughn, Delphie
Silks and Satins 1920,Jl 16,19:1
Daughtry, Harriet
Louisiana 1933,F 28,15:5
Daum, Margaret
Mikado, The 1935,Jl 16,24:4
Pirates of Penzance, The 1935,Jl 23,24:2
Yeomen of the Guard, The 1935,Jl 30,16:4
Gondoliers, The 1935,Ag 6,20:5
H M S Pinafore 1935,Ag 13,20:6
H M S Pinafore 1936,Ap 28,17:2
Dauphin, Claude
Voyage, Le 1937,F 28,XI,2:1
No Exit 1946,N 27,21:1
Soif, La 1949,F 9,33:2
Happy Time, The 1950,Ja 25,24:1
Mister Roberts 1951,F 9,20:7
Janus 1955,N 25,37:2
Clerambard 1957,N 8,22:3
Clerambard 1957,N 17,II,1:1
Infernal Machine, The 1958,F 4,33:1
Deadly Game, The 1960,F 3,27:2
Giants, Sons of Giants 1962,Ja 8,26:2
Hedda Gabler 1962,D 13,8:5
Dauphin, William
Along Came a Spider 1963,My 28,33:1
Dauphin, William E (Miscellaneous)
Billygoat Eddie 1964,Ap 21,43:2

Dauphinais, John
Ice Capades 1957,S 5,33:2
Daussmond, Betty
Masque et Visage 1927,Ap 3,VIII,4:7
d'Autremont, Ann
Great Campaign, The 1947,Ap 1,33:2
Dautun, Berengere
Troupe Du Roi, La 1970,F 4,38:1
Amphitryon 1970,F 4,38:1
Don Juan 1970,F 7,24:2
Malade Imaginaire, Le 1970,F 18,40:2
Davalos, Ellen
World of Suzie Wong, The 1958,O 15,47:1
Davalos, Richard
View From the Bridge, A 1955,Ag 31,16:8
View From the Bridge, A 1955,S 30,21:1
Memory of Two Mondays, A 1955,S 30,21:1
Davel, Mark Wing
Twelfth Night 1970,Ja 1,18:1
Davenant, William (Sir) (Playwright)
Tempest, The: or, The Enchanted Forest 1959,Je 10,42:2
Davenny, Hollis
Blossom Time 1922,O 24,18:2
Blossom Time 1923,My 22,14:3
Student Prince, The 1931,Ja 30,18:1
Davenport, Alice
Remote Control 1929,S 11,24:5
Dora Mobridge 1930,Ap 21,20:2
Davenport, Basil
Faun, The 1924,Mr 28,17:2
Orestes 1926,Je 20,II,3:6
Davenport, Basil (Translator)
Aiglon, L' 1925,O 31,20:3
Davenport, Butler
Passing of the Third Floor Back, The 1928,Ja 17,22:7
Passing of the Third Floor Back, The 1928,F 21,18:2
Tenth Man, The 1929,Mr 21,29:2
David Garrick 1929,Ag 2,17:5
Davenport, Butler (Director)
Passing of the Third Floor Back, The 1928,F 21,18:2
Tenth Man, The 1929,Mr 21,29:2
David Garrick 1929,Ag 2,17:5
Davenport, Butler (Producer)
Passing of the Third Floor Back, The 1928,F 21,18:2
Tenth Man, The 1929,Mr 21,29:2
David Garrick 1929,Ag 2,17:5
Davenport, Carson
School for Scandal, The 1923,Mr 13,19:2
Simon Called Peter 1924,N 11,20:2
Play, A 1925,F 11,19:2
Perfect Alibi, The 1928,N 28,24:2
Little Women 1931,D 8,36:2
Davenport, Charles (Director)
Brother Cain 1941,S 13,21:5
Davenport, Edward L
Move on, Sister 1933,O 25,22:4
Richelieu 1934,My 22,28:1
Davenport, Eva
Love Birds 1921,Mr 16,12:1
Davenport, Fanny
Six Characters in Search of an Author 1931,Ap 16,29:2
Davenport, Frank
Cherry Blossoms 1927,Mr 29,22:3
Satellite 1935,N 21,27:5
Davenport, Harry
Thank You 1921,O 4,10:2
Cock o' the Roost 1924,O 14,23:1
Hay Fever 1925,O 5,25:1
Makropoulos Secret, The 1926,Ja 22,12:4
Lost 1927,Mr 29,22:2
Julius Caesar 1927,Je 7,27:2
Jealous Moon, The 1928,N 21,32:2
Topaze 1930,F 13,25:3
Melo 1931,Ap 17,26:6
Melo 1931,O 20,29:3
Happy Landing 1932,Mr 28,10:5
Move on, Sister 1933,O 25,22:4
Re-Echo 1934,Ja 12,28:4
Battleship Gertie 1935,Ja 19,9:2
Davenport, Joan
Doll's House, A 1954,N 15,32:2
Auntie Mame 1958,Ag 12,33:2
Follies of 1910, The 1960,Ja 15,37:3
Davenport, La Noue
Play of Daniel, The 1960,D 27,23:6
Davenport, La Noue (Miscellaneous)
Marco Millions 1964,F 21,33:1
Davenport, M L (Playwright)
Davy Jones's Locker 1959,Mr 30,25:1
Davy Jones's Locker 1959,D 28,18:1
Davenport, Marie
Great Broxopp, The 1921,N 16,22:1
Davenport, Millia (Costume Designer)
Patience 1925,Ja 4,VII,1:1
Shoemaker's Holiday, The 1938,Ja 3,17:2
Love for Love 1940,Je 4,19:5
Journey to Jerusalem 1940,O 7,21:2

Davenport, Millia (Costume Designer)—Cont
Truckline Cafe 1946,F 28,19:4
Davenport, Nigel
Taste of Honey, A 1960,O 5,46:1
Taste of Honey, A 1960,N 6,II,1:1
Taste of Honey, A 1961,My 17,43:1
Davenport, Pembroke (Composer)
Dr Willy Nilly 1959,Je 5,18:2
Long Dream, The 1960,F 18,36:2
Davenport, Pembroke (Miscellaneous)
Sweethearts 1947,Ja 22,31:2
Sally 1948,My 7,31:2
Arabian Nights 1954,Je 25,15:2
Dr Willy Nilly 1959,Je 5,18:2
13 Daughters 1961,Mr 3,17:2
Paradise Island 1961,Je 24,11:1
Kean 1961,N 3,28:2
Davenport, Pembroke (Musical Director)
Carib Song 1945,S 28,17:2
Look, Ma, I'm Dancin' 1948,Ja 30,20:2
Kiss Me, Kate 1948,D 31,10:3
Out of This World 1950,D 22,17:3
Hazel Flagg 1953,F 12,22:2
Arabian Nights 1954,Je 25,15:2
Arabian Nights 1955,Je 24,16:1
King and I, The 1960,My 12,40:1
King and I, The 1960,My 22,II,1:1
Hit the Deck 1960,Je 24,32:1
13 Daughters 1961,Mr 3,17:2
Paradise Island 1961,Je 24,11:1
Kean 1961,N 3,28:2
Eddie Fisher at the Winter Garden 1962,O 3,47:1
Pal Joey 1963,My 30,21:1
King and I, The 1963,Je 13,30:2
I Had a Ball 1964,D 16,50:1
Kiss Me, Kate 1965,My 13,31:1
Oklahoma! 1965,D 16,62:1
Where's Charley? 1966,My 26,57:1
Davenport, Velle
Curious Savage, The 1956,Mr 17,12:3
Daver, Minoo
Prescott Proposals, The 1953,D 17,53:1
Prescott Proposals, The 1953,D 27,II,3:1
Daveris, George (Miscellaneous)
Tragical Historie of Doctor Faustus, The 1964,O 6,34:2
Davey, Leon (Scenic Designer)
Don't Listen, Ladies 1948,D 29,16:2
Davi, Cherleaes
Ghost of Elsinore, The 1949,Ap 16,10:2
Davia
Lulu 1927,O 2,VIII,2:4
David, Baruch
Dybbuk, The 1964,F 4,30:2
David, Benjamin (Producer)
Affair of State, An 1930,N 20,30:3
David, Bob
By Hex 1956,Je 19,25:1
David, Bob (Miscellaneous)
By Hex 1956,Je 19,25:1
David, Clifford
Burning Bright 1959,O 17,27:2
Caligula 1960,F 17,31:1
Caligula 1960,F 28,II,1:1
Wildcat 1960,D 17,20:2
Aspern Papers, The 1962,F 8,26:1
Boys From Syracuse, The 1963,Ap 16,31:1
Boys From Syracuse, The 1963,Je 2,II,1:1
Hamlet 1964,Je 17,49:1
Cradle Will Rock, The 1964,N 9,40:4
On a Clear Day You Can See Forever 1965,O 18,44:1
Joyful Noise, A 1966,D 16,57:1
1776 1969,Mr 17,46:2
1776 1969,Mr 23,II,1:1
Camino Real 1970,Ja 9,42:1
David, Frank
Macbeth 1936,Ap 15,25:4
David, Hal (Lyricist)
Promises, Promises 1968,D 2,59:3
Promises, Promises 1968,D 15,II,3:1
David, Jay
Lonesome West, The 1936,Je 30,15:1
David, Jean
Now You See It 1967,N 20,59:1
Beclch 1968,D 17,59:1
Moondreamers, The 1969,D 9,68:1
Dark of the Moon 1970,Ap 4,21:2
David, Jeff
Bacchae, The 1963,Ap 25,39:5
Arms and the Man 1965,Je 24,32:5
Butter and Egg Man, The 1966,O 18,49:1
Francesca da Rimini 1967,S 12,54:1
Hamlet 1967,D 27,45:1
Pequod 1969,Je 30,33:1
Memory Bank, The 1970,Ja 12,24:3
David, Jules
Farewell to Arms, A 1930,S 23,30:3
David, Lee (Composer)
Padlocks of 1927 1927,Jl 6,23:4
Night in Venice, A 1929,My 22,30:2
Broadway Nights 1929,Jl 16,23:2
David, Lee (Playwright)
Little Miss Door-Step 1924,Ap 1,18:1

David, Lou
Hooray!! It's a Glorious Day. . .And All That 1966,Mr 10,28:1
David, Lulla
Gentle People, The 1939,Ja 6,25:1
David, Mack (Lyricist)
Brights Lights of 1944 1943,S 17,27:4
David, Martin
Violet 1944,O 25,16:1
Farther Off From Heaven 1947,Je 4,33:3
David, Michael
Lark, The 1955,My 13,21:2
David, Michael (Director)
Slave Ship 1969,N 22,46:1
Brass Butterfly, The 1970,Ja 31,34:1
Universal Nigger, The 1970,Mr 21,18:1
Saved 1970,O 29,57:1
David, Miriam
Partition 1948,O 29,31:2
David, Sam (Playwright)
Of V We Sing 1941,O 26,I,39:1
David, Thayer
Relapse, The 1950,N 23,54:2
Taming of the Shrew, The 1951,Ap 26,35:2
Way of the World, The 1954,S 30,38:2
Way of the World, The 1954,O 17,II,1:1
White Devil, The 1955,Mr 15,32:5
Moby Dick 1955,Ap 26,25:3
Othello 1955,S 8,27:2
Henry IV, Part I 1955,S 22,34:2
Carefree Tree, The 1955,O 12,37:2
King Lear 1956,Ja 13,17:1
Mister Johnson 1956,Mr 30,11:1
Henry V 1956,Jl 7,11:2
Saint Joan 1956,S 12,42:1
Saint Joan 1956,S 16,II,1:1
Protective Custody 1956,D 29,8:7
Oscar Wilde 1957,Ap 20,21:3
Golden Six, The 1958,O 27,31:2
Andorra 1963,F 11,5:5
Seagull, The 1964,Ap 6,36:1
Crucible, The 1964,Ap 7,30:2
Royal Hunt of the Sun, The 1965,O 27,36:2
Those That Play the Clowns 1966,N 25,48:1
Bench, The 1968,Mr 5,35:2
David, William
Marry the Poor Girl 1920,S 27,18:3
Gentle Grafters 1926,O 28,23:1
Tonight at 12 1928,N 16,28:1
Ladies All 1930,Jl 29,25:2
Happy Landing 1932,Mr 28,10:5
Bad Manners 1933,Ja 31,15:5
I Myself 1934,My 10,24:6
Lady Detained, A 1935,Ja 10,23:3
Knock on Wood 1935,My 29,16:2
Sweet Mystery of Life 1935,O 12,13:3
Whatever Goes Up 1935,N 26,28:2
Tomorrow's a Holiday! 1935,D 31,10:2
Fulton of Oak Falls 1937,Ja 2,15:3
Fulton of Oak Falls 1937,F 11,18:2
Miss Quis 1937,Ap 8,20:5
Reno 1937,Ag 10,22:7
Prodigal Father, The 1937,Ag 17,23:1
Love in My Fashion 1937,D 4,21:4
Empress of Destiny 1938,Mr 10,16:2
Skylark 1939,O 12,32:2
Night Before Christmas, The 1941,Ap 11,25:2
All the Comforts of Home 1942,My 26,24:5
Million Dollar Baby 1945,D 22,17:2
Tenting Tonight 1947,Ap 3,32:2
Open House 1947,Je 4,33:4
High Button Shoes 1947,O 10,32:2
Mrs Gibsons' Boys 1949,My 5,35:2
Call Me Madam 1950,O 13,25:1
Pajama Game, The 1954,My 14,20:2
Pajama Game, The 1957,My 16,27:1
David, Worton (Playwright)
Afgar 1920,N 9,13:2
David (dog)
Double Door 1935,Ag 21,22:2
Davidge, William
Appearances 1925,O 15,27:3
Davidoff
Chauve-Souris 1922,Je 6,17:4
Chauve-Souris 1925,Ja 15,25:1
Davidoff, Judith
Play of Daniel, The 1966,Ja 2,64:4
Davidoss, Georg
Vaudeville (Hippodrome) 1926,My 8,29:2
Davidow, Edward (Producer)
Satellite 1935,N 21,27:5
Davids, Nancy (Producer)
Pin to See the Peepshow, A 1953,S 18,17:2
Davidsohn, George
Enchanting Melody 1964,N 25,40:1
Davidson, David Jr (Playwright)
Mountain Fury 1929,S 26,27:2
Davidson, Dore
Rollo's Wild Oat 1920,N 24,14:1
Davidson, Gordon (Director)
In the Matter of J Robert Oppenheimer 1968,My 27,55:1

Davidson, Gordon (Director)—Cont
In the Matter of J Robert Oppenheimer 1968,Je 7,31:1
In the Matter of J Robert Oppenheimer 1968,Je 9,II,1:1
In the Matter of J Robert Oppenheimer 1969,Mr 7,28:1
Murderous Angels 1970,F 8,70:1
Murderous Angels 1970,Mr 15,II,1:4
Trial of the Catonsville Nine, The 1970,Ag 16,II,1:7
Story Theater 1970,O 27,54:1
Davidson, Gordon (Miscellaneous)
From the Second City 1961,S 27,32:1
Next Time I'll Sing to You 1963,N 28,69:2
Right You Are (If You Think You Are) 1964,Mr 5,37:1
Tavern, The 1964,Mr 6,39:2
Scapin 1964,Mr 10,43:1
Impromptu at Versailles 1964,Mr 10,43:1
Lower Depths, The 1964,Mr 31,30:1
Davidson, Gretchen
Many Mansions 1937,O 28,28:6
Return of the Vagabond, The 1940,My 14,27:2
Davidson, Gustav (Playwright)
Night in Spring, A 1935,Ag 7,22:2
Davidson, Gustav (Translator)
Rapid Transit 1927,Ap 8,21:2
Davidson, H E S (Playwright)
Truth Game, The 1928,O 21,IX,1:3
Davidson, Helen
Ice Capades 1952,S 12,18:1
Ice Capades 1953,S 11,25:1
Ice Capades 1954,S 16,37:1
Ice Capades 1955,S 15,38:1
Ice Capades 1956,S 13,41:2
Ice Capades 1957,S 5,33:2
Davidson, Irwin
Bolls of Cotton 1925,D 22,18:3
Yo Ho Hum 1927,My 7,15:1
Davidson, Irwin (Playwright)
Yo Ho Hum 1927,My 7,15:1
Davidson, James
Traitor, The 1949,Ap 1,30:2
Davidson, Jo (Costume Designer)
Grand Street Follies, The 1924,My 21,22:2
Davidson, John
Business Widow, The 1923,D 11,27:1
Locked Door, The 1924,Je 20,17:2
Clubs Are Trumps 1924,O 15,27:1
Loves of Lulu, The 1925,My 12,26:1
It Is to Laugh 1927,D 27,24:2
Foxy 1964,F 17,26:1
Oklahoma! 1965,D 16,62:1
Davidson, Joseph
New Freedom, The 1930,My 15,32:4
New Freedom, The 1930,My 17,21:4
Davidson, Ken
Laugh, Town, Laugh! 1942,Je 23,22:2
Davidson, Madeline
Four in Hand 1923,S 7,10:2
Gift, The 1924,Ja 23,15:4
Flesh 1925,My 8,22:3
Davidson, Margaret
Nights of Wrath; Nuits de la Colere, Les 1947,D 1,26:4
Davidson, Michael (Lighting Director)
Bench, The 1968,Mr 5,35:2
Get Thee to Canterbury 1969,Ja 26,74:1
Next 1969,F 11,27:1
Adaptation 1969,F 11,27:1
Corner of the Bed, A 1969,F 27,35:2
No Place to Be Somebody 1969,My 5,53:3
World of Mrs Solomon, The; Another Chance 1969,Je 4,37:1
World of Mrs Solomon, The; Second Mrs Aarons, The 1969,Je 4,37:1
Rose 1969,O 29,30:1
No Place to Be Somebody 1969,D 31,17:1
Davidson, Michael (Scenic Designer)
Collision Course; Camera Obscura 1968,My 9,55:2
Collision Course; Skywriting 1968,My 9,55:2
Collision Course; Unexpurgated Memoirs of Bernard Mergendeiler, The 1968,My 9,55:2
Collision Course; Thoughts on the Instant of Greeting a Friend on the Street 1968,My 9,55:2
Collision Course; Rats 1968,My 9,55:2
Collision Course; Chuck 1968,My 9,55:2
Collision Course; Jew! 1968,My 9,55:2
Collision Course; Tour 1968,My 9,55:2
Collision Course; Stars and Stripes 1968,My 9,55:2
Collision Course; Metaphors 1968,My 9,55:2
Collision Course; Wandering 1968,My 9,55:2
No Place to Be Somebody 1969,My 5,53:3
No Place to Be Somebody 1969,D 31,17:1
Davidson, Milton (Composer)
Traveling Lady 1954,O 28,45:2
Davidson, Mr
Merry Wives of West Point, The 1932,Mr 20,II,7:7
Davidson, N R (Playwright)
Hajj Malik, El 1970,O 4,II,5:1
Davidson, Richard
Nobody's Child 1956,Ag 23,25:2
Henry VI 1966,Je 9,55:2

Davidson, Richard (Playwright)
Nobody's Child 1956,Ag 23,25:2
Davidson, Richard (Producer)
Enchanted, The 1950,Ja 19,34:2
Davidson, Roy (Playwright)
Right of Happiness 1931,Ap 3,34:2
Davidson, Sam E (Translator)
To Damascus 1961,F 15,40:2
Davidson, Sue (Miscellaneous)
Sally 1948,My 7,31:2
Enchanted, The 1950,Ja 19,34:2
Davidson, Sybil
Nine Till Six 1930,S 29,17:2
Davidson, W B
June Love 1921,Ap 26,20:1
Davidson, William
Listening In 1922,D 5,24:1
Davidson, William (Miscellaneous)
Javelin 1966,N 10,63:1
Davie, Cedric Thorpe (Composer)
Oedipus Rex 1954,Jl 17,6:6
Davies, Arthur
Chivalry 1925,D 16,22:3
Oh, Promise Me 1930,N 25,31:1
Mr Papavert 1932,Ja 23,18:6
Davies, Betty Ann
Women of Twilight 1952,Mr 4,22:2
Davies, Blair
Chalked Out 1937,Mr 26,24:2
Blow Ye Winds 1937,S 24,17:4
Solitaire 1942,Ja 28,22:2
Hidden Horizon 1946,S 20,42:2
Temporary Island, A 1948,Mr 15,27:3
Davies, Brian
Sound of Music, The 1959,N 17,40:2
Funny Thing Happened on the Way to the Forum,
A 1962,My 9,49:1
Davies, Carlotta
Squealer, The 1928,N 13,36:3
Davies, Dai
Midsummer Night's Dream, A 1968,D 9,59:1
Davies, Dawn
Pirates of Penzance, The 1964,N 27,43:1
Davies, Edgar (Producer)
Gates of Summer, The 1970,Je 16,53:2
Davies, Elaine
Nobody's Business 1923,O 23,17:1
Puppets of Passion 1927,F 25,24:4
Davies, Fanille
Natja 1925,F 17,19:2
Davies, Harry
Drifting 1922,Ja 3,20:3
That Awful Mrs Eaton! 1924,S 30,27:1
Davies, Harry Parr (Composer)
Dear Miss Phoebe 1950,O 14,13:8
Davies, Henry
Opportunity 1920,Jl 31,5:1
Leah Kleschna 1924,Ap 22,19:2
Davies, Irving
Joyce Grenfell Requests the Pleasure
1955,O 11,48:1
Davies, Irving (Choreographer)
Joyce Grenfell Requests the Pleasure
1955,O 11,48:1
Davies, James
Utopia, Limited 1960,Ap 8,27:2
Davies, Joe
Long Voyage Home, The 1961,D 5,49:1
Time of the Key, A 1963,S 12,33:3
Davies, Joe (Costume Designer)
Goose, The 1960,Mr 16,44:1
Long Voyage Home, The 1961,D 5,49:1
Creditors 1962,Ja 26,19:1
Davies, John
Whatever Goes Up 1935,N 26,28:2
Davies, Joseph
Good Soldier Schweik, The 1963,Ap 9,57:1
Davies, Joseph C
Open 24 Hours 1969,F 12,31:1
Gandhi 1970,O 21,37:1
Davies, Joseph C (Costume Designer)
Silhouettes 1969,S 9,41:1
Davies, Joseph C (Scenic Designer)
Silhouettes 1969,S 9,41:1
Davies, Kitty
Midsummer Night's Dream, A 1957,Je 27,21:3
Davies, Lilian
Katja 1926,O 19,27:3
Davies, Margaret
Greenwich Village Follies 1920,Ag 31,7:3
Earl Carroll's Vanities 1923,Jl 6,8:2
Earl Carroll's Vanities 1924,S 11,23:6
Davies, Marjorie
Highland Fling, A 1944,Ap 29,13:2
Davies, Patricia
Witchfinders, The 1956,My 11,22:6
Davies, Ridler
Passion Flower, The 1920,Ja 14,12:1
Davies, Rita
Blind Mice 1930,O 16,28:2
Love on the Dole 1936,F 25,23:3
Davies, Robertson (Playwright)
Love and Libel 1960,D 8,44:1

Davies, Rupert
Troilus and Cressida 1956,D 27,21:1
Davies, Sarah
Twelfth Night 1966,Je 10,51:2
Davies, Spencer (Scenic Designer)
Billy Barnes People, The 1961,Je 14,10:3
Davies, Timothy
Measure for Measure 1967,F 15,37:1
Hamlet 1967,F 17,44:1
Romeo and Juliet 1967,F 22,18:1
Davies, Tom Trio
Vaudeville (Palace) 1924,Ap 29,12:2
Vaudeville (Palace) 1924,S 30,27:5
Vaudeville (Hippodrome) 1926,Ap 27,22:3
Davies, Valentine (Lyricist)
Tambourine 1925,D 30,10:2
Davies, Valentine (Original Author)
Here's Love 1963,O 4,28:1
Davies, Valentine (Playwright)
Tambourine 1925,D 30,10:2
Three Times the Hour 1931,Ag 26,15:5
Keeper of the Keys 1933,O 19,23:2
Blow Ye Winds 1937,S 8,20:5
Blow Ye Winds 1937,S 24,17:4
Davila, Diana
Midsummer Night's Dream, A 1967,Je 19,42:1
Song of the Grasshopper 1967,S 29,52:2
Prime of Miss Jean Brodie, The 1968,Ja 17,39:1
What the Butler Saw 1970,My 5,56:1
Davila, Raul
Vida es Sueno, La 1964,Mr 18,49:1
Davin, Paul
Sweethearts 1929,S 23,25:1
Davini, Davide
Giuochi di Prestigio 1931,N 2,26:1
Davini, Mr
Civil Death, The 1932,Ja 25,20:3
Davion, Alexander
Matchmaker, The 1955,D 6,45:6
Daviot, Gordon (Playwright)
Richard of Bordeaux 1933,F 26,IX,3:1
Richard of Bordeaux 1934,F 4,IX,2:2
Richard of Bordeaux 1934,F 15,16:2
Richard of Bordeaux 1934,F 25,IX,1:1
Laughing Woman, The 1934,Ap 8,33:6
Laughing Lady, The 1934,My 6,IX,2:5
Queen of Scots 1934,Je 9,18:5
Queen of Scots 1934,Jl 15,X,1:3
Laughing Woman, The 1936,Jl 8,14:7
Laughing Woman, The 1936,O 14,30:1
Davis, Agnes
Variations of 1940 1940,Ja 29,12:1
Davis, Alan
Seven 1929,D 28,10:5
I Want My Wife 1930,Mr 21,30:7
Life Is Like That 1930,D 23,24:3
Arms for Venus 1937,Mr 12,18:7
Davis, Alida
Kai Khosru 1925,Ap 27,14:2
Davis, Allan
Skull, The 1928,Ap 24,28:3
Davis, Allan (Composer)
From Here to There; Otherwise Engaged
1958,Ap 24,37:3
Davis, Allan (Director)
Someone Waiting 1956,F 15,26:1
Keep It in the Family 1967,S 28,59:1
Come as You Are 1970,Ag 12,32:1
Davis, Allan (Playwright)
Gypsy Fires 1925,D 8,28:3
From Here to There; Otherwise Engaged
1958,Ap 24,37:3
Davis, Allan S
Tragedy of the Ages, The 1933,Ap 7,22:7
Davis, Allen 3d
Merry Wives of Windsor, The 1954,F 17,27:1
Davis, Allen 3d (Director)
Clandestine on the Morning Line 1961,O 31,28:1
Davis, Allen 3d (Miscellaneous)
When Did You Last See My Mother?
1967,Ja 5,27:5
Golden Streets, The 1970,Ag 14,21:1
Davis, Amon
Pansy 1929,My 15,36:3
Kilpatrick's Old-Time Minstrels 1930,Ap 21,20:2
Hot Rhythm 1930,Ag 22,18:5
Davis, Anis
Second Comin', The 1931,D 9,32:4
Davis, Ann
Beware of Dogs 1921,O 4,10:1
Not so Fast 1923,My 23,18:4
Catskill Dutch 1924,My 7,18:1
Virgin of Bethulia, The 1925,F 24,17:2
Accused 1925,S 20,VIII,2:4
Accused 1925,S 30,20:1
Love Is Like That 1927,Ap 19,24:1
Mid-Channel 1928,S 16,IX,1:4
Marriage Bed, The 1929,Ja 8,35:1
Bon Voyage 1929,D 29,VIII,4:3
She Means Business 1931,Ja 27,21:2
Davis, Audrey
Stepping Out 1929,My 21,29:1
Sex Fable, The 1931,O 21,26:1

Davis, Audrey—Cont
Through the Years 1932,Ja 29,13:3
Little Black Book, The 1932,D 27,11:2
Merrily We Roll Along 1936,Je 30,15:1
Davis, Augusta
Bulldog Drummond 1921,D 27,10:2
Davis, Bancroft G (Playwright)
Assorted Nuts 1940,Ap 7,I,44:6
Davis, Barbara
Bring Me a Warm Body 1962,Ap 17,29:3
Davis, Barry (Director)
Would You Look At Them Smashing All the
Lovely Windows! 1969,S 5,30:1
Davis, Benny
Vaudeville (Palace) 1928,O 2,35:1
Vaudeville (Palace) 1929,Mr 18,30:5
Vaudeville (Palace) 1930,S 22,23:2
Vaudeville (Loew's State) 1932,Jl 18,9:7
Davis, Benny (Composer)
Carry On 1929,N 3,IX,1:7
Sons o' Guns 1929,N 27,30:4
Take a Bow 1944,Je 16,15:3
Davis, Benny (Director)
Cotton Club Revue of 1957 1957,Jl 10,23:4
Davis, Benny (Lyricist)
Artists and Models 1927,N 16,28:2
Sons o' Guns 1929,N 27,30:4
Davis, Benny (Playwright)
Cotton Club Revue of 1957 1957,Jl 10,23:4
Davis, Berton
Louisiana Lady 1947,Je 3,35:2
Davis, Bertram (Playwright)
Katinka 1923,Ag 31,15:4
Davis, Bessie McCoy (Director)
What Next 1920,Ja 27,7:2
Davis, Bette
Earth Between, The 1929,Mr 6,33:1
Broken Dishes 1929,N 6,28:3
Nina Rosa 1930,My 31,19:3
Solid South 1930,O 15,27:1
Marching By 1932,Mr 4,17:1
Music Hath Charms 1934,D 31,8:2
Roberta 1937,Je 27,II,6:1
Blossom Time 1938,D 27,12:2
Two's Company 1952,D 16,43:5
Two's Company 1952,D 21,II,3:1
World of Carl Sandburg, The 1959,O 13,44:6
World of Carl Sandburg, The 1959,O 26,53:3
World of Carl Sandburg, The 1960,S 15,44:1
World of Carl Sandburg, The 1960,S 25,II,1:1
Night of the Iguana, The 1961,D 29,10:1
Night of the Iguana, The 1962,Ja 7,II,1:1
Davis, Blevins (Director)
Attack 1942,S 8,13:4
Merchant of Venice, The 1950,My 3,37:2
Davis, Blevins (Lyricist)
Rhapsody 1944,N 23,37:2
Davis, Blevins (Miscellaneous)
Hamlet 1949,Je 18,9:6
Davis, Blevins (Playwright)
Attack 1942,S 8,13:4
Davis, Blevins (Producer)
Rhapsody 1944,N 23,37:2
Joy Forever, A 1946,Ja 8,20:2
Porgy and Bess 1952,Ag 6,17:7
Porgy and Bess 1953,F 17,21:1
Porgy and Bess 1953,Mr 10,25:5
Porgy and Bess 1954,S 23,42:6
Porgy and Bess 1954,D 17,36:7
Porgy and Bess 1955,F 8,23:4
Davis, Bob
Let Freedom Sing 1942,O 6,18:2
Davis, Bootsie
Rain 1948,F 2,15:2
Davis, Boyd
Fake, The 1924,O 7,26:3
Arabesque 1925,O 21,20:2
Girl Trouble 1928,O 26,22:3
Meet My Sister 1930,D 31,11:1
Smiling Faces 1931,D 13,VIII,2:5
Smiling Faces 1932,Ag 31,12:3
Conquest 1933,F 20,11:3
No More Ladies 1934,Ja 24,20:3
No More Ladies 1934,S 4,23:2
Living Dangerously 1935,Ja 14,10:3
If This Be Treason 1935,Jl 30,17:1
If This Be Treason 1935,S 24,28:2
There's Wisdom in Women 1935,O 31,17:1
Fresh Fields 1936,F 11,19:2
Fresh Fields 1936,Je 23,27:3
White Christmas 1936,Jl 7,22:2
Seen But Not Heard 1936,S 18,19:2
Virginian, The 1937,Ag 10,22:7
Yes, My Darling Daughter 1938,Je 14,17:1
What Every Woman Knows 1938,Ag 30,14:5
Lorelei 1938,N 30,21:2
Slightly Scandalous 1944,Je 14,16:2
Davis, Brian
You Said It 1931,Ja 20,21:3
Bitter Sweet 1934,My 8,28:4
Davis, Buster (Miscellaneous)
Make a Wish 1951,Ap 19,38:1
Bells Are Ringing 1956,N 29,43:4
Bells Are Ringing 1956,N 30,18:2

Davis, Buster (Miscellaneous)—Cont
First Impressions 1959,Mr 20,28:1
Do Re Mi 1960,D 27,23:2
Funny Girl 1964,Mr 27,15:1
Fade Out--Fade In 1964,My 27,45:1
Something More! 1964,N 11,36:1
Look to the Lilies 1970,Mr 30,59:1
Davis, Buster (Musical Director)
John Murray Anderson's Almanac 1953,D 11,42:2
Phoenix '55 1955,Ap 25,20:2
Best Foot Forward 1963,Ap 3,43:1
Hallelujah, Baby! 1967,Ap 27,51:1
Darling of the Day 1968,Ja 29,26:2
Davis, Buster (Producer)
Best Foot Forward 1963,Ap 3,43:1
Davis, C H
Pure in Heart, The 1934,Mr 21,24:3
Davis, C M Bootsie
Native Son 1941,Mr 25,26:5
Native Son 1942,O 24,10:6
Davis, C T
House Divided, The 1923,N 12,14:1
Old Bill, M P 1926,N 11,22:2
Romancing 'Round 1927,O 4,32:4
Davis, C T (Director)
Romancing 'Round 1927,O 4,32:4
Davis, Carl (Composer)
Diversions 1958,N 8,14:4
Davis, Carl E
Many a Slip 1940,N 16,12:7
Davis, Carl E Jr (Composer)
Fol-De-Rol 1937,D 11,22:4
Once Over Lightly 1938,D 10,13:4
Davis, Carl E Jr (Lyricist)
Fol-De-Rol 1937,D 11,22:4
Once Over Lightly 1938,D 10,13:4
Davis, Carl F (Playwright)
Any Moment Now 1939,N 25,13:6
Davis, Carlos E
Romeo y Julieta 1965,Ag 28,13:3
Davis, Carroll J
Criminal Code, The 1929,O 3,28:2
Davis, Charles
Bachelor's Brides 1925,My 29,20:2
Honeymoon Lane 1926,S 21,32:3
Desert Song, The 1926,D 1,24:2
Rosalie 1928,Ja 11,26:3
If I Were You 1931,S 24,21:1
Bloody Laughter 1931,D 5,20:6
Birthright 1933,N 22,22:3
Slave Ship 1969,N 22,46:1
Davis, Charles (Choreographer)
My Magnolia 1926,Jl 13,19:2
Rang Tang 1927,Jl 13,20:1
Davis, Charles (Director)
Brown Buddies 1930,O 8,29:1
Davis, Charles H
We the People 1933,Ja 23,9:5
Davis, Charlotte
Bye Bye, Barbara 1924,Ag 26,6:3
Davis, Cherry
Damn Yankees 1955,My 6,17:1
As You Like It 1958,Ja 21,33:6
She Shall Have Music 1959,Ja 23,18:4
Miss Emily Adam 1960,Mr 30,43:1
Madame Aphrodite 1961,D 30,13:1
Oliver 1963,Ja 8,5:5
Beggar on Horseback 1970,My 15,47:2
Davis, Christopher (Original Author)
There Was a Little Girl 1960,Mr 1,28:1
Davis, Cleland
Saint's Parade 1930,N 1,23:4
Davis, Clifford
Cradle Will Rock, The 1964,N 9,40:4
Davis, Clifton
How to Steal an Election 1968,O 14,56:1
Horseman, Pass By 1969,Ja 16,46:4
Engagement Baby, The 1970,My 22,40:1
Davis, Constance
Men in White 1955,F 26,13:2
Davis, Courtlandt
Young Madame Conti 1937,Ap 1,18:4
Davis, D
Pansy 1929,My 15,36:3
Davis, Daniel
Wild Oats Lane 1922,S 7,12:1
Davis, Danny
Henry V 1969,Je 9,57:1
Hamlet 1969,Je 30,33:1
Henry V 1969,N 11,43:1
All's Well That Ends Well 1970,Je 16,53:1
Othello 1970,Je 22,43:1
Othello 1970,S 15,51:1
Davis, David
Mister Roberts 1956,D 6,46:2
Annie Get Your Gun 1957,Mr 9,15:5
Davis, Diane
New Faces of 1943 1942,D 23,22:2
Davis, Dona (Producer)
It's an Ill Wind 1957,Ap 24,28:1
Davis, Donald
Oedipus Rex 1954,Jl 17,6:6
Julius Caesar 1955,Je 29,23:3
Tamburlaine the Great 1956,Ja 20,19:1

Henry V 1956,Je 20,27:2
Merry Wives of Windsor, The 1956,Je 21,34:4
Glass Cage, The 1957,Mr 11,21:2
Krapp's Last Tape 1960,Ja 15,37:2
Krapp's Last Tape 1960,Ja 31,II,1:1
Twelfth Night 1960,Je 9,29:4
Antony and Cleopatra 1960,Ag 1,19:1
As You Like It 1961,Je 17,13:2
Macbeth 1961,Je 19,31:1
As You Like It 1961,Je 25,II,1:1
Troilus and Cressida 1961,Jl 24,15:1
Creditors 1962,Ja 26,19:1
Photo Finish 1963,F 14,5:2
Evening's Frost, An 1965,O 12,56:1
Oresteia 1966,Je 30,29:1
Birds, The 1966,Jl 1,40:1
Elizabeth the Queen 1966,N 4,30:1
American Dream, The 1968,O 3,55:1
Zoo Story, The 1968,O 11,41:1
Krapp's Last Tape 1968,O 11,41:1
Merchant of Venice, The 1970,Je 10,39:1
Hedda Gabler 1970,Je 12,28:1
Merchant of Venice, The 1970,Je 21,II,1:1
Davis, Donald (Miscellaneous)
Donovan Affair, The 1926,Ag 31,15:2
Ethan Frome 1936,Ja 22,15:2
Davis, Donald (Playwright)
Gone Hollywood 1930,D 28,VIII,2:1
Good Earth, The 1932,S 25,IX,1:6
Good Earth, The 1932,O 18,23:4
Good Earth, The 1932,O 23,IX,1:1
Haunch, Paunch and Jowl 1935,D 27,22:4
Ethan Frome 1936,Ja 7,24:7
Ethan Frome 1936,F 2,IX,1:1
Davis, Donald (Producer)
Glass Cage, The 1957,Mr 11,21:2
Davis, Doris
Saint of Bleecker Street, The 1954,D 28,21:1
Young and Beautiful, The 1959,My 29,13:1
Davis, Dorrance (Playwright)
Sable Coat, The 1924,Jl 6,VII,1:1
Busybody, The 1924,S 30,27:5
Shelf, The 1926,S 28,31:1
Lady in Love, A 1927,F 22,22:1
Lady in Love, A 1927,F 27,VII,1:1
Apron Strings 1930,F 18,28:2
Apron Strings 1930,F 27,JI 13,22:3
Davis, E H (Miscellaneous)
Leader, The 1969,Ap 22,40:2
Honest-to-God Schnozzola, The 1969,Ap 22,40:2
Davis, Eddie (Original Author)
Hold On to Your Hats 1940,S 12,30:3
Davis, Eddie (Playwright)
Bare Facts of Today 1930,Ap 17,24:4
Scandals 1939,Ag 29,17:2
Follow the Girls 1944,Ap 10,15:2
Follow the Girls 1944,Ap 16,II,1:2
Ankles Aweigh 1955,Ap 19,27:1
Ankles Aweigh 1955,Ap 24,II,1:1
Davis, Edgar B (Producer)
Ladder, The 1927,O 7,24:2
Davis, Edith
Tell Her the Truth 1932,O 29,18:2
Davis, Edward
Policy Kings 1938,D 31,6:2
Davis, Edward H (Miscellaneous)
Pleasure of His Company, The 1958,O 23,36:1
Gazebo, The 1958,D 13,2:7
Davis, Edward H (Producer)
Great Scot! 1965,N 12,56:3
Davis, Elizabeth
Julius Caesar 1962,F 22,19:6
Davis, Emery
Cave Dwellers, The 1957,O 21,29:2
Davis, Estelle H (Director)
Contrast, The 1926,O 1,26:2
Davis, Ethel
Greenwich Village Follies 1924,S 17,16:1
Vaudeville (Palace) 1926,Ap 27,22:3
Vaudeville (Palace) 1927,S 13,36:3
Vaudeville (Palace) 1929,F 11,26:2
Davis, Eugene (Playwright)
Ten Per Cent 1927,S 14,29:3
Davis, Evelyn
Vickie 1942,S 23,28:1
Perfect Marriage, The 1944,O 27,17:6
Flamingo Road 1946,Mr 20,18:2
How Long Till Summer 1949,D 28,30:3
Southern Exposure 1950,S 27,36:3
Wisteria Trees, The 1955,F 3,20:2
Sound of Silence, A 1965,Mr 9,30:1
Davis, Fay
Second Mrs Tanqueray, The 1922,Jl 9,VI,1:1
Davis, Fitzroy K
Good Hunting 1938,N 22,26:5
Davis, Foster
Reclining Figure 1954,O 8,26:5
Davis, Frank
Frivolities of 1920 1920,Ja 9,22:2
Romeo and Juliet 1923,Ja 25,16:1
Vaudeville (Palace) 1927,N 22,33:2
Hear! Hear! 1955,S 28,38:1
Judy Garland's New Variety Show 1956,S 27,43:2

Davis, Franklin
How Beautiful With Shoes 1935,N 29,24:1
Wingless Victory, The 1936,D 24,20:2
Davis, Fred
Kiss Me, Kate 1948,D 31,10:3
Davis, Garry
Three to Make Ready 1946,Mr 8,16:2
Bless You All 1950,D 15,42:2
Stalag 17 1951,My 9,41:2
Davis, George
Good Times 1920,Ag 10,10:1
Doughgirls, The 1942,D 31,19:2
Davis, Geri (Scenic Designer)
Phedre 1966,F 11,36:1
Davis, Gertrude
Prince and the Pauper, The 1920,N 2,15:1
Aiglon, L' 1927,D 27,24:3
Divided by Three 1934,O 3,24:2
Davis, Grosvenor
Lid's Off, The 1936,Ap 4,11:6
Davis, Gwen (Playwright)
Best Laid Plans, The 1966,Mr 26,15:2
Davis, H Tyrrell
Simon Called Peter 1924,N 11,20:2
She Had to Know 1925,F 3,25:3
Antonia 1925,O 21,20:1
Davis, Hallie Flanagan (Playwright)
E-MC2 1948,Je 16,36:2
Davis, Harris
Yeomen of the Guard, The 1968,My 9,53:1
Davis, Harry
Bitter Stream 1936,Mr 31,16:6
Fifth Column, The 1940,Mr 7,18:2
Jacobowsky and the Colonel 1944,Mr 15,17:2
All You Need Is One Good Break 1950,F 10,20:3
Bravo Giovanni 1962,My 21,41:2
West Side Story 1964,Ap 9,24:2
Masks of Angels 1965,Ja 20,33:1
Anna Kleiber 1965,Ja 20,33:1
Davis, Hazel (Choreographer)
Swing Mikado, The 1939,Mr 2,18:2
Davis, Henry
Young Alexander 1929,Mr 13,28:2
Change Your Luck 1930,Je 7,10:2
Sailor, Beware! 1935,My 7,28:4
Porgy and Bess 1935,O 11,30:2
Porgy and Bess 1942,Ja 23,16:2
Porgy and Bess 1943,S 14,26:2
Porgy and Bess 1944,F 8,13:2
Davis, Herb
Entertain a Ghost 1962,Ap 10,48:1
Raisin' Hell in the Son 1962,Jl 3,13:2
Volpone 1967,Je 30,29:1
Henry IV, Part I 1968,Je 30,54:7
Henry IV, Part II 1968,Jl 2,33:1
Henry V 1969,Je 9,57:1
Hamlet 1969,Je 30,33:1
Davis, Humphrey
First American Dictator 1939,Mr 15,18:2
Hook'n Ladder 1952,Ap 30,31:2
Corn Is Green, The 1954,F 27,10:2
Jolly's Progress 1959,D 7,42:2
Saving Grace, The 1963,Ap 19,28:1
Once for the Asking 1963,N 21,42:2
Dream of Swallows, A 1964,Ap 15,46:1
Who's Who, Baby? 1968,Ja 30,36:1
Davis, Humphrey (Director)
First American Dictator 1939,Mr 15,18:2
Davis, Irving Kaye (Playwright)
Right to Dream, The 1924,My 27,14:2
Veils 1928,Mr 14,28:5
Diana 1929,D 10,37:1
Courtesan 1930,Ap 30,29:3
All Rights Reserved 1934,N 7,33:5
So Many Paths 1934,D 7,26:5
Last Stop 1944,S 6,17:2
Davis, Irving Kaye (Producer)
With a Silk Thread 1950,Ap 13,34:3
Davis, J Frank (Playwright)
Ladder, The 1926,Je 27,VII,3:1
Ladder, The 1926,S 26,VIII,2:7
Ladder, The 1926,O 23,15:1
Ladder, The 1927,O 7,24:2
Davis, J P (Translator)
Cherry Orchard, The 1970,My 7,63:2
Davis, Jack
Rendezvous 1932,O 13,22:3
Pardon My English 1933,Ja 21,11:4
Tragedy of the Ages, The 1933,Ap 7,22:7
They All Come to Moscow 1933,My 12,20:6
Every Thursday 1934,My 11,25:5
Paths of Glory 1935,S 27,24:2
Whatever Goes Up 1935,N 26,28:2
So Proudly We Hail 1936,S 23,28:4
Greatest Show on Earth, The 1938,Ja 6,22:2
Rosalie 1957,Je 26,28:2
Davis, James
Change Your Luck 1930,Je 7,10:2
Louisiana 1933,F 28,15:5
Serjeant Musgrave's Dance 1966,Mr 9,44:1
Riot 1968,D 20,64:1
Davis, James E (Costume Designer)
Man From Earth, The 1923,Ja 3,6:2

Davis, James P (Playwright)
Run, Thief, Run 1957,My 2,27:1
Davis, James P (Producer)
Run, Thief, Run 1957,My 2,27:1
Davis, Jane
Dear Judas 1947,O 6,26:4
Davis, Jay
Sweet Genevieve 1945,Mr 21,27:3
Davis, Jean
Vaudeville (Palace) 1932,S 12,13:5
Gondoliers, The 1944,F 22,26:3
Davis, Jennie
Tonight We Improvise 1959,N 7,27:4
Marrying Maiden, The 1960,Je 23,18:3
Dance of Death, The 1960,S 14,51:1
Davis, Joan
Vaudeville (Palace) 1931,O 19,28:5
Davis, Joe (Lighting Director)
Irma la Douce 1960,S 30,31:2
Marlene Dietrich 1967,O 10,52:1
Marlene Dietrich 1968,O 4,36:1
Davis, Joe (Producer)
Bill Noname 1970,Mr 3,37:1
Davis, John
Sam Abramovitch 1927,Ja 20,20:5
Mimie Scheller 1936,O 1,28:4
Davis, John (Lighting Director)
Burning Glass, The 1954,Mr 5,15:2
Davis, John C
Romeo and Juliet 1922,D 28,20:1
What Price Glory 1924,S 6,14:3
Volpone 1928,Ap 10,32:1
Marco Millions 1930,Mr 4,24:4
Volpone 1930,Mr 11,24:5
If Booth Had Missed 1932,F 5,24:2
Davis, John W
Wars of the Roses, The (Part II) 1970,Jl 3,15:1
Davis, Joseph C
Satisfaction Guaranteed 1969,F 12,31:1
Davis, Joyce
Time of the Key, A 1963,S 12,33:3
Davis, Jud
Tree Witch, The 1961,Je 5,39:4
Life and Times of J Walter Smintheus, The
1970,D 10,59:1
Davis, Judith (Costume Designer)
Galileo 1963,Ja 5,5:2
Davis, Judith (Scenic Designer)
Galileo 1963,Ja 5,5:2
Davis, Julia (Playwright)
Anvil, The 1962,O 31,33:3
Davis, Ken
Kongi's Harvest 1968,Ap 15,49:1
Davis, Kenneth
Sign of the Leopard 1928,D 12,34:4
Peter Pan 1950,Ap 25,27:2
Davis, Lanier
Tenderloin 1960,O 18,47:2
Davis, Lanier (Miscellaneous)
Wait a Minim! 1966,Mr 8,43:1
Davis, Lauman
Taps 1925,Ap 15,16:2
Davis, Lee
Follow the Girls 1944,Ap 10,15:2
Davis, Luther (Playwright)
Kiss Them for Me 1945,Mr 21,27:2
Kiss Them for Me 1945,Mr 25,II,1:1
Kismet 1953,D 4,2:4
At the Grand 1958,Ag 13,24:3
Kismet 1965,Je 23,45:1
Davis, M S
Espanola 1921,D 30,13:1
Davis, Mack (Playwright)
Crazy With the Heat 1941,Ja 15,18:2
Davis, Mae
Nativity Play, The 1937,D 21,29:1
Davis, Mag
Dead End 1935,O 29,17:2
Davis, Mallory
Grey Fox, The 1928,O 23,32:3
Davis, Marguerite
417 1961,Mr 6,30:1
Salad of the Mad Cafe, The 1964,Ap 1,43:1
Davis, Marianne
Red Cat, The 1934,S 20,21:1
Davis, Marion
Ed Wynn's Carnival 1920,Ap 6,18:2
Davis, Mary Jo
John Turner Davis 1958,Jl 2,25:1
Davis, Mary Newnham
And So to Bed 1927,N 10,23:1
Cherry Orchard, The 1928,Mr 6,20:1
Musical Chairs 1934,Jl 31,20:7
Davis, Maude
Keep Off the Grass 1940,My 5,X,1:6
Keep Off the Grass 1940,My 24,22:6
Davis, Melvin
Injury Sustained 1940,O 24,30:3
Night Watch In Syria 1943,Ja 5,15:5
Familiar Pattern 1943,S 3,15:6
Davis, Meyer (Miscellaneous)
Hollywood Pinafore 1945,Je 1,20:1

Davis, Meyer (Producer)
Run, Little Chillun 1943,Ag 14,6:1
Wallflower 1944,Ja 27,14:2
Dark Hammock 1944,D 12,27:8
Sophie 1944,D 26,22:7
Davis, Meyer and His Orchestra
Vaudeville (Palace) 1929,Jl 8,17:6
Davis, Michael
Most Happy Fella, The 1959,F 11,50:2
All in Love 1961,N 11,15:2
Pilgrim's Progress 1962,Mr 21,36:2
Sweet Charity 1966,Ja 31,22:1
Lady or the Tiger?, The 1966,O 19,53:1
Passionella 1966,O 19,53:1
Dear World 1969,F 7,33:1
Promenade 1969,Je 5,56:1
Look to the Lilies 1970,Mr 30,59:1
Davis, Michael (Producer)
Come Play With Me 1959,My 1,33:5
Thurber Carnival, A 1960,F 27,13:2
Davis, Mildred
Child of the Morning 1958,Ap 22,40:2
Davis, Murray
Glass Cage, The 1957,Mr 11,21:2
Davis, Murray (Director)
Long and the Short and the Tall, The
1962,Mr 30,28:2
Davis, Murray (Producer)
Glass Cage, The 1957,Mr 11,21:2
Davis, Nancy
Lute Song 1946,F 7,29:2
Davis, Naomi
Anthony on Overtime 1961,O 21,13:2
Davis, Nat
Room of Dreams 1930,N 6,22:4
Davis, Nathaniel
School for Scandal, The 1923,Mr 13,19:2
Davis, Nathaniel (Playwright)
Air-Minded 1932,F 11,17:3
Davis, Nesther
Little Inn, The 1935,Ag 20,25:1
Davis, Noel
One Way Pendulum 1961,S 19,38:2
Passage to India, A 1962,F 1,23:1
Creeper, The 1965,Jl 15,21:1
Davis, Ossie
Jeb 1946,F 22,20:2
Leading Lady 1948,O 19,33:1
Smile of the World, The 1949,Ja 13,26:5
Stevedore 1949,F 23,30:2
Wisteria Trees, The 1950,Mr 30,39:1
Royal Family, The 1951,Ja 11,28:2
Green Pastures, The 1951,Mr 16,35:2
Green Pastures, The 1951,Ap 1,II,1:1
Remains to Be Seen 1951,O 4,37:1
Touchstone 1953,F 4,33:2
Wisteria Trees, The 1955,F 3,20:2
Jamaica 1957,N 1,32:2
Purlie Victorious 1961,S 29,29:1
Purlie Victorious 1961,O 8,II,1:1
Ballad for Bimshire 1963,O 16,54:1
Zulu and the Zayda, The 1965,N 11,59:1
Davis, Ossie (Playwright)
Big Deal, The 1953,Mr 7,13:6
Purlie Victorious 1961,S 29,29:1
Purlie Victorious 1961,O 8,II,1:1
Purlie Victorious 1962,Ap 29,II,1:1
Purlie 1970,Mr 16,53:1
Purlie Victorious 1970,Mr 22,II,3:1
Davis, Ossie (Producer)
Ballad for Bimshire 1963,O 16,54:1
Davis, Owen (Director)
9th Street Guest, The 1930,Ag 26,24:3
Spring Freshet 1934,O 5,28:3
No Way Out 1944,O 31,23:1
Davis, Owen (Miscellaneous)
Ethan Frome 1936,Ja 22,15:2
Davis, Owen (Original Author)
Lady Fingers 1929,F 1,22:4
Whoopee 1929,Ag 6,29:4
Virginia 1937,S 3,13:2
Virginia 1937,O 5,29:1
Davis, Owen (Playwright)
Opportunity 1920,Jl 31,5:1
Marry the Poor Girl 1920,S 27,18:3
Detour, The 1921,Jl 17,VI,1:1
Detour, The 1921,Ag 24,12:2
Detour, The 1921,S 4,VI,1:1
Up the Ladder 1922,Mr 7,11:2
Bronx Express 1922,Ap 27,12:2
Dreams for Sale 1922,S 14,24:1
World We Live In, The 1922,N 1,16:1
Ice-Bound 1923,Ja 21,VII,1:6
Ice-Bound 1923,F 12,16:2
Ice-Bound 1923,F 18,VII,1:1
Home Fires 1923,Ag 21,12:1
Home Fires 1923,S 2,VI,1:1
Nervous Wreck, The 1923,O 10,16:1
Nervous Wreck, The 1923,O 21,VIII,1:1
Peacocks 1924,Mr 2,VIII,2:7
Lazybones 1924,Je 1,VII,4:3
Haunted House, The 1924,S 3,12:1
Lazybones 1924,S 23,23:1

Davis, Owen (Playwright)—Cont
Nervous Wreck, The 1924,O 19,VIII,2:1
Easy Come, Easy Go 1925,O 27,20:2
Beware of Widows 1925,N 8,VIII,2:1
Beware of Widows 1925,D 2,22:3
Great Gatsby, The 1926,F 3,22:1
Great Gatsby, The 1926,F 7,VII,1:1
Phantom Ship, The 1926,Je 27,VII,3:1
Shelf, The 1926,Jl 4,VII,3:2
Donovan Affair, The 1926,Ag 31,15:2
Sandalwood 1926,S 23,23:1
Sandalwood 1926,O 3,VIII,1:1
Gentle Grafters 1926,O 17,VIII,2:4
Gentle Grafters 1926,O 28,23:1
Triumphant Bachelor, The 1927,S 16,21:1
Carry On 1928,Ja 24,26:1
Tonight at 12 1928,N 16,28:1
Whoopee 1928,D 5,34:3
Lady Fingers 1929,Ja 13,VIII,2:4
Spring Is Here 1929,Mr 12,26:1
Me for You 1929,S 22,IX,2:6
Dread 1929,O 27,IX,2:1
9th Street Guest, The 1930,Ag 26,24:3
Wife's Away, The 1930,N 23,IX,3:5
Just to Remind You 1931,S 8,39:1
Harbor Light, The 1932,Ag 7,IX,2:2
Good Earth, The 1932,S 25,IX,1:6
Good Earth, The 1932,O 18,23:4
Good Earth, The 1932,O 23,IX,1:1
Saturday Night 1933,Mr 1,13:2
Saturday Night 1933,Mr 19,IX,1:1
Jezebel 1933,D 20,26:3
Too Many Boats 1934,S 12,26:3
Coming Spring 1934,S 23,X,2:4
Spring Freshet 1934,O 5,28:3
Ethan Frome 1936,Ja 7,24:7
Ethan Frome 1936,F 2,IX,1:1
Two Time Mary 1937,Ag 3,20:5
Virginia 1937,S 12,XI,1:1
Mr and Mrs North 1941,Ja 13,11:2
Mr and Mrs North 1941,F 23,IX,1:1
Snark Was a Boojum, The 1943,S 2,14:4
No Way Out 1944,O 31,23:1
Insect Comedy, The 1948,Je 4,26:3
Davis, Owen Jr
Carry On 1928,Ja 24,26:1
Tonight at 12 1928,N 16,28:1
Solid South 1930,My 11,IX,2:6
9th Street Guest, The 1930,Ag 26,24:3
Solid South 1930,O 15,27:1
Just to Remind You 1931,S 8,39:1
Sentinels 1931,D 26,15:1
Evensong 1933,F 1,13:4
Saturday Night 1933,Mr 1,13:2
Noble Prize, The 1933,Jl 4,16:4
Jezebel 1933,D 20,26:3
Shatter'd Lamp, The 1934,Mr 22,26:3
Spring Freshet 1934,O 5,28:3
Times Have Changed 1935,F 26,16:1
Ten Minute Alibi 1935,Je 11,24:4
Remember the Day 1935,Jl 9,24:3
Stag at Bay, The 1935,Jl 30,17:1
Little Inn, The 1935,Ag 20,25:1
Rain 1935,Ag 27,23:4
Two Time Mary 1937,Ag 3,20:5
Mr and Mrs North 1941,Ja 13,11:2
Davis, Pat
Poupees de Paris, Les 1962,D 13,8:2
Davis, Patti
How Now, Dow Jones 1967,D 8,53:1
Davis, Paul
Devil's Disciple, The 1950,Ja 26,23:2
Mary Stuart 1956,Ap 28,10:2
Teahouse of the August Moon, The 1956,N 9,33:2
Davis, Paul (Miscellaneous)
Hot Spot 1963,Ap 20,17:2
Davis, Paul E (Director)
Miss Emily Adam 1960,Mr 30,43:1
Noontide 1961,Je 2,37:1
Matter of Like Life and Death, A 1963,O 3,28:2
Opening Night 1963,O 3,28:2
Davis, Paul E (Producer)
Obbligato 1958,F 19,22:2
Guests of the Nation 1958,Ag 31,II,1:1
Confederates, The 1959,S 29,45:1
Miss Emily Adam 1960,Mr 30,43:1
Davis, Paula May
Off Your Marx 1936,Ap 2,28:2
Davis, Peter (Director)
Golden Journey, The 1936,S 16,28:6
Davis, Peter (Producer)
Doctors Disagree 1943,D 29,15:2
Davis, Philip H (Professor) (Playwright)
Trojan Incident 1938,Ap 22,15:2
Davis, Pierrepont
Wolf! Wolf! 1925,O 30,21:1
Davis, Prentiss
Red, Hot and Blue! 1936,O 30,26:3
Davis, R P
Just Married 1921,Ap 27,21:1
Davis, Richard
If Booth Had Missed 1931,My 14,27:1
Kiss Them for Me 1945,Mr 21,27:2

Davis, Richard (Scenic Designer)
This Happy Breed 1952,Ap 4,23:2
Mrs Moonlight 1952,N 21,21:1
Cherry Orchard, The 1970,My 7,63:2
Davis, Richard Harding (Original Author)
Girl From Home, The 1920,My 4,9:2
Davis, Richard Harding (Playwright)
Galloper, The 1924,D 19,26:2
Davis, Robert
First Love 1926,N 9,31:2
Kith and Kin 1930,My 14,31:1
Yoshe Kalb 1933,D 29,27:2
This Our House 1935,D 12,33:3
Meet the People 1940,D 26,22:2
Lamp at Midnight 1947,D 22,29:2
Blood Wedding 1949,F 7,16:2
Villa of Madame Vidac, The 1959,O 1,40:1
Big Knife, The 1959,N 13,25:1
Davis, Roger
Love Letter, The 1921,O 5,20:1
Bunch and Judy, The 1922,N 29,20:1
Davis, Rookie
Deep Harlem 1929,Ja 8,35:2
Davis, Ruth
Days of Our Youth, The 1941,N 29,15:2
Alive and Kicking 1950,Ja 18,25:5
Davis, Sammy Jr
Mr Wonderful 1956,Mr 23,23:2
Golden Boy 1964,O 21,56:1
Golden Boy 1964,N 1,II,1:1
Davis, Sammy Sr
Mr Wonderful 1956,Mr 23,23:2
Davis, Samuel
Green Pastures, The 1931,Mr 1,VIII,1:1
Davis, Saul
Quick Years, The 1953,N 26,51:2
Davis, Sheldon (Playwright)
Good-Bye to Love 1940,Je 8,18:1
Try and Get It 1943,Ag 3,13:2
Earth Journey 1944,Ap 28,24:2
Davis, Shirley
Dick Whittington and His Remarkable Cat
  1950,N 25,10:5
Davis, Stephen
Bab 1920,O 19,12:1
Davis, Stringer
Importance of Being Earnest, The 1947,Mr 4,30:2
Time Remembered 1955,My 4,35:1
Farewell, Farewell Eugene 1960,S 28,35:1
Davis, Susan (Miscellaneous)
Conversation at Midnight 1964,N 13,27:1
Davis, Sylvia
Blood Wedding 1949,F 7,16:2
Bruno and Sidney 1949,My 4,38:2
Boy With a Cart, The 1954,Ap 5,19:2
Sands of the Negev 1954,O 20,32:1
Orpheus Descending 1959,O 6,45:2
Tobacco Road 1960,My 11,44:2
Book of Job, The 1962,F 10,13:1
Nathan Weinstein, Mystic, Connecticut
  1966,F 26,15:2
Davis, Tom Trio
Vaudeville (Palace) 1930,Mr 24,24:5
Davis, Tony (Lighting Director)
Last Pad, The 1970,D 8,61:1
Davis, Tony (Miscellaneous)
Last Pad, The 1970,D 8,61:1
Davis, Tyrrell
Creaking Chair, The 1926,F 23,26:1
Serena Blandish 1929,Ja 24,30:3
Davis, W Boyd
Wild Westcotts, The 1923,D 25,26:2
Little Minister, The 1925,Mr 24,21:1
Davis, Walder
Black Rhythm 1936,D 21,19:2
Davis, Wallace (Producer)
Make Me Know It 1929,N 5,32:5
Davis, Walter
Easy Terms 1925,S 23,22:2
Uninvited Guest, The 1927,S 28,28:2
Little Orchard Annie 1930,Ap 22,33:1
Tragedy of the Ages, The 1933,Ap 7,22:7
Black Widow 1936,F 13,24:3
Stage Door 1936,O 23,26:3
Waltz in Goose Step 1938,N 2,26:2
Holy Night 1941,D 22,23:3
Kiss and Tell 1943,Mr 18,22:1
Davis, Wilba
War 1929,S 19,37:3
Davis, Will
Mayor of Zalamea, The 1946,Ja 28,15:5
Velvet Glove, The 1949,D 27,26:2
Richard III 1953,D 10,65:2
Davis, William
Romance 1921,Mr 1,18:2
All God's Chillun Got Wings 1924,My 16,22:3
All God's Chillun Got Wings 1924,Ag 19,9:1
Night in Paris, A 1926,Ja 6,16:3
Artists and Models 1927,N 16,28:2
Davis, William O
Run, Little Chillun 1943,Ag 14,6:1
Green Pastures, The 1951,Mr 16,35:2

Davis, Wilva
Decision 1929,My 28,37:3
Davis, Winifred
Conversation Piece 1934,O 24,24:1
Davis and Carey (Choreographer)
Shuffle Along of 1933 1932,D 27,11:3
Davis and Darnell
Vaudeville (Palace) 1924,Ja 22,15:6
Vaudeville (Palace) 1927,N 22,33:2
Davis and Pelle
Vaudeville (Palace) 1923,F 13,25:1
Davis-Rose-Udell (Playwright)
Purlie 1970,Mr 16,53:1
Davison, Alan
Guests of the Nation 1958,Je 27,18:5
Davison, Arthur
Ghost of Yankee Doodle, The 1937,N 23,26:3
Davison, Bob (Costume Designer)
Hand in Glove 1944,D 5,19:1
Davison, Bruce
Tiger at the Gates 1968,Mr 1,30:1
Home Away From, A 1969,Ap 29,40:3
Davison, Frank (Playwright)
Women of Property 1937,Ag 1,X,1:7
Davison, Frank (Translator)
Women of Property 1937,Jl 9,18:3
Davison, Jack
Mame 1966,My 25,41:1
Davison, Lesley (Playwright)
That Thing at the Cherry Lane 1965,My 19,42:1
Davison, Robert (Costume Designer)
Song of Norway 1944,Ag 22,20:2
Miracle in the Mountains 1947,Ap 26,10:2
Galileo 1947,D 8,34:2
Davison, Robert (Scenic Designer)
Day Before Spring, The 1945,N 23,27:2
O Mistress Mine 1946,Ja 24,25:2
Around the World 1946,Je 1,9:5
Flag Is Born, A 1946,S 7,10:6
Great Campaign, The 1947,Ap 1,33:2
Miracle in the Mountains 1947,Ap 26,10:2
Galileo 1947,Ag 1,21:4
Galileo 1947,D 8,34:2
Davisson, Charles
Gay Divorce 1960,Ap 4,37:1
Better Luck Next Time 1966,Ja 28,21:1
Davisson, Charles (Miscellaneous)
No Trifling With Love 1959,N 10,55:3
Merry Death, A 1959,N 10,55:3
Bella 1961,N 17,40:1
Sweet Miani 1962,S 26,33:2
d'Avray, Tania
Midsummer Night's Dream, A 1954,S 22,33:1
Davy, Floria
Porgy and Bess 1955,Ja 21,19:6
Davy, Fred
Aiglon, L' 1924,O 21,21:1
Madame Sans-Gene 1924,N 4,30:1
Caprice, Un 1924,N 25,26:2
Amoureuse 1924,N 28,13:1
Davy, Gloria
Porgy and Bess 1954,D 17,36:7
Daw, Mae
Ziegfeld Follies 1924,Je 25,26:1
Dawdy, Jo Ann
Ice Follies 1959,Ja 14,30:1
Dawe, Janice
Ebb Tide 1931,Je 9,33:6
Dawe, Virginia
House Afire 1930,Ap 1,34:7
Mystery Moon 1930,Je 24,23:4
Dawes, Wetmore (Miscellaneous)
Fratricide Punished 1925,Ap 21,19:1
Romio and Julietta 1925,Ap 21,19:1
Dawforth, Mr
Ruddigore 1920,Ja 20,11:2
Dawforth, William
Lambs Gambol 1925,Ap 27,15:1
Dawkins, Cecil (Playwright)
Displaced Person, The 1966,D 30,15:1
Dawkins, Paul
Afore Night Come 1964,Je 26,34:1
Dawley, Herbert
Play Without a Name, A 1928,N 26,30:5
Dawn, Eleanor
Ladies' Night 1920,Ag 10,10:1
Getting Gertie's Garter 1921,Ag 2,16:2
Gingham Girl, The 1922,Ag 29,15:5
Clinging Vine, The 1922,S 25,20:2
No, No, Nanette 1925,S 17,20:2
Ramblers, The 1926,S 21,32:2
Dawn, Gloria
Lollipop 1924,Ja 22,15:3
Paradise Alley 1924,Ap 2,17:3
Ziegfeld Follies 1924,Je 25,26:1
Dawn, Hazel
Getting Gertie's Garter 1921,Ag 2,16:2
Demi-Virgin, The 1921,O 19,22:1
Nifties of 1923 1923,S 26,10:1
Keep Kool 1924,My 23,16:4
Great Temptations, The 1926,My 19,29:1
Wonder Boy 1931,O 24,20:1

Dawn, Hazel Jr
My Romance 1948,O 20,38:5
Dawn, Hope
Joker, The 1925,N 17,29:1
Dawn, Isabel
Bells, The 1926,Ap 14,20:3
Scarlet Lily, The 1927,Ja 31,12:3
Scalawag, The 1927,Mr 30,22:3
He Loved the Ladies 1927,My 11,29:2
Skidding 1928,My 22,18:5
Lawyers' Dilemma, The 1928,Jl 10,17:2
Marathon 1933,Ja 28,8:8
Dawn, Isabel (Playwright)
Marathon 1933,Ja 28,8:8
Dawn, Leo
Broadway Shadows 1930,Ap 1,34:6
Dawn, Marpessa
Jardin des Delices, Le 1969,N 4,54:1
Dawn, Michael
Dancing Mothers 1924,Ag 12,12:2
Dawn, Thera
Enchanted Isle 1927,S 20,33:2
Dawson, Ailsa
Joan of Lorraine 1955,Mr 26,12:2
Augustus Does His Bit 1958,F 22,8:3
Cock-A-Doodle Dandy 1958,N 13,39:2
Rivalry, The 1959,F 9,24:2
Dawson, Anne
Gondoliers, The 1940,O 1,29:2
Rosalinda; Fledermaus, Die 1942,O 29,26:5
Dawson, Anthony
Dial 'M' for Murder 1952,O 30,41:2
Dawson, Beatrice (Costume Designer)
Three Sisters, The 1970,F 12,30:1
Dawson, Betty Jane
Merry Wives of Windsor, The 1954,F 17,27:1
Dawson, Clay
Movie Man 1959,O 28,40:4
Dawson, Colin
All That Glitters 1938,Ja 20,18:2
Dawson, Curt
And People All Around 1968,F 12,46:1
Not Now Darling 1970,O 30,33:1
Dawson, Dan
Daddy Dumplins 1920,N 23,11:1
Dawson, David
In the Groove 1938,Ap 22,14:5
Hogan's Goat 1965,N 12,56:1
Dawson, David (Playwright)
In the Groove 1938,Ap 22,14:5
Dawson, Don
Antigone 1962,D 29,5:5
Orthee 1962,D 29,5:5
Dawson, Donald
Tall Story 1959,Ja 30,33:2
Dawson, Earl
Story of Mary Surratt, The 1947,F 10,25:2
Dawson, Earl (Director)
Blithe Spirit 1952,F 23,7:5
Dawson, Edward Colin (Scenic Designer)
Trojan Horse, The 1940,O 31,28:3
Dawson, F Eckhard
Johannes Kreisler 1922,D 25,20:3
Dawson, Forbes
Cymbeline 1923,O 3,12:1
Starlight 1925,Mr 4,17:2
Loves of Lulu, The 1925,My 12,26:1
Patriot, The 1928,Ja 20,15:1
One, Two, Three! 1930,S 30,24:2
Truth Game, The 1930,D 29,19:1
Don't Look Now! 1936,N 4,41:3
Dawson, Forbes (Producer)
Day in the Sun 1939,My 17,29:2
Dawson, Frank
Martinique 1920,Ap 27,18:2
Romance 1921,Mr 1,18:2
Starlight 1925,Mr 4,17:2
Dawson, Gregory (Playwright)
Great Scot! 1965,N 12,56:3
Dawson, Hal K
Machinal 1928,S 8,10:3
Bedfellows 1929,Jl 3,19:2
Half Gods 1929,D 23,18:5
Torch Song 1930,Ag 3,VIII,3:4
Torch Song 1930,Ag 28,23:1
Three Times the Hour 1931,Ag 26,15:5
Another Language 1932,Ap 26,25:3
Another Language 1933,My 9,20:2
Dodsworth 1934,F 26,20:4
Ladies' Money 1934,N 2,26:6
Ode to Liberty 1934,D 22,20:2
But Not Goodbye 1944,Ap 12,19:2
Dawson, Ida Fowler
Myself and I 1929,Ag 31,13:6
Dawson, Janice
Broadway Interlude 1934,Ap 20,16:3
Dawson, Jennifer (Playwright)
Ha-Ha, The 1968,Je 15,38:2
Dawson, John
Rain Before Seven 1935,Ag 13,20:3
Dawson, Jon
Russian People, The 1942,D 30,17:2
Maid in the Ozarks 1946,Jl 16,20:3

Dawson, Jon—Cont
Medea 1947,O 21,27:2
Dawson, Leonia
Black Souls 1932,Mr 31,25:1
Dawson, Mark
By Jupiter 1942,Je 4,22:1
Sweethearts 1947,Ja 22,31:2
High Button Shoes 1947,O 10,32:2
Great to Be Alive! 1950,Mr 24,28:2
Me and Juliet 1953,My 29,17:1
Me and Juliet 1953,Je 7,II,1:1
Ankles Aweigh 1955,Ap 19,27:1
Ankles Aweigh 1955,Ap 24,II,1:1
New Girl in Town 1957,My 15,40:1
Fiorello! 1959,N 24,45:3
Fiorello! 1959,N 29,II,1:1
Riot Act, The 1963,Mr 9,5:2
Dawson, Preston Jr
Tom Sawyer 1931,D 26,15:3
Dawson, Robert F
Great Guns 1939,N 18,23:4
Dawson, Ronald
Witness for the Prosecution 1954,D 17,35:2
Sleeping Prince, The 1956,N 2,31:1
Penny Change 1963,O 25,37:1
Traveller Without Luggage 1964,S 18,26:2
Dawson, Rudolph
Kilpatrick's Old-Time Minstrels 1930,Ap 21,20:2
Dawson, Sara
Cradle Song 1921,Mr 1,18:2
Dawson, Shirley
Born Yesterday 1954,Ja 1,16:6
Dawson, Steve
Nat Turner 1960,N 7,46:3
Dawson, Steve P
Cockeyed Kite 1961,S 14,27:1
Day, Alexander
Winter Soldiers 1942,N 30,19:2
Day, Bernard (Choreographer)
Faust 1928,O 9,34:1
Day, Carol
Loose Moments 1935,F 5,22:3
Day, Charles
Criminal Code, The 1929,O 3,28:2
Day, Clarence (Original Author)
Life With Father 1939,Ag 15,14:4
Life With Father 1939,N 9,26:2
Life With Father 1939,N 19,X,1:1
Life With Father 1940,Ag 18,IX,1:1
Life With Mother 1948,Je 9,36:3
Life With Mother 1948,O 21,32:2
Life With Mother 1948,O 31,II,1:1
Day, Dan
Lilies of the Field 1921,O 5,20:1
Day, David
Man Who Married a Dumb Wife, The 1930,My 9,20:5
Day, Diana
Twinkle Twinkle 1926,N 17,22:2
Day, Doris
Women, The 1936,D 28,13:1
Susan and God 1943,D 14,30:2
Day, Dorothy
When We Are Young 1920,N 23,11:1
Lilies of the Field 1921,O 5,20:1
Great Music 1924,O 6,24:1
Dove, The 1925,F 12,17:3
Fifty Million Frenchmen 1929,N 28,34:4
Gone Hollywood 1930,D 28,VIII,2:1
Left Bank, The 1931,O 6,35:3
Counsellor-at-Law 1932,S 13,17:2
Day, Edith
Orange Blossoms 1922,S 20,18:1
Wildflower 1923,F 8,17:2
Rose Marie 1925,Mr 21,16:2
Desert Song, The 1927,My 8,VII,1:5
Show Boat 1928,My 4,31:3
Day, Edmund (Playwright)
Round-Up, The 1932,Mr 8,19:4
Day, Elizabeth
Comedy of Women, A 1929,S 14,17:4
Web, The 1932,Je 28,24:4
Day, Eugene
Greenwich Villagers, The 1927,Ag 19,20:2
Day, Frances
How D'you Do? 1933,Ap 26,13:4
Jill Darling 1934,D 20,29:8
Floodlight 1937,Je 24,30:3
Du Barry 1942,N 1,VIII,2:2
Buoyant Billions 1949,O 24,18:3
Day, Frances (Producer)
Blind Man's Buff 1953,N 15,II,3:1
Day, Francis H
Two by Two 1925,F 24,17:1
Twelve Miles Out 1925,N 17,29:2
Henry IV, Part I 1926,Je 1,29:1
Old Bill, M P 1926,N 11,22:2
Interference 1927,O 19,24:3
Beaux' Stratagem, The 1928,Je 5,20:1
Potiphar's Wife 1928,D 24,10:7
Sweet Stranger 1930,O 22,23:3
Uncle Tom's Cabin 1933,My 30,13:4
Slight Case of Murder, A 1935,S 12,28:5
County Chairman, The 1936,My 26,26:5

Day, Frederick Lansing (Playwright)
Makers of Light 1922,My 24,22:3
Day, Janet
Golden Screw, The 1967,Ja 31,52:1
Day, Juliette
Scrambled Wives 1920,Ag 6,16:1
We Girls 1921,N 10,26:3
Pride 1923,My 3,22:3
Sharlee 1923,N 23,20:1
Matinee Girl, The 1926,F 2,20:3
No Trespassing! 1926,S 8,19:1
Dark, The 1927,F 24,22:5
Katy Did 1927,My 10,24:3
This Thing Called Love 1928,S 18,32:7
Sun Kissed 1937,Mr 11,20:2
Day, June
Jotham Valley 1951,F 7,37:2
Day, June (Choreographer)
Jotham Valley 1951,F 7,37:2
Day, Lillian (Playwright)
Our Wife 1933,Mr 3,13:2
Collector's Item 1952,F 9,11:2
Day, Lois
Lady Behave 1943,N 17,30:1
Day, Lynda
Devils, The 1965,N 17,51:2
Day, Marie (Costume Designer)
Macbeth 1959,Ag 1,9:2
Love and Libel 1960,D 8,44:1
Day, Marie (Scenic Designer)
Glass Cage, The 1957,Mr 11,21:2
Henry IV, Part I 1958,Je 25,23:3
Day, Marie L
First Man, The 1922,Mr 6,9:2
Spite Corner 1922,S 26,18:1
Chicken Feed 1923,S 25,10:2
Day, Marilyn
If the Shoe Fits 1946,D 6,29:4
Small Wonder 1948,S 16,33:5
Kiss Me, Kate 1952,Ja 9,24:6
Day, Marion
Diamond Lil 1928,Ap 10,32:1
Day, Nola
Golden Apple, The 1954,Mr 12,15:2
Day, Paul (Miscellaneous)
Pretender, The 1960,My 25,42:1
Day, Sonny
Hayride 1954,S 14,24:2
Day, Wilson
Nightcap, The 1921,Ag 16,18:3
Rose Bernd 1922,S 27,17:1
Dayde, Bernard (Costume Designer)
Love Doctor, The 1959,O 14,52:4
Andromaque 1964,F 29,13:2
Dayde, Bernard (Scenic Designer)
Love Doctor, The 1959,O 14,52:4
Andromaque 1964,F 29,13:2
Daye, Dorothy
New Yorkers, The 1927,Mr 11,24:3
Daye, Ruth
Leave It to Me! 1938,N 10,32:2
Daykarhanova, Tamara
Chauve-Souris 1922,Je 6,17:4
Chauve-Souris 1925,Ja 15,25:1
Chauve-Souris 1929,Ja 23,20:2
House of Bernarda Alba, The 1951,Ja 8,14:6
Emperor's Clothes, The 1953,F 10,24:2
Bullfight 1954,Ja 13,25:2
Three Sisters, The 1964,Je 23,24:1
Dayne, Marie
Madcap, The 1928,F 1,31:2
Dayton, Frank
Merchants of Venus 1920,S 28,14:2
Dayton, Helena Smith (Playwright)
Hot Water 1929,Ja 22,22:3
Dayton, June
Lovely Me 1946,D 26,30:4
Tenting Tonight 1947,Ap 3,32:2
Ivy Green, The 1949,Ap 6,37:2
Dayton, Katharine (Playwright)
First Lady 1935,N 11,21:3
First Lady 1935,N 27,17:4
First Lady 1935,D 8,X,3:1
First Lady 1937,O 9,17:2
Save Me the Waltz 1938,Mr 1,19:2
First Lady 1952,My 29,18:5
Dayton, Lewis
Firebird 1932,N 22,25:2
Red Cat, The 1934,S 20,21:1
Dark Victory 1934,N 10,18:2
Libel! 1935,D 21,10:5
St Helena 1936,O 7,32:1
Country Wife, The 1936,D 2,34:1
Many Mansions 1937,O 28,28:6
Once Is Enough 1938,F 16,16:2
Oscar Wilde 1938,O 11,20:2
Dayton, Maude
Chippies 1929,My 30,23:3
Dayton, Ruth
Tiger Cats 1924,O 22,18:1
Dove, The 1925,F 12,17:3
Fanny 1926,S 22,30:1
Mima 1928,D 13,24:2

Dazey, Frank (Playwright)
Peter Weston 1923,S 20,5:2
Peter Weston 1923,S 30,II,1:1
Peter Weston 1924,Je 15,VII,1:4
Black Boy 1926,S 26,VIII,2:7
Black Boy 1926,O 7,30:2
Sweet Stranger 1930,O 22,23:3
Dazil, Claude (Mrs) (Playwright)
Untitled-Play 1929,Mr 10,X,1:8
D'Castro, B N
Teahouse of the August Moon, The 1955,My 10,24:1
De Abaldia, Rene (Playwright)
Grand Vizir, Le 1970,Ap 8,38:3
Cosmonaute Agricole, Le 1970,Ap 8,38:3
de Acosta, Mercedes (Playwright)
Sandro Botticelli 1923,Mr 27,24:2
Jacob Slovak 1927,O 6,28:4
de Acosta, Natica
One, Two, Three! 1930,S 30,24:2
Violet, The 1930,S 30,24:2
Marseilles 1930,N 18,28:2
De Aguenta, Juan
To Quito and Back 1937,O 7,30:4
de Alarcon, Pedro A (Original Author)
Revenge With Music 1934,N 29,33:5
de Anchoriz, Alba
Light of the World, The 1920,Ja 7,17:1
Passion Flower, The 1920,Ja 14,12:1
De Angelis, Arthur
Tom Sawyer 1931,D 26,15:3
de Angelis, Jefferson
Merry Widow, The 1921,S 6,13:1
Some Party 1922,Ap 17,22:1
School for Scandal, The 1925,D 7,18:2
Girofle-Girofla 1926,N 24,26:2
Revelry 1927,S 13,37:1
Royal Family, The 1927,D 29,26:4
Royal Family, The 1928,Ja 8,VIII,1:1
Diana 1929,D 10,37:1
Apron Strings 1930,F 18,28:2
de Angelis, John
Tide Rising 1937,Ja 26,17:2
de Angelis, Marshall
Riff-Raff 1926,F 9,18:6
de Angelis, Ricardo
Rockbound 1929,Ap 20,23:2
Incubator 1932,N 2,23:3
De Angelis, Rosemarie
Time of Vengeance 1959,D 11,39:1
De Angelo, Carlo
Bells, The 1926,Ap 14,20:3
Ringside 1928,Ag 30,13:2
Best House in Naples, The 1956,O 27,16:2
De Angelo, Carlo (Director)
Run, Thief, Run 1957,My 2,27:1
de Anguera, Marguerite
Green Table, The 1942,Ja 22,12:2
Prodigal Son, The 1942,F 18,22:2
Dark of the Moon 1945,Mr 15,27:2
De Avila, Rosa
Cabalgata 1949,Jl 8,14:2
de Azertis, Lorenzo (Playwright)
Casanova 1923,S 27,10:2
de Banfield, Raffaello (Composer)
Much Ado About Nothing 1952,My 2,20:1
de Banfield, Raffaello (Playwright)
Lord Byron's Love Letter 1955,Ja 19,23:2
de Banzie, Brenda
Murder Mistaken 1952,D 7,II,7:1
Speaking of Murder 1956,D 20,37:1
Entertainer, The 1958,F 13,22:2
Entertainer, The 1958,F 23,II,1:1
de Barros, Theo
Arena Conta Zumbi 1969,Ag 19,31:1
de Barros, Theo (Musical Director)
Arena Conta Zumbi 1969,Ag 19,31:1
De Bary, Harold
Challenge of Youth 1930,Ja 21,28:5
de Battle, Carlos (Playwright)
Spanish Love 1920,Ag 18,6:1
de Battle, John
Lysistrata 1946,O 18,27:5
De Beck, Billy
Untitled-Revue 1923,My 12,15:4
De Becker, Ernestine
Late One Evening 1933,Ja 10,27:3
Taming of the Shrew, The 1935,O 1,27:3
Idiot's Delight 1936,Mr 25,25:2
Amphitryon 38 1937,Je 24,30:2
Amphitryon 38 1937,N 2,32:2
Sea Gull, The 1938,Mr 29,19:2
de Becker, Harold
Marry the Poor Girl 1920,S 27,18:3
In the Night Watch 1921,Ja 31,10:1
Imaginary Invalid, The 1922,Jl 26,26:2
Blue Bird, The 1923,D 26,13:3
Simon Called Peter 1924,N 11,20:2
Blonde Sinner, The 1926,Jl 15,21:2
Witch, The 1926,N 19,22:5
Savages Under the Skin 1927,Mr 25,25:2
Blood Money 1927,Ag 23,29:2
Maya 1928,F 22,19:1

de Becker, Harold—Cont
Silent Witness, The 1931,Mr 24,31:5
Miss Gulliver Travels 1931,N 26,36:4
Web, The 1932,Je 28,24:4
Silent House, The 1932,N 9,28:3
Hangman's Whip 1933,F 25,20:2
Her Man of Wax 1933,O 12,32:3
Rain 1935,F 13,24:1
Weather Permitting 1935,My 24,24:5
Ringside Seat 1938,N 23,24:5
Foreigners 1939,D 6,30:2
Woman Brown, The 1939,D 9,18:5
Charley's Aunt 1940,O 18,24:2
Delicate Story 1940,D 5,32:2

De Becker, Kate
Humble, The 1926,O 14,22:2

de Becker, Marie
Madras House, The 1921,O 31,18:2
Love on the Dole 1936,F 25,23:3
And Now Goodbye 1937,F 3,26:4
If I Were You 1938,Ja 25,24:2
Bright Rebel 1938,D 28,24:2

de Beer, Gerrit
Illya Darling 1967,Ap 12,37:1
Zorba 1968,N 18,58:1

de Belleval, Jean Fournier (Costume Designer)
Ti-Coq 1951,F 10,10:2

de Belleval, Jean Fournier (Scenic Designer)
Ti-Coq 1951,F 10,10:2

De Belleville, Frederic
Guest of Honor, The 1920,S 21,12:1
Humming Bird, The 1923,Ja 16,16:2

de Benedictus, Richard (Miscellaneous)
Fade Out--Fade In 1964,My 27,45:1
Bajour 1964,N 24,42:1
Do I Hear a Waltz? 1965,Mr 19,28:1
Annie Get Your Gun 1966,Je 1,42:2
Show Boat 1966,Jl 20,48:1

de Bergh, Karen
Princess Ida 1967,Ap 17,46:2
Sacco-Vanzetti 1969,F 9,78:1

de Bethel, David (Scenic Designer)
Joyce Grenfell Requests the Pleasure
1955,O 11,48:1

de Bethel, Joan (Scenic Designer)
Joyce Grenfell Requests the Pleasure
1955,O 11,48:1

De Bevoise, Charles
Henry-Behave 1926,Ag 24,19:4

de Bien, Thomas
Shadow of Heroes 1961,D 6,59:1

de Bordes, Arnoud
Curtain Call 1937,Ap 23,24:7

de Bouvier, Simone
Louie the 14th 1925,Mr 4,17:1

de Bresson, Christian
Innocents, The 1959,Ap 21,41:2

de Brett, Diane
Lute Song 1946,F 7,29:2
Land's End 1946,D 12,37:5
Lute Song 1959,Mr 13,24:1

de Briac, Jean
Slightly Scandalous 1944,Je 14,16:2

De Bries, Magda
Earl Carroll's Vanities 1926,Ag 25,19:4

de Brossard, Boyd
Catherine Was Great 1944,Ag 3,16:1

de Bruin, Valentina
Oedipus Rex 1954,Jl 17,6:6

De Bus, Phyllis
Strange Fruit 1945,N 30,18:6

de Caillaux, Pierre (Musical Director)
Broken Hearts of Broadway 1944,Je 13,16:2

de Caillavet, G A (Playwright)
Fan, The 1921,O 4,10:1
Monsieur Brotonneau 1924,Mr 13,14:1
Bois Sacre, Le 1924,Mr 23,VIII,1:3
Monsieur Brotonneau 1930,O 5,IX,2:4

De Cardi, Laura
Mary Jane McKane 1923,D 26,13:2

De Carion, Philip
Man of Destiny, The 1926,My 1,10:1

De Carlton, Grace
Tangerine 1921,Ag 10,8:2

De Caro, Paula
Frugal Noon 1964,My 23,15:2

de Casalis, Jeanne
Tidings Brought to Mary, The 1922,D 25,20:1
Potiphar's Wife 1927,Ag 19,20:6
Out Goes She 1928,D 30,VIII,4:1
Tidings Brought to Mary, The 1929,Ap 7,X,2:7
Colonel Satan 1931,F 8,VIII,3:3
Success Story 1934,Ja 2,17:4
Mask of Virtue, The 1935,My 16,20:1
Mask of Virtue, The 1935,Je 9,IX,1:1

de Casalis, Jeanne (Playwright)
St Helena 1936,F 5,15:8
St Helena 1936,Mr 8,IX,1:1
St Helena 1936,S 29,35:1
St Helena 1936,O 7,32:1
St Helena 1936,O 11,X,1:1

de Casenave, Myrna
Vida es Sueno, La 1964,Mr 18,49:1

De Cenzo, Arthur (Lighting Director)
From Here to There; Otherwise Engaged
1958,Ap 24,37:3
From Here to There; Real Strange One, A
1958,Ap 24,37:3
From Here to There; Slow Dusk 1958,Ap 24,37:3

De Cenzo, Arthur (Scenic Designer)
From Here to There; Real Strange One, A
1958,Ap 24,37:3
From Here to There; Otherwise Engaged
1958,Ap 24,37:3
From Here to There; Slow Dusk 1958,Ap 24,37:3

de Cerami, Ami
Devil's Host, The 1931,N 20,27:2

de Chantal, Anne
Liliom 1921,Ap 21,18:1

De Claris, Vincent
Ruy Blas 1957,D 14,16:3

De Cordoba, Mercedes
As You Like It 1923,Ap 24,24:1

de Cordoba, Pedro
Light of the World, The 1920,Ja 7,17:1
Nemesis 1921,Ap 5,24:3
Lancelot and Elaine 1921,S 13,12:1
Marie Antoinette 1921,N 23,16:1
Rivals, The 1922,Je 6,18:2
Jolly Roger, The 1923,Ag 31,10:4
Jolly Roger, The 1923,S 9,VII,1:1
Gift, The 1924,Ja 23,15:4
Candida 1924,D 13,12:3
Servant in the House, The 1925,Ap 8,24:2
Arms and the Man 1925,S 15,28:1
Arms and the Man 1925,O 4,IX,1:1
Sam Abramovitch 1927,Ja 20,20:5
Julius Caesar 1927,Je 7,27:2
Woman of Bronze, The 1927,Je 16,25:4
Arms and the Man 1929,Ag 13,23:4
See Naples and Die 1929,S 27,30:4
Rivals, The 1930,Mr 14,24:4
Merchant of Venice, The 1931,N 17,31:1
Julius Caesar 1931,N 18,26:3
Hamlet 1931,N 19,26:6
Too True to Be Good 1932,Mr 1,19:2
Too True to Be Good 1932,Mr 6,VIII,1:1
Lucrece 1932,N 30,22:8
Lucrece 1932,D 21,22:2
Lucrece 1933,Ja 1,IX,1:1
Uncle Tom's Cabin 1933,My 30,13:4
First Legion, The 1934,O 2,18:2
Spring in Autumn 1937,Ag 17,23:1

de Cordova, Fred
Elmer the Great 1928,S 25,29:1
Piper Paid 1934,D 26,19:1
Symphony 1935,Ap 27,20:3
Beverly Hills 1940,N 8,24:2

de Cordova, Fred (Director)
Keep Off the Grass 1940,My 24,22:6

de Cordova, Fred (Miscellaneous)
Ziegfeld Follies 1943,Ap 2,16:2

De Cormier, Robert
Sandhog 1954,N 24,17:1

De Cormier, Robert (Composer)
World of Sholom Aleichem, The 1953,S 12,13:2
Merry-Go-Rounders, The 1956,N 22,50:1

De Cormier, Robert (Miscellaneous)
Wall, The 1960,O 12,44:4
Milk and Honey 1961,O 11,52:1
110 in the Shade 1963,O 25,37:1

De Cormier, Robert (Musical Director)
Happiest Girl in the World, The 1961,Ap 4,42:1

De Corsia, Theodore
Little Theatre Tournament; Father Returns, The
1929,My 7,28:1
Scarlet Sister Mary 1930,N 26,19:2
Symphony 1935,Ap 27,20:3

De Cost, Robert
Thor, With Angels 1956,O 15,29:4
Oscar Wilde 1957,Ap 20,21:3

De Costa, Leon (Playwright)
Kosher Kitty Kelly 1925,Je 16,24:2
Blonde Sinner, The 1926,Jl 15,21:2

de Costa, Mercedes (Lyricist)
What Next 1920,Ja 27,7:2

de Costa, Mercedes (Playwright)
What Next 1920,Ja 27,7:2

de Courville, Albert (Director)
At the Stroke of Eight 1940,My 21,29:2
Ten Little Indians 1944,Je 28,21:2
Wind Is Ninety, The 1945,Je 22,12:2
Hidden Horizon 1946,S 20,42:2

de Courville, Albert (Miscellaneous)
Merry World, The 1926,Je 9,18:3
Wind Is Ninety, The 1945,Je 22,12:2
Ryan Girl, The 1945,S 25,28:2
Hidden Horizon 1946,S 20,42:2

de Courville, Albert (Playwright)
Pins and Needles 1922,F 2,20:1

de Courville, Albert (Producer)
Rainbow, The 1923,Ap 8,VIII,1:7
At the Stroke of Eight 1940,My 21,29:2
Ten Little Indians 1944,Je 28,21:2
Lute Song 1948,O 12,32:3

de Crespo, Helena
Antony and Cleopatra 1959,Ja 14,28:1

de Crignis, Natalie
Contrast, The 1926,O 1,26:2

de Croisset, Francis (Playwright)
Orange Blossoms 1922,S 20,18:1

de Decker, Harold
Among Those Sailing 1936,F 12,24:4

de Dome, Agnes
Tonight or Never 1930,N 19,19:3

De Elmo, Betty
Lady Comes Across, The 1942,Ja 10,10:2

de Fay, Jack
Rat, The 1925,F 11,19:3

de Faye-Jozin (Mme)
Untitled-One Woman Show 1928,Je 24,VIII,4:2

De Felice, Aurelia
Scarlet Lullaby 1968,Mr 11,48:1
Transgressor Rides Again, The 1969,My 21,42:1

de Felice, James
Tree Witch, The 1961,Je 5,39:4

de Feraudy, Maurice
Monsieur Brotonneau 1923,Ap 8,VIII,1:7
Avare, L'; Miser, The 1924,Mr 12,17:3
Monsieur Brotonneau 1924,Mr 13,14:1
Cette Vieille Canaille 1930,D 7,IX,4:2
Michel 1932,Ap 3,VIII,2:1

de Filippi, Armando
Arzigogolo, L'; Whim, The 1931,Ap 27,24:4
Giuochi di Prestigio 1931,N 2,26:1
Piccolo Santo, Il; Little Saint, The 1931,D 14,16:4
Casa di Tutti, La; Everybody's Home 1932,D 5,21:4
Cardinale, Il 1933,Ja 9,24:2
Zia Morta, La; Dead Aunt, The 1933,F 13,11:3

de Filippo, Eduardo (Playwright)
Best House in Naples, The 1956,O 27,16:2
Fortuna 1962,Ja 4,26:1

de Flers, Robert (Playwright)
Transplanting Jean 1921,Ja 4,11:2
Fan, The 1921,O 4,10:1
Monsieur Brotonneau 1923,Ap 8,VIII,1:7
Monsieur Brotonneau 1924,Mr 13,14:1
Bois Sacre, Le 1924,Mr 23,VIII,1:3
Monsieur Brotonneau 1930,O 5,IX,2:4

de Forest, Marian (Playwright)
Little Women 1931,D 8,36:2
Little Women 1944,D 13,29:2

de Forrest, Edward (Scenic Designer)
Victory Belles 1943,O 27,26:3

de Forrest, Louise
Pal Joey 1940,D 26,22:2

De Forrest, Muriel
Florodora 1920,Ap 6,18:1
Century Revue and the Midnight Rounders, The
1920,Jl 13,9:1
Make It Snappy 1922,Ap 14,20:2
Vaudeville (Palace) 1926,My 11,25:3

De Forrest, William (Scenic Designer)
Rats of Norway, The 1948,Ap 16,27:6
Diamond Lil 1948,N 30,33:2
Diamond Lil 1949,F 7,16:2

De Francis, Karen (Miscellaneous)
Marie Vison, La 1970,Jl 15,29:1

de Friis, Inger
Maitresse de Roi 1926,D 1,24:1

De Gaetani, Tom (Lighting Director)
Floydada to Matador 1955,D 22,19:1
Hello Out There 1955,D 22,19:1
Opera Opera 1955,D 22,19:1
Hungerers, The 1955,D 22,19:1

de Garcin, M
Deburau 1926,D 28,16:1
Mozart 1926,D 28,16:1
Illusioniste, L' 1927,Ja 11,36:5

de Gaw, Boyce (Playwright)
Marathon 1933,Ja 28,8:8

de Ghelder, Stephan
Celebration 1969,Ja 23,55:2

de Ghelderode, Michel (Playwright)
Escurial 1956,O 3,29:2
Escurial 1960,Jl 22,13:1
Women at the Tomb, The 1961,Ap 25,41:1
Hop, Signor! 1962,My 8,45:2
Pantagleize 1967,D 1,54:1
Victims, The; Escurial 1968,Mr 6,34:1
Chronicles of Hell, The 1969,O 19,II,12:1

de Give, Paul (Miscellaneous)
Lid's Off, The 1936,Ap 4,11:6

de Glauco, Scilla (Playwright)
My Wife Is Different 1931,Ap 27,24:4

De Gore, Janet
Member of the Wedding, The 1950,Ja 6,26:6

de Gorsse, Henry (Playwright)
Procureur Hallers, Le 1924,N 13,18:1

De Graaff, Alfred
Under the Sycamore Tree 1960,Mr 8,37:2

de Graffenried, Kent (Miscellaneous)
Tartuffe 1957,O 9,39:1

De Gresac, Fred (Playwright)
Orange Blossoms 1922,S 20,18:1
Sweethearts 1929,S 23,25:1
Sweethearts 1947,Ja 22,31:2

De Groot
Vaudeville (Palace) 1928,Ja 24,26:4
de Groot, Pauline
Eccentricities of Davy Crockett, The 1961,Ja 4,26:1
de Guzman, Dylan Stephen
Babes Don't Cry Anymore 1968,F 21,55:1
De Hart, Gail
Henry-Behave 1926,Ag 24,19:4
One Glorious Hour 1927,Ap 15,27:2
Very Wise Virgin, A 1927,Je 3,25:3
Belt, The 1927,O 20,33:1
Mystery Man, The 1928,Ja 27,14:2
Night Hostess 1928,S 13,31:2
Heat Lightning 1933,S 16,9:6
Dance Night 1938,O 15,20:5
de Hartog, Jan (Original Author)
I Do! I Do! 1966,D 18,II,3:1
I Do! I Do! 1967,N 28,54:1
de Hartog, Jan (Playwright)
This Time Tomorrow 1947,N 4,31:2
Skipper Next to God 1948,Ja 5,14:5
Fourposter, The 1951,O 25,34:2
Fourposter, The 1951,N 25,II,1:1
Fourposter, The 1955,Ja 6,23:3
I Do! I Do! 1966,D 6,58:1
De Haven, Gloria
Seventh Heaven 1955,My 27,16:2
Have I Got One for You 1968,Ja 8,32:1
De Haven and Nice
Puzzles of 1925 1925,F 3,25:3
de Havilland, Olivia
Romeo and Juliet 1951,Ja 23,24:8
Romeo and Juliet 1951,Mr 12,21:2
Romeo and Juliet 1951,Mr 25,II,1:1
Candida 1952,Ap 23,23:6
Gift of Time, A 1962,F 23,34:1
Gift of Time, A 1962,Mr 4,II,1:1
de Hetre, Katherine
Story Theater Repertory; Saint Julian the
Hospitaler 1970,O 21,40:1
Story Theater Repertory; Gimpel the Food
1970,O 21,40:1
de Hierapolis, Leo
Mikado, The 1925,Ap 13,25:1
de Jari, M
Fashions of 1924 1923,Jl 19,18:2
Earl Carroll's Vanities 1925,Jl 7,24:1
Earl Carroll's Vanities 1925,D 29,20:3
Earl Carroll's Vanities 1926,Ag 25,19:4
De Jerez, Jesus
Handful of Fire 1958,O 2,45:3
de Jong, Betty
Eccentricities of Davy Crockett, The 1961,Ja 4,26:1
de Jonge, Frank (Translator)
Mystery of the Finding of the Cross, The
1959,Ja 16,35:2
Way of the Cross, The 1959,Ja 16,35:2
De Kanelba, Zita Gomez (Scenic Designer)
Pericas, Las 1969,N 2,86:5
de Kay, Drake
Royal Fandango, A 1923,N 13,25:1
Wise-Crackers, The 1925,D 17,26:1
De Knight, Fannie Belle
Taboo 1922,Ap 5,22:1
Lulu Belle 1926,F 10,20:1
House of Connelly, The 1931,S 29,22:4
Carry Nation 1932,O 31,18:2
De Knight, Rene
Memphis Bound 1945,My 25,23:2
De Kos Brothers
Vaudeville (Hippodrome) 1926,Ap 13,28:2
de Kova, Frank
Heads or Tails 1947,My 3,10:6
De Koven, Henry
Marseilles 1930,N 18,28:2
Hot Money 1931,N 9,22:2
All Good Americans 1933,D 6,29:2
Nowhere Bound 1935,Ja 23,20:2
de Koven, Jean
Threepenny Opera, The 1933,Ap 14,22:4
de Koven, Reginald (Composer)
Robin Hood 1929,N 20,26:5
Robin Hood 1932,Ja 28,25:4
Robin Hood 1935,Jl 15,20:6
Fencing Master, The 1936,Ap 1,29:1
Robin Hood 1944,N 8,28:2
De Koven, Roger
Mystery Man, The 1928,Ja 27,14:2
Murder in the Cathedral 1936,Mr 21,13:5
Eternal Road, The 1937,Ja 8,14:2
King Lear 1940,D 16,27:2
Brooklyn, U S A 1941,D 22,24:2
Assassin, The 1945,O 18,20:2
Joan of Lorraine 1946,N 19,40:2
Abie's Irish Rose 1954,N 19,19:1
Three Sisters, The 1955,F 26,13:2
Three Sisters, The 1955,Mr 20,II,1:1
Lark, The 1955,N 18,20:1
Hidden River, The 1957,Ja 24,32:1
Compulsion 1957,O 25,21:1
Making of Moo, The 1958,Je 12,34:1
Miracle Worker, The 1959,O 20,44:1
Fighting Cock, The 1959,D 9,57:3

Arturo Ui 1963,N 12,49:1
Funny Girl 1964,Mr 27,15:1
Deadly Game, The 1966,F 14,34:1
Walking to Waldheim 1967,N 11,25:2
Saint Joan 1968,Ja 5,42:1
Tiger at the Gates 1968,Mr 1,30:1
Cyrano de Bergerac 1968,Ap 26,30:1
Steal the Old Man's Bundle 1970,My 16,30:1
de Kruif, Paul (Playwright)
Yellow Jack 1934,Mr 7,22:6
Yellow Jack 1934,Mr 18,IX,1:1
Yellow Jack 1944,Ap 7,23:3
Yellow Jack 1944,Ap 16,II,1:1
Yellow Jack 1947,F 28,26:2
de la Cruz, J Morety
Strange Prince, The 1926,D 8,24:2
de la Cruz, Juan
Great Way, The 1921,N 8,28:2
Tendresse, La 1922,S 26,18:1
Apache, The 1923,My 9,14:3
Peace Palace 1933,Je 6,30:2
de la Fontaine, Gerald
Horse Play 1937,Ag 28,8:3
Swingin' the Dream 1939,N 30,24:2
De La Fuente, Alfred
And the Wind Blows 1959,Ap 29,28:1
De La Madrid, Rodolfo
Vida es Sueno, La 1964,Mr 18,49:1
de la Passardiere, Guy (Producer)
Pousse-Cafe 1966,Mr 19,19:2
de la Roche, Mazo (Original Author)
Whiteoaks 1936,Ap 15,25:2
Whiteoaks 1938,Mr 24,20:2
de la Roche, Mazo (Playwright)
Whiteoaks 1936,Ap 15,25:2
Whiteoaks 1938,Mr 24,20:2
de la Torre, Rosario
Don Juan Tenorio 1953,N 20,18:5
de la Tour, Evelyn
Optimists, The 1928,Ja 31,28:2
de Lacy, Julia
Birds, The 1966,Jl 1,40:1
de Lacy, Philippe
Growing Pains 1933,N 24,24:2
Strangers at Home 1934,S 15,20:5
de Lalama, Luis
Pluma en el Viento; Feather in the Wind
1932,Ap 2,13:4
de Landa, Maria
Golden Streets, The 1970,Ag 14,21:1
De Langis, Arthur
Scaramouche 1923,O 25,14:2
de Lano, Allen (Director)
Adams' Wife 1931,D 29,27:1
de Lano, Allen (Playwright)
For Better or Worse 1927,F 1,24:3
De Lano, Walter
Happiness Cage, The 1970,O 5,56:4
de Lany, Dorothy
Caesar and Cleopatra 1935,Ag 22,21:1
De Lany, Gwendolyn
Hail and Farewell 1923,F 20,12:1
Primer for Lovers, A 1929,N 19,26:5
De Lany, Robert
Tom Sawyer 1931,D 26,15:3
Man Who Killed Lincoln, The 1940,Ja 18,26:4
de Lappe, Gemze
Oklahoma! 1943,N 14,II,1:1
Paint Your Wagon 1951,N 13,32:2
Paint Your Wagon 1951,N 18,II,1:1
Phoenix '55 1955,Ap 25,20:2
Oklahoma! 1958,Mr 20,32:3
Juno 1959,Mr 10,41:1
King and I, The 1960,My 12,40:1
Brigadoon 1962,My 31,21:4
Oklahoma! 1963,F 28,8:2
Brigadoon 1964,D 24,9:1
de Lappe, Gemze (Choreographer)
Birds, The 1966,Jl 1,40:1
Oklahoma! 1969,Je 24,37:1
de Lappe, Gemze (Miscellaneous)
Oklahoma! 1958,Mr 20,32:3
Oklahoma! 1963,F 28,8:2
Carousel 1965,Ag 11,39:1
Oklahoma! 1965,D 16,62:1
Carousel 1966,D 16,56:2
Brigadoon 1967,D 14,59:2
Oklahoma! 1969,Jl 6,II,1:1
de Laval, Mario
Carousel 1949,Ja 26,28:2
Carousel 1949,F 6,II,1:1
de Lavallade, Carmen (Miscellaneous)
Revenger's Tragedy, The 1970,D 2,58:1
de Lavallade, Carmen
House of Flowers 1954,D 31,11:2
Eccentricities of Davy Crockett, The 1961,Ja 4,26:1
Willie the Weeper 1961,Ja 4,26:1
Hot Spot 1963,Ap 20,17:2
Metamorphoses 1969,D 12,69:1
Crimes and Crimes 1970,Ja 19,35:1
Don Juan 1970,My 26,32:1
Don Juan 1970,My 31,II,1:6

de Lavallade, Carmen—Cont
Three Philip Roth Stories; Conversion of the Jews
1970,Jl 31,14:1
Cops and Horrors; Dracula 1970,Ag 11,27:1
Cops and Horrors; Fly Paper 1970,Ag 11,27:1
Story Theater Repertory; Gimpel the Food
1970,O 21,40:1
Story Theater Repertory; Saint Julian the
Hospitaler 1970,O 21,40:1
Revenger's Tragedy, The 1970,D 2,58:1
de le Traz, Jean (Playwright)
Pajama Tops 1963,Je 1,15:1
De Leath, Vaughn
Laugh, Clown, Laugh! 1923,N 29,30:1
Three Plays of the Sea 1970,Ag 20,39:1
De Ledger, Stephane
Great Music 1924,O 6,24:1
de Leeuw, Reinbert (Composer)
Reconstruction 1969,Jl 8,36:1
de Leger, Stephane
Lady, The 1923,D 5,23:2
De Lellis, Giovanni
Venetian Twins, The 1968,My 29,23:1
De Leo, Don
Catherine Was Great 1944,Ag 3,16:1
Million Dollar Baby 1945,D 22,17:2
Single Man at a Party 1959,Ap 22,30:4
De Leon, Jack (Original Author)
Silent Witness, The 1931,My 10,VIII,3:5
De Leon, Jack (Playwright)
Silent Witness, The 1931,F 22,VIII,4:4
Silent Witness, The 1931,Mr 24,31:5
Line Engaged 1934,O 25,28:5
de Leon, L Perez
Road to Happiness, The 1927,My 3,24:1
Girl and the Cat, The 1927,My 6,21:2
Blind Heart, The 1927,My 8,30:2
Fragila Rosina 1927,My 10,24:4
Pygmalion 1927,My 12,25:2
De Leon, Raoul
Creoles 1927,S 23,33:3
Dorian Gray 1928,My 22,18:4
De Leon, Walter (Lyricist)
Lollipop 1924,Ja 22,15:3
Rainbow Rose 1926,Mr 17,28:2
De Leon, Walter (Playwright)
Dew Drop Inn 1923,My 18,26:4
Dixie to Broadway 1924,O 30,22:1
Rainbow Rose 1926,Mr 17,28:2
K Guy, The 1928,O 16,28:4
Hello, Yourself 1928,O 31,28:2
de Leoni, Aristides
Colonel Satan 1931,Ja 12,24:1
Adam Had Two Sons 1932,Ja 21,17:1
Nona 1932,O 5,26:4
Keeper of the Keys 1933,O 19,23:2
Hook-Up, The 1935,My 9,24:6
Squaring the Circle 1935,S 22,X,3:2
Squaring the Circle 1935,O 4,24:6
Hallowe'en 1936,F 21,20:3
Tovarich 1936,O 16,31:4
Foreigners 1939,D 6,30:2
de Letrez, Jean (Playwright)
Bichon; Little Dear 1936,D 31,20:5
de Lette, Bruce
Way of the World, The 1924,N 18,23:4
Right to Kill, The 1926,F 16,22:2
de Liagre, Alfred Jr (Director)
Three-Cornered Moon 1933,Mr 17,20:6
By Your Leave 1934,Ja 25,15:3
Petticoat Fever 1935,Mr 5,22:2
Fresh Fields 1936,F 11,19:2
Yes, My Darling Daughter 1937,F 10,19:2
Yes, My Darling Daughter 1937,Je 4,26:2
I Am My Youth 1938,Mr 8,22:4
Mr and Mrs North 1941,Ja 13,11:2
Walrus and the Carpenter, The 1941,N 10,20:2
Little Darling 1942,O 28,26:2
Ask My Friend Sandy 1943,F 5,16:2
Madwoman of Chaillot, The 1950,Je 14,41:2
Second Threshold 1951,Ja 3,23:2
Second Threshold 1951,Ja 14,II,1:1
Escapade 1953,N 19,40:1
Nature's Way 1957,O 17,42:2
de Liagre, Alfred Jr (Miscellaneous)
Front Page, The 1968,O 20,85:5
de Liagre, Alfred Jr (Producer)
Three-Cornered Moon 1933,Mr 17,20:6
By Your Leave 1934,Ja 25,15:3
Pure in Heart, The 1934,Mr 21,24:3
Petticoat Fever 1935,Mr 5,22:2
Fresh Fields 1936,F 11,19:2
Yes, My Darling Daughter 1937,F 10,19:2
I Am My Youth 1938,Mr 8,22:4
Mr and Mrs North 1941,Ja 13,11:2
Walrus and the Carpenter, The 1941,N 10,20:2
Ask My Friend Sandy 1943,F 5,16:2
Voice of the Turtle 1943,D 9,30:3
Voice of the Turtle, The 1944,D 10,II,6:4
Mermaids Singing, The 1945,N 29,26:6
Druid Circle, The 1947,O 23,29:5
Madwoman of Chaillot, The 1948,D 26,II,3:1
Madwoman of Chaillot, The 1949,Ja 9,II,1:1
Madwoman of Chaillot, The 1950,Je 14,41:2

de Liagre, Alfred Jr (Producer)—Cont
Second Threshold 1951,Ja 3,23:2
Deep Blue Sea, The 1952,N 6,38:3
Escapade 1953,N 19,40:1
Janus 1955,N 25,37:2
Nature's Way 1957,O 17,42:2
Girls in 509, The 1958,O 16,47:1
J B 1958,D 12,2:7
Tumbler, The 1960,F 25,32:2
Kwamina 1961,O 24,42:1
Photo Finish 1963,F 14,5:2
Irregular Verb to Love, The 1963,S 19,22:2
Love in E Flat 1967,F 14,38:1
Tiny Alice 1969,S 30,42:1
Flea in Her Ear, A 1969,O 4,25:1
Three Sisters, The 1969,O 10,38:1
Henry V 1969,N 11,43:1
Our Town 1969,N 28,50:1
No Place to Be Somebody 1969,D 31,17:1
Songs From Milk Wood 1970,Ja 13,41:1
Watercolor 1970,Ja 22,30:1
Criss-Crossing 1970,Ja 22,30:1
Harvey 1970,F 25,41:1
Cherry Orchard, The 1970,My 7,63:2
Wilson in the Promise Land 1970,My 27,41:1
De Lima, Charles (Director)
Bare Facts 1927,Ag 17,27:5
de Lima, Luis
Overcoat, The 1960,S 7,45:1
De Loach, Buddy
Carry Nation 1932,O 31,18:2
de Loache, Benjamin
Variations of 1940 1940,Ja 29,12:1
De Lon, Jack
Beggar's Opera, The 1957,Mr 14,35:1
Body Beautiful, The 1958,Ja 24,15:2
Most Happy Fella, The 1959,F 11,50:2
Most Happy Fella, The 1960,Ap 22,25:3
Family Affair, A 1962,Ja 29,17:1
Jennie 1963,O 18,35:2
Guys and Dolls 1965,Ap 29,39:1
Most Happy Fella, The 1966,My 12,55:1
Carousel 1966,D 16,56:2
Mahagonny 1970,Ap 29,51:1
Mahagonny 1970,My 10,II,15:1
de Loos, Polly
Autumn Crocus 1932,N 21,20:2
Between Two Worlds 1934,O 26,24:2
de Lorde, Andre (Playwright)
Au Rat Mort, Cabinet No 6 1923,O 16,18:1
Horrible Experience, L' 1923,O 23,16:1
Laboratoire des Hallucinations, Le 1923,N 20,23:3
Padre, The 1926,D 28,16:3
de Loville, Aljan
Homme Que J'Ai Tue, L'; Man Whom I Have Killed, The 1936,O 10,34:3
Bichon; Little Dear 1936,D 31,20:5
Sexe Fort, Le; Strong Sex, The 1937,Ja 14,17:4
Babes in Arms 1937,Ap 15,18:4
de Lozier, S Bouvet (Mme) (Playwright)
Gods We Make, The 1934,Ja 4,16:4
de Luca, Giuseppe (Musical Director)
Figlia del Dragone Rosso, La; Red Dragon's Daughter, The 1933,D 10,11:7
De Lucas, Cecile
Maid in the Ozarks 1946,Jl 16,20:3
de Luce, Virginia
New Faces of 1952 1952,My 17,23:2
Who Was That Lady I Saw You With? 1958,Mr 4,33:2
Chic 1959,My 19,28:2
De Luise, Dom
Jackass, The 1960,Mr 24,39:2
Another Evening With Harry Stoones 1961,O 23,22:2
All in Love 1961,N 11,15:2
Half-Past Wednesday 1962,Ap 7,16:2
Around the World in 80 Days 1963,Je 24,22:1
Student Gypsy, The; Prince of Liederkranz, The 1963,O 1,34:1
Too Much Johnson 1964,Ja 16,29:1
Around the World in 80 Days 1964,Je 29,33:2
De Luz, Trudy
Miss Liberty 1949,Jl 16,6:5
de Lyon, Leo
Vaudeville (Palace) 1952,F 27,22:2
de Lys, Derna
Medium, The 1948,D 8,41:6
Medium, The 1950,Jl 20,22:5
Medium, The 1950,S 3,II,1:1
de Lys, William (Playwright)
Mistress of the House, The 1950,Ja 31,19:1
de Lys, William (Producer)
Frankie and Johnny 1952,O 29,37:2
De Maio, Peter
Secret Life of Walter Mitty, The 1964,O 27,44:5
Billy 1969,Mr 24,56:1
Dark of the Moon 1970,Ap 4,21:2
De Mal, Carl
Chicago 1926,D 31,11:1
De Malo, Peter
Golden Apple, The 1954,Mr 12,15:2
de Mangus, Louis
Sweethearts 1947,Ja 22,31:2

De Mann, Ronald (Miscellaneous)
Auntie Mame 1956,N 1,47:2
Candide 1956,D 3,40:2
New Girl in Town 1957,My 15,40:1
Music Man, The 1957,D 20,31:1
Redhead 1959,F 6,21:1
Harlequinade 1959,F 14,15:1
Electra 1959,F 14,15:1
There Was a Little Girl 1960,Mr 1,28:1
Gay Divorce 1960,Ap 4,37:1
Tenderloin 1960,O 18,47:2
13 Daughters 1961,Mr 3,17:2
Happiest Girl in the World, The 1961,Ap 4,42:1
Hot Spot 1963,Ap 20,17:2
Roar Like a Dove 1964,My 22,40:2
Mame 1966,My 25,41:1
Fig Leaves Are Falling, The 1969,Ja 3,19:1
De Mar, Ramsey
Love Birds 1921,Mr 16,12:1
De Marco, Antonio
Girl Crazy 1930,O 15,27:1
Casino Varieties 1934,Ap 3,26:4
Boys and Girls Together 1940,O 2,19:2
De Marco, Dominic (Miscellaneous)
Blood Wedding 1958,Ap 1,35:1
de Marco, Jimmy
Boys and Girls Together 1940,S 5,28:6
de Marco, Michael (Costume Designer)
Mandragola 1958,My 29,23:2
Royal Gambit 1959,Mr 5,34:2
de Marco, Michael (Scenic Designer)
Mandragola 1958,My 29,23:2
De Marco, Renee
Girl Crazy 1930,O 15,27:1
Casino Varieties 1934,Ap 3,26:4
Boys and Girls Together 1940,S 5,28:6
Boys and Girls Together 1940,O 2,19:2
De Marco, Sally
Banjo Eyes 1941,N 8,10:6
Banjo Eyes 1941,D 26,20:2
Star Time 1944,S 13,16:2
Star Time 1944,S 17,II,1:1
De Marco, Tony
Banjo Eyes 1941,N 8,10:6
Banjo Eyes 1941,D 26,20:2
Star Time 1944,S 13,16:2
Star Time 1944,S 17,II,1:1
De Marcos, The
Scandals 1924,Jl 1,16:1
Vaudeville (Palace) 1928,Ap 24,29:2
Girl Crazy 1930,O 5,IX,4:6
Actors Fund Fete 1942,F 23,24:5
Show Time 1942,S 17,20:2
Show Time 1942,O 4,VIII,1:1
de Marhanno, Marguerite
Drifting 1922,Ja 3,20:3
De Marinis, Constance
Lower Depths, The 1956,O 3,29:2
de Marney, Derrick
Matriarch, The 1930,Mr 19,24:5
Last Enemy, The 1930,O 31,21:1
Tudor Wench, The 1933,N 12,IX,3:6
Young Mr Disraeli 1934,N 13,22:2
Young Mr Disraeli 1937,N 10,30:5
Importance of Wearing Clothes, The 1951,D 11,44:7
de Marney, Terence
Wanted for Murder 1937,Je 29,18:1
de Marney, Terence (Playwright)
Whispering Gallery, The 1929,Ja 6,VIII,4:4
Whispering Gallery, The 1929,F 12,22:2
Wanted for Murder 1937,Je 29,18:1
Wanted for Murder 1937,Ag 26,25:3
De Marrais, Joan
Enemy of the People, An 1959,F 5,24:4
De Marse, James
Twelfth Night 1969,Ag 14,29:2
Happiness Cage, The 1970,O 5,56:4
De Martin, Imelda
South Pacific 1957,Ap 25,35:1
Girls Against the Boys, The 1959,N 3,26:1
Girls Against the Boys, The 1959,N 8,II,1:1
Jennie 1963,O 18,35:2
Amorous Flea, The 1964,F 18,26:1
Brigadoon 1964,D 24,9:1
de Martino, Leonard
Miss Julie 1965,N 11,59:1
de Martinprey, Floria
Marie Antoinette 1921,N 23,16:1
de Mattos, Alexander Teixera (Translator)
Burgomaster of Stilemonde, The 1923,N 16,15:3
Blue Bird, The 1923,D 26,13:3
De Mause, Alan (Composer)
World of Illusion 1964,Je 25,26:2
De May, Sally
We're Civilized? 1962,N 9,30:1
How Now, Dow Jones 1967,D 8,53:1
De Me, Jeanne
Loose Ankles 1926,Ag 17,15:1
Divided Honors 1929,O 1,28:2
American, Very Early 1934,Ja 31,21:2
De Me, Shirley
Nobody's Money 1921,Ag 18,9:3

De Mel, Carl
Big Fight, The 1928,S 19,33:1
de Mendoza, Fernando Diaz
Pluma en el Viento; Feather in the Wind 1932,Ap 2,13:4
Tambor y Cascabel; Drum and Bell 1932,Ap 21,25:4
De Muy Buena Familia; Of Very Good Family 1932,Ap 29,13:3
De Mette, Stella
Scrap Book 1932,Ag 2,20:3
de Mille, Agnes
Finta Giardiniera, La 1927,Ja 19,20:5
Black Crook, The 1929,Mr 17,X,8:1
Untitled-Dance 1930,F 13,25:2
de Mille, Agnes (Choreographer)
Black Crook, The 1929,Mr 17,X,8:1
Black Crook, The 1929,Ap 7,X,1:1
Swingin' the Dream 1939,N 30,24:2
American Legend 1941,My 12,13:2
Oklahoma! 1943,Ap 1,27:1
Oklahoma! 1943,Ap 11,II,1:1
Oklahoma! 1943,My 9,II,6:4
One Touch of Venus 1943,O 8,14:1
One Touch of Venus 1943,O 17,II,1:1
Bloomer Girl 1944,O 6,18:5
Bloomer Girl 1944,O 8,II,1:1
Carousel 1945,Ap 20,24:2
Carousel 1945,Ap 29,II,1:1
Brigadoon 1947,Mr 14,28:2
Brigadoon 1947,Mr 23,II,1:1
Allegro 1947,O 11,10:2
Allegro 1947,N 2,II,1:1
Carousel 1949,Ja 26,28:2
Carousel 1949,F 6,II,1:1
Gentlemen Prefer Blondes 1949,D 9,35:3
Gentlemen Prefer Blondes 1949,D 18,II,3:1
Brigadoon 1950,My 3,36:2
Carousel 1950,Je 8,37:2
Oklahoma! 1951,My 30,15:2
Paint Your Wagon 1951,N 13,32:2
Paint Your Wagon 1951,N 18,II,1:1
Oklahoma! 1953,S 1,19:1
Girl in Pink Tights, The 1954,Mr 6,13:2
Carousel 1954,Je 3,32:2
Oklahoma! 1955,Je 21,37:7
Brigadoon 1957,Mr 28,37:1
Carousel 1957,S 12,38:2
Oklahoma! 1958,Mr 20,32:3
Goldilocks 1958,O 13,33:1
Goldilocks 1958,O 19,II,1:1
Juno 1959,Mr 10,41:1
Juno 1959,Mr 15,II,1:1
Kwamina 1961,O 24,42:1
Brigadoon 1962,My 31,21:4
Brigadoon 1963,F 1,6:2
Oklahoma! 1963,F 28,8:2
Oklahoma! 1963,My 16,40:1
110 in the Shade 1963,O 25,37:1
Brigadoon 1964,D 24,9:1
Carousel 1965,Ag 11,39:1
Oklahoma! 1965,D 16,62:1
Carousel 1966,D 16,56:2
Brigadoon 1967,D 14,59:2
Oklahoma! 1969,Jl 6,II,1:1
de Mille, Agnes (Director)
Allegro 1947,O 11,10:2
Allegro 1948,Ja 18,II,3:5
Rape of Lucretia, The 1948,D 30,24:2
Out of This World 1950,D 22,17:3
Come Summer 1969,Mr 19,43:1
de Mille, Margaret
When Crummles Played 1928,O 2,34:3
de Mille, William (Director)
Hallowe'en 1936,F 21,20:3
de Mille, William (Playwright)
Man Higher Up, The 1926,N 23,27:3
Little Theatre Tournament; Poor Old Jim 1929,My 10,32:2
Forest Ring, The 1930,Ap 26,11:2
de Mille, William (Producer)
Hallowe'en 1936,F 21,20:3
De Milt, Joe (Producer)
Bidding High 1932,S 29,17:2
de Min, Jacqueline
Zizi 1964,N 23,51:1
De Monde, Miss
Dear Love 1930,My 18,VIII,3:1
De Monde, Belle
Keep Kool 1924,My 23,16:4
De Monde, Dolores
Artists and Models 1930,Je 11,33:2
Paging Danger 1931,F 27,19:2
de Monvil, Renee
Sacred and Profane Love 1920,F 24,11:1
de Moor, Jacqueline
Jazz a La Carte 1922,Je 3,8:3
De Mora, Robert (Costume Designer)
Susannah and the Elders 1959,O 19,37:3
Coach With the Six Insides, The 1962,N 27,44:1
Babu 1967,D 23,28:1
De Mora, Robert (Scenic Designer)
Susannah and the Elders 1959,O 19,37:3

De Mora, Robert (Scenic Designer)—Cont
Long and the Short and the Tall, The
1962,Mr 30,28:2
Coach With the Six Insides, The 1962,N 27,44:1
Babu 1967,D 23,28:1
de Mosa, Noelle
Green Table, The 1942,Ja 22,12:2
Prodigal Son, The 1942,F 18,22:2
De Mossin, Charlotte
Cinderella on Broadway 1920,Je 25,18:1
De Moya, Manuel
To Quito and Back 1937,O 7,30:4
de Munoz, Onda
Career 1943,O 29,22:6
de Musset, Alfred (Original Author)
Night's Candles 1933,S 21,22:1
de Musset, Alfred (Playwright)
Caprice, Un 1924,N 25,26:2
Fantasio 1938,F 8,17:2
Caprice, Un 1938,F 8,17:2
Caprice, Un 1955,N 16,42:4
No Trifling With Love 1959,N 10,55:3
de Navarro, Carlos (Playwright)
Love Scandal, A 1923,N 7,14:1
de Neergaard, Beatrice
John Gabriel Borkman 1926,Ja 30,13:1
Saturday Night 1926,O 26,25:1
Three Sisters, The 1926,O 27,24:1
Locandiera, La; Mistress of the Inn, The
1926,N 23,26:1
Cradle Song 1927,Ja 25,18:2
Good Hope, The 1927,O 19,24:2
2 + 2 = 5 1927,N 29,30:3
Would-Be Gentleman, The 1928,O 2,34:1
Cherry Orchard, The 1928,O 16,28:5
Peter Pan; Boy Who Would Not Grow Up, The
1928,N 27,36:3
Lady From Alfaqueque, The; Consulesa, La
1929,Ja 15,22:3
Lady of the Camellias, The 1931,Ja 27,21:2
Liliom 1932,O 27,23:2
Camille 1932,O 28,23:2
Dear Jane 1932,N 15,24:3
Cherry Orchard, The 1933,Mr 7,20:3
Doctor Monica 1933,N 7,29:3
Hedda Gabler 1934,D 4,22:5
Cradle Song 1934,D 11,28:4
Squaring the Circle 1935,S 22,X,3:2
Squaring the Circle 1935,O 4,24:6
Ghosts 1936,My 12,26:8
Arms for Venus 1937,Mr 12,18:7
Mistress of the Inn, The 1937,Je 22,26:3
One Flight Down 1937,D 14,32:4
Land of Fame 1943,S 22,31:5
Live Life Again 1945,O 1,14:7
Whole World Over, The 1947,Mr 28,28:2
de Nicola, Peter
West Side Story 1968,Je 25,32:1
de Nobili, Lila (Costume Designer)
Love for Love 1967,O 21,17:1
de Nobili, Lila (Scenic Designer)
Love for Love 1967,O 21,17:1
Love for Love 1967,O 30,59:1
de Novellis, Max
Great Big Doorstep, The 1950,Mr 18,8:6
American Mime Theatre 1958,S 25,28:4
de Obaldia, Rene (Playwright)
Grand Vizier, The 1961,D 13,55:5
Cayenne Pepper 1961,D 13,55:5
French Way, The; Grand Vizier, The
1962,Mr 21,36:2
French Way, The; Deceased, The 1962,Mr 21,36:2
French Way, The; Edward and Agrippina
1962,Mr 21,36:2
Rockefeller and the Red Indians 1968,O 25,37:1
de Oca, Montes
Most Happy Fella, The 1966,My 12,55:1
De Pace, Bernardo
George White's Scandals 1926,Je 15,23:2
De Paolo, Dan
Student Prince, The 1943,Je 9,16:2
Hollywood Pinafore 1945,Je 1,20:1
de Paris, Wilbur
Pirate, The 1942,N 26,39:2
Mardi Gras! 1965,Je 28,33:2
de Pascue, Betty
This Man's Town 1930,Mr 11,24:4
de Paul, Gene (Composer)
Li'l Abner 1956,N 16,24:2
Li'l Abner 1956,N 25,II,1:1
De Paul, Justine
Cape Cod Follies 1929,S 19,37:2
De Paule, Hendryk
Farewell to Arms, A 1930,S 23,30:3
de Paur, Leonard
Susanna, Don't You Cry 1939,My 23,27:2
de Paur, Leonard (Miscellaneous)
Haiti 1938,Mr 3,16:1
Winged Victory 1943,N 22,24:1
Carmen Jones 1956,Je 1,28:2
de Paur, Leonard (Musical Director)
John Henry 1940,Ja 11,18:2
De Pauw, Billie
Stars on Ice (2d Edition) 1943,Je 25,13:2

de Peri, Panchita
Zizi 1964,N 23,51:1
de Philippe, Edith
Motel Peissi, The Contor's Kid 1934,N 29,33:3
de Phillippe, Dora
Beggar Student, The 1921,Ja 8,9:3
de Porot-Riche, Georges (Playwright)
Tyranny of Love, The 1921,Mr 2,7:3
Amoureuse 1924,N 28,13:1
De Poumayrac, Jane
Trois Jeunes Filles Nues; Three Young Maids From
the Folies Bergere 1929,Mr 5,28:2
Passionement; Passionately 1929,Mr 8,31:4
Comte Obligado 1929,Mr 12,26:2
Ta Bouche 1929,Mr 15,28:5
Bon Garcon, Un 1929,Mr 19,36:2
Pas Sur La Bouche; Not on the Lips
1929,Mr 26,34:3
De Poyster, Paul
Song of Norway 1944,Ag 22,20:2
De Priest, Margaret
Crucible, The 1958,Mr 12,36:1
Buffalo Skinner, The 1959,F 20,18:1
Picnic on the Battlefield 1960,My 17,42:2
Portrait of the Artist as a Young Man, A
1962,My 29,21:1
Place for Chance, The 1964,My 15,44:2
Friday Night; River, The 1965,F 9,42:5
de Pury, Marianne (Composer)
Viet Rock 1966,N 11,38:1
de Pury, Marianne (Director)
Terminal 1970,Ap 15,51:2
Serpent, The 1970,Je 2,35:1
de Pury, Marianne (Miscellaneous)
Viet Rock 1966,N 11,38:1
de Putti, Lya
Made in France 1930,O 19,IX,3:4
Made in France 1930,N 12,21:1
de Ramey, Pierre
Marathon 1933,Ja 28,8:8
Drums Begin, The 1933,N 25,10:5
Nowhere Bound 1935,Ja 23,20:2
De Luxe 1935,Mr 6,22:2
De Re, Michael
Architruc 1970,Ap 16,55:1
De Re, Michael (Director)
Lettre Morte 1970,Ap 16,55:1
de Reeder, Pierre (Composer)
Singing Girl, The 1952,Je 4,31:8
de Reeder, Pierre (Musical Director)
My Maryland 1936,Ag 12,14:2
Florodora 1936,Ag 23,II,8:2
Blossom Time 1936,Ag 30,II,5:8
Roberta 1937,S 7,16:4
Student Prince, The 1943,Je 9,16:2
de Reeder, Pierre (Producer)
If a Body 1935,My 1,25:3
De Renty, Germaine
Dancing Partner 1930,Ag 6,24:2
De Reszke Singers, The
Untitled-One Man Show 1926,Ap 12,18:1
de Rham, S W
1776 1926,Ap 24,11:2
de Richelieu, Duchesse
Clouds of the Sun 1922,My 6,11:2
de Rigault, Jean (Miscellaneous)
Marcel Marceau 1956,F 2,18:1
Otage, L' 1959,O 27,42:1
Femmes Savantes, Les 1967,F 7,34:2
de Rigault, Jean (Producer)
Ecole des Femmes, L' 1961,Ap 28,23:1
Cantatrice Chauve, La 1962,Ja 16,30:1
Huis Clos 1962,Ja 16,30:1
Diary of a Madman 1967,Mr 24,25:1
Cosmonaute Agricole, Le 1970,Ap 8,38:3
Grand Vizir, Le 1970,Ap 8,38:3
Architruc 1970,Ap 16,55:1
Lettre Morte 1970,Ap 16,55:1
Chaises, Les 1970,My 6,49:1
Lacune, La 1970,My 6,49:1
Jeune Fille a Marier, La 1970,My 6,49:1
de Rigoult, Pierre
Affaires Son les Affaires, Les 1924,Mr 11,17:1
Avare, L'; Miser, The 1924,Mr 12,17:3
Monsieur Brotonneau 1924,Mr 13,14:1
Blanchette 1924,Mr 19,19:4
Vierge Folle, La; Foolish Virgin, The
1924,Mr 22,12:2
de Roche, Rene
Vanderbilt Revue, The 1930,N 6,22:6
de Rochemont, Ren
Zizi 1964,N 23,51:1
De Rome, Lola
Aloma of the South Seas 1925,Ap 21,18:1
de Rosa, Ascanio
Barbara 1929,N 18,24:5
Marchese di Priola, Il 1931,Mr 2,19:3
My Wife Is Different 1931,Ap 27,24:4
De Rosa, William
Straight Thru the Door 1928,O 5,17:2
de Rosas, Enrique
Todo un Hombre 1937,Ap 28,19:2

de Rosas, Enrique—Cont
Cuando Los Hijos De Eva No Son Los Hijos De
Adan 1937,My 1,17:4
Tierra Baja 1937,My 8,22:4
Sirena Varada, La 1937,O 23,15:3
de Rosas, Enrique (Director)
Sirena Varada, La 1937,O 23,15:3
de Rosas, Enrique (Producer)
Sirena Varada, La 1937,O 23,15:3
de Rose, Peter (Composer)
It Happens on Ice 1940,O 11,24:3
de Rose, Peter (Lyricist)
Ziegfeld Follies 1934,Ja 5,24:3
de Rose, Peter (Playwright)
Ziegfeld Follies 1934,Ja 5,24:3
de Rosier, G Philippe (Scenic Designer)
Right You Are (If You Think You Are)
1950,Je 29,37:2
De Roze
Continental Varieties 1934,N 15,24:3
De Ruth, Jan
House in Berlin, A (Als der Kreig zu Ende War);
Als der Krieg zu Ende War (A House in Berlin)
1950,D 27,32:3
Prescott Proposals, The 1953,D 17,53:1
de Sade, Marquis (Original Author)
De Sade Illustrated 1969,My 13,42:4
de Sade, Marquis (Playwright)
Philosophy in the Boudoir 1969,My 22,55:2
de Saint-Phalle, Niki
Tinguely Machine Mystery, or the Love Suicide at
Kaluka, The 1965,D 24,15:5
De Sales, Francis
Dead End 1935,O 29,17:2
Thanks for Tomorrow 1938,S 28,28:2
Liliom 1940,Mr 26,17:2
Man With Blonde Hair, The 1941,N 5,30:2
Men in Shadow 1943,Mr 11,16:2
Three's a Family 1943,My 6,24:2
In Bed We Cry 1944,N 15,20:2
Christopher Blake 1946,D 2,33:2
de San Marzano, Robert
Oliver Twist 1934,Ag 11,16:5
Crab Apple 1936,Jl 8,14:2
Pursuit of Happiness, The 1936,Jl 15,14:1
Post Road 1936,Ag 5,15:4
Royal Family, The 1936,Ag 12,15:1
Art and Mrs Bottle 1936,S 2,18:1
Bachelor Born 1938,Ag 17,23:1
Springtime for Henry 1938,Ag 31,12:5
de San Marzano, Roger
Truth About Blayds, The 1936,Ag 19,18:5
de Santi, Giuseppe
Susannah and the Elders 1959,O 19,37:3
de Santis, Giuseppe
Colonello Bridall, L' 1934,Ap 16,20:3
Romanticismo 1934,My 14,20:2
Miserabili I, 1934,O 1,14:2
Signora Dalle Camelie, La; Camille 1934,O 22,13:2
Processo dei Veleni, Il; Case of Poisons, The
1935,Ja 21,18:2
De Santis, Joseph
Cyrano de Bergerac 1932,D 27,11:2
St Helena 1936,O 7,32:1
Journey to Jerusalem 1940,O 7,21:2
Walk Into My Parlor 1941,N 20,38:2
Men in Shadow 1943,Mr 11,16:2
Storm Operation 1944,Ja 12,28:2
Searching Wind, The 1944,Ap 13,25:2
Front Page, The 1946,S 5,22:4
In Any Language 1952,O 9,40:2
Highest Tree, The 1959,N 5,41:1
Daughter of Silence 1961,D 1,28:1
de Sapio, Francesca
And I Met a Man 1970,Ap 11,20:3
De Sax, G
Maitresse de Roi 1926,D 1,24:1
Misanthrope, Le 1926,D 10,31:2
Aventuriere, L' 1926,D 17,27:3
de Schipper, C'Mari
Faun 1935,N 25,23:5
De Sheim, Charles
My Heart's in the Highlands 1939,Ap 14,29:2
As You Like It 1939,My 9,28:4
As You Like It; Midsummer Night's Dream, A;
Comedy of Errors, The; Taming of the Shrew,
The 1939,My 9,28:4
Time of Your Life, The 1939,O 26,26:2
Journey to Jerusalem 1940,O 7,21:2
De Silva, Bill (Choreographer)
Chief Thing, The 1963,Ap 30,27:2
De Silva, Clarence
Rosalie 1928,Ja 11,26:3
De Silva, Frank
Savages Under the Skin 1927,Mr 25,25:2
Congai 1928,N 28,24:3
Chinese O'Neill 1929,My 23,27:1
Soldiers and Women 1929,S 3,25:1
Singapore 1932,N 15,24:2
Queer People 1934,F 16,16:2
Rain 1935,F 13,24:1
He Who Gets Slapped 1946,Mr 21,31:4
De Silva, J Marshall
Congai 1928,N 28,24:3

De Silva, J Marshall—Cont
Singapore 1932,N 15,24:2
de Silva, John
Goldfish, The 1922,Ap 18,15:3
De Silva, John
Singapore 1932,N 15,24:2
de Silva, N
Via Crucis 1923,N 13,25:2
Burgomaster of Stilemonde, The 1923,N 16,15:3
de Silva, Nancy
Old Bill, M P 1926,N 11,22:2
Royal Virgin, The 1930,Mr 18,30:5
Forest Ring, The 1930,Ap 26,11:2
De Sisto, David
Fiesta 1929,S 18,35:1
Pelican, The 1929,N 14,25:1
Drunkard, The; Fallen Saved, The 1929,D 31,14:6
de Solis, Luchino Solito
Waiting for Godot 1956,Ap 20,21:2
de Soto, Anita
Innkeepers, The 1956,F 3,19:1
de Souiny, Leonie (Playwright)
Musk 1920,Mr 15,13:1
de Souza, Edward
All's Well That Ends Well 1959,Ap 22,30:3
De Spirito, Romolo
Wind Remains, The 1943,Mr 31,16:6
de Statera, Henri
Marie Antoinette 1921,N 23,16:1
De Stefani, Joseph
It Is the Law 1922,N 30,28:2
De Stefanis, Alberto
Subway Express 1929,S 25,34:3
de Stefano, Salvator
Clouds of the Sun 1922,My 6,11:2
De Sylva, B G (Composer)
Manhattan Mary 1927,S 27,30:3
George White's Scandals 1928,Jl 3,19:1
Follow Thru 1929,Ja 10,24:3
Humpty Dumpty 1932,S 18,IX,2:1
De Sylva, B G (Lyricist)
Ziegfeld Follies 1921,Je 22,10:1
George White's Scandals 1922,Ag 29,10:1
Orange Blossoms 1922,S 20,18:1
Yankee Princess, The 1922,O 3,22:1
George White's Scandals 1923,Je 19,22:5
Sweet Little Devil 1924,Ja 22,15:4
Scandals 1924,Jl 1,16:1
Big Boy 1925,Ja 8,28:2
Tell Me More 1925,Ap 14,27:3
George White's Scandals 1925,Je 23,24:2
George White's Scandals 1926,Je 15,23:2
Queen High 1926,S 9,21:2
Good News 1927,S 7,35:4
Manhattan Mary 1927,S 27,30:3
George White's Scandals 1928,Jl 3,19:1
Follow Thru 1929,Ja 10,24:3
Flying High 1930,Mr 4,24:4
De Sylva, B G (Original Author)
Du Barry Was a Lady 1939,D 7,34:2
Louisiana Purchase 1940,My 29,19:2
Panama Hattie 1940,O 31,28:2
De Sylva, B G (Playwright)
Queen High 1926,S 9,21:2
Good News 1927,S 7,35:4
Manhattan Mary 1927,S 27,30:3
Hold Everything 1928,O 11,24:2
Follow Thru 1929,Ja 10,24:3
Flying High 1930,F 9,VIII,4:2
Flying High 1930,Mr 4,24:4
Take a Chance 1932,N 28,11:2
Du Barry 1939,N 19,X,3:4
Panama Hattie 1940,O 4,28:4
Panama Hattie 1940,N 10,IX,1:1
De Sylva, B G (Producer)
Take a Chance 1932,N 28,11:2
Du Barry Was a Lady 1939,D 7,34:2
Louisiana Purchase 1940,My 29,19:2
Panama Hattie 1940,O 31,28:2
de Sylva, Riccardo
Simon Called Peter 1924,N 11,20:2
De Tisne, Edward
King Can Do No Wrong, The 1927,N 17,28:4
Mr Moneypenny 1928,O 17,26:2
De Tisne, Raoul
Scotland Yard 1929,S 28,16:6
Sons o' Guns 1929,N 27,30:4
Prince Charming 1930,O 14,31:1
America's Sweetheart 1931,F 11,23:1
de Toma, Vincenzo
Servant of Two Masters, The 1960,F 24,42:2
De Traumont
Madame Sans-Gene 1924,N 4,30:1
de Troia, Garet
West Side Story 1968,Je 25,32:1
de Vadetzky, Boris
There's Always a Breeze 1938,Mr 3,16:2
De Valat, Regine
Everything's Jake 1930,Ja 17,20:4
de Valery, Leo
Comedy of Women, A 1929,S 14,17:4
de Valery, Leo (Playwright)
Comedy of Women, A 1929,S 14,17:4

de Valery, Leo (Producer)
Comedy of Women, A 1929,S 14,17:4
De Vaudray, William
Lido Girl, The 1928,Ag 24,23:2
de Vaultier, Richard
Carmen Jones 1946,Ap 8,32:2
Carmen Jones 1951,S 22,8:6
de Vecchi, Anthony
Man of La Mancha 1965,N 23,52:1
Golden Rainbow 1968,F 5,27:1
de Ved, Charmion
Across the Board on Tomorrow Morning
1942,Mr 21,13:5
Theatre of the Soul 1942,Mr 21,13:5
de Vega, Lope (Original Author)
Gardener's Dog, The 1927,O 21,27:1
de Vega, Lope (Playwright)
Fuente Ovejuna; Sheep Well, The 1936,My 3,II,4:1
Dog in the Manger, The 1944,Je 18,II,1:1
Chien du Jardinier, Le; Gardener's Dog, The
1957,F 19,36:1
De Velde, Edward
Tenting Tonight 1947,Ap 3,32:2
De Vere, Frisco
Yankee Princess, The 1922,O 3,22:1
de Vestel, Guy
Huitieme Femme de Barbe-Bleue, La
1936,Ja 27,20:5
Homme Que J'Ai Tue, L'; Man Whom I Have
Killed, The 1936,D 10,34:3
Bichon; Little Dear 1936,D 31,20:5
Sexe Fort, Le; Strong Sex, The 1937,Ja 14,17:4
Si Je Voulais; If I Wished to 1937,Ja 28,22:5
Dans Le Noir; In the Dark 1937,F 11,18:3
Christian 1937,F 25,18:6
Foreigners 1939,D 6,30:2
de Vestel, Guy (Director)
Martine 1936,N 26,38:2
Homme Que J'Ai Tue, L'; Man Whom I Have
Killed, The 1936,D 10,34:3
Bichon; Little Dear 1936,D 31,20:5
Sexe Fort, Le; Strong Sex, The 1937,Ja 14,17:4
Si Je Voulais; If I Wished to 1937,Ja 28,22:5
Dans Le Noir; In the Dark 1937,F 11,18:3
Christian 1937,F 25,18:6
de Vestel, Guy (Producer)
Huitieme Femme de Barbe-Bleue, La
1936,Ja 27,20:5
de Villard, Joseph M
Baby Pompadour 1934,D 28,24:2
Nowhere Bound 1935,Ja 23,20:2
Life's Too Short 1935,S 21,18:5
To Quito and Back 1937,O 7,30:4
Tortilla Flat 1938,Ja 13,16:2
De Vine, Claire
High Flyers 1927,Je 26,VIII,1:1
De Vinny, H B
Somebody's Lion 1921,Ap 13,20:1
de Vise, Peter
Silent Night, Lonely Night 1959,D 4,36:1
Camelot 1960,D 5,42:1
Journey to the Day 1963,N 12,49:1
De Vito, Anthony
Lady From Maxim's, The 1970,Je 1,41:1
De Vito, Danny
Shoot Anything With Hair That Moves
1969,F 3,29:1
License, The 1969,Ap 23,42:1
Jar, The 1969,Ap 23,42:1
De Vito, Dorothy
Creeping Fire 1935,Ja 17,22:3
de Vito, Eleanor (Costume Designer)
Merry-Go-Rounders, The 1956,N 22,50:1
De Voe, Louise
Outrageous Mrs Palmer, The 1920,O 13,18:1
De Voe, Marjorie
Cinderelative 1930,S 19,18:4
Born Yesterday 1958,Mr 22,12:6
De Voe, Mlle
Cloches de Cornville, Les; Chimes of Normandy,
The 1926,D 14,24:4
De Vonde, Chester (Director)
Kongo 1926,Mr 31,20:5
Tia Juana 1927,N 16,28:4
De Vonde, Chester (Playwright)
Kongo 1926,Mr 31,20:5
Tia Juana 1927,N 16,28:4
De Vries, Beppe
Merry Widow, The 1929,D 3,29:1
Merry Widow, The 1932,F 21,VIII,23:3
De Vries, Henry
How Revolting! 1932,Mr 11,14:6
de Vries, Henry P
Great Shakes 1931,Mr 12,22:2
De Vries, Jan
Major Barbara 1965,My 18,33:1
de Vries, Robert
Diary of Anne Frank, The 1956,N 29,43:1
De Vries, Wim (Miscellaneous)
World of Cilli Wang, The 1957,O 15,38:4
De Werth, Ernest (Costume Designer)
Midsummer Night's Dream, A 1927,Ag 8,6:1

De Whirst, Chester
Night Hostess 1928,S 13,31:2
de Wilde, Brandon
Member of the Wedding, The 1950,Ja 6,26:6
Member of the Wedding, The 1950,Ja 15,II,1:1
Member of the Wedding, The 1950,S 17,II,1:1
Mrs McThing 1952,F 21,22:1
Mrs McThing 1952,Mr 2,II,1:1
Emperor's Clothes, The 1953,F 10,24:2
Comes a Day 1958,N 7,22:1
Race of Hairy Men!, A 1965,Ap 30,42:1
Race of Hairy Men!, A 1965,My 9,II,1:2
de Wilde, Frederic
Brother Cain 1941,S 13,21:5
Lamp at Midnight 1947,D 22,29:2
de Wilde, Frederic (Miscellaneous)
Separate Tables 1956,O 26,33:1
Day the Money Stopped, The 1958,F 21,19:4
Visit, The 1958,My 6,40:1
Distant Bell, A 1960,Ja 14,29:1
Farewell, Farewell Eugene 1960,S 28,35:1
Rape of the Belt, The 1960,N 7,46:1
Come Blow Your Horn 1961,F 23,31:3
Man for All Seasons, A 1961,N 23,51:1
After the Fall 1964,Ja 24,18:1
Marco Millions 1964,F 21,33:1
But for Whom Charlie 1964,Mr 13,42:2
Incident at Vichy 1964,D 4,44:1
Utbu 1966,Ja 5,24:1
Where's Daddy? 1966,Mr 3,27:1
Watering Place, The 1969,Mr 13,51:1
Conduct Unbecoming 1970,O 13,50:1
De Winter, George
Richard III 1920,Mr 8,7:1
de Wit, Jacqueline
Romeo and Juliet 1934,D 21,30:3
Country Wife, The 1935,Jl 2,24:2
Caesar and Cleopatra 1935,Ag 22,21:1
Kind Lady 1937,Jl 6,23:1
Madame Bovary 1937,N 17,26:2
Empress of Destiny 1938,Mr 10,16:2
Day in the Sun 1939,My 17,29:2
Come of Age 1952,Ja 24,22:2
de Witt, Camilla
Annie Get Your Gun 1946,My 17,14:2
Jenny Kissed Me 1948,D 24,12:2
Bernardine 1952,O 17,33:4
De Witt, Fay
Pardon Our French 1950,O 6,22:4
Flahooley 1951,My 15,39:1
Shoestring '57 1956,N 6,31:1
Vintage '60 1960,S 13,41:1
Oklahoma! 1963,My 16,40:1
De Witt, Francis (Lyricist)
Oh, Ernest! 1927,My 10,24:3
De Witt, Francis (Playwright)
90 Horse Power 1926,Mr 16,22:4
Oh, Ernest! 1927,My 10,24:3
Absent Father 1932,O 18,23:5
De Witt, June
Jacob Slovak 1927,O 6,28:4
De Witte, Daisy
Sun-Kist 1921,My 24,20:2
de Wohl, Louis (Playwright)
Restless Flame, The 1952,Ap 15,30:6
De Wolf, Ward
Anna Ascends 1920,S 23,14:1
De Wolfe, Billy
Actors Fund Fete 1942,F 23,24:5
John Murray Anderson's Almanac 1953,D 11,42:2
Almanac 1954,Ja 3,II,1:1
Ziegfeld Follies 1957,Mr 2,19:2
How to Succeed in Business Without Really Trying
1966,Ap 21,45:1
De Wolfe, J S
Clair de Lune 1921,Ap 19,15:1
de Wolfe, Jacques
Comedian, The 1923,Mr 14,14:1
De Wolfe, Stanley
Juarez and Maximilian 1926,O 12,31:1
Katy Did 1927,My 10,24:3
Porgy 1927,O 11,26:2
Ladies Don't Lie 1929,O 11,36:3
Hotel Alimony 1934,Ja 30,16:2
de Wolfe, Vera
Orange Blossoms 1922,S 20,18:1
de Wolfe, Warde
Merchant of Venice, The 1922,D 22,13:1
de Zogheb, Jacques (Playwright)
Sport 1930,F 16,IX,4:4
de Zogheb, Madeline (Playwright)
Sport 1930,F 16,IX,4:4
De Zramont
Aiglon, L' 1924,O 21,21:1
Deacon, Richard
Hello, Dolly! 1970,Ja 25,70:6
Deagon, Arthur
Little Nellie Kelly 1922,N 14,16:1
Rose Marie 1924,S 3,12:2
Deagon, Gracie
Cinderella on Broadway 1920,Je 25,18:1
Deakins, June
Son, The 1950,Ag 16,24:6

Deal, Borden (Playwright)
Joyful Noise, A 1966,D 16,57:1
DeAlbrew, Peppy
De Luxe 1935,Mr 6,22:2
Dean, Abner (Miscellaneous)
Too True to Be Good 1963,Mr 14,8:2
Dean, Alex (Producer)
Beware of the Bull 1933,My 30,13:7
Dean, Alexander (Director)
Roof, The 1930,Je 14,9:2
Saint's Parade 1930,N 1,23:4
Racket, The 1930,N 20,30:6
Russet Mantle 1936,Ja 17,15:5
Russet Mantle 1936,Ja 26,IX,1:1
Laughing Woman, The 1936,Jl 8,14:7
Laughing Woman, The 1936,O 14,30:1
In Clover 1937,O 14,23:1
Dean, Alexander (Miscellaneous)
In Clover 1937,O 14,23:1
Dean, Alfred
Wandering Jew, The 1927,F 2,22:4
Dean, Barbara
Sally 1920,D 22,16:1
Dean, Basil (Director)
Hassan 1923,O 14,VIII,2:6
Peter Pan 1924,N 7,16:2
Little Minister, The 1925,Mr 24,21:1
Young Woodley 1925,N 3,34:1
School for Scandal, The 1925,D 7,18:2
Easy Virtue 1925,D 8,28:2
This Was a Man 1926,N 24,27:1
Constant Nymph, The 1926,D 10,31:1
Constant Nymph, The 1926,D 19,VII,3:1
Autumn Crocus 1932,N 21,20:2
Follow Your Saint 1936,S 25,20:3
Day of Glory, The 1946,D 22,II,2:1
Dean, Basil (Miscellaneous)
Hassan 1924,S 23,23:1
Easy Virtue 1925,D 8,28:2
Autumn Crocus 1932,N 21,20:2
Dean, Basil (Playwright)
Constant Nymph, The 1926,D 10,31:1
Come With Me 1928,My 20,VIII,2:3
Beau Geste 1929,F 17,IX,2:1
Tessa 1935,Ja 6,IX,2:1
Murder Gang 1935,N 16,19:2
Murder Gang 1935,D 15,XI,5:6
Dean, Basil (Producer)
Constant Nymph, The 1926,D 10,31:1
Second Man, The 1928,F 12,VIII,2:1
Young Woodley 1928,Mr 11,VIII,1:3
Moving Finger, The 1928,S 16,IX,1:4
Circle of Chalk, The 1929,Mr 31,VIII,2:6
Roof, The 1929,N 6,30:4
Healthy, Wealthy and Wise 1930,Mr 2,26:3
Autumn Crocus 1931,Ap 26,VIII,2:4
Queer Cattle 1932,My 19,24:2
Inside the Room 1934,D 23,15:3
Sun Never Sets, The 1938,Je 26,IX,2:1
Dean, Dot
Vaudeville (Palace) 1927,Mr 22,31:1
Vaudeville (Palace) 1928,O 30,27:3
Dean, Douglas
Johnny 2X4 1942,Mr 17,24:6
Dean, Eddie
Little Orchard Annie 1930,Ap 22,33:1
Dean, Gerri
Sambo 1969,D 22,42:1
Me Nobody Knows, The 1970,My 19,42:1
Me Nobody Knows, The 1970,My 31,II,1:6
Dean, Horme (Choreographer)
Aqua Carnival 1962,Je 29,15:1
Dean, Irene
Utopia, Limited; Flowers of Progress, The 1957,F 27,21:1
Mikado, The 1957,Ap 24,28:2
H M S Pinafore 1957,My 1,42:6
Pirates of Penzance, The 1957,My 8,43:1
Yeomen of the Guard, The 1957,My 22,28:3
Gondoliers, The 1957,My 29,34:2
Dean, Isabel
Hotel in Amsterdam, The 1968,Jl 21,II,12:1
Dean, Jacque
Drat! the Cat! 1965,O 11,54:2
Dean, James
See the Jaguar 1952,D 4,46:2
Immoralist, The 1954,F 9,22:1
Immoralist, The 1954,F 14,II,1:1
Dean, Janice
Adding Machine, The 1970,D 5,40:1
Dean, Jerold
Jazz Singer, The 1925,S 15,29:2
Dean, Jo Ann
It Happens on Ice 1940,O 11,24:3
It Happens on Ice 1941,Ap 5,13:2
Dean, John
Gondoliers, The 1934,S 4,23:1
Cox and Box 1934,S 7,24:3
Gondoliers, The 1934,S 9,IX,1:1
Yeomen of the Guard, The 1934,S 21,28:3
Ruddigore 1934,S 25,25:2
Princess Ida; Castle Adamant 1934,S 28,26:3
Patience 1934,O 12,32:2

Pirates of Penzance, The 1936,S 1,24:4
Gondoliers, The 1936,S 8,23:1
Cox and Box 1936,S 29,34:2
Patience 1936,O 6,28:6
Princess Ida 1936,O 13,32:2
Ruddigore 1936,O 23,26:4
Pirates of Penzance, The 1939,Ja 6,25:1
Iolanthe 1939,Ja 13,16:3
Cox and Box 1939,Ja 17,27:5
Yeomen of the Guard, The 1939,Ja 24,17:1
Patience 1939,Ja 27,16:3
Dean, Julia
Poldekin 1920,S 10,12:1
Dean, Kathi
Gay Divorce 1960,Ap 4,37:1
Dean, Leamond
Conversation Piece 1957,N 19,38:2
Dean, Libby
Marathon '33 1963,D 23,20:1
Dean, Man Mountain Jr
Teahouse of the August Moon, The 1956,N 9,33:2
Dean, Mary Jennings
Reunion of Sorts 1969,O 15,40:1
Dean, Maysie
Trial by Jury 1939,Ja 6,25:1
Pirates of Penzance, The 1939,Ja 6,25:1
Mikado, The 1939,Ja 10,16:3
Iolanthe 1939,Ja 13,16:3
Gondoliers, The 1939,Ja 20,14:2
Dean, Nina
Mikado, The 1935,Jl 16,24:4
Pirates of Penzance, The 1935,Jl 23,24:2
Yeomen of the Guard, The 1935,Jl 30,16:4
Dean, Norma
Hell'z-A-Splashin' 1959,Je 25,22:2
Dean, Norman (Composer)
Autumn's Here 1966,O 26,40:1
Dean, Norman (Lyricist)
Autumn's Here 1966,O 26,40:1
Dean, Norman (Miscellaneous)
Autumn's Here 1966,O 26,40:1
Dean, Norman (Musical Director)
Greenwillow 1970,D 8,60:1
Dean, Norman (Playwright)
Autumn's Here 1966,O 26,40:1
Dean, Paula
Arms and the Man 1956,O 2,39:4
Pink String and Sealing Wax 1957,S 6,13:1
Dean, Paula (Producer)
Pink String and Sealing Wax 1957,S 6,13:1
Dean, Philip
Wisteria Trees, The 1955,F 3,20:2
Dean, Philip (Playwright)
This Bird of Dawning Singeth All Night Long 1968,D 31,19:1
This Bird of Dawning Singeth All Night Long 1969,Ja 12,II,1:1
Dean, Priscilla
Pierre of the Plains 1929,Ja 6,VIII,4:4
Dean, Ray
Vaudeville (Palace) 1927,Mr 22,31:1
Vaudeville (Palace) 1928,O 30,27:3
Dean, Robert
Point of Honor, A 1937,F 12,26:2
Dean, Roy
Merchant of Venice, The 1955,Ja 8,9:7
King Lear 1956,Ja 13,17:1
King Lear 1956,Ja 22,II,1:1
Dean, Shannon
Abie's Irish Rose 1937,My 13,30:2
Knights of Song 1938,O 18,29:2
Laffing Room Only 1944,D 25,15:4
Michael Todd's Peep Show 1950,Je 29,37:2
Auntie Mame 1958,Ag 12,33:2
Dean, Steve
Hair 1967,O 30,55:1
Dean, Susan
Idiot's Delight 1957,F 23,14:2
Dean, Verna
Humble, The 1926,O 14,22:2
Dean, Viola
Never No More 1932,Ja 8,27:1
Brain Sweat 1934,Ap 5,24:4
Macbeth 1936,Ap 15,25:4
Turpentine 1936,Je 27,21:6
Out From Under 1940,My 6,13:2
Skin of Our Teeth, The 1942,N 19,29:5
Chicken Every Sunday 1944,Ap 6,27:2
And Be My Love 1945,F 22,30:4
Round Trip 1945,My 30,16:4
Dean, Violet
90 Horse Power 1926,Mr 16,22:4
Dean, Will
Where Do We Go From Here? 1938,N 16,26:2
Dean, William
Bronx Express 1922,Ap 27,12:2
Flame of Love 1924,Ap 22,19:2
Peter Pan 1924,N 7,16:2
Dean, William (Producer)
Rape of the Belt, The 1960,N 7,46:1
DeAnda, Peter
Sound of Silence, A 1965,Mr 9,30:1
Zulu and the Zayda, The 1965,N 11,59:1

DeAnda, Peter—Cont
Kitchen, The 1966,Je 14,50:1
Inherit the Wind 1967,Je 23,50:1
Guide, The 1968,Mr 7,50:1
Passing Through From Exotic Places; Sunstroke 1969,D 8,60:4
House of Leather, The 1970,Mr 19,56:1
Deane, Berna
Love Call, The 1927,O 25,33:1
Deane, Christopher
Child's Play 1970,F 18,39:1
Deane, Doris
Vagabond King, The 1935,N 29,22:7
Love Is No Heaven 1943,Mr 16,15:3
Deane, Douglas
Million Dollar Baby 1945,D 22,17:2
Where's Charley? 1948,O 12,33:2
Guys and Dolls 1950,N 25,11:2
Boy Friend, The 1954,O 1,20:1
Deane, Gregory
We the People 1933,Ja 23,9:5
Hilda Cassidy 1933,My 5,18:3
Order Please 1934,O 10,21:2
Deane, Gregory (Director)
Few Are Chosen 1935,S 18,19:3
Greater Lust, The 1936,Jl 14,22:4
Amateur Hour 1936,Jl 21,13:1
Call Me Ziggy 1937,F 13,9:6
Deane, Gregory (Producer)
Greater Lust, The 1936,Jl 14,22:4
Amateur Hour 1936,Jl 21,13:1
Deane, Hamilton (Playwright)
Dracula 1927,O 6,29:1
Dracula 1931,Ap 14,33:3
Deane, Katherine
Susan and God 1937,O 8,26:4
Eye on the Sparrow 1938,My 4,26:3
Deane, Melba
I Must Love Someone 1939,F 8,18:7
Deane, Richard
Sophie 1944,D 26,22:7
Corn Is Green, The 1950,Ja 12,33:2
Deane, Toby
Hit the Trail 1954,D 3,31:2
Deane, Vera
Everywhere I Roam 1938,D 30,10:4
Deane, Virginia
Baby Pompadour 1934,D 28,24:2
Deane, William
Fuente Ovejuna; Sheep Well, The 1936,My 3,II,4:1
Deaner, George
Polly Preferred 1923,Ja 12,13:3
DeAngelis, Rosemary
In the Summer House 1964,Mr 26,43:1
Deans, Harris (Playwright)
Husbands Are a Problem 1922,Ag 27,VI,1:5
Dear, George W
Great Way, The 1921,N 8,28:2
Dearborn, Dalton
Burning Bush, The 1949,D 17,15:5
Mary Stuart 1957,O 9,39:1
Makropoulos Secret, The 1957,D 4,52:4
Emperor, The 1963,Ap 17,30:1
MacBird! 1967,F 23,38:1
Dearborn, Dorothy
Fruehlingsluft 1921,N 29,17:4
Dearborn, Elwyn
Desire Under the Elms 1952,Ja 17,23:4
Dearborn, Hal
Night Remembers, The 1934,N 28,24:3
Dearborn, L
Gentlemen, the Queen 1927,Ap 23,14:3
Dearden, Anthony
Dock Brief, The 1961,N 22,24:2
What Shall We Tell Caroline? 1961,N 22,24:2
Dearden, Audrey
Trial by Jury 1952,N 4,32:2
Iolanthe 1952,N 11,26:3
Dearden, Harold (Playwright)
Interference 1927,F 20,VII,1:4
Interference 1927,F 27,VII,1:3
Interference 1927,O 19,24:3
Interference 1927,D 18,IX,1:1
Happy Medium 1936,My 4,17:7
To Kill a Cat 1939,Jl 2,IX,1:6
Dearden, Peg
Iolanthe 1965,My 19,42:1
DeArechaga, Frederic M (Miscellaneous)
Lysistrata 1959,My 20,40:2
Dearing, Ann
Cellar and the Well, The 1950,D 11,30:2
Dearing, Peter
Much Ado About Nothing 1929,N 17,30:4
Hamlet 1931,Ap 24,26:4
Hamlet 1954,Ap 24,15:2
Dearing, Peter (Director)
Much Ado About Nothing 1929,N 17,30:4
Dearly, Max
Baby Mine 1921,S 4,13:2
Potash and Perlmutter 1926,N 14,VIII,2:1
Coiffeur Pour Dames 1928,Ja 1,VIII,2:3
Roi, Le 1931,Ap 5,VIII,3:1
DeArment, Daniel C
Everyman Today 1958,Ja 16,32:4

Dearring, Mary Lee
Anniversary Waltz 1954,Ap 8,34:1
Dears, Francis
Bonds of Interest, The 1929,O 15,34:2
Dearth, John
Midsummer Night's Dream, A 1954,S 22,33:1
Deas, Lawrence (Choreographer)
Change Your Luck 1930,Je 7,10:2
Deasey, Dillon M
Woman of Destiny, A 1936,Mr 3,25:2
Deasy, Ann
Brigadoon 1950,My 3,36:2
Deasy, Dillon
Post Road 1934,D 5,28:3
Deasy, Mary (Playwright)
Morning Sun 1963,O 7,36:2
deBanzie, Los
Elizabeth the Queen 1966,N 4,30:1
DeBarr, Margo
What a Killing 1961,Mr 28,41:1
Debary, Jacques
Tartuffe 1968,Jl 3,28:2
DeBella, Richard
Body Beautiful, The 1958,Ja 24,15:2
Debenham, Cicely
9 O'Clock Revue 1923,O 5,22:1
Debenham, Dorothy
9 O'Clock Revue 1923,O 5,22:1
Bitter Sweet 1929,N 6,30:2
Debenning, Burris
Thistle in My Bed 1963,N 20,48:1
Debin, Lenny (Producer)
Can-Can 1959,Ag 26,25:4
DeBoer, Franklin (Producer)
Peace 1969,Ja 28,49:1
deBoer, Fritz (Lighting Director)
Walk Together Children 1968,N 12,54:1
Debonairs, The
You Never Know 1938,S 22,26:3
Nellie Bly 1946,Ja 22,32:2
Nellie Bly 1946,Ja 27,II,1:1
Tidbits of 1946 1946,Jl 9,17:2
Debonera, N
Electra 1961,S 20,23:4
Choephori 1961,S 27,32:4
DeBruce, Robert
Suspect 1940,Ap 10,30:4
Debucourt
Dompteur, Le, ou L'Anglais Tel Qu' On La Mange
1926,Ja 10,VII,1:3
As You Like It 1934,N 11,IX,3:6
Debussy, Claude (Composer)
Pelleas et Melisande 1939,Ap 2,X,7:4
Toy Box 1955,D 18,95:3
deCamo, Charles
Jumbo 1935,N 18,20:2
DeCarlo, Anthony
Phaedra 1967,My 22,50:2
DeCarlos, Juan
Open 24 Hours 1969,F 12,31:1
Decart, Andre
Trois Jeunes Filles Nues; Three Young Maids From
the Folies Bergere 1929,Mr 5,28:2
Comte Obligado 1929,Mr 12,26:2
Bon Garcon, Un 1929,Mr 19,36:2
Dechaux, George
Agent 666, L' 1923,My 30,10:5
Dechazza, Pepe (Choreographer)
Cabin in the Sky 1964,Ja 22,32:1
Deckard, Diane
Sweeney Todd 1957,Ag 28,21:4
Decker, Edith
Two Little Girls in Blue 1921,My 4,10:3
Decker, Elma
Right Girl, The 1921,Mr 16,12:1
Decker, Elsie
Yankee Princess, The 1922,O 3,22:1
Decker, John (Producer)
Before I Wake 1968,O 14,56:1
Decker, Lionel
There Is No End 1950,F 17,27:4
Decker, Marceline
Man of La Mancha 1965,N 23,52:1
Decker, Nancy
Vaudeville (Palace) 1929,O 7,22:4
Decker, Norma
Will and the Way, The 1957,D 3,46:5
Decoin, Henri (Playwright)
Hector 1932,Mr 20,VIII,2:2
Untitled-Play 1937,Ja 24,X,2:1
DeCosta, Wilfred
Roll Sweet Chariot 1934,O 3,24:3
deCoursey, Patricia
Wisteria Trees, The 1950,Mr 30,39:1
Decroux, Etienne
Mime Theatre of Etienne Decroux, The
1959,D 24,15:1
Decroux, Etienne (Composer)
Mime Theatre of Etienne Decroux, The
1959,D 24,15:1
Decroux, Etienne (Director)
Mime Theatre of Etienne Decroux, The
1959,D 24,15:1

Deddens, Helen
Lombardi, Ltd 1927,Je 7,27:3
Late One Evening 1933,Ja 10,27:3
Dedovitch
Chauve-Souris 1929,Ja 23,20:2
Dee, Billie
Let's Face It 1941,O 30,26:2
Dee, Blanche
Rimers of Eldritch, The 1967,F 21,53:1
Homo 1969,Ap 12,40:2
Grin and Bare It 1970,Mr 17,36:1
Dee, Frances
Secret Room, The 1945,N 8,16:2
Dee, H B
Lancelot and Elaine 1921,S 13,12:1
Dee, Harry
Page Miss Glory 1934,N 28,24:2
Dee, Mel 'n' (Composer)
Fun City 1968,Mr 7,53:2
Dee, Pauline
Burlesque 1927,S 2,15:3
Houseboat on the Styx, The 1928,D 26,14:3
Mystery Moon 1930,Je 24,23:4
Dee, Ruby
South Pacific 1943,D 30,11:2
Walk Hard 1944,D 1,28:2
Jeb 1946,F 22,20:2
Long Way From Home, A 1948,F 9,25:2
Smile of the World, The 1949,Ja 13,26:5
World of Sholom Aleichem, The 1953,S 12,13:2
Raisin in the Sun, A 1959,Mr 12,27:1
Purlie Victorious 1961,S 29,29:1
Purlie Victorious 1961,O 8,II,1:1
Taming of the Shrew, The 1965,Je 24,32:2
King Lear 1965,Je 25,39:1
Oresteia 1966,Je 30,29:1
Birds, The 1966,Jl 1,40:1
Boesman and Lena 1970,Je 23,35:1
Boesman and Lena 1970,Jl 5,II,1:3
Dee, Sylvia (Lyricist)
Barefoot Boy With Cheek 1947,Ap 4,20:2
Deebank, Felix
Deep Blue Sea, The 1952,N 6,38:3
Escapade 1953,N 19,40:1
Dandy Dick 1956,Ja 11,37:2
In Good King Charles's Golden Days
1957,Ja 25,16:1
In Good King Charles's Golden Days
1957,F 3,II,1:1
Epitaph for George Dillon 1958,N 5,44:1
Duel of Angels 1960,Ap 20,42:2
Deeble, Deborah
Up Eden 1968,N 27,42:1
Deedee
Sea Legs 1937,My 19,26:5
Deeder, Dorothy
Americana 1926,Jl 27,15:3
White Lights 1927,O 12,30:4
Deeds, Tony (Lighting Director)
You Can't Take It With You 1951,Ap 7,8:6
Deeds, Tony (Scenic Designer)
You Can't Take It With You 1951,Ap 7,8:6
Lady's Not for Burning, The 1959,Ja 31,13:2
Deegan, Denis (Director)
Last Minstrel, The 1963,My 9,40:2
Save Me a Place at Forest Lawn 1963,My 9,40:2
Deegan, Denis (Producer)
Last Minstrel, The 1963,My 9,40:2
Save Me a Place at Forest Lawn 1963,My 9,40:2
Deei, Kaie
Passenger to Bali, A 1940,Mr 15,26:2
Family, The 1943,Mr 31,22:4
South Pacific 1943,D 30,11:2
Teahouse of the August Moon, The 1953,O 16,32:1
Time Limit! 1956,Ja 25,27:2
Shangri-La 1956,Je 14,40:1
Deeks, Jean
Boys From Syracuse, The 1963,Ap 16,31:1
That Hat! 1964,S 24,45:1
Deel, Sandra
Look, Ma, I'm Dancin' 1948,Ja 30,20:2
South Pacific 1949,Ap 8,30:2
Grey-Eyed People, The 1952,D 18,41:2
South Pacific 1955,My 5,39:5
Deeming, Marianne
Romanoff and Juliet 1957,O 11,24:1
Deems, Mickey
Alive and Kicking 1950,Ja 18,25:5
Kaleidoscope 1957,Je 14,20:2
Golden Fleecing 1959,O 16,24:5
Vintage '60 1960,S 13,41:1
Anything Goes 1962,My 16,35:1
Little Me 1962,N 19,41:3
Deep River Boys, The
How Come Lawd? 1937,O 1,18:5
Deer Horn, Dorothy
Thais 1931,Je 19,21:3
Deer Horn, Dorothy (Director)
Thais 1931,Je 19,21:3
Deering, D V
Lady of the Rose 1925,My 20,26:4
Honor of the Family, The 1926,D 27,21:1

Deering, Diane
Salvation on a String; No Count Boy, The
1954,Jl 7,23:1
110 in the Shade 1963,O 25,37:1
Our Town 1969,N 28,50:1
Deering, Gladyce
Woof, Woof 1929,D 26,20:4
Deering, Jane
Early to Bed 1943,Je 18,16:2
Are You With It? 1945,N 12,17:3
Three to Make Ready 1946,Mr 8,16:2
Deering, John
Strangers at Home 1934,S 15,20:5
Deering, Olive
Searching for the Sun 1936,F 20,22:6
Daughters of Atreus 1936,O 15,33:1
Eternal Road, The 1937,Ja 8,14:2
Richard II 1937,F 6,14:2
Medicine Show 1940,Ap 13,20:6
No for an Answer 1941,Ja 6,10:6
They Walk Alone 1941,Mr 13,24:2
Nathan the Wise 1942,Mr 12,25:4
Nathan the Wise 1942,Ap 4,18:4
Counsellor-at-Law 1942,N 25,17:2
Winged Victory 1943,N 22,24:1
Yellow Jack 1944,Ap 7,23:3
Sky Drift 1945,N 14,25:2
Dark Legend 1952,Mr 25,24:2
Trojan Women, The 1957,Mr 19,42:7
Othello 1957,Je 24,19:2
Devil's Advocate, The 1961,Mr 10,20:1
Devil's Advocate, The 1961,Mr 19,II,1:1
Marathon '33 1963,D 23,20:1
Murder in the Cathedral 1966,Je 21,38:1
Ceremony of Innocence, The 1968,Ja 2,33:1
Deering, Patricia
Nowhere Bound 1935,Ja 23,20:2
Lady in the Dark 1941,Ja 24,14:2
Lady in the Dark 1941,S 3,26:6
Deering, Rosemary
International Revue 1930,F 26,22:2
Everybody's Welcome 1931,S 20,VIII,3:2
Deering, William Rogers (Producer)
Out of the Frying Pan 1941,F 12,24:2
Dees, Milton S
Taboo 1922,Ap 5,22:1
Deeter, Jasper
World We Live In, The 1922,N 1,16:1
Princess Turandot 1926,N 13,14:2
Heartbreak House 1935,Jl 23,24:3
Arms and the Man 1937,Jl 20,19:3
Emperor Jones, The 1945,Ja 17,18:4
Deeter, Jasper (Director)
In Abraham's Bosom 1926,D 31,10:2
Blue and the Gray, The; War Is Hell Gray, The
1929,D 27,26:4
Cherokee Night, The 1932,Je 21,19:4
Cherokee Night, The 1932,Je 26,IX,1:1
Heartbreak House 1935,Jl 23,24:3
One Way to Heaven 1936,S 29,35:1
Arms and the Man 1937,Jl 20,19:3
Too True to Be Good 1937,Jl 27,24:2
Too True to Be Good 1937,Ag 15,II,5:8
Bystander 1937,S 15,27:1
Emperor Jones, The 1945,Ja 17,18:4
Emperor Jones, The 1945,Ja 28,II,1:1
Deeter, Jasper (Producer)
Behold Your God 1936,Ap 22,28:3
Deevy, Teresa (Playwright)
Disciple, The 1931,S 27,VIII,2:8
Katie Roche 1937,O 4,17:4
Deffry, Josephine
Clubs Are Trumps 1924,O 15,27:1
Dove, The 1925,F 12,17:3
Crime 1927,F 23,27:3
Booster, The 1929,O 25,26:2
Sing High, Sing Low 1931,N 13,26:4
Hilda Cassidy 1933,My 5,18:3
DeFilippi, Dino (Director)
Imaginary Invalid, The 1968,My 28,41:1
DeFore, Don
Where Do We Go From Here? 1938,N 16,26:2
Steel 1939,D 20,30:2
Male Animal, The 1940,Ja 10,17:2
Dream Girl 1951,My 10,39:1
DeForest, Marie
Meet the People 1940,D 26,22:2
Defresne, Louis
Nuit au Bouge, Une 1923,O 16,18:1
Au Rat Mort, Cabinet No 6 1923,O 16,18:1
Au Coin Joli 1923,O 23,16:1
Sur la Dalle 1923,O 30,17:2
Crucifies, Les 1923,O 30,17:2
Alcide Pepis 1923,O 30,17:2
Trois Masques, Les 1923,N 6,22:1
Catherine Goulden 1923,N 6,22:1
Bonheur, Le 1923,N 20,23:3
Laboratoire des Hallucinations, Le 1923,N 20,23:3
Petite Bonnie Serieuse 1923,N 27,23:5
Griffe, La 1923,N 27,23:5
Defresne, Louise
Sol Hyam's Brocanteur 1923,N 27,23:5

Defrey, Josephine
Biography 1934,F 6,24:4
Defries, Amelia (Translator)
Commedia Dell' Arte 1927,Ap 6,24:3
Degand, Michel
Pique-Nique en Campagne 1969,My 1,50:1
Jeune Fille a Marier, La 1970,My 6,49:1
Degen, John A Jr
Caesar and Cleopatra 1927,N 6,IX,2:1
Degen, Michael
Tenth Man, The 1962,O 3,46:1
Degenshen, Braun (Miscellaneous)
Adding Machine, The 1970,D 5,40:1
Degidon, J Thomas
Enemy of the People, An 1959,F 5,24:4
DeHart, Jon
Playroom, The 1965,D 6,49:1
Dehelly
Turcaret 1928,Mr 4,IX,4:5
Dehelly, Drawem
Soeurs Hortensias, Les 1934,My 13,IX,2:2
Dehelly, Suzanne
Soeurs Hortensias, Les 1934,My 13,IX,2:2
Dehn, Mura
Manhattan Varieties 1932,O 22,18:3
Deibat, Germaine
Annonce Faite a Marie, L' 1965,Ap 6,33:2
Deiber, Paul-Emile
Cid, Le 1966,F 12,17:1
Reine Morte, La 1966,F 16,52:1
Fil a la Paite, Un 1966,F 18,25:1
Deiber, Paul-Emile (Director)
Cid, Le 1963,N 8,36:2
Phedre 1966,F 11,36:1
Cid, Le 1966,F 12,17:1
Deiber, Paul-Emile (Producer)
Troupe Du Roi, La 1970,F 4,38:1
Deicke, Irene
Right of Possession 1930,My 9,20:5
Twelfth Disciple, The 1930,My 17,21:4
Deighton, Ann
Masks and Faces 1933,Mr 20,18:5
It Happened Tomorrow 1933,My 6,11:5
Then Came the Dawn 1935,Ag 29,25:4
Deighton, Marga Ann
Love on the Dole 1936,F 25,23:3
Laughing Woman, The 1936,O 14,30:1
Fly Away Home 1937,Jl 27,24:3
Summer and Smoke 1947,Jl 9,18:5
Summer and Smoke 1948,O 7,33:2
Summer and Smoke 1948,O 17,II,1:1
Major Barbara 1951,F 24,10:2
Mrs McThing 1952,F 21,22:1
Dein, Joel (Miscellaneous)
Postmark Zero 1965,N 2,28:1
Deininger, William H
Grey Heir, The 1926,Ap 6,29:2
Deis, Carol
Lady in the Dark 1941,Ja 24,14:2
Deitch, Burtress
Blossom Time 1921,S 30,10:1
Deitch, Dan
Critic, The 1965,Jl 26,15:2
Deitrich, F Y
Tiger Smiles, The 1930,D 18,29:1
Deja, Lora (Composer)
Tobias and the Angel 1937,Ap 29,16:5
DeJagers, Dorothy (Playwright)
Cinderelative 1930,S 19,18:4
Dejmek, Kazimierz (Director)
Story of the Glorious Resurrection of Our Lord,
The 1962,Je 10,II,1:1
DeJoie, Norman
Peter Pan 1950,Ap 25,27:2
DeJoria, Nicholas
Twelfth Night 1968,Je 15,40:1
Resistible Rise of Arturo Ui, The 1968,Ag 8,25:1
Merton of the Movies 1968,S 26,62:1
House of Atreus, The 1968,D 18,55:1
Resistible Rise of Arturo Ui, The 1968,D 23,44:1
Dekany, Laszlo
Kek Roka; Blue Fox 1957,D 5,47:2
Egerfogo; Mousetrap, The 1958,Ja 30,18:6
DeKarlo, Sergio
Mexican Hayride 1944,Ja 29,9:6
Dekker, Albert
Troika 1930,Ap 2,32:6
Lysistrata 1930,Je 6,20:1
Passionate Pilgrim, The 1932,O 20,24:3
Journey by Night 1935,Ap 7,IX,2:1
Squaring the Circle 1935,S 22,X,3:2
Bitter Stream 1936,Mr 31,16:6
Gertie 1952,Ja 31,23:1
Andersonville Trial, The 1959,D 30,15:1
Andersonville Trial, The 1960,Ja 10,II,1:1
Face of a Hero 1960,O 21,29:5
Man for All Seasons, A 1961,N 23,51:1
Man for All Seasons, A 1961,D 3,II,1:1
Man for All Seasons, A 1962,S 23,II,1:1
Man for All Seasons, A 1964,Ja 28,24:2
Devils, The 1965,N 17,51:2
Sorrow of Frederick, The 1967,Jl 8,14:2

Dekker, Albert (Director)
Angels of Anadarko 1962,O 11,47:1
Dekker, Thomas (Playwright)
Witch of Edmonton, The 1936,D 9,34:1
Witch of Edmonton, The 1937,Ja 3,X,3:6
Shoemaker's Holiday, The 1938,Ja 3,17:2
Shoemaker's Holiday, The 1938,Ja 9,X,1:1
Shoemaker's Holiday, The 1938,Ja 23,XI,1:6
Witch of Edmonton, The 1962,N 23,32:2
Shoemaker's Holiday, The 1967,Mr 3,25:1
Shoemaker's Holiday, The 1967,Je 3,19:1
Dekobra, Maurice (Original Author)
Mon Coeur au Ralenti 1927,Je 12,VII,2:1
Madone des Sleepings, La 1928,O 14,X,5:1
Dekobra, Maurice (Playwright)
Epinard Gagne le Grand Steeple 1926,D 19,VII,3:3
Mon Coeur au Ralenti 1927,Je 12,VII,2:1
Dekova, Margit
Mr Strauss Goes to Boston 1945,S 7,20:2
DeKoven, Harry
Adam Had Two Sons 1932,Ja 21,17:1
Dekoven, Lenore
Entertain a Ghost 1962,Ap 10,48:1
Whisper in God's Ear, A 1962,O 12,27:2
Dekum, Frank
Outrageous Mrs Palmer, The 1920,O 13,18:1
March Hares 1921,Ag 12,8:3
March Hares 1923,Mr 13,19:5
Del Bondio, J H (Miscellaneous)
House of Shadows, The 1927,Ap 22,18:4
Chocolate Soldier, The 1947,Mr 13,34:2
Del Bondio, J H (Producer)
Hey, Nonny, Nonny! 1932,Je 7,22:3
It's You I Want 1935,F 6,23:3
To See Ourselves 1935,My 1,25:2
Great Lady 1938,D 2,26:6
Murder Without Crime 1943,Ag 19,24:6
Suds in Your Eye 1944,Ja 13,15:5
Goodbye Again 1956,Ap 25,38:1
del C Gil, M
Road to Happiness, The 1927,My 3,24:1
Girl and the Cat, The 1927,My 6,21:2
Cradle Song 1927,My 10,24:4
Del Carmen Gil, M
Blind Heart, The 1927,My 8,30:2
del Cerro, Enrique
El Alcalde De Zalamea 1953,N 23,32:5
Del Drigo, George
Top Speed 1929,D 26,20:1
Del Gatto, Tony
Hasty Heart, The 1959,S 15,45:2
Del Maestro, Lorna
Carnival in Flanders 1953,S 9,38:2
Del Mar, Josephine
Meet the People 1940,D 26,22:2
del Mar, Juan
Sirena Varada, La 1937,O 23,15:3
Del Mar, Norman
Let's Make an Opera 1950,D 14,50:2
Del Mar, Norman (Miscellaneous)
Let's Make an Opera 1950,D 14,50:2
Del Mar, Norman (Musical Director)
Let's Make an Opera 1950,D 14,50:2
Del Marga, Rita
Sweetheart Time 1926,Ja 20,23:2
Del Medico, Michael
Disenchanted, The 1958,D 4,53:4
Cicero 1961,F 9,37:2
Go Show Me a Dragon 1961,O 28,18:1
Witches' Sabbath 1962,Ap 20,22:2
Burn Me to Ashes 1963,N 20,48:1
Del Mel, Carl
One, Two, Three! 1930,S 30,24:2
Del Monte, George
Irma la Douce 1960,S 30,31:2
Del Pozo, J G (Miscellaneous)
Don Juan Tenorio 1953,N 20,18:5
El Alcalde De Zalamea 1953,N 23,32:5
del Rey, Isobel
Great Way, The 1921,N 8,28:2
Dove, The 1925,F 12,17:3
Del Rigo, George
Student Prince, The 1931,Ja 30,18:1
Little Racketeer, The 1932,Ja 19,24:4
Del Rio, Bobbie
Challenge of Youth 1930,Ja 21,28:5
Del Rossi, Angelo
Pale Horse, Pale Rider 1957,O 30,26:1
Cheri 1959,O 13,44:1
Del Santi, Giuseppe (Miscellaneous)
Miracle, The 1960,D 5,42:3
Oldest Trick in the World, The 1961,F 21,40:1
Bible Salesman, The 1961,F 21,40:1
Del Val, Jean
Lulu Belle 1926,F 10,20:1
Play Without a Name, A 1928,N 26,30:5
Fifty Million Frenchmen 1929,N 28,34:4
Oscar Wilde 1938,O 11,20:2
Del Varo, Lucille
Robin Hood 1935,Jl 15,20:6
Del Vecchio, Ethel
Thunder on the Left 1933,N 1,25:2

Del Vecchio, Thomas (Playwright)
Feast of Panthers 1961,Mr 21,32:1
Delacre, Jules (Playwright)
Revisor 1927,My 1,VIII,2:4
Delacruz, Chester (Scenic Designer)
Parasite, The 1965,D 17,43:2
Delafield, Ann
Hassan 1924,S 23,23:1
Peter Pan 1924,N 7,16:2
Bachelor's Brides 1925,My 29,20:2
Two Orphans, The 1926,Ap 6,26:2
Potiphar's Wife 1928,D 24,10:7
Delafield, E M (Playwright)
To See Ourselves 1930,D 28,VIII,2:6
Glass Wall, The 1933,F 21,17:2
To See Ourselves 1935,My 1,25:2
Delage, Jean-Pierre
Misanthrope, Le 1960,Mr 9,38:3
Ecole des Femmes, L' 1961,Ap 28,23:1
Delair, Paul (Playwright)
Megere Apprivoisee, La 1922,N 20,21:2
Delair, Suzy
Vie Parisienne, La 1964,Mr 11,34:2
Delamare, Lise
Impromptu de Versailles, L' 1961,F 22,30:1
Tartuffe 1961,Mr 1,28:1
Dindon, Le 1961,Mr 8,38:1
Avare, L', L'; Miser, The 1966,F 9,32:1
Cid, Le 1966,F 12,17:1
Fil a la Paite, Un 1966,F 18,25:1
Delamercie
Cloches de Cornville, Les; Chimes of Normandy,
The 1926,D 14,24:4
Perichole, La 1926,D 29,24:4
Delamere, Margaret
Rope's End 1929,S 20,34:5
Delance, Georges (Playwright)
Equipage, L' 1930,Ap 13,X,2:7
Bluff 1932,Ja 3,VIII,2:4
Deland, Eugene (Playwright)
Woman of Bronze, The 1920,S 8,9:2
Delaney, Geraldine
Silk Stockings 1955,F 25,17:3
Delaney, Jack
Vaudeville (Hippodrome) 1926,My 4,31:2
Delaney, Jere
Mercenary Mary 1925,Ap 14,27:3
Vaudeville (Palace) 1929,O 21,31:2
Babes in Arms 1937,Ap 15,18:4
Delaney, Merri
Year Round, The 1953,My 6,38:7
Delaney, Patsy
Love Birds 1921,Mr 16,12:1
Delaney, Sean
Bead-Tangle 1970,Jl 16,38:1
Delaney, Shelagh (Playwright)
Taste of Honey, A 1959,F 12,24:7
Taste of Honey, A 1959,Mr 15,II,3:1
Taste of Honey, A 1960,O 5,46:1
Taste of Honey, A 1960,N 6,II,1:1
Lion in Love, The 1960,D 31,10:7
Taste of Honey, A 1961,My 17,43:1
Lion in Love, The 1963,Ap 26,28:3
deLange, Eddie (Lyricist)
Swingin' the Dream 1939,N 30,24:2
DeLangton, Frank
Assassin, The 1945,O 18,20:2
Delannoy, Henriette
Ma Tante d' Honfleur 1920,Ja 27,18:3
Delannoy, Marcel (Composer)
Paix, La 1933,Ja 15,IX,2:1
Philippine 1937,N 14,XI,7:5
Delano, Abigail
Unto Such Glory 1937,My 7,28:2
Delano, Allen
Seven Keys to Baldpate 1935,My 28,30:2
Delano, Allen (Playwright)
Illustrators' Show, The 1936,Ja 23,25:3
Delano, Ben
False Dreams, Farewell 1934,Ja 16,18:3
Delano, Helen (Costume Designer)
Nine Till Six 1936,Mr 14,10:3
Delany, Maureen
White-Headed Boy, The 1921,S 16,20:1
Plough and the Stars, The 1926,Mr 21,VIII,2:6
Things That Are Caesar's, The 1932,O 18,23:4
Far-Off Hills, The 1932,O 19,22:4
Juno and the Paycock 1932,O 20,24:3
Playboy of the Western World, The 1932,O 21,25:1
New Gossoon, The 1932,O 22,18:2
Cathleen ni Houlihan 1932,O 31,18:1
Shadow of a Gunman, The 1932,O 31,18:1
Birthright 1932,N 4,25:1
Crabbed Youth and Age 1932,N 4,25:1
Autumn Fire 1932,D 29,16:3
Plough and the Stars, The 1934,N 13,22:2
Drama at Inish 1934,N 15,24:2
Look at the Heffernans 1934,N 17,13:2
Church Street 1934,N 20,24:5
Coiner, The 1934,N 22,26:2
Bridgehead 1935,Ag 7,22:3
Katie Roche 1937,O 4,17:4
Plough and the Stars, The 1937,O 8,26:5

Delany, Maureen—Cont
Far-Off Hills, The 1937,O 12,30:4
In the Train 1937,N 22,14:5
Playboy of the Western World, The 1937,N 22,14:5
New Gossoon, The 1937,N 30,26:2
Juno and the Paycock 1937,D 7,32:5
Drama at Inish 1937,D 14,33:2
God and Kate Murphy 1959,F 27,21:2
Delany, Patsy
Rise of Rosie O'Reilly, The 1923,D 26,13:4
Delapenha, Denise
Walk Down Mah Street! 1968,Je 13,54:1
Delaquereere
Vierge Folle, La; Foolish Virgin, The 1924,Mr 22,12:2
Delard, Eugene (Playwright)
Woman of Bronze, The 1927,Je 16,25:4
Delaro, Genevieve
Blood and Sand 1921,S 21,16:2
Delarova, Eugenia
Lady Comes Across, The 1942,Ja 10,10:2
Snafu 1944,O 26,19:5
Dark Eyes 1948,Mr 25,34:4
Delasser, Jean
Operation Sidewinder 1970,Mr 22,II,1:4
Delaunois, Raymond (Mme)
Retablo de Maese Pedro, El 1925,D 30,10:1
Delaunois, Raymonde
Odeon-Revue 1927,My 22,VIII,2:7
Delavaivre, Madeleine
Misanthrope, Le 1960,Mr 9,38:3
Delbee, Pierre (Miscellaneous)
Mariage de Figaro, Le 1964,F 26,41:2
Delbee, Pierre (Scenic Designer)
Misanthrope, Le 1957,F 8,19:1
Delbert, Robert
Penny Wars, The 1969,O 16,52:1
Delbet, Pierre (Playwright)
Vocation, La 1926,D 19,VII,3:3
Delbridge, Ed
Anything Goes 1934,N 22,26:1
Delbridge, Edward
Anything Goes 1934,N 22,26:1
Delbridge, Edwin
My Maryland 1927,S 13,37:2
Saluta 1934,Ag 29,13:4
Delbruyere, Daniele
Dejeuner d'Amoureax, Un; Lovers Breakfast, A 1936,N 26,38:2
Martine 1936,N 26,38:2
Homme Que J'Ai Tue, L'; Man Whom I Have Killed, The 1936,D 10,34:3
Bichon; Little Dear 1936,D 31,20:5
Sexe Fort, Le; Strong Sex, The 1937,Ja 14,17:4
Dans Le Noir; In the Dark 1937,F 11,18:3
Christian 1937,F 25,18:6
DeLeath, Vaughn
Easy Come, Easy Go 1925,O 27,20:2
Delegall, Bob
Moon on a Rainbow Shawl 1970,D 18,52:1
Delehante, Dhoris
Geisha, The 1931,O 6,35:4
Chimes of Normandy, The 1931,N 3,31:3
Naughty Marietta 1931,N 17,31:2
Delehanty, Isabel
Journey by Night, A 1935,Ap 17,26:3
Delehente, Denise
Merry Widow, The 1931,S 8,39:1
D'Elena, L (Composer)
It's the Valet 1933,D 15,25:4
D'Elena, L (Lyricist)
It's the Valet 1933,D 15,25:4
DeLeon, Grayce
Doctored Wife, The 1950,Jl 12,33:2
Delerfield, R F (Playwright)
Peace Comes to Peckham 1947,Ap 20,II,3:7
Delerue, Georges (Composer)
Red Roses for Me 1961,F 11,26:5
Salut a Moliere 1964,Mr 4,33:2
Pieton de L'Air, Le 1964,Mr 4,33:2
Diary of a Madman 1964,Ap 17,29:2
Diary of a Madman 1967,Mr 24,25:1
Deley, Yvan
Watch on the Rhine 1942,My 3,VIII,1:7
Delf, Harry
Jimmie 1920,N 18,15:3
Sun Showers 1923,F 6,14:2
Vaudeville (Palace) 1926,Jl 6,19:3
Earl Carroll's Vanities 1926,Ag 25,19:4
Atlas and Eva 1928,F 7,30:2
Delf, Harry (Composer)
Sun Showers 1923,F 6,14:2
Delf, Harry (Lyricist)
Sun Showers 1923,F 6,14:2
Delf, Harry (Playwright)
Sun Showers 1923,F 6,14:2
Family Upstairs, The 1925,My 3,VIII,2:1
Family Upstairs, The 1925,Ag 18,14:2
Family Upstairs, The 1925,Ag 23,VII,1:1
Unsophisticates, The 1926,Ag 8,VII,3:1
Six Feet under 1928,Ja 22,VIII,4:7
Atlas and Eva 1928,F 7,30:2
Unsophisticates, The 1929,D 31,14:5
She Lived Next to the Firehouse 1931,F 11,23:1

Family Upstairs, The 1933,O 28,20:6
Delf, Harry (Producer)
Atlas and Eva 1928,F 7,30:2
Unsophisticates, The 1929,D 31,14:5
Delfau, Andre (Costume Designer)
Avare, L', L'; Miser, The 1966,F 9,32:1
Cid, Le 1966,F 12,17:1
Delfau, Andre (Scenic Designer)
Cid, Le 1966,N 8,36:2
Avare, L', L'; Miser, The 1966,F 9,32:1
Cid, Le 1966,F 12,17:1
Delfino, Frank
No Mother to Guide Her 1933,D 26,18:5
Delfont, Bernard (Miscellaneous)
Stop the World-I Want to Get Off 1962,O 4,45:4
Roar of the Greasepaint-the Smell of the Crowd 1965,My 17,46:2
Killing of Sister George, The 1966,O 6,57:1
Delgado, Camilo
Shakuntala 1959,S 10,41:2
Delgardo, Louis
Heads Up! 1929,N 12,34:1
Smiles 1930,N 19,19:2
Hot-Cha! 1932,Mr 9,17:3
Delhem, Lolita
Blue Butterfly, The 1929,F 17,29:3
D'Elia, Maria
Moondreamers, The 1969,D 9,68:1
deLille, Lola
Five O'Clock Girl, The 1927,O 11,26:3
Delius, Frederick (Composer)
Hassan 1923,S 30,II,1:6
Hassan 1923,O 14,VIII,2:6
Hassan 1924,S 23,23:1
Deliyanni, V
Electra 1952,N 20,38:2
Deliyannis, Al
Electra 1952,N 20,38:2
Oedipus Tyrannus 1952,N 25,35:2
Dell, Betty
Say When 1934,N 9,24:2
Sketch Book 1935,Je 5,22:2
Dell, Claudia
Rosalie 1928,Ja 11,26:3
Dell, Delano
Bunch and Judy, The 1922,N 29,20:1
Topics of 1923 1923,N 21,23:2
Dell, Dorothy
Tattle Tales 1933,Je 2,22:6
Dell, Ethel
Dead End 1935,O 29,17:2
Dell, Floyd (Original Author)
Little Accident 1928,S 16,IX,2:4
Dell, Floyd (Playwright)
Little Accident 1928,O 10,32:3
Little Accident 1929,S 22,IX,4:1
Cloudy With Showers 1931,Ag 23,VIII,2:5
Cloudy With Showers 1931,S 2,17:5
Dell, Gabriel
Dead End 1935,O 29,17:2
Ankles Aweigh 1955,Ap 19,27:1
Can-Can 1959,Ag 26,25:4
Automobile Graveyard, The 1961,N 14,46:2
Fortuna 1962,Ja 4,26:1
Man Out Loud, Girl Quiet 1962,Ap 4,38:1
Spanish Armada, The 1962,Ap 4,38:1
Can-Can 1962,My 17,32:2
Wonderful Town 1963,F 15,10:2
Oklahoma! 1963,F 28,8:2
Marathon '33 1963,D 23,20:1
Anyone Can Whistle 1964,Ap 6,36:1
Sign in Sidney Brustein's Window, The 1964,O 16,32:1
Chocolates 1967,Ap 11,51:1
Something Different 1967,N 29,52:1
Adaptation 1969,F 11,27:1
Dell, Jack Holton (Playwright)
Duel, The 1968,Ap 18,56:1
Dell, Jeffrey (Playwright)
Payment Deferred 1931,O 1,24:2
Firebird 1932,S 25,IX,1:3
Business With America 1933,Ja 1,IX,1:3
Dell, Jeffrey (Translator)
Firebird 1932,N 22,25:2
Dell, Marie
Dead End 1935,O 29,17:2
Dell, Marlene
On the Town 1959,Ja 16,36:1
della Cioppa, Guy
This Mad Whirl 1937,Ja 10,II,4:8
Della Santina, Bruno
Passion Play 1937,Mr 22,26:6
Dellafiora, Barrie
Pigeon, The 1957,My 17,19:2
Dellasorte, Joseph
Billy 1969,Mr 24,56:1
Delli, Ceil
Milk and Honey 1961,O 11,52:1
Skyscraper 1965,N 15,48:1
Dell'Isola, Salvatore (Musical Director)
Allegro 1947,O 11,10:2
South Pacific 1949,Ap 8,30:2

Dell'Isola, Salvatore (Musical Director)—Cont
Me and Juliet 1953,My 29,17:1
On Your Toes 1954,O 12,24:4
Ankles Aweigh 1955,Ap 19,27:1
Pipe Dream 1955,D 1,44:1
Flower Drum Song 1958,D 2,44:1
Dello Joio, Nurman (Composer)
Tall Kentuckian, The 1953,Je 17,30:1
Island of Goats 1955,O 5,40:1
Antony and Cleopatra 1960,Ag 1,19:1
Dellysia, Alice
At the Silver Swan 1936,F 20,22:2
Delman, Kenny
Texas Li'l Darlin' 1949,N 26,10:5
Delmar, Ethel
Scandals 1920,Je 8,9:1
Delmar, Frank
Thumbs Up! 1934,D 28,24:1
Johnny Belinda 1940,S 19,26:2
Delmar, Gray (Director)
Confederates, The 1959,S 29,45:1
Delmar, Gray (Producer)
Confederates, The 1959,S 29,45:1
Delmar, Harry
Vaudeville (Palace) 1926,My 8,29:2
Vaudeville (Palace) 1926,N 9,30:3
Delmar, Harry (Choreographer)
Harry Delmar's Revels 1927,N 29,30:2
Delmar, Harry (Director)
Follow the Girls 1944,Ap 10,15:2
Follow the Girls 1944,Ap 16,II,1:2
Delmar, Harry (Producer)
Harry Delmar's Revels 1927,N 29,30:2
Delmar, John
Thumbs Up! 1934,D 28,24:1
Johnny Belinda 1940,S 19,26:2
Delmar, Madeline
His Chinese Wife 1920,My 18,9:3
Blood and Sand 1921,S 21,16:2
Comedienne 1924,O 22,18:1
Jest, The 1926,F 5,22:2
Jest, The 1926,F 14,VIII,1:1
One for All 1927,My 14,25:5
Aiglon, L' 1927,D 27,24:3
Kingdom of God, The 1928,D 21,30:2
Delmar, Vicky
Johnny Belinda 1940,S 19,26:2
Delmar, Vina (Original Author)
Bad Girl 1930,O 3,30:2
Confederates, The 1959,S 29,45:1
Delmar, Vina (Playwright)
Bad Girl 1930,O 3,30:2
Rich Full Life, The 1945,N 10,9:2
Mid-Summer 1953,Ja 22,19:1
Confederates, The 1959,S 29,45:1
Delmar Twins
Keep Moving 1934,Ag 24,10:2
Delmas, Christian
Ecole des Femmes, L' 1961,Ap 28,23:1
Delmont, Gene
Mimic World of 1921, The 1921,Ag 18,9:2
Fashions of 1924 1923,Jl 19,18:2
Delmonte, Jack
Right You Are (If You Think You Are) 1950,Je 29,37:2
You Never Can Tell 1958,Je 17,25:1
Old Tune, The 1961,Mr 24,37:1
Delmonto, Donald
Mikado, The 1935,Ag 24,17:5
Delmore, Herbert
Sancho Panza 1923,N 27,23:1
Life Line, The 1930,D 29,19:3
Wolves 1932,Ja 7,26:3
Dark Hours, The 1932,N 15,24:2
Delmore and Lee
Earl Carroll's Vanities 1923,Jl 6,8:2
Delno, Lee
Picture of Dorian Gray, The 1956,Ag 18,15:5
Androcles and the Lion 1958,F 22,8:3
Delnunzio, Richard (Composer)
Life Begins in '40 1940,Ap 5,24:2
Hit the Road 1941,Ap 4,18:3
DeLong, Georgia
Masked Woman, The 1922,D 23,14:2
Delores Twins, The
Schoen und Schick 1928,Ag 26,II,1:2
deLorez, Thelma
Wann und Wo 1927,D 18,IX,1:8
Delorme, Daniele
Annonce Faite a Marie, L' 1965,Ap 6,33:2
Delorme, Hugues (Lyricist)
Divin Mensonge 1926,N 14,VIII,2:1
Temps d'Aimer, Le 1926,D 12,VIII,3:4
Delroy, Irene
Greenwich Village Follies 1923,S 21,4:6
Vogues of 1924 1924,Mr 28,14:3
Round the Town 1924,My 22,14:3
Greenwich Village Follies 1925,D 25,23:3
Greenwich Village Follies 1926,Mr 16,22:2
Ziegfeld Follies 1927,Ag 17,27:3
Here's Howe! 1928,My 2,19:3
Follow Thru 1929,Ja 10,24:3
Top Speed 1929,D 26,20:1

Dels, Carol
Knickerbocker Holiday 1938,O 20,26:2
Delson, Jeff
Oresteia 1966,Je 30,29:1
Delson, Pril Smiley (Miscellaneous)
Increased Difficulty of Concentration, The 1969,D 5,48:1
Delu, Dahl (Lighting Director)
Ofay Watcher, The 1969,S 16,40:1
Delu, Dahl
House of Atreus, The; Bringers of Offerings, The 1967,Jl 24,23:1
House of Atreus, The; Agamemnon 1967,Jl 24,23:1
House of Atreus, The; Furies, The 1967,Jl 24,23:1
Delu, Dahl (Scenic Designer)
Shoemaker's Holiday, The 1967,Je 3,19:1
Ofay Watcher, The 1969,S 16,40:1
Ofay Watcher, The 1969,S 21,II,1:2
Delubac, Jacqueline
Chateaux en Espagne 1933,Ap 30,IX,2:3
Deluca, Frank
Apollo of Bellac, The 1954,My 29,12:1
Purification, The 1954,My 29,12:1
Delueese, Joan
Othello 1964,O 13,48:1
Delugg, Milton
Very Warm for May 1939,N 18,23:2
DeLuise, Jerry
Red Eye of Love 1961,Je 13,28:1
Fortuna 1962,Ja 4,26:1
Deluna, Walter
House of Doom, The 1932,Ja 26,20:4
Delval, Jean
Dancers, The 1923,O 18,17:2
Delvin, William
Twelfth Night 1950,D 3,II,3:1
Delysia, Alice
Afgar 1920,N 9,13:2
Afgar 1920,N 14,VI,1:1
Topics of 1923 1923,N 21,23:2
On With the Dance 1925,My 1,22:4
Her Past 1929,F 10,IX,4:7
Mother of Pearl 1933,F 26,IX,3:1
At the Silver Swan 1936,Mr 15,X,2:1
French for Love 1939,N 12,IX,1:8
Delza, Sophia
Fiesta 1929,S 18,35:1
DeMagnus, Louis
Desert Song, The 1946,Ja 9,20:2
Demarest, Mary E
Contrast, The 1926,O 1,26:2
Demarest, William
Silks and Satins 1920,Jl 16,19:1
Vaudeville (Palace) 1929,Je 3,27:4
Sketch Book 1929,Jl 2,33:5
Vanities 1931,Ag 11,28:4
Vanities 1931,Ag 16,VIII,1:1
Earl Carroll's Vanities 1931,Ag 28,18:7
Vaudeville (Palace) 1932,My 9,19:3
Demarest, William (Producer)
Woof, Woof 1929,D 26,20:4
DeMaria, Paul (Miscellaneous)
Moon Over Mulberry Street 1935,S 5,24:6
DeMaris, Aida
Yours Truly 1927,Ja 26,16:5
Demas, Carole
Morning Sun 1963,O 7,36:2
How to Steal an Election 1968,O 14,56:1
Rondelay 1969,N 6,55:1
Demasy, Paul (Playwright)
Untitled-Play 1933,N 12,IX,3:4
DeMave, Jack
Mister Roberts 1956,D 6,46:2
Sweeney Todd 1957,Ag 28,21:4
Visit, The 1960,Mr 9,38:3
Demazis
Marius 1929,Mr 31,VIII,2:7
Demazis, Orane
Fanny 1931,D 27,VIII,3:4
Demby, Claude
Angelic Doctor 1953,Ap 14,30:2
Comedian, The 1956,O 18,36:4
D'Emidio, Michael
Moon on a Rainbow Shawl 1970,D 18,52:1
Demidoff
Palace aux Femmes 1926,O 10,VIII,2:1
Demier, Joseph
Passing of the Third Floor Back, The 1928,F 21,18:2
DeMilt, Aida Rodman (Playwright)
Values 1927,My 5,30:1
Deming, Will
Breakfast in Bed 1920,F 4,12:1
Nobody's Money 1921,My 22,VI,1:6
Nobody's Money 1921,Ag 18,9:3
Her Salary Man 1921,N 29,20:1
French Doll, The 1922,F 21,20:2
Go Easy Mabel 1922,My 9,22:2
Barnum Was Right 1923,Mr 13,19:3
Tantrum, The 1924,S 5,20:2
Demitriou, D
Screwball, The 1957,My 25,24:7

Demming, Ellen
Family Portrait 1959,My 6,48:2
Demnati, Liazeed
Vaudeville (Palace) 1931,My 11,15:5
Demnati, Liazeed Company
Vaudeville (Palace) 1930,Mr 3,18:5
Demone, Richard (Musical Director)
Dames at Sea 1970,S 24,60:1
Demont, Billy
Kilpatrick's Old-Time Minstrels 1930,Ap 21,20:2
Man Who Killed Lincoln, The 1940,Ja 18,26:4
Demos, Bill (Costume Designer)
Cradle of Willow, A 1961,D 16,20:2
Demos, Bill (Scenic Designer)
Christmas in the Market Place 1960,D 10,26:1
King of the Dark Chamber 1961,F 10,21:1
Cradle of Willow, A 1961,D 16,20:2
Beyond the Horizon 1962,O 26,27:2
DeMotte, Josie
Jumbo 1935,N 18,20:2
Dempsey, Clifford
All Soul's Eve 1920,My 13,9:1
Opportunity 1920,Jl 31,5:1
Honors Are Even 1921,Ag 11,8:2
Lawbreaker, The 1922,F 7,12:1
Gorilla, The 1925,Ap 29,24:2
Sh! The Octopus 1928,F 22,19:2
Order Please 1934,O 10,21:2
Trial of Dr Beck, The 1937,Ag 10,22:2
Dempsey, David
Cure for Matrimony 1939,O 26,26:3
Dempsey, Jack
Big Fight, The 1928,Ag 31,23:1
Big Fight, The 1928,S 19,33:1
Big Fight, The 1928,S 23,IX,1:1
Vaudeville (Palace) 1929,D 9,33:2
Dempsey, Jerome
Love Nest, The 1963,Ja 28,7:6
Phaedra 1967,My 22,50:2
Spofford 1967,D 15,54:3
Ordinary Man, An 1968,S 10,39:1
Cry of Players, A 1968,N 15,40:1
Evening for Merlin Finch, An 1968,D 30,25:1
Year Boston Won the Pennant, The 1969,My 23,38:1
Room Service 1970,My 13,49:1
Sunday Dinner 1970,N 3,28:1
Dempsey, Mark
Oh! Calcutta! 1969,Je 18,33:1
Dempsey, William (Producer)
Fashion 1959,Ja 21,27:1
Moon in the Yellow River, The 1961,F 7,40:2
Colombe 1965,F 24,33:1
Dempster, Curt
View From the Bridge, A 1965,Ja 29,24:1
Dempster, Curt (Director)
Not a Way of Life 1967,Mr 23,28:1
Sunday Dinner 1970,N 3,28:1
Dempster, Curt (Miscellaneous)
Salvation 1969,S 25,55:1
Dempster, Hugh
Rope's End 1929,S 20,34:5
Denbeaux, Jacques
Private Life of the Master Race, The 1956,Ja 31,33:3
Denberg, Irwin T (Miscellaneous)
Her First Roman 1968,O 21,53:3
Denby, Edwin (Choreographer)
Knickerbocker Holiday 1938,O 20,26:2
Denby, Edwin (Playwright)
Horse Eats Hat 1936,S 28,14:2
Second Hurricane 1937,Ap 22,18:4
Denby, Edwin (Translator)
Criminals, The 1941,D 22,24:3
Dench, Judi
Twelfth Night 1958,D 10,54:2
Henry V 1958,D 26,2:7
Measure for Measure 1962,Ap 11,47:4
Midsummer Night's Dream, A 1962,Ap 18,30:3
Winter's Tale, The 1969,My 17,18:1
Winter's Tale, The 1969,Je 1,II,4:5
Twelfth Night 1969,S 1,13:1
Winter's Tale, The 1969,S 1,13:1
London Assurance 1970,Je 25,55:2
London Assurance 1970,Ag 7,26:1
Dench, Robert (Choreographer)
Ice Capades 1952,S 12,18:1
Ice Capades 1953,S 11,25:1
Ice Capades 1955,S 15,38:1
Ice Capades 1957,S 5,33:2
Ice Capades 1960,S 1,30:1
Ice Capades 1961,Ag 31,24:4
Dench, Robert (Director)
Ice Capades 1964,Ag 27,27:2
Dench, Robert (Miscellaneous)
Ice Capades 1958,S 4,33:2
Ice Capades 1959,S 4,12:1
Ice Capades 1960,S 1,30:1
Ice Capades 1962,Ag 30,34:1
Dencyger, Henry (Lighting Director)
Enemy of the People, An 1958,F 26,24:2
Dendy, Mike
Macbeth 1968,N 30,49:3

Denehy, Anna May
Wonderful Night, A; Fledermaus, Die 1929,N 1,23:3
Denenbourg
Aiglon, L' 1924,O 21,21:1
Madame Sans-Gene 1924,N 4,30:1
Denes, Jules (Director)
Eternal Cage 1945,Mr 22,19:7
Denes, Jules (Playwright)
Eternal Cage 1945,Mr 22,19:7
Denese, Dorothy
Show Boat 1927,D 28,26:1
Show Boat 1932,My 20,22:2
Dengate, Dennis
R U R 1942,D 4,30:2
Student Prince, The 1943,Je 9,16:2
Merry Widow, The 1944,O 9,17:1
Mr Strauss Goes to Boston 1945,S 7,20:2
Dengel, Jake
Midsummer Night's Dream, A 1960,Je 30,23:5
Romeo and Juliet 1960,Jl 1,14:1
Fortuna 1962,Ja 4,26:1
Abe Lincoln in Illinois 1963,Ja 23,5:2
Cyrano de Bergerac 1963,Je 20,30:1
Tragical Historie of Doctor Faustus, The 1964,O 6,34:2
Royal Hunt of the Sun, The 1965,O 27,36:2
Cock-A-Doodle Dandy 1969,Ja 21,40:1
Hamlet 1969,Mr 4,34:1
Dengel, Roni
Remarkable Mr Pennypacker, The 1953,D 31,11:2
Sunrise at Campobello 1958,Ja 31,25:1
Merry Widow, The 1961,O 27,28:2
Not Now Darling 1970,O 30,33:1
Dengel, Roni (Choreographer)
Merry Widow, The 1961,O 27,28:2
Vagabond King, The 1961,N 24,36:1
Gondoliers, The 1961,D 8,44:1
Denger (Playwright)
I Only Want an Answer 1968,F 6,36:1
Dengg, Irmi
Passion of Christ, The 1960,My 18,46:1
Denham, George
Victoria Regina 1938,O 4,20:2
Denham, Reginald (Director)
Rope's End 1929,S 20,34:5
Josef Suss 1930,Ja 21,28:5
Suspense 1930,Ap 27,IX,1:8
Suspense 1930,Ag 13,22:3
Ladies in Retirement 1940,Mr 27,24:3
Jupiter Laughs 1940,S 10,27:1
Guest in the House 1942,F 25,25:2
Yesterday's Magic 1942,Ap 15,27:2
Malice Domestic 1942,Jl 21,22:1
Nine Girls 1943,Ja 14,26:2
Two Mrs Carrolls, The 1943,Ag 4,14:1
Wallflower 1944,Ja 27,14:2
Dark Hammock 1944,D 12,27:8
Round Trip 1945,My 30,16:4
Joy Forever, A 1946,Ja 8,20:2
Obsession 1946,O 2,39:2
Temper the Wind 1946,D 28,10:2
Portrait in Black 1947,My 15,30:2
Duet for Two Hands 1947,O 8,28:3
Gramercy Ghost 1951,Ap 27,20:2
Dial 'M' for Murder 1952,O 30,41:2
Be Your Age 1953,Ja 15,24:2
Date With April, A 1953,Ap 16,36:2
Sherlock Holmes 1953,O 31,11:2
Bad Seed, The 1954,D 9,42:1
Bad Seed, The 1954,D 19,II,3:1
Janus 1955,N 25,37:2
Hide and Seek 1957,Ap 3,26:1
Mighty Man Is He, A 1960,Ja 7,25:2
Once for the Asking 1963,N 21,42:2
Hostile Witness 1966,F 18,26:1
Denham, Reginald (Playwright)
Suspect 1937,F 17,16:2
Ladies in Retirement 1939,D 24,IX,1:7
Ladies in Retirement 1940,Mr 27,24:3
Suspect 1940,Ap 10,30:4
Malice Domestic 1942,Jl 21,22:1
Wallflower 1944,Ja 27,14:2
Dark Hammock 1944,D 12,27:8
Round Trip 1945,My 30,16:4
Be Your Age 1953,Ja 15,24:2
DeNiro, Robert
One Night Stands of a Noisy Passenger; Last Stand 1970,D 31,8:3
Denis, Joseph (Playwright)
Veritable Histoire de Mignon, La 1927,F 20,VII,2:1
Denis, Michael
Lifeline 1942,D 1,20:3
Denis, Ray
Caesar and Cleopatra 1935,Ag 22,21:1
Denise, Diane
Priorities of 1942 1942,Mr 13,23:2
Denise, Dorotha
Aloma of the South Seas 1925,Ap 21,18:1
Denise, Patricia
Pardon Our French 1950,O 6,22:4
Denison, Leslie
Made in France 1930,N 12,21:1

Denison, Leslie—Cont
Barretts of Wimpole Street, The 1931,F 10,25:1
Only the Young 1932,S 22,25:2
As Husbands Go 1933,Ja 20,20:5
Strange Orchestra 1933,N 29,23:2
Broadway Interlude 1934,Ap 20,16:3
Roman Servant, A 1934,D 3,14:5
Kind Lady 1937,Jl 6,23:1
On Location 1937,S 28,19:1
Robin Landing 1937,N 19,26:4
Gloriana 1938,N 26,18:4
Denison, Lewis
Ten Nights in a Barroom 1928,Mr 28,31:2
Denison, Lewis (Director)
Yeomen of the Guard, The 1941,D 19,34:3
Pirates of Penzance, The 1942,F 20,20:2
Denison, Michael
Twelfth Night 1955,Je 7,37:4
Village Wooing 1956,S 5,22:6
Denison, Vivian
Yeomen of the Guard, The 1941,D 19,34:3
Denisova, Alexandra
Rhapsody 1944,N 23,37:2
Denizon, Helene
Vaudeville (Palace) 1929,Mr 25,33:2
Denker, Henry (Playwright)
Time Limit! 1956,Ja 25,27:2
Time Limit! 1956,F 5,II,1:1
Far Country, A 1961,Ap 5,32:1
Far Country, A 1961,Ap 16,II,1:1
Venus at Large 1962,Ap 13,30:1
Case of Libel, A 1963,O 11,43:2
Case of Libel, A 1963,O 27,II,1:1
What Did We Do Wrong? 1967,O 23,56:1
What Did We Do Wrong? 1967,N 12,II,5:6
What Did We Do Wrong? 1967,N 19,II,1:1
Denlea, Martyn (Miscellaneous)
Camille 1956,S 19,33:1
Denman, Florence
Busybody, The 1924,S 30,27:5
Denman, Philip
Victory Belles 1943,O 27,26:3
Dennen, Barre
Henry V 1960,Je 30,23:1
Fourth Avenue North 1961,S 28,50:2
Dennen, Leon (Playwright)
Bed Bug, The 1931,Mr 20,28:6
Dennen, Leon (Translator)
Bed Bug, The 1931,Mr 20,28:6
D'Ennery, A (Playwright)
Two Orphans, The 1926,Ap 6,26:2
D'Ennery, Guy
Show-Off, The 1924,F 6,16:2
Show-Off, The 1932,D 13,25:4
Big Hearted Herbert 1934,Ja 2,17:3
d'Ennery, Pierre
Rebound 1930,F 4,29:1
Order Please 1934,O 10,21:2
American Landscape 1938,D 5,19:2
d'Ennery (Original Author)
Due Orfanelle, Le; Two Orphans, The
1936,O 5,24:4
d'Ennery (Playwright)
Faiseur, Le 1936,Ja 12,IX,3:7
Dennett, Walker
Sporting Thing to Do, The 1923,F 20,12:2
Inspector General, The 1923,My 1,24:1
Denney, Dodo
Bella 1961,N 17,40:1
Denney, John
Cock-A-Doodle Dandy 1950,F 1,26:2
Denni, Lucien (Composer)
Happy-Go-Lucky 1926,O 1,27:2
Dennie
In Clover 1937,S 21,29:1
Denning, Denise
Jubilee 1935,O 14,20:1
Denning, Edwin
Laugh It Off 1934,Ap 5,24:2
Denning, James E
Flair-Flair the Idol of Paree 1935,Mr 13,16:1
Denning, Paula
Potash and Perlmutter 1935,Ap 6,11:3
Dennis, Alfred
That Hat! 1964,S 24,45:1
Square in the Eye 1965,My 20,54:1
Play That on Your Old Piano 1965,O 15,49:1
Dennis, Amy
Mandarin, The 1920,N 10,18:2
Matrimonial Bed, The 1927,O 13,23:2
Five Star Final 1930,D 31,11:1
Dennis, Beverly
Charley's Aunt 1953,D 23,22:2
Dennis, Danny
Magic and the Loss, The 1954,Ap 10,10:3
Queen After Death 1956,Mr 13,33:2
Dennis, Dorothy
New Faces of 1943 1942,D 23,22:2
Dennis, Estelle
Patience 1928,Je 26,29:3
Dennis, John
Peter Pan 1950,Ap 25,27:2
By the Beautiful Sea 1954,Ap 9,20:1
Plain and Fancy 1955,Ja 28,14:2

Dennis, Nick
Slight Case of Murder, A 1935,S 12,28:5
On Your Toes 1936,Ap 13,14:4
On Borrowed Time 1938,F 4,16:4
World We Make, The 1939,N 21,19:1
Love's Old Sweet Song 1940,My 3,16:3
What Big Ears! 1942,Ap 21,18:5
Innocent Voyage, The 1943,N 16,27:2
Storm Operation 1944,Ja 12,28:2
Rugged Path, The 1945,N 12,17:2
Cyrano de Bergerac 1946,O 9,33:2
Cyrano de Bergerac 1947,Ja 17,27:2
Streetcar Named Desire, A 1947,D 4,42:2
Dennis, Nigel (Playwright)
Making of Moo, The 1958,Je 12,34:1
August for the People 1961,S 5,41:6
Dennis, Nikolas
Food for Midas 1942,Ja 31,12:7
Dennis, Patrick (Original Author)
Auntie Mame 1956,N 1,47:2
Auntie Mame 1956,N 11,II,1:1
Auntie Mame 1958,Je 8,II,1:1
Auntie Mame 1958,Ag 12,33:2
Little Me 1962,N 19,41:3
Little Me 1962,D 2,II,1:1
Mame 1966,My 25,41:1
Mame 1968,Ap 20,25:1
Dennis, Ray
Please Do Not Disturb 1936,Je 23,27:1
Romance 1937,Ag 17,23:1
You Never Know 1938,S 22,26:3
Dennis, Richard
Barrier, The 1950,N 3,32:2
Dennis, Robert
Oh! Calcutta! 1969,Je 18,33:1
Dennis, Robert (Composer)
Endecott and the Red Cross 1968,My 7,50:1
Dennis, Ronald
Of Thee I Sing 1969,Mr 8,19:1
Moon Walk 1970,N 27,52:1
Dennis, Sandy
Lady From the Sea, The 1956,D 13,49:5
Burning Bright 1959,O 17,27:2
Port-Royal 1960,Ap 26,41:1
Face of a Hero 1960,O 21,29:5
Complaisant Lover, The 1961,N 2,43:2
Thousand Clowns, A 1962,Ap 6,31:2
Thousand Clowns, A 1962,Ap 15,II,1:1
Any Wednesday 1964,F 19,34:1
Daphne in Cottage D 1967,O 16,56:1
Daphne in Cottage D 1967,N 5,II,3:1
Dennis, Shirley
Star Time 1944,S 13,16:2
Star Time 1944,S 17,II,1:1
Dennis, Stephan
This Our House 1935,D 12,33:3
Dennis, Vincent
Breakfast in Bed 1920,F 4,12:1
Skirt, The 1921,N 8,28:1
Dennison, Billy (Musical Director)
Jimmy Roselli Show, The 1969,My 3,39:1
Dennison, John
All in Love 1961,N 11,15:2
Dennison, L H
Silver Tassie, The 1929,O 25,26:1
Dennison, Leslie
Passionate Pilgrim, The 1932,O 20,24:3
Dennison, Loretta
Between the Devil 1937,D 23,24:5
Dennison, Mac
This Was Burlesque 1962,Mr 7,29:1
This Was Burlesque 1965,Mr 17,55:3
Dennison, Malcolm
Antonia 1925,O 21,20:1
Denniston, Charlotte
2 Girls Wanted 1926,S 10,25:3
Revolt 1928,N 1,25:3
Monkey 1932,F 12,25:2
Denniston, Reynolds
Fake, The 1924,O 7,26:3
Suspense 1930,Ag 13,22:3
Roar China! 1930,O 28,23:1
Man Who Changed His Name, The 1932,My 3,25:3
Pigeons and People 1933,Ja 17,22:3
Ten Minute Alibi 1933,O 18,24:3
Errant Lady 1934,S 18,18:2
Laburnum Grove 1935,Ja 15,23:5
Bishop Misbehaves, The 1935,F 21,22:4
Caesar and Cleopatra 1935,Ag 22,21:1
Dear Old Darling 1936,Mr 3,25:1
White Christmas 1936,Jl 7,22:2
Whiteoaks 1938,Mr 24,20:2
Leave Her to Heaven 1940,F 28,16:2
At the Stroke of Eight 1940,My 21,29:2
School for Scandal, The 1940,Je 18,29:5
School for Scandal, The 1940,Je 23,IX,1:1
Charley's Aunt 1940,O 18,24:2
Plan M 1942,F 21,15:2
Flare Path 1942,D 24,20:2
Denny, Christine (Director)
Tree Witch, The 1961,Je 5,39:4
Denny, Doreen
Gondoliers, The 1934,S 4,23:1

Denny, Doreen—Cont
Trial by Jury 1934,S 14,24:3
Princess Ida; Castle Adamant 1934,S 28,26:3
Denny, Ernest (Playwright)
Mountebank, The 1923,My 8,22:2
Denny, George
If Booth Had Missed 1931,My 14,27:1
If Booth Had Missed 1932,F 5,24:2
Denny, George V
Junk 1927,Ja 6,25:1
Denny, George V Jr
Old Bill, M P 1926,N 11,22:2
Denny, Harry
Footlights 1927,Ag 20,8:2
Denny, Jack
Vaudeville (Palace) 1932,My 16,19:2
Denny, John
Silver Tassie, The 1949,Jl 22,16:5
Denny, Loren
Nights of Wrath; Nuits de la Colere, Les
1947,D 1,26:4
Denny, Norman (Playwright)
Clerambard 1957,N 8,22:3
Denny, Reginald
Richard III 1920,Mr 8,7:1
All Men Are Alike 1941,O 7,27:2
Larger Than Life 1950,F 8,33:2
My Fair Lady 1958,Mr 9,II,1:1
Deno and Rochelle
Vaudeville (Hippodrome) 1924,Ap 1,18:1
Denor, Evelyn
Go, Go, Go, God is Dead! 1966,O 12,37:1
Denoux, Francois
Annonce Faite a Marie, L'; Tidings Brought to
Mary, The 1942,My 21,24:1
Dent, Edward (Translator)
Servant of Two Masters, The 1958,F 11,35:2
Dent, Nellie Graham
Fanny Hawthorn 1922,My 12,22:2
Top Hole 1924,S 2,22:3
Dent, Wade
Native Ground 1937,Mr 24,28:4
Denti, Emilio
Pirate, The 1942,N 26,39:2
Dentler, Pell
Big Blow 1938,O 3,11:2
Denton, Crahan
Man in Possession, The 1939,S 26,21:4
Key Largo 1939,N 28,30:2
Fragile Fox 1954,O 13,27:1
Bus Stop 1955,Mr 3,23:2
Bus Stop 1955,Mr 13,II,1:1
Orpheus Descending 1957,Mr 22,28:1
Orpheus Descending 1957,Mr 31,II,1:1
Winesburg, Ohio 1958,F 6,22:2
Buffalo Skinner, The 1959,F 20,18:1
Denton, Dan
Tobacco Road 1943,S 6,21:3
Denton, Graham
Story of Mary Surratt, The 1947,F 10,25:2
Denton, Judi
Ice Follies 1965,Ja 13,35:1
Ice Follies 1966,Ja 12,27:6
Denton, Pauline
Most Immoral Lady, A 1928,N 27,36:1
Denton, Vicki
Ice Follies 1965,Ja 13,35:1
Ice Follies 1966,Ja 12,27:6
Denver, Bob
Play It Again, Sam 1970,F 7,25:2
Denys, Marguerite
Comedian, The 1923,Mr 14,14:1
Deosy, Ernst (Original Author)
Cissy 1932,D 24,10:5
dePakch, Maurice (Composer)
Glory 1922,D 26,10:1
Depew, Joseph
Hero, The 1921,S 6,13:2
dePeyster, Alice
Sonya's Search for the Christmas Star
1929,D 14,24:6
Depillo, James
Town Boy 1929,O 5,22:4
DePinna, Connie (Costume Designer)
Jubilee 1935,O 14,20:1
Three Waltzes 1937,D 27,10:2
Deppe, Lois
Great Day! 1929,O 18,24:3
Hello Paris 1930,N 17,29:3
Depres, Suzanne
Mademoiselle le Feu 1924,My 18,VII,2:8
Der Linden, Mme Van
Faiseur, Le; Promoter, The 1938,D 27,12:3
Dera, Alyce
Brothers 1928,D 26,14:3
Derayville, Jean
Cynara 1931,N 3,31:1
Derbas, Frank
Kiss Me, Kate 1952,Ja 9,24:6
Derbas, Frank (Choreographer)
Ernest in Love 1960,My 5,39:4
Derby, Carol Field (Director)
First Lady 1937,O 9,17:2

Derby, Dermot (Playwright)
Maid of All Work 1927,Ja 13,28:4
Cocktail Impromptu 1927,Ja 13,28:4
Claw, The 1927,Ja 13,28:4
Derby, Jack
Vaudeville (Palace) 1923,N 20,23:4
Derby, Joan
Blancs, Les 1970,N 16,48:4
Derby, Rhy
Goldfish, The 1922,Ap 18,15:3
Mister Malatesta 1923,F 27,14:2
Dere, Ann
Marry the Man! 1929,Ap 23,26:3
It Never Rains 1929,N 20,26:4
Paging Danger 1931,F 27,19:2
Perfectly Scandalous 1931,My 14,27:2
Pillars of Society, The 1931,O 15,19:1
Give Us This Day 1933,O 28,20:6
Mahogany Hall 1934,Ja 18,18:5
Ragged Army 1934,F 27,16:5
Every Thursday 1934,My 11,25:5
Portrait of Gilbert 1934,D 29,11:5
Journey by Night, A 1935,Ap 17,26:3
Wild Justice 1935,Jl 9,24:3
Thy People 1935,Ag 13,20:3
Paths of Glory 1935,S 27,24:2
Timber House 1936,S 21,27:5
Farm of Three Echoes 1939,N 29,18:3
Village Green 1941,Je 17,24:7
Viva O'Brien 1941,O 10,27:2
Yankee Point 1942,N 24,28:2
Snark Was a Boojum, The 1943,S 2,14:4
Wallflower 1944,Ja 27,14:2
Snafu 1944,O 26,19:5
Open House 1947,Je 4,33:4
Alice Adams 1947,Ag 5,26:1
Streetcar Named Desire, A 1947,D 4,42:2
Touchstone 1953,F 4,33:2
Late Love 1953,O 14,35:2
Red Roses for Me 1955,D 29,15:2
Red Roses for Me 1956,Ja 8,II,1:1
Too Late the Phalarope 1956,O 12,35:1
Dereeder, Pierre (Miscellaneous)
Bitter Sweet 1934,My 8,28:4
Derefinko, Rod (Musical Director)
Persecution and Assassination of Marat As
Performed by the Inmates of the Asylum of
Charenton Under the Direction of the Marquis de
Sade, The 1967,Ja 4,34:1
Celebration 1969,Ja 23,55:2
Dergurian, Jack
Tragicomedy of Don Cristobita and Dona Rosita,
The 1958,My 30,12:2
Derickson, Charles
Clinging Vine, The 1922,D 25,20:2
Paradise Alley 1924,Ap 2,17:3
Vaudeville (Palace) 1926,Mr 16,22:2
Vaudeville (Palace) 1928,O 30,27:3
Vaudeville (Palace) 1929,O 7,22:4
Derig, Klaus
Minna von Barnhelm 1968,N 13,37:1
Derigo, Ainos
Aqua Carnival 1962,Je 29,15:1
Derives, Jacques
Au Rat Mort, Cabinet No 6 1923,O 16,18:1
Crucifies, Les 1923,O 30,17:2
Sur la Dalle 1923,O 30,17:2
Peu de Musique, Un 1923,N 6,22:1
Bonheur, Le 1923,N 20,23:3
Laboratoire des Hallucinations, Le 1923,N 20,23:3
Sol Hyam's Brocanteur 1923,N 27,23:5
Griffe, La 1923,N 27,23:5
Derlin, William
Mr Gladstone 1937,O 17,XI,3:5
Derman, Alex
We've Got to Have Money 1923,Ag 21,12:1
Dermody, Frank (Director)
Long Day's Journey Into Night 1959,Ap 29,30:2
Juno and the Paycock 1964,My 6,41:1
Dermoz, Germaine
Berlioz 1927,F 20,VII,2:1
Mon Coeur au Ralenti 1927,Je 12,VII,2:1
Exaltation, L' 1929,Mr 10,X,1:8
Roi, Deux Dames et un Valet, Un
1935,Mr 3,VIII,2:3
Dern, Bruce
Shadow of a Gunman, The 1958,N 21,26:1
Sweet Bird of Youth 1959,Mr 11,39:2
DeRolph, S I (Scenic Designer)
Pelican, The 1929,N 14,25:1
DeRoss, Frank
Panama Hattie 1940,O 31,28:2
DeRouge, Wilbur
Passing Show of 1922, The 1922,S 21,18:2
Ruint 1925,Ap 8,24:2
Drift 1925,N 25,15:3
Greenwich Villagers, The 1927,Ag 19,20:2
57 Bowery 1928,Ja 27,14:3
Enemy Within 1931,O 6,35:3
Jefferson Davis 1936,F 19,17:2
Derr, Gene
Doctor in Spite of Himself, The 1957,F 28,18:4

Derr, Hume
Bad Habits of 1926 1926,My 1,11:1
Derr, Richard
Traitor, The 1949,Ap 1,30:2
Fundamental George, The 1949,Ag 17,19:4
Closing Door, The 1949,D 2,36:2
Phoenix Too Frequent, A 1950,Ap 27,36:2
Grand Tour, The 1951,D 11,45:2
Dial 'M' for Murder 1952,O 30,41:2
Plain and Fancy 1955,Ja 28,14:2
Plain and Fancy 1955,F 6,II,1:1
Plain and Fancy 1956,F 5,II,3:1
Maybe Tuesday 1958,Ja 30,18:3
Invitation to a March 1960,O 31,27:2
Derrick, Fred
Circus Princess, The 1927,Ap 26,32:2
Derring, Rosemary
Artists and Models 1930,Je 11,33:2
Derringer, William (Director)
Perfect Match, The 1970,N 18,41:1
Derringer, William (Playwright)
Perfect Match, The 1970,N 18,41:1
Derro, John (Costume Designer)
Small Wonder 1948,S 16,33:5
Town House 1948,S 24,31:2
Now I Lay Me Down to Sleep 1950,Mr 3,21:2
Glad Tidings 1951,O 12,33:2
Derrow, Don
Yeomen of the Guard, The 1965,Jl 8,34:1
Trial by Jury 1966,Je 8,41:2
Gondoliers, The 1967,O 29,83:1
Derst, Ralph
Sweetheart Shop, The 1920,S 1,13:4
Derver, Janet Van
Show Boat 1948,S 9,33:2
Derwent, Clarence
Letter of the Law, The; Robe Rouge, La
1920,F 24,11:1
Unwritten Chapter, The 1920,O 12,18:1
Rosa Machree 1922,Ja 10,15:2
Last Warning, The 1922,O 25,23:1
Queen Victoria 1923,N 16,15:1
Garden of Weeds 1924,Ap 29,12:3
Habitual Husband, The 1924,D 25,27:3
Pierrot the Prodigal; Enfant Prodigue, L'
1925,Mr 7,8:1
Love for Love 1925,S 15,29:3
House of Ussher, The 1926,Ja 14,18:4
Beau-Strings 1926,Ap 27,22:2
Florentine Tragedy, A 1927,F 2,22:4
Napoleon's Barber 1927,F 2,22:4
Rapid Transit 1927,Ap 8,21:2
Woman of Bronze, The 1927,Je 16,25:4
Stairs, The 1927,N 8,32:7
Electra 1927,D 2,20:6
Patriot, The 1928,Ja 20,15:1
Three Musketeers, The 1928,Mr 4,IX,2:3
Three Musketeers, The 1928,Mr 14,28:1
Three Musketeers, The 1928,Mr 25,IX,1:1
Serena Blandish 1929,Ja 24,30:3
Serena Blandish 1929,F 3,VIII,1:1
Ghost Parade, The 1929,O 31,28:4
Topaze 1930,F 13,25:3
Topaze 1930,Mr 2,IX,1:1
Jewel Robbery 1932,Ja 14,17:2
Broadway Boy 1932,My 4,23:5
Late Christopher Bean, The 1932,N 1,24:3
False Dreams, Farewell 1934,Ja 16,18:3
Field of Ermine 1935,F 9,10:4
Play, Genius, Play! 1935,O 31,17:2
Tulips Are Blooming, The 1935,D 4,27:6
Lady Precious Stream 1936,Ja 28,15:2
Lady Precious Stream 1936,F 23,X,1:1
Amazing Dr. Clitterhouse, The 1937,Mr 3,26:4
Princess Turandot 1937,Ag 3,20:5
Romance 1937,Ag 17,23:1
Soliloquy 1938,N 29,26:4
Kind Lady 1940,S 4,28:3
Doctor's Dilemma, The 1941,Mr 12,18:2
Rose Burke 1942,Ja 25,IX,2:5
Walking Gentleman, The 1942,My 8,26:2
I Killed the Count 1942,S 4,18:1
Pirate, The 1942,N 26,39:2
Innocent Voyage, The 1943,N 16,27:2
Rebecca 1944,Ap 30,II,1:1
Lady in Danger 1945,Mr 30,18:6
Private Life of the Master Race, The
1945,Je 13,28:3
Private Life of the Master Race, The
1945,Je 17,II,1:1
Lute Song 1946,F 7,29:2
Gypsy Lady 1946,S 18,25:6
Eagle Has Two Heads, The 1947,Mr 20,39:2
Topaze 1947,D 29,21:5
Minnie and Mr Williams 1948,O 28,37:2
Madwoman of Chaillot, The 1949,Ja 9,II,1:1
Merchant of Venice, The 1950,My 3,37:2
Merchant of Venice, The 1955,Ja 8,9:7
Deadfall 1955,O 28,20:1
Uncle Vanya 1956,F 1,25:2
Uncle Vanya 1956,F 12,II,1:1
Hamlet 1957,Ja 29,27:1
First Gentleman, The 1957,Ap 26,22:2

Derwent, Clarence—Cont
Prometheus Bound 1957,Ag 9,11:6
Edward II 1958,F 12,32:5
Lulu 1958,S 30,24:1
Lute Song 1959,Mr 13,24:1
Derwent, Clarence (Director)
Wise-Crackers, The 1925,D 17,26:1
Tales of Rigo 1927,My 31,25:3
Sing High, Sing Low 1931,N 13,26:4
Mademoiselle 1932,O 19,22:4
Brittle Heaven 1934,N 14,22:5
Baby Pompadour 1934,D 28,24:2
House in Paris, The 1944,Mr 21,17:1
Rebecca 1945,Ja 19,17:2
Lady in Danger 1945,Mr 30,18:6
Haven, The 1946,N 14,39:4
Laura 1947,Je 27,16:1
Derwent, Clarence (Playwright)
We're All in the Gutter 1927,Mr 5,12:2
Derwent, Elfrida
Near to the Stars 1932,F 23,23:2
Kind Lady 1935,Ap 24,24:5
At Mrs Beam's 1937,Jl 27,24:2
Kind Lady 1940,S 4,28:3
Lady in Danger 1945,Mr 30,18:6
Derwent, Elfrida (Playwright)
We're All in the Gutter 1927,Mr 5,12:2
des Barres, Michael
Girlfriend 1970,F 19,59:1
Des Jardins, Lang
How to Succeed in Business Without Really Trying
1966,Ap 21,45:1
des Mazes, Marcel
Court Circuit, Le 1923,O 16,18:1
Sur le Banc 1923,O 16,18:1
Nounouche 1923,O 23,16:1
Alcide Pepis 1923,O 30,17:2
Fiole, La 1923,N 20,23:3
Laboratoire des Hallucinations, Le 1923,N 20,23:3
Prenez Ma Dame 1923,N 27,23:5
Sol Hyam's Brocanteur 1923,N 27,23:5
Petite Bonnie Serieuse 1923,N 27,23:5
Des Verney, Harold
Earth 1927,Mr 10,23:1
Set My People Free 1948,N 4,38:2
Desai, Shelly
Golden Streets, The 1970,Ag 14,21:1
Gandhi 1970,O 21,37:1
Desailly, Jean
Baptiste 1952,N 13,34:2
Fausses Confidences, Les 1952,N 13,34:2
Proces, Le; Trial, The 1952,N 18,36:2
Amphitryon 1952,N 21,21:2
Occupe-Toi d'Amelie; Keep Your Eyes on Amelie
1952,N 25,35:2
Hamlet 1952,D 2,39:1
Christophe Colomb 1957,Ja 31,20:5
Volpone 1957,F 5,27:2
Misanthrope, Le 1957,F 8,19:1
Nuits de La Colere, Les; Nights of Fury
1957,F 12,31:1
Intermezzo 1957,F 15,20:4
Mariage de Figaro, Le 1964,F 26,41:2
Andromaque 1964,F 29,13:2
Vie Parisienne, La 1964,Mr 11,34:2
DeSal, Frank
How Now, Dow Jones 1967,D 8,53:1
Fig Leaves Are Falling, The 1969,Ja 3,19:1
Billy 1969,Mr 24,56:1
DeSaussure, Bessie
Policy Kings 1938,D 31,6:2
Desboro, Dana
Tantrum, The 1924,S 5,20:2
Bluffing Bluffers 1924,D 23,17:2
Rat, The 1925,F 11,19:3
Lady Screams, The 1927,My 3,24:2
Banshee, The 1927,D 6,26:2
Desborough, Philip
One 1920,S 15,12:2
Country Wife, The 1927,Ja 2,VII,2:5
Desca, Eva
Dear Judas 1947,O 6,26:4
Desca, Eva (Choreographer)
Merry-Go-Rounders, The 1956,N 22,50:1
Descaves, Lucien (Playwright)
Coeur Ebloui, Le 1926,N 21,VIII,2:1
Untitled-Play 1928,Mr 18,IX,2:1
Ascension de Virginie, L' 1929,N 3,IX,4:2
Deschamps, Jean
Lorenzaccio 1958,O 15,44:2
Deschamps, Sylvain (Costume Designer)
Ecole des Femmes, L' 1961,Ap 28,23:1
Deschamps, Sylvain (Scenic Designer)
Ecole des Femmes, L' 1961,Ap 28,23:1
Descombes, Paul
Annonce Faite a Marie, L' 1965,Ap 6,33:2
Descrieres, Georges
Impromptu de Versailles, L' 1961,F 22,30:1
Fourberies de Scapin, Les 1961,F 22,30:1
Tartuffe 1961,Mr 1,28:1
Dindon, Le 1961,Mr 8,38:1
Amphitryon 1970,F 4,38:1
Troupe Du Roi, La 1970,F 4,38:1
Don Juan 1970,F 7,24:2

Descrieres, Georges—Cont
Femmes Savaantes, Les 1970,F 14,12:1
Deseta, William (Director)
Open 24 Hours 1969,F 12,31:1
Satisfaction Guaranteed 1969,F 12,31:1
Deseta, William (Miscellaneous)
Ticket-of-Leave Man, The 1961,D 23,15:1
Penny Change 1963,O 25,37:1
Deseta, William (Producer)
Ticket-of-Leave Man, The 1961,D 23,15:1
Candyapple, The 1970,N 24,33:1
Desha, Lora
Rose of Stamboul, The 1922,Mr 8,11:2
Ziegfeld Follies 1927,Ag 17,27:3
Music in the Air 1932,N 9,28:2
DeShay, John
Othello 1943,O 20,18:1
Decision 1944,My 21,II,1:1
Desheim, Charles
Hamlet 1930,Mr 25,34:4
Twelfth Night 1930,Mr 27,24:7
Merchant of Venice, The 1930,Mr 27,24:7
Richard III 1930,Mr 31,24:1
King Lear 1930,Ap 1,34:6
Julius Caesar 1930,Ap 4,22:3
deShields, Henry
Andorra 1963,F 11,5:5
Desiderato, E
Tutto Per Bene; All's Well That Ends Well
1929,Je 3,27:1
DeSimone, B J
West Side Story 1964,Ap 9,24:2
Unknown Soldier and His Wife, The 1967,Jl 7,22:1
Rosencrantz and Guildenstern Are Dead
1967,O 17,53:1
Madwoman of Chaillot, The 1970,Mr 23,48:3
DeSimone, Michael
Walk in Darkness 1963,O 29,30:2
DeSio, Al
West Side Story 1957,S 27,14:4
Donnybrook! 1961,My 19,23:1
Kean 1961,N 3,28:2
I'm Solomon 1968,Ap 24,51:1
Zorba 1968,N 18,58:1
Coco 1969,D 19,66:1
Desjardins
Paquebot Tenacity, Le 1930,Mr 9,IX,2:7
Desjardins, Pete
Viva O'Brien 1941,O 10,27:2
Deslys
Continental Varieties 1934,N 15,24:3
Deslys, Marie
Pearl of Great Price, The 1926,N 2,34:3
Desmarais, Marie (Producer)
Mirele Efros 1967,O 20,55:1
Mother Courage 1967,N 17,55:1
Desmarets, Sophie
Four Pieces sur Jardin 1969,F 18,35:1
Desmond, Brian
Measure for Measure 1957,Ja 23,24:1
Delightful Season, A 1960,S 29,30:1
Desmond, Bruce
Black Widow 1936,F 13,24:3
Desmond, Cullen
Wayward Saint, The 1955,F 18,17:1
Desmond, Denny
Catch a Star! 1955,S 7,35:2
Desmond, Florence
This Year of Grace 1928,N 8,27:1
Seeing Stars 1935,N 1,25:5
Let's Raise the Curtain 1936,S 29,34:3
If the Shoe Fits 1946,D 6,29:4
Desmond, Gerald
Plan M 1942,F 21,15:2
Desmond, Johnny
Romeo and Juliet 1955,D 16,36:3
Say Darling 1958,Ap 4,17:1
Say Darling 1958,Ap 13,II,1:1
Desmond, Mae
Five Little Peppers, The 1952,My 19,13:1
Desmond, Nora
White-Headed Boy, The 1921,S 16,20:1
Desmond, Patrick
Front Page, The 1969,My 12,54:2
Desmond, Ralph
Farewell to Arms, A 1930,S 23,30:3
Desmond, Shelia
Garden of Weeds 1924,Ap 29,12:3
Desmond, William
Three Men and a Woman 1932,Ja 12,29:2
Desmore, Mercedes
Three Live Ghosts 1920,S 30,12:1
Hedda Gabler 1920,O 5,12:2
Bombasters Furioso 1924,Jl 19,10:4
Sweeney Todd 1924,Jl 19,10:4
Lancashire Lass, The 1931,D 31,16:3
DeSoria, Finita
O'Brien Girl, The 1921,O 4,10:2
Despa, Jeanne
Maitresse de Roi 1926,D 1,24:1
Despo
Illya Darling 1967,Ap 12,37:1
Illya Darling 1967,N 2,58:1

Despres, Suzanne
Gioconda 1926,N 14,VIII,2:1
Image, L' 1928,Ja 1,VIII,2:3
Amours 1929,Ja 13,VIII,2:7
Cyclone, Le 1931,O 25,VIII,1:6
Dessau, Paul (Composer)
Good Woman of Setzuan, The 1956,D 19,41:2
Good Woman of Setzuan, The 1956,D 30,II,1:1
Mother Courage and Her Children 1963,Mr 30,5:5
Mother Courage and Her Children 1964,My 12,32:2
Mother Courage 1967,N 17,55:1
Desta, Dena
Seven Mirrors 1945,O 26,17:2
Destal, Frederick
Variations of 1940 1940,Ja 29,12:1
Gypsy Baron, The 1942,Je 20,8:5
Gypsy Baron, The 1942,Ag 7,12:4
Destazio, Michael (Lighting Director)
Eternal Sabbath 1963,O 19,17:2
Ah, Wilderness! 1969,N 9,86:1
d'Este, Iolanda
Cardinale, Il 1933,Ja 9,24:2
Istruttoria, L'; Judicial Inquiry, The 1933,F 13,11:3
Curioso Accidente, Un 1933,Mr 6,16:3
Romanticismo 1933,My 1,10:5
Liane, Le (Ties That Bind) 1933,Je 12,20:3
Ingeborg 1933,D 11,23:3
Conte di Monte Cristo, Il 1934,Ja 22,13:2
Padrone Delle Ferriere, Il 1934,Mr 19,13:5
Colonello Bridall, L' 1934,Ap 16,20:3
Romanticismo 1934,My 14,20:2
Miserabili I, 1934,S 24,15:1
Miserabili I, 1934,O 1,14:2
Signora Dalle Camelie, La; Camille 1934,O 22,13:2
Processo dei Veleni, Il; Case of Poisons, The
1935,Ja 21,18:2
Romanzo di un Giovane Povero, Il 1935,F 25,12:3
Conte di Monte Cristo, Il 1935,Ap 1,17:6
Signo Della Croce, Il 1935,O 7,11:1
Adventurer, The 1935,N 11,21:1
Cardinale Giovanni de Medici, Il 1935,D 9,24:8
Three Guardsmen, The 1936,F 17,21:3
Religione e Patria 1936,Mr 23,22:4
Feudalismo Oppure La Terra Bassa; Feudalism or
the Lowland 1937,Mr 8,22:2
Fantasmi 1937,Mr 22,26:5
Medico Delle Pazze, Il; Physician of Mad Woman,
The 1937,S 27,24:2
Signora Dalle Camelie, La; Dame aux Camelias, La
1937,O 9,16:3
D'Este, Stephanie
Hamlet 1922,N 17,14:1
Destine, Jean Leon and Dancers
Anna Russell and Her Little Show 1953,S 8,27:2
Destinn, Francesca
Through the Night 1930,Ag 19,19:1
Destoop, Jacques
Cid, Le 1963,N 8,36:2
Cid, Le 1966,F 12,17:1
Reine Morte, La 1966,F 16,52:1
Fil a la Paite, Un 1966,F 18,25:1
Desurmont, Nicole
Ecole des Femmes, L' 1961,Ap 28,23:1
Desvallieres, Maurice (Playwright)
Hotel Paradiso 1957,Ap 12,22:2
Hotel Paradiso 1957,Ap 21,II,1:1
Desy, Victor
Malade Imaginaire, Le; Imaginary Invalid, The
1958,Ap 30,28:2
Sganarelle; Imaginary Cuckold, The 1958,My 7,43:1
Detchon, Eileen
My Heart's in the Highlands 1939,Ap 14,29:2
Everyman 1941,My 9,19:2
Dettori, Giancarlo
Servant of Two Masters, The 1960,F 24,42:2
DeTuscans, The
Keep Off the Grass 1940,My 24,22:6
Deuel Sisters
Music Box Revue 1924,D 2,23:3
Great Temptations, The 1926,My 19,29:1
Deutsch, Armand (Producer)
Wooden Dish, The 1955,O 7,20:1
World of Carl Sandburg, The 1960,S 15,44:1
Deutsch, Ernst
Escape 1928,My 20,VIII,2:1
Ursache, Die 1929,My 12,IX,1:8
Road to Rome, The 1929,N 10,X,4:8
Jud Suess 1930,N 30,IX,2:1
Amphitryon 38 1931,Mr 15,IX,2:4
Page From a Diary 1936,Ja 17,14:6
Page From a Diary 1936,F 9,X,3:1
I Have Been Here Before 1938,O 14,26:2
Talley Method, The 1941,F 25,26:3
Nathan the Wise 1962,Mr 7,29:1
Before Sundown 1962,Mr 14,43:1
Don Carlos 1964,N 25,40:1
Professor Bernhardi 1968,Mr 20,38:1
Deutsch, Gregory
Red Eye of Love 1961,Je 13,28:1
Deutsch, Helen (Playwright)
Love on an Island 1934,Jl 24,20:5
Carnival! 1961,Ap 14,22:2
Carnival! 1968,D 13,58:1

Deutsch, June
Love Me Little 1958,Ap 15,42:2
Deval, Jacques (Director)
Mademoiselle 1932,O 19,22:4
Lorelei 1938,N 30,21:2
Boudoir 1941,F 8,18:4
Deval, Jacques (Lyricist)
Whores, Wars & Tin Pan Alley 1969,Je 17,37:1
Deval, Jacques (Original Author)
Another Love 1934,Mr 20,26:3
Tovarich 1936,S 29,35:2
Mademoiselle 1936,O 4,IX,3:7
Tovarich 1936,O 16,31:4
Tovarich 1936,O 25,X,1:1
Deval, Jacques (Playwright)
Weak Woman, A 1926,Ja 27,16:3
Viens Avec Nous Petit! 1927,F 20,VII,2:1
Her Cardboard Lover 1927,Mr 22,30:5
Ventose 1927,D 18,IX,4:4
Her Cardboard Lover 1928,S 9,IX,2:7
Debauche 1929,Mr 24,X,2:1
Barricou 1930,Ap 20,VIII,2:8
Etienne 1930,Ap 27,IX,2:1
Mademoiselle 1932,Ja 31,VIII,3:1
Onzieme Commandement 1932,My 15,VIII,2:2
Signor Bracoli 1932,O 2,IX,2:3
Mademoiselle 1932,O 19,22:4
Priere Pour les Vivants 1933,O 29,IX,2:5
Tovarich 1933,D 3,IX,7:7
Age de Juliette, L' 1935,Ja 13,IX,2:1
Tovarich 1935,My 19,IX,1:1
Lorelei 1938,N 30,21:2
Behold the Bride 1939,My 24,28:3
Behold the Bride 1939,Je 11,IX,2:5
Boudoir 1941,F 8,18:4
Oh, Herbert! 1945,Je 20,26:3
Bathsheba 1947,Mr 27,40:2
Tovarich 1952,My 15,39:2
Tovarich 1953,N 29,II,3:1
Tonight in Samarkand 1955,F 17,22:2
Tovarich 1963,Mr 20,5:1
Et l'Enfer, Isabelle 1963,S 21,13:3
Deval, Marguerite
Untitled-Revue 1927,O 9,VIII,2:4
Fleur des Pois, La 1932,O 30,IX,3:7
Devallieres, Maurice (Playwright)
Hotel Paradiso 1956,My 3,34:8
Devan, Harold
Electra 1958,My 10,17:7
Devane, William
Othello 1964,Jl 15,29:1
Tragical Historie of Doctor Faustus, The
1964,O 6,34:2
Coriolanus 1965,Jl 15,23:1
MacBird! 1967,F 23,38:1
MacBird! 1967,Mr 12,II,1:1
Ceremony of Innocence, The 1968,Ja 2,33:1
Hamlet 1968,Jl 4,15:1
Romeo and Juliet 1968,Ag 16,19:1
People vs Ranchman, The 1968,O 28,56:1
Watering Place, The 1969,Mr 13,51:1
Chinese, The 1970,Mr 11,42:2
Chinese, The 1970,Mr 22,II,3:1
Devani-Bernae Dancers
Mermaid's Holiday 1961,Jl 1,8:1
Devanny, Hollis
Blossom Time 1923,Je 1,22:2
Devany, Ed (Lighting Director)
Pets 1969,My 15,41:2
Baby With a Knife 1969,My 15,41:2
Silver Grey Toy Poodle 1969,My 15,41:2
DeVarney, E J
Mountain Man, The 1921,D 13,24:2
Sex Fable, The 1931,O 21,26:1
Berlin 1931,D 31,16:1
Devegh, Diana
Bacchae, The 1969,Mr 15,24:1
Devel, Marguerite
Poulette et Son Poulain 1924,Je 15,VII,1:4
Develin, John
Lid's Off, The 1936,Ap 4,11:6
Devello, Peggy
Land Beyond the River, A 1957,Mr 29,15:7
Devenport, Janice
Fledermaus, Die 1933,My 14,II,3:8
Deveraux, Kam (Costume Designer)
International Playgirls '64 1964,My 22,40:2
Devere, Kitty
O'Brien Girl, The 1921,O 4,10:2
DeVere, Mitty
Burlesque 1927,S 2,15:3
Devereaux, Jack
New Brooms 1924,N 18,23:5
Devereaux, James B
Young Alexander 1929,Mr 13,28:2
Devereaux, Jean
Vaudeville (Palladium) 1935,O 30,16:8
Devereaux, John Drew
Little Inn, The 1935,Ag 20,25:1
Remember the Day 1935,S 26,19:3
Feather in the Breeze 1936,Jl 14,22:2
Bright Honor 1936,S 28,14:1

Devereaux, John Drew—Cont
Prodigal Father, The 1937,Ag 17,23:1
Ghost of Yankee Doodle, The 1937,N 23,26:3
Life With Father 1939,Ag 15,14:4
Life With Father 1939,N 9,26:2
Life With Father 1939,N 19,X,1:1
Life With Mother 1948,O 21,32:2
King of Friday's Men, The 1951,F 22,26:2
To Be Continued 1952,Ap 24,37:2
Prescott Proposals, The 1953,D 17,53:1
King of Hearts 1954,Ap 2,23:1
Devereaux, John Drew (Miscellaneous)
Miss Lonelyhearts 1957,O 4,26:2
Private Ear, The 1963,O 10,51:1
Public Eye, The 1963,O 10,51:1
Poor Richard 1964,D 3,59:1
Race of Hairy Men!, A 1965,Ap 30,42:1
3 Bags Full 1966,Mr 7,22:1
How's the World Treating You? 1966,O 25,50:1
Birthday Party, The 1967,O 4,40:2
Man in the Glass Booth, The 1968,S 27,41:1
Devereaux, May
Passing Show of 1921, The 1920,D 30,16:2
Devereaux, Michael (Director)
And Puppy Dog Tails 1969,O 20,60:1
Devereaux, Michael (Producer)
And Puppy Dog Tails 1969,O 20,60:1
Deverell, Francis (Playwright)
Future That Was, The 1936,Ap 23,21:3
Deverell, Hilda (Playwright)
Future That Was, The 1936,Ap 23,21:3
Deverell, John
Dover Road, The 1924,My 4,VIII,2:4
Naughty Cinderella 1925,N 10,23:6
He Walked in Her Sleep 1929,F 3,VIII,2:1
Devereux, William
Respect for Riches, The 1920,My 12,9:1
Czarina, The 1922,F 1,22:1
R U R 1922,O 10,16:1
Devereux, William (Playwright)
Respect for Riches, The 1920,My 12,9:1
Elton Case, The 1921,Jl 5,15:1
Elton Case, The 1921,Jl 17,VI,1:1
Elton Case, The 1921,S 12,16:2
Devers, Joseph
Magistrate, The 1959,My 14,30:6
Hamlet 1959,S 11,21:4
DeVerter, John
This Way to the Tomb 1961,D 9,21:1
Devilin, Joyce
Autumn's Here 1966,O 26,40:1
Deville, Roland (Scenic Designer)
Cosmonaute Agricole, Le 1970,Ap 8,38:3
Grand Vizir, Le 1970,Ap 8,38:3
Devillers, Renee
Yes 1928,F 19,VIII,4:4
Ascension de Virginie, L' 1929,N 3,IX,4:2
Teddy and Partner 1933,F 12,IX,3:4
Homme, L' 1934,F 25,IX,2:3
DeVincent, Jerry
Power of Darkness, The 1959,S 30,33:1
Devine, Andy
Show Boat 1957,Je 28,30:2
Devine, Barry
Noble Rogue, A 1929,Ag 20,31:2
Devine, Claire
Privilege Car 1931,Mr 4,33:1
Devil's Host, The 1931,N 20,27:2
Incubator 1932,N 2,23:3
Places, Please 1937,N 13,10:6
Devine, Emily
Tell Me Pretty Maiden 1937,D 17,33:5
Devine, Eugene
Hero of Santa Maria, The 1926,My 1,10:1
Devine, George
Patriot for Me, A 1965,Jl 11,II,1:4
Devine, George (Director)
Crucible, The 1956,Ap 11,28:3
Country Wife, The 1957,N 28,56:1
Taste of Honey, A 1960,O 5,46:1
Taste of Honey, A 1960,N 6,II,1:1
Day of the Prince 1963,My 15,33:4
Devine, James A
Bad Man, The 1920,Ag 31,7:1
What Price Glory 1924,S 6,14:3
Devine, Jean
Pimpernel! 1964,Ja 7,26:6
Anna Kleiber 1965,Ja 20,33:1
Masks of Angels 1965,Ja 20,33:1
Anna Kleiber 1965,Ja 20,33:1
Devine, Jerry
Melody Man, The 1924,My 14,14:2
Deacon, The 1925,N 25,14:3
Married-And How! 1928,Je 15,30:2
Sap Runs High, The 1936,F 5,15:3
Devine, Jerry (Playwright)
Amorous Flea, The 1964,F 18,26:1
Never Live Over a Pretzel Factory 1964,Mr 30,37:1
Devine, Jerry (Producer)
Amorous Flea, The 1964,F 18,26:1
Devine, Michael (Director)
Anna Kleiber 1965,Ja 20,33:1
Masks of Angels 1965,Ja 20,33:1

Devine, Michael (Miscellaneous)
Story Theater 1970,O 27,54:1
Devine, Michael (Scenic Designer)
Arms and the Man 1964,Ap 28,41:1
Story Theater 1970,O 27,54:1
Devine, Mickey
Elliott Murphy's Aquashow 1955,Je 23,25:1
Devine, Mr
Romeo and Juliet 1932,F 28,VIII,2:4
Devinny, H B
Here's Howe 1923,Ap 26,19:3
Devitt, Alan
Get Me in the Movies 1928,My 22,18:3
He Understood Women 1928,Ag 16,25:1
Diana 1929,D 10,37:1
Gold Braid 1930,My 14,31:2
Devlin, Cory
Nude With Violin 1957,N 15,36:1
Devlin, Donald
Star Spangled Family 1945,Ap 11,18:6
Wind Is Ninety, The 1945,Je 22,12:2
Devlin, Helen
Let's Face It 1941,O 30,26:2
Devlin, Jay
Littlest Circus, The 1959,D 26,5:6
Little Murders 1969,O 2,54:1
Unfair to Goliath 1970,Ja 26,27:1
Devlin, John
King Lear 1963,Je 10,37:1
Henry V 1963,Je 14,37:1
Caesar and Cleopatra 1963,Ag 1,18:2
Richard III 1964,Je 12,44:2
Hamlet 1964,Jl 4,9:1
Poor Bitos 1964,N 16,40:2
Richard III 1966,Ag 11,26:1
Antigone 1967,Je 19,43:1
Merchant of Venice, The 1967,Je 22,46:2
Macbeth 1967,Jl 31,21:1
Concept, The 1968,My 7,51:1
King Lear 1968,N 8,43:1
Billy 1969,Mr 24,56:1
Devlin, John (Lyricist)
Antigone 1967,Je 19,43:1
Devlin, Jon (Choreographer)
Tango 1969,Ja 20,33:1
Devlin, Leianna
Right of Possession 1930,My 9,20:5
Twelfth Disciple, The 1930,My 17,21:4
Devlin, Nancy
Remarkable Mr Pennypacker, The 1953,D 31,11:2
Loud Red Patrick, The 1956,O 4,28:1
Mrs Patterson 1957,F 6,20:2
Hotel Paradiso 1957,Ap 12,22:2
Devlin, Ray
Slight Case of Murder, A 1935,S 12,28:5
Devlin, Sandra
Carnival in Flanders 1953,S 9,38:2
Devlin, Sandra (Choreographer)
Hooray!! It's a Glorious Day. . .And All That
1966,Mr 10,28:1
Devlin, Sandra (Miscellaneous)
Pimpernel! 1964,Ja 7,26:6
That 5 A.M. Jazz 1964,O 20,42:2
Devlin, William
King Lear 1934,N 4,IX,3:1
Peer Gynt 1935,S 24,28:2
Peer Gynt 1935,O 20,XI,3:7
Tiger, The 1936,S 15,36:5
Tiger, The 1936,O 4,IX,3:7
Expedition 1936,O 13,32:4
Mr Gladstone 1937,O 1,18:4
You Never Can Tell 1948,Mr 17,31:2
Devol, James
Tall Kentuckian, The 1953,Je 17,30:1
DeVoll, Ray
Play of Herod, The 1963,D 10,55:2
Play of Daniel, The 1966,Ja 2,64:4
Play of Risen Christ, The 1970,Mr 9,44:1
Devon, Jack
Fall 1957,N 22,19:1
Devon, Larry
My Fair Lady 1968,Je 14,42:1
Devon, Marc
Trumpets and Drums 1969,O 13,52:1
Macbeth 1969,D 23,25:1
Devon, Patricia
Under Milk Wood 1957,O 16,42:5
Devon, Suzan
Yes, Yes, No No 1969,Ja 1,16:1
DeVore, Jesse (Producer)
Believers, The 1968,My 10,57:4
Devorin, Ruth
Carousel 1949,Ja 26,28:2
Devrient-Reinhold (Frau)
Kyrill Reist ins Abendland 1933,Ja 8,IX,2:1
DeVries, Jan
Spofford 1967,D 15,54:3
DeVries, Peter (Original Author)
Tunnel of Love, The 1957,F 14,31:4
Spofford 1967,D 15,54:3
Spofford 1967,D 24,II,3:2
DeVries, Peter (Playwright)
New Faces of 1952 1952,My 17,23:2

DeVries, Peter (Playwright)—Cont
Two's Company 1952,D 16,43:5
Tunnel of Love, The 1957,F 14,31:4
Tunnel of Love, The 1957,D 5,47:2
Leonard Sillman's New Faces of 1968
1968,My 3,43:1
Dew, Edward
Red Mill, The 1945,O 17,16:2
If the Shoe Fits 1946,D 6,29:4
Dewald, Shirley
Full Moon in March, A 1960,S 20,48:1
Dewar, Patrick
Too Late the Phalarope 1956,O 12,35:1
Dewart, Russell
Laugh It Off 1925,Ap 25,18:4
DeWeese, Joan
Blithe Spirit 1946,Je 5,17:3
Afternoon Storm 1948,Ap 12,24:2
Madame Is Served 1949,F 15,28:1
Macbeth 1962,N 17,16:2
Othello 1964,Jl 15,29:1
Baal 1965,My 7,33:2
Dewell, Michael (Director)
Seagull, The 1964,Ap 6,36:1
Crucible, The 1964,Ap 7,30:2
Dewell, Michael (Producer)
Imaginary Invalid, The 1967,My 2,53:1
Touch of the Poet, A 1967,My 3,38:2
Ways and Means 1967,My 4,34:1
Still Life 1967,My 4,34:1
Fumed Oak 1967,My 4,34:1
Comedy of Errors, The 1968,F 28,40:2
She Stoops to Conquer 1968,Ap 1,58:3
Dewes, Carl
Count of Luxembourg, The 1930,F 18,28:2
Dewey, Allan
Contrast, The 1926,O 1,26:2
Dewey, Arline
Imaginary Invalid, The 1922,Jl 26,26:2
Dewey, Earle S
Jonica 1930,Ap 8,27:1
Dewey, Frances
Shoot the Works! 1931,Jl 22,19:5
New Faces 1934,Mr 16,24:5
Dewey, George
Off Your Marx 1936,Ap 2,28:2
Off to Buffalo! 1939,F 22,18:2
Dewey, Gus
House of Leather, The 1970,Mr 19,56:1
Dewey, Jane
Be So Kindly 1937,F 9,19:4
Dewey, John
Mikado, The 1944,F 12,11:3
Dewey, Kenneth (Playwright)
Gift, The 1963,Jl 9,27:2
Dewey, Lottie
Imaginary Invalid, The 1922,Jl 26,26:2
Dewey, Walter
Cure for Matrimony 1939,O 26,26:3
Dewey, William
Off to Buffalo! 1939,F 22,18:2
Dewhurst, Colleen
Desire Under the Elms 1952,Ja 17,23:4
Taming of the Shrew, The 1956,Ag 11,11:2
Taming of the Shrew, The 1956,Ag 26,II,1:1
Camille 1956,S 19,33:1
Titus Andronicus 1956,D 3,40:2
Eagle Has Two Heads, The 1956,D 14,37:2
Macbeth 1957,Ag 16,11:2
Country Wife, The 1957,N 28,56:1
Children of Darkness 1958,Mr 1,11:4
Moon for the Misbegotten, A 1958,Je 7,10:6
Antony and Cleopatra 1959,Ja 14,28:1
Caligula 1960,F 17,31:1
Caligula 1960,F 28,II,1:1
All the Way Home 1960,D 1,42:1
All the Way Home 1960,D 18,II,3:1
All the Way Home 1960,D 27,26:7
Great Day in the Morning 1962,Mr 29,29:1
Desire Under the Elms 1963,Ja 11,5:6
Antony and Cleopatra 1963,Je 21,33:1
Ballad of the Sad Cafe, The 1963,O 31,27:1
Ballad of the Sad Cafe, The 1963,N 10,II,1:1
More Stately Mansions 1967,S 14,54:1
More Stately Mansions 1967,N 1,40:1
More Stately Mansions 1967,N 12,II,1:1
Hello and Goodbye 1969,S 19,54:1
Good Woman of Setzuan, The 1970,N 6,51:1
Good Woman of Setzuan, The 1970,N 15,II,1:5
Dewhurst, Dorothy
Young Madame Conti 1937,Ap 1,18:4
Dewhurst, William
Young Madame Conti 1937,Ap 1,18:4
DeWindt, Hal
Entertain a Ghost 1962,Ap 10,48:1
DeWindt, Hal (Director)
Raisin' Hell in the Son 1962,Jl 3,13:2
DeWindt, Hal (Miscellaneous)
Day of Absence 1965,N 16,56:1
Happy Ending 1965,N 16,56:1
Volpone 1967,Je 30,29:1
DeWindt, Hal (Playwright)
Raisin' Hell in the Son 1962,Jl 3,13:2

Dewing, E B
Don't Bother Mother 1925,F 4,18:2
Dewing, E B (Playwright)
Don't Bother Mother 1925,F 4,18:2
Dewing, Elizabeth
Rain 1935,F 13,24:1
Something Gay 1935,Ap 30,12:2
Achilles Had a Heel 1935,O 14,20:2
County Chairman, The 1936,My 26,26:5
Circle, The 1939,Jl 12,17:2
Circle, The 1939,Jl 13,17:1
What a Life 1939,Ag 2,17:5
White Steed, The 1939,Ag 16,21:3
New Life, A 1943,S 16,26:6
Peepshow 1944,F 4,12:2
Town House 1948,S 24,31:2
Leading Lady 1948,O 19,33:1
Smile of the World, The 1949,Ja 13,26:5
Dewing, Mary
County Chairman, The 1936,My 26,26:5
Dews, Carl
Prince of Pilsen, The 1930,Ja 14,24:3
Serenade, The 1930,Mr 5,26:7
Dews, Peter
King Lear 1950,Ag 30,26:2
Alchemist, The 1970,Ag 26,36:1
Dews, Peter (Director)
Hadrian VII 1968,Jl 4,14:1
Hadrian VII 1969,Ja 9,22:1
Hadrian VII 1969,S 20,20:1
Vivat! Vivat Regina! 1970,Jl 20,21:2
Alchemist, The 1970,Ag 26,36:1
Dews, Peter (Original Author)
Antony and Cleopatra 1969,Ag 30,10:3
Dews, Peter (Producer)
Vivat! Vivat Regina! 1970,My 24,80:1
Dexter, Alan
Music Man, The 1965,Je 17,26:4
Dexter, Alven
Dancing Mothers 1924,Ag 12,12:2
One Man's Woman 1926,My 26,25:1
Black Souls 1932,Mr 31,25:1
Peace on Earth 1933,N 30,39:2
Creeping Fire 1935,Ja 17,22:3
Let Freedom Ring 1935,N 7,26:2
Dexter, Aubrey
Many Waters 1929,S 26,27:1
Dexter, Brad
Magnolia Alley 1949,Ap 19,29:2
Dexter, Brina
High Button Shoes 1955,Mr 12,10:6
Dexter, F
1776 1926,Ap 24,11:2
Gentlemen, the Queen 1927,Ap 23,14:3
Dexter, Joan
Let Freedom Sing 1942,O 6,18:2
Dexter, John
Our Town 1944,Ja 11,24:5
Dexter, John (Director)
Saint Joan 1963,Je 25,23:1
Chips With Everything 1963,O 2,49:1
Royal Hunt of the Sun, The 1964,Jl 8,40:6
Do I Hear a Waltz? 1965,Mr 19,28:1
Royal Hunt of the Sun, The 1965,O 27,36:2
Royal Hunt of the Sun, The 1965,N 14,II,1:1
Black Comedy; White Lies 1967,F 13,42:1
Black Comedy 1967,F 13,42:1
Unknown Soldier and His Wife, The 1967,Jl 7,22:1
Black Comedy 1967,O 19,58:1
Hamlet 1969,Je 30,33:1
Hamlet 1969,Jl 6,II,1:1
Dexter, John (Producer)
Othello 1964,Ap 22,56:1
Dexter, Ronald
Jade God, The 1929,My 14,28:3
Lost Sheep 1930,My 6,33:2
Family, The 1943,Mr 31,22:4
Dexter, Rose
New Faces of 1936 1936,My 20,24:5
Dexter, Sidney
Man and the Masses 1924,Ap 15,25:1
Dexter, Van
Coach With the Six Insides, The 1962,N 27,44:1
Crime and Crime 1963,D 17,51:2
Coach With the Six Insides, The 1967,My 12,50:1
Dey, James (Playwright)
What Did You Say "What" For? 1959,My 5,40:1
Redemptor, The 1959,My 5,40:1
Dey, James (Scenic Designer)
What Did You Say "What" For? 1959,My 5,40:1
Redemptor, The 1959,My 5,40:1
Deylin, Judy
Beaux' Stratagem, The 1957,Jl 9,25:4
Dezseran, Louis John
Bacchae, The 1963,Ap 25,39:5
Dheran, Bernard (Director)
Misanthrope, Le 1960,Mr 9,38:3
Dhery, Robert
Plume de Ma Tante, La 1958,N 12,42:1
Plume de Ma Tante, La 1959,S 13,II,1:1
Dhery, Robert (Director)
Plume de Ma Tante, La 1958,N 12,42:1
Grosse Valise, La 1965,D 15,52:1

Dhery, Robert (Playwright)
Plume de Ma Tante, La 1958,N 12,42:1
Plume de Ma Tante, La 1958,N 16,II,1:1
Grosse Valise, La 1965,D 15,52:1
Dhery, Robert (Producer)
Plume de Ma Tante, La 1959,S 13,II,1:1
Dhiegh, Khigh
In the Jungle of Cities 1960,D 21,39:1
Seven Scenes for Yeni 1963,My 13,36:2
Life Is a Dream 1964,Mr 20,24:1
Queen and the Rebels, The 1965,F 26,16:1
Dhomnail, Marie N
Well of the Saints, The 1970,Ag 10,34:1
D'Honau, Lillian
Show Boat 1956,Je 22,16:1
D'Honau, Marilyn
West Side Story 1957,S 27,14:4
di Bella, Angelo
Padrone Delle Ferriere, Il 1934,Mr 19,13:5
di Bella, Giovanna
Padrone Delle Ferriere, Il 1934,Mr 19,13:5
Di Beni, John
These Are the Times 1950,My 11,37:2
di Carpio, Tony
Medea 1965,N 29,46:1
di Cosmi, Bruno (Producer)
Once for the Asking 1963,N 21,42:2
di Dolcini, Dolores
Ora di Diana, L' 1937,My 17,22:3
di Dolcini, Dolores (Miscellaneous)
Ora di Diana, L' 1937,My 17,22:3
Di Gatano, Adam
Laugh Time 1943,S 9,35:2
Di Gatano, Jane
Laugh Time 1943,S 9,35:2
Di Gatanos, The
Laugh Parade, The 1931,N 3,31:2
Di Genova, Eddy
Nellie Bly 1946,Ja 22,32:2
Around the World 1946,Je 1,9:5
Di Gerlando, Maria
Night in Venice, A 1953,Je 26,15:2
Saint of Bleecker Street, The 1954,D 28,21:1
Saint of Bleecker Street, The 1955,Ja 2,II,1:1
Di Guiseppe, Enrico
Saint of Bleecker Street, The 1965,Mr 19,28:1
Di Leo, Peter (Playwright)
Beautiful Jailer, The 1957,My 17,19:2
Di Martino, Robert
School for Scandal, The 1953,Je 24,29:2
Di Mattiazzis, The
Aquashow 1952,Je 25,25:1
Di Noto, Andrea
Demon Mirror, The 1968,Mr 13,42:1
Di Palazzo, Anthony
Child of Fortune 1956,N 14,41:1
Di San Secondo, Rosso (Playwright)
Stairs, The 1927,N 8,32:7
Di Stinti, Francesca
Lancelot and Elaine 1921,S 13,12:1
Dia, Richard
Macbeth 1969,N 21,51:1
Diakonova, (Mlle)
Chauve-Souris; Romantic Adventure of an Italian
Ballerina and a Marquis, A 1931,O 22,27:1
Diallina, Rica
Cute Gata.....Oute Zhmia; Neither Cat . . . Nor
Damage 1957,D 20,31:1
Diamant, Sherry Lynn
West Side Story 1968,Je 25,32:1
Diamond, Aaron
From Morn Till Midnight 1948,D 7,41:6
Diamond, B
Cute Gata.....Oute Zhmia; Neither Cat . . . Nor
Damage 1957,D 20,31:1
Diamond, Barry (Miscellaneous)
Fourth Wall, The 1968,S 5,53:1
Diamond, Barry (Producer)
Leader, The 1969,Ap 22,40:2
Honest-to-God Schnozzola, The 1969,Ap 22,40:2
Diamond, Bernard
Adding Machine, The 1948,N 18,35:2
Coriolanus 1953,Ag 21,9:2
Billy Budd 1955,My 4,35:1
Diamond, Carlina
Earl Carroll's Vanities 1923,Jl 6,8:2
Diamond, Charles
Marion Show, The 1923,My 8,22:3
Diamond, David (Composer)
Tempest, The 1945,Ja 26,17:2
Romeo and Juliet 1951,Ja 23,24:8
Rose Tattoo, The 1951,F 5,19:2
Romeo and Juliet 1951,Mr 12,21:2
Diamond, Frances
Liliom 1921,Ap 21,18:1
Green Ring, The 1922,Ap 5,22:1
Diamond, Harold
Viva O'Brien 1941,O 10,27:2
Diamond, Hugh
Viva O'Brien 1941,O 10,27:2
Diamond, I A L (Lyricist)
Life Begins in '40 1940,Ap 5,24:2
Hit the Road 1941,Ap 4,18:3

Diamond, I A L (Miscellaneous)
Alive and Kicking 1950,Ja 18,25:5
Diamond, I A L (Original Author)
Promises, Promises 1968,D 2,59:3
Promises, Promises 1968,D 15,II,3:1
Diamond, I A L (Playwright)
Life Begins in '40 1940,Ap 5,24:2
Hit the Road 1941,Ap 4,18:3
Diamond, Jack
Tidbits of 1946 1946,Jl 9,17:2
Happy Birthday 1946,N 1,31:2
Kiss Me, Kate 1948,D 31,10:3
Diamond, Jess
Hamlet 1939,D 5,35:2
Diamond, Jim
Lady Fingers 1929,F 1,22:4
Diamond, Louis
Babes in Toyland 1929,D 24,15:3
Diamond, Mel
Caucasian Chalk Circle, The 1961,N 1,35:1
Diamond, Michael
Ballad of John Ogilvie, The 1968,O 9,42:4
Diamond, Muni
Living Corpse, The 1929,D 7,19:1
Lost Boy 1932,Ja 6,24:4
Incubator 1932,N 2,23:3
Little Ol' Boy 1933,Ap 25,15:5
Hotel Alimony 1934,Ja 30,16:2
Diamond, Richard
Man of Destiny, The 1926,My 1,10:1
Diamond, Sidney A
If Booth Had Missed 1931,My 14,27:1
Diamond, Tom
Viva O'Brien 1941,O 10,27:2
Diamond, William
Don't Go Away Mad 1949,My 10,28:2
Edge of the Sword, The 1949,N 10,40:3
Diamond Boys
Vaudeville (Palace) 1930,N 17,21:2
Vaudeville (Palace) 1931,Je 15,23:5
Vaudeville (Palace) 1932,Ja 4,27:4
Vaudeville (Palace) 1932,Je 13,19:7
Diamond Brothers
Vaudeville (Palace) 1932,Jl 11,11:6
Vaudeville (Palladium) 1935,O 30,16:8
Diamonds, The Four
Vaudeville (Palace) 1923,O 23,18:2
Diana G
Eva the Fifth 1928,Ag 29,19:3
Diane, Dorothy
Virtue's Bed 1930,Ap 16,26:5
Young Sinners 1933,Mr 7,20:4
Dianina
Chauve-Souris 1922,Je 6,17:4
Diano, Lucia
Roberta 1937,Je 27,II,6:1
Diard, William
Gondoliers, The 1961,Ja 26,33:2
Gondoliers, The 1962,Ap 19,34:2
Mikado, The 1965,Ap 17,11:3
Pirates of Penzance, The 1965,Ap 21,50:6
Diaz, Frank
Saint Wench 1933,Ja 3,19:3
Diaz, Freddy
Walk Down Mah Street! 1968,Je 13,54:1
Diaz, Jorge (Playwright)
Toothbrush, The 1970,S 27,84:5
Diaz, Joseph M (Miscellaneous)
But Never Jam Today 1969,Ap 24,40:1
Diaz, Rafael (Choreographer)
Mexicana 1939,My 7,X,3:1
Diaz, Rafaelo
Retablo de Maese Pedro, El 1925,D 30,10:1
Diaz, Rosita
Teahouse of the August Moon, The 1956,N 9,33:2
Diaz, Tony
Cruce de Vias 1969,N 2,86:5
Dice, George
Land of Fame 1943,S 22,31:5
Deep Are the Roots 1945,S 27,24:4
Dicenta, Joaquin Jr (Playwright)
Pluma en el Viento; Feather in the Wind
1932,Ap 2,13:4
DiCenzo, George R Jr
Simple Life, A 1964,My 18,36:1
Dick, Richard
Best Foot Forward 1941,O 2,28:2
Dick, William
Deluge, The 1922,Ja 28,14:2
Dickens, Alfred
Macbeth 1928,N 20,28:3
Dickens, C Stafford
Old English 1924,D 24,11:2
Hamlet 1925,N 10,23:1
Chief Thing, The 1926,Mr 23,24:2
Beau-Strings 1926,Ap 27,22:2
Garden of Eden, The 1927,S 28,28:1
Freddy 1929,Jl 17,23:4
Many Waters 1929,S 26,27:1
Bon Voyage 1929,D 29,VIII,4:3
Child of Fortune 1956,N 14,41:1
Sail Away 1961,O 4,48:5
Affair, The 1962,S 21,34:2

Dickens, C Stafford—Cont
Hostile Witness 1966,F 18,26:1
Dickens, C Stafford (Director)
Freddy 1929,Jl 17,23:4
Dickens, C Stafford (Playwright)
Command Performance, The 1928,S 23,IX,2:2
Command Performance, The 1928,O 4,27:1
Freddy 1929,Jl 17,23:4
Quitter, The 1934,F 6,24:4
Love and Let Love 1935,Mr 26,23:4
Dickens, Carol
Empress of Destiny 1938,Mr 10,16:2
Dickens, Charles (Original Author)
Cricket on the Hearth, The 1925,My 29,20:2
Pickwick 1927,F 16,17:4
Mr Pickwick 1927,F 20,VII,2:6
Pickwick 1927,Mr 13,VII,1:1
Pickwick 1927,S 6,35:2
Pickwick 1927,S 11,VIII,1:1
Pickwick 1927,O 2,VIII,1:1
Lady Dedlock 1929,Ja 1,61:2
Mr Pickwick 1931,Ja 11,VIII,3:5
Oliver Twist 1934,Ag 11,16:5
Convict, The 1935,F 5,23:2
Pikvikski Klub; Pickwick Club, The 1936,O 4,IX,1:8
Oliver Twist 1937,F 21,II,4:4
Great Expectations 1939,D 17,IX,4:5
Untitled-Reading 1952,Ja 30,20:2
Emlyn Williams 1952,F 5,25:2
Untitled-Reading 1952,F 17,II,1:1
Bleak House 1952,S 4,24:7
Mr Pickwick 1952,S 18,36:3
Mr Pickwick 1952,S 28,II,1:1
Bleak House 1953,Ap 21,33:2
Oliver 1962,S 27,32:3
Oliver 1963,Ja 8,5:5
Pickwick 1963,Jl 5,13:2
Pickwick 1965,O 6,5:3
Oliver 1966,F 5,32:2
Christmas Carol, A 1967,D 23,28:1
Two Cities 1969,Mr 1,22:1
Dickens, Dean
Fortune Teller, The 1929,N 5,32:3
Merry Widow, The 1929,D 3,29:1
Babes in Toyland 1929,D 24,15:3
Prince of Pilsen, The 1930,Ja 14,24:3
Babes in Toyland 1930,D 22,17:1
Patience 1931,Je 16,30:4
Iolanthe 1931,Jl 14,21:5
Merry Widow, The 1931,S 8,39:1
Iolanthe 1932,Ja 5,20:2
Patience 1933,My 23,22:6
Iolanthe 1934,My 1,26:4
H M S Pinafore 1935,Ag 13,20:6
Mikado, The 1936,Ap 11,18:4
Pirates of Penzance, The 1936,Ap 21,27:5
H M S Pinafore 1936,Ap 28,17:2
Iolanthe 1936,My 5,26:2
Roberta 1937,Je 27,II,6:1
Roberta 1937,S 7,16:4
Sally, Irene and Mary 1938,Jl 5,13:4
Firefly, The 1938,Jl 12,15:4
Dickens, Ethel (Playwright)
Convict, The 1935,F 5,23:2
Dickens, Gene
Babes in Toyland 1929,D 24,15:3
Dickens, John
Blackberries of 1932 1932,Ap 5,27:5
Everywhere I Roam 1938,D 30,10:4
Dickenson, Margaret
Injury Sustained 1940,O 24,30:3
Dickerson, Jenny
Nemesis 1921,Ap 5,24:3
Pot-Luck 1921,S 30,10:1
Steamship Tenacity 1922,Ja 3,20:2
Laugh, Clown, Laugh! 1923,N 29,30:1
Quarantine 1924,D 17,19:7
Magda 1926,Ja 27,16:2
Wolf's Cub, The 1927,Ag 30,21:2
Dickerson, Nathaniel
Finian's Rainbow 1947,Ja 11,23:2
Dickey, Annamary
Poisoned Kiss, The 1937,Ap 22,19:1
Rhapsody 1944,N 23,37:2
Hollywood Pinafore 1945,Je 1,20:1
Allegro 1947,O 11,10:2
Dickey, Paul (Director)
Yours Truly 1927,Ja 26,16:5
Shannons of Broadway, The 1927,S 27,30:4
New York 1927,N 15,26:2
Excess Baggage 1927,D 27,24:2
Dickey, Paul (Playwright)
Broken Wing, The 1920,N 30,14:1
Lights Out 1922,Ag 18,8:4
Dust Heap, The 1924,F 24,VII,2:5
Dust Heap, The 1924,Ap 25,20:2
Backslapper, The 1925,Ap 13,25:2
Through the Night 1930,Ag 19,19:1
Dickinson, Angie
Perfect Setup, The 1962,O 25,47:1
Dickinson, Bishop
Wandering Jew, The 1921,O 27,22:1
Dickinson, Don M (Director)
Frankie and Johnny 1952,O 29,37:2

Dickinson, Dorothy
Italian Straw Hat, The 1957,O 1,37:2
Dickinson, Homer
Cinderella on Broadway 1920,Je 25,18:1
Dickinson, Thomas H (Playwright)
Winter Bound 1929,N 13,24:6
Dicks, Joseph (Producer)
Career Angel 1944,My 24,23:7
Dicks, Terry
Mexican Mural; Miracle Painting 1942,Ap 27,19:2
Dickson, Alma
Flying Blind 1930,My 16,20:2
Macbeth 1936,Ap 15,25:4
Angel Island 1937,O 21,26:2
Dickson, Artells
Vagabond King, The 1943,Je 30,24:2
Nellie Bly 1946,Ja 22,32:2
Dickson, Charles
Great Gatsby, The 1926,F 3,22:1
Look, Ma, I'm Dancin' 1948,F 8,II,2:1
Dickson, Charles (Musical Director)
Mermaid's Holiday 1961,Jl 1,8:1
Dickson, Dorothy
Lassie 1920,Ap 7,9:2
Sally 1921,S 11,20:2
Tip-Toes 1926,S 1,27:4
Sunshine Sisters 1933,N 26,IX,3:6
Stop Press 1935,F 22,26:4
Spread It Abroad 1936,Ap 2,29:5
Careless Rapture 1936,S 12,20:6
Crest of the Wave 1937,S 19,XI,3:1
Our Betters 1946,N 10,II,3:1
Red Letter Day 1952,Mr 16,II,3:7
Dickson, George
John Henry 1940,Ja 11,18:2
Dickson, Gloria
Wise Tomorrow 1937,O 5,29:2
Wise Tomorrow 1937,O 16,22:5
Dickson, Harry
Flying Blind 1930,My 16,20:2
Dickson, Marian
Sitting Pretty 1924,Ap 9,24:2
Dickson, Mary
That Old Devil 1944,Je 6,14:2
Dickson, Miles
R U R 1942,D 4,30:2
Threepenny Opera, The 1954,Mr 11,26:5
Dickson, Miles (Director)
Comrades 1956,Je 6,38:1
Eagle Has Two Heads, The 1956,D 14,37:2
Dickson, Miles (Playwright)
Comrades 1956,Je 6,38:1
Dickson, Miles (Translator)
Eagle Has Two Heads, The 1956,D 14,37:2
Dickson, Muriel
Gondoliers, The 1934,S 4,23:1
Gondoliers, The 1934,S 9,IX,1:1
Iolanthe 1934,S 11,24:3
H M S Pinafore 1934,S 14,24:3
Yeomen of the Guard, The 1934,S 21,28:3
Princess Ida; Castle Adamant 1934,S 28,26:3
Patience 1934,O 12,32:2
Dickson, Owen
Respectfully Yours 1947,My 14,29:4
Dickson, W Lee (Playwright)
Clubs Are Trumps 1924,O 15,27:1
Dickstein, Sol (Producer)
Honeymoon in Israel, A 1962,O 15,33:5
Don't Worry Brother! 1963,O 14,35:2
Light, Lively and Yiddish 1970,O 28,58:1
Dicky, Alevel D (Director)
David's Crown 1948,My 10,26:2
Diderot (Original Author)
Mask of Virtue, The 1935,My 16,20:1
Didinato, Peter (Producer)
Sweet Shadow 1935,Ag 7,22:2
Didjah, Belle
Gypsy Blonde 1934,Je 26,22:5
Didjah, Belle (Choreographer)
Yosele the Nightingale 1949,O 21,30:4
Borscht Capades 1951,S 18,38:3
King And the Cobbler, The 1954,D 13,33:6
Shepherd King, The 1955,O 13,36:2
Devil's Game, A 1959,N 9,35:6
Diedrichs, Deslyn
Cradle of Willow, A 1961,D 16,20:2
Diegelmann, Wilhelm
Redemption: Lebende Leichnam, Der; Living
Corpse, The 1928,N 20,28:2
Diehl, Bill Jr (Miscellaneous)
Red, White and Maddox 1969,Ja 27,27:1
Diehl, Crandall
Gentlemen Prefer Blondes 1949,D 9,35:3
Golden Apple, The 1954,Mr 12,15:2
Plain and Fancy 1955,F 6,II,6:6
Diehl, D Altman
Untitled-Nativity Play 1950,D 25,15:2
Diehl, Karl Ludwig
Redemption: Lebende Leichnam, Der; Living
Corpse, The 1928,N 20,28:2
Diehl, Robert
Enchanted, The 1958,Ap 23,41:1
Ivanov 1958,O 8,42:1

Diehl, William
Gentlemen Prefer Blondes 1949,D 9,35:3
Dieley, James
Taming of the Shrew, The 1925,D 19,14:1
Dielhenn, J C (Composer)
It's the Valet 1933,D 15,25:4
Dielhenn, J C (Lyricist)
It's the Valet 1933,D 15,25:4
Diemer, Christine
Rapid Transit 1927,Ap 8,21:2
Diener, Joan
Small Wonder 1948,S 16,33:5
Season in the Sun 1950,S 29,31:2
Kismet 1953,D 4,2:4
Kismet 1955,My 1,II,3:1
Kismet 1955,My 17,33:4
Man of La Mancha 1965,N 23,52:1
Man of La Mancha 1968,D 12,61:1
Cry for Us All 1970,Ap 9,48:2
Dienstag, Isidore
Mikado, The 1935,Ag 24,17:5
Dierig, Klaus
Schloss, Das 1968,N 20,35:3
Dierking, Sharon
Walking Happy 1966,N 28,47:1
Diers, Dippy
New Hellzapoppin, The 1939,D 12,36:4
Diesel, Leota
House of Remsen 1934,Ap 3,26:4
Dieter, George
Music in the Air 1932,N 9,28:2
Dieter, Georgina
Pirates of Penzance, The; Slave of Duty, The
1931,Je 30,23:6
Iolanthe 1931,Jl 14,21:5
Chimes of Normandy, The 1931,N 3,31:3
Firefly, The 1931,D 1,23:2
Pirates of Penzance, The 1936,Ap 21,27:5
Iolanthe 1936,My 5,26:2
Dietl, Fritz
Stars on Ice 1942,Jl 3,12:2
Stars on Ice (2d Edition) 1943,Je 25,13:2
Icetime 1947,My 29,28:2
Dietrich, Daniel P
Adding Machine, The 1970,D 5,40:1
Dietrich, Dena
Cindy 1964,Mr 20,24:1
Rimers of Eldritch, The 1967,F 21,53:1
Here's Where I Belong 1968,Mr 4,32:1
Dietrich, Janette
Bombo 1921,O 7,20:2
Dietrich, Marlene
Marlene Dietrich 1967,O 10,52:1
Marlene Dietrich 1968,O 4,36:1
Dietsch, Burnell
Judy Garland's New Variety Show 1956,S 27,43:2
Dietz, Carl L
Unwritten Chapter, The 1920,O 12,18:1
Dietz, David (Producer)
Minnie and Mr Williams 1948,O 28,37:2
Dietz, Eileen
Steambath 1970,Jl 1,49:1
Dietz, Elizabeth
Passion of Christ, The 1960,My 18,46:1
Dietz, Fritz
It Happens on Ice 1941,Ap 5,13:2
Icetime 1946,Je 21,20:5
Dietz, Howard (Composer)
Three's a Crowd 1930,O 16,28:3
Flying Colors 1932,S 16,24:2
Revenge With Music 1934,N 29,33:5
It's All Yours 1942,Mr 26,26:2
Ziegfeld Follies 1957,Mr 2,19:2
Jennie 1963,O 18,35:2
Dietz, Howard (Director)
Flying Colors 1932,S 16,24:2
Dietz, Howard (Lyricist)
Dear Sir 1924,S 24,21:3
Merry-Go-Round 1927,Je 1,25:4
Little Show, The 1929,My 1,28:5
Little Show, The 1929,My 12,IX,1:2
Second Little Show, The 1930,Ag 17,VIII,2:2
Second Little Show, The 1930,S 3,36:1
Three's a Crowd 1930,O 16,28:3
Flying Colors 1932,S 16,24:2
Revenge With Music 1934,N 29,33:5
Show Is On, The 1937,S 20,18:4
It's All Yours 1942,Mr 26,26:2
Jackpot 1944,Ja 14,15:2
Tars and Spars 1944,Ap 7,23:1
Sadie Thompson 1944,N 17,25:2
Sadie Thompson 1944,N 26,II,1:1
Inside U S A 1948,Mr 30,27:3
Inside U S A 1948,My 1,19:2
Inside U S A 1948,My 23,II,1:1
Ziegfeld Follies 1957,Mr 2,19:2
Gay Life, The 1961,N 20,38:1
Jennie 1963,O 18,35:2
Dietz, Howard (Miscellaneous)
Three's a Crowd 1930,O 26,VIII,1:1
Band Wagon, The 1931,My 17,VIII,3:2
Dietz, Howard (Mrs)
Variations of 1940 1940,Ja 29,12:1

Dietz, Howard (Playwright)
Merry-Go-Round 1927,Je 1,25:4
Three's a Crowd 1930,O 5,IX,4:6
Three's a Crowd 1930,O 16,28:3
Band Wagon, The 1931,Je 4,31:3
Band Wagon, The 1931,Je 14,VIII,1:1
Flying Colors 1932,O 9,IX,1:1
Revenge With Music 1934,N 29,33:5
At Home Abroad 1935,S 20,17:4
At Home Abroad 1935,O 27,IX,1:1
Between the Devil 1937,O 24,XI,2:1
Between the Devil 1937,D 23,24:5
Tars and Spars 1944,Ap 7,23:1
Sadie Thompson 1944,N 17,25:2
Dietz, J Robert
Admirable Bashville, The 1956,F 21,38:1
Comedian, The 1956,O 18,36:4
School for Wives 1957,Je 20,23:4
Caucasian Chalk Circle, The 1961,N 1,35:1
Burning of the Lepers, The 1962,Ap 5,29:1
Once in a Lifetime 1962,O 30,30:1
Devils, The 1963,N 5,25:1
Dietz, J Robert (Director)
You Never Can Tell 1958,Je 17,25:1
Dietz, J Robert (Playwright)
School for Wives 1957,Je 20,23:4
Dietz, John A (Producer)
Cross-Town 1937,Mr 18,21:5
Dietz, Norman
Little Baloney, A 1968,Ja 9,34:1
Dietz, Norman D (Director)
Christmas in the Market Place 1960,D 10,26:1
Cradle of Willow, A 1961,D 16,20:2
Dietz, Norman D (Producer)
Christmas in the Market Place 1960,D 10,26:1
Cradle of Willow, A 1961,D 16,20:2
Dietz, Paul
Shadow, The 1923,D 15,16:2
Fedora 1924,Ja 24,14:2
Armseligen Besenbinder, Die 1928,N 19,16:2
Eight Bells 1933,O 30,14:2
Dietz, Sandra
Little Baloney, A 1968,Ja 9,34:1
Dietz, Sandra (Miscellaneous)
Cradle of Willow, A 1961,D 16,20:2
Dieu, Nicole
Zizi 1964,N 23,51:1
Diezenschmidt (Playwright)
Beloved Augustine, The 1931,Ap 26,VIII,2:6
Diffen, Ray (Costume Designer)
Under the Yum-Yum Tree 1960,N 17,45:1
Thracian Horses, The 1961,S 28,58:2
Fun Couple, The 1962,O 27,15:2
Andorra 1963,F 11,5:5
Importance of Being Earnest, The 1963,F 27,5:2
Hamlet 1963,My 9,41:1
Miser, The 1963,My 10,39:1
Three Sisters, The 1964,Je 23,24:1
Hamlet 1964,Jl 4,9:1
Coriolanus 1965,Jl 15,23:1
Dinner at Eight 1966,S 28,38:1
Richard II 1968,Je 24,42:3
Diffen, Ray (Miscellaneous)
Much Ado About Nothing 1961,Jl 7,17:1
Right Honourable Gentleman, The 1965,O 20,50:2
Diffring, Anton
Winners and Losers 1947,F 27,27:2
Deputy of Paris, The 1947,Mr 22,9:5
Faust 1947,N 29,9:2
Difley, James
World We Live In, The 1922,N 1,16:1
Antony and Cleopatra 1924,F 20,22:1
Digatanos, The
Follow the Girls 1944,Ap 10,15:2
Digges, Dudley
Jane Clegg 1920,F 25,14:1
Treasure, The 1920,O 5,13:1
Heartbreak House 1920,N 11,11:1
Mr Pim Passes By 1921,Mr 1,18:1
Liliom 1921,Ap 21,18:1
Liliom 1921,My 1,VII,1:1
John Ferguson 1921,My 24,20:1
Rose Bernd 1922,S 27,17:1
Rose Bernd 1922,O 8,VI,1:2
Dragon, The 1922,D 27,12:1
Peer Gynt 1923,F 6,14:1
Adding Machine, The 1923,Mr 20,24:1
Failures, The 1923,N 23,20:1
Outward Bound 1924,Ja 8,26:1
Hedda Gabler 1924,My 17,18:4
She Stoops to Conquer 1924,Je 10,24:3
Guardsman, The 1924,O 14,23:1
Morals 1925,D 1,22:2
Hedda Gabler 1926,Ja 27,16:5
Hedda Gabler 1926,F 21,VII,1:2
Importance of Being Earnest, The 1926,My 4,30:1
Juarez and Maximilian 1926,O 12,31:1
Juarez and Maximilian 1926,O 17,VIII,1:1
Brothers Karamazov, The 1927,Ja 4,20:1
Mr Pim Passes By 1927,Ap 19,24:1
Mr Pim Passes By 1927,My 22,VIII,1:1
Doctor's Dilemma, The 1927,N 22,33:1
Marco Millions 1928,Ja 10,28:2

Volpone 1928,Ap 10,32:1
Volpone 1928,Ap 22,IX,1:1
Faust 1928,O 9,34:1
Faust 1928,N 4,IX,4:1
Major Barbara 1928,N 20,28:4
Major Barbara 1928,D 2,X,1:1
Dynamo 1929,F 12,22:1
Man's Estate 1929,Ap 2,28:2
Man's Estate 1929,Ap 28,IX,1:1
Month in the Country, A 1930,Mr 18,30:5
Hour Glass, The 1930,O 26,VIII,4:6
Marseilles; Marius 1930,N 9,IX,3:2
Marseilles 1930,N 18,28:2
Masque of Kings, The 1937,Ja 31,XI,2:1
Masque of the Kings, The 1937,F 9,19:4
Ghost of Yankee Doodle, The 1937,O 28,28:5
Ghost of Yankee Doodle, The 1937,N 7,XI,2:4
Ghost of Yankee Doodle, The 1937,N 23,26:3
On Borrowed Time 1938,F 4,16:4
On Borrowed Time 1938,N 6,IX,1:1
Love for Love 1940,Je 4,19:5
George Washington Slept Here 1940,O 19,20:3
George Washington Slept Here 1940,O 27,IX,1:1
Somewhere in France 1941,Ap 29,16:8
Candida 1942,Ap 28,24:4
Candida 1942,My 3,VIII,1:1
Lifeline 1942,D 1,20:3
Listen Professor! 1943,D 23,22:1
Searching Wind, The 1944,Ap 13,25:2
Searching Wind, The 1944,Ap 23,II,1:1
Iceman Cometh, The 1946,O 10,31:3
Iceman Cometh, The 1946,O 20,II,1:1
Digges, Dudley (Director)
Candida 1924,D 13,12:3
Habitual Husband, The 1924,D 25,27:3
Wild Duck, The 1925,F 25,16:4
Call of Life, The 1925,O 10,10:1
Morals 1925,D 1,22:2
Hedda Gabler 1926,Ja 27,16:5
Ghosts 1926,Mr 17,28:2
Importance of Being Earnest, The 1926,My 4,30:1
Love Is Like That 1927,Ap 19,24:1
Doctor's Dilemma, The 1927,N 22,33:1
Doctor's Dilemma, The 1927,D 4,X,1:1
Man's Estate 1929,Ap 2,28:2
Becky Sharp 1929,Je 4,29:1
Solitaire 1942,Ja 28,22:2
Lifeline 1942,D 1,20:3
Diggs, Alfreda
Mistress of the House, The 1950,Ja 31,19:1
Diggs, John
New Brooms 1924,N 18,23:5
Patsy, The 1925,D 24,8:5
Money From Home 1927,Mr 1,30:2
Porgy and Bess 1935,O 11,30:2
Sweet River 1936,O 29,30:2
Porgy and Bess 1942,Ja 23,16:2
Barrier, The 1950,N 3,32:2
Diggs, Leon
Power of Darkness, The 1948,O 11,28:2
Diggs, Mabel
Run, Little Chillun! 1933,Mr 2,21:3
Dight, Kenneth
Chemmy Circle, The 1968,Ag 10,17:2
Doctor's Dilemma, The 1969,Je 24,37:1
DiGiacoma, Jerry
Moon Walk 1970,N 27,52:1
DiGitanos, The
Laugh Parade, The 1931,S 20,VIII,3:1
Dignam, George (Lighting Director)
Victims of Duty 1960,Ja 20,26:1
Gay Apprentice, The 1960,F 3,27:2
Too Close for Comfort 1960,F 3,27:2
Coggerers, The 1960,Mr 23,33:1
Time to Go 1960,Mr 23,33:1
Embers 1960,O 26,44:1
Nekros 1960,O 26,44:1
Fam and Yam 1960,O 26,44:1
Hanjo 1960,N 16,51:4
Lady Akane, The 1960,N 16,51:4
Shepherd's Chameleon, The 1960,N 30,41:1
Dignam, Mark
Oscar Wilde 1938,O 11,20:2
Love's Labour's Lost 1949,O 24,18:3
Twelfth Night 1950,D 3,II,3:1
World of Sholom Aleichem, The 1955,Ja 12,22:4
Hamlet 1969,Mr 2,II,3:1
Hamlet 1969,My 2,38:1
Voyage Round My Father, A 1970,N 28,20:2
Dignan, John
Caucasian Chalk Circle, The 1961,N 1,35:1
Diiroe, Dorothy A (Composer)
Ododo 1970,N 25,26:1
Diiroe, Dorothy A (Musical Director)
Ododo 1970,N 25,26:1
Dilks, Arthur
My 3 Angels 1953,Mr 12,23:2
Dill, Charles
Lady Dedlock 1929,Ja 1,61:2
Stepping Out 1929,My 21,29:1
Houseparty 1929,S 10,26:5
Suspense 1930,Ag 13,22:3

Dill, David
Tempest, The 1950,S 17,II,3:7
Dill, Dorothy
Truce of the Bear 1957,O 24,39:1
Child of the Morning 1958,Ap 22,40:2
Many Loves 1959,Ja 14,28:1
Orpheus Descending 1959,O 6,45:2
Secret Concubine, The 1960,Mr 22,29:2
Cockeyed Kite 1961,S 14,27:1
Dill, George
Four Flusher, The 1925,Ap 14,27:4
Let and Sub-Let 1930,My 20,32:2
We Are No Longer Children 1932,Ap 1,17:2
Rose Marie 1936,Jl 22,22:6
My Maryland 1936,Ag 12,14:2
Countess Maritza 1936,Ag 19,18:2
Dill, George V
My Maryland 1927,S 13,37:2
Antony and Cleopatra 1937,N 11,30:2
Dill, George V (Playwright)
Top Hole 1924,S 2,22:3
Dill, Leo
Ziegfeld Follies 1927,Ag 17,27:3
Dill, Marcel
Jolly Roger, The 1923,Ag 31,10:4
Cyrano de Bergerac 1923,N 2,14:1
Othello 1925,Ja 12,11:1
Hamlet 1925,O 12,19:2
Merchant of Venice, The 1925,D 28,12:1
Immortal Thief, The 1926,O 4,21:1
Kingdom of God, The 1928,D 21,30:2
Love Duel, The 1929,Ap 16,32:3
Scarlet Sister Mary 1930,N 26,19:2
School for Scandal, The 1931,N 11,26:4
Cyrano de Bergerac 1936,Ap 28,17:1
Embezzled Heaven 1944,N 1,20:2
Ring Around the Moon 1950,N 24,30:1
Dill, Mary Alice
Cyrano de Bergerac 1932,D 27,11:2
Dillard, Bill
Temporary Island, A 1948,Mr 15,27:3
Dillard, Phyllis
Poet's Follies of 1955 1955,My 15,II,3:1
Dillard, Pierre
Green Pastures, The 1951,Mr 16,35:2
Dillard, William
Carmen Jones 1943,D 3,26:2
Memphis Bound 1945,My 25,23:2
Power of Darkness, The 1948,O 11,28:2
Regina 1949,N 1,32:2
Regina 1949,N 13,II,1:1
Green Pastures, The 1951,Mr 16,35:2
Carmen Jones 1951,S 22,8:6
Shuffle Along 1952,My 9,20:5
Regina 1952,Je 2,25:4
My Darlin' Aida 1952,O 28,36:4
Porgy and Bess 1964,My 7,32:1
Dillaway, Don
Backslapper, The 1925,Ap 13,25:2
Still Waters 1926,Mr 2,23:1
Virgin Man, The 1927,Ja 19,20:4
Atlas and Eva 1928,F 7,30:2
Fast Life 1928,S 27,35:2
Flight 1929,F 19,22:3
Mid-West 1936,Ja 8,22:4
Feather in the Breeze 1936,Jl 14,22:2
Holmeses of Baker Street, The 1936,D 10,34:3
Without Warning 1937,My 3,23:2
Reno 1937,Ag 10,22:7
Places, Please 1937,N 13,10:6
Dille, Marjorie
Yellow Jacket, The 1928,N 8,27:3
Octoroon, The 1929,Mr 13,28:3
East Wind 1931,O 28,19:1
Melody 1933,F 15,17:4
Threepenny Opera, The 1933,Ap 14,22:4
Hotel Alimony 1934,Ja 30,16:2
Diller, Britton
Three Sisters, The 1930,Ja 9,22:2
Glass of Water, A 1930,Mr 6,16:3
First Night 1930,N 27,32:3
Diller, Phyllis
Hello, Dolly! 1970,Ja 25,70:6
Dilley, Dorothy
Music Box Revue 1923,S 24,5:3
Kitty's Kisses 1926,My 7,12:2
Oh, Ernest! 1927,My 10,24:3
Take the Air 1927,N 23,28:2
Dillinger, Michael
Front Page, The 1968,O 20,85:5
Dillingham, Benjamin
So Proudly We Hail 1938,Ap 9,11:1
Dillingham, Charles (Miscellaneous)
Good Woman, Poor Thing, A 1933,Ja 10,27:3
Dillingham, Charles (Producer)
Girl From Home, The 1920,My 4,9:2
Bunch and Judy, The 1922,N 12,VIII,1:6
Peter Pan 1924,N 7,16:2
Madame Pompadour 1924,N 12,20:6
Little Minister, The 1925,Mr 24,21:1
Sunny 1925,S 23,22:1
These Charming People 1925,O 7,31:2
City Chap, The 1925,O 27,21:1

Dillingham, Charles (Producer)—Cont

Last of Mrs Cheyney, The 1925,N 10,23:5
Criss Cross 1926,O 13,20:2
On Approval 1926,O 19,27:1
Oh, Please! 1926,D 22,24:3
Lucky 1927,Mr 23,28:3
Sidewalks of New York 1927,O 4,33:1
Mulberry Bush, The 1927,O 27,33:1
She's My Baby 1928,Ja 4,22:2
High Road, The 1928,S 11,31:1
Three Cheers 1928,O 16,28:1
Stepping Out 1929,My 21,29:1
Waterloo Bridge 1930,Ja 7,29:2
Josef Suss 1930,Ja 21,28:5
Ripples 1930,F 2,VIII,2:7
Ripples 1930,F 12,26:1
Suspense 1930,Ag 13,22:3
That's the Woman 1930,S 4,27:2
As Good as new 1930,O 19,IX,3:4
Canaries Sometimes Sing 1930,O 21,34:2
As Good As New 1930,N 18,32:2
Merchant of Venice, The 1930,N 16,VIII,3:1
Merchant of Venice, The 1930,D 3,29:2
Bad Penny, A 1931,Ag 23,VIII,2:4
Stella Brady 1931,O 11,VIII,4:3
Maurice Chevalier 1932,F 10,26:6
New Faces 1934,Mr 16,24:5
New Faces 1934,Ap 1,X,1:1

Dillingham, Joy

Cherry Orchard, The 1960,Je 4,17:2

Dillion, Conway

Up She Goes 1922,N 7,14:2

Dillman, Bradford

Scarecrow, The 1953,Je 17,31:1
Third Person 1955,D 30,13:4
Long Day's Journey Into Night 1956,N 8,47:2
Long Day's Journey Into Night 1956,N 18,II,1:1
Long Day's Journey Into Night 1957,Jl 3,14:1
Fun Couple, The 1962,O 27,15:2

Dillman, Hugh

Daddy's Gone A-Hunting 1921,S 1,18:3

Dillon, Barbara

Transit of Venus, The 1927,My 22,VIII,2:1

Dillon, Brendan

This Island Is Mine 1959,Jl 1,26:4

Dillon, Charles

Twelfth Disciple, The 1930,My 17,21:4

Dillon, Charles (Mrs) (Producer)

Beggar's Opera, The 1952,S 26,17:4

Dillon, Charles (Producer)

Beggar's Opera, The 1952,S 26,17:4

Dillon, Elizabeth

Front Page, The 1946,S 5,22:4
Tovarich 1952,My 15,39:2

Dillon, George

Juno and the Paycock 1927,D 20,32:2

Dillon, Irving

Adding Machine, The 1923,Mr 20,24:1

Dillon, Irwin

Zaporogetz Za Dunayem 1937,My 9,II,5:3

Dillon, Maureen

Peter Pan 1924,N 7,16:2
Strange Prince, The 1926,D 8,24:2
Pickwick 1927,S 6,35:2

Dillon, Melinda

Caucasian Chalk Circle, The 1961,N 1,35:1
Burning of the Lepers, The 1962,Ap 5,29:1
Who's Afraid of Virginia Woolf? 1962,O 15,33:1
Who's Afraid of Virginia Woolf? 1962,O 28,II,1:1
You Know I Can't Hear You When the Water's Running; Shock of Recognition, The 1967,Mr 14,54:1
You Know I Can't Hear You When the Water's Running; I'll Be Home for Christmas 1967,Mr 14,54:1
You Know I Can't Hear You When the Water's Running; Footsteps of Doves, The 1967,Mr 14,54:1
Round With Ring, A 1969,O 30,56:1
Story Theater 1970,O 27,54:1
Story Theater 1970,N 8,II,1:1

Dillon, Richard Jr

Father, The 1937,Ap 21,18:5

Dillon, Sara

Show Boat 1948,S 9,33:2
Top Banana 1951,N 2,19:2
On the Town 1959,F 14,15:1

Dillon, Sean

Silver Tassie, The 1929,O 25,26:1
Playboy of the Western World, The 1930,Ja 3,20:4
Siegfried 1930,O 21,34:1
Pipe in the Fields, The 1931,Mr 14,23:4
O'Flaherty, V C 1931,Ap 11,17:6
Well of the Saints, The 1932,Ja 22,15:2
Mr Jiggins of Jigginstown 1936,D 18,30:2
Old Foolishness, The 1940,D 21,20:2
Wookey, The 1941,S 11,20:5
Ulysses in Nighttown 1958,Je 6,30:1
Mundy Scheme, The 1969,D 12,75:1

Dillon, Thomas

Cloudy With Showers 1931,S 2,17:5
Rendezvous 1932,O 13,22:3
Hotel Alimony 1934,Ja 30,16:2
Pre-Honeymoon 1936,My 1,19:4

Young Madame Conti 1937,Ap 1,18:4
Father Malachy's Miracle 1937,N 18,26:4
30 Days Hath September 1938,O 1,10:5
White Steed, The 1939,Ja 11,16:2
Juno and the Paycock 1940,Ja 17,24:2
My Sister Eileen 1940,D 27,23:2
Patriots, The 1943,Ja 30,11:2
Winged Victory 1943,N 22,24:1
This Was Burlesque 1970,F 12,31:1

Dillon, William

Silver Swan, The 1929,N 28,34:5

Dillson, Jay

K Guy, The 1928,O 16,28:4

Dillworth, Mary

Bedrock 1934,N 18,II,6:3

Dilman, Gwen (Producer)

Whisper in God's Ear, A 1962,O 12,27:2

Dilson, Clyde

Two Blocks Away 1921,Ag 31,8:3
Tia Juana 1927,N 16,28:4
Adventure 1928,S 26,25:2
Buckaroo 1929,Mr 18,31:1

Dilson, John

I Must Love Someone 1939,F 8,18:7

Dilson, John H

Ink 1927,N 2,24:2
Excess Baggage 1927,D 27,24:2

DiLuca, Dino

Time of the Cuckoo, The 1952,O 16,37:4
Time of the Cuckoo, The 1952,N 2,II,1:1
House of Flowers 1954,D 31,11:2

Dilworth, Gordon

Sunny River 1941,D 5,28:2
Helen Goes to Troy 1944,Ap 25,17:2
Merry Widow, The 1944,O 9,17:1
Paint Your Wagon 1951,N 13,32:2
Night in Venice, A 1953,Je 26,15:2
Sandhog 1954,N 24,17:1
My Fair Lady 1956,Mr 16,20:2
Flora, the Red Menace 1965,My 12,41:2
On a Clear Day You Can See Forever 1965,O 18,44:1
Walking Happy 1966,N 28,47:1

Dilworth, Hugh

Bloomer Girl 1944,O 6,18:5
Bloomer Girl 1947,Ja 7,33:2
Porgy and Bess 1953,Mr 10,25:5
Jamaica 1957,N 1,32:2
Kiss Me, Kate 1959,Ag 10,24:1

DiMaggio, Vincenza

Moondreamers, The 1969,D 9,68:1

Dimitri, James

Semi-Detached 1960,Mr 11,20:2
Merchant of Venice, The 1962,Je 22,1:4

Dimitri, Richard

Guide, The 1968,Mr 7,50:1

Dimond, Edward P (Director)

Candida 1942,Ap 28,24:4

Dimond, Jack

Closing Door, The 1949,D 2,36:2
Peter Pan 1950,Ap 25,27:2

Dimopoulos, D

Oedipus Tyrannus 1952,N 25,35:2

Dinan, James

Hamlet 1936,O 9,30:2

Dinarzade

Fashions of 1924 1923,Jl 19,18:2
Casanova 1923,S 27,10:2

Dinay, Monette

Mes Amours 1940,My 3,16:5

D'Incecco, Joan (Producer)

Best Foot Forward 1963,Ap 3,43:1

Dine, Jim (Miscellaneous)

Midsummer Night's Dream, A 1967,Je 30,23:1

Dinehart, Allan

Big Game 1920,Ja 22,23:1
Blue Flame, The 1920,Mr 16,18:1
Mirage, The 1920,O 1,14:1
Lawful Larceny 1922,Ja 3,20:2
Exciters, The 1922,S 23,10:4
Rose Briar 1922,D 26,11:3
Two Fellows and a Girl 1923,Jl 20,8:2
Vaudeville (Palace) 1924,F 19,12:1
Cheaper to Marry 1924,Ap 16,26:1
Applesauce 1924,S 7,VII,1:4
Applesauce 1925,S 29,31:2
Treat 'Em Rough 1926,O 5,26:2
Sinner 1927,F 8,20:2
Creoles 1927,S 23,33:3
Silent House, The 1928,F 8,28:5
Vaudeville (Palace) 1928,Ag 28,27:3
Girl Trouble 1928,O 7,IX,2:3
Girl Trouble 1928,O 26,22:3
Marriage Bed, The 1929,Ja 8,35:1
9th Street Guest, The 1930,Ag 26,24:3
Alley Cat 1934,S 18,18:1
Seperate Rooms 1940,Mr 25,10:3

Dinehart, Allan (Director)

Applesauce 1924,S 7,VII,1:4
Applesauce 1925,S 29,31:2
Patsy, The 1925,D 24,8:5
Americana 1926,Jl 27,15:3
Treat 'Em Rough 1926,O 5,26:2

Dinehart, Allan (Director)—Cont

Up the Line 1926,N 23,26:1
Sinner 1927,F 8,20:2
Merry-Go-Round 1927,Je 1,25:4
Father, The 1928,My 12,9:4
Girl Trouble 1928,O 26,22:3
Queen Bee 1929,N 13,25:1
Alley Cat 1934,S 18,18:1

Dinehart, Allan (Playwright)

Alley Cat 1934,S 18,18:1
Seperate Rooms 1940,Mr 25,10:3

Dinelli, Mel (Playwright)

Man, The 1950,Ja 20,28:2
Man, The 1953,Ja 25,II,3:1
Man, The 1953,F 15,II,2:1

Dingenary, Gene (Director)

Darker Flower, A 1963,Mr 11,7:2

Dingenary, Gene (Producer)

Heloise 1958,S 25,28:4
Darker Flower, A 1963,Mr 11,7:2
Saving Grace, The 1963,Ap 19,28:1
Streets of New York, The 1963,O 30,47:1
Song of the Grasshopper 1967,S 29,52:2

Dingle, Charles

Killers 1928,Mr 14,28:3
Midsummer Night's Dream, A 1932,N 18,22:2
Twelfth Night 1932,N 19,20:5
Comedy of Errors, The 1932,N 22,25:3
Merchant of Venice, The 1932,N 24,34:5
Yesterday's Orchids 1934,O 6,20:4
Let Freedom Ring 1935,N 7,26:2
Hymn to the Rising Sun 1936,Ja 13,14:4
So Proudly We Hail 1936,S 23,28:4
Sweet River 1936,O 29,30:2
Days to Come 1936,D 16,35:1
Petticoat Fever 1937,Jl 6,23:1
Casey Jones 1938,F 21,14:2
All the Living 1938,Mr 25,14:4
American Landscape 1938,D 5,19:2
Little Foxes, The 1939,F 16,16:2
Little Foxes, The 1939,F 26,IX,1:1
Miss Liberty 1949,Jl 16,6:5
Immoralist, The 1954,F 2,18:7
Immoralist, The 1954,F 9,22:1
Immoralist, The 1954,F 14,II,1:1

Dingle, Tom

Love Birds 1921,Mr 16,12:1
Sun Showers 1923,F 6,14:2
Rise of Rosie O'Reilly, The 1923,D 26,13:4

Dinkin, Herm

Cherry Orchard, The 1955,O 19,38:1

Dinnell, Patty

Doctor Faustus Lights the Lights 1951,D 3,23:4

Dinner, William (Playwright)

Edwina Black 1950,N 22,20:5

Dinoff, Eva

Chocolate Soldier, The 1932,F 9,30:3

Dinroe, Dorothy A (Composer)

Believers, The 1968,My 10,57:4

Dinroe, Dorothy A (Costume Designer)

Ododo 1970,N 25,26:1

Dinroe, Dorothy A (Musical Director)

Harangues, The 1970,Ja 14,42:1

Dinsmore, Ed

Let's Laugh Again 1937,Ag 24,24:5

Dinsmore, R B

Drake's Drum 1923,D 26,17:7

Dinwiddie, Harry

Teahouse of the August Moon, The 1955,Ag 7,60:3

Dione, John

Christmas Eve 1939,D 28,17:2

Dior, Christian (Costume Designer)

Duel of Angels 1960,Ap 20,42:2
Duel of Angels 1960,My 1,II,1:1

Dira, Obed

Sponono 1964,Ap 3,28:1

Dirga, Andrew

Merry Widow, The 1961,O 27,28:2
Iolanthe 1962,Ag 8,34:2
Gondoliers, The 1963,Je 5,33:2

Dirichs, Ursula

Minna von Barnhelm 1968,N 13,37:1
Schloss, Das 1968,N 20,35:3

Dirksen, Richard (Musical Director)

Faith of Our Fathers 1950,Ag 6,72:2

Dirkson, Sherman

Swing It 1937,Jl 23,17:2

Diserio, Eugene

Lazarus Laughed 1948,Ap 9,27:4

Dishy, Bob

Chic 1959,My 19,28:2
From A to Z 1960,Ap 21,23:2
There Is a Play Tonight 1961,F 16,24:2
Can-Can 1962,My 17,32:2
Open Season at Second City 1964,Ja 23,25:1
Flora, the Red Menace 1965,My 12,41:2
By Jupiter 1967,Ja 20,28:2
Unknown Soldier and His Wife, The 1967,Jl 7,22:1
Something Different 1967,N 29,52:1
Something Different 1967,D 10,II,15:6
Something Different 1968,Ja 7,II,1:5
Goodbye People, The 1968,D 4,52:1
Goodbye People, The 1968,D 15,II,3:1

Diskin, Ellyn
Earthlight Theater 1970,N 4,38:2
Disney, Walt (Miscellaneous)
Swingin' the Dream 1939,N 30,24:2
Disney-Roebuck, Claude
Evensong 1933,F 1,13:4
Disque, Brice Jr
Judgment Day 1934,S 13,26:4
Disraeli, Joe
Frere Jacques 1968,Je 8,23:2
Disraeli (Original Author)
Tancred 1923,Jl 17,14:4
DiStefano, Joseph
Familiar Pattern 1943,S 3,15:6
Career 1943,O 29,22:6
Spring Production 1944,My 20,12:4
DiStefano, Joseph (Playwright)
Evangelist, The 1967,Ap 28,30:3
Ditmer, Carl
Fedora 1924,Ja 24,14:2
Ditrichstein, Leo
Purple Mask, The 1920,Ja 6,18:1
Toto 1921,Mr 22,15:2
Face Value 1921,Jl 24,VI,1:1
Face Value 1921,D 27,10:2
Egotist, The 1922,D 27,12:1
Egotist, The 1922,D 31,VII,1:1
Business Widow, The 1923,D 11,27:1
Ditrichstein, Leo (Playwright)
Purple Mask, The 1920,Ja 11,VIII,2:1
Great Lover, The 1932,O 12,27:3
Dittmann, Dean
Sunday Man, The 1964,My 14,41:3
Cradle Will Rock, The 1964,N 9,40:4
Dittmar, Margaret
Riff-Raff 1926,F 9,18:6
Dittmer, David
Othello 1937,Ja 7,16:4
Diven, Kenneth
Shore Leave 1922,Ag 9,20:2
Flame of Love 1924,Ap 22,19:2
Diveny, Mary
Playboy of the Western World, The 1946,O 28,18:3
Life With Mother 1948,O 21,32:2
Divine, Charles (Playwright)
Strangers at Home 1934,S 15,20:5
Dix, Beulah Marie (Playwright)
Ragged Army 1934,F 27,16:5
Dix, Dorothy
Father, The 1927,S 4,VII,2:1
Lad, The 1929,Ja 13,VIII,4:5
Father, The 1931,O 9,21:1
Soldier and the Gentlewoman, The
1933,My 7,IX,1:4
Dix, Elizabeth
Fuente Ovejuna; Sheep Well, The 1936,My 3,II,4:1
Dix, Franklin J
Lovely Lady 1927,D 30,22:1
Dix, Lillian
Swords 1921,S 2,9:3
Dix, Mae
Scrap Book 1932,Ag 2,20:3
Dix, Richard
Night Lodging 1920,Ap 14,18:2
Lambs Gambol 1925,Ap 27,15:1
Dix, Rollo
Deep River 1926,O 5,26:2
Dix, Tommy
Best Foot Forward 1941,O 2,28:2
Dixey, Henry E
Outrageous Mrs Palmer, The 1920,O 13,18:1
Personality 1921,Ag 29,14:3
Rivals, The 1922,Je 6,18:2
School for Scandal, The 1923,Je 5,24:3
She Stoops to Conquer 1924,Je 10,24:3
Two Orphans, The 1926,Ap 6,26:2
Two Orphans, The 1926,Ap 11,VIII,1:1
Dixie Four, The
Vaudeville (Palace) 1926,Ag 17,21:2
Dixon, Adele
Caste 1929,F 24,IX,4:3
Marriage a la Mode 1930,O 26,VIII,2:1
Good Companions, The 1931,My 15,20:8
Good Companions, The 1931,My 31,VIII,2:6
Between the Devil 1937,O 15,19:1
Between the Devil 1937,O 24,XI,2:1
Between the Devil 1937,D 23,24:5
Don't Listen, Ladies 1948,D 29,16:2
Dixon, Alma
Cradle Will Rock, The 1937,D 6,19:4
Cradle Will Rock, The 1938,Ja 4,19:3
Dixon, Beryl
Iolanthe 1955,S 28,38:1
Mikado, The 1955,S 30,20:2
Princess Ida 1955,O 14,22:3
Dixon, Beth
Brown Sugar 1937,D 3,29:2
Dixon, Billie
Beard, The 1967,O 25,40:1
Dixon, Bob
Redhead 1959,F 6,21:1
Conquering Hero, The 1961,Ja 17,40:2

Dixon, Brenda
Terminal 1970,Ap 15,51:2
Serpent, The 1970,Je 2,35:1
Dixon, Campbell (Playwright)
This Way to Paradise 1930,F 16,IX,2:1
Money! Money! 1931,Mr 15,IX,2:8
Dixon, Campbell (Producer)
This Way to Paradise 1930,Ja 31,24:2
Dixon, Cecile
Old English 1924,D 24,11:2
Adventurous Age, The 1927,F 8,20:1
Spellbound 1927,N 15,26:2
Meet the Prince 1929,F 26,30:5
Dixon, Dorothy
Vanderbilt Revue, The 1930,O 26,VIII,3:5
Vanderbilt Revue, The 1930,N 6,22:6
Vaudeville (Palace) 1931,Jl 6,24:6
Scandals 1931,Ag 16,VIII,1:1
Dixon, Eleanora
Naughty-Naught '00 1937,Ja 25,23:2
Fireman's Flame, The 1937,O 11,26:2
Dixon, Frank
Vaudeville (Palace) 1923,Mr 13,19:2
Dixon, Gale
Jimmy Shine 1968,D 6,52:1
Coco 1969,D 19,66:1
Coco 1970,Ag 7,28:1
Dixon, Harland
Vaudeville (Palace) 1921,Je 14,18:2
Good Morning, Dearie 1921,N 2,20:2
Wildflower 1923,F 8,17:2
Ziegfeld Follies 1923,O 22,17:2
Kid Boots 1924,Ja 1,21:3
Lambs Gambol 1925,Ap 27,15:1
Vaudeville (Hippodrome) 1926,My 11,25:3
Oh, Kay! 1926,N 9,31:3
Manhattan Mary 1927,S 27,30:3
Rainbow 1928,N 22,25:1
Rainbow 1928,D 16,IX,1:1
Vaudeville (Palace) 1929,Jl 8,17:6
Top Speed 1929,D 26,20:1
Vaudeville (Palace) 1931,Ja 5,20:3
Lambs Gambol 1932,Ap 25,18:2
Vaudeville (Palace) 1932,Je 6,18:2
Actors Fund Fete 1942,F 23,24:5
Tree Grows in Brooklyn, A 1951,Ap 20,24:3
Old Bucks and New Wings 1962,N 6,39:4
Dixon, Harry
Vanderbilt Revue, The 1930,O 26,VIII,3:5
Vanderbilt Revue, The 1930,N 6,22:6
Scandals 1931,Ag 16,VIII,1:1
Dixon, Ivan
Wedding in Japan 1957,Mr 12,37:7
Cave Dwellers, The 1957,O 21,29:2
Raisin in the Sun, A 1959,Mr 12,27:1
Dixon, J Mac
Antigone 1930,Ap 25,28:4
Dixon, Jean
Wooden Kimono 1926,D 28,16:2
Behold the Bridegroom 1927,D 27,24:1
Anna 1928,My 17,25:2
Heavy Traffic 1928,S 6,23:3
Final Fling, The 1928,O 7,IX,2:3
Back Here 1928,N 27,36:3
June Moon 1929,O 10,34:5
Divorce Me, Dear 1930,Ag 3,VIII,3:4
Once in a Lifetime 1930,S 7,IX,2:4
Once in a Lifetime 1930,S 25,22:3
Once in a Lifetime 1930,D 7,IX,1:1
Dangerous Corner 1932,O 28,23:1
Heat Lightning 1933,S 16,9:6
Bright Star 1935,O 16,26:2
George Washington Slept Here 1940,S 24,27:3
George Washington Slept Here 1940,O 19,20:3
George Washington Slept Here 1940,O 27,IX,1:1
Deep Mrs Sykes, The 1945,Mr 20,22:6
Deep Mrs Sykes, The 1945,Mr 25,II,1:1
Velvet Glove, The 1949,D 27,26:2
To Be Continued 1952,Ap 24,37:2
Square Root of Wonderful, The 1957,O 31,40:1
Gang's All Here, The 1959,O 2,23:1
Gang's All Here, The 1959,O 11,II,1:1
Dixon, John
Pirate, The 1942,N 26,39:2
Dixon, Joseph
Revolt of the Beavers, The 1937,My 21,19:2
Circle, The 1939,Jl 12,17:2
What a Life 1939,Ag 2,17:5
White Steed, The 1939,Ag 16,21:3
Blind Alley 1939,Ag 23,18:8
Good Fairy, The 1939,Ag 30,15:5
Dixon, Joseph M
Medicine Show 1940,Ap 13,20:6
Dixon, Lee
Sally, Irene and Mary 1938,Jl 5,13:4
Higher and Higher 1940,Mr 17,X,2:5
Higher and Higher 1940,Ap 5,24:3
Oklahoma! 1943,Ap 1,27:1
Dixon, MacIntyre
Stewed Prunes 1960,N 15,47:1
Infancy 1962,Ja 12,28:1
Three Times Three; George Washington Crossing
the Delaware 1962,Mr 2,24:1

Dixon, MacIntyre—Cont
Three Times Three; Twenty-Five Cent White Cap,
The 1962,Mr 2,24:1
Cats' Pajamas, The 1962,Je 1,16:2
Xmas in Las Vegas 1965,N 5,31:1
Mad Show, The 1966,Ja 10,16:1
Home Fires 1969,Ap 8,42:1
Dixon, MacIntyre (Playwright)
Stewed Prunes 1960,N 15,47:1
Cats' Pajamas, The 1962,Je 1,16:2
Dixon, Mort (Lyricist)
Laugh Parade, The 1931,N 3,31:2
Dixon, Oliver
Love's Labour's Lost 1965,Je 16,46:1
Dixon, Osborne B
Little Theatre Tournament; Man Who Died at
Twelve O'Clock, The 1929,My 11,22:2
Dixon, R C (Composer)
Kid Himself, The 1925,D 25,23:2
Dixon, Robert
Heaven on Earth 1948,S 17,29:2
Lend an Ear 1948,D 17,38:2
Wish You Were Here 1952,Je 26,26:6
Dixon, Roberta
Family Reunion, The 1947,N 29,9:2
Dixon, Roy (Lyricist)
Suzette 1921,N 25,18:3
Dixon, Roy (Playwright)
Suzette 1921,N 25,18:3
Dixon, Thomas (Playwright)
Man of the People, A 1920,S 8,9:2
Dixson, Phil (Lighting Director)
Prometheus Bound 1967,My 11,52:1
Dizenzo, Charles (Playwright)
Evening for Merlin Finch, An 1968,D 30,25:1
Great Career, A 1968,D 30,25:1
Evening for Merlin Finch, An 1969,Ja 26,II,1:1
Two Times One; Last Straw, The 1970,Ap 5,76:4
Djimos, George
Sweet Adeline 1929,S 4,33:1
Luana 1930,S 18,28:1
Roberta 1933,N 20,18:4
Djury, Vladimir (Miscellaneous)
Arabian Nights 1967,Jl 3,12:1
D'Lugoff, Art (Producer)
Zany Evening With Elsa Lanchester, A
1960,N 5,27:2
O, Oysters! 1961,Ja 31,23:1
Love and Maple Syrup 1970,Ja 8,47:1
D'Lugoff, Burt (Original Author)
Postmark Zero 1965,N 2,28:1
D'Lugoff, Burt (Producer)
Sign in Sidney Brustein's Window, The
1964,O 16,32:1
Love and Maple Syrup 1970,Ja 8,47:1
Dlugoszewski, Lucia (Composer)
Women of Trachis 1960,Je 23,18:3
Dluznowsky, Moshe (Original Author)
Eleventh Inheritor, The 1962,N 22,43:5
Dluznowsky, Moshe (Playwright)
Lonesome Ship, The 1956,D 7,32:6
Eleventh Inheritor, The 1962,N 22,43:5
Dmitri, Richard
Zorba 1968,N 18,58:1
Dmitrieff, Athy
Roar China! 1930,O 28,23:1
Dmitriev, V V (Scenic Designer)
Three Sisters, The 1965,F 12,15:1
Kremlin Chimes 1965,F 25,23:1
Dneproff, Ivan
Nightingale, The 1927,Ja 4,20:4
Dniestroff, Gregory
See Naples and Die 1929,S 27,30:4
Dniestroff, M
Revue Russe, The 1922,O 6,28:1
Doan, Miriam
Doctor X 1930,Jl 31,12:4
Saint's Parade 1930,N 1,23:4
Doan and Ormsby
Ice Follies 1965,Ja 13,35:1
Doane, Frank
Kissing Time 1920,O 12,18:2
Montmartre 1922,F 14,20:1
Yankee Princess, The 1922,O 3,22:1
Chiffon Girl, The 1924,F 20,23:2
Magnolia Lady, The 1924,N 26,17:2
City Chap, The 1925,O 27,21:1
Girl Friend, The 1926,Mr 18,26:5
She's My Baby 1928,Ja 4,22:2
Doba, Aurelio
Passenger to Bali, A 1940,Mr 15,26:2
Dobbie, Donald A
Betty Behave 1927,Mr 9,28:4
Dobbie, Vyvyan
Sam Abramovitch 1927,Ja 20,20:5
Dobbins, Bert
Tragedy of the Ages, The 1933,Ap 7,22:7
Dobbins, Herbert
Right to Love, The 1925,Je 9,16:4
Tragedy of the Ages, The 1933,Ap 7,22:7
Sellout, The 1933,S 7,17:2
In Heaven and Earth 1936,Mr 27,24:8
Dobbins, Shelley (Playwright)
Babes in Arms 1951,Mr 10,7:3

Dobbs, Bryan
Romeo and Juliet 1960,Jl 1,14:1
Dobbs, Elsie
Glory in the Flower 1959,D 9,57:5
Dobbs, George
June Days 1925,Ag 7,12:5
Night in Paris, A 1926,Ja 6,16:3
Red Robe, The 1928,D 26,15:1
Broadway Nights 1929,Jl 16,23:2
Three Little Girls 1930,Ap 15,29:1
Countess Maritza 1936,Ag 19,18:2
Frederika 1937,F 5,16:5
Roberta 1937,Je 27,II,6:1
Roberta 1937,S 7,16:4
Dobbs, Irving (Playwright)
Belle of New York, The 1948,D 2,36:6
Dobbs, Kenneth
Big Two, The 1947,Ja 9,21:2
Dobbs, Randolph
Cage, The 1970,Je 19,25:1
Dober, Arthur
Fatal Wedding, The 1924,Je 3,22:3
Dobert, Frank
Music in the Air 1932,N 9,28:2
Dobie, Alan
Chips With Everything 1963,O 2,49:1
Dobie, Frances
Sirocco 1927,N 25,24:4
Dobie, Frances (Miscellaneous)
Goose-Feather Bed 1935,D 17,30:7
Dobkin, Ronald
Night Is Black Bottles, The 1962,D 5,56:1
Doble, Frances
Sirocco 1927,D 18,IX,4:1
Ballerina 1933,O 11,26:3
Ballerina 1933,O 29,IX,1:6
Dobos, Viola
International Revue 1930,F 26,22:2
Dobricanin, Dragutin
Progress of Bora, The Tailor, The 1968,Je 27,49:2
Dobrinin, N
Blue Bird, The 1932,Ap 22,23:2
Dobronravoff, Boris
Tsar Fyodor Ivanovitch 1923,Ja 9,26:1
Lady From the Provinces, The 1923,F 27,14:2
Brothers Karamazov, The 1923,F 27,14:2
Brothers Karamazov, The 1923,N 20,23:4
Mistress of the Inn, The; Locandiera, La 1923,N 22,16:1
Ivanoff 1923,N 27,23:2
In the Claws of Life 1923,N 30,23:4
Enough Stupidity in Every Wise Man 1923,D 6,23:1
Brothers Karamazov, The 1924,My 6,25:2
Dobsb, Kenneth
Ali Baba 1951,Mr 27,34:2
Dobson, Frank
Lady Butterfly 1923,Ja 23,18:1
Innocent Eyes 1924,My 21,22:2
Face the Music 1933,F 1,13:4
Dobson, James
Love on Leave 1944,Je 21,23:4
Day Will Come, The 1944,S 8,17:2
Firebird of Florence 1945,Mr 23,13:4
Wind Is Ninety, The 1945,Je 12,12:2
Story for Strangers, A 1948,S 22,39:2
Mr Adam 1949,My 26,34:6
Design For A Stained Glass Window 1950,Ja 24,26:2
Dobson, Margaret
Iolanthe 1955,S 28,38:1
Pirates of Penzance, The 1955,O 7,21:1
Princess Ida 1955,O 14,22:3
Trial by Jury 1955,O 18,48:1
Dobson, Nan
Ladies Night in a Turkish Bath 1961,Mr 22,38:1
Dobson, Phyllis
Censored 1938,F 28,18:2
Dobson, Shedrack
Porgy and Bess 1935,O 11,30:2
Dobujinsky, Mstislav (Costume Designer)
Month in the Country, A 1930,Mr 18,30:5
Possessed, The 1939,O 25,26:2
Anne of England 1941,O 8,26:2
After the Theatre 1942,S 28,13:1
Story of Miss N N, The 1942,S 28,13:1
Witch, The 1942,S 28,13:1
Happy Ending 1942,S 28,13:1
I Forgot 1942,S 28,13:1
Dobujinsky, Mstislav (Scenic Designer)
Month in the Country, A 1930,Mr 18,30:5
Possessed, The 1939,O 25,26:2
Anne of England 1941,O 8,26:2
Story of Miss N N, The 1942,S 28,13:1
I Forgot 1942,S 28,13:1
Happy Ending 1942,S 28,13:1
After the Theatre 1942,S 28,13:1
Witch, The 1942,S 28,13:1
Doby, Dora
Bombo 1921,O 7,20:2
Dobycheff, Vernon
Boys in the Band, The 1969,S 20,21:2

Dockrell, Samuel
Did I Say No? 1931,S 23,19:4
Dockstader, Lew
Some Party 1922,Ap 17,22:1
Black and White Revue, The 1923,O 28,VIII,2:1
Docky, Rudy
Aquacircus 1958,Je 30,24:6
Dodd, Clare
Smiles 1930,N 19,19:2
Dodd, Emily
Book of Charm, The 1925,S 4,26:3
Dodd, Gerry
Tempest, The 1955,S 3,8:6
Dodd, John P (Lighting Director)
Only a Countess May Dance When She's Crazy (An Almost Historical Camp) 1968,Mr 19,41:1
Last Triangle, The (An Embroidered Camp) 1968,Mr 19,41:1
Tom Paine 1968,Mr 26,38:1
Red Cross 1968,Ap 29,47:2
Muzeeka 1968,Ap 29,47:2
Futz 1968,Je 14,39:1
Rat's Mass, A 1969,N 1,39:1
Moondreamers, The 1969,D 9,68:1
Ubu Roi 1970,F 17,33:1
Arden of Faversham 1970,F 17,33:1
Dodd, Lee Wilson (Playwright)
Changelings, The 1923,Ag 26,VI,2:1
Changelings, The 1923,S 18,16:3
Changelings, The 1923,S 30,II,1:1
Strong Man's House, A 1929,S 17,34:3
Dodds, Ethel
Side-Show 1931,My 16,13:1
Dodds, Jack
Kismet 1953,D 4,2:4
Dodds, William (Costume Designer)
Write Me a Murder 1961,O 27,28:2
Dodds, William (Miscellaneous)
Ben Franklin in Paris 1964,O 28,52:1
Happily Never After 1966,Mr 11,37:1
Star-Spangled Girl, The 1966,D 22,38:1
Henry, Sweet Henry 1967,O 24,51:2
Great White Hope, The 1968,O 4,40:1
Engagement Baby, The 1970,My 22,40:1
Dodge, Betty
Night in Venice, A 1929,My 22,30:2
Vaudeville (Palace) 1930,Mr 24,24:5
Vaudeville (Palace) 1931,Ap 20,16:2
Dodge, Dorothy
Counsellor-at-Law 1931,N 7,17:2
Dodge, H W Jr
Front Page, The 1937,N 12,27:2
Dodge, Helen
Houseparty 1929,S 10,26:5
White Flame 1929,N 5,32:7
Man on Stilts, The 1931,S 10,23:2
Dodge, Jacqueline
High Button Shoes 1947,O 10,32:2
Dodge, Jerry
Sap of Life, The 1961,O 3,44:1
110 in the Shade 1963,O 25,37:1
Hello, Dolly! 1964,Ja 17,22:1
Hello, Dolly! 1965,Ag 10,17:2
Those That Play the Clowns 1966,N 25,48:1
Shoemaker's Holiday, The 1967,Mr 3,25:1
Midsummer Night's Dream, A 1967,Je 19,42:1
Merchant of Venice, The 1967,Je 22,46:2
Macbeth 1967,Jl 31,21:1
George M! 1968,Ap 11,48:1
Dodge, Jerry (Director)
Sensations 1970,O 26,48:2
Dodge, Jimmy
You're a Good Man, Charlie Brown 1969,N 14,39:1
Dodge, L V
Rose, The 1922,D 30,13:4
Dodge, Wendell Phillips (Director)
Way, The 1940,O 12,20:3
Dodge, Wendell Phillips (Producer)
Way, The 1940,O 12,20:3
Fiddler's House, The 1941,Mr 28,27:5
Dodge Sisters, The
An und Aus 1926,D 5,VIII,8:7
Dodge Twins
Vaudeville (Palace) 1927,Mr 22,31:1
Untitled-Revue 1928,Mr 11,VIII,2:7
Dodimead, David
King Lear 1947,F 19,32:2
As You Like It 1947,F 21,16:2
Merchant of Venice, The 1947,F 24,16:2
Volpone 1947,F 25,32:2
Hamlet 1947,F 27,27:2
Hamlet 1958,D 17,2:7
Henry V 1958,D 26,2:7
Dods, Marcus (Musical Director)
Kiss Me, Kate 1970,D 26,10:4
Dodson, Charles
Sons o' Guns 1929,N 27,30:4

Dodson, Daryl
Utopia, Limited; Flowers of Progress, The 1957,F 27,21:1
Dodson, Jack
Under Milk Wood 1961,Mr 30,25:1
Infancy 1962,Ja 12,28:1
Under Milk Wood 1962,O 6,13:4
Pullman Car Hiawatha 1962,D 4,46:2
Hughie 1964,D 23,21:2
Dodson, John
Country Wife, The 1957,Je 27,22:1
Trial of Dmitri Karamazov, The 1958,Ja 28,30:1
Our Town 1959,Mr 24,46:2
Dodson, John S
Balcony, The 1960,Mr 4,21:1
Dodson, Owen (Director)
Garden of Time 1945,Mr 10,13:7
Hamlet 1951,Jl 20,13:6
Dodson, Owen (Playwright)
Garden of Time 1945,Mr 10,13:7
Dodson, St Clair
Hot Rhythm 1930,Ag 22,18:5
Dodson's Monkeys
Keep Off the Grass 1940,My 24,22:6
Dodsworth, John
Sherlock Holmes 1953,O 31,11:2
Dodsworth, Wilkie
Burlesque 1927,S 2,15:3
Doeblin, Alfred (Playwright)
Lusitania 1926,Ja 20,22:1
Doench, Clarence
Shannons of Broadway, The 1927,S 27,30:4
Doenhoff, A Edward von
Betty Behave 1927,Mr 9,28:4
Doepp, John (Costume Designer)
Bacchae, The 1963,Ap 25,39:5
Doepper, John
Second Hurricane 1937,Ap 22,18:4
Doerfler, Ernst
Alt Heidelberg 1926,My 31,10:5
Doerr, Jim
Journey of the Fifth Horse, The 1966,Ap 22,36:1
Doerr, Mary
Centuries, The 1927,N 30,23:1
Hoboken Blues 1928,F 18,10:1
Doerr, Mary Jane
Gay Divorce 1960,Ap 4,37:1
Doerr, Mary Jane (Choreographer)
Leave It to Jane 1959,My 26,30:2
Doesky's Russian Choir
Vanderbilt Revue, The 1930,O 26,VIII,3:5
Doff, Gerard S
Touch 1970,N 9,52:1
Dogan, Vivian Hall
On Strivers' Row 1946,Mr 1,17:2
Doggett, Norma
By Jupiter 1967,Ja 20,28:2
Dogim, Izaak
Mother Courage 1967,N 17,55:1
Dohanos, Peter (Lighting Director)
Ernest in Love 1960,My 5,39:4
Dohanos, Peter (Scenic Designer)
Kataki 1959,Ap 10,24:1
Ernest in Love 1960,My 5,39:4
Arabian Nights 1967,Jl 3,12:1
Doherr, Florence
Merry Duchess, The 1943,Je 24,25:1
Doherty, Barbara
Bye Bye Birdie 1960,Ap 15,13:4
Doherty, Brian (Miscellaneous)
John Bull's Other Island 1948,F 11,33:4
Old Lady Says No, The 1948,F 18,35:1
Where Stars Walk 1948,F 25,27:2
Macbeth 1948,Ap 1,30:2
Doherty, Brian (Playwright)
Father Malachy's Miracle 1937,N 18,26:4
Father Malachy's Miracle 1937,D 5,XII,5:1
Doherty, Chester
Taming of the Shrew, The 1956,Ag 11,11:2
Marvellous History of Saint Bernard, The 1958,F 24,16:3
Billy Budd 1959,F 28,13:3
Roman Candle 1960,F 4,34:2
Rules of the Game, The 1960,D 20,44:1
Philoktetes 1961,Ap 25,41:1
Doherty, Don
Traitor, The 1949,Ap 1,30:2
Anyone Can Whistle 1964,Ap 6,36:1
Her Master's Voice 1964,D 28,33:2
Doherty, Don (Director)
Her Master's Voice 1964,D 28,33:2
Doherty, Don (Miscellaneous)
Playroom, The 1965,D 6,49:1
Illya Darling 1967,Ap 12,37:1
Happiness Is Just a Little Thing Called a Rolls Royce 1968,My 13,54:7
Doherty, Felix (Playwright)
Song Out of Sorrow 1941,D 12,34:5
Song Out of Sorrow 1955,N 1,27:3
Doherty, John Jr
Fuente Ovejuna; Sheep Well, The 1936,My 3,II,4:1
Doherty, Lindy
Top Banana 1951,N 2,19:2

Doherty, Tom Jr (Scenic Designer)
Purple Canary, The 1963,Ap 23,31:1
Dohn, Robert
Sons o' Guns 1929,N 27,30:4
Doig, Len
Man on Stilts, The 1931,S 10,23:2
Doini, Giovanni
They Knew What They Wanted 1939,O 3,19:1
D'Oize, Edward
Blue Monday 1932,Je 3,23:2
Dolan, Al
Apollo of Bellac, The 1957,Ap 10,39:1
Virtuous Island, The 1957,Ap 10,39:1
Dolan, Bobby
East Wind 1931,O 28,19:1
Dolan, Catherine
Under Milk Wood 1957,O 16,42:5
Dolan, Charles
Minstrel Boy, The 1948,O 15,28:2
Dolan, Clinton
Beautiful Dreamer 1960,D 28,22:1
Dolan, James
Lady Killer, The 1924,Mr 13,14:2
Dolan, Joann
Years Between, The 1942,F 7,13:2
Eve of St Mark, The 1942,O 8,30:2
Love on Leave 1944,Je 21,23:4
Truckline Cafe 1946,F 28,19:4
Story for Strangers, A 1948,S 22,39:2
Dolan, M J
New Gossoon, The 1937,N 30,26:2
Juno and the Paycock 1937,D 7,32:5
Drama at Inish 1937,D 14,33:2
Dolan, Michael
Marks and Mabel 1945,S 9,II,1:4
Heel, The 1954,My 27,33:2
Purification, The 1954,My 29,12:1
Apollo of Bellac, The 1954,My 29,12:1
Dolan, Michael (Producer)
Aries Is Rising 1939,N 22,16:5
Dolan, Michael J
Things That Are Caesar's, The 1932,O 18,23:4
Far-Off Hills, The 1932,O 19,22:4
Juno and the Paycock 1932,O 20,24:3
Playboy of the Western World, The 1932,O 21,25:1
Rising of the Moon, The 1932,O 21,25:1
New Gossoon, The 1932,O 22,18:2
Words Upon the Window Pane, The
1932,O 29,18:2
Shadow of a Gunman, The 1932,O 31,18:1
Birthright 1932,N 4,25:1
Autumn Fire 1932,D 29,16:3
Big House, The 1933,Ja 5,19:3
King Oedipus 1933,Ja 16,12:4
Days Without End 1934,Ap 24,26:7
Plough and the Stars, The 1934,N 13,22:2
Drama at Inish 1934,N 15,24:2
Look at the Heffernans 1934,N 17,13:2
Church Street 1934,N 20,24:5
Resurrection 1934,N 20,24:5
Noah 1935,D 1,XI,6:4
Saint in a Hurry, A 1935,D 29,IX,2:1
Katie Roche 1937,O 4,17:4
Far-Off Hills, The 1937,O 12,30:4
Playboy of the Western World, The 1937,N 22,14:5
In the Train 1937,N 22,14:5
Righteous Are Bold, The 1946,O 27,II,1:3
Bugle in the Blood, The 1949,Mr 15,34:5
Dolan, Peggy
Scandals 1920,Je 8,9:1
George White's Scandals 1922,Ag 29,10:1
Red Robe, The 1928,D 26,15:1
Dolun, Robert
Soliloquy 1938,N 29,26:4
Dolun, Robert (Composer)
Foxy 1962,Jl 4,12:2
Dolan, Robert (Lyricist)
Ziegfeld Follies 1934,Ja 5,24:3
Dolan, Robert (Playwright)
Ziegfeld Follies 1934,Ja 5,24:3
Dolan, Robert Emmett (Composer)
Texas Li'l Darlin' 1949,N 26,10:5
Not for Children 1951,F 14,35:2
Foxy 1964,F 17,26:1
Dolan, Robert Emmett (Miscellaneous)
Loss of Roses, A 1959,N 30,27:1
Dolan, Robert Emmett (Musical Director)
Juno 1959,Mr 10,41:1
Coco 1969,D 19,66:1
Dolarea, Angel
Pluma en el Viento; Feather in the Wind
1932,Ap 2,13:4
Tambor y Cascabel; Drum and Bell
1932,Ap 21,25:4
De Muy Buena Familia; Of Very Good Family
1932,Ap 29,13:3
Dolaro, Genevieve
Mecca 1920,O 5,12:2
Witch, The 1926,N 19,22:5
Lally 1927,F 9,16:3
Nona 1932,O 5,26:4
Dole, Barbara
Lady From the Sea, The 1935,D 14,11:3

Dole, Charles
Engaged! or Cheviot's Choice 1965,Ap 24,19:2
Dole, Oscar
Adding Machine, The 1970,D 5,40:1
Dolen, Jim
Family Portrait 1959,My 6,48:2
Doley, Ray
Nifties of 1923 1923,S 26,10:1
Dolgova, Nina
Clear All Wires! 1932,S 15,19:1
Dolin, Anton
White Birds 1927,Je 26,VIII,1:3
International Revue 1930,F 26,22:2
Tales of Hoffmann 1932,Ja 10,VIII,1:6
Ballerina 1933,O 29,IX,1:6
Precipice 1934,Je 6,24:4
Players' Masque for Marie Tempest, The
1935,Je 23,IX,1:3
Seven Lively Arts 1944,D 8,26:6
Seven Lively Arts 1944,D 17,II,3:1
Dancer, The 1946,Je 6,16:5
Dolin, Anton (Choreographer)
Ballerina 1933,O 11,26:3
Walk With Music 1940,Je 5,33:2
Seven Lively Arts 1944,D 8,26:6
Dolin, Gerald (Composer)
Smile at Me 1935,Ag 24,18:4
Dolin, Gerry (Composer)
Where's Charley? 1948,O 12,33:2
Dolin, Gerry (Miscellaneous)
Where's Charley? 1948,O 12,33:2
Dolinoff, Alexis (Choreographer)
Student Prince, The 1943,Je 9,16:2
Dolinoff, M
Chauve-Souris; Romantic Adventure of an Italian
Ballerina and a Marquis, A 1931,O 22,27:1
Dolinoff and Raya Sisters
Vaudeville (Palace) 1949,My 20,32:4
Dolinski, Voytek
Flight Into Egypt 1952,Mr 19,33:2
Dolive, William
Unknown Soldier and His Wife, The 1967,Jl 7,22:1
Ah, Wilderness! 1969,N 9,86:1
Doll, Bill (Producer)
Evening With Cecilia Loftus, An 1938,Mr 28,19:2
????? 1939,Ja 2,28:2
Sherlock Holmes 1953,O 31,11:2
Doll, James (Costume Designer)
Mrs Warren's Profession 1956,Je 7,35:2
Doll, Nina
Mr Big 1941,S 7,I,51:3
Mr Big 1941,O 1,24:2
Dollar, William
Rosalinda; Fledermaus, Die 1942,O 29,26:5
Dollar, William (Choreographer)
Great Lady 1938,D 2,26:6
Four Saints in Three Acts 1952,Ap 17,35:1
Dollarhide, Don
Zany Evening With Elsa Lanchester, A
1960,N 5,27:2
Elsa Lanchester-Herself 1961,F 6,28:1
Dolley, Georges (Playwright)
Untitled-Play 1928,Je 17,VIII,1:4
Untitled-Play 1928,N 11,X,2:7
Dolly Sisters, The
Greenwich Village Follies 1924,S 17,16:1
A Vol d'Oiseau 1926,D 5,VIII,8:7
Dolman, Dorothy
Charlot's Revue 1924,Ja 10,18:1
Dolores
Ziegfeld Midnight Frolic 1920,Mr 17,14:2
Sally 1920,D 22,16:1
Broadway Nights 1929,Je 23,VIII,2:4
Broadway Nights 1929,Jl 16,23:2
Untitled-Stage Show 1931,Ap 7,31:2
Dolph, Jack (Composer)
Hear! Hear! 1955,S 28,38:1
Dolph, Jack (Playwright)
Hear! Hear! 1955,S 28,38:1
Dolphin, Eileen
Tiger at the Gates 1968,Mr 1,30:1
Possibilities 1968,D 5,60:1
Dolphin, Joseph
Along Came a Spider 1963,My 28,33:1
Dolson, Bertrand O
Beggar on Horseback 1924,F 13,17:2
Dolson, Robert
Passion, Poison and Petrifaction 1959,Ag 21,13:1
Shewing-Up of Blanco Posnet, The 1959,S 19,26:7
Dolting, Renee
Cinderella on Broadway 1920,Je 25,18:1
Dolton, Matthew
Apple Cart, The 1929,Ag 20,30:2
Domaninska, Libuse
Laterna Magika 1964,Ag 4,21:1
Dombrowski, Jacques
Zizi 1964,N 23,51:1
Domgraf-Fassbaender, Willi
Alt Heidelberg; Student Prince, The
1932,N 20,IX,3:3
Domingo, Marcelino (Playwright)
Dona Maria de Castilla 1933,Mr 19,IV,2:2

Dominick, Liz (Costume Designer)
Basement, The 1967,O 3,56:1
Fragments 1967,O 3,56:1
Dominico, Michael
New Faces of 1952 1952,My 17,23:2
Show Boat 1956,Je 22,16:1
Russell Patterson's Sketch-Book 1960,F 8,35:1
Golden Apple, The 1962,F 13,38:2
Dominique, Pierre (Playwright)
Feu du Ciel 1930,Mr 16,IX,4:3
Dompietrini, Colette
Three Musketeers, The 1968,Je 26,43:1
Tartuffe 1968,Jl 3,28:2
Don, Carl
Relapse, The 1950,N 23,54:2
Romanoff and Juliet 1957,O 11,24:1
Dear Me, the Sky Is Falling 1963,Mr 4,9:1
Twelfth Night 1963,O 9,47:1
Arms and the Man 1964,Ap 28,41:1
Midsummer Night's Dream, A 1967,Je 19,42:1
Don, Hal
Raw Meat 1933,Mr 23,13:2
Don, Stuart W
What a Relief 1935,D 14,10:6
Don Ritz Favorettes
Wine, Women and Song 1942,S 29,18:3
Dona, Sarah B (Miscellaneous)
Triumph of Robert Emmet, The 1969,My 8,54:1
Donaghy, Harry
Half a Widow 1927,S 13,37:3
Rosalie 1928,Ja 11,26:3
Donah, Paul
Music in the Air 1932,N 9,28:2
Bathsheba 1947,Mr 27,40:2
Donahoe, John O'Day
Without the Walls 1920,Je 7,20:1
Little Town of Bethlehem, The 1920,D 27,11:1
Without the Walls 1921,Mr 28,8:1
Without the Walls 1922,Ap 17,17:1
Donahue, Alice
Criss Cross 1926,O 13,20:2
Donahue, Bonnie
Canteen Show, The 1942,S 4,18:1
Donahue, Jack
Ziegfeld Follies 1920,Je 23,14:1
Vaudeville (Palace) 1921,Je 14,18:2
Molly Darling 1922,S 2,10:2
Be Yourself! 1924,Ag 24,VII,1:8
Be Yourself! 1924,S 4,13:3
Sunny 1925,S 23,22:1
Vaudeville (Palace) 1927,Ag 23,29:3
Rosalie 1927,D 18,IX,2:3
Rosalie 1928,Ja 11,26:3
Carry On 1929,N 3,IX,1:7
Sons o' Guns 1929,N 27,30:4
Sons o' Guns 1930,Ja 12,VIII,1:1
Here's How 1934,F 23,22:4
Higher and Higher 1940,Ag 6,15:4
Panama Hattie 1940,O 31,28:2
Donahue, Jack (Choreographer)
Shady Lady 1933,Jl 6,26:3
Of Thee I Sing 1952,My 6,34:2
Donahue, Jack (Director)
Top Banana 1951,N 2,19:2
Night in Venice, A 1952,Je 27,18:6
Jollyanna; Flahooley 1952,Ag 13,17:7
Mr Wonderful 1956,Mr 23,23:2
Rumple 1957,N 7,42:2
Donahue, Jack (Miscellaneous)
Seven Lively Arts 1944,D 8,26:6
Donahue, Jack (Musical Director)
Are You With It? 1945,N 12,17:3
Donahue, Jack (Playwright)
Carry On 1929,N 3,IX,1:7
Sons o' Guns 1929,N 27,30:4
Sons o' Guns 1930,Ag 24,VIII,1:1
Prince Charming 1930,O 14,31:1
Donahue, Jack (Producer)
Lost Sheep 1930,My 6,33:2
Donahue, Jimmy (Playwright)
Transatlantic Rhythm 1936,O 2,16:3
Donahue, Joe
Vaudeville (Palace) 1923,O 23,18:2
Vaudeville (Palace) 1928,S 4,21:3
Americana 1928,O 31,28:2
Donahue, John
Free for All 1931,S 9,25:1
Donahue, Joseph A
Commodore Marries, The 1929,S 15,IX,1:1
Donahue, Michael
Story Teller, The 1951,D 15,11:3
Donahue, Robert
Gantry 1970,F 16,44:1
Donahue, Tom
Minstrel Boy, The 1948,O 15,28:2
Donahue, Vincent
Cyrano de Bergerac 1946,O 9,33:2
Cyrano de Bergerac 1947,Ja 17,27:2
Twentieth Century 1950,D 25,23:6
Shrike, The 1952,Ja 16,20:2
Cyrano de Bergerac 1953,N 13,24:3
Shrike, The 1953,N 26,51:2
Richard III 1953,D 10,65:2

Donahue, Walter
Oklahoma! 1951,My 30,15:2
Oklahoma! 1951,S 13,38:2
Donahue, William F
Take the Air 1927,N 23,28:2
Donal Sisters
Vaudeville (Palace) 1926,N 23,27:3
Vaudeville (Palace) 1929,N 25,22:4
Donald, Edmund
Gasoline Gypsies 1931,Je 8,21:3
Donald, Frew
Orchids Preferred 1937,My 12,26:5
Donald, Isobel
To Quito and Back 1937,O 7,30:4
Donald, James
Heiress, The 1949,F 3,26:2
Face of a Hero 1960,O 21,29:5
Write Me a Murder 1961,O 27,28:2
Donald, Mark (Miscellaneous)
One-Woman Show, A 1962,My 22,31:1
Donald, Peter
Bitter Sweet 1929,N 6,30:2
Donald, Peter Jr
Would-Be Gentleman, The 1930,Ap 30,29:2
Give Me Yesterday 1931,Mr 5,32:1
Pure in Heart, The 1934,Mr 21,24:3
Donaldson, Ann
Earth Journey 1944,Ap 28,24:2
Donaldson, Arthur
What's the Big Idea? 1926,Mr 24,20:3
Straight Thru the Door 1928,O 5,17:2
Little Women 1931,D 8,36:2
Achilles Had a Heel 1935,O 14,20:2
Donaldson, Arthur (Director)
Green Stick 1934,O 10,21:2
Donaldson, Jack
Jubilee 1935,O 14,20:1
Donaldson, John
Orchids Preferred 1937,My 12,26:5
Steps Leading Up 1941,Ap 19,20:6
Donaldson, Midge
Shadow Years, The 1957,Ja 9,26:2
Donaldson, Norma
Happiest Girl in the World, The 1961,Ap 4,42:1
Until the Monkey Comes 1966,Je 21,38:1
Great White Hope, The 1967,D 14,58:1
Great White Hope, The 1967,D 24,II,3:1
Great White Hope, The 1969,S 27,26:1
Donaldson, Robert
Power of Darkness, The 1920,Ja 22,22:1
Boubouroche 1921,N 29,20:1
Infinite Shoeblack, The 1930,F 18,28:1
Donaldson, Ted
Sons and Soldiers 1943,My 5,22:2
Donaldson, Virginia
Curious Savage, The 1956,Mr 17,12:3
Skin of Our Teeth, The 1960,O 14,24:1
Walk in Darkness 1963,O 29,30:2
Donaldson, Walter (Composer)
Sweetheart Time 1926,Ja 20,23:2
Whoopee 1928,D 5,34:3
Whoopee 1929,Ag 6,29:4
Ziegfeld Follies 1931,Jl 2,30:5
Donaldson, Walter (Playwright)
Ed Wynn's Carnival 1920,Ap 6,18:2
Ziegfeld Follies 1931,Jl 2,30:5
Donaldson, Wharton Landell Jr
This Mad Whirl 1937,Ja 10,II,4:8
Donaldson, William (Miscellaneous)
Beyond the Fringe 1962,O 29,36:1
Donat, Peter
Julius Caesar 1955,Jl 13,20:1
God Slept Here, A 1957,F 20,38:1
First Gentleman, The 1957,Ap 26,22:2
Country Wife, The 1957,N 28,56:1
Entertainer, The 1958,F 13,22:2
Henry IV, Part I 1958,Je 25,23:3
Winter's Tale, The 1958,Jl 23,34:3
Three Sisters, The 1959,S 22,46:1
Three Sisters, The 1959,O 4,II,1:1
King John 1960,Je 29,26:2
Midsummer Night's Dream, A 1960,Je 30,23:5
Henry VIII 1961,Je 22,22:1
Love's Labour's Lost 1961,Je 23,19:1
Taming of the Shrew, The 1962,Je 21,25:1
Tempest, The 1962,Je 22,14:1
Cyrano de Bergerac 1962,Ag 1,21:1
Troilus and Cressida 1963,Je 19,40:2
Cyrano de Bergerac 1963,Je 20,30:1
Comedy of Errors, The 1963,Je 21,35:3
Chinese Prime Minister, The 1964,Ja 3,14:1
Falstaff; Henry IV, Part II 1965,Jl 1,35:1
Julius Caesar 1965,Jl 2,18:1
Donat, Robert
Bluestone Quarry 1931,N 29,VIII,2:2
Precious Bane 1932,Ap 24,VIII,1:1
Sleeping Clergyman, A 1933,O 8,X,2:4
Mary Read 1934,N 22,26:7
Red Night 1936,Mr 5,25:1
Cure For Love, The 1945,Ag 5,II,1:4
Murder in the Cathedral 1953,Ap 26,II,1:1
Donat, Robert (Miscellaneous)
Red Night 1936,Mr 5,25:1

Donat, Robert (Producer)
Red Night 1936,Ap 5,IX,1:2
Donatella, Joseph
Music Hall Varieties 1932,N 23,15:3
Donatello, Joe
Illustrators' Show, The 1936,Ja 23,25:3
Donath, Ludwig
Four Twelves Are 48 1951,Ja 18,30:2
Dybbuk, The 1954,O 27,33:6
Abie's Irish Rose 1954,N 19,19:1
Sea Gull, The 1956,O 23,38:1
Only in America 1959,N 20,35:1
Deadly Game, The 1960,F 3,27:2
She Loves Me 1963,Ap 24,39:1
She Loves Me 1963,My 5,II,1:1
Donati, Danilo (Costume Designer)
Festa Italiana 1966,S 30,55:1
Donaudy, Alberto (Playwright)
Incendio Doloso, L'; False Flame, The
1931,N 16,22:4
Doncaster, Stephen (Scenic Designer)
Epitaph for George Dillon 1958,N 5,44:1
Doncourt, Joseph
Lost Horizons 1934,O 16,31:2
Donegan, Francis X
No Other Girl 1924,Ag 14,10:4
City Chap, The 1925,O 27,21:1
Girl Friend, The 1926,Mr 18,26:5
Donegan, John
Walrus and the Carpenter, The 1941,N 10,20:2
Donegan, Martin
Before I Wake 1968,O 14,56:1
Donehue, Vincent
Christmas Eve 1939,D 28,17:2
My Fair Ladies 1941,Mr 24,12:7
Donehue, Vincent J
Old Foolishness, The 1940,D 21,20:2
Donehue, Vincent J (Director)
Trip to Bountiful, The 1953,N 4,30:3
Trip to Bountiful, The 1953,N 15,II,1:1
Traveling Lady 1954,O 28,45:2
All in One; 27 Wagons Full of Cotton
1955,Ap 20,40:3
Annie Get Your Gun 1957,Ag 31,18:2
Sunrise at Campobello 1958,Ja 31,25:1
Sunrise at Campobello 1958,F 9,II,1:1
Sound of Music, The 1959,N 17,40:2
Sound of Music, The 1959,N 22,II,1:1
Daughter of Silence 1961,D 1,28:1
Lord Pengo 1962,N 20,41:2
Jennie 1963,O 18,35:2
Catch Me if You Can 1965,Mr 10,50:1
Donen, Stanley
Pal Joey 1940,D 26,22:2
Best Foot Forward 1941,O 2,28:2
Doner, Jack
Billy Budd 1959,F 28,13:3
Doner, Kitty
Dancing Girl, The 1923,Ja 25,16:2
Vaudeville (Palace) 1924,Ap 1,18:1
Vaudeville (Palace) 1926,My 4,31:2
Vaudeville (Palace) 1926,D 28,12:3
Vaudeville (Palace) 1928,D 17,23:3
Vaudeville (Palace) 1932,Je 13,19:7
Vaudeville (Palace) 1933,Ja 16,13:2
Doner, Maurice
Storm Operation 1944,Ja 12,28:2
Doner, Rose
Dancing Girl, The 1923,Ja 25,16:2
Doner, Ted
Dancing Girl, The 1923,Ja 25,16:2
Innocent Eyes 1924,My 21,22:2
Circus Princess, The 1927,Ap 26,32:2
Doney, Melva
Deputy of Paris, The 1947,Mr 22,9:5
Donhanyi, Ernst von (Composer)
Bridal Veil, The 1928,Ja 27,15:2
Donhowe, Gwyda
Clandestine on the Morning Line 1959,D 5,18:2
Laterna Magika 1964,Ag 4,21:1
Show-Off, The 1967,D 6,40:2
Flip Side, The 1968,O 11,36:1
Philosophy in the Boudoir 1969,My 22,55:2
Rondelay 1969,N 6,55:1
Paris Is Out! 1970,F 3,35:1
Donicht, Mark
Jack Jack 1968,Je 23,74:5
Doniger, Paul E
Man and Superman 1970,F 24,48:1
Hamlet 1970,O 27,54:2
Rosencrantz and Guildenstern Are Dead
1970,N 19,39:3
Doniger, Paul E (Musical Director)
Hamlet 1970,O 27,54:2
Rosencrantz and Guildenstern Are Dead
1970,N 19,39:3
Donisthorpe, Sheila (Playwright)
Guests at Lancaster Gate 1937,My 4,28:6
Donkin, Eric
Henry V 1966,Je 8,38:1
Henry VI 1966,Je 9,55:2
Twelfth Night 1966,Je 10,51:2
Government Inspector, The 1967,Je 15,55:1

Donkin, Eric—Cont
Antony and Cleopatra 1967,Ag 2,25:1
Government Inspector, The 1967,O 28,34:1
Midsummer Night's Dream, A 1968,Je 13,54:1
Three Musketeers, The 1968,Jl 24,49:2
Hamlet 1969,Je 11,37:1
Alchemist, The 1969,Je 12,51:1
Merchant of Venice, The 1970,Je 10,39:1
School for Scandal, The 1970,Je 11,51:1
Donlan, Yolande
School for Brides 1944,Ag 2,19:4
Born Yesterday 1947,F 9,II,3:7
Rocket to the Moon 1948,Mr 23,30:4
Rocket to the Moon 1948,Ap 11,II,3:1
Cage Me a Peacock 1948,Jl 11,II,1:2
Red-Headed Blonde 1953,Ap 20,22:4
Donleavy, J P (Lyricist)
Ginger Man, The 1963,N 22,42:1
Donleavy, J P (Playwright)
Fairy Tales of New York 1961,Ja 26,33:1
Ginger Man, The 1963,N 22,42:1
Donlevy, Brian
What Price Glory 1924,S 6,14:3
Hit the Deck! 1927,Ap 26,32:1
Ringside 1928,Ag 30,13:2
Rainbow 1928,N 22,25:1
Queen Bee 1929,N 13,25:1
Up Pops the Devil 1930,S 2,19:1
Peter Flies High 1931,N 10,28:3
Society Girl 1931,D 31,16:1
Inside Story, The 1932,F 23,23:2
Boy Friend, The 1932,Je 8,22:3
Three-Cornered Moon 1933,Mr 17,20:6
Three and One 1933,O 26,22:6
No Questions Asked 1934,F 6,24:3
Perfumed Lady, The 1934,Mr 13,27:2
Milky Way, The 1934,My 9,23:2
Life Begins at 8:40 1934,Ag 7,20:7
Life Begins at 8:40 1934,Ag 28,24:2
Donley, Robert
Hall of Healing 1952,My 8,35:6
Bedtime Story 1952,My 8,35:6
Finian's Rainbow 1953,Mr 7,13:2
Visit, The 1958,My 6,40:1
Friends and Lovers; In the Zone; Bound East for
Cardiff 1961,My 11,43:1
Friends and Lovers; End of the Beginning, The
1961,My 11,43:1
Something About a Soldier 1962,Ja 5,36:2
Donlin, James
Dreams for Sale 1922,S 14,24:1
Donlin, Mike
This One Man 1930,O 22,32:3
Donn, Berta
Snapshots of 1921 1921,Je 3,19:2
Sun Showers 1923,F 6,14:2
Magnolia Lady, The 1924,N 26,17:2
June Days 1925,Ag 7,12:5
My Maryland 1927,S 13,37:2
There You Are! 1932,My 17,25:4
Tell Her the Truth 1932,O 29,18:2
Revenge With Music 1934,N 29,33:5
Donna, Margaret
Daddy Dumplins 1920,N 23,11:1
Donnay, Maurice (Playwright)
Amants 1928,Mr 4,IX,4:5
Retour de Jerusalem 1929,F 3,VIII,2:3
Ascension de Virginie, L' 1929,N 3,IX,4:2
Lysistrata 1930,D 14,IX,2:7
Donne, Berta
Sonny 1921,Ag 17,12:2
Donnegan, Thomas
Betty Behave 1927,Mr 9,28:4
Donneley, Guerita
Black Souls 1932,Mr 31,25:1
Donnell, Cushing (Captain) (Costume Designer)
Chinese O'Neill 1929,My 23,27:1
Donnell, Cushing (Captain) (Playwright)
Chinese O'Neill 1929,My 23,27:1
Donnell, Cushing (Captain) (Producer)
Chinese O'Neill 1929,My 23,27:1
Donnell, Cushing (Captain) (Scenic Designer)
Chinese O'Neill 1929,My 23,27:1
Donnelly, Charles
Solid Ivory 1925,N 17,29:3
Donnelly, Cornelius
Walk Together Chillun 1936,F 5,15:2
Donnelly, Donal
Philadelphia, Here I Come! 1966,F 17,28:1
Joe Egg 1968,Ap 27,43:2
Donnelly, Donald (Director)
Mundy Scheme, The 1969,D 12,75:1
Donnelly, Dorothy (Lyricist)
Blossom Time 1923,My 22,14:3
Poppy 1923,S 4,14:2
Student Prince, The 1924,D 3,25:3
Hello, Lola! 1926,Ja 13,30:1
My Maryland 1927,S 13,37:2
My Princess 1927,O 7,24:2
Student Prince, The 1931,Ja 30,18:1
Blossom Time 1931,Mr 5,32:1
Blossom Time 1938,D 27,12:2
Student Prince, The 1943,Je 9,16:2
Blossom Time 1943,S 6,21:2

Donnelly, Dorothy (Original Author)
My Princess 1927,O 7,24:2
Donnelly, Dorothy (Playwright)
Blossom Time 1921,S 30,10:1
Blossom Time 1921,O 9,VI,1:1
Blossom Time 1923,My 22,14:3
Poppy 1923,S 4,14:2
Proud Princess, The 1924,F 17,VII,2:8
Student Prince, The 1924,D 3,25:3
Call of Life, The 1925,O 10,10:1
Hello, Lola! 1926,Ja 13,30:1
My Golden Girl 1927,S 11,VIII,1:3
My Maryland 1927,S 13,37:2
My Princess 1927,O 7,24:2
Student Prince, The 1931,Ja 30,18:1
Blossom Time 1931,Mr 5,32:1
Alt Heidelberg; Student Prince, The
1932,N 20,IX,3:3
Blossom Time 1938,D 27,12:2
Student Prince, The 1943,Je 9,16:2
Blossom Time 1943,S 6,21:2
Student Prince, The 1961,Jl 14,14:1
Donnelly, Edward
Merchants of Venus 1920,S 28,14:2
Ambush 1921,O 11,22:1
Ambush 1921,O 16,VI,1:1
Up the Ladder 1922,Mr 7,11:2
Cock o' the Roost 1924,O 14,23:1
One of the Family 1925,D 23,22:3
Behold This Dreamer 1927,N 1,20:4
Young Alexander 1929,Mr 13,28:2
Everything's Jake 1930,Ja 17,20:4
Donnelly, Elizabeth
Titus Andronicus 1956,D 3,40:2
Man and Superman 1960,Ag 17,35:3
Donnelly, Guerita
Old Foolishness, The 1940,D 21,20:2
Brooklyn Biarritz 1941,F 28,16:2
Life of Reilly, The 1942,Ap 30,13:2
Donnelly, Hazel
Scandals 1924,Jl 1,16:1
Donnelly, J Joseph
Moon for the Misbegotten, A 1947,F 21,16:2
Donnelly, James
Keep Kool 1924,My 23,16:4
Donnelly, Jamie
Flora, the Red Menace 1965,My 12,41:2
George M! 1968,Ap 11,48:1
Donnelly, Ken
Hasty Heart, The 1954,Mr 13,10:1
Donnelly, Leo
No More Blondes 1920,Ja 8,22:1
Meanest Man in the World, The 1920,O 13,18:2
Back Pay 1921,Ag 31,8:2
We've Got to Have Money 1923,Ag 21,12:1
Vaudeville (Palace) 1924,Ja 22,15:6
Big Boy 1925,Ja 8,28:2
Money From Home 1927,Mr 1,30:2
White Lights 1927,O 12,30:4
Crooks' Convention, The 1929,S 19,37:4
Spook House 1930,My 25,IX,3:1
Spook House 1930,Je 4,33:3
Pagan Lady 1930,S 28,VIII,4:1
Pagan Lady 1930,O 21,34:2
Hot Money 1931,N 9,22:2
Man Bites Dog 1933,Ap 26,11:2
Milky Way, The 1934,My 9,23:2
Donnelly, Leo (Playwright)
White Lights 1927,O 12,30:4
Donnelly, Leon (Director)
Crooks' Convention, The 1929,S 19,37:4
Donnelly, Mary
Everyday 1921,N 17,15:1
Red Geranium, The 1922,My 9,22:3
Donnelly, Patricia
Lady Comes Across, The 1942,Ja 10,10:2
Priorities of 1942 1942,Mr 13,23:2
Donnelly, Richard
Laughing Woman, The 1936,O 14,30:1
Donnelly, Robert (Scenic Designer)
Much Ado About Nothing 1963,Jl 15,25:2
Donnelly, Ruth
As You Were 1920,Ja 28,22:3
Meanest Man in the World, The 1920,O 13,18:2
Madeleine and the Movies 1922,Mr 7,11:1
Crooked Square, The 1923,S 11,10:2
Cheaper to Marry 1924,Ap 16,26:1
If I Was Rich 1926,S 3,15:2
So Was Napoleon 1930,Ja 9,22:2
She Means Business 1931,Ja 27,21:2
Riot Act, The 1963,Mr 9,5:2
Donnelly, Thomas
Ruined Lady, The 1920,Ja 21,10:2
Taming of the Shrew, The 1927,O 26,26:4
Donnenwirth, Diana
Madame Capet 1938,O 26,26:2
Donner, Jane
Boudoir 1941,F 8,18:4
Donnet, Jacqueline (Miscellaneous)
Save Me a Place at Forest Lawn 1963,My 9,40:2
Last Minstrel, The 1963,My 9,40:2
I Knock at the Door 1964,N 26,53:2
Pictures in the Hallway 1964,D 17,51:1

Donnet, Jacqueline (Producer)
Fireworks; Report, The 1969,Je 12,51:1
Fireworks; Fireworks for a Hot Fourth
1969,Je 12,51:1
Fireworks; Football 1969,Je 12,51:1
Donnet, Marie
Master Builder Solness 1950,My 26,19:3
Daughters of the Late Colonel, The 1951,O 15,21:2
Donnet, Marie (Playwright)
Master Builder Solness 1950,My 26,19:3
Donnio
Procureur Hallers, Le 1924,N 13,18:1
Homme et Ses Fantomes, L' 1924,N 14,16:1
Merchant of Venice, The 1924,N 18,23:2
Bourgeois Gentilhomme, Le 1924,N 20,21:2
Taming of the Shrew, The 1924,N 25,27:3
Donnovan, Gertrude (Sgt)
Swing Sister Wac Swing 1944,Ja 4,20:4
Dono, Vati
Farewell to Arms, A 1930,S 23,30:3
Donoghue, Dennis (Playwright)
Malinda 1929,D 4,37:2
Legal Murder 1934,F 16,16:2
Donohue, Joe
Vaudeville (Hippodrome) 1924,Mr 18,25:1
Donohue, Joseph A
Commodore Marries, The 1929,S 5,26:3
Donohue, Master J
Under the Gaslight 1929,Ap 3,27:1
Donohue, Thomas
Henry V 1966,Je 8,38:1
Twelfth Night 1966,Je 10,51:2
Donovan, Eugene
Where's Your Husband? 1927,Ja 15,10:3
Bless You, Sister 1927,D 27,24:5
Napoleon 1928,Mr 9,21:1
Mima 1928,D 13,24:2
Donovan, F X
Derryowen 1946,O 29,34:2
Donovan, Harriet
Cafe de Danse 1929,Ja 16,22:2
Before You're 25 1929,Ap 17,30:2
Donovan, Joan
Seven Year Itch, The 1952,N 21,21:2
Donovan, Joe (Director)
Hair 1970,Ja 13,39:1
Donovan, John (Playwright)
All My Pretty Little Ones 1964,F 5,30:1
Damn You, Scarlett O'Hara 1964,F 5,30:1
Donovan, King
Vigil, The 1948,My 22,8:6
Girls in 509, The 1958,O 16,47:1
Donovan, Linda
This Was Burlesque 1965,Mr 17,55:3
Donovan, Mary
Royal Family, The 1936,Jl 16,15:4
Donovan, Patrick (Director)
Children in the Rain 1970,O 3,14:1
Donovan, Patrick (Scenic Designer)
Children in the Rain 1970,O 3,14:1
Donovan, Tom
Vigil, The 1948,My 22,8:6
Goodbye My Fancy 1948,N 18,35:2
Donovan, Warde
Toplitzky of Notre Dame 1946,D 27,13:4
By the Beautiful Sea 1954,Ap 9,20:1
Merry Widow, The 1957,Ap 11,36:6
Saratoga 1959,D 8,59:4
Donovan, William J
Dancers, The 1923,O 18,17:2
Donsu, H L
Roar China! 1930,O 28,23:1
Singapore 1932,N 15,24:2
Bad Manners 1933,Ja 31,15:5
Threepenny Opera, The 1933,Ap 14,22:4
Peace Palace 1933,Je 6,30:2
Her Man of Wax 1933,O 12,32:3
Donsue
Ten Million Ghosts 1936,O 24,23:7
Dontzoff, Nicholas
Chauve-Souris of 1943 1943,Ag 13,13:2
Dood, Lee Wilson (Playwright)
Strong Man's House, A 1929,Je 30,VIII,1:2
Doodles and Spider
Vaudeville (Palace) 1951,O 17,36:6
Doody, James
Petrified Forest, The 1935,Ja 8,26:1
Blow Ye Winds 1937,S 24,17:4
Doohan, James
Rehearsal, The 1952,My 27,30:5
Doolan, James
Penny Wars, The 1969,O 16,52:1
Doolan, James (Miscellaneous)
Oh, Pioneers 1969,N 12,41:1
Exchange 1970,F 9,47:2
Dooley, Carol
Tragical Historie of Doctor Faustus, The
1964,O 6,34:2
Dooley, Gordon
Midnight Frolic 1920,Ag 4,7:1
Honeymoon Lane 1926,S 21,32:3
Earl Carroll's Vanities 1928,Ag 7,25:2
Vaudeville (Palace) 1929,Mr 11,22:5

Dooley, Hy
Veronica's Veil 1934,F 19,20:7
Dooley, Hyacinth (Director)
Veronica's Veil 1950,F 12,II,1:5
Dooley, Jed
Vaudeville (Palace) 1927,S 20,33:3
Vaudeville (Palace) 1929,Jl 1,31:4
Mr Sycamore 1942,N 14,13:2
Dooley, Jim
Anvil, The 1962,O 31,33:3
Dooley, John (Composer)
Hobo 1961,Ap 11,41:2
Dooley, John (Lyricist)
Hobo 1961,Ap 11,41:2
Dooley, John (Playwright)
Hobo 1961,Ap 11,41:2
Dooley, Johnny
Girl in the Spotlight, The 1920,Jl 13,9:3
June Love 1921,Ap 26,20:1
Bunch and Judy, The 1922,N 29,20:1
George White's Scandals 1923,Je 19,22:5
Keep Kool 1924,My 23,16:4
Vaudeville (Palace) 1926,Je 22,21:3
Vanities 1927,F 22,19:1
Vaudeville (Palace) 1927,Jl 5,19:3
Vaudeville (Palace) 1927,S 13,36:3
Dooley, Joseph
Richard II 1951,Ja 25,21:2
Dream Girl 1951,My 10,39:1
Strong Are Lonely, The 1953,S 30,38:3
Good as Gold 1957,Mr 8,22:2
Dooley, Joseph (Miscellaneous)
Beg, Borrow or Steal 1960,F 11,39:4
Dooley, Muriel
Restless Flame, The 1952,Ap 15,30:6
In Good King Charles's Golden Days
1957,Ja 25,16:1
Beaux' Stratagem, The 1957,Jl 9,25:4
Fools Are Passing Through 1958,Ap 3,24:2
Hole, The 1961,Ap 4,42:2
Dooley, Paul
Threepenny Opera, The 1954,Mr 11,26:5
Fallout 1959,My 21,36:2
Dr Willy Nilly 1959,Je 5,18:2
'Toinette 1961,N 21,46:1
Odd Couple, The 1965,Mr 11,36:1
Adaptation 1969,F 11,27:1
White House Murder Case, The 1970,F 19,59:1
Dooley, Ray
Ziegfeld Follies 1920,Je 23,14:1
Ziegfeld Follies 1921,Je 22,10:1
Bunch and Judy, The 1922,N 12,VIII,1:6
Bunch and Judy, The 1922,N 29,20:1
Vaudeville (Palace) 1924,F 12,20:2
Comic Supplement, The 1925,Ja 25,VII,1:4
Follies 1925,Mr 11,19:2
Follies 1925,Jl 7,24:3
No Foolin' 1926,Je 25,25:1
Sidewalks of New York 1927,O 4,33:1
Earl Carroll's Vanities 1928,Ag 7,25:2
Thumbs Up! 1934,D 28,24:1
Home Life of a Buffalo; Hope's the Thing
1948,My 12,34:6
Gone Tomorrow; Hope's the Thing
1948,My 12,34:6
Hope Is the Thing With Feathers; Hope's the
Thing 1948,My 12,34:6
Dooley, William
Midnight Frolic 1920,Ag 4,7:1
Dooley and Morton
George White's Scandals 1925,Je 23,24:2
Dooley and Sales
Vaudeville (Hippodrome) 1925,D 8,28:6
Doolittle, James A (Director)
Electra 1961,S 20,23:4
Eumenides 1961,S 27,32:4
Choephori 1961,S 27,32:4
Doolittle, James A (Producer)
Show Girl 1961,Ja 13,37:1
Wiener Blut 1964,S 12,14:1
Doonan, Patric
All Kinds of Men 1957,S 20,20:3
Doonan, Tony
Grosse Valise, La 1965,D 15,52:1
Doone, Rupert (Director)
Sweeney Agonistes 1935,O 2,26:2
Dance of Death, The 1935,O 2,26:2
Doorly, Margaret
Master of the Revels 1935,Ag 14,16:2
Dopp, Pat
Book of Job, The 1962,F 10,13:1
DoQuui, Robert
Murderous Angels 1970,F 8,70:1
Dor, Christiane
Lulu 1927,O 2,VIII,2:4
Doraldina
Frivolities of 1920 1920,Ja 9,22:2
Doran, D A (Producer)
Mad Morning 1935,Je 25,14:1
There's Wisdom in Women 1935,O 31,17:1
Please Do Not Disturb 1936,Je 23,27:1
Seen But Not Heard 1936,S 18,19:2
Sunup to Sundown 1938,F 2,14:3

Doran, D A Jr (Miscellaneous)
Gentlewoman 1934,Mr 23,28:4
Gold Eagle Guy 1934,N 29,33:4
Doran, John
Mecca 1920,O 5,12:2
Doran, Peggy
Advertising of Kate, The 1922,My 9,22:2
Mr Gilhooley 1930,O 1,26:1
Doran (Producer)
Wild Waves 1932,Ja 24,VIII,3:3
Seen But Not Heard 1936,Jl 22,23:4
Dorati, Antal (Miscellaneous)
Vie Parisienne, La 1945,Ja 13,14:5
Dorati, Antal (Musical Director)
Vie Parisienne, La 1941,N 6,20:3
Doray, Delphine
Order Please 1934,O 10,21:2
Doray, Gloria
Swing Your Lady 1936,O 19,22:4
Dorazio, Ralph (Scenic Designer)
Purgatory 1960,S 20,48:1
Dorbin, William
Her Friend the King 1929,O 8,34:5
Inspector General, The 1930,D 24,19:2
Paging Danger 1931,F 27,19:2
Triplets 1932,S 22,25:2
Foolscap 1933,Ja 12,21:2
One Sunday Afternoon 1933,F 16,23:5
Mahogany Hall 1934,Ja 18,18:5
Ragged Army 1934,F 27,16:5
Rain Before Seven 1935,Ag 13,20:3
Merrily We Roll Along 1936,Je 30,15:1
Dorce, Roburte
Big White Fog 1940,O 23,26:2
Dordoni, Ester
Signora Dalle Camelie, La; Camille 1934,O 22,13:2
Processo dei Veleni, Il; Case of Poisons, The 1935,Ja 21,18:2
Romanzo di un Giovane Povero, Il 1935,F 25,12:3
Due Orfanelle, Le; Two Orphans, The 1936,O 5,24:4
Asino di Buridano, L' 1936,N 30,25:2
Dore, Alexander (Director)
Sunday Man, The 1964,My 14,41:3
Dore, Doremus
Present Arms 1928,Ap 27,16:2
Dore, Lynne
Nine Fifteen Revue, The 1930,F 12,26:2
Dore, Richard
My Golden Girl 1920,F 3,18:2
Dew Drop Inn 1923,My 18,26:4
Dore, Thea
Three Cheers 1928,O 16,28:1
Doree, Betty
Tattle Tales 1933,Je 2,22:6
Doremus, Thomas
Betty Behave 1927,Mr 9,28:4
Dorey, Milnor (Playwright)
Under Conviction 1923,My 9,14:4
Dorf, Ethel
Mazal Darf Men; You Need Luck 1938,My 18,16:5
Dorf, Morris
Awake and Sing! 1938,D 23,16:6
Dorfman, Herbert (Producer)
Blitzstein! 1966,D 1,58:2
Dorfman, Irvin (Producer)
Lion in Love, The 1963,Ap 26,28:3
Dorfman, Nat N (Playwright)
International Revue 1930,F 26,22:2
Take My Tip 1932,Ap 12,25:2
Blackbirds 1933,D 4,22:3
Errant Lady 1934,S 18,18:2
Lew Leslie's Blackbirds of 1939 1939,F 13,12:2
Dorfman, Sidney (Playwright)
Go Fly a Kite! 1969,O 20,60:1
Dori, Adriana
Bachelor Father, The 1928,F 29,28:2
Cena Delle Beffe, La; Jest, The 1930,N 24,26:4
Gli Spettri 1930,D 22,16:4
Cardinale, Il; Cardinal, The 1931,Ja 12,24:2
Marchese di Priola, Il 1931,Mr 2,19:3
Wonder Bar, The 1931,Mr 18,23:4
Cantico dei Cantici, Il; Song of Songs 1931,Ap 13,17:3
Cantico dei Cantici, Il; Song of Songs 1931,My 18,21:4
Zia Morta, La; Dead Aunt, The 1931,N 30,16:3
Profumo di Mia Moglie, Il; My Wife's Perfume 1932,Ja 11,29:5
Civil Death, The 1932,Ja 25,20:3
Doria, Fredric
Mother Courage and Her Children 1964,My 12,32:2
Doria, Lotte (Costume Designer)
Fourth Avenue North 1961,S 28,50:2
Dorian, Philip (Miscellaneous)
Uncommon Denominator, The 1963,My 8,35:2
Dorian, Ray
Wonderful Town 1953,F 26,22:3
Dorin, Denise
Goodbye Again 1956,Ap 25,38:1
Holiday for Lovers 1957,F 15,20:1
Dorin, Francoise (Playwright)
Play on Love 1970,Ja 16,31:1

Dorin, Phoebe
Burn Me to Ashes 1963,N 20,48:1
Happiness Is Just a Little Thing Called a Rolls Royce 1968,My 13,54:5
Awake and Sing! 1970,My 28,35:1
Awake and Sing! 1970,Je 7,II,1:1
Doriss, Bernard
Fashion 1937,Mr 21,II,7:8
Dorival
Moloch 1929,Ja 27,IX,2:8
Dorkin, Marvyn
Venice Preserv'd 1955,D 13,54:4
Witchfinders, The 1956,My 11,22:6
Dorlen, Susan
Kitchen, The 1966,Je 14,50:1
Dorly, Leah Trio
New Music Hall of Israel, The 1969,O 3,40:1
Dorman, Celeste
Nautical but Nice 1931,Ap 19,31:6
Dorman, Harry
Circle of Chalk, The 1950,D 2,8:3
Dorman, Joanna
Cyrano de Bergerac 1932,D 27,11:2
Cyrano de Bergerac 1936,Ap 28,17:1
Dorman, John
Finian's Rainbow 1953,Mr 7,13:2
Adding Machine, The 1956,F 10,17:1
Requiem for a Nun 1959,Ja 31,13:2
Midsummer Night's Dream, A 1961,Ag 3,13:1
Night Is Black Bottles, The 1962,D 5,56:1
Hogan's Goat 1965,N 12,56:1
Acquisition, The 1968,D 31,19:1
Dorman, Wyllis (Miscellaneous)
Many Loves 1959,Ja 14,28:1
Dormer, Venetia
Middle Watch, The 1929,O 17,27:1
Dormonde, George
Edith Piaf 1947,O 30,30:2
Dormonde, Tim
Edith Piaf 1947,O 30,30:2
Dormondes, The
Vaudeville (Palace) 1927,Je 14,33:3
Dormont, Eli
Playing With Love 1929,F 27,16:4
Dorn, Augusta
Paul Bunyan 1941,My 6,25:1
Dorn, Dolores
Someone From Assisi 1962,Ja 12,28:1
Dorn, Harding
Arabian Nights 1954,Je 25,15:2
Dorn, Joseph
Storm Operation 1944,Ja 12,28:2
Dorn, Julia
Yoshe Kalb 1933,D 29,27:2
Dorn, Patricia
Walk a Little Faster 1932,D 8,24:4
Dorn, Paul
Fiesta 1929,S 18,35:1
Channel Road, The 1929,O 18,24:2
Everything's Jake 1930,Ja 17,20:4
Dorn, Philip
Big Two, The 1947,Ja 9,21:2
Dorn, Robert
Antigone 1962,D 29,5:5
Dorn-Heft, Dolores
Hide and Seek 1957,Ap 3,26:1
To Damascus 1961,F 15,40:2
Khaki Blue 1969,Mr 27,54:2
Dorne, Cyrilla
Squaring the Circle 1935,O 4,24:6
Call Me Ziggy 1937,F 13,9:6
Bough Breaks, The 1937,N 20,21:4
Everyman 1941,My 9,19:2
Dorne, Mary
Man Who Killed Lincoln, The 1940,Ja 18,26:4
Dorne, Phyllis
Pal Joey 1952,Ja 4,17:6
Almost Crazy 1955,Je 21,37:1
Vamp, The 1955,N 11,30:1
Dornes, Roger (Director)
Otage, L' 1959,O 27,42:1
Dornes, Roger (Scenic Designer)
Britannicus 1958,N 29,17:2
Misanthrope, Le 1960,Mr 9,38:3
Dorney, Joseph R
Sharlee 1923,N 23,20:1
Dornfeld, W
Elsie Janis and Her Gang 1922,Ja 17,13:2
Dornhurst, Paul (Playwright)
Stubble Before Swords 1936,Mr 24,26:8
Dorning, Charles
Mikado, The 1947,D 30,18:2
Trial by Jury 1948,Ja 6,27:2
Iolanthe 1948,Ja 13,29:3
H M S Pinafore 1948,Ja 20,26:2
Gondoliers, The 1948,Ja 27,31:2
Patience 1948,F 10,27:2
Dornton, Henry
Dope 1926,Ja 4,16:3
Dorny, Therese
Untitled-Play 1925,D 27,VII,2:1
Doro, Marie
Lilies of the Field 1921,O 5,20:1

Doronne, Dina
Merchant of Venice, The 1957,Jl 11,19:5
Doroshow, Jack (Director)
Last Pad, The 1970,D 8,61:1
Dorothy, Esther (Miscellaneous)
Cup of Trembling, The 1948,Ap 21,33:5
Dorp, Alice
Schoolmaster, The 1928,Mr 21,30:1
Dorr, Ellen
Prunella; Love in a Garden 1926,Je 16,23:3
Free Soul, A 1928,Ja 13,26:5
Merry Andrew 1929,Ja 22,22:2
Dorr, Lester
LeMaire's Affairs 1927,Mr 29,22:4
New Moon, The 1928,S 20,33:1
Dorr, Nelson (Playwright)
Pericas, Las 1969,N 2,86:5
Dorr, William (Producer)
Tom Paine 1968,Mr 26,38:1
Dorrey, Charles
Winners and Losers 1947,F 27,27:2
Dorriani, William
Tickle Me 1920,Ag 18,9:1
Dorrin, John
Brigadoon 1957,Mr 28,37:1
What Makes Sammy Run? 1964,F 28,19:1
Carousel 1965,Ag 11,39:1
Annie Get Your Gun 1966,Je 1,42:2
Finian's Rainbow 1967,Ap 6,44:1
I'm Solomon 1968,Ap 24,51:1
Dorris, Hubert (Composer)
White Rose and the Red, The 1964,Mr 17,31:1
Dors, Diana
Remains to Be Seen 1952,D 17,44:4
Three Months Gone 1970,S 10,59:1
Dorsay, Colette
Phedre 1969,Mr 1,20:1
Dorsay, Edmund
Stage Door 1936,O 23,26:3
Michael Drops In 1938,D 28,24:3
Off to Buffalo! 1939,F 22,18:2
Aries Is Rising 1939,N 22,16:5
Weak Link, The 1940,Mr 5,19:2
Ah, Wilderness! 1941,O 3,26:2
Criminals, The 1941,D 22,24:3
Lily of the Valley 1942,Ja 27,25:2
Three's a Family 1943,My 6,24:2
Gypsy Lady 1946,S 18,25:6
Allegro 1952,S 18,36:3
D'Orsay, Fifi
Vaudeville (Palace) 1932,Ap 18,19:5
D'Orsay, Lawrence
So This Is London 1922,Ag 31,18:2
Two by Two 1925,F 24,17:1
American Born 1925,S 27,VII,2:1
American Born 1925,O 6,31:3
Old Bill, M P 1926,N 11,22:2
Trelawney of the 'Wells' 1927,F 1,24:4
White Eagle, The 1927,D 27,24:4
She Stoops to Conquer 1928,My 15,17:1
She Stoops to Conquer 1928,My 20,VIII,1:1
Dorsch, Kaethe
Kiki 1921,D 11,VI,1:4
Rain 1925,N 25,23:5
Friederike 1929,F 17,IX,2:3
Karl und Anna 1929,Mr 10,X,2:1
Blue Beard 1929,Jl 7,VIII,2:1
Marietta 1929,D 8,X,4:4
Kat 1931,O 4,VIII,4:1
Rebound 1931,N 1,VIII,4:1
Liselott 1932,My 22,VIII,2:3
Maria Stuart 1933,D 10,X,5:1
Family Portrait; Familie, Eine 1946,N 11,44:1
Dorsett, Wilbur (Director)
Lost Colony, The 1937,Jl 11,X,2:1
Dorsey, Abner
Walk Together Chillun 1936,F 5,15:2
Cradle Will Rock, The 1937,D 6,19:4
Dorsey, Earl
Nathan the Wise 1962,Mr 23,29:1
Dorsey, Edmund
Summer Night 1939,N 3,17:1
Days of Our Youth, The 1941,N 29,15:2
Dorsey, Frances
Ice Follies 1957,Ja 16,36:1
Ice Follies 1958,Ja 15,26:2
Dorsey, Joe
Fortune and Men's Eyes 1969,O 23,55:1
Dorsey, Leslie (Scenic Designer)
Only the Heart 1942,D 7,22:3
D'Orso, Wisa
Kaleidoscope 1957,Je 14,20:2
On the Town 1959,Ja 16,36:1
On the Town 1959,Ja 25,II,1:1
Not While I'm Eating 1961,D 20,37:1
Mr President 1962,O 22,34:2
D'Orso, Wisa (Miscellaneous)
Ice Capades 1966,Je 2,50:2
Dorst, Tankred (Playwright)
Kurve, Die 1970,N 25,25:1
Dortch, Helen
Journeyman 1938,Ja 31,14:2

Dortch, Sam
Winners and Losers 1947,F 27,27:2
Dorville
A la Mode de Chez Nous 1929,My 26,IX,4:1
Paris 1932,F 14,VIII,2:5
Dorziat, Gabrielle
Comedienne 1924,F 24,VII,1:4
Dame de Chambre, La 1924,Je 1,VII,1:7
Je T'Attendais 1929,Ja 20,VIII,1:8
Trois et Une 1933,Ja 1,IX,3:4
Espoir 1935,Ja 6,IX,2:1
Espoir 1935,F 3,VIII,3:3
Dos Passos, John (Original Author)
U S A 1956,D 19,41:4
U S A 1959,O 29,38:1
U S A 1959,N 8,II,1:1
Dos Passos, John (Playwright)
Moon Is a Gong, The 1926,Mr 13,21:3
Moon Is a Gong, The 1926,Mr 21,VIII,1:1
Airways, Inc 1929,F 21,30:5
U S A 1959,O 29,38:1
U S A 1959,N 8,II,1:1
Dos Passos, John (Scenic Designer)
Moon Is a Gong, The 1926,Mr 13,21:3
Belt, The 1927,O 20,33:1
Centuries, The 1927,N 30,23:1
International, The 1928,Ja 16,24:4
Airways, Inc 1929,F 21,30:5
Dosch, Charles
On Call 1928,N 10,20:7
Doscher, Richard (Miscellaneous)
Springtime for Henry 1951,Mr 15,36:2
Dose, Louise
Passing Show of 1923, The 1923,Je 15,24:6
Dosher, George
Set My People Free 1948,N 4,38:2
Doss, Leonard (Miscellaneous)
Ice Follies 1967,Ja 11,51:1
D'Ossetynski, Leonidas (Director)
Policemen, The 1961,N 22,24:2
Alcestis Comes Back 1962,Ap 24,33:1
At Sea 1962,Ap 24,33:1
D'Ossetynski, Leonidas (Miscellaneous)
Policemen, The 1961,N 22,24:2
D'Ossetynski, Leonidas (Playwright)
Policemen, The 1961,N 22,24:2
D'Ossetynski, Leonidas (Producer)
Alcestis Comes Back 1962,Ap 24,33:1
At Sea 1962,Ap 24,33:1
Dossey, Earl
Five Posts in the Market Place 1961,Mr 6,30:1
Dossey, Earl (Miscellaneous)
Noontide 1961,Je 2,37:1
Dostal, Karel (Producer)
Desire Under the Elms 1925,N 1,VIII,1:3
Dostal, Nico (Composer)
Vielgeliebte, Die 1935,My 19,IX,2:5
Dostis, Isaac
Wicked Cooks, The 1967,Ja 24,42:1
Dostoievsky, Fyodor (Original Author)
Brothers Karamazov, The 1923,F 27,14:2
Brothers Karamazov, The 1923,Mr 4,VII,1:1
Brothers Karamazov, The 1923,N 20,23:4
Brothers Karamazov, The 1924,My 6,25:2
Idiot, The 1926,S 26,VIII,2:1
Humble, The 1926,O 14,22:2
Brothers Karamazov, The 1926,D 12,VIII,3:4
Brothers Karamazov, The 1927,Ja 4,20:1
Crime and Punishment 1927,Mr 6,VIII,2:1
Brass Paperweight, The 1928,N 4,IX,2:4
Possessed, The 1939,O 25,26:2
Crime and Punishment 1946,Jl 21,II,1:5
Crime and Punishment 1947,D 23,29:3
Crime and Punishment 1948,Ja 4,II,1:1
Brothers Karamazov, The 1957,D 9,39:4
Brothers Karamazov, The 1957,D 22,II,3:1
Trial of Dmitri Karamazov, The 1958,Ja 28,30:1
Possessed, The 1959,Ja 31,13:7
Eternal Husband, The 1962,O 18,46:4
Idiot, The 1970,Jl 17,18:1
Idiot, The 1970,Jl 30,39:1
Dostoievsky, Fyodor (Playwright)
Strange Prince, The 1926,D 8,24:2
Crime and Punishment 1935,Ja 23,20:3
Doten, Jay (Playwright)
Green Stick 1934,O 10,21:2
Dotrice, Roy
Tempest, The 1963,Ap 3,43:1
Brief Lives 1967,D 19,60:4
God Bless 1968,N 3,II,1:1
Twist of Sand, A 1969,F 22,36:1
Dotson, Josie
Amen Corner, The 1965,Ap 16,35:1
Dotson, Melinda
Confederacy, The 1958,Jl 3,20:1
Doty, Helen
Elsie 1923,Ap 3,26:1
Doty, Judith
Romeo and Juliet 1960,Jl 1,14:1
Witches' Sabbath 1962,Ap 20,22:2
Moby Dick 1962,N 29,45:1
Miser, The 1963,My 10,39:1
Death of a Salesman 1963,Jl 20,11:2

Thistle in My Bed 1963,N 20,48:1
Doty, Margaret
War 1929,S 19,37:3
Humbug, The 1929,N 28,34:5
Doubinsky
Chauve-Souris 1922,Je 6,17:4
Doubleday, Kay
Boo Hoo! East Lynne 1959,S 9,50:4
Dinny and the Witches 1959,D 10,53:3
Doubrava, Kenneth
Mikado, The 1957,Ap 24,28:2
H M S Pinafore 1957,My 1,42:6
Pirates of Penzance, The 1957,My 8,43:1
Yeomen of the Guard, The 1957,My 22,28:3
Gondoliers, The 1957,My 29,34:2
Doubrovsky, Georges
Chauve-Souris of 1943 1943,Ag 13,13:2
Doucet, Catherine
Miss Lulu Bett 1920,D 28,9:1
Dolly Jordan 1922,O 4,26:1
Cold Feet 1923,My 22,14:2
Potters, The 1923,D 10,21:4
Louie the 14th 1925,Mr 4,17:1
Devil in the Cheese, The 1926,D 30,22:4
Royal Family, The 1927,D 29,26:4
Perfect Alibi 1928,N 28,24:2
Dynamo 1929,F 12,22:1
Camel Through the Needle's Eye, The
  1929,Ap 16,32:2
Camel Through the Needle's Eye, The
  1929,Ap 28,IX,1:1
Ladies Leave 1929,O 2,28:3
Topaze 1930,F 13,25:3
As Husbands Go 1931,Mr 6,26:5
Border-Land 1932,Mr 30,15:5
Whatever Possessed Her 1934,Ja 26,21:2
Eye on the Sparrow 1938,My 4,26:3
Rose Burke 1942,Ja 25,IX,2:5
Last Stop 1944,S 6,17:2
Oh, Herbert! 1945,Je 20,26:3
Doucet, H Paul
Marie Antoinette 1921,N 23,16:1
Salome 1922,My 23,12:4
Rose Briar 1922,D 26,11:3
Comedian, The 1923,Mr 14,14:1
Agent 666, L' 1923,My 30,10:5
Loves of Lulu, The 1925,My 12,26:1
Yellow 1926,S 22,30:1
Half a Widow 1927,S 13,37:3
India 1928,Ja 17,23:3
Vaudeville (Palace) 1928,Ja 17,23:3
Napoleon 1928,Mr 9,21:1
Doucet, Theeodore
Hail and Farewell 1923,F 20,12:1
Doucette, Arthur (Costume Designer)
Ardele 1958,Ap 9,39:4
Douday, Salo
Good Fairy, The 1931,N 25,17:1
Good Fairy, The 1932,N 18,22:3
Country Wife, The 1936,D 2,34:1
Roosty 1938,F 15,21:2
Douday, Sol
Journey's End 1930,Ja 27,24:7
Journey's End 1930,Ag 5,26:4
Dougall, Thomas J
Front Page Stuff 1926,D 29,24:4
Dougherty, Anne
When the Bough Breaks 1950,Mr 9,25:5
Dougherty, Dennis (Lighting Director)
Evening With Max Morath at the Turn of the
  Century, An 1969,F 18,35:1
Dougherty, Dennis (Scenic Designer)
Evening With Max Morath at the Turn of the
  Century, An 1969,F 18,35:1
Dougherty, Ed
Kongi's Harvest 1968,Ap 15,49:1
Dougherty, Frances Ann (Director)
Seagull, The 1964,Ap 6,36:1
Crucible, The 1964,Ap 7,30:2
Dougherty, Frances Ann (Producer)
Imaginary Invalid, The 1967,My 2,53:1
Touch of the Poet, A 1967,My 3,38:2
Ways and Means 1967,My 4,34:1
Fumed Oak 1967,My 4,34:1
Still Life 1967,My 4,34:1
Comedy of Errors, The 1968,F 28,40:2
She Stoops to Conquer 1968,Ap 1,58:3
Dougherty, Grace
Opportunity 1920,Jl 31,5:1
Young Visitors, The 1920,N 30,14:1
World We Live In, The 1922,N 1,16:1
Kind Lady 1940,S 4,28:3
Dougherty, John
Caesar and Cleopatra 1935,Ag 22,21:1
Dougherty, Richard (Playwright)
Fair Game for Lovers 1964,F 11,43:2
Dougherty, William
Ice Capades 1954,S 16,37:1
Ice Capades 1955,S 15,38:1
Douglas, Althea (Costume Designer)
Misanthrope, The 1956,N 13,44:1
Country Wife, The 1957,Je 27,22:1

Douglas, Audrey
Slightly Delirious 1935,Ja 1,25:3
Douglas, Betty
Lady Comes Across, The 1942,Ja 10,10:2
Douglas, Bill
Howdy, Mr Ice of 1950 1949,My 27,24:2
Douglas, Bob
By Jupiter 1942,Je 4,22:1
Marinka 1945,Jl 19,19:2
Douglas, Buddy
Dream With Music 1944,My 19,15:2
Douglas, Burt
Macbeth 1955,O 20,42:2
Midsummer Night's Dream, A 1956,Ja 14,12:2
Romeo and Juliet 1956,F 24,20:4
Douglas, Charles
Dragon, The 1922,D 27,12:1
Merchant of Venice, The 1931,N 9,22:2
Douglas, Charles E
Peace Palace 1933,Je 6,30:2
Douglas, Charles L
Pigeon, The 1922,F 3,13:1
Douglas, Dan
Cherry Blossoms 1927,Mr 29,22:3
Douglas, Diana
Highest Tree, The 1959,N 5,41:1
Douglas, Donald
Rio Rita 1927,F 3,18:3
Woman Denied, A 1931,F 26,21:1
Piper Paid 1934,D 26,19:1
Jubilee 1935,O 14,20:1
Douglas, Edward
No More Blondes 1920,Ja 8,22:1
Ladies' Night 1920,Ag 10,10:1
Sky High 1925,Mr 3,21:4
Hearts Are Trumps! 1927,Ap 8,21:1
Douglas, Eileen
Lolly 1929,O 17,26:2
Douglas, Emmet
H M S Pinafore 1926,Ap 7,26:3
Douglas, Gerald
Madame Lafayette 1960,Mr 4,21:1
Douglas, Gilbert
Not So Long Ago 1920,My 5,14:1
Dulcy 1921,Ag 15,14:1
Vaudeville (Palace) 1925,Ap 7,16:3
Enchanted April, The 1925,Ag 25,12:3
Creaking Chair, The 1926,F 23,26:1
Outsider, The 1928,Ap 10,32:2
High Hatters, The 1928,My 11,28:2
Let Us Be Gay 1929,F 22,19:1
Devil's Host, The 1931,N 20,27:2
Christopher Comes Across 1932,Je 1,19:2
Great Magoo, The 1932,D 3,20:7
Fresh Fields 1934,Jl 15,X,1:1
Douglas, Hazel
All in Good Time 1965,F 19,25:1
Douglas, James
Long and the Short and the Tall, The
  1962,Mr 30,28:2
Troilus and Cressida 1963,Je 19,40:2
Cyrano de Bergerac 1963,Je 20,30:1
Comedy of Errors, The 1963,Je 21,35:3
Day the Whores Came Out to Play Tennis, The
  1965,Mr 16,45:1
Douglas, Jeffery (Miscellaneous)
Bald Soprano, The 1963,S 18,35:4
Lesson, The 1963,S 18,35:4
Douglas, Jerry
Golden Six, The 1958,O 27,31:2
Douglas, Jerry (Director)
Score 1970,O 29,57:4
Douglas, Jerry (Lyricist)
Rondelay 1969,N 6,55:1
Douglas, Jerry (Playwright)
Rondelay 1969,N 6,55:1
Score 1970,O 29,57:4
Douglas, Johanna
Eternal Cage 1945,Mr 22,19:7
Mame 1966,My 25,41:1
Douglas, Johanne
Adam Had Two Sons 1932,Ja 21,17:1
Douglas, John C
Bronx Express 1922,Ap 27,12:2
Douglas, John E
Erminie 1921,Ja 4,11:1
Douglas, Joy
Broken Chain, The 1929,F 21,30:4
Douglas, Kenneth
Demi-Virgin, The 1921,O 19,22:1
Douglas, Kirk
Spring Again 1941,N 11,28:2
Three Sisters, The 1942,D 22,31:2
Alice in Arms 1945,F 1,18:4
Wind Is Ninety, The 1945,Je 22,12:2
Woman Bites Dog 1946,Ap 18,21:2
One Flew Over the Cuckoo's Nest 1963,N 14,40:2
One Flew Over the Cuckoo's Nest 1963,D 1,II,1:1
Douglas, Larry
What's Up 1943,N 12,24:6
Duchess Misbehaves 1946,F 14,32:2
Hold It! 1948,My 6,31:5
Hilarities 1948,S 10,20:2

Douglas, Larry—Cont
King and I, The 1951,Mr 30,26:2
Pajama Game, The 1957,My 16,27:1
Pajama Game, The 1957,My 26,II,1:1
Here's Love 1963,O 4,28:1
Her First Roman 1968,O 21,53:3
Jimmy 1969,O 24,38:1
Douglas, Laura V
Joyous Season, The 1935,N 24,II,9:2
Douglas, Louis
Von Mund zu Mund 1926,D 5,VIII,8:7
Douglas, Louis (Choreographer)
Franziska 1927,Ja 30,VII,4:3
Africana 1927,Jl 12,29:2
Douglas, M K
Paradise Gardens East 1969,Mr 11,39:1
Conerico Was Here to Stay 1969,Mr 11,39:1
Douglas, Margaret
Love for Love 1925,S 15,29:3
Wall Street 1927,Ap 21,24:4
Fatal Witness, The 1946,N 20,43:2
Douglas, Mary
Summer Wives 1936,Ap 14,18:1
Douglas, Melvyn
Free Soul, A 1928,Ja 13,26:5
Back Here 1928,N 27,36:3
Now-A-Days 1929,Ag 6,29:3
Recapture 1930,Ja 19,VIII,2:6
Recapture 1930,Ja 30,16:4
Tonight or Never 1930,N 9,IX,3:2
Tonight or Never 1930,N 19,19:3
No More Ladies 1934,Ja 24,20:3
Mother Lode 1934,D 24,16:5
De Luxe 1935,Mr 6,22:2
Tapestry in Gray 1935,D 28,10:2
Two Blind Mice 1949,Mr 3,32:2
Bird Cage, The 1950,F 23,32:2
Little Blue Light, The 1951,Ap 30,17:2
Glad Tidings 1951,O 12,33:2
Time Out for Ginger 1952,N 27,50:4
Inherit the Wind 1955,S 25,II,1:1
Waltz of the Toreadors, The 1958,Mr 5,37:1
Juno 1959,Mr 10,41:1
Juno 1959,Mr 15,II,1:1
Gang's All Here, The 1959,O 2,23:1
Gang's All Here, The 1959,O 11,II,1:1
Best Man, The 1960,Ap 1,39:1
Best Man, The 1960,Ap 10,II,1:1
Spofford 1967,D 15,54:3
Spofford 1967,D 24,II,3:2
Douglas, Melvyn (Director)
Moor Born 1934,Ap 4,26:4
Moor Born 1934,Ap 8,X,2:7
Within the Gates 1934,O 23,23:1
Mother Lode 1934,D 24,16:5
Glad Tidings 1951,O 12,33:2
Douglas, Melvyn (Producer)
Call Me Mister 1946,Ap 19,26:2
Call Me Mister 1946,Ap 28,II,1:1
Douglas, Milton
Melody 1933,F 15,17:4
Summer Wives 1936,Ap 14,18:1
Douglas, Nancy
Great Airplane Snatch, The 1969,My 28,36:1
Douglas, Norma
Hear! Hear! 1955,S 28,38:1
Copper and Brass 1957,O 18,19:2
Douglas, Paul
Double Dummy 1936,N 12,30:1
Born Yesterday 1946,F 5,18:2
Born Yesterday 1946,F 10,II,1:1
Born Yesterday 1947,My 18,II,1:1
Hole in the Head, A 1957,Mr 1,15:1
Hole in the Head, A 1957,Mr 10,II,1:1
Douglas, Ralph
Quiet, Please! 1940,N 9,20:3
Duke in Darkness, The 1944,Ja 25,15:2
Harriet 1944,S 28,26:1
Douglas, Robert
Many Waters 1929,S 26,27:1
Many Waters 1929,O 6,IX,1:1
Last Enemy, The 1930,O 31,21:1
Brief Moment 1931,N 10,28:2
Men in White 1934,Je 29,16:3
Inside the Room 1934,D 23,15:3
Most of the Game 1935,O 2,27:4
No Exit 1936,Ja 22,15:3
Stubble Before Swords 1936,Mr 24,26:8
Douglas, Robert (Director)
Ponder Heart, The 1956,F 17,14:2
Ponder Heart, The 1956,F 26,II,1:1
Affair of Honor 1956,Ap 7,12:3
Loud Red Patrick, The 1956,O 4,28:1
Uncle Willie 1956,D 21,17:1
Douglas, Robert (Producer)
Loud Red Patrick, The 1956,O 4,28:1
Douglas, Rodney K
Scuba Duba 1967,O 11,36:1
Douglas, Ronnie
Cry for Us All 1970,Ap 9,48:2
Douglas, Scott
You Never Can Tell 1948,Mr 17,31:2
Douglas, Stephen
110 in the Shade 1963,S 12,33:2

Douglas, Susan
He Who Gets Slapped 1946,Mr 21,31:4
He Who Gets Slapped 1946,Mr 31,II,1:1
Druid Circle, The 1947,O 23,29:5
Taming of the Shrew, The 1951,Ap 26,35:2
Douglas, Tom
Vaudeville (Palace) 1923,Ja 23,18:2
Young Love 1928,O 31,28:1
Town Boy 1929,O 5,22:4
Seven 1929,D 28,10:5
Divine Moment, A 1934,Ja 8,21:8
Douglas, Tony
Guys and Dolls 1959,Jl 22,22:2
Douglas, W A S (Playwright)
Minstrel Boy, The 1948,O 15,28:2
Douglas, Wallace (Director)
Love Goes to Press 1947,Ja 2,22:2
Douglas, Warren
Elizabeth the Queen 1941,O 17,27:2
Happily Ever After 1945,Mr 16,21:2
Douglas, William
Howdy Mr Ice 1948,Je 25,28:5
Douglas, Winston (Director)
Policy Kings 1938,D 31,6:2
Douglass, Amy
Kiss Them for Me 1945,Mr 21,27:2
Life With Mother 1948,O 21,32:2
Mr Barry's Etchings 1950,F 1,26:2
Douglass, Charles
Jefferson Davis 1936,F 19,17:2
Douglass, Charles E
Reunion in Vienna 1931,N 17,31:1
Douglass, Charles L
Johnny 2X4 1942,Mr 17,24:6
Douglass, Donald
Forty-Four Below 1935,Jl 23,24:3
Douglass, Dudley
Vaudeville (Palace) 1926,Je 15,23:3
Douglass, Eileen
Buckaroo 1929,Mr 18,31:1
Douglass, Gilbert
Mariners 1927,Mr 29,22:2
Douglass, Jane (Composer)
Bella 1961,N 17,40:1
Douglass, Jane (Miscellaneous)
Bella 1961,N 17,40:1
Douglass, Jane (Musical Director)
Bella 1961,N 17,40:1
Douglass, Jim
Good Soldier Schweik, The 1963,Ap 9,57:1
Douglass, Lewis
Miss Gulliver Travels 1931,N 26,36:4
Douglass, Margaret
Devil to Pay, The 1925,D 4,26:2
Unchastened Woman, The 1926,F 17,12:1
Off Key 1927,F 9,16:2
Loud Speaker 1927,Mr 3,27:2
Russet Mantle 1936,Ja 17,15:5
Russet Mantle 1936,Ja 26,IX,1:1
Russet Mantle 1936,Ag 18,15:2
Women, The 1936,D 28,13:1
Out From Under 1940,My 6,13:2
Eight O'Clock Tuesday 1941,Ja 7,18:2
Yesterday's Magic 1942,Ap 15,27:2
Damask Cheek, The 1942,O 23,24:2
Bloomer Girl 1944,O 6,18:5
Douglass, Milton
Good Boy 1928,S 6,23:2
Douglass, Nancy
Out of the Frying Pan 1941,F 12,24:2
Bloomer Girl 1944,O 6,18:5
Douglass, Stephen
Carousel 1949,Ja 26,28:2
Carousel 1949,F 6,II,1:1
Make a Wish 1951,Ap 19,38:1
Golden Apple, The 1954,Mr 12,15:2
Damn Yankees 1955,My 6,17:1
Rumple 1957,N 7,42:2
Song of Norway 1958,Je 23,19:2
110 in the Shade 1963,O 25,37:1
Show Boat 1966,Jl 20,48:1
Dournel, Gerard
Misanthrope, Le 1957,F 8,19:1
Intermezzo 1957,F 15,20:4
Adieux, Les 1957,F 19,36:1
Chien du Jardinier, Le; Gardener's Dog, The 1957,F 19,36:1
Douzelli, Mme
Untitled-Passion Play 1925,Ag 17,8:1
Dova, Ben
Greenwich Village Follies 1928,Ap 10,32:2
Revels of 1936 1935,S 30,12:4
Streets of Paris, The 1939,Je 20,25:2
Hell'z-A-Splashin' 1959,Je 25,22:2
Dova, Dick
Ice Follies 1959,Ja 14,30:1
Ice Follies 1961,Ja 11,25:2
Ice Follies 1962,Ja 10,24:6
Ice Follies 1966,Ja 12,27:6
Dova, Nina
I Feel Wonderful 1954,O 19,22:5
Yerma 1966,D 9,60:1
Frere Jacques 1968,Je 8,23:2

Dova, Nina—Cont
Zorba 1968,N 18,58:1
Rothschilds, The 1970,O 20,40:1
Dove, Johnny
Gay Paree 1925,Ag 19,14:3
Dove, Larry
Sweet Enemy, The 1965,F 16,39:1
Dove, Marie
Keep Shufflin' 1928,F 28,18:3
Dover, Nancy
Too Many Boats 1934,S 12,26:3
Ragged Edge, The 1935,N 26,28:3
Dow, Bonnie
Little Theatre Tournament; White Peacock, The 1928,My 11,28:1
Dow, Gene
Silver Tassie, The 1949,Jl 22,16:5
Silver Tassle, The 1949,S 4,II,1:1
Dow, Maree
Patriots, The 1943,D 21,22:5
No Time for Sergeants 1955,O 21,32:2
Dow, R A
Dirtiest Show in Town, The 1970,Je 29,43:2
Dowaliby, James
Gondoliers, The 1963,Je 5,33:2
Dowd, Harrison
Trip to Scarborough, A 1929,Mr 18,31:2
Dragon, The 1929,Mr 26,34:2
Patience 1935,S 3,24:4
Night of Love 1941,Ja 8,14:2
Harriet 1943,Mr 4,24:2
Little Women 1944,D 13,29:2
Assassin, The 1945,O 18,20:2
Temporary Island, A 1948,Mr 15,27:3
Dinosaur Wharf 1951,N 9,23:2
See the Jaguar 1952,D 4,46:2
Morning's at Seven 1955,Je 23,25:1
Kiss Me, Kate 1956,My 10,27:2
Italian Straw Hat, The 1957,O 1,37:2
Blood Wedding 1958,Ap 1,35:1
Visit, The 1958,My 6,40:1
Our Town 1959,Mr 24,46:2
Caligula 1960,F 17,31:1
Dowd, Harrison (Miscellaneous)
Finta Giardiniera, La 1927,Ja 19,20:5
Dowd, James
Touch of Brimstone, A 1935,S 23,20:1
Dowd, Janet
Hickory Stick 1944,My 9,15:6
Pygmalion 1945,D 27,16:1
Saint Joan 1956,S 12,42:1
Hamlet 1957,Ja 29,27:1
Electra 1964,Ag 12,42:1
To Bury a Cousin 1967,My 17,38:3
Invitation to a Beheading 1969,Mr 18,36:1
Colette 1970,O 15,58:1
Dowd, M'el
Macbeth 1955,O 20,42:2
Midsummer Night's Dream, A 1956,Ja 14,12:2
Romeo and Juliet 1956,F 24,20:4
Julius Caesar 1957,O 24,39:1
Back to Methuselah 1958,Mr 27,41:5
Back to Methuselah 1958,Ap 6,II,1:1
Royal Gambit 1959,Mr 5,34:2
Royal Gambit 1959,Mr 15,II,1:1
Camelot 1960,D 5,42:1
Emperor, The 1963,Ap 17,30:1
Case of Libel, A 1963,O 11,43:2
Right Honourable Gentleman, The 1965,O 20,50:2
Sound of Music, The 1967,Ap 27,52:1
Unknown Soldier and His Wife, The 1967,Jl 7,22:1
Everything in the Garden 1967,N 30,60:1
Tiger at the Gates 1968,Mr 1,30:1
Mercy Street 1969,O 28,43:1
Not Now Darling 1970,O 30,33:1
Dowdall, Ann
Yeomen of the Guard, The 1962,Jl 11,28:1
Dowday, Sol
Journey's End 1929,Mr 23,23:1
Dowdell, Robert
Dybbuk, The 1954,O 27,33:6
Love Me Little 1958,Ap 15,42:2
Viva Madison Avenue 1960,Ap 7,42:1
Dowdney, Louise
Occasion, L' 1939,Ja 10,16:4
Jacobowsky and the Colonel 1944,Mr 15,17:2
Dowdy, Helen
Porgy and Bess 1935,O 11,30:2
Mamba's Daughters 1939,Ja 4,24:2
Porgy and Bess 1942,Ja 23,16:2
Run, Little Chillun 1943,Ag 14,6:1
Show Boat 1946,Ja 7,17:2
Show Boat 1948,S 9,33:2
Porgy and Bess 1953,Mr 10,25:5
Mrs Patterson 1954,D 2,37:1
Show Boat 1956,Je 22,16:1
Show Boat 1957,Je 28,30:2
Porgy and Bess 1965,Mr 6,17:1
Dowell, Coleman (Composer)
Tattooed Countess, The 1961,My 4,40:2
Dowell, Coleman (Lyricist)
Tattooed Countess, The 1961,My 4,40:2
Dowell, Coleman (Playwright)
Tattooed Countess, The 1961,My 4,40:2

Dowell, Edgar
Broadway Boy 1932,My 4,23:5
Dowell, George (Playwright)
God Innis 1937,Ag 25,24:3
Dowell, George B
Sisters' Tragedy, The 1930,My 6,33:1
Dowling, Constance
Strings, My Lord, Are False, The 1942,My 20,24:2
Only the Heart 1942,D 7,22:3
Dowling, Doris
Banjo Eyes 1941,D 26,20:2
Beat the Band 1942,O 15,26:1
New Faces of 1943 1942,D 23,22:2
Dowling, Eddie
Sally, Irene and Mary 1922,S 5,21:2
Honeymoon Lane 1926,S 21,32:3
Vaudeville (Palace) 1931,Mr 2,19:2
Thumbs Up! 1934,D 28,24:1
Here Come the Clowns 1938,D 8,36:2
Time of Your Life, The 1939,O 26,26:2
Time of Your Life, The 1939,N 5,IX,1:1
Time of Your Life, The 1940,S 24,27:2
Life, Laughter And Tears 1942,F 26,15:2
Magic 1942,S 30,28:2
Hello Out There 1942,S 30,28:2
Manhattan Nocturne 1943,O 27,26:2
Glass Menagerie, The 1945,Ja 14,II,2:4
Glass Menagerie, The 1945,Ap 2,15:5
Glass Menagerie, The 1945,Ap 8,II,1:1
Home Life of a Buffalo; Hope's the Thing
   1948,My 12,34:6
Hope Is the Thing With Feathers; Hope's the
   Thing 1948,My 12,34:6
Gone Tomorrow; Hope's the Thing
   1948,My 12,34:6
Minnie and Mr Williams 1948,O 28,37:2
Angel in the Pawnshop 1951,Ja 19,20:3
Dowling, Eddie (Composer)
Honeymoon Lane 1926,S 21,32:3
Sidewalks of New York 1927,O 4,33:1
Dowling, Eddie (Director)
Time of Your Life, The 1939,O 26,26:2
Love's Old Sweet Song 1940,My 3,16:3
Time of Your Life, The 1940,S 24,27:2
Magic 1942,S 30,28:2
Hello Out There 1942,S 30,28:2
This Rock 1943,F 19,23:2
Men to the Sea 1944,O 4,25:2
Glass Menagerie, The 1945,Ap 2,15:5
Iceman Cometh, The 1946,O 10,31:3
Iceman Cometh, The 1946,O 20,II,1:1
Our Lan' 1947,S 29,16:5
Hope Is the Thing With Feathers; Hope's the
   Thing 1948,My 12,34:6
Gone Tomorrow; Hope's the Thing
   1948,My 12,34:6
Home Life of a Buffalo; Hope's the Thing
   1948,My 12,34:6
Minnie and Mr Williams 1948,O 28,37:2
Righteous Are Bold, The 1955,D 23,12:1
Seven Scenes for Yeni 1963,My 13,36:2
Dowling, Eddie (Lyricist)
Honeymoon Lane 1926,S 21,32:3
Sidewalks of New York 1927,O 4,33:1
Dowling, Eddie (Miscellaneous)
Stepping Out 1929,My 21,29:1
Time of Your Life, The 1939,O 26,26:2
Love's Old Sweet Song 1940,My 3,16:3
Time of Your Life, The 1940,S 24,27:2
Dowling, Eddie (Playwright)
Sally, Irene and Mary 1922,S 5,21:2
Honeymoon Lane 1926,S 21,32:3
Sidewalks of New York 1927,O 4,33:1
Dowling, Eddie (Producer)
Big Hearted Herbert 1934,Ja 2,17:3
Thumbs Up! 1934,D 28,24:1
Agatha Calling 1935,O 1,27:5
Richard II 1937,F 6,14:2
Richard II 1937,S 16,28:2
Shadow and Substance 1938,Ja 27,16:2
Madame Capet 1938,O 26,26:2
Here Come the Clowns 1938,D 8,36:2
White Steed, The 1939,Ja 11,16:2
Love's Old Sweet Song 1940,Ap 14,IX,3:3
Life, Laughter And Tears 1942,F 26,15:2
Hello Out There 1942,S 30,28:2
Magic 1942,S 30,28:2
This Rock 1943,F 19,23:2
Little Women 1944,D 13,29:2
Glass Menagerie, The 1945,Ja 14,II,2:4
Glass Menagerie, The 1945,Ap 2,15:5
Our Lan' 1947,S 29,16:5
Hope Is the Thing With Feathers; Hope's the
   Thing 1948,My 12,34:6
Gone Tomorrow; Hope's the Thing
   1948,My 12,34:6
Home Life of a Buffalo; Hope's the Thing
   1948,My 12,34:6
Heaven on Earth 1948,S 17,29:2
Angel in the Pawnshop 1951,Ja 19,20:3
Child of the Morning 1951,N 17,9:7
Righteous Are Bold, The 1955,D 23,12:1

Dowling, Eddie Jr
Tell Me More 1925,Ap 14,27:3
Dowling, Edward
All-Star Jamboree 1921,Jl 14,18:1
Dowling, Edward Duryea (Director)
Ziegfeld Follies 1936,S 15,37:1
Streets of Paris, The 1939,Je 20,25:2
New Hellzapoppin, The 1939,D 12,36:4
Keep Off the Grass 1940,My 24,22:6
Sons o' Fun 1941,D 2,28:2
It's All Yours 1942,Mr 26,26:2
Evening With Beatrice Lillie, An 1952,O 3,17:2
Dowling, Edward Duryea (Lighting Director)
Streets of Paris, The 1939,Je 20,25:2
Keep Off the Grass 1940,My 24,22:6
Sons o' Fun 1941,D 2,28:2
Dowling, Edward Duryea (Producer)
Evening With Beatrice Lillie, An 1952,O 3,17:2
Dowling, Frank
Ruddigore 1931,Ag 11,28:3
Dowling, Henry
Sidewalks of New York 1927,O 4,33:1
Dowling, Jennette
As We Forgive Our Debtors 1947,Mr 11,37:2
Shrike, The 1952,Ja 16,20:2
Dowling, Jennette (Playwright)
Young Elizabeth, The 1952,Ap 3,45:1
Young Elizabeth, The 1952,Ap 13,II,3:8
Dowling, John
Master of the Revels 1935,Ag 14,16:2
Dowling, Robert W (Miscellaneous)
Tamburlaine the Great 1956,Ja 20,19:1
Major Barbara 1956,O 31,27:1
Visit, The 1958,My 6,40:1
Price, The 1968,F 8,37:1
Dowling, Robert W (Playwright)
Sleeping Prince, The 1956,N 2,31:1
Dowling, Robert W (Producer)
Remarkable Mr Pennypacker, The 1953,D 31,11:2
Goldilocks 1958,O 13,33:1
Cold Wind and the Warm, The 1958,D 9,55:1
Much Ado About Nothing 1959,S 18,25:2
Prime of Miss Jean Brodie, The 1968,Ja 17,39:1
Sheep on the Runway 1970,F 2,28:3
Dowling, Tony
Vigil, The 1948,My 22,8:6
Julius Caesar 1950,Je 21,30:1
Marching Song 1959,D 29,20:1
Mummers and Men 1962,Mr 27,41:6
Dowling, Vincent
Passion of Gross, The 1955,Ja 24,20:2
Billy Budd 1955,My 4,35:1
Red Roses for Me 1955,D 29,15:2
Mary Stuart 1957,O 9,39:1
Sunrise at Campobello 1958,Ja 31,25:1
Mister Roberts 1962,O 12,27:2
More Stately Mansions 1967,N 1,40:1
Playboy of the Western World, The 1968,S 4,40:1
Downdey, Louise
Possessed, The 1939,O 25,26:2
Downer, Stephen West
Cradle Will Rock, The 1947,D 27,11:2
Downes, Annette
Journey by Night, A 1935,Ap 17,26:3
Downes, Edward
They All Want Something 1926,O 13,20:2
Street Scene 1929,Ja 11,20:4
Left Bank, The 1931,O 6,35:3
Black Sheep 1932,O 14,22:6
Judgment Day 1934,S 13,26:4
All the Living 1938,Mr 25,14:4
Two on an Island 1940,Ja 23,17:2
Downes, Martha
Medea 1947,O 21,27:2
Medea 1949,My 3,31:2
Tower Beyond Tragedy, The 1950,N 27,29:1
Downes, Viola
Month in the Country, A 1959,Mr 2,32:2
Downey, Catherine
Big Mogul, The 1925,My 12,26:3
Downey, Libbie
Old Maid, The 1949,Ja 27,20:6
Downey, Morton
Vaudeville (Palace) 1927,My 10,25:3
Excess Baggage 1927,O 27,24:2
Vaudeville (Palace) 1929,S 30,22:3
Vaudeville (Palace) 1931,F 2,23:3
Let's Play Fair 1938,Ja 19,26:4
Aquacade 1939,My 5,26:2
Downey, Muriel
Red, Hot and Blue! 1936,O 30,26:3
Downey, Norma
Sky's the Limit, The 1934,D 18,25:5
Few Are Chosen 1935,S 18,19:3
Tapestry in Gray 1935,D 28,10:2
Pygmalion 1938,Ja 27,16:3
Captain Jinks of the Horse Marines 1938,Ja 28,16:2
No More Peace 1938,Ja 29,13:2
Coriolanus 1938,F 2,14:5
Downey, Norman
Pygmalion 1937,Jl 7,26:3

Downey, Robert (Miscellaneous)
Experiment, The 1967,My 9,54:2
Downie, Andrew
H M S Pinafore 1960,S 8,41:1
Pirates of Penzance, The 1961,S 7,41:1
Pirates of Penzance, The 1961,S 17,II,1:1
Downing, Al
Follow Thru 1929,Ja 10,24:3
Ballyhoo 1930,D 23,24:1
America's Sweetheart 1931,F 11,23:1
Free for All 1931,S 9,25:1
Take a Chance 1932,N 28,11:2
New Hellzapoppin, The 1939,D 12,36:4
Panama Hattie 1940,O 31,28:2
Duchess Misbehaves, The 1946,F 14,32:2
Downing, David
Song of the Lusitanian Bogey, The 1968,Ja 3,52:1
Kongi's Harvest 1968,Ap 15,49:1
Daddy Goodness 1968,Je 5,37:1
God Is a (Guess What?) 1968,D 18,56:1
Ceremonies in Dark Old Men 1969,F 6,33:1
Man Better Man 1969,Jl 3,22:1
Man Better Man 1969,Jl 13,II,3:6
Harangues, The 1970,Ja 14,42:1
Day of Absence 1970,Mr 18,39:1
Downing, Edward
Master of the Revels 1935,Ag 14,16:2
Downing, Eliza (Director)
New York Idea, The 1948,Ag 18,29:2
Peg o' My Heart 1948,Ag 25,29:2
Downing, Evelyn
Adam Had Two Sons 1932,Ja 21,17:1
Downing, Frank
Man From Cairo, The 1938,My 5,26:5
If You Get It, Do You Want It? 1938,D 1,28:2
Circle, The 1939,Jl 12,17:2
What a Life 1939,Ag 2,17:5
White Steed, The 1939,Ag 16,21:3
Blind Alley 1939,Ag 23,18:8
Burning Deck, The 1940,Mr 2,9:2
Romeo and Juliet 1940,My 10,27:1
West Side Story 1964,Ap 9,24:2
Downing, Franklin
Masque of the Kings, The 1937,F 9,19:4
Downing, Joe
Ramshackle Inn 1944,Ja 6,17:5
Adding Machine, The 1970,D 5,40:1
Downing, Joe (Miscellaneous)
Wuziz! 1970,O 2,25:2
Downing, John
Royal Family, The 1940,Ag 13,15:3
Downing, Joseph
Prunella; Love in a Garden 1926,Je 16,23:3
Farewell to Arms, A 1930,S 23,30:3
Shooting Star 1933,Je 13,22:2
Heat Lightning 1933,S 16,9:6
Drums Begin, The 1933,N 25,10:5
Page Miss Glory 1934,N 28,24:2
Ceiling Zero 1935,Ap 11,26:2
Dead End 1935,O 29,17:2
Cross-Town 1937,Mr 18,21:5
Downing, Patricia
Pirates of Penzance, The 1970,Jl 26,49:5
Downing, Robert
There Shall Be No Night 1940,Ap 30,25:2
Naked Genius, The 1943,O 22,20:5
Wake Up, Darling 1956,My 3,34:2
Say Darling 1958,Ap 4,17:1
Butter and Egg Man, The 1966,O 18,49:1
Downing, Robert (Miscellaneous)
Cat on a Hot Tin Roof 1955,Mr 25,18:2
Happy Hunting 1956,D 7,30:1
Say Darling 1958,Ap 4,17:1
J B 1958,D 12,2:7
Cheri 1959,O 13,44:1
Camelot 1960,D 5,42:1
Natural Affection 1963,F 2,5:2
After the Fall 1964,Ja 24,18:1
Marco Millions 1964,F 21,33:1
But for Whom Charlie 1964,Mr 13,42:2
Changeling, The 1964,O 30,32:2
Great Indoors, The 1966,F 2,23:1
Downing, Todd (Original Author)
Cat Screams, The 1942,Je 17,26:5
Downing, Vernon
Barretts of Wimpole Street, The 1931,F 10,25:1
Downing, Virginia
Juno and the Paycock 1955,F 24,20:4
Man With the Golden Arm, The 1956,My 22,28:1
Mrs Warren's Profession 1958,Je 26,22:1
Idiot, The 1960,S 26,38:1
Play With a Tiger 1964,D 31,14:2
Mercy Street 1969,O 28,43:1
Downing, W A
Merry Wives of West Point, The 1932,Mr 20,II,7:7
Downing, Walter
Taboo 1922,Ap 5,22:1
19th Hole, The 1927,O 12,30:3
Downs, Frederic
Oedipus Rex 1945,D 17,16:7
Mayor of Zalamea, The 1946,Ja 28,15:5
Duchess of Malfi, The 1946,O 16,35:2
Frankie and Johnny 1952,O 29,37:2

Downs, Frederic—Cont
Grass Harp, The 1953,Ap 28,32:2
Grass Harp, The 1953,My 24,II,1:1
Trip to Bountiful, The 1953,N 4,30:3
Threepenny Opera, The 1955,S 21,38:1
Julius Caesar 1959,Ag 4,30:1
Fiorello! 1959,N 24,45:3
Threepenny Opera, The 1960,S 15,44:3
Downs, James E
Marriage of Cana, The 1932,F 3,22:4
Downs, Jane
Twelfth Night 1958,D 10,54:2
Henry V 1958,D 26,2:7
Man and Boy 1963,N 13,34:1
Downs, Jean
Comedy of Women, A 1929,S 14,17:4
Downs, Johnny
Vaudeville (Palace) 1929,Je 17,29:3
Strike Me Pink 1933,Mr 6,16:3
Growing Pains 1933,N 24,24:2
Ragged Army 1934,F 27,16:5
Are You With It? 1945,N 12,17:3
Hold It! 1948,My 6,31:5
Downs, Oliphant (Playwright)
Maker of Dreams, The 1920,Ap 28,9:3
Downs, Robert C
On the Level 1937,Mr 26,24:4
Doxie, Devona
May Wine 1935,D 6,30:3
Doyl, Ollor
She Couldn't Say No! 1926,S 1,27:3
Doyle, Agnes
Fresh Fields 1936,F 11,19:2
That Old Devil 1944,Je 6,14:2
Doyle, Arthur Conan (Sir) (Original Author)
Return of Sherlock Holmes 1923,O 11,23:7
Sherlock Holmes 1953,O 31,11:2
Sherlock Holmes 1953,N 8,II,1:1
Baker Street 1965,F 17,36:1
Doyle, Arthur Conan (Sir) (Playwright)
Sherlock Holmes 1929,N 26,28:3
Doyle, Brian
Minstrel Boy, The 1948,O 15,28:2
Saint Joan 1950,Mr 4,10:6
Doyle, Buddy
Artists and Models 1923,Ag 21,12:2
Doyle, Charles
Bottomland 1927,Je 28,29:3
Jonica 1930,Ap 8,27:1
Doyle, Charles H
Mr Samuel 1930,N 11,28:4
Honor Code, The 1931,My 19,25:3
Doyle, David
Mandragola 1956,Mr 1,36:4
Bonds of Interest, The 1958,My 7,43:1
Beg, Borrow or Steal 1960,F 11,39:4
Under the Sycamore Tree 1960,Mr 8,37:2
Camino Real 1960,My 17,42:2
Camino Real 1960,My 29,II,1:1
Something About a Soldier 1962,Ja 5,36:2
Beauty Part, The 1962,D 28,5:2
Here's Love 1963,O 4,28:1
I Was Dancing 1964,N 9,40:4
Serjeant Musgrave's Dance 1966,Mr 9,44:1
Elizabeth the Queen 1966,N 4,30:1
South Pacific 1967,Je 13,56:1
Doyle, David (Director)
Beg, Borrow or Steal 1960,F 11,39:4
Doyle, Deirdre
Mob, The 1920,O 11,18:1
Whispering Well, The 1920,D 6,19:1
Great Adventure, The 1921,F 26,9:2
Doyle, J H
Badges 1924,D 4,25:1
Doyle, J W
Louie the 14th 1925,Mr 4,17:1
Doyle, James
Wildflower 1923,F 8,17:2
Medea 1949,My 3,31:2
Doyle, James H (Director)
Pressing Business 1930,N 18,28:5
Doyle, Jay
Beyond the Horizon 1962,O 26,27:2
My Kinsman, Major Molineux 1964,N 2,62:2
Hamlet 1968,Je 10,59:1
Three Sisters, The 1969,O 10,38:1
Doyle, John
Breaking Point, The 1923,Jl 1,VI,1:4
Breaking Point, The 1923,Ag 17,8:4
Doyle, John T
Meanest Man in the World, The 1920,O 13,18:2
Cold Feet 1923,My 22,14:2
Bluffing Bluffers 1924,D 23,17:2
If I Was Rich 1926,S 3,15:2
Love Is Like That 1927,Ap 19,24:1
Baby Cyclone, The 1927,S 13,37:4
Great Power, The 1928,S 12,25:1
Vermont 1929,Ja 9,28:1
Congratulations 1929,My 1,28:4
Unsophisticates, The 1929,D 31,14:5
Boundry Line, The 1930,F 6,21:1
Rhapsody, The 1930,S 16,30:3
Tomorrow and Tomorrow 1931,Ja 14,26:3
Move on, Sister 1933,O 25,22:4

Dark Tower, The 1933,N 27,20:3
Doyle, Joseph
Pastorale 1936,Mr 5,24:6
Doyle, Katherine
County Chairman, The 1936,My 26,26:5
Doyle, Kathleen
Tom Paine 1969,Mr 30,71:2
Doyle, Len
Ladies' Money 1934,N 2,26:6
Weather Permitting 1935,My 24,24:5
Play, Genius, Play! 1935,O 31,17:2
On Location 1937,S 28,19:1
Shadow and Substance 1938,Ja 27,16:2
Time of Your Life, The 1939,O 26,26:2
Time of Your Life, The 1939,N 5,IX,1:1
Distant City, The 1941,S 23,27:5
Plan M 1942,F 21,15:2
I'll Take the High Road 1943,N 10,28:3
Streets Are Guarded, The 1944,N 21,19:7
Righteous Are Bold, The 1955,D 23,12:1
Run, Thief, Run 1957,My 2,27:1
Doyle, Leonard
Bonehead, The 1920,Ap 13,12:1
Crooked Gamblers 1920,Ag 2,12:1
Nature's Nobleman 1921,N 15,23:2
Gringo 1922,D 15,26:3
Square Peg, A 1923,Ja 29,10:2
Within Four Walls 1923,Ap 18,24:1
Night Hawk 1925,F 25,16:4
Black Velvet 1927,S 28,28:1
King Can Do No Wrong, The 1927,N 17,28:4
Buzzard, The 1928,Mr 15,29:1
Family Upstairs 1933,O 28,20:6
Doyle, Leonard (Director)
Family Upstairs, The 1933,O 28,20:6
Doyle, Leonard (Producer)
Family Upstairs, The 1933,O 28,20:6
Doyle, Lynn (Playwright)
Love and Land 1931,F 1,VIII,3:3
Doyle, Major
White Gold 1925,N 3,34:5
Doyle, Mary
House of Breath, The 1957,Ap 15,23:2
Roots 1961,Mr 7,40:2
Roots 1961,Mr 19,II,1:1
Infancy 1962,Ja 12,28:1
Limb of Snow 1967,D 13,55:1
Henry V 1969,Je 9,57:1
Henry V 1969,Je 15,II,3:1
Much Ado About Nothing 1969,Je 16,57:1
Three Sisters, The 1969,Ag 4,29:1
Henry V 1969,N 11,43:1
Doyle, Michael
Meet the People 1940,D 26,22:2
Doyle, Miriam
Innocent Idea, An 1920,My 26,9:4
Return of Peter Grimm, The 1921,S 22,12:2
Goose Hangs High, The 1924,Ja 30,16:1
Out of Step 1925,Ja 30,12:1
Still Waters 1926,Mr 2,23:1
Donovan Affair, The 1926,Ag 31,15:2
Jacob Slovak 1927,O 6,28:4
Dread 1929,O 27,IX,2:1
Doyle, Miriam (Director)
Pursuit of Happiness, The 1933,O 10,24:4
Tight Britches 1934,S 12,26:2
Black Widow 1936,F 13,24:3
Merely Murder 1937,D 4,21:4
Doyle, Peggy
House of Bernarda Alba, The 1963,N 25,23:2
Doyle, Peter
Pearl of Great Price, The 1926,N 2,34:3
Doyle, Robert
King Lear 1961,My 15,34:6
King Lear 1964,Jl 28,18:2
Doyle, William (Playwright)
Carnival 1929,Ap 25,32:5
Lady Beyond the Moon 1931,Ap 1,36:5
D'Oyly Carte, Bridget
Pirates of Penzance, The 1948,Ja 11,II,1:1
D'Oyly Carte, Bridget (Miscellaneous)
Pirates of Penzance, The 1966,N 16,54:1
Mikado, The 1966,N 18,36:1
H M S Pinafore 1966,N 24,64:1
Patience 1966,N 30,58:1
H M S Pinafore 1968,O 30,35:1
Mikado, The 1968,N 2,29:4
Pirates of Penzance, The 1968,N 7,54:1
Iolanthe 1968,N 9,37:3
Dozer, David (Playwright)
Plot Against the Chase Manhattan Bank, The
1963,N 27,29:1
Draak, Tom
Of Thee I Sing 1931,D 28,20:1
Draghi, Priscilla
Bobino 1944,Ap 7,23:4
Drago, Cathleen
Plough and the Stars, The 1927,N 29,30:2
Juno and the Paycock 1927,D 20,32:2
Dragonette, Jessica
Earl Carroll's Vanities 1925,Jl 7,24:1
Dragovic, Biliana (Costume Designer)
Progress of Bora, The Tailor, The 1968,Je 27,49:2

Drahos, Mary (Playwright)
Eternal Sabbath 1963,O 19,17:2
Go, Go, Go, God is Dead! 1966,O 12,37:1
Reunion of Sorts 1969,O 15,40:1
Drake, Alfred
Babes in Arms 1937,Ap 15,18:4
Two Bouquets, The 1938,Je 1,19:2
One for the Money 1939,F 6,9:2
Straw Hat, The 1939,S 30,10:6
Two for the Show 1940,F 9,14:2
Two for the Show 1940,F 18,IX,1:1
Out of the Frying Pan 1941,F 12,24:2
As You Like It 1941,O 21,29:2
Yesterday's Magic 1942,Ap 15,27:2
Oklahoma! 1943,Ap 1,27:1
Oklahoma! 1943,Ap 11,II,1:1
Sing Out, Sweet Land! 1944,Ja 7,II,1:1
Swing Out, Sweet Land! 1944,N 10,24:6
Sing Out, Sweet Land! 1944,D 28,24:2
Beggar's Holiday 1946,D 27,13:3
Beggar's Holiday 1947,Ja 26,II,1:1
Promised Valley 1947,Jl 23,18:3
Cradle Will Rock, The 1947,D 27,11:2
Joy to the World 1948,My 19,28:2
Kiss Me, Kate 1948,D 31,10:3
Kiss Me, Kate 1949,Ja 16,II,1:1
Kiss Me, Kate 1949,Ja 30,II,6:5
Gambler, The 1952,O 14,40:1
Kismet 1953,D 4,2:4
Kismet 1955,My 1,II,3:1
Kismet 1955,My 17,33:4
Othello 1957,Je 24,19:2
Othello 1957,Je 30,II,1:1
Much Ado About Nothing 1957,Ag 8,15:2
Much Ado About Nothing 1957,Ag 18,II,1:1
Kean 1961,N 3,28:2
Kean 1961,N 12,II,1:1
Lorenzo 1963,F 16,5:2
Hamlet 1964,F 28,17:5
Hamlet 1964,Ap 10,30:1
Kismet 1965,Je 23,45:1
Those That Play the Clowns 1966,N 25,48:1
Song of the Grasshopper 1967,S 29,52:2
Drake, Alfred (Director)
Courtin' Time 1951,Je 14,30:2
Love Me Little 1958,Ap 15,42:2
Dr Willy Nilly 1959,Je 5,18:2
Drake, Alfred (Playwright)
Liar, The 1950,My 19,30:2
Gambler, The 1952,O 14,40:1
Dr Willy Nilly 1959,Je 5,18:2
Rugantino 1964,F 7,34:1
Drake, Alfred (Producer)
Liar, The 1950,My 19,30:2
Dr Willy Nilly 1959,Je 5,18:2
Drake, Alfred (Translator)
Rugantino 1964,F 2,II,1:4
Drake, Alice
Blossom Time 1943,S 6,21:2
Drake, Allan
International Playgirls '64 1964,My 22,40:2
Drake, Alma
Lady in the Dark 1952,Mr 8,11:3
Drake, Christopher
Madwoman of Chaillot, The 1950,Je 14,41:2
'Tis Pity She's a Whore 1958,D 6,21:1
Drake, Diana
Show Boat 1954,My 6,44:1
Hit the Trail 1954,D 3,31:2
Drake, Doris
Seven Keys to Baldpate 1930,Ja 8,25:2
Drake, Dorothy
Wooden Slipper, The 1934,Ja 4,16:3
Jericho-Jim Crow 1964,Ja 13,25:3
Prodigal Son, The 1965,My 21,19:1
Jericho-Jim Crow 1968,Mr 23,22:2
Drake, Elizabeth
What a Life 1939,Ag 2,17:5
White Steed, The 1939,Ag 16,21:3
Blind Alley 1939,Ag 23,18:8
Good Fairy, The 1939,Ag 30,15:5
Drake, Ervin (Composer)
Love, Honor and Oh Baby 1940,Mr 29,25:2
What Makes Sammy Run? 1964,F 28,19:1
Her First Roman 1968,N 3,II,1:1
Drake, Ervin (Lyricist)
What Makes Sammy Run? 1964,F 28,19:1
Drake, Ervin (Playwright)
Heads or Tails 1947,My 3,10:6
Her First Roman 1968,O 21,53:3
Drake, Fabia
Scarlet Lady, The 1926,O 17,VIII,2:1
Loyalties 1928,Ag 26,VII,1:3
Anthony and Anna 1935,D 8,X,5:1
Indian Summer 1936,Ap 20,17:5
Drake, George
Brigadoon 1947,Mr 14,28:2
Drake, Henry
Policy Kings 1938,D 31,6:2
Drake, Josephine
Lilies of the Field 1921,O 5,20:1
Passing Show of 1923, The 1923,Je 15,24:6
Nobody's Business 1923,O 23,17:1

Drake, Josephine—Cont
Sweet Seventeen 1924,Mr 18,24:2
Busybody, The 1924,S 30,27:5
No Trespassing! 1926,S 8,19:1
Luckee Girl 1928,S 17,28:6
Drake, Judith
Masks of Angels 1965,Ja 20,33:1
Drake, Marty
Hold On to Your Hats 1940,S 12,30:3
Bagels and Yox 1951,S 13,38:2
Drake, Pauline
Laff That Off 1925,N 3,34:2
Her Unborn Child 1928,Mr 7,28:3
Flight 1929,F 19,22:3
It Never Rains 1929,N 20,26:4
Drake, Phyllis
Would-Be Gentleman, The 1930,Ap 30,29:2
Drake, Ronald
Blood Red Roses 1970,Mr 23,48:1
Conduct Unbecoming 1970,O 13,50:1
Drake, Stuart (Producer)
Something for Nothing 1937,D 10,33:5
Drake, William A (Playwright)
In Command 1930,Mr 9,IX,4:3
Drake, William A (Producer)
Eternal Road, The 1937,Ja 8,14:2
Drake, William A (Translator)
Schweiger 1926,Mr 24,20:4
Twelve Thousand 1928,Mr 13,23:1
Grand Hotel 1930,N 14,30:4
Hat, a Coat, a Glove, A 1934,F 1,15:2
Drake, Wilma
Johnny 2X4 1942,Mr 17,24:6
Drakeley, Ray
Sleepy Hollow 1948,Je 4,26:3
Drakert, William
Myself and I 1929,Ag 31,13:6
Drama Repertoire Players
Thais 1931,Je 19,21:3
Drancourt, Arsene
Bourgeois Gentilhomme, Le 1955,O 26,26:1
Barbier de Seville, Le 1955,N 9,40:1
Arlequin Poli par l'Amour 1955,N 16,42:4
Jeu de l'Amour et du Hasard, Le 1955,N 16,42:4
Caprice, Un 1955,N 16,42:4
Dranem
Palace aux Femmes 1926,O 10,VIII,2:1
Diable a Paris, Le 1927,N 13,IX,4:2
Untitled-Revue 1928,Mr 18,III,3:1
1928 1928,Ap 8,VIII,4:1
Draney, John Jr
Fuente Ovejuna; Sheep Well, The 1936,My 3,II,4:1
Drange, Emily
Orange Blossoms 1922,S 20,18:1
Dranova, Nadya
My Little Girl 1931,F 2,22:4
Night in the Woods, A 1931,Mr 2,19:3
Great Miracle, The 1931,D 12,23:5
Rich Paupers 1932,Mr 14,13:4
Big Surprise, The 1932,O 17,18:3
Traveling Salesman, The 1932,N 1,24:4
Jewish Melody, The 1933,Mr 27,12:4
Three in Love 1933,N 8,32:5
Little Giants 1933,D 2,9:5
Organ Grinder, The 1934,Ja 1,28:3
Happy Days 1934,Ap 2,12:5
Secret of Love, The 1936,F 24,15:2
Draper, Anne
King Lear 1963,Je 10,37:1
Comedy of Errors, The 1963,Je 13,28:1
Caesar and Cleopatra 1963,Ag 1,18:2
Much Ado About Nothing 1964,Je 11,26:2
Richard III 1964,Je 12,44:2
Phedre 1966,F 11,36:1
Butterfly Dream, The 1966,My 20,41:1
Carricknabauna 1967,Mr 31,30:1
John Brown's Body 1968,F 13,49:2
Comedy of Errors, The 1968,F 28,40:2
Draper, Don
Man and Superman 1953,F 21,11:2
Scrapbooks 1953,N 6,24:2
Madam Will You Walk 1953,D 2,2:4
Draper, Dorothy
Peter Pan 1941,D 31,22:3
Draper, Emily
O Evening Star 1936,Ja 9,24:6
Draper, Jane
Those That Play the Clowns 1966,N 25,48:1
Draper, Jessie
Sketch Book 1935,Je 5,22:2
Draper, John
Land Is Bright, The 1941,O 29,26:2
Draper, Josef
Murder in the Cathedral 1936,Mr 21,13:5
Iron Men 1936,O 20,30:6
Native Ground 1937,Mr 24,28:4
Polonaise 1945,O 8,20:2
Draper, Margaret
For Heaven's Sake Mother 1948,N 17,33:4
Me, The Sleeper 1949,My 16,18:6
Gambler, The 1952,O 14,40:1
Edward II 1958,F 12,32:5
Cherry Orchard, The 1960,Je 4,17:2
Minor Adjustment, A 1967,O 7,33:3

Draper, Natalie
Johnny 2X4 1942,Mr 17,24:6
Draper, Paul
Thumbs Up! 1934,D 28,24:1
Ruth and Paul Draper 1940,D 27,23:2
Priorities of 1942 1942,Mr 13,23:2
Priorities of 1942 1942,Mr 29,VIII,1:1
Priorities of 1942 1942,My 10,VIII,8:3
Untitled-Recital 1954,D 27,21:2
Untitled-Recital 1955,Ja 9,II,7:1
All in One; Paul Draper Dance Program
   1955,Ap 20,40:3
All in One 1955,Ap 24,II,1:1
Draper, Ruth
Untitled-One Woman Show 1921,Ja 28,16:2
Untitled-One Woman Show 1921,N 12,18:2
Untitled-One Woman Show 1921,N 19,11:2
Untitled-One Woman Show 1921,N 28,16:2
Untitled-One Woman Show 1921,D 4,VIII,1:2
Untitled-One Woman Show 1922,Mr 17,20:2
Untitled-One Woman Show 1923,Ja 15,15:3
Untitled-One Woman Show 1923,O 29,18:2
Untitled-One Woman Show 1923,N 4,VIII,1:2
Vaudeville (Palace) 1924,S 16,26:5
Untitled-One Woman Show 1925,N 9,25:2
Untitled-One Woman Show 1926,Ap 12,18:1
Untitled-One Woman Show 1926,Ap 19,24:4
Untitled-One Woman Show 1926,Je 20,VII,1:1
Untitled-One Woman Show 1926,O 18,18:2
Untitled-One Woman Show 1928,Mr 4,IX,2:1
Untitled-One Woman Show 1928,Je 10,VIII,1:3
Ruth Draper 1928,D 26,14:5
Untitled-One Woman Show 1929,Ja 6,VIII,1:1
Untitled-One Woman Show 1929,D 27,26:6
Untitled-One Woman Show 1930,D 27,16:3
Three Women and Mr. Clifford 1931,Ja 4,VIII,1:1
Untitled-One Woman Show 1931,Je 21,VIII,1:3
Untitled-One Woman Show 1932,N 15,24:2
Untitled-One Woman Show 1934,D 27,24:3
Untitled-One Woman Show 1936,Ja 20,23:3
Untitled-One Woman Show 1936,D 28,13:1
Untitled-One Woman Show 1937,D 1,27:1
Untitled-One Woman Show 1938,D 27,12:2
Ruth and Paul Draper 1940,D 27,23:2
Untitled-One Woman Show 1942,D 26,14:3
Untitled-One Woman Show 1947,Ja 13,18:2
At an Art Exhibition 1947,D 29,21:5
In County Kerry 1947,D 29,21:5
Actress, The 1947,D 29,21:5
Three Breakfasts 1947,D 29,21:5
Children's Party, A 1947,D 29,21:5
Ruth Draper 1954,Ja 26,21:2
Untitled-Recital 1954,D 27,21:2
Untitled-Recital 1955,Ja 9,II,7:1
Untitled-One Woman Show 1956,D 26,32:1
Draper, Ruth (Playwright)
Three Women and Mr. Clifford 1931,Ja 4,VIII,1:1
Untitled-One Woman Show 1938,D 27,12:2
Draper, Stephen
Sun-Up 1929,F 19,22:6
Draper, Tom
Chocolate Soldier, The 1932,F 9,30:3
Draper, Walt
Rivals, The 1942,Ja 15,24:2
Drasin, Tamara
New Yorkers, The 1927,Mr 11,24:3
Draswell, John
Gertrude 1970,N 13,29:1
Dratch, Sam
Pins and Needles 1939,Ap 21,26:2
Draw, Inez
Rang Tang 1927,Jl 13,20:1
Drawbell, James Wedgwood (Playwright)
Who Goes Next? 1931,Mr 8,VIII,2:4
Drayson, Danny
Heaven on Earth 1948,S 17,29:2
Drayton, Alfred
These Charming People 1925,O 7,31:2
Double Dan 1927,Je 5,VII,2:1
High Road, The 1928,S 11,31:1
Aren't Men Beasts? 1936,My 15,29:1
Spot of Bother 1937,Jl 7,26:2
Women Aren't Angels 1941,Ap 27,IX,1:6
Drayton, Mary
Few Are Chosen 1935,S 18,19:3
On Location 1937,S 28,19:1
Thanks for Tomorrow 1938,S 28,28:2
Drayton, Mary (Playwright)
Debut 1956,F 23,32:1
Playroom, The 1965,D 6,49:1
Drayton, Thaddeus
Liza 1922,N 28,24:1
Drayton, Thelma
But Never Jam Today 1969,Ap 24,40:1
Drdla, Franz
Vaudeville (Palace) 1924,Ja 15,17:3
Dreeben, Alan
Dark Hammock 1944,D 12,27:8
Assassin, The 1945,O 18,20:2
Hamlet 1945,D 14,25:2
Julius Caesar 1950,Je 21,30:1
Dregely (Playwright)
Youngest Verebezy Girl, The 1928,D 2,X,4:7

Dregge, John
Blue Blood 1924,Ap 3,21:2
Dreher, Walter
See Naples and Die 1929,S 27,30:4
Troika 1930,Ap 2,32:6
Once in a Lifetime 1930,S 25,22:3
Dreiblatt, A L
Yes is for a Very Young Man 1949,Je 7,27:2
Dreifuss, Arthur (Choreographer)
Nautical but Nice 1931,Ap 19,31:6
Dreifuss, Arthur (Producer)
Allure 1934,O 30,22:6
Baby Pompadour 1934,D 28,24:2
Dreiser, Theodore (Original Author)
American Tragedy, An 1926,O 12,31:2
American Tragedy, An 1926,O 24,VIII,1:1
American Tragedy, An 1931,F 21,15:5
American Tragedy, An 1932,Ap 17,I,19:1
Sandhog 1954,N 24,17:1
Dreiser, Theodore (Playwright)
Girl in the Coffin, The 1920,F 10,10:2
Case of Clyde Griffiths 1936,Mr 14,10:4
Dremak, W P
Jonah! 1967,S 22,52:2
Dremann, Janis
I Married an Angel 1938,My 12,26:2
Drenova, Felicia
Princess Flavia 1925,N 3,34:3
Dresbach, James
Cotton Stockings 1923,D 19,16:2
Dresdel, Sonia
This Was a Woman 1944,Ap 30,II,1:3
Mourning Becomes Electra 1961,N 22,24:3
Man in the Glass Booth, The 1967,Jl 29,12:1
Dresher, Paul
Tarot 1970,D 12,19:1
Dressel, Erwin (Composer)
Armer Columbus 1928,Ap 22,IX,6:7
Dressel, Walter
Eight Bells 1933,O 30,14:2
Shatter'd Lamp, The 1934,Mr 22,26:3
Versunkene Glocke, Die 1936,N 20,26:3
Dresselhuys, Cornelius (Mrs)
Variations of 1940 1940,Ja 29,12:1
Dresselhuys, Lorraine Manville (Miscellaneous)
Rhapsody 1944,N 23,37:2
Dressler, Eric
Goose Hangs High, The 1924,Ja 30,16:1
Out of Step 1925,Ja 30,12:1
Young Blood 1925,N 25,15:1
Young Blood 1925,N 29,VIII,1:1
Adorable Liar, The 1926,Ag 31,15:2
Ballyhoo 1927,Ja 5,18:1
Trelawney of the 'Wells' 1927,F 1,24:4
Excess Baggage 1927,D 27,24:2
Exceeding Small 1928,O 23,32:2
Exceeding Small 1928,N 4,IX,1:1
Before You're 25 1929,Ap 17,30:2
Parade 1929,S 1,VIII,1:1
Nigger Rich 1929,S 21,16:7
Cross Roads 1929,N 12,34:2
Penny Arcade 1930,Mr 11,24:5
Lysistrata 1930,Ap 29,30:5
Lysistrata 1930,Je 1,VIII,1:1
Lysistrata 1930,Je 6,20:1
Paging Danger 1931,F 27,19:2
Adams' Wife 1931,D 29,27:1
All Good Americans 1933,D 6,29:2
Joyous Season, The 1934,Ja 30,16:3
Are You Decent? 1934,Ap 20,16:2
Good-Bye Please 1934,O 25,26:6
Creeping Fire 1935,Ja 17,22:3
Dominant Sex, The 1935,Ap 2,24:5
Squaring the Circle 1935,S 22,X,3:2
Squaring the Circle 1935,O 4,24:6
Three Sisters, The 1942,D 22,31:2
Three Sisters, The 1942,D 27,VIII,1:1
Dressler, Marie
Passing Show of 1921, The 1920,D 30,16:2
Dancing Girl, The 1923,Ja 25,16:2
Untitled-Play 1923,O 7,IX,2:2
Vaudeville (Palace) 1925,O 20,29:2
Dretzin, David (Producer)
Great Airplane Snatch, The 1969,My 28,36:1
Arf 1969,My 28,36:1
Drew, Alex
Marvellous History of Saint Bernard, The
   1958,F 24,16:3
Drew, Bill
Penny Friend, The 1966,D 27,46:1
Drew, David (Choreographer)
Canterbury Tales 1968,S 7,23:3
Drew, Dennis
Right You Are (If You Think You Are)
   1957,Mr 5,37:1
Androcles and the Lion 1958,F 22,8:3
Cock-A-Doodle Dandy 1958,N 13,39:2
Drew, Elizabeth (Playwright)
Genius at Home 1934,Ja 16,18:3
Genius at Home 1934,F 11,IX,3:1
Drew, Elsie
Play, A 1925,F 11,19:2

Drew, George
Relapse, The 1950,N 23,54:2
Drew, George (Costume Designer)
Mikado, The 1967,D 4,65:3
Drew, George (Scenic Designer)
Tenth of an Inch Makes the Difference, A
1962,N 13,44:1
Drew, John
Cat-Bird, The 1920,F 17,18:1
Cat-Bird, The 1920,F 22,III,6:1
Untitled-Benefit 1921,My 2,12:3
Circle, The 1921,S 13,12:1
Circle, The 1921,S 18,VI,1:1
School for Scandal, The 1923,Je 5,24:3
Trelawney of the 'Wells' 1925,Je 2,16:2
Henry IV, Part I 1926,Je 1,29:1
Trelawney of the 'Wells' 1927,F 1,24:4
Trelawney of the 'Wells' 1927,F 6,VII,1:1
Sophie 1963,Ap 16,32:1
Drew, Louise
Little Inn, The 1935,Ag 20,25:1
Drew, Richard
Mulatto 1967,N 16,61:4
Drew, Robert
Time Limit! 1956,Ja 25,27:2
Drew, Roland
Shooting Star 1933,Je 13,22:2
Whatever Possessed Her 1934,Ja 26,21:2
Paths of Glory 1935,S 19,29:1
Paths of Glory 1935,S 27,24:2
Drew, Warren Bill
Sextet 1958,N 27,53:1
Drew-Wilkinson, Katie
Oh! Calcutta! 1969,Je 18,33:1
Drewes, Russell W (Cpl)
Winged Victory 1943,N 22,24:1
Drewitt, Stanley
Slaves All 1926,D 7,24:4
Josef Suss 1930,Ja 21,28:5
Drexel, Todd
Much Ado About Nothing 1964,Je 11,26:2
Richard III 1964,Je 12,44:2
Hamlet 1964,Jl 4,9:1
Coriolanus 1965,Je 21,36:1
Romeo and Juliet 1965,Je 21,36:3
Taming of the Shrew, The 1965,Je 24,32:2
King Lear 1965,Je 25,39:1
Falstaff 1966,Je 20,27:1
Murder in the Cathedral 1966,Je 21,38:1
Julius Caesar 1966,Je 24,29:2
Comedy of Errors, The 1968,F 28,40:2
Drexler, Eleanor
Love's Old Sweet Song 1940,My 3,16:3
Drexler, Rosalyn (Lyricist)
Home Movies 1964,My 12,32:1
Softly, and Consider the Nearness 1964,My 12,32:1
Drexler, Rosalyn (Playwright)
Softly, and Consider the Nearness 1964,My 12,32:1
Home Movies 1964,My 12,32:1
Line of Least Existence, The 1968,Mr 25,53:1
Collision Course; Skywriting 1968,My 9,55:2
Skywriting 1968,My 19,II,1:1
Drey, Walter (Producer)
Manhattan Nocturne 1943,O 27,26:2
Dreyden, George
Sweet Chariot 1930,O 24,30:2
Dreyer, Gisela
Kleinburgerhochzeit, Die 1970,N 25,25:1
Dreyfuss, Henry (Director)
Continental Varieties 1934,O 4,18:3
Dreyfuss, Henry (Scenic Designer)
Beau Gallant 1926,Ap 6,26:3
Hold Everything 1928,O 11,24:2
Remote Control 1929,S 11,24:5
Boundry Line, The 1930,F 6,21:1
Last Mile, The 1930,F 14,21:2
Fine and Dandy 1930,S 24,26:1
Blind Mice 1930,O 16,28:2
Pagan Lady 1930,O 21,34:2
Sweet Stranger 1930,O 22,23:3
Affair of State, An 1930,N 20,30:3
This Is New York 1930,N 29,21:1
Kiss of Importance, A 1930,D 2,31:3
Philip Goes Forth 1931,Ja 13,35:4
Gang's All Here, The 1931,F 19,21:3
Man on Stilts, The 1931,S 10,23:2
Cat and the Fiddle, The 1931,O 16,26:4
Strike Me Pink 1933,Mr 6,16:3
Continental Varieties 1934,O 4,18:3
Paths of Glory 1935,S 19,29:1
Paths of Glory 1935,S 27,24:2
Dreyfuss, Michael
Listen Professor! 1943,D 23,22:1
Bright Boy 1944,Mr 3,19:5
Career Angel 1944,My 24,23:7
Many Happy Returns 1945,Ja 6,15:5
Too Hot for Maneuvers 1945,My 3,26:5
Bees and the Flowers, The 1946,S 27,19:3
Joy to the World 1948,Mr 19,28:2
Traitor, The 1949,Ap 1,30:2
Babes in Arms 1951,Mr 10,7:3
Dreyfuss, Richard
But, Seriously... 1969,F 28,29:1

Drierley, David (Miscellaneous)
Comedy of Errors, The 1964,My 21,43:1
Driers, Richard
Hamp 1964,Ag 18,25:1
Drinkwater, John (Director)
Bird in Hand 1929,Ap 5,28:2
Drinkwater, John (Playwright)
Abraham Lincoln 1920,Mr 14,V,5:1
Abraham Lincoln 1920,My 23,VI,8:2
Mary Queen of Scots 1921,F 6,VI,1:2
Mary Stuart 1921,Mr 22,15:1
Mary Stuart 1921,Ap 3,VII,1:1
Mary Stuart 1921,Ap 17,VI,1:1
Oliver Cromwell 1923,F 25,VII,1:7
Oliver Cromwell 1923,My 30,10:5
Robert E Lee 1923,Je 21,22:4
Robert E Lee 1923,Jl 8,VI,1:1
Robert E Lee 1923,N 21,23:1
Robert E Lee 1923,N 25,VIII,1:1
Mayor of Casterbridge, The 1926,S 9,20:1
Mayor of Casterbridge, The 1926,O 3,VIII,2:1
Abraham Lincoln 1927,Ja 21,12:3
Bird in Hand 1928,My 13,IX,2:7
Bird in Hand 1929,Ap 5,28:2
Bird in Hand 1929,Ap 14,X,1:1
Abraham Lincoln 1929,O 22,26:3
Napoleon: The Hundred Days 1932,Ap 19,25:2
Napoleon: The Hundred Days 1932,My 8,VIII,1:3
Laying the Devil 1933,Jl 23,IX,1:3
Man's House, A 1934,S 13,26:3
Abraham Lincoln 1934,D 1,8:6
Players' Masque for Marie Tempest, The
1935,Je 23,IX,1:3
Abraham Lincoln 1940,My 5,X,1:2
Bird in Hand 1942,O 20,24:2
Man's House, A 1943,Ap 3,10:4
Man's House, A 1943,Ap 4,II,2:1
Drinkwater, John (Translator)
Napoleon: The Hundred Days 1932,Ap 19,25:2
Drisch, Russell
Until the Monkey Comes 1966,Je 21,38:1
Drischell, Ralph
Playboy of the Western World, The 1958,My 9,19:2
Merry Death, A 1959,N 10,55:3
No Trifling With Love 1959,N 10,55:3
Slight Ache, A 1964,D 10,62:1
Room, The 1964,D 10,62:1
King John 1967,Jl 14,19:1
Rosencrantz and Guildenstern Are Dead
1967,O 17,53:1
Year Boston Won the Pennant, The
1969,My 23,38:1
Time of Your Life, The 1969,N 7,37:1
Camino Real 1970,Ja 9,42:1
Operation Sidewinder 1970,Mr 13,33:1
Driscoll, Ann
Skylark 1939,O 12,32:2
Hello Out There 1942,S 30,28:2
New Life, A 1943,S 16,26:6
Death of a Salesman 1949,F 11,27:2
Blithe Spirit 1952,F 23,7:5
View From the Bridge, A 1955,S 30,21:1
Driscoll, Bobby
Ah, Wilderness! 1954,Ag 21,20:4
Driscoll, David (Playwright)
All Desirable Young Men 1936,Jl 22,22:5
Driscoll, J Emmett
Suppressed Desires 1920,F 10,10:2
Magnanimous Lover, The 1920,F 10,10:2
Girl in the Coffin, The 1920,F 10,10:2
Driscoll, John
Big Mogul, The 1925,My 12,26:3
Driscoll, Loren
Juno 1959,Mr 10,41:1
Driscoll, Maxwell
Drifting 1922,Ja 3,20:3
First Mortgage 1929,O 11,36:1
Cortez 1929,N 5,32:2
Driscoll, Ralph
Comedy of Errors, The 1967,Je 15,58:4
Drivas, Robert
Firstborn, The 1958,My 1,35:1
Firstborn, The 1958,My 11,II,1:1
One More River 1960,Mr 19,12:2
Wall, The 1960,O 12,44:4
Diff'rent 1961,O 18,52:1
Mrs Dally Has a Lover 1962,O 2,47:1
Lorenzo 1963,F 16,5:2
Irregular Verb to Love, The 1963,S 19,22:2
And Things That Go Bump in the Night
1965,Ap 27,27:5
Sweet Eros 1968,N 22,38:1
Cops and Horrors; Fly Paper 1970,Ag 11,27:1
Cops and Horrors; Dracula 1970,Ag 11,27:1
Driver, Anne
Cranmer of Canterbury 1959,D 4,36:1
Driver, Donald
Buttrio Square 1952,O 15,40:2
Finian's Rainbow 1953,Mr 7,13:2
Show Boat 1954,My 6,44:1
Hit the Trail 1954,D 3,31:2
Finian's Rainbow 1955,My 19,25:1

Driver, Donald (Director)
Persecution and Assassination of Marat As
Performed by the Inmates of the Asylum of
Charenton Under the Direction of the Marquis de
Sade, The 1967,Ap 4,34:1
Persecution and Assassination of Marat As
Performed by the Inmates of the Asylum of
Charenton Under the Direction of the Marquis de
Sade, The 1967,Ja 15,II,1:1
Your Own Thing 1968,Ja 15,33:1
Your Own Thing 1968,Ja 28,II,3:1
Mike Downstairs 1968,Ap 19,35:1
Jimmy Shine 1968,D 6,52:1
Our Town 1969,N 28,50:1
Our Town 1969,D 7,II,7:1
Driver, Donald (Miscellaneous)
Taming of the Shrew, The 1965,Je 24,32:2
Driver, Donald (Playwright)
Your Own Thing 1968,Ja 15,33:1
Your Own Thing 1968,Ja 28,II,3:1
Your Own Thing 1969,Mr 29,39:1
Driver, Tom F (Director)
York Nativity Play, The 1956,D 5,49:2
Cup of Trembling, The 1959,My 1,33:5
Drix, Walter (Composer)
From Vienna 1939,Je 21,26:2
Droge, Wendell Phillips (Producer)
Seeniaya Ptitza 1924,D 29,11:1
Drohan, Kevin
Egghead, The 1957,O 10,39:1
Drop Dead
Moon Vine, The 1943,F 12,22:2
Dropkin, Norman (Miscellaneous)
Swing Sister Wac Swing 1944,Ja 4,20:4
D'Rosa, Guglielmo
Traitor, The 1930,My 3,23:4
Drouet, J A (Composer)
Jardin des Delices, Le 1969,N 4,54:1
Drouot, Jean-Claude
Jardin des Delices, Le 1969,N 4,54:1
Drover, Dorothy
Conversation Piece 1934,O 24,24:1
Drown, Hope
Peter Weston 1923,S 20,5:2
Best People, The 1924,Ag 20,8:1
Move On 1926,Ja 19,30:1
Security 1929,Mr 29,20:1
Nice Women 1929,Je 11,27:4
Dru, Joanne
Deadfall 1955,O 28,20:1
Druce, Hubert
Unwritten Chapter, The 1920,O 12,18:1
Deburau 1920,D 24,14:3
Pigeon, The 1922,F 3,13:1
Manhattan 1922,Ag 16,7:5
Seventh Heaven 1922,O 31,11:1
Little Minister, The 1925,Mr 24,21:1
School for Scandal, The 1925,O 24,19:1
Play's the Thing, The 1926,N 4,25:1
Command Performance, The 1928,O 4,27:1
Lady Dedlock 1929,Ja 1,61:2
Mystery Square 1929,Ap 5,28:3
Uncle Vanya 1929,My 25,17:1
Freddy 1929,Jl 17,23:4
Topaze 1930,F 13,25:3
Marseilles 1930,N 18,28:2
Admirable Crichton, The 1931,Mr 10,23:2
Druce, Hubert (Director)
Little Angel, The 1924,S 29,10:3
School for Scandal, The 1925,O 24,19:1
Master of the Inn, The 1925,D 23,22:2
You Can't Win 1926,F 17,12:1
Druce, Hubert (Producer)
School for Scandal, The 1925,O 24,19:1
Master of the Inn, The 1925,D 23,22:2
Druce, Jeff
Five Star Saint 1970,F 11,41:2
Druce, Olga
Judgment Day 1934,S 13,26:4
Moon Over Mulberry Street 1935,S 5,24:6
Druce, Olga (Playwright)
Constant Heckler, The 1948,Ag 21,8:5
Druck, Murray
All the King's Men 1950,Jl 19,25:6
Drucker, Frances (Miscellaneous)
Ballad of Jazz Street, The 1959,N 12,28:1
All in Love 1961,N 11,15:2
Walk in Darkness 1963,O 29,30:2
Drucker, Frances (Producer)
Oh, Say Can You See L A 1968,F 9,50:1
Other Man, The 1968,F 9,50:1
Drucker, Nathan (Lighting Director)
Three Philip Roth Stories; Defender of the Faith
1970,Jl 31,14:1
Three Philip Roth Stories; Conversion of the Jews
1970,Jl 31,14:1
Three Philip Roth Stories; Epstein 1970,Jl 31,14:1
Drulie, Sylvia (Miscellaneous)
Girls of Summer 1956,N 20,45:1
Good as Gold 1957,Mr 8,22:2
Livin' the Life 1957,Ap 29,20:1
West Side Story 1957,S 27,14:4
Music Man, The 1957,D 20,31:1

Drulie, Sylvia (Miscellaneous)—Cont
Oh Captain! 1958,F 5,21:2
Gang's All Here, The 1959,O 2,23:1
West Side Story 1960,Ap 28,31:1
Drulie, Sylvia (Producer)
Auntie Mame 1958,Ag 12,33:2
Drum, Dorothy
Pleasure Bound 1929,F 19,22:4
Drum, Leonard
Kaleidoscope 1957,Je 14,20:2
On the Town 1959,Ja 16,36:1
O Marry Me 1961,O 28,13:1
Giants' Dance, The 1964,N 17,48:2
Persecution and Assassination of Marat As
  Performed by the Inmates of the Asylum of
  Charenton Under the Direction of the Marquis de
  Sade, The 1967,Ja 4,34:1
Drumm, Julia
Blue Butterfly, The 1929,F 17,29:3
Drumm, Robert (Musical Director)
Kiss Me, Kate 1954,Mr 27,13:2
Drummond, A M (Professor) (Playwright)
Traffic Signals 1937,Ag 7,7:4
Drummond, Alice
Fortunato 1956,Mr 24,15:2
Royal Gambit 1959,Mr 5,34:2
Lysistrata 1959,N 25,19:4
Sudden End of Anne Cinquefoil, The
  1961,Ja 11,25:2
Cicero 1961,F 9,37:2
Go Show Me a Dragon 1961,O 28,18:1
Bertha 1962,F 12,27:1
Toy for the Clowns, A 1962,S 13,31:2
Doll's House, A 1963,F 4,5:6
Blue Boy in Black, The 1963,My 1,32:1
American Dream, The 1963,My 29,39:6
Play 1964,Mr 25,46:2
Giants' Dance, The 1964,N 17,48:2
Malcolm 1966,Ja 12,29:1
Chinese, The 1970,Mr 11,42:2
Chinese, The 1970,Mr 22,II,3:1
In 3 Zones 1970,N 3,28:1
Carpenters, The 1970,D 22,40:1
Drummond, Bob
Ice Capades 1956,S 13,41:2
Drummond, Cecil
Hamlet 1932,N 13,IX,3:8
Drummond, Charles
Valley Forge 1934,D 11,28:3
Drummond, Jack
Pajama Game, The 1954,My 14,20:2
Madame Aphrodite 1961,D 30,13:1
Drummond, T K
Espanola 1921,D 30,13:1
Drummond, Vivienne
Look Back in Anger 1957,O 2,28:2
Look Back in Anger 1957,O 13,II,1:1
Drummond-Grant, Ann
Trial by Jury 1936,S 1,24:4
Gondoliers, The 1936,S 8,23:1
Iolanthe 1936,S 22,30:3
Princess Ida 1936,O 13,32:2
Ruddigore 1936,O 23,26:4
Iolanthe 1955,S 28,38:1
Mikado, The 1955,S 30,20:2
Yeomen of the Guard, The 1955,O 4,39:2
Pirates of Penzance, The 1955,O 7,21:1
Princess Ida 1955,O 14,22:3
H M S Pinafore 1955,O 18,48:1
Ruddigore 1955,O 21,32:2
Drury, Allen (Original Author)
Advise and Consent 1960,O 19,57:3
Advise and Consent 1960,N 18,25:1
Advise and Consent 1960,N 27,II,1:1
Drury, Ann
Romantic Mr Dickens 1940,D 3,33:2
Drury, Charles (Musical Director)
Nellie Bly 1946,Ja 22,32:2
Drury, DeWitt
Creditors 1949,N 22,36:5
Drury, Hazel
Golden Dawn 1927,D 1,32:3
Riddle Me This! 1933,Mr 15,21:3
Potash and Perlmutter 1935,Ap 6,11:3
Drury, J T
Schoolmaster, The 1928,Mr 21,30:1
Drury, Maude
Elsie Janis and Her Gang 1922,Ja 17,13:2
Drute, D
Yegor Bulevitch 1934,Ja 8,21:7
Aristocrats 1935,My 2,16:2
Druyanof, Yael
Children of the Shadows 1964,F 27,26:1
Dryden, Draja
Stage Door 1936,O 23,26:3
Dryden, John (Playwright)
Marriage a la Mode 1930,O 26,VIII,2:1
Tempest, The: or, The Enchanted Forest
  1959,Je 10,42:2
King Arthur 1968,N 3,87:1
Dryden, Robert
Hill Between, The 1938,Mr 12,12:5
Clerambard 1957,N 8,22:3
Night Life 1962,O 24,44:1

Passage to E M Forster, A 1970,O 28,62:1
Dryden, Wheeler
Bridge of Distances, The 1925,S 29,30:1
Morals 1925,D 1,22:2
Great Adventure, The 1926,D 23,23:1
Wings Over Europe 1928,D 11,35:1
Humbug, The 1929,N 28,34:5
Oh, Professor 1930,My 2,19:6
Come of Age 1934,Ja 13,16:6
Touch of Brimstone, A 1935,S 23,20:1
Frederika 1937,F 5,16:5
Three Waltzes 1937,D 27,10:2
Blossom Time 1938,D 27,12:2
Dryden, Wheeler (Director)
Oh, Professor 1930,My 2,19:6
Dryer, Jay (Miscellaneous)
How to Steal an Election 1968,O 14,56:1
Drylie, Pat (Choreographer)
My Fair Lady 1959,Ja 27,26:1
Dryni, Acti
Hippolytus 1968,N 20,38:3
Drysdale, Robert
Hunky Dory 1922,S 5,21:2
Little Minister, The 1925,Mr 24,21:1
Drzic, Marin (Playwright)
Tirena 1959,Ag 19,34:1
D'Sylva, Allan
You Said It 1931,Ja 20,21:3
D'tyl, Utoy
Lulu Belle 1926,F 10,20:1
du Bard, Raphael
Four Saints in Three Acts 1952,Ap 17,35:1
Du Bief, Jacqueline
Ice Capades 1952,S 12,18:1
Hollywood Ice Revue 1954,Ja 15,16:2
du Bois, Albert (Comte) (Playwright)
Herodienne, L' 1924,S 7,III,12:4
Femme d'Amour, La 1927,Je 5,VII,2:1
Du Bois, Raoul Pene (Costume Designer)
Ziegfeld Follies 1934,Ja 5,24:3
Thumbs Up! 1934,D 28,24:1
Jumbo 1935,N 18,20:2
Jumbo 1935,N 24,IX,1:1
Ziegfeld Follies 1936,Ja 5,IX,3:1
Hooray for What! 1937,D 2,32:5
Let's Play Fair 1938,Ja 19,26:4
Two Bouquets, The 1938,Je 1,19:2
Leave It to Me! 1938,N 10,32:2
One for the Money 1939,F 6,9:2
Aquacade 1939,My 5,26:2
Too Many Girls 1939,O 19,26:2
Du Barry 1939,N 19,X,3:4
Du Barry Was a Lady 1939,D 7,34:2
Two for the Show 1940,F 9,14:2
New Aquacade Revue, The 1940,My 13,20:5
Hold On to Your Hats 1940,S 12,30:3
Panama Hattie 1940,O 31,28:2
Liberty Jones 1941,F 6,24:2
Sons o' Fun 1941,D 2,28:2
Carmen Jones 1943,D 3,26:2
Carmen Jones 1943,D 12,II,3:1
Firebird of Florence 1945,Mr 23,13:4
Carmen Jones 1945,My 3,26:5
Carmen Jones 1946,Ap 8,32:2
Heaven on Earth 1948,S 17,29:2
Lend an Ear 1948,D 17,38:2
Alive and Kicking 1950,Ja 18,25:5
Call Me Madam 1950,O 22,II,1:1
Make a Wish 1951,Ap 19,38:1
Night in Venice, A 1952,Je 27,18:6
In Any Language 1952,O 9,40:2
Maggie 1953,F 19,20:2
Wonderful Town 1953,F 26,22:3
Night in Venice, A 1953,Je 26,15:2
Mrs Patterson 1954,D 2,37:1
Hollywood Ice Revue 1955 1955,Ja 14,16:1
Plain and Fancy 1955,Ja 28,14:2
Vamp, The 1955,N 11,30:1
Hollywood Ice Revue 1956,Ja 13,17:1
Carmen Jones 1956,Je 1,28:2
Bells Are Ringing 1956,N 29,43:4
Bells Are Ringing 1956,N 30,18:2
Ziegfeld Follies 1957,Mr 2,19:2
Rosalie 1957,Je 26,28:2
Music Man, The 1957,D 20,31:1
Wonderful Town 1958,Mr 6,32:4
Music Man, The 1958,S 28,II,1:1
Gypsy 1959,My 22,31:6
Gypsy 1959,My 31,II,1:1
Carmen Jones 1959,Ag 18,25:1
Student Gypsy, The; Prince of Liederkranz, The
  1963,O 1,34:1
P S I Love You 1964,N 20,40:1
Music Man, The 1965,Je 17,26:4
Darling of the Day 1968,Ja 29,26:2
Rondelay 1969,N 6,55:1
Du Bois, Raoul Pene (Director)
Alive and Kicking 1950,Ja 18,25:5
Du Bois, Raoul Pene (Lighting Director)
Lend an Ear 1948,D 17,38:2
Maurice Chevalier 1963,Ja 30,7:2
Du Bois, Raoul Pene (Miscellaneous)
Are You With It? 1945,N 12,17:3

Du Bois, Raoul Pene (Scenic Designer)
Thumbs Up! 1934,D 28,24:1
Let's Play Fair 1938,Ja 19,26:4
One for the Money 1939,F 6,9:2
Du Barry Was a Lady 1939,D 7,34:2
Two for the Show 1940,F 9,14:2
New Aquacade Revue, The 1940,My 13,20:5
Hold On to Your Hats 1940,S 12,30:3
Panama Hattie 1940,O 31,28:2
Liberty Jones 1941,F 6,24:2
Sons o' Fun 1941,D 2,28:2
Heaven on Earth 1948,S 17,29:2
Lend an Ear 1948,D 17,38:2
Call Me Madam 1950,O 13,25:1
Call Me Madam 1950,O 22,II,1:1
Make a Wish 1951,Ap 19,38:1
New Faces of 1952 1952,My 17,23:2
New Faces of 1952 1952,My 25,II,1:1
Night in Venice, A 1952,Je 27,18:6
Night in Venice, A 1952,Jl 13,II,1:1
In Any Language 1952,O 9,40:2
Maggie 1953,F 19,20:2
Wonderful Town 1953,Mr 8,II,1:1
Night in Venice, A 1953,Je 26,15:2
John Murray Anderson's Almanac 1953,D 11,42:2
Charley's Aunt 1953,D 23,22:2
Almanac 1954,Ja 3,II,1:1
Mrs Patterson 1954,D 2,37:1
Plain and Fancy 1955,Ja 28,14:2
Vamp, The 1955,N 11,30:1
Bells Are Ringing 1956,N 29,43:4
Bells Are Ringing 1956,N 30,18:2
Ziegfeld Follies 1957,Mr 2,19:2
Rosalie 1957,Je 26,28:2
Wonderful Town 1958,Mr 6,32:4
Maurice Chevalier 1963,Ja 30,7:2
Wonderful Town 1963,F 15,10:2
Student Gypsy, The; Prince of Liederkranz, The
  1963,O 1,34:1
P S I Love You 1964,N 20,40:1
Where's Charley? 1966,My 26,57:1
Wonderful Town 1967,My 18,50:1
Rondelay 1969,N 6,55:1
Du Bois, William (Playwright)
Pirate, The 1929,Ap 21,IX,1:4
Pagan Lady 1930,S 28,VIII,4:1
Pagan Lady 1930,O 21,34:2
I Loved You Wednesday 1932,O 12,27:1
Curse You, Jack Dalton 1935,Jl 16,24:1
Left Turn 1936,Jl 7,22:3
Haiti 1938,Mr 3,16:1
Michael Drops In 1938,D 28,24:3
Du Brock, Neal (Producer)
Box-Mao-Box; Quotations From Chairman Mao
  Tse-Tung 1968,Mr 8,48:1
Box-Mao-Box; Box 1968,Mr 8,48:1
du Chailu-Dalton, F
Dove, The 1925,F 12,17:3
Du Chette, Marie
Two Orphans, The 1926,Ap 6,26:2
Du-For, Denis (Producer)
Thoroughbred 1933,N 7,29:2
Broadway Interlude 1934,Ap 20,16:3
Popsy 1941,F 11,26:2
Du For Brothers, The
Vaudeville (Palace) 1924,Ja 1,21:1
Du Frayne, Jane
Four Twelves Are 48 1951,Ja 18,30:2
Du Kore, Lawrence
Automobile Graveyard, The 1961,N 14,46:2
du Maurier, Daphne (Original Author)
Rebecca 1945,Ja 19,17:2
Rebecca 1945,Ja 28,II,1:2
du Maurier, Daphne (Playwright)
Rebecca 1942,My 31,VIII,2:3
Rebecca 1944,Ap 30,II,1:1
Rebecca 1945,Ja 19,17:2
Rebecca 1945,Ja 28,II,1:2
September Tide 1948,D 16,39:5
September Tide 1949,Ja 9,II,3:7
du Maurier, George (Original Author)
Peter Ibbetson 1926,Mr 26,24:7
Peter Ibbetson 1931,Ap 9,30:3
Trilby 1958,Ja 9,40:3
du Maurier, Gerald
Not in Our Stars 1924,F 10,VII,2:4
Interference 1927,F 27,VII,1:3
Return Journey 1928,S 9,III,3:5
Return Journey, The 1928,S 23,IX,1:3
Play's the Thing, The 1928,D 23,VIII,4:7
Fame 1929,Mr 10,X,4:6
Cynara 1930,Jl 13,VIII,1:3
Behold We Live 1932,Ag 17,13:2
Behold We Live 1932,S 11,IX,1:1
du Maurier, Gerald (Playwright)
Dancers, The 1923,F 25,VII,1:7
Dancers, The 1923,O 18,17:2
Dancers, The 1923,O 28,VIII,1:1
du Maurier, Gerald (Producer)
Interference 1927,F 20,VII,1:4
Fame 1929,Mr 10,X,4:6
Du Moulin, Francoise
Katerina 1929,F 26,30:3

Du Plantier, T D
If Booth Had Missed 1931,My 14,27:1
du Pont, Paul
Royal Family, The 1940,Ag 13,15:3
Five Alarm Waltz 1941,Mr 14,16:2
Porgy and Bess 1942,Ja 23,16:2
du Pont, Paul (Costume Designer)
Johnny Johnson 1936,N 20,26:3
Another Sun 1940,F 24,8:6
Retreat to Pleasure 1940,D 18,32:2
Kiss for Cinderella, A 1942,Mr 11,22:2
Strings, My Lord, Are False, The 1942,My 20,24:2
All the Comforts of Home 1942,My 26,24:5
Chocolate Soldier, The 1942,Je 24,22:2
Let Freedom Sing 1942,O 6,18:2
Time, Place and the Girl, The 1942,O 22,24:3
Stars on Ice (2d Edition) 1943,Je 25,13:2
Porgy and Bess 1943,S 14,26:2
One Touch of Venus 1943,O 8,14:1
Porgy and Bess 1944,F 8,13:2
Pretty Little Parlor 1944,Ap 18,24:8
Anna Lucasta 1944,Ag 31,15:1
Diamond Lil 1948,N 30,33:2
Diamond Lil 1949,F 7,16:2
All You Need Is One Good Break 1950,F 10,20:3
Parisienne 1950,Jl 25,24:2
Lady From the Sea, The 1950,Ag 8,23:2
Borned in Texas 1950,Ag 22,30:6
Oh, Men! Oh, Women! 1953,D 18,37:2
Brigadoon 1957,Mr 28,37:1
Merry Widow, The 1957,Ap 11,36:6
du Pont, Paul (Miscellaneous)
Porgy and Bess 1942,Ja 23,16:2
du Pont, Paul (Scenic Designer)
Royal Family, The 1940,Ag 13,15:3
Du Pont, William
Pearl of Great Price, The 1926,N 2,34:3
Wild Duck, The 1928,N 19,17:1
Subway Express 1929,S 25,34:3
du Ponts, The
Vaudeville (Palace) 1926,My 8,29:2
Vaudeville (Loew's State) 1932,Jl 18,9:7
du Pury, Marianne (Composer)
Motel 1966,N 7,66:1
TV 1966,N 7,66:1
Interview 1966,N 7,66:1
du Reis, Costa (Playwright)
King's Standards, The 1958,F 14,19:1
du Rodier, Jacqueline
Jane-Our Stranger 1925,O 9,27:2
Du Sablon
Bourgeois Gentilhomme, Le 1955,O 26,26:1
Duane, Dick (Producer)
Stop, You're Killing Me; Terrible Jim Fitch 1969,Mr 20,53:1
Stop, You're Killing Me; Laughs, Etc 1969,Mr 20,53:1
Stop, You're Killing Me; Bad Bad Jo-Jo 1969,Mr 20,53:1
Duane, E L
Like a King 1921,O 4,10:1
Duane, Edward
Romance 1921,Mr 1,18:2
Duane, Frank (Playwright)
Guitar 1959,N 11,42:5
Duane, Jed
Cyanamide 1954,Mr 26,17:6
Comrades 1956,Je 6,38:1
Duane, Jed (Director)
He Who Gets Slapped 1956,F 2,18:1
World's My Oyster, The 1956,Ag 10,10:4
Duane, Jed (Producer)
Out of This World 1955,O 13,35:2
Comrades 1956,Je 6,38:1
Duane, Jed (Translator)
He Who Gets Slapped 1956,F 2,18:1
Duane, Jerry
Are You With It? 1945,N 12,17:3
Duane, Margaret
Ten Nights in a Barroom 1928,Mr 28,31:2
Duane, Michael (Pvt)
Winged Victory 1943,N 22,24:1
Duart, Carl
Smiling Faces 1932,Ag 31,12:3
Duarte, Lima
Arena Conta Zumbi 1969,Ag 19,31:1
Duarte, Manuel
Tavern, The 1930,My 20,32:1
Song and Dance Man, The 1930,Je 17,25:5
Frankie and Johnny 1930,S 26,16:5
Duberman, Martin (Playwright)
In White America 1963,N 1,26:1
In White America 1965,F 9,42:5
Collision Course; Metaphors 1968,My 9,55:2
Memory Bank, The 1970,Ja 12,24:3
Memory Bank, The 1970,Ja 25,II,1:4
Duberstein, Wilbur
Cocktails of 1934 1934,My 5,22:1
Dubey, Matt (Composer)
New Faces of 1956 1956,Je 15,32:1
Dubey, Matt (Lyricist)
New Faces of 1956 1956,Je 15,32:1
Happy Hunting 1956,D 7,30:1

Happy Hunting 1956,D 16,II,3:1
Dubin, Al (Composer)
Streets of Paris, The 1939,Je 20,25:2
Star and Garter 1942,Je 25,26:2
Dubin, Al (Lyricist)
White Lights 1927,O 12,30:4
Keep Off the Grass 1940,My 24,22:6
Star and Garter 1942,Je 25,26:2
Dubin, Charles S
Secret Room, The 1945,N 8,16:2
Dubin, Charles S (Director)
Semi-Detached 1960,Mr 11,20:2
Dubin, Jeannette
Gods Are Wise, The 1930,My 6,33:1
Dubinsky, Vladimir
Excess Baggage 1927,D 27,24:2
Dubinsky, Yudel
Witch of Castile, The 1930,O 25,21:1
Man With the Portfolio, The 1931,F 12,24:6
Yoina Seeks a Bride 1936,O 20,31:1
'Round the Family Table 1938,O 8,10:3
Chaver, Nachman 1939,O 2,15:2
Song of Dnieper 1946,O 26,10:5
Shylock and His Daughter 1947,S 30,22:2
Voice of Israel, The 1948,O 26,40:2
Hershel, The Jester 1948,D 14,39:2
Yosele the Nightingale 1949,O 21,30:4
Shepherd King, The 1955,O 13,36:2
Brothers Ashkenazi, The 1955,N 12,24:4
Devil's Game, A 1959,N 9,35:6
Going to America 1961,O 30,33:7
Dublin, Charles S
Signature 1945,F 15,25:2
Dublin, Elizabeth
Knight of the Burning Pestle, The 1927,Ap 23,15:1
Dublin, Mary
Knight of the Burning Pestle, The 1927,Ap 23,15:1
What of It? 1929,Mr 9,24:2
Dublyn, Darren
Nathan the Wise 1942,Mr 12,25:4
Nathan the Wise 1944,F 22,26:3
Duboc, Zezinha
Arena Conta Zumbi 1969,Ag 19,31:1
DuBois, Jeannette
Golden Boy 1964,O 21,56:1
Reckoning, The 1969,S 5,28:1
Reckoning, The 1969,S 14,II,1:3
Reckoning, The 1969,S 14,II,1:1
Dubois, Lona
Professor Bernhardi 1968,Mr 20,38:1
Konzert, Das 1968,Mr 25,52:1
Maria Stuart 1968,Mr 27,38:1
DuBois, Wilfred
Vaudeville (Loew's State) 1932,O 3,15:5
Dubosq, Lucien
Procureur Hallers, Le 1924,N 13,18:1
Homme et Ses Fantomes, L' 1924,N 14,16:1
Bourgeois Gentilhomme, Le 1924,N 20,21:2
Taming of the Shrew, The 1924,N 25,27:3
Dubravina, Xenia
Uncle Vanya 1960,F 13,13:4
Dubro, Bette
My Darlin' Aida 1952,O 28,36:4
Dubrow, Esther
Farblondjete Honeymoon 1955,S 27,42:1
Going to America 1961,O 30,33:7
Honeymoon in Israel, A 1962,O 15,33:5
Don't Worry Brother! 1963,O 14,35:2
Oh What a Wedding! 1969,O 20,60:1
Dubrow, Vity
Devil's Game, A 1959,N 9,35:6
Going to America 1961,O 30,33:7
Honeymoon in Israel, A 1962,O 15,33:5
Don't Worry Brother! 1963,O 14,35:2
Duby, Jacques
How to Succeed in Business Without Really Trying; Comment Reussir Dans les Affaires Sans Vraiment Se Fatiguer 1964,F 12,30:1
Ducaux, Annie
Tombeau Sous l'Arc de Triomphe 1929,Je 16,VIII,2:3
Napoleon Unique 1936,N 13,27:3
Tartuffe 1961,Mr 1,28:1
Britannicus 1961,Mr 3,17:1
Duchaussoy, Michel
Avare, L', L'; Miser, The 1966,F 9,32:1
Cid, Le 1966,F 12,17:1
Reine Morte, La 1966,F 16,52:1
Fil a la Paite, Un 1966,F 18,25:1
Duchesne, Andree
Court Circuit, Le 1923,O 16,18:1
Au Coin Joli 1923,O 23,16:1
Duchinsky (Original Author)
Statisterna 1931,O 11,VIII,4:6
Duckat, Lipman
Panama Hattie 1940,O 31,28:2
Duckler, Marvin (Lighting Director)
Opening of a Window, The 1961,S 26,32:2
Duckworth, Dortha
White Flame 1929,N 5,32:7
Caught Wet 1931,N 5,29:1
Goodbye Again 1932,D 29,16:4
Stork Mad 1936,O 1,28:4

Apron Strings 1937,Jl 13,22:3
Ten Minute Alibi 1937,Jl 20,19:3
She Gave Him All She Had 1939,D 2,20:7
Little Women 1945,D 24,18:2
Craig's Wife 1947,F 13,35:2
Craig's Wife 1947,Mr 30,II,1:1
Hot Corner, The 1956,Ja 26,25:2
Greenwillow 1960,Mr 9,38:1
Call Me by My Rightful Name 1961,F 1,31:1
Oliver 1963,Ja 8,5:5
Flora, the Red Menace 1965,My 12,41:2
Indians 1969,O 14,51:1
Place for Polly, A 1970,Ap 20,45:1
Duckworth, Joe
Backslapper, The 1925,Ap 13,25:2
First Flight 1925,S 18,26:2
Duckworth, Loretta
Ruy Blas 1957,D 14,16:3
Duckworth, Willard
Bridal Crown, The 1938,F 7,11:2
Duclos, Albert
Love's Labour's Lost 1953,F 5,20:3
Merchant of Venice, The 1953,Mr 5,20:2
Duclos, Estelle
Au Rat Mort, Cabinet No 6 1923,O 16,18:1
Duclow, Douglas C
Burning Bush, The 1949,D 17,15:5
Scapegoat, The 1950,Ap 20,36:5
Home Is Tomorrow 1950,Je 2,27:2
Ducovny, Amram (Playwright)
Trial of Lee Harvey Oswald, The 1967,N 6,64:1
Ducret, Mauricette
Dancing Partner 1930,Ag 6,24:2
Belmont Varieties 1932,S 29,17:2
Ducrox, Pierre (Playwright)
Van Dyck, The 1921,O 12,18:2
Duddy, James
Riddle Me This! 1932,F 26,22:5
Duddy, Lyn (Composer)
Tickets, Please! 1950,Ap 28,25:2
Duddy, Lyn (Lyricist)
Tickets, Please! 1950,Ap 28,25:2
Duddy, Neil
My Beginning 1962,Ja 31,21:1
Dudek, Stan
Aquashow 1954,Je 23,20:4
Elliott Murphy's Aquashow 1955,Je 23,25:1
Elliott Murphy's Aquashow 1955,Je 20,26:2
Aquarama 1960 1960,Jl 1,14:6
Dudeney (Mrs) (Original Author)
Old House, The 1920,Jl 11,VI,1:6
Dudgeon, Dorothy
Evil Doers of Good, The 1923,Ja 17,22:2
Dudgeon, Elspeth
Bellamy Trial, The 1928,Ag 20,21:1
Dudicourt, Marc
Jeune Fille a Marier, La 1970,My 6,49:1
Dudley, Alice
Caviar 1934,Je 8,19:2
Thumbs Up! 1934,D 28,24:1
May Wine 1935,D 30,3
Walk With Music 1940,Je 5,33:2
Count Me In 1942,O 9,24:2
Dudley, Arthur
Good Hunting 1938,N 22,26:5
Dudley, Bernard
Merry World, The 1926,Je 9,18:3
Earl Carroll's Vanities 1926,Ag 25,19:4
Dudley, Bessie
Vaudeville (Hollywood) 1932,F 16,24:3
Vaudeville (Palace) 1932,My 23,18:7
Dudley, Bide (Lyricist)
Sue, Dear 1922,Jl 11,16:2
Dudley, Bide (Playwright)
Oh, Henry! 1920,My 6,14:2
Sue, Dear 1922,Jl 11,16:2
Bye Bye Bonnie 1927,Ja 14,15:3
Borrowed Love 1929,Je 18,29:2
Dudley, Bronson
Set to Music 1939,Ja 19,16:2
Dudley, Doris
Stick-in-the-Mud 1935,D 2,18:2
Season Changes, The 1935,D 24,10:2
End of Summer 1936,Ja 31,17:1
End of Summer 1936,F 18,26:4
Here Come the Clowns 1938,D 8,36:2
My Dear Children 1939,My 3,26:4
My Dear Children 1939,S 10,IX,1:6
My Dear Children 1940,F 1,16:2
Rose Burke 1942,Ja 25,IX,2:5
Dudley, Frank
Rose in the Wilderness 1949,Ja 5,21:2
Dudley, George Jr
Medea 1960,Jl 26,25:2
Dudley, Helen
Man on Stilts, The 1931,S 10,23:2
Dudley, Jacqueline
Cretan Woman, The 1954,My 21,17:2
Dudley, Jane
Manhattan Varieties 1932,O 22,18:3
Dudley, John
Mikado, The 1939,Ja 10,16:3
H. M. S. Pinafore 1939,Ja 17,27:5

Dudley, John—Cont
Gondoliers, The 1939,Ja 20,14:2
Pirates of Penzance, The 1946,My 17,14:6
Pirates of Penzance, The 1946,S 21,19:2
Madame Is Served 1949,F 15,28:1
Dudley, Mrs
Poisoned Kiss, The 1937,Ap 22,19:1
Dudley, Renee
110 in the Shade 1963,O 25,37:1
Dudley, Robert
Billy Budd 1951,F 12,18:3
Dudley, Sidney
Exciters, The 1922,S 23,10:4
Dudley-Ward, Penelope
Victoria Regina 1937,Je 22,26:2
Victoria Regina 1937,Jl 11,X,1:7
Due, Auda
Valley of Content, The 1925,Ja 14,19:2
Duell, William
Threepenny Opera, The 1954,Mr 11,26:5
Threepenny Opera, The 1955,S 21,38:1
Threepenny Opera, The 1956,Mr 11,II,1:1
Cook for Mr General, A 1961,O 20,39:1
Ballad of the Sad Cafe, The 1963,O 31,27:1
Midsummer Night's Dream, A 1964,Je 30,23:2
Henry V 1965,Je 29,27:2
Illya Darling 1967,Ap 12,37:1
Memorandum, The 1968,My 6,55:1
Romeo and Juliet 1968,Ag 16,19:1
Front Page, The 1968,O 20,85:5
1776 1969,Mr 17,46:2
Duenwihe, Robert
Hit the Deck! 1927,Ap 26,32:1
Duer, Shoshana
Dybbuk, The 1948,My 3,26:3
David's Crown 1948,My 10,26:2
Golem, The 1948,My 17,22:3
Oedipus Rex 1948,My 24,23:2
Duerr, Donald
Tree Grows in Brooklyn, A 1951,Ap 20,24:3
Duerrenmatt, Friedrich (Original Author)
Deadly Game, The 1960,Ja 31,II,1:7
Deadly Game, The 1960,F 3,27:2
Duerrenmatt, Friedrich (Playwright)
Fools Are Passing Through 1958,Ap 3,24:2
Visit, The 1958,My 6,40:1
Visit, The 1958,My 18,II,1:1
Visit, The 1958,S 7,II,1:1
Visit, The 1958,N 16,II,1:1
Visit, The 1960,Mr 9,38:3
Jackass, The 1960,Mr 24,39:2
Visit, The 1960,Je 25,13:5
Romulus the Great 1960,Ag 25,24:3
Romulus 1962,Ja 11,27:1
Angel Comes to Babylon, An 1962,S 29,15:2
Romulus the Great 1964,Ap 30,29:1
Physicists, The 1964,O 14,52:1
Physicists, The 1964,O 25,II,1:1
Deadly Game, The 1966,F 14,34:1
Visit, The 1967,S 13,41:1
Marriage of Mr Mississippi, The 1969,N 20,60:5
Dueth, Celeste
Connecticut Yankee, A 1927,N 4,24:2
Dufac
Cloches de Cornville, Les; Chimes of Normandy,
The 1926,D 14,24:4
Dufallo, Richard (Miscellaneous)
Peter and the Wolf 1969,N 30,85:5
Duff, Amanda
Tovarich 1936,O 16,31:4
Duff, Cara
Watch-Pit 1969,Ja 30,39:1
Duff, Donald
Wild Birds 1925,Ap 10,16:1
Makropoulos Secret, The 1926,Ja 22,12:4
Stigma 1927,F 11,19:1
Duff, Donald (Playwright)
Stigma 1927,F 11,19:1
Duff, Donald (Producer)
Stigma 1927,F 11,19:1
Duff, Gordon
Mr and Mrs North 1941,Ja 13,11:2
Duff, Sadie
Innocent Idea, An 1920,My 26,9:4
Duff, William
With a Silk Thread 1950,Ap 13,34:3
Duffey, Gordon (Composer)
Happy Town 1959,O 8,49:2
Duffey, Gordon (Director)
Flight of Lindbergh, The 1969,My 26,55:2
Lesson in Consent, A 1969,My 26,55:2
Ceremonial Dance to Which There Is No End, A
1969,My 26,55:2
Persians, The 1970,Ap 16,53:1
Duffey, Gordon (Playwright)
Ceremonial Dance to Which There Is No End, A
1969,My 26,55:2
Duffey, Gordon (Producer)
Persians, The 1970,Ap 26,II,1:3
Duffey, J Humbird
Three Musketeers, The 1921,My 20,18:5
Chocolate Soldier, The 1921,D 13,24:2
Iolanthe 1926,Ap 20,24:2

Pirates of Penzance, The; Slave of Duty, The
1926,D 7,25:1
Mikado, The; Town of Titipu, The 1927,S 19,30:1
Sari 1930,Ja 29,27:1
Duffey, Vincent (Playwright)
Mystery Man, The 1928,Ja 27,14:2
Greatest Show on Earth, The 1938,Ja 6,22:2
Duffield, Brainerd
Private Life of the Master Race, The
1945,Je 13,28:3
Around the World 1946,Je 1,9:5
Macbeth 1947,My 30,25:1
Duffield, Malcolm
Pickwick 1927,S 6,35:2
Duffield, Pitts (Playwright)
Fan, The 1921,O 4,10:1
Duffin, Joan B
Greenwillow 1970,D 8,60:1
Duffin, Matt
Sketch Book 1935,Je 5,22:2
Duffy, Benedict A Jr
Once Over Lightly 1938,D 10,13:4
Duffy, Benedict J
Many a Slip 1940,N 16,12:7
Duffy, Bernard (Playwright)
Cupboard Love 1929,D 1,X,4:4
Spell, The 1930,Mr 23,4:3
Coiner, The 1934,N 22,26:2
Duffy, Elsie
Everybody's Welcome 1931,O 14,26:3
Duffy, Gus (Scenic Designer)
She Gave Him All She Had 1939,D 2,20:7
Duffy, Henry
Wonderful Thing, The 1920,F 18,9:1
Wait Till We're Married 1921,S 27,14:1
Duffy, Henry (Producer)
Coquette 1935,My 22,23:4
Quiet, Please! 1940,O 20,IX,2:3
Music in My Heart 1947,O 3,30:2
Duffy, Herbert
Diamond Lil 1928,Ap 10,32:1
Passing Present, The 1931,D 8,36:2
Blessed Event 1932,F 13,23:2
Another Language 1932,Ap 26,25:3
Another Language 1933,My 9,20:2
Small Miracle 1934,S 27,24:3
Caesar and Cleopatra 1935,Ag 22,21:1
Tomorrow's a Holiday! 1935,D 31,10:2
Fields Beyond, The 1936,Mr 7,11:2
Sweet River 1936,O 29,30:2
Call Me Ziggy 1937,F 13,9:6
Boy Meets Girl 1937,Jl 6,23:1
There's Always a Breeze 1938,Mr 3,16:2
Case of Youth, A 1940,Mr 25,10:3
More the Merrier, The 1941,S 16,19:3
Land Is Bright, The 1941,O 29,26:2
What Big Ears! 1942,Ap 21,18:5
Sun Field, The 1942,D 10,33:2
Duffy, Jimmy
Earl Carroll's Vanities 1923,Jl 6,8:2
Keep It Clean 1929,Je 25,35:5
Duffy, Jimmy (Composer)
Keep It Clean 1929,Je 25,35:5
Duffy, Jimmy (Lyricist)
Keep It Clean 1929,Je 25,35:5
Duffy, Jimmy (Playwright)
Earl Carroll's Vanities 1925,Jl 7,24:1
Keep It Clean 1929,Je 25,35:5
Duffy, John (Composer)
Ginger Man, The 1963,N 22,42:1
Hamlet 1964,Jl 4,9:1
Taming of the Shrew, The 1965,Je 24,32:2
Falstaff 1966,Je 20,27:1
MacBird! 1967,F 23,38:1
Antigone 1967,Je 19,43:1
Macbeth 1967,Jl 31,21:1
Carving a Statue 1968,My 1,43:1
Richard II 1968,Je 24,42:3
Horseman, Pass By 1969,Ja 16,46:4
Dream of a Blacklisted Actor 1969,D 18,64:1
Duffy, John (Lyricist)
Ginger Man, The 1963,N 22,42:1
Taming of the Shrew, The 1965,Je 24,32:2
Falstaff 1966,Je 20,27:1
MacBird! 1967,F 23,38:1
Duffy, John (Musical Director)
Midsummer Night's Dream, A 1967,Je 19,42:1
Merchant of Venice, The 1967,Je 22,46:2
Macbeth 1967,Jl 31,21:1
Richard II 1968,Je 24,42:3
Androcles and the Lion 1968,Je 27,47:1
Love's Labour's Lost 1968,Je 28,36:1
Duffy, John (Playwright)
Horseman, Pass By 1969,Ja 16,46:4
Duffy, Ray
All the King's Men 1963,Jl 12,12:1
Duffy, Ray (Miscellaneous)
All the King's Men 1963,Jl 12,12:1
Duffy, William
Caution: A Love Story 1969,Ap 4,45:1
Duffy, William (Producer)
Keep It Clean 1929,Je 25,35:5

Duffy, William Griffin
Ubu Roi 1970,F 17,33:1
Arden of Faversham 1970,F 17,33:1
Duffy (Mr) (Producer)
Autumn Crocus 1934,Ja 21,X,1:6
DuFine, Herbert (Miscellaneous)
Threepenny Opera, The 1955,S 21,38:1
Roots 1961,Mr 7,40:2
Duflac
Perichole, La 1926,D 29,24:4
Duflos, Huguette (Mme)
Nicole et Sa Vertu 1927,O 30,IX,4:7
Miss France 1930,Ap 13,X,2:7
DuFor, Denis (Producer)
Howdy Stranger 1937,Ja 15,17:5
Dufors, The
Vaudeville (Palace) 1926,N 2,35:2
Dufour, Val
Babes in Arms 1951,Mr 10,7:3
Grass Harp, The 1952,Mr 28,26:2
Frankie and Johnny 1952,O 29,37:2
Abie's Irish Rose 1954,N 19,19:1
Dufrann, Georges
Merry Widow, The 1921,S 6,13:1
Dufrene, Alice
Pas Avec l'Amour 1926,Ap 14,20:2
Dufton, Bill (Playwright)
Boswell's Life of Johnson 1970,S 4,19:1
Dufy, Henry (Producer)
Quiet, Please! 1940,N 9,20:3
Dufy, Raoul (Miscellaneous)
Ring Around the Moon 1950,N 24,30:1
Duga, Don (Miscellaneous)
Moon Walk 1970,N 27,52:1
Duga, Irene (Miscellaneous)
Moon Walk 1970,N 27,52:1
Dugan, Dan (Miscellaneous)
Hamlet 1968,Je 10,59:1
Dugan, Dennis
Tom Paine 1969,Mr 30,71:2
Dugan, Jack
Lady Fingers 1929,F 1,22:4
Dugan, John
Lazarus Laughed 1948,Ap 9,27:4
Dugan, John T (Playwright)
Martyr Without Tears 1942,N 23,19:2
Dugan, Lawrence (Playwright)
Dick Whittington and His Remarkable Cat
1950,N 25,10:5
Dugan, Lawrence Joseph (Playwright)
Once Upon a Time 1939,D 21,28:2
Dugan, Leo
Rainbow 1928,N 22,25:1
Dugan, Virginia (Playwright)
Dick Whittington and His Remarkable Cat
1950,N 25,10:5
Dugan, William
Fuente Ovejuna; Sheep Well, The 1936,My 3,II,4:1
Dugan, William F (Playwright)
Tantrum, The 1924,My 18,VII,2:4
Tantrum, The 1924,S 5,20:2
Dugan, William Francis (Director)
Virgin Man, The 1927,Ja 19,20:4
Dugan, William Francis (Playwright)
Thrills 1925,Ap 17,24:3
Virgin Man, The 1927,Ja 19,20:4
Dugas, Katherine
Country Wife, The 1955,Ap 6,35:1
Comic Strip 1958,My 15,26:2
Duggan, Andrew
Innocents, The 1950,F 2,30:2
Rose Tattoo, The 1951,F 5,19:2
Gently Does It 1953,O 29,43:4
Anniversary Waltz 1954,Ap 8,34:1
Fragile Fox 1954,O 13,27:1
Third Best Sport 1958,D 31,15:3
Duggan, Dan (Miscellaneous)
Hair 1970,Ja 13,39:1
Duggan, Henry
Broken Wing, The 1920,N 30,14:1
Duggan, Jan
Drunkard, The 1936,S 20,IX,3:4
Duggan, Norman
Chauve-Souris; Queen of Spades, The
1931,O 22,27:1
Hotel Alimony 1934,Ja 30,16:2
Duggan, Thomas
Silks and Satins 1920,Jl 16,19:1
Duggan, Thomas (Playwright)
Silks and Satins 1920,Jl 16,19:1
Barber Had Two Sons, The 1943,F 2,22:2
Duggan, Walter
Scarlet Letter, The 1926,Ja 8,16:5
Trumpet Shall Sound, The 1926,D 11,15:2
Duguid, Peter
Lark, The 1955,My 13,21:2
Duhamel, Marcel (Translator)
Mister Roberts 1951,F 9,20:7
Dukakis, Olympia
Breaking Wall, The 1960,Ja 26,27:5
Opening of a Window, The 1961,S 26,32:2
Man's a Man, A 1962,S 20,30:2
Crime and Crime 1963,D 17,51:2

Dukakis, Olympia—Cont

Abraham Cochrane 1964,F 18,26:1
Electra 1964,Ag 12,42:1
Titus Andronicus 1967,Ag 10,43:2
Father Uxbridge Wants to Marry 1967,O 30,57:1
Memorandum, The 1968,My 6,55:1
Peer Gynt 1969,Jl 17,56:1

Dukas, James

Passion of Gross, The 1955,Ja 24,20:2
Tartuffe 1957,O 9,39:1
Last Analysis, The 1964,O 2,30:1
Incident at Vichy 1964,D 4,44:1
Condemned of Altona, The 1966,F 4,21:1
Don't Drink the Water 1966,N 18,37:1
Patriot for Me, A 1969,O 6,58:1

Duke, Bill

Slave Ship 1969,N 22,46:1
Day of Absence 1970,Mr 18,39:1

Duke, Harriett

Americans in France, The 1920,Ag 4,14:1

Duke, Milton (Lighting Director)

That 5 A.M. Jazz 1964,O 20,42:2

Duke, Milton (Scenic Designer)

Local Stigmatic, The 1969,N 4,55:2
Local Stigmatic, The; Applicant 1969,N 4,55:2
Local Stigmatic, The; That's Your Trouble 1969,N 4,55:2
Local Stigmatic, The; Interview 1969,N 4,55:2
Local Stigmatic, The; Request Stop 1969,N 4,55:2
Local Stigmatic, The; That's All 1969,N 4,55:2
Local Stigmatic, The; Trouble in the Works 1969,N 4,55:2
Local Stigmatic, The; Last to Go 1969,N 4,55:2

Duke, Patty

Miracle Worker, The 1959,O 20,44:1
Miracle Worker, The 1959,N 1,II,1:1
Miracle Worker, The 1959,D 20,II,5:1
Miracle Worker, The 1961,F 7,40:2
Isle of Children 1962,Mr 17,16:2

Duke, Paul

Stars on Ice 1942,Jl 3,12:2
Stars on Ice (2d Edition) 1943,Je 25,13:2
Anna Russell and Her Little Show 1953,S 8,27:2

Duke, Robert

Winter's Tale, The 1946,Ja 16,18:6
Antony and Cleopatra 1947,N 27,49:2
Anne of the Thousand Days 1948,D 9,49:2
Romeo and Juliet 1951,Mr 12,21:2
Gertie 1952,Ja 31,23:1
Sabrina Fair 1953,N 12,37:1
Henry V 1956,Jl 7,11:2
Eugenia 1957,Ja 31,20:1
Miss Isobel 1957,D 27,22:1

Duke, Robert (Playwright)

If the Shoe Fits 1946,D 6,29:4

Duke, Vernon

Tars and Spars 1944,Ap 7,23:1

Duke, Vernon (Composer)

Garrick Gaieties 1930,Je 5,29:2
Walk a Little Faster 1932,D 8,24:4
Ziegfeld Follies 1936,Ja 5,IX,3:1
Ziegfeld Follies 1936,Ja 31,17:2
Ziegfeld Follies 1936,S 15,37:1
Show Is On, The 1936,N 15,XI,2:1
Show Is On, The 1936,D 26,14:2
White Plume, The 1939,D 27,16:1
It Happens on Ice 1940,O 11,24:3
Cabin in the Sky 1940,O 26,19:2
Cabin in the Sky 1940,N 3,IX,1:1
Banjo Eyes 1941,N 8,10:6
Banjo Eyes 1941,D 26,20:2
Lady Comes Across, The 1942,Ja 10,10:2
Jackpot 1944,Ja 14,15:2
Sadie Thompson 1944,N 17,25:2
Sadie Thompson 1944,N 26,II,1:1
Two's Company 1952,D 16,43:5
Two's Company 1952,D 21,II,3:1
Littlest Revue, The 1956,My 23,37:2
Time Remembered 1957,N 13,41:2
Cabin in the Sky 1964,Ja 22,32:1

Duke, Vernon (Lyricist)

Ziegfeld Follies 1934,Ja 5,24:3
Show Is On, The 1936,D 26,14:2
Show Is On, The 1937,S 20,18:4
Banjo Eyes 1941,N 8,10:6
Lady Comes Across, The 1942,Ja 10,10:2
Littlest Revue, The 1956,My 23,37:2
Time Remembered 1957,N 13,41:2

Duke, Vernon (Playwright)

Ziegfeld Follies 1934,Ja 5,24:3

Duke, Walter

Make Me Know It 1929,N 5,32:5
Conjur' Man Dies 1936,Mr 12,18:5
Case of Philip Lawrence, The 1937,Je 9,31:1
One-Act Plays of the Sea; In the Zone 1937,O 30,23:2
One-Act Plays of the Sea; Moon of the Caribbees 1937,O 30,23:2
One-Act Plays of the Sea; Long Voyage Home, The 1937,O 30,23:2

Duke Ellington and his orchestra

Elliott Murphy's Aquashow 1955,Je 23,25:1

Duke of Iron

Caribbean Carnival 1947,D 6,12:2

Dukes, Ashley (Director)

Mandragola 1949,Ja 25,26:6

Dukes, Ashley (Playwright)

Man With a Load of Mischief, The 1925,O 27,20:1
Man With a Load of Mischief, The 1925,N 1,VIII,1:1
Mozart 1926,N 23,26:2
Patriot, The 1928,Ja 20,15:1
Such Men Are Dangerous 1928,O 7,IX,2:7
Jew Suess 1929,O 6,IX,1:3
Josef Suss 1930,Ja 21,28:5
Elizabeth of England 1931,O 18,VIII,1:3
Vintage Wine 1934,Je 24,IX,1:4
Mask of Virtue, The 1935,My 16,20:1
Mask of Virtue, The 1935,Je 9,IX,1:1
Parisienne 1950,Jl 25,24:2
Mandragola 1956,Mr 1,36:4
Man With a Load of Mischief, The 1966,N 7,65:1

Dukes, Ashley (Producer)

Murder in the Cathedral 1935,N 2,12:2
In Theatre Street 1937,Ap 29,17:5
Murder in the Cathedral 1938,F 17,16:2

Dukes, Ashley (Translator)

From Morn to Midnight 1922,My 22,17:2
From Morn Till Midnight 1948,D 7,41:6

Dukes, David

Hamlet 1968,Je 10,59:1
Murderous Angels 1970,F 8,70:1
In 3 Zones 1970,N 3,28:1

Dukore, Lawrence

Lower Depths, The 1956,O 3,29:2
Kumquat in the Persimmon Tree, The 1962,Je 19,27:2

Dukore, Phyllis (Miscellaneous)

Applause 1970,Mr 31,35:1

Dulac, Simone

Sexe Fort, Le 1927,F 13,VII,4:1
Femme Dans un Lit, Une 1928,Ja 15,VIII,2:3

Dulaski, Ilona

Stephen D 1966,Ag 5,17:1

Dullaghan, John

Recruiting Officer, The 1958,F 8,12:2

Dullea, Keir

Season of Choice 1959,Ap 14,40:1
Dr Cook's Garden 1967,S 26,52:1
Butterflies Are Free 1969,O 22,30:1
Butterflies Are Free 1969,N 2,II,1:1
Butterflies Are Free 1970,N 5,60:4

Dullin, Charles

Volpone 1928,D 9,X,2:7
Carnaval des Enfants, Le 1930,Mr 2,IX,4:2
Fils de Don Quichotte, Le 1930,N 2,VIII,2:1
Musse 1930,D 14,IX,2:7
Untitled-Play 1931,N 15,VIII,2:1
Paix, La 1933,Ja 15,IX,2:1
Richard III 1933,D 3,IX,7:7
Frenetiques, Les 1935,Ja 13,IX,2:1
Faiseur, Le 1936,Ja 12,IX,3:7

Dullin, Charles (Producer)

Veau Gras, Le 1924,Mr 23,VIII,1:3
Dance of Life, The 1927,N 27,IX,4:7
Birds, The 1928,F 19,VIII,4:4
A Quoi Penses-Tu? 1928,O 28,IX,2:7
Volpone 1928,D 9,X,2:7
Patchouli 1930,F 16,IX,4:4
Beaux' Stratagem, The 1930,Ap 13,X,2:7
Fils de Don Quichotte, Le 1930,N 2,VIII,2:1
Untitled-Play 1931,N 15,VIII,2:1
Tricheurs, Les 1932,Ap 3,VIII,2:2
Chateau des Papes, Le 1932,N 13,IX,2:5
Paix, La 1933,Ja 15,IX,2:1
Medecin de Son Honneur 1935,Mr 3,VIII,2:3
Untitled-Play 1935,N 24,IX,3:7
Faiseur, Le 1936,Ja 12,IX,3:7

Dulo, Jane

Are You With It? 1945,N 12,17:3
Pal Joey 1949,Mr 7,17:2

Duls, Louisa

Little Theatre Tournament; Pink and Patches 1928,My 11,28:1

Dulud, Michel (Playwright)

Dans Le Noir; In the Dark 1937,F 11,18:3

Dumaresq, William (Playwright)

Isabel's a Jezebel 1970,D 27,II,3:1

Dumas, Alexander (fils) (Miscellaneous)

Rings on Her Fingers 1932,My 22,VIII,1:3

Dumas, Alexander (fils) (Original Author)

Lady of the Camellias, The 1963,Mr 22,7:1

Dumas, Alexander (fils) (Playwright)

Demi-Monde, Le 1922,N 15,22:3
Dame aux Camelias, La 1922,N 16,22:2
Dame aux Camelias, La 1926,D 7,24:2
Lady of the Camellias, The 1930,Mr 6,16:4
Lady of the Camellias, The 1930,Mr 23,IX,2:3
Lady of the Camellias, The 1931,Ja 27,21:2
Camille 1931,F 15,VIII,1:1
Camille 1932,O 28,23:2
Camille 1932,N 2,23:3
Dame aux Camelias, La 1934,Je 10,IX,2:5
Camille 1935,Jl 31,21:1
Signora Dalle Camelie, La; Dame aux Camelias, La 1937,O 9,16:3
Camille 1956,S 19,33:1

Dumas, Alexander (Original Author)

Kean 1921,D 11,VI,1:4
Three Musketeers, The 1928,Mr 4,IX,2:3
Three Musketeers, The 1928,Mr 14,28:1
Three Musketeers, The 1928,Mr 25,IX,1:1
Three Musketeers 1929,O 13,IX,4:7
Conte di Monte Cristo, Il 1934,Ja 22,13:2
Conte di Monte Cristo, Il 1935,Ap 1,17:6
Three Guardsmen, The 1936,F 17,21:3
Three Musketeers, The 1968,Je 26,43:1
Three Musketeers, The 1968,Jl 24,49:2
Corsican Brothers, The 1970,Mr 20,56:2

Dumas, Alexander (Playwright)

Royal Box, The 1928,N 21,32:3
Tour de Nesle, La 1930,S 7,IX,1:3
Tour de Nesle, La 1932,S 25,IX,2:5
Signora Dalle Camelie, La; Camille 1934,O 22,13:2
Kean 1961,N 3,28:2

Dumas, Francez

Old Rascal, The 1930,Mr 25,34:4
Singing Rabbi, The 1931,S 11,24:4

Dumas, Helene

Under the Gaslight 1929,Ap 3,27:1
Crooks' Convention, The 1929,S 19,37:4
Mendel, Inc 1929,N 26,28:5
Betty, Be Careful 1931,My 5,33:3
All Rights Reserved 1934,N 7,33:5
Audition of the Apprentice Theatre 1939,Je 2,26:2
Brass Ring, The 1952,Ap 11,19:2

Dumbrille, Douglas

Macbeth 1924,Mr 17,18:1
Call of Life, The 1925,O 10,10:1
Princess Flavia 1925,N 3,34:3
Three Musketeers, The 1928,Mr 4,IX,2:3
Three Musketeers, The 1928,Mr 14,28:1
Three Musketeers, The 1928,Mr 25,IX,1:1
Chinese O'Neill 1929,My 23,27:1
Tabloid 1929,S 29,IX,5:1
Joseph 1930,F 13,25:3
Month in the Country, A 1930,Mr 18,30:5
Prince Charming 1930,O 14,31:1
As You Desire Me 1931,Ja 29,21:2
Child of Manhattan 1932,Mr 2,15:1

Dumcke, Ernst

Story of the Wolf 1932,N 6,IX,3:4

Dumesnil, Jacques

Misanthrope, Le 1960,Mr 9,38:3

Dumke, Ralph

By Jupiter 1942,Je 4,22:1
Merry Widow, The 1943,Ag 5,19:2
Merry Widow, The 1943,Ag 22,II,5:1
Helen Goes to Troy 1944,Ap 25,17:2
Helen Goes to Troy 1944,Ap 30,II,1:1
Sadie Thompson 1944,N 17,25:2
Mr Strauss Goes to Boston 1945,S 7,20:2
Show Boat 1946,Ja 7,17:2
Show Boat 1946,Ja 13,II,1:1

Dumont, Andre

Deep River 1926,O 5,26:2
Mima 1928,D 13,24:2

Dumont, Margaret

Fan, The 1921,O 4,10:1
Go Easy Mabel 1922,My 9,22:2
Rise of Rosie O'Reilly, The 1923,D 26,13:4
Four Flusher, The 1925,Ap 14,27:4
Cocoanuts, The 1925,D 9,30:1
Animal Crackers 1928,O 24,26:2
Shoot the Works! 1931,Ag 21,20:2
Tell Her the Truth 1932,O 29,18:2

Dumont, Paul

Coco 1969,D 19,66:1

Dumont, Thomas

Processional 1937,O 14,23:1

Dumper, Robert S

What a Relief 1935,D 14,10:6

Dumrose, Boyd (Costume Designer)

Bivouac at Lucca 1957,O 30,26:1

Dumrose, Boyd (Lighting Director)

Bivouac at Lucca 1957,O 30,26:1
Under Milk Wood 1961,Mr 30,25:1
Seven at Dawn, The 1961,Ap 18,43:1
Diff'rent 1961,O 18,52:1
Sing Muse 1961,D 7,52:1
Living Room, The 1962,N 22,43:5
Dream of Swallows, A 1964,Ap 15,46:1

Dumrose, Boyd (Scenic Designer)

Bivouac at Lucca 1957,O 30,26:1
John Turner Davis 1958,Jl 2,25:1
Midnight Caller, The 1958,Jl 2,25:1
Time of the Cuckoo, The 1958,O 28,40:2
Clearing in the Woods, A 1959,F 13,32:1
Come Share My House 1960,F 19,20:2
Here Come the Clowns 1960,S 20,48:1
Whisper to Me 1960,N 22,38:6
Under Milk Wood 1961,Mr 30,25:1
Seven at Dawn, The 1961,Ap 18,43:1
Diff'rent 1961,O 18,52:1
Sing Muse 1961,D 7,52:1
Living Room, The 1962,N 22,43:5
Dream of Swallows, A 1964,Ap 15,46:1
Dirty Old Man, The 1964,My 5,53:1
Sarah and the Sax 1964,My 5,53:1
Other Man, The 1968,F 9,50:1

Dumrose, Boyd (Scenic Designer)—Cont
Oh, Say Can You See L A 1968,F 9,50:1
Three Men on a Horse 1969,O 17,35:1
Dun, Rubin
Wandering Stars 1966,N 14,52:2
Duna, Steffi
Threepenny Opera, The 1933,Ap 14,22:4
Dunai, Ferenc (Original Author)
Sunday Man, The 1964,My 14,41:3
Dunaway, Faye
Man for All Seasons, A 1962,S 23,II,1:1
After the Fall 1964,Ja 24,18:1
But for Whom Charlie 1964,Mr 13,42:2
Changeling, The 1964,O 30,32:2
Hogan's Goat 1965,N 12,56:1
Dunbar, Andrew
Color of Darkness: An Evening in the World of
   James Purdy; Cracks 1963,O 1,24:1
Matty and the Moron and Madonna
   1965,Mr 30,53:1
Dunbar, Ann
Sleepy Hollow 1948,Je 4,26:3
Kiss Me, Kate 1949,Ja 30,II,6:5
Peace 1969,Ja 28,49:1
Dunbar, Barre (Translator)
Purity 1930,D 26,18:2
Dunbar, Brooks
Fencing Master, The 1936,Ap 1,29:1
Variations of 1940 1940,Ja 29,12:1
Cradle Will Rock, The 1947,D 27,11:2
Dunbar, Dixie
Life Begins at 8:40 1934,Ag 7,20:7
Life Begins at 8:40 1934,Ag 28,24:2
Yokel Boy 1939,Jl 7,12:2
Dunbar, Edward
Sunny River 1941,D 5,28:2
Dunbar, Madeline
Twinkle Twinkle 1926,N 17,22:2
Dunbar, Olive
From Morn Till Midnight 1948,D 7,41:6
Butter and Egg Man, The 1949,Ap 29,27:1
She Stoops to Conquer 1949,D 29,21:3
Devil's Disciple, The 1950,Ja 26,23:2
Heiress, The 1950,F 9,34:2
Cretan Woman, The 1954,My 21,17:2
Dandy Dick 1956,Ja 11,37:2
Misanthrope, The 1956,N 13,44:1
Box of Watercolors, A 1957,F 18,22:2
Country Wife, The 1957,Je 27,22:1
Under Milk Wood 1957,O 16,42:5
Port-Royal 1960,Ap 26,41:1
Dunbar, Ralph
Folly Town 1920,My 18,9:2
Dunbar, Ted
Sambo 1970,Jl 23,24:1
Duncan, Alastair
Under Milk Wood 1957,O 16,42:5
Duncan, Andrea
Trojan Horse, The 1940,O 31,28:3
Homecoming 1942,N 17,28:5
Duncan, Andrew
From the Second City 1961,S 27,32:1
Untitled-Revue; Second City 1962,Ja 12,30:2
Little Murders 1969,Ja 6,38:1
White House Murder Case, The 1970,F 19,59:1
Duncan, Angus
Dark Hours, The 1932,N 15,24:2
John Ferguson 1933,Jl 11,15:7
Romeo and Juliet 1934,D 21,30:3
So Proudly We Hail 1936,S 23,28:4
Duncan, Anna
Arabesque 1925,O 21,20:2
John 1927,N 5,16:4
Ladies All 1930,Jl 20,VIII,2:1
Electra 1932,Ja 9,21:4
Duncan, Anna (Miscellaneous)
Electra 1932,Ja 9,21:4
Duncan, Archie
Vivat! Vivat Regina! 1970,Jl 20,21:2
Duncan, Augustin
Mixed Marriage 1920,D 15,18:2
Cradle Song 1921,Mr 1,18:2
John Ferguson 1921,My 24,20:1
John Ferguson 1921,Je 21,20:2
Detour, The 1921,Jl 17,VI,1:1
Detour, The 1921,Ag 24,12:2
Steamship Tenacity 1922,Ja 3,20:2
First Man, The 1922,Mr 6,9:2
For Value Received 1923,My 8,22:3
Hell-Bent Fer Heaven 1924,Ja 5,10:1
Hell-Bent Fer Heaven 1924,F 10,VII,1:1
She Stoops to Conquer 1924,Je 10,24:3
Harvest 1925,Ap 19,IX,2:1
Harvest 1925,S 21,16:2
Last Night of Don Juan, The 1925,N 10,23:2
Pilgrimage, The; Pelerin, Le 1925,N 10,23:2
Merchants of Glory 1925,D 15,28:3
Merchants of Glory 1925,D 27,VII,1:1
Juno and the Paycock 1926,Mr 16,22:1
Juno and the Paycock 1926,Mr 21,VIII,1:1
Naked 1926,N 9,31:2
John Ferguson 1928,Ja 18,23:1
Ledge, A 1929,N 19,26:3
Little Father of the Wilderness, The 1930,Je 3,27:1

Lottery, The 1930,N 23,IX,3:5
Well of the Saints, The 1932,Ja 22,15:2
Troilus and Cressida 1932,Je 7,22:3
John Ferguson 1933,Jl 11,15:7
Richard II 1937,F 6,14:2
Richard II 1937,F 14,X,1:1
Hamlet 1938,O 13,28:1
Fiddler's House, The 1941,Mr 28,27:5
Homecoming 1942,N 17,28:5
Man's House, A 1943,Ap 3,10:4
Lute Song 1946,F 7,29:2
Duncan, Augustin (Director)
Nancy Ann 1924,Ap 1,18:1
Outside Looking In 1925,S 8,28:1
Pilgrimage, The; Pelerin, Le 1925,N 10,23:2
Move On 1926,Ja 19,30:1
Juno and the Paycock 1926,Mr 16,22:1
Juno and the Paycock 1926,Mr 21,VIII,1:1
Naked 1926,N 9,31:2
John Ferguson 1928,Ja 18,23:1
Breaks, The 1928,Ap 17,26:3
John Ferguson 1933,Jl 11,15:7
Ship Comes in, A 1934,S 20,21:1
Homecoming 1942,N 17,28:5
Duncan, Augustin (Miscellaneous)
Hell-Bent Fer Heaven 1924,F 10,VII,1:1
Duncan, Augustin (Producer)
Roger Bloomer 1923,Mr 11,VIII,1:3
Naked 1926,N 9,31:2
Duncan, Bessie
Little Theatre Tournament; Another Room for
   Rent 1929,My 7,28:1
Duncan, Bruce
Three Sisters, The 1930,Ja 9,22:2
Man on Stilts, The 1931,S 10,23:2
Duncan, Charles R
Dead End 1935,O 29,17:2
Bright Honor 1936,S 28,14:1
Duncan, Danny
Blackouts of 1949 1949,S 7,39:2
Duncan, Doris
Flossie 1924,Je 4,25:2
Duncan, Dorothy
Merry Widow, The 1931,S 8,39:1
Duncan, Evelyn
Lilies of the Field 1921,O 5,20:1
Duncan, Frank
Henry IV, Part I 1946,My 7,25:2
Henry IV, Part II 1946,My 8,33:4
Oedipus; Critic, The 1946,My 21,19:2
Duncan, Harry
Pinocchio 1939,Ja 3,19:2
Duncan, Herbert (Producer)
In the Penal Colony 1962,My 4,27:2
Come Out, Carlo! 1962,My 4,27:2
Duncan, Ina
Runnin' Wild 1923,O 30,17:3
Hot Rhythm 1930,Ag 22,18:5
Sugar Hill 1931,D 26,15:2
Black Rhythm 1936,D 21,19:2
Duncan, Jeff
Red Roses for Me 1955,D 29,15:2
Metamorphosis 1957,F 20,38:1
Duncan, Jenny
Donogoo 1961,Ja 19,25:3
Duncan, Jesse (Producer)
All in Favor 1942,Ja 21,20:6
Duncan, Jimmie
Orpheus Descending 1959,O 6,45:2
Duncan, Joanna
Plan M 1942,F 21,15:2
Duncan, John
Courting 1925,S 14,17:1
Duncan, Julia
Stronger Than Love 1925,D 29,20:2
Duncan, Kenn (Miscellaneous)
Local Stigmatic, The; Last to Go 1969,N 4,55:2
Local Stigmatic, The; Request Stop 1969,N 4,55:2
Local Stigmatic, The; Interview 1969,N 4,55:2
Local Stigmatic, The; That's All 1969,N 4,55:2
Local Stigmatic, The; Trouble in the Works
   1969,N 4,55:2
Local Stigmatic, The; Applicant 1969,N 4,55:2
Local Stigmatic, The; That's Your Trouble
   1969,N 4,55:2
Local Stigmatic, The 1969,N 4,55:2
Duncan, Laura
Hot Rhythm 1930,Ag 22,18:5
Set to Music 1939,Ja 19,16:2
'Tis of Thee 1940,O 28,21:3
It's About Time 1942,Mr 31,28:3
Duncan, Malcolm
Your Woman and Mine 1922,F 28,17:2
Whispering Wires 1922,Ag 8,26:2
Out of Step 1925,Ja 30,12:1
Backslapper, The 1925,Ap 13,25:2
All Dressed Up 1925,S 10,28:1
Young Blood 1925,N 25,15:1
Glory Hallelujah 1926,Ap 7,26:2
Buy, Buy Baby 1926,O 8,26:2
Spread Eagle 1927,Ap 5,30:2
Blood Money 1927,Ag 23,29:2
This Thing Called Love 1928,S 18,32:7

Duncan, Malcolm—Cont
Cross Roads 1929,N 12,34:2
Many a Slip 1930,F 4,29:2
Five Star Final 1930,D 31,11:1
When the Bough Breaks 1932,F 17,19:2
Dinner at Eight 1932,O 24,18:2
Uncle Tom's Cabin 1933,My 30,13:4
Merrily We Roll Along 1934,O 1,14:1
Slight Case of Murder, A 1935,S 12,28:5
Duncan, Mary
Face Value 1921,D 27,10:2
Egotist, The 1922,D 27,12:1
New Toys 1924,F 19,12:1
New Toys 1924,F 24,VII,1:1
Nervous Wreck, The 1924,O 19,VIII,2:1
All Wet 1925,Jl 7,24:1
Human Nature 1925,S 25,24:3
Shanghai Gesture, The 1926,F 2,20:2
Roamin' Gentleman, A 1930,F 23,VIII,2:5
Duncan, Pamela
Satisfaction Guaranteed 1969,F 12,31:1
Open 24 Hours 1969,F 12,31:1
Duncan, Richard
Patience 1967,O 13,32:1
Iolanthe 1967,O 18,40:1
Mikado, The 1967,O 25,42:2
Gondoliers, The 1967,O 29,83:1
H M S Pinafore 1967,N 1,40:1
Duncan, Rita
Bird Cage, The 1950,F 23,32:2
Duncan, Ronald (Original Author)
Rape of Lucretia, The 1948,D 30,24:2
Duncan, Ronald (Playwright)
Azrael; Eagle Has Two Heads, The 1946,S 16,9:7
Eagle Has Two Heads, The 1947,Mr 20,39:2
Death of Satan, The 1960,Ap 6,49:1
Death of Satan, The 1960,Ap 17,II,1:1
Duncan, Ronald (Translator)
Typewriter, The 1955,Jl 29,8:3
Duncan, Rosetta
Tip-Top 1920,O 6,13:2
Topsy and Eva 1924,D 24,11:1
Vaudeville (Palace) 1927,N 15,27:2
Vaudeville (Palace) 1927,D 20,33:4
Vaudeville (Palace) 1931,My 4,15:2
Duncan, Rosetta (Composer)
Topsy and Eva 1924,D 24,11:1
Duncan, Rosetta (Lyricist)
Topsy and Eva 1924,D 24,11:1
Duncan, Rosetta (Topsy)
Vaudeville (Palace) 1932,My 9,19:3
Duncan, Sandy
Music Man, The 1965,Je 17,26:4
Carousel 1966,D 16,56:2
Finian's Rainbow 1967,Ap 6,44:1
Sound of Music, The 1967,Ap 27,52:1
Life With Father 1967,O 20,53:2
Ceremony of Innocence, The 1968,Ja 2,33:1
Canterbury Tales; Pilgrims, The 1969,F 4,34:1
Canterbury Tales; Steward's Tale, The
   1969,F 4,34:1
Canterbury Tales; Wife of Bath's Tale, The
   1969,F 4,34:1
Canterbury Tales; Merchant's Tale, The
   1969,F 4,34:1
Canterbury Tales; Miller's Tale, The 1969,F 4,34:1
Love Is a Time of Day 1969,D 23,21:3
Love Is a Time of Day 1970,Ja 4,II,5:1
Boy Friend, The 1970,Ap 15,54:1
Boy Friend, The 1970,Ap 26,II,5:7
Duncan, Spencer
Enemy of the People, An 1959,F 5,24:4
Duncan, Stuart (Producer)
Under the Sycamore Tree 1960,Mr 8,37:2
Misalliance 1961,S 26,32:2
Yes is for a Very Young Man 1963,Mr 6,7:5
Alchemist, The 1964,S 15,33:1
Arms and the Man 1967,Je 23,44:2
Duncan, Todd
Porgy and Bess 1935,O 1,27:2
Porgy and Bess 1935,O 11,30:2
Cabin in the Sky 1940,O 26,19:2
Cabin in the Sky 1940,N 3,IX,1:1
Porgy and Bess 1942,Ja 23,16:2
Porgy and Bess 1943,S 14,26:2
Lost in the Stars 1949,O 31,21:2
Lost in the Stars 1949,N 6,II,1:1
ANTA Album 1951,My 7,22:7
Duncan, Vivian
Tip-Top 1920,O 6,13:2
Topsy and Eva 1924,D 24,11:1
Duncan, Vivian (Composer)
Topsy and Eva 1924,D 24,11:1
Duncan, Vivian (Lyricist)
Topsy and Eva 1924,D 24,11:1
Duncan, William (Director)
Peer Gynt 1937,Mr 14,II,7:8
Duncan, William (Producer)
Pan Pipes and Donkeys' Ears 1929,D 27,26:5
Duncan, William Cary (Lyricist)
Rose Girl, The 1921,F 12,11:1
Mary Jane McKane 1923,D 26,13:2
Sunny Days 1928,F 9,29:1

Duncan, William Cary (Playwright)
Three Showers 1920,Ap 6,18:1
Rose Girl, The 1921,F 12,11:1
Blue Kitten, The 1922,Ja 14,9:3
Molly Darling 1922,S 2,10:2
Mary Jane McKane 1923,D 26,13:2
Princess April 1924,D 2,23:2
Talk About Girls 1927,Je 15,31:3
Yes, Yes, Yvette 1927,O 4,32:3
Sunny Days 1928,F 9,29:1
Great Day! 1929,O 18,24:3
Duncan, Willis
Dead End 1935,O 29,17:2
Victoria Regina 1935,D 27,15:2
Too Many Girls 1939,O 19,26:2
Duncan-Jones, Elsie Elizabeth (Translator)
Misanthrope, The 1937,F 24,18:6
Duncan Sisters, The
Untitled-Benefit 1921,My 2,12:3
Untitled-Benefit 1922,My 8,14:5
Vaudeville (Palace) 1923,Mr 6,26:1
Vaudeville (Palace) 1927,N 15,27:2
Vaudeville (Palace) 1927,N 22,33:2
Vaudeville (Palace) 1927,D 20,33:4
Vaudeville (Palace) 1927,D 27,25:2
Uncle Tom's Cabin 1928,O 21,IX,1:3
Ziegfeld's Midnight Frolic 1929,F 19,22:4
Vaudeville (Palace) 1930,N 10,17:1
Duncklee, W S (Lyricist)
1776 1926,Ap 24,11:2
Dunckley, Joseph
Pirates of Penzance, The 1942,F 18,22:2
Iolanthe 1942,F 24,26:4
Gondoliers, The 1942,Mr 4,22:3
Dunckley, Mary
Lovely Lady 1927,D 30,22:1
Dundee
X Has No Value 1970,F 17,35:1
Dundee, Fredi
Lion in Love, The 1963,Ap 26,28:3
Dundy, Elaine (Playwright)
My Place 1962,F 14,40:2
Dunfee, Katharine
Under Milk Wood 1957,O 16,42:5
Mod Donna 1970,My 4,48:1
Dunfee, Nora
Madam Will You Walk 1953,D 2,2:4
John Turner Davis 1958,Jl 2,25:1
Midnight Caller, The 1958,Jl 2,25:1
John Turner Davis 1958,Jl 2,25:1
Visit, The 1960,Mr 9,38:3
Last Days of Lincoln, The 1961,O 19,39:7
Dunfee, Susan
Ballad of the Sad Cafe, The 1963,O 31,27:1
Dunford, Judith
On the Town 1959,Ja 16,36:1
Dunham, Clarke (Lighting Director)
Match-Play 1966,O 12,37:1
Party for Divorce, A 1966,O 12,37:1
Infantry, The 1966,N 15,51:1
Wicked Cooks, The 1967,Ja 24,42:1
Girl in the Freudian Slip, The 1967,My 19,34:3
Ninety Day Mistress, The 1967,N 7,49:1
How to Steal an Election 1968,O 14,56:1
Philosophy in the Boudoir 1969,My 22,55:2
Contributions; Shoes 1970,Mr 10,53:1
Contributions; Plantation 1970,Mr 10,53:1
Contributions; Contribution 1970,Mr 10,53:1
Place for Polly, A 1970,Ap 20,45:1
Me Nobody Knows, The 1970,My 19,42:1
Dunham, Clarke (Scenic Designer)
Party for Divorce, A 1966,O 12,37:1
Match-Play 1966,O 12,37:1
Infantry, The 1966,N 15,51:1
Wicked Cooks, The 1967,Ja 24,42:1
MacBird! 1967,F 23,38:1
How to Steal an Election 1968,O 14,56:1
Philosophy in the Boudoir 1969,My 22,55:2
Contributions; Plantation 1970,Mr 10,53:1
Contributions; Shoes 1970,Mr 10,53:1
Contributions; Contribution 1970,Mr 10,53:1
Place for Polly, A 1970,Ap 20,45:1
Me Nobody Knows, The 1970,My 19,42:1
Dunham, David (Director)
I Dreamt I Dwelt in Bloomingdale's 1970,F 13,26:1
Dunham, H H
Tiger Smiles, The 1930,D 18,29:1
It's the Valet 1933,D 15,25:4
Dunham, Harry
Tiger Smiles, The 1930,D 18,29:1
Dunham, Joanna
Romeo and Juliet 1962,F 14,39:1
Romeo and Juliet 1962,F 25,II,1:1
Dunham, Katherine
Cabin in the Sky 1940,O 26,19:2
Cabin in the Sky 1940,N 3,IX,1:1
Cabin in the Sky 1940,N 10,IX,2:1
Concert Varieties 1945,Je 2,10:7
Carib Song 1945,S 28,17:2
Dunham, Katherine (Choreographer)
Carib Song 1945,S 28,17:2
Dunham, Katherine (Director)
Carib Song 1945,S 28,17:2

Dunham, Katherine Dancers
Blue Holiday 1945,My 22,13:3
Dunham, Richard
Traffic Signals 1937,Ag 7,7:4
Dunham, T C
First Episode 1934,S 18,18:1
Dunham Brothers
I Married an Angel 1938,My 12,26:2
Dunhills, The
Danny Kaye's International Show 1953,Ja 19,20:2
Danny Kaye Show 1963,Ap 11,28:2
Dunkel, Eugene (Scenic Designer)
One Sunday Afternoon 1933,F 16,23:5
Scorpion, The 1933,N 28,28:4
Fools Rush In 1934,D 26,19:2
Naughty-Naught '00 1937,Ja 25,23:2
Fireman's Flame, The 1937,O 11,26:2
Bridal Crown, The 1938,F 7,11:2
Girl From Wyoming, The 1938,O 31,12:1
Man Who Killed Lincoln, The 1940,Ja 18,26:4
Uncle Vanya 1960,F 13,13:4
Dunkel, Irene
Bronx Express, 1968 1968,N 16,43:3
Dunkels, Dorothy
Matriarch, The 1930,Mr 19,24:5
Dunkley, Billy
Bitter Stream 1936,Mr 31,16:6
Dunkley, Joseph
Mikado, The 1942,F 4,22:2
Dunlap, Florence
One Touch of Venus 1943,O 8,14:1
Fanny 1954,N 5,16:1
Happy Hunting 1956,D 7,30:1
Dunlap, Lucy Ann
Mystery of the Finding of the Cross, The 1959,Ja 16,35:2
Dunlap, Pamela
Yerma 1966,D 9,60:1
Dunlop, Charles L (Scenic Designer)
Love and Maple Syrup 1970,Ja 8,47:1
Dunlop, Frank (Director)
Edward II 1968,My 2,58:4
Zoo, Zoo, Widdershins, Zoo 1969,S 5,30:1
Three Sisters, The 1970,F 12,30:1
Dunlop, Frank (Miscellaneous)
Beaux' Stratagem, The 1970,F 10,50:2
Dunlop, Frank (Producer)
White Devil, The 1969,N 14,38:2
Dunlop, Geoffrey (Translator)
Danton's Death 1938,N 3,26:2
Dunlop, Helen
Elizabeth the Queen 1941,O 17,27:2
Dunlop, Peter
Sweet Miani 1962,S 26,33:2
Dunmore, James
In Abraham's Bosom 1926,D 31,10:2
In Abraham's Bosom 1927,F 20,VII,1:1
Rope 1928,F 23,18:3
Make Me Know It 1929,N 5,32:5
Constant Sinner, The 1931,S 15,30:1
Never No More 1932,Ja 8,27:1
Blue Monday 1932,Je 3,23:2
Incubator 1932,N 2,23:3
Black Diamond 1933,F 24,12:2
Raw Meat 1933,Mr 23,13:2
Sailor, Beware! 1935,My 7,28:4
Dunn, Alice
Whole Town's Talking, The 1923,Ag 30,8:2
Cape Smoke 1925,F 17,19:1
Mama Loves Papa 1926,F 23,26:2
Dunn, Arthur
Potash and Perlmutter, Detectives; Poisoned by Pictures 1926,S 1,27:3
Dunn, B F (Playwright)
Snow Maiden, The 1960,Ap 5,43:3
Dunn, Billie
Bridge, The 1930,My 6,33:1
Dunn, Caesar (Playwright)
King for a Day, A 1923,D 2,VIII,2:1
Four Flusher, The 1925,S,IX,2:4
Four Flusher, The 1925,Ap 14,27:4
What the Doctor Ordered 1927,Ag 19,20:2
Dunn, Charles
Kean 1961,N 3,28:2
Dunn, E Malcolm
Antony and Cleopatra 1937,N 11,30:2
Dunn, Edward
And Puppy Dog Tails 1969,O 20,60:1
Dunn, Edward D
County Chairman, The 1936,My 26,26:5
Dunn, Edward Delaney (Lyricist)
Phoebe of Quality Street 1921,My 10,20:1
Dunn, Edward Delaney (Playwright)
Phoebe of Quality Street 1921,My 10,20:1
Last Waltz, The 1921,My 11,20:3
Claw, The 1921,O 18,20:1
Caroline 1923,F 1,13:2
Dew Drop Inn 1923,My 18,26:4
Red Robe, The 1928,D 26,15:1
Dunn, Elaine
John Murray Anderson's Almanac 1953,D 11,42:2
Catch a Star! 1955,S 7,35:2
Pal Joey 1963,My 30,21:1

Dunn, Emma
Sonny 1921,Ag 17,12:2
Her Happiness 1922,O 8,VI,1:6
Dawn 1924,O 19,VIII,2:6
Dawn 1924,N 25,27:1
Rip Van Winkle 1925,N 24,28:5
Junk 1927,Ja 6,25:1
Dunn, Francis
Red Light Annie 1923,Ag 22,10:3
Dunn, Geoffrey
Time Remembered 1955,My 4,35:1
Dunn, Henry
Vaudeville (Palace) 1929,Jl 8,17:6
Vaudeville (New Amsterdam Theatre) 1931,Je 22,17:3
Take a Bow 1944,Je 16,15:3
Dunn, Isabel (Original Author)
Debut 1956,F 23,32:1
Dunn, J Colville
Hamlet 1923,N 27,23:6
Second Mrs Tanqueray, The 1924,O 28,27:1
Buccaneer, The 1925,O 3,10:2
Josef Suss 1930,Ja 21,28:5
Admirable Crichton, The 1931,Mr 10,23:2
Sleeping Clergyman, A 1934,O 9,16:1
Tovarich 1936,O 16,31:4
Leave It to Me! 1938,N 10,32:2
At the Stroke of Eight 1940,My 21,29:2
Theatre 1941,N 13,34:2
Uncle Harry 1942,My 21,24:1
That Old Devil 1944,Je 6,14:2
Sleep, My Pretty One 1944,N 3,26:8
Hasty Heart, The 1945,Ja 4,14:2
Dunn, J Malcolm
Poppy God, The 1921,Ag 30,10:1
Squaw Man, The 1921,D 27,10:3
What the Public Wants 1922,My 2,22:3
Banco 1922,S 21,18:1
Lady Cristilinda, The 1922,D 26,11:2
As You Like It 1923,Ap 24,24:1
White Cargo 1923,N 6,22:2
Up the Line 1926,N 23,26:1
Savages Under the Skin 1927,Mr 25,25:2
Midsummer Night's Dream, A 1927,Je 27,25:1
Silver Box, The 1928,Ja 18,23:1
Napoleon 1928,Mr 9,21:1
Anna 1928,My 17,25:2
Damn Your Honor 1929,D 31,14:3
Great Barrington, The 1931,F 20,18:1
Midsummer Night's Dream, A 1932,Jl 13,15:1
Men Must Fight 1932,O 15,13:4
Scorpion, The 1933,N 28,28:4
Sleeping Clergyman, A 1934,O 9,16:1
It's You I Want 1935,F 6,23:3
Murder With Pen and Ink 1935,Jl 30,17:2
Middle Man 1936,S 8,23:1
Black Limelight 1936,N 10,31:1
If I Were You 1938,Ja 25,24:2
Foreigners 1939,D 6,30:2
Leave Her to Heaven 1940,F 28,16:2
This Rock 1943,F 19,23:2
Dunn, Jackson
Fan, The 1921,O 4,10:1
Dunn, James
His Majesty's Car 1930,O 24,30:1
Panama Hattie 1940,O 4,28:4
Panama Hattie 1940,O 31,28:2
Moon for the Misbegotten, A 1947,F 21,16:2
Dunn, Janice
Cat on a Hot Tin Roof 1955,Mr 25,18:2
Dunn, Jimmie
One Shot Fired 1927,N 8,32:5
Dunn, John
Great Temptations, The 1926,My 19,29:1
Wings Over Europe 1928,D 11,35:1
Apple Cart, The 1930,F 25,30:1
Country Wife, The 1931,Ap 19,31:5
I Love an Actress 1931,S 18,29:2
Evensong 1933,F 1,13:4
Dunn, John (Sir)
Merry-Go-Round 1927,Jl 5,19:4
Dunn, Johnnie
Plantation Revue, The 1922,Jl 18,18:4
Dixie to Broadway 1924,O 30,22:1
Dunn, Joseph H
At Sea 1962,Ap 24,33:1
Alcestis Comes Back 1962,Ap 24,33:1
Dunn, Josephine
Pickwick 1927,S 6,35:2
Take a Chance 1932,N 28,11:2
Between Two Worlds 1934,O 26,24:2
Accent on Youth 1935,Jl 9,24:4
She Cried for the Moon 1935,Jl 23,24:3
Dunn, Kathy
Uncle Willie 1956,D 21,17:1
Sound of Music, The 1959,N 17,40:2
Dunn, Liam
Up the Rebels 1941,O 31,21:1
Savonarola 1942,Ap 24,20:2
Career Angel 1943,N 19,24:2
Bright Boy 1944,Mr 3,19:5
Dunn, Michael
Here Come the Clowns 1960,S 20,48:1

Dunn, Michael—Cont
How to Make a Man 1961,F 3,16:1
Talking to You 1961,O 23,22:5
Hop, Signor! 1962,My 8,45:2
Ballad of the Sad Cafe, The 1963,O 31,27:1
Ballad of the Sad Cafe, The 1963,N 10,II,1:1
Inner Journey, The 1969,Mr 21,42:1
Dunn, Mignon
Saint of Bleecker Street, The 1954,D 28,21:1
Dunn, Patricia
Kismet 1953,D 4,2:4
Dunn, Patsy
Kitty's Kisses 1926,My 7,12:2
Dunn, Peter
Dear Ruth 1944,D 14,29:2
Dunn, Quinn
Out of the Seven Seas 1923,N 20,23:3
Dunn, Ralph
Seventh Heart, The 1927,My 3,24:4
Enemy of the People, An 1950,D 29,14:1
Moon Is Blue, The 1951,Mr 9,29:2
Room Service 1953,Ap 7,34:1
Pajama Game, The 1954,My 14,20:2
Make a Million 1958,O 24,39:2
Happy Town 1959,O 8,49:2
Tenderloin 1960,O 18,47:2
Once for the Asking 1963,N 21,42:2
Dunn, Richard
Gondoliers, The 1936,S 8,23:1
Cox and Box 1936,S 29,34:2
Gondoliers, The 1939,Ja 20,14:2
Pirates of Penzance, The 1948,Ja 6,27:2
Iolanthe 1948,Ja 13,29:3
Cox and Box 1948,Ja 20,26:2
Gondoliers, The 1948,Ja 27,31:2
Yeomen of the Guard, The 1948,F 3,30:2
Dunn, Vera
Stolen Fruit 1925,O 8,31:4
Anything Goes 1934,N 22,26:1
Anything Goes 1937,Ag 26,24:3
Dunn, Violet
Within Four Walls 1923,Ap 18,24:1
Whole Town's Talking, The 1923,Ag 30,8:2
Hell's Bells! 1925,Ja 27,14:2
Buckaroo 1929,Mr 18,31:1
Bicycle Ride to Nevada 1963,S 25,38:1
Dunn, W B
Tiger Smiles, The 1930,D 18,29:1
Dunn, Willim
Forbidden Melody 1936,N 3,33:1
Dunne, Eithne
Playboy of the Western World, The 1946,O 28,18:3
Othello 1962,S 28,27:1
Dunne, Elizabeth
Tangletoes 1925,F 18,17:1
All Wet 1925,Jl 7,24:1
Reflected Glory 1936,S 18,19:5
Reflected Glory 1936,S 22,30:2
Dunne, George H (Rev) (Playwright)
Trial by Fire 1947,D 5,31:5
Dunne, Irene
Clinging Vine, The 1922,D 25,20:2
City Chap, The 1925,O 27,21:1
Yours Truly 1927,Ja 26,16:5
She's My Baby 1928,Ja 4,22:2
Luckee Girl 1928,S 17,28:6
Dunne, Murphy
From the Second City 1969,O 15,34:1
Dunne, S Liam (Director)
Silver Tassie, The 1929,O 25,26:1
Dunne, William
Royal Box, The 1928,N 21,32:3
Sakura 1928,D 26,14:4
Dunnett, Walter A 3d
Butter and Egg Man, The 1966,O 18,49:1
Dunnigan, Ann
Lord Blesses the Bishop, The 1934,N 28,24:5
Dunning, Carol
Earth Journey 1944,Ap 28,24:2
Don't, George! 1944,N 4,18:6
Dunning, Elizabeth
Saint of Bleecker Street, The 1954,D 28,21:1
Dunning, Frances Fox (Original Author)
Lilly Turner 1932,S 20,26:1
Dunning, Philip
Wonderful Thing, The 1920,F 18,9:1
Beware of Dogs 1921,O 4,10:1
For All of Us 1923,O 16,19:4
Dunning, Philip (Director)
Broadway 1926,S 17,19:3
Sweet Land of Liberty 1929,S 24,29:2
Lilly Turner 1932,S 20,26:1
Schoolhouse on the Lot 1938,Mr 23,18:4
Dunning, Philip (Playwright)
Broadway 1926,S 17,19:3
Broadway 1926,S 26,VIII,1:1
Broadway 1928,Mr 11,5:3
Get Me in the Movies 1928,My 22,18:3
Get Me in the Movies 1928,My 27,VIII,1:1
Night Hostess 1928,Jl 29,VII,2:2
Night Hostess 1928,S 13,31:2
Sweet Land of Liberty 1929,S 24,29:2
Lilly Turner 1932,S 20,26:1
Kill That Story 1934,Ag 30,22:2

Page Miss Glory 1934,N 28,24:2
Remember the Day 1935,Jl 9,24:3
Remember the Day 1935,S 26,19:3
Remember the Day 1935,O 13,IX,1:1
Dunning, Philip (Producer)
Those We Love 1930,F 20,22:2
Lilly Turner 1932,S 20,26:1
20th Century 1932,D 30,15:1
Heat Lightning 1933,S 16,9:6
Drums Begin, The 1933,N 25,10:5
Kill That Story 1934,Ag 30,22:2
Page Miss Glory 1934,N 28,24:2
Remember the Day 1935,S 26,19:3
Schoolhouse on the Lot 1938,Mr 23,18:4
Dunning, Virginia
Remember the Day 1935,Jl 9,24:3
Remember the Day 1935,S 26,19:3
Schoolhouse on the Lot 1938,Mr 23,18:4
Life With Father 1939,Ag 15,14:4
Unconquered, The 1940,F 14,25:2
Dunningan, Ann
All the Living 1938,Mr 25,14:4
Dunninger
Vaudeville (Palace) 1926,N 30,27:2
Dunno, Glenn
Bella 1961,N 17,40:1
Dunnock, Mildred
Midsummer Night's Dream, A 1931,Ag 19,19:3
Life Begins 1932,Mr 29,23:2
Elizabeth Sleeps Out 1935,Ag 27,23:4
Trojan Women, The 1938,Ja 25,24:2
Hill Between, The 1938,Mr 12,12:5
Comedy of Good and Evil, A 1938,Ap 8,16:3
Candida 1938,Ag 31,13:2
Corn Is Green, The 1940,N 27,27:2
War and Peace 1942,My 22,26:3
Cat Screams, The 1942,Je 17,26:5
Vickie 1942,S 23,28:1
Richard III 1943,Mr 27,8:3
Foolish Notion 1945,Mr 14,23:2
Lute Song 1946,F 7,29:2
Another Part of the Forest 1946,N 21,42:2
Hallams, The 1948,Mr 5,18:2
Leading Lady 1948,O 19,33:1
Death of a Salesman 1949,F 11,27:2
Death of a Salesman 1949,F 20,II,1:1
ANTA Album 1950,Ja 30,13:2
Death of a Salesman 1950,Mr 12,II,1:1
Pride's Crossing 1950,N 21,37:5
Peer Gynt 1951,Ja 29,15:2
Red Roses for Me 1951,Ap 26,35:8
Wild Duck, The 1951,D 27,17:1
International Set, The 1953,Je 12,19:3
In the Summer House 1953,D 30,17:1
In the Summer House 1954,Ja 10,II,1:1
Cat on a Hot Tin Roof 1955,Mr 25,18:2
Cat on a Hot Tin Roof 1955,Ap 3,II,1:1
King John 1956,Je 28,33:5
Child of Fortune 1956,N 14,41:1
Pictures in the Hallway 1959,D 28,19:1
Crystal Heart, The 1960,F 16,31:2
Farewell, Farewell Eugene 1960,S 28,35:1
Cantilevered Terrace, The 1962,Ja 18,24:1
Milk Train Doesn't Stop Here Anymore, The 1962,Jl 12,19:8
Milk Train Doesn't Stop Here Anymore, The 1963,Ja 18,7:1
Trojan Women, The 1963,D 24,7:6
Traveller Without Luggage 1964,S 18,26:2
Phedre 1966,F 11,36:1
Willie Doesn't Live Here Anymore 1967,F 8,20:2
Bacchae, The 1969,Mr 15,24:1
Bacchae, The 1969,Mr 23,II,11:1
Crimes and Crimes 1970,Ja 19,35:1
Colette 1970,My 7,60:1
Colette 1970,My 17,II,1:1
Place Without Doors, A 1970,D 1,60:1
DuNouy, Daphne Lecomte
Intermezzo 1957,F 15,20:4
Dunphy, Agnes
Marie Antoinette 1921,N 23,16:1
Dunphy, Jack
Green Table, The 1942,Ja 22,12:2
Prodigal Son, The 1942,F 18,22:2
It's About Time 1942,Mr 31,28:3
Dunphy, Jack (Playwright)
Saturday Night Kid, The 1958,My 16,22:1
Gay Apprentice, The 1960,F 3,27:2
Too Close for Comfort 1960,F 3,27:2
Dunsany, Lord (Playwright)
If 1921,Je 26,VI,1:1
Gods of the Mountain, The 1925,Ap 4,20:2
Gods of the Mountain, The 1925,Ap 26,VIII,1:3
If 1927,O 26,26:2
If 1927,O 30,IX,1:1
Night at an Inn, A 1930,My 10,25:1
Lord Adrian 1937,Ap 17,14:8
Alexander 1938,Ag 5,11:2
Alexander 1938,Ag 14,IX,2:2
Gods of the Mountain, The 1950,My 25,36:2
Dunsby, Dorothy
Life and Death of an American 1939,My 20,11:2

Dunsmore, Elspeth
Myself and I 1929,Ag 31,13:6
Dunsmore, John
Honeydew 1920,S 7,20:1
Dunsmore, Margaret
Don't Tell 1920,S 29,12:1
Dunsmuir, Eleanor (Composer)
Sunny Days 1928,F 9,29:1
Dunsmuir, John
Treasure Girl 1928,N 9,22:1
Dunsmure, John
Chocolate Soldier, The 1921,D 13,24:2
Love Song, The 1925,Ja 14,19:4
Chocolate Soldier, The 1930,Ja 28,28:1
Chocolate Soldier, The 1934,My 3,15:3
Gypsy Blonde 1934,Je 26,22:5
Dunstan, Cliff
Round-Up, The 1932,Mr 8,19:4
Room Service 1937,My 20,16:1
Boys From Syracuse, The 1938,N 24,36:1
Aries Is Rising 1939,N 22,16:5
Unconquered, The 1940,F 14,25:2
Pal Joey 1940,D 26,22:2
Beat the Band 1942,O 15,26:1
Snafu 1944,O 26,19:5
Annie Get Your Gun 1946,My 17,14:2
Arms and the Girl 1950,F 3,28:2
Out West of Eighth 1951,S 21,20:3
Duntiere, Victor
Kiss Me, Kate 1949,Ja 30,II,6:5
South Pacific 1965,Je 3,25:1
Dunwell, William K
Our Betters 1937,Jl 22,16:2
Dupius
Vierge Folle, La; Foolish Virgin, The 1924,Mr 22,12:2
Dupont, Edwin
Grand Duke, The 1921,N 2,20:1
Dupont, Jacques (Costume Designer)
Phedre 1963,O 21,39:1
Grosse Valise, La 1965,D 15,52:1
Piano Dans l'Herbe, Un 1970,S 17,56:1
Dupont, Jacques (Miscellaneous)
Phedre 1963,O 21,39:1
Dupont, Jacques (Scenic Designer)
Grosse Valise, La 1965,D 15,52:1
Piano Dans l'Herbe, Un 1970,S 17,56:1
Dupont, Richard
Americans in France, The 1920,Ag 4,14:1
Return of Peter Grimm, The 1921,S 22,12:2
Seventeen 1924,Ap 12,18:2
Dupree, Frank (Lyricist)
Half a Widow 1927,S 13,37:3
Dupree, Frank (Playwright)
Half a Widow 1927,S 13,37:3
Dupree, Minnie
Charm School, The 1920,Ag 3,12:1
Detour, The 1921,Jl 17,VI,1:1
Everyday 1921,N 17,15:1
Your Woman and Mine 1922,F 28,17:2
Old Soak, The 1922,Ag 23,14:5
Shame Woman, The 1923,O 17,14:1
Catskill Dutch 1924,My 7,18:1
Catskill Dutch 1924,My 11,VIII,1:1
His Queen 1925,My 12,26:1
Schweiger 1926,Mr 24,20:4
Kept 1926,S 18,13:3
Paradise 1927,D 26,26:4
Clutching Claw, The 1928,F 15,20:1
Uncle Tom's Cabin 1933,My 30,13:4
Sellout, The 1933,S 7,17:2
Eldest, The 1935,F 12,24:3
Rag Picker of Paris, The: or, Modest Modiste 1935,N 12,23:7
Kind Lady 1935,N 19,27:3
Story to Be Whispered 1937,Ag 20,21:4
Lily of the Valley 1942,Ja 27,25:2
Dark Eyes 1943,Ja 15,20:2
Last Stop 1944,S 6,17:2
Land's End 1946,D 12,37:5
Dupree, Roland
New Meet the People, The 1943,Ag 22,II,1:6
Dupree, Vivienne
Miser, The 1950,Mr 27,19:5
DuPree, William
Carmen Jones 1956,Je 1,28:2
Carmen Jones 1959,Ag 18,25:1
Duprez, June
We Were Dancing; Tonight at Eight 1940,Ag 6,15:3
Henry VIII 1946,N 7,42:2
What Every Woman Knows 1946,N 9,13:2
Androcles and the Lion 1946,D 20,29:2
Town House 1948,S 24,31:2
Dupuy, Rene
Voyage de Monsieur Perrichon, Le 1937,N 2,32:3
Knock 1937,N 17,26:3
Roi Cerf, Le 1937,N 30,26:3
Y'Avait un Prisonnier 1938,Ja 25,24:3
DuQuan, Doreese
Oldest Trick in the World, The 1961,F 21,40:1
Porgy and Bess 1961,My 18,40:1
Duquesnal, Felix (Playwright)
Toto 1921,Mr 22,15:2

Duquet, Wallace
Ballad of John Ogilvie, The 1968,O 9,42:4
Duquette, Adrian (Costume Designer)
Camelot 1960,D 5,42:1
Camelot 1960,D 11,II,5:1
Duquette, Tony (Costume Designer)
Camelot 1960,D 5,42:1
Camelot 1960,D 11,II,5:1
Duran, Darryl
Peter Pan 1954,O 21,30:2
Duran, Michel
Grandee Penitence, La 1926,N 14,VIII,2:1
Duran, Michel (Original Author)
Ode to Liberty 1934,D 22,20:2
Duran, Michel (Playwright)
Liberte Provisoire 1934,My 27,X,2:1
Ode to Liberty 1934,D 11,28:2
Trois, Six, Neuf 1936,Je 21,IX,2:4
Ode to Liberty 1937,Ag 18,15:2
Duran-Reynals, Francisca (Miscellaneous)
Interview 1966,N 7,66:1
TV 1966,N 7,66:1
Motel 1966,N 7,66:1
Durand, Albert
Moon Is a Gong, The 1926,Mr 13,21:3
Men in White 1955,F 26,13:2
Durand, Charles
Judgment Day 1934,S 13,26:4
Durand, Charles (Miscellaneous)
Righteous Are Bold, The 1955,D 23,12:1
Affair of Honor 1956,Ap 7,12:3
Speaking of Murder 1956,D 20,37:1
Jane Eyre 1958,My 2,31:1
Howie 1958,S 18,35:2
Golden Fleecing 1959,O 16,24:5
Cool World, The 1960,F 23,38:2
Send Me No Flowers 1960,D 6,54:1
Cactus Flower 1965,D 9,60:2
Durand, Edouard
French Doll, The 1922,F 21,20:2
Her Way Out 1924,Je 24,18:3
Louie the 14th 1925,Mr 4,17:1
Durand, Juliette
Zorba 1968,N 18,58:1
Durand, Madeleine
Americans in France, The 1920,Ag 4,14:1
Durand, Marie
Dancing Partner 1930,Ag 6,24:2
Durand, Mark
Child Buyer, The 1964,D 22,35:1
Durand, Mark (Producer)
Steal the Old Man's Bundle 1970,My 16,30:1
Shepherd of Avenue B, The 1970,My 16,30:1
Durand, Maud
Her Way Out 1924,Je 24,18:3
Mask and the Face, The 1924,S 11,27:3
Two by Two 1925,F 24,17:1
Barefoot 1925,O 20,29:2
Jest, The 1926,F 14,VIII,1:1
Menace 1927,Mr 15,28:2
Bottled 1928,Ap 11,25:1
Strange Interlude 1928,D 18,37:3
When the Bough Breaks 1932,F 17,19:2
Two Strange Women 1933,Ja 11,23:3
Strangers at Home 1934,S 15,20:5
Durant, Al
Johnny 2X4 1942,Mr 17,24:6
Durant, Harry (Playwright)
Imaginative Girl, The 1926,Ag 8,VII,3:1
Adorable Liar, The 1926,Ag 31,15:2
Durant, Jack
Vaudeville (Palace) 1928,D 31,9:3
Earl Carroll's Vanities 1931,Ag 28,18:7
Pal Joey 1940,D 26,22:2
Girl From Nantucket, The 1945,N 9,17:2
Pal Joey 1963,My 30,21:1
Durante, Jimmy
Vaudeville (Palace) 1928,Ap 17,26:2
Vaudeville (Palace) 1928,Je 5,21:3
Show Girl 1929,Jl 3,19:3
New Yorkers, The 1930,D 9,31:1
New Yorkers, The 1930,D 28,VIII,1:1
Vaudeville (Palace) 1931,My 11,15:5
Strike Me Pink 1933,Mr 6,16:3
Friars Club Frolic 1933,My 15,16:4
Jumbo 1935,N 18,20:2
Jumbo 1935,N 24,IX,1:1
Red, Hot and Blue! 1936,O 8,26:1
Red, Hot and Blue! 1936,O 11,X,3:1
Red, Hot and Blue! 1936,O 30,26:3
Stars in Your Eyes 1939,F 10,18:2
Stars in Your Eyes 1939,Mr 5,X,1:2
Keep Off the Grass 1940,My 5,X,1:6
Keep Off the Grass 1940,My 24,22:6
Keep Off the Grass 1940,Je 16,IX,1:1
Durante, Vito
Bajour 1964,N 24,42:1
Wonderful Town 1967,My 18,50:1
Duras, Marguerite (Playwright)
Square, The 1961,Mr 24,37:1
Miracle Worker, The 1961,O 8,II,3:4
Journees Entieres dans les Arbres, Des
1965,D 4,20:1

Place Without Doors, A 1970,D 1,60:1
Durask, Norman
Mlle Modiste 1937,My 5,28:5
Durasova, Nina
Lysistrata 1925,D 15,28:2
Duree, Meurisse
Judy Garland's New Variety Show 1956,S 27,43:2
Duren, Fred
Peace 1970,S 2,30:2
Durgeon, Augusta
God Loves Us 1926,O 20,22:2
Lally 1927,F 9,16:3
Mourning Becomes Electra; Hunted, The
1931,O 27,22:1
Professor Mamlock 1937,Ap 14,30:3
Durham, Earl (Director)
In the Nick of Time 1967,Je 2,36:1
Durham, Richard
King John 1956,Je 28,33:5
Measure for Measure 1956,Je 29,16:1
Romeo and Juliet 1957,Je 28,30:2
Two Gentlemen of Verona 1957,Jl 23,21:5
Macbeth 1957,Ag 16,11:2
Legend of Lizzie, The 1959,F 10,39:1
Geranium Hat, The 1959,Mr 18,45:1
Step on a Crack 1962,O 18,48:1
Durham, T C Jr
Nerves 1924,S 2,22:2
Durham, Tom
Measure for Measure 1967,F 15,37:1
Hamlet 1967,F 17,44:1
Romeo and Juliet 1967,F 22,18:1
Durieux, Tilla
Robe Rouge, La 1922,F 5,VI,1:7
Shadow, The 1923,D 15,16:2
Fedora 1924,Ja 24,14:2
Franziska 1927,Ja 30,VII,4:3
Iphigenia in Aulis; Agamemnon's Death; Electra;
Iphigenia in Delphi 1962,N 11,82:4
Durkee, Dorothy
Mexican Hayride 1944,Ja 29,9:6
Durkin, Bernard
Squaw Man, The 1921,D 27,10:3
Paid 1925,N 26,32:1
Durkin, Betsy
Athenian Touch, The 1964,Ja 15,25:4
Durkin, Gertrude
Courage 1928,O 9,34:2
Durkin, Grace
Paid 1925,N 26,32:1
Street Wolf, The 1929,Ja 1,61:1
Durkin, James
Robert E Lee 1923,N 21,23:1
Durkin, James (Director)
Chivalry 1925,D 16,22:3
Durkin, Junior
Lady, The 1923,D 5,23:2
Courage 1928,O 9,34:2
Vaudeville (Palace) 1929,S 16,30:4
Lottery, The 1930,N 23,IX,3:5
Growing Pains 1933,N 24,24:2
Durkin, Lillian
Ed Wynn's Carnival 1920,Ap 6,18:2
Durkin, Master
H M S Pinafore 1926,Ap 7,26:3
Durling, Ronald
Billy Budd 1955,My 4,35:1
Venice Preserv'd 1955,D 13,54:4
Lower Depths, The 1956,O 3,29:2
Many Loves 1959,Ja 14,28:1
Little Hut, The 1961,Jl 26,34:2
Durning, Charles
In April Once 1955,Mr 14,29:3
Hour Glass, The 1955,O 17,33:1
Julius Caesar 1962,F 22,19:6
Tempest, The 1962,Jl 17,18:2
As You Like It 1963,Jl 17,19:2
Winter's Tale, The 1963,Ag 16,14:1
Twelfth Night 1963,O 9,47:1
Child Buyer, The 1964,D 22,35:1
Henry V 1965,Je 29,27:2
Taming of the Shrew, The 1965,Jl 3,10:5
Drat! the Cat! 1965,O 11,54:2
Pousse-Cafe 1966,Mr 19,19:2
World of Gunter Grass, The 1966,Ap 27,38:1
All's Well That Ends Well 1966,Je 17,39:1
Measure for Measure 1966,Jl 14,27:1
Comedy of Errors, The 1967,Je 15,58:4
King John 1967,Jl 14,19:1
Titus Andronicus 1967,Ag 10,43:2
Happy Time, The 1968,Ja 19,32:2
Huui, Huui 1968,N 25,58:1
Invitation to a Beheading 1969,Mr 18,36:1
Twelfth Night 1969,Ag 14,29:2
Indians 1969,O 14,51:1
Lemon Sky 1970,My 18,40:1
Wars of the Roses, The (Part II) 1970,Jl 3,15:1
Happiness Cage, The 1970,O 5,56:4
Durning, Dan
Simpleton of the Unexpected Isles, The
1954,Ja 12,19:1
Taming of the Shrew, The 1956,Ag 11,11:2
Camille 1956,S 19,33:1

Durning, Dan—Cont
Richard III 1957,N 26,41:1
As You Like It 1958,Ja 21,33:6
Othello 1958,Jl 4,16:1
Herne's Egg, The 1960,S 20,48:1
Taming of the Shrew, The 1963,Mr 8,9:1
Love's Labour's Lost 1965,Je 16,46:1
Serjeant Musgrave's Dance 1966,Mr 9,44:1
Gloria and Esperanza 1970,F 5,32:1
Trelawny of the 'Wells' 1970,O 12,48:1
DuRoy, Robert
Right of Happiness 1931,Ap 3,34:2
Durrant, Hugh (Scenic Designer)
Midsummer Night's Dream, A 1968,D 9,59:1
Twelfth Night 1970,Ja 1,18:1
Durrant, Regan
King of the Dark Chamber 1961,F 10,21:1
Durrell, Katherine
Antigone 1923,My 4,18:4
Durrell, Lawrence (Playwright)
Sappho 1961,Ag 23,28:5
Actis 1961,N 23,50:2
Irish Faustus, An 1963,D 19,40:1
Durrell, Michael
Phedre 1966,F 11,36:1
Butterfly Dream, The 1966,My 20,41:1
Cherry Orchard, The 1968,Mr 20,41:1
Misanthrope, The 1968,O 10,59:1
Cock-A-Doodle Dandy 1969,Ja 21,40:1
Hamlet 1969,Mr 4,34:1
Durrence, Betty
Polonaise 1945,O 8,20:2
Durston, David
How to Make a Man 1961,F 3,16:1
Durston, David (Sgt)
Winged Victory 1943,N 22,24:1
Duryea, Dan
Caesar and Cleopatra 1935,Ag 22,21:1
Dead End 1935,O 29,17:2
Virginian, The 1937,Ag 10,22:7
Many Mansions 1937,O 28,28:6
Missouri Legend 1938,S 20,27:2
Little Foxes, The 1939,F 16,16:2
Little Foxes, The 1939,F 26,IX,1:1
Duryea, Edward (Director)
Between the Devil 1937,D 23,24:5
Duryea, May
2 Girls Wanted 1926,S 10,25:3
Eva the Fifth 1928,Ag 29,19:3
Dusch, Barnardine (Rev) (Playwright)
Veronica's Veil 1950,F 12,II,1:5
Veronica's Veil 1954,F 28,I,78:5
Duschinsky, Richard (Playwright)
Stempellbrueder 1929,N 24,X,2:4
Dole Brothers 1932,Mr 26,17:7
Komparserie 1933,Mr 19,IX,2:2
Duse, Eleonora
Donna Del Mare, La; Lady From the Sea, The
1923,O 30,17:1
Lady of the Sea 1923,N 3,8:2
Lady of the Sea 1923,N 4,VIII,1:2
Spretti; Ghosts 1923,N 7,14:1
Cosi Sia; Thy Will be Done 1923,N 14,29:2
Porta Chiusa, La; Closed Door, The 1923,N 21,23:1
Citta Morta, La; Dead City, The 1923,N 28,14:1
Locandiera, La 1923,D 9,IX,1:1
Duse, Eleonora (Producer)
Lady of the Sea 1923,N 3,8:2
Dusenbury, Delwin
Confederacy, The 1958,Jl 3,20:1
Dushell, Lilian
Lady Precious Stream 1936,Ja 28,15:2
Duskin, Joyce
Between the Devil 1937,D 23,24:5
Saint of Bleecker Street, The 1954,D 28,21:1
Dussault, Nancy
Diversions 1958,N 8,14:4
Dr Willy Nilly 1959,Je 5,18:2
Mikado, The 1959,O 2,24:1
Do Re Mi 1960,D 27,23:2
Do Re Mi 1961,Ja 8,II,1:1
Bajour 1964,N 24,42:1
Carousel 1966,D 16,56:2
Finian's Rainbow 1967,Ap 6,44:1
South Pacific 1969,Jl 7,27:1
Whispers on the Wind 1970,Je 4,50:1
Trelawny of the 'Wells' 1970,O 12,48:1
Trelawney of the 'Wells' 1970,O 25,II,16:1
d'Usseau, Arnaud (Playwright)
Tomorrow the World 1943,Ap 15,22:2
Tomorrow the World 1943,Ap 25,II,1:1
Deep Are the Roots 1945,S 27,24:4
Deep Are the Roots 1945,O 7,II,1:1
Deep Are the Roots 1947,Ap 28,26:3
Deep Are the Roots 1947,Jl 10,17:1
Legend of Sarah 1950,O 12,42:4
Ladies of the Corridor, The 1953,O 22,33:5
Ladies of the Corridor, The 1953,N 1,II,1:1
Deep Are the Roots 1960,O 4,47:1
Dusseau, Oscar
Ice Follies 1961,Ja 11,25:2
Ice Follies 1963,Ja 10,5:2
Duthers, Lou
Fifty Million Frenchmen 1929,N 28,34:4

Duthie, George
Jefferson Davis 1936,F 19,17:2
Horse Eats Hat 1936,S 28,14:2
Doctor Faustus 1937,Ja 9,21:2
Julius Caesar 1937,N 12,26:6
Shoemaker's Holiday, The 1938,Ja 3,17:2
Dutra, John
Comes a Day 1958,N 7,22:1
Physicists, The 1964,O 14,52:1
Dutt, Utpal
Ayeya Vietnam 1966,D 21,2:4
Dutt, Utpal (Director)
Ayeya Vietnam 1966,D 21,2:4
Dutt, Utpal (Playwright)
Ayeya Vietnam 1966,D 21,2:4
Kallol 1966,D 21,2:4
Dutton, Jimmy
Seeds in the Wind 1948,Ap 26,27:2
Seeds in the Wind 1948,My 26,29:2
Anybody Home 1949,F 26,10:5
Member of the Wedding, The 1950,Ja 6,26:6
Dutton, Laura Deane
New Faces of 1943 1942,D 23,22:2
Duval, Darlean
Porgy and Bess 1935,O 11,30:2
Sweet River 1936,O 29,30:2
Duval, Edna
Hotel Mouse, The 1922,Mr 14,11:3
Caroline 1923,F 1,13:2
Duval, Franca
Maria Golovin 1958,N 6,43:1
Duval, Gabrielle
Pinocchio 1939,Ja 3,19:2
DuVal, Herbert
Five Star Saint 1970,F 11,41:2
Duval, Immanuel
Homecoming 1942,N 17,28:5
Duval, Jack
Soliloquy 1938,N 29,26:4
Duval, Jose
Merry Widow, The 1957,Ap 11,36:6
Shoemaker and the Peddler, The 1960,O 15,27:4
That Hat! 1964,S 24,45:1
Duval, Josephine
Mayflowers 1925,N 25,14:2
Duval, Margaret K
Vagabond King, The 1935,N 29,22:7
Duval, Paulette
Ziegfeld Follies 1923,O 22,17:2
Duval, Viola
Caroline 1923,F 1,13:2
Duval, Violet
Hotel Mouse, The 1922,Mr 14,11:3
Duvall, Robert
Mrs Warren's Profession 1958,Je 26,22:1
Call Me by My Rightful Name 1961,F 1,31:1
Days and Nights of Beebee Fenstermaker, The 1962,S 18,33:1
View from the Bridge, A 1965,Ja 29,24:1
Wait Until Dark 1966,F 3,21:1
Duvernois, Henri (Original Author)
Jacqueline 1921,N 20,VI,1:3
Eunuque, L' 1927,Ap 3,VIII,4:7
Soeurs Hortensias, Les 1934,My 13,IX,2:2
Duvernois, Henri (Playwright)
Nounouche 1923,O 23,16:1
Seul 1923,N 13,24:2
Apres l'Amour 1924,Mr 2,VIII,1:3
Embers 1926,F 2,20:3
Temps d'Aimer, Le 1926,D 12,VIII,3:4
Eunuque, L' 1927,Ap 3,VIII,4:7
Untitled-Play 1928,F 5,VIII,2:1
Eusebe 1928,N 25,X,4:7
Hermonie 1929,Mr 3,VIII,4:8
Coeur 1930,O 26,VIII,2:1
Jeanne 1932,N 27,IX,3:1
Soeurs Hortensias, Les 1934,My 13,IX,2:2
Duvey, Eliot (Lighting Director)
An Evening With G B S; Press Cuttings 1957,F 19,35:7
Evening With G B S, An; O'Flaherty, V C 1957,F 19,35:7
Duvoisin, Willi (Original Author)
Fanny 1955,D 17,19:6
Dux, Francis
An Evening With G B S; Press Cuttings 1957,F 19,35:7
Fashion 1959,Ja 21,27:1
Susannah and the Elders 1959,O 19,37:3
Miss Emily Adam 1960,Mr 30,43:1
Sudden End of Anne Cinquefoil, The 1961,Ja 11,25:2
I Want You 1961,S 15,29:1
Dux, Pierre
Absence of a Cello; Mal de Test, Le 1965,S 9,36:3
Dvonch, Frederick (Musical Director)
Arms and the Girl 1950,F 3,28:2
King and I, The 1951,Mr 30,26:2
King and I, The 1951,Ap 8,II,1:1
Guys and Dolls 1955,Ap 21,32:2
South Pacific 1955,My 5,39:5
King and I, The 1956,Ap 19,35:4
Kiss Me, Kate 1956,My 10,27:2

Show Boat 1956,Je 22,16:1
South Pacific 1957,Ap 25,35:1
Pajama Game, The 1957,My 16,27:1
Pajama Game, The 1957,My 26,II,1:1
Show Boat 1957,Je 28,30:2
Rumple 1957,N 7,42:2
Annie Get Your Gun 1958,F 20,29:2
Oklahoma! 1958,Mr 20,32:3
Song of Norway 1958,Je 23,19:2
First Impressions 1959,Mr 20,28:1
Song of Norway 1959,Je 26,16:2
Sound of Music, The 1959,N 17,40:2
Do I Hear a Waltz? 1965,Mr 19,28:1
Sound of Music, The 1967,Ap 27,52:1
South Pacific 1969,Jl 7,27:1
Dvorak, Elsie
As You Like It 1939,My 9,28:4
Dvorak, Jeraldine
Boudoir 1941,F 8,18:4
All Men Are Alike 1941,O 7,27:2
Dvorikin, Judith (Miscellaneous)
Way of the World, The 1950,Ap 9,73:5
Dweck, Samuel
Nights of Wrath; Nuits de la Colere, Les 1947,D 1,26:4
Dweir (Musical Director)
Month of Sundays 1968,S 17,50:1
Dwellers, Cliff (Miscellaneous)
Thracian Horses, The 1961,S 28,58:2
Dwight, Everett
Uniform of Flesh 1949,Ja 31,15:2
Saint Joan 1950,Mr 4,10:6
Lucky Sam McCarver 1950,Ap 15,10:6
Dwight, Maquita
Comedian, The 1923,Mr 14,14:1
Dwight, Sally
Lucky Sam McCarver 1950,Ap 15,10:6
Dwork, Kermit (Composer)
How Revolting! 1932,Mr 11,14:6
Dworken, Frances
Sunup to Sundown 1938,F 2,14:3
Red Velvet Goat, The 1939,Ja 21,18:4
Dworkin, Harry (Scenic Designer)
Slightly Scandalous 1944,Je 14,16:2
Dworkin, Stan
Hamlet 1959,S 11,21:4
Antony and Cleopatra 1963,Je 21,33:1
As You Like It 1963,Jl 17,19:2
Measure for Measure 1966,Jl 14,27:1
Richard III 1966,Ag 11,26:1
King John 1967,Jl 14,19:1
Dworshak, Lois
Ice Follies 1937,D 22,29:1
Dwyer, Allys
Five O'Clock Girl, The 1927,O 11,26:3
Regular Guy, A; Man's Man, A 1931,Je 5,27:1
Hot Money 1931,N 9,22:2
Dwyer, Anthony
Dance Night 1938,O 15,20:5
Dwyer, Erik
Peg o' My Heart 1948,Ag 25,29:2
Dwyer, Ethel
Tarzan of the Apes 1921,S 8,14:3
Dwyer, Frank
Moby Dick 1970,Je 3,52:1
Hamlet 1970,O 27,54:2
Rosencrantz and Guildenstern Are Dead 1970,N 19,39:3
Dwyer, Frank (Director)
Rosencrantz and Guildenstern Are Dead 1970,N 19,39:3
Dwyer, Frank (Miscellaneous)
Hamlet 1970,O 27,54:2
Dwyer, Frank (Scenic Designer)
Twelfth Night 1932,N 19,20:5
Dwyer, James (Director)
War Games 1969,Ap 18,37:1
Dwyer, James (Lighting Director)
Motel 1966,N 7,66:1
TV 1966,N 7,66:1
Interview 1966,N 7,66:1
Dwyer, James (Miscellaneous)
Niggerlovers, The; Demonstration, The 1967,O 2,54:2
Niggerlovers, The; Man and Dog 1967,O 2,54:2
Little Murders 1969,Ja 6,38:1
Dwyer, John
Road Together, The 1924,Ja 18,21:2
Dwyer, John (Scenic Designer)
Nic-Nax of 1926 1926,Ag 5,19:1
Dwyer, John D
Jack in the Pulpit 1925,Ja 7,33:1
Dwyer, John T
Back Pay 1921,Ag 31,8:2
Partners Again 1922,My 2,22:2
Spring Fever 1925,Ag 4,14:2
Don Q Jr 1926,Ja 28,16:3
Judy 1927,F 8,20:2
Brass Buttons 1927,D 6,26:3
Congai 1928,N 28,24:3
Top Speed 1929,D 26,20:1
You Said It 1931,Ja 20,21:3
Monkey 1932,F 12,25:2

Dwyer, John T—Cont
Take My Tip 1932,Ap 12,25:2
Best People, The 1933,Mr 16,21:5
She Loves Me Not 1933,N 21,22:4
Mother Lode 1934,D 24,16:5
Play, Genius, Play! 1935,O 31,17:2
Bright Honor 1936,S 28,14:1
Dwyer, Lou
Days of Our Youth, The 1941,N 29,15:2
Dwyer, Marlo
Good Night Ladies 1945,Ja 18,16:2
Loco 1946,O 17,29:2
Dwyer, Phil
Ziegfeld Follies 1921,Je 22,10:1
Dwyer, R Corcoran
New York Idea, The 1948,Ag 18,29:2
Dwyer, Richard
Ice Follies 1957,Ja 16,36:1
Ice Follies 1958,Ja 15,26:2
Ice Follies 1959,Ja 14,30:1
Ice Follies 1960,Ja 13,20:1
Ice Follies 1961,Ja 11,25:2
Ice Follies 1963,Ja 10,5:2
Ice Follies 1964,Ja 8,41:2
Ice Follies 1965,Ja 13,35:1
Ice Follies 1966,Ja 12,27:6
Ice Follies 1967,Ja 11,51:1
Ice Follies 1969,My 23,38:1
Ice Follies 1970,My 23,27:1
Dwyer, Virginia
Home Is the Hero 1945,Ja 20,16:4
Craig's Wife 1947,F 13,35:2
Craig's Wife 1947,Mr 30,II,1:1
Dawn's Early Light 1950,O 25,44:3
Dwyer, William
Ponder Heart, The 1956,F 17,14:2
Dyall, Franklin
Silent House, The 1927,Jl 3,VII,1:4
Last Hour, The 1929,Ja 6,VIII,1:4
Toy Cart, The 1930,D 7,IX,2:7
Black Magic 1931,S 6,VIII,2:1
Great Van Dyn, The 1935,Mr 6,22:2
Butterfly on the Wheel 1935,N 10,IX,3:1
Dyas, James (Director)
Trouble in July 1949,D 2,36:2
Send Me No Flowers 1960,D 6,54:1
Dyas, Mary Alma (Lighting Director)
In the Shadow of the Glen 1957,Mr 7,24:1
Tinker's Wedding, The 1957,Mr 7,24:1
Riders to the Sea 1957,Mr 7,24:1
Blood Wedding 1958,Ap 1,35:1
Dybas, James
Do I Hear a Waltz? 1965,Mr 19,28:1
George M! 1968,Ap 11,48:1
Dycke, Tom Van (Producer)
Out of a Blue Sky 1930,F 10,20:6
Dye, Carol
Servant of Two Masters, The 1958,F 11,35:2
Dye, Robert
Treat 'Em Rough 1926,O 5,26:2
Dyer, Charles (Playwright)
Rattle of a Simple Man 1963,Ap 18,39:1
Staircase 1968,Ja 11,41:2
Staircase 1968,Ja 21,II,3:7
Dyer, Chouteau
Merrily We Roll Along 1934,O 1,14:1
To See Ourselves 1935,My 1,25:2
Return to Folly 1935,Jl 23,24:3
Pride and Prejudice 1935,N 6,32:4
Criminals, The 1941,D 22,24:3
Dyer, Chouteau (Director)
Wedding in Japan 1949,N 11,29:1
Dyer, Elizabeth
Little Theatre Tournament; Monkey's Paw, The 1929,My 10,32:2
Dyer, G B
Galloper, The 1924,D 19,26:2
Dyer, John
Tattle Tales 1933,Je 2,22:6
Dyer, Johnny
Vaudeville (Palace) 1926,Je 15,23:3
Dyer, Mansel
Yeomen of the Guard, The 1936,S 15,37:2
Yeomen of the Guard, The 1939,Ja 24,17:1
Dyer, Marion
Martinique 1920,Ap 27,18:2
So This Is Politics 1924,Je 17,22:2
Dyer, Robert E Jr (Producer)
Pirates of Penzance, The 1967,Ag 7,34:2
Dyer, Sammy (Choreographer)
Swing Mikado, The 1939,Mr 2,18:2
Dyer, Virginia
Harriet 1944,S 28,26:1
Dyer, William (Composer)
From A to Z 1960,Ap 21,23:2
Jo 1964,F 13,25:1
Dyer, William (Lyricist)
Jo 1964,F 13,25:1
Dyer, William (Playwright)
Jo 1964,F 13,25:1
Dyer-Bennett, Richard
Second Best Bed 1946,Je 4,20:2
Evening With Will Shakespeare, An 1952,D 7,86:5

Dyington, H
Plain Dealer, The 1929,My 23,27:1
Dykes, Hazel
Natural Man 1941,My 8,20:4
Dymally, Amentha
Amen Corner, The 1965,Ap 16,35:1
Dymov, Ossip
Salt and Pepper 1933,Ap 24,10:2
Dymov, Ossip (Director)
Once Upon a Time 1933,S 22,15:1
Germany Aflame 1933,O 28,20:5
Dymov, Ossip (Playwright)
Bronx Express 1922,Ap 27,12:2
Bronx Express 1927,D 4,31:4
Europa A G 1932,O 2,IX,1:2
Bread 1932,D 14,27:3
Town Lunatics 1933,F 6,11:4
Salt and Pepper 1933,Ap 24,10:2
Germany Aflame 1933,O 28,20:5
Slaves of the Public 1934,Mr 10,18:6
Here Runs the Bride 1934,S 20,21:3
Here Runs the Bride 1934,N 4,IX,2:1
East Side Professor, The 1938,F 12,19:7
Bronx Express, 1968 1968,N 16,43:3
Dyne, Michael (Playwright)
Right Honourable Gentleman, The 1965,O 20,50:2
Dyneforth, James
Business Widow, The 1923,D 11,27:1
Dyneley, Peter
Millionairess, The 1952,O 18,17:2
Dyrenforth, Harald
Flight to the West 1940,D 31,19:1
Letters to Lucerne 1941,D 24,14:2
Russian People, The 1942,D 30,17:2
Dyrenforth, James
Not so Fast 1923,My 23,18:4
Dyrenforth, James (Lyricist)
Glory 1922,D 26,10:1
Nikki 1931,S 30,23:4
Dysart, Max (Producer)
Mrs Patterson 1957,F 6,20:2
Dysart, Richard
Our Town 1959,Mr 24,46:2
Epitaph for George Dillon 1960,D 29,17:1
Our Town 1961,N 4,14:7
Six Characters in Search of an Author
1963,Mr 11,7:2
Man for All Seasons, A 1964,Ja 28,24:2
All in Good Time 1965,F 19,25:1
Little Foxes, The 1967,O 27,53:1
Crimes of Passion; Ruffian on the Stair, The
1969,O 27,54:1
Crimes of Passion; Erpingham Camp, The
1969,O 27,54:1
Crimes of Passion; Erpingham Camp, The; Ruffian
on the Stair, The 1969,N 9,II,1:1
Place Without Doors, A 1970,D 1,60:1
Dyson, Ronald
Hair 1968,Ap 30,40:2
Dyson, Wynn
Patience 1936,O 6,28:6
Patience 1939,Ja 27,16:3
Dyville, Jack
Light, Lively and Yiddish 1970,O 28,58:1
Dzeduszycka, Teresa (Translator)
Tango 1969,Ja 20,33:1
Dziewonski, Edward
Visit With the Family, A 1957,O 17,42:5
Dzigan, Shimen
Hut a Yid a Landele 1968,O 19,28:1
From Israel With Laughter 1969,O 17,34:1

E

Eadie, Dennis
Love at Second Sight 1927,S 11,VIII,2:4
Eadie, Dennis (Producer)
Half a Loaf 1926,N 28,VIII,1:4
Eadie and Rack
Evening With Beatrice Lillie, An 1952,O 3,17:2
Eads, Harold M (Rev) (Director)
Man Dies, A 1968,Jl 16,35:1
Eady, Joseph
St Louis Woman 1946,Ap 1,22:2
Eagan, Allen
Princess Virtue 1921,My 5,20:2
Eagan, Biron
Trimmed in Scarlet 1920,F 3,18:1
Eagan, Raymond B (Lyricist)
Holka Polka 1925,O 15,27:2
Eagels, Jeanne
Wonderful Thing, The 1920,F 18,9:1
Wonderful Thing, The 1920,F 22,III,6:1
In the Night Watch 1921,Ja 31,10:1
Rain 1922,N 8,18:2
Rain 1922,N 12,VIII,1:1
Untitled-Recital 1923,D 29,8:2
Rain 1926,O 12,27:1
Her Cardboard Lover 1927,Mr 22,30:5
Eager, Edward (Lyricist)
Dream With Music 1944,My 19,15:2
Liar, The 1950,My 19,30:2

Dr Willy Nilly 1959,Je 5,18:2
Happy Hypocrite, The 1968,S 6,38:1
Eager, Edward (Playwright)
Two Misers, The 1943,D 9,30:5
Liar, The 1950,My 19,30:2
Gambler, The 1952,O 14,40:1
Dr Willy Nilly 1959,Je 5,18:2
Happy Hypocrite, The 1968,S 6,38:1
Eager, Edward (Translator)
Call It Virtue 1963,Mr 28,8:2
Rugantino 1964,F 7,34:1
Eager, Johnny
Girl From Nantucket, The 1945,N 9,17:2
Eagle, Oscar (Director)
Topsy and Eva 1924,D 24,11:1
Cocoanuts, The 1925,D 9,30:1
Matinee Girl, The 1926,F 2,20:3
Just Life 1926,S 15,33:3
Katy Did 1927,My 10,24:3
Enchanted Isle 1927,S 20,33:2
Animal Crackers 1928,O 24,26:2
Houseboat on the Styx, The 1928,D 26,14:3
Borrowed Love 1929,Je 18,29:2
Eagles, James
Bad Penny, A 1931,Ag 23,VIII,2:4
Eakin, J H
Merchant of Venice, The 1930,D 3,29:2
Eames, Clare
Prince and the Pauper, The 1920,N 2,15:1
Mary Stuart 1921,Mr 22,15:1
Mary Stuart 1921,Ap 3,VII,1:1
Swords 1921,S 2,9:3
Swords 1921,S 11,VI,1:1
Aglavaine and Selysette 1922,Ja 4,11:1
First Fifty Years, The 1922,Mr 14,11:2
Clouds of the Sun 1922,My 6,11:2
Spook Sonata, The 1924,Ja 7,23:3
Fashion 1924,F 5,21:2
Macbeth 1924,Mr 17,18:1
Hedda Gabler 1924,My 17,18:4
Little Angel, The 1924,S 29,10:3
Candida 1924,D 13,12:3
Candida 1924,D 21,VII,1:1
Lucky Sam McCarver 1925,O 22,22:1
Lucky Sam McCarver 1925,N 1,VIII,1:1
Androcles and the Lion 1925,N 24,28:1
Man of Destiny, The 1925,N 24,28:1
Little Eyolf 1926,F 3,22:1
Juarez and Maximilian 1926,O 12,31:1
Juarez and Maximilian 1926,O 17,VIII,1:1
Ned McCobb's Daughter 1926,N 30,26:2
Ned McCobb's Daughter 1926,D 5,VIII,5:1
Brothers Karamazov, The 1927,Ja 4,20:1
Silver Cord, The 1927,S 14,29:2
Silver Cord, The 1927,O 2,VIII,1:3
Ame en Peine, L' 1928,F 12,VIII,2:1
Sacred Flame, The 1928,N 20,28:2
Sacred Flame, The 1929,Mr 3,VIII,2:5
Eames, Clare (Director)
Wild Duck, The 1925,F 25,16:4
Eames, Ernest
Gondoliers, The 1940,O 1,29:2
Eames, Florence
Tobias and the Angel 1937,Ap 29,16:5
Eames, Howard
Peggy-Ann 1926,D 28,16:3
Eames, Kathryn
Lamp at Midnight 1947,D 22,29:2
Book of Job, The 1962,F 10,13:1
Eames, Peggy
Vaudeville (Palace) 1927,Ap 12,25:4
Earing, June
Mr Winkle's Holliday 1946,Je 24,27:6
Aquashow 1952,Je 25,25:1
Aquashow 1953,Je 24,29:2
Aquashow 1954,Je 23,20:4
Elliott Murphy's Aquashow 1955,Je 23,25:1
Elliott Murphy's Aquashow 1956,Je 20,26:2
Earl, Donna
Moroni 1936,Ag 19,19:1
Earl, Eugene
Searching Wind, The 1944,Ap 13,25:2
Earl, Florence
Wild Oats Lane 1922,S 7,12:1
Earl, Jane
Fundamental George, The 1949,Ag 17,19:4
Earl, Marshall (Producer)
Lady's Not for Burning, The 1957,F 22,26:2
Cloud 7 1958,F 15,15:2
Earl, William
Grab Bag, The 1924,O 7,26:2
Earle, Arthur
From Morn Till Midnight 1948,D 7,41:6
Earle, Edward
Viva Madison Avenue 1960,Ap 7,42:1
Sweet Miani 1962,S 26,33:2
Show Me Where the Good Times Are
1970,Mr 6,32:1
Earle, Edward (Choreographer)
Decameron, The 1961,Ap 13,32:1
Sweet Miani 1962,S 26,33:2
Earle, Edward (Composer)
Decameron, The 1961,Ap 13,32:1

Earle, Eileen
Murder in the Cathedral 1958,Mr 22,12:4
House of Bernarda Alba, The 1963,N 25,23:2
Earle, Emily
Peek-A-Boo 1921,My 17,20:3
Money Business 1926,Ja 21,18:1
Earle, Florence
It's Up to You 1921,Mr 29,20:1
Golden Days 1921,N 2,20:1
Anathema 1923,Ap 11,16:2
Inspector General, The 1923,My 1,24:1
Connie Goes Home 1923,S 7,10:1
So This Is Politics 1924,Je 17,22:2
Good Bad Woman, A 1925,F 10,21:1
Backslapper, The 1925,Ap 13,25:2
Home Towners, The 1926,Ag 24,19:3
Talk About Girls 1927,Je 15,31:3
Weather Clear, Track Fast 1927,O 19,24:5
Hello, Daddy! 1928,D 27,26:5
House Afire 1930,Ap 1,34:7
Farewell to Arms, A 1930,S 23,30:3
Anything Goes 1934,N 22,26:1
Alice Takat 1936,F 11,19:2
Earle, Frederick
Old English 1924,D 24,11:2
Tale of the Wolf, The 1925,O 8,31:2
Fast Life 1928,S 27,35:2
Earle, George
What Ann Brought Home 1927,F 22,22:2
Earle, George H 4th
Come Across 1937,Ap 10,10:7
Earle, Gordon
Sex 1926,Ap 27,22:4
Gang War 1928,Ag 21,27:2
Earle, Jane
Secret Room, The 1945,N 8,16:2
Earle, Nick
Everyman Today 1958,Ja 16,32:4
Earle, Robert
Danton's Death 1938,N 3,26:2
Earle, William
Game of Love and Death, The 1929,N 26,28:4
Earles, Ray
First Mortgage 1929,O 11,36:1
Troika 1930,Ap 2,32:6
Find the Fox 1930,Je 21,20:4
Long Road, The 1930,S 10,30:2
Gasoline Gypsies 1931,Je 8,21:3
House of Doom, The 1932,Ja 26,20:4
Decoy, The 1932,Ap 2,13:4
Earley, Jackie
Slave Ship 1969,N 22,46:1
Early, Enez
Pal Joey 1940,D 26,22:2
Early, Margaret
Try and Get It 1943,Ag 3,13:2
Early, Robert
Oklahoma! 1951,My 30,15:2
Earp, Mary
Importance of Being Earnest, The 1936,O 22,31:2
Earp, Shelton
Hipper's Holiday 1934,O 19,26:2
Easdale, Brian (Composer)
Romeo and Juliet 1956,O 25,41:1
Macbeth 1956,O 30,42:2
Easley, Douglas
Elizabeth the Queen 1966,N 4,30:1
Easley, Holmes (Scenic Designer)
Hamlet 1970,O 19,51:1
Easman, Manuel (Scenic Designer)
Conjur' Man Dies 1936,Mr 12,18:5
Eason, Myles
Visit, The 1958,My 6,40:1
Visit, The 1960,Mr 9,38:3
Julia, Jake, and Uncle Joe 1961,Ja 30,19:1
My Fair Lady 1964,My 21,43:2
Midsummer Night's Dream, A 1967,Je 19,42:1
Eason, Myles (Miscellaneous)
Much Ado About Nothing 1959,S 18,25:2
Midsummer Night's Dream, A 1967,Je 19,42:1
East, Ron
Alchemist, The 1969,Je 12,51:1
Merchant of Venice, The 1970,Je 10,39:1
School for Scandal, The 1970,Je 11,51:1
Eastburn, E C
Wedding in Japan 1957,Mr 12,37:7
Easteal, Rita
Ice Capades 1958,S 4,33:2
Easterly, Tom
Earthlight Theater 1970,N 4,38:2
Eastham, Richard
South Pacific 1949,Je 5,II,1:1
South Pacific 1950,Ap 26,36:5
Eastland, Edward
Flies, The 1954,S 10,18:2
Eastman, Edgar
Elmer the Great 1928,S 25,29:1
Eastman, Jean
Marie Antoinette 1921,N 23,16:1
Eastman, Joan
Hooray!! It's a Glorious Day. . .And All That
1966,Mr 10,28:1

Eastman, Virginia
How's Your Health? 1929,N 27,30:3
Easton, Edward
Party on Greenwich Avenue, The 1967,My 11,52:1
Easton, Jack
Undesirable Lady, An 1933,O 10,24:4
Sap Runs High, The 1936,F 5,15:3
Easton, Jack (Miscellaneous)
Smiling the Boy Fell Dead 1961,Ap 20,28:1
Easton, Jack (Musical Director)
Skits-Oh-Frantics 1967,Ap 3,39:2
Easton, Jay
Shadow and Substance 1956,Mr 14,38:1
Easton, Richard
Richard III 1953,Jl 15,22:2
Henry V 1956,Je 20,27:2
Merry Wives of Windsor, The 1956,Je 21,34:4
Measure for Measure 1957,Ja 23,24:1
Taming of the Shrew, The 1957,F 21,30:2
Duchess of Malfi, The 1957,Mr 20,33:1
Othello 1957,Je 24,19:2
Merchant of Venice, The 1957,Jl 11,19:5
Much Ado About Nothing 1957,Ag 8,15:2
Country Wife, The 1957,N 28,56:1
Back to Methuselah 1958,Mr 27,41:5
Back to Methuselah 1958,Ap 6,II,1:1
Hamlet 1958,Je 21,11:1
Midsummer Night's Dream, A 1958,Je 23,19:1
Winter's Tale, The 1958,Jl 21,17:4
Winter's Tale, The 1958,Jl 27,II,1:1
Salad Days 1958,N 11,24:1
Romeo and Juliet 1959,Je 15,31:1
Romeo and Juliet 1959,Je 15,31:1
Merry Wives of Windsor, The 1959,Jl 9,23:2
All's Well That Ends Well 1959,Ag 3,20:4
School for Scandal, The 1963,Ja 26,5:2
Who's Afraid of Virginia Woolf? 1964,F 8,15:1
Pantagleize 1967,D 1,54:1
Exit the King 1968,Ja 10,48:1
Exit the King 1968,Ja 21,II,1:2
Cherry Orchard, The 1968,Mr 20,41:1
Misanthrope, The 1968,O 10,59:1
Misanthrope, The 1968,O 20,II,1:1
Cock-A-Doodle Dandy 1969,Ja 21,40:1
Cock-A-Doodle Dandy 1969,F 2,II,1:1
Hamlet 1969,Mr 4,34:1
Murderous Angels 1970,F 8,70:1
Easton, Ruth
Head First 1926,Ja 7,22:4
Friend Indeed 1926,Ap 27,22:3
One Shot Fired 1927,N 8,32:5
Exceeding Small 1928,O 23,32:2
Exceeding Small 1928,N 4,IX,1:1
Buckaroo 1929,Mr 18,31:1
Town Boy 1929,O 5,22:4
Privilege Car 1931,Mr 4,33:1
Keeper of the Keys 1933,O 19,23:2
Easton, Sidney
Kilpatrick's Old-Time Minstrels 1930,Ap 21,20:2
Case of Philip Lawrence, The 1937,Je 9,31:1
Easton, William R
Betty Behave 1927,Mr 9,28:4
Eastwood, Oliver (Playwright)
Piker, The 1925,Ja 16,14:1
Eastwood, Thomas (Composer)
Look Back in Anger 1957,O 2,28:2
Country Wife, The 1957,N 28,56:1
Eatman, Tom
Who's Who, Baby? 1968,Ja 30,36:1
Eaton, Charles
Royal Fandango, A 1923,N 13,25:1
Peter Pan 1924,N 7,16:2
Lucky 1927,Mr 23,28:3
Skidding 1928,My 22,18:5
Incubator 1932,N 2,23:3
Tommy 1933,Ag 8,22:5
Growing Pains 1933,N 24,24:2
White Hell 1935,Ag 13,20:3
Lady Luck 1936,Ap 16,21:2
Eaton, Delephene
Chameleon, The 1932,Jl 19,20:4
Eaton, Doris
Ziegfeld Follies 1920,Je 23,14:1
No Other Girl 1924,Ag 14,10:4
Sap, The 1924,D 16,28:3
Excess Baggage 1927,D 27,24:2
Cross My Heart 1928,S 18,32:7
Hollywood Music Box Revue, The
 1929,Ja 6,VIII,4:4
Page Pygmalion 1932,Ag 4,17:5
Merrily We Roll Along 1934,O 1,14:1
Eaton, Dorothy
Murder in the Cathedral 1935,D 21,11:3
Trojan Horse, The 1940,O 31,28:3
Trojan Women, The 1941,Ag 9,32:5
Sun Field, The 1942,D 10,33:2
Right Next to Broadway 1944,F 22,26:2
Parlor Story 1947,Mr 5,29:2
Man and Superman 1949,My 17,28:6
Eaton, Elwyn
Bombasters Furioso 1924,Jl 19,10:4
Sweeney Todd 1924,Jl 19,10:4
Padre, The 1926,D 28,16:3

Royal Box, The 1928,N 21,32:3
Sakura 1928,D 26,14:4
Eaton, Evelyn
Show Boat 1932,My 20,22:2
Man Who Reclaimed His Head 1932,S 9,17:3
Jubilee 1935,O 14,20:1
Eaton, Ewing
Artists and Models 1924,O 16,33:3
Eaton, F M
Laugh It Off 1925,Ap 25,18:4
1776 1926,Ap 24,11:2
Eaton, John
Champion, The 1925,Ap 24,16:4
Robin Hood 1932,Ja 28,25:4
Pirates of Penzance, The 1936,Ap 21,27:5
H M S Pinafore 1936,Ap 28,17:2
Trial by Jury 1936,Ap 28,17:2
Iolanthe 1936,My 5,26:2
Great Campaign, The 1947,Ap 1,33:2
Eaton, Joseph S
This Way Out 1929,Ap 28,24:4
Eaton, Macdonald (Scenic Designer)
Macbeth 1955,O 8,12:6
Last Love of Don Juan, The 1955,N 24,40:1
Eaton, Marjorie
Shakespeare's Merchant 1939 1939,Ja 10,16:3
In the Summer House 1953,D 30,17:1
One Eye Closed 1954,N 25,45:2
Eaton, Mary
Ziegfeld Follies 1920,Je 23,14:1
Ziegfeld Follies 1921,Je 22,10:1
Ziegfeld Follies 1922,Je 6,18:2
Kid Boots 1923,D 16,IX,2:4
Kid Boots 1924,Ja 1,21:3
Lucky 1927,Mr 23,28:3
Julius Caesar 1927,Je 7,27:2
Five O'Clock Girl, The 1927,O 11,26:3
Audition of the Apprentice Theatre 1939,Je 2,26:2
Eaton, Nancy
Sound of Music, The 1970,Jl 3,13:1
Eaton, Paul
King's Standards, The 1958,F 14,19:1
Eaton, Pearl
Tick-Tack-Toe 1920,F 24,11:2
Earl Carroll's Vanities 1925,Jl 7,24:1
City Chap, The 1925,O 27,21:1
Criss Cross 1926,O 13,20:2
She's My Baby 1928,Ja 4,22:2
Eaton, Pearl (Choreographer)
Black Crook, The 1929,Mr 17,X,8:1
Eaton, Robert
Maker of Images, The 1927,Mr 5,12:2
Eaton, Sally
Hair 1967,O 30,55:1
Hair 1967,N 14,50:1
Hair 1968,Ap 30,40:2
Eaton, Walter Prichard (Playwright)
Queen Victoria 1923,N 16,15:1
Queen Victoria 1923,N 25,VIII,1:1
Eaton, Warren
Jubilee 1935,O 14,20:1
Eaton, William (Miscellaneous)
To Be Young Gifted and Black; World of Lorraine
 Hansberry, The 1969,Ja 3,15:1
Eaves, Hilary
Gentleman Unknown 1938,D 4,X,7:5
Eaves (Costume Designer)
If I Were You 1931,S 24,21:1
Ebb, Fred (Composer)
Put It in Writing 1963,My 14,31:1
Cabaret 1969,F 2,74:2
Ebb, Fred (Lyricist)
From A to Z 1960,Ap 21,23:2
Morning Sun 1963,O 7,36:2
Flora, the Red Menace 1965,My 12,41:2
Cabaret 1966,N 21,62:1
Cabaret 1966,D 4,II,5:1
Cabaret 1968,Ja 12,19:1
Happy Time, The 1968,Ja 19,32:2
Happy Time, The 1968,Ja 28,II,3:1
Cabaret 1968,Mr 1,32:1
Zorba 1968,N 18,58:1
Zorba 1968,N 24,II,1:1
Ebb, Fred (Playwright)
Put It in Writing 1963,My 14,31:1
Morning Sun 1963,O 7,36:2
By Jupiter 1967,Ja 20,28:2
Mister Mayor! 1967,Ap 4,36:3
Ebeling, George
Climate of Eden, The 1953,N 21,11:2
Wise Have Not Spoken, The 1954,F 11,35:2
Three Sisters, The 1955,F 26,13:2
Three Sisters, The 1955,Mr 20,II,1:1
Cherry Orchard, The 1955,O 19,38:1
Lovers 1956,My 11,23:1
Good Woman of Setzuan, The 1956,D 19,41:2
Romeo and Juliet 1957,Je 28,30:2
Macbeth 1957,Ag 16,11:2
Time Remembered 1957,N 13,41:2
Cock-A-Doodle Dandy 1958,N 13,39:2
Measure for Measure 1960,Jl 27,33:1
Rendezvous at Senlis 1961,F 28,39:2
Nathan the Wise 1962,Mr 23,29:1

Ebeling, George—Cont
Last Minstrel, The 1963,My 9,40:2
Devils, The 1963,N 5,25:1
Lonesome Train, The 1965,Je 17,25:1
Great White Hope, The 1967,D 14,58:1
Great White Hope, The 1967,D 24,II,3:1
Iceman Cometh, The 1968,Ap 1,58:1
Great White Hope, The 1968,O 4,40:1
Ebeling, Thatcher George
Hard Travelin' 1965,Je 17,25:1
Eben, Al
Pins and Needles 1939,Ap 21,26:2
New Pins and Needles 1939,N 21,19:2
New Meet the People, The 1943,Ag 22,II,1:6
Ebenhack, Arthur
Dream Maker, The 1921,N 22,17:1
Ebenhack, Arthur (Playwright)
School for Virtue 1931,Mr 11,23:4
School for Virtue 1931,Ap 22,29:2
Cinderella's Brothers 1933,Ja 30,9:6
Marilyn's Affairs 1933,Mr 16,21:5
Eberhart, Herd
Hymn to the Rising Sun 1937,My 7,28:2
Eberhart, Mignon G (Original Author)
Eight O'Clock Tuesday 1941,Ja 7,18:2
Eberhart, Mignon G (Playwright)
Eight O'Clock Tuesday 1941,Ja 7,18:2
Eberle, Eleanor
Sing Out the News 1938,S 26,12:5
Lady in the Dark 1941,Ja 24,14:2
Ebermayer (Playwright)
Bargold Lacht 1932,N 6,IX,3:2
Ebert, Betty
Point of No Return 1957,Mr 23,17:2
Ebert, George
Yeomen of the Guard, The 1935,Jl 30,16:4
Ebert, Joyce
Hamlet 1957,Ja 29,27:1
Country Wife, The 1957,Je 27,22:1
Asmodee 1958,Mr 26,42:2
Sign of Winter 1958,My 8,35:1
King Lear 1959,Ja 3,11:2
No Trifling With Love 1959,N 10,55:3
Tempest, The 1960,Je 20,35:1
Hamlet 1961,Mr 17,17:1
Trojan Women, The 1963,D 24,7:6
Tartuffe 1965,Ja 15,23:1
Country People 1970,Ja 19,35:1
Ebert, Karl
Robbers, The 1926,N 21,VIII,1:3
Ebert, Michael
Twelfth Night 1957,Ja 5,12:2
Trojan Women, The 1957,Mr 19,42:7
Asmodee 1958,Mr 26,42:2
Sign of Winter 1958,My 8,35:1
Wall, The 1960,O 12,44:4
Beyond the Horizon 1962,O 26,27:2
Hamlet 1964,Ap 10,30:1
Man in the Glass Booth, The 1968,S 27,41:1
Ebi, Earl
Behind the Red Lights 1937,Ja 14,17:4
Ebin, Gala (Playwright)
Five Evenings 1963,My 10,37:3
Ebin, Petruchio
Cherry Orchard, The 1960,Je 4,17:2
Ebner, Jacques
Grosse Valise, La 1965,D 15,52:1
Ebony Scandals
Vaudeville (Palace) 1929,Je 10,22:6
Ebsen, Buddy
Flying Colors 1932,S 16,24:2
Flying Colors 1932,O 9,IX,1:1
Ziegfeld Follies 1934,Ja 5,24:3
Yokel Boy 1939,Jl 7,12:2
Show Boat 1946,Ja 7,17:2
Ebsen, Vilma
Vaudeville (Palace) 1930,S 22,23:2
Flying Colors 1932,S 16,24:2
Flying Colors 1932,O 9,IX,1:1
Ziegfeld Follies 1934,Ja 5,24:3
Between the Devil 1937,O 15,19:1
Between the Devil 1937,D 23,24:5
Ebsens, The
Follies 1933,N 19,IX,2:5
Eburne, Maude
Half-Moon, The 1920,N 2,15:2
Love Dreams 1921,O 11,22:2
Bavu 1922,F 27,16:1
Lady Butterfly 1923,Ja 23,18:1
Puppy Love 1926,Ja 28,16:3
Storm Center 1927,D 1,33:2
Three Cheers 1928,O 16,28:1
Three Cheers 1928,O 21,IX,1:1
Great Day! 1929,O 18,24:3
Many a Slip 1930,F 4,29:2
Eby, Earl
Chameleon, The 1932,Jl 19,20:4
Eby, Helyn
Silks and Satins 1920,Jl 16,19:1
Eby, James Jr
Triplets 1932,S 22,25:2
Eby-Rock, Helyn
Honeymoon Lane 1926,S 21,32:3
That's the Woman 1930,S 4,27:2

Eccles, Donald
Last Enemy, The 1930,O 31,21:1
Duchess of Malfi, The 1946,O 16,35:2
Eccles, James
Good Soldier Schweik, The 1963,Ap 9,57:1
Eccles, Jane
Separate Tables 1955,My 22,II,1:1
Separate Tables 1956,O 26,33:1
Eccles, Peggy
Last Enemy, The 1930,O 31,21:1
Echlin, Robert
Home Is the Hero 1945,Ja 20,16:4
Echnation
Antigone 1968,O 11,36:1
Echnation (Miscellaneous)
Frankenstein 1968,O 3,54:1
Echols, Frank
Thesmophoriazusae, The; Goddesses of Athens,
The 1955,D 14,52:4
Drunkard, The; Fallen Saved, The 1959,Je 24,37:2
Jackass, The 1960,Mr 24,39:2
Idiot, The 1960,S 26,38:1
Man and Superman 1960,N 7,46:2
Emmanuel 1960,D 5,42:2
Montserrat 1961,Ja 9,30:5
Merchant of Venice, The 1962,F 3,13:2
Seven Scenes for Yeni 1963,My 13,36:2
Echols, Frank (Director)
I Got Shoes 1963,Ja 25,12:2
Echols, Randolph
Little Ol' Boy 1933,Ap 25,15:5
Richard II 1937,F 6,14:2
King Lear 1940,D 16,27:2
As You Like It 1941,O 21,29:2
Russian People, The 1942,D 30,17:2
Men to the Sea 1944,O 4,25:2
Closing Door, The 1949,D 2,36:2
Flight Into Egypt 1952,Mr 19,33:2
Apollo of Bellac, The 1957,Ap 10,39:1
Puntila 1959,My 15,26:2
Echols, Randolph (Scenic Designer)
Death of a Salesman 1963,Jl 20,11:2
Echols, Weyland
Finta Giardiniera, La 1927,Ja 19,20:5
Eck, Marsha (Costume Designer)
Sound of Silence, A 1965,Mr 9,30:1
Arf 1969,My 28,36:1
Great Airplane Snatch, The 1969,My 28,36:1
Eck, Marsha (Scenic Designer)
Moon for the Misbegotten, A 1968,Je 13,55:2
Trumpets of the Lord 1969,Ap 30,37:1
Great Airplane Snatch, The 1969,My 28,36:1
Arf 1969,My 28,36:1
Ah, Wilderness! 1969,N 9,86:1
Seven Days of Mourning 1969,D 17,64:1
White House Murder Case, The 1970,F 19,59:1
All's Well That Ends Well 1970,Je 16,53:1
Arsenic and Old Lace 1970,N 5,59:1
Eckart, Dietrich (Playwright)
Dark Roads 1935,O 6,XI,3:7
Eckart, Jean (Costume Designer)
Damn Yankees 1955,My 6,17:1
Mister Johnson 1956,Mr 30,11:1
Once Upon a Mattress 1959,My 12,40:1
Fiorello! 1959,N 24,45:3
Eckart, Jean (Lighting Director)
Wedding Breakfast 1954,N 22,29:2
Portrait of a Lady 1954,D 22,27:6
Mister Johnson 1956,Mr 30,11:1
Li'l Abner 1956,N 16,24:2
Copper and Brass 1957,O 18,19:2
Body Beautiful, The 1958,Ja 24,15:2
Fiorello! 1959,N 24,45:3
Viva Madison Avenue 1960,Ap 7,42:1
Happiest Girl in the World, The 1961,Ap 4,42:1
Let It Ride 1961,O 13,27:4
Take Her, She's Mine 1961,D 22,19:1
Fiorello! 1962,Je 14,24:1
Never Too Late 1962,N 28,42:1
She Loves Me 1963,Ap 24,39:1
Fade Out--Fade In 1964,My 27,45:1
Zulu and the Zayda, The 1965,N 11,59:1
Agatha Sue, I Love You 1966,D 15,61:1
Eckart, Jean (Producer)
Once Upon a Mattress 1959,My 12,40:1
Once Upon a Mattress 1959,My 17,II,1:1
Eckart, Jean (Scenic Designer)
Glad Tidings 1951,O 12,33:2
To Dorothy, A Son 1951,N 20,37:2
Gertie 1952,Ja 31,23:1
Maya 1953,Je 10,35:1
Scarecrow, The 1953,Je 17,31:1
School for Scandal, The 1953,Je 24,29:2
Little Clay Cart, The 1953,Jl 1,25:1
Oh, Men! Oh, Women! 1953,D 18,37:2
Dead Pigeon 1953,D 24,10:2
Golden Apple, The 1954,Mr 12,15:2
Golden Apple, The 1954,Mr 21,II,1:1
Wedding Breakfast 1954,N 22,29:2
Portrait of a Lady 1954,D 22,27:6
Damn Yankees 1955,My 6,17:1
Mister Johnson 1956,Mr 30,11:1
Mister Johnson 1956,Ap 8,II,1:1

Li'l Abner 1956,N 16,24:2
Li'l Abner 1956,N 25,II,1:1
Livin' the Life 1957,Ap 29,20:1
Copper and Brass 1957,O 18,19:2
Body Beautiful, The 1958,Ja 24,15:2
Once Upon a Mattress 1959,My 12,40:1
Fiorello! 1959,N 24,45:3
Viva Madison Avenue 1960,Ap 7,42:1
Happiest Girl in the World, The 1961,Ap 4,42:1
Let It Ride 1961,O 13,27:4
Take Her, She's Mine 1961,D 22,19:1
Oh Dad, Poor Dad, Mamma's Hung You in the
Closet and I'm Feelin' So Sad 1962,F 27,28:1
Oh Dad, Poor Dad, Mamma's Hung You in the
Closet and I'm Feelin' So Sad 1962,Ap 29,II,3:1
Fiorello! 1962,Je 14,24:1
Never Too Late 1962,N 28,42:1
She Loves Me 1963,Ap 24,39:1
Oh Dad, Poor Dad, Mamma's Hung You in the
Closet and I'm Feelin' So Sad 1963,Ag 28,28:2
Here's Love 1963,O 4,28:1
Too Much Johnson 1964,Ja 16,29:1
Anyone Can Whistle 1964,Ap 6,36:1
Fade Out--Fade In 1964,My 27,45:1
Flora, the Red Menace 1965,My 12,41:2
Zulu and the Zayda, The 1965,N 11,59:1
Mame 1966,My 25,41:1
Agatha Sue, I Love You 1966,D 15,61:1
Hallelujah, Baby! 1967,Ap 27,51:1
Midsummer Night's Dream, A 1967,Je 19,42:1
Education of H*Y*M*A*N K*A*P*L*A*N, The
1968,Ap 5,57:1
Maggie Flynn 1968,O 24,52:1
Maggie Flynn 1968,N 3,II,1:1
Fig Leaves Are Falling, The 1969,Ja 3,19:1
Norman, Is That You? 1970,F 20,30:1
Sensations 1970,O 26,48:2
Eckart, William (Costume Designer)
Damn Yankees 1955,My 6,17:1
Mister Johnson 1956,Mr 30,11:1
Once Upon a Mattress 1959,My 12,40:1
Fiorello! 1959,N 24,45:3
Eckart, William (Lighting Director)
Wedding Breakfast 1954,N 22,29:2
Portrait of a Lady 1954,D 22,27:6
Mister Johnson 1956,Mr 30,11:1
Li'l Abner 1956,N 16,24:2
Copper and Brass 1957,O 18,19:2
Body Beautiful, The 1958,Ja 24,15:2
Fiorello! 1959,N 24,45:3
Viva Madison Avenue 1960,Ap 7,42:1
Happiest Girl in the World, The 1961,Ap 4,42:1
Let It Ride 1961,O 13,27:4
Take Her, She's Mine 1961,D 22,19:1
Fiorello! 1962,Je 14,24:1
Never Too Late 1962,N 28,42:1
She Loves Me 1963,Ap 24,39:1
Fade Out--Fade In 1964,My 27,45:1
Zulu and the Zayda, The 1965,N 11,59:1
Agatha Sue, I Love You 1966,D 15,61:1
Eckart, William (Producer)
Once Upon a Mattress 1959,My 12,40:1
Once Upon a Mattress 1959,My 17,II,1:1
Eckart, William (Scenic Designer)
Glad Tidings 1951,O 12,33:2
To Dorothy, A Son 1951,N 20,37:2
Gertie 1952,Ja 31,23:1
Maya 1953,Je 10,35:1
Scarecrow, The 1953,Je 17,31:1
School for Scandal, The 1953,Je 24,29:2
Little Clay Cart, The 1953,Jl 1,25:1
Oh, Men! Oh, Women! 1953,D 18,37:2
Dead Pigeon 1953,D 24,10:2
Golden Apple, The 1954,Mr 12,15:2
Golden Apple, The 1954,Mr 21,II,1:1
Wedding Breakfast 1954,N 22,29:2
Portrait of a Lady 1954,D 22,27:6
Damn Yankees 1955,My 6,17:1
Mister Johnson 1956,Mr 30,11:1
Mister Johnson 1956,Ap 8,II,1:1
Li'l Abner 1956,N 16,24:2
Li'l Abner 1956,N 25,II,1:1
Livin' the Life 1957,Ap 29,20:1
Copper and Brass 1957,O 18,19:2
Body Beautiful, The 1958,Ja 24,15:2
Once Upon a Mattress 1959,My 12,40:1
Fiorello! 1959,N 24,45:3
Viva Madison Avenue 1960,Ap 7,42:1
Happiest Girl in the World, The 1961,Ap 4,42:1
Let It Ride 1961,O 13,27:4
Take Her, She's Mine 1961,D 22,19:1
Oh Dad, Poor Dad, Mamma's Hung You in the
Closet and I'm Feelin' So Sad 1962,F 27,28:1
Oh Dad, Poor Dad, Mamma's Hung You in the
Closet and I'm Feelin' So Sad 1962,Ap 29,II,3:1
Fiorello! 1962,Je 14,24:1
Never Too Late 1962,N 28,42:1
She Loves Me 1963,Ap 24,39:1
Oh Dad, Poor Dad, Mamma's Hung You in the
Closet and I'm Feelin' So Sad 1963,Ag 28,28:2
Here's Love 1963,O 4,28:1
Too Much Johnson 1964,Ja 16,29:1
Anyone Can Whistle 1964,Ap 6,36:1

Eckart, William (Scenic Designer)—Cont
Fade Out--Fade In 1964,My 27,45:1
Flora, the Red Menace 1965,My 12,41:2
Zulu and the Zayda, The 1965,N 11,59:1
Mame 1966,My 25,41:1
Agatha Sue, I Love You 1966,D 15,61:1
Hallelujah, Baby! 1967,Ap 27,51:1
Midsummer Night's Dream, A 1967,Je 19,42:1
Education of H*Y*M*A*N K*A*P*L*A*N, The
1968,Ap 5,57:1
Maggie Flynn 1968,O 24,52:1
Maggie Flynn 1968,N 3,II,1:1
Fig Leaves Are Falling, The 1969,Ja 3,19:1
Norman, Is That You? 1970,F 20,30:1
Sensations 1970,O 26,48:2
Eckels, Lew
Enemy Within 1931,O 6,35:3
Steel 1931,N 19,26:5
Murder at the Vanities 1933,S 13,22:4
Let Freedom Ring 1935,N 7,26:2
Too Many Heroes 1937,N 16,26:2
On Borrowed Time 1938,F 4,16:4
I Must Love Someone 1939,F 8,18:7
Hold On to Your Hats 1940,S 12,30:3
Night Before Christmas, The 1941,Ap 11,25:2
Johnny 2X4 1942,Mr 17,24:6
Are You With It? 1945,N 12,17:3
Ecker, Leo
On the Level 1937,Mr 26,24:4
Eckert, Ella
Would-Be Gentleman, The 1930,Ap 30,29:2
Eckert, Royal
Point of No Return 1957,Mr 23,17:2
Eckhard, Fred
Your Woman and Mine 1922,F 28,17:2
Eckhardt, Fritz (Playwright)
Rendezvous in Wien 1956,S 5,23:1
Eckhart, Fred
Grand Hotel 1930,N 14,30:4
Eckhart, Lois
George White's Scandals 1931,S 15,30:1
George White's Scandals 1935,D 26,20:2
Eckhart, Paul-Matthew
Dirtiest Show in Town, The 1970,My 2,21:1
Dirtiest Show in Town, The 1970,Je 29,43:2
Eckl, Shirley
Kiss Me, Kate 1949,Ja 30,II,6:5
Eckles, R B (Composer)
Pudding on the Ritz 1932,Ap 9,18:3
Eckles, R B (Lyricist)
Pudding on the Ritz 1932,Ap 9,18:3
Eckles, Robert
Gondoliers, The 1940,O 1,29:2
Mikado, The 1944,F 12,11:3
Trial by Jury 1944,F 15,14:4
H M S Pinafore 1944,F 15,14:4
Cox and Box 1944,F 18,15:5
Pirates of Penzance, The 1944,F 18,15:5
Gondoliers, The 1944,F 22,26:3
Iolanthe 1944,F 23,17:1
Ruddigore 1944,Mr 3,19:5
Yeomen of the Guard, The 1944,Mr 5,34:3
Mikado, The 1949,O 5,35:2
Pirates of Penzance, The 1949,O 11,41:2
H M S Pinafore 1949,O 18,34:2
Trial by Jury 1949,O 18,34:2
Singing Girl, The 1952,Je 4,31:8
Mikado, The 1952,O 21,35:2
Pirates of Penzance, The 1952,O 28,36:4
Trial by Jury 1952,N 4,32:2
H M S Pinafore 1952,N 4,32:2
Iolanthe 1952,N 11,26:3
Lady's Not for Burning, The 1957,F 22,26:2
Carousel 1957,S 12,38:2
Cloud 7 1958,F 15,15:2
Becket 1960,O 6,50:1
Becket 1961,My 9,44:1
Pequod 1969,Je 30,33:1
Eckley, Dan (Choreographer)
Let Freedom Sing 1942,O 6,18:2
Eckley, Dan (Director)
Brights Lights of 1944 1943,S 17,27:4
Ecklund, Lillian
Lightnin' 1938,S 16,17:2
Eckman, Margaret
Victory Belles 1943,O 27,26:3
Eckstein, George (Producer)
Billy Barnes Revue, The 1959,Je 10,42:2
Eckstein, Gustav (Dr) (Playwright)
Christmas Eve 1939,D 28,17:2
Eckstrom, Carl
Blue Eyes 1921,F 22,11:2
Processional 1925,Ja 13,17:1
Chicago 1926,D 31,11:1
Solitaire 1929,Mr 13,28:3
They Shall Not Die 1934,F 22,24:4
They Shall Not Die 1934,Mr 4,IX,1:3
Economides, John
Love's Old Sweet Song 1940,My 3,16:3
Economos, John (Miscellaneous)
Phedre 1969,Mr 1,20:1
Ecton, Richard (Miscellaneous)
Cup of Trembling, The 1959,My 1,33:5

Ecton, Robert
Porgy and Bess 1942,Ja 23,16:2
eda-Young, Barbara
Hawk, The 1968,Ap 18,54:1
Time of Your Life, The 1969,N 7,37:1
Camino Real 1970,Ja 9,42:1
Operation Sidewinder 1970,Mr 13,33:1
Eddie, George Woof
Bitter Sweet 1929,N 6,30:2
Eddie and Douglas
Broadway Nights 1929,Jl 16,23:2
Eddinger, Lawrence
Just Suppose 1920,N 2,15:1
Mountain Man, The 1921,D 13,24:2
Ice-Bound 1923,F 12,16:2
Stolen Fruit 1925,O 8,31:4
Lulu Belle 1926,F 10,20:1
Eddinger, Wallace
Nobody's Money 1921,Ag 18,9:3
Captain Applejack 1921,D 31,14:2
Naked Man, The 1923,D 16,IX,2:4
Haunted House, The 1924,S 3,12:1
Tale of the Wolf, The 1925,O 8,31:2
Tale of the Wolf, The 1925,O 18,IX,1:2
Long Island Love 1926,Ag 1,VII,4:1
Vaudeville (Palace) 1926,Ag 10,19:4
On Approval 1926,O 19,27:1
Zoo, The 1927,O 9,VIII,1:3
And So to Bed 1927,N 10,23:1
Eddinger, Young
Tale of the Wolf, The 1925,S 27,VII,2:1
Eddington, Mary (Playwright)
Secrets 1922,D 31,VII,1:1
Eddington, Paul
Severed Head, A 1964,O 29,40:1
Eddins, Homer
Old King's 1924,Mr 12,19:3
Half Moon Inn 1925,Mr 10,14:1
Eddison, Robert
Midsummer Night's Dream, A 1939,Jl 23,IX,1:3
Ridgeway's Late Joys 1939,O 22,IX,3:5
Twelfth Night 1950,D 3,II,3:1
Doctor Faustus 1961,Ag 22,23:1
Eddleman, Jack
Annie Get Your Gun 1957,Mr 9,15:5
Shinbone Alley 1957,Ap 15,23:2
Oh Captain! 1958,F 5,21:2
Lend an Ear 1959,S 25,20:5
Hot Spot 1963,Ap 20,17:2
Girl Who Came to Supper, The 1963,D 9,49:1
My Fair Lady 1964,My 21,43:2
Oh What a Lovely War 1964,O 1,30:1
Great Scot! 1965,N 12,56:3
Eddy, David (Lyricist)
Athenian Touch, The 1964,Ja 15,25:4
Eddy, Edward (Scenic Designer)
57 Bowery 1928,Ja 27,14:3
Indiscretion 1929,Mr 5,28:1
Town's Woman, The 1929,Mr 12,26:2
Come-On Man, The 1929,Ap 23,26:2
Comedy of Women, A 1929,S 14,17:4
Broken Dishes 1929,N 6,28:3
Patriarch, The 1929,N 26,28:5
Nancy's Private Affair 1930,Ja 14,24:3
Troika 1930,Ap 2,32:6
Room 349 1930,Ap 23,24:5
Room of Dreams 1930,N 6,22:4
Privilege Car 1931,Mr 4,33:1
Singapore 1932,N 15,24:2
Late One Evening 1933,Ja 10,27:3
First Legion, The 1934,O 2,18:2
This Our House 1935,D 12,33:3
Eddy, George A
Coriolanus 1927,Je 18,8:3
Eddy, Junes
Cure for Matrimony 1939,O 26,26:3
Eddy, Marion
Vaudeville (Palace) 1931,O 26,22:3
Eddy, Max (Playwright)
Poulette et Son Poulain 1924,Je 15,VII,1:4
Palace aux Femmes 1926,O 10,VIII,2:1
Paris-Capucines 1927,Ja 16,VII,2:1
Eddy, William
Delightful Season, A 1960,S 29,30:1
Ede, Christopher (Director)
King Lear 1947,F 19,32:2
As You Like It 1947,F 21,16:2
Merchant of Venice, The 1947,F 24,16:2
Volpone 1947,F 25,32:2
Hamlet 1947,F 27,27:2
Ede, George
Flea in Her Ear, A 1969,O 4,25:1
Edelheit, M (Playwright)
Motel Peissi, The Contor's Kid 1934,N 29,33:3
Secret of Love, The 1936,F 24,15:2
Edell, Frederick (Miscellaneous)
Cabin in the Sky 1964,Ja 22,32:1
Edell, Ruth
Noble Experiment, The 1930,O 28,21:4
Rap, The 1931,Ap 7,31:2
House of Doom, The 1932,Ja 26,20:4
Triplets 1932,S 22,25:2
One Wife or Another 1933,F 7,23:6

Smile at Me 1935,Ag 24,18:4
Edelman, Charles
Golem, The 1927,F 5,13:2
Edelman, Daniel J
Life Begins in '40 1940,Ap 5,24:2
Edelman, David
Rat Race, The 1949,D 23,16:2
Edelman, Enid
Caution: A Love Story 1969,Ap 4,45:1
Edelman, Herbert
Barefoot in the Park 1963,O 24,36:2
Bajour 1964,N 24,42:1
Two Times One; Duet for Solo Voice 1970,Ap 5,76:4
Edelman, Maurice (Original Author)
Call on Kuprin, A 1961,My 26,29:3
Call on Kuprin, A 1961,Je 4,II,1:1
Edelsack, May
Gods Are Wise, The 1930,My 6,33:1
Edelstein, Ray
Candyapple, The 1970,N 24,33:1
Edem, Carl
Music in the Air 1932,N 9,28:2
Eden, Beatrice
Yours Is My Heart 1946,S 6,16:5
Eden, Carol
Great Big Doorstep, The 1950,Mr 18,8:6
Eden, Dorothy
Best Foot Forward 1941,O 2,28:2
Eden, Evelyn Swenson
Trojan Incident 1938,Ap 22,15:2
Eden, Susan (Producer)
Tour De Four 1963,Je 19,41:1
Eden, Suzanne
Right You Are (If You Think You Are) 1957,Mr 5,37:1
Eden, Tony
Dark of the Moon 1945,Mr 15,27:2
Devils Galore 1945,S 13,27:2
Edendorf Choral Society
Music in the Air 1932,N 20,IX,1:1
Edens, Roger
Vaudeville (Palace) 1931,Jl 20,20:3
Edens, Roger (Composer)
Judy Garland's New Variety Show 1956,S 27,43:2
Party With Betty Comden and Adolph Green, A 1958,D 24,2:7
Judy Garland 1959,My 12,40:1
Edens, Roger (Lyricist)
Judy Garland's New Variety Show 1956,S 27,43:2
Judy Garland 1959,My 12,40:1
Eder, Linda
Cynara 1931,N 3,31:1
Marilyn's Affairs 1933,Mr 16,21:5
Eder, Robert
Macbeth 1969,D 23,25:1
Ederle, Gertrude
Vaudeville (Hippodrome) 1926,My 4,31:2
Vaudeville (Hippodrome) 1926,My 8,29:2
Vaudeville (Hippodrome) 1926,My 11,25:3
Aquacade 1939,My 5,26:2
Edeson, Elinor
Patience 1927,My 24,23:2
Edeson, Robert
Mamma's Affair 1920,Ja 20,10:1
World We Live In, The 1922,N 1,16:1
Edgar, Day
Scarlet Coat, The 1924,D 24,11:1
Edgar, Day (Lyricist)
Scarlet Coat, The 1924,D 24,11:1
Edgar, Day (Playwright)
Scarlet Coat, The 1924,D 24,11:1
Edgar, George (Producer)
Blacks, The 1961,My 5,23:1
Ox Cart, The 1966,D 20,58:1
Edgar, Marriott (Playwright)
Jill Darling 1934,D 20,29:8
Edgar, Michael
Beaux' Stratagem, The 1970,F 10,50:2
Three Sisters, The 1970,F 12,30:1
Edge, Jack
Rainbow, The 1923,Ap 8,VIII,1:7
Edge, Wilfred
Plan M 1942,F 21,15:2
Edgecomb, Gladys
Mary of Magdala 1946,Mr 26,24:5
Edgell, David
Leader, The 1969,Ap 22,40:2
Honest-to-God Schnozzola, The 1969,Ap 22,40:2
Edgerly, Serge (Scenic Designer)
Tree, The 1932,Ap 13,23:5
Edgerton, Earle
Doctor and the Devils, The 1959,Ja 21,27:8
Three Plays of the Sea 1970,Ag 20,39:1
Edginton, May (Original Author)
His Wife's Castle 1939,O 1,IX,2:2
Edginton, May (Playwright)
Secrets 1922,O 8,VI,1:7
Secrets 1922,D 26,11:1
Captain Briquet 1923,S 16,VII,2:8
Lesson in Love, A 1923,S 25,10:1
Lesson in Love, A 1923,S 30,II,1:1
Deadlock 1928,O 28,IX,1:3

Edinborough, Oswald
Lulu Belle 1926,F 10,20:1
Edington, Ralph
Pygmalion 1945,D 27,16:1
Edison, Arthur (Producer)
Incubator 1932,N 2,23:3
Hand in Glove 1944,D 5,19:1
Hand in Glove 1944,D 10,II,5:1
Edison, Edith
Revolt of the Beavers, The 1937,My 21,19:2
Ediss, May
Potiphar's Wife 1928,D 24,10:7
Venetian, The 1931,N 2,26:1
Girls in Uniform 1932,D 31,10:3
Editorial Staff of the Living Newspaper /(Miscellaneous)
1935 1936,My 13,28:2
Edloe
Salvation 1969,Mr 13,53:1
Edlund, Harold A
Hoot Mon, or Clans Across the Sea 1927,My 8,29:4
Edmond, Gay
It's a Bird . . . It's a Plane . . . It's Superman 1966,Mr 30,34:1
Edmond, James
Glass Cage, The 1957,Mr 11,21:2
Love and Libel 1960,D 8,44:1
Doctor's Dilemma, The 1969,Je 24,37:1
Edmonds, Audrey
Girl From Wyoming, The 1938,O 31,12:1
Edmonds, Bentley
Walk Hard 1944,D 1,28:2
Edmonds, Beulah E
Brown Sugar 1937,D 3,29:2
Edmonds, Louis
Way of the World, The 1954,S 30,38:2
Tempest, The 1955,S 3,8:6
Cherry Orchard, The 1955,O 19,38:1
Queen After Death 1956,Mr 13,33:2
Candide 1956,D 3,40:2
Taming of the Shrew, The 1957,F 21,30:2
Duchess of Malfi, The 1957,Mr 20,33:1
Maybe Tuesday 1958,Ja 30,18:3
Asmodee 1958,Mr 26,42:2
Killer, The 1960,Mr 23,33:1
Ernest in Love 1960,My 5,39:4
Decameron, The 1961,Ap 13,32:1
Passage to India, A 1962,F 1,23:1
Passage to India, A 1962,F 11,II,1:1
Importance of Being Earnest, The 1963,F 27,5:2
Winter's Tale, The 1963,Je 29,13:1
Midsummer Night's Dream, A 1963,Jl 1,19:2
Fire! 1969,Ja 29,26:1
Edmonds, Mitchell
Red, White and Maddox 1969,Ja 27,27:1
Edmonds, Phil
Midsummer Night's Dream, A 1968,D 9,59:1
Edmonds, Walter D (Original Author)
Low Bridge 1933,F 10,13:4
Farmer Takes a Wife, The 1934,O 31,17:1
Farmer Takes a Wife, The 1934,N 11,IX,1:1
Edmondston, D B (Composer)
Bulls and Belles 1931,Ap 18,17:2
Edmonson, William
Marco Millions 1928,Ja 10,28:2
Deep Harlem 1929,Ja 8,35:2
2 for Fun; Switch in Time, A 1955,My 26,34:1
2 for Fun; Anniversary, The 1955,My 26,34:1
Iceman Cometh, The 1956,My 8,38:1
Rope Dancers, The 1957,N 21,39:1
Handful of Fire 1958,O 2,45:3
Edmunds, Dallas
It's a Bird . . . It's a Plane . . . It's Superman 1966,Mr 30,34:1
Edmunds, William
Salt Water 1929,N 27,30:3
Friars Club Frolic 1933,My 15,16:4
Saluta 1934,Ag 29,13:4
Moon Over Mulberry Street 1935,S 5,24:6
Siege 1937,D 9,31:4
Edney, Florence
Outrageous Mrs Palmer, The 1920,O 13,18:1
Marie Antoinette 1921,N 23,16:1
Guilty One, The 1923,Mr 21,19:1
Mary, Mary, Quite Contrary 1923,S 12,14:1
Outsider, The 1924,Mr 4,16:4
Dark Angel, The 1925,F 11,19:2
School for Scandal, The 1925,O 24,19:1
Countess Maritza 1926,Mr 30,20:3
Countess Maritza 1926,S 20,21:1
Murray Hill 1927,S 30,29:1
Paris 1928,O 9,34:3
Murder on the Second Floor 1929,S 12,35:1
Waterloo Bridge 1929,D 1,X,4:7
Waterloo Bridge 1930,Ja 7,29:2
In The Best of Families 1931,F 3,29:1
Widow in Green, A 1931,N 21,21:4
Thousand Summers, A 1932,My 25,23:4
20th Century 1932,D 30,15:1
Mackerel Skies 1934,Ja 24,20:4
Red Cat, The 1934,S 20,21:1
Birthday 1934,D 27,24:2
De Luxe 1935,Mr 6,22:2

Edney, Florence—Cont
Call It a Day 1936,Ja 29,15:2
Wise Tomorrow 1937,O 16,22:5
Barchester Towers 1937,D 1,27:1
Billy Draws a Horse 1939,D 22,14:5
Ladies in Retirement 1940,Mr 27,24:3
Angel Street 1941,D 6,15:2

Edomy, Patricia A
Five on the Black Hand Side 1970,Ja 2,32:2

Edouin, Walter
Fanny Hawthorn 1922,My 12,22:2

Edreich, Jack (Miscellaneous)
Something Different 1967,N 29,52:1

Edschmidt, Casimir (Playwright)
Kean 1921,D 11,VI,1:4

Edson, Marjory
Minnie's Boys 1970,Mr 27,27:1

Edthofer, Anton
Anatol 1922,F 5,VI,1:7
Hannibal Ante Portas 1929,Ap 15,22:2
Story of the Wolf 1932,N 6,IX,3:4
Death of a Salesman 1950,Mr 4,10:7

Edwall, Allan
Hughie 1958,S 9,24:5

Edward, Ian
Hamp 1967,Mr 10,32:1
Stephen D 1967,S 25,58:1
Guide, The 1968,Mr 7,50:1

Edward, Leslie
Homo 1969,Ap 12,40:2

Edward, Nathan
Blood and Sand 1921,S 21,16:2

Edward, Sherman (Composer)
Mighty Man Is He, A 1960,Ja 7,25:2

Edwardes, Felix (Director)
Lady Be Good 1924,D 2,23:4

Edwardes, Howard
Fedora 1922,F 11,18:1

Edwardes, Kathleen
Marching By 1932,Mr 4,17:1

Edwards, Alan
Her Family Tree 1920,D 28,9:2
Snapshots of 1921 1921,Je 3,19:2
Gingham Girl, The 1922,Ag 29,15:5
Poppy 1923,S 4,14:2
Lady Be Good 1924,D 2,23:4
Beware of Widows 1925,N 8,VIII,2:1
Beware of Widows 1925,D 2,22:3
Twinkle Twinkle 1926,N 17,22:2
Merry Malones, The 1927,S 27,30:2
Three Cheers 1928,O 16,28:1
Simple Simon 1930,F 19,22:1
Social Register, The 1931,N 10,28:2

Edwards, Albert V
Matriarch, The 1930,Mr 19,24:5

Edwards, Alice
All the King's Men 1950,Jl 19,25:6
Pony Cart, The 1954,S 15,39:2

Edwards, Anne
Venice Preserv'd 1955,D 13,54:4

Edwards, Bart
Hear That Trumpet 1946,O 8,19:2

Edwards, Ben
Daughters of Atreus 1936,O 15,33:1

Edwards, Ben (Costume Designer)
Diff'rent 1938,Ja 26,26:4
Pygmalion 1938,Ja 27,16:3
Captain Jinks of the Horse Marines 1938,Ja 28,16:2
Coriolanus 1938,F 2,14:5
Bird Cage, The 1950,F 23,32:2
Legend of Sarah 1950,O 12,42:4
Desire Under the Elms 1952,Ja 17,23:4
Sunday Breakfast 1952,My 30,12:2
Emperor's Clothes, The 1953,F 10,24:2
Remarkable Mr Pennypacker, The 1953,D 31,11:2
Sing Me No Lullaby 1954,O 15,17:2
Traveling Lady 1954,O 28,45:2
Changeling, The 1964,O 30,32:2

Edwards, Ben (Lighting Director)
Royal Family, The 1951,Ja 11,28:2
Richard II 1951,Ja 25,21:2
Taming of the Shrew, The 1951,Ap 26,35:2
Time of the Cuckoo, The 1952,O 16,37:4
Lullaby 1954,F 4,21:2
Traveling Lady 1954,O 28,45:2
Tonight in Samarkand 1955,F 17,22:2
Someone Waiting 1956,F 15,26:1
Ponder Heart, The 1956,F 17,14:2
Ages of Man 1958,D 29,21:1
God and Kate Murphy 1959,F 27,21:2
Second String, A 1960,Ap 14,36:2
Face of a Hero 1960,O 21,29:5
Midgie Purvis 1961,F 2,25:3
Big Fish, Little Fish 1961,Mr 16,42:2
Purlie Victorious 1961,S 29,29:1
Shot in the Dark, A 1961,O 19,40:1
Aspern Papers, The 1962,F 8,26:1
Harold 1962,N 30,27:1
Family Way, The 1965,Ja 14,44:5
Race of Hairy Men!, A 1965,Ap 30,42:1
Nathan Weinstein, Mystic, Connecticut 1966,F 26,15:2
Where's Daddy? 1966,Mr 3,27:1
How's the World Treating You? 1966,O 25,50:1

Mother Lover, The 1969,F 3,28:1
Hay Fever 1970,N 10,55:1

Edwards, Ben (Miscellaneous)
Harold 1962,N 30,27:1
Royal Hunt of the Sun, The 1965,O 27,36:2

Edwards, Ben (Producer)
Big Fish, Little Fish 1961,Mr 16,42:2
Ballad of the Sad Cafe, The 1963,O 31,27:1
Race of Hairy Men!, A 1965,Ap 30,42:1

Edwards, Ben (Scenic Designer)
Diff'rent 1938,Ja 26,26:4
Pygmalion 1938,Ja 27,16:3
Captain Jinks of the Horse Marines 1938,Ja 28,16:2
Coriolanus 1938,F 2,14:5
Another Sun 1940,F 24,8:6
Medea 1947,O 21,27:2
Sundown Beach 1948,S 8,37:1
Diamond Lil 1949,F 7,16:2
Sister Oakes 1949,Ap 25,19:4
Medea 1949,My 3,31:2
Lucky Sam McCarver 1950,Ap 15,10:6
Captain Brassbound's Conversion 1950,D 28,21:1
Royal Family, The 1951,Ja 11,28:2
Richard II 1951,Ja 25,21:2
Taming of the Shrew, The 1951,Ap 26,35:2
Sunday Breakfast 1952,My 30,12:2
Time of the Cuckoo, The 1952,O 16,37:4
Remarkable Mr Pennypacker, The 1953,D 31,11:2
Lullaby 1954,F 4,21:2
Traveling Lady 1954,O 28,45:2
Anastasia 1954,D 30,13:1
Tonight in Samarkand 1955,F 17,22:2
Honeys, The 1955,Ap 29,26:1
Someone Waiting 1956,F 15,26:1
Ponder Heart, The 1956,F 17,14:2
Waltz of the Toreadors, The 1957,Ja 18,17:2
Dark at the Top of the Stairs, The 1957,D 6,38:1
Waltz of the Toreadors, The 1958,Mr 5,37:1
Jane Eyre 1958,My 2,31:1
Touch of the Poet, A 1958,O 3,23:2
Disenchanted, The 1958,D 4,53:4
God and Kate Murphy 1959,F 27,21:2
Heartbreak House 1959,O 19,37:1
Second String, A 1960,Ap 14,36:2
Face of a Hero 1960,O 21,29:5
Midgie Purvis 1961,F 2,25:3
Big Fish, Little Fish 1961,Mr 16,42:2
Purlie Victorious 1961,S 29,29:1
Shot in the Dark, A 1961,O 19,40:1
Aspern Papers, The 1962,F 8,26:1
Harold 1962,N 30,27:1
Ballad of the Sad Cafe, The 1963,O 31,27:1
Hamlet 1964,Ap 10,30:1
Family Way, The 1965,Ja 14,44:5
Race of Hairy Men!, A 1965,Ap 30,42:1
Nathan Weinstein, Mystic, Connecticut 1966,F 26,15:2
Where's Daddy? 1966,Mr 3,27:1
How's the World Treating You? 1966,O 25,50:1
More Stately Mansions 1967,N 1,40:1
More Stately Mansions 1967,N 12,II,1:1
Twelfth Night 1968,Je 15,40:1
Master Builder, The 1968,Je 22,26:1
Mother Lover, The 1969,F 3,28:1
Purlie 1970,Mr 16,53:1
Hay Fever 1970,N 10,55:1

Edwards, Bruce
Riot 1968,D 20,64:1
Marie Vison, La 1970,Jl 15,29:1

Edwards, Charles
Kissing Time 1920,O 12,18:2
Two Blocks Away 1921,Ag 31,8:3
Trial of Mary Dugan, The 1927,S 20,33:1
Criminal Code, The 1929,O 3,28:2
Doctor X 1931,F 10,25:1

Edwards, Clair
Smyth With a Y 1937,Je 30,19:5

Edwards, Cliff
Mimic World of 1921, The 1921,Ag 18,9:2
Vaudeville (Palace) 1924,Ap 29,12:2
Lady Be Good 1924,D 2,23:4
Lambs Gambol 1925,Ap 27,15:1
Sunny 1925,S 23,22:1
Vaudeville (Palace) 1932,Ag 1,11:5
Scandals 1935,O 30,17:1
George White's Scandals 1935,D 26,20:2

Edwards, Earl
Cabin in the Sky 1940,O 26,19:2

Edwards, Earle
Cinderella on Broadway 1920,Je 25,18:1

Edwards, Eddie
Mystery Square 1929,Ap 5,28:3

Edwards, Elizabeth
Bridal Crown, The 1938,F 7,11:2

Edwards, Erwin
World We Make, The 1939,N 21,19:1

Edwards, Eugene
Ballad for Bimshire 1963,O 16,54:1
Porgy and Bess 1964,My 7,32:1
It's a Bird . . . It's a Plane . . . It's Superman 1966,Mr 30,34:1
Bill Noname 1970,Mr 3,37:1

Edwards, Evan
Bootleggers, The 1922,N 28,24:1

Edwards, George
Brother Cain 1941,S 13,21:5

Edwards, George (Composer)
Lady XX 1928,O 28,IX,2:1

Edwards, George (Playwright)
Girl Friend, The 1928,O 28,IX,2:1

Edwards, Glynn
Hostage, The 1960,S 21,42:1
Hostage, The 1960,O 2,II,1:1

Edwards, Gus
Vaudeville (Palace) 1927,D 6,26:3
Radio Carnival 1932,Mr 14,13:3
Vaudeville (Palace) 1932,My 16,19:2
Vaudeville (Palace) 1932,O 3,15:5

Edwards, Gus (Composer)
Broadway Sho-Window 1936,Ap 13,14:5

Edwards, Gus Annual Revue
Vaudeville (Palace) 1923,Ja 30,12:2

Edwards, H Robert
Lady in the Dark 1941,S 3,26:6

Edwards, Hazel
Lady in the Dark 1941,Ja 24,14:2

Edwards, Helen
Having Wonderful Time 1937,F 22,12:5

Edwards, Henry
Bulldog Drummond Hits Out 1937,D 22,33:2
Hamlet 1938,O 13,28:1
Henry IV, Part I 1939,Ja 31,17:2
Henry IV 1939,F 5,IX,1:1
Hamlet 1939,D 5,35:2

Edwards, Hilton
Hairy Ape, The 1928,D 2,X,2:1
Anna Christie 1930,My 4,XI,3:1
Merchant of Venice, The 1931,F 1,VIII,3:3
Jew Suss 1931,N 8,VIII,4:4
Mogul of the Desert 1932,F 7,VIII,3:2
Julius Caesar 1934,O 24,25:2
Drunkard, The 1934,D 6,26:3
Ascendancy 1935,Ja 31,22:3
Yahoo 1935,Jl 28,X,1:1
Not for Children 1935,D 29,IX,2:1
Skin of Our Teeth, The 1945,N 18,II,2:5
John Bull's Other Island 1948,F 11,33:4
Abdication 1948,S 28,32:5

Edwards, Hilton (Director)
Ten Nights in a Barroom 1930,My 25,IX,2:3
Archdupe 1931,D 27,VIII,4:1
Mogul of the Desert 1932,F 7,VIII,3:2
Lady of the Sea 1945,S 9,II,1:5
John Bull's Other Island 1948,F 11,33:4
Old Lady Says No, The 1948,F 18,35:1
Where Stars Walk 1948,F 25,27:2
Importance of Being Oscar, The 1961,Mr 15,45:2
Othello 1962,S 28,27:1
Philadelphia, Here I Come! 1966,F 17,28:1
Loves of Cass McGuire, The 1966,O 7,36:1
I Must Be Talking to My Friends 1967,N 17,59:1
Lovers; Winners 1968,Jl 26,21:4
Lovers; Losers 1968,Jl 26,21:4

Edwards, Hilton (Lighting Director)
Old Lady Says No, The 1948,F 18,35:1

Edwards, Hilton (Miscellaneous)
Bernard Shaw Story, The 1965,N 19,31:1

Edwards, Hilton (Producer)
Hairy Ape, The 1928,D 2,X,2:1
Peer Gynt 1928,D 2,X,2:1
Faust 1930,Mr 23,4:3
Terrible Meek, The 1930,My 4,XI,3:1
Merchant of Venice, The 1931,F 1,VIII,3:3
Jew Suss 1931,N 8,VIII,4:4
Julius Caesar 1934,O 24,25:2
Old Lady Says No, The 1935,Jl 28,X,1:1
Skin of Our Teeth, The 1945,N 18,II,2:5
Abdication 1948,S 28,32:5

Edwards, Hilton (Scenic Designer)
I Must Be Talking to My Friends 1967,N 17,59:1

Edwards, Irving
Merry World, The 1926,Je 9,18:3
Vanities 1927,F 22,19:1

Edwards, Jack
Garrick Gaieties 1926,My 11,25:2
Barrister, The 1932,N 22,25:2
All the King's Horses 1934,Ja 31,21:3
Merrily We Roll Along 1934,O 1,14:1
Jubilee 1935,O 14,20:1

Edwards, Jack (Costume Designer)
To Clothe the Naked 1967,Ap 28,30:1
What Did We Do Wrong? 1967,O 23,56:1

Edwards, Jack (Director)
King Midas and the Golden Touch 1948,O 25,28:3

Edwards, Jack (Miscellaneous)
Love's Labour's Lost 1968,Je 28,36:1

Edwards, Jane Ann
Pirates of Penzance, The 1936,Ap 21,27:5

Edwards, Joan
It Happens on Ice 1940,O 11,24:3

Edwards, Joan (Composer)
Tickets, Please! 1950,Ap 28,25:2

Edwards, Joan (Lyricist)
Tickets, Please! 1950,Ap 28,25:2

Edwards, John
Straight Thru the Door 1928,O 5,17:2
Three Little Girls 1930,Ap 15,29:1
New Moon, The 1942,Ag 19,14:2
Aquashow 1954,Je 23,20:4
Elliott Murphy's Aquashow 1955,Je 23,25:1
Aquarama 1960 1960,Jl 1,14:6
Aqua Carnival 1962,Je 29,15:1
Edwards, June
Ladies Night in a Turkish Bath 1961,Mr 22,38:1
Edwards, Kathleen
Bad Habits of 1926 1926,My 1,11:1
Music in the Air 1932,N 9,28:2
Edwards, Keith
Anatomist, The 1957,F 27,21:5
Making of Moo, The 1958,Je 12,34:1
Edwards, Kenneth
Henry IV, Part I 1946,My 7,25:2
Henry IV, Part II 1946,My 8,33:4
Oedipus; Critic, The 1946,My 21,19:2
Edwards, Kent
New Faces of 1943 1942,D 23,22:2
Song of Norway 1944,Ag 22,20:2
Edwards, Lee
Vie Parisienne, La 1945,Ja 13,14:5
Mr Strauss Goes to Boston 1945,S 7,20:2
Edwards, Leo (Composer)
You'll See Stars 1943,Ja 1,26:6
Edwards, Lou
Mimic World of 1921, The 1921,Ag 18,9:2
Edwards, Lydia
Pirates of Penzance, The 1946,S 21,19:2
Edwards, Lynn
Marilyn's Affairs 1933,Mr 16,21:5
Edwards, Marcelle
Vanities 1932,S 28,22:4
Edwards, Margaret
Earl Carroll's Vanities 1923,Jl 6,8:2
Canteen Show, The 1942,S 4,18:1
Edwards, Marian
George Washington Slept Here 1940,O 19,20:3
Edwards, Martha
Kibitzer, The 1929,F 19,22:5
Edwards, Mattie
Main Line, The 1924,Mr 26,19:4
Edwards, Maurice
Silver Tassie, The 1949,Jl 22,16:5
Happy as Larry 1950,Ja 7,11:2
Rehearsal, The 1952,My 27,30:5
Golden Apple, The 1954,Mr 12,15:2
Bil and Cora Baird's Marionette Theater; Ali Baba
    and the Forty Thieves 1956,S 3,10:1
Johnny Johnson 1956,O 22,24:1
Beggar's Opera, The 1957,Mr 14,35:1
Enchanted, The 1958,Ap 23,41:1
Hamlet of Stepney Green 1958,N 14,21:1
Drunkard, The; Fallen Saved, The 1959,Je 24,37:2
Miss Emily Adam 1960,Mr 30,43:1
Man and Superman 1960,N 7,46:2
Emmanuel 1960,D 5,42:2
Man's a Man, A 1962,S 20,30:2
Fiddler on the Roof 1964,S 23,56:2
Edwards, Maurice (Director)
Take It From the Top 1967,N 23,59:2
Edwards, Maurice (Miscellaneous)
Rehearsal, The 1952,My 27,30:5
Merchant of Venice, The 1962,F 3,13:2
Edwards, Max
Lady in the Dark 1941,Ja 24,14:2
Edwards, Melvin
Fun City 1968,Mr 7,53:2
Edwards, Melvin (Scenic Designer)
X Has No Value 1970,F 17,35:1
Edwards, Michael
Diamond Lil 1949,F 7,16:2
Edwards, Nonnie
Black Pit 1935,Mr 21,26:6
Crime Marches on 1935,O 24,19:1
Sunup to Sundown 1938,F 2,14:3
Edwards, Norman (Costume Designer)
Try and Get It 1943,Ag 3,13:2
Edwards, Osman (Translator)
Cloister, The 1921,Je 6,16:3
Edwards, Paddy
Egg, The 1962,Ja 9,23:2
Baker Street 1965,F 17,36:1
Edwards, Paige
Embezzled Heaven 1944,N 1,20:2
Edwards, Patty
Photo Finish 1963,F 14,5:2
Edwards, Penny
Ziegfeld Follies 1943,Ap 2,16:2
Laffing Room Only 1944,D 25,15:4
Duchess Misbehaves, The 1946,F 14,32:2
Edwards, Peter (Miscellaneous)
Single Man at a Party 1959,Ap 22,30:4
Edwards, Robert
Fantastic Fricassee, A 1922,S 12,24:1
Edwards, Robert (Lyricist)
Fantastic Fricassee, A 1922,S 12,24:1
Edwards, Roland G (Director)
Popsy 1941,F 11,26:2

Edwards, Ronnie
Tickets, Please! 1950,Ap 28,25:2
Season of the Beast 1958,Mr 14,29:2
Seven Scenes for Yeni 1963,My 13,36:2
Edwards, Rowland G (Director)
Money Mad 1937,My 25,32:5
Edwards, Ryan (Composer)
World of Gunter Grass, The 1966,Ap 27,38:1
Edwards, Sally (Costume Designer)
Night Is Black Bottles, The 1962,D 5,56:1
Edwards, Sam
Bab 1920,O 19,12:1
Edwards, Sarah
Iolanthe 1920,Ja 6,13:3
H M S Pinafore 1920,Ja 13,10:2
Ruddigore 1920,Ja 20,11:2
Ruddigore 1920,F 1,VIII,2:2
Princess Virtue 1921,My 5,20:2
Mikado, The 1925,Ap 13,25:1
Ruddigore 1927,My 21,25:2
Merry Malones, The 1927,S 27,30:2
Ruddigore 1931,Ag 11,28:3
Edwards, Seth
Cat on a Hot Tin Roof 1955,Mr 25,18:2
Edwards, Sherman (Composer)
1776 1969,Mr 17,46:2
1776 1969,Mr 23,II,1:1
Edwards, Sherman (Lyricist)
1776 1969,Mr 17,46:2
Edwards, Sherman (Playwright)
1776 1969,Mr 17,46:2
Edwards, Stewart
Rainbow 1928,N 22,25:1
Edwards, Thelma
Just Fancy! 1927,O 12,30:2
Edwards, Virginia
Mexican Hayride 1944,Ja 29,9:6
Edwards, Waldo
Henry-Behave 1926,Ag 24,19:4
Gertie 1926,N 16,24:2
Houseparty 1929,S 10,26:5
Wooden Soldier, The 1931,Je 23,28:4
Hired Husband 1932,Je 4,9:5
Potash and Perlmutter 1935,Ap 6,11:3
Edwards, William
Moon Is a Gong, The 1926,Mr 13,21:3
Meek Mose 1928,F 7,30:1
Troika 1930,Ap 2,32:6
Long Road, The 1930,S 10,30:2
Edwin, Robert
Million Dollar Baby 1945,D 22,17:2
It Takes Two 1947,F 4,33:4
Edwin, Walter
Paddy the Next Best Thing 1920,Ag 28,5:5
Rise of Rosie O'Reilly, The 1923,D 26,13:4
Farmer's Wife, The 1924,O 10,22:3
Castles in the Air 1926,S 7,19:2
Pickwick 1927,S 6,35:2
Whispering Friends 1928,F 21,18:3
Yellow Jacket, The 1928,N 8,27:3
Falstaff 1928,D 26,14:2
Plutocrat, The 1930,F 21,23:3
Edymar (Playwright)
Marie Antoinette 1921,N 23,16:1
Eells, Harriet
Warrior's Husband, The 1932,Mr 12,19:4
Mad Hopes, The 1932,D 2,26:3
Efelia and Pimento
Life Begins at 8:40 1934,Ag 28,24:2
Effah, Tony
Madmen and Specialists 1970,Ag 3,38:1
Effrat, John
In Heaven and Earth 1936,Mr 27,24:8
Steps Leading Up 1941,Ap 19,20:6
Autumn Hill 1942,Ap 14,17:4
Odds on Mrs Oakley 1944,O 3,18:8
Streets Are Guarded, The 1944,N 21,19:7
I Like It Here 1946,Mr 23,8:6
Effrat, John (Director)
Dawn's Early Light 1950,O 25,44:3
Effrat, John (Miscellaneous)
Mister Johnson 1956,Mr 30,11:1
Cloud 7 1958,F 15,15:2
Evening With Yves Montand, An 1961,O 25,30:1
Effrat, John (Producer)
Talent '49 1949,Ap 13,39:4
Efird, Mel
Everything's Jake 1930,Ja 17,20:4
Sweet Stranger 1930,O 22,23:3
In The Best of Families 1931,F 3,29:1
Efron, Eric
Summer Night 1939,N 3,17:1
Efron, Marshall
Midsummer Night's Dream, A 1967,Je 30,23:1
Efroni, Yehuda
Dybbuk, The 1964,F 4,30:2
Children of the Shadows 1964,F 27,26:1
Efros, Anatoly (Producer)
Romeo and Juliet 1970,My 28,28:1
Egan, Bill
Henry V 1965,Je 29,27:2
Egan, Frank (Producer)
Starlight 1925,Mr 4,17:2

Egan, George
Hero of Santa Maria, The 1926,My 1,10:1
Egan, Jack
Kansas City Kitty 1929,S 26,27:4
American Holiday 1936,F 22,13:3
Sun and I, The 1937,F 27,9:5
Egan, James
Corn Is Green, The 1954,F 27,10:2
Egan, Jenny
Crucible, The 1953,Ja 23,15:2
Crucible, The 1953,Jl 2,20:2
Mary Stuart 1956,Ap 28,10:2
Good Woman of Setzuan, The 1956,D 19,41:2
Bald Soprano, The 1958,Je 4,39:2
Jack 1958,Je 4,39:2
Port-Royal 1960,Ap 26,41:1
Two Executioners, The 1960,My 17,42:2
Henry V 1960,Je 30,23:1
Plough and the Stars, The 1960,D 7,56:2
Under Milk Wood 1961,Mr 30,25:1
Ballad of the Sad Cafe, The 1963,O 31,27:1
Box-Mao-Box; Quotations From Chairman Mao
    Tse-Tung 1968,Mr 8,48:1
Cuban Thing, The 1968,S 25,36:2
Egan, Jenny (Director)
Triumph of Delight 1965,My 1,19:1
Unto Thee a Garden 1968,O 28,55:3
Egan, Jenny (Miscellaneous)
Antony and Cleopatra 1959,Ja 14,28:1
Egan, Michael
Great Sebastians, The 1956,Ja 5,27:1
House of Breath, The 1957,Ap 15,23:2
Call It Virtue 1963,Mr 28,8:2
Luther 1963,S 26,41:1
Drums in the Night 1967,My 18,54:1
Cry of Players, A 1968,N 15,40:1
Egan, Michael (Playwright)
Dominant Sex, The 1934,D 4,23:1
Dominant Sex, The 1935,Ap 2,24:5
Private Company 1936,F 11,19:3
Art and Craft 1936,D 1,30:4
Dominant Sex, The 1937,O 24,XI,3:2
Egan, Peter (Lighting Director)
Peter and the Wolf 1969,N 30,85:5
Egan, Raymond B (Composer)
Moon Over Mulberry Street 1935,S 5,24:6
Egan, Richard
Go, Go, Go, God is Dead! 1966,O 12,37:1
Egan, Thomas
Lazarus Laughed 1948,Ap 9,27:4
Egbert, Charles
Apollo of Bellac, The 1958,Mr 7,17:2
Egbert, Jane
Love Call, The 1927,O 25,33:1
Egbert, Leslie Floyd (Playwright)
Boy Who Lived Twice, A 1945,S 12,31:2
Eger, Rudolph (Playwright)
Machen Sie Das Nicht Mit Ihrer Frau
    1932,Je 19,IX,1:5
Egerton, Francis
Kiss Me, Kate 1970,D 26,10:4
Egerton, George (Playwright)
Camilla States Her Case 1925,F 1,VII,2:1
Egg, Lois (Scenic Designer)
Professor Bernhardi 1968,Mr 20,38:1
Konzert, Das 1968,Mr 25,52:1
Maria Stuart 1968,Mr 27,38:1
Jux Will Er Sich Machen, Einen 1968,Ap 3,41:1
Eggenton, Joseph
Adventure 1928,S 26,25:2
Dora Mobridge 1930,Ap 21,20:2
Lost Boy 1932,Ja 6,24:4
Panic 1935,Mr 16,18:4
Sweet Mystery of Life 1935,O 12,13:3
Egger, Jill
Fireman's Flame, The 1937,O 11,26:2
Eggerth, Marta
Higher and Higher 1940,Mr 17,X,2:5
Higher and Higher 1940,Ap 5,24:3
Merry Widow, The 1943,My 5,19:2
Merry Widow, The 1943,Ag 22,II,5:1
Merry Widow, The 1944,O 9,17:1
Polonaise 1945,O 8,20:2
Polonaise 1945,O 14,II,1:1
Merry Widow, The 1957,Ap 11,36:6
Eggerton, Joseph
Come Angel Band 1936,F 19,17:1
Egginton, Joseph
American Tragedy, An 1931,F 21,15:5
Eggleston, Clark
Banjo Eyes 1941,D 26,20:2
Eggleston, Marjorie
Polly Preferred 1923,Ja 12,13:3
Sitting Pretty 1924,Ap 9,24:2
Eggleston, Shirley
Church Street 1948,F 10,27:2
Blood Wedding 1949,F 7,16:2
Eggleston, William (Lighting Director)
Great White Hope, The 1967,D 14,58:1
Iceman Cometh, The 1968,Ap 1,58:1
Indians 1969,My 27,43:1
Eggleton, Larry (Scenic Designer)
Black Chiffon 1950,S 28,39:2

Eglevsky, Andre
  Great Lady 1938,D 2,26:6
  Peter and the Wolf 1969,N 30,85:5
Eglevsky, Andre (Choreographer)
  Peter and the Wolf 1969,N 30,85:5
Egly, Allan (Scenic Designer)
  My 3 Angels 1956,F 4,24:2
Egner, Philip (Lieutenant) (Composer)
  Merry Wives of West Point, The 1932,Mr 20,II,7:7
Egolf, Clarence (Scenic Designer)
  Animal Kingdom, The 1938,Jl 27,14:5
  Arms and the Man 1938,Ag 10,14:1
Egri, Lajos N (Playwright)
  Rapid Transit 1927,Ap 8,21:2
Egyed, Zoltan (Playwright)
  Az Ego Szoknya 1928,S 30,IX,4:4
Egypt, Lorraine
  Gideon 1961,N 10,38:1
Ehara, Mary
  Cabaret 1966,N 21,62:1
Eheman, Joan
  Carousel 1957,S 12,38:2
Ehler, Ernest
  White Eagle, The 1927,D 27,24:4
Ehlert, Fay (Playwright)
  Undercurrent, The 1929,Ja 21,18:3
Ehmann, F H
  Somebody's Lion 1921,Ap 13,20:1
Ehrenburg, Ilya (Playwright)
  Lion in the Square 1948,Mr 27,9:4
Ehrenfreund, Heinz
  Maria Stuart 1968,Mr 27,38:1
  Jux Will Er Sich Machen, Einen 1968,Ap 3,41:1
Ehrenfreund, Norbert
  Macbeth 1955,O 8,12:6
  Last Love of Don Juan, The 1955,N 24,40:1
Ehrenfried, Jean
  Fuente Ovejuna; Sheep Well, The 1936,My 3,II,4:1
Ehrenman, Howard (Director)
  Floydada to Matador 1955,D 22,19:1
  Hungerers, The 1955,D 22,19:1
  Opera Opera 1955,D 22,19:1
  Hello Out There 1955,D 22,19:1
Ehrenman, Howard (Producer)
  Opera Opera 1955,D 22,19:1
  Hello Out There 1955,D 22,19:1
  Hungerers, The 1955,D 22,19:1
  Floydada to Matador 1955,D 22,19:1
Ehrhardt, Anna
  Untitled-Passion Play 1927,Jl 31,VII,1:6
Ehrhardt, Bess
  Ice Follies 1937,D 22,29:1
  Ice Follies 1939,D 5,38:2
  Ice Follies 1941,D 2,32:2
Ehrhardt, Willie
  Passion Play, The 1929,Ap 30,32:1
Ehrle, John
  Fine and Dandy 1930,S 24,26:1
  Face the Music 1933,F 1,13:4
Ehrlich, Estelle
  Nativity Play, The 1937,D 21,29:1
Ehrlich, Ida Lublenski (Costume Designer)
  Girl From Samos, The 1954,N 24,17:1
Ehrlich, Ida Lublenski (Director)
  Everyman 1953,O 12,30:2
  Top Secret 1960,S 6,40:1
Ehrlich, Ida Lublenski (Playwright)
  Helena's Boys 1924,Ap 8,22:2
  Love Kills 1934,My 2,25:3
  Girl From Samos, The 1954,N 24,17:1
  Top Secret 1960,S 6,40:1
Ehrlich, Ida Lublenski (Producer)
  Love Kills 1934,My 2,25:3
  Top Secret 1960,S 6,40:1
Ehrlich, Max
  An und Aus 1926,D 5,VIII,8:7
  On the Spot 1931,Ja 18,VIII,3:1
Ehrlich, Milton
  Home Is Tomorrow 1950,Je 2,27:2
Ehrlich, Paul
  Play of Daniel, The 1960,D 27,23:6
  Play of Daniel, The 1961,D 28,22:6
Ehrlicher, Jay
  Oedipus Rex 1959,Ap 30,36:1
Ehrman, A L
  Merton of the Movies 1922,N 14,16:2
Eiben, Conrad (Rev) (Playwright)
  Veronica's Veil 1950,F 12,II,1:5
  Veronica's Veil 1954,F 28,I,78:5
Eiben, Conrad (Rev) (Producer)
  Veronica's Veil 1940,F 12,2:7
Eichberg, Richard (Miscellaneous)
  New Moon, The 1942,Ag 19,14:2
Eichel, Leslie P (Playwright)
  Downstream 1926,Ja 12,28:1
Eichel, Paul
  Finian's Rainbow 1967,Ap 6,44:1
  Darling of the Day 1968,Ja 29,26:2
  Look to the Lilies 1970,Mr 30,59:1
Eichelberger, James
  Brother to Dragons 1968,D 8,86:1
  Wilson in the Promise Land 1970,Ja 11,78:1
  Wilson in the Promise Land 1970,My 27,41:1

Eichheim, Henry (Composer)
  Burmese Pwe, A 1926,Mr 17,28:1
Eidelman, M
  Golem, The 1927,F 5,13:2
Eidelseim, Harold
  Journey by Night, A 1935,Ap 17,26:3
Eidenberg, David (Miscellaneous)
  Saved 1970,O 29,57:1
Eidman, Earl (Lighting Director)
  Kill the One-Eyed Man 1965,O 21,56:1
  Man and Superman 1970,F 24,48:1
Eien, Simon
  Troupe Du Roi, La 1970,F 4,38:1
Eigerman, Sarah
  Instructions for the Running of Trains, etc on the
    Erie Railway to Go Into Effect January 1,1862
    1970,Ja 7,36:2
Eigerman, Sarah (Composer)
  Instructions for the Running of Trains, etc on the
    Erie Railway to Go Into Effect January 1,1862
    1970,Ja 7,36:2
Eiges, Marilyn
  Adding Machine, The 1970,D 5,40:1
Eigsti, Karl (Costume Designer)
  Serjeant Musgrave's Dance 1968,Je 16,52:4
Eigsti, Karl (Scenic Designer)
  Serjeant Musgrave's Dance 1968,Je 16,52:4
  Merton of the Movies 1968,S 26,62:1
  Bananas 1968,D 5,60:1
  Henry V 1969,Je 9,57:1
  Hamlet 1969,Je 30,33:1
  Henry V 1969,N 11,43:1
  Instructions for the Running of Trains, etc on the
    Erie Railway to Go Into Effect January 1,1862
    1970,Ja 7,36:2
  Inquest 1970,Ap 24,38:1
  Othello 1970,Je 22,43:1
  Boesman and Lena 1970,Je 23,35:1
  Othello 1970,S 15,51:1
Eigsti, Molly (Costume Designer)
  Happiness 1967,N 11,25:2
  Walking to Waldheim 1967,N 11,25:2
Eikenberry, Jill
  Night Thoreau Spent in Jail, The 1970,N 2,66:1
Eine, Simon
  Troupe Du Roi, La 1970,F 4,38:1
  Don Juan 1970,F 7,24:2
  Malade Imaginaire, Le 1970,F 18,40:2
Einenkel, Robert
  Volpone 1967,Je 30,29:1
Einhorn, Abe (Playwright)
  Agatha Sue, I Love You 1966,D 15,61:1
Einhorn, Carl
  Antigone 1968,O 11,36:1
Einhorn, Sam
  Trial of Dr Beck, The 1937,Ag 10,22:2
Einstein, Doris (Lighting Director)
  Nights of Wrath; Nuits de la Colere, Les
    1947,D 1,26:4
  Burning Bush, The 1949,D 17,15:5
  Circle of Chalk, The 1950,D 2,8:3
Einstein, Doris (Miscellaneous)
  Rich Man, Poor Man 1950,F 13,15:4
  How to Make a Man 1961,F 3,16:1
Eis, Elizabeth
  Comedy of Errors, The 1967,Je 15,58:4
  King John 1967,Jl 14,19:1
  Brother to Dragons 1968,D 8,86:1
  Jungle of Cities 1970,Mr 1,75:2
Eis, Gordon (Composer)
  Cockeyed Kite 1961,S 14,27:1
Eis, Heinrich
  Professor Bernhardi 1968,Mr 20,38:1
  Maria Stuart 1968,Mr 27,38:1
Eis, Maria
  Elizabeth and Essex 1935,N 9,18:8
  Millionairess, The 1936,Ja 5,39:3
Eisele, Lou (Costume Designer)
  Follow the Girls 1944,Ap 10,15:2
  Lady Says Yes, A 1945,Ja 11,18:5
  Star Spangled Family 1945,Ap 11,18:6
  Too Hot for Maneuvers 1945,My 3,26:5
  Girl From Nantucket, The 1945,N 9,17:2
  Icetime 1946,Je 21,20:5
  Young Man's Fancy, A 1947,Ap 30,33:2
  Icetime 1947,My 29,28:2
  Caribbean Carnival 1947,D 6,12:2
  My Romance 1948,O 20,38:5
Eisemann, Michel (Composer)
  Kuss-und Sonst Gar Nichts, Ein 1933,N 19,IX,3:1
Eisen, Anne (Miscellaneous)
  Virtuous Island, The 1957,Ap 10,39:1
  Apollo of Bellac, The 1957,Ap 10,39:1
Eisen, Michela
  Prodigal, The 1960,F 12,23:1
Eisen, Rose
  Jazz a La Carte 1922,Je 3,8:3
Eisenberg, Ellen
  When Differences Disappear 1941,Je 3,17:4
Eisenberg, Emanuel (Playwright)
  Pins and Needles 1936,Je 15,24:6
  Pins and Needles 1937,N 29,18:6

Eisenberg, Jack
  Come of Age 1952,Ja 24,22:2
Eisenberg, Lawrence B (Playwright)
  Plot Against the Chase Manhattan Bank, The
    1963,N 27,29:1
Eisenborg, M
  Chains 1937,Ja 22,25:1
Eisenbud, Gertrude
  39 Steps 1938,Mr 12,13:1
Eisenbud, Jule
  Upon My Soul 1927,Ap 22,19:1
Eisenhauer, Lette
  Originale 1964,S 9,46:1
Eisensmith, Bruce Paul (Miscellaneous)
  Papp 1969,My 6,39:1
Eisenstadt, Maurice
  Brigadoon 1964,D 24,9:1
  Brigadoon 1967,D 14,59:2
Eisikoff, Sol
  Parnosseh 1939,F 20,12:5
Eisinberg, Joseph (Playwright)
  Jane Brady-Editor 1935,Jl 2,24:3
Eisinger, Jo (Playwright)
  Point of Honor, A 1937,Ja 31,II,10:4
  Point of Honor 1937,F 12,26:2
  What Big Ears! 1942,Ap 21,18:5
Eisler, Chuck (Lighting Director)
  Iolanthe 1965,My 19,42:1
Eisler, Chuck (Miscellaneous)
  Iolanthe 1965,My 19,42:1
  Moon Walk 1970,N 27,52:1
Eisler, Edmund (Playwright)
  Bruder Straubinger 1921,N 16,22:3
Eisler, Hanns (Composer)
  Mother, The 1935,N 20,26:3
  Night Music 1940,F 23,18:2
  Medicine Show 1940,Ap 13,20:6
  Private Life of the Master Race, The
    1945,Je 13,28:3
  Galileo 1947,Ag 1,21:4
  Galileo 1947,D 8,34:2
  Days of the Commune, The 1956,N 20,44:4
  Galileo 1967,Ap 14,31:1
  Schweik in the Second World War
    1967,N 12,II,17:1
  Galileo 1968,D 1,88:4
Eisley, Fred
  Desperate Hours, The 1955,F 11,20:2
  Goodbye Again 1956,Ap 25,38:1
Eisman, Fred (Playwright)
  At Your Service 1937,Ag 17,23:1
Eisman, Goldie
  Love and Politics 1929,O 21,30:7
  Slaves of Luxury 1930,F 8,13:3
  Sonitchka 1930,Mr 8,21:3
  Song of the Ghetto, The 1932,O 3,15:5
  Schlemihl 1936,S 19,20:4
  Yossel and His Wives 1937,S 19,II,8:3
  Little Tailor, The 1938,Mr 21,18:2
  Long Live America 1939,Ja 2,28:3
Eisman, Michael
  Song of Dnieper 1946,O 26,10:5
Eisner, Helen (Playwright)
  Penny Change 1963,O 25,37:1
Eistenstadter, Peter
  Moby Dick 1970,Je 3,52:1
Eistenstadter, Peter (Miscellaneous)
  Moby Dick 1970,Je 3,52:1
Ek, Malin
  Dream Play 1970,Ap 17,45:1
Ekerot, Bengt
  Father, The 1962,My 15,49:1
Ekerot, Bengt (Director)
  Father, The 1962,My 15,49:1
  Long Day's Journey Into Night 1962,My 16,35:4
Eklund, Bengt
  Hughie 1958,S 9,24:5
Ekman, Gosta
  Henry VIII 1930,Jl 13,VIII,2:1
  Gustav Vasa 1930,N 2,VIII,3:2
  Merry Widow, The 1931,O 11,VIII,4:4
  Hamlet 1934,F 11,IX,3:7
Ekman, Gosta (Director)
  Merry Widow, The 1931,O 11,VIII,4:4
Ekman, Gosta (Producer)
  Merry Widow, The 1931,O 11,VIII,4:4
  His Excellency's Last Will and Testament
    1931,O 11,VIII,4:5
Ekson, Larrio
  Jonah! 1966,F 16,52:1
Ekstrom, Marta
  Dear Octopus 1939,N 12,IX,2:5
Elaine, Mabel
  Red Pepper 1922,My 30,8:3
Elaine, Ruth
  Fools Errant 1922,Ag 22,12:3
Elaine, Sybil
  Jumbo 1935,N 18,20:2
Elan, Joan
  Lark, The 1955,N 18,20:1
Elbershagen, Frithiof (Lighting Director)
  Mitschuldigen, Die 1966,Ap 6,34:1
  Wozzeck 1966,Ap 6,34:1

Elbert, Harold
Eyes 1930,My 10,25:1
Elberton, Sam
Aries Is Rising 1939,N 22,16:5
Elcar, Dana
Knight of the Burning Pestle, The 1953,O 24,13:2
Moon in Capricorn 1953,O 28,37:2
Honeys, The 1955,Ap 29,26:1
Venice Preserv'd 1955,D 13,54:4
Good as Gold 1957,Mr 8,22:2
Richard III 1957,N 26,41:1
As You Like It 1958,Ja 21,33:6
Augustus Does His Bit 1958,F 22,8:3
Androcles and the Lion 1958,F 22,8:3
Power and the Glory, The 1958,D 12,2:7
Our Town 1959,Mr 24,46:2
Summer of the Seventeenth Doll 1959,O 14,52:1
Semi-Detached 1960,Mr 11,20:2
Drums Under the Windows 1960,O 14,26:1
Under Milk Wood 1961,Mr 30,25:1
Androcles and the Lion 1961,N 22,24:2
Childhood 1962,Ja 12,28:1
Dumbwaiter, The 1962,N 27,44:1
Murderer Among Us, A 1964,Mr 26,43:1
Eh? 1966,O 17,47:1
Elder, Althea
Red, Hot and Blue! 1936,O 30,26:3
I Married an Angel 1938,My 12,26:2
Jackpot 1944,Ja 14,15:2
Million Dollar Baby 1945,D 22,17:2
Three to Make Ready 1946,Mr 8,16:2
Elder, Dorothy
News Item 1935,Ag 6,20:3
I Remember Mama 1944,O 20,16:2
Leaf and Bough 1949,Ja 22,10:2
Southern Exposure 1950,S 27,36:3
Three by Thurber; Middle Years, The
  1955,Mr 8,23:2
Three by Thurber; Imperturbable Spirit, The
  1955,Mr 8,23:2
Elder, Eldon (Costume Designer)
Othello 1958,Jl 4,16:1
Twelfth Night 1958,Ag 7,21:4
Julius Caesar 1959,Ag 4,30:1
Henry V 1960,Je 30,23:1
Taming of the Shrew, The 1960,Ag 20,17:1
Drums Under the Windows 1960,O 14,26:1
Julius Caesar 1962,F 22,19:6
Birds, The 1966,Jl 1,40:1
Elder, Eldon (Lighting Director)
Long Days, The 1951,Ap 21,10:5
Dream Girl 1951,My 10,39:1
Idiot's Delight 1951,My 24,46:3
Hook'n Ladder 1952,Ap 30,31:2
Time Out for Ginger 1952,N 27,50:4
Grey-Eyed People, The 1952,D 18,41:2
Girl in Pink Tights, The 1954,Mr 6,13:2
One Eye Closed 1954,N 25,45:2
All in One; Trouble in Tahiti 1955,Ap 20,40:3
All in One; 27 Wagons Full of Cotton
  1955,Ap 20,40:3
Young and Beautiful, The 1955,O 3,23:2
Heavenly Twins, The 1955,N 5,23:2
Fallen Angels 1956,Ja 18,27:1
Drums Under the Windows 1960,O 14,26:1
Affair, The 1962,S 21,34:2
Fun Couple, The 1962,O 27,15:2
Morning Sun 1963,O 7,36:2
Child Buyer, The 1964,D 22,35:1
Whitman Portrait, A 1966,O 12,37:1
Of Love Remembered 1967,F 20,46:5
Megilla of Itzik Manger, The 1968,O 10,60:1
Megilla of Itzik Manger, The 1969,Ap 21,55:1
Elder, Eldon (Miscellaneous)
Fun Couple, The 1962,O 27,15:2
Rugantino 1964,F 7,34:1
Elder, Eldon (Scenic Designer)
Earth Spirit 1950,Je 7,33:4
Long Days, The 1951,Ap 21,10:5
Dream Girl 1951,My 10,39:1
Idiot's Delight 1951,My 24,46:3
Legend of Lovers 1951,D 27,17:1
Hook'n Ladder 1952,Ap 30,31:2
Time Out for Ginger 1952,N 27,50:4
Grey-Eyed People, The 1952,D 18,41:2
Girl in Pink Tights, The 1954,Mr 6,13:2
One Eye Closed 1954,N 25,45:2
All in One; 27 Wagons Full of Cotton
  1955,Ap 20,40:3
All in One; Trouble in Tahiti 1955,Ap 20,40:3
Phoenix '55 1955,Ap 25,20:2
Young and Beautiful, The 1955,O 3,23:2
Heavenly Twins, The 1955,N 5,23:2
Fallen Angels 1956,Ja 18,27:1
Shinbone Alley 1957,Ap 15,23:2
Othello 1958,Jl 4,16:1
Twelfth Night 1958,Ag 7,21:4
Lulu 1958,S 30,24:1
Julius Caesar 1959,Ag 4,30:1
Julius Caesar 1959,Ag 16,II,1:1
Henry V 1960,Je 30,23:1
Measure for Measure 1960,Jl 27,33:1
Taming of the Shrew, The 1960,Ag 20,17:1

Drums Under the Windows 1960,O 14,26:1
Much Ado About Nothing 1961,Jl 7,17:1
Midsummer Night's Dream, A 1961,Ag 3,13:1
Richard II 1961,Ag 30,25:1
Richard II 1962,Je 18,20:2
Henry IV, Part I 1962,Je 18,20:4
Affair, The 1962,S 21,34:2
Fun Couple, The 1962,O 27,15:2
Morning Sun 1963,O 7,36:2
I Knock at the Door 1964,N 26,53:2
Pictures in the Hallway 1964,D 17,51:1
Child Buyer, The 1964,D 22,35:1
Mating Dance 1965,N 4,58:1
Oresteia 1966,Je 30,29:1
Birds, The 1966,Jl 1,40:1
Whitman Portrait, A 1966,O 12,37:1
Of Love Remembered 1967,F 20,46:5
Amazing Grace 1967,D 10,82:1
Spiro Who? 1969,My 19,55:1
Elder, Judith
Merchant of Venice, The 1930,D 3,29:2
Murder in the Old Red Barn, The 1936,F 3,20:4
Elder, Judyann
Song of the Lusitanian Bogey, The 1969,My 13,41:1
Five on the Black Hand Side 1970,Ja 2,32:2
Elder, Lonne 3d
Raisin in the Sun, A 1959,Mr 12,27:1
Day of Absence 1965,N 16,56:1
Elder, Lonne 3d (Playwright)
Ceremonies in Dark Old Men 1969,F 6,33:1
Ceremonies in Dark Old Men 1969,F 23,II,5:1
Ceremonies in Dark Old Men 1969,O 11,42:1
Eldershaw, Thomas B
Smyth With a Y 1937,Je 30,19:5
Eldred, Arthur
Bab 1920,O 19,12:1
Eldredge, John
Would-Be Gentleman, The 1928,O 2,34:1
Cherry Orchard, The 1928,O 16,28:5
Katerina 1929,F 26,30:3
Good Fairy, The 1932,N 18,22:3
Three-Cornered Moon 1933,Mr 17,20:6
Three and One 1933,O 26,22:6
Joyous Season, The 1934,Ja 30,16:3
Eldridge, Elaine
Gabrielle 1941,Mr 26,26:2
All the King's Men 1948,Ja 19,19:2
Outside the Door 1949,Mr 2,33:2
Circle of Chalk, The 1950,D 2,8:3
Beaver Coat, The 1956,Mr 29,22:5
In Good King Charles's Golden Days
  1957,Ja 25,16:1
Johnny Summit 1957,S 25,23:4
Every Other Evil 1961,Ja 23,20:2
Trelawny of the 'Wells' 1970,O 12,48:1
Trelawney of the 'Wells' 1970,O 25,II,16:1
Eldridge, Florence
Ambush 1921,O 11,22:1
Ambush 1921,O 16,VI,1:1
Cat and the Canary, The 1922,F 8,13:1
Six Characters in Search of an Author
  1922,O 31,11:2
Love Habit, The 1923,Mr 15,17:1
Dancers, The 1923,O 18,17:2
Cheaper to Marry 1924,Ap 16,26:1
Bewitched 1924,O 2,26:3
Bewitched 1924,O 5,VIII,1:1
Bewitched 1924,O 19,VIII,1:1
Young Blood 1925,N 25,15:1
Young Blood 1925,N 29,VIII,1:1
Great Gatsby, The 1926,F 3,22:1
Proud Woman, A 1926,N 16,24:1
Off Key 1927,F 9,16:2
Among the Married 1929,D 8,X,2:7
Affair of State, An 1930,N 20,30:3
Days to Come 1936,D 16,35:1
Yr Obedient Husband 1937,N 27,21:2
Yr Obedient Husband 1938,Ja 11,26:5
American Way, The 1939,Ja 23,9:2
Hope for a Harvest 1941,Ap 5,18:4
Hope for a Harvest 1941,N 27,28:2
Hope for a Harvest 1941,D 7,X,5:1
Skin of Our Teeth, The 1942,N 19,29:5
Skin of Our Teeth, The 1942,N 22,VIII,1:1
Years Ago 1946,D 4,44:2
Now I Lay Me Down to Sleep 1950,Mr 3,21:2
Now I Lay Me Down to Sleep 1950,Mr 19,II,1:1
Enemy of the People, An 1950,D 29,14:1
Enemy of the People, An 1951,Ja 7,II,1:1
Autumn Garden, The 1951,Mr 8,36:2
Autumn Garden, The 1951,Mr 18,II,1:1
Long Day's Journey Into Night 1956,O 17,40:1
Long Day's Journey Into Night 1956,N 8,47:2
Long Day's Journey Into Night 1956,N 18,II,1:1
Long Day's Journey Into Night 1957,Jl 3,14:1
Eldridge, Frances
Red Poppy, The 1922,D 21,18:2
Eldridge, H E
Dearest Enemy 1925,S 19,9:2
Eldridge, John
Inheritors 1927,Mr 8,23:1
Good Hope, The 1927,O 19,24:2
2 + 2 = 5 1927,N 29,30:3

Eldridge, John—Cont
Improvisations in June 1928,F 27,16:5
Peter Pan; Boy Who Would Not Grow Up, The
  1928,N 27,36:3
Eldridge, Mr
Will Morrissey's Folies Bergere Revue
  1930,Ap 16,26:6
Eldridge, Paul (Playwright)
Intruder, The 1928,Jl 26,25:4
Elek, Marie
Savages Under the Skin 1927,Mr 25,25:2
Elenitsa (Costume Designer)
Cretan Woman, The 1954,My 21,17:2
Eleven
Bluebeard 1970,My 5,58:1
Eley, Helen
Battling Buttler 1923,O 9,17:2
Eley, Jean
Hear! Hear! 1955,S 28,38:1
Eley, Lou
Hear! Hear! 1955,S 28,38:1
Eley, Robert (Director)
Adding Machine, The 1948,N 18,35:2
Hamlet 1948,D 4,9:2
Maya 1951,Ag 9,17:4
Eley, Wallace
Portofino 1958,F 22,8:3
Elfenbein, Beatrice
What of It? 1929,Mr 9,24:2
Elg, Taina
Look to the Lilies 1970,Mr 30,59:1
Elgar, Anne
H M S Pinafore 1964,Mr 21,13:4
H M S Pinafore 1965,Ap 15,39:1
Pirates of Penzance, The 1965,Ap 21,50:6
Elgar, Avril
Epitaph for George Dillon 1958,N 5,44:1
Elgar, Edward (Sir) (Composer)
Arthur 1923,Mr 18,VII,1:1
Elgart, Isadore (Miscellaneous)
Go Fight City Hall 1961,N 3,28:5
Elgart, Jeanne
Possessed, The 1939,O 25,26:2
Elgas, Priscilla
Lady From the Sea, The 1935,D 14,11:3
Fuente Ovejuna; Sheep Well, The 1936,My 3,II,4:1
Elgin, Claire
Earl Carroll's Vanities 1923,Jl 6,8:2
Elgin, Janice
Open House 1925,D 15,28:3
Elhajaji
Ali Baba 1951,Mr 27,34:2
Elias, Alix
As You Like It 1963,Jl 17,19:2
Oh Dad, Poor Dad, Mamma's Hung You in the
  Closet and I'm Feelin' So Sad 1963,Ag 28,28:2
Last Analysis, The 1964,O 2,30:1
Falstaff 1966,Je 20,27:1
Increased Difficulty of Concentration, The
  1969,D 5,48:1
Early Morning 1970,N 26,57:1
Elias, Bert V
Merry Widow, The 1921,S 6,13:1
Elias, Erica (Costume Designer)
Salvation 1969,S 25,55:1
Elias, Hector
Susie Is a Good Girl 1968,N 5,53:2
Subscriber, The 1968,N 5,53:2
Grab Bag, The 1968,N 5,53:2
Elias, Michael
Brig, The 1963,My 16,40:1
Elias, Miriam
God Man and Devil 1928,D 22,14:8
Othello 1929,F 4,21:2
Untitled-Recital 1931,Ap 13,17:4
Salt and Pepper 1933,Ap 24,10:2
Elias, Robert Downey
Failures, The 1959,Ja 6,30:2
Elias, Sylvia
Princess Virtue 1921,My 5,20:2
Elias, Vincente
Guide, The 1968,Mr 7,50:1
Eliashevitch, Nina
Cricket on the Hearth, The 1925,My 29,20:2
Elic, Josip
Three by Thurber; Imperturbable Spirit, The
  1955,Mr 8,23:2
Three by Thurber; Middle Years, The
  1955,Mr 8,23:2
Safari! 1955,My 12,32:6
Threepenny Opera, The 1955,S 21,38:1
Threepenny Opera, The 1956,Mr 11,II,1:1
Girl of the Golden West, The 1957,N 6,44:1
Comic Strip 1958,My 15,26:2
Leave It to Jane 1959,My 26,30:2
Death of Satan 1960,Ap 6,49:1
Dragon, The 1963,Ap 10,32:1
Too Much Johnson 1964,Ja 16,29:1
Sign in Sidney Brustein's Window, The
  1964,O 16,32:1
West Side Story 1968,Je 25,32:1
Elin, Sedonia
Fashions for Men 1922,D 6,22:1

Elinore, Kate
Vaudeville (Palace) 1924,Ja 1,21:1
Elinson, Izzy (Playwright)
Banjo Eyes 1941,D 26,20:2
Eliot, Ann
Church Street 1948,F 10,27:2
Eliot, Constance
O Nightingale 1925,Ap 16,25:2
Eliot, David
Wisteria Trees, The 1955,F 3,20:2
Eliot, Day
Two Time Mary 1937,Ag 3,20:5
Reno 1937,Ag 10,22:7
Love in My Fashion 1937,D 4,21:4
Eliot, Drew
Doctor Faustus 1957,F 19,35:7
Physicists, The 1964,O 14,52:1
Henry V 1965,Je 29,27:2
Elizabeth the Queen 1966,N 4,30:1
Stephen D 1967,S 25,58:1
Eliot, George (Original Author)
Daniel Deronda 1969,Ja 11,22:2
Eliot, John
Louisiana Purchase 1940,My 29,19:2
Eliot, Marc
Macbeth 1969,D 23,25:1
Eliot, Marge
No Place to Be Somebody 1969,My 5,53:3
No Place to Be Somebody 1969,D 31,17:1
Eliot, Miriam
Outrageous Mrs Palmer, The 1920,O 13,18:1
Eliot, Samuel A Jr (Translator)
Loves of Lulu, The 1925,My 12,26:1
Eliot, Sidney
Ebb Tide 1931,Je 9,33:6
Eliot, T S (Original Author)
Practical Cats 1954,Ag 27,11:5
Eliot, T S (Playwright)
Sweeney Agonistes 1935,O 2,26:2
Murder in the Cathedral 1935,N 2,12:2
Murder in the Cathedral 1935,D 21,11:3
Murder in the Cathedral 1936,Ja 12,IX,1:5
Murder in the Cathedral 1936,Mr 11,13:5
Murder in the Cathedral 1936,Mr 29,IX,1:1
Murder in the Cathedral 1938,F 17,16:2
Family Reunion, The 1939,Ap 9,X,1:5
Family Reunion, The 1947,N 29,9:2
Cocktail Party, The 1949,Ag 23,28:6
Cocktail Party, The 1949,S 11,II,2:1
Cocktail Party, The 1950,Ja 23,17:2
Cocktail Party, The 1950,Ja 29,II,1:1
Cocktail Party, The 1950,My 4,33:2
Cocktail Party, The 1950,My 7,II,2:5
Cocktail Party, The 1950,My 14,II,1:1
Cocktail Party, The 1950,My 21,II,3:2
Murder in the Cathedral 1953,Ap 26,II,1:1
Confidential Clerk, The 1953,Ag 26,22:2
Confidential Clerk, The 1953,Ag 27,21:7
Confidential Clerk, The 1953,Ag 30,II,2:1
Confidential Clerk, The 1953,O 11,II,3:7
Confidential Clerk, The 1954,F 12,22:1
Confidential Clerk, The 1954,F 21,VI,16:1
Confidential Clerk, The 1954,F 21,II,1:1
Family Reunion, The 1956,Je 9,13:6
Murder in the Cathedral 1958,Mr 22,12:4
Elder Statesman, The 1958,Ag 20,21:5
Elder Statesman, The 1958,Ag 26,35:1
Elder Statesman, The 1958,Ag 31,II,3:1
Family Reunion, The 1958,O 21,39:1
Family Reunion, The 1958,O 26,II,1:1
Family Reunion, The 1960,D 10,26:1
Murder in the Cathedral 1966,Je 21,38:1
Cocktail Party, The 1968,O 8,42:1
Cocktail Party, The 1968,O 20,II,1:1
Eliran, Ron
Holiday in Israel 1968,O 14,55:2
Eliscu, David (Director)
Harry, Noon and Night 1965,My 6,44:1
Eliscu, David (Miscellaneous)
Grand Vizier, The 1961,D 13,55:5
Cayenne Pepper 1961,D 13,55:5
Moon on a Rainbow Shawl 1962,Ja 16,30:1
Me and Thee 1965,D 8,58:4
Eliscu, Edward
Quarantine 1924,D 17,19:7
Drift 1925,N 25,15:3
Don Q Jr 1926,Ja 28,16:3
Racket, The 1927,N 23,28:3
Eliscu, Edward (Composer)
Nine Fifteen Revue, The 1930,F 12,26:2
Tattle Tales 1933,Je 2,22:6
Meet the People 1940,D 26,22:2
Eliscu, Edward (Director)
Mister Romeo 1927,S 6,35:3
Eliscu, Edward (Lyricist)
Loud Speaker 1927,Mr 3,27:2
Lady Fingers 1929,F 1,22:4
Murray Anderson's Almanac 1929,Ag 15,20:3
Great Day! 1929,O 18,24:3
Nine Fifteen Revue, The 1930,F 12,26:2
Little Racketeer, The 1931,O 11,VIII,4:7
Little Racketeer, The 1932,Ja 19,24:4
Tattle Tales 1933,Je 2,22:6

Frederika 1937,F 5,16:5
Meet the People 1940,O 20,IX,3:3
Meet the People 1940,D 26,22:2
These Are the Times 1950,My 11,37:2
Banker's Daughter, The 1962,Ja 23,37:1
Eliscu, Edward (Miscellaneous)
Frederika 1937,F 5,16:5
Eliscu, Edward (Playwright)
Meet the People 1940,D 26,22:2
They Can't Get You Down 1941,N 2,IX,3:5
These Are the Times 1950,My 11,37:2
Banker's Daughter, The 1962,Ja 23,37:1
Eliscu, Edward (Producer)
New Meet the People, The 1943,Ag 22,II,1:6
Eliscu, Fernanda
Outsider, The 1924,Mr 4,16:4
Outsider, The 1928,Ap 10,32:2
If I Were You 1931,S 24,21:1
Triplets 1932,S 22,25:2
Creeping Fire 1935,Ja 17,22:3
Winterset 1935,S 26,19:2
Elizabeth
Pietro 1920,Ja 20,10:2
Elizondo, Hector
Kill the One-Eyed Man 1965,O 21,56:1
Drums in the Night 1967,My 18,54:1
Great White Hope, The 1967,D 14,58:1
Steambath 1970,Jl 1,49:1
Steambath 1970,Jl 12,II,1:3
Steambath 1970,O 11,II,1:1
Elkan, Henri (Miscellaneous)
East Lynne Goes West 1931,My 3,I,26:5
Elkas, Edward
Tale of the Wolf, The 1925,O 8,31:2
Elkenberry, Jill
Don Juan 1970,My 26,32:1
Elkin, Saul
Floydada to Matador 1955,D 22,19:1
Hello Out There 1955,D 22,19:1
Opera Opera 1955,D 22,19:1
Hungerers, The 1955,D 22,19:1
Elkins, Alfredo
Sojourner Truth 1948,Ap 22,35:2
Elkins, Bob (Musical Director)
Hatfields & McCoys 1970,Je 23,34:1
Elkins, Feltin
Patience 1924,D 30,15:1
Elkins, Flora
Ardele 1958,Ap 9,39:4
Geranium Hat, The 1959,Mr 18,45:1
Rhinoceros 1961,Ja 10,27:1
Baal 1965,My 7,33:2
Troilus and Cressida 1965,Ag 13,17:1
Stephen D 1967,S 25,58:1
Elkins, H Webster
Earth 1927,Mr 10,23:1
Elkins, Hanson W
Strange Fruit 1945,N 30,18:6
Elkins, Hillard (Producer)
Come on Strong 1962,O 5,29:1
Golden Boy 1964,O 21,56:1
Best Laid Plans, The 1966,Mr 26,15:2
Oh! Calcutta! 1969,Je 18,33:1
Rothschilds, The 1970,O 20,40:1
Elkins, Judie
Another City, Another Land 1968,O 9,42:1
Elkins, Marie Louise (Miscellaneous)
Blind Alley 1940,O 16,28:2
Elkins, Marie Louise (Producer)
Michael Drops In 1938,D 28,24:3
Brooklyn Biarritz 1941,F 28,16:2
Yankee Point 1942,N 24,28:2
Hickory Stick 1944,My 9,15:6
Alice in Arms 1945,F 1,18:4
Elkins, Maybelle
Mirage, The 1920,O 1,14:1
Elkins, William C
Stevedore 1934,Ap 19,33:2
Ellen, Mary
Rosalinda; Fledermaus, Die 1942,O 29,26:5
Ellen, Sandy
Drat! the Cat! 1965,O 11,54:2
Illya Darling 1967,Ap 12,37:1
Ellenstein, Robert
Long Moment, The 1950,My 22,16:6
Tempest, The 1955,S 3,8:6
Thor, With Angels 1956,O 15,29:4
Eller, Dorothea
Happiest Days, The 1939,Ap 12,26:2
Eller, Gloria
Honor Code, The 1931,My 19,25:3
Ellerbe, Harry
Philip Goes Forth 1931,Ja 4,VIII,2:2
Philip Goes Forth 1931,Ja 13,35:4
Man on Stilts, The 1931,S 10,23:2
Tadpole, The 1931,D 6,VIII,2:7
Mad Hopes, The 1932,D 2,26:3
Her Tin Soldier 1933,Ap 7,22:6
Thoroughbred 1933,N 7,29:2
Strange Orchestra 1933,N 29,23:2
Ghosts 1935,D 13,30:6
Ghosts 1936,My 12,26:8
Book of Charm, The 1936,Je 30,15:1

Ellerbe, Harry—Cont
Hedda Gabler 1936,N 17,34:4
Petticoat Fever 1937,Jl 6,23:1
Feathers in a Gale 1943,D 22,26:2
Sleep, My Pretty One 1944,N 3,26:8
Oh, Mr Meadowbrook! 1948,D 27,17:2
One Eye Closed 1954,N 25,45:2
Desk Set, The 1955,O 25,36:7
Ellerbe, Harry (Director)
For Love or Money 1947,N 5,36:2
Oh, Mr Meadowbrook! 1948,D 27,17:2
Pink Elephant, The 1953,Ap 23,37:2
Ellers, Barbara
What a Killing 1961,Mr 28,41:1
Ellery, Arthur
Trial of Dr Beck, The 1937,Ag 10,22:2
Ellestein, Abraham (Composer)
Motel Peissi, The Contor's Kid 1934,N 29,33:3
Great to Be Alive! 1950,Mr 24,28:2
Ellfeldt, William (Miscellaneous)
Three Wishes for Jamie 1952,Mr 22,9:2
Ellias, Miriam
Shakespeare and Company 1925,O 22,22:5
Ellin, David
Swan Song 1946,My 16,29:2
Shepherd King, The 1955,O 13,36:2
Brothers Ashkenazi, The 1955,N 12,24:4
Go Fight City Hall 1961,N 3,28:5
Education of H*Y*M*A*N K*A*P*L*A*N, The
1968,Ap 5,57:1
End of All Things Natural, The 1969,S 12,38:1
Trees Die Standing, The 1969,O 13,52:1
Mirele Efros 1969,D 26,41:1
Light, Lively and Yiddish 1970,O 28,58:1
Ellin, Dorothy
Hurricane 1923,D 26,13:4
Fog-Bound 1927,Ap 2,21:2
Three 1928,D 4,28:2
Ellin, Ruth
Melody Lingers On, The 1969,N 17,55:1
Brothers Ashkenazi, The 1970,N 17,53:2
Ellinger, Desiree
Wild Rose, The 1926,O 21,23:1
Cherry Blossoms 1927,Mr 29,22:3
Kiss Me! 1927,Jl 22,17:1
Mississippi 1929,Ap 14,X,2:1
Eldorado 1930,S 4,26:3
Rose of Persia 1935,Mr 1,17:4
Ellinger, Larry
Incubator 1932,N 2,23:3
Ellington, Dick
Hipper's Holiday 1934,O 19,26:2
Ellington, Duke
Vaudeville (Palace) 1930,My 26,25:2
Vaudeville (Palace) 1930,S 8,17:3
Ellington, Duke (Composer)
Beggar's Holiday 1946,D 27,13:3
Beggar's Holiday 1947,Ja 26,II,1:1
Timon of Athens 1963,Jl 31,19:2
Pousse-Cafe 1966,Mr 19,19:2
Ellington, Duke and His Cotton Club Orchestra
Vaudeville (Palace) 1929,Ap 22,22:6
Untitled-One Man Show 1930,Mr 31,24:1
Ellington, Edna
Make Me Know It 1929,N 5,32:5
Ellington, Richard
Cyrano de Bergerac 1936,Ap 28,17:1
Hill Between, The 1938,Mr 12,12:5
Love for Love 1940,Je 4,19:5
Elliot, Arthur
Fool, The 1922,O 24,18:1
Elliot, Clint
Mahagonny 1970,Ap 29,51:1
Elliot, Dan (Composer)
Only Game in Town, The 1968,My 21,42:1
Elliot, Daniel
Five Queens 1963,S 11,46:2
Elliot, Frank
Wings Over Europe 1928,D 11,35:1
Family Affairs 1929,D 11,34:6
Lady Jane 1934,S 11,24:2
Elliot, Jane
Impossible Years, The 1965,O 14,55:1
Elliot, Lance
Johnny 2X4 1942,Mr 17,24:6
Elliot, Lorna
Bride of the Lamb 1926,Mr 31,20:3
Elliot, Maurice
Anything Goes 1934,N 22,26:1
Elliot, Rand
Would-Be Gentleman, The 1946,Ja 10,29:2
Swan Song 1946,My 16,29:2
Vigil, The 1948,My 22,8:6
Elliot, Sidney
Lulu Belle 1926,F 10,20:1
Social Register, The 1931,N 10,28:2
Elliot, Stephanie
Trouble in Mind 1955,N 5,23:2
Elliot, Walter
Fly Away Home 1937,Ap 27,18:1

Elliott, Ada
O Evening Star 1936,Ja 9,24:6
Elliott, Arthur
He and She 1920,F 13,16:3
Champion, The 1921,Ja 4,11:1
Champion, The 1921,Ja 9,VI,1:1
Fool, The 1922,O 24,18:1
Elliott, Audrey
Orchids Preferred 1937,My 12,26:5
Elliott, Bernice
Napi 1931,Mr 12,22:5
Mourning Becomes Electra; Homecoming 1931,O 27,22:1
Mourning Becomes Electra; Hunted, The 1932,My 10,25:2
Mourning Becomes Electra; Haunted, The 1932,My 10,25:2
Mourning Becomes Electra; Homecoming 1932,My 10,25:2
Conquest 1933,F 20,11:3
Elliott, Beth
Jitta's Atonement 1923,Ja 18,16:3
Artists and Models 1923,Ag 21,12:2
Gay Paree 1925,Ag 19,14:3
Elliott, Bill (Composer)
Daniel Boone 1967,D 23,28:1
Elliott, Bob (Playwright)
Bob and Ray-The Two and Only 1970,S 25,36:1
Elliott, Cecil
Boy Who Lived Twice, A 1945,S 12,31:2
Elliott, Clyde (Producer)
Marry the Man! 1929,Ap 23,26:3
Sleep No More 1944,S 1,11:5
Elliott, Collyer
Rogues and Vagabonds 1930,My 8,32:5
Elliott, David
Trip to Scarborough, A 1929,Mr 18,31:2
Dragon, The 1929,Mr 26,34:2
Tower Beyond Tragedy, The 1950,N 27,29:1
Blithe Spirit 1952,F 23,7:5
Hamlet 1956,O 29,34:1
Julius Caesar 1957,O 24,39:1
Crucible, The 1958,Mr 12,36:1
Golem, The 1959,F 26,38:2
Elliott, David (Director)
Trip to Scarborough, A 1929,Mr 18,31:2
Dragon, The 1929,Mr 26,34:2
Elliott, Denholm
Buoyant Billions 1949,O 24,18:3
Ring Around the Moon 1950,N 24,30:1
Green Bay Tree, The 1951,F 2,18:2
Confidential Clerk, The 1953,O 11,II,3:7
South 1955,My 2,17:4
Monique 1957,O 23,38:1
Write Me a Murder 1961,O 27,28:2
Seagull, The 1964,Ap 6,36:1
Crucible, The 1964,Ap 7,30:2
Imaginary Invalid, The 1967,My 2,53:1
Touch of the Poet, A 1967,My 3,38:2
Still Life 1967,My 4,34:1
Come as You Are 1970,Ag 12,32:1
Elliott, Dick
Happy Town 1959,O 8,49:2
Elliott, Dix (Costume Designer)
What's Up 1953,O 28,37:2
Elliott, Dix (Scenic Designer)
What's Up 1953,O 28,37:2
Elliott, Don
Thurber Carnival, A 1960,F 27,13:2
Elliott, Don (Composer)
Thurber Carnival, A 1960,F 27,13:2
Thurber Carnival, A 1960,Mr 6,II,1:1
Beast in Me, The 1963,My 17,29:1
Elliott, Don (Miscellaneous)
Private Lives 1968,My 20,59:1
Elliott, Don and Orchestra
Beast in Me, The 1963,My 17,29:1
Elliott, Edward
George Washington Slept Here 1940,O 19,20:3
Elliott, Edythe
Salt Water 1929,N 27,30:3
After Tomorrow 1930,Ag 10,VIII,2:3
After Tomorrow 1931,Ag 27,22:4
Mother Lode 1934,D 24,16:5
Elliott, Eric
First Mrs Fraser, The 1929,D 30,16:2
Elliott, Eunice
Paddy the Next Best Thing 1920,Ag 28,5:5
Elliott, Frank
Patriot, The 1928,Ja 20,15:1
Seven Year Love 1929,O 27,IX,2:1
Elliott, Gertrude
Come Out of the Kitchen 1920,Mr 16,17:7
Folly Town 1920,My 18,9:2
Old House, The 1920,Jl 11,VI,1:6
Twelfth Night 1927,Je 12,VII,2:1
Elliott, Gladys
Betty, Be Good 1920,My 5,14:2
Elliott, Grace
Love Dreams 1921,O 11,22:2
Sancho Panza 1923,N 27,23:1
Elliott, H (Composer)
It's Only Natural 1922,Ap 21,13:2

Elliott, H (Lyricist)
It's Only Natural 1922,Ap 21,13:2
Elliott, Hank
On the Town 1959,F 14,15:1
Elliott, Harold
Family Upstairs, The 1925,Ag 18,14:2
Trouper, The 1926,Mr 9,21:1
Seed of the Brute 1926,N 2,34:3
Wild Man of Borneo, The 1927,S 14,29:2
Tia Juana 1927,N 16,28:4
Distant Drum, A 1928,Ja 21,13:1
Box Seats 1928,Ap 20,27:2
Cyclone Lover, The 1928,Je 6,23:3
Common Sin, The 1928,O 16,28:2
Tomorrow 1928,D 29,20:2
Indiscretion 1929,Mr 5,28:1
Birthright 1933,N 22,22:3
Valley Forge 1934,D 11,28:3
Elliott, Howard Jr (Composer)
Wetward Ho 1921,Ap 22,13:2
Elliott, Howard Jr (Lyricist)
Wetward Ho 1921,Ap 22,13:2
Elliott, Jack (Miscellaneous)
Fiorello! 1959,N 24,45:3
Tenderloin 1960,O 18,47:2
Mr President 1962,O 22,34:2
She Loves Me 1963,Ap 24,39:1
Elliott, James
Mr Big 1941,O 1,24:2
Junior Miss 1941,N 19,28:2
I'll Take the High Road 1943,N 10,28:3
Men to the Sea 1944,O 4,25:2
Elliott, James (Producer)
27 Wagons Full of Cotton 1955,Ja 19,23:2
Elliott, James E (Producer)
First Million, The 1943,Ap 29,27:4
Elliott, James S
Love's Old Sweet Song 1940,My 3,16:3
Elliott, James S (Director)
Rats of Norway, The 1948,Ap 16,27:6
Elliott, James S (Miscellaneous)
Electra 1961,S 20,23:4
Eumenides 1961,S 27,32:4
Choephori 1961,S 27,32:4
Elliott, James S (Producer)
Too Hot for Maneuvers 1945,My 3,26:5
Rats of Norway, The 1948,Ap 16,27:6
Prometheus Bound 1957,Ag 9,11:6
Elliott, James W (Playwright)
Man in the Making, The 1921,S 21,16:2
Man in the Making, The 1921,O 2,VII,1:1
Elliott, James W (Producer)
Fool's Bells 1925,D 24,8:3
Castles in the Air 1926,S 7,19:2
King Can Do No Wrong, The 1927,N 17,28:4
Rope 1928,F 23,18:3
Napoleon 1928,Mr 9,21:1
Scarlet Fox, The 1928,Mr 28,31:1
Hobo 1931,F 12,24:4
Brass Ankle 1931,Ap 24,26:4
Hot Money 1931,N 9,22:2
Widow in Green, A 1931,N 21,21:4
Elliott, James Withers (Producer)
Bat, The 1953,Ja 21,28:2
Elliott, Jessie
Annie Get Your Gun 1957,Mr 9,15:5
Elliott, John (Pvt)
Winged Victory 1943,N 22,24:1
Elliott, Judith
Quiet, Please! 1940,N 9,20:3
Elliott, Keith
Thieves' Carnival 1955,F 2,21:1
Elliott, Leonard
Right This Way 1938,Ja 6,22:3
Family Portrait 1939,Mr 9,18:4
As You Like It 1941,O 21,29:2
It's About Time 1942,Mr 31,28:3
Dream With Music 1944,My 19,15:2
Marinka 1945,Jl 19,19:2
Would-Be Gentleman, The 1946,Ja 10,29:2
Grandma's Diary 1948,S 23,36:2
Right You Are (If You Think You Are) 1957,Mr 5,37:1
Song of Norway 1958,Je 23,19:2
Dr Willy Nilly 1959,Je 5,18:2
Guitar 1959,N 11,42:5
Gay Life, The 1961,N 20,38:1
Contributions; Plantation 1970,Mr 10,53:1
Elliott, Leonore
Lady Windermere's Fan 1946,O 15,29:2
Elliott, Linda
Tall Kentuckian, The 1953,Je 17,30:1
Elliott, Lorna
Red Poppy, The 1922,D 21,18:2
Connie Goes Home 1923,S 7,10:1
Goose Hangs High, The 1924,Ja 30,16:1
Howdy King 1926,D 14,24:4
Stepping Sisters 1930,Ap 23,24:2
Sing High, Sing Low 1931,N 13,26:4
Decoy, The 1932,Ap 2,13:4
Elliott, Madge
Sigh No More 1945,S 2,II,1:2
Relapse, The 1950,N 23,54:2
Elliott, Maggie
Second Comin', The 1931,D 9,32:4

Elliott, Marianna (Costume Designer)
Kaleidoscope 1957,Je 14,20:2
Month in the Country, A 1959,Mr 2,32:2
Clandestine on the Morning Line 1959,D 5,18:2
Caucasian Chalk Circle, The 1961,N 1,35:1
Burning of the Lepers, The 1962,Ap 5,29:1
Once in a Lifetime 1962,O 30,30:1
Devils, The 1963,N 5,25:1
Hard Travelin' 1965,Je 17,25:1
Lonesome Train, The 1965,Je 17,25:1
In the Matter of J Robert Oppenheimer 1968,Je 7,31:1
Elliott, Maxine
Trimmed in Scarlet 1920,F 3,18:1
Elliott, Michael (Director)
As You Like It 1961,Jl 5,30:1
Peer Gynt 1962,S 27,33:7
Miss Julie 1965,Jl 29,19:1
Peer Gynt 1970,D 23,12:5
Elliott, Mildred
Pressing Business 1930,N 18,28:5
East of Broadway 1932,Ja 27,19:3
Elliott, Miriam
Romance 1921,Mr 1,18:2
Lass O' Laughter 1925,Ja 9,13:2
Elliott, Patricia
Skin of Our Teeth, The 1966,Je 2,51:1
Dance of Death, The 1966,Je 3,31:1
As You Like It 1966,Je 4,19:1
Shoemaker's Holiday, The 1967,Je 3,19:1
Thieves' Carnival 1967,Je 5,52:1
She Stoops to Conquer 1968,Ja 1,11:1
King Lear 1968,N 8,43:1
Henry V 1969,Je 9,57:1
Much Ado About Nothing 1969,Je 16,57:1
Henry V 1969,N 11,43:1
Persians, The 1970,Ap 16,53:1
Elliott, Robert
Rain 1922,N 8,18:2
Elliott, Rose Marie
Lady in the Dark 1943,Mr 1,14:2
Firebird of Florence 1945,Mr 23,13:4
Elliott, Ross
Danton's Death 1938,N 3,26:2
Morning Star 1940,Ap 17,26:4
Elliott, Shawn
Jacques Brel Is Alive and Well and Living in Paris 1968,Ja 23,25:2
Rondelay 1969,N 6,55:1
Elliott, Sidney
Merchant of Venice, The 1920,D 30,16:2
What Price Glory 1924,S 6,14:3
Elliott, Stephen
Tempest, The 1945,Ja 26,17:2
Walk Hard 1946,Mr 28,34:2
Wonderful Journey 1946,D 26,30:2
Command Decision 1947,O 2,30:2
Shrike, The 1952,Ja 16,20:2
Purple Dust 1956,D 28,15:1
Livin' the Life 1957,Ap 29,20:1
Roman Candle 1960,F 4,34:2
Traveller Without Luggage 1964,S 18,26:2
I Knock at the Door 1964,N 26,53:2
Pictures in the Hallway 1964,D 17,51:1
Persecution and Assassination of Marat As Performed by the Inmates of the Asylum of Charenton Under the Direction of the Marquis de Sade, The 1967,Ja 4,34:1
Henry IV, Part I 1968,Je 30,54:7
Henry IV, Part II 1968,Jl 2,33:1
Henry IV, Part II 1968,Jl 14,II,1:1
King Lear 1968,N 8,43:1
Cry of Players, A 1968,N 15,40:1
King Lear 1968,N 17,II,1:3
Cry of Players, A 1968,N 24,II,9:4
In the Matter of J Robert Oppenheimer 1969,Mr 7,28:1
Miser, The 1969,My 9,35:1
Twelfth Night 1969,Ag 14,29:2
Whistle in the Dark, A 1969,O 9,55:1
Whistle in the Dark, A 1969,N 9,II,3:1
Georgy 1970,F 27,26:1
Good Woman of Setzuan, The 1970,N 6,51:1
Good Woman of Setzuan, The 1970,N 15,II,1:5
Elliott, Sumner Locke (Playwright)
Buy Me Blue Ribbons 1951,O 18,33:2
John Murray Anderson's Almanac 1953,D 11,42:2
Elliott, Walter
Remember the Day 1936,Je 30,15:1
Elliott, William
Home Towners, The 1926,Ag 24,19:3
Fiesta 1933,D 16,12:2
Ellis, Anita
Flower Drum Song 1958,D 2,44:1
Ellis, Anthony (Producer)
Great Possessions 1937,F 9,18:3
Ellis, Barbara
Touch 1970,N 9,52:1
Ellis, Bayne
Wicked Cooks, The 1967,Ja 24,42:1
Ellis, Brobury
Ode to Liberty 1937,Ag 18,15:2
Elizabeth the Queen 1937,Ag 25,24:3

Ellis, Charles
Diff'rent 1920,D 29,8:1
Ambush 1921,O 11,22:1
Ambush 1921,O 16,VI,1:1
Deluge, The 1922,Ja 28,14:2
Ever Green Lady, The 1922,O 12,25:2
Spook Sonata, The 1924,Ja 7,23:3
Fashion 1924,F 5,21:2
Assumption of Hannele, The 1924,F 16,16:2
George Dandin 1924,Ap 7,15:5
Emperor Jones, The 1924,My 7,18:1
All God's Chillun Got Wings 1924,My 16,22:3
Saint, The 1924,O 13,20:3
Desire Under the Elms 1924,N 12,20:7
We Americans 1926,O 13,20:4
Revelry 1927,S 13,37:1
Show Boat 1927,D 28,26:1
Show Boat 1932,My 20,22:2
Liliom 1932,O 27,23:2
Camille 1932,O 28,23:2
Alice in Wonderland 1932,D 12,18:3
Valley Forge 1934,D 11,28:3
Call Me Ziggy 1937,F 13,9:6
Key Largo 1939,N 28,30:2
Journey to Jerusalem 1940,O 7,21:2
Eve of St Mark, The 1942,O 8,30:2
Storm Operation 1944,Ja 12,28:2
Joan of Lorraine 1946,N 19,40:2
Anne of the Thousand Days 1948,D 9,49:2
Ellis, Craig
Marie Antoinette 1921,N 23,16:1
Ellis, David
Porgy and Bess 1935,O 11,30:2
Confederacy, The 1958,Jl 3,20:1
Mike Downstairs 1968,Ap 19,35:1
Ellis, David (Producer)
Royal Gambit 1959,Mr 5,34:2
Ellis, Diane
Nine Fifteen Revue, The 1930,F 12,26:2
Ellis, Edith (Director)
Starlight 1925,Mr 4,17:2
Gala Night 1930,F 26,22:4
Ellis, Edith (Playwright)
Mrs Jimmie Thompson 1920,Mr 30,9:1
White Villa, The 1921,F 15,7:1
White Villa, The 1921,F 20,VI,1:1
White Collars 1925,F 24,17:2
Moon and Sixpence, The 1933,D 17,IX,4:3
Dangerous Age, The 1937,O 6,29:1
Ellis, Edward
Ouija Board, The 1920,Mr 30,9:1
Bat, The 1920,Ag 24,6:1
White Villa, The 1921,F 15,7:1
Red Light Annie 1923,Ag 22,10:3
Paid 1925,N 26,32:1
Chicago 1926,D 31,11:1
Cock Robin 1928,Ja 13,26:6
Subway Express 1929,S 25,34:3
Distant Drums 1932,Ja 19,24:3
Distant Drums 1932,Ja 31,VIII,1:1
Inside Story, The 1932,F 23,23:2
Ellis, Edwin
Plough and the Stars, The 1927,N 29,30:2
Juno and the Paycock 1927,D 20,32:2
Ellis, Elaine
Merry Widow, The 1942,Jl 16,22:1
Down to Miami 1944,S 12,23:5
Ellis, Evelyn
Goat Alley 1927,Ap 21,24:3
Porgy 1927,O 11,26:2
Native Son 1941,Mr 25,26:5
Native Son 1942,O 24,10:6
Deep Are the Roots 1945,S 27,24:4
Tobacco Road 1950,Mr 7,23:2
Royal Family, The 1951,Ja 11,28:2
Touchstone 1953,F 4,33:2
Salvation on a String; Supper for the Dead 1954,Jl 7,23:1
Ellis, Evelyn (Director)
Horse Play 1937,Ag 28,8:3
Tobacco Road 1950,Mr 7,23:2
Ellis, Frank
Without Warning 1937,My 3,23:2
Ellis, Garrison
Jim Dandy 1941,N 8,10:5
Ellis, Helen
Electronic Nigger, The 1968,Mr 9,23:2
Clara's Ole Man 1968,Mr 9,23:2
Ellis, Helene
Barrier, The 1950,N 3,32:2
Ellis, Herbert
Kongo 1926,Mr 31,20:5
Ol' Man Satan 1932,O 4,26:3
Ellis, Irving
Conjur' Man Dies 1936,Mr 12,18:5
Ellis, Jacqueline
Red Mill, The 1945,O 17,16:2
Richard II 1956,Jl 4,15:1
Ellis, James
My Maryland 1927,S 13,37:2
Ellis, John
Wild Oats Lane 1922,S 7,12:1

Ellis, Kathleen
Red Mill, The 1945,O 17,16:2
Ellis, Lucille
Carib Song 1945,S 28,17:2
Ellis, Mabel
Wonderful Night, A; Fledermaus, Die 1929,N 1,23:3
Ellis, Marge
Allah Be Praised! 1944,Ap 21,14:2
Boy Friend, The 1954,O 1,20:1
Ellis, Mary
Merchant of Venice, The 1922,D 22,13:1
Casanova 1923,S 27,10:2
Fanshastics 1924,Ja 17,13:2
Rose Marie 1924,S 3,12:2
Dybbuk, The 1925,D 16,22:2
Romantic Young Lady, The 1926,My 5,24:3
Humble, The 1926,O 14,22:2
Crown Prince, The 1927,F 27,VII,4:6
Crown Prince, The 1927,Mr 24,23:2
Taming of the Shrew, The 1927,O 26,26:4
Taming of the Shrew, The 1927,N 13,IX,1:1
Twelve Thousand 1928,Mr 13,23:1
Twelve Thousand 1928,Mr 31,IX,1:1
Meet the Prince 1929,F 26,30:5
Meet the Prince 1929,Mr 10,X,1:1
Becky Sharp 1929,Je 4,29:1
Children of Darkness 1930,Ja 8,25:1
Children of Darkness 1930,Ja 19,VIII,1:1
Strange Interlude 1931,F 4,21:2
Strange Interlude 1931,F 22,VIII,1:3
Jewel Robbery 1932,Ja 14,17:2
Jewel Robbery 1932,F 10,27:1
Queer Cattle 1932,My 19,24:2
Double Harness 1933,Ja 13,18:5
Music in the Air 1933,My 20,11:3
Josephine 1934,S 26,17:5
Josephine 1934,O 14,X,3:1
Glamorous Night 1935,My 3,23:6
Farewell Performance 1936,S 11,28:3
Farewell Performance 1936,S 27,X,3:5
Farewell Performance 1936,O 4,IX,1:1
Innocent Party, The 1938,F 13,X,3:3
Dancing Years, The 1939,Ap 16,X,2:3
Harlequinade 1948,O 10,II,3:7
Coriolanus 1952,Mr 14,26:2
After The Ball 1954,Je 11,19:3
Dark Halo 1959,Ap 15,28:4
Look Homeward, Angel 1962,Ap 4,38:3
Ellis, Maurice
Brown Buddies 1930,O 8,29:1
Macbeth 1936,Ap 15,25:4
Case of Philip Lawrence, The 1937,Je 9,31:1
Androcles and the Lion 1938,D 17,10:5
Hot Mikado, The 1939,Mr 24,26:2
Cabin in the Sky 1940,O 26,19:2
Pirate, The 1942,N 26,39:2
Early to Bed 1943,Je 18,16:2
Men to the Sea 1944,O 4,25:2
Private Life of the Master Race, The 1945,Je 13,28:3
Jeb 1946,F 22,20:2
Lysistrata 1946,O 18,27:5
Long Way From Home, A 1948,F 9,25:2
Wisteria Trees, The 1950,Mr 30,39:1
Seventeen 1951,Je 22,16:6
Wisteria Trees, The 1955,F 3,20:2
Miss Lonelyhearts 1957,O 4,26:2
Ellis, Michael
Duchess of Malfi, The 1946,O 16,35:2
Ellis, Michael (Miscellaneous)
Last Dance, The 1948,Ja 28,27:2
Play's the Thing, The 1948,Ap 29,19:2
Play's the Thing, The 1948,My 9,II,1:1
Body Beautiful, The 1958,Ja 24,15:2
Ellis, Michael (Producer)
Jenny Kissed Me 1948,D 24,12:2
Courtin' Time 1951,Je 14,30:2
Two's Company 1952,D 16,43:5
Come Blow Your Horn 1961,F 23,31:3
Beauty Part, The 1962,D 28,5:2
Advocate, The 1963,O 15,46:7
Absence of a Cello 1964,S 22,45:1
Paisley Convertible, The 1967,F 13,42:1
Girl in the Freudian Slip, The 1967,My 19,34:3
Sweet Eros 1968,N 22,38:1
Witness 1968,N 22,38:1
Angela 1969,O 31,33:1
Who's Happy Now? 1969,N 18,39:1
Ellis, Milton
When Differences Disappear 1941,Je 3,17:4
Ellis, Osian
Flower of Cities All 1962,Jl 12,21:2
Ellis, Patrick
Chips With Everything 1963,O 2,49:1
Ellis, Peggy
Cape Cod Follies 1929,S 19,37:2
Ellis, Phil
Vaudeville (Palace) 1926,S 28,30:4
Ellis, Ray (Miscellaneous)
Arturo Ui 1963,N 12,49:1
Wonder World 1964,My 18,32:1
Fade Out--Fade In 1964,My 27,45:1

Ellis, Ray (Miscellaneous)—Cont
Secret Life of Walter Mitty, The 1964,O 27,44:5
Ellis, Robert S
Way of the World, The 1950,Ap 9,73:5
Ellis, Ruth
Meek Mose 1928,F 7,30:1
Ellis, Selma
As You Like It 1936,Ap 24,18:4
Ellis, Sydney
Fedora 1922,F 11,18:1
Ellis, Terry
Republic, The 1970,Ap 28,49:1
Ellis, Tom
Eugenia 1957,Ja 31,20:1
Ellis, Vivian (Composer)
By the Way 1925,D 29,20:3
Cochran's 1930 Revue 1930,Ap 13,X,1:6
Streamline 1934,O 21,IX,1:3
Jill Darling 1934,D 20,29:8
Big Ben 1946,Ag 4,II,1:4
Bless the Bride 1947,My 11,II,3:7
Tough at the Top 1949,Jl 17,58:5
Tough at the Top 1949,Ag 7,II,1:4
Sleeping Prince, The 1956,N 2,31:1
Ellis, Vivian (Lyricist)
Sleeping Prince, The 1956,N 2,31:1
Ellis, Vivian (Playwright)
Streamline 1934,S 29,13:1
Ellis, Walker
Beggar on Horseback 1924,F 13,17:2
Youngest, The 1924,D 23,17:1
Tangletoes 1925,F 18,17:1
Ellis, Walter (Playwright)
Actresses Will Happen 1941,Je 15,IX,2:6
Ellis, Yetta Samuels
Rutherford and Son 1927,Ap 13,29:2
Ellison, Anderson
Sacco-Vanzetti 1969,F 9,78:1
Ellison, George
Florodora 1920,Ap 6,18:1
Ellison, James
Good Night Ladies 1945,Ja 18,16:2
Good Night Ladies 1945,Ja 28,II,1:1
Ellison, Jane
Fanny 1926,S 22,30:1
Town Boy 1929,O 5,22:4
Ellison, Margie
Policy Kings 1938,D 31,6:2
Ellison, True
Come on Strong 1962,O 5,29:1
Elliston, Grace
Lucky One, The 1922,N 21,15:2
Ellovich, Rosa (Director)
Rehearsal, The 1952,My 27,30:5
Ellsler, Effie
Bat, The 1920,Ag 24,6:1
Ellsperman, Jean
Music in the Air 1951,O 9,32:2
Ellsperman, Joanne
Oedipus Rex 1959,Ap 30,36:1
Lysistrata 1959,N 25,19:4
Ellstein, Abe (Composer)
Broken Chain, The 1929,F 21,30:4
His Wife's Lover 1929,O 21,30:6
If the Rabbi Wants 1929,D 23,18:5
Jolly World, A 1931,Ja 24,15:3
One in a Million 1934,N 17,13:2
My Malkele 1937,S 20,18:6
Bublitchki 1938,Ja 17,11:2
Family Mishmash, A 1958,O 20,36:1
Ellstein, Abe (Lyricist)
One in a Million 1934,N 17,13:2
Ellstein, Abe (Musical Director)
Hello Grandpa! 1931,Ja 2,25:3
Women of New York 1931,Mr 23,24:3
Ellstein, Abe (Playwright)
Berdichever Bridegroom, The 1930,S 24,26:2
My Pal Sasha 1941,O 23,24:4
Ellsworth, Elton (Director)
My Beginning 1962,Ja 31,21:1
Ellsworth, Grace
Century Revue and the Midnight Rounders, The 1920,Jl 13,9:1
Love Birds 1921,Mr 16,12:1
Dew Drop Inn 1923,My 18,26:4
Ellsworth, Harry
Dew Drop Inn 1923,My 18,26:4
Ellsworth, John
Elizabeth the Queen 1930,N 4,37:1
Ellsworth, Lee
Jamboree 1932,N 25,18:4
Between Two Worlds 1934,O 26,24:2
Ellsworth, Ursula
Lucky Break 1925,Ag 12,16:2
Ellwood, Paul (Playwright)
Three by Thurber; Mr Montoe Holds the Fort 1955,Mr 8,23:2
Three by Thurber; Imperturbable Spirit, The 1955,Mr 8,23:2
Three by Thurber; Middle Years, The 1955,Mr 8,23:2
Elly, Cornelia
Fireworks on the James 1940,My 15,30:2

Ellyn, Glenn
Burlesque; Artisten 1928,Je 10,17:2
Ellyn, Jean
Immortal Husband, The 1955,F 15,32:2
Streetcar Named Desire, A 1956,F 16,24:1
Ellys, France
Saison d'Amour 1926,O 31,VIII,2:4
Mixture 1927,N 20,IX,4:4
Elm City Quartet, The
Nifties of 1923 1923,S 26,10:1
Vaudeville (Hippodrome) 1924,Ja 1,21:1
Scandals 1924,Jl 1,16:1
George White's Scandals 1929,S 24,29:1
Elman, Esta
Virginia 1937,S 3,13:2
Elman, Gene
Projection Room, The 1969,Ja 15,38:2
Elman, Irving (Playwright)
First Million, The 1943,Ap 29,27:4
Brass Ring, The 1952,Ap 11,19:2
Uncle Willie 1956,D 21,17:1
Elmer, Arthur
It's About Time 1942,Mr 31,28:3
Elmer, Arthur (Playwright)
It's About Time 1942,Mr 31,28:3
Elmer, Robert Potter
This Mad Whirl 1937,Ja 10,II,4:8
Elmore, Bruce
Teaser, The 1921,Jl 28,8:3
Nest, The 1922,F 2,20:1
Neighbors 1923,D 27,11:1
Dr David's Dad 1924,Ag 14,10:3
90 Horse Power 1926,Mr 16,22:4
This Thing Called Love 1928,S 18,32:7
Devil in the Mind 1931,My 2,23:2
Elmore, Florence
Cinderella on Broadway 1920,Je 25,18:1
Elmore, Howard
Deep Harlem 1929,Ja 8,35:2
Elmore, Lee
When Crummles Played 1928,O 2,34:3
Elmore, Lee (Director)
Frankie and Johnny 1930,S 26,16:5
Woman Denied, A 1931,F 26,21:1
Singapore 1932,N 15,24:2
Day Will Come, The 1944,S 8,17:2
Elmore, Lucille
Stepping Stones 1923,N 7,14:3
Elmore, Stephen
Madame Aphrodite 1961,D 30,13:1
Elmore, Steve
Kelly 1965,F 8,28:2
Dames at Sea 1968,D 21,46:1
Dames at Sea 1970,Ja 5,46:3
Company 1970,Ap 27,40:1
Company 1970,My 3,II,1:4
Elmquist, Carl
Blue Blood 1924,Ap 3,21:2
Elmslie, Kenward
Tinguely Machine Mystery, or the Love Suicide at
Kaluka, The 1965,D 24,15:5
Elmslie, Kenward (Lyricist)
Automobile Graveyard, The 1961,N 14,46:2
Elmslie, Kenward (Playwright)
Shoestring '57 1956,N 6,31:1
Elphick, Michael
Hamlet 1969,My 2,38:1
Elross, Robert
Confederates, The 1959,S 29,45:1
Elser, Frank B (Playwright)
Mr Gilhooley 1930,O 1,26:1
Low Bridge 1933,F 10,13:4
Farmer Takes a Wife, The 1934,O 9,17:2
Farmer Takes a Wife, The 1934,O 28,IX,3:1
Farmer Takes a Wife, The 1934,O 31,17:1
Farmer Takes a Wife, The 1934,N 11,IX,1:1
Elsie, Lily
Blue Train, The 1927,Je 5,VII,2:1
Truth Game, The 1928,O 21,IX,1:3
Elsner, Edward (Director)
Cousin Sonia 1925,D 8,28:3
House of Usshher, The 1926,Ja 14,18:4
Sex 1926,Ap 27,22:4
Legend of Leonora, The 1927,Mr 30,22:4
Seventh Heart, The 1927,My 3,24:4
Kiss Me! 1927,Jl 22,17:1
Wicked Age, The 1927,N 5,16:6
57 Bowery 1928,Ja 27,14:3
Veils 1928,Mr 14,28:5
Lido Girl, The 1928,Ag 24,23:2
She Got What She Wanted 1929,Mr 5,28:1
Comedy of Women, A 1929,S 14,17:4
Elsner, Edward (Miscellaneous)
Comedy of Women, A 1929,S 14,17:4
Elsner, Edward (Playwright)
Lido Girl, The 1928,Ag 24,23:2
Elsner, Maira
Alt Heidelberg; Student Prince, The
1932,N 20,IX,3:3
Elsom, Isobel
Outsider, The 1923,Je 10,VII,1:4
Ghost Train, The 1926,Ag 26,17:2
Mulberry Bush, The 1927,O 27,33:1

People Don't Do Such Things 1927,N 24,28:3
Silver Box, The 1928,Ja 18,23:1
Behavior of Mrs Crane, The 1928,Mr 21,30:1
Outsider, The 1928,Ap 10,32:2
Behavior of Mrs Crane, The 1928,My 27,VIII,1:1
American Landscape 1938,D 5,19:2
Ladies in Retirement 1940,Mr 27,24:3
Flowers of Virtue, The 1942,F 6,22:2
Hand in Glove 1944,D 5,19:1
Innocents, The 1950,F 2,30:2
Innocents, The 1950,F 12,II,1:1
Curious Savage, The 1950,O 25,44:3
Romeo and Juliet 1951,Mr 12,21:2
Climate of Eden, The 1952,N 7,20:2
Burning Glass, The 1954,Mr 5,15:2
Burning Glass, The 1954,Mr 14,II,1:1
Hide and Seek 1957,Ap 3,26:1
First Gentleman, The 1957,Ap 26,22:2
Elson, Charles
Streets of New York, The 1934,Jl 21,14:5
Elson, Charles (Lighting Director)
Orphee 1935,Mr 23,10:3
Duet for Two Hands 1947,O 8,28:3
Regina 1949,N 1,32:2
Enemy of the People, An 1950,D 29,14:1
Rose Tattoo, The 1951,F 5,19:2
Borscht Capades 1951,S 18,38:3
Music in the Air 1951,O 9,32:2
Lovers 1956,My 11,23:1
Compulsion 1957,O 25,21:1
Blue Denim 1958,F 28,17:1
Maria Golovin 1958,N 6,43:1
Plume de Ma Tante, La 1958,N 12,42:1
First Impressions 1959,Mr 20,28:1
Wildcat 1960,D 17,20:2
Troilus and Cressida 1961,Jl 24,15:1
Henry IV, Part I 1962,Je 18,20:4
Richard II 1962,Je 18,20:2
Shakespeare Revisited 1962,Jl 19,19:2
Perfect Setup, The 1962,O 25,47:1
Photo Finish 1963,F 14,5:2
Elson, Charles (Miscellaneous)
Collector's Item 1952,F 9,11:2
Deep Blue Sea, The 1952,N 6,38:3
Elson, Charles (Scenic Designer)
As You Like It 1945,Jl 4,10:4
Hidden Horizon 1946,S 20,42:2
Duet for Two Hands 1947,O 8,28:3
First Mrs Fraser, The 1947,N 6,36:2
Power Without Glory 1948,Ja 14,30:2
Kathleen 1948,F 4,26:2
Cup of Trembling, The 1948,Ap 21,33:5
Private Lives 1948,O 5,30:2
Borscht Capades 1951,S 18,38:3
Nina 1951,D 6,44:3
His and Hers 1954,Ja 8,18:2
Qudrille 1954,N 4,39:2
Champagne Complex 1955,Ap 13,33:1
Lovers 1956,My 11,23:1
Plume de Ma Tante, La 1958,N 12,42:1
Lysistrata 1968,N 15,42:1
Elson, Donald
Desire Under the Elms 1952,Ja 17,23:4
Threepenny Opera, The 1954,Mr 11,26:5
Inherit the Wind 1955,Ap 22,20:2
Elson, Elizabeth (Director)
Trachiniae 1931,Ja 27,21:2
Elson, Joseph (Composer)
Trachiniae 1931,Ja 27,21:2
Elstner, Anne
Sun-Up 1923,My 25,28:1
Elston, Gerhard (Translator)
Sign of Jonah, The 1957,My 2,27:1
Elston, Robert
Camille 1956,S 19,33:1
Maybe Tuesday 1958,Ja 30,18:3
Tall Story 1959,Ja 30,33:2
Twelfth Night 1959,Jl 11,10:2
Golden Fleecing 1959,O 16,24:5
Spoon River Anthology 1963,My 2,40:5
Spoon River Anthology 1963,S 30,23:2
Undercover Man 1966,Je 3,30:2
Come Slowly, Eden 1966,D 7,56:1
Conditioned Reflex 1967,Ja 11,51:1
Elston, Robert (Director)
Harold Arlen Songbook, The 1967,Mr 1,48:1
Elston, Robert (Playwright)
Harold Arlen Songbook, The 1967,Mr 1,48:1
Elston, Robert (Producer)
Harold Arlen Songbook, The 1967,Mr 1,48:1
Eltheir, Jean D'Avila R (Abbe) (Director)
Untitled-Passion Play 1925,Ag 17,8:1
Elthier, Jancy
Untitled-Passion Play 1925,Ag 17,8:1
Eltinge, Julian
Black and White Revue, The 1923,O 28,VIII,2:1
Vaudeville (Palace) 1927,N 1,20:3
Elton, Edmund
Alias Jimmy Valentine 1921,D 9,20:3
Cat and the Canary, The 1922,F 8,13:1
Green Beetle, The 1924,S 3,12:3
Shipwrecked 1924,N 13,18:1
Out of Step 1925,Ja 30,12:1

Elton, Edmund—Cont
Caesar and Cleopatra 1925,Ap 14,27:1
Bride of the Lamb 1926,Mr 31,20:3
Kept 1926,S 18,13:3
Desert Song, The 1926,D 1,24:2
Hold Everything 1928,O 11,24:2
Betty, Be Careful 1931,My 5,33:3
Bloody Laughter 1931,D 5,20:6
Heigh-Ho, Everybody 1932,My 26,31:2
Elton, Ernest A
Light of the World, The 1920,Ja 7,17:1
Elton, George
Skin Game, The 1920,My 23,VI,1:3
Elverson, Louis Henry
This Mad Whirl 1937,Ja 10,II,4:8
Elvidge, June
Girl in the Spotlight, The 1920,Jl 13,9:3
Elward, James
Finian's Rainbow 1955,My 19,25:1
Elward, James (Playwright)
Friday Night; Mary Agnes Is Thirty-Five
1965,F 9,42:5
Friday Night; Passport 1965,F 9,42:5
Friday Night; River, The 1965,F 9,42:5
Best of Friends 1970,F 21,22:1
Elwell, George D
Little Town of Bethlehem, The 1922,D 26,15:4
Elwell, Richard
Bird Cage, The 1925,Je 3,26:2
Elwood, Walter (Playwright)
Spellbound 1927,F 16,17:2
Elwyn, Robert
Night Remembers, The 1934,N 28,24:3
Hook-Up, The 1935,My 9,24:6
Ely, Lewis B (Playwright)
Horse-Thief, The 1924,Ap 27,VIII,2:3
Thoroughbreds 1924,S 9,12:1
Sporting Blood 1929,Jl 28,VIII,1:6
Ely, Lyn (Producer)
Worlds of Shakespeare, The 1963,D 5,58:1
Ely, William S
Breakfast in Bed 1920,F 4,12:1
Crooked Gamblers 1920,Ag 2,12:1
Elyas, Miriam
Dybbuk, The 1954,O 27,33:6
Elythe, Betty
Man Who Came to Dinner, The 1940,F 10,19:5
Elzer, Karl
Wetter Fuer Morgen-Veranderlich 1932,Je 19,IX,1:3
Elzy, Ruby
Porgy and Bess 1935,O 1,27:2
Porgy and Bess 1935,O 11,30:2
Brown Sugar 1937,D 3,29:2
John Henry 1939,D 12,36:4
John Henry 1939,D 17,IX,5:6
John Henry 1940,Ja 11,18:2
Porgy and Bess 1942,Ja 23,16:2
Emanuel, Arnold
If I Were You 1931,S 24,21:1
Emanuel-Gatti, G (Director)
Barbara 1929,N 18,24:5
My Wife Is Different 1931,Ap 27,24:4
Emanule, Kenneth (Costume Designer)
Crimes and Crimes 1970,Ja 19,35:1
Embert, Grace
Don't Tell 1920,S 29,12:1
Embie, A J
My Beginning 1962,Ja 31,21:1
Finis for Oscar Wilde 1964,F 15,15:1
Comforter, The 1964,O 22,42:1
Embree, Katherine
Country Wife, The 1936,D 2,34:1
Emerald, Connie
Naughty Riquette 1926,S 14,25:2
Emerson, C L
Listening In 1922,D 5,24:1
Emerson, C P (Composer)
It's the Valet 1933,D 15,25:4
Emerson, C P (Lyricist)
It's the Valet 1933,D 15,25:4
Emerson, C P (Miscellaneous)
It's the Valet 1933,D 15,25:4
Emerson, Dorothy
Jimmy Shine 1968,D 6,52:1
Emerson, Edith
Ah, Wilderness! 1934,O 30,23:1
Emerson, Edward
Spring Fever 1925,Ag 4,14:2
Heigh-Ho, Everybody 1932,My 26,31:2
Hilda Cassidy 1933,My 5,18:3
Milky Way, The 1934,My 9,23:2
Crime Marches on 1935,O 24,19:1
O Evening Star 1936,Ja 9,24:6
Emerson, Faye
State of the Union 1947,Jl 15,26:2
Profile 1947,Ag 12,26:1
Play's the Thing, The 1948,Ap 29,19:2
Play's the Thing, The 1948,My 9,II,1:1
Parisienne 1950,Jl 25,24:2
Evening With Will Shakespeare, An 1952,D 7,86:5
Heavenly Twins, The 1955,N 5,23:2
Protective Custody 1956,D 29,8:7
Back to Methuselah 1958,Mr 27,41:5
Back to Methuselah 1958,Ap 6,II,1:1

Emerson, Frank
Persecution and Assassination of Marat As
Performed by the Inmates of the Asylum of
Charenton Under the Direction of the Marquis de
Sade, The 1967,Ja 4,34:1
Emerson, Geraldine B (Mrs) (Playwright)
But Not for Love 1934,N 27,26:2
Emerson, Ginnie
Allegro 1952,S 18,36:3
Emerson, Gordon (Miscellaneous)
All Kinds of Giants 1961,D 19,40:1
Emerson, Gwen
Please, Mrs. Garibaldi 1939,Mr 17,24:3
Emerson, Harry A
Come Seven 1920,Jl 20,10:1
Emerson, Hope
Lysistrata 1930,Ap 29,30:5
Lysistrata 1930,Je 6,20:1
Smiling Faces 1931,D 13,VIII,2:5
Smiling Faces 1932,Ag 31,12:3
Student Prince, The 1936,Jl 12,II,5:2
Rose Marie 1936,Jl 22,22:6
My Maryland 1936,Ag 12,14:2
Florodora 1936,Ag 23,II,8:2
Naughty Marietta 1936,S 2,19:5
Swing Your Lady 1936,O 19,22:4
Roberta 1937,Je 27,II,6:1
Gay Divorce 1937,Jl 20,19:4
Student Prince, The 1937,Jl 28,15:1
On Your Toes 1937,Ag 3,21:2
Gay Divorce 1937,Ag 11,27:2
Nina Rosa 1937,Ag 26,24:3
Roberta 1937,S 7,16:4
White Plume, The 1939,D 27,16:1
New Moon, The 1942,Ag 19,14:2
Chicken Every Sunday 1944,Ap 6,27:2
Chicken Every Sunday 1944,Ap 16,II,1:1
Street Scene 1947,Ja 10,17:2
Magic Touch, The 1947,S 4,30:1
Cup of Trembling, The 1948,Ap 21,33:5
Emerson, Hugh
Julius Caesar 1957,O 24,39:1
Emerson, J H
Young Madame Conti 1937,Ap 1,18:4
Emerson, John (Director)
Social Register, The 1931,O 4,VIII,2:3
Social Register, The 1931,N 10,28:2
Emerson, John (Playwright)
Whole Town's Talking, The 1923,Ag 30,8:2
Whole Town's Talking, The 1923,S 9,VII,1:1
Fall of Eve, The 1925,S 1,18:1
Fall of Eve, The 1925,S 6,VII,1:1
Whole Town's Talking, The 1926,S 8,19:3
Gentlemen Prefer Blondes 1926,S 29,23:1
Gentlemen Prefer Blondes 1928,Ap 3,32:3
Nine Fifteen Revue, The 1930,F 12,26:2
Social Register, The 1931,O 4,VIII,2:3
Social Register, The 1931,N 10,28:2
Emerson, Lillian
Man on Stilts, The 1931,S 10,23:2
Passing Present, The 1931,D 8,36:2
Tell Her the Truth 1932,O 29,18:2
Thoroughbred 1933,N 7,29:2
Wife Insurance 1934,Ap 13,24:5
Say When 1934,N 9,24:2
Thy People 1935,Ag 13,20:3
Ragged Edge, The 1935,N 26,28:3
Arrest That Woman 1936,S 19,20:4
Around the Corner 1936,D 29,17:2
Point of Honor, A 1937,Ja 31,II,10:4
Point of Honor, A 1937,F 12,26:2
Places, Please 1937,N 13,10:6
Spring Thaw 1938,Mr 22,18:1
Emerson, Mary
Street Scene 1929,Ja 11,20:4
Decoy, The 1932,Ap 2,13:4
Emerton, Roy
Good Companions, The 1931,O 2,31:1
Antony and Cleopatra 1935,Ap 16,26:7
Emery, Curtis W (Producer)
Life Is Like That 1930,D 23,24:3
Emery, Dorothy
Please, Mrs. Garibaldi 1939,Mr 17,24:3
Emery, Edward
Three Musketeers, The 1921,My 20,18:5
Sonya 1921,Ag 16,18:3
Dreams for Sale 1922,S 14,24:1
Lesson in Love, A 1923,S 25,10:1
Little Angel, The 1924,S 29,10:3
His Queen 1925,My 12,26:1
All Wet 1925,Jl 7,24:1
Still Waters 1926,Mr 2,23:1
Constant Nymph, The 1926,D 10,31:1
Good News 1927,Ag 14,VII,2:1
Good News 1927,S 7,35:4
Marriage Bed, The 1929,Ja 8,35:1
Dinner Is Served 1929,Ag 16,18:4
Meteor 1929,D 24,15:1
Free for All 1931,S 9,25:1
Late One Evening 1933,Ja 10,27:3
These Two 1934,My 8,28:3
Emery, Edward Jr
Mrs Partridge Presents 1925,Ja 6,23:3

Emery, Edwin T
Julius Caesar 1927,Je 7,27:2
Little Father of the Wilderness, The 1930,Je 3,27:1
Troilus and Cressida 1932,Je 7,22:3
Uncle Tom's Cabin 1933,My 30,13:4
County Chairman, The 1936,My 26,26:5
Emery, Edwin T (Director)
Half a Widow 1927,S 13,37:3
H M S Pinafore 1935,Ag 17,18:4
Pirates of Penzance, The 1938,Je 3,16:2
Emery, Edwin T (Producer)
H M S Pinafore 1935,Ag 17,18:4
Emery, Eleanor
Days of Our Youth, The 1941,N 29,15:2
Emery, Essie
Little Father of the Wilderness, The 1930,Je 3,27:1
County Chairman, The 1936,My 26,26:5
Emery, Ethel
Merry Merry 1925,S 25,24:3
Emery, Gilbert
Truth About Blayds, The 1922,Mr 15,22:1
Dagmar 1923,Ja 23,18:2
Enchanted Cottage, The 1923,Ap 2,22:3
Enchanted Cottage, The 1923,Ap 8,VIII,1:1
Chains 1923,S 20,5:2
New Englander, The 1924,F 8,22:2
Episode 1925,F 5,23:2
Henry IV, Part I 1926,Je 1,29:1
Thief, The 1927,Ap 23,15:2
Paris Bound 1927,D 28,26:3
Paris Bound 1928,Ja 15,VIII,1:1
Men Must Fight 1932,O 15,13:4
Emery, Gilbert (Director)
Love in a Mist 1926,Ap 13,28:3
Far Away Horses 1933,Mr 22,21:6
Emery, Gilbert (Original Author)
Far Away Horses 1933,Mr 22,21:6
Emery, Gilbert (Playwright)
Hero, The 1921,S 6,13:2
Hero, The 1921,S 11,VI,1:1
Tarnish 1923,O 2,10:1
Episode 1925,F 5,23:2
Episode 1925,F 8,VII,1:1
Episode 1925,F 15,VII,1:1
Love in a Mist 1926,Ap 13,28:3
Say When 1928,Je 27,29:3
Housewarming 1932,Ap 8,25:1
Emery, Ian
Three Sisters, The 1926,O 27,24:1
Bellamy Trial, The 1928,Ag 20,21:1
Bellamy Trial, The 1931,Ap 23,28:6
Strange Orchestra 1933,N 29,23:2
Emery, John
John Brown 1934,Ja 23,22:3
Romeo and Juliet 1934,D 21,30:3
Barretts of Wimpole Street, The 1935,F 26,16:2
Flowers of the Forest 1935,Ap 9,25:2
Parnell 1935,N 12,24:2
Alice Takat 1936,F 11,19:2
Sweet Aloes 1936,F 25,23:5
Sweet Aloes 1936,Mr 5,24:5
Parnell 1936,My 5,26:2
Hamlet 1936,O 9,30:2
Antony and Cleopatra 1937,O 14,23:2
Antony and Cleopatra 1937,N 11,30:2
Save Me the Waltz 1938,Mr 1,19:2
Circle, The 1938,Ap 19,24:2
I Am Different 1938,Ag 28,IX,2:5
Five Kings 1939,Mr 5,X,3:1
Wuthering Heights 1939,Ap 28,30:4
Gas Light 1939,Ag 30,20:8
Unconquered, The 1940,F 14,25:2
Liliom 1940,Mr 26,17:2
Retreat to Pleasure 1940,D 18,32:2
Peepshow 1944,F 4,12:2
Relapse, The 1950,N 23,54:2
Royal Family, The 1951,Ja 11,28:2
Constant Wife, The 1951,D 10,34:3
Coriolanus 1954,Ja 20,34:2
Coriolanus 1954,Ja 24,II,1:1
King John 1956,Je 28,33:5
Hotel Paradiso 1957,Ap 12,22:2
Hotel Paradiso 1957,Ap 21,II,1:1
Rape of the Belt, The 1960,N 7,46:1
Emery, June
Tea Time 1968,O 16,40:1
Emery, Karl
Red, White and Maddox 1969,Ja 27,27:1
Emery, Katherine
Carry Nation 1932,O 31,18:2
Strangers at Home 1934,S 15,20:5
Children's Hour, The 1934,N 21,23:2
As You Like It 1937,N 1,25:2
As You Like It 1937,N 8,18:2
Roosty 1938,F 15,21:2
Everywhere I Roam 1938,D 30,10:4
Everywhere I Roam 1939,Ja 8,IX,1:1
Three Sisters, The 1939,O 16,23:1
Proof Thro' the Night 1942,D 26,14:2
Cherry Orchard, The 1944,Ja 26,22:1
Cherry Orchard, The 1944,F 6,II,1:1
Emery, Lin (Scenic Designer)
Kaleidoscope 1957,Je 14,20:2

Emery, Louie
Lassie 1920,Ap 7,9:2
Helena's Boys 1924,Ap 8,22:2
Little Minister, The 1925,Mr 24,21:1
Shanghai Gesture, The 1926,F 2,20:2
Emery, Peter
Patriots, The 1943,D 21,22:5
Emery, Ted
Pie in the Sky 1941,D 23,26:5
Emery, Winifred
Enchanted Cottage, The 1922,Mr 2,21:4
Emhardt, Robert
Pirate, The 1942,N 26,39:2
Harriet 1944,S 28,26:1
Virginia Reel 1947,Ap 15,28:2
Ghosts 1948,F 17,31:2
Hedda Gabler 1948,F 25,27:2
Life With Mother 1948,O 21,32:2
Life With Mother 1949,Mr 27,II,1:1
Man, The 1950,Ja 20,28:2
Curious Savage, The 1950,O 25,44:3
Seven Year Itch, The 1952,N 21,21:2
Janus 1955,N 25,37:2
Good as Gold 1957,Mr 8,22:2
Nature's Way 1957,O 17,42:2
Girls in 509, The 1958,O 16,47:1
Emimory (Playwright)
Petite Bonnie Serieuse 1923,N 27,23:5
Emlott, Irving
Holy Night 1941,D 22,23:3
Emma, Tommy
Creeping Fire 1935,Ja 17,22:3
Emmanuel, Ivor
Trial by Jury 1951,F 6,24:2
Time for Singing, A 1966,My 23,48:2
Emmer, Irwin
As You Were 1920,Ja 28,22:3
Immoral Isabella 1927,O 28,20:3
Emmerson, Dorothy
Education of H*Y*M*A*N K*A*P*L*A*N, The
1968,Ap 5,57:1
Norman, Is That You? 1970,F 20,30:1
Emmet, Barton H (Director)
Brother to Dragons 1968,D 8,86:1
Wilson in the Promise Land 1970,Ja 11,78:1
Emmet, Katherine
Laughing Lady, The 1923,F 13,25:1
New Englander, The 1924,F 8,22:2
Thoroughbreds 1924,S 9,12:1
Hangman's House 1926,D 17,27:2
Paolo and Francesca 1929,Ap 2,28:2
Jenny 1929,O 9,34:4
Widow in Green, A 1931,N 21,21:4
We the People 1933,Ja 23,9:5
Children's Hour, The 1934,N 21,23:2
Ring Around Elizabeth 1941,N 18,32:2
Guest in the House 1942,F 25,25:2
Pygmalion 1945,D 27,16:1
Children's Hour, The 1952,D 19,35:2
Children's Hour, The 1952,D 28,II,1:1
Emmett, Elizabeth
What Next 1920,Ja 27,7:2
Emmett, Frank
What's Your Wife Doing? 1923,O 2,10:3
Emmett, Joseph
Richard II 1951,Ja 25,21:2
Emmett, Robert
Minstrel Boy, The 1948,O 15,28:2
Mid-Summer 1953,Ja 22,19:1
Knight of the Burning Pestle, The 1953,O 24,13:2
Madam Will You Walk 1953,D 2,2:4
Madam Will You Walk 1953,D 20,II,3:1
Emmons, Beverly (Lighting Director)
Dracula Sabbat 1970,O 2,28:2
Sensations 1970,O 26,48:2
Gertrude 1970,N 13,29:1
Emmons, Don
Hooray!! It's a Glorious Day. . .And All That
1966,Mr 10,28:1
Curley McDimple 1969,N 25,53:1
Emmy, Carlton
Vaudeville (Palace) 1926,Je 15,23:3
Dance of Death, The 1932,Ja 11,29:5
Emmy, Carlton Mad Wags
Vaudeville (Palace) 1930,S 15,29:2
Emney, Fred
Seeing Stars 1935,N 1,25:5
Swing Along 1936,S 20,IX,1:4
Going Greek 1937,S 17,28:4
Emo, Maria
Rendezvous in Wien 1956,S 5,23:1
Emod (Playwright)
Romance of Ida, The 1929,F 3,VIII,2:1
Emory, Carl
Lady Windermere's Fan 1932,Ja 27,19:3
In Heaven and Earth 1936,Mr 27,24:8
Emory, Carlton
Charm 1929,N 29,24:5
Emory, Ian
Twelfth Night 1926,D 21,21:4
Emory, Richard
Green Pastures, The 1935,F 27,16:2

Emory, Robert
Lingering Past, The 1932,Je 30,26:5
Empey, Georgia
Big Blow 1938,O 3,11:2
Empire Girls
Ziegfeld Follies 1924,Je 25,26:1
Emrek, Jack
Brigadoon 1957,Mr 28,37:1
Annie Get Your Gun 1958,F 20,29:2
Emshoff, Carol
Death of a Salesman 1963,Jl 20,11:2
Emslie, Jean
Slice It Thin 1945,My 11,22:5
Respectfully Yours 1947,My 14,29:4
Enbach, Richard
Tom Sawyer 1931,D 26,15:3
Passionate Pilgrim, The 1932,O 20,24:3
Wooden Slipper, The 1934,Ja 4,16:3
Enck, Gary
Life With Father 1967,O 20,53:2
Enderle, Edith
Our Town 1944,Ja 11,24:5
Enders, Elvia
Little Accident 1928,O 10,32:3
Nigger Rich 1929,S 21,16:7
Enders, Paul
Young Go First, The 1935,My 29,16:2
Enders, Ruth
Twelfth Night 1949,O 4,33:2
Twelfth Night 1949,O 9,II,1:1
Endfield, Cyril
In the Days of the Turbins 1934,Mr 7,22:5
Endicott, Carl
By Your Leave 1934,Ja 25,15:3
Endicott, Harry
Strada, La 1969,D 15,63:1
Light, Lively and Yiddish 1970,O 28,58:1
Endres, Alice
Two Blocks Away 1921,Ag 31,8:3
Endrey, Eugene (Director)
Smell the Sweet Savor 1940,F 3,8:4
Many Things 1940,F 3,8:4
One-Act Variety Theatre; According to Law
  1940,Mr 20,36:2
Time to Burn 1940,D 4,34:3
Reaper 1940,D 4,34:3
Strange Play, A 1944,Je 2,20:3
According to Law 1944,Je 2,20:3
Endrey, Eugene (Miscellaneous)
Doing Nicely 1940,D 4,34:3
Man-Hunt 1940,D 4,34:3
Endrey, Eugene (Producer)
Sari 1930,Ja 29,27:1
Smell the Sweet Savor 1940,F 3,8:4
Many Things 1940,F 3,8:4
One-Act Variety Theatre; Devil Is a Good Man,
  The 1940,Mr 20,36:2
This Earth Is Ours 1940,Ap 26,24:2
Fireworks on the James 1940,My 15,30:2
Strange Play, A 1944,Je 2,20:3
According to Law 1944,Je 2,20:3
Enesco, Georges (Composer)
Rumanian Rhapsody, No 1 1929,Ap 27,16:4
Enet, Georges Jr
Martine 1936,N 26,38:2
Dejeuner d'Amoureax, Un; Lovers Breakfast, A
  1936,N 26,38:2
Enet, Simone
Bal des Voleurs, Le 1938,N 29,26:4
Enfield, Hugh
Coquette 1935,My 22,23:4
Engalitcheff, N (Prince)
Wonder Bar, The 1931,Mr 18,23:4
Enge, Walter
Faust 1947,N 29,9:2
Engel, Alexander (Playwright)
What Never Dies 1926,D 29,24:2
What Never Dies 1927,Ja 16,VII,1:1
Dancing Partner 1930,Jl 27,VIII,2:3
Dancing Partner 1930,Ag 6,24:2
Engel, Arthur
Monkey Talks, The 1925,D 29,20:1
Engel, Bernerd
J B 1958,Ap 24,37:1
J B 1958,My 4,II,1:1
John Brown's Body 1960,Je 22,31:1
Merchant of Venice, The 1970,Je 10,39:1
Engel, Bette
J B 1958,Ap 24,37:1
Engel, Charles
Merrily We Roll Along 1934,O 1,14:1
Engel, Ellen Bogen
Dinny and the Witches 1959,D 10,53:3
Engel, Erich (Director)
Lulu 1927,Ja 30,VII,4:3
Five From the Jazz Band; Fuenf von der Jazzband
  1927,N 20,IX,4:7
Mann Ist Mann 1928,Ap 15,IX,4:7
Threepenny Opera, The 1928,D 2,X,4:4
Rote General, Der 1928,D 23,VIII,4:1
London Prodigal, The 1928,D 23,VIII,4:1
Karl und Anna 1929,Mr 10,X,2:1

Wie Werde Ich Reich und Gluecklich?
  1930,Ag 31,VIII,2:1
Engel, Fred (Producer)
Twist of Sand, A 1969,F 22,36:1
Engel, Georgia
Lend an Ear 1969,O 29,32:1
Hello, Dolly! 1970,Ap 12,II,3:7
Engel, I (Composer)
Dybbuk, The 1926,D 14,24:2
Dybbuk, The 1948,My 3,26:3
Dybbuk, The 1964,F 4,30:2
Engel, Joan
O Evening Star 1936,Ja 9,24:6
Off to Buffalo! 1939,F 22,18:2
Out of This World 1950,D 22,17:3
Engel, Joel (Composer)
Dybbuk, The 1925,D 16,22:2
Engel, Lehman (Composer)
Within the Gates 1934,O 23,23:1
Murder in the Cathedral 1936,Mr 21,13:5
Murder in the Cathedral 1936,Mr 29,IX,1:1
Hero Is Born, A 1937,O 2,18:6
Shoemaker's Holiday, The 1938,Ja 3,17:2
Hamlet 1938,O 13,28:1
Everywhere I Roam 1938,D 30,10:4
Everywhere I Roam 1939,Ja 8,IX,1:1
Family Portrait 1939,Mr 9,18:4
Time of Your Life, The 1939,N 5,IX,1:1
Hamlet 1939,D 5,35:2
Heavenly Express 1940,Ap 19,24:2
Trojan Women, The 1941,Ap 9,32:5
Macbeth 1941,N 12,30:2
Henry VIII 1946,N 7,42:2
John Gabriel Borkman 1946,N 13,33:2
Yellow Jack 1947,F 28,26:2
Me and Molly 1948,F 27,27:2
Temporary Island, A 1948,Mr 15,27:3
Anne of the Thousand Days 1948,D 9,49:2
Uniform of Flesh 1949,Ja 31,15:2
Mikado, The 1949,O 5,35:2
Wisteria Trees, The 1950,Mr 30,39:1
Saint Joan 1951,O 5,23:2
Strong Are Lonely, The 1953,S 30,38:3
Fanny 1954,N 5,16:1
Julius Caesar 1955,Jl 13,20:1
Middle of the Night 1956,F 9,39:1
Ponder Heart, The 1956,F 17,14:2
There Was a Little Girl 1960,Mr 1,28:1
Engel, Lehman (Director)
Beggar's Opera, The 1941,Ag 12,14:6
Engel, Lehman (Miscellaneous)
Alive and Kicking 1950,Ja 18,25:5
Liar, The 1950,My 19,30:2
Taming of the Shrew, The 1951,Ap 26,35:2
Pirates of Penzance, The 1952,O 28,36:4
Wonderful Town 1953,F 26,22:3
Jamaica 1957,N 1,32:2
Jane Eyre 1958,My 2,31:1
Take Me Along 1959,O 23,22:2
I Can Get It for You Wholesale 1962,Mr 23,29:1
Beast in Me, The 1963,My 17,29:1
Engel, Lehman (Musical Director)
Second Hurricane 1937,Ap 22,18:4
Shadow Play 1939,Ag 15,14:5
Heavenly Express 1940,Ap 19,24:2
Beggar's Opera, The 1941,Ag 12,14:6
Call Me Mister 1946,Ap 19,26:2
Mr Winkle's Holliday 1946,Je 24,27:6
Dear Judas 1947,Ag 5,26:1
Dear Judas 1947,O 6,26:4
Macbeth 1948,Ap 1,30:2
Uniform of Flesh 1949,Ja 31,15:2
Pirates of Penzance, The 1949,O 11,41:2
Trial by Jury 1949,O 18,34:2
H M S Pinafore 1949,O 18,34:2
Consul, The 1950,Mr 16,41:1
Consul, The 1950,Mr 26,II,1:1
Liar, The 1950,My 19,30:2
Bless You All 1950,D 15,42:2
Mikado, The 1952,O 21,35:2
H M S Pinafore 1952,N 4,32:2
Trial by Jury 1952,N 4,32:2
H M S Pinafore 1952,N 4,32:2
Iolanthe 1952,N 11,26:3
Wonderful Town 1953,F 26,22:3
Fanny 1954,N 5,16:1
Shangri-La 1956,Je 14,40:1
Li'l Abner 1956,N 16,24:2
Consul, The 1957,S 4,40:3
Jamaica 1957,N 1,32:2
Wonderful Town 1958,Mr 6,32:4
Goldilocks 1958,O 13,33:1
Destry Rides Again 1959,Ap 24,24:1
Take Me Along 1959,O 23,22:2
Do Re Mi 1960,D 27,23:2
Do Re Mi 1961,Ja 8,II,1:1
I Can Get It for You Wholesale 1962,Mr 23,29:1
Wonderful Town 1963,F 15,10:2
What Makes Sammy Run? 1964,F 28,19:1
Bajour 1964,N 24,42:1
Grosse Valise, La 1965,D 15,52:1
Engel, Mary
Italian Straw Hat, The 1957,O 1,37:2

Engel, S Sanford (Scenic Designer)
Natural Man 1941,My 8,20:4
Engel, Sadie (Playwright)
Squaring the Circle 1931,Ap 27,24:4
Engel, Scotty
Plain and Fancy 1955,Ja 28,14:2
Pipe Dream 1955,D 1,44:1
Engel, Susan
Hotel in Amsterdam, The 1968,Jl 21,II,12:1
Engel, Walter
Rape of the Sabine Women, The 1949,F 5,10:5
Engel, Walter (Director)
Rape of the Sabine Women, The 1949,F 5,10:5
Iphigenie in Tauris 1949,O 22,11:2
Engelhardt, Wallace
Buskers, The 1961,O 31,28:1
Never Too Late 1962,N 28,42:1
Education of H*Y*M*A*N K*A*P*L*A*N, The
  1968,Ap 5,57:1
Three Men on a Horse 1969,O 17,35:1
Engelman, Irving J
Button Your Lip 1943,Je 15,16:1
Engels, Catherine
Young Go First, The 1935,My 29,16:2
Engels, Heinz (Director)
Tango 1969,Ja 20,33:1
Engels, Jacqueline
House of Bernarda Alba, The 1963,N 25,23:2
Engerbretson, Ollie
Call Me Madam 1950,O 13,25:1
England, Barry (Playwright)
Conduct Unbecoming 1969,Jl 26,14:1
Conduct Unbecoming 1970,O 13,50:1
Conduct Unbecoming 1970,O 25,II,16:2
England, Edward
Waltz of the Dogs, The 1928,Ap 26,31:3
England, Hal
Trouble in Mind 1955,N 5,23:2
Candida 1957,F 9,14:1
Beggar's Opera, The 1957,Mr 14,35:1
Romeo and Juliet 1957,Je 28,30:2
Two Gentlemen of Verona 1957,Jl 23,21:5
Macbeth 1957,Ag 16,11:2
Love Me Little 1958,Ap 15,42:2
Conversation at Midnight 1964,N 13,27:1
England, Helen
Judge, The 1958,My 14,36:2
Puntila 1959,My 15,26:2
England, Paul
Where's Charley? 1948,O 12,33:2
Where's Charley? 1951,Ja 30,21:7
Englander, Alec
Willow and I, The 1942,D 11,32:2
Family, The 1943,Mr 31,22:4
Englander, Ludwig (Original Author)
Piggy 1927,Ja 12,22:2
Englander, Roger (Director)
Music Man, The 1963,Ag 15,24:1
Englander, Roger (Producer)
Music Man, The 1963,Ag 15,24:1
Engle, Morris
Night Thoreau Spent in Jail, The 1970,N 2,66:1
Engle, Peter
Bystander 1937,S 15,27:1
Englebach, Jerry
Hamlet 1970,O 27,54:2
Englefield, Violet
Sky High 1925,Mr 3,21:4
Engleman, Norman
Caucasian Chalk Circle, The 1961,N 1,35:1
Engler, James (Pvt)
Winged Victory 1943,N 22,24:1
Engler, Sam (Miscellaneous)
Reckoning, The 1969,S 5,28:1
Engleson, Liz
Millionairess, The 1969,Mr 3,28:1
Englich, Ivan (Miscellaneous)
Apparition Theater of Prague, The 1966,N 17,56:2
English, Anna
Tambourines to Glory 1963,N 4,47:1
English, Anne
Moral Fabric 1932,N 22,25:3
English, Bessie
Field God, The 1927,Ap 22,18:2
American Holiday 1936,F 22,13:3
Murder in the Cathedral 1936,Mr 21,13:5
English, Floyd
How's Your Health? 1929,N 27,30:3
English, Genora
Swing It 1937,Jl 23,17:2
English, Harry
Don Juan 1921,S 8,14:2
Kongo 1926,Mr 31,20:5
Honor Be Damned! 1927,Ja 27,13:1
Racket, The 1927,N 23,28:3
English, June
Berkeley Square 1929,N 5,32:4
English, Kay
Rio Rita 1927,F 3,18:3
English, Logan
Girl of the Golden West, The 1957,N 6,44:1
English, Margaret
Lady From the Sea, The 1934,My 2,25:2

English, Margaret—Cont

Othello 1935,S 28,13:2
Macbeth 1935,O 8,26:4
English, Robert
Candle-Light 1929,O 1,28:2
English, Virginia (Miscellaneous)
Spots of the Leopard, The 1963,S 25,38:1
English Bull
Beware of Dogs 1921,O 4,10:1
Englund, George
Lo and Behold! 1951,D 13,45:2
Englund, George (Director)
High Named Today 1954,D 11,11:2
Brigadoon 1957,Mr 28,37:1
Englund, Hilda
Ghosts 1925,D 2,23:2
Ghosts 1933,My 24,24:5
Englund, Hilda (Director)
Ghosts 1925,D 2,23:2
Englund, Patricia
As You Like It 1950,Ja 27,27:2
Long Watch, The 1952,Mr 21,19:5
Festival 1955,Ja 19,22:1
Beauty Part, The 1962,D 28,5:2
Engrav, Elizabeth (Costume Designer)
Arms and the Man 1956,O 2,39:4
In Good King Charles's Golden Days
1957,Ja 25,16:1
Beaux' Stratagem, The 1957,Jl 9,25:4
Engstrom, Robert (Lighting Director)
Geese 1969,Ja 13,26:6
Parents and Children 1969,Ja 13,26:6
My House Is Your House 1970,O 16,53:2
Engstrom, Robert (Scenic Designer)
My House Is Your House 1970,O 16,53:2
Engvick, William (Composer)
Once Over Lightly 1955,Mr 16,39:1
Engvick, William (Lyricist)
Once Over Lightly 1955,Mr 16,39:1
Engvick, William (Playwright)
Beautiful Dreamer 1960,D 28,22:1
Enjaku, Toyozawa
Chushingura; Treasury of Loyal Retainers, The
1969,S 11,53:1
Kumagai Jinya 1969,S 18,64:1
Ennery, Florence
Phedre 1963,O 21,39:1
Berenice 1963,O 30,46:1
Ennio, Mr (Playwright)
Princess Liana 1929,Jl 14,IX,6:8
Ennis, Luce
Sound of Music, The 1959,N 17,40:2
Merry Widow, The 1964,Ag 18,24:2
Eno, Harry
Mother Courage and Her Children 1963,Mr 30,5:5
My House Is Your House 1970,O 16,53:2
Eno, Harry (Miscellaneous)
Friday Night; Mary Agnes Is Thirty-Five
1965,F 9,42:5
Friday Night; River, The 1965,F 9,42:5
Friday Night; Passport 1965,F 9,42:5
Eno, Terry
Canterbury Tales; Miller's Tale, The 1969,F 4,34:1
Enright, Harold
Man on Stilts, The 1931,S 10,23:2
Enright, Sara
Mrs Jimmie Thompson 1920,Mr 30,9:1
Dragon, The 1922,D 27,12:1
Wild Man of Borneo, The 1927,S 14,29:2
Ensemble, The
Queen of Greece, The 1969,Ap 12,40:2
Enserro, Michael
Me and Molly 1948,F 27,27:2
Miracle, The 1960,D 5,42:3
Penny Change 1963,O 25,37:1
Kitchen, The 1966,Je 14,50:1
Song of the Grasshopper 1967,S 29,52:2
Camino Real 1970,Ja 9,42:1
Ensslen, Dick
Anyone Can Whistle 1964,Ap 6,36:1
Bajour 1964,N 24,42:1
Most Happy Fella, The 1966,My 12,55:1
Education of H*Y*M*A*N K*A*P*L*A*N, The
1968,Ap 5,57:1
Canterbury Tales; Pilgrims, The 1969,F 4,34:1
Enten, Boni
Oh! Calcutta! 1969,Je 18,33:1
Salvation 1969,S 25,55:1
Salvation 1969,O 5,II,1:1
Salvation 1970,F 15,II,1:1
Enters, Angna
Theatre of Angna Enters, The 1955,Ja 25,22:2
Enters, Marjorie
Manhattan Varieties 1932,O 22,18:3
Enters, Warren (Director)
Way of the World, The 1954,S 30,38:2
Thieves' Carnival 1955,F 2,21:1
Morning's at Seven 1955,Je 23,25:1
Dragon's Mouth 1955,N 17,45:1
Dandy Dick 1956,Ja 11,37:2
Palm Tree in a Rose Garden, A 1957,N 27,26:2
Warm Peninsula, The 1959,O 21,46:2
Not While I'm Eating 1961,D 20,37:1
Shakespeare Revisited 1962,Jl 19,19:2

Emperor, The 1963,Ap 17,30:1
Lemon Sky 1970,My 18,40:1
Enters, Warren (Miscellaneous)
Dandy Dick 1956,Ja 11,37:2
Enters, Warren (Producer)
Thieves' Carnival 1955,F 2,21:1
Morning's at Seven 1955,Je 23,25:1
Entman, Fred (Producer)
Transgressor Rides Again, The 1969,My 21,42:1
Enton, David
Sun and I, The 1937,F 27,9:5
Haiti 1938,Mr 3,16:1
Entrikin, Knowles
Pillars of Society, The 1931,O 15,19:1
Entrikin, Knowles (Director)
Wolf! Wolf! 1925,O 30,21:1
Seed of the Brute 1926,N 2,34:3
Streets of New York, The 1931,O 7,29:1
Bride the Sun Shines On, The 1931,D 28,20:2
Entrikin, Knowles (Playwright)
Small Timers, The 1925,Ja 28,15:3
Seed of the Brute 1926,O 17,VIII,2:4
Seed of the Brute 1926,N 2,34:3
Seed of the Brute 1926,N 7,VIII,1:1
Ali Baba and the Forty Thieves 1926,D 23,23:2
Entwhistle, John
Tommy 1969,O 26,82:1
Entwisle, Robert
What a Relief 1935,D 14,10:6
Entwistle, Agatha
Processional 1937,O 14,23:1
Entwistle, Peg
Man From Toronto, The 1926,Je 18,27:2
Home Towners, The 1926,Ag 24,19:3
Tommy 1927,Ja 11,36:4
Uninvited Guest, The 1927,S 28,28:2
Sherlock Holmes 1929,N 26,28:3
She Means Business 1931,Ja 27,21:2
Getting Married 1931,Mr 31,25:5
Just to Remind You 1931,S 8,39:1
Little Women 1931,D 8,36:2
Alice Sit-By-The-Fire 1932,Mr 8,19:3
Mad Hopes, The 1932,My 29,VIII,2:2
Enzensberger, Hans Magnus (Playwright)
Verhoer von Habana, Das 1970,O 13,52:2
Epailly, Jules
Breakfast in Bed 1920,F 4,12:1
Princess Virtue 1921,My 5,20:2
Bluebeard's Eighth Wife 1921,S 20,12:2
Lovely Lady 1927,D 30,22:1
By Request 1928,S 28,30:2
Precious 1929,Ja 15,22:5
Gala Night 1930,F 26,22:4
Ada Beats the Drum 1930,My 9,20:4
Dancing Partner 1930,Jl 27,VIII,2:3
Dancing Partner 1930,Ag 6,24:2
Woman Denied, A 1931,F 26,21:1
Miracle at Verdun 1931,Mr 17,34:6
East Wind 1931,O 28,19:1
Papavert 1931,D 30,25:1
Hot-Cha! 1932,My 9,17:3
Before Morning 1933,F 10,13:4
Her Man of Wax 1933,O 12,32:3
Broomsticks Amen! 1934,F 10,20:4
Any Woman 1934,Ag 28,24:4
O'Flynn, The 1934,D 28,24:1
Kind Lady 1935,Ap 24,24:5
Bonfire to Glory 1936,Jl 28,23:4
St Helena 1936,O 7,32:1
Between the Devil 1937,O 15,19:1
Between the Devil 1937,D 23,24:5
Great Lady 1938,D 2,26:6
Billy Draws a Horse 1939,D 22,14:5
Johnny Belinda 1940,S 19,26:2
Ephraim, Armand (Playwright)
Maitresse de Roi 1926,D 1,24:1
Ephraim, Lee (Director)
On the Spot 1930,O 30,33:3
Ephraim, Lee (Miscellaneous)
On the Spot 1930,O 30,33:3
Call It a Day 1936,Ja 29,15:2
Spring Meeting 1938,D 9,30:4
Ephraim, Lee (Producer)
Call It a Day 1936,Ja 21,26:7
Sweet Aloes 1936,Mr 5,24:5
All Men Are Alike 1941,O 7,27:2
Claudia 1942,S 27,VIII,2:2
Under the Counter 1947,O 4,10:2
Don't Listen, Ladies 1948,D 29,16:2
Ephram, Bobby
Old Bucks and New Wings 1962,N 6,39:4
Ephron, Henry
Merrily We Roll Along 1934,O 1,14:1
Ephron, Henry (Director)
Three's a Family 1943,My 6,24:2
Ephron, Henry (Playwright)
Three's a Family 1943,My 6,24:2
Take Her, She's Mine 1961,D 22,19:1
My Daughter, Your Son 1969,My 14,36:2
Ephron, Phoebe (Playwright)
Three's a Family 1943,My 6,24:2
Howie 1958,S 18,35:2
Take Her, She's Mine 1961,D 22,19:1

Ephron, Phoebe (Playwright)—Cont

My Daughter, Your Son 1969,My 14,36:2
Eppens, Phil
Naughty-Naught 'OO 1937,Ja 25,23:2
Epperly, Verna
My Romance 1948,O 20,38:5
Epstein, Alvin
Evening of Pantomime, An 1955,S 21,38:1
King Lear 1956,Ja 13,17:1
King Lear 1956,Ja 22,II,1:1
Waiting for Godot 1956,Ap 20,21:2
Waiting for Godot 1956,Ap 29,II,1:2
Purple Dust 1956,D 28,15:1
Clerambard 1957,N 8,22:3
Clerambard 1957,N 17,II,1:1
Endgame 1958,Ja 29,32:4
Endgame 1958,F 16,II,1:1
Golden Six, The 1958,O 27,31:2
Play of Daniel, The 1959,Ja 6,30:2
Twelfth Night 1959,Jl 11,10:2
Play of Daniel, The 1959,D 28,17:6
From A to Z 1960,Ap 21,23:2
Play of Daniel, The 1960,D 27,23:6
No Strings 1962,Mr 16,24:1
Passion of Josef D, The 1964,F 12,29:1
Postmark Zero 1965,N 2,28:1
Dynamite Tonight 1967,Mr 16,52:2
Midsummer Night's Dream, A 1967,Je 30,23:1
Bacchae, The 1969,Mr 15,24:1
Bacchae, The 1969,Mr 23,II,11:1
Greatshot 1969,My 18,II,3:1
Whores, Wars & Tin Pan Alley 1969,Je 17,37:1
Metamorphoses 1969,D 12,69:1
Crimes and Crimes 1970,Ja 19,35:1
Don Juan 1970,My 26,32:1
Don Juan 1970,My 31,II,1:6
Three Philip Roth Stories; Defender of the Faith
1970,Jl 31,14:1
Three Philip Roth Stories; Epstein 1970,Jl 31,14:1
Story Theater Repertory; Gimpel the Food
1970,O 21,40:1
Place Without Doors, A 1970,D 1,60:1
Epstein, Alvin (Director)
Rivals, The 1969,O 18,37:1
Epstein, Barnett
In the Matter of J Robert Oppenheimer
1969,Mr 7,28:1
Epstein, Eppie
Commedia Dell' Arte 1927,Ap 6,24:3
Epstein, Jerry (Miscellaneous)
Son, The 1950,Ap 1,12:4
Epstein, Jerry (Producer)
Caligula 1949,Ap 23,10:2
Epstein, Julius J (Playwright)
And Stars Remain 1936,S 29,35:2
And Stars Remain 1936,O 13,32:2
Chicken Every Sunday 1944,Ap 6,27:2
Chicken Every Sunday 1944,Ap 16,II,1:1
But, Seriously... 1969,F 28,29:1
Epstein, L (Playwright)
Victims of Life 1931,O 21,26:2
Epstein, Marion
Twelfth Disciple, The 1930,My 17,21:4
Epstein, Mark
Dynamite Tonight 1967,Mr 16,52:2
Epstein, Mark (Director)
Scaffold for Marionettes, A 1968,Mr 24,II,16:5
Epstein, Philip
Hoboken Blues 1928,F 18,10:1
Epstein, Philip G (Playwright)
And Stars Remain 1936,S 29,35:2
And Stars Remain 1936,O 13,32:2
Chicken Every Sunday 1944,Ap 6,27:2
Chicken Every Sunday 1944,Ap 16,II,1:1
Epstein, Pierre
Private Life of the Master Race, The
1956,Ja 31,33:3
Jeannette 1960,Mr 25,20:2
Shot in the Dark, A 1961,O 19,40:1
Enter Laughing 1963,Mr 15,8:1
Too Much Johnson 1964,Ja 16,29:1
Incident at Vichy 1964,D 4,44:1
Black Comedy 1967,F 13,42:1
People vs Ranchman, The 1968,O 28,56:1
Promenade 1969,Je 5,56:1
Epstein, Pierre (Miscellaneous)
Too Close for Comfort 1960,F 3,27:2
Gay Apprentice, The 1960,F 3,27:2
Jeannette 1960,Mr 25,20:2
Drums Under the Windows 1960,O 14,26:1
Epstein, S Walter (Miscellaneous)
Before You Go 1968,Ja 12,20:1
Epstein, Sabin
Arden of Faversham 1970,F 17,33:1
Ubu Roi 1970,F 17,33:1
Erbach, Paul
Plough and the Stars, The 1956,Ap 6,14:1
Erbacher, Richard
Yeomen of the Guard, The 1965,Jl 8,34:1
Ruddigore 1965,Ag 27,16:1
Erbele, Carl
Banjo Eyes 1941,D 26,20:2
Erben, Dey (Lighting Director)
Adding Machine, The 1948,N 18,35:2

Erber, A
Three Little Business Men, The 1923,S 4,12:1
Erber, Anna
He, She and the Ox 1934,F 21,22:7
Berl and Shmerl Corporation 1934,Ap 2,12:5
Erber, M
Hello Grandpa! 1931,Ja 2,25:3
Erber, Ursula
Amphitryon 1970,N 18,40:1
Erby, Morris
Hamlet 1964,Je 17,49:1
Coriolanus 1965,Jl 15,23:1
Troilus and Cressida 1965,Ag 13,17:1
Kitchen, The 1966,Je 14,50:1
Erdenberg, Gabrielle
Dream Play 1960,N 23,22:1
Erdman, Jean
Wind Remains, The 1943,Mr 31,16:6
Coach With the Six Insides, The 1962,N 27,44:1
Coach With the Six Insides, The 1967,My 12,50:1
Erdman, Jean (Choreographer)
Enchanted, The 1950,Ja 19,34:2
Yerma 1966,D 9,60:1
Coach With the Six Insides, The 1967,My 12,50:1
Erdman, Jean (Director)
Coach With the Six Insides, The 1962,N 27,44:1
Coach With the Six Insides, The 1967,My 12,50:1
Erdman, Jean (Playwright)
Coach With the Six Insides, The 1962,N 27,44:1
Coach With the Six Insides, The 1967,My 12,50:1
Erdman, N (Playwright)
Moscow Circus on Ice 1970,D 9,63:1
Erdman (Playwright)
Mandate 1926,F 15,19:1
Erdmann, Jane
Sonya's Search for the Christmas Star
1929,D 14,24:6
Erdos, Irving
Song of Songs 1958,O 29,31:1
Erenborg (Original Author)
Destruction of Europe, The 1925,Ja 11,VII,2:7
Erens, Joseph (Miscellaneous)
Ziegfeld Follies 1943,Ap 2,16:2
Erens, Joseph (Playwright)
Brights Lights of 1944 1943,S 17,27:4
Erfords, The
Vaudeville (Palace) 1926,S 21,32:5
Ergotti, Herman
Fine and Dandy 1930,S 24,26:1
Summer Night 1939,N 3,17:1
Erhardt, Alice
Playboy of the Western World, The 1930,Ja 3,20:4
Eri, Chiemi
My Fair Lady 1963,S 2,19:4
Kiss Me, Kate 1966,F 5,32:1
Eric, Betsy Lous
Woman Bites Dog 1946,Ap 18,21:2
Eric, Elspeth
Small Miracle 1934,S 27,24:3
Dead End 1935,O 29,17:2
Too Many Heroes 1937,N 16,26:2
Margin for Error 1939,O 15,48:7
Margin for Error 1939,N 4,11:3
Snafu 1944,O 26,19:5
Live Wire, The 1950,Ag 18,16:2
Eric, Fred
Treasure, The 1920,O 5,13:1
Heartbreak House 1920,N 11,11:1
Trial of Joan of Arc, The 1921,Mr 28,8:2
Skylark 1921,Jl 26,10:6
Marie Antoinette 1921,N 23,16:1
Salome 1922,My 23,12:4
Number 7 1926,S 9,21:3
Beaux' Stratagem, The 1928,Je 5,20:1
Bellamy Trial, The 1928,Ag 20,21:1
Bellamy Trial, The 1931,Ap 23,28:6
Bloody Laughter 1931,D 5,20:6
Wolves 1932,Ja 7,26:3
If Booth Had Missed 1932,F 5,24:2
Yellow Jacket, The 1934,F 25,IX,2:6
Eric, Fred (Director)
Mountain, The 1933,S 12,28:6
Eric, James
Walk-Up 1961,F 24,24:1
Ericks, Eileen
Few Wild Oats, A 1932,Mr 25,22:6
Ericksen, Ed
I'm Solomon 1968,Ap 24,51:1
Ericksen, Eddie
Donnybrook! 1961,My 19,23:1
Erickson, Arthur
Howdy, Mr Ice of 1950 1949,My 27,24:2
Erickson, Claris
Little Eyolf 1964,Mr 17,31:1
Erickson, Corydon
Great God Brown, The 1959,O 7,48:1
Erickson, Eddie
Hear! Hear! 1955,S 28,38:1
Erickson, Leif
All the Living 1938,Mr 25,14:4
Rocket to the Moon 1938,N 25,18:2
Sarah Adler Testimonial 1939,Mr 15,18:2
Margin for Error 1939,N 4,11:3

Higher and Higher 1940,Mr 17,X,2:5
Higher and Higher 1940,Ap 5,24:3
Higher and Higher 1940,Ag 6,15:4
Higher and Higher 1940,Ag 11,IX,1:1
Retreat to Pleasure 1940,D 18,32:2
Cream in the Well, The 1941,Ja 21,19:2
Tea and Sympathy 1953,O 1,35:1
Tea and Sympathy 1953,O 11,II,1:1
Tea and Sympathy 1954,Ag 15,II,1:1
World of Carl Sandburg, The 1960,S 15,44:1
World of Carl Sandburg, The 1960,S 25,II,1:1
Glass Menagerie, The 1961,Mr 6,30:1
Skin of Our Teeth, The 1961,Mr 6,30:1
Skin of Our Teeth, The 1961,Mr 20,32:6
Skin of Our Teeth, The 1961,Mr 28,40:2
Glass Menagerie, The 1961,Ap 21,29:1
Skin of Our Teeth, The 1961,Ap 21,29:1
Glass Menagerie, The 1961,My 1,35:3
Skin of Our Teeth, The 1961,My 1,35:3
Skin of Our Teeth, The 1961,My 19,22:2
Glass Menagerie, The 1961,Je 16,27:3
Erickson, Lorna
Picture of Dorian Gray, The 1956,Ag 18,15:5
Fall 1957,N 22,19:1
Erickson, Louise
Hole in the Head, A 1957,Mr 1,15:1
Erickson, Mitchell
Protective Custody 1956,D 29,8:7
Affair, The 1962,S 21,34:2
Erickson, Mitchell (Director)
Streetcar Named Desire, A 1955,Mr 4,18:2
Erickson, Mitchell (Miscellaneous)
Luther 1963,S 26,41:1
Rosencrantz and Guildenstern Are Dead
1967,O 17,53:1
Rockefeller and the Red Indians 1968,O 25,37:1
Play It Again, Sam 1969,F 13,52:3
Child's Play 1970,F 18,39:1
Erickson, Stanley
Visit, The 1958,My 6,40:1
Ericksson, John (Director)
Dunungen 1939,F 26,IX,2:3
Ericson, Brenda
Shoemaker's Prodigious Wife, The 1949,Je 15,38:2
Ericson, John
Stalag 17 1951,My 9,41:2
Ericson, June
Once Over Lightly 1955,Mr 16,39:1
Midsummer Night's Dream, A 1958,Je 23,19:1
Winter's Tale, The 1958,Jl 21,17:4
Fashion 1959,Ja 21,27:1
Eringer, Elliot
He Who Gets Slapped 1946,Mr 21,31:4
Mister Roberts 1948,F 19,27:2
Erion, Hope
Yellow Jacket, The 1923,Ap 20,20:3
Erlanger, A L (Producer)
Hassan 1924,S 23,23:1
Service for Two 1926,Ag 31,15:1
Honeymoon Lane 1926,S 21,32:3
Happy-Go-Lucky 1926,O 1,27:2
Money From Home 1927,Mr 1,30:2
19th Hole, The 1927,O 12,30:3
Houseparty 1929,S 10,26:5
Sweet Land of Liberty 1929,S 24,29:2
Ladies of the Jury 1929,O 6,IX,1:4
Ladies of the Jury 1929,O 22,26:2
Your Uncle Dudley 1929,N 19,26:4
Sherlock Holmes 1929,N 26,28:3
It's a Grand Life 1930,F 11,30:3
Erlanger, Aline (Playwright)
Manhatters, The 1927,Ag 4,25:4
Erlanger, Annette
Winners and Losers 1947,F 27,27:2
Deputy of Paris, The 1947,Mr 22,9:5
Erlanger, Arlene (Playwright)
Manhatters, The 1927,Jl 19,27:3
Erlanger Productions, Inc (Director)
Merchant of Venice, The 1931,N 9,22:2
Ermansons, Taiga
Lysistrata 1968,N 15,42:1
Ermoloff, (Messr)
Chauve-Souris 1925,Ja 15,25:1
Ermoloff, George
Clear All Wires! 1932,S 15,19:1
Ermoloff, George (Director)
Vagabond King, The 1943,Je 30,24:2
Ernest, Ingrid
Before Sundown 1962,Mr 14,43:1
Ernest, Paul
Comforter, The 1964,O 22,42:1
Ernst, Aileen
Mrs O'Brien Entertains 1939,F 9,16:3
Ernst, Connie
Having Wonderful Time 1937,F 22,12:5
Ernst, Jessie (Playwright)
Storm Center 1927,D 1,33:2
Red Cat, The 1934,S 20,21:1
Ernst, Leila
Too Many Girls 1939,O 19,26:2
Pal Joey 1940,D 26,22:2
Truckline Cafe 1946,F 28,19:4
If the Shoe Fits 1946,D 6,29:4

Ernst, Paul (Playwright)
Heilige Crispin, Der 1933,Je 25,IX,1:2
Ernst, Russell
Murder in the Cathedral 1958,Mr 22,12:4
Ernst, Ruth
Red, Hot and Blue! 1936,O 30,26:3
Ernst, Walter (Producer)
Death of Satan, The 1960,Ap 6,49:1
Errett, Geoffrey
Red, Hot and Blue! 1936,O 30,26:3
Errico, Joseph
Jane-Our Stranger 1925,O 9,27:2
Paging Danger 1931,F 27,19:2
Errol, Bert
Vaudeville (Palace) 1926,Je 8,23:1
Vaudeville (Palace) 1927,Ja 18,23:2
Errol, Doreen (Costume Designer)
Much Ado About Nothing 1929,N 17,30:4
Errol, Katherine
Yankee Princess, The 1922,O 3,22:1
Errol, Leon
Sally 1920,D 22,16:1
Midnight Frolic 1921,N 19,11:3
Louie the 14th 1925,Mr 4,17:1
Lambs Gambol 1925,Ap 27,15:1
Yours Truly 1927,Ja 26,16:5
Fioretta 1929,Ja 6,VIII,4:6
Fioretta 1929,F 6,30:3
Lambs Gambol 1933,Ap 24,10:1
Errol, Leon (Playwright)
Partners 1927,Jl 26,16:5
Errolle, Marthe
Night of Love 1940,O 29,32:6
Night of Love 1941,Ja 8,14:2
Park Avenue 1946,N 5,31:2
Lady From Paris, The 1950,S 27,36:1
Errolle, Ralph
Nightingale, The 1927,Ja 4,20:4
Ershova
Chauve-Souris 1922,Je 6,17:4
Chauve-Souris 1923,S 4,12:1
Chauve-Souris 1925,Ja 15,25:1
Chauve-Souris 1929,Ja 23,20:2
Ersi, Elsa
Moonlight 1924,Ja 31,13:7
Vaudeville (Palace) 1927,F 8,20:3
Vaudeville (Palace) 1928,Ap 10,32:4
So Was Napoleon 1930,Ja 9,22:2
Fabulous Invalid, The 1938,O 10,15:1
Erskin, Chester
Puppets of Passion 1927,F 25,24:4
What Do We Know 1927,D 24,8:1
Erskin, Chester (Director)
Harlem 1929,F 21,30:3
Subway Express 1929,S 25,34:3
Last Mile, The 1930,F 14,21:2
Stepdaughters of War 1930,O 7,27:1
I Love an Actress 1931,S 18,29:2
He 1931,S 22,33:1
De Luxe 1935,Mr 6,22:2
Puritan, The 1936,Ja 24,14:3
Siege 1937,D 9,31:4
Good, The 1938,O 6,27:2
Weak Link, The 1940,Mr 5,19:2
Moon Is Down, The 1942,Ap 8,22:2
Erskin, Chester (Playwright)
I Love an Actress 1931,S 18,29:2
He 1931,S 22,33:1
Puritan, The 1936,Ja 24,14:3
Good, The 1938,O 6,27:2
Into Thin Air 1955,My 25,39:1
Erskin, Chester (Producer)
I Love an Actress 1931,S 18,29:2
De Luxe 1935,F 24,VIII,3:4
De Luxe 1935,Mr 6,22:2
Puritan, The 1936,Ja 24,14:3
Weak Link, The 1940,Mr 5,19:2
Erskine, Anna
Growing Pains 1933,N 24,24:2
Naughty-Naught '00 1937,Ja 25,23:2
Fireman's Flame, The 1937,O 11,26:2
Erskine, Drummond
Antony and Cleopatra 1947,N 27,49:2
Trial, The 1955,Je 15,35:2
Jolly's Progress 1959,D 7,42:2
Anvil, The 1962,O 31,33:3
Erskine, Eileen
Faithfully Yours 1951,O 19,22:5
Erskine, Howard
Private Lives 1968,My 20,59:1
Erskine, Howard (Director)
Happiest Millionaire, The 1956,N 21,21:
Minor Miracle 1965,O 8,4:3
Erskine, Howard (Miscellaneous)
Late Love 1953,O 14,35:2
Erskine, Howard (Producer)
Desperate Hours, The 1955,F 11,20:2
Happiest Millionaire, The 1956,N 21,21:3
Calculated Risk 1962,N 1,35:1
Erskine, John (Original Author)
Helen 1952,D 15,22:6
Erskine, Marilyn
Excursion 1937,Ap 10,11:4

Erskine, Marilyn—Cont
Ghost of Yankee Doodle, The 1937,N 23,26:3
Our Town 1938,F 5,18:3
Primrose Path, The 1939,Ja 5,16:3
Primrose Path, The 1939,Ja 16,11:2
Goodbye in the Night 1940,Mr 19,31:2
Ring Around Elizabeth 1941,N 18,32:2
What Big Ears! 1942,Ap 21,18:5
Nine Girls 1943,Ja 14,26:2
Pretty Little Parlor 1944,Ap 18,24:8
Linden Tree, The 1948,Mr 3,28:2
Erskine, Milton (Playwright)
Time of the Key, A 1963,S 12,33:3
Erskine, Sara
My Son's My Son 1936,My 27,26:4
Erskine, Wallace
Two Blocks Away 1921,Ag 31,8:3
Harvest 1925,S 21,16:2
Beaten Track, The 1926,F 9,23:2
Beau Gallant 1926,Ap 6,26:3
Lally 1927,F 9,16:3
Mystery Ship, The 1927,Mr 15,28:2
Outsider, The 1928,Ap 10,32:2
Bellamy Trial, The 1928,Ag 20,21:1
Girl Trouble 1928,O 26,22:3
Serena Blandish 1929,Ja 24,30:3
Ladies Don't Lie 1929,O 11,36:3
Death Takes a Holiday 1929,D 27,26:4
Church Mouse, A 1931,O 13,26:4
Unto the Third 1933,Ap 21,24:8
Home Sweet Home 1936,Jl 1,29:2
Erskine, Walter
Death Takes a Holiday 1931,F 17,29:1
Erte (Miscellaneous)
Wonder World 1964,My 18,32:1
Ertell, George
Joseph 1930,F 13,25:3
Ervesun, Ernrique A
Flair-Flair the Idol of Paree 1935,Mr 13,16:1
Laugh It Off 1934,Ap 5,24:2
Ervin, Goldie
One Way to Heaven 1936,S 29,35:1
Ervin, John
Banjo Eyes 1941,D 26,20:2
Ervine, St John (Playwright)
Magnanimous Lover, The 1920,F 10,10:2
Jane Clegg 1920,F 25,14:1
Jane Clegg 1920,F 29,V,5:1
Jane Clegg 1920,Mr 28,V,6:1
Mixed Marriage 1920,D 15,18:2
Wonderful Visit, The 1921,Ap 3,VII,1:3
John Ferguson 1921,My 24,20:1
Mary, Mary, Quite Contrary 1923,S 2,VI,2:6
Mary, Mary, Quite Contrary 1923,S 12,14:1
Mary, Mary, Quite Contrary 1923,S 16,VII,1:1
Wonderful Visit, The 1924,F 13,17:3
Wonderful Visit, The 1924,My 18,VII,1:1
Jane Clegg 1926,D 12,VIII,4:7
John Ferguson 1928,Ja 18,23:1
Ship, The 1929,F 17,IX,2:1
First Mrs Fraser, The 1929,Jl 21,VIII,1:4
First Mrs Fraser, The 1929,N 17,IX,4:1
Ship, The 1929,N 21,24:7
First Mrs Fraser, The 1929,D 30,16:2
First Mrs Fraser, The 1930,Mr 9,IX,4:3
Lady of Belmont, The 1931,F 1,VIII,3:3
Magnanimous Lover, The 1933,F 1,13:5
John Ferguson 1933,Jl 11,15:7
Anthony and Anna 1934,N 13,22:2
Anthony and Anna 1935,N 9,18:2
Anthony and Anna 1935,D 8,X,5:1
Boyd's Shop 1936,F 21,20:5
Robert's Wife 1937,N 24,20:2
Robert's Wife 1937,D 19,XI,3:7
People of our Class 1938,My 13,16:6
Boyd's Daughter 1940,O 12,20:2
First Mrs Fraser, The 1947,N 6,36:2
Private Enterprise 1947,D 7,II,7:1
Erwin, Frank
Love Call, The 1927,O 25,33:1
Erwin, Grant
Yesterday's Orchids 1934,O 6,20:4
Erwin, Stuart
Mr Sycamore 1942,N 14,13:2
Mr Sycamore 1942,N 29,VIII,1:1
Great to Be Alive! 1950,Mr 24,28:2
Erwin, Ted
Paths of Glory 1935,S 27,24:2
I Gotta Get Out 1947,S 26,27:2
Erwin, Thomas
Catskill Dutch 1924,My 7,18:1
Erwin, Will
High Named Today 1954,D 11,11:2
Esa, Carol
Love's Old Sweet Song 1940,My 3,16:3
Escalante, Elieser
Vida es Sueno, La 1964,Mr 18,49:1
Escamilio
Red Pepper 1922,My 30,8:3
Escande, Maurice
Dans l'Ombre du Harem 1927,My 29,VII,2:7
Bourgeois Gentilhomme, Le 1955,O 26,26:1
Bourgeois Gentilhomme, Le 1955,O 30,II,1:1

Jeu de l'Amour et du Hasard, Le 1955,N 16,42:4
Caprice, Un 1955,N 16,42:4
Escande, Maurice (Director)
Jeu de l'Amour et du Hasard, Le 1955,N 16,42:4
Escariz, Emilina
Show Boat 1966,Jl 20,48:1
Esch, Ursula (Miscellaneous)
Amphitryon 1970,N 18,40:1
Kleinburgerhochzeit, Die 1970,N 25,25:1
Kurve, Die 1970,N 25,25:1
Eschbach, Victor
Henry IV, Part II 1968,Jl 2,33:1
Perfect Party. The 1969,Mr 21,42:1
Esckilsen, Richard
Birds, The 1966,Jl 1,40:1
Escobar (Playwright)
Pibe de Corralon, El 1927,D 23,16:4
Escoffier, Marcel (Costume Designer)
Misanthrope, Le 1957,F 8,19:1
Lady of the Camellias, The 1963,Mr 22,7:1
Escott, T J
Picture of Dorian Gray, The 1963,Ag 29,37:4
Escudero, Vicente
Americana 1932,O 16,IX,11:2
Continental Varieties 1934,O 4,18:3
Continental Varieties 1934,N 15,24:3
Esdale, Charles
Like a King 1921,O 4,10:1
Rosa Machree 1922,Ja 10,15:2
Fedora 1922,F 11,18:1
Dolly Jordan 1922,O 4,26:1
Ashes 1924,O 21,21:2
Quarantine 1924,D 17,19:7
Carolinian, The 1925,N 3,34:2
Right Age to Marry, The 1926,F 16,22:3
Her Cardboard Lover 1927,Mr 22,30:5
Money Lender, The 1928,Ag 28,27:3
Polly 1929,Ja 9,28:3
Whispering Gallery, The 1929,F 12,22:2
Her Friend the King 1929,O 8,34:5
Bellamy Trial, The 1931,Ap 23,28:6
Lean Harvest 1931,O 14,26:3
Peace on Earth 1933,N 30,39:2
Living Dangerously 1935,Ja 14,10:3
American Holiday 1936,F 22,13:3
Mr Jiggins of Jigginstown 1936,D 18,30:2
Esden, Alice
Happy-Go-Lucky 1920,Ag 25,6:1
Eshbach, Harry
Potash and Perlmutter 1935,Ap 6,11:3
Esherick, Mary
Trojan Horse, The 1940,O 31,28:3
Esherick, Ruth (Lighting Director)
Playboy of the Western World, The 1958,My 9,19:2
When I Was a Child 1960,D 9,38:1
Eshley, Norman
Measure for Measure 1967,F 15,37:1
Romeo and Juliet 1967,F 22,18:1
Eshrick, Mary
Arms and the Man 1937,Jl 20,19:3
Eskell, Dick
Vamp, The 1955,N 11,30:1
Esker, Victor
Scarlet Fox, The 1928,Mr 28,31:1
Josef Suss 1930,Ja 21,28:5
Sweet Chariot 1930,O 24,30:2
Come Angel Band 1936,Jl 19,17:1
Farm of Three Echoes 1939,N 29,18:3
Eskow, Jerome (Director)
Of Mice and Men 1958,D 5,38:1
Most Happy Fella, The 1960,Ap 22,25:3
Fly Blackbird 1962,F 6,26:2
Cafe Crown 1964,Ap 18,32:1
Esler, Lemist (Director)
Grey Fox, The 1928,O 23,32:3
Flight 1929,F 19,22:3
Troika 1930,Ap 2,32:6
Esler, Lemist (Playwright)
Grey Fox, The 1928,O 23,32:3
Esmond, Annie
Middle Watch, The 1929,O 17,27:1
Esmond, Carl
Victoria Regina 1937,Jl 11,X,1:7
Lady Maria, The 1947,Ag 5,26:1
Four Winds 1957,S 26,21:2
Esmond, Diane (Costume Designer)
Berenice 1963,O 30,46:1
Esmond, Diane (Scenic Designer)
Berenice 1963,O 30,46:1
Esmond, Elsie
Lancelot and Elaine 1921,S 13,12:1
Ever Green Lady, The 1922,O 12,25:2
Main Line, The 1924,Mr 26,19:4
Undercurrent, The 1925,F 4,18:2
You Can't Beat a Woman 1925,Mr 24,26:5
Book of Charm, The 1925,S 4,26:3
Esmond, H V (Playwright)
House of Ussher, The 1926,Ja 14,18:4
Esmond, Harry
Sweet Adeline 1929,S 4,33:1
Esmond, Jack
Havoc 1924,S 2,22:2

Esmond, Jill
Private Lives 1931,Ja 28,24:1
Green Bay Tree, The 1933,O 21,11:5
Green Bay Tree, The 1933,O 29,IX,1:1
Men in White 1934,Je 29,16:3
Ringmaster, The 1935,Mr 12,24:5
Black Eye, The 1935,O 12,13:5
Morning Star, The 1942,S 15,18:4
Morning Star, The 1942,S 20,VIII,1:1
Esmonde, Diane
Tonight at 12 1928,N 16,28:1
Esmonde, Merceita
First Year, The 1920,O 21,11:2
Esmone, Charlotte
Tell Me More 1925,Ap 14,27:3
Espanol, Teatro (Miscellaneous)
Vida es Sueno, La 1964,Mr 18,49:1
Espe, Andrea
On the Town 1959,F 14,15:1
Esper, William (Miscellaneous)
Another Evening With Harry Stoones 1961,O 23,22:2
Espero, Sidonie
Honey Girl 1920,My 4,9:1
Dead End 1935,O 29,17:2
To Quito and Back 1937,O 7,30:4
Espiau, Marcel (Playwright)
Miroir Qui Fait Rire, Le 1927,My 1,VIII,2:4
Espinosa, Edward Luis
Matty and the Moron and Madonna 1965,Mr 30,53:1
Strong Breed, The 1967,N 10,60:1
Trials of Brother Jero, The 1967,N 10,60:1
Espinosa, Louis
Akokawe 1970,Je 5,21:1
Espinosa, Phyllis
Slave Ship 1969,N 22,46:1
Espinosa, Ralph
Slave Ship 1969,N 22,46:1
Esposito, Charles
Instructions for the Running of Trains, etc on the Erie Railway to Go Into Effect January 1,1862 1970,Ja 7,36:2
Esposito, Terry
Paradise 1931,My 12,29:2
Espri, August
Son, The 1950,Ag 16,24:6
Essen, Viola
New Moon, The 1942,Ag 19,14:2
Hollywood Pinafore 1945,Je 1,20:1
Hollywood Pinafore 1945,Je 17,II,4:5
Along Fifth Avenue 1949,Ja 14,28:2
Esser, Carl
Whisper to Me 1960,N 22,38:6
Alcestis Comes Back 1962,Ap 24,33:1
At Sea 1962,Ap 24,33:1
Stone Tower, The 1962,Ag 24,14:2
Esser, Peter
Before Sundown 1962,Mr 14,43:1
Essex, Harry J (Playwright)
Something for Nothing 1937,D 10,33:5
Essin, Max
S S Glencairn 1929,Ja 10,24:5
Essler, Fred
From Vienna 1939,Je 21,26:2
Essley, Charmine
Love Dreams 1921,O 11,22:2
Esslin, Martin (Playwright)
Baal 1965,My 7,33:2
Esslin, Martin (Translator)
Brecht on Brecht 1962,Ja 14,II,1:1
Essman, Manuel (Scenic Designer)
Singing Jailbirds 1928,D 5,34:4
Turpentine 1936,Je 27,21:6
Processional 1937,O 14,23:1
Processional 1937,O 24,XI,1:1
Androcles and the Lion 1938,D 17,10:5
Coggerers, The 1939,Ja 21,18:4
Mr Banks of Birmingham 1939,Ja 21,18:4
Red Velvet Goat, The 1939,Ja 21,18:4
Estabrook, Dorothy
Kept 1926,S 18,13:3
Up the Line 1926,N 23,26:1
Lady in Love, A 1927,F 22,22:1
Bless You, Sister 1927,D 27,24:5
Este, Evelyn
Dark Hours, The 1932,N 15,24:2
Este, Iolanda d'
Sparviero, Lo 1934,N 12,16:1
Estela
Mexicana 1939,Ap 22,14:4
Mexicana 1939,My 7,X,3:1
Estelle and LeRoy
Variations of 1940 1940,Ja 29,12:1
Esterman, Laura
New York Idea, The 1963,Jl 13,12:2
Time of Your Life, The 1969,N 7,37:1
Carpenters, The 1970,D 22,40:1
Esteve, Rafael (Costume Designer)
Pique-Nique en Campagne 1969,My 1,50:1
Guernica 1969,My 1,50:1
Esteve, Rafael (Scenic Designer)
Guernica 1969,My 1,50:1

Esteve, Rafael (Scenic Designer)—Cont
  Pique-Nique en Campagne 1969,My 1,50:1
Estevez, George (Musical Director)
  Mother Courage and Her Children 1964,My 12,32:2
Estrada, Herbert
  Joan of Arkansas 1925,Ap 5,16:1
Estrada, La Rosa
  Carib Song 1945,S 28,17:2
Estrada, Roy
  Absolutely Freeee 1967,My 25,58:1
Estrange, David L' (Playwright)
  Rat, The 1924,Je 29,VII,1:8
Estreich, Basil (Miscellaneous)
  Wonder World 1964,My 18,32:1
Estremera, Felix
  Vida es Sueno, La 1964,Mr 18,49:1
Estrin, Slava (Translator)
  Fifth Commandment, The 1965,N 15,48:4
Estrow, Herbert
  Partition 1948,O 29,31:2
  Arabian Nights 1954,Je 25,15:2
  Arabian Nights 1955,Je 24,16:1
Estry, Joseph L (Playwright)
  Doctor Social 1948,F 12,29:5
Esty, Robert (Musical Director)
  Lyle 1970,Mr 21,16:2
Eswood, Lynn
  Spring 3100 1928,F 16,14:2
  Ghost Writer, The 1933,Je 20,22:4
Etchepare (M)
  Mauvais Ange, Le 1927,Je 5,VII,2:1
Etcheverry, Alfred
  Crab Apple 1936,Jl 8,14:2
  Key Largo 1939,N 28,30:2
  Delicate Story 1940,D 5,32:2
  My Fair Ladies 1941,Mr 24,12:7
Etcheverry, Michel
  Ecole des Femmes, L'; School for Wives 1951,Mr 19,22:1
Etehli, Edgar
  Love for Love 1925,Ap 1,21:2
Etheridge, Dorothy
  Music in My Heart 1947,O 3,30:2
Etheridge, Eleanor
  Gay Divorce 1932,N 30,23:4
Etheridge, H P
  Monkey's Paw, The 1922,D 30,13:4
Etheridge, Helen
  Merry Widow, The 1929,D 3,29:1
  Babes in Toyland 1929,D 24,15:3
Etheridge, Jeffrey
  Pirate, The 1942,N 26,39:2
Etherton, Frank
  Men to the Sea 1944,O 4,25:2
Ethier, Alphonz
  Broken Wing, The 1920,N 30,14:1
  Dolly Jordan 1922,O 4,26:1
  Jest, The 1926,F 5,22:2
  Jest, The 1926,F 14,VIII,1:1
Ethridge, Vic
  You Said It 1931,Ja 20,21:3
Etienne, H
  Cherry Orchard, The 1944,Ja 26,22:1
Etlinger, Anne
  Eternal Sabbath 1963,O 19,17:2
Eton, Ewing
  Vaudeville (Palace) 1930,Mr 3,18:5
Ettel, Friedrich
  General Percy Gruendet ein Koenigreich 1932,N 6,IX,3:1
Etter, J Wesley (Lyricist)
  Kid Himself, The 1925,D 25,23:2
Etter, J Wesley (Playwright)
  Kid Himself, The 1925,D 25,23:2
Etting, Ruth
  Ziegfeld Follies 1927,Ag 17,27:3
  Whoopee 1928,D 5,34:3
  Nine Fifteen Revue, The 1930,F 12,26:2
  Simple Simon 1930,F 19,22:1
  Vaudeville (Palace) 1930,Jl 7,22:2
  Ziegfeld Follies 1931,Jl 2,30:5
  Transatlantic Rhythm 1936,O 2,16:3
Ettinger, Georgette
  Vaudeville (Palace) 1926,Ap 13,28:3
Ettlinger, Karl
  Three Sisters, The 1927,Mr 13,VII,2:4
Ettlinger, Norman
  Billy Budd 1951,F 12,18:3
Ettore, Matthew
  Good Times 1920,Ag 10,10:1
Eubank, Eloise
  This Is Today 1935,Jl 30,17:2
Eubonks, Dennis (Miscellaneous)
  Walk in Dark Places, A 1966,Ja 28,21:1
  Better Luck Next Time 1966,Ja 28,21:1
Eula, Joe (Scenic Designer)
  Black Nativity 1961,D 12,54:2
Eulo, Ken
  Neighbors 1966,N 15,51:4
  March March, The 1966,N 15,51:4
Eunson, Dale (Original Author)
  Loco 1946,O 17,29:2
Eunson, Dale (Playwright)
  Guest in the House 1942,F 25,25:2

Public Relations 1944,Ap 7,23:3
  Loco 1946,O 17,29:2
Eura, Joe (Costume Designer)
  Private Lives 1969,D 5,52:1
Eure, Ella
  Trumpets of the Lord 1969,Ap 30,37:1
Euringer, Alfred
  Coriolanus 1961,Je 21,31:2
  Henry VIII 1961,Je 22,22:1
Euringer, Fred
  Timon of Athens 1963,Jl 31,19:2
Euringer, J A
  Twelfth Night 1957,Jl 4,16:4
Euringer, Richard (Playwright)
  Deutsche Passion 1933 1934,S 16,X,1:6
Euripides (Original Author)
  Medea 1948,S 30,32:4
  Cretan Woman, The 1954,S 5,II,1:1
  Medea 1955,Je 16,35:4
  Electra 1962,Mr 22,42:1
  Medea 1964,S 1,31:1
  Medea 1965,N 29,46:1
  Dionysus in 69 1968,Je 16,II,1:1
  Dionysus in 69 1968,N 19,52:1
Euripides (Playwright)
  Iphigenie in Tauris 1915,Je 1,15:5
  Medea 1920,Mr 23,12:2
  Iphigenia in Aulis 1921,Ap 8,18:2
  Iphigenia in Aulis 1921,Ap 17,VI,1:1
  Trojan Women, The 1923,My 27,10:2
  Trojan Women, The 1923,N 8,17:6
  Hecuba 1926,My 31,19:1
  Medea 1926,D 19,VII,3:3
  Alcestis 1927,My 22,II,8:4
  Iphigenia 1931,Ja 6,24:1
  Hippolytus 1935,F 12,25:4
  Hippolytus 1935,Je 15,20:4
  Trojan Women, The 1941,Ap 9,32:5
  Medea 1941,Ag 3,IX,2:2
  Medea 1947,O 21,27:2
  Medea 1947,O 26,II,1:1
  Medea 1951,S 14,22:5
  Trojan Women, The 1957,Mr 19,42:7
  Electra 1958,My 10,17:7
  Elsa Lanchester-Herself 1961,F 6,28:1
  Bacchae, The 1962,Je 19,30:1
  Trojan Women, The 1963,D 24,7:6
  Trojan Women, The 1965,Mr 18,25:1
  Bacchants, The 1967,F 25,14:1
  Trojan Women, The 1967,Ag 27,II,4:8
  Iphigenia in Aulis 1967,D 3,II,1:1
  Orestes 1968,F 17,32:5
  Iphigenia in Aulis 1968,Ap 6,43:1
  Iphigenia in Aulis 1968,N 13,40:1
  Hippolytus 1968,N 20,38:3
  Bacchae, The 1969,Mr 15,24:1
  Bacchae, The 1969,Mr 23,II,11:1
Europe, Rudolph
  Legal Murder 1934,F 16,16:2
European Ballet Twelve
  Ice Capades 1956,S 13,41:2
Eury, Peggy F
  Lady of the Camellias, The 1963,Mr 22,7:1
Eustace, Jennie A
  Floriani's Wife 1923,O 1,10:1
  Blue Bird, The 1923,D 26,13:3
  Sweet Seventeen 1924,Mr 18,24:2
  Depths, The 1925,Ja 28,15:3
  Edgar Allan Poe 1925,O 6,31:1
  Morals 1925,D 1,22:2
  Dope 1926,Ja 4,16:3
  Tragic 18 1926,O 11,18:2
  Scarlet Lily, The 1927,Ja 31,12:3
  One for All 1927,My 14,25:5
  Sherlock Holmes 1928,F 21,18:4
  Judas 1929,Ja 25,20:4
  Mrs Bumpstead-Leigh 1929,Ap 2,28:3
Eustein, Abe (Composer)
  Eretz Israel 1930,N 7,32:3
Euster, Roger (Producer)
  Evening With the Times Square Two, An 1967,My 21,83:6
Eustis, Eleanor (Scenic Designer)
  Paolo and Francesca 1929,Ap 2,28:2
Eustis, Elizabeth
  Angel Street 1941,D 6,15:2
  Second Best Bed 1946,Je 4,20:2
  Hippolytus 1948,N 22,25:5
  Once an Actor 1950,Ag 1,19:8
  Orpheus Descending 1957,Mr 22,28:1
Eustrel, Antony
  Much Ado About Nothing 1952,My 2,20:1
Eustrel, Antony (Director)
  Much Ado About Nothing 1952,My 2,20:1
Evan, Harvey
  Boy Friend, The 1970,Ap 26,II,5:7
Evane, Kathleen
  Lido Girl, The 1928,Ag 24,23:2
Evangelidou, Agapi (Choreographer)
  Oedipus Tyrannus 1952,N 25,35:2
Evanko, Ed
  Canterbury Tales; Merchant's Tale, The 1969,F 4,34:1

Evanko, Ed—Cont
  Canterbury Tales; Steward's Tale, The 1969,F 4,34:1
  Canterbury Tales; Miller's Tale, The 1969,F 4,34:1
  Canterbury Tales; Pilgrims, The 1969,F 4,34:1
Evanof, Sonia
  It Is to Laugh 1927,D 27,24:2
Evans, Alfred (Miscellaneous)
  Oklahoma! 1958,Mr 8,15:2
Evans, Alfred (Musical Director)
  Oklahoma! 1958,Mr 8,15:2
Evans, Alice
  I'm Solomon 1968,Ap 24,51:1
Evans, Art
  Amen Corner, The 1965,Ap 16,35:1
  Amen Corner, The 1965,Ap 25,II,1:2
Evans, Barbara
  Mis-Guided Tour 1959,O 13,44:7
Evans, Barry
  Chips With Everything 1963,O 2,49:1
Evans, Beverly
  Gondoliers, The 1961,Ja 26,33:2
  Gondoliers, The 1963,Je 5,33:2
  Help! Help! the Globolinks 1970,D 24,10:2
Evans, Bobby
  Lew Leslie's Blackbirds of 1939 1939,F 13,12:2
  Hi Yank 1944,Ap 8,14:2
Evans, Bonnie
  Kismet 1953,D 4,2:4
Evans, Brandon
  Made in America 1925,O 15,27:2
  Proud Woman, A 1926,N 16,24:1
  Set a Thief 1927,F 22,22:1
  Ink 1927,N 2,24:2
  We Never Learn 1928,Ja 24,26:1
  Uncle Tom's Cabin 1933,O 10,24:3
Evans, Bruce
  Servant in the House, The 1925,Ap 8,24:2
  Joker, The 1925,N 17,29:1
  Mirrors 1928,Ja 19,17:1
  March Hares 1928,Ap 3,32:6
  These Days 1928,N 13,36:2
  Tomorrow 1928,D 29,20:2
  Family Affairs 1929,D 11,34:6
  Come Easy 1933,Ag 30,22:5
  Crime Marches on 1935,O 24,19:1
  Black Limelight 1936,N 10,31:1
  Knights of Song 1938,O 18,29:2
  Glorious Morning 1938,N 28,10:3
  Mrs Kimball Presents 1944,Mr 1,17:3
  Laffing Room Only 1944,D 25,15:4
  Sound of Hunting, A 1945,N 21,16:6
  One Bright Day 1952,Mr 20,37:2
  Sixth Finger in a Five Finger Glove 1956,O 9,31:4
Evans, Candasa
  Magistrate, The 1959,My 14,30:6
Evans, Celia
  Morning Star 1940,Ap 17,26:4
Evans, Charles
  Ballyhoo 1930,D 23,24:1
Evans, Charles (Costume Designer)
  Me and Thee 1965,D 8,58:4
Evans, Charles (Lighting Director)
  Journey to the Day 1963,N 12,49:1
Evans, Charles (Scenic Designer)
  Carmen Jones 1951,S 22,8:6
  Call Me by My Rightful Name 1961,F 1,31:1
  This Side of Paradise 1962,F 22,19:6
  Journey to the Day 1963,N 12,49:1
  Harry, Noon and Night 1965,My 6,44:1
  Me and Thee 1965,D 8,58:4
Evans, Claire (Miscellaneous)
  Comedy of Good and Evil, A 1938,Ap 8,16:3
Evans, Claire Louise
  As the Girls Go 1948,N 15,21:2
Evans, Clarence
  White Man 1936,O 19,22:4
Evans, Clifford
  Distaff Side, The 1933,S 24,X,1:6
  Distaff Side, The 1934,S 26,17:2
  Hamlet 1936,O 20,31:3
  Hamlet 1936,N 11,54:2
  Ghosts 1937,N 28,XI,2:1
Evans, Constance
  Will Morrissey's Newcomers 1923,Ag 9,16:2
Evans, Dan
  I Gotta Get Out 1947,S 26,27:2
Evans, David
  30 Days Hath September 1938,O 1,10:5
  Lady's Not for Burning, The 1950,N 9,42:2
  Come Summer 1969,Mr 19,43:1
Evans, Dillon
  School for Scandal, The 1963,Ja 26,5:2
  Hamlet 1964,Ap 10,30:1
  Giants' Dance, The 1964,N 17,48:2
  Ivanov 1966,My 4,50:1
  Rondelay 1969,N 6,55:1
  Little Boxes; Trevor 1969,D 4,71:2
Evans, Dillon (Director)
  Doctor's Dilemma, The 1969,Je 24,37:1
Evans, Dina Rees (Miscellaneous)
  Midsummer Night's Dream, A 1950,Je 22,33:2
Evans, Don (Musical Director)
  Signs Along the Cynic Route 1961,D 15,49:5

Evans, Edith
Tiger Cats 1924,Ag 17,VII,1:8
Beaux' Stratagem, The 1927,F 13,VII,2:1
Untitled-Play 1927,O 2,II,7:2
Lady-in-Law, The 1927,O 23,VIII,4:1
Vaudeville (Palace) 1928,D 31,9:3
Lady With a Lamp, The 1929,Ja 27,IX,2:1
Humours of the Court, The 1930,Ja 26,VIII,1:8
Plus ca Change 1930,F 26,22:3
Vaudeville (Palace) 1930,Mr 31,24:2
Delilah 1930,O 12,VIII,1:8
O H M S 1931,Mr 29,VIII,2:1
Lady With a Lamp, The 1931,N 20,27:2
Romeo and Juliet 1932,F 28,VIII,2:4
Evensong 1932,Jl 1,19:6
Evensong 1932,Jl 24,IX,2:1
Evensong 1933,F 1,13:4
Late Christopher Bean, The 1933,My 17,15:2
Tattle Tales 1933,Je 2,22:6
Viceroy Sarah 1934,Je 24,IX,1:4
Romeo and Juliet 1934,D 4,23:2
Romeo and Juliet 1934,D 21,30:3
Romeo and Juliet 1934,D 30,IX,1:1
Old Ladies, The 1935,Ap 4,21:2
Romeo and Juliet 1935,O 18,27:5
Romeo and Juliet 1935,N 17,IX,2:4
Romeo and Juliet 1935,D 29,IX,1:3
Seagull, The 1936,My 21,19:2
Seagull, The 1936,Je 21,IX,1:5
Seagull, The 1936,Ag 30,IX,1:1
Country Wife, The 1936,O 7,32:3
Country Wife, The 1936,O 25,X,2:4
Witch of Edmonton, The 1937,Ja 3,X,3:6
As You Like It 1937,Ja 3,X,3:6
Taming of the Shrew, The 1937,Ap 11,XI,2:1
Robert's Wife 1937,N 24,20:2
Robert's Wife 1937,D 19,XI,3:7
Importance of Being Earnest, The 1939,S 17,X,2:3
Cousin Muriel 1940,Mr 17,X,1:6
Old Acquaintance 1941,D 28,IX,2:3
Crime and Punishment 1946,Jl 21,II,1:5
Way of the World, The 1948,N 7,II,3:1
Daphne Laureola 1950,S 19,38:6
Daphne Laureola 1950,S 24,II,1:1
Waters of the Moon 1951,My 6,II,3:7
Consul, The 1952,O 30,41:2
Waters of the Moon 1953,Ap 2,34:3
Dark Is Light Enough, The 1954,My 1,12:4
Chalk Garden, The 1956,Ap 12,26:8
Chalk Garden, The 1956,My 13,II,3:1
All's Well That Ends Well 1959,Ap 22,30:3
Coriolanus 1959,Jl 8,24:5
Richard III 1961,My 25,32:3
Romeo and Juliet 1961,Ag 16,36:3
Gentle Jack 1963,N 29,50:7
Homage to Shakespeare 1964,Mr 16,36:2
Chinese Prime Minister, The 1965,My 21,21:1

Evans, Edith (Producer)
Untitled-Play 1927,O 2,II,7:2
Lady-in-Law, The 1927,O 23,VIII,4:1
Delilah 1930,O 12,VIII,1:8

Evans, Edwin
Bootleggers, The 1922,N 28,24:1
Slightly Delirious 1935,Ja 1,25:3

Evans, Edwin (Musical Director)
Joan of Arkansas 1925,Ap 5,16:1

Evans, Eleanor (Director)
H M S Pinafore 1951,F 6,24:2

Evans, Eleanor Vishno
Hippolytus 1935,Je 15,20:4

Evans, Elizabeth
Revolt of the Beavers, The 1937,My 21,19:2

Evans, Ellen
Tender Trap, The 1961,Ag 26,15:1

Evans, Ellwin
Johnny 2X4 1942,Mr 17,24:6

Evans, Estelle
Our Lan' 1947,Ap 19,11:2
Our Lan' 1947,S 29,16:5
Take a Giant Step 1953,O 4,II,1:1
Who's Got His Own 1966,O 13,52:1
Who's Got His Own 1967,O 14,13:3
Clara's Ole Man 1968,Mr 9,23:2
Son, Come Home, A 1968,Mr 9,23:2

Evans, Evans
Coggerers, The 1939,Ja 21,18:4
Love for Love 1940,Je 4,19:5
Cock-A-Doodle Dandy 1955,N 4,26:5
Dark at the Top of the Stairs, The 1957,D 6,38:1
Dark at the Top of the Stairs, The 1957,D 15,II,3:1
Distant Bell, A 1960,Ja 14,29:1
49th Cousin, The 1960,O 28,22:1

Evans, Frank (Miscellaneous)
Pastry Shop, The 1970,Je 12,28:1
Young Among Themselves, The 1970,Je 12,28:1

Evans, Frieda (Costume Designer)
I Want You 1961,S 15,29:1
Blind Angel, The 1965,Ap 2,26:1
Bitch of Waverly Place, The 1965,Ap 2,26:1

Evans, G Douglas
Connecticut Yankee, A 1927,N 4,24:2

Evans, George
Last Waltz, The 1921,My 11,20:3

Evans, Geraldine
Earth 1927,Mr 10,23:1

Evans, Gloria
Long Watch, The 1952,Mr 21,19:5

Evans, Greek
Student Prince, The 1924,D 3,25:3
Song of the Flame 1925,D 31,10:2
Yours Truly 1927,Ja 26,16:5
Enchanted Isle 1927,S 20,33:2
Take the Air 1927,N 23,28:2
Music in May 1929,Ap 2,29:1
Robin Hood 1929,N 20,26:5
Serenade, The 1930,Mr 5,26:7
East Wind 1931,O 28,19:1
Robin Hood 1935,Jl 15,20:6

Evans, Griff
I Gotta Get Out 1947,S 26,27:2
Son, The 1950,Ag 16,24:6
Ballad of the Sad Cafe, The 1963,O 31,27:1
This Here Nice Place 1966,N 2,35:2

Evans, Gwyllum
Carousel 1965,Ag 11,39:1
Blancs, Les 1970,N 16,48:4

Evans, Harold
God Loves Us 1926,O 20,22:2

Evans, Harry
Cross My Heart 1928,S 18,32:7

Evans, Harry (Playwright)
Illustrators' Show, The 1936,Ja 23,25:3

Evans, Harvey
Anyone Can Whistle 1964,Ap 6,36:1
George M! 1968,Ap 11,48:1
Our Town 1969,N 28,50:1
Boy Friend, The 1970,Ap 15,54:1

Evans, Helena Phillips (Lyricist)
Happy-Go-Lucky 1926,O 1,27:2

Evans, Helena Phillips (Playwright)
Happy-Go-Lucky 1926,O 1,27:2

Evans, Herbert
Varying Shore, The 1921,D 6,24:1
Policy Kings 1938,D 31,6:2

Evans, Hugh
Good as Gold 1957,Mr 8,22:2

Evans, J W (Miscellaneous)
Philanderer, The 1958,My 13,26:2

Evans, Jack
Scarlet Coat, The 1924,D 24,11:1
Tartuffe 1957,O 9,39:1

Evans, James
Vaudeville (Palace) 1932,Je 13,19:7

Evans, James & Co
Virginia 1937,S 3,13:2

Evans, Jane
Outrageous Mrs Palmer, The 1920,O 13,18:1
Evensong 1933,F 1,13:4
Jubilee 1935,O 14,20:1

Evans, Jessie
Love for Love 1947,My 27,30:2
Lily of Little India, A 1966,Ja 22,17:2
Canterbury Tales 1968,S 7,23:3
Cannibal Crackers 1969,N 25,52:2

Evans, John
Trelawney of the 'Wells' 1925,Je 2,16:2

Evans, John Wynn
'Tis Pity She's a Whore 1958,D 6,21:1
Candida 1962,N 12,35:5

Evans, Johnny
Mike Downstairs 1968,Ap 19,35:1
Jimmy Shine 1968,D 6,52:1

Evans, Jonathan
Nobody's Child 1956,Ag 23,25:2

Evans, Joseph
Sonny 1921,Ag 17,12:2

Evans, Josephine
Simon Called Peter 1924,N 11,20:2
Great Gatsby, The 1926,F 3,22:1
Carnival 1929,Ap 25,32:5
Chinese O'Neill 1929,My 23,27:1
Ritzy 1930,F 11,30:4
Frankie and Johnny 1930,S 26,16:5
Hobo 1931,F 12,24:4
Sailor, Beware! 1933,S 29,24:4
Flying Gerardos, The 1940,D 30,21:4

Evans, Julius
Too True to Be Good 1932,Mr 1,19:2
Too True to Be Good 1932,Ap 5,27:5

Evans, Julius (Director)
Dream Child 1934,S 28,26:2
Searching for the Sun 1936,F 20,22:6
Mr Shaddy 1936,Jl 15,14:4
Infernal Machine, The 1937,D 13,22:7

Evans, Kathleen
Sign of the Leopard 1928,D 12,34:4

Evans, Lillian
Galileo 1968,D 1,88:4

Evans, Lloyd (Costume Designer)
Color of Darkness: An Evening in the World of James Purdy; Sermon 1963,O 1,34:1
Color of Darkness: An Evening in the World of James Purdy; Everything Under the Sun 1963,O 1,34:1
Color of Darkness: An Evening in the World of James Purdy; Encore 1963,O 1,34:1

Evans, Lloyd (Costume Designer)—Cont
Color of Darkness: An Evening in the World of James Purdy; Don't Call Me By My Right Name 1963,O 1,34:1
Color of Darkness: An Evening in the World of James Purdy; Cracks 1963,O 1,24:1
Color of Darkness: An Evening in the World of James Purdy; You Reach for Your Hat 1963,O 1,34:1

Evans, Lloyd (Scenic Designer)
Color of Darkness: An Evening in the World of James Purdy; Everything Under the Sun 1963,O 1,34:1
Color of Darkness: An Evening in the World of James Purdy; You Reach for Your Hat 1963,O 1,34:1
Color of Darkness: An Evening in the World of James Purdy; Encore 1963,O 1,34:1
Color of Darkness: An Evening in the World of James Purdy; Don't Call Me By My Right Name 1963,O 1,34:1
Color of Darkness: An Evening in the World of James Purdy; Cracks 1963,O 1,24:1
Color of Darkness: An Evening in the World of James Purdy; Sermon 1963,O 1,34:1
Pirates of Penzance, The 1968,Ap 26,32:1

Evans, Lonnie (Director)
Curley McDimple 1967,N 23,59:2

Evans, Louise (Costume Designer)
2 for Fun; Anniversary, The 1955,My 26,34:1
2 for Fun; Switch in Time, A 1955,My 26,34:1

Evans, Lydia (Scenic Designer)
Nine Till Six 1936,Mr 14,10:3

Evans, Lyle
Desert Song, The 1926,D 1,24:2
New Moon, The 1928,S 20,33:1
Melody 1933,F 15,17:4
Spread It Abroad 1936,Ap 2,29:5

Evans, Madge
Daisy Mayme 1926,O 26,24:2
Marquise, The 1927,N 15,26:4
Our Betters 1928,F 21,18:2
Dread 1929,O 27,IX,2:1
Philip Goes Forth 1931,Ja 13,35:4
Here Come the Clowns 1938,D 8,36:2
Patriots, The 1943,Ja 30,11:2

Evans, Margie
Artists and Models 1927,N 16,28:2
Let's Face It 1941,O 30,26:2

Evans, Martha
Our Lan' 1947,Ap 19,11:2
Our Lan' 1947,S 29,16:5

Evans, Maurice
Journey's End 1929,Jl 14,IX,5:1
To See Ourselves 1930,D 28,VIII,2:6
Dark Hester 1931,My 17,VIII,1:3
Avalanche 1932,F 14,VIII,1:8
Soldier and the Gentlewoman, The 1933,My 7,IX,1:4
Richard II 1934,N 4,IX,3:1
Romeo and Juliet 1935,D 24,10:2
Saint Joan 1936,Mr 10,27:4
St Helena 1936,S 29,35:1
St Helena 1936,O 7,32:1
St Helena 1936,O 11,X,1:1
Richard II 1937,F 6,14:2
Richard II 1937,F 14,X,1:1
Richard II 1937,S 16,28:2
Richard II 1937,S 26,XI,1:1
Hamlet 1938,O 13,28:1
Hamlet 1938,O 30,IX,1:1
Henry IV, Part I 1939,Ja 31,17:2
Henry IV 1939,F 5,IX,1:1
Hamlet 1939,D 5,35:2
Hamlet 1939,D 10,X,3:1
Richard II 1940,Ap 2,31:2
Twelfth Night 1940,O 18,26:7
Twelfth Night 1940,O 27,IX,1:5
Twelfth Night 1940,N 20,26:3
Twelfth Night 1940,N 24,IX,1:1
Macbeth 1941,N 12,30:2
Macbeth 1941,N 23,IX,1:1
Macbeth 1942,Je 3,26:4
Hamlet 1945,D 14,25:2
Hamlet 1945,D 23,II,3:1
Hamlet 1946,Je 4,18:4
Man and Superman 1947,O 9,31:2
Man and Superman 1947,O 19,II,1:1
Man and Superman 1949,My 17,28:6
Harlequinade 1949,O 13,32:2
Browning Version, The 1949,O 13,32:2
Harlequinade 1949,O 23,II,1:1
Browning Version, The 1949,O 23,II,1:1
Devil's Disciple, The 1950,Ja 26,23:2
Devil's Disciple, The 1950,F 5,II,1:1
Richard II 1951,Ja 25,21:2
Wild Duck, The 1951,D 27,17:1
Dial 'M' for Murder 1952,O 14,41:5
Dial 'M' for Murder 1952,O 30,41:2
Dial 'M' for Murder 1952,N 30,II,1:1
Dial 'M' for Murder 1953,N 8,II,1:1
Apple Cart, The 1956,O 19,23:1
Apple Cart, The 1956,O 28,II,1:1
Heartbreak House 1959,O 19,37:1

Evans, Maurice—Cont

Heartbreak House 1959,O 25,II,1:1
Tenderloin 1960,O 18,47:2
Tenderloin 1960,O 30,II,1:1
Aspern Papers, The 1962,F 8,26:1
Aspern Papers, The 1962,F 18,II,1:1
Shakespeare Revisited 1962,Jl 19,19:2

Evans, Maurice (Director)

Man and Superman 1947,O 9,31:2
Man and Superman 1947,O 19,II,1:1
Man and Superman 1949,My 17,28:6

Evans, Maurice (Miscellaneous)

Linden Tree, The 1948,Mr 3,28:2
Corn Is Green, The 1950,Ja 12,33:2
Devil's Disciple, The 1950,Ja 26,23:2
Heiress, The 1950,F 9,34:2
Captain Brassbound's Conversion 1950,D 28,21:1
Royal Family, The 1951,Ja 11,28:2
Richard II 1951,Ja 25,21:2
Taming of the Shrew, The 1951,Ap 26,35:2
Dream Girl 1951,My 10,39:1
Idiot's Delight 1951,My 24,46:3

Evans, Maurice (Producer)

Hamlet 1938,O 13,28:1
Henry IV, Part I 1939,Ja 31,17:2
Hamlet 1939,D 5,35:2
Richard II 1940,Ap 2,31:2
Macbeth 1941,N 12,30:2
Macbeth 1942,Je 3,26:4
Hamlet 1945,D 23,II,3:1
Man and Superman 1947,O 9,31:2
Man and Superman 1949,My 17,28:6
Harlequinade 1949,O 13,32:2
Browning Version, The 1949,O 13,32:2
Teahouse of the August Moon, The 1953,O 16,32:1
No Time for Sergeants 1955,O 21,32:2
Apple Cart, The 1956,O 28,II,1:1
Heartbreak House 1959,O 19,37:1

Evans, Max (Miscellaneous)

Boys From Syracuse, The 1963,Ap 16,31:1

Evans, Michael

White Eagle, The 1927,D 27,24:4
Ring Around the Moon 1950,N 24,30:1
Gigi 1951,N 26,20:4
River Line, The 1957,Ja 3,29:2

Evans, Michele

Kismet 1965,Je 23,45:1
Those That Play the Clowns 1966,N 25,48:1

Evans, Monica

Odd Couple, The 1965,Mr 11,36:1
Flip Side, The 1968,O 11,36:1

Evans, Morley

Sleepy Hollow 1948,Je 4,26:3

Evans, Nancy

Hotel Alimony 1934,Ja 30,16:2
Come What May 1934,My 16,23:4
Potash and Perlmutter 1935,Ap 6,11:3
All Editions 1936,D 23,17:2
Popsy 1941,F 11,26:2

Evans, Neal

Anything Goes 1934,N 22,26:1

Evans, Neil

Lady in Ermine, The 1922,O 3,22:2

Evans, Nell

Pirates of Penzance, The 1966,My 24,54:1
H M S Pinafore 1966,Je 8,41:2

Evans, Nina

Murder in the Cathedral 1938,F 17,16:2

Evans, Norman

Vaudeville (Palace) 1949,My 20,32:4

Evans, Ray (Composer)

Oh Captain! 1958,F 5,21:2
Let It Ride 1961,O 13,27:4

Evans, Ray (Lyricist)

Oh Captain! 1958,F 5,21:2
Let It Ride 1961,O 13,27:4

Evans, Rex

Threepenny Opera, The 1933,Ap 14,22:4
Lady Windermere's Fan 1946,O 15,29:2
My Romance 1948,O 20,38:5
Gentlemen Prefer Blondes 1949,D 9,35:3

Evans, Reynolds

Jolly Roger, The 1923,Ag 31,10:4
Cyrano de Bergerac 1923,N 2,14:1
Othello 1925,Ja 12,11:1
Hamlet 1925,O 12,19:2
Merchant of Venice, The 1925,D 28,12:1
Cyrano de Bergerac 1926,F 19,18:1
Joan of Arc 1926,Ap 24,21:2
Henry V 1928,Mr 16,26:2
Grey Fox, The 1928,O 23,32:3
Troilus and Cressida 1932,Je 7,22:3
Cyrano de Bergerac 1932,D 27,11:2
Romeo and Juliet 1934,D 21,30:3
Romeo and Juliet 1934,D 30,IX,1:1
Barretts of Wimpole Street, The 1935,F 26,16:2
Romeo and Juliet 1935,D 24,10:2
Richard II 1937,F 6,14:2
Richard II 1937,S 16,28:2
Hamlet 1938,O 13,28:1
Henry IV, Part I 1939,Ja 31,17:2
I Know What I Like 1939,N 25,13:5
Out of the Frying Pan 1941,F 12,24:2
Elizabeth the Queen 1941,O 17,27:2

What Big Ears! 1942,Ap 21,18:5
Strings, My Lord, Are False, The 1942,My 20,24:2
Doughgirls, The 1942,D 31,19:2
Late George Apley, The 1944,O 20,16:4
Late George Apley, The 1944,N 22,26:2
Late George Apley, The 1944,D 3,II,1:1
Lovely Me 1946,D 26,30:4
Metropole 1949,D 7,43:2
Richard II 1951,Ja 25,21:2
Taming of the Shrew, The 1951,Ap 26,35:2
Fancy Meeting You Again 1952,Ja 15,23:2
Solid Gold Cadillac, The 1953,N 6,24:2
Eugenia 1957,Ja 31,20:1
Compulsion 1957,O 25,21:1
First Love 1961,D 26,20:2
Lord Pengo 1962,N 20,41:2
Deputy, The 1964,F 27,26:1

Evans, Richard (Miscellaneous)

Maria Golovin 1958,N 6,43:1
Caligula 1960,F 17,31:1
As You Like It 1961,Je 17,13:2
Macbeth 1961,Je 19,31:1
Family Affair, A 1962,Ja 29,17:1
Riot Act, The 1963,Mr 9,5:2
Abraham Cochrane 1964,F 18,26:1
Funny Girl 1964,Mr 27,15:1

Evans, Robert Rees

All the King's Men 1963,Jl 12,12:1

Evans, Ross (Playwright)

Coast of Illyria, The 1949,Ap 5,37:4
Coast of Illyria, The 1949,Ap 13,39:2

Evans, Samuel

Drunkard, The; Fallen Saved, The 1929,D 31,14:6

Evans, Stephen (Miscellaneous)

Vagabond King, The 1961,N 24,36:1
Gondoliers, The 1961,D 8,44:1

Evans, Sticks

Carmen Jones 1959,Ag 18,25:1

Evans, Suzannah

Hair 1967,O 30,55:1

Evans, Sylvan

Vie Parisienne, La 1945,Ja 13,14:5

Evans, Wilbur

Merry Widow, The 1942,Jl 16,22:1
New Moon, The 1942,Ag 19,14:2
Mexican Hayride 1944,Ja 29,9:6
Mexican Hayride 1944,F 6,II,1:1
Up in Central Park 1945,Ja 29,17:2
South Pacific 1951,N 2,19:1
South Pacific 1951,N 11,II,3:1
By the Beautiful Sea 1954,Ap 9,20:1

Evans, Will (Playwright)

Tons of Money 1922,My 21,VI,1:6

Evans, William A

Sweeney Todd 1924,Jl 19,10:4
Bombasters Furioso 1924,Jl 19,10:4
Bells, The 1926,Ap 14,20:3
Constant Nymph, The 1926,D 10,31:1
Skull, The 1928,Ap 24,28:3
Waterloo Bridge 1930,Ja 7,29:2
Crucible 1933,S 5,22:4

Evans Four, The

Elliott Murphy's Aquashow 1956,Je 20,26:2

Evarts, William

Time 1923,N 27,23:3

Eveling, Stanley (Playwright)

Strange Case of Martin Richter, The 1968,N 6,34:2
Lunatic the Secret Sportsman and the Woman
    Next 1968,D 5,58:4
Jakey Fat Boy 1970,Ap 6,46:1
Dear Janet Rosenberg, Dear Mr Kooning
    1970,Ap 6,46:1
Dear Janet Rosenberg, Dear Mr Kooning
    1970,Ap 26,II,5:7

Evelyn, Fay

Florodora 1920,Ap 6,18:1
Afgar 1920,N 9,13:2
Orange Blossoms 1922,S 20,18:1

Evelyn, John

Bitter Sweet 1929,O 27,IX,2:1
Bitter Sweet 1929,N 6,30:2

Evelyn, Judith

Angel Street 1941,D 6,15:2
Rich Full Life, The 1945,N 10,9:2
Craig's Wife 1947,F 13,35:2
Craig's Wife 1947,Mr 30,II,1:1
Ivy Green, The 1949,Ap 6,37:2
Getting Married 1950,Je 14,41:2
Shrike, The 1952,Ja 16,20:2
Shrike, The 1952,Ja 27,II,1:1
Shrike, The 1953,N 26,51:2
Sea Gull, The 1954,My 12,38:1
Sea Gull, The 1954,My 23,II,1:1
Electra 1959,F 14,15:1

Even, Jean

Fig Leaves Are Falling, The 1969,Ja 3,19:1

Evennett, Wallace

Good Companions, The 1931,O 2,31:1
They Came by Night 1937,Jl 25,X,1:3

Evensen, Maren

Paolo and Francesca 1929,Ap 2,28:2

Evensen, Marion

Antony and Cleopatra 1924,F 20,22:1

Evensen, Marion—Cont

Depths, The 1925,Ja 28,15:3
Easy Virtue 1925,D 8,28:2
Behold the Bridegroom 1927,D 27,24:1
Jealous Moon, The 1928,N 21,32:2
Thousand Summers, A 1932,My 25,23:4
Sophisticrats, The 1933,F 14,19:5
Aiglon, L' 1934,N 5,22:2
Hedda Gabler 1934,D 4,22:5
Love for Love 1936,Je 30,15:4
Mistress of the Inn, The 1937,Je 22,26:3
Madame Capet 1938,O 26,26:2
Family, The 1943,Mr 31,22:4
Henry VIII 1946,N 7,42:2
John Gabriel Borkman 1946,N 13,33:2
Androcles and the Lion 1946,D 20,29:2
Hedda Gabler 1948,F 25,27:2

Everest, Barbara

Viceroy Sarah 1935,F 13,27:4
Viceroy Sarah 1935,Mr 10,VIII,2:1
Flora 1935,O 30,17:4
Anne of England 1941,O 8,26:2
Sheppey 1944,Ap 19,27:2
Linden Tree, The 1948,Mr 3,28:2

Everett, Clara

Mr Moneypenny 1928,O 17,26:2

Everett, Cleon

Thomas Paine 1930,Mr 21,30:7

Everett, Durwood

Nobody's Child 1956,Ag 23,25:2

Everett, Elise

What Next 1920,Ja 27,7:2

Everett, Ethel

Sunrise at Campobello 1958,Ja 31,25:1

Everett, Frances

Swing It 1937,Jl 23,17:2

Everett, Michael

God Strikes Back 1943,F 27,11:2
As You Like It 1950,Ja 27,27:2

Everett, Richard

Hamlet 1969,My 2,38:1

Everett, Sophie

Nightingale, The 1927,Ja 4,20:4

Everett, Stephen

Magistrate, The 1959,My 14,30:6

Everett, Tanya

Fiddler on the Roof 1964,S 23,56:2

Everett, Timmy

Livin' the Life 1957,Ap 29,20:1
Dark at the Top of the Stairs, The 1957,D 6,38:1
Dark at the Top of the Stairs, The 1957,D 15,II,3:1
Cold Wind and the Warm, The 1958,D 9,55:1
Cold Wind and the Warm, The 1959,Ja 18,II,1:1
Marathon '33 1963,D 23,20:1

Everett, Timmy (Director)

And I Met a Man 1970,Ap 11,20:3

Everett, Timmy (Miscellaneous)

Marathon '33 1963,D 23,20:1
Leader, The 1969,Ap 22,40:2
Honest-to-God Schnozzola, The 1969,Ap 22,40:2

Everett, Walker G (Lyricist)

Tambourine 1925,D 30,10:2

Everett, Walker G (Playwright)

Tambourine 1925,D 30,10:2

Everett, William (Playwright)

Virtue (?) 1922,N 17,14:1

Everhart, Douglas

Bacchae, The 1969,Mr 15,24:1

Everhart, Henry

Cage, The 1970,Je 19,25:1

Everhart, Rex

Julius Caesar 1955,Jl 13,20:1
Tempest, The 1955,Ag 2,18:2
Tempest, The 1955,Ag 7,II,1:1
Much Ado About Nothing 1955,Ag 20,20:4
No Time for Sergeants 1955,O 21,32:2
Tall Story 1959,Ja 30,33:2
Julius Caesar 1959,Ag 4,30:1
Julius Caesar 1959,Ag 16,II,1:1
Moonbirds 1959,O 10,13:1
Lysistrata 1959,N 25,19:4
Pictures in the Hallway 1959,D 28,19:1
Peer Gynt 1960,Ja 13,21:1
Henry IV 1960,Mr 2,42:1
Henry IV 1960,Mr 13,II,1:1
Henry IV 1960,Ap 19,41:1
Tenderloin 1960,O 18,47:2
Henry IV, Part I 1962,Je 18,20:4
Comedy of Errors, The 1963,Je 13,28:1
Henry V 1963,Je 14,37:1
Caesar and Cleopatra 1963,Ag 1,18:2
Rainy Day in Newark, A 1963,O 23,35:1
Much Ado About Nothing 1964,Je 11,26:2
Richard III 1964,Je 12,44:2
Hamlet 1964,Jl 4,9:1
Coriolanus 1965,Je 21,36:1
Taming of the Shrew, The 1965,Je 24,32:2
Skyscraper 1965,N 15,48:1
How Now, Dow Jones 1967,D 8,53:1
As You Like It 1968,Je 24,42:3
Androcles and the Lion 1968,Je 27,47:1
Love's Labour's Lost 1968,Je 28,36:1

Everhart, Richard

One Eye Closed 1954,N 25,45:2

Everingham, Joseph
Othello 1955,S 8,27:2
Everingham, Joseph D (Playwright)
Doctor and the Devils, The 1959,Ja 21,27:8
Evers, Ann
Mr Big 1941,S 7,I,51:3
Mr Big 1941,O 1,24:2
Evers, Evelyn
Cure for Matrimony 1939,O 26,26:3
Steel 1939,D 20,30:2
Evers, Florence
Merry Duchess, The 1943,Je 24,25:1
Evers, Herbert
Popsy 1941,F 11,26:2
Pie in the Sky 1941,D 23,26:5
Janie 1942,S 11,24:2
Grandma's Diary 1948,S 23,36:2
Angel in the Pawnshop 1951,Ja 19,20:3
Date With April, A 1953,Ap 16,36:2
Fair Game 1957,N 4,39:1
Evers, Jean Joseph
Merry Wives of Windsor, The 1954,F 17,27:1
Evers, Karry
Carousel 1945,Ap 20,24:2
Evers, Larry
Dream With Music 1944,My 19,15:2
Tempest, The 1945,Ja 26,17:2
Evers, Sybil
Lily Maid, The 1937,Ja 13,20:4
Everton, Paul
Man in the Making, The 1921,S 21,16:2
Varying Shore, The 1921,D 6,24:1
Drums of Jeopardy, The 1922,My 30,8:4
Why Men Leave Home 1922,S 13,18:2
Peter Weston 1923,S 20,5:2
Kid Boots 1924,Ja 1,21:3
Lucky 1927,Mr 23,28:3
Connecticut Yankee, A 1927,N 4,24:2
Vanderbilt Revue, The 1930,N 6,22:6
Inside Story, The 1932,F 23,23:2
Lambs Gambol 1932,Ap 25,18:2
Hired Husband 1932,Je 4,9:5
Theodora, the Queen 1934,F 1,15:3
Broadway Interlude 1934,Ap 20,16:3
Anything Goes 1934,N 22,26:1
Eville, William
Checkerboard, The 1920,Ag 20,7:2
My Aunt From Ypsilanti 1923,My 2,22:6
Little Miss Bluebeard 1923,Ag 29,12:1
Dearest Enemy 1925,S 19,9:2
Mixed Doubles 1927,Ap 27,22:3
Lady Dedlock 1929,Ja 1,61:2
Before You're 25 1929,Ap 17,30:2
Evily, Helen
Minute's Wait, A 1920,Je 22,9:1
Eviston, Walter
Carry Nation 1932,O 31,18:2
Evnas, Richard
King Lear 1950,Ag 30,26:2
Evrard, Marcelle
Girofle-Girofla 1926,N 23,26:3
Evrard, Mlle
Cloches de Cornville, Les; Chimes of Normandy,
The 1926,D 14,24:4
Evreinoff, Nicholas (Director)
Chief Thing, The 1926,Mr 23,24:2
Evreinoff, Nicholas (Playwright)
Chief Thing, The 1926,Mr 23,24:2
Chief Thing, The 1926,Mr 28,VIII,1:1
Comedie du Bonheur, La 1926,D 12,VIII,3:4
Theatre of the Soul 1942,Mr 21,13:5
Merry Death, A 1959,N 10,55:3
Chief Thing, The 1963,Ap 30,27:2
Evslin, Bernard (Playwright)
Geranium Hat, The 1959,Mr 18,45:1
Step on a Crack 1962,O 18,48:1
Ewart, Philip
Carousel 1966,D 16,56:2
Ewell, Patricia
Founders, The 1957,My 14,39:1
Ewell, Richard
Little Princess, The 1931,F 7,11:3
Jamboree 1932,N 25,18:4
Strange Gods 1933,Ap 17,16:6
Halfway to Hell 1934,Ja 3,22:3
Ewell, Tom
They Shall Not Die 1934,F 22,24:4
Geraniums in My Window 1934,O 27,20:6
De Luxe 1935,Mr 6,22:2
Let Freedom Ring 1935,N 7,26:2
Ethan Frome 1936,Ja 22,15:2
Stage Door 1936,O 23,26:3
Merchant of Yonkers, The 1938,D 13,30:1
Merchant of Yonkers, The 1938,D 29,14:2
Family Portrait 1939,Mr 9,18:4
Susannah and the Elders 1940,O 30,28:2
Liberty Jones 1941,F 6,24:2
Sunny River 1941,D 5,28:2
Apple of His Eye 1946,F 6,18:2
John Loves Mary 1947,F 5,29:2
Small Wonder 1948,S 16,33:5
Seven Year Itch, The 1952,N 21,21:2
Seven Year Itch, The 1952,N 30,II,1:1

Tunnel of Love, The 1957,F 14,31:4
Thurber Carnival, A 1960,F 27,13:2
Thurber Carnival, A 1960,Mr 6,II,1:1
Thurber Carnival, A 1960,Ap 12,42:1
Xmas in Las Vegas 1965,N 5,31:1
Ewell, Tom (Playwright)
Small Wonder 1948,S 26,II,1:1
Ewen, Frederic (Playwright)
Portrait of the Artist as a Young Man, A
1962,My 29,21:1
Ewen, Frederick (Miscellaneous)
Man of Destiny, The 1926,My 1,10:1
Hero of Santa Maria, The 1926,My 1,10:1
Ewer, Donald
Under Milk Wood 1957,O 16,42:5
This Island Is Mine 1959,Jl 1,26:4
Alfie 1964,D 18,27:1
Billy Liar 1965,Mr 18,26:1
Vatzlav 1970,Ag 23,II,1:6
Saved 1970,O 29,57:1
Saved 1970,N 1,II,10:1
Ewing, B
Front Page, The 1937,N 12,27:2
Ewing, Eleanor
Moon Is a Gong, The 1926,Mr 13,21:3
Ewing, George
Run Sheep Run 1938,N 4,26:2
Ewing, Jan (Director)
Pirates of Penzance, The 1970,D 6,84:6
Ewing, Katherine E (Producer)
Lady From the Sea, The 1935,D 14,11:3
Ewing, Lucia
Sonya's Search for the Christmas Star
1929,D 14,24:6
Ewing, Marjorie (Producer)
Hickory Stick 1944,My 9,15:6
Angel in the Wings 1947,D 12,36:4
Rape of Lucretia, The 1948,D 30,24:2
Getting Married 1951,My 14,28:5
Certain Young Man, A 1967,D 27,45:1
Ewing, Max (Composer)
Grand Street Follies, The 1927,My 20,23:3
Grand Street Follies, The 1928,My 29,16:2
Grand Street Follies, The 1929,My 2,20:4
Ewing, Sherman (Director)
Certain Young Man, A 1967,D 27,45:1
Ewing, Sherman (Producer)
Angel in the Wings 1947,D 12,36:4
Rape of Lucretia, The 1948,D 30,24:2
Getting Married 1951,My 14,28:5
Certain Young Man, A 1967,D 27,45:1
Eybner, Richard
Professor Bernhardi 1968,Mr 20,38:1
Eyen, Jerome (Director)
Dirtiest Show in Town, The 1970,My 2,21:1
Eyen, Tom (Director)
Tour De Four 1963,Je 19,41:1
Caution: A Love Story 1969,Ap 4,45:1
Dirtiest Show in Town, The 1970,Je 29,43:2
Dirtiest Show in Town, The 1970,Jl 5,II,14:5
Eyen, Tom (Playwright)
Tour De Four 1963,Je 19,41:1
Give My Regards to Off Off Broadway
1966,D 9,57:1
Alice Through the Glass Lightly 1968,Ap 15,41:1
Caution: A Love Story 1969,Ap 4,45:1
Dirtiest Show in Town, The 1970,My 2,21:1
Dirtiest Show in Town, The 1970,Je 29,43:2
Dirtiest Show in Town, The 1970,Jl 5,II,14:5
Eyen, Tom (Producer)
Tour De Four 1963,Je 19,41:1
Eyles, Mary
Aaron Slick From Punkin Crick 1935,Ap 6,11:4
Eyre, Alice
Service for Two 1935,Ag 20,25:1
Eyre, John (Director)
Puntila 1959,My 15,26:2
Eyre, John (Miscellaneous)
Jackass, The 1960,Mr 24,39:2
Death of Bessie Smith, The 1961,Mr 2,19:1
Eyre, John (Producer)
Machinal 1960,Ap 8,27:1
Eyre, Laurence (Director)
Mayfair 1930,Mr 18,30:5
Eyre, Laurence (Playwright)
Martinique 1920,Ap 27,18:2
Martinique 1920,My 2,VI,2:2
Fanshastics 1924,Ja 17,13:2
Merry Wives of Gotham 1924,Ja 27,VII,1:1
Steam Roller, The 1924,O 26,VIII,2:1
Steam Roller, The 1924,N 11,20:2
One Trip of the Silver Star 1925,Jl 12,VII,1:8
Forcing Bed, The 1929,Ag 4,VIII,1:6
Escapade 1929,S 29,IX,5:1
Gala Night 1930,F 26,22:4
Mayfair 1930,Mr 18,30:5
Service for Two 1935,Ag 20,25:1
Eyre, Marjorie
Gondoliers, The 1934,S 4,23:1
Pirates of Penzance, The; Slave of Duty, The
1934,S 7,24:3
Gondoliers, The 1934,S 9,IX,1:1
H M S Pinafore 1934,S 14,24:3

Eyre, Marjorie—Cont
Mikado, The; Town of Titipu, The 1934,S 18,18:1
Yeomen of the Guard, The 1934,S 21,28:3
Ruddigore 1934,S 25,25:2
Princess Ida; Castle Adamant 1934,S 28,26:3
Patience 1934,O 12,32:2
Mikado, The 1936,Ag 21,13:2
Pirates of Penzance, The 1936,S 1,24:4
Gondoliers, The 1936,S 8,23:1
Yeomen of the Guard, The 1936,S 15,37:2
H M S Pinafore 1936,S 29,34:2
Patience 1936,O 6,28:6
Princess Ida 1936,O 13,32:2
Ruddigore 1936,O 23,26:4
Pirates of Penzance, The 1939,Ja 6,25:1
Mikado, The 1939,Ja 10,16:3
Iolanthe 1939,Ja 13,16:3
H. M. S. Pinafore 1939,Ja 17,27:5
Gondoliers, The 1939,Ja 20,14:2
Yeomen of the Guard, The 1939,Ja 24,17:1
Patience 1939,Ja 27,16:3
Eyre, Richard (Playwright)
Ha-Ha, The 1968,Je 15,38:2
Eyre, Ronald
King Lear 1950,Ag 30,26:2
Eyre, Ronald (Director)
London Assurance 1970,Ag 7,26:1
Eyre, Ronald (Producer)
London Assurance 1970,Je 25,55:2
Eyser, Jacques
Troupe Du Roi, La 1970,F 4,38:1
Amphitryon 1970,F 4,38:1
Don Juan 1970,F 7,24:2
Femmes Savaantes, Les 1970,F 14,12:1
Malade Imaginaire, Le 1970,F 18,40:2
Eysler, Edmund (Composer)
Goldne Meisterin, Die 1927,S 16,21:1
Goldne Meisterin 1927,O 25,33:4
Ihr Erster Ball 1930,N 25,30:3
Eythe, William
Moon Is Down, The 1942,Ap 8,22:2
Lend an Ear 1948,D 17,38:2
Liar, The 1950,My 19,30:2
Out of This World 1950,D 22,17:3
Eythe, William (Producer)
Lend an Ear 1948,D 17,38:2
Eyton, Frank (Lyricist)
Good Companions, The 1931,O 2,31:1
Twenty to One 1935,N 13,24:3
Eyton, Frank (Playwright)
Streets of Paris, The 1939,Je 20,25:2
Ezequelle, Marjorie
Marriage for Three 1931,N 12,30:5

F

Fabbri, Diego (Playwright)
Between Two Thieves 1960,F 12,23:1
Fabbri, Jacques (Director)
Midsummer Night's Dream, A 1965,N 21,123:1
Faber, Erwin
Robbers, The 1926,N 21,VIII,1:3
Wozzeck 1966,Ap 6,34:1
Faber, Frederic
Signature 1945,F 15,25:2
Faber, Leslie
Outsider, The 1923,Je 10,VII,1:4
Letter, The 1927,Mr 27,VII,1:2
Patriot, The 1928,Ja 20,15:1
Patriot, The 1928,Ja 29,VIII,1:1
Making of an Immortal, The 1928,Ap 29,IX,1:3
By Candle Light 1928,O 7,IX,2:7
Faber, Max (Playwright)
Wild Duck, The 1951,D 27,17:1
Master Builder, The 1955,Mr 2,23:2
Master Builder, The 1955,Mr 20,II,1:1
Faber, Ron
Spots of the Leopard, The 1963,S 25,38:1
America Hurrah; Interview; TV; Motel
1967,O 10,55:2
Terminal 1970,Ap 15,51:2
Serpent, The 1970,Je 2,35:1
Faber, Ruth
New Hellzapoppin, The 1939,D 12,36:4
Fabian, Olga
Big Two, The 1947,Ja 9,21:2
Come Back, Little Sheba 1950,F 16,28:5
I Am a Camera 1951,N 29,39:6
Genius and the Goddess, The 1957,D 11,41:1
Fabian, T (Lighting Director)
Happy Faculty, The 1967,Ap 19,50:1
Priest in the Cellar, The 1969,F 19,39:1
Reunion of Sorts 1969,O 15,40:1
Five Star Saint 1970,F 11,41:2
Fabian, T (Scenic Designer)
Eternal Sabbath 1963,O 19,17:2
Go, Go, Go, God is Dead! 1966,O 12,37:1
Happy Faculty, The 1967,Ap 19,50:1
Priest in the Cellar, The 1969,F 19,39:1
Reunion of Sorts 1969,O 15,40:1
Five Star Saint 1970,F 11,41:2
Fabian, Thomas (Scenic Designer)
Caukey 1944,F 18,15:4

Fabiani, Joel
One Way Pendulum 1961,S 19,38:2
Richard II 1962,Je 18,20:2
Mr Grossman 1964,My 6,43:1
Beyond the Fringe, '65 1964,D 16,49:2
Fabien, Louis
Storm Operation 1944,Ja 12,28:2
Thank You Svoboda 1944,Mr 2,13:2
Fabing, Jolyn
Oliver Oliver 1934,Ja 6,18:5
Fabiolo
Decent People Frighten Me 1964,Ja 26,82:3
Fables, Helen
Keep Kool 1924,My 23,16:4
Fabray, Nanette
Meet the People 1940,D 26,22:2
Let's Face It 1941,O 30,26:2
My Dear Public 1943,S 10,28:1
Jackpot 1944,Ja 14,15:2
Bloomer Girl 1947,Ja 7,33:2
High Button Shoes 1947,O 10,32:2
High Button Shoes 1947,N 23,II,1:1
Love Life 1948,O 8,31:2
Arms and the Girl 1950,F 3,28:2
Make a Wish 1951,Ap 19,38:1
Mr President 1962,Ag 29,18:4
Mr President 1962,S 26,36:1
Mr President 1962,O 14,II,1:7
Mr President 1962,O 22,34:2
Fabre, Emile (Original Author)
Colonello Bridall, L' 1934,Ap 16,20:3
Fabre, Emile (Playwright)
Honor of the Family, The 1926,D 27,21:1
Ventres Dores, Les 1929,N 17,IX,2:6
Fabre, Saturnin
Tu m'ePouseras 1927,Mr 13,VII,2:7
Guignol 1930,Mr 30,VIII,2:4
Fabre-Luce, Alfred (Jacques Sindral) (Playwright)
Double 1929,Ja 13,VIII,2:7
Transfuges, Les 1929,N 10,X,4:1
Fabregas, Manolo
King and I, The 1963,Je 13,30:2
Fabretti, Giorgio
Rugantino 1964,F 7,34:1
Fabricant, Gwen (Costume Designer)
Terminal 1970,Ap 15,51:2
Endgame 1970,My 6,47:1
Fabricatore, Gene (Scenic Designer)
Here Comes Santa Claus 1962,My 18,34:1
Fabricius, Jan (Original Author)
Insult 1930,S 16,30:2
Fabricius, Jan (Playwright)
Insult; Dolle Hans 1930,My 4,XI,1:3
At Eight AM 1935,F 12,25:4
Fabrizi, Aldo
Rugantino 1964,F 2,II,1:4
Rugantino 1964,F 7,34:1
Fabrizi, Bernard
Paths of Glory 1935,S 27,24:2
Cyrano de Bergerac 1936,Ap 28,17:1
Fabry, Vera
Americans on the Rhine 1934,O 11,28:4
Facey, Stephen
Anna Kleiber 1965,Ja 20,33:1
Masks of Angels 1965,Ja 20,33:1
Factorowitch, Elisheva
Dybbuk, The 1926,D 14,24:2
Jacob's Dream 1927,Ja 4,20:2
Golem, The 1927,F 5,13:2
Fadden, Tom
Wonderful Visit, The 1924,F 13,17:3
Nocturne 1925,F 17,19:1
Butter and Egg Man, The 1925,S 24,28:1
Elmer Gantry 1928,Ag 10,9:4
Squealer, The 1928,N 13,36:3
Kibitzer, The 1929,F 19,22:5
This Is New York 1930,N 29,21:1
Just to Remind You 1931,S 8,39:1
Rendezvous 1932,O 13,22:3
Marathon 1933,Ja 28,8:8
Little Ol' Boy 1933,Ap 25,15:5
Ghost Writer, The 1933,Je 20,22:4
Theodora, the Queen 1934,F 1,15:3
Jayhawker 1934,N 6,34:2
Petrified Forest, The 1935,Ja 8,26:1
Tide Rising 1937,Ja 26,17:2
Miss Quis 1937,Ap 8,20:5
Our Town 1938,F 5,18:3
Vigil, The 1948,My 22,8:6
Fadeuilhe, Andre
Trois Jeunes Filles Nues; Three Young Maids From the Folies Bergere 1929,Mr 5,28:2
Passionement; Passionately 1929,Mr 8,31:4
Comte Obligado 1929,Mr 12,26:2
Ta Bouche 1929,Mr 15,28:5
Bon Garcon, Un 1929,Mr 19,36:2
Pas Sur La Bouche; Not on the Lips 1929,Mr 26,34:3
Faffin, Toni
Enchaines; Welded 1965,Mr 13,17:1
Fagan, Allen
49ers, The 1922,N 7,14:1
Stepping Out 1929,My 21,29:1

Waterloo Bridge 1930,Ja 7,29:2
Ode to Liberty 1934,D 22,20:2
Abide With Me 1935,N 22,19:2
Among Those Sailing 1936,F 12,24:4
Fagan, Barney
Jazz Singer, The 1925,S 15,29:2
Sidewalks of New York 1927,O 4,33:1
Friars Club Frolic 1933,My 15,16:4
Fagan, Bruce V (Producer)
Red Rainbow, A 1953,S 15,37:4
Fagan, Gemma
And So to Bed 1927,N 10,23:1
Cherry Orchard, The 1928,Mr 6,20:1
Fagan, J B (Director)
Professor Tim 1927,Ap 17,VII,1:4
Fagan, J B (Miscellaneous)
Heartbreak House 1921,N 18,20:3
Fagan, J B (Playwright)
Greater Love, The 1927,Ap 3,VIII,1:4
Improper Duchess, The 1931,F 8,VIII,3:3
Fagan, J B (Producer)
Spook Sonata, The 1927,Jl 10,VII,2:3
Fagan, James B
Cherry Orchard, The 1928,Mr 6,20:1
Fagan, James B (Director)
And So to Bed 1927,N 10,23:1
Cherry Orchard, The 1928,Mr 6,20:1
Fagan, James B (Playwright)
And So to Bed 1927,N 10,23:1
Improper Duchess, The 1931,Ja 23,28:1
Fagan, James B (Producer)
Cherry Orchard, The 1928,Mr 6,20:1
Fagan, James B (Scenic Designer)
And So to Bed 1927,N 10,23:1
Cherry Orchard, The 1928,Mr 6,20:1
Fagan, Joan
Donnybrook! 1961,My 19,23:1
Donnybrook! 1961,My 28,II,1:1
Fagan, Myron C (Director)
Jimmie's Women 1927,S 27,30:3
Great Power, The 1928,S 12,25:1
Indiscretion 1929,Mr 5,28:1
Nancy's Private Affair 1930,Ja 14,24:3
Red Rainbow, A 1953,S 15,37:4
Fagan, Myron C (Playwright)
Thumbs Down 1923,Ag 7,20:1
Two Strangers From Nowhere 1924,Ap 8,22:2
Mismates 1925,Ap 14,27:2
Little Spitfire, The 1926,Ag 17,15:2
Jimmie's Women 1927,S 27,30:3
Great Power, The 1928,Jl 8,VII,1:2
Indiscretion 1929,Mr 5,28:1
Nancy's Private Affair 1930,Ja 14,24:3
Peter Flies High 1931,S 20,VIII,3:1
Peter Flies High 1931,N 10,28:3
Memory 1934,My 13,IX,2:6
Red Rainbow, A 1953,S 15,37:4
Fagan, Myron C (Producer)
Great Power, The 1928,S 12,25:1
Indiscretion 1929,Mr 5,28:1
Nancy's Private Affair 1930,Ja 14,24:3
Faggen, Jay (Producer)
Snark Was a Boojum, The 1943,S 2,14:4
Fago, Jack
Bitter Sweet 1934,My 8,28:4
Fahey, Bob (Miscellaneous)
Iolanthe 1967,O 18,40:1
Mikado, The 1967,O 25,42:2
Gondoliers, The 1967,O 29,83:1
Fahey, Lee Anne
Play It Again, Sam 1969,F 13,52:3
Fahlstedt, Sven (Scenic Designer)
Father, The 1962,My 15,49:1
Faier, Billy
In White America 1963,N 1,26:1
Faiko, Alexis (Playwright)
Man With the Portfolio, The 1931,F 12,24:6
Fain, Pauline (Playwright)
What's the Use? 1926,S 7,19:1
Fain, Sammy (Composer)
Everybody's Welcome 1931,S 20,VIII,3:2
Everybody's Welcome 1931,O 14,26:3
Right This Way 1938,Ja 6,22:3
Lew Leslie's Blackbirds of 1939 1939,F 13,12:2
Scandals 1939,Ag 29,17:2
New Hellzapoppin, The 1939,D 12,36:4
Boys and Girls Together 1940,O 2,19:2
Sons o' Fun 1941,D 2,28:2
Toplitzky of Notre Dame 1946,D 27,13:4
Alive and Kicking 1950,Ja 18,25:5
Michael Todd's Peep Show 1950,Je 29,37:2
Flahooley 1951,My 15,39:1
Flahooley 1951,My 20,II,1:1
My L A 1951,D 9,87:1
Jollyanna; Flahooley 1952,Ag 13,17:7
Ankles Aweigh 1955,Ap 19,27:1
Catch a Star! 1955,S 7,35:2
Ziegfeld Follies 1957,Mr 2,19:2
Christine 1960,Ap 29,27:1
Around the World in 80 Days 1963,Je 24,22:1
Around the World in 80 Days 1964,Je 29,33:2
Something More! 1964,N 11,36:1

Fain, Sammy (Lyricist)
Hellzapoppin 1938,S 23,34:2
Lew Leslie's Blackbirds of 1939 1939,F 13,12:2
Michael Todd's Peep Show 1950,Je 29,37:2
Ziegfeld Follies 1957,Mr 2,19:2
Fainsilber, Samson
Prometheide 1926,N 21,VIII,2:1
Oedipus and the Sphinx 1928,Mr 11,VIII,2:7
Histoires de France 1929,O 27,IX,2:4
Fair, Florence
Elton Case, The 1921,S 12,16:2
Tendresse, La 1922,S 26,18:1
Cymbeline 1923,O 3,12:1
Green Beetle, The 1924,S 3,12:3
Gay Paree 1925,Ag 19,14:3
Service for Two 1926,Ag 31,15:1
Little Father of the Wilderness, The 1930,Je 3,27:1
Yoshe Kalb 1933,D 29,27:2
Boys From Syracuse, The 1938,N 24,36:1
Delicate Story 1940,D 5,32:2
Fair, Joyce
Bootleggers, The 1922,N 28,24:1
Fair, Nancy
No More Blondes 1920,Ja 8,22:1
Fairbanks, Douglas Jr
Winding Journey, The 1934,My 8,28:6
Here Lies Truth 1934,Ag 28,24:6
Moonlight Is Silver 1934,S 20,21:1
Moonlight Is Silver 1934,O 7,IX,3:7
We Were Dancing; Tonight at Eight 1940,Ag 6,15:3
Tonight at 8:30 1940,Ag 11,IX,11:2
Fairbanks, Fred
Little Old New York 1920,S 9,9:2
Sam Abramovitch 1927,Ja 20,20:5
Fairbanks, Madeleine
Two Little Girls in Blue 1921,My 4,10:3
King for a Day, A 1923,D 2,VIII,2:1
Hassard Short's Ritz Revue 1924,S 18,19:1
Mercenary Mary 1925,Ap 14,27:3
Oh, Kay! 1926,N 9,31:3
Allez-Opp! 1927,Ag 3,29:3
Happy 1927,D 6,26:3
Fairbanks, Marion
Two Little Girls in Blue 1921,My 4,10:3
Grab Bag, The 1924,O 7,26:2
Oh, Kay! 1926,N 9,31:3
Fairbanks, Nola
Icetime 1947,My 29,28:2
Howdy Mr Ice 1948,Je 25,28:5
Howdy, Mr Ice of 1950 1949,My 27,24:2
Out of This World 1950,D 22,17:3
Night in Venice, A 1952,Je 27,18:6
Night in Venice, A 1952,Jl 13,II,1:1
Night in Venice, A 1953,Je 26,15:2
Fairbanks Sisters
George White's Scandals 1926,Je 15,23:2
Fairbanks Twins
Midnight Frolic 1920,Ag 4,7:1
Nine O'Clock Revue 1921,F 9,7:5
Irving Berlin's New Music Box Revue 1922,O 24,18:1
Fairbrother, Sydney
Charm School, The 1921,F 27,VI,1:6
Fairchild, C A
Half Moon Inn 1925,Mr 10,14:1
Fairchild, Charlotte
Mr President 1962,O 22,34:2
Penny Friend, The 1966,D 27,46:1
Fairchild, Dona
Singing Rabbi, The 1931,S 11,24:4
Lingering Past, The 1932,Je 30,26:5
Fairchild, Edgar (Composer)
New Yorkers, The 1927,Mr 11,24:3
Illustrators' Show, The 1936,Ja 23,25:3
Fairchild, Eleanor
Out of This World 1950,D 22,17:3
Fairchild, George
Collision 1932,F 17,19:2
Processional 1937,O 14,23:1
Cradle Will Rock, The 1937,D 6,19:4
Cradle Will Rock, The 1938,Ja 4,19:3
Journey to Jerusalem 1940,O 7,21:2
No for an Answer 1941,Ja 6,10:6
Fairchild, Jackson
Sweet Adeline 1929,S 4,33:1
Faire, Rosanna
Wonderful World of Burlesque, The 1965,Ap 29,38:1
Fairfax, Virginia
Charm 1929,N 29,24:5
Fairleigh, Paul
Lady in Danger 1945,Mr 30,18:6
Fairley, Freeman
Ol' Man Satan 1932,O 4,26:3
Fairley, George
Blancs, Les 1970,N 16,48:4
Fairley, Lillian
Harlem 1929,F 21,30:3
Fairlie, Dolly
Topaze 1931,F 17,29:1
Fairman, Austin
Lady, The 1923,D 5,23:2
Mask and the Face, The 1924,S 11,27:3

Fairman, Austin—Cont
Artistic Temperament 1924,D 10,20:2
Lucky Sam McCarver 1925,O 22,22:1
Ashes of Love 1926,Mr 23,24:3
Number 7 1926,S 9,21:3
Lady Alone 1927,Ja 21,12:5
We Never Learn 1928,Ja 24,26:1
Most Immoral Lady, A 1928,N 27,36:1
Show Girl 1929,Jl 3,19:3
That's the Woman 1930,S 4,27:2
Vaudeville (Palace) 1931,Ap 20,16:2
Roof, The 1931,O 31,22:4
Dinner at Eight 1932,O 24,18:2
Halfway to Hell 1934,Ja 3,22:3
Distaff Side, The 1934,S 26,17:2
Cross-Town 1937,Mr 18,21:5
Seperate Rooms 1940,Mr 25,10:3
Ghost for Sale 1941,S 30,27:4
Heart of a City 1942,F 13,24:6
Beggars Are Comming to Town 1945,O 29,16:2

Fairman, Churton
Lark, The 1955,My 13,21:2

Fairman, Derek
Cinderelative 1930,S 19,18:4
Twelfth Night 1930,O 16,28:2
In The Best of Families 1931,F 3,29:1
Man Who Changed His Name, The 1932,My 3,25:3
Best People, The 1933,Mr 16,21:5
Fresh Fields 1934,Jl 15,X,1:1
Fresh Fields 1936,F 11,19:2
Springtime for Henry 1936,Je 30,15:1
Susan and God 1937,Ap 25,X,2:6
Sea Legs 1937,My 19,26:5
Lady Has a Heart, The 1937,S 27,24:1
Save Me the Waltz 1938,Mr 1,19:2

Fairman, Michael
Cactus Flower 1965,D 9,60:2
Night Thoreau Spent in Jail, The 1970,N 2,66:1

Fairmont, Walter
Strike Up the Band 1930,Ja 15,29:1

Fairweather, Caswell
Miracle Worker, The 1959,O 20,44:1

Faison, Clyde
Ol' Man Satan 1932,O 4,26:3

Faison, George William
Here's Josephine Premice 1966,Ap 26,54:4

Faita, Josef
Button, Button 1970,O 20,41:1

Faithfull, Marianne
Early Morning 1968,Ap 9,58:1
Hamlet 1969,F 19,38:1
Hamlet 1969,Mr 2,II,3:1

Falana, Lola
Golden Boy 1964,O 21,56:1

Falasca, Edward A (Composer)
Life Begins in '40 1940,Ap 5,24:2
Hit the Road 1941,Ap 4,18:3

Falasco, Don
High Button Shoes 1955,Mr 12,10:6

Falbel, Rita
Student Prince, The 1961,Jl 14,14:1

Falckenberg, Gina
Gestern und Heute 1931,My 24,VIII,2:1

Falco, Anthony
Ben Franklin in Paris 1964,O 28,52:1
Flora, the Red Menace 1965,My 12,41:2

Falcon, Andre
Cardinal of Spain, The 1960,D 22,16:6

Falcone, Rina
Buttrio Square 1952,O 15,40:2

Falconer, Edna
Lady of the Lamp, The 1920,Ag 18,6:4

Falconer, Martha
Othello 1943,O 20,18:1

Falconer, Mary
Annie Get Your Gun 1966,Je 1,42:2

Falconetti, Mlle
Trio 1929,Mr 17,X,2:7
Phedre 1930,F 2,VIII,4:1

Falconetti, Mlle (Producer)
Rouille, La 1929,D 29,VIII,2:6
Phedre 1930,F 2,VIII,4:1
Juliette, ou La Cle des Songes 1930,Mr 30,VIII,2:4
Mais n'te Promene Donc pas Toute Nue 1930,Mr 30,VIII,2:4

Falconi, Dino (Playwright)
Casa di Tutti, La; Everybody's Home 1932,D 5,21:4

Fales, Margaret
Iolanthe 1964,N 18,52:1

Falk, Alfred
To the Ladies! 1922,F 21,20:1

Falk, Henri (Playwright)
Naughty Cinderella 1925,N 10,23:6
Untitled-Play 1928,F 5,VIII,2:1

Falk, Lee (Director)
Winkelberg 1958,Ja 15,26:2

Falk, Lee (Producer)
Winkelberg 1958,Ja 15,26:2

Falk, Paul
Hollywood Ice Revue 1956,Ja 13,17:1

Falk, Peter
Don Juan; Feast With the Statue, The 1956,Ja 4,21:4
Iceman Cometh, The 1956,My 8,38:1

Saint Joan 1956,S 12,42:1
Diary of a Scoundrel 1956,N 5,41:1
Lady's Not for Burning, The 1957,F 22,26:2
Bonds of Interest, The 1958,My 7,43:1
Passion of Josef D, The 1964,F 12,29:1
Passion of Josef D, The 1964,F 23,II,1:1

Falk, R R (Scenic Designer)
Jacob's Dream 1927,Ja 4,20:2

Falk, Sawyer (Director)
Live Life Again 1945,O 1,14:7

Falkenberg, Gerhardt (Playwright)
One Glorious Hour 1927,Ap 15,27:2

Falkenburg, Jinx
Hold On to Your Hats 1940,S 12,30:3

Falkenhain, Patricia
Romeo and Juliet 1956,F 24,20:4
Capacity for Wings 1957,Ja 10,25:2
Romeo and Juliet 1957,Je 28,30:2
Two Gentlemen of Verona 1957,Jl 23,21:5
Macbeth 1957,Ag 16,11:2
Othello 1958,Jl 4,16:1
Power and the Glory, The 1958,D 12,2:7
Beaux' Stratagem, The 1959,F 25,35:4
Buoyant Billions 1959,My 27,32:2
Getting Married 1959,Je 5,18:2
Lysistrata 1959,N 25,19:4
Peer Gynt 1960,Ja 13,21:1
Henry IV 1960,Ap 19,41:1
Henry IV, Part II 1960,Ap 24,II,1:1
She Stoops to Conquer 1960,N 2,42:5
Plough and the Stars, The 1960,D 7,56:2
Hamlet 1961,Mr 17,17:1
Androcles and the Lion 1961,N 22,24:2
Dark Lady of the Sonnets, The 1961,D 15,48:1
Saving Grace, The 1963,Ap 19,28:1

Falkenstein, Julius
Escape 1928,My 20,VIII,2:1
Menschen im Hotel 1930,Mr 16,IX,4:1

Falkner, William (Miscellaneous)
Young Abe Lincoln 1961,Ap 26,36:1

Fall, Leo (Composer)
Spanische Nachtigall, Die 1920,D 12,VI,1:4
Rose of Stamboul, The 1922,Mr 8,11:2
Madame Pompadour 1924,N 2,VII,2:3
Madame Pompadour 1924,N 12,20:6
Jugend im Mai 1927,Ja 23,VII,4:5
Rose of Florida, The 1929,F 23,17:1

Fall, Leo (Original Author)
Dollar Princess 1949,Je 2,32:1

Falla, Manuel de (Composer)
Retablo de Maese Pedro, El 1925,D 30,10:1

Falla Sisters
Thumbs Up! 1934,D 28,24:1

Faller, James (Playwright)
Hotheads, The 1921,Je 12,VI,1:6
Play, A 1925,F 11,19:2

Fallet, Maurice
Processional 1937,O 14,23:1
Big Blow 1938,O 3,11:2

Fallon, James
Little Ol' Boy 1933,Ap 25,15:5
Queer People 1934,F 16,16:2
American Holiday 1936,F 22,13:3
Johnny 2X4 1942,Mr 17,24:6
Tenting Tonight 1947,Ap 3,32:2
Diamond Lil 1948,N 30,33:2
Diamond Lil 1949,F 7,16:2
Diamond Lil 1951,S 15,8:2

Fallon, Joseph
Sundown Beach 1948,S 8,37:1
Design For A Stained Glass Window 1950,Ja 24,26:2

Fallon, Richard (Director)
Last Days of Lincoln, The 1961,O 19,39:7

Fallon, Sheila
Late Arrival 1953,O 20,35:5

Fallon, Thomas F (Playwright)
Last Warning, The 1922,O 25,23:1
Wasp, The 1923,Mr 28,14:3
Last Warning, The 1927,Ap 3,VIII,2:1
Lovebound 1929,My 19,IX,2:1

Fallows, Gordon
Second Comin', The 1931,D 9,32:4
Lady Remembers, The 1932,My 11,15:3

Fallows, Ruth
Dishonored Lady 1930,F 5,27:1
On the Make 1932,My 24,23:2
Rendezvous 1932,O 13,22:3
Hook-Up, The 1935,My 9,24:6
Blind Alley 1935,S 25,19:6

Falls, Bedelia
County Chairman, The 1936,My 26,26:5

Falls, Charles B (Costume Designer)
Troilus and Cressida 1932,Je 7,22:3
Macbeth 1935,O 8,26:4

Falls, Charles B (Miscellaneous)
Troilus and Cressida 1932,Je 7,22:3

Falls, Marie
Dodsworth 1934,F 26,20:4
Ethan Frome 1936,Ja 22,15:2
Places, Please 1937,N 13,10:6

Falls, Nathan (Costume Designer)
In-Laws 1960,O 17,32:4

Falls (Mae), Reading and Royce
Vaudeville (Palace) 1929,Jl 15,25:4

Falzone, Peter
Yearling, The 1965,D 11,25:1
Rose Tattoo, The 1966,O 21,36:2

Fananas, Jean (Miscellaneous)
Zizi 1964,N 23,51:1

Fanchon, Miss
Sun-Kist 1921,My 24,20:2

Fanchon (Composer)
Sun-Kist 1921,My 24,20:2

Fanchon (Lyricist)
Sun-Kist 1921,My 24,20:2

Fancourt, Darrell
Pirates of Penzance, The; Slave of Duty, The 1934,S 7,24:3
Cox and Box 1934,S 7,24:3
Iolanthe 1934,S 11,24:3
H M S Pinafore 1934,S 14,24:3
Mikado, The; Town of Titipu, The 1934,S 18,18:1
Yeomen of the Guard, The 1934,S 21,28:3
Ruddigore 1934,S 25,25:2
Princess Ida; Castle Adamant 1934,S 28,26:3
Patience 1934,O 12,32:2
Mikado, The 1936,Ag 21,13:2
Pirates of Penzance, The 1936,S 1,24:4
Yeomen of the Guard, The 1936,S 15,37:2
Iolanthe 1936,S 22,30:3
H M S Pinafore 1936,S 29,34:2
Patience 1936,O 6,28:6
Princess Ida 1936,O 13,32:2
Ruddigore 1936,O 23,26:4
Pirates of Penzance, The 1939,Ja 6,25:1
Mikado, The 1939,Ja 10,16:3
Iolanthe 1939,Ja 13,16:3
H. M. S. Pinafore 1939,Ja 17,27:5
Yeomen of the Guard, The 1939,Ja 24,17:1
Patience 1939,Ja 27,16:3
Mikado, The 1947,D 30,18:2
Pirates of Penzance, The 1948,Ja 6,27:2
Pirates of Penzance, The 1948,Ja 11,II,1:1
H M S Pinafore 1948,Ja 20,26:2
Yeomen of the Guard, The 1948,F 3,30:2
Mikado, The 1951,Ja 30,21:2
H M S Pinafore 1951,F 6,24:2
Pirates of Penzance, The 1951,F 20,21:2

Fane, Caryl
Gondoliers, The 1948,Ja 27,31:2
Gondoliers, The 1951,F 13,27:2

Fane, Eric (Miscellaneous)
Great Music 1924,O 6,24:1

Fanelle, Sara
Ghost for Sale 1941,S 30,27:4

Fanfarillo, Joy
Emerald Slippers, The 1970,S 2,31:2

Fang, Charlie
Gold Braid 1930,My 14,31:2
Roar China! 1930,O 28,23:1
Just to Remind You 1931,S 8,39:1
Anything Goes 1934,N 22,26:1

Fang, Chiao-Chin
First Wife, The 1945,N 28,21:5

Fann, Al
Porgy and Bess 1964,My 7,32:1

Fanning, A P (Playwright)
Vigil 1932,D 11,IX,4:5

Fanning, Frank
Skirt, The 1921,N 8,28:1
Easy Terms 1925,S 23,22:2

Fanning, George
Half Moon Inn 1925,Mr 10,14:1
His Majesty the Queen 1926,Mr 9,8:1
Betty Behave 1927,Mr 9,28:4
Zuleika 1928,Mr 7,28:7

Fanning, Lotta
Yours Truly 1927,Ja 26,16:5

Fanny
Rainbow 1928,N 22,25:1

Fanny and Kitty (Watson Sisters)
Vaudeville (Palace) 1930,N 17,21:2

Fanson, Arthur
Wise-Crackers, The 1925,D 17,26:1

Fant, Lou
Gianni Schicci 1969,F 25,36:1
On the Harmfulness of Tobacco 1969,Mr 9,76:5
Sganarelle 1970,Ja 13,41:1
Songs From Milk Wood 1970,Ja 13,41:1

Fant, Lou (Playwright)
Critic, The 1969,Mr 9,76:5

Fant, Roy
Daisy Mayme 1926,O 26,24:2
A la Carte 1927,Ag 18,25:3
Chicken Every Sunday 1944,Ap 6,27:2
Dark of the Moon 1945,Mr 15,27:2
Apple of His Eye 1946,F 6,18:2
See the Jaguar 1952,D 4,46:2
Tenderloin 1960,O 18,47:2

Fant, Tom
Vaudeville (Palace) 1923,My 15,22:2

Fantoni, Gino
Donna Del Mare, La; Lady From the Sea, The 1923,O 30,17:1
Cosi Sia; Thy Will be Done 1923,N 14,29:2
Citta Morta, La; Dead City, The 1923,N 28,14:1
Fantoni, Italia
Nemica, La 1926,S 7,24:6
Faraday, Mr (Producer)
Enchanted Cottage, The 1922,Mr 2,21:4
Farago, Sandor (Playwright)
Berkaszarnya 1928,O 28,IX,2:1
Faragoh, Francis Edwards (Playwright)
Pinwheel 1927,F 4,16:4
Pinwheel 1927,F 13,VII,1:1
Ritornell 1927,Ap 6,24:3
Sunup to Sundown 1938,F 2,14:3
Faragoh, Francis Edwards (Translator)
Rapid Transit 1927,Ap 8,21:2
Farah, Helen
Bamboo Cross 1955,F 22,17:2
Farani (Miscellaneous)
Festa Italiana 1966,S 30,55:1
Farbar, Bernard
Deer Park, The 1967,F 1,27:2
Farber, Constance
Demi-Virgin, The 1921,O 19,22:1
Farber, Joan
Women at the Tomb, The 1961,Ap 25,41:1
Farber, Norman (Miscellaneous)
Salad of the Mad Cafe, The 1964,Ap 1,43:1
Farber, Sam (Miscellaneous)
Christine 1960,Ap 29,27:1
Farber, Sandy (Producer)
Student Gypsy, The; Prince of Liederkranz, The 1963,O 1,34:1
Damn You, Scarlett O'Hara 1964,F 5,30:1
All My Pretty Little Ones 1964,F 5,30:1
Babes in the Wood 1964,D 29,21:2
Family Way, The 1965,Ja 14,44:5
Summertree 1969,D 10,60:1
Farbman, Abel (Producer)
Tovarich 1963,Mr 20,5:1
Farebrother, Violet
King Lear 1947,F 19,32:2
Hamlet 1947,F 27,27:2
Living Room, The 1953,Ap 17,29:5
Fareed, Badry
Mother Courage and Her Children 1964,My 12,32:2
Fareleigh, Margaret
Lancelot and Elaine 1921,S 13,12:1
Malvaloca 1922,O 3,22:1
Roger Bloomer 1923,Mr 2,18:3
Farentino, James
Night of the Iguana, The 1961,D 29,10:1
In the Summer House 1964,Mr 26,43:1
Fargas, Antonio
Toilet, The 1964,D 17,51:1
Amen Corner, The 1965,Je 13,82:4
Great White Hope, The 1967,D 14,58:1
Hamlet 1968,Jl 4,15:1
Romeo and Juliet 1968,Ag 16,19:1
Ceremonies in Dark Old Men 1969,O 11,42:1
Fargo, Evelyn Wells
Maid in the Ozarks 1946,Jl 16,20:3
Faria, Arthur
Boy Friend, The 1970,Ap 15,54:1
Faricy, Robert
Show Boat 1927,D 28,26:1
Fariello, Alfred
Dreaming Dust, The 1955,D 8,46:5
Sable Brush, The 1956,N 28,41:1
Farinon, Catherine (Miscellaneous)
Macbeth 1969,N 21,51:1
Farjeon, Eleanor (Playwright)
Two Bouquets, The 1936,S 13,X,1:5
Two Bouquets, The 1938,Je 1,19:2
Farjeon, Herbert
Squaw Man, The 1921,D 27,10:3
Listening In 1922,D 5,24:1
Queen Victoria 1923,N 16,15:1
Fanshastics 1924,Ja 17,13:2
Dust Heap, The 1924,Ap 25,20:2
Tale of the Wolf, The 1925,O 8,31:2
Find Daddy 1926,Mr 9,21:3
Farjeon, Herbert (Playwright)
Advertising April 1923,F 4,VII,1:4
Spread It Abroad 1936,My 3,X,1:2
Two Bouquets, The 1936,S 13,X,1:5
Nine Sharp 1938,Ap 24,X,2:1
Two Bouquets, The 1938,Je 1,19:2
Big Top 1942,My 17,VIII,1:3
John Murray Anderson's Almanac 1953,D 11,42:2
From A to Z 1960,Ap 21,23:2
Elsa Lanchester-Herself 1961,F 6,28:1
Farjeon, J Jefferson (Playwright)
Number 7 1926,S 9,21:3
After Dark 1926,O 10,VIII,2:1
Enchantment 1927,Ap 28,27:3
Philomel 1932,D 4,IX,3:8
Farkas, Karl
Gypsy Baron, The 1942,Je 20,8:5
Gypsy Baron, The 1942,Ag 7,12:4
Merry Widow, The 1943,Ag 5,19:2

Merry Widow, The 1944,O 9,17:1
Vienna at Night 1945,Ap 30,12:4
Farkas, Karl (Lyricist)
Vienna at Night 1945,Ap 30,12:4
Yours Is My Heart 1946,S 6,16:5
Farkas, Karl (Original Author)
Wonder Bar, The 1931,Mr 8,VIII,3:5
Wonder Bar, The 1931,Mr 18,23:4
You Never Know 1938,S 22,26:3
Yours Is My Heart 1946,S 6,16:5
Farkas, Karl (Playwright)
Vienna at Night 1945,Ap 30,12:4
Marinka 1945,Jl 19,19:2
Farker, Thomas (Scenic Designer)
Michael and Mary 1929,D 14,23:3
Farleigh, Lynn
Exiles 1970,N 19,42:4
Farley, Albert
Ghost of Yankee Doodle, The 1937,O 28,28:5
Farley, Buddy
Between Two Worlds 1934,O 26,24:2
Farley, Duke
Sweet Bird of Youth 1959,Mr 11,39:2
Mandingo 1961,My 23,43:6
Farley, Frederick
Under the Counter 1947,O 4,10:2
Farley, Leonard
Living Corpse, The 1929,D 7,19:1
Farley, Mary
Manhattan Mary 1927,S 27,30:3
Farley, Morgan
Charm School, The 1920,Ag 3,12:1
Deburau 1920,D 24,14:3
Grand Duke, The 1921,N 2,20:1
Mary the 3d 1923,F 6,14:2
Home Fires 1923,Ag 21,12:1
Wild Westcotts, The 1923,D 25,26:2
Fata Morgana 1924,Mr 4,16:3
Fata Morgana 1924,Mr 9,VIII,1:1
Fata Morgana 1924,Ag 24,VII,1:1
Paolo and Francesca 1924,D 3,24:2
Tangletoes 1925,F 18,17:1
Candida 1925,N 10,23:4
Unchastened Woman, The 1926,F 17,12:1
Easter 1926,Mr 19,24:3
American Tragedy, An 1926,O 12,31:2
American Tragedy, An 1926,O 24,VIII,1:1
Lady of the Camellias, The 1931,Ja 27,21:2
Passing Present, The 1931,D 8,36:2
Crime and Punishment 1935,Ja 23,20:3
Candida 1935,Ag 20,25:1
Julie the Great 1936,Ja 15,15:3
Hamlet 1936,O 9,30:2
Candida 1937,Mr 11,20:2
Danton's Death 1938,N 3,26:2
Outward Bound 1938,D 23,16:5
Distant City, The 1941,S 23,27:5
Savonarola 1942,Ap 24,20:2
Galileo 1947,Ag 1,21:4
Farley, Robert
Show Boat 1932,My 20,22:2
Farley, William
Anatomist, The 1957,F 27,21:5
Shewing-Up of Blanco Posnet, The 1959,S 19,26:7
Farlow, Robert
Betty Behave 1927,Mr 9,28:4
Farman, M
Yoshe Kalb 1933,D 29,27:2
Farmer, Frances
At Mrs Beam's 1937,Jl 27,24:2
Golden Boy 1937,N 5,18:5
Sarah Adler Testimonial 1939,Mr 15,18:2
Thunder Rock 1939,N 15,18:1
Farmer, Frank
Richard II 1961,Ag 30,25:1
Night of the Auk 1963,My 22,35:2
Farmer, Loren
Best House in Naples, The 1956,O 27,16:2
Farmer, Mary Virginia
Men in White 1933,S 27,24:2
Farmer, Peggy
Yes, My Darling Daughter 1938,Jl 13,19:2
Animal Kingdom, The 1938,Jl 27,14:5
Biography 1938,Ag 3,14:7
Arms and the Man 1938,Ag 10,14:1
Bachelor Born 1938,Ag 17,23:1
Farmer, Richard
Caine Mutiny Court-Martial, The 1953,O 14,35:1
Man Who Never Died, The 1958,N 22,27:2
Farmer, Shirley (Miscellaneous)
Major Barbara 1956,O 31,27:1
Farmer, Virginia
Stolen Fruit 1925,O 8,31:4
Damn the Tears 1927,Ja 22,11:1
Spread Eagle 1927,Ap 5,30:2
1931 1931,D 11,34:3
Night Over Taos 1932,Mr 10,25:3
Listen Professor! 1943,D 23,22:1
Farmer, Virginia (Playwright)
Spring Song 1927,D 22,26:3
Farnam, George B
Hippolytus 1935,Je 15,20:4

Farnel, Mme
Tartuffe 1922,N 23,21:3
Maitresse de Roi 1926,D 1,24:1
Dame aux Camelias, La 1926,D 7,24:2
Farnese, Sylva
Back Seat Drivers 1928,D 26,14:4
Farney, Evelyn
Actors Fund Fete 1942,F 23,24:5
Wine, Women and Song 1942,S 29,18:3
Farnham, Sylvia
Saint Joan 1951,O 5,23:2
Farnol, Jane
Midsummer Night's Dream, A 1967,Je 19,42:1
Antigone 1967,Je 19,43:1
Richard II 1968,Je 24,42:3
As You Like It 1968,Je 24,42:3
Androcles and the Lion 1968,Je 27,47:1
Farnoli, Barry (Costume Designer)
Bassa Moona 1936,D 9,35:4
Farnoli, Barry (Scenic Designer)
Bassa Moona 1936,D 9,35:4
Farnsworth, Elizabeth
Nine Till Six 1936,Mr 14,10:3
Farnsworth, Robert
Cradle Will Rock, The 1937,D 6,19:4
Cradle Will Rock, The 1938,Ja 4,19:3
Farnsworth, W P (Producer)
Big Pond, The 1928,Ag 22,25:1
First Mortgage 1929,O 11,36:1
Farnum, Bee
Best Foot Forward 1941,O 2,28:2
Farnum, Frank
Nine O'Clock Revue 1921,F 9,7:5
Keep It Clean 1929,Je 25,35:5
Farnum, Frank and Orchestra
Vaudeville (Palace) 1923,Ja 23,18:2
Farnum, Hilda (Costume Designer)
Ginger Snaps 1930,Ja 1,30:5
Farnum, William
Untitled-Benefit 1922,My 8,14:5
Buccaneer, The 1925,O 3,10:2
Julius Caesar 1926,S 19,28:5
Macbeth 1928,N 20,28:3
Headquarters 1929,N 24,X,4:5
Headquarters 1929,D 5,32:4
Farnworth, Donald
Best Foot Forward 1956,Mr 3,16:1
Show Boat 1957,Je 28,30:2
Farnworth, Ralph
Pajama Game, The 1954,My 14,20:2
Bajour 1964,N 24,42:1
Farquhar, Camilla
Small Timers, The 1925,Ja 28,15:3
Farquhar, George (Playwright)
Beaux' Stratagem, The 1927,F 13,VII,2:1
Beaux' Stratagem, The 1928,Je 5,20:1
Beaux' Stratagem, The 1928,Je 10,VIII,1:1
Beaux' Stratagem, The 1930,Ap 13,X,2:7
Recruiting Officer, The 1931,O 18,I,30:1
Beaux' Stratagem, The 1935,Jl 17,22:5
Recruiting Officer, The 1937,N 27,20:3
Beaux' Stratagem, The 1957,Jl 9,25:4
Recruiting Officer, The 1958,F 8,12:2
Beaux' Stratagem, The 1959,F 25,35:4
Beaux' Stratagem, The 1959,Mr 1,II,1:1
Beaux' Stratagem, The 1970,F 10,50:2
Beaux' Stratagem, The 1970,F 22,II,1:1
Farquhar, Malcolm (Director)
Lady Frederick 1970,S 17,57:1
Farquhar, Marlan (Lyricist)
Vie Parisienne, La 1945,Ja 13,14:5
Farquharson, Robert
Such Men Are Dangerous 1928,O 7,IX,2:7
Cenci, The 1935,Ag 18,IX,1:4
Farr, Derek
Odd Man In 1957,Jl 17,21:3
Farr, Gary
Exception and the Rule, The 1965,My 21,19:1
Farr, Helen
Kai Khosru 1925,Ap 27,14:2
Farr, Inga
Hamlet 1921,Je 21,20:2
Farr, Lowell (Musical Director)
O Marry Me 1961,O 28,13:1
Farr, Paxton (Playwright)
What's Your Number? 1929,Ag 16,18:3
Farra, Martha
Vaudeville (Hippodrome) 1924,Ap 1,18:1
Farrah, Abdel Kader (Costume Designer)
Othello 1964,Ag 3,16:6
Farrah, Abdel Kader (Scenic Designer)
Dr Faustus 1968,Je 29,20:1
Farrah, Farid
Mira 1970,Je 3,51:1
Farrand, Jan
Relapse, The 1950,N 23,54:2
Love's Labour's Lost 1953,F 5,20:3
Misalliance 1953,F 19,20:1
Portrait of a Lady 1954,D 22,27:6
Tonight in Samarkand 1955,F 17,22:2
Othello 1955,S 8,27:2
Othello 1955,S 18,II,1:1
Henry IV, Part I 1955,S 22,34:2

Farrand, Jan—Cont
Duchess of Malfi, The 1957,Mr 20,33:1
Right You Are (If You Think You Are) 1964,Mr 5,37:1
Impromptu at Versailles 1964,Mr 10,43:1
Lower Depths, The 1964,Mr 31,30:1
Umbrella, The 1965,My 27,31:1
Song of the Grasshopper 1967,S 29,52:2
What the Butler Saw 1970,My 5,56:1
What the Butler Saw 1970,My 17,II,1:1
Farrar, Elizabeth
Electra 1932,Ja 9,21:4
Ship Comes in, A 1934,S 20,21:1
Enemy of the People, An 1937,F 16,19:1
Cherry Orchard, The 1955,O 19,38:1
Asmodee 1958,Mr 26,42:2
Sign of Winter 1958,My 8,35:1
Song of Songs 1958,O 29,31:1
Farrar, Geraldine
Love Spell, The 1925,N 25,14:2
Farrar, Gwen
Louie the 14th 1925,N 17,29:3
Vaudeville (Palace) 1925,D 29,21:2
Farrar, John (Playwright)
Awful Mrs Eaton, The 1924,Jl 20,VII,1:7
Nerves 1924,S 2,22:2
That Awful Mrs Eaton! 1924,S 30,27:1
Farrar, Jules
That's the Woman 1930,S 4,27:2
Farrar, Karl
Admirable Bashville, The 1956,F 21,38:1
Farrar, Martha
Pin to See the Peepshow, A 1953,S 18,17:2
Cretan Woman, The 1954,Jl 8,18:2
Farrar, Matthew
One Touch of Venus 1943,O 8,14:1
Farrar, Phillip
Sleuth 1970,N 13,25:1
Farrar, Ruth
Merry Merry 1925,S 25,24:3
Farrar, Thomas (Scenic Designer)
Perfect Alibi, The 1928,N 28,24:2
Neighborhood Playhouse Program 1930,F 21,23:1
Mrs Moonlight 1930,S 30,24:3
Give Me Yesterday 1931,Mr 5,32:1
Roof, The 1931,O 31,22:4
Mahogany Hall 1934,Ja 18,18:5
Farrar, Tony
New Faces of 1943 1942,D 23,22:2
Farrara, Frank
Farewell to Arms, A 1930,S 23,30:3
Farrel, James
Upon My Soul 1927,Ap 22,19:1
Farrell, Anthony B (Miscellaneous)
Arms and the Girl 1950,F 3,28:2
Pal Joey 1952,Ja 4,17:6
Hazel Flagg 1953,F 12,22:2
Girl in Pink Tights, The 1954,Mr 6,13:2
Farrell, Anthony B (Producer)
All for Love 1949,Ja 24,16:5
Angel in the Pawnshop 1951,Ja 19,20:3
Billy Budd 1951,F 12,18:3
Love and Let Love 1951,O 20,11:2
Long Watch, The 1952,Mr 21,19:5
Farrell, Charles
Two Time Mary 1937,Ag 3,20:5
Reno 1937,Ag 10,22:7
Farrell, Clara
It Happened Tomorrow 1933,My 6,11:5
Farrell, Dorothy
Firebugs, The 1963,F 13,7:2
Farrell, Edward
White Gold 1925,N 3,34:5
Farrell, Eugene
Headquarters 1929,D 5,32:4
Farrell, Eve
Stork Is Dead, The 1932,S 24,18:2
Hotel Alimony 1934,Ja 30,16:2
Farrell, Frank
Robin Hood 1944,N 8,28:2
Farrell, George
Mongolia 1927,D 27,24:5
Farrell, Glenda
Third Day, The 1929,Ag 13,23:4
Divided Honors 1929,O 1,28:2
Recapture 1930,Ja 19,VIII,2:6
Recapture 1930,Ja 30,16:4
Fatal Woman, The 1930,Mr 2,IX,4:7
Love, Honor and Betray 1930,Mr 13,22:2
On the Spot 1930,O 30,33:3
Life Begins; Birth 1932,Mr 20,VIII,2:4
Life Begins 1932,Mr 29,23:2
Seperate Rooms 1940,Mr 25,10:3
Life of Reilly, The 1942,Ap 30,13:2
Overtons, The 1945,F 7,16:6
Mrs Gibsons' Boys 1949,My 5,35:2
Home Is the Hero 1954,S 23,42:2
Masquerade 1959,Mr 17,42:1
Forty Carats 1968,D 27,45:1
Forty Carats 1969,Ja 5,II,1:3
Farrell, Isabelle
From A to Z 1960,Ap 21,23:2
13 Daughters 1961,Mr 3,17:2
Sweet Miani 1962,S 26,33:2

Farrell, James
Ziegfeld Follies 1936,S 15,37:1
Banjo Eyes 1941,D 26,20:2
Farrell, Jane
Mima 1928,D 13,24:2
Social Register, The 1931,N 10,28:2
To My Husband 1936,Je 2,35:2
Farrell, John
Time of Your Life, The 1939,O 26,26:2
Time of Your Life, The 1940,S 24,27:2
Hello Out There 1942,S 30,28:2
This Rock 1943,F 19,23:2
Manhattan Nocturne 1943,O 27,26:2
Love on Leave 1944,Je 21,23:4
Lower North 1944,Ag 26,15:4
Angel in the Pawnshop 1951,Ja 19,20:3
Farrell, Johnny
Vaudeville (Hippodrome) 1926,My 4,31:2
Vaudeville (Palace) 1931,Ap 20,16:2
Farrell, M J (Playwright)
Spring Meeting 1938,Je 19,IX,2:1
Spring Meeting 1938,D 9,30:4
Ducks and Drakes 1941,D 14,IX,4:3
Farrell, Marie
Phoebe of Quality Street 1921,My 10,20:1
Farrell, Mary
After Such Pleasures 1934,Ja 6,18:6
After Such Pleasures 1934,F 8,15:2
Ponder Heart, The 1956,F 17,14:2
Loud Red Patrick, The 1956,O 4,28:1
Orpheus Descending 1957,Mr 22,28:1
Look Homeward, Angel 1957,N 29,33:1
Face of a Hero 1960,O 21,29:5
Midgie Purvis 1961,F 2,25:3
Days and Nights of Beebee Fenstermaker, The 1962,S 18,33:1
Farrell, Minerva (Costume Designer)
Come Slowly, Eden 1966,D 7,56:1
Farrell, Patsy
Aquarama 1960 1960,Jl 1,14:6
Farrell, Paul
Bishop's Bonfire, The 1955,Mr 1,22:8
Farrell, Paul (Producer)
Second Man, The 1930,My 25,IX,2:3
Bystander 1931,F 1,VIII,3:4
Farrell, Richard
Ruined Lady, The 1920,Ja 21,10:2
Elton Case, The 1921,S 12,16:2
Made for Each Other 1924,S 30,27:2
Nica 1926,Ja 26,19:1
Castles in the Air 1926,S 7,19:2
Lucky 1927,Mr 23,28:3
Forbidden Roads 1928,Ap 17,26:4
Farrell, Robert
Seventh Heart, The 1927,My 3,24:4
Aiglon, L' 1927,D 27,24:3
Mystery Man, The 1928,Ja 27,14:2
Congratulations 1929,My 1,28:4
Farrell, Rose
What Never Dies 1926,D 29,24:2
Farrell, T J
Fly With Me 1920,Mr 25,11:4
Farrell, Thomas
Up the Rebels 1941,O 31,21:1
Farrell, Tommy
Strip for Action 1942,O 1,26:2
Barefoot Boy With Cheek 1947,Ap 4,20:2
Farrell, Vessie
Out of the Night 1927,O 18,32:3
Farrell, Walter
Adam Had Two Sons 1932,Ja 21,17:1
Conquering Hero, The 1961,Ja 17,40:2
Paradise Island 1962,Je 28,22:1
Farrell, Walter S
You'll Never Know 1921,Ap 21,9:2
Farrell, William
Walk-Up 1961,F 24,24:1
Farren, George
Straw, The 1921,N 11,16:2
Alias Jimmy Valentine 1921,D 9,20:3
Up the Ladder 1922,Mr 7,11:2
Tweedles 1923,Ag 14,10:1
Queen Victoria 1923,N 16,15:1
Gypsy Jim 1924,Ja 15,17:4
Dust Heap, The 1924,Ap 25,20:2
In the Near Future 1925,Mr 11,19:1
Wild Birds 1925,Ap 10,16:1
Shannons of Broadway, The 1927,S 27,30:4
Money Lender, The 1928,Ag 28,27:3
Ladies of the Jury 1929,O 22,26:2
Precedent 1931,Ap 15,24:5
Farren, Jack (Miscellaneous)
Take a Giant Step 1956,S 26,30:1
Farren, Jack (Producer)
You Know I Can't Hear You When the Water's Running; Footsteps of Doves, The 1967,Mr 14,54:1
You Know I Can't Hear You When the Water's Running; I'm Herbert 1967,Mr 14,54:1
You Know I Can't Hear You When the Water's Running; I'll Be Home for Christmas 1967,Mr 14,54:1

Farren, Jack (Producer)—Cont
You Know I Can't Hear You When the Water's Running; Shock of Recognition, The 1967,Mr 14,54:1
Education of H*Y*M*A*N K*A*P*L*A*N, The 1968,Ap 5,57:1
Up Eden 1968,N 27,42:1
Farren, Vivian (Miscellaneous)
Education of H*Y*M*A*N K*A*P*L*A*N, The 1968,Ap 5,57:1
Up Eden 1968,N 27,42:1
Farrer, Joyce
Ruddigore 1955,O 21,32:2
Farrere, Claude (Playwright)
In the Night Watch 1921,Ja 31,10:1
Homme Qui Assassina, L' 1924,N 11,20:1
Farrill, Laritta
New York Exchange 1926,D 31,11:2
Farrington, Coleen
Chiaroscuro; Judges, The 1963,Je 6,40:8
Chiaroscuro; Maggie French Understands 1963,Je 6,40:8
Chiaroscuro; Kitty, I Hardly Knew You 1963,Je 6,40:8
Farrington, Eleanor (Scenic Designer)
Michael Drops In 1938,D 28,24:3
Deep Mrs Sykes, The 1945,Mr 20,22:6
Farrington, Mark
Merry Widow, The 1943,Ag 5,19:2
Farris, Dolores
Oh, Please! 1926,D 22,24:3
Farris, John
Hollywood Ice Revue 1950,Ja 21,13:4
Farris, John (Miscellaneous)
Hollywood Ice Revue 1955 1955,Ja 14,16:1
Farris, John (Playwright)
Death of the Well-Loved Boy, The 1967,My 16,48:1
Farriss, Carter
Trojan Women, The 1941,Ap 9,32:5
Farrow, Claude
Conversation Piece 1934,O 24,24:1
Farrow, Edward
Bottomland 1927,Je 28,29:3
Farss, Hassan
Marseilles 1930,N 18,28:2
Farster, Ned (Miscellaneous)
Getting Married 1970,Ja 20,46:1
Farwell, Jonathan
Coming Forth by Day of Osiris Jones, The; Kid, The 1961,Mr 15,45:2
Midsummer Night's Dream, A 1961,Ag 3,13:1
Tristram 1962,O 29,36:1
Devils, The 1963,N 5,25:1
Farwell, Sara
Here Come the Clowns 1954,My 5,36:2
Fasce, Tony (Miscellaneous)
After the Angels 1961,F 11,27:5
Fasciano, Marcia
Nativity, The 1965,D 3,44:2
Fascinato, Jack (Composer)
Kukla, Burr and Ollie 1960,N 1,47:2
Fass, Robert
Walk in Darkness 1963,O 29,30:2
Fass, Robert (Miscellaneous)
Walk in Darkness 1963,O 29,30:2
Fassett, Aubrey
Skin of Our Teeth, The 1942,N 19,29:5
Fassett, Jacob S Jr (Translator)
Malvaloca 1922,O 3,22:1
Fassett, Jay
Sonya 1921,Ag 16,18:3
Rita Coventry 1923,F 20,12:2
Cyrano de Bergerac 1923,N 2,14:1
Othello 1925,Ja 12,11:1
Don't Bother Mother 1925,F 4,18:2
Engaged! or Cheviot's Choice 1925,Je 19,24:2
Joker, The 1925,N 17,29:1
Bunk of 1926 1926,F 17,12:3
Bunk of 1926 1926,Ap 23,25:2
Henry IV, Part I 1926,Je 1,29:1
Junk 1927,Ja 6,25:1
One Glorious Hour 1927,Ap 15,27:2
Tales of Rigo 1927,My 31,25:3
Midsummer Night's Dream, A 1927,Je 27,25:1
White Eagle, The 1927,D 27,24:4
Becky Sharp 1929,Je 4,29:1
Milestones 1930,Je 3,27:1
As Husbands Go 1931,Mr 6,26:5
Biography 1932,D 13,25:3
Biography 1934,F 6,24:4
Late Wisdom 1934,Ap 24,27:4
Cross Ruff 1935,F 20,23:3
Declassee 1935,Ag 6,20:3
Russet Mantle 1936,Ja 17,15:5
County Chairman, The 1936,My 26,26:5
Russet Mantle 1936,Ag 18,15:2
Tovarich 1936,O 16,31:4
Our Town 1938,Ja 23,II,10:6
Our Town 1938,Ja 26,27:4
Our Town 1938,Ja 30,X,3:1
Our Town 1938,F 5,18:3
Our Town 1938,F 13,X,1:1
Delicate Story 1940,D 5,32:2

Fassett, Jay—Cont
Your Loving Son 1941,Ap 5,13:2
Dark Eyes 1943,Ja 15,20:2
Dark Eyes 1943,Ja 31,II,1:1
Loco 1946,O 17,29:2
Command Decision 1947,S 21,I,59:7
Command Decision 1947,O 2,30:2
Command Decision 1947,O 12,II,1:1
Fassett, Julia
American Holiday 1936,F 22,13:3
Fassett, Malcolm
White Peacock, The 1921,D 27,10:2
Little Clay Cart, The 1924,D 6,13:3
Exiles 1925,F 20,20:2
Pearl of Great Price, The 1926,N 2,34:3
Scarlet Lily, The 1927,Ja 31,12:3
Fassnacht, Adolph
Passion Play, The 1929,Ap 30,32:1
Passion Play, The 1929,My 5,IX,1:1
Fassnacht, Amalie
Passion Play, The 1929,Ap 30,32:1
Fassnacht, Augusta
Passion Play, The 1929,Ap 30,32:1
Fassnacht, Elsa
Passion Play, The 1929,Ap 30,32:1
Fassnacht, Georg
Passion Play, The 1929,Ap 30,32:1
Passion Play, The 1929,My 5,IX,1:1
Fassnacht, Georg Jr
Passion Play, The 1929,Ap 30,32:1
Fassy, Mark
Mummers and Men 1962,Mr 27,41:6
Fast, Howard (Playwright)
Thirty Pieces of Silver 1951,Mr 18,42:1
Fastre, Eddie
Maitresse de Roi 1926,D 1,24:1
Dame aux Camelias, La 1926,D 7,24:2
Fately, Midgie
Vaudeville (Palace) 1929,N 11,20:5
Fates, Gilbert
Hill Between, The 1938,Mr 12,12:5
Where Do We Go From Here? 1938,N 16,26:2
Stop Press 1939,Mr 20,13:2
Fatone, Charles (Costume Designer)
Decline and Fall of the Entire World As Seen
Through the Eyes of Cole Porter Revisited, The
1965,Mr 31,24:2
Ben Bagley's New Cole Porter Revue
1965,D 23,20:1
Fatoni, Italia
Onda e lo Scoglio, L'; Wave and the Rock, The
1931,Ap 13,17:3
Fatt, Chan
Teahouse of the August Moon, The
1955,My 10,24:1
Fauchild, Nora
Jazz a La Carte 1922,Je 3,8:3
Fauchois, Rene (Original Author)
Late Christopher Bean, The 1932,N 1,24:3
Fauchois, Rene (Playwright)
Monkey Talks, The 1925,D 29,20:1
Monkey Talks, The 1926,Ja 3,VII,1:1
Lecon de Talma, La 1926,N 14,VIII,2:1
Mademoiselle Jockey 1926,D 5,VIII,6:1
Faulkner, Caroline
Winterset 1966,F 10,32:2
Faulkner, David
Blood Wedding 1958,Ap 1,35:1
Cock-A-Doodle Dandy 1958,N 13,39:2
Faulkner, John (Lighting Director)
Chicago 70 1970,My 26,33:1
Faulkner, John (Miscellaneous)
Chicago 70 1970,My 26,33:1
Faulkner, Maurice (Musical Director)
Yanqui and the Senorita, The 1952,Ag 8,8:7
Faulkner, Virginia (Playwright)
All in Fun 1940,D 28,11:2
It Takes Two 1947,F 4,33:4
Faulkner, William (Miscellaneous)
Banquet for the Moon, A 1961,Ja 20,24:2
Faulkner, William (Original Author)
Journey to Jefferson 1964,Jl 9,24:3
Faulkner, William (Playwright)
Requiem for a Nun 1956,S 24,23:6
Requiem for a Nun 1959,Ja 31,13:2
Requiem for a Nun 1959,F 8,II,1:1
Faulkner, Worthe
Marjolaine 1922,Ja 25,16:1
Magic Ring, The 1923,O 2,10:1
Magnolia Lady, The 1924,N 26,17:2
Honeymoon Lane 1926,S 21,32:3
Faure, Gabriel (Miscellaneous)
Pelleas et Melisande 1939,Ap 2,X,7:4
Faurkauf, Betty
Uncle Moses 1930,N 29,21:3
Faussett, Hudson
Royal Family, The 1936,Jl 16,15:4
Criminals, The 1941,D 22,24:3
Lady in Danger 1945,Mr 30,18:6
Faussett, Hudson (Director)
Night in Spring, A 1935,Ag 7,22:2
Tenting Tonight 1947,Ap 3,32:2
Russell Patterson's Sketch-Book 1960,F 8,35:1

Faussett, Hudson (Producer)
Russell Patterson's Sketch-Book 1960,F 8,35:1
Faust, Gilberta
Peg o' My Dreams 1924,My 6,25:3
Jack in the Pulpit 1925,Ja 7,33:1
Scarlet Pages 1929,S 10,26:3
Fulton of Oak Falls 1937,Ja 2,15:3
Fulton of Oak Falls 1937,F 11,18:2
Faust, Jean
Rosalinda; Fledermaus, Die 1942,O 29,26:5
Faust, Vic
Ten Nights in a Barroom 1932,Ja 21,17:1
Faust, Walter Livingston (Playwright)
This Rock 1943,F 19,23:2
Faustine, Cosette
Paolo and Francesca 1924,D 3,24:2
Favart, Edmee
Ciboulette 1926,O 31,VIII,2:4
Diable a Paris, Le 1927,N 13,IX,4:2
Faversham, Edith
Skin of Our Teeth, The 1942,N 19,29:5
Faversham, Judith
Macbeth 1955,O 8,12:6
Faversham, Philip
Fly Away Home 1935,Ja 16,20:4
Boy Meets Girl 1935,N 28,38:2
Chalked Out 1937,Mr 26,24:2
Fly Away Home 1937,Ap 27,18:1
Boy Meets Girl 1937,Jl 6,23:1
Hill Between, The 1938,Mr 12,12:5
Gloriana 1938,N 26,18:4
Cue for Passion 1940,D 20,33:4
Faversham, William
Prince and the Pauper, The 1920,N 2,15:1
Prince and the Pauper, The 1920,N 7,VII,1:1
Prince and the Pauper, The 1920,N 21,VI,1:4
Silver Fox, The 1921,S 6,13:1
Squaw Man, The 1921,D 27,10:3
Captain Briquet 1923,S 16,VII,2:8
Lesson in Love, A 1923,S 25,10:1
Lesson in Love, A 1923,S 30,II,1:1
Leah Kleschna 1924,Ap 22,19:2
Leah Kleschna 1924,Ap 27,VIII,1:1
Mask and the Face, The 1924,S 11,27:3
Vaudeville (Palace) 1927,My 17,27:4
Diplomacy 1928,My 29,16:3
Diplomacy 1928,Je 3,VIII,1:1
Her Friend the King 1929,O 8,34:5
Merchant of Venice, The 1931,N 17,31:1
Julius Caesar 1931,N 18,26:3
Hamlet 1931,N 19,26:6
Faversham, William (Mrs)
Pearl of Great Price, The 1926,N 2,34:3
Faversham, William (Producer)
Prince and the Pauper, The 1920,N 21,VI,1:4
Favia, Raffaele
Roberta 1937,Je 27,II,6:1
Favieres, Guy
Maitresse de Roi 1926,D 1,24:1
Dame aux Camelias, La 1926,D 7,24:2
Aventuriere, L' 1926,D 17,27:3
Favor, Edward
Three Musketeers, The 1921,My 20,18:5
Bulldog Drummond 1921,D 27,10:2
Merton of the Movies 1922,N 14,16:2
Shooting Shadows 1924,Je 27,16:5
Pearl of Great Price, The 1926,N 2,34:3
Banshee, The 1927,D 6,26:2
John Ferguson 1928,Ja 18,23:1
Eva the Fifth 1928,Ag 29,19:3
Man's Estate 1929,Ap 2,28:2
Purity 1930,D 26,18:2
Lancashire Lass, The 1931,D 31,16:3
Round-Up, The 1932,Mr 8,19:4
John Ferguson 1933,Jl 11,15:7
American, Very Early 1934,Ja 31,21:2
Favor, Toni
Eve of St Mark, The 1942,O 8,30:2
Pick-Up Girl 1944,My 4,25:2
Place of Our Own, A 1945,Ap 3,23:7
Favre, Lucienne (Playwright)
Prosper 1935,Ja 13,IX,2:1
Favreau, Didi (Composer)
Dark of the Moon 1970,Ap 4,21:2
Fawcett, Frances (Translator)
Lulu 1958,S 30,24:1
Fawcett, George
Wren, The 1921,O 11,22:1
Mountain Man, The 1921,D 13,24:2
Peacock 1932,O 12,27:1
Fawcett, George (Director)
Peacock 1932,O 12,27:1
Fawcett, George (Producer)
Peacock 1932,O 12,27:1
Fawcett, Marion (Playwright)
Quince Bush, The 1932,Ag 21,IX,1:1
Fawkes, Conrad
That Thing at the Cherry Lane 1965,My 19,42:1
Fay, Alice
Skin of Our Teeth, The 1955,Ag 18,16:1
Fay, Billy
Plutocrat, The 1930,F 21,23:3

Fay, Billy—Cont
This One Man 1930,O 22,32:3
Fay, Brendan
Heloise 1958,S 25,28:4
Legend of Lizzie, The 1959,F 10,39:1
Donogoo 1961,Ja 19,25:3
King of the Whole Damn World 1962,Ap 16,32:2
Wretched the Lionhearted 1962,S 13,31:2
Time of the Key, A 1963,S 12,33:3
Thistle in My Bed 1963,N 20,48:1
Stephen D 1967,S 25,58:1
King Lear 1968,N 8,43:1
Cry of Players, A 1968,N 15,40:1
Borstal Boy 1970,Ap 1,38:1
Fay, E Ford (Miscellaneous)
And the Wind Blows 1959,Ap 29,28:1
Fay, Elaine
Broken Chain, The 1929,F 21,30:4
Fay, Frances C (Translator)
Mongrel, The 1924,D 16,28:2
Fay, Frank
Jim Jam Jems 1920,O 5,13:2
Fables 1922,F 7,12:2
Pinwheel Revel 1922,Je 16,20:6
Artists and Models 1923,Ag 21,12:2
Vaudeville (Palace) 1926,Je 1,29:5
Vaudeville (Palace) 1926,Je 8,23:1
Vaudeville (Palace) 1926,Je 15,23:3
Vaudeville (Palace) 1926,Je 22,21:3
Vaudeville (Palace) 1926,Je 29,21:3
Vaudeville (Palace) 1926,Jl 6,19:3
Vaudeville (Palace) 1926,Jl 13,19:4
Vaudeville (Palace) 1926,Jl 20,17:4
Vaudeville (Palace) 1926,S 7,24:6
Vaudeville (Palace) 1926,S 14,25:3
Vaudeville (Palace) 1927,Jl 5,19:3
Vaudeville (Palace) 1927,Jl 12,29:3
Vaudeville (Palace) 1927,Jl 19,27:6
Harry Delmar's Revels 1927,N 29,30:2
Vaudeville (Palace) 1928,My 1,33:2
Vaudeville (Palace) 1928,My 8,25:2
Vaudeville (Palace) 1929,F 4,21:4
Vaudeville (Palace) 1929,F 11,26:2
Conflict, The 1929,F 11,26:2
Vaudeville (Palace) 1929,Mr 18,30:5
Vaudeville (Palace) 1930,S 8,17:3
Vaudeville (Palace) 1932,Mr 7,13:4
Tattle Tales 1933,Je 2,22:6
Frank Fay's Vaudeville 1939,Mr 3,20:4
Laugh Time 1943,S 9,35:2
Laugh Time 1943,S 19,II,1:1
Harvey 1944,N 2,23:2
Harvey 1944,N 12,II,1:1
Harvey 1947,Jl 15,27:3
Fay, Frank (Director)
Tattle Tales 1933,Je 2,22:6
Fay, Frank (Playwright)
Fables 1922,F 7,12:2
Tattle Tales 1933,Je 2,22:6
Fay, Frank (Producer)
Tattle Tales 1933,Je 2,22:6
Frank Fay's Vaudeville 1939,Mr 3,20:4
Fay, Gaby
Murray Hill 1927,S 30,29:1
Bellamy Trial, The 1928,Ag 20,21:1
Dinner Is Served 1929,Ag 16,18:4
Fay, George
Mr Jiggins of Jigginstown 1936,D 18,30:2
Big Blow 1938,O 3,11:2
Fay, Joseph
Hello, Yourself 1928,O 31,28:2
Jerry for Short 1929,Ag 13,23:4
Fay, Larry (Producer)
Under the Gaslight 1929,Ap 3,27:1
Fay, Letitia
He Who Gets Slapped 1946,Mr 21,31:4
Blithe Spirit 1952,F 23,7:5
Fay, Marilyn
Late Arrival 1953,O 20,35:5
Fay, Marion
Late Arrival 1953,O 20,35:5
Fay, Mary Helen (Playwright)
Embezzled Heaven 1944,N 1,20:2
Embezzled Heaven 1944,N 5,II,1:2
Alice in Arms 1945,F 1,18:4
Big Two, The 1947,Ja 9,21:2
Faithfully Yours 1951,O 19,22:5
Fay, Olive
Woof, Woof 1929,D 26,20:4
Fay, Patricia
Flowering Peach, The 1954,D 29,19:2
Hotel Paradiso 1957,Ap 12,22:2
Waltz of the Toreadors, The 1958,Mr 5,37:1
Darwin's Theories 1960,O 19,53:2
Coop, The 1966,Mr 2,48:1
Fay, Terry
Dance Night 1938,O 15,20:5
Girl From Wyoming, The 1938,O 31,12:1
Heart of a City 1942,F 13,24:6
Fay, Terry (Miscellaneous)
Dozens, The 1969,Mr 14,51:1
Fay, Vivian
Earl Carroll's Vanities 1930,Jl 2,28:3
Music Hall Varieties 1932,N 23,15:3

Fay, Vivian—Cont

Melody 1933,F 15,17:4

Fay, William
Murder at the Vanities 1933,S 13,22:4
Play, Genius, Play! 1935,O 31,17:2
Abie's Irish Rose 1937,My 13,30:2
Roosty 1938,F 15,21:2

Fayde, Gertrude
Promis' Lan', De 1930,My 28,31:2

Fayde, Gertrude (Director)
Promis' Lan', De 1930,My 28,31:2

Faye, Blanche
Kiss for Cinderella, A 1942,Mr 11,22:2
Lower North 1944,Ag 26,15:4

Faye, Bobby
Hi Yank 1944,Ap 8,14:2

Faye, Frances
Artists and Models 1943,N 6,16:6

Faye, Herbie
Wine, Women and Song 1942,S 29,18:3
Top Banana 1951,N 2,19:2

Faye, Janina
Miracle Worker, The 1961,Mr 10,19:4
Dance of Death, The 1967,O 20,50:1

Faye, Joey
Sing Out the News 1938,S 26,12:5
Laughter Over Broadway 1939,Ja 16,10:3
Strip for Action 1942,O 1,26:2
Strip for Action 1942,O 11,VIII,1:1
Milky Way, The 1943,Je 10,17:2
Boy Meets Girl 1943,Je 23,15:5
Allah Be Praised! 1944,Ap 21,14:2
Duchess Misbehaves, The 1946,F 14,32:2
Tidbits of 1946 1946,Jl 9,17:2
High Button Shoes 1947,O 10,32:2
High Button Shoes 1947,N 23,II,1:1
Top Banana 1951,N 2,19:2
Tender Trap, The 1954,O 14,37:2
Little Me 1962,N 19,41:3
Guys and Dolls 1965,Ap 29,39:1
Man of La Mancha 1969,My 3,38:4
Lyle 1970,Mr 21,16:2

Faye, Tina
It's a Bird . . . It's a Plane . . . It's Superman
1966,Mr 30,34:1

Faye, Vini
Best of Burlesque 1957,S 30,27:2

Faye, Vini (Miscellaneous)
Best of Burlesque 1957,S 30,27:2

Fayer, Art
Tarot 1970,D 12,19:1

Fayer, Theresa
Jazz a La Carte 1922,Je 3,8:3

Fayne and Foster
Mr Winkle's Holliday 1946,Je 24,27:6

Faystone, Anne
All Soul's Eve 1920,My 13,9:1

Fayth, Roger
Young and Beautiful, The 1959,My 29,13:1

Fazakas, Franz
Davy Jones's Locker 1959,Mr 30,25:1
Davy Jones's Locker 1966,D 25,48:5
People Is the Thing That the World Is Fullest Of
1967,F 21,53:1
Wizard of Oz, The 1968,N 28,69:2

Fazan, Eleanor (Director)
Beyond the Fringe 1962,O 29,36:1

Fazekas, Imre (Playwright)
Troika 1928,Mr 4,IX,2:7
Troika 1930,Ap 2,32:6

Fazio, Dino
Advocate, The 1963,O 15,46:7
Advocate, The 1963,O 27,II,1:1

Feagin, Hugh
Richard II 1962,Je 18,20:2

Feagins, Joe (Miscellaneous)
Ruy Blas 1957,D 14,16:3

Fear, Arthur
Lily Maid, The 1937,Ja 13,20:4

Fearing, Gordon
Philosophy in the Boudoir 1969,My 22,55:2

Fearl, Clifford
South Pacific 1955,My 5,39:5
Mame 1966,My 25,41:1
Dear World 1969,F 7,33:1
Jimmy 1969,O 24,38:1

Fearnley, John
Key Largo 1939,N 28,30:2

Fearnley, John (Director)
King and I, The 1956,Ap 19,35:4
South Pacific 1957,Ap 25,35:1
Carousel 1957,S 12,38:2
Oklahoma! 1958,Mr 20,32:3
King and I, The 1960,My 12,40:1
King and I, The 1960,My 22,II,1:1
South Pacific 1961,Ap 27,26:3
Brigadoon 1962,My 31,21:4
Eddie Fisher at the Winter Garden 1962,O 3,47:1
Brigadoon 1963,F 1,6:2
Oklahoma! 1963,F 28,8:2
Oklahoma! 1963,My 16,40:1
King and I, The 1963,Je 13,30:2
Porgy and Bess 1964,My 7,32:1
Brigadoon 1964,D 24,9:1

Kiss Me, Kate 1965,My 13,31:1
Oklahoma! 1965,D 16,62:1
Sound of Music, The 1967,Ap 27,52:1
King and I, The 1968,My 24,39:1
Sound of Music, The 1970,Jl 3,13:1

Fearnley, John (Miscellaneous)
Maggie 1953,F 19,20:2

Fearnley, John (Producer)
Talent '49 1949,Ap 13,39:4
Maggie 1953,F 19,20:2

Fearon, Edward
Shunned 1960,D 21,39:1

Fearon, W R (Playwright)
Parnell of Avondale 1934,O 3,24:4

Fears, Peggy
No Foolin' 1926,Je 25,25:1
LeMaire's Affairs 1927,Mr 29,22:4
Divine Moment, A 1934,Ja 8,21:8

Fears, Peggy (Producer)
Child of Manhattan 1932,Mr 2,15:1
Nona 1932,O 5,26:4
Music in the Air 1932,O 23,IX,3:3
Music in the Air 1932,N 9,28:2
Divine Moment, A 1934,Ja 8,21:8

Feaster, Gwendolyn
Chocolate Dandies, The 1924,S 2,22:2

Feather, Lorraine
Walk Down Mah Street! 1968,Je 13,54:1

Feather, William A Jr
What a Relief 1935,D 14,10:6

Featherston, Vane
Voice From the Minaret, The 1922,Ja 31,11:2
Fedora 1922,F 11,18:1

Featherstone, Kevin
Finian's Rainbow 1967,Ap 6,44:1

Featherstone, Vane
Truth About Blayds, The 1922,Mr 15,22:1

Fechner, Antonina
Cricket on the Hearth, The 1925,My 29,20:2
Wonder Bar, The 1931,Mr 18,23:4

Fechner, Mme
Chauve-Souris 1922,Je 6,17:4
Chauve-Souris 1925,Ja 15,25:1

Fedak, Sari
Twin Stars 1928,Ja 15,VIII,2:1

Fedak-Molnar, Mrs
Dream Queen 1930,F 23,III,7:2

Fede, Val
Movie Man 1959,O 28,40:4

Feder, A H (Lighting Director)
Gentlewoman 1934,Mr 23,28:4
Hook-Up, The 1935,My 9,24:6
Ghosts 1935,D 13,30:6
Conjur' Man Dies 1936,Mr 12,18:5
Macbeth 1936,Ap 15,25:4
New Faces of 1936 1936,My 20,24:5
Horse Eats Hat 1936,S 28,14:2
Hedda Gabler 1936,N 17,34:4
Tragical Historie of Doctor Faustus, The
1937,Ja 31,XI,1:1
Native Ground 1937,Mr 24,28:4
Without Warning 1937,My 3,23:2
Diff'rent 1938,Ja 26,26:4
Pygmalion 1938,Ja 27,16:3
Captain Jinks of the Horse Marines 1938,Ja 28,16:2
Prologue to Glory 1938,Mr 18,22:2
Big Blow 1938,O 3,11:2
Here Come the Clowns 1938,D 8,36:2
Sing for Your Supper 1939,Ap 25,18:6
Speak of the Devil! 1939,O 7,21:7
Passenger to Bali, A 1940,Mr 15,26:2
Hold On to Your Hats 1940,S 12,30:3
Johnny Belinda 1940,S 19,26:2
Autumn Hill 1942,Ap 14,17:4
Magic 1942,S 30,28:2
Hello Out There 1942,S 30,28:2
Winged Victory 1943,N 22,24:1
Tower Beyond Tragedy, The 1950,N 27,29:1
Mary Rose 1951,Mr 5,25:2
Sleep of Prisoners, A 1951,O 17,36:2
Three Wishes for Jamie 1952,Mr 22,9:2
Pin to See the Peepshow, A 1953,S 18,17:2
Immoralist, The 1954,F 9,22:1
Immoralist, The 1954,F 14,II,1:1
Boy Friend, The 1954,O 1,20:1
What Every Woman Knows 1954,D 23,16:2
Flowering Peach, The 1954,D 29,19:2
Flowering Peach, The 1955,Ja 9,II,1:1
Wisteria Trees, The 1955,F 3,20:2
Inherit the Wind 1955,Ap 22,20:2
Seventh Heaven 1955,My 27,16:2
Skin of Our Teeth, The 1955,Ag 18,16:1
My Fair Lady 1956,Mr 16,20:2
Clearing in the Woods, A 1957,Ja 11,20:2
Clearing in the Woods, A 1957,Ja 20,II,1:1
Visit to a Small Planet 1957,F 8,18:1
Orpheus Descending 1957,Mr 22,28:1
Orpheus Descending 1957,Mr 31,II,1:1
Time Remembered 1957,N 13,41:2
Goldilocks 1958,O 13,33:1
Cold Wind and the Warm, The 1958,D 9,55:1
Come Play With Me 1959,My 1,33:5

Feder, A H (Lighting Director)—Cont
Can-Can 1959,Ag 26,25:4
Loss of Roses, A 1959,N 30,27:1
Loss of Roses, A 1959,D 6,II,5:1
Greenwillow 1960,Mr 9,38:1
Camelot 1960,D 5,42:1
Tiger Tiger Burning Bright 1962,D 24,5:2
My Fair Lady 1964,My 21,43:2
Three Sisters, The 1964,Je 23,24:1
On a Clear Day You Can See Forever
1965,O 18,44:1
Country Girl, The 1966,S 30,55:1
Elizabeth the Queen 1966,N 4,30:1
Carousel 1966,D 16,56:2
Beyond Desire 1967,O 11,36:1
Carnival! 1968,D 13,58:1

Feder, A H (Scenic Designer)
Gioconda Smile, The 1950,O 9,21:2
Boy Friend, The 1954,O 1,20:1
Come Play With Me 1959,My 1,33:5
Country Girl, The 1966,S 30,55:1
Elizabeth the Queen 1966,N 4,30:1
Beyond Desire 1967,O 11,36:1

Feder, Blanche
Nautical but Nice 1931,Ap 19,31:6

Feder, M
Germany Aflame 1933,O 28,20:5
Happy Days 1934,Ap 2,12:5
Schlemihl 1936,S 19,20:4

Feder, Miriam
Abi Gezunt 1949,O 10,19:4
Sadie Is a Lady 1950,Ja 28,9:2

Feder, Moishe
Once Upon a Time 1933,S 22,15:1
Little Giants 1933,D 2,9:5
House on Grand Street, A 1953,O 10,12:6

Feder, Morris
Mazal Darf Men; You Need Luck 1938,My 18,16:5

Feder, Moses
Dybbuk, The 1924,Ja 29,17:7
Kibitzer, The 1931,N 7,17:3
Mother's Son 1931,N 26,36:4
Under One Roof 1932,F 8,21:2
Three in Love 1933,N 8,32:5
Organ Grinder, The 1934,Ja 1,28:3
One in a Million 1934,N 17,13:2
What Girls Do 1935,Ja 14,10:4
Stranger, The 1935,N 7,26:2
Saint and Sinners 1935,D 30,15:2
Warson at Night 1938,Ja 31,14:3

Feder, Sylvia
Abi Gezunt 1949,O 10,19:4
Sadie Is a Lady 1950,Ja 28,9:2
Family Mishmash, A 1958,O 20,36:1

Federici, Marietta
Another City, Another Land 1968,O 9,42:1

Federoff, George (Scenic Designer)
What Every Woman Knows 1938,Ag 30,14:5

Fedor, Tania
Sidna 1926,Jl 23,11:2

Fedorova, Nina (Original Author)
Family, The 1943,Mr 31,22:4

Fee, Eileen
Blue Butterfly, The 1929,F 17,29:3

Fee, John G
Good Old Days, The 1923,Ag 15,21:2

Feeley, Danny
Too Many Heroes 1937,N 16,26:2

Feeney, George
Happy Hypocrite, The 1968,S 6,38:1

Feffer, Itzik (Miscellaneous)
Untitled-Poetry Reading 1967,Jl 18,29:1

Fehdmer, Helene
Blaue Boll, Der 1931,Ja 25,VIII,4:1

Feher, Milton
Noah 1935,F 14,25:2

Fehl, Walter
Fine and Dandy 1930,S 24,26:1

Fehlhaber, Fred R (Producer)
Anya 1965,N 30,48:1

Fehling, Ilse (Scenic Designer)
Lauter Luegen 1937,O 24,XI,3:1

Fehling, Juergen (Director)
Three Sisters, The 1927,Mr 13,VII,2:4
Measure for Measure 1927,S 18,VII,2:2
Outside Looking In 1929,Je 23,VIII,2:1
Love in the Country 1930,S 28,VIII,4:4
Rauhnacht 1932,F 21,VIII,2:1
Egmont 1932,Je 19,IX,1:3
Princess of Trapezunt 1933,F 19,IX,3:1
Siebenstein 1933,My 28,IX,1:3
Heilige Crispin, Der 1933,Je 25,IX,1:2
Mensch aus Erde Gemacht 1933,N 5,IX,3:1
Glass Wasser, Das 1934,D 30,IX,2:1
Revisor 1935,O 6,XI,3:7
Donna Diana 1936,Je 28,IX,2:1
Gefesselte Phantasie, Die 1936,N 8,X,2:1
Richard III 1937,My 30,X,2:2
Flies, The 1948,F 29,II,2:1

Fehling, Juergen (Producer)
Merchant of Venice, The 1928,Ap 1,IX,2:4
Blaue Boll, Der 1931,Ja 25,VIII,4:1
Marriage 1931,N 1,VIII,4:3
Don Karlos 1935,Jl 28,X,1:6

Fehling, Juergen (Producer)—Cont
Glass Wasser, Das 1935,Jl 28,X,1:6
Fehr, Carl A (Musical Director)
Common Glory, The 1947,Jl 27,II,1:1
Founders, The 1957,My 14,39:1
Feibleman, Peter S (Original Author)
Tiger Tiger Burning Bright 1962,D 24,5:2
Feibleman, Peter S (Playwright)
Tiger Tiger Burning Bright 1962,D 24,5:2
Feid, Eliot
Sandhog 1954,N 24,17:1
Feiffer, Jules (Miscellaneous)
Oh! Calcutta! 1969,Je 18,33:1
Feiffer, Jules (Playwright)
Passionella 1966,O 19,53:1
Little Murders 1967,Ap 26,38:1
Little Murders 1967,Je 4,II,1:1
Little Murders 1967,Jl 23,II,5:4
Collision Course; Unexpurgated Memoirs of
Bernard Mergendeiler, The 1968,My 9,55:2
God Bless 1968,N 3,II,1:1
Little Murders 1969,Ja 6,38:1
Little Murders 1969,Ja 26,II,1:1
Oh! Calcutta! 1969,Je 29,II,1:7
Little Murders 1969,O 2,54:1
White House Murder Case, The 1970,F 19,59:1
White House Murder Case, The 1970,Mr 1,II,1:4
White House Murder Case, The 1970,Mr 15,II,3:1
Feigay, Paul (Producer)
On the Town 1944,D 29,11:4
Million Dollar Baby 1945,D 22,17:2
Land's End 1946,D 12,37:5
Me and Molly 1948,F 27,27:2
Do You Know the Milky Way? 1961,O 17,45:1
Feigenbaum, Naomi
Flies, The; Mouches, Les 1947,Ap 18,26:3
Feil, Gerald (Lighting Director)
Macbeth 1955,O 8,12:6
Dark Lady of the Sonnets, The 1956,F 21,38:1
Admirable Bashville, The 1956,F 21,38:1
Ballad of Jazz Street, The 1959,N 12,28:1
Rosemary 1960,N 15,47:1
Alligators, The 1960,N 15,47:1
Traveller Without Luggage 1964,S 18,26:2
Feil, Gerald (Miscellaneous)
Fallout 1959,My 21,36:2
Alligators, The 1960,N 15,47:1
Rosemary 1960,N 15,47:1
Feil, Pat
Little Theatre Tournament; Man in the Stalls, The
1929,My 8,34:4
Feilbert, Ed (Playwright)
Pajama Tops 1963,Je 1,15:1
Feilbert, Edward Allen (Playwright)
House in Paris, The 1944,Mr 21,17:1
Fein, Bernie
Threepenny Opera, The 1955,S 21,38:1
Fein, Claire
Aunt Caroline's Will 1954,Ag 11,21:1
Fein, Irving (Producer)
Jack Benny 1963,Mr 1,10:5
Fein, Maria
Verbrecher, Die 1928,D 23,VIII,4:1
Evening of European Theatre, An 1960,Ap 26,41:1
Fein, Maurice
Humble, The 1926,O 14,22:2
Loud Speaker 1927,Mr 3,27:2
Tales of Rigo 1927,My 31,25:3
Feinberg, Joseph M
Little Theatre Tournement; Where The Cross Is
Made 1928,My 10,31:1
Feinberg, L (Translator)
Yegor Bulevitch 1934,Ja 8,21:7
Dostigayev 1935,Ja 14,10:5
Feiner, Benjamin F
His Majesty the Queen 1926,Mr 9,8:1
Feiner, Benjamin Jr (Playwright)
Bursting the Barriers 1930,My 7,25:1
Feiner, Herman (Playwright)
Three Little Girls 1930,Mr 30,VIII,2:7
Three Little Girls 1930,Ap 15,29:1
Feinman, Diana
Longing for Home 1933,S 22,15:1
Feinstein, Ashley (Director)
Blue Boy in Black, The 1963,My 1,32:1
Feinstein, Ashley (Producer)
Blue Boy in Black, The 1963,My 1,32:1
How Much, How Much? 1970,Ap 21,49:1
Feinstein, Florence
Honeymoon in Israel, A 1962,O 15,33:5
Feinstein, Laurence
Shoot Anything With Hair That Moves
1969,F 3,29:1
Feirstein, Frederick (Playwright)
Sondra 1967,My 10,39:1
Harold 1967,My 10,39:1
Feist, Babette
Crime and Punishment 1935,Ja 23,20:3
Victoria Regina 1935,D 27,15:2
Victoria Regina 1938,O 4,20:2
Case of Youth, A 1940,Mr 25,10:3
Criminals, The 1941,D 22,24:3
Feist, Eugene (Playwright)
Building Blocks 1954,My 8,14:4

Feist, Frances (Costume Designer)
Lew Leslie's Blackbirds of 1939 1939,F 13,12:2
Yokel Boy 1939,Jl 7,12:2
Feist, Gene (Director)
Wretched the Lionhearted 1962,S 13,31:2
Pins and Needles 1967,Je 9,51:2
Waiting for Lefty 1967,D 19,58:2
King Lear 1968,Je 3,55:4
Journey's End 1968,O 28,55:3
Candida 1969,F 3,29:1
Dance of Death, The 1969,My 26,53:1
Trumpets and Drums 1969,O 13,52:1
Macbeth 1969,D 23,25:1
Oedipus 1970,F 23,30:1
Hamlet 1970,O 19,51:1
Feist, Gene (Playwright)
Toy for the Clowns, A 1962,S 13,31:2
Wretched the Lionhearted 1962,S 13,31:2
Dance of Death, The 1969,My 26,53:1
Lady From Maxim's, The 1970,Je 1,41:1
Feist, Gene (Producer)
Lady From Maxim's, The 1970,Je 1,41:1
Feist, Milton (Translator)
Aunt Caroline's Will 1954,Ag 11,21:1
Feistel, John
Shadow, The 1923,D 15,16:2
Anneliese von Dessau 1926,F 26,24:3
Dantons Tod 1927,D 21,28:3
Armseligen Besenbinder, Die 1928,N 19,16:2
Berlin 1931,D 31,16:1
Feivelowitz, Ben
Mother's Sabbath Days 1960,N 21,33:2
Eleventh Inheritor, The 1962,N 22,43:5
Bronx Express, 1968 1968,N 16,43:3
Brothers Ashkenazi, The 1970,N 17,53:2
Fejer, Joe
Vaudeville (Palace) 1927,F 8,20:3
Fejer, Joe and His Orchestra
Vaudeville (Palace) 1927,Jl 5,19:3
Vaudeville (Loew's State) 1932,O 3,15:5
Feld, Fritz
Miracle, The 1924,Ag 19,9:1
Miracle, The 1926,D 28,16:2
Miracle, The 1927,F 1,24:5
Feld, Fritz (Director)
Berlin 1931,D 31,16:1
Feld, Harry
Love Thief, The 1931,Ja 19,24:5
Feld, Isadore
Golden Ring, The 1930,F 1,14:7
Motke From Slobodke 1930,Ap 12,23:3
Russian Love 1930,N 27,32:3
Big Surprise, The 1932,O 17,18:3
Itche Mayer of Warsaw 1935,Ja 31,22:4
Lovka Maladetz 1935,Mr 27,25:5
Feld, Itzik
My Little Girl 1931,F 2,22:4
Night in the Woods, A 1931,Mr 2,19:3
Victims of Life 1931,O 21,26:2
Great Miracle, The 1931,D 12,23:5
Rich Paupers 1932,Mr 14,13:4
Love for Sale 1932,D 5,21:4
Untitled-Benefit 1933,Ja 25,13:3
Honeymoon for Three, A 1933,Ja 30,9:6
Jewish Melody, The 1933,Mr 27,12:4
Happy Family, A 1934,S 24,15:2
East Side Wedding, An 1935,Ja 21,18:2
Heaven on Earth 1935,O 8,26:2
Love for Sale 1936,Ja 24,14:2
Pinye of Pinchev 1936,S 21,27:5
Night in Budapest, A 1936,N 3,33:2
His Jewish Girl 1936,D 9,34:1
Let's Get Married 1937,Ja 11,16:2
My Baby's Wedding 1938,O 10,15:3
Long Live America 1939,Ja 2,28:3
Polish Rabbi, The 1939,Mr 20,13:3
Feld, Lee Neil
Judith 1965,Mr 25,42:2
Feld, Morris (Miscellaneous)
Desert Incident, A 1959,Mr 25,40:1
Feld, Norman
Bonds of Interest, The 1951,D 1,7:2
Frankie and Johnny 1952,O 29,37:2
Uncle Willie 1956,D 21,17:1
Feld, Rose C (Original Author)
Sophie 1944,D 26,22:7
Feld, Rose C (Playwright)
Sophie 1944,D 26,22:7
Felder, Clarence
Room, The 1964,D 10,62:1
Red, White and Maddox 1969,Ja 27,27:1
In 3 Zones 1970,N 3,28:1
Felder, Victor (Playwright)
Jacques Bergson 1936,O 31,24:6
Jacques Bergson 1936,N 29,XII,3:3
Feldman, Arthur
Little Cantor, The 1930,S 24,26:2
Feldman, David
Summer of Daisy Miller, The 1963,My 28,33:1
Feldman, Dick (Miscellaneous)
Orlando Furioso 1970,N 5,59:1
Feldman, Gene (Playwright)
Go Show Me a Dragon 1961,O 28,18:1

Feldman, Gladys
Merton of the Movies 1922,N 14,16:2
Thrills 1925,Ap 17,24:3
Great Gatsby, The 1926,F 3,22:1
Set a Thief 1927,F 22,22:1
Mating Season, The 1927,Jl 19,27:6
What Do We Know 1927,D 24,8:1
Lady for a Night, A 1928,Ap 17,26:4
Counsellor-at-Law 1931,N 7,17:2
Between Two Worlds 1934,O 26,24:2
Baby Pompadour 1934,D 28,24:2
Good Men and True 1935,O 26,12:4
Feldman, Harry
Will, The 1930,My 6,33:1
Feldman, Ida
Naomi 1920,My 7,12:2
Feldman, Jerry (Miscellaneous)
Go Show Me a Dragon 1961,O 28,18:1
Feldman, Joan
Country Wife, The 1957,Je 27,22:1
Feldman, Justin N (Miscellaneous)
Life Begins in '40 1940,Ap 5,24:2
Feldman, Laurence (Producer)
I Am a Camera 1961,Jl 10,26:1
Miss Julie 1961,Jl 10,26:1
Zoo Story, The 1961,Jl 10,26:1
Girl Could Get Lucky, A 1964,S 21,36:1
Feldman, Mildred
Boutique Fantasque, La 1929,D 28,10:6
Feldman, Morton
Tinguely Machine Mystery, or the Love Suicide at
Kaluka, The 1965,D 24,15:5
Feldman, Peter
Diversions 1958,N 8,14:4
In the Jungle of Cities 1960,D 21,39:1
Feldman, Peter (Miscellaneous)
Cave at Machpelah, The 1959,Jl 1,25:1
Connection, The 1959,Jl 16,30:2
Tonight We Improvise 1959,N 7,27:4
Feldman, Shellie
Balls 1965,F 11,45:1
Persecution and Assassination of Marat As
Performed by the Inmates of the Asylum of
Charenton Under the Direction of the Marquis de
Sade, The 1967,Ja 4,34:1
Feldmann, Benno
Rape of the Sabine Women, The 1949,F 5,10:5
Feldshuh, David
Twelfth Night 1968,Je 15,40:1
Serjeant Musgrave's Dance 1968,Je 16,52:4
Merton of the Movies 1968,S 26,62:1
Feldstein, Charlotte
Chaver, Nachman 1939,O 2,15:2
Feldstein, Robert D (Miscellaneous)
Tattooed Countess, The 1961,My 4,40:2
Ordinary Man, An 1968,S 10,39:1
Feldstein, Robert D (Producer)
Mousetrap, The 1960,N 7,46:1
Sing Muse 1961,D 7,52:1
Papers 1968,D 3,54:1
Felgemacher, Olga
Whistling Wizard and the Sultan of Tuffet
1970,F 1,70:1
Felikamp, Walter
Bye Bye Bonnie 1927,Ja 14,15:3
Felix, A J
Escape Me Never! 1935,Ja 22,22:2
Felix, Hugo (Composer)
Lassie 1920,F 7,9:2
Sweetheart Shop, The 1920,S 1,13:4
Marjolaine 1922,Ja 25,16:1
Peg o' My Dreams 1924,My 6,25:3
Jealous Moon, The 1928,N 21,32:2
Felix, Seymour (Choreographer)
Hello, Lola! 1926,Ja 13,30:1
Gay Paree 1926,N 10,24:2
Peggy-Ann 1926,D 28,16:3
Hit the Deck! 1927,Ap 26,32:1
Rosalie 1928,Ja 11,26:3
Whoopee 1928,D 5,34:3
Simple Simon 1931,Mr 10,23:2
Forward March 1932,O 23,IX,3:5
Strike Me Pink 1933,Mr 6,16:3
Felix, Seymour (Director)
Simple Simon 1930,F 19,22:1
Fell, Isidore
Seven Against One 1930,My 7,25:1
Fell, Patricia
Is Zat So? 1925,Ap 25,18:2
Fell, Walden 2d
Espanola 1921,D 30,13:1
Fellegi, Theresa
Natja 1925,F 17,19:2
Feller, Catherine
Lark, The 1955,My 13,21:2
Fellini, Federico (Playwright)
Sweet Charity 1966,Ja 31,22:1
Fellowes, Rockliffe
Pot-Luck 1921,S 30,10:1
Fellows, Don
South Pacific 1949,Ap 8,30:2
Troublemakers, The 1954,D 31,11:3
South Pacific 1955,My 5,39:5

Fellows, Don—Cont
Lulu 1958,S 30,24:1
Only in America 1959,N 20,35:1
Coming Forth by Day of Osiris Jones, The; Kid, The 1961,Mr 15,45:2
Marathon '33 1963,D 23,20:1
Friday Night; Mary Agnes Is Thirty-Five 1965,F 9,42:5
Friday Night; Passport 1965,F 9,42:5
Limb of Snow 1967,D 13,55:1
My House Is Your House 1970,O 16,53:2

Fellows, Doris
Macbeth 1921,F 18,16:1

Fellows, Edith
Louisiana Lady 1947,Je 3,35:2
Uncle Willie 1956,D 21,17:1

Fellows, Robert
Unknown Lady, The 1923,N 6,22:1

Fells, George
Billy Budd 1951,F 12,18:3
Coriolanus 1954,Ja 20,34:2

Fells, Richard
Slave Ship 1969,N 22,46:1

Felouis
Vaudeville (Palace) 1928,O 2,35:1
Vaudeville (Palace) 1929,D 16,34:4

Felsmann, Christiane
Lady From the Sea, The 1956,D 13,49:5

Felstiner, Helen
What of It? 1929,Mr 9,24:2

Felt, Eugene
Here's Howe 1923,Ap 26,19:3
That's That 1924,Ap 30,19:2

Felton, Francis
Seventh Heart, The 1927,My 3,24:4

Felton, Francis J
Flamingo Road 1946,Mr 20,18:2

Felton, John
South Pacific 1968,Je 30,54:2
South Pacific 1969,Jl 7,27:1

Felton, Selma
Mr Strauss Goes to Boston 1945,S 7,20:2

Fen, Elisaveta (Playwright)
Ivanov 1958,O 8,42:1

Fender, Harry
Florodora 1920,Ap 6,18:1
Last Waltz, The 1921,My 11,20:3
Lady in Ermine, The 1922,O 3,22:2
Adrienne 1923,My 29,10:4
Kid Boots 1924,Ja 1,21:3
Louie the 14th 1925,Mr 4,17:1

Fender, Michael
Duchess of Malfi, The 1962,Mr 5,27:1

Fenderson, Alonzo
Liza 1922,N 28,24:1
Fall of Eve, The 1925,S 1,18:1
Green Pastures, The 1930,F 27,26:1
Stevedore 1934,Ap 19,33:2

Fenderson, Reginald
Green Pastures, The 1935,F 27,16:2
Sailor, Beware! 1935,My 7,28:4

Fenet, Mabel
Strings, My Lord, Are False, The 1942,My 20,24:2

Fenington, Sylvia
Centuries, The 1927,N 30,23:1
Maya 1928,F 22,19:1
Night Over Taos 1932,Mr 10,25:3

Fenn, Converse
Stag at Bay, The 1935,Jl 30,17:1

Fenn, Jean
Liberace's Variety Bill 1957,Ap 22,29:5

Fenn, John (Miscellaneous)
Automobile Graveyard, The 1961,N 14,46:2
Julius Caesar 1962,F 22,19:6
Merchant of Venice, The 1962,Je 22,1:4
Tempest, The 1962,Jl 17,18:2
Macbeth 1962,N 17,16:2
Amorous Flea, The 1964,F 18,26:1
Othello 1964,Jl 15,29:1
Othello 1964,O 13,48:1
Baal 1965,My 7,33:2
Love's Labour's Lost 1965,Je 16,46:1

Fennelly, Parker
Mister Pitt 1924,Ja 23,15:3
Small Timers, The 1925,Ja 28,15:3
Florida Girl 1925,N 3,34:1
Faust 1927,Ja 4,20:1
Babbling Brookes 1927,F 26,13:2
Black Velvet 1927,S 28,28:1
County Chairman, The 1936,My 26,26:5
Our Town 1944,Ja 11,24:5
Happily Ever After 1945,Mr 16,21:2
Live Life Again 1945,O 1,14:7
Loco 1946,O 17,29:2
Southwest Corner, The 1955,F 4,18:2
Southwest Corner, The 1955,F 13,II,1:1
Carousel 1966,D 16,56:2

Fennelly, Parker (Director)
Technique 1931,My 15,21:1

Fennelly, Parker (Playwright)
Fulton of Oak Falls 1937,Ja 2,15:3
Fulton of Oak Falls 1937,F 11,18:2
Two Story House 1941,S 2,20:3
Cuckoos on the Hearth 1941,S 17,26:2

Fennelly, Porter
Fog-Bound 1927,Ap 2,21:2

Fenner, Janise
Who's Got His Own 1967,O 14,13:3

Fenner, Walter
Carnival 1929,Ap 25,32:5
Cortez 1929,N 5,32:2
Purity 1930,D 26,18:2
Heigh-Ho, Everybody 1932,My 26,31:2
Queer People 1934,F 16,16:2
Potash and Perlmutter 1935,Ap 6,11:3
Play, Genius, Play! 1935,O 31,17:2
Money Mad 1937,My 25,32:5

Fennessy, John
Greenwillow 1970,D 8,60:1

Fennington, Sylvia
1931 1931,D 11,34:3

Fenron, Dorothy
Scandals 1924,Jl 1,16:1
If I Was Rich 1926,S 3,15:2

Fenton, Babe
Vaudeville (Palace) 1930,Mr 31,24:2

Fenton, Calvin
Shakespeare in Harlem 1959,O 28,40:7

Fenton, Carl Gypsy Orchestra
Vaudeville (Palace) 1926,Ap 20,24:6

Fenton, Frank
O'Flynn, The 1934,D 28,24:1
O Evening Star 1936,Ja 9,24:6
Philadelphia Story, The 1939,Mr 29,21:1

Fenton, Frank (Playwright)
Stork Mad 1936,O 1,28:4

Fenton, Howard (Composer)
Americana Pastoral 1968,D 11,51:1

Fenton, Lucille
Broadway Shadows 1930,Ap 1,34:6
Decoy, The 1932,Ap 2,13:4
Dodsworth 1934,F 26,20:4
Women, The 1936,D 28,13:1
Painted Days, The 1961,Ap 7,24:1

Fenton, Mildred
Leave It to Me! 1939,S 10,IX,1:1

Fenton, Peter
Alfie 1964,D 18,27:1

Fenton, William
Green Pastures, The 1935,F 27,16:2

Fentress, David
Fratricide Punished 1925,Ap 21,19:1

Fenwick, Ellen
Trial Honeymoon 1947,N 4,31:2

Fenwick, Fred
Biff, Bing, Bang 1921,My 10,20:1

Fenwick, Gillie
Salad Days 1958,N 11,24:1
Hadrian VII 1969,Ja 9,22:1

Fenwick, Irene
Claw, The 1921,O 18,20:1
Laugh, Clown, Laugh! 1923,N 29,30:1
Piker, The 1925,Ja 16,14:1
Taps 1925,Ap 15,16:2

Fenwick, John (Miscellaneous)
Salad Days 1958,N 11,24:1

Feodorova, Irina
Tovarich 1936,O 16,31:4

Ferago, Eugene (Playwright)
Love Song, The 1925,Ja 14,19:4

Ferai, Donald
Scapegoat, The 1950,Ap 20,36:5

Feraudy, Maurice de
Affaires Son les Affaires, Les 1924,Mr 11,17:1
Affaires Sont les Affaires, Les 1924,Mr 16,VIII,1:1
Blanchette 1924,Mr 19,19:4
Bonheur du Jour, Le 1926,D 5,VIII,6:1

Ferber, Edna
Royal Family, The 1940,Ag 13,15:3

Ferber, Edna (Original Author)
Old Man Minick 1924,Ag 24,VII,1:8
Show Boat 1927,D 28,26:1
Show Boat 1928,Ja 8,VIII,1:1
Show Boat 1932,My 20,22:2
Show Boat 1946,Ja 7,17:2
Show Boat 1946,Ja 13,II,1:1
Show Boat 1948,S 9,33:2
Show Boat 1948,S 19,II,1:1
Show Boat 1954,My 6,44:1
Show Boat 1956,Je 22,16:1
Show Boat 1957,Je 28,30:2
Saratoga 1959,D 8,59:4
Show Boat 1961,Ap 13,32:1
Show Boat 1966,Jl 20,48:1

Ferber, Edna (Playwright)
Old Man Minick 1924,Ag 24,VII,1:8
Minick 1924,S 25,20:1
Royal Family, The 1927,D 29,26:4
Royal Family, The 1928,Ja 8,VIII,1:1
Royal Family, The 1928,Jl 1,VIII,3:5
Royal Family, The 1931,Ap 12,IX,1:3
Dinner at Eight 1932,O 24,18:2
Dinner at Eight 1932,N 6,IX,1:1
Dinner at Eight 1933,Ja 7,11:5
Dinner at Eight 1933,Ja 29,IX,1:3
Dinner at Eight 1933,Ap 9,IX,1:7
Dinner at Eight 1933,O 17,26:2

Ferber, Edna (Playwright)—Cont
Theatre Royal 1934,N 11,IX,1:1
Royal Family, The 1936,Jl 16,15:4
Royal Family, The 1936,Ag 12,15:1
Stage Door 1936,S 29,35:1
Stage Door 1936,O 4,IX,2:1
Stage Door 1936,O 23,26:3
Stage Door 1936,N 1,X,1:1
Royal Family, The 1940,Ag 13,15:3
Land Is Bright, The 1941,O 21,28:5
Land Is Bright, The 1941,O 29,26:2
Land Is Bright, The 1941,N 9,IX,1:1
Bravo! 1948,N 12,31:2
Royal Family, The 1951,Ja 11,28:2
Dinner at Eight 1966,S 28,38:1
Dinner at Eight 1966,O 9,II,1:1

Ferber, Samuel
Com Zaa 1945,Ja 10,28:2

Ferber, Samuel (Director)
Com Zaa 1945,Ja 10,28:2

Ferdinand, Edmund J (Producer)
Who's Who, Baby? 1968,Ja 30,36:1

Ferdinand, Roger (Playwright)
Homme En Or, Un 1927,Mr 13,VII,2:7
7 Rue de la Paroisse 1927,Ap 3,VIII,4:7
Chotard et Cie 1928,N 11,X,2:7
Man of Gold, A; Uomo d'Oro, Un 1929,My 6,30:2
Touche-A-Tout 1929,O 20,IX,4:4
Cabrioles 1932,N 20,IX,2:1

Ferdinando, Felix (Lieutenant) Havana Band
Vaudeville (Hippodrome) 1926,My 11,25:3

Ferenzo, Mischa
Romancing 'Round 1927,O 4,32:4
Moon Over Mulberry Street 1935,S 5,24:6

Fergan, J R
Espanola 1921,D 30,13:1

Fergan, J R (Playwright)
Espanola 1921,D 30,13:1

Ferguson, Adela
Hamlet 1931,Ap 24,26:4

Ferguson, Adele
Folly Town 1920,My 18,9:2

Ferguson, Allyn (Miscellaneous)
Vintage '60 1960,S 13,41:1

Ferguson, Bill
Small Wonder 1948,S 16,33:5

Ferguson, Carol
Resistible Rise of Arturo Ui, The 1968,Ag 8,25:1

Ferguson, Dave
All-Star Jamboree 1921,Jl 14,18:1
Polly of Hollywood 1927,F 22,22:3

Ferguson, Doris
Nirvana 1926,Mr 4,19:1

Ferguson, Dorothy
Shakespeare's Merchant 1939 1939,Ja 10,16:3

Ferguson, Douglas
Barchester Towers 1937,D 1,27:1

Ferguson, Edre
Faith of Our Fathers 1950,Ag 6,72:2

Ferguson, Edward
Hook-Up, The 1935,My 9,24:6
Marching Song 1937,F 18,18:2

Ferguson, Elsie
Sacred and Profane Love 1920,F 24,11:1
Sacred and Profane Love 1920,F 29,V,5:2
Varying Shore, The 1921,D 6,24:1
Untitled-Benefit 1922,My 8,14:5
Moon-Flower, The 1924,Ja 27,VII,2:7
Moon-Flower, The 1924,F 26,15:1
Moon-Flower, The 1924,Mr 2,VIII,1:1
She Stoops to Conquer 1924,Je 10,24:3
Carnival 1924,N 30,VIII,2:1
Carnaval 1924,D 30,15:1
Grand Duchess and the Waiter, The 1925,O 14,31:1
House of Women, The 1927,S 11,VIII,1:3
House of Women, The 1927,O 4,32:2
House of Women, The 1927,O 9,VIII,1:1
Scarlet Pages 1929,S 1,VIII,1:1
Scarlet Pages 1929,S 10,26:3
Scarlet Pages 1929,S 22,IX,1:1
Outrageous Fortune 1943,N 4,28:5

Ferguson, Francis (Playwright)
King and the Duke, The 1955,Je 2,25:2

Ferguson, Frank
Trial of Dr Beck, The 1937,Ag 10,22:2

Ferguson, Helen
World's My Oyster, The 1956,Ag 10,10:4
Take a Giant Step 1956,S 26,30:1
Cabin in the Sky 1964,Ja 22,32:1

Ferguson, Hilda
Ziegfeld Follies 1923,O 22,17:2
Yours Truly 1927,Ja 26,16:5

Ferguson, Howard
Night Remembers, The 1934,N 28,24:3
Pursuit of Happiness, The 1936,Jl 15,14:1
Post Road 1936,Ag 5,15:4
Royal Family, The 1936,Ag 12,15:1
Truth About Blayds, The 1936,Ag 19,18:5
Art and Mrs Bottle 1936,S 2,18:1
Boy Meets Girl 1937,Jl 6,23:1
Man Who Killed Lincoln, The 1940,Ja 18,26:4
Rugged Path, The 1945,N 12,17:2

Ferguson, Jean
Clinging Vine, The 1922,D 25,20:2
Peg o' My Dreams 1924,My 6,25:3
Ferguson, John
Three Doors 1925,Ap 24,16:4
So That's That 1925,D 15,28:3
One Shot Fired 1927,N 8,32:5
Kidding Kidders 1928,Ap 24,28:3
Guinea Pig, The 1929,Ja 8,35:1
Under the Gaslight 1929,Ap 3,27:1
Ferguson, John H
Hippolytus 1935,Je 15,20:4
Ferguson, Larry
Twelfth Night 1968,Je 15,40:1
Serjeant Musgrave's Dance 1968,Je 16,52:4
Resistible Rise of Arturo Ui, The 1968,D 23,44:1
Ferguson, Laura
Yeomen of the Guard, The 1933,My 2,20:4
H M S Pinafore 1933,My 9,20:3
Yeomen of the Guard, The 1933,Ag 15,20:5
Mikado, The 1934,Ap 3,26:3
Pirates of Penzance, The 1934,Ap 10,26:5
H M S Pinafore 1934,Ap 17,27:2
Ferguson, Libby
Blind Mice 1930,O 16,28:2
Ferguson, Marie
Once in a Lifetime 1930,S 25,22:3
Ferguson, Marlow
Arsenic and Old Lace 1970,N 5,59:1
Ferguson, Mattie
Unwritten Chapter, The 1920,O 12,18:1
Ferguson, Myrtle
Topsy and Eva 1924,D 24,11:1
Young Man's Fancy, A 1947,Ap 30,33:2
Ferguson, Neil (Scenic Designer)
No Laughter in Heaven 1938,My 17,26:5
Ferguson, Patrick
Billy Budd 1959,F 28,13:3
Ferguson, Sally
Lady in the Dark 1941,Ja 24,14:2
It's A Gift 1945,Mr 13,18:7
Ferguson, Samuel
Lost Boy 1932,Ja 6,24:4
Ferguson, William
Sleepy Hollow 1948,Je 4,26:3
Ferguson, William H Jr (Producer)
Bill Noname 1970,Mr 3,37:1
Fergusson, Denise
Whistle in the Dark, A 1968,F 17,32:2
Fergusson, Francis
Big Lake 1927,Ap 9,17:2
Doctor Knock 1928,F 24,15:2
Three Sisters, The 1930,Ja 9,22:2
Boeuf sur le Toit, Le 1930,Ap 25,28:4
Fergusson, Francis (Director)
Antigone 1930,Ap 25,28:4
Fergusson, Francis (Playwright)
Electra 1959,F 14,15:1
Fergusson, Francis (Translator)
Antigone 1930,Ap 25,28:4
Fergusson, Stuart
Ten Million Ghosts 1936,O 24,23:7
Ferjac, Anouk
Misanthrope, Le 1960,Mr 9,38:3
Ferleger, Alvin (Miscellaneous)
Scuba Duba 1967,O 11,36:1
Ferling, Lawrence
Poet's Follies of 1955 1955,My 15,II,3:1
Ferlinghetti, Lawrence (Playwright)
Three by Ferlinghetti; Victims of Amnesia, The
1970,S 23,43:1
Three by Ferlinghetti; Alligation, The
1970,S 23,43:1
Three by Ferlinghetti; Three Thousand Red Ants
1970,S 23,43:1
Ferlita, Ernest (Playwright)
Ballad of John Ogilvie, The 1968,O 9,42:4
Fern, Dan
Lower Depths, The 1956,O 3,29:2
Idiot's Delight 1957,F 23,14:2
Nat Turner 1960,N 7,46:3
Fern, Vera
Too Many Girls 1939,O 19,26:2
Fernald, Bruce
Candle in the Wind 1941,O 23,26:2
Fernald, Chester Bailey (Playwright)
Married Woman, The 1921,D 26,21:1
Married Woman, The 1922,F 5,VI,1:1
Mask and the Face, The 1924,S 11,27:3
Princess in the Cage, The 1933,Mr 19,IX,2:2
Fernald, J B (Translator)
Fourteenth of July, The 1928,Mr 11,VIII,1:3
Fernald, Jeff
Mrs Warren's Profession 1956,Je 7,35:2
Fernald, John (Director)
Gooseberry Fool 1929,N 2,14:8
Murder Gang 1935,N 16,19:2
Tea and Sympathy 1957,Ap 26,22:5
Seagull, The 1960,Ag 24,33:2
Affair, The 1962,S 21,34:2
Cherry Orchard, The 1970,My 7,63:2
Fernald, John (Miscellaneous)
And People All Around 1968,F 12,46:1

Fernald, John (Producer)
Seagull, The 1960,Ag 24,33:2
Fernald, Karin
Measure for Measure 1969,Je 13,41:3
Measure for Measure 1969,Je 22,II,1:7
Fernandez, Bijou
Masque of the Kings, The 1937,F 9,19:4
I'd Rather Be Right 1937,N 3,28:2
Small Hours, The 1951,F 16,22:1
Prescott Proposals, The 1953,D 17,53:1
Fernandez, C
Road to Happiness, The 1927,My 3,24:1
Girl and the Cat, The 1927,My 6,21:2
Blind Heart, The 1927,My 8,30:2
Cradle Song 1927,My 10,24:4
Fernandez, Concepcion
Romantic Young Lady, The 1927,My 5,30:2
Fernandez, Conchita
Pygmalion 1927,My 12,25:2
Fernandez, D
Sirena Varada, La 1937,O 23,15:3
Fernandez, E L
White Peacock, The 1921,D 27,10:2
My Son 1924,S 18,18:2
Honor Code, The 1931,My 19,25:3
Fernandez, Edward
Embezzled Heaven 1944,N 1,20:2
Fernandez, F
Road to Happiness, The 1927,My 3,24:1
Romantic Young Lady, The 1927,My 5,30:2
Girl and the Cat, The 1927,My 6,21:2
Blind Heart, The 1927,My 8,30:2
Fernandez, Jose
Mexicana 1939,Ap 22,14:4
Mexicana 1939,My 7,X,3:1
Me Nobody Knows, The 1970,My 19,42:1
Me Nobody Knows, The 1970,My 31,II,1:6
Fernandez, Jose (Choreographer)
Mexicana 1939,My 7,X,3:1
Fernandez, Paco
Cabalgata 1949,Jl 8,14:2
Fernandez, Peter
Whiteoaks 1938,Mr 24,20:2
Love's Old Sweet Song 1940,Ap 14,IX,3:3
Love's Old Sweet Song 1940,My 3,16:3
Watch on the Rhine 1941,Ap 2,26:2
Damask Cheek, The 1942,O 23,24:2
Listen Professor! 1943,D 23,22:1
Once Upon a Tailor 1955,My 24,36:2
Fernandez, T
Road to Happiness, The 1927,My 3,24:1
Girl and the Cat, The 1927,My 6,21:2
Blind Heart, The 1927,My 8,30:2
Cradle Song 1927,My 10,24:4
Pygmalion 1927,My 12,25:2
Fernando, K A
Dorian Gray 1928,My 22,18:4
Heat Wave 1931,F 18,14:6
Rain 1935,F 13,24:1
Fernau, Rudolf
Don Carlos 1964,N 25,40:1
Fernhoff, Rosina
Fashion 1959,Ja 21,27:1
Geranium Hat, The 1959,Mr 18,45:1
Rendezvous at Senlis 1961,F 28,39:2
Fernlock, John
Within Four Walls 1923,Ap 18,24:1
Fernold, Bruce
Audition of the Apprentice Theatre 1939,Je 2,26:2
Fernow, Donald
Passion of Gross, The 1955,Ja 24,20:2
Ferns, Nellie
LeMaire's Affairs 1927,Mr 29,22:4
Fero, James J (Producer)
Love in My Fashion 1937,D 4,21:4
Ferra, Max (Director)
Toothbrush, The 1970,S 27,84:5
Ferrada, Teenyson
Remolienda, La; Bawdy Party 1968,F 3,20:1
Ferrall, Charles
Wicked Cooks, The 1967,Ja 24,42:1
Ferrall, Michael (Director)
Under the Yum-Yum Tree 1964,My 29,18:1
Ferrand, Katherine
Resistible Rise of Arturo Ui, The 1968,Ag 8,25:1
Merton of the Movies 1968,S 26,62:1
House of Atreus, The 1968,D 18,55:1
Resistible Rise of Arturo Ui, The 1968,D 23,44:1
Ferrandiz, Francisca
Don Juan Tenorio 1953,N 20,18:5
El Alcalde De Zalamea 1953,N 23,32:5
Ferrante, Dino
Colonello Bridall, L' 1934,Ap 16,20:3
Ferrante, John
Play of Herod, The 1963,D 10,55:2
Cry for Us All 1970,Ap 9,48:2
Ferrar, Jules
Woman on the Jury, The 1923,Ag 16,10:4
Gods of the Lightning 1928,O 25,27:2
Ferrara, Mercedes
Elizabeth Sleeps Out 1936,Ap 21,27:6
Ferrara, Peter
Line of Least Existence, The 1968,Mr 25,53:1

Ferrard, Buddy
Say Darling 1959,F 26,38:2
Ferrari
Folly Town 1920,My 18,9:2
Ferrario, Florindo
Fuerza Ciega, La 1927,D 6,26:1
Ferraro, John
Instructions for the Running of Trains, etc on the
Erie Railway to Go Into Effect January 1,1862
1970,Ja 7,36:2
Ferras, Edouard (Playwright)
Paradis Perdu, Le 1923,D 12,VIII,3:4
Ferrau, A
Cena Delle Beffe, La; Jest, The 1930,N 24,26:4
Ferre, Cliff
Dance Me a Song 1950,Ja 21,10:5
Ferreira, Bibi
My Fair Lady 1962,Ag 23,24:6
Ferreira, Maria
Flowers of Virtue, The 1942,F 6,22:2
Ferreira, Maria (Costume Designer)
Golden Streets, The 1970,Ag 14,21:1
Ferrell, Jane
Lulu Belle 1926,F 10,20:1
Mima 1928,D 13,24:2
Pagan Lady 1930,O 21,34:2
Nona 1932,O 5,26:4
Her Man of Wax 1933,O 12,32:3
Trial of Dr Beck, The 1937,Ag 10,22:2
Ferrell, Walter
Wall Street 1927,Ap 21,24:4
Ten Per Cent 1927,S 14,29:3
Ferrend, Lionel
Man Who Ate the Popomack, The 1924,Mr 25,24:1
Two by Two 1925,F 24,17:1
Belt, The 1927,O 20,33:1
Centuries, The 1927,N 30,23:1
International, The 1928,Ja 16,24:4
Singing Jailbirds 1928,D 5,34:4
Ferrentino, Henry
Sunset 1966,My 13,34:1
Ferrer, J V (Composer)
It's the Valet 1933,D 15,25:4
Ferrer, J V (Lyricist)
It's the Valet 1933,D 15,25:4
Ferrer, Jose
Caesar and Cleopatra 1935,Ag 22,21:1
Slight Case of Murder, A 1935,S 12,28:5
Stick-in-the-Mud 1935,D 2,18:2
Spring Dance 1936,Jl 7,22:2
Spring Dance 1936,Ag 26,17:4
Brother Rat 1936,D 17,34:5
Kind Lady 1937,Jl 6,23:1
Night of January 16 1937,Jl 20,19:3
Pride and Prejudice 1937,Ag 3,20:5
Idiot's Delight 1937,Ag 10,22:7
Worse Things Happen at Sea 1937,S 1,15:3
In Clover 1937,S 21,29:1
In Clover 1937,O 14,23:1
How to Get Tough About It 1938,F 9,16:2
Missouri Legend 1938,S 20,27:2
Missouri Legend 1938,S 25,IX,1:1
Mamba's Daughters 1939,Ja 4,24:2
Mamba's Daughters 1939,Ja 15,IX,1:1
Flight Into China 1939,S 12,28:1
Key Largo 1939,O 31,26:6
Key Largo 1939,N 28,30:2
Charley's Aunt 1940,O 18,24:2
It's All Yours 1942,Mr 26,26:2
Othello 1942,Ag 16,VIII,1:7
Vickie 1942,S 23,28:1
Othello 1943,O 20,18:1
Othello 1943,O 24,II,1:1
Othello 1945,My 23,25:4
Cyrano de Bergerac 1946,O 9,33:2
Cyrano de Bergerac 1946,N 3,II,1:1
Cyrano de Bergerac 1947,Ja 17,27:2
Volpone 1948,Ja 9,24:6
Angel Street 1948,Ja 23,26:6
Alchemist, The 1948,My 7,31:4
S S Glencairn; Long Voyage Home, The
1948,My 21,21:2
Insect Comedy, The 1948,Je 4,26:3
Silver Whistle, The 1948,N 25,49:2
Twentieth Century 1950,D 25,23:6
Shrike, The 1952,Ja 16,20:2
Shrike, The 1952,Ja 27,II,1:1
Cyrano de Bergerac 1953,N 13,24:3
Shrike, The 1953,N 26,51:2
Richard III 1953,D 10,65:2
Charley's Aunt 1953,D 23,22:2
This Is Edwin Booth 1958,Ag 27,32:7
Edwin Booth 1958,N 25,37:1
Edwin Booth 1958,N 30,II,1:1
Girl Who Came to Supper, The 1963,D 9,49:1
Ferrer, Jose (Director)
Vickie 1942,S 23,28:1
Strange Fruit 1945,N 30,18:6
Cyrano de Bergerac 1947,Ja 17,27:2
As We Forgive Our Debtors 1947,Mr 11,37:2
Tragedian in Spite of Himself, A 1948,F 6,29:2
Bear, The 1948,F 6,29:2
On the Harmfulness of Tobacco 1948,F 6,29:2

Ferrer, Jose (Director)—Cont
Wedding, The 1948,F 6,29:2
S S Glencairn; Moon of the Caribbees 1948,My 21,21:2
S S Glencairn; Long Voyage Home, The 1948,My 21,21:2
S S Glencairn; Bound East for Cardiff 1948,My 21,21:2
S S Glencairn; In the Zone 1948,My 21,21:2
S S Glencairn; Long Voyage Home, The; Moon of the Caribbees; In the Zone; Bound East for Cardiff 1948,My 30,II,1:1
Insect Comedy, The 1948,Je 4,26:3
Twentieth Century 1950,D 25,23:6
Stalag 17 1951,My 9,41:2
Fourposter, The 1951,O 25,34:2
Fourposter, The 1951,N 25,II,1:1
Shrike, The 1952,Ja 16,20:2
Shrike, The 1952,Ja 27,II,1:1
Chase, The 1952,Ap 16,30:2
My 3 Angels 1953,Mr 12,23:2
Cyrano de Bergerac 1953,N 13,24:3
Shrike, The 1953,N 26,51:2
Charley's Aunt 1953,D 23,22:2
Fourposter, The 1955,Ja 6,23:3
Oh Captain! 1958,F 5,21:2
This Is Edwin Booth 1958,Ag 27,32:7
Edwin Booth 1958,N 25,37:1
Juno 1959,Mr 10,41:1
Juno 1959,Mr 15,II,1:1
Andersonville Trial, The 1959,D 30,15:1
Andersonville Trial, The 1960,Ja 10,II,1:1
Ferrer, Jose (Miscellaneous)
Cyrano de Bergerac 1946,O 9,33:2
Ferrer, Jose (Playwright)
Oh Captain! 1958,F 5,21:2
Ferrer, Jose (Producer)
Strange Fruit 1945,N 30,18:6
Cyrano de Bergerac 1947,Ja 17,27:2
Twentieth Century 1950,D 25,23:6
Stalag 17 1951,My 9,41:2
Shrike, The 1952,Ja 16,20:2
Shrike, The 1952,Ja 27,II,1:1
Chase, The 1952,Ap 16,30:2
Edwin Booth 1958,N 25,37:1
Ferrer, Mel
Importance of Being Earnest, The 1936,O 22,31:2
Awhile to Work 1937,Mr 20,23:1
Kind Lady 1940,S 4,28:3
Cue for Passion 1940,D 20,33:4
Strange Fruit 1945,N 30,18:6
On the Harmfulness of Tobacco 1948,F 6,29:2
Wedding, The 1948,F 6,29:2
Bear, The 1948,F 6,29:2
Tragedian in Spite of Himself, A 1948,F 6,29:2
Ondine 1954,F 19,23:1
Ondine 1954,F 28,II,1:1
Ferrer, Mel (Director)
Awhile to Work 1937,Mr 20,23:1
Cyrano de Bergerac 1946,O 9,33:2
Eurydice 1948,O 17,I,67:4
Ferrer, Mel (Playwright)
Awhile to Work 1937,Mr 20,23:1
Ferrer, Mel (Translator)
Eurydice 1948,O 17,I,67:4
Ferrero, Leo (Playwright)
Angelica 1937,Ap 13,31:2
Ferrerra, Everaldo
Joy 1970,Ja 28,50:1
Ferretti, Carlo
Roberta 1937,Je 27,II,6:1
Ferriano, Frank (Musical Director)
Safari! 1955,My 12,32:6
Ferriday, Carolyn
Merchant of Venice, The 1921,N 22,17:1
Love Set, The 1923,Mr 20,24:2
Two Orphans, The 1926,Ap 6,26:2
What Never Dies 1926,D 29,24:2
Tia Juana 1927,N 16,28:4
Before You're 25 1929,Ap 17,30:2
Midsummer Night's Dream, A 1932,N 18,22:2
Twelfth Night 1932,N 19,20:5
Comedy of Errors, The 1932,N 22,25:3
Merchant of Venice, The 1932,N 24,34:5
Huitieme Femme de Barbe-Bleue, La 1936,Ja 27,20:5
Ferrier, Pat
Redhead 1959,F 6,21:1
Ferril, Kenneth
As You Like It 1939,My 9,28:4
Ferrio, Gianni (Composer)
Festa Italiana 1966,S 30,55:1
Ferris, Anne
Dear Judas 1947,O 6,26:4
Make Mine Manhattan 1948,Ja 16,26:2
Ferris, Barbara
There's a Girl in My Soup 1967,O 19,58:1
There's a Girl in My Soup 1967,N 12,II,5:6
Ferris, Benjamin G
Assorted Nuts 1940,Ap 7,I,44:6
Ferris, Elizabeth Delmore
Deep Channels 1929,O 19,22:3
Ferris, Evelyn
Mirage, The 1920,O 1,14:1

Ferris, Hugh (Scenic Designer)
Neighborhood Playhouse Program 1930,F 21,23:1
Ferris, John
Tenth Man, The 1929,Mr 21,29:2
Silver Tassie, The 1929,O 25,26:1
Ferris, Noah
Pinocchio 1939,Ja 3,19:2
Ferris, Peggy
Sleepy Hollow 1948,Je 4,26:3
Ferris, Walter (Playwright)
First Stone, The 1928,Ja 14,12:2
Judas 1929,Ja 25,20:4
Death Takes a Holiday 1929,N 24,X,4:5
Death Takes a Holiday 1929,D 27,26:4
Death Takes a Holiday 1931,F 17,29:1
Dark Hester 1931,My 17,VIII,1:3
Ferro, Albert
Nancy's Private Affair 1930,Ja 14,24:3
Farewell to Arms, A 1930,S 23,30:3
Ferro, Maurishka
Mandingo 1961,My 23,43:6
Ferrolle, Michel
Cocktail Impromptu 1927,Ja 13,28:4
Ferrone, Dan
Step on a Crack 1962,O 18,48:1
Ferry, Elizabeth
Tree Witch, The 1961,Je 5,39:4
Ferry, Lucille
Little Theatre Tournament; Thirst 1929,My 10,32:2
Ladies Leave 1929,O 2,28:3
Ferry, Mabel
Glory 1922,D 26,10:1
Adrienne 1923,My 29,10:4
Ferry, Will
Jumbo 1935,N 18,20:2
Hooray for What! 1937,D 2,32:5
Fersen, Christine
Cid, Le 1966,F 12,17:1
Reine Morte, La 1966,F 16,52:1
Fil a la Paite, Un 1966,F 18,25:1
Fershko, Shmuel (Composer)
Sands of the Negev 1952,O 20,32:1
Devil's Game, A 1959,N 9,35:6
It's Never Too Late for Happiness 1968,O 21,59:3
Fertig, Robert
Quo Vadis 1932,O 17,18:2
Veronica's Veil 1936,F 10,19:6
Fertik, Fannie (Playwright)
World of Mrs Solomon, The; Second Mrs Aarons, The 1969,Je 4,37:1
World of Mrs Solomon, The; Another Chance 1969,Je 4,37:1
Fesco, Michael
Mis-Guided Tour 1959,O 13,44:7
Follies of 1910, The 1960,Ja 15,37:3
From A to Z 1960,Ap 21,23:2
New Faces of 1962 1962,F 2,25:1
Fesette, Doris
Great Sebastians, The 1956,Ja 5,27:1
Fessenden, Benjamin
Gods of the Lightning 1928,O 25,27:2
Festival Company of Stratford, Canada
Tamburlaine the Great 1956,Ja 29,II,1:1
Fetbroth, Edward
Red Geranium, The 1922,My 9,22:3
Lady, The 1923,D 5,23:2
Puppets of Passion 1927,F 25,24:4
Fetchit, Stepin
Three After Three 1939,N 25,13:5
Walk With Music 1940,Je 5,33:2
Fetherston, Edward
Flossie 1924,Je 4,25:2
Fetler, Paul (Composer)
Miser, The 1963,My 10,39:1
As You Like It 1966,Je 4,19:1
Fetter, Ted
Peter Pan; Boy Who Would Not Grow Up, The 1928,N 27,36:3
Marseilles 1930,N 18,28:2
Creeping Fire 1935,Ja 17,22:3
Jubilee 1935,O 14,20:1
Many Mansions 1937,O 28,28:6
Fetter, Ted (Composer)
Show Is On, The 1936,N 15,XI,2:1
Show Is On, The 1936,D 26,14:2
It's All Yours 1942,Mr 26,26:2
Fetter, Ted (Director)
One on the House 1941,Mr 30,I,47:3
Naughty-Naught '00 1946,O 21,27:5
Fetter, Ted (Lyricist)
Show Is On, The 1936,D 26,14:2
Naughty-Naught '00 1937,Ja 25,23:2
Show Is On, The 1937,S 20,18:4
Fireman's Flame, The 1937,O 11,26:2
Let's Play Fair 1938,Ja 19,26:4
Girl From Wyoming, The 1938,O 31,12:1
It's All Yours 1942,Mr 26,26:2
Naughty-Naught '00 1946,O 21,27:5
Fetter, Ted (Producer)
Two Weeks With Pay 1940,Je 25,28:3
Fetzko, Donald C (Producer)
Difficult Woman, The 1962,Ap 26,22:7

Feuchtwanger, Lion (Original Author)
Jew Suess 1929,O 6,IX,1:3
Jew Suss 1929,O 19,22:3
Josef Suss 1930,Ja 21,28:5
Ugly Duchess, The 1930,Je 1,VIII,2:8
Josephus 1933,D 1,22:5
Jew Suss 1936,Ag 16,X,2:5
Feuchtwanger, Lion (Playwright)
Will Hill Be Pardoned; Wird Hill Amnestiert? 1930,Je 1,VIII,2:1
Feuer, Cy (Director)
Silk Stockings 1955,F 25,17:3
Whoop-Up 1958,D 23,2:7
Little Me 1962,N 19,41:3
Little Me 1962,D 2,II,1:1
Skyscraper 1965,N 15,48:1
Walking Happy 1966,N 28,47:1
Feuer, Cy (Playwright)
Whoop-Up 1958,D 23,2:7
Feuer, Cy (Producer)
Where's Charley? 1948,O 12,33:2
Guys and Dolls 1950,N 25,11:2
Where's Charley? 1951,Ja 30,21:7
Can-Can 1953,My 8,28:1
Silk Stockings 1955,F 25,17:3
Whoop-Up 1958,D 23,2:7
How to Succeed in Business Without Really Trying 1961,O 16,34:1
Little Me 1962,N 19,41:3
Skyscraper 1965,N 15,48:1
Goodbye People, The 1968,D 4,52:1
Feuer and Martin (Producer)
Boy Friend, The 1954,O 1,20:1
Feuilet, Octave (Playwright)
Romanzo di un Giovane Povero, Il 1935,F 25,12:3
Feuillere, Edwige
Pour Lucrece 1953,N 29,II,3:1
Feury, Peggy
Me and Molly 1948,F 27,27:2
Cock-A-Doodle-Doo 1949,F 28,16:5
Earth Spirit 1950,Je 7,33:4
Sunday Breakfast 1952,My 30,12:2
Man With the Golden Arm, The 1956,My 22,28:1
Innocents, The 1959,Ap 21,41:2
Antony and Cleopatra 1963,Je 21,33:1
Drums in the Night 1967,My 18,54:1
Fey, Frank H
Broadway Shadows 1930,Ap 1,34:6
Feydeau, Alain
Avare, L', L'; Miser, The 1966,F 9,32:1
Fil a la Paite, Un 1966,F 18,25:1
Feydeau, Georges (Original Author)
Look After Lulu 1959,Mr 4,35:1
Look After Lulu 1959,Jl 30,20:1
Feydeau, Georges (Playwright)
Breakfast in Bed 1920,F 4,12:1
Mais n'te Promene Donc pas Toute Nue 1930,Mr 30,VIII,2:4
Occupe-Toi d'Amelie; Keep Your Eyes on Amelie 1952,N 25,35:2
Hotel Paradiso 1956,My 3,34:8
Feu la Mere de Madame; Dear Departed Mother-in-Law 1957,F 12,31:1
Hotel Paradiso 1957,Ap 12,22:2
Hotel Paradiso 1957,Ap 21,II,1:1
Dindon, Le 1961,Mr 8,38:1
File a la Patte, Il 1962,Jl 8,II,1:1
Fil a la Paite, Un; How to Cut the Thread That Ties You to Your Mistress 1966,F 9,32:1
Fil a la Paite, Un 1966,F 18,25:1
Flea in Her Ear, A 1967,O 29,II,5:1
Flea in Her Ear, A 1967,O 30,59:1
Chemmy Circle, The 1968,Ag 10,17:2
Flea in Her Ear, A 1969,O 4,25:1
Flea in Her Ear, A 1969,O 12,II,9:1
Lady From Maxim's, The 1970,Je 1,41:1
Feyder, Jacques (Original Author)
Carnival in Flanders 1953,S 9,38:2
Feyti, Robert
Familiar Pattern 1943,S 3,15:6
Career 1943,O 29,22:6
Spring Production 1944,My 20,12:4
Sweethearts 1947,Ja 22,31:2
Ffolkes, David (Costume Designer)
Richard II 1937,F 6,14:2
Richard II 1937,S 16,28:2
Young Mr Disraeli 1937,N 10,30:5
Hamlet 1938,O 13,28:1
As You Like It 1939,My 9,28:4
As You Like It; Midsummer Night's Dream, A; Comedy of Errors, The; Taming of the Shrew, The 1939,My 9,28:4
Hamlet 1939,D 5,35:2
Richard II 1940,Ap 2,31:2
Henry VIII 1946,N 7,42:2
What Every Woman Knows 1946,N 9,13:2
Brigadoon 1947,Mr 14,28:2
Man and Superman 1947,O 9,31:2
Sleepy Hollow 1948,Je 4,26:3
Where's Charley? 1948,O 12,33:2
Along Fifth Avenue 1949,Ja 14,28:2
Man and Superman 1949,My 17,28:6
Browning Version, The 1949,O 13,32:2

Ffolkes, David (Costume Designer)—Cont
Harlequinade 1949,O 13,32:2
Browning Version, The 1949,O 23,II,1:1
Brigadoon 1950,My 3,36:2
Springtime for Henry 1951,Mr 15,36:2
Flahooley 1951,My 15,39:1
Flahooley 1951,My 20,II,1:1
Seventeen 1951,Je 22,16:6
Ffolkes, David (Lighting Director)
Men of Distinction 1953,My 1,18:4
Ffolkes, David (Scenic Designer)
Young Mr Disraeli 1937,N 10,30:5
Hamlet 1938,O 13,28:1
Henry IV, Part I 1939,Ja 31,17:2
Hamlet 1939,D 5,35:2
Richard II 1940,Ap 2,31:2
Henry VIII 1946,N 7,42:2
Where's Charley? 1948,O 12,33:2
Men of Distinction 1953,My 1,18:4
Ffolliott, Gladys
Ghost Train, The 1926,Ag 26,17:2
Ffrangcon-Davies, Gwen
Rates, Les; Might-Have-Beens, The
1927,Je 19,VII,2:3
Lady With a Lamp, The 1929,Ja 27,IX,2:1
Macbeth 1930,F 13,9:6
Macbeth 1930,Mr 2,IX,2:4
Magda 1930,Je 1,VIII,2:8
Barretts of Wimpole Street, The 1930,Ag 21,13:4
Barretts of Wimpole Street, The 1930,S 7,IX,2:1
Precious Bane 1932,Ap 24,VIII,1:1
Way to the Stars, The 1932,O 2,IX,2:5
Queen of Scots 1934,Je 9,18:5
Queen of Scots 1934,Jl 15,X,1:3
Flowers of the Forest 1934,N 21,23:2
Flowers of the Forest 1934,D 9,X,3:1
Return to Yesterday 1936,Ap 29,19:1
Return to Yesterday 1936,My 31,X,1:5
Charles the King 1936,O 10,20:6
He Was Born Gay 1937,My 27,20:5
He Was Born Gay 1937,Je 13,XI,1:7
Three Sisters, The 1938,F 13,X,3:3
Gas Light 1939,F 19,IX,3:1
Importance of Being Earnest, The 1939,S 17,X,2:3
Macbeth 1942,Jl 26,VIII,1:7
Long Day's Journey Into Night 1958,S 9,40:4
Long Day's Journey Into Night 1958,S 26,21:2
School for Scandal, The 1963,Ja 26,5:2
Uncle Vanya 1970,Mr 15,II,7:3
Fialka, Ladislav
Pierrot's Journey 1964,Ag 5,23:1
Button, Button 1970,O 20,41:1
Button, Button 1970,N 1,II,26:1
Fialka, Ladislav (Director)
Twenty-four Inventions 1964,Ag 11,37:5
Button, Button 1970,O 20,41:1
Fialka, Ladislav (Original Author)
Pierrot's Journey 1964,Ag 5,23:1
Fialkov, Max (Miscellaneous)
Sophie 1963,Ap 16,32:1
Fiander, Lewis
Duel, The 1968,Ap 18,56:1
1776 1970,Je 18,54:4
Fibich, Felix (Choreographer)
Golem, The 1959,F 26,38:2
Enchanting Melody 1964,N 25,40:1
Let's Sing Yiddish 1966,N 10,63:1
Sing Israel Sing 1967,My 12,50:1
Bride Got Farblondjet, The 1967,N 6,61:6
Light, Lively and Yiddish 1970,O 28,58:1
Fibich, Felix (Director)
From Israel With Laughter 1969,O 17,34:1
Light, Lively and Yiddish 1970,O 28,58:1
Fibich, Felix (Miscellaneous)
Let's Sing Yiddish 1966,N 10,63:1
Sing Israel Sing 1967,My 12,50:1
Fibich, Judith (Miscellaneous)
Let's Sing Yiddish 1966,N 10,63:1
Sing Israel Sing 1967,My 12,50:1
Fibich, Yehudith (Choreographer)
Enchanting Melody 1964,N 25,40:1
Fichandler, Thomas C (Director)
Great White Hope, The 1967,D 14,58:1
Indians 1969,My 27,43:1
Night Thoreau Spent in Jail, The 1970,N 2,66:1
Fichandler, Thomas C (Miscellaneous)
Month in the Country, A 1959,Mr 2,32:2
Clandestine on the Morning Line 1959,D 5,18:2
Fichandler, Zelda (Director)
Portrait of a Madonna 1957,Ap 1,21:2
Man of Destiny, The 1957,Ap 1,21:2
Browning Version, The 1958,Mr 7,17:2
Month in the Country, A 1959,Mr 2,32:2
Summer of the Seventeenth Doll 1959,O 14,52:1
Clandestine on the Morning Line 1959,D 5,18:2
Burning of the Lepers, The 1962,Ap 5,29:1
Once in a Lifetime 1962,O 30,30:1
Devils, The 1963,N 5,25:1
Devils, The 1963,N 17,II,1:1
Great White Hope, The 1967,D 14,58:1
Iceman Cometh, The 1968,Ap 1,58:1
Indians 1969,My 27,43:1
Night Thoreau Spent in Jail, The 1970,N 2,66:1

Fichandler, Zelda (Miscellaneous)
View From the Bridge, A 1956,N 9,34:4
Bedtime Story 1957,Ap 1,21:2
Prodigal Son, The 1965,My 21,19:1
Lonesome Train, The 1965,Je 17,25:1
Hard Travelin' 1965,Je 17,25:1
Fichandler, Zelda (Producer)
Caucasian Chalk Circle, The 1961,N 1,35:1
Devils, The 1963,N 5,25:1
Hard Travelin' 1965,Je 27,II,1:1
Ficke, Arthur Davison (Playwright)
Mr Faust 1922,Ja 31,11:2
Fickett, Homer (Playwright)
Calling All Stars 1934,N 22,26:1
Calling All Stars 1934,D 14,28:2
Fickett, Mary
I Know My Love 1949,N 3,36:1
Sunrise at Campobello 1958,Ja 31,25:1
Sunrise at Campobello 1958,F 9,II,1:1
Love and Kisses 1963,D 19,39:1
Fiddler, Harry
Yeah-Man 1932,My 27,27:3
Fidesser, Hans
Tales of Hoffmann 1932,Ja 10,VIII,1:6
Fiebig, Eva
Fedora 1924,Ja 24,14:2
Fiedler, John
Cock-A-Doodle-Doo 1949,F 28,16:5
Sea Gull, The 1954,My 12,38:1
One Eye Closed 1954,N 25,45:2
Billy Budd 1955,My 4,35:1
Terrible Swift Sword, The 1955,N 16,42:1
Howie 1958,S 18,35:2
Harold 1962,N 30,27:1
Odd Couple, The 1965,Mr 11,36:1
Our Town 1969,N 28,50:1
Field, Alexander
Journey's End 1929,Jl 14,IX,5:1
Amazing Dr. Clitterhouse, The 1937,Mr 3,26:4
Field, Alice
Trois et Une 1933,Ja 1,IX,3:4
Field, Alice (Playwright)
Untitled-Play 1935,O 27,IX,2:1
Field, Ben
School for Scandal, The 1925,D 7,18:2
Field, Betty
Page Miss Glory 1934,N 28,24:2
Room Service 1937,My 20,16:1
Angel Island 1937,O 21,26:2
If I Were You 1938,Ja 9,II,3:2
If I Were You 1938,Ja 25,24:2
What a Life 1938,Ap 14,26:2
Primrose Path, The 1939,Ja 5,16:3
Primrose Path, The 1939,Ja 16,11:2
Ring Two 1939,N 14,20:3
Ring Two 1939,N 23,38:2
Two on an Island 1940,Ja 16,18:4
Two on an Island 1940,Ja 23,17:2
Two on an Island 1940,Ja 28,IX,1:2
Two on an Island 1940,F 4,IX,1:1
Flight to the West 1940,D 15,I,59:5
Flight to the West 1940,D 31,19:1
New Life, A 1943,S 12,VI,14:4
New Life, A 1943,S 16,26:6
Voice of the Turtle, The 1944,D 19,27:2
Dream Girl 1945,D 15,13:2
Dream Girl 1945,D 23,II,3:1
Twelfth Night 1949,O 8,9:4
Rat Race, The 1949,D 23,16:2
Not for Children 1951,F 14,35:2
Ladies of the Corridor, The 1953,O 22,33:5
Ladies of the Corridor, The 1953,N 1,II,1:1
Festival 1955,Ja 19,22:1
Sea Gull, The 1956,O 23,38:1
Waltz of the Toreadors, The 1958,Mr 5,37:1
Touch of the Poet, A 1958,O 3,23:2
Touch of the Poet, A 1958,O 12,II,1:1
Loss of Roses, A 1959,N 30,27:1
Loss of Roses, A 1959,D 6,II,5:1
Strange Interlude 1963,Mr 13,5:2
Where's Daddy? 1966,Mr 3,27:1
Field, Bill (Miscellaneous)
Say Darling 1959,F 26,38:2
King and I, The 1960,My 12,40:1
Porgy and Bess 1961,My 18,40:1
Porgy and Bess 1964,My 7,32:1
Field, Catherine
$25 an Hour 1933,My 11,14:4
Field, Charles (Miscellaneous)
Private Life of the Master Race, The
1945,Je 13,28:3
Field, Crystal
Vincent 1959,O 1,40:1
Country Scandal, A 1960,My 6,21:8
When I Was a Child 1960,D 9,38:1
After the Fall 1964,Ja 24,18:1
Marco Millions 1964,F 21,33:1
Changeling, The 1964,O 30,32:2
Line of Least Existence, The 1968,Mr 25,53:1
Dracula Sabbat 1970,O 2,28:2
Field, Crystal (Choreographer)
Changeling, The 1964,O 30,32:2

Field, Elvin
Let Freedom Ring 1935,N 7,26:2
This Our House 1935,D 12,33:3
Come Angel Band 1936,F 19,17:1
County Chairman, The 1936,My 26,26:5
Brooklyn Biarritz 1941,F 28,16:2
Field, James
Heel, The 1954,My 27,33:2
Apollo of Bellac, The 1954,My 29,12:1
Purification, The 1954,My 29,12:1
Field, Joan
Slice It Thin 1945,My 11,22:5
Young American, A 1946,Ja 18,14:5
Field, Jules (Producer)
John Gabriel Borkman 1959,N 26,57:4
Field, Lelo
Faust 1947,N 29,9:2
Field, Leonard (Miscellaneous)
Virginia Reel 1947,Ap 15,28:2
Field, Leonard (Producer)
Lend Me Your Ears! 1936,O 6,28:5
Good Hunting 1938,N 22,26:5
Field, Leonard S (Producer)
Hostage, The 1960,S 21,42:1
3 Bags Full 1966,Mr 7,22:1
Birthday Party, The 1967,O 4,40:2
Little Boxes; Coffee Lace, The 1969,D 4,71:2
Little Boxes; Trevor 1969,D 4,71:2
Field, Malcolm
Keating 1927,D 26,26:6
Field, Marshall 3d
Lid's Off, The 1936,Ap 4,11:6
Field, Mary
Story to Be Whispered 1937,Ag 20,21:4
Field, Miss
Broadway 1926,S 26,VIII,1:1
Field, Mr (Playwright)
America's Sweetheart 1931,Ja 25,VIII,2:4
Field, Olin
Gringo 1922,D 15,26:3
We Moderns 1924,Mr 12,17:2
Field, R P
It's Only Natural 1922,Ap 21,13:2
Field, Rachel Lyman (Playwright)
Three Pills in a Bottle 1935,My 12,15:4
Sentimental Scarecrow 1934,Mr 22,24:6
Field, Ray (Playwright)
Under One Roof 1932,F 8,21:2
Field, Richard Dryden
This Mad Whirl 1937,Ja 10,II,4:8
Field, Robert
Merry Widow, The 1943,Ag 5,19:2
Robin Hood 1944,N 8,28:2
Up in Central Park 1945,Ja 29,17:2
Day Before Spring, The 1945,N 23,27:2
Field, Roberta
Town House 1948,S 24,31:2
Field, Ron   (Choreographer)
Anything Goes 1962,My 16,35:1
Nowhere to Go But Up 1962,N 12,36:2
Cafe Crown 1964,Ap 18,32:1
Show Boat 1966,Jl 20,48:1
Cabaret 1966,D 4,II,5:1
Zorba 1968,N 18,58:1
Applause 1970,Mr 31,35:1
Applause 1970,Ap 5,II,1:1
Field, Ron   (Costume Designer)
Cabaret 1966,N 21,62:1
Field, Ron   (Director)
Applause 1970,Mr 31,35:1
Applause 1970,Ap 5,II,1:1
Field, Salisbury (Playwright)
Zander the Great 1923,Ap 10,24:2
Zander the Great 1923,Ap 15,VII,1:1
Field, Sid
Harvey 1949,Ja 6,29:2
Harvey 1949,F 13,II,3:7
Field, Sylvia
Connie Goes Home 1923,S 7,10:1
Rabbit's Foot, The 1924,Ap 27,VIII,2:3
Cock o' the Roost 1924,O 14,23:1
Mrs Partridge Presents 1925,Ja 6,23:3
Something to Brag About 1925,Ag 14,14:3
Butter and Egg Man, The 1925,S 24,28:1
Little Spitfire, The 1926,Ag 17,15:2
Broadway 1926,S 17,19:3
Behold This Dreamer 1927,N 1,20:4
Royal Family, The 1927,D 29,26:4
Royal Family, The 1928,Ja 8,VIII,1:1
R U R 1930,F 18,28:1
Marco Millions 1930,Mr 4,24:4
Volpone 1930,Mr 11,24:5
Up and Up, The 1930,S 9,25:2
Queen at Home 1930,N 2,VIII,3:5
Queen at Home 1930,D 30,25:2
Give Me Yesterday 1931,Mr 5,32:1
Just to Remind You 1931,S 8,39:1
Caught Wet 1931,N 5,29:1
Adams' Wife 1931,D 29,27:1
Hilda Cassidy 1933,My 5,18:3
Uncle Tom's Cabin 1933,My 30,13:4
Birthright 1933,N 22,22:3
Sing and Whistle 1934,F 12,18:3

Field, Sylvia—Cont

Distant Shore, The 1935,F 22,26:2
Is This a Zither? 1935,Je 11,24:3
Three-Cornered Moon 1935,Je 25,14:5
All This While 1935,Jl 30,17:2
Achilles Had a Heel 1935,O 14,20:2
Stick-in-the-Mud 1935,D 2,18:2
I Want a Policeman! 1936,Ja 15,15:5
Pre-Honeymoon 1936,My 1,19:4
Crab Apple 1936,Jl 8,14:2
White Man 1936,O 19,22:4
Matrimony, PFD 1936,N 6,28:4
Matrimony, PFD 1936,N 13,26:3
Something for Nothing 1937,D 10,33:5
Popsy 1941,F 11,26:2
But Not Goodbye 1944,Ap 12,19:2
Oh, Mr Meadowbrook! 1948,D 27,17:2
ANTA Album 1951,My 7,22:7
Child of the Morning 1951,N 17,9:7

Field, Ted

As You Like It 1945,Jl 4,10:4

Field, Theodore

Pygmalion 1952,F 9,11:2

Field, Virginia

Doughgirls, The 1942,D 31,19:2
Doughgirls, The 1943,Ja 10,VIII,1:1
Light Up the Sky 1948,N 19,34:2

Field Sisters

Sharlee 1923,N 23,20:1

Fielden-Kaye, Beatrix

Evensong 1933,F 1,13:4

Fielder, Frank

Five Little Peppers, The 1952,My 19,13:1

Fielder, Frank Ray (Playwright)

Five Little Peppers, The 1952,My 19,13:1

Fielder, John

Sing Me No Lullaby 1954,O 15,17:2
Raisin in the Sun, A 1959,Mr 12,27:1

Fielder, Richard (Director)

Five Little Peppers, The 1952,My 19,13:1

Fielder, Ronald

Earl Carroll's Vanities 1930,Jl 2,28:3

Fielder, Sheila

And the Wind Blows 1959,Ap 29,28:1

Fielder, William

Five Little Peppers, The 1952,My 19,13:1

Fielding, Anne

Time of Storm 1954,F 26,14:2
Major Barbara 1954,Je 30,23:2
Juno and the Paycock 1955,F 24,20:4
Beaver Coat, The 1956,Mr 29,22:5
Tevya and His Daughters 1957,S 17,38:2
Ivanov 1958,O 8,42:1
Ivanov 1958,O 19,II,1:1
Tempest, The 1960,Je 20,35:1
Antony and Cleopatra 1960,Ag 1,19:1
Montserrat 1961,Ja 9,30:5
Midsummer Night's Dream, A 1961,Ag 3,13:1
Don Carlos 1962,F 28,27:5
Richard II 1962,Je 18,20:2
Henry IV, Part I 1962,Je 18,20:4
Hedda Gabler 1970,Ja 18,78:1

Fielding, Clayton

Macbeth 1928,N 20,28:3

Fielding, Edward

Crooked Gamblers 1920,Ag 2,12:1
Cornered 1920,D 9,18:2
We Girls 1921,N 10,26:3
That Day 1922,Jl 9,VI,1:4
That Day 1922,O 4,27:3
Pasteur 1923,Mr 13,19:1
Queen Victoria 1923,N 16,15:1
Rising Son, The 1924,O 28,27:2
Glass Slipper, The 1925,O 20,29:1
Merchants of Glory 1925,D 15,28:3
Goat Song 1926,Ja 26,18:1
Ghosts 1926,Mr 17,28:2
Porgy 1927,O 11,26:2
Lady From the Sea, The 1929,Mr 19,36:1
Soldiers and Women 1929,S 3,25:1
I Want My Wife 1930,Mr 21,30:7
Richard III 1930,Mr 31,24:1
Reunion in Vienna 1931,N 17,31:1
Peace Palace 1933,Je 6,30:2
Iron Flowers 1933,Je 13,22:2
No More Ladies 1934,Ja 24,20:3
Post Road 1934,D 5,28:3
St Helena 1936,O 7,32:1
Othello 1937,Ja 7,16:4
Amazing Dr. Clitterhouse, The 1937,Mr 3,26:4
Merely Murder 1937,D 4,21:4
Brown Danube, The 1939,My 18,30:4

Fielding, Fenella

Colette 1970,O 15,58:1

Fielding, Harold (Producer)

Half a Sixpence 1965,Ap 26,38:2

Fielding, Henry (Original Author)

Children of Darkness 1930,Ja 19,VIII,1:1

Fielding, Henry (Playwright)

Tom Thumb the Great 1932,Ag 28,IX,1:1
Covent Garden Tragedy, The 1968,Jl 9,30:2
Covent Garden Tragedy, The 1968,Jl 14,II,4:5

Fielding, Jerry (Miscellaneous)

Eddie Fisher at the Winter Garden 1962,O 3,47:1

Fielding, Marjery

Shining Hour, The 1934,F 14,22:6
Quiet Wedding 1938,N 6,IX,3:5

Fielding, Marjery (Choreographer)

Jumbo 1935,N 18,20:2
On Your Toes 1937,Ag 3,21:2
Right This Way 1938,Ja 6,22:3
Sally, Irene and Mary 1938,Jl 5,13:4
All in Fun 1940,D 28,11:2
Priorities of 1942 1942,Mr 13,23:2
Take a Bow 1944,Je 16,15:3

Fielding, Marjery (Composer)

Priorities of 1942 1942,Mr 13,23:2

Fielding, Marjery (Lyricist)

Priorities of 1942 1942,Mr 13,23:2

Fielding, Robert

When Did You Last See My Mother?
1967,Ja 5,27:5
Antigone 1967,Ja 14,18:1

Fields, Al

Will Morrissey's Newcomers 1923,Ag 9,16:2
O Evening Star 1936,Ja 9,24:6

Fields, Benny

Vaudeville (Palace) 1921,Jl 5,15:1
Vaudeville (Palace) 1923,Mr 13,19:2
Vaudeville (Palace) 1926,My 4,31:2
Vaudeville (Palace) 1926,S 28,30:4
Vaudeville (Palace) 1927,S 20,33:3
Vaudeville (Palace) 1927,O 18,32:4
Vaudeville (Palace) 1927,O 25,33:2
Greenwich Village Follies 1928,Ap 10,32:2
Vaudeville (Palace) 1929,N 18,22:4
Vaudeville (Palace) 1931,Ap 20,16:2
Vaudeville (Hollywood) 1932,Ap 19,25:5
Star Time 1944,S 13,16:2
Star Time 1944,S 17,II,1:1

Fields, David

Fiesta 1929,S 18,35:1

Fields, Donald

Liza 1922,N 28,24:1

Fields, Dorothy (Composer)

International Revue 1930,F 26,22:2
Rhapsody in Black 1931,My 5,33:2
Singin' the Blues 1931,S 17,21:3
Sweet Charity 1967,Jl 1,13:1

Fields, Dorothy (Lyricist)

Blackbirds 1928,My 10,31:3
Hello, Daddy! 1928,D 27,26:5
International Revue 1930,F 26,22:2
Singin' the Blues 1931,Ap 12,IX,2:1
Rhapsody in Black 1931,My 5,33:2
Stars in Your Eyes 1939,F 10,18:2
Up in Central Park 1945,Ja 29,17:2
Up in Central Park 1947,My 20,29:2
Arms and the Girl 1950,F 3,28:2
Tree Grows in Brooklyn, A 1951,Ap 20,24:3
Tree Grows in Brooklyn, A 1951,Ap 29,II,1:1
Tree Grows in Brooklyn, A 1951,My 20,II,1:1
By the Beautiful Sea 1954,Ap 9,20:1
By the Beautiful Sea 1954,Ap 18,II,1:1
Redhead 1959,F 6,21:1
Redhead 1959,F 15,II,1:1
Sweet Charity 1966,Ja 31,22:1
Harold Arlen Songbook, The 1967,Mr 1,48:1

Fields, Dorothy (Miscellaneous)

Annie Get Your Gun 1946,S 29,II,1:1

Fields, Dorothy (Original Author)

Up in Central Park 1945,Ja 29,17:2
Annie Get Your Gun 1946,My 17,14:2

Fields, Dorothy (Playwright)

Let's Face It 1941,O 10,27:1
Let's Face It 1941,O 30,26:2
Something for the Boys 1943,Ja 17,VIII,1:1
Mexican Hayride 1944,Ja 29,9:6
Mexican Hayride 1944,F 6,II,1:1
Annie Get Your Gun 1946,My 26,II,1:1
Up in Central Park 1947,My 20,29:2
Arms and the Girl 1950,F 3,28:2
By the Beautiful Sea 1954,Ap 9,20:1
By the Beautiful Sea 1954,Ap 18,II,1:1
Annie Get Your Gun 1957,Mr 9,15:5
Annie Get Your Gun 1957,Ag 31,18:2
Annie Get Your Gun 1958,F 20,29:2
Redhead 1959,F 6,21:1
Annie Get Your Gun 1966,Je 1,42:2

Fields, Dorothy G (Producer)

Kiss Mama 1964,O 2,30:1

Fields, Eddy

Barber Had Two Sons, The 1943,F 2,22:2

Fields, Florence

Green Pastures, The 1935,F 27,16:2

Fields, Frank (Composer)

Shoemaker and the Peddler, The 1960,O 15,27:4
Sacco-Vanzetti 1969,F 9,78:1

Fields, Freddie (Producer)

Judy Garland 1961,Ap 24,36:1

Fields, Gracie

Vaudeville (Palace) 1930,S 29,19:1
Top-Notchers 1942,My 30,8:5
Vaudeville (Palladium) 1953,Ap 24,29:4

Fields, Harvey

Have You Heard This One 1953,N 9,23:4

Fields, Helen

Great Way, The 1921,N 8,28:2

Fields, Herbert

Ankles Aweigh 1955,Ap 19,27:1
Hit the Deck 1960,Je 24,32:1
Show Boat 1961,Ap 13,32:1
Foxy 1964,F 17,26:1

Fields, Herbert (Choreographer)

Jazz a La Carte 1922,Je 3,8:3
Garrick Gaieties 1926,My 11,25:2

Fields, Herbert (Director)

You'll Never Know 1921,Ap 21,9:2

Fields, Herbert (Miscellaneous)

Connecticut Yankee 1927,N 21,II,1:1
Annie Get Your Gun 1946,S 29,II,1:1

Fields, Herbert (Original Author)

Du Barry 1939,N 19,X,3:4
Du Barry Was a Lady 1939,D 7,34:2
Panama Hattie 1940,O 31,28:2
Up in Central Park 1945,Ja 29,17:2
Annie Get Your Gun 1946,My 17,14:2

Fields, Herbert (Playwright)

Dearest Enemy 1925,S 19,9:2
Girl Friend, The 1926,Mr 18,26:5
Peggy-Ann 1926,D 28,16:3
Hit the Deck! 1927,Ap 26,32:1
Connecticut Yankee, A 1927,O 9,VIII,1:3
Connecticut Yankee, A 1927,N 4,24:2
Present Arms 1928,Ap 27,16:2
Chee-Chee 1928,S 26,25:1
Hello, Daddy! 1928,D 27,26:5
Fifty Million Frenchmen 1929,N 28,34:4
New Yorkers, The 1930,N 16,VIII,3:1
New Yorkers, The 1930,D 9,31:1
America's Sweetheart 1931,F 11,23:1
Pardon My English 1932,D 11,IX,5:2
Pardon My English 1933,Ja 21,11:4
Panama Hattie 1940,N 10,IX,1:1
Let's Face It 1941,O 10,27:1
Let's Face It 1941,O 30,26:2
Something for the Boys 1943,Ja 17,VIII,1:1
Connecticut Yankee, A 1943,N 18,30:2
Mexican Hayride 1944,Ja 29,9:6
Mexican Hayride 1944,F 6,II,1:1
Annie Get Your Gun 1946,My 26,II,1:1
Up in Central Park 1947,My 20,29:2
Arms and the Girl 1950,F 3,28:2
By the Beautiful Sea 1954,Ap 9,20:1
By the Beautiful Sea 1954,Ap 18,II,1:1
Annie Get Your Gun 1957,Mr 9,15:5
Annie Get Your Gun 1957,Ag 31,18:2
Annie Get Your Gun 1958,F 20,29:2
Redhead 1959,F 6,21:1
Hit the Deck 1960,Je 24,32:1
Annie Get Your Gun 1966,Je 1,42:2

Fields, Jeanne

Reunion of Sorts 1969,O 15,40:1

Fields, Jimmie (Choreographer)

World of My America, The 1966,O 4,53:1

Fields, Joan

Top Banana 1951,N 2,19:2

Fields, Joe

Great Magoo, The 1932,D 3,20:7
It Pays to Sin 1933,N 4,18:6
Farmer Takes a Wife, The 1934,O 31,17:1
O Evening Star 1936,Ja 9,24:6

Fields, Johnny

Houseboat on the Styx, The 1928,D 26,14:3

Fields, Joseph (Director)

Man Who Had All the Luck, The 1944,N 24,18:5
I Gotta Get Out 1947,S 26,27:2
Desk Set, The 1955,O 25,36:7
Tunnel of Love, The 1957,F 14,31:4

Fields, Joseph (Miscellaneous)

Flower Drum Song 1958,D 2,44:1

Fields, Joseph (Original Author)

Gentlemen Prefer Blondes 1949,D 9,35:3
Wonderful Town 1953,F 26,22:3

Fields, Joseph (Playwright)

Schoolhouse on the Lot 1938,Mr 23,18:4
My Sister Eileen 1940,D 27,23:2
My Sister Eileen 1941,Ja 5,IX,1:1
Junior Miss 1941,N 19,28:2
Junior Miss 1941,N 30,IX,1:1
Doughgirls, The 1942,D 31,19:2
Doughgirls, The 1943,Ja 10,VIII,1:1
French Touch, The 1945,D 10,18:2
I Gotta Get Out 1947,S 26,27:2
Gentlemen Prefer Blondes 1949,D 18,II,3:1
Wonderful Town 1953,F 26,22:3
Wonderful Town 1953,Mr 8,II,1:1
Girl in Pink Tights, The 1954,Mr 6,13:2
Anniversary Waltz 1954,Ap 8,34:1
Anniversary Waltz 1954,Ap 25,II,1:1
Wonderful Town 1954,My 7,II,1:1
Anniversary Waltz 1955,D 2,31:3
Anniversary Waltz 1955,D 11,II,7:1
Ponder Heart, The 1956,F 17,14:2
Ponder Heart, The 1956,F 26,II,1:1
Tunnel of Love, The 1957,F 14,31:4
Tunnel of Love, The 1957,D 5,47:2
Wonderful Town 1958,Mr 6,32:4
Flower Drum Song 1958,D 2,44:1

Fields, Joseph (Playwright)—Cont
Flower Drum Song 1958,D 7,II,5:1
Wonderful Town 1963,F 15,10:2
Wonderful Town 1967,My 18,50:1
Fields, Julius
Kismet 1965,Je 23,45:1
Fields, Leo
Devil's Host, The 1931,N 20,27:2
Fields, Lew
Blue Eyes 1921,F 22,11:2
Snapshots of 1921 1921,Je 3,19:2
Friars Club Frolic 1921,Je 13,16:2
Friar's Club Frolic 1922,Je 5,16:1
Vaudeville (Central) 1922,S 19,14:1
Jazz King, The 1924,Ap 6,VIII,2:1
Henky 1924,Ap 27,VIII,2:3
Melody Man, The 1924,My 14,14:2
Melody Man, The 1924,My 18,VII,1:1
Money Business 1926,Ja 21,18:1
High Cost of Loving, The 1928,D 16,IX,2:1
Hello, Daddy! 1928,D 27,26:5
Fields, Lew (Director)
Vanderbilt Revue, The 1930,N 6,22:6
Fields, Lew (Playwright)
Poor Little Ritz Girl 1920,Jl 29,7:1
Fields, Lew (Producer)
Girl Friend, The 1926,Mr 18,26:5
Peggy-Ann 1926,D 28,16:3
Hit the Deck! 1927,Ap 26,32:1
Connecticut Yankee, A 1927,N 4,24:2
Present Arms 1928,Ap 27,16:2
Chee-Chee 1928,S 26,25:1
Hello, Daddy! 1928,D 27,26:5
Vanderbilt Revue, The 1930,N 6,22:6
Fields, Lilian
Beautiful Dreamer 1960,D 28,22:1
Sap of Life, The 1961,O 3,44:1
Fields, Michael (Miscellaneous)
Hamlet 1970,O 19,51:1
Fields, Nancy
God and Kate Murphy 1959,F 27,21:2
Fields, Norman (Musical Director)
Kiss Me, Kate 1954,Mr 27,13:2
Fields, Peter
Magdalena 1948,S 21,31:2
Fields, R P
It's Only Natural 1922,Ap 21,13:2
Fields, Ric
Immoralist, The 1963,N 8,36:2
Fields, Robert
And the Wind Blows 1959,Ap 29,28:1
Deirdre of the Sorrows 1959,O 15,46:1
Between Two Thieves 1960,F 12,23:1
Iolanthe 1965,My 19,42:1
Live Like Pigs 1965,Je 8,48:2
Yeomen of the Guard, The 1965,Jl 8,34:1
Ruddigore 1965,Ag 27,16:1
Persecution and Assassination of Marat As
    Performed by the Inmates of the Asylum of
    Charenton Under the Direction of the Marquis de
    Sade, The 1967,Ja 4,34:1
Cuban Thing, The 1968,S 25,36:2
Fields, Ruth
Devil's Little Game, The 1932,Ag 2,20:4
Fields, Sally
Dancing Girl, The 1923,Ja 25,16:2
Fields, Sandie
Maggie Flynn 1968,O 24,52:1
Fields, W C
Ziegfeld 9 o'clock Follies 1920,Mr 9,18:1
Ziegfeld Midnight Frolic 1920,Mr 17,14:2
Ziegfeld Follies 1920,Je 23,14:1
Ziegfeld Follies 1921,Je 22,10:1
George White's Scandals 1922,Ag 29,10:1
Poppy 1923,S 4,14:2
Comic Supplement, The 1925,Ja 25,VII,1:4
Follies 1925,Mr 11,19:2
Lambs Gambol 1925,Ap 27,15:1
Ziegfeld Follies 1925,Je 28,VIII,1:1
Follies 1925,Jl 7,24:3
Earl Carroll's Vanities 1928,Ag 7,25:2
Vaudeville (Palace) 1930,Mr 24,24:5
Ballyhoo 1930,D 14,IX,3:1
Ballyhoo 1930,D 23,24:1
Fields, W C (Composer)
Ziegfeld Follies 1920,Je 23,14:1
Fields, W C (Lyricist)
Ziegfeld Follies 1920,Je 23,14:1
Fields, W C (Playwright)
Ziegfeld Follies 1920,Je 23,14:1
George White's Scandals 1922,Ag 29,10:1
Earl Carroll's Vanities 1928,Ag 7,25:2
Fields, William (Producer)
Privilege Car 1931,Mr 4,33:1
How I Wonder 1947,O 1,34:2
Leading Lady 1948,O 19,33:1
Fien, Lupin (Composer)
Some of the People 1937,Mr 11,20:1
Fierce, Louis
Your Woman and Mine 1922,F 28,17:2
Advertising of Kate, The 1922,My 9,22:2
Fierman, Robert
Come Marching Home 1946,My 20,18:6
Winners and Losers 1947,F 27,27:2

Fierron, Ernest
White Cargo 1960,D 30,12:1
Fiers, Robert de (Playwright)
Transplanting Jean 1921,Ja 9,VI,1:1
Fiester, Elaine
Scapegoat, The 1950,Ap 20,36:5
Home Is Tomorrow 1950,Je 2,27:2
Fievelowitz, Ben
Enchanting Melody 1964,N 25,40:1
Fife, George Buchanan
Little Father of the Wilderness, The 1930,Je 3,27:1
Fife, George Buchanan (Playwright)
Ask Your Wife 1929,O 14,20:4
Fife, Reginald
Button, Button 1929,O 24,26:1
City Haul 1929,D 31,14:4
Fifer Trio, The
Fables 1922,F 7,12:2
Fifield, Ruth M
Merry Wives of Windsor, The 1954,F 17,27:1
Figel-Hartman, Dorothy (Playwright)
Spoken English and Broken English; Don Quixote
    Meets the Puppet-Master 1959,Ja 27,27:5
Figlmiller, John
Macbeth 1968,N 30,49:3
Figlmiller, John (Miscellaneous)
Macbeth 1968,N 30,49:3
Figman, Felix
Inspector Kennedy 1929,D 21,16:3
Figman, Max
In the Night Watch 1921,Ja 31,10:1
Kiki 1921,N 30,13:1
Parasites 1924,N 20,21:1
Vagabond King, The 1925,S 22,23:3
New Moon, The 1928,S 20,33:1
Well of Romance, The 1930,N 8,21:2
Papavert 1931,D 30,25:1
Mr Papavert 1932,Ja 23,18:6
Du Barry 1932,N 23,15:2
Mackerel Skies 1934,Ja 24,20:4
Figman, Max (Director)
Vagabond King, The 1925,S 22,23:3
Mr Papavert 1932,Ja 23,18:6
Figman, Oscar
Peg o' My Dreams 1924,My 6,25:3
Madame Pompadour 1924,N 12,20:6
Katja 1926,O 19,27:3
Angela 1928,D 4,28:2
Figueiredo, Guilherme (Playwright)
God Slept Here, A 1957,F 20,38:1
Figueroa, Laura
Does a Tiger Wear a Necktie? 1969,F 26,38:1
Figueroa, Ruben
Ox Cart, The 1966,D 20,58:1
Fijalkowska, Dina
Mirele Efros 1967,O 20,55:1
Mother Courage 1967,N 17,55:1
Fila, Eugene
Firebird 1932,N 22,25:2
Filauri, Antonio
Honor Code, The 1931,My 19,25:3
Berretto a Songali, Il; Cap With Bells, The
    1931,N 30,16:3
Piccolo Santo, Il; Little Saint, The 1931,D 14,16:4
Profumo di Mia Moglie, Il; My Wife's Perfume
    1932,Ja 11,29:5
Civil Death, The 1932,Ja 25,20:3
Trio 1932,F 8,21:1
Ladro, Il; Thief, The 1932,F 22,23:4
Fileding, Edward
Eye on the Sparrow 1938,My 4,26:3
Filett, Louis
Winners and Losers 1947,F 27,27:2
Filiatreault, Adrien
Untitled-Passion Play 1925,Ag 17,8:1
Filippo, Budd (Producer)
Three Men on a Horse 1969,O 17,35:1
Filkins, Ada
Unto Such Glory 1937,My 7,28:2
Filkins, Grace
Rita Coventry 1923,F 20,12:2
Sweet Seventeen 1924,Mr 18,24:2
Head or Tail 1926,N 10,24:1
In The Best of Families 1931,F 3,29:1
Fill, Albert I (Miscellaneous)
Home Fires 1969,Ap 8,42:1
Cop-Out 1969,Ap 8,42:1
Fill, Albert I (Producer)
Hamlet 1969,My 2,38:1
Charles Aznavour 1970,F 5,32:4
Filler, Martin
Mikado, The 1935,Ag 24,17:5
Filler, Sarah
Soul of a Woman, The 1930,F 22,13:1
Motke From Slobodke 1930,Ap 12,23:3
Filley, Mary G
Variations of 1940 1940,Ja 29,12:1
Fillinger, Johan (Director)
Arms and the Man 1964,Ap 28,41:1
Fillini, Mel
Trial, The 1955,Je 15,35:2
Spring's Awakening 1955,O 10,30:2

Fillmore, Blaine
If This Be Treason 1935,Jl 30,17:1
What a Life 1938,Ap 14,26:2
Janie 1942,S 11,24:2
Fillmore, Clyde
Sea Woman, The 1925,Ag 25,12:2
Right to Kill, The 1926,F 16,22:2
Just Life 1926,S 15,33:3
Love Nest, The 1927,D 23,17:1
Buzzard, The 1928,Mr 15,29:1
Tomorrow 1928,D 29,20:2
Sweet Stranger 1930,O 22,23:3
Face the Music 1932,F 18,24:5
Absent Father 1932,O 18,23:5
Before Morning 1933,F 10,13:4
Thoroughbred 1933,N 7,29:2
False Dreams, Farewell 1934,Ja 16,18:3
Between Two Worlds 1934,O 26,24:2
De Luxe 1935,Mr 6,22:2
If This Be Treason 1935,Jl 30,17:1
Night of January 16 1935,S 17,26:4
Pre-Honeymoon 1936,My 1,19:4
Tide Rising 1937,Ja 26,17:2
Angel Island 1937,O 21,26:2
Primrose Path, The 1939,Ja 5,16:3
Primrose Path, The 1939,Ja 16,11:2
Too Many Girls 1939,O 19,26:2
Fillmore, John Eldon (Playwright)
Fantasia 1933,Ja 4,22:4
Fillmore, Nellie
Ladies' Night 1920,Ag 10,10:1
Myrtie 1924,F 5,21:2
Magnolia Lady, The 1924,N 26,17:2
Set a Thief 1927,F 22,22:1
Fillmore, Russell
Innocent Idea, An 1920,My 26,9:4
Masked Woman, The 1922,D 23,14:2
Fillmore, Russell (Director)
Coquette 1935,My 22,23:4
Quiet, Please! 1940,N 9,20:3
Filos, Joseph
Mikado, The 1944,F 12,11:3
Ruddigore 1944,Mr 3,19:5
Filsinger, Gary
Hole, The 1961,Ap 4,42:2
Finch, Flora
We've Got to Have Money 1923,Ag 21,12:1
Finch, John (Playwright)
Wanhope Building, The 1947,F 11,36:5
Finch, Palmer
Backslapper, The 1925,Ap 13,25:2
Finch, Patricia
Oklahoma! 1958,Mr 20,32:3
Tall Story 1959,Ja 30,33:2
Kiss Me, Kate 1965,My 13,31:1
Finch, Robert
Mighty Nimrod, The 1931,My 13,23:1
Lord Blesses the Bishop, The 1934,N 28,24:5
Crime and Punishment 1935,Ja 23,20:3
Lost Colony, The 1937,Jl 11,X,2:1
Finch, Robert (Playwright)
Whistler's Grandmother 1952,D 12,40:2
Finch, Thomas
Three Plays of the Sea 1970,Ag 20,39:1
Finci, Mara (Costume Designer)
Who's Afraid of Virginia Woolf? 1968,Jl 4,13:1
Finck, Harold (Composer)
Nine to Eleven, The 1925,Jl 12,VII,1:1
Finck, Herman (Composer)
Decameron Nights 1922,Ap 21,14:5
Finckel, Edwin (Composer)
Red Roses for Me 1955,D 29,15:2
Findlay, Agnes
Merton of the Movies 1922,N 14,16:2
Findlay, Denise
Mikado, The 1947,D 30,18:2
Iolanthe 1948,Ja 13,29:3
Gondoliers, The 1948,Ja 27,31:2
Yeomen of the Guard, The 1948,F 3,30:2
Findlay, Diane
We're Civilized? 1962,N 9,30:1
Findlay, Elsa (Choreographer)
Within the Gates 1934,O 23,23:1
Mother Lode 1934,D 24,16:5
Findlay, Grace Francis
Old Foolishness, The 1940,D 21,20:2
Findlay, Hal
Wicked Age, The 1927,N 5,16:6
Findlay, John (Mrs)
Night Boat, The 1920,F 3,18:1
Findlay, Ruth
Cat-Bird, The 1920,F 17,18:1
Prince and the Pauper, The 1920,N 2,15:1
Prince and the Pauper, The 1920,N 7,VII,1:1
Anything Might Happen 1921,F 21,22:3
Man or Devil 1925,My 22,22:4
Window Panes 1927,F 22,22:2
Gypsy 1929,Ja 15,22:2
Land Is Bright, The 1941,O 29,26:2
Findlay, Thomas
Kiki 1921,N 30,13:1
Little Minister, The 1925,Mr 24,21:1
Spider, The 1927,Mr 23,29:1

Findlay, Thomas—Cont
Criminal Code, The 1929,O 3,28:2
Pagan Lady 1930,O 21,34:2
Distant Drums 1932,Ja 19,24:3
Distant Drums 1932,Ja 31,VIII,1:1
Thousand Summers, A 1932,My 25,23:4
Best Years 1932,S 8,16:2
Moor Born 1934,Ap 4,26:4
Moor Born 1934,Ap 8,X,2:7
First Legion, The 1934,O 2,18:2
First Lady 1935,N 27,17:4
Of Mice and Men 1937,N 24,20:5
Kindred 1939,D 27,17:2

Findley, Timothy
Richard III 1953,Jl 15,22:2

Fine, Aaron
Trial, The 1955,Je 15,35:2

Fine, Aaron (Playwright)
Trial, The 1955,Je 15,35:2

Fine, Al
Cocktails of 1934 1934,My 5,22:1

Fine, Harry
Moon Is Blue, The 1953,Jl 8,24:1

Fine, Larry
Night in Venice, A 1929,My 22,30:2

Fine, Miriam
Song of the Ghetto, The 1932,O 3,15:5

Fine, Ruth (Playwright)
This Is Today 1935,Jl 30,17:2

Fine, Sylvia (Composer)
Straw Hat, The 1939,S 30,10:6

Fineberg, Lawrence W (Miscellaneous)
Ballad for a Firing Squad 1968,D 12,64:2

Finell, Alyce (Lyricist)
Ivanov 1958,O 8,42:1

Finer, Louis (Translator)
Masks of Angels 1965,Ja 20,33:1

Finfree, Sarah
All the Living 1938,Mr 25,14:4

Fingar, Thelma (Producer)
Sixth Finger in a Five Finger Glove 1956,O 9,31:4

Finin, Charles
Merry Malones, The 1927,S 27,30:2

Fink, Alfred
Deep Channels 1929,O 19,22:3

Fink, Anna Marie
Blue Butterfly, The 1929,F 17,29:3

Fink, Mitchell (Miscellaneous)
Someone's Comin' Hungry 1969,Ap 1,51:1

Fink, Mitchell (Producer)
Whispers on the Wind 1970,Je 4,50:1

Fink, Richard E
Republic, The 1970,Ap 28,49:1

Fink and Busher
Ice Follies 1937,D 22,29:1

Finkel, Alicia (Costume Designer)
Tempest, The 1970,F 15,67:1

Finkel, Fyvush
Go Fight City Hall 1961,N 3,28:5
Good Luck 1964,O 19,38:3

Finkel, Ian
Dames at Sea 1970,Ja 5,46:3

Finkel, Lucy
Salt and Pepper 1933,Ap 24,10:2
Happy Days 1934,Ap 2,12:5

Finkel, Shimon
Dybbuk, The 1948,My 3,26:3
David's Crown 1948,My 10,26:2
Golem, The 1948,My 17,22:3
Oedipus Rex 1948,My 24,23:2
Dybbuk, The 1964,F 4,30:2

Finkelstein, Daniel
Sign of Jonah, The 1960,S 9,35:1

Finkelstien, Norman (Lighting Director)
Sweet Miani 1962,S 26,33:2

Finkl, Fred (Producer)
Have You Heard This One 1953,N 9,23:4

Finkle, Bella
Four Walls 1927,S 20,33:1
Four Walls 1927,O 2,VIII,1:1

Finkle, David (Miscellaneous)
I'm Solomon 1968,Ap 24,51:1

Finkle, Lucy
Honeymoon for Three, A 1933,Ja 30,9:6

Finklehoffe, Fred F (Director)
Ankles Aweigh 1955,Ap 19,27:1
Ankles Aweigh 1955,Ap 24,II,1:1

Finklehoffe, Fred F (Miscellaneous)
Affairs of State 1950,S 26,37:2

Finklehoffe, Fred F (Playwright)
Brother Rat 1936,D 8,30:6
Brother Rat 1936,D 17,34:5
Lew Leslie's Blackbirds of 1939 1939,F 13,12:2

Finklehoffe, Fred F (Producer)
Show Time 1942,S 17,20:2
Laugh Time 1943,S 9,35:2
Heiress, The 1947,S 30,22:2
Ankles Aweigh 1955,Ap 19,27:1
Hide and Seek 1957,Ap 3,26:1

Fink's Mules
Vaudeville (Hippodrome) 1926,Ap 13,28:2

Finlay, Frank
Epitaph for George Dillon 1958,N 5,44:1
Othello 1964,Ap 22,56:1

Othello 1964,Jl 23,18:4

Finlay, Vera
Paddy the Next Best Thing 1920,Ag 28,5:5
Bachelor's Night, A 1921,O 18,20:1

Finlayson, Donald (Costume Designer)
Burning Bush, The 1949,D 17,15:5

Finlayson, M J
Pudding on the Ritz 1932,Ap 9,18:3

Finletter, Gretchen Damrosch (Playwright)
Runaway Road, The 1926,N 14,VIII,5:1
Garrick Gaieties 1930,Je 5,29:2
Picnic 1934,My 3,15:2

Finley, Edward
Sitting Pretty 1924,Ap 9,24:2
Brass Buttons 1927,D 6,26:3

Finley, George
All God's Chillun Got Wings 1924,My 16,22:3
All God's Chillun Got Wings 1924,Ag 19,9:1

Finley, John (Director)
Holiday on Ice 1968,Ag 29,44:1
Holiday on Ice 1969,Ag 28,44:1

Finley, John (Miscellaneous)
Holiday on Ice 1965,S 2,38:4

Finley, John (Producer)
Holiday on Ice 1966,S 1,30:1
Holiday on Ice 1967,Ag 31,29:2

Finley, Margie
Broadway Whirl, The 1921,Je 9,10:4
Gay Paree 1925,Ag 19,14:3
Night in Paris, A 1926,Jl 27,15:4
Gay Paree 1926,N 10,24:2
Sunny Days 1928,F 9,29:1
Hold Your Horses 1933,S 26,26:4

Finley, Muriel
Whoopee 1928,D 5,34:3

Finley, Pat
Greenwich Village U S A 1960,S 29,30:5
Hello, Dolly! 1965,Ag 10,17:2

Finley, Robert
Eve's Leaves 1925,Mr 27,22:2

Finley, William
Macbeth 1969,N 21,51:1
Makbeth 1969,N 30,II,3:1
Renard 1970,Mr 25,36:4
Only Jealousy of Emer, The 1970,Mr 25,36:4
Gertrude 1970,N 13,29:1

Finn, Caroline
Variations of 1940 1940,Ja 29,12:1

Finn, Elfin
Beyond the Horizon 1920,F 4,12:1
Eyvind of the Hills 1921,F 2,14:1
Lilies of the Field 1921,O 5,20:1
Great Way, The 1921,N 8,28:2
Tendresse, La 1922,S 26,18:1
Plain Jane 1924,My 13,24:2

Finn, Frank
Mr Strauss Goes to Boston 1945,S 7,20:2

Finn, Helen
Doctor's Dilemma, The 1969,Je 24,37:1

Finn, Irving S
Marjolaine 1922,Ja 25,16:1

Finn, John
Boy David, The 1936,N 22,VI,7:1

Finn, Jonathan (Playwright)
Chalked Out 1937,Mr 26,24:2

Finn, Konstantin (Composer)
Dollar Princess 1949,Je 2,32:1

Finn, Konstantin (Lyricist)
Dollar Princess 1949,Je 2,32:1

Finnan, Tommy 3d
Follies of 1910, The 1960,Ja 15,37:3

Finnegan, Arthur
Elmer the Great 1928,S 25,29:1

Finnegan, Jack
Follies of 1910, The 1960,Ja 15,37:3

Finnegan, Lynn
Ice Capades 1959,S 4,12:1
Ice Capades 1960,S 1,30:1
Ice Capades 1960,S 1,30:1
Ice Capades 1961,Ag 31,24:4
Ice Capades 1962,Ag 30,34:1
Ice Capades 1964,Ag 27,27:2
Ice Capades 1966,Je 2,50:2

Finnell, Carrie
Star and Garter 1942,Je 25,26:2

Finneran, Timothy (Lighting Director)
Shadow and Substance 1959,N 4,42:1

Finnerty, Mary
Lazarus Laughed 1948,Ap 9,27:4

Finnerty, Warren
Connection, The 1959,Jl 16,30:2
Tonight We Improvise 1959,N 7,27:4
Connection, The 1960,F 7,II,1:1
Women of Trachis 1960,Je 23,18:3
Man Is Man 1962,S 19,31:1
Brig, The 1963,My 16,40:1

Finney, Albert
Luther 1961,Jl 8,9:2
Luther 1961,Jl 28,10:2
Luther 1963,S 11,46:3
Luther 1963,S 26,41:1
Luther 1963,O 6,II,1:1
Armstrong's Last Goodnight 1965,Jl 7,26:1

Finney, Albert—Cont
Black Comedy 1965,Jl 29,19:1
Miss Julie 1965,Jl 29,19:1
Joe Egg 1968,F 2,26:1
Joe Egg 1968,F 11,II,1:1
Joe Egg 1968,Ap 27,43:2

Finney, Mary
Throng o' Scarlet 1947,D 2,37:2
Coast of Illyria, The 1949,Ap 5,37:4
Cock-A-Doodle Dandy 1950,F 1,26:2
Southern Exposure 1950,S 27,36:3
Cellar and the Well, The 1950,D 11,30:2
Make a Wish 1951,Ap 19,38:1
Children's Hour, The 1952,D 19,35:2
Corn Is Green, The 1954,F 27,10:2
Honeys, The 1955,Ap 29,26:1
Janus 1955,N 25,37:2
Happy Hunting 1956,D 7,30:1
First Impressions 1959,Mr 20,28:1
Whisper to Me 1960,N 22,38:6
Milk Train Doesn't Stop Here Anymore, The 1963,S 18,32:1
Too Much Johnson 1964,Ja 16,29:1

Finney, Victor
Johnny 2X4 1942,Mr 17,24:6
Catherine Was Great 1944,Ag 3,16:1

Finsterwald, Maxine (Playwright)
Little Theatre Tournament; Severed Cord, The 1929,My 9,34:3
Seven Against One 1930,My 7,25:1

Fiondella, Jay (Miscellaneous)
Go Fly a Kite! 1969,O 20,60:1

Fiorato, Hugo
Would-Be Gentleman, The 1930,Ap 30,29:2

Fiore
Donogoo 1961,Ja 19,25:3

Fiore, Frank
Child's Play 1970,F 18,39:1

Fiore, Roland
Untitled-One Woman Show 1938,O 31,12:2

Fiore, Roland (Musical Director)
My Romance 1948,O 20,38:5

Fiore, Rosa
Abisso 1920,O 10,VI,1:8

Fiorella, Mario
Countess Maritza 1936,Ag 19,18:2

Fiorentino, Imero (Lighting Director)
Orlando Furioso 1970,N 5,59:1

Fiory, Mariana
Dans Le Noir; In the Dark 1937,F 11,18:3
Christian 1937,F 25,18:6
Waltz in Goose Step 1938,N 2,26:2

Fiory, Marina
No Tears for Tony 1954,Je 3,32:6

Fippinger, Lynne (Choreographer)
Will the Mail Train Run Tonight? 1964,Ja 10,18:1

Firbank, Ann
All Kinds of Men 1957,S 20,20:3
Richard III 1967,Je 14,43:1
Government Inspector, The 1967,Je 15,55:1
Antony and Cleopatra 1967,Ag 2,25:1
Government Inspector, The 1967,O 28,34:1
Antony and Cleopatra 1967,O 29,83:4

Firbank, Ronald (Playwright)
Valmouth 1960,O 7,29:1

Fire Department Glee Club
Off the Record; Mayor Answers the Newspapers! Wow! 1935,Je 19,23:3

Firestone, Eddie
Caine Mutiny Court-Martial, The 1954,Ja 21,27:2
Roman Candle 1960,F 4,34:2

Firestone, Lee
Banquet for the Moon, A 1961,Ja 20,24:2

Firko, Vivian
Sundown Beach 1948,S 8,37:1

Firmbach, Charles Jr
Laugh, Clown, Laugh! 1923,N 29,30:1

Firner, Walter (Director)
Strange Interlude 1937,Ja 5,19:1
Everyman 1941,My 9,19:2

Firsow, Eugene
Diary of a Scoundrel 1956,N 5,41:1

Firstbrook, Peter
Hollywood Ice Revue 1954,Ja 15,16:2

Firth, Ann
Crooked Cross 1937,F 7,X,3:5

Fischbein, Lyn (Lighting Director)
Dream Play 1960,N 23,22:1
Feast of Panthers 1961,Mr 21,32:1

Fischbein, Saul (Producer)
Tenting Tonight 1947,Ap 3,32:2

Fischel, Arthur
Trojan Women, The 1923,My 27,10:2

Fischelli, Camille
Rosalinda; Fledermaus, Die 1942,O 29,26:5

Fischer, Alice
Pagans 1921,Ja 5,11:1
My Aunt From Ypsilanti 1923,My 2,22:6
Bride Retires, The 1925,My 18,12:3
Gypsy Fires 1925,D 8,28:3
Where's Your Husband? 1927,Ja 15,10:3
Hearts Are Trumps! 1927,Ap 8,21:1
Love Call, The 1927,O 25,33:1
Hello, Daddy! 1928,D 27,26:5

Fischer, Alice—Cont
Old Rascal, The 1930,Mr 25,34:4
Way of the World, The 1931,Je 2,34:3
Golden Cinderella, A 1931,O 4,VIII,2:2
Come Easy 1933,Ag 30,22:5
Symphony 1935,Ap 27,20:3
Fischer, Alice (Pvt)
Swing Sister Wac Swing 1944,Ja 4,20:4
Fischer, Betty
Goldne Meisterin 1927,O 25,33:4
Fischer, Bob
Christopher's Wonders 1960,S 27,41:1
Fischer, Charles
Victims, The; Escurial 1968,Mr 6,34:1
Victims, The; On the Hazards of Smoking Tobacco
1968,Mr 6,34:1
Fischer, Charles (Director)
Victims, The; Escurial 1968,Mr 6,34:1
Victims, The; On the Hazards of Smoking Tobacco
1968,Mr 6,34:1
Victims, The; Victims of Duty 1968,Mr 6,34:1
Fischer, Charles (Translator)
Victims, The; On the Hazards of Smoking Tobacco
1968,Mr 6,34:1
Fischer, Clifford C (Producer)
Folies Bergere 1939,D 25,28:2
Priorities of 1942 1942,Mr 13,23:2
Keep 'Em Laughing 1942,Ap 25,9:2
Top-Notchers 1942,My 30,8:5
New Priorities of 1943 1942,S 16,28:2
Edith Piaf 1947,O 30,30:2
Fischer, Donn (Costume Designer)
Innocents, The 1959,Ap 21,41:2
Fischer, Doris
Virginia 1937,S 3,13:2
Fischer, Harry
Tragedy of the Ages, The 1933,Ap 7,22:7
Fischer, Herbert
Low Bridge 1933,F 10,13:4
Fischer, Howard
Naughty-Naught '00 1937,Ja 25,23:2
Private Lives 1937,Jl 14,17:4
Kind Lady 1937,Jl 21,19:3
Fly Away Home 1937,Jl 28,15:1
Candida 1937,Ag 4,14:5
Whiteheaded Boy, The 1937,Ag 11,27:3
Elizabeth the Queen 1937,Ag 25,24:3
Goodbye Again 1937,S 1,15:1
Fireman's Flame, The 1937,O 11,26:2
Yes, My Darling Daughter 1938,Jl 13,19:2
Animal Kingdom, The 1938,Jl 27,14:5
Arms and the Man 1938,Ag 10,14:1
Bachelor Born 1938,Ag 17,23:1
Waltz in Goose Step 1938,N 2,26:2
Good Neighbor 1941,O 22,26:2
Second Best Bed 1946,Je 4,20:2
Crime and Punishment 1947,D 23,29:3
Two Blind Mice 1949,Mr 3,32:2
Remarkable Mr Pennypacker, The 1953,D 31,11:2
Skin of Our Teeth, The 1955,Ag 18,16:1
Visit, The 1958,My 6,40:1
Best Man, The 1960,Ap 1,39:1
Wildcat 1960,D 17,20:2
Finian's Rainbow 1967,Ap 6,44:1
Fischer, Howard (Miscellaneous)
Sheep on the Runway 1970,F 2,28:3
Fischer, Howard H
Desire Under the Elms 1952,Ja 17,23:4
Emperor's Clothes, The 1953,F 10,24:2
Fischer, Loretta
Priorities of 1942 1942,Mr 13,23:2
Take a Bow 1944,Je 16,15:3
Fischer, Margaret
Mikado, The 1942,F 4,22:2
Iolanthe 1942,F 24,26:4
Fischer, Preston (Producer)
Someone's Comin' Hungry 1969,Ap 1,51:1
Opium 1970,O 6,58:1
Fischer, Robert
Passion Flower, The 1920,Ja 14,12:1
Dear Me 1921,Ja 18,14:1
Fair Circassian, The 1921,D 7,22:3
Orange Blossoms 1922,S 20,18:1
Harem, The 1924,D 3,24:1
Sweet Adeline 1929,S 4,33:1
Tall Kentuckian, The 1953,Je 17,30:1
Fischer, Robert C
Vikings, The 1930,My 13,27:3
Friendship 1931,S 1,30:2
Friendship 1931,S 13,IX,1:1
Divorce Me, Dear 1931,O 7,29:2
Hot Money 1931,N 9,22:2
Autumn Crocus 1932,N 21,20:2
Shooting Star 1933,Je 13,22:2
Great Waltz, The 1934,S 24,14:4
May Wine 1935,D 6,30:3
Fischer, Robert C (Director)
Hat, a Coat, a Glove, A 1934,F 1,15:2
Fischer, Ruth
Simon's Wife 1945,Mr 9,16:4
Fischer, Sam
One Heluva Night 1924,Je 5,18:1
Fischer, Sebastian
Faust, Part I; Prologue in Heaven 1961,F 5,27:2

Faust, Part I; Play, The 1961,F 5,27:2
Maria Stuart 1968,Mr 27,38:1
Fischer, Thomas
Little Ol' Boy 1933,Ap 25,15:5
Fischetti, Michael
Montserrat 1961,Ja 9,30:5
Viewing, The 1967,Ja 11,51:1
Fischman, Iver
Mary Stuart 1956,Ap 28,10:2
Eagle Has Two Heads, The 1956,D 14,37:2
Right You Are (If You Think You Are)
1957,Mr 5,37:1
Two Gentlemen of Verona 1957,Jl 23,21:5
Macbeth 1957,Ag 16,11:2
Richard III 1957,N 26,41:1
Enemy of the People, An 1958,F 26,24:2
Fischoff, George (Composer)
If Five Years Pass 1962,My 11,37:1
Anvil, The 1962,O 31,33:3
Abe Lincoln in Illinois 1963,Ja 23,5:2
Awakening of Spring, The 1964,My 13,50:1
Me and Thee 1965,D 8,58:4
Georgy 1970,F 27,26:1
Fischoff, George (Miscellaneous)
Walk in Darkness 1963,O 29,30:2
Fiser, Don
Mr Strauss Goes to Boston 1945,S 7,20:2
Fish, Horace (Original Author)
Great Way, The 1921,N 8,28:2
Great Way, The 1921,N 13,VI,1:1
Fish, Horace (Playwright)
Great Way, The 1921,N 8,28:2
Fish, John
Macbeth 1968,N 30,49:3
Fish, Mr (Costume Designer)
Opium 1970,O 6,58:1
Fish, Peggy
Child of Manhattan 1932,Mr 2,15:1
Fish, Wille
Bronx Express 1922,Ap 27,12:2
Fishback, Joe
Trumpets and Drums 1969,O 13,52:1
Five Star Saint 1970,F 11,41:2
Fishbein, Benjamin
He, She and the Ox 1934,F 21,22:7
Fishbein, Carrie (Costume Designer)
Acquisition, The 1968,D 31,19:1
This Bird of Dawning Singeth All Night Long
1968,D 31,19:1
Young Master Dante, The 1968,D 31,19:1
Fishbein, Lynn (Lighting Director)
Every Other Evil 1961,Ja 23,20:2
Fishbein, Zenon (Miscellaneous)
Italian Straw Hat, The 1957,O 1,37:2
Fishberg, Jacob (Playwright)
One Sabbath Afternoon 1939,Ja 17,27:5
Fishberg, Louis
Backlane Center 1961,N 23,51:1
Fishberg, Z (Playwright)
Verdict, The 1934,S 22,12:5
Fishburn, Alan (Director)
Murder in the Cathedral 1935,D 21,11:3
Fishburn, Hummel (Lyricist)
Kid Himself, The 1925,D 25,23:2
Fishburn, Hummel (Playwright)
Kid Himself, The 1925,D 25,23:2
Fishelson, Bob
Babes in Arms 1937,Ap 15,18:4
Fisher, Alex
Strike Me Pink 1933,Mr 6,16:3
Vaudeville (Palladium) 1935,O 30,16:8
Ziegfeld Follies 1936,S 15,37:1
Shadow Play 1939,Ag 15,14:5
Would-Be Gentleman, The 1946,Ja 10,29:2
Fisher, Alice
Bit o' Love, A 1925,My 13,24:2
Fisher, Arthur (Composer)
Bewitched 1924,O 2,26:3
Fisher, Arthur (Producer)
House Afire 1930,Ap 1,34:7
Fisher, Bob (Playwright)
Impossible Years, The 1965,O 14,55:1
Fisher, Charlotte
Wolf! Wolf! 1925,O 30,21:1
Fisher, Daisy (Playwright)
Cave Man, The 1928,Ja 1,VIII,1:3
Ship Comes Home, A 1937,My 18,27:1
Fisher, Dan (Miscellaneous)
Second String, A 1960,Ap 14,36:2
Fisher, Dan (Producer)
Lady in Danger 1945,Mr 30,18:6
Fisher, Dorothy (Playwright)
Ship Comes Home, A 1937,Je 6,XI,1:3
Fisher, Dothea
White Villa, The 1921,F 15,7:1
Straw, The 1921,N 11,16:2
Fisher, Douglas
Frere Jacques 1968,Je 8,23:2
Straight Up 1970,S 2,30:2
Ben Bagley's Shoestring Revues 1970,O 24,22:1
Fisher, Eddie
Eddie Fisher at the Winter Garden 1962,O 3,47:1
Untitled-Revue 1967,Ag 29,26:1

Fisher, Edward
Patience 1935,S 3,24:4
Eternal Road, The 1937,Ja 8,14:2
Mr Big 1941,O 1,24:2
Fisher, Elliott
Peace on Earth 1933,N 30,39:2
Black Pit 1935,Mr 21,26:6
Fisher, Ethel
Buccaneer, The 1925,O 3,10:2
Lido Girl, The 1928,Ag 24,23:2
Fisher, F S
Julia, Jake, and Uncle Joe 1961,Ja 30,19:1
Fisher, Fred (Producer)
Only the Young 1932,S 22,25:2
Fisher, Fred Y
Hamlet 1927,Ap 7,23:3
Fisher, Gail
Susan Slept Here 1961,Jl 12,35:2
Danton's Death 1965,O 22,46:1
Fisher, George
Headquarters 1929,D 5,32:4
Country Wife, The 1931,Ap 19,31:5
South Pacific 1943,D 30,11:2
Year Round, The 1953,My 6,38:7
Fisher, Harrison (Composer)
Round With Ring, A 1969,O 30,56:1
Fisher, Harry J
Escape This Night 1938,Ap 23,18:1
Fisher, Herbert
Chinese Nightingale, The 1934,O 6,20:4
Fisher, Howard
Biography 1938,Ag 3,14:7
Fisher, Irving
Sally 1920,D 22,16:1
Ziegfeld Follies 1924,Je 25,26:1
Follies 1925,Mr 11,19:2
Lambs Gambol 1925,Ap 27,15:1
Follies 1925,Jl 7,24:3
No Foolin' 1926,Je 25,25:1
Luckee Girl 1928,S 17,28:6
Christopher Blake 1946,D 2,33:2
Fisher, Jack
Florida Girl 1925,N 3,34:1
Macbeth 1955,O 8,12:6
Private Life of the Master Race, The
1956,Ja 31,33:3
Fisher, Jack (Miscellaneous)
Private Life of the Master Race, The
1956,Ja 31,33:3
Fisher, Jacob
Shepherd King, The 1955,O 13,36:2
Brothers Ashkenazi, The 1955,N 12,24:4
Fisher, John
Uniform of Flesh 1949,Ja 31,15:2
My Beginning 1962,Ja 31,21:1
Fisher, Judy (Lighting Director)
Salvation 1969,Mr 13,53:1
Fisher, Judy (Miscellaneous)
Tarot 1970,D 12,19:1
Fisher, Judy (Scenic Designer)
Salvation 1969,Mr 13,53:1
Fisher, Jules (Lighting Director)
All the King's Men 1959,O 17,27:2
Tobacco Road 1960,My 11,44:2
Here Come the Clowns 1960,S 20,48:1
Greenwich Village U S A 1960,S 29,30:5
Marcus in the High Grass 1960,N 22,38:6
Eccentricities of Davy Crockett, The 1961,Ja 4,26:1
Riding Hood Revisited 1961,Ja 4,26:1
Willie the Weeper 1961,Ja 4,26:1
Donogoo 1961,Ja 19,25:3
Cicero 1961,F 9,37:2
Tiger Rag, The 1961,F 17,20:2
Go Show Me a Dragon 1961,O 28,18:1
All in Love 1961,N 11,15:2
Red Roses for Me 1961,N 28,41:1
Moon on a Rainbow Shawl 1962,Ja 16,30:1
Banker's Daughter, The 1962,Ja 23,37:1
Creditors 1962,Ja 26,19:1
Fly Blackbird 1962,F 6,26:2
Book of Job, The 1962,F 10,13:1
Golden Apple, The 1962,F 13,38:2
This Side of Paradise 1962,F 22,19:6
Nathan the Wise 1962,Mr 23,29:1
Half-Past Wednesday 1962,Ap 7,16:2
O Say Can You See! 1962,O 9,45:1
Riverwind 1962,D 14,5:5
Love Nest, The 1963,Ja 28,7:6
Six Characters in Search of an Author
1963,Mr 11,7:2
Best Foot Forward 1963,Ap 3,43:1
Dragon, The 1963,Ap 10,32:1
Spoon River Anthology 1963,S 30,23:2
Telemachus Clay 1963,N 16,17:2
Ginger Man, The 1963,N 22,42:1
Trojan Women, The 1963,D 24,7:6
Anyone Can Whistle 1964,Ap 6,36:1
High Spirits 1964,Ap 8,34:1
Wonder World 1964,My 18,32:1
White House, The 1964,My 20,39:1
Subject Was Roses, The 1964,My 26,45:1
Girl Could Get Lucky, A 1964,S 21,36:1

Fisher, Jules (Lighting Director)—Cont

Tragical Historie of Doctor Faustus, The
1964,O 6,34:2
Gogo Loves You 1964,O 10,19:2
Sign in Sidney Brustein's Window, The
1964,O 16,32:1
P S I Love You 1964,N 20,40:1
Do I Hear a Waltz? 1965,Mr 19,28:1
Decline and Fall of the Entire World As Seen
Through the Eyes of Cole Porter Revisited, The
1965,Mr 31,24:2
Half a Sixpence 1965,Ap 26,38:2
And Things That Go Bump in the Night
1965,Ap 27,27:5
Square in the Eye 1965,My 20,54:1
Leonard Bernstein's Theater Songs 1965,Je 29,27:2
Devils, The 1965,N 17,51:2
White Devil, The 1965,D 7,56:1
Yearling, The 1965,D 11,25:1
Ben Bagley's New Cole Porter Revue
1965,D 23,20:1
Suburban Tragedy 1966,Mr 7,22:1
Make Like a Dog 1966,Mr 7,22:1
Princess Rebecca Birnbaum 1966,Mr 7,22:1
Young Marrieds Play Monopoly 1966,Mr 7,22:1
Serjeant Musgrave's Dance 1966,Mr 9,44:1
Hooray!! It's a Glorious Day. . .And All That
1966,Mr 10,28:1
Kitchen, The 1966,Je 14,50:1
Hand Is on the Gate, A 1966,S 22,54:1
Eh? 1966,O 17,47:1
Threepenny Opera, The 1966,O 28,33:1
Hail Scrawdyke! 1966,N 29,50:1
Black Comedy 1967,F 13,42:1
Black Comedy; White Lies 1967,F 13,42:1
You're a Good Man, Charlie Brown 1967,Mr 8,51:1
Natural Look, The 1967,Mr 13,45:2
You Know I Can't Hear You When the Water's
Running; I'll Be Home for Christmas
1967,Mr 14,54:1
You Know I Can't Hear You When the Water's
Running; Shock of Recognition, The
1967,Mr 14,54:1
You Know I Can't Hear You When the Water's
Running; I'm Herbert 1967,Mr 14,54:1
You Know I Can't Hear You When the Water's
Running; Footsteps of Doves, The
1967,Mr 14,54:1
Little Murders 1967,Ap 26,38:1
South Pacific 1967,Je 13,56:1
Unknown Soldier and His Wife, The 1967,Jl 7,22:1
Minor Adjustment, A 1967,O 7,33:3
Scuba Duba 1967,O 11,36:1
Trial of Lee Harvey Oswald, The 1967,N 6,64:1
Iphigenia in Aulis 1967,N 22,40:2
Before You Go 1968,Ja 12,20:1
Grand Music Hall of Israel, The 1968,F 7,42:1
Here's Where I Belong 1968,Mr 4,32:1
Kongi's Harvest 1968,Ap 15,49:1
Hair 1968,Ap 30,40:2
Only Game in Town, The 1968,My 21,42:1
Moon for the Misbegotten, A 1968,Je 13,55:2
Happy Hypocrite, The 1968,S 6,38:1
Cuban Thing, The 1968,S 25,36:2
Man in the Glass Booth, The 1968,S 27,41:1
But, Seriously... 1969,F 28,29:1
Watering Place, The 1969,Mr 13,51:1
Someone's Comin' Hungry 1969,Ap 1,51:1
Trumpets of the Lord 1969,Ap 30,37:1
Promenade 1969,Je 5,56:1
Butterflies Are Free 1969,O 22,30:1
Hair 1970,Ja 13,39:1
Sheep on the Runway 1970,F 2,28:3
Gantry 1970,F 16,44:1
Minnie's Boys 1970,Mr 27,27:1
Jakey Fat Boy 1970,Ap 6,46:1
Dear Janet Rosenberg, Dear Mr Kooning
1970,Ap 6,46:1
Inquest 1970,Ap 24,38:1
Engagement Baby, The 1970,My 22,40:1
Steambath 1970,Jl 1,49:1
Home 1970,N 18,41:1
Fisher, Kim
Streetcar Named Desire, A 1955,Mr 4,18:2
Fisher, L W (Composer)
Kid Himself, The 1925,D 25,23:2
Fisher, Lewis
First American Dictator 1939,Mr 15,18:2
Fisher, Lewis (Producer)
Foursome 1965,Mr 8,34:1
Leader, The 1965,Mr 8,34:1
Impromptu, L' 1965,Mr 8,34:1
Bedlam Galore, for Two or More 1965,Mr 8,34:1
Fisher, Linda (Costume Designer)
Three Sisters, The 1968,Mr 18,56:1
Brass Butterfly, The 1970,Ja 31,34:1
Forensic and the Navigators 1970,Ap 2,43:1
Unseen Hand, The 1970,Ap 2,43:1
Fisher, Lola
All Soul's Eve 1920,My 13,9:1
Honors Are Even 1921,Ag 11,8:2
Banco 1922,S 21,18:1
Business Widow, The 1923,D 11,27:1
Fiorello! 1962,Je 14,24:1

Fisher, Lydia
'Tis Pity She's a Whore 1967,O 21,15:2
Rivals, The 1969,O 18,37:1
Metamorphoses 1969,D 12,69:1
Don Juan 1970,My 26,32:1
Three Philip Roth Stories; Epstein 1970,Jl 31,14:1
Cops and Horrors; Fly Paper 1970,Ag 11,27:1
Cops and Horrors; Dracula 1970,Ag 11,27:1
Story Theater Repertory; Gimpel the Food
1970,O 21,40:1
Story Theater Repertory; Saint Julian the
Hospitaler 1970,O 21,40:1
Revenger's Tragedy, The 1970,D 2,58:1
Fisher, Lynne
Children's Hour, The 1934,N 21,23:2
Fisher, Madeleine
Happy Faculty, The 1967,Ap 19,50:1
Spitting Image 1969,Mr 3,28:1
Fisher, Margaret
Pirates of Penzance, The 1942,F 18,22:2
Gondoliers, The 1942,Mr 4,22:3
Fisher, Marion
Ah! Wah! 1932,My 11,15:2
Fisher, Mary
Sporting Thing to Do, The 1923,F 20,12:2
Pride 1923,My 3,22:3
Fisher, Mary-Louise
Alt Heidelberg 1926,My 31,10:5
Fisher, Nelle
On the Town 1944,D 29,11:4
Make Mine Manhattan 1948,Ja 16,26:2
Make Mine Manhattan 1948,F 8,II,2:1
Best of Burlesque 1957,S 30,27:2
Fisher, Nelle (Choreographer)
Razzle Dazzle 1951,F 20,21:1
Best of Burlesque 1957,S 30,27:2
Littlest Circus, The 1959,D 26,5:6
Russell Patterson's Sketch-Book 1960,F 8,35:1
Golden Apple, The 1962,F 13,38:2
Fisher, Nelle (Director)
Littlest Circus, The 1959,D 26,5:6
Fisher, Nelle (Miscellaneous)
Tobias and the Angel 1937,Ap 29,16:5
Fisher, Ray
Eternal Sabbath 1963,O 19,17:2
Finis for Oscar Wilde 1964,F 15,15:1
Fisher, Robert
Pride 1923,My 3,22:3
Fisher, Robert (Playwright)
Happiness Is Just a Little Thing Called a Rolls
Royce 1968,My 13,54:5
Minnie's Boys 1970,Mr 27,27:1
Fisher, Rudolph (Playwright)
Conjur' Man Dies 1936,Mr 12,18:5
Fisher, Sallie
Chinese Love 1921,Mr 1,18:1
Fisher, Steve (Playwright)
Susan Slept Here 1961,Jl 12,35:2
Fisher, Susan
Grand Duchess 1929,D 17,29:2
Fisher, Thomas
Red Rust 1929,D 18,31:1
Spring in Autumn 1933,O 25,22:5
Searching for the Sun 1936,F 20,22:6
Days to Come 1936,D 16,35:1
Too Many Heroes 1937,N 16,26:2
Sunup to Sundown 1938,F 2,14:3
Fisher, Thomas (Miscellaneous)
Chair, The 1930,O 4,15:4
Fisher, Walter
Dreaming Dust, The 1955,D 8,46:5
Sixth Finger in a Five Finger Glove 1956,O 9,31:4
Fisher, William
Cocktails of 1934 1934,My 5,22:1
Fisher, William (Composer)
Place for Polly, A 1970,Ap 20,45:1
Fisher and Bray Scenic Studios (Scenic Designer)
Tom Sawyer 1931,D 26,15:3
Fisher and Gillmore
Vaudeville (Palace) 1928,Je 5,21:3
Fisherman, Pichas
Brothers Ashkenazi, The 1955,N 12,24:4
Fishkind, Abraham
Tenth Commandment, The 1926,N 18,27:1
Witch of Castile, The 1930,O 25,21:1
Fishko, Robert S (Producer)
Cradle Will Rock, The 1964,N 9,40:4
Fishman, Sarah
Anathema 1923,Ap 11,16:2
Fishman, Sylvia
Berl and Shmerl Corporation 1934,Ap 2,12:5
Topsy-Turvy 1939,F 13,12:3
Fishon, Misha
Matinee Wife 1936,Ap 25,21:3
Song of Dnieper 1946,O 26,10:5
Shylock and His Daughter 1947,S 30,22:2
Voice of Israel, The 1948,O 26,40:2
Hershel, The Jester 1948,D 14,39:2
Fiske, Clinton E (Producer)
Timber House 1936,S 21,27:5
Fiske, Dwight
Dark Victory 1934,N 10,18:2

Fiske, Edith
Love in Our Time 1952,O 4,14:3
Fiske, Harrison Grey
Ladies of the Jury 1929,O 22,26:2
Fiske, Harrison Grey (Director)
We Moderns 1924,Mr 12,17:2
Helena's Boys 1924,Ap 8,22:2
Ghosts 1927,Ja 11,36:3
Merry Wives of Windsor, The 1928,Mr 20,20:1
Mrs Bumpstead-Leigh 1929,Ap 2,28:3
Ladies of the Jury 1929,O 22,26:2
It's a Grand Life 1930,F 11,30:3
Rivals, The 1930,Mr 14,24:4
Fiske, Harrison Grey (Mrs)
Rivals, The 1930,Mr 14,24:4
Fiske, Harrison Grey (Playwright)
Ghosts 1927,Ja 11,36:3
Fiske, Harrison Grey (Producer)
Merry Wives of Windsor, The 1928,Mr 20,20:1
Fiske, Kate Woods
Scrap Book 1932,Ag 2,20:3
Fiske, Loise
My Dear Public 1943,S 10,28:1
Fiske, Margo
As Husbands Go 1933,Ja 20,20:5
Fiske, Mianna
Off Your Marx 1936,Ap 2,28:2
Fiske, Minnie Maddern
Wake Up, Jonathan 1921,Ja 18,14:1
Wake Up, Jonathan 1921,Ja 23,VI,1:1
Dice of the Gods, The 1923,Ap 6,20:2
Dice of the Gods, The 1923,Ap 15,VII,1:1
Mary, Mary, Quite Contrary 1923,S 2,VI,2:6
Mary, Mary, Quite Contrary 1923,S 12,14:1
Mary, Mary, Quite Contrary 1923,S 16,VII,1:1
Helena's Boys 1924,Ap 6,VIII,2:1
Helena's Boys 1924,Ap 8,22:2
Helena's Boys 1924,Ap 13,VIII,1:1
Ghosts 1927,Ja 11,36:3
Ghosts 1927,Ja 16,VII,1:1
Merry Wives of Windsor, The 1928,Mr 20,20:1
Much Ado About Nothing 1928,N 18,IX,2:6
Mrs Bumpstead-Leigh 1929,Ap 2,28:3
Ladies of the Jury 1929,O 6,IX,1:4
It's a Grand Life 1930,F 2,VIII,2:7
It's a Grand Life 1930,F 11,30:3
Rivals, The 1930,Mr 23,IX,1:1
Fiske, Perry
Inherit the Wind 1955,Ap 22,20:2
Fiske, Robert
Man in the Making, The 1921,S 21,16:2
Golden Days 1921,N 2,20:1
To the Ladies! 1922,F 21,20:1
Fitch, Betty
Earl Carroll's Vanities 1924,S 11,23:6
Fitch, Bob
Crystal Heart, The 1960,F 16,31:2
Miss Emily Adam 1960,Mr 30,43:1
Fitch, Charlotte
Romeo and Juliet 1935,D 24,10:2
Fitch, Clyde (Playwright)
Captain Jinks 1925,S 9,22:1
Captain Jinks of the Horse Marines 1938,Ja 28,16:2
Fitch, Dorothy
Riff-Raff 1926,F 9,18:6
Fitch, Elizabeth (Composer)
Recruiting Officer, The 1958,F 8,12:2
Fitch, Eugene (Scenic Designer)
All Bow Down 1935,Ag 6,20:4
Fitch, Geneva
Rain 1948,F 2,15:2
Power of Darkness, The 1948,O 11,28:2
Fitch, George
Racket, The 1930,N 20,30:6
Fitch, Margaret
Poor Nut, The 1925,Ap 28,18:1
Fitch, Robert
Lend an Ear 1959,S 25,20:5
Anything Goes 1962,My 16,35:1
We're Civilized? 1962,N 9,30:1
Flora, the Red Menace 1965,My 12,41:2
Coco 1969,D 19,66:1
Fitch, Sonia B
Gay Divorce 1932,N 30,23:4
Fite, Harvey
Bedrock 1934,N 18,II,6:3
Fitelberg (Composer)
Mikado, The 1927,O 30,IX,4:6
Fith, George
Roof, The 1930,Je 14,9:2
Fitsch, Eugene (Scenic Designer)
Winter Bound 1929,N 13,24:6
Ladies of Creation 1931,S 9,25:1
When Ladies Meet 1932,O 7,19:1
Whatever Possessed Her 1934,Ja 26,21:2
Petrified Forest, The 1935,N 24,II,9:3
Western Union 1937,Ag 10,22:7
Damn Deborah 1937,Ag 17,23:1
Good Housekeeping 1949,Ag 17,19:3
Fitter, Joey
Around the World in 80 Days 1963,Je 24,22:1
Fitts, Dudley (Playwright)
Lysistrata 1959,N 25,19:4

Fitts, Dudley (Playwright)—Cont
Antigone 1967,Ja 14,18:1
Fitts, Dudley (Translator)
Lysistrata 1959,D 6,II,5:1
Fitts, Eugene
Love's Old Sweet Song 1940,My 3,16:3
Fitz, Erica
There's a Girl in My Soup 1967,O 19,58:1
Fitz, Kathleen
Iron Men 1936,O 20,30:6
Brother Rat 1936,D 17,34:5
One Thing After Another 1937,D 29,17:2
Fitz, Richard
Bananas 1968,D 5,60:1
Fitz-Allen, Adelaide
Woman on the Jury, The 1923,Ag 16,10:4
Mister Pitt 1924,Ja 23,15:3
Immortal Thief, The 1926,O 4,21:1
Witch, The 1926,N 19,22:5
Spellbound 1927,F 16,17:2
Thou Desperate Pilot 1927,Mr 8,23:1
Field God, The 1927,Ap 22,18:2
Fitz-Gibbons, Bert
Will Morrissey's Folies Bergere Revue
1930,Ap 16,26:6
Fitz-Patrick, Harry
Drifting 1922,Ja 3,20:3
Fitzgerald, Arthur
Light of the World, The 1920,Ja 7,17:1
Fools Errant 1922,Ag 22,12:3
Fitzgerald, Barry
Cartney and Kevney 1928,Ja 1,VIII,2:8
Peter 1930,Mr 2,IX,4:4
New Gossoon, The 1931,Ap 27,24:5
Things That Are Caesar's, The 1932,O 18,23:4
Far-Off Hills, The 1932,O 19,22:4
Juno and the Paycock 1932,O 20,24:3
Playboy of the Western World, The 1932,O 21,25:1
Shadow of a Gunman, The 1932,O 31,18:1
Shadow of the Glen, The 1932,N 4,25:1
Big House, The 1933,Ja 5,19:3
King Oedipus 1933,Ja 16,12:4
Bridgehead 1934,Je 20,24:1
On the Rocks 1934,Jl 11,20:4
Plough and the Stars, The 1934,N 13,22:2
Drama at Inish 1934,N 15,24:2
Look at the Heffernans 1934,N 17,13:2
Church Street 1934,N 20,24:5
Well of the Saints, The 1934,N 22,26:2
Bridgehead 1935,Ag 7,22:3
Silver Tassie, The 1935,Ag 14,16:1
Saint in a Hurry, A 1935,D 29,IX,2:1
White Steed, The 1939,Ja 11,16:2
White Steed, The 1939,Ja 22,IX,1:1
Kindred 1939,D 27,17:2
Juno and the Paycock 1940,Ja 17,24:2
Juno and the Paycock 1940,Ja 21,IX,1:2
Juno and the Paycock 1940,Ja 28,IX,1:1
Tanyard Street 1941,F 5,16:2
Fitzgerald, Brydon
Lonesome Train, The 1965,Je 17,25:1
Hard Travelin' 1965,Je 17,25:1
Fitzgerald, Edith
Wake Up, Jonathan 1921,Ja 18,14:1
Chicago 1926,D 31,11:1
Fitzgerald, Edith (Playwright)
Many a Slip 1930,F 4,29:2
Fitzgerald, Edward (Translator)
Mayor of Zalamea, The 1946,Ja 28,15:5
Fitzgerald, F Scott (Original Author)
Great Gatsby, The 1926,F 3,22:1
Great Gatsby, The 1926,F 7,VII,1:1
Young and Beautiful, The 1959,My 29,13:1
This Side of Paradise 1962,F 22,19:6
Fitzgerald, F Scott (Playwright)
Vegetable, The, or From President to Postman
1929,Ap 11,32:3
Young and Beautiful, The 1955,O 3,23:2
Fitzgerald, Fred
Sojourner Truth 1948,Ap 22,35:2
Orpheus Descending 1959,O 6,45:2
Fitzgerald, George
Great Adventure, The 1921,F 26,9:2
Old Bill, M P 1926,N 11,22:2
Great Adventure, The 1926,D 23,23:1
Courage 1927,Ja 20,20:1
Mariners 1927,Mr 29,22:2
Merry-Go-Round 1927,Je 1,25:4
Fitzgerald, Geraldine
She's My Baby 1928,Ja 4,22:2
Heartbreak House 1938,Ap 30,18:2
Lottie Dundass 1941,Ag 22,19:5
Sons and Soldiers 1943,My 5,22:2
Doctor's Dilemma, The 1955,Ja 12,22:1
Doctor's Dilemma, The 1955,Ja 23,II,1:1
King Lear 1956,Ja 13,17:1
Hide and Seek 1957,Ap 3,26:1
Hamlet 1958,Je 21,11:1
Cave Dwellers, The 1961,O 16,34:2
Pigeons 1965,Mr 4,37:1
Ah, Wilderness! 1969,N 9,86:1
Fitzgerald, Harry
Sancho's Master 1927,Ap 10,VIII,4:7

Fitzgerald, Henry
Cyrano de Bergerac 1923,N 2,14:1
Fitzgerald, J
Slight Case of Murder, A 1935,S 12,28:5
Fitzgerald, Jim (Director)
Stephen D 1962,S 25,31:3
Death and Resurrection of Mr Roche, The
1968,O 11,44:4
Fitzgerald, Lillian
Ed Wynn's Carnival 1920,Ap 6,18:2
Make It Snappy 1922,Ap 14,20:2
Bye Bye, Barbara 1924,Ag 26,6:3
Americana 1932,O 6,19:3
Blue Holiday 1945,My 22,13:3
Fitzgerald, M Eleanor (Producer)
Black Souls 1932,Mr 31,25:1
Fitzgerald, Margaret
Beyond the Horizon 1962,O 26,27:2
Fitzgerald, Maureen
Coriolanus 1961,Je 21,31:2
Henry VIII 1961,Je 22,22:1
Falstaff; Henry IV, Part II 1965,Jl 1,35:1
Julius Caesar 1965,Jl 2,18:1
Reunion of Sorts 1969,O 15,40:1
Fitzgerald, Maurice
Springtime Folly 1951,F 27,23:4
Fitzgerald, Neil
Miles of Heaven, The 1937,Ag 31,27:4
Leave Her to Heaven 1940,F 28,16:2
Wookey, The 1941,S 11,20:5
Plan M 1942,F 21,15:2
Merry Widow, The 1942,Jl 16,22:1
Without Love 1942,N 11,28:1
Ten Little Indians 1944,Je 28,21:2
You Touched Me! 1945,S 26,27:2
Survivors, The 1948,Ja 20,24:2
Design For A Stained Glass Window
1950,Ja 24,26:2
High Ground, The 1951,F 21,31:2
To Dorothy, A Son 1951,N 20,37:2
Mr Pickwick 1952,S 18,36:3
Abie's Irish Rose 1954,N 19,19:1
Tinker's Wedding, The 1957,Mr 7,24:1
Oscar Wilde 1957,Ap 20,21:3
Monique 1957,O 23,38:1
On Baile's Strand 1959,Ap 13,34:4
Death of Cuchulain, The 1959,Ap 13,34:4
Little Moon of Alban 1960,D 2,34:1
Moon in the Yellow River, The 1961,F 7,40:2
Portrait of the Artist as a Young Man, A
1962,My 29,21:1
Barroom Monks, The 1962,My 29,21:1
Roar Like a Dove 1964,My 22,40:2
Bridal Night, The 1966,N 8,45:1
Eternal Triangle 1966,N 8,45:1
Carricknabauna 1967,Mr 31,30:1
Stephen D 1967,S 25,58:1
Hadrian VII 1969,Ja 9,22:1
Mundy Scheme, The 1969,D 12,75:1
Fitzgerald, Rita
Me and Juliet 1970,My 15,42:1
Fitzgerald, Robert (Playwright)
Antigone 1967,Ja 14,18:1
Fitzgerald, Walter
Evensong 1933,F 1,13:4
Living Room, The 1954,N 18,41:1
Living Room, The 1954,N 28,II,1:1
Tiger at the Gates 1955,Je 12,II,1:1
Tiger at the Gates 1955,O 4,40:1
Fitzgibbon, Bert
Hoboken Hoboes 1929,D 28,10:8
Fitzgibbon, Dave
Wake Up and Dream 1929,D 31,14:3
Wake Up and Dream 1930,Ja 12,9:1
Fitzgibbon, David (Producer)
Hi Yank 1944,Ap 8,14:2
Fitzgibbon, Dorothy
Say When 1928,Je 27,29:3
Third Little Show, The 1931,Je 2,34:3
Walk a Little Faster 1932,D 8,24:4
Fitzgibbon, Henry
Mikado, The 1954,Mr 24,31:1
Fitzgibbons, Grace
Veronica's Veil 1933,F 20,11:7
Fitzgibbons, John
Veronica's Veil 1934,F 19,20:7
Fitzhugh, Edward
Dear Brutus 1926,Jl 15,21:3
Fitzhugh, Ida
Lady Bug 1922,Ap 18,15:3
Six Characters in Search of an Author
1922,O 31,11:2
Mister Malatesta 1923,F 27,14:2
Apache, The 1923,My 9,14:3
Fitziu, Anna
Vaudeville (Palace) 1926,S 28,30:4
Fitzmaurice, George (Playwright)
Dandy Dolls, The 1970,Ag 10,34:1
Fitzmaurice, Michael
Chocolate Soldier, The 1942,Je 24,22:2
Merry Widow, The 1942,Jl 16,22:1
Swing Out, Sweet Land! 1944,N 10,24:6

Fitzpatrick, Bettye
Three Love Affairs; Phoenix Too Frequent, A
1958,Mr 11,33:1
Three Love Affairs; Still Life 1958,Mr 11,33:1
Phoenix Too Frequent, A 1958,Mr 16,II,1:1
Friends and Lovers; End of the Beginning, The
1961,My 11,43:1
Six Characters in Search of an Author
1961,My 11,43:1
Long Day's Journey Into Night 1963,Je 27,25:1
Effect of Gamma Rays on Man-in-the-Moon
Marigolds, The 1965,Je 7,48:1
Fitzpatrick, Bettye (Miscellaneous)
Six Characters in Search of an Author
1961,My 11,43:1
Long Day's Journey Into Night 1963,Je 27,25:1
Fitzpatrick, Edmund
Dream Girl, The 1924,Ag 21,12:2
Fitzpatrick, Edward
Cure for Matrimony 1939,O 26,26:3
Steel 1939,D 20,30:2
Fitzpatrick, Edward (Lighting Director)
Cure for Matrimony 1939,O 26,26:3
Steel 1939,D 20,30:2
Fitzpatrick, George
Brown Sugar 1937,D 3,29:2
Fitzpatrick, Marybeth
Music in the Air 1951,O 9,32:2
Fitzpatrick, Paul
Arms and the Girl 1950,F 3,28:2
Fitzpatrick, Sally
Beggarman, Thief 1935,Jl 16,24:1
Lady Precious Stream 1936,Ja 28,15:2
Aged 26 1936,D 22,32:1
Bachelor Born 1938,Ja 26,26:3
Fitzpatrick, Stanley
Once in a Lifetime 1930,S 25,22:3
Fitzpatrick, Thomas
Love Letter, The 1921,O 5,20:1
Cinders 1923,Ap 4,22:1
Fitzroy, Emily
What the Public Wants 1922,My 2,22:3
Fitzsimmons, Alice
Jubilee 1935,O 14,20:1
Fitzsimmons, Robert
Abe Lincoln in Illinois 1938,O 17,12:2
Legal Grounds 1940,D 2,18:4
Tread the Green Grass 1950,Ap 21,19:4
Macbeth 1967,Jl 31,21:1
Five Amandis
Aquashow 1952,Je 25,25:1
Five Crackerjacks
Harlem Cavalcade 1942,My 2,11:2
Five Kaeths, The
Get Together 1921,S 5,12:2
Five Spinnettes, The
Vaudeville (Hippodrome) 1924,O 21,21:2
Fix, Jack
Sold to the Movies; Life Size 1970,Je 18,54:2
Sold to the Movies; Type 424 Meet Type Oh-Oh,
No! 1970,Je 18,54:2
Sold to the Movies; Crossing the Gap
1970,Je 18,54:2
Fjellman, Richard
Call Me Madam 1950,O 13,25:1
Flack, Nanette
Good Times 1920,Ag 10,10:1
Some Party 1922,Ap 17,22:1
Better Times 1922,S 4,14:2
Hello, Lola! 1926,Ja 13,30:1
Noble Rogue, A 1929,Ag 20,31:2
Flacks, Niki
Way of the World, The 1965,Je 2,40:1
Dinner at Eight 1966,S 28,38:1
Flagg, Clay
Grey-Eyed People, The 1952,D 18,41:2
Flagg, Eleanor
Schoolhouse on the Lot 1938,Mr 23,18:4
Yes, My Darling Daughter 1938,Jl 13,19:2
Animal Kingdom, The 1938,Jl 27,14:5
Biography 1938,Ag 3,14:7
Arms and the Man 1938,Ag 10,14:1
Bachelor Born 1938,Ag 17,23:1
Springtime for Henry 1938,Ag 31,12:5
Flagg, James Montgomery (Playwright)
Untitled-Revue 1923,My 12,15:4
Flagg, Stephanie
Street Sounds 1970,O 23,32:1
Flaherty, Joseph X
Priest in the Cellar, The 1969,F 19,39:1
Flaherty, William C
Faith of Our Fathers 1950,Ag 6,72:2
Flaiano, Ennio (Playwright)
Sweet Charity 1966,Ja 31,22:1
Flamm, Donald (Miscellaneous)
Brass Ring, The 1952,Ap 11,19:2
Spitting Image 1969,Mr 3,28:1
Flamm, Donald (Producer)
Edwina Black 1950,N 22,20:5
What Did We Do Wrong? 1967,O 23,56:1
Flamm, Morton
Locked Room, The 1933,D 26,18:5

Flamma, Ario (Playwright)
Mask of Hamlet, The 1921,Ag 23,10:3
Potenza, La 1926,Je 29,21:3
Flanagan, Celine
Tree Grows in Brooklyn, A 1951,Ap 20,24:3
Flanagan, D J
Spider, The 1927,Mr 23,29:1
Flanagan, Fionnuala
Lovers; Finders 1967,S 24,II,1:4
Lovers; Winners 1968,Jl 26,21:4
Flanagan, Flannusia
Tempest, The 1970,F 15,67:1
Flanagan, Frederic
Lady From the Sea, The 1935,D 14,11:3
Fuente Ovejuna; Sheep Well, The 1936,My 3,II,4:1
Flanagan, Harriet
Petticoat Fever 1937,Mr 21,II,7:3
Flanagan, Karin
In Any Language 1952,O 9,40:2
Flanagan, Michael
Murderer Among Us, A 1964,Mr 26,43:1
Flanagan, Mike
Racket, The 1927,N 23,28:3
Grey Fox, The 1928,O 23,32:3
Flanagan, Neil
Haunted Host, The 1969,O 28,43:1
Sheep on the Runway 1970,F 2,28:3
Adding Machine, The 1970,D 5,40:1
Flanagan, Neil (Director)
Triumph of Robert Emmet, The 1969,My 8,54:1
Flanagan, Pauline
Midsummer Night's Dream, A 1957,Je 27,21:3
Under Milk Wood 1957,O 16,42:5
Ulysses in Nighttown 1958,Je 6,30:1
God and Kate Murphy 1959,F 27,21:2
Drums Under the Windows 1960,O 14,26:1
Step on a Crack 1962,O 18,48:1
King Lear 1963,N 23,22:1
Flanagan, Phyllis (Composer)
London Assurance 1937,F 19,14:5
Flanagan, Walter
Five Posts in the Market Place 1961,Mr 6,30:1
Opening of a Window, The 1961,S 26,32:2
Once for the Asking 1963,N 21,42:2
Laughwind 1966,Mr 3,27:1
Dodo Bird, The 1967,D 9,62:1
Rate of Exchange 1968,Ap 2,50:1
Front Page, The 1969,My 12,54:2
Front Page, The 1969,N 2,86:1
Arsenic and Old Lace 1970,N 5,59:1
Flanagan, William
Sandbox, The 1960,My 17,42:2
Moon Is Blue, The 1961,Ag 9,29:1
Flanagan, William (Composer)
Bartleby 1961,Ja 25,28:1
Death of Bessie Smith, The 1961,Mr 2,19:1
Ballad of the Sad Cafe, The 1963,O 31,27:1
Ballad of the Sad Cafe, The 1963,N 10,II,1:1
Malcolm 1966,Ja 12,29:1
Death of Bessie Smith, The 1968,O 3,55:1
American Dream, The 1968,O 3,55:1
Flanagan, William J
Little Theatre Tournament; Rhythm of the City, The 1929,My 7,28:1
Flanagan and Allen
Happy Returns 1938,My 20,16:6
Flanagan and Morrison
Vaudeville (Palace) 1923,Ja 16,16:3
Passing Show of 1923, The 1923,Je 15,24:6
Flanders, Alfred
Lean Harvest 1931,O 14,26:3
Flanders, Christian
Requiem for a Nun 1959,Ja 31,13:2
Flanders, Dolores
Forbidden Melody 1936,N 3,33:1
Flanders, Ed
Winter's Tale, The 1963,Je 29,13:1
Midsummer Night's Dream, A 1963,Jl 1,19:2
Henry V 1964,My 13,52:1
Saint Joan 1964,My 14,41:1
Glass Menagerie, The 1964,Jl 20,18:3
Way of the World, The 1965,Je 2,40:1
Cherry Orchard, The 1965,Ag 2,17:2
Skin of Our Teeth, The 1966,Je 2,51:1
Birthday Party, The 1967,O 4,40:2
Flanders, Michael
At the Drop of a Hat 1959,O 9,22:2
Glimpse of the Domesticity of Franklyn Barnabas, A 1960,Mr 7,24:2
Caucasian Chalk Circle, The 1962,Mr 30,28:1
At the Drop of Another Hat 1966,D 28,30:2
At the Drop of Another Hat 1967,Ja 8,II,1:5
Flanders, Michael (Lyricist)
At the Drop of a Hat 1959,O 9,22:2
Flanders, Michael (Playwright)
At the Drop of Another Hat 1966,D 28,30:2
Flanigen, Betty
Babes in Toyland 1930,D 22,17:1
Flannery, Maud (Playwright)
Man Who Had Nothing, The 1937,Je 8,30:1
Flannery, Olive
Tidings Brought to Mary, The 1922,D 25,20:1

Flash, Serge
Vaudeville (Palace) 1931,My 4,15:2
Vaudeville (Palace) 1931,N 2,26:2
Flaszen, Ludwik (Miscellaneous)
Constant Prince, The 1969,O 18,36:1
Acropolis 1969,N 5,40:1
Apocalypsis cum Figuris 1969,N 20,60:2
Flateau, Georges
Tyranny of Love, The 1921,Mr 2,7:3
Flath, Edwin (Miscellaneous)
Bible Salesman, The 1960,F 22,12:2
Flath, Edwin (Musical Director)
Bible Salesman, The 1960,F 22,12:2
Flatley, William
Ah, Wilderness! 1953,F 7,10:6
Flatt, Ernest (Choreographer)
Fade Out--Fade In 1964,My 27,45:1
It's a Bird . . . It's a Plane . . . It's Superman 1966,Mr 30,34:1
Flatt, Lester
Hayride 1954,S 14,24:2
Flatt, Robyn Baker
Macbeth 1968,N 30,49:3
Flaubert, Gustave (Original Author)
Madame Bovary 1936,N 8,X,3:6
Madame Bovary 1937,O 6,28:4
Story Theater Repertory; Saint Julian the Hospitaler 1970,O 21,40:1
Flaum, Marshall
Don't Go Away Mad 1949,My 10,28:2
Flavelle, Robert
Golden Apple, The 1954,Mr 12,15:2
Flavin, James
Front Page, The 1969,My 12,54:2
Front Page, The 1969,N 2,86:1
Flavin, Martin (Playwright)
Children of the Moon 1923,Ag 18,10:3
Children of the Moon 1923,Ag 26,VI,1:1
Children of the Moon 1923,S 9,VII,1:1
Lady of the Rose 1925,My 20,26:4
Little Theatre Tournament; Brains 1926,My 4,30:2
Service for Two 1926,Ag 31,15:1
Children of the Moon 1926,N 7,VIII,1:3
Casualties 1927,Mr 5,12:2
Criminal Code, The 1929,O 3,28:2
Criminal Code, The 1929,O 13,IX,1:1
Broken Dishes 1929,N 6,28:3
Cross Roads 1929,N 12,34:2
Children of the Moon 1930,My 4,XI,3:1
Achilles Had a Heel 1935,Ap 28,X,1:1
Achilles Had a Heel 1935,O 14,20:2
Tapestry in Gray 1935,D 28,10:2
Around the Corner 1936,D 29,17:2
Flaxman, John (Miscellaneous)
Maggie Flynn 1968,O 24,52:1
Flaxman, John (Producer)
Dear Janet Rosenberg, Dear Mr Kooning 1970,Ap 6,46:1
Jakey Fat Boy 1970,Ap 6,46:1
Fleao, Bruno
Emerald Slippers, The 1970,S 2,31:2
Fleck, Frances
Tree Witch, The 1961,Je 5,39:4
Fleck, William
Patience 1967,O 13,32:1
Iolanthe 1967,O 18,40:1
Mikado, The 1967,O 25,42:2
Gondoliers, The 1967,O 29,83:1
H M S Pinafore 1967,N 1,40:1
Flecker, James Elroy (Playwright)
Hassan 1923,S 30,II,1:6
Hassan 1924,S 23,23:1
Don Juan 1927,Ap 10,VIII,4:7
Hassan 1931,Mr 8,VIII,2:6
Fleer, Harry
Toplitzky of Notre Dame 1946,D 27,13:4
Fleeson, Neville
Vaudeville (Palace) 1927,Ap 5,30:2
Vaudeville (Palace) 1927,Ap 12,25:4
Vaudeville (Palace) 1927,N 8,33:3
Vaudeville (Palace) 1929,Jl 15,25:4
Vaudeville (Palace) 1929,O 7,22:4
Vaudeville (Palace) 1930,Ag 18,24:3
Vaudeville (Palace) 1931,My 11,15:5
Fleeson, Neville (Lyricist)
Gingham Girl, The 1922,Ag 29,15:5
Bye Bye Bonnie 1927,Ja 14,15:3
Fleet, Biddy
Moon Vine, The 1943,F 12,22:2
Fleet, Jenna
Rose in the Wilderness 1949,Ja 5,21:2
Fleet, Phil
Merry Death, A 1959,N 10,55:3
Fleetwood, James
Help! Help! the Globolinks 1970,D 24,10:2
Fleetwood, Susan
Criminals, The 1967,O 15,II,9:3
King Lear 1968,Ap 12,42:5
Pericles 1969,Ap 11,36:1
Pericles 1969,Je 1,II,4:5
Fleetwood, Tom
Yearling, The 1965,D 11,25:1

Fleg, Edmond (Playwright)
Mr Samuel 1930,O 26,VIII,3:5
Faust 1937,Ag 29,X,1:3
Fleg, Edward (Playwright)
Mr Samuel 1930,N 11,28:4
Fleischer, Bob (Playwright)
Egg in Your Beer 1945,My 13,II,1:3
Fleischer, Editha
Tanzgraefin, Die 1925,S 18,26:3
Fleischer, Edward
Case of Philip Lawrence, The 1937,Je 9,31:1
One-Act Plays of the Sea; Moon of the Caribbees 1937,O 30,23:2
One-Act Plays of the Sea; Bound East for Cardiff 1937,O 30,23:2
Big Blow 1938,O 3,11:2
Fleischer, Richard (Producer)
Laterna Magika 1964,Ag 4,21:1
Fleischman, Earl
Plumes in the Dust 1936,N 7,14:2
Fleischman, Emanuel (Musical Director)
Grass Is Always Greener, The 1955,F 16,25:2
Miser, The 1955,Mr 18,34:2
Fleischman, Manny (Composer)
Second Marriage 1953,O 12,30:1
Fleischman, Manny (Musical Director)
Stone for Danny Fisher, A 1954,O 22,24:2
Fleischman, Mark
Venice Preserv'd 1955,D 13,54:4
Distant Bell, A 1960,Ja 14,29:1
Fleischman, Mark (Miscellaneous)
Pequod 1969,Je 30,33:1
Fleischman, Maxine (Playwright)
God Bless You, Harold Fineberg 1969,Mr 31,30:2
Fleischmann, Julius (Miscellaneous)
Caesar and Cleopatra 1949,D 22,28:2
Moon Is Blue, The 1951,My 9,29:2
Girl Can Tell, A 1953,O 30,28:2
Dear Charles 1954,S 16,37:2
Little Glass Clock, The 1956,Mr 27,40:2
Fleischmann, Julius (Producer)
Four Twelves Are 48 1951,Ja 18,30:2
Hotel Paradiso 1957,Ap 12,22:2
Interlock 1958,F 7,18:1
Requiem for a Nun 1959,Ja 31,13:2
Fleiser, Joseph R (Playwright)
Road to Rio, The 1930,My 7,25:1
Fleishman, Dave (Musical Director)
Oh What a Wedding! 1969,O 20,60:1
Fleisig, Moss
Princess Turandot 1926,N 13,14:2
Rapid Transit 1927,Ap 8,21:2
Belt, The 1927,O 20,33:1
Gods of the Lightning 1928,O 25,27:2
With Privileges 1930,S 16,30:2
Fleisman, M (Composer)
Papirossen 1936,S 18,19:3
Fleisser, Marieluise (Playwright)
Pioniere in Ingolstadt 1929,My 12,IX,1:8
Fleming, Alan
Once Upon a Time 1939,D 21,28:2
Fleming, Alice
Masked Woman, The 1922,D 23,14:2
Morphia 1923,Mr 7,20:2
So This Is Politics 1924,Je 17,22:2
Thrills 1925,Ap 17,24:3
Pelican, The 1925,S 22,23:2
One More Honeymoon 1934,Ap 2,13:5
Stick-in-the-Mud 1935,D 2,18:2
30 Days Hath September 1938,O 1,10:5
Window Shopping 1938,D 24,13:2
When We Are Married 1939,D 26,22:3
Fleming, Allan (Playwright)
This Our House 1935,D 12,33:3
Fleming, Blanche
Garrick Gaieties 1926,My 11,25:2
White Eagle, The 1927,D 27,24:4
So Many Paths 1934,D 7,26:5
Fleming, Brandon (Playwright)
As Bad as I Am 1935,S 29,X,1:6
Fleming, Bud
Oklahoma! 1958,Mr 8,15:2
Fleming, Charles
Man Who Died Twice, The 1925,D 14,19:1
Dream Play 1926,Ja 21,18:2
East Lynne 1926,Mr 11,18:4
Fleming, Eric
Tower Beyond Tragedy, The 1950,N 27,29:1
Stalag 17 1951,My 9,41:2
My 3 Angels 1953,Mr 12,23:2
Portrait of a Lady 1954,D 22,27:6
Fleming, Gerry
Way of the World, The 1954,S 30,38:2
Way of the World, The 1954,O 17,II,1:1
Thieves' Carnival 1955,F 2,21:1
Fleming, Gus
Operation Sidewinder 1970,Mr 13,33:1
Fleming, Howard
So's Your Old Manhattan 1927,My 5,30:5
Fleming, Ian
Madame X 1927,Ap 3,VIII,1:4
Rising Sun, The 1929,O 27,IX,2:2
School for Scandal, The 1929,D 15,X,4:2

Fleming, Ian—Cont
Passing of the Essenes, The 1930,O 19,IX,4:1
Fleming, Ingrid
Winners and Losers 1947,F 27,27:2
Fleming, John
Page Miss Glory 1934,N 28,24:2
Mamba's Daughters 1953,Mr 21,12:6
Fleming, Leopoldo
Slave Ship 1969,N 22,46:1
Fleming, Leopoldo (Musical Director)
Slave Ship 1969,N 22,46:1
Fleming, Marion
Make Me Know It 1929,N 5,32:5
Fleming, Peggy
Ice Follies 1969,My 23,38:1
Ice Follies 1970,My 23,27:1
Fleming, Peter J (Producer)
Pigeon, The 1957,My 17,19:2
Fleming, Richard
Noah 1935,F 14,25:2
Fleming, Suzanne
No Foolin' 1926,Je 25,25:1
Manhattan Mary 1927,S 27,30:3
Fleming, Tom
Macbeth 1962,Je 6,35:2
Tempest, The 1963,Ap 3,43:1
King Lear 1964,My 19,43:2
Fleming, Tony Jr
Carmen Jones 1943,D 3,26:2
Fleming, Una
Sweetheart Shop, The 1920,S 1,13:4
Her Family Tree 1920,D 28,9:2
Flemming, Carol
On a Clear Day You Can See Forever 1965,O 18,44:1
Hallelujah, Baby! 1967,Ap 27,51:1
Flemming, John
Of V We Sing 1942,F 16,20:3
Flemyng, Robert
Lady Fingers 1929,F 1,22:4
Spring Meeting 1938,D 9,30:4
No Time for Comedy 1939,Ap 18,26:4
Importance of Being Earnest, The 1947,Ja 24,18:6
Importance of Being Earnest, The 1947,Mr 4,30:2
Importance of Being Earnest, The 1947,Mr 9,II,1:1
Love for Love 1947,My 27,30:2
Show Boat 1948,S 9,33:2
Cocktail Party, The 1950,Ja 23,17:2
Moon Is Blue, The 1953,Jl 8,24:1
Moon Is Blue, The 1953,Ag 9,II,1:2
Portrait of a Lady 1954,D 22,27:6
Potting Shed, The 1957,Ja 30,32:1
Potting Shed, The 1957,F 10,II,1:1
Doctor's Dilemma, The 1969,Je 24,37:1
Flers, Robert de (Playwright)
Ciboulette 1926,O 31,VIII,2:4
Habit Vert, L' 1927,Ja 16,VII,2:1
Diable a Paris, Le 1927,N 13,IX,4:2
Flesh, Ed (Costume Designer)
Hour Glass, The 1955,O 17,33:1
Flesh, Ed (Scenic Designer)
By Hex 1956,Je 19,25:1
Box of Watercolors, A 1957,F 18,22:2
Oscar Wilde 1957,Ap 20,21:3
Flesig, Moss
Stairs, The 1927,N 8,32:7
Fleson, Neville
Vaudeville (Palace) 1927,Je 14,33:3
Fletcher, Allen (Director)
Borak 1960,D 14,51:1
H M S Pinafore 1961,F 2,26:6
Richard II 1962,Je 18,20:2
Richard II 1962,Je 24,II,1:1
King Lear 1963,Je 10,37:1
Yeomen of the Guard, The 1964,Mr 19,29:2
H M S Pinafore 1964,Mr 21,13:4
Much Ado About Nothing 1964,Je 11,26:2
Richard III 1964,Je 12,44:2
Hamlet 1964,Jl 4,9:1
Measure for Measure 1964,Jl 27,22:3
Romeo and Juliet 1965,Je 21,36:3
Coriolanus 1965,Je 21,36:1
King Lear 1965,Je 25,39:1
Pirates of Penzance, The 1968,Ap 26,32:1
H M S Pinafore 1968,Ap 29,47:2
Yeomen of the Guard, The 1968,My 9,53:1
Fletcher, Bill
Fall 1957,N 22,19:1
Painted Days, The 1961,Ap 7,24:1
Macbeth 1961,Je 19,31:1
Moby Dick 1962,N 29,45:1
Student Gypsy, The; Prince of Liederkranz, The 1963,O 1,34:1
Midsummer Night's Dream, A 1964,Je 30,23:2
Giants' Dance, The 1964,N 17,48:2
Henry V 1965,Je 29,27:2
Fletcher, Bramwell
Scotland Yard 1929,S 28,16:6
Red Planet 1932,D 19,19:2
Ten Minute Alibi 1933,O 18,24:3
These Two 1934,My 8,28:3
Within the Gates 1934,O 23,23:1
Within the Gates 1934,O 28,IX,1:1
Dominant Sex, The 1935,Ap 2,24:5

Tulips Are Blooming, The 1935,D 4,27:6
Lady Precious Stream 1936,Ja 28,15:2
Lady Precious Stream 1936,F 23,X,1:1
Boy Meets Girl 1936,My 28,18:8
Circle, The 1938,Ap 19,24:2
Ruy Blas 1938,Jl 24,IX,2:1
Outward Bound 1938,D 23,16:5
Outward Bound 1939,Ja 1,IX,1:1
Margin for Error 1939,O 15,48:7
Margin for Error 1939,N 4,11:3
Eight O'Clock Tuesday 1941,Ja 7,18:2
Doctor's Dilemma, The 1941,Mr 12,18:2
Storm Operation 1944,Ja 12,28:2
Rebecca 1944,Ap 30,II,1:1
Rebecca 1945,Ja 19,17:2
Rebecca 1945,Ja 28,II,1:2
Day After Tomorrow 1950,O 27,25:2
Getting Married 1951,My 14,28:5
Candida 1952,Ap 23,23:6
Maggie 1953,F 19,20:2
Wisteria Trees, The 1955,F 3,20:2
Little Glass Clock, The 1956,Mr 27,40:2
Lovers 1956,My 11,23:1
Candida 1957,Mr 29,18:5
Rosmersholm 1962,Ap 12,42:1
Rosmersholm 1962,Ap 22,II,1:1
Cherry Orchard, The 1962,N 15,46:2
Major Barbara 1965,My 18,33:1
Bernard Shaw Story, The 1965,N 19,31:1
Fletcher, Bramwell (Playwright)
Bernard Shaw Story, The 1965,N 19,31:1
Fletcher, Bramwell (Producer)
Outward Bound 1938,D 23,16:5
Fletcher, Bruz (Playwright)
Commuting Distance 1936,Je 30,15:1
Fletcher, Charlotte
Ghost of Elsinore, The 1949,Ap 16,10:2
Serpent in the Orchard, The 1949,Ap 24,II,1:1
Fletcher, Dorothy
Port O' London 1926,F 10,20:2
At Mrs Beam's 1926,Ap 26,24:3
Brothers Karamazov, The 1927,Ja 4,20:1
Right You Are (If You Think You Are) 1927,F 24,27:1
Fletcher, Dusty
Bomboola 1929,Je 27,17:3
Fletcher, J (Producer)
Taming of the Shrew, The 1925,D 19,14:1
Fletcher, Jack
Trial Honeymoon 1947,N 4,31:2
She Stoops to Conquer 1949,D 29,21:3
Romeo and Juliet 1951,Mr 12,21:2
Cyrano de Bergerac 1953,N 13,24:3
Richard III 1953,D 10,65:2
Way of the World, The 1954,S 30,38:2
Way of the World, The 1954,O 17,II,1:1
Comic Strip 1958,My 15,26:2
Can-Can 1962,My 17,32:2
Amorous Flea, The 1964,F 18,26:1
Ben Franklin in Paris 1964,O 28,52:1
Drat! the Cat! 1965,O 11,54:2
Birds, The 1966,Jl 1,40:1
Joyful Noise, A 1966,D 16,57:1
Wonderful Town 1967,My 18,50:1
My Fair Lady 1968,Je 14,42:1
American Hamburger League, The 1969,S 17,51:1
Time of Your Life, The 1969,N 7,37:1
Lyle 1970,Mr 21,16:2
Arsenic and Old Lace 1970,N 5,59:1
Fletcher, Jay
Street Sounds 1970,O 23,32:1
Fletcher, John (Playwright)
Two Noble Kinsmen, The 1928,Ap 8,VIII,2:7
Fletcher, John J
Frogs, The 1941,N 14,25:3
Fletcher, Juanita
Little Miss Charity 1920,S 3,6:3
Fletcher, Larry
King Can Do No Wrong, The 1927,N 17,28:4
Marriage on Approval 1928,Mr 2,28:2
Karl and Anna 1929,O 8,34:1
Holiday 1930,F 6,21:2
Sailor, Beware! 1933,S 29,24:4
Fletcher, Lawrence
Old Lady Shows Her Medals, The 1932,Mr 8,19:3
Boy Meets Girl 1937,Jl 6,23:1
Antony and Cleopatra 1937,N 11,30:2
Merely Murder 1937,D 4,21:4
Romantic Mr Dickens 1940,D 3,33:2
Spring Again 1941,N 11,28:2
Tinker's Dam 1943,Ja 29,22:2
Hickory Stick 1944,My 9,15:6
Man Who Had All the Luck, The 1944,N 24,18:5
Signature 1945,F 15,25:2
Too Hot for Maneuvers 1945,My 3,26:5
Rugged Path, The 1945,N 12,17:2
Made in Heaven 1946,O 25,28:2
Allegro 1947,O 11,10:2
Silver Whistle, The 1948,N 25,49:2
My Name is Aquilon 1949,F 10,38:2
Mister Johnson 1956,Mr 30,11:1
Fletcher, Mary
This Is Today 1935,Jl 30,17:2

Fletcher, Mary—Cont
How Beautiful With Shoes 1935,N 29,24:1
Co-Respondent Unknown 1936,Ag 19,18:5
Sun Kissed 1937,N 11,20:2
Strange Fruit 1945,N 30,18:6
As We Forgive Our Debtors 1947,Mr 11,37:2
I Am a Camera 1956,O 10,47:2
Fletcher, Percy (Composer)
Mecca 1920,O 5,12:2
Fletcher, Raymond (Miscellaneous)
Oh What a Lovely War 1964,O 1,30:1
Fletcher, Robert
Embezzled Heaven 1944,N 1,20:2
Dream Girl 1945,D 15,13:2
Twelfth Night 1949,O 8,9:4
Relapse, The 1950,N 23,54:2
Love's Labour's Lost 1953,F 5,20:3
Merchant of Venice, The 1953,Mr 5,20:2
King Lear 1956,Ja 13,17:1
Fletcher, Robert (Costume Designer)
Little Blue Light, The 1951,Ap 30,17:2
Love's Labour's Lost 1953,F 5,20:3
Misalliance 1953,F 19,20:1
Julius Caesar 1955,Jl 13,20:1
Tempest, The 1955,Ag 2,18:2
Tempest, The 1955,Ag 7,II,1:1
Much Ado About Nothing 1955,Ag 20,20:4
Othello 1955,S 8,27:2
Henry IV, Part I 1955,S 22,34:2
King Lear 1956,Ja 13,17:1
Absalom 1956,My 17,37:2
Henry V 1956,Jl 7,11:2
Saint Joan 1956,S 12,42:1
Beggar's Opera, The 1957,Mr 14,35:1
Play of Daniel, The 1958,Ja 3,15:3
Firstborn, The 1958,My 1,35:1
Firstborn, The 1958,My 11,II,1:1
Play of Daniel, The 1959,Ja 6,30:2
Tempest, The 1960,Je 26,II,1:1
Farewell, Farewell Eugene 1960,S 28,35:1
Happiest Girl in the World, The 1961,Ap 4,42:1
How to Succeed in Business Without Really Trying 1961,O 16,34:1
Family Affair, A 1962,Ja 29,17:1
Half-Past Wednesday 1962,Ap 7,16:2
Charlatans; On Circe's Island 1962,Ap 27,26:1
Nowhere to Go But Up 1962,N 12,36:2
Little Me 1962,N 19,41:3
Moon Besieged, The 1962,D 6,54:1
Best Foot Forward 1963,Ap 3,43:1
Foxy 1964,F 17,26:1
High Spirits 1964,Ap 8,34:1
Walking Happy 1966,N 28,47:1
Midsummer Night's Dream, A 1967,Je 19,42:1
Hamlet 1968,Je 10,59:1
Hadrian VII 1969,Ja 9,22:1
Borstal Boy 1970,Ap 1,38:1
Cry for Us All 1970,Ap 9,48:2
Fletcher, Robert (Producer)
High Spirits 1964,Ap 8,34:1
Queen and the Rebels, The 1965,F 26,16:1
Fletcher, Robert (Scenic Designer)
Doll's House, A 1954,N 15,32:2
Much Ado About Nothing 1955,Ag 20,20:4
Absalom 1956,My 17,37:2
Play of Daniel, The 1958,Ja 26,II,1:1
Geranium Hat, The 1959,Mr 18,45:1
Tempest, The 1960,Je 20,35:1
Farewell, Farewell Eugene 1960,S 28,35:1
Dear Liar 1962,Mr 19,36:1
Best Foot Forward 1963,Ap 3,43:1
High Spirits 1964,Ap 8,34:1
Hadrian VII 1969,Ja 9,22:1
Madwoman of Chaillot, The 1970,Mr 23,48:3
Fletcher, Ron (Choreographer)
Top Banana 1951,N 2,19:2
Ice Capades 1953,S 11,25:1
Ice Capades 1954,S 16,37:1
Ice Capades 1955,S 15,38:1
Ice Capades 1956,S 13,41:2
Ice Capades 1957,S 5,33:2
Ice Capades 1959,S 4,12:1
Ice Capades 1960,S 1,30:1
Ice Capades 1962,Ag 30,34:1
Ice Capades 1963,Ag 29,37:2
Ice Capades 1964,Ag 27,27:2
Ice Capades 1966,Je 2,50:2
Fletcher, Ron (Miscellaneous)
Ice Capades 1964,Ag 27,27:2
Ice Capades 1966,Je 2,50:2
Fletcher, Ronald
Lute Song 1946,F 7,29:2
Fletcher, Ronnie
Last Love of Don Juan, The 1955,N 24,40:1
Fletcher, Tex
Howdy Stranger 1937,Ja 15,17:5
Fletcher, Tom
Harlem Cavalcade 1942,My 2,11:2
Flett, Julian
Broken Jug, The 1958,Ap 2,36:1
Fleury, Baby
Business Widow, The 1923,D 11,27:1
Fleury, Gaby
Whispering Wires 1922,Ag 8,26:2

Fleury, Gaby—Cont
Werewolf, The 1924,Ag 26,6:1
Fleury, Vanni
Edith Piaf 1947,O 30,30:2
Flexner, Anne Crawford (Playwright)
All Soul's Eve 1920,My 13,9:1
Aged 26 1936,D 22,32:1
Flick, Harold
She Loves Me Not 1933,N 21,22:4
Hide and Seek 1934,Ag 7,20:2
Flick, Pat (Playwright)
Boys and Girls Together 1940,S 5,28:6
Boys and Girls Together 1940,O 2,19:2
Flick, Patsy
Calling All Stars 1934,D 14,28:2
Flicker, J (Director)
Nervous Set, The 1959,My 13,43:1
Flicker, Joan Patsy
This Rock 1943,F 19,23:2
Flicker, Theodore
Once Around the Block 1956,O 29,34:1
Flicker, Theodore J
Premise, The 1962,Jl 27,15:5
Flicker, Theodore J (Director)
I Want You 1961,S 15,29:1
Living Premise, The 1963,Je 14,34:1
Flicker, Theodore J (Miscellaneous)
Premise, The 1962,Jl 27,15:5
Flicker, Theodore J (Playwright)
Nervous Set, The 1959,My 13,43:1
Flicker, Theodore J (Producer)
I Want You 1961,S 15,29:1
Flink, Stanley (Producer)
Salad Days 1958,N 11,24:1
Flinn, Florence
Daddy Dumplins 1920,N 23,11:1
Cradle Song 1921,Mr 1,18:2
Exciters, The 1922,S 23,10:4
Woman on the Jury, The 1923,Ag 16,10:4
Flinn, Marjorie
Gondoliers, The 1939,Ja 20,14:2
Flint, Eva Kay (Playwright)
Subway Express 1929,S 25,34:3
Up and Up, The 1930,S 9,25:2
Under Glass 1933,O 31,24:3
Flint, Helen
Demi-Virgin, The 1921,O 19,22:1
Listening In 1922,D 5,24:1
Alarm Clock, The 1923,D 25,26:2
Noose, The 1926,O 21,23:3
Paradise 1927,D 26,26:4
These Modern Women 1928,F 14,26:2
Gentlemen of the Press 1928,Ag 28,27:2
Marriage Bed, The 1929,Ja 8,35:1
Parade 1929,S 1,VIII,1:1
Nigger Rich 1929,S 21,16:7
Those We Love 1930,F 20,22:2
London Calling 1930,O 20,29:1
House Beautiful, The 1931,Mr 13,20:4
Melo 1931,O 20,29:3
Hangman's Whip 1933,F 25,20:2
Blue Widow, The 1933,Ag 31,20:2
Ah, Wilderness! 1934,My 1,26:3
Too Many Boats 1934,S 12,26:3
Summer Night 1939,N 3,17:1
Theatre 1941,N 13,34:2
Perfect Marriage, The 1944,O 27,17:6
Dancer, The 1946,Je 6,16:5
Flint, J G
It's Only Natural 1922,Ap 21,13:2
Flint, Kay (Playwright)
Up and Up, The 1930,S 14,VIII,1:1
Flint, Samuel
Ebb Tide 1931,Je 9,33:6
Flippen, Jay C
June Days 1925,Ag 7,12:5
June Days 1925,Ag 23,VII,1:1
Hello, Lola! 1926,Ja 13,30:1
Vaudeville (Palace) 1926,Mr 23,24:3
Great Temptations, The 1926,My 19,29:1
Great Temptations, The 1926,My 23,VIII,1:1
Vaudeville (Palace) 1926,S 21,32:5
Vaudeville (Palace) 1927,My 17,27:4
Padlocks of 1927 1927,Jl 6,23:4
Vaudeville (Palace) 1928,Ja 10,28:5
Vaudeville (Palace) 1929,Je 24,27:4
Second Little Show, The 1930,S 3,36:1
Vaudeville (Palace) 1931,F 2,23:3
Vaudeville (New Amsterdam Theatre)
  1931,Je 22,17:3
Variety Anthology 1932,Mr 21,19:4
Friars Club Frolic 1933,My 15,16:4
Take a Bow 1944,Je 16,15:3
Flippin, Lucy Lee
Ben Bagley's Shoestring Revues 1970,O 24,22:1
Knack With Horses, A 1970,D 21,52:1
Floetman, Lucille
Day Before Spring, The 1945,N 23,27:2
Flon, Suzanne
Little Foxes, The 1962,D 6,56:1
Flood, Alice Wikoff
Time of Their Lives 1937,O 26,19:1
Flood, Ann
Holiday for Lovers 1957,F 15,20:1

Flood, James
Jubilee 1935,O 14,20:1
Flood, John
Wren, The 1921,O 11,22:1
Italian Straw Hat, The 1957,O 1,37:2
Flood, Maxine
Garden of Weeds 1924,Ap 29,12:3
Don Q Jr 1926,Ja 28,16:3
Intimate Relations 1932,Mr 29,23:2
Flood, Richard R (Director)
On the Level 1937,Mr 26,24:4
Floppit (Dog)
Vaudeville (Palace) 1926,Ag 17,21:2
Florance, Marian
American Tragedy, An 1926,O 12,31:2
Florant, Lester
Sunup to Sundown 1938,F 2,14:3
Florant, Sylvia
Sunup to Sundown 1938,F 2,14:3
Florath, Albert
Heilige Crispin, Der 1933,Je 25,IX,1:2
Florell, Walter (Choreographer)
Mr Strauss Goes to Boston 1945,S 7,20:2
Florell, Walter (Costume Designer)
Merry Widow, The 1943,Ag 5,19:2
Merry Widow, The 1944,O 9,17:1
Beggar's Holiday 1946,D 27,13:3
Beggar's Holiday 1947,Ja 26,II,1:1
Florence, Carol
Winterset 1966,F 10,32:2
Florence, Louis A
Truckline Cafe 1946,F 28,19:4
Florence, Mildred
Busybody, The 1924,S 30,27:5
Sapphire Ring, The 1925,Ap 16,25:2
Oh! Mama 1925,Ag 20,22:2
Twelve Miles Out 1925,N 17,29:2
Mongolia 1927,D 27,24:5
Florence, Miss
Artists and Models 1930,Je 11,33:2
Florence, William J
Personality 1921,Ag 29,14:3
Florentine Singers
Vaudeville (Palace) 1928,F 28,18:7
Florenz, Paul (Choreographer)
Smile at Me 1935,Ag 24,18:4
Flores, Marissa
Mexicana 1939,Ap 22,14:4
Mexicana 1939,My 7,X,3:1
Flores, Paul
King and I, The 1963,Je 13,30:2
Deputy, The 1964,F 27,26:1
King and I, The 1968,My 24,39:1
South Pacific 1969,Jl 7,27:1
Flores, Sam
Enemy of the People, An 1958,F 26,24:2
Florestano, Joseph
Bloomer Girl 1944,O 6,18:5
Florian, Myra
Comedian, The 1923,Mr 14,14:1
Laugh, Clown, Laugh! 1923,N 29,30:1
Mima 1928,D 13,24:2
Florianne, Mlle
Ziegfeld Follies 1923,O 22,17:2
Floriet, Bernard (Scenic Designer)
Waiting for Godot 1968,Ap 23,38:1
Florman, Irving (Lyricist)
Chauve-Souris of 1943 1943,Ag 13,13:2
Floud, Alan
Tyrants 1924,Mr 5,14:1
Blue Peter, The 1925,Mr 25,25:3
Veils 1928,Mr 14,28:5
Pleased to Meet You 1928,O 30,27:2
Second Mate, The 1930,Mr 25,34:5
Wrong Number 1934,Mr 14,23:6
Floud, Ruth
Right of Happiness 1931,Ap 3,34:2
Flournoy, Peter (Director)
Single Man at a Party 1959,Ap 22,30:4
Flournoy, Peter (Miscellaneous)
Innkeepers, The 1956,F 3,19:1
Flournoy, Richard F (Original Author)
Ladies' Money 1934,N 2,26:6
Flournoy, Richard F (Playwright)
Fly by Night 1933,Je 3,16:2
Come What May 1934,My 16,23:4
Flower, Belle
Gondoliers, The 1931,Je 2,34:4
Flower, Belle
Rat Race, The 1949,D 23,16:2
Flower, C S (Playwright)
Twelfth Night's Tune, A 1967,D 23,28:1
Flower, Carol
Bunch and Judy, The 1922,N 29,20:1
Flowers, Barbara (Costume Designer)
Mikado, The 1967,D 4,65:3
Flowers, Martha
Four Saints in Three Acts 1952,Ap 17,35:1
Porgy and Bess 1955,Jl 9,9:5
Porgy and Bess 1955,O 13,37:4
Free and Easy 1959,D 15,51:4
Free and Easy 1959,D 20,II,3:2

Flowers, Max
Orphee 1935,Mr 23,10:3
Flowers, Priscilla (Playwright)
Little Theatre Tournament; May Night
  1926,My 5,24:5
Little Theatre Tournament; White Peacock, The
  1928,My 11,28:1
Flowerton, Consuelo
Remote Control 1929,S 11,24:5
American Tragedy, An 1931,F 21,15:5
Six Characters in Search of an Author
  1931,Ap 16,29:2
Sex Fable, The 1931,O 21,26:1
Melody 1933,F 15,17:4
Let 'Em Eat Cake 1933,O 23,18:1
Floyd, Carlisle (Composer)
Susannah 1955,F 25,18:4
Floyd, Carlisle (Playwright)
From Here to There; Slow Dusk 1958,Ap 24,37:3
Floyd, Cecily
Trumpets and Drums 1969,O 13,52:1
Oedipus 1970,F 23,30:1
Young Among Themselves, The 1970,Je 12,28:1
Floyd, Charles
Mis-Guided Tour 1959,O 13,44:7
Floyd, Emily
Glass of Water, A 1930,Mr 6,16:3
Antigone 1930,Ap 25,28:4
Boeuf sur le Toit, Le 1930,Ap 25,28:4
Floyd, Estelle
My Magnolia 1926,Jl 13,19:2
Show Boat 1927,D 28,26:1
Show Boat 1932,My 20,22:2
Sweet River 1936,O 29,30:2
Floyd, Hal
Beautiful Jailer, The 1957,My 17,19:2
Floyd, John
Demi-Virgin, The 1921,O 19,22:1
Floyd, John (Playwright)
Wooden Kimono 1926,D 28,16:2
Queer People 1934,F 16,16:2
Floyd, Paul C
Runnin' Wild 1923,O 30,17:3
Messin' Around 1929,Ap 23,26:3
Make Me Know It 1929,N 5,32:5
Budget, The 1932,S 21,26:4
Floyd, Sara
Atlas and Eva 1928,F 7,30:2
Tin Pan Alley 1928,N 2,29:1
Broken Chain, The 1929,F 21,30:4
Dream Child 1934,S 28,26:2
Bedrock 1934,N 18,II,6:3
Achilles Had a Heel 1935,O 14,20:4
Lady From the Sea, The 1935,D 14,11:3
O Evening Star 1936,Ja 9,24:6
Merrily We Roll Along 1936,Je 30,15:1
One More Genius 1936,Ag 11,24:6
Lend Me Your Ears! 1936,O 6,28:5
Our Betters 1937,Jl 22,16:2
There's Always a Breeze 1938,Mr 3,16:2
Medicine Show 1940,Ap 13,20:6
Mr Big 1941,O 1,24:2
Comes the Revelation 1942,My 27,26:2
Take It As It Comes 1944,F 11,17:2
Hickory Stick 1944,My 9,15:6
Show Boat 1946,Ja 7,17:2
As We Forgive Our Debtors 1947,Mr 11,37:2
Show Boat 1948,S 9,33:2
Show Boat 1954,My 6,44:1
Show Boat 1954,O 29,28:4
Inherit the Wind 1955,Ap 22,20:2
Show Boat 1956,Je 22,16:1
Show Boat 1957,Je 28,30:2
Show Boat 1961,Ap 13,32:1
Floyd, Sara (Playwright)
Fuente Ovejuna; Sheep Well, The 1936,My 3,II,4:1
Fluegelmen, Arthur
You'll Never Know 1921,Ap 21,9:2
Fluggers, Mr
George Barnwell; London Merchant, The
  1928,O 2,34:3
Flush
Barretts of Wimpole Street, The 1931,F 10,25:1
Barretts of Wimpole Street, The 1935,F 26,16:2
Barretts of Wimpole Street, The 1945,Mr 27,23:6
Flushing, Loretta
Little Jessie James 1923,Ag 16,10:4
Flynn, Barney
Hobo 1931,F 12,24:4
Flynn, Bina
Kathleen ni Houlihan 1920,Je 29,9:2
Flynn, Charles J
Sound of Hunting, A 1945,N 21,16:6
Flynn, Denise
Winter's Tale, The 1946,Ja 16,18:6
Flynn, Eamon
Red Roses for Me 1955,D 29,15:2
Red Roses for Me 1956,Ja 8,II,1:1
Anatomist, The 1957,F 27,21:5
Flynn, Elinor
American Holiday 1936,F 22,13:3
Sun and I, The 1937,F 27,9:5

Flynn, F R (Playwright)
Bulls and Belles 1931,Ap 18,17:2
Flynn, Florence
Lilies of the Field 1921,O 5,20:1
Masked Woman, The 1922,D 23,14:2
Flynn, Gertrude
Penal Law 2010 1930,Ap 19,14:2
Gasoline Gypsies 1931,Je 8,21:3
Three Times the Hour 1931,Ag 26,15:5
Racketty Packetty House 1931,N 7,16:1
Moon in the Yellow River, The 1932,Mr 1,19:3
Moon in the Yellow River, The
1932,Mr 13,VIII,1:1
Good Earth, The 1932,O 18,23:4
American Dream; 1933 1933,F 22,24:5
American Dream; 1650 1933,F 22,24:5
Man Bites Dog 1933,Ap 26,11:2
Biography 1934,F 6,24:4
Jig Saw 1934,My 1,26:3
Sleeping Clergyman, A 1934,O 9,16:1
Mother Lode 1934,D 24,16:5
Noah 1935,F 14,25:2
One Good Year 1935,N 28,38:3
Puritan, The 1936,Ja 24,14:3
Marching Song 1937,F 18,18:2
Wind in the Sails 1940,Ag 1,24:6
Romantic Mr Dickens 1940,D 3,33:2
Distant City, The 1941,S 23,27:5
Grass Harp, The 1952,Mr 28,26:2
Flynn, Hazel (Playwright)
Three's a Crowd 1930,O 26,VIII,1:1
Flynn, Jane
Hamlet 1945,D 14,25:2
On the Town 1959,F 14,15:1
Flynn, Jim
Wise Have Not Spoken, The 1954,F 11,35:2
Flynn, John
Frivolities of 1920 1920,Ja 9,22:2
Possessed, The 1939,O 25,26:2
Twelfth Night 1941,D 3,32:2
Flynn, John W
Easy Mark, The 1924,Ag 27,14:2
Flynn, Kathleen
Rotters, The 1922,My 23,12:4
Flynn, Kitty
Blushing Bride, The 1922,F 7,12:1
Sally, Irene and Mary 1922,S 5,21:2
Flynn, L Radley
H M S Pinafore 1948,Ja 20,26:2
Flynn, Marjorie
Silks and Satins 1920,Jl 16,19:1
Flynn, Martha
Singing Girl, The 1952,Je 4,31:8
Music Man, The 1957,D 20,31:1
Flynn, Maryellen
Guimpes and Saddles 1967,O 11,36:3
Babes Don't Cry Anymore 1968,F 21,55:1
Flynn, Philip
Juno and the Paycock 1964,My 6,41:1
Flynn, Radley
Gondoliers, The 1934,S 4,23:1
H M S Pinafore 1934,S 14,24:3
Mikado, The; Town of Titipu, The 1934,S 18,18:1
Ruddigore 1934,S 25,25:2
Princess Ida; Castle Adamant 1934,S 28,26:3
Mikado, The 1936,Ag 21,13:2
Gondoliers, The 1936,S 8,23:1
H M S Pinafore 1936,S 29,34:2
Princess Ida 1936,O 13,32:2
Ruddigore 1936,O 23,26:4
Mikado, The 1939,Ja 10,16:3
H. M. S. Pinafore 1939,Ja 17,27:5
Gondoliers, The 1939,Ja 20,14:2
Trial by Jury 1948,Ja 6,27:2
Gondoliers, The 1948,Ja 27,31:2
H M S Pinafore 1951,F 6,24:2
Trial by Jury 1951,F 6,24:2
Gondoliers, The 1951,F 13,27:2
Mikado, The 1952,O 21,35:2
Trial by Jury 1952,N 4,32:2
H M S Pinafore 1952,N 4,32:2
Flynn, Rose
Damaged Goods 1937,My 18,27:2
30 Days Hath September 1938,O 1,10:5
Flynn, Sarah
Up the Rebels 1941,O 31,21:1
Flynn, Seumas
Skin of Our Teeth, The 1942,N 19,29:5
Flynn, Thomas
Paul Bunyan 1941,My 6,25:1
Foa, George R (Director)
Gondoliers, The 1962,N 16,25:2
Foch, Leon (Scenic Designer)
Yosele the Nightingale 1949,O 21,30:4
Foch, Nina
John Loves Mary 1947,F 5,29:2
Twelfth Night 1949,O 4,33:2
Twelfth Night 1949,O 9,II,1:1
Phoenix Too Frequent, A 1950,Ap 27,36:2
King Lear 1950,D 26,18:1
King Lear 1950,D 31,II,1:1
Evening With Will Shakespeare, An 1952,D 7,86:5
Measure for Measure 1956,Je 29,16:1

Taming of the Shrew, The 1956,Ag 6,20:1
Measure for Measure 1957,Ja 23,24:1
Taming of the Shrew, The 1957,F 21,30:2
Second String, A 1960,Ap 14,36:2
Foch, Nina (Director)
Ways and Means 1967,My 4,34:1
Foch, Nina (Miscellaneous)
Imaginary Invalid, The 1967,My 2,53:1
Fodor, Joleen
Student Gypsy, The; Prince of Liederkranz, The
1963,O 1,34:1
Babes in the Wood 1964,D 29,21:2
Great Scot! 1965,N 12,56:3
Grin and Bare It 1970,Mr 17,36:1
Fodor, Ladislaus (Composer)
Luck of the Devil 1936,Ja 14,25:1
Fodor, Ladislaus (Miscellaneous)
Good Morning, Bill! 1927,D 25,VIII,1:4
Grand Hotel 1929,D 22,VIII,4:6
Fodor, Ladislaus (Original Author)
Church Mouse, A 1931,My 3,VIII,2:1
Orchard Walls 1937,F 4,17:3
Orchard Walls 1937,F 21,X,2:1
Fodor, Ladislaus (Playwright)
Roulette 1932,Ja 17,VIII,2:2
Jewel Robbery; Juwelenraub am Kurfurstendamm
1932,F 21,VIII,2:3
Roulette 1932,Mr 27,VIII,3:1
Unguarded Hour, The 1935,Ag 25,X,1:3
Love Is Not So Simple 1935,N 5,33:1
Love Is Not So Simple 1935,N 10,IX,1:6
Love Is Not So Simple 1935,N 20,26:7
Luck of the Devil 1936,Ja 14,25:1
Vigil, The 1948,My 11,28:1
Vigil, The 1948,My 22,8:6
Fodor, Laszlo (Playwright)
Stork, The 1925,Ja 27,14:2
Church Mouse, A 1927,D 4,X,2:3
Cradle Song 1928,D 9,X,2:7
I Love an Actress 1931,S 18,29:2
Church Mouse, A 1931,O 13,26:4
Kiss Before the Mirror, The 1932,N 13,IX,3:7
Church Mouse, A 1933,Je 27,13:7
Roulette 1935,Je 16,X,1:1
Fodor, Laszlo (Translator)
Jewel Robbery 1932,Ja 14,17:2
Foeides (Playwright)
Victoria and Her Hussar 1930,S 21,IX,2:6
Fogarty, Alexander (Composer)
Cape Cod Follies 1929,S 19,37:2
New Faces of 1936 1936,My 20,24:5
Fogarty, Jack Patrick
Sweeney Todd 1957,Ag 28,21:4
Fogarty, Martin
Mother Sings 1935,N 13,24:1
Fogarty, Mary
Well of the Saints, The 1959,Ap 11,15:4
Nathan the Wise 1962,Mr 23,29:1
Fogel, Jacqueline (Miscellaneous)
Paradise Gardens East 1969,Mr 11,39:1
Conerico Was Here to Stay 1969,Mr 11,39:1
Fogel, Mortie
Spring 3100 1928,F 16,14:2
Fogelson, E E (Producer)
Golden Age, The 1963,N 19,49:2
Passion of Josef D, The 1964,F 12,29:1
Foggy Mountain Boys
Hayride 1954,S 14,24:2
Fogle, George
One, Two, Three! 1930,S 30,24:2
Fogle, George L
Mongrel, The 1924,D 16,28:2
Foix, Georges
Girofle-Girofla 1926,N 23,26:3
Cloches de Cornville, Les; Chimes of Normandy,
The 1926,D 14,24:4
Perichole, La 1926,D 29,24:4
Trois Jeunes Filles Nues; Three Young Maids From
the Folies Bergere 1929,Mr 5,28:2
Passionement; Passionately 1929,Mr 8,31:4
Comte Obligado 1929,Mr 12,26:2
Ta Bouche 1929,Mr 15,28:5
Bon Garcon, Un 1929,Mr 19,36:2
Pas Sur La Bouche; Not on the Lips
1929,Mr 26,34:3
Fokina, Vera
Vaudeville (Hippodrome) 1926,Ap 27,22:3
Fokine, Leon
Paese dei Campanelli, Il; Land of Bells, The
1935,My 10,25:4
Fokine, Michel (Choreographer)
Johannes Kreisler 1923,Ja 21,VII,1:1
Casanova 1923,S 16,VII,2:8
Hassan 1923,S 30,II,1:6
Casanova 1923,O 2,10:3
Hassan 1923,O 14,VIII,2:6
Hassan 1924,S 23,23:1
Tenth Commandment, The 1926,N 18,27:1
Florodora 1936,Ag 23,II,8:2
Blossom Time 1936,Ag 30,II,5:8
Fokine, Michel (Miscellaneous)
Vaudeville (Hippodrome) 1926,Ap 27,22:3

Fokine and Fokina
Get Together 1921,S 5,12:2
Folair, Mr
George Barnwell; London Merchant, The
1928,O 2,34:3
Foldes, Emery (Playwright)
Fires in the Night 1928,D 2,X,4:7
Flower of Hawaii; Blume von Hawaii, Die
1931,O 4,VIII,4:1
Foldes, Lew
Carousel 1945,Ap 20,24:2
Folds, Lou
Icetime 1947,My 29,28:2
Foldsmith, Jechiel
Dybbuk, The 1921,S 2,9:2
Foley, Adrian
Jane Eyre 1958,My 2,31:1
Foley, Charles
You Can't Take It With You 1945,Mr 27,23:7
Foley, Chotzi
Gypsy 1959,My 22,31:6
Foley, Clare
Janie 1942,S 11,24:2
Foley, Cynthia
Three Cheers 1928,O 16,28:1
Foley, Frances
Idiot's Delight 1936,Mr 25,25:2
Foley, Hattie
Laff That Off 1925,N 3,34:2
Foley, Janice
Titus Andronicus 1956,D 3,40:2
Foley, Joseph
Retreat to Pleasure 1940,D 18,32:2
Land's End 1946,D 12,37:5
Richard III 1949,F 9,33:2
Master Builder, The 1955,Mr 2,23:2
Foley, Ken
Sleepy Hollow 1948,Je 4,26:3
Foley, Lee (Choreographer)
Tempest, The 1959,D 28,19:2
Foley, Lee (Director)
Stone Tower, The 1962,Ag 24,14:2
Foley, Margaret
Psychological Moment, The 1931,Mr 4,33:2
Divina Pastora, La 1931,Mr 4,33:2
Sparkin' 1931,Mr 4,33:2
This Happy Breed 1952,Ap 4,23:2
Foley, Michael
Mr Barry's Etchings 1950,F 1,26:2
Sweet Confession 1959,Ap 15,30:1
Foley, Michael (Miscellaneous)
Man of Destiny, The 1957,Ap 1,21:2
Bedtime Story 1957,Ap 1,21:2
Portrait of a Madonna 1957,Ap 1,21:2
Family Portrait 1959,My 6,48:2
Susannah and the Elders 1959,O 19,37:3
Peh Shuh Tchuwan; White Snake, The 1963,Ja 4,5:2
Foley, Paul A
Triumph 1935,O 15,18:5
Foley, Paul A (Director)
Steps Leading Up 1941,Ap 19,20:6
Boy Who Lived Twice, A 1945,S 12,31:2
Foley, Paul A (Miscellaneous)
Day by the Sea, A 1955,S 27,42:1
Waltz of the Toreadors, The 1958,Mr 5,37:1
Man in the Dog Suit, The 1958,O 31,34:2
On the Harmful Effects of Tobacco
1959,Ap 16,28:1
Portrait of a Madonna 1959,Ap 16,28:1
Pound on Demand, A 1959,Ap 16,28:1
Bedtime Story 1959,Ap 16,28:1
Man for All Seasons, A 1964,Ja 28,24:2
Physicists, The 1964,O 14,52:1
I Never Sang for My Father 1968,Ja 26,30:1
Foley, Peggy
This Happy Breed 1952,Ap 4,23:2
Foley, Tom (Scenic Designer)
Toothbrush, The 1970,S 27,84:5
Folinet, W F
They Never Come Back 1920,D 19,I,22:3
Folk Singers, The
Next President, The 1958,Ap 10,34:3
Folks Quintet
Kibbetzers, Inc 1935,My 13,18:5
Folland, Gloria
Return of Ulysses, The 1943,F 7,II,1:6
Follansbee, Julie
Fifth Horseman, The 1949,Je 14,26:6
Brothers Karamazov, The 1957,D 9,39:4
Our Town 1959,Mr 24,46:2
Epitaph for George Dillon 1960,D 29,17:1
Willie Doesn't Live Here Anymore 1967,F 8,20:2
Follett, Charron
Country Wife, The 1955,Ap 6,35:1
Follette, Grace
Susannah and the Elders 1940,O 30,28:2
Follies Quartette
Ziegfeld Follies 1922,Je 6,18:2
Follis, Dorothy
Honeydew 1920,S 7,20:1
Follmann, Anne
Respectfully Yours 1947,My 14,29:4

Follmann, Joseph F Jr (Musical Director)
Red Rhumba 1936,Ap 14,18:1
This Mad Whirl 1937,Ja 10,II,4:8
Follows, Ruth
Comedy of Women, A 1929,S 14,17:4
Follows, Ted
Merchant of Venice, The 1955,Jl 1,13:1
Tamburlaine the Great 1956,Ja 20,19:1
Henry V 1956,Je 20,27:2
Merry Wives of Windsor, The 1956,Je 21,34:4
Hamlet 1957,Jl 3,15:2
Twelfth Night 1957,Jl 4,16:4
Henry IV, Part I 1958,Je 25,23:3
Much Ado About Nothing 1958,Je 26,22:1
As You Like It 1959,Jl 1,27:1
Othello 1959,Jl 2,17:2
Folmer, Richard S
Sacco-Vanzetti 1969,F 9,78:1
Folsom, Bobby
Vaudeville (Palace) 1923,N 20,23:4
Earl Carroll's Vanities 1925,Jl 7,24:1
Vaudeville (Palace) 1927,Je 14,33:3
Vaudeville (Palace) 1927,N 8,33:3
Fomeen, Basil (Composer)
Garrick Gaieties 1930,Je 5,29:2
Fond, Miriam (Choreographer)
Ben Bagley's Shoestring Revues 1970,O 24,22:1
Fond, Miriam (Director)
Ben Bagley's Shoestring Revues 1970,O 24,22:1
Fonda, Dow
Knickerbocker Holiday 1938,O 20,26:2
Fonda, Henry
I Loved You Wednesday 1932,O 12,27:1
Forsaking All Others 1933,Mr 2,21:2
New Faces 1934,Mr 16,24:5
Farmer Takes a Wife, The 1934,O 9,17:2
Farmer Takes a Wife, The 1934,O 28,IX,3:1
Farmer Takes a Wife, The 1934,O 31,17:1
Farmer Takes a Wife, The 1934,N 11,IX,1:1
Virginian, The 1937,Ag 10,22:7
Blow Ye Winds 1937,S 8,20:5
Blow Ye Winds 1937,S 24,17:4
Mister Roberts 1948,F 19,27:2
Mister Roberts 1948,F 29,II,1:1
Mister Roberts 1950,My 21,II,1:1
Point of No Return 1951,O 31,32:2
Point of No Return 1951,D 14,35:2
Point of No Return 1951,D 23,II,3:1
Caine Mutiny Court-Martial, The 1953,O 14,35:1
Caine Mutiny Court-Martial, The 1953,D 15,52:8
Caine Mutiny Court-Martial, The 1954,Ja 21,27:2
Caine Mutiny Court-Martial, The 1954,Ja 31,II,1:1
Two for the Seesaw 1958,Ja 17,15:1
Two for the Seesaw 1958,Ja 26,II,1:1
Silent Night, Lonely Night 1959,D 4,36:1
Silent Night, Lonely Night 1959,D 13,II,3:1
Critic's Choice 1960,D 15,61:3
Gift of Time, A 1962,F 23,34:1
Gift of Time, A 1962,Mr 4,II,1:1
Generation 1965,O 8,5:6
Our Town 1968,S 29,77:4
Front Page, The 1968,O 20,85:5
Our Town 1969,N 28,50:1
Our Town 1969,D 7,II,7:1
Fonda, Jane
There Was a Little Girl 1960,Mr 1,28:1
Invitation to a March 1960,O 31,27:2
Fun Couple, The 1962,O 27,15:2
Strange Interlude 1963,Mr 13,5:2
Fonda, Jeanne
Sunny 1925,S 23,22:1
Fonda, Peter
Blood, Sweat & Stanley Poole 1961,O 6,31:1
Fong, Frances
Pajama Tops 1963,Je 1,15:1
Fonnesbeck, Lujah
Suds in Your Eye 1944,Ja 13,15:5
Fonsgaines, George
Fool's Bells 1925,D 24,8:3
Font, Alida
Burning Bush, The 1949,D 17,15:5
Fontaine, Evan Burrows
Ed Wynn's Carnival 1920,Ap 6,18:2
Fontaine, Helene
Warrior's Husband, The 1932,Mr 12,19:4
Fontaine, Joan
Tea and Sympathy 1954,Ag 15,II,1:1
Fontaine, R Carlton (Director)
Untitled-Nativity Play 1946,D 25,46:1
Pageant of the Nativity of Christ 1948,D 25,6:7
Untitled-Nativity Play 1950,D 25,15:2
Fontaine, Robert (Original Author)
Happy Time, The 1950,Ja 25,24:1
Fontaine, Robert (Playwright)
Happy Time, The 1968,Ja 19,32:2
Fontan, Natalia
Fuerza Ciega, La 1927,D 6,26:1
Fontana, Georges
City Chap, The 1925,O 27,21:1
Diable 1926,O 31,VIII,2:4
Vaudeville (Palace) 1928,Ja 31,29:2
This Year of Grace 1928,N 8,27:1

Fontana (Miscellaneous)
Wonder World 1964,My 18,32:1
Fontanals (Scenic Designer)
Dama Boba, La; Villano En Su Rincon, El;
Fuenteovejuna 1935,S 22,X,2:5
Fontanel, Genevieve
Impromptu de Versailles, L' 1961,F 22,30:1
Fourberies de Scapin, Les 1961,F 22,30:1
Dindon, Le 1961,Mr 8,38:1
Fontanes (Playwright)
Plein aux As 1926,O 31,VIII,2:4
Fontanne, Lynn
Dulcy 1921,Ag 15,14:1
Dulcy 1921,Ag 21,VI,1:1
Sweet Nell of Old Drury 1923,My 19,16:4
In Love With Love 1923,Ag 7,20:1
In Love With Love 1923,Ag 12,VI,1:1
Guardsman, The 1924,O 14,23:1
Arms and the Man 1925,S 15,28:1
Arms and the Man 1925,O 4,IX,1:1
Goat Song 1926,Ja 26,18:1
At Mrs Beam's 1926,Ap 26,24:3
At Mrs Beam's 1926,My 2,VIII,1:1
Pygmalion 1926,N 16,24:1
Brothers Karamazov, The 1927,Ja 4,20:1
Second Man, The 1927,Ap 12,24:3
Doctor's Dilemma, The 1927,N 22,33:1
Strange Interlude 1928,Ja 31,28:1
Strange Interlude 1928,F 5,VIII,1:1
Caprice 1928,D 23,VIII,4:1
Caprice 1929,Ja 1,61:1
Caprice 1929,Ja 13,VIII,1:1
Caprice 1929,Je 23,VIII,1:3
Meteor 1929,D 8,X,2:1
Meteor 1929,D 24,15:1
Elizabeth the Queen 1930,O 5,IX,4:6
Elizabeth the Queen 1930,N 4,37:1
Elizabeth the Queen 1930,N 9,IX,1:1
Reunion in Vienna 1931,O 11,VIII,4:6
Reunion in Vienna 1931,N 17,31:1
Reunion in Vienna 1931,N 29,VIII,1:1
Design for Living 1933,Ja 3,19:5
Design for Living 1933,Ja 8,IX,3:2
Design for Living 1933,Ja 25,13:2
Design for Living 1933,Ja 29,IX,1:1
Reunion in Vienna 1934,Ja 4,17:1
Reunion in Vienna 1934,Ja 28,IX,3:4
Point Valaine 1934,D 30,IX,1:6
Point Valaine 1935,Ja 17,22:2
Point Valaine 1935,F 3,VIII,1:1
Taming of the Shrew, The 1935,Ap 23,24:1
Taming of the Shrew, The 1935,S 22,X,3:2
Taming of the Shrew, The 1935,S 29,X,3:1
Taming of the Shrew, The 1935,O 1,27:3
Taming of the Shrew, The 1935,O 20,X,1:1
Idiot's Delight 1936,Mr 10,26:7
Idiot's Delight 1936,Mr 25,25:2
Idiot's Delight 1936,Ap 12,IX,1:1
Idiot's Delight 1936,S 1,24:5
Amphitryon 38 1937,Je 24,30:2
Amphitryon 38 1937,N 2,32:2
Amphitryon 38 1937,N 7,XI,1:1
Amphitryon 1938,Ja 23,XI,1:6
Sea Gull, The 1938,Mr 17,16:5
Sea Gull, The 1938,Mr 29,19:2
Amphitryon 38 1938,My 18,17:2
Amphitryon 38 1938,Je 5,IX,2:6
Taming of the Shrew, The 1940,F 6,17:2
There Shall Be No Night 1940,Mr 30,11:2
There Shall Be No Night 1940,Ap 30,25:2
There Shall Be No Night 1940,My 5,X,1:1
There Shall Be No Night 1940,S 10,27:3
There Shall Be No Night 1940,S 22,IX,1:1
Pirate, The 1942,S 15,18:6
Pirate, The 1942,N 26,39:2
Pirate, The 1942,D 6,VIII,1:1
There Shall Be No Night 1943,D 16,34:5
There Shall Be No Night 1944,Ja 2,II,1:5
Love in Idleness 1944,D 22,13:2
Love in Idleness 1945,Ja 7,II,2:3
O Mistress Mine 1946,Ja 24,25:2
O Mistress Mine 1946,F 3,II,1:1
O Mistress Mine 1946,S 1,II,1:1
I Know My Love 1949,F 24,29:2
I Know My Love 1949,Ap 23,10:2
I Know My Love 1949,N 3,36:1
I Know My Love 1949,N 20,II,1:1
Quadrille 1952,Jl 17,20:4
Quadrille 1952,S 13,10:7
Quadrille 1952,O 12,II,3:7
Quadrille 1953,Ap 5,II,1:1
Qudrille 1954,N 4,39:2
Quadrille 1954,N 14,II,1:1
Great Sebastians, The 1956,Ja 5,27:1
Great Sebastians, The 1956,Ja 15,II,1:1
Visit, The 1958,My 6,40:1
Visit, The 1958,My 18,II,1:1
Visit, The 1958,S 7,II,1:1
Visit, The 1958,N 16,II,1:1
Visit, The 1960,Mr 9,38:3
Visit, The 1960,Je 25,13:5
Fontanne, Lynn (Miscellaneous)
Taming of the Shrew, The 1935,O 1,27:3

Idiot's Delight 1936,Mr 10,26:7
Amphitryon 38 1937,N 2,32:2
Taming of the Shrew, The 1940,F 6,17:2
Fontanne, Lynn (Producer)
Point Valaine 1935,Ja 17,22:2
Idiot's Delight 1936,Mr 25,25:2
Amphitryon 38 1937,Je 24,30:2
Amphitryon 38 1937,N 2,32:2
Fonte, Adriana
Processo dei Veleni, Il; Case of Poisons, The
1935,Ja 21,18:2
Due Orfanelle, Le; Two Orphans, The
1936,O 5,24:4
Fontenay, Catherine
Moloch 1929,Ja 27,IX,2:8
Fooshee, Gladys
Red Pepper 1922,My 30,8:3
Fooshee, Sybil
Red Pepper 1922,My 30,8:3
Fooshee Sisters
Passing Show of 1922, The 1922,S 21,18:2
Foote, Courtenay
Lady Cristilinda, The 1922,D 26,11:2
Foote, Dick
Three Wishes for Jamie 1952,Mr 22,9:2
Foote, Donald (Costume Designer)
Athenian Touch, The 1964,Ja 15,25:4
Subject Was Roses, The 1964,My 26,45:1
Foote, Gene
Sweet Charity 1966,Ja 31,22:1
Foote, Horton
Coggerers, The 1939,Ja 21,18:4
Mr Banks of Birmingham 1939,Ja 21,18:4
Red Velvet Goat, The 1939,Ja 21,18:4
Texas Town 1941,Ap 30,22:3
Foote, Horton (Director)
Out of My House 1942,Ja 8,28:6
Foote, Horton (Playwright)
Texas Town 1941,Ap 30,22:3
Out of My House 1942,Ja 8,28:6
Only the Heart 1942,D 7,22:3
Only the Heart 1944,Ap 5,17:2
Celebration 1948,Ap 12,24:2
Chase, The 1952,Ap 16,30:2
Trip to Bountiful, The 1953,N 4,30:3
Trip to Bountiful, The 1953,N 15,II,1:1
Traveling Lady 1954,O 28,45:2
Trip to Bountiful, The 1956,Jl 5,25:1
Midnight Caller, The 1958,Jl 2,25:1
John Turner Davis 1958,Jl 2,25:1
Trip to Bountiful, The 1959,F 27,20:4
Foote, John Taintor (Original Author)
Julie the Great 1936,Ja 15,15:3
Foote, John Taintor (Playwright)
Tight Britches 1934,S 12,26:2
Julie the Great 1936,Ja 15,15:3
Foote, Sterling
Prunella 1929,Ap 10,23:3
Foote, Tom Brooks
Out of My House 1942,Ja 8,28:6
Footlight Players
Recruiting Officer, The 1937,N 27,20:3
Footner, Hulbert (Playwright)
Open Fire, The 1921,Ag 21,VI,1:8
Foran, Arthur
He Who Gets Slapped 1946,Mr 21,31:4
Mr Peebles and Mr Hooker 1946,O 11,29:2
Foran, Dick
Connecticut Yankee, A 1943,N 18,30:2
Foran, Edward J (Playwright)
Privilege Car 1931,Mr 4,33:1
Foran, J F
What a Relief 1935,D 14,10:6
Foran, Tom
Vaudeville (Hippodrome) 1926,My 4,31:2
Foran, William
Florida Girl 1925,N 3,34:1
Wisdom Tooth, The 1926,F 16,22:2
Broadway 1926,S 17,19:3
Front Page, The 1928,Ag 15,19:2
Remote Control 1929,S 11,24:5
Up and Up, The 1930,S 9,25:2
Overture 1930,N 25,31:2
Overture 1930,D 8,26:4
Privilege Car 1931,Mr 4,33:1
Both Your Houses 1933,Mr 7,20:3
Double Door 1933,S 22,15:5
Drums Begin, The 1933,N 25,10:5
Mahogany Hall 1934,Ja 18,18:5
Milky Way, The 1934,My 9,23:2
Kill That Story 1934,Ag 30,22:2
Call Me Ziggy 1937,F 13,9:6
Excursion 1937,Ap 10,11:4
One Thing After Another 1937,D 29,17:2
Schoolhouse on the Lot 1938,Mr 23,18:4
Knights of Song 1938,O 18,29:2
Window Shopping 1938,D 24,13:2
Family Portrait 1939,Mr 9,18:4
Johnny on the Spot 1942,Ja 9,24:2
They Should Have Stood in Bed 1942,F 14,18:5
Three Men on a Horse 1942,O 10,10:2
Innocent Voyage, The 1943,N 16,27:2
Pick-Up Girl 1944,My 4,25:2

Forber, Martha
Three Little Girls 1930,Ap 15,29:1
Forbes, Ben
Girl in the Spotlight, The 1920,Jl 13,9:3
Forbes, Brenda
Barretts of Wimpole Street, The 1931,F 10,25:1
Lucrece 1932,D 21,22:2
Lucrece 1933,Ja 1,IX,1:1
Party, A 1933,Ag 24,18:4
Romeo and Juliet 1934,D 21,30:3
Barretts of Wimpole Street, The 1935,F 26,16:2
Flowers of the Forest 1935,Ap 9,25:2
Pride and Prejudice 1935,N 6,32:4
Black Limelight 1936,N 10,31:1
Storm Over Patsy 1937,Mr 9,26:4
Yr Obedient Husband 1938,Ja 11,26:5
Save Me the Waltz 1938,Mr 1,19:2
Heartbreak House 1938,Ap 30,18:2
One for the Money 1939,F 6,9:2
Two for the Show 1940,F 9,14:2
Yesterday's Magic 1942,Ap 15,27:2
Morning Star, The 1942,S 15,18:4
Morning Star, The 1942,S 20,VIII,1:1
Suds in Your Eye 1944,Ja 13,15:5
Barretts of Wimpole Street, The 1945,Mr 27,23:6
Barretts of Wimpole Street, The 1945,Ap 1,II,1:1
Candida 1945,Ag 7,25:3
Three to Make Ready 1946,Mr 8,16:2
ANTA Album 1950,Ja 30,13:2
Ring Around the Moon 1950,N 24,30:1
Qudrille 1954,N 4,39:2
Quadrille 1954,N 14,II,1:1
Medea 1955,Je 16,35:4
Reluctant Debutante, The 1956,O 11,50:1
Loves of Cass McGuire, The 1966,O 7,36:1
Darling of the Day 1968,Ja 29,26:2
Forbes, Charlotte
Oedipus 1970,F 23,30:1
Forbes, Edward
Assumption of Hannele, The 1924,F 16,16:2
Master of the Inn, The 1925,D 23,22:2
Schweiger 1926,Mr 24,20:4
Black Cockatoo, The 1926,D 31,11:1
King Can Do No Wrong, The 1927,N 17,28:4
False Dreams, Farewell 1934,Ja 16,18:3
Hipper's Holiday 1934,O 19,26:2
Crime and Punishment 1935,Ja 23,20:3
American Holiday 1936,F 22,13:3
Class of '29 1936,My 16,10:3
Help Yourself! 1936,Jl 15,15:1
On the Rocks 1938,Je 16,20:2
Cue for Passion 1940,D 20,33:4
Sons and Soldiers 1943,My 5,22:2
Jeb 1946,F 22,20:2
Forbes, Esther (Original Author)
Come Summer 1969,Mr 19,43:1
Forbes, G A
Madame X 1927,Jl 7,29:3
Forbes, Hazel
Rosalie 1928,Ja 11,26:3
Simple Simon 1930,F 19,22:1
Forbes, Henry (Director)
Wild Duck, The 1938,Ap 16,16:5
Forbes, Henry (Producer)
Tin Pan Alley 1928,N 2,29:1
Schoolgirl 1930,N 21,31:1
Intimate Relations 1932,Mr 29,23:2
Thunder on the Left 1933,N 1,25:2
Wild Duck, The 1938,Ap 16,16:5
Forbes, James (Director)
Cock o' the Roost 1924,O 14,23:1
Young Blood 1925,N 25,15:1
Forbes, James (Playwright)
Endless Chain, The 1922,S 5,21:2
Young Blood 1925,N 25,15:1
Young Blood 1925,N 29,VIII,1:1
Final Fling, The 1928,O 7,IX,2:3
Precious 1929,Ja 15,22:5
Matrimony, PFD 1936,N 6,28:4
Matrimony, PFD 1936,N 13,26:3
Forbes, Jane
Walking Gentleman, The 1942,My 8,26:2
Forbes, Juliet
Stage Door 1936,O 23,26:3
Young Couple Wanted 1940,Ja 25,16:2
Forbes, Kathryn (Original Author)
I Remember Mama 1944,O 20,16:2
I Remember Mama 1944,O 29,II,1:1
Forbes, Kenneth
Junior Miss 1941,N 19,28:2
Winged Victory 1943,N 22,24:1
Naughty-Naught '00 1946,O 21,27:5
I Gotta Get Out 1947,S 26,27:2
At War With the Army 1949,Mr 9,32:2
Forbes, Leon
As You Like It 1945,Jl 4,10:4
Mermaids Singing, The 1945,N 29,26:6
Forbes, Mary
Merton of the Movies 1922,N 14,16:2
Trelawney of the 'Wells' 1925,Je 2,16:2
Sport of Kings, The 1926,My 5,24:2
Silver Box, The 1928,Ja 18,23:1
Tomorrow and Tomorrow 1931,Ja 14,26:3

Victoria Regina 1935,D 27,15:2
Tovarich 1937,Ap 25,X,2:4
Forbes, Meriel
Millionairess, The 1952,Je 28,12:2
Waltz of the Toreadors, The 1957,Ja 18,17:2
Waltz of the Toreadors, The 1957,Ja 27,II,1:1
School for Scandal, The 1963,Ja 26,5:2
Forbes, Myra
Deep Mrs Sykes, The 1945,Mr 20,22:6
Forbes, Norman
Shall We Join the Ladies? 1921,Je 26,VI,1:1
Twelfth Night 1927,Je 12,VII,2:1
Twelfth Night 1932,Ag 7,IX,1:6
Forbes, Ralph
Havoc 1924,S 2,22:2
Magnolia Lady, The 1924,N 26,17:2
Little Minister, The 1925,Mr 24,21:1
Man With a Load of Mischief, The 1925,O 27,20:1
Man With a Load of Mischief, The
1925,N 1,VIII,1:1
Stronger Than Love 1925,D 29,20:2
Let Us Divorce; Counsel's Opinion
1932,Ap 17,VIII,2:6
Doctor's Dilemma, The 1941,F 18,26:6
Doctor's Dilemma, The 1941,Mr 12,18:2
Hedda Gabler 1942,Ja 30,22:2
Kiss for Cinderella, A 1942,Mr 11,22:2
Highland Fling, A 1944,Ap 29,13:2
Visitor, The 1944,O 18,24:5
Second Best Bed 1946,Je 4,20:2
You Never Can Tell 1948,Mr 17,31:2
Caesar and Cleopatra 1949,D 22,28:2
Getting Married 1950,Je 14,41:2
Forbes, Ralph (Director)
Anybody Home 1949,F 26,10:5
Forbes, Scott
Horses in Midstream 1953,Ap 3,18:7
Burning Glass, The 1954,Mr 5,15:2
Burning Glass, The 1954,Mr 14,II,1:1
Lover, The 1963,S 19,21:1
Forbes-Robertson, Jean
Berkeley Square 1926,O 7,19:6
Berkeley Square 1926,O 24,VIII,2:1
Romeo and Juliet 1927,Ja 2,VII,2:5
Dybbuk, The 1927,My 1,VIII,2:7
Twelfth Night 1927,Je 12,VII,2:1
Peter Pan 1928,Ja 15,VIII,4:6
Berkeley, Square 1929,Mr 24,X,4:5
Little Eyolf 1930,N 2,VIII,2:6
Object of Virtue, An 1930,N 5,28:3
Object of Virtue, An 1930,N 23,IX,2:4
Hedda Gabler 1931,Ap 5,VIII,4:1
Dark Hester 1931,My 17,VIII,1:3
Measure for Measure 1931,Ag 9,VIII,1:3
Twelfth Night 1932,Ag 7,IX,1:6
As You Desire Me 1934,O 2,18:3
As You Desire Me 1934,O 28,IX,3:4
Promise 1936,D 31,20:4
Forbes-Robertson, Jean (Producer)
As You Desire Me 1934,O 2,18:3
Forbes-Robertson, Johnston (Sir)
Twelfth Night 1927,Je 12,VII,2:1
Force, Joan
Still Life 1967,My 4,34:1
Ways and Means 1967,My 4,34:1
Fumed Oak 1967,My 4,34:1
Ford, Barbara
John Brown's Body 1953,F 16,17:2
Show Boat 1954,My 6,44:1
Ford, Bette
First Lady 1952,My 29,18:5
Ford, Bill
Vaudeville (Palace) 1932,O 3,15:5
Ford, Cadet
Merry Wives of West Point, The 1932,Mr 20,II,7:7
Ford, Carl
Black Nativity 1961,D 12,54:2
Ford, Ciel
Me and Harry 1942,Ap 3,24:6
Ford, Clebert
Cool World, The 1960,F 23,38:2
Romeo and Juliet 1961,F 24,24:1
Ballad for Bimshire 1963,O 16,54:1
Blancs, Les 1970,N 16,48:4
Blancs, Les 1970,N 29,II,3:5
Blancs, Les 1970,N 29,II,3:1
Ford, Constance
Death of a Salesman 1949,F 11,27:2
See the Jaguar 1952,D 4,46:2
Say Darling 1958,Ap 4,17:1
Say Darling 1958,Ap 13,II,1:1
Golden Fleecing 1959,O 16,24:5
Nobody Loves an Albatross 1963,D 20,20:1
Nobody Loves an Albatross 1964,Ja 5,II,1:1
Utbu 1966,Ja 5,24:1
Ford, Corey (Lyricist)
Old King's 1924,Mr 12,19:3
Ford, Corey (Playwright)
Half Moon Inn 1923,Mr 21,19:2
Old King's 1924,Mr 12,19:3
Half Moon Inn 1925,Mr 10,14:1
Three's a Crowd 1930,O 5,IX,4:6
Hold Your Horses 1933,Ag 31,20:4

Ford, Corey (Playwright)—Cont
Hold Your Horses 1933,S 26,26:4
Ford, David
Billy Budd 1955,My 4,35:1
Mary Stuart 1957,O 9,39:1
Journey With Strangers, A 1958,N 27,53:1
Sign of Jonah, The 1960,S 9,35:1
Marcus in the High Grass 1960,N 22,38:6
Vagrant, The 1962,F 16,35:2
Witch, The 1962,F 16,35:2
Abe Lincoln in Illinois 1963,Ja 23,5:2
White Rose and the Red, The 1964,Mr 17,31:1
Physicists, The 1964,O 14,52:1
Tea Party 1968,O 16,40:1
Tea Party 1968,N 3,II,7:4
1776 1969,Mr 17,46:2
Ford, Della
Doctor Faustus 1937,Ja 9,21:2
Ford, Dora
Vaudeville (Palace) 1924,S 16,26:5
Ford, Earl
Peace on Earth 1933,N 30,39:2
Ford, Ed
Vaudeville (Palace) 1924,S 16,26:5
Vaudeville (Palace) 1929,N 4,29:1
Ford, Edith
Cornered 1920,D 9,18:2
Ford, Frances
Hold Your Horses 1933,S 26,26:4
Sacco-Vanzetti 1969,F 9,78:1
Ford, Frank
Los Angeles 1927,D 20,32:3
Precedent 1931,Ap 15,24:5
Come Marching Home 1946,My 20,18:6
Wild Duck, The 1951,O 27,17:1
Drink to Me Only 1958,O 9,47:4
Ford, Frank (Miscellaneous)
Lazarus Laughed 1948,Ap 9,27:4
Ford, Frank (Producer)
Catch Me if You Can 1965,Mr 10,50:1
Sherry! 1967,Mr 29,39:1
Ford, Frederick (Playwright)
Food for Midas 1942,Ja 31,12:7
Ford, Friendly
House of Connelly, The 1931,S 29,22:4
1931 1931,D 11,34:3
Night Over Taos 1932,Mr 10,25:3
Ford, Gene
George White's Scandals 1921,Jl 12,14:1
Ford, George (Playwright)
Miss Gulliver Travels 1931,N 26,36:4
Ford, George (Producer)
Dearest Enemy 1925,S 19,9:2
Miss Gulliver Travels 1931,N 26,36:4
Ford, Gwyllyn
Soliloquy 1938,N 29,26:4
Ford, Harriet (Playwright)
Wrong Number, The 1921,Jl 17,VI,1:8
Main Street 1921,Jl 24,VI,1:1
Main Street 1921,O 6,21:1
In the Next Room 1923,O 3,15:3
In the Next Room 1923,N 28,14:1
Sweet Seventeen 1924,Mr 18,24:2
In the Next Room 1924,Je 7,16:5
Ford, Harry Chapman (Playwright)
Anna Ascends 1920,S 23,14:1
Eve's Leaves 1925,Mr 27,22:2
Shelter 1926,Ja 26,18:2
Ebb Tide 1931,Je 9,33:6
Ford, Helen
Always You 1920,Ja 6,18:2
Sweetheart Shop, The 1920,S 1,13:4
For Goodness Sake 1922,F 22,13:1
Gingham Girl, The 1922,Ag 29,15:5
Helen of Troy, New York 1923,Je 20,22:6
No Other Girl 1924,Ag 14,10:4
Dearest Enemy 1925,S 19,9:2
Peggy-Ann 1926,D 28,16:3
Peggy-Ann 1927,Jl 3,VII,1:1
Chee-Chee 1928,S 26,25:1
Patsy, The 1929,Ja 6,VIII,1:4
Vaudeville (Palace) 1929,D 23,19:1
Other One, The 1932,O 4,26:3
Champagne, Sec 1933,O 16,20:2
Chimes of Corneville, The 1934,Je 29,16:2
Patsy, The 1935,Jl 16,24:1
Patience 1935,S 3,24:4
Mariette 1937,Je 29,18:3
Great Lady 1938,D 2,26:6
Retreat to Pleasure 1940,D 18,32:2
Rivals, The 1941,N 18,32:2
Rivals, The 1942,Ja 15,24:2
Ford, Hugh (Director)
Diana 1929,D 10,37:1
Budget, The 1932,S 21,26:4
Ford, Hugh (Miscellaneous)
Diana 1929,D 10,37:1
Ford, Hugh (Playwright)
Bunch and Judy, The 1922,N 12,VIII,1:6
Bunch and Judy, The 1922,N 29,20:1
It Makes a Difference 1928,Ja 22,VIII,4:7
Ford, Hugh (Producer)
Budget, The 1932,S 21,26:4

Ford, James T
Gingham Girl, The 1922,Ag 29,15:5
Zeno 1923,Ag 27,14:2
What Women Do? 1925,Jl 21,26:4
Black Boy 1926,O 7,30:2
Within the Law 1928,Mr 6,20:1
Getting Even 1929,Ag 20,31:1
Crooks' Convention, The 1929,S 19,37:4
Damn Your Honor 1929,D 31,14:3
Privilege Car 1931,Mr 4,33:1
Man on Stilts, The 1931,S 10,23:2
Ford, Jean
Romantic Age, The 1922,N 15,22:1
Ford, Joan (Lyricist)
Goldilocks 1958,O 13,33:1
Ford, John
New Girl in Town 1957,My 15,40:1
Gazebo, The 1958,D 13,2:7
Ford, John (Playwright)
'Tis Pity She's a Whore 1926,Ja 24,VII,1:3
'Tis Pity She's a Whore 1934,My 13,IX,2:2
'Tis Pity She's a Whore 1958,D 6,21:1
Broken Heart, The 1962,Jl 10,28:2
Witch of Edmonton, The 1962,N 23,32:2
'Tis Pity She's a Whore 1967,O 21,15:2
Ford, John (Producer)
What Price Glory 1949,Mr 3,33:2
Ford, Judith
Lady Comes Across, The 1942,Ja 10,10:2
Ford, Larkin
Othello 1955,S 8,27:2
Henry IV, Part I 1955,S 22,34:2
Ford, Lester
Much Ado About Nothing 1927,N 19,14:6
Ford, Mabel
Vaudeville (Palace) 1922,F 14,21:1
Vaudeville (Hippodrome) 1924,Ap 1,18:1
Ford, Marjorie
Blossom Time 1938,D 27,12:2
Ford, Melbourne
But for the Grace of God 1937,Ja 13,21:4
Straw Hat, The 1937,D 31,8:2
Dance Night 1938,O 15,20:5
Medicine Show 1940,Ap 13,20:6
Ford, Montgomery (Producer)
Devil Takes a Bride, The 1938,O 8,10:3
Passenger to Bali, A 1940,Mr 15,26:2
Ford, Nancy (Composer)
Now Is the Time for all Good Men 1967,S 27,42:1
Last Sweet Days of Isaac, The 1970,Ja 27,49:1
Last Sweet Days of Isaac, The 1970,F 8,II,1:6
Ford, Nancy (Miscellaneous)
Now Is the Time for all Good Men 1967,S 27,42:1
Now Is the Time for All Good Men 1967,O 27,49:1
Ford, Paul
Decision 1944,F 3,23:2
War President 1944,Ap 25,17:3
Lower North 1944,Ag 26,15:4
Kiss Them for Me 1945,Mr 21,27:2
Flamingo Road 1946,Mr 20,18:2
Another Part of the Forest 1946,N 21,42:2
As We Forgive Our Debtors 1947,Mr 11,37:2
Command Decision 1947,O 2,30:2
Brass Ring, The 1952,Ap 11,19:2
Teahouse of the August Moon, The 1953,O 16,32:1
Teahouse of the August Moon, The
1953,O 25,II,1:1
Teahouse of the August Moon, The 1954,S 12,II,1:1
Good as Gold 1957,Mr 8,22:2
Whoop-Up 1958,D 23,2:7
Thurber Carnival, A 1960,F 27,13:2
Thurber Carnival, A 1960,Mr 6,II,1:1
Never Too Late 1962,N 28,42:1
3 Bags Full 1966,Mr 7,22:1
What Did We Do Wrong? 1967,O 23,56:1
What Did We Do Wrong? 1967,N 12,II,5:6
What Did We Do Wrong? 1967,N 19,II,1:1
Three Men on a Horse 1969,O 17,35:1
Ford, Pearl
Women at the Tomb, The 1961,Ap 25,41:1
Ford, Phyllis
Russell Patterson's Sketch-Book 1960,F 8,35:1
Ford, Richard
Peg o' My Dreams 1924,My 6,25:3
Grand Street Follies, The 1928,My 29,16:2
Ford, Robert
Caesar and Cleopatra 1935,Ag 22,21:1
Ford, Ruth
Shoemaker's Holiday, The 1938,Ja 3,17:2
Danton's Death 1938,N 3,26:2
Swingin' the Dream 1939,N 30,24:2
No Exit 1946,N 27,21:1
This Time Tomorrow 1947,N 4,31:2
Clutterbuck 1949,D 5,29:2
House of Bernarda Alba, The 1951,Ja 8,14:6
Island of Goats 1955,O 5,40:1
Stronger, The 1956,F 22,23:2
Miss Julie 1956,F 22,23:2
Miss Julie 1956,Mr 4,II,1:1
Requiem for a Nun 1959,Ja 31,13:2
Requiem for a Nun 1959,F 8,II,1:1
Milk Train Doesn't Stop Here Anymore, The
1964,Ja 2,33:1

Lovey 1965,Mr 26,27:1
Dinner at Eight 1966,S 28,38:1
Ninety Day Mistress, The 1967,N 7,49:1
Ford, Ruth Thea
Walking Gentleman, The 1942,My 8,26:2
Ford, Saville T
This Mad Whirl 1937,Ja 10,II,4:8
Ford, Simon (Producer)
Marigold 1930,O 9,23:1
Ford, Stanley
Sally, Irene and Mary 1922,S 5,21:2
Ford, Stephen
Out of This World 1955,N 10,44:2
Ford, Sylvia
Love Birds 1921,Mr 16,12:1
Ford, Thomas
Caesar and Cleopatra 1935,Ag 22,21:1
Ford, Vernon
Natural Man 1941,My 8,20:4
Ford, Wallace
Poppy God, The 1921,Ag 30,10:1
Broken Branches 1922,Mr 7,11:1
Nobody's Business 1923,O 23,17:1
Gypsy Jim 1924,Ja 15,17:4
Nancy Ann 1924,Ap 1,18:1
Pigs 1924,S 2,22:5
Lambs Gambol 1925,Ap 27,15:1
Gypsy 1929,Ja 15,22:2
Nut Farm, The 1929,O 15,34:3
Of Mice and Men 1937,N 24,20:5
Of Mice and Men 1937,D 12,XI,3:1
Of Mice and Men 1938,Ja 23,XI,1:6
Kindred 1939,D 27,17:2
What Price Glory 1949,Mr 3,33:2
Ford and Price
Vaudeville (Palace) 1924,F 19,12:1
Vaudeville (Palace) 1929,D 9,33:2
Forde, Edmund
Tyrants 1924,Mr 5,14:1
Way of the World, The 1924,N 18,23:4
Wild Birds 1925,Ap 10,16:1
Polly 1925,O 12,19:1
Caravan 1928,Ag 30,13:3
Singing Jailbirds 1928,D 5,34:4
Airways, Inc 1929,F 21,30:5
Forde, Hal
Honeydew 1920,S 7,20:1
Molly Darling 1922,S 2,10:2
Hassard Short's Ritz Revue 1924,S 18,19:1
Oh, Ernest! 1927,My 10,24:3
Houseboat on the Styx, The 1928,D 16,IX,2:1
Houseboat on the Styx, The 1928,D 26,14:3
Wonderful Night, A; Fledermaus, Die
1929,N 1,23:3
Merry Widow, The 1931,S 8,39:1
Chocolate Soldier, The 1931,S 22,33:3
As Thousands Cheer 1933,O 2,22:1
George White's Scandals 1935,D 26,20:2
Forde, Hal (Composer)
19th Hole, The 1927,O 12,30:3
Forde, Marvin
Pick-Up Girl 1944,My 4,25:2
Forde, Stanley
Jim Jam Jems 1920,O 5,13:2
Green Ring, The 1922,Ap 5,22:1
Princess April 1924,D 2,23:2
Mikado, The 1925,Ap 13,25:1
Castles in the Air 1926,S 7,19:2
Fordred, Dorice
Payment Deferred 1931,O 1,24:2
Sleeping Clergyman, A 1933,O 8,X,2:4
Fordrung, Rita
Hero of Santa Maria, The 1926,My 1,10:1
Fordyce, Miss (Playwright)
Corps a Corps 1932,O 30,IX,3:8
Foreman, Edward
Young Sinners 1929,N 29,24:4
Foreman, Richard (Miscellaneous)
Butterfly Dream, The 1966,My 20,41:1
Forer, Daniel (Lighting Director)
Cabin in the Sky 1964,Ja 22,32:1
Forer, Daniel (Miscellaneous)
Blue Boy in Black, The 1963,My 1,32:1
Forest, Anne
Black Cockatoo, The 1926,D 31,11:1
Forest, Janeen
Patrick--The First 1965,F 19,25:1
Forest, John
Merchant of Venice, The 1930,Mr 27,24:7
Taming of the Shrew, The 1930,Mr 28,22:8
King Lear 1930,Ap 1,34:6
As You Like It 1930,Ap 3,32:5
Julius Caesar 1930,Ap 4,22:3
Forest, Louis (Playwright)
Procureur Hallers, Le 1924,N 13,18:1
Forest, Peter
Romeo and Juliet 1962,F 14,39:1
Forester, C S (Original Author)
Payment Deferred 1931,O 1,24:2
Forester, C S (Playwright)
Nurse Cavell 1934,Ap 1,X,1:7
Forester, R (Scenic Designer)
Chivalry 1925,D 16,22:3

Forester, William
Johnny 2X4 1942,Mr 17,24:6
Savonarola 1942,Ap 24,20:2
Petrified Forest, The 1943,N 2,30:6
Signature 1945,F 15,25:2
Detective Story 1954,F 13,11:2
Foret, Lilas
Salome 1922,My 23,12:4
Forgan, J R
They Never Come Back 1920,D 19,I,22:3
Forgie, Heather
Jack and the Beanstalk 1947,N 3,28:2
Forgie, Hugh
Laugh, Town, Laugh! 1942,Je 23,22:2
Ice Capades 1953,S 11,25:1
Ice Capades 1954,S 16,37:1
Ice Capades 1955,S 15,38:1
Ice Capades 1956,S 13,41:2
Ice Capades 1957,S 5,33:2
Ice Capades 1963,Ag 29,37:2
Ice Capades 1964,Ag 27,27:2
Forgie & Larson
Ice Capades 1952,S 12,18:1
Ice Capades 1958,S 4,33:2
Forgues, Jean Jus (Miscellaneous)
Lettre Morte 1970,Ap 16,55:1
Architruc 1970,Ap 16,55:1
Forhan, Diane (Choreographer)
Tempest, The 1960,Je 20,35:1
Forhan, Diane (Director)
Tableaux 1961,D 18,41:3
Forkins, Marty (Producer)
Brown Buddies 1930,O 8,29:1
Forkum, Debner
Bridal Crown, The 1938,F 7,11:2
Forlow, Ted
Hit the Deck 1960,Je 24,32:1
To Broadway With Love 1964,Ap 30,28:6
Forman, Arthur Ed
Tango 1969,Ja 20,33:1
Forman, Frederic
Damn Your Honor 1929,D 31,14:3
Money in the Air 1932,Mr 8,19:3
Whatever Possessed Her 1934,Ja 26,21:2
Curse You, Jack Dalton 1935,Jl 16,24:1
Forman, Hilda
America's Sweetheart 1931,F 11,23:1
Forman, Kathie
Body Beautiful, The 1958,Ja 24,15:2
Forman, Lou
Vaudeville (Palace) 1931,My·25,17:4
Forman, Lou (Musical Director)
Vaudeville (Palace) 1930,S 15,29:2
Priorities of 1942 1942,Mr 13,23:2
Forman, Lou and His Orchestra
Vaudeville (Palace) 1929,F 11,26:2
Forman, Louise
America's Sweetheart 1931,F 11,23:1
Forman, Lynn
Devil's Advocate, The 1961,Mr 10,20:1
Forman, Maxine
America's Sweetheart 1931,F 11,23:1
Forman, Milton
If Booth Had Missed 1931,My 14,27:1
Forman, Norman (Miscellaneous)
Girl of the Golden West, The 1957,N 6,44:1
Forman, Norman (Producer)
Comic Strip 1958,My 15,26:2
King of the Whole Damn World 1962,Ap 16,32:2
Forman, Terry
Penny Friend, The 1966,D 27,46:1
Forman, William
Tomorrow's a Holiday! 1935,D 31,10:2
Forman Sisters
Vanities 1931,Ag 16,VIII,1:1
Formes, Carl
Eternal Road, The 1937,Ja 8,14:2
Formosa, Daniel (Dr)
Veronica's Veil 1950,F 12,II,1:5
Fornadel, Jeanne
Sea Gull, The 1956,O 23,38:1
Fornes, Maria Irene (Costume Designer)
Only a Countess May Dance When She's Crazy
(An Almost Historical Camp) 1968,Mr 19,41:1
Last Triangle, The (An Embroidered Camp)
1968,Mr 19,41:1
Fornes, Maria Irene (Lyricist)
Promenade 1969,Je 5,56:1
Promenade 1969,Je 15,II,1:1
Fornes, Maria Irene (Playwright)
Promenade 1969,Je 5,56:1
Forness, Cameron
Petticoat Fever 1937,Mr 21,II,7:3
Forno, Rosemarie
Lovers in the Metro, The 1962,Ja 31,21:1
Forrai, Miss
Abie's Irish Rose 1928,Je 10,VIII,2:8
Forrest, Alma
Big White Fog 1940,O 23,26:2
Forrest, Anne
Quicksand 1928,F 14,26:3
Gang War 1928,Ag 21,27:2
Carnival 1929,Ap 25,32:5

Forrest, Anne—Cont
Sweet Land of Liberty 1929,S 24,29:2
Channel Road, The 1929,O 18,24:2
Channel Road, The 1929,O 27,IX,1:1
Frankie and Johnny 1930,S 26,16:5
Anatol 1931,Ja 17,23:3
Enemy Within 1931,O 6,35:3
Roof, The 1931,O 31,22:4
Roof, The 1931,N 8,VIII,1:1
Forrest, Arthur
Carolinian, The 1925,N 3,34:2
Forrest, Belford (Playwright)
Lost Sheep 1930,My 6,33:2
Forrest, Fred
And Be My Love 1934,Ja 19,25:2
Viet Rock 1966,N 11,38:1
Futz 1968,Je 14,39:1
Silhouettes 1969,S 9,41:1
Forrest, George (Composer)
Song of Norway 1944,Ag 22,20:2
Song of Norway 1944,Ag 27,II,1:1
Kismet 1953,D 4,2:4
Song of Norway 1958,Je 23,19:2
At the Grand 1958,Ag 13,24:3
Song of Norway 1959,Je 26,16:2
Kean 1961,N 3,28:2
Kean 1961,N 12,II,1:1
Kismet 1965,Je 23,45:1
Anya 1965,N 30,48:1
Forrest, George (Director)
Gypsy Lady 1946,S 18,25:6
Forrest, George (Lyricist)
Song of Norway 1944,Ag 22,20:2
Song of Norway 1944,Ag 27,II,1:1
Gypsy Lady 1946,S 18,25:6
Magdalena 1948,S 21,31:2
Magdalena 1948,S 26,II,1:1
Kismet 1953,D 4,2:4
At the Grand 1958,Ag 13,24:3
Song of Norway 1959,Je 26,16:2
Kean 1961,N 3,28:2
Kean 1961,N 12,II,1:1
Kismet 1965,Je 23,45:1
Anya 1965,N 30,48:1
Forrest, George (Miscellaneous)
Magdalena 1948,S 21,31:2
Forrest, George (Playwright)
Love Doctor, The 1959,O 14,52:4
Forrest, Helen
Swords 1921,S 2,9:3
Forrest, Ingrid
Under the Counter 1947,O 4,10:2
Forrest, Iris
Tartuffe 1957,O 9,39:1
Forrest, Iris (Miscellaneous)
Night of the Auk 1963,My 22,35:2
Forrest, Iris (Producer)
Night of the Auk 1963,My 22,35:2
Forrest, Joan
Women of Twilight 1952,Mr 4,22:2
Forrest, John
Richard III 1930,Mr 31,24:1
King Lear 1930,D 26,18:2
Merchant of Venice, The 1931,N 17,31:1
Julius Caesar 1931,N 18,26:3
Hamlet 1931,N 19,26:6
Forrest, Marguerite
We Girls 1921,N 10,26:3
Steamship Tenacity 1922,Ja 3,20:2
Voltaire 1922,Mr 21,17:1
Sancho Panza 1923,N 27,23:1
Treat 'Em Rough 1926,O 5,26:2
Forrest, Mary
Bagels and Yox 1951,S 13,38:2
Forrest, Mary (Director)
Spellbound 1927,F 16,17:2
Forrest, Mary (Producer)
Friend Indeed 1926,Ap 27,22:3
Spellbound 1927,F 16,17:2
One Shot Fired 1927,N 8,32:5
Forrest, Michael
Hostage, The 1960,S 21,42:1
Forrest, Milton Earl
David Show, The 1968,N 1,34:2
Forrest, Miranee
Jack and the Beanstalk 1947,N 3,28:2
Forrest, Paul
Jimmy 1969,O 24,38:1
Forrest, Sam (Director)
Acquittal, The 1920,Ja 6,18:2
Acquittal, The 1920,Ja 11,VIII,2:1
Hero, The 1921,Mr 20,VI,1:1
Cradle Snatchers 1925,S 8,28:2
Paid 1925,N 26,32:1
Virgin, The 1926,F 23,26:1
We Americans 1926,O 13,20:4
Gentle Grafters 1926,O 28,23:1
Gossipy Sex, The 1927,Ap 20,28:3
Baby Cyclone, The 1927,S 13,37:4
My Princess 1927,O 7,24:2
19th Hole, The 1927,O 12,30:3
Los Angeles 1927,D 20,32:3
Whispering Friends 1928,F 21,18:3
Elmer the Great 1928,S 25,29:1

By Request 1928,S 28,30:2
Billie 1928,O 2,34:2
Vermont 1929,Ja 9,28:1
Gambling 1929,Ag 27,31:2
Tavern, The 1930,My 20,32:1
Song and Dance Man, The 1930,Je 17,25:5
Rhapsody, The 1930,S 16,30:3
Friendship 1931,S 1,30:2
Pigeons and People 1933,Ja 17,22:3
Rain 1935,F 13,24:1
Seven Keys to Baldpate 1935,My 28,30:2
Dear Old Darling 1936,Mr 3,25:1
County Chairman, The 1936,My 26,26:5
Fulton of Oak Falls 1937,F 11,18:2
Return of the Vagabond, The 1940,My 14,27:2
Forrest, Sam (Playwright)
Red Light Annie 1923,Ag 22,10:3
Horse-Thief, The 1924,Ap 27,VIII,2:3
Thoroughbreds 1924,S 9,12:1
Winner Loses, The 1925,N 8,VIII,2:1
Paid 1925,N 26,32:1
Forrest, Steve
Body Beautiful, The 1958,Ja 24,15:2
Forrest, Undine
My Heart's in the Highlands 1939,Ap 14,29:2
Carnival in Flanders 1953,S 9,38:2
Catch a Star! 1955,S 7,35:2
Drink to Me Only 1958,O 9,47:4
Forrest, Velma
Nightstick 1927,N 11,20:4
Forrest, William
Day Will Come, The 1944,S 8,17:2
Eternal Cage 1945,Mr 22,19:7
Forrester, Charles
High Tor 1937,Ja 11,15:2
Star-Wagon, The 1937,S 30,18:5
Forrester, Frederick
Animal Kingdom, The 1932,Ja 13,26:4
Scorpion, The 1933,N 28,28:4
Days Without End 1934,Ja 9,19:1
Every Thursday 1934,My 11,25:5
Portrait of Gilbert 1934,D 29,11:5
Tapestry in Gray 1935,D 28,10:2
Forrester, Hugh
Dynamo 1929,F 12,22:1
Forrester, Iazzolla (Playwright)
Greatness Comes to the Maronies 1937,Ag 18,15:2
Forrester, Jack
Captain Jinks 1925,S 9,22:1
Forrester, Joseph
As You Like It 1936,Ap 24,18:4
Forrester, Lynne
Desert Incident, A 1959,Mr 25,40:1
Forrester, Ross
They Shall Not Die 1934,F 22,24:4
Love on an Island 1934,Jl 24,20:5
Jackson White 1935,Ap 22,14:6
Forsberg, Edwin
O'Brien Girl, The 1921,O 4,10:2
Marjorie 1924,Ag 12,12:2
Talk About Girls 1927,Je 15,31:3
Spook House 1930,Je 4,33:3
Forsberg, Henry
Mulatto 1935,O 25,25:2
Forsberg, Rolf
Tempest, The 1959,D 28,19:2
Forsberg, Rolf (Director)
Tempest, The 1959,D 28,19:2
Tenth of an Inch Makes the Difference, A
1962,N 13,44:1
Forsberg, Rolf (Mrs) (Producer)
Tempest, The 1959,D 28,19:2
Forsberg, Rolf (Playwright)
Tenth of an Inch Makes the Difference, A
1962,N 13,44:1
Forsberg, Rolf (Producer)
Tempest, The 1959,D 28,19:2
Forshaw, Arthur
Side-Show 1931,My 16,13:1
Forsht, John
Trojan Women, The 1938,Ja 25,24:2
Forslund, R V (Translator)
Little Eyolf 1964,Mr 17,31:1
Forsman, Harry
Seventh Heaven 1922,O 31,11:1
Gossipy Sex, The 1927,Ap 20,28:3
Julius Caesar 1927,Je 7,27:2
Little Accident 1928,O 10,32:3
Little Father of the Wilderness, The 1930,Je 3,27:1
Forsman, Henry
Trelawney of the 'Wells' 1925,Je 2,16:2
Forssen, David
Annie Get Your Gun 1966,Je 1,42:2
Forssgren, Margit
Sherlock Holmes 1953,O 31,11:2
Forst, William
Little Theatre Tournament; Sightseers
1929,My 8,34:4
Forster, E M (Original Author)
Passage to India, A 1960,Ap 21,23:1
Passage to India, A 1962,F 1,23:1
Passage to India, A 1962,F 11,II,1:1
Where Angels Fear to Tread 1963,Je 8,14:6

Forster, E M (Playwright)
Passage to E M Forster, A 1970,O 28,62:1
Forster, James
Man and Superman 1960,Ag 17,35:3
Don Juan in Hell 1960,O 4,47:3
Cicero 1961,F 9,37:2
Ticket-of-Leave Man, The 1961,D 23,15:1
Forster, John
Proposition, The 1968,Ap 20,25:3
Forster, Margaret (Miscellaneous)
Georgy 1970,F 27,26:1
Forster, Margaret (Original Author)
Georgy 1970,F 27,26:1
Forster, Peter
Pink String and Sealing Wax 1957,S 6,13:1
Forster, Robert
Mrs Dally 1965,S 25,5:7
Forster, Rudolf
Saint Joan 1924,N 9,VII,2:3
King John 1929,Je 23,VIII,2:1
Front Page, The 1929,Jl 14,IX,2:1
Kreatur, Die 1930,My 25,IX,1:8
Will Hill Be Pardoned; Wird Hill Amnestiert?
1930,Je 1,VIII,2:1
Kabale und Liebe 1931,N 1,VIII,4:2
Egmont 1932,Je 19,IX,1:3
World We Make, The 1939,N 21,19:1
Forster-Larrinaga
Constant Wife, The 1928,My 20,VIII,2:1
Forster-Larrinaga (Director)
Constant Wife, The 1928,My 20,VIII,2:1
Strictly Dishonorable 1931,Ap 12,IX,1:3
Forsyne, Ida
Malinda 1929,D 4,37:2
Emperor Jones, The 1936,Ag 11,24:6
Conjur 1938,N 1,27:2
Forsyth, Bertram (Director)
Humble, The 1926,O 14,22:2
Forsyth, James (Playwright)
Other Heart, The 1952,My 11,II,3:7
Heloise 1958,S 25,28:4
Heloise 1958,O 5,II,1:1
Emmanuel 1960,D 5,42:2
Seven Scenes for Yeni 1963,My 13,36:2
Cyrano de Bergerac 1968,Ap 26,30:1
Forsyth, Miss
Secretary Bird, The 1968,O 18,40:5
Forsyth, Richard
Cock-A-Doodle Dandy 1955,N 4,26:5
J B 1958,Ap 24,37:1
Major Barbara 1965,My 18,33:1
Forsyth, Robert
Opportunity 1920,Jl 31,5:1
Cornered 1920,D 9,18:2
Green Ring, The 1922,Ap 5,22:1
Forsythe, Charles
Twelfth Night 1954,N 10,42:2
Merchant of Venice, The 1955,F 23,23:2
Twelfth Night 1957,Ja 5,12:2
Forsythe, Charles (Director)
King Lear 1959,Ja 3,11:2
Forsythe, Charles (Miscellaneous)
Roomful of Roses, A 1955,O 18,48:1
Andorra 1963,F 11,5:5
Oh Dad, Poor Dad, Mamma's Hung You in the
Closet and I'm Feelin' So Sad 1963,Ag 28,28:2
Beekman Place 1964,O 8,50:1
Alfie 1964,D 18,27:1
Forsythe, Charles (Producer)
Flip Side, The 1968,O 11,36:1
Forsythe, Christine
Scandals 1939,Ag 29,17:2
Forsythe, Dorothy
Pirates of Penzance, The 1936,Ap 21,27:5
Forbidden Melody 1936,N 3,33:1
Forsythe, Henderson
Cellar and the Well, The 1950,D 11,30:2
Miss Lonelyhearts 1957,O 4,26:2
Enemy of the People, An 1959,F 5,24:4
Macbeth 1959,Ag 1,9:2
Fig Leaf in Her Bonnet, A 1961,Je 15,50:1
Collection, The 1962,N 27,44:1
Dark Corners 1964,My 6,43:1
Slight Ache, A 1964,D 10,62:1
Right Honourable Gentleman, The 1965,O 20,50:2
Malcolm 1966,Ja 12,29:1
Delicate Balance, A 1966,S 23,44:1
Birthday Party, The 1967,O 4,40:2
Birthday Party, The 1967,O 15,II,1:1
Harvey 1970,F 25,41:1
Engagement Baby, The 1970,My 22,40:1
Happiness Cage, The 1970,O 5,56:4
Happiness Cage, The 1970,O 11,II,1:1
Forsythe, Henderson (Director)
Cellar and the Well, The 1950,D 11,30:2
Forsythe, John
Yankee Point 1942,N 24,28:2
Yellow Jack 1944,Ap 7,23:3
It Takes Two 1947,F 4,33:4
Teahouse of the August Moon, The 1953,O 16,32:1
Teahouse of the August Moon, The
1953,O 25,II,1:1
Teahouse of the August Moon, The 1954,S 12,II,1:

Forsythe, John—Cont
Weekend 1968,Mr 14,50:2
Weekend 1968,Mr 31,II,1:1
Forsythe, John (Director)
Mister Roberts 1956,D 6,46:2
Forsythe, Lawrence
Too Many Heroes 1937,N 16,26:2
Forsythe, Melba
Du Barry 1932,N 23,15:2
Forsythe, Robert
Steamship Tenacity 1922,Ja 3,20:2
Roger Bloomer 1923,Mr 2,18:3
Bewitched 1924,O 2,26:3
Fort, Garrett (Playwright)
Jarnegan 1928,S 25,29:2
Fort, Stanley (Scenic Designer)
Mountain, The 1933,S 12,28:6
Fort, Syvilla (Choreographer)
Prodigal Son, The 1965,My 21,19:1
Ododo 1970,N 25,26:1
Fort, William
Sunrise at Campobello 1958,Ja 31,25:1
Andorra 1963,F 11,5:5
Forte, Mozelle (Costume Designer)
Ballad for Bimshire 1963,O 16,54:1
Fortelle, Victor de la (Playwright)
Demon de la Chair, Le 1927,N 20,IX,4:4
Fortello, Fredericka
To Quito and Back 1937,O 7,30:4
Fortescue, Viola
Mud Turtle, The 1925,Ag 21,8:2
Made in America 1925,O 15,27:2
Bells, The 1926,Ap 14,20:3
New York 1927,N 15,26:2
Forth, Allen
Chameleon, The 1932,Jl 19,20:4
Fortier, Bob
Me and Juliet 1953,My 29,17:1
Me and Juliet 1953,Je 7,II,1:1
Fortier, Frank
Power of Dreams, A 1958,Mr 11,33:1
Fortier, Herbert
He Loved the Ladies 1927,My 11,29:2
Atlas and Eva 1928,F 7,30:2
Fortier, Robert
Pal Joey 1952,Ja 4,17:6
Pal Joey 1952,F 17,II,13:5
Fortin, Adele
My Heart's in the Highlands 1950,F 18,8:4
Crucible, The 1953,Ja 23,15:2
Crucible, The 1953,Jl 2,20:2
Fortin, Robert
Moby Dick 1955,Ap 26,25:3
Fortis, John (Composer)
Hats Off to Ice 1944,Je 23,15:2
Icetime 1946,Je 21,20:5
Icetime 1947,My 29,28:2
Fortney, Ann
Good Night Ladies 1945,Ja 18,16:2
Fortseitz-Mendez Troupe
Elliott Murphy's Aquashow 1956,Je 20,26:2
Fortson, Carmelita
Flowers of Virtue, The 1942,F 6,22:2
Fortune, Antony
Catherine Was Great 1944,Ag 3,16:1
Fortune, Gae
Lady Detained, A 1935,Ja 10,23:3
Fortune, James
Sun and I, The 1937,F 27,9:5
Fortune, John
Swing It 1937,Jl 23,17:2
Fortune, Wallace
Firebrand, The 1924,O 16,33:1
Fortune Players
Recruiting Officer, The 1931,O 18,I,30:1
Tiara, The 1932,D 12,18:3
Fortunello
Vaudeville (Hippodrome) 1924,Mr 18,25:1
Fortunello and Cirillino
Greenwich Village Follies 1922,S 13,18:2
Vaudeville (Hippodrome) 1926,My 8,29:2
Fortus, Barry
Awakening of Spring, The 1964,My 13,50:1
Fortus, Daniel
Minnie's Boys 1970,Mr 27,27:1
Minnie's Boys 1970,Ap 5,II,3:1
Forward, Peter M (Lighting Director)
Voice of the Turtle, The 1961,Je 28,41:1
Love of Two Hours, The 1962,O 27,16:2
Forward, Peter M (Miscellaneous)
Witch, The 1962,F 16,35:2
Music Shop, The 1962,F 16,35:2
Vagrant, The 1962,F 16,35:2
Forward, Peter M (Scenic Designer)
Voice of the Turtle, The 1961,Je 28,41:1
Susan Slept Here 1961,Jl 12,35:2
Love of Two Hours, The 1962,O 27,16:2
Forza, Dario (Playwright)
Stairs, The 1927,N 8,32:7
Forzano, Giovacchino (Director)
Daughter of Iorio 1927,S 12,6:4
Forzano, Giovacchino (Playwright)
Campo di Maggio; Hundred Days 1932,F 7,III,3:7
Villa Franca 1932,Mr 17,16:5

Napoleon: The Hundred Days 1932,Ap 19,25:2
Napoleon: The Hundred Days 1932,My 8,VIII,1:3
Cabbages and Kings 1933,N 22,22:3
Hundred Days 1934,Ap 29,IX,2:3
Foshko (Scenic Designer)
Golem, The 1931,N 6,28:5
Foskett, Harry
Little Theatre Tournament; Shall We Join the Ladies? 1929,My 9,34:3
Shall We Join the Ladies? 1929,My 12,28:3
Foskett, Mary
Cradle Song 1955,D 2,32:2
Child of Fortune 1956,N 14,41:1
Foss, Jack
It Can't Happen Here 1936,O 28,30:1
Foss, John
Black Rhythm 1936,D 21,19:2
Foss, Nat
Bellamy Trial, The 1931,Ap 23,28:6
Foss, Patricia
Variations of 1940 1940,Ja 29,12:1
Foss, William (Producer)
Hamlet 1925,F 20,20:1
Fosse, Bob
Pal Joey 1961,Je 1,32:1
Pal Joey 1963,My 30,21:1
Fosse, Bob (Choreographer)
Pajama Game, The 1954,My 14,20:2
Pajama Game, The 1954,My 30,II,1:1
Damn Yankees 1955,My 6,17:1
Bells Are Ringing 1956,N 29,43:4
Bells Are Ringing 1956,N 30,18:2
New Girl in Town 1957,My 15,40:1
Pajama Game, The 1957,My 16,27:1
Pajama Game, The 1957,My 26,II,1:1
New Girl in Town 1957,My 26,II,1:1
Redhead 1959,F 6,21:1
Little Me 1962,N 19,41:3
Sweet Charity 1966,Ja 31,22:1
Sweet Charity 1967,Jl 1,13:1
Fosse, Bob (Director)
Redhead 1959,F 6,21:1
How to Succeed in Business Without Really Trying 1961,O 16,34:1
Little Me 1962,N 19,41:3
Little Me 1962,D 2,II,1:1
Sweet Charity 1966,Ja 31,22:1
Sweet Charity 1967,Jl 1,13:1
Fosse & Niles
Dance Me a Song 1950,Ja 21,10:5
Foster, Allan K (Choreographer)
Circus Princess, The 1927,Ap 26,32:2
Jumbo 1935,N 18,20:2
Foster, Allan K (Director)
Hummin' Sam 1933,Ap 10,8:8
Foster, Allan K (Producer)
Hummin' Sam 1933,Ap 10,8:8
Foster, Barry
Private Ear, The 1963,O 10,51:1
Public Eye, The 1963,O 10,51:1
Semi-Detached 1963,O 20,II,1:1
Foster, Basil
Damsel in Distress, A 1928,S 2,VII,2:1
Foster, Ben
Tableaux 1961,D 18,41:3
Foster, Beno
Annie Get Your Gun 1966,Je 1,42:2
Foster, Betsy
From Morn Till Midnight 1948,D 7,41:6
Foster, Claiborne
Ladies' Night 1920,Ag 10,10:1
Two Fellows and a Girl 1923,Jl 20,8:2
Lady Killer, The 1924,F 24,VII,2:5
Lady Killer, The 1924,Mr 13,14:2
Cheaper to Marry 1924,Ap 16,26:1
Applesauce 1924,S 7,VII,1:4
Patsy, The 1925,D 24,8:5
Sinner 1927,F 8,20:2
Trigger 1927,D 7,32:1
Vaudeville (Palace) 1928,Mr 27,30:5
Eva the Fifth 1928,Ag 29,19:3
Gypsy 1929,Ja 15,22:2
Gypsy 1929,Ja 27,IX,1:1
Other Men's Wives 1929,N 13,24:4
Marriage Recipe, The 1930,Ag 4,13:2
Vaudeville (Palace) 1930,Ag 4,13:2
Blind Mice 1930,S 7,IX,2:4
Blind Mice 1930,O 16,28:2
Widow in Green, A 1931,N 21,21:4
Foster, Claiborne (Playwright)
Pretty Little Parlor 1944,Ap 18,24:8
Foster, Clarence Q
Caukey 1944,F 18,15:4
Foster, Dan
Utopia, Limited; Flowers of Progress, The 1957,F 27,21:1
Foster, Daniel
George Washington 1920,Mr 2,9:1
Foster, David
Midsummer Night's Dream, A 1968,Je 13,54:1
Foster, Deborah (Costume Designer)
Sourball 1969,Ag 6,29:2

Foster, Deborah (Costume Designer)—Cont
Three by Ferlinghetti; Alligation, The 1970,S 23,43:1
Three by Ferlinghetti; Victims of Amnesia, The 1970,S 23,43:1
Three by Ferlinghetti; Three Thousand Red Ants 1970,S 23,43:1
Foster, Desiree
She Means Business 1931,Ja 27,21:2
Foster, Donald
Thank You 1921,O 4,10:2
Thank You 1921,O 16,VI,1:1
Connie Goes Home 1923,S 7,10:1
Suicide Love 1924,S 7,VII,1:4
Cock o' the Roost 1924,O 14,23:1
Artistic Temperament 1924,D 10,20:2
Morning After, The 1925,Jl 28,24:2
Crooked Friday, The 1925,O 9,27:3
Deacon, The 1925,N 25,14:3
Headquarters 1929,D 5,32:4
Girl Crazy 1930,O 15,27:1
Carry Nation 1932,O 31,18:2
Little Black Book, The 1932,D 27,11:2
Masks and Faces 1933,Mr 20,18:5
Curtain Rises, The 1933,O 20,15:2
All Bow Down 1935,Ag 6,20:4
Tomorrow's a Holiday! 1935,D 31,10:2
Woman's a Fool-To Be Clever, A 1938,O 19,18:6
My Sister Eileen 1940,D 27,23:2
Career Angel 1944,My 24,23:7
Good Morning, Corporal 1944,Ag 9,13:7
No Way Out 1944,O 31,23:1
I Gotta Get Out 1947,S 26,27:2
Doctor Social 1948,F 12,29:5
Twentieth Century 1950,D 25,23:6
Of Thee I Sing 1952,My 6,34:2
Men of Distinction 1953,My 1,18:4
Shrike, The 1953,N 26,51:2
Ponder Heart, The 1956,F 17,14:2
Foster, Dwight
Angels Kiss Me 1951,Ap 18,37:6
Foster, Elizabeth
Porgy and Bess 1952,Ag 6,17:7
Porgy and Bess 1953,Mr 10,25:5
Foster, Fagan and Cox
Vaudeville (Palace) 1929,D 9,33:2
Vaudeville (Palace) 1930,N 3,19:2
Foster, Florence
Green Hat, The 1925,S 16,23:2
Boys and Girls Together 1940,O 2,19:2
Banjo Eyes 1941,D 26,20:2
Foster, Frances
Wisteria Trees, The 1955,F 3,20:2
Take a Giant Step 1956,S 26,30:1
Last Minstrel, The 1963,My 9,40:2
Day of Absence 1965,N 16,56:1
Happy Ending 1965,N 16,56:1
Summer of the Seventeenth Doll 1968,F 21,59:1
Summer of the Seventeenth Doll 1968,Mr 3,II,3:1
Kongi's Harvest 1968,Ap 15,49:1
God Is a (Guess What?) 1968,D 18,56:1
God Is a (Guess What?) 1968,D 19,63:6
God Is a (Guess What?) 1968,D 29,II,1:1
String 1969,Ap 2,37:1
Malcochon 1969,Ap 2,37:1
Song of the Lusitanian Bogey, The 1969,My 13,41:1
Man Better Man 1969,Jl 3,22:1
Brotherhood 1970,Mr 18,39:1
Day of Absence 1970,Mr 18,39:1
Akokawe 1970,Je 5,21:1
Good Woman of Setzuan, The 1970,N 6,51:1
Foster, Gae (Choreographer)
New Hellzapoppin, The 1939,D 12,36:4
New Aquacade Revue, The 1940,My 13,20:5
Foster, George
Out of Step 1925,Ja 30,12:1
Foster, George (Choreographer)
Ice Capades 1970,Ja 7,35:1
Foster, George (Playwright)
Two's Company 1952,D 16,43:5
Foster, Gladys S (Playwright)
Brownstone Urge, The 1969,D 18,63:1
Foster, Gloria
In White America 1963,N 1,26:1
Medea 1965,N 29,46:1
Hand Is on the Gate, A 1966,S 22,54:1
Yerma 1966,D 9,60:1
Midsummer Night's Dream, A 1967,Je 30,23:1
Foster, Harry L (Playwright)
Savages Under the Skin 1927,Mr 25,25:2
Foster, Herbert
Major Barbara 1965,My 18,33:1
Imaginary Invalid, The 1967,My 2,53:1
Touch of the Poet, A 1967,My 3,38:2
Ways and Means 1967,My 4,34:1
Papers 1968,D 3,54:1
Good Woman of Setzuan, The 1970,N 6,51:1
Foster, Horace
Romeo and Juliet 1961,F 24,24:1
Foster, Horace Jr
Hamlet 1959,S 11,21:4
Foster, J F
Trelawney of the 'Wells' 1927,F 1,24:4
New Freedom, The 1930,My 15,32:4

Foster, J F—Cont

New Freedom, The 1930,My 17,21:4
Foster, Joel (Miscellaneous)
Transgressor Rides Again, The 1969,My 21,42:1
Foster, John
Bright Honor 1936,S 28,14:1
Bet Your Life 1937,Ap 6,20:2
Money Mad 1937,My 25,32:5
Once Upon a Time 1939,D 21,28:2
Billy Budd 1959,F 28,13:3
John Gabriel Borkman 1959,N 26,57:4
Foster, John (Miscellaneous)
Maidens and Mistresses at Home at the Zoo
1958,O 29,31:1
Song of Songs 1958,O 29,31:1
Foster, Judy
Beautiful Dreamer 1960,D 28,22:1
Young Abe Lincoln 1961,Ap 26,36:1
Foster, Julia
Flint 1970,Jl 26,49:2
Foster, Justin (Playwright)
Picture of Dorian Gray, The 1956,Ag 18,15:5
Foster, Kendall
Roadside 1930,S 27,21:1
In The Best of Families 1931,F 3,29:1
Foster, Leesa
Porgy and Bess 1961,My 18,40:1
Foster, Lillian
Conscience 1924,S 12,19:3
Gypsy Fires 1925,D 8,28:3
Courage 1927,Ja 20,20:1
Paradise 1927,D 26,26:4
Conscience 1929,O 25,26:1
Eldest, The 1935,F 12,24:3
Immoral Support 1935,S 3,24:3
At the Theatre 1937,Ag 4,14:1
Abe Lincoln in Illinois 1938,O 17,12:2
American Landscape 1938,D 5,19:2
Morning's at Seven 1939,N 7,30:2
Goodbye My Fancy 1948,N 18,35:2
Foster, Lillian (Producer)
Conscience 1929,O 25,26:1
Foster, Lloyd
Passing of the Third Floor Back, The
1928,Ja 17,22:7
Foster, Marel
Good Earth, The 1932,O 18,23:4
Foster, Marie
Where's Charley? 1948,O 12,33:2
Show Boat 1956,Je 22,16:1
Show Boat 1957,Je 28,30:2
Foster, Meg
Empire Builders, The 1968,O 2,34:1
Foster, Melissa
Birds, The 1966,Jl 1,40:1
Foster, Norman
Just Life 1926,S 15,33:3
Sure Fire! 1926,O 21,23:1
Barker, The 1927,Ja 19,20:6
Barker, The 1927,Ja 23,VII,1:1
Racket, The 1927,N 23,28:3
Racket, The 1927,D 18,IX,1:1
Night Hostess 1928,S 13,31:2
Tin Pan Alley 1928,N 2,29:1
Carnival 1929,Ap 25,32:5
June Moon 1929,Ag 4,VIII,1:6
June Moon 1929,O 10,34:5
Foster, Norman (Playwright)
Savage Rhythm 1932,Ja 1,30:4
Foster, Oliver
Bomboola 1929,Je 27,17:3
Walk Together Chillun 1936,F 5,15:2
One-Act Plays of the Sea; Long Voyage Home,
The 1937,O 30,23:2
One-Act Plays of the Sea; In the Zone
1937,O 30,23:2
One-Act Plays of the Sea; Moon of the Caribbees
1937,O 30,23:2
Foster, Oliver (Director)
Green Pastures, The 1935,F 27,16:2
Foster, Paul
Hamlet 1936,N 11,54:2
Foster, Paul (Playwright)
Balls 1965,F 11,45:1
Recluse, The 1966,Ap 13,36:1
Tom Paine 1967,N 12,II,17:6
Tom Paine 1968,Mr 26,38:1
Tom Paine 1968,My 12,II,1:1
Tom Paine 1969,Mr 30,71:2
Foster, Peg (Musical Director)
Madame Aphrodite 1961,D 30,13:1
Foster, Phil
Borscht Capades 1951,S 18,38:3
Elliott Murphy's Aquashow 1955,Je 23,25:1
Day the Whores Came Out to Play Tennis, The
1965,Mr 16,45:1
Foster, Philip
R U R 1930,F 18,28:1
Marco Millions 1930,Mr 4,24:4
Volpone 1930,Mr 11,24:5
Elizabeth the Queen 1930,N 4,37:1
Mourning Becomes Electra; Hunted, The
1931,O 27,22:1

Mourning Becomes Electra; Haunted, The
1931,O 27,22:1
Mourning Becomes Electra; Homecoming
1931,O 27,22:1
Mary of Scotland 1933,N 28,28:3
Othello 1934,Jl 22,23:4
Othello 1937,Ja 7,16:4
Philadelphia Story, The 1939,Mr 29,21:1
Moon Is Down, The 1942,Ap 8,22:2
Foster, Phoebe
Toto 1921,Mr 22,15:2
Captain Applejack 1921,D 31,14:2
Garden of Weeds 1924,Ap 29,12:3
High Stakes 1924,S 10,21:3
Jazz Singer, The 1925,S 15,29:2
Donovan Affair, The 1926,Ag 31,15:2
Interference 1927,O 19,24:3
Scotland Yard 1929,S 28,16:6
Amorous Antic, The 1929,D 3,29:2
Topaze 1930,F 13,25:3
That's the Woman 1930,S 4,27:2
Truth Game, The 1930,D 29,19:1
Cynara 1931,N 3,31:1
Living Dangerously 1935,Ja 14,10:3
Bachelor Born 1938,Ja 26,26:3
American Landscape 1938,D 5,19:2
Foster, Preston
Congratulations 1929,My 1,28:4
Seven 1929,D 28,10:5
Ladies All 1930,Jl 29,25:2
Two Seconds 1931,O 10,20:6
Adam Had Two Sons 1932,Ja 21,17:1
Foster, Quentin
Long Way From Home, A 1948,F 9,25:2
Foster, R
They Never Come Back 1920,D 19,I,22:3
Foster, Robert
As You Like It 1950,Ja 27,27:2
Foster, Robert (Director)
Mrs Moonlight 1952,N 21,21:1
Foster, Roy
Just Married 1921,Ap 27,21:1
Foster, Royal (Composer)
Blackouts of 1949 1949,S 7,39:2
Foster, Royal (Lyricist)
Blackouts of 1949 1949,S 7,39:2
Foster, Royal (Playwright)
Sketch Book 1935,Je 5,22:2
Foster, Stephanie
Strange Bedfellows 1948,Ja 15,27:3
Foster, Stephen (Composer)
Susanna, Don't You Cry 1939,My 23,27:2
Beautiful Dreamer 1960,D 28,22:1
I Dream of Jeanie 1963,Je 25,23:1
Foster, Willard
Women Go on Forever 1927,S 8,25:1
Pygmalion 1938,Ja 27,16:3
Captain Jinks of the Horse Marines 1938,Ja 28,16:2
Coriolanus 1938,F 2,14:5
Man Who Killed Lincoln, The 1940,Ja 18,26:4
Foster, William
Coriolanus 1938,F 2,14:5
Foster Girls
Vaudeville (Hippodrome) 1925,D 29,21:2
Fostini, John
Enemies Don't Send Flowers 1957,F 20,38:1
Hidden Stranger 1963,Ja 10,5:5
Fostini, John (Miscellaneous)
Enemies Don't Send Flowers 1957,F 20,38:1
God Slept Here, A 1957,F 20,38:1
Fostini, John (Playwright)
Enemies Don't Send Flowers 1957,F 20,38:1
God Slept Here, A 1957,F 20,38:1
Fostini, John (Translator)
Enemies Don't Send Flowers 1957,F 20,38:1
God Slept Here, A 1957,F 20,38:1
Fotakis, K
Screwball, The 1957,My 25,24:7
Fotez, Marko (Dr) (Director)
Hamlet 1959,Ag 19,34:1
Fouchardiere, Georges de la (Playwright)
Paris-Capucines 1927,Ja 16,VII,2:1
Fouche, Betty
How Beautiful With Shoes 1935,N 29,24:1
Foulger, Byron
Medea 1920,Mr 23,12:2
Trial of Joan of Arc, The 1921,Mr 28,8:2
Iphigenia in Aulis 1921,Ap 8,18:2
Mr Faust 1922,Ja 31,11:2
Foulk, Robert
As Husbands Go 1931,Mr 6,26:5
As Husbands Go 1933,Ja 20,20:5
John Brown 1934,Ja 23,22:3
Boy Meets Girl 1935,N 28,38:2
Brother Rat 1936,D 17,34:5
Fountain, Brooks (Miscellaneous)
Fitz 1966,My 17,51:2
Biscuit 1966,My 17,51:2
Fountaine, William E
Brown Buddies 1930,O 8,29:1
Four American Aces and a Queen
Vaudeville (Hippodrome) 1926,Mr 16,22:2
Vaudeville (Palace) 1930,D 29,19:3

Four Bruises, The
It Happens on Ice 1941,Ap 5,13:2
Stars on Ice 1942,Jl 3,12:2
Four Camerons, The
Vaudeville (Palace) 1928,D 3,30:6
Four Cansinos, The
Greenwich Village Follies 1923,S 21,4:6
Four Carltons, The
Vaudeville (Palace) 1930,My 26,25:2
Four Diamonds, The
Vaudeville (Palace) 1924,S 16,26:5
Four Fays, The
Vaudeville (Loew's State) 1932,O 3,15:5
Four Flash Devils, The
Singin' the Blues 1931,S 17,21:3
"Four Golden Blondes"
Vaudeville (Palace) 1932,F 15,13:3
Four Mortons, The
Vaudeville (Palace) 1923,Ja 23,18:2
Vaudeville (Hippodrome) 1924,Ap 1,18:1
Four Mullen Sisters
Music Hall Varieties 1932,N 23,15:3
Four Nelsons, The
Good Times 1920,Ag 10,10:1
Four Ortons, The
Vaudeville (Palace) 1930,D 1,19:1
Four Roses
Good Times 1920,Ag 10,10:1
Four Step Brothers, The
Liberace's Variety Bill 1957,Ap 22,29:5
Fouret, Maurice (Composer)
Locus Solus 1922,D 9,11:4
Fournel, Max
Reine Morte, La; Dead Queen, The 1966,F 9,32:1
Cid, Le 1966,F 9,32:1
Avare, L', L'; Miser, The 1966,F 9,32:1
Fil a la Paite, Un; How to Cut the Thread That
Ties You to Your Mistress 1966,F 9,32:1
Cid, Le 1966,F 12,17:1
Reine Morte, La 1966,F 16,52:1
Fil a la Paite, Un 1966,F 18,25:1
Fowble, Helen
Tantrum, The 1924,S 5,20:2
Fowkes, Conrad
Howie 1958,S 18,35:2
TV 1966,N 7,66:1
Motel 1966,N 7,66:1
Interview 1966,N 7,66:1
Reckoning, The 1969,S 5,28:1
Fowlds, Derek
Chips With Everything 1963,O 2,49:1
Spitting Image 1968,S 11,42:1
Fowler
Cochran's 1930 Revue 1930,Ap 13,X,1:6
Fowler, Addison
Lollipop 1924,Ja 22,15:3
Fowler, Beth
Gantry 1970,F 16,44:1
Fowler, Clement
Richard II 1951,Ja 25,21:2
Legend of Lovers 1951,D 27,17:1
Fragile Fox 1954,O 13,27:1
Titus Andronicus 1956,D 3,40:2
Eagle Has Two Heads, The 1956,D 14,37:2
God Slept Here, A 1957,F 20,38:1
Power of Darkness, The 1959,S 30,33:1
Hamlet 1964,Ap 10,30:1
Fowler, Dorothy (Miscellaneous)
Call Me by My Rightful Name 1961,F 1,31:1
Darker Flower, A 1963,Mr 11,7:2
Streets of New York, The 1963,O 30,47:1
Fowler, Edwin
Rosalinda; Fledermaus, Die 1942,O 29,26:5
Fowler, Gene (Original Author)
Jimmy 1969,O 24,38:1
Fowler, Gene (Playwright)
Great Magoo, The 1932,D 3,20:7
Fowler, Gertrude
He Loved the Ladies 1927,My 11,29:2
Wasp's Nest, The 1927,O 26,26:3
Let and Sub-Let 1930,My 20,32:2
Old Man Murphy 1931,My 19,25:2
We Are No Longer Children 1932,Ap 1,17:2
Mountain, The 1933,S 12,28:6
Big Hearted Herbert 1934,Ja 2,17:3
Fowler, Gus
Vaudeville (Palace) 1928,Jl 3,19:2
Fowler, Harriet
Untitled-Revue 1926,N 21,VIII,2:1
Fowler, Jean
Winter Journey 1968,Mr 13,39:1
Play It Again, Sam 1969,F 13,52:3
Fowler, Keith
Here Comes Santa Claus 1962,My 18,34:1
Fowler, Mary
Woman of Bronze, The 1920,S 8,9:2
Iphigenia in Aulis 1921,Ap 8,18:2
Tendresse, La 1922,S 26,18:1
Tidings Brought to Mary, The 1922,D 25,20:1
Roger Bloomer 1923,Mr 2,18:3
Backslapper, The 1925,Ap 13,25:2
Dream Play 1926,Ja 21,18:2
Squall, The 1926,N 12,20:1

Fowler, Mary—Cont
Sam Abramovitch 1927,Ja 20,20:5
Rapid Transit 1927,Ap 8,21:2
Woman of Bronze, The 1927,Je 16,25:4
Broken Chain, The 1929,F 21,30:4
Borrowed Love 1929,Je 18,29:2
Hawk Island 1929,S 17,34:7
They Never Grow Up 1930,Ap 8,27:1
Thunder Rock 1939,N 15,18:1
Fowler, Neva
Gift of Fury, A 1958,Mr 24,21:4
Fowler, Pat
Seven Year Itch, The 1952,N 21,21:2
Fowler, Pat (Miscellaneous)
Garden of Sweets, The 1961,N 1,35:1
Fowler, Pat (Producer)
Owl and the Pussycat, The 1964,N 19,48:1
Fowler, Robert (Producer)
Experiment, The 1967,My 9,54:2
Fowler, Truman
Old King's 1924,Mr 12,19:3
Fowler and Tamara
George White's Scandals 1926,Je 15,23:2
Vaudeville (Palace) 1928,My 29,17:4
Vaudeville (Palace) 1928,O 30,27:3
Fowley, Douglas
Earthlight Theater 1970,N 4,38:2
Fowlkes, Joseph
Brother to Dragons 1968,D 8,86:1
Fownes, Henry (Producer)
Joe Egg 1968,F 2,26:1
Her First Roman 1968,O 21,53:3
Crimes of Passion; Ruffian on the Stair, The 1969,O 27,54:1
Crimes of Passion; Erpingham Camp, The 1969,O 27,54:1
Fox, Al
Scandals 1920,Je 8,9:1
Greenwich Villagers, The 1927,Ag 19,20:2
Fox, Alan
Ups-A-Daisy 1928,O 9,34:2
Fox, Allen (Miscellaneous)
Theatre of Robert Frost, The; Masque of Reason, The; Bonfire, The; Masque of Mercy, The; Generations of Men, The 1962,My 31,23:6
Fox, Andrew J Jr
Reunion 1938,Ap 12,26:4
Fox, Anne
When the Bough Breaks 1950,Mr 9,25:5
Fox, Arthur
Taming of the Shrew, The 1921,My 12,20:2
Merchant of Venice, The 1921,My 14,10:4
Little Poor Man, The 1925,Ag 6,14:1
Fox, Bernard
Heartbreak House 1963,Je 28,24:1
Fox, Carol
Tour De Four 1963,Je 19,41:1
Fox, Colin
Henry VI 1966,Je 9,55:2
Richard III 1967,Je 14,43:1
Government Inspector, The 1967,Je 15,55:1
Merry Wives of Windsor, The 1967,Ag 4,18:1
Government Inspector, The 1967,O 28,34:1
Soldiers 1968,My 2,58:1
Fox, Dorothy
New Faces 1934,Mr 16,24:5
Parade 1935,My 21,22:2
Jubilee 1935,O 14,20:1
Jubilee 1935,N 24,IX,8:1
Sing Out the News 1938,S 26,12:5
Fox, Dulce
Divine Moment, A 1934,Ja 8,21:8
Cradle Will Rock, The 1937,D 6,19:4
Cradle Will Rock, The 1938,Ja 4,19:3
Fox, Ernest
Gambling 1929,Ag 27,31:2
Fox, Florence
Caukey 1944,F 18,15:4
Fox, Fontaine
Untitled-Revue 1923,My 12,15:4
Fox, Franklyn
Drifting 1922,Ja 3,20:3
That Awful Mrs Eaton! 1924,S 30,27:1
Carnaval 1924,D 30,15:1
Gypsy Fires 1925,D 8,28:3
Humble, The 1926,O 14,22:2
Mirrors 1928,Ja 19,17:1
Straight Thru the Door 1928,O 5,17:2
Skyrocket, The 1929,Ja 12,14:7
Nigger Rich 1929,S 21,16:7
So Was Napoleon 1930,Ja 9,22:2
Those We Love 1930,F 20,22:2
Queen at Home 1930,D 30,25:2
Riddle Me This! 1933,Mr 15,21:3
Caviar 1934,Je 8,19:2
Menagerie 1935,Jl 2,24:3
Accent on Youth 1935,Jl 9,24:5
Bishop Misbehaves, The 1935,Ag 27,23:4
Sweet Mystery of Life 1935,O 12,13:3
Tapestry in Gray 1935,D 28,10:2
Pre-Honeymoon 1936,My 1,19:4
Without Warning 1937,My 3,23:2
Hooray for What! 1937,D 2,32:5
Lightnin' 1938,S 16,17:2

Day in the Sun 1939,My 17,29:2
Leave Her to Heaven 1940,F 28,16:2
Royal Family, The 1940,Ag 13,15:3
High Kickers 1941,N 1,21:2
Mr Sycamore 1942,N 14,13:2
Ask My Friend Sandy 1943,F 5,16:2
Early to Bed 1943,Je 18,16:2
Pillar to Post 1943,D 11,11:2
Rebecca 1945,Ja 19,17:2
Carousel 1945,Ap 20,24:2
Song of Norway 1958,Je 23,19:2
Fox, Frederic E
Take It Away 1936,D 15,30:5
Once Over Lightly 1938,D 10,13:4
Fox, Frederick (Costume Designer)
Johnny on the Spot 1942,Ja 9,24:2
Only the Heart 1944,Ap 5,17:2
Julia, Jake, and Uncle Joe 1961,Ja 30,19:1
Fox, Frederick (Lighting Director)
Men in Shadow 1943,Mr 11,16:2
Career Angel 1944,My 24,23:7
Good Night Ladies 1945,Ja 18,16:2
Alice in Arms 1945,F 1,18:4
Secret Room, The 1945,N 8,16:2
Little Brown Jug 1946,Mr 7,32:2
John Loves Mary 1947,F 5,29:2
They Knew What They Wanted 1949,F 17,28:2
Southern Exposure 1950,S 27,36:3
Darkness at Noon 1951,Ja 15,13:4
Never Say Never 1951,N 21,21:2
Seven Year Itch, The 1952,N 21,21:2
Room Service 1953,Ap 7,34:1
King of Hearts 1954,Ap 2,23:1
Anniversary Waltz 1954,Ap 8,34:1
Reclining Figure 1954,O 8,26:5
Lunatics and Lovers 1954,D 14,44:2
Wayward Saint, The 1955,F 18,17:1
Speaking of Murder 1956,D 20,37:1
Greatest Man Alive!, The 1957,My 9,37:2
Howie 1958,S 18,35:2
Golden Fleecing 1959,O 16,24:5
Warm Peninsula, The 1959,O 21,46:2
Mighty Man Is He, A 1960,Ja 7,25:2
Hostage, The 1960,S 21,42:1
Send Me No Flowers 1960,D 6,54:1
Julia, Jake, and Uncle Joe 1961,Ja 30,19:1
Mandingo 1961,My 23,43:6
From the Second City 1961,S 27,32:1
Fox, Frederick (Miscellaneous)
Hostage, The 1960,S 21,42:1
Fox, Frederick (Producer)
Land of Fame 1943,S 22,31:5
Greatest Man Alive!, The 1957,My 9,37:2
Fox, Frederick (Scenic Designer)
Farewell Summer 1937,Mr 30,20:2
Bat, The 1937,Je 1,27:5
There's Always a Breeze 1938,Mr 3,16:2
Man From Cairo, The 1938,My 5,26:5
Strangler Fig, The 1940,My 7,31:2
Johnny Belinda 1940,S 19,26:2
Blind Alley 1940,O 16,28:2
Brooklyn Biarritz 1941,F 28,16:2
Snookie 1941,Je 4,26:2
All Men Are Alike 1941,O 7,27:2
Good Neighbor 1941,O 22,26:2
Junior Miss 1941,N 19,28:2
Johnny on the Spot 1942,Ja 9,24:2
Wine, Women and Song 1942,S 29,18:3
Yankee Point 1942,N 24,28:2
Doughgirls, The 1942,D 31,19:2
Men in Shadow 1943,Mr 11,16:2
Those Endearing Young Charms 1943,Je 17,16:3
Two Mrs Carrolls, The 1943,Ag 4,14:1
Snark Was a Boojum, The 1943,S 2,14:4
Land of Fame 1943,S 22,31:5
Naked Genius, The 1943,O 22,20:5
Lady Behave 1943,N 17,30:1
Ramshackle Inn 1944,Ja 6,17:5
Decision 1944,F 3,23:2
Only the Heart 1944,Ap 5,17:2
Hickory Stick 1944,My 9,15:6
Anna Lucasta 1944,Ag 31,15:1
Day Will Come, The 1944,S 8,17:2
Odds on Mrs Oakley, The 1944,O 3,18:8
Man Who Had All the Luck, The 1944,N 24,18:5
Dear Ruth 1944,D 14,29:2
Good Night Ladies 1945,Ja 18,16:2
Goose for the Gander, A 1945,Ja 24,16:4
Alice in Arms 1945,F 1,18:4
Calico Wedding 1945,Mr 8,18:6
Kiss Them for Me 1945,Mr 21,27:2
Wind Is Ninety, The 1945,Ap 22,12:2
Marriage Is for Single People 1945,N 22,38:2
Little Brown Jug 1946,Mr 7,32:2
Mr Peebles and Mr Hooker 1946,O 11,29:2
John Loves Mary 1947,F 5,29:2
Make Mine Manhattan 1948,Ja 16,26:2
Light Up the Sky 1948,N 19,34:2
They Knew What They Wanted 1949,F 17,28:2
Southern Exposure 1950,S 27,36:3
Darkness at Noon 1951,Ja 15,13:4
Darkness at Noon 1951,Ja 21,II,1:1
Angels Kiss Me 1951,Ap 18,37:6

Fox, Frederick (Scenic Designer)—Cont
Never Say Never 1951,N 21,21:2
Climate of Eden, The 1952,N 7,20:2
Climate of Eden, The 1952,N 16,II,1:1
Seven Year Itch, The 1952,N 21,21:2
Room Service 1953,Ap 7,34:1
King of Hearts 1954,Ap 2,23:1
Anniversary Waltz 1954,Ap 8,34:1
Reclining Figure 1954,O 8,26:5
Lunatics and Lovers 1954,D 14,44:2
Wayward Saint 1955,F 18,17:1
Speaking of Murder 1956,D 20,37:1
Greatest Man Alive!, The 1957,My 9,37:2
Fair Game 1957,N 4,39:1
Howie 1958,S 18,35:2
Golden Fleecing 1959,O 16,24:5
Warm Peninsula, The 1959,O 21,46:2
Mighty Man Is He, A 1960,Ja 7,25:2
Hostage, The 1960,S 21,42:1
Send Me No Flowers 1960,D 6,54:1
Julia, Jake, and Uncle Joe 1961,Ja 30,19:1
Mandingo 1961,My 23,43:6
From the Second City 1961,S 27,32:1
Fox, Gladys
Minskey the Magnificent 1936,D 26,14:3
Fox, Grace
O Evening Star 1936,Ja 9,24:6
Seen But Not Heard 1936,S 18,19:2
Case History 1938,O 22,15:2
Fox, H C
Gentlemen, the Queen 1927,Ap 23,14:3
Fox, Harry
All-Star Jamboree 1921,Jl 14,18:1
Round the Town 1924,My 22,14:3
George White's Scandals 1925,Je 23,24:2
Vaudeville (Palace) 1926,Je 29,21:3
Vaudeville (Palace) 1926,D 21,20:5
Vaudeville (Palace) 1927,O 11,27:2
Vaudeville (Palace) 1928,N 26,31:2
Fox, Helen
Child of the Morning 1958,Ap 22,40:2
Fox, Henry
By Your Leave 1934,Ja 25,15:3
Fox, Jack
Sonny 1921,Ag 17,12:2
Fox, James J
Show Boat 1957,Je 28,30:2
Song of Norway 1958,Je 23,19:2
Fox, Janet
Dinner at Eight 1932,O 24,18:2
Between Two Worlds 1934,O 26,24:2
Fools Rush In 1934,D 26,19:2
Cross Ruff 1935,F 20,23:3
Life's Too Short 1935,S 21,18:5
Tomorrow's a Holiday! 1935,D 31,10:2
Stage Door 1936,O 23,26:3
Having Wonderful Time 1937,F 22,12:5
American Way, The 1939,Ja 23,9:2
Higher and Higher 1940,Ap 5,24:3
Two Story House 1941,S 2,20:3
Cuckoos on the Hearth 1941,S 17,26:2
Bravo! 1948,N 12,31:2
Tall Story 1959,Ja 30,33:2
Tattooed Countess, The 1961,My 4,40:2
Once for the Asking 1963,N 21,42:2
Sherry! 1967,Mr 29,39:1
Fox, Jeannette
Love on an Island 1934,Jl 24,20:5
Fox, Jimmy
Hold Your Horses 1933,S 26,26:4
Drums Professor, The 1955,Jl 30,17:2
Arabian Nights 1955,Je 24,16:1
Fox, John
Savonarola 1942,Ap 24,20:2
City of Kings 1949,F 18,27:2
Fox, Kenneth
Lady of the Rose 1925,My 20,26:4
Fox, Margery (Miscellaneous)
Greatest Man Alive!, The 1957,My 9,37:2
Fox, Mary
Don't Bother Mother 1925,F 4,18:2
Gambling 1929,Ag 27,31:2
Fox, Maxine (Producer)
Fortune and Men's Eyes 1969,O 23,55:1
Fox, Melvin
Tom Sawyer 1931,D 26,15:3
Fox, Michael
Story of Mary Surratt, The 1947,F 10,25:2
Fox, Patrick
Whispers on the Wind 1970,Je 4,50:1
Fox, Paul Hervey (Playwright)
Odd Man Out 1925,My 26,24:3
Soldiers and Women 1929,Ag 25,VIII,3:1
Soldiers and Women 1929,S 3,25:1
Great Man, The 1931,Ap 8,20:6
Foreign Affairs 1932,Ap 14,25:5
If I Were You 1938,Ja 9,II,3:2
If I Were You 1938,Ja 25,24:2
Fox, Paul Hervey (Producer)
If I Were You 1938,Ja 9,II,3:2
Fox, Philip
Poppa Is Home 1961,D 20,37:1
Fox, Roger
Many Mansions 1937,O 28,28:6

Fox, Rose D
  Midsummer Night's Dream, A 1932,N 18,22:2
Fox, Sidney
  It Never Rains 1929,N 20,26:4
  Lost Sheep 1930,My 6,33:2
Fox, Sonny
  Littlest Circus, The 1959,D 26,5:6
Fox, Stephen
  Amazing Dr. Clitterhouse, The 1937,Mr 3,26:4
  Antony and Cleopatra 1937,N 11,30:2
Fox, Stuart
  Wheel, The 1921,Ag 30,10:1
  Chicken Feed 1923,S 25,10:2
  Puppy Love 1926,Ja 28,16:3
  Storm Center 1927,D 1,33:2
  Crooks' Convention, The 1929,S 19,37:4
  Errant Lady 1934,S 18,18:2
Fox, Susan
  Petticoat Fever 1937,Jl 6,23:1
  Summer Night 1939,N 3,17:1
Fox, Virginia
  Iolanthe 1927,N 15,26:3
Fox, William
  Delusion 1935,Mr 29,26:4
  Dusty Ermine 1936,Mr 7,11:6
  Young Madame Conti 1936,D 6,XII,7:6
  Young Madame Conti 1937,Ap 1,18:4
  Call Home the Heart 1947,Ap 13,I,54:2
Fox, William (Miscellaneous)
  Billy Barnes People, The 1961,Je 14,10:3
Fox-Lee, Jeanette
  Tia Juana 1927,N 16,28:4
  Straight Thru the Door 1928,O 5,17:2
  Long Road, The 1930,S 10,30:2
  On the Make 1932,My 24,23:2
  Barrister, The 1932,N 22,25:2
  Hotel Alimony 1934,Ja 30,16:2
Foxall, Arthur J (Playwright)
  Trilby 1958,Ja 9,40:3
Foxe, Earle
  Come Seven 1920,Jl 20,10:1
  Princess Virtue 1921,My 5,20:2
Foxhall, Florence
  Veils 1928,Mr 14,28:5
Foxman, Aaron (Director)
  Hymn to the Rising Sun 1937,My 7,28:2
Foxman, Aaron (Miscellaneous)
  Battle Hymn 1936,My 23,12:1
Foxworth, Bob
  Friends and Lovers; In the Zone; Bound East for
    Cardiff 1961,My 11,43:1
  Six Characters in Search of an Author
    1961,My 11,43:1
Foxworth, Robert
  Great White Hope, The 1967,D 14,58:1
  Iceman Cometh, The 1968,Ap 1,58:1
  Much Ado About Nothing 1969,Je 16,57:1
  Hamlet 1969,Je 30,33:1
  Henry V 1969,N 11,43:1
Foy, Charles
  Friars Club Frolic 1933,My 15,16:4
Foy, Eddie Jr
  Vaudeville (Palace) 1927,S 20,33:3
  Vaudeville (Palace) 1927,D 27,25:2
  Show Girl 1929,Jl 3,19:3
  Ripples 1930,F 2,VIII,2:7
  Ripples 1930,F 12,26:1
  Smiles 1930,N 19,19:2
  Cat and the Fiddle, The 1931,O 16,26:4
  Humpty Dumpty 1932,S 18,IX,2:1
  At Home Abroad 1935,S 4,22:3
  At Home Abroad 1935,S 20,17:4
  Orchids Preferred 1937,Ap 29,16:6
  Orchids Preferred 1937,My 12,26:5
  Red Mill, The 1945,O 17,16:2
  Red Mill, The 1945,O 28,II,1:1
  Pajama Game, The 1954,My 14,20:2
  Pajama Game, The 1954,My 15,12:1
  Pajama Game, The 1954,My 30,II,1:1
  Rumple 1957,N 7,42:2
  Donnybrook! 1961,My 19,23:1
  Donnybrook! 1961,My 28,II,1:1
Foy, Gloria
  What's in a Name? 1920,Mr 20,14:2
  Up She Goes 1922,N 7,14:2
  Round the Town 1924,My 22,14:3
  Betty Lee 1924,D 26,18:2
  Circus Princess, The 1927,Ap 26,32:2
  Vaudeville (Palace) 1930,Jl 7,22:2
Foye, Hope
  Dance Me a Song 1950,Ja 21,10:5
Foyer, Bernie (Producer)
  Seventeen 1951,Je 22,16:6
Fraccaroli, Arnaldo (Playwright)
  Plot Thickens, The 1922,S 6,16:1
Fracht, J Albert (Playwright)
  Athenian Touch, The 1964,Ja 15,25:4
Fraction, Edward
  Swing Mikado, The 1939,Mr 2,18:2
  Big White Fog 1940,O 23,26:2
Fradkin, Philip (Musical Director)
  Tattooed Countess, The 1961,My 4,40:2
  Golden Apple, The 1962,F 13,38:2

Frael, Virginia
  Dope 1926,Ja 4,16:3
Fraenkel, Helene (Playwright)
  Dark Legend 1952,Mr 25,24:2
Fraenzel, Willy
  Diable 1926,O 31,VIII,2:4
Fraiberg, Lawrence P (Producer)
  Khaki Blue 1969,Mr 27,54:2
  Lime Green 1969,Mr 27,54:2
Frakson
  Vaudeville (Palace) 1926,N 23,27:3
Fralick, (Mrs)
  Slight Case of Murder, A 1935,S 12,28:5
Fram, Robert
  Sinbad the Sailor 1929,D 27,26:5
Frame, Elsa (Scenic Designer)
  Our Betters 1937,Jl 22,16:2
Framer, Walt (Miscellaneous)
  Big Knife, The 1959,N 13,25:1
Franc, Jacqueline
  Jubilee 1935,O 14,20:1
Franc-Nohain (Playwright)
  March Indienne, La 1927,Mr 27,VIII,4:8
  Chapeau Chinois, Le 1930,Ap 27,IX,2:1
France, Alexis
  Apple Cart, The 1953,My 8,29:3
  Lark, The 1955,My 13,21:2
France, Alois
  Money Business 1926,Ja 21,18:1
France, Anatole (Original Author)
  Thais 1931,Je 19,21:3
France, Anatole (Playwright)
  Man Who Married a Dumb Wife, The
    1923,My 10,22:3
  Man Who Married a Dumb Wife, The
    1923,My 26,8:4
  Man Who Married a Dumb Wife, The
    1930,My 9,20:5
  Doctored Wife, The 1950,Jl 12,33:2
France, Anna
  Sage of Rottenburg, The 1963,N 20,48:1
France, C V
  Unknown, The 1920,Ag 29,VI,1:4
  Dover Road, The 1924,My 4,VIII,2:4
  Lady of the Camellias, The 1930,Mr 23,IX,2:3
  Dishonored Lady 1930,My 25,IX,2:4
  Object of Virtue, An 1930,N 23,IX,2:4
  Man of Yesterday 1935,Mr 17,VIII,1:4
France, Dawson
  Caesar and Cleopatra 1951,D 20,43:2
France, Nicole
  Gentlemen Prefer Blondes 1949,D 9,35:3
France, Richard
  Seventeen 1951,Je 22,16:6
  Wish You Were Here 1952,Je 26,26:6
  By the Beautiful Sea 1954,Ap 9,20:1
  Kiss Me, Kate 1956,My 10,27:2
  Pajama Game, The 1957,My 16,27:1
  Annie Get Your Gun 1958,F 20,29:2
  Tom Sawyer 1958,Jl 15,21:8
  Girls Against the Boys, The 1959,N 3,26:1
  Girls Against the Boys, The 1959,N 8,II,1:1
  Show Boat 1961,Ap 13,32:1
  Fiorello! 1962,Je 14,24:1
  Oklahoma! 1963,F 28,8:2
  Oklahoma! 1963,My 16,40:1
  What Makes Sammy Run? 1964,F 28,19:1
  Oklahoma! 1965,D 16,62:1
  Wonderful Town 1967,My 18,50:1
  Carnival! 1968,D 13,58:1
France, Suzanne
  Ben Franklin in Paris 1964,O 28,52:1
Francen, Victor
  Cyrano de Bergerac 1926,Ja 24,II,8:5
  Dictateur, Le 1926,N 7,VIII,2:7
  Chantecler 1927,N 6,IX,4:1
  Tombeau Sous l'Arc de Triomphe
    1929,Je 16,VIII,2:3
  Trois Chambres, Les 1931,Mr 15,IX,1:6
  Espoir 1935,F 3,VIII,3:3
  Walking Gentleman, The 1942,My 8,26:2
  Strong Are Lonely, The 1953,S 30,38:3
Francen, Victor (Playwright)
  Bourgeoise, La 1927,O 2,VIII,2:4
Frances, Charles
  Rose Bernd 1922,O 8,VI,1:2
Frances, Helen
  Tangerine 1921,Ag 10,8:2
Frances, Josephine
  Happy Ending 1936,Jl 15,14:3
Frances, Kathleen
  Pirates of Penzance, The; Slave of Duty, The
    1934,S 7,24:3
  Iolanthe 1934,S 11,24:3
  Trial by Jury 1934,S 14,24:3
  Yeomen of the Guard, The 1934,S 21,28:3
  Ruddigore 1934,S 25,25:2
  Princess Ida; Castle Adamant 1934,S 28,26:3
  Patience 1934,O 12,32:2
Frances, Mary
  Green Pastures, The 1935,F 27,16:2

Frances, Norma
  Private Life of the Master Race, The
    1956,Ja 31,33:3
Frances, Norma (Director)
  Private Life of the Master Race, The
    1956,Ja 31,33:3
Frances, Norma (Miscellaneous)
  Private Life of the Master Race, The
    1956,Ja 31,33:3
Frances, Norma (Producer)
  Hostage, The 1961,D 13,55:4
  Billy Liar 1965,Mr 18,26:1
Francesco, Tony
  Vaudeville (Palace) 1926,N 30,27:2
Franchi, Sergio
  Do I Hear a Waltz? 1965,Mr 19,28:1
  Do I Hear a Waltz? 1965,Mr 28,II,1:1
Franchot, Richard
  Tea and Sympathy 1953,O 1,35:1
  Tall Story 1959,Ja 30,33:2
Francine, Anne
  Lunchtime Follies, The 1942,Je 23,22:3
  Marriage Is for Single People 1945,N 22,38:2
  You Can't Take It With You 1951,Ap 7,8:6
  By the Beautiful Sea 1954,Ap 9,20:1
  Great Sebastians, The 1956,Ja 5,27:1
  Guitar 1959,N 11,42:5
  Innocent as Hell 1960,Je 30,2:6
  Valmouth 1960,O 7,29:1
  If Five Years Pass 1962,My 11,37:1
  Mame 1967,Ag 15,31:2
  Mame 1969,Ja 5,79:4
  Mame 1969,Je 20,36:1
Franciosa, Anthony
  Hamlet 1948,D 4,9:2
  City of Kings 1949,F 18,27:2
  Yes is for a Very Young Man 1949,Je 7,27:2
  End as a Man 1953,S 16,39:1
  Wedding Breakfast 1954,N 22,29:2
  Wedding Breakfast 1954,D 5,II,5:1
  Hatful of Rain, A 1955,N 10,44:1
  Hatful of Rain, A 1955,D 4,II,1:1
Franciosa, Massimo (Playwright)
  Rugantino 1964,F 7,34:1
Francis, Amadeo
  Medea 1960,Jl 26,25:2
Francis, Anne
  Remote Asylum 1970,D 13,II,3:1
Francis, Arlene
  Gringa, La 1928,F 2,17:1
  I Loved You Wednesday 1932,O 12,27:1
  Body Beautiful, The 1935,N 1,24:3
  Horse Eats Hat 1936,S 28,14:2
  Women, The 1936,D 28,13:1
  Angel Island 1937,O 21,26:2
  All That Glitters 1938,Ja 20,18:2
  Danton's Death 1938,N 3,26:2
  Michael Drops In 1938,D 28,24:3
  Young Couple Wanted 1940,Ja 25,16:2
  Journey to Jerusalem 1940,O 7,21:2
  Somewhere in France 1941,Ap 29,16:8
  Walking Gentleman, The 1942,My 8,26:2
  Doughgirls, The 1942,D 31,19:2
  Doughgirls, The 1943,Ja 10,VIII,1:1
  Overtons, The 1945,F 7,16:6
  French Touch, The 1945,D 10,18:2
  Cup of Trembling, The 1948,Ap 21,33:5
  My Name is Aquilon 1949,F 10,38:2
  Metropole 1949,D 7,43:2
  Little Blue Light, The 1951,Ap 30,17:2
  Late Love 1953,O 14,35:2
  Once More With Feeling 1958,O 22,39:1
  Beekman Place 1964,O 8,50:1
  Mrs Dally 1965,S 25,5:7
  Dinner at Eight 1966,S 28,38:1
  Dinner at Eight 1966,O 9,II,1:1
Francis, Arthur (Lyricist)
  Two Little Girls in Blue 1921,My 4,10:3
Francis, Carl
  Sidewalks of New York 1927,O 4,33:1
  Billie 1928,O 2,34:2
Francis, Charles
  Tragedy of Nan, The 1920,F 18,9:1
  Mary Stuart 1921,Mr 22,15:1
  Gold 1921,Je 2,14:2
  Varying Shore, The 1921,D 6,24:1
  Rose Bernd 1922,S 27,17:1
  Tidings Brought to Mary, The 1922,D 25,20:1
  Rita Coventry 1923,F 20,12:2
  Cyrano de Bergerac 1923,N 2,14:1
  Assumption of Hannele, The 1924,F 16,16:2
  Othello 1925,Ja 12,11:1
  Cyrano de Bergerac 1926,F 19,18:1
  Wings Over Europe 1928,D 11,35:1
  Royal Virgin, The 1930,Mr 18,30:5
  Lonely Way, The 1931,F 22,VIII,4:1
  Merchant of Venice, The 1931,N 9,22:2
  Good Fairy, The 1932,N 18,22:3
  Valley Forge 1934,D 11,28:3
  Othello 1935,S 28,13:2
  Macbeth 1935,O 8,26:4
  Libel! 1935,D 21,10:5
  Victoria Regina 1936,S 1,24:5

Francis, Charles—Cont

Merchant of Venice, The 1938,Ja 15,18:8
Victoria Regina 1938,O 4,20:2
Flying Gerardos, The 1940,D 30,21:4
Trojan Women, The 1941,Ap 9,32:5
Wookey, The 1941,S 11,20:5
Signature 1945,F 15,25:2
Winter's Tale, The 1946,Ja 16,18:6
Haven, The 1946,N 14,39:4
Anne of the Thousand Days 1948,D 9,49:2
Gioconda Smile, The 1950,O 9,21:2
King and I, The 1951,Mr 30,26:2

Francis, Charlotte (Playwright)
Western Wind 1949,Ag 9,20:6

Francis, Claire
All in Favor 1942,Ja 21,20:6

Francis, Dean (Miscellaneous)
Arms and the Man 1956,O 2,39:4
In Good King Charles's Golden Days
1957,Ja 25,16:1
Hobo 1961,Ap 11,41:2

Francis, Dorothy
Merry Widow, The 1921,S 6,13:1
Rita Coventry 1923,F 20,12:2
Time 1923,N 27,23:3
Love Song, The 1925,Ja 14,19:4
Sunny 1925,S 23,22:1
Climax, The 1926,My 18,29:3
Criss Cross 1926,O 13,20:2
Eye on the Sparrow 1938,My 4,26:3

Francis, Emily
Main Line, The 1924,Mr 26,19:4
Wicked Age, The 1927,N 5,16:6

Francis, Eugene
Hamlet 1936,N 11,54:2
Glorious Morning 1938,N 28,10:3
Man Who Killed Lincoln, The 1940,Ja 18,26:4

Francis, Franklin
Weak Woman, A 1926,Ja 27,16:3

Francis, Grace
Moor Born 1934,Ap 4,26:4
Moor Born 1934,Ap 8,X,2:7

Francis, Harold
Would-Be Gentleman, The 1928,O 2,34:1

Francis, Helen
Alternate Current 1939,D 23,8:3

Francis, Ivor
Will and the Way, The 1957,D 3,46:5
J B 1958,D 12,2:7
Fun Couple, The 1962,O 27,15:2
Rainy Day in Newark, A 1963,O 23,35:1
Investigation, The 1966,O 5,40:1

Francis, J O (Playwright)
Dark Little People, The 1924,Mr 2,VIII,2:7
Beaten Track, The 1926,F 9,23:2

Francis, Jack
Brown Danube, The 1939,My 18,30:4

Francis, James X
High Flyers 1927,Je 26,VIII,1:1

Francis, Jean
Susie Is a Good Girl 1968,N 5,53:2
Grab Bag, The 1968,N 5,53:2
Subscriber, The 1968,N 5,53:2

Francis, Jean (Playwright)
Dallas, Nov 22, 1963 1966,N 13,80:1

Francis, John
Career 1943,O 29,22:6
Spring Production 1944,My 20,12:4
Partition 1948,O 29,31:2

Francis, Judson
Hamlet 1959,S 11,21:4

Francis, Katharine
Hamlet 1925,N 10,23:1
Venus 1927,D 26,26:5
Elmer the Great 1928,S 25,29:1

Francis, Katherine
Crime 1927,F 23,27:3

Francis, Kay
Web and the Rock, The 1950,Ag 20,II,1:1

Francis, Mary (Sister) (Lyricist)
Lady of Mexico 1962,O 20,13:2

Francis, Mary (Sister) (Playwright)
Madre, La 1959,F 12,24:1

Francis, Mona
Trojan Horse, The 1940,O 31,28:3

Francis, Nick (Miscellaneous)
This Was Burlesque 1970,F 12,31:1

Francis, Nick (Musical Director)
Hell'z-A-Splashin' 1959,Je 25,22:2

Francis, Noel
No Foolin' 1926,Je 25,25:1
Rio Rita 1927,F 3,18:3
Show Girl 1929,Jl 3,19:3
Satellite 1935,N 21,27:5

Francis, Stephen
Treasure Girl 1928,N 9,22:1

Francis, William
Merry Wives of Windsor, The 1954,F 17,27:1

Francis, William (Composer)
Portrait of a Queen 1968,F 29,29:1

Francis, William (Playwright)
Portrait of a Queen 1965,My 7,35:5
Portrait of a Queen 1968,F 29,29:1

Francis-Robertson, James
Broken Dishes 1929,N 6,28:3
Man Bites Dog 1933,Ap 26,11:2
Farmer Takes a Wife, The 1934,O 31,17:1
Achilles Had a Heel 1935,O 14,20:2

Francisco, Dick
Poupees de Paris, Les 1962,D 13,8:2

Francisco, Hale (Playwright)
Angeline Moves In 1932,Ap 20,27:5

Francisco, Hale (Producer)
Angeline Moves In 1932,Ap 20,27:5

Francisco, William (Director)
O, Oysters! 1961,Ja 31,23:1
Sap of Life, The 1961,O 3,44:1
Color of Darkness: An Evening in the World of
James Purdy; You Reach for Your Hat
1963,O 1,34:1
Color of Darkness: An Evening in the World of
James Purdy; Sermon 1963,O 1,34:1
Color of Darkness: An Evening in the World of
James Purdy; Everything Under the Sun
1963,O 1,34:1
Color of Darkness: An Evening in the World of
James Purdy; Cracks 1963,O 1,24:1
Color of Darkness: An Evening in the World of
James Purdy; Don't Call Me By My Right Name
1963,O 1,34:1
Color of Darkness: An Evening in the World of
James Purdy; Encore 1963,O 1,34:1
Rondelay 1969,N 6,55:1

Francisco, William (Miscellaneous)
J B 1958,Ap 24,37:1
Sap of Life, The 1961,O 3,44:1

Francisco, William (Producer)
Sap of Life, The 1961,O 3,44:1

Franck, Edward A (Producer)
Mike Downstairs 1968,Ap 19,35:1

Franck, Eric (Producer)
Black Nativity 1961,D 12,54:2

Franck, Frederic (Scenic Designer)
Bed Time 1958,Ap 11,20:2

Franck, Nelly
From Vienna 1939,Je 21,26:2
Reunion in New York 1940,F 22,28:4

Franck, Pierre (Director)
Annonce Faite a Marie, L' 1965,Ap 6,33:2
Reine Morte, La 1966,F 16,52:1

Franck, Vanya
Alfie 1964,D 18,27:1
Conduct Unbecoming 1970,O 13,50:1

Franck, Virginia
Criss Cross 1926,O 13,20:2
Treasure Girl 1928,N 9,22:1

Franck, Walter
Richard III 1937,My 30,X,2:2

Franck, Walther
Persians, The 1927,F 27,VII,2:3

Francke, Caroline (Playwright)
Exceeding Small 1928,O 23,32:2
Exceeding Small 1928,N 4,IX,1:1
49th Cousin, The 1960,O 28,22:1

Francks, Don
Kelly 1965,F 8,28:2
Leonard Bernstein's Theater Songs 1965,Je 29,27:2
Flip Side, The 1968,O 11,36:1

Francks, Marienne
Man's Man, A 1925,O 14,31:2
Gertie 1926,N 16,24:2
Spring Song 1927,D 22,26:3
That Ferguson Family 1928,D 24,10:7

Franco, Tony
Ziegfeld Follies 1957,Mr 2,19:2

Francois, Jacques
Britannicus 1958,N 29,17:2
Otage, L' 1959,O 27,42:1
Misanthrope, Le 1960,Mr 9,38:3

Francois and Denmore
Vaudeville (Palace) 1930,My 26,25:2

Francon, Victor (Playwright)
Bourgeoise, La 1927,O 16,IX,4:7

Franda, Charles
Babu 1967,D 23,28:1

Franekl, Daniel T (Lighting Director)
Spots of the Leopard, The 1963,S 25,38:1

Frangipane, Ronald (Miscellaneous)
Billy 1969,Mr 24,56:1

Frangos, Aria
Good Soldier Schweik, The 1963,Ap 9,57:1

Frangos, Christos
Iphigenia in Aulis 1968,N 13,40:1
Hippolytus 1968,N 20,38:3

Frangos, Stefani
Breaking Wall, The 1960,Ja 26,27:5

Frank, Addie
No Mother to Guide Her 1933,D 26,18:5

Frank, Alexander
Passing Show of 1922, The 1922,S 21,18:2
Artists and Models 1924,O 16,33:3
Jest, The 1926,F 5,22:2
Royal Box, The 1928,N 21,32:3
Sakura 1928,D 26,14:4
Waterloo Bridge 1930,Ja 7,29:2
Absent Father 1932,O 18,23:5

Frank, Alexander—Cont
Richard of Bordeaux 1934,F 15,16:2
Allure 1934,O 30,22:6
Parnell 1935,N 12,24:2
Parnell 1936,My 5,26:2
Point of Honor, A 1937,F 12,26:2

Frank, Allan
Revolt of the Beavers, The 1937,My 21,19:2
Pinocchio 1939,Ja 3,19:2
Steel 1939,D 20,30:2
Skipper Next to God 1948,Ja 5,14:5
I Never Sang for My Father 1968,Ja 26,30:1

Frank, Allan (Producer)
Whitman Portrait, A 1966,O 12,37:1

Frank, Amy
Tick-Tack-Toe 1920,F 24,11:2
Hotel Mouse, The 1922,Mr 14,11:3

Frank, Anne (Miscellaneous)
Diary of Anne Frank, The 1955,O 16,II,1:1

Frank, Anne (Original Author)
Diary of Anne Frank, The 1956,N 29,43:1
Diary of Anne Frank, The 1963,Ap 12,33:1
Diary, The 1966,N 27,159:3

Frank, Arlyne
Let's Make an Opera 1950,D 14,50:2

Frank, Art
Vaudeville (Hippodrome) 1926,Mr 30,20:4
Vaudeville (Palace) 1926,Ap 27,22:3
Vaudeville (Palace) 1926,D 28,12:3
Vaudeville (Palace) 1930,My 26,25:2
Vaudeville (Palace) 1930,N 24,26:3

Frank, Barry
Old Bucks and New Wings 1962,N 6,39:4

Frank, Benno (Dr) (Miscellaneous)
Midsummer Night's Dream, A 1950,Je 22,33:2

Frank, Benno D (Director)
Penny Friend, The 1966,D 27,46:1

Frank, Bernard
Anya 1965,N 30,48:1

Frank, Betty
Village Wedding, A 1930,S 24,26:2
My Little Girl 1931,F 2,22:4
Night in the Woods, A 1931,Mr 2,19:3

Frank, Bruno (Original Author)
Storm in a Teacup 1936,F 6,23:1
Young Madame Conti 1937,Ap 1,18:4

Frank, Bruno (Playwright)
Twelve Thousand 1928,Mr 13,23:1
Twelve Thousand 1928,Mr 18,IX,1:1
Perlenkomoedie 1929,Ap 7,X,4:4
Sturm im Wasserglas 1930,D 28,VIII,2:4
Nina 1935,S 18,19:6
Nina 1935,O 13,IX,3:1
Nina 1935,N 3,X,3:8
Young Madame Conti 1936,N 20,26:4
Young Madame Conti 1936,D 6,XII,7:6
Storm Over Patsy 1937,Mr 2,16:4
Storm Over Patsy 1937,Mr 9,26:4

Frank, Carl
Paths of Glory 1935,S 27,24:2
Sound of Hunting, A 1945,N 21,16:6
Shrike, The 1953,N 26,51:2

Frank, Charles (Translator)
Intimate Relations 1962,N 2,27:1

Frank, David
Life With Mother 1948,Je 9,36:3
Life With Mother 1948,O 21,32:2

Frank, Dottie
Leonard Sillman's New Faces of 1968
1968,My 3,43:1

Frank, Eileen
Come Out, Carlo! 1962,My 4,27:2

Frank, Elsie
Tick-Tack-Toe 1920,F 24,11:2

Frank, Ethel
Fuente Ovejuna; Sheep Well, The 1936,My 3,II,4:1

Frank, Ethel (Director)
Nine Till Six 1936,Mr 14,10:3

Frank, Gerald A
Flying Blind 1930,My 16,20:2

Frank, Gerold (Playwright)
Who's Who, Baby? 1968,Ja 30,36:1

Frank, H
Roaming Stars 1930,Ja 25,12:2

Frank, Howard
Show Boat 1946,Ja 7,17:2
Show Boat 1948,S 9,33:2

Frank, J Herbert
Don Juan 1921,S 8,14:2

Frank, Jacob
Four Walls 1927,S 20,33:1
Street Wolf, The 1929,Ja 1,61:1
Up and Up, The 1930,S 9,25:2

Frank, Janet
Sign of Jonah, The 1957,My 2,27:1

Frank, Joanna
Hey You, Light Man! 1963,Mr 2,5:2

Frank, Josephine
Veronica's Veil 1933,F 20,11:7

Frank, Judy
Xmas in Las Vegas 1965,N 5,31:1
Now Is the Time for all Good Men 1967,S 27,42:1

Frank, Lee
Guest of Honor, The 1920,S 21,12:1

Frank, Len
Lady in the Dark 1941,Ja 24,14:2
Frank, Leonhard (Original Author)
Karl and Anna 1935,O 13,IX,3:1
Frank, Leonhard (Playwright)
Karl und Anna 1929,Mr 10,X,2:1
Karl und Anna 1929,My 5,IX,2:4
Ursache, Die 1929,My 12,IX,1:8
Karl and Anna 1929,O 8,34:1
Karl and Anna 1935,O 13,IX,3:1
Frank, Mary K (Miscellaneous)
Tea and Sympathy 1953,O 1,35:1
Frank, Mary K (Producer)
Too Late the Phalarope 1956,O 12,35:1
One More River 1960,Mr 19,12:2
Sponono 1964,Ap 3,28:1
Frank, Melvin (Playwright)
Li'l Abner 1956,N 16,24:2
Li'l Abner 1956,N 25,II,1:1
Frank, Melvin (Producer)
Li'l Abner 1956,N 16,24:2
Frank, Michael (Miscellaneous)
People vs Ranchman, The 1968,O 28,56:1
Perfect Party, The 1969,Mr 21,42:1
End of All Things Natural, The 1969,S 12,38:1
Frank, Neal
Nightingale, The 1927,Ja 4,20:4
Frank, Nelson
Centuries, The 1927,N 30,23:1
Frank, Nino (Playwright)
Ex-Napoleon 1960,D 29,16:3
Frank, Pat (Original Author)
Mr Adam 1949,My 26,34:6
Frank, Paul (Original Author)
Mandarin, The 1920,N 10,18:2
Frank, Paul (Playwright)
Four in Hand 1923,S 7,10:2
Ladies Don't Lie 1929,O 11,36:3
Grand Hotel 1929,D 22,VIII,4:6
Frank, Perry (Producer)
New Moon, The 1944,My 18,16:2
Frank, Robert
Riverside Drive 1931,Ja 6,24:2
Frank, Ruth
Laughing Woman, The 1936,O 14,30:1
Frank, Sherman (Choreographer)
Conquering Hero, The 1961,Ja 17,40:2
Frank, Sherman (Musical Director)
Conquering Hero, The 1961,Ja 17,40:2
Pousse-Cafe 1966,Mr 19,19:2
Frank, Stanley
Sound of Hunting, A 1954,Ap 7,41:1
Frank, Susan
Great Sebastians, The 1956,Ja 5,27:1
Frank, Thomas
Curtain Call 1937,Ap 23,24:7
Frank, Vanya
Bourgeois Gentilhomme, Le 1964,Je 18,28:2
Frank, Virginia
Ethan Frome 1936,Ja 22,15:2
Frank, Yasha (Director)
Pinocchio 1939,Ja 3,19:2
Frank, Yasha (Playwright)
Pinocchio 1939,Ja 3,19:2
Frank (Playwright)
Musik um Susi 1933,Ja 1,IX,1:1
Frank-Hirschfeld (Original Author)
Business With America 1933,Ja 1,IX,1:3
Frankau, Edla
Taming of the Shrew, The 1927,O 26,26:4
Elizabeth the Queen 1930,N 4,37:1
Frankau, Pamela (Playwright)
Who's Taking Liberty 1939,D 17,IX,4:4
Franke, Anthony
Making of Moo, The 1958,Je 12,34:1
Franke, Nick
Titus Andronicus 1956,D 3,40:2
Oscar Wilde 1957,Ap 20,21:3
Frankel, Aaron M (Director)
Ah, Wilderness! 1953,F 7,10:6
Ah, Wilderness! 1953,F 15,II,1:1
Viva Madison Avenue 1960,Ap 7,42:1
Frankel, Beulah (Costume Designer)
Show-Off, The 1950,Je 1,24:5
Julius Caesar 1950,Je 21,30:1
Frankel, Beulah (Lighting Director)
Show-Off, The 1950,Je 1,24:5
Frankel, Beulah (Miscellaneous)
Me, The Sleeper 1949,My 16,18:6
Frankel, Daniel
'Toinette 1961,N 21,46:1
Pocket Watch, The 1966,Ja 6,18:1
Kitchen, The 1966,Je 14,50:1
Frankel, Doris (Playwright)
Don't Throw Glass Houses 1938,D 28,24:4
Love Me Long 1949,N 8,34:5
Frankel, Eddie
Tick-Tack-Toe 1920,F 24,11:2
Frankel, Evan M (Miscellaneous)
Gramercy Ghost 1951,Ap 27,20:2
Frankel, Gene (Director)
John Brown 1950,My 4,32:7
Volpone 1957,Ja 8,27:1

Volpone 1957,Ja 13,II,10:1
Enemy of the People, An 1959,F 5,24:4
Machinal 1960,Ap 8,27:1
Machinal 1960,Ap 17,II,1:1
Once There Was a Russian 1961,F 20,32:2
Blacks, The 1961,My 5,23:1
Blacks, The 1961,My 14,II,1:1
Brecht on Brecht 1961,N 15,52:2
Brecht on Brecht 1962,Ja 4,26:1
Brecht on Brecht 1962,Ja 14,II,1:1
Firebugs, The 1963,F 13,7:2
Niggerlovers, The; Demonstration, The
1967,O 2,54:2
Niggerlovers, The; Man and Dog 1967,O 2,54:2
Niggerlovers, The 1967,O 15,II,3:3
Cry of Players, A 1968,N 15,40:1
To Be Young Gifted and Black; World of Lorraine
Hansberry, The 1969,Ja 3,15:1
Indians 1969,My 18,II,3:5
To Be Young, Gifted and Black: The World of
Lorraine Hansberry 1969,My 25,II,1:5
Indians 1969,My 27,43:1
Indians 1969,O 14,51:1
Indians 1969,O 19,II,1:1
Engagement Baby, The 1970,My 22,40:1
Frankel, Gene (Producer)
Volpone 1957,Ja 8,27:1
Enemy of the People, An 1959,F 5,24:4
Frankel, Kenneth
Richard III 1965,Je 3,26:1
Dinner at Eight 1966,S 28,38:1
Frankel, Kenneth (Miscellaneous)
Doctor's Dilemma, The 1969,Je 24,37:1
Frankel, Leo
Unwritten Chapter, The 1920,O 12,18:1
Blue Eyes 1921,F 22,11:2
Frankel, Richard (Miscellaneous)
Street Sounds 1970,O 23,32:1
Franken, Edgar
Flight Into Egypt 1952,Mr 19,33:2
Lulu 1958,S 30,24:1
Franken, Rose (Director)
Claudia 1941,F 13,24:2
Outrageous Fortune 1943,N 4,28:5
Doctors Disagree 1943,D 29,15:2
Soldier's Wife 1944,O 5,18:6
Hallams, The 1948,Mr 5,18:2
Franken, Rose (Playwright)
Another Language 1932,Ap 26,25:3
Another Language 1932,My 15,VIII,1:1
Another Language 1932,D 25,IX,1:6
Another Language 1933,My 9,20:2
Claudia 1941,F 13,24:2
Claudia 1941,Mr 9,IX,1:1
Claudia 1942,My 25,11:3
Claudia 1942,S 27,VIII,2:2
Claudia 1942,O 4,VIII,2:1
Outrageous Fortune 1943,N 4,28:5
Doctors Disagree 1943,D 29,15:2
Soldier's Wife 1944,O 5,18:6
Soldier's Wife 1944,O 15,II,1:1
Soldier's Wife 1946,S 2,13:2
Hallams, The 1948,Mr 5,18:2
Franken, Stephen
Edwin Booth 1958,N 25,37:1
Say Darling 1959,F 26,38:2
Frankenstein, Alfred V
Trachiniae 1931,Ja 27,21:2
Franklin, Anna
Sweet River 1936,O 29,30:2
Brother Rat 1936,D 17,34:5
Old Acquaintance 1940,D 24,18:3
Solitaire 1942,Ja 28,22:2
Ask My Friend Sandy 1943,F 5,16:2
Down to Miami 1944,S 12,23:5
Franklin, Barbara
Salad Days 1958,N 11,24:1
Franklin, Ben
Hello, Lola! 1926,Ja 13,30:1
Franklin, Bennie
Passing Show of 1924, The 1924,S 4,13:4
Franklin, Bonnie
Applause 1970,Mr 31,35:1
Applause 1970,Ap 5,II,1:1
Franklin, Booth
Pearl of Great Price, The 1926,N 2,34:3
Franklin, C Lester (Playwright)
Scaffold for Marionettes, A 1968,Mr 24,II,16:5
Franklin, Clyde
Up and Up, The 1930,S 9,25:2
Precedent 1931,Ap 15,24:5
Lost Boy 1932,Ja 6,24:4
When the Bough Breaks 1932,F 17,19:2
Bloodstream 1932,Mr 31,25:1
Good Earth, The 1932,O 18,23:4
Peace on Earth 1933,N 30,39:2
Hide and Seek 1934,Ag 7,20:2
Strangers at Home 1934,S 15,20:5
Hipper's Holiday 1934,O 19,26:2
Black Pit 1935,Mr 21,26:6
Slight Case of Murder, A 1935,S 12,28:5
Lend Me Your Ears! 1936,O 6,28:5
All Editions 1936,D 23,17:2

Franklin, Clyde—Cont
Too Many Heroes 1937,N 16,26:2
On Borrowed Time 1938,F 4,16:4
Days of Our Youth, The 1941,N 29,15:2
Autumn Hill 1942,Ap 14,17:4
Franklin, Daniel
Sing Israel Sing 1967,My 12,50:1
Of Thee I Sing 1969,Mr 8,19:1
Franklin, Earl
Wann und Wo 1927,D 18,IX,1:8
Franklin, Edgar (Original Author)
No More Blondes 1920,Ja 8,22:1
Franklin, Edgar (Playwright)
White Collars 1925,F 24,17:2
Franklin, Eva
Creoles 1927,S 23,33:3
Franklin, Eva (Costume Designer)
Year Round, The 1953,My 6,38:7
Franklin, Eva (Translator)
From Vienna 1939,Je 21,26:2
Franklin, Frederic
Song of Norway 1944,Ag 22,20:2
Franklin, George
Bonds of Interest, The 1951,D 1,7:2
Franklin, Harold B (Producer)
Lady Jane 1934,S 11,24:2
Continental Varieties 1934,O 4,18:3
Conversation Piece 1934,O 24,24:1
Aiglon, L' 1934,N 5,22:2
Revenge With Music 1934,N 29,33:5
Franklin, Hugh
Harriet 1943,Mr 4,24:2
One-Man Show 1945,F 9,21:2
Medea 1947,O 21,27:2
I Know My Love 1949,F 24,29:2
I Know My Love 1949,N 3,36:1
Best Man, The 1960,Ap 1,39:1
Shot in the Dark, A 1961,O 19,40:1
Arturo Ui 1963,N 12,49:1
Devils, The 1965,N 17,51:2
What Did We Do Wrong? 1967,O 23,56:1
Possibilities 1968,D 5,60:1
How Much, How Much? 1970,Ap 21,49:1
Franklin, Irene
Greenwich Village Follies 1921,S 1,18:3
Vaudeville (Palace) 1925,O 6,31:3
Vaudeville (Palace) 1926,My 8,29:2
Vaudeville (Palace) 1929,Mr 11,22:5
Sweet Adeline 1929,Ag 25,VIII,3:1
Sweet Adeline 1929,S 4,33:1
Vaudeville (Palace) 1930,Mr 7,21:2
Franklin, Irving P (Director)
Hotel Alimony 1934,Ja 30,16:2
Franklin, Irving P (Producer)
Hotel Alimony 1934,Ja 30,16:2
Franklin, Jane
Man Who Married a Dumb Wife, The
1930,My 9,20:5
Franklin, Joyce
Bright Boy 1944,Mr 3,19:5
Franklin, Lee
Rothschilds, The 1970,O 20,40:1
Franklin, Leonard
Nautical but Nice 1931,Ap 19,31:6
Porgy and Bess 1935,O 11,30:2
Franklin, Lidija
Brigadoon 1947,Mr 14,28:2
Brigadoon 1947,Mr 23,II,1:1
Rape of Lucretia, The 1948,D 30,24:2
Fledermaus, Die 1954,My 20,38:5
Brigadoon 1957,Mr 28,37:1
Franklin, Marion
Prodigal Son, The 1965,My 21,19:1
Franklin, Marion (Composer)
Prodigal Son, The 1965,My 21,19:1
Franklin, Marion (Musical Director)
Prodigal Son, The 1965,My 21,19:1
Franklin, Maude
Bully, The 1924,D 26,18:1
Franklin, Miriam
Let's Face It 1941,O 30,26:2
Franklin, Murray
Belt, The 1927,O 20,33:1
Centuries, The 1927,N 30,23:1
Hoboken Blues 1928,F 18,10:1
Franklin, Nancy
Temporary Island, A 1948,Mr 15,27:3
Lend an Ear 1948,D 17,38:2
Rose Tattoo, The 1951,F 5,19:2
Wish You Were Here 1952,Je 26,26:6
Buffalo Skinner, The 1959,F 20,18:1
Power of Darkness, The 1959,S 30,33:1
Theater of Peretz, The 1963,N 6,35:2
Never Live Over a Pretzel Factory 1964,Mr 30,37:1
White House, The 1964,My 20,39:1
Seven Days of Mourning 1969,D 17,64:1
Bad Place to Get Your Head, A 1970,Jl 16,38:1
Here Be Dragons 1970,D 21,52:1
Franklin, Nony
Red Mill, The 1945,O 17,16:2
Sweethearts 1947,Ja 22,31:2
Franklin, Norman (Playwright)
These Are the Times 1950,My 11,37:2

Franklin, Pearl
Rise of Rosie O'Reilly, The 1923,D 26,13:4
Franklin, Pearl (Playwright)
Cowboy Crazy 1926,Ag 1,VII,4:1
Franklin, Roger
Trial by Jury 1952,N 4,32:2
Vamp, The 1955,N 11,30:1
West Side Story 1960,Ap 28,31:1
Canterbury Tales; Wife of Bath's Tale, The
1969,F 4,34:1
Franklin, Roy (Miscellaneous)
Miss Emily Adam 1960,Mr 30,43:1
Franklin, Susie
Creoles 1927,S 23,33:3
Franklin, William
John Hawthorne 1921,Ja 24,16:1
Merchant of Venice, The 1921,Ap 2,14:2
Liliom 1921,Ap 21,18:1
Cloister, The 1921,Je 6,16:3
Peer Gynt 1923,F 6,14:1
Man and the Masses 1924,Ap 15,25:1
Ringside 1928,Ag 30,13:2
Final Balance, The 1928,O 31,28:3
Criminal Code, The 1929,O 3,28:2
This One Man 1930,O 22,32:3
I Love an Actress 1931,S 18,29:2
Broadway Boy 1932,My 4,23:5
Good Earth, The 1932,O 18,23:4
Mother Lode 1934,D 24,16:5
Siege 1937,D 9,31:4
All the Living 1938,Mr 25,14:4
Swing Mikado, The 1939,Mr 2,18:2
As You Like It 1939,My 9,28:4
Porgy and Bess 1944,F 8,13:2
Carib Song 1945,S 28,17:2
Franklyn, Barry
As You Like It 1936,Ap 24,18:4
Franklyn, Beth
Pot-Luck 1921,S 30,10:1
Cat and the Canary, The 1922,F 8,13:1
New Poor, The 1924,Ja 8,26:1
Slight Case of Murder, A 1935,S 12,28:5
Franklyn, Clyde
War Song, The 1928,S 25,29:3
Franklyn, Roy (Director)
Nathan the Wise 1962,Mr 23,29:1
Franklyn, Roy (Miscellaneous)
Obbligato 1958,F 19,22:2
Comic Strip 1958,My 15,26:2
Ronde, La 1960,My 10,44:2
Franklyn, Roy (Playwright)
Nathan the Wise 1962,Mr 23,29:1
Franklyn, Roy (Producer)
Nathan the Wise 1962,Mr 23,29:1
Brownstone Urge, The 1969,D 18,63:1
Franklyn, Walter
Merry Widow, The 1931,S 8,39:1
Franklyn, William
Berlin 1931,D 31,16:1
Straight Up 1970,S 2,30:2
Franklyn and Charles
Vaudeville (Palace) 1921,Jl 5,15:1
Franks, Dobbs (Musical Director)
King of the Whole Damn World 1962,Ap 16,32:2
Franks, Laurie
Around the World in 80 Days 1963,Je 24,22:1
Something More! 1964,N 11,36:1
Anya 1965,N 30,48:1
Franks, Mack
Ten Nights in a Barroom 1932,Ja 21,17:1
Franks, Thetta Quay (Playwright)
Money in the Air 1932,Mr 8,19:3
Frann, Mary
Story Theater 1970,O 27,54:1
Franqui, Hermes
Retabilillo de Don Cristobal, El; Puppet Theater of
Don Cristobal, The; Zapatera Prodigiosa, La;
Shoemaker's Prodigious Wife, The 1964,S 3,23:2
Fransioli, Flora
Dodsworth 1934,F 26,20:4
Fransioli, Margaret
Medea 1920,Mr 23,12:2
Franson, Eric
Wild Duck, The 1938,Ap 16,16:5
Franz, Arthur
Hope for a Harvest 1941,N 27,28:2
Witch, The 1942,S 28,13:1
Little Darling 1942,O 28,26:2
Moon Vine, The 1943,F 12,22:2
Little Brown Jug 1946,Mr 7,32:2
Rip Van Winkle 1947,Jl 16,28:2
Command Decision 1947,O 2,30:2
Franz, Eduard
Rapid Transit 1927,Ap 8,21:2
Belt, The 1927,O 20,33:1
Centuries, The 1927,N 30,23:1
International, The 1928,Ja 16,24:4
Hot Pan 1928,F 16,14:1
Three 1928,D 4,28:2
Broken Chain, The 1929,F 21,30:4
Shakespeare's Merchant 1939 1939,Ja 10,16:3
Miss Swan Expects 1939,F 21,15:2
Brown Danube, The 1939,My 18,30:4

Farm of Three Echoes 1939,N 29,18:3
First Stop to Heaven 1941,Ja 6,10:7
Cafe Crown 1942,Ja 24,12:5
Russian People, The 1942,D 16,21:3
Russian People, The 1942,D 30,17:2
Outrageous Fortune 1943,N 4,28:5
Cherry Orchard, The 1944,Ja 26,22:1
Cherry Orchard, The 1944,F 6,II,1:1
Embezzled Heaven 1944,N 1,20:2
Stranger, The 1945,F 13,21:2
Home of the Brave 1945,D 28,13:2
Home of the Brave 1946,Ja 6,II,1:1
Big Two, The 1947,Ja 9,21:2
Egghead, The 1957,O 10,39:1
Conversation at Midnight 1964,N 13,27:1
Those That Play the Clowns 1966,N 25,48:1
In the Matter of J Robert Oppenheimer
1968,Je 7,31:1
In the Matter of J Robert Oppenheimer
1968,Je 9,II,1:1
In the Matter of J Robert Oppenheimer
1969,Mr 7,28:1
Uncle Vanya 1969,Ag 31,II,4:1
Franz, Elizabeth
Death of the Well-Loved Boy, The
1967,My 16,48:1
One Night Stands of a Noisy Passenger; Passage,
Un 1970,D 31,8:3
Franz, Joy
Of Thee I Sing 1969,Mr 8,19:1
Franz, Miss
Folly Town 1920,My 18,9:2
Franz, Victor
Harriet 1943,Mr 4,24:2
Franzell, Carlotta
Carmen Jones 1943,D 3,26:2
Carmen Jones 1945,My 3,26:5
Franzos, Leslie
110 in the Shade 1963,O 25,37:1
Sherry! 1967,Mr 29,39:1
Brigadoon 1967,D 14,59:2
Frasca, Mary A
Off the Record; Mayor Answers the Newspapers!
Wow! 1935,Je 19,23:3
Fraser, Andrew
Verge, The 1921,N 15,23:2
Fraser, Ann
Brigadoon 1962,My 31,21:4
Brigadoon 1963,F 1,6:2
Oklahoma! 1963,F 28,8:2
Fraser, Anne (Scenic Designer)
Summer of the Seventeenth Doll 1958,Ja 23,23:2
Fraser, Bill
Heartbreak House 1967,Ag 27,II,1:1
Heartbreak House 1968,Jl 6,9:1
Twelfth Night 1969,S 1,13:1
Fraser, Bryant
Poor Bitos 1964,N 16,40:2
Our Town 1969,N 28,50:1
Child's Play 1970,F 18,39:1
Fraser, Elisabeth
There Shall Be No Night 1940,Ap 30,25:2
Russian People, The 1942,D 16,21:3
Russian People, The 1942,D 30,17:2
Family, The 1943,Mr 31,22:4
Winged Victory 1943,N 22,24:1
Mr Adam 1949,My 26,34:6
Tunnel of Love, The 1957,F 14,31:4
Great Day in the Morning 1962,Mr 29,29:1
Fraser, Ferrin L
His Majesty the Queen 1926,Mr 9,8:1
Fraser, Harry
All-Star Jamboree 1921,Jl 14,18:1
Fraser, Helen
Beaux' Stratagem, The 1970,F 10,50:2
Beaux' Stratagem, The 1970,F 22,II,1:1
Fraser, Ian (Miscellaneous)
Stop the World-I Want to Get Off 1962,O 4,45:4
Fraser, Jane
Sing Out the News 1938,S 26,12:5
Pal Joey 1940,D 26,22:2
Fraser, John (Playwright)
Cannibal Crackers 1969,N 25,52:2
Fraser, June
Trouble in July 1949,D 2,36:2
Fraser, Pamela
On an Open Roof 1963,Ja 30,7:3
Fraser, Ronald
Grosse Valise, La 1965,D 15,52:1
Fraser, Simon
Twelfth Night 1958,D 10,54:2
Fraser, Stuart
Anything Goes 1934,N 22,26:1
Fraser, Winifred
Mary Rose 1920,D 23,9:2
Mary, Mary, Quite Contrary 1923,S 12,14:1
Captive, The 1926,S 30,23:1
Interference 1927,O 19,24:3
Stepdaughters of War 1930,O 7,27:1
Frasher, James
Susannah and the Elders 1959,O 19,37:3
Tobacco Road 1960,My 11,44:2

Frasher, James (Miscellaneous)
Thor, With Angels 1956,O 15,29:4
Box of Watercolors, A 1957,F 18,22:2
Frasier, Sudworth
Princess Ida 1925,Ap 14,27:2
Merry World, The 1926,Je 9,18:3
Gondoliers, The 1931,Je 2,34:4
Frass-Wolfsburg, Peter (Lighting Director)
Why Do I Deserve This? 1966,Ja 19,31:2
Fratellini, The
Untitled-Revue 1928,S 23,IX,2:1
Fratus, Estelle
Sketch Book 1929,Jl 2,33:5
Fraunberger, George S
Hoot Mon, or Clans Across the Sea 1927,My 8,29:4
Fraunie, Francis
Any Woman 1934,Ag 28,24:4
Fraunie, Francis (Director)
Babies a La Carte 1927,Ag 16,31:1
Frawley, Bernard
All's Well That Ends Well 1970,Je 16,53:1
Othello 1970,Je 22,43:1
Devil's Disciple, The 1970,Je 30,48:1
Othello 1970,S 15,51:1
Greenwillow 1970,D 8,60:1
Frawley, Daniel (Director)
March Hares 1928,Ap 3,32:6
Frawley, James
Golden Six, The 1958,O 27,31:2
Antony and Cleopatra 1959,Ja 14,28:1
Time of Vengeance 1959,D 11,39:1
Between Two Thieves 1960,F 12,23:1
Becket 1961,My 9,44:1
Untitled-Revue 1961,Je 18,II,1:1
Premise, The 1962,Jl 27,15:5
Anyone Can Whistle 1964,Ap 6,36:1
Frawley, Paul
Three Showers 1920,Ap 6,18:1
Kissing Time 1920,O 12,18:2
Irving Berlin's Music Box Revue 1921,S 23,18:2
Helen of Troy, New York 1923,Je 20,22:6
Sunny 1925,S 23,22:1
Piggy 1927,Ja 12,22:2
Manhattan Mary 1927,S 27,30:3
Treasure Girl 1928,N 9,22:1
Top Speed 1929,D 26,20:1
Here Goes the Bride 1931,N 4,31:2
Frawley, T Daniel (Director)
Springboard, The 1927,O 13,23:1
Ink 1927,N 2,24:2
Frawley, William
Merry Merry 1925,S 25,24:3
Bye Bye Bonnie 1927,Ja 14,15:3
She's My Baby 1928,Ja 4,22:2
Here's Howe! 1928,My 2,19:3
Carry On 1929,N 3,IX,1:7
Sons o' Guns 1929,N 27,30:4
She Lived Next to the Firehouse 1931,F 11,23:1
Tell Her the Truth 1932,O 29,18:2
20th Century 1932,D 30,15:1
Twentieth Century 1933,F 12,IX,1:1
Ghost Writer, The 1933,Je 20,22:4
Fray, Gilberti
Adam Had Two Sons 1932,Ja 21,17:1
Fray, Jacques
Vaudeville (Carnegie Hall) 1931,Ap 12,I,30:4
Maurice Chevalier 1932,F 10,26:6
Fray, Jacques (Composer)
Vanderbilt Revue, The 1930,N 6,22:6
Fray, Ray
Danton's Death 1965,O 22,46:1
Frayn, Michael (Playwright)
Two of Us, The 1970,Ag 1,13:2
Two of Us, The 1970,S 11,33:2
Frayne, Frank I
Malvaloca 1922,O 3,22:1
Leap, The 1924,My 23,16:5
Made for Each Other 1924,S 30,27:2
Two by Two 1925,F 24,17:1
Made in America 1925,O 15,27:2
Move On 1926,Ja 19,30:1
Faust 1927,Ja 4,20:1
Exceeding Small 1928,O 23,32:2
Wild Duck, The 1928,N 19,17:1
Whispering Gallery, The 1929,F 12,22:2
Roadside 1930,S 27,21:1
Near to the Stars 1932,F 23,23:2
Frayne, Frank I (Mrs)
Pilgrimage, The; Pelerin, Le 1925,N 10,23:2
Frayne, Viola
Intruder, The 1928,Jl 26,25:4
Tonight at 12 1928,N 16,28:1
This Man's Town 1930,Mr 11,24:4
Stepdaughters of War 1930,O 7,27:1
He 1931,S 22,33:1
Merry-Go-Round 1932,Ap 23,11:2
Spring Freshet 1934,O 5,28:3
Weather Permitting 1935,My 24,24:5
Lady Luck 1936,Ap 16,21:2
Hedda Gabler 1936,N 17,34:4
Listen Professor! 1943,D 23,22:1
No Way Out 1944,O 31,23:1

Frazee, H H (Producer)
Yes, Yes, Yvette 1927,O 4,32:3
Frazee, Treva
Sundown Beach 1948,S 8,37:1
Frazee Sisters
Revels of 1936 1935,S 30,12:4
Frazer, Dan
Grass Is Always Greener, The 1955,F 16,25:2
Who Was That Lady I Saw You With?
1958,Mr 4,33:2
Once More With Feeling 1958,O 22,39:1
Goodbye Charlie 1959,D 17,50:1
Frazer, Winifred
Enchanted Cottage, The 1923,Ap 2,22:3
Frazier, Bob
March March, The 1966,N 15,51:4
Frazier, Cliff
Boy; Job; The; Study in Color 1964,Ag 1,13:1
Frazier, Eloise
Right of Possession 1930,My 9,20:5
Twelfth Disciple, The 1930,My 17,21:4
Frazier, Harry
Winter's Tale, The 1963,Je 29,13:1
Midsummer Night's Dream, A 1963,Jl 1,19:2
Much Ado About Nothing 1964,Je 11,26:2
Richard III 1964,Je 12,44:2
Hamlet 1964,Jl 4,9:1
Tiny Alice 1969,S 30,42:1
Flea in Her Ear, A 1969,O 4,25:1
Three Sisters, The 1969,O 10,38:1
Tiny Alice 1969,O 12,II,9:1
Frazier, Kay
Snow Maiden, The 1960,Ap 5,43:3
Frazier, Ronald
Brother to Dragons 1968,D 8,86:1
Wilson in the Promise Land 1970,Ja 11,78:1
Wilson in the Promise Land 1970,My 27,41:1
Frazier, Smith E
Ballyhoo 1927,Ja 5,18:1
Frazin, Gladys
Masked Woman, The 1922,D 23,14:2
Marriage Is No Joke 1934,F 7,16:2
Frazzi, Vito (Musical Director)
Strega, La 1939,Jl 23,IX,5:3
Frech, Albert
Quo Vadis 1932,O 17,18:2
Passion Play 1934,F 12,15:1
Veronica's Veil 1936,F 10,19:6
Frechette, Marilyn
Miss Liberty 1949,Jl 16,6:5
Frechtman, Bernard (Translator)
Deathwatch 1958,O 10,34:2
Balcony, The 1960,Mr 4,21:1
Balcony, The 1960,Mr 20,II,1:1
Blacks, The 1961,My 5,23:1
Blacks, The 1961,My 14,II,1:1
Maids, The 1963,N 15,29:1
Freda, Steve
Vaudeville (Palace) 1926,O 19,27:5
Vaudeville (Palace) 1927,Je 7,27:3
Frede, Lazor
Wolves 1924,D 31,9:4
Frederic, Agatha
Spring Fever 1925,Ag 4,14:2
Frederic, George
Mongolia 1927,D 27,24:5
Frederic, Joe
Viva O'Brien 1941,O 10,27:2
Frederic, Marion
Field God, The 1927,Ap 22,18:2
One Sunday Afternoon 1933,F 16,23:5
Slight Case of Murder, A 1935,S 12,28:5
Frederic, Willa (Playwright)
Feather in the Breeze 1936,Jl 14,22:2
Inconstant Moon, The 1937,Ag 18,15:2
Frederic, William
Squaw Man, The 1921,D 27,10:3
Sam Abramovitch 1927,Ja 20,20:5
Babbling Brookes 1927,F 26,13:2
Frankie and Johnny 1930,S 26,16:5
Frederick, G
Nowhere Bound 1935,Ja 23,20:2
Frederick, Hal
Dutchman; Slave, The 1965,N 17,53:7
Frederick, John
Miracle in the Mountains 1947,Ap 26,10:2
Frederick, Lee
More the Merrier, The 1941,S 16,19:3
Frederick, Leonard
Five Star Saint 1970,F 11,41:2
Frederick, Norman
Around the World in 80 Days 1964,Je 29,33:2
Frederick, Otto
Machinal 1928,S 8,10:3
Little Ol' Boy 1933,Ap 25,15:5
Frederick, Pauline
Guilty One, The 1922,Ag 13,VI,1:3
Guilty One, The 1923,Mr 21,19:1
Madame X 1927,Mr 11,24:3
Madame X 1927,Ap 3,VIII,1:4
Scarlet Woman, The 1929,Ja 27,IX,1:3
When the Bough Breaks 1932,F 17,19:2
Her Majesty the Widow 1934,Je 19,24:5

Masque of Kings, The 1937,Ja 31,XI,2:1
Masque of the Kings, The 1937,F 9,19:4
Across the Blue 1937,Je 1,27:1
Her Majesty the Widow 1937,Jl 14,16:2
Frederick, Pauline (Director)
Housewarming 1932,Ap 8,25:1
Her Majesty the Widow 1934,Je 19,24:5
Frederick, Philis
Babbling Brookes 1927,F 26,13:2
Frederick, William
Sam Abramovitch 1927,Ja 20,20:5
Fredericks, Arline
Kiki 1921,N 30,13:1
Fredericks, Charles
Show Boat 1946,Ja 7,17:2
Show Boat 1946,Ja 13,II,1:1
Music in My Heart 1947,O 3,30:2
Lady From Paris, The 1950,S 27,36:1
Fredericks, Chester
Earl Carroll's Vanities 1924,S 11,23:6
Florida Girl 1925,N 3,34:1
Gay Paree 1926,N 10,24:2
Fredericks, Claude (Playwright)
Charlatans; On Circe's Island 1962,Ap 27,26:1
Charlatans; Summer Ghost, A 1962,Ap 27,26:1
Fredericks, Claude (Translator)
Tonight We Improvise 1959,N 7,27:4
Fredericks, G
Oedipus Rex 1923,O 26,14:1
Fredericks, George
Immodest Violet 1920,Ag 25,6:2
Happy 1927,D 6,26:3
Fredericks, Lydia
Up in Central Park 1945,Ja 29,17:2
Show Boat 1946,Ja 7,17:2
Girl in Pink Tights, The 1954,Mr 6,13:2
Fredericks, Lydia S
Funny Girl 1964,Mr 27,15:1
Fredericks, Norman
Song of Norway 1959,Je 26,16:2
Fredericks, Padjet
Caribbean Carnival 1947,D 6,12:2
Fredericks, Richard
200 Were Chosen 1936,N 21,21:1
H M S Pinafore 1961,F 2,26:6
H M S Pinafore 1968,Ap 29,47:2
Fredericks, Rita (Miscellaneous)
Sunset 1966,My 13,34:1
Hand Is on the Gate, A 1966,S 22,54:1
Fredericks, Rita (Producer)
Kitchen, The 1966,Je 14,50:1
Fredericks, Saul
Volpone 1967,Je 30,29:1
Frederics, Marion
Silent Witness, The 1931,Mr 24,31:5
Fredrick, Millie Bruhl (Playwright)
Thorntons, The 1956,F 15,26:1
Fredricks, Richard
Gondoliers, The 1961,Ja 26,33:2
Iolanthe 1962,Ap 12,42:4
South Pacific 1968,Je 30,54:2
Fredricks, Rita (Miscellaneous)
Slave, The 1964,D 17,51:1
Toilet, The 1964,D 17,51:1
Fredrik, Burry (Director)
Decameron, The 1961,Ap 13,32:1
Fredrik, Burry (Miscellaneous)
Loss of Roses, A 1959,N 30,27:1
Viva Madison Avenue 1960,Ap 7,42:1
Harold 1962,N 30,27:1
Never Live Over a Pretzel Factory 1964,Mr 30,37:1
But, Seriously... 1969,F 28,29:1
Show Me Where the Good Times Are
1970,Mr 6,32:1
Fredrik, Burry (Producer)
Thieves' Carnival 1955,F 2,21:1
Exiles 1957,Mr 13,27:1
Girl of the Golden West, The 1957,N 6,44:1
Too True to Be Good 1963,Mr 14,8:2
Possibilities 1968,D 5,60:1
Fredrik, John
World Waits, The 1933,O 26,22:5
Free, James S
Star of Bengal 1929,S 26,27:2
Free, Michael
Grey-Eyed People, The 1952,D 18,41:2
Freeborn, Frances
Little Theatre Tournament; Pink and Patches
1928,My 11,28:1
Freeborn, Harriet
Theodora, the Queen 1934,F 1,15:3
Freed, Bert
Counterattack 1943,F 4,27:2
One Touch of Venus 1943,O 8,14:1
Love on Leave 1944,Je 21,23:4
Firebird of Florence 1945,Mr 23,13:4
Day Before Spring, The 1945,N 23,27:2
Joy to the World 1948,Mr 19,28:2
Stone for Danny Fisher, A 1954,O 22,24:2
In the Matter of J Robert Oppenheimer
1968,Je 7,31:1
In the Matter of J Robert Oppenheimer
1968,Je 9,II,1:1

Freed, Burt
Pirates of Penzance, The 1942,F 20,20:2
Freed, Carl
Vaudeville (Palace) 1928,Ag 21,27:5
Freed, Donald (Playwright)
United States vs Julius and Ethel Rosenberg, The
1969,Ap 20,II,3:1
United States vs Julius and Ethel Rosenberg, The
1969,Ap 27,92:1
Inquest 1970,Ap 24,38:1
Inquest 1970,My 3,II,3:1
Freed, Dorothea
Eve of St Mark, The 1942,O 8,30:2
Storm Operation 1944,Ja 12,28:2
Freed, Elsa
Mrs McThing 1952,F 21,22:1
Rashomon 1959,Ja 28,36:2
Freed, Fred
Songs and Impressions 1955,S 29,38:2
Untitled-One Man Show 1967,N 20,61:1
Freed, Lazar
Silent Forces 1920,Ag 30,12:1
King Saul 1925,S 18,26:3
Tenth Commandment, The 1926,N 18,27:1
Gardener's Dog, The 1927,O 21,27:1
Gold Diggers, The 1927,D 3,19:2
On Foreign Soil 1927,D 24,8:2
Alexander Pushkin 1928,Ja 27,14:2
American Chasidim 1928,Mr 17,8:8
God Man and Devil 1928,D 22,14:8
Major Noah 1929,F 23,17:2
Jew Suss 1929,O 19,22:3
Angels on Earth 1929,D 11,34:7
Chains 1930,F 23,29:2
Witch of Castile, The 1930,O 25,21:1
Uncle Moses 1930,N 29,21:3
Man With the Portfolio, The 1931,F 12,24:6
Golem, The 1931,N 6,28:5
Armored Train No 1469 1931,N 28,20:3
New Man, The 1932,Ap 22,23:2
Yoshe Kalb 1932,O 3,15:5
Yoshe Kalb 1932,N 6,IX,2:1
Chayim Lederer 1932,N 15,24:4
Revolt 1933,Ja 12,21:3
Wise Men of Chelm, The 1933,O 18,24:4
Josephus 1933,D 1,22:5
Treasure, The 1934,D 18,25:5
60,000 Heroes 1935,Ja 28,11:5
God Man and Devil 1935,Mr 6,22:3
Power That Builds, The 1935,Mr 9,18:4
Jacques Bergson 1936,O 31,24:6
Jacques Bergson 1936,N 29,XII,3:3
Yoshe Kalb 1939,F 6,9:2
Chaver, Nachman 1939,O 2,15:2
Day of Judgement, The 1941,O 9,27:3
Freed, Les
Flora, the Red Menace 1965,My 12,41:2
It's a Bird . . . It's a Plane . . . It's Superman
1966,Mr 30,34:1
Autumn's Here 1966,O 26,40:1
Freedlander, Max
Jacques Bergson 1936,O 31,24:6
Freedley, George
Camel Through the Needle's Eye, The
1929,Ap 16,32:2
Everything's Jake 1930,Ja 17,20:4
Freedley, George (Producer)
Cellar and the Well, The 1950,D 11,30:2
Freedley, Vinton
For Goodness Sake 1922,F 22,13:1
World We Live In, The 1922,N 1,16:1
Elsie 1923,Ap 3,26:1
Freedley, Vinton (Director)
Pardon My English 1933,Ja 21,11:4
Freedley, Vinton (Miscellaneous)
Liliom 1940,Mr 26,17:2
Cabin in the Sky 1940,O 26,19:2
Memphis Bound 1945,My 25,23:2
Freedley, Vinton (Producer)
Oh, Kay! 1926,N 9,31:3
Funny Face 1927,N 23,28:2
Here's Howe! 1928,My 2,19:3
Hold Everything 1928,O 11,24:2
Treasure Girl 1928,N 9,22:1
Spring Is Here 1929,Mr 12,26:1
Heads Up! 1929,N 12,34:1
Girl Crazy 1930,O 15,27:1
Singin' the Blues 1931,Ap 12,IX,2:1
Singin' the Blues 1931,S 17,21:3
Adam Had Two Sons 1932,Ja 17,VIII,3:5
Pardon My English 1933,Ja 21,11:4
Anything Goes 1934,N 22,26:1
Red, Hot and Blue! 1936,O 8,26:1
Red, Hot and Blue! 1936,O 30,26:3
Miss Quis 1937,Ap 2,18:5
Miss Quis 1937,Ap 8,20:5
Leave It to Me! 1938,O 23,IX,3:5
Leave It to Me! 1938,N 10,32:2
Flying Ginzburgs, The 1938,N 13,IX,2:2
Liliom 1940,Mr 31,IX,1:1
Delicate Story 1940,D 5,32:2
Let's Face It 1941,O 10,27:1
Let's Face It 1941,O 30,26:2

Freedley, Vinton (Producer)—Cont
Jackpot 1944,Ja 14,15:2
Young and Fair, The 1948,N 23,35:2
Great to Be Alive! 1950,Mr 24,28:2
Freedley, Vinton Jr
So Proudly We Hail 1938,Mr 30,18:5
So Proudly We Hail 1938,Ap 9,11:1
Freedman, Benedict (Playwright)
Off Your Marx 1936,Ap 2,28:2
Freedman, Betty (Playwright)
Plot Against the Chase Manhattan Bank, The 1963,N 27,29:1
Freedman, Bill (Producer)
Staircase 1968,Ja 11,41:2
Hadrian VII 1969,Ja 9,22:1
Freedman, Carol
County Chairman, The 1936,My 26,26:5
Freedman, David (Lyricist)
Ziegfeld Follies 1934,Ja 5,24:3
Freedman, David (Miscellaneous)
Show Is On, The 1937,S 20,18:4
Freedman, David (Original Author)
Mendel, Inc 1929,S 1,VIII,1:1
Mendel, Inc 1929,N 26,28:5
Freedman, David (Playwright)
Betsy 1926,D 29,24:3
Mendel, Inc 1929,S 1,VIII,1:1
Mendel, Inc 1929,N 26,28:5
Sweet and Low 1930,N 18,28:5
Crazy Quilt 1931,My 20,28:4
Ziegfeld Follies 1934,Ja 5,24:3
Life Begins at 8:40 1934,Ag 28,24:2
Ziegfeld Follies 1936,Ja 31,17:2
Ziegfeld Follies 1936,S 15,37:1
White Horse Inn 1936,O 2,28:5
Show Is On, The 1936,D 26,14:2
Freedman, Estelle (Lighting Director)
All the King's Men 1950,Jl 19,25:6
Freedman, Gerald (Composer)
Alligators, The 1960,N 15,47:1
Rosemary 1960,N 15,47:1
Freedman, Gerald (Director)
On the Town 1959,Ja 16,36:1
On the Town 1959,Ja 25,II,1:1
Taming of the Shrew, The 1960,Ag 20,17:1
Rosemary 1960,N 15,47:1
Alligators, The 1960,N 15,47:1
Gay Life, The 1961,N 20,38:1
Tempest, The 1962,Jl 17,18:2
Bil and Cora Baird's Marionette Theater 1963,Ap 12,34:2
As You Like It 1963,Jl 17,19:2
West Side Story 1964,Ap 9,24:2
Electra 1964,Ag 12,42:1
Sing to Me Through Open Windows 1965,Mr 16,45:1
Day the Whores Came Out to Play Tennis, The 1965,Mr 16,45:1
Love's Labour's Lost 1965,Je 16,46:1
Time for Singing, A 1966,My 23,48:2
Richard III 1966,Ag 11,26:1
Comedy of Errors, The 1967,Je 15,58:4
Titus Andronicus 1967,Ag 10,43:2
Hair 1967,O 30,55:1
Hamlet 1967,D 27,45:1
Ergo 1968,Mr 4,29:1
Memorandum, The 1968,My 6,55:1
Henry IV, Part I 1968,Je 30,54:7
Henry IV, Part II 1968,Jl 2,33:1
Henry IV, Part II 1968,Jl 14,II,1:1
King Lear 1968,N 8,43:1
King Lear 1968,N 17,II,1:3
Huui, Huui 1968,N 25,58:1
Cities in Bezique; Owl Answers, The 1969,Ja 13,26:1
Cities in Bezique; Beast's Story, A 1969,Ja 13,26:1
Cities in Bezique; Owl Answers, The 1969,Ja 13,26:1
Cities in Bezique 1969,Ja 19,II,3:5
Invitation to a Beheading 1969,Mr 18,36:1
No Place to Be Somebody 1969,My 5,53:3
Peer Gynt 1969,Jl 17,56:1
Electra 1969,Ag 8,14:1
Twelfth Night 1969,Ag 14,29:2
Sambo 1969,D 22,42:1
No Place to Be Somebody 1969,D 31,17:1
Colette 1970,My 7,60:1
Colette 1970,My 17,II,1:1
Colette 1970,O 15,58:1
Freedman, Gerald (Lyricist)
Time for Singing, A 1966,My 23,48:2
Take One Step 1968,Jl 5,17:1
Peer Gynt 1969,Jl 17,56:1
Freedman, Gerald (Miscellaneous)
Gypsy 1959,My 22,31:6
All's Well That Ends Well 1966,Je 17,39:1
Hamlet 1968,Jl 4,15:1
Romeo and Juliet 1968,Ag 16,19:1
Electra 1969,Ag 8,14:1
Sambo 1969,D 22,42:1
Freedman, Gerald (Playwright)
Time for Singing, A 1966,My 23,48:2
Take One Step 1968,Jl 5,17:1

Freedman, Gerald (Producer)
Henry IV, Part II 1968,Jl 2,33:1
Freedman, Herman
G-II 1948,My 28,27:3
Freedman, Irvin
Capacity for Wings 1957,Ja 10,25:2
Freedman, Lester
Carousel 1945,Ap 20,24:2
Freedman, Norma
Right You Are (If You Think You Are) 1950,Je 29,37:2
Freedman, Phil (Miscellaneous)
First Impressions 1959,Mr 20,28:1
Freedman, Robert (Composer)
Tree Witch, The 1961,Je 5,39:4
Freedman, Robert A (Lighting Director)
Hedda Gabler 1970,Ja 18,78:1
Freedman, William (Miscellaneous)
Salad Days 1958,N 11,24:1
Freel, Aleta
Three Times the Hour 1931,Ag 26,15:5
Louder, Please! 1931,N 13,26:4
Both Your Houses 1933,Mr 7,20:3
Both Your Houses 1933,My 23,22:2
Double Door 1933,S 22,15:5
Freeland, Kathleen
Round Table, The 1930,F 28,20:5
Freeman, Al Jr
Long Dream, The 1960,F 18,36:2
Tiger Tiger Burning Bright 1962,D 24,5:2
Living Premise, The 1963,Je 14,34:1
Trumpets of the Lord 1963,D 23,22:3
Blues for Mister Charlie 1964,Ap 24,24:1
Blues for Mister Charlie 1964,My 3,II,1:1
Conversation at Midnight 1964,N 13,27:1
Slave, The 1964,D 17,51:1
Troilus and Cressida 1965,Ag 13,17:1
All's Well That Ends Well 1966,Je 17,39:1
Measure for Measure 1966,Jl 14,27:1
Dozens, The 1969,Mr 14,51:1
Look to the Lilies 1970,Mr 30,59:1
Look to the Lilies 1970,Ap 12,II,3:7
Freeman, Ann
Life With Father 1967,O 20,53:2
Freeman, Arny
Streetcar Named Desire, A 1950,My 24,36:1
Dream Girl 1951,My 10,39:1
Dark Legend 1952,Mr 25,24:2
Tovarich 1952,My 15,39:2
Shrike, The 1953,N 26,51:2
Great Sebastians, The 1956,Ja 5,27:1
Gay Divorce 1960,Ap 4,37:1
Hot Spot 1963,Ap 20,17:2
What Makes Sammy Run? 1964,F 28,19:1
Cactus Flower 1965,D 9,60:2
Minnie's Boys 1970,Mr 27,27:1
Freeman, Bee
Malinda 1929,D 4,37:2
Ol' Man Satan 1932,O 4,26:3
Freeman, Beryl
And So to Bed 1927,N 10,23:1
Freeman, Bud (Lyricist)
Beg, Borrow or Steal 1960,F 11,39:4
Freeman, Bud (Original Author)
Beg, Borrow or Steal 1960,F 11,39:4
Freeman, Bud (Playwright)
Beg, Borrow or Steal 1960,F 11,39:4
Freeman, C Denis (Playwright)
Melody That Got Lost, The 1938,F 6,X,1:2
Freeman, Charles
You and I 1925,O 20,29:1
Freeman, Charles K (Director)
Merry-Go-Round 1932,N 27,IX,1:1
Life and Death of an American 1939,My 20,11:2
Morning Star 1940,Ap 17,26:4
I Like It Here 1946,Mr 23,8:6
Diamond Lil 1948,N 30,33:2
Diamond Lil 1951,S 15,8:2
Freeman, Charles K (Miscellaneous)
Song of Norway 1944,Ag 22,20:2
Freeman, Charles K (Playwright)
Hand in Glove 1944,D 5,19:1
Hand in Glove 1944,D 10,II,5:1
Freeman, Charles K (Producer)
Life and Death of an American 1939,My 20,11:2
Freeman, David (Producer)
Pirates of Penzance, The 1967,Ag 7,34:2
Freeman, Dick
Cretan Woman, The 1954,My 21,17:2
Freeman, Don
Beautiful People, The 1941,Ap 22,27:2
Freeman, Don (Miscellaneous)
Beautiful People, The 1941,My 4,IX,1:1
Freeman, Doris
Good Bad Woman, A 1925,F 10,21:1
Home Towners, The 1926,Ag 24,19:3
Baby Cyclone, The 1927,S 13,37:4
Mrs Bumpstead-Leigh 1929,Ap 2,28:3
Divided Honors 1929,O 1,28:2
House Afire 1930,Ap 1,34:7
Freeman, Edward
Purification, The 1954,My 29,12:1
Apollo of Bellac, The 1954,My 29,12:1

Freeman, Frances
Young and Fair, The 1948,N 23,35:2
Freeman, Francis
Silver Tassie, The 1949,Jl 22,16:5
Freeman, G Alan
In the Matter of J Robert Oppenheimer 1968,Je 7,31:1
Freeman, Gerald (Producer)
World War 2 1/2 1969,Mr 25,40:1
Freeman, Helen
Beyond the Horizon 1920,Mr 10,9:2
Great Way, The 1921,N 8,28:2
Great Way, The 1921,N 13,VI,1:1
Bavu 1922,F 27,16:1
Spook Sonata, The 1924,Ja 7,23:3
Fashion 1924,F 5,21:2
Saint, The 1924,O 13,20:3
S S Glencairn 1924,N 4,31:4
Patience 1924,D 30,15:1
Michel Auclair 1925,Mr 5,23:1
Love for Love 1925,Ap 1,21:2
House of Women, The 1927,O 4,32:2
House of Women, The 1927,O 9,VIII,1:1
These Days 1928,N 13,36:2
Becky Sharp 1929,Je 4,29:1
Camille 1932,N 2,23:3
Othello 1934,Jl 22,23:4
Othello 1934,Jl 29,IX,1:3
Mother Lode 1934,D 24,16:5
Freeman, Helen (Director)
Finta Giardiniera, La 1927,Ja 19,20:5
Freeman, Helen (Playwright)
Great Way, The 1921,N 8,28:2
Great Way, The 1921,N 13,VI,1:1
Freeman, Helen (Producer)
Great Way, The 1921,N 13,VI,1:1
Freeman, Howard
Serpent's Tooth, A 1922,Ag 25,8:5
All Wet 1925,Jl 7,24:1
Clouds 1925,S 3,32:1
Cock Robin 1928,Ja 13,26:6
Skyrocket, The 1929,Ja 12,14:7
Star-Wagon, The 1937,S 30,18:5
Knickerbocker Holiday 1938,O 20,26:2
Unconquered, The 1940,F 14,25:2
Liliom 1940,Mr 26,17:2
Love's Old Sweet Song 1940,My 3,16:3
Susannah and the Elders 1940,O 13,47:7
Susannah and the Elders 1940,O 30,28:2
Liberty Jones 1941,F 6,24:2
Five Alarm Waltz 1941,Mr 14,16:2
Cuckoos on the Hearth 1941,S 17,26:2
Sunny River 1941,D 5,28:2
Mr Adam 1949,My 26,34:6
Of Thee I Sing 1952,My 6,34:2
No Time for Sergeants 1955,O 21,32:2
Hot Spot 1963,Ap 20,17:2
Freeman, Irene
Man in Evening Clothes, The 1924,D 6,13:4
Buccaneer, The 1925,O 3,10:2
Freeman, Irving
You'll See Stars 1943,Ja 1,26:6
Freeman, Jerry
When Differences Disappear 1941,Je 3,17:4
Freeman, Ken
Stevedore 1949,F 23,30:2
Freeman, Ken (Director)
Anna Lucasta 1956,Ap 13,21:8
Freeman, Lea D (Playwright)
Widow Shannon, The 1923,Jl 15,VI,1:2
All Alone Susie 1923,N 4,VIII,2:7
Widow in Green, A 1931,N 21,21:4
Freeman, Maurice
Vaudeville (Palace) 1926,Ag 31,15:3
Celebrity 1927,D 27,24:3
Night Hostess 1928,S 13,31:2
Octoroon, The 1929,Mr 13,28:3
Did I Say No? 1931,S 23,19:4
When in Rome 1934,F 28,22:6
Play, Genius, Play! 1935,O 31,17:2
Tomorrow's a Holiday! 1935,D 31,10:2
Freeman, Mavis
Last Stop 1944,S 6,17:2
Freeman, Millie
Blossom Time 1931,Mr 5,32:1
Freeman, Morgan
Niggerlovers, The; Demonstration, The 1967,O 2,54:2
Niggerlovers, The; Man and Dog 1967,O 2,54:2
Hello, Dolly! 1967,N 13,61:1
Dozens, The 1969,Mr 14,51:1
Exhibition 1969,My 16,41:1
Jungle of Cities 1970,Mr 1,75:2
Freeman, Morris
Mendel, Inc 1929,N 26,28:5
Freeman, Nancy
No More Peace 1937,F 27,9:1
Freeman, Ona (Wac Pfc)
Swing Sister Wac Swing 1944,Ja 4,20:4
Freeman, Richard
Yellow 1926,S 22,30:1
Sam Abramovitch 1927,Ja 20,20:5
Overture 1930,D 8,26:4

Freeman, Richard—Cont
Enemy of the People, An 1937,F 16,19:1
Escape This Night 1938,Ap 23,18:1
Freeman, Stan (Composer)
I Had a Ball 1964,D 16,50:1
Lovely Ladies, Kind Gentlemen 1970,D 29,38:1
Freeman, Stan (Lyricist)
I Had a Ball 1964,D 16,50:1
Lovely Ladies, Kind Gentlemen 1970,D 29,38:1
Freeman, Stan (Miscellaneous)
Marlene Dietrich 1968,O 4,36:1
Freeman, Susan
Hello, Dolly! 1965,O 10,3:3
Freeman, Suzanne
These Days 1928,N 13,36:2
Freeman, Virginia (Choreographer)
Indians 1969,My 27,43:1
Freeman, Waller (Playwright)
Conjur 1938,N 1,27:2
Frees, Natalie
Crooks' Convention, The 1929,S 19,37:4
Freezer, Herbert J (Producer)
Diamond Lil 1949,F 7,16:2
Frei, Ann-Margret
Ice Capades 1966,Je 2,50:2
Ice Capades 1967,Je 2,33:1
Ice Capades 1969,Ja 8,42:1
Freiburger, Jim (Scenic Designer)
Promises to Keep 1965,Jl 22,25:1
Freiden, Eddy (Musical Director)
Hate Planters 1933,My 26,24:5
Freifeld, Harry
Mother's Sabbath Days 1960,N 21,33:2
Backlane Center 1961,N 23,51:1
Eleventh Inheritor, The 1962,N 22,43:5
Sage of Rottenburg, The 1963,N 20,48:1
Enchanting Melody 1964,N 25,40:1
Wandering Stars 1966,N 14,52:2
Melody Lingers On, The 1969,N 17,55:1
Freifeld, Harry (Miscellaneous)
Bronx Express, 1968 1968,N 16,43:3
Melody Lingers On, The 1969,N 17,55:1
Brothers Ashkenazi, The 1970,N 17,53:2
Freilich, Jovana
Jack in the Box 1960,My 19,43:3
Freilich, Louis
Aristocrats 1935,My 2,16:2
Clinton Street 1939,O 13,27:2
Winners and Losers 1947,F 27,27:2
Freilicher, Jane
Tinguely Machine Mystery, or the Love Suicide at
Kaluka, The 1965,D 24,15:5
Freiman, F (Playwright)
Secret of Love, The 1936,F 24,15:2
Freiman, Flora
Street Singers 1938,D 12,25:6
Queen Mother 1938,D 26,29:4
Schwartse Mamme 1939,Ja 16,11:3
Freiman, Louis (Director)
Second Marriage 1953,O 12,30:1
Freiman, Louis (Lyricist)
Yossel and His Wives 1937,S 19,II,8:3
Freiman, Louis (Playwright)
Radio Girl, The 1929,O 19,22:4
Traveling Salesman, The 1932,N 1,24:4
Three in Love 1933,N 8,32:5
Organ Grinder, The 1934,Ja 1,28:3
Happy Days 1934,Ap 2,12:5
Perfect Fishel, The 1935,S 30,12:4
Pinye of Pinchev 1936,S 21,27:5
Straw Hero, The 1936,N 24,35:1
Galician Rabbi, The 1937,F 13,9:7
Yossel and His Wives 1937,S 19,II,8:3
Little Tailor, The 1938,Mr 21,18:2
Wise Fool, The 1938,O 10,15:3
David and Esther 1938,O 12,34:3
Should a Mother Tell? 1938,N 25,18:3
Street Singers 1938,D 12,25:6
Schwartse Mamme 1939,Ja 16,11:3
Sadie Is a Lady 1950,Ja 28,9:2
Second Marriage 1953,O 12,30:1
It Could Happen to You 1957,O 28,30:5
Nice People 1958,O 20,36:1
Kosher Widow, The 1959,N 2,40:2
Bei Mir Bistu Schoen 1961,O 23,22:2
Cowboy in Israel, A 1962,O 29,36:2
Good Luck 1964,O 19,38:3
Freimann, John Raymond (Scenic Designer)
Mamba's Daughters 1953,Mr 21,12:6
Burning of the Lepers, The 1962,Ap 5,29:1
Freisinger, Leo
Stars on Ice (2d Edition) 1943,Je 25,13:2
Freitag, Dorothea
Gantry 1970,F 16,44:1
Freitag, Dorothea (Choreographer)
I'm Solomon 1968,Ap 24,51:1
Dear World 1969,F 7,33:1
Gantry 1970,F 16,44:1
Freitag, Dorothea (Composer)
Autobiography 1956,O 3,29:2
Mask and Gown 1957,S 11,29:1
Freitag, Dorothea (Lyricist)
Mask and Gown 1957,S 11,29:1

Freitag, Dorothea (Miscellaneous)
Oh, Kay! 1960,Ap 18,37:2
Zorba 1968,N 18,58:1
Freitag, Dorothea (Musical Director)
Shoestring '57 1956,N 6,31:1
Chic 1959,My 19,28:2
Oh, Kay! 1960,Ap 18,37:2
Mod Donna 1970,My 4,48:1
Freitag, Lee (Musical Director)
Mask and Gown 1957,S 11,29:1
Freitag, Otto
Marriage of Mr Mississippi, The 1969,N 20,60:5
Philipp Hotz 1969,N 27,52:1
Firebugs, The 1969,N 27,52:1
Freitag, Robert
Marriage of Mr Mississippi, The 1969,N 20,60:5
Firebugs, The 1969,N 27,52:1
Philipp Hotz 1969,N 27,52:1
Freitag, Robert (Director)
Marriage of Mr Mississippi, The 1969,N 20,60:5
Freitas, Richard (Composer)
Difficult Woman, The 1962,Ap 26,22:7
Freitas, Richard (Musical Director)
Difficult Woman, The 1962,Ap 26,22:7
Frejomieh, Exavier
Emerald Slippers, The 1970,S 2,31:2
Frelich, Phyllis
Songs From Milk Wood 1970,Ja 13,41:1
Sganarelle 1970,Ja 13,41:1
Frelinghuysen, Estelle
Middletown 1934,Ap 23,24:6
Fremed, Charles
Mikado, The 1939,Mr 11,15:6
Fremont, Juliet
Plumes in the Dust 1936,N 7,14:2
Fremont, Louis (Director)
Cosmonaute Agricole, Le 1970,Ap 8,38:3
Fremont, Louis (Miscellaneous)
Grand Vizir, Le 1970,Ap 8,38:3
French, Arthur
Raisin' Hell in the Son 1962,Jl 3,13:2
Day of Absence 1965,N 16,56:1
Jonah! 1967,S 22,52:2
Song of the Lusitanian Bogey, The 1968,Ja 3,52:1
Kongi's Harvest 1968,Ap 15,49:1
Daddy Goodness 1968,Je 5,37:1
God Is a (Guess What?) 1968,D 18,56:1
Ceremonies in Dark Old Men 1969,F 6,33:1
String 1969,Ap 2,37:1
Malcochon 1969,Ap 2,37:1
Man Better Man 1969,Jl 3,22:1
Day of Absence 1970,Mr 18,39:1
French, Augusta
Mr Jiggins of Jigginstown 1936,D 18,30:2
Last Stop 1944,S 6,17:2
French, Briggs
Polly Preferred 1923,Ja 12,13:3
French, Carroll (Costume Designer)
Valley Forge 1934,D 11,28:3
French, Elsie
Ridgeway's Late Joys 1939,O 22,IX,3:5
French, Francis
Field of Ermine 1935,F 9,10:4
French, George S
Half Moon Inn 1925,Mr 10,14:1
French, Harold
Blue Lagoon, The 1921,S 15,16:1
By the Way 1925,D 29,20:3
By the Way 1926,Ap 16,20:3
French, Harold (Director)
French Without Tears 1937,S 29,19:1
New Men, The 1962,S 7,35:2
French, Hilda
Macbeth 1936,Ap 15,25:4
French, Hugh
Set to Music 1939,Ja 19,16:2
French, Jacqueline
Tree Witch, The 1961,Je 5,39:4
French, James E (Scenic Designer)
Sacco-Vanzetti 1969,F 9,78:1
Trees Die Standing, The 1969,O 13,52:1
Adding Machine, The 1970,D 5,40:1
French, Joseph
Plough and the Stars, The 1927,N 29,30:2
French, Judd
Engaged! or Cheviot's Choice 1965,Ap 24,19:2
French, Laverne
Show Boat 1946,Ja 7,17:2
Show Boat 1946,Ja 11,11:1
Show Boat 1948,S 9,33:2
French, Leslie
Fritzi 1935,D 21,10:3
Home and Beauty 1937,F 3,26:2
Two Bouquets, The 1938,Je 1,19:2
Midsummer Night's Dream, A 1939,Jl 23,IX,1:3
French, Peggy
Weak Link, The 1940,Mr 5,19:2
George Washington Slept Here 1940,O 19,20:3
Town House 1948,S 24,31:2
French, Percy
Dearest Enemy 1925,S 19,9:2
French, Peter
Semi-Detached 1963,O 8,49:1

French, Richard
Night of January 16 1935,S 17,26:4
French, Richard E (Miscellaneous)
Hallams, The 1948,Mr 5,18:2
French, S G
Who's Who 1924,Ap 18,19:2
French, Sadie
Heel, The 1954,My 27,33:2
Season of the Beast 1958,Mr 14,29:2
French, Valerie
Inadmissible Evidence 1965,D 1,52:1
Help Stamp Out Marriage 1966,S 30,50:1
Tea Party 1968,O 16,40:1
Mother Lover, The 1969,F 3,28:1
Trelawny of the 'Wells' 1970,O 12,48:1
French, Ward M
East Lynne Goes West 1931,My 3,I,26:5
French Wonderwheels, The
Wonder World 1964,My 18,32:1
Frenger, George
Purple Mask, The 1920,Ja 6,18:1
John Hawthorne 1921,Ja 24,16:1
Liliom 1921,Ap 21,18:1
Cloister, The 1921,Je 6,16:3
What the Public Wants 1922,My 2,22:3
Drums of Jeopardy, The 1922,My 30,8:4
Fashions for Men 1922,D 6,22:1
Freni, Pat
Cherry Orchard, The 1970,My 7,63:2
Frenyear, Mabel
Montmartre 1922,F 14,20:1
Frenzel, Susanne
Emperor's New Clothes, The 1950,Je 20,23:2
Frere, Andre
Voyage de Monsieur Perrichon, Le 1937,N 2,32:3
Knock 1937,N 17,26:3
Roi Cerf, Le 1937,N 30,26:3
Medecin Malgre Lui, Le 1937,D 28,28:7
Jalousie du Barbouille, La 1937,D 28,28:7
Y'Avait un Prisonnier 1938,Ja 25,24:3
Fantasio 1938,F 8,17:2
Caprice, Un 1938,F 8,17:2
Bal des Voleurs, Le 1938,N 29,26:4
Fourberies de Scapin, Les 1938,D 13,30:3
Precieuses Ridicules, Les 1938,D 13,30:3
Faiseur, Le; Promoter, The 1938,D 27,12:3
Chacun Sa Verite 1939,Ja 24,17:1
37 Sous de M Montaudoin, Les 1939,F 7,17:2
Enterrement, L' 1939,F 7,17:2
Siegfried 1939,F 21,15:2
Barbier de Seville, Le 1939,Mr 7,19:2
Freschard
Avare, L'; Miser, The 1924,Mr 12,17:3
Monsieur Brotonneau 1924,Mr 13,14:1
Blanchette 1924,Mr 19,19:4
Freschi, Bob
Of Thee I Sing 1969,Mr 8,19:1
Freschmann, Ann
Daughters of Atreus 1936,O 15,33:1
Madame Bovary 1937,N 17,26:2
Frescott, Norman
Earl Carroll's Vanities 1927,Ja 5,18:1
Vaudeville (Hollywood) 1932,Mr 22,17:5
Freshman, Ann
Berkeley Square 1929,N 5,32:4
Freshman, William (Playwright)
Last of the Ladies, The 1936,Mr 26,26:7
Fresnay, Pierre
Chatterton 1926,O 3,VIII,2:1
Miracle, Un 1927,D 25,VIII,4:3
Je T'Attendais 1929,Ja 20,VIII,1:8
Marius 1929,Mr 31,VIII,2:7
Bloomfield 1930,O 12,VIII,4:2
Cette Vieille Canaille 1930,D 7,IX,4:2
Hermine, L' 1932,My 29,VIII,1:7
Teddy and Partner 1933,F 12,IX,3:4
Don Juan 1934,F 27,16:5
Conversation Piece 1934,O 24,24:1
Conversation Piece 1934,N 18,IX,1:1
Noah 1935,F 14,25:2
O Mistress Mine 1936,D 4,30:3
Cyclones, Les 1955,F 27,II,3:1
Ross; Lawrence d'Arabie 1961,O 8,II,3:4
Fresnay, Pierre (Producer)
Hermine, L' 1932,My 29,VIII,1:7
Cyclones, Les 1955,F 27,II,3:1
Fresson, Bernard
Jardin des Delices, Le 1969,N 4,54:1
Frett, Kenneth
Walk Down Mah Street! 1968,Je 13,54:1
Fretwell, Joseph 3d (Costume Designer)
Flowers of Virtue, The 1942,F 6,22:2
Traitor, The 1949,Ap 1,30:2
Rat Race, The 1949,D 23,16:2
Freud, Ralph
Growing Pains 1933,N 24,24:2
Freudenberger, Daniel (Miscellaneous)
Persians, The 1970,Ap 16,53:1
Freund, Alois (Original Author)
One Flight Down 1937,D 14,32:4
Freund, Kim
Happy Time, The 1968,Ja 19,32:2

Frey, Alice
Slight Case of Murder, A 1935,S 12,28:5
Frey, Bob
Love in Our Time 1952,O 4,14:3
Frey, Fran
Good News 1927,S 7,35:4
Frey, Fran (Composer)
Ice Capades 1952,S 12,18:1
Ice Capades 1953,S 11,25:1
Ice Capades 1954,S 16,37:1
Ice Capades 1955,S 15,38:1
Ice Capades 1956,S 13,41:2
Ice Capades 1958,S 4,33:2
Ice Capades 1959,S 4,12:1
Frey, Fran (Miscellaneous)
Ice Capades 1957,S 5,33:2
Ice Capades 1960,S 1,30:1
Frey, Frank
Whoopee 1928,D 5,34:3
Frey, Gilberte
Chrysalis 1932,N 16,15:2
Frey, Gladys
Women at the Tomb, The 1961,Ap 25,41:1
Frey, Gloria
Sari 1930,Ja 29,27:1
Frey, Harry
Mother's Sabbath Days 1960,N 21,33:2
Frey, Jean
Bees and the Flowers, The 1946,S 27,19:3
Frey, Jeanne
Guys and Dolls 1966,Je 9,55:2
West Side Story 1968,Je 25,32:1
Frey, Katherine
Betty Lee 1924,D 26,18:2
Frey, Kay
In the Summer House 1964,Mr 26,43:1
Frey, Leonard
Coach With the Six Insides, The 1962,N 27,44:1
Funnyhouse of a Negro 1964,Ja 15,25:3
Fiddler on the Roof 1964,S 23,56:2
Boys in the Band, The 1968,Ap 15,48:1
Boys in the Band, The 1968,Ap 28,II,1:6
Time of Your Life, The 1969,N 7,37:1
Time of Your Life, The 1969,N 16,II,1:4
Beggar on Horseback 1970,My 15,47:2
Beggar on Horseback 1970,My 24,II,1:1
Frey, Mary
Strawberry Blonde, The 1927,F 8,20:3
Maggie, the Magnificent 1929,O 22,26:1
Frey, Nathaniel
Barefoot Boy With Cheek 1947,Ap 4,20:2
High Button Shoes 1947,O 10,32:2
Tree Grows in Brooklyn, A 1951,Ap 20,24:3
Tree Grows in Brooklyn, A 1951,Ap 29,II,1:1
Wonderful Town 1953,F 26,22:3
On Your Toes 1954,O 12,24:4
Damn Yankees 1955,My 6,17:1
Goldilocks 1958,O 13,33:1
Goldilocks 1958,O 19,II,1:1
Fiorello! 1959,N 24,45:3
Fiorello! 1959,N 29,II,1:1
Harold 1962,N 30,27:1
She Loves Me 1963,Ap 24,39:1
She Loves Me 1963,My 5,II,1:1
Odd Couple, The 1965,Mr 11,36:1
Education of H*Y*M*A*N K*A*P*L*A*N, The
1968,Ap 5,57:1
Frey, Steven
Once There Was a Russian 1961,F 20,32:2
Freye, Richard
Legal Murder 1934,F 16,16:2
Freyer, Nat
Jazz Singer, The 1925,S 15,29:2
Freytag, Gustav (Playwright)
Journalisten, Die 1932,Jl 17,IX,1:1
Friar, Kimon (Translator)
Burn Me to Ashes 1963,N 20,48:1
Friar, Ralph
Praise Of Folly 1954,F 24,23:2
Tartuffe 1957,O 9,39:1
Friar, Ralph (Director)
Tartuffe 1957,O 9,39:1
Friberg, Carl (Composer)
Leonard Sillman's New Faces of 1968
1968,My 3,43:1
Friberg, Carl (Lyricist)
Leonard Sillman's New Faces of 1968
1968,My 3,43:1
Fribourg, Nathan
Bursting the Barriers 1930,My 7,25:1
Frick, Max
Dear Me 1921,Ja 18,14:1
Frick, Mr
Ice Follies 1957,Ja 16,36:1
Ice Follies 1958,Ja 15,26:2
Ice Follies 1959,Ja 14,30:1
Ice Follies 1960,Ja 13,20:1
Ice Follies 1961,Ja 11,25:2
Ice Follies 1962,Ja 10,24:6
Ice Follies 1963,Ja 10,5:2
Ice Follies 1965,Ja 13,35:1
Ice Follies 1966,Ja 12,27:6
Ice Follies 1967,Ja 11,51:1

Ice Follies 1969,My 23,38:1
Ice Follies 1970,My 23,27:1
Frick, Willie
Vaudeville (Palace) 1928,Jl 24,13:4
Frick and Frack
Ice Follies 1939,D 5,38:2
Ice Follies 1941,D 2,32:2
Fricke, Ed (Costume Designer)
Fourth Pig, The 1965,Ja 27,24:6
Fisherman, The 1965,Ja 27,24:6
Fricke, Peter
Wozzeck 1966,Ap 6,34:1
Ratten, Die 1966,Ap 13,36:1
Frid, Jonathan
King John 1956,Je 28,33:5
Measure for Measure 1956,Je 29,16:1
Othello 1957,Je 24,19:2
Merchant of Venice, The 1957,Jl 11,19:5
Much Ado About Nothing 1957,Ag 8,15:2
Golem, The 1959,F 26,38:2
Henry IV 1960,Ap 19,41:1
Moon in the Yellow River, The 1961,F 7,40:2
Don Carlos 1962,F 28,27:5
Storm, The 1962,Mr 31,17:2
Burning, The 1963,D 4,57:1
White Rose and the Red, The 1964,Mr 17,31:1
Fridel, Howard
Last Enemy, The 1934,Jl 13,14:4
Fridel, Robert (Director)
Macbeth 1959,Je 7,124:3
Friderici, Blanche
Hero, The 1921,Mr 15,14:1
Hero, The 1921,S 6,13:2
Cat and the Canary, The 1922,F 8,13:1
Green Beetle, The 1924,S 3,12:3
Processional 1925,Ja 13,17:1
Rain 1926,O 12,27:1
Julie 1927,My 10,24:4
Fridge, Mary Sue
Days Between, The 1965,Je 4,39:1
Fridh, Gertrud
Hedda Gabler 1968,Je 5,39:1
Fridman, Maria
Mirele Efros 1967,O 20,55:1
Mother Courage 1967,N 17,55:1
Fridolin
Ti-Coq 1951,F 10,10:2
Ti-Coq 1951,F 25,II,1:1
Friebus, Florida
Lady From the Sea, The 1929,Mr 19,36:1
Mademoiselle Bourrat 1929,O 8,34:3
Living Corpse, The 1929,D 7,19:1
Alison's House 1930,D 2,31:2
Liliom 1932,O 27,23:2
Camille 1932,O 28,23:2
Alice in Wonderland 1932,D 12,18:3
Primrose Path, The 1939,Ja 5,16:3
Primrose Path, The 1939,Ja 16,11:2
Church Street 1948,F 10,27:2
Victors, The 1948,D 27,17:2
Collector's Item 1952,F 9,11:2
Tea and Sympathy 1953,O 1,35:1
Boy With a Cart, The 1954,Ap 5,19:2
Friebus, Florida (Miscellaneous)
Alice in Wonderland 1932,D 25,IX,1:1
Friebus, Florida (Playwright)
Alice in Wonderland 1932,D 12,18:3
Alice in Wonderland 1947,Ap 7,19:2
Alice in Wonderland 1947,Ap 13,II,1:1
Fried, Barbara (Playwright)
In the Nick of Time 1967,Je 2,36:1
Fried, Elsa
Silver Tassie, The 1949,Jl 22,16:5
Fried, Emanuel (Playwright)
Peddler, The 1967,D 9,62:1
Dodo Bird, The 1967,D 9,62:1
Rose 1969,O 29,30:1
Fried, Franklin (Producer)
Postmark Zero 1965,N 2,28:1
Fried, Gerald (Composer)
Egg, The 1962,Ja 9,23:2
Fried, J M (Miscellaneous)
Secret Life of Walter Mitty, The 1964,O 27,44:5
Fried, Lazar
Green Fields 1920,Mr 26,11:2
One Life for Another 1920,D 18,11:2
Stempenu, the Fiddler 1929,Mr 9,24:7
Roaming Stars 1930,Ja 25,12:2
Riverside Drive 1931,Ja 6,24:2
Fried, Martin
Best Man, The 1960,Ap 1,39:1
Fried, Martin (Director)
Coop, The 1966,Mr 2,48:1
Country Girl, The 1966,S 30,55:1
Natural Look, The 1967,Mr 13,45:2
Daphne in Cottage D 1967,O 16,56:1
Cannibals, The 1968,N 4,60:1
Cannibals, The 1968,N 10,II,5:1
This Bird of Dawning Singeth All Night Long
1968,D 31,19:1
Papp 1969,My 6,39:1
Two Times One; Duet for Solo Voice
1970,Ap 5,76:4

Fried, Martin (Miscellaneous)
Affair, The 1962,S 21,34:2
Three Sisters, The 1964,Je 23,24:1
Fried, S K
Anna Ascends 1920,S 23,14:1
Fried, Walter (Producer)
All My Sons 1947,Ja 30,21:2
Whole World Over, The 1947,Mr 28,28:2
Death of a Salesman 1949,F 11,27:2
Bird Cage, The 1950,F 23,32:2
Time of the Cuckoo, The 1952,O 16,37:4
Ladies of the Corridor, The 1953,O 22,33:5
Festival 1955,Ja 19,22:1
Abraham Cochrane 1964,F 18,26:1
Friedberg, Billy (Playwright)
Littlest Revue, The 1956,My 23,37:2
Friedberg, Martin Harvey
From the Second City 1969,O 15,34:1
Friedberg, Sidney (Playwright)
Nautical but Nice 1931,Ap 19,31:6
Friedberg, William (Playwright)
Two on the Aisle 1951,Jl 29,II,1:1
Two's Company 1952,D 16,43:5
Friedburg, Marion
Burmese Pwe, A 1926,Mr 17,28:1
Friede, Jo Ann
Here Come the Clowns 1954,My 5,36:2
Friedel, Molly (Lighting Director)
Local Stigmatic, The; Trouble in the Works
1969,N 4,55:2
Local Stigmatic, The; Applicant 1969,N 4,55:2
Local Stigmatic, The; Interview 1969,N 4,55:2
Local Stigmatic, The; Last to Go 1969,N 4,55:2
Local Stigmatic, The; That's All 1969,N 4,55:2
Local Stigmatic, The; That's Your Trouble
1969,N 4,55:2
Local Stigmatic, The; Request Stop 1969,N 4,55:2
Local Stigmatic, The 1969,N 4,55:2
Little Boxes; Coffee Lace, The 1969,D 4,71:2
Little Boxes; Trevor 1969,D 4,71:2
Instructions for the Running of Trains, etc on the
Erie Railway to Go Into Effect January 1,1862
1970,Ja 7,36:2
Dark of the Moon 1970,Ap 4,21:2
Awake and Sing! 1970,My 28,35:1
Friedell, Egon (Playwright)
Tales of Hoffmann 1932,Ja 10,VIII,1:6
Fair Helen 1932,Jl 17,IX,1:2
Frieder, Sol
Song of Songs 1958,O 29,31:1
Wall, The 1960,O 12,44:4
In the Counting House 1962,D 15,5:5
Dreigroschenoper, Die 1965,Mr 12,24:1
Cabaret 1966,N 21,62:1
Friedkin, David
Noah 1935,F 14,25:2
Murder in the Cathedral 1936,Mr 21,13:5
Friedland, Adele
Cherry Pie 1926,Ap 15,24:4
Friedland, Anatole
Vaudeville (Palace) 1921,My 17,20:3
Vaudeville (Palace) 1924,Ja 1,21:1
Vaudeville (Palace) 1926,My 11,25:3
Vaudeville (Palace) 1929,S 16,30:4
Vaudeville (Palace) 1932,My 23,18:7
Friedland, Z
Eternal Jew, The 1926,D 21,21:2
Deluge, The 1927,Ja 11,36:2
Friedland, Zvi
Dybbuk, The 1948,My 3,26:3
David's Crown 1948,My 10,26:2
Golem, The 1948,My 17,22:3
Friedland, Zvi (Miscellaneous)
Dybbuk, The 1964,F 4,30:2
Friedlander, Eddie
Soul of a Woman, The 1930,F 22,13:1
Borderline 1937,F 10,18:6
Friedlander, Jane (Miscellaneous)
Lord Pengo 1962,N 20,41:2
Friedlander, Jane (Producer)
Anything Goes 1962,My 16,35:1
Friedlander, Martin
Thomas Paine 1930,Mr 21,30:7
Friedlander, Miriam
Cocktails of 1934 1934,My 5,22:1
Friedlander, Sylvia (Costume Designer)
Mirele Efros 1969,D 26,41:1
Light, Lively and Yiddish 1970,O 28,58:1
Friedlander, Sylvia (Miscellaneous)
Burlesque 1946,D 26,30:3
Bathsheba 1947,Mr 27,40:2
Friedlander, William B (Composer)
Frivolities of 1920 1920,Ja 9,22:2
Pitter Patter 1920,S 29,12:2
Mercenary Mary 1925,Ap 14,27:3
Snookie 1941,Je 4,26:2
Friedlander, William B (Director)
Sea Woman, The 1925,Ag 25,12:2
Dagger, The 1925,S 10,28:1
Hush Money 1926,Mr 16,22:3
Shelf, The 1926,S 28,31:1
Speakeasy 1927,S 27,30:1
We Never Learn 1928,Ja 24,26:1

Friedlander, William B (Director)—Cont

Nice Women 1929,Je 11,27:4
Divided Honors 1929,O 1,28:2
Jonica 1930,Ap 8,27:1
She Lived Next to the Firehouse 1931,F 11,23:1
Nikki 1931,S 30,23:4
Before Morning 1933,F 10,13:4
Under Glass 1933,O 31,24:3
Locked Room, The 1933,D 26,18:5
Too Much Party 1934,Mr 6,28:4
Roman Servant, A 1934,D 3,14:5
Cross-Town 1937,Mr 18,21:5
Seperate Rooms 1940,Mr 25,10:3
Snookie 1941,Je 4,26:2
Time, Place and the Girl, The 1942,O 22,24:3
Right Next to Broadway 1944,F 22,26:2
Good Morning, Corporal 1944,Ag 9,13:7

Friedlander, William B (Lyricist)

Frivolities of 1920 1920,Ja 9,22:2
Pitter Patter 1920,S 29,12:2
Moonlight 1924,Ja 31,13:7
Mercenary Mary 1925,Ap 14,27:3
Time, Place and the Girl, The 1942,O 22,24:3

Friedlander, William B (Playwright)

Mercenary Mary 1925,Ap 14,27:3

Friedlander, William B (Producer)

Shelf, The 1926,S 28,31:1
Piggy 1927,Ja 12,22:2
Speakeasy 1927,S 27,30:1
We Never Learn 1928,Ja 24,26:1
Jonica 1930,Mr 30,VIII,2:7
Jonica 1930,Ap 8,27:1
Under Glass 1933,O 31,24:3
Locked Room, The 1933,D 26,18:5
Good Morning, Corporal 1944,Ag 9,13:7

Friedlander, Zwi

Dybbuk, The 1926,D 14,24:2

Friedlich, Kate

Banjo Eyes 1941,D 26,20:2
Oklahoma! 1943,Ap 1,27:1
Small Wonder 1948,S 16,33:5
Razzle Dazzle 1951,F 20,21:1
Death of Cuchulain, The 1959,Ap 13,34:4

Friedman, Armin (Original Author)

One Flight Down 1937,D 14,32:4

Friedman, Armin (Playwright)

Dr David's Dad 1924,Ag 14,10:3

Friedman, Bruce Jay (Playwright)

Scuba Duba 1967,O 11,36:1
Scuba Duba 1967,O 22,II,3:7
Scuba Duba 1969,Ap 7,51:1
Steambath 1970,Jl 1,49:1
Steambath 1970,Jl 2,30:3
Steambath 1970,Jl 12,II,1:3
Steambath 1970,O 11,II,1:1

Friedman, Charles (Composer)

Carmen Jones 1945,My 3,26:5

Friedman, Charles (Director)

Rutherford and Son 1927,Ap 13,29:2
Jamboree 1932,N 25,18:4
Bitter Stream 1936,Mr 31,16:6
Pins and Needles 1937,N 29,18:6
Sing Out the News 1938,S 26,12:5
John Henry 1940,Ja 11,18:2
Carmen Jones 1943,D 3,26:2
Carmen Jones 1946,Ap 8,32:2
Street Scene 1947,Ja 10,17:2
Street Scene 1947,Ja 19,II,1:1
My Darlin' Aida 1952,O 28,36:4

Friedman, Charles (Lighting Director)

Mother, The 1935,N 20,26:3

Friedman, Charles (Lyricist)

My Darlin' Aida 1952,O 28,36:4

Friedman, Charles (Miscellaneous)

Sing Out the News 1938,S 26,12:5
From Vienna 1939,Je 21,26:2

Friedman, Charles (Playwright)

Young Go First, The 1935,My 29,16:2
Pins and Needles 1937,N 29,18:6
Sing Out the News 1938,O 2,IX,1:1
Pins and Needles 1939,Ap 21,26:2
My Darlin' Aida 1952,O 28,36:4

Friedman, Charles (Scenic Designer)

Waltz of the Dogs, The 1928,Ap 26,31:3
Three 1928,D 4,28:2
Silver Tassie, The 1929,O 25,26:1

Friedman, David

Anatomist, The 1957,F 27,21:5

Friedman, David (Miscellaneous)

Have I Got One for You 1968,Ja 8,32:1

Friedman, David (Producer)

Anatomist, The 1957,F 27,21:5

Friedman, Edward (Producer)

Mandingo 1961,My 23,43:6

Friedman, Frederica

Nautical but Nice 1931,Ap 19,31:6

Friedman, Gary William (Composer)

Blind Angel, The 1965,Ap 2,26:1
Bitch of Waverly Place, The 1965,Ap 2,26:1
Kill the One-Eyed Man 1965,O 21,56:1
Macbeth 1966,Ag 30,34:1
Me Nobody Knows, The 1970,My 19,42:1

Friedman, Gary William (Miscellaneous)

Me Nobody Knows, The 1970,My 19,42:1

Friedman, Isidor

Yoina Seeks a Bride 1936,O 20,31:1

Friedman, Isidor (Playwright)

Papirossen 1936,S 18,19:3
Yoina Seeks a Bride 1936,O 20,31:1
Give Me Back My Heart 1937,O 4,17:6
Jolly Village, The 1937,N 15,15:5
Jolly Wedding, The 1937,N 17,26:3

Friedman, Jerome (Miscellaneous)

Endgame 1958,Ja 29,32:4

Friedman, Joel (Composer)

As You Like It 1955,O 29,12:2

Friedman, Joel (Director)

As You Like It 1955,O 29,12:2
Romeo and Juliet 1955,D 16,36:3
Pelleas and Melisande 1957,F 20,38:1
Midsummer Night's Dream, A 1961,Ag 3,13:1
Limb of Snow 1967,D 13,55:1
Meeting, The 1967,D 13,55:1

Friedman, Joel (Playwright)

Mr and Mrs Lyman 1968,Mr 6,35:1

Friedman, Kenneth (Playwright)

March March, The 1966,N 15,51:4
Neighbors 1966,N 15,51:4

Friedman, Larry

Night Thoreau Spent in Jail, The 1970,N 2,66:1

Friedman, Lee

Doctored Wife, The 1950,Jl 12,33:2

Friedman, Leo (Producer)

Cabin in the Sky 1964,Ja 22,32:1

Friedman, Leon (Playwright)

Trial of Lee Harvey Oswald, The 1967,N 6,64:1

Friedman, Lisa

In 3 Zones 1970,N 3,28:1

Friedman, Nathan (Miscellaneous)

Those That Play the Clowns 1966,N 25,48:1

Friedman, Phil (Miscellaneous)

Whoop-Up 1958,D 23,2:7
Cut of the Axe 1960,F 2,38:2
Conquering Hero, The 1961,Ja 17,40:2
How to Succeed in Business Without Really Trying 1961,O 16,34:1
Little Me 1962,N 19,41:3
Skyscraper 1965,N 15,48:1
Walking Happy 1966,N 28,47:1
Darling of the Day 1968,Ja 29,26:2
Come Summer 1969,Mr 19,43:1
Boy Friend, The 1970,Ap 15,54:1
Lovely Ladies, Kind Gentlemen 1970,D 29,38:1

Friedman, Ralph

Right of Possession 1930,My 9,20:5
Twelfth Disciple, The 1930,My 17,21:4

Friedman, Samuel J (Producer)

In Circles 1968,Je 28,36:1

Friedman, Sanford (Miscellaneous)

Antigone 1956,Ap 3,32:2
Tevya and His Daughters 1957,S 17,38:2

Friedman, Sanford (Producer)

River Line, The 1957,Ja 3,29:2
Best of Burlesque 1957,S 30,27:2
All That Fall 1957,O 8,41:2
Quare Fellow, The 1958,N 28,34:1

Friedman, Shraga

Oliver 1966,F 5,32:2

Friedman, Shraga (Director)

My Fair Lady 1964,F 20,24:4

Friedman, Shraga (Translator)

My Fair Lady 1964,F 20,24:4

Friedman, Sol

49ers, The 1922,N 7,14:1
Commedia Dell' Arte 1927,Ap 6,24:3

Friedman, Stanley P

Amedee: or, How to Disentangle Yourself 1955,N 1,27:3

Friedman, Virginia (Miscellaneous)

Three by Ferlinghetti; Three Thousand Red Ants 1970,S 23,43:1
Three by Ferlinghetti; Victims of Amnesia, The 1970,S 23,43:1
Three by Ferlinghetti; Alligation, The 1970,S 23,43:1

Friedman-Friedrich (Director)

Nass Oder Trocken? 1929,Jl 7,VIII,2:1

Friedmann, Armand (Playwright)

Booster, The 1929,O 25,26:2

Friedrichsen, Uwe

Faust, Part I; Play, The 1961,F 5,27:2
Faust, Part I; Prologue in Heaven 1961,F 5,27:2

Friel, Brian (Playwright)

Philadelphia, Here I Come! 1966,F 17,28:1
Loves of Cass McGuire, The 1966,O 7,36:1
Loves of Cass McGuire, The 1967,Je 4,II,1:1
Lovers; Finders 1967,S 24,II,1:4
Losers 1967,S 24,II,1:4
Lovers; Losers 1968,Jl 26,21:4
Lovers; Winners 1968,Jl 26,21:4
Lovers 1968,N 24,II,9:4
Lovers 1968,N 26,43:1
Mundy Scheme, The 1969,D 12,75:1

Frieling, Gustave

One Woman's Husband 1920,Mr 23,9:3

Frielinghaus, Henry 3d

Once Over Lightly 1938,D 10,13:4

Frielinghaus, Henry 3d—Cont

Any Moment Now 1939,N 25,13:6

Friemen, L (Playwright)

Jolly World, A 1931,Ja 24,15:3

Friemann, John Raymond (Scenic Designer)

Land Beyond the River, A 1957,Mr 29,15:7

Friend, Arthur S (Miscellaneous)

Strange Fruit 1945,N 30,18:6
Cyrano de Bergerac 1946,O 9,33:2

Friend, Cliff (Miscellaneous)

Piggy 1927,Ja 12,22:2
George White's Scandals 1929,S 24,29:1

Friend, Cliff (Lyricist)

George White's Scandals 1929,S 24,29:1

Friend, Constance

Hamlet 1938,O 13,28:1
Hamlet 1939,D 5,35:2

Friend, Irma

Noble Rogue, A 1929,Ag 20,31:2

Friend, Jack

Where's Charley? 1948,O 12,33:2

Friend, Joel

Pal Joey 1949,Mr 7,17:2

Friend, John Edward (Miscellaneous)

On the Town 1959,Ja 16,36:1

Friend, Philip

French Without Tears 1937,S 29,19:1
Jane 1952,F 2,10:2
Jane 1952,F 10,II,1:1

Friend, William

Skirt, The 1921,N 8,28:1
White Desert 1923,O 19,17:3

Frierson, Andrew

Show Boat 1961,Ap 13,32:1
Porgy and Bess 1965,Mr 6,17:1

Frierson, George

Garrick Gaieties 1926,My 11,25:2

Frierson, Monte L (Producer)

Buffalo Skinner, The 1959,F 20,18:1

Fries, K T (Costume Designer)

But Never Jam Today 1969,Ap 24,40:1

Fries, Margarethe

Strange Interlude 1937,Ja 5,19:1

Friesen, Dick (Composer)

Ice Follies 1967,Ja 11,51:1
Ice Follies 1969,My 23,38:1
Ice Follies 1970,My 23,27:1

Friesen, Dick (Lyricist)

Ice Follies 1967,Ja 11,51:1
Ice Follies 1969,My 23,38:1

Friesen, Dick (Miscellaneous)

Ice Follies 1967,Ja 11,51:1

Friesen, Norman

Blitzstein! 1966,D 1,58:2

Friganza, Trixie

Vaudeville (Palace) 1924,Ap 29,12:2
Vaudeville (Palace) 1927,My 10,25:3
Vaudeville (Palace) 1927,My 17,27:4
Vaudeville (Palace) 1928,Ap 10,32:4
Vaudeville (Palace) 1928,S 4,21:3
Vaudeville (Palace) 1929,Ap 22,22:6
Murray Anderson's Almanac 1929,Ag 4,VIII,1:6
Murray Anderson's Almanac 1929,Ag 15,20:3

Frigerio, Ezio (Costume Designer)

Servant of Two Masters, The 1960,F 24,42:2

Frigerio, Ezio (Scenic Designer)

Servant of Two Masters, The 1960,F 24,42:2

Friia, Donna

Enchanted, The 1958,Ap 23,41:1

Friman, Karen

Six Characters in Search of an Author 1961,My 11,43:1

Friml, Rudolf (Composer)

June Love 1921,Ap 26,20:1
Ziegfeld Follies 1921,Je 22,10:1
Blue Kitten, The 1922,Ja 14,9:3
Cinders 1923,Ap 4,22:1
Katinka 1923,Ag 31,15:4
Rose Marie 1924,Ag 24,VII,1:8
Rose Marie 1924,S 3,12:2
Vagabond King, The 1925,S 22,23:3
No Foolin' 1926,Je 25,25:1
Wild Rose, The 1926,O 21,23:1
White Eagle, The 1927,D 27,24:4
Three Musketeers, The 1928,Mr 14,28:1
Three Musketeers, The 1928,Mr 25,IX,1:1
Rose Marie 1928,Ap 29,IX,2:8
Nine Fifteen Revue, The 1930,F 12,26:2
Luana 1930,S 18,28:1
Firefly, The 1931,D 1,23:2
Annina 1934,Mr 12,21:6
Music Hath Charms 1934,D 31,8:2
Vagabond King, The 1935,N 29,22:7
Rose Marie 1936,Jl 22,22:6
Firefly, The 1937,Ag 4,14:1
Vagabond King, The 1943,Je 30,24:2

Friml, Rudolf (Lyricist)

Nine Fifteen Revue, The 1930,F 12,26:2

Friml, Rudolf (Playwright)

Vagabond King, The 1961,N 24,36:1

Friml, William (Composer)

Jollyanna; Flahooley 1952,Ag 13,17:7

Frind, Annie

Casanova 1928,N 4,IX,2:1

Frings, Ketti (Playwright)
Mr Sycamore 1942,N 14,13:2
Mr Sycamore 1942,N 29,VIII,1:1
Look Homeward, Angel 1957,N 29,33:1
Look Homeward, Angel 1957,D 8,II,5:1
Look Homeward, Angel 1958,Ag 31,II,1:1
Long Dream, The 1960,F 18,36:2
Look Homeward, Angel 1962,Ap 4,38:3
Walking Happy 1966,N 28,47:1
Frink, Robert
Jonah! 1966,F 16,52:1
Measure for Measure 1966,Jl 14,27:1
Midsummer Night's Dream, A 1967,Je 19,42:1
Huui, Huui 1968,N 25,58:1
Frisa, Lucille
Sold to the Movies; Type 424 Meet Type Oh-Oh,
No! 1970,Je 18,54:2
Sold to the Movies; Crossing the Gap
1970,Je 18,54:2
Frisbee, Edith
Hoboken Blues 1928,F 18,10:1
Frisby, Terence (Playwright)
There's a Girl in My Soup 1967,O 19,58:1
There's a Girl in My Soup 1967,N 12,II,5:6
Frisch, Max (Playwright)
House in Berlin, A (Als der Kreig zu Ende War);
Als der Krieg zu Ende War (A House in Berlin)
1950,D 27,32:3
Andorra 1963,F 11,5:5
Firebugs, The 1963,F 13,7:2
Andorra 1963,F 25,7:5
Firebugs, The 1963,N 22,41:1
Firebugs, The 1968,Jl 2,36:1
Firebugs, The 1969,N 27,52:1
Philipp Hotz 1969,N 27,52:1
Frisch, Richard
Jonah! 1966,F 16,52:1
Frisco
Ziegfeld Midnight Frolic 1920,Mr 17,14:2
Vaudeville (Palace) 1927,F 8,20:3
Vaudeville (Palace) 1927,F 13,VII,1:1
Vaudeville (Palace) 1929,Je 17,29:3
Vaudeville (New Amsterdam Theatre)
1931,Je 22,17:3
Frisco, Al
Pansy 1929,My 15,36:3
Frisco, Eddie
Just a Minute 1928,O 9,34:3
Frisco, Joe
Vaudeville (Palace) 1927,S 13,36:3
Vaudeville (Palace) 1927,O 18,32:4
Earl Carroll's Vanities 1928,Ag 7,25:2
Vaudeville (Palace) 1929,Je 10,22:6
Vaudeville (Palace) 1930,D 22,16:5
Vaudeville (Palace) 1930,D 29,19:3
Vaudeville (Broadway) 1932,D 27,11:4
Frison, Jeanne
Maitresse de Roi 1926,D 1,24:1
Frith, Alfred
Dracula 1927,O 6,29:1
King Can Do No Wrong, The 1927,N 17,28:4
Frith, John Leslie (Playwright)
Fresh Fruit 1927,S 11,VIII,2:4
Desire 1930,Jl 27,VIII,1:8
Ame en Peine, L'; Unquiet Spirit, The
1937,N 14,XI,3:1
Frith, John Leslie (Translator)
Ame en Peine, L' 1928,F 12,VIII,2:1
Frith, Leslie
Frau Jitta's Suehne 1930,My 18,VIII,2:6
Fritz, Anna Mae
Green Pastures, The 1930,F 27,26:1
Green Pastures, The 1935,F 27,16:2
Fritz, Bruno
My Fair Lady 1962,Je 14,24:1
Fritz, Jerry
My 3 Angels 1956,F 4,24:2
Fritz, Maureen
Valmouth 1960,O 7,29:1
Fritzell, Alix
Lord of the Manor, The 1928,O 14,X,2:1
Fritzius, Harry
Dinny and the Witches 1959,D 10,53:3
Frizell, Cornelius
Hamlet 1959,S 11,21:4
Comforter, The 1964,O 22,42:1
Frizzell, Genevieve
Adam Had Two Sons 1932,Ja 21,17:1
Another Language 1933,My 9,20:2
Winged Victory 1943,N 22,24:1
Winter's Tale, The 1946,Ja 16,18:6
Twilight Walk 1951,S 25,25:4
First Lady 1952,My 29,18:5
Frizzell, Lou
Red Roses for Me 1955,D 29,15:2
Quare Fellow, The 1958,N 28,34:1
Great Day in the Morning 1962,Mr 29,29:1
Pullman Car Hiawatha 1962,D 4,46:2
Desire Under the Elms 1963,Ja 11,5:6
After the Fall 1964,Ja 24,18:1
Marco Millions 1964,F 21,33:1
Froehlich, Jacques (Producer)
Wooden Kimono 1926,D 28,16:2

Froehlich, Rico
Most Happy Fella, The 1956,My 4,20:1
Most Happy Fella, The 1956,My 13,II,1:1
Juno 1959,Mr 10,41:1
Happy Town 1959,O 8,49:2
Irma la Douce 1960,S 30,31:2
Gay Life, The 1961,N 20,38:1
Bravo Giovanni 1962,My 21,41:2
Passion of Josef D, The 1964,F 12,29:1
Something More! 1964,N 11,36:1
Froelich, Bill
Billy Budd 1951,F 12,18:3
Froelich, Gustaf
Kat 1931,O 4,VIII,4:1
Dominant Sex, The 1937,O 24,XI,3:2
Froelich, Max
Genius and the Crowd 1920,S 7,20:1
Froelick, Anne
Romeo and Juliet 1935,D 24,10:2
Saint Joan 1936,Mr 10,27:4
Froeschel, George (Original Author)
Papavert 1931,D 30,25:1
Mr Papavert 1932,Ja 23,18:6
Frohlich, Henry
Saint of Bleecker Street, The 1954,D 28,21:1
Frohliger, Clarence
Little Theatre Tournament; Edna 1929,My 11,22:2
Frohman, Alice
George White's Scandals 1931,S 15,30:1
Frohman, Bert
Johnny 2X4 1942,Mr 17,24:6
Frohman, Daniel
Untitled-One Man Show 1928,D 12,34:5
Frohman, Daniel (Producer)
Yoshe Kalb 1933,D 29,27:2
Frohman, Louis M (Composer)
Broken Chain, The 1929,F 21,30:4
Frohoff, Joseph
Good Times 1920,Ag 10,10:1
Frohoff, Louis
Immodest Violet 1920,Ag 25,6:2
Appearances 1925,O 15,27:3
Howdy King 1926,D 14,24:4
Racket, The 1927,N 23,28:3
So Was Napoleon 1930,Ja 9,22:2
American Holiday 1936,F 22,13:3
Murder in the Cathedral 1936,Mr 21,13:5
Froissart (Original Author)
Six of Calais, The 1934,Jl 18,20:3
Six of Calais, The 1934,Ag 12,IX,1:3
Froman, Ann (Costume Designer)
Harold 1967,My 10,39:1
Sondra 1967,My 10,39:1
Froman, Jane
Ziegfeld Follies 1934,Ja 5,24:3
Keep Off the Grass 1940,My 5,X,1:6
Keep Off the Grass 1940,My 24,22:6
Laugh, Town, Laugh! 1942,Je 20,9:1
Laugh, Town, Laugh! 1942,Je 23,22:2
Laugh, Town, Laugh! 1942,Jl 23,15:3
Artists and Models 1943,N 6,16:6
Artists and Models 1943,N 21,II,1:1
Froman, Valentin
Oklahoma! 1951,My 30,15:2
Frome, Milton
All for Love 1949,Ja 24,16:5
Fromen, Betty
Polly Preferred 1923,Ja 12,13:3
Weak Sisters 1925,O 14,31:3
Fromkes, Harry (Miscellaneous)
Green Pastures, The 1951,Mr 16,35:2
Frondaie, Pierre (Playwright)
Montmartre 1922,F 14,20:1
Montmartre 1924,Je 15,VII,1:4
Homme Qui Assassina, L' 1924,N 11,20:1
Amants de Paris, Les 1927,N 6,IX,4:1
Fils de Don Quichotte, Le 1930,N 2,VIII,2:1
Frontal, Eugenie
Once in a Lifetime 1930,S 25,22:3
Frontal, Jean
Gay Divorce 1932,N 30,23:4
Froom, Albert
Good Times 1920,Ag 10,10:1
Pearl of Great Price, The 1926,N 2,34:3
Padre, The 1926,D 28,16:3
Half a Widow 1927,S 13,37:3
King Can Do No Wrong, The 1927,N 17,28:4
Billie 1928,O 2,34:2
Farewell to Arms, A 1930,S 23,30:3
School for Scandal, The 1931,N 11,26:4
Her Man of Wax 1933,O 12,32:3
Victoria Regina 1937,D 27,15:2
Victoria Regina 1938,O 4,20:2
Froom, Charles
Just Because 1922,Mr 23,11:1
Red Robe, The 1928,D 26,15:1
Froos, Sylvia
Vaudeville (Palace) 1932,Ja 4,27:4
Frost, Alan
Richard III 1949,F 9,33:2
Frost, Alice
Great Lover, The 1932,O 12,27:3
As Husbands Go 1933,Ja 20,20:5

Frost, Alice—Cont
It's a Wise Child 1933,My 17,15:2
Shoemaker's Holiday, The 1938,Ja 3,17:2
Frost, Eddie
Bourgeois Gentleman, The 1949,Ag 31,27:2
Frost, Jack (Composer)
Keep Kool 1924,My 23,16:4
Frost, Jack (Lyricist)
Keep Kool 1924,My 23,16:4
Frost, Leila
Ruined Lady, The 1920,Ja 21,10:2
Bachelor's Night, A 1921,O 18,20:1
Lady Bug 1922,Ap 18,15:3
I Will IF You Will 1922,Ag 30,10:4
Backslapper, The 1925,Ap 13,25:2
One of the Family 1925,D 23,22:3
Restless Women 1927,D 27,24:1
Golden Age, The 1928,Ap 25,31:3
House Unguarded 1929,Ja 16,22:2
Frost, Robert (Playwright)
Masque of Reason, The 1959,N 25,19:4
Theatre of Robert Frost, The; Masque of Reason,
The; Bonfire, The; Masque of Mercy, The;
Generations of Men, The 1962,My 31,23:6
Frost, Tony
Evening With Shaw, An; Excerpts From Shaw
1955,Ag 13,6:6
Frost, Walter Archer (Playwright)
Cape Smoke 1925,F 17,19:1
Frost, Warren (Director)
Mother Said No 1951,Ap 17,34:2
Frost, Warren (Scenic Designer)
Mother Said No 1951,Ap 17,34:2
Frothingham, Diana
Magistrate, The 1959,My 14,30:6
Froy, Elaine
Life Begins 1932,Mr 29,23:2
Fruchtman, Oscar
Different Kick, A 1969,Ja 5,76:2
Fruges, Thalie
Matter of Days, A 1969,My 20,40:1
Frumkin, Peter
Golden Bat 1970,Je 27,18:2
Fry, Alex (Composer)
Do You Know the Milky Way? 1961,O 17,45:1
Fry, Ben
Twelfth Disciple, The 1930,My 17,21:4
Fry, Christopher (Playwright)
Lady's Not for Burning, The 1949,Je 12,II,3:1
Venus Observed 1950,Ja 19,35:2
Phoenix Too Frequent, A 1950,Ap 27,36:2
Lady's Not for Burning, The 1950,N 9,42:2
Lady's Not for Burning, The 1950,N 26,II,1:1
Venus Observed 1950,N 26,II,1:1
Sleep of Prisoners, A 1951,My 16,46:6
Sleep of Prisoners, A 1951,O 17,36:2
Sleep of Prisoners, A 1951,O 28,II,1:1
Sleep of Prisoners, A 1952,Ja 2,21:7
Firstborn, The 1952,Ja 30,22:5
Firstborn, The 1952,F 10,II,2:1
Venus Observed 1952,F 14,24:2
Venus Observed 1952,F 24,II,1:1
Boy With a Cart, The 1954,Ap 5,19:2
Dark Is Light Enough, The 1954,My 1,12:4
Sleep of Prisoners, A 1955,Ja 15,10:5
Dark Is Light Enough, The 1955,F 24,20:1
Sleep of Prisoners, A 1955,F 27,II,1:1
Dark Is Light Enough, The 1955,Mr 6,II,1:1
Lark, The 1955,My 29,II,1:1
Tiger at the Gates 1955,Je 12,II,1:1
Tiger at the Gates 1955,O 23,II,1:1
Thor, With Angels 1956,O 15,29:4
Firstborn, The 1957,Ja 7,29:2
Lady's Not for Burning, The 1957,F 22,26:2
Three Love Affairs; Phoenix Too Frequent, A
1958,Mr 11,33:1
Phoenix Too Frequent, A 1958,Mr 16,II,1:1
Firstborn, The 1958,My 1,35:1
Firstborn, The 1958,My 11,II,1:1
Firstborn, The 1958,Jl 4,16:3
Lady's Not for Burning, The 1959,Ja 31,13:2
Duel of Angels 1960,My 1,II,1:1
Judith 1962,Je 21,25:4
Curtmantle 1962,S 5,44:3
Tiger at the Gates 1968,Mr 1,30:1
Ring Around the Moon 1968,N 2,28:1
Fry, Christopher (Translator)
Ring Around the Moon 1950,Ja 27,29:2
Ring Around the Moon 1950,N 24,30:1
Lark, The 1955,My 13,21:2
Tiger at the Gates 1955,Je 3,27:1
Tiger at the Gates 1955,O 4,40:1
Duel of Angels 1960,Ap 20,42:2
Fry, Emma Sheridan
Clouds of the Sun 1922,My 6,11:2
Fry, Eva M (Director)
Kiss for Cinderella, A 1930,F 1,14:6
Madame Pepita 1931,Mr 7,17:1
Mighty Nimrod, The 1931,My 13,23:1
Murder Has Been Arranged, A 1931,D 12,23:5
Fry, Horace B (Playwright)
Little Theatre Tournament; Little Italy
1928,My 10,31:1

Fry, Ray
Hickory Stick 1944,My 9,15:6
Cradle Will Rock, The 1947,D 27,11:2
Country Wife, The 1965,D 10,58:2
Caucasian Chalk Circle, The 1966,Mr 25,35:1
Alchemist, The 1966,O 14,48:1
Saint Joan 1968,Ja 5,42:1
Tiger at the Gates 1968,Mr 1,30:1
Cyrano de Bergerac 1968,Ap 26,30:1
Cry of Players, A 1968,N 15,40:1
Bananas 1968,D 5,60:1
Miser, The 1969,My 9,35:1
Miser, The 1969,My 25,II,1:1
Operation Sidewinder 1970,Mr 13,33:1
Good Woman of Setzuan, The 1970,N 6,51:1
Fry, Willard C
Just Fancy! 1927,O 12,30:2
Fryatt, John
Yeomen of the Guard, The 1955,O 4,39:2
Princess Ida 1955,O 14,22:3
Trial by Jury 1955,O 18,48:1
Frycz, Charles (Costume Designer)
Julius Caesar 1928,Ap 8,VIII,4:3
Frycz, Charles (Scenic Designer)
Julius Caesar 1928,Ap 8,VIII,4:3
Frye, Ben (Miscellaneous)
Christine 1960,Ap 29,27:1
Frye, Ben (Producer)
Garden of Sweets, The 1961,N 1,35:1
Frye, Dwight
Plot Thickens, The 1922,S 6,16:1
Six Characters in Search of an Author
1922,O 31,11:2
Rita Coventry 1923,F 20,12:2
Love Habit, The 1923,Mr 15,17:1
Sitting Pretty 1924,Ap 9,24:2
So This Is Politics 1924,Je 17,22:2
Puppets 1925,Mr 10,19:1
Man's Man, A 1925,O 14,31:2
Man's Man, A 1925,O 25,VIII,1:1
Goat Song 1926,Ja 26,18:1
Chief Thing, The 1926,Mr 23,24:2
Devil in the Cheese, The 1926,D 30,22:4
Ink 1927,N 2,24:2
Queen's Husband, The 1928,Ja 26,17:2
Mima 1928,D 13,24:2
Keeper of the Keys 1933,O 19,23:2
Queer People 1934,F 16,16:2
Crucible, The 1958,Mr 17,21:1
Frye, Edward
Swing It 1937,Jl 23,17:2
Frye, G Clayton
Nemesis 1921,Ap 5,24:3
Frye, Gilbert (Sgt)
Winged Victory 1943,N 22,24:1
Frye, Hal
Music in the Air 1951,O 9,32:2
Frye, Patricia
Midnight Caller, The 1958,Jl 2,25:1
Frye, Peter
Medicine Show 1940,Ap 13,20:6
Frye, Peter (Director)
Forward the Heart 1949,Ja 29,9:2
Getting Married 1951,My 14,28:5
Diary, The 1966,N 27,159:3
Frye, Peter (Playwright)
Shylock '47 1947,My 28,30:5
Frye, Peter (Producer)
200,000 1966,F 15,33:5
Fryer, Randall
Rainbow 1928,N 22,25:1
Merchant of Venice, The 1930,D 3,29:2
Fryer, Robert (Miscellaneous)
Tree Grows in Brooklyn, A 1951,Ap 20,24:3
Fryer, Robert (Producer)
Wonderful Town 1953,F 26,22:3
By the Beautiful Sea 1954,Ap 9,20:1
Desk Set, The 1955,O 25,36:7
Shangri-La 1956,Je 14,40:1
Auntie Mame 1956,N 1,47:2
Redhead 1959,F 6,21:1
Saratoga 1959,D 8,59:4
There Was a Little Girl 1960,Mr 1,28:1
Advise and Consent 1960,N 18,25:1
Passage to India, A 1962,F 1,23:1
Hot Spot 1963,Ap 20,17:2
Sweet Charity 1966,Ja 31,22:1
Mame 1966,My 25,41:1
Frymire, Jack (Director)
Mikado, The 1967,D 4,65:3
Mikado, The 1968,My 2,59:1
Frymire, Virginia (Director)
Mikado, The 1967,D 4,65:3
Mikado, The 1968,My 2,59:1
Fu, Lee Tong
Roar China! 1930,O 28,23:1
Fu-chi, Lin
Tio Ch'an; Beautiful Bait, The 1962,N 13,44:1
Fu-chien, Chang
Tio Ch'an; Beautiful Bait, The 1962,N 13,44:1
Peh Shuh Tchuwan; White Snake, The 1963,Ja 4,5:2
Fu-chien, Mao
Tio Ch'an; Beautiful Bait, The 1962,N 13,44:1

Peh Shuh Tchuwan; White Snake, The 1963,Ja 4,5:2
Fu-hsiao, Chen
Tio Ch'an; Beautiful Bait, The 1962,N 13,44:1
Peh Shuh Tchuwan; White Snake, The 1963,Ja 4,5:2
Fu-hsin, Hsieh
Tio Ch'an; Beautiful Bait, The 1962,N 13,44:1
Fu-hua, Feng
Tio Ch'an; Beautiful Bait, The 1962,N 13,44:1
Fu-shan, Hsiao
Tio Ch'an; Beautiful Bait, The 1962,N 13,44:1
Peh Shuh Tchuwan; White Snake, The 1963,Ja 4,5:2
Fu-wen, Chen
Tio Ch'an; Beautiful Bait, The 1962,N 13,44:1
Fu-Yung, Feh
Tio Ch'an; Beautiful Bait, The 1962,N 13,44:1
Fu-yung, Tsao
Tio Ch'an; Beautiful Bait, The 1962,N 13,44:1
Peh Shuh Tchuwan; White Snake, The 1963,Ja 4,5:2
Fu-yung, Wang
Tio Ch'an; Beautiful Bait, The 1962,N 13,44:1
Peh Shuh Tchuwan; White Snake, The 1963,Ja 4,5:2
Fuccello, Tom
Saint Joan 1968,Ja 5,42:1
Grin and Bare It 1970,Mr 17,36:1
Fuchs, Jay (Miscellaneous)
Trial of Lee Harvey Oswald, The 1967,N 6,64:1
Fuchs, Jay H (Producer)
Fourth Wall, The 1968,S 5,53:1
Leader, The 1969,Ap 22,40:2
Honest-to-God Schnozzola, The 1969,Ap 22,40:2
Room Service 1970,My 13,49:1
Charley's Aunt 1970,Jl 6,38:1
Fuchs, Leo
Lucky Boy 1935,D 2,19:5
Papirossen 1936,S 18,19:3
Yoina Seeks a Bride 1936,O 20,31:1
Give Me Back My Heart 1937,O 4,17:6
Jolly Wedding, The 1937,N 17,26:3
Semele's Bar Mitzvah 1938,Ja 17,11:2
David and Esther 1938,O 12,34:3
Schwartse Mamme 1939,Ja 16,11:3
Salvation 1939,S 29,19:2
If I Were Rothschild 1940,Ja 1,28:7
Family Mishmash, A 1958,O 20,36:1
Bei Mir Bistu Schoen 1961,O 23,22:2
Cowboy in Israel, A 1962,O 29,36:2
My Wife With Conditions 1963,O 21,39:1
Poor Millionaire, The 1966,O 24,48:2
Fuchs, Leo (Director)
Family Mishmash, A 1958,O 20,36:1
Bei Mir Bistu Schoen 1961,O 23,22:2
My Wife With Conditions 1963,O 21,39:1
Fuchs, Leo (Miscellaneous)
My Wife With Conditions 1963,O 21,39:1
Fuchs, Leo (Playwright)
Cowboy in Israel, A 1962,O 29,36:2
Fuchs, Lillian
Jazz a La Carte 1922,Je 3,8:3
Fuchs, Peter (Miscellaneous)
Hooray!! It's a Glorious Day. . .And All That
1966,Mr 10,28:1
Fuchs, Theodore (Scenic Designer)
Path of Flowers, The 1936,S 18,19:3
Hymn to the Rising Sun 1937,My 7,28:2
Unto Such Glory 1937,My 7,28:2
Fudge, Alan
School for Scandal, The 1966,N 22,33:2
War and Peace 1967,Mr 22,42:1
Pantagleize 1967,D 1,54:1
Show-Off, The 1967,D 6,40:2
Cherry Orchard, The 1968,Mr 20,41:1
Hamlet 1969,Mr 4,34:1
In 3 Zones 1970,N 3,28:1
Fuend, William
Polly of Hollywood 1927,F 22,22:3
Fuentes, Francisco
Pluma en el Viento; Feather in the Wind
1932,Ap 2,13:4
Cuando Los Hijos De Eva No Son Los Hijos De
Adan; When Eve's Children Are Not Adam's
1932,Ap 23,11:2
De Muy Buena Familia; Of Very Good Family
1932,Ap 29,13:3
Fuentes, Pancho
Jest, The 1926,F 5,22:2
Fugard, Athol (Playwright)
Blood Knot, The 1964,Mr 3,30:2
Hello and Goodbye 1968,N 13,36:2
Hello and Goodbye 1969,S 19,54:1
Boesman and Lena 1970,Je 23,35:1
Boesman and Lena 1970,Jl 5,II,1:3
Fugazy, Anita
Game of Love and Death, The 1929,N 26,28:4
Fugmann, Andreas (Director)
Tanzgraefin, Die 1925,S 18,26:3
Fuguet, Guy
Rapid Transit 1927,Ap 8,21:2
Fuhrman, Lee (Playwright)
Local Angle, The 1952,Ja 26,9:2
Fuhrman, Richard (Miscellaneous)
Carnival! 1968,D 13,58:1
Fuhs, Julian (Musical Director)
Vaudeville Marches On 1938,D 30,11:1

Fujikawa, Jerry
Teahouse of the August Moon, The 1956,N 9,33:2
Wedding in Japan 1957,Mr 12,37:7
Pleasure of His Company, The 1958,O 23,36:1
It's a Bird . . . It's a Plane . . . It's Superman
1966,Mr 30,34:1
Fujima, Masaya
Azuma Kabuki Dancers and Musicians
1954,F 19,22:3
Azuma Kabuki Dancers and Musicians
1954,F 28,II,4:1
Azuma Kabuki Dancers and Musicians
1954,Mr 10,29:4
Azuma Kabuki Dancers and Musicians
1955,D 27,31:4
Azuma Kabuki Dancers and Musicians
1956,Ja 8,II,3:1
Fujima, Masaya (Choreographer)
Azuma Kabuki Dancers and Musicians
1954,Mr 10,29:4
Azuma Kabuki Dancers and Musicians
1955,D 27,31:4
Fujima, Masaya (Director)
Azuma Kabuki Dancers and Musicians
1955,D 27,31:4
Fujima, Shusai
Azuma Kabuki Dancers and Musicians
1955,D 27,31:4
Azuma Kabuki Dancers and Musicians
1956,Ja 8,II,3:1
Fujimoto, Haruki
It's a Bird . . . It's a Plane . . . It's Superman
1966,Mr 30,34:1
Fukuda, Tsuneari (Director)
Othello 1960,S 11,II,7:1
Taming of the Shrew, The 1966,F 5,32:1
Fukuda, Tsuneari (Translator)
Taming of the Shrew, The 1966,F 5,32:1
Fulco, Giovanni
Paese dei Campanelli, Il; Land of Bells, The
1935,My 10,25:4
Fulco, John
Lady, The 1923,D 5,23:2
Gray Shadow 1931,Mr 11,23:4
Hot-Cha! 1932,Mr 9,17:3
Fulda, Ludwig (Miscellaneous)
Pirate, The 1942,N 26,39:2
Fulda, Ludwig (Original Author)
Pirate, The 1942,S 15,18:6
Pirate, The 1942,D 6,VIII,1:1
Fulda, Ludwig (Playwright)
Vertrag von Nizza, Der 1922,Ap 2,VI,1:2
Fulford, David
Dear Judas 1947,O 6,26:4
Fulford, David (Director)
Fashion 1959,Ja 21,27:1
Moon in the Yellow River, The 1961,F 7,40:2
Colombe 1965,F 24,33:1
Fulford, David (Producer)
Fashion 1959,Ja 21,27:1
Moon in the Yellow River, The 1961,F 7,40:2
Colombe 1965,F 24,33:1
Fulham, William H (Playwright)
To My Husband 1936,Je 2,35:2
Fullar, Darley
Life Begins 1932,Mr 29,23:2
Fullarton, Jean
Truth Game, The 1930,D 29,19:1
Peter Ibbetson 1931,Ap 9,30:3
Life Begins 1932,Mr 29,23:2
Saint Wench 1933,Ja 3,19:3
Fullemann, Lizbeth (Costume Designer)
Nest, The 1970,Ap 10,46:1
Fuller, Albert C (Playwright)
Remote Control 1929,S 11,24:5
Fuller, Barbara
Anatomist, The 1957,F 27,21:5
Fuller, Bobby
Gondoliers, The 1931,Je 2,34:4
Fuller, Charles (Playwright)
Village, The: A Party 1968,N 13,39:1
Perfect Party, The 1969,Mr 21,42:1
Fuller, Daphne
Hamlet 1934,D 26,19:3
Fuller, Dean
Pal Joey 1949,Mr 7,17:2
Fuller, Dean (Composer)
Once Over Lightly 1955,Mr 16,39:1
New Faces of 1956 1956,Je 15,32:1
Ziegfeld Follies 1957,Mr 2,19:2
Imaginary Invalid, The 1967,My 2,53:1
Ways and Means 1967,My 4,34:1
Fumed Oak 1967,My 4,34:1
Still Life 1967,My 4,34:1
She Stoops to Conquer 1968,Ap 1,58:3
Fuller, Dean (Lyricist)
Once Over Lightly 1955,Mr 16,39:1
New Faces of 1956 1956,Je 15,32:1
Ziegfeld Follies 1957,Mr 2,19:2
Fuller, Dean (Miscellaneous)
Maggie 1953,F 19,20:2
Fuller, Dean (Musical Director)
Seagull, The 1964,Ap 6,36:1

Fuller, Dean (Musical Director)—Cont
Crucible, The 1964,Ap 7,30:2
Fuller, Dean (Playwright)
Once Upon a Mattress 1959,My 12,40:1
Once Upon a Mattress 1959,My 17,II,1:1
Fuller, Eddie
Sing for Your Supper 1939,Ap 25,18:6
Fuller, Edmund (Playwright)
Amateur Hour 1936,Jl 21,13:1
Fuller, Eduard (Miscellaneous)
Gypsy 1959,My 22,31:6
Take Me Along 1959,O 23,22:2
Fuller, Edward
Whatever Possessed Her 1934,Ja 26,21:2
Cradle Will Rock, The 1937,D 6,19:4
Cradle Will Rock, The 1938,Ja 4,19:3
Good as Gold 1957,Mr 8,22:2
Guys and Dolls 1959,Jl 22,22:2
Fuller, Elsbeth
Seven Mirrors 1945,O 26,17:2
He Who Gets Slapped 1946,Mr 21,31:4
Fuller, Frances
Front Page, The 1928,Ag 15,19:2
Cafe 1930,Ag 29,11:1
Five Star Final 1930,D 31,11:1
Animal Kingdom, The 1932,Ja 13,26:4
Animal Kingdom, The 1932,Ja 24,1:1
I Loved You Wednesday 1932,O 12,27:1
Her Master's Voice 1933,O 24,24:3
Country Wife, The 1935,Jl 2,24:2
Coward, The 1935,Jl 16,24:1
Stage Door 1936,S 29,35:1
Stage Door 1936,O 23,26:3
Excursion 1937,Ap 10,11:4
Home Is the Hero 1954,S 23,42:2
Lady of the Camellias, The 1963,Mr 22,7:1
Fuller, Gene
Fifth Horseman, The 1949,Je 14,26:6
Fuller, George
Simon Called Peter 1924,N 11,20:2
Fuller, Harrison
Ruddigore 1931,Ag 11,28:3
Yeomen of the Guard, The 1933,My 2,20:4
Yeomen of the Guard, The 1933,Ag 15,20:5
Fuller, Harry
Porgy and Bess 1955,Jl 9,9:5
Fuller, James
Green Pastures, The 1930,F 27,26:1
Green Pastures, The 1935,F 27,16:2
How Come Lawd? 1937,O 1,18:5
Where Do We Go From Here? 1938,N 16,26:2
Green Pastures, The 1951,Mr 16,35:2
Fuller, Janice (Miscellaneous)
Annie Get Your Gun 1957,Mr 9,15:5
Fuller, Jeff
Love's Labour's Lost 1968,Je 28,36:1
Fuller, John G (Playwright)
Pink Elephant, The 1953,Ap 23,37:2
Love Me Little 1958,Ap 15,42:2
Fuller, Larry
Porgy and Bess 1954,D 17,36:7
Carousel 1957,S 12,38:2
Fuller, Larry (Director)
Blood Red Roses 1970,Mr 23,48:1
Fuller, Lester (Director)
Foreign Affairs 1932,Ap 14,25:5
Fuller, Lester (Producer)
Foreign Affairs 1932,Ap 14,25:5
Fuller, Lorenzo
St Louis Woman 1946,Ap 1,22:2
Kiss Me, Kate 1948,D 31,10:3
World's My Oyster, The 1956,Ag 10,10:4
Time of Your Life, The 1969,N 7,37:1
Time of Your Life, The 1969,N 16,II,1:4
Fuller, Lorenzo (Composer)
Temporary Island, A 1948,Mr 15,27:3
Fuller, Lorenzo (Musical Director)
World's My Oyster, The 1956,Ag 10,10:4
Fuller, Lorenzo (Playwright)
World's My Oyster, The 1956,Ag 10,10:4
Fuller, Lydia
Accent on Youth 1935,Jl 2,24:3
Fuller, Penny
Oh, Kay! 1960,Ap 18,37:2
As You Like It 1963,Jl 17,19:2
Richard III 1966,Ag 11,26:1
Henry IV, Part I 1968,Je 30,54:7
Henry IV, Part II 1968,Jl 2,33:1
Applause 1970,Mr 31,35:1
Applause 1970,Ap 5,II,1:1
Fuller, Robert
Wedding in Japan 1949,N 11,29:1
Burning Bush, The 1949,D 17,15:5
Scapegoat, The 1950,Ap 20,36:5
Circle of Chalk, The 1950,D 2,8:3
Fuller, Rosalinde
What's in a Name? 1920,Mr 20,14:2
Christmas Carol, A 1921,D 23,18:3
Hamlet 1922,N 17,14:1
Hamlet 1923,N 27,23:6
Farmer's Wife, The 1924,O 10,22:3
Patience 1924,D 30,15:1
Love for Love 1925,Ap 1,21:2
Call of Life, The 1925,O 10,10:1

Fountain, The 1925,D 11,26:1
House of Ussher, The 1926,Ja 14,18:4
Scotch Mist 1926,S 21,32:3
What Never Dies 1926,D 29,24:2
Lost 1927,Mr 29,22:2
Squall, The 1927,D 4,X,1:3
Unknown Warrior, The 1931,O 23,28:4
Son of Man 1933,O 22,IX,2:2
Murder on Account 1936,S 26,11:2
Fuller-Mellish, Vera
Traitor, The 1930,My 3,23:4
Late One Evening 1933,Ja 10,27:3
Lake, The 1933,D 27,24:2
Fulling, Edna
Americana 1926,Jl 27,15:3
Fulling, Ednor
Merry Merry 1925,S 25,24:3
Fullum, Clay (Musical Director)
Last Sweet Days of Isaac, The 1970,Ja 27,49:1
Rothschilds, The 1970,O 20,40:1
Fulmer, Ray
Happiness Is Just a Little Thing Called a Rolls
  Royce 1968,My 13,54:5
Fulmer, Richard
Fuente Ovejuna; Sheep Well, The 1936,My 3,II,4:1
No More Peace 1937,F 27,9:1
Fulton, Barbara
Plumes in the Dust 1936,N 7,14:2
Fulton, Bobby
Cape Cod Follies 1929,S 19,37:2
Fulton, Eileen
Many Loves 1959,Ja 14,28:1
Summer of the Seventeenth Doll 1959,O 14,52:1
Abe Lincoln in Illinois 1963,Ja 23,5:2
Fulton, Frances
Tom Sawyer 1931,D 26,15:3
Fulton, Future
Safari! 1955,My 12,32:6
Fulton, Jack
Variety Anthology 1932,Mr 21,19:4
Fulton, James R
Black Cockatoo, The 1926,D 31,11:1
Fulton, Maude
Humming Bird, The 1923,Ja 16,16:2
Fulton, Maude (Playwright)
Humming Bird, The 1923,Ja 16,16:2
Fulton, Robert
Gypsy Baron, The 1944,Je 15,17:3
Fun-yun, Yeh
Peh Shuh Tchuwan; White Snake, The 1963,Ja 4,5:2
Funakoshi, Mitsuko
Ice Capades 1964,Ag 27,27:2
Ice Capades 1969,Ja 8,42:1
Ice Capades 1970,Ja 7,35:1
Fung, Paul
Roar China! 1930,O 28,23:1
Funk, Emmy
Porgy and Bess 1950,N 26,II,7:8
Funk, Jerald (Miscellaneous)
Worlds of Shakespeare, The 1963,D 5,58:1
Funston, Beverly
Thesmophoriazusae, The; Goddesses of Athens,
  The 1955,D 14,52:4
Funt, Julian (Playwright)
Dancer, The 1946,Je 6,16:5
Magic and the Loss, The 1954,Ap 10,10:3
Fuorry, Michael
Fall 1957,N 22,19:1
Fuqua, V C (Lighting Director)
New Tenant, The 1964,My 28,40:2
Victims of Duty 1964,My 28,40:2
Sweet Enemy, The 1965,F 16,39:1
Colombe 1965,F 24,33:1
Glass Menagerie, The 1965,My 5,53:2
Good Day 1965,O 19,51:1
Exhaustion of Our Son's Love, The 1965,O 19,51:1
Me and Thee 1965,D 8,58:4
Mad Show, The 1966,Ja 10,16:1
Pousse-Cafe 1966,Mr 19,19:2
Death of the Well-Loved Boy, The
  1967,My 16,48:1
Make Me Disappear 1969,My 14,34:1
Furber, Douglas
Charlot's Revue 1924,Ja 10,18:1
Furber, Douglas (Miscellaneous)
Wake Up and Dream 1929,D 31,14:3
Furber, Douglas (Playwright)
Toni 1924,My 18,VII,2:8
Ladies' Night 1933,N 19,IX,3:7
Lucky Break 1934,O 3,25:3
Lucky Break 1934,O 28,IX,3:4
Furcolo, Foster (Gov) (Playwright)
Ballots Up 1960,Ag 24,34:4
Furcolowe, Charles
Father Malachy's Miracle 1937,N 18,26:4
Waltz in Goose Step 1938,N 2,26:2
Jeremiah 1939,F 4,11:2
Summer Night 1939,N 3,17:1
Susannah and the Elders 1940,O 30,28:2
My Fair Ladies 1941,Mr 24,12:7
Night Before Christmas, The 1941,Ap 11,25:2
First Crocus, The 1942,Ja 3,14:6

Furher, Douglas (Lyricist)
Afgar 1920,N 9,13:2
Furhman, Richard (Costume Designer)
God Bless You, Harold Fineberg 1969,Mr 31,30:2
Furhman, Richard (Scenic Designer)
God Bless You, Harold Fineberg 1969,Mr 31,30:2
Furie, Wallace
Lido Girl, The 1928,Ag 24,23:2
Furlan, Alan
Romeo and Juliet 1951,Mr 12,21:2
Furlaud, Maxine (Playwright)
Biscuit 1966,My 17,51:2
Fitz 1966,My 17,51:2
Furlow, Brown (Composer)
From Morn Till Midnight 1948,D 7,41:6
Furman, Ariel
Megilla of Itzik Manger, The 1968,O 10,60:1
Megilla of Itzik Manger, The 1969,Ap 21,55:1
Furman, Charles
Me and Molly 1948,F 27,27:2
Furman, Edward
Dead End 1936,S 20,IX,3:7
Furman, Jacque
Earthlight Theater 1970,N 4,38:2
Furman, Roger (Costume Designer)
Freight 1949,F 4,30:2
Riders to the Sea 1949,F 4,30:2
Furman, Roger (Scenic Designer)
Tin Top Valley 1947,Mr 1,11:2
Rain 1948,F 2,15:2
Furness, Betty
Off the Record 1940,D 1,63:5
My Fair Ladies 1941,Mr 24,12:7
Mr Big 1941,S 14,IX,2:5
Mr Big 1941,O 1,24:2
Furness, James
Orphee 1935,Mr 23,10:3
Not in Our Stars 1941,Ap 26,20:5
Furness, Mark (Miscellaneous)
Salad Days 1958,N 11,24:1
Thracian Horses, The 1961,S 28,58:2
Pimpernel! 1964,Ja 7,26:6
Furrell, Ann
Oedipus Rex 1923,O 26,14:1
Furse, Celia
Empress of Destiny 1938,Mr 10,16:2
Furse, Jill
Goodness, How Sad 1938,O 19,18:6
Goodness, How Sad 1938,N 6,IX,3:5
Rebecca 1942,My 31,VIII,2:3
Furse, Judith
Goodness, How Sad 1938,N 6,IX,3:5
Furse, Roger (Costume Designer)
Henry IV, Part I 1946,My 7,25:2
Henry IV, Part II 1946,My 8,33:4
Broken Heart, The 1962,Jl 10,28:2
Pickwick 1965,O 6,5:3
Furse, Roger (Miscellaneous)
Daphne Laureola 1950,S 19,38:6
Furse, Roger (Scenic Designer)
Spring Meeting 1938,D 9,30:4
Caesar and Cleopatra 1951,D 20,43:2
Antony and Cleopatra 1951,D 21,22:2
Caesar and Cleopatra 1951,D 30,II,1:1
Antony and Cleopatra 1951,D 30,II,1:1
Venus Observed 1952,F 14,24:2
Venus Observed 1952,F 24,II,1:1
Macbeth 1955,Je 19,II,1:1
Tumbler, The 1960,F 25,32:2
Duel of Angels 1960,Ap 20,42:2
Duel of Angels 1960,My 1,II,1:1
Broken Heart, The 1962,Jl 10,28:2
Furshard, John (Playwright)
Public Savior Number One 1935,Je 11,23:2
Furst, Jeff
Digging for Apples 1962,S 28,29:4
Furst, Myra (Producer)
Little Orchard Annie 1930,Ap 22,33:1
Furst, William (Composer)
Yellow Jacket, The 1928,N 8,27:3
Furtado, Ernie
Copper and Brass 1957,O 18,19:2
Furth, George
Cook for Mr General, A 1961,O 20,39:1
Hot Spot 1963,Ap 20,17:2
Furth, George (Playwright)
Company 1970,Ap 27,40:1
Company 1970,My 3,II,1:4
Company 1970,Jl 29,31:1
Furth, Seymour (Composer)
Bringing Up Father 1925,Mr 31,16:1
Furuhashi, Takeshi (Translator)
Kiss Me, Kate 1966,F 5,32:1
Fury, Loretta
Comic Strip 1958,My 15,26:2
Mike Downstairs 1968,Ap 19,35:1
Fusier-Gir, Jeanne
Attachee, L' 1929,My 19,IX,2:1
Futrelle, Virginia
Good Times 1920,Ag 10,10:1
Some Party 1922,Ap 17,22:1
Fuumer, John C
Zuider Zee 1928,D 19,24:4

Fyfe, Clyde
Mrs Warren's Profession 1956,Je 7,35:2
Fyffe, Will
Vaudeville (Palace) 1927,Ap 5,30:2
Vaudeville (Palace) 1927,Ap 12,25:4
Vaudeville (Palace) 1927,Ap 19,24:3
Vaudeville (Palace) 1928,F 28,18:7
Vaudeville (Palace) 1928,Mr 6,20:5
Vaudeville (Palace) 1929,Ja 14,20:3
Vaudeville (Palace) 1929,Ja 21,18:3
Vanities 1932,S 18,IX,2:1
Vanities 1932,S 28,22:4
Fyler, Herbert
Hobo 1961,Ap 11,41:2

G

Gaal, Francisca
Case of the Noszty Boy and Mary Toth, The
  1927,Mr 20,VIII,4:3
Church Mouse, A 1927,D 4,X,2:3
Postmistress, The 1928,Ja 15,VIII,2:1
Youngest Verebezy Girl, The 1928,D 2,X,4:7
Romance of Ida, The 1929,F 3,VIII,2:1
Good Fairy, The 1930,O 13,31:2
Woman Brown, The 1939,D 9,18:5
Gaar, Frances
Skipper Next to God 1948,Ja 5,14:5
Gaard, David (Playwright)
And Puppy Dog Tails 1969,O 20,60:1
And Puppy Dog Tails 1969,O 26,II,3:7
Gabanyi, Boske
Egerfogo; Mousetrap, The 1958,Ja 30,18:6
Gabel, Martin
Man Bites Dog 1933,Ap 26,11:2
Sky's the Limit, The 1934,D 18,25:5
Dead End 1935,O 29,17:2
Ten Million Ghosts 1936,O 24,23:7
Julius Caesar 1937,N 12,26:6
Danton's Death 1938,N 3,26:2
Medicine Show 1940,Ap 13,20:6
King Lear 1950,D 26,18:1
King Lear 1950,D 31,II,1:1
Little Blue Light, The 1951,Ap 30,17:2
Reclining Figure 1954,O 8,26:5
Will Success Spoil Rock Hunter? 1955,O 14,22:2
Rivalry, The 1959,F 9,24:2
Rivalry, The 1959,F 15,II,1:1
Big Fish, Little Fish 1961,Mr 16,42:2
Big Fish, Little Fish 1961,Mr 26,II,1:1
Children From Their Games 1963,Ap 12,33:1
Baker Street 1965,F 17,36:1
Baker Street 1965,F 28,II,1:1
Sheep on the Runway 1970,F 2,28:3
Sheep on the Runway 1970,F 8,II,5:5
Gabel, Martin (Director)
Young Couple Wanted 1940,Ja 25,16:2
Cream in the Well, The 1941,Ja 21,19:2
Assassin, The 1945,O 18,20:2
Survivors, The 1948,Ja 20,27:2
Survivors, The 1948,Ja 25,II,1:1
Men of Distinction 1953,My 1,18:4
Gabel, Martin (Miscellaneous)
King Lear 1956,Ja 13,17:1
Gabel, Martin (Producer)
Medicine Show 1940,Ap 13,20:6
Cream in the Well, The 1941,Ja 21,19:2
Cafe Crown 1942,Ja 24,12:5
Assassin, The 1945,O 18,20:2
Survivors, The 1948,Ja 20,27:2
Men of Distinction 1953,My 1,18:4
Reclining Figure 1954,O 8,26:5
Hidden River, The 1957,Ja 24,32:1
Once More With Feeling 1958,O 22,39:1
Gabel, Max
Love and Politics 1929,O 21,30:7
Slaves of Luxury 1930,F 8,13:3
Sonitchka 1930,Mr 8,21:3
Gabel, Max (Director)
Love and Politics 1929,O 21,30:7
Gabel, Max (Playwright)
Love and Politics 1929,O 21,30:7
Slaves of Luxury 1930,F 8,13:3
Girls of Today 1935,N 20,26:5
Gabel, Max (Producer)
Love and Politics 1929,O 21,30:7
Slaves of Luxury 1930,F 8,13:3
Sonitchka 1930,Mr 8,21:3
Gabel, Ruby C (Playwright)
Horse Fever 1940,N 25,21:2
Gabel, Zac H (Playwright)
Horse Fever 1940,N 25,21:2
Gabelman, Cyprienne
Canteen Show, The 1942,S 4,18:1
Gaber, Munro
Billy Budd 1955,My 4,35:1
Gabest, Charles
Peter Flies High 1931,N 10,28:3
Gabet (Playwright)
Cloches de Cornville, Les; Chimes of Normandy,
  The 1926,D 14,24:4

Gabin, Jean
Soif, La 1949,F 9,33:2
Gable, Bonnie (Miscellaneous)
Dirtiest Show in Town, The 1970,Je 29,43:2
Gable, Chris (Playwright)
Littlest Crown, The 1968,Ap 15,41:1
Gable, Clark
Machinal 1928,S 8,10:3
Machinal 1928,S 16,IX,1:1
Scars 1929,F 10,IX,2:1
Gambling 1929,My 19,IX,2:1
Hawk Island 1929,S 17,34:7
Love, Honor and Betray 1930,Mr 13,22:2
Gable, June
Jacques Brel Is Alive and Well and Living in Paris
  1970,Ja 21,34:1
Mod Donna 1970,My 4,48:1
In 3 Zones 1970,N 3,28:1
Gabler, Carl
Eh? 1966,O 17,47:1
Gabler, Deneen
Point of No Return 1957,Mr 23,17:2
Gabler, Sally
Beauty and the Beast 1932,Ja 10,I,29:2
In Clover 1937,O 14,23:1
Odds on Mrs Oakley, The 1944,O 3,18:8
Gabler, Sarah
Mister Romeo 1927,S 6,35:3
Gabor, Eva
Happy Time, The 1950,Ja 25,24:1
Little Glass Clock, The 1956,Mr 27,40:2
Lulu 1958,S 30,24:1
Gabriel, Ethel
Summer of the Seventeenth Doll 1958,Ja 23,23:2
Gabriel, Francois
Three Musketeers, The 1968,Je 26,43:1
Gabriel, Gilbert W (Miscellaneous)
Clap Hands 1934,Ag 21,12:7
Gabriel, Master
Letty Pepper 1922,Ap 11,22:2
Solitaire 1929,Mr 13,28:3
Gabrieli, Andrea (Composer)
Oedipus Rex 1937,My 9,XI,7:5
Gabrielson, Frank
Stevedore 1934,Ap 19,33:2
Whatever Goes Up 1935,N 26,28:2
But for the Grace of God 1937,Ja 13,21:4
Gabrielson, Frank (Lyricist)
Gypsy Blonde 1934,Je 26,22:5
Gabrielson, Frank (Playwright)
Life Begins at 8:40 1934,Ag 28,24:2
Parade 1935,My 7,26:1
Parade 1935,My 12,X,2:5
Parade 1935,My 21,22:2
Illustrators' Show, The 1936,Ja 23,25:3
More the Merrier, The 1941,S 16,19:3
Days of Our Youth, The 1941,N 29,15:2
Gabrielson, Hale
Don Juan in the Russian Manner 1954,Ap 23,23:2
Six Characters in Search of an Author
  1955,D 12,38:1
Julius Caesar 1957,O 24,39:1
Gaburo, Kenneth (Composer)
Tiger Rag, The 1961,F 17,20:2
Tiger Rag, The 1961,Mr 5,II,1:1
Gaby, Frank
Will Morrissey's Newcomers 1923,Ag 9,16:2
Artists and Models 1924,O 16,33:3
Gay Paree 1926,N 10,24:2
Vaudeville (Palace) 1928,Ag 7,25:5
Vaudeville (Palace) 1928,S 18,34:6
Broadway Nights 1929,Jl 16,23:2
Here Come the Clowns 1938,D 8,36:2
Gaby, Yvonne (Mlle)
Girofle-Girofla 1926,N 23,26:3
Gadd, May (Choreographer)
As You Like It 1937,N 1,25:2
Gadd, Renee
And Be My Love 1934,Ja 19,25:2
Living Dangerously 1935,Ja 14,10:3
They Came to a City 1943,Je 6,II,1:6
Third Person 1955,D 30,13:4
Reluctant Debutante, The 1956,O 11,50:1
Gade, Willy
Armseligen Besenbinder, Die 1928,N 19,16:2
Gadsden, Emma
Roseanne 1923,D 31,9:5
Gadsden, Lionel
Marigold 1930,O 9,23:1
Gae, Nadine
One for the Money 1939,F 6,9:2
Two for the Show 1940,F 9,14:2
Two for the Show 1940,F 18,IX,2:1
Panama Hattie 1940,O 31,28:2
Ziegfeld Follies 1943,Ap 2,16:2
Angel in the Wings 1947,D 12,36:4
Angel in the Wings 1948,F 8,II,2:1
Gaertner, Lillian (Costume Designer)
Straw Hat, The 1926,O 15,20:2
Gaertner, Lillian (Scenic Designer)
Straw Hat, The 1926,O 15,20:2
Gaetha, Vincent
Originale 1964,S 9,46:1

Gaffield, Dick (Director)
Adding Machine, The 1970,D 5,40:1
Gaffigan, Catherine
Journey of the Fifth Horse, The 1966,Ap 22,36:1
Kicking the Castle Down 1967,Ja 19,43:1
Gaffney, Archie A
Old King's 1924,Mr 12,19:3
Gaffney, M S
It's the Valet 1933,D 15,25:4
Gagan, Myron C (Playwright)
Great Power, The 1928,S 12,25:1
Gage, Erford
Coriolanus 1937,O 10,VI,4:7
Diff'rent 1937,N 21,II,10:7
Diff'rent 1938,Ja 26,26:4
Pygmalion 1938,Ja 27,16:3
Captain Jinks of the Horse Marines 1938,Ja 28,16:2
No More Peace 1938,Ja 29,13:2
Coriolanus 1938,F 2,14:5
As You Like It 1939,My 9,28:4
As You Like It; Midsummer Night's Dream, A;
  Comedy of Errors, The; Taming of the Shrew,
  The 1939,My 9,28:4
King Lear 1940,D 16,27:2
They Walk Alone 1941,Mr 13,24:2
Macbeth 1941,N 12,30:2
Gage, Faith
Made for Each Other 1924,S 30,27:2
Gage, Gary
Red, White and Maddox 1969,Ja 27,27:1
Gage, John
Sea Dogs 1939,N 7,30:3
International Incident, An 1940,Ap 3,18:2
Gage, John Gordon
Romeo and Juliet 1934,D 21,30:3
Gage, Loren
Tomorrow's a Holiday! 1935,D 31,10:2
My Heart's in the Highlands 1939,Ap 14,29:2
Gage, Margaret
Chastening, The 1923,F 17,9:2
Antigone 1923,My 4,18:4
Admiral, The 1924,Ap 25,20:2
Admiral, The 1924,My 4,VIII,1:1
Gage, Margaret (Choreographer)
Antigone 1923,My 4,18:4
Gage, Margaret (Producer)
Admiral, The 1929,Ja 23,21:1
Gage, Martin
Best Foot Forward 1956,Mr 3,16:1
On the Town 1959,F 14,15:1
Gage, Patricia
Chemmy Circle, The 1968,Ag 10,17:2
Gage, Richard North
Orphee 1935,Mr 23,10:3
Gagen, Frank
Spring Is Here 1929,Mr 12,26:1
Street Singer, The 1929,S 18,35:2
Between the Devil 1937,D 23,24:5
Gagen, Frank (Choreographer)
Life Begins in '40 1940,Ap 5,24:2
Hit the Road 1941,Ap 4,18:3
Gagliano, B (Composer)
Tragedy of the Ages, The 1933,Ap 7,22:7
Gagliano, Frank (Lyricist)
Prince of Peasantmania 1970,F 22,88:1
Gagliano, Frank (Playwright)
Conerico Was Here to Stay 1965,Mr 4,37:1
Night of the Dunce 1966,D 29,21:1
Father Uxbridge Wants to Marry 1967,O 30,57:1
Conerico Was Here to Stay 1969,Mr 11,39:1
Paradise Gardens East 1969,Mr 11,39:1
Prince of Peasantmania 1970,F 22,88:1
Gagnon, Chick
Banjo Eyes 1941,D 26,20:2
Gagnon, Marie Louise
Ora di Diana, L' 1937,My 17,22:3
Gagnon, Roland (Musical Director)
Galileo 1967,Ap 14,31:1
Gahagan, Helen
Shoot 1922,Je 8,14:2
Manhattan 1922,Ag 16,7:5
Dreams for Sale 1922,S 14,24:1
Fashions for Men 1922,D 6,22:1
Fashions for Men 1922,D 24,VII,1:1
Chains 1923,S 20,5:2
Leah Kleschna 1924,Ap 22,19:2
Leah Kleschna 1924,Ap 27,VIII,1:1
Beyond 1925,Ja 27,14:1
Sapphire Ring, The 1925,Ap 16,25:2
Enchanted April, The 1925,Ag 25,12:3
Young Woodley 1925,N 3,34:1
Trelawney of the 'Wells' 1927,F 1,24:4
Diplomacy 1928,My 29,16:3
Diplomacy 1928,Je 3,VIII,1:1
Tonight or Never 1930,N 9,IX,3:2
Tonight or Never 1930,N 19,19:3
Dance of Death, The 1932,Ja 11,29:5
Moor Born 1934,Ap 4,26:4
Moor Born 1934,Ap 8,X,2:7
Mother Lode 1934,D 24,16:5
And Stars Remain 1936,S 29,35:2
And Stars Remain 1936,O 13,32:2
Wind in the Sails 1940,Ag 1,24:6

Gahagan, Helen—Cont
First Lady 1952,My 23,16:5
First Lady 1952,My 29,18:5
Untitled-Dramatic Reading 1955,O 7,21:1
Gahagan, Herbert (Scenic Designer)
Wisteria Trees, The 1955,F 3,20:2
Gaige, Crosby (Director)
Hat, a Coat, a Glove, A 1934,F 1,15:2
Ragged Army 1934,F 27,16:5
Gaige, Crosby (Miscellaneous)
Coquette 1927,N 9,23:1
Gaige, Crosby (Playwright)
Larger Than Life 1936,Mr 17,25:3
Gaige, Crosby (Producer)
Butter and Egg Man, The 1925,S 24,28:1
Enemy, The 1925,O 21,20:1
Beware of Widows 1925,D 2,22:3
Good Fellow, The 1926,O 6,22:1
Road to Happiness, The 1927,My 3,24:1
Romantic Young Lady, The 1927,My 5,30:2
Girl and the Cat, The 1927,My 6,21:2
Blind Heart, The 1927,My 8,30:2
Fragila Rosina 1927,My 10,24:4
Cradle Song 1927,My 10,24:4
Pygmalion 1927,My 12,25:2
Shannons of Broadway, The 1927,S 27,30:4
Nightstick 1927,N 11,20:4
Little Accident 1928,O 10,32:3
Blind Mice 1930,S 7,IX,2:4
Blind Mice 1930,O 16,28:2
House Beautiful, The 1931,Mr 13,20:4
I Loved You Wednesday 1932,O 12,27:1
Shooting Star 1933,Je 13,22:2
Ten Minute Alibi 1933,O 18,24:3
Hat, a Coat, a Glove, A 1934,F 1,15:2
Ragged Army 1934,F 27,16:5
Accent on Youth 1934,D 26,19:1
On to Fortune 1935,Ja 15,23:2
On to Fortune 1935,F 5,22:2
Field of Ermine 1935,F 9,10:4
Othello 1935,S 13,19:2
Othello 1935,S 28,13:2
Macbeth 1935,O 8,26:4
Whatever Goes Up 1935,N 26,28:2
Eternal Road, The 1937,Ja 8,14:2
Time and the Conways 1938,Ja 4,19:2
Gaige, Russell
Violet 1944,O 25,16:1
Barretts of Wimpole Street, The 1945,Mr 27,23:6
Anne of the Thousand Days 1948,D 9,49:2
Desire Under the Elms 1952,Ja 17,23:4
Brigadoon 1957,Mr 28,37:1
Italian Straw Hat, The 1957,O 1,37:2
Cue for Passion 1958,N 26,25:2
Gaige, Truman
Blossom Time 1931,Mr 5,32:1
Bitter Sweet 1934,My 8,28:4
Music Hath Charms 1934,D 31,8:2
Roberta 1937,Je 27,II,6:1
Three Waltzes 1937,D 27,10:2
You Never Know 1938,S 22,26:3
Song of Norway 1951,Ja 11,28:5
Kismet 1953,D 4,2:4
Time Remembered 1957,N 13,41:2
Song of Norway 1959,Je 26,16:2
Saratoga 1959,D 8,59:4
Wall, The 1960,O 12,44:4
Kismet 1965,Je 23,45:1
Hadrian VII 1969,Ja 9,22:1
Gaile, Evelyn
Mendel, Inc 1929,N 26,28:5
Gailhard, Andre (Composer)
Beux Billes de Cadix, Les 1923,Ja 21,VII,1:3
Gailing, Ben
Of One Mother 1937,Ja 18,21:3
Gaillard, Margaret
Ivory Door, The 1927,O 19,24:5
Gaillard, Marion
Trois Jeunes Filles Nues; Three Young Maids From
the Folies Bergere 1929,Mr 5,28:2
Comte Obligado 1929,Mr 12,26:2
Ta Bouche 1929,Mr 15,28:5
Bon Garcon, Un 1929,Mr 19,36:2
Pas Sur La Bouche; Not on the Lips
1929,Mr 26,34:3
Gaine, Jim
Earthlight Theater 1970,N 4,38:2
Gainer, Joan (Choreographer)
Play That on Your Old Piano 1965,O 15,49:1
Gaines, Coulter
George Washington 1920,Mr 2,9:1
Gaines, Ernestine
Such Is Life 1927,S 1,27:3
Kingdom of God, The 1928,D 21,30:2
Gaines, Frederick (Lyricist)
House of Leather, The 1970,Mr 19,56:1
Gaines, Frederick (Playwright)
House of Leather, The 1970,Mr 19,56:1
Gaines, Gordon
Trojan Women, The 1941,Ap 9,32:5
Gaines, John
Nightingale, The 1927,Ja 4,20:4
March March, The 1966,N 15,51:4

Gaines, Lee
Memphis Bound 1945,My 25,23:2
Gaines, Marjorie
Mystery Moon 1930,Je 24,23:4
Gaines, Muriel
Tidbits of 1946 1946,Jl 9,17:2
Gaines, Pearl
Conjur 1938,N 1,27:2
Medicine Show 1940,Ap 13,20:6
Lysistrata 1946,O 18,27:5
Gaines, Richard
S S Glencairn 1929,Ja 10,24:5
Three Sisters, The 1930,Ja 9,22:2
Glass of Water, A 1930,Mr 6,16:3
Antigone 1930,Ap 25,28:4
Abe Lincoln in Illinois 1939,Jl 30,IX,1:1
In Time to Come 1941,D 29,20:2
In Time to Come 1942,Ja 4,IX,1:1
Walking Gentleman, The 1942,My 8,26:2
Child of the Morning 1951,N 17,9:7
Gaines, Thomas
O Say Can You See! 1962,O 9,45:1
Gains, Ardis
On the Rocks 1938,Je 16,20:2
Gains, Frederica (Director)
What of It? 1929,Mr 9,24:2
Gaipman, Nathan (Costume Designer)
Going to America 1961,O 30,33:7
Gairdner, Christabel
Hamlet 1970,D 28,40:1
Gaites, Joseph M (Producer)
Up in the Clouds 1922,Ja 3,20:3
Americana 1932,O 6,19:3
I Am Different 1938,Ag 28,IX,2:5
Man Who Killed Lincoln, The 1940,Ja 18,26:4
At the Stroke of Eight 1940,My 21,29:2
Boyd's Daughter 1940,O 12,20:2
Return Engagement 1940,N 2,19:2
Gaither, David S (Scenic Designer)
Ghosts 1927,Ja 11,36:3
Queen Bee 1929,N 13,25:1
Forest Ring, The 1930,Ap 26,11:2
Gold Braid 1930,My 14,31:2
Riddle Me This! 1932,F 26,22:5
Two Strange Women 1933,Ja 11,23:3
Foolscap 1933,Ja 12,21:2
Riddle Me This! 1933,Mr 15,21:3
Twelfth Night 1934,Jl 17,24:5
Gaither, Gant (Director)
Dear Barbarians 1952,F 22,15:2
Gaither, Gant (Miscellaneous)
Craig's Wife 1947,F 13,35:2
Gaither, Gant (Producer)
First Mrs Fraser, The 1947,N 6,36:2
Shop at Sly Corner, The 1949,Ja 19,35:2
Gayden 1949,My 11,34:4
Dear Barbarians 1952,F 22,15:2
Seventh Heaven 1955,My 27,16:2
Gaither, Mareda
Sandhog 1954,N 24,17:1
Gaitman, Nathan (Costume Designer)
Life Is a Dream 1962,Ja 15,22:3
Gal, Jeanne
Heel, The 1954,My 27,33:2
Purification, The 1954,My 29,12:1
Apollo of Bellac, The 1954,My 29,12:1
Gal, Julius
Campo di Maggio 1931,Je 5,4:3
Galabru, Michel
Bourgeois Gentilhomme, Le 1955,O 26,26:1
Bourgeois Gentilhomme, Le 1955,O 30,II,1:1
Barbier de Seville, Le 1955,N 9,40:1
Galagher, Charles
Wild Rose, The 1926,O 21,23:1
White Eagle, The 1927,D 27,24:4
Robin Hood 1929,N 20,26:5
O'Flynn, The 1934,D 28,24:1
Firefly, The 1937,Ag 4,14:1
Galahoff, Basil
On Your Toes 1936,Ap 13,14:4
Galambos, Peter (Director)
Romeo and Jeanette 1969,D 16,53:1
Steal the Old Man's Bundle 1970,My 16,30:1
Shepherd of Avenue B, The 1970,My 16,30:1
Galambos, Peter (Miscellaneous)
Benito Cereno 1964,N 2,62:2
My Kinsman, Major Molineux 1964,N 2,62:2
Hogan's Goat 1965,N 12,56:1
Who's Got His Own 1966,O 13,52:1
Displaced Person, The 1966,D 30,15:1
Ceremony of Innocence, The 1968,Ja 2,33:1
Clara's Ole Man 1968,Mr 9,23:2
Son, Come Home, A 1968,Mr 9,23:2
Electronic Nigger, The 1968,Mr 9,23:2
Endecott and the Red Cross 1968,My 7,50:1
Galan, Gilda
Soles Truncos, Los; House on Cristo Street, The
1959,Ag 31,15:2
Galanakis, Costis
Medea 1964,S 1,31:1
Electra 1964,S 8,33:1
Hippolytus 1968,N 20,38:3

Galante, Elaine
Saint of Bleecker Street, The 1954,D 28,21:1
Galantiere, Lewis (Playwright)
Woman Kind 1933,S 28,25:2
Three and One 1933,O 26,22:6
And Be My Love 1934,Ja 19,25:2
Antigone 1946,F 19,21:3
Antigone 1946,F 24,II,1:1
Antigone 1959,S 16,46:2
Galantiere, Lewis (Translator)
Antigone 1946,Ja 10,28:2
Antigone 1956,Ap 3,32:2
Antigone 1967,Je 19,43:1
Galarno, Bill
Nathan the Wise 1962,Mr 23,29:1
Galbraith, Davida
Candida 1925,D 19,14:2
Galbraith, Richard
On the Level 1937,Mr 26,24:4
Galbreaith, Sally
Sweethearts 1929,S 23,25:1
Gale, David
Othello 1964,Jl 15,29:1
Othello 1964,O 13,48:1
Baal 1965,My 7,33:2
Gale, E C
Gentlemen, the Queen 1927,Ap 23,14:3
Gale, Edra
Babes in Arms 1951,Mr 10,7:3
Gale, Edward
Between the Devil 1937,D 23,24:5
You Never Know 1938,S 22,26:3
Gale, Gerri (Choreographer)
Safari! 1955,My 12,32:6
Gale, Jean
George White's Scandals 1935,D 26,20:2
Gale, Joan
John Gabriel Borkman 1959,N 26,57:4
Gale, Marie
Victory Belles 1943,O 27,26:3
I Remember Mama 1944,O 20,16:2
Gale, Martha
Babes in Toyland 1929,D 24,15:3
Gale, Peter
Hamlet 1969,My 2,38:1
Gale, Richard
Black Chiffon 1950,S 28,39:2
Gale, Richmond (Miscellaneous)
Laughs and Other Events 1960,O 11,57:1
Gale, Robert
Johnny Doodle 1942,Mr 19,28:2
Gale, Rona
Miracle Worker, The 1961,Mr 10,22:4
Miracle Worker, The 1961,Ap 1,11:2
Miracle Worker, The 1961,Ap 21,29:1
Miracle Worker, The 1961,My 1,35:3
Miracle Worker, The 1961,My 31,28:1
Gale, Rose
Jubilee 1935,O 14,20:1
Gale, Sandra
Third Little Show, The 1931,Je 2,34:3
Gale, Shirley
Skin Game, The 1920,O 21,11:1
Clair de Lune 1921,Ap 19,15:1
Blood and Sand 1921,S 21,16:2
Dolly Jordan 1922,O 4,26:1
Farmer's Wife, The 1924,O 10,22:3
Shall We Join the Ladies? 1925,Ja 14,19:1
Ostriches 1925,Mr 31,16:1
Weak Woman, A 1926,Ja 27,16:3
Thou Desperate Pilot 1927,Mr 8,23:1
Maya 1928,F 22,19:1
Virtue's Bed 1930,Ap 16,26:5
Cynara 1931,N 3,31:1
All Rights Reserved 1934,N 7,33:5
Victoria Regina 1935,D 27,15:2
Night Must Fall 1936,S 29,34:1
Knights of Song 1938,O 18,29:2
New Life, A 1943,S 16,26:6
Pin to See the Peepshow, A 1953,S 18,17:2
Three Sisters, The 1955,F 26,13:2
Gale, Wesley
One Flew Over the Cuckoo's Nest 1963,N 14,40:2
Gale, Zona (Original Author)
Miss Lulu Bett 1920,D 28,9:1
Miss Lulu Bett 1921,Ja 2,VI,3:1
Miss Lulu Bett 1921,Ja 9,VI,1:1
Miss Lulu Bett 1921,F 20,VI,1:1
Mister Pitt 1924,Ja 6,VII,1:4
Gale, Zona (Playwright)
Miss Lulu Bett 1920,D 28,9:1
Miss Lulu Bett 1921,Ja 2,VI,3:1
Miss Lulu Bett 1921,Ja 9,VI,1:1
Miss Lulu Bett 1921,F 20,VI,1:1
Mister Pitt 1924,Ja 6,VII,1:4
Mister Pitt 1924,Ja 23,15:3
Neighbors 1924,Je 18,23:3
Gale Quadruplets, The
Flying High 1930,Mr 4,24:4
Scandals 1931,Ag 11,28:4
Galedon, John
Jackson White 1935,Ap 22,14:6
Hitch Your Wagon! 1937,Ap 9,18:2

Galen, Diana
Countess Maritza 1936,Ag 19,18:2
Galen, Hetty
Chameleon, The 1949,F 7,16:2
Galenos, The
Vaudeville (Palace) 1930,N 3,19:2
Gales, Judith
Forbidden Melody 1936,N 3,33:1
Galetti and Kokin
Vaudeville (Palace) 1924,S 16,26:5
Gali-Gali
Continental Varieties 1934,N 15,24:3
Hilarities 1948,S 10,20:2
Galiano, Joseph
Amahl and the Night Visitors 1970,D 24,10:2
Galiber, Doris
Carmen Jones 1959,Ag 18,25:1
South Pacific 1968,Je 30,54:2
Galina, Gita
Honeymoon in Israel, A 1962,O 15,33:5
Don't Worry Brother! 1963,O 14,35:2
Good Luck 1964,O 19,38:3
Hello Charlie 1965,O 25,47:2
It's Never Too Late for Happiness 1968,O 21,59:3
Galina, Gita (Lyricist)
Don't Worry Brother! 1963,O 14,35:2
Galipeau, Jacques
Henry V 1966,Je 8,38:1
Henry VI 1966,Je 9,55:2
Galjour, Warren
Dear Judas 1947,O 6,26:4
Wonderful Town 1953,F 26,22:3
Gall, Wanda
Hello, Daddy! 1928,D 27,26:5
Galla-Rini and Sisters
Vaudeville (Palace) 1925,D 8,28:6
Gallagher, Alfred
Merchant of Venice, The 1970,Je 10,39:1
School for Scandal, The 1970,Je 11,51:1
Gallagher, Bernard
Beaux' Stratagem, The 1970,F 10,50:2
Three Sisters, The 1970,F 12,30:1
Gallagher, Betty
Happy-Go-Lucky 1926,O 1,27:2
Prince Charming 1930,O 14,31:1
Gallagher, Charles E
H M S Pinafore 1926,Ap 7,26:3
Fortune Teller, The 1929,N 5,32:3
Serenade, The 1930,Mr 5,26:7
Gallagher, Dan
Vagabond King, The 1943,Je 30,24:2
Bloomer Girl 1944,O 6,18:5
Gallagher, David
De Sade Illustrated 1969,My 13,42:4
Gallagher, Desmond
True to Form 1921,S 13,12:1
Cock o' the Roost 1924,O 14,23:1
Kongo 1926,Mr 31,20:5
Hotel Alimony 1934,Ja 30,16:2
Gallagher, Donald
Yellow Jacket, The 1921,Ja 5,11:1
Man in the Making, The 1921,S 21,16:2
Airways, Inc 1929,F 21,30:5
Gallagher, Edward
Frivolities of 1920 1920,Ja 9,22:2
Ziegfeld Follies 1923,Ja 30,12:2
Gallagher, Francis (Playwright)
Iron Men 1936,O 20,30:6
Vincent 1959,O 1,40:1
Gallagher, Frank
Babes in Toyland 1929,D 24,15:3
Gallagher, Helen
Million Dollar Baby 1945,D 22,17:2
High Button Shoes 1947,O 10,32:2
Touch and Go 1949,O 14,34:2
Make a Wish 1951,Ap 19,38:1
Pal Joey 1952,Ja 4,17:6
Pal Joey 1952,Ja 13,II,1:1
Pal Joey 1952,F 17,II,13:5
Hazel Flagg 1953,F 12,22:2
Guys and Dolls 1955,Ap 21,32:2
Finian's Rainbow 1955,My 19,25:1
Brigadoon 1957,Mr 28,37:1
Portofino 1958,F 22,8:3
Oklahoma! 1958,Mr 20,32:3
Sweet Charity 1966,Ja 31,22:1
Sweet Charity 1967,Jl 1,13:1
Mame 1968,Ap 20,25:1
Mame 1969,Je 20,36:1
Cry for Us All 1970,Ap 9,48:2
Gallagher, Julia
Well of the Saints, The 1932,Ja 22,15:2
Gallagher, Margaret
Blue Butterfly, The 1929,F 17,29:3
Gallagher, Mary
Well of the Saints, The 1932,Ja 22,15:2
Gallagher, Peggy
Well of the Saints, The 1932,Ja 22,15:2
Gallagher, Richard Skeets
Up in the Clouds 1922,Ja 3,20:3
Up She Goes 1922,N 7,14:2
Marjorie 1924,Ag 12,12:2
Magnolia Lady, The 1924,N 26,17:2

City Chap, The 1925,O 27,21:1
Lucky 1927,Mr 23,28:3
Good Night Ladies 1945,Ja 18,16:2
Good Night Ladies 1945,Ja 28,II,1:1
Gallagher, Robert
I Gotta Get Out 1947,S 26,27:2
Two on the Aisle 1951,Jl 20,13:6
Show Boat 1954,My 6,44:1
Show Boat 1954,O 29,28:4
Gallagher, Walter Bedloe
This Mad Whirl 1937,Ja 10,II,4:8
Gallagher, William
Big Blow 1938,O 3,11:2
Gallagher and Shean
Ziegfeld Follies 1922,Je 6,18:2
In Dutch 1924,O 26,VIII,2:1
Gallaher, Donald
Blue Flame, The 1920,Mr 16,18:1
Man in the Making, The 1921,O 2,VII,1:1
Golden Days 1921,N 2,20:1
So This Is London 1922,Ag 31,18:2
Melody Man, The 1924,My 14,14:2
Judy Drops In 1924,O 6,24:2
Fool's Bells 1925,D 24,8:3
Salvation 1928,F 1,31:1
Golden Age, The 1928,Ap 25,31:3
Back Fire 1932,Je 14,26:3
World Waits, The 1933,O 26,22:5
Gallaher, Donald (Director)
Sh! The Octopus 1928,F 22,19:2
Gallaher, Donald (Playwright)
Sh! The Octopus 1928,F 22,19:2
Gallaher, Donald (Producer)
Fool's Bells 1925,D 24,8:3
Sh! The Octopus 1928,F 22,19:2
Galland, E
Golem, The 1927,F 5,13:2
Galland, Jacques
Fausses Confidences, Les 1952,N 13,34:2
Baptiste 1952,N 13,34:2
Proces, Le; Trial, The 1952,N 18,36:2
Occupe-Toi d'Amelie; Keep Your Eyes on Amelie
1952,N 25,35:2
Hamlet 1952,D 2,39:1
Christophe Colómb 1957,Ja 31,20:5
Misanthrope, Le 1957,F 8,19:1
Intermezzo 1957,F 15,20:4
Adieux, Les 1957,F 19,36:1
Chien du Jardinier, Le; Gardener's Dog, The
1957,F 19,36:1
Galland, John
Hamlet 1936,O 9,30:2
Gallarati-Scotti, Tommaso (Count) (Playwright)
Cosi Sia; Thy Will be Done 1923,N 14,29:2
Gallare, Dan
Man's House, A 1943,Ap 3,10:4
Gallatin, Alberta
Lord Byron's Cain 1925,Ap 9,20:3
Gallaudet, John
When You Smile 1925,O 6,31:2
Don Q Jr 1926,Ja 28,16:3
Vaudeville (Palace) 1928,Jl 31,13:5
Saturday Night 1928,Jl 31,13:5
On the Spot 1930,O 30,33:3
Gang's All Here, The 1931,F 19,21:3
Here Goes the Bride 1931,N 4,31:2
Lost Horizons 1934,O 16,31:2
Is This a Zither? 1935,Je 11,24:3
Menagerie 1935,Jl 2,24:3
Accent on Youth 1935,Jl 9,24:5
White Hell 1935,Ag 13,20:3
Good Men and True 1935,O 26,12:4
Every Man for Himself 1940,D 10,32:3
Galle, Myrna (Choreographer)
Shoemaker's Holiday, The 1967,Mr 3,25:1
Gallegher, Desmond (Playwright)
Suicide Love 1924,S 7,VII,1:4
Gallegher, Francis (Playwright)
Vincent 1959,O 11,II,1:1
Galleher, Alice Gray
Eyes 1930,My 10,25:1
Gallenstein, Leo (Lighting Director)
All Summer Long 1953,Ja 29,23:1
Cretan Woman, The 1954,My 21,17:2
View From the Bridge, A 1956,N 9,34:4
Portrait of a Madonna 1957,Ap 1,21:2
Man of Destiny, The 1957,Ap 1,21:2
Bedtime Story 1957,Ap 1,21:2
Browning Version, The 1958,Mr 7,17:2
Month in the Country, A 1959,Mr 2,32:2
Summer of the Seventeenth Doll 1959,O 14,52:1
Clandestine on the Morning Line 1959,D 5,18:2
Caucasian Chalk Circle, The 1961,N 1,35:1
Burning of the Lepers, The 1962,Ap 5,29:1
Once in a Lifetime 1962,O 30,30:1
Devils, The 1963,N 5,25:1
Lonesome Train, The 1965,Je 17,25:1
Hard Travelin' 1965,Je 17,25:1
Gallery, James
Daddy Come Home 1963,Ap 17,33:1
Brother to Dragons 1968,D 8,86:1
Wilson in the Promise Land 1970,Ja 11,78:1
Wilson in the Promise Land 1970,My 27,41:1

Gallet
Nuit, Une 1935,Je 16,X,1:1
Galley, Miriam
Home Is the Hero 1945,Ja 20,16:4
Galli, Mario
Cosi Sia; Thy Will be Done 1923,N 14,29:2
Porta Chiusa, La; Closed Door, The 1923,N 21,23:1
Galli, Richard
Sing High, Sing Low 1931,N 13,26:4
Galli, Rosina
Walk Into My Parlor 1941,N 20,38:2
Galli, Rosina (Choreographer)
Blue Butterfly, The 1929,F 17,29:3
Gallian, Ketty
Ace, The 1933,Ag 25,12:4
Galliard-Rissler, Francine (Mme) (Costume Designer)
Britannicus 1961,Mr 3,17:1
Galliard-Rissler, Francine (Mme) (Scenic Designer)
Britannicus 1961,Mr 3,17:1
Gallick, Muriel
Days to Come 1936,D 16,35:1
Gallico, Paul (Original Author)
Carnival! 1961,Ap 14,22:2
Gallico, Paul (Playwright)
Saturday It Rained 1932,D 14,27:3
Galliher, W H
It's the Valet 1933,D 15,25:4
Gallimore, Catherine
Night in Paris, A 1926,Jl 27,15:4
Artists and Models 1927,N 16,28:2
Gallimore, Ferrell
Tall Kentuckian, The 1953,Je 17,30:1
Gallimore, Peggy
George White's Scandals 1926,Je 15,23:2
Gallipaux
Locus Solus 1922,D 9,11:4
Gallivan, Gerry (Playwright)
Stepping Stone, The 1963,My 24,16:2
Gallo, A Raymond (Miscellaneous)
Philadelphia 1929,S 17,34:5
Gallo, Al
Camille 1956,S 19,33:1
Gallo, Al (Miscellaneous)
Cradle Song 1955,D 2,32:2
Gallo, Fortune (Director)
Student Prince, The 1936,Jl 12,II,5:2
Blossom Time 1936,Jl 29,23:1
My Maryland 1936,Ag 12,14:2
Countess Maritza 1936,Ag 19,18:2
Blossom Time 1936,Ag 30,II,5:8
Roberta 1937,Je 27,II,6:1
Maytime 1937,Jl 6,23:4
Gallo, Fortune (Producer)
Rose Marie 1936,Jl 22,22:6
Florodora 1936,Ag 23,II,8:2
Bitter Sweet 1936,Ag 26,17:3
Naughty Marietta 1936,S 2,19:5
Wonderful Night, A; Fledermaus, Die
1937,Jl 14,17:1
Gay Divorce 1937,Jl 20,19:4
Student Prince, The 1937,Jl 28,15:1
On Your Toes 1937,Ag 3,21:2
Firefly, The 1937,Ag 4,14:1
Of Thee I Sing 1937,Ag 10,22:3
Gay Divorce 1937,Ag 11,27:2
Anything Goes 1937,Ag 17,23:4
Of Thee I Sing 1937,Ag 18,14:4
Nina Rosa 1937,Ag 26,24:3
Circus Princess, The 1937,Ag 31,26:6
Roberta 1937,S 7,16:4
Show Boat 1938,Je 30,21:1
Sally, Irene and Mary 1938,Jl 5,13:4
Firefly, The 1938,Jl 12,15:4
Gallo, Leo
Femme Dans un Lit, Une 1928,Ja 15,VIII,2:3
Gallo, Lew
Troublemakers, The 1954,D 31,11:3
Will Success Spoil Rock Hunter? 1955,O 14,22:2
Gallo, Mario
Comic Strip 1958,My 15,26:2
Gallo, Nora
Cinderella on Broadway 1920,Je 25,18:1
Gallo, Norma
Vaudeville (Palace) 1926,My 11,25:3
Ramblers, The 1926,S 21,32:2
Gallo, Nunzio
Rugantino 1964,F 7,34:1
Gallo, Paul
Tapestry in Gray 1935,D 28,10:2
Gallo, Ray (Producer)
Perfectly Scandalous 1931,My 14,27:2
Gallois, Germaine
Mozart 1925,D 27,VII,6:7
Mozart 1926,D 28,16:1
Galloway, Don
Bring Me a Warm Body 1962,Ap 17,29:3
Galloway, Edward
May Wine 1935,D 6,30:3
Galloway, Goodie
Cherry Blossoms 1927,Mr 29,22:3
Galloway, Hunter
Censored 1938,F 28,18:2

Galloway, Louise
Clinging Vine, The 1922,D 25,20:2
Lucky Break 1925,Ag 12,16:2
Weak Sisters 1925,O 14,31:3
Rainbow Rose 1926,Mr 17,28:2
Lady Alone 1927,Ja 21,12:5
Let's Laugh Again 1937,Ag 24,24:5
Galloway, Louise (Director)
Let's Laugh Again 1937,Ag 24,24:5
Galloway, Pat
Midsummer Night's Dream, A 1960,Je 30,23:5
Coriolanus 1961,Je 21,31:2
Henry VIII 1961,Je 22,22:1
Macbeth 1962,Je 20,41:1
Tempest, The 1962,Je 22,14:1
Cyrano de Bergerac 1962,Ag 1,21:1
Tartuffe 1968,Je 12,39:1
Tartuffe 1968,Je 23,II,1:1
Three Musketeers, The 1968,Jl 24,49:2
School for Scandal, The 1970,Je 11,51:1
School for Scandal, The 1970,Je 21,II,1:1
Cymbeline 1970,Ag 23,II,1:6
Galloway, William
If This Be Treason 1935,S 24,28:2
Galman, Peter
Henry IV, Part II 1968,Jl 2,33:1
Galmarini, Anna
Holiday on Ice 1967,Ag 31,29:2
Holiday on Ice 1968,Ag 29,44:1
Galo, Alberto
Vaudeville (Palace) 1926,Je 1,29:5
Galper, Sam
Hush Money 1926,Mr 16,22:3
Galpern, Lasar (Director)
Chinese Nightingale, The 1934,O 6,20:4
Galpern, Lasar (Playwright)
Chinese Nightingale, The 1934,O 6,20:4
Galphin, Martha
Penny Wars, The 1969,O 16,52:1
Brightower 1970,Ja 29,32:1
Galster, Robert (Scenic Designer)
Man and Superman 1953,F 21,11:2
Galsworthy, John (Original Author)
Old English 1924,O 26,VIII,1:1
Old English 1924,N 9,VIII,2:3
Galsworthy, John (Playwright)
Skin Game, The 1920,My 23,VI,1:3
Mob, The 1920,O 11,18:1
Skin Game, The 1920,O 21,11:1
Skin Game, The 1920,O 31,VI,1:2
Mob, The 1920,D 12,VI,1:3
First and the Last, The 1921,Je 26,VI,1:1
Family Man, A 1921,Je 26,VI,1:1
Pigeon, The 1922,F 3,13:1
Loyalties 1922,Mr 26,VI,1:2
Windows 1922,My 21,VI,1:6
Loyalties 1922,Jl 9,VI,1:1
Loyalties 1922,S 28,18:1
Loyalties 1922,O 8,VI,1:1
Windows 1923,O 9,17:2
Windows 1923,O 14,VIII,1:1
Forest, The 1924,Mr 16,VIII,1:7
Old English 1924,O 26,VIII,1:1
Old English 1924,N 9,VIII,2:3
Old English 1924,D 24,11:2
Bit o' Love, A 1925,My 13,24:2
Show, The 1925,Jl 12,VII,1:1
Escape 1926,Ag 22,VII,1:2
Escape 1926,Ag 29,VII,2:4
Escape 1926,S 12,VIII,2:1
Escape 1926,D 12,VIII,3:4
Joy 1927,Ag 14,VII,1:7
Escape 1927,O 27,33:1
Escape 1927,N 6,IX,1:1
Silver Box, The 1928,Ja 18,23:1
Escape 1928,My 20,VIII,2:1
Loyalties 1928,Ag 26,VII,1:3
Silver Box, The 1928,N 25,X,2:3
Exile 1929,Je 21,17:5
Exiled 1929,Jl 7,VIII,1:3
Roof, The 1929,N 6,30:4
Roof, The 1929,N 24,X,1:6
Roof, The 1930,Je 14,9:2
Pigeon, The 1930,O 15,26:2
Roof, The 1931,O 31,22:4
Roof, The 1931,N 8,VIII,1:1
Little Man, The 1934,Je 20,24:3
Silver Box, The 1935,Jl 16,24:2
Family Man, A 1936,Jl 8,14:2
Galt, Florella
Gods of the Mountain, The 1950,My 25,36:2
Galt, Howard
Cyrano de Bergerac 1926,F 19,18:1
Bonds of Interest, The 1929,O 15,34:2
Cyrano de Bergerac 1932,D 27,11:2
Hamlet 1934,D 26,19:3
Richard III 1934,D 28,24:3
Cyrano de Bergerac 1936,Ap 28,17:1
Galton, Ray (Playwright)
Rockefeller and the Red Indians 1968,O 25,37:1
Galuback, Helen
Pinocchio 1939,Ja 3,19:2

Galuska, Edward
Sound of Hunting, A 1954,Ap 7,41:1
Galvan, Gil
Viva O'Brien 1941,O 10,27:2
Galvan, Pedro
Page Miss Glory 1934,N 28,24:2
Mad Morning 1935,Je 25,14:1
Caesar and Cleopatra 1935,Ag 22,21:1
Galvan, Peter
If This Be Treason 1935,S 24,28:2
Galvani, Ciro
Spretti; Ghosts 1923,N 7,14:1
Cosi Sia; Thy Will be Done 1923,N 14,29:2
Porta Chiusa, La; Closed Door, The 1923,N 21,23:1
Galvann, Roc
Ringside Seat 1938,N 23,24:5
Mr Banks of Birmingham 1939,Ja 21,18:4
Red Velvet Goat, The 1939,Ja 21,18:4
Coggerers, The 1939,Ja 21,18:4
Galvin, Gene
Lute Song 1946,F 7,29:2
Temporary Island, A 1948,Mr 15,27:3
Born Yesterday 1954,Ja 1,16:6
Lute Song 1959,Mr 13,24:1
Curley McDimple 1967,N 23,59:2
Galvin, Gene (Costume Designer)
Silver Grey Toy Poodle 1969,My 15,41:2
Baby With a Knife 1969,My 15,41:2
Pets 1969,My 15,41:2
Galvin, Patrick (Playwright)
And Him Stretched 1962,S 26,33:1
Galvin, Randolph (Playwright)
Immaculate Misconception, The 1970,O 28,63:3
Galvin, Randolph (Producer)
Immaculate Misconception, The 1970,O 28,63:3
Galvin, Randolph (Scenic Designer)
Immaculate Misconception, The 1970,O 28,63:3
Galyer, May
Mary the 3d 1923,F 6,14:2
Gam, Rita
Temporary Island, A 1948,Mr 15,27:3
Insect Comedy, The 1948,Je 4,26:3
Young and Fair, The 1948,N 23,35:2
For the Time Being 1957,D 18,42:7
I Am a Camera 1961,Jl 10,26:1
Miser, The 1963,My 10,39:1
Three Sisters, The 1963,Je 20,30:7
Three Sisters, The 1963,Jl 22,19:2
There's a Girl in My Soup 1967,O 19,58:1
Gambarelli, Eole
They Knew What They Wanted 1949,F 17,28:2
Gambarelli, Maria
Vaudeville (Palace) 1929,S 30,22:3
To Damascus 1961,F 15,40:2
Gambino, Pete
On the Town 1959,F 14,15:1
Gamble, Albert
Nativity Play, The 1937,D 21,29:1
Gamble, David G
What a Relief 1935,D 14,10:6
Gamble, Glenn
Afgar 1920,N 9,13:2
Gamble, Warburton
New Morality, The 1921,Ja 31,10:1
Madras House, The 1921,O 31,18:2
Rubicon, The 1922,F 22,13:1
Why Not? 1922,D 25,20:1
Living Mask, The 1924,Ja 22,15:1
Garden of Weeds 1924,Ap 29,12:3
Ashes 1924,O 21,21:2
Wild Duck, The 1925,F 25,16:4
Magda 1926,Ja 27,16:2
Milestones 1930,Je 3,27:1
Tonight or Never 1930,N 19,19:3
Gamble Boys and Bache
Vaudeville (Palace) 1928,Ag 7,25:5
Gamboa, Marcelo
Grosse Valise, La 1965,D 15,52:1
Minnie's Boys 1970,Mr 27,27:1
Boy Friend, The 1970,Ap 15,54:1
Gammell, Robin
Henry V 1956,Je 20,27:2
Merry Wives of Windsor, The 1956,Je 21,34:4
Henry VIII 1961,Je 22,22:1
Tempest, The 1962,Jl 17,18:2
Hamlet 1964,Je 17,49:1
Shoemaker's Holiday, The 1967,Je 3,19:1
Thieves' Carnival 1967,Je 5,52:1
House of Atreus, The; Agamemnon 1967,Jl 24,23:1
House of Atreus, The; Bringers of Offerings, The 1967,Jl 24,23:1
Visit, The 1967,S 13,41:1
Tango 1968,Ja 1,11:1
Serjeant Musgrave's Dance 1968,Je 16,52:4
Resistible Rise of Arturo Ui, The 1968,Ag 8,25:1
Merton of the Movies 1968,S 26,62:1
House of Atreus, The 1968,D 18,55:1
Resistible Rise of Arturo Ui, The 1968,D 23,44:1
School for Scandal, The 1970,Je 11,51:1
Cymbeline 1970,Jl 24,17:2
Gammon, Dorothy
Revolt of the Beavers, The 1937,My 21,19:2

Gammon, Everett
Pursuit of Happiness, The 1936,Jl 15,14:1
Post Road 1936,Ag 5,15:4
Royal Family, The 1936,Ag 12,15:1
Gammon, William
Red, White and Maddox 1969,Ja 27,27:1
Gamnon, Everett
As You Like It 1950,Ja 27,27:2
Gampel, C M
Pocket Watch, The 1966,Ja 6,18:1
Gampel, Chris
Captain Brassbound's Conversion 1950,D 28,21:1
Royal Family, The 1951,Ja 11,28:2
Richard II 1951,Ja 25,21:2
Flight Into Egypt 1952,Mr 19,33:2
Crucible, The 1953,Jl 2,20:2
Saint Joan 1956,S 12,42:1
Firstborn, The 1958,My 1,35:1
Borak 1960,D 14,51:1
Girl Who Came to Supper, The 1963,D 9,49:1
Gampel, Morison
Front Page, The 1969,My 12,54:2
Gamsakouidia
Palace aux Femmes 1926,O 10,VIII,2:1
Ganahl, Joe de (Playwright)
Who's Who 1924,Ap 18,19:2
Gandera, Felix (Playwright)
Dame de Chambre, La 1924,Je 1,VII,1:7
Bride Retires, The 1925,My 18,12:3
Facon de Se Donner, La 1925,D 27,VII,2:1
Paris-Capucines 1927,Ja 16,VII,2:1
Hearts Are Trumps! 1927,Ap 8,21:1
Vingt ans, Madame 1928,Ap 8,VIII,4:1
Manquait un Homme, Il 1929,Ap 14,X,2:1
Quick 1930,N 23,IX,1:1
Youki 1932,O 16,IX,2:3
Atout... Coeur 1936,Mr 27,25:4
Ganduglia, Jose
Fuerza Ciega, La 1927,D 6,26:1
Ganeau, Wilda
Moon Is a Gong, The 1926,Mr 13,21:3
Gang, Mario
Candle in the Wind 1941,O 23,26:2
Family Carnovsky, The 1943,O 19,16:7
Gangadharan, S
Mahabharata 1970,N 28,22:1
Ganimian, Charles (Chick)
Moths, The 1970,My 12,46:1
Ganley, Mary
Best Foot Forward 1941,O 2,28:2
Ziegfeld Follies 1943,Ap 2,16:2
Gann, Ernest
Saint's Parade 1930,N 1,23:4
Firebird 1932,N 22,25:2
Sailors of Cattaro 1934,D 11,28:4
Gannon, Gerlad
Shake Hands With the Devil 1949,O 21,30:4
Gannon, James
Carousel 1957,S 12,38:2
Camelot 1960,D 5,42:1
Donnybrook! 1961,My 19,23:1
Gannon, Jane
What Next 1920,Ja 27,7:2
Woman of Bronze, The 1920,S 8,9:2
Gannon, Kim (Lyricist)
Seventeen 1951,Je 22,16:6
Seventeen 1951,Jl 1,II,1:1
Gannon, Liam
John Bull's Other Island 1948,F 11,33:4
Old Lady Says No, The 1948,F 18,35:1
Righteous Are Bold, The 1955,D 23,12:1
Bridal Night, The 1966,N 8,45:1
Frying Pan, The 1966,N 8,45:1
Eternal Triangle 1966,N 8,45:1
Mundy Scheme, The 1969,D 12,75:1
Borstal Boy 1970,Ap 1,38:1
Gannon, Paul
Ice Follies 1958,Ja 15,26:2
Gannon, Paul (Miscellaneous)
Ice Follies 1959,Ja 14,30:1
Ice Follies 1960,Ja 13,20:1
Ice Follies 1962,Ja 10,24:6
Ice Follies 1963,Ja 10,5:2
Ice Follies 1965,Ja 13,35:1
Gano, Norman
York Nativity Play, The 1956,D 5,49:2
Sign of Jonah, The 1957,My 2,27:1
Everyman Today 1958,Ja 16,32:4
Ganon, James
I Killed the Count 1942,S 4,18:1
Tinker's Dam 1943,Ja 29,22:2
Dark Hammock 1944,D 12,27:8
Lady in Danger 1945,Mr 30,18:6
Restless Flame, The 1952,Ap 15,30:6
Gans, Louis
Wooden Idol, The 1930,My 13,27:2
Gans, Sharon
Clerambard 1957,N 8,22:3
Victims of Duty 1964,My 28,40:2
3 Bags Full 1966,Mr 7,22:1
Viet Rock 1966,N 11,38:1
Nest, The 1970,Ap 10,46:1

Gansert, Jack
Green Table, The 1942,Ja 22,12:2
Prodigal Son, The 1942,F 18,22:2
Rosalinda; Fledermaus, Die 1942,O 29,26:5
Chauve-Souris of 1943 1943,Ag 13,13:2
Merry Widow, The 1944,O 9,17:1
Marinka 1945,Jl 19,19:2
Gant, Mabel
My Magnolia 1926,Jl 13,19:2
Change Your Luck 1930,Je 7,10:2
Gantillon, Simon (Playwright)
Maya 1927,F 13,VII,4:1
Maya 1927,D 11,IX,2:1
Maya 1928,F 22,19:1
Departs 1928,D 23,VIII,2:1
Cocktail 328 1930,Ap 13,X,2:7
Bifur 1932,F 28,VIII,1:1
Cyclone 1934,D 2,X,2:1
Notre Dame du Cinema 1936,Ja 19,IX,3:4
Maya 1951,Ag 9,17:4
Maya 1953,Je 10,35:1
Gantry, Donald
One More River 1960,Mr 19,12:2
Here Come the Clowns 1960,S 20,48:1
Seven at Dawn, The 1961,Ap 18,43:1
Jackhammer, The 1962,F 6,26:2
Henry V 1963,Je 14,37:1
Much Ado About Nothing 1964,Je 11,26:2
Richard III 1964,Je 12,44:2
Hamlet 1964,Jl 4,9:1
Cruising Speed 600 MPH 1970,Ja 6,48:3
Gantt, Cora Dick (Playwright)
Tavern, The 1920,S 28,14:1
Tavern, The 1962,Ap 5,29:1
Gantvoort, Herman (Director)
Long Road, The 1930,Jl 20,VIII,2:1
Gantvoort, Herman (Miscellaneous)
Makropoulos Secret, The 1926,Ja 22,12:4
Gantvoort, Herman (Producer)
Jane-Our Stranger 1925,O 9,27:2
They All Want Something 1926,O 13,20:2
Bottled 1928,Ap 11,25:1
Silver Swan, The 1929,N 3,IX,1:7
Primer for Lovers, A 1929,N 19,26:5
Silver Swan, The 1929,N 28,34:5
Long Road, The 1930,S 10,30:2
Ganzenmuller, Dieter (Director)
Mitschuldigen, Die 1966,Ap 6,34:1
Wozzeck 1966,Ap 6,34:1
Ratten, Die 1966,Ap 13,36:1
Ganzert, Albert (Playwright)
Borderline 1937,F 10,18:6
Garabedian, John
John Brown 1950,My 4,32:7
Cyanamide 1954,Mr 26,17:6
Garabedian, John (Producer)
Homeward Look, The 1954,Je 4,26:2
Garan, Barbara (Costume Designer)
Hasty Heart, The 1954,Mr 13,10:1
Garard, John
Abe Lincoln in Illinois 1938,O 17,12:2
Garas, Kazimer
Wives, The 1965,My 18,35:4
Garber, Jan
Vaudeville (Palace) 1928,Jl 31,13:5
Garber, Jan Orchestra
Vaudeville (Palace) 1929,Ja 14,20:3
Garbett, George
Pickwick 1927,S 6,35:2
Garbiel, Inia
Tiger Rag, The 1961,F 17,20:2
Garbo, Latzo
Wonderful Night, A; Fledermaus, Die 1937,Jl 14,17:1
Garceau, Roger
Henry V 1956,Je 20,27:2
Henry V 1956,Je 24,II,1:1
Garces, John
King and I, The 1963,Je 13,30:2
Diamond Orchid 1965,F 11,44:4
Garchery, Gaston
Trois Jeunes Filles Nues; Three Young Maids From the Folies Bergere 1929,Mr 5,28:2
Comte Obligado 1929,Mr 12,26:2
Bon Garcon, Un 1929,Mr 19,36:2
Pas Sur La Bouche; Not on the Lips 1929,Mr 26,34:3
Garcia, A
Cradle Song 1927,My 10,24:4
Garcia, David
This Is Edwin Booth 1958,Ag 27,32:7
Garcia, Louis
Zorba 1968,N 18,58:1
Lend an Ear 1969,O 29,32:1
Garcia, Luis
Don Juan Tenorio 1953,N 20,18:5
Garcia, Miguel
Don Juan Tenorio 1953,N 20,18:5
El Alcalde De Zalamea 1953,N 23,32:5
Garcia, Pilar
Dandelion 1969,D 24,12:1
Hot Feet 1970,D 22,38:1

Garcia, Rita
Rain or Shine 1928,F 10,26:3
Garcia, Ruben
Thumbs Up! 1934,D 28,24:1
Garcia, Tuan
To Quito and Back 1937,O 7,30:4
Garcya, Marguerite
Topaze 1931,F 17,29:1
Gard, David
Infernal Machine, The 1954,Mr 22,22:2
Merchant of Venice, The 1955,Ja 8,9:7
Gard, Roger Martin du (Playwright)
Taciturne, Un 1931,N 22,VIII,1:6
Gard, Sumner
Hawk Island 1929,S 17,34:7
Garde, Beth
Beaver Coat, The 1956,Mr 29,22:5
Garde, Betty
Easy Come, Easy Go 1925,O 27,20:2
Social Register, The 1931,N 10,28:2
Best People, The 1933,Mr 16,21:5
Primrose Path, The 1939,Ja 5,16:3
Primrose Path, The 1939,Ja 16,11:2
Oklahoma! 1943,Ap 1,27:1
Oklahoma! 1943,Ap 11,II,1:1
Miser, The 1955,Mr 18,34:2
Oklahoma! 1958,Mr 20,32:3
Oklahoma! 1963,F 28,8:2
Oklahoma! 1963,My 16,40:1
Agatha Sue, I Love You 1966,D 15,61:1
Stephen D 1967,S 25,58:1
Gardeen, Gertrude
Deep Harlem 1929,Ja 8,35:2
Gardell, Tess
Radio Carnival 1932,Mr 14,13:3
Show Boat 1932,My 20,22:2
Gardell, Tony
Million Dollar Baby 1945,D 22,17:2
Guys and Dolls 1950,N 25,11:2
Silk Stockings 1955,F 25,17:3
Garden, Douglas
Musk 1920,Mr 15,13:1
Skin Game, The 1920,O 21,11:1
Torch Bearers, The 1922,Ag 30,10:2
Expressing Willie 1924,Ap 17,22:1
Claw, The 1927,Ja 13,28:4
Last Torture, The 1927,Ja 13,28:4
We're All in the Gutter 1927,Mr 5,12:2
Aiglon, L' 1927,D 27,24:3
Wrecker, The 1928,F 28,18:2
Serena Blandish 1929,Ja 24,30:3
Waterloo Bridge 1930,Ja 7,29:2
Lake, The 1933,D 27,24:2
Garden, Douglas (Mrs)
Elizabeth Sleeps Out 1935,Ag 27,23:4
Garden, Elizabeth
Last Enemy, The 1934,Jl 13,14:4
Garden, Larry
It Can't Happen Here 1936,O 28,30:1
Garden, Louis (Lyricist)
Once Over Lightly 1942,N 20,26:2
Garden, Reba
This Fine-Pretty World 1923,D 27,11:1
Maid of All Work 1927,Ja 13,28:4
Last Torture, The 1927,Ja 13,28:4
Garden, Rebekah
Gray Shadow 1931,Mr 11,23:4
Gardenia, Vincent
In April Once 1955,Mr 14,29:3
Man With the Golden Arm, The 1956,My 22,28:1
Volpone 1957,Ja 8,27:1
Right You Are (If You Think You Are) 1957,Mr 5,37:1
Brothers Karamazov, The 1957,D 9,39:4
Brothers Karamazov, The 1957,D 22,II,3:1
Visit, The 1958,My 6,40:1
Cold Wind and the Warm, The 1958,D 9,55:1
Power of Darkness, The 1959,S 30,33:1
Only in America 1959,N 20,35:1
Machinal 1960,Ap 8,27:1
Machinal 1960,Ap 17,II,1:1
Wall, The 1960,O 12,44:4
Gallows Humor 1961,Ap 19,35:1
Daughter of Silence 1961,D 1,28:1
Endgame 1962,F 12,27:1
Seidman and Son 1962,O 16,32:2
Little Murders 1969,Ja 6,38:1
Little Murders 1969,Ja 26,II,1:1
Passing Through From Exotic Places; Son Who Hunted Tigers in Jakarta, The 1969,D 8,60:4
Passing Through From Exotic Places; Burial of Esposito, The 1969,D 8,60:4
Passing Through From Exotic Places 1969,D 21,II,3:1
Dr Fish 1970,Mr 11,42:2
Dr Fish 1970,Mr 22,II,3:1
Carpenters, The 1970,D 22,40:1
Carpenters, The 1970,D 27,II,1:1
Gardet, Mr
Trois Jeunes Filles Nues; Three Young Maids From the Folies Bergere 1929,Mr 5,28:2
Gardet, Robert
Live Life Again 1945,O 1,14:7

Gardet, Robert—Cont
Mayor of Zalamea, The 1946,Ja 28,15:5
Gardiner, Becky (Director)
Damn Your Honor 1929,D 31,14:3
Gardiner, Becky (Playwright)
Damn Your Honor 1929,D 31,14:3
Gardiner, Brenda
Gondoliers, The 1967,O 29,83:1
Gardiner, Cyril
Geneva 1940,Ja 31,15:2
Gardiner, Edgar
I'll Say She Is 1924,My 20,15:1
Americana 1926,Jl 27,15:3
Rain or Shine 1928,F 10,26:3
Gardiner, Evelyn
Mikado, The 1936,Ag 21,13:2
Pirates of Penzance, The 1936,S 1,24:4
Gondoliers, The 1936,S 8,23:1
Yeomen of the Guard, The 1936,S 15,37:2
Iolanthe 1936,S 22,30:3
H M S Pinafore 1936,S 29,34:2
Patience 1936,O 6,28:6
Princess Ida 1936,O 13,32:2
Ruddigore 1936,O 23,26:4
Pirates of Penzance, The 1939,Ja 6,25:1
Mikado, The 1939,Ja 10,16:3
Iolanthe 1939,Ja 13,16:3
H. M. S. Pinafore 1939,Ja 17,27:5
Gondoliers, The 1939,Ja 20,14:2
Yeomen of the Guard, The 1939,Ja 24,17:1
Patience 1939,Ja 27,16:3
Gardiner, Frank
Oh, Kay! 1926,N 9,31:3
Gardiner, James W (Producer)
Are You With It? 1945,N 12,17:3
Plain and Fancy 1955,Ja 28,14:2
Gardiner, John
Hamlet 1957,Jl 3,15:2
Twelfth Night 1957,Jl 4,16:4
Broken Jug, The 1958,Ap 2,36:1
Henry IV, Part I 1958,Je 25,23:3
Winter's Tale, The 1958,Jl 23,34:3
Government Inspector, The 1967,Je 15,55:1
Antony and Cleopatra 1967,Ag 2,25:1
Government Inspector, The 1967,O 28,34:1
Hamlet 1969,Je 11,37:1
Alchemist, The 1969,Je 12,51:1
Measure for Measure 1969,Je 13,41:3
Gardiner, Kevin
Twelfth Night 1969,Ag 14,29:2
Gardiner, Max
Antony and Cleopatra 1951,D 21,22:2
Gardiner, Reginald
Flat to Let 1931,D 20,VIII,3:6
Char-A-Bang 1935,My 5,IX,1:7
At Home Abroad 1935,S 4,22:3
At Home Abroad 1935,S 8,IX,1:1
At Home Abroad 1935,S 20,17:4
Show Is On, The 1936,N 9,22:2
Show Is On, The 1936,N 15,XI,2:1
Show Is On, The 1936,D 26,14:2
Red Peppers; Tonight at Eight 1940,Ag 6,15:3
Evening With Beatrice Lillie, An 1952,O 3,17:2
Evening With Beatrice Lillie, An 1952,O 12,II,1:1
Little Glass Clock, The 1956,Mr 27,40:2
My Fair Lady 1964,My 21,43:2
Gardino, Jerome
Dark Is Light Enough, The 1955,F 24,20:1
Gardner, Amelia
Cornered 1920,D 9,18:2
Dolly Jordan 1922,O 4,26:1
Lazybones 1924,S 23,23:1
You Can't Beat a Woman 1925,Mr 24,26:5
Gardner, Ann
Canterbury Tales; Pilgrims, The 1969,F 4,34:1
Canterbury Tales; Merchant's Tale, The 1969,F 4,34:1
Canterbury Tales; Wife of Bath's Tale, The 1969,F 4,34:1
Gardner, Arron (Producer)
Hi, Paisano 1961,O 2,36:2
Gardner, Bernice
Pearl of Great Price, The 1926,N 2,34:3
Gardner, Bert
Hello, Lola! 1926,Ja 13,30:1
Night in Spain, A 1927,My 4,28:2
Dodsworth 1934,F 26,20:4
Gardner, Bunk
Absolutely Freee 1967,My 25,58:1
Gardner, Dale
Two Seconds 1931,O 10,20:6
Gardner, David
Tamburlaine the Great 1956,Ja 20,19:1
Henry V 1956,Je 20,27:2
Merry Wives of Windsor, The 1956,Je 21,34:4
Twelfth Night 1958,D 10,54:2
Hamlet 1958,D 17,2:7
Henry V 1958,D 26,2:7
Gardner, Diane
Gingham Dog, The 1968,O 13,II,18:6
Gardner, Dorothy (Playwright)
Eastward in Eden 1947,N 19,33:2
Eastward in Eden 1956,Ap 18,25:4

Gardner, E Sewall
Foemen of the Yard 1935,Ap 6,10:4
Gardner, Edward F (Director)
After Such Pleasures 1934,F 8,15:2
Gardner, Edward F (Playwright)
After Such Pleasures 1934,Ja 6,18:6
After Such Pleasures 1934,F 8,15:2
Gardner, Edward F (Producer)
Coastwise 1931,D 1,23:1
After Such Pleasures 1934,Ja 6,18:6
Gardner, Florence
Dora Mobridge 1930,Ap 21,20:2
Gardner, George N
Betty Behave 1927,Mr 9,28:4
Gardner, Gil
Beauty Part, The 1962,D 28,5:2
Gardner, Helen
Sunny 1925,S 23,22:1
Man Who Married a Dumb Wife, The
  1930,My 9,20:5
Small Miracle 1934,S 27,24:3
Country Wife, The 1935,Jl 2,24:2
Boy Meets Girl 1935,N 28,38:2
Our Betters 1937,Jl 22,16:2
All That Glitters 1938,Ja 20,18:2
Gardner, Herb (Director)
Goodbye People, The 1968,D 4,52:1
Goodbye People, The 1968,D 15,II,3:1
Gardner, Herb (Playwright)
Thousand Clowns, A 1962,Ap 6,31:2
Thousand Clowns, A 1962,Ap 15,II,1:1
Goodbye People, The 1968,D 4,52:1
Goodbye People, The 1968,D 15,II,3:1
Gardner, Hunter
Zombie 1932,F 11,17:2
Pursuit of Happiness, The 1933,O 10,24:4
Divided by Three 1934,O 3,24:2
If This Be Treason 1935,Jl 30,17:1
If This Be Treason 1935,S 24,28:2
Siege 1937,D 9,31:4
Jeannie 1940,N 13,29:2
Old Acquaintance 1940,D 24,18:3
R U R 1942,D 4,30:2
Land of Fame 1943,S 22,31:5
Gardner, Hy
Pins and Needles 1939,Ap 21,26:2
New Pins and Needles 1939,N 21,19:2
Gardner, Isabella
Crime at Blossoms, The 1937,Jl 17,12:8
Gardner, Joan
Kid Boots 1924,Ja 1,21:3
Gardner, John (Composer)
Tamburlaine the Great 1956,Ja 20,19:1
Gardner, John G
Frogs, The 1941,N 14,25:3
Gardner, Laine
Thesmophoriazusae, The; Goddesses of Athens,
  The 1955,D 14,52:4
Gardner, Lynn
What's Up 1943,N 12,24:6
Gardner, Mark
Legitimate Steal, The 1958,Ap 1,35:1
Doctor Faustus 1961,Ap 26,36:1
Gardner, Michael (Producer)
American Mime Theatre 1958,S 25,28:4
Gardner, Patricia
Red Mill, The 1945,O 17,16:2
Gardner, Perita West
Widow in Green, A 1931,N 21,21:4
Gardner, Peter
Faithful Heart, The 1922,O 11,22:1
Gardner, Reba
Loud Speaker 1927,Mr 3,27:2
Gardner, Rita
Fantasticks, The 1960,My 4,55:2
Family Affair, A 1962,Ja 29,17:1
Pal Joey 1963,My 30,21:1
Yeomen of the Guard, The 1964,Ag 3,16:1
Cradle Will Rock, The 1964,N 9,40:4
To Be Young Gifted and Black; World of Lorraine
  Hansberry, The 1969,Ja 3,15:1
Gardner, Sammy
Black Rhythm 1936,D 21,19:2
Gardner, Sandra
Spots of the Leopard, The 1963,S 25,38:1
Gardner, Shayle
Wandering Jew, The 1927,F 2,22:4
Gardner, Stephen (Miscellaneous)
Put It in Writing 1963,My 14,31:1
Sign in Sidney Brustein's Window, The
  1964,O 16,32:1
Of Love Remembered 1967,F 20,46:5
Gardner, Stuart
Play of Daniel, The 1960,D 27,23:6
Play of Daniel, The 1961,D 28,22:6
Gardner, Stuart (Miscellaneous)
Play of Daniel, The 1966,Ja 2,64:4
Gardner, Tom (Miscellaneous)
Riot 1968,D 20,64:1
Gardner, Vincent
Daughters of Atreus 1936,O 15,33:1
Many Happy Returns 1945,Ja 6,15:5
Calico Wedding 1945,Mr 8,18:6

Gardner's Maniacs
Vaudeville (Palace) 1926,Je 29,21:3
Gardon, George
Mima 1928,D 13,24:2
Gardonyi (Original Author)
Romance of Ida, The 1929,F 3,VIII,2:1
Gare, Maryanna
Angels Kiss Me 1951,Ap 18,37:6
Garen, Leo (Director)
Deathwatch 1958,O 10,34:2
Ginger Man, The 1963,N 22,42:1
Slave, The 1964,D 17,51:1
Toilet, The 1964,D 17,51:1
Sunset 1966,My 13,34:1
Deer Park, The 1967,F 1,27:2
Garen, Leo (Lighting Director)
Wise Have Not Spoken, The 1954,F 11,35:2
Garen, Leo (Producer)
Deathwatch 1958,O 10,34:2
Ginger Man, The 1963,N 22,42:1
Slave, The 1964,D 17,51:1
Toilet, The 1964,D 17,51:1
Garett, Daisy
Goat Alley 1921,Je 21,20:2
Garey, James R
Decoy, The 1932,Ap 2,13:4
Garey, Peter
Return Engagement 1940,N 2,19:2
Pirate, The 1942,N 26,39:2
Garfein, Jack (Director)
End as a Man 1953,S 16,39:1
Girls of Summer 1956,N 20,45:1
Sin of Pat Muldoon, The 1957,Mr 14,35:1
Shadow of a Gunman, The 1958,N 21,26:1
Shadow of a Gunman, The 1958,N 30,II,1:1
Garfield, Allen
Dream of a Blacklisted Actor 1969,D 18,64:1
Inquest 1970,Ap 24,38:1
Garfield, David
Hang Down Your Head and Die 1964,O 19,38:1
Fiddler on the Roof 1970,F 28,20:1
Rothschilds, The 1970,O 20,40:1
Garfield, George
Candida 1925,D 19,14:2
Garfield, Gil (Miscellaneous)
Hail Scrawdyke! 1966,N 29,50:1
Garfield, Irving MacD
Hades, the Ladies 1934,Mr 29,25:3
Garfield, John
Lost Boy 1932,Ja 6,24:4
Waiting for Lefty 1935,F 11,14:5
Awake and Sing! 1935,F 20,23:2
Weep for the Virgins 1935,D 2,18:1
Case of Clyde Griffiths 1936,Mr 14,10:4
Johnny Johnson 1936,N 20,26:3
Having Wonderful Time 1937,F 22,12:5
Having Wonderful Time 1937,F 28,XI,1:1
Golden Boy 1937,N 5,18:5
Golden Boy 1938,Ja 23,XI,1:6
Heavenly Express 1940,Ap 19,24:2
Heavenly Express 1940,Ap 28,IX,1:1
Skipper Next to God 1948,Ja 5,14:5
Big Knife, The 1949,F 25,27:5
Big Knife, The 1949,Mr 6,II,1:1
Peer Gynt 1951,Ja 29,15:2
Peer Gynt 1951,F 4,II,1:1
Golden Boy 1952,Mr 13,24:3
Golden Boy 1952,Mr 23,II,1:1
Garfield, Julian
Processional 1937,O 14,23:1
Big Blow 1938,O 3,11:2
Garfield, Julie
Leader, The 1969,Ap 22,40:2
Honest-to-God Schnozzola, The 1969,Ap 22,40:2
Garfield, Kurt
Sheep on the Runway 1970,F 2,28:3
Garfield, Mason
Nantucket Follies 1927,Jl 30,13:2
Garfield, Mason (Mrs)
Clarence 1923,My 14,18:4
Gargan, Edward
Black Boy 1926,O 7,30:2
Polly of Hollywood 1927,F 22,22:3
Face the Music 1932,F 18,24:5
Gargan, William
Aloma of the South Seas 1925,Ap 21,18:1
War Song, The 1928,S 25,29:3
Headquarters 1929,D 5,32:4
Out of a Blue Sky 1930,My 17,20:6
Roar China! 1930,O 28,23:1
She Lived Next to the Firehouse 1931,F 11,23:1
He 1931,S 22,33:1
Animal Kingdom, The 1932,Ja 13,26:4
Garin, Pierre
Lorenzaccio 1958,O 15,44:2
Garinei, Pietro (Director)
Rugantino 1964,F 7,34:1
Garinei, Pietro (Lyricist)
Rugantino 1964,F 2,II,1:4
Rugantino 1964,F 7,34:1
Garinei, Pietro (Playwright)
Rugantino 1964,F 2,II,1:4
Rugantino 1964,F 7,34:1

Garinei, Pietro (Playwright)—Cont
Ciao, Rudy 1966,Ja 8,15:3
Garis, Roger (Playwright)
Pony Cart, The 1954,S 15,39:2
Garl, Janet (Composer)
Lyle 1970,Mr 21,16:2
Garland, Charles
Seventh Heart, The 1927,My 3,24:4
Hello Paris 1930,N 17,29:3
Everybody's Welcome 1931,O 14,26:3
Garland, Geoff
Hostage, The 1961,D 13,55:4
Hamlet 1964,Ap 10,30:1
Imaginary Invalid, The 1967,My 2,53:1
Touch of the Poet, A 1967,My 3,38:2
Still Life 1967,My 4,34:1
Fumed Oak 1967,My 4,34:1
John Brown's Body 1968,F 13,49:2
Comedy of Errors, The 1968,F 28,40:2
She Stoops to Conquer 1968,Ap 1,58:3
Front Page, The 1969,My 12,54:2
Trelawny of the 'Wells' 1970,O 12,48:1
Garland, Isabel
Cyrano de Bergerac 1923,N 2,14:1
Garland, Judy
Vaudeville (Palace) 1951,O 17,36:6
Vaudeville (Palace) 1951,N 17,9:6
Judy Garland's New Variety Show 1956,S 27,43:2
Judy Garland 1959,My 12,40:1
Judy Garland 1961,Ap 24,36:1
Untitled-Revue 1964,N 10,56:2
At Home at the Palace 1967,Ag 1,23:1
Untitled-Judy Garland 1967,D 26,45:1
Garland, Lenore
Goodbye My Fancy 1948,N 18,35:2
Garland, Margaret
Family Affair, A 1946,N 28,41:2
Anne of the Thousand Days 1948,D 9,49:2
Garland, Michel
Femmes Savantes, Les 1967,F 7,34:2
Garland, Nicholas (Director)
Photo Finish 1963,F 14,5:2
Garland, Patrick (Director)
Rebel, The 1964,F 22,14:5
Brief Lives 1967,D 19,60:4
40 Years On 1968,N 5,53:3
Garland, Patrick (Playwright)
Brief Lives 1967,D 19,60:4
Garland, Patrick (Producer)
Stiffkey Scandals of 1932, The 1969,Je 14,24:3
Garland, Peter (Playwright)
Eternal Spring, The 1924,F 3,VII,1:4
Basalik 1935,Ap 8,22:5
Garland, Ruth
Out of Step 1925,Ja 30,12:1
This Thing Called Love 1928,S 18,32:7
Lysistrata 1930,Ap 29,30:5
Lysistrata 1930,Je 6,20:1
Troilus and Cressida 1932,Je 7,22:3
Garland, Victor
Treasure Girl 1928,N 9,22:1
Garletts, Frank
Gala Night 1930,F 26,22:4
Garley, John
Henry IV, Part I 1946,My 7,25:2
Henry IV, Part II 1946,My 8,33:4
Oedipus; Critic, The 1946,My 21,19:2
Garlinger, Barry (Lighting Director)
Conversation at Midnight 1964,N 13,27:1
Garn, Jack (Choreographer)
Manhatters, The 1927,Jl 19,27:3
Garner, Don
Camino Real 1960,My 17,42:2
Pullman Car Hiawatha 1962,D 4,46:2
Garner, Don (Miscellaneous)
Pullman Car Hiawatha 1962,D 4,46:2
Desire Under the Elms 1963,Ja 11,5:6
Garner, Jay
Red, White and Maddox 1969,Ja 27,27:1
Disintegration of James Cherry, The
  1970,Ja 30,33:3
Contributions; Plantation 1970,Mr 10,53:1
Beggar on Horseback 1970,My 15,47:2
Beggar on Horseback 1970,My 24,II,1:1
Garner, Martin
Dybbuk, The 1954,O 27,33:6
Jackknife 1958,S 23,36:2
Golem, The 1959,F 26,38:2
Tenth Man, The 1959,N 6,24:2
Tenth Man, The 1959,N 15,II,1:1
Gideon 1961,N 10,38:1
Seidman and Son 1962,O 16,32:2
Dylan 1964,Ja 20,18:1
Kitchen, The 1966,Je 14,50:1
Garner, Mitzi
Gay Divorce 1932,N 30,23:4
Caviar 1934,Je 8,19:2
Garner, Paul
Gang's All Here, The 1931,F 19,21:3
Garner, Peggy Ann
Man, The 1950,Ja 20,28:2
Royal Family, The 1951,Ja 11,28:2
First Lady 1952,My 29,18:5
Home Is the Hero 1954,S 23,42:2

Garner, Rex
Not Now Darling 1970,O 30,33:1
Garner, Sylvia
Tobias and the Angel 1937,Ap 29,16:5
Garner, Ward
Sleepy Hollow 1948,Je 4,26:3
Garner, William
Star-Wagon, The 1937,S 30,18:5
Garnett, Catherine
Twelfth Night 1968,Je 15,40:1
Garnett, Constance (Translator)
Cherry Orchard, The 1928,O 16,28:5
On the High Road 1929,Ja 15,22:3
Sea Gull, The 1929,S 17,34:1
Cherry Orchard, The 1933,Mr 7,20:3
Uncle Vanya 1946,My 14,18:2
Sea Gull, The 1956,O 23,38:1
Storm, The 1962,Mr 31,17:2
Cherry Orchard, The 1962,N 15,46:2
Month in the Country, A 1963,My 29,39:2
Garnett, Gale
Hair 1970,Ja 13,39:1
Garnett, Katherine
Merton of the Movies 1968,S 26,62:1
Garnett, Richard (Original Author)
Poisoned Kiss, The 1937,Ap 22,19:1
Garnett, Susana
Pillar to Post 1943,D 11,11:2
Mrs January & Mr Ex 1944,Ap 1,10:2
Men to the Sea 1944,O 4,25:2
Little Women 1944,D 13,29:2
Oh, Herbert! 1945,Je 20,26:3
Garnier, Dorothy
American Tragedy, An 1931,F 21,15:5
Garon, Jay (Miscellaneous)
Kataki 1959,D 16,55:1
Garon, Jay (Producer)
Kataki 1959,Ap 10,24:1
Evening of Rare Pleasures, An 1959,Je 4,26:2
Garon, Pauline
Lilies of the Field 1921,O 5,20:1
Vaudeville (Palace) 1927,Ap 5,30:2
Garr, Alfred
For Heaven's Sake Mother 1948,N 17,33:4
Garr, Eddie
Vaudeville (Palace) 1932,My 16,19:2
Strike Me Pink 1933,Mr 6,16:3
Friars Club Frolic 1933,My 15,16:4
Thumbs Up! 1934,D 28,24:1
Vaudeville Marches On 1938,D 30,11:1
Laughter Over Broadway 1939,Ja 16,10:3
Merry Widow, The 1942,Jl 16,22:1
Garran, Gabriel (Director)
Stars Turn Red, The 1962,O 25,47:1
Garrard, Henry
Billy Budd 1951,F 12,18:3
Glad Tidings 1951,O 12,33:2
Garrard, Henry (Miscellaneous)
Park 1970,Ap 23,47:1
Garreau, Claude (Miscellaneous)
Shuffle Along 1952,My 9,20:5
Garrel, Maurice (Director)
Luv 1965,N 16,56:4
Garrel, Sofia
Kremlin Chimes 1965,F 25,23:1
Garren, Joseph J (Playwright)
Dr David's Dad 1924,Ag 14,10:3
Garren, Lois
Founders, The 1957,My 14,39:1
Garrett, Ann
Three Sisters, The 1939,O 16,23:1
Garrett, Betty
Danton's Death 1938,N 3,26:2
You Can't Sleep Here 1941,My 11,I,42:6
Of V We Sing 1941,O 26,I,39:1
Of V We Sing 1942,F 16,20:3
Let Freedom Sing 1942,O 6,18:2
Something for the Boys 1943,Ja 17,VIII,1:1
Jackpot 1944,Ja 14,15:2
Laffing Room Only 1944,D 25,15:4
Call Me Mister 1946,Ap 19,26:2
Call Me Mister 1946,Ap 28,II,1:1
Beg, Borrow or Steal 1960,F 11,39:4
Spoon River Anthology 1963,My 2,40:5
Spoon River Anthology 1963,S 30,23:2
Girl Could Get Lucky, A 1964,S 21,36:1
Garrett, Charlcie (Playwright)
Sleep, My Pretty One 1944,N 3,26:8
Garrett, Cleve
Kick Back, The 1936,Je 23,27:3
Garrett, Hank
Wet Paint 1965,Ap 13,33:1
Garrett, James
Oh, Please! 1926,D 22,24:3
Garrett, John
Crucible, The 1958,Mr 17,21:1
Garrett, Joy
Gertrude Stein's First Reader 1969,D 16,56:1
Drunkard, The 1970,Ap 14,54:1
Candyapple, The 1970,N 24,33:1
Garrett, Lloyd
Scandals 1920,Je 8,9:1
George White's Scandals 1921,Jl 12,14:1

George White's Scandals 1926,Je 15,23:2
Garrett, Marjorie
After Tomorrow 1931,Ag 27,22:4
Riddle Me This! 1932,F 26,22:5
Divine Drudge 1933,O 27,22:3
No Questions Asked 1934,F 6,24:3
Lightnin' 1938,S 16,17:2
Garrett, Oliver (Playwright)
Waltz in Goose Step 1938,N 2,26:2
Sleep, My Pretty One 1944,N 3,26:8
Garrick, Beulah
Auntie Mame 1956,N 1,47:2
Juno 1959,Mr 10,41:1
Shadow and Substance 1959,N 4,42:1
Little Moon of Alban 1960,D 2,34:1
Lovers; Losers 1968,Je 26,21:4
Little Boxes; Coffee Lace, The 1969,D 4,71:2
Little Boxes; Trevor 1969,D 4,71:2
Garrick, David (Playwright)
She Stoops to Conquer 1928,My 15,17:1
Clandestine Marriage, The 1954,O 4,23:2
Clandestine Marriage, The 1954,O 17,II,1:1
Garrick, John
Little Racketeer, The 1932,Ja 19,24:4
Garrick, Lillian
Humoresque 1923,F 28,13:2
Family Upstairs, The 1925,Ag 18,14:2
Garrick, Richard
Feathers in a Gale 1943,D 22,26:2
Streetcar Named Desire, A 1947,D 4,42:2
Garrick, Yvonne
Musk 1920,Mr 15,13:1
Garrigan, Gerald
Conversation Piece 1957,N 19,38:2
Garringer, Nelson (Miscellaneous)
Fun City 1968,Mr 7,53:2
Garris, John
Gypsy Baron, The 1942,Je 20,8:5
Gypsy Baron, The 1942,Ag 7,12:4
Beggar Student, The 1942,S 26,11:4
Garrison, Isabel
Anything Might Happen 1923,F 21,22:3
Garrison, Jack
Confederacy, The 1958,Jl 3,20:1
Garrison, James
Guys and Dolls 1959,Jl 22,22:2
Garrison, John
Buoyant Billions 1959,My 27,32:2
Garrison, Sean
There Was a Little Girl 1960,Mr 1,28:1
Half-Past Wednesday 1962,Ap 7,16:2
Beauty Part, The 1962,D 28,5:2
Garrubbo, Filippo
Casa di Tutti, La; Everybody's Home 1932,D 5,21:4
Cardinale, Il 1933,Ja 9,24:2
Romanticismo 1933,My 1,10:5
Liane, Le (Ties That Bind) 1933,Je 12,20:3
Garry, Harold
Fiesta 1929,S 18,35:1
Garry, Ian
Walking Happy 1966,N 28,47:1
Garry, Joseph R
Shipwrecked 1924,N 13,18:1
Fall Guy, The 1925,Mr 11,19:1
Mystery Ship, The 1927,Mr 15,28:2
Round-Up, The 1932,Mr 8,19:4
Order Please 1934,O 10,21:2
Dear Old Darling 1936,Mr 3,25:1
Village Green 1941,S 4,24:4
For Keeps 1944,Je 15,17:5
Garry, Sid
Vaudeville (Palace) 1923,O 30,16:1
Garry, William (Miscellaneous)
Place Without Doors, A 1970,D 1,60:1
Garson, Barbara (Playwright)
MacBird! 1967,F 23,38:1
MacBird! 1967,Mr 12,II,1:1
MacBird! 1967,Ap 11,54:5
MacBird! 1967,Ap 16,II,3:6
Garson, Betty
Flossie 1924,Je 4,25:2
Garson, Eddie
Liberace's Variety Bill 1957,Ap 22,29:5
Garson, Greer
Accent on Youth 1935,S 29,X,1:6
Butterfly on the Wheel 1935,N 10,IX,3:1
Page From a Diary 1936,F 9,X,3:1
Old Music 1937,S 5,X,2:1
Garson, Henry (Original Author)
In Any Language 1952,O 9,40:2
Garson, Henry (Playwright)
In Any Language 1952,O 9,40:2
In Any Language 1952,O 19,II,1:1
Garson, John
Call on Kuprin, A 1961,My 26,29:3
Dreigroschenoper, Die 1965,Mr 12,24:1
Garson, Marilyn
Sacco-Vanzetti 1969,F 9,78:1
Garson, Toby (Lyricist)
Lyle 1970,Mr 21,16:2
Garstin, Gertrude
Carry Nation 1932,O 31,18:2

Garstin, Herbert
Virginia 1937,S 3,13:2
Garth, Caswell (Original Author)
Great Waltz, The 1934,S 24,14:4
Garth, John
Porgy and Bess 1935,O 11,30:2
Porgy and Bess 1942,Ja 23,16:2
Garth, John 3d
Belle Helene, La 1941,Jl 8,14:1
Annie Get Your Gun 1946,My 17,14:2
Long Dream, The 1960,F 18,36:2
Garton, Mr
Merchant of Venice, The 1921,Ap 2,14:2
Gartrell, Claire
Mystery of the Finding of the Cross, The 1959,Ja 16,35:2
Garuffi, Carlo
Paese dei Campanelli, Il; Land of Bells, The 1935,My 10,25:4
Garuffi, Maria
Paese dei Campanelli, Il; Land of Bells, The 1935,My 10,25:4
Garvey, Joseph (Composer)
Buffalo Skinner, The 1959,F 20,18:1
Nathan Weinstein, Mystic, Connecticut 1966,F 26,15:2
Garvie, Eddie
Betty, Be Good 1920,My 5,14:2
Hell's Bells! 1925,Ja 27,14:2
Exceeding Small 1928,O 23,32:2
Street Singer, The 1929,S 18,35:2
Smiling Faces 1932,Ag 31,12:3
Loose Moments 1935,F 5,22:3
Achilles Had a Heel 1935,O 14,20:2
Home Sweet Home 1936,Jl 1,29:2
Garwood, Kelton
Carefree Tree, The 1955,O 12,37:2
Last Love of Don Juan, The 1955,N 24,40:1
Thesmophoriazusae, The; Goddesses of Athens, The 1955,D 14,52:4
Misanthrope, The 1956,N 13,44:1
Midsummer Night's Dream, A 1957,Je 27,21:3
Chairs, The 1958,Ja 10,20:3
Garwood, Kelton (Miscellaneous)
Richard III 1957,N 26,41:1
Gary, Bill
For Your Pleasure 1943,F 6,9:2
Gary, Charles
School for Brides 1944,Ag 2,19:4
Gary, Franklin
Romio and Julietta 1925,Ap 21,19:1
Fortuno 1925,D 23,22:1
Dover Road, The 1926,Ap 29,20:3
Samarkand 1926,D 22,24:4
Hamlet 1927,Ap 7,23:3
Gary, Franklin (Director)
Dover Road, The 1926,Ap 29,20:3
Gary, Franklin (Playwright)
Samarkand 1926,D 22,24:4
Gary, Gene
Slightly Scandalous 1944,Je 14,16:2
Gary, Harold
World We Make, The 1939,N 21,19:1
Flag Is Born, A 1946,S 7,10:6
Rosalie 1957,Je 26,28:2
How to Make a Man 1961,F 3,16:1
Paradise Island 1961,Je 24,11:1
Let It Ride 1961,O 13,27:4
In the Counting House 1962,D 15,5:5
Illya Darling 1967,Ap 12,37:1
Price, The 1968,F 8,37:1
Price, The 1968,F 18,II,1:1
Gary, John
Processional 1937,O 14,23:1
Gary, Kellogg (Producer)
Gods of the Lightning 1928,O 25,27:2
Gary, Nadia
Wake Up, Jonathan 1921,Ja 18,14:1
Gary, Romain (Original Author)
First Love 1961,D 26,20:2
Gary, Sheila
Parasite, The 1965,D 17,43:2
Gary, Ted
Stars in Your Eyes 1939,F 10,18:2
Walk With Music 1940,Je 5,33:2
Crazy With the Heat 1940,D 26,22:1
Crazy With the Heat 1941,Ja 15,18:2
Crazy With the Heat 1941,Ja 31,15:2
Gary, Theodora
Othello 1964,Ag 3,16:6
Gary, Willard
Two for the Show 1940,F 9,14:2
Garzera, Edward (Lighting Director)
Ticket-of-Leave Man, The 1961,D 23,15:1
Garzera, Edward (Scenic Designer)
Ticket-of-Leave Man, The 1961,D 23,15:1
Garzone, Jean (Costume Designer)
Pigeon, The 1957,My 17,19:2
Garzone, Tullio
In the Jungle of Cities 1960,D 21,39:1
Garzonne, Tullio (Miscellaneous)
Soul Gone Home 1959,O 28,40:7
Shakespeare in Harlem 1959,O 28,40:7

Gasc, Yves
Lorenzaccio 1958,O 15,44:2
Gascoigne, Cleo
Vaudeville (Lexington) 1921,O 18,20:2
Gascom, Jean (Director)
Malade Imaginaire, Le; Imaginary Invalid, The 1958,Ap 30,28:2
Gascon, Andre
Malade Imaginaire, Le; Imaginary Invalid, The 1958,Ap 30,28:2
Gascon, Gabriel
Malade Imaginaire, Le; Imaginary Invalid, The 1958,Ap 30,28:2
Jalousie du Barbouille, La; Jealousy of the Barbouille, The 1958,My 7,43:1
Mariage Force, Le; Forced Wedding, The 1958,My 7,43:1
Sganarelle; Imaginary Cuckold, The 1958,My 7,43:1
Love and Maple Syrup 1970,Ja 8,47:1
Gascon, Jean
Henry V 1956,Je 20,27:2
Henry V 1956,Je 24,II,1:1
Malade Imaginaire, Le; Imaginary Invalid, The 1958,Ap 30,28:2
Mariage Force, Le; Forced Wedding, The 1958,My 7,43:1
Jalousie du Barbouille, La; Jealousy of the Barbouille, The 1958,My 7,43:1
Richard II 1962,Ag 8,36:1
Henry V 1966,Je 8,38:1
Merry Wives of Windsor, The 1967,Ag 4,18:1
Gascon, Jean (Director)
Mariage Force, Le; Forced Wedding, The 1958,My 7,43:1
Sganarelle; Imaginary Cuckold, The 1958,My 7,43:1
Jalousie du Barbouille, La; Jealousy of the Barbouille, The 1958,My 7,43:1
Othello 1959,Jl 2,17:2
Othello 1959,Jl 5,II,1:1
Lysistrata 1959,N 25,19:4
Lysistrata 1959,D 6,II,5:1
Richard II 1962,Ag 8,36:1
Comedy of Errors, The 1963,Je 21,35:3
Bourgeois Gentilhomme, Le 1964,Je 18,28:2
Tartuffe 1968,Je 12,39:1
Seagull, The 1968,Jl 25,27:2
Alchemist, The 1969,Je 12,51:1
Merchant of Venice, The 1970,Je 10,39:1
Merchant of Venice, The 1970,Je 21,II,1:1
Cymbeline 1970,Ag 23,II,1:6
Gascon, Jean (Producer)
Tartuffe 1968,Je 23,II,1:1
Alchemist, The 1969,Je 22,II,1:7
Gaselli, Silva
Time of the Cuckoo, The 1952,O 16,37:4
Gasgoines, The Royal
Vaudeville (Palace) 1926,Jl 6,19:3
Gaskill, Clarence (Composer)
Fables 1922,F 7,12:2
Earl Carroll's Vanities 1925,Jl 7,24:1
Earl Carroll's Vanities 1925,D 29,20:3
Keep It Clean 1929,Je 25,35:5
Gaskill, Clarence (Lyricist)
Keep It Clean 1929,Je 25,35:5
Gaskill, Helen (Playwright)
Caviar and Wine 1932,Ap 17,VIII,2:6
Gaskill, Norma
Thesmophoriazusae, The; Goddesses of Athens, The 1955,D 14,52:4
Gaskill, William (Director)
Epitaph for George Dillon 1958,N 5,44:1
Deadly Game, The 1960,F 3,27:2
Richard III 1961,My 25,32:3
Richard III 1961,Je 25,II,3:5
Caucasian Chalk Circle, The 1962,Mr 30,28:1
Cymbeline 1962,Jl 18,21:2
Double Dealer, The 1969,Ag 7,29:1
Beaux' Stratagem, The 1970,F 10,50:2
Beaux' Stratagem, The 1970,F 22,II,1:1
Gaskin, Leonard
All in One; Trouble in Tahiti 1955,Ap 20,40:3
Gaskin, William (Scenic Designer)
Hoboken Blues 1928,F 18,10:1
Playboy of the Western World, The 1930,Ja 3,20:4
General John Regan 1930,Ja 30,16:5
Gaskins, Deloris
Electra 1969,Ag 8,14:1
Mod Donna 1970,My 4,48:1
Ododo 1970,N 25,26:1
Gaskins, Pauline
Here Goes the Bride 1931,N 4,31:2
Gaspar, Edd
Anna Kleiber 1965,Ja 20,33:1
Gaspar, Marie
Vaudeville (Palace) 1924,Mr 18,25:1
Gasper, Eddie
Irma la Douce 1960,S 30,31:2
Bacchae, The 1963,Ap 25,39:5
Burning, The 1963,D 4,57:1
Sweet Charity 1966,Ja 31,22:1
Gasper, Eddie (Choreographer)
Fig Leaves Are Falling, The 1969,Ja 3,19:1

Gasper, Marie
Vaudeville (Palace) 1923,N 20,23:4
Gassel, Sylvia
As You Like It 1955,O 29,12:2
Romeo and Juliet 1955,D 16,36:3
Henry V 1956,Jl 7,11:2
Beyond the Horizon 1962,O 26,27:2
Darker Flower, A 1963,Mr 11,7:2
Fair Game for Lovers 1964,F 11,43:2
Basement, The 1967,O 3,56:1
Goa 1968,F 23,46:1
Mr and Mrs Lyman 1968,Mr 6,35:1
God Bless You, Harold Fineberg 1969,Mr 31,30:2
Philosophy in the Boudoir 1969,My 22,55:2
Inquest 1970,Ap 24,38:1
Gassel, Sylvia (Miscellaneous)
E-MC2 1948,Je 16,36:2
Gasser, Wolfgang
Professor Bernhardi 1968,Mr 20,38:1
Maria Stuart 1968,Mr 27,38:1
Jux Will Er Sich Machen, Einen 1968,Ap 3,41:1
Gassman, Vittorio
Game of Heroes, The 1966,F 22,14:2
Gassman, Vittorio (Producer)
Heroes, The 1963,My 22,36:1
Gassner, Florence
Nervous Set, The 1959,My 13,43:1
Gassner, John (Producer)
Minnie and Mr Williams 1948,O 28,37:2
Gassner, John W (Playwright)
Peace Palace 1933,Je 6,30:2
Jeremiah 1939,F 4,11:2
Gassner, Mordi (Costume Designer)
Minnie and Mr Williams 1948,O 28,37:2
Gassner, Mordi (Lighting Director)
Mrs Warren's Profession 1950,O 26,39:2
Sands of the Negev 1954,O 20,32:1
Gassner, Mordi (Scenic Designer)
Minnie and Mr Williams 1948,O 28,37:2
Sands of the Negev 1954,O 20,32:1
Gast, Florence
Good Times 1920,Ag 10,10:1
Rose Girl, The 1921,F 12,11:1
Gaston, Anne
Married Woman, The 1921,D 26,21:1
Gaston, Billy
Harry Delmar's Revels 1927,N 29,30:2
Gaston, George
Transplanting Jean 1921,Ja 4,11:2
Listening In 1922,D 5,24:1
Gaston, John M
Hamlet 1927,Ap 7,23:3
Gaston, Ken (Producer)
Three Men on a Horse 1969,O 17,35:1
Place for Polly, A 1970,Ap 20,45:1
Gaston, Penny
Shoemaker's Holiday, The 1967,Mr 3,25:1
Gaston, Robert (Miscellaneous)
Macbeth 1962,F 7,32:2
Romeo and Juliet 1962,F 14,39:1
Saint Joan 1962,F 21,57:4
Gaston, William (Playwright)
Damn the Tears 1927,Ja 22,11:1
Damn the Tears 1927,Ja 30,VII,1:1
Gaston and Andree
Vaudeville (Palace) 1927,Jl 12,29:3
Vaudeville (Palace) 1927,N 15,27:2
Vaudeville (Palace) 1928,S 18,34:6
Gatch, Merriman
Time of Vengeance 1959,D 11,39:1
Time of Vengeance 1959,D 27,II,1:1
Gateley, Jacqueline
Kiss for Cinderella, A 1942,Mr 11,22:2
Gately, Kathleen
Remarkable Mr Pennypacker, The 1953,D 31,11:2
Gately, Virginia
Meet the Prince 1935,Jl 9,24:5
Gates, Aaron (Director)
Bottomland 1927,Je 28,29:3
Gates, Crawford (Composer)
Promised Valley 1947,Jl 23,18:3
Gates, Crawford (Musical Director)
Promised Valley 1947,Jl 23,18:3
Gates, Dorothy
Good Times 1920,Ag 10,10:1
Gates, Helen
Girl in the Spotlight, The 1920,Jl 13,9:3
Gates, J M
1776 1926,Ap 24,11:2
Gates, J W Jr
Tiger Smiles, The 1930,D 18,29:1
Gates, Jane Hinton (Playwright)
Obbligato 1958,F 19,22:2
Gates, Jim
Brig, The 1963,My 16,40:1
Moon Walk 1970,N 27,52:1
Gates, Joseph M
Don't Tell George 1928,Jl 22,VII,1:1
Gates, Joyce
Come Angel Band 1936,F 19,17:1
Gates, Larry
Bell, Book and Candle 1950,N 15,37:4
Bell, Book and Candle 1950,D 17,II,3:1

Gates, Larry—Cont
Taming of the Shrew, The 1951,Ap 26,35:2
Love of Four Colonels, The 1953,Ja 16,17:2
Teahouse of the August Moon, The 1953,O 16,32:1
Teahouse of the August Moon, The 1953,O 25,II,1:1
Teahouse of the August Moon, The 1954,S 12,II,1:1
Sing Me No Lullaby 1954,O 15,17:2
Sing Me No Lullaby 1954,O 24,II,1:1
Carefree Tree, The 1955,O 12,37:2
Othello 1957,Je 24,19:2
Merchant of Venice, The 1957,Jl 11,19:5
Much Ado About Nothing 1957,Ag 8,15:2
Romeo and Juliet 1959,Je 15,31:1
Merry Wives of Windsor, The 1959,Jl 9,23:2
All's Well That Ends Well 1959,Ag 3,20:4
Highest Tree, The 1959,N 5,41:1
Case of Libel, A 1963,O 11,43:2
Case of Libel, A 1963,O 27,II,1:1
Conversation at Midnight 1964,N 13,27:1
Tartuffe 1965,Ja 15,23:1
Carving a Statue 1968,My 1,43:1
Ah, Wilderness! 1969,N 9,86:1
Gates, Marion
Diamond Lil 1951,S 15,8:2
Gates, McLain
Light Wines and Beer 1930,N 11,28:6
Lend Me Your Ears! 1936,O 6,28:5
Gates, Melvin
Flight to the West 1940,D 31,19:1
Gates, Ruth
Not Herbert 1926,Ja 27,16:2
Straight Thru the Door 1928,O 5,17:2
Brass Ankle 1931,Ap 24,26:4
Too Many Boats 1934,S 12,26:3
Substitute for Murder 1935,O 23,18:6
Crab Apple 1936,Jl 8,14:2
Now You've Done It 1937,Mr 6,10:4
Pillar to Post 1943,D 11,11:2
Ramshackle Inn 1944,Ja 6,17:5
That Old Devil 1944,Je 6,14:2
I Remember Mama 1944,O 20,16:2
Show Boat 1948,S 9,33:2
Opening Night 1963,O 3,28:2
Gates, W N
Take a Brace 1923,Ap 20,20:3
Gates & Morange (Scenic Designer)
Colonel Satan 1931,Ja 12,24:1
Gateson, Marjorie
Little Miss Charity 1920,S 3,6:3
Rose Girl, The 1921,F 12,11:1
Love Letter, The 1921,O 5,20:1
For Goodness Sake 1922,F 22,13:1
Lady Butterfly 1923,Ja 23,18:1
Sweet Little Devil 1924,Ja 22,15:4
So This Is Politics 1924,Je 17,22:2
Man in Evening Clothes, The 1924,D 6,13:4
Blonde Sinner, The 1926,Jl 15,21:2
Oh, Ernest! 1927,My 10,24:3
Midsummer Night's Dream, A 1927,Je 27,25:1
Hidden 1927,O 5,30:4
Great Necker, The 1928,Mr 7,28:2
Security 1929,Mr 29,20:1
Cafe 1930,Ag 29,11:1
As Good as new 1930,O 19,IX,3:4
As Good As New 1930,N 4,37:3
Sweethearts 1947,Ja 22,31:2
Show Boat 1954,My 6,44:1
Gathright, Margaret
Russell Patterson's Sketch-Book 1960,F 8,35:1
Kean 1961,N 3,28:2
Gatlin, George
Clandestine on the Morning Line 1961,O 31,28:1
Gatteys, Bennye
Behind the Wall 1960,N 1,47:1
Gatti, Emanuel
Abisso 1920,O 10,VI,1:8
Gatti, Ettore
Barbara 1929,N 18,24:5
My Wife Is Different 1931,Ap 27,24:4
Romanticismo 1933,My 1,10:5
Gatti, Giannina
Age of Innocence, The 1928,N 28,24:2
Gatti, Giorgio
Testamento della Zia d'America, Il; American Aunt's Will, The 1936,Mr 23,22:4
Gatti, Guglielmo E (Cav) (Director)
Nica 1926,Ja 26,19:1
Gatti, Rossana
My Wife Is Different 1931,Ap 27,24:4
Gatti, Sylvia
God's Thieves 1930,O 27,17:4
Gatti, Virginia
Barbara 1929,N 18,24:5
Gatts, George (Producer)
Her Happiness 1922,O 8,VI,1:6
For Your Pleasure 1943,F 6,9:2
Gaubert, Helen A (Translator)
King's Standards, The 1958,F 14,19:1
Gaudel, Marcelle
Maid in the Ozarks 1946,Jl 16,20:3
Gaudio, Carlo
Colonello Bridall, L' 1934,Ap 16,20:3
Romanticismo 1934,My 14,20:2

Gaudio, Carlo—Cont
Promessi Sposi I,; Betrothed, The 1934,O 22,13:2
Romanzo di un Giovane Povero, Il 1935,F 25,12:3
Vita Nuova; Life Begins Again 1935,F 26,16:2
Signo Della Croce, Il 1935,O 7,11:1
Three Guardsmen, The 1936,F 17,21:3
Religione e Patria 1936,Mr 23,22:4
Due Orfanelle, Le; Two Orphans, The 1936,O 5,24:4
Feudalismo Oppure La Terra Bassa; Feudalism or the Lowland 1937,Mr 8,22:2
Fantasmi 1937,Mr 22,26:5
Medico Delle Pazze, Il; Physician of Mad Woman, The 1937,S 27,24:2
Signora Dalle Camelie, La; Dame aux Camelias, La 1937,O 9,16:3

Gaudio, Silvia
Signora Dalle Camelie, La; Dame aux Camelias, La 1937,O 9,16:3

Gaudreau, Hazel
I'll Say She Is 1924,My 20,15:1

Gaudry, John
Pink String and Sealing Wax 1957,S 6,13:1

Gaudsmith Brothers
Untitled-Revue 1924,F 19,12:1
Vaudeville (Hippodrome) 1924,Ap 1,18:1
Vaudeville (Palace) 1927,Ja 18,23:2
Vaudeville (Palace) 1927,O 25,33:2

Gauge, Alexander
Eden End 1935,O 22,17:1
King Lear 1947,F 19,32:2
As You Like It 1947,F 21,16:2
Merchant of Venice, The 1947,F 24,16:2
Volpone 1947,F 25,32:2
Hamlet 1947,F 27,27:2

Gaul, George
Big Game 1920,Ja 22,23:1
Big Game 1920,Ja 25,VIII,2:2
Ouija Board, The 1920,Mr 30,9:1
Lady of the Lamp, The 1920,Ag 18,6:4
Lady of the Lamp, The 1920,Ag 22,VI,1:2
Steamship Tenacity 1922,Ja 3,20:2
Back to Methuselah (Part I: In the Beginning) 1922,F 28,17:2
Back to Methuselah (Part V: As Far as Thought Can Reach) 1922,Mr 14,11:2
Seventh Heaven 1922,O 31,11:1
Two Married Men 1925,Ja 14,19:1
Aloma of the South Seas 1925,Ap 21,18:1
Goat Song 1926,Ja 26,18:1
Brothers Karamazov, The 1927,Ja 4,20:1
Faust 1928,O 9,34:1
Dynamo 1929,F 12,22:1
Troilus and Cressida 1932,Je 7,22:3
Perfect Marriage, The 1932,N 17,23:2

Gaul, Patricia
Street Sounds 1970,O 23,32:1

Gauld, Carlton
Gypsy Baron, The 1944,N 15,20:3

Gault, Warner
Broadway Whirl, The 1921,Je 9,10:4

Gaument, Jean (Playwright)
Boucheur N'Est Pas de ce Monde, Le 1926,D 26,VII,2:1

Gaumont, Irving (Playwright)
30 Days Hath September 1938,O 1,10:5

Gaumont, Irving (Producer)
Shuffle Along 1952,My 9,20:5

Gaunt, William
Tavern, The 1920,S 28,14:1

Gaus, Robert
Doctor Faustus 1961,Ap 26,36:1
Candida 1961,Ap 27,26:1
1776 1969,Mr 17,46:2

Gaut, Lou
Vaudeville (Palace) 1923,Ja 30,12:2

Gauthier, Donat
Marjorie 1924,Ag 12,12:2

Gauthier Sisters, The
Vaudeville (Palace) 1928,N 6,35:2

Gauthron, Bernard
Grosse Valise, La 1965,D 15,52:1

Gautier, Dick
Bye Bye Birdie 1960,Ap 15,13:4

Gautiers Bricklayers
Vaudeville (Palace) 1924,Ja 1,21:1

Gautier's Dogs
Vaudeville (Palace) 1926,Ag 3,19:2

Gauvault, Paul (Playwright)
Mademoiselle Josette Ma Femme 1924,Je 1,VII,1:7

Gauvin, J A (Miscellaneous)
Passionement; Passionately 1929,Mr 8,31:4
Comte Obligado 1929,Mr 12,26:2
Ta Bouche 1929,Mr 15,28:5
Bon Garcon 1929,Mr 19,36:2
Pas Sur La Bouche; Not on the Lips 1929,Mr 26,34:3

Gauvin, J A (Playwright)
Topaze 1931,F 17,29:1

Gauvin, J A (Producer)
Trois Jeunes Filles Nues; Three Young Maids From the Folies Bergere 1929,Mr 5,28:2

Gavault, Paul (Playwright)
Ma Tante d' Honfleur 1920,Ja 27,18:3

My Aunt From Ypsilanti 1923,My 2,22:6
Yeux du Coeur, Les 1927,O 16,IX,4:7

Gavin
Bourgeois Gentilhomme, Le 1955,O 26,26:1

Gavin, Gene
West Side Story 1957,S 27,14:4

Gavin, Jimmy
Venice Preserv'd 1955,D 13,54:4
Mime and Me, The 1960,Ap 8,27:3
Automobile Graveyard, The 1961,N 14,46:2

Gavin, Jimmy (Composer)
Mime and Me, The 1960,Ap 8,27:3

Gavin, Tommy
White Horse Inn 1936,O 2,28:5

Gavlin, Fredric
Crucible, The 1958,Mr 17,21:1

Gavon, Igors
Carnival! 1961,Ap 14,22:2
Hello, Dolly! 1964,Ja 17,22:1
Persecution and Assassination of Marat As Performed by the Inmates of the Asylum of Charenton Under the Direction of the Marquis de Sade, The 1967,Ja 4,34:1
Your Own Thing 1968,Ja 15,33:1
Billy 1969,Mr 24,56:1
Exchange 1970,F 9,47:2

Gavrilithis, Eihs
Cute Gata.....Oute Zhmia; Neither Cat . . . Nor Damage 1957,D 20,31:1

Gawel, Karen
Trumpets and Drums 1969,O 13,52:1

Gaxton, William
Irving Berlin's New Music Box Revue 1922,O 24,18:1
Partners 1927,Jl 26,16:5
Connecticut Yankee, A 1927,N 4,24:2
Fifty Million Frenchmen 1929,N 28,34:4
Fifty Million Frenchmen 1930,Ja 5,VIII,1:8
Vaudeville (Palace) 1930,N 3,19:2
Vaudeville (Palace) 1931,Jl 13,13:4
Vaudeville (Palace) 1931,Jl 20,20:3
Vaudeville (Palace) 1931,Ag 3,15:7
Vaudeville (Palace) 1931,S 7,19:2
Of Thee I Sing 1931,D 28,20:1
Lambs Gambol 1932,Ap 25,18:2
Let 'Em Eat Cake 1933,O 23,18:1
Anything Goes 1934,N 18,IX,1:7
Anything Goes 1934,N 22,26:1
Anything Goes 1935,S 15,IX,1:1
White Horse Inn 1936,O 2,28:5
Leave It to Me! 1938,O 23,IX,3:5
Leave It to Me! 1938,N 10,32:2
Leave It to Me! 1939,S 10,IX,1:1
Leave It to Me! 1940,Ja 18,27:2
Louisiana Purchase 1940,My 29,19:2
Keep 'Em Laughing 1942,Ap 25,9:2
Hollywood Pinafore 1945,Je 1,20:1
Hollywood Pinafore 1945,Je 10,II,1:1
Nellie Bly 1946,Ja 22,32:2
Nellie Bly 1946,Ja 27,II,1:1
ANTA Album 1951,My 7,22:7
Paradise Island 1961,Je 24,11:1
Paradise Island 1962,Je 28,22:1

Gay
Jim Jam Jems 1920,O 5,13:2

Gay, Alden
Greenwich Village Follies 1920,Ag 31,7:3
Fashions of 1924 1923,Jl 19,18:2
One Kiss 1923,N 28,14:2
Man in Evening Clothes, The 1924,D 6,13:4
Dearest Enemy 1925,S 19,9:2
House of Shadows, The 1927,Ap 22,18:4
Lady for a Night, A 1928,Ap 17,26:4

Gay, Charles
Lady Billy 1920,D 15,18:2

Gay, Christopher
Great Big Doorstep, The 1950,Mr 18,8:6

Gay, Colette
Variations of 1940 1940,Ja 29,12:1

Gay, Dorthy
Kosher Kitty Kelly 1925,Je 16,24:2

Gay, G Hamilton (Director)
Truth Game, The 1930,D 29,19:1

Gay, G Hamilton (Scenic Designer)
Symphony in Two Flats 1930,S 17,30:4

Gay, Janet
Subway Express 1929,S 25,34:3

Gay, John
Second Best Bed 1946,Je 4,20:2
Twelfth Night 1958,D 10,54:2
Henry V 1958,D 26,2:7

Gay, John (Lyricist)
Polly 1925,O 12,19:1

Gay, John (Original Author)
Threepenny Opera, The 1928,D 2,X,4:4
Threepenny Opera, The 1933,Ap 14,22:4
Beggar's Holiday 1947,Ja 26,II,1:1
Threepenny Opera, The 1954,Mr 21,II,1:1
Threepenny Opera, The 1956,Ap 8,II,3:1

Gay, John (Playwright)
Polly 1925,O 12,19:1
Beggar's Opera, The 1934,Jl 17,24:5
Beggar's Opera, The 1940,Mr 17,X,1:8

Gay, John (Playwright)—Cont
Beggar's Opera, The 1941,Ag 12,14:6
Beggar's Opera, The 1952,S 26,17:4
Beggar's Opera, The 1957,Mr 14,35:1
Beggar's Opera, The 1965,Mr 21,II,13:1

Gay, Louise
Vaudeville (Palace) 1932,My 30,16:7

Gay, Maisie
Pins and Needles 1922,F 2,20:1
Cochran's 1930 Revue 1930,Ap 13,X,1:6

Gay, Noel (Composer)
Jack o' Diamonds 1935,F 26,17:3

Gay, Noel (Miscellaneous)
Earl Carroll's Vanities 1927,Ja 5,18:1

Gaye, Albie
I Feel Wonderful 1954,O 19,22:5
Harbor Lights 1956,O 5,20:1
Darwin's Theories 1960,O 19,53:2

Gaye, Barbara
Doodle Dandy of the U S A 1942,O 19,15:2
Peer Gynt 1951,Ja 29,15:2

Gaye, Freda
Evensong 1933,F 1,13:4

Gaye, Gregory
Through the Years 1932,Ja 29,13:3
Christopher Comes Across 1932,Je 1,19:2
Dinner at Eight 1932,O 24,18:2
Burning Deck, The 1940,Mr 2,9:2

Gayer, Anne-Marie
Temporary Island, A 1948,Mr 15,27:3
Desk Set, The 1955,O 25,36:7

Gayer, Echlin
Fair Circassian, The 1921,D 7,22:3
Exciters, The 1922,S 23,10:4
If Winter Comes 1923,Ap 3,26:1
For All of Us 1923,O 16,19:4
Stronger Than Love 1925,D 29,20:2

Gayle, Peter (Miscellaneous)
Follies of 1910, The 1960,Ja 15,37:3

Gaylen, Diana
Blossom Time 1936,Jl 29,23:1
Blossom Time 1936,Ag 30,II,5:8
Frederika 1937,F 5,16:5
Frederika 1937,Jl 28,15:2
Of Thee I Sing 1937,Ag 10,22:3
Of Thee I Sing 1937,Ag 18,14:4
I Married an Angel 1938,My 12,26:2

Gayley, Mary
Truth About Blayds, The 1922,Mr 15,22:1

Gaylor, Anna
Turlututu 1962,S 29,14:2

Gaylor, James
Spice of 1922 1922,Jl 7,12:4

Gaylor, May
Mary the 3d 1923,F 11,VII,1:1

Gaylord, Janet
Angel in the Wings 1947,D 12,36:4
Sophie 1963,Ap 16,32:1

Gaylord, William
Blood and Sand 1921,S 21,16:2

Gaynes, Edmund
Body Beautiful, The 1958,Ja 24,15:2
Bartleby 1961,Ja 25,28:1
Best Foot Forward 1963,Ap 3,43:1
Promenade 1969,Je 5,56:1

Gaynes, George
Consul, The 1950,Mr 16,41:1
Consul, The 1950,Mr 26,II,1:1
Out of This World 1950,D 22,17:3
Consul, The 1952,O 30,41:2
Wonderful Town 1953,F 26,22:3
Absalom 1956,My 17,37:2
Beggar's Opera, The 1957,Mr 14,35:1
Consul, The 1957,S 4,40:3
Mikado, The 1959,O 2,24:1
Mikado, The 1961,Ja 18,26:1
Gondoliers, The 1961,Ja 26,33:2
Brecht on Brecht 1961,N 15,52:2
Shadow of Heroes 1961,D 6,59:1
Gondoliers, The 1962,Ap 19,34:2
Can-Can 1962,My 17,32:2
Lady of the Camellias, The 1963,Mr 22,7:1
Dynamite Tonight 1964,Mr 16,36:2
Yeomen of the Guard, The 1964,Mr 19,29:2
Gondoliers, The 1964,Mr 28,14:1
Mikado, The 1965,Ap 17,11:3
Yeomen of the Guard, The 1965,Ap 22,26:1
Of Love Remembered 1967,F 20,46:5
Dynamite Tonight 1967,Mr 16,52:2

Gaynes, Kathy
Girl From Nantucket, The 1945,N 9,17:2

Gaynes, Kim
Girl From Nantucket, The 1945,N 9,17:2

Gaynes, Larry
Adding Machine, The 1956,F 10,17:1

Gaynor, Charles (Composer)
Lend an Ear 1948,D 17,38:2
Lend an Ear 1959,S 25,20:5
Show Girl 1961,Ja 13,37:1
Show Girl 1961,Ja 29,II,1:1
Lend an Ear 1969,O 29,32:1

Gaynor, Charles (Director)
Show Girl 1961,Ja 13,37:1

Gaynor, Charles (Lyricist)
Lend an Ear 1948,D 17,38:2
Lend an Ear 1959,S 25,20:5
Show Girl 1961,Ja 13,37:1
Show Girl 1961,Ja 29,II,1:1
Lend an Ear 1969,O 29,32:1
Gaynor, Charles (Playwright)
Lend an Ear 1948,D 17,38:2
Lend an Ear 1959,S 25,20:5
Show Girl 1961,Ja 13,37:1
Lend an Ear 1969,O 29,32:1
Gaynor, Gay
Hairpin Harmony 1943,O 2,18:5
Gaynor, Grace
Look After Lulu 1959,Mr 4,35:1
Gaynor, Janet
Devil's Disciple, The 1941,S 11,20:6
Gaynor, Jock (Lighting Director)
Liliom 1956,F 18,12:5
Gaynor, Mitzi
Jollyanna; Flahooley 1952,Ag 13,17:7
Gaynor, Winifred
Gypsy Fires 1925,D 8,28:3
Gaynor and Byron
Vaudeville (Palace) 1929,Jl 1,31:4
Gaythorne, Pamela
Great Broxopp, The 1921,N 16,22:1
Green Ring, The 1922,Ap 5,22:1
Pinch Hitter, A 1922,Je 2,20:4
Fool, The 1922,O 24,18:1
Shewing-Up of Blanco Posnet, The 1923,O 17,14:2
This Fine-Pretty World 1923,D 27,11:1
Gazetas, Aristides (Lighting Director)
Beautiful Jailer, The 1957,My 17,19:2
Gazetas, Aristides (Scenic Designer)
Beautiful Jailer, The 1957,My 17,19:2
Gazzara, Ben
Circle of Chalk, The 1950,D 2,8:3
End as a Man 1953,S 16,39:1
End As a Man 1953,S 27,II,1:1
Cat on a Hot Tin Roof 1955,Mr 25,18:2
Cat on a Hot Tin Roof 1955,Ap 3,II,1:1
Hatful of Rain, A 1955,N 10,44:1
Hatful of Rain, A 1955,D 4,II,1:1
Night Circus, The 1958,D 3,44:1
Strange Interlude 1963,Mr 13,5:2
Traveller Without Luggage 1964,S 18,26:2
Gazzo, Michael V
Yes is for a Very Young Man 1949,Je 7,27:2
Night Music 1951,Ap 9,29:6
Camino Real 1953,Mr 20,26:1
Gazzo, Michael V (Playwright)
Hatful of Rain, A 1955,N 10,44:1
Hatful of Rain, A 1955,D 4,II,1:1
Night Circus, The 1958,D 3,44:1
Geandreau, Louis (Playwright)
Gualtier l'Oyseau 1926,D 5,VIII,6:1
Gear, Arthur
Countess Maritza 1926,S 20,21:1
Gear, Luella
Bachelor's Night, A 1921,O 18,20:1
Elsie 1923,Ap 3,26:1
Poppy 1923,S 4,14:2
Queen High 1926,S 9,21:2
Optimists, The 1928,Ja 31,28:2
Ups-A-Daisy 1928,O 9,34:2
Gay Divorce 1932,N 13,IX,1:7
Gay Divorce 1932,N 30,23:4
Life Begins at 8:40 1934,Ag 7,20:7
Life Begins at 8:40 1934,Ag 28,24:2
Life Begins at 8:40 1934,S 2,IX,1:1
On Your Toes 1936,Ap 13,14:4
Love in My Fashion 1937,D 4,21:4
Streets of Paris, The 1939,Je 20,25:2
Streets of Paris, The 1939,Je 25,IX,1:1
Crazy With the Heat 1940,D 26,22:1
Crazy With the Heat 1941,Ja 15,18:2
Crazy With the Heat 1941,Ja 31,15:2
Pie in the Sky 1941,D 23,26:5
Count Me In 1942,O 9,24:2
That Old Devil 1944,Je 6,14:2
My Romance 1948,O 20,38:5
To Be Continued 1952,Ap 24,37:2
Sabrina Fair 1953,N 12,37:1
Sabrina Fair 1953,N 22,II,1:1
Four Winds 1957,S 26,21:2
Gearey, Dorothy
This Way to the Tomb 1961,D 9,21:1
Gearhart, William
Volpone 1967,Je 30,29:1
Gearon, John (Playwright)
De Luxe 1935,F 20,22:1
De Luxe 1935,F 24,VIII,3:4
De Luxe 1935,Mr 6,22:2
Gearon, Valerie
Tenth Man, The 1961,Ap 14,23:4
Geary, Arthur
Good Times 1920,Ag 10,10:1
Tyrant, The 1930,N 13,33:1
Marching By 1932,Mr 4,17:1
Geary, Paul
Take Her, She's Mine 1961,D 22,19:1

Gebhardt, George (Miscellaneous)
Eternal Road, The 1937,Ap 25,X,1:6
Gebirtig, Mordecai (Playwright)
Let's Sing Yiddish 1966,N 10,63:1
Gecker, Sidney (Miscellaneous)
Curate's Play, The 1961,D 18,41:3
Tableaux 1961,D 18,41:3
Geddes, Stuart R
Storm, The 1962,Mr 31,17:2
Lion in Love, The 1963,Ap 26,28:3
Geddes, Virgil (Playwright)
Earth Between, The 1929,Mr 6,33:1
Native Ground 1937,Mr 24,28:4
Geddes, Virgil (Producer)
Chalk Dust 1936,Mr 5,24:5
Geddis, John Ralph
If 1927,O 26,26:2
Gedeon, Mila
Armseligen Besenbinder, Die 1928,N 19,16:2
Gedit, Jeremy
Trigon, The 1965,O 11,62:2
Gedrgi, Mali
Italienische Nacht 1931,My 10,VIII,1:5
Gedzel, Morris
Dear Judas 1947,O 6,26:4
Gee, Anne
Duchess of Malfi, The 1962,Mr 5,27:1
Gee, Donald
Semi-Detached 1963,O 8,49:1
Gee, Lottie
Chocolate Dandies, The 1924,S 2,22:2
Geer, Ellen
School for Scandal, The 1962,Mr 19,36:1
Tavern, The 1962,Ap 5,29:1
Hamlet 1963,My 9,41:1
Miser, The 1963,My 10,39:1
Hamlet 1963,My 19,II,1:1
Three Sisters, The 1963,Je 20,30:7
Saint Joan 1964,My 14,41:1
Way of the World, The 1965,Je 2,40:1
Richard III 1965,Je 3,26:1
Cherry Orchard, The 1965,Ag 2,17:2
Skin of Our Teeth, The 1966,Je 2,51:1
As You Like It 1966,Je 4,19:1
Geer, Jack
Junior Miss 1941,N 19,28:2
Geer, Langdon
At the Theatre 1937,Ag 4,14:1
Geer, Shippen (Producer)
Fourth Avenue North 1961,S 28,50:2
Geer, Walter
Dybbuk, The 1926,D 17,27:2
Garden of Eden, The 1927,S 28,28:1
Broken Chain, The 1929,F 21,30:4
Much Ado About Nothing 1929,N 17,30:4
Geer, Will
Merry Wives of Windsor, The 1928,Mr 20,20:1
Let Freedom Ring 1935,N 7,26:2
Bury the Dead 1936,Ap 20,17:4
Prelude 1936,Ap 20,17:4
200 Were Chosen 1936,N 21,21:1
House in the Country, A 1937,Ja 12,18:3
Unto Such Glory 1937,My 7,28:2
Of Mice and Men 1937,N 24,20:5
Cradle Will Rock, The 1937,D 6,19:4
Town and Country Jig, A 1937,D 13,22:8
Cradle Will Rock, The 1938,Ja 4,19:3
Journeyman 1938,Ja 31,14:2
Washington Jitters 1938,My 3,19:1
Sing Out the News 1938,S 24,12:5
Tobacco Road 1940,D 5,32:3
More the Merrier, The 1941,S 16,19:3
Johnny on the Spot 1942,Ja 9,24:2
Comes the Revelation 1942,My 27,26:2
Moon Vine, The 1943,F 12,22:2
Sophie 1944,D 26,22:7
Flamingo Road 1946,Mr 20,18:2
On Whitman Avenue 1946,My 9,28:2
Alice Adams 1947,Ag 5,26:1
Cradle Will Rock, The 1947,D 27,11:2
Hope Is the Thing With Feathers 1948,Ap 12,24:2
Gone Tomorrow; Hope's the Thing
1948,My 12,34:6
Home Life of a Buffalo; Hope's the Thing
1948,My 12,34:6
Hope Is the Thing With Feathers; Hope's the
Thing 1948,My 12,34:6
Coriolanus 1954,Ja 20,34:2
Sea Gull, The 1954,My 12,38:1
Wisteria Trees, The 1955,F 3,20:2
Vamp, The 1955,N 11,30:1
Ponder Heart, The 1956,F 17,14:2
Hamlet 1958,Je 21,11:1
Midsummer Night's Dream, A 1958,Je 23,19:1
Winter's Tale, The 1958,Jl 21,17:4
Cock-A-Doodle Dandy 1958,N 13,39:2
Cock-A-Doodle Dandy 1958,N 23,II,1:1
Fashion 1959,Ja 21,27:1
Merry Wives of Windsor, The 1959,Jl 9,23:2
All's Well That Ends Well 1959,Ag 3,20:4
Twelfth Night 1960,Je 9,29:4
Antony and Cleopatra 1960,Ag 1,19:1
As You Like It 1961,Je 17,13:2

Geer, Will—Cont
Macbeth 1961,Je 19,31:1
School for Scandal, The 1962,Mr 19,36:1
Henry IV, Part I 1962,Je 18,20:4
Richard II 1962,Je 18,20:2
We Comrades Three 1962,O 12,26:1
110 in the Shade 1963,O 25,37:1
Evening's Frost, An 1965,O 12,56:1
We Comrades Three 1966,D 21,46:1
Horseman, Pass By 1969,Ja 16,46:4
Geery, William
Gondoliers, The 1940,O 1,29:2
Geffe, Anne
Occupe-Toi d'Amelie; Keep Your Eyes on Amelie
1952,N 25,35:2
Geffen, Freddie
All in Favor 1942,Ja 21,20:6
Geffen, Jetta
You and I 1925,O 20,29:1
Geffen, Joy
All in Favor 1942,Ja 21,20:6
Great Big Doorstep, The 1942,N 27,26:2
Calico Wedding 1945,Mr 8,18:6
Five Evenings 1963,My 10,37:3
Geffen, Roger
Bitter Tulips 1936,Mr 5,24:6
Geherin, Jean C
Joyous Season, The 1935,N 24,II,9:2
Gehlert, Gerald
Red Robe, The 1928,D 26,15:1
Gehman, Murrell
Renard 1970,Mr 25,36:4
Only Jealousy of Emer, The 1970,Mr 25,36:4
Only Jealousy of Emer, The 1970,Ap 26,II,1:3
Gertrude 1970,N 13,29:1
Carmilla 1970,D 1,61:2
Gehman, Richard (Miscellaneous)
By Hex 1956,Je 19,25:1
Gehman, Richard (Playwright)
By Hex 1956,Je 19,25:1
Gehr, Robert
Processional 1937,O 14,23:1
Gehrecke, Frank (Lyricist)
Greenwich Village U S A 1960,S 29,30:5
Gehrecke, Frank (Playwright)
Greenwich Village U S A 1960,S 29,30:5
Gehri, Alfred (Original Author)
Sixth Floor 1939,Je 11,IX,2:5
Gehrman, Lucy
Yosele the Nightingale 1949,O 21,30:4
Second Marriage 1953,O 12,30:1
Geidt, Jeremy
Alfie 1964,D 18,27:1
Rivals, The 1969,O 18,37:1
Story Theater Repertory; Saint Julian the
Hospitaler 1970,O 21,40:1
Revenger's Tragedy, The 1970,D 2,58:1
Geiger, Josef G (Producer)
Hedda Gabler 1934,Je 5,28:3
Geiger, Milton (Playwright)
This Is Edwin Booth 1958,Ag 27,32:7
Edwin Booth 1958,N 25,37:1
Edwin Booth 1958,N 30,II,1:1
Geijerstam, Gustav (Playwright)
Big Claus and Little Claus 1931,Mr 1,VIII,3:1
Geirasch, Stefan
Medal for Willie, A 1951,O 16,35:2
Geiringer, Robert
Thieves' Carnival 1955,F 2,21:1
Julius Caesar 1955,Jl 13,20:1
Tempest, The 1955,Ag 2,18:2
Macbeth 1955,O 20,42:2
I Knock at the Door 1956,Mr 19,27:5
Pictures in the Hallway 1956,My 28,23:1
Pictures in the Hallway 1956,S 17,23:2
Pictures in the Hallway 1956,S 23,II,1:1
Purple Dust 1956,D 28,15:1
Two Gentlemen of Verona 1957,Jl 23,21:5
Macbeth 1957,Ag 16,11:2
Waltz of the Toreadors, The 1958,Mr 5,37:1
Guests of the Nation 1958,My 21,40:1
Othello 1958,Jl 4,16:1
This Is Edwin Booth 1958,Ag 27,32:7
Family Reunion, The 1958,O 21,39:1
Power and the Glory, The 1958,D 12,2:7
Geis, Wayne
Kicking the Castle Down 1967,Ja 19,43:1
Me and Juliet 1970,My 15,42:1
Geison, Vivian
Romeo and Juliet 1922,D 28,20:1
Geiss, Jacob (Director)
Pioniere in Ingolstadt 1929,My 12,IX,1:8
Geiss, Tony (Composer)
Leonard Sillman's New Faces of 1968
1968,My 3,43:1
Geiss, Tony (Lyricist)
Leonard Sillman's New Faces of 1968
1968,My 3,43:1
Geist, Irvin
It Can't Happen Here 1936,O 28,30:1
Geist, Kenneth (Miscellaneous)
Happy Days 1961,S 18,36:1
Geist, Marie
Skin of Our Teeth, The 1966,Je 2,51:1

Geist, Marie—Cont
Dance of Death, The 1966,Je 3,31:1
As You Like It 1966,Je 4,19:1
Geither, David S (Scenic Designer)
Closed Room, The 1934,Jl 24,20:2
Gelasseu, Al
Daddy Come Home 1963,Ap 17,33:1
Gelatt, Charles (Costume Designer)
Moon on a Rainbow Shawl 1962,Ja 16,30:1
Gelb, James (Miscellaneous)
Once Upon a Tailor 1955,My 24,36:2
Tiger at the Gates 1955,O 4,40:1
Sleeping Prince, The 1956,N 2,31:1
Orpheus Descending 1957,Mr 22,28:1
Time Remembered 1957,N 13,41:2
Goldilocks 1958,O 13,33:1
Cold Wind and the Warm, The 1958,D 9,55:1
Flowering Cherry 1959,O 22,46:1
Invitation to a March 1960,O 31,27:2
Mandingo 1961,My 23,43:6
Milk and Honey 1961,O 11,52:1
Rainy Day in Newark, A 1963,O 23,35:1
Anyone Can Whistle 1964,Ap 6,36:1
Girl Could Get Lucky, A 1964,S 21,36:1
Amen Corner, The 1965,Ap 16,35:1
Portrait of a Queen 1968,F 29,29:1
Cry for Us All 1970,Ap 9,48:2
Gelb, Philip (Scenic Designer)
Life Is Like That 1930,D 23,24:3
Jamboree 1932,N 25,18:4
Anybody's Game 1932,D 22,21:4
Come Easy 1933,Ag 30,22:5
Halfway to Hell 1934,Ja 3,22:3
Wind and the Rain, The 1934,F 2,20:6
Geraniums in My Window 1934,O 27,20:6
Triumph 1935,O 15,18:5
Gelb, Phillip S (Director)
God, Man & You, Baby! 1963,O 30,47:1
Gelb, Phillip S (Playwright)
God, Man & You, Baby! 1963,O 30,47:1
Gelbart, Larry (Playwright)
Conquering Hero, The 1961,Ja 17,40:2
Funny Thing Happened on the Way to the Forum,
  A 1962,My 9,49:1
Funny Thing Happened on the Way to the Forum,
  A 1962,My 20,II,1:1
Funny Thing Happened on the Way to the Forum,
  A 1963,Je 2,II,1:1
Gelbart, Sima
Antigone 1967,Ja 14,18:1
Gelber, Jack (Director)
Kitchen, The 1966,Je 14,50:1
Indians 1968,Jl 9,30:2
Indians 1968,Jl 21,II,12:1
Cuban Thing, The 1968,S 25,36:2
Gelber, Jack (Playwright)
Connection, The 1959,Jl 16,30:2
Connection, The 1960,F 7,II,1:1
Connection, The 1961,F 23,30:2
Connection, The 1961,Je 16,29:1
Apple, The 1961,D 8,44:1
Apple, The 1962,Ap 20,22:1
Apple, The 1962,Ap 23,33:3
Square in the Eye 1965,My 20,54:1
Square in the Eye 1965,Je 6,II,1:1
Cuban Thing, The 1968,S 25,36:2
Gelber, Stanley Jay (Composer)
Love and Let Love 1968,Ja 4,30:1
Gelbert, Larry (Playwright)
My L A 1951,D 9,87:1
Gelbort, Gunnar (Costume Designer)
Long Day's Journey Into Night 1962,My 16,35:4
Miss Julie 1962,My 17,31:1
Geld, Gary (Composer)
Purlie 1970,Mr 16,53:1
Geleznova, Katia
Helen Goes to Troy 1944,Ap 25,17:2
Girl in Pink Tights, The 1954,Mr 6,13:2
Gelfand, Carol
Company 1970,Ap 27,40:1
Gelfer, Steven
West Side Story 1968,Je 25,32:1
Gelfman, Sam W (Producer)
I Want You 1961,S 15,29:1
Gelhausen, Herman
Beggar's Opera, The 1934,Jl 17,24:5
Gelikhovsky, Nicholas
Chauve-Souris 1929,Ja 23,20:2
Diana 1929,D 10,37:1
Gelin, Daniel
Bonheur, Impair et Passe 1964,Ja 17,23:3
Gelinas, Gratien
Henry V 1956,Je 20,27:2
Merry Wives of Windsor, The 1956,Je 21,34:4
Henry V 1956,Je 24,II,1:1
Gelinas, Gratien (Director)
Ti-Coq 1951,F 10,10:2
Gelinas, Gratien (Playwright)
Ti-Coq 1951,F 10,10:2
Gellatly, William B
Passing of the Third Floor Back, The 1924,F 8,19:4
Gellen, Audrey
Don Juan in the Russian Manner 1954,Ap 23,23:2

Gellendre, Herbert V
Scarlet Letter, The 1926,Ja 8,16:5
Trumpet Shall Sound, The 1926,D 11,15:2
Granite 1927,F 12,13:1
Much Ado About Nothing 1927,N 19,14:6
At the Gate of the Kingdom 1927,D 9,28:5
Doctor Knock 1928,F 24,15:2
Martine 1928,Ap 5,19:3
Gellendre, Herbert V (Director)
Portrait of Gilbert 1934,D 29,11:5
Edge of the Sword, The 1949,N 10,40:3
Gellendre, Herbert V (Playwright)
Tread the Green Grass 1950,Ap 21,19:4
Geller, Bruce (Lyricist)
Livin' the Life 1957,Ap 29,20:1
All in Love 1961,N 11,15:2
Geller, Bruce (Playwright)
Livin' the Life 1957,Ap 29,20:1
All in Love 1961,N 11,15:2
Geller, Evelyn
Time of Your Life, The 1939,O 26,26:2
Time of Your Life, The 1940,S 24,27:2
Geller, Joe
Nautical but Nice 1931,Ap 19,31:6
Gellhorn, Martha (Playwright)
Love Goes to Press 1946,Je 19,16:2
Love Goes to Press 1947,Ja 2,22:2
Gelli, Cesare
Rugantino 1964,F 7,34:1
Gelli, Nicholai
Hide and Seek 1934,Ag 7,20:2
Gellis, Les
Vaudeville (Palace) 1932,O 3,15:5
Gelman, Mary (Lighting Director)
Son, The 1950,Ag 16,24:6
Gemier, Firmin
Merchant of Venice, The 1921,Je 9,10:2
Homme Qui Assassina, L' 1924,N 11,20:1
Procureur Hallers, Le 1924,N 13,18:1
Homme et Ses Fantomes, L' 1924,N 14,16:1
Merchant of Venice, The 1924,N 18,23:2
Bourgeois Gentilhomme, Le 1924,N 20,21:2
Taming of the Shrew, The 1924,N 25,27:3
Parmi les Loups 1926,N 7,VIII,2:7
Client Serieux, Un 1927,Mr 27,VII,4:8
March Indienne, La 1927,Mr 27,VIII,4:8
Hundred Days 1931,N 17,31:3
Gemier, Firmin (Director)
Rain 1927,Mr 27,VII,4:8
Gemier, Firmin (Producer)
Arms and the Man 1921,Ap 10,VI,1:1
Emperor Jones, The 1923,N 18,VIII,2:8
Homme et Ses Fantomes, L' 1924,Je 29,VII,1:8
Merchant of Venice, The 1924,N 23,VIII,1:1
Hundred Days 1931,N 17,31:3
Gemignani, Rhoda
House of Bernarda Alba, The 1963,N 25,23:2
Cabaret 1969,F 2,74:2
Gemma, Iris
No Place to Be Somebody 1969,My 5,53:3
Genaro, Dave
Vaudeville (Palace) 1931,Mr 2,19:2
Genaro, John
Farewell to Arms, A 1930,S 23,30:3
Gence, Denise
Fourberies de Scapin, Les 1961,F 22,30:1
Impromptu de Versailles, L' 1961,F 22,30:1
Tartuffe 1961,Mr 1,28:1
Britannicus 1961,Mr 3,17:1
Dindon, Le 1961,Mr 8,38:1
Amphitryon 1970,F 4,38:1
Troupe Du Roi, La 1970,F 4,38:1
Femmes Savantes, Les 1970,F 14,12:1
Gendel, H
Aristocrats 1935,My 2,16:2
Haunch, Paunch and Jowl 1935,D 27,22:4
Gendell, Gary
Jimmy 1969,O 24,38:1
Gendron, Pierre
What's the Big Idea? 1926,Mr 24,20:3
Gendron, Pierre (Playwright)
Cold Feet 1923,My 22,14:2
Cold Feet 1923,My 22,14:3
Kept 1926,S 18,13:3
Gene, Juan Carlos
Projimos, Los 1966,Je 29,38:5
Genee, Richard (Miscellaneous)
Fledermaus, Die 1954,My 20,38:5
Genesko
No Foolin' 1926,Je 25,25:1
Geness, Marcy
Sniper, The 1959,O 28,40:4
Genet, Jean (Playwright)
Deathwatch 1957,Mr 7,25:4
Deathwatch 1958,O 10,34:2
Balcony, The 1960,Mr 4,21:1
Balcony, The 1960,Mr 20,II,1:1
Blacks, The 1961,My 5,23:1
Blacks, The 1961,My 14,II,1:1
Bonnes, Les 1963,S 4,34:3
Maids, The 1963,N 15,29:1
Paravents, Les 1966,Ap 22,36:3

Geneva, Alice
Green Pastures, The 1935,F 27,16:2
Genevieve
Can-Can 1959,Ag 26,25:4
Can-Can 1962,My 17,32:2
Genevrino, Louis
Fiddler on the Roof 1964,S 23,56:2
Genge, Paul
Panic 1935,Mr 16,18:4
Hamlet 1936,N 11,54:2
Journey to Jerusalem 1940,O 7,21:2
Romeo and Juliet 1951,Mr 12,21:2
Bernardine 1952,O 17,33:4
Genia, Claude
Jeune Fille a Marier, La 1970,My 6,49:1
Lacune, La 1970,My 6,49:1
Genn, Leo
Flashing Stream, The 1938,S 2,21:4
Flashing Stream, The 1939,Ap 11,19:2
Another Part of the Forest 1946,N 21,42:2
Small War on Murray Hill 1957,Ja 4,19:1
Small War on Murray Hill 1957,Ja 13,II,1:1
Hidden River, The 1959,Ap 14,41:2
Devil's Advocate, The 1961,Mr 10,20:1
Devil's Advocate, The 1961,Mr 19,II,1:1
Fair Game for Lovers 1964,F 11,43:2
Only Game in Town, The 1968,My 21,42:1
Gennaro, Peter
Pajama Game, The 1954,My 14,20:2
Pajama Game, The 1954,My 30,II,1:1
Bells Are Ringing 1956,N 29,43:4
Bells Are Ringing 1956,N 30,18:2
Gennaro, Peter (Choreographer)
Seventh Heaven 1955,My 27,16:2
West Side Story 1957,O 27,II,15:3
Fiorello! 1959,N 24,45:3
Fiorello! 1959,N 29,II,1:1
Unsinkable Molly Brown, The 1960,N 4,28:1
Mr President 1962,O 22,34:2
West Side Story 1964,Ap 9,24:2
Bajour 1964,N 24,42:1
Gennaro, Peter (Miscellaneous)
West Side Story 1957,S 27,14:4
West Side Story 1960,Ap 28,31:1
Jimmy 1969,O 24,38:1
Gennel, Paul
Immoralist, The 1963,N 8,36:2
Genovese, Gen (Lyricist)
Buttrio Square 1952,O 15,40:2
Genovese, Gen (Playwright)
Buttrio Square 1952,O 15,40:2
Genovese, Gen (Producer)
Buttrio Square 1952,O 15,40:2
Gens, Oskar (Playwright)
Spring Production 1944,My 20,12:4
Gensel, Jimmy
Cradle of Willow, A 1961,D 16,20:2
Gensel, Johnny
Cradle of Willow, A 1961,D 16,20:2
Gensler, Lewis E (Composer)
Queen O' Hearts 1922,O 11,22:1
49ers, The 1922,N 7,14:1
Be Yourself! 1924,S 4,13:3
Captain Jinks 1925,S 9,22:1
Queen High 1926,S 9,21:2
Ups-A-Daisy 1928,O 9,34:2
Gang's All Here, The 1931,F 19,21:3
Ballyhoo of 1932 1932,S 7,14:2
Gensler, Lewis E (Director)
Ballyhoo of 1932 1932,S 7,14:2
Gensler, Lewis E (Producer)
Ups-A-Daisy 1928,O 9,34:2
See Naples and Die 1929,S 27,30:4
Cross Roads 1929,N 12,34:2
Fine and Dandy 1930,S 24,26:1
Pagan Lady 1930,O 21,34:2
Rock Me, Julie 1931,Ja 4,VIII,2:3
Rock Me, Julie 1931,F 4,21:1
Gang's All Here, The 1931,F 19,21:3
Collision 1932,F 17,19:2
Ballyhoo of 1932 1932,S 7,14:2
Summer Night 1939,N 3,17:1
Genteel, Grace
Time of the Cuckoo, The 1958,O 28,40:2
Gentile, Michael
Chameleon, The 1949,F 7,16:2
Gentile, Robert
Chiaroscuro; Maggie French Understands
  1963,Je 6,40:8
Chiaroscuro; Judges, The 1963,Je 6,40:8
Chiaroscuro; Kitty, I Hardly Knew You
  1963,Je 6,40:8
Gentile, Robert (Playwright)
Chiaroscuro; Judges, The 1963,Je 6,40:8
Chiaroscuro; Maggie French Understands
  1963,Je 6,40:8
Chiaroscuro; Kitty, I Hardly Knew You
  1963,Je 6,40:8
Gentle, Alice
Vaudeville (Hippodrome) 1926,Ap 13,28:2
Gentles, Avril
Dinny and the Witches 1959,D 10,53:3
My Mother, My Father and Me 1963,Mr 25,5:5

Gentles, Avril—Cont
Route 1 1964,N 18,52:3
Wives, The 1965,My 18,35:4
Grin and Bare It 1970,Mr 17,36:1
Gentles, Avril (Scenic Designer)
Derryowen 1946,O 29,34:2
If in the Green Wood 1947,Ja 17,27:6
Gentner, Norma
Firebird of Florence 1945,Mr 23,13:4
Gentry, Alain H
Tableaux 1961,D 18,41:3
Gentry, Bob
Angels of Anadarko 1962,O 11,47:1
Gentry, Herbert
Scarlet Sister Mary 1930,N 26,19:2
Gentry, Joseph
All American 1962,Mr 20,44:1
It's a Bird . . . It's a Plane . . . It's Superman 1966,Mr 30,34:1
Gentry, Michael
All American 1962,Mr 20,44:1
It's a Bird . . . It's a Plane . . . It's Superman 1966,Mr 30,34:1
Gentry, Minnie
Junebug Graduates Tonight! 1967,F 27,35:1
Gentleman Caller, The 1969,Ap 27,92:1
Warning, The-A Theme for Linda 1969,Ap 27,92:1
Black Quartet, A; Warning, The-A Theme for Linda 1969,Jl 31,28:1
Black Quartet, A; Gentleman Caller, The 1969,Jl 31,28:1
Warning, The-A Theme for Linda 1969,Ag 3,II,1:4
Gentry Brothers
Around the World in 80 Days 1963,Je 24,22:1
Genus, Karl (Director)
Portofino 1958,F 22,8:3
Geoffrey, Madeleine
37 Sous de M Montaudoin, Les 1939,F 7,17:2
Enterrement, L' 1939,F 7,17:2
Geoffrey, Myles
Ten Million Ghosts 1936,O 24,23:7
Geoffroy, Madeleine
Voyage de Monsieur Perrichon, Le 1937,N 2,32:3
Knock 1937,N 17,26:3
Roi Cerf, Le 1937,N 30,26:3
Nationale 6 1938,Ja 11,26:6
Y'Avait un Prisonnier 1938,Ja 25,24:3
Caprice, Un 1938,F 8,17:2
Fantasio 1938,F 8,17:2
Bal des Voleurs, Le 1938,N 29,26:4
Faiseur, Le; Promoter, The 1938,D 27,12:3
Paquebot Tenacity, Le 1939,Ja 10,16:4
Chacun Sa Verite 1939,Ja 24,17:1
Siegfried 1939,F 21,15:2
Geoppinger, Susan
Ruddigore 1965,Ag 27,16:1
Georg, Rita
Evelyne 1928,F 19,VIII,2:1
Rose of Florida, The 1929,F 23,17:1
Farmer General, The 1931,Mr 31,24:8
Georgala, M
Electra 1952,N 20,38:2
Georgas, Evangeline
From Morn Till Midnight 1948,D 7,41:6
George
Are You With It? 1945,N 12,17:3
George, (Mr) (Miscellaneous)
Fun City 1968,Mr 7,53:2
George, Agnes
Dangerous Corner 1933,Jl 18,20:4
George, Alice
Poisoned Kiss, The 1937,Ap 22,19:1
George, Andrew
Vigil, The 1948,My 22,8:6
Goodbye My Fancy 1948,N 18,35:2
Caesar and Cleopatra 1949,D 22,28:2
Witness for the Prosecution 1954,D 17,35:2
George, Anthony
Front Page, The 1968,O 20,85:5
George, Betty
Heaven on Earth 1948,S 17,29:2
Ankles Aweigh 1955,Ap 19,27:1
George, Bopo
Madmen and Specialists 1970,Ag 3,38:1
George, Charles
Solitaire 1942,Ja 28,22:2
George, Charles (Composer)
Go Easy Mabel 1922,My 9,22:2
George, Charles (Lyricist)
Go Easy Mabel 1922,My 9,22:2
George, Charles (Playwright)
Go Easy Mabel 1922,My 9,22:2
Love in My Fashion 1937,D 4,21:4
George, Colin (Director)
Vatzlav 1970,Ag 23,II,1:6
George, Dwight
School for Scandal, The 1925,O 24,19:1
George, Earl
Lamp at Midnight 1947,D 22,29:2
Stevedore 1949,F 23,30:2
Skin of Our Teeth, The 1955,Ag 18,16:1
Beaver Coat, The 1956,Mr 29,22:5
Fair Game 1957,N 4,39:1
Night Is Black Bottles, The 1962,D 5,56:1

Scarlet Lullaby 1968,Mr 11,48:1
George, Edmund
Banshee, The 1927,D 6,26:2
Bellamy Trial, The 1928,Ag 20,21:1
Whispering Gallery, The 1929,F 12,22:2
Mrs Bumpstead-Leigh 1929,Ap 2,28:3
Family Affairs 1929,D 11,34:6
Milestones 1930,Je 3,27:1
Great Barrington, The 1931,F 20,18:1
After All 1931,D 4,28:4
Journey by Night, A 1935,Ap 17,26:3
Cat and the Canary, The 1935,Jl 9,24:4
Trelawney of the 'Wells' 1935,Jl 16,24:1
All This While 1935,Jl 30,17:2
Declassee 1935,Ag 6,20:3
Accent on Youth 1935,Ag 13,20:3
They Knew What They Wanted 1936,Jl 7,17:2
Octoroon, The 1936,S 1,24:2
Many Mansions 1937,Ag 3,20:5
I Know What I Like 1939,N 25,13:5
George, Edwin
Vaudeville (Palace) 1928,Jl 24,13:4
Liliom 1940,Mr 26,17:2
George, Ernest (Playwright)
Low Tide 1924,Ag 17,VII,1:8
George, Franklin
Americans in France, The 1920,Ag 4,14:1
Outrageous Mrs Palmer, The 1920,O 13,18:1
Window Shopping 1938,D 24,13:2
George, George
Patience 1924,D 30,15:1
George, George (Director)
Private Life of the Master Race, The 1945,Je 13,28:3
George, George S (Playwright)
Caviar to the General 1947,Ja 14,30:3
George, George W (Miscellaneous)
Murderous Angels 1970,F 8,70:1
George, George W (Producer)
Dylan 1964,Ja 20,18:1
Any Wednesday 1964,F 19,34:1
Ben Franklin in Paris 1964,O 28,52:1
Great Indoors, The 1966,F 2,23:1
Happily Never After 1966,Mr 11,37:1
George, Gladys
Queer People 1934,F 16,16:2
Milky Way, The 1934,My 9,23:2
Personal Appearance 1934,O 18,26:7
Lady in Waiting 1940,Mr 28,19:1
Distant City, The 1941,S 23,27:5
George, Grace
Ruined Lady, The 1920,Ja 21,10:2
Ruined Lady, The 1920,Ja 25,VIII,2:2
New Morality, The 1921,Ja 31,10:1
Marie Antoinette 1921,N 23,16:1
To Love 1922,O 18,16:2
All Alone Susie 1923,N 4,VIII,2:7
Fanshastics 1924,Ja 17,13:2
Merry Wives of Gotham 1924,Ja 27,VII,1:1
She Wanted to Know 1925,Ja 25,VII,1:4
She Had to Know 1925,F 3,25:3
She Had to Know 1925,F 8,VII,1:1
Arlene Adair 1926,Jl 4,VII,3:2
Legend of Leonora, The 1927,Mr 30,22:4
Legend of Leonora, The 1927,Ap 3,VIII,1:1
All the King's Horses 1928,Je 17,VIII,1:6
First Mrs Fraser, The 1929,N 17,IX,4:1
First Mrs Fraser, The 1929,D 30,16:2
Golden Cinderella, A 1931,O 4,VIII,2:2
Mademoiselle 1932,O 9,IX,3:6
Mademoiselle 1932,O 19,22:4
Kind Lady 1935,Ap 24,24:5
Kind Lady 1935,Ap 28,X,1:1
Difficulty of Getting Married, The 1936,Jl 7,22:1
Matrimony, PFD 1936,N 6,28:4
Matrimony, PFD 1936,N 13,26:3
Circle, The 1938,Ap 19,24:2
Billy Draws a Horse 1939,D 22,14:5
Kind Lady 1940,S 4,28:3
Spring Again 1941,O 28,28:3
Spring Again 1941,N 11,28:2
Velvet Glove, The 1949,D 27,26:2
Constant Wife, The 1951,D 10,34:3
Constant Wife, The 1951,D 16,II,6:1
George, Grace (Director)
First Mrs Fraser, The 1929,D 30,16:2
George, Grace (Playwright)
Nest, The 1922,F 2,20:1
She Wanted to Know 1925,Ja 25,VII,1:4
She Had to Know 1925,F 3,25:3
She Had to Know 1925,F 8,VII,1:1
Husband Habit, The 1929,Mr 24,X,4:7
Domino 1932,Ag 7,IX,1:1
Matrimony, PFD 1936,N 6,28:4
Matrimony, PFD 1936,N 13,26:3
George, Grace (Translator)
Domino 1932,Ag 17,13:2
Mademoiselle 1932,O 19,22:4
George, Hal (Costume Designer)
Lysistrata 1959,My 20,40:2
Antigone 1959,S 16,46:2
Eccentricities of Davy Crockett, The 1961,Ja 4,26:1
Willie the Weeper 1961,Ja 4,26:1

George, Hal (Costume Designer)—Cont
Riding Hood Revisited 1961,Ja 4,26:1
West of the Moon 1961,Je 29,26:1
Blood Bugle, The 1961,Je 29,26:1
Sing Muse 1961,D 7,52:1
Emperor, The 1963,Ap 17,30:1
Taming of the Shrew, The 1965,Je 24,32:2
Mike Downstairs 1968,Ap 19,35:1
George, Hal (Director)
We Comrades Three 1966,D 21,46:1
George, Hal (Miscellaneous)
School for Scandal, The 1966,N 22,33:2
George, Heinrich
Broadway 1928,Ap 15,IX,4:7
Karl und Anna 1929,N X,2:1
Submarine S-4 1929,My 26,IX,2:3
Nass Oder Trocken? 1929,Jl 7,VIII,2:1
Stempellbrueder 1929,N 24,X,2:4
Phaea 1930,Ag 31,VIII,2:1
Goetz von Berlichingen 1930,D 14,IX,4:1
Blaue Boll, Der 1931,Ja 25,VIII,4:1
Othello 1932,Mr 6,VIII,2:1
Mensch aus Erde Gemacht 1933,N 5,IX,3:1
George, John
King and I, The 1956,Ap 19,35:4
George, Joseph
'Toinette 1961,N 21,46:1
George, Kathleen
Sancho Panza 1923,N 27,23:1
George, Lloyd (Playwright)
God Slept Here, A 1957,F 20,38:1
George, Lloyd (Translator)
God Slept Here, A 1957,F 20,38:1
George, Mareta
Weak Sisters 1925,O 14,31:3
George, Margaret
Taming of the Shrew, The 1927,O 26,26:4
George, Mary
Dybbuk, The 1926,D 17,27:2
Pinwheel 1927,F 4,16:4
Professor Mamlock 1937,Ap 14,30:3
George, McKay
Deep Tangled Wildwood, The 1923,N 6,22:1
George, Nathan
No Place to Be Somebody 1969,My 5,53:3
No Place to Be Somebody 1969,My 18,II,1:1
No Place to Be Somebody 1969,My 18,II,22:1
No Place to Be Somebody 1969,D 31,17:1
George, Paul
Maitresse de Roi 1926,D 1,24:1
George, Phillip
Vie Parisienne, La 1945,Ja 13,14:5
George, Ray
It's Up to You 1921,Mr 29,20:1
George, Richard (Miscellaneous)
And Life Burns On 1938,Jl 31,IX,1:4
George, Rita
Zarewitsch, Der 1927,Ap 3,VIII,2:1
George, Russell
Sleepy Hollow 1948,Je 4,26:3
George, Stephen
Mourners' Bench, The 1950,S 22,35:7
George, Steven
Listen to the Quiet 1958,O 28,40:2
George, Theodore
Little Glass Clock, The 1956,Mr 27,40:2
George, Theseus
Night of the Iguana, The 1961,D 29,10:1
George, Vaughn
War and Peace 1942,My 22,26:3
Winter Soldiers 1942,N 30,19:2
George, Walter
Mikado, The 1944,F 12,11:3
Ruddigore 1944,Mr 3,19:5
Yeomen of the Guard, The 1944,Mr 5,34:3
George, William
Short Cut, The 1930,Ja 28,28:2
George, Yvonne
Greenwich Village Follies 1922,S 13,18:2
Night in Paris, A 1926,Ja 6,16:3
Montmarte aux Nues 1926,O 3,VIII,2:1
George, Zelma
Medium, The 1950,Jl 20,22:5
Medium, The 1950,S 3,II,1:1
George and Betty
Singin' the Blues 1931,S 17,21:3
George Sisters, The
Scandals 1924,Jl 1,16:1
Allez-Opp! 1927,Ag 3,29:3
Georges, Mr
Trois Jeunes Filles Nues; Three Young Maids From the Folies Bergere 1929,Mr 5,28:2
Georgie, Leyla
What Price Glory 1924,S 6,14:3
Evensong 1933,F 1,13:4
Georgie, Leyla (Playwright)
$25 an Hour 1933,My 11,14:4
I Must Love Someone 1939,F 8,18:7
Georgievskaya, Anastasiya
Kremlin Chimes 1965,F 25,23:1
Georginna, Lillie
Fatal Wedding, The 1924,Je 3,22:3
Georgiou, Despina
Electra 1930,D 27,16:1

Georgiou, Paul
Che! 1969,Mr 24,56:1
Georgiou, Vilma
Consul, The 1952,O 30,41:2
Georgoussopoulos, K
Electra 1961,S 20,23:4
Choephori 1961,S 27,32:4
Gephart, Starr
Road to Rio, The 1930,My 7,25:1
Geraci, Frank
Mr Grossman 1964,My 6,43:1
End of All Things Natural, The 1969,S 12,38:1
Geraci, Frank (Miscellaneous)
Color of Darkness: An Evening in the World of
James Purdy; You Reach for Your Hat
1963,O 1,34:1
Color of Darkness: An Evening in the World of
James Purdy; Cracks 1963,O 1,24:1
Color of Darkness: An Evening in the World of
James Purdy; Encore 1963,O 1,34:1
Color of Darkness: An Evening in the World of
James Purdy; Don't Call Me By My Right Name
1963,O 1,34:1
Color of Darkness: An Evening in the World of
James Purdy; Sermon 1963,O 1,34:1
Color of Darkness: An Evening in the World of
James Purdy; Everything Under the Sun
1963,O 1,34:1
Mr Grossman 1964,My 6,43:1
Dark Corners 1964,My 6,43:1
Geraghty, B J
Orpheus Descending 1959,O 6,45:2
Time to Go 1960,Mr 23,33:1
Gerald, Ara
Great Temptations, The 1926,My 19,29:1
Congai 1928,N 28,24:3
Uncle Vanya 1929,My 25,17:1
Her Friend the King 1929,O 8,34:5
Even in Egypt 1930,Ja 19,VIII,2:6
Joseph 1930,F 13,25:3
Virtue's Bed 1930,Ap 16,26:5
She Lived Next to the Firehouse 1931,F 11,23:1
Fata Morgana 1931,D 26,15:3
Passionate Pilgrim, The 1932,O 20,24:3
Four O'Clock 1933,F 14,19:6
Little Ol' Boy 1933,Ap 25,15:5
Ghost Writer, The 1933,Je 20,22:4
Gods We Make, The 1934,Ja 4,16:4
Pure in Heart, The 1934,Mr 21,24:3
Few Are Chosen 1935,S 18,19:3
Mimie Scheller 1936,O 1,28:4
Curtain Call 1937,Ap 23,24:7
I Am Different 1938,Ag 28,IX,2:5
Gerald, Charles
Liliom 1956,F 18,12:5
Comedian, The 1956,O 18,36:4
Desert Incident, A 1959,Mr 25,40:1
Ignorants Abroad, The 1960,My 24,43:2
One Way Pendulum 1961,S 19,38:2
Darling of the Day 1968,Ja 29,26:2
Gerald, Florence
Innocent Idea, An 1920,My 26,9:4
Immodest Violet 1920,Ag 25,6:2
Within Four Walls 1923,Ap 18,24:1
Shame Woman, The 1923,O 17,14:1
Rat, The 1925,F 11,19:3
Lily Sue 1926,N 17,22:2
Barker, The 1927,Ja 19,20:6
Heaven-Tappers, The 1927,Mr 9,28:3
Maya 1928,F 22,19:1
Wild Birds 1929,Je 23,VIII,2:3
Saint Wench 1933,Ja 3,19:3
Valley Forge 1934,D 11,28:3
Gerald, Kenneth
Building 222 1950,F 3,28:2
Gerald, May
Six Characters in Search of an Author
1931,Ap 16,29:2
Crucible 1933,S 5,22:4
Green Stick 1934,O 10,21:2
Gerald, Robert
Founders, The 1957,My 14,39:1
Gerald, William
Mad Honeymoon, The 1923,Ag 8,10:1
Bottled 1928,Ap 11,25:1
Geraldo, Gerry (Miscellaneous)
Homecoming, The 1967,Ja 6,29:1
Geraldy, Paul (Playwright)
Nest, The 1922,F 2,20:1
To Love 1922,O 18,16:2
She Wanted to Know 1925,Ja 25,VII,1:4
She Had to Know 1925,F 3,25:3
She Had to Know 1925,F 8,VII,1:1
Noces d'Argent, Les 1928,Ap 8,VIII,4:1
Homme de Joie, L' 1929,Mr 17,X,2:7
Bryllupsdager; Noces d'Argent, Les
1930,D 28,VIII,3:5
Christine 1932,N 27,IX,3:2
Do, Mi, Sol, Do 1935,F 3,VIII,3:3
Son Mari 1936,Ap 17,17:3
Si Je Voulais; If I Wished to 1937,Ja 28,22:5
Gerard, Barney (Director)
What Does the Public Want? 1923,Jl 16,14:3

Gerard, Ben
By Jupiter 1967,Ja 20,28:2
Gerard, Carl
Honor Be Damned! 1927,Ja 27,13:1
Gerard, Charles
Yellow Jack 1934,Mr 7,22:6
Gerard, Douglas
Scorpion, The 1933,N 28,28:4
Gerard, Eddie
No Other Girl 1924,Ag 14,10:4
Gerard, Emanuel
Merry Wives of Windsor, The 1954,F 17,27:1
Gerard, Harry
Young American, A 1946,Ja 18,14:5
Gerard, J N
Front Page, The 1937,N 12,27:2
Gerard, James
H M S Pinafore 1944,F 15,14:4
Yeomen of the Guard, The 1944,Mr 5,34:3
Gerard, John
Expressing Willie 1924,Ap 17,22:1
Young Woodley 1925,N 3,34:1
Play's the Thing, The 1926,N 4,25:1
Dantons Tod 1927,D 21,28:3
Greatest Show on Earth, The 1938,Ja 6,22:2
Fifth Column, The 1940,Mr 7,18:2
Suds in Your Eye 1944,Ja 13,15:5
Gerard, John (Playwright)
Princess Turandot 1937,Ag 3,20:5
Gerard, Ken
Aria Da Capo 1950,My 25,36:2
Gerard, Louise
Dear Judas 1947,O 6,26:4
Gerard, Philippe (Composer)
Folies Bergere 1964,Je 3,36:1
Gerard, Rolf
Robin Hood 1935,Jl 15,20:6
Gerard, Rolf (Costume Designer)
That Lady 1949,N 23,18:4
Caesar and Cleopatra 1949,D 22,28:2
Love of Four Colonels, The 1953,Ja 16,17:2
Strong Are Lonely, The 1953,S 30,38:3
Fighting Cock, The 1959,D 9,57:3
Irma la Douce 1960,S 30,31:2
Gerard, Rolf (Scenic Designer)
That Lady 1949,N 23,18:4
Caesar and Cleopatra 1949,D 22,28:2
Evening With Beatrice Lillie, An 1952,O 3,17:2
Love of Four Colonels, The 1953,Ja 16,17:2
Strong Are Lonely, The 1953,S 30,38:3
Fighting Cock, The 1959,D 9,57:3
Irma la Douce 1960,S 30,31:2
Tovarich 1963,Mr 20,5:1
Gerard, Rosemonde (Playwright)
Accordeur, L' 1928,D 30,VIII,1:3
Gerard, Sumner Jr
Variations of 1940 1940,Ja 29,12:1
Gerard, Teddy
Midnight Frolic 1920,Ag 4,7:1
Rat, The 1925,F 11,19:3
Geray, Steven
Folies Bergere 1939,D 25,28:2
Eurydice 1948,O 17,I,67:4
Gerber, Alex (Lyricist)
Poor Little Ritz Girl 1920,Jl 29,7:1
Gerber, Billie
Murray Anderson's Almanac 1929,Ag 15,20:3
Gerber, Ella (Director)
Design For A Stained Glass Window
1950,Ja 24,26:2
Dial 'M' for Murder 1958,F 8,12:2
Tiger Rag, The 1961,F 17,20:2
Gerber, Ella (Miscellaneous)
Porgy and Bess 1965,Mr 6,17:1
Gerber, Jay
Annie Get Your Gun 1957,Mr 9,15:5
Caucasian Chalk Circle, The 1961,N 1,35:1
Toy for the Clowns, A 1962,S 13,31:2
Wretched the Lionhearted 1962,S 13,31:2
Jonah! 1967,S 22,52:2
Jumping Fool, The 1970,F 10,53:1
Gerbidon, Marcel (Playwright)
French Doll, The 1922,F 21,20:2
Hotel Mouse, The 1922,Mr 14,11:3
Goldfish, The 1922,Ap 18,15:3
Monsieur de Cleopatre, Le 1927,Ja 16,VII,2:1
Enlevement, L' 1927,O 2,VIII,2:4
Coiffeur Pour Dames 1928,Ja 1,VIII,2:3
Excelsior 1928,S 30,IX,1:3
Amoureuse Aventure, L' 1929,F 10,IX,4:6
Fleurs de Luxe 1930,Mr 23,IX,2:1
Gerbino, Vincent
Night Remembers, The 1934,N 28,24:3
Gerc, Gaby
Across the Board on Tomorrow Morning
1942,Mr 21,13:5
Theatre of the Soul 1942,Mr 21,13:5
Gerdago (Costume Designer)
Eisrevue 1969,O 23,55:1
Gerdesmann, Karl-Heinz
Why Do I Deserve This? 1966,Ja 19,31:2

Gerdt, Zinovy
Obratsov Russian Pupper Theater in an Unusual
Concert 1963,O 3,28:1
Aladdin and His Wonderful Lamp 1963,O 21,39:1
Gerdt, Zinovy (Playwright)
Obratsov Russian Pupper Theater in an Unusual
Concert 1963,O 3,28:1
Gerety, Anne
All the King's Men 1963,Jl 12,12:1
Gerety, Peter
In the Summer House 1964,Mr 26,43:1
Brother to Dragons 1968,D 8,86:1
Gergely, Eliz
No More Blondes 1920,Ja 8,22:1
Just Married 1921,Ap 27,21:1
Nine Till Six 1930,S 29,17:2
Student Prince, The 1931,Ja 30,18:1
Gerguson, Harry F
Vaudeville (Palace) 1933,Ja 16,13:2
Gericke, Eugene
Sunup to Sundown 1938,F 2,14:3
30 Days Hath September 1938,O 1,10:5
Where Do We Go From Here? 1938,N 16,26:2
Gering, Marion (Director)
So Am I 1928,Ja 28,9:1
Skidding 1928,My 22,18:5
Solitaire 1929,Mr 13,28:3
Tired Business Man, The 1929,Je 5,32:5
Broken Dishes 1929,N 6,28:3
Lost Sheep 1930,My 6,33:2
Bad Girl 1930,O 3,30:2
Tapestry in Gray 1935,D 28,10:2
Plan M 1942,F 21,15:2
Walking Gentleman, The 1942,My 8,26:2
Gering, Marion (Miscellaneous)
Lost Sheep 1930,My 6,33:2
Gering, Marion (Producer)
Skidding 1928,My 22,18:5
Broken Dishes 1929,N 6,28:3
Walking Gentleman, The 1942,My 8,26:2
Gering, Marion (Translator)
Ragged Edge, The 1927,F 13,VII,1:4
Gerken, Ted (Producer)
Mrs Kimball Presents 1944,Mr 1,17:3
Gerlach, Fritz
Iron Men 1936,O 20,30:6
Gerlach, Ginger
Great Scot! 1965,N 12,56:3
Gerlette, Anne
Crime and Punishment 1935,Ja 23,20:3
Bridal Crown, The 1938,F 7,11:2
Case of Youth, A 1940,Mr 25,10:3
Lady of Larkspur Lotion, The 1949,Jl 9,9:2
Hortense, to Bed With You 1949,Jl 9,9:2
Happy Journey to Trenton and Camden, The
1949,Jl 9,9:2
Germain, Bill
Poupees de Paris, Les 1962,D 13,8:2
Germain, Stuart
Desire Under the Elms 1951,N 22,45:1
Anastasia 1954,D 30,13:1
Well of the Saints, The 1959,Ap 11,15:4
Who's Happy Now? 1969,N 18,39:1
German, Lucy
Naomi 1920,My 7,12:2
Andersh; New Worlds 1922,S 26,18:2
One Woman 1931,D 14,16:4
In a Tenement House 1932,Ja 25,20:4
Pioneers 1932,F 26,22:5
Wedding Chains 1932,Mr 28,10:5
Worlds Apart 1941,Ja 23,19:3
German, Misha
Green Fields 1920,Mr 26,11:2
Fortune 1920,Ap 22,11:3
Andersh; New Worlds 1922,S 26,18:2
One Woman 1931,D 14,16:4
In a Tenement House 1932,Ja 25,20:4
Pioneers 1932,F 26,22:5
Wedding Chains 1932,Mr 28,10:5
German, Misha (Producer)
One Woman 1931,D 14,16:4
Wedding Chains 1932,Mr 28,10:5
Germanova, Maria
Three Sisters, The 1930,Ja 9,22:2
Glass of Water, A 1930,Mr 6,16:3
Germanova, Maria (Director)
Three Sisters, The 1930,Ja 9,22:2
Glass of Water, A 1930,Mr 6,16:3
Germanova, Maria (Miscellaneous)
Brothers Karamazov, The; Cherry Orchard, The
1928,My 6,IX,2:4
Poverty Is No Crime 1928,Je 3,VIII,2:1
Germonde, Perle
Florodora 1920,Ap 6,18:1
Dancing Girl, The 1923,Ja 25,16:2
Gernaat, Jan
Venice Preserv'd 1955,D 13,54:4
Shadow Years, The 1957,Ja 9,26:2
Gernau, Mischa
Mute, The 1920,Ap 9,11:4

Gernet, Nina (Playwright)
Aladdin and His Wonderful Lamp 1963,O 21,39:1
Gernhardt, Willard G (Producer)
Allure 1934,O 30,22:6
Baby Pompadour 1934,D 28,24:2
Gero, Frank
Major Barbara 1956,O 31,27:1
Geranium Hat, The 1959,Mr 18,45:1
Gero, Frank (Miscellaneous)
Abe Lincoln in Illinois 1963,Ja 23,5:2
Don't Shoot Mable It's Your Husband
1968,O 23,34:1
Gero, Frank (Producer)
Dear Liar 1962,Mr 19,36:1
Gero, Jason
Queen and the Rebels, The 1965,F 26,16:1
Hunting the Jingo Birds 1965,Mr 26,27:1
Geroge, George Bergen
Floriani's Wife 1923,O 1,10:1
Gerold, Hermann
Unwritten Chapter, The 1920,O 12,18:1
Gerome, Raymond
Britannicus 1958,N 29,17:2
Gerome, Raymond (Director)
Britannicus 1958,N 29,17:2
Second String, A 1960,Ap 14,36:2
Phedre 1963,O 21,39:1
Gerould, Dan (Playwright)
Candaules, Commissioner 1970,My 29,15:1
Gerould, Florence
Man's Estate 1929,Ap 2,28:2
Geroule (Playwright)
Quand Je Voudrais 1924,Je 29,VII,1:8
Gerr, Walter
Power of Darkness, The 1920,Ja 22,22:1
Gerrard, Alfred
Sally, Irene and Mary 1922,S 5,21:2
Betty Lee 1924,D 26,18:2
Gerrard, Charles
World Waits, The 1933,O 26,22:5
Puritan, The 1936,Ja 24,14:3
Plan M 1942,F 21,15:2
Catherine Was Great 1944,Ag 3,16:1
Gioconda Smile, The 1950,O 9,21:2
Gerrard, Gene
Desert Song, The 1927,My 8,VII,1:5
Gerrick, Ruth
Little Poor Man, The 1925,Ag 6,14:1
Gerringer, Robert
Beaux' Stratagem, The 1959,F 25,35:4
Andersonville Trial, The 1959,D 30,15:1
Under Milk Wood 1961,Mr 30,25:1
Long Voyage Home, The 1961,D 5,49:1
Tristram 1962,O 29,36:1
Taming of the Shrew, The 1963,Mr 8,9:1
Flea in Her Ear, A 1969,O 4,25:1
Flea in Her Ear, A 1969,O 12,II,9:1
Wars of the Roses, The (Part I) 1970,Jl 2,30:1
Wars of the Roses, The (Part II) 1970,Jl 3,15:1
Richard III 1970,Jl 4,11:1
Henry VI, Parts I, II, III 1970,Jl 5,II,3:1
Gerrish, Paul
Murder at the Vanities 1933,S 13,22:4
Gerrits, Paul
All in Fun 1940,D 28,11:2
Gerrity, Maggie
Journey With Strangers, A 1958,N 27,53:1
Gerron, Kurt
Threepenny Opera, The 1928,D 2,X,4:4
Front Page, The 1929,Jl 14,IX,2:1
Gerry, Alexander
Seventeen 1926,My 1,10:1
Gerry, Alexander (Playwright)
Penal Law 2010 1930,Ap 19,14:2
Gerry, Alexander (Producer)
Penal Law 2010 1930,Ap 19,14:2
Gerry, Arthur
Prelude to Exile 1936,N 22,XI,3:2
Prelude to Exile 1936,D 1,31:1
Gerry, Roger
Panama Hattie 1940,O 31,28:2
Gerry, Virginia
Speaking of Murder 1956,D 20,37:1
Gersene, Claude
Fighting Cock, The 1959,D 9,57:3
Behind the Wall 1960,N 1,47:1
First Love 1961,D 26,20:2
Come Out, Carlo! 1962,My 4,27:2
Aqua Carnival 1962,Je 29,15:1
Call It Virtue 1963,Mr 28,8:2
Gersene, Georges D (Producer)
Time, Place and the Girl, The 1942,O 22,24:3
Gershe, Leonard
Canteen Show, The 1942,S 4,18:1
Gershe, Leonard (Composer)
Alive and Kicking 1950,Ja 18,25:5
Gershe, Leonard (Lyricist)
Alive and Kicking 1950,Ja 18,25:5
Gershe, Leonard (Playwright)
Destry Rides Again 1959,Ap 24,24:1
Butterflies Are Free 1969,O 22,30:1
Butterflies Are Free 1969,N 2,II,1:1
Butterflies Are Free 1970,N 5,60:4

Butterflies Are Free 1970,D 3,60:2
Gershenson, M (Playwright)
Light, Lively and Yiddish 1970,O 28,58:1
Gershenzwitz, Morris
Mikado, The 1939,Mr 11,15:6
Gershick, William
Winners and Losers 1947,F 27,27:2
Our Lan' 1947,Ap 19,11:2
Gershwin, Arthur (Composer)
Lady Says Yes, A 1945,Ja 11,18:5
Gershwin, Dolly
Lower Depths, The 1956,O 3,29:2
Gershwin, Frances
Americana 1928,O 31,28:2
Vaudeville (Palace) 1929,O 14,20:4
Gershwin, George
Spring Tonic 1936,My 11,16:1
Gershwin, George (Composer)
Scandals 1920,Je 8,9:1
George White's Scandals 1921,Jl 12,14:1
George White's Scandals 1922,Ag 29,10:1
Our Nell 1922,D 5,24:1
George White's Scandals 1923,Je 19,22:5
Sweet Little Devil 1924,Ja 22,15:4
Scandals 1924,Jl 1,16:1
Lady Be Good 1924,D 2,23:4
Tell Me More 1925,Ap 14,27:3
Tip-Toes 1925,D 29,20:2
Song of the Flame 1925,D 11,26:4
Song of the Flame 1925,D 31,10:2
Americana 1926,Jl 27,15:3
Oh, Kay! 1926,N 9,31:3
Funny Face 1927,N 23,28:2
Rosalie 1927,D 18,IX,2:3
Rosalie 1928,Ja 11,26:3
Treasure Girl 1928,O 21,IX,2:1
Treasure Girl 1928,N 9,22:1
Funny Face 1928,N 9,22:3
Show Girl 1929,Jl 3,19:3
Show Girl 1929,Ag 25,VIII,1:1
Strike Up the Band 1929,D 29,VIII,4:3
Strike Up the Band 1930,Ja 15,29:1
Nine Fifteen Revue, The 1930,F 12,26:2
Girl Crazy 1930,O 15,27:1
Girl Crazy 1930,D 28,VIII,1:1
Of Thee I Sing 1931,D 13,VIII,2:4
Of Thee I Sing 1931,D 28,20:1
Of Thee I Sing 1932,My 8,VIII,1:1
Pardon My English 1932,D 11,IX,5:2
Pardon My English 1933,Ja 21,11:4
Let 'Em Eat Cake 1933,O 3,26:5
Let 'Em Eat Cake 1933,O 23,18:1
Let 'Em Eat Cake 1933,N 12,IX,1:1
Porgy and Bess 1935,O 1,27:2
Porgy and Bess 1935,O 11,30:2
Porgy and Bess 1935,O 20,XI,7:1
Porgy and Bess 1936,F 2,IX,1:3
Of Thee I Sing 1937,Ag 10,22:3
Of Thee I Sing 1937,Ag 18,14:4
Porgy and Bess 1942,Ja 23,16:2
Porgy and Bess 1942,F 1,IX,1:1
Porgy and Bess 1943,S 14,26:2
Porgy and Bess 1944,F 8,13:2
Porgy and Bess 1945,Je 17,II,4:3
Of Thee I Sing 1952,My 6,34:2
Of Thee I Sing 1952,My 11,II,1:1
Porgy and Bess 1952,S 8,18:2
Porgy and Bess 1952,S 18,36:5
Porgy and Bess 1952,O 10,21:4
Porgy and Bess 1953,F 17,21:1
Porgy and Bess 1953,Mr 10,25:5
Porgy and Bess 1953,Mr 15,II,1:1
Porgy and Bess 1954,Jl 15,24:2
Porgy and Bess 1954,S 23,42:6
Porgy and Bess 1954,D 17,36:7
Porgy and Bess 1954,D 22,30:2
Porgy and Bess 1955,Ja 13,31:1
Porgy and Bess 1955,Ja 21,19:6
Porgy and Bess 1955,F 8,23:4
Porgy and Bess 1955,F 16,26:4
Porgy and Bess 1955,F 23,23:8
Porgy and Bess 1955,Ap 22,20:6
Porgy and Bess 1955,Jl 9,9:5
Porgy and Bess 1955,Ag 5,14:5
Porgy and Bess 1956,Ja 11,36:1
Porgy and Bess 1956,Ja 15,II,3:1
Rosalie 1957,Je 26,28:2
Oh, Kay! 1960,Ap 18,37:2
Porgy and Bess 1965,O 20,53:3
Of Thee I Sing 1969,Mr 8,19:1
Gershwin, George (Director)
Of Thee I Sing 1952,My 11,II,1:1
Gershwin, George (Lyricist)
Nine Fifteen Revue, The 1930,F 12,26:2
Rhapsody in Black 1931,My 5,33:2
Show Is On, The 1937,S 20,18:4
Gershwin, George (Musical Director)
Rhapsody in Black 1931,My 5,33:2
Gershwin, George (Playwright)
Broadway Brevities, 1920 1920,S 30,12:2
Porgy and Bess 1961,My 18,40:1
Porgy and Bess 1964,My 7,32:1
Porgy and Bess 1965,Mr 6,17:1

Gershwin, Ira (Lyricist)
Be Yourself! 1924,S 4,13:3
Lady Be Good 1924,D 2,23:4
Tell Me More 1925,Ap 14,27:3
Tip-Toes 1925,D 29,20:2
Americana 1926,Jl 27,15:3
Oh, Kay! 1926,N 9,31:3
Funny Face 1927,N 23,28:2
Rosalie 1928,Ja 11,26:3
Treasure Girl 1928,N 9,22:1
Funny Face 1928,N 9,22:3
Show Girl 1929,Jl 3,19:3
Strike Up the Band 1929,D 29,VIII,4:3
Strike Up the Band 1930,Ja 15,29:1
Nine Fifteen Revue, The 1930,F 12,26:2
Garrick Gaieties 1930,Je 5,29:2
Girl Crazy 1930,O 15,27:1
Girl Crazy 1930,D 28,VIII,1:1
Of Thee I Sing 1931,D 13,VIII,2:4
Of Thee I Sing 1931,D 28,20:1
Of Thee I Sing 1932,My 8,VIII,1:1
Pardon My English 1933,Ja 21,11:4
Let 'Em Eat Cake 1933,O 3,26:5
Let 'Em Eat Cake 1933,O 23,18:1
Let 'Em Eat Cake 1933,N 12,IX,1:1
Life Begins at 8:40 1934,Ag 28,24:2
Porgy and Bess 1935,O 1,27:2
Porgy and Bess 1935,O 11,30:2
Ziegfeld Follies 1936,Ja 31,17:2
Ziegfeld Follies 1936,S 15,37:1
Of Thee I Sing 1937,Ag 10,22:3
Show Is On, The 1937,S 20,18:4
Lady in the Dark 1940,D 31,18:6
Lady in the Dark 1941,Ja 5,IX,1:7
Lady in the Dark 1941,Ja 24,14:2
Lady in the Dark 1941,S 3,26:6
Porgy and Bess 1942,Ja 23,16:2
Porgy and Bess 1942,F 1,IX,1:1
Lady in the Dark 1943,Mr 1,14:2
Porgy and Bess 1943,S 14,26:2
Porgy and Bess 1944,F 8,13:2
Firebird of Florence 1945,Mr 23,13:4
Park Avenue 1946,N 5,31:2
Porgy and Bess 1950,N 26,II,7:8
Lady in the Dark 1952,Mr 8,11:3
Of Thee I Sing 1952,My 6,34:2
Of Thee I Sing 1952,My 11,II,1:1
Porgy and Bess 1953,F 17,21:1
Porgy and Bess 1953,Mr 10,25:5
Porgy and Bess 1954,Jl 15,24:2
Porgy and Bess 1954,S 23,42:6
Porgy and Bess 1954,D 17,36:7
Porgy and Bess 1954,D 22,30:2
Porgy and Bess 1955,Ja 13,31:1
Porgy and Bess 1955,Ja 21,19:6
Porgy and Bess 1955,F 8,23:4
Porgy and Bess 1955,F 16,26:4
Porgy and Bess 1955,F 23,23:8
Porgy and Bess 1955,Ap 22,20:6
Porgy and Bess 1955,Jl 9,9:5
Porgy and Bess 1955,Ag 5,14:5
Rosalie 1957,Je 26,28:2
Oh, Kay! 1960,Ap 18,37:2
Porgy and Bess 1964,My 7,32:1
Porgy and Bess 1965,Mr 6,17:1
Porgy and Bess 1965,O 20,53:3
Harold Arlen Songbook, The 1967,Mr 1,48:1
Of Thee I Sing 1969,Mr 8,19:1
Whores, Wars & Tin Pan Alley 1969,Je 17,37:1
Gershwin, Ira (Miscellaneous)
Two Weeks With Pay 1940,Je 25,28:3
Gershwin, Ira (Playwright)
Life Begins at 8:40 1934,Ag 28,24:2
Porgy and Bess 1961,My 18,40:1
Gerson, Betty Lou (Miscellaneous)
Ice Capades 1960,S 1,30:1
Gerson, Eva
High Named Today 1954,D 11,11:2
Gerson, Hal
Joy to the World 1948,Mr 19,28:2
Gerson, Hal (Director)
Lend an Ear 1948,D 17,38:2
Gerson, Joe
Camels Are Coming, The 1931,O 3,20:4
Gerson, Theresa
Gypsy Baron, The 1942,Je 20,8:5
Gypsy Baron, The 1942,Ag 7,12:4
Beggar Student, The 1942,S 26,11:4
Gerstad, John
Othello 1943,O 20,18:1
Not for Children 1951,F 14,35:2
Male Animal, The 1952,My 1,35:1
Male Animal, The 1952,My 18,II,1:1
Trial of Lee Harvey Oswald, The 1967,N 6,64:1
Come Summer 1969,Mr 19,43:1
Oklahoma! 1969,Je 24,37:1
Penny Wars, The 1969,O 16,52:1
Gerstad, John (Director)
Seven Year Itch, The 1952,N 21,21:2
Wayward Saint, The 1955,F 18,17:1
Debut 1956,F 23,32:1
Double in Hearts 1956,O 17,41:7
Howie 1958,S 18,35:2

Gerstad, John (Director)—Cont
Play That on Your Old Piano 1965,O 15,49:1
Gerstad, John (Miscellaneous)
Greatest Man Alive!, The 1957,My 9,37:2
Redhead 1959,F 6,21:1
Captains and the Kings, The 1962,Ja 3,25:2
Gerstad, John (Playwright)
When the Bough Breaks 1950,Mr 9,25:5
Gerstad, John (Producer)
Howie 1958,S 18,35:2
Gerstein, E L (Playwright)
Four in Hand 1923,S 7,10:2
Gerstein, Robert
Whistling Wizard and the Sultan of Tuffet 1970,F 1,70:1
Gersten, Bernard
Hamlet 1968,Jl 4,15:1
Gersten, Bernard (Director)
Untitled-Poetry Reading 1967,Jl 18,29:1
Gersten, Bernard (Lighting Director)
World of Sholom Aleichem, The 1953,S 12,13:2
Gersten, Bernard (Miscellaneous)
Time to Go 1952,My 8,35:6
Hall of Healing 1952,My 8,35:6
Bedtime Story 1952,My 8,35:6
Brigadoon 1957,Mr 28,37:1
Edwin Booth 1958,N 25,37:1
Legend of Lizzie, The 1959,F 10,39:1
Merry Wives of Windsor, The 1959,Jl 9,23:2
Roman Candle 1960,F 4,34:2
Do Re Mi 1960,D 27,23:2
Much Ado About Nothing 1961,Jl 7,17:1
Arturo Ui 1963,N 12,49:1
Midsummer Night's Dream, A 1964,Je 30,23:2
Coriolanus 1965,Jl 15,23:1
Troilus and Cressida 1965,Ag 13,17:1
All's Well That Ends Well 1966,Je 17,39:1
Comedy of Errors, The 1967,Je 15,58:4
Hair 1967,O 30,55:1
Memorandum, The 1968,My 6,55:1
Henry IV, Part I 1968,Je 30,54:7
Romeo and Juliet 1968,Ag 16,19:1
Huui, Huui 1968,N 25,58:1
Cities in Bezique; Beast's Story, A 1969,Ja 13,26:1
Cities in Bezique; Owl Answers, The 1969,Ja 13,26:1
Invitation to a Beheading 1969,Mr 18,36:1
No Place to Be Somebody 1969,My 5,53:3
Peer Gynt 1969,Jl 17,56:1
Twelfth Night 1969,Ag 14,29:2
Sambo 1969,D 22,42:1
No Place to Be Somebody 1969,D 31,17:1
Mod Donna 1970,My 4,48:1
Wars of the Roses, The (Part I) 1970,Jl 2,30:1
Wars of the Roses, The (Part II) 1970,Jl 3,15:1
Richard III 1970,Jl 4,11:1
Sambo 1970,Jl 23,24:1
Happiness Cage, The 1970,O 5,56:4
Trelawny of the 'Wells' 1970,O 12,48:1
Jack MacGowran in the Works of Samuel Beckett 1970,N 20,32:1
Gersten, Bernard (Producer)
Henry IV, Part II 1968,Jl 2,33:1
Gersten, Berta
Andersh; New Worlds 1922,S 26,18:2
Tenth Commandment, The 1926,N 18,27:1
Gardener's Dog, The 1927,O 21,27:1
Gold Diggers, The 1927,D 3,19:2
On Foreign Soil 1927,D 24,8:2
Alexander Pushkin 1928,Ja 27,14:2
Jew Suss 1929,O 19,22:3
Angels on Earth 1929,D 11,34:7
Roaming Stars 1930,Ja 25,12:2
Untitled-Benefit 1933,Ja 25,13:3
Jacques Bergson 1936,O 31,24:6
Jacques Bergson 1936,N 29,XII,3:3
Water Carrier, The 1936,D 25,20:2
Borderline 1937,F 10,18:6
Warson at Night 1938,Ja 31,14:3
Three Cities 1938,O 11,20:3
Yoshe Kalb 1939,F 6,9:2
Day of Judgement, The 1941,O 9,27:3
Doctor Herzl 1945,D 21,25:4
Yosele the Nightingale 1949,O 21,30:4
Second Marriage 1953,O 12,30:1
Flowering Peach, The 1954,D 29,19:2
Flowering Peach, The 1955,Ja 9,II,1:1
Sophie 1963,Ap 16,32:1
Bride Got Farblondjet, The 1967,N 6,61:6
Gersten, Leon (Miscellaneous)
Best of Burlesque 1957,S 30,27:2
Evening of European Theatre, An 1960,Ap 26,41:1
Much Ado About Nothing 1961,Jl 7,17:1
Midsummer Night's Dream, A 1961,Ag 3,13:1
Richard II 1961,Ag 30,25:1
Gerstenberg, Alice (Playwright)
Pot Boiler, The 1923,My 11,20:3
When Chicago Was Young 1932,N 13,IX,3:8
Victory Belles 1943,O 27,26:3
Gerstenberger, Emil (Composer)
Lace Petticoat 1927,Ja 5,18:2
Gerstman, Felix G (Director)
Faust 1947,N 29,9:2
Rape of the Sabine Women, The 1949,F 5,10:5

Josephine Baker and Her Company 1964,F 5,30:1
Gerstman, Felix G (Miscellaneous)
Nathan the Wise 1962,Mr 7,29:1
Before Sundown 1962,Mr 14,43:1
Josephine Baker and Her Company 1964,F 5,30:1
Nathan der Weise 1966,D 10,45:2
Gerstman, Felix G (Producer)
Rendezvous in Wien 1956,S 5,23:1
Faust, Part I; Prelude in the Theater 1961,F 5,27:2
Faust, Part I; Play, The 1961,F 5,27:2
Faust, Part I; Prologue in Heaven 1961,F 5,27:2
Satiric Evening 1963,O 24,36:2
Wiener Blut 1964,S 12,14:1
Don Carlos 1964,N 25,40:1
Captain of Koepenick, The 1964,D 2,60:1
Why Do I Deserve This? 1966,Ja 19,31:2
Wozzeck 1966,Ap 6,34:1
Mitschuldigen, Die 1966,Ap 6,34:1
Ratten, Die 1966,Ap 13,36:1
Gertler, Sam
Love and Politics 1929,O 21,30:7
Sonitchka 1930,Mr 8,21:3
My Little Girl 1931,F 2,22:4
Night in the Woods, A 1931,Mr 2,19:3
Victims of Life 1931,O 21,26:2
Big Surprise, The 1932,O 17,18:3
Traveling Salesman, The 1932,N 1,24:4
Jewish Melody, The 1933,Mr 27,12:4
Street Singers 1938,D 12,25:6
Queen Mother 1938,D 26,29:4
Gertner, Eric (Lighting Director)
World of Illusion 1964,Je 25,26:2
Sacco-Vanzetti 1969,F 9,78:1
Gerton, Philip (Producer)
With Privileges 1930,S 16,30:2
Her Supporting Cast 1931,My 5,33:3
Border-Land 1932,Mr 30,15:5
Gertrude Hoffman Girls
Artists and Models 1925,Je 25,16:2
Gerussi, Bruno
Taming of the Shrew, The 1954,Jl 1,22:2
Merchant of Venice, The 1955,Jl 1,13:1
Henry V 1956,Je 20,27:2
Merry Wives of Windsor, The 1956,Je 21,34:4
Henry V 1956,Je 24,II,1:1
Hamlet 1957,Jl 3,15:2
Twelfth Night 1957,Jl 4,16:4
Twelfth Night 1957,Jl 7,II,1:1
Two Gentlemen of Verona 1958,Mr 19,35:1
Broken Jug, The 1958,Ap 2,36:1
Much Ado About Nothing 1958,Je 26,22:1
Winter's Tale, The 1958,Jl 23,34:3
Winter's Tale, The 1958,Jl 27,II,1:1
Midsummer Night's Dream, A 1960,Je 30,23:5
Romeo and Juliet 1960,Jl 1,14:1
Coriolanus 1961,Je 21,31:2
Henry VIII 1961,Je 22,22:1
Coriolanus 1961,Jl 5,30:1
Macbeth 1962,Je 20,41:1
Tempest, The 1962,Je 22,14:1
Cyrano de Bergerac 1962,Ag 1,21:1
Moby Dick 1962,N 29,45:1
Richard II 1964,Je 17,47:1
Bourgeois Gentilhomme, Le 1964,Je 18,28:2
King Lear 1964,Je 19,36:1
Henry IV, Part I 1965,Je 30,42:1
Julius Caesar 1965,Jl 2,18:1
Cherry Orchard, The 1965,Ag 2,17:2
Gervais, Blanche
Six Characters in Search of an Author 1922,O 31,11:2
Gerval, Charlie
Aventuriere, L' 1922,N 14,16:1
Maitresse de Roi 1926,D 1,24:1
Dame aux Camelias, La 1926,D 7,24:2
Misanthrope, Le 1926,D 10,31:2
Gerwig, George (Playwright)
Yanqui and the Senorita, The 1952,Ag 8,8:7
Gesek, Tad (Costume Designer)
Come Out, Carlo! 1962,My 4,27:2
In the Penal Colony 1962,My 4,27:2
Gesek, Tad (Lighting Director)
In the Penal Colony 1962,My 4,27:2
Come Out, Carlo! 1962,My 4,27:2
Gesek, Tad (Scenic Designer)
Come Out, Carlo! 1962,My 4,27:2
In the Penal Colony 1962,My 4,27:2
Bohikee Creek 1966,Ap 29,39:1
Javelin 1966,N 10,63:1
Gesell, Morris
Heimkehr aus der Fremde, Die; Stranger, The 1949,S 2,14:1
Shadow of My Enemy, A 1957,D 12,35:4
Gesmar (Costume Designer)
Ca. . . C'Est Paris 1927,F 6,VII,4:1
Gesner, Clark (Composer)
You're a Good Man, Charlie Brown 1967,Mr 8,51:1
You're a Good Man, Charlie Brown 1967,Ap 9,II,1:1
Leonard Sillman's New Faces of 1968 1968,My 3,43:1
You're a Good Man, Charlie Brown 1969,N 14,39:1

Gesner, Clark (Lyricist)
You're a Good Man, Charlie Brown 1967,Mr 8,51:1
Leonard Sillman's New Faces of 1968 1968,My 3,43:1
You're a Good Man, Charlie Brown 1969,N 14,39:1
Gesner, Clark (Miscellaneous)
You're a Good Man, Charlie Brown 1967,N 19,30:1
Gessner, Adrienne
Another Sun 1940,F 24,8:6
Claudia 1941,F 13,24:2
Thank You Svoboda 1944,Mr 2,13:2
I Remember Mama 1944,O 20,16:2
Harvey 1949,Mr 24,34:1
Death of a Salesman 1950,Mr 4,10:7
Jux Will Er Sich Machen, Einen 1968,Ap 3,41:1
Gest, Morris (Director)
Miracle, The 1927,Je 8,23:2
Merry Wives of Windsor, The 1928,O 2,24:5
Gest, Morris (Producer)
Afgar 1920,N 14,VI,1:1
Chauve-Souris 1922,F 6,9:2
Chauve-Souris 1922,F 12,VI,1:1
Miracle, The 1924,Ja 16,17:1
Miracle, The 1924,Ja 20,VII,1:1
Miracle, The 1924,F 17,4:3
Miracle, The 1924,My 22,14:3
Miracle, The 1924,Ag 19,9:1
Miracle, The 1925,S 29,31:6
Miracle, The 1925,O 29,29:1
Lysistrata 1925,D 15,28:2
Miracle, The 1926,D 28,16:2
Chauve-Souris 1927,O 23,VIII,1:1
Merry Wives of Windsor, The 1928,O 2,24:5
Redemption: Lebende Leichnam, Der; Living Corpse, The 1928,N 20,28:2
Chauve-Souris 1929,Ja 23,20:2
Ghosts; Gespenster 1929,F 6,30:3
Passion Play, The 1929,Ap 30,32:1
Passion Play, The 1929,My 5,IX,1:1
Wonder Bar, The 1931,Mr 6,26:6
Wonder Bar, The 1931,Mr 8,VIII,3:5
Wonder Bar, The 1931,Mr 18,23:4
Chauve-Souris; Romantic Adventure of an Italian Ballerina and a Marquis, A 1931,O 22,27:1
Chauve-Souris; Queen of Spades, The 1931,O 22,27:1
1860: or, Aris; 1860, or an Interrupted Festival 1931,O 22,27:1
Lady Precious Stream 1936,Ja 28,15:2
Lady Precious Stream 1936,F 23,X,1:1
Gethers, Steven
Open House 1947,Je 4,33:4
Gethers, Steven (Playwright)
Cook for Mr General, A 1961,O 20,39:1
Gethins, Mildred
Du Barry 1932,N 23,15:2
Getlin, Jules
Caesar and Cleopatra 1949,D 22,28:2
Geto, Al (Playwright)
Of V We Sing 1941,O 26,I,39:1
Of V We Sing 1942,F 16,20:3
Pack Up Your Troubles 1943,Je 15,16:1
Gettinger, Sylvia (Composer)
What of It? 1929,Mr 9,24:2
Getz, Ilse (Miscellaneous)
Killer, The 1960,Mr 23,33:1
Getz, Robert
Never Live Over a Pretzel Factory 1964,Mr 30,37:1
Getz, Stuart
Ben Franklin in Paris 1964,O 28,52:1
Mame 1967,Ag 15,31:2
Getze, Tilda
Between the Devil 1937,D 23,24:5
Pal Joey 1940,D 26,22:2
Geva, Tamara
Whoopee 1928,D 5,34:3
Three's a Crowd 1930,O 16,28:3
Three's a Crowd 1930,O 26,VIII,1:1
Flying Colors 1932,S 16,24:2
Flying Colors 1932,O 9,IX,1:1
Divine Drudge 1933,Jl 4,16:4
Divine Drudge 1933,O 27,22:3
Red Cat, The 1934,S 20,21:1
On Your Toes 1936,Ap 13,14:4
Idiot's Delight 1937,Ag 10,22:7
Idiot's Delight 1938,Mr 23,19:3
Idiot's Delight 1938,Ap 10,X,2:1
Trojan Women, The 1941,Ap 9,32:5
Peepshow 1944,F 4,12:2
Pride's Crossing 1950,N 21,37:5
Misalliance 1953,F 19,20:1
Misalliance 1953,Mr 22,II,1:1
Queen and the Rebels, The 1965,F 26,16:1
Geva, Tamara (Playwright)
Come Play With Me 1959,My 1,33:5
Gevanthor, Norman (Director)
Night Thoreau Spent in Jail, The 1970,N 2,66:1
Gevel, Claude (Playwright)
Vingt ans, Madame 1928,Ap 8,VIII,4:1
Geyer, Paul
Groove Tube 1969,O 12,88:3
Geyer, S (Playwright)
Four in Hand 1923,S 7,10:2

Geyer, Siegfried (Original Author)
Church Mouse, A 1931,My 3,VIII,2:1
You Never Know 1938,S 22,26:3
Geyer, Siegfried (Playwright)
By Candle Light 1928,O 7,IX,2:7
Kleine Komodie 1928,D 2,X,4:7
Serata D'Inverno; Winter Evening, A
1929,Ap 8,32:5
Candle Light 1929,S 22,IX,2:6
Candle-Light 1929,O 1,28:2
Geyra, Ellida (Choreographer)
Cherry Orchard, The 1955,O 19,38:1
Italian Straw Hat, The 1957,O 1,37:2
Geyra, Zvi (Lighting Director)
Cherry Orchard, The 1955,O 19,38:1
Uncle Vanya 1956,F 1,25:2
Uncle Vanya 1956,F 12,II,1:1
Sea Gull, The 1956,O 23,38:1
This Is Edwin Booth 1958,Ag 27,32:7
Edwin Booth 1958,N 25,37:1
Roots 1961,Mr 7,40:2
Hey You, Light Man! 1963,Mr 2,5:2
Geyra, Zvi (Scenic Designer)
Cherry Orchard, The 1955,O 19,38:1
Uncle Vanya 1956,F 1,25:2
Uncle Vanya 1956,F 12,II,1:1
Three Times Three; Merrye Playe, A
1956,My 24,27:2
Three Times Three; Box and Cox 1956,My 24,27:2
Three Times Three; How He Lied to Her Husband
1956,My 24,27:2
Sea Gull, The 1956,O 23,38:1
This Is Edwin Booth 1958,Ag 27,32:7
Edwin Booth 1958,N 25,37:1
Long Dream, The 1960,F 18,36:2
Roots 1961,Mr 7,40:2
Hey You, Light Man! 1963,Mr 2,5:2
Ghabrit, Si Kaddour Ben (Playwright)
Sidna 1926,Jl 23,11:2
Ghar, Francos (Choreographer)
Aqua Carnival 1962,Je 29,15:1
Gheduzzi, Giannina
In Fondo Al Cuore; Depths of the Heart, The
1930,D 8,27:1
Cardinale, Il; Cardinal, The 1931,Ja 12,24:2
Sansone; Samson 1931,F 9,25:1
My Wife Is Different 1931,Ap 27,24:4
Berretto a Songali, Il; Cap With Bells, The
1931,N 30,16:3
Zia Morta, La; Dead Aunt, The 1931,N 30,16:3
Canto Della Vita, Il; Song of Life, The
1932,Ap 4,13:3
Cardinale, Il 1933,Ja 9,24:2
Zia Morta, La; Dead Aunt, The 1933,F 13,11:3
Romanticismo 1933,My 1,10:5
Padrone Delle Ferriere, Il 1934,Mr 19,13:5
Colonello Bridall, L' 1934,Ap 16,20:3
Romanticismo 1934,My 14,20:2
Miserabili I, 1934,S 24,15:1
Miserabili I, 1934,O 1,14:2
Signora Dalle Camelie, La; Camille 1934,O 22,13:2
Processo dei Veleni, Il; Case of Poisons, The
1935,Ja 21,18:2
Romanzo di un Giovane Povero, Il 1935,F 25,12:3
Signo Della Croce, Il 1935,O 7,11:1
Religione e Patria 1936,Mr 23,22:4
Testamento della Zia d'America, Il; American
Aunt's Will, The 1936,Mr 23,22:4
Due Orfanelle, Le; Two Orphans, The
1936,O 5,24:4
Sansone; Samson 1936,N 30,25:2
Asino di Buridano, L' 1936,N 30,25:2
Medico Delle Pazze, Il; Physician of Mad Woman,
The 1937,S 27,24:2
Signora Dalle Camelie, La; Dame aux Camelias, La
1937,O 9,16:3
Ghee, Iruen (Composer)
Laugh It Off 1934,Ap 5,24:2
Ghelderode, Michael de (Playwright)
Pantagleize 1967,D 17,II,3:7
Gheon, Henri (Playwright)
Marriage of St Francis, The 1935,D 1,XI,6:4
Comedian, The 1956,O 18,36:4
Parade at the Devil's Bridge 1957,F 19,35:7
Marvellous History of Saint Bernard, The
1958,F 24,16:3
Mystery of the Finding of the Cross, The
1959,Ja 16,35:2
Way of the Cross, The 1959,Ja 16,35:2
Christmas in the Market Place 1960,D 10,26:1
Gheri, Alfred (Playwright)
Sixieme Etage 1938,Je 12,X,2:3
Six Flights Up 1939,F 26,IX,2:3
Ghezzi Brothers, The
Vaudeville (Palace) 1927,Je 28,29:2
Vaudeville (Palace) 1928,F 28,18:7
Vaudeville (Palace) 1929,Jl 8,17:6
Ghigi, Renato
Rugantino 1964,F 7,34:1
Ghisi, Federico (Musical Director)
Clizia 1939,Jl 23,IX,6:3
Ghostley, Alice
New Faces of 1952 1952,My 17,23:2

New Faces of 1952 1952,My 25,II,1:1
Sandhog 1954,N 24,17:1
All in One; Trouble in Tahiti 1955,Ap 20,40:3
All in One 1955,Ap 24,II,1:1
Shangri-La 1956,Je 14,40:1
Livin' the Life 1957,Ap 29,20:1
Thurber Carnival, A 1960,F 27,13:2
Thurber Carnival, A 1960,Mr 6,II,1:1
Beauty Part, The 1962,D 28,5:2
Sign in Sidney Brustein's Window, The
1964,O 16,32:1
Ghostley, Alice (Miscellaneous)
Box of Watercolors, A 1957,F 18,22:2
Ghriskey, H William
Fiesta 1933,D 16,12:2
Giaccone, Leonard
Buoyant Billions 1959,My 27,32:2
Getting Married 1959,Je 5,18:2
Passion, Poison and Petrifaction 1959,Ag 21,13:1
Giacometti, Paolo (Playwright)
Civil Death, The 1932,Ja 25,20:3
Morte Civile, La; Civic Death 1936,N 9,23:4
Giacosa, Giuseppe (Playwright)
Tristi Amori; Unhappy Loves 1930,O 27,17:6
Giagolin, Boris (Director)
Legend of the Golem, The 1931,My 27,25:2
Giancapo (Playwright)
Delitto e Castigo; Crime and Punishment
1931,Ja 26,20:5
Gianino, Jack
Henry V 1965,Je 29,27:2
Taming of the Shrew, The 1965,Jl 3,10:5
Giannakouros, Anthea (Costume Designer)
PS 193 1962,O 31,33:1
Chief Thing, The 1963,Ap 30,27:2
Giannini, A Christina (Costume Designer)
Make Me Disappear 1969,My 14,34:1
Three Men on a Horse 1969,O 17,35:1
Giannini, A Christina (Miscellaneous)
Me and Thee 1965,D 8,58:4
Giannini, Allessandro
Bride in the Morning, A 1960,My 26,38:2
Gianotti, Mafalda
Barbara 1929,N 18,24:5
Gianville, Maxwell
Freight 1949,F 4,30:2
We Bombed in New Haven 1968,O 17,51:1
Giasi, John
Pygmalion 1938,Ja 27,16:3
Captain Jinks of the Horse Marines 1938,Ja 28,16:2
No More Peace 1938,Ja 29,13:2
Giasson, Paul
What's Up 1953,O 28,37:2
Giasson, Paul (Composer)
What's Up 1953,O 28,37:2
Gibb, A
Plain Dealer, The 1929,My 23,27:1
Gibb, MacGregor
Victim, The 1952,My 3,17:5
Time of Storm 1954,F 26,14:2
Gibb, MacGregor (Director)
Enemies Don't Send Flowers 1957,F 20,38:1
Gibb, MacGregor (Miscellaneous)
God Slept Here, A 1957,F 20,38:1
Enemies Don't Send Flowers 1957,F 20,38:1
Gibbens, Bill
Blood Red Roses 1970,Mr 23,48:1
Gibberson, William
Mr Barry's Etchings 1950,F 1,26:2
Gibbes, Frances Grugnard (Playwright)
Face, The 1941,N 29,15:3
Gibbin, Rosaleen
Joyous Season, The 1935,N 24,II,9:2
Gibbon, J Murray (Playwright)
Prince Charlie and Flora 1931,Ag 29,16:5
Gibbons, Arthur (Playwright)
Tarzan of the Apes 1921,S 8,14:3
Gibbons, Daniel (Playwright)
After All That 1931,F 22,VIII,3:5
Gibbons, Floyd
Vaudeville (Palace) 1932,My 9,19:3
Gibbons, Kate
Home Is the Hero 1945,Ja 20,16:4
Gibbons, L M
Rose Tattoo, The 1966,O 21,36:2
Gibbons, Robert
All the King's Men 1950,Jl 19,25:6
Missouri Legend 1951,F 10,10:4
Stone for Danny Fisher, A 1954,O 22,24:2
Gibbons, Stella (Original Author)
Cold Comfort Farm 1936,Mr 2,13:7
Gibbs, Ann
You're a Good Man, Charlie Brown 1969,N 14,39:1
Gibbs, Anthony (Playwright)
Aunt of England 1935,Mr 28,25:4
Aunt of England 1935,Ap 21,IX,2:2
Gibbs, Eddie
Pirate, The 1942,N 26,39:2
Gibbs, H H
Napi 1931,Mr 12,22:5
Gibbs, Harry
Love Child, The 1922,N 15,22:1

Gibbs, John (Playwright)
Good Morning 1937,D 4,20:7
Fundamental George, The 1949,Ag 17,19:4
Gibbs, Judy
Concept, The 1968,My 7,51:1
Gibbs, Louis
Jefferson Davis 1936,F 19,17:2
Gibbs, MacGregor
Danton's Death 1938,N 3,26:2
Gibbs, Nancy
Artists and Models 1923,Ag 21,12:2
Artists and Models 1924,O 16,33:3
Nic-Nax of 1926 1926,Ag 5,19:1
Vaudeville (Palace) 1927,Jl 19,27:6
Gibbs, Norman
Street Sounds 1970,O 23,32:1
Gibbs, Orvie
Middletown 1934,Ap 23,24:6
Gibbs, Phyllis
Touch 1970,N 9,52:1
Gibbs, Richard
Ryan Girl, The 1945,S 25,28:2
Gibbs, Robert Paton
Blossom Time 1921,S 30,10:1
Ashes of Love 1926,Mr 23,24:3
Immortal Thief, The 1926,O 4,21:1
Caponsacchi 1926,O 27,24:2
Golden Dawn 1927,D 1,32:3
Gibbs, Ruth
Vaudeville (Palace) 1929,S 23,24:6
Gibbs, Shirley
Too Many Boats 1934,S 12,26:3
All Rights Reserved 1934,N 7,33:5
Lady Detained, A 1935,Ja 10,23:3
Remember the Day 1935,Jl 9,24:3
Little Inn, The 1935,Ag 20,25:1
Rain 1935,Ag 27,23:4
Gibbs, William Francis (Mrs)
Variations of 1940 1940,Ja 29,12:1
Gibbs, Wolcott (Playwright)
Season in the Sun 1950,S 29,31:2
Season in the Sun 1950,O 8,II,1:1
Gibney, Charles
Bad Man, The 1920,Ag 31,7:1
Lord Byron's Cain 1925,Ap 9,20:3
God Loves Us 1926,O 20,22:2
Babbling Brookes 1927,F 26,13:2
Lucky 1927,Mr 23,28:3
Houseboat on the Styx, The 1928,D 26,14:3
Coastwise 1931,D 1,23:1
Gibney, Charles (Director)
Babbling Brookes 1927,F 26,13:2
Gibney, Frank
Straw Hat, The 1937,D 31,8:2
Savonarola 1942,Ap 24,20:2
Man's House, A 1943,Ap 3,10:4
Eternal Cage 1945,Mr 22,19:7
Gibney, Sheridan (Director)
Calico Wedding 1945,Mr 8,18:6
Gibney, Sheridan (Playwright)
When Father Smiles 1931,Mr 22,VIII,4:4
Wiser They Are, The 1931,Ap 7,31:1
Calico Wedding 1945,Mr 8,18:6
Gibson, Albert L
Deep Are the Roots 1960,O 4,47:1
Gibson, Albert L (Miscellaneous)
Deirdre of the Sorrows 1959,O 15,46:1
Kataki 1959,D 16,55:1
Deep Are the Roots 1960,O 4,47:1
Indians 1969,My 27,43:1
Gibson, Alice (Costume Designer)
Heads or Tails 1947,My 3,10:6
Small Hours, The 1951,F 16,22:1
Never Say Never 1951,N 21,21:2
Bat, The 1953,Ja 21,28:2
Speaking of Murder 1956,D 20,37:1
Cloud 7 1958,F 15,15:2
Night Life 1962,O 24,44:1
Gibson, Bonnie
Tall Kentuckian, The 1953,Je 17,30:1
Gibson, Chloe (Director)
Power Without Glory 1948,Ja 14,30:2
Gibson, David (Lighting Director)
Days Between, The 1965,Je 4,39:1
Gibson, Don
Catherine Was Great 1944,Ag 3,16:1
Sleep, My Pretty One 1944,N 3,26:8
Many Happy Returns 1945,Ja 6,15:5
Oh, Herbert! 1945,Je 20,26:3
Love Goes to Press 1947,Ja 2,22:2
Open House 1947,Je 4,33:4
Gibson, Edith
Gondoliers, The 1935,Ag 6,20:5
Gibson, Ethel
Masked Woman, The 1922,D 23,14:2
Gibson, Frederic
Case of Philip Lawrence, The 1937,Je 9,31:1
Horse Play 1937,Ag 28,8:3
Haiti 1938,Mr 3,16:1
Gibson, Henry
My Mother, My Father and Me 1963,Mr 25,5:5
Gibson, Howard Hull
Hottentot, The 1920,Mr 2,9:1

Gibson, Howard Hull—Cont
Six-Cylinder Love 1921,Ag 26,8:2
Paid 1925,N 26,32:1
If I Was Rich 1926,S 3,15:2
Friendship 1931,S 1,30:2
Pigeons and People 1933,Ja 17,22:3
Gibson, Jack
Blue Flame, The 1920,Mr 16,18:1
Gibson, James
Fratricide Punished 1925,Ap 21,19:1
Victoria Regina 1938,O 4,20:2
Jacob 1942,Je 14,VIII,1:7
Arms and the Man 1956,O 2,39:4
Gibson, John
Greatest Man Alive!, The 1957,My 9,37:2
Cut of the Axe 1960,F 2,38:2
Riot 1968,D 20,64:1
Gibson, John (Director)
Hamp 1964,Ag 18,25:1
Gibson, Judy
Sensations 1970,O 26,48:2
Gibson, Lester A (Lighting Director)
Curate's Play, The 1961,D 18,41:3
Tableaux 1961,D 18,41:3
Gibson, Lillian
Jarnegan 1928,S 25,29:2
Seven Keys to Baldpate 1930,Ja 8,25:2
Gibson, M
Alexander Pushkin 1928,Ja 27,14:2
Gibson, Madeline
This Year of Grace 1928,N 8,27:1
Gibson, Margaret
Lady in the Dark 1943,Mr 1,14:2
Gibson, Marie
Three Wishes for Jamie 1952,Mr 22,9:2
Buttrio Square 1952,O 15,40:2
Gibson, Michael
Othello 1929,F 4,21:2
Major Noah 1929,F 23,17:2
Jew Suss 1929,O 19,22:3
Angels on Earth 1929,D 11,34:7
Roaming Stars 1930,Ja 25,12:2
Chains 1930,F 23,29:2
Witch of Castile, The 1930,O 25,21:1
Man With the Portfolio, The 1931,F 12,24:6
Josephus 1933,D 1,22:5
Verdict, The 1934,S 22,12:5
In-Laws 1934,O 25,28:2
Jealousy 1934,D 20,31:4
60,000 Heroes 1935,Ja 28,11:5
Parnosseh 1935,F 16,8:8
Sappho 1935,Mr 22,26:4
Gibson, Millard (Miscellaneous)
Sadie Thompson 1944,N 17,25:2
Gibson, Richard (Miscellaneous)
Frere Jacques 1968,Je 8,23:2
Gibson, Robert
Tempest, The 1959,D 28,19:2
Gibson, Robert A (Director)
Iolanthe 1955,S 28,38:1
Mikado, The 1955,S 30,20:2
Pirates of Penzance, The 1955,O 7,21:1
Princess Ida 1955,O 14,22:3
Gibson, Robert J (Miscellaneous)
Hamp 1967,Mr 10,32:1
Adaptation 1969,F 11,27:1
Next 1969,F 11,27:1
Gibson, Robert J (Producer)
Awake and Sing! 1970,My 28,35:1
Gibson, Rosalyn Kay
X Has No Value 1970,F 17,35:1
Gibson, Sandra
Hoofers, The 1969,Jl 30,23:4
Gibson, Ted W
Try It With Alice 1924,Je 24,18:4
Easy Mark, The 1924,Ag 27,14:2
Gibson, Virginia
Happy Hunting 1956,D 7,30:1
Tom Sawyer 1958,Jl 15,21:8
Gibson, William (Composer)
Dinny and the Witches 1959,D 10,53:3
Gibson, William (Playwright)
Two for the Seesaw 1958,Ja 17,15:1
Two for the Seesaw 1958,Ja 26,II,1:1
Miracle Worker, The 1959,O 20,44:1
Miracle Worker, The 1959,N 1,II,1:1
Dinny and the Witches 1959,D 10,53:3
Miracle Worker, The 1959,D 20,II,5:1
Miracle Worker, The 1961,Mr 10,19:4
Miracle Worker, The 1961,Ap 1,11:2
Miracle Worker, The 1961,Ap 11,43:5
Miracle Worker, The 1961,Ap 21,29:1
Miracle Worker, The 1961,My 1,35:3
Miracle Worker, The 1961,My 19,22:2
Miracle Worker, The 1961,My 31,28:1
Miracle Worker, The 1961,O 8,II,3:4
Two for the Seesaw 1963,S 4,34:1
Golden Boy 1964,O 21,56:1
Golden Boy 1964,N 1,II,1:1
Cry of Players, A 1968,N 15,40:1
Cry of Players, A 1968,N 24,II,9:4
Gibson, Wynne
When You Smile 1925,O 6,31:2
Jarnegan 1928,S 25,29:2

Silk Hat Harry 1943,Ag 22,II,1:6
Gichner, Ted (Pvt) (Composer)
Swing Sister Wac Swing 1944,Ja 4,20:4
Gichner, Ted (Pvt) (Lyricist)
Swing Sister Wac Swing 1944,Ja 4,20:4
Gick, Judith
Catiline 1936,Ja 28,14:6
Gidaly, Walter (Miscellaneous)
Your Own Thing 1968,Ja 15,33:1
Giddens, George
Respect for Riches, The 1920,My 12,9:1
Happy-Go-Lucky 1920,Ag 25,6:1
Gide, Andre (Original Author)
Immoralist, The 1954,F 2,18:7
Immoralist, The 1954,F 9,22:1
Immoralist, The 1954,F 14,II,1:1
Immoralist, The 1954,N 4,39:5
Gide, Andre (Playwright)
Trial, The 1947,N 2,II,3:7
On Trial 1949,D 9,35:5
Proces, Le; Trial, The 1952,N 18,36:2
Philoctetes 1959,Ja 14,28:1
Immoralist, The 1963,N 8,36:2
Gide, Andre (Translator)
Trial, The 1947,N 2,II,3:7
Hamlet 1948,S 11,13:3
Hamlet 1952,D 2,39:1
Gideon, Melville
Optimists, The 1928,Ja 31,28:2
Gideon, Melville (Composer)
Optimists, The 1928,Ja 31,28:2
Gideon, Melville (Producer)
Optimists, The 1928,Ja 31,28:2
Gideon, William
Kilgo Run, The 1953,D 13,105:1
Gidney, James B (Translator)
Donogoo 1961,Ja 19,25:3
Giehse, Therese
Pepper Mill 1937,Ja 6,19:4
Giehse, Therese (Director)
Pepper Mill 1937,Ja 6,19:4
Gielgud, John
Patriot, The 1928,Ja 20,15:1
Importance of Being Earnest, The
  1930,Jl 27,VIII,1:8
Jealous Wife, The 1930,N 16,VIII,4:1
Antony and Cleopatra 1930,D 14,IX,3:1
Good Companions, The 1931,My 15,20:8
Good Companions, The 1931,My 31,VIII,2:6
Musical Chairs 1931,D 6,VIII,2:7
Richard of Bordeaux 1933,F 26,IX,3:1
Maitlands, The 1934,Jl 22,IX,1:3
Hamlet 1934,N 15,25:1
Hamlet 1934,D 2,X,3:6
Noah 1935,Ag 4,IX,1:3
Romeo and Juliet 1935,O 18,27:5
Romeo and Juliet 1935,N 17,IX,2:4
Romeo and Juliet 1935,D 29,IX,1:3
Seagull, The 1936,My 21,19:2
Seagull, The 1936,Je 21,IX,1:5
Hamlet 1936,O 1,28:3
Hamlet 1936,O 9,30:2
Hamlet 1936,O 18,X,1:1
He Was Born Gay 1937,My 27,20:5
He Was Born Gay 1937,Je 13,XI,1:7
Richard II 1937,S 7,16:3
Three Sisters, The 1938,F 13,X,3:3
Merchant of Venice, The 1938,My 15,X,1:5
Dear Octopus 1938,O 2,IX,2:1
Hamlet 1939,Jl 7,12:2
Hamlet 1939,Jl 16,IX,2:1
Importance of Being Earnest, The 1939,S 17,X,2:3
King Lear 1940,Ap 28,IX,1:7
Macbeth 1942,Jl 26,VIII,1:7
Hamlet 1944,N 19,II,2:4
Midsummer Night's Dream, A 1945,Mr 25,II,2:4
Crime and Punishment 1946,Jl 21,II,1:5
Importance of Being Earnest, The 1947,Ja 24,18:6
Importance of Being Earnest, The 1947,Mr 4,30:2
Importance of Being Earnest, The 1947,Mr 9,II,1:1
Richard II 1947,My 11,II,3:7
Love for Love 1947,My 27,30:2
Love for Love 1947,Je 1,II,1:1
Medea 1947,O 21,27:2
Medea 1947,O 26,II,1:1
Crime and Punishment 1947,D 23,29:3
Crime and Punishment 1948,Ja 4,II,1:1
Lady's Not for Burning, The 1949,Je 12,II,3:1
Measure for Measure 1950,Mr 10,33:5
King Lear 1950,Jl 19,26:7
Lady's Not for Burning, The 1950,N 9,42:2
Lady's Not for Burning, The 1950,N 26,II,1:1
Much Ado About Nothing 1952,F 10,II,2:1
Way of the World, The 1953,Ap 10,17:1
Day by the Sea, A 1953,N 27,22:3
Day by the Sea, A 1953,D 20,II,4:2
King Lear 1955,Jl 28,19:2
Nude With Violin 1956,D 2,II,3:1
Tempest, The 1957,Ag 14,21:1
Potting Shed, The 1958,Mr 16,II,3:1
Ages of Man 1958,S 22,26:1
Ages of Man 1958,D 29,21:1
Ages of Man 1959,Jl 10,28:2

Gielgud, John—Cont
Much Ado About Nothing 1959,S 18,25:2
Much Ado About Nothing 1959,S 27,II,1:1
Othello 1961,O 11,53:6
Cherry Orchard, The 1961,D 15,49:1
School for Scandal, The 1962,N 30,27:1
School for Scandal, The 1963,Ja 26,5:2
Ages of Man 1963,Ap 15,36:1
Ides of March, The 1963,Ag 9,12:1
Homage to Shakespeare 1964,Mr 16,36:2
Hamlet 1964,Ap 10,30:1
Tiny Alice 1964,D 30,14:2
Tiny Alice 1965,Ja 10,II,1:1
Ivanov 1966,My 4,50:1
Ivanov 1966,My 15,II,1:1
Oedipus 1968,Mr 31,II,5:1
Oedipus 1968,Ap 2,54:1
Oedipus 1968,Jl 31,29:1
40 Years On 1968,N 5,53:3
40 Years On 1969,Jl 26,14:1
Battle of Shrivings, The 1970,F 7,23:1
Home 1970,Je 20,23:1
Home 1970,Ag 17,32:1
Home 1970,N 18,41:1
Home 1970,N 29,II,1:1
Gielgud, John (Director)
Romeo and Juliet 1932,F 28,VIII,2:4
Spring, 1600 1934,F 1,14:1
Spring, 1600 1934,Mr 4,IX,3:8
Queen of Scots 1934,Jl 15,X,1:3
Hamlet 1934,N 15,25:1
Hamlet 1934,D 2,X,3:6
Old Ladies, The 1935,Ap 4,21:2
Richard II 1937,S 7,16:3
Spring Meeting 1938,D 9,30:4
Beggar's Opera, The 1940,Mr 17,X,1:8
Macbeth 1942,Jl 26,VIII,1:7
Importance of Being Earnest, The 1947,Mr 4,30:2
Importance of Being Earnest, The 1947,Mr 9,II,1:1
Love for Love 1947,My 27,30:2
Medea 1947,O 21,27:2
Medea 1947,O 26,II,1:1
Heiress, The 1949,F 3,26:2
Lady's Not for Burning, The 1950,N 9,42:2
Richard II 1953,Ja 25,II,3:1
Way of the World, The 1953,Ap 10,17:1
Twelfth Night 1955,Je 7,37:4
Chalk Garden, The 1956,Ap 12,26:8
Chalk Garden, The 1956,My 13,II,3:1
Complaisant Lover, The 1959,Je 19,28:3
Much Ado About Nothing 1959,S 18,25:2
Five Finger Exercise 1959,D 3,45:4
Five Finger Exercise 1959,D 13,II,3:1
Big Fish, Little Fish 1961,Mr 16,42:2
Big Fish, Little Fish 1961,Mr 26,II,1:1
School for Scandal, The 1963,Ja 26,5:2
Hamlet 1964,Ap 10,30:1
Hamlet 1964,Ap 19,II,1:1
Ivanov 1966,My 4,50:1
Halfway up the Tree 1967,N 24,60:4
Gielgud, John (Miscellaneous)
Ivanov 1966,My 4,50:1
Gielgud, John (Producer)
Spring, 1600 1934,F 1,14:1
Spring, 1600 1934,Mr 4,IX,3:8
Queen of Scots 1934,Je 9,18:5
Hamlet 1934,N 15,25:1
Old Ladies, The 1935,Ap 28,X,2:3
Romeo and Juliet 1935,O 18,27:5
Romeo and Juliet 1935,N 17,IX,2:4
Richard II 1937,S 7,16:3
Merchant of Venice, The 1938,My 15,X,1:5
Spring Meeting 1938,Je 19,IX,2:1
Rhondda Roundabout 1939,Je 18,IX,1:7
Hamlet 1939,Jl 16,IX,2:1
Macbeth 1942,Jl 26,VIII,1:7
Importance of Being Earnest, The 1947,Mr 9,II,1:1
Love for Love 1947,Je 1,II,1:1
Medea 1948,S 30,32:4
Much Ado About Nothing 1952,F 10,II,2:1
Richard II 1953,Ja 1,19:1
Way of the World, The 1953,Ap 10,17:1
Day by the Sea, A 1953,N 27,22:3
Twelfth Night 1955,My 1,II,3:1
Much Ado About Nothing 1959,S 27,II,1:1
School for Scandal, The 1962,Ap 6,31:3
Hamlet 1964,F 28,17:5
Gielgud, Val (Director)
Heartbreak House 1968,Jl 6,9:1
Gierasch, Stefan
Snafu 1944,O 26,19:5
Silver Tassie, The 1949,Jl 22,16:5
Montserrat 1949,O 31,21:4
Night Music 1951,Ap 9,29:6
Time to Go 1952,My 8,35:6
Maya 1953,Je 10,35:1
Scarecrow, The 1953,Je 17,31:1
Little Clay Cart, The 1953,Jl 1,25:1
Homeward Look, The 1954,Je 4,26:2
Men in White 1955,F 26,13:2
Threepenny Opera, The 1956,Mr 11,II,1:1
Month in the Country, A 1956,Ap 4,23:1
Purple Dust 1956,D 28,15:1
Mrs Patterson 1957,F 6,20:2

Gierasch, Stefan—Cont
Deathwatch 1958,O 10,34:2
Shadow of a Gunman, The 1958,N 21,26:1
Sound of Music, The 1959,N 17,40:2
Little Moon of Alban 1960,D 2,34:1
Roots 1961,Mr 7,40:2
Isle of Children 1962,Mr 17,16:2
Ginger Man, The 1963,N 22,42:1
Deputy, The 1964,F 27,26:1
War and Peace 1967,Mr 22,42:1
Richard II 1968,Je 24,42:3
As You Like It 1968,Je 24,42:3
Love's Labour's Lost 1968,Je 28,36:1
Ah, Wilderness! 1969,N 9,86:1
Seven Days of Mourning 1969,D 17,64:1
Seven Days of Mourning 1970,Ja 4,II,5:1
Arsenic and Old Lace 1970,N 5,59:1
Giermann, Frederick
Nowhere Bound 1935,Ja 23,20:2
Gierow, Karl Ragnar (Miscellaneous)
More Stately Mansions 1962,N 10,16:4
Gierow, Karl Ragnar (Producer)
Long Day's Journey Into Night 1956,F 19,II,1:6
Giersberg, Max (Playwright)
All the King's Horses 1934,Ja 31,21:3
Giersdorf Sisters
A la Carte 1927,Ag 18,25:3
Hello, Daddy! 1928,D 27,26:5
Vaudeville (Palace) 1931,F 16,16:3
Gierymski, Tadeusz (Playwright)
Tango 1968,Ja 1,11:1
Giesen, Vivian
Mima 1928,D 13,24:2
Love Kills 1934,My 2,25:3
Gieser, Harold
Love Birds 1921,Mr 16,12:1
Giffard, Ingaret (Playwright)
Because We Must 1937,F 6,14:4
Giffin, Herbert
Familiar Pattern 1943,S 3,15:6
Gifford, Albert
Poisoned Kiss, The 1937,Ap 22,19:1
Adventures of Marco Polo, The 1941,D 28,I,31:7
Gifford, Bette (Costume Designer)
Happy as Larry 1961,Ap 26,36:1
Gifford, Catherine
Masks of Angels 1965,Ja 20,33:1
Gifford, Edwin (Costume Designer)
Pony Cart, The 1954,S 15,39:2
Gifford, Eleanor
Vickie 1942,S 23,28:1
Gifford, Ezra
Purple Canary, The 1963,Ap 23,31:1
Gifford, Gordon
Lady in the Dark 1941,Ja 24,14:2
My Dear Public 1943,S 10,28:1
Gifford, Hazen
Armor of Light 1950,F 24,26:4
No Time for Sergeants 1955,O 21,32:2
Night Circus, The 1958,D 3,44:1
Tall Story 1959,Ja 30,33:2
Under the Weather 1966,O 28,35:1
Gifford, Jack
Whoopee 1928,D 5,34:3
Gifford, John
Dark of the Moon 1945,Mr 15,27:2
Gifford, Joseph (Choreographer)
Lysistrata 1959,My 20,40:2
Gifford, Louise (Choreographer)
Iolanthe 1926,Ap 20,24:2
Pirates of Penzance, The; Slave of Duty, The
1926,D 7,25:1
Gifford, Ross
Will the Mail Train Run Tonight? 1964,Ja 10,18:1
Gifft, Sally (Costume Designer)
Billygoat Eddie 1964,Ap 21,43:2
Awakening of Spring, The 1964,My 13,50:1
Giftos, Elaine
Leonard Sillman's New Faces of 1968
1968,My 3,43:1
Giger, Edward
Finian's Rainbow 1953,Mr 7,13:2
Giglio, Adelina
Mother Martyr 1935,Ja 28,10:3
Giglio, Clemente
Figlia del Dragone Rosso, La; Red Dragon's
Daughter, The 1933,D 10,11:7
Uncle Tom's Cabin; Popolo Senza Dio
1934,F 19,19:2
Pasquale Never Knew 1938,Mr 31,14:2
Giglio, Clemente (Director)
Uncle Tom's Cabin; Popolo Senza Dio
1934,F 19,19:2
Mother Martyr 1935,Ja 28,10:3
Giglio, Clemente (Playwright)
Figlia del Dragone Rosso, La; Red Dragon's
Daughter, The 1933,D 10,11:7
Uncle Tom's Cabin; Popolo Senza Dio
1934,F 19,19:2
Mother Martyr 1935,Ja 28,10:3
Figlia Brutta, La; Ugly Daughter, The
1937,Ag 30,24:6
Pasquale Never Knew 1938,Mr 31,14:2

Giglio, Clemente (Producer)
Figlia del Dragone Rosso, La; Red Dragon's
Daughter, The 1933,D 10,11:7
Giglio, Gemma
Mother Martyr 1935,Ja 28,10:3
Giglio, Sandrino
Mother Martyr 1935,Ja 28,10:3
Giglio, Sandro
Madwoman of Chaillot, The 1950,Je 14,41:2
Gignoux, Edward T
On the Level 1937,Mr 26,24:4
Gignoux, Regis (Playwright)
Fresh Fruit 1927,S 11,VIII,2:4
Prof' d'Anglais, Le 1930,My 25,IX,2:8
Giil, Michael (Director)
Spitting Image 1969,Mr 3,28:1
Gil, Pedro
Don Juan Tenorio 1953,N 20,18:5
El Alcalde De Zalamea 1953,N 23,32:5
Gil, Ray
Little Hut, The 1953,O 8,37:2
Gilabert, Henri
Mariage de Figaro, Le 1964,F 26,41:2
Andromaque 1964,F 29,13:2
Gilad, Ami (Miscellaneous)
Sing Israel Sing 1967,My 12,50:1
Grand Music Hall of Israel, The 1968,F 7,42:1
Giladi, Moti
To Be or Not to Be-What Kind of a Question Is
That? 1970,O 20,39:1
Gilberg, Jo
Knight of the Burning Pestle, The 1953,O 24,13:2
Moon in Capricorn 1953,O 28,37:2
Gilbert, Adele
Carnival 1929,Ap 25,32:5
Broadway Shadows 1930,Ap 1,34:6
Constant Sinner, The 1931,S 15,30:1
Gilbert, Alan
Tide Rising 1937,Ja 26,17:2
Audition of the Apprentice Theatre 1939,Je 2,26:2
Million Dollar Baby 1945,D 22,17:2
Finian's Rainbow 1947,Ja 11,23:2
Finian's Rainbow 1947,O 22,38:4
Tree Grows in Brooklyn, A 1951,Ap 20,24:3
Most Happy Fella, The 1956,My 4,20:1
Gilbert, Andre
Maitresse de Roi 1926,D 1,24:1
Gilbert, Anthony (Original Author)
Haven, The 1946,N 14,39:4
Gilbert, Barbara
Put It in Writing 1963,My 14,31:1
Gilbert, Bebe
Six Characters in Search of an Author
1931,Ap 16,29:2
Gilbert, Billy
Chocolate Soldier, The 1947,Mr 13,34:2
Buttrio Square 1952,O 15,40:2
Gilbert, Billy (Director)
Red Mill, The 1945,O 17,16:2
Sally 1948,My 7,31:2
Gilbert, Billy (Playwright)
Buttrio Square 1952,O 15,40:2
Gilbert, Bob
Passing Show of 1921, The 1920,D 30,16:2
Passing Show of 1923, The 1923,Je 15,24:6
Gilbert, Brennan
School for Wives 1957,Je 20,23:4
Gilbert, Brian
Trojan Horse, The 1940,O 31,28:3
Gilbert, C Walter
Rain 1935,F 13,24:1
Gilbert, E A (Producer)
World of Kurt Weill in Song, The 1964,My 13,53:1
Entertaining Mr Sloane 1965,O 13,41:1
Gilbert, E Reid (Miscellaneous)
Everyman Today 1958,Ja 16,32:4
Gilbert, Earl
Gang's All Here, The 1931,F 19,21:3
Gilbert, Earl Jay
Out West of Eighth 1951,S 21,20:3
Gilbert, Edward (Costume Designer)
New Faces of 1943 1942,D 23,22:2
Yes, M'Lord 1949,O 5,35:2
Gilbert, Edward (Lighting Director)
Bees and the Flowers, The 1946,S 27,19:3
Gilbert, Edward (Scenic Designer)
Straw Hat, The 1939,S 30,10:6
All in Fun 1940,D 28,11:2
New Faces of 1943 1942,D 23,22:2
While the Sun Shines 1944,S 20,21:3
No Way Out 1944,O 31,23:1
Overtons, The 1945,F 7,16:6
Star Spangled Family 1945,Ap 11,18:6
Next Half Hour, The 1945,O 30,14:6
Icetime 1946,Je 21,20:5
Bees and the Flowers, The 1946,S 27,19:3
If the Shoe Fits 1946,D 6,29:4
Toplitzky of Notre Dame 1946,D 27,13:4
Icetime 1947,My 29,28:2
Hold It! 1948,My 6,31:5
All for Love 1949,Ja 24,16:5
Magnolia Alley 1949,Ap 19,29:2
Yes, M'Lord 1949,O 5,35:2

Gilbert, Edward (Scenic Designer)—Cont
Metropole 1949,D 7,43:2
Day After Tomorrow 1950,O 27,25:2
Solid Gold Cadillac, The 1953,N 6,24:2
Gilbert, Edward M (Producer)
How Long Till Summer 1949,D 28,30:3
Gilbert, Edwin (Lyricist)
New Faces of 1936 1936,My 20,24:5
Gilbert, Edwin (Playwright)
Golden Journey, The 1936,S 16,28:6
Gilbert, Elizabeth (Choreographer)
Lady in the Dark 1952,Mr 8,11:3
Gilbert, Emily
Libel! 1935,D 21,10:5
Gilbert, Enid (Costume Designer)
Bees and the Flowers, The 1946,S 27,19:3
Gilbert, Erskine F (Playwright)
Lawrence of Arabia 1954,D 10,35:3
Gilbert, Everett
Lucky Break 1925,Ag 12,16:2
Gilbert, Franklin (Producer)
Lend an Ear 1948,D 17,38:2
Maggie 1953,F 19,20:2
Gilbert, Fraye
Small Miracle 1934,S 27,24:3
Noah 1935,F 14,25:2
Squaring the Circle 1935,S 22,X,3:2
Squaring the Circle 1935,O 4,24:6
Cross-Town 1937,Mr 18,21:5
Trojan Women, The 1941,Ap 9,32:5
Gilbert, George (Miscellaneous)
Say Darling 1958,Ap 4,17:1
Gilbert, George (Producer)
Mr Wonderful 1956,Mr 23,23:2
First Impressions 1959,Mr 20,28:1
How Much, How Much? 1970,Ap 21,49:1
Gilbert, Gerald
Woman of Bronze, The 1920,S 8,9:2
Stepping Stones 1923,N 7,14:3
Gilbert, Gladys
Breakfast in Bed 1920,F 4,12:1
Gilbert, Gloria
Five O'Clock Girl, The 1927,O 11,26:3
Ballyhoo of 1932 1932,S 7,14:2
Funzapoppin 1949,Jl 1,16:2
Night in Venice, A 1952,Je 27,18:6
Night in Venice, A 1953,Je 26,15:2
Gilbert, H Arthur (Miscellaneous)
Machinal 1960,Ap 8,27:1
Gilbert, Harry Y
Fiesta 1933,D 16,12:2
Gilbert, J Charles
Count of Luxembourg, The 1930,F 18,28:2
Firefly, The 1937,Ag 4,14:1
Gilbert, Jean (Composer)
Braut von Lucullus, Die 1921,D 11,VI,1:4
Prinzessin Olala 1921,D 11,VI,1:4
Lady in Ermine, The 1922,O 3,22:2
Katja 1926,O 19,27:3
Red Robe, The 1928,D 26,15:1
Marching By 1932,Mr 4,17:1
Lovely Lady 1932,Mr 20,VIII,1:8
Gilbert, Jody
If the Shoe Fits 1946,D 6,29:4
Gilbert, John Charles
Blossom Time 1931,Mr 5,32:1
Blossom Time 1936,Ag 30,II,5:8
Gilbert, Joseph
Mary of Magdala 1946,Mr 26,24:5
Armor of Light 1950,F 24,26:4
Gilbert, L Wolfe
Vaudeville (Palace) 1927,Je 14,33:3
Gilbert, L Wolfe (Lyricist)
Singing Rabbi, The 1931,S 11,24:4
Gilbert, Larry
Mr Strauss Goes to Boston 1945,S 7,20:2
Gilbert, Lauren
God Innis 1937,Ag 25,24:3
Save Me the Waltz 1938,Mr 1,19:2
Hamlet 1939,D 5,35:2
Richard II 1940,Ap 2,31:2
Cue for Passion 1940,D 20,33:4
Flamingo Road 1946,Mr 20,18:2
Street Scene 1947,Ja 10,17:2
Vigil, The 1948,My 22,8:6
Story for Strangers, A 1948,S 22,39:2
Dragon's Mouth 1955,N 17,45:1
Roman Candle 1960,F 4,34:2
Gilbert, Lewis
Stop Press 1939,Mr 20,13:2
Gilbert, Lou
John Henry 1940,Ja 11,18:2
Common Ground 1945,Ap 26,27:2
Beggars Are Comming to Town 1945,O 29,16:2
Truckline Cafe 1946,F 28,19:4
Volpone 1948,Ja 9,24:6
Hope Is the Thing With Feathers 1948,Ap 12,24:2
Home Life of a Buffalo; Hope's the Thing
1948,My 12,34:6
Hope Is the Thing With Feathers; Hope's the
Thing 1948,My 12,34:6
Gone Tomorrow; Hope's the Thing
1948,My 12,34:6
Sundown Beach 1948,S 8,37:1

Gilbert, Lou—Cont

Detective Story 1949,Mr 24,34:2
Enemy of the People, An 1950,D 29,14:1
Anna Christie 1952,Ja 10,33:1
Victim, The 1952,My 3,17:5
Whistler's Grandmother 1952,D 12,40:2
His and Hers 1954,Ja 8,18:2
Dybbuk, The 1954,O 27,33:6
Abie's Irish Rose 1954,N 19,19:1
Highway Robbery 1955,N 8,36:1
Streetcar Named Desire, A 1956,F 16,24:1
Month in the Country, A 1956,Ap 4,23:1
Good as Gold 1957,Mr 8,22:2
Sweet Confession 1959,Ap 15,30:1
Time of Vengeance 1959,D 11,39:1
Time of Vengeance 1959,D 27,II,1:1
Coming Forth by Day of Osiris Jones, The; Kid,
  The 1961,Mr 15,45:2
Egg, The 1962,Ja 9,23:2
Tempest, The 1962,Jl 17,18:2
King Lear 1962,Ag 14,35:1
In the Counting House 1962,D 15,5:5
Dynamite Tonight 1964,Mr 16,36:2
Day the Whores Came Out to Play Tennis, The
  1965,Mr 16,45:1
Sing to Me Through Open Windows
  1965,Mr 16,45:1
Big Man 1966,My 20,41:1
Dynamite Tonight 1967,Mr 16,52:2
Great White Hope, The 1967,D 14,58:1
Great White Hope, The 1967,D 24,II,3:1
Iceman Cometh, The 1968,Ap 1,58:1
Great White Hope, The 1968,O 4,40:1
Good Woman of Setzuan, The 1970,N 6,51:1

Gilbert, Mercedes

Lace Petticoat 1927,Ja 5,18:2
Lost 1927,Mr 29,22:2
Bomboola 1929,Je 27,17:3
Malinda 1929,D 4,37:2
Green Pastures, The 1930,F 27,26:1
Green Pastures, The 1935,F 27,16:2
Play, Genius, Play! 1935,O 31,17:2
How Come Lawd? 1937,O 1,18:5
Searching Wind, The 1944,Ap 13,25:2
Carib Song 1945,S 28,17:2
Lysistrata 1946,O 18,27:5
Tobacco Road 1950,Mr 7,23:2

Gilbert, Mira

Blitzstein! 1966,D 1,58:2

Gilbert, Pia (Composer)

Murderous Angels 1970,F 8,70:1

Gilbert, Ray

Utopia! 1963,My 7,47:4

Gilbert, Robert

Solitaire 1942,Ja 28,22:2

Gilbert, Robert (Composer)

Prosit Gypsy 1929,Je 2,VIII,2:6

Gilbert, Robert (Lyricist)

Merry Widow, The 1943,Ag 5,19:2

Gilbert, Robert (Translator)

My Fair Lady 1962,Je 14,24:1

Gilbert, Ronald

Lulu; Earth Spirit 1970,Mr 28,32:1

Gilbert, Ronnie

Interview 1966,N 7,66:1
TV 1966,N 7,66:1
Man in the Glass Booth, The 1968,S 27,41:1

Gilbert, Russ

Good Girl, The 1934,Je 26,22:5

Gilbert, Ruth

Girls in Uniform 1932,D 31,10:3
Ah, Wilderness! 1933,O 3,28:2
Bright Honor 1936,S 28,14:1
Processional 1937,O 14,23:1
Processional 1937,O 24,XI,1:1
Ghost for Sale 1941,S 30,27:4
Suds in Your Eye 1944,Ja 13,15:5
That Old Devil 1944,Je 6,14:2
Iceman Cometh, The 1946,O 10,31:3

Gilbert, Stuart (Playwright)

Flies, The 1954,S 10,18:2

Gilbert, Stuart (Translator)

Flies, The; Mouches, Les 1947,Ap 18,26:3

Gilbert, Suzanne

Caution: A Love Story 1969,Ap 4,45:1

Gilbert, W S (Lyricist)

Yeomen of the Guard, The 1933,Ag 15,20:5
Iolanthe 1934,My 1,26:4
Gondoliers, The 1934,S 4,23:1
Iolanthe 1934,S 11,24:3
Trial by Jury 1934,S 14,24:3
H M S Pinafore 1934,S 14,24:3
Mikado, The; Town of Titipu, The 1934,S 18,18:1
Yeomen of the Guard, The 1934,S 21,28:3
Ruddigore 1934,S 25,25:2
Princess Ida; Castle Adamant 1934,S 28,26:3
Patience 1934,O 12,32:2
Ruddigore 1936,O 23,26:4
Yeomen of the Guard, The 1948,F 3,30:2
Pirates of Penzance, The 1949,O 11,41:2
Mikado, The 1952,O 21,35:2
Pirates of Penzance, The 1952,O 28,36:4
H M S Pinafore 1952,N 4,32:2
Trial by Jury 1952,N 4,32:2

Iolanthe 1952,N 11,26:3
H M S Pinafore 1960,Ja 29,14:1
Gondoliers, The 1961,Ja 26,33:2
Yeomen of the Guard, The 1964,Mr 19,29:2
Patience 1964,Mr 26,42:1

Gilbert, W S (Miscellaneous)

Ruddigore 1936,O 23,26:4
Memphis Bound 1945,My 25,23:2
Hollywood Pinafore 1945,Je 1,20:1

Gilbert, W S (Original Author)

Rise and Shine 1936,My 8,21:4
Pirates of Penzance, The 1936,S 1,24:4
Trial by Jury 1936,S 1,24:4
H M S Pinafore 1936,S 29,34:2
Hollywood Pinafore 1945,Je 1,20:1
Iolanthe 1965,My 19,42:1

Gilbert, W S (Playwright)

Iolanthe 1920,Ja 6,13:3
H M S Pinafore 1920,Ja 13,10:2
Ruddigore 1920,Ja 20,11:2
Ruddigore 1920,F 1,VIII,2:2
Pygmalion and Galatea 1920,Ap 28,9:3
Mikado, The 1924,Jl 29,9:1
Patience 1924,D 30,15:1
Patience 1925,Ja 4,VII,1:1
Patience 1925,F 1,VII,1:1
Mikado, The 1925,Ap 13,25:1
Princess Ida 1925,Ap 14,27:2
Engaged! or Cheviot's Choice 1925,Je 19,24:2
H M S Pinafore 1926,Ap 7,26:3
Iolanthe 1926,Ap 20,24:2
Iolanthe 1926,Ap 25,VIII,1:1
Mikado, The 1926,S 22,13:1
Mikado, The 1926,O 10,VIII,2:1
Pirates of Penzance, The; Slave of Duty, The
  1926,D 7,25:1
Pirates of Penzance, The 1926,D 12,VIII,3:1
Ruddigore 1927,My 21,25:2
Patience 1927,My 24,23:2
Mikado, The; Town of Titipu, The 1927,S 19,30:1
Mikado, The 1927,S 25,VIII,1:1
Mikado, The 1927,O 30,IX,4:6
Iolanthe 1927,N 15,26:3
Sorcerer, The 1928,Je 24,VIII,1:1
Patience 1928,Je 26,29:3
Gondoliers 1929,O 22,26:3
Patience 1929,D 16,34:5
Mikado, The; Town of Titipu, The 1931,My 5,33:2
H M S Pinafore 1931,My 19,25:2
H M S Pinafore 1931,My 31,II,1:2
Patience 1931,Je 16,30:4
Pirates of Penzance, The; Slave of Duty, The
  1931,Je 30,23:6
Iolanthe 1931,Jl 14,21:5
Ruddigore 1931,Ag 11,28:3
Mikado, The 1931,Ag 25,17:7
Iolanthe 1932,Ja 5,20:2
Gondoliers, The 1932,Ja 12,29:1
Mikado, The 1932,Jl 29,18:4
Mikado, The 1933,Ap 18,13:4
Yeomen of the Guard, The 1933,My 2,20:4
H M S Pinafore 1933,My 9,20:3
Trial by Jury 1933,My 9,20:3
Patience 1933,My 23,22:6
Pirates of Penzance, The 1933,Ag 8,22:4
Yeomen of the Guard, The 1933,Ag 15,20:5
Mikado, The 1934,Ap 3,26:3
Pirates of Penzance, The 1934,Ap 10,26:5
Trial by Jury 1934,Ap 17,27:2
H M S Pinafore 1934,Ap 17,27:2
Mikado, The 1934,Ap 24,27:5
Mikado, The 1934,My 22,28:2
Pirates of Penzance, The; Slave of Duty, The
  1934,S 7,24:3
Gondoliers, The 1934,S 9,IX,1:1
Mikado, The 1935,Jl 16,24:4
Pirates of Penzance, The 1935,Jl 23,24:2
Yeomen of the Guard, The 1935,Jl 30,16:4
Gondoliers, The 1935,Ag 6,20:5
Trial by Jury 1935,Ag 13,20:6
H M S Pinafore 1935,Ag 13,20:6
H M S Pinafore 1935,Ag 17,18:4
Mikado, The 1935,Ag 24,17:5
Patience 1935,S 3,24:4
Utopia, Limited 1936,My 23,10:6
Gondoliers, The 1936,Jl 19,12:5
Mikado, The 1936,Ag 21,13:2
Gondoliers, The 1936,S 8,23:1
Yeomen of the Guard, The 1936,S 15,37:2
Iolanthe 1936,S 22,30:3
Patience 1936,O 6,28:6
Princess Ida 1936,O 13,32:2
Mikado, The 1939,Mr 11,15:6
Swing Mikado, The 1939,Mr 12,XI,1:1
Hot Mikado, The 1939,Ap 2,X,1:3
Hot Mikado, The 1939,Je 23,23:4
Yeomen of the Guard, The 1939,Jl 16,30:4
Yeomen of the Guard, The 1939,Jl 23,IX,2:1
Yeomen of the Guard, The 1941,D 19,34:3
Pirates of Penzance, The 1946,My 17,14:6
Mikado, The 1946,Ag 12,9:2
Pirates of Penzance, The 1946,S 21,19:2
Pirates of Penzance, The 1948,Ja 11,II,1:1

Gilbert, W S (Playwright)—Cont

Yeomen of the Guard, The 1948,F 3,30:2
Pirates of Penzance, The 1949,O 11,41:2
H M S Pinafore 1949,O 18,34:2
Trial by Jury 1949,O 18,34:2
Mikado, The 1951,Ja 30,21:2
Trial by Jury 1951,F 6,24:2
H M S Pinafore 1951,F 6,24:2
Gondoliers, The 1951,F 13,27:2
Iolanthe 1951,F 16,22:1
Pirates of Penzance, The 1951,F 20,21:2
H M S Pinafore 1952,N 4,32:2
Thespis 1953,Ja 17,13:5
Pirates of Penzance, The 1954,Mr 31,32:5
Patience 1954,Ap 7,41:1
Ruddigore 1954,Ap 21,36:4
Iolanthe 1954,Ap 28,36:8
Yeomen of the Guard, The 1954,My 5,36:2
H M S Pinafore 1954,My 19,36:8
Sorcerer, The 1954,My 26,34:3
Iolanthe 1955,S 28,38:1
Mikado, The 1955,S 30,20:2
Yeomen of the Guard, The 1955,O 4,39:2
Pirates of Penzance, The 1955,O 7,21:1
Princess Ida 1955,O 14,22:3
Trial by Jury 1955,O 18,48:1
H M S Pinafore 1955,O 18,48:1
Ruddigore 1955,O 21,32:2
Mountebanks, The 1955,D 2,32:3
Utopia, Limited; Flowers of Progress, The
  1957,F 27,21:1
Utopia, Limited 1957,Mr 17,II,1:1
Mikado, The 1957,Ap 24,28:2
Pirates of Penzance, The 1957,My 8,43:1
Yeomen of the Guard, The 1957,My 22,28:3
Gondoliers, The 1957,My 29,34:2
H M S Pinafore; Trial by Jury 1957,Jl 29,16:1
Mikado, The 1959,O 2,24:1
Gondoliers, The 1960,F 7,II,1:1
Utopia, Limited 1960,Ap 8,27:2
H M S Pinafore 1960,Jl 17,51:1
H M S Pinafore 1960,S 8,41:1
Pirates of Penzance, The 1960,O 7,29:1
Mikado, The 1961,Ja 18,26:1
Pirates of Penzance, The 1961,Ja 20,24:5
H M S Pinafore 1961,F 2,26:6
Yeomen of the Guard, The 1961,Ap 28,23:1
Mikado, The 1961,My 5,23:1
Grand Duke, The 1961,My 12,24:1
Princess Ida 1961,My 19,23:1
Iolanthe 1961,My 26,29:6
H M S Pinafore 1961,Je 9,29:5
Pirates of Penzance, The 1961,S 7,41:1
Pirates of Penzance, The 1961,S 17,II,1:1
Gondoliers, The 1961,D 8,44:1
Iolanthe 1962,Ap 12,42:4
Gondoliers, The 1962,Ap 19,34:2
Gondoliers, The 1962,Jl 7,9:4
Yeomen of the Guard, The 1962,Jl 11,28:1
Gondoliers, The 1963,Je 5,33:2
H M S Pinafore 1964,Mr 21,13:4
Gondoliers, The 1964,Mr 28,14:1
Yeomen of the Guard, The 1964,Ag 3,16:1
Iolanthe 1964,N 18,52:1
Trial by Jury 1964,N 20,40:1
H M S Pinafore 1964,N 20,40:1
Pirates of Penzance, The 1964,N 27,43:1
Mikado, The 1964,N 27,43:1
Ruddigore 1964,D 4,44:1
H M S Pinafore 1965,Ap 15,39:1
Patience 1965,Ap 16,34:1
Mikado, The 1965,Ap 17,11:3
Pirates of Penzance, The 1965,Ap 21,50:6
Engaged! or Cheviot's Choice 1965,Ap 24,19:2
Yeomen of the Guard, The 1965,Jl 8,34:1
Ruddigore 1965,Ag 27,16:1
Pirates of Penzance, The 1966,My 24,54:1
Trial by Jury 1966,Je 8,41:2
H M S Pinafore 1966,Je 8,41:2
Pirates of Penzance, The 1966,N 16,54:1
Mikado, The 1966,N 18,36:1
Ruddigore 1966,N 23,28:1
H M S Pinafore 1966,N 24,64:1
Patience 1966,N 30,58:1
Princess Ida 1967,Ap 17,46:2
Pirates of Penzance, The 1967,Ag 7,34:2
Patience 1967,O 13,32:1
Iolanthe 1967,O 18,40:1
Mikado, The 1967,O 25,42:2
Gondoliers, The 1967,O 29,83:1
H M S Pinafore 1967,N 1,40:1
Mikado, The 1967,D 4,65:3
Pirates of Penzance, The 1968,Ap 26,32:1
H M S Pinafore 1968,Ap 29,47:2
Yeomen of the Guard, The 1968,My 9,53:1
Patience 1968,My 16,52:1
Patience 1968,N 1,34:1
Mikado, The 1968,N 2,29:4
Pirates of Penzance, The 1968,N 7,54:1
Iolanthe 1968,N 9,37:3
Gondoliers, The 1969,My 10,35:1
H M S Pinafore 1969,D 8,61:2
Patience 1970,My 10,72:4
Pirates of Penzance, The 1970,Jl 26,49:5

Gilbert, W S (Playwright)—Cont

Pirates of Penzance, The 1970,D 6,84:6

Gilbert, Walter
Joker, The 1925,N 17,29:1
Gang War 1928,Ag 21,27:2
Scarlet Sister Mary 1930,N 26,19:2
School for Scandal, The 1931,N 11,26:4
Pigeons and People 1933,Ja 17,22:3
Divine Drudge 1933,Jl 4,16:4
Locked Room, The 1933,D 26,18:5
Wednesday's Child 1934,Ja 17,23:2
Lost Horizons 1934,O 16,31:2
As Husbands Go 1935,Jl 10,24:1
Strip Girl 1935,O 21,22:6
Dear Old Darling 1936,Mr 3,25:1
Bonfire to Glory 1936,Jl 28,23:4
Eternal Road, The 1937,Ja 8,14:2
Farewell Summer 1937,Mr 30,20:2
Lightnin' 1938,S 16,17:2
Skylark 1939,O 12,32:2

Gilbert, Willie (Playwright)
How to Succeed in Business Without Really Trying 1961,O 16,34:1
Hot Spot 1963,Ap 20,17:2
Catch Me if You Can 1965,Mr 10,50:1
How to Succeed in Business Without Really Trying 1966,Ap 21,45:1

Gilbert and French
Vaudeville (Palace) 1928,Ja 24,26:4

Gilborn, Steven
Othello 1958,Jl 4,16:1
Twelfth Night 1958,Ag 7,21:4

Gilbreath, George
Troublemakers, The 1954,D 31,11:3

Gilbricht, Walter (Playwright)
Oliver Cromwells Sendung 1933,Mr 19,IX,2:2

Gilcher, Edward
Incubator 1932,N 2,23:3

Gilcher, Peggy Anne
On the Town 1959,F 14,15:1

Gilchrist, Connie
Mulatto 1935,O 25,25:2
Excursion 1937,Ap 10,11:4
Work Is for Horses 1937,N 22,14:6
How to Get Tough About It 1938,F 9,16:2
Ladies and Gentlemen 1939,O 18,30:2

Gilchrist, Connie (Miscellaneous)
Accent on Youth 1935,Jl 11,24:3

Gilchrist, Dorothy
Yankee Point 1942,N 24,28:2
Three's a Family 1943,My 6,24:2
Mr Peebles and Mr Hooker 1946,O 11,29:2

Gilchrist, J N (Director)
Unto the Third 1933,Ap 21,24:8

Gilchrist, J N (Original Author)
Unto the Third 1933,Ap 21,24:8

Gilchrist, J N (Producer)
Unto the Third 1933,Ap 21,24:8

Gilchrist, Jack
Henry V 1928,Mr 16,26:2
Fields Beyond, The 1936,Mr 7,11:2
Right This Way 1938,Ja 6,22:3
Sea Dogs 1939,N 7,30:3

Gilchrist, John
Christopher Comes Across 1932,Je 1,19:2

Gilday, George
Big Boy 1925,Ja 8,28:2
Taps 1925,Ap 15,16:2
Pleasure Bound 1929,F 19,22:4
Light Wines and Beer 1930,N 11,28:6

Gildea, Agnes
Moon Is a Gong, The 1926,Mr 13,21:3
Baby Cyclone, The 1927,S 13,37:4
Big Blow 1938,O 3,11:2

Gildea, Mary
Torch Bearers, The 1922,Ag 30,10:2
Craig's Wife 1925,O 13,21:2
Behold the Bridegroom 1927,D 27,24:1
Button, Button 1929,O 24,26:1
Let and Sub-Let 1930,My 20,32:2
Philip Goes Forth 1931,Ja 13,35:4
Reunion in Vienna 1931,N 17,31:1
Miss Quis 1937,Ap 8,20:5
Deep Mrs Sykes, The 1945,Mr 20,22:6
Fatal Witness, The 1946,N 20,43:2
To Be Continued 1952,Ap 24,37:2
Desk Set, The 1955,O 25,36:7

Gilden, Richard
World of Illusion 1964,Je 25,26:2

Gildersleeve, Allen
Bartleby 1961,Ja 25,28:1

Gildersleeve, James
Bedrock 1934,N 18,II,6:3
Major Barbara 1951,F 24,10:2

Giler, Berne (Original Author)
Girl From Nantucket, The 1945,N 9,17:2

Giles, David (Director)
Measure for Measure 1969,Je 13,41:3
Measure for Measure 1969,Je 22,II,1:7

Giles, John Martin (Miscellaneous)
Before I Wake 1968,O 14,56:1

Giles, Paul Kirk
Trojan Women, The 1941,Ap 9,32:5
Pillar to Post 1943,D 11,11:2

Small Hours, The 1951,F 16,22:1
Ah, Wilderness! 1953,F 7,10:6

Giles, Willard
Dandy Dick 1956,Ja 11,37:2
Well of the Saints, The 1959,Ap 11,15:4

Gilfillan, Sue Ann
Merry Wives of Windsor, The 1954,F 17,27:1
Servant of Two Masters, The 1958,F 11,35:2

Gilfond, Edythe (Costume Designer)
Fifth Season, The 1953,Ja 24,13:2

Gilford, Jack
Meet the People 1940,O 20,IX,3:3
Meet the People 1940,D 26,22:2
Meet the People 1941,Ja 3,24,1:1
They Should Have Stood in Bed 1942,F 14,18:5
It's All Yours 1942,Mr 26,26:2
New Meet the People, The 1943,Ag 22,II,1:6
Alive and Kicking 1950,Ja 18,25:5
Live Wire, The 1950,Ag 18,16:2
Live Wire, The 1950,Ag 27,II,1:1
World of Sholom Aleichem, The 1953,S 12,13:2
World of Sholom Aleichem, The 1953,S 20,II,1:1
Passion of Gross, The 1955,Ja 24,20:2
Once Over Lightly 1955,Mr 16,39:1
Diary of Anne Frank, The 1955,O 6,24:2
Romanoff and Juliet 1957,O 11,24:1
Drink to Me Only 1958,O 9,47:4
Look After Lulu 1959,Mr 4,35:1
Once Upon a Mattress 1959,My 12,40:1
Tenth Man, The 1959,N 6,24:2
Tenth Man, The 1959,N 15,II,1:1
Policemen, The 1961,N 22,24:2
Funny Thing Happened on the Way to the Forum, A 1962,My 9,49:1
Funny Thing Happened on the Way to the Forum, A 1962,My 20,II,1:1
Funny Thing Happened on the Way to the Forum, A 1962,Jl 6,22:5
Cabaret 1966,N 21,62:1
Cabaret 1966,D 4,II,5:1
Cabaret 1968,Ja 12,19:1
Three Men on a Horse 1969,O 17,35:1

Gilford, Madeline Lee (Miscellaneous)
But, Seriously... 1969,F 28,29:1

Gilford, Michael
Finian's Rainbow 1955,My 19,25:1

Gilford, Stephen
Purgatory 1960,S 20,48:1

Gilford, Stephen (Miscellaneous)
Purgatory 1960,S 20,48:1
Full Moon in March, A 1960,S 20,48:1

Gilkey, Stanley
Age of Innocence, The 1928,N 28,24:2

Gilkey, Stanley (Producer)
One for the Money 1939,F 6,9:2
Two for the Show 1940,F 9,14:2
Deep Mrs Sykes, The 1945,Mr 20,22:6
Three to Make Ready 1946,Mr 8,16:2
Message for Margaret 1947,Ap 17,34:2
John Murray Anderson's Almanac 1953,D 11,42:2
Roomful of Roses, A 1955,O 18,48:1
Day the Money Stopped, The 1958,F 21,19:4

Gilkinson, Jane
Good Morning 1937,D 4,20:7

Gill, Basil
Greater Love, The 1927,Ap 3,VIII,1:4
Macbeth 1928,N 20,28:3
Julius Caesar 1932,F 9,30:7
Julius Caesar 1932,F 28,VIII,2:4
Julius Caesar 1934,O 24,25:2

Gill, Brendan (Original Author)
Day the Money Stopped, The 1958,F 21,19:4

Gill, Brendan (Playwright)
Day the Money Stopped, The 1958,F 21,19:4

Gill, Brian
Taming of the Shrew, The 1954,Jl 1,22:2

Gill, C C
Singin' the Blues 1931,S 17,21:3

Gill, David
Murder in the Cathedral 1938,F 17,16:2

Gill, Dorothy
Gondoliers, The 1934,S 4,23:1
Pirates of Penzance, The; Slave of Duty, The 1934,S 7,24:3
Gondoliers, The 1934,S 9,IX,1:1
Iolanthe 1934,S 11,24:3
H M S Pinafore 1934,S 14,24:3
Mikado, The; Town of Titipu, The 1934,S 18,18:1
Yeomen of the Guard, The 1934,S 21,28:3
Ruddigore 1934,S 25,25:2
Princess Ida; Castle Adamant 1934,S 28,26:3
Patience 1934,O 12,32:2

Gill, Frank
Irving Berlin's Music Box Revue 1921,S 23,18:2

Gill, Frank Jr (Playwright)
School for Brides 1944,Ag 2,19:4

Gill, George
Thespis 1953,Ja 17,13:5

Gill, Geula
Grand Music Hall of Israel, The 1968,F 7,42:1
New Music Hall of Israel, The 1969,O 3,40:1

Gill, Helen
Your Woman and Mine 1922,F 28,17:2

Gill, Helen—Cont

Advertising of Kate, The 1922,My 9,22:2
Zeno 1923,Ag 27,14:2

Gill, John
Lark, The 1955,My 13,21:2

Gill, Nellie
Decision 1929,My 28,37:3

Gill, Paul
Fanatics, The 1927,N 8,32:4
Many Waters 1929,S 26,27:1
Man in Possession, The 1930,N 3,19:1
Queen's Husband, The 1931,N 15,VIII,2:1

Gill, Peter (Director)
Life Price 1969,Ja 14,36:2
Much Ado About Nothing 1969,Je 16,57:1
Landscape 1970,Ap 3,43:1
Silence 1970,Ap 3,43:1
Hedda Gabler 1970,Je 12,28:1

Gill, Philippa
Love for Love 1947,My 27,30:2

Gillam, Dorothy Fowler
Kith and Kin 1930,My 14,31:1

Gillam, Lucie
By Hex 1956,Je 19,25:1

Gillard, Allen
Make Me Know It 1929,N 5,32:5

Gillard, Emanuel
South Pacific 1943,D 30,11:2

Gillard, William
Gambling 1929,Ag 27,31:2

Gillen, Billy
Red Light Annie 1923,Ag 22,10:3

Gillen, Girard
Bernardine 1952,O 17,33:4

Gillen, Thomas
Bulldog Drummond 1921,D 27,10:2
Faithful Heart, The 1922,O 11,22:1
Elmer the Great 1928,S 25,29:1
Vermont 1929,Ja 9,28:1
Cortez 1929,N 5,32:2
Friendship 1931,S 1,30:2
June Moon 1933,My 16,15:5

Gilleran, Tom
There Was a Little Girl 1960,Mr 1,28:1

Gillern, Grace
Red, Hot and Blue! 1936,O 30,26:3

Gillespie, Ben
Brigadoon 1964,D 24,9:1
Kiss Me, Kate 1965,My 13,31:1

Gillespie, Ben (Choreographer)
Picnic on the Battlefield 1967,S 9,25:2

Gillespie, Christie
Fireman's Flame, The 1937,O 11,26:2

Gillespie, Christina
Reluctant Debutante, The 1956,O 11,50:1
Boy Friend, The 1958,Ja 27,24:4
Ernest in Love 1960,My 5,39:4
Camelot 1960,D 5,42:1
All in Love 1961,N 11,15:2

Gillespie, Frank M (Director)
Great Day! 1929,O 18,24:3

Gillespie, Jean
Chicken Every Sunday 1944,Ap 6,27:2
Chicken Every Sunday 1944,Ap 16,II,1:1
Happy Journey to Trenton and Camden, The 1948,Mr 21,II,1:1
To Tell You the Truth 1948,Ap 19,28:6
Blood Wedding 1949,F 7,16:2
Southwest Corner, The 1955,F 4,18:2

Gillespie, Kevin
Ame en Peine, L' 1950,My 31,25:2
You Can't Take It With You 1951,Ap 7,8:6

Gillespie, Lucile
Penny Arcade 1930,Mr 11,24:5

Gillespie, Marian (Lyricist)
Greenwich Villagers, The 1927,Ag 19,20:2

Gillespie, Ruth C (Translator)
Difficult Woman, The 1962,Ap 26,22:7

Gillette, Abram
Tenth Man, The 1929,Mr 21,29:2
Silver Tassie, The 1929,O 25,26:1
It Never Rains 1929,N 20,26:4
Penal Law 2010 1930,Ap 19,14:2
Little Father of the Wilderness, The 1930,Je 3,27:1
O'Flaherty, V C 1931,Ap 11,17:6
It Never Rains 1931,D 25,29:3

Gillette, Anita
Russell Patterson's Sketch-Book 1960,F 8,35:1
All American 1962,Mr 20,44:1
Mr President 1962,Ag 29,18:4
Mr President 1962,O 22,34:2
Kelly 1965,F 8,28:2
Guys and Dolls 1965,Ap 29,39:1
Don't Drink the Water 1966,N 18,37:1
Cabaret 1969,F 2,74:2
Jimmy 1969,O 24,38:1

Gillette, Arnold (Scenic Designer)
Tread the Green Grass 1932,Jl 24,IX,1:3

Gillette, Betty
Caesar and Cleopatra 1935,Ag 22,21:1

Gillette, Bobby
Shoot the Works! 1931,Jl 22,19:5

Gillette, Don Carle (Playwright)
In the Bag 1936,D 18,30:2

Gillette, Guy
Pillar to Post 1943,D 11,11:2
Gillette, Helen
Milky Way, The 1943,Je 10,17:2
Gillette, Priscilla
Regina 1949,N 1,32:2
Out of This World 1950,D 22,17:3
Regina 1952,Je 2,25:4
Golden Apple, The 1954,Mr 12,15:2
Golden Apple, The 1954,Mr 21,II,1:1
Gillette, Ruth
Gay Paree 1925,Ag 19,14:3
Babes in Toyland 1930,D 22,17:1
Gazebo, The 1958,D 13,2:7
Gillette, Viola
Caroline 1923,F 1,13:2
China Rose 1925,Ja 20,18:1
Lucky Break 1925,Ag 12,16:2
Rainbow Rose 1926,Mr 17,28:2
Gillette, William
Dream Maker, The 1921,N 22,17:1
Sherlock Holmes 1929,N 26,28:3
Three Wise Fools 1936,Ja 14,25:2
Three Wise Fools 1936,F 2,IX,1:3
Three Wise Fools 1936,Mr 2,12:2
Gillette, William (Original Author)
Too Much Johnson 1964,Ja 16,29:1
Gillette, William (Playwright)
Dream Maker, The 1921,N 22,17:1
Sherlock Holmes 1928,F 21,18:4
Sherlock Holmes 1929,N 26,28:3
All the Comforts of Home 1942,My 26,24:5
Gilliam, Barbara Jean
Ponder Heart, The 1956,F 17,14:2
Gilliland, Don (Miscellaneous)
Brecht on Brecht 1961,N 15,52:2
Brecht on Brecht 1962,Ja 4,26:1
Gilliland, Helen
Red Robe, The 1928,D 26,15:1
Red Robe, The 1929,Ja 13,VIII,1:1
Dear Love 1930,My 18,VIII,3:1
Gay Masquerade 1935,My 15,26:1
Gilliland, Jane (Producer)
Darker Flower, A 1963,Mr 11,7:2
Saving Grace, The 1963,Ap 19,28:1
Streets of New York, The 1963,O 30,47:1
Gilliland, Jill (Miscellaneous)
One Is a Lonely Number 1964,Je 19,37:3
Gilliland, Max
Simpleton of the Unexpected Isles, The
  1954,Ja 12,19:1
Gillin, Caryl
Nobody's Business 1923,O 23,17:1
Padre, The 1926,D 28,16:3
What the Doctor Ordered 1927,Ag 19,20:2
Commodore Marries, The 1929,S 5,26:3
Divine Drudge 1933,Jl 4,16:4
It Pays to Sin 1933,N 4,18:6
Gillingham, Joan
Mikado, The 1947,D 30,18:2
Pirates of Penzance, The 1948,Ja 6,27:2
Iolanthe 1948,Ja 13,29:3
H M S Pinafore 1948,Ja 20,26:2
Gondoliers, The 1948,Ja 27,31:2
Patience 1948,F 10,27:2
Mikado, The 1951,Ja 30,21:2
H M S Pinafore 1951,F 6,24:2
Gondoliers, The 1951,F 13,27:2
Iolanthe 1951,F 16,22:1
Pirates of Penzance, The 1951,F 20,21:2
Gillis, Eugene
Child of the Morning 1958,Ap 22,40:2
Gillis, James
Babes in Arms 1937,Ap 15,18:4
Devil and Daniel Webster, The 1939,My 19,26:1
Gillis, Mary Jo
Great Scot! 1965,N 12,56:3
Gillis, Roland
Policy Kings 1938,D 31,6:2
Gillis, Verna
But Never Jam Today 1969,Ap 24,40:1
Gillman, Charles
Little Theatre Tournament; Monkey's Paw, The
  1929,My 10,32:2
Gillman, Sam
Black Eye, The 1938,Mr 8,22:4
How Long Till Summer 1949,D 28,30:3
Gillmore, Douglas
Greater Love 1931,Mr 3,39:1
Gillmore, Eleanor
Mikado, The 1931,Ag 25,17:7
Professor Mamlock 1937,Ap 14,30:3
Gillmore, Margalo
Straw, The 1921,N 11,16:2
Alias Jimmy Valentine 1921,D 9,20:3
He Who Gets Slapped 1922,Ja 10,15:1
Romantic Age, The 1922,N 15,22:1
As You Like It 1923,Ap 24,24:1
Scaramouche 1923,O 25,14:2
Outward Bound 1924,Ja 8,26:1
Outward Bound 1924,Ja 13,VII,1:1
Hedda Gabler 1924,My 17,18:4
Far Cry, The 1924,S 28,VII,2:1

Far Cry, The 1924,O 1,24:1
Habitual Husband, The 1924,D 25,27:3
Green Hat, The 1925,S 16,23:2
Green Hat, The 1925,S 20,VIII,1:1
Little Eyolf 1926,F 3,22:1
Juarez and Maximilian 1926,O 12,31:1
Juarez and Maximilian 1926,O 17,VIII,1:1
Ned McCobb's Daughter 1926,N 30,26:2
Silver Cord, The 1926,D 21,21:1
Second Man, The 1927,Ap 12,24:3
Marco Millions 1928,Ja 10,28:2
Volpone 1928,Ap 10,32:1
Man's Estate 1929,Ap 2,28:2
Man's Estate 1929,Ap 28,IX,1:1
Berkeley Square 1929,N 5,32:4
Berkeley Square 1929,D 1,X,1:1
Little Father of the Wilderness, The 1930,Je 3,27:1
Dark Tower, The 1933,N 27,20:3
Valley Forge 1934,N 27,26:4
Valley Forge 1934,D 11,28:3
Barretts of Wimpole Street, The 1935,F 26,16:2
Flowers of the Forest 1935,Ap 9,25:2
Remember the Day 1935,Je 30,15:1
Women, The 1936,D 8,30:6
Women, The 1936,D 28,13:1
No Time for Comedy 1939,Ap 18,26:4
No Time for Comedy 1939,Ap 30,XI,1:1
Outrageous Fortune 1943,N 4,28:5
State of the Union 1946,S 8,II,1:1
All My Sons 1948,My 12,33:3
Kind Sir 1953,S 28,21:2
Kind Sir 1953,N 5,41:2
Peter Pan 1954,O 21,30:2
Peter Pan 1954,O 31,II,1:1
Bad Seed, The 1955,My 1,II,3:1
Sail Away 1961,O 4,48:5
Gillmore, Ruth
Robbery, The 1921,Mr 1,18:1
49ers, The 1922,N 7,14:1
No More Frontier 1931,O 22,27:1
Farmer Takes a Wife, The 1934,O 31,17:1
Gillon, Marion
Wonderful Night, A; Fledermaus, Die
  1929,N 1,23:3
Gillyn, Allyn
Macushla 1920,My 18,9:3
Nature's Nobleman 1921,N 15,23:2
Ladies of the Evening 1924,D 24,11:2
Pleased to Meet You 1928,O 30,27:2
Silver Tassie, The 1929,O 25,26:1
Silver Tassie, The 1929,N 10,X,1:1
Gilman, Albert
Centuries, The 1927,N 30,23:1
Hoboken Blues 1928,F 18,10:1
Gilman, Judith
Kittiwake Island 1960,O 13,43:1
Sacco-Vanzetti 1969,F 9,78:1
Gilman, Sam
Nineteenth Hole of Europe, The 1949,Mr 28,16:2
Gilman, Toni
Let Freedom Ring 1935,N 7,26:2
My Fair Ladies 1941,Mr 24,12:7
Walking Gentleman, The 1942,My 8,26:2
Beat the Band 1942,O 15,26:1
Follow the Girls 1944,Ap 10,15:2
Men to the Sea 1944,O 4,25:2
Gilmore, Art (Miscellaneous)
Ice Capades 1962,Ag 30,34:1
Gilmore, Arthur
Infinite Shoeblack, The 1930,F 18,28:1
Gilmore, Douglas
Passing Present, The 1931,D 8,36:2
Two Strange Women 1933,Ja 11,23:3
Hold Your Horses 1933,S 26,26:4
Susan and God 1937,Ap 11,II,12:3
Susan and God 1937,Ap 25,X,2:6
Susan and God 1937,O 8,26:4
Cue for Passion 1940,D 20,33:4
Plan M 1942,F 21,15:2
Vagabond King, The 1943,Je 30,24:2
Susan and God 1943,D 14,30:2
Gilmore, Edward (Playwright)
Building 222 1950,F 3,28:2
Gilmore, Eleanor
Merry Widow, The 1929,D 3,29:1
Babes in Toyland 1929,D 24,15:3
Babes in Toyland 1930,D 22,17:1
Iolanthe 1931,Jl 14,21:5
Iolanthe 1934,My 1,26:4
Gondoliers, The 1935,Ag 6,20:5
Gilmore, Harris
Varying Shore, The 1921,D 6,24:1
White Cargo 1923,N 6,22:2
We Moderns 1924,Mr 12,17:2
Gilmore, Helen
When We Are Young 1920,N 23,11:1
Gilmore, Jeanette
Passing Show of 1923, The 1923,Je 15,24:6
Earl Carroll's Vanities 1925,Jl 7,24:1
Florida Girl 1925,N 3,34:1
Oh, Kay! 1926,N 9,31:3
Gilmore, Jeanne
Father Malachy's Miracle 1937,N 18,26:4

Gilmore, Lester
Wedding in Japan 1949,N 11,29:1
There Is No End 1950,F 17,27:4
John Brown 1950,My 4,32:7
Gilmore, Lowell
Fatal Alibi, The 1932,F 10,26:6
Autumn Crocus 1932,N 21,20:2
Wind and the Rain, The 1934,F 2,20:6
Lady Jane 1934,S 11,24:2
Prisoners of War 1935,Ja 29,24:1
Taming of the Shrew, The 1935,O 1,27:3
Leave Her to Heaven 1940,F 28,16:2
School for Scandal, The 1940,Je 23,IX,1:1
Golden Wings 1941,D 9,46:6
Family, The 1943,Mr 31,22:4
Gilmore, Paul
Hotbed 1928,N 10,20:7
Gilmore, Paul (Director)
Noble Rogue, A 1929,Ag 20,31:2
Gilmore, Paul (Producer)
Passion of Judas, The 1930,D 2,31:2
Gilmore, Peter
Fantasticks, The 1961,S 8,36:5
Gilmore, Ruth
Nest, The 1922,F 2,20:1
Gilmore, Virginia
Those Endearing Young Charms 1943,Je 17,16:3
World's Full of Girls, The 1943,D 7,31:2
Dear Ruth 1944,D 14,23:2
Dear Ruth 1944,D 31,II,1:1
Truckline Cafe 1946,F 28,19:4
Grey-Eyed People, The 1952,D 18,41:2
Critic's Choice 1960,D 15,61:3
Gilmore, William H (Director)
Naughty Cinderella 1925,N 10,23:6
Mozart 1926,N 23,26:2
Paris 1928,O 9,34:3
Lady of the Orchids, The 1928,D 14,37:3
Gilmour, Ailes
Iron Flowers 1933,Je 13,22:2
Gilmour, Arthur
Cyrano de Bergerac 1936,Ap 28,17:1
Enemy of the People, An 1937,F 16,19:1
Gilmour, Brian
Berkeley Square 1929,N 5,32:4
Gilner, Elias (Playwright)
Voice of Israel, The 1948,O 26,40:2
Backlane Center 1961,N 23,51:1
Gilner, Margaret
Patience 1928,Je 26,29:3
Gilpatrick, Betty
Sunny River 1941,D 5,28:2
Gilpin, Charles (Composer)
Don Quixote, Esquire 1920,My 7,12:6
Somebody's Lion 1921,Ap 13,20:1
Here's Howe 1923,Ap 26,19:3
That's That 1924,Ap 30,19:2
Joan of Arkansas 1925,Ap 5,16:1
Sale and a Sailor, A, or Glory! What Price!
  1926,Ap 25,30:4
This Way Out 1929,Ap 28,24:4
East Lynne Goes West 1931,My 3,I,26:5
Gilpin, Charles (Lyricist)
Don Quixote, Esquire 1920,My 7,12:6
Somebody's Lion 1921,Ap 13,20:1
Here's Howe 1923,Ap 26,19:3
That's That 1924,Ap 30,19:2
Joan of Arkansas 1925,Ap 5,16:1
This Way Out 1929,Ap 28,24:4
Gilpin, Charles S
Emperor Jones, The 1920,N 7,VII,1:3
Emperor Jones, The 1920,D 28,9:1
Roseanne 1924,Mr 11,16:3
So That's That 1925,D 15,28:3
Gilpin, Gertrude
Criminals, The 1941,D 22,24:3
Mexican Mural; Miracle Painting 1942,Ap 27,19:2
Gilpin, Richard B
Petticoat Fever 1937,Mr 21,II,7:3
Gilren, Grace
Banjo Eyes 1941,D 26,20:2
Gilrod, L (Lyricist)
Jolly Orphan, The 1929,D 23,18:6
Gilrod, Minnie
Love and Politics 1929,O 21,30:7
Gilroy, Frank D (Playwright)
Who'll Save the Plowboy? 1962,Ja 10,24:2
Who'll Save the Plowboy? 1962,Ja 28,II,1:1
Subject Was Roses, The 1964,My 26,45:1
Subject Was Roses, The 1964,Je 7,II,1:1
That Summer-That Fall 1967,Mr 17,33:1
Phedre 1967,Ap 2,II,1:1
Only Game in Town, The 1968,My 21,42:1
Gilson, Paul (Playwright)
Ex-Napoleon 1960,D 29,16:3
Gilson, Tom
Nobody's Child 1956,Ag 23,25:2
Gilvey, John
Passion Play 1938,Mr 7,11:2
Gilzinger, Poldi
Versunkene Glocke, Die 1936,N 20,26:3
Gimbel, Harriet
Greenwich Village Follies 1922,S 13,18:2

Gimbel, Harriet—Cont
Artists and Models 1923,Ag 21,12:2
Gimbel, Norman (Lyricist)
Shoestring '57 1956,N 6,31:1
Whoop-Up 1958,D 23,2:7
Conquering Hero, The 1961,Ja 17,40:2
Gimeno, Rosita Diaz
Teahouse of the August Moon, The 1956,Ap 20,22:1
Teahouse of the August Moon, The 1956,My 7,31:8
Gines, Jesse
Too Many Boats 1934,S 12,26:3
Ginger
Daddy Dumplins 1920,N 23,11:1
Cheri 1959,O 13,44:1
Gingersnaps, The
Harlem Cavalcade 1942,My 2,11:2
Gingles, Keith
Desert Song, The 1946,Ja 9,20:2
Gingold, Hermione
John Murray Anderson's Almanac 1953,D 11,42:2
Almanac 1954,Ja 3,II,1:1
First Impressions 1959,Mr 20,28:1
From A to Z 1960,Ap 21,23:2
Oh Dad, Poor Dad, Mamma's Hung You in the Closet and I'm Feelin' So Sad 1963,Ag 28,28:2
Gingold, Hermione (Playwright)
From A to Z 1960,Ap 21,23:2
Gingold, Marc (Scenic Designer)
Undercover Man 1966,Je 3,30:2
Gingold, Marvin (Lighting Director)
Enchanting Melody 1964,N 25,40:1
Gingold, Marvin (Scenic Designer)
Enchanting Melody 1964,N 25,40:1
Gingold, Sara
Voice of Israel, The 1948,O 26,40:2
Hershel, The Jester 1948,D 14,39:2
Wish Me Luck! 1954,N 1,37:2
Shepherd King, The 1955,O 13,36:2
Brothers Ashkenazi, The 1955,N 12,24:4
Devil's Game, A 1959,N 9,35:6
In-Laws 1960,O 17,32:4
Country Boy, The 1963,O 28,20:1
Gingrich, Susan (Costume Designer)
Beclch 1968,D 17,59:1
Ginn, Robert
'Tis Pity She's a Whore 1967,O 21,15:2
Ginnes, Abram S (Playwright)
Drink to Me Only 1958,O 9,47:4
Let It Ride 1961,O 13,27:4
Ginnett Family, The
Better Times 1922,S 4,14:2
Ginnosuke
Kumagai Jinya 1969,S 18,64:1
Gino, George
Bad Seed, The 1954,D 9,42:1
Ginsberg, Allen
Originale 1964,S 9,46:1
Ginsberg, Arthur (Lighting Director)
Great Goodness of Life (A Coon Show) 1969,Ap 27,92:1
Gentleman Caller, The 1969,Ap 27,92:1
Prayer Meeting: or, The First Militant Minister 1969,Ap 27,92:1
Warning, The-A Theme for Linda 1969,Ap 27,92:1
Ginsberg, Edward (Miscellaneous)
Not Now Darling 1970,O 30,33:1
Ginsberg, Gerald M (Miscellaneous)
Matty and the Moron and Madonna 1965,Mr 30,53:1
Ginsburg, Hilda (Playwright)
Yo Ho Hum 1927,My 7,15:1
Ginsburg, Mirra (Translator)
Sunset 1966,My 13,34:1
Ginsbury, Norman (Playwright)
Viceroy Sarah 1934,Je 24,IX,1:4
Viceroy Sarah 1935,F 13,27:4
Viceroy Sarah 1935,Mr 10,VIII,2:1
Ghosts 1937,N 28,XI,2:1
Viceroy Sarah 1939,Ag 15,14:4
Anne of England 1941,O 8,26:2
First Gentleman, The 1945,Jl 19,18:8
First Gentleman, The 1945,Ag 5,II,1:2
First Gentleman, The 1957,Ap 26,22:2
First Gentleman, The 1957,My 5,II,1:1
Peer Gynt 1960,Ja 13,21:1
Ginsbury, Norman (Translator)
Peer Gynt 1960,Ja 24,II,1:1
Dance of Death, The 1966,Je 3,31:1
Gintaro
Untitled-Revue 1924,F 19,12:1
Ginty, Elizabeth B (Playwright)
Missouri Legend 1938,S 20,27:2
Missouri Legend 1938,S 25,IX,1:1
Missouri Legend 1951,F 10,10:4
Gintzburger, Andre (Director)
On Ne Badine Pas Avec l'Amour; No Trifling With Love 1968,Mr 5,35:1
Ginzburg, Kalman (Miscellaneous)
I'm Solomon 1968,Ap 24,51:1
Ginzler, Robert (Miscellaneous)
Gypsy 1959,My 22,31:6
Girls Against the Boys, The 1959,N 3,26:1
Bye Bye Birdie 1960,Ap 15,13:4

Irma la Douce 1960,S 30,31:2
Wildcat 1960,D 17,20:2
Conquering Hero, The 1961,Ja 17,40:2
Donnybrook! 1961,My 19,23:1
How to Succeed in Business Without Really Trying 1961,O 16,34:1
Family Affair, A 1962,Ja 29,17:1
All American 1962,Mr 20,44:1
Bravo Giovanni 1962,My 21,41:2
Nowhere to Go But Up 1962,N 12,36:2
Giono (Playwright)
Lanceurs des Graines 1933,Jl 23,IX,1:3
Giordano, Frank R
Gertrude Stein's First Reader 1969,D 16,56:1
Children in the Rain 1970,O 3,14:1
Giordano, Frank R (Director)
Children in the Rain 1970,O 3,14:1
Giordano, Gus
Babes in Arms 1951,Mr 10,7:3
Giordano, Tony (Miscellaneous)
Glorious Ruler, The 1969,Jl 1,31:1
Giorloff, Ruth
Pirates of Penzance, The 1942,F 20,20:2
Giorloff, Ruth (Playwright)
Jazz and Minuet 1927,My 6,20:3
Giovanelli, Elvira
Passion Play 1937,Mr 22,26:6
Giovanni, Guy Bon
Serjeant Musgrave's Dance 1966,Mr 9,44:1
Giovanni, Paul
School for Wives 1957,Je 20,23:4
West of the Moon 1961,Je 29,26:1
Viet Rock 1966,N 11,38:1
Giovannini, Caesar (Composer)
Kukla, Burr and Ollie 1960,N 1,47:2
Giovannini, Sandro (Director)
Rugantino 1964,F 7,34:1
Giovannini, Sandro (Lyricist)
Rugantino 1964,F 2,II,1:4
Rugantino 1964,F 7,34:1
Ciao, Rudy 1966,Ja 8,15:3
Giovannini, Sandro (Playwright)
Rugantino 1964,F 2,II,1:4
Rugantino 1964,F 7,34:1
Gippner, Erika
Three Sisters, The 1955,F 26,13:2
Sea Gull, The 1956,O 23,38:1
Gipson, Karl
Sacco-Vanzetti 1969,F 9,78:1
Giquel, Bernard (Playwright)
Boys in the Band, The 1969,S 20,21:2
Girard, Andre (Miscellaneous)
Vie Parisienne, La 1964,Mr 11,34:2
Girard, Eddie
Marion Show, The 1923,My 8,22:3
City Chap, The 1925,O 27,21:1
Girard, Gilbert
Twelve Miles Out 1925,N 17,29:2
Girard, Helene
Purity 1930,D 26,18:2
Girard, Isabel
Great Lady 1938,D 2,26:6
Girard, Lois
Let Freedom Sing 1942,O 6,18:2
Girard, Louis
Mamba's Daughters 1953,Mr 21,12:6
Point of No Return 1957,Mr 23,17:2
Time of the Cuckoo, The 1958,O 28,40:2
Distant Bell, A 1960,Ja 14,29:1
Come Share My House 1960,F 19,20:2
Purple Canary, The 1963,Ap 23,31:1
Girard, Maxime (Playwright)
Prenez Ma Dame 1923,N 27,23:5
Girard, Paulette
Boy Friend, The 1954,O 1,20:1
Girard, Pauline
Little Theatre Tournament; White Peacock, The 1928,My 11,28:1
Girardot, Annie
Idiote, L' 1960,S 16,39:4
Girardot, Etienne
Two Little Girls in Blue 1921,My 4,10:3
World We Live In, The 1922,N 1,16:1
Exile, The 1923,Ap 10,24:2
School for Scandal, The 1923,Je 5,24:3
Farmer's Wife, The 1924,O 10,22:3
Arabesque 1925,O 21,20:2
Merry-Go-Round 1927,Je 1,25:4
Becky Sharp 1929,Je 4,29:1
Bonds of Interest, The 1929,O 15,34:2
Lysistrata 1930,Ap 29,30:5
Lysistrata 1930,Je 6,20:1
I Love an Actress 1931,S 18,29:2
House of Doom, The 1932,Ja 26,20:4
20th Century 1932,D 30,15:1
Girasoli, Italo
Arzigogolo, L'; Whim, The 1931,Ap 27,24:4
Giraud, Anna (Mme) (Scenic Designer)
Dear Jane 1932,N 15,24:3
Giraud, Claude
Phedre 1963,O 21,39:1
Berenice 1963,O 30,46:1

Giraudoux, Jean (Original Author)
Siegfried 1928,My 20,VIII,1:3
Siegfried 1939,F 21,15:2
Enchanted, The 1950,Ja 19,34:2
Madwoman of Chaillot, The 1950,Je 14,41:2
Dear World 1969,F 16,II,1:1
Giraudoux, Jean (Playwright)
Siegfried 1928,My 20,VIII,1:3
Amphitryon 38 1929,D 1,X,4:1
Siegfried 1930,O 21,34:1
Amphitryon 38 1931,Mr 15,IX,2:4
Judith 1931,N 29,VIII,3:1
Intermezzo 1933,Mr 26,IX,2:1
Amphitryon 38 1934,F 11,IX,3:7
Tessa 1935,Ja 6,IX,2:1
Guerre de Troie N'Aura pas Lieu, La 1935,D 29,IX,2:1
Amphitryon 38 1937,Je 24,30:2
Electra 1937,Jl 4,X,2:1
Amphitryon 38 1937,N 2,32:2
Amphitryon 38 1938,Je 5,IX,2:6
Mr Banks of Birmingham 1939,Ja 21,18:4
Folle de Chaillot, La 1945,D 20,17:4
Madwoman of Chaillot, The 1948,D 26,II,3:1
Madwoman of Chaillot, The 1949,Ja 9,II,1:1
Madwoman of Chaillot, The 1949,S 11,II,1:1
Pour Lucrece 1953,N 29,II,3:1
Ondine 1954,F 19,23:1
Ondine 1954,F 28,II,1:1
Apollo of Bellac, The 1954,My 29,12:1
Apollo of Bellac, The 1954,Je 6,II,1:1
Tiger at the Gates 1955,Je 3,27:1
Tiger at the Gates 1955,Je 12,II,1:1
Tiger at the Gates 1955,O 4,40:1
Tiger at the Gates 1955,O 23,II,1:1
Intermezzo 1957,F 15,20:4
Apollo of Bellac, The 1957,Ap 10,39:1
Virtuous Island, The 1957,Ap 10,39:1
Apollo of Bellac, The 1958,Mr 7,17:2
Enchanted, The 1958,Ap 23,41:1
Song of Songs 1958,O 29,31:1
Duel of Angels 1960,Ap 20,42:2
Duel of Angels 1960,My 1,II,1:1
Judith 1962,Je 21,25:4
Judith 1965,Mr 25,42:2
Judith 1965,Ap 4,II,1:1
Tiger at the Gates 1968,Mr 1,30:1
Tiger at the Gates 1968,Mr 10,II,1:1
Dear World 1969,F 7,33:1
Madwoman of Chaillot, The 1970,Mr 23,48:3
Girel, Denise
H M S Pinafore 1961,Je 9,29:5
Girod, Roger
Hot Money 1931,N 9,22:2
Girouard, Tina (Miscellaneous)
Red Horse Animation, The 1970,N 20,32:1
Giroux, Claude (Producer)
Rendezvous at Senlis 1961,F 28,39:2
Six Characters in Search of an Author 1963,Mr 11,7:2
Glass Menagerie, The 1965,My 5,53:2
Giroux, Germaine
Spider, The 1927,Mr 23,29:1
Carnival 1929,Ap 25,32:5
Ladies of the Jury 1929,O 6,IX,1:4
Ladies of the Jury 1929,O 22,26:2
It's a Grand Life 1930,F 11,30:3
Ladies All 1930,Jl 20,VIII,2:1
Ladies All 1930,Jl 29,25:2
Miracle at Verdun 1931,Mr 17,34:6
Henry V 1956,Je 20,27:2
Giroux, John
Much Ado About Nothing 1952,My 2,20:1
Girsdansky, Barbara
Mascaiada 1929,D 28,10:6
Giruso, Benny
Great Big Doorstep, The 1950,Mr 18,8:6
Girvan, Pat
Man Who Washed His Hands, The 1967,F 16,33:1
Girven, Howard
Happy Hypocrite, The 1968,S 6,38:1
Billy 1969,Mr 24,56:1
Girvin, Brenda (Playwright)
Cautious Campbell 1927,Ag 14,VII,1:7
Madame Plays Nap 1929,D 18,31:2
Girvin, Virginia
Macbeth 1936,Ap 15,25:4
Out of My House 1942,Ja 8,28:6
Long Way From Home, A 1948,F 9,25:2
Gischia, Leon (Costume Designer)
Triomphe de l'Amour, Le 1958,O 17,32:1
Marie Tudor 1958,O 22,39:1
Don Juan 1958,O 29,29:1
Cid, Le 1958,O 31,35:2
Gischia, Leon (Scenic Designer)
Lorenzaccio 1958,O 15,44:2
Triomphe de l'Amour, Le 1958,O 17,32:1
Marie Tudor 1958,O 22,39:1
Gish, Dorothy
Young Love 1928,Ag 12,VII,1:2
Young Love 1928,S 30,IX,2:7
Young Love 1928,O 31,28:1
Young Love 1929,Jl 4,8:4

Inspector General, The 1930,D 24,19:2
Getting Married 1931,Mr 31,25:5
Streets of New York, The 1931,O 7,29:1
Pillars of Society, The 1931,O 15,19:1
Bride the Sun Shines On, The 1931,D 28,20:2
Foreign Affairs 1932,Ap 14,25:5
By Your Leave 1934,Ja 25,15:3
Brittle Heaven 1934,N 14,22:5
Mainly for Lovers 1936,F 11,19:5
Mainly for Lovers 1936,F 22,13:2
Russet Mantle 1936,Ag 18,15:2
Missouri Legend 1938,S 20,27:2
Morning's at Seven 1939,D 1,26:2
Morning's at Seven 1939,D 17,IX,3:1
Love for Love 1940,Je 4,19:5
Great Big Doorstep, The 1942,N 27,26:2
Magnificent Yankee, The 1946,Ja 18,25:2
Magnificent Yankee, The 1946,Ja 23,21:2
Magnificent Yankee, The 1946,F 3,II,1:2
Story of Mary Surratt, The 1947,F 10,25:2
Man, The 1950,Ja 20,28:2

Gish, Lillian
Uncle Vanya 1930,Ap 16,26:5
Uncle Vanya 1930,My 4,XI,1:1
Uncle Vanya 1930,S 23,30:3
Camille 1932,N 2,23:3
Nine Pine Street 1933,Ap 28,15:5
Joyous Season, The 1934,Ja 30,16:3
Within the Gates 1934,O 23,23:1
Within the Gates 1934,O 28,IX,1:1
Hamlet 1936,O 1,28:3
Hamlet 1936,O 9,30:2
Star-Wagon, The 1937,S 17,28:5
Star-Wagon, The 1937,S 30,18:5
Star-Wagon, The 1937,O 10,XI,1:1
Dear Octopus 1939,Ja 12,22:2
Life With Father 1940,Mr 3,X,2:5
Mr Sycamore 1942,N 14,13:2
Mr Sycamore 1942,N 29,VIII,1:1
Crime and Punishment 1947,D 23,29:3
Crime and Punishment 1948,Ja 4,II,1:1
Curious Savage, The 1950,O 25,44:3
Trip to Bountiful, The 1953,N 4,30:3
Trip to Bountiful, The 1953,N 15,II,1:1
Family Reunion, The 1958,O 21,39:1
Family Reunion, The 1958,O 26,II,1:1
All the Way Home 1960,D 1,42:1
All the Way Home 1960,D 18,II,3:1
All the Way Home 1960,D 27,26:7
Too True to Be Good 1963,Mr 14,8:2
Too True to Be Good 1963,Mr 23,5:6
Romeo and Juliet 1965,Je 21,36:3
Anya 1965,N 30,48:1
I Never Sang for My Father 1968,Ja 26,30:1
I Never Sang for My Father 1968,F 4,II,1:1

Gissentanner, Joyce
Green Pastures, The 1951,Mr 16,35:2

Gist, Robert
Harvey 1944,N 2,23:2
Caine Mutiny Court-Martial, The 1954,Ja 21,27:2

Gist, Robert (Director)
Conversation at Midnight 1964,N 13,27:1

Gistirak, Joseph (Director)
Playboy of the Western World, The 1958,My 9,19:2
Shadow and Substance 1959,N 4,42:1

Gitlin, Murray
Finian's Rainbow 1953,Mr 7,13:2
Golden Apple, The 1954,Mr 12,15:2
Guitar 1959,N 11,42:5
King and I, The 1960,My 12,40:1

Gitlin, Murray (Miscellaneous)
Minor Adjustment, A 1967,O 7,33:3
Private Lives 1968,My 20,59:1
What the Butler Saw 1970,My 5,56:1

Gitlitz, Benny
Hershel, The Jester 1948,D 14,39:2

Gittens, Clarence E
Hit the Road 1941,Ap 4,18:3

Gittens, Hugh (Director)
Street Sounds 1970,O 23,32:1

Gittens, Hugh (Miscellaneous)
Evening With the Times Square Two, An 1967,My 21,83:6

Gitter, Dean
Doctor and the Devils, The 1959,Ja 21,27:8

Gitter, Dean (Director)
Puntila 1959,My 15,26:2

Gittings, John
Spoon River Anthology 1964,Je 27,15:2

Gitz-Rice
Vaudeville (Palace) 1924,S 16,26:5
Vaudeville (Palace) 1927,O 11,27:2

Giudici, Ann (Director)
Lovers in the Metro, The 1962,Ja 31,21:1
Lion in Love, The 1963,Ap 26,28:3

Giudici, Ann (Lyricist)
Lion in Love, The 1963,Ap 26,28:3

Giudici, Ann (Producer)
Information Bureau, The 1962,Ja 31,21:1
Keyhole, The 1962,Ja 31,21:1
Lovers in the Metro, The 1962,Ja 31,21:1

Giuffre, Jimmy
Next President, The 1958,Ap 10,34:3

Giuffre, Jimmy Quartet
Apparition Theater of Prague, The 1966,N 17,56:2

Giuliano, Frederic
Crime and Punishment 1935,Ja 23,20:3
Chalk Dust 1936,Mr 5,24:5
Tell My Story 1939,Mr 16,26:6

Giuliano, Peter
Life and Times of J Walter Smintheus, The 1970,D 10,59:1

Giunta, Aldo (Playwright)
Transgressor Rides Again, The 1969,My 21,42:1

Giuran and Marguerite
Last Waltz, The 1921,My 11,20:3

Given, Susan
Tragedy of Nan, The 1920,F 18,9:1

Givens, Charles G (Original Author)
Mr Peebles and Mr Hooker 1946,O 11,29:2

Givens, Wesley
Jamboree 1932,N 25,18:4
Queer People 1934,F 16,16:2
Every Man for Himself 1940,D 10,32:3

Givney, Kathryn
Ballyhoo 1927,Ja 5,18:1
We All Do 1927,Mr 1,30:3
Nightstick 1927,N 11,20:4
Behavior of Mrs Crane, The 1928,Mr 21,30:1
Peter Flies High 1931,N 10,28:3
Absent Father 1932,O 18,23:5
Lost Horizons 1934,O 16,31:2
If This Be Treason 1935,S 24,28:2
Fulton of Oak Falls 1937,Ja 2,15:3
Fulton of Oak Falls 1937,F 11,18:2
One Thing After Another 1937,D 29,17:2
Happiest Days, The 1939,Ap 12,26:2
Life With Father 1939,Ag 15,14:4
Royal Family, The 1940,Ag 13,15:3
Little Dark Horse 1941,N 17,14:4
Flowers of Virtue, The 1942,F 6,22:2
Wallflower 1944,Ja 27,14:2
Good Night Ladies 1945,Ja 18,16:2
This, Too, Shall Pass 1946,My 1,32:4

Givnoux, Regis (Playwright)
Kama Sutra, Le 1923,N 13,24:2

Givot, George
Constant Sinner, The 1931,Ag 30,VIII,1:6
Constant Sinner, The 1931,S 15,30:1
Americana 1932,S 25,IX,1:6
Americana 1932,O 6,19:3
Pardon My English 1933,Ja 21,11:4
Mexican Hayride 1944,Ja 29,9:6
Mexican Hayride 1944,F 6,II,1:1
Wonderful Town 1958,Mr 6,32:4
Do Re Mi 1960,D 27,23:2
Do Re Mi 1961,Ja 8,II,1:1

Glad, Gladys
Rio Rita 1927,F 3,18:3
Rosalie 1928,Ja 11,26:3
Whoopee 1928,D 5,34:3
Ziegfeld Follies 1931,Jl 2,30:5

Gladding, Hazel
Moon Is a Gong, The 1926,Mr 13,21:3

Gladdings, Helen
Buzzin' Around 1920,Jl 7,14:1

Glade, Carol
Babes in the Wood 1964,D 29,21:2

Gladiov, Alexander (Playwright)
Deathless, The 1943,Jl 11,II,1:2

Gladke, Peter
Paradise Island 1961,Je 24,11:1
Around the World in 80 Days 1963,Je 24,22:1
Around the World in 80 Days 1964,Je 29,33:2
Mardi Gras! 1965,Je 28,33:2
Mardi Gras! 1966,Jl 11,32:2

Gladstone, Blanche
Paradise Lost 1935,D 10,31:5
Please Do Not Disturb 1936,Je 23,27:1
Lower North 1944,Ag 26,15:4

Gladstone, Christopher
Night Thoreau Spent in Jail, The 1970,N 2,66:1

Gladstone, Gail
Set My People Free 1948,N 4,38:2

Gladstone, Isaac
Salt and Pepper 1933,Ap 24,10:2
Untitled-Revue 1935,S 23,20:2

Gladstone, Timoney
Bomboola 1929,Je 27,17:3

Glaenzer, Doris
Cape Cod Follies 1929,S 19,37:2

Glaenzer, Marion
Cape Cod Follies 1929,S 19,37:2

Glaeser, Gaye
When I Was a Child 1960,D 9,38:1

Glagolin, B S (Director)
Gardener's Dog, The 1927,O 21,27:1

Glagolin, B S (Playwright)
Gardener's Dog, The 1927,O 21,27:1

Glagolin, Boris (Director)
Turandot 1929,Ja 12,14:4
Othello 1929,F 4,21:2

Glancey, Alfred R Jr (Miscellaneous)
Midgie Purvis 1961,F 2,25:3

Glancy, Alfred R Jr (Producer)
Miss Lonelyhearts 1957,O 4,26:2

Glanternik, Toby
Matty and the Moron and Madonna 1965,Mr 30,53:1

Glanville, Maxwell
Natural Man 1941,My 8,20:4
Home Is the Hunter 1945,D 21,25:4
Walk Hard 1946,Mr 28,34:2
Rain 1948,F 2,15:2
How Long Till Summer 1949,D 28,30:3
Freight 1950,Ap 27,36:2
Son, The 1950,Ag 16,24:6
Autumn Garden, The 1951,Mr 8,36:2
In Splendid Error 1954,O 27,33:6
Cat on a Hot Tin Roof 1955,Mr 25,18:2
Cool World, The 1960,F 23,38:2
Golden Boy 1964,O 21,56:1
Zelda 1969,Mr 6,38:1

Glanville, Maxwell (Miscellaneous)
Blacks, The 1961,My 5,23:1

Glasco, Joseph (Miscellaneous)
House of Breath, The 1957,Ap 15,23:2

Glascow, George
If Booth Had Missed 1931,My 14,27:1

Glaser, Darel
Wozzeck 1966,Ap 6,34:1
Cry for Us All 1970,Ap 9,48:2

Glaser, Michael
Butterflies Are Free 1969,O 22,30:1

Glaser, Milton (Miscellaneous)
Signs Along the Cynic Route 1961,D 15,49:5

Glaser, Paul M
Hamlet 1967,D 27,45:1

Glaser, Vaughan
Cross-Town 1937,Mr 18,21:5
Many Mansions 1937,O 28,28:6
What a Life 1938,Ap 14,26:2
Boy Who Lived Twice, A 1945,S 12,31:2
Throng o' Scarlet 1947,D 2,37:2

Glasgow, Bonnie
Merry Widow, The 1961,O 27,28:2
Vagabond King, The 1961,N 24,36:1

Glasgow, Patrick
Getting Even 1929,Ag 20,31:1
Silver Tassie, The 1929,O 25,26:1
Tyrant, The 1930,N 13,33:1
Peter Ibbetson 1931,Ap 9,30:3
Venetian, The 1931,N 2,26:1
Christopher Comes Across 1932,Je 1,19:2

Glaspell, Susan (Director)
Trifles 1932,Ja 30,13:6

Glaspell, Susan (Playwright)
Inheritors 1921,Mr 27,VII,1:2
Verge, The 1921,N 15,23:2
Verge, The 1921,N 20,VI,1:1
Chains of Dew 1922,Ap 28,20:2
Inheritors 1925,S 28,24:3
Inheritors 1926,Ja 3,VII,2:8
Trifles 1927,F 13,VII,4:6
Inheritors 1927,Mr 8,23:1
Inheritors 1927,Mr 20,VIII,1:1
Little Theatre Tournament; Trifles 1928,My 11,28:1
Comic Artist, The 1928,Jl 22,VII,1:3
Comic Artist, The 1929,N 23,19:3
Alison's House 1930,D 2,31:2
Alison's House 1931,My 10,VIII,1:1
Alison's House 1931,My 12,29:2
Trifles 1932,Ja 30,13:6
Alison's House 1932,N 13,IX,3:4
Comic Artist, The 1933,Ap 20,20:3

Glass, Frank
Finian's Rainbow 1953,Mr 7,13:2
Shakespeare in Harlem 1959,O 28,40:7
Soul Gone Home 1959,O 28,40:7
God's Trombones 1960,F 10,43:4
Shakespeare in Harlem 1960,F 10,43:4

Glass, George
Panic 1935,Mr 16,18:4
Stork Mad 1936,O 1,28:4

Glass, Mary Ellen
Innocent Voyage, The 1943,N 16,27:2

Glass, Montague (Playwright)
Potasch und Perlmutter 1921,Je 5,VI,1:3
Partners Again 1922,My 2,22:2
Partners Again 1922,My 14,VII,1:1
49ers, The 1922,N 7,14:1
49ers, The 1922,N 12,VIII,1:1
Potash and Perlmutter, Detectives; Poisoned by Pictures 1926,S 1,27:3
Potash and Perlmutter, Detectives 1926,S 5,VII,1:1
Keeping Expenses Down 1932,O 21,25:2
Potash and Perlmutter 1935,Ap 6,11:3

Glass, Ned
Counsellor-at-Law 1931,N 7,17:2
Between Two Worlds 1934,O 26,24:2
Hot Corner, The 1956,Ja 26,25:2

Glass, Philip (Composer)
Red Horse Animation, The 1970,N 20,32:1

Glass, Ron
Serjeant Musgrave's Dance 1968,Je 16,52:4
Resistible Rise of Arturo Ui, The 1968,Ag 8,25:1
Resistible Rise of Arturo Ui, The 1968,D 23,44:1

Glass, Shelley
Mother Courage and Her Children 1964,My 12,32:2

Glass, Walter
Aloma of the South Seas 1925,Ap 21,18:1
Little Spitfire, The 1926,Ag 17,15:2
This Man's Town 1930,Mr 11,24:4
Constant Sinner, The 1931,S 15,30:1
Boy Friend, The 1932,Je 8,22:3
Lambs Gambol 1933,Ap 24,10:1

Glasser, Leonard (Miscellaneous)
Square in the Eye 1965,My 20,54:1

Glassford, David
Lassie 1920,Ap 7,9:2
Pagans 1921,Ja 5,11:1
Blue Lagoon, The 1921,S 15,16:1
Vortex, The 1925,S 17,20:1
Henry IV, Part I 1926,Je 1,29:1
Seed of the Brute 1926,N 2,34:3
Julius Caesar 1927,Je 7,27:2
Command to Love, The 1927,S 21,27:1
Bachelor Father, The 1928,F 29,28:2
Michael and Mary 1929,D 14,23:3
Criminal at Large 1932,O 11,26:3
For Services Rendered 1933,Ap 13,15:5
Taming of the Shrew, The 1935,O 1,27:3

Glassman, Stephen (Director)
Summertree 1969,D 10,60:1

Glassman, Stephen (Playwright)
Billy 1969,Mr 24,56:1

Glassman, William
Music Man, The 1965,Je 17,26:4
Come Summer 1969,Mr 19,43:1

Glassmeyer, Edward Jr
What a Relief 1935,D 14,10:6

Glassoff, Charles
Henri Christophe 1945,Je 7,24:5

Glattstein, Jacob (Miscellaneous)
Untitled-Poetry Reading 1967,Jl 18,29:1

Glaze, Sugar
Best of Burlesque 1957,S 30,27:2

Glazebrook, G Truxton (Mrs)
Our Betters 1937,Jl 22,16:2

Glazer, Benjamin F (Miscellaneous)
Liliom 1932,O 27,23:2
Liliom 1940,Mr 26,17:2
Carousel 1945,Ap 20,24:2
Carousel 1954,Je 13,II,1:1

Glazer, Benjamin F (Playwright)
Thy Name Is Woman 1920,N 16,19:1
Liliom 1921,Ap 21,18:1
Children's Tragedy, The 1921,O 12,18:2
Montmartre 1922,F 14,20:1
Fashions for Men 1922,D 6,22:1
Tyrants 1924,Mr 5,14:1
Summer Night 1939,N 3,17:1
Fifth Column, The 1940,Ja 27,9:1
Fifth Column, The 1940,F 4,IX,1:6
Fifth Column, The 1940,Mr 7,18:2
Fifth Column, The 1940,Mr 17,X,1:1
Carousel 1954,Je 3,32:2
Liliom 1956,F 18,12:5
Carousel 1957,S 12,38:2

Glazer, Benjamin F (Translator)
Liliom 1921,Ap 24,VI,1:1

Glazer, Darel
Tea Party 1968,O 16,40:1

Glazer, Maurice (Director)
Montserrat 1954,My 26,34:2

Glazer, Maurice (Miscellaneous)
Making of Moo, The 1958,Je 12,34:1
Harlequinade 1959,F 14,15:1
Electra 1959,F 14,15:1

Glazer, Maurice (Producer)
Montserrat 1954,My 26,34:2

Glazer, Tom
Robin Hood 1950,N 6,32:2

Gleason, Adda
Dust Heap, The 1924,Ap 25,20:2

Gleason, Ellen
Show Boat 1954,My 6,44:1

Gleason, Helen
Frederika 1937,F 5,16:5
Night of Love 1940,O 29,32:6
Night of Love 1941,Ja 8,14:2
Merry Widow, The 1942,Jl 16,22:1

Gleason, Jackie
Keep Off the Grass 1940,My 24,22:6
Artists and Models 1943,N 6,16:6
Follow the Girls 1944,Ap 10,15:2
Follow the Girls 1944,Ap 16,II,1:2
Along Fifth Avenue 1949,Ja 14,28:2
Take Me Along 1959,O 23,22:2
Take Me Along 1959,N 1,II,1:1

Gleason, James
Charm School, The 1920,Ag 3,12:1
Like a King 1921,O 4,10:1
Deep Tangled Wildwood, The 1923,N 6,22:1
Lady Killer, The 1924,Mr 13,14:2
Is Zat So? 1925,Ja 6,23:4
Is Zat So? 1925,F 1,VII,1:1
Lambs Gambol 1925,Ap 27,15:1
Shannons of Broadway, The 1927,S 11,VIII,1:3
Shannons of Broadway, The 1927,S 27,30:4

Shannons of Broadway, The 1927,O 9,VIII,1:1

Gleason, James (Director)
Butter and Egg Man, The 1925,S 24,28:1

Gleason, James (Playwright)
Fall Guy, The 1924,Jl 20,VII,1:7
Is Zat So? 1925,Ja 6,23:4
Fall Guy, The 1925,Mr 11,19:1
Fall Guy, The 1926,O 10,VIII,2:1
Shannons of Broadway, The 1927,S 27,30:4
Shannons of Broadway, The 1927,O 9,VIII,1:1
Rain or Shine 1928,F 10,26:3
Puffy 1928,Jl 29,VII,2:2

Gleason, John (Lighting Director)
Tartuffe 1965,Ja 15,23:1
Grosse Valise, La 1965,D 15,52:1
Alchemist, The 1966,O 14,48:1
Father Uxbridge Wants to Marry 1967,O 30,57:1
Happiness 1967,N 11,25:2
Walking to Waldheim 1967,N 11,25:2
Saint Joan 1968,Ja 5,42:1
Tiger at the Gates 1968,Mr 1,30:1
Summertree 1968,Mr 4,29:1
Cyrano de Bergerac 1968,Ap 26,30:1
Lovers and Other Strangers 1968,S 19,63:1
Great White Hope, The 1968,O 4,40:1
We Bombed in New Haven 1968,O 17,51:1
King Lear 1968,N 8,43:1
Cry of Players, A 1968,N 15,40:1
Bananas 1968,D 5,60:1
Great Career, A 1968,D 30,25:1
Evening for Merlin Finch, An 1968,D 30,25:1
Blueprints 1969,F 25,36:1
Tale of Kasane, The 1969,F 25,36:1
Gianni Schicci 1969,F 25,36:1
In the Matter of J Robert Oppenheimer
 1969,Mr 7,28:1
Inner Journey, The 1969,Mr 21,42:1
Home Fires 1969,Ap 8,42:1
Cop-Out 1969,Ap 8,42:1
Hamlet 1969,My 2,38:1
Miser, The 1969,My 9,35:1
Year Boston Won the Pennant, The
 1969,My 23,38:1
Time of Your Life, The 1969,N 7,37:1
Increased Difficulty of Concentration, The
 1969,D 5,48:1
Camino Real 1970,Ja 9,42:1
Songs From Milk Wood 1970,Ja 13,41:1
Sganarelle 1970,Ja 13,41:1
Brightower 1970,Ja 29,32:1
Disintegration of James Cherry, The
 1970,Ja 30,33:3
Operation Sidewinder 1970,Mr 13,33:1
Operation Sidewinder 1970,Mr 22,II,1:4
Silence 1970,Ap 3,43:1
Landscape 1970,Ap 3,43:1
Candida 1970,Ap 7,41:1
Amphitryon 1970,My 29,13:1
All's Well That Ends Well 1970,Je 16,53:1
Othello 1970,Je 22,43:1
Devil's Disciple, The 1970,Je 30,48:1
Othello 1970,S 15,51:1
Good Woman of Setzuan, The 1970,N 6,51:1
Two by Two 1970,N 11,37:1

Gleason, Marguerite
Lady Windermere's Fan 1946,O 15,29:2

Gleason, Mary Elizabeth (La Americana)
Farandula, La 1930,Mr 25,34:6

Gleason, Michael
Distant Bell, A 1960,Ja 14,29:1

Gleason, Mina
Like a King 1921,O 4,10:1
Her Salary Man 1921,N 29,20:1
Red Geranium, The 1922,My 9,22:3
Zeno 1923,Ag 27,14:2
Wild Birds 1925,Ap 10,16:1
Sure Fire! 1926,O 21,23:1

Gleason, Pat
Clean Beds 1939,My 26,21:2

Gleason, Thomas
By the Beautiful Sea 1954,Ap 9,20:1
Fanny 1954,N 5,16:1

Gleason, Tommy
Let's Face It 1941,O 30,26:2

Gleason, Tommy and His Royal Guards
Brights Lights of 1944 1943,S 17,27:4

Gleason, Violet
One Shot Fired 1927,N 8,32:5

Gleason, William
Pullman Car Hiawatha 1962,D 4,46:2
One Flew Over the Cuckoo's Nest 1963,N 14,40:2

Gleaton, David
Moon Walk 1970,N 27,52:1

Gleckler, Robert
Partners Again 1922,My 2,22:2
Love's Call 1925,S 11,20:1
Man's Man, A 1925,O 14,31:2
Beau Gallant 1926,Ap 6,26:3
Broadway 1926,S 17,19:3
Broadway 1926,S 26,VIII,1:1
Ringside 1928,Ag 30,13:2
Strong Man's House, A 1929,Je 30,VIII,1:2
Tabloid 1929,S 29,IX,5:1

Gleckler, Robert—Cont
Heads Up! 1929,N 12,34:1
Louder, Please! 1931,N 13,26:4
Hot-Cha! 1932,Mr 9,17:3
Take a Chance 1932,N 28,11:2
Marathon 1933,Ja 28,8:8
Shooting Star 1933,Je 13,22:2
Heat Lightning 1933,S 16,9:6
Drums Begin, The 1933,N 25,10:5
Locked Room, The 1933,D 26,18:5

Gledern, Harold van
Help! Help! the Globolinks 1970,D 24,10:2

Glee, Martin
Fiesta 1929,S 18,35:1

Gleissner, Vicki
Midsummer Night's Dream, A 1963,Jl 1,19:2

Glen, Cunningham
Bitter Sweet 1929,N 6,30:2

Glen, Hazel
Stepping Stones 1923,N 7,14:3
White Eagle, The 1927,D 27,24:4

Glendinning, Ernest
Little Old New York 1920,S 9,9:2
Sonny 1921,Ag 17,12:2
Untitled-Benefit 1922,My 8,14:5
Listening In 1922,D 5,24:1
Anathema 1923,Ap 11,16:2
Moonlight 1924,Ja 31,13:7
She Stoops to Conquer 1924,Je 10,24:3
Top Hole 1924,S 2,22:3
Flight 1929,F 19,22:3
Before You're 25 1929,Ap 17,30:2
Third Day, The 1929,Ag 13,23:4
Greeks Had a Word for It, The 1930,S 26,16:5
She Means Business 1931,Ja 27,21:2
Admirable Crichton, The 1931,Mr 10,23:2
Admirable Crichton, The 1931,Mr 29,VIII,1:1
I Love an Actress 1931,S 18,29:2
Widow in Green, A 1931,N 21,21:4
Uncle Tom's Cabin 1933,My 30,13:4
Move on, Sister 1933,O 25,22:4
By Your Leave 1934,Ja 25,15:3
Roman Servant, A 1934,D 3,14:5
Seven Keys to Baldpate 1935,My 28,30:2

Glendinning, John
From Morn Till Midnight 1948,D 7,41:6
Metropole 1949,D 7,43:2
Julius Caesar 1950,Je 21,30:1
Twentieth Century 1950,D 25,23:6

Glenister, Lionel
Great Adventure, The 1921,F 26,9:2
Squaring the Triangle 1921,Je 14,15:2
Tarzan of the Apes 1921,S 8,14:3
On the Stairs 1922,S 26,18:2

Glenn, Alice
By Jupiter 1967,Ja 20,28:2

Glenn, Allan
Ice Follies 1959,Ja 14,30:1

Glenn, Carrie
Scotch Mist 1926,S 21,32:3
Knights of Song 1938,O 18,29:2

Glenn, Cinda
Vaudeville Marches On 1938,D 30,11:1

Glenn, Dana
Not a Way of Life 1967,Mr 23,28:1

Glenn, Fredric
Richard II 1968,Je 24,42:3
Henry V 1969,N 11,43:1

Glenn, Helena
Venetian, The 1931,N 2,26:1
Adam Had Two Sons 1932,Ja 21,17:1
Triplets 1932,S 22,25:2
Aiglon, L' 1934,N 5,22:2
Yr Obedient Husband 1938,Ja 11,26:5
Bright Rebel 1938,D 28,24:2

Glenn, Jack
Blue and the Gray, The; War Is Hell Gray, The
 1929,D 27,26:4
Second Mate, The 1930,Mr 25,34:5

Glenn, James
Titus Andronicus 1956,D 3,40:2
Julius Caesar 1957,O 24,39:1
Immaculate Misconception, The 1970,O 28,63:3

Glenn, Peter (Miscellaneous)
Children's Hour, The 1952,D 19,35:2

Glenn, Robert (Director)
Soul Gone Home 1959,O 28,40:7
Shakespeare in Harlem 1959,O 28,40:7
Victims of Duty 1960,Ja 20,26:1
God's Trombones 1960,F 10,43:4
Shakespeare in Harlem 1960,F 10,43:4
Shakespeare in Harlem 1960,F 21,II,1:1
Time to Go 1960,Mr 23,33:1
Coggerers, The 1960,Mr 23,33:1

Glenn, Robert (Playwright)
Shakespeare in Harlem 1959,O 28,40:7
God's Trombones 1960,F 10,43:4
Shakespeare in Harlem 1960,F 10,43:4
Shakespeare in Harlem 1960,F 21,II,1:1
God's Trombones 1960,F 21,II,1:1

Glenn, Roy
Golden Boy 1964,O 21,56:1

Glenn, Scott
Impossible Years, The 1965,O 14,55:1
Collision Course; Metaphors 1968,My 9,55:2
Collision Course; Rats 1968,My 9,55:2
Collision Course; Wandering 1968,My 9,55:2
Collision Course; Tour 1968,My 9,55:2
Collision Course; Jew! 1968,My 9,55:2
Collision Course; Stars and Stripes 1968,My 9,55:2
Glenn, Tom (Miscellaneous)
Tender Trap, The 1961,Ag 26,15:1
Glenn, Vivian
Tell Me More 1925,Ap 14,27:3
Glenn, Wilfred
Robin Hood 1944,N 8,28:2
Glenn & Colleen
Ice Follies 1960,Ja 13,20:1
Glenn and Jenkins
Frivolities of 1920 1920,Ja 9,22:2
Vaudeville (Hippodrome) 1924,O 21,21:2
Vaudeville (Palace) 1925,O 6,31:3
Vaudeville (Hippodrome) 1926,My 4,31:2
Africana 1927,S 4,VII,1:1
Vaudeville (Palace) 1929,Ja 14,20:3
Vaudeville (Palace) 1929,D 23,19:1
Vaudeville (Palace) 1930,O 20,29:1
Glenn-Smith, Michael
Celebration 1969,Ja 23,55:2
Glennon, David
King John 1967,Jl 14,19:1
Glennon, John
Richard II 1951,Ja 25,21:2
Taming of the Shrew, The 1951,Ap 26,35:2
Gordon Reilly 1952,N 26,20:5
Cyrano de Bergerac 1953,N 13,24:3
Richard III 1953,D 10,65:2
Troublemakers, The 1954,D 31,11:3
Six Characters in Search of an Author
1955,D 12,38:1
Bil and Cora Baird's Marionette Theater
1955,D 27,29:2
Saint Joan 1956,S 12,42:1
Invitation to a Beheading 1969,Mr 18,36:1
Glennon, John (Miscellaneous)
I Only Want an Answer 1968,F 6,36:1
Glennon, Tom
High Button Shoes 1947,O 10,32:2
Glenny, Peter (Playwright)
New York Exchange 1926,D 31,11:3
Such Is Life 1927,S 1,27:3
Glenville, Peter (Director)
Browning Version, The 1949,O 13,32:2
Harlequinade 1949,O 13,32:2
Browning Version, The 1949,O 23,II,1:1
Innocents, The 1950,F 2,30:2
Innocents, The 1950,F 12,II,1:1
Curious Savage, The 1950,O 25,44:3
Romeo and Juliet 1951,Ja 23,24:8
Romeo and Juliet 1951,Mr 12,21:2
Romeo and Juliet 1951,Mr 25,II,1:1
Living Room, The 1953,Ap 17,29:5
Separate Tables 1955,My 22,II,1:1
Island of Goats 1955,O 5,40:1
Hotel Paradiso 1956,My 3,34:8
Separate Tables 1956,O 26,33:1
Hotel Paradiso 1957,Ap 12,22:2
Hotel Paradiso 1957,Ap 21,II,1:1
Rashomon 1959,Ja 28,36:2
Rashomon 1959,F 8,II,1:1
Take Me Along 1959,O 23,22:2
Silent Night, Lonely Night 1959,D 4,36:1
Silent Night, Lonely Night 1959,D 13,II,3:1
Becket 1960,O 6,50:1
Becket 1961,My 9,44:1
Tchin-Tchin 1962,O 26,26:2
Tovarich 1963,Mr 20,5:1
Dylan 1964,Ja 20,18:1
Foxy 1964,Mr 20,30:1
Everything in the Garden 1967,N 30,60:1
Patriot for Me, A 1969,O 6,58:1
Glenville, Peter (Playwright)
Hotel Paradiso 1957,Ap 12,22:2
Glenville, Peter (Producer)
Adventure Story 1949,Mr 19,11:2
Island of Goats 1955,O 5,40:1
Becket 1960,O 16,II,1:1
Bequest to the Nation, A 1970,S 25,36:1
Glenville, Peter (Translator)
Hotel Paradiso 1956,My 3,34:8
Glenville, Shaun
Phoebe of Quality Street 1921,My 10,20:1
Whirl of New York, The 1921,Je 14,18:1
Gleson, Vivian
Chinese Nightingale, The 1934,O 6,20:4
Glespen, Marian
Joan of Arc-The Warrior Maid 1931,N 9,21:6
Glick, Ben (Scenic Designer)
Ginger Snaps 1930,Ja 1,30:5
Glick, Carl
Sylvia 1923,Ap 26,22:1
Glick, Carl (Playwright)
Devil's Host, The 1928,S 9,IX,2:7
Devil's Host, The 1931,N 20,27:2

Glick, Harold (Composer)
Moby Dick 1962,N 29,45:1
Glick, Joseph B (Producer)
Queen Bee 1929,N 13,25:1
Glick, Ronald (Miscellaneous)
Antigone 1959,S 16,46:2
Glickfeld, Ken (Lighting Director)
TV 1966,N 7,66:1
Interview 1966,N 7,66:1
Motel 1966,N 7,66:1
Glickfeld, Ken (Miscellaneous)
Candaules, Commissioner 1970,My 29,15:1
Sambo 1970,Jl 23,24:1
Glickman, Paul (Scenic Designer)
Nat Turner 1960,N 7,46:3
Glickman, Will (Miscellaneous)
Lend an Ear 1948,D 17,38:2
Alive and Kicking 1950,Ja 18,25:5
Glickman, Will (Playwright)
Mrs Gibsons' Boys 1949,My 5,35:2
Plain and Fancy 1955,Ja 28,14:2
Plain and Fancy 1955,F 6,II,1:1
Mr Wonderful 1956,Mr 23,23:2
Body Beautiful, The 1958,Ja 24,15:2
Glickson, Zipora
House on Grand Street, A 1953,O 10,12:6
Glickstein, Haim (Translator)
Children of the Shadows 1964,F 27,26:1
Glidden, David
Anything Goes 1934,N 22,26:1
Glidden, Ivan (Scenic Designer)
Jefferson Davis 1936,F 19,17:2
Gliere, Reinhold (Composer)
Lysistrata 1925,D 15,28:2
Gliese, Rochus (Scenic Designer)
Outside Looking In 1929,Je 23,VIII,2:1
Blaue Boll, Der 1931,Ja 25,VIII,4:1
Siebenstein 1933,My 28,IX,1:3
Gliman, Mary
Career 1943,O 29,22:6
Glineur, Irene
Avare, L'; Miser, The 1924,Mr 12,17:3
Monsieur Brotonneau 1924,Mr 13,14:1
Blanchette 1924,Mr 19,19:4
Glizer, J C
Circle, The 1946,Mr 17,II,1:3
Gloer, Carla
Theodora, the Queen 1934,F 1,15:3
Gloer, Charlotte
Few Are Chosen 1935,S 18,19:3
Play, Genius, Play! 1935,O 31,17:2
Murder in the Cathedral 1936,Mr 21,13:5
On the Rocks 1938,Je 16,20:2
Gloninger, Irving L W
Sale and a Sailor, A, or Glory! What Price!
1926,Ap 25,30:4
Gloria, Adelaide
Rise of Rosie O'Reilly, The 1923,D 26,13:4
Gloria, Albert
Rise of Rosie O'Reilly, The 1923,D 26,13:4
Her Man of Wax 1933,O 12,32:3
Glorias, The
Cinderella on Broadway 1920,Je 25,18:1
Glover, Bill
Ross 1961,D 27,20:2
Trumpets of the Lord 1963,D 23,22:3
Trumpets of the Lord 1969,Ap 30,37:1
Glover, Bruce
Billy Budd 1959,F 28,13:3
King of the Dark Chamber 1961,F 10,21:1
Little Hut, The 1961,Jl 26,34:2
Night of the Iguana, The 1961,D 29,10:1
Mother Courage and Her Children 1963,Mr 30,5:5
Harry, Noon and Night 1965,My 6,44:1
Glover, David
Private Lives 1969,D 5,52:1
Glover, Doreen
Boom Boom 1929,Ja 29,26:4
Glover, Edmund
Where Do We Go From Here? 1938,N 16,26:2
Vickie 1942,S 23,28:1
Glover, Ernest (Scenic Designer)
Suspect 1940,Ap 10,30:4
Every Man for Himself 1940,D 10,32:3
Vickie 1942,S 23,28:1
Sun Field, The 1942,D 10,33:2
School for Brides 1944,Ag 2,19:4
Glover, Grace
Merry World, The 1926,Je 9,18:3
Glover, Halcott (Playwright)
Bellairs 1933,Ap 23,X,1:3
Glover, Harry
Love Song, The 1925,Ja 14,19:4
Glover, Hileary
Our Lan' 1947,Ap 19,11:2
Glover, Joe (Miscellaneous)
Tree Grows in Brooklyn, A 1951,Ap 20,24:3
New Faces of 1956 1956,Je 15,32:1
Ziegfeld Follies 1957,Mr 2,19:2
Livin' the Life 1957,Ap 29,20:1
Dr Willy Nilly 1959,Je 5,18:2
13 Daughters 1961,Mr 3,17:2
Paradise Island 1961,Je 24,11:1

Glover, Joe (Miscellaneous)—Cont
Paradise Island 1962,Je 28,22:1
Arabian Nights 1967,Jl 3,12:1
Glover, Joe (Musical Director)
Arabian Nights 1954,Je 25,15:2
Arabian Nights 1955,Je 24,16:1
Glover, John
Junebug Graduates Tonight! 1967,F 27,35:1
Scent of Flowers, A 1969,O 21,42:1
Prince of Peasantmania 1970,F 22,88:1
Glover, Julian
Boswell's Life of Johnson 1970,S 4,19:1
Glover, Louise
Thoroughbred 1933,N 7,29:2
Bitter Oleander 1935,F 12,24:3
Glover, Omar
Vaudeville (Palace) 1928,Ja 31,29:2
Chippies 1929,My 30,23:3
Glover, Ralph
Demi-Virgin, The 1921,O 19,22:1
Chee-Chee 1928,S 26,25:1
New Yorkers, The 1930,D 9,31:1
Great Waltz, The 1934,S 24,14:4
I'd Rather Be Right 1937,N 3,28:2
Naked Genius, The 1943,O 22,20:5
Deep Mrs Sykes, The 1945,Mr 20,22:6
Day Before Spring, The 1945,N 23,27:2
Music in My Heart 1947,O 3,30:2
Glover, Rita (Director)
Stairs to the Roof 1947,F 26,35:4
Glover, Rita (Scenic Designer)
Return of Ulysses, The 1943,F 7,II,1:6
Glover, T J
First Flight 1925,S 18,26:2
Glover, William
Henry IV, Part I 1958,Je 25,23:3
Winter's Tale, The 1958,Jl 23,34:3
Hamlet 1968,Jl 21,II,21:2
Henry V 1969,Je 9,57:1
Much Ado About Nothing 1969,Je 16,57:1
Glucas, Carroll
Hello, Daddy! 1928,D 27,26:5
Gluck, Arnold
Little Jessie James 1923,Ag 16,10:4
Gluck, C W von (Composer)
Mum's the Word 1940,D 6,28:5
Gluck, Senia
Pinwheel Revel 1922,Je 16,20:6
Pinwheel Revel 1922,Ag 1,14:2
Earl Carroll's Vanities 1925,Jl 7,24:1
Gluck, Wally (Producer)
Half a Widow 1927,S 13,37:3
Gluck-Sandor (Choreographer)
Vanities 1932,S 28,22:4
Gluckman, Leon (Director)
Wait a Minim! 1966,Mr 8,43:1
Gluckman, Leon (Lighting Director)
Wait a Minim! 1966,Mr 8,43:1
Gluckman, Leon (Playwright)
Wait a Minim! 1966,Mr 8,43:1
Gluckman, Leon (Scenic Designer)
Wait a Minim! 1966,Mr 8,43:1
Glueck, David
On the Level 1937,Mr 26,24:4
Glukhareva, Olga
Uncle Vanya 1960,F 13,13:4
Glukoff, Sigmund
Geisha, The 1931,O 6,35:4
Glyn, Trevor
Bitter Sweet 1929,N 6,30:2
Glynde, Rita
Black Crook, The 1929,Mr 17,X,8:1
How's Your Health? 1929,N 27,30:3
Glynn, Celia
By the Way 1925,D 29,20:3
By the Way 1926,Ap 16,20:3
Glynn, Thomas
Story of Mary Surratt, The 1947,F 10,25:2
Glynne, Derek
Call of Life, The 1925,O 10,10:1
Soldiers and Women 1929,S 3,25:1
Mayfair 1930,Mr 18,30:5
Glynne, Howell
Pirates of Penzance, The 1961,S 7,41:1
Yeomen of the Guard, The 1964,Ag 3,16:1
Glynne, Mary
Crooked Friday, The 1925,O 9,27:3
Offence, The 1925,N 16,25:1
Untitled-Play 1933,Ap 2,IX,2:4
Gmuer, Alexander
David Garrick 1929,Ag 2,17:5
Gnaralia, Thomas
Screwball, The 1957,My 25,24:7
Gnessin, David
Tobias and the Angel 1937,Ap 29,16:5
Gnireg, Mar
Plan M 1942,F 21,15:2
Gnys, Charles (Director)
Up to Thursday 1965,F 11,45:1
Hunting the Jingo Birds 1965,Mr 26,27:1
Criss-Crossing 1970,Ja 22,30:1
Watercolor 1970,Ja 22,30:1
Gnys, Charles (Producer)
Exhaustion of Our Son's Love, The 1965,O 19,51:1

Gnys, Charles (Producer)—Cont

Good Day 1965,O 19,51:1

Goas, T W (Composer)
It's the Valet 1933,D 15,25:4

Goas, T W (Lyricist)
It's the Valet 1933,D 15,25:4

Gobel, George
Let It Ride 1961,O 13,27:4

Gobel, Heini
Amphitryon 1970,N 18,40:1
Kleinburgerhochzeit, Die 1970,N 25,25:1

Goberman, Max (Composer)
Where's Charley? 1948,O 12,33:2

Goberman, Max (Musical Director)
On the Town 1944,D 29,11:4
Tree Grows in Brooklyn, A 1951,Ap 20,24:3
West Side Story 1957,S 27,14:4
Milk and Honey 1961,O 11,52:1

Gobian, Carlos and His Argentinian Orchestra
Vaudeville (Hippodrome) 1924,O 21,21:2

Goble, Diana
Up Eden 1968,N 27,42:1

Gochman, Len
How to Succeed in Business Without Really Trying
1966,Ap 21,45:1
Finian's Rainbow 1967,Ap 6,44:1

Gochman, Len (Producer)
Local Stigmatic, The 1969,N 4,55:2
Local Stigmatic, The; Applicant 1969,N 4,55:2
Local Stigmatic, The; That's Your Trouble
1969,N 4,55:2
Local Stigmatic, The; Request Stop 1969,N 4,55:2
Local Stigmatic, The; That's All 1969,N 4,55:2
Local Stigmatic, The; Trouble in the Works
1969,N 4,55:2
Local Stigmatic, The; Last to Go 1969,N 4,55:2
Local Stigmatic, The; Interview 1969,N 4,55:2

Gockel, Fred
Autumn's Here 1966,O 26,40:1

Godard, Lucile
Sue, Dear 1922,Jl 11,16:2

Godart, Louise
Heure du Berger, L'; Propitious Moment, The
1936,N 12,30:1

Goddard, Charles W (Playwright)
Broken Wing, The 1920,N 30,14:1

Goddard, Elizabeth
Passing Present, The 1931,D 8,36:2
Trojan Women, The 1938,Ja 25,24:2

Goddard, Malcolm (Choreographer)
Persecution and Assassination of Marat As
Performed by the Inmates of the Asylum of
Charenton Under the Direction of the Marquis de
Sade, The 1965,D 28,35:1

Goddard, Nevill
Great Music 1924,O 6,24:1
Hello Paris 1930,N 17,29:3

Goddard, Paulette
No Foolin' 1926,Je 25,25:1

Goddard, Pauline
Music in My Heart 1947,O 3,30:2

Goddard, Samuel
Right of Possession 1930,My 9,20:5
Twelfth Disciple, The 1930,My 17,21:4

Goddard, Selwyn
On Call 1928,N 10,20:7

Goddard, Victor
Poppy God, The 1921,Ag 30,10:1

Goddard, Warren
What Big Ears! 1942,Ap 21,18:5

Goddard, William
Will and the Way, The 1957,D 3,46:5

Goddard, Willoughby
Oliver 1963,Ja 8,5:5

Godden, Reginald (Composer)
Doll's House, A 1956,My 8,29:2

Godett, Hal
Cage, The 1961,Mr 6,30:1

Godfernaux, Andre (Playwright)
Triplepatte 1926,N 14,VIII,2:1

Godfrey, Arthur
Three to Make Ready 1946,Mr 8,16:2

Godfrey, Derek
Henry VI (Part III) 1957,O 18,19:5
Taming of the Shrew, The 1962,Ap 24,33:3
Curtmantle 1962,S 5,44:3
Roar Like a Dove 1964,My 22,40:2
Ruling Class, The 1969,F 28,31:1
Travails of Sancho Panza, The 1969,D 20,35:1

Godfrey, E W
It's the Valet 1933,D 15,25:4

Godfrey, Ilene
Jotham Valley 1951,F 7,37:2

Godfrey, Isidore (Miscellaneous)
Gondoliers, The 1934,S 4,23:1
Cox and Box 1934,S 7,24:3
Pirates of Penzance, The; Slave of Duty, The
1934,S 7,24:3
Iolanthe 1934,S 11,24:3
H M S Pinafore 1934,S 14,24:3
Trial by Jury 1934,S 14,24:3
Mikado, The; Town of Titipu, The 1934,S 18,18:1
Yeomen of the Guard, The 1934,S 21,28:3
Ruddigore 1934,S 25,25:2

Princess Ida; Castle Adamant 1934,S 28,26:3
Patience 1934,O 12,32:2
Mikado, The 1947,D 30,18:2
Mikado, The 1962,N 14,43:1
Pirates of Penzance, The 1962,N 21,28:1
H M S Pinafore 1962,N 23,32:4
Trial by Jury 1962,N 23,32:4
Iolanthe 1962,N 28,42:1
H M S Pinafore 1964,N 20,40:1
Mikado, The 1964,N 27,43:1
Ruddigore 1964,D 4,44:1

Godfrey, Isidore (Musical Director)
Mikado, The 1936,Ag 21,13:2
Gondoliers, The 1936,S 8,23:1
Yeomen of the Guard, The 1936,S 15,37:2
Ruddigore 1936,O 23,26:4
Trial by Jury 1948,Ja 6,27:2
Pirates of Penzance, The 1948,Ja 6,27:2
Pirates of Penzance, The 1948,Ja 11,II,1:1
Cox and Box 1948,Ja 20,26:2
H M S Pinafore 1948,Ja 20,26:2
Gondoliers, The 1948,Ja 27,31:2
Yeomen of the Guard, The 1948,F 3,30:2
Patience 1948,F 10,27:2
Mikado, The 1951,Ja 30,21:2
Trial by Jury 1951,F 6,24:2
H M S Pinafore 1951,F 6,24:2
Gondoliers, The 1951,F 13,27:2
Iolanthe 1951,F 16,22:1
Iolanthe 1955,S 28,38:1
Mikado, The 1955,S 30,20:2
Yeomen of the Guard, The 1955,O 4,39:2
Pirates of Penzance, The 1955,O 7,21:1
Princess Ida 1955,O 14,22:3
H M S Pinafore 1955,O 18,48:1
Trial by Jury 1955,O 18,48:1
Ruddigore 1955,O 21,32:2
Mikado, The 1962,N 14,43:1
Iolanthe 1964,N 18,52:1
H M S Pinafore 1964,N 20,40:1
Trial by Jury 1964,N 20,40:1
Pirates of Penzance, The 1964,N 27,43:1
Pirates of Penzance, The 1966,N 16,54:1
Mikado, The 1966,N 18,36:1
Ruddigore 1966,N 23,28:1
H M S Pinafore 1966,N 24,64:1
Patience 1966,N 30,58:1

Godfrey, Patricia
Flashing Stream, The 1939,Ap 11,19:2

Godfrey, Peter (Director)
Close Quarters 1937,Ap 18,II,3:5
Shadow and Substance 1938,Ja 27,16:2

Godfrey, Peter (Miscellaneous)
Salome 1931,Je 21,VIII,1:4

Godfrey, Peter (Producer)
Hairy Ape, The 1928,F 19,VIII,4:1
Hoopla! 1929,Mr 10,X,4:6
As You Desire Me 1934,O 2,18:3
Red Rover's Revenge 1934,D 22,21:3

Godfrey, Samuel
Will Shakespeare 1923,Ja 2,14:1
Kibitzer, The 1929,F 19,22:5

Godfrey, Vaughn
Play, Genius, Play! 1935,O 31,17:2

Godfrey, Vaughn (Choreographer)
White Lilacs 1928,S 11,31:2
There You Are! 1932,My 17,25:4

Godick, Willy
Girl From Warsaw, The 1931,S 14,15:5
Pleasure 1931,D 28,20:2

Godik, Giora (Producer)
My Fair Lady 1964,F 20,24:4
Fiddler on the Roof 1965,Je 9,40:1
Fiddler on the Roof 1965,Ag 15,II,2:5

Godin, Emmerich
Wiener Blut 1964,S 12,14:1

Godin, Jacques
Henry V 1956,Je 20,27:2

Godiner, Shin (Playwright)
Jim Cooperkop 1930,O 18,23:1

Godkin, Paul
High Button Shoes 1947,O 10,32:2

Godkin, Paul (Miscellaneous)
Maggie 1953,F 19,20:2

Godreau, Miguel
Dear World 1969,F 7,33:1

Godwin, Carol
Nina Rosa 1930,My 31,19:3

Goe, Bernie
Matinee Girl, The 1926,F 2,20:3

Goe, Lady Chong
Letter, The 1927,S 27,30:1

Goe, Peter Chong
Twelve Miles Out 1925,N 17,29:2

Goehr, Rudolph (Miscellaneous)
Happy as Larry 1950,Ja 7,11:2

Goelet, O
Gentlemen, the Queen 1927,Ap 23,14:3

Goener, Christine
Fanny 1955,D 17,19:6

Goeppinger, Susan
Strada, La 1969,D 15,63:1

Goethe (Miscellaneous)
Friederike 1929,F 17,IX,2:3

Goethe (Original Author)
Veritable Histoire de Mignon, La 1927,F 20,VII,2:1
Faust 1937,Ag 29,X,1:3
Speak of the Devil! 1939,O 7,21:7

Goethe (Playwright)
Faust 1927,Ja 4,20:1
Scherz, List und Rache 1928,Ap 22,IX,6:7
Faust 1928,O 9,34:1
Faust 1928,N 4,IX,4:1
Egmont 1929,Mr 24,X,2:3
Faust 1930,Mr 23,4:3
Goetz von Berlichingen 1930,D 14,IX,4:1
Faust 1932,Je 19,IX,1:3
Unnaturliche Tochter, Die 1932,Je 19,IX,1:3
Egmont 1932,Je 19,IX,1:3
Faust 1933,Ja 22,IX,1:1
Faust 1947,N 29,9:2
Iphigenie in Tauris 1949,Ap 9,8:1
Iphigenie in Tauris 1949,O 22,11:2
Faust, Part I; Play, The 1961,F 5,27:2
Faust, Part I; Prologue in Heaven 1961,F 5,27:2
Faust, Part I; Prelude in the Theater 1961,F 5,27:2
Mitschuldigen, Die 1966,Ap 6,34:1
After-Dinner Evening With Oskar Werner, An
1967,Mr 27,39:1

Goetz, Augustus (Playwright)
One-Man Show 1945,F 9,21:2
One-Man Show 1945,F 18,II,1:1
Heiress, The 1947,S 30,22:2
Heiress, The 1947,O 5,II,1:1
Heiress, The 1949,F 3,26:2
Heiress, The 1950,F 9,34:2
Heiress, The 1950,F 12,II,1:1
Immoralist, The 1954,F 2,18:7
Immoralist, The 1954,F 9,22:1
Immoralist, The 1954,F 14,II,1:1
Immoralist, The 1954,N 4,39:5
Hidden River, The 1957,Ja 24,32:1
Hidden River, The 1959,Ap 14,41:2
Immoralist, The 1963,N 8,36:2

Goetz, Carl (Playwright)
Logneren og Nonnen 1930,D 28,VIII,3:5

Goetz, Curt
Ballerina des Koenigs, Die 1921,Jl 24,VI,1:7
Hokus Pokus 1928,Ja 29,VIII,4:1
Perlenkomoedie 1929,Ap 7,X,4:4
Circus Aimee 1932,My 22,VIII,2:2
Dr med Hiob Praetorius 1934,My 6,IX,2:2
It's A Gift 1945,Mr 13,18:7

Goetz, Curt (Director)
Dr med Hiob Praetorius 1934,My 6,IX,2:2

Goetz, Curt (Lyricist)
Circus Aimee 1932,My 22,VIII,2:2

Goetz, Curt (Miscellaneous)
Hokus Pokus 1928,Ja 29,VIII,4:1
Giuochi di Prestigio 1931,N 2,26:1

Goetz, Curt (Playwright)
Isabel 1925,Ja 14,19:1
Zia Morta, La; Dead Aunt, The 1931,N 30,16:3
Circus Aimee 1932,My 22,VIII,2:2
Zia Morta, La; Dead Aunt, The 1933,F 13,11:3
Ingeborg 1933,D 11,23:3
Dr med Hiob Praetorius 1934,My 6,IX,2:2
It's A Gift 1945,Mr 13,18:7

Goetz, Curt (Producer)
Dr med Hiob Praetorius 1934,My 6,IX,2:2

Goetz, E Ray (Composer)
As You Were 1920,Ja 28,22:3
Paris 1928,O 9,34:3

Goetz, E Ray (Director)
Fifty Million Frenchmen 1929,N 28,34:4
New Yorkers, The 1930,D 9,31:1

Goetz, E Ray (Lyricist)
George White's Scandals 1923,Je 19,22:5

Goetz, E Ray (Miscellaneous)
Naughty Cinderella 1925,N 10,23:6
Paris 1928,O 9,34:3

Goetz, E Ray (Original Author)
New Yorkers, The 1930,N 16,VIII,3:1

Goetz, E Ray (Playwright)
George White's Scandals 1922,Ag 29,10:1
Lady of the Orchids, The 1928,D 14,37:3
New Yorkers, The 1930,D 9,31:1

Goetz, E Ray (Producer)
Raquel Meller 1926,Ap 15,24:1
Mozart 1926,N 23,26:2
Lady of the Orchids, The 1928,D 14,37:3
Fifty Million Frenchmen 1929,N 28,34:4
New Yorkers, The 1930,N 16,VIII,3:1
New Yorkers, The 1930,D 9,31:1

Goetz, George
If Booth Had Missed 1931,My 14,27:1

Goetz, Ruth (Playwright)
Heiress, The 1947,S 30,22:2
Heiress, The 1947,O 5,II,1:1
Heiress, The 1949,F 3,26:2
Heiress, The 1950,F 9,34:2
Heiress, The 1950,F 12,II,1:1
Immoralist, The 1954,F 2,18:7
Immoralist, The 1954,F 9,22:1
Immoralist, The 1954,F 14,II,1:1

Goetz, Ruth (Playwright)—Cont
Immoralist, The 1954,N 4,39:5
Hidden River, The 1957,Ja 24,32:1
Hidden River, The 1959,Ap 14,41:2
Immoralist, The 1963,N 8,36:2
Play on Love 1970,Ja 16,31:1
Goetz, Theo
Everyman 1941,My 9,19:2
Winter Soldiers 1942,N 30,19:2
Land of Fame 1943,S 22,31:5
Swan Song 1946,My 16,29:2
Iphigenie in Tauris 1949,Ap 9,8:1
Deadfall 1955,O 28,20:1
Golem, The 1959,F 26,38:2
Family Portrait 1959,My 6,48:2
Poppa Is Home 1961,D 20,37:1
Goetz, Wolfgang (Playwright)
Neidhardt von Gneisenau 1927,Ja 23,VII,4:5
Minister-Praesident, Der 1936,Je 28,IX,2:1
Goetze, Walter W (Composer)
Manon 1929,Je 2,VIII,2:6
Goetzl, Anselm (Composer)
Rose Girl, The 1921,F 12,11:1
Goff, Charles
Hamlet 1945,D 14,25:2
Enchanted, The 1958,Ap 23,41:1
My Fair Lady 1968,Je 14,42:1
Goff, Edward
Gertie 1926,N 16,24:2
Goff, Herbert
Elsie Janis and Her Gang 1922,Ja 17,13:2
Goff, Ivan (Playwright)
Portrait in Black 1947,My 15,30:2
Goff, Jerry
Strike Up the Band 1930,Ja 15,29:1
Goff, Marie
Immodest Violet 1920,Ag 25,6:2
Young Visitors, The 1920,N 30,14:1
Nemesis 1921,Ap 5,24:3
Danger 1921,D 23,18:3
Winter Bound 1929,N 13,24:6
Goff, Michael
Love of Women 1937,D 14,33:2
Goff, Mr
Manhattan Mary 1927,S 27,30:3
Goffin, Peter (Costume Designer)
Yeoman of the Guard, The 1948,F 3,30:2
Yeoman of the Guard, The 1955,O 4,39:2
Ruddigore 1955,O 21,32:2
Gondoliers, The 1962,N 16,25:2
H M S Pinafore 1962,N 23,32:4
H M S Pinafore 1964,N 20,40:1
Ruddigore 1964,D 4,44:1
H M S Pinafore 1968,O 30,35:1
Goffin, Peter (Director)
Patience 1966,N 30,58:1
Goffin, Peter (Musical Director)
Iolanthe 1964,N 18,52:1
Goffin, Peter (Scenic Designer)
Yeomen of the Guard, The 1948,F 3,30:2
Mikado, The 1955,S 30,20:2
Yeomen of the Guard, The 1955,O 4,39:2
Ruddigore 1955,O 21,32:2
Mikado, The 1962,N 14,43:1
Pirates of Penzance, The 1962,N 21,28:1
Trial by Jury 1962,N 23,32:4
H M S Pinafore 1962,N 23,32:4
Iolanthe 1962,N 28,42:1
Iolanthe 1964,N 18,52:1
Trial by Jury 1964,N 20,40:1
H M S Pinafore 1964,N 20,40:1
Pirates of Penzance, The 1964,N 27,43:1
Ruddigore 1964,D 4,44:1
Pirates of Penzance, The 1966,N 16,54:1
Mikado, The 1966,N 18,36:1
Ruddigore 1966,N 23,28:1
H M S Pinafore 1966,N 24,64:1
Patience 1966,N 30,58:1
H M S Pinafore 1968,O 30,35:1
Mikado, The 1968,N 2,29:4
Pirates of Penzance, The 1968,N 7,54:1
Iolanthe 1968,N 9,37:3
Goforth, Frances
Dark of the Moon 1945,Mr 15,27:2
Gogan, Warren
Hamlet 1954,Ap 24,15:2
Gogol, Nikolai (Original Author)
Dead Souls 1936,S 27,X,1:1
Diary of a Madman 1964,Ap 17,29:2
Gogol, Nikolai (Playwright)
Inspector General, The 1922,O 9,15:4
Inspector General, The 1923,My 1,24:1
Revisor 1927,My 1,VIII,2:4
Revisor 1927,My 1,II,6:8
Inspector General, The 1930,D 24,19:2
Marriage 1931,N 1,VIII,4:3
Revisor; Inspector General, The 1935,F 18,19:6
Inspector General, The 1935,F 24,VIII,3:1
Marriage 1935,F 24,VIII,3:1
Marriage 1935,Mr 12,24:8
Revisor 1935,O 6,XI,3:7
Dead Souls 1965,F 5,34:1
Diary of a Madman 1967,Mr 24,25:1
Government Inspector, The 1967,Je 15,55:1

Government Inspector, The 1967,Je 25,II,1:2
Government Inspector, The 1967,O 28,34:1
Gogotsky, M (Musical Director)
Blue Bird, The 1925,Ja 30,10:2
Gohl, James F (Lighting Director)
Nobody Hears A Broken Drum 1970,Mr 20,55:1
Gohl, James F (Miscellaneous)
Country Wife, The 1965,D 10,58:2
Caucasian Chalk Circle, The 1966,Mr 25,35:1
Gohl, James F (Scenic Designer)
East Wind, The 1967,F 10,30:1
Get Thee to Canterbury 1969,Ja 26,74:1
Nobody Hears A Broken Drum 1970,Mr 20,55:1
Gohring, Russell
Tambourine 1925,D 30,10:2
Front Page Stuff 1926,D 29,24:4
Goines, Clyde
South Pacific 1943,D 30,11:2
Going, Frederica
His Chinese Wife 1920,My 18,9:3
Jeweled Tree, The 1926,O 8,26:2
Street Scene 1929,Ja 11,20:4
Black Sheep 1932,O 14,22:6
Midsummer Night's Dream, A 1932,N 18,22:2
Comedy of Errors, The 1932,N 22,25:3
Merchant of Venice, The 1932,N 24,34:5
Romeo and Juliet 1933,F 3,21:5
Chinese Nightingale, The 1934,O 6,20:4
For Valor 1935,N 19,27:5
Two on an Island 1940,Ja 23,17:2
New Life, A 1943,S 16,26:6
Our Town 1944,Ja 11,24:5
Last Stop 1944,S 6,17:2
Harvey 1944,N 2,23:2
Righteous Are Bold, The 1955,D 23,12:1
Going, John
Oedipus Rex 1959,Ap 30,36:1
Goins, Bobby
Africana 1927,Jl 12,29:2
Africana 1927,Jl 12,29:2
Gokcer, Cuneyt
Kiss Me, Kate 1964,F 16,29:1
Fiddler on the Roof 1970,Jl 8,34:1
Goland, Arnold (Composer)
Babes in the Wood 1964,D 29,21:2
Goland, Arnold (Miscellaneous)
Student Gypsy, The; Prince of Liederkranz, The 1963,O 1,34:1
What Makes Sammy Run? 1964,F 28,19:1
Golar, Martin
Cool World, The 1960,F 23,38:2
Golberg, Stan (Miscellaneous)
Me Nobody Knows, The 1970,My 19,42:1
Gold, Annabelle
Make Mine Manhattan 1948,Ja 16,26:2
Pipe Dream 1955,D 1,44:1
Gold, Anne
Johnny Doodle 1942,Mr 19,28:2
Gold, Clara
Little Cantor, The 1930,S 24,26:2
Berl and Shmerl Corporation 1934,Ap 2,12:5
Gold, Dave (Choreographer)
Grand Street Follies, The 1929,My 2,20:4
Gold, David
Carefree Tree, The 1955,O 12,37:2
Red Roses for Me 1955,D 29,15:2
Metamorphosis 1957,F 20,38:1
Midsummer Night's Dream, A 1957,Je 27,21:3
If Five Years Pass 1962,My 11,37:1
Drat! the Cat! 1965,O 11,54:2
Sweet Charity 1966,Ja 31,22:1
Education of H*Y*M*A*N K*A*P*L*A*N, The 1968,Ap 5,57:1
Gold, Ernest (Composer)
I'm Solomon 1968,Ap 24,51:1
Gold, Felice
Enchanting Melody 1964,N 25,40:1
Gold, Harry
Mirele Efros 1967,O 20,55:1
Gold, Kaethe
Faust 1933,Ja 22,IX,1:1
Gefesselte Phantasie, Die 1936,N 8,X,2:1
Gold, Leon
His Wife's Lover 1929,O 21,30:6
Love Thief, The 1931,Ja 19,24:5
Girl From Warsaw, The 1931,S 14,15:5
Shulamith 1931,O 14,26:4
Kibitzer, The 1931,N 7,17:3
Mother's Son 1931,N 26,36:4
Under One Roof 1932,F 8,21:2
Song of the Ghetto, The 1932,O 3,15:5
Untitled-Benefit 1933,Ja 25,13:3
Germany Aflame 1933,O 28,20:5
Three in Love 1933,N 8,32:5
Little Giants 1933,D 2,9:5
Organ Grinder, The 1934,Ja 1,28:3
Happy Days 1934,Ap 2,12:5
Here Runs the Bride 1934,S 20,21:3
Here Runs the Bride 1934,N 4,IX,2:1
One in a Million 1934,N 17,13:2
What Girls Do 1935,Ja 14,10:4
Heaven on Earth 1935,O 8,26:2
Tevye the Dairyman 1935,O 25,25:1

Gold, Leon—Cont
Schlemihl 1936,S 19,20:4
Straw Hero, The 1936,N 24,35:1
Yossel and His Wives 1937,S 19,II,8:3
Warson at Night 1938,Ja 31,14:3
Mazel Tov, Rabbi 1938,N 28,10:4
Jewish Heart, The 1939,Ja 25,16:6
If I Were Rothschild 1940,Ja 1,28:7
Oy, Is Dus a Leben!; Oh, What a Life! 1942,O 13,19:2
Gold, Marilyn
Enchanting Melody 1964,N 25,40:1
Gold, Martin (Miscellaneous)
Jack in the Box 1960,My 19,43:3
Buck White 1969,D 3,63:1
Dr Fish 1970,Mr 11,42:2
Chinese, The 1970,Mr 11,42:2
Blancs, Les 1970,N 16,48:4
Gold, Mervin
Silk Stockings 1955,F 25,17:3
Gold, Michael (Playwright)
Hoboken Blues 1928,F 18,10:1
Hoboken Blues 1928,F 26,VIII,1:1
Fiesta 1928,D 13,25:2
Fiesta 1929,S 18,35:1
Hoboken Blues 1930,Ap 1,10:1
Battle Hymn 1936,My 23,12:1
Gold, Mirele
Enchanting Melody 1964,N 25,40:1
Gold, Mitzi
Cocktails of 1934 1934,My 5,22:1
Gold, Muriel
Death of Satan, The 1960,Ap 6,49:1
Gold, Muriel (Miscellaneous)
Herne's Egg, The 1960,S 20,48:1
Gold, Robert Alan (Miscellaneous)
Fantasticks, The 1960,My 4,55:2
Celebration 1969,Ja 23,55:2
Gold, Robert Alan (Producer)
Buffalo Skinner, The 1959,F 20,18:1
Gold, Rochelle
Enchanting Melody 1964,N 25,40:1
Gold, Russell
Lady in the Dark 1952,Mr 8,11:3
Capacity for Wings 1957,Ja 10,25:2
Royal Gambit 1959,Mr 5,34:2
Royal Gambit 1959,Mr 15,II,1:1
Prodigal, The 1960,F 12,23:1
Prodigal, The 1960,F 21,II,1:1
Rendezvous at Senlis 1961,F 28,39:2
We Comrades Three 1962,O 12,26:1
Corruption in the Palace of Justice 1963,O 9,49:2
Place for Chance, The 1964,My 15,44:2
Gold, Sam
Cinderella on Broadway 1920,Je 25,18:1
Gold, Sanford (Musical Director)
Gay Blades 1937,N 16,27:1
Gold, Zisha
Father and Son 1956,O 20,17:4
Honeymoon in Israel, A 1962,O 15,33:5
Megilla of Itzik Manger, The 1968,O 10,60:1
Megilla of Itzik Manger, The 1969,Ap 21,55:1
Gold and Raye
Vaudeville (Palace) 1930,Ag 18,24:3
Vaudeville (Palace) 1932,S 12,13:5
Golday, George
Love and Politics 1929,O 21,30:7
Goldbaum, Peter (Playwright)
Last Dance, The 1948,Ja 28,27:2
Goldberg, Alan (Composer)
Life Begins in '40 1940,Ap 5,24:2
Goldberg, Beryl
Private Life of the Master Race, The 1956,Ja 31,33:3
Goldberg, Dan (Playwright)
Call Me Ziggy 1937,F 13,9:6
Man From Cairo, The 1938,My 5,26:5
Goldberg, David S (Lyricist)
Bare Facts 1927,Ag 17,27:5
Goldberg, Diana
Perfect Fishel, The 1935,S 30,12:4
Pinye of Pinchev 1936,S 21,27:5
Night in Budapest, A 1936,N 3,33:2
His Jewish Girl 1936,D 9,34:1
Let's Get Married 1937,Ja 11,16:2
Warson at Night 1938,Ja 31,14:3
David and Esther 1938,O 12,34:3
Street Singers 1938,D 12,25:6
Wish Me Luck! 1954,N 1,37:2
Wedding March, The 1955,O 17,33:1
It's a Funny World 1956,O 22,24:1
It Could Happen to You 1957,O 28,30:5
Nice People 1958,O 20,36:1
Milk and Honey 1961,O 11,52:1
President's Daughter, The 1970,N 4,41:2
Goldberg, Dina
Longing for Home 1933,S 22,15:1
Goldberg, Dinah
Jolly World, A 1931,Ja 24,15:3
Singing Thief, The 1933,D 4,22:4
Goldberg, Fannie
Andersh; New Worlds 1922,S 26,18:2
Goldberg, Herman (Playwright)
Angels of Anadarko 1962,O 11,47:1

Goldberg, Isaac (Playwright)
Idle Inn, The 1921,D 21,26:2
God of Vengeance, The 1922,D 20,22:5
Goldberg, Isaac (Translator)
Zwie Family, The 1934,Mr 2,22:8
Goldberg, Jerry (Musical Director)
Sing Muse 1961,D 7,52:1
Boy Friend, The 1970,Ap 15,54:1
Goldberg, Leonard (Producer)
Three Men on a Horse 1969,O 17,35:1
Place for Polly, A 1970,Ap 20,45:1
Goldberg, Maxwell
Cocktails of 1934 1934,My 5,22:1
Goldberg, Nathan
All in a Lifetime 1934,Ap 2,12:5
Sins of Mothers 1937,Mr 30,20:2
Goldberg, Reuben (Lighting Director)
Does a Tiger Wear a Necktie? 1967,F 4,17:1
Goldberg, Rosa
Sins of Mothers 1937,Mr 30,20:2
Goldberg, Rose
All in a Lifetime 1934,Ap 2,12:5
Goldberg, Rube
Untitled-Revue 1923,My 12,15:4
Goldberg, Rube (Miscellaneous)
Untitled-Revue 1923,My 12,15:4
Goldberg, Rube (Playwright)
Murray Anderson's Almanac 1929,Ag 15,20:3
Russell Patterson's Sketch-Book 1960,F 8,35:1
Goldberg, Rubin
Right Next to Broadway 1944,F 22,26:2
Goldberg, Zina
Sonitchka 1930,Mr 8,21:3
Goldblatt, Aaron (Miscellaneous)
And the Wind Blows 1959,Ap 29,28:1
O Say Can You See! 1962,O 9,45:1
Goldby, Derek (Director)
Rosencrantz and Guildenstern Are Dead
1967,O 17,53:1
Rosencrantz and Guildenstern Are Dead
1967,O 29,II,1:1
Loot 1968,Mr 19,40:2
Goldby, Derek (Miscellaneous)
Her First Roman 1968,O 21,53:3
Goldby, Derek (Producer)
Loot 1968,Mr 31,II,1:1
Golden, Alfred L (Director)
Lady Behave 1943,N 17,30:1
Collector's Item 1952,F 9,11:2
Golden, Alfred L (Playwright)
Mimie Scheller 1936,O 1,28:4
Lady Behave 1943,N 17,30:1
Young Man's Fancy, A 1947,Ap 30,33:2
Collector's Item 1952,F 9,11:2
Golden, August
Deep Harlem 1929,Ja 8,35:2
Golden, Carole J
Anthony on Overtime 1961,O 21,13:2
Golden, Daniel (Composer)
Volpone 1957,Ja 8,27:1
Golden, Daniel (Musical Director)
Volpone 1957,Ja 13,II,10:1
Golden, Edward
John Bull's Other Island 1948,F 11,33:4
Where Stars Walk 1948,F 25,27:2
Golden, Eleanor (Original Author)
Spring Dance 1936,Ag 26,17:4
Golden, Eleanor (Playwright)
Little Theatre Tournament; Puppet-Play, A
1926,My 8,21:2
Spring Dance 1936,Jl 7,22:2
Golden, Ernie (Composer)
Artists and Models 1930,Je 11,33:2
Golden, Ernie and His Orchestra
Vaudeville (Palace) 1926,D 21,20:5
Golden, Florence
Mima 1928,D 13,24:2
Death Takes a Holiday 1929,D 27,26:4
Golden, George
Drums of Jeopardy, The 1922,My 30,8:4
Golden, Harry (Original Author)
Only in America 1959,N 20,35:1
Golden, Helen
Having Wonderful Time 1937,F 22,12:5
Escape This Night 1938,Ap 23,18:1
Golden, I J (Playwright)
Precedent 1931,Ap 15,24:5
Precedent 1931,Ap 26,VIII,1:1
Re-Echo 1934,Ja 12,28:4
Golden, John (Director)
Eva the Fifth 1928,Ag 29,19:3
Salt Water 1929,N 27,30:3
After Tomorrow 1931,Ag 27,22:4
Divine Drudge 1933,O 27,22:3
No Questions Asked 1934,F 6,24:3
Lightnin' 1938,S 16,17:2
Theatre 1941,N 13,34:2
Golden, John (Miscellaneous)
All Bow Down 1935,Ag 6,20:4
Three Wise Fools 1936,Mr 2,12:2
Golden, John (Playwright)
Eva the Fifth 1928,Ag 29,19:3
After Tomorrow 1930,Ag 10,VIII,2:3

After Tomorrow 1931,Ag 27,22:4
Divine Drudge 1933,Jl 4,16:4
Divine Drudge 1933,O 27,22:3
Dawn's Early Light 1950,O 25,44:3
Golden, John (Producer)
Pigs 1924,Je 8,VII,1:8
Holy Terror, A 1925,S 29,31:2
Wisdom Tooth, The 1926,F 16,22:2
2 Girls Wanted 1926,S 10,25:3
Gossipy Sex, The 1927,Ap 20,28:3
Four Walls 1927,S 20,33:1
Eva the Fifth 1928,Jl 22,VII,1:7
Eva the Fifth 1928,Ag 29,19:3
Night Hostess 1928,S 13,31:2
Let Us Be Gay 1929,F 22,19:1
When in Rome 1929,Je 16,VIII,2:1
Salt Water 1929,N 27,30:3
Bon Voyage 1929,D 29,VIII,4:3
Even in Egypt 1930,Ja 19,VIII,2:6
Joseph 1930,F 13,25:3
Ada Beats the Drum 1930,My 9,20:4
After Tomorrow 1930,Ag 10,VIII,2:3
That's Gratitude 1930,S 12,28:1
London Calling 1930,S 28,VIII,4:1
London Calling 1930,O 20,29:1
As Husbands Go 1931,Mr 6,26:5
After Tomorrow 1931,Ag 27,22:4
Caught Wet 1931,N 5,29:1
Savage Rhythm 1932,Ja 1,30:4
Riddle Me This! 1932,F 26,22:5
When Ladies Meet 1932,O 7,19:1
Divine Drudge 1933,Jl 4,16:4
Divine Drudge 1933,O 27,22:3
No Questions Asked 1934,F 6,24:3
Bishop Misbehaves, The 1935,F 21,22:4
Touch of Brimstone, A 1935,S 23,20:1
Tomorrow's a Holiday! 1935,D 31,10:2
And Now Goodbye 1937,Ja 19,29:1
And Now Goodbye 1937,F 3,26:4
Susan and God 1937,Ap 11,II,12:3
Never Trouble Trouble 1937,Ag 18,15:2
Susan and God 1937,O 8,26:4
Lightnin' 1938,S 16,17:2
Skylark 1939,Mr 19,XI,2:5
Skylark 1939,O 12,32:2
Old Foolishness, The 1940,D 21,20:2
Claudia 1941,F 13,24:2
Theatre 1941,O 26,IX,2:3
Theatre 1941,N 13,34:2
Claudia 1942,My 25,11:3
Counsellor-at-Law 1942,N 25,17:2
Three's a Family 1943,My 6,24:2
Army Play by Play, The 1943,Ag 3,13:3
Susan and God 1943,D 14,30:2
But Not Goodbye 1944,Ap 12,19:2
Place of Our Own, A 1945,Ap 3,23:7
Made in Heaven 1946,O 25,28:2
Belle of New York, The 1948,D 2,36:6
They Knew What They Wanted 1949,F 17,28:2
Golden, Mart Fuller
Chicken Feed 1923,S 25,10:2
Golden, Meyer
Vaudeville (Palace) 1929,N 18,22:4
Golden, N Lawrence (Producer)
Little Boxes; Coffee Lace, The 1969,D 4,71:2
Little Boxes; Trevor 1969,D 4,71:2
Golden, Ray (Composer)
Meet the People 1940,O 20,IX,3:3
Meet the People 1940,D 26,22:2
Golden, Ray (Lyricist)
Meet the People 1940,D 26,22:2
Alive and Kicking 1950,Ja 18,25:5
Catch a Star! 1955,S 7,35:2
Golden, Ray (Miscellaneous)
Ziegfeld Follies 1943,Ap 2,16:2
Alive and Kicking 1950,Ja 18,25:5
Catch a Star! 1955,S 7,35:2
Golden, Ray (Playwright)
Meet the People 1940,D 26,22:2
Golden, Ray (Producer)
Alive and Kicking 1950,Ja 18,25:5
Golden, Raymond (Producer)
Sky's the Limit, The 1934,D 18,25:5
Golden, Richard
As You Like It 1936,Ap 24,18:4
Golden, Rosalind
Would-Be Gentleman, The 1930,Ap 30,29:2
Golden Gate Quartet, The
For Your Pleasure 1943,F 6,9:2
Goldenberg, Billy (Miscellaneous)
Let It Ride 1961,O 13,27:4
Goldenberg, Samuel
American Dream; 1933 1933,F 22,24:5
Shooting Star 1933,Je 13,22:2
Once Upon a Time 1933,S 22,15:1
Germany Aflame 1933,O 28,20:5
Little Giants 1933,D 2,9:5
Eternal Road, The 1937,Ja 8,14:2
Who Is Who? 1938,D 24,13:3
Royal Family, The 1940,Ag 13,15:3
Goldenberg, William (Choreographer)
Best Foot Forward 1963,Ap 3,43:1

Goldenberg, William (Composer)
Evening With Mike Nichols and Elaine May, An
1960,O 10,37:1
Shout From the Rooftops 1964,O 29,40:1
Goldenberg, William (Miscellaneous)
110 in the Shade 1963,O 25,37:1
High Spirits 1964,Ap 8,34:1
Henry, Sweet Henry 1967,O 24,51:2
Goldenburg, Samuel
Jew Suss 1929,O 19,22:3
Angels on Earth 1929,D 11,34:7
Under One Roof 1932,F 8,21:2
Madame Pagliacci 1935,S 30,12:3
Brothers Ashkenazi, The 1937,S 21,28:6
Three Cities 1938,O 11,20:3
Worlds Apart 1941,Ja 23,19:3
Goldenburg, Samuel (Director)
Under One Roof 1932,F 8,21:2
Golder, Jenny
Palace aux Femmes 1926,O 10,VIII,2:1
Vive la Femme 1927,My 29,VII,2:1
Goldes, Sheila
Henry V 1964,My 13,52:1
Goldfaden, Abraham (Composer)
Tenth Commandment, The 1926,N 18,27:1
Wandering Stars 1946,D 14,18:2
Goldfaden, Abraham (Playwright)
Tenth Commandment, The 1926,N 18,27:1
Shulamith 1931,O 14,26:4
Sacrifice of Isaac, The 1933,N 22,22:4
Both Kooney Lemels 1964,O 12,37:2
Goldfaden, Wolf
Wolves 1924,D 31,9:4
Tenth Commandment, The 1926,N 18,27:1
Gardener's Dog, The 1927,O 21,27:1
Gold Diggers, The 1927,D 3,19:2
On Foreign Soil 1927,D 24,8:2
Alexander Pushkin 1928,Ja 27,14:2
Witch of Castile, The 1930,O 25,21:1
Uncle Moses 1930,N 29,21:3
Riverside Drive 1931,Ja 6,24:2
Man With the Portfolio, The 1931,F 12,24:6
New Man, The 1932,Ap 22,23:2
Bread 1932,D 14,27:3
Motke Ganef 1932,D 30,15:2
Revolt 1933,Ja 12,21:3
Wise Men of Chelm, The 1933,O 18,24:4
Josephus 1933,D 1,22:5
Jacques Bergson 1936,O 31,24:6
If I Were Rothschild 1940,Ja 1,28:7
Goldfarb, Belle
Out of This World 1955,N 10,44:2
Goldfarb, Helene D (Producer)
Toy for the Clowns, A 1962,S 13,31:2
Wretched the Lionhearted 1962,S 13,31:2
Goldfarb, Peter (Producer)
In the Summer House 1964,Mr 26,43:1
Goldfein, Abraham L (Playwright)
Fifth Horseman, The 1949,Je 14,26:6
Goldgran, Henry (Miscellaneous)
World of Charles Aznavour, The 1965,O 15,49:1
Goldgran, Henry (Producer)
From Israel With Laughter 1969,O 17,34:1
To Be or Not to Be-What Kind of a Question Is
That? 1970,O 20,39:1
Goldhurst, Richard
Career 1957,My 1,42:6
Goldie, Alfred
Spider, The 1927,Mr 23,29:1
Goldie, Hugh (Miscellaneous)
Sleep of Prisoners, A 1951,O 17,36:2
Goldie, Jack
Girl From Wyoming, The 1938,O 31,12:1
Goldie, Wyndham
Basalik 1935,Ap 8,22:5
Parnell 1936,Ap 24,19:5
Parnell 1936,My 24,IX,1:7
Parnell 1936,N 22,XI,1:3
King's Pirate, The 1937,Je 11,26:1
King's Pirate, The 1937,Je 27,X,1:3
Saint Joan 1954,S 18,12:1
Tiger at the Gates 1955,O 4,40:1
Goldin, Al (Miscellaneous)
Funny Girl 1964,Mr 27,15:1
Goldin, Al (Producer)
Come on Strong 1962,O 5,29:1
Goldin, Miriam
Eternal Jew, The 1926,D 21,21:2
Jacob's Dream 1927,Ja 4,20:2
Turandot 1929,Ja 12,14:4
Goldina, Miriam
Within the Gates 1934,O 23,23:1
Nowhere Bound 1935,Ja 23,20:2
Heart of a City 1942,F 13,24:6
Winter Soldiers 1942,N 30,19:2
Bell for Adano, A 1944,D 7,21:2
Diamond Lil 1948,N 30,33:2
Diamond Lil 1949,F 7,16:2
Right You Are (If You Think You Are)
1957,Mr 5,37:1
Highest Tree, The 1959,N 5,41:1
Crossroads 1969,Ag 7,28:1

Goldina, Miriam (Director)
Doll's House, A 1956,My 8,29:2
Courageous One, The 1958,Ja 21,33:6
Courageous One, The 1958,F 2,II,1:1
Goldina, Miriam (Playwright)
Doll's House, A 1956,My 8,29:2
Courageous One, The 1958,Ja 21,33:6
Golding, Edgar
Solid Ivory 1925,N 17,29:3
Golding, Louis (Original Author)
Magnolia Street 1934,Mr 9,22:6
Magnolia Street 1934,Ap 1,X,1:7
Golding, Louis (Playwright)
Magnolia Street 1934,Mr 9,22:6
Magnolia Street 1934,Ap 1,X,1:7
Golding, Richard
Hollow Crown, The 1963,Ja 31,5:1
Golding, Samuel Ruskin (Director)
Divorce a la Carte 1928,Mr 27,30:3
Through the Night 1930,Ag 19,19:1
Puppet Show 1930,O 29,26:5
Golding, Samuel Ruskin (Playwright)
Open House 1925,D 15,28:3
Pyramids 1926,Jl 20,17:2
Black Cockatoo, The 1926,D 31,11:1
New York 1927,N 15,26:2
Divorce a la Carte 1928,Mr 27,30:3
Through the Night 1930,Ag 19,19:1
Puppet Show 1930,O 29,26:5
Golding, Samuel Ruskin (Producer)
Open House 1925,D 15,28:3
Golding, William (Playwright)
Brass Butterfly, The 1970,Ja 31,34:1
Goldknopf, Abraham (Playwright)
In the Near Future 1925,Mr 11,19:1
Goldman, Blanche
Bursting the Barriers 1930,My 7,25:1
Goldman, Byron (Miscellaneous)
Maria Golovin 1958,N 6,43:1
Goldman, Byron (Producer)
Butterflies Are Free 1969,O 22,30:1
Minnie's Boys 1970,Mr 27,27:1
Goldman, Carl
Revolt of the Beavers, The 1937,My 21,19:2
Goldman, Daniel (Miscellaneous)
Theater of Peretz, The 1963,N 6,35:2
Goldman, David (Director)
Shoot Anything With Hair That Moves
1969,F 3,29:1
Goldman, Donald H (Costume Designer)
Othello 1953,O 30,28:2
Twelfth Night 1957,Ja 5,12:2
Goldman, Donald H (Lighting Designer)
Othello 1953,O 30,28:2
Goldman, Donald H (Miscellaneous)
H M S Pinafore 1957,My 1,42:6
Goldman, Donald H (Producer)
Twelfth Night 1954,N 10,42:2
Merchant of Venice, The 1955,F 23,23:2
Macbeth 1955,O 20,42:2
Midsummer Night's Dream, A 1956,Ja 14,12:2
Romeo and Juliet 1956,F 24,20:4
Hamlet 1956,O 29,34:1
Twelfth Night 1957,Ja 5,12:2
Utopia, Limited; Flowers of Progress, The
1957,F 27,21:1
Mikado, The 1957,Ap 24,28:2
Pirates of Penzance, The 1957,My 8,43:1
Yeomen of the Guard, The 1957,My 22,28:3
Gondoliers, The 1957,My 29,34:2
Julius Caesar 1957,O 24,39:1
King Lear 1959,Ja 3,11:2
Sign of Jonah, The 1960,S 9,35:1
Electra 1962,Mr 22,42:1
Man With a Load of Mischief, The 1966,N 7,65:1
David Show, The 1968,N 1,34:2
Goldman, Donald H (Scenic Designer)
Major Barbara 1951,F 24,10:2
Othello 1953,O 30,28:2
Twelfth Night 1954,N 10,42:2
Twelfth Night 1954,D 12,II,3:1
Merchant of Venice, The 1955,F 23,23:2
Midsummer Night's Dream, A 1956,Ja 14,12:2
Romeo and Juliet 1956,F 24,20:4
Twelfth Night 1957,Ja 5,12:2
Goldman, Harold (Composer)
Garrick Gaieties 1930,Je 5,29:2
Goldman, Harold (Playwright)
Co-Respondent Unknown 1936,F 12,24:4
Goldman, James (Lyricist)
Family Affair, A 1962,Ja 29,17:1
Goldman, James (Playwright)
Blood, Sweat & Stanley Poole 1961,O 6,31:1
Family Affair, A 1962,Ja 29,17:1
Lion in Winter, The 1966,Mr 4,23:1
Lion in Winter, The 1966,Mr 13,II,1:1
Goldman, Jerry (Miscellaneous)
Fallout 1959,My 21,36:2
Goldman, Jerry (Playwright)
Fallout 1959,My 21,36:2
Goldman, Lee (Lighting Director)
Immaculate Misconception, The 1970,O 28,63:3

Goldman, Leon
Love Nest, The 1927,D 23,17:1
Goldman, Louis S (Producer)
Blood Red Roses 1970,Mr 23,48:1
Goldman, Rachel
Brothers Ashkenazi, The 1955,N 12,24:4
Goldman, Robert
Never Say Horses 1951,D 7,34:4
Goldman, Robert (Composer)
First Impressions 1959,Mr 20,28:1
Goldman, Robert (Lyricist)
First Impressions 1959,Mr 20,28:1
Goldman, William (Playwright)
Blood, Sweat & Stanley Poole 1961,O 6,31:1
Family Affair, A 1962,Ja 29,17:1
Goldner, Charles
Moment of Truth 1951,D 9,II,7:7
Dear Charles 1952,D 21,44:5
Dear Charles 1953,Ap 20,22:4
Girl in Pink Tights, The 1954,Mr 6,13:2
Goldoni, Carlo (Original Author)
Four Brawlers, The 1928,Mr 4,IX,2:7
Liar, The 1950,My 19,30:2
Goldoni, Carlo (Playwright)
Locandiera, La 1923,N 1,24:1
Mistress of the Inn, The; Locandiera, La
1923,N 22,16:1
Locandiera, La 1923,D 9,IX,1:1
Locandiera, La; Mistress of the Inn, The
1926,N 23,26:1
Diener Zweier Herren; Servant of Two Masters,
The 1928,Ja 10,28:3
Servant of Two Masters, The 1928,Ja 22,VIII,6:1
Curioso Accidente, Un 1933,Mr 6,16:3
Good Girl, The 1934,Je 26,22:5
Impresario From Smyrna 1935,D 24,10:3
Mistress of the Inn, The 1937,Je 22,26:3
Arlecchino, the Servant of Two Masters
1956,Ag 28,31:1
Servant of Two Masters, The 1958,F 11,35:2
Servant of Two Masters, The 1960,F 24,42:2
Servant of Two Masters, The 1960,F 29,31:5
Servant of Two Masters, The 1966,Je 28,51:1
Venetian Twins, The 1968,My 29,23:1
Goldreyer, Michael (Producer)
Praying Curve 1927,Ja 25,18:2
Goldsborough, Ellen (Costume Designer)
I Am a Camera 1951,N 29,39:6
Goldsbury, Christopher
What a Relief 1935,D 14,10:6
Goldsby, Algela
Antony and Cleopatra 1963,S 14,12:4
Goldschmidt, Lina (Original Author)
Case of Clyde Griffiths 1936,Mr 14,10:4
Goldschmidt, Nicholas (Musical Director)
Two Misers, The 1943,D 9,30:5
Goldsmith, Abe (Miscellaneous)
Fallout 1959,My 21,36:2
Goldsmith, Abe (Playwright)
Fallout 1959,My 21,36:2
Goldsmith, Bea (Lyricist)
Of V We Sing 1942,F 16,20:3
Goldsmith, C Gerald (Miscellaneous)
Cry for Us All 1970,Ap 9,48:2
Goldsmith, Castillo (Costume Designer)
Inside U S A 1948,My 23,II,1:1
Goldsmith, Clifford (Playwright)
What a Life 1938,Ap 14,26:2
What a Life 1939,Ag 2,17:5
Goldsmith, Eleanor (Costume Designer)
Mr Peebles and Mr Hooker 1946,O 11,29:2
Lovely Me 1946,D 26,30:4
Finian's Rainbow 1947,Ja 11,23:2
Inside U S A 1948,My 1,19:2
Inside U S A 1948,My 23,II,1:1
Young and Fair, The 1948,N 23,35:2
Jenny Kissed Me 1948,D 24,12:2
Biggest Thief in Town 1949,Mr 31,31:2
Father, The 1949,N 17,36:2
Texas Li'l Darlin' 1949,N 26,10:5
Goldsmith, Jack (Producer)
Let Freedom Ring 1935,N 7,26:2
Goldsmith, James
Country Wife, The 1957,Je 27,22:1
Ivanov 1958,O 8,42:1
Philoctetes 1959,Ja 14,28:1
Goldsmith, Jechiel
Green Fields 1920,Mr 26,11:2
Fortune 1920,Ap 22,11:3
Naomi 1920,My 7,12:2
One Life for Another 1920,D 18,11:2
Andersh; New Worlds 1922,S 26,18:2
Gardener's Dog, The 1927,O 21,27:1
Gold Diggers, The 1927,D 3,19:2
On Foreign Soil 1927,D 24,8:2
Alexander Pushkin 1928,Ja 27,14:2
American Chasidim 1928,Mr 17,8:8
Poppa 1928,D 25,31:1
Goldsmith, Joan
Hamlet 1970,O 27,54:2
Goldsmith, Lester M (Producer)
Happy Birthday, Wanda June 1970,O 8,58:2

Goldsmith, Margie (Costume Designer)
Boesman and Lena 1970,Je 23,35:1
Goldsmith, Merwin
Phaedra 1967,My 22,50:2
Hamlet 1967,D 27,45:1
Minnie's Boys 1970,Mr 27,27:1
Goldsmith, Oliver (Original Author)
O Marry Me 1961,O 28,13:1
Goldsmith, Oliver (Playwright)
She Stoops to Conquer 1924,Je 10,24:3
She Stoops to Conquer 1928,My 15,17:1
She Stoops to Conquer 1928,My 20,VIII,1:1
She Stoops to Conquer 1928,S 2,VII,2:1
She Stoops to Conquer 1949,D 29,21:3
She Stoops to Conquer 1950,Je 18,34:4
She Stoops to Conquer 1960,N 2,42:5
She Stoops to Conquer 1960,N 13,II,1:1
She Stoops to Conquer 1960,N 15,36:3
She Stoops to Conquer 1968,Ja 1,11:1
She Stoops to Conquer 1968,Ap 1,58:3
She Stoops to Conquer 1969,Ag 18,28:1
Goldsmith, Peter (Playwright)
Spring Tide 1936,Ag 9,IX,1:5
Goldstein, Charlotte
Yoshe Kalb 1932,N 6,IX,2:1
Revolt 1933,Ja 12,21:3
Doctor Herzl 1945,D 21,25:4
Song of Dnieper 1946,O 26,10:5
Shylock and His Daughter 1947,S 30,22:2
Voice of Israel, The 1948,O 26,40:2
Yosele the Nightingale 1949,O 21,30:4
Goldstein, David
Rosalinda; Fledermaus, Die 1942,O 29,26:5
Goldstein, Florence
Storm, The 1962,Mr 31,17:2
Goldstein, Izzie
Secret of Love, The 1936,F 24,15:2
Her Great Mistake 1940,F 5,12:6
Goldstein, Jacob
Gardener's Dog, The 1927,O 21,27:1
Gold Diggers, The 1927,D 3,19:2
Alexander Pushkin 1928,Ja 27,14:2
Goldstein, Jennie
Love and Politics 1929,O 21,30:7
Slaves of Luxury 1930,F 8,13:3
Sonitchka 1930,Mr 8,21:3
Untitled-Benefit 1933,Ja 25,13:3
Madame Pagliacci 1935,S 30,12:3
Girls of Today 1935,N 20,26:5
Saint and Sinners 1935,D 30,15:2
Freidel Becomes a Bride 1936,F 10,14:3
Golden Stream, The 1936,F 13,25:1
Souls for Sale 1936,S 21,27:6
Stepsisters 1936,O 13,32:3
Of One Mother 1937,Ja 18,21:3
Should a Mother Tell? 1938,N 25,18:3
Number, The 1951,O 31,33:2
Camino Real 1953,Mr 20,26:1
Camino Real 1953,Mr 29,II,1:1
Goldstein, Jennie (Playwright)
Madame Pagliacci 1935,S 30,12:3
Goldstein, Jennie (Producer)
Girls of Today 1935,N 20,26:5
Saint and Sinners 1935,D 30,15:2
Stepsisters 1936,O 13,32:3
Goldstein, Katherine
Broken Engagement, The 1921,My 12,20:2
Goldstein, Laurence (Producer)
Vida es Sueno, La 1964,Mr 18,49:1
Life Is a Dream 1964,Mr 20,24:1
Goldstein, Louis (Miscellaneous)
Devil's Game, A 1959,N 9,35:6
Goldstein, Michael
Yegor Bulevitch 1934,Ja 8,21:7
Aristocrats 1935,My 2,16:2
Haunch, Paunch and Jowl 1935,D 27,22:4
Chains 1937,Ja 22,25:1
Outlaw, The 1937,O 6,28:1
Good Soldier Schweik, The 1937,D 22,33:2
Far-Away Corner, A 1939,F 15,15:2
Clinton Street 1939,O 13,27:2
Uriel Acosta 1939,D 31,18:3
Goldstein, Robert
Brothers Ashkenazi, The 1970,N 17,53:2
Goldstein, Robert (Miscellaneous)
Howdy Stranger 1937,Ja 15,17:5
Goldstein, Ruth (Lyricist)
Dutchman's Farm, A 1941,My 11,I,43:3
Goldstein, Ruth (Playwright)
Dutchman's Farm, A 1941,My 11,I,43:3
Goldstein, Shmulik
World Is a Stage, The 1962,N 5,37:4
Don't Worry Brother! 1963,O 14,35:2
Both Kooney Lemels 1964,O 12,37:2
Untitled-Revue 1966,O 3,62:5
Let's Sing Yiddish 1966,N 10,63:1
Sing Israel Sing 1967,My 12,50:1
Hut a Yid a Landele 1968,O 19,28:1
From Israel With Laughter 1969,O 17,34:1
To Be or Not to Be-What Kind of a Question Is
That? 1970,O 20,39:1
Goldstein, Solomon
Processional 1937,O 14,23:1

Goldstein, Zina
Parisian Love 1927,Ja 28,15:5
Berdichever Bridegroom, The 1930,S 24,26:2
Jolly World, A 1931,Ja 24,15:3
Women of New York 1931,Mr 23,24:3
Goldstone, Jean Stock (Playwright)
Mary Stuart 1957,O 9,39:1
Mary Stuart 1957,O 20,II,1:1
Goldstone, Nat (Miscellaneous)
Bloomer Girl 1944,O 6,18:5
Goldstone, Nat (Producer)
Bloomer Girl 1947,Ja 7,33:2
Goldsworthy, John
Whitewashed 1924,Ap 24,22:2
Leap, The 1924,My 23,16:5
This Woman Business 1926,D 8,25:1
Red Robe, The 1928,D 26,15:1
Three Little Girls 1930,Ap 15,29:1
Lady Beyond the Moon 1931,Ap 1,36:5
Goldsworthy, John (Playwright)
Whitewashed 1924,Ap 24,22:2
Goldthwaite, Eaton
Betty Behave 1927,Mr 9,28:4
Goldwasser, Lawrence (Lighting Director)
Temporary Island, A 1948,Mr 15,27:3
Goldwasser, Lawrence (Scenic Designer)
Washington Jitters 1938,My 3,19:1
Devil Takes a Bride, The 1938,O 8,10:3
Ringside Seat 1938,N 23,24:5
Streets of Paris, The 1939,Je 20,25:2
Emperor Jones, The 1939,Je 20,25:2
Passenger to Bali, A 1940,Mr 15,26:2
At the Stroke of Eight 1940,My 21,29:2
Made in Heaven 1946,O 25,28:2
Temporary Island, A 1948,Mr 15,27:3
Goldwater, Erwin
Not for Children 1935,D 29,IX,2:1
Goldwater, Irving
War and Peace 1942,My 22,26:3
Golea, Francoise
Intermezzo 1957,F 15,20:4
Goleeke, Bill
Annie Get Your Gun 1957,Mr 9,15:5
Golightly, John
Rockefeller and the Red Indians 1968,O 25,37:1
Golikov, Victor
Moscow Circus on Ice 1970,D 9,63:1
Golkin, Dewey
Penny Friend, The 1966,D 27,46:1
Golkin, Jeffrey
Penny Friend, The 1966,D 27,46:1
Goll, Barbara
Modern Statuary 1968,My 28,41:1
Golland, I
Jacob's Dream 1927,Ja 4,20:2
Golle, Hans (Lieut)
War Song, The 1928,S 25,29:3
Gollins, Margaret
Comedy of Women, A 1929,S 14,17:4
Golomb, Sheldon
King of the Whole Damn World 1962,Ap 16,32:2
Golonka, Arlene
Night Circus, The 1958,D 3,44:1
Take Me Along 1959,O 23,22:2
Come Blow Your Horn 1961,F 23,31:3
One Flew Over the Cuckoo's Nest 1963,N 14,40:2
Ready When You Are, C. B.! 1964,D 8,55:1
Wayward Stork, The 1966,Ja 20,27:1
Golovko, Kira
Three Sisters, The 1965,F 12,15:1
Golson, Harry
Jefferson Davis 1936,F 19,17:2
Treasure Island 1938,My 15,II,2:3
Golstein, Milton E
Thomas Paine 1930,Mr 21,30:7
Goltz, Arnold (Playwright)
Queen Mother 1938,D 26,29:4
Goltz, Emil (Playwright)
Queen Mother 1938,D 26,29:4
Golub, Frances
Riverside Drive 1931,Ja 6,24:2
Golub, Selvin
Riverside Drive 1931,Ja 6,24:2
Gombaszogi, Frida
Letter, The 1927,O 30,IX,4:1
Postmistress, The 1928,Ja 15,VIII,2:1
Olympia 1928,Mr 25,IX,4:1
A Farkas 1928,O 28,IX,2:1
Constant Wife, The 1928,D 30,VIII,4:4
Constant Wife, The 1929,F 3,VIII,2:1
Romance of Ida, The 1929,F 3,VIII,2:1
Alice Takat 1930,F 23,III,7:2
Gombell, Minna
Listening In 1922,D 5,24:1
Mister Pitt 1924,Ja 23,15:3
Alloy 1924,O 28,27:1
Ballyhoo 1927,Ja 5,18:1
Jimmie's Women 1927,S 27,30:3
Great Power, The 1928,S 12,25:1
Indiscretion 1929,Mr 5,28:1
Nancy's Private Affair 1930,Ja 14,24:3
Gomberg, Leo
Blood Wedding 1949,F 7,16:2

Gombrowicz, Witold (Playwright)
Operetta 1970,Mr 9,42:1
Gomer, Geoffrey (Playwright)
Anteroom, The 1936,Ag 15,6:7
Anteroom, The 1936,S 6,IX,1:1
Gomez
Gang's All Here, The 1931,F 19,21:3
Gomez, Augie
Buckaroo 1929,Mr 18,31:1
Gomez, Perla
Trojan Women, The 1938,Ja 25,24:2
Gomez, Thomas
Hamlet 1925,O 12,19:2
Hamlet 1928,Ja 5,33:2
Caponsacchi 1928,Ja 25,20:3
Henry V 1928,Mr 16,26:2
Light of Asia, The 1928,O 10,32:2
Becky Sharp 1929,Je 4,29:1
Bonds of Interest, The 1929,O 15,34:2
Richelieu 1929,D 26,20:3
Hamlet 1934,D 26,19:3
Richard III 1934,D 28,24:3
Caesar and Cleopatra 1935,Ag 22,21:1
Taming of the Shrew, The 1935,O 1,27:3
Idiot's Delight 1936,Mr 25,25:2
Hamlet 1937,Ag 24,24:4
Robin Landing 1937,N 19,26:4
Western Waters 1937,D 29,17:1
Sea Gull, The 1938,Mr 29,19:2
Taming of the Shrew, The 1940,F 6,17:2
There Shall Be No Night 1940,Ap 30,25:2
Flowers of Virtue, The 1942,F 6,22:2
Hamlet 1945,D 14,25:2
Hamlet 1946,Je 4,18:4
Sherlock Holmes 1953,O 31,11:2
Visit, The 1960,Mr 9,38:3
Man for All Seasons, A 1962,S 23,II,1:1
Gomez, Tommy
Carib Song 1945,S 28,17:2
Gomez, Vincente
Mexicana 1939,Ap 22,14:4
For Your Pleasure 1943,F 6,9:2
Gomez, Vincente (Musical Director)
Mexicana 1939,My 7,X,3:1
Gomez and Winona
Crazy Quilt 1931,My 20,28:4
        1936,Ja 23,25:3
Gomez Trio
Vaudeville (Palace) 1923,O 23,18:2
Wake Up and Dream 1929,D 31,14:3
Gon, Zamira (Choreographer)
Flag Is Born, A 1946,S 7,10:6
Goncharov, Andrei (Director)
Man Alive 1965,My 23,13:1
Gondell, Harris
Barefoot Boy With Cheek 1947,Ap 4,20:2
Gondra, Arthur
Mexican Hayride 1944,Ja 29,9:6
Common Ground 1945,Ap 26,27:2
Dunnigan's Daughter 1945,D 27,16:1
Gonos, Jenny
Private Life of the Master Race, The
        1956,Ja 31,33:3
Gontacharoff
Chauve-Souris 1922,Je 6,17:4
Gontard, G V (Director)
Rape of the Sabine Women, The 1949,F 5,10:5
Gontard, G V (Miscellaneous)
Faust 1947,N 29,9:2
Gontard, Gert von (Producer)
Why Do I Deserve This? 1966,Ja 19,31:2
Gonzales, Alfonso
King and the Duke, The 1955,Je 2,25:2
Gonzales, Enrique
Leyenda del Beso, La 1942,N 20,26:4
Gonzales, Jorge
Handful of Fire 1958,O 2,45:3
Gonzales, Max
Wildcat, The 1921,N 28,16:2
Gonzalez, Ernesto
Camino Real 1953,Mr 20,26:1
Saint of Bleecker Street, The 1954,D 28,21:1
Innkeepers, The 1956,F 3,19:1
Secret Concubine, The 1960,Mr 22,29:2
Kitchen, The 1966,Je 14,50:1
Que Vida de Perro 1968,Ag 2,24:1
Gonzalez, Ernesto (Playwright)
Que Vida de Perro 1968,Ag 2,24:1
Gonzalez, Pedro
Cuando Los Hijos De Eva No Son Los Hijos De
        Adan 1937,My 1,17:4
Tierra Baja 1937,My 8,22:4
Good, J S
Affair, The 1962,S 21,34:2
Good, Jack
Hello Paris 1930,N 17,29:3
Face the Music 1932,F 18,24:5
Face the Music 1933,F 1,13:4
Show Is On, The 1937,S 20,18:4
Good, Kip
Pillar to Post 1943,D 11,11:2
Pretty Little Parlor 1944,Ap 18,24:8

Good, Kip (Miscellaneous)
Live Wire, The 1950,Ag 18,16:2
Small War on Murray Hill 1957,Ja 4,19:1
Hole in the Head, A 1957,Mr 1,15:1
Good, Maggi
Master Builder, The 1968,Je 22,26:1
Goodbody, Buzz (Director)
King John 1970,Je 19,27:2
Goodchild, George (Playwright)
No Exit 1936,Ja 22,15:3
Goode, Alan
Rope 1928,F 23,18:3
Salt Water 1929,N 27,30:3
Betty, Be Careful 1931,My 5,33:3
Geraniums in My Window 1934,O 27,20:6
Goode, Herbert
Sing High, Sing Low 1931,N 13,26:4
Goode, Jack
So This Is Paris 1930,Ap 27,IX,2:3
Desert Song, The 1946,Ja 9,20:2
Sally 1948,My 7,31:2
Hello, Dolly! 1970,Mr 30,52:1
Goode, James
Innocent Voyage, The 1943,N 16,27:2
Goode, Jimmy
Biff, Bing, Bang 1921,My 10,20:1
Goode, Peter (Playwright)
Two for Fun 1961,F 14,45:3
Goode, Reginald
Merchant of Venice, The 1922,D 22,13:1
Sandro Botticelli 1923,Mr 27,24:2
Devil's Disciple, The 1923,Ap 24,24:1
Midsummer Night's Dream, A 1927,Je 27,25:1
Madame X 1927,Jl 7,29:3
Prisoner, The 1927,D 30,22:2
Vaudeville (Palace) 1928,My 8,25:2
Wild Duck, The 1928,N 19,17:1
First Law, The 1929,My 7,28:4
Puppet Show 1930,O 29,26:5
Goode, Reginald (Playwright)
Ashes 1924,Je 1,VII,4:3
Ashes 1924,O 21,21:2
Just Beyond 1925,D 2,22:4
Goode, William
Inside Story, The 1932,F 23,23:2
Goodell, Danzi
Criss Cross 1926,O 13,20:2
Vaudeville (Palace) 1930,S 29,19:1
Vaudeville (Palace) 1932,Ap 25,18:3
Goodell, John
Paradise 1931,My 12,29:2
Goodell, Ted
Out of This World 1955,N 10,44:2
Goodelle, Niela
Only Girl, The 1934,My 22,28:2
Illustrators' Show, The 1936,Ja 23,25:3
Goodem, Gladys
Porgy and Bess 1942,Ja 23,16:2
Goodhall, Grace
Swifty 1922,O 17,14:1
Goodhart, Ernest
Red Robe, The 1928,D 26,15:1
Countess Maritza 1936,Ag 19,18:2
Blossom Time 1938,D 27,12:2
Follow the Girls 1944,Ap 10,15:2
Goodhart, William (Playwright)
Generation 1965,O 8,5:6
Goodhead, Jimmy
Aquarama 1960 1960,Jl 1,14:6
Aqua Carnival 1962,Je 29,15:1
Goodhue, Helen
Hello, Yourself 1928,O 31,28:2
Woof, Woof 1929,D 26,20:4
Goodhue, Kenneth
Master of the Inn, The 1925,D 23,22:2
Goodhue, Willis Maxwell (Playwright)
Myrtie 1924,F 5,21:2
All Wet 1925,Jl 7,24:1
Head First 1926,Ja 7,22:4
Katy Did 1927,My 10,24:3
Betty, Be Careful 1931,My 5,33:3
Goodier, Henry
Gondoliers, The 1951,F 13,27:2
Goodier, Robert
All's Well That Ends Well 1953,Jl 16,18:2
Measure for Measure 1954,Je 30,23:1
Taming of the Shrew, The 1954,Jl 1,22:2
Oedipus Rex 1954,Jl 17,6:6
Saint Joan 1954,S 18,12:1
Merchant of Venice, The 1955,Jl 1,13:1
Tamburlaine the Great 1956,Ja 20,19:1
Henry V 1956,Je 20,27:2
Merry Wives of Windsor, The 1956,Je 21,34:4
First Gentleman, The 1957,Ap 26,22:2
Mary Stuart 1957,O 9,39:1
Mary Stuart 1957,O 20,II,1:1
King John 1960,Je 29,26:2
Romeo and Juliet 1960,Jl 1,14:1
Coriolanus 1961,Je 21,31:2
Henry VIII 1961,Je 22,22:1
Gooding, Geraldine
Green Pastures, The 1935,F 27,16:2

Goodis, Marvin
  Around the World in 80 Days 1964,Je 29,33:2
  Guys and Dolls 1966,Je 9,55:2
  Wonderful Town 1967,My 18,50:1
Goodjohn, Arlouine
  Day Before Spring, The 1945,N 23,27:2
Goodkin, Lennie (Lighting Director)
  Servant of Two Masters, The 1958,F 11,35:2
Goodlake, Richard H
  My Fair Lady 1964,My 21,43:2
Goodliffe, Michael
  Living Room, The 1954,N 18,41:1
  Living Room, The 1954,N 28,II,1:1
  Lark, The 1955,My 13,21:2
  Doctor Faustus 1961,Ag 22,23:1
  Sponono 1964,Ap 3,28:1
Goodman, Alfred (Composer)
  Cinderella on Broadway 1920,Je 25,18:1
  Whirl of New York, The 1921,Je 14,18:1
  Passing Show of 1922, The 1922,S 21,18:2
  Lady in Ermine, The 1922,O 3,22:2
  Dew Drop Inn 1923,My 18,26:4
  Topics of 1923 1923,N 21,23:2
  Sky High 1925,Mr 3,21:4
  Artists and Models 1925,Je 25,16:2
  Gay Paree 1925,Ag 19,14:3
Goodman, Alfred Grant (Composer)
  Bride in the Morning, A 1960,My 26,38:2
Goodman, Arthur
  If Booth Had Missed 1931,My 14,27:1
Goodman, Arthur (Playwright)
  If Booth Had Missed 1931,My 14,27:1
  If Booth Had Missed 1932,F 5,24:2
  If Booth Had Missed 1932,F 14,VIII,1:1
  In Heaven and Earth 1936,Mr 27,24:8
  Seeds in the Wind 1948,Ap 26,27:2
  Seeds in the Wind 1948,My 26,29:2
  Athenian Touch, The 1964,Ja 15,25:4
Goodman, Benny
  Seven Lively Arts 1944,D 8,26:6
Goodman, Benny (Musical Director)
  Swingin' the Dream 1939,N 30,24:2
Goodman, Benny and His Band
  Seven Lively Arts 1944,D 17,II,3:1
Goodman, Bernard
  Othello 1937,Ja 7,16:4
Goodman, David Zelag (Playwright)
  High Named Today 1954,D 11,11:2
Goodman, Davis
  Topsy and Eva 1924,D 24,11:1
Goodman, Dody
  Wonderful Town 1953,F 26,22:3
  Shoestring Revue 1955,Mr 1,22:2
  Shoestring '57 1956,N 6,31:1
  Parade 1960,Ja 21,27:4
  Fiorello! 1962,Je 14,24:1
  Rainy Day in Newark, A 1963,O 23,35:1
  Ben Bagley's New Cole Porter Revue
    1965,D 23,20:1
  My Daughter, Your Son 1969,My 14,36:2
  Front Page, The 1969,N 2,86:1
Goodman, Eckert (Playwright)
  Many Mansions 1937,Ag 3,20:5
  Many Mansions 1937,O 28,28:6
Goodman, Edward (Director)
  Blue Peter, The 1925,Mr 25,25:3
  Rosmersholm 1925,My 6,27:2
  Man's Man, A 1925,O 14,31:2
  Devil to Pay, The 1925,D 4,26:2
  Unchastened Woman, The 1926,F 17,12:1
  One Day More 1926,Mr 19,24:3
  Easter 1926,Mr 19,24:3
  American Tragedy, An 1926,O 12,31:2
  Wall Street 1927,Ap 21,24:4
  Celebrity 1927,D 27,24:3
  Americana 1928,O 31,28:2
  No Questions Asked 1934,F 6,24:3
  Class of '29 1936,My 16,10:3
  Sun and I, The 1937,F 27,9:5
Goodman, Edward (Playwright)
  Other Lives 1921,S 11,VI,1:6
Goodman, Edward (Producer)
  American Holiday 1936,F 22,13:3
  Murder in the Cathedral 1936,Mr 21,13:5
Goodman, Esther
  Tobias and the Angel 1937,Ap 29,16:5
Goodman, George
  Four Saints in Three Acts 1952,Ap 17,35:1
Goodman, Gerald
  As You Like It 1963,Jl 17,19:2
Goodman, Gerald (Composer)
  'Tis Pity She's a Whore 1958,D 6,21:1
Goodman, Gordon
  Aquashow 1952,Je 25,25:1
  Hear! Hear! 1955,S 28,38:1
Goodman, Hallie
  World of Illusion 1964,Je 25,26:2
Goodman, Harry (Musical Director)
  Frere Jacques 1968,Je 8,23:2
Goodman, Jack
  Broadway Shadows 1930,Ap 1,34:6
Goodman, James (Miscellaneous)
  Black-Eyed Susan 1954,D 24,7:5

Goodman, Jules Eckert (Playwright)
  Pietro 1920,Ja 20,10:2
  Lawbreaker, The 1922,F 7,12:1
  Partners Again 1922,My 2,22:2
  Chains 1923,S 20,5:2
  Simon Called Peter 1924,My 4,VIII,2:1
  Simon Called Peter 1924,N 11,20:2
  Potash and Perlmutter, Detectives; Poisoned by
    Pictures 1926,S 1,27:3
  Potash and Perlmutter, Detectives 1926,S 5,VII,1:1
  Great Romancer, The 1937,Je 16,26:3
  Great Romancer, The 1937,Jl 4,X,1:4
  Many Mansions 1937,Ag 3,20:5
  Many Mansions 1937,O 28,28:6
  Treasure Island 1938,My 15,II,2:3
Goodman, Kim
  Love for Love 1967,O 21,17:1
Goodman, Lee
  Dance Me a Song 1950,Ja 21,10:5
  Razzle Dazzle 1951,F 20,21:1
  Carnival in Flanders 1953,S 9,38:2
  How to Succeed in Business Without Really Trying
    1966,Ap 21,45:1
  Alchemist, The 1966,O 14,48:1
  Criss-Crossing 1970,Ja 22,30:1
Goodman, Lee (Playwright)
  Dance Me a Song 1950,Ja 21,10:5
Goodman, Leonard
  Conversation Piece 1934,O 24,24:1
Goodman, Martin (Producer)
  Love on Leave 1944,Je 21,23:4
  Deadfall 1955,O 28,20:1
Goodman, Paul (Playwright)
  Faustina 1952,My 26,19:5
  Cave at Machpelah, The 1959,Jl 1,25:1
  Jonah! 1966,F 16,52:1
Goodman, Peter (Miscellaneous)
  Courtyard 1960,Mr 1,28:1
  Magnificent Hugo, The 1961,Ap 8,12:2
Goodman, Philip (Director)
  Washington Heights 1931,S 30,23:4
Goodman, Philip (Producer)
  Dear Sir 1924,S 24,21:3
  Ramblers, The 1926,S 21,32:2
  Wild Man of Borneo, The 1927,S 14,29:2
  Five O'Clock Girl, The 1927,O 11,26:3
  Rainbow 1928,N 22,25:1
  Rainbow 1928,D 16,IX,1:1
  Among the Married 1929,O 4,24:3
  Washington Heights 1931,S 30,23:4
Goodman, Philip S
  Joan of Lorraine 1955,Mr 26,12:2
Goodman, Ralph
  Young and Beautiful, The 1959,My 29,13:1
Goodman, Randolph (Playwright)
  Long Way From Home, A 1948,F 9,25:2
Goodman, Ruth (Playwright)
  One-Man Show 1945,F 9,21:2
  One-Man Show 1945,F 18,II,1:1
Goodman, Stuart (Producer)
  Nobody Hears A Broken Drum 1970,Mr 20,55:1
Goodman, Willard W (Producer)
  Awake and Sing! 1970,My 28,35:1
Goodner, Carol
  Great Gatsby, The 1926,F 3,22:1
  First Mrs Fraser, The 1929,D 30,16:2
  Musical Chairs 1931,D 6,VIII,2:7
  Dinner at Eight 1933,Ja 7,11:5
  Dinner at Eight 1933,Ja 29,IX,1:3
  Success Story 1934,Ja 2,17:4
  Nineties; Double Door 1934,Mr 22,24:6
  Double Door 1934,Ap 15,X,2:2
  Rose and Glove 1934,S 9,35:5
  Anthony and Anna 1934,N 13,22:2
  He Was Born Gay 1937,Je 13,XI,1:7
  Great Romancer, The 1937,Jl 4,X,1:4
  Gertie Maude 1937,Ag 18,14:5
  Gertie Maude 1937,S 5,X,2:1
  Three Sisters, The 1938,F 13,X,3:3
  They Walk Alone 1939,F 5,IX,3:2
  Man Who Came to Dinner, The 1939,O 17,31:1
  They Walk Alone 1941,Mr 13,24:2
  Wookey, The 1941,Ag 26,23:2
  Wookey, The 1941,S 11,20:5
  Family, The 1943,Mr 31,22:4
  Lovers and Friends 1943,N 30,23:2
  Lovers and Friends 1943,D 5,II,5:1
  Deep Are the Roots 1945,S 27,24:4
  Deep Are the Roots 1945,O 7,II,1:1
  Farther Off From Heaven 1947,Je 4,33:3
  How I Wonder 1947,O 1,34:2
  Autumn Garden, The 1951,Mr 8,36:2
  Autumn Garden, The 1951,Mr 18,II,1:1
  Brass Ring, The 1952,Ap 11,19:2
  Horses in Midstream 1953,Ap 3,18:7
  Living Room, The 1954,N 18,41:1
  Living Room, The 1954,N 28,II,1:1
  Man for All Seasons, A 1961,N 23,51:1
  Man for All Seasons, A 1961,D 3,II,1:1
  Man for All Seasons, A 1962,S 23,II,1:1
Goodnow, Edward A (Director)
  B J One 1931,My 7,21:3

Goodnow, Edward P
  Dead End 1935,O 29,17:2
Goodrich, Alton
  Neighbors 1923,D 27,11:1
  Silence 1924,N 13,18:2
Goodrich, Arthur (Director)
  Richelieu 1929,D 26,20:3
  Plutocrat, The 1930,F 21,23:3
  Richelieu 1934,My 22,28:1
Goodrich, Arthur (Playwright)
  So This Is London 1922,Ag 31,18:2
  Joker, The 1925,N 17,29:1
  Caponsacchi 1926,O 27,24:2
  Caponsacchi 1927,F 20,VII,1:1
  Caponsacchi 1928,Ja 25,20:3
  Richelieu 1929,D 26,20:3
  Plutocrat, The 1930,F 21,23:3
  Perfect Marriage, The 1932,N 17,23:2
  Richelieu 1934,My 22,28:1
  Journey by Night 1935,Ap 7,IX,2:1
  Journey by Night, A 1935,Ap 17,26:3
Goodrich, Charles
  Thank You 1921,O 4,10:2
  It Is the Law 1922,N 30,28:2
  Show-Off, The 1924,F 6,16:2
Goodrich, Eleanor
  Electra 1932,Ja 9,21:4
  Midsummer Night's Dream, A 1932,Jl 13,15:1
  Dark Hours, The 1932,N 15,24:2
  Uncle Tom's Cabin 1933,My 30,13:4
  Hamlet 1934,D 26,19:3
  Richard III 1934,D 28,24:3
  Plumes in the Dust 1936,N 7,14:2
Goodrich, Evelyn
  Light of Asia, The 1928,O 10,32:2
  Enemy of the People, An 1928,N 6,34:3
  Becky Sharp 1929,Je 4,29:1
  Bonds of Interest, The 1929,O 15,34:2
  Richelieu 1929,D 26,20:3
  Cyrano de Bergerac 1932,D 27,11:2
Goodrich, Frances
  Fashions for Men 1922,D 6,22:1
  Queen Victoria 1923,N 16,15:1
  Skin Deep 1927,O 18,32:1
  Excess Baggage 1927,D 27,24:2
Goodrich, Frances (Original Author)
  Everybody's Welcome 1931,O 14,26:3
Goodrich, Frances (Playwright)
  Up Pops the Devil 1930,S 2,19:1
  Up Pops the Devil 1930,S 14,VIII,1:1
  Bridal Wise 1932,My 31,15:5
  Great Big Doorstep, The 1942,N 27,26:2
  Great Big Doorstep, The 1950,Mr 18,8:6
  Diary of Anne Frank, The 1955,O 6,24:2
  Diary of Anne Frank, The 1955,O 16,II,1:1
  Diary of Anne Frank, The 1956,O 14,II,3:1
  Diary of Anne Frank, The 1956,N 29,43:1
  Diary of Anne Frank, The 1963,Ap 12,33:1
Goodrich, Trudi
  Sing for Your Supper 1939,Ap 25,18:6
Goodrich, Virginia
  Logia a la Natividad de Nuestro Senor Jesucristo,
    El 1937,D 14,33:4
Goodridge, Lillie
  Deirdre of the Sorrows 1949,D 15,51:2
  When the Bough Breaks 1950,Mr 9,25:5
  Major Barbara 1951,F 24,10:2
Goodrow, Freddie
  Wake Up, Jonathan 1921,Ja 18,14:1
  Good Earth, The 1932,O 18,23:4
  Taming of the Shrew, The 1935,O 1,27:3
  Taming of the Shrew, The 1940,F 6,17:2
Goodrow, Garry
  Cave at Machpelah, The 1959,Jl 1,25:1
  Connection, The 1959,Jl 16,30:2
  Tonight We Improvise 1959,N 7,27:4
  Women of Trachis 1960,Je 23,18:3
  Committee, The 1964,S 17,53:1
  Critic, The 1965,Jl 26,15:2
Goods, Jack
  Gypsy Lady 1946,S 18,25:6
Goodsell, Dean (Director)
  Thy Kingdom Come 1957,Je 25,24:6
Goodsitt, Hortense
  Peter Ibbetson 1926,Mr 26,24:7
Goodstein, Gerald
  Cyanamide 1954,Mr 26,17:6
Goodwich, Frances (Playwright)
  Western Union 1937,Ag 10,22:7
Goodwin, Bill
  Summer and Smoke 1952,Ap 25,19:5
  Pullman Car Hiawatha 1962,D 4,46:2
Goodwin, Coburn
  Jealous Moon, The 1928,N 21,32:2
  Paolo and Francesca 1929,Ap 2,28:2
  Jenny 1929,O 9,34:4
  Twelfth Night 1930,S 14,VIII,2:8
  Twelfth Night 1930,O 16,28:2
  Did I Say No? 1931,S 23,19:4
  Sophisticrats, The 1933,F 14,19:5
  Heat Lightning 1933,S 16,9:6
  All Good Americans 1933,D 6,29:2

Goodwin, Coburn—Cont

Few Are Chosen 1935,S 18,19:3
Infernal Machine, The 1937,D 13,22:7
Medicine Show 1940,Ap 13,20:6
Catherine Was Great 1944,Ag 3,16:1

Goodwin, Doris
Beggar's Holiday 1946,D 27,13:3

Goodwin, Dwight
Strip Girl 1935,O 21,22:6

Goodwin, Geena
Russian Bank 1940,My 25,20:2
Shepherd King, The 1955,O 13,36:2
Brothers Ashkenazi, The 1955,N 12,24:4
Me, Candido! 1956,O 16,36:2
Pigeon, The 1957,My 17,19:2

Goodwin, Harry
Compulsion 1957,O 25,21:1

Goodwin, Henrietta
Clair de Lune 1921,Ap 19,15:1
Old English 1924,D 24,11:2
Escape 1927,O 27,33:1
Escape 1927,N 6,IX,1:1
These Few Ashes 1928,O 31,28:1

Goodwin, James
Happiest Years, The 1949,Ap 26,29:8

Goodwin, Lesley
Ice Follies 1957,Ja 16,36:1
Ice Follies 1958,Ja 15,26:2
Ice Follies 1959,Ja 14,30:1
Ice Follies 1960,Ja 13,20:1
Ice Follies 1961,Ja 11,25:2

Goodwin, Mary
Would-Be Gentleman, The 1946,Ja 10,29:2

Goodwin, Michael
Patriot for Me, A 1969,O 6,58:1
Charley's Aunt 1970,Jl 6,38:1
Colette 1970,O 15,58:1

Goodwin, Nate
Sonny 1921,Ag 17,12:2

Goodwin, Patricia
Thunder on the Left 1933,N 1,25:2

Goodwin, Phyllis
Straw Hat, The 1937,D 31,8:2

Goodwin, Regina
Hedda Gabler 1936,Ag 19,18:5

Goodwin, Russell
Carousel 1954,Je 3,32:2
Saint of Bleecker Street, The 1954,D 28,21:1
Most Happy Fella, The 1956,My 4,20:1

Goodwin, Ruth
George White's Scandals 1928,Jl 3,19:1
Jonica 1930,Ap 8,27:1

Goodwin, Sandy
Hot Money 1931,N 9,22:2

Goodwin, Tabitha
Back Seat Drivers 1928,D 26,14:4

Goodwin, Thelma
Three Little Girls 1930,Ap 15,29:1

Goodwin, William
Grass Harp, The 1953,Ap 28,32:2
Balcony, The 1960,Mr 4,21:1

Goodyear, Elizabeth
Half Gods 1929,D 23,18:5

Goodyear, T
Front Page, The 1937,N 12,27:2

Goofers, The
Liberace's Variety Bill 1957,Ap 22,29:5

Goolden, Richard
Time Remembered 1955,My 4,35:1

Goon, Henry
Trio 1944,D 30,13:4

Goorney, Howard
School for Scandal, The 1963,Ja 26,5:2

Goossen, Lawrence (Producer)
Scent of Flowers, A 1969,O 21,42:1
One Night Stands of a Noisy Passenger; Passage, Un 1970,D 31,8:3
One Night Stands of a Noisy Passenger; Last Stand 1970,D 31,8:3
One Night Stands of a Noisy Passenger; Noisy Passenger, The 1970,D 31,8:3

Goossens, Eugene (Composer)
Constant Nymph, The 1926,D 10,31:1
Constant Nymph, The 1927,Mr 6,VIII,1:4
Autumn Crocus 1932,N 21,20:2

Goozee, Sherwood (Miscellaneous)
Kreutzer Sonata, The 1961,F 16,24:2

Gorall, Leslie
Patience 1935,S 3,24:4
Daughters of Atreus 1936,O 15,33:1
High Tor 1937,Ja 11,15:2
Mistress of the Inn, The 1937,Je 22,26:3
Petticoat Fever 1937,Jl 6,23:1
Lysistrata 1937,Jl 20,19:3
Once Upon a Time 1939,D 21,28:2

Gorbea, Carlos
Time of Storm 1954,F 26,14:2

Gorber, Carl
Making of Moo, The 1958,Je 12,34:1

Gorcey, Bernard
Abie's Irish Rose 1922,My 24,22:4
Song of the Flame 1925,D 11,26:4
Song of the Flame 1925,D 31,10:2
Cherry Blossoms 1927,Mr 29,22:3

Pressing Business 1930,N 18,28:5
Joy of Living 1931,Ap 7,31:1
Wonder Boy 1931,O 24,20:1
Keeping Expenses Down 1932,O 21,25:2
Creeping Fire 1935,Ja 17,22:3
Satellite 1935,N 21,27:5
Abie's Irish Rose 1937,My 13,30:2

Gorcey, David
Dead End 1935,O 29,17:2

Gorcey, Leo
Dead End 1935,O 29,17:2

Gordan, Bruce
Girl From Wyoming, The 1938,O 31,12:1

Gordan, Grant
Meet the Wife 1937,Jl 6,23:1

Gordan, Mel
South Pacific 1965,Je 3,25:1

Gordan, Ruby
Young Visitors, The 1920,N 30,14:1

Gordani, Nina
Vaudeville (Palace) 1929,Jl 15,25:4
Nina Rosa 1930,My 31,19:3

Gordin, Jacob (Original Author)
Family Mishmash, A 1958,O 20,36:1

Gordin, Jacob (Playwright)
Kreutzer Sonata, The 1924,My 15,22:3
God Man and Devil 1928,D 22,14:8
Wild Man, The 1930,My 17,21:5
God Man and Devil 1935,Mr 6,22:3
Stranger, The 1935,N 7,26:2
Mirele Efros 1967,O 20,55:1
Mirele Efros 1969,D 26,41:1
Beyond the Ocean 1970,Ag 19,30:1

Gordon, Agnes (Lighting Director)
Wretched the Lionhearted 1962,S 13,31:2
Toy for the Clowns, A 1962,S 13,31:2

Gordon, Al (His Dogs)
Music Hall Varieties 1932,N 23,15:3
Hooray for What! 1937,D 2,32:5

Gordon, Alastair
Cops and Horrors; Fly Paper 1970,Ag 11,27:1
Cops and Horrors; Dracula 1970,Ag 11,27:1

Gordon, Alex (Playwright)
Here's Where I Belong 1968,Mr 4,32:1

Gordon, Alice
June Love 1921,Ap 26,20:1

Gordon, Alicia
Flying Blind 1930,My 16,20:2

Gordon, Alvin
How Revolting! 1932,Mr 11,14:6
Laugh It Off 1934,Ap 5,24:2

Gordon, Anne
Live Like Pigs 1965,Je 8,48:2

Gordon, Arthur (Composer)
Hooray!! It's a Glorious Day. . .And All That 1966,Mr 10,28:1

Gordon, Barry
Thousand Clowns, A 1962,Ap 6,31:2
Thousand Clowns, A 1962,Ap 15,II,1:1

Gordon, Barry (Miscellaneous)
Happy Time, The 1968,Ja 19,32:2

Gordon, Barry (Producer)
Across the Board on Tomorrow Morning 1961,O 23,22:5
Talking to You 1961,O 23,22:5
Laundry, The 1963,F 19,5:2

Gordon, Barry (Scenic Designer)
Sappho 1960,Ja 12,22:1

Gordon, Bert
George White's Scandals 1921,Jl 12,14:1
Vaudeville (Palace) 1927,Ja 4,21:2
Hold On to Your Hats 1940,Jl 17,25:3
Hold On to Your Hats 1940,S 12,30:3
Hold On to Your Hats 1940,S 29,IX,1:1

Gordon, Blanche
Lady Refuses, The 1933,Mr 8,18:6

Gordon, Brenda
Hair 1970,Ja 13,39:1

Gordon, Bruce
Fireman's Flame, The 1937,O 11,26:2
Arsenic and Old Lace 1941,Ja 11,13:2
Antony and Cleopatra 1947,N 27,49:2
Medea 1949,My 3,31:2
Captain Brassbound's Conversion 1950,D 28,21:1
Richard II 1951,Ja 25,21:2
Legend of Lovers 1951,D 27,17:1
Pink Elephant, The 1953,Ap 23,37:2
Lark, The 1955,N 18,20:1
Nowhere to Go But Up 1962,N 12,36:2
Man for All Seasons, A 1964,Ja 28,24:2
Diamond Orchid 1965,F 11,44:4
Murderous Angels 1970,F 8,70:1

Gordon, C Henry
Drums of Jeopardy, The 1922,My 30,8:4
Lights Out 1922,Ag 18,8:4
Thin Ice 1922,O 2,20:1
Crooked Square, The 1923,S 11,10:2
Mister Pitt 1924,Ja 23,15:3
Saint, The 1924,O 13,20:3
Puppets 1925,Mr 10,19:1
Mismates 1925,Ap 14,27:2
Shanghai Gesture, The 1926,F 2,20:2

Gordon, Carl
Kongi's Harvest 1968,Ap 15,49:1

Gordon, Carol
Priorities of 1942 1942,Mr 13,23:2

Gordon, Charles
Journeyman 1938,Ja 31,14:2
Washington Jitters 1938,My 3,19:1
Johnny on the Spot 1942,Ja 9,24:2
Moon Is Down, The 1942,Ap 8,22:2
Happy Birthday 1946,N 1,31:2
Climate of Eden, The 1953,N 21,11:2

Gordon, Charles K (Director)
Ghost Parade, The 1929,O 31,28:4
Papavert 1931,D 30,25:1

Gordon, Charles K (Playwright)
Papavert 1931,D 30,25:1

Gordon, Charles K (Producer)
Just Beyond 1925,D 2,22:4
Hush Money 1926,Mr 16,22:3
Jarnegan 1928,S 25,29:2
Ghost Parade, The 1929,O 31,28:4

Gordon, Clarke
Son, The 1950,Ap 1,12:4
Son, The 1950,Ag 16,24:6
Night Music 1951,Ap 9,29:6
Pal Joey 1952,Ja 4,17:6

Gordon, Colin
Little Hut, The 1953,O 8,37:2

Gordon, Daniel
Girl From Samos, The 1954,N 24,17:1
Beautiful Changes, The 1956,Mr 24,15:2
Idiot's Delight 1957,F 23,14:2
Androcles and the Lion 1958,F 22,8:3

Gordon, Daniel (Miscellaneous)
On the Town 1959,F 14,15:1
Hobo 1961,Ap 11,41:2

Gordon, Deborah
MacBird! 1967,F 23,38:1

Gordon, Diana
George White's Scandals 1922,Ag 29,10:1

Gordon, Don
Stockade 1954,F 5,14:2
On an Open Roof 1963,Ja 30,7:3

Gordon, Donald
Bitter Sweet 1929,N 6,30:2

Gordon, Douglas
Mary of Magdala 1946,Mr 26,24:5

Gordon, Ed
Let's Laugh Again 1937,Ag 24,24:5

Gordon, Edith
Paolo and Francesca 1924,D 3,24:2
High Gear 1927,O 7,24:3
Telephone, The 1950,Jl 20,22:5
Medium, The 1950,Jl 20,22:5
Medium, The 1950,S 3,II,1:1

Gordon, Edwin
Tide Rising 1937,Ja 26,17:2
Cue for Passion 1940,D 20,33:4
Your Loving Son 1941,Ap 5,13:2
Moon Is Down, The 1942,Ap 8,22:2
Crucible, The 1953,Jl 2,20:2
Here Come the Clowns 1954,My 5,36:2
Major Barbara 1954,Je 30,23:2

Gordon, Elaine
Wish You Were Here 1952,Je 26,26:6

Gordon, Eleanor
Six-Cylinder Love 1921,Ag 26,8:2
Merry Wives of Windsor, The 1928,Mr 20,20:1
Love on Leave 1944,Je 21,23:4

Gordon, Ella
Bridal Wise 1932,My 31,15:5

Gordon, Elmer (Composer)
Thieves' Carnival 1955,F 2,21:1

Gordon, Elsie May
Glamour Preferred 1940,N 16,13:2
Gentleman From Athens, The 1947,D 10,42:4

Gordon, Eugene
Brouhaha 1960,Ap 27,31:2

Gordon, Everett (Musical Director)
Gogo Loves You 1964,O 10,19:2

Gordon, Frank
Theatre of the Soul 1942,Mr 21,13:5
Across the Board on Tomorrow Morning 1942,Mr 21,13:5

Gordon, G Swayne
Room 349 1930,Ap 23,24:5
Noble Experiment, The 1930,O 28,21:4
Nowhere Bound 1935,Ja 23,20:2
Kick Back, The 1936,Je 23,27:3
Young Madame Conti 1937,Ap 1,18:4
Not in Our Stars 1941,Ap 26,20:5
Johnny on the Spot 1942,Ja 9,24:2
Comes the Revelation 1942,My 27,26:2
I'll Take the High Road 1943,N 10,28:3
Sleep No More 1944,S 1,11:5
It's A Gift 1945,Mr 13,18:7
Topaze 1947,D 29,21:5

Gordon, G Swayne (Director)
No Mother to Guide Her 1933,D 26,18:5

Gordon, Gale
Daughters of Atreus 1936,O 15,33:1

Gordon, Garry
Golden Apple, The 1954,Mr 12,15:2

Gordon, Garry—Cont
Saint of Bleecker Street, The 1954,D 28,21:1
Gordon, Gavin
Annie Dear 1924,N 5,25:3
Lady in Love, A 1927,F 22,22:1
Vaudeville (Palace) 1927,Ap 19,24:3
Celebrity 1927,D 11,IX,2:5
Celebrity 1927,D 27,24:3
Sh! The Octopus 1928,F 22,19:2
Crashing Through 1928,O 30,26:5
Coquette 1935,My 22,23:4
Gentleman From Athens, The 1947,D 10,42:4
Metropole 1949,D 7,43:2
Devil's Disciple, The 1950,Ja 26,23:2
Devil's Disciple, The 1950,F 5,II,1:1
Buy Me Blue Ribbons 1951,O 18,33:2
Gordon, Genevieve
Pirates of Penzance, The 1961,S 7,41:1
Gordon, George
Caviar 1934,Je 8,19:2
Gordon, Gerald
Nature of the Crime 1970,Mr 24,41:1
Gordon, Glen
Freight 1949,F 4,30:2
Freight 1950,Ap 27,36:2
Gordon, Glenn (Director)
Disintegration of James Cherry, The
    1970,Ja 30,33:3
Gordon, Grace
Valley of Content, The 1925,Ja 14,19:2
Gordon, Grant
Hamlet 1930,Mr 25,34:4
Macbeth 1930,Mr 26,24:6
Twelfth Night 1930,Mr 27,24:7
Merchant of Venice, The 1930,Mr 27,24:7
Taming of the Shrew, The 1930,Mr 28,22:8
Richard III 1930,Mr 31,24:1
King Lear 1930,Ap 1,34:6
As You Like It 1930,Ap 3,32:5
Julius Caesar 1930,Ap 4,22:3
Perfectly Scandalous 1931,My 14,27:2
Mourning Becomes Electra; Haunted, The
    1931,O 27,22:1
Great Lover, The 1932,O 12,27:3
Monster, The 1933,F 11,11:5
Brittle Heaven 1934,N 14,22:5
Loose Moments 1935,F 5,22:3
Romeo and Juliet 1935,D 24,10:2
Fly Away Home 1937,Jl 27,24:3
Great Sebastians, The 1956,Ja 5,27:1
Julia, Jake, and Uncle Joe 1961,Ja 30,19:1
Sound of Music, The 1967,Ap 27,52:1
Gordon, Gustave
It Can't Happen Here 1936,O 28,30:1
Sun and I, The 1937,F 27,9:5
Prologue to Glory 1938,Mr 18,22:2
Gordon, Guy
Brigadoon 1957,Mr 28,37:1
Gordon, Gwyneth
Green Hat, The 1925,S 16,23:2
Skyrocket, The 1929,Ja 12,14:7
Whispering Gallery, The 1929,F 12,22:2
Jade God, The 1929,My 14,28:3
Gordon, H Sheldon (Producer)
Laundry, The 1963,F 19,5:2
Gordon, Harold
Rosalinda; Fledermaus, Die 1942,O 29,26:5
New Moon, The 1944,My 18,16:2
John Brown 1950,My 4,32:7
Gordon, Harron
Land of Fame 1943,S 22,31:5
Innocent Voyage, The 1943,N 16,27:2
Gordon, Harry
Sunny Days 1928,F 9,29:1
Ten Nights in a Barroom 1928,Mr 28,31:2
Sign of the Leopard 1928,D 12,34:4
Airways, Inc 1929,F 21,30:5
Injury Sustained 1940,O 24,30:3
Gordon, Hayes
Oklahoma! 1943,Ap 1,27:1
Winged Victory 1943,N 22,24:1
Brigadoon 1947,Mr 14,28:2
Sleepy Hollow 1948,Je 4,26:3
Small Wonder 1948,S 16,33:5
Gordon, Helen
Music Hall Varieties 1932,N 23,15:3
Gordon, Hugh
Tyrant, The 1930,N 13,33:1
Gordon, Huntley
Dinner at Eight 1933,Ap 9,IX,1:7
Gordon, Irving
Stevedore 1934,Ap 19,33:2
Gordon, Irving (Composer)
Star and Garter 1942,Je 25,26:2
Gordon, Irving (Director)
Stevedore 1934,Ap 19,33:2
Sailors of Cattaro 1934,D 11,28:4
Black Pit 1935,Mr 21,26:6
Gordon, Irving (Lyricist)
Star and Garter 1942,Je 25,26:2
Gordon, Jack
Climate of Eden, The 1953,N 21,11:2
Gordon, Jacob (Playwright)
Sappho 1935,Mr 22,26:4

Gordon, Jane
Private Lives 1937,Jl 14,17:4
Kind Lady 1937,Jl 21,19:3
Fly Away Home 1937,Jl 28,15:1
Whiteheaded Boy, The 1937,Ag 11,27:3
Ode to Liberty 1937,Ag 18,15:2
Elizabeth the Queen 1937,Ag 25,24:3
Goodbye Again 1937,S 1,15:1
Spring Thaw 1938,Mr 22,18:1
Biography 1938,Ag 3,14:7
Arms and the Man 1938,Ag 10,14:1
Bachelor Born 1938,Ag 17,23:1
Springtime for Henry 1938,Ag 31,12:5
Lady in the Dark 1941,S 3,26:6
Theatre 1941,N 13,34:2
Gordon, Jean
Lass O' Laughter 1925,Ja 9,13:2
Gordon, Jeanne
Two Misers, The 1943,D 9,30:5
On the Town 1944,D 29,11:4
Gordon, Joan
My Son 1924,S 18,18:2
Very Wise Virgin, A 1927,Je 3,25:3
Guest Room, The 1931,O 7,29:2
It's A Gift 1945,Mr 13,18:7
Gordon, Jocelyn
Peter Pan; Boy Who Would Not Grow Up, The
    1928,N 27,36:3
Lady From Alfaqueque, The; Consulesa, La
    1929,Ja 15,22:3
New York to Cherbourg 1932,F 20,11:4
Gordon, John
Dance With Your Gods 1934,O 8,14:3
Gordon, John (Playwright)
You're a Good Man, Charlie Brown 1967,Mr 8,51:1
Gordon, Joy
Billy Liar 1965,Mr 18,26:1
Gordon, Julius M (Miscellaneous)
Deadfall 1955,O 28,20:1
Gordon, Kilbourn (Director)
Kongo 1926,Mr 31,20:5
Tia Juana 1927,N 16,28:4
Gordon, Kilbourn (Playwright)
Big Game 1920,Ja 22,23:1
Out of the Seven Seas 1923,N 4,VIII,2:7
Out of the Seven Seas 1923,N 20,23:3
Kongo 1926,Mr 31,20:5
Tia Juana 1927,N 16,28:4
Gordon, Kilbourn (Producer)
Green Beetle, The 1924,Jl 20,VII,1:7
Kongo 1926,Mr 31,20:5
Tia Juana 1927,N 16,28:4
Gordon, Kurt
Trumpeter of Sakkingen 1921,Ja 15,11:3
Gordon, Lee X
Sweet Bird of Youth 1956,Ap 17,27:2
Gordon, Leon
Breakfast in Bed 1920,F 4,12:1
White Peacock, The 1921,D 27,10:2
Lady Bug 1922,Ap 18,15:3
Red Poppy, The 1922,D 21,18:2
Pride 1923,My 3,22:3
Not so Fast 1923,My 23,18:4
Gordon, Leon (Director)
Undesirable Lady, An 1933,O 10,24:4
Gordon, Leon (Playwright)
Blue Eyes 1921,F 22,11:2
Poppy God, The 1921,Ag 30,10:1
White Cargo 1923,N 6,22:2
White Cargo 1923,D 23,VII,1:1
Garden of Weeds 1924,Ap 29,12:3
Garden of Weeds 1924,My 4,VIII,1:1
Piker, The 1925,Ja 16,14:1
Undesirable Lady, An 1933,O 10,24:4
White Cargo 1941,My 14,24:3
White Cargo 1960,D 30,12:1
Gordon, Leon (Producer)
Garden of Weeds 1924,My 4,VIII,1:1
Undesirable Lady, An 1933,O 10,24:4
Gordon, Leslie Howard (Playwright)
Borderer, The 1923,Mr 18,VII,1:1
Gordon, Lewis
Taming of the Shrew, The 1962,Je 21,25:1
Richard II 1964,Je 17,47:1
Bourgeois Gentilhomme, Le 1964,Je 18,28:2
Henry IV, Part I 1965,Je 30,42:1
Falstaff; Henry IV, Part II 1965,Jl 1,35:1
Henry V 1966,Je 8,38:1
Henry VI 1966,Je 9,55:2
Gordon, Mack (Composer)
Ziegfeld Follies 1931,Jl 2,30:5
Marching By 1932,Mr 4,17:1
Gordon, Mack (Lyricist)
Marching By 1932,Mr 4,17:1
Smiling Faces 1932,Ag 31,12:3
Gordon, Mack (Playwright)
Ziegfeld Follies 1931,Jl 2,30:5
Strike Me Pink 1933,Mr 6,16:3
Gordon, Madge (Playwright)
Borderer, The 1923,Mr 18,VII,1:1
Gordon, Marjorie
Flirting 1923,My 31,12:5

Gordon, Mark
Desire Under the Elms 1952,Ja 17,23:4
Wedding in Japan 1957,Mr 12,37:7
Man Who Never Died, The 1958,N 22,27:2
Deep Are the Roots 1960,O 4,47:1
Third Ear, The 1964,My 29,16:1
Conerico Was Here to Stay 1965,Mr 4,37:1
Devils, The 1965,N 17,51:2
Adaptation 1970,Mr 12,46:1
Gordon, Mark (Director)
Homeward Look, The 1954,Je 4,26:2
Ever Since Paradise 1957,Jl 12,18:4
Before You Go 1968,Ja 12,20:1
Gordon, Marvin
Thieves' Carnival 1955,F 2,21:1
Gordon, Marvin (Choreographer)
Taming of the Shrew, The 1956,Ag 11,11:2
Camille 1956,S 19,33:1
Trojan Women, The 1957,Mr 19,42:7
Cindy 1964,Mr 20,24:1
Gogo Loves You 1964,O 10,19:2
Who's Who, Baby? 1968,Ja 30,36:1
Gordon, Marvin (Director)
Cindy 1964,Mr 20,24:1
Who's Who, Baby? 1968,Ja 30,36:1
Now 1968,Je 6,53:1
Of Thee I Sing 1969,Mr 8,19:1
Lyle 1970,Mr 21,16:2
To Be or Not to Be-What Kind of a Question Is
    That? 1970,O 20,39:1
Gordon, Marvin (Miscellaneous)
Now 1968,Je 6,53:1
Gordon, Mary
Cradle Song 1955,D 2,32:2
Gordon, Mary McKenzie
Yes is for a Very Young Man 1963,Mr 6,7:5
Gordon, Maude Turner
Wait Till We're Married 1921,S 27,14:1
Elsie 1923,Ap 3,26:1
Chains 1923,S 20,5:2
Big Boy 1925,Ja 8,28:2
Gordon, Maurice
Pirates of Penzance, The 1942,F 20,20:2
Gordon, Maurice (Director)
In a Jewish Grocery 1939,O 2,15:2
Gordon, Maurice (Scenic Designer)
Billy the Kid 1951,Ag 21,23:2
Gordon, Max (Miscellaneous)
Cat and the Fiddle, The 1931,O 16,26:4
Great Waltz, The 1935,Ag 6,20:5
Missouri Legend 1938,S 20,27:2
Gordon, Max (Producer)
Three's a Crowd 1930,O 5,IX,4:6
Three's a Crowd 1930,O 16,28:3
Wife's Away, The 1930,N 23,IX,3:5
Band Wagon, The 1931,My 17,VIII,3:2
Band Wagon, The 1931,Je 4,31:3
Cat and the Fiddle, The 1931,S 27,VIII,3:1
Flying Colors 1932,S 16,24:2
Flying Colors 1932,O 9,IX,1:1
Design for Living 1933,Ja 3,19:5
Design for Living 1933,Ja 8,IX,3:2
Design for Living 1933,Ja 25,13:2
Her Master's Voice 1933,O 24,24:3
Roberta 1933,N 20,18:4
Shining Hour, The 1934,F 14,22:6
Dodsworth 1934,F 26,20:4
Great Waltz, The 1934,S 24,14:4
Great Waltz, The 1934,S 30,IX,1:1
Spring Song 1934,O 2,18:2
Farmer Takes a Wife, The 1934,O 31,17:1
Gather Ye Rosebuds 1934,N 29,33:2
Gather Ye Rosebuds 1934,D 2,X,1:1
Long Frontier, The 1935,Jl 23,24:4
Jubilee 1935,S 23,20:3
Jubilee 1935,S 29,X,1:1
Jubilee 1935,O 14,20:1
Pride and Prejudice 1935,O 23,19:2
Great Waltz, The 1935,N 3,X,1:5
Pride and Prejudice 1935,N 3,X,1:5
Pride and Prejudice 1935,N 6,32:4
Pride and Prejudice 1935,N 10,IX,2:5
Ethan Frome 1936,Ja 7,24:7
Ethan Frome 1936,Ja 22,15:2
Ethan Frome 1936,F 2,IX,1:1
As We Forgive Our Debtors 1936,Ag 11,24:6
St Helena 1936,S 29,35:1
St Helena 1936,O 7,32:1
St Helena 1936,O 11,X,1:1
Othello 1936,N 27,26:5
Othello 1936,D 6,XII,6:1
Women, The 1936,D 8,30:6
Women, The 1936,D 28,13:1
Othello 1937,Ja 7,16:4
Save Me the Waltz 1938,Mr 1,19:2
Spring Thaw 1938,Mr 22,18:1
Sing Out the News 1938,S 26,12:5
American Way, The 1939,Ja 23,9:2
Very Warm for May 1939,N 18,23:2
My Sister Eileen 1940,D 27,23:2
Land Is Bright, The 1941,O 21,28:5
Land Is Bright, The 1941,O 29,26:2
Junior Miss 1941,N 19,28:2

Gordon, Max (Producer)—Cont
Sunny River 1941,D 5,28:2
Doughgirls, The 1942,D 31,19:2
Doughgirls, The 1943,Ja 10,VIII,1:1
Men in Shadow 1943,Mr 11,16:2
Those Endearing Young Charms 1943,Je 17,16:3
Over Twenty-One 1944,Ja 4,20:2
While the Sun Shines 1944,S 20,21:3
While the Sun Shines 1944,S 24,II,1:1
Late George Apley, The 1944,N 22,26:2
Late George Apley, The 1944,D 3,II,1:1
Firebird of Florence 1945,Mr 23,13:4
Hollywood Pinafore 1945,Je 1,20:1
Next Half Hour, The 1945,O 30,14:6
Born Yesterday 1946,F 5,18:2
Years Ago 1946,D 4,44:2
Town House 1948,S 24,31:2
Bravo! 1948,N 12,31:2
Metropole 1949,D 7,43:2
Small Hours, The 1951,F 16,22:1
Solid Gold Cadillac, The 1953,N 6,24:2
Solid Gold Cadillac, The 1954,Ag 16,13:4
Gordon, Meg
Country Wife, The 1936,D 13,XI,3:1
Gordon, Mel
Fourth Pig, The 1965,Ja 27,24:6
Gordon, Michael
Golden Boy 1937,N 5,18:5
Gordon, Michael (Director)
Storm Operation 1944,Ja 12,28:2
Sophie 1944,D 26,22:7
Home of the Brave 1945,D 28,13:2
Anna Christie 1952,Ja 10,33:1
Anna Christie 1952,Ja 20,II,1:1
One Bright Day 1952,Mr 20,37:2
Male Animal, The 1952,My 1,35:1
Male Animal, The 1952,My 18,II,1:1
See the Jaguar 1952,D 4,46:2
Maggie 1953,F 19,20:2
His and Hers 1954,Ja 8,18:2
Magic and the Loss, The 1954,Ap 10,10:3
Tender Trap, The 1954,O 14,37:2
Champagne Complex 1955,Ap 13,33:1
Deadfall 1955,O 28,20:1
Lovers 1956,My 11,23:1
Family Way, The 1965,Ja 14,44:5
Gordon, Michael (Lighting Director)
Thunder Rock 1939,N 15,18:1
Gordon, Milton
Catherine Was Great 1944,Ag 3,16:1
Walk Hard 1944,D 1,28:2
Gordon, Myron P
Oh, Hector! 1929,Mr 6,33:2
Gordon, Nancy
Hippolytus 1948,N 22,25:5
Gordon, Noel
Marinka 1945,Jl 19,19:2
Bless You All 1950,D 15,42:2
Call Me Madam 1952,D 16,44:4
Gordon, Pamela
John Loves Mary 1947,F 5,29:2
Gordon, Paul
Hail and Farewell 1923,F 20,12:1
My Aunt From Ypsilanti 1923,My 2,22:6
Children of the Moon 1923,Ag 18,10:3
Children of the Moon 1923,Ag 26,VI,1:1
Vaudeville (Palace) 1926,S 7,24:6
Gordon, Paul Vincent (Director)
Major Barbara 1954,Je 30,23:2
Passion of Gross, The 1955,Ja 24,20:2
Gordon, Paula
Mourners' Bench, The 1950,S 22,35:7
Gordon, Philip
Counsellor-at-Law 1942,N 25,17:2
Mayor of Zalamea, The 1946,Ja 28,15:5
Happy Birthday 1946,N 1,31:2
Now I Lay Me Down to Sleep 1950,Mr 3,21:2
Gordon, Ramon (Director)
Winterset 1968,Jl 23,28:2
Gordon, Ray
Hide and Seek 1934,Ag 7,20:2
Peer Gynt 1951,Ja 29,15:2
Gordon, Richard
Two Strangers From Nowhere 1924,Ap 8,22:2
Aloma of the South Seas 1925,Ap 21,18:1
Crooked Friday, The 1925,O 9,27:3
Offence, The 1925,N 16,25:1
Hush Money 1926,Mr 16,22:3
Judge's Husband, The 1926,S 28,31:1
Wasp's Nest, The 1927,O 26,26:3
Intruder, The 1928,Jl 26,25:4
Borrowed Love 1929,Je 18,29:2
International Revue 1930,F 26,22:2
Battleship Gertie 1935,Ja 19,9:2
Fabulous Invalid, The 1938,O 10,15:1
Actors Fund Fete 1942,F 23,24:5
Sun Field, The 1942,D 10,33:2
Strange Play, A 1944,Je 2,20:3
Day After Tomorrow 1950,O 27,25:2
Gordon, Richard H
Hamlet 1938,N 8,26:1
Carousel 1945,Ap 20,24:2
Gordon, Richard H Jr (Composer)
Once Over Lightly 1938,D 10,13:4

Gordon, Richard H Jr (Lyricist)
Once Over Lightly 1938,D 10,13:4
Gordon, Robert H
Straw Hat, The 1926,O 15,20:2
Trumpet Shall Sound, The 1926,D 11,15:2
Granite 1927,F 12,13:1
Much Ado About Nothing 1927,N 19,14:6
At the Gate of the Kingdom 1927,D 9,28:5
Doctor Knock 1928,F 24,15:2
Peter Pan; Boy Who Would Not Grow Up, The 1928,N 27,36:3
On the High Road 1929,Ja 15,22:3
Lady From Alfaqueque, The; Consulesa, La 1929,Ja 15,22:3
Katerina 1929,F 26,30:3
Living Corpse, The 1929,D 7,19:1
Romeo and Juliet 1930,Ap 22,33:1
Siegfried 1930,O 21,34:1
Lady of the Camellias, The 1931,Ja 27,21:2
Merry-Go-Round 1932,Ap 23,11:2
Scrap Book 1932,Ag 2,20:3
Liliom 1932,O 27,23:2
Camille 1932,O 28,23:2
Dear Jane 1932,N 15,24:3
Alice in Wonderland 1932,D 12,18:3
Cherry Orchard, The 1933,Mr 7,20:3
Sellout, The 1933,S 7,17:2
Granite 1936,Ja 14,24:6
But for the Grace of God 1937,Ja 13,21:4
Gordon, Robert H (Director)
Constant Wife, The 1935,Jl 3,20:2
Stardust 1935,Jl 17,22:4
Pins and Needles 1939,Ap 21,26:2
Sing for Your Supper 1939,Ap 25,18:6
New Pins and Needles 1939,N 21,19:2
Let Freedom Sing 1942,O 6,18:2
Once Over Lightly 1942,N 20,26:2
What's Up 1943,N 12,24:6
Allah Be Praised! 1944,Ap 21,14:2
Call Me Mister 1946,Ap 19,26:2
Inside U S A 1948,My 1,19:2
Alive and Kicking 1950,Ja 18,25:5
Stockade 1954,F 5,14:2
Arabian Nights 1954,Je 25,15:2
Gordon, Robert H (Original Author)
Call Me Mister 1946,Ap 28,II,1:1
Gordon, Roderick
What's Your Number? 1929,Ag 16,18:3
Gordon, Rose (Choreographer)
Little Clown, The 1930,Mr 15,23:3
Gordon, Roy
Sweetheart Shop, The 1920,S 1,13:4
Exciters, The 1922,S 23,10:4
Tantrum, The 1924,S 5,20:2
Bluffing Bluffers 1924,D 23,17:2
Spooks 1925,Je 2,16:4
Chivalry 1925,D 16,22:3
Pyramids 1926,Jl 20,17:2
New York Exchange 1926,D 31,11:2
Jimmie's Women 1927,S 27,30:3
Red Robe, The 1928,D 26,15:1
Prince Charming 1930,O 14,31:1
House Beautiful, The 1931,Mr 13,20:4
Divine Moment, A 1934,Ja 8,21:8
Ragged Army 1934,F 27,16:5
Page Miss Glory 1934,N 28,24:2
Something Gay 1935,Ap 30,12:2
May Wine 1935,D 6,30:3
Left Turn 1936,Jl 7,22:3
Fly Away Home 1936,Jl 21,13:1
House in the Country, A 1937,Ja 12,18:3
Gordon, Ruby
Poppy God, The 1921,Ag 30,10:1
Garden of Weeds 1924,Ap 29,12:3
Ashes of Love 1926,Mr 23,24:3
If This Be Treason 1935,S 24,28:2
Gordon, Ruth
Tweedles 1923,Ag 14,10:1
Tweedles 1923,Ag 19,VI,1:1
Mrs Partridge Presents 1925,Ja 6,23:3
Mrs Partridge Presents 1925,Ja 11,VII,1:2
Fall of Eve, The 1925,S 1,18:1
Fall of Eve, The 1925,S 6,VII,1:1
Phantom Ship, The 1926,Je 27,VII,3:1
Saturday's Children 1927,Ja 27,13:1
Saturday's Children 1927,F 6,VII,1:1
Lovely Lady 1927,D 30,22:1
Serena Blandish 1929,Ja 13,VIII,2:4
Serena Blandish 1929,Ja 24,30:3
Lady Fingers 1929,F 1,22:4
Serena Blandish 1929,F 3,VIII,1:1
Hotel Universe 1930,Ap 15,29:1
Violet, The 1930,S 30,33:2
Wiser They Are, The 1931,Ap 7,31:1
Church Mouse, A 1931,O 13,26:4
Here Today 1932,S 7,14:2
Here Today 1932,S 18,IX,1:1
Three-Cornered Moon 1933,Mr 17,20:6
They Shall Not Die 1934,F 22,24:4
They Shall Not Die 1934,Mr 4,IX,1:3
They Shall Not Die 1934,Mr 11,X,1:1
Sleeping Clergyman, A 1934,O 9,16:1
Country Wife, The 1935,Jl 2,24:2

Gordon, Ruth—Cont
Saturday's Children 1935,Jl 30,17:2
Ethan Frome 1936,Ja 7,24:7
Ethan Frome 1936,Ja 22,15:2
Ethan Frome 1936,F 2,IX,1:1
Saturday's Children 1936,Jl 7,22:5
Country Wife, The 1936,O 7,32:3
Country Wife, The 1936,O 25,X,2:4
Country Wife, The 1936,D 2,34:1
Doll's House, A 1937,Jl 18,II,6:8
Doll's House, A 1937,Jl 25,X,2:3
Doll's House, A 1937,D 28,28:6
Strings, My Lord, Are False, The 1942,My 20,24:2
Three Sisters, The 1942,D 22,31:2
Three Sisters, The 1942,D 27,VIII,1:1
Over Twenty-One 1944,Ja 4,20:2
Leading Lady 1948,S 15,38:1
Leading Lady 1948,O 19,33:1
Smile of the World, The 1949,Ja 13,26:5
ANTA Album 1950,Ja 30,13:2
Matchmaker, The 1954,Ag 24,18:1
Matchmaker, The 1954,S 5,II,3:7
Matchmaker, The 1954,N 14,II,3:1
Matchmaker, The 1955,My 8,II,1:1
Matchmaker, The 1955,D 6,45:6
Matchmaker, The 1955,D 18,II,3:1
Good Soup, The 1960,Mr 3,26:4
Time to Laugh, A 1962,Ap 25,31:4
My Mother, My Father and Me 1963,Mr 25,5:5
Very Rich Woman, A 1965,O 5,5:8
Loves of Cass McGuire, The 1966,O 7,36:1
Gordon, Ruth (Playwright)
Over Twenty-One 1944,Ja 4,20:2
Years Ago 1946,D 4,44:2
Years Ago 1946,D 15,II,3:1
Leading Lady 1948,S 15,38:1
Leading Lady 1948,O 19,33:1
Very Rich Woman, A 1965,O 5,5:8
Gordon, Ruth (Producer)
How I Wonder 1947,O 1,34:2
Gordon, Sada
Princess Turandot 1926,N 13,14:2
Gordon, Samson
Sailors of Cattaro 1934,D 11,28:4
Bitter Stream 1936,Mr 31,16:6
Bury the Dead 1936,Ap 20,17:4
Prelude 1936,Ap 20,17:4
Tortilla Flat 1938,Ja 13,16:2
Flowers of Virtue, The 1942,F 6,22:2
Gordon, Samuel
Life Is a Dream 1962,Ja 15,22:3
Gordon, Shelly (Producer)
Talking to You 1961,O 23,22:5
Across the Board on Tomorrow Morning 1961,O 23,22:5
Gordon, Sid
High Named Today 1954,D 11,11:2
Gordon, Sonya (Miscellaneous)
Pygmalion 1952,F 9,11:2
Gordon, Stanley (Producer)
Riot Act, The 1963,Mr 9,5:2
Possibilities 1968,D 5,60:1
Gordon, Stephanie
Up to Thursday 1965,F 11,45:1
Chicago 1966,Ap 13,36:1
Gordon, Taylor
Untitled-Revue 1928,N 19,16:2
Ol' Man Satan 1932,O 4,26:3
Gay Divorce 1932,N 30,23:4
After Such Pleasures 1934,F 8,15:2
Gordon, Thabo Quinland R
Five on the Black Hand Side 1970,Ja 2,32:2
Gordon, Vincent
Shake Hands With the Devil 1949,O 21,30:4
Gordon, Virginia
Yellow Jacket, The 1928,N 8,27:3
Falstaff 1928,D 26,14:2
Park Avenue 1946,N 5,31:2
Gordon, William C
Clinging Vine, The 1922,D 25,20:2
Iolanthe 1926,Ap 20,24:2
Pirates of Penzance, The; Slave of Duty, The 1926,D 7,25:1
Mikado, The; Town of Titipu, The 1927,S 19,30:1
Chocolate Soldier, The 1930,Ja 28,28:1
Luana 1930,S 18,28:1
Mikado, The; Town of Titipu, The 1931,My 5,33:2
H M S Pinafore 1931,My 19,25:2
Patience 1931,Je 16,30:4
Gordon, Yaro
Golden Six, The 1958,O 27,31:2
Gordon, Zoe
Bitter Sweet 1929,N 6,30:2
Gordon (Producer)
Nervous Wreck, The 1924,O 19,VIII,2:1
Gordon and Harris
Vaudeville (Palace) 1929,F 11,26:2
Gordon and King
White Lights 1927,O 12,30:4
Vaudeville (Palace) 1929,Ap 22,22:6
Gordon-Gage, John
Barretts of Wimpole Street, The 1935,F 26,16:2
Gordone, Charles
Fortunato 1956,Mr 24,15:2

Gordone, Charles—Cont
Blacks, The 1961,My 5,23:1
Gordone, Charles (Playwright)
No Place to Be Somebody 1969,My 5,53:3
No Place to Be Somebody 1969,My 18,II,1:1
No Place to Be Somebody 1969,My 18,II,22:1
No Place to Be Somebody 1969,D 31,17:1
Gordoni, Arthur
George White's Scandals 1926,Je 15,23:2
Gordon's Circus
Vaudeville (Palace) 1921,Jl 5,15:1
Gore, Dorothy Holmes
Miracle in America 1934,O 2,18:4
Gore, Edward F
East Lynne Goes West 1931,My 3,I,26:5
Gore, James
Young Provincials, The 1958,S 19,22:4
Gore, James (Lighting Director)
Prodigal Son, The 1965,My 21,19:1
Exception and the Rule, The 1965,My 21,19:1
Javelin 1966,N 10,63:1
Ox Cart, The 1966,D 20,58:1
To Bury a Cousin 1967,My 17,38:3
Gore, James (Miscellaneous)
Prodigal Son, The 1965,My 21,19:1
Exception and the Rule, The 1965,My 21,19:1
To Bury a Cousin 1967,My 17,38:3
Gore, James (Scenic Designer)
Butterfly Dream, The 1966,My 20,41:1
Gore, Lance
Finis for Oscar Wilde 1964,F 15,15:1
Gore, Mabel
Jonica 1930,Ap 8,27:1
Peter Ibbetson 1931,Ap 9,30:3
For Services Rendered 1933,Ap 13,15:5
Come of Age 1934,Ja 13,16:6
Distant Shore, The 1935,F 22,26:2
Gore, Nina
Sign of the Leopard 1928,D 12,34:4
Gore-Browne, R F (Original Author)
Cynara 1931,N 3,31:1
Gore-Browne, R F (Playwright)
Cynara 1931,N 3,31:1
Key, The 1933,S 7,17:5
Can We Tell? 1938,O 9,X,3:2
Gorecki, Leon
Post Office, The 1965,Ja 6,32:1
Kernel and the Shell, The 1965,Ja 6,32:1
Jacob and the Angel 1965,Ja 6,32:1
Jaselka 1965,Ja 6,32:1
Book, The 1965,Ja 6,32:1
Woman, The 1965,Ja 6,32:1
Labyrinth, The 1965,Ja 6,32:1
Nightmare, The 1965,Ja 6,32:1
Gorelick, Bob (Miscellaneous)
Bead-Tangle 1970,Jl 16,38:1
Bad Place to Get Your Head, A 1970,Jl 16,38:1
Gorelik, Alexander
Moscow Circus on Ice 1970,D 9,63:1
Gorelik, Michael (Costume Designer)
Saint Joan 1954,S 18,12:1
Gorelik, Michael (Scenic Designer)
Saint Joan 1954,S 18,12:1
Gorelik, Mordecai (Costume Designer)
Processional 1925,Ja 13,17:1
Gorelik, Mordecai (Director)
Plough and the Stars, The 1956,Ap 6,14:1
Gorelik, Mordecai (Lighting Director)
All My Sons 1947,Ja 30,21:2
Desire Under the Elms 1952,Ja 17,23:4
Plough and the Stars, The 1956,Ap 6,14:1
Gorelik, Mordecai (Playwright)
Firebugs, The 1963,F 13,7:2
Gorelik, Mordecai (Producer)
Guests of the Nation 1958,Je 27,18:5
Gorelik, Mordecai (Scenic Designer)
Processional 1925,Ja 13,17:1
Nirvana 1926,Mr 4,19:1
Moon Is a Gong, The 1926,Mr 13,21:3
Loud Speaker 1927,Mr 3,27:2
Final Balance, The 1928,O 31,28:3
1931 1931,D 11,34:3
1931- 1931,D 20,VIII,1:1
Success Story 1932,S 27,24:4
Big Night 1933,Ja 18,16:2
Little Ol' Boy 1933,Ap 25,15:5
Men in White 1933,S 27,24:2
All Good Americans 1933,D 6,29:2
Gentlewoman 1934,Mr 23,28:4
Sailors of Cattaro 1934,D 11,28:4
Young Go First, The 1935,My 29,16:2
Let Freedom Ring 1935,N 7,26:2
Mother, The 1935,N 20,26:3
Golden Boy 1937,N 5,18:5
Tortilla Flat 1938,Ja 13,16:2
Casey Jones 1938,F 21,14:2
Rocket to the Moon 1938,N 25,18:2
Thunder Rock 1939,N 15,18:1
Night Music 1940,F 23,18:2
All My Sons 1947,Ja 30,21:2
Desire Under the Elms 1952,Ja 17,23:4
Desire Under the Elms 1952,Ja 20,II,1:1
Flowering Peach, The 1954,D 29,19:2
Flowering Peach, The 1955,Ja 9,II,1:1

Hatful of Rain, A 1955,N 10,44:1
Hatful of Rain, A 1955,D 4,II,1:1
Plough and the Stars, The 1956,Ap 6,14:1
Volpone 1957,Ja 8,27:1
Volpone 1957,Ja 13,II,10:1
Sin of Pat Muldoon, The 1957,Mr 14,35:1
Distant Bell, A 1960,Ja 14,29:1
Gorelik, Mordecai (Translator)
Firebugs, The 1968,Jl 2,36:1
Gorgal, J Wellington
Dracula Sabbat 1970,O 2,28:2
Gorgas, Alice
Marriage of Cana, The 1932,F 3,22:4
Gorgas, Jennifer
Take a Giant Step 1956,S 26,30:1
Gorge, George S (Satovsky, Youacca G) (Playwright)
Clean Beds 1939,My 26,21:2
Gorgoni, Al
Recruiting Officer, The 1958,F 8,12:2
Gorham, Roy
Gentlemen Prefer Blondes 1926,S 29,23:1
Gorin, Igor
Once Over Lightly 1942,N 20,26:2
Gorin, Pavel
Uncle Vanya 1960,F 13,13:4
Goring, Marius
Mary Tudor 1935,D 13,30:6
Mary Tudor 1936,Ja 12,IX,1:5
Satyr 1937,Je 17,18:5
Satyr 1937,Jl 4,X,1:4
Richard III 1953,My 10,II,1:1
Measure for Measure 1962,Ap 11,47:4
Poker Session, The 1964,F 12,30:4
Demonstration, The 1969,N 20,60:1
Goritz, George
Henry IV, Part I 1958,Je 25,23:3
Gorky, Maxim (Original Author)
Mother, The 1935,N 20,26:3
Mother, The 1937,Ag 29,X,1:3
Long Way From Home, A 1948,F 9,25:2
Gorky, Maxim (Playwright)
Night Lodging 1920,Ap 14,18:2
Night Lodging 1920,Ap 18,VI,2:1
Lodging for the Night, A 1922,O 2,10:2
Lower Depths, The 1923,Ja 16,16:1
Lower Depths, The 1923,Ja 21,VII,1:1
Lower Depths, The 1923,D 9,IX,1:1
Lower Depths, The 1928,My 13,IX,2:7
At the Bottom 1930,Ja 10,24:3
Yegor Bulevitch 1934,Ja 8,21:7
Dostigayev 1935,Ja 14,10:5
Lower Depths, The 1956,O 3,29:2
Courageous One, The 1958,Ja 21,33:6
Courageous One, The 1958,F 2,II,1:1
Children of the Sun 1963,D 11,56:3
Lower Depths, The 1964,Mr 31,30:1
Lower Depths, The 1964,Ap 12,II,1:1
Country People 1970,Ja 19,35:1
Gorman, Bert
Don Q Jr 1926,Ja 28,16:3
Scarlet Lily, The 1927,Ja 31,12:3
Gorman, Bob
How Now, Dow Jones 1967,D 8,53:1
Gantry 1970,F 16,44:1
Gorman, Brant
Fly Away Home 1937,Ap 27,18:1
Gorman, Cliff
Hogan's Goat 1965,N 12,56:1
Boys in the Band, The 1968,Ap 15,48:1
Boys in the Band, The 1968,Ap 28,II,1:6
Gorman, Edward
Castles in the Air 1926,S 7,19:2
Gorman, Eric
School for Wives 1934,N 14,22:2
Gorman, George
Spite Corner 1922,S 26,18:1
Gorman, Julia
First Flight 1925,S 18,26:2
Gorman, Manuel (Producer)
Many Mansions 1937,O 28,28:6
Gorman, Mari
Kitchen, The 1966,Je 14,50:1
Walking to Waldheim 1967,N 11,25:2
Memorandum, The 1968,My 6,55:1
Gorman, Pat
Judy Garland's New Variety Show 1956,S 27,43:2
Gorman, Patrick
Henry V 1965,Je 29,27:2
Those That Play the Clowns 1966,N 25,48:1
Gorman, Robert
Half a Sixpence 1965,Ap 26,38:2
Gorman, Ross and Band
Vaudeville (Hippodrome) 1926,My 8,29:2
Gorman, Tom
Clean Beds 1939,My 26,21:2
Late Arrival 1953,O 20,35:5
Point of No Return 1957,Mr 23,17:2
Shadow of My Enemy, A 1957,D 12,35:4
Enter Laughing 1963,Mr 15,8:1
Investigation, The 1966,O 5,40:1
Gorman, Walter (Director)
Notes From the Underground 1960,Ja 20,26:1

Gorman, Walter (Playwright)
Notes From the Underground 1960,Ja 20,26:1
Gorme, Eydie
Jerry Lewis' Variety Show 1957,F 8,18:5
Golden Rainbow 1968,F 5,27:1
Golden Rainbow 1968,Mr 3,II,3:1
Gormley, James
In the Jungle of Cities 1960,D 21,39:1
Red Eye of Love 1961,Je 13,28:1
Gormly, Pat (Wac Pvt)
Swing Sister Wac Swing 1944,Ja 4,20:4
Gormly, Ruth
Red, Hot and Blue! 1936,O 30,26:3
Gorney, Camille
Grandee Penitence, La 1926,N 14,VIII,2:1
Gorney, Jay (Composer)
Top Hole 1924,S 2,22:3
Merry-Go-Round 1927,Je 1,25:4
Caravan 1928,Ag 30,13:3
Sketch Book 1929,Jl 2,33:5
Earl Carroll's Vanities 1930,Jl 2,28:3
Americana 1932,O 6,19:3
Meet the People 1940,O 20,IX,3:3
Meet the People 1940,D 26,22:2
Meet the People 1941,Ja 12,IX,1:1
Heaven on Earth 1948,S 17,29:2
Touch and Go 1949,O 14,34:2
Touch and Go 1949,O 30,II,1:1
These Are the Times 1950,My 11,37:2
Gorney, Jay (Lyricist)
Top Hole 1924,S 2,22:3
Sketch Book 1929,Jl 2,33:5
Earl Carroll's Vanities 1930,Jl 2,28:3
Meet the People 1940,D 26,22:2
Meet the People 1941,Ja 12,IX,1:1
Gorney, Jay (Miscellaneous)
They Can't Get You Down 1941,N 2,IX,3:5
Happiest Girl in the World, The 1961,Ap 4,42:1
Gorney, Jay (Playwright)
Earl Carroll's Vanities 1925,Jl 7,24:1
Meet the People 1940,D 26,22:2
Gorney, Jay (Producer)
New Meet the People, The 1943,Ag 22,II,1:6
These Are the Times 1950,My 11,37:2
Gorney, Walter
'Tis Pity She's a Whore 1958,D 6,21:1
Cockeyed Kite 1961,S 14,27:1
Gorodetsky
Chauve-Souris 1922,Je 6,17:4
Chauve-Souris 1925,Ja 15,25:1
Chauve-Souris 1929,Ja 23,20:2
Gorostiza, Carlos (Director)
Neighbors 1966,D 3,45:3
Gorostiza, Carlos (Playwright)
Projimos, Los 1966,Je 29,38:5
Neighbors 1966,D 3,45:3
Gorostiza, Celestino (Producer)
Mexicana 1939,Ap 22,14:4
Gorrall, Leslie
Menonite 1936,Mr 20,29:6
Gorrell, Jerrold (Lighting Director)
Tom Paine 1969,Mr 30,71:2
Tempest, The 1970,F 15,67:1
Gorrill, Liz
Mod Donna 1970,My 4,48:1
Gorrin, Michael
Cafe Crown 1942,Ja 24,12:5
Tonight in Samarkand 1955,F 17,22:2
Hamlet of Stepney Green 1958,N 14,21:1
Sound of Music, The 1959,N 17,40:2
Have I Got a Girl for You! 1963,D 3,53:2
Pocket Watch, The 1966,Ja 6,18:1
East Wind, The 1967,F 10,30:1
Untitled-Poetry Reading 1967,Jl 18,29:1
Tenth Man, The 1967,N 9,54:1
Gorsch, Martin G (Producer)
Gentleman From Athens, The 1947,N 30,I,78:2
Gorsey, Renee
Plot Against the Chase Manhattan Bank, The 1963,N 27,29:1
South Pacific 1965,Je 3,25:1
Gorshin, Frank
Jimmy 1969,O 24,38:1
Jimmy 1969,N 9,II,1:1
Gorskaya, Sonia
Green Fields 1920,Mr 26,11:2
Fortune 1920,Ap 22,11:3
Gorski, Virginia
Million Dollar Baby 1945,D 22,17:2
Look, Ma, I'm Dancin' 1948,Ja 30,20:2
Along Fifth Avenue 1949,Ja 14,28:2
Gorsse, Henry de (Playwright)
Femme au Chat, La 1929,Je 9,VIII,2:4
Gorst, Eldon
Leave Her to Heaven 1940,F 28,16:2
Gorsten, Leon (Miscellaneous)
Valmouth 1960,O 7,29:1
Gorton, Arthur
Villa of Madame Vidac, The 1959,O 1,40:1
Gorunov
Hamlet 1932,Je 26,IX,1:3
Gosch, Martin (Producer)
Gentleman From Athens, The 1947,D 10,42:4

Gose, Carl
Good Hunting 1938,N 22,26:5
Three Sisters, The 1939,O 16,23:1
Night Before Christmas, The 1941,Ap 11,25:2
Letters to Lucerne 1941,D 24,14:2
Moon Is Down, The 1942,Ap 8,22:2
Eve of St Mark, The 1942,O 8,30:2
Dark Eyes 1943,Ja 15,20:2
Pillar to Post 1943,D 11,11:2
Gosfield, Maurice
Siege 1937,D 9,31:4
Darkness at Noon 1951,Ja 15,13:4
In Any Language 1952,O 9,40:2
Stone for Danny Fisher, A 1954,O 22,24:2
Goshal, Kumar
Golden Dawn 1927,D 1,32:3
Flowers of Virtue, The 1942,F 6,22:2
Goslar, Lotte
Pepper Mill 1937,Ja 6,19:4
Who's Who 1938,Mr 2,16:2
Reunion in New York 1940,F 22,28:4
Lotte Goslar's Pantomime Circus-For Humans
Only 1957,D 17,45:1
Goslar, Lotte (Choreographer)
Reunion in New York 1940,F 22,28:4
Galileo 1947,Ag 1,21:4
Galileo 1947,D 8,34:2
Goslar, Lotte and Her Dance Group
King Lear 1940,D 16,27:2
Gosling, Pat
Cabaret 1966,N 21,62:1
Gosnell, Evelyn
Ladies' Night 1920,Ag 10,10:1
Comedian, The 1923,Mr 14,14:1
Naughty Cinderella 1925,N 10,23:6
Gosnova, Florentine
Louie the 14th 1925,Mr 4,17:1
Honeymoon Lane 1926,S 21,32:3
Gospel Starlets
God Is Back, Black and Singing Gospel at the
Fortune Theater 1969,N 19,48:1
Goss, Bick
It's a Bird . . . It's a Plane . . . It's Superman
1966,Mr 30,34:1
Goss, Bick (Choreographer)
Plot Against the Chase Manhattan Bank, The
1963,N 27,29:1
I Dreamt I Dwelt in Bloomingdale's 1970,F 13,26:1
Ben Bagley's Shoestring Revues 1970,O 24,22:1
Goss, Don
Young Alexander 1929,Mr 13,28:2
Goss, Dorothy
Would-Be Gentleman, The 1930,Ap 30,29:2
Goss, George
Ghost of Yankee Doodle, The 1937,N 23,26:3
Goss, Helen
Karl and Anna 1935,O 13,IX,3:1
Libel! 1935,D 21,10:5
Goss, Julia
Pirates of Penzance, The 1968,N 7,54:1
Goss, Robert
Merry Widow, The 1964,Ag 18,24:2
Yearling, The 1965,D 11,25:1
Gossage, Sally Kemp
Life Is a Dream 1964,Mr 20,24:1
Gosselin, Mlle
Bourgeois Gentilhomme, Le 1955,O 26,26:1
Gossett, Lou
Take a Giant Step 1953,O 4,II,1:1
Desk Set, The 1955,O 25,36:7
Raisin in the Sun, A 1959,Mr 12,27:1
Blacks, The 1961,My 5,23:1
Tambourines to Glory 1963,N 4,47:1
Golden Boy 1964,O 21,56:1
Zulu and the Zayda, The 1965,N 11,59:1
My Sweet Charlie 1966,D 7,56:1
Tartuffe 1967,S 18,60:1
Carry Me Back to Morningside Heights
1968,F 28,41:1
Murderous Angels 1970,F 8,70:1
Murderous Angels 1970,Mr 15,II,1:4
Gossman, Gertrude M
Patience 1928,Je 26,29:3
Gossman, Irving H
Half Moon Inn 1925,Mr 10,14:1
Gostelow, Gordon
Country Wife, The 1969,Ag 30,10:3
Gostinsky, J
Yegor Bulevitch 1934,Ja 8,21:7
Aristocrats 1935,My 2,16:2
Gostony, Adam (Playwright)
Chameleon, The 1932,Jl 19,20:4
Gotch, Stanley
Loves of Lulu, The 1925,My 12,26:1
Gotesfeld, Chune (Playwright)
American Chasidim 1928,Mr 17,8:8
Goth
Olympia 1928,Mr 25,IX,4:1
Constant Wife, The 1928,D 30,VIII,4:4
Siege of Besztercze, The 1929,F 3,VIII,2:1
One, Two, Three 1929,N 17,IX,4:7
Good Fairy, The 1930,O 13,31:2

Goth, Mrs
Olympia 1928,Mr 25,IX,4:1
Constant Wife, The 1928,D 30,VIII,4:4
Siege of Besztercze, The 1929,F 3,VIII,2:1
Goth, Trudy
War and Peace 1942,My 22,26:3
Gotham City Four
Blossom Time 1921,S 30,10:1
Gothie, Bob
Visit to a Small Planet 1957,F 8,18:1
Gott, Barbara
Tovarich 1936,O 16,31:4
Gott, Tom
Love Birds 1921,Mr 16,12:1
Gottermeyer, Eileen
Touch 1970,N 9,52:1
Gottesfeld, Charles (Playwright)
My Dear Public 1943,S 10,28:1
Gottesfeld, Chono (Director)
In-Laws 1960,O 17,32:4
World Is a Stage, The 1962,N 5,37:4
Gottesfeld, Chono (Playwright)
Angels on Earth 1929,D 11,34:7
God's Thieves 1930,O 27,17:4
In-Laws 1934,O 25,28:2
Parnosseh 1935,F 16,8:8
Topsy-Turvy 1939,F 13,12:3
Parnosseh 1939,F 20,12:5
In-Laws 1960,O 17,32:4
World Is a Stage, The 1962,N 5,37:4
Gottfried, Emanuel
Wooden Idol, The 1930,My 13,27:2
Gottfried, Howard (Miscellaneous)
Major Barbara 1951,F 24,10:2
Gottfried, Howard (Producer)
Purple Dust 1956,D 28,15:1
I Know at the Door 1957,S 30,27:2
Cock-A-Doodle Dandy 1958,N 13,39:2
U S A 1959,O 29,38:1
God's Trombones 1960,F 10,43:4
Shakespeare in Harlem 1960,F 10,43:4
Gottfried, Ruth
Wooden Idol, The 1930,My 13,27:2
Gotthold, Charles
Potash and Perlmutter, Detectives; Poisoned by
Pictures 1926,S 1,27:3
Rosalie 1928,Ja 11,26:3
Gotthold, Philip (Scenic Designer)
Sign of Jonah, The 1957,My 2,27:1
Gotthold, Philip M
Everyman Today 1958,Ja 16,32:4
Gottleb, Anne (Lighting Director)
Moby Dick 1970,Je 3,52:1
Gottler, Archie (Playwright)
Broadway Brevities, 1920 1920,S 30,12:2
Gottlieb, Alex (Miscellaneous)
Seperate Rooms 1940,Mr 25,10:3
Gottlieb, Alex (Playwright)
Wake Up, Darling 1956,My 3,34:2
Susan Slept Here 1961,Jl 12,35:2
Gottlieb, Bernard L
Loud Speaker 1927,Mr 3,27:2
Gottlieb, Grance
39 Steps 1938,Mr 12,13:1
Gottlieb, Harry
Hairy Ape, The 1922,Mr 10,18:2
Gottlieb, Herbert
John Brown 1950,My 4,32:7
Night Music 1951,Ap 9,29:6
Gottlieb, Iris
Finian's Rainbow 1953,Mr 7,13:2
Gottlieb, Morton (Producer)
His and Hers 1954,Ja 8,18:2
Enter Laughing 1963,Mr 15,8:1
Enter Laughing 1963,Je 16,II,1:1
Chips With Everything 1963,O 2,49:1
White House, The 1964,My 20,39:1
P S I Love You 1964,N 20,40:1
Killing of Sister George, The 1966,O 6,57:1
Come Live With Me 1967,Ja 27,29:1
Promise, The 1967,N 15,38:1
Lovers; Winners 1968,Jl 26,21:4
Lovers; Losers 1968,Jl 26,21:4
We Bombed in New Haven 1968,O 17,51:1
Mundy Scheme, The 1969,D 12,75:1
Sleuth 1970,N 13,25:1
Gottlieb, Saul (Director)
Evening With the Times Square Two, An
1967,My 21,83:6
Gottlieb, Saul (Miscellaneous)
Brig, The 1963,My 16,40:1
Gottlieb, Saul (Producer)
Saintliness of Margery Kempe, The 1959,F 3,35:6
Geranium Hat, The 1959,Mr 18,45:1
Gottlieb, W H
If Booth Had Missed 1931,My 14,27:1
Gottowt, John
Liebestrank 1927,Ja 30,VII,4:3
Gottschalk, Ferdinand
Captain Applejack 1921,D 31,14:2
Truth About Blayds, The 1922,Mr 15,22:1
Lady Cristilinda, The 1922,D 26,11:2
You and I 1923,F 20,12:1

Gottschalk, Ferdinand—Cont

Bride, The 1924,My 6,25:1
Stork, The 1925,Ja 27,14:2
Buccaneer, The 1925,O 3,10:2
In a Garden 1925,N 17,29:1
Jest, The 1926,F 5,22:2
Crown Prince, The 1927,Mr 24,23:2
Command to Love, The 1927,S 21,27:1
Love Duel, The 1929,Ap 16,32:3
Even in Egypt 1930,Ja 19,VIII,2:6
Joseph 1930,F 13,25:3
Lost Sheep 1930,My 6,33:2
Tonight or Never 1930,N 9,IX,3:2
Tonight or Never 1930,N 19,19:3
Play, Genius, Play! 1935,O 31,17:2
Gottschlich, Hugo
Konzert, Das 1968,Mr 25,52:1
Jux Will Er Sich Machen, Einen 1968,Ap 3,41:1
Gottwald, Fritz (Original Author)
Command to Love, The 1927,S 21,27:1
Goudal, Jetta
Hero, The 1921,Mr 15,14:1
Elton Case, The 1921,S 12,16:2
Gouderc
Affaires Son les Affaires, Les 1924,Mr 11,17:1
Goudge, Elizabeth (Playwright)
Joy Will Come Back 1937,Mr 22,27:3
Goudvis, Helena
Jackpot 1944,Ja 14,15:2
Gough, Dan
Three Plays of the Sea 1970,Ag 20,39:1
Gough, Lloyd
Yellow Jack 1934,Mr 7,22:6
Laburnum Grove 1935,Ja 15,23:5
With All My Heart 1935,Jl 30,17:1
Alice Takat 1936,F 11,19:2
Laughing Woman, The 1936,O 14,30:1
Aged 26 1936,D 22,32:1
Point of Honor, A 1937,Ja 31,II,10:4
Point of Honor, A 1937,F 12,26:2
Red Harvest 1937,Mr 31,29:2
Ghost of Yankee Doodle, The 1937,N 23,26:3
Shadow and Substance 1938,Ja 27,16:2
Shadow and Substance 1938,F 6,X,1:1
My Dear Children 1939,Mr 25,19:6
Young Couple Wanted 1940,Ja 25,16:2
Weak Link, The 1940,Mr 5,19:2
Love's Old Sweet Song 1940,My 3,16:3
No for an Answer 1941,Ja 6,10:6
Tanyard Street 1941,F 5,16:2
Golden Wings 1941,N 25,33:3
Golden Wings 1941,D 9,46:6
Heart of a City 1942,F 13,24:6
Cat Screams, The 1942,Je 17,26:5
Deep Are the Roots 1945,S 27,24:4
Deep Are the Roots 1945,O 7,II,1:1
Victim, The 1952,My 3,17:5
Ondine 1954,F 19,23:1
Ondine 1954,F 28,II,1:1
Bad Seed, The 1954,D 9,42:1
Compulsion 1957,O 25,21:1
Cue for Passion 1958,N 26,25:2
Roman Candle 1960,F 4,34:2
Banker's Daughter, The 1962,Ja 23,37:1
Gough, Michael
But for the Grace of God 1946,S 4,27:2
Way Things Go, The 1950,Mr 3,19:8
Colombe 1951,D 15,13:2
Immoralist, The 1954,N 4,39:5
Fighting Cock, The 1959,D 9,57:3
Gough, Sylvia
Varying Shore, The 1921,D 6,24:1
Gould, Allan
Birthright 1933,N 22,22:3
Gould, Amy Kennedy (Playwright)
Retreat From Folly 1937,F 25,18:2
Retreat From Folly 1937,Je 29,18:3
Gould, Beatrice (Playwright)
Man's Estate 1929,Ap 28,IX,1:1
Gould, Berni
New Pins and Needles 1939,N 21,19:2
By Jupiter 1942,Je 4,22:1
Let Freedom Sing 1942,O 6,18:2
Gould, Bert
Lucky 1927,Mr 23,28:3
Gould, Bradley
Many Moons 1947,D 15,35:2
Gould, Bruce (Playwright)
Man's Estate 1929,Ap 2,28:2
Man's Estate 1929,Ap 28,IX,1:1
Terrible Turk, The 1934,F 25,IX,1:6
Gould, Cara
Lady Lies, The 1928,N 27,36:2
Gould, Chuck (Composer)
Funzapoppin 1949,Jl 1,16:2
Gould, Chuck (Lyricist)
Funzapoppin 1949,Jl 1,16:2
Gould, Dave
Vaudeville (Hollywood) 1932,F 16,24:3
Gould, Dave (Choreographer)
Hello, Yourself 1928,O 31,28:2
Second Little Show, The 1930,S 3,36:1
Fine and Dandy 1930,S 24,26:1
Gang's All Here, The 1931,F 19,21:3

Gould, Dave (Choreographer)—Cont
Third Little Show, The 1931,Je 2,34:3
Hey, Nonny, Nonny! 1932,Je 7,22:3
Sing Out the News 1938,S 26,12:5
Gould, Diane
Midsummer Night's Dream, A 1964,Je 30,23:2
Gould, Edith Kelly
Pins and Needles 1922,F 2,20:1
Gould, Elliott
Rumple 1957,N 7,42:2
Say Darling 1959,F 26,38:2
Irma la Douce 1960,S 30,31:2
I Can Get It for You Wholesale 1962,Mr 23,29:1
Drat! the Cat! 1965,O 11,54:2
Little Murders 1967,Ap 26,38:1
Gould, Frank
Having Wonderful Time 1937,F 22,12:5
Escape This Night 1938,Ap 23,18:1
Cafe Crown 1942,Ja 24,12:5
Gould, Frank (Playwright)
Scene of the Crime, The 1940,Mr 29,24:1
Tenting Tonight 1947,Ap 3,32:2
Gould, Gordon
Within the Gates 1934,O 23,23:1
Creeping Fire 1935,Ja 17,22:3
Right You Are (If You Think You Are) 1964,Mr 5,37:1
Tavern, The 1964,Mr 6,39:2
Scapin 1964,Mr 10,43:1
Lower Depths, The 1964,Mr 31,30:1
Man and Superman 1964,D 7,45:2
Judith 1965,Mr 25,42:2
You Can't Take It With You 1965,N 24,32:1
Right You Are (If You Think You Are) 1966,N 23,34:2
Wild Duck, The 1967,Ja 12,49:1
War and Peace 1967,Mr 22,42:1
Pantagleize 1967,D 1,54:1
Show-Off, The 1967,D 6,40:2
Gould, Harold
Passing of the Third Floor Back, The 1924,F 8,19:4
Prunella 1929,Ap 10,23:3
Perfect Marriage, The 1932,N 17,23:2
Uncle Tom's Cabin 1933,My 30,13:4
John Brown 1934,Ja 23,22:3
Valley Forge 1934,D 11,28:3
Othello 1935,S 28,13:2
Macbeth 1935,O 8,26:4
White Man 1936,O 19,22:4
Madame Capet 1938,O 26,26:2
Increased Difficulty of Concentration, The 1969,D 5,48:1
Increased Difficulty of Concentration, The 1969,D 21,II,3:1
Amphitryon 1970,My 29,13:1
Gould, Harold W (Mrs)
Passing of the Third Floor Back, The 1924,F 8,19:4
Gould, Herbert
Chimes of Normandy, The 1931,N 3,31:3
Fledermaus, Die 1933,My 14,II,3:8
Gould, Howard
Nobody's Money 1921,Ag 18,9:3
Home Fires 1923,Ag 21,12:1
Gould, Hull (Playwright)
Tomorrow 1928,D 29,20:2
Gould, J P
Overture 1930,D 8,26:4
Gould, Jay
Tick-Tack-Toe 1920,F 24,11:2
Broadway Whirl, The 1921,Je 9,10:4
Molly Darling 1922,S 2,10:2
Topics of 1923 1923,N 21,23:2
Plain Jane 1924,My 13,24:2
Gould, John
Down to Miami 1944,S 12,23:5
Gould, Lucielle
Grand Vizier, The 1961,D 13,55:5
Gould, Lucretia
Gift of Time, A 1962,F 23,34:1
Sweet Miani 1962,S 26,33:2
Gould, Maggie
Men to the Sea 1944,O 4,25:2
Season in the Sun 1950,S 29,31:2
Gould, Marguerite
Faithfully Yours 1951,O 19,22:5
Gould, Martha (Costume Designer)
Blood Knot, The 1964,Mr 3,30:2
Place for Chance, The 1964,My 15,44:2
Tragical Historie of Doctor Faustus, The 1964,O 6,34:2
Gould, Molly
Myself and I 1929,Ag 31,13:6
Gould, Morton (Composer)
Million Dollar Baby 1945,D 22,17:2
Billion Dollar Baby 1945,D 30,II,1:1
Arms and the Girl 1950,F 3,28:2
Party With Betty Comden and Adolph Green, A 1958,D 24,2:7
Gould, Morton (Miscellaneous)
Let Freedom Sing 1942,O 6,18:2
Arms and the Girl 1950,F 3,28:2

Gould, Mr
Will Morrissey's Folies Bergere Revue 1930,Ap 16,26:6
Gould, Peggy
Goodbye in the Night 1940,Mr 19,31:2
Gould, Rita Burgess
Vaudeville (Palace) 1929,N 11,20:5
Gould, Sandra
Having Wonderful Time 1937,F 22,12:5
Gould, Sol
Vaudeville (Palace) 1929,N 4,29:1
Gould, Stanley
Winterset 1935,S 26,19:2
Hamlet 1936,O 9,30:2
Gould, Stanley (Director)
Brass Ring, The 1952,Ap 11,19:2
Gould, Toby
Little Red Riding Hood 1948,Ja 12,15:3
Gould, Val
Diamond Lil 1951,S 15,8:2
Gould, Venita
Greenwich Village Follies 1920,Ag 31,7:3
Vaudeville (Palace) 1923,Mr 13,19:2
Vaudeville (Palace) 1926,D 21,20:5
Vaudeville (Palace) 1927,O 4,34:3
Vaudeville (Palace) 1929,D 30,16:3
Vaudeville (Palace) 1930,N 3,19:2
Vaudeville (Hollywood) 1932,F 16,24:3
Gould, Willis
King Lear 1940,D 16,27:2
Gould, Willis E (Miscellaneous)
Innocents, The 1959,Ap 21,41:2
Gould, Zelda
Bread 1932,D 14,27:3
Gould-Porter, Arthur
New York to Cherbourg 1932,F 20,11:4
Victoria Regina 1935,D 27,15:2
Bachelor Born 1938,Ja 26,26:3
Oscar Wilde 1938,O 11,20:2
Contrast, The 1940,Mr 26,17:2
Rats of Norway, The 1948,Ap 16,27:6
Goulden, Harold
Princess Virtue 1921,My 5,20:2
Drift 1925,N 25,15:3
Goulding, Edmund (Director)
Ryan Girl, The 1945,S 25,28:2
Ryan Girl, The 1945,S 30,II,1:2
Goulding, Edmund (Playwright)
Dancing Mothers 1924,My 4,VIII,2:1
Dancing Mothers 1924,Ag 12,12:2
Ryan Girl, The 1945,S 25,28:2
Ryan Girl, The 1945,S 30,II,1:2
Goulding, Ellott (Playwright)
Bob and Ray-The Two and Only 1970,S 25,36:1
Goulding, Ivis
Mid-Channel 1928,S 16,IX,1:4
Goulding, Lawrence
Simpleton of the Unexpected Isles, The 1954,Ja 12,19:1
Goulding, Ray
Bob and Ray-The Two and Only 1970,S 25,36:1
Goulding, Ray (Playwright)
Bob and Ray-The Two and Only 1970,S 25,36:1
Goulding, Reginald (Director)
We Were Dancing; Tonight at Eight 1940,Ag 6,15:3
Goulet, Edgar
Untitled-Passion Play 1925,Ag 17,8:1
Goulet, Jean (Prof) (Musical Director)
Untitled-Passion Play 1925,Ag 17,8:1
Goulet, Robert
Camelot 1960,D 5,42:1
Camelot 1960,D 11,II,5:1
Happy Time, The 1968,Ja 19,32:2
Happy Time, The 1968,Ja 28,II,3:1
Goulston, Andre (Miscellaneous)
Fun Couple, The 1962,O 27,15:2
Beyond the Fringe 1962,O 29,36:1
Man and Boy 1963,N 13,34:1
Rugantino 1964,F 7,34:1
Hamlet 1964,Ap 10,30:1
Cambridge Circus 1964,O 7,53:1
Goulston, Andre (Producer)
Legend of Lovers 1959,O 28,40:3
Hostile Witness 1966,F 18,26:1
Education of H*Y*M*A*N K*A*P*L*A*N, The 1968,Ap 5,57:1
Gounod, Charles (Composer)
Man and Superman 1970,F 24,48:1
Gour, Betty (Miscellaneous)
Oklahoma! 1953,S 1,19:1
Gourard, Yvonne
No More Blondes 1920,Ja 8,22:1
Gouraud, Claude
Blood and Sand 1921,S 21,16:2
Desert Flower, The 1924,N 19,18:2
Gouraud, George
Pickwick 1927,S 6,35:2
Gouraud, Powers (Composer)
Dear Love 1930,My 18,VIII,3:1
Gouraud, Powers (Lyricist)
Dear Love 1930,My 18,VIII,3:1
Gouriadec, Loic Le (Playwright)
Jeune Fille a Reve, Une 1935,My 5,IX,2:4

Gove, Fiske
Saturday's Children 1936,Jl 7,22:5
Gover, Aithna
Time Remembered 1955,My 4,35:1
Govind, Arjun
Little Clay Cart, The 1924,D 6,13:3
Govindan, V M
Mahabharata 1970,N 28,22:1
Govinska, Ianna
Dybbuk, The 1948,My 3,26:3
Golem, The 1948,My 17,22:3
Govinskaya, Ina
Dybbuk, The 1926,D 14,24:2
Eternal Jew, The 1926,D 21,21:2
Jacob's Dream 1927,Ja 4,20:2
Gow, James (Playwright)
Drums Professor, The 1935,Jl 30,17:2
Tomorrow the World 1943,Ap 15,22:2
Tomorrow the World 1943,Ap 25,II,1:1
Deep Are the Roots 1945,S 27,24:4
Deep Are the Roots 1945,O 7,II,1:1
Deep Are the Roots 1947,Ap 28,26:3
Deep Are the Roots 1947,Jl 10,17:1
Legend of Sarah 1950,O 12,42:4
Deep Are the Roots 1960,O 4,47:1
Gow, Ronald (Playwright)
Gallows Glorious 1933,My 1,10:5
Gallows Glorious 1933,My 21,IX,1:3
John Brown 1934,Ja 23,22:3
Love on the Dole 1935,F 17,VIII,3:1
Love on the Dole 1936,F 25,23:3
Love on the Dole 1936,Mr 8,IX,1:1
Ann Veronica 1949,My 21,9:2
Boston Story, A 1968,S 21,26:2
Gowen, John (Director)
Good Morning 1937,D 4,20:7
Gower, Mary
Crucible, The 1958,Mr 12,36:1
Saintliness of Margery Kempe, The 1959,F 3,35:6
Gower & Jeanne
Count Me In 1942,O 9,24:2
Gowing, Almerin
Dancers, The 1923,O 18,17:2
Two by Two 1925,F 24,17:1
Gowing, Gene
Courage 1928,O 9,34:2
It's a Grand Life 1930,F 11,30:3
Great Barrington, The 1931,F 20,18:1
Gowing, Gene (Director)
Gold Braid 1930,My 14,31:2
Goya, Carola (Choreographer)
Becky Sharp 1929,Je 4,29:1
Goyen, William (Lyricist)
House of Breath, The 1957,Ap 15,23:2
Goyen, William (Playwright)
House of Breath, The 1957,Ap 15,23:2
Whisper to Me 1960,N 22,38:6
Goz, Harry
Utopia, Limited; Flowers of Progress, The 1957,F 27,21:1
Hit the Deck 1960,Je 24,32:1
Around the World in 80 Days 1963,Je 24,22:1
Bajour 1964,N 24,42:1
Fiddler on the Roof 1967,N 16,61:5
Two by Two 1970,N 11,37:1
Gozez Trio
Wake Up and Dream 1930,Ja 12,9:1
Gozzi, Carlo (Original Author)
Princess Turandot 1937,Ag 3,20:5
Roi Cerf, Le 1937,N 30,26:3
Gozzi, Carlo (Playwright)
Princess Turandot 1926,N 13,14:2
Turandot 1929,Ja 12,14:4
Roi Cerf, Le 1937,O 27,28:7
Grable, Betty
Du Barry Was a Lady 1939,D 7,34:2
Hello, Dolly! 1967,Je 14,38:1
Belle Starr 1969,My 3,40:2
Grablen, Tom
Private Life of the Master Race, The 1956,Ja 31,33:3
Grace, Barbara
Queen High 1926,S 9,21:2
Grace, Buster
Stars on Ice 1942,Jl 3,12:2
Howdy Mr Ice 1948,Je 25,28:5
Howdy, Mr Ice of 1950 1949,My 27,24:2
Grace, Carol
Time of Your Life, The 1955,Ja 20,34:1
Will Success Spoil Rock Hunter? 1955,O 14,22:2
Cold Wind and the Warm, The 1958,D 9,55:1
Once There Was a Russian 1961,F 20,32:2
Grace, Charity
Biggest Thief in Town 1949,Mr 31,31:2
Pygmalion 1952,F 9,11:2
Matchmaker, The 1955,D 6,45:6
Grace, Edward
Dark of the Moon 1958,F 27,22:2
Grace, Edward M
Inspector General, The 1923,My 1,24:1
Strings, My Lord, Are False, The 1942,My 20,24:2
Grace, Jerry (Miscellaneous)
Cindy 1964,Mr 20,24:1

Grace, Kathryn
Excursion 1937,Ap 10,11:4
Grace, Michael (Producer)
John Murray Anderson's Almanac 1953,D 11,42:2
Grace, Michael P (Director)
Consul, The 1957,S 4,40:3
Grace, Michael P (Producer)
Rosalie 1957,Je 26,28:2
Grace, Robb
Red Eye of Love 1961,Je 13,28:1
Grace, Robert
Child of the Morning 1958,Ap 22,40:2
Antony and Cleopatra 1959,Ja 14,28:1
Grace, Timothy
Memphis Bound 1945,My 25,23:2
Grace, Wayne
Midsummer Night's Dream, A 1967,Je 30,23:1
Grace and Berkes
Century Revue and the Midnight Rounders, The
1920,Jl 13,9:1
Passing Show of 1921, The 1920,D 30,16:2
Grace and Slagle
Icetime 1946,Je 21,20:5
Icetime 1947,My 29,28:2
Gracella
Florida Girl 1925,N 3,34:1
Gracella and Theodore
Vaudeville (Palace) 1926,S 28,30:4
Nine Fifteen Revue, The 1930,F 12,26:2
Grachev, Anatoli
Man Alive 1965,My 23,13:1
Romeo and Juliet 1970,My 28,28:1
Gracie, Sally
Let Freedom Sing 1942,O 6,18:2
Victory Belles 1943,O 27,26:3
Celebration 1948,Ap 12,24:2
At War With the Army 1949,Mr 9,32:2
Dinosaur Wharf 1951,N 9,23:2
Goodbye Again 1956,Ap 25,38:1
Major Barbara 1956,O 31,27:1
Fair Game 1957,N 4,39:1
Venus at Large 1962,Ap 13,30:1
Helen 1964,D 11,55:4
But, Seriously... 1969,F 28,29:1
Grad, Peter N (Miscellaneous)
Minnie's Boys 1970,Mr 27,27:1
Grade, Chaim (Original Author)
Mother's Sabbath Days 1960,N 21,33:2
Grady, Blanche
Lady Says Yes, A 1945,Ja 11,18:5
Grady, Chester
Elsie Janis and Her Gang 1922,Ja 17,13:2
Grady, James
Lily Sue 1926,N 17,22:2
Grady, James (Playwright)
Billygoat Eddie 1964,Ap 21,43:2
Grady, Nancy
Juno and the Paycock 1940,Ja 17,24:2
Grady, Stanley
Father Malachy's Miracle 1937,N 18,26:4
Graeber, Ted
Taming of the Shrew, The 1963,Mr 8,9:1
Much Ado About Nothing 1964,Je 11,26:2
Richard III 1964,Je 12,44:2
Hamlet 1964,Jl 4,9:1
Coriolanus 1965,Je 21,36:1
Taming of the Shrew, The 1965,Je 24,32:2
King Lear 1965,Je 25,39:1
Midsummer Night's Dream, A 1967,Je 19,42:1
Merchant of Venice, The 1967,Je 22,46:2
Macbeth 1967,Jl 31,21:1
As You Like It 1968,Je 24,42:3
Androcles and the Lion 1968,Je 27,47:1
Love's Labour's Lost 1968,Je 28,36:1
Graef, Bernard (Director)
Period of Adjustment 1962,Je 4,24:2
Grael, Barry Alan
I Feel Wonderful 1954,O 19,22:5
Streets of New York, The 1963,O 30,47:1
Grael, Barry Alan (Lyricist)
Streets of New York, The 1963,O 30,47:1
Grael, Barry Alan (Playwright)
I Feel Wonderful 1954,O 19,22:5
Streets of New York, The 1963,O 30,47:1
Graeme, Kenneth (Original Author)
Toad of Toad Hall 1929,D 23,5:2
Graeme-Brook, Douglas
Bitter Sweet 1929,N 6,30:2
Graetz, Paul
Kean 1921,D 11,VI,1:4
Spread Eagle 1929,N 10,X,4:8
Tales of Hoffmann 1932,Ja 10,VIII,1:6
Alt Heidelberg; Student Prince, The
1932,N 20,IX,3:3
Graf, Fritz (Director)
Satiric Evening 1963,O 24,36:2
Graf, Fritz (Miscellaneous)
Satiric Evening 1963,O 24,36:2
Graf, Herbert (Director)
Gypsy Baron, The 1942,Je 20,8:5
Helen Goes to Troy 1944,Ap 25,17:2
Graf, James M (Producer)
Mystery Moon 1930,Je 24,23:4

Graf, Raymond
Recruiting Officer, The 1958,F 8,12:2
Graf, Walter
Paul Bunyan 1941,My 6,25:1
Firebird of Florence 1945,Mr 23,13:4
Graff, Ellen
Eccentricities of Davy Crockett, The 1961,Ja 4,26:1
Graff, Frederick
King Lear 1940,D 16,27:2
Graff, Peter
His Wife's Lover 1929,O 21,30:6
Russian Love 1930,N 27,32:3
My Little Girl 1931,F 2,22:4
Night in the Woods, A 1931,Mr 2,19:3
Victims of Life 1931,O 21,26:2
Great Miracle, The 1931,D 12,23:5
Big Surprise, The 1932,O 17,18:3
Traveling Salesman, The 1932,N 1,24:4
Sins of Mothers 1937,Mr 30,20:2
Graff, Wilton
Beauty and the Beast 1932,Ja 10,I,29:2
American Dream; 1650 1933,F 22,24:5
American Dream; 1933 1933,F 22,24:5
Mary of Scotland 1933,N 28,28:3
Lord Blesses the Bishop, The 1934,N 28,24:5
Cyrano de Bergerac 1936,Ap 28,17:1
Antony and Cleopatra 1937,N 11,30:2
Millionairess, The 1938,Ag 16,22:5
Dame Nature 1938,S 27,24:3
Pastoral 1939,N 2,26:2
Romeo and Juliet 1940,My 10,27:1
Cue for Passion 1940,D 20,33:4
Gabrielle 1941,Mr 26,26:2
Graff (Playwright)
Endlose Strasse, Die 1932,Mr 27,VIII,3:1
Grafrath, David
Mother Courage and Her Children 1964,My 12,32:2
Graft, Barbara
School for Virtue 1931,Ap 22,29:2
Grafton, Beryl
Murder in the Cathedral 1958,Mr 22,12:4
Grafton, Gloria
Second Little Show, The 1930,Ag 17,VIII,2:2
Second Little Show, The 1930,S 3,36:1
Vaudeville (Hollywood) 1932,Mr 22,17:5
Kill That Story 1934,Ag 30,22:2
Jumbo 1935,N 18,20:2
Grahal, Fernando
Man of La Mancha 1965,N 23,52:1
Graham, Ann
Panama Hattie 1940,O 31,28:2
Banjo Eyes 1941,D 26,20:2
Graham, Anne (Costume Designer)
Kataki 1959,Ap 10,24:1
Graham, Beatrice
Accent on Youth 1935,Jl 9,24:5
Meet the Prince 1935,Ag 6,20:4
Ethan Frome 1936,Ja 22,15:2
Holmeses of Baker Street, The 1936,D 10,34:3
Two Time Mary 1937,Ag 3,20:5
Who's Who 1938,Mr 2,16:2
Graham, Benjamin (Playwright)
Baby Pompadour 1934,D 28,24:2
Graham, Bette
Redhead 1959,F 6,21:1
Graham, Bruce
From Here to There; Otherwise Engaged
1958,Ap 24,37:3
Graham, Buddy
Off Your Marx 1936,Ap 2,28:2
Graham, Carroll (Original Author)
Queer People 1934,F 16,16:2
Graham, Chele
Pajama Game, The 1957,My 16,27:1
Graham, Clive
Hamlet 1969,My 2,38:1
Graham, David
Lower North 1944,Ag 26,15:4
Graham, David B (Producer)
Salvation on a String; Supper for the Dead
1954,Jl 7,23:1
Salvation on a String; Chair Endowed 1954,Jl 7,23:1
Salvation on a String; No Count Boy, The
1954,Jl 7,23:1
Graham, Dorothy
Caribbean Carnival 1947,D 6,12:2
Graham, Douglas (Miscellaneous)
Vincent 1959,O 1,40:1
Graham, E Savage (Playwright)
Those Naughty Nineties 1931,S 13,IX,2:7.
Graham, Edward
Earl Carroll's Vanities 1928,Ag 7,25:2
Graham, Emily
Cyclone Lover, The 1928,Je 6,23:3
Final Balance, The 1928,O 31,28:3
Plutocrat, The 1930,F 21,23:3
Forest Ring, The 1930,Ap 26,11:2
Little Father of the Wilderness, The 1930,Je 3,27:1
Bad Girl 1930,O 3,30:2
First Night 1930,N 27,32:3
Man Who Changed His Name, The 1932,My 3,25:3
Boy Friend, The 1932,Je 8,22:3

Graham, Frank
Fast Life 1928,S 27,35:2
Graham, Frederick
Bill of Divorcement, A 1921,O 11,22:2
Up She Goes 1922,N 7,14:2
Louie the 14th 1925,Mr 4,17:1
Lambs Gambol 1925,Ap 27,15:1
Money From Home 1927,Mr 1,30:2
Red Cat, The 1934,S 20,21:1
Hook-Up, The 1935,My 9,24:6
Petticoat Fever 1935,Je 25,14:5
Ragged Edge, The 1935,N 26,28:3
I Want a Policeman! 1936,Ja 15,15:5
White Horse Inn 1936,O 2,28:5
Barchester Towers 1937,D 1,27:1
Oscar Wilde 1938,O 11,20:2
Graham, Garrett (Original Author)
Queer People 1934,F 16,16:2
Graham, Gary
Touch 1970,N 9,52:1
Graham, Genine
Millionairess, The 1952,O 18,17:2
Graham, George
Transplanting Jean 1921,Ja 4,11:2
True to Form 1921,S 13,12:1
Great Broxopp, The 1921,N 16,22:1
Yankee Princess, The 1922,O 3,22:1
Best People, The 1924,Ag 20,8:1
Kiss in a Taxi, The 1925,Ag 26,14:1
Man From Toronto, The 1926,Je 18,27:2
This Woman Business 1926,D 8,25:1
John 1927,N 5,16:4
Merchant of Venice, The 1928,Ja 17,22:2
Possession 1928,O 3,35:1
Wings Over Europe 1928,D 11,35:1
Apple Cart, The 1930,F 25,30:1
Silent Witness, The 1931,Mr 24,31:5
Wild Waves 1932,F 20,11:4
Party's Over, The 1933,Mr 28,23:3
Taming of the Shrew, The 1935,S 22,X,3:2
Taming of the Shrew, The 1935,O 1,27:3
Private Affair, A 1936,My 15,28:7
Eastwood Ho 1936,Jl 8,14:2
Love From a Stranger 1936,S 30,28:1
Country Wife, The 1936,D 2,34:1
Hamlet 1937,Ag 24,24:4
Candida 1938,Ag 31,13:2
Hamlet 1938,O 13,28:1
Hamlet 1938,O 30,IX,1:1
Henry IV, Part I 1939,Ja 31,17:2
Graham, Georgia
Dark Hours, The 1932,N 15,24:2
Noah 1935,F 14,25:2
Path of Flowers, The 1936,S 18,19:3
Graham, Georgia (Choreographer)
Battle Hymn 1936,My 23,12:1
Graham, Glenn
Melody 1933,F 15,17:4
Graham, H Gordon (Director)
1935 1936,My 13,28:2
Sing for Your Supper 1939,Ap 25,18:6
Graham, Harry (Lyricist)
Lady in Ermine, The 1922,O 3,22:2
Katja 1926,O 19,27:3
Good Companions, The 1931,O 2,31:1
Casanova 1932,Je 19,IX,2:1
Graham, Harry (Playwright)
Toni 1924,My 18,VII,2:8
Sky High 1925,Mr 3,21:4
By Candle Light 1928,O 7,IX,2:7
Casanova 1932,Je 19,IX,2:1
Roulette 1935,Je 16,X,1:1
Rise and Shine 1936,My 8,21:4
Graham, Hedley Gordon (Director)
Nativity Play, The 1937,D 21,29:1
Graham, Herbert
Lucky Sam McCarver 1950,Ap 15,10:6
Graham, Howard
State of the Union 1945,N 15,25:2
Graham, Hugh
Lonesome West, The 1936,Je 30,15:1
Graham, Irvin (Composer)
New Faces of 1936 1936,My 20,24:5
Who's Who 1938,Mr 2,16:2
All in Fun 1940,D 28,11:2
Crazy With the Heat 1941,Ja 15,18:2
Crazy With the Heat 1941,Ja 31,15:2
Wine, Women and Song 1942,S 29,18:3
New Faces of 1956 1956,Je 15,32:1
Graham, Irvin (Lyricist)
Who's Who 1938,Mr 2,16:2
All in Fun 1940,D 28,11:2
Crazy With the Heat 1941,Ja 15,18:2
Crazy With the Heat 1941,Ja 31,15:2
New Faces of 1956 1956,Je 15,32:1
Graham, Jack
Juno and the Paycock 1940,Ja 17,24:2
Journey With Strangers, A 1958,N 27,53:1
Graham, James
Saintliness of Margery Kempe, The 1959,F 3,35:6
Graham, Jane (Scenic Designer)
Rehearsal, The 1963,S 24,45:2

Graham, Jessie
Shame Woman, The 1923,O 17,14:1
Minick 1924,S 25,20:1
White Wings 1926,O 16,15:1
Gringa, La 1928,F 2,17:1
Pleased to Meet You 1928,O 30,27:2
Houseboat on the Styx, The 1928,D 16,IX,2:1
Houseboat on the Styx, The 1928,D 26,14:3
Just to Remind You 1931,S 8,39:1
Chrysalis 1932,N 16,15:2
Far Away Horses 1933,Mr 22,21:6
Move on, Sister 1933,O 25,22:4
May Wine 1935,D 6,30:3
Merry Wives of Windsor, The 1938,Ap 15,22:3
Graham, Jo
Two Seconds 1931,O 10,20:6
Ah, Wilderness! 1953,F 7,10:6
Eastward in Eden 1956,Ap 18,25:4
Graham, Jo (Director)
Virtue's Bed 1930,Ap 16,26:5
In The Best of Families 1931,F 3,29:1
Great Man, The 1931,Ap 8,20:6
Ghost Writer, The 1933,Je 20,22:4
Theodora, the Queen 1934,F 1,15:3
Play, Genius, Play! 1935,O 31,17:2
Graham, Jo (Producer)
Theodora, the Queen 1934,F 1,15:3
Graham, Joan
Out of a Blue Sky 1930,F 10,20:6
Graham, John
French Touch, The 1945,D 10,18:2
Man Who Never Died, The 1958,N 22,27:2
Family Portrait 1959,My 6,48:2
Graham, John (Playwright)
So Proudly We Hail 1938,Mr 30,18:5
So Proudly We Hail 1938,Ap 9,11:1
There Was an Old Woman... 1969,O 16,56:4
Graham, John Maxtone (Miscellaneous)
Kiss Me, Kate 1965,My 13,31:1
Graham, Joseph
Heads or Tails 1947,My 3,10:6
Graham, Joseph H (Director)
Solid Ivory 1925,My 17,29:3
Spring 3100 1928,F 16,14:2
Elmer Gantry 1928,Ag 10,9:4
Little Accident 1928,O 10,32:3
Soldiers and Women 1929,S 3,25:1
Headquarters 1929,D 5,32:4
Graham, Joseph H (Playwright)
Spring 3100 1928,F 16,14:2
Graham, Joseph L
Story for Strangers, A 1948,S 22,39:2
Graham, June
Lady Comes Across, The 1942,Ja 10,10:2
Look, Ma, I'm Dancin' 1948,F 8,II,2:1
All for Love 1949,Ja 24,16:5
Dance Me a Song 1950,Ja 21,10:5
War Games 1969,Ap 18,37:1
My House Is Your House 1970,O 16,53:2
Graham, June (Choreographer)
Maggie 1953,F 19,20:2
Graham, June (Miscellaneous)
King and I, The 1956,Ap 19,35:4
Graham, Kathleen
Six Characters in Search of an Author
1922,O 31,11:2
All Gummed Up 1923,Ja 29,11:2
Thoroughbreds 1924,S 9,12:1
Wise-Crackers, The 1925,D 17,26:1
Graham, Lee
Seeds in the Wind 1948,Ap 26,27:2
Seeds in the Wind 1948,My 26,29:2
Infernal Machine, The 1954,Mr 22,22:2
Graham, Martha
Greenwich Village Follies 1923,S 21,4:6
Heldenleben, Ein 1929,Ap 27,16:4
Neighborhood Playhouse Program 1930,F 21,23:1
Six Miracle Plays; Miraculous Birth and the
Midwives, The; Lamentation of the Virgin Mary,
The; Magdalen, The; Trois Rois, Les; Trois
Maries, Les; Nativite, La 1933,F 12,IX,2:1
Graham, Martha (Choreographer)
Iron Flowers 1933,Je 13,22:2
Iron Flowers 1933,Je 18,VIII,5:2
Romeo and Juliet 1934,D 21,30:3
Graham, Martha (Director)
Electra 1931,My 24,VIII,3:5
Nativite, La; Miraculous Birth and the Midwives,
The; Trois Rois, Les; Trois Maries, Les;
Lamentation of the Virgin Mary, The; Magdalen,
The; Six Miracle Plays 1933,F 6,11:3
Six Miracle Plays; Miraculous Birth and the
Midwives, The; Lamentation of the Virgin Mary,
The; Magdalen, The; Trois Rois, Les; Trois
Maries, Les; Nativite, La 1933,F 12,IX,2:1
Graham, Martha (Miscellaneous)
Panic 1935,Mr 16,18:4
Graham, Michael
Anvil, The 1962,O 31,33:3
Graham, Mona
I'll Take the High Road 1943,N 10,28:3
Graham, Moni
Ice Follies 1969,My 23,38:1

Graham, Morland
George and Margaret 1937,S 23,32:2
Graham, Paul
Naughty Marietta 1931,N 17,31:2
Graham, R W
Kid Himself, The 1925,D 25,23:2
Graham, Ranald (Director)
Opium 1970,O 6,58:1
Graham, Richard
Romeo and Juliet 1935,D 24,10:2
Saint Joan 1936,N 10,27:4
Arms for Venus 1937,Mr 12,18:7
Trojan Horse, The 1940,O 31,28:3
Julius Caesar 1959,Ag 4,30:1
Saratoga 1959,D 8,59:4
Richard II 1961,Ag 30,25:1
King Lear 1964,Jl 23,18:1
Scarlet Lullaby 1968,Mr 11,48:1
Romeo and Jeanette 1969,D 16,53:1
Look to the Lilies 1970,Mr 30,59:1
Graham, Robert C
Front Page Stuff 1926,D 29,24:4
Graham, Ronald
Virginia 1937,S 3,13:2
Boys From Syracuse, The 1938,N 24,36:1
Du Barry Was a Lady 1939,D 7,34:2
Lady Comes Across, The 1942,Ja 10,10:2
By Jupiter 1942,Je 4,22:1
By Jupiter 1942,Ag 30,VIII,1:1
Dream With Music 1944,My 19,15:2
Graham, Ronny
New Faces of 1952 1952,My 17,23:2
New Faces of 1952 1952,My 25,II,1:1
Tender Trap, The 1954,O 14,37:2
Something More! 1964,N 11,36:1
Graham, Ronny (Composer)
New Faces of 1952 1952,My 17,23:2
New Faces of 1956 1956,Je 15,32:1
Mask and Gown 1957,S 11,29:1
New Faces of 1962 1962,F 2,25:1
Cats' Pajamas, The 1962,Je 1,16:2
Leonard Sillman's New Faces of 1968
1968,My 3,43:1
Graham, Ronny (Director)
Mating Dance 1965,N 4,58:1
Postcards 1970,Mr 17,36:1
Place for Polly, A 1970,Ap 20,45:1
Graham, Ronny (Lyricist)
New Faces of 1952 1952,My 17,23:2
New Faces of 1952 1952,My 25,II,1:1
Shoestring Revue 1955,Mr 1,22:2
New Faces of 1956 1956,Je 15,32:1
Mask and Gown 1957,S 11,29:1
New Faces of 1962 1962,F 2,25:1
Bravo Giovanni 1962,My 21,41:2
Bravo Giovanni 1962,My 27,II,1:1
Cats' Pajamas, The 1962,Je 1,16:2
Leonard Sillman's New Faces of 1968
1968,My 3,43:1
Graham, Ronny (Miscellaneous)
Mask and Gown 1957,S 11,29:1
Let It Ride 1961,O 13,27:4
Graham, Ronny (Playwright)
New Faces of 1952 1952,My 17,23:2
New Faces of 1962 1962,F 2,25:1
Leonard Sillman's New Faces of 1968
1968,My 3,43:1
Graham, Schuyler
Fuente Ovejuna; Sheep Well, The 1936,My 3,II,4:1
Graham, Stacy
Ondine 1954,F 19,23:1
Graham, Thomas H
Angel Island 1937,O 21,26:2
Graham, Tracy
Wrecker, The 1928,F 28,18:2
Graham, Ulysses
Mob, The 1920,O 11,18:1
Great Adventure, The 1921,F 26,9:2
Graham, William
Little Mary Sunshine 1959,N 19,49:3
Little Mary Sunshine 1959,N 29,II,1:1
Graham (Cadet)
Merry Wives of West Point, The 1932,Mr 20,II,7:7
Graham-Browne, W
Old Folks at Home 1934,Ja 14,IX,1:8
Retreat From Folly 1937,F 25,18:2
Graham-Dent, Nellie
Fair Circassian, The 1921,D 7,22:3
Just Because 1922,Mr 23,11:1
Wonderful Visit, The 1924,F 13,17:3
Graham-Lujan, James (Translator)
Blood Wedding 1949,F 7,16:2
Yerma 1952,F 8,18:4
Blood Wedding 1958,Ap 1,35:1
House of Bernarda Alba, The 1963,N 25,23:2
Graham Trio
Greenwich Village Follies 1928,Ap 10,32:2
Grahame, John F (Director)
Lady Remembers, The 1932,My 11,15:3
Moral Fabric 1932,N 22,25:3
Wrong Number 1934,Mr 14,23:6
Familiar Pattern 1943,S 3,15:6
Career 1943,O 29,22:6

Grahame, John F (Director)—Cont
Spring Production 1944,My 20,12:4
Partition 1948,O 29,31:2
Grahame, John F (Lyricist)
What's It to You? 1932,Mr 18,25:4
Grahame, John F (Playwright)
What's It to You? 1932,Mr 18,25:4
Grahame, John P (Playwright)
Rip Van Wrinkle 1967,D 23,28:1
Grahame, Kenneth (Original Author)
Toad of Toad Hall 1931,Ja 4,VIII,2:5
Grahame, Margot
Heart of a City 1942,F 13,24:6
Strings, My Lord, Are False, The 1942,My 20,24:2
Grahl, Arthur
Banjo Eyes 1941,D 26,20:2
On Your Toes 1954,O 12,24:4
Grahn, Mary
Airways, Inc 1929,F 21,30:5
Round Table, The 1930,F 28,20:5
Grainger, Gawn
Measure for Measure 1967,F 15,37:1
Hamlet 1967,F 17,44:1
Romeo and Juliet 1967,F 22,18:1
There's a Girl in My Soup 1967,O 19,58:1
Grainger, James
Lake, The 1933,D 27,24:2
Grainger, Mabel
Up and Up, The 1930,S 9,25:2
Black Tower 1932,Ja 12,29:2
Grainger, Percy
Vaudeville (Hippodrome) 1926,Mr 30,20:4
Grainger, Porter (Composer)
Hot Rhythm 1930,Ag 22,18:5
Brown Buddies 1930,O 8,29:1
Grainger, Porter (Lyricist)
Hot Rhythm 1930,Ag 22,18:5
Gramatica, Emma
Old Lady Shows Her Medals, The
1926,O 31,VIII,2:4
Camille 1928,Ja 29,VIII,4:1
Citta Morta, La 1935,S 22,X,7:7
Gramm, Donald
Fledermaus, Die 1954,My 20,38:5
Grammer, Sidney
Conversation Piece 1934,O 24,24:1
Gramovto, Doris
Republic, The 1970,Ap 28,49:1
Gran, Albert
Trimmed in Scarlet 1920,F 3,18:1
Trial of Joan of Arc, The 1921,Mr 28,8:2
Manhattan 1922,Ag 16,7:5
Comedian, The 1923,Mr 14,14:1
Tarnish 1923,O 2,10:1
Canary Dutch 1925,S 9,22:1
Granach, Alexander
Hoppla, Wir Leben! 1927,D 11,IX,4:1
Singing Jailbirds 1928,My 20,VIII,2:1
King John 1929,Je 23,VIII,2:1
Love in the Country 1930,S 28,VIII,4:4
From Morn to Midnight 1931,S 22,30:4
From Morn to Midnight 1931,S 26,25:5
Golem, The 1931,N 6,28:5
Bell for Adano, A 1944,N 10,24:6
Bell for Adano, A 1944,D 7,21:2
Granat, Frank (Miscellaneous)
Murderous Angels 1970,F 8,70:1
Granat, Frank (Producer)
Dylan 1964,Ja 20,18:1
Any Wednesday 1964,F 19,34:1
Ben Franklin in Paris 1964,O 28,52:1
Great Indoors, The 1966,F 2,23:1
Happily Never After 1966,Mr 11,37:1
Granby, Joseph
Claw, The 1921,O 18,20:1
We've Got to Have Money 1923,Ag 21,12:1
Hurricane 1923,D 26,13:4
Lally 1927,F 9,16:3
Menace 1927,Mr 15,28:2
He Understood Women 1928,Ag 16,25:1
Town's Woman, The 1929,Mr 12,26:2
Hawk Island 1929,S 17,34:7
Grand, Arthur (Lighting Director)
Mikado, The 1967,D 4,65:3
Grand, Bert (Composer)
Cinderella on Broadway 1920,Je 25,18:1
Grand, Murray (Composer)
Once Over Lightly 1955,Mr 16,39:1
New Faces of 1956 1956,Je 15,32:1
Chic 1959,My 19,28:2
Leonard Sillman's New Faces of 1968
1968,My 3,43:1
Grand, Murray (Lyricist)
Once Over Lightly 1955,Mr 16,39:1
New Faces of 1956 1956,Je 15,32:1
Leonard Sillman's New Faces of 1968
1968,My 3,43:1
Grand, Stanley
Puppets 1925,Mr 10,19:1
Love's Call 1925,S 11,20:1
Grandais
Cloches de Cornville, Les; Chimes of Normandy,
The 1926,D 14,24:4
Perichole, La 1926,D 29,24:4

Grandi, Lois
Decameron, The 1961,Ap 13,32:1
Grandi, Oliver
Henri Christophe 1945,Je 7,24:5
Small Hours, The 1951,F 16,22:1
Grandin, Elmer
Main Street 1921,O 6,21:1
Secrets 1922,D 26,11:1
Across the Street 1924,Mr 25,24:1
That Awful Mrs Eaton! 1924,S 30,27:1
Jack in the Pulpit 1925,Ja 7,33:1
Pearl of Great Price, The 1926,N 2,34:3
Uninvited Guest, The 1927,S 28,28:2
Wild Birds 1929,Je 23,VIII,2:3
Round-Up, The 1932,Mr 8,19:4
Grandison, Alexander
Love on the Dole 1936,F 25,23:3
Love on the Dole 1936,Mr 8,IX,1:1
Grandjean, Michel
Ice Capades 1954,S 16,37:1
Grandjean, Silvia
Ice Capades 1954,S 16,37:1
Grandsted, Greta
One More Genius 1936,Ag 11,24:6
Grandy, Fred
Proposition, The 1968,Ap 20,25:3
Granet, Bert
Airways, Inc 1929,F 21,30:5
Graney, Tom
High Button Shoes 1955,Mr 12,10:6
Grange, Doug
Noah 1954,O 11,32:2
Granger, Dorothy
Ah, Wilderness! 1954,Ag 21,20:4
Granger, Farley
Carefree Tree, The 1955,O 12,37:2
First Impressions 1959,Mr 20,28:1
First Impressions 1959,Mr 29,II,1:1
Warm Peninsula, The 1959,O 21,46:2
King and I, The 1960,My 12,40:1
King and I, The 1960,My 22,II,1:1
Brigadoon 1962,My 31,21:4
Seagull, The 1964,Ap 6,36:1
Crucible, The 1964,Ap 7,30:2
Granger, John
Othello 1945,My 23,25:4
Auntie Mame 1958,Ag 12,33:2
Cheri 1959,O 13,44:1
Hop, Signor! 1962,My 8,45:2
Cat and the Canary, The 1965,Ja 5,26:1
Granger, Maude
First Year, The 1920,O 21,11:2
First Year, The 1920,O 31,VI,1:1
Pigs 1924,Je 8,VII,1:8
Pigs 1924,S 2,22:5
Granger, Michael
Whisper in God's Ear, A 1962,O 12,27:2
Fiddler on the Roof 1964,S 23,56:2
Danton's Death 1965,O 22,46:1
Country Wife, The 1965,D 10,58:2
Caucasian Chalk Circle, The 1966,Mr 25,35:1
Alchemist, The 1966,O 14,48:1
East Wind, The 1967,F 10,30:1
Granger, Neville
Long and the Short and the Tall, The
1962,Mr 30,28:2
Granger, Red
Golden Fleecing 1959,O 16,24:5
Midgie Purvis 1961,F 2,25:3
Granger, William F
Honor of the Family, The 1926,D 27,21:1
Granichstaedten, Bruno (Composer)
Evelyne 1928,F 19,VIII,2:1
Granick, Harry (Playwright)
Witches' Sabbath 1962,Ap 20,22:2
Granier, Jeanne
Bois Sacre, Le 1924,Mr 23,VIII,1:3
Granite, Judith
Keyhole, The 1962,Ja 31,21:1
Lovers in the Metro, The 1962,Ja 31,21:1
World of Gunter Grass, The 1966,Ap 27,38:1
Criss-Crossing 1970,Ja 22,30:1
Granlund, Nils T
Vaudeville (Palace) 1932,Ap 18,19:5
Grannell, William
Silver Grey Toy Poodle 1969,My 15,41:2
Pets 1969,My 15,41:2
Grannis, Anita (Director)
Love in Our Time 1952,O 4,14:3
Grannis, Anita (Playwright)
Love in Our Time 1952,O 4,14:3
Granowsky, Alexander (Director)
Bourgeois Gentilhomme, Le 1929,Mr 24,X,2:3
Granstedt, Greta
Tomorrow's Harvest 1934,D 6,26:5
If a Body 1935,My 1,25:3
Thirsty Soil 1937,F 4,16:2
Grant, A Rockefeller
Early Morning 1970,N 26,57:1
Grant, Albert
Land Beyond the River, A 1957,Mr 29,15:7
Grant, Alberta
Seidman and Son 1962,O 16,32:2

Love and Kisses 1963,D 19,39:1
Grant, Alma
Lady of the Lamp, The 1920,Ag 18,6:4
Grant, Belle
Bad Habits of 1925 1925,F 9,17:1
Grant, Bernard
Trial of Dmitri Karamazov, The 1958,Ja 28,30:1
Shadow of Heroes 1961,D 6,59:1
Veronica 1965,N 19,31:1
Grant, Bernice
Earth Journey 1944,Ap 28,24:2
Grant, Bob
MacBird! 1967,Ap 16,II,3:6
Grant, Calvin
Three Love Affairs; Still Life 1958,Mr 11,33:1
Grant, Cameron
Song of Norway 1944,Ag 22,20:2
Grant, Carol
Patience 1967,O 13,32:1
Iolanthe 1967,O 18,40:1
Grant, Charles
Contributions; Shoes 1970,Mr 10,53:1
Grant, Cy
Antony and Cleopatra 1951,D 21,22:2
Grant, Diane
Chicago 70 1970,My 26,33:1
Grant, Douglas
Me Nobody Knows, The 1970,My 19,42:1
Grant, Elinor
Out of My House 1942,Ja 8,28:6
Grant, Elsie
Victoria Regina 1938,O 4,20:2
Grant, Ernest
Prince and the Pauper, The 1920,N 2,15:1
Grant, Frances
Betty, Be Good 1920,My 5,14:2
Tickle Me 1920,Ag 18,9:1
Cold in Sables 1931,D 24,20:7
Grant, Gordon (Mrs)
Passing of the Third Floor Back, The 1924,F 8,19:4
Grant, Grayce
Great White Hope, The 1967,D 14,58:1
Night Thoreau Spent in Jail, The 1970,N 2,66:1
Grant, Gretchen
O'Brien Girl, The 1921,O 4,10:2
Merry Merry 1925,S 25,24:3
Grant, Henry A
Half Moon Inn 1925,Mr 10,14:1
His Majesty the Queen 1926,Mr 9,8:1
Betty Behave 1927,Mr 9,28:4
Zuleika 1928,Mr 7,28:7
Grant, James Edward (Playwright)
Plan M 1942,F 21,15:2
Plan M 1942,Mr 1,VIII,1:1
Grant, Jeanne
Saint of Bleecker Street, The 1954,D 28,21:1
Grant, John
Good News 1927,Ag 14,VII,2:1
Good News 1927,S 7,35:4
Take a Chance 1932,N 28,11:2
Grant, Joyce
Rockefeller and the Red Indians 1968,O 25,37:1
Grant, Karen
Most Happy Fella, The 1966,My 12,55:1
Grant, Kirby, Inc (Producer)
30 Days Hath September 1938,O 1,10:5
Grant, Lackaye
We Americans 1926,O 13,20:4
Joseph 1930,F 13,25:3
Zombie 1932,F 11,17:2
Grant, Lawrence
Lady Cristilinda, The 1922,D 26,11:2
Grant, Lee
Detective Story 1949,Mr 24,34:2
Detective Story 1949,Ap 3,II,1:1
All You Need Is One Good Break 1950,F 10,20:3
Arms and the Man 1950,O 20,34:2
Lo and Behold! 1951,D 13,45:2
Wedding Breakfast 1954,N 22,29:2
Wedding Breakfast 1954,D 5,II,5:1
Hole in the Head, A 1957,Mr 1,15:1
Hole in the Head, A 1957,Mr 10,II,1:1
Captains and the Kings, The 1962,Ja 3,25:2
Maids, The 1963,N 15,29:1
Electra 1964,Ag 12,42:1
Grant, Leonard (Miscellaneous)
Big Time Buck White 1968,D 9,58:1
Grant, Lillian Ward
Chains of Dew 1922,Ap 28,20:2
Grant, Lyman
Salome 1922,My 23,12:4
Grant, Madge
Madame Lafayette 1960,Mr 4,21:1
Finis for Oscar Wilde 1964,F 15,15:1
Grant, Marian
Veneer 1929,N 13,24:5
Patriarch, The 1929,N 26,28:5
Nancy's Private Affair 1930,Ja 14,24:3
Grant, Marshall
Rain From Heaven 1934,D 25,28:4
Grant, Mary
Bonds of Interest, The 1958,My 7,43:1
You Never Can Tell 1958,Je 17,25:1

Grant, Mary—Cont
Under the Sycamore Tree 1960,Mr 8,37:2
Grant, Mary (Costume Designer)
Cat Screams, The 1942,Je 17,26:5
Mexican Hayride 1944,Ja 29,9:6
Seven Lively Arts 1944,D 17,II,3:1
Marinka 1945,Jl 19,19:2
Polonaise 1945,O 8,20:2
Woman Bites Dog 1946,Ap 18,21:1
Big Fish, Little Fish 1961,Mr 16,42:2
Grant, Maxwell
Shoestring Revue 1955,Mr 1,22:2
Grant, Maxwell (Playwright)
Ziegfeld Follies 1957,Mr 2,19:2
Vintage '60 1960,S 13,41:1
Grant, Micki
Fly Blackbird 1962,F 6,26:2
Tambourines to Glory 1963,N 4,47:1
Cradle Will Rock, The 1964,N 9,40:4
Leonard Bernstein's Theater Songs 1965,Je 29,27:2
Scaffold for Marionettes, A 1968,Mr 24,II,16:5
Gingham Dog, The 1968,O 13,II,18:6
Don't Bother Me, I Can't Cope 1970,O 8,60:3
Grant, Micki (Composer)
Don't Bother Me, I Can't Cope 1970,O 8,60:3
Moon on a Rainbow Shawl 1970,D 18,52:1
Grant, Micki (Lyricist)
Don't Bother Me, I Can't Cope 1970,O 8,60:3
Grant, Neil (Playwright)
Petticoat Influence 1930,D 16,34:6
Nelson Touch, The 1931,S 20,VIII,2:6
Women in Politics 1933,O 22,IX,2:3
Dusty Ermine 1935,S 25,19:6
Dusty Ermine 1936,Mr 7,11:6
Grant, Nelson
Little Poor Man, The 1925,Ag 6,14:1
Grant, Pauline (Choreographer)
Much Ado About Nothing 1959,S 18,25:2
Grant, Roddy
Family Portrait 1959,My 6,48:2
Grant, Sterling
Deep Harlem 1929,Ja 8,35:2
Messin' Around 1929,Ap 23,26:3
Change Your Luck 1930,Je 7,10:2
Grant, Sydney
Sharlee 1923,N 23,20:1
Flossie 1924,Je 4,25:2
Fabulous Invalid, The 1938,O 10,15:1
American Way, The 1939,Ja 23,9:2
Man Who Came to Dinner, The 1940,F 10,19:5
Doughgirls, The 1942,D 31,19:2
Man Who Had All the Luck, The 1944,N 24,18:5
And Be My Love 1945,F 22,30:4
Mr Strauss Goes to Boston 1945,S 7,20:2
Grant, William
Some Party 1922,Ap 17,22:1
Grant, William Coley
White Man 1936,O 19,22:4
Grantham, Wilfred (Playwright)
Mary Tudor 1935,D 13,30:6
Mary Tudor 1936,Ja 12,IX,1:5
Grantoff, Lili Christiane
No More Peace 1936,Je 12,19:4
Granval
Turcaret 1928,Mr 4,IX,4:5
Granval, Charles (Scenic Designer)
Roi Dagobert, Le 1926,N 14,VIII,2:1
Great Catherine, The 1927,Ap 3,VIII,4:7
Flambeaux de la Noce, Les 1927,Ap 17,VII,2:3
Granval, Jean-Pierre
Baptiste 1952,N 13,34:2
Fausses Confidences, Les 1952,N 13,34:2
Baptiste 1952,N 13,34:2
Proces, Le; Trial, The 1952,N 18,36:2
Amphitryon 1952,N 21,21:2
Occupe-Toi d'Amelie; Keep Your Eyes on Amelie
1952,N 25,35:2
Hamlet 1952,D 2,39:1
Christophe Colomb 1957,Ja 31,20:5
Misanthrope, Le 1957,F 8,19:1
Intermezzo 1957,F 15,20:4
Adieux, Les 1957,F 19,36:1
Chien du Jardinier, Le; Gardener's Dog, The
1957,F 19,36:1
Vie Parisienne, La 1964,Mr 11,34:2
Granval, Jeannette
Femmes Savantes, Les 1967,F 7,34:2
Granville, Bernard
Ziegfeld Follies 1920,Je 23,14:1
Fables 1922,F 7,12:2
Go-Go 1923,Mr 13,19:4
Castles in the Air 1926,S 7,19:2
Whistling in the Dark 1932,N 4,25:2
Granville, Charlotte
Great Way, The 1921,N 8,28:2
Shoot 1922,Je 8,14:2
Banco 1922,S 21,18:1
Romeo and Juliet 1922,D 28,20:1
March Hares 1923,Mr 13,19:5
Love Scandal, A 1923,N 7,14:1
Outward Bound 1924,Ja 8,26:1
Gentle Grafters 1926,O 28,23:1
Veils 1928,Mr 14,28:5
Command Performance, The 1928,O 4,27:1

Granville, Charlotte—Cont
Let Us Be Gay 1929,F 22,19:1
Dancing Partner 1930,Jl 27,VIII,2:3
Dancing Partner 1930,Ag 6,24:2
Roof, The 1931,O 31,22:4
Roof, The 1931,N 8,VIII,1:1
Berlin 1931,D 31,16:1
Here Today 1932,S 7,14:2
Here Today 1932,S 18,IX,1:1
Great Magoo, The 1932,D 3,20:7
Divine Moment, A 1934,Ja 8,21:8
Granville, Joseph
Higher and Higher 1940,Ap 5,24:3
Granville, Renay
Enemy of the People, An 1958,F 26,24:2
Granville, Sydney
Gondoliers, The 1934,S 4,23:1
Pirates of Penzance, The; Slave of Duty, The
   1934,S 7,24:3
Gondoliers, The 1934,S 9,IX,1:1
Iolanthe 1934,S 11,24:3
Trial by Jury 1934,S 14,24:3
Mikado, The; Town of Titipu, The 1934,S 18,18:1
Yeomen of the Guard, The 1934,S 21,28:3
Ruddigore 1934,S 25,25:2
Princess Ida; Castle Adamant 1934,S 28,26:3
Mikado, The 1936,Ag 21,13:2
Pirates of Penzance, The 1936,S 1,24:4
Trial by Jury 1936,S 1,24:4
Gondoliers, The 1936,S 8,23:1
Yeomen of the Guard, The 1936,S 15,37:2
Iolanthe 1936,S 22,30:3
Princess Ida 1936,O 13,32:2
Ruddigore 1936,O 23,26:4
Pirates of Penzance, The 1939,Ja 6,25:1
Mikado, The 1939,Ja 10,16:3
Iolanthe 1939,Ja 13,16:3
Gondoliers, The 1939,Ja 20,14:2
Yeomen of the Guard, The 1939,Ja 24,17:1
Granville, V L
Twelfth Night 1921,N 1,17:1
Merchant of Venice, The 1921,N 22,17:1
Cymbeline 1923,O 3,12:1
Coriolanus 1938,F 2,14:5
Granville-Barker, Harley (Miscellaneous)
Anatol 1931,Ja 17,23:3
Granville-Barker, Harley (Playwright)
Kingdom of God, The 1927,N 20,IX,2:7
Hundred Years Old, A 1929,O 2,28:2
Waste 1936,D 20,XI,3:3
Granville-Barker, Harley (Producer)
Voysey Inheritance, The 1934,Je 3,IX,2:5
Granville-Barker, Harley (Translator)
Hundred Years Old, A 1928,D 9,X,2:1
Lady From Alfaqueque, The; Consulesa, La
   1929,Ja 15,22:3
Women Have Their Way, The 1930,Ja 28,28:1
Take Two From One 1931,O 4,VIII,2:6
Granville-Barker, Helen (Playwright)
Kingdom of God, The 1927,N 20,IX,2:7
Hundred Years Old, A 1929,O 2,28:2
Granville-Barker, Helen (Translator)
Hundred Years Old, A 1928,D 9,X,2:1
Lady From Alfaqueque, The; Consulesa, La
   1929,Ja 15,22:3
Women Have Their Way, The 1930,Ja 28,28:1
Take Two From One 1931,O 4,VIII,2:6
Granz, Norman (Producer)
Evening With Yves Montand, An 1959,S 23,45:1
Evening With Yves Montand, An 1961,O 25,30:1
Granzow, Sarah
Night in Venice, A 1929,My 22,30:2
Grapewin, Charles
Bad Penny, A 1931,Ag 23,VIII,2:4
Grasby, Dorothy (Sgt)
Swing Sister Wac Swing 1944,Ja 4,20:4
Grasch, Charles
Delightful Season, A 1960,S 29,30:1
Grass, Guenther (Playwright)
Plebejer Proben Den Aufstand, Die 1966,Ja 18,32:1
Wicked Cooks, The 1967,Ja 24,42:1
Wicked Cooks, The 1967,F 5,II,1:1
Plebeians Rehearse the Uprising, The
   1968,S 8,II,11:1
Plebeians Rehearse the Uprising, The
   1970,Jl 23,26:1
Grassi, Joseph
Midgie Purvis 1961,F 2,25:3
Grassi, Paolo (Director)
Servant of Two Masters, The 1960,F 24,42:2
Grassle, Karen
Gingham Dog, The 1969,Ap 24,41:1
Grasso, Arthur (Producer)
Darwin's Theories 1960,O 19,53:2
Grasso, Carlo
Babes Don't Cry Anymore 1968,F 21,55:1
Grasso, Giovanni (Comm)
Malia 1921,S 10,12:3
'Il Tesoro D'Isacco; Treasure of Isaac, The
   1928,Ja 26,17:1
Grasson, Carlo
Dark of the Moon 1970,Ap 4,21:2
Grattan, Jack
Tarzan of the Apes 1921,S 8,14:3

Marie Antoinette 1921,N 23,16:1
Drifting 1922,Ja 3,20:3
Peter Pan 1924,N 7,16:2
Half-Naked Truth, The 1926,Je 8,23:1
Woman Disputed, A 1926,S 29,23:2
Sellout, The 1933,S 7,17:2
Grattan, Lawrence
Take My Advice 1927,N 2,24:3
Crucible 1933,S 5,22:4
Grattan, Lawrence (Playwright)
Gossipy Sex, The 1927,Ap 20,28:3
Gratz, Rudolph
Sing High, Sing Low 1931,N 13,26:4
Grau, Dorothy
Abie's Irish Rose 1922,My 24,22:4
Grau, Harold
Padre, The 1926,D 28,16:3
19th Hole, The 1927,O 12,30:3
Gentlemen of the Press 1928,Ag 28,27:2
Once in a Lifetime 1930,S 25,22:3
Mr Papavert 1932,Ja 23,18:6
Little Ol' Boy 1933,Ap 25,15:5
Strangers at Home 1934,S 15,20:5
Page Miss Glory 1934,N 28,24:2
High Tor 1937,Ja 11,15:2
Cue for Passion 1940,D 20,33:4
Mr and Mrs North 1941,Ja 13,11:2
Mr Big 1941,O 1,24:2
Clash by Night 1941,D 29,20:2
Doughgirls, The 1942,D 31,19:2
Kiss Them for Me 1945,MR 21,27:2
Woman Bites Dog 1946,Ap 18,21:2
Front Page, The 1946,S 5,22:4
Open House 1947,Je 4,33:4
Madwoman of Chaillot, The 1950,Je 14,41:2
Collector's Item 1952,F 9,11:2
Ponder Heart, The 1956,F 17,14:2
Graubart, Judy
Return of Second City in "20,000 Frozen
   Grenadiers," The 1966,Ap 22,36:1
Grauer, Ben
Blue Bird, The 1923,D 26,13:3
Processional 1925,Ja 13,17:1
Grauer, Ben (Playwright)
Mrs Warren's Profession 1950,O 26,39:2
Grautoff, Christiane
Kreatur, Die 1930,My 25,IX,1:8
Bravo! 1948,N 12,31:2
Graveley, George (Translator)
Miser, The 1963,My 10,39:1
Gravenor, Barbara
Twelfth Night 1970,Ja 1,18:1
Gravers, Steve
Outside the Door 1949,Mr 2,33:2
Scapegoat, The 1950,Ap 20,36:5
All the King's Men 1950,Jl 19,25:6
Hatful of Rain, A 1955,N 10,44:1
But, Seriously... 1969,F 28,29:1
Graves, Allison
Mandragola 1958,My 29,23:2
Graves, Arthur
Untitled-Passion Play 1926,Mr 30,20:2
Graves, Avery
Woman Brown, The 1939,D 9,18:5
Graves, Beatrice E
Joyous Season, The 1935,N 24,II,9:2
Graves, Cebra
Prunella; Love in a Garden 1926,Je 16,23:3
God Loves Us 1926,O 20,22:2
Tightwad, The 1927,Ap 18,18:2
Graves, Dorothy
Jubilee 1935,O 14,20:1
Graves, Ernest
Macbeth 1941,N 12,30:2
Russian People, The 1942,D 30,17:2
Men in Shadow 1943,Mr 11,16:2
Cyrano de Bergerac 1946,O 9,33:2
Cyrano de Bergerac 1947,Ja 17,27:2
Eastward in Eden 1947,N 19,33:2
As You Like It 1950,Ja 27,27:2
Much Ado About Nothing 1952,My 2,20:1
Tiger at the Gates 1955,O 4,40:1
Firstborn, The 1957,Ja 7,29:2
Prometheus Bound 1957,Ag 9,11:6
Julius Caesar 1957,O 24,39:1
Three Love Affairs; Phoenix Too Frequent, A
   1958,Mr 11,33:1
Three Love Affairs; Still Life 1958,Mr 11,33:1
Phoenix Too Frequent, A 1958,Mr 16,II,1:1
Julius Caesar 1959,Ag 4,30:1
Julius Caesar 1959,Ag 16,II,1:1
Dylan 1964,Ja 20,18:1
Macbeth 1967,Jl 31,21:1
Ceremony of Innocence, The 1968,Ja 2,33:1
Graves, George
Paolo and Francesca 1929,Ap 2,28:2
Riddle Me This! 1933,Mr 15,21:3
Tommy 1933,Ag 8,22:5
Graves, George L (Director)
House of Doom, The 1932,Ja 26,20:4
Graves, Gloria
Originale 1964,S 9,46:1

Graves, James
Song for a Certain Midnight 1959,S 17,49:1
Graves, Joan
Tom Paine 1969,Mr 30,71:2
Graves, Judith
Liliom 1956,F 18,12:5
Graves, Leonard
King and I, The 1951,Mr 30,26:2
King and I, The 1956,Ap 19,35:4
Graves, Michael
Triumph of Robert Emmet, The 1969,My 8,54:1
Graves, Nancy
Jack and the Beanstalk 1947,N 3,28:2
Indian Captive, The 1949,Ja 31,15:2
Graves, Peter
After The Ball 1954,Je 11,19:3
Captains and the Kings, The 1962,Ja 3,25:2
Graves, Phillip
Her First Roman 1968,O 21,53:3
Graves, Ralph
Thomas Paine 1930,Mr 21,30:7
Graves, Robert (Miscellaneous)
Richard II 1951,Ja 25,21:2
Graves, Rupert (Composer)
Henry IV, Part I 1939,Ja 31,17:2
Richard II 1940,Ap 2,31:2
Graves, Russell
Yeah-Man 1932,My 27,27:3
Graves, Taylor
Bride Retires, The 1925,My 18,12:3
Shelter 1926,Ja 26,18:2
Lorelei 1938,N 30,21:2
Temporary Island, A 1948,Mr 15,27:3
Makropoulos Secret, The 1957,D 4,52:4
Asmodee 1958,Mr 26,42:2
Gravet, Fernand
Pierre ou Jack? 1931,Ap 19,VIII,2:7
Harvey 1950,O 21,10:4
Harvey 1950,D 31,II,3:7
Beekman Place 1964,O 8,50:1
Graveure, Louis
Valliere, La 1933,Ap 16,IX,2:5
Grawowsky, Alexis (Director)
Journey of Benjamin III, The 1928,Je 24,VIII,1:4
Grawowsky, Alexis (Playwright)
Journey of Benjamin III, The 1928,Je 24,VIII,1:4
Gray, Adrienne
Sing Out, Sweet Land! 1944,D 28,24:2
Marinka 1945,Jl 19,19:2
Gray, Alexander
Ziegfeld Follies 1922,Je 6,18:2
Annie Dear 1924,N 5,25:3
Tell Me More 1925,Ap 14,27:3
Merry World, The 1926,Je 9,18:3
Naughty Riquette 1926,S 14,25:2
Vaudeville (Palace) 1930,N 17,21:2
John Henry 1939,D 17,IX,5:6
John Henry 1940,Ja 11,18:2
Blossom Time 1943,S 6,21:2
Pirates of Penzance, The 1961,S 7,41:1
Gray, Anna
Carnaval 1924,D 30,15:1
Gray, Anthony
Howdy Stranger 1937,Ja 15,17:5
Heads or Tails 1947,My 3,10:6
Gray, Arthur
Humble, The 1926,O 14,22:2
Witch, The 1926,N 19,22:5
Spellbound 1927,F 16,17:2
Gray, Barbara
Loose Ankles 1926,Ag 17,15:1
House of Fear, The 1929,O 8,34:2
Gray, Barbara Ann
Safari! 1955,My 12,32:6
Jack in the Box 1960,My 19,43:3
Gray, Bee Ho
Red Pepper 1922,My 30,8:3
Gray, C B
Philoktetes 1961,Ap 25,41:1
Gray, C B (Miscellaneous)
Women at the Tomb, The 1961,Ap 25,41:1
Philoktetes 1961,Ap 25,41:1
Red Eye of Love 1961,Je 13,28:1
Fortuna 1962,Ja 4,26:1
Laundry, The 1963,F 19,5:2
Gray, Caleb
Counsellor-at-Law 1942,N 25,17:2
Gray, Carlos N
Blood and Sand 1921,S 21,16:2
Gray, Cecilia
Unto Such Glory 1937,My 7,28:2
Gray, Charles
Hang Down Your Head and Die 1964,O 19,38:1
Gray, Charles (Miscellaneous)
Here Come the Clowns 1960,S 20,48:1
Coop, The 1966,Mr 2,48:1
Fire! 1969,Ja 29,26:1
Dozens, The 1969,Mr 14,51:1
Rothschilds, The 1970,O 20,40:1
Gray, Charles D
Richard II 1956,Jl 4,15:1
Richard II 1956,O 24,44:1
Romeo and Juliet 1956,O 25,41:1

Gray, Charles D—Cont
Macbeth 1956,O 30,42:2
Troilus and Cressida 1956,D 27,21:1
Troilus and Cressida 1957,Ja 6,II,1:1
Poor Bitos 1964,N 16,40:2
Right Honourable Gentleman, The 1965,O 20,50:2
Gray, Clifford (Choreographer)
Annie Dear 1924,N 5,25:3
Gray, Coleen
Leaf and Bough 1949,Ja 22,10:2
Gray, David
Country Wife, The 1936,D 2,34:1
Gray, David (Playwright)
Best People, The 1924,Ag 20,8:1
Best People, The 1933,Mr 16,21:5
Gray, David (Producer)
Detective Story 1950,Mr 27,18:2
Gray, David Jr (Miscellaneous)
Your Young Men 1935,Ag 8,13:2
Great Sebastians, The 1956,Ja 5,27:1
Who Was That Lady I Saw You With?
1958,Mr 4,33:2
Goodbye Charlie 1959,D 17,50:1
Shot in the Dark, A 1961,O 19,40:1
Tiger Tiger Burning Bright 1962,D 24,5:2
Gray, Diane
Elizabeth the Queen 1966,N 4,30:1
Gray, Dolle
Blue Peter, The 1925,Mr 25,25:3
Engaged! or Cheviot's Choice 1925,Je 19,24:2
Beaten Track, The 1926,F 9,23:2
Gray, Dolores
Seven Lively Arts 1944,D 8,26:6
Are You With It? 1945,N 12,17:3
Annie Get Your Gun 1947,Je 8,I,63:2
ANTA Album 1951,My 7,22:7
Two on the Aisle 1951,Jl 20,13:6
Two on the Aisle 1951,Jl 29,II,1:1
Carnival in Flanders 1953,S 9,38:2
Destry Rides Again 1959,Ap 24,24:1
Destry Rides Again 1959,My 3,II,1:1
Sherry! 1967,Mr 29,39:1
Sherry! 1967,Ap 9,II,1:1
Gray, Dulcie
Dear Ruth 1946,Mr 1,17:3
Where Angels Fear to Tread 1963,Je 8,14:6
Gray, Earl
Robert E Lee 1923,N 21,23:1
Gray, Earnest
Dracula Sabbat 1970,O 2,28:2
Gray, Eddie
Runnin' Wild 1923,O 30,17:3
Gray, Eden
Deburau 1920,D 24,14:3
Orange Blossoms 1922,S 20,18:1
We've Got to Have Money 1923,Ag 21,12:1
Firebrand, The 1924,O 16,33:1
Number 7 1926,S 9,21:3
What the Doctor Ordered 1927,Ag 19,20:2
Age of Innocence, The 1928,N 28,24:2
Second Mate, The 1930,Mr 25,34:5
Doctor X 1931,F 10,25:1
Dangerous Corner 1933,Jl 18,20:4
Gray, Edward (Tech Sgt)
Swing Sister Wac Swing 1944,Ja 4,20:4
Gray, Enid
Go West, Young Man 1923,N 13,25:2
Family Upstairs, The 1925,Ag 18,14:2
Strawberry Blonde, The 1927,F 8,20:3
Unsophisticates, The 1929,D 31,14:5
Gray, Ethel
Vaudeville (Palace) 1927,N 8,33:3
Gray, Frank (Composer)
Happy 1927,D 6,26:3
Gray, Franklin
Romeo and Juliet 1934,D 21,30:3
Simpleton of the Unexpected Isles, The
1935,F 19,27:5
Be So Kindly 1937,F 9,19:4
Many Mansions 1937,O 28,28:6
Gray, Gilda
Ziegfeld Follies 1922,Je 6,18:2
Vaudeville (Palace) 1929,Mr 25,33:2
Gray, Gillian
John Brown's Body 1953,F 16,17:2
Gray, Glorian
Merry-Go-Round 1932,Ap 23,11:2
Gray, Gynia
In Bed We Cry 1944,N 15,20:2
Gray, Helen
Seventh Heart, The 1927,My 3,24:4
Nine Fifteen Revue, The 1930,F 12,26:2
Second Little Show, The 1930,Ag 17,VIII,2:2
Second Little Show, The 1930,S 3,36:1
Roberta 1933,N 20,18:4
Continental Varieties 1935,D 27,15:3
Forbidden Melody 1936,N 3,33:1
Gray, Hitous
Theodora, the Queen 1934,F 1,15:3
Small Miracle 1934,S 27,24:3
Young Madame Conti 1937,Ap 1,18:4
Victoria Regina 1938,O 4,20:2
Gray, Jabez
As You Like It 1937,N 1,25:2

Shakespeare's Merchant 1939 1939,Ja 10,16:3
Three Sisters, The 1939,O 16,23:1
Male Animal, The 1941,Jl 9,24:6
Holiday 1941,Jl 23,15:2
Skipper Next to God 1948,Ja 5,14:5
Hope Is the Thing With Feathers 1948,Ap 12,24:2
Home Life of a Buffalo; Hope's the Thing
1948,My 12,34:6
Gone Tomorrow; Hope's the Thing
1948,My 12,34:6
Hope Is the Thing With Feathers; Hope's the
Thing 1948,My 12,34:6
Madame Is Served 1949,F 15,28:1
Gray, Joan
Story for Strangers, A 1948,S 22,39:2
Oh, Men! Oh, Women! 1953,D 18,37:2
Cheri 1959,O 13,44:1
Gray, John
Not So Long Ago 1920,My 5,14:1
New Morality, The 1921,Ja 31,10:1
Scarlet Man, The 1921,Ag 23,10:3
Captain Applejack 1921,D 31,14:2
Nerves 1924,S 22,22:2
Simon Called Peter 1924,N 11,20:2
Half-Caste, The 1926,Mr 30,20:4
Twinkle Twinkle 1926,N 17,22:2
Serena Blandish 1929,Ja 24,30:3
Sweet Adeline 1929,S 4,33:1
Plutocrat, The 1930,F 21,23:3
Lady Clara 1930,Ap 18,28:7
Insult 1930,S 16,30:2
Church Mouse, A 1931,O 13,26:4
Gray, John (Miscellaneous)
Ice Capades 1963,Ag 29,37:2
Gray, John (Playwright)
Two Worlds 1926,Je 27,VII,3:1
Bright Sun at Midnight 1957,N 29,32:4
Gray, Johnny
Ice Capades 1956,S 13,41:2
Ice Capades 1957,S 5,33:2
Gray, Katharine
Gypsy Baron, The 1944,Je 15,17:3
Gray, Katherine
Little Theatre Tournament; Edna 1929,My 11,22:2
Gray, Kitty
Bachelor Father, The 1928,F 29,28:2
Mima 1928,D 13,24:2
Gray, Lawrence
Laugh Parade, The 1931,N 3,31:2
Gray, Leslie
Porgy and Bess 1942,Ja 23,16:2
Porgy and Bess 1944,F 8,13:2
Gray, Linda
Accounting for Love 1954,D 2,37:6
Gray, Lloyd
Porgy 1927,O 11,26:2
Gray, Margery
Dark of the Moon 1958,F 27,22:2
Tovarich 1963,Mr 20,5:1
Gray, Marion
Come Live With Me 1967,Ja 27,29:1
Gray, Marvin M
Jim Dandy 1941,N 8,10:5
Gray, Mary
Oedipus Rex 1923,O 26,14:1
Via Crucis 1923,N 13,25:2
Hamlet 1923,N 20,23:3
Gray, Maurine
Hamlet 1954,Ap 24,15:2
Gray, Michael
Hot Pan 1928,F 16,14:1
Pure in Heart, The 1934,Mr 21,24:3
Cherry Orchard, The 1944,Ja 26,22:1
Gray, Minerva
Girl in the Spotlight, The 1920,Jl 13,9:3
Gray, Monita
Red Light Annie 1923,Ag 22,10:3
Gray, Nellie
Singing Jailbirds 1928,D 5,34:4
Gray, Nicholas
Miracle, The 1924,Ag 19,9:1
Gray, Nicholas Stuart (Playwright)
Stone Tower, The 1962,Ag 24,14:2
Gray, Norman
Knights of Song 1938,O 18,29:2
Gray, Oliver
Kean 1961,N 3,28:2
Gray, Peter
Hamlet 1936,O 9,30:2
Gray, Richard
Two on the Aisle 1951,Jl 20,13:6
Wilde Evening with Shaw, A 1963,Mr 7,8:2
Gray, Richard (Playwright)
Wilde Evening with Shaw, A 1963,Mr 7,8:2
Gray, Robert
Knock on Wood 1935,My 29,16:2
Lorelei 1938,N 30,21:2
More the Merrier, The 1941,S 16,19:3
In Time to Come 1941,D 29,20:2
Mr Adam 1949,My 26,34:6
Nighthawks 1967,D 30,14:2
Gray, Roger
Little Jessie James 1923,Ag 16,10:4

Gray, Roger—Cont
My Girl 1924,N 25,27:2
Nic-Nax of 1926 1926,Ag 5,19:1
Hit the Deck! 1927,Ap 26,32:1
Say When 1928,Je 27,29:3
Ned Wayburn's Gambols 1929,Ja 16,22:3
She Lived Next to the Firehouse 1931,F 11,23:1
Gray, Roger (Playwright)
Nic-Nax of 1926 1926,Ag 5,19:1
Ned Wayburn's Gambols 1929,Ja 16,22:3
On the Make 1932,My 24,23:2
Gray, Ruth
Sue, Dear 1922,Jl 11,16:2
Gray, Sam
Deadfall 1955,O 28,20:1
Sixth Finger in a Five Finger Glove 1956,O 9,31:4
Family Portrait 1959,My 6,48:2
Shadow of Heroes 1961,D 6,59:1
Gray, Simon (Playwright)
Dutch Uncle 1969,Mr 28,41:1
Idiot, The 1970,Jl 17,18:1
Idiot, The 1970,Jl 30,39:1
Gray, Spalding
Endecott and the Red Cross 1968,My 7,50:1
Gray, Stephen
Detective Story 1954,F 13,11:2
High Button Shoes 1955,Mr 12,10:6
Greatest Man Alive!, The 1957,My 9,37:2
Howie 1958,S 18,35:2
Man Who Never Died, The 1958,N 22,27:2
Gray, Stokely
My Fair Lady 1964,My 21,43:2
Wonderful Town 1967,My 18,50:1
My Fair Lady 1968,Je 14,42:1
Gray, Thad
Springboard, The 1927,O 13,23:1
Town Boy 1929,O 5,22:4
Gray, Thomas J (Lyricist)
Greenwich Village Follies 1920,Ag 31,7:3
Gray, Thomas J (Playwright)
Greenwich Village Follies 1920,Ag 31,7:3
Irving Berlin's Music Box Revue 1921,S 23,18:2
Gray, Timothy (Composer)
High Spirits 1964,Ap 8,34:1
Gray, Timothy (Director)
Cast of Characters 1959,Je 11,37:2
Gray, Timothy (Lyricist)
Cast of Characters 1959,Je 11,37:2
High Spirits 1964,Ap 8,34:1
Gray, Timothy (Miscellaneous)
High Spirits 1964,Ap 8,34:1
Gray, Timothy (Playwright)
Cast of Characters 1959,Je 11,37:2
High Spirits 1964,Ap 8,34:1
High Spirits 1964,N 4,46:4
Gray, Violet
Sonny 1921,Ag 17,12:2
Gray, Virginia
Achilles Had a Heel 1935,O 14,20:2
Gray, Wallace (Playwright)
Helen 1964,D 11,55:4
Gray, Willa
Out of a Blue Sky 1930,F 10,20:6
Gray, William
Taming of the Shrew, The 1935,O 1,27:3
Grayam, Penny
Annie Get Your Gun 1958,F 20,29:2
Graybill, Patrick
Sganarelle 1970,Ja 13,41:1
Songs From Milk Wood 1970,Ja 13,41:1
Grayce, Helen
Kongo 1926,Mr 31,20:5
Grayer, Jules
Squaring the Circle 1936,Ag 12,15:3
Grayson, Bette
Night Music 1940,F 23,18:2
Night Music 1951,Ap 9,29:6
Golden Boy 1952,Mr 13,24:3
Golden Boy 1952,Mr 23,II,1:1
Grayson, Frank
Cornered 1920,D 9,18:2
Grayson, George
Firebird 1932,N 22,25:2
Grayson, Helen (Translator)
Martine 1928,Ap 5,19:3
Grayson, Lucille
Career 1943,O 29,22:6
Grayson, Millicent
Morals 1925,D 1,22:2
Lady Screams, The 1927,My 3,24:2
Grayson, Milton
Trumpets of the Lord 1969,Ap 30,37:1
Grayson, Mitchell
Young Go First, The 1935,My 29,16:2
Chalk Dust 1936,Mr 5,24:5
Having Wonderful Time 1937,F 22,12:5
Grayson, Richard (Miscellaneous)
Apple Cart, The 1956,O 19,23:1
Grayson, Rick
Hello Charlie 1965,O 25,47:2
Grayson, Shirley
Man and Superman 1953,F 21,11:2
Ronde, La 1955,Je 28,24:2

Grayson, Shirley—Cont

Six Characters in Search of an Author
1955,D 12,38:1

Grayson, William
Fedora 1922,F 11,18:1

Graziani, Itzchak (Musical Director)
Grand Music Hall of Israel, The 1968,F 7,42:1

Graziano, John (Composer)
Sweeney Todd 1957,Ag 28,21:4

Graziano, Victor (Scenic Designer)
Errant Lady 1934,S 18,18:2

Grazzini, Anton Francesco (Playwright)
Strega, La 1939,Jl 23,IX,5:3

Greaham, Harry
Great Music 1924,O 6,24:1

Greaney, Mary
Loves of Cass McGuire, The 1966,O 7,36:1

Greanin, Leon
Chauve-Souris of 1943 1943,Ag 13,13:2

Greanin, Leon (Producer)
Chauve-Souris of 1943 1943,Ag 13,13:2

Great Arturo, The
Circus-Madison Square Garden 1939,Ap 6,23:5

Greaves, William
Garden of Time 1945,Mr 10,13:7
Henri Christophe 1945,Je 7,24:5
Finian's Rainbow 1947,Ja 11,23:2
Freight 1949,F 4,30:2

Greaves, William (Composer)
Garden of Time 1945,Mr 10,13:7

Greaza, Mary Young
Comedy of Good and Evil, A 1938,Ap 8,16:3

Greaza, Walter N
Love in the Tropics 1927,O 19,24:3
Remote Control 1929,S 11,24:5
Remote Control 1929,S 22,IX,1:1
Enemy Within 1931,O 6,35:3
In Times Square 1931,N 24,29:3
We the People 1933,Ja 23,9:5
Lambs Gambol 1933,Ap 24,10:1
Wednesday's Child 1934,Ja 17,23:2
Love on an Island 1934,Jl 24,20:5
Judgment Day 1934,S 13,26:4
Judgment Day 1934,S 23,X,1:1
But Not for Love 1934,N 27,26:2
Ceiling Zero 1935,Ap 11,26:2
Return to Folly 1935,Jl 23,24:3
Candida 1935,Ag 20,25:1
If This Be Treason 1935,S 24,28:2
Arrest That Woman 1936,N 19,20:4
All Editions 1936,D 23,17:2
Now You've Done It 1937,Mr 6,10:4
Sea Legs 1937,My 19,26:5
To Quito and Back 1937,S 21,29:1
To Quito and Back 1937,O 7,30:4
One Flight Down 1937,D 14,32:4
Sunup to Sundown 1938,F 2,14:3
Red Velvet Goat, The 1939,Ja 21,18:4
Mr Banks of Birmingham 1939,Ja 21,18:4
New Life, A 1943,S 16,26:6
Wallflower 1944,Ja 27,14:2
Visitor, The 1944,O 18,24:5
Overtons, The 1945,F 7,16:6
Temper the Wind 1946,D 28,10:2
Temper the Wind 1947,Ja 12,II,1:1
Roman Candle 1960,F 4,34:2

Grebanier, Jerry
Big White Fog 1940,O 23,26:2

Greben, Michael
Russian People, The 1942,D 30,17:2

Grebenetsky
Chauve-Souris 1929,Ja 23,20:2

Grechtman, S (Composer)
Matinee Wife 1936,Ap 25,21:3

Grecia, Neva
Land of Fame 1943,S 22,31:5

Greco, Frank
Follow the Girls 1944,Ap 10,15:2

Greco, Jose (Choreographer)
Ice Capades 1957,S 5,33:2

Greco, Jose and His Spanish Dancers
Vaudeville (Palace) 1952,Mr 12,31:2
Vaudeville (Palace) 1952,Mr 16,II,1:1

Greco, Juliette
Bonheur, Impair et Passe 1964,Ja 17,23:3

Greco, Vincent A
Babes Don't Cry Anymore 1968,F 21,55:1

Gredy, Jean-Pierre (Original Author)
Cactus Flower 1965,D 9,60:2
Forty Carats 1969,Ja 5,II,1:3

Gredy, Jean-Pierre (Playwright)
Four Pieces sur Jardin 1969,F 18,35:1

Greek, James (Lighting Director)
Macbeth 1969,D 23,25:1

Greek, James (Miscellaneous)
Fireworks; Report, The 1969,Je 12,51:1
Fireworks; Fireworks for a Hot Fourth
1969,Je 12,51:1
Fireworks; Football 1969,Je 12,51:1
And Puppy Dog Tails 1969,O 20,60:1

Greel, Muriel
Good Boy 1928,S 6,23:2

Greeley, Dana Watterson (Playwright)
Ink 1927,N 2,24:2

Greeley, Jack
Tom Sawyer - Ballad of the Mississippi
1947,D 27,11:3

Greely, Augusta (Director)
Penal Law 2010 1930,Ap 19,14:2

Greely, Augusta (Playwright)
Penal Law 2010 1930,Ap 19,14:2

Green, Adolph
On the Town 1944,D 29,11:4
Party With Betty Comden and Adolph Green, A
1958,D 24,2:7

Green, Adolph (Lyricist)
On the Town 1944,D 29,11:4
Million Dollar Baby 1945,D 22,17:2
Two on the Aisle 1951,Jl 20,13:6
Wonderful Town 1953,F 26,22:3
Wonderful Town 1953,Mr 8,II,1:1
Wonderful Town 1953,Ap 5,II,1:5
Peter Pan 1954,O 21,30:2
Bells Are Ringing 1956,N 29,43:4
Bells Are Ringing 1956,N 30,18:2
Wonderful Town 1958,Mr 6,32:4
Say Darling 1958,Ap 4,17:1
Say Darling 1958,Ap 13,II,1:1
On the Town 1959,Ja 16,36:1
On the Town 1959,Ja 25,II,1:1
On the Town 1959,F 14,15:1
Say Darling 1959,F 26,38:2
Do Re Mi 1960,D 27,23:2
Do Re Mi 1961,Ja 8,II,1:1
Subways Are for Sleeping 1961,D 28,22:1
Wonderful Town 1963,F 15,10:2
On the Town 1963,My 31,30:7
Fade Out--Fade In 1964,My 27,45:1
Leonard Bernstein's Theater Songs 1965,Je 29,27:2
Hallelujah, Baby! 1967,Ap 27,51:1
Hallelujah, Baby! 1967,My 7,II,1:1
Wonderful Town 1967,My 18,50:1

Green, Adolph (Playwright)
On the Town 1944,D 29,11:4
On the Town 1945,Ja 7,II,1:1
Million Dollar Baby 1945,D 22,17:2
Billion Dollar Baby 1945,D 30,II,1:1
Two on the Aisle 1951,Jl 20,13:6
Two on the Aisle 1951,Jl 29,II,1:1
Bells Are Ringing 1956,N 29,43:4
Bells Are Ringing 1956,N 30,18:2
On the Town 1959,Ja 16,36:1
On the Town 1959,Ja 25,II,1:1
On the Town 1959,F 14,15:1
Subways Are for Sleeping 1961,D 28,22:1
On the Town 1963,My 31,30:7
Fade Out--Fade In 1964,My 27,45:1
Applause 1970,Mr 31,35:1
Applause 1970,Ap 5,II,1:1

Green, Alan
Angel in the Wings 1947,D 12,36:4

Green, Alan (Miscellaneous)
Beggar's Opera, The 1957,Mr 14,35:1
Brigadoon 1957,Mr 28,37:1
Merry Widow, The 1957,Ap 11,36:6
South Pacific 1957,Ap 25,35:1
Pajama Game, The 1957,My 16,27:1
Carousel 1957,S 12,38:2

Green, Alice
Changeling, The 1956,My 4,20:3

Green, Alice (Choreographer)
Twelfth Night 1958,Ag 7,21:4

Green, Aline
Present Arms 1928,Ap 27,16:2

Green, Almeina
Big White Fog 1940,O 23,26:2

Green, Bambi Lee
Me, Candido! 1956,O 16,36:2

Green, Belle
Henry's Harem 1926,S 14,25:2

Green, Bernard (Composer)
Who Was That Lady I Saw You With?
1958,Mr 4,33:2

Green, Bigelow (Miscellaneous)
Who'll Save the Plowboy? 1962,Ja 10,24:2

Green, Billie
Gay Divorce 1932,N 30,23:4

Green, Bud (Composer)
Shady Lady 1933,Jl 6,26:3

Green, Bud (Lyricist)
Shady Lady 1933,Jl 6,26:3

Green, Carolyn (Playwright)
Janus 1955,N 25,37:2
Janus 1956,Je 12,39:6
Janus 1957,Ap 25,34:2

Green, Chuck
Tap Happening 1969,Je 20,36:1
Hoofers, The 1969,Jl 30,23:4

Green, Cora
Dixie to Broadway 1924,O 30,22:1
Vaudeville (Palace) 1927,D 13,33:5
Policy Kings 1938,D 31,6:2

Green, David
It's A Gift 1945,Mr 13,18:7
Life and Times of J Walter Smintheus, The
1970,D 10,59:1

Green, Del
How to Succeed in Business Without Really Trying
1966,Ap 21,45:1
Illya Darling 1967,Ap 12,37:1

Green, Denis
Hamlet 1936,N 11,54:2
Murder in the Cathedral 1938,F 17,16:2
Kiss Me, Kate 1948,D 31,10:3

Green, Diana (Miscellaneous)
Miss Lonelyhearts 1957,O 4,26:2

Green, Diana (Producer)
Date With April, A 1953,Ap 16,36:2
Stockade 1954,F 5,14:2
Mighty Man Is He, A 1960,Ja 7,25:2

Green, Doe Doe
Liza 1922,N 28,24:1
Appearances 1925,O 15,27:3
If 1927,O 26,26:2
Appearances 1929,Ap 2,28:1
Miss Gulliver Travels 1931,N 26,36:4
Horse Play 1937,Ag 28,8:3
Big Blow 1938,O 3,11:2
I Know What I Like 1939,N 25,13:5

Green, Dorothy
King Lear 1927,Mr 13,VII,1:4
Jealous Wife, The 1930,N 16,VIII,4:1
Antony and Cleopatra 1930,D 14,IX,3:1
Julius Caesar 1932,F 28,VIII,2:4

Green, Dylan
Tragical Historie of Doctor Faustus, The
1964,O 6,34:2
Veronica 1965,N 19,31:1
Bugs 1965,N 19,31:1
Scaffold for Marionettes, A 1968,Mr 24,II,16:5

Green, E Mawby (Playwright)
House in Paris, The 1944,Mr 21,17:1

Green, Eddie
Hot Chocolates 1929,Je 21,17:4
Blackberries of 1932 1932,Ap 5,27:5
Woman's a Fool-To Be Clever, A 1938,O 19,18:6
Hot Mikado, The 1939,Mr 24,26:2

Green, Eddie (Original Author)
Blackberries of 1932 1932,Ap 5,27:5

Green, Ellen
Watched Pot, The 1947,O 29,31:4

Green, Ethel (Scenic Designer)
Awake and Sing! 1970,My 28,35:1

Green, Forrest
Silk Stockings 1955,F 25,17:3

Green, Frank
Hotel Mouse, The 1922,Mr 14,11:3
Topics of 1923 1923,N 21,23:2
Pearl of Great Price, The 1926,N 2,34:3
Stag at Bay, The 1935,Jl 30,17:1
St Louis Woman 1946,Ap 1,22:2
West Side Story 1957,S 27,14:4

Green, Frank (Playwright)
Nass Oder Trocken? 1929,Jl 7,VIII,2:1

Green, Gary
Polonaise 1945,O 8,20:2

Green, Gerald (Original Author)
Something More! 1964,N 11,36:1

Green, Gilbert
First American Dictator 1939,Mr 15,18:2
Hall of Healing 1952,My 8,35:6
World of Sholom Aleichem, The 1953,S 12,13:2
Tevya and His Daughters 1957,S 17,38:2
Tevya and His Daughters 1957,S 29,II,1:1
Murderous Angels 1970,F 8,70:1

Green, H F
New Girl in Town 1957,My 15,40:1
Fiorello! 1959,N 24,45:3
Wildcat 1960,D 17,20:2
Nowhere to Go But Up 1962,N 12,36:2

Green, Hal
Rat Race, The 1949,D 23,16:2

Green, Harry
Welcome Stranger 1921,O 21,18:2
Fair Circassian, The 1921,D 7,22:3
Rosa Machree 1922,Ja 10,15:2
Clubs Are Trumps 1924,O 15,27:1
Hamlet 1925,N 10,23:1
Great Adventure, The 1926,D 23,23:1
Possibilities 1927,F 19,13:3
Music Master, The 1927,S 7,34:4
Music Master, The 1927,S 25,VIII,2:1
If 1927,O 26,26:2
Diversion 1928,Ja 12,25:1
K Guy, The 1928,O 16,28:4
Life Line, The 1930,D 29,19:3
Dance of Death, The 1932,Ja 11,29:5
Great Magoo, The 1932,D 3,20:7
Red Planet 1932,D 19,19:2
False Dreams, Farewell 1934,Ja 16,18:3
Piper Paid 1934,D 26,19:1
Distant Shore, The 1935,F 22,26:2
All for All 1943,S 30,25:2
Day Will Come, The 1944,S 8,17:2

Green, Harry (Director)
All for All 1943,S 30,25:2

Green, Harry (Producer)
Day Will Come, The 1944,S 8,17:2

Green, Herman
Swingin' the Dream 1939,N 30,24:2
Green, Howard
Romeo and Juliet 1962,Ap 3,42:1
Ceremony of Innocence, The 1968,Ja 2,33:1
Wars of the Roses, The (Part II) 1970,Jl 3,15:1
Green, Howard J (Playwright)
Beverly Hills 1940,N 8,24:2
Green, Hugh
Captain Brassbound's Conversion 1950,D 28,21:1
Green, Hughie
Golden Wings 1941,N 25,33:3
Golden Wings 1941,D 9,46:6
Green, Isaac Jr (Playwright)
Louisiana Lady 1947,Je 3,35:2
Green, Jackie
You'll See Stars 1943,Ja 1,26:6
Green, Jacquelyn
Doctor X 1930,Jl 31,12:4
Ringside Seat 1938,N 23,24:5
Green, James
Ballyhoo 1927,Ja 5,18:1
Swing It 1937,Jl 23,17:2
Green, Jane
Century Revue and the Midnight Rounders, The
1920,Jl 13,9:1
Nifties of 1923 1923,S 26,10:1
Green, Janet (Playwright)
Murder Mistaken 1952,D 7,II,7:1
Gently Does It 1953,O 29,43:4
Green, Jess
Show Boat 1966,Jl 20,48:1
Sacco-Vanzetti 1969,F 9,78:1
South Pacific 1969,Jl 7,27:1
Green, John
Midsummer Night's Dream, A 1968,D 9,59:1
Green, John W
Vaudeville (Palace) 1931,Jl 20,20:3
Green, John W (Composer)
Here Goes the Bride 1931,N 4,31:2
Green, Johnny
Actors Fund Fete 1942,F 23,24:5
Green, Johnny (Composer)
Beat the Band 1942,O 15,26:1
Green, Johnny (Miscellaneous)
Two Weeks With Pay 1940,Je 25,28:3
Green, Julien (Playwright)
South 1955,My 2,17:4
Green, Keith (Miscellaneous)
Hamlet 1969,Je 11,37:1
Alchemist, The 1969,Je 12,51:1
Measure for Measure 1969,Je 13,41:3
Green, Kenneth (Playwright)
Behind the Wall 1960,N 1,47:1
Green, Laurence
By the Way 1925,D 29,20:3
Green, Lillian
Symphony 1935,Ap 27,20:3
Dance Night 1938,O 15,20:5
Green, Marion
Wildcat, The 1921,N 28,16:2
Rose of Stamboul, The 1922,Mr 8,11:2
Greenwich Village Follies 1923,S 21,4:6
Annie Dear 1924,N 5,25:3
H M S Pinafore 1926,Ap 7,26:3
Du Barry 1932,N 23,15:2
Mahogany Hall 1934,Ja 18,18:5
Love Kills 1934,My 2,25:3
I'd Rather Be Right 1937,N 3,28:2
Firebird of Florence 1945,Mr 23,13:4
Green, Martyn
Gondoliers, The 1934,S 4,23:1
Cox and Box 1934,S 7,24:3
Pirates of Penzance, The; Slave of Duty, The
1934,S 7,24:3
Gondoliers, The 1934,S 9,IX,1:1
Iolanthe 1934,S 11,24:3
H M S Pinafore 1934,S 14,24:3
Mikado, The; Town of Titipu, The 1934,S 18,18:1
Yeomen of the Guard, The 1934,S 21,28:3
Ruddigore 1934,S 25,25:2
Princess Ida; Castle Adamant 1934,S 28,26:3
Patience 1934,O 12,32:2
Mikado, The 1936,Ag 21,13:2
Pirates of Penzance, The 1936,S 1,24:4
Gondoliers, The 1936,S 8,23:1
Yeomen of the Guard, The 1936,S 15,37:2
Iolanthe 1936,S 22,30:3
H M S Pinafore 1936,S 29,34:2
Patience 1936,O 6,28:6
Princess Ida 1936,O 13,32:2
Ruddigore 1936,O 23,26:4
Pirates of Penzance, The 1939,Ja 6,25:1
Mikado, The 1939,Ja 10,16:3
Iolanthe 1939,Ja 13,16:3
H. M. S. Pinafore 1939,Ja 17,27:5
Gondoliers, The 1939,Ja 20,14:2
Yeomen of the Guard, The 1939,Ja 24,17:1
Patience 1939,Ja 27,16:3

Lights Up 1940,F 18,IX,2:5
Mikado, The 1947,D 30,18:2
Pirates of Penzance, The 1948,Ja 6,27:2
Pirates of Penzance, The 1948,Ja 11,II,1:1
Iolanthe 1948,Ja 13,29:3
H M S Pinafore 1948,Ja 20,26:2
Gondoliers, The 1948,Ja 27,31:2
Yeomen of the Guard, The 1948,F 3,30:2
Patience 1948,F 10,27:2
Mikado, The 1951,Ja 30,21:2
H M S Pinafore 1951,F 6,24:2
Gondoliers, The 1951,F 13,27:2
Iolanthe 1951,F 16,22:1
Pirates of Penzance, The 1951,F 20,21:2
Mikado, The 1952,O 21,35:2
Pirates of Penzance, The 1952,O 28,36:4
Trial by Jury 1952,N 4,32:2
H M S Pinafore 1952,N 4,32:2
Iolanthe 1952,N 11,26:3
Shangri-La 1956,Je 14,40:1
Child of Fortune 1956,N 14,41:1
Virtuous Island, The 1957,Ap 10,39:1
Apollo of Bellac 1957,Ap 10,39:1
Drums Under the Windows 1960,O 14,26:1
Red Roses for Me 1961,N 28,41:1
Living Room, The 1962,N 22,43:5
Carricknabauna 1967,Mr 31,30:1
Black Comedy 1967,O 19,58:1
Canterbury Tales; Merchant's Tale, The
1969,F 4,34:1
Canterbury Tales; Pilgrims, The 1969,F 4,34:1
Charley's Aunt 1970,Jl 6,38:1
Green, Martyn (Miscellaneous)
Mikado, The 1952,O 21,35:2
Pirates of Penzance, The 1952,O 28,36:4
H M S Pinafore 1952,N 4,32:2
Trial by Jury 1952,N 4,32:2
H M S Pinafore 1952,N 4,32:2
Iolanthe 1952,N 11,26:3
Green, Mary
Bare Facts 1927,Je 30,35:1
Green, Mawby (Playwright)
Pajama Tops 1963,Je 1,15:1
Green, Melody
Visit, The 1967,S 13,41:1
Green, Michael
Fools Are Passing Through 1958,Ap 3,24:2
Green, Millicent
Intruder, The 1928,Jl 26,25:4
Machinal 1928,S 8,10:3
Machinal 1928,S 16,IX,1:1
Street Scene 1929,Ja 11,20:4
Left Bank, The 1931,O 6,35:3
Peace on Earth 1933,N 30,39:2
Stevedore 1934,Ap 19,33:2
Black Pit 1935,Mr 21,26:6
Mother, The 1935,N 20,26:3
Bitter Stream 1936,Mr 31,16:6
Tomorrow's Monday 1936,Jl 16,15:6
Hitch Your Wagon! 1937,Ap 9,18:2
If You Get It, Do You Want It? 1938,D 1,28:2
Green, Miriam
Bonds of Interest, The 1951,D 1,7:2
Yerma 1952,F 8,18:4
Cradle Song 1955,D 2,32:2
Courageous One, The 1958,Ja 21,33:6
Green, Mitzi
Murder With Pen and Ink 1935,Jl 30,17:2
Service for Two 1935,Ag 20,25:1
Babes in Arms 1937,Ap 15,18:4
Three After Three 1939,N 25,13:5
Walk With Music 1940,Je 5,33:2
Let Freedom Sing 1942,O 6,18:2
Million Dollar Baby 1945,D 22,17:2
Billion Dollar Baby 1945,D 30,II,1:1
Liberace's Variety Bill 1957,Ap 22,29:5
Green, Morris (Director)
Fine and Dandy 1930,S 24,26:1
Tell Her the Truth 1932,O 29,18:2
Du Barry 1932,N 23,15:2
Green, Morris (Miscellaneous)
Fountain, The 1925,D 11,26:1
Du Barry 1932,N 23,15:2
Green, Morris (Producer)
Love for Love 1925,S 15,29:3
Squall, The 1926,N 12,20:1
That French Lady 1927,Mr 16,29:3
Love Is Like That 1927,Ap 19,24:1
People Don't Do Such Things 1927,N 24,28:3
Rain or Shine 1928,F 10,26:3
Remote Control 1929,S 11,24:5
Boundry Line, The 1930,F 6,21:1
Fine and Dandy 1930,S 24,26:1
Pagan Lady 1930,O 21,34:2
Rock Me, Julie 1931,F 4,21:1
Gang's All Here, The 1931,F 19,21:3
Love and Babies 1933,Ag 23,21:4
Curtain Rises, The 1933,O 20,15:2
Love in My Fashion 1937,D 4,21:4
Green, Mort (Playwright)
Two's Company 1952,D 16,43:5
Green, Nancy W (Producer)
Jackhammer, The 1962,F 6,26:2

Green, Natalye
Trial by Jury 1949,O 18,34:2
Green, Nigel
Mr Pickwick 1952,S 18,36:3
Mr Pickwick 1952,S 28,II,1:1
Green, Norma
Two on an Island 1940,Ja 23,17:2
Medicine Show 1940,Ap 13,20:6
No for an Answer 1941,Ja 6,10:6
Green, Norman
Faun 1935,N 25,23:5
Green, Paul (Composer)
Tread the Green Grass 1950,Ap 21,19:4
Green, Paul (Director)
Common Glory, The 1947,Jl 19,11:2
Green, Paul (Lyricist)
Whores, Wars & Tin Pan Alley 1969,Je 17,37:1
Green, Paul (Miscellaneous)
Peer Gynt 1951,F 4,II,1:1
Green, Paul (Playwright)
In Abraham's Bosom 1926,D 31,10:2
In Abraham's Bosom 1927,F 20,VII,1:1
Field God, The 1927,Ap 22,18:2
Field God, The 1927,My 1,VIII,1:1
Little Theatre Tournament; Man Who Died at
Twelve O'Clock, The 1929,My 11,22:2
House of Connelly, The 1931,S 29,22:4
House of Connelly, The 1931,O 4,VIII,1:1
Tread the Green Grass 1932,Jl 24,IX,1:3
Potter's Field 1934,Ap 22,IX,1:1
Roll Sweet Chariot 1934,O 3,24:3
Roll Sweet Chariot 1934,O 14,X,1:1
Shroud My Body Down 1934,D 9,II,1:6
Enchanted Maze, The 1935,D 14,10:4
Enchanted Maze, The 1935,D 15,XI,5:4
Hymn to the Rising Sun 1936,Ja 13,14:4
Unto Such Glory 1936,Ja 13,14:4
Johnny Johnson 1936,N 19,XII,1:1
Johnny Johnson 1936,N 20,26:3
Hymn to the Rising Sun 1937,My 7,28:2
Unto Such Glory 1937,My 7,28:2
Lost Colony, The 1937,Jl 11,X,2:1
Highland Call, The 1939,N 21,19:1
Native Son 1941,Mr 25,26:5
Native Son 1941,Ap 6,IX,1:1
Johnny Johnson 1941,My 3,20:2
Native Son 1942,O 24,10:6
Native Son 1942,N 1,VIII,1:1
Common Glory, The 1947,Jl 19,11:2
Common Glory, The 1947,Jl 27,II,1:1
Tread the Green Grass 1950,Ap 21,19:4
Faith of Our Fathers 1950,Ag 6,72:2
Faith of Our Fathers 1950,Ag 13,II,1:1
Peer Gynt 1951,Ja 29,15:2
Salvation on a String; No Count Boy, The
1954,Jl 7,23:1
Salvation on a String; Supper for the Dead
1954,Jl 7,23:1
Salvation on a String; Chair Endowed 1954,Jl 7,23:1
Wilderness Road 1955,Je 30,20:4
Johnny Johnson 1956,O 22,24:1
Founders, The 1957,My 14,39:1
Confederacy, The 1958,Jl 3,20:1
Confederacy, The 1958,Jl 13,II,1:1
Cross and the Sword, The 1965,Je 28,32:6
Green, Phil (Producer)
First Legion, The 1934,O 2,18:2
Green, Ragna Wetter
League of Youth 1928,Mr 17,9:1
Green, Reginald
Love for Love 1967,O 21,17:1
Green, Robert
Empress of Destiny 1938,Mr 10,16:2
Green, Robert (Lighting Director)
Notes From the Underground 1960,Ja 20,26:1
My Wife and I 1966,O 11,53:2
Green, Robert (Scenic Designer)
Once in a Lifetime 1962,O 30,30:1
My Wife and I 1966,O 11,53:2
Green, Roland
It's A Gift 1945,Mr 13,18:7
Green, Rosie
Whirl of New York, The 1921,Je 14,18:1
Green, Solomon Earl
House of Flowers 1954,D 31,11:2
Green, Sylvan (Composer)
Provincetown Follies, The 1935,N 4,24:3
Green, Teddy
Pickwick 1963,Jl 5,13:2
Baker Street 1965,F 17,36:1
Darling of the Day 1968,Ja 29,26:2
Kiss Me, Kate 1970,D 26,10:4
Green, Tessie
Trial of Dr Beck, The 1937,Ag 10,22:2

Green, Tim
Latent Heterosexual, The 1968,Mr 22,52:1
Macbeth 1968,N 30,49:3
Green, Tom
Katja 1926,O 19,27:3
Green, W Jr (Composer)
It's the Valet 1933,D 15,25:4
Green, W Jr (Lyricist)
It's the Valet 1933,D 15,25:4
Green, Walter
Woman of Destiny, A 1936,Mr 3,25:2
Green, William
Chiffon Girl, The 1924,F 20,23:2
Fortuno 1925,D 23,22:1
Second Mate, The 1930,Mr 25,34:5
Sisters of the Chorus 1930,My 18,VIII,3:1
Sisters of the Chorus 1930,O 21,34:3
Two Seconds 1931,O 10,20:6
Cold in Sables 1931,D 24,20:7
Green (Producer)
Rock Me, Julie 1931,Ja 4,VIII,2:3
Green and Blyler
Century Revue and the Midnight Rounders, The
1920,Jl 13,9:1
Century Review, The 1920,Jl 22,9:5
Greenbank, Harry (Lyricist)
Geisha, The 1931,O 6,35:4
Greenbaum, Fritz (Playwright)
Sari 1930,Ja 29,27:1
Greenberg, Edward (Director)
Billy Budd 1959,F 28,13:3
Hit the Deck 1960,Je 24,32:1
King and I, The 1964,Jl 7,26:1
Merry Widow, The 1964,Ag 18,24:2
Kismet 1965,Je 23,45:1
Carousel 1965,Ag 11,39:1
Greenberg, Edward (Lighting Director)
Romeo and Jeanette 1969,D 16,53:1
Me and Juliet 1970,My 15,42:1
Greenberg, Edwin (Playwright)
Pilgrim's Progress 1962,Mr 21,36:2
Greenberg, George
Tale of the Wolf, The 1925,O 8,31:2
Antonia 1925,O 21,20:1
Blessed Event 1932,F 13,23:2
Greenberg, George (Director)
American Tragedy, An 1931,F 21,15:5
Greenberg, George (Miscellaneous)
Child of Fortune 1956,N 14,41:1
Greenberg, Gerald
Hit the Road 1941,Ap 4,18:3
Greenberg, Isaac
Chair, The 1930,O 4,15:4
Greenberg, Jacob
Tenth Commandment, The 1926,N 18,27:1
Greenberg, Joseph
Dybbuk, The 1924,Ja 29,17:7
Othello 1929,F 4,21:2
Major Noah 1929,F 23,17:2
Jew Suss 1929,O 19,22:3
Angels on Earth 1929,D 11,34:7
Roaming Stars 1930,Ja 25,12:2
Chains 1930,F 23,29:2
Armored Train No 1469 1931,N 28,20:3
Greenberg, Jules
Rivalry, The 1959,F 9,24:2
Greenberg, Lloyd (Miscellaneous)
Wicked Cooks, The 1967,Ja 24,42:1
Greenberg, Noah (Miscellaneous)
Shadow of My Enemy, A 1957,D 12,35:4
Greenberg, Noah (Musical Director)
Play of Daniel, The 1958,Ja 3,15:3
Play of Daniel, The 1958,Ja 26,II,1:1
Play of Daniel, The 1959,Ja 6,30:2
Play of Daniel, The 1960,Jl 13,30:6
Play of Daniel, The 1960,D 27,23:6
Play of Daniel, The 1961,D 28,22:6
Play of Herod, The 1963,D 10,55:2
Play of Herod, The 1965,D 29,24:2
Play of Herod, The 1966,Ja 2,64:4
Greenbie, Barrie (Scenic Designer)
Lysistrata 1959,My 20,40:2
Greenburg, Dan (Miscellaneous)
Oh! Calcutta! 1969,Je 18,33:1
Greenburg, Dan (Original Author)
How to Be a Jewish Mother 1967,D 29,18:1
Greenburg, Dan (Playwright)
Arf 1969,My 28,36:1
Great Airplane Snatch, The 1969,My 28,36:1
Greendale, Alexander (Playwright)
Walk Into My Parlor 1941,N 20,38:2
Greene, Alexis
Oedipus 1970,F 23,30:1
Greene, Angela
Early to Bed 1943,Je 18,16:2
Greene, Belle
Mongolia 1927,D 27,24:5
Greene, Bert (Playwright)
Trial, The 1955,Je 15,35:2
Spring's Awakening 1955,O 10,30:2
Summer of Daisy Miller, The 1963,My 28,33:1
Greene, Bert (Scenic Designer)
Flies, The 1954,S 10,18:2

Trial, The 1955,Je 15,35:2
Spring's Awakening 1955,O 10,30:2
Greene, Billy B
Bye Bye, Barbara 1924,Ag 26,6:3
Greene, Billy M
Furnished Rooms 1934,My 30,14:6
Provincetown Follies, The 1935,N 4,24:3
Girl From Wyoming, The 1938,O 31,12:1
O'Daniel 1947,F 25,32:2
Me, The Sleeper 1949,My 16,18:6
Shrike, The 1952,Ja 16,20:2
Shrike, The 1953,N 26,51:2
Time of Your Life, The 1955,Ja 20,34:1
Age and Grace 1956,F 21,38:2
Greene, Brad (Composer)
Right This Way 1938,Ja 6,22:3
Greene, Charles Jr
Kongi's Harvest 1968,Ap 15,49:1
Greene, Charles N
Letter of the Law, The; Robe Rouge, La
1920,F 24,11:1
Blood and Sand 1921,S 21,16:2
Four Flusher, The 1925,Ap 14,27:4
Greene, Danny
Life and Death of an American 1939,My 20,11:2
Greene, David
Caesar and Cleopatra 1951,D 20,43:2
Antony and Cleopatra 1951,D 21,22:2
Greene, Dixie Jan
Faith of Our Fathers 1950,Ag 6,72:2
Greene, Dorothy
Jerry for Short 1929,Ag 13,23:4
Greene, Frances Nemo (Playwright)
Last Enemy, The 1934,Jl 13,14:4
Greene, Frank
Princess Virtue 1921,My 5,20:2
Dancing Girl, The 1923,Ja 25,16:2
Rose Marie 1924,S 3,12:2
Cherry Blossoms 1927,Mr 29,22:3
Lovely Lady 1927,D 30,22:1
Death Takes a Holiday 1929,D 27,26:4
Death Takes a Holiday 1931,F 17,29:1
All the King's Horses 1934,Ja 31,21:3
Father Malachy's Miracle 1937,N 18,26:4
Greene, Frederick S (Colonel)
County Chairman, The 1936,My 26,26:5
Greene, Graham (Original Author)
Brighton Rock 1943,Ap 18,II,1:1
Power and the Glory, The 1956,Ap 6,14:3
Power and the Glory, The 1956,My 13,II,3:1
Power and the Glory, The 1958,D 12,2:7
Greene, Graham (Playwright)
Living Room, The 1953,Ap 17,29:5
Living Room, The 1954,N 18,41:1
Living Room, The 1954,N 28,II,1:1
Potting Shed, The 1957,Ja 30,32:1
Potting Shed, The 1957,F 10,II,1:1
Potting Shed, The 1958,Mr 16,II,3:1
Potting Shed, The 1958,N 3,49:2
Complaisant Lover, The 1959,Je 19,28:3
Complaisant Lover, The 1961,N 2,43:2
Living Room, The 1962,N 22,43:5
Carving a Statue 1964,S 18,25:1
Carving a Statue 1968,My 1,43:1
Greene, H C (Director)
Just a Minute 1928,O 9,34:3
Greene, H C (Playwright)
Just a Minute 1928,O 9,34:3
Greene, H C (Producer)
Just a Minute 1928,O 9,34:3
Greene, Harriet
Paul Bunyan 1941,My 6,25:1
Greene, Herbert
On the Town 1944,D 29,11:4
Greene, Herbert (Composer)
Small Wonder 1948,S 16,33:5
Greene, Herbert (Miscellaneous)
Happy as Larry 1950,Ja 7,11:2
Guys and Dolls 1950,N 25,11:2
Two on the Aisle 1951,Jl 20,13:6
Bells Are Ringing 1956,N 29,43:4
Bells Are Ringing 1956,N 30,18:2
Saratoga 1959,D 8,59:4
Music Man, The 1965,Je 17,26:4
Greene, Herbert (Musical Director)
Silk Stockings 1955,F 25,17:3
Guys and Dolls 1955,Ap 21,32:2
Most Happy Fella, The 1956,My 4,20:1
Music Man, The 1957,D 20,31:1
Unsinkable Molly Brown, The 1960,N 4,28:1
Gay Life, The 1961,N 20,38:1
Nowhere to Go But Up 1962,N 12,36:2
Anyone Can Whistle 1964,Ap 6,36:1
Greene, Herbert (Producer)
Music Man, The 1957,D 20,31:1
Nowhere to Go But Up 1962,N 12,36:2
Greene, Herman
Swing Mikado, The 1939,Mr 2,18:2
Greene, Jaclynne
City of Kings 1949,F 18,27:2
Greene, James
American Gothic 1953,N 11,35:6
Girl on the Via Flaminia, The 1954,F 10,37:1
King and the Duke, The 1955,Je 2,25:2

Greene, James—Cont
Iceman Cometh, The 1956,My 8,38:1
Shadow of a Gunman, The 1958,N 21,26:1
Andersonville Trial, The 1959,D 30,15:1
Moon in the Yellow River, The 1961,F 7,40:2
Misalliance 1961,S 26,32:2
In White America 1963,N 1,26:1
After the Fall 1964,Ja 24,18:1
Marco Millions 1964,F 21,33:1
Changeling, The 1964,O 30,32:2
Incident at Vichy 1964,D 4,44:1
You Can't Take It With You 1965,N 24,32:1
School for Scandal, The 1966,N 22,33:2
Right You Are (If You Think You Are)
1966,N 23,34:2
War and Peace 1967,Mr 22,42:1
Show-Off, The 1967,D 6,40:2
Henry V 1969,Je 9,57:1
Much Ado About Nothing 1969,Je 16,57:1
Three Sisters, The 1969,Ag 4,29:1
Greene, Javotte S
Simply Heavenly 1957,My 22,28:2
Greene, Jeanne
Not so Fast 1923,My 23,18:4
Whole Town's Talking, The 1923,Ag 30,8:2
Milgrim's Progress 1924,D 23,17:1
Buccaneer, The 1925,O 3,10:2
Offence, The 1925,N 16,25:1
Bunk of 1926 1926,Ap 23,25:2
Mozart 1926,N 23,26:2
Four Walls 1927,S 20,33:1
Four Walls 1927,O 2,VIII,1:1
K Guy, The 1928,O 16,28:4
Back Here 1928,N 27,36:3
Kibitzer, The 1929,F 19,22:5
Veneer 1929,N 13,24:5
Oh, Promise Me 1930,N 25,31:1
Perfectly Scandalous 1931,My 14,27:2
Wonder Boy 1931,O 24,20:1
Mulatto 1935,O 25,25:2
Be So Kindly 1937,F 9,19:4
Morning Star 1940,Ap 17,26:4
Greene, Joseph
Hell's Bells! 1925,Ja 27,14:2
Jane-Our Stranger 1925,O 9,27:2
They All Want Something 1926,O 13,20:2
Black Velvet 1927,S 28,28:1
Primer for Lovers, A 1929,N 19,26:5
Virtue's Bed 1930,Ap 16,26:5
Long Road, The 1930,S 10,30:2
Greene, Josephine
Comedy of Errors, The 1932,N 22,25:3
Greene, Lillian
All God's Chillun Got Wings 1924,My 16,22:3
All God's Chillun Got Wings 1924,Ag 19,9:1
Greene, Loretta
Warning, The-A Theme for Linda 1969,Ap 27,92:1
Black Quartet, A; Warning, The-A Theme for
Linda 1969,Jl 31,28:1
Greene, Lorne
Prescott Proposals, The 1953,D 17,53:1
Julius Caesar 1955,Je 29,23:3
Merchant of Venice, The 1955,Jl 1,13:1
Speaking of Murder 1956,D 20,37:1
This Is Edwin Booth 1958,Ag 27,32:7
Edwin Booth 1958,N 25,37:1
Greene, Luther (Director)
Point of Honor, A 1937,Ja 31,II,10:4
Point of Honor, A 1937,F 12,26:2
Triple Play 1937,Ag 24,24:4
Eight O'Clock Tuesday 1941,Ja 7,18:2
Walk Into My Parlor 1941,N 20,38:2
Hedda Gabler 1942,Ja 30,22:2
Greene, Luther (Miscellaneous)
Pursuit of Happiness, The 1935,Jl 16,24:2
Greene, Luther (Producer)
Ghosts 1935,D 13,30:6
Personal Appearance 1936,Jl 9,17:4
Point of Honor, A 1937,Ja 31,II,10:4
Point of Honor, A 1937,F 12,26:2
Eight O'Clock Tuesday 1941,Ja 7,18:2
Walk Into My Parlor 1941,N 20,38:2
Hedda Gabler 1942,Ja 30,22:2
Tower Beyond Tragedy, The 1950,N 27,29:1
Sleep of Prisoners, A 1951,O 17,36:2
Much Ado About Nothing 1952,My 2,20:1
Greene, Margie
Hold On to Your Hats 1940,S 12,30:3
Greene, Martin
Summer Night 1939,N 3,17:1
Johnny Doodle 1942,Mr 19,28:2
Night Music 1951,Ap 9,29:6
Out West of Eighth 1951,S 21,20:3
Golden Boy 1952,Mr 13,24:3
Greene, Marty
Enter Laughing 1963,Mr 15,8:1
Enter Laughing 1963,Je 16,II,1:1
God Bless You, Harold Fineberg 1969,Mr 31,30:2
Greene, Melville
Porgy 1927,O 11,26:2
Greene, Melvin
In Abraham's Bosom 1926,D 31,10:2
Greene, Milton (Miscellaneous)
Body Beautiful, The 1958,Ja 24,15:2

Greene, Milton (Musical Director)
Catch a Star! 1955,S 7,35:2
Body Beautiful, The 1958,Ja 24,15:2
From A to Z 1960,Ap 21,23:2
Not While I'm Eating 1961,D 20,37:1
Fiddler on the Roof 1964,S 23,56:2
Rothschilds, The 1970,O 20,40:1
Greene, Myra
Flies, The 1954,S 10,18:2
Trial, The 1955,Je 15,35:2
Spring's Awakening 1955,O 10,30:2
Summer of Daisy Miller, The 1963,My 28,33:1
Greene, Natalye
Yours Is My Heart 1946,S 6,16:5
Greene, Niki
Shoemaker's Prodigious Wife, The 1949,Je 15,38:2
Lower Depths, The 1956,O 3,29:2
Greene, Patterson
O Evening Star 1936,Ja 9,24:6
Greene, Patterson (Playwright)
Closed Room, The 1934,Jl 24,20:2
Papa Is All 1942,Ja 7,22:2
Papa Is All 1942,Ja 18,IX,1:1
Greene, Reuben
Boys in the Band, The 1968,Ap 15,48:1
Boys in the Band, The 1968,Ap 28,II,1:6
Pantagleize 1967,D 1,54:1
Greene, Robert (Original Author)
Winter's Tale, The 1958,Jl 27,II,1:1
Greene, Ruby
Set to Music 1939,Ja 19,16:2
Pirate, The 1942,N 26,39:2
Greene, Ruth
Witness for the Prosecution 1954,D 17,35:2
Greene, Sam
Crucible, The 1958,Mr 12,36:1
Crucible, The 1958,Je 1,II,1:1
Goldilocks 1958,O 13,33:1
Tobacco Road 1960,My 11,44:2
As You Like It 1961,Je 17,13:2
Month in the Country, A 1963,My 29,39:2
Place for Chance, The 1964,My 15,44:2
Ben Franklin in Paris 1964,O 28,52:1
Greene, Stanley
In Abraham's Bosom 1926,D 31,10:2
Natural Man 1941,My 8,20:4
On Strivers' Row 1946,Mr 1,17:2
Another Part of the Forest 1946,N 21,42:2
Big Deal, The 1953,Mr 7,13:6
King and the Duke, The 1955,Je 2,25:2
Take a Giant Step 1956,S 26,30:1
Simply Heavenly 1957,My 22,28:2
And the Wind Blows 1959,Ap 29,28:1
Long Dream, The 1960,F 18,36:2
Contributions; Plantation 1970,Mr 10,53:1
Contributions; Shoes 1970,Mr 10,53:1
Greene, Stanley (Miscellaneous)
Wedding in Japan 1957,Mr 12,37:7
Greene, Stanley (Producer)
Wedding in Japan 1957,Mr 12,37:7
Deathwatch 1958,O 10,34:2
Greene, Walter D
Crime 1927,F 23,27:3
Precedent 1931,Ap 15,24:5
Re-Echo 1934,Ja 12,28:4
Greene, Will (Playwright)
Riot Act, The 1963,Mr 9,5:2
Greene, William
Haiti 1938,Mr 3,16:1
Romanoff and Juliet 1957,O 11,24:1
Yeomen of the Guard, The 1965,Ap 22,26:1
Harpers Ferry 1967,Je 6,52:2
Greener, Dorothy
Razzle Dazzle 1951,F 20,21:1
Shoestring Revue 1955,Mr 1,22:2
Shoestring '57 1956,N 6,31:1
Leave It to Jane 1959,My 26,30:2
My Mother, My Father and Me 1963,Mr 25,5:5
Gogo Loves You 1964,O 10,19:2
War Games 1969,Ap 18,37:1
Greenfeld, Josh (Playwright)
Clandestine on the Morning Line 1959,D 5,18:2
Clandestine on the Morning Line 1961,O 31,28:1
Greenfield, Anne
Everyman 1941,My 9,19:2
Greenfield, Lawrence
Hamlet 1956,O 29,34:1
Greenfield, Richard (Miscellaneous)
Postmark Zero 1965,N 2,28:1
Greenfield, Rose
Radio Girl, The 1929,O 19,22:4
Jolly Orphan, The 1929,D 23,18:6
Mother's Son 1931,N 26,36:4
Under One Roof 1932,F 8,21:2
Germany Aflame 1933,O 28,20:5
What Girls Do 1935,Ja 14,10:4
His Jewish Girl 1936,D 9,34:1
Jewish Heart, The 1939,Ja 25,16:6
Oy, Is Dus a Leben!; Oh, What a Life!
1942,O 13,19:2
Abi Gezunt 1949,O 10,19:4
Sadie Is a Lady 1950,Ja 28,9:2
Farblondjete Honeymoon 1955,S 27,42:1
Family Mishmash, A 1958,O 20,36:1
Bei Mir Bistu Schoen 1961,O 23,22:2

Cowboy in Israel, A 1962,O 29,36:2
My Wife With Conditions 1963,O 21,39:1
Good Luck 1964,O 19,38:3
Greenhalgh, Dawn
Antony and Cleopatra 1967,Ag 2,25:1
Greenhalgh, Edward
Foxy 1964,F 17,26:1
Greenhaw, Art
Days Between, The 1965,Je 4,39:1
Greenhill, Wendy
Midsummer Night's Dream, A 1968,D 9,59:1
Greenhouse, Martha
Sons and Soldiers 1943,My 5,22:2
Clerambard 1957,N 8,22:3
Our Town 1959,Mr 24,46:2
Dear Me, the Sky Is Falling 1963,Mr 4,9:1
Family Way, The 1965,Ja 14,44:5
Journey of the Fifth Horse, The 1966,Ap 22,36:1
Woman Is My Idea 1968,S 26,61:1
Three by Ferlinghetti; Three Thousand Red Ants
1970,S 23,43:1
Three by Ferlinghetti; Victims of Amnesia, The
1970,S 23,43:1
Three by Ferlinghetti; Alligation, The
1970,S 23,43:1
Greenhut, Andrew Jay (Costume Designer)
De Sade Illustrated 1969,My 13,42:4
Greenhut, Andrew Jay (Lighting Director)
Patience 1967,O 13,32:1
Iolanthe 1967,O 18,40:1
Mikado, The 1967,O 25,42:2
Gondoliers, The 1967,O 29,83:1
H M S Pinafore 1967,N 1,40:1
Greening, Arlene
Little Theatre Tournament; Shall We Join the
Ladies? 1929,My 9,34:3
Shall We Join the Ladies? 1929,My 12,28:3
Greening, George (Miscellaneous)
Time and the Conways 1938,Ja 4,19:2
Greenlaw, Gene
Jumbo 1935,N 18,20:2
Greenleaf, Lewis Stone 3d (Scenic Designer)
Colombe 1965,F 24,33:1
Greenleaf, Raymond
Your Loving Son 1941,Ap 5,13:2
Jason 1942,Ja 22,12:2
Decision 1944,F 3,23:2
Decision 1944,F 13,II,1:1
Foxhole in the Parlor 1945,My 24,15:4
Henry VIII 1946,N 7,42:2
Androcles and the Lion 1946,D 20,29:2
Yellow Jack 1947,F 28,26:2
Alice in Wonderland 1947,Ap 7,19:2
Greenlee, Martin
Tom Sawyer - Ballad of the Mississippi
1947,D 27,11:3
Greenlee, R Eddie
Liza 1922,N 28,24:1
Greenman, Jean
Dole Brothers 1932,Mr 26,17:7
Greeno, Lucy
Singing Girl, The 1952,Je 4,31:8
Greenough, Walter
Hotbed 1928,N 10,20:7
Room of Dreams 1930,N 6,22:4
Greenough, Walter (Director)
Guinea Pig, The 1929,Ja 8,35:1
Jade God, The 1929,My 14,28:3
Ledge, A 1929,N 19,26:3
Everything's Jake 1930,Ja 17,20:4
They Never Grow Up 1930,Ap 8,27:1
Venetian Glass Nephew, The 1931,F 24,26:3
Greenough, Walter (Miscellaneous)
Lolly 1929,O 17,26:2
Greenough, Walter (Producer)
Venetian Glass Nephew, The 1931,F 24,26:3
Greensfelder, Elmer (Playwright)
Crocodile Chuckles, The 1929,F 24,IX,4:1
Broomsticks Amen! 1934,F 10,20:4
Greenspon, Muriel
O Marry Me 1961,O 28,13:1
H M S Pinafore 1964,Mr 21,13:4
Yeomen of the Guard, The 1964,Ag 3,16:1
Saint of Bleecker Street, The 1965,Mr 19,28:1
H M S Pinafore 1965,Ap 15,39:1
Pirates of Penzance, The 1965,Ap 21,50:6
Pirates of Penzance, The 1965,Ap 26,32:1
Mikado, The 1968,My 2,59:1
Fiesta in Madrid 1969,My 29,49:1
Greenstein, Ilise
Women at the Tomb, The 1961,Ap 25,41:1
Greenstein, Stephen
Hamlet 1970,O 19,51:1
Greenstreet, Sydney
Lady Billy 1920,D 15,18:2
Her Happiness 1920,O 8,VI,1:6
Magic Ring, The 1923,O 2,10:1
Humble, The 1926,O 14,22:2
Junk 1927,Ja 6,25:1
Lady in Love, A 1927,F 22,22:1
Madcap, The 1928,F 1,31:2
R U R 1930,F 18,28:1
Marco Millions 1930,Mr 4,24:4
Volpone 1930,Mr 11,24:5

Lysistrata 1930,Ap 29,30:5
Lysistrata 1930,Je 1,VIII,1:1
Lysistrata 1930,Je 6,20:1
Berlin 1931,D 31,16:1
Good Earth, The 1932,O 18,23:4
Roberta 1933,N 20,18:4
Taming of the Shrew, The 1935,S 22,X,3:2
Taming of the Shrew, The 1935,O 1,27:3
Idiot's Delight 1936,Mr 10,26:7
Idiot's Delight 1936,Mr 25,25:2
Amphitryon 38 1937,Je 24,30:2
Amphitryon 38 1937,N 2,32:2
Sea Gull, The 1938,Mr 29,19:2
Sea Gull, The 1938,Ap 3,XI,1:1
Taming of the Shrew, The 1940,F 6,17:2
There Shall Be No Night 1940,Ap 30,25:2
Greenwald, Jack (Producer)
Long and the Short and the Tall, The
1962,Mr 30,28:2
Greenwald, Joseph
Abie's Irish Rose 1927,Mr 29,23:3
Camels Are Coming, The 1931,O 3,20:4
Bulls, Bears and Asses 1932,My 7,11:3
Keeping Expenses Down 1932,O 21,25:2
Great Magoo, The 1932,D 3,20:7
Spring Song 1934,O 2,18:2
Eldest, The 1935,F 12,24:3
Postman Always Rings Twice, The 1936,F 7,14:4
Postman Always Rings Twice, The 1936,F 26,17:2
Forbidden Melody 1936,N 3,33:1
But for the Grace of God 1937,Ja 13,21:4
Hitch Your Wagon! 1937,Ap 9,18:2
Greenwald, Robert
Tragical Historie of Doctor Faustus, The
1964,O 6,34:2
Greenwald, Robert (Director)
Picnic on the Battlefield 1967,S 9,25:2
People vs Ranchman, The 1968,O 28,56:1
Calling in Crazy 1969,O 7,42:2
Greenway, Ann
Vaudeville (Palace) 1928,Ap 24,29:2
Vaudeville (Palace) 1928,Ag 21,27:5
Greenway, Tom
American Holiday 1936,F 22,13:3
Murder in the Cathedral 1936,Mr 21,13:5
It Can't Happen Here 1936,O 28,30:1
Sun and I, The 1937,F 27,9:5
Greenwell, Gean
Poisoned Kiss, The 1937,Ap 22,19:1
Pirates of Penzance, The 1946,My 17,14:6
Greenwood, Anna
Book of Charm, The 1925,S 4,26:3
Greenwood, Barrett
Love Birds 1921,Mr 16,12:1
Red Pepper 1922,My 30,8:3
Little Nellie Kelly 1922,N 14,16:1
Be Yourself! 1924,S 4,13:3
Greenwood, Charlotte
Letty Pepper 1922,Ap 11,22:2
Irving Berlin's New Music Box Revue
1922,O 24,18:1
Hassard Short's Ritz Revue 1924,S 18,19:1
Vaudeville (Palace) 1926,My 4,31:2
LeMaire's Affairs 1927,Mr 29,22:4
Rufus Le Maire's Affairs 1927,Ap 10,VIII,1:1
Vaudeville (Palace) 1927,Je 28,29:2
Out of This World 1950,D 22,17:3
Greenwood, James (Costume Designer)
Twelfth Night 1968,Je 15,40:1
Crimes of Passion; Ruffian on the Stair, The
1969,O 27,54:1
Crimes of Passion; Erpingham Camp, The
1969,O 27,54:1
Othello 1970,S 15,51:1
Greenwood, Jane (Costume Designer)
Ballad of the Sad Cafe, The 1963,O 31,27:1
Hamlet 1964,Ap 10,30:1
Incident at Vichy 1964,D 4,44:1
Tartuffe 1965,Ja 15,23:1
Race of Hairy Men!, A 1965,Ap 30,42:1
Nathan Weinstein, Mystic, Connecticut
1966,F 26,15:2
Where's Daddy? 1966,Mr 3,27:1
Murder in the Cathedral 1966,Je 21,38:1
Twelfth Night 1966,Je 23,28:1
How's the World Treating You? 1966,O 25,50:1
More Stately Mansions 1967,N 1,40:1
Prime of Miss Jean Brodie, The 1968,Ja 17,39:1
Comedy of Errors, The 1968,F 28,40:2
Seven Descents of Myrtle, The 1968,Mr 28,54:1
I'm Solomon 1968,Ap 24,51:1
Master Builder, The 1968,Je 22,26:1
Androcles and the Lion 1968,Je 27,47:1
Love's Labour's Lost 1968,Je 28,36:1
Mother Lover, The 1969,F 3,28:1
Wrong Way Light Bulb, The 1969,Mr 5,40:1
Much Ado About Nothing 1969,Je 16,57:1
Hamlet 1969,Je 30,33:1
Three Sisters, The 1969,Ag 4,29:1
Penny Wars, The 1969,O 16,52:1
Angela 1969,O 31,33:1
Sheep on the Runway 1970,F 2,28:3
All's Well That Ends Well 1970,Je 16,53:1
Othello 1970,Je 22,43:1

Greenwood, Jane (Costume Designer)—Cont
Devil's Disciple, The 1970,Je 30,48:1
Gandhi 1970,O 21,37:1
Hay Fever 1970,N 10,55:1
Blancs, Les 1970,N 16,48:4
Greenwood, Joan
Confidential Clerk, The 1954,F 12,22:1
Broken Heart, The 1962,Jl 10,28:2
Uncle Vanya 1962,Jl 17,18:4
Those That Play the Clowns 1966,N 25,48:1
Greenwood, John
Carmen Jones 1956,Je 1,28:2
Richard II 1956,O 24,44:1
Romeo and Juliet 1956,O 25,41:1
Macbeth 1956,O 30,42:2
Troilus and Cressida 1956,D 27,21:1
Carmen Jones 1959,Ag 18,25:1
Greenwood, John (Lighting Director)
Romeo and Juliet 1956,O 25,41:1
Greenwood, John (Miscellaneous)
Macbeth 1956,O 30,42:2
Troilus and Cressida 1956,D 27,21:1
Greenwood, Leila
Hostage, The 1960,S 21,42:1
Greenwood, Reva
Jeweled Tree, The 1926,O 8,26:2
Greenwood, Rosamund
Matchmaker, The 1955,D 6,45:6
Matchmaker, The 1955,D 18,II,3:1
Greenwood, Walter (Original Author)
Love on the Dole 1936,F 25,23:3
Love on the Dole 1936,Mr 8,IX,1:1
Greenwood, Walter (Playwright)
Love on the Dole 1935,F 17,VIII,3:1
Love on the Dole 1936,F 25,23:3
Love on the Dole 1936,Mr 8,IX,1:1
My Son's My Son 1936,My 27,26:4
Cure For Love, The 1945,Ag 5,II,1:4
Greer, Ben
Man Who Washed His Hands, The 1967,F 16,33:1
Greer, Edward
Aladdin and His Wonderful Lamp 1963,O 21,39:1
Greer, Edward (Director)
Little Clay Cart, The 1953,Jl 1,25:1
All That Fall 1957,O 8,41:2
Edward II 1958,F 12,32:5
Greer, Edward (Translator)
Three Sisters, The 1965,F 12,15:1
Kremlin Chimes 1965,F 25,23:1
Greer, Ellen
Three Sisters, The 1963,Jl 22,19:2
Glass Menagerie, The 1964,Jl 20,18:3
Greer, J J
Red Poppy, The 1922,D 21,18:2
Greer, Jesse (Composer)
Folly Town 1920,My 18,9:2
Padlocks of 1927 1927,Jl 6,23:4
Harry Delmar's Revels 1927,N 29,30:2
Shady Lady 1933,Jl 6,26:3
Greer, Jesse (Lyricist)
Shady Lady 1933,Jl 6,26:3
Greer, Julian
Hamlet 1925,N 10,23:1
Greer, Melody
Harpers Ferry 1967,Je 6,52:2
Greer, Michael
Fortune and Men's Eyes 1969,O 23,55:1
Greer, Simeon
Shatter'd Lamp, The 1934,Mr 22,26:3
Greet, Ben
Much Ado About Nothing 1929,N 17,30:4
Hamlet 1931,Ap 24,26:4
Greet, Ben (Director)
Much Ado About Nothing 1929,N 17,30:4
Hamlet 1931,Ap 24,26:4
Greet, Ben (Producer)
Much Ado About Nothing 1929,N 17,30:4
Greet, Clare
Old House, The 1920,Jl 11,VI,1:6
Mariners 1929,My 19,IX,1:8
Greet, Frances
Country Wife, The 1936,D 2,34:1
Audition of the Apprentice Theatre 1939,Je 2,26:2
Getting Married 1951,My 14,28:5
First Gentleman, The 1957,Ap 26,22:2
Greet, Maurice
Man Who Changed His Name, The 1932,My 3,25:3
Midsummer Night's Dream, A 1932,N 18,22:2
Twelfth Night 1932,N 19,20:5
Comedy of Errors, The 1932,N 22,25:3
Merchant of Venice, The 1932,N 24,34:5
Greet, Maurice (Producer)
In Times Square 1931,N 24,29:3
Greet, Philip Ben (Sir)
Miracle Man, The 1935,My 14,17:5
Greet, Philip Ben (Sir) (Director)
Midsummer Night's Dream, A 1932,Jl 13,15:1
Greeves, Vernon
Millionairess, The 1952,O 18,17:2
Greeves, William
Lost in the Stars 1949,O 31,21:2
Gregg, Bud
Not for Children 1951,F 14,35:2

Gregg, Bud (Composer)
Dance Me a Song 1950,Ja 21,10:5
Gregg, Everley
Point Valaine 1935,Ja 17,22:2
Gregg, Hubert
French Without Tears 1937,S 26,II,4:3
French Without Tears 1937,S 29,19:1
Gregg, Jess (Playwright)
Shout From the Rooftops 1964,O 29,40:1
Gregg, John
Keep Shufflin' 1928,F 28,18:3
Gregg, Julie
Happy Time, The 1968,Ja 19,32:2
Gregg, Mitchell
Music in the Air 1951,O 9,32:2
Music in the Air 1951,O 21,II,1:1
Say Darling 1958,Ap 4,17:1
Say Darling 1958,Ap 13,II,1:1
Say Darling 1959,F 26,38:2
Unsinkable Molly Brown, The 1960,N 4,28:1
No Strings 1962,Mr 16,24:1
Gregg, Norma (Composer)
A la Carte 1927,Ag 18,25:3
Gregg, Norma (Lyricist)
A la Carte 1927,Ag 18,25:3
Gregg, Peter
War President 1944,Ap 25,17:3
Assassin, The 1945,O 18,20:2
Gregg, Richard N
Creoles 1927,S 23,33:3
Meek Mose 1928,F 7,30:1
Girl Trouble 1928,O 26,22:3
First Night 1930,N 27,32:3
Rap, The 1931,Ap 7,31:2
Going Gay 1933,Ag 4,18:5
Audition of the Apprentice Theatre 1939,Je 2,26:2
Ring Two 1939,N 23,38:2
Gregg, Royal D
East Lynne Goes West 1931,My 3,I,26:5
Gregg, Sydney (Miscellaneous)
Sometime Jam Today 1967,F 13,41:1
Greggory, David
It's About Time 1942,Mr 31,28:3
Greggory, David (Composer)
Reunion in New York 1940,F 22,28:4
It's All Yours 1942,Mr 26,26:2
Greggory, David (Director)
It's About Time 1942,Mr 31,28:3
Greggory, David (Lyricist)
It's All Yours 1942,Mr 26,26:2
It's About Time 1942,Mr 31,28:3
Greggory, David (Miscellaneous)
'Tis of Thee 1940,O 28,21:3
Greggory, David (Playwright)
It's About Time 1942,Mr 31,28:3
Gregoera, A
Electra 1952,N 20,38:2
Gregor, Nora
Weaker Sex, The 1931,Mr 1,VIII,1:3
Old Maid, The; Two Mothers, The 1937,F 24,19:3
Gregori, Virginia
Broken Chain, The 1929,F 21,30:4
O Evening Star 1936,Ja 9,24:6
To Quito and Back 1937,O 7,30:4
Gregorio, Rose
Bivouac at Lucca 1957,O 30,26:1
Days and Nights of Beebee Fenstermaker, The 1962,S 18,33:1
Journey to the Day 1963,N 12,49:1
Kiss Mama 1964,O 2,30:1
Cuban Thing, The 1968,S 25,36:2
Jimmy Shine 1968,D 6,52:1
Gregory, Alex
Anvil, The 1962,O 31,33:3
Call It Virtue 1963,Mr 28,8:2
Gregory, Andre
Time to Go 1960,Mr 23,33:1
Gregory, Andre (Director)
PS 193 1962,O 31,33:1
Firebugs, The 1963,N 22,41:1
Tartuffe 1967,S 18,60:1
Bacchae, The 1969,Mr 15,24:1
Bacchae, The 1969,Mr 23,II,11:1
Alice in Wonderland 1970,O 9,43:1
Alice in Wonderland 1970,O 18,II,3:1
Gregory, Andre (Producer)
Deirdre of the Sorrows 1959,O 15,46:1
Blacks, The 1961,My 5,23:1
Gregory, Anne
So That's That 1925,D 15,28:3
Gregory, Arnold
Fireworks on the James 1940,My 15,30:2
Gregory, Celia
Madwoman of Chaillot, The 1970,Mr 23,48:3
Gregory, Charles
Time of Vengeance 1959,D 11,39:1
Time of Vengeance 1959,D 27,II,1:1
Three by Ferlinghetti; Three Thousand Red Ants 1970,S 23,43:1
Three by Ferlinghetti; Alligation, The 1970,S 23,43:1
Three by Ferlinghetti; Victims of Amnesia, The 1970,S 23,43:1

Gregory, Count
This Was Burlesque 1970,F 12,31:1
Gregory, David (Lyricist)
From Vienna 1939,Je 21,26:2
Gregory, David (Playwright)
Pins and Needles 1939,Ap 21,26:2
Gregory, Dick
Untitled-Revue 1961,Je 18,II,1:1
Eddie Fisher at the Winter Garden 1962,O 3,47:1
Gregory, Douglas
They Shall Not Die 1934,F 22,24:4
Page Miss Glory 1934,N 28,24:2
Hook-Up, The 1935,My 9,24:6
Triumph 1935,O 15,18:5
In Bed We Cry 1944,N 15,20:2
Gregory, Edna
Founders, The 1957,My 14,39:1
Gregory, Frances (Playwright)
Precipice 1934,Je 6,24:4
Gregory, Frank
Tragedy of Nan, The 1920,F 18,9:1
Gregory, Frank (Director)
Girls in Uniform 1932,D 31,10:3
Eight Bells 1933,O 30,14:2
Gregory, Frank (Playwright)
Living Dangerously 1934,Je 8,19:3
Moon Is Red, The 1934,D 5,29:1
Moon Is Red, The 1934,D 23,IX,1:8
Living Dangerously 1935,Ja 14,10:3
Gentle Rain 1936,S 2,18:2
Gentle Rain 1936,S 20,IX,1:4
Gregory, Huguette
Joies du Capitole, Les 1935,Ap 21,IX,2:1
Gregory, James
Rain or Shine 1928,F 10,26:3
Play's the Thing, The 1935,Jl 24,20:4
Key Largo 1939,N 28,30:2
Journey to Jerusalem 1940,O 7,21:2
Glamour Preferred 1940,N 16,13:2
Steps Leading Up 1941,Ap 19,20:6
Man With Blonde Hair, The 1941,N 5,30:2
In Time to Come 1941,D 29,20:2
Autumn Hill 1942,Ap 14,17:4
Dream Girl 1945,D 15,13:2
Dinosaur Wharf 1951,N 9,23:2
Collector's Item 1952,F 9,11:2
Dead Pigeon 1953,D 24,10:2
Fragile Fox 1954,O 13,27:1
Desperate Hours, The 1955,F 11,20:2
Gregory, Jay
Time for Singing, A 1966,My 23,48:2
Blood Red Roses 1970,Mr 23,48:1
Gregory, Jo
Malinda 1929,D 4,37:2
Gregory, John
Under the Counter 1947,O 4,10:2
King and the Duke, The 1955,Je 2,25:2
Gregory, Lady (Playwright)
Rising of the Moon, The 1920,Je 22,9:1
Rising of the Moon, The 1920,Je 29,9:2
Dragon, The 1922,D 27,12:1
Sancho's Master 1927,Ap 10,VIII,4:7
Dave 1927,Je 5,VII,2:3
Rising of the Moon, The 1928,Je 6,23:4
Dragon, The 1929,Mr 26,34:2
Rising of the Moon, The 1932,O 21,25:1
Workhouse Ward, The 1937,F 15,13:2
Rising of the Moon, The 1937,F 15,13:2
Workhouse Ward, The 1959,Ap 11,15:4
Gregory, Maia
Theatre of the Soul 1942,Mr 21,13:5
Across the Board on Tomorrow Morning 1942,Mr 21,13:5
Gregory, Paul
Great Way, The 1921,N 8,28:2
Golden Dawn 1927,D 1,32:3
Whoopee 1928,D 5,34:3
Smiles 1930,N 19,19:2
If in the Green Wood 1947,Ja 17,27:6
Gregory, Paul (Director)
Caine Mutiny Court-Martial, The 1953,O 14,35:1
Gregory, Paul (Producer)
Don Juan in Hell 1951,O 23,34:4
John Brown's Body 1952,N 3,25:8
John Brown's Body 1953,F 16,17:2
Caine Mutiny Court-Martial, The 1953,O 14,35:1
Caine Mutiny Court-Martial, The 1953,D 15,52:8
Caine Mutiny Court-Martial, The 1954,Ja 21,27:2
3 for Tonight 1955,Ap 7,23:2
3 for Tonight 1955,Ap 17,II,1:1
Marriage-Go-Round, The 1958,O 30,37:1
Captains and the Kings, The 1962,Ja 3,25:2
Lord Pengo 1962,N 20,41:2
Gregory, Robin (Choreographer)
Rehearsal, The 1952,My 27,30:5
Gregory, Ruth
Song of Bernadette 1946,Mr 27,22:2
Enemies Don't Send Flowers 1957,F 20,38:1
Gregory, Shirley
Years Between, The 1942,F 7,13:2
Gregory, Vahan (Miscellaneous)
Big Time Buck White 1968,D 9,58:1

Gregory, Will
Cactus Flower 1965,D 9,60:2
Warm Body, A 1967,Ap 17,44:2
Front Page, The 1969,My 12,54:2
Gregory, William
Buccaneer, The 1925,O 3,10:2
Number 7 1926,S 9,21:3
Precedent 1931,Ap 15,24:5
Eastward in Eden 1956,Ap 18,25:4
Gregson, Hartley
Patience 1927,My 24,23:2
Gregson, James R (Playwright)
Young Imeson 1924,Mr 23,VIII,1:3
Greig, Evelyn
No Foolin' 1926,Je 25,25:1
Greig, Robert
Animal Crackers 1928,O 24,26:2
Berkeley Square 1929,N 5,32:4
Tonight or Never 1930,N 9,IX,3:2
Tonight or Never 1930,N 19,19:3
Great Lady 1938,D 2,26:6
Greiling, John
Coney Island Play 1970,O 31,34:2
Grein, J T (Producer)
Parisienne, La 1929,Mr 10,X,4:6
Grenelle, Helen
Sancho Panza 1923,N 27,23:1
Vagabond King, The 1925,S 22,23:3
O'Flynn, The 1934,D 28,24:1
Grenfell, Joyce
Sigh No More 1945,S 2,II,1:2
Joyce Grenfell Requests the Pleasure 1955,O 11,48:1
Joyce Grenfell 1958,Ap 8,32:1
Grenfell, Joyce (Lyricist)
Joyce Grenfell Requests the Pleasure 1955,O 11,48:1
Joyce Grenfell 1958,Ap 8,32:1
Grenfell, Joyce (Playwright)
Joyce Grenfell Requests the Pleasure 1955,O 11,48:1
Joyce Grenfell 1958,Ap 8,32:1
Grenidge, Lisle
Macbeth 1936,Ap 15,25:4
Grenier, Aileen
Mister Romeo 1927,S 6,35:3
Grenier, Arthur S
What a Relief 1935,D 14,10:6
Grenier, Richard (Playwright)
Puntila 1959,My 15,26:2
Grenville, Claire
Sun Showers 1923,F 6,14:2
Natja 1925,F 17,19:2
June Days 1925,Ag 7,12:5
Ladies of the Jury 1929,O 22,26:2
Fata Morgana 1931,D 26,15:3
Too Much Party 1934,Mr 6,28:4
As the Girls Go 1948,N 15,21:2
Grenville, Robert
Shake Hands With the Devil 1949,O 21,30:4
Grenzeback, Joe (Playwright)
Madame Is Served 1949,F 15,28:1
Gres, Francoise
Folies Bergere 1964,Je 3,36:1
Gresen, Harry M (Miscellaneous)
Montserrat 1954,My 26,34:2
Gresen, Jack (Miscellaneous)
Montserrat 1954,My 26,34:2
Gresham, Edith
Whispering Friends 1928,F 21,18:3
Girls in Uniform 1932,D 31,10:3
Frederika 1937,F 5,16:5
Run Sheep Run 1938,N 4,26:2
Debut 1956,F 23,32:1
Visit, The 1960,Mr 9,38:3
Conquering Hero, The 1961,Ja 17,40:2
Country Wife, The 1965,D 10,58:2
Gresham, Gloria (Costume Designer)
Prayer Meeting: or, The First Militant Minister 1969,Ap 27,92:1
Gentleman Caller, The 1969,Ap 27,92:1
Warning, The-A Theme for Linda 1969,Ap 27,92:1
Great Goodness of Life (A Coon Show) 1969,Ap 27,92:1
Black Quartet, A; Great Goodness of Life (A Coon Show) 1969,Jl 31,28:1
Black Quartet, A; Prayer Meeting or The First Militant Minister 1969,Jl 31,28:1
Black Quartet, A; Gentleman Caller, The 1969,Jl 31,28:1
Black Quartet, A; Warning, The-A Theme for Linda 1969,Jl 31,28:1
Show Me Where the Good Times Are 1970,Mr 6,32:1
Gresham, Harry
Out of Step 1925,Ja 30,12:1
Penny Arcade 1930,Mr 11,24:5
Philip Goes Forth 1931,Ja 13,35:4
I Loved You Wednesday 1932,O 12,27:1
Uncle Tom's Cabin 1933,My 30,13:4
Give Us This Day 1933,O 28,20:6
On Stage 1935,O 30,16:6
Solitaire 1942,Ja 28,22:2
Man With the Golden Arm, The 1956,My 22,28:1

Obbligato 1958,F 19,22:2
Giants, Sons of Giants 1962,Ja 8,26:2
Gresham, Herbert (Mrs)
Triumph of X, The 1921,Ag 25,8:2
Gress, David
Twelfth Night 1960,Je 9,29:4
Gresset (Playwright)
Untitled-Play 1935,N 24,IX,3:7
Gressieker, Hermann (Playwright)
Royal Gambit 1959,Mr 5,34:2
Royal Gambit 1959,Mr 15,II,1:1
Emperor, The 1963,Ap 17,30:1
Gretch, Vera
Revisor; Inspector General, The 1935,F 18,19:6
Poverty Is No Crime 1935,F 21,22:5
Strange Child 1935,F 26,16:1
White Guard, The; Days of the Turbins 1935,Mr 7,27:5
Marriage 1935,Mr 12,24:8
Gretch, Vera (Director)
Poverty Is No Crime 1935,F 21,22:5
Strange Child 1935,F 26,16:1
White Guard, The; Days of the Turbins 1935,Mr 7,27:5
Gretillat, Jacques
Dans l'Ombre du Harem 1927,My 29,VII,2:7
Yeux du Coeur, Les 1927,O 16,IX,4:7
Gretry, Andre (Composer)
Two Misers, The 1943,D 9,30:5
Grevatt, Bonnie
H M S Pinafore 1952,N 4,32:2
Grever, Maria (Composer)
Viva O'Brien 1941,O 10,27:2
Grever, Maria (Lyricist)
Viva O'Brien 1941,O 10,27:2
Greville, Fredericka
Young Visitors, The 1920,N 30,14:1
Grew, William A
Mating Season, The 1927,Jl 19,27:6
My Girl Friday! 1929,F 13,20:2
Grew, William A (Director)
Mating Season, The 1927,Jl 19,27:6
My Girl Friday! 1929,F 13,20:2
Jerry for Short 1929,Ag 13,23:4
Grew, William A (Lyricist)
Florida Girl 1925,N 3,34:1
Grew, William A (Playwright)
Sap, The 1924,D 16,28:3
Earl Carroll's Vanities 1925,Jl 7,24:1
Florida Girl 1925,N 3,34:1
Earl Carroll's Vanities 1925,D 29,20:3
Earl Carroll's Vanities 1926,Ag 25,19:4
Mating Season, The 1927,Jl 19,27:6
My Girl Friday! 1929,F 13,20:2
Nice Women 1929,Je 11,27:4
Jerry for Short 1929,Ag 13,23:4
She Lived Next to the Firehouse 1931,F 11,23:1
Grey, Anthony
Pelican, The 1929,N 14,25:1
Drunkard, The; Fallen Saved, The 1929,D 31,14:6
Joy of Serpents 1930,Ap 4,22:4
Sun and I, The 1937,F 27,9:5
Wanhope Building, The 1947,F 11,36:5
Andorra 1963,F 11,5:5
Grey, Christian
Secret Life of Walter Mitty, The 1964,O 27,44:5
Grey, Clifford (Lyricist)
Sally 1920,D 22,16:1
Hotel Mouse, The 1922,Mr 14,11:3
Lady Butterfly 1923,Ja 23,18:1
Vogues of 1924 1924,Mr 28,14:3
Marjorie 1924,Ag 12,12:2
Artists and Models 1924,O 16,33:3
Sky High 1925,Mr 3,21:4
Artists and Models 1925,Je 25,16:2
June Days 1925,Ag 7,12:5
Gay Paree 1925,Ag 19,14:3
Mayflowers 1925,N 25,14:2
Night in Paris, A 1926,Ja 6,16:3
Great Temptations, The 1926,My 19,29:1
Merry World, The 1926,Je 9,18:3
Hit the Deck! 1927,Ap 26,32:1
Optimists, The 1928,Ja 31,28:2
Madcap, The 1928,F 1,31:2
Sunny Days 1928,F 9,29:1
Three Musketeers, The 1928,Mr 14,28:1
Ups-A-Daisy 1928,O 9,34:2
Ned Wayburn's Gambols 1929,Ja 16,22:3
Smiles 1930,N 19,19:2
Jack o' Diamonds 1935,F 26,17:3
Sally 1948,My 7,31:2
Hit the Deck 1960,Je 24,32:1
Grey, Clifford (Playwright)
Lady Butterfly 1923,Ja 23,18:1
Vogues of 1924 1924,Mr 28,14:3
Marjorie 1924,Ag 12,12:2
Kiss in a Taxi, The 1925,Ag 26,14:1
Mayflowers 1925,N 25,14:2
Optimists, The 1928,Ja 31,28:2
Sunny Days 1928,F 9,29:1
Ups-A-Daisy 1928,O 9,34:2
Jack o' Diamonds 1935,F 26,17:3
At the Silver Swan 1936,F 20,22:2

Grey, Diana
Pirates of Penzance, The 1942,F 20,20:2
Grey, Earle
Matriarch, The 1930,Mr 19,24:5
Geneva 1940,Ja 31,15:2
Romeo and Juliet 1940,My 10,27:1
Grey, Elsa
Humoresque 1923,F 28,13:2
Grey, Frank (Composer)
Sue, Dear 1922,Jl 11,16:2
Matinee Girl, The 1926,F 2,20:3
Grey, Gina
Piper, The 1920,Mr 20,14:2
Grey, Isabel
Fall and Rise of Susan Lenox, The 1920,Je 11,11:2
Grey, Jack C
Partners Again 1922,My 2,22:2
Grey, Jane
Teaser, The 1921,Jl 28,8:3
Why Not? 1922,D 25,20:1
Lord Byron's Cain 1925,Ap 9,20:3
It All Depends 1925,Ag 11,16:4
Lady Detained, A 1935,Ja 10,23:3
Wild Justice 1935,Jl 9,24:3
Grey, Jean
Afgar 1920,N 9,13:2
Grey, Joel
Littlest Revue, The 1956,My 23,37:2
Cabaret 1966,N 21,62:1
Cabaret 1966,D 4,II,5:1
George M! 1968,Ap 11,48:1
George M! 1968,Ap 21,II,1:5
Grey, John
Wall Street 1927,Ap 21,24:4
Grey, Katherine
Gold 1921,Je 2,14:2
Straw, The 1921,N 11,16:2
Dreams for Sale 1922,S 14,24:1
House Divided, The 1923,N 12,14:1
Goose Hangs High, The 1924,Ja 30,16:1
Bridge of Distances, The 1925,S 29,30:1
Bridge of Distances, The 1925,O 4,IX,1:1
Stronger Than Love 1925,D 29,20:2
Hundred Years Old, A 1929,O 2,28:2
Bright Star 1935,O 16,26:2
Delicate Story 1940,D 5,32:2
Grey, Laura
Lancashire Lass, The 1931,D 31,16:3
Grey, Liana
Furnished Rooms 1934,My 30,14:6
Grey, Madeline
Sue, Dear 1922,Jl 11,16:2
Matinee Girl, The 1926,F 2,20:3
Pyramids 1926,Jl 20,17:2
Tales of Rigo 1927,My 31,25:3
Enchanted Isle 1927,S 20,33:2
Restless Women 1927,D 27,24:1
Just a Minute 1928,O 9,34:3
Hello, Daddy! 1928,D 27,26:5
Woof, Woof 1929,D 26,20:4
Jonica 1930,Ap 8,27:1
With Privileges 1930,S 16,30:2
Great Man, The 1931,Ap 8,20:6
Social Register, The 1931,N 10,28:2
Ghost Writer, The 1933,Je 20,22:4
Kultur 1933,S 27,24:3
Few Are Chosen 1935,S 18,19:3
To My Husband 1936,Je 2,35:2
Grey, Marion
Poppy God, The 1921,Ag 30,10:1
So This Is London 1922,Ag 31,18:2
Money Lender, The 1928,Ag 28,27:3
Serena Blandish 1929,Ja 24,30:3
Grey, Mary
And So to Bed 1927,N 10,23:1
Cherry Orchard, The 1928,Mr 6,20:1
Firebird of Florence 1945,Mr 23,13:4
Grey, Nicholas
Diana 1929,D 10,37:1
Grey, Pamela
Happiness Cage, The 1970,O 5,56:4
Grey, Penelope
From Morn Till Midnight 1948,D 7,41:6
Changeling, The 1956,My 4,20:3
Grey, Yvonne
Rosalie 1928,Ja 11,26:3
Ringside 1928,Ag 30,13:4
Follow Thru 1929,Ja 10,24:3
Prince Charming 1930,O 14,31:1
Gribbin, Eve (Costume Designer)
Exception and the Rule, The 1965,My 21,19:1
Prodigal Son, The 1965,My 21,19:1
Gribble, George Dunning (Playwright)
Masque of Venice, The 1926,Mr 3,27:3
Masque of Venice, The 1926,Mr 7,VIII,1:2
Masque of Venice, The 1928,F 12,VIII,2:1
Artist and the Shadow, The 1930,Ap 6,IX,2:1
Gribble, Harry Wagstaff
Merchant of Venice, The 1921,Ap 2,14:2
Tyrants 1924,Mr 5,14:1
All Men Are Alike 1941,O 7,27:2
Thorntons, The 1956,F 15,26:1

Gribble, Harry Wagstaff (Director)
Cherry Pie 1926,Ap 15,24:4
Loud Speaker 1927,Mr 3,27:2
Pleased to Meet You 1928,O 30,27:2
Revolt 1928,N 1,25:3
After Dark 1928,D 11,35:2
Houseparty 1929,S 10,26:5
City Haul 1929,D 31,14:4
Royal Virgin, The 1930,Mr 18,30:5
Last Enemy, The 1930,O 31,21:1
Silent Witness, The 1931,Mr 24,31:5
Old Man Murphy 1931,My 19,25:2
Cynara 1931,N 3,31:1
Trick for Trick 1932,F 19,14:2
No More Ladies 1934,Ja 24,20:3
Perfumed Lady, The 1934,Mr 13,27:2
No More Ladies 1934,S 4,23:2
Living Dangerously 1935,Ja 14,10:3
Simpleton of the Unexpected Isles, The
    1935,F 19,27:5
There's Wisdom in Women 1935,Jl 16,24:1
If This Be Treason 1935,Jl 30,17:1
If This Be Treason 1935,S 24,28:2
Taming of the Shrew, The 1935,O 1,27:3
There's Wisdom in Women 1935,O 31,17:1
Mainly for Lovers 1936,F 22,13:2
White Christmas 1936,Jl 7,22:2
Aged 26 1936,D 22,32:1
Something for Nothing 1937,D 10,33:5
There's Always a Breeze 1938,Mr 3,16:2
Man From Cairo, The 1938,My 5,26:5
Millionairess, The 1938,Ag 16,22:5
Billy Draws a Horse 1939,D 22,14:5
Taming of the Shrew, The 1940,F 6,17:2
Johnny Belinda 1940,S 19,26:2
All Men Are Alike 1941,O 7,27:2
Anna Lucasta 1944,Je 17,10:1
Anna Lucasta 1944,Ag 31,15:1
Anna Lucasta 1944,S 10,II,1:1
Almost Faithful 1948,Je 5,9:2
Wise Have Not Spoken, The 1954,F 11,35:2
Gribble, Harry Wagstaff (Miscellaneous)
Memphis Bound 1945,My 25,23:2
Gribble, Harry Wagstaff (Playwright)
Outrageous Mrs Palmer, The 1920,O 13,18:1
Juliet and Romeo 1921,My 17,20:3
March Hares 1921,Ag 12,8:3
March Hares 1921,Ag 21,VI,1:1
Shoot 1922,Je 8,14:2
All Gummed Up 1923,Ja 29,11:2
March Hares 1923,Mr 13,19:5
Topics of 1923 1923,N 21,23:2
Artists and Models 1925,Je 25,16:2
Oh! Mama 1925,Ag 20,22:2
Oh! Mama 1925,Ag 30,VII,1:1
Cherry Pie 1926,Ap 15,24:4
Mister Romeo 1927,S 6,35:3
March Hares 1928,Ja 1,VIII,1:3
March Hares 1928,Ap 3,32:6
Revolt 1928,O 21,IX,2:1
Revolt 1928,N 1,25:3
Elizabeth and Essex 1930,Mr 2,IX,4:7
Royal Virgin, The 1930,Mr 18,30:5
Meet My Sister 1930,D 31,11:1
Silent Witness, The 1931,My 10,VIII,3:5
Old Man Murphy 1931,My 19,25:2
Trick for Trick 1932,F 19,14:2
Perfumed Lady, The 1934,Mr 13,27:2
Anna Lucasta 1944,Je 17,10:1
Almost Faithful 1948,Je 5,9:2
Gribble, Harry Wagstaff (Producer)
Black Crook, The 1929,Mr 12,26:5
Johnny Belinda 1940,S 19,26:2
Gribbon, Harry
Alley Cat 1934,S 18,18:1
Delicate Story 1940,D 5,32:2
Mr Big 1941,S 7,I,51:3
Mr Big 1941,S 14,IX,2:5
Mr Big 1941,O 1,24:2
Meet a Body 1944,O 17,19:5
Gribkov, V V
Pikvikski Klub; Pickwick Club, The 1936,O 4,IX,1:8
Gribov, Aleksei
Cherry Orchard, The 1964,Je 18,29:5
Dead Souls 1965,F 5,34:1
Cherry Orchard, The 1965,F 10,46:1
Three Sisters, The 1965,F 12,15:1
Griboyedov (Playwright)
Woe to Wit 1936,S 13,X,1:1
Gribunin, Vladimir
Tsar Fyodor Ivanovitch 1923,Ja 9,26:1
Lower Depths, The 1923,Ja 16,16:1
Cherry Orchard, The 1923,Ja 23,18:1
Three Sisters, The 1923,Ja 30,12:2
Lady From the Provinces, The 1923,F 27,14:2
Brothers Karamazov, The 1923,N 20,23:4
Ivanoff 1923,N 27,23:2
Enemy of the People, An 1923,D 4,25:1
Death of Pazukhin, The 1924,F 12,20:1
Brothers Karamazov, The 1924,My 6,25:2
Grice, Wayne
Moon on a Rainbow Shawl 1962,Ja 16,30:1
Walk in Darkness 1963,O 29,30:2

Blues for Mister Charlie 1964,Ap 24,24:1
Bohikee Creek 1966,Ap 29,39:1
Electronic Nigger, The 1968,Mr 9,23:2
Son, Come Home, A 1968,Mr 9,23:2
Gridier, Patrice
Dancing Partner 1930,Ag 6,24:2
Grieco, Rose (Playwright)
Anthony on Overtime 1961,O 21,13:2
Daddy Come Home 1963,Ap 17,33:1
Grieff, Joseph N (Rev) (Director)
Untitled-Passion Play 1925,Mr 2,5:6
Passion Play 1934,F 12,15:1
Grieff, Joseph N (Rev) (Playwright)
Quo Vadis 1932,O 17,18:2
Passion Play 1934,F 12,15:1
Passion Play 1940,F 12,2:7
Grieff, Joseph N (Rev) (Producer)
Untitled-Passion Play 1936,Mr 2,4:3
Grieff, Joseph N (Rev) (Translator)
Untitled-Passion Play 1925,Mr 2,5:6
Grieg, Evelyn
Girl in the Spotlight, The 1920,Jl 13,9:3
Grieg, Michael
Poet's Follies of 1955 1955,My 15,II,3:1
Grieg, Nordal (Playwright)
Our Honor and Our Power 1936,Je 28,IX,1:6
Grieg, Weldon (Producer)
Poet's Follies of 1955 1955,My 15,II,3:1
Grieg (Composer)
Peer Gynt 1928,Mr 24,4:6
Peer Gynt 1935,S 24,28:2
Peer Gynt 1937,Mr 14,II,7:8
Song of Norway 1944,Ag 27,II,1:1
Song of Norway 1946,Mr 8,17:1
Grier, Bill
Porgy and Bess 1965,Mr 6,17:1
Grier, Carolyn
Enchanted, The 1950,Ja 19,34:2
Grier, William
Cyrano de Bergerac 1936,Ap 28,17:1
Mimie Scheller 1936,O 1,28:4
Griese, Friedrich (Playwright)
Mensch aus Erde Gemacht 1933,N 5,IX,3:1
Griess, Otto
Before Sundown 1962,Mr 14,43:1
Griethuysen, Ted van
Tempest, The 1960,Je 20,35:1
Inadmissible Evidence 1965,D 1,52:1
Grieve, Frederick
Yeomen of the Guard, The 1933,My 2,20:4
Yeomen of the Guard, The 1933,Ag 15,20:5
Griffen, Arthur
Mahogany Hall 1934,Ja 18,18:5
Griffen, Edward G
Without the Walls 1922,Ap 17,17:1
Griffen, Nellie
March Hares 1921,Ag 12,8:3
Griffes, Charles (Composer)
White Peacock, The 1929,Ap 27,16:4
Griffes, Charles (Playwright)
Tone Pictures and the White Peacock
    1927,Ap 6,24:3
Griffeth, Linda
Banjo Eyes 1941,D 26,20:2
Griffies, Ethel
Havoc 1924,S 2,22:2
Old English 1924,D 24,11:2
Loose Ends 1926,N 2,34:2
Mariners 1927,Mr 29,22:2
Interference 1927,O 19,24:3
Cherry Orchard, The 1928,Mr 6,20:1
Lady Dedlock 1929,Ja 1,61:2
Criminal Code, The 1929,O 3,28:2
Stepdaughters of War 1930,O 7,27:1
Druid Circle, The 1947,O 23,29:5
Druid Circle, The 1947,N 16,II,1:1
Hallams, The 1948,Mr 5,18:2
Leading Lady 1948,O 19,33:1
Shop at Sly Corner, The 1949,Ja 19,35:2
Miss Liberty 1949,Jl 16,6:5
Miss Liberty 1949,Jl 24,II,1:1
Legend of Sarah 1950,O 12,42:4
Royal Family, The 1951,Ja 11,28:2
Autumn Garden, The 1951,Mr 8,36:2
Autumn Garden, The 1951,Mr 18,II,1:1
Write Me a Murder 1961,O 27,28:2
Billy Liar 1965,Mr 18,26:1
Very Rich Woman, A 1965,O 5,5:8
Ivanov 1966,My 4,50:1
Natural Look, The 1967,Mr 13,45:2
Griffin
High Kickers 1941,N 1,21:2
Griffin, Arthur
Frankie and Johnny 1930,S 26,16:5
Little Black Book, The 1932,D 27,11:2
Sketch Book 1935,Je 5,22:2
Come Angel Band 1936,F 19,17:1
Stork Mad 1936,O 1,28:4
Madame Bovary 1937,N 17,26:2
Greatest Show on Earth, The 1938,Ja 6,22:2
Escape This Night 1938,Ap 23,18:1
Abe Lincoln in Illinois 1938,O 4,20:1
Abe Lincoln in Illinois 1938,O 17,12:2

Griffin, Arthur—Cont
Across the Board on Tomorrow Morning
    1942,Ag 18,17:1
Skin of Our Teeth, The 1942,N 19,29:5
New Life, A 1943,S 16,26:6
Take It As It Comes 1944,F 11,17:2
Mermaids Singing, The 1945,N 29,26:6
Griffin, Bill (Costume Designer)
Parade at the Devil's Bridge 1957,F 19,35:7
Doctor Faustus 1957,F 19,35:7
Truce of the Bear 1957,O 24,39:1
King's Standards, The 1958,F 14,19:1
Child of the Morning 1958,Ap 22,40:2
Listen to the Quiet 1958,O 28,40:2
Madre, La 1959,F 12,24:1
Egoists, The 1959,O 14,52:2
Griffin, Charles
Our Lan' 1947,S 29,16:5
Land Beyond the River, A 1957,Mr 29,15:7
Griffin, Denise
Wish You Were Here 1952,Je 26,26:6
Griffin, Dorothea
No Trifling With Love 1959,N 10,55:3
Eternal Sabbath 1963,O 19,17:2
Griffin, Edmund (Translator)
Queen After Death 1956,Mr 13,33:2
Griffin, Genevieve
Watched Pot, The 1947,O 29,31:4
Griffin, Hayden (Costume Designer)
Rockefeller and the Red Indians 1968,O 25,37:1
Griffin, Hayden (Scenic Designer)
Rockefeller and the Red Indians 1968,O 25,37:1
Griffin, Irene (Costume Designer)
Minstrel Boy, The 1948,O 15,28:2
City of Kings 1949,F 18,27:2
Armor of Light 1950,F 24,26:4
Restless Flame, The 1952,Ap 15,30:6
Angelic Doctor 1953,Ap 14,30:2
Late Arrival 1953,O 20,35:5
Griffin, Jenne
Bamboo Cross 1955,F 22,17:2
Griffin, Jonathan (Translator)
Port-Royal 1960,Ap 26,41:1
Griffin, Joseph (Playwright)
Hidden King, The 1957,Ag 21,21:1
Griffin, Josephine
Merry Widow, The 1943,Ag 5,19:2
Griffin, Merv
Finian's Rainbow 1955,My 19,25:1
Griffin, Nannie
Fanny Hawthorn 1922,My 12,22:2
Lucky One, The 1922,N 21,15:2
Griffin, Peter
Edgar Allan Poe 1925,O 6,31:1
Griffin, Robert
This One Man 1930,O 22,32:3
Bivouac at Lucca 1957,O 30,26:1
Griffin, Robert E
Grandma's Diary 1948,S 23,36:2
Griffin, Russell
Street Scene 1929,Ja 11,20:4
Griffin, Scott
New York Idea, The 1948,Ag 18,29:2
Griffin, Wee
Sweethearts 1929,S 23,25:1
Naughty Marietta 1929,O 22,26:2
Merry Widow, The 1929,D 3,29:1
Babes in Toyland 1929,D 24,15:3
Prince of Pilsen, The 1930,Ja 14,24:3
Chocolate Soldier, The 1930,Ja 28,28:1
Count of Luxembourg, The 1930,F 18,28:2
Serenade, The 1930,Mr 5,26:7
Singing Rabbi, The 1931,S 11,24:4
Griffin, William (Costume Designer)
Madame Lafayette 1960,Mr 4,21:1
Griffis, William
Major Barbara 1951,F 24,10:2
Babes in Arms 1951,Mr 10,7:3
Pin to See the Peepshow, A 1953,S 18,17:2
Corn Is Green, The 1954,F 27,10:2
Capacity for Wings 1957,Ja 10,25:2
Oscar Wilde 1957,Ap 20,21:3
Trial of Dmitri Karamazov, The 1958,Ja 28,30:1
Look After Lulu 1959,Mr 4,35:1
No Trifling With Love 1959,N 10,55:3
Here's Love 1963,O 4,28:1
Philadelphia, Here I Come! 1966,F 17,28:1
Oklahoma! 1969,Je 24,37:1
Jimmy 1969,O 24,38:1
Cry for Us All 1970,Ap 9,48:2
Griffith
Decoy, The 1932,Ap 2,13:4
Griffith, A M
Sellout, The 1933,S 7,17:2
Griffith, Andy
No Time for Sergeants 1955,O 21,32:2
No Time for Sergeants 1955,N 6,II,1:1
Destry Rides Again 1959,Ap 24,24:1
Destry Rides Again 1959,My 3,II,1:1
Griffith, Antoinette
Shrike, The 1953,N 26,51:2
Griffith, Billy
Red Mill, The 1945,O 17,16:2

Griffith, Byron
Streets Are Guarded, The 1944,N 21,19:7
Star Spangled Family 1945,Ap 11,18:6
Griffith, Corinne
Design for Living 1933,N 19,IX,2:5
Griffith, Diane
By Hex 1956,Je 19,25:1
Griffith, Donald
Pigeon, The 1930,O 15,26:2
Contributions; Shoes 1970,Mr 10,53:1
Contributions; Contribution 1970,Mr 10,53:1
Griffith, E E (Director)
Virgin and the Fawn, The 1949,Mr 18,33:2
Griffith, Ed
Never Too Late 1962,N 28,42:1
Griffith, Eleanor
Poor Little Ritz Girl 1920,Jl 29,7:1
Last Waltz, The 1921,My 11,20:3
Springtime of Youth 1922,O 27,15:1
For Value Received 1923,My 8,22:3
Meet the Wife 1923,N 27,23:4
Creaking Chair, The 1926,F 23,26:1
Sunshine 1926,Ag 18,15:2
Damn the Tears 1927,Ja 22,11:1
Spider, The 1927,Mr 23,29:1
Mrs Bumpstead-Leigh 1929,Ap 2,28:3
Humbug, The 1929,N 28,34:5
Griffith, Fred
Great Guns 1939,N 18,23:4
Griffith, Gladys
Country Wife, The 1936,D 2,34:1
Griffith, Hubert (Playwright)
Tragic Muse, The 1928,Jl 22,VII,1:3
Tunnel Trench 1929,N 26,28:7
Tunnel Trench 1929,D 15,X,4:2
Youth at the Helm 1935,F 21,22:1
Nina 1935,S 18,19:6
Return to Yesterday 1936,Ap 29,19:1
Return to Yesterday 1936,My 31,X,1:5
Young Madame Conti 1936,D 6,XII,7:6
Young Madame Conti 1937,Ap 1,18:4
Griffith, Hubert (Translator)
Distant Point 1941,N 9,IX,3:6
Griffith, Hugh
Richard II 1951,Mr 25,75:3
Legend of Lovers 1951,D 27,17:1
Dark Is Light Enough, The 1954,My 1,12:4
Waltz of the Toreadors, The 1956,Mr 11,II,3:1
Look Homeward, Angel 1957,N 29,33:1
Look Homeward, Angel 1957,D 8,II,5:1
Caucasian Chalk Circle, The 1962,Mr 30,28:1
Andorra 1963,F 11,5:5
Griffith, Kay
Up in Central Park 1945,Ja 29,17:2
Griffith, Leroy C (Director)
Wonderful World of Burlesque, The
1965,Ap 29,38:1
Griffith, Leroy C (Producer)
Wonderful World of Burlesque, The
1965,Ap 29,38:1
Fractured Follies of 1966 1965,D 18,35:1
Griffith, Linda
Panama Hattie 1940,O 31,28:2
Griffith, Mark
Hamlet 1969,My 2,38:1
Griffith, Maxine
Kongi's Harvest 1968,Ap 15,49:1
Griffith, Peter
Harriet 1944,S 28,26:1
Strange Fruit 1945,N 30,18:6
Street Scene 1947,Ja 10,17:2
Griffith, Robert
Under the Gaslight 1929,Ap 3,27:1
Dinner at Eight 1932,O 24,18:2
Merrily We Roll Along 1934,O 1,14:1
Brother Rat 1936,D 17,34:5
See My Lawyer 1939,S 28,29:1
Best Foot Forward 1941,O 2,28:2
Griffith, Robert (Miscellaneous)
Land's End 1946,D 12,37:5
Griffith, Robert E (Miscellaneous)
On Your Toes 1954,O 12,24:4
Griffith, Robert E (Producer)
Pajama Game, The 1954,My 14,20:2
Damn Yankees 1955,My 6,17:1
New Girl in Town 1957,My 15,40:1
West Side Story 1957,S 27,14:4
Fiorello! 1959,N 24,45:3
West Side Story 1960,Ap 28,31:1
Tenderloin 1960,O 18,47:2
Call on Kuprin, A 1961,My 26,29:3
Griffith, William
Peer Gynt 1923,F 6,14:1
Adding Machine, The 1923,Mr 20,24:1
Saint Joan 1923,D 29,8:4
Bewitched 1924,O 2,26:3
Caesar and Cleopatra 1925,Ap 14,27:1
Androcles and the Lion 1925,N 24,28:1
Chief Thing, The 1926,Mr 23,24:2
Garrick Gaieties 1926,My 11,25:2
Chee-Chee 1928,S 26,25:1
Lady Fingers 1929,F 1,22:4
Murray Anderson's Almanac 1929,Ag 4,VIII,1:6

Murray Anderson's Almanac 1929,Ag 15,20:3
Third Little Show, The 1931,Je 2,34:3
Griffiths, Hubert (Playwright)
Youth at the Helm 1934,N 25,IX,3:1
Griffiths, James
Galileo 1968,D 1,88:4
Narrow Road to the Deep North 1969,D 2,64:1
Griffiths, Mary
Beaux' Stratagem, The 1970,F 10,50:2
Three Sisters, The 1970,F 12,30:1
Griffiths, Neville
Mikado, The 1951,Ja 30,21:2
H M S Pinafore 1951,F 6,24:2
Pirates of Penzance, The 1951,F 20,21:2
Mikado, The 1955,S 30,20:2
Pirates of Penzance, The 1955,O 7,21:1
H M S Pinafore 1955,O 18,48:1
Griffiths Family
Wake Up and Dream 1929,D 31,14:3
Griffo, Guy
From Morn Till Midnight 1948,D 7,41:6
Butter and Egg Man, The 1949,Ap 29,27:1
Grigas, John
It's a Bird . . . It's a Plane . . . It's Superman
1966,Mr 30,34:1
Griggs, John
Truth About Blayds, The 1932,Ap 12,25:2
Two Strange Women 1933,Ja 11,23:3
Man Bites Dog 1933,Ap 26,11:2
Dark Tower, The 1933,N 27,20:3
Mackerel Skies 1934,Ja 24,20:4
Wild Justice 1935,Jl 9,24:3
Slight Case of Murder, A 1935,S 12,28:5
Saturday's Children 1936,Jl 7,22:5
Lightnin' 1938,S 16,17:4
Farm of Three Echoes 1939,N 29,18:3
Fifth Season, The 1953,Ja 24,13:2
Man in the Dog Suit, The 1958,O 31,34:2
Abraham Cochrane 1964,F 18,26:1
Slave Ship 1969,N 22,46:1
Griggs, Nelson
No More Peace 1937,F 27,9:1
Grigorova, Romayne (Choreographer)
Dance of Death, The 1967,O 20,50:1
Grilikhes, Michael M (Miscellaneous)
Disney on Parade 1970,S 24,63:1
Grill, Franklin (Lighting Director)
Forever This Land 1952,Je 30,14:6
Grill, Kathryn
Prelude 1936,Ap 20,17:4
Bury the Dead 1936,Ap 20,17:4
200 Were Chosen 1936,N 21,21:1
But for the Grace of God 1937,Ja 13,21:4
Robin Landing 1937,N 19,26:4
Washington Jitters 1938,My 3,19:1
Dame Nature 1938,S 27,24:3
Jeremiah 1939,F 4,11:2
Family Portrait 1939,Mr 9,18:4
Trojan Women, The 1941,Ap 9,32:5
Mexican Mural; Vera Cruz Interior 1942,Ap 27,19:2
Pick-Up Girl 1944,My 4,25:2
Medea 1947,O 21,27:2
Grill, Mitzi
Blue Monday 1932,Je 3,23:2
Grilley, Don
West Side Story 1961,Mr 31,22:3
Grillo, Evelio
Home Is the Hunter 1945,D 21,25:4
Grillparzer (Playwright)
Weh dem der Luegt 1928,Ap 1,IX,2:4
Grimaldi, Joseph
Me and Juliet 1970,My 15,42:1
Grimaldi, M J
Bertha 1962,F 12,27:1
Grime, Leonard S
Marching Song 1937,F 18,18:2
Grimes, Daryl
Hot Corner, The 1956,Ja 26,25:2
Affair of Honor 1956,Ap 7,12:3
Grimes, Frank
Borstal Boy 1967,O 12,55:2
Borstal Boy 1970,Ap 1,38:1
Borstal Boy 1970,Ap 12,II,9:6
Grimes, Jackie
Stork Mad 1936,O 1,28:4
Excursion 1937,Ap 10,11:4
Western Waters 1937,D 29,17:1
Grimes, Jeffrey
Golden Streets, The 1970,Ag 14,21:1
Grimes, Mae
Excursion 1937,Ap 10,11:4
Everywhere I Roam 1938,D 30,10:4
My Heart's in the Highlands 1939,Ap 14,29:2
Love's Old Sweet Song 1940,My 3,16:3
Grimes, Nichols
Cradle Will Rock, The 1964,N 9,40:4
Grimes, Rollin
My Maryland 1927,S 13,37:2
Three Little Girls 1930,Ap 15,29:1
If a Body 1935,My 1,25:3
Grimes, Tammy
Littlest Revue, The 1956,My 23,37:2
Clerambard 1957,N 8,22:3

Grimes, Tammy—Cont
Clerambard 1957,N 17,II,1:1
Henry IV, Part I 1958,Je 25,23:3
Winter's Tale, The 1958,Jl 23,34:3
Look After Lulu 1959,N 4,35:1
Twelfth Night 1959,Jl 11,10:2
Unsinkable Molly Brown, The 1960,N 4,28:1
Rattle of a Simple Man 1963,Ap 18,39:1
High Spirits 1964,Ap 8,34:1
Only Game in Town, The 1968,My 21,42:1
Private Lives 1969,D 5,52:1
Private Lives 1969,D 14,II,3:3
Grimes, Tiny (Musical Director)
Hoofers, The 1969,Jl 30,23:4
Grimm, David
Richard III 1964,Je 12,44:2
Coriolanus 1965,Je 21,36:1
Romeo and Juliet 1965,Je 21,36:3
Taming of the Shrew, The 1965,Je 24,32:2
King Lear 1965,Je 25,39:1
Grimm Brothers (Original Author)
Stone Tower, The 1962,Ag 24,14:2
Grimshaw, John
Daughters of Atreus 1936,O 15,33:1
Grimwood, Herbert
Mecca 1920,O 5,12:2
Clair de Lune 1921,Ap 19,15:1
Merchant of Venice, The 1922,D 22,13:1
Sweet Nell of Old Drury 1923,My 19,16:4
Grindell, Maggie
Howie 1958,S 18,35:2
Grinell, Robert
Foemen of the Yard 1935,Ap 6,10:4
Griner, Barbara (Miscellaneous)
Deadly Game, The 1960,F 3,27:2
Griner, Barbara (Producer)
Valmouth 1960,O 7,29:1
Voice of the Turtle, The 1961,Je 28,41:1
Susan Slept Here 1961,Jl 12,35:2
Little Hut, The 1961,Jl 26,34:2
Moon Is Blue, The 1961,Ag 9,29:1
Tender Trap, The 1961,Ag 26,15:1
Black Nativity 1961,D 12,54:2
Griner, Georgi
My Fair Lady 1964,D 29,22:1
Grinnage, Jack
Billy Barnes People, The 1961,Je 14,10:3
Grinnell, Frank
Bitter Sweet 1934,My 8,28:4
Grinnell, George
Don Juan; Feast With the Statue, The
1956,Ja 4,21:4
Grioux, Germaine
Henry V 1956,Je 24,II,1:1
Griscom, Bert
Possessed, The 1939,O 25,26:2
Griscom, Lloyd (Playwright)
Tenth Avenue 1927,Ag 16,31:1
Grisewood, Harman
King Lear 1927,Mr 13,VII,1:4
Grisha and Brona
Elliott Murphy's Aquashow 1956,Je 20,26:2
Griska, Susan
Pirates of Penzance, The 1946,My 17,14:6
Grismaijer, Michael (Playwright)
Noble Experiment, The 1930,O 28,21:4
Grisman, Sam H (Miscellaneous)
Red Velvet Goat, The 1939,Ja 21,18:4
Mr Banks of Birmingham 1939,Ja 21,18:4
Coggerers, The 1939,Ja 21,18:4
Grisman, Sam H (Producer)
Talk About Girls 1927,Je 15,31:3
Deep Harlem 1929,Ja 8,35:2
Portrait of Gilbert 1934,D 29,11:5
Eldest, The 1935,F 12,24:3
Bright Honor 1936,S 28,14:1
Forbidden Melody 1936,O 13,30:3
Forbidden Melody 1936,N 3,33:1
Cradle Will Rock, The 1938,Ja 4,19:3
Tortilla Flat 1938,Ja 13,16:2
They Should Have Stood in Bed 1942,F 14,18:5
Dark Hammock 1944,D 12,27:8
Griso, Frank
Time for Singing, A 1966,My 23,48:2
Grissmer, John (Playwright)
Candyapple, The 1970,N 24,33:1
Grissmer, John (Producer)
Ticket-of-Leave Man, The 1961,D 23,15:1
Open 24 Hours 1969,F 12,31:1
Satisfaction Guaranteed 1969,F 12,31:1
Grist, Reri
Jeb 1946,F 22,20:2
Wisteria Trees, The 1950,Mr 30,39:1
Barrier, The 1950,N 3,32:2
Carmen Jones 1956,Je 1,28:2
Shinbone Alley 1957,Ap 15,23:2
West Side Story 1957,S 27,14:4
West Side Story 1957,O 6,II,1:1
Griswold, Alice
Dodsworth 1934,F 26,20:4
Griswold, Gladys
Town's Woman, The 1929,Mr 12,26:2
Order Please 1934,O 10,21:2
Battleship Gertie 1935,Ja 19,9:2

Griswold, Gladys—Cont

Ceiling Zero 1935,Ap 11,26:2
Triumph 1935,O 15,18:5
All Editions 1936,D 23,17:2

Griswold, Grace

Red Poppy, The 1922,D 21,18:2
House Divided, The 1923,N 12,14:1
Main Line, The 1924,Mr 26,19:4
Main Line, The 1924,Mr 30,VIII,1:1
Service for Two 1926,Ag 31,15:1
American Tragedy, An 1926,O 12,31:2

Griswold, Grace (Director)

Billeted 1922,My 10,22:4

Griswold, Grace (Playwright)

Main Line, The 1924,Mr 26,19:4
Main Line, The 1924,Mr 30,VIII,1:1

Grizunoff, Alexander

Lower Depths, The 1923,Ja 16,16:1

Grizzard, George

All Summer Long 1953,Ja 29,23:1
Cretan Woman, The 1954,My 21,17:2
Desperate Hours, The 1955,F 11,20:2
Happiest Millionaire, The 1956,N 21,21:3
Happiest Millionaire, The 1956,D 2,II,1:1
Disenchanted, The 1958,D 4,53:4
Disenchanted, The 1959,Ja 11,II,1:1
Face of a Hero 1960,O 21,29:5
Big Fish, Little Fish 1961,Mr 16,42:2
Big Fish, Little Fish 1961,Mr 26,II,1:1
Curate's Play, The 1961,D 18,41:3
School for Scandal, The 1962,Mr 19,36:1
Tavern, The 1962,Ap 5,29:1
Who's Afraid of Virginia Woolf? 1962,O 15,33:1
Who's Afraid of Virginia Woolf? 1962,O 28,II,1:1
Hamlet 1963,My 9,41:1
Miser, The 1963,My 10,39:1
Hamlet 1963,My 19,II,1:1
Miser, The 1963,My 19,II,1:1
Three Sisters, The 1963,Jl 22,19:2
Henry V 1964,My 13,52:1
Saint Joan 1964,My 14,41:1
Volpone 1964,Jl 20,18:3
Glass Menagerie, The 1965,My 5,53:2
Glass Menagerie, The 1965,My 16,II,1:1
Stephen D 1966,Ag 5,17:1
You Know I Can't Hear You When the Water's
  Running; Shock of Recognition, The
  1967,Mr 14,54:1
You Know I Can't Hear You When the Water's
  Running; Footsteps of Doves, The
  1967,Mr 14,54:1
You Know I Can't Hear You When the Water's
  Running; I'm Herbert 1967,Mr 14,54:1
You Know I Can't Hear You When the Water's
  Running 1967,Mr 26,II,1:1
Noel Coward's Sweet Potato 1968,S 30,59:1
Noel Coward's Sweet Potato 1968,O 13,II,5:1
Gingham Dog, The 1969,Ap 24,41:1
Gingham Dog, The 1969,My 4,II,1:5
Gingham Dog, The 1969,Jl 13,II,1:1
Inquest 1970,Ap 24,38:1
Inquest 1970,My 3,II,3:1

Groag, Edward

Yours Is My Heart 1946,S 6,16:5
Montserrat 1949,O 31,21:4
Barefoot in Athens 1951,N 1,35:2
Strong Are Lonely, The 1953,S 30,38:3
Prescott Proposals, The 1953,D 17,53:1
Snow Maiden, The 1960,Ap 5,43:3

Grobard, Auram

Holiday in Israel 1968,O 14,55:2

Grobe, Donald

Saint of Bleecker Street, The 1954,D 28,21:1

Grobe, Edouard

Circus Princess, The 1927,Ap 26,32:2
Whoopee 1928,D 5,34:3

Grober, Ch

Dybbuk, The 1926,D 14,24:2
Eternal Jew, The 1926,D 21,21:2

Grod, Fred

Sonny 1921,Ag 17,12:2

Groday, Doris

Free for All 1931,S 9,25:1
Humpty Dumpty 1932,S 18,IX,2:1

Grodin, Charles

Tchin-Tchin 1962,O 26,26:2
Absence of a Cello 1964,S 22,45:1

Grodin, Charles (Director)

Hooray!! It's a Glorious Day. . .And All That
  1966,Mr 10,28:1
Lovers and Other Strangers 1968,S 19,63:1
Lovers and Other Strangers 1968,S 29,II,1:1

Grodin, Charles (Lyricist)

Hooray!! It's a Glorious Day. . .And All That
  1966,Mr 10,28:1

Grodin, Charles (Playwright)

Hooray!! It's a Glorious Day. . .And All That
  1966,Mr 10,28:1

Groelhesl, Paul (Playwright)

Untitled-Passion Play 1927,Jl 31,VII,1:6

Groetzinger, Edward

This Mad Whirl 1937,Ja 10,II,4:8

Grogan, Diane

Ice Capades 1958,S 4,33:2

Ice Capades 1959,S 4,12:1

Grogan, Jimmy

Hollywood Ice Revue 1955 1955,Ja 14,16:1
Hollywood Ice Revue 1956,Ja 13,17:1
Ice Capades 1957,S 5,33:2
Ice Capades 1958,S 4,33:2
Ice Capades 1959,S 4,12:1
Ice Capades 1962,Ag 30,34:1

Grogan, Norman

Gondoliers, The 1961,Ja 26,33:2
Show Boat 1961,Ap 13,32:1

Grogan, Norman (Miscellaneous)

My Sweet Charlie 1966,D 7,56:1

Grogan, Oscar

You Said It 1931,Ja 20,21:3

Grolius, Louise

Shannons of Broadway, The 1927,S 27,30:4

Groll, Paul (Producer)

Kick Back, The 1936,Je 23,27:3

Grombach, Jean V (Miscellaneous)

Time and the Conways 1938,Ja 4,19:2

Grona, Eugene Von (Choreographer)

Fine and Dandy 1930,S 24,26:1
Let 'Em Eat Cake 1933,O 23,18:1

Gronau, Ilse

Hamlet 1931,N 6,28:4

Gronemann, Sammy (Playwright)

King And the Cobbler, The 1954,D 13,33:6
I'm Solomon 1968,Ap 24,51:1

Groob, Michael

Oedipus 1970,F 23,30:1

Groody, Helen

Fables 1922,F 7,12:2
Glory 1922,D 26,10:1

Groody, Louise

Night Boat, The 1920,F 3,18:1
Good Morning, Dearie 1921,N 2,20:2
One Kiss 1923,N 28,14:2
No, No, Nanette 1925,S 17,20:2
Hit the Deck! 1927,Ap 26,32:1
Vaudeville (Palace) 1928,S 18,34:6
Vaudeville (Palace) 1930,Ag 18,24:3
Vaudeville (Palace) 1931,My 11,15:5
Saturday It Rained 1932,D 14,27:3
Church Mouse, A 1933,Je 27,13:7

Groom, Sam

Not a Way of Life 1967,Mr 23,28:1
Collision Course; Chuck 1968,My 9,55:2
Collision Course; Jew! 1968,My 9,55:2
Collision Course; Thoughts on the Instant of
  Greeting a Friend on the Street 1968,My 9,55:2
Collision Course; Unexpurgated Memoirs of
  Bernard Mergendeiler, The 1968,My 9,55:2
Collision Course; Camera Obscura 1968,My 9,55:2
Collision Course; Metaphors 1968,My 9,55:2
Collision Course; Stars and Stripes 1968,My 9,55:2
Collision Course; Tour 1968,My 9,55:2

Gropper, A (Costume Designer)

Rich Man, Poor Man 1950,F 13,15:4

Gropper, Gabriele

Untitled-Passion Play 1950,My 19,29:6

Gropper, Ida

What's the Use? 1926,S 7,19:1

Gropper, Milton Herbert (Playwright)

Gypsy Jim 1924,Ja 6,VII,1:4
Gypsy Jim 1924,Ja 15,17:4
New Toys 1924,Ja 20,VII,2:8
New Toys 1924,F 19,12:1
New Toys 1924,F 24,VII,1:1
Ladies of the Evening 1924,D 24,11:2
We Americans 1926,O 13,20:4
Mirrors 1928,Ja 19,17:1
Big Fight, The 1928,Ag 31,23:1
Big Fight, The 1928,S 19,33:1
Big Fight, The 1928,S 23,IX,1:1
Inspector Kennedy 1929,D 21,16:3
Bulls, Bears and Asses 1932,My 7,11:3
Sing and Whistle 1934,F 12,18:3
Good Morning, Corporal 1944,Ag 9,13:7

Gropper, Milton Herbert (Producer)

Bulls, Bears and Asses 1932,My 7,11:3
Sing and Whistle 1934,F 12,18:3

Gros, Theodore

Processional 1937,O 14,23:1

Grosbard, Ulu (Director)

Days and Nights of Beebee Fenstermaker, The
  1962,S 18,33:1
Subject Was Roses, The 1964,My 26,45:1
Subject Was Roses, The 1964,Je 7,II,1:1
View From the Bridge, A 1965,Ja 29,24:1
Investigation, The 1966,O 5,40:1
That Summer-That Fall 1967,Mr 17,33:1
Price, The 1968,F 8,37:1
Price, The 1968,F 18,II,1:1
Price, The 1968,O 30,39:1

Grosbard, Ulu (Playwright)

Investigation, The 1966,O 5,40:1

Grosbard, Ulu (Producer)

Days and Nights of Beebee Fenstermaker, The
  1962,S 18,33:1
View From the Bridge, A 1965,Ja 29,24:1

Grosberg, Chana

World Trembles, The 1939,F 28,17:3

Grosberg, Lassor H (Producer)

Inspector Calls, An 1947,O 22,38:2

Groscup, Marie

Magdalena 1948,S 21,31:2
Magdalena 1948,N 7,II,6:5
Alive and Kicking 1950,Ja 18,25:5

Grose, Robert Paine (Miscellaneous)

Darwin's Theories 1960,O 19,53:2

Grose, Robert Paine (Scenic Designer)

Darwin's Theories 1960,O 19,53:2

Groseclose, Frank

Trial of Dmitri Karamazov, The 1958,Ja 28,30:1
Cock-A-Doodle Dandy 1958,N 13,39:2
Buffalo Skinner, The 1959,F 20,18:1
Three Sisters, The 1959,S 22,46:1
Shepherd's Chameleon, The 1960,N 30,41:1
Merchant of Venice, The 1962,Je 22,1:4
King Lear 1962,Ag 14,35:1
Midsummer Night's Dream, A 1964,Je 30,23:2
Exception and the Rule, The 1965,My 21,19:1
Henry V 1965,Je 29,27:2
Ergo 1968,Mr 4,29:1

Groseclose, Frank (Composer)

Cry of the Raindrop 1961,Mr 8,38:1

Gross, Abe

Golden Ring, The 1930,F 1,14:7
Jolly World, A 1931,Ja 24,15:3

Gross, Abe (Director)

Golden Ring, The 1930,F 1,14:7
Soul of a Woman, The 1930,F 22,13:1
Motke From Slobodke 1930,Ap 12,23:3

Gross, Alfred

Wise-Crackers, The 1925,D 17,26:1

Gross, Ben S (Playwright)

Where's Your Husband? 1927,Ja 15,10:3

Gross, C S

Laugh It Off 1925,Ap 25,18:4
1776 1926,Ap 24,11:2

Gross, Chaim (Scenic Designer)

Heroic Years 1934,Ja 12,28:4

Gross, Charles (Composer)

Deirdre of the Sorrows 1959,O 15,46:1
Time of Vengeance 1959,D 11,39:1
Plough and the Stars, The 1960,D 7,56:2
Hop, Signor! 1962,My 8,45:2
Firebugs, The 1963,F 13,7:2
Lonesome Train, The 1965,Je 17,25:1
Hard Travelin' 1965,Je 17,25:1
Great White Hope, The 1967,D 14,58:1
Great White Hope, The 1968,O 4,40:1
Engagement Baby, The 1970,My 22,40:1

Gross, Charles (Miscellaneous)

Blacks, The 1961,My 5,23:1
Hi, Paisano 1961,O 2,36:2
Condemned of Altona, The 1966,F 4,21:1
Deer Park, The 1967,F 1,27:2

Gross, Edward (Producer)

Chicken Every Sunday 1944,Ap 6,27:2
St Louis Woman 1946,Ap 1,22:2

Gross, Gene

Joan of Lorraine 1955,Mr 26,12:2
View From the Bridge, A 1956,N 9,34:4
Handful of Fire 1958,O 2,45:3
Month in the Country, A 1959,Mr 2,32:2
Shepherd's Chameleon, The 1960,N 30,41:1
Passion of Josef D, The 1964,F 12,29:1
Tenth Man, The 1967,N 9,54:1
Cannibals, The 1968,N 4,60:1

Gross, Georg (Miscellaneous)

Adventures of the Worthy Soldier Schwejk, The
  1928,Mr 4,IX,2:1

Gross, Harry

How Revolting! 1932,Mr 11,14:6

Gross, Jerry B

From Morn Till Midnight 1948,D 7,41:6

Gross, Laurence (Playwright)

Whistling in the Dark 1932,Ja 20,16:6
Whistling in the Dark 1932,N 4,25:2

Gross, Milt (Composer)

Meet the People 1940,D 26,22:2

Gross, Milt (Lyricist)

Meet the People 1940,D 26,22:2

Gross, Milt (Playwright)

Fireman, The 1938,Ap 24,II,2:8
Meet the People 1940,D 26,22:2

Gross, Philip (Director)

Kith and Kin 1930,My 14,31:1

Gross, Robert (Producer)

Only the Young 1932,S 22,25:2

Gross, Seymour

Strip Girl 1935,O 21,22:6
Storm Over Patsy 1937,Mr 9,26:4
Time of Your Life, The 1940,S 24,27:2

Gross, Shelly (Producer)

Catch Me if You Can 1965,Mr 10,50:1
Sherry! 1967,Mr 29,39:1
Grand Music Hall of Israel, The 1968,F 7,42:1
Inquest 1970,Ap 24,38:1

Gross, Sid R

Man Who Never Died, The 1958,N 22,27:2

Gross, Stephen (Playwright)

Hook-Up, The 1935,My 9,24:6
One Good Year 1935,N 28,38:3

Grossberg, Chana
  Untitled-Revue 1939,Ap 5,31:2
Grossel, Ira
  Trojan Horse, The 1940,O 31,28:3
Grosselfinger, Burt
  Last Pad, The 1970,D 8,61:1
Grosser, Maurice (Director)
  Four Saints in Three Acts 1952,Ap 17,35:1
Grosset, Vera
  Broadway Brevities, 1920 1920,S 30,12:2
Grossett, Jeanne
  Eastwood Ho 1936,Jl 8,14:2
Grosskurth, Kurt
  Fanny 1955,D 17,19:6
Grossman, Hal (Producer)
  Sophie 1963,Ap 16,32:1
Grossman, Harvey
  Measure for Measure 1956,Je 29,16:1
Grossman, Henry
  Magistrate, The 1959,My 14,30:6
Grossman, Herbert (Miscellaneous)
  Maria Golovin 1958,N 6,43:1
Grossman, Herbert (Musical Director)
  Roar of the Greasepaint-the Smell of the Crowd
    1965,My 17,46:2
  Drat! the Cat! 1965,O 11,54:2
  Walking Happy 1966,N 28,47:1
  Cry for Us All 1970,Ap 9,48:2
Grossman, Hertha
  Stars on Ice 1942,Jl 3,12:2
  Stars on Ice (2d Edition) 1943,Je 25,13:2
Grossman, Irving
  Three Little Business Men, The 1923,S 4,12:1
  Some Girl 1927,D 24,8:2
  Motke From Slobodke 1930,Ap 12,23:3
  Berdichever Bridegroom, The 1930,S 24,26:2
  Jolly World, A 1931,Ja 24,15:3
  Women of New York 1931,Mr 23,24:3
  Longing for Home 1933,S 22,15:1
  Singing Thief, The 1933,D 4,22:4
  Slaves of the Public 1934,Mr 10,18:6
  Perfect Fishel, The 1935,S 30,12:4
  Pinye of Pinchev 1936,S 21,27:5
  Night in Budapest, A 1936,N 3,33:2
  His Jewish Girl 1936,D 9,34:1
  Warson at Night 1938,Ja 31,14:3
  David and Esther 1938,O 12,34:3
  My Pal Sasha 1941,O 23,24:4
  Wish Me Luck! 1954,N 1,37:2
  Wedding March, The 1955,O 17,33:1
  It's a Funny World 1956,O 22,24:1
  It Could Happen to You 1957,O 28,30:5
Grossman, Irving (Director)
  Wedding March, The 1955,O 17,33:1
Grossman, Irving (Producer)
  My Pal Sasha 1941,O 23,24:4
  Wish Me Luck! 1954,N 1,37:2
  Wedding March, The 1955,O 17,33:1
  It's a Funny World 1956,O 22,24:1
  It Could Happen to You 1957,O 28,30:5
  Nice People 1958,O 20,36:1
Grossman, Larry (Composer)
  Mating Dance 1965,N 4,58:1
  Minnie's Boys 1970,Mr 27,27:1
Grossman, Rickie
  Wish Me Luck! 1954,N 1,37:2
  It's a Funny World 1956,O 22,24:1
Grossman, Samuel S (Translator)
  Samson and Delilah 1920,N 18,18:1
  Inspector General, The 1923,My 1,24:1
Grossman, Shirley (Composer)
  Political Party, A 1963,S 27,17:5
Grossman, Shirley (Lyricist)
  Political Party, A 1963,S 27,17:5
Grossman, Shirley (Playwright)
  Political Party, A 1963,S 27,17:5
Grossmann, Suzanne
  Richard II 1964,Je 17,47:1
  Country Wife, The 1964,Ag 3,16:1
  Lion in Winter, The 1966,Mr 4,23:1
  Cyrano de Bergerac 1968,Ap 26,30:1
  Private Lives 1969,D 5,52:1
Grossmann, Suzanne (Translator)
  Chemmy Circle, The 1968,Ag 10,17:2
Grossmith, George
  Sally 1921,S 11,20:2
  Gay Lord Quex 1923,Ap 8,VIII,1:7
  Prince Charming 1930,O 14,31:1
  Meet My Sister 1930,D 31,11:1
  Josephine 1934,S 26,17:5
Grossmith, George (Producer)
  Sally 1921,S 11,20:2
Grossmith, Lawrence
  Foot-Loose 1920,Ag 15,VI,1:1
  New Morality, The 1921,Ja 31,10:1
  Silver Fox, The 1921,S 6,13:1
  Happy Husband, The 1927,Jl 10,VII,2:3
  Good Morning, Bill! 1927,D 25,VIII,1:4
  Happy Husband, The 1928,My 8,25:2
  Happy Husband, The 1928,My 27,VIII,1:1
  First Mrs Fraser, The 1929,D 30,16:2
  Cat and the Fiddle, The 1931,S 27,VIII,3:1
  Cat and the Fiddle, The 1931,O 16,26:4

Simpleton of the Unexpected Isles, The
    1935,F 19,27:5
  Slight Case of Murder, A 1935,S 12,28:5
  Love Is Not So Simple 1935,N 5,33:1
  Love Is Not So Simple 1935,N 10,IX,1:6
  Call It a Day 1936,Ja 29,15:2
  Call It a Day 1936,F 9,X,1:1
  Yes, My Darling Daughter 1938,Je 14,17:1
Grossmith, Weedon (Playwright)
  Night of the Party, The 1921,Jl 17,VI,1:8
Grosso, Guy
  Grosse Valise, La 1965,D 15,52:1
Grosso, Paolo
  To the Ladies! 1922,F 21,20:1
Grosso, Tony
  Doctor Faustus Lights the Lights 1951,D 3,23:4
Groth, Gordon
  Romio and Julietta 1925,Ap 21,19:1
Grotowski, Jerzy (Director)
  Acropolis 1968,Ag 24,24:3
  Constant Prince, The 1969,O 18,36:1
  Constant Prince, The 1969,O 26,II,1:1
  Acropolis 1969,N 5,40:1
  Apocalypsis cum Figuris 1969,N 20,60:2
  Acropolis; Apocalypsis cum Figuris
    1969,N 30,II,1:4
Grotowski, Jerzy (Miscellaneous)
  Acropolis 1969,N 5,40:1
Grotowski, Jerzy (Scenic Designer)
  Constant Prince, The 1969,O 18,36:1
  Apocalypsis cum Figuris 1969,N 20,60:2
Groubert, Louis
  Soul Gone Home 1959,O 28,40:7
Groulx, Georges
  Malade Imaginaire, Le; Imaginary Invalid, The
    1958,Ap 30,28:2
  Jalousie du Barbouille, La; Jealousy of the
    Barbouille, The 1958,My 7,43:1
  Sganarelle; Imaginary Cuckold, The 1958,My 7,43:1
  Mariage Force, Le; Forced Wedding, The
    1958,My 7,43:1
Group Theatre
  House of Connelly, The 1931,O 4,VIII,1:1
Grout, James
  Half a Sixpence 1965,Ap 26,38:2
Grout, Philip (Director)
  How's the World Treating You? 1966,O 25,50:1
  Little Boxes; Coffee Lace, The; Trevor
    1968,Jl 5,20:1
Grove, Betty Ann
  Hit the Deck 1960,Je 24,32:1
  George M! 1968,Ap 11,48:1
Grove, Eddy
  Catherine Was Great 1944,Ag 3,16:1
Grove, Fred
  Oedipus Rex 1923,O 26,14:1
  Burgomaster of Stilemonde, The 1923,N 16,15:3
  Hamlet 1923,N 20,23:3
Grove, H C (Playwright)
  Foot-Loose 1920,My 11,12:1
Grove, James (Director)
  Golden Screw, The 1967,Ja 31,52:1
Grover, Edward
  Trip to Bountiful, The 1959,F 27,20:4
  Misalliance 1961,S 26,32:2
  Alchemist, The 1964,S 15,33:1
  Postmark Zero 1965,N 2,28:1
Grover, Loraine
  Sabrina Fair 1953,N 12,37:1
Grover, Stanley
  Time Remembered 1957,N 13,41:2
  13 Daughters 1961,Mr 3,17:2
  South Pacific 1961,Ap 26,26:3
  Let It Ride 1961,O 13,27:4
  Mr President 1962,O 22,34:2
  Finian's Rainbow 1967,Ap 6,44:1
  King and I, The 1968,My 24,39:1
  Lyle 1970,Mr 21,16:2
Grover, Ted
  Emmanuel 1960,D 5,42:2
Groves, Charles
  Hen Upon a Steeple 1927,Ap 24,VII,2:3
Groves, Dinwiddie (Mrs) (Costume Designer)
  Merchant of Venice, The 1950,My 3,37:2
Groves, Evelyn
  Vaudeville (Palace) 1926,Jl 20,17:4
Groves, Jane
  All's Well That Ends Well 1955,Je 7,37:4
  Macbeth 1955,O 8,12:6
  Thesmophoriazusae, The; Goddesses of Athens,
    The 1955,D 14,52:4
  Trojan Women, The 1957,Mr 19,42:7
  Man and Superman 1960,N 7,46:2
Growden, Graham
  Love for Love 1967,O 21,17:1
Grower, Edgar
  Cellar and the Well, The 1950,D 11,30:2
Grozier, David
  City of Kings 1949,F 18,27:2
  Shake Hands With the Devil 1949,O 21,30:4
Grubbs, Ruth
  Sweet Genevieve 1945,Mr 21,27:3

Gruber, Edward
  Final Balance, The 1928,O 31,28:3
Gruber, H
  Deluge, The 1927,Ja 11,36:2
Gruber, Mirele
  Stranger, The 1935,N 7,26:2
  Freidel Becomes a Bride 1936,F 10,14:3
  Give Me Back My Heart 1937,O 4,17:6
  One Sabbath Afternoon 1939,Ja 17,27:5
  Her Great Mistake 1940,F 5,12:6
Gruber, Muriel
  Family Carnovsky, The 1943,O 19,16:7
  Doctor Herzl 1945,D 21,25:4
Grubinski, W (Playwright)
  Pecheresse Innocent, La 1927,Ja 9,VII,2:5
Grubler, Ekkehard (Costume Designer)
  Nathan der Weise 1966,D 10,45:2
Grubman, Anton
  Mob, The 1920,O 11,18:1
  Whispering Well, The 1920,D 6,19:1
Grubman, Jimmie
  Life With Father 1967,O 20,53:2
Grudden, Mrs
  George Barnwell; London Merchant, The
    1928,O 2,34:3
Grudeff, Marian (Composer)
  Baker Street 1965,F 17,36:1
Grudeff, Marian (Lyricist)
  Baker Street 1965,F 17,36:1
Gruden, Alexander
  Progress of Bora, The Tailor, The 1968,Je 27,49:2
Grudier, James
  Antony and Cleopatra 1947,N 27,49:2
Gruen, Bernhard (Composer)
  Musik um Susi 1933,Ja 1,IX,1:1
Gruen, John (Composer)
  Absalom 1956,My 17,37:2
  Escurial 1956,O 3,29:2
Gruen, John (Playwright)
  Soap Opera 1968,My 10,54:7
  Treatment, The 1968,My 10,54:7
Gruen, Pamela
  Crucible, The 1964,Ap 7,30:2
  Midsummer Night's Dream, A 1968,Je 13,54:1
Gruenberg, Len S (Miscellaneous)
  Compulsion 1957,O 25,21:1
Gruenberg (Composer)
  Emperor Jones, The 1933,Mr 15,21:4
Gruendgens, Gustaf
  Verbrecher, Die 1928,D 23,VIII,4:1
  Alles Schwindel 1931,Je 7,VIII,2:5
  Faust 1933,Ja 22,IX,1:1
  Hundred Days 1934,Ap 29,IX,2:3
  Glass Wasser, Das 1934,D 30,IX,2:1
  Hans Sonnenstoessers Hoellenfahrt 1937,Ja 3,X,2:6
  Manor House 1953,D 27,53:4
  Faust, Part I; Prologue in Heaven 1961,F 5,27:2
  Faust, Part I; Play, The 1961,F 5,27:2
  Faust, Part I; Prelude in the Theater 1961,F 5,27:2
Gruendgens, Gustaf (Director)
  Menschen im Hotel 1930,Mr 16,IX,4:1
  Alles Schwindel 1931,Je 7,VIII,2:5
  Hans Sonnenstoessers Hoellenfahrt 1937,Ja 3,X,2:6
  Manor House 1953,D 27,53:4
  Faust, Part I; Prelude in the Theater 1961,F 5,27:2
  Faust, Part I; Prologue in Heaven 1961,F 5,27:2
  Faust, Part I; Play, The 1961,F 5,27:2
Gruendgens, Gustaf (Playwright)
  Hans Sonnenstoessers Hoellenfahrt 1937,Ja 3,X,2:6
Gruendgens, Gustaf (Producer)
  Actis 1961,N 23,50:2
Gruenewald, Tom
  Henry IV 1960,Ap 19,41:1
Gruenewald, Tom (Director)
  Androcles and the Lion 1961,N 22,24:2
  Dark Lady of the Sonnets, The 1961,D 15,48:1
  Plot Against the Chase Manhattan Bank, The
    1963,N 27,29:1
  Man With a Load of Mischief, The 1966,N 7,65:1
  Philosophy in the Boudoir 1969,My 22,55:2
Gruenewald, Tom (Miscellaneous)
  Julius Caesar 1959,Ag 4,30:1
Gruening, Hunt S
  On the Level 1937,Mr 26,24:4
Gruening, Ilka
  Trial of Mary Dugan, The 1928,Je 24,VIII,1:4
Gruenwald, Alfred (Lyricist)
  Countess Maritza 1926,S 20,21:1
  Circus Princess, The 1927,Ap 26,32:2
Gruenwald, Alfred (Original Author)
  Circus Princess, The 1937,Ag 31,26:6
  Mr Strauss Goes to Boston 1945,S 7,20:2
Gruenwald, Alfred (Playwright)
  Yankee Princess, The 1922,O 3,22:1
  Countess Maritza 1926,Mr 30,20:3
  Countess Maritza 1926,S 20,21:1
  Countess Maritza 1927,Ja 30,VII,4:3
  Circus Princess, The 1927,Ap 26,32:2
  Herzogin von Chicago, Die 1929,F 17,IX,2:3
  Marietta 1929,D 8,X,4:4
  Dancing Partner 1930,Jl 27,VIII,2:3
  Dancing Partner 1930,Ag 6,24:2
  Victoria and Her Hussar 1930,S 21,IX,2:6

Gruenwald, Alfred (Playwright)—Cont
Veilchen von Montmartre 1931,Mr 29,VIII,3:1
Flower of Hawaii; Blume von Hawaii, Die
1931,O 4,VIII,4:1
Frau Die Weiss Was Sie Will, Eine 1932,O 9,IX,3:7
Ball at the Savoy 1933,F 19,IX,3:1
Ball at the Savoy 1933,S 9,9:7

Gruenwald, John
Zeppelin 1929,Ja 15,22:3

Gruet, Allan
Rothschilds, The 1970,O 20,40:1

Gruette, Ruth
County Chairman, The 1936,My 26,26:5

Grumbach, Jeanne
Sujet de Roman, Un 1923,Je 10,VII,1:4
Aiglon, L' 1924,O 21,21:1
Naked 1924,O 28,27:2
Naked 1924,N 2,VII,1:1
Madame Sans-Gene 1924,N 4,30:1
Famille Lavolette, La 1926,O 10,VIII,2:1

Grun, Bernard (Composer)
Balalaika 1936,D 23,17:4

Grund, Leo
Armseligen Besenbinder, Die 1928,N 19,16:2

Grunden, Wayne
Betty Behave 1927,Mr 9,28:4

Grundjoan, Tove
I Shall Have a Child; Jeg Skal Ha' et Barn
1939,Ap 2,X,2:4

Grundman, Clare (Composer)
Lend an Ear 1948,D 17,38:2

Grundman, Clare (Miscellaneous)
Show Girl 1961,Ja 13,37:1
Drat! the Cat! 1965,O 11,54:2

Grundman, Clare (Musical Director)
Phoenix '55 1955,Ap 25,20:2
Joyce Grenfell Requests the Pleasure
1955,O 11,48:1

Grundy, Sidney (Lyricist)
Engaged! or Cheviot's Choice 1965,Ap 24,19:2

Grundy, William
Chocolate Dandies, The 1924,S 2,22:2

Grunewald, Isaac (Costume Designer)
Fiesco 1930,Jl 13,VIII,2:1

Grunewald, Isaac (Scenic Designer)
Fiesco 1930,Jl 13,VIII,2:1

Grunwald, A de (Playwright)
Bridge of Sighs 1939,Jl 2,IX,1:4

Grunwald, Willy (Director)
Christus 1922,My 28,VI,1:6

Grunwell, Charles
Lost in the Stars 1949,O 31,21:2
Pursuit of Happiness, The 1952,Mr 22,9:2

Gruskin, Shelley
Play of Daniel, The 1961,D 28,22:6
Play of Daniel, The 1966,Ja 2,64:4

Grusso, Don
Lower North 1944,Ag 26,15:4
I Gotta Get Out 1947,S 26,27:2
Collector's Item 1952,F 9,11:2
Anniversary Waltz 1954,Ap 8,34:1
Gazebo, The 1958,D 13,2:7

Gruver, Elbert
Saint's Parade 1930,N 1,23:4
Double Door 1933,S 22,15:5

Grylls, John R
Cotton Stockings 1923,D 19,16:2

Grymes, Oliver
He Who Gets Slapped 1922,Ja 10,15:1

Grynberg, Henryk
Mirele Efros 1967,O 20,55:1
Mother Courage 1967,N 17,55:1

Gryparis, J (Translator)
Electra 1952,N 20,38:2
Electra 1961,S 20,23:4
Choephori 1961,S 27,32:4
Eumenides 1961,S 27,32:4
Electra 1964,S 8,33:1

Gstettenbaur, Gustl Stark
Im Weissen Roessel 1930,D 28,VIII,2:4

Guadagno, George
Belafonte at the Palace 1959,D 16,55:1

Guard, Audrey
Song of Norway 1944,Ag 22,20:2
Oklahoma! 1958,Mr 8,15:2

Guard, Philip
Midsummer Night's Dream, A 1954,S 22,33:1

Guardino, Harry
Hatful of Rain, A 1955,N 10,44:1
One More River 1960,Mr 19,12:2
Natural Affection 1963,F 2,5:2
Anyone Can Whistle 1964,Ap 6,36:1
Rose Tattoo, The 1966,O 21,36:2
Rose Tattoo, The 1966,N 20,II,1:1
Seven Descents of Myrtle, The 1968,Mr 28,54:1
Seven Descents of Myrtle, The 1968,Ap 7,II,1:5

Guardino, Jerome
Breaking Wall, The 1960,Ja 26,27:5
Opening of a Window, The 1961,S 26,32:2
Hop, Signor! 1962,My 8,45:2
Yes is for a Very Young Man 1963,Mr 6,7:5
Burning, The 1963,D 4,57:1
Shout From the Rooftops 1964,O 29,40:1

Guardino, Jerome (Producer)
Opening of a Window, The 1961,S 26,32:2

Guare, John (Playwright)
Muzeeka 1968,Ap 29,47:2
Cop-Out 1969,Ap 8,42:1
Home Fires 1969,Ap 8,42:1
Cop-Out 1969,Ap 20,II,11:4

Guarnieri, Anna-Maria
Hamlet 1964,Je 2,32:8

Guarnieri, Gianfrancesco (Playwright)
Arena Conta Zumbi 1969,Ag 19,31:1

Gubanov, Leonid
Cherry Orchard, The 1965,F 10,46:1
Three Sisters, The 1965,F 12,15:1
Kremlin Chimes 1965,F 25,23:1

Gubelman, Herbert
Dark Hours, The 1932,N 15,24:2

Gubelman, Johnny
All Good Americans 1933,D 6,29:2

Guber, Lee (Producer)
Happiest Girl in the World, The 1961,Ap 4,42:1
Catch Me if You Can 1965,Mr 10,50:1
Sherry! 1967,Mr 29,39:1
Grand Music Hall of Israel, The 1968,F 7,42:1
Inquest 1970,Ap 24,38:1

Guberman, Ruth
Adding Machine, The 1956,F 10,17:1

Gubernick, Hy
Full Moon in March, A 1960,S 20,48:1

Gubernick, Hy (Composer)
Full Moon in March, A 1960,S 20,48:1

Gudde, Lynda
Hair 1967,O 30,55:1

Gude, Jack
Mr Faust 1922,Ja 31,11:2
Hairy Ape, The 1922,Mr 10,18:2

Gude, O J Jr
Little Theatre Tournament; Prison Bars
1928,My 10,31:1

Gudegast, Hans
Great Indoors, The 1966,F 2,23:1

Gudin, Michel
Otage, L' 1959,O 27,42:1

Gudinsky, Bella (Mme)
It Is to Laugh 1927,D 27,24:2

Gudrun and Galloway
Merry World, The 1926,Je 9,18:3

Gudzin, Maryann
Stage Affair, A 1962,Ja 17,30:2

Guelis, Jean
Firebird of Florence 1945,Mr 23,13:4

Guelis, John
Helen Goes to Troy 1944,Ap 25,17:2

Guelma, Andre
On Ne Badine Pas Avec l'Amour; No Trifling With
Love 1968,Mr 5,35:1

Guelpli, Gabrielle
Music in the Air 1932,N 9,28:2

Guelstdorf, Max
Peripherie 1926,D 19,VII,4:4
Timon 1932,Mr 6,VIII,2:1
Alt Heidelberg; Student Prince, The
1932,N 20,IX,3:3

Guenther, Felix (Composer)
Saint Joan 1940,Mr 11,10:6
Yours Is My Heart 1946,S 6,16:5

Guenther, Skeet
Ankles Aweigh 1955,Ap 19,27:1

Gueral, Vladimir
Paese dei Campanelli, Il; Land of Bells, The
1935,My 10,25:4

Guerard, Roland
Brigadoon 1947,Mr 14,28:2

Guerden, Keith (Costume Designer)
Golem, The 1959,F 26,38:2

Guerden, Keith (Scenic Designer)
Golem, The 1959,F 26,38:2

Guerdon, Barbara
Marching Song 1937,F 18,18:2

Guerdon, David (Playwright)
Laundry, The 1963,F 19,5:2

Guerin, John
Low Bridge 1933,F 10,13:4

Guerin, Jules (Costume Designer)
Beaux' Stratagem, The 1928,Je 5,20:1

Guerin, Jules (Scenic Designer)
Beaux' Stratagem, The 1928,Je 5,20:1

Guerini, Therese
Starlight 1925,Mr 4,17:2
R U R 1930,F 18,28:1
Marco Millions 1930,Mr 4,24:4
Laughing Woman, The 1936,O 14,30:1

Guerlac, Anne
Riot 1968,D 20,64:1

Guerman
Chauve-Souris 1929,Ja 23,20:2

Guermanova, Marie
Brothers Karamazov, The 1926,D 12,VIII,3:4
Medea 1926,D 19,VII,3:3

Guermanova, Marie (Miscellaneous)
Lower Depths, The 1928,My 13,IX,2:7
Poverty Is No Crime 1928,My 13,IX,2:7

Guerney, Bernard Guilbert (Translator)
Three Sisters, The 1939,O 16,23:1

Guerney, Celia
Orpheus in Hades 1930,D 16,30:1

Guerra, Francesco
Promessi Sposi I,; Betrothed, The 1934,O 22,13:2

Guerra, Francesco (Playwright)
Promessi Sposi I,; Betrothed, The 1934,O 22,13:2

Guerra, Robert (Scenic Designer)
Your Own Thing 1968,Ja 15,33:1
Transgressor Rides Again, The 1969,My 21,42:1

Guerrasio, John
Macbeth 1969,D 23,25:1
Oedipus 1970,F 23,30:1
Hamlet 1970,O 19,51:1

Guerreri, Giovanni
Fioretta 1929,F 6,30:3

Guerrero, Danny
Who's Who, Baby? 1968,Ja 30,36:1

Guerrero, Maria
Pluma en el Viento; Feather in the Wind
1932,Ap 2,13:4
Tambor y Cascabel; Drum and Bell
1932,Ap 21,25:4
Cuando Los Hijos De Eva No Son Los Hijos De
Adan; When Eve's Children Are Not Adam's
1932,Ap 23,11:2

Guest, Christopher
Room Service 1970,My 13,49:1

Guest, Clifford
Michael Todd's Peep Show 1950,Je 29,37:2

Guest, Pam
And People All Around 1968,F 12,46:1

Guest, Richard
Streets of New York, The 1934,Jl 21,14:5
Oliver Twist 1934,Ag 11,16:5

Guest, Val (Playwright)
Red-Headed Blonde 1953,Ap 20,22:4

Guetary, Georges
Bless the Bride 1947,My 5,31:2
Arms and the Girl 1950,F 3,28:2
Portofino 1958,F 22,8:3

Guettel, Henry (Miscellaneous)
Romulus 1962,Ja 11,27:1

Guggenheimer, Randolph (Mrs)
Variations of 1940 1940,Ja 29,12:1

Gugleotti, Vincent
Love Life 1948,O 8,31:2

Guhl, Edwin
Hold Your Horses 1933,S 26,26:4

Guhl, William
Scapegoat, The 1950,Ap 20,36:5

Guhlke, Antoinette
Lend an Ear 1948,D 17,38:2

Guidall, George
And People All Around 1968,F 12,46:1
Wrong Way Light Bulb, The 1969,Mr 5,40:1
Trees Die Standing, The 1969,O 13,52:1
President's Daughter, The 1970,N 4,41:2

Guidall, George (Director)
And People All Around 1968,F 12,46:1

Guidi, Robert
In the Matter of J Robert Oppenheimer
1968,Je 7,31:1

Guier, Anne
Best Foot Forward 1941,O 2,28:2

Guier, Kay
Best Foot Forward 1941,O 2,28:2

Guilbert, Ann
Billy Barnes Revue, The 1959,Je 10,42:2

Guilbert, Warburton
Virgin of Bethulia, The 1925,F 24,17:2
Three Doors 1925,Ap 24,16:4

Guilbert, Warburton (Composer)
New Faces 1934,Mr 16,24:5

Guilbert, Yvette
Untitled-One Woman Show 1928,Je 24,VIII,4:2
A la Mode de Chez Nous 1929,My 26,IX,4:1

Guile, Helen
Patience 1964,Mr 26,42:1
Pirates of Penzance, The 1965,Ap 21,50:6
Patience 1968,My 16,52:1

Guiles, Fred Lawrence (Playwright)
Song for a Certain Midnight 1959,S 17,49:1

Guiles, Fred Lawrence (Scenic Designer)
Song for a Certain Midnight 1959,S 17,49:1

Guilet, Helene
Utopia, Limited; Flowers of Progress, The
1957,F 27,21:1
Pirates of Penzance, The 1957,My 8,43:1
Gondoliers, The 1957,My 29,34:2
From Here to There; Real Strange One, A
1958,Ap 24,37:3

Guilet, Helene (Miscellaneous)
Utopia, Limited; Flowers of Progress, The
1957,F 27,21:1

Guilford, Carol
Italian Straw Hat, The 1957,O 1,37:2
Walk-Up 1961,F 24,24:1

Guilford, Nanette
Vaudeville (Palace) 1932,Ap 4,13:4
Caviar 1934,Je 8,19:2

377

Guilford, William
Family Reunion, The 1960,D 10,26:1
Guilford, Willor
Policy Kings 1938,D 31,6:2
Guilfoyle, Emmet
Hoboken Hoboes 1929,D 28,10:8
Guilfoyle, J
Tick-Tack-Toe 1920,F 24,11:2
Guilfoyle, Paul
Jolly Roger, The 1923,Ag 31,10:4
Othello 1925,Ja 12,11:1
Green Hat, The 1925,S 16,23:2
Box Seats 1928,Ap 20,27:2
Revolt 1928,N 1,25:3
Zeppelin 1929,Ja 15,22:3
Penny Arcade 1930,Mr 11,24:5
This One Man 1930,O 22,32:3
Privilege Car 1931,Mr 4,33:1
Six Characters in Search of an Author
1931,Ap 16,29:2
Steel 1931,N 19,26:5
Marathon 1933,Ja 28,8:8
Fly by Night 1933,Je 3,16:2
Give Us This Day 1933,O 28,20:6
Wooden Slipper, The 1934,Ja 4,16:3
Jayhawker 1934,N 6,34:2
Guillaumat, Gerard
Three Musketeers, The 1968,Je 26,43:1
George Dandin 1968,Je 28,36:1
Tartuffe 1968,Jl 3,28:2
Guillaume, Robert
Kwamina 1961,O 24,42:1
Fly Blackbird 1962,F 6,26:2
Fly Blackbird 1962,Ap 29,II,1:1
Tambourines to Glory 1963,N 4,47:1
Porgy and Bess 1964,My 7,32:1
Porgy and Bess 1965,O 20,53:3
Life and Times of J Walter Smintheus, The
1970,D 10,59:1
Guilliatt, Lee
In Circles 1968,Je 28,36:1
Guilloton, Alain
Tall Kentuckian, The 1953,Je 17,30:1
Guillott, Gilles
Grand Vizir, Le 1970,Ap 8,38:3
Guimera, Angel (Playwright)
Feudalismo Oppure La Terra Bassa; Feudalism or
the Lowland 1937,Mr 8,22:2
Tierra Baja 1937,My 8,22:4
Guin, Al
First Night 1930,N 27,32:3
Jamboree 1932,N 25,18:4
Big Blow 1938,O 3,11:2
Guiname, James
Topaze 1930,F 13,25:3
Guinan, John (Playwright)
Black Oliver 1927,Je 5,VII,2:3
Rune of Healing, The 1931,Mr 22,VIII,3:1
Guinan, Patricia
Major Barbara 1965,My 18,33:1
Imaginary Invalid, The 1967,My 2,53:1
Fumed Oak 1967,My 4,34:1
Still Life 1967,My 4,34:1
Ways and Means 1967,My 4,34:1
John Brown's Body 1968,F 13,49:2
Comedy of Errors, The 1968,F 28,40:2
She Stoops to Conquer 1968,Ap 1,58:3
Guinan, Robert A
Waiting for Lefty 1967,D 19,58:2
Guinan, Texas
Padlocks of 1927 1927,Jl 6,23:4
Vaudeville (Palace) 1932,Mr 7,13:4
Guinee, Christopher
Heritage and Its History, A 1965,My 19,42:1
Guinevere, Camelot
Great Scot! 1965,N 12,56:3
Guinness, Alec
Great Expectations 1939,D 17,IX,4:5
Flare Path 1942,D 24,20:2
King Lear 1946,S 25,39:4
King Lear 1946,O 13,II,2:3
Cyrano de Bergerac 1946,N 3,I,54:6
Richard II 1947,My 11,II,3:7
Cocktail Party, The 1949,Ag 23,28:6
Cocktail Party, The 1950,Ja 23,17:2
Cocktail Party, The 1950,Ja 29,II,1:1
Cocktail Party, The 1950,My 21,II,3:2
Under the Sycamore Tree 1952,Ap 24,38:4
Under the Sycamore Tree 1952,My 11,II,3:7
Richard III 1953,Jl 15,22:2
All's Well That Ends Well 1953,Jl 16,18:2
All's Well That Ends Well 1953,Jl 19,II,1:1
Richard III 1953,Jl 19,II,1:1
Hotel Paradiso 1956,My 3,34:8
Ross 1960,My 13,26:4
Exit the King 1963,S 13,19:4
Dylan 1964,Ja 20,18:1
Incident at Vichy 1966,Ja 27,28:5
Time Out of Mind 1970,Jl 15,29:1
Guinness, Alec (Playwright)
Great Expectations 1939,D 17,IX,4:5
Guion, Marion
Potters, The 1923,D 10,21:4

Guion, Raymond
Piper, The 1920,Mr 20,14:2
Eyvind of the Hills 1921,F 2,14:1
Why Not? 1922,D 25,20:1
Cradle Snatchers 1925,S 8,28:2
Take My Advice 1927,N 2,24:3
Mirrors 1928,Ja 19,17:1
Sherlock Holmes 1928,F 21,18:4
Say When 1928,Je 27,29:3
War Song, The 1928,S 25,29:3
Jonesy 1929,Ap 10,32:2
Young Sinners 1929,N 29,24:4
Guion, Robert
Unexpected Husband 1931,Je 3,29:4
Guiran and Marguerite
Showboat Revue 1934,Ag 18,13:2
Guiraud, Edmund (Playwright)
Black Divan 1921,Ap 10,VI,1:1
Bonheur du Jour, Le 1926,D 5,VIII,6:1
Guise, Florence
Silver Box, The 1928,Ja 18,23:1
Guise, Jeanne
Peter Ibbetson 1931,Ap 9,30:3
Guisti, Roy
Earl Carroll's Vanities 1923,Jl 6,8:2
Guiterman, Arthur (Composer)
Rivals, The 1942,Ja 15,24:2
Guiterman, Arthur (Lyricist)
School for Husbands, The 1933,O 17,26:5
Dream of Sganarelle, The 1933,O 17,26:5
Mariette 1937,Je 29,18:3
Guiterman, Arthur (Miscellaneous)
Rivals, The 1942,Ja 15,24:2
Guiterman, Arthur (Playwright)
School for Husbands, The 1933,O 17,26:5
Dream of Sganarelle, The 1933,O 17,26:5
Chimes of Corneville, The 1934,Je 29,16:2
Guiterman, Arthur (Translator)
Mariette 1937,Je 29,18:3
Guiterman, Ruth
Electra 1932,Ja 9,21:4
Guiterrez, Carmen
West Side Story 1957,S 27,14:4
Guitterez, Ernesto
Sex Fable, The 1931,O 21,26:1
Guiterson, Waldemar (Miscellaneous)
Star Time 1944,S 13,16:2
Guitry, Lucien
Grand Duke, The 1921,Ap 17,VI,1:8
Grand Duc, Le 1922,Jl 30,VI,1:7
Sujet de Roman, Un 1923,Ja 14,VII,1:1
Sujet de Roman, Un 1923,Je 10,VII,1:4
Lion et la Poule, Le 1923,N 21,23:2
Apres l'Amour 1924,Mr 2,VIII,1:3
Guitry, Sacha
Jacqueline 1921,N 20,VI,1:3
Grand Duc, Le 1922,Jl 30,VI,1:7
Mozart 1925,D 27,VII,6:7
Deburau 1926,D 28,16:1
Mozart 1926,D 28,16:1
Mozart 1927,Ja 2,VII,1:1
Illusioniste, L' 1927,Ja 11,36:5
Desire 1927,My 29,VII,2:7
Mariette 1928,O 21,IX,5:6
Et Vive le Theatre! 1930,Ap 20,VIII,2:8
Rapide de Minuit, Le; Last Mile, The
1932,Ap 3,VIII,2:1
Jalousie, La 1932,D 4,IX,3:6
Chateaux en Espagne 1933,Ap 30,IX,2:3
Illusioniste, L' 1933,D 3,IX,7:7
Fin du Monde, La 1935,N 3,X,3:8
Mon Pere Avait Raison 1936,Je 21,IX,2:4
Mot de Cambronne, Le 1936,O 25,X,3:8
Genevieve 1936,O 25,X,3:8
Limping Devil, The 1948,Ja 22,36:4
Guitry, Sacha (Director)
Springtime 1924,My 11,VIII,1:4
Guitry, Sacha (Lyricist)
Mozart 1926,N 23,26:2
Guitry, Sacha (Original Author)
Where There's a Will 1939,Ja 18,16:6
Guitry, Sacha (Playwright)
Deburau 1920,D 24,14:3
Deburau 1921,Ja 2,VI,3:1
Deburau 1921,Ja 16,VI,1:1
Grand Duke, The 1921,Ap 17,VI,1:8
Grand Duke, The 1921,N 2,20:1
Grand Duke, The 1921,N 6,VI,1:1
Jacqueline 1921,N 20,VI,1:3
Grand Duke, The 1921,N 27,VI,1:1
Petite Main Qui Se Place, Une 1922,Jl 2,VI,1:1
Grand Duc, Le 1922,Jl 30,VI,1:7
Sujet de Roman, Un 1923,Ja 14,VII,1:1
Pasteur 1923,Mr 13,19:1
Comedian, The 1923,Mr 14,14:1
Pasteur 1923,Mr 18,VII,1:1
Pasteur 1923,Mr 25,VIII,1:1
Comedian, The 1923,Mr 25,VIII,1:1
Comedian, The 1923,Ap 8,VIII,1:1
Beranger 1923,Ap 20,20:3
Lion et la Poule, Le 1923,N 21,23:2
Mozart 1925,D 27,VII,6:7
Mozart 1925,D 27,VII,2:1

Guitry, Sacha (Playwright)—Cont
Mozart 1926,Jl 4,VII,1:3
Deburau 1926,N 14,VIII,2:1
Mozart 1926,N 23,26:2
A Vol d'Oiseau 1926,D 5,VIII,8:7
Mozart 1926,D 28,16:1
Deburau 1926,D 28,16:1
Mozart 1927,Ja 2,VII,1:1
Illusioniste, L' 1927,Ja 11,36:5
Desire 1927,My 29,VII,2:7
Miracle, Un 1927,D 25,VIII,4:3
Mariette 1928,O 21,IX,5:6
Untitled-Play 1928,D 9,III,3:8
Attore, L' 1929,Mr 11,29:5
Histoires de France 1929,O 27,IX,2:4
IIIe Chambre, La 1929,N 24,X,2:1
Marietta 1929,D 8,X,4:4
Et Vive le Theatre! 1930,Ap 20,VIII,2:8
Fall of Berg-Op-Zoom, The 1930,Je 8,IX,2:7
Desire 1930,Jl 27,VIII,1:8
Jalousie, La 1930,N 23,IX,1:1
Frans Hals 1931,Ap 26,VIII,2:5
Untitled-Play 1932,Ja 31,VIII,3:1
Jalousie, La 1932,Jl 3,IX,1:3
Chateaux en Espagne 1933,Ap 30,IX,2:3
Untitled-Play 1933,Je 4,IX,1:6
Tour au Paradis, Un 1933,D 3,IX,7:7
Illusioniste, L' 1933,D 3,IX,7:7
Florestan Ier, Prince de Monaco 1933,D 31,IX,2:2
Nouveau Testament 1934,N 11,IX,3:6
Quand Jouons-Nous La Comedie? 1935,O 27,IX,2:1
Fin du Monde, La 1935,N 3,X,3:8
Mon Pere Avait Raison 1936,Je 21,IX,2:4
Mot de Cambronne, Le 1936,O 25,X,3:8
Genevieve 1936,O 25,X,3:8
Mariette 1937,Je 29,18:3
S A D M P, La 1937,N 14,XI,7:5
Limping Devil, The 1948,Ja 22,36:4
Don't Listen, Ladies 1948,D 29,16:2
Guitry, Sacha (Producer)
Mariette 1928,O 21,IX,5:6
Rapide de Minuit, Le; Last Mile, The
1932,Ap 3,VIII,2:1
Jalousie, La 1932,D 4,IX,3:6
Mot de Cambronne, Le 1936,O 25,X,3:8
Genevieve 1936,O 25,X,3:8
Guittard, Laurence
Chronicles of Hell, The 1969,O 19,II,12:1
Guitton, Jean (Playwright)
Jeune Homme Venait de Se Pendre, Un
1926,O 31,VIII,2:4
Baigneuse du Lido, La 1928,Jl 1,VIII,1:8
Monsieur Qui Se Regrette, Un 1928,D 9,X,2:7
Femme Sous la Pluie, Llne 1929,My 26,IX,4:1
Gulack, Max
Country Scandal, A 1960,My 6,21:8
Worm in Horseradish, A 1961,Mr 14,32:3
Poppa Is Home 1961,D 20,37:1
Gulager, Clu
Long Gallery, The 1958,Mr 7,17:2
Gulak, Max
Bonds of Interest, The 1951,D 1,7:2
Gulbrandsen, Signe
Captain Jinks of the Horse Marines 1938,Ja 28,16:2
Gulbrandson, Signe
Poisoned Kiss, The 1937,Ap 22,19:1
Guldemeister, Horst (Miscellaneous)
Don Carlos 1964,N 25,40:1
Captain of Koepenick, The 1964,D 2,60:1
Gulden, F Byron
Brown Danube, The 1939,My 18,30:4
Gulesian, M H (Mrs) (Playwright)
Made in America 1925,O 15,27:2
Gulesian, M H (Playwright)
Made in America 1925,O 15,27:2
Guliaeva, Nina
Kremlin Chimes 1965,F 25,23:1
Gulick, Elizabeth
Daddy Dumplins 1920,N 23,11:1
Gullan, Campbell
Red Blinds 1926,O 1,27:1
What Never Dies 1926,D 29,24:2
Spellbound 1927,N 15,26:2
Caste 1927,D 24,8:1
Sign of the Leopard 1928,D 12,34:4
Design for Living 1933,Ja 3,19:5
Design for Living 1933,Ja 25,13:2
Gullan, Campbell (Director)
Pickwick 1927,S 6,35:2
Interference 1927,O 19,24:3
Diplomacy 1928,My 29,16:3
Diplomacy 1928,Je 3,VIII,1:1
Gullestad, Anne
Othello 1963,Ap 13,10:4
Gulliksen, J Walter
Grey Heir, The 1926,Ap 6,29:2
Gulliksen, J Walter (Playwright)
Grey Heir, The 1926,Ap 6,29:2
Gulliver, Robert
Reunion of Sorts 1969,O 15,40:1
Gulliver, Vincent
Fast Life 1928,S 27,35:2
Gumble, Albert (Composer)
Red Pepper 1922,My 30,8:3

Gumble, Miriam
Centuries, The 1927,N 30,23:1
International, The 1928,Ja 16,24:4

Gumeny, Peter
Billy Budd 1955,My 4,35:1
Great Sebastians, The 1956,Ja 5,27:1
Who Was That Lady I Saw You With?
  1958,Mr 4,33:2
Jolly's Progress 1959,D 7,42:2
One Flew Over the Cuckoo's Nest 1963,N 14,40:2

Gums, Reuben
Way of the Cross, The 1959,Ja 16,35:2
Mystery of the Finding of the Cross, The
  1959,Ja 16,35:2

Gunderman, Claire
Rumple 1957,N 7,42:2

Gunderson, Don
Othello 1958,Jl 4,16:1
Twelfth Night 1958,Ag 7,21:4
Borak 1960,D 14,51:1
Beautiful Dreamer 1960,D 28,22:1
Richard II 1961,Ag 30,25:1
Pilgrim's Progress 1962,Mr 21,36:2
Witches' Sabbath 1962,Ap 20,22:2
Macbeth 1962,N 17,16:2
Burn Me to Ashes 1963,N 20,48:1

Gundlach, Reinhold (Scenic Designer)
Versunkene Glocke, Die 1936,N 20,26:3

Gundlach, Robert (Lighting Director)
Sun and I, The 1949,Mr 21,18:4
Bruno and Sidney 1949,My 4,38:2

Gundlach, Robert (Scenic Designer)
Lamp at Midnight 1947,D 22,29:2
Church Street 1948,F 10,27:2
Respectful Prostitute, The 1948,F 10,27:2
Respectful Prostitute, The 1948,F 15,II,1:1
Victors, The 1948,D 27,17:2
Sun and I, The 1949,Mr 21,18:4
Bruno and Sidney 1949,My 4,38:2
Fifth Horseman, The 1949,Je 14,26:6

Gundunas, Lewis
Zorba 1968,N 18,58:1

Gundy, Cletus L (Producer)
Typewriter, The 1955,Jl 29,8:3

Gundy, Leon
Love in Our Time 1952,O 4,14:3

Gunn, Bill
Immoralist, The 1954,F 9,22:1
Take a Giant Step 1956,S 26,30:1
Sign of Winter 1958,My 8,35:1
Moon on a Rainbow Shawl 1962,Ja 16,30:1
Antony and Cleopatra 1963,Je 21,33:1
Troilus and Cressida 1965,Ag 13,17:1

Gunn, Bill (Playwright)
Marcus in the High Grass 1960,N 22,38:6

Gunn, John
Family Reunion, The 1960,D 10,26:1

Gunn, Moses
In White America 1963,N 1,26:1
Lonesome Train, The 1965,Je 17,25:1
Hard Travelin' 1965,Je 17,25:1
Day of Absence 1965,N 16,56:1
Bohikee Creek 1966,Ap 29,39:1
Measure for Measure 1966,Jl 14,27:1
Hand Is on the Gate, A 1966,S 22,54:1
Junebug Graduates Tonight! 1967,F 27,35:1
Titus Andronicus 1967,Ag 10,43:2
Song of the Lusitanian Bogey, The 1968,Ja 3,52:1
Summer of the Seventeenth Doll 1968,F 21,59:1
Summer of the Seventeenth Doll 1968,Mr 3,II,3:1
Kongi's Harvest 1968,Ap 15,49:1
Kongi's Harvest 1968,Ap 21,II,5:3
Daddy Goodness 1968,Je 5,37:1
Romeo and Juliet 1968,Ag 16,19:1
Cities in Bezique; Beast's Story, A 1969,Ja 13,26:1
Cities in Bezique; Owl Answers, The
  1969,Ja 13,26:1
Perfect Party, The 1969,Mr 21,42:1
Othello 1970,Je 22,43:1
Othello 1970,Je 28,II,1:1
Othello 1970,S 15,51:1

Gunn, Moses (Director)
Contributions; Plantation 1970,Mr 10,53:1
Contributions; Contribution 1970,Mr 10,53:1
Contributions; Shoes 1970,Mr 10,53:1

Gunn, Thomas
Come Seven 1920,Jl 20,10:1
Cornered 1920,D 9,18:2
Wild Oats Lane 1922,S 7,12:1
Zeno 1923,Ag 27,14:2
Green Beetle, The 1924,S 3,12:3
Edgar Allan Poe 1925,O 6,31:1
Virgin, The 1926,F 23,26:1
Heaven-Tappers, The 1927,Mr 9,28:3
Show Boat 1927,D 28,26:1
Show Boat 1932,My 20,22:2

Gunnell, John
Murder in the Cathedral 1935,D 21,11:3

Gunner, Paul (Producer)
Two Mrs Carrolls, The 1943,Ag 4,14:1

Gunnersen, Mickey
Girl in Pink Tights, The 1954,Mr 6,13:2

Gunning, John D (Producer)
Four O'Clock 1933,F 14,19:6

Gunnis, Gordon
Pinch Hitter, A 1922,Je 2,20:4
John 1927,N 5,16:4
Privilege Car 1931,Mr 4,33:1

Gunter, Herman
Susannah 1955,F 25,18:4

Gunter, John (Miscellaneous)
Silence 1970,Ap 3,43:1
Landscape 1970,Ap 3,43:1

Gunther, Alec
Blood Wedding 1958,Ap 1,35:1

Gunther, Gabriele
Susannah and the Elders 1959,O 19,37:3

Gunther, Hanna
Winners and Losers 1947,F 27,27:2

Gunther, Helene
Seven 1929,D 28,10:5

Gunther, John (Original Author)
Inside U S A 1948,My 23,II,1:1

Gunther, Ted
Dark Is Light Enough, The 1955,F 24,20:1
Great Sebastians, The 1956,Ja 5,27:1
West Side Story 1960,Ap 28,31:1
Ross 1961,D 27,20:2
West Side Story 1964,Ap 9,24:2

Gunthy, William
Bedfellows 1929,Jl 3,19:2

Gunty, Morty
Love in E Flat 1967,F 14,38:1

Guren, Sheldon B (Miscellaneous)
Not Now Darling 1970,O 30,33:1

Gurgone, Frances
Legal Grounds 1940,D 2,18:4

Gurian, Manning (Producer)
Southern Exposure 1950,S 27,36:3
Warm Peninsula, The 1959,O 21,46:2

Gurin, Ellen
Caution: A Love Story 1969,Ap 4,45:1
Dirtiest Show in Town, The 1970,Je 29,43:2

Gurion, Israel
Overcoat, The 1960,S 7,45:1

Gurkin, Konstantin
Aladdin and His Wonderful Lamp 1963,O 21,39:1

Gurley, Walker
Way, The 1940,O 12,20:3

Gurlitz, Eugene (Scenic Designer)
Anatomist, The 1957,F 27,21:5

Gurman, Jamey
Moby Dick 1970,Je 3,52:1
Hamlet 1970,O 27,54:2
Rosencrantz and Guildenstern Are Dead
  1970,N 19,39:3

Gurney, A R Jr (Playwright)
David Show, The 1968,N 1,34:2
Tonight in Living Color; Golden Fleece, The
  1969,Je 11,43:1
Tonight in Living Color; David Show, The
  1969,Je 11,43:1

Gurney, Claud
They Came by Night 1937,Jl 25,X,1:3

Gurney, Claud (Playwright)
Mary Read 1934,N 22,26:7
Mary Read 1934,D 16,XI,3:4

Gurney, Claud (Producer)
Hell for Leather 1936,N 27,27:2

Gurney, Dennis
Aren't We All? 1923,My 22,14:2
Havoc 1924,S 2,22:2
Shall We Join the Ladies? 1925,Ja 14,19:1
Aloma of the South Seas 1925,Ap 21,18:1
Maid of All Work 1927,Ja 13,28:4
Last Torture, The 1927,Ja 13,28:4
Cocktail Impromptu 1927,Ja 13,28:4
Butterflies 1927,F 2,22:4
Morgue, The 1927,F 2,22:4
Minuet, A 1927,Mr 5,12:2
We're All in the Gutter 1927,Mr 5,12:2
Maker of Images, The 1927,Mr 5,12:2
Bless You, Sister 1927,D 27,24:5
Grey Fox, The 1928,O 23,32:3
Prince of Pilsen, The 1930,Ja 14,24:3
Affair of State, An 1930,N 20,30:3
Anatomist, The 1932,O 25,24:3
Late One Evening 1933,Ja 10,27:3
Hotel Alimony 1934,Ja 30,16:2
Distant Shore, The 1935,F 22,26:2
Bishop Misbehaves, The 1935,Ag 27,23:4
Good Hunting 1938,N 22,26:5
Man's House, A 1943,Ap 3,10:4

Gurney, Dennis (Director)
Years Between, The 1942,F 7,13:2
Savonarola 1942,Ap 24,20:2
Inside Story 1942,O 30,22:2
Tinker's Dam 1943,Ja 29,22:2
Man's House, A 1943,Ap 3,10:4
Moment Musical 1943,Je 1,18:1
Career Angel 1943,N 19,24:2
Caukey 1944,F 18,15:4
Earth Journey 1944,Ap 28,24:2
Don't, George! 1944,N 4,18:6
Home Is the Hero 1945,Ja 20,16:4

Gurney, Dennis (Director)—Cont
Simon's Wife 1945,Mr 9,16:4
Slice It Thin 1945,My 11,22:5
Seven Mirrors 1945,O 26,17:2
Young American, A 1946,Ja 18,14:5
Mary of Magdala 1946,Mr 26,24:5
Come Marching Home 1946,My 20,18:6
Derryowen 1946,O 29,34:2
If in the Green Wood 1947,Ja 17,27:6
Lady of Fatima 1948,F 13,27:4
Minstrel Boy, The 1948,O 15,28:2
City of Kings 1949,F 18,27:2
Shake Hands With the Devil 1949,O 21,30:4
Armor of Light 1950,F 24,26:4
Faith and Prudence 1952,O 15,40:2
Angelic Doctor 1953,Ap 14,30:2
Slightly Delinquent 1954,O 26,32:5
Bamboo Cross 1955,F 22,17:2
Song Out of Sorrow 1955,N 1,27:3
Age and Grace 1956,F 21,38:2
Comedian, The 1956,O 18,36:4
Parade at the Devil's Bridge 1957,F 19,35:7
Doctor Faustus 1957,F 19,35:7
Truce of the Bear 1957,O 24,39:1
Child of the Morning 1958,Ap 22,40:2
Madre, La 1959,F 12,24:1
Egoists, The 1959,O 14,52:2

Gurney, Dennis (Miscellaneous)
Listen to the Quiet 1958,O 28,40:2

Gurney, Edmund
Deburau 1920,D 24,14:3
Blue Lagoon, The 1921,S 15,16:1
If Winter Comes 1923,Ap 3,26:1
Dancers, The 1923,O 18,17:2

Gurney, Edmund (Mrs)
Happy-Go-Lucky 1920,Ag 25,6:1
Married Woman, The 1921,D 26,21:1
Secrets 1922,D 26,11:1
Assumption of Hannele, The 1924,F 16,16:2

Gurney, Helen
Bab 1920,O 19,12:1

Gurney, Henry
Maker of Images, The 1927,Mr 5,12:2

Gurney, John
Devil and Daniel Webster, The 1939,My 19,26:1

Gurney, Mr (Producer)
Taming of the Shrew, The 1937,Ap 11,XI,2:1

Gurney, Peter (Playwright)
Tom Sawyer 1958,Jl 15,21:8

Gurney, Priscilla
Jonica 1930,Ap 8,27:1

Gurnie-Butler, G
Find the Fox 1930,Je 21,20:4

Gurrey, Nicola
Midsummer Night's Dream, A 1968,D 9,59:1

Gurskaya, Sonia
Major Noah 1929,F 23,17:2
Roaming Stars 1930,Ja 25,12:2
Riverside Drive 1931,Ja 6,24:2
Man With the Portfolio, The 1931,F 12,24:6
Who Is Who? 1938,D 24,13:3
Far-Away Corner, A 1939,F 15,15:2

Gurster, Eugen (Playwright)
Wetter Fuer Morgen-Veranderlich 1932,Je 19,IX,1:3

Gurt, Joseph (Miscellaneous)
Riding Hood Revisited 1961,Ja 4,26:1
Eccentricities of Davy Crockett, The 1961,Ja 4,26:1
Willie the Weeper 1961,Ja 4,26:1

Gurvey, Henry
God Loves Us 1926,O 20,22:2
One Shot Fired 1927,N 8,32:5

Gus
Sweet Adeline 1929,S 4,33:1

Gusakova, L
Aristocrats 1935,My 2,16:2

Gushee, Philip
Galileo 1968,D 1,88:4
Narrow Road to the Deep North 1969,D 2,64:1

Gushee, Stephen L (Director)
Bed Bug, The 1931,Mr 20,28:6

Gushee, Stephen L (Original Author)
Bed Bug, The 1931,Mr 20,28:6

Guske, William
Conquering Hero, The 1961,Ja 17,40:2

Gusky, Shirley
Reunion of Sorts 1969,O 15,40:1

Guslin, Gertrude
Passion Flower, The 1920,Ja 14,12:1

Gusman, Alfred
Tom Sawyer - Ballad of the Mississippi
  1947,D 27,11:3

Guss, Jack Raphael (Playwright)
Umbrella, The 1965,My 27,31:1

Guss, Lew
Man With the Golden Arm, The 1956,My 22,28:1

Guss, Louis
Girl on the Via Flaminia, The 1954,F 10,37:1
In Splendid Error 1954,O 27,33:6
He Who Gets Slapped 1956,F 2,18:1
Mandragola 1956,Mr 1,36:4
Bonds of Interest, The 1958,My 7,43:1
Handful of Fire 1958,O 2,45:3
And the Wind Blows 1959,Ap 29,28:1
One More River 1960,Mr 19,12:2

Guss, Louis—Cont

Camino Real 1960,My 17,42:2
Once There Was a Russian 1961,F 20,32:2
Night of the Iguana, The 1961,D 29,10:1
Mother Courage and Her Children 1963,Mr 30,5:5
Diamond Orchid 1965,F 11,44:4
Flora, the Red Menace 1965,My 12,41:2
But, Seriously... 1969,F 28,29:1
Gandhi 1970,O 21,37:1

Gustafson, Carol

Seven Mirrors 1945,O 26,17:2
Flies, The; Mouches, Les 1947,Ap 18,26:3
Three Sisters, The 1955,F 26,13:2
Twelfth Night 1958,Ag 7,21:4
Three Sisters, The 1959,S 22,46:1
Merchant of Venice, The 1962,F 3,13:2
Dylan 1964,Ja 20,18:1
Serjeant Musgrave's Dance 1968,Je 16,52:4
Resistible Rise of Arturo Ui, The 1968,Ag 8,25:1
Merton of the Movies 1968,S 26,62:1
Resistible Rise of Arturo Ui, The 1968,D 23,44:1

Gustafson, Elsie

Inside Story 1942,O 30,22:2

Gustafson, Karen (Musical Director)

Illya Darling 1967,Ap 12,37:1
Rondelay 1969,N 6,55:1
Show Me Where the Good Times Are 1970,Mr 6,32:1

Gustafson, Lillian

Jazz a La Carte 1922,Je 3,8:3

Gustafson, Stephen

Our Town 1969,N 28,50:1

Gustafson, Walter (Miscellaneous)

Transgressor Rides Again, The 1969,My 21,42:1

Gustavson, Tylar

Earthlight Theater 1970,N 4,38:2

Gustin, Edward

Matty and the Moron and Madonna 1965,Mr 30,53:1

Gustin, Gertrude

Extra 1923,Ja 24,22:3
Solid Ivory 1925,N 17,29:3

Gustin, Oskar (Costume Designer)

Don Juan 1970,F 7,24:2

Gustin, Oskar (Scenic Designer)

Don Juan 1970,F 7,24:2

Gustke, Marie

Side-Show 1931,My 16,13:1

Guterson, Waldemar (Musical Director)

Desert Song, The 1946,Ja 9,20:2

Guthern, Dorothy

Yellow Jacket, The 1928,N 8,27:3
Solitaire 1929,Mr 13,28:3
Getting Even 1929,Ag 20,31:1

Guthman, Louise (Lighting Director)

Iolanthe 1962,Ag 8,34:2
Up Eden 1968,N 27,42:1

Guthman, Louise (Miscellaneous)

Santa Claus 1960,Jl 22,13:1
Calvary 1960,Jl 22,13:1
Escurial 1960,Jl 22,13:1
Iolanthe 1962,Ag 8,34:2

Guthrie, Charles W

Road Together, The 1924,Ja 18,21:2

Guthrie, Ian

Killer, The 1960,Mr 23,33:1

Guthrie, Joseph

Tavern, The 1920,S 28,14:1
Man in the Making, The 1921,S 21,16:2
Busybody, The 1924,S 30,27:5
Gorilla, The 1925,Ap 29,24:2
Yellow 1926,S 22,30:1
Woman of Destiny, A 1936,Mr 3,25:2
Treasure Island 1938,My 15,II,2:3

Guthrie, Judith (Miscellaneous)

He Who Gets Slapped 1946,Mr 21,31:4

Guthrie, Tyrone

Paganini 1937,Je 6,XI,1:2

Guthrie, Tyrone (Director)

Sweet Aloes 1934,N 1,24:1
Mary Read 1934,N 22,26:7
Mary Read 1934,D 16,XI,3:4
Hervey House 1935,My 18,21:2
Sweeney Agonistes 1935,O 2,26:2
Dance of Death, The 1935,O 2,26:2
Call It a Day 1936,Ja 29,15:2
Sweet Aloes 1936,Mr 5,24:5
Paganini 1937,My 21,18:6
Hamlet 1937,Je 4,26:6
Cherry Orchard, The 1941,S 7,IX,2:5
He Who Gets Slapped 1946,Mr 21,31:4
He Who Gets Slapped 1946,Mr 31,II,1:1
Oedipus Rex 1948,My 24,23:2
Tamburlaine the Great 1951,O 14,II,3:7
Timon of Athens 1952,Je 8,II,3:1
Richard III 1953,Jl 15,22:2
All's Well That Ends Well 1953,Jl 16,18:2
Richard III 1953,Jl 19,II,1:1
All's Well That Ends Well 1953,Jl 19,II,1:1
Taming of the Shrew, The 1954,Jl 1,22:2
Taming of the Shrew, The 1954,Jl 4,II,1:1
Oedipus Rex 1954,Jl 17,6:6
Matchmaker, The 1954,S 5,II,3:7
Matchmaker, The 1954,N 14,II,3:1

Bishop's Bonfire, The 1955,Mr 6,II,3:1
Matchmaker, The 1955,My 8,II,1:1
Life in the Sun, A 1955,Ag 24,24:7
Life in the Sun, A 1955,Ag 28,II,1:6
Matchmaker, The 1955,D 6,45:6
Six Characters in Search of an Author 1955,D 12,38:1
Matchmaker, The 1955,D 18,II,3:1
Six Characters in Search of an Author 1955,D 25,II,3:1
Tamburlaine the Great 1956,Ja 20,19:1
Tamburlaine the Great 1956,Ja 29,II,1:1
Oedipus Rex 1956,S 4,32:6
Candide 1956,D 3,40:2
Candide 1956,D 9,II,5:1
Troilus and Cressida 1956,D 27,21:1
First Gentleman, The 1957,Ap 26,22:2
First Gentleman, The 1957,My 5,II,1:1
Twelfth Night 1957,Jl 4,16:4
Mary Stuart 1957,O 9,39:1
Mary Stuart 1957,O 20,II,1:1
Makropoulos Secret, The 1957,D 4,52:4
Tenth Man, The 1959,N 6,24:2
Tenth Man, The 1959,N 15,II,1:1
H M S Pinafore 1960,Jl 17,51:1
H M S Pinafore 1960,S 8,41:1
Love and Libel 1960,D 8,44:1
Pirates of Penzance, The 1961,S 7,41:1
Gideon 1961,N 10,38:1
Gideon 1961,N 19,II,1:1
Time to Laugh, A 1962,Ap 25,31:4
Alchemist, The 1962,N 29,44:1
Hamlet 1963,My 9,41:1
Hamlet 1963,My 19,II,1:1
Three Sisters, The 1963,Jl 22,19:2
Henry V 1964,My 13,52:1
Volpone 1964,Jl 20,18:3
Richard III 1965,Je 3,26:1
Cherry Orchard, The 1965,Ag 2,17:2
Dinner at Eight 1966,S 28,38:1
Dinner at Eight 1966,O 9,II,1:1
Measure for Measure 1967,F 15,37:1
Harpers Ferry 1967,Je 6,52:2
House of Atreus, The; Bringers of Offerings, The 1967,Jl 24,23:1
House of Atreus, The; Furies, The 1967,Jl 24,23:1
House of Atreus, The; Agamemnon 1967,Jl 24,23:1
House of Atreus, The 1968,D 18,55:1

Guthrie, Tyrone (Miscellaneous)

Saint Joan 1964,My 14,41:1

Guthrie, Tyrone (Playwright)

Follow Me 1932,D 11,IX,5:3
Haste To The Wedding 1954,My 6,44:6
Six Characters in Search of an Author 1955,D 12,38:1
Tamburlaine the Great 1956,Ja 20,19:1
Makropoulos Secret, The 1957,D 4,52:4

Guthrie, Tyrone (Producer)

Love's Labour's Lost 1932,Ag 7,IX,1:7
Tempest, The 1934,F 4,IX,3:4
Mrs Nobby Clark 1935,F 28,16:2
Players' Masque for Marie Tempest, The 1935,Je 23,IX,1:3
Othello 1938,F 27,X,1:4
Matchmaker, The 1954,N 5,16:4
Merchant of Venice, The 1955,Jl 1,13:1
Troilus and Cressida 1956,Ap 4,22:7
Troilus and Cressida 1957,Ja 6,II,1:1
Twelfth Night 1957,Jl 7,II,1:1
All's Well That Ends Well 1959,Ap 22,30:3
Three Estates, The 1959,Ag 26,25:3
Pirates of Penzance, The 1961,S 17,II,1:1
Alchemist, The 1962,N 29,44:1
Coriolanus 1963,D 17,52:1
Dinner at Eight 1966,O 9,II,1:1

Guthrie, Tyrone (Translator)

Three Sisters, The 1963,Jl 22,19:2
Cherry Orchard, The 1965,Ag 2,17:2
Three Sisters, The 1968,Mr 18,56:1

Guthrie, William A (Playwright)

Ignorants Abroad, The 1960,My 24,43:2

Gutierrez, Carmen

Shinbone Alley 1957,Ap 15,23:2

Gutierrez, Fernando (Miscellaneous)

Along Came a Spider 1963,My 28,33:1

Gutierrez, Isaura

Cuando Los Hijos De Eva No Son Los Hijos De Adan 1937,My 1,17:4
Tierra Baja 1937,My 8,22:4

Gutierrez, Leopoldo

Evensong 1933,F 1,13:4

Gutierrez, Lolina

Difunta, La 1969,N 2,86:5

Gutman, Arthur H (Composer)

Suzette 1921,N 25,18:3

Gutman, John (Translator)

Heimkehr aus der Fremde, Die; Stranger, The 1949,S 2,14:1

Guttenberg (Costume Designer)

Gods of the Mountain, The 1950,My 25,36:2
Aria Da Capo 1950,My 25,36:2
Once Around the Block 1950,My 25,36:2

Gutterman, Marley

Whispering Well, The 1920,D 6,19:1

Gutterson, Wilder (Mrs)

Riff-Raff 1926,F 9,18:6

Guttmann, Karl (Director)

Diary of Anne Frank, The 1956,N 29,43:1

Guttmann-Horch, Maria

Faust 1947,N 29,9:2

Gutzkow, Karl (Playwright)

Uriel Acosta 1939,D 31,18:3

Guy

Affaires Son les Affaires, Les 1924,Mr 11,17:1
Avare, L'; Miser, The 1924,Mr 12,17:3
Monsieur Brotonneau 1924,Mr 13,14:1
Blanchette 1924,Mr 19,19:4

Guy, Barrington

Comedy of Errors, The 1923,My 16,22:5
Make Me Know It 1929,N 5,32:5
Ginger Snaps 1930,Ja 1,30:5
Brain Sweat 1934,Ap 5,24:4
Black Rhythm 1936,D 21,19:2

Guy, Bessie

Run, Little Chillun! 1933,Mr 2,21:3

Guy, Bette

Darwin's Theories 1960,O 19,53:2

Guy, Eula

Dear Me 1921,Ja 18,14:1
Great Broxopp, The 1921,N 16,22:1
Personal Appearance 1934,O 18,26:7
Work Is for Horses 1937,N 22,14:6
Work Is for Horses 1937,N 22,14:6
Sunup to Sundown 1938,F 2,14:3
Family Portrait 1939,Mr 9,18:4

Guy, Mr

Roi, Le 1931,Ap 5,VIII,3:1

Guy, Nathaniel

Comedy of Errors, The 1923,My 16,22:5

Guy, Shirley

Francesca da Rimini 1967,S 12,54:1

Guy Sisters

Great Temptations, The 1926,My 19,29:1

Guyll, Judy

On the Town 1959,F 14,15:1
Fallout 1959,My 21,36:2
Greenwich Village U S A 1960,S 29,30:5
Tattooed Countess, The 1961,My 4,40:2
Make Me Disappear 1969,My 14,34:1

Guyse, Sheila

Memphis Bound 1945,My 25,23:2
Lost in the Stars 1949,O 31,21:2

Guzman, Senor

Farandula, La 1930,Mr 25,34:6

Guzzetti, Joseph Jr (Producer)

Salome 1956,F 14,24:4
Florentine Tragedy, The 1956,F 14,24:4

Guzzinati, Margherita

Venetian Twins, The 1968,My 29,23:1

Gvida, Marcelle

Crucifies, Les 1923,O 30,17:2

Gwardian, Richard

When Differences Disappear 1941,Je 3,17:4

Gwathney, Harry

Moon Is a Gong, The 1926,Mr 13,21:3

Gwathney, Tonice

Ododo 1970,N 25,26:1

Gwenn, Edmund

Skin Game, The 1920,My 23,VI,1:3
Skin Game, The 1920,O 31,VI,1:2
Voice From the Minaret, The 1922,Ja 31,11:2
Fedora 1922,F 11,18:1
Old Bill, M P 1922,Ag 13,VI,1:8
Great Broxopp, The 1923,Mr 11,VIII,2:4
Making of an Immortal, The 1928,Ap 29,IX,1:3
Devil's Disciple, The 1930,S 21,IX,2:1
Laburnum Grove 1933,N 29,23:4
Laburnum Grove 1933,D 17,IX,4:2
Laburnum Grove 1935,Ja 15,23:5
Laburnum Grove 1935,Ja 20,X,1:1
Thank You, Mr Pepys; Ninety Sail 1937,D 1,27:2
She, Too, Was Young 1938,S 4,X,2:1
Wookey, The 1941,Ag 26,23:2
Wookey, The 1941,S 11,20:5
Wookey, The 1941,S 21,IX,1:1
Three Sisters, The 1942,D 22,31:2
Three Sisters, The 1942,D 27,VIII,1:1
Sheppey 1944,Ap 19,27:2
You Touched Me! 1945,S 26,27:2
You Touched Me! 1945,S 30,II,1:1

Gwillim, Jack

Romeo and Juliet 1956,S 19,34:6
Richard II 1956,O 24,44:1
Romeo and Juliet 1956,O 25,41:1
Macbeth 1956,O 30,42:2
Troilus and Cressida 1956,D 27,21:1

Gwinn, Miriam

Banjo Eyes 1941,D 26,20:2

Gwinn, R L

It's the Valet 1933,D 15,25:4

GWS

Instructions for the Running of Trains, etc on the Erie Railway to Go Into Effect January 1,1862 1970,Ja 7,36:2

Gwyer, Mace
Miracle in the Mountains 1947,Ap 26,10:2
Gwyn, Peter
Subway, The 1929,Ja 26,15:1
Gwynn, Harold
Romance 1921,Mr 1,18:2
Gwynn, Michael
I Am a Camera 1954,Mr 13,11:1
Crucible, The 1956,Ap 11,28:3
Gwynne, Coates
Devil Within, The 1925,Mr 17,19:4
Gwynne, Fred
Mrs McThing 1952,F 21,22:1
Love's Labour's Lost 1953,F 5,20:3
Frogs of Spring, The 1953,O 21,36:2
Irma la Douce 1960,S 30,31:2
Here's Love 1963,O 4,28:1
Gwynne, Georgia
Houseboat on the Styx, The 1928,D 26,14:3
Wonderful Night, A; Fledermaus, Die
1929,N 1,23:3
Gwynne, Harold
Blushing Bride, The 1922,F 7,12:1
Gyarmathy, Michel (Costume Designer)
Folies Bergere 1964,Je 3,36:1
Gyarmathy, Michel (Director)
Folies Bergere 1964,Je 3,36:1
Gyarmathy, Michel (Playwright)
Folies Bergere 1964,Je 3,36:1
Gyarmathy, Michel (Scenic Designer)
Folies Bergere 1964,Je 3,36:1
Gygi, Ota
Vaudeville (Palace) 1927,Je 28,29:2
Gyimes, William (Director)
Lady From the Sea, The 1956,D 13,49:5
Hole, The 1961,Ap 4,42:2
Gyimes, William (Miscellaneous)
Resounding Tinkle, The 1961,Ap 4,42:2
Gyimes, William (Producer)
Lady From the Sea, The 1956,D 13,49:5
Fools Are Passing Through 1958,Ap 3,24:2
Egg and I, The 1958,S 11,43:4
Don Juan in Hell 1960,O 4,47:3
Gylda, Marcelle
Nuit au Bouge, Une 1923,O 16,18:1
Catherine Goulden 1923,N 6,22:1
Laboratoire des Hallucinations, Le 1923,N 20,23:3
Gynt, Greta
Lysistrata 1938,Ag 7,IX,1:5
Gynt, Kaj (Playwright)
Rang Tang 1927,Jl 13,20:1
Gyseghem, Andre Van (Director)
Stevedore 1935,My 7,26:2
Gyula (Scenic Designer)
Man of Destiny, The 1956,Ap 26,38:1
On the Harmfulness of Tobacco 1956,Ap 26,38:1
West of the Moon 1961,Je 29,26:1
Blood Bugle, The 1961,Je 29,26:1

H

Haack, Bruce (Composer)
Kumquat in the Persimmon Tree, The
1962,Je 19,27:2
Haack, Kaethe
Race With the Shadow, The 1927,Ap 7,23:1
Jewel Robbery; Juwelenraub am Kurfurstendamm
1932,F 21,VIII,2:3
Lauter Luegen 1937,O 24,XI,3:1
Haack, Morton (Costume Designer)
Strange Bedfellows 1948,Ja 15,27:3
Make Mine Manhattan 1948,Ja 16,26:2
Haade, William
Iron Men 1936,O 20,30:6
Haag, J Robert
Lady Luck 1936,Ap 16,21:2
Bet Your Life 1937,Ap 6,20:2
Haakon, Paul
Champagne, Sec 1933,O 16,20:2
Music Hath Charms 1934,D 31,8:2
At Home Abroad 1935,S 4,22:3
At Home Abroad 1935,S 8,IX,1:1
At Home Abroad 1935,S 20,17:4
At Home Abroad 1935,O 27,IX,8:1
At Home Abroad 1935,O 27,IX,1:1
Florodora 1936,Ag 23,II,8:2
Show Is On, The 1936,N 9,22:2
Show Is On, The 1936,N 15,XI,2:1
Show Is On, The 1936,D 26,14:2
Hooray for What! 1937,N 7,XI,2:4
Hooray for What! 1937,D 2,32:5
American Jubilee 1940,My 13,20:5
Mexican Hayride 1944,Ja 29,9:6
Haakon, Paul (Choreographer)
Mexican Hayride 1944,Ja 29,9:6
Mexican Hayride 1944,F 6,II,1:1
Haals, Ione
Gondoliers, The 1935,Ag 6,20:5
Haas, Alexander (Composer)
Battleship Gertie 1935,Ja 19,9:2
Haas, Alexander (Musical Director)
Play's the Thing, The 1948,My 9,II,1:1

Haas, Amelia
Bye Bye Birdie 1960,Ap 15,13:4
Hello, Dolly! 1964,Ja 17,22:1
Haas, Dolly
Wie Werde Ich Reich und Gluecklich?
1930,Ag 31,VIII,2:1
Circle of Chalk, The 1941,Mr 27,28:4
War and Peace 1942,My 22,26:3
Winter Soldiers 1942,N 30,19:2
Doctors Disagree 1943,D 29,15:2
Crime and Punishment 1947,D 23,29:3
Crime and Punishment 1948,Ja 4,II,1:1
Lute Song 1948,O 12,32:3
Circle of Chalk, The 1950,D 2,8:3
Lute Song 1959,Mr 13,24:1
Brecht on Brecht 1961,N 15,52:2
Haas, Holly (Costume Designer)
Bananas 1968,D 5,60:1
Great Career, A 1968,D 30,25:1
Evening for Merlin Finch, An 1968,D 30,25:1
Haas, Holly (Scenic Designer)
Now Is the Time for all Good Men 1967,S 27,42:1
Year Boston Won the Pennant, The
1969,My 23,38:1
Haas, Hugo
First Crocus, The 1942,Ja 3,14:6
War and Peace 1942,My 22,26:3
R U R 1942,D 4,30:2
Galileo 1947,Ag 1,21:4
Magdalena 1948,Jl 28,27:2
Magdalena 1948,S 21,31:2
Haas, Roland (Producer)
Temper the Wind 1946,D 28,10:2
Temper the Wind 1947,Ja 12,II,1:1
Haase, Alfred
Great Music 1924,O 6,24:1
Haase, John (Original Author)
Fun Couple, The 1962,O 27,15:2
Haase, John (Playwright)
Fun Couple, The 1962,O 27,15:2
Haase, Oscar
Musical Mishaps 1949,Mr 21,18:2
Habart, Michel (Translator)
Red Roses for Me 1961,F 11,26:5
Habas, Lionel
Land Beyond the River, A 1957,Mr 29,15:7
Enemy of the People, An 1958,F 26,24:2
Golem, The 1959,F 26,38:2
Habberstad, Claude (Playwright)
Cat Comes Back, The 1923,Ja 29,11:2
Habberton, John
Fireworks on the James 1940,My 15,30:2
Habbick, Jack (Miscellaneous)
Mikado, The 1962,N 14,43:1
Gondoliers, The 1962,N 16,25:2
Pirates of Penzance, The 1962,N 21,28:1
Trial by Jury 1962,N 23,32:4
H M S Pinafore 1962,N 23,32:4
Iolanthe 1962,N 28,42:1
Habe, Hans (Original Author)
Walk in Darkness 1963,O 29,30:2
Haber, Arlene
Wild Duck, The 1938,Ap 16,16:5
Haber, David (Miscellaneous)
Ages of Man 1958,D 29,21:1
Laughs and Other Events 1960,O 11,57:1
Haber, Janet (Costume Designer)
Don Carlos 1962,F 28,27:5
Haber, John (Costume Designer)
Candida 1969,F 3,29:1
Haber, John (Scenic Designer)
Candida 1969,F 3,29:1
And Puppy Dog Tails 1969,O 20,60:1
Haber, Louis (Composer)
Lew Leslie's Blackbirds of 1939 1939,F 13,12:2
Haber, Louis (Lyricist)
Lew Leslie's Blackbirds of 1939 1939,F 13,12:2
Haber, Sheldon (Costume Designer)
Don Carlos 1962,F 28,27:5
Haber, Sheldon (Lighting Director)
Burning Bright 1959,O 17,27:2
Haber, Sheldon (Scenic Designer)
Burning Bright 1959,O 17,27:2
Haber-Hirsch, David
Have You Heard This One 1953,N 9,23:4
Habib, George
Sun and I, The 1949,Mr 21,18:4
Habimah (Miscellaneous)
Each Had Six Wings 1964,Mr 12,39:1
Habos
Abie's Irish Rose 1928,Je 10,VIII,2:8
Habunek, Vlado (Director)
Canterbury Tales 1968,S 7,23:3
Hacha, Robert
Julius Caesar 1955,Jl 13,20:1
Tempest, The 1955,Ag 2,18:2
Richard III 1957,N 26,41:1
Hachfeld, Eckart (Playwright)
Why Do I Deserve This? 1966,Ja 19,31:2
Hachmeister, Albert
Othello 1943,O 20,18:1
Hack, Mac (Lighting Director)
Pinocchio 1939,Ja 3,19:2

Hack, Moe (Director)
Thank You Svoboda 1944,Mr 2,13:2
Hack, Moe (Lighting Director)
One-Third of a Nation 1938,Ja 18,27:2
Life and Death of an American 1939,My 20,11:2
Clinton Street 1939,O 13,27:2
Brooklyn, U S A 1941,D 28,IX,1:1
Eve of St Mark, The 1942,O 8,30:2
Family, The 1943,Mr 31,22:4
Patriots, The 1943,D 21,22:5
Storm Operation 1944,Ja 12,28:2
Tempest, The 1945,Ja 26,17:2
Hack, Monroe B (Director)
Phantoms 1930,Ja 14,24:3
Blue Holiday 1945,My 22,13:3
E-MC2 1948,Je 16,8:6
Hack, Monroe B (Producer)
Seeds in the Wind 1948,Ap 26,27:2
Talent '49 1949,Ap 13,39:4
Hackady, Hal (Composer)
Leonard Sillman's New Faces of 1968
1968,My 3,43:1
Hackady, Hal (Lyricist)
Leonard Sillman's New Faces of 1968
1968,My 3,43:1
Minnie's Boys 1970,Mr 27,27:1
Minnie's Boys 1970,Ap 5,II,3:1
Hackady, Hal (Playwright)
Almost Crazy 1955,Je 21,37:1
Hackenberg, Wolfgang
Wiener Blut 1964,S 12,14:1
Hacker, Alfred
Passion Play, The 1929,Ap 30,32:1
Hacker, Seymour (Producer)
New Tenant, The 1964,My 28,40:2
Victims of Duty 1964,My 28,40:2
Hackett, Albert
Up the Ladder 1922,Mr 7,11:2
Nervous Wreck, The 1923,O 10,16:1
Twelve Miles Out 1925,N 17,29:2
Off Key 1927,F 9,16:2
Ten Per Cent 1927,S 14,29:3
Mirrors 1928,Ja 19,17:1
Whoopee 1928,D 5,34:3
Up Pops the Devil 1930,S 2,19:1
Up Pops the Devil 1930,S 14,VIII,1:1
Mr and Mrs North 1941,Ja 13,11:2
Mr and Mrs North 1941,F 23,IX,1:1
Hackett, Albert (Original Author)
Everybody's Welcome 1931,O 14,26:3
Hackett, Albert (Playwright)
Up Pops the Devil 1930,S 2,19:1
Up Pops the Devil 1930,S 14,VIII,1:1
Bridal Wise 1932,My 31,15:5
Western Union 1937,Ag 10,22:7
Great Big Doorstep, The 1942,N 27,26:2
Great Big Doorstep, The 1950,Mr 18,8:6
Diary of Anne Frank, The 1955,O 6,24:2
Diary of Anne Frank, The 1955,O 16,II,1:1
Diary of Anne Frank, The 1956,O 14,II,3:1
Diary of Anne Frank, The 1956,N 29,43:1
Diary of Anne Frank, The 1963,Ap 12,33:1
Hackett, Arleen
Unwritten Chapter, The 1920,O 12,18:1
Hackett, Buddy
Lunatics and Lovers 1954,D 14,44:2
Viva Madison Avenue 1960,Ap 7,42:1
I Had a Ball 1964,D 16,50:1
Untitled-Revue 1967,Ag 29,26:1
Hackett, Charles
Variations of 1940 1940,Ja 29,12:1
Hackett, Dolly
Passing Show of 1921, The 1920,D 30,16:2
Make It Snappy 1922,Ap 14,20:2
Hackett, Edward
Seven Lively Arts 1944,D 8,26:6
Hackett, George (Musical Director)
Ice Follies 1957,Ja 16,36:1
Ice Follies 1958,Ja 15,26:2
Ice Follies 1959,Ja 14,30:1
Ice Follies 1960,Ja 13,20:1
Ice Follies 1961,Ja 11,25:2
Ice Follies 1962,Ja 10,24:6
Ice Follies 1963,Ja 10,5:2
Ice Follies 1965,Ja 13,35:1
Ice Follies 1966,Ja 12,27:6
Ice Follies 1967,Ja 11,51:1
Ice Follies 1969,My 23,38:1
Ice Follies 1970,My 23,27:1
Hackett, Hal
Kismet 1953,D 4,2:4
Lady's Not for Burning, The 1957,F 22,26:2
Book of Job, The 1962,F 10,13:1
Hackett, Harley (Miscellaneous)
Exit the King 1968,Ja 10,48:1
Cocktail Party, The 1968,O 8,42:1
Misanthrope, The 1968,O 10,59:1
Hackett, James K
Macbeth 1920,N 3,14:2
Macbeth 1921,Je 7,20:2
Othello 1921,Je 9,10:2
Macbeth 1924,Mr 17,18:1
Macbeth 1924,Mr 23,VIII,1:1

Hackett, Jeanette
Vaudeville (Palace) 1926,My 8,29:2
Vaudeville (Palace) 1926,N 9,30:3
Vaudeville (Palace) 1929,F 18,29:1
Vaudeville (Palace) 1929,D 30,16:3
Vaudeville (Palace) 1931,F 2,23:3
Hackett, Jeanne
Harry Delmar's Revels 1927,N 29,30:2
Hackett, Joan
Call Me by My Rightful Name 1961,F 1,31:1
Peterpat 1965,Ja 7,27:1
Park 1970,Ap 23,47:1
Hackett, Lester (Costume Designer)
Typewriter, The 1955,Jl 29,8:3
Amedee: or, How to Disentangle Yourself
  1955,N 1,27:3
Hackett, Lester (Miscellaneous)
Escurial 1956,O 3,29:2
Lesson, The 1956,O 3,29:2
Hackett, Lester (Producer)
By Hex 1956,Je 19,25:1
Hackett, Lester (Scenic Designer)
Typewriter, The 1955,Jl 29,8:3
Amedee: or, How to Disentangle Yourself
  1955,N 1,27:3
Admirable Bashville, The 1956,F 21,38:1
Dark Lady of the Sonnets, The 1956,F 21,38:1
Hackett, Norman
What's Your Wife Doing? 1923,O 2,10:3
Garden of Weeds 1924,Ap 29,12:3
Hackett, Ralph
Holy Terror, A 1925,S 29,31:2
Hackett, Raymond
Outrageous Mrs Palmer, The 1920,O 13,18:1
Man in the Making, The 1921,S 21,16:2
Broken Branches 1922,Mr 7,11:1
Dreams for Sale 1922,S 14,24:1
Glory 1922,D 26,10:1
Play, A 1925,F 11,19:2
Cradle Snatchers 1925,S 8,28:2
Nightstick 1927,N 11,20:4
Adam Had Two Sons 1932,Ja 17,VIII,3:5
Adam Had Two Sons 1932,Ja 21,17:1
Camille 1932,N 2,23:3
Conquest 1933,F 20,11:3
Nine Pine Street 1933,Ap 28,15:5
Piper Paid 1934,D 26,19:1
Hackett, W J
Judgment Day 1934,S 13,26:4
Call Me Ziggy 1937,F 13,9:6
Window Shopping 1938,D 24,13:2
Jeb 1946,F 22,20:2
Hackett, Walter (Original Author)
Order Please 1934,O 10,21:2
Hackett, Walter (Playwright)
Captain Applejack 1921,D 31,14:2
Pansy's Arabian Night 1924,Ag 24,VII,1:3
Wicked Earl, The 1927,Mr 20,VIII,2:7
Sorry You've Been Troubled 1929,O 13,IX,4:1
Other Men's Wives 1929,N 13,24:4
Gay Adventure, The 1932,Ja 24,VIII,3:5
Road House 1932,O 30,IX,2:3
Afterwards 1933,N 26,IX,3:6
Hyde Park Corner 1934,O 6,20:1
Hyde Park Corner 1934,O 28,IX,3:4
Espionage 1935,O 16,27:5
Espionage 1935,N 10,IX,3:1
Fugitive, The 1936,Je 28,IX,1:8
London After Dark 1937,Ap 8,21:2
Hackett and Delmar
Vaudeville (Hippodrome) 1924,Ja 1,21:1
Hackforth, Norman (Composer)
Sigh No More 1945,Jl 12,8:4
Hackins, Dick
Gang's All Here, The 1931,F 19,21:3
Hackman, Gene
Chaparral 1958,S 10,38:2
Saintliness of Margery Kempe, The 1959,F 3,35:6
Children From Their Games 1963,Ap 12,33:1
Rainy Day in Newark, A 1963,O 23,35:1
Any Wednesday 1964,F 19,34:1
Poor Richard 1964,D 3,59:1
Natural Look, The 1967,Mr 13,45:2
Basement, The 1967,O 3,56:1
Fragments 1967,O 3,56:1
Fragments; Basement, The 1967,O 15,II,3:3
Hacks, Peter (Playwright)
Amphitryon 1970,My 29,13:1
Hadassah Badoch
Sing Israel Sing 1967,My 12,50:1
Hadaway, Tom
Merton of the Movies 1922,N 14,16:2
Haddad, Bob
Babes in Arms 1951,Mr 10,7:3
Haddad, Bob (Choreographer)
Best Foot Forward 1956,Mr 3,16:1
Haddad, Robert (Director)
Until the Monkey Comes 1966,Je 21,38:1
Pastry Shop, The 1970,Je 12,28:1
Young Among Themselves, The 1970,Je 12,28:1
Hadden, Frances (Composer)
Jotham Valley 1951,F 7,37:2

Hadden, George
Beyond the Horizon 1920,F 4,12:1
Haddon, Laurence
Bat, The 1953,Ja 21,28:2
Billy Budd 1955,My 4,35:1
Idiot's Delight 1957,F 23,14:2
Warm Peninsula, The 1959,O 21,46:2
Haddon, Pauline
Tomorrow's a Holiday! 1935,D 31,10:2
Haddon, Peter
Double Dan 1927,Je 5,VII,2:1
No Sleep for the Wicked 1937,Jl 1,32:5
No Sleep for the Wicked 1937,Jl 18,X,1:5
Haden, Katherine
Hamlet 1920,Mr 17,14:2
Fashions for Men 1922,D 6,22:1
Haden, Sara
Merchant of Venice, The 1921,My 14,10:4
Lawful Larceny 1922,Ja 3,20:2
Trigger 1927,D 7,32:1
Wrecker, The 1928,F 28,18:2
Girl Trouble 1928,O 26,22:3
Hot Water 1929,Ja 22,22:3
First Mortgage 1929,O 11,36:1
Hill Between, The 1938,Mr 12,12:5
Haderer, Frank B (Producer)
Single Man at a Party 1959,Ap 22,30:4
Hadfield, Patricia
Iolanthe 1948,Ja 13,29:3
Hadge, Michael
Sweet Enemy, The 1965,F 16,39:1
Impossible Years, The 1965,O 14,55:1
Local Stigmatic, The 1969,N 4,55:2
Hadjidakis, Manos (Composer)
Illya Darling 1967,N 2,58:1
Hadjidakis, Manos (Composer)
Illya Darling 1967,Ap 12,37:1
Hadler, Walter
Patrick--The First 1965,F 19,25:1
Serjeant Musgrave's Dance 1966,Mr 9,44:1
Rimers of Eldritch, The 1967,F 21,53:1
Hawk, The 1968,Ap 18,54:1
Hadley, Bob (Producer)
Autumn's Here 1966,O 26,40:1
Skits-Oh-Frantics 1967,Ap 3,39:2
Hadley, Hap
Greenwich Village Follies 1920,Ag 31,7:3
Hadley, Henry (Playwright)
Lambs Gambol 1925,Ap 27,15:1
Hadley, Sally
Mikado, The 1942,F 4,22:2
Pirates of Penzance, The 1942,F 18,22:2
Iolanthe 1942,F 24,26:4
Gondoliers, The 1942,Mr 4,22:3
Hadra, Phyllis (Composer)
39 Steps 1938,Mr 12,13:1
Hadra, Phyllis (Costume Designer)
39 Steps 1938,Mr 12,13:1
Hadreas, Jimmy
Fine and Dandy 1930,S 24,26:1
Hadreas, Peter
Narrow Road to the Deep North 1969,D 2,64:1
Hadreas, Peter (Composer)
Time for Bed 1969,Je 14,24:1
Take Me to Bed 1969,Je 14,24:1
Hadziscos, N
Electra 1952,N 20,38:2
Oedipus Tyrannus 1952,N 25,35:2
Haedrich, Rolf (Producer)
Tenth Man, The 1962,O 3,46:1
Haffner, Alfred
Mother Sings 1935,N 13,24:1
Haffner, C (Composer)
Fledermaus, Die 1954,My 20,38:5
Hafid, Ali
Zorba 1968,N 18,58:1
Haflin, Dan
Bride of Torozko, The 1934,Jl 10,24:7
Haflin, Harry
Petticoat Fever 1935,Jl 2,24:4
As Husbands Go 1935,Jl 10,24:1
Hafsten, Gunnar
High Named Today 1954,D 11,11:2
Haft, Betty
Pirates of Penzance, The 1942,F 20,20:2
Hagan, Edna
Diana 1929,D 10,37:1
Far Away Horses 1933,Mr 22,21:6
Hilda Cassidy 1933,My 5,18:3
Thunder on the Left 1933,N 1,25:2
John Brown 1934,Ja 23,22:3
Small Miracle 1934,S 27,24:3
Return to Folly 1935,Ja 23,24:3
Remember the Day 1935,S 26,19:3
Hagan, James
Collision 1932,F 17,19:2
Here Come the Clowns 1938,D 8,36:2
Hagan, James (Original Author)
One Sabbath Afternoon 1939,Ja 17,27:5
Hagan, James (Playwright)
Guns 1928,Ag 7,25:2
One Sunday Afternoon 1933,F 16,23:5
One Sunday Afternoon 1933,Mr 19,IX,1:1

Hagan, James (Playwright)—Cont
One Sunday Afternoon 1933,S 17,X,2:4
Mid-West 1936,Ja 2,21:2
Mid-West 1936,Ja 5,IX,3:1
Mid-West 1936,Ja 8,22:4
Hagan, Oliver
Naughty Riquette 1926,S 14,25:2
Hagan, R H
Poet's Follies of 1955 1955,My 15,II,3:1
Hagar, Oma
Steel 1939,D 20,30:2
Hagen, Christian A
Antigone 1930,Ap 25,28:4
Hagen, Hans (Composer)
Wiener Blut 1964,S 12,14:1
Hagen, James
Twelfth Night 1921,N 1,17:1
Merchant of Venice, The 1921,N 22,17:1
Fashions for Men 1922,D 6,22:1
Hagen, James P
Letter of the Law, The; Robe Rouge, La
  1920,F 24,11:1
Hagen, Jean
Another Part of the Forest 1946,N 21,42:2
Ghosts 1948,F 17,31:2
Traitor, The 1949,Ap 1,30:2
Hagen, John Milton (Composer)
Greenwich Villagers, The 1927,Ag 19,20:2
Hagen, John Milton (Lyricist)
Greenwich Villagers, The 1927,Ag 19,20:2
Hagen, John Milton (Playwright)
Bare Facts 1927,Je 30,35:1
Hagen, Reigh
Moondreamers, The 1969,D 9,68:1
Gloria and Esperanza 1970,F 5,32:1
Hagen, Rick
Front Page, The 1969,My 12,54:2
Hagen, Scott
Front Page, The 1969,My 12,54:2
Hagen, Uta
Hamlet 1937,Ag 24,24:4
Sea Gull, The 1938,Mr 29,19:2
Happiest Days, The 1939,Ap 12,26:2
Happiest Days, The 1939,Ap 16,X,1:2
Flight Into China 1939,S 12,28:1
Key Largo 1939,O 31,26:6
Key Largo 1939,N 28,30:2
Othello 1942,Ag 16,VIII,1:7
Vickie 1942,S 23,28:1
Othello 1943,O 20,18:1
Othello 1943,O 24,II,1:1
Othello 1945,My 23,25:4
Whole World Over, The 1947,Mr 28,28:2
Whole World Over, The 1947,Ap 6,II,1:1
Faust 1947,N 29,9:2
Angel Street 1948,Ja 23,26:6
Streetcar Named Desire, A 1949,Je 12,II,1:1
Streetcar Named Desire, A 1950,My 24,36:1
Country Girl, The 1950,N 11,10:6
Country Girl, The 1950,N 19,II,1:1
ANTA Album 1951,My 7,22:7
Saint Joan 1951,O 5,23:2
Saint Joan 1951,O 14,II,1:1
Tovarich 1952,My 15,39:2
In Any Language 1952,O 9,40:2
In Any Language 1952,O 19,II,1:1
Magic and the Loss, The 1954,Ap 10,10:3
Island of Goats 1955,O 5,40:1
Month in the Country, A 1956,Ap 4,23:1
Month in the Country, A 1956,Ap 15,II,1:1
Good Woman of Setzuan, The 1956,D 19,41:2
Good Woman of Setzuan, The 1956,D 30,II,1:1
Port-Royal 1960,Ap 26,41:1
Who's Afraid of Virginia Woolf? 1962,O 15,33:1
Who's Afraid of Virginia Woolf? 1962,O 28,II,1:1
Who's Afraid of Virginia Woolf? 1964,F 8,15:1
Cherry Orchard, The 1968,Mr 20,41:1
Cherry Orchard, The 1968,Ap 7,II,3:7
Hagen, Winston
Prunella 1929,Ap 10,23:3
Hager, Clyde
Keep Moving 1934,Ag 24,10:2
Hager, David (Director)
Doctor Faustus 1961,Ap 26,36:1
Hager, David (Miscellaneous)
Doctor Faustus 1961,Ap 26,36:1
Candida 1961,Ap 27,26:1
Hager, David (Scenic Designer)
Doctor Faustus 1961,Ap 26,36:1
Candida 1961,Ap 27,26:1
Hager, John
Apollo of Bellac, The 1958,Mr 7,17:2
Hager, Linda Rae
I Dreamt I Dwelt in Bloomingdale's 1970,F 13,26:1
Hagerman, James
Glad Tidings 1951,O 12,33:2
Hagerman, James (Miscellaneous)
Come Play With Me 1959,My 1,33:5
Hagerty, Tim
Three Plays of the Sea 1970,Ag 20,39:1
Haggard, Paul
Jungle of Cities 1970,Mr 1,75:2
Haggard, Stephen
Come of Age 1934,Ja 13,16:6

Haggard, Stephen—Cont
Laughing Woman, The 1934,Ap 8,33:6
Laughing Lady, The 1934,My 6,IX,2:5
Maitlands, The 1934,Jl 22,IX,1:3
Flowers of the Forest 1934,D 9,X,3:1
Black Eye, The 1935,O 12,13:5
Black Eye, The 1935,N 10,IX,3:1
Whiteoaks 1936,Ap 15,25:2
Seagull, The 1936,My 21,19:2
Seagull, The 1936,Je 21,IX,1:5
Seagull, The 1936,Ag 30,IX,1:1
Whiteoaks 1938,F 23,26:2
Whiteoaks 1938,Mr 24,20:2
King Lear 1940,Ap 28,IX,1:7

Haggard, Stephen (Director)
Whiteoaks 1938,Mr 24,20:2

Haggart, John (Playwright)
Mackerel Skies 1934,Ja 24,20:4
Reno 1937,Ag 10,22:7

Haggarty, Marion
Lady From the Sea, The 1935,D 14,11:3

Haggert, John D (Playwright)
Seven Year Love 1929,O 27,IX,2:1

Haggerty, Don
Mr and Mrs North 1941,Ja 13,11:2

Haggerty, Elizabeth
Little Theatre Tournament; White Peacock, The 1928,My 11,28:1

Haggerty, George
Hello, Yourself 1928,O 31,28:2
Woof, Woof 1929,D 26,20:4
Vaudeville (Palace) 1930,S 8,17:3
You Said It 1931,Ja 20,21:3

Haggerty, John
Oedipus Rex 1959,Ap 30,36:1

Haggin, Ben Ali (Director)
What Next 1920,Ja 27,7:2
Ziegfeld 9 o'clock Follies 1920,Mr 9,18:1
Field of Ermine 1935,F 9,10:4

Haggin, Ben Ali (Miscellaneous)
Vaudeville (Palace) 1923,Mr 6,26:1
Ziegfeld Follies 1924,Mr 18,25:2

Haggin, Ben Ali (Playwright)
No Foolin' 1926,Je 25,25:1

Haggin, Ben Ali (Scenic Designer)
Ziegfeld Midnight Frolic 1920,Mr 17,14:2
Midnight Frolic 1920,Ag 4,7:1

Haggott, John (Director)
Streets Are Guarded, The 1944,N 21,19:7
Firebird of Florence 1945,Mr 23,13:4

Haggott, John (Miscellaneous)
Macbeth 1941,N 12,30:2
Othello 1945,My 23,25:4
Affairs of State 1950,S 26,37:2

Haggott, John (Producer)
Othello 1943,O 20,18:1

Hagin, Booth
Zombie 1932,F 11,17:2

Hagman, Larry
Cock-A-Doodle Dandy 1950,F 1,26:2
Taming of the Shrew, The 1951,Ap 26,35:2
Once Around the Block 1956,O 29,34:1
Career 1957,My 1,42:6
Career 1957,My 19,II,1:1
Comes a Day 1958,N 7,22:1
God and Kate Murphy 1959,F 27,21:2
Nervous Set, The 1959,My 13,43:1
Warm Peninsula, The 1959,O 21,46:2
Beauty Part, The 1962,D 28,5:2

Hagon, Garrick
King John 1960,Je 29,26:2
Henry VIII 1961,Je 22,22:1
Taming of the Shrew, The 1962,Je 21,25:1
Troilus and Cressida 1963,Je 19,40:2
Cyrano de Bergerac 1963,Je 20,30:1
Timon of Athens 1963,Jl 31,19:2
Richard II 1964,Je 17,47:1
Bourgeois Gentilhomme, Le 1964,Je 18,28:2
King Lear 1964,Je 19,36:1

Hagood, Brown
Nat Turner 1960,N 7,46:3

Hague, Albert (Composer)
Dance Me a Song 1950,Ja 21,10:5
Great Magician, The 1951,N 22,45:1
All Summer Long 1954,S 24,26:2
Plain and Fancy 1955,Ja 28,14:2
Plain and Fancy 1955,F 6,II,1:1
Redhead 1959,F 6,21:1
Redhead 1959,F 15,II,1:1
Girls Against the Boys, The 1959,N 3,26:1
Fun Couple, The 1962,O 27,15:2
Cafe Crown 1964,Ap 18,32:1
Oh, Say Can You See L A 1968,F 9,50:1
Other Man, The 1968,F 9,50:1
Fig Leaves Are Falling, The 1969,Ja 3,19:1

Hague, Albert (Musical Director)
Enchanted, The 1950,Ja 19,34:2

Hague, William E Jr
Once Over Lightly 1938,D 10,13:4

Hahn, Harry
Roger Bloomer 1923,Mr 2,18:3

Hahn, Herbie
Me and Molly 1948,F 27,27:2

Hahn, Milton C (Playwright)
Joan of Arkansas 1925,Ap 5,16:1

Hahn, Pauline
As the Girls Go 1948,N 15,21:2
Twilight Walk 1951,S 25,25:4
Cat on a Hot Tin Roof 1955,Mr 25,18:2

Hahn, Reynaldo (Composer)
Mozart 1925,D 27,VII,2:1
Mozart 1925,D 27,VII,6:7
Ciboulette 1926,O 31,VIII,2:4
Mozart 1926,N 23,26:2
Temps d'Aimer, Le 1926,D 12,VIII,3:4
Mozart 1926,D 28,16:1

Haiduk, Peter J (Miscellaneous)
Country People 1970,Ja 19,35:1

Haig, Emma
Irving Berlin's Music Box Revue 1921,S 23,18:2
Our Nell 1922,D 5,24:1
Rise of Rosie O'Reilly, The 1923,D 26,13:4
Tell Me More 1925,Ap 14,27:3
Vaudeville (Palace) 1926,Jl 13,19:4

Haig, Peter
Romeo and Jeanette 1969,D 16,53:1
Mod Donna 1970,My 4,48:1

Haig, Robert
Sleeping Clergyman, A 1934,O 9,16:1

Haigh, Kenneth
Look Back in Anger 1957,O 2,28:2
Look Back in Anger 1957,O 13,II,1:1
Caligula 1960,F 17,31:1
Caligula 1960,F 28,II,1:1
Altona; Sequestres d'Altona, Les 1961,Je 25,II,3:5
Prometheus Bound 1967,My 11,52:1
Prometheus Bound 1967,Je 11,II,1:1
Henry IV 1968,F 7,40:1
Endecott and the Red Cross 1968,My 7,50:1
Revenger's Tragedy, The 1970,D 2,58:1
Revenger's Tragedy, The 1970,D 6,II,5:1

Haigh, Kenneth (Director)
'Tis Pity She's a Whore 1967,O 21,15:2

Haigh, Richard H
Fiesta 1933,D 16,12:2

Haight, George
Command Performance, The 1928,O 4,27:1

Haight, George (Miscellaneous)
Button, Button 1929,O 24,26:1

Haight, George (Playwright)
Ned Wayburn's Gambols 1929,Ja 16,22:3
Goodbye Again 1932,D 29,16:4
Kind Lady 1935,Ap 24,24:5
Sweet Mystery of Life 1935,O 12,13:3
Goodbye Again 1937,S 1,15:1
Kind Lady 1940,S 4,28:3
Goodbye Again 1943,N 10,28:4
Goodbye Again 1956,Ap 25,38:1

Haight, George (Producer)
Double Door 1933,S 22,15:5
Wednesday's Child 1934,Ja 17,23:2
Post Road 1934,D 5,28:3
Kind Lady 1935,Ap 24,24:5

Haight, Mark
Rose Briar 1922,D 26,11:3
Where's Your Husband? 1927,Ja 15,10:3
Lady for a Night, A 1928,Ap 17,26:4
Sonya's Search for the Christmas Star 1929,D 14,24:6

Haijo, Michael (Composer)
Gay Masquerade 1935,My 15,26:1

Hail, William
Call Me Madam 1950,O 13,25:1

Haile, Eugen (Composer)
Richard III 1920,Mr 21,VI,6:1

Hailey, Marian
Under the Yum-Yum Tree 1964,My 29,18:1
Mating Dance 1965,N 4,58:1
Best Laid Plans, The 1966,Mr 26,15:2
All's Well That Ends Well 1966,Je 17,39:1
Queens of France 1966,S 7,53:1
Long Christmas Dinner, The 1966,S 7,53:1
Antigone 1967,Je 19,43:1
Merchant of Venice, The 1967,Je 22,46:2
Keep It in the Family 1967,S 28,59:1
As You Like It 1968,Je 24,42:3
Love's Labour's Lost 1968,Je 28,36:1
Harvey 1970,F 25,41:1
Castro Complex, The 1970,N 19,40:1

Hailey, Oliver (Playwright)
Hey You, Light Man! 1963,Mr 2,5:2
First One Asleep, Whistle 1966,F 28,19:1
Who's Happy Now? 1969,N 18,39:1

Hailton, Barbara
Anne of Green Gables 1969,Ap 18,39:1

Haimowitz, Oscar
Shakespeare's Merchant 1939 1939,Ja 10,16:3

Haimsohn, George (Lyricist)
Now 1968,Je 6,53:1
Dames at Sea 1968,D 21,46:1
Dames at Sea 1970,S 24,60:1

Haimsohn, George (Playwright)
Now 1968,Je 6,53:1
Dames at Sea 1968,D 21,46:1
Dames at Sea 1970,S 24,60:1

Hain, Charles
It Happens on Ice 1941,Ap 5,13:2

Hain, William
Grand Duchess 1929,D 17,29:2
Gypsy Baron, The 1930,Ap 22,22:8
Chocolate Soldier, The 1932,F 9,30:3
Du Barry 1932,N 23,15:2
Fledermaus, Die 1933,My 14,II,3:8
Roberta 1933,N 20,18:4

Haine, David
I Want You 1961,S 15,29:1
Elizabeth the Queen 1966,N 4,30:1

Haines, A Larry
Thousand Clowns, A 1962,Ap 6,31:2
Thousand Clowns, A 1962,Ap 15,II,1:1
Promises, Promises 1968,D 2,59:3
Promises, Promises 1968,D 15,III,3:1

Haines, Donal (Playwright)
Joan of Arc 1926,Ap 24,21:2

Haines, Helen
Peg o' My Dreams 1924,My 6,25:3

Haines, Hilda
Almost Faithful 1948,Je 5,9:2

Haines, Louis
She Couldn't Say No! 1926,S 1,27:3

Haines, Mervyn Jr
Boy; Job, The; Study in Color 1964,Ag 1,13:1
All's Well That Ends Well 1966,Je 17,39:1
Much Ado About Nothing 1969,Je 16,57:1
Hamlet 1969,Je 30,33:1
Henry V 1969,N 11,43:1

Haines, Mildred
Doughgirls, The 1942,D 31,19:2

Haines, Nat C
So This Is Paris 1930,Ap 27,IX,2:3
Hello Paris 1930,N 17,29:3

Haines, Robert
Nobody Hears A Broken Drum 1970,Mr 20,55:1

Haines, Robert T
Fall and Rise of Susan Lenox, The 1920,Je 11,11:2
Samson and Delilah 1920,N 18,18:1
Samson and Delilah 1920,D 26,VI,3:2
Goldfish, The 1922,Ap 18,15:3
Ever Green Lady, The 1922,O 12,25:2
Vagabond, The 1923,D 28,13:4
Garden of Weeds 1924,Ap 29,12:3
Dope 1926,Ja 4,16:3
Trouper, The 1926,Mr 9,21:1
Donovan Affair, The 1926,Ag 31,15:2
This Is New York 1930,N 29,21:1
Good Fairy, The 1932,N 18,22:3
Allure 1934,O 30,22:6
On to Fortune 1935,F 5,22:2
Hallowe'en 1936,F 21,20:3
Places, Please 1937,N 13,10:6

Haines, Stanley
Patience 1935,S 3,24:4

Haines, William Wister (Original Author)
Command Decision 1947,S 21,I,59:7

Haines, William Wister (Playwright)
Command Decision 1947,O 2,30:2
Command Decision 1947,O 12,II,1:1

Hainesworth, James
Moon on a Rainbow Shawl 1970,D 18,52:1

Hainesworth, Lorna (Scenic Designer)
Lady From Maxim's, The 1970,Je 1,41:1

Hains, Frank (Scenic Designer)
Home Away From, A 1969,Ap 29,40:3

Haire, James (Miscellaneous)
Little Eyolf 1964,Mr 17,31:1

Hairston, Jacqueline
Finian's Rainbow 1953,Mr 7,13:2

Hairston, William (Playwright)
Walk in Darkness 1963,O 29,30:2

Haislip, Bill
De Sade Illustrated 1969,My 13,42:4
Silhouettes 1969,S 9,41:1

Haislip, Bill (Miscellaneous)
De Sade Illustrated 1969,My 13,42:4

Haislip, Bill (Scenic Designer)
De Sade Illustrated 1969,My 13,42:4

Haislip, Harvey (Playwright)
Long Watch, The 1952,Mr 21,19:5

Haiyna
Shakuntala 1959,S 10,41:2

Haizlip, Ellis (Producer)
Amen Corner, The 1965,Je 13,82:4

Hajos, Karl (Composer)
Natja 1925,F 17,19:2
Pearl of Great Price, The 1926,N 2,34:3
White Lilacs 1928,S 11,31:2

Hajos, Mitzi
You Can't Take It With You 1936,D 15,31:1
Mr Big 1941,O 1,24:2
Cafe Crown 1942,Ja 24,12:5

Hajos, Mitzi (Director)
Sari 1930,Ja 29,27:1

Hakim, Raphael (Producer)
Happy Days 1941,My 14,24:2

Hakim, Robert (Producer)
Happy Days 1941,My 14,24:2

Haks, Frederick J (Director)
This Mad Whirl 1937,Ja 10,II,4:8

Halaman-Daris, Frederic (Director)
Sextet 1958,N 27,53:1
Halaman-Daris, Frederic (Lighting Director)
Cast of Characters 1959,Je 11,37:2
Halaman-Daris, Frederic (Producer)
Cast of Characters 1959,Je 11,37:2
Halaman-Daris, Frederic (Scenic Designer)
Cast of Characters 1959,Je 11,37:2
Halare, Vera
Endless Chain, The 1922,S 5,21:2
Halasz, Andreij
Wiener Blut 1964,S 12,14:1
Halasz, Emery (Playwright)
How Long Will You Love Me? 1931,Jl 19,VIII,2:3
Halasz, Laszlo (Miscellaneous)
Once Over Lightly 1942,N 20,26:2
Halasz, Laszlo (Musical Director)
Gypsy Baron, The 1944,N 15,20:3
Halasz, Laszlo (Playwright)
Once Over Lightly 1942,N 20,26:2
Halasz, Peter (Playwright)
Egerfogo; Mousetrap, The 1958,Ja 30,18:6
Halbe, Max (Playwright)
Youth 1920,O 27,14:3
Haldane, Harry M (Lyricist)
Happy Town 1959,O 8,49:2
Haldorn, Georgine
Daddy Dumplins 1920,N 23,11:1
Hale, Allan
Mima 1928,D 13,24:2
Caught Wet 1931,N 5,29:1
Small Miracle 1934,S 27,24:3
Ceiling Zero 1935,Ap 11,26:2
Red Harvest 1937,Mr 31,29:2
Scene of the Crime, The 1940,Mr 29,24:1
Hook'n Ladder 1952,Ap 30,31:2
Hale, Betty
Night Boat, The 1920,F 3,18:1
Rise of Rosie O'Reilly, The 1923,D 26,13:4
Hale, Binnie
Katinka 1923,Ag 31,15:4
Rise and Shine 1936,My 8,21:4
Home and Beauty 1937,F 3,26:2
Home and Beauty 1937,F 21,X,2:1
Hale, Chanin
Idiot's Delight 1957,F 23,14:2
What a Killing 1961,Mr 28,41:1
Hale, Charles
Eternal Road, The 1937,Ja 8,14:2
Hale, Charles E (Miscellaneous)
Papers 1968,D 3,54:1
Hale, Chester
Untitled-Benefit 1922,My 8,14:5
Peg o' My Dreams 1924,My 6,25:3
Hassard Short's Ritz Revue 1924,S 18,19:1
Hale, Chester (Choreographer)
Angela 1928,D 4,28:2
Houseboat on the Styx, The 1928,D 26,14:3
Music in May 1929,Ap 2,29:1
Wonderful Night, A; Fledermaus, Die
1929,N 1,23:3
Murder at the Vanities 1933,S 13,22:4
Three Waltzes 1937,D 27,10:2
Viva O'Brien 1941,O 10,27:2
Ice Capades 1952,S 12,18:1
Holiday on Ice 1966,S 1,30:1
Holiday on Ice 1967,Ag 31,29:2
Hale, Chester (Director)
Holiday on Ice 1965,S 2,38:4
Holiday on Ice 1966,S 1,30:1
Holiday on Ice 1967,Ag 31,29:2
Hale, Chester (Producer)
Viva O'Brien 1941,O 10,27:2
Hale, Claire
Beggar's Holiday 1946,D 27,13:3
Insect Comedy, The 1948,Je 4,26:3
Hale, Eastern (Miscellaneous)
Lulu; Earth Spirit 1970,Mr 28,32:1
Hale, Edmond
Lingering Past, The 1932,Je 30,26:5
Devil's Little Game, The 1932,Ag 2,20:4
Hale, Edward Everett
Manhatters, The 1927,Ag 4,25:4
Father, The 1928,My 12,9:4
Cyrano de Bergerac 1932,D 27,11:2
Richelieu 1934,My 22,28:1
Declassee 1935,Ag 6,20:3
Cyrano de Bergerac 1936,Ap 28,17:1
Marching Song 1937,F 18,18:2
Hale, Franc
Arabian, The 1927,N 1,20:5
Royal Box, The 1928,N 21,32:3
Sakura 1928,D 26,14:4
Three Men and a Woman 1932,Ja 12,29:2
Nona 1932,O 5,26:4
Late Wisdom 1934,Ap 24,27:4
My 3 Angels 1956,F 4,24:2
Hale, Frank J (Producer)
Mid-Summer 1953,Ja 22,19:1
Girl in the Freudian Slip, The 1967,My 19,34:3
Hale, George
Bye Bye Bonnie 1927,Ja 14,15:3

Hale, George (Choreographer)
Heads Up! 1929,N 12,34:1
Strike Up the Band 1930,Ja 15,29:1
New Yorkers, The 1930,D 9,31:1
Earl Carroll's Vanities 1931,Ag 28,18:7
Red, Hot and Blue! 1936,O 30,26:3
Hale, George (Director)
International Ice Frolics, The 1938,My 7,18:3
Shuffle Along 1952,My 9,20:5
Hale, George (Miscellaneous)
Pardon My English 1933,Ja 21,11:4
Evening With G B S, An; O'Flaherty, V C
1957,F 19,35:7
An Evening With G B S; Press Cuttings
1957,F 19,35:7
Hale, George (Producer)
Hold On to Your Hats 1940,S 12,30:3
Lady Comes Across, The 1942,Ja 10,10:2
Hale, George
Rise of Rosie O'Reilly, The 1923,D 26,13:4
Greenwich Village Follies 1924,S 17,16:1
Puzzles of 1925 1925,F 3,25:3
Cocoanuts, The 1925,D 9,30:1
Hale, Georgie (Choreographer)
Of Thee I Sing 1931,D 28,20:1
Hale, Gordon (Choreographer)
Girl Crazy 1930,O 15,27:1
Hale, Helen
Fashion 1937,Mr 21,II,7:8
Hale, J R (Translator)
Mandragola 1958,My 29,23:2
Hale, Jane
Doctor Faustus 1937,Ja 9,21:2
Hale, John
Earl Carroll's Vanities 1930,Jl 2,28:3
Vanities 1932,S 28,22:4
Wedding in Japan 1957,Mr 12,37:7
Hale, John (Director)
John Gabriel Borkman 1959,N 26,57:4
Hale, John (Playwright)
Spithead 1969,N 22,46:3
Hale, Jonathan
Midsummer Night's Dream, A 1932,Jl 13,15:1
Hale, Juno
Here Come the Clowns 1960,S 20,48:1
Hale, Kurt (Producer)
Here Come the Clowns 1960,S 20,48:1
Hale, Lionel (Playwright)
These Two 1933,Mr 5,IX,1:6
Mocking Bird, The 1933,Je 23,18:2
These Two 1934,My 8,28:3
Hale, Louise Closser
Beyond the Horizon 1920,F 4,12:1
Beyond the Horizon 1920,F 8,VIII,2:1
Miss Lulu Bett 1920,D 28,9:1
Miss Lulu Bett 1921,Ja 9,VI,1:1
Malvaloca 1922,O 3,22:1
Hospitality 1922,N 14,16:1
Hospitality 1922,D 3,VIII,1:1
Peer Gynt 1923,F 6,14:1
Camel's Back, The 1923,N 4,19:2
New Toys 1924,F 19,12:1
New Toys 1924,F 24,VII,1:1
Expressing Willie 1924,Ap 17,22:1
Expressing Willie 1924,Ap 27,VIII,1:1
Expressing Willie 1924,My 4,VIII,1:1
Harvest 1925,Ap 19,IX,2:1
Harvest 1925,S 21,16:2
One of the Family 1925,D 23,22:3
Ivory Door, The 1927,O 19,24:5
Paris 1928,O 9,34:3
Hale, Margaret
Who Cares 1930,Jl 9,27:1
Hale, Marian
National Anthem, The 1922,F 5,VI,1:1
Hale, Marshall
Red Falcon, The 1924,O 8,22:1
Small Timers, The 1925,Ja 28,15:3
Pickwick 1927,S 6,35:2
Storm Center 1927,D 1,33:2
Penny Arcade 1930,Mr 11,24:5
Adam Had Two Sons 1932,Ja 21,17:1
Man Who Reclaimed His Head 1932,S 9,17:3
Dark Hours, The 1932,N 15,24:2
Nowhere Bound 1935,Ja 23,20:2
Hale, Minna
Crime Marches on 1935,O 24,19:1
Hale, Mr
Mr Whistler 1931,D 6,VIII,2:6
Hale, Nancy (Lyricist)
Best of Everything, The 1952,My 8,35:4
Hale, Nancy (Playwright)
Best of Everything, The 1952,My 8,35:4
Hale, Natalie
Knights of Song 1938,O 18,29:2
Hale, Pat
What's Up 1953,O 28,37:2
Hale, Peter
Twelfth Night 1957,Jl 4,16:4
Electra 1962,Mr 22,42:1
Hale, Randolph
Happy Landing 1932,Mr 28,10:5

Hale, Randolph (Miscellaneous)
Bicycle Ride to Nevada 1963,S 25,38:1
Hale, Randolph (Producer)
On Borrowed Time 1953,Ja 1,19:1
On Borrowed Time 1953,F 11,34:1
Hale, Richard
Finta Giardiniera, La 1927,Ja 19,20:5
Goin' Home 1928,Ag 24,23:2
At the Bottom 1930,Ja 10,24:3
Vikings, The 1930,My 13,27:3
Green Grow the Lilacs 1931,Ja 27,21:2
Housewarming 1932,Ap 8,25:1
Comic Artist, The 1933,Ap 20,20:3
Peace Palace 1933,Je 6,30:2
Spring in Autumn 1933,O 25,22:5
As Husbands Go 1935,Jl 2,24:3
Cat and the Canary, The 1935,Jl 9,24:4
Trelawney of the 'Wells' 1935,Jl 16,24:1
All This While 1935,Jl 30,17:2
Accent on Youth 1935,Ag 13,20:3
Berkeley Square 1935,Ag 20,25:1
In Old Kentucky 1935,Ag 27,23:4
They Knew What They Wanted 1936,Jl 7,17:2
Shining Hour, The 1936,Ag 12,15:3
Mariette 1937,Je 29,18:3
Yeomen of the Guard, The 1939,Jl 23,IX,2:1
Bicentennial 1939,Ag 29,18:2
Beggar's Opera, The 1941,Ag 12,14:6
Attack 1942,S 8,13:4
Lady in the Dark 1943,Mr 1,14:2
Hale, Robert
H M S Pinafore 1968,Ap 29,47:2
Yeomen of the Guard, The 1968,My 9,53:1
Hale, Rodney (Director)
Milky Way, The 1943,Je 10,17:2
Boy Meets Girl 1943,Je 23,15:5
Hale, Ronald
Time of Your Life, The 1969,N 7,37:1
Hale, Ruth
Poor Little Ritz Girl 1920,Jl 29,7:1
Hale, Ruth (Lyricist)
Venetian Glass Nephew, The 1931,F 24,26:3
Hale, Scott
Nights of Wrath; Nuits de la Colere, Les
1947,D 1,26:4
Outside the Door 1949,Mr 2,33:2
Scapegoat, The 1950,Ap 20,36:5
All the King's Men 1950,Jl 19,25:6
How to Make a Man 1961,F 3,16:1
Hale, Sonnie
Wake Up and Dream 1929,Ap 14,X,1:8
Evergreen 1930,D 21,VIII,1:6
Hale, Sonnie (Choreographer)
Wake Up and Dream 1929,D 31,14:3
Hale, Walter
Yellow 1926,S 22,30:1
Hale, William
Top Speed 1929,D 26,20:1
Hale, William J
Father, The 1937,Ap 21,18:5
Halenke, Gustl
Ratten, Die 1966,Ap 13,36:1
Hales, Ethelbert
Lady Cristilinda, The 1922,D 26,11:2
Lady, The 1923,D 5,23:2
Houses of Sand 1925,F 18,17:1
Rain 1926,O 12,27:1
Hales, N St Clair
Skin Game, The 1920,O 21,11:1
World We Live In, The 1922,N 1,16:1
Old Bill, M P 1926,N 11,22:2
Grey Fox, The 1928,O 23,32:3
Yellow Jacket, The 1928,N 8,27:3
Falstaff 1928,D 26,14:2
Halevy, Ludovic (Lyricist)
Vie Parisienne, La 1941,N 6,20:3
Halevy, Ludovic (Original Author)
Carmen Jones 1943,D 19,II,9:1
Halevy, Ludovic (Playwright)
Perichole, La 1926,D 29,24:4
Blue Beard 1929,Jl 7,VIII,2:1
Fledermaus, Die 1929,Jl 14,IX,2:1
Fair Helen 1931,Ag 30,VIII,2:1
Fair Helen 1932,Jl 17,IX,1:2
Carmen Jones 1943,D 3,26:2
Carmen Jones 1945,My 3,26:5
Carmen Jones 1946,Ap 8,32:2
Carmen Jones 1959,Ag 18,25:1
Vie Parisienne, La 1964,Mr 11,34:2
Haley, Alex (Miscellaneous)
Hajj Malik, El 1970,O 4,II,5:1
Haley, Jack
Round the Town 1924,My 22,14:3
Gay Paree 1925,Ag 19,14:3
Gay Paree 1926,N 10,24:2
Follow Thru 1929,Ja 10,24:3
Free for All 1931,Ag 16,VIII,1:1
Free for All 1931,S 9,25:1
Radio Carnival 1932,Mr 14,13:3
Vaudeville (Palace) 1932,Ap 25,18:3
Take a Chance 1932,N 28,11:2
Higher and Higher 1940,Mr 17,X,2:5
Higher and Higher 1940,Ap 5,24:3

Haley, Jack—Cont
Higher and Higher 1940,Ag 6,15:4
Higher and Higher 1940,Ag 11,IX,1:1
Show Time 1942,S 17,20:2
Show Time 1942,O 4,VIII,1:1
Inside U S A 1948,Mr 30,27:3
Inside U S A 1948,My 1,19:2
Inside U S A 1948,My 23,II,1:1
Inside U S A 1948,Ag 29,II,1:1

Haley, Rosemary
Tender Trap, The 1961,Ag 26,15:1

Haley, Selma
Myrtie 1924,F 5,21:2

Haley, Whitney
All the King's Men 1963,Jl 12,12:1

Half Brothers, The
Jack Benny 1963,Mr 1,10:5

Halicka, Alice (Costume Designer)
I Married an Angel 1938,My 22,XI,1:1

Haliday, Bryant
Relapse, The 1950,N 23,54:2
Henry IV, Part I 1955,S 22,34:2

Haliday, Bryant (Miscellaneous)
Henry V 1956,Jl 7,11:2
Saint Joan 1956,S 12,42:1

Haliday, Bryant (Producer)
Henry IV, Part I 1955,S 22,34:2
Mask and Gown 1957,S 11,29:1

Haliet, Louis
Verge, The 1921,N 15,23:2

Halkin, Simon (Translator)
Shylock '47 1947,My 28,30:5

Hall, Adelaide
Runnin' Wild 1923,O 30,17:3
Blackbirds 1928,My 10,31:3
Vaudeville (Palace) 1930,F 10,20:3
Vaudeville (Palace) 1930,Ag 11,13:3
Brown Buddies 1930,O 8,29:1
Vaudeville (Palace) 1931,Ap 6,24:3
Vaudeville (Palace) 1931,Jl 13,13:4
Jamaica 1957,N 1,32:2
Jamaica 1957,N 10,II,1:1

Hall, Adrian (Director)
Long Gallery, The 1958,Mr 7,17:2
Journey With Strangers, A 1958,N 27,53:1
Trip to Bountiful, The 1959,F 27,20:4
Orpheus Descending 1959,O 6,45:2
Ballad of Jazz Street, The 1959,N 12,28:1
Mousetrap, The 1960,N 7,46:1
Donogoo 1961,Ja 19,25:3
Red Roses for Me 1961,N 28,41:1
Riverwind 1962,D 14,5:5
Milk Train Doesn't Stop Here Anymore, The 1963,S 18,32:1
Brother to Dragons 1968,D 8,86:1
Wilson in the Promise Land 1970,Ja 11,78:1
Lovecraft's Follies 1970,Ap 19,II,12:1
Wilson in the Promise Land 1970,My 27,41:1

Hall, Adrian (Lighting Director)
Doll's House, A 1956,My 8,29:2

Hall, Al
Evening With Yves Montand, An 1959,S 23,45:1

Hall, Al K
Earl Carroll's Vanities 1924,S 11,23:6
Vaudeville (Palace) 1930,My 5,27:5

Hall, Alan (Miscellaneous)
Beyond the Fringe 1962,O 29,36:1
Patriot for Me, A 1969,O 6,58:1

Hall, Albert
Bewitched 1924,O 2,26:3

Hall, Amelia
Richard III 1953,Jl 15,22:2
All's Well That Ends Well 1953,Jl 16,18:2
Merry Wives of Windsor, The 1956,Je 21,34:4
Twelfth Night 1957,Jl 4,16:4
Twelfth Night 1957,Jl 7,II,1:1
Two Gentlemen of Verona 1957,Mr 19,35:1
Broken Jug, The 1958,Ap 2,36:1
Love and Libel 1960,D 8,44:1
Macbeth 1962,Je 20,41:1
Tempest, The 1962,Je 22,14:1
Cyrano de Bergerac 1962,Ag 1,21:1
Troilus and Cressida 1963,Je 19,40:2
Cyrano de Bergerac 1963,Je 20,30:1
Comedy of Errors, The 1963,Je 21,35:3
Richard II 1964,Je 17,47:1
Country Wife, The 1964,Ag 3,16:1
Henry V 1966,Je 8,38:1
Henry VI 1966,Je 9,55:2
Government Inspector, The 1967,Je 15,55:1
Government Inspector, The 1967,O 28,34:1
Romeo and Juliet 1968,Je 11,55:2
Seagull, The 1968,Jl 25,27:2
Forty Years On 1970,Ag 30,II,1:1

Hall, Anmer (Producer)
Women of Property 1937,Ag 1,X,1:7
Mourning Becomes Electra 1937,D 12,XI,3:8

Hall, Austin Briggs Jr
Strong Breed, The 1967,N 10,60:1

Hall, Bernice
Year Round, The 1953,My 6,38:7

Hall, Berniece
Trumpets of the Lord 1963,D 23,22:3
Trumpets of the Lord 1969,Ap 30,37:1

Hall, Bettina
Mikado, The; Town of Titipu, The 1927,S 19,30:1
Iolanthe 1927,N 15,26:3
Little Show, The 1929,My 1,28:5
Three Little Girls 1930,Mr 30,VIII,2:7
Three Little Girls 1930,Ap 15,29:1
Meet My Sister 1930,D 31,11:1
Cat and the Fiddle, The 1931,S 27,VIII,3:1
Cat and the Fiddle, The 1931,O 16,26:4
Only Girl, The 1934,My 22,28:2
Anything Goes 1934,N 18,IX,1:7
Anything Goes 1934,N 22,26:1
Show Boat 1938,Je 30,21:1
Susanna, Don't You Cry 1939,My 23,27:2

Hall, Bill
Dark of the Moon 1970,Ap 4,21:2

Hall, Bruce
Song of Bernadette 1946,Mr 27,22:2
Joan of Lorraine 1946,N 19,40:2
Building 222 1950,F 3,28:2
Barefoot in Athens 1951,N 1,35:2
Seagulls Over Sorrento 1952,S 12,18:4
Season of the Beast 1958,Mr 14,29:2

Hall, Bryant
They Shall Not Die 1934,F 22,24:4

Hall, C Porter
Dragon, The 1922,D 27,12:1
Peer Gynt 1923,F 6,14:1
Flame of Love 1924,Ap 22,19:2

Hall, Cameron
Young Madame Conti 1937,Ap 1,18:4
Come Across 1938,S 15,28:3

Hall, Carlyle (Miscellaneous)
Come Summer 1969,Mr 19,43:1

Hall, Carlyle (Musical Director)
Cry for Us All 1970,Ap 9,48:2

Hall, Carol
Sing Out, Sweet Land! 1944,D 28,24:2

Hall, Chester
Irving Berlin's Music Box Revue 1921,S 23,18:2

Hall, Clay
All Summer Long 1953,Ja 29,23:1
All Summer Long 1954,S 24,26:2
All Summer Long 1954,O 3,II,1:1
Gang's All Here, The 1959,O 2,23:1
Gang's All Here, The 1959,O 11,II,1:1
Courtyard 1960,Mr 1,28:1

Hall, Cliff
Lord Pengo 1962,N 20,41:2
Here's Love 1963,O 4,28:1
Sherry! 1967,Mr 29,39:1

Hall, Cliff (Charlie)
Pardon My English 1933,Ja 21,11:4

Hall, David (Miscellaneous)
Play 1964,Ja 6,35:1
Lover, The 1964,Ja 6,35:1

Hall, Donald
Back Pay 1921,Ag 31,8:2
Her Salary Man 1921,N 29,20:1

Hall, Donald (Playwright)
Evening's Frost, An 1965,O 12,56:1

Hall, Doris
Distaff Side, The 1934,S 26,17:2

Hall, Dorothy
Complex, The 1925,Mr 4,17:2
Virgin Man, The 1927,Ja 19,20:4
Speakeasy 1927,S 27,30:1
Lady for a Night, A 1928,Ap 17,26:4
Final Fling, The 1928,O 7,IX,2:3
Girl Trouble 1928,O 26,22:3
Precious 1929,Ja 15,22:5
Love Duel, The 1929,Ap 16,32:3
Other Men's Wives 1929,N 13,24:4
Flying High 1930,Mr 4,24:4
Greeks Had a Word for It, The 1930,S 26,16:5
Child of Manhattan 1932,Mr 2,15:1
Lilly Turner 1932,S 20,26:1
Day I Forgot, The 1933,My 13,16:6
Wooden Slipper, The 1934,Ja 4,16:3
Pure in Heart, The 1934,Mr 21,24:3
Page Miss Glory 1934,N 28,24:2
As We Forgive Our Debtors 1936,Ag 11,24:6
Behind the Red Lights 1937,Ja 14,17:4

Hall, Ed
Raisin in the Sun, A 1959,Mr 12,27:1
Brother to Dragons 1968,D 8,86:1
Wilson in the Promise Land 1970,Ja 11,78:1
Wilson in the Promise Land 1970,My 27,41:1

Hall, Edsley
Mr Papavert 1932,Ja 23,18:6

Hall, Edward
Climate of Eden, The 1952,N 7,20:2

Hall, Eileen
Fashion 1937,Mr 21,II,7:8

Hall, Eleanor
Allah Be Praised! 1944,Ap 21,14:2

Hall, Ellen
Precedent 1931,Ap 15,24:5
Cat and the Canary, The 1935,Jl 9,24:4
Trelawney of the 'Wells' 1935,Jl 16,24:1
All This While 1935,Jl 30,17:2
Declassee 1935,Ag 6,20:3
Night in the House 1935,N 8,19:5

Hall, Ellen—Cont
Shining Hour, The 1936,Ag 12,15:3
Octoroon, The 1936,S 1,24:2
Many Mansions 1937,O 28,28:6
Escape This Night 1938,Ap 23,18:1
Unconquered, The 1940,F 14,25:2
Night Before Christmas, The 1941,Ap 11,25:2
Jason 1942,Ja 22,12:2
Born Yesterday 1946,F 5,18:2

Hall, Elmer
Little Inn, The 1935,Ag 20,25:1

Hall, Enid
Out of This World 1950,D 22,17:3

Hall, Erle
Othello 1953,O 30,28:2

Hall, Evelyn Walsh
Richard III 1920,Mr 8,7:1
Fake, The 1924,O 7,26:3
Mariners 1927,Mr 29,22:2

Hall, Fifi Louise
Clean Beds 1939,My 26,21:2

Hall, Francis (Playwright)
Jazz Age 1937,Jl 20,19:3

Hall, Frank
Acquittal, The 1920,Ja 6,18:2
Daddy Dumplins 1920,N 23,11:1

Hall, Fred
Two Little Girls in Blue 1921,My 4,10:3
Bombo 1921,O 7,20:2
Wandering Jew, The 1927,F 2,22:4

Hall, Frederick (Professor) (Director)
Pearly Gates 1931,S 1,30:3

Hall, Frederick (Professor) (Musical Director)
Pearly Gates 1931,S 1,30:3

Hall, George
Theophilus 1942,Ja 7,23:2
Call Me Mister 1946,Ap 19,26:2
Insect Comedy, The 1948,Je 4,26:3
Lend an Ear 1948,D 17,38:2
Touch and Go 1949,O 14,34:1
Touch and Go 1949,O 30,II,1:1
Night in Venice, A 1953,Je 26,15:2
Stockade 1954,F 5,14:2
Ernest in Love 1960,My 5,39:4
There's a Girl in My Soup 1967,O 19,58:1
Round With Ring, A 1969,O 30,56:1

Hall, George F
Sweet River 1936,O 29,30:2

Hall, Georgia Lee
Donovan Affair, The 1926,Ag 31,15:2
Clutching Claw, The 1928,F 15,20:1
Girl Trouble 1928,O 26,22:3
Top O' the Hill 1929,N 27,30:4

Hall, Georgine
Duchess of Malfi, The 1962,Mr 5,27:1

Hall, Grayson
Balcony, The 1960,Mr 4,21:1
Buskers, The 1961,O 31,28:1
Subways Are for Sleeping 1961,D 28,22:1
Love Nest, The 1963,Ja 28,7:6
Shout From the Rooftops 1964,O 29,40:1
Those That Play the Clowns 1966,N 25,48:1

Hall, Harrison (Producer)
Nikki 1931,S 30,23:4

Hall, Hedley
Three Musketeers, The 1921,My 20,18:5
Her Salary Man 1921,N 29,20:1

Hall, Henry
Other Rose, The 1923,D 16,IX,2:4

Hall, Holworthy (Playwright)
Little Theatre Tournament; Valiant, The 1926,My 5,24:5
Valiant, The 1927,F 22,22:5
Valiant, The 1929,S 22,24:6

Hall, Homer W
John Brown's Body 1953,F 16,17:2

Hall, Howard
Man of the People, A 1920,S 8,9:2
Chinese O'Neill 1929,My 23,27:1
Second Mate, The 1930,Mr 25,34:5
That's Gratitude 1932,Je 17,24:3
Riddle Me This! 1933,Mr 15,21:3
John Ferguson 1933,Jl 11,15:7
Woman of Destiny, A 1936,Mr 3,25:2

Hall, Howard (Director)
Riddle Me This! 1933,Mr 15,21:3

Hall, Howard Jr
Nowhere Bound 1935,Ja 23,20:2

Hall, Huntz
Dead End 1935,O 29,17:2

Hall, Iris
Three Men on a Horse 1942,O 10,10:2
Try and Get It 1943,Ag 3,13:2

Hall, J Jeff
Easy Come, Easy Go 1925,O 27,20:2

Hall, Jack
Passing Show of 1923, The 1923,Je 15,24:6
Laugh Parade, The 1931,S 20,VIII,3:1

Hall, James
Folly Town 1920,My 18,9:2
Tragical Historie of Doctor Faustus, The 1964,O 6,34:2
Displaced Person, The 1966,D 30,15:1
Party on Greenwich Avenue, The 1967,My 11,52:1

Hall, James—Cont
Transgressor Rides Again, The 1969,My 21,42:1
Hall, James Thornton (Producer)
Legend of Lovers 1959,O 28,40:3
Hall, Jeannette
Jazz a La Carte 1922,Je 3,8:3
Hall, Jefferson
Donovan Affair, The 1926,Ag 31,15:2
Big Fight, The 1928,S 19,33:1
Gypsy 1929,Ja 15,22:2
Hall, Jim
Next President, The 1958,Ap 10,34:3
Evening With Yves Montand, An 1959,S 23,45:1
Hall, John
Last Warning, The 1922,O 25,23:1
Crooked Square, The 1923,S 11,10:2
Hall, John (Composer)
Morning 1968,N 29,52:1
Night 1968,N 29,52:1
Noon 1968,N 29,52:1
Honest-to-God Schnozzola, The 1969,Ap 22,40:2
Leader, The 1969,Ap 22,40:2
Hall, Joseph
Nativity Play, The 1937,D 21,29:1
Hall, Josephine
Rang Tang 1927,Jl 13,20:1
Keep Shufflin' 1928,F 28,18:3
Hall, Juanita
Sailor, Beware! 1935,My 7,28:4
Conjur 1938,N 1,27:2
Pirate, The 1942,N 26,39:2
Secret Room, The 1945,N 8,16:2
St Louis Woman 1946,Ap 1,22:2
Mr Peebles and Mr Hooker 1946,O 11,29:2
S S Glencairn; Moon of the Caribbees
   1948,My 21,21:2
South Pacific 1949,Ap 8,30:2
South Pacific 1949,Ap 17,II,1:1
South Pacific 1949,Je 5,II,1:1
House of Flowers 1954,D 31,11:2
Ponder Heart, The 1956,F 17,14:2
South Pacific 1957,Ap 25,35:1
Flower Drum Song 1958,D 2,44:1
Flower Drum Song 1958,D 7,II,5:1
Mardi Gras! 1965,Je 28,33:2
Woman and the Blues, A 1966,Mr 29,35:2
Mardi Gras! 1966,Jl 11,32:2
Hall, Juanita (Composer)
Sweet River 1936,O 29,30:2
Hall, Juanita (Director)
Sweet River 1936,O 29,30:2
Hall, Juanita (Musical Director)
Conjur 1938,N 1,27:2
Hall, Judson Best
Everywhere I Roam 1938,D 30,10:4
Hall, Judy
Collector's Item 1952,F 9,11:2
Hall, Kate
Porgy and Bess 1935,O 11,30:2
Lew Leslie's Blackbirds of 1939 1939,F 13,12:2
Hall, Katharine
Walk a Little Faster 1932,D 8,24:4
Hall, Laura Nelson
Survival of the Fittest 1921,Mr 15,14:1
Easiest Way, The 1921,S 7,14:1
Hall, Leonne
Beggar's Holiday 1946,D 27,13:3
Hall, Lewis
If This Be Treason 1935,S 24,28:2
Hall, Lois
Meet the Prince 1935,Jl 9,24:5
Laughing Woman, The 1936,O 14,30:1
Infernal Machine, The 1937,D 13,22:7
Dame Nature 1938,S 27,24:3
My Dear Children 1939,Mr 25,19:6
My Dear Children 1940,F 1,16:2
Susannah and the Elders 1940,O 13,47:7
Susannah and the Elders 1940,O 30,28:2
Flying Gerardos, The 1940,D 30,21:4
First Million, The 1943,Ap 29,27:4
Cherry Orchard, The 1944,Ja 26,22:1
Joy to the World 1948,Mr 19,28:2
Curious Savage, The 1950,O 25,44:3
Hall, Louis
Patience 1935,S 3,24:4
Hall, Louis Leon
Merchant of Venice, The 1920,D 30,16:2
Julius Caesar 1929,N 19,26:5
Hall, Lyle Weaver (Playwright)
Tired Business Man, The 1929,Je 5,32:5
Hall, Malcolm
Dance of Death, The 1967,O 20,50:1
Hall, Margaret
Fallout 1959,My 21,36:2
Jackass, The 1960,Mr 24,39:2
Becket 1960,O 6,50:1
Becket 1961,My 9,44:1
Midsummer Night's Dream, A 1961,Ag 3,13:1
High Spirits 1964,Ap 8,34:1
Mame 1966,My 25,41:1
Hall, Marian
As You Like It 1945,Jl 4,10:4
Hall, Mark
Child's Play 1970,F 18,39:1

Hall, Mary
Hamlet 1920,Mr 17,14:2
Macbeth 1921,Ap 20,11:1
Taming of the Shrew, The 1921,My 12,20:2
Merchant of Venice, The 1921,My 14,10:4
Cyrano de Bergerac 1923,N 2,14:1
Othello 1925,Ja 12,11:1
Don't Bother Mother 1925,F 4,18:2
Devil Within, The 1925,Mr 17,19:4
Hamlet 1925,O 12,19:2
These Days 1928,N 13,36:2
Airways, Inc 1929,F 21,30:5
Hall, Mary Louise
Contrast, The 1940,Mr 26,17:2
Hall, Mary Porter (Miscellaneous)
Calling in Crazy 1969,O 7,42:2
Candida 1970,Ap 7,41:1
Hall, Maud Edna
Bidding High 1932,S 29,17:2
Hall, Michael
Strange Bedfellows 1948,Ja 15,27:3
Hall, Mildred
Lulu Belle 1926,F 10,20:1
Hall, Misses
Three Little Girls 1930,S 28,VIII,2:5
Hall, Nadea
Daisy Mayme 1926,O 26,24:2
Black Velvet 1927,S 28,28:1
Stairs, The 1927,N 8,32:7
Hall, Nancy
All Summer Long 1953,Ja 29,23:1
Hall, Natalie
Three Little Girls 1930,Mr 30,VIII,2:7
Three Little Girls 1930,Ap 15,29:1
Through the Years 1932,Ja 29,13:3
Music in the Air 1932,N 9,28:2
Music in the Air 1932,N 20,IX,1:1
Merry Widow, The 1933,Ag 13,IX,1:3
Ball at the Savoy 1933,S 9,9:7
Music Hath Charms 1934,D 31,8:2
Othello 1936,D 6,XII,6:1
Othello 1937,Ja 7,16:4
Show Boat 1938,Je 30,21:1
Yeomen of the Guard, The 1939,Jl 16,30:4
Yeomen of the Guard, The 1939,Jl 23,IX,2:1
Man in Possession, The 1939,S 26,21:4
Hall, Norman (Director)
Son, The 1950,Ag 16,24:6
Joan of Lorraine 1955,Mr 26,12:2
U S A 1956,D 19,41:4
Trial of Dmitri Karamazov, The 1958,Ja 28,30:1
Hall, Norman (Miscellaneous)
Trial of Dmitri Karamazov, The 1958,Ja 28,30:1
Hall, Norman (Playwright)
Doctored Wife, The 1950,Jl 12,33:2
Hall, Oliver
When We Are Young 1920,N 23,11:1
Hall, Owen
Walk a Little Faster 1932,D 8,24:4
Hall, Owen (Playwright)
Florodora 1920,Ap 6,18:1
Geisha, The 1931,O 6,35:4
Florodora 1936,Ag 23,II,8:2
Hall, Pamela
Harold Arlen Songbook, The 1967,Mr 1,48:1
Littlest Crown, The 1968,Ap 15,41:1
Frere Jacques 1968,Je 8,23:2
Month of Sundays 1968,S 17,50:1
Dear World 1969,F 7,33:1
Hall, Pat
Gondoliers, The 1963,Je 5,33:2
Hall, Patricia
Ziegfeld Follies 1943,Ap 2,16:2
Annie Get Your Gun 1966,Je 1,42:2
Hall, Patti
Louisiana Lady 1947,Je 3,35:2
Hall, Pauline
Tip-Top 1920,O 6,13:2
Good Morning, Dearie 1921,N 2,20:2
One Kiss 1923,N 28,14:2
Hall, Peter (Costume Designer)
Romeo and Juliet 1962,F 14,39:1
Hall, Peter (Director)
South 1955,My 2,17:4
Rope Dancers, The 1957,N 21,39:1
Rope Dancers, The 1957,D 1,II,1:1
Cat on a Hot Tin Roof 1958,Ja 31,24:2
Midsummer Night's Dream, A 1959,Je 3,30:1
Coriolanus 1959,Jl 8,24:5
Two Gentlemen of Verona 1960,Ap 6,47:3
Twelfth Night 1960,My 18,48:6
Much Ado About Nothing 1961,Ap 5,31:1
Becket 1961,Jl 12,35:6
Romeo and Juliet 1961,Ag 16,36:3
Midsummer Night's Dream, A 1962,Ap 18,30:3
Wars of the Roses, The; Henry VI; Richard III
   1964,Ja 14,24:7
King Lear 1964,My 19,43:2
Hamlet 1965,Ag 20,18:2
Homecoming, The 1967,Ja 6,29:1
Homecoming, The 1967,Ja 22,II,1:4
Criminals, The 1967,O 15,II,9:3
Landscape 1969,Jl 13,II,8:1

Hall, Peter (Miscellaneous)
Taming of the Shrew, The 1962,Ap 24,33:3
Milk Train Doesn't Stop Here Anymore, The
   1963,Ja 18,7:1
Wars of the Roses, The 1963,Jl 18,14:1
Hall, Peter (Producer)
Two Gentlemen of Verona 1960,Ap 6,47:3
Dutch Uncle 1969,Mr 28,41:1
Battle of Shrivings, The 1970,F 7,23:1
Hall, Philip Baker
World of Gunter Grass, The 1966,Ap 27,38:1
Hall, Porter
Great Gatsby, The 1926,F 3,22:1
Naked 1926,N 9,31:2
Loud Speaker 1927,Mr 3,27:2
Night Hostess 1928,S 13,31:2
It's a Wise Child 1929,Ag 7,29:1
It's a Wise Child 1929,Ag 25,VIII,1:1
Collision 1932,F 17,19:2
Warrior's Husband, The 1932,Mr 12,19:4
Dark Tower, The 1933,N 27,20:3
Red Cat, The 1934,S 20,21:1
Bring on the Girls 1934,O 23,23:2
Hall, Randy
Me and Juliet 1953,My 29,17:1
Hall, Richard
Up Eden 1968,N 27,42:1
Hall, Richard B W (Mrs)
Variations of 1940 1940,Ja 29,12:1
Hall, Roy
Conversation Piece 1934,O 24,24:1
Hall, Selma
Blue Lagoon, The 1921,S 15,16:1
Rotters, The 1922,My 23,12:4
Live and Learn 1930,Ap 10,24:6
Love on the Dole 1936,F 25,23:3
Hall, Spalding
Good Morning, Dearie 1921,N 2,20:2
Blue and the Gray, The; War Is Hell Gray, The
   1929,D 27,26:4
Hall, Stephen J
All the King's Men 1959,O 17,27:2
Hall, Sterling
Arms and the Girl 1950,F 3,28:2
Hall, Susan
Master of the Revels 1935,Ag 14,16:2
Octoroon, The 1936,S 1,24:2
Hall, Thurston
Mary Stuart 1921,Mr 22,15:1
Mary Stuart 1921,Ap 3,VII,1:1
French Doll, The 1922,F 21,20:2
Civilian Clothes 1923,Jl 26,13:2
Still Waters 1926,F 26,24:2
Still Waters 1926,Mr 2,23:1
Buy, Buy Baby 1926,O 8,26:2
Mixed Doubles 1927,Ap 27,22:3
Behold the Bridegroom 1927,D 27,24:1
Common Sin, The 1928,O 16,28:2
Sign of the Leopard 1928,D 12,34:4
Security 1929,Mr 29,20:1
Fifty Million Frenchmen 1929,N 28,34:4
Everything's Jake 1930,Ja 17,20:4
Philip Goes Forth 1931,Ja 13,35:4
Mourning Becomes Electra; Homecoming
   1932,My 10,25:2
Chrysalis 1932,N 16,15:2
Thoroughbred 1933,N 7,29:2
Re-Echo 1934,Ja 12,28:4
They Shall Not Die 1934,F 22,24:4
Spring Freshet 1934,O 5,28:3
All Rights Reserved 1934,N 7,33:5
Rain From Heaven 1934,D 25,28:4
Hall, Valerie
Murder in the Cathedral 1938,F 17,16:2
Hall, Wilbur
Laugh Parade, The 1931,S 20,VIII,3:1
Laugh Parade, The 1931,N 3,31:2
Laugh Parade, The 1931,D 6,VIII,1:1
Hall, Willard
High Hatters, The 1928,My 11,28:2
Hall, Willis (Playwright)
Long and the Short and the Tall, The
   1962,Mr 30,28:2
Squat Betty 1964,F 25,24:1
Sponge Room, The 1964,F 25,24:1
Billy Liar 1965,Mr 18,26:1
Help Stamp Out Marriage 1966,S 30,50:1
Whoops-A-Daisy 1968,D 13,61:1
Hall Johnson Choir
Susanna, Don't You Cry 1939,My 23,27:2
Hallahan, Harry
Seven Keys to Baldpate 1930,Ja 8,25:2
Hallam, Grace
Betty, Be Good 1920,My 5,14:2
Hallant, Uta
Don Carlos 1964,N 25,40:1
Hallaran, Francis
Empress of Destiny 1938,Mr 10,16:2
Hallaran, Toni
Children's Hour, The 1952,D 19,35:2
Hallard, C M
Voice From the Minaret, The 1922,Ja 31,11:2
Fedora 1922,F 11,18:1

Hallard, C M—Cont
Rudolph of Austria 1932,Ap 10,VIII,3:7
Hallatt, Henry
Good Companions, The 1931,O 2,31:1
Good Companions, The 1931,O 11,VIII,1:1
Hallatt, May
Separate Tables 1955,My 22,II,1:1
Separate Tables 1956,O 26,33:1
Halle, Abe H (Producer)
Our Wife 1933,Mr 3,13:2
Halle, Cliff
Pajama Tops 1963,Je 1,15:1
Halle, Walter
Samarkand 1926,D 22,24:4
Halleck, Dan
Parents and Children 1969,Ja 13,26:6
Hallee, Royal
Clinging Vine, The 1922,D 25,20:2
Hallenborg, Anne
Gypsy Baron, The 1944,Je 15,17:3
Haller, Bernard
Untitled-Revue 1968,O 21,55:4
Cabaret Rive Gauche 1969,S 5,30:1
Haller, Gretchen
Gypsy Baron, The 1930,Ap 22,22:8
Venetian Glass Nephew, The 1931,F 24,26:3
Haller, Herman (Playwright)
Caroline 1923,F 1,13:2
Haller, Herman (Producer)
An und Aus 1926,D 5,VIII,8:7
Wann und Wo 1927,D 18,IX,1:8
Schoen und Schick 1928,Ag 26,II,1:2
Schoen und Schick 1928,N 4,IX,2:1
Haller, Ward
Oh, Hector! 1929,Mr 6,33:2
Halleran, Patrick
Then Came the Dawn 1935,Ag 29,25:4
Hallett, Cleda
Reunion 1938,Ap 12,26:4
Hallett, Ralph
King Lear 1950,Ag 30,26:2
Halley, Beryl
LeMaire's Affairs 1927,Mr 29,22:4
Half a Widow 1927,S 13,37:3
Earl Carroll's Vanities 1928,Ag 7,25:2
Halley, William
Out of This World 1955,N 10,44:2
Hallhuber, Heino (Choreographer)
Wozzeck 1966,Ap 6,34:1
Mitschuldigen, Die 1966,Ap 6,34:1
Halli, Tom
New York Idea, The 1948,Ag 18,29:2
Halliburton, Isabel M (Producer)
Yes is for a Very Young Man 1963,Mr 6,7:5
Halliday, Buzz
Idiot's Delight 1957,F 23,14:2
Shinbone Alley 1957,Ap 15,23:2
Girls Against the Boys, The 1959,N 3,26:1
Girls Against the Boys, The 1959,N 8,II,1:1
Not While I'm Eating 1961,D 20,37:1
Put It in Writing 1963,My 14,31:1
Halliday, Frances
Blossom Time 1921,S 30,10:1
Battling Buttler 1923,O 9,17:2
Lady Screams, The 1927,My 3,24:2
Half a Widow 1927,S 13,37:3
Buckaroo 1929,Mr 18,31:1
Face the Music 1932,F 18,24:5
Amourette 1933,S 28,25:2
Halliday, Heller
Peter Pan 1954,Jl 20,15:3
Peter Pan 1954,O 21,30:2
Peter Pan 1954,O 31,II,1:1
Skin of Our Teeth, The 1955,Je 29,25:3
Skin of Our Teeth, The 1955,Ag 18,16:1
Skin of Our Teeth, The 1955,Ag 28,II,1:1
Halliday, Hildegarde
Failures, The 1923,N 23,20:1
Garrick Gaieties 1925,My 18,12:2
Chief Thing, The 1926,Mr 23,24:2
Garrick Gaieties 1926,My 11,25:2
Garrick Gaieties 1930,Je 5,29:2
New Faces 1934,Mr 16,24:5
Crazy With the Heat 1941,Ja 15,18:2
Walk Into My Parlor 1941,N 20,38:2
Odds on Mrs Oakley, The 1944,O 3,18:8
My Romance 1948,O 20,38:5
Halliday, Jack
Dora Mobridge 1930,Ap 21,20:2
Halliday, Jackson
Young Sinners 1931,Ap 21,35:5
Child of Manhattan 1932,Mr 2,15:1
Rendezvous 1932,O 13,22:3
Young Sinners 1933,Mr 7,20:4
Miss Temple Is Willing 1936,Jl 21,13:1
Suddenly a Stranger 1936,Ag 4,15:2
High Tor 1937,Ja 11,15:2
Siege 1937,D 9,31:4
Halliday, Janis
Taming of the Shrew, The 1956,Ag 11,11:2
Halliday, John
Hole in the Wall, The 1920,Mr 27,11:1
Woman of Bronze, The 1920,S 8,9:2
Circle, The 1921,S 13,12:1

East of Suez 1922,S 22,16:3
Masked Woman, The 1922,D 23,14:2
Two Fellows and a Girl 1923,Jl 20,8:2
Dancing Mothers 1924,Ag 12,12:2
Sour Grapes 1926,Jl 4,VII,3:2
Sour Grapes 1926,S 7,19:1
Sour Grapes 1926,S 12,VIII,1:1
Spider, The 1927,Mr 23,29:1
Jealousy 1928,O 23,32:2
Humbug, The 1929,N 28,34:5
Damn Your Honor 1929,D 31,14:3
Rain From Heaven 1934,D 11,26:5
Rain From Heaven 1934,D 16,XI,2:1
Rain From Heaven 1934,D 25,28:4
Rain From Heaven 1935,Ja 6,IX,1:1
Tovarich 1936,S 29,35:2
Tovarich 1936,O 16,31:4
Tovarich 1936,O 25,X,1:1
Halliday, John (Producer)
Women, The 1928,S 16,IX,2:4
Halliday, Mary
Easy Come, Easy Go 1925,O 27,20:2
Halliday, Richard
Holiday 1930,F 6,21:2
Halliday, Richard (Miscellaneous)
Peter Pan 1954,O 21,30:2
Halliday, Richard (Producer)
Annie Get Your Gun 1957,Ag 31,18:2
Sound of Music, The 1959,N 17,40:2
Daughter of Silence 1961,D 1,28:1
Jennie 1963,O 18,35:2
Halliday, Robert
Dew Drop Inn 1923,My 18,26:4
Holka Polka 1925,O 15,27:2
Tip-Toes 1925,D 29,20:2
Desert Song, The 1926,D 1,24:2
New Moon, The 1928,S 20,33:1
Prince Charming 1930,O 14,31:1
Only Girl, The 1934,My 22,28:2
Music Hath Charms 1934,D 31,8:2
White Horse Inn 1936,O 2,28:5
Three Wishes for Jamie 1952,Mr 22,9:2
Hallier, Ruby
Talking Parrot, The 1923,D 4,25:3
Pickwick 1927,Mr 13,VII,1:1
Pickwick 1927,S 6,35:2
Diversion 1928,Ja 12,25:1
Lost Sheep 1930,My 6,33:2
Halligan, Billy
Vaudeville (Hippodrome) 1926,My 4,31:2
Halligan, Joseph (Choreographer)
Grey Heir, The 1926,Ap 6,29:2
Halligan, T J
Pal Joey 1952,Ja 4,17:6
Mr Wonderful 1956,Mr 23,23:2
Auntie Mame 1958,Ag 12,33:2
Conquering Hero, The 1961,Ja 17,40:2
O Say Can You See! 1962,O 9,45:1
Halligan, Tom
Red Mill, The 1945,O 17,16:2
Halligan, William
All-Star Jamboree 1921,Jl 14,18:1
LeMaire's Affairs 1927,Mr 29,22:4
Halligan, William (Director)
LeMaire's Affairs 1927,Mr 29,22:4
Halliwell, David (Playwright)
Little Malcolm and His Struggle Against the
  Eunuchs 1966,F 5,32:3
Hail Scrawdyke! 1966,N 29,50:1
Experiment, The 1967,My 9,54:2
Hallman, Nancy
Five Little Peppers, The 1952,My 19,13:1
Hallman, William
Enter Madame 1920,Ag 17,11:2
Mr Jiggins of Jigginstown 1936,D 18,30:2
Hallock, Carol
Kismet 1965,Je 23,45:1
Hallor, Edith
Broadway Brevities, 1920 1920,S 30,12:2
Halloran, John
First Mrs Fraser, The 1929,D 30,16:2
Suspense 1930,Ag 13,22:3
Merchant of Venice, The 1930,D 3,29:2
Barretts of Wimpole Street, The 1931,F 10,25:1
Mad Hopes, The 1932,D 2,26:3
Wooden Slipper, The 1934,Ja 4,16:3
First Episode 1934,S 18,18:1
Pride and Prejudice 1935,N 3,X,1:5
Pride and Prejudice 1935,N 6,32:4
Escape This Night 1938,Ap 23,18:1
Man in Possession, The 1939,S 26,21:4
Halloran, John (Playwright)
Why We Misbehave 1935,Jl 25,14:8
Halloran, Tommy
Body Beautiful, The 1958,Ja 24,15:2
Hallow, John
Hamlet 1956,O 29,34:1
Visit to a Small Planet 1957,F 8,18:1
Oh Dad, Poor Dad, Mamma's Hung You in the
  Closet and I'm Feelin' So Sad 1963,Ag 28,28:2
Foxy 1964,F 17,26:1
Don't Drink the Water 1966,N 18,37:1
Hadrian VII 1969,Ja 9,22:1

Hallowell, William
Brown Danube, The 1939,My 18,30:4
Hallparn, Dorothy (Playwright)
Horse Play 1937,Ag 28,8:3
Hallums, Lilia
Cradle Will Rock, The 1937,D 6,19:4
Cradle Will Rock, The 1938,Ja 4,19:3
Hallward, Gloria
World's Full of Girls, The 1943,D 7,31:2
Highland Fling, A 1944,Ap 29,13:2
Halman, Ella
Gondoliers, The 1939,Ja 20,14:2
Mikado, The 1947,D 30,18:2
Pirates of Penzance, The 1948,Ja 6,27:2
Pirates of Penzance, The 1948,Ja 11,II,1:1
Iolanthe 1948,Ja 13,29:3
H M S Pinafore 1948,Ja 20,26:2
Gondoliers, The 1948,Ja 27,31:2
Yeomen of the Guard, The 1948,F 3,30:2
Patience 1948,F 10,27:2
Mikado, The 1951,Ja 30,21:2
H M S Pinafore 1951,F 6,24:2
Gondoliers, The 1951,F 13,27:2
Iolanthe 1951,F 16,22:1
Pirates of Penzance, The 1951,F 20,21:2
Mikado, The 1952,O 21,35:2
Pirates of Penzance, The 1952,O 28,36:4
H M S Pinafore 1952,N 4,32:2
Iolanthe 1952,N 11,26:3
Halmy, Tibor von
Fledermaus, Die 1929,Jl 14,IX,2:1
Halop, Billy
Dead End 1935,O 29,17:2
Halperin, Nan
Frivolities of 1920 1920,Ja 9,22:2
Make It Snappy 1922,Ap 14,20:2
Little Jessie James 1923,Ag 16,10:4
Vaudeville (Palace) 1924,Ja 1,21:1
Vaudeville (Palace) 1926,Mr 16,22:2
Vaudeville (Palace) 1927,My 24,23:1
Vaudeville (Palace) 1929,D 2,28:6
Vaudeville (Palace) 1930,D 22,16:5
Halperin, Dinah
With Open Eyes 1938,O 27,27:2
Long Live America 1939,Ja 2,28:3
In a Jewish Grocery 1939,O 2,15:2
Her Great Mistake 1940,F 5,12:6
Shylock and His Daughter 1947,S 30,22:2
Halperin, Evelyn
When Differences Disappear 1941,Je 3,17:4
Halperin, Fred
Tom Sawyer - Ballad of the Mississippi
  1947,D 27,11:3
Halpern, M L (Miscellaneous)
Untitled-Poetry Reading 1967,Jl 18,29:1
Halpern, Marty (Miscellaneous)
Sophie 1963,Ap 16,32:1
Halpern, Mortimer
Kith and Kin 1930,My 14,31:1
Halpern, Mortimer (Miscellaneous)
E-MC2 1948,Je 16,36:2
New Faces of 1956 1956,Je 15,32:1
Shinbone Alley 1957,Ap 15,23:2
Miss Isobel 1957,D 27,22:1
Disenchanted, The 1958,D 4,53:4
Song of Norway 1959,Je 26,16:2
Andersonville Trial, The 1959,D 30,15:1
Paradise Island 1961,Je 24,11:1
Cook for Mr General, A 1961,O 20,39:1
Paradise Island 1962,Je 28,22:1
Moon Besieged, The 1962,D 6,54:1
Around the World in 80 Days 1963,Je 24,22:1
Once for the Asking 1963,N 21,42:2
Around the World in 80 Days 1964,Je 29,33:2
I Had a Ball 1964,D 16,50:1
Mardi Gras! 1965,Je 28,33:2
Yearling, The 1965,D 11,25:1
Arabian Nights 1967,Jl 3,12:1
Dr Cook's Garden 1967,S 26,52:1
I'm Solomon 1968,Ap 24,51:1
South Pacific 1968,Je 30,54:2
South Pacific 1969,Jl 7,27:1
Sound of Music, The 1970,Jl 3,13:1
Hay Fever 1970,N 10,55:1
Halpern, Oscar (Saul, Oscar) (Playwright)
Medicine Show 1940,Ap 13,20:6
Halpern, Selma
Highway Robbery 1955,N 8,36:1
Majority of One, A 1959,F 17,28:2
Halpin, Hebe
Good Morning, Dearie 1921,N 2,20:2
Halpin, Helen
Catch a Star! 1955,S 7,35:2
Halpin, Luke
Take Me Along 1959,O 23,22:2
Halprin, Louis
Gentlemen of the Press 1928,Ag 28,27:2
To Quito and Back 1937,O 7,30:4
Halsey, Bruce
Innocent Voyage, The 1943,N 16,27:2
War President 1944,Ap 25,17:3
Day Will Come, The 1944,S 8,17:2
Signature 1945,F 15,25:2

Halsey, Bruce—Cont

Live Life Again 1945,O 1,14:7
Halsey, Forrest (Original Author)
His Chinese Wife 1920,My 18,9:3
Halsey, Forrest (Playwright)
His Chinese Wife 1920,My 18,9:3
Halsey, Joseph
Gambling 1929,Ag 27,31:2
Halsey, Lena
Haiti 1938,Mr 3,16:1
Halstead, Byron
Mexican Hayride 1944,Ja 29,9:6
Halsted, Mary Jane
Gay Blades 1937,N 16,27:1
Halsted, Ruth
Beggarman, Thief 1935,Jl 16,24:1
Haltiner, Fred
Marriage of Mr Mississippi, The 1969,N 20,60:5
Firebugs, The 1969,N 27,52:1
Haltiner, Fred (Director)
Philipp Hotz 1969,N 27,52:1
Halton, Charles
Hole in the Wall, The 1920,Mr 27,11:1
Smooth as Silk 1921,F 23,18:3
Madeleine and the Movies 1922,Mr 7,11:1
Peer Gynt 1923,F 6,14:1
Sancho Panza 1923,N 27,23:1
Milgrim's Progress 1924,D 23,17:1
Processional 1925,Ja 13,17:1
Sea Woman, The 1925,Ag 25,12:2
Merchants of Glory 1925,D 15,28:3
Head or Tail 1926,N 10,24:1
Chicago 1926,D 31,11:1
By Request 1928,S 28,30:2
Judas 1929,Ja 25,20:4
Hawk Island 1929,S 17,34:7
Once in a Lifetime 1930,S 7,IX,2:4
Once in a Lifetime 1930,S 25,22:3
Once in a Lifetime 1930,D 7,IX,1:1
Whistling in the Dark 1932,Ja 20,16:6
Going Gay 1933,Ag 4,18:5
Dodsworth 1934,F 26,20:4
Othello 1934,Jl 22,23:4
Merrily We Roll Along 1934,O 1,14:1
Crime Marches on 1935,O 24,19:1
Room Service 1935,N 17,II,7:7
Tomorrow's a Holiday! 1935,D 31,10:2
Postman Always Rings Twice, The 1936,F 26,17:2
Vickie 1942,S 23,28:1
Enchanted, The 1950,Ja 19,34:2
Halverson, Richard
Doctor Faustus 1961,Ap 26,36:1
Candida 1961,Ap 27,26:1
Halvorsen, Finn (Playwright)
Abraham's Offering 1938,D 18,IX,4:2
Halvorsen, Hal (Miscellaneous)
Mother Lover, The 1969,F 3,28:1
Hama, Yukiko
Teahouse of the August Moon, The 1954,Ap 23,23:6
Hamblen, Bernard (Composer)
Pickwick 1927,S 6,35:2
Hamblen, Bernard (Lyricist)
Pickwick 1927,S 6,35:2
Hambleton, John (Costume Designer)
Save Me the Waltz 1938,Mr 1,19:2
I Married an Angel 1938,My 12,26:2
Sing Out the News 1938,S 26,12:5
Fabulous Invalid, The 1938,O 10,15:1
Stars in Your Eyes 1939,F 10,18:2
John Henry 1940,Ja 11,18:2
Hambleton, T Edward
In the Days of the Turbins 1934,Mr 7,22:5
Hambleton, T Edward (Director)
Mary Stuart 1957,O 9,39:1
World of Cilli Wang, The 1957,O 15,38:4
Makropoulos Secret, The 1957,D 4,52:4
Infernal Machine, The 1958,F 4,33:1
Two Gentlemen of Verona 1958,Mr 19,35:1
Family Reunion, The 1958,O 21,39:1
Power and the Glory, The 1958,D 12,2:7
Great God Brown, The 1959,O 7,48:1
Lysistrata 1959,N 25,19:4
Peer Gynt 1960,Ja 13,21:1
Henry IV 1960,Ap 19,41:1
She Stoops to Conquer 1960,N 2,42:5
Plough and the Stars, The 1960,D 7,56:2
Octoroon, The 1961,Ja 28,13:1
Hamlet 1961,Mr 17,17:1
Taming of the Shrew, The 1963,Mr 8,9:1
Next Time I'll Sing to You 1963,N 28,69:2
Right You Are (If You Think You Are) 1964,Mr 5,37:1
Tavern, The 1964,Mr 6,39:2
Scapin 1964,Mr 10,43:1
Impromptu at Versailles 1964,Mr 10,43:1
Lower Depths, The 1964,Mr 31,30:1
Tragical Historie of Doctor Faustus, The 1964,O 6,34:2
You Can't Take It With You 1965,N 24,32:1
School for Scandal, The 1966,N 22,33:2
Right You Are (If You Think You Are) 1966,N 23,34:2
We Comrades Three 1966,D 21,46:1

War and Peace 1967,Mr 22,42:1
Show-Off, The 1967,D 6,40:2
Exit the King 1968,Ja 10,48:1
Cherry Orchard, The 1968,Mr 20,41:1
Cock-A-Doodle Dandy 1969,Ja 21,40:1
Hamlet 1969,Mr 4,34:1
Harvey 1970,F 25,41:1
Criminals, The 1970,F 26,33:2
Persians, The 1970,Ap 16,53:1
Hambleton, T Edward (Miscellaneous)
Coriolanus 1954,Ja 20,34:2
Venice Preserv'd 1955,D 13,54:4
Cocktail Party, The 1968,O 8,42:1
Misanthrope, The 1968,O 10,59:1
Hambleton, T Edward (Producer)
Robin Landing 1937,N 19,26:4
I Know What I Like 1939,N 25,13:5
First Crocus, The 1942,Ja 3,14:6
Galileo 1947,Ag 1,21:4
Temporary Island, A 1948,Mr 15,27:3
Pride's Crossing 1950,N 21,37:5
Golden Apple, The 1954,Mr 12,15:2
Sandhog 1954,N 24,17:1
Doctor's Dilemma, The 1955,Ja 12,22:1
Master Builder, The 1955,Mr 2,23:2
Phoenix '55 1955,Ap 25,20:2
Carefree Tree, The 1955,O 12,37:2
Anna Christie 1955,N 22,41:1
Six Characters in Search of an Author 1955,D 12,38:1
Stronger, The 1956,F 22,23:2
Miss Julie 1956,F 22,23:2
Queen After Death 1956,Mr 13,33:2
Month in the Country, A 1956,Ap 4,23:1
Littlest Revue, The 1956,My 23,37:2
Saint Joan 1956,S 12,42:1
Diary of a Scoundrel 1956,N 5,41:1
Good Woman of Setzuan, The 1956,D 19,41:2
Measure for Measure 1957,Ja 23,24:1
Duchess of Malfi, The 1957,Mr 20,33:1
Livin' the Life 1957,Ap 29,20:1
Beaux' Stratagem, The 1959,F 25,35:4
Once Upon a Mattress 1959,My 12,40:1
Pirates of Penzance, The 1961,S 7,41:1
Androcles and the Lion 1961,N 22,24:2
Who'll Save the Plowboy? 1962,Ja 10,24:2
Oh Dad, Poor Dad, Mamma's Hung You in the Closet and I'm Feelin' So Sad 1962,F 27,28:1
Abe Lincoln in Illinois 1963,Ja 23,5:2
Dragon, The 1963,Ap 10,32:1
Oh Dad, Poor Dad, Mamma's Hung You in the Closet and I'm Feelin' So Sad 1963,Ag 28,28:2
Morning Sun 1963,O 7,36:2
Too Much Johnson 1964,Ja 16,29:1
Hambleton, Thomas
I Want a Policeman! 1936,Ja 15,15:5
Hambling, Arthur (Scenic Designer)
School for Scandal, The 1929,D 15,X,4:2
Hambro, Leonid
Comedy in Music, Opus 2 1964,N 10,54:1
Comedy in Music 1964,N 22,II,1:1
Hambro, Madelon
Arrow-Maker, The 1956,O 5,20:1
Hambur, Pierre (Miscellaneous)
Not Now Darling 1970,O 30,33:1
Hamburger, Sylvia (Scenic Designer)
Flying Blind 1930,My 16,20:2
Hamdown, John
Processional 1937,O 14,23:1
Hamer, Gerald
George Washington 1920,Mr 2,9:1
Champion, The 1921,Ja 4,11:1
Red Poppy, The 1922,D 21,18:2
Devil's Disciple, The 1923,Ap 24,24:1
Devil's Disciple, The 1923,My 6,VII,1:1
Living Mask, The 1924,Ja 22,15:1
Candida 1924,D 13,12:3
Importance of Being Earnest, The 1926,My 4,30:1
Henry IV, Part I 1926,Je 1,29:1
Lally 1927,F 9,16:3
Taming of the Shrew, The 1927,O 26,26:4
Fallen Angels 1927,D 2,20:4
Becky Sharp 1929,Je 4,29:1
Hundred Years Old, A 1929,O 2,28:2
Milestones 1930,Je 3,27:1
Admirable Crichton, The 1931,Mr 10,23:2
Way of the World, The 1931,Je 2,34:3
One Wife or Another 1933,F 7,23:6
Threepenny Opera, The 1933,Ap 14,22:4
Hamer, Janet
Song of Norway 1944,Ag 22,20:2
Hamer, Joseph
White Cargo 1960,D 30,12:1
Cicero 1961,F 9,37:2
Month in the Country, A 1963,My 29,39:2
Hamid, George A (Producer)
Aquacircus 1958,Je 30,24:6
Hell'z-A-Splashin' 1959,Je 25,22:2
Hamil, Harriet
Bad Habits of 1926 1926,My 1,11:1
Hamil, John
Jackpot 1944,Ja 14,15:2

Hamil, Kathryn
Bad Habits of 1926 1926,My 1,11:1
Hamilin, Jack
Scarlet Coat, The 1924,D 24,11:1
Hamill, Emily
Back Here 1928,N 27,36:3
Street Scene 1929,Ja 11,20:4
First Mrs Fraser, The 1929,D 30,16:2
Hamill, Gwen Jo (Lighting Director)
Ben Bagley's Shoestring Revues 1970,O 24,22:1
Hamill, John
New Moon, The 1944,My 18,16:2
Rhapsody 1944,N 23,37:2
Pirates of Penzance, The 1946,My 17,14:6
Pirates of Penzance, The 1946,S 21,19:2
Hamill, Kathryn
Lucky 1927,Mr 23,28:3
Second Little Show, The 1930,S 3,36:1
Hamill, Mary
Spiro Who? 1969,My 19,55:1
Hamill, Stuart (Playwright)
Bare Facts 1927,Je 30,35:1
Hamill, Virginia
Comrades 1956,Je 6,38:1
Hamilton, Aileen
Lady of the Lamp, The 1920,Ag 18,6:4
Hamilton, Alice
Greenwich Village Follies 1920,Ag 31,7:3
Hamilton, Allen
Twelfth Night 1968,Je 15,40:1
Serjeant Musgrave's Dance 1968,Je 16,52:4
Resistible Rise of Arturo Ui, The 1968,Ag 8,25:1
House of Atreus, The 1968,D 18,55:1
Resistible Rise of Arturo Ui, The 1968,D 23,44:1
Jungle of Cities 1970,Mr 1,75:2
Hamilton, Ann
Chaparral 1958,S 10,38:2
Orpheus Descending 1959,O 6,45:2
Rockefeller and the Red Indians 1968,O 25,37:1
Hamilton, Barbara
Razzle Dazzle 1951,F 20,21:1
Love and Libel 1960,D 8,44:1
Anne of Green Gables 1969,Ag 25,41:1
Hamilton, Betty
Pardon My English 1933,Ja 21,11:4
Hamilton, Bob (Choreographer)
Rumple 1957,N 7,42:2
What a Killing 1961,Mr 28,41:1
Hamilton, Bruce
Knickerbocker Holiday 1938,O 20,26:2
Hamilton, Bruce (Original Author)
Hanging Judge 1952,S 24,40:4
Hamilton, Carl
Behold the Bridegroom 1927,D 27,24:1
Hamilton, Charles
Iceman Cometh, The 1956,My 8,38:1
Hamilton, Charles (Miscellaneous)
Drums in the Night 1967,My 18,54:1
Hamilton, Christabel
Mikado, The 1924,Jl 29,9:1
Hamilton, Clayton (Playwright)
Friend Indeed 1926,Ap 27,22:3
Hamilton, Cosmo (Playwright)
Silver Fox, The 1921,S 6,13:1
Danger 1921,D 23,18:3
New Poor, The 1923,D 30,VII,2:1
New Poor, The 1924,Ja 8,26:1
New Poor, The 1924,Ja 20,VII,1:1
Parasites 1924,N 20,21:1
Parasites 1924,N 23,VIII,1:1
Women and Ladies 1925,My 10,VIII,4:4
Pickwick 1927,F 16,17:4
Mr Pickwick 1927,F 20,VII,2:6
Pickwick 1927,Mr 13,VII,1:1
Pickwick 1927,S 6,35:2
Pickwick 1927,O 2,VIII,1:1
Caste 1927,D 24,8:1
Aunt of England 1935,Mr 28,25:4
Aunt of England 1935,Ap 21,IX,2:2
Hamilton, D J
Sex 1926,Ap 27,22:4
Napoleon 1928,Mr 9,21:1
Elmer the Great 1928,S 25,29:1
Headquarters 1929,D 5,32:4
Papavert 1931,D 30,25:1
Iron Men 1936,O 20,30:6
Hamilton, Dan
Conduct Unbecoming 1970,O 13,50:1
Hamilton, Daniel
Adding Machine, The 1923,Mr 20,24:1
Overture 1930,D 8,26:4
Tree, The 1932,Ap 13,23:5
Man Who Reclaimed His Head 1932,S 9,17:3
Hamilton, Dave
My Dear Public 1943,S 10,28:1
Hamilton, Donald
Gypsy Baron, The 1944,Je 15,17:3
Hamilton, Dorothy
Winslow Boy, The 1947,O 30,32:2
Hamilton, Edgar
Gingham Girl, The 1922,Ag 29,15:5
Hamilton, Edith (Translator)
Trojan Women, The 1938,Ja 25,24:2

Hamilton, Edith (Translator)—Cont
Prometheus Bound 1957,Ag 9,11:6
Trojan Women, The 1963,D 24,7:6
Hamilton, Eric
Sound of Music, The 1967,Ap 27,52:1
King and I, The 1968,My 24,39:1
Hamilton, Ethel
Greeks Had a Word for It, The 1930,S 26,16:5
Hamilton, Frank
Skin of Our Teeth, The 1955,Ag 18,16:1
Visit, The 1960,Mr 9,38:3
Barroom Monks, The 1962,My 29,21:1
Portrait of the Artist as a Young Man, A
1962,My 29,21:1
Hallelujah, Baby! 1967,Ap 27,51:1
Hamilton, Frank (Director)
Arms and the Man 1965,Je 24,32:5
Hamilton, Frank (Miscellaneous)
Step on a Crack 1962,O 18,48:1
Rondelay 1969,N 6,55:1
Minnie's Boys 1970,Mr 27,27:1
Hamilton, G Gordon
Noble Experiment, The 1930,O 28,21:4
Hamilton, G T
Hamlet 1920,Mr 17,14:2
Hamilton, Gary
Sound of Music, The 1967,Ap 27,52:1
Hamilton, Gloria
Chocolate Soldier, The 1947,Mr 13,34:2
Lend an Ear 1948,D 17,38:2
Courtin' Time 1951,Je 14,30:2
Show Boat 1956,Je 22,16:1
Show Boat 1957,Je 28,30:2
Hamilton, Gordon
Shipwrecked 1924,N 13,18:1
Subway Express 1929,S 25,34:3
Honor Code, The 1931,My 19,25:3
Did I Say No? 1931,S 23,19:4
Coastwise 1931,D 1,23:1
Crucible 1933,S 5,22:4
Ladies' Money 1934,N 2,26:6
Whatever Goes Up 1935,N 26,28:2
Two on the Aisle 1951,Jl 20,13:6
My Darlin' Aida 1952,O 28,36:4
Hamilton, Grace
Wildcat, The 1921,N 28,16:2
Springtime of Youth 1922,O 27,15:1
Artists and Models 1923,Ag 21,12:2
Hamilton, Guy
I Loved You Wednesday 1932,O 12,27:1
Hamilton, Hal
Liliom 1956,F 18,12:5
Hamilton, Hale
Dear Me 1921,Ja 18,14:1
Swifty 1922,O 17,14:1
Vaudeville (Palace) 1924,Ja 22,15:6
Yellow 1926,S 22,30:1
What the Doctor Ordered 1927,Ag 19,20:2
Mirrors 1928,Ja 19,17:1
Divorce a la Carte 1928,Mr 27,30:3
Mr Moneypenny 1928,O 17,26:2
Precious 1929,Ja 15,22:5
Stepping Out 1929,My 21,29:1
Hamilton, Hale (Playwright)
Dear Me 1921,Ja 18,14:1
Dear Me 1921,Ja 30,VI,1:1
Hamilton, Harry (Playwright)
Savage Rhythm 1932,Ja 1,30:4
Hamilton, Henry
Buttrio Square 1952,O 15,40:2
Maggie 1953,F 19,20:2
Me and Juliet 1953,My 29,17:1
Hamilton, J Allen
Wild Duck, The 1938,Ap 16,16:5
Hamilton, Jack (Miscellaneous)
Time for Singing, A 1966,My 23,48:2
Hamilton, Jake (Miscellaneous)
Homecoming, The 1967,Ja 6,29:1
Halfway up the Tree 1967,N 8,52:1
Hamilton, James
Passing Show of 1923, The 1923,Je 15,24:6
Matinee Girl, The 1926,F 2,20:3
Hamilton, James (Miscellaneous)
Jimmy 1969,O 24,38:1
Hamilton, James (Scenic Designer)
Allegro 1952,S 18,36:3
Hamilton, Jane
Subway, The 1929,Ja 26,15:1
Little Father of the Wilderness, The 1930,Je 3,27:1
Counsellor-at-Law 1931,N 7,17:2
Black Sheep 1932,O 14,22:6
Counsellor-at-Law 1942,N 25,17:2
Hamilton, Jeffrey
Penny Wars, The 1969,O 16,52:1
Hamilton, Joan
Child of Manhattan 1932,Mr 2,15:1
Hamilton, John
Macushla 1920,My 18,9:3
LeMaire's Affairs 1927,Mr 29,22:4
Heads Up! 1929,N 12,34:1
Fresh Fields 1934,Jl 15,X,1:1
Dr Knock 1936,Jl 14,22:1
Feathers in a Gale 1943,D 22,26:2
Child of the Morning 1951,N 17,9:7

Hamilton, John F
Shore Leave 1922,Ag 9,20:2
Hell-Bent Fer Heaven 1924,Ja 5,10:1
Mongrel, The 1924,D 16,28:2
Dagger, The 1925,S 10,28:1
Americana 1928,O 31,28:2
Rockbound 1929,Ap 20,23:2
Alchemist, The 1931,Je 5,27:1
Black Tower 1932,Ja 12,29:2
Pursuit of Happiness, The 1934,Je 24,IX,1:4
Ceiling Zero 1935,Ap 2,24:3
Ceiling Zero 1935,Ap 11,26:2
Iron Men 1936,O 20,30:6
Of Mice and Men 1937,N 24,20:5
Of Mice and Men 1937,D 12,XI,3:1
Clash by Night 1941,D 29,20:2
Day Will Come, The 1944,S 8,17:2
Therese 1945,O 10,24:2
Of Mice and Men 1958,D 5,38:1
Hamilton, John R
Stolen Fruit 1925,O 8,31:4
Gods of the Lightning 1928,O 25,27:2
One Way Street 1928,D 25,31:2
Rhapsody, The 1930,S 16,30:3
Heigh-Ho, Everybody 1932,My 26,31:2
Hamilton, Julie
Devil Came From Dublin, The! 1955,Je 3,27:2
Hamilton, Katherine
If in the Green Wood 1947,Ja 17,27:6
Hamilton, Lance (Producer)
Nude With Violin 1957,N 15,36:1
Look After Lulu 1959,Mr 4,35:1
Hamilton, Laura
Half Gods 1929,D 23,18:5
Hamilton, Lavinia
Carmen Jones 1956,Je 1,28:2
Hamilton, Leland
Hidden Horizon 1946,S 20,42:2
Hamilton, Leon
Catherine Was Great 1944,Ag 3,16:1
Hamilton, Lynn
Only in America 1959,N 20,35:1
Cool World, The 1960,F 23,38:2
Face of a Hero 1960,O 21,29:5
Midsummer Night's Dream, A 1964,Je 30,23:2
Henry V 1965,Je 29,27:2
Hamilton, Marc
Big Two, The 1947,Ja 9,21:2
Hamilton, Margaret
Another Language 1932,Ap 26,25:3
Another Language 1932,My 15,VIII,1:1
Dark Tower, The 1933,N 27,20:3
Farmer Takes a Wife, The 1934,O 31,17:1
Outrageous Fortune 1943,N 4,28:5
Men We Marry, The 1948,Ja 17,11:2
Fancy Meeting You Again 1952,Ja 15,23:2
Adding Machine, The 1956,F 10,17:1
Diary of a Scoundrel 1956,N 5,41:1
Annie Get Your Gun 1958,F 20,29:2
Goldilocks 1958,O 13,33:1
Goldilocks 1958,O 19,II,1:1
Save Me a Place at Forest Lawn 1963,My 9,40:2
Utbu 1966,Ja 5,24:1
Show Boat 1966,Jl 20,48:1
Come Summer 1969,Mr 19,43:1
Oklahoma! 1969,Je 24,37:1
Oklahoma! 1969,Jl 6,II,1:1
Our Town 1969,N 28,50:1
Our Town 1969,D 7,II,7:1
Devil's Disciple, The 1970,Je 30,48:1
Hamilton, Marion
Lady Butterfly 1923,Ja 23,18:1
Billie 1928,O 2,34:2
Hamilton, May
Little Theatre Tournament; Old Lady Shows Her
Medals, The 1928,My 11,28:1
Hamilton, Morris (Composer)
Riff-Raff 1926,F 9,18:6
Earl Carroll's Vanities 1926,Ag 25,19:4
Earl Carroll's Vanities 1927,Ja 5,18:1
Earl Carroll's Vanities 1928,Ag 7,25:2
Hamilton, Morris (Lyricist)
Earl Carroll's Vanities 1926,Ag 25,19:4
Earl Carroll's Vanities 1927,Ja 5,18:1
Earl Carroll's Vanities 1928,Ag 7,25:2
Hamilton, Morris W (Musical Director)
Riff-Raff 1926,F 9,18:6
Hamilton, Murray
Strange Fruit 1945,N 30,18:6
Mister Roberts 1948,F 19,27:2
Mister Roberts 1950,My 21,II,1:1
Chase, The 1952,Ap 16,30:2
Stockade 1954,F 5,14:2
Critic's Choice 1960,D 15,61:3
Heroine, The 1963,F 21,5:5
Absence of a Cello 1964,S 22,45:1
Forty Carats 1968,D 27,45:1
Forty Carats 1969,Ja 5,II,1:3
Hamilton, Nancy
New Faces 1934,Mr 16,24:5
Pride and Prejudice 1935,N 6,32:4
One for the Money 1939,F 9,9:2

Hamilton, Nancy (Composer)
It's All Yours 1942,Mr 26,26:2
Hamilton, Nancy (Lyricist)
New Faces 1934,Mr 16,24:5
One for the Money 1939,F 6,9:2
Two for the Show 1940,F 9,14:2
It's All Yours 1942,Mr 26,26:2
Three to Make Ready 1946,Mr 8,16:2
Hamilton, Nancy (Playwright)
New Faces 1934,Mr 16,24:5
One for the Money 1939,F 6,9:2
Two for the Show 1940,F 9,14:2
Two for the Show 1940,F 18,IX,1:1
Three to Make Ready 1946,Mr 8,16:2
Three to Make Ready 1946,Mr 17,II,1:1
Hamilton, Neil
Many Happy Returns 1945,Ja 6,15:5
Deep Mrs Sykes, The 1945,Mr 20,22:6
Deep Mrs Sykes, The 1945,Mr 25,II,1:1
Men We Marry, The 1948,Ja 17,11:2
To Be Continued 1952,Ap 24,37:2
Late Love 1953,O 14,35:2
Hamilton, Patricia
Pullman Car Hiawatha 1962,D 4,46:2
Much Ado About Nothing 1964,Je 11,26:2
Hamlet 1964,Jl 4,9:1
Coriolanus 1965,Je 21,36:1
Romeo and Juliet 1965,Je 21,36:3
King Lear 1965,Je 25,39:1
Yes, Yes, No No 1969,Ja 1,16:1
Hamilton, Patrick (Playwright)
Rope's End 1929,S 20,34:5
John Brown's Body 1931,Ja 12,24:2
John Brown's Body 1931,F 1,VIII,2:4
Angel Street 1941,D 6,15:2
Duke in Darkness, The 1942,O 18,VIII,1:4
Duke in Darkness, The 1944,Ja 25,15:2
Angel Street 1944,Jl 9,II,1:1
Angel Street 1948,Ja 23,26:6
Hamilton, Peter
New Moon, The 1944,My 18,16:2
Swing Out, Sweet Land! 1944,N 10,24:6
Sing Out, Sweet Land! 1944,D 28,24:2
Angel in the Wings 1947,D 12,36:4
Angel in the Wings 1948,F 8,II,2:1
Hamilton, Peter (Choreographer)
Spree de Corps 1955,D 9,33:8
Take a Gander 1956,D 14,36:4
Can-Can 1959,Ag 26,25:4
Beg, Borrow or Steal 1960,F 11,39:4
Kittiwake Island 1960,O 13,43:1
Hamilton, Phyllis
Censored 1938,F 28,18:2
Hamilton, Reed
Paris 1928,O 9,34:3
Hamilton, Richard
First Lady 1952,My 29,18:5
Cloud 7 1958,F 15,15:2
Blood, Sweat & Stanley Poole 1961,O 6,31:1
Exception and the Rule, The 1965,My 21,19:1
Bench, The 1968,Mr 5,35:2
Hamilton, Richard (Miscellaneous)
Laughwind 1966,Mr 3,27:1
Infantry, The 1966,N 15,51:1
Hamilton, Rick
Galileo 1968,D 1,88:4
Hamilton, Robert
Midsummer Night's Dream, A 1932,N 18,22:2
Twelfth Night 1932,N 19,20:5
Merchant of Venice, The 1932,N 24,34:5
Romeo and Juliet 1933,F 3,21:5
Hamilton, Robert Hugh
Little Theatre Tournament; Tale Retold, A
1928,My 10,31:1
Hamilton, Roger
Merchant of Venice, The 1955,Ja 8,9:7
Grass Is Always Greener, The 1955,F 16,25:2
Miser, The 1955,Mr 18,34:2
Julius Caesar 1955,Jl 13,20:1
Tempest, The 1955,Ag 2,18:2
Much Ado About Nothing 1955,Ag 20,20:4
Hamlet 1956,O 29,34:1
Founders, The 1957,My 14,39:1
Deputy, The 1964,F 27,26:1
Live Like Pigs 1965,Je 8,48:2
Serjeant Musgrave's Dance 1966,Mr 9,44:1
Rosencrantz and Guildenstern Are Dead
1967,O 17,53:1
Hamilton, Ronald
Hall of Healing 1952,My 8,35:6
Hamilton, Ross
Biff, Bing, Bang 1921,My 10,20:1
Hamilton, Scott
Simpleton of the Unexpected Isles, The
1954,Ja 12,19:1
Private Life of the Master Race, The
1956,Ja 31,33:3
Hamilton, Spike
Michael Todd's Peep Show 1950,Je 29,37:2
Hamilton, T A
Beau-Strings 1926,Ap 27,22:2
Hamilton, T Edward (Producer)
Great Campaign, The 1947,Ap 1,33:2

Hamilton, Thale
Wonderful Night, A; Fledermaus, Die
1929,N 1,23:3
Hamilton, Thomas
Saint Wench 1933,Ja 3,19:3
Her Tin Soldier 1933,Ap 7,22:6
As Thousands Cheer 1933,O 2,22:1
Hamilton, Vonn (Choreographer)
Frankie and Johnny 1952,O 29,37:2
Hamilton, Wallace (Playwright)
Burning of the Lepers, The 1962,Ap 5,29:1
Burning, The 1963,D 4,57:1
Hamizrachi, Ezra
Melody Lingers On, The 1969,N 17,55:1
Hamlett, Dilys
Miracle Worker, The 1961,Mr 10,19:4
Hamlin, Charles
Spider, The 1927,Mr 23,29:1
Hamlin, Frances
Cup of Trembling, The 1959,My 1,33:5
Hamlin, George (Director)
New York Idea, The 1963,Jl 13,12:2
Hamlin, George (Miscellaneous)
Miss Lonelyhearts 1957,O 4,26:2
Time Remembered 1957,N 13,41:2
Firstborn, The 1958,My 1,35:1
Hamlin, Hannibal
Coriolanus 1927,Je 18,8:3
Hamlin, Joanne
New York Idea, The 1963,Jl 13,12:2
Hamlin, John
Cup of Trembling, The 1959,My 1,33:5
Hamlin, Robert (Scenic Designer)
Alcestis Comes Back 1962,Ap 24,33:1
At Sea 1962,Ap 24,33:1
Stone Tower, The 1962,Ag 24,14:2
Hamlisch, Marvin (Choreographer)
Minnie's Boys 1970,Mr 27,27:1
Hamlisch, Marvin (Composer)
Minnie's Boys 1970,Mr 27,27:1
Hamlisch, Marvin (Miscellaneous)
Henry, Sweet Henry 1967,O 24,51:2
Golden Rainbow 1968,F 5,27:1
Hamm, Peter von (Translator)
Family Portrait; Familie, Eine 1946,N 11,44:1
Hammack, Warren
Book of Job, The 1962,F 10,13:1
Hamme, Benjamin
Mother Courage and Her Children 1963,Mr 30,5:5
Hammel, Fritz
Versunkene Glocke, Die 1936,N 20,26:3
Hammel, Harry
Unsophisticates, The 1929,D 31,14:5
Hammer, Ben
Silver Tassie, The 1949,Jl 22,16:5
Trouble in July 1949,D 2,36:2
Montserrat 1954,My 26,34:2
Moby Dick 1955,Ap 26,25:3
Great Sebastians, The 1956,Ja 5,27:1
Two Executioners, The 1960,My 17,42:2
Picnic on the Battlefield 1960,My 17,42:2
Deputy, The 1964,F 27,26:1
Royal Hunt of the Sun, The 1965,O 27,36:2
Murderous Angels 1970,F 8,70:1
Hammer, Borgny
Hedda Gabler 1920,O 5,12:2
Hammer, Eleanor
Shadow and Substance 1959,N 4,42:1
Man and Superman 1960,Ag 17,35:3
Hammer, Jay
Passing Through From Exotic Places; Burial of
Esposito, The 1969,D 8,60:4
Hammer, Joseph
White Rose and the Red, The 1964,Mr 17,31:1
Hammer, Josephine
Face Value 1921,D 27,10:2
Hammer, Mark
Journey of the Fifth Horse, The 1966,Ap 22,36:1
Stephen D 1966,Ag 5,17:1
Hammer, Robert (Miscellaneous)
Hobo 1961,Ap 11,41:2
Hammer, Vernon
Jubilee 1935,O 14,20:1
Between the Devil 1937,D 23,24:5
Hammerlee, Patricia
New Faces of 1952 1952,My 17,23:2
Seventh Heaven 1955,My 27,16:2
Vamp, The 1955,N 11,30:1
Shoestring '57 1956,N 6,31:1
Hammerman, Dan (Playwright)
Henri Christophe 1945,Je 7,24:5
Henri Christophe 1945,Je 17,II,1:1
Hammerschlag, Peter (Lyricist)
From Vienna 1939,Je 21,26:2
Hammerslough, Charles (Director)
Granite 1936,Ja 14,24:6
Hammerslough, Charles (Miscellaneous)
Granite 1936,Ja 14,24:6
Hammersmith (Producer)
Azrael; Eagle Has Two Heads, The 1946,S 16,9:7
Hammerstein, Arthur (Director)
Rose Marie 1928,Mr 31,23:2

Hammerstein, Arthur (Producer)
Always You 1920,Ja 6,18:2
Tickle Me 1920,Ag 18,9:1
Front Seat, The 1921,My 22,VI,1:6
Rose Marie 1924,Ag 24,VII,1:8
Rose Marie 1925,Mr 21,16:2
Song of the Flame 1925,D 11,26:4
Song of the Flame 1925,D 31,10:2
Wild Rose, The 1926,O 21,23:1
Golden Dawn 1927,D 1,32:3
Good Boy 1928,S 6,23:2
Polly 1928,N 11,X,2:4
Polly 1929,Ja 9,28:3
Sweet Adeline 1929,Ag 25,VIII,3:1
Sweet Adeline 1929,S 4,33:1
Luana 1930,S 18,28:1
Ballyhoo 1930,D 14,IX,3:1
Ballyhoo 1930,D 23,24:1
Man Who Reclaimed His Head 1932,S 9,17:3
Hammerstein, James (Director)
Absence of a Cello 1964,S 22,45:1
South Pacific 1965,Je 3,25:1
Paisley Convertible, The 1967,F 13,42:1
It's Called the Sugar Plum 1968,Ja 18,47:2
Indian Wants the Bronx, The 1968,Ja 18,47:2
Indian Wants the Bronx, The 1968,Je 30,II,1:1
Tea Party 1968,O 16,40:1
Basement, The 1968,O 16,40:1
Tea Party 1968,N 3,II,7:4
Hammerstein, James (Miscellaneous)
Flower Drum Song 1958,D 2,44:1
Hammerstein, James (Producer)
Blue Denim 1958,F 28,17:1
Hammerstein, Oscar 2d (Composer)
Carousel 1949,Ja 26,28:2
Show Boat 1954,My 6,44:1
Carousel 1954,Je 3,32:2
Hammerstein, Oscar 2d (Director)
You'll Never Know 1921,Ap 21,9:2
Rainbow 1928,N 22,25:1
Ballyhoo 1930,D 23,24:1
Free for All 1931,S 9,25:1
East Wind 1931,O 28,19:1
Music in the Air 1932,N 9,28:2
Knights of Song 1938,O 18,29:2
Glorious Morning 1938,N 28,10:3
Very Warm for May 1939,N 18,23:2
Sunny River 1941,D 5,28:2
Show Boat 1946,Ja 7,17:2
Show Boat 1948,S 9,33:2
Show Boat 1948,S 19,II,1:1
Music in the Air 1951,O 9,32:2
Hammerstein, Oscar 2d (Lyricist)
Always You 1920,Ja 6,18:2
Tickle Me 1920,Ag 18,9:1
Jimmie 1920,N 18,15:3
Daffy Dill 1922,Ag 23,14:5
Mary Jane McKane 1923,D 26,13:2
Rose Marie 1924,S 3,12:2
Sunny 1925,S 23,22:1
Song of the Flame 1925,D 31,10:2
Wild Rose, The 1926,O 21,23:1
Show Boat 1927,D 28,26:1
Rainbow 1928,N 22,25:1
Sweet Adeline 1929,Ag 25,VIII,3:1
Sweet Adeline 1929,S 4,33:1
Sweet Adeline 1929,S 15,IX,1:8
Show Boat 1932,My 20,22:2
Music in the Air 1932,O 23,IX,3:3
Music in the Air 1932,N 9,28:2
Music in the Air 1932,N 20,IX,1:1
May Wine 1935,N 23,23:1
May Wine 1935,D 6,30:3
Very Warm for May 1939,N 12,IX,2:3
American Jubilee 1940,My 13,20:5
Sunny River 1941,D 5,28:2
Oklahoma! 1943,Ap 1,27:1
Oklahoma! 1943,My 9,II,6:4
Carmen Jones 1943,D 3,26:2
Carmen Jones 1943,D 12,II,3:1
Carousel 1945,Ap 20,24:2
Carousel 1945,Ap 29,II,1:1
Desert Song, The 1946,Ja 9,20:2
Show Boat 1946,Ja 13,II,1:1
Happy Birthday 1946,N 1,31:2
Allegro 1947,O 11,10:2
Allegro 1947,N 2,II,1:1
Carousel 1949,F 6,II,1:1
South Pacific 1949,Ap 8,30:2
South Pacific 1949,Ap 17,II,1:1
South Pacific 1949,Je 5,II,1:1
South Pacific 1950,Ap 26,36:5
King and I, The 1951,Mr 30,26:2
King and I, The 1951,Ap 8,II,1:1
Oklahoma! 1951,My 30,15:2
South Pacific 1951,Jl 10,30:5
South Pacific 1951,S 2,II,1:1
Oklahoma! 1951,S 13,38:2
Music in the Air 1951,O 9,32:2
South Pacific 1951,N 2,19:1
South Pacific 1951,N 11,II,3:1
King and I, The 1952,Ap 14,23:1
Allegro 1952,S 18,36:3

Hammerstein, Oscar 2d (Lyricist)—Cont
Carousel 1953,My 6,38:1
Me and Juliet 1953,My 29,17:1
Me and Juliet 1953,Je 7,II,1:1
Oklahoma! 1953,S 1,19:1
Oklahoma! 1953,S 6,II,1:1
King and I, The 1953,O 9,33:3
King and I, The 1953,O 18,II,3:1
Show Boat 1954,My 6,44:1
Carousel 1954,Je 13,II,1:1
Show Boat 1954,N 1,27:2
South Pacific 1955,My 5,39:5
Pipe Dream 1955,D 1,44:1
Pipe Dream 1955,D 11,II,5:1
King and I, The 1956,Ap 19,35:4
Show Boat 1956,Je 22,16:1
South Pacific 1957,Ap 25,35:1
Oklahoma! 1958,Mr 8,15:2
Oklahoma! 1958,Mr 20,32:3
Flower Drum Song 1958,D 2,44:1
Flower Drum Song 1958,D 7,II,5:1
Sound of Music, The 1959,N 17,40:2
Sound of Music, The 1959,N 22,II,1:1
Flower Drum Song 1960,Mr 25,20:4
King and I, The 1960,My 12,40:1
King and I, The 1960,My 22,II,1:1
Oklahoma! 1963,My 16,40:1
King and I, The 1964,Jl 7,26:1
South Pacific 1965,Je 3,25:1
Carousel 1965,Ag 11,39:1
Oklahoma! 1965,D 16,62:1
Carousel 1966,D 16,56:2
Sound of Music, The 1967,Ap 27,52:1
South Pacific 1967,Je 13,56:1
King and I, The 1968,My 24,39:1
South Pacific 1968,Je 30,54:2
Oklahoma! 1969,Je 24,37:1
South Pacific 1969,Jl 7,27:1
Sound of Music, The 1970,Jl 3,13:1
Hammerstein, Oscar 2d (Miscellaneous)
9 O'Clock Revue 1923,O 5,22:1
Golden Dawn 1927,O 2,VIII,4:6
Rainbow 1928,N 4,IX,1:3
Show Boat 1946,Ja 7,17:2
Hammerstein, Oscar 2d (Musical Director)
Gang's All Here, The 1931,F 19,21:3
Hammerstein, Oscar 2d (Original Author)
Show Boat 1932,My 20,22:2
American Jubilee 1940,My 13,20:5
Carousel 1945,Ap 20,24:2
Desert Song, The 1946,Ja 9,20:2
Hammerstein, Oscar 2d (Playwright)
Always You 1920,Ja 6,18:2
Tickle Me 1920,Ag 18,9:1
Jimmie 1920,N 18,15:3
Daffy Dill 1922,Ag 23,14:5
Queen O' Hearts 1922,O 11,22:1
Wildflower 1923,F 8,17:2
Mary Jane McKane 1923,D 26,13:2
Gypsy Jim 1924,Ja 6,VII,1:4
Gypsy Jim 1924,Ja 15,17:4
New Toys 1924,Ja 20,VII,2:8
New Toys 1924,F 19,12:1
New Toys 1924,F 24,VII,1:1
Rose Marie 1924,Ag 24,VII,1:8
Rose Marie 1924,S 3,12:2
Sunny 1925,S 23,22:1
Song of the Flame 1925,D 11,26:4
Song of the Flame 1925,D 31,10:2
Wild Rose, The 1926,O 21,23:1
Desert Song, The 1926,D 1,24:2
Golden Dawn 1927,D 1,32:3
Show Boat 1927,D 28,26:1
Show Boat 1928,Ja 8,VIII,1:1
Rose Marie 1928,Ap 29,IX,2:8
Good Boy 1928,S 6,23:2
New Moon, The 1928,S 20,33:1
Rainbow 1928,N 22,25:1
Rainbow 1928,D 16,IX,1:1
Sweet Adeline 1929,Ag 25,VIII,3:1
Sweet Adeline 1929,S 4,33:1
Sweet Adeline 1929,S 15,IX,1:8
Free for All 1931,S 9,25:1
East Wind 1931,O 28,19:1
East Wind 1931,D 11,VIII,4:3
Music in the Air 1932,O 23,IX,3:3
Music in the Air 1932,N 9,28:2
Music in the Air 1932,N 20,IX,1:1
Ball at the Savoy 1933,S 9,9:7
Gentlemen Unafraid 1938,Je 5,II,6:8
Very Warm for May 1939,N 18,23:2
Sunny River 1941,D 5,28:2
New Moon, The 1942,Ag 19,14:2
Hay-Foot, Straw-Foot 1942,O 24,11:6
Oklahoma! 1943,Ap 1,27:1
Carmen Jones 1943,O 20,17:2
Carmen Jones 1943,D 3,26:2
Carmen Jones 1943,D 12,II,3:1
Carmen Jones 1943,D 19,II,9:1
New Moon, The 1944,My 18,16:2
Show Boat 1946,Ja 7,17:2
Carmen Jones 1946,Ap 8,32:2
Allegro 1947,N 2,II,1:1
Show Boat 1948,S 9,33:2

Hammerstein, Oscar 2d (Playwright)—Cont

Show Boat 1948,S 19,II,1:1
South Pacific 1949,Ap 8,30:2
King and I, The 1951,Mr 30,26:2
King and I, The 1951,Ap 8,II,1:1
Oklahoma! 1951,My 30,15:2
Carmen Jones 1951,S 22,8:6
Music in the Air 1951,O 9,32:2
Music in the Air 1951,O 21,II,1:1
Allegro 1952,S 18,36:3
Me and Juliet 1953,My 29,17:1
Oklahoma! 1953,S 1,19:1
Carousel 1954,Je 13,II,1:1
South Pacific 1955,My 5,39:5
King and I, The 1955,My 17,33:4
Oklahoma! 1955,Je 21,37:7
Pipe Dream 1955,D 1,44:1
King and I, The 1956,Ap 19,35:4
Carmen Jones 1956,Je 1,28:2
Show Boat 1956,Je 22,16:1
South Pacific 1957,Ap 25,35:1
Show Boat 1957,Je 28,30:2
Carousel 1957,S 12,38:2
Oklahoma! 1958,Mr 8,15:2
Oklahoma! 1958,Mr 20,32:3
Flower Drum Song 1958,D 2,44:1
Flower Drum Song 1958,D 7,II,5:1
Carmen Jones 1959,Ag 18,25:1
King and I, The 1960,My 12,40:1
King and I, The 1960,My 22,II,1:1
King and I, The 1961,Mr 19,22:5
Show Boat 1961,Ap 13,32:1
South Pacific 1961,Ap 27,26:3
Sound of Music, The 1961,My 19,22:6
Oklahoma! 1963,F 28,8:2
Oklahoma! 1963,My 16,40:1
King and I, The 1963,Je 13,30:2
King and I, The 1964,Jl 7,26:1
South Pacific 1965,Je 3,25:1
Carousel 1965,Ag 11,39:1
Oklahoma! 1965,D 16,62:1
Show Boat 1966,Jl 20,48:1
Carousel 1966,D 16,56:2
South Pacific 1967,Je 13,56:1
King and I, The 1968,My 24,39:1
South Pacific 1968,Je 30,54:2
Oklahoma! 1969,Je 24,37:1
South Pacific 1969,Jl 7,27:1
Me and Juliet 1970,My 15,42:1

Hammerstein, Oscar 2d (Producer)

Where Do We Go From Here? 1938,N 16,26:2
Glorious Morning 1938,N 28,10:3
I Remember Mama 1944,O 20,16:2
I Remember Mama 1944,O 29,II,1:1
Annie Get Your Gun 1946,Mr 29,18:2
Annie Get Your Gun 1946,My 17,14:2
Happy Birthday 1946,N 1,31:2
John Loves Mary 1947,F 5,29:2
Show Boat 1948,S 9,33:2
Show Boat 1948,S 19,II,1:1
South Pacific 1949,Ap 8,30:2
Happy Time, The 1950,Ja 25,24:1
Burning Bright 1950,O 19,40:2
King and I, The 1951,Mr 30,26:2
South Pacific 1952,Ap 14,23:1
Me and Juliet 1953,My 29,17:1
Oklahoma! 1953,S 1,19:1
Flower Drum Song 1958,D 2,44:1
Sound of Music, The 1959,N 17,40:2

Hammerstein, Reginald (Director)

Golden Dawn 1927,D 1,32:3
Good Boy 1928,S 6,23:2
Sweet Adeline 1929,S 4,33:1
Ballyhoo 1930,D 23,24:1
Show Boat 1956,Je 22,16:1
Show Boat 1957,Je 28,30:2

Hammerstein, Reginald (Producer)

Music in the Air 1951,O 9,32:2
Ankles Aweigh 1955,Ap 19,27:1

Hammerstein, Theodore J (Director)

Shoot the Works! 1931,Jl 26,VIII,2:1
Anybody's Game 1932,D 22,21:4
Shady Lady 1933,Jl 6,26:3
Thoroughbred 1933,N 7,29:2
Broadway Interlude 1934,Ap 20,16:3
Sap Runs High, The 1936,F 5,15:3

Hammerstein, Theodore J (Miscellaneous)

Vanderbilt Revue, The 1930,N 6,22:6
Shoot the Works! 1931,Jl 22,19:5

Hammerstein, Theodore J (Producer)

Thoroughbred 1933,N 7,29:2
Broadway Interlude 1934,Ap 20,16:3
Howdy Stranger 1937,Ja 15,17:5
Popsy 1941,F 11,26:2

Hammerstein, William (Director)

Show Boat 1954,My 6,44:1
Carousel 1954,Je 3,32:2
Carousel 1954,Je 13,II,1:1
Guys and Dolls 1955,Ap 21,32:2
Finian's Rainbow 1955,My 19,25:1
King and I, The 1956,Ap 19,35:4
Kiss Me, Kate 1956,My 10,27:2
Carmen Jones 1956,Je 1,28:2
Carmen Jones 1959,Ag 18,25:1

South Pacific 1968,Je 30,54:2
South Pacific 1969,Jl 7,27:1

Hammerstein, William (Miscellaneous)

Diary of Anne Frank, The 1955,O 6,24:2
Do Re Mi 1960,D 27,23:2

Hammerstein, William (Producer)

Talent '49 1949,Ap 13,39:4
Fledermaus, Die 1954,My 20,38:5
Come Blow Your Horn 1961,F 23,31:3
Gift of Time, A 1962,F 23,34:1
Advocate, The 1963,O 15,46:7

Hammerton, Frank

Parade at the Devil's Bridge 1957,F 19,35:7
Doctor Faustus 1957,F 19,35:7

Hammett, Dashiell (Playwright)

Cops and Horrors; Fly Paper 1970,Ag 11,27:1

Hammil, Arthur

Headquarters 1929,D 5,32:4

Hammill, Bernard Jr

Man Who Married a Dumb Wife, The
1930,My 9,20:5

Hammill, Gordon

I'll Take the High Road 1943,N 10,28:3

Hammill, Harry

Six-Cylinder Love 1921,Ag 26,8:2
Red Light Annie 1923,Ag 22,10:3

Hammond, Aubrey (Scenic Designer)

Josef Suss 1930,Ja 21,28:5
Colonel Satan 1931,Ja 18,I,28:6
Acropolis 1933,N 24,25:8
Shining Hour, The 1934,F 14,22:6
Tempest, The 1934,Ap 17,26:6

Hammond, Blair

Funny Girl 1964,Mr 27,15:1

Hammond, C Norman

Jolly Roger, The 1923,Ag 31,10:4
Cyrano de Bergerac 1923,N 2,14:1
Immortal Thief, The 1926,O 4,21:1
Enemy of the People, An 1927,O 4,32:5
Hamlet 1928,Ja 5,33:2
Henry V 1928,Mr 16,26:2
Light of Asia, The 1928,O 10,32:2
Cyrano de Bergerac 1928,D 26,14:4
Bonds of Interest, The 1929,O 15,34:2
Richelieu 1929,D 26,20:3
Cyrano de Bergerac 1932,D 27,11:2
Twelfth Night 1934,Jl 17,24:5
Cyrano de Bergerac 1936,Ap 28,17:1
Enemy of the People, An 1937,F 16,19:1
Miss Quis 1937,Ap 8,20:5
Empress of Destiny 1938,Mr 10,16:2
Miss Swan Expects 1939,F 21,15:2

Hammond, Charles

Lady Killer, The 1924,Mr 13,14:2
Blue Bandanna, The 1924,Je 24,18:4
Woman Disputed, A 1926,S 29,23:2
Tia Juana 1927,N 16,28:4
Kibitzer, The 1929,F 19,22:5
Launcelot and Elaine 1930,Mr 10,24:3
On the Make 1932,My 24,23:2
Bamboo Cross 1955,F 22,17:2

Hammond, Daga

World We Make, The 1939,N 21,19:1

Hammond, Dorothea

View From the Bridge, A 1956,N 9,34:4
Portrait of a Madonna 1957,Ap 1,21:2

Hammond, Dorothy

Country Wife, The 1931,Ap 19,31:5

Hammond, Dowuona

Next Phase, The 1957,Ag 4,38:3

Hammond, Earl

Lamp at Midnight 1947,D 22,29:2
Church Street 1948,F 10,27:2
Blood Wedding 1949,F 7,16:2
Juno 1959,Mr 10,41:1

Hammond, Edward (Playwright)

Badges 1924,D 4,25:1

Hammond, Frances

Madwoman of Chaillot, The 1950,Je 14,41:2
Legend of Lizzie, The 1959,F 10,39:1

Hammond, Freeman

Greatness Comes to the Maronies 1937,Ag 18,15:2
Only the Heart 1942,D 7,22:3
Patriots, The 1943,D 21,22:5
You Touched Me! 1945,S 26,27:2

Hammond, Freeman (Director)

Greatness Comes to the Maronies 1937,Ag 18,15:2
Reunion 1938,Ap 12,26:4

Hammond, George V

Tableaux 1961,D 18,41:3

Hammond, Gwendolyn

Nine Till Six 1930,S 29,17:2

Hammond, Jane

Naughty-Naught '00 1937,Ja 25,23:2

Hammond, Kay

Woman Kind 1933,S 28,25:2
Sugar Plum 1939,Ap 2,X,1:7
Blithe Spirit 1941,Jl 13,IX,1:4
Happy Marriage, The 1952,Ag 8,9:2
On Borrowed Time 1953,F 11,34:1
Little Glass Clock, The 1954,D 12,II,5:1

Hammond, Lionel

Antony and Cleopatra 1924,F 20,22:1

Hammond, Natalie Hays (Costume Designer)

Nativite, La; Miraculous Birth and the Midwives,
The; Trois Rois, Les; Trois Maries, Les;
Lamentation of the Virgin Mary, The; Magdalen,
The; Six Miracle Plays 1933,F 6,11:3

Hammond, Natalie Hays (Miscellaneous)

Six Miracle Plays; Miraculous Birth and the
Midwives, The; Magdalen, The; Trois Rois, Les; Trois
Maries, Les; Nativite, La 1933,F 12,IX,2:1

Hammond, Natalie Hays (Scenic Designer)

Social Register, The 1931,N 10,28:2

Hammond, Nicholas

Complaisant Lover, The 1961,N 2,43:2
Conduct Unbecoming 1970,O 13,50:1

Hammond, Norman

Caponsacchi 1926,O 27,24:2

Hammond, Norman C

Yoshe Kalb 1933,D 29,27:2

Hammond, Paul

Timber House 1936,S 21,27:5
Eternal Road, The 1937,Ja 8,14:2
Where Do We Go From Here? 1938,N 16,26:2

Hammond, Paul (Director)

Happy Valley, Limited 1936,Je 30,15:1
They Knew What They Wanted 1936,Jl 8,14:2

Hammond, Paul (Producer)

Timber House 1936,S 21,27:5

Hammond, Ronald

Boy Friend, The 1932,Je 8,22:3
Family Portrait 1939,Mr 9,18:4

Hammond, Ronald (Director)

My Dear Children 1941,Jl 22,22:6
Autumn Hill 1942,Ap 14,17:4
Bird in Hand 1942,O 20,24:2

Hammond, Ronald (Producer)

Bird in Hand 1942,O 20,24:2

Hammond, Ruth

Ouija Board, The 1920,Mr 30,9:1
Skirt, The 1921,N 8,28:1
Danger 1921,D 23,18:3
Antonia 1925,O 21,20:1
Saturday's Children 1927,Ja 27,13:1
Beaux' Stratagem, The 1928,Je 5,20:1
Karl and Anna 1929,O 8,34:1
This Is New York 1930,N 29,21:1
Good Fairy, The 1931,N 25,17:1
Good-Bye Please 1934,O 25,26:6
Winterset 1935,S 26,19:2
Saturday's Children 1936,Jl 7,22:5
Women, The 1936,D 28,13:1
Life With Father 1939,N 9,26:2
Life With Mother 1948,O 21,33:2
Mr Barry's Etchings 1950,F 1,26:2
Small Hours, The 1951,F 16,22:1
Candida 1957,Mr 29,18:5
Comes a Day 1958,N 7,22:1

Hammond, T W

Magistrate, The 1959,My 14,30:6

Hammond, Thomas (Miscellaneous)

Candide 1956,D 3,40:2

Hammond, Thomas (Producer)

Liar, The 1950,My 19,30:2
Candida 1952,Ap 23,23:6
Gambler, The 1952,O 14,40:1
Penny Friend, The 1966,D 27,46:1

Hammond, Tom

Witchfinders, The 1956,My 11,22:6
Three Sisters, The 1959,S 22,46:1
Case of Libel, A 1963,O 11,43:2

Hammond, Victor

Spanish Love 1920,Ag 18,6:1
Blood and Sand 1921,S 21,16:2
Arabesque 1925,O 21,20:2

Hammond, Virginia

Desert Sands 1922,F 14,20:1
Blue Bird, The 1923,D 26,13:3
Harem, The 1924,N 16,VIII,2:8
Harem, The 1924,D 3,24:1
Top O' the Hill 1929,N 27,30:4
You Can't Take It With You 1936,D 15,31:1
Man Who Came to Dinner, The 1939,O 17,31:1
Winged Victory 1943,N 22,24:1
Craig's Wife 1947,F 13,35:2
Craig's Wife 1947,Mr 30,II,1:1

Hamner, Josephine

Toto 1921,Mr 22,15:2

Hamon, Augustin (Translator)

Great Catherine, The 1927,Ap 3,VIII,4:7

Hamon, Henriette (Translator)

Great Catherine, The 1927,Ap 3,VIII,4:7

Hamor, Gerald

Lucky Sam McCarver 1925,O 22,22:1

Hamowitz, Ruth

Sisters' Tragedy, The 1930,My 6,33:1
Mighty Nimrod, The 1931,My 13,23:1

Hamp, Pierre (Henri Bourillon) (Playwright)

Deraillement du T P 33 1927,F 13,VII,4:1

Hampden, Burford

Richard III 1920,Mr 8,7:1
Macbeth 1921,F 18,16:1

Hampden, Burford—Cont

Sally, Irene and Mary 1922,S 5,21:2
Merry Wives of Windsor, The 1928,Mr 20,20:1
Macbeth 1928,N 20,28:3
Sherlock Holmes 1929,N 26,28:3
Troilus and Cressida 1932,Je 7,22:3
Passionate Pilgrim, The 1932,O 20,24:3
Uncle Tom's Cabin 1933,My 30,13:4
One More Honeymoon 1934,Ap 2,13:5

Hampden, Charles

Mask and the Face, The 1924,S 11,27:3
Black Cockatoo, The 1926,D 31,11:1
Butterflies 1927,F 2,22:4
Venus 1927,D 26,26:5
Silver Box, The 1928,Ja 18,23:1
Novice and the Duke, The 1929,D 11,37:2

Hampden, Paul

Fratricide Punished 1925,Ap 21,19:1

Hampden, Walter

George Washington 1920,Mr 2,9:1
Hamlet 1920,Mr 17,14:2
Merchant of Venice, The 1920,My 9,VI,1:7
Macbeth 1921,Ap 20,11:1
Macbeth 1921,Ap 24,VI,1:1
Servant in the House, The 1921,My 3,20:1
Taming of the Shrew, The 1921,My 12,20:2
Merchant of Venice, The 1921,My 14,10:4
School for Scandal, The 1923,Je 5,24:3
Cyrano de Bergerac 1923,N 2,14:1
Cyrano de Bergerac 1923,N 11,VIII,1:1
Othello 1925,Ja 12,11:1
Othello 1925,Ja 18,VII,1:1
Hamlet 1925,O 12,19:2
Hamlet 1925,N 22,VIII,1:1
Merchant of Venice, The 1925,D 28,12:1
Hamlet; Merchant of Venice, The 1926,Ja 3,VII,1:1
Cyrano de Bergerac 1926,F 19,18:1
Cyrano de Bergerac 1926,F 28,VIII,1:1
Servant in the House, The 1926,My 4,30:1
Immortal Thief, The 1926,O 4,21:1
Caponsacchi 1926,O 27,24:2
Caponsacchi 1927,F 20,VII,1:1
Enemy of the People, An 1927,O 4,32:5
Hamlet 1928,Ja 5,33:2
Caponsacchi 1928,Ja 25,20:3
Henry V 1928,Mr 16,26:2
Light of Asia, The 1928,O 10,32:2
Enemy of the People, An 1928,N 6,34:3
Cyrano de Bergerac 1928,D 26,14:4
Bonds of Interest, The 1929,O 15,34:2
Richelieu 1929,D 26,20:3
Little Father of the Wilderness, The 1930,Je 3,27:1
Admirable Crichton, The 1931,Mr 10,23:2
Admirable Crichton, The 1931,Mr 29,VIII,1:1
Way of the World, The 1931,Je 2,34:3
Cyrano de Bergerac 1932,D 27,11:2
Ruy Blas 1933,O 10,24:4
Richelieu 1934,My 22,28:1
Hamlet 1934,D 26,19:3
Richard III 1934,D 28,24:3
Achilles Had a Heel 1935,Ap 28,X,1:1
Seven Keys to Baldpate 1935,My 28,30:2
Achilles Had a Heel 1935,O 14,20:2
Cyrano de Bergerac 1936,Ap 28,17:1
Enemy of the People, An 1937,F 16,19:1
Passing of the Third Floor Back, The
    1937,Ag 3,20:6
Love for Love 1940,Je 4,19:5
Rivals, The 1941,N 18,32:2
Rivals, The 1942,Ja 15,24:2
Strings, My Lord, Are False, The 1942,My 20,24:2
Patriots, The 1943,D 21,22:5
And Be My Love 1945,F 22,30:4
Henry VIII 1946,N 7,42:2
What Every Woman Knows 1946,N 9,13:2
Traitor, The 1949,Ap 1,30:2
Traitor, The 1949,Ap 10,II,1:1
Velvet Glove, The 1949,D 27,26:2
Crucible, The 1953,Ja 23,15:2
Crucible, The 1953,F 1,II,1:1

Hampden, Walter (Director)

Othello 1925,Ja 12,11:1
Hamlet 1925,O 12,19:2
Merchant of Venice, The 1925,D 28,12:1
Immortal Thief, The 1926,O 4,21:1
Enemy of the People, An 1927,O 4,32:5
Out of the Sea 1927,D 6,26:2
Hamlet 1928,Ja 5,33:2
Henry V 1928,Mr 16,26:2
Light of Asia, The 1928,O 10,32:2
Bonds of Interest, The 1929,O 15,34:2
Richelieu 1929,D 26,20:3
Cyrano de Bergerac 1932,D 27,11:2
Richelieu 1934,My 22,28:1
Hamlet 1934,D 26,19:3
Achilles Had a Heel 1935,O 14,20:2
Cyrano de Bergerac 1936,Ap 28,17:1
Enemy of the People, An 1937,F 16,19:1

Hampden, Walter (Miscellaneous)

Cyrano de Bergerac 1926,F 19,18:1
Beaux' Stratagem, The 1928,Je 5,20:1
Cyrano de Bergerac 1936,Ap 28,17:1

Hampden, Walter (Producer)

Jolly Roger, The 1923,S 9,VII,1:1

Hamlet 1925,O 12,19:2
Merchant of Venice, The 1925,D 28,12:1
Servant in the House, The 1926,My 4,30:1
Immortal Thief, The 1926,O 4,21:1
Enemy of the People, An 1927,O 4,32:5
Hamlet 1928,Ja 5,33:2
Caponsacchi 1928,Ja 25,20:3
Henry V 1928,Mr 16,26:2
Light of Asia, The 1928,O 10,32:2
Enemy of the People, An 1928,N 6,34:3
Cyrano de Bergerac 1928,D 26,14:4
Bonds of Interest, The 1929,O 15,34:2
Richelieu 1929,D 26,20:3
Cyrano de Bergerac 1932,D 27,11:2
Richelieu 1934,My 22,28:1
Hamlet 1934,D 26,19:3
Richard III 1934,D 28,24:3
Achilles Had a Heel 1935,O 14,20:2
Enemy of the People, An 1937,F 16,19:1

Hampf, Dagmar

World We Make, The 1939,N 21,19:1

Hampshire, Bernice

Half-Caste, The 1926,Mr 30,20:4

Hampshire, John

Texas Town 1941,Ap 30,22:3

Hampshire, Michael Allen (Lighting Director)

Chocolates 1967,Ap 11,51:1

Hampshire, Michael Allen (Scenic Designer)

Night Is Black Bottles, The 1962,D 5,56:1
Chief Thing, The 1963,Ap 30,27:2
Chocolates 1967,Ap 11,51:1

Hampton, Betsy

Chivalry 1925,D 16,22:3

Hampton, Christopher (Playwright)

When Did You Last See My Mother?
    1967,Ja 5,27:5
Hedda Gabler 1970,Je 12,28:1
Philanthropist, The 1970,Ag 5,20:1
Philanthropist, The 1970,S 10,59:1

Hampton, Christopher (Translator)

Uncle Vanya 1970,Mr 15,II,7:3
Hedda Gabler 1970,Je 21,II,1:1

Hampton, Craig (Costume Designer)

Gift of Fury, A 1958,Mr 24,21:4

Hampton, Dawn

Greenwich Village U S A 1960,S 29,30:5

Hampton, Earl

Funny Face 1927,N 23,28:2

Hampton, Ethel

Gay Divorce 1932,N 30,23:4
Dodsworth 1934,F 26,20:4
On Your Toes 1936,Ap 13,14:4

Hampton, Grace

Fall and Rise of Susan Lenox, The 1920,Je 11,11:2
Malvaloca 1922,O 3,22:1
Romeo and Juliet 1923,Ja 25,16:1
Pelleas and Melisande 1923,D 5,23:2
Antony and Cleopatra 1924,F 20,22:1
Easy Virtue 1925,D 8,28:2
Gentlemen Prefer Blondes 1926,S 29,23:1
Her Majesty the Widow 1934,Je 19,24:5
Point Valaine 1935,Ja 17,22:2
Suspect 1940,Ap 10,30:4

Hampton, Hope

My Golden Girl 1927,S 11,VIII,1:3
My Princess 1927,O 7,24:2

Hampton, Jay

Fantasticks, The 1960,My 4,55:2

Hampton, Joy

Forbidden Melody 1936,N 3,33:1

Hampton, Louise

Old English 1924,N 9,VIII,2:3
Habit 1926,N 4,VIII,4:7
Mariners 1929,My 19,IX,1:8
Quince Bush, The 1932,Ag 21,IX,1:1
For Services Rendered 1932,N 27,IX,1:3
My Son's My Son 1936,My 27,26:4
Spring Tide 1936,Ag 9,IX,1:5
Wanted for Murder 1937,Je 29,18:1

Hampton, Mary

Cradle Song 1921,Mr 1,18:2
John Ferguson 1921,My 24,20:1

Hampton, Max (Playwright)

Happy Town 1959,O 8,49:2

Hampton, Myra

New Poor, The 1924,Ja 8,26:1
Sitting Pretty 1924,Ap 9,24:2
Minick 1924,S 25,20:1
Cradle Snatchers 1925,S 8,28:2
Ten Per Cent 1927,S 14,29:3
Dark Victory 1934,N 10,18:2
Sweet Aloes 1936,Mr 5,24:5

Hampton, Rawls

Love's Call 1925,S 11,20:1

Hampton, Stewart

Black Scandals 1928,O 27,23:2

Hamsa, Hans

Bajadere, Die 1925,O 2,26:2
20th Century 1932,D 30,15:1
How to Get Tough About It 1938,F 9,16:2

Hamsa, John

Clear All Wires! 1932,S 15,19:1

Hamsun, Knut (Playwright)

In the Claws of Life 1923,N 30,23:4
In the Claws of Life 1923,D 9,IX,1:1
At the Gate of the Kingdom 1927,D 9,28:5

Hanaford, Maude

Crooked Gamblers 1920,Ag 2,12:1
Egotist, The 1922,D 27,12:1
For Value Received 1923,My 8,22:3
Tragic 18 1926,O 11,18:2

Hanan, Marcia

Pleased to Meet You 1928,O 30,27:2
After Dark 1928,D 11,35:2
Royal Virgin, The 1930,Mr 18,30:5

Hanau, John (Director)

Picnic 1957,F 21,32:1

Hanauer, Bertram

Romance 1921,Mr 1,18:2

Hanayagi, Isami

Azuma Kabuki Dancers and Musicians
    1954,Mr 10,29:4

Hanbury, Basil

Carnaval 1924,D 30,15:1
Pickwick 1927,S 6,35:2
Soldiers and Women 1929,S 3,25:1
Good Companions, The 1931,O 2,31:1
Touch of Brimstone, A 1935,S 23,20:1

Hancock, Carolyn

Tangerine 1921,Ag 10,8:2

Hancock, Carolyn (Costume Designer)

They Knew What They Wanted 1924,N 25,27:1
Ariadne 1925,F 24,17:1
Man of Destiny, The 1925,N 24,28:1
At Mrs Beam's 1926,Ap 26,24:3
Family, The 1943,Mr 31,22:4

Hancock, Carolyn (Scenic Designer)

They Knew What They Wanted 1924,N 25,27:1
Ariadne 1925,F 24,17:1
Man of Destiny, The 1925,N 24,28:1
At Mrs Beam's 1926,Ap 26,24:3
American Tragedy, An 1926,O 12,31:2
Taming of the Shrew, The 1935,O 1,27:3
Taming of the Shrew, The 1940,F 6,17:2
Secret Room, The 1945,N 8,16:2

Hancock, John

In the Matter of J Robert Oppenheimer
    1968,Je 7,31:1

Hancock, John (Director)

Storm, The 1962,Mr 31,17:2
Man's a Man, A 1962,S 20,30:2
Milk Train Doesn't Stop Here Anymore, The
    1965,Jl 27,25:1
Midsummer Night's Dream, A 1967,Je 30,23:1
Endecott and the Red Cross 1968,My 7,50:1

Hancock, Sheila

Entertaining Mr Sloane 1965,O 13,41:1

Hancock, Thomas

Yeomen of the Guard, The 1939,Ja 24,17:1
Gondoliers, The 1948,Ja 27,31:2
Yeomen of the Guard, The 1948,F 3,30:2
Gondoliers, The 1951,F 13,27:2

Hancock, Wyley

Foenix in Choir 1958,O 28,40:2

Hand, John (Director)

Mlle Modiste 1937,My 5,28:5
Merry Duchess, The 1943,Je 24,25:1
Gypsy Baron, The 1944,Je 15,17:3

Hand, John (Musical Director)

Mlle Modiste 1937,My 5,28:5
Merry Duchess, The 1943,Je 24,25:1

Hand, Margot

Fashion 1959,Ja 21,27:1
Streets of New York, The 1963,O 30,47:1

Handers and Millis

Flossie 1924,Je 4,25:2

Handin, Helene

Dove, The 1925,F 12,17:3
Scarlet Fox, The 1928,Mr 28,31:1

Handke, Peter (Playwright)

Quodlibet 1970,O 13,52:2

Handleman, Stanley

Great White Hope, The 1967,D 14,58:1

Handler, Helen

Mascaiada 1929,D 28,10:6

Handler, Leonard

Twelfth Night 1969,Ag 14,29:2

Handler, Pauline

Injury Sustained 1940,O 24,30:3
When Differences Disappear 1941,Je 3,17:4

Handley, Alan

New Faces 1934,Mr 16,24:5
Truly Valiant 1936,Ja 10,17:3
Naughty-Naught 'OO 1937,Ja 25,23:2
Fireman's Flame, The 1937,O 11,26:2
As You Like It 1937,N 1,25:2
Greatest Show on Earth, The 1938,Ja 6,22:2
Seventh Trumpet, The 1941,N 22,10:6

Handman, Barbara (Playwright)

Power of Darkness, The 1959,S 30,33:1

Handman, Lou

Vaudeville (Palace) 1926,N 16,24:3

Handman, Wynn

Uniform of Flesh 1949,Ja 31,15:2

Handman, Wynn (Director)
Power of Darkness, The 1959,S 30,33:1
Jonah! 1966,F 16,52:1
Who's Got His Own 1966,O 13,52:1
Father Uxbridge Wants to Marry 1967,O 30,57:1
Ceremony of Innocence, The 1968,Ja 2,33:1
Son, Come Home, A 1968,Mr 9,23:2
Electronic Nigger, The 1968,Mr 9,23:2
Clara's Ole Man 1968,Mr 9,23:2
Endecott and the Red Cross 1968,My 7,50:1
Cannibals, The 1968,N 4,60:1
Young Master Dante, The 1968,D 31,19:1
Acquisition, The 1968,D 31,19:1
This Bird of Dawning Singeth All Night Long
1968,D 31,19:1
Boy on the Straight-Back Chair 1969,Mr 18,36:1
Papp 1969,My 6,39:1
Mercy Street 1969,O 28,43:1
Five on the Black Hand Side 1970,Ja 2,32:2
Two Times One; Last Straw, The 1970,Ap 5,76:4
Two Times One; Duet for Solo Voice
1970,Ap 5,76:4
Sunday Dinner 1970,N 3,28:1
Carpenters, The 1970,D 22,40:1
Handon, R Henry
Piper, The 1920,Mr 20,14:2
Minute's Wait, A 1920,Je 22,9:1
Rising of the Moon, The 1920,Je 22,9:1
Cradle Song 1921,Mr 1,18:2
John Ferguson 1921,My 24,20:1
Steamship Tenacity 1922,Ja 3,20:2
Hangman's House 1926,D 17,27:2
Battle Hymn 1936,My 23,12:1
Liliom 1940,Mr 26,17:2
Handrah, Michael
Birds, The 1966,Jl 1,40:1
Hands, Divers (Playwright)
People Is the Thing That the World Is Fullest Of
1967,F 21,53:1
Hands, Terry (Director)
Merry Wives of Windsor, The 1968,My 4,45:5
Merry Wives of Windsor, The 1968,Jl 31,29:1
Pericles 1969,Je 1,II,4:5
Richard III 1970,Ag 3,37:3
Hands, Terry (Producer)
Pericles 1969,Ap 11,36:1
Handt-Warden (Playwright)
Three Little Girls 1930,Mr 30,VIII,2:7
Handy, John
Child's Play 1970,F 18,39:1
Handy, W C
Friars Club Frolic 1933,My 15,16:4
Handy, W C (Composer)
Rhapsody in Black 1931,My 5,33:2
Handy, W C (Lyricist)
Rhapsody in Black 1931,My 5,33:2
Handysides, Clarence
Virtue (?) 1922,N 17,14:1
New Brooms 1924,N 18,23:5
Furies, The 1928,Mr 8,23:1
Handzlik, Anna
Gondoliers, The 1940,O 1,29:2
Handzlik, Jean
Duchess Misbehaves, The 1946,F 14,32:2
Music in My Heart 1947,O 3,30:2
Sleepy Hollow 1948,Je 4,26:3
Mikado, The 1949,O 5,35:2
Pirates of Penzance, The 1949,O 11,41:2
H M S Pinafore 1949,O 18,34:2
Liar, The 1950,My 19,30:2
Carousel 1954,Je 3,32:2
Show Boat 1954,O 29,28:4
New Girl in Town 1957,My 15,40:1
Hanefey, Mary
Alfie 1964,D 18,27:1
Haneman, Judith
Thunder in the Air 1929,N 12,34:3
Hanemann, H W (Playwright)
You'll Never Know 1921,Ap 21,9:2
Nine Fifteen Revue, The 1930,F 12,26:2
Haney, Carol
Pajama Game, The 1954,My 14,20:2
Pajama Game, The 1954,My 15,12:1
Pajama Game, The 1954,My 30,II,1:1
Loss of Roses, A 1959,N 30,27:1
Loss of Roses, A 1959,D 6,II,5:1
Haney, Carol (Choreographer)
Flower Drum Song 1958,D 2,44:1
Flower Drum Song 1958,D 7,II,5:1
Bravo Giovanni 1962,My 21,41:2
Bravo Giovanni 1962,My 27,II,1:1
She Loves Me 1963,Ap 24,39:1
She Loves Me 1963,My 5,II,1:1
Funny Girl 1964,Mr 27,15:1
Haney, Felix
Hangman's House 1926,D 17,27:2
Haney, Paul
Arsenic and Old Lace 1970,N 5,59:1
Haney, Ray (Composer)
We're Civilized? 1962,N 9,30:1
Hanford, Charles (Costume Designer)
Diversions 1958,N 8,14:4

Hanford, Janice
Kind Lady 1937,Jl 6,23:1
Night of January 16 1937,Jl 20,19:3
Bright Rebel 1938,D 28,24:2
Hanft, Karl
Wozzeck 1966,Ap 6,34:1
Hanighen, Bernard (Lyricist)
Lute Song 1946,F 7,29:2
Chocolate Soldier, The 1947,Mr 13,34:2
Lute Song 1959,Mr 13,24:1
Hanighen, Bernard (Miscellaneous)
Chocolate Soldier, The 1947,Mr 13,34:2
Hanily, Kevin
Rate of Exchange 1968,Ap 2,50:1
Hankel, Edward
Pygmalion 1938,Ja 27,16:3
Captain Jinks of the Horse Marines 1938,Ja 28,16:2
Coriolanus 1938,F 2,14:5
Hankey, Adele (Miscellaneous)
King Lear 1964,My 19,43:2
Hankey, Anthony
Symphony in Two Flats 1930,S 17,30:4
Hankin, Larry
Pilgrim's Progress 1962,Mr 21,36:2
Committee, The 1964,S 17,53:1
Committee, The 1964,S 27,II,1:1
Hankle, Hans (Composer)
Americans on the Rhine 1934,O 11,28:4
Hankle, Hans (Lyricist)
Americans on the Rhine 1934,O 11,28:4
Hanley, Ed
Top Banana 1951,N 2,19:2
Ankles Aweigh 1955,Ap 19,27:1
Hanley, Ellen
Barefoot Boy With Cheek 1947,Ap 4,20:2
Two's Company 1952,D 16,43:5
First Impressions 1959,Mr 20,28:1
Fiorello! 1959,N 24,45:3
Fiorello! 1959,N 29,II,1:1
Boys From Syracuse, The 1963,Ap 16,31:1
Boys From Syracuse, The 1963,Je 2,II,1:1
Hanley, Jack
Midnight Frolic 1920,Ag 4,7:1
Nine O'Clock Revue 1921,F 9,7:5
Vaudeville (Palace) 1927,My 31,25:1
Hanley, James
Deep Blue Sea, The 1952,N 6,38:3
Deep Blue Sea, The 1952,D 14,II,3:1
Hanley, James (Composer)
Jim Jam Jems 1920,O 5,13:2
Pins and Needles 1922,F 2,20:1
Spice of 1922 1922,Jl 7,12:4
Big Boy 1925,Ja 8,28:2
Honeymoon Lane 1926,S 21,32:3
Sidewalks of New York 1927,O 4,33:1
Keep It Clean 1929,Je 25,35:5
Thumbs Up! 1934,D 28,24:1
Hanley, James (Lyricist)
No Foolin' 1926,Je 25,25:1
Honeymoon Lane 1926,S 21,32:3
Sidewalks of New York 1927,O 4,33:1
Keep It Clean 1929,Je 25,35:5
Hanley, James (Playwright)
No Foolin' 1926,Je 25,25:1
Honeymoon Lane 1926,S 21,32:3
Sidewalks of New York 1927,O 4,33:1
Say Nothing 1965,Ja 28,21:2
Inner Journey, The 1969,Mr 21,42:1
Hanley, Jerome (Lighting Director)
Much Ado About Nothing 1963,Jl 15,25:2
Hanley, John
Anna Christie 1921,N 3,22:1
Aiglon, L' 1927,D 27,24:3
Machinal 1928,S 8,10:3
Hanley, Matt
Bye Bye, Barbara 1924,Ag 26,6:3
Natja 1925,F 17,19:2
Blonde Sinner, The 1926,Jl 15,21:2
Hanley, Millicent
It's a Boy! 1922,S 20,18:3
Peter Weston 1923,S 20,5:2
Valley of Content, The 1925,Ja 14,19:2
People Don't Do Such Things 1927,N 24,28:3
Sisters 1927,D 26,26:5
Common Sin, The 1928,O 16,28:2
Fast Service 1931,N 18,26:3
Good Woman, Poor Thing, A 1933,Ja 10,27:3
Forsaking All Others 1933,Mr 2,21:2
Curtain Rises, The 1933,O 20,15:2
Tomorrow's a Holiday! 1935,D 31,10:2
Hanley, Robert
Danton's Death 1938,N 3,26:2
As You Like It 1939,My 9,28:4
Hanley, William
Tendresse, La 1922,S 26,18:1
Mary the 3d 1923,F 6,14:2
Fanshastics 1924,Ja 17,13:2
Dust Heap, The 1924,Ap 25,20:2
Lovely Lady 1925,O 15,27:1
Puppy Love 1926,Ja 28,16:3
2 Girls Wanted 1926,S 10,25:3
What Ann Brought Home 1927,F 22,22:2

Hanley, William (Playwright)
Whisper Into My Good Ear 1962,O 2,47:1
Mrs Dally Has a Lover 1962,O 2,47:1
Slow Dance on the Killing Ground 1964,D 1,50:1
Mrs Dally 1965,S 25,5:7
Slow Dance on the Killing Ground 1968,N 3,87:1
Slow Dance on the Killing Ground
1970,My 14,43:1
Hanley, Winifred
Queen Victoria 1923,N 16,15:1
Pygmalion 1926,N 16,24:1
Roar China! 1930,O 28,23:1
Hanlin, Henry
Come Seven 1920,Jl 20,10:1
Hanlon, Alice
Erminie 1921,Ja 4,11:1
Hanlon, Bert
All-Star Jamboree 1921,Jl 14,18:1
Vaudeville (New Amsterdam Theatre)
1931,Je 22,17:3
Hanlon, Brendan
Jumping Fool, The 1970,F 10,53:1
Hanlon, Dan E
Red Falcon, The 1924,O 8,22:1
Ringside 1928,Ag 30,13:2
Hanlon, Edward
Don Juan; Feast With the Statue, The
1956,Ja 4,21:4
Hanlon, Harry
Breakfast in Bed 1920,F 4,12:1
Squaw Man, The 1921,D 27,10:3
Kiss in a Taxi, The 1925,Ag 26,14:1
Potash and Perlmutter, Detectives; Poisoned by
Pictures 1926,S 1,27:3
Headquarters 1929,D 5,32:4
Grand Hotel 1930,N 14,30:4
Hilda Cassidy 1933,My 5,18:3
Wednesday's Child 1934,Ja 17,23:2
One More Honeymoon 1934,Ap 2,13:5
Love Kills 1934,My 2,25:3
Arrest That Woman 1936,S 19,20:4
Fledgling 1940,N 28,29:2
Hanlon, Helen
Old Bill, M P 1926,N 11,22:2
Hanlon, Henry H
John Ferguson 1928,Ja 18,23:1
Hanmer, Don
Winged Victory 1943,N 22,24:1
Yellow Jack 1944,Ap 7,23:3
Sundown Beach 1948,S 8,37:1
My Name is Aquilon 1949,F 10,38:2
Man, The 1950,Ja 20,28:2
Ponder Heart, The 1956,F 17,14:2
Hann, W A
Chocolate Dandies, The 1924,S 2,22:2
Hanna, Arthur (Producer)
All Paris Knows 1934,Jl 24,20:1
Musical Chairs 1934,Jl 31,20:7
Nude in Washington Square, The 1934,Ag 7,20:1
Clap Hands 1934,Ag 21,12:7
Mad Morning 1935,Je 25,14:1
Please Do Not Disturb 1936,Je 23,27:1
Hanna, Betty
Mr Samuel 1930,N 11,28:4
Rock Me, Julie 1931,F 4,21:1
Joy of Living 1931,Ap 7,31:1
In Times Square 1931,N 24,29:3
Potash and Perlmutter 1935,Ap 6,11:3
Hanna, Charles
Trimmed in Scarlet 1920,F 3,18:1
Young Visitors, The 1920,N 30,14:1
Atlas and Eva 1928,F 7,30:2
Get Me in the Movies 1928,My 22,18:3
Merchant of Venice, The 1930,D 3,29:2
Hanna, Franklyn
Cave Girl, The 1920,Ag 19,12:2
Daddy Dumplins 1920,N 23,11:1
John Hawthorne 1921,Ja 24,16:1
Tidings Brought to Mary, The 1922,D 25,20:1
Crooked Square, The 1923,S 11,10:2
Bluffing Bluffers 1924,D 23,17:2
Hanna, Hazel
Chrysalis 1932,N 16,15:2
Madame Bovary 1937,N 17,26:2
Hanna, J R
Here's Howe 1923,Ap 26,19:3
Hanna, James E
Joan of Arkansas 1925,Ap 5,16:1
Hanna, Jay
Night Call, The 1922,Ap 27,12:2
Daffy Dill 1922,Ag 23,14:5
Peter Weston 1923,S 20,5:2
Myrtie 1924,F 5,21:2
Praying Curve 1927,Ja 25,18:2
Hanna, Mark (Producer)
Kiss Them for Me 1945,Mr 21,27:2
Hanna, Philip
Brigadoon 1949,Ap 16,11:1
Brigadoon 1950,My 3,36:2
Hanna (Producer)
Seen But Not Heard 1936,Jl 22,23:4
Hannafin, Daniel P
Oklahoma! 1963,F 28,8:2

Hannafin, Daniel P—Cont
Oklahoma! 1963,My 16,40:1
Brigadoon 1964,D 24,9:1
Flora, the Red Menace 1965,My 12,41:2
Oklahoma! 1965,D 16,62:1
Tenth Man, The 1967,N 9,54:1

Hannaford, R O
Front Page, The 1937,N 12,27:2

Hannah, Link (Playwright)
Woman's a Fool-To Be Clever, A 1938,O 19,18:6

Hannam-Clark, G F
George Washington 1920,Mr 2,9:1
Hamlet 1920,Mr 17,14:2

Hannan, Chick
Buckaroo 1929,Mr 18,31:1

Hannan, Peggy
Buckaroo 1929,Mr 18,31:1

Hanneford, George
Vaudeville (Hippodrome) 1926,Mr 16,22:2
Vaudeville (Palace) 1928,Ja 3,29:3
Frank Fay's Vaudeville 1939,Mr 3,20:4

Hanneford, Grace Elizabeth
Jumbo 1935,N 18,20:2

Hanneford, Poodles
Vaudeville (Hippodrome) 1924,F 12,20:2
Vaudeville (Hippodrome) 1924,F 19,12:1
Circus Princess, The 1927,Ap 26,32:2
Jumbo 1935,N 18,20:2

Hannefords, The
Good Times 1920,Ag 10,10:1

Hannelin, Goldie
Key Largo 1939,N 28,30:2

Hannen, Mr
To See Ourselves 1930,D 28,VIII,2:6

Hannen, Nicholas
Conquering Hero, The 1924,Ap 13,VIII,1:3
Escape 1926,Ag 29,VII,2:4
Escape 1926,S 12,VIII,2:1
Transit of Venus, The 1927,My 22,VIII,2:1
Golden Calf, The 1927,O 2,VIII,1:3
Listeners 1928,Mr 11,VIII,1:3
Last Enemy, The 1930,Ja 5,VIII,2:2
Max and Mr Max 1932,Ja 24,VIII,3:5
On the Rocks 1933,N 26,II,2:8
Big House, The 1934,Mr 18,IX,2:3
Winding Journey, The 1934,My 8,28:6
Accent on Youth 1934,D 26,19:1
Hervey House 1935,My 18,21:2
Accent on Youth 1935,S 29,X,1:6
Page From a Diary 1936,F 9,X,3:1
Last of the Ladies, The 1936,Mr 26,26:7
Follow Your Saint 1936,O 11,X,3:1
Waste 1936,D 20,XI,3:3
King Lear 1940,Ap 28,IX,1:7
Cherry Orchard, The 1941,S 7,IX,2:5
Richard III 1944,O 1,II,1:3
Arms and the Man 1944,O 1,II,1:3
Peer Gynt 1944,O 1,II,1:3
Henry IV, Part I 1946,My 7,25:2
Henry IV, Part II 1946,My 8,33:4
Henry IV 1946,My 12,II,1:1
Uncle Vanya 1946,My 14,18:2
Oedipus; Critic, The 1946,My 21,19:2
Oedipus 1946,My 21,19:2
King Lear 1946,S 25,39:4
King Lear 1946,O 13,II,2:3
Cyrano de Bergerac 1946,N 3,I,54:6

Hanner, James
Belle Helene, La 1941,Jl 8,14:1

Hannigan, Erdine
Midsummer Night's Dream, A 1931,Ag 19,19:3

Hanning, Dorothy
South Pacific 1965,Je 3,25:1

Hanning, Geraldine
In Good King Charles's Golden Days
1957,Ja 25,16:1
Philanderer, The 1958,My 13,26:2
Lysistrata 1959,My 20,40:2
Alcestis Comes Back 1962,Ap 24,33:1

Hanoteau, Guillaume (Miscellaneous)
Detour After Dark 1959,Je 9,11:4

Hanov, A A
Circle, The 1946,Mr 17,II,1:3

Hanover, Elsie
Pillar to Post 1943,D 11,11:2

Hanrahan, Joseph
Trial of Dmitri Karamazov, The 1958,Ja 28,30:1
Asmodee 1958,Mr 26,42:2

Hanray, Lawrence
Loyalties 1922,S 28,18:1
School for Scandal, The 1923,Mr 13,19:2
Old English 1924,N 9,VIII,2:3
Escape 1927,O 27,33:1
Escape 1927,N 6,IX,1:1
Rasputin 1929,My 12,IX,2:3
Hairy Ape, The 1931,My 12,29:4
Father, The 1931,O 9,21:1
Geneva 1940,Ja 31,15:2

Hanray, Lawrence (Director)
Silver Box, The 1928,Ja 18,23:1

Hansberry, Lorraine (Original Author)
To Be Young, Gifted and Black: The World of
Lorraine Hansberry 1969,My 25,II,1:5

To Be Young, Gifted and Black: The World of
Lorraine Hansberry 1969,S 22,36:1

Hansberry, Lorraine (Playwright)
Raisin in the Sun, A 1959,Mr 12,27:1
Raisin in the Sun, A 1959,Mr 29,II,1:1
Raisin in the Sun, A 1959,Ag 5,32:3
Sign in Sidney Brustein's Window, The
1964,O 16,32:1
Sign in Sidney Brustein's Window, The
1964,N 1,II,1:1
Blancs, Les 1970,N 16,48:4
Blancs, Les 1970,N 29,II,3:5
Blancs, Les 1970,N 29,II,3:1

Hanschi, Fred
Antony and Cleopatra 1937,N 11,30:2

Hansen, Gudrun
R U R 1942,D 4,30:2

Hansen, Hans
Anna Christie 1921,N 3,22:1
Nature's Nobleman 1921,N 15,23:2
Lenz 1926,Ap 29,20:4
Storm Center 1927,D 1,33:2
Miracle at Verdun 1931,Mr 17,34:6
Social Register, The 1931,N 10,28:2
Broadway Boy 1932,My 4,23:5
Nona 1932,O 5,26:4
Anybody's Game 1932,D 22,21:4
Late One Evening 1933,Ja 10,27:3
Kultur 1933,S 27,24:3
Broadway Interlude 1934,Ap 20,16:3
Valley Forge 1934,D 11,28:3
O Evening Star 1935,D 26,20:1
O Evening Star 1936,Ja 9,24:6
Leave It to Me! 1938,N 10,32:2

Hansen, Harold
Patience 1927,My 24,23:2

Hansen, Janis
Riot Act, The 1963,Mr 9,5:2

Hansen, Joseph (Scenic Designer)
Fly by Night 1933,Je 3,16:2

Hansen, Juanita
High Hatters, The 1928,My 11,28:2

Hansen, Kai
Caviar 1934,Je 8,19:2

Hansen, Louise
Everybody's Welcome 1931,O 14,26:3

Hansen, Marvin
Othello 1937,Ja 7,16:4

Hansen, Max
Wieder Metropol 1926,D 5,VIII,8:7
Countess Maritza 1927,Ja 30,VII,4:3
Evelyne 1928,F 19,VIII,2:1
Merry Widow, The 1929,F 17,IX,2:3
Three Musketeers 1929,O 13,IX,4:7
Im Weissen Roessel 1930,D 28,VIII,2:4
Bezauberndes Fraeulein 1933,N 19,IX,3:1

Hansen, Olga C
Triplets 1932,S 22,25:2

Hansen, Peter Brett
Hedda Gabler 1970,Ja 18,78:1

Hansen, Ronn
Athenian Touch, The 1964,Ja 15,25:4
Minnie's Boys 1970,Mr 27,27:1

Hansen, Tom (Miscellaneous)
From A to Z 1960,Ap 21,23:2

Hansen, Vaugn
Town Boy 1929,O 5,22:4

Hansen, Waldemar (Playwright)
Garden of Sweets, The 1961,N 1,35:1

Hansen, William
My Heart's in the Highlands 1939,Ap 14,29:2
I Know What I Like 1939,N 25,13:5
Night Music 1940,F 23,18:2
Medicine Show 1940,Ap 13,20:6
Twelfth Night 1940,N 20,26:3
Macbeth 1941,N 12,30:2
Assassin, The 1945,O 18,20:2
Brigadoon 1947,Mr 14,28:2
Montserrat 1949,O 31,21:4
Member of the Wedding, The 1950,Ja 6,26:6
Barefoot in Athens 1951,N 1,35:2
Golden Boy 1952,Mr 13,24:3
Golden Boy 1952,Mr 23,II,1:1
Teahouse of the August Moon, The 1953,O 16,32:1
Teahouse of the August Moon, The
1953,O 25,II,1:1
Waltz of the Toreadors, The 1957,Ja 18,17:2
Waltz of the Toreadors, The 1957,Ja 27,II,1:1
Day the Money Stopped, The 1958,F 21,19:4
Visit, The 1958,My 6,40:1
Visit, The 1960,Mr 9,38:3
Roots 1961,Mr 7,40:2
Roots 1961,Mr 19,II,1:1
Daughter of Silence 1961,D 1,28:1
Lorenzo 1963,F 16,5:2
Slow Dance on the Killing Ground 1968,N 3,87:1

Hanson, Allen (Lighting Director)
Cradle of Willow, A 1961,D 16,20:2

Hanson, Allen (Miscellaneous)
Cradle of Willow, A 1961,D 16,20:2

Hanson, Arthur
Emperor Jones, The 1945,Ja 17,18:4

Hanson, Gladys
Mecca 1920,O 5,12:2
Crooked Square, The 1923,S 11,10:2
Blue Bird, The 1923,D 26,13:3
Houses of Sand 1925,F 18,17:1
Trelawney of the 'Wells' 1925,Je 2,16:2
Judge's Husband, The 1926,S 28,31:1
Queen's Husband, The 1928,Ja 26,17:2
Dear Old England 1930,Mr 26,24:6
Give Me Yesterday 1931,Mr 5,32:1
Evensong 1933,F 1,13:4
Brown Danube, The 1939,My 18,30:4

Hanson, John
Free Soul, A 1928,Ja 13,26:5

Hanson, Lars
Macbeth 1931,O 11,VIII,4:5
Mourning Becomes Electra 1933,My 7,IX,2:3
Desire Under the Elms 1933,N 12,IX,1:1
Dream Play 1935,D 8,X,4:5
Long Day's Journey Into Night 1956,F 19,II,1:6
Father, The 1962,My 15,49:1

Hanson, Leona
Trial of Dr Beck, The 1937,Ag 10,22:2

Hanson, Leslie
Lady of the Lamp, The 1920,Ag 18,6:4

Hanson, Margot
Now Is the Time for all Good Men 1967,S 27,42:1

Hanson, Olga
Little Accident 1928,O 10,32:3

Hanson, Paul
Yellow 1926,S 22,30:1
Cynara 1931,N 3,31:1

Hanson, Peter
Bat, The 1953,Ja 21,28:2

Hanson, Philip
Moby Dick 1961,Ap 11,41:2

Hanson, Philip (Director)
Moby Dick 1961,Ap 11,41:2

Hanson, Philip (Playwright)
Moby Dick 1961,Ap 11,41:2

Hanson, Preston
Uniform of Flesh 1949,Ja 31,15:2
Billy Budd 1951,F 12,18:3
Saint Joan 1951,O 5,23:2
Much Ado About Nothing 1952,My 2,20:1

Hanzel, Carol
Show Boat 1966,Jl 20,48:1
West Side Story 1968,Je 25,32:1

Hapgood, Althea
Partition 1948,O 29,31:2

Hapgood, Elizabeth Reynolds (Translator)
Possessed, The 1939,O 25,26:2
Dragon, The 1963,Ap 10,32:1

Happa, Mutoshi
My Fair Lady 1963,S 2,19:4

Har, Vivian
Countess Maritza 1926,S 20,21:1

Hara, Mary
Building Blocks 1954,My 8,14:4
Men in White 1955,F 26,13:2
Purification, The 1959,D 9,57:5
Crucible, The 1964,Ap 7,30:2
Romeo and Juliet 1965,Je 21,36:3
Taming of the Shrew, The 1965,Je 24,32:2
King Lear 1965,Je 25,39:1
Kitchen, The 1966,Je 14,50:1
Glorious Ruler, The 1969,Jl 1,31:1

Harahan, Bill
Age and Grace 1956,F 21,38:2

Haraldson, Marian
Girl Who Came to Supper, The 1963,D 9,49:1
Merry Widow, The 1964,Ag 18,24:2
Drat! the Cat! 1965,O 11,54:2

Haran, Ronnie
Step on a Crack 1962,O 18,48:1

Harary, Nina
Pins and Needles 1939,Ap 21,26:2

Haraucourt, Edmond (Playwright)
Passion, La 1930,My 11,IX,2:4

Harbach, Otto (Lyricist)
Tickle Me 1920,Ag 18,9:1
Jimmie 1920,N 18,15:3
O'Brien Girl, The 1921,O 4,10:2
Jack and Jill 1923,Mr 23,17:2
Rose Marie 1924,S 3,12:2
Betty Lee 1924,D 26,18:2
No, No, Nanette 1925,S 17,20:2
Sunny 1925,S 23,22:1
Song of the Flame 1925,D 31,10:2
Wild Rose, The 1926,O 21,23:1
Lucky 1927,Mr 23,28:3
Firefly, The 1931,D 1,23:2
Roberta 1933,N 20,18:4
Forbidden Melody 1936,O 13,30:3
Forbidden Melody 1936,N 3,33:1
Desert Song, The 1946,Ja 9,20:2

Harbach, Otto (Miscellaneous)
Cat and the Fiddle, The 1931,O 16,26:4

Harbach, Otto (Original Author)
Desert Song, The 1946,Ja 9,20:2

Harbach, Otto (Playwright)
No More Blondes 1920,Ja 8,22:1
Tickle Me 1920,Ag 18,9:1

Harbach, Otto (Playwright)—Cont

Mary 1920,O 19,12:1
Jimmie 1920,N 18,15:3
June Love 1921,Ap 26,20:1
O'Brien Girl, The 1921,O 4,10:2
Blue Kitten, The 1922,Ja 14,9:3
Molly Darling 1922,S 2,10:2
Wildflower 1923,F 8,17:2
Jack and Jill 1923,Mr 23,17:2
Katinka 1923,Ag 31,15:4
Kid Boots 1924,Ja 1,21:3
Rose Marie 1924,Ag 24,VII,1:8
Rose Marie 1924,S 3,12:2
Betty Lee 1924,D 26,18:2
No, No, Nanette 1925,S 17,20:2
Sunny 1925,S 23,22:1
Song of the Flame 1925,D 11,26:4
Song of the Flame 1925,D 31,10:2
Kitty's Kisses 1926,My 7,12:2
Criss Cross 1926,O 13,20:2
Wild Rose, The 1926,O 21,23:1
Desert Song, The 1926,D 1,24:2
Oh, Please! 1926,D 22,24:3
Lucky 1927,Mr 23,28:3
Golden Dawn 1927,D 1,32:3
Rose Marie 1928,Ap 29,IX,2:8
Good Boy 1928,S 6,23:2
Nina Rosa 1929,O 27,IX,2:1
Nina Rosa 1930,My 31,19:3
Nina Rosa 1930,S 22,22:5
Cat and the Fiddle, The 1931,S 27,VIII,3:1
Firefly, The 1931,D 1,23:2
Roberta 1933,N 20,18:4
Forbidden Melody 1936,O 13,30:3
Forbidden Melody 1936,N 3,33:1
Roberta 1937,Je 27,II,6:1
Gentlemen Unafraid 1938,Je 5,II,6:8
Hay-Foot, Straw-Foot 1942,O 24,11:6

Harbaugh, Harriet
In the Near Future 1925,Mr 11,19:1
Honest Liars 1926,Jl 20,17:2

Harben, Hubert
Dover Road, The 1924,My 4,VIII,2:4
Rates, Les; Might-Have-Beens, The 1927,Je 19,VII,2:3
Sacred Flame, The 1928,N 20,28:2

Harbert, James (Composer)
Ice Capades 1967,Je 2,33:1
Ice Capades 1969,Ja 8,42:1
Ice Capades 1970,Ja 7,35:1

Harbert, James (Lyricist)
Ice Capades 1967,Je 2,33:1
Ice Capades 1969,Ja 8,42:1
Ice Capades 1970,Ja 7,35:1

Harbert, James (Miscellaneous)
Ice Capades 1967,Je 2,33:1

Harbeson, Georgiana (Scenic Designer)
Strange Prince, The 1926,D 8,24:2

Harbison, E Harris (Composer)
Samarkand 1926,D 22,24:4
Napoleon Passes 1927,D 21,29:2

Harbison, E Harris (Lyricist)
Napoleon Passes 1927,D 21,29:2

Harbord, Carl
Last Enemy, The 1930,Ja 5,VIII,2:2
Conversation Piece 1934,O 24,24:1
Madame Bovary 1937,N 17,26:2
Jupiter Laughs 1940,S 10,27:1
Romeo and Juliet 1951,Mr 12,21:2
Much Ado About Nothing 1952,My 2,20:1
Hide and Seek 1957,Ap 3,26:1

Harburg, E Y (Composer)
Sketch Book 1929,Jl 2,33:5
Earl Carroll's Vanities 1930,Jl 2,28:3
It's All Yours 1942,Mr 26,26:2
Blue Holiday 1945,My 22,13:3

Harburg, E Y (Director)
Bloomer Girl 1944,O 6,18:5
Flahooley 1951,My 15,39:1

Harburg, E Y (Lyricist)
Sketch Book 1929,Jl 2,33:5
Garrick Gaieties 1930,Je 5,29:2
Earl Carroll's Vanities 1930,Jl 2,28:3
Vanderbilt Revue, The 1930,N 6,22:6
Ballyhoo of 1932 1932,S 7,14:2
Americana 1932,O 6,19:3
Walk a Little Faster 1932,D 8,24:4
Ziegfeld Follies 1934,Ja 5,24:3
Life Begins at 8:40 1934,Ag 28,24:2
Show Is On, The 1937,S 20,18:4
Hooray for What! 1937,D 2,32:5
Hold On to Your Hats 1940,S 12,30:3
It's All Yours 1942,Mr 26,26:2
Bloomer Girl 1944,O 6,18:5
Bloomer Girl 1944,O 8,II,1:1
Finian's Rainbow 1947,Ja 11,23:2
Flahooley 1951,My 15,39:1
Finian's Rainbow 1953,Mr 7,13:2
Finian's Rainbow 1955,My 19,25:1
Jamaica 1957,N 1,32:2
Finian's Rainbow 1960,Ap 28,31:1
Happiest Girl in the World, The 1961,Ap 4,42:1
Harold Arlen Songbook, The 1967,Mr 1,48:1
Finian's Rainbow 1967,Ap 6,44:1

Darling of the Day 1968,Ja 29,26:2
Darling of the Day 1968,F 11,II,3:1
Wizard of Oz, The 1968,N 28,69:2

Harburg, E Y (Miscellaneous)
Bloomer Girl 1947,Ja 7,33:2
Flahooley 1951,My 15,39:1

Harburg, E Y (Playwright)
Ziegfeld Follies 1934,Ja 5,24:3
Life Begins at 8:40 1934,Ag 28,24:2
Hooray for What! 1937,N 7,XI,2:4
Hooray for What! 1937,D 2,32:5
Finian's Rainbow 1947,Ja 11,23:2
Finian's Rainbow 1947,Ja 26,II,1:1
Flahooley 1951,My 15,39:1
Flahooley 1951,My 20,II,1:1
Jollyanna; Flahooley 1952,Ag 13,17:7
Finian's Rainbow 1953,Mr 7,13:2
Finian's Rainbow 1955,My 19,25:1
Jamaica 1957,N 1,32:2
Jamaica 1957,N 10,II,1:1
Finian's Rainbow 1960,Ap 28,31:1
Finian's Rainbow 1967,Ap 6,44:1

Harbury, Charles
Lancelot and Elaine 1921,S 13,12:1
Merchant of Venice, The 1922,D 22,13:1
School for Scandal, The 1923,Mr 13,19:2

Harcott, Joseph
Mrs Warren's Profession 1963,Ap 25,39:1

Harcourt, Cyril (Playwright)
Will You Kiss Me? 1920,D 5,VII,1:4

Harcourt, Edith
Thunder in the Air 1929,N 12,34:3
Nine Till Six 1930,S 29,17:2
In Heaven and Earth 1936,Mr 27,24:8

Harcourt, George
Pietro 1920,Ja 20,10:2
Dancing Mothers 1924,Ag 12,12:2
Vortex, The 1925,S 17,20:1
Just Fancy! 1927,O 12,30:2
Straight Thru the Door 1928,O 5,17:2

Harcourt, Halyna
Call on Kuprin, A 1961,My 26,29:3

Harcourt, James
Anthony and Anna 1935,D 8,X,5:1

Harcourt, William
Mad Dog, The 1921,N 9,20:1

Hardeen, Theo
Hellzapoppin 1938,S 23,34:2
New Hellzapoppin, The 1939,D 12,36:4

Harden, Dan
You Never Know 1938,S 22,26:3
Lady in the Dark 1941,Ja 24,14:2
Lady in the Dark 1941,S 3,26:6
Singing Girl, The 1952,Je 4,31:8

Harden, Douglas
Dear Judas 1947,O 6,26:4

Harder, James
Never Say Horses 1951,D 7,34:4
Bonds of Interest, The 1958,My 7,43:1
On the Town 1959,F 14,15:1
Athenian Touch, The 1964,Ja 15,25:4
Kitchen, The 1966,Je 14,50:1
Lend an Ear 1969,O 29,32:1

Hardie, Marcella
I'll Say She Is 1924,My 20,15:1

Hardie, Russell
Criminal Code, The 1929,O 3,28:2
Pagan Lady 1930,O 21,34:2
Constant Sinner, The 1931,Ag 30,VIII,1:6
Constant Sinner, The 1931,S 15,30:1
Society Girl 1931,D 31,16:1
Happy Landing 1932,Mr 28,10:5
Saint Wench 1933,Ja 3,19:3
Remember the Day 1935,S 26,19:3
Alice Takat 1936,F 11,19:2
Sun Kissed 1937,Mr 11,20:2
Ghost of Yankee Doodle, The 1937,O 28,28:5
Ghost of Yankee Doodle, The 1937,N 7,XI,2:4
Ghost of Yankee Doodle, The 1937,N 23,26:3
Roosty 1938,F 15,21:2
Primrose Path, The 1939,Ja 5,16:3
Primrose Path, The 1939,Ja 16,11:2
Sea Dogs 1939,N 7,30:3
Burning Deck, The 1940,Mr 2,9:2
My Fair Ladies 1941,Mr 24,12:7
Good Morning, Corporal 1944,Ag 9,13:7
Snafu 1944,O 26,19:5
Foxhole in the Parlor 1945,My 24,15:4
Home of the Brave 1945,D 28,13:2
Home of the Brave 1946,Ja 6,II,1:1
Bees and the Flowers, The 1946,S 27,19:3
Harvest of Years 1948,Ja 13,29:2
Love Me Long 1949,N 8,34:5
Andersonville Trial, The 1959,D 30,15:1
Midgie Purvis 1961,F 2,25:3

Hardin, Jerry
9 by Six: A Cry of Players 1956,D 5,49:2
This Island Is Mine 1959,Jl 1,26:4
Henry IV 1960,Mr 2,42:1
Henry IV 1960,Ap 19,41:1
Rendezvous at Senlis 1961,F 28,39:2

Hardin, Lo (Miscellaneous)
On an Open Roof 1963,Ja 30,7:3

Hardin, Lo (Miscellaneous)—Cont

Taming of the Shrew, The 1965,Je 24,32:2
Richard II 1968,Je 24,42:3
As You Like It 1968,Je 24,42:3
Androcles and the Lion 1968,Je 27,47:1
Love's Labour's Lost 1968,Je 28,36:1
Hamlet 1969,Je 30,33:1
Private Lives 1969,D 5,52:1
Othello 1970,S 15,51:1

Harding, Ann
Like a King 1921,O 4,10:1
Tarnish 1923,O 2,10:1
Horse-Thief, The 1924,Ap 27,VIII,2:3
Thoroughbreds 1924,S 9,12:1
Stolen Fruit 1925,O 8,31:4
Stolen Fruit 1925,N 8,VIII,1:1
Taming of the Shrew, The 1925,D 19,14:1
Taming of the Shrew, The 1925,D 27,VII,1:1
Schweiger 1926,Mr 24,20:4
Eskimo, The 1926,Je 20,VII,3:1
Woman Disputed, A 1926,S 29,23:2
Trial of Mary Dugan, The 1927,S 20,33:1
Trial of Mary Dugan, The 1927,O 9,VIII,1:1
Candida 1937,F 11,19:3
Candida 1937,F 28,XI,1:5
General Seeger 1962,Mr 1,26:2
Abraham Cochrane 1964,F 18,26:1

Harding, Annette
Show Boat 1927,D 28,26:1

Harding, Enid
Oklahoma! 1955,Ag 15,19:1

Harding, John
Emperor Jones, The 1936,Ag 11,24:6
Ten Million Ghosts 1936,O 24,23:7

Harding, June
Ignorants Abroad, The 1960,My 24,43:2
Cry of the Raindrop 1961,Mr 8,38:1
Take Her, She's Mine 1961,D 22,19:1

Harding, Lyn
New Poor, The 1924,Ja 8,26:1
Mayor of Casterbridge, The 1926,S 9,20:1
Mayor of Casterbridge, The 1926,O 3,VIII,2:1
12 Miles Out 1927,F 20,VII,1:4
Out of the Sea 1927,D 6,26:2
Patriot, The 1928,Ja 20,15:1
Patriot, The 1928,Ja 29,VIII,1:1
She Stoops to Conquer 1928,My 15,17:1
She Stoops to Conquer 1928,My 20,VIII,1:1
Beaux' Stratagem, The 1928,Je 5,20:1
Macbeth 1928,N 4,IX,1:3
Macbeth 1928,N 20,28:3
Grand Hotel 1931,S 27,VIII,1:4
Julius Caesar 1932,F 9,30:7
Julius Caesar 1932,F 28,VIII,2:4
Dinner at Eight 1933,Ja 7,11:5
Dinner at Eight 1933,Ja 29,IX,1:3
Josephine 1934,S 26,17:5
Glamorous Night 1935,My 3,23:6

Harding, Marguerite
Roseanne 1923,D 31,9:5

Harding, Miss
Green Hat, The 1925,Ap 5,IX,2:4

Harding, Muriel
Patience 1948,F 10,27:2
H M S Pinafore 1951,F 6,24:2
Gondoliers, The 1951,F 13,27:2
Pirates of Penzance, The 1951,F 20,21:2
Yeomen of the Guard, The 1955,O 4,39:2
Pirates of Penzance, The 1955,O 7,21:1
Princess Ida 1955,O 14,22:3
H M S Pinafore 1955,O 18,48:1

Harding, Norman
Chemmy Circle, The 1968,Ag 10,17:2

Harding, Paul
Conduct Unbecoming 1970,O 13,50:1

Harding, Peter
New York Idea, The 1948,Ag 18,29:2

Harding, Phoebe
Job's Kinfolks 1929,N 24,31:1

Harding, Phyllis
Mongolia 1927,D 27,24:5
Wrecker, The 1928,F 28,18:2
This Year of Grace 1928,N 8,27:1
Conversation Piece 1934,O 24,24:1
Point Valaine 1935,Ja 17,22:2

Harding, R P
Rose, The 1922,D 30,13:4

Harding, Ruth
Golden Days 1921,N 2,20:1
One Heluva Night 1924,Je 5,18:1
Valley of Content, The 1925,Ja 14,19:2

Harding, Vince
Praise Of Folly 1954,F 24,23:2
Foenix in Choir 1958,O 28,40:2

Hardison, Inge
Sweet River 1936,O 29,30:2
Country Wife, The 1936,D 2,34:1
Almost Faithful 1948,Je 5,9:2

Hards, Ina
Wolf! Wolf! 1925,O 30,21:1

Hards, Ira (Director)
Twelve Miles Out 1925,N 17,29:2
Kept 1926,S 18,13:3
Blood Money 1927,Ag 23,29:2

Hards, Ira (Director)—Cont
Dracula 1927,O 6,29:1
Red Dust 1928,Ja 3,29:2
Atlas and Eva 1928,F 7,30:2
Jarnegan 1928,S 25,29:2
Be Your Age 1929,F 5,27:1
Young Alexander 1929,Mr 13,28:2
Scarlet Pages 1929,S 10,26:3
Cortez 1929,N 5,32:2
Bishop Misbehaves, The 1935,F 21,22:4
Summer Wives 1936,Ap 14,18:1
Arrest That Woman 1936,S 19,20:4

Hardt, Erich
As You Like It 1936,Ap 24,18:4

Hardt, Hanna
Home Is Tomorrow 1950,Je 2,27:2

Hardt-Warden, Bruno (Playwright)
Three Little Girls 1930,Ap 15,29:1

Hardtap, Hale
Like a King 1921,O 4,10:1

Hardwick, Mary
Family Reunion, The 1960,D 10,26:1

Hardwick, Paul
Cymbeline 1962,Jl 18,21:2
Hollow Crown, The 1963,Ja 31,5:1

Hardwick, Thelma
Stripped 1929,O 13,IX,5:1
Stripped 1929,O 22,26:1
Warrior's Husband, The 1932,Mr 12,19:4

Hardwick, W Dana
Ethan Frome 1936,Ja 22,15:2
Pursuit of Happiness, The 1936,Jl 15,14:1
Post Road 1936,Ag 5,15:4
Royal Family, The 1936,Ag 12,15:1
Truth About Blayds, The 1936,Ag 19,18:5
Art and Mrs Bottle 1936,S 2,18:1

Hardwicke, Cedric
Show Boat 1928,My 27,VIII,1:8
Apple Cart, The 1929,Ag 20,30:2
Apple Cart, The 1929,S 8,IX,1:8
Barretts of Wimpole Street, The 1930,Ag 21,13:4
Barretts of Wimpole Street, The 1930,S 7,IX,2:1
Widowers' Houses 1931,Ap 12,IX,2:1
Caravan 1932,My 1,VIII,2:2
Too True to Be Good 1932,Ag 7,I,23:2
For Services Rendered 1932,N 2,23:5
For Services Rendered 1932,N 27,IX,1:3
Late Christopher Bean, The 1933,My 17,15:2
Tovarich 1935,Ap 25,19:8
Tovarich 1935,My 19,IX,1:1
Promise 1936,D 31,20:4
Amazing Dr. Clitterhouse, The 1937,Mr 3,26:4
Shadow and Substance 1938,Ja 23,XI,1:6
Shadow and Substance 1938,Ja 27,16:2
Shadow and Substance 1938,F 6,X,1:1
Devil's Disciple, The 1941,S 11,20:6
Antigone 1946,Ja 10,28:2
Antigone 1946,F 19,21:3
Antigone 1946,F 24,II,1:1
Candida 1946,Ap 4,33:2
Candida 1946,Ap 14,II,1:1
Caesar and Cleopatra 1949,D 22,28:2
Caesar and Cleopatra 1950,Ja 8,II,1:1
Getting Married 1950,Je 14,41:2
Don Juan in Hell 1951,O 23,34:4
Don Juan in Hell 1951,N 4,II,1:1
Horses in Midstream 1953,Ap 3,18:7
Burning Glass, The 1954,Mr 5,15:2
Burning Glass, The 1954,Mr 14,II,1:1
Majority of One, A 1959,F 17,28:2
Majority of One, A 1959,F 22,II,1:1
Too True to Be Good 1963,Mr 14,8:2
Too True to Be Good 1963,Mr 23,5:6

Hardwicke, Cedric (Director)
Laburnum Grove 1933,N 29,23:4
Duet in Floodlight 1935,Je 5,22:1
Lorelei 1938,N 30,21:2
Devil's Disciple, The 1941,S 11,20:6
Sheppey 1944,Ap 19,27:2
Pygmalion 1945,D 27,16:1
Inspector Calls, An 1947,O 22,38:2
Caesar and Cleopatra 1949,D 22,28:2
Getting Married 1950,Je 14,41:2
Horses in Midstream 1953,Ap 3,18:7
Day by the Sea, A 1955,S 27,42:1
Day by the Sea, A 1955,O 2,II,1:1
Miss Isobel 1957,D 27,22:1
Wilde Evening with Shaw, A 1963,Mr 7,8:2

Hardwicke, Cedric (Producer)
Lorelei 1938,N 30,21:2

Hardwicke, Clarice
Rose Marie 1925,Mr 21,16:2
Desert Song, The 1927,My 8,VII,1:5
Baa, Baa, Black Sheep 1929,My 12,IX,2:3

Hardwicke, Cyril
Side-Show 1931,My 16,13:1

Hardwicke, Edward
Love for Love 1967,O 21,17:1
Dance of Death 1967,O 29,II,5:1
Love for Love 1967,O 30,59:1
Flea in Her Ear, A 1967,O 30,59:1
Way of the World, The 1969,Ag 7,29:1

Hardwicke, Paul
Midsummer Night's Dream, A 1962,Ap 18,30:3

Hardwicke, Thelma
Stripped 1929,Je 9,VIII,1:2

Hardwicke, W Dana
Iron Men 1936,O 20,30:6
Babes in Arms 1937,Ap 15,18:4

Hardy, Betty
Anatomist, The 1931,O 25,VIII,2:6

Hardy, Cherry
Victoria Regina 1935,D 27,15:2
Anne of England 1941,O 8,26:2
Druid Circle, The 1947,O 23,29:5
Make Way for Lucia 1948,D 23,23:5
Conversation Piece 1957,N 19,38:2

Hardy, Donald L (Playwright)
Merry Wives of West Point, The 1932,Mr 20,II,7:7

Hardy, Edward Roche Jr
You'll Never Know 1921,Ap 21,9:2

Hardy, Hugh (Lighting Director)
Bonds of Interest, The 1958,My 7,43:1
Under the Sycamore Tree 1960,Mr 8,37:2

Hardy, Hugh (Scenic Designer)
Bonds of Interest, The 1958,My 7,43:1
Under the Sycamore Tree 1960,Mr 8,37:2

Hardy, J L (Playwright)
Key, The 1933,S 7,17:5

Hardy, Jack
Marvellous History of Saint Bernard, The 1958,F 24,16:3

Hardy, Jim (Lighting Director)
Caution: A Love Story 1969,Ap 4,45:1
Queen of Greece, The 1969,Ap 12,40:2
Homo 1969,Ap 12,40:2
I Dreamt I Dwelt in Bloomingdale's 1970,F 13,26:1
Young Among Themselves, The 1970,Je 12,28:1
Pastry Shop, The 1970,Je 12,28:1

Hardy, Jim (Scenic Designer)
Homo 1969,Ap 12,40:2
Queen of Greece, The 1969,Ap 12,40:2
Pastry Shop, The 1970,Je 12,28:1
Young Among Themselves, The 1970,Je 12,28:1

Hardy, Joseph
Tempest, The 1945,Ja 26,17:2
Small Hours, The 1951,F 16,22:1
Mister Roberts 1956,D 6,46:2
J B 1958,Ap 24,37:1

Hardy, Joseph (Director)
Streets of New York, The 1963,O 30,47:1
Mr Grossman 1964,My 6,43:1
Dark Corners 1964,My 6,43:1
Night of the Dunce 1966,D 29,21:1
You're a Good Man, Charlie Brown 1967,Mr 8,51:1
You're a Good Man, Charlie Brown 1967,Ap 9,II,1:1
Johnny No-Trump 1967,O 9,60:2
House of Flowers 1968,Ja 29,26:2
Play It Again, Sam 1969,F 13,52:3
You're a Good Man, Charlie Brown 1969,N 14,39:1
Child's Play 1970,F 18,39:1
What the Butler Saw 1970,My 5,56:1
What the Butler Saw 1970,My 17,II,1:1
Bob and Ray-The Two and Only 1970,S 25,36:1
Bob and Ray-The Two and Only 1970,O 4,II,3:1
What the Butler Saw 1970,O 14,38:1

Hardy, Laurence
Hamlet 1953,Ag 25,18:6
Love and Libel 1960,D 8,44:1

Hardy, Michele
Half a Sixpence 1965,Ap 26,38:2

Hardy, Oliver
What Price Glory 1949,Mr 3,33:2

Hardy, Robert
Henry IV 1955,My 15,II,1:1
Someone Waiting 1956,F 15,26:1
Four Winds 1957,S 26,21:2
All's Well That Ends Well 1959,Ap 22,30:3

Hardy, Sam
Charm School, The 1920,Ag 3,12:1
Kiki 1921,N 30,13:1
Lambs Gambol 1925,Ap 27,15:1

Hardy, Sarah
Picnic 1957,F 21,32:1
Love Me Little 1958,Ap 15,42:2

Hardy, Thomas (Original Author)
Mayor of Casterbridge, The 1926,S 9,20:1
Mayor of Casterbridge, The 1926,O 3,VIII,2:1
Tess of the d'Urbervilles 1929,Ag 18,VIII,1:3

Hardy, Thomas (Playwright)
Famous Tragedy of the Queen of Cornwall, The 1923,D 2,VIII,2:8
Tess of the d'Urbervilles 1929,Ag 18,VIII,1:3

Hardy, William
Three Love Affairs; Bedtime Story 1958,Mr 11,33:1
Three Love Affairs; Still Life 1958,Mr 11,33:1
Galileo 1968,D 1,88:4

Hardy, William M
What a Relief 1935,D 14,10:6

Hare, Amory (Hutchinson, James P Mrs) (Playwright)
Return of Hannibal, The 1937,F 2,21:1

Hare, Betty
Still Life 1936,D 1,31:1

Hare, Doris
Night Must Fall 1936,S 29,34:1

Hare, Ernest
Richard II 1956,O 24,44:1
Romeo and Juliet 1956,O 25,41:1
Macbeth 1956,O 30,42:2
Troilus and Cressida 1956,D 27,21:1
Troilus and Cressida 1957,Ja 6,II,1:1

Hare, George
Little Poor Man, The 1925,Ag 6,14:1
Much Ado About Nothing 1929,N 17,30:4
Hamlet 1931,Ap 24,26:4

Hare, Lumsden
Trimmed in Scarlet 1920,F 3,18:1
Title, The 1921,N 15,23:3
Drifting 1922,Ja 3,20:3
Billeted 1922,My 10,22:4
Mask and the Face, The 1924,S 11,27:3
His Queen 1925,My 12,26:1
Antonia 1925,O 21,20:1
Ashes of Love 1926,Mr 23,24:3
What Every Woman Knows 1926,Ap 14,20:2
Patriot, The 1928,Ja 20,15:1
Twelve Thousand 1928,Mr 13,23:1
Elmer Gantry 1928,Ag 10,9:4
Lady Has a Heart, The 1937,S 27,24:1
Billy Draws a Horse 1939,D 22,14:5
Plan M 1942,F 21,15:2

Hare, Lumsden (Director)
What Every Woman Knows 1926,Ap 14,20:2
Slaves All 1926,D 7,24:4

Hare, Lumsden (Producer)
Slaves All 1926,D 7,24:4

Hare, Mary Ida
Little Town of Bethlehem, The 1920,D 27,11:1
Without the Walls 1921,Mr 28,8:1
Without the Walls 1922,Ap 17,17:1
Little Town of Bethlehem, The 1922,D 26,15:4

Hare, Montgomery (Playwright)
Venus-Shot 1966,Je 24,30:2
Child and the Dragon, The 1966,Je 24,30:2
Miracle in Brooklyn 1966,Je 24,30:2
Pin Up 1966,Je 24,30:2

Hare, Richard V (Costume Designer)
Immortal Husband, The 1955,F 15,32:2

Hare, Richard V (Scenic Designer)
Immortal Husband, The 1955,F 15,32:2

Hare, Robertson
Aren't Men Beasts? 1936,My 15,29:1
Spot of Bother 1937,Jl 7,26:2
Women Aren't Angels 1941,Ap 27,IX,1:6

Hare, Walter (Playwright)
Over Here 1936,Mr 16,21:2

Hare, Will
Playboy of Newark, The 1943,Mr 20,11:2
Suds in Your Eye 1944,Ja 13,15:5
Only the Heart 1944,Ap 5,17:2
Visitor, The 1944,O 18,24:5
Little Clay Cart, The 1953,Jl 1,25:1
Trip to Bountiful, The 1953,N 4,30:3
Marathon '33 1963,D 23,20:1
Live Like Pigs 1965,Je 8,48:2
Viewing, The 1967,Ja 11,51:1
Winter Journey 1968,Mr 13,39:1

Hare, Will (Director)
French Way, The; Deceased, The 1962,Mr 21,36:2
French Way, The; Grand Vizier, The 1962,Mr 21,36:2
French Way, The; Edward and Agrippina 1962,Mr 21,36:2

Hare, William
Mad Morning 1935,Je 25,14:1
Texas Town 1941,Ap 30,22:3
Out of My House 1942,Ja 8,28:6

Harens, Dean
Talley Method, The 1941,F 25,26:3
Men in Shadow 1943,Mr 11,16:2
Those Endearing Young Charms 1943,Je 17,16:3
Candida 1945,Ag 7,25:3
Tenting Tonight 1947,Ap 3,32:2
Be Your Age 1953,Ja 15,24:2
Girl Can Tell, A 1953,O 30,28:2

Harford, Alec
Red Blinds 1926,O 1,27:1

Harford, Betty
King Lear 1964,Jl 28,18:2

Harford, Burton (Producer)
Lost Boy 1932,Ja 6,24:4

Hargadon, Frank
Long Gallery, The 1958,Mr 7,17:2

Hargan, Elizabeth
Point of No Return 1957,Mr 23,17:2

Hargarther, Peta
America Hurrah; Interview; TV; Motel 1967,O 10,55:2

Hargate, Bill (Costume Designer)
Billy Budd 1959,F 28,13:3
Ballad of Jazz Street, The 1959,N 12,28:1
Jackass, The 1960,Mr 24,39:2
Marcus in the High Grass 1960,N 22,38:6
Cicero 1961,F 9,37:2
Tattooed Countess, The 1961,My 4,40:2
Golden Apple, The 1962,F 13,38:2
Anything Goes 1962,My 16,35:1
That Hat! 1964,S 24,45:1

Hargate, Bill (Scenic Designer)
Golden Apple, The 1962,F 13,38:2
Amorous Flea, The 1964,F 18,26:1
That Hat! 1964,S 24,45:1
Hargate, William (Miscellaneous)
Saintliness of Margery Kempe, The 1959,F 3,35:6
Hargatee, Bill (Costume Designer)
Black Nativity 1961,D 12,54:2
Harger, Burt
Merry-Go-Round 1927,Je 1,25:4
Just a Minute 1928,O 9,34:3
Early to Bed 1943,Je 18,16:2
Harger, Solon
Merry Wives of Windsor, The 1938,Ap 15,22:3
Hargis, Rebecca
Farther Off From Heaven 1947,Je 4,33:3
Summer and Smoke 1947,Jl 9,18:5
Hargrave, Edith
Houseparty 1929,S 10,26:5
Hargrave, Roy
Spider, The 1927,Mr 23,29:1
Big Fight, The 1928,S 19,33:1
Houseparty 1929,S 10,26:5
With Privileges 1930,S 16,30:2
American Tragedy, An 1931,F 21,15:5
Blind Alley 1935,S 25,19:6
Blind Alley 1940,O 16,28:2
Men in Shadow 1943,Mr 11,16:2
Dear Judas 1947,O 6,26:4
Hargrave, Roy (Director)
Room in Red and White, A 1936,Ja 20,23:3
Life of Reilly, The 1942,Ap 30,13:2
Men in Shadow 1943,Mr 11,16:2
Jackpot 1944,Ja 14,15:2
Pick-Up Girl 1944,My 4,25:2
Catherine Was Great 1944,Ag 3,16:1
Sleep, My Pretty One 1944,N 3,26:8
Signature 1945,F 15,25:2
Sky Drift 1945,N 14,25:2
Ivy Green, The 1949,Ap 6,37:2
Hargrave, Roy (Playwright)
Houseparty 1929,S 10,26:5
Dance With Your Gods 1934,O 8,14:3
Room in Red and White, A 1936,Ja 20,23:3
Hargrave, William
Tattle Tales 1933,Je 2,22:6
Saluta 1934,Ag 29,13:4
Hargraves, Adele
Yeah-Man 1932,My 27,27:3
Hargraves, Donald
Sign of the Leopard 1928,D 12,34:4
Hargreaves, Norman
Critic, The 1965,Jl 26,15:2
Hargrove, Halcyone
Blue Peter, The 1925,Mr 25,25:3
Hari, Eugene
Two for Fun 1961,F 14,45:3
Hari, Eugene (Director)
Two for Fun 1961,F 14,45:3
Hari, Sara
Evening With the Times Square Two, An 1967,My 21,83:6
Haring, Blanche
Happy Ending 1936,Jl 15,14:3
So Proudly We Hail 1936,S 23,28:4
Bet Your Life 1937,Ap 6,20:2
Reunion 1938,Ap 12,26:4
Haring, Forrest C
Bad Manners 1933,Ja 31,15:5
Haring, Forrest C (Director)
It's You I Want 1935,F 6,23:3
Haring, Forrest C (Producer)
Apron Strings 1930,F 18,28:2
Hey, Nonny, Nonny! 1932,Je 7,22:3
It's You I Want 1935,F 6,23:3
Harington, Joy
Murder in the Cathedral 1938,F 17,16:2
Sarah Simple 1940,N 18,22:5
Haris, Ellyn
Lyle 1970,Mr 21,16:2
Harison, Frances
Madame Bovary 1937,N 17,26:2
Merchant of Yonkers, The 1938,D 29,14:2
Hariss, Lillian (Playwright)
Prima Donna 1929,D 12,36:4
Hariston, William (Director)
Jericho-Jim Crow 1964,Ja 13,25:3
Harker, Gordon
Persons Unknown 1929,Je 2,VIII,2:7
Road House 1932,O 30,IX,2:3
Hyde Park Corner 1934,O 28,IX,3:4
Frog, The 1936,Ap 12,II,8:4
Saloon Bar 1939,N 26,IX,3:6
Once a Crook 1940,S 1,IX,2:4
Warn That Man 1942,Ja 4,IX,1:4
Harker, James
Family Portrait 1939,Mr 9,18:4
Harker, Joseph (Miscellaneous)
Decameron Nights 1922,Ap 21,14:5
Harker, Joseph (Scenic Designer)
Sally 1921,S 11,20:2
Barbara's Wedding 1931,O 9,21:1
H M S Pinafore 1948,Ja 20,26:2

Trial by Jury 1951,F 6,24:2
H M S Pinafore 1951,F 6,24:2
H M S Pinafore 1955,O 18,48:1
Trial by Jury 1955,O 18,48:1
H M S Pinafore 1964,N 20,40:1
Harker, L Allen (Playwright)
Marigold 1927,My 29,VII,1:3
Marigold 1930,O 9,23:1
Harker, Phil (Scenic Designer)
Sally 1921,S 11,20:2
Barbara's Wedding 1931,O 9,21:1
H M S Pinafore 1948,Ja 20,26:2
H M S Pinafore 1951,F 6,24:2
Trial by Jury 1951,F 6,24:2
Trial by Jury 1955,O 18,48:1
H M S Pinafore 1955,O 18,48:1
H M S Pinafore 1964,N 20,40:1
Harkers, The (Scenic Designer)
Flashing Stream, The 1939,Ap 11,19:2
Harkin, Kate
Bird Cage, The 1950,F 23,32:2
Ladies of the Corridor, The 1953,O 22,33:5
Harkins, Barbara
Alternate Current 1939,D 23,8:3
Harkins, Charlene
Pal Joey 1940,D 26,22:2
Harkins, Dolla
Tell Me More 1925,Ap 14,27:3
Harkins, Jim
Will Morrissey's Folies Bergere Revue 1930,Ap 16,26:6
Harkins, John
Cretan Woman, The 1954,Jl 8,18:2
Clandestine Marriage, The 1954,O 4,23:2
White Devil, The 1955,Mr 15,32:5
Othello 1955,S 8,27:2
Henry IV, Part I 1955,S 22,34:2
Terrible Swift Sword, The 1955,N 16,42:1
Henry V 1956,Jl 7,11:2
Girls of Summer 1956,N 20,45:1
Good as Gold 1957,Mr 8,22:2
West Side Story 1957,S 27,14:4
Night Circus, The 1958,D 3,44:1
Julius Caesar 1959,Ag 4,30:1
Julius Caesar 1959,Ag 16,II,1:1
Gang's All Here, The 1959,O 2,23:1
Twelfth Night 1960,Je 9,29:4
Antony and Cleopatra 1960,Ag 1,19:1
Under Milk Wood 1961,Mr 30,25:1
Cantilevered Terrace, The 1962,Ja 18,24:1
Mother Courage and Her Children 1963,Mr 30,5:5
Dynamite Tonight 1964,Mr 16,36:2
Three Sisters, The 1964,Je 23,24:1
Biscuit 1966,My 17,51:2
Endecott and the Red Cross 1968,My 7,50:1
Early Morning 1970,N 26,57:1
Harkness, Alan
Twelfth Night 1941,D 3,32:2
Harkness, Percy
Narrow Road to the Deep North 1969,D 2,64:1
Harkrider, John (Costume Designer)
Rio Rita 1927,F 3,18:3
Ziegfeld Follies 1927,Ag 17,27:3
Rosalie 1927,D 18,IX,2:3
Show Boat 1927,D 28,26:1
Three Musketeers, The 1928,Mr 4,IX,2:3
Three Musketeers, The 1928,Mr 14,28:1
Whoopee 1928,D 5,34:3
Show Girl 1929,Jl 3,19:3
Show Boat 1932,My 20,22:2
Music in the Air 1932,N 9,28:2
Let's Face It 1941,O 30,26:2
Harlan, J F
Espanola 1921,D 30,13:1
Harlan, Ken
Student Prince, The 1943,Je 9,16:2
Harlan, Kenneth
Vaudeville (Palace) 1928,O 23,32:5
White Flame 1929,N 5,32:7
Curtain Rises, The 1933,O 20,15:2
Harlan, Rita
Blonde Beast, The 1923,Mr 3,9:3
Harlan, Warren (Costume Designer)
Naked 1950,S 7,39:2
Harland, Frances
Nature's Nobleman 1921,N 15,23:2
Harless, Arthur
Getting Even 1929,Ag 20,31:1
Harless, Dee
Oh Captain! 1958,F 5,21:2
Harley, Margot
Crystal Heart, The 1960,F 16,31:2
Ernest in Love 1960,My 5,39:4
Harling, Colt
London Assurance 1937,F 19,14:5
Harling, Frank (Composer)
Deep River 1926,S 26,VIII,2:7
Deep River 1926,O 5,26:2
Deep River 1926,O 10,VIII,1:1
Deep River 1926,O 10,VIII,4:8
Machinal 1928,S 8,10:3

Harling, Jack
Achilles Had a Heel 1935,O 14,20:2
Cyrano de Bergerac 1936,Ap 28,17:1
Tide Rising 1937,Ja 26,17:2
Harling, LuGarda
Lancelot and Elaine 1921,S 13,12:1
Harling, Sheila
Music Hath Charms 1934,D 31,8:2
Harlow, Leola
Flies, The; Mouches, Les 1947,Ap 18,26:3
Millionairess, The 1949,Ap 7,38:5
Harlow, Nicholas
Paths of Glory 1935,S 27,24:2
Harlowe, Beatrice
Bringing Up Father 1925,Mr 31,16:1
Harmati, Sandor (Composer)
Jeweled Tree, The 1926,O 8,26:2
Harmer, Ralf (Miscellaneous)
Muzeeka 1968,Ap 29,47:2
Harmon, April
By the Way 1925,D 29,20:3
Harmon, Betty
Huui, Huui 1968,N 25,58:1
Harmon, Erv
Gypsy 1959,My 22,31:6
Harmon, Gay
Susan Slept Here 1961,Jl 12,35:2
Harmon, Gwen
Me and Juliet 1953,My 29,17:1
Shinbone Alley 1957,Ap 15,23:2
Harmon, Helen
Glamour Preferred 1940,N 16,13:2
Harmon, Irv
Skits-Oh-Frantics 1967,Ap 3,39:2
Harmon, Irv (Playwright)
Skits-Oh-Frantics 1967,Ap 3,39:2
Harmon, Jennifer
Man and Superman 1964,D 7,45:2
War and Peace 1965,Ja 12,32:1
You Can't Take It With You 1965,N 24,32:1
School for Scandal, The 1966,N 22,33:2
Right You Are (If You Think You Are) 1966,N 23,34:2
Wild Duck, The 1967,Ja 12,49:1
Cherry Orchard, The 1968,Mr 20,41:1
Jungle of Cities 1970,Mr 1,75:2
Harmon, Jill
Rate of Exchange 1968,Ap 2,50:1
Fiddler on the Roof 1970,F 28,20:1
Harmon, Joan
Bad Girl 1930,O 3,30:2
Hobo 1931,F 12,24:4
Harmon, John
Sophie 1944,D 26,22:7
Harmon, Johnny
Cindy 1964,Mr 20,24:1
Harmon, Josephine
Vaudeville (Palace) 1928,F 21,19:2
Vaudeville (Palace) 1928,O 23,32:5
Harmon, Joy
Make a Million 1958,O 24,39:2
Susan Slept Here 1961,Jl 12,35:2
Harmon, Lois
Diamond Lil 1951,S 15,8:2
Long Watch, The 1952,Mr 21,19:5
Harmon, Lucille
Sun-Kist 1921,My 24,20:2
Harmon, Mary
Top Banana 1951,N 2,19:2
By the Beautiful Sea 1954,Ap 9,20:1
Mrs Patterson 1954,D 2,37:1
Harmon, May
Inspector General, The 1923,My 1,24:1
Harmon, Myles
Promises to Keep 1965,Jl 22,25:1
Harmon, Myles (Miscellaneous)
Promises to Keep 1965,Jl 22,25:1
Harmon, Myles (Scenic Designer)
Heartbreak House 1963,Je 28,24:1
Harmon, Natalie
Weep for the Virgins 1935,D 2,18:1
Harmon, Sidney (Miscellaneous)
Men in White 1933,S 27,24:2
But for the Grace of God 1937,Ja 13,21:4
Harmon, Sidney (Producer)
Precedent 1931,Ap 15,24:5
Bloodstream 1932,Mr 31,25:1
Far Away Horses 1933,Mr 22,21:6
Milky Way, The 1934,My 9,23:2
Birthday 1934,D 27,24:2
Body Beautiful, The 1935,N 1,24:3
200 Were Chosen 1936,N 21,21:1
But for the Grace of God 1937,Ja 13,21:4
Robin Landing 1937,N 19,26:4
Harmon, Steve
Lyle 1970,Mr 21,16:2
Harmon, William
Born Yesterday 1946,F 5,18:2
Harmonica Rogues
Aquarama 1960 1960,Jl 1,14:6
Harmonica Symphony Orchestra
Betsy 1926,D 29,24:3

Harms, Carl
Sojourner Truth 1948,Ap 22,35:2
Wild Duck, The 1951,D 27,17:1
Much Ado About Nothing 1952,My 2,20:1
Girl on the Via Flaminia, The 1954,F 10,37:1
Girl on the Via Flaminia, The 1954,Ap 6,35:5
Davy Jones's Locker 1959,Mr 30,25:1
People Is the Thing That the World Is Fullest Of
1967,F 21,53:1

Harms, Carl (Miscellaneous)
Davy Jones's Locker 1959,Mr 30,25:1
Davy Jones's Locker 1966,D 25,48:5
Wizard of Oz, The 1968,N 28,69:2
Whistling Wizard and the Sultan of Tuffet
1970,F 1,70:1

Harnden, Red
Lady Fingers 1929,F 1,22:4

Harnett, Sunny
Seidman and Son 1962,O 16,32:2

Harnick, Jay
Alive and Kicking 1950,Ja 18,25:5

Harnick, Jay (Director)
On the Town 1959,F 14,15:1
Young Abe Lincoln 1961,Ap 26,36:1

Harnick, Jay (Miscellaneous)
Tartuffe 1965,Ja 15,23:1

Harnick, Jay (Producer)
Sudden and Accidental Re-education of Horse
Johnson, The 1968,D 19,63:1

Harnick, Sheldon (Composer)
New Faces of 1952 1952,My 17,23:2
Littlest Revue, The 1956,My 23,37:2
Oh, Johnny: or, Jonny Spielt Auf 1970,Mr 15,88:4

Harnick, Sheldon (Lyricist)
New Faces of 1952 1952,My 17,23:2
New Faces of 1952 1952,My 25,II,1:1
Littlest Revue, The 1956,My 23,37:2
Body Beautiful, The 1958,Ja 24,15:2
Portofino 1958,F 22,8:3
Fiorello! 1959,N 24,45:3
Fiorello! 1959,N 29,II,1:1
Tenderloin 1960,O 18,47:2
Smiling the Boy Fell Dead 1961,Ap 20,28:1
Fiorello! 1962,Je 14,24:1
Bil and Cora Baird's Marionette Theater
1963,Ap 12,34:2
She Loves Me 1963,Ap 24,39:1
She Loves Me 1963,My 5,II,1:1
Fiddler on the Roof 1964,S 23,56:2
Fiddler on the Roof 1964,O 4,II,1:1
Lady or the Tiger?, The 1966,O 19,53:1
Diary of Adam and Eve, The 1966,O 19,53:1
Passionella 1966,O 19,53:1
Apple Tree, The 1966,O 30,II,1:1
Fiddler on the Roof 1967,F 17,50:1
Fiddler on the Roof 1967,S 7,50:1
Fiddler on the Roof 1967,S 28,59:2
Fiddler on the Roof 1970,F 28,20:1
Oh, Johnny: or, Jonny Spielt Auf 1970,Mr 15,88:4
Rothschilds, The 1970,O 20,40:1
Rothschilds, The 1970,N 1,II,1:1

Harnick, Sheldon (Playwright)
Almanac 1954,Ja 3,II,1:1
Shoestring Revue 1955,Mr 1,22:2
To Broadway With Love 1964,Ap 30,28:6
Diary of Adam and Eve, The 1966,O 19,53:1
Lady or the Tiger?, The 1966,O 19,53:1
Passionella 1966,O 19,53:1

Harnley, Leslie (Musical Director)
Fourth Avenue North 1961,S 28,50:2
Who's Who, Baby? 1968,Ja 30,36:1
Of Thee I Sing 1969,Mr 8,19:1

Harold and Lola
Artists and Models 1943,N 6,16:6
Hilarities 1948,S 10,20:2

Haroldson, Ann
Ice Follies 1937,D 22,29:1

Harout
Maitresse de Roi 1926,D 1,24:1
Dame aux Camelias, La 1926,D 7,24:2
Misanthrope, Le 1926,D 10,31:2

Harout, Magda
Moths, The 1970,My 12,46:1

Harper, Barbara
Hello, Dolly! 1967,N 13,61:1

Harper, Bob (Director)
Servant of Two Masters, The 1958,F 11,35:2

Harper, David (Miscellaneous)
Cry of the Raindrop 1961,Mr 8,38:1

Harper, Dolores
House of Flowers 1954,D 31,11:2

Harper, Edward
Great Big Doorstep, The 1950,Mr 18,8:6

Harper, Fred
Merry World, The 1926,Je 9,18:3
Cherry Blossoms 1927,Mr 29,22:3
Allegro 1952,S 18,36:3

Harper, Gerald
Truce of the Bear 1957,O 24,39:1

Twelfth Night 1958,D 10,54:2
Hamlet 1958,D 17,2:7
Henry V 1958,D 26,2:7
Boeing-Boeing 1965,F 3,30:1
Corsican Brothers, The 1970,Mr 20,56:2

Harper, Henry H (Playwright)
Devil's Mistress, The 1929,Mr 10,X,4:5
Romantic Mr Dickens 1940,D 3,33:2

Harper, Herb
School for Wives 1957,Je 20,23:4

Harper, Herbert (Choreographer)
Walk With Music 1940,Je 5,33:2
Year Round, The 1953,My 6,38:7

Harper, James
Hamlet 1937,Ag 24,24:4

Harper, Jean
Young Go First, The 1935,My 29,16:2

Harper, Leonard (Director)
Hot Chocolates 1929,Je 21,17:4

Harper, Marguerite (Playwright)
Romantic Mr Dickens 1940,D 3,33:2

Harper, Mary
Sweetheart Shop, The 1920,S 1,13:4
Four in Hand 1923,S 7,10:2

Harper, Otis
Good Morning, Dearie 1921,N 2,20:2

Harper, Ray
Great Scott! 1929,S 3,25:1
Phantoms 1930,Ja 14,24:3
Man Who Reclaimed His Head 1932,S 9,17:3
But Not for Love 1934,N 27,26:2
Ten Million Ghosts 1936,O 24,23:7

Harper, Robert
Nightingale, The 1927,Ja 4,20:4
Cock-A-Doodle Dandy 1955,N 4,26:5

Harper, Ron
Sweet Bird of Youth 1959,Mr 11,39:2

Harper, Valerie
Story Theater 1970,O 27,54:1

Harper, Ves (Costume Designer)
Jericho-Jim Crow 1964,Ja 13,25:3

Harper, Ves (Lighting Director)
Jericho-Jim Crow 1964,Ja 13,25:3

Harper, Wally (Composer)
Company 1970,Ap 27,40:1

Harper, Wally (Miscellaneous)
Up Eden 1968,N 27,42:1
Billy 1969,Mr 24,56:1

Harper, Wally (Musical Director)
Whispers on the Wind 1970,Je 4,50:1

Harper, William P
Tidings Brought to Mary, The 1922,D 25,20:1

Harr, George (Playwright)
Steps Leading Up 1941,Ap 19,20:6

Harr, Warren
Carousel 1949,Ja 26,28:2

Harraday, Richard
Made for Each Other 1924,S 30,27:2

Harragan, Robert
That Day 1922,O 4,27:3

Harrell, Bobby
Best Foot Forward 1941,O 2,28:2
You Can't Take It With You 1951,Ap 7,8:6

Harrell, James Nelson
Journey to Jefferson 1964,Jl 9,24:3
Macbeth 1968,N 30,49:3

Harrell, James Nelson (Miscellaneous)
Macbeth 1968,N 30,49:3

Harrell, Mack
Susannah 1955,F 25,18:4

Harrell, Maurice
Latent Heterosexual, The 1968,Mr 22,52:1

Harrell, Nelson
Twelfth Night 1941,D 3,32:2

Harrell, Wilma
Tall Kentuckian, The 1953,Je 17,30:1

Harrelson, Helen
Cellar and the Well, The 1950,D 11,30:2
One Bright Day 1952,Mr 20,37:2
His and Hers 1954,Ja 8,18:2
Our Town 1959,Mr 24,46:2
Way of the World, The 1965,Je 2,40:1
Richard III 1965,Je 3,26:1
Master Builder, The 1968,Je 22,26:1

Harrett, Lee
World We Make, The 1939,N 21,19:1

Harrice, Lincoln
Groove Tube 1969,O 12,88:3

Harrie, Morgan
Master of the Revels 1935,Ag 14,16:2

Harrigan, Charles
In Splendid Error 1954,O 27,33:6
Juno and the Paycock 1955,F 24,20:4
Simply Heavenly 1957,My 22,28:2
White Cargo 1960,D 30,12:1

Harrigan, Dorothy L
Some Party 1922,Ap 17,22:1

Harrigan, Mary
Ticket-of-Leave Man, The 1961,D 23,15:1

Harrigan, Nedda
Children's Tragedy, The 1921,O 12,18:2
Treat 'Em Rough 1926,O 5,26:2
Dracula 1927,O 6,29:1

Harrigan, Nedda—Cont
Merry Andrew 1929,Ja 22,22:2
Becky Sharp 1929,Je 4,29:1
Paris Bound 1929,Jl 20,8:3
Great Man, The 1931,Ap 8,20:6
Monkey 1932,F 12,25:2
Bidding High 1932,S 29,17:2
Hat, a Coat, a Glove, A 1934,F 1,15:2
Field of Ermine 1935,F 9,10:4
Spring in Autumn 1937,Ag 17,23:1
Charley's Aunt 1940,O 18,24:2
In Time to Come 1941,D 29,20:2

Harrigan, Robert
Just Married 1921,Ap 27,21:1
Title, The 1921,N 15,23:3
One Shot Fired 1927,N 8,32:5
Elmer Gantry 1928,Ag 10,9:4
Crashing Through 1928,O 30,26:5
Lady Dedlock 1929,Ja 1,61:2
Security 1929,Mr 29,20:1
Infinite Shoeblack, The 1930,F 18,28:1
Good Companions, The 1931,O 2,31:1
Alice Sit-By-The-Fire 1932,Mr 8,19:3
Mrs Warren's Profession 1956,Je 7,35:2

Harrigan, William
Acquittal, The 1920,Ja 6,18:2
Acquittal, The 1920,Ja 11,VIII,2:1
Bought and Paid For 1921,D 8,17:5
Polly Preferred 1923,Ja 12,13:3
Schemers 1924,S 16,27:1
Dove, The 1925,F 12,17:3
Great God Brown, The 1926,Ja 25,26:1
Sandalwood 1926,S 23,23:1
Vaudeville (Palace) 1927,Jl 12,29:3
Ink 1927,N 2,24:2
Whispering Friends 1928,F 21,18:3
Washington Heights 1931,S 30,23:4
Moon in the Yellow River, The 1932,F 21,VIII,2:1
Moon in the Yellow River, The 1932,Mr 1,19:3
Moon in the Yellow River, The
1932,Mr 13,VIII,1:1
Criminal at Large 1932,O 11,26:3
Keeper of the Keys 1933,O 19,23:2
Dark Tower, The 1933,N 27,20:3
She Loves Me Not 1934,My 27,X,2:5
All Rights Reserved 1934,N 7,33:5
Portrait of Gilbert 1934,D 29,11:5
Paths of Glory 1935,S 19,29:1
Paths of Glory 1935,S 27,24:2
Among Those Sailing 1936,F 12,24:4
Days to Come 1936,D 16,35:1
Roosty 1938,F 15,21:2
Happiest Days, The 1939,Ap 12,26:2
Passenger to Bali, A 1940,Mr 15,26:2
Snookie 1941,Je 4,26:2
In Time to Come 1941,D 29,20:2
Pick-Up Girl 1944,My 4,25:2
Mister Roberts 1948,F 19,27:2
Mister Roberts 1948,F 29,II,1:1
Mister Roberts 1950,My 21,II,1:1
Wayward Saint, The 1955,F 18,17:1
Wayward Saint, The 1955,F 27,II,1:1
Mister Roberts 1956,D 6,46:2
Shadow of My Enemy, A 1957,D 12,35:4

Harriman, Borden
Queen Victoria 1923,N 16,15:1
Mister Pitt 1924,Ja 23,15:3
Don't Bother Mother 1925,F 4,18:2
Starlight 1925,Mr 4,17:2
Stronger Than Love 1925,D 29,20:2

Harrington, Agnes
Vaudeville (Palace) 1926,Mr 23,24:3

Harrington, Cecil
Her Family Tree 1920,D 28,9:2

Harrington, Donal
Singing Jailbirds 1928,D 5,34:4

Harrington, Donald
Only Jealousy of Emer, The 1970,Mr 25,36:4
Renard 1970,Mr 25,36:4
Gertrude 1970,N 13,29:1
Carmilla 1970,D 1,61:2

Harrington, Donald (Director)
Nautical but Nice 1931,Ap 19,31:6

Harrington, Dorothy
Saint Joan 1950,Mr 4,10:6

Harrington, Frank
Trial of Dr Beck, The 1937,Ag 10,22:2

Harrington, Guy
Squealer, The 1928,N 13,36:3

Harrington, Hal
Silks and Satins 1920,Jl 16,19:1

Harrington, Hamtree
Dixie to Broadway 1924,O 30,22:1
Vaudeville (Palace) 1927,D 13,33:5
Change Your Luck 1930,Je 7,10:2
Little Racketeer, The 1932,Ja 19,24:4
As Thousands Cheer 1933,O 2,22:1
Lew Leslie's Blackbirds of 1939 1939,F 13,12:2
Belle Helene, La 1941,Jl 8,14:1
Pillar to Post 1943,D 11,11:2
Shuffle Along 1952,My 9,20:5

Harrington, Helen
Vaudeville (Palace) 1926,Mr 23,24:3

Harrington, John
Bad Man, The 1920,Ag 31,7:1
Magnolia 1923,Ag 28,12:3
Roseanne 1923,D 31,9:5
Dove, The 1925,F 12,17:3
Canary Dutch 1925,S 9,22:1
Lulu Belle 1926,F 10,20:1
Young Sinners 1929,N 29,24:4
Living Dangerously 1935,Ja 14,10:3
Slight Case of Murder, A 1935,S 12,28:5

Harrington, Kate
Slightly Married 1943,O 26,19:2
Buy Me Blue Ribbons 1951,O 18,33:2
Morning's at Seven 1955,Je 23,25:1
Plough and the Stars, The 1956,Ap 6,14:1
Happiest Millionaire, The 1956,N 21,21:3
Courtyard 1960,Mr 1,28:1
Days and Nights of Beebee Fenstermaker, The
  1962,S 18,33:1
Dream of Swallows, A 1964,Ap 15,46:1
Stephen D 1966,Ag 5,17:1
Not a Way of Life 1967,Mr 23,28:1

Harrington, Pat
Ladies and Gentlemen 1939,O 18,30:2
Panama Hattie 1940,O 31,28:2
Panama Hattie 1940,N 10,IX,1:1
Star and Garter 1942,Je 25,26:2
Front Page, The 1946,S 5,22:4
Rat Race, The 1949,D 23,16:2
Live Wire, The 1950,Ag 18,16:2
Live·Wire, The 1950,Ag 27,II,1:1
Call Me Madam 1950,O 13,25:1
Harbor Lights 1956,O 5,20:1
Good Soup, The 1960,Mr 3,26:4
Happiness Is Just a Little Thing Called a Rolls
  Royce 1968,My 13,54:5

Harrington, Pat Sr
Sunday in New York 1961,N 10,40:1

Harrington, Robert
Peter Pan 1954,O 21,30:2

Harrington, Tony Jr
Riot 1968,D 20,64:1

Harrington Sisters
Passing Show of 1924, The 1924,S 4,13:4
Vaudeville (Palace) 1928,S 4,21:3
Vaudeville (Palace) 1930,Ap 21,20:7

Harriot, Elinor
Bonds of Interest, The 1929,O 15,34:2

Harris, Adrian Sayre (Scenic Designer)
Faith of Our Fathers 1950,Ag 6,72:2

Harris, Al
Country Boy, The 1963,O 28,20:1

Harris, Al (Miscellaneous)
Country Boy, The 1963,O 28,20:1

Harris, Alexander
Daphne Laureola 1950,S 19,38:6

Harris, Alice
Blackberries of 1932 1932,Ap 5,27:5

Harris, Anthony Burtt
Tobacco Road 1960,My 11,44:2

Harris, Art (Miscellaneous)
O, Oysters! 1961,Ja 31,23:1

Harris, Arthur
Anna Russell and Her Little Show 1953,S 8,27:2

Harris, Arthur (Miscellaneous)
Anna Russell and Her Little Show 1953,S 8,27:2

Harris, Averell
Pearls 1921,Je 14,15:2
Squaring the Triangle 1921,Je 14,15:2
Persons Unknown 1922,O 26,12:1
Gypsy Jim 1924,Ja 15,17:4
Deacon, The 1925,N 25,14:3
Four Walls 1927,S 20,33:1
Night Hostess 1928,S 13,31:2
Mouthpiece, The 1929,Je 16,VIII,2:1
Third Day, The 1929,Ag 13,23:4
Tyrant, The 1930,N 13,33:1
Napi 1931,Mr 12,22:5
Trick for Trick 1932,F 19,14:2
Errant Lady 1934,S 18,18:2
Rosmersholm 1935,D 3,32:5
Greater Lust, The 1936,Jl 14,22:4
Amateur Hour 1936,Jl 21,13:1
Antony and Cleopatra 1937,N 11,30:2
Schoolhouse on the Lot 1938,Mr 23,18:4
Key Largo 1939,N 28,30:2
Pal Joey 1940,D 26,22:2
Beat the Band 1942,O 15,26:1
Othello 1943,O 20,18:1
Therese 1945,O 10,24:2

Harris, Barbara
From the Second City 1961,S 27,32:1
Untitled-Revue; Second City 1962,Ja 12,30:2
Oh Dad, Poor Dad, Mamma's Hung You in the
  Closet and I'm Feelin' So Sad 1962,F 27,28:1
Mother Courage and Her Children 1963,Mr 30,5:5
Open Season at Second City 1964,Ja 23,25:1
Dynamite Tonight 1964,Mr 16,36:2
On a Clear Day You Can See Forever
  1965,O 18,44:1
Diary of Adam and Eve, The 1966,O 19,53:1
Lady or the Tiger?, The 1966,O 19,53:1
Passionella 1966,O 19,53:1

Apple Tree, The 1966,O 30,II,1:1
Mahagonny 1970,Ap 29,51:1
Mahagonny 1970,My 10,II,1:1
Mahagonny 1970,My 10,II,15:1

Harris, Barbara (Director)
Penny Wars, The 1969,O 16,52:1
Penny Wars, The 1969,O 26,II,1:1

Harris, Bill
Sojourner Truth 1948,Ap 22,35:2

Harris, Billy
Master Builder, The 1955,Mr 2,23:2

Harris, Blaney
Johnny Belinda 1940,S 19,26:2

Harris, Bob (Composer)
Dream of Swallows, A 1964,Ap 15,46:1

Harris, Bud and Radcliff
Vaudeville (Palace) 1930,Mr 10,24:4

Harris, Byron
Merchant of Venice, The 1931,N 9,22:2

Harris, Calvin
Merry Duchess, The 1943,Je 24,25:1

Harris, Charlene
Bless You All 1950,D 15,42:2

Harris, Charles (Producer)
Town Boy 1929,O 5,22:4

Harris, Charles Mitchell
Her Majesty the Widow 1934,Je 19,24:5

Harris, Cleo
Ol' Man Satan 1932,O 4,26:3

Harris, Clyde
Connection, The 1959,Jl 16,30:2

Harris, Cynthia
Best Laid Plans, The 1966,Mr 26,15:2
Long Christmas Dinner, The 1966,S 7,53:1
Happy Journey to Trenton and Camden, The
  1966,S 7,53:1
TV 1966,N 7,66:1
Interview 1966,N 7,66:1
White House Murder Case, The 1970,F 19,59:1
Slow Memories 1970,N 18,41:1

Harris, Daniel
Fencing Master, The 1936,Ap 1,29:1
Forbidden Melody 1936,N 3,33:1

Harris, David
Shylock and His Daughter 1947,S 30,22:2
Life Is a Dream 1964,Mr 20,24:1

Harris, Desiree
Town Boy 1929,O 5,22:4
Penny Arcade 1930,Mr 11,24:5

Harris, Dina
Vaudeville (Palace) 1926,Ap 20,24:6
Vaudeville (Palace) 1926,Jl 6,19:3

Harris, Dina (Costume Designer)
Wedding, The 1961,Ap 21,26:2
Anniversary, The 1961,Ap 21,26:2
On the High Road 1961,Ap 21,26:2
Buskers, The 1961,O 31,28:1
Poppa Is Home 1961,D 20,37:1
French Way, The; Grand Vizier, The
  1962,Mr 21,36:2
French Way, The; Edward and Agrippina
  1962,Mr 21,36:2
French Way, The; Deceased, The 1962,Mr 21,36:2
Call It Virtue 1963,Mr 28,8:2
Enchanting Melody 1964,N 25,40:1
Winterset 1966,F 10,32:2

Harris, Donald
High Button Shoes 1947,O 10,32:2
As the Girls Go 1948,N 15,21:2
Caesar and Cleopatra 1949,D 22,28:2
Pride's Crossing 1950,N 21,37:5
Mikado, The 1951,Ja 30,21:2
H M S Pinafore 1951,F 6,24:2
Trial by Jury 1951,F 6,24:2

Harris, Douglas
Henry V 1958,D 26,2:7

Harris, Duncan
Man in the Making, The 1921,S 21,16:2

Harris, Edith
Legend of Leonora, The 1926,My 1,10:1

Harris, Edna Mae
Green Pastures, The 1930,F 27,26:1
Green Pastures, The 1935,F 27,16:2
Good Neighbor 1941,O 22,26:2
Run, Little Chillun 1943,Ag 14,6:1
Long Way From Home, A 1948,F 9,25:2

Harris, Edward
Hamlet 1968,Jl 4,15:1
Romeo and Juliet 1968,Ag 16,19:1
Riot 1968,D 20,64:1

Harris, Edward H (Producer)
Oh, Professor 1930,My 2,19:6

Harris, Edward Peyton (Director)
Homecoming 1942,N 17,28:5

Harris, Edward Peyton (Playwright)
Homecoming 1942,N 17,28:5

Harris, Edward W (Playwright)
Oh, Professor 1930,My 2,19:6

Harris, Elaine
Red, White and Maddox 1969,Ja 27,27:1

Harris, Ellyn
Lyle 1970,Mr 21,16:2

Harris, Elmer (?laywright)
Great Necker, The 1928,Mr 7,28:2
Stepping Out 1929,My 21,29:1
Young Sinners 1929,N 29,24:4
Ladies All 1930,Jl 20,VIII,2:1
Ladies All 1930,Jl 29,25:2
Young Sinners 1931,Ap 21,35:5
Modern Virgin, A 1931,My 21,33:4
Marriage for Three 1931,N 12,30:5
Young Sinners 1933,Mr 7,20:4
Man Who Killed Lincoln, The 1939,D 30,9:1
Man Who Killed Lincoln, The 1940,Ja 18,26:4
Johnny Belinda 1940,S 19,26:2

Harris, Eloise
Invitation to a Beheading 1969,Mr 18,36:1

Harris, Erona
Carmen Jones 1945,My 3,26:5
Carmen Jones 1946,Ap 8,32:2

Harris, Ethel
Potash and Perlmutter 1935,Ap 6,11:3

Harris, Frances
Nautical but Nice 1931,Ap 19,31:6

Harris, Frederick
High Road, The 1928,S 11,31:1

Harris, G Spencer
Blue Jeans 1933,Ap 9,31:5

Harris, Gary
Originale 1964,S 9,46:1

Harris, Gary (Lighting Director)
Evening's Frost, An 1965,O 12,56:1
Sunset 1966,My 13,34:1
From the Second City 1969,O 15,34:1

Harris, Gary (Miscellaneous)
Sunset 1966,My 13,34:1
From the Second City 1969,O 15,34:1
Fortune and Men's Eyes 1969,O 23,55:1
Rose 1969,O 29,30:1
Memory Bank, The 1970,Ja 12,24:3
Child's Play 1970,F 18,39:1
Nature of the Crime 1970,Mr 24,41:1
Dark of the Moon 1970,Ap 4,21:2
Inquest 1970,Ap 24,38:1
Happy Birthday, Wanda June 1970,O 8,58:2

Harris, George W (Costume Designer)
Hassan 1924,S 23,23:1

Harris, George W (Scenic Designer)
Hassan 1924,S 23,23:1
School for Scandal, The 1925,D 7,18:2
Constant Nymph, The 1926,D 10,31:1

Harris, H Blanche
Trial of Dr Beck, The 1937,Ag 10,22:2

Harris, Hazel
Lovely Lady 1927,D 30,22:1
Dear Love 1930,My 18,VIII,3:1
Artists and Models 1930,Je 11,33:2

Harris, Henry B (Mrs) (Producer)
Noose, The 1926,O 21,23:3
Blood Money 1927,Ag 23,29:2

Harris, Herbert (Composer)
White Devil, The 1965,D 7,56:1

Harris, Herbert (Miscellaneous)
U S A 1959,O 29,38:1
Those That Play the Clowns 1966,N 25,48:1

Harris, Herbert (Musical Director)
Best of Burlesque 1957,S 30,27:2
U S A 1959,O 29,38:1
Drums Under the Windows 1960,O 14,26:1
Royal Hunt of the Sun, The 1965,O 27,36:2

Harris, Herbert H (Miscellaneous)
All My Sons 1947,Ja 30,21:2

Harris, Herbert H (Producer)
Man Who Had All the Luck, The 1944,N 24,18:5
French Touch, The 1945,D 10,18:2
I Gotta Get Out 1947,S 26,27:2

Harris, Hilda
Ballad for Bimshire 1963,O 16,54:1
Jericho-Jim Crow 1964,Ja 13,25:3

Harris, Holly
Love Life 1948,O 8,31:2
Kiss Me, Kate 1952,Ja 9,24:6

Harris, Howard (Miscellaneous)
Hilarities 1948,S 10,20:2

Harris, James
Hajj Malik, El 1970,O 4,II,5:1
Hamlet 1970,D 28,40:1

Harris, Jean
County Chairman, The 1936,My 26,26:5
Schoolhouse on the Lot 1938,Mr 23,18:4
Polonaise 1945,O 8,20:2
Alive and Kicking 1950,Ja 18,25:5

Harris, Jed (Director)
Uncle Vanya 1930,My 4,XI,1:1
Uncle Vanya 1930,S 23,30:3
Mr Gilhooley 1930,O 1,26:1
Wonder Boy 1931,O 24,20:1
Green Bay Tree, The 1933,O 21,11:5
Green Bay Tree, The 1933,O 29,IX,1:1
Lake, The 1933,D 27,24:2
Life's Too Short 1935,S 21,18:5
Doll's House, A 1937,D 28,28:6
Our Town 1938,Ja 23,II,10:6
Our Town 1938,F 5,18:3
Dark Eyes 1943,Ja 15,20:2

Harris, Jed (Director)—Cont
World's Full of Girls, The 1943,D 7,31:2
Our Town 1944,Ja 11,24:5
One-Man Show 1945,F 9,21:2
One-Man Show 1945,F 18,II,1:1
Apple of His Eye 1946,F 6,18:2
Loco 1946,O 17,29:2
Heiress, The 1947,S 30,22:2
Heiress, The 1947,O 5,II,1:1
Red Gloves 1948,D 6,28:2
Traitor, The 1949,Ap 1,30:2
Traitor, The 1949,Ap 10,II,1:1
Heiress, The 1950,F 9,34:2
Crucible, The 1953,Ja 23,15:2
Crucible, The 1953,F 1,II,1:1
Crucible, The 1953,Jl 2,20:2
Child of Fortune 1956,N 14,41:1
Harris, Jed (Producer)
Weak Sisters 1925,O 14,31:3
Love 'Em and Leave 'Em 1926,F 4,20:4
Broadway 1926,S 17,19:3
Spread Eagle 1927,Ap 5,30:2
Spread Eagle 1927,Ap 10,VIII,1:1
Coquette 1927,N 9,23:1
Coquette 1927,N 13,IX,1:1
Royal Family, The 1927,D 29,26:4
Royal Family, The 1928,Ja 8,VIII,1:1
Front Page, The 1928,Ag 15,19:2
Serena Blandish 1929,Ja 13,VIII,2:4
Serena Blandish 1929,Ja 24,30:3
Serena Blandish 1929,F 3,VIII,1:1
Uncle Vanya 1930,Ap 16,26:5
Uncle Vanya 1930,S 23,30:3
Mr Gilhooley 1930,O 1,26:1
Inspector General, The 1930,D 24,19:2
Wiser They Are, The 1931,Ap 7,31:1
Wonder Boy 1931,O 24,20:1
Fatal Alibi, The 1932,F 10,26:6
Green Bay Tree, The 1933,O 21,11:5
Green Bay Tree, The 1933,O 29,IX,1:1
Lake, The 1933,D 19,26:3
Lake, The 1933,D 27,24:2
Lake, The 1934,Ja 7,X,1:1
Life's Too Short 1935,S 21,18:5
Spring Dance 1936,Ag 26,17:4
Doll's House, A 1937,D 28,28:6
Our Town 1938,Ja 23,II,10:6
Our Town 1938,Ja 26,27:4
Our Town 1938,Ja 30,X,3:1
Our Town 1938,F 5,18:3
Our Town 1938,F 13,X,1:1
Dark Eyes 1943,Ja 15,20:2
Dark Eyes 1943,Ja 31,II,1:1
World's Full of Girls, The 1943,D 7,31:2
Our Town 1944,Ja 11,24:5
One-Man Show 1945,F 9,21:2
One-Man Show 1945,F 18,II,1:1
Apple of His Eye 1946,F 6,18:2
Our Town 1946,My 2,27:3
Loco 1946,O 17,29:2
Traitor, The 1949,Ap 1,30:2
Child of Fortune 1956,N 14,41:1
Harris, Jed (Scenic Designer)
Spring Dance 1936,Ag 26,17:4
Harris, Jeff
Mister Roberts 1956,D 6,46:2
Winesburg, Ohio 1958,F 6,22:2
Tall Story 1959,Ja 30,33:2
South Pacific 1961,Ap 27,26:3
Harris, Jeff (Composer)
Another Evening With Harry Stoones 1961,O 23,22:2
Harris, Jeff (Lyricist)
Another Evening With Harry Stoones 1961,O 23,22:2
Harris, Jeff (Playwright)
Another Evening With Harry Stoones 1961,O 23,22:2
That Thing at the Cherry Lane 1965,My 19,42:1
Harris, Joan
Cities in Bezique; Owl Answers, The 1969,Ja 13,26:1
Electra 1969,Ag 8,14:1
Harris, John
Our Town 1940,Je 30,35:5
Harris, John (Playwright)
Autumn Hill 1942,Ap 14,17:4
Harris, John H (Director)
Ice Capades 1952,S 12,18:1
Ice Capades 1953,S 11,25:1
Ice Capades 1960,S 1,30:1
Ice Capades 1961,Ag 31,24:4
Ice Capades 1962,Ag 30,34:1
Ice Capades 1963,Ag 29,37:2
Harris, John H (Lighting Director)
Ice Capades 1961,Ag 31,24:4
Harris, John H (Miscellaneous)
Ice Capades 1954,S 16,37:1
Harris, John H (Playwright)
Ice Capades 1953,S 11,25:1
Ice Capades 1956,S 13,41:2
Ice Capades 1957,S 5,33:2
Ice Capades 1960,S 1,30:1
Ice Capades 1961,Ag 31,24:4

Harris, John H (Producer)
Ice Capades 1952,S 12,18:1
Ice Capades 1953,S 11,25:1
Ice Capades 1955,S 15,38:1
Ice Capades 1956,S 13,41:2
Ice Capades 1957,S 5,33:2
Ice Capades 1958,S 4,33:2
Ice Capades 1959,S 4,12:1
Ice Capades 1960,S 1,30:1
Ice Capades 1961,Ag 31,24:4
Ice Capades 1962,Ag 30,34:1
Ice Capades 1963,Ag 29,37:2
Harris, Johnny
Prodigal Son, The 1965,My 21,19:1
Exception and the Rule, The 1965,My 21,19:1
But Never Jam Today 1969,Ap 24,40:1
Harris, Jonathan
Heart of a City 1942,F 13,24:6
Right Next to Broadway 1944,F 22,26:2
Flag Is Born, A 1946,S 7,10:6
Madwoman of Chaillot, The 1949,S 11,II,1:1
Madwoman of Chaillot, The 1950,Je 14,41:2
Grass Harp, The 1952,Mr 28,26:2
Hazel Flagg 1953,F 12,22:2
Harris, Jones (Miscellaneous)
Do Re Mi 1960,D 27,23:2
Harris, Jones (Producer)
Billygoat Eddie 1964,Ap 21,43:2
Harris, Joseph (Miscellaneous)
Tovarich 1963,Mr 20,5:1
Harris, Joseph (Producer)
Davy Jones's Locker 1959,Mr 30,25:1
Fig Leaves Are Falling, The 1969,Ja 3,19:1
Harris, Joseph P
All Good Americans 1933,D 6,29:2
Battleship Gertie 1935,Ja 19,9:2
Harris, Joseph P (Miscellaneous)
Georgy 1970,F 27,26:1
Harris, Joseph P (Producer)
Sweet Charity 1966,Ja 31,22:1
Mame 1966,My 25,41:1
Golden Rainbow 1968,F 5,27:1
Harris, Josephine
Guimpes and Saddles 1967,O 11,36:3
Harris, Julie
It's A Gift 1945,Mr 13,18:7
Playboy of the Western World, The 1946,O 28,18:3
Alice in Wonderland 1947,Ap 7,19:2
Sundown Beach 1948,S 8,37:1
Young and Fair, The 1948,N 23,35:2
Magnolia Alley 1949,Ap 19,29:2
Montserrat 1949,O 31,21:4
Member of the Wedding, The 1950,Ja 6,26:6
Member of the Wedding, The 1950,Ja 15,II,1:1
Member of the Wedding, The 1950,My 14,II,1:1
Member of the Wedding, The 1950,S 17,II,1:1
I Am a Camera 1951,N 29,39:6
I Am a Camera 1951,D 9,II,5:1
Mademoiselle Colombe 1954,Ja 7,26:1
Mademoiselle Colombe 1954,Ja 17,II,1:1
Lark, The 1955,N 18,20:1
Lark, The 1955,N 27,II,1:1
Lark, The 1956,Ja 8,II,3:1
Country Wife, The 1957,N 28,56:1
Warm Peninsula, The 1959,O 21,46:2
King John 1960,Je 29,26:2
Romeo and Juliet 1960,Jl 1,14:1
Little Moon of Alban 1960,D 2,34:1
Shot in the Dark, A 1961,O 19,40:1
Marathon '33 1963,D 23,20:1
Hamlet 1964,Je 17,49:1
Hamlet 1964,Je 18,28:1
Ready When You Are, C. B.! 1964,D 8,55:1
Skyscraper 1965,N 15,48:1
Forty Carats 1968,D 27,45:1
Forty Carats 1969,Ja 5,II,1:3
Harris, Julius W
Amen Corner, The 1965,Je 13,82:4
Bohikee Creek 1966,Ap 29,39:1
God Is a (Guess What?) 1968,D 18,56:1
String 1969,Ap 2,37:1
Man Better Man 1969,Jl 3,22:1
Harangues, The 1970,Ja 14,42:1
Harris, Kathryn
Don't Look Now! 1936,N 4,41:3
Harris, Lawrence (Miscellaneous)
Lysistrata 1959,My 20,40:2
Curtains Up! 1959,N 3,26:3
Harris, Leland Stanford
Hook'n Ladder 1952,Ap 30,31:2
Harris, Leonard
Don Carlos 1962,F 28,27:5
Harris, Leonore
Tyranny of Love, The 1921,My 3,20:2
Tyranny of Love, The 1921,My 8,VI,1:1
Bluebeard's Eighth Wife 1920,D 12:2
Crooked Square, The 1923,S 11,10:2
Far Cry, The 1924,O 1,24:1
Badges 1924,D 4,25:1
Creaking Chair, The 1926,F 23,26:1
Wooden Kimono 1926,D 28,16:2
Dodsworth 1934,F 26,20:4
Present Laughter 1946,O 30,31:2

Harris, Linda
Hamlet 1954,Ap 24,15:2
Put It in Writing 1963,My 14,31:1
Harris, Lloyd
Tempest, The 1955,S 3,8:6
Around the World in 80 Days 1963,Je 24,22:1
Around the World in 80 Days 1964,Je 29,33:2
Mardi Gras! 1965,Je 28,33:2
Oresteia 1966,Je 30,29:1
Birds, The 1966,Jl 1,40:1
Mike Downstairs 1968,Ap 19,35:1
Harris, Lord
Loyalties 1928,Ag 26,VII,1:3
Harris, Lowell
Twelfth Night 1954,N 10,42:2
West Side Story 1957,S 27,14:4
Romeo and Juliet 1959,Je 15,31:1
Merry Wives of Windsor, The 1959,Jl 9,23:2
Jo 1964,F 13,25:1
Blood Red Roses 1970,Mr 23,48:1
Harris, M H (Composer)
Who's Who 1924,Ap 18,19:2
Harris, Marcia
Adding Machine, The 1923,Mr 20,24:1
Harris, Margaret
Sambo 1970,Jl 23,24:1
Harris, Margaret (Musical Director)
Harangues, The 1970,Ja 14,42:1
Sambo 1970,Jl 23,24:1
Harris, Marion
Vaudeville (Palace) 1926,Jl 27,15:4
Vaudeville (Palace) 1926,Ag 3,19:2
Yours Truly 1927,Ja 26,16:5
Vaudeville (Palace) 1927,Jl 26,16:5
Vaudeville (Palace) 1928,Mr 27,30:5
Vaudeville (Palace) 1928,D 24,10:8
Great Day! 1929,Je 9,VIII,1:2
Vaudeville (Palace) 1930,D 29,19:3
Vaudeville (Palace) 1931,Ja 5,20:3
Harris, Mark (Original Author)
Something About a Soldier 1962,Ja 5,36:2
Harris, Mildred
Vaudeville (Palace) 1923,F 13,25:1
Harris, Mildred (Playwright)
Co-Respondent Unknown 1936,F 12,24:4
Harris, Mimi
Here Come the Clowns 1960,S 20,48:1
Harris, Mitchell
Shavings 1920,F 17,18:1
Love's Call 1925,S 11,20:1
Trouper, The 1926,Mr 9,21:1
World Waits, The 1933,O 26,22:5
Halfway to Hell 1934,Ja 3,22:3
Too Many Boats 1934,S 12,26:3
If This Be Treason 1935,Jl 30,17:1
If This Be Treason 1935,S 24,28:2
May Wine 1935,D 6,30:3
Puritan, The 1936,Ja 24,14:3
Johnny on the Spot 1942,Ja 9,24:2
Comes the Revelation 1942,My 27,26:2
One-Man Show 1945,F 9,21:2
Harris, Nat (Playwright)
Tin Waltz 1954,Ap 23,23:2
Harris, Natalie
Doctor Faustus 1937,Ja 9,21:2
Russian Bank 1940,My 25,20:2
City of Kings 1949,F 18,27:2
Harris, Orville
Scarlet Fox, The 1928,Mr 28,31:1
Merry Andrew 1929,Ja 22,22:2
So Was Napoleon 1930,Ja 9,22:2
Last Mile, The 1930,F 14,21:2
Late One Evening 1933,Ja 10,27:3
Harris, Paul
Free and Easy 1959,D 15,51:4
Harris, Pearl
Nautical but Nice 1931,Ap 19,31:6
Harris, Peggy (Costume Designer)
Doctor's Dilemma, The 1941,Mr 12,18:2
Harris, Peter
Corn Is Green, The 1943,My 4,18:3
Male Animal, The 1952,My 1,35:1
Richard III 1953,D 10,65:2
God, Man & You, Baby! 1963,O 30,47:1
Harris, Philip
America Hurrah; Interview; TV; Motel 1967,O 10,55:2
Twelfth Night 1969,Ag 14,29:2
Harris, R J
Port-Royal 1960,Ap 26,41:1
Harris, Ralph
Pansy 1929,My 15,36:3
Harris, Rhett
Young and Beautiful, The 1959,My 29,13:1
Harris, Richard
Guys and Dolls 1968,S 2,14:2
Harris, Richard W (Playwright)
Fourth Pig, The 1965,Ja 27,24:6
Fisherman, The 1965,Ja 27,24:6
Harris, Robert
Easy Virtue 1925,D 8,28:2
Sacred Flame, The 1928.N 20,28:2
Humours of the Court, The 1930,Ja 26,VIII,1:8

Harris, Robert—Cont

Yoshe Kalb 1933,D 29,27:2
Promise 1936,Mr 22,XI,1:7
Bitter Stream 1936,Mr 31,16:6
Happy Valley, Limited 1936,Je 30,15:1
They Knew What They Wanted 1936,Jl 8,14:2
Aged 26 1936,D 22,32:1
Candida 1937,Mr 11,20:2
Mourning Becomes Electra 1937,D 12,XI,3:8
Marco Millions 1939,Ja 15,IX,3:1
After the Dance 1939,Jl 16,IX,2:3
King Lear 1940,Ap 28,IX,1:7
Oedipus Rex 1945,D 17,16:7
Edwina Black 1950,N 22,20:5
Forty Years On 1970,Ag 30,II,1:1

Harris, Robert H

Many Mansions 1937,Ag 3,20:5
Schoolhouse on the Lot 1938,Mr 23,18:4
Tell My Story 1939,Mr 16,26:6
Any Day Now 1941,Je 10,28:2
Brooklyn, U S A 1941,D 22,24:2
Look, Ma, I'm Dancin' 1948,Ja 30,20:2
Richard III 1949,F 9,33:2
Foxy 1964,F 17,26:1
Minor Miracle 1965,O 8,4:3
Xmas in Las Vegas 1965,N 5,31:1

Harris, Rosalind

Now 1968,Je 6,53:1
Fiddler on the Roof 1970,F 28,20:1

Harris, Rosemary

Climate of Eden, The 1952,N 7,20:2
Climate of Eden, The 1952,N 16,II,1:1
Troilus and Cressida 1956,D 27,21:1
Interlock 1958,F 7,18:1
Disenchanted, The 1958,D 4,53:4
Disenchanted, The 1959,Ja 11,II,1:1
Tumbler, The 1960,F 25,32:2
School for Scandal, The 1962,Mr 19,36:1
Seagull, The 1962,Mr 22,42:1
Tavern, The 1962,Ap 5,29:1
Chances, The 1962,Jl 4,11:2
Broken Heart, The 1962,Jl 10,28:2
We Comrades Three 1962,O 12,26:1
Uncle Vanya 1963,Jl 2,16:2
Man and Superman 1964,D 7,45:2
War and Peace 1965,Ja 12,32:1
War and Peace 1965,Ja 31,II,1:1
Man and Superman 1965,Ja 31,II,1:1
Judith 1965,Mr 25,42:2
Judith 1965,Ap 4,II,1:1
You Can't Take It With You 1965,N 24,32:1
You Can't Take It With You 1965,D 5,II,5:1
Lion in Winter, The 1966,Mr 4,23:1
Lion in Winter, The 1966,Mr 13,II,1:1
School for Scandal, The 1966,N 22,33:2
Right You Are (If You Think You Are)
  1966,D 11,II,3:1
School for Scandal, The 1966,D 11,II,3:1
War and Peace 1967,Mr 22,42:1
War and Peace 1967,Ap 2,II,1:1
Idiot's Delight 1970,Mr 24,39:1

Harris, Ruth (Choreographer)

Brothers Karamazov, The 1957,D 9,39:4

Harris, Sam H (Miscellaneous)

Easy Come, Easy Go 1925,O 27,20:2
Sandalwood 1926,S 23,23:1
Save Me the Waltz 1938,Mr 1,19:2

Harris, Sam H (Producer)

Mary Queen of Scots 1921,F 6,VI,1:2
Turn in the Road, A 1921,Je 12,VI,1:6
Six-Cylinder Love 1921,Jl 24,VI,1:1
It's a Boy! 1922,Jl 23,VI,1:6
Rain 1922,O 15,VIII,1:8
Horse-Thief, The 1924,Ap 27,VIII,2:3
Lazybones 1924,Je 1,VII,4:3
Lazybones 1924,S 23,23:1
In His Arms 1924,O 14,23:1
Nervous Wreck, The 1924,O 19,VIII,2:1
Money Lender, The 1924,N 23,VIII,2:4
Music Box Revue 1924,D 2,23:3
Cradle Snatchers 1925,S 8,28:2
Paid 1925,N 26,32:1
Cocoanuts, The 1925,D 9,30:1
Fever of Youth, The 1926,Ag 8,VII,3:1
Unsophisticates 1926,Ag 8,VII,3:1
We Americans 1926,O 13,20:4
Gentle Grafters 1926,O 28,23:1
Loose Ends 1926,N 2,34:2
Chicago 1926,D 31,11:1
Spider, The 1927,Mr 23,29:1
Big Fight, The 1928,S 19,33:1
War Song, The 1928,S 25,29:3
Animal Crackers 1928,O 24,26:2
Congai 1928,N 28,24:3
Marriage Bed, The 1929,Ja 8,35:1
June Moon 1929,O 10,34:5
Amorous Antic, The 1929,D 3,29:2
Once in a Lifetime 1930,S 25,22:3
Oh, Promise Me 1930,N 25,31:1
Just to Remind You 1931,S 8,39:1
Of Thee I Sing 1931,D 13,VIII,2:4
Of Thee I Sing 1931,D 28,20:1
Face the Music 1932,F 18,24:5
Of Thee I Sing 1932,My 8,VIII,1:1

Here Today 1932,S 7,14:2
Dinner at Eight 1932,O 24,18:2
For Services Rendered 1933,Ap 13,15:5
As Thousands Cheer 1933,O 2,22:1
Let 'Em Eat Cake 1933,O 23,18:1
Dark Tower, The 1933,N 27,20:3
Merrily We Roll Along 1934,O 1,14:1
Rain 1935,F 13,24:1
Jubilee 1935,S 23,20:3
Jubilee 1935,S 29,X,1:1
Jubilee 1935,O 14,20:1
Room Service 1935,N 17,II,7:7
First Lady 1935,N 27,17:4
As We Forgive Our Debtors 1936,Ag 11,24:6
Night Must Fall 1936,S 29,34:1
Stage Door 1936,S 29,35:1
Stage Door 1936,O 23,26:3
You Can't Take It With You 1936,D 15,31:1
Fulton of Oak Falls 1937,Ja 2,15:3
Fulton of Oak Falls 1937,F 11,18:2
I'd Rather Be Right 1937,O 12,27:6
I'd Rather Be Right 1937,N 3,28:2
Of Mice and Men 1937,N 24,20:5
Of Mice and Men 1937,D 12,XI,3:1
Fabulous Invalid, The 1938,O 10,15:1
American Way, The 1939,Ja 23,9:2
Man Who Came to Dinner, The 1939,O 1,IX,2:5
Man Who Came to Dinner, The 1939,O 17,31:1
Man Who Came to Dinner, The 1940,F 10,19:5
George Washington Slept Here 1940,O 19,20:3
Lady in the Dark 1941,Ja 5,IX,1:7
Lady in the Dark 1941,Ja 24,14:2

Harris, Sammie

Charm 1929,N 29,24:5

Harris, Sara Lee

Sons and Soldiers 1943,My 5,22:2
Boy Meets Girl 1943,Je 23,15:5

Harris, Sara Lou

Shuffle Along 1952,My 9,20:5

Harris, Sayre

Servant of Two Masters, The 1958,F 11,35:2

Harris, Stacy

Song Out of Sorrow 1941,D 12,34:5
Sound of Hunting, A 1945,N 21,16:6

Harris, Stephen

Journey With Strangers, A 1958,N 27,53:1
Backlane Center 1961,N 23,51:1

Harris, Susan

Long Days, The 1951,Ap 21,10:5
Point of No Return 1951,D 14,35:2

Harris, Susan (Miscellaneous)

Mummers and Men 1962,Mr 27,41:6

Harris, Sylvia (Producer)

Make a Million 1958,O 24,39:2
Tovarich 1963,Mr 20,5:1

Harris, Ted

Amedee: or, How to Disentangle Yourself
  1955,N 1,27:3
Red, White and Maddox 1969,Ja 27,27:1

Harris, Ted (Composer)

Meet Peter Grant 1961,My 11,41:4

Harris, Ted (Playwright)

Silhouettes 1969,S 9,41:1

Harris, Ted (Producer)

Spring Dance 1936,Jl 7,22:2

Harris, Terry

Two on an Island 1940,Ja 23,17:2
New Life, A 1943,S 16,26:6

Harris, Thomas

York Nativity Play, The 1956,D 5,49:2

Harris, Timmy (Lighting Director)

Kataki 1959,D 16,55:1
Tempest, The 1959,D 28,19:2
Come Slowly, Eden 1966,D 7,56:1

Harris, Tom

Vaudeville (Palace) 1931,Mr 2,19:2

Harris, W C

1776 1926,Ap 24,11:2
Gentlemen, the Queen 1927,Ap 23,14:3

Harris, W C (Composer)

1776 1926,Ap 24,11:2

Harris, Walter

Berlin 1931,D 31,16:1

Harris, Walter (Composer)

Give My Regards to Off Off Broadway
  1966,D 9,57:1

Harris, William

Porgy and Bess 1964,My 7,32:1

Harris, William (Producer)

Two Married Men 1925,Ja 14,19:1

Harris, William Howard (Playwright)

Greater Lust, The 1936,Jl 14,22:4

Harris, William Jr (Director)

Distant Drum, A 1928,Ja 21,13:1
Criminal Code, The 1929,O 3,28:2
Greeks Had a Word for It, The 1930,S 26,16:5
Three and One 1933,O 26,22:6
Substitute for Murder 1935,O 23,18:6
Silk Hat Harry 1943,Ag 22,II,1:6

Harris, William Jr (Producer)

Bad Man, The 1921,O 2,VII,1:3
Outward Bound 1924,Ja 8,26:1
Outward Bound 1924,Ja 13,VII,1:1

Harris, William Jr (Producer)—Cont

Outsider, The 1924,Mr 4,16:4
Sour Grapes 1926,S 7,19:1
Distant Drum, A 1928,Ja 21,13:1
Criminal Code, The 1929,O 3,28:2
Abraham Lincoln 1929,O 22,26:3
Greeks Had a Word for It, The 1930,S 26,16:5
Three and One 1933,O 26,22:6
Substitute for Murder 1935,O 23,18:6
Miss Swan Expects 1939,F 21,15:2
Silk Hat Harry 1943,Ag 22,II,1:6

Harris, Winifred

Squaw Man, The 1921,D 27,10:3
Sally, Irene and Mary 1922,S 5,21:2
Little Jessie James 1923,Ag 16,10:4
Far Cry, The 1924,S 28,VII,2:1
Far Cry, The 1924,O 1,24:1
June Days 1925,Ag 7,12:5
Tale of the Wolf, The 1925,O 8,31:2
Last of Mrs Cheyney, The 1925,N 10,23:5
Sidewalks of New York 1927,O 4,33:1
High Road, The 1928,S 11,31:1
So This Is Paris 1930,Ap 27,IX,2:3
Life Begins 1932,N 29,23:2
Late One Evening 1933,Ja 10,27:3
Party, A 1933,Ag 24,18:4
While Parents Sleep 1934,Je 5,28:2
Life Begins at 8:40 1934,Ag 28,24:2

Harris (Scenic Designer)

Hassan 1923,O 14,VIII,2:6

Harris and Holley

Vaudeville (Palace) 1926,S 28,30:4

Harris and Radcliffe

Vaudeville (Palace) 1929,F 11,26:2
Vaudeville (Palace) 1929,Mr 25,33:2
Vaudeville (Palace) 1929,Jl 8,17:6
Vaudeville (Palace) 1929,Jl 15,25:4

Harris and Shore

Blackouts of 1949 1949,S 7,39:2

Harrison, Adele

Steps Leading Up 1941,Ap 19,20:6

Harrison, Al

Good Times 1920,Ag 10,10:1

Harrison, Alfred

Promis' Lan', De 1930,My 28,31:2

Harrison, B J (Costume Designer)

Lower Depths, The 1956,O 3,29:2

Harrison, Bertram (Director)

Best People, The 1924,Ag 20,8:1
Kiss in a Taxi, The 1925,Ag 26,14:1
Potash and Perlmutter, Detectives; Poisoned by
  Pictures 1926,S 1,27:3
Matrimonial Bed, The 1927,O 13,23:2
Skin Deep 1927,O 18,32:1
Behavior of Mrs Crane, The 1928,Mr 21,30:1
Say When 1928,Je 27,29:3
Heavy Traffic 1928,S 6,23:3
Treasure Girl 1928,N 9,22:1
Singin' the Blues 1931,S 17,21:3
Hot Money 1931,N 9,22:2
Keeping Expenses Down 1932,O 21,25:2
Red Cat, The 1934,S 20,21:1
Just Suppose 1935,Jl 2,24:3
Swing Your Lady 1936,O 19,22:4
Around the Corner 1936,D 29,17:2
Miss Quis 1937,Ap 8,20:5
30 Days Hath September 1938,O 1,10:5

Harrison, Bertram (Producer)

Buy, Buy Baby 1926,O 8,26:2

Harrison, Betty

Aquashow 1953,Je 24,29:2
Aquashow 1954,Je 23,20:4

Harrison, Bob

Volpone 1948,Ja 9,24:6

Harrison, Charles

This One Man 1930,O 22,32:3
Precedent 1931,Ap 15,24:5
S..llout, The 1933,S 7,17:2
One More Honeymoon 1934,Ap 2,13:5

Harrison, Dennis

Seven Mirrors 1945,O 26,17:2
Derryowen 1946,O 29,34:2
Cock-A-Doodle-Doo 1949,F 28,16:5

Harrison, Dorothy

New Pins and Needles 1939,N 21,19:2

Harrison, Edward

Earl Carroll's Vanities 1930,Jl 2,28:3

Harrison, Francis

Susannah and the Elders 1940,O 30,28:2

Harrison, Frank

Deep River 1926,O 5,26:2
Saint Joan 1950,Mr 4,10:6

Harrison, Frederick (Producer)

Mary Rose 1920,My 16,VI,1:7

Harrison, Geneva

Taming of the Shrew, The 1921,My 12,20:2
Merchant of Venice, The 1921,My 14,10:4
Love Child, The 1922,N 15,22:1
Polly 1925,O 12,19:1
Shelter 1926,Ja 28,18:2
Caprice 1929,Ja 1,61:1
Mr Samuel 1930,N 11,28:4

Harrison, Harold

Nautical but Nice 1931,Ap 19,31:6

Harrison, Jean
Phaedra 1967,My 22,50:2
Harrison, Joan
Trial, The 1955,Je 15,35:2
Harrison, John
South 1955,My 2,17:4
Harrison, Kathleen
Waters of the Moon 1953,Ap 2,34:3
Chances, The 1962,Jl 4,11:2
Harrison, Lanny
Moondreamers, The 1969,D 9,68:1
Harrison, Louis
Madame Pompadour 1924,N 12,20:6
Sunny 1925,S 23,22:1
Harrison, M
Wonderful Town 1967,My 18,50:1
Harrison, Michael
Get Thee to Canterbury 1969,Ja 26,74:1
Harrison, Muriel
Good Morning, Dearie 1921,N 2,20:2
Harrison, Neil
Hill Between, The 1938,Mr 12,12:5
Crucible, The 1953,Jl 2,20:2
Harrison, Nell
Precedent 1931,Ap 15,24:5
How Beautiful With Shoes 1935,N 29,24:1
Native Son 1941,Mr 25,26:5
Candle in the Wind 1941,O 23,26:2
Native Son 1942,O 24,10:6
Last Stop 1944,S 6,17:2
Orpheus Descending 1957,Mr 22,28:1
Ballad of the Sad Cafe, The 1963,O 31,27:1
Harrison, Pat (Miscellaneous)
Oh, Kay! 1960,Ap 18,37:2
Harrison, Patrick
Persecution and Assassination of Marat As Performed by the Inmates of the Asylum of Charenton Under the Direction of the Marquis de Sade, The 1967,Ja 4,34:1
Harrison, Pendleton
Silver Tassie, The 1929,O 25,26:1
Everything's Jake 1930,Ja 17,20:4
London Assurance 1937,F 19,14:5
As You Like It 1937,N 1,25:2
Man Who Killed Lincoln, The 1940,Ja 18,26:4
Harrison, Penn
Steps Leading Up 1941,Ap 19,20:6
Harrison, R A
Simple Life, A 1964,My 18,36:1
Harrison, Ray
Banjo Eyes 1941,D 26,20:2
On the Town 1944,D 29,11:4
Allegro 1947,O 11,10:2
Make Mine Manhattan 1948,Ja 16,26:2
Make Mine Manhattan 1948,F 8,II,2:1
Out of This World 1950,D 22,17:3
Harrison, Ray (Choreographer)
Naughty-Naught '00 1946,O 21,27:5
Kiss Me, Kate 1956,My 10,27:2
Portofino 1958,F 22,8:3
Come Play With Me 1959,My 1,33:5
Little Mary Sunshine 1959,N 19,49:3
From A to Z 1960,Ap 21,23:2
O Say Can You See! 1962,O 9,45:1
Student Gypsy, The; Prince of Liederkranz, The 1963,O 1,34:1
Harrison, Ray (Director)
Little Mary Sunshine 1959,N 19,49:3
Little Mary Sunshine 1959,N 29,II,1:1
O Say Can You See! 1962,O 9,45:1
Harrison, Rex
Anthony and Anna 1934,N 13,22:2
Sweet Aloes 1936,F 25,23:5
Sweet Aloes 1936,Mr 5,24:5
Anne of the Thousand Days 1948,D 9,49:2
Anne of the Thousand Days 1948,D 19,II,3:1
Anne of the Thousand Days 1949,S 18,II,1:1
ANTA Album 1950,Ja 30,13:2
Cocktail Party, The 1950,My 4,33:2
Cocktail Party, The 1950,My 7,II,2:5
Cocktail Party, The 1950,My 21,II,3:2
Bell, Book and Candle 1950,N 15,37:4
Bell, Book and Candle 1950,D 17,II,3:1
Venus Observed 1952,F 14,24:2
Venus Observed 1952,F 24,II,1:1
Love of Four Colonels, The 1953,Ja 16,17:2
Bell, Book and Candle 1954,O 6,30:8
My Fair Lady 1956,Mr 16,20:2
My Fair Lady 1956,Mr 25,II,1:1
My Fair Lady 1956,Je 3,II,1:1
My Fair Lady 1958,My 1,34:5
My Fair Lady 1958,My 4,II,3:1
Fighting Cock, The 1959,D 9,57:3
Fighting Cock, The 1959,D 20,II,3:1
August for the People 1961,S 5,41:6
Lionel Touch, The 1969,N 6,57:2
Harrison, Rex (Director)
Love of Four Colonels, The 1953,Ja 16,17:2
Harrison, Richard B
Green Pastures, The 1930,F 27,26:1
Green Pastures, The 1930,Mr 9,IX,1:1
Green Pastures, The 1931,Mr 1,VIII,1:1
Green Pastures, The 1933,O 5,24:5

Green Pastures, The 1933,O 22,IX,1:6
Green Pastures, The 1935,F 27,16:2
Green Pastures, The 1935,Mr 24,VIII,1:1
Harrison, Robert
Blue Bonnet 1920,Ag 30,12:1
Samson and Delilah 1920,N 18,18:1
Bride, The 1924,My 6,25:1
Complex, The 1925,Mr 4,17:2
Caught 1925,O 6,31:2
Honor of the Family, The 1926,D 27,21:1
Squealer, The 1928,N 13,36:3
Sweet Land of Liberty 1929,S 24,29:2
Cortez 1929,N 5,32:2
Melo 1931,Ap 17,26:6
Merchant of Venice, The 1931,N 9,22:2
Nine Pine Street 1933,Ap 28,15:5
Move on, Sister 1933,O 25,22:4
Tight Britches 1934,S 12,26:2
Ragged Edge, The 1935,N 26,28:3
Woman of Destiny, A 1936,Mr 3,25:2
Kick Back, The 1936,Je 23,27:3
It Can't Happen Here 1936,O 28,30:1
Eternal Road, The 1937,Ja 8,14:2
Father Malachy's Miracle 1937,N 18,26:4
Jeremiah 1939,F 4,11:2
Popsy 1941,F 11,26:2
Candle in the Wind 1941,O 23,26:2
Willow and I, The 1942,D 11,32:2
Harriet 1943,Mr 4,24:2
According to Law 1944,Je 2,20:3
Harriet 1944,S 28,26:1
Tempest, The 1945,N 13,24:6
Christopher Blake 1946,D 2,33:2
Alexander Hamilton 1949,Mr 30,29:2
Tower Beyond Tragedy, The 1950,N 27,29:1
Come of Age 1952,Ja 24,22:2
Harrison, Ruth
Bird Cage, The 1925,Je 3,26:2
Strike Me Pink 1933,Mr 6,16:3
Vaudeville (Palladium) 1935,O 30,16:8
Ziegfeld Follies 1936,S 15,37:1
Would-Be Gentleman, The 1946,Ja 10,29:2
Song of Norway 1959,Je 26,16:2
Harrison, Stanley
As You Were 1920,Ja 28,22:3
Whispering Wires 1922,Ag 8,26:2
Creaking Chair, The 1926,F 23,26:1
Circus Princess, The 1927,Ap 26,32:2
Midsummer Night's Dream, A 1927,Je 27,25:1
Mulberry Bush, The 1927,O 27,33:1
Jade God, The 1929,My 14,28:3
Artists and Models 1930,Je 11,33:2
New Yorkers, The 1930,D 9,31:1
Payment Deferred 1931,O 1,24:2
$25 an Hour 1933,My 11,14:4
School for Husbands, The 1933,O 17,26:5
First Episode 1934,S 18,18:1
Music Hath Charms 1934,D 31,8:2
Theatre 1941,O 26,IX,2:3
Theatre 1941,N 13,34:2
Magic 1942,S 30,28:2
Harrison, Stephen
Triumph of Robert Emmet, The 1969,My 8,54:1
Harrison, Susan
Cave Dwellers, The 1957,O 21,29:2
Cave Dwellers, The 1957,O 27,II,1:1
Harrison, Victor
Drums of Jeopardy, The 1922,My 30,8:4
Harrison, William H
Fiesta 1933,D 16,12:2
Harrison and Fisher
Lunchtime Follies, The 1942,Je 23,22:3
New Priorities of 1943 1942,S 16,28:2
Harrison and Kossi
Elliott Murphy's Aquashow 1955,Je 23,25:1
Harriss, Wayne (Producer)
Gambler, The 1952,O 14,40:1
Harritan, David
Road to Rio, The 1930,My 7,25:1
Harriton, Maria
Million Dollar Baby 1945,D 22,17:2
Harrity, Richard (Playwright)
Hope Is the Thing With Feathers 1948,Ap 12,24:2
Harrity, Rory
Look After Lulu 1959,Mr 4,35:1
Fourth Avenue North 1961,S 28,50:2
Harrold, Jack
Vamp, The 1955,N 11,30:1
Unsinkable Molly Brown, The 1960,N 4,28:1
Good Woman of Setzuan, The 1970,N 6,51:1
Harrold, John
Merry Widow, The 1944,O 9,17:1
Mr Strauss Goes to Boston 1945,S 7,20:2
Harrold, Orville
Holka Polka 1925,O 15,27:2
Vaudeville (Palace) 1927,Mr 1,31:2
Harrold, Patti
Glory 1922,D 26,10:1
Big Boy 1925,Ja 8,28:2
Holka Polka 1925,O 15,27:2
Vaudeville (Palace) 1927,Mr 1,31:2
Harrold, William
Cicero 1961,F 9,37:2

Harron, Donald
Sleep of Prisoners, A 1951,O 17,36:2
All's Well That Ends Well 1953,Jl 16,18:2
Measure for Measure 1954,Je 30,23:1
Taming of the Shrew, The 1954,Jl 1,22:2
Home Is the Hero 1954,S 23,42:2
Dark Is Light Enough, The 1955,F 24,20:1
Merchant of Venice, The 1955,Jl 1,13:1
King John 1956,Je 28,33:5
Measure for Measure 1956,Je 29,16:1
Taming of the Shrew, The 1956,Ag 6,20:1
Separate Tables 1956,O 26,33:1
Merchant of Venice, The 1957,Jl 11,19:5
Much Ado About Nothing 1957,Ag 8,15:2
Tenth Man, The 1959,N 6,24:2
Tenth Man, The 1959,N 15,II,1:1
As You Like It 1961,Je 17,13:2
Macbeth 1961,Je 19,31:1
As You Like It 1961,Je 25,II,1:1
Troilus and Cressida 1961,Jl 24,15:1
Everybody Loves Opal 1961,O 12,40:2
King Lear 1962,Ag 14,35:1
Harron, Donald (Playwright)
Broken Jug, The 1958,Ap 2,36:1
Anne 1965,Ag 22,82:2
Anne of Green Gables 1969,Ap 18,39:1
Anne of Green Gables 1969,Ag 25,41:1
Harron, Peter (Producer)
Good Day 1965,O 19,51:1
Exhaustion of Our Son's Love, The 1965,O 19,51:1
Harroun, Hazel
Main Line, The 1924,Mr 26,19:4
Harrow, Bruce (Costume Designer)
Bacchants, The 1967,F 25,14:1
Harrow, Bruce (Miscellaneous)
Tiny Alice 1969,S 30,42:1
Harrow, Charles (Producer)
Before I Wake 1968,O 14,56:1
Harrow, Donald
Julius Caesar 1955,Je 29,23:3
King Lear 1964,Jl 28,18:2
Harrow, Joseph
Paul Bunyan 1941,My 6,25:1
Harrow, Joseph (Producer)
Mystery of Theodosia Burr, The 1947,Mr 10,24:7
Harrow, Lisa
Twelfth Night 1969,S 1,13:1
Harrow, Ronda
Doll's House, A 1954,N 15,32:2
Harry, Curtis
Stevedore 1949,F 23,30:2
Freight 1950,Ap 27,36:2
Harry, Master
Fatal Wedding, The 1924,Je 3,22:3
Harryett, Miss
Revue des Femmes Nouvelles, La 1926,D 5,VIII,6:1
Harryman, Elizabeth
Children in the Rain 1970,O 3,14:1
Harsanyi, Zsolt
Fires in the Night 1928,D 2,X,4:7
Harsanyi, Zsolt (Playwright)
Case of the Noszty Boy and Mary Toth, The 1927,Mr 20,VIII,4:3
Cuckoo Clock, The 1927,O 30,IX,4:1
Siege of Besztercze, The 1929,F 3,VIII,2:1
Harsfai, Gustav
Davy Jones's Locker 1966,D 25,48:5
Harshbarger, Karl
Bacchae, The 1963,Ap 25,39:5
Hart, Anita (Playwright)
In The Best of Families 1931,F 3,29:1
In the Best of Families 1937,Jl 1,32:5
Hart, Annie
Show Boat 1927,D 28,26:1
Vaudeville (Palace) 1931,Mr 2,19:2
Show Boat 1932,My 20,22:2
Hart, Audrey
Why Men Leave Home 1922,S 13,18:2
Connie Goes Home 1923,S 7,10:1
Out of the Seven Seas 1923,N 20,23:3
Hart, Bernard (Miscellaneous)
Christopher Blake 1946,D 2,33:2
Hart, Bernard (Producer)
Evening With Cecilia Loftus, An 1938,Mr 28,19:2
????? 1939,Ja 2,28:2
Dear Ruth 1944,D 14,29:2
Secret Room, The 1945,N 8,16:2
Survivors, The 1948,Ja 20,27:2
Light Up the Sky 1948,N 19,34:2
Climate of Eden, The 1952,N 7,20:2
Room Service 1953,Ap 7,34:1
Anniversary Waltz 1954,Ap 8,34:1
Hart, Bernice
Silks and Satins 1920,Jl 16,19:1
Bombo 1921,O 7,20:2
Ziegfeld Follies 1923,Ja 30,12:2
Hart, Bertha
Far-Away Corner, A 1939,F 15,15:2
Hart, Charles
Lambs Gambol 1925,Ap 27,15:1
Girofle-Girofla 1926,N 24,26:2
Sing Out, Sweet Land! 1944,D 28,24:2
Iceman Cometh, The 1946,O 10,31:3

Hart, Charles—Cont
Silver Whistle, The 1948,N 25,49:2
Oklahoma! 1953,S 1,19:1
Hart, David
Pursuit of Happiness, The 1933,O 10,24:4
Hart, Diane
Yes, M'Lord 1949,O 5,35:2
Hart, Dolores
Pleasure of His Company, The 1958,O 23,36:1
Pleasure of His Company, The 1958,N 2,II,1:1
Hart, Edward
Bystander 1937,S 15,27:1
Hart, Edward S (Producer)
Family Affair, A 1946,N 28,41:2
Hart, Elizabeth (Playwright)
Where Angels Fear to Tread 1963,Je 8,14:6
Hart, Ervil
Maid in the Ozarks 1946,Jl 16,20:3
Hart, Ethel
Mikado, The 1924,Jl 29,9:1
Hart, Everett (Miscellaneous)
Black-Eyed Susan 1954,D 24,7:5
Hart, Florence
Damn the Tears 1927,Ja 22,11:1
Hart, Frances Noyes (Original Author)
Bellamy Trial, The 1931,Ap 23,28:6
Hart, Frances Noyes (Playwright)
Bellamy Trial, The 1928,Ag 20,21:1
Bellamy Trial, The 1931,Ap 23,28:6
Hart, George Drury
Firebrand, The 1924,O 16,33:1
New York 1927,N 15,26:2
Divorce a la Carte 1928,Mr 27,30:3
Tired Business Man, The 1929,Je 5,32:5
On the Spot 1930,O 30,33:3
Hart, Gordon
Hamlet 1925,O 12,19:2
Merchant of Venice, The 1925,D 28,12:1
Immortal Thief, The 1926,O 4,21:1
Hamlet 1928,Ja 5,33:2
Henry V 1928,Mr 16,26:2
Light of Asia, The 1928,O 10,32:2
Becky Sharp 1929,Je 4,29:1
Bonds of Interest, The 1929,O 15,34:2
Richelieu 1929,D 26,20:3
Troilus and Cressida 1932,Je 7,22:3
Cyrano de Bergerac 1932,D 27,11:2
Hart, Hariot
Heartbreak House 1950,Mr 22,33:2
Hart, Harrison
Awakening of Spring, The 1964,My 13,50:1
Hart, Harry
Sing for Your Supper 1939,Ap 25,18:6
Hart, Henry
Respectfully Yours 1947,My 14,29:4
G-II 1948,My 28,27:3
With a Silk Thread 1950,Ap 13,34:3
Man and Superman 1953,F 21,11:2
Girl Can Tell, A 1953,O 30,28:2
Hart, Howard (Playwright)
Noontide 1961,Je 2,37:1
Cayenne Pepper 1961,D 13,55:5
Grand Vizier, The 1961,D 13,55:5
Hart, Irene
Silks and Satins 1920,Jl 16,19:1
Bombo 1921,O 7,20:2
Hart, Jean
New Cambridge Circus, The 1965,Ja 15,22:2
Hart, Jeanne
Red Harvest 1937,Mr 31,29:2
There's Always a Breeze 1938,Mr 3,16:2
Hart, Jerry
Nemesis 1921,Ap 5,24:3
Exciters, The 1922,S 23,10:4
Hart, Jewel
Bright Honor 1936,S 28,14:1
Audition of the Apprentice Theatre 1939,Je 2,26:2
Once Upon a Time 1939,D 21,28:2
Hart, John Patrick
Guide, The 1968,Mr 7,50:1
Hart, Josephine
Tenth Man, The 1929,Mr 21,29:2
Hart, Josie
Passing of the Third Floor Back, The 1928,Ja 17,22:7
Passing of the Third Floor Back, The 1928,F 21,18:2
Hart, June
Streamline 1934,O 21,IX,1:3
Laughter Over Broadway 1939,Ja 16,10:3
Hart, Justina
Fool's Bells 1925,D 24,8:3
Hart, Kathleen
On Location 1937,S 28,19:1
Hart, Larry
Hole in the Head, A 1957,Mr 1,15:1
Hart, Lorenz (Director)
Blonde Beast, The 1923,Mr 3,9:3
Hart, Lorenz (Lyricist)
Fly With Me 1920,Mr 25,11:4
Poor Little Ritz Girl 1920,Jl 29,7:1
You'll Never Know 1921,Ap 21,9:2
Bad Habits of 1925 1925,F 9,17:1
Garrick Gaieties 1925,My 18,12:2

Dearest Enemy 1925,S 19,9:2
Girl Friend, The 1926,Mr 18,26:5
Garrick Gaieties 1926,My 11,25:2
Peggy-Ann 1926,D 28,16:3
Betsy 1926,D 29,24:3
Connecticut Yankee, A 1927,O 9,VIII,1:3
Connecticut Yankee, A 1927,N 4,24:2
She's My Baby 1928,Ja 4,22:2
Present Arms 1928,Ap 27,16:2
Chee-Chee 1928,S 26,25:1
Spring Is Here 1929,Mr 12,26:1
Me for You 1929,S 22,IX,2:6
Heads Up! 1929,N 12,34:1
Simple Simon 1930,F 19,22:1
America's Sweetheart 1931,F 11,23:1
Simple Simon 1931,Mr 10,23:2
Jumbo 1935,N 18,20:2
Jumbo 1935,N 24,IX,1:1
On Your Toes 1936,Ap 13,14:4
Babes in Arms 1937,Ap 15,18:4
Show Is On, The 1937,S 20,18:4
I'd Rather Be Right 1937,O 12,27:6
I'd Rather Be Right 1937,O 17,XI,2:1
I'd Rather Be Right 1937,N 3,28:2
I'd Rather Be Right 1937,N 14,XI,1:1
I Married an Angel 1938,My 12,26:2
Boys From Syracuse, The 1938,N 13,IX,2:2
Boys From Syracuse, The 1938,N 24,36:1
Too Many Girls 1939,O 19,26:2
Too Many Girls 1939,O 29,IX,1:6
Higher and Higher 1940,Mr 17,X,2:5
Higher and Higher 1940,Ap 5,24:3
Two Weeks With Pay 1940,Je 25,28:3
Higher and Higher 1940,Ag 6,15:4
Higher and Higher 1940,Ag 11,IX,1:1
Pal Joey 1940,D 26,22:2
It's All Yours 1942,Mr 26,26:2
By Jupiter 1942,Je 4,22:1
Connecticut Yankee, A 1943,N 18,30:2
Connecticut Yankee, A 1943,N 21,II,1:1
Babes in Arms 1951,Mr 10,7:3
Pal Joey 1952,Ja 4,17:6
Pal Joey 1952,Ja 13,II,1:1
On Your Toes 1954,O 12,24:4
Boys From Syracuse, The 1963,Ap 16,31:1
Pal Joey 1963,My 30,21:1
Boys From Syracuse, The 1963,Je 2,II,1:1
Boys From Syracuse, The 1963,N 9,14:3
By Jupiter 1967,Ja 20,28:2
Hart, Lorenz (Original Author)
Babes in Arms 1937,Ap 15,18:4
I Married an Angel 1938,My 12,26:2
On Your Toes 1954,O 12,24:4
Hart, Lorenz (Playwright)
Evergreen 1930,O 14,31:2
America's Sweetheart 1931,Ja 25,VIII,2:4
On Your Toes 1936,Mr 23,22:4
On Your Toes 1936,Ap 13,14:4
On Your Toes 1937,Ag 3,21:2
I'd Rather Be Right 1937,N 14,XI,1:1
I Married an Angel 1938,My 22,XI,1:1
Man Who Came to Dinner, The 1940,F 18,IX,3:6
By Jupiter 1942,Je 4,22:1
By Jupiter 1942,Ag 30,VIII,1:1
Babes in Arms 1951,Mr 10,7:3
Pal Joey 1954,Ap 1,40:5
Pal Joey 1961,Je 1,32:1
By Jupiter 1967,Ja 20,28:2
Hart, Lorenz (Producer)
By Jupiter 1942,Ag 30,VIII,1:1
Hart, Margaret
She's My Baby 1928,Ja 4,22:2
Hart, Margie
Wine, Women and Song 1942,S 29,18:3
Hart, Mario
Pinocchio 1939,Ja 3,19:2
Hart, Max
Kiss Me, Kate 1952,Ja 9,24:6
Hart, Michael
Anatomist, The 1957,F 27,21:5
Hart, Moss
Man Who Came to Dinner, The 1941,Jl 29,13:5
Hart, Moss (Director)
Once in a Lifetime 1931,F 1,VIII,1:3
Lady in the Dark 1941,Ja 24,14:2
Lady in the Dark 1941,S 3,26:6
Junior Miss 1941,N 19,28:2
Junior Miss 1941,N 30,IX,1:1
Lady in the Dark 1943,Mr 1,14:2
Winged Victory 1943,N 22,24:1
Dear Ruth 1944,D 14,29:2
Dear Ruth 1944,D 31,II,1:1
Secret Room, The 1945,N 8,16:2
Christopher Blake 1946,D 2,33:2
Christopher Blake 1946,D 8,II,5:1
Light Up the Sky 1948,N 19,34:2
Miss Liberty 1949,Je 14,26:6
Miss Liberty 1949,Jl 16,6:5
Miss Liberty 1949,Jl 24,II,1:1
Climate of Eden, The 1952,N 7,20:2
Climate of Eden, The 1952,N 16,II,1:1
Anniversary Waltz 1954,Ap 8,34:1
My Fair Lady 1956,Mr 16,20:2

Hart, Moss (Director)—Cont
My Fair Lady 1956,Mr 25,II,1:1
My Fair Lady 1956,Ap 29,II,17:1
My Fair Lady 1956,Je 3,II,1:1
My Fair Lady 1958,Mr 9,II,1:1
My Fair Lady 1958,My 1,34:5
Camelot 1960,O 3,35:1
Camelot 1960,D 5,42:1
My Fair Lady 1964,My 21,43:2
My Fair Lady 1968,Je 14,42:1
Hart, Moss (Miscellaneous)
Show Is On, The 1937,S 20,18:4
Sing Out the News 1938,S 26,12:5
Hart, Moss (Original Author)
Face the Music 1932,F 18,24:5
Camelot 1960,D 11,II,5:1
Sherry! 1967,Ap 9,II,1:1
Hart, Moss (Playwright)
Jonica 1930,Mr 30,VIII,2:7
Jonica 1930,Ap 8,27:1
Once in a Lifetime 1930,S 7,IX,2:4
Once in a Lifetime 1930,S 25,22:3
Garrick Gaieties 1930,O 17,21:2
Once in a Lifetime 1930,D 7,IX,1:1
Once in a Lifetime 1931,F 1,VIII,1:3
Face the Music 1932,F 4,25:4
Face the Music 1932,Mr 20,VIII,1:1
Face the Music 1933,F 1,13:4
Once in a Lifetime 1933,F 24,13:1
Once in a Lifetime 1933,Mr 19,IX,2:2
As Thousands Cheer 1933,S 10,II,5:3
As Thousands Cheer 1933,O 2,22:1
As Thousands Cheer 1933,O 15,IX,1:1
Great Waltz, The 1934,S 24,14:4
Great Waltz, The 1934,S 30,IX,1:1
Merrily We Roll Along 1934,O 1,14:1
Merrily We Roll Along 1934,O 7,IX,1:1
Jubilee 1935,S 23,20:3
Jubilee 1935,S 29,X,1:1
Jubilee 1935,O 14,20:1
Jubilee 1935,O 27,IX,1:1
Merrily We Roll Along 1936,Je 30,15:1
You Can't Take It With You 1936,D 1,30:8
You Can't Take It With You 1936,D 6,XII,6:2
You Can't Take It With You 1936,D 15,31:1
You Can't Take It With You 1936,D 20,XI,3:1
Show Is On, The 1936,D 26,14:2
You Can't Take It With You 1937,Ag 29,X,1:1
I'd Rather Be Right 1937,O 12,27:6
I'd Rather Be Right 1937,O 17,XI,2:1
I'd Rather Be Right 1937,N 3,28:2
You Can't Take It With You 1937,D 23,25:5
You Can't Take It With You 1938,Ja 9,X,1:7
You Can't Take It With You 1938,Ja 16,X,1:6
Sing Out the News 1938,S 26,12:5
Fabulous Invalid, The 1938,O 10,15:1
American Way, The 1939,Ja 23,9:2
American Way, The 1939,Ja 29,IX,1:1
Man Who Came to Dinner, The 1939,S 26,21:3
Man Who Came to Dinner, The 1939,O 1,IX,2:5
Man Who Came to Dinner, The 1939,O 17,31:1
Man Who Came to Dinner, The 1939,O 22,IX,1:1
Man Who Came to Dinner, The 1940,F 10,19:5
George Washington Slept Here 1940,S 24,27:3
George Washington Slept Here 1940,O 19,20:3
George Washington Slept Here 1940,O 27,IX,1:1
Lady in the Dark 1940,D 31,18:6
Lady in the Dark 1941,Ja 5,IX,1:7
Lady in the Dark 1941,Ja 24,14:2
Lady in the Dark 1941,F 2,IX,1:1
Man Who Came to Dinner, The 1941,Jl 29,13:5
Lady in the Dark 1941,S 3,26:6
Lady in the Dark 1941,S 7,IX,1:1
Man Who Came to Dinner, The 1941,D 14,IX,4:3
Lunchtime Follies, The 1942,Je 23,22:3
Lady in the Dark 1943,Mr 1,14:2
Winged Victory 1943,N 22,24:1
Winged Victory 1943,N 28,II,1:1
Seven Lively Arts 1944,D 8,26:6
Seven Lively Arts 1944,D 17,II,3:1
You Can't Take It With You 1945,Mr 27,23:7
Christopher Blake 1946,D 2,33:2
Christopher Blake 1946,D 8,II,5:1
Inside U S A 1948,My 1,19:2
Inside U S A 1948,Ag 29,II,1:1
Light Up the Sky 1948,N 19,34:2
Light Up the Sky 1948,D 5,II,5:1
You Can't Take It With You 1951,Ap 7,8:6
Lady in the Dark 1952,Mr 8,11:3
Climate of Eden, The 1952,N 7,20:2
Climate of Eden, The 1952,N 16,II,1:1
Climate of Eden, The 1953,N 21,11:2
Once in a Lifetime 1962,O 30,30:1
Once in a Lifetime 1964,Ja 29,20:1
You Can't Take It With You 1965,N 24,32:1
You Can't Take It With You 1965,D 5,II,5:1
Sherry! 1967,Mr 29,39:1
Hart, Moss (Producer)
Miss Liberty 1949,Jl 16,6:5
Camelot 1960,D 5,42:1
Hart, Nat (Miscellaneous)
Poupees de Paris, Les 1962,D 13,8:2
Hart, Peggy
Will Morrissey's Newcomers 1923,Ag 9,16:2

Hart, Peggy—Cont

Page Miss Glory 1934,N 28,24:2
Boy Meets Girl 1935,N 28,38:2
Hart, Ray
Out of the Seven Seas 1923,N 20,23:3
Hart, Richard
Only the Heart 1942,D 7,22:3
Pillar to Post 1943,D 11,11:2
Dark of the Moon 1945,Mr 15,27:2
Dark of the Moon 1945,Mr 25,II,1:1
Leaf and Bough 1949,Ja 22,10:2
· Happy Time, The 1950,Ja 25,24:1
Hart, Sheila
Narrow Road to the Deep North 1969,D 2,64:1
Jungle of Cities 1970,Mr 1,75:2
Hart, Stan
Let Them Down, Gently; On Vacation
1968,Ja 31,28:2
Hart, Stan (Playwright)
Mad Show, The 1966,Ja 10,16:1
Hart, Stephen
Grand Vizier, The 1961,D 13,55:5
Hart, Suzanna (Costume Designer)
Murder in the Cathedral 1958,Mr 22,12:4
Hart, Suzanna (Scenic Designer)
Murder in the Cathedral 1958,Mr 22,12:4
Hart, Teddy
Innocent Idea, An 1920,My 26,9:4
Guns 1928,Ag 7,25:2
East of Broadway 1932,Ja 27,19:3
Three Men on a Horse 1935,Ja 31,22:3
Room Service 1937,My 20,16:1
Boys From Syracuse, The 1938,N 24,36:1
See My Lawyer 1939,S 28,29:1
More the Merrier, The 1941,S 16,19:3
New Moon, The 1942,Ag 19,14:2
Three Men on a Horse 1942,O 10,10:2
One Touch of Venus 1943,O 8,14:1
Naughty-Naught '00 1946,O 21,27:5
Hart, Theodore
Inspector General, The 1930,D 24,19:2
Hart, Thomas A (Director)
Night in Venice, A 1929,My 22,30:2
Hart, Tom (Pfc)
Swing Sister Wac Swing 1944,Ja 4,20:4
Hart, Toni
Bloomer Girl 1944,O 6,18:5
Hart, Virginia
Italian Straw Hat, The 1957,O 1,37:2
Hart, Vivian
Earl Carroll's Vanities 1925,Jl 7,24:1
Earl Carroll's Vanities 1925,D 29,20:3
Countess Maritza 1926,Mr 30,20:3
Lace Petticoat 1927,Ja 5,18:2
Patience 1927,My 24,23:2
Vaudeville (Palace) 1927,Jl 5,19:3
Vaudeville (Palace) 1928,Ja 3,29:3
Silver Swan, The 1929,N 28,34:5
Prince of Pilsen, The 1930,Ja 14,24:3
Chocolate Soldier, The 1930,Ja 28,28:1
Patience 1931,Je 16,30:4
Pirates of Penzance, The; Slave of Duty, The
1931,Je 30,23:6
Iolanthe 1931,Jl 14,21:5
Chocolate Soldier, The 1931,S 22,33:3
Chimes of Normandy, The 1931,N 3,31:3
Iolanthe 1932,Ja 5,20:2
Gondoliers, The 1932,Ja 12,29:1
Robin Hood 1932,Ja 28,25:4
Yeomen of the Guard, The 1933,My 2,20:4
Patience 1933,My 23,22:6
Mikado, The 1934,Ap 3,26:3
Pirates of Penzance, The 1934,Ap 10,26:5
H M S Pinafore 1934,Ap 17,27:2
Trial by Jury 1934,Ap 17,27:2
Iolanthe 1934,My 1,26:4
Mikado, The 1935,Jl 16,24:4
Pirates of Penzance, The 1935,Jl 23,24:2
Yeomen of the Guard, The 1935,Jl 30,16:4
Gondoliers, The 1935,Ag 6,20:5
Trial by Jury 1935,Ag 13,20:6
Mikado, The 1936,Ap 11,18:4
Pirates of Penzance, The 1936,Ap 21,27:5
Trial by Jury 1936,Ap 28,17:2
Iolanthe 1936,My 5,26:2
Hart, W S
Lambs Gambol 1925,Ap 27,15:1
Hart, Walter (Director)
Precedent 1931,Ap 15,24:5
Merry-Go-Round 1932,Ap 23,11:2
Wind and the Rain, The 1934,F 2,20:6
Strangers at Home 1934,S 15,20:5
Bury the Dead 1936,Mr 16,21:2
Prelude 1936,Ap 20,17:4
Bury the Dead 1936,Ap 20,17:4
Washington Jitters 1938,My 3,19:1
Hart, Walter (Playwright)
Washington Jitters 1938,My 3,19:1
Primrose Path, The 1939,Ja 5,16:3
Primrose Path, The 1939,Ja 16,11:2
Hart, Walter (Producer)
Merry-Go-Round 1932,Ap 23,11:2
Wind and the Rain, The 1934,F 2,20:6

Hart, Whitey
Aquashow 1954,Je 23,20:4
Elliott Murphy's Aquashow 1955,Je 23,25:1
Elliott Murphy's Aquashow 1956,Je 20,26:2
Hart, William
Kilpatrick's Old-Time Minstrels 1930,Ap 21,20:2
Frankie and Johnny 1930,S 26,16:5
Hartberg, Carl
Swan, The 1923,O 24,15:3
Harte, Julian
So Was Napoleon 1930,Ja 9,22:2
Harten, Lenn
Shoemaker and the Peddler, The 1960,O 15,27:4
Hartenstein, P B
Somebody's Lion 1921,Ap 13,20:1
Here's Howe 1923,Ap 26,19:3
Hartenstein, P B (Original Author)
Hoot Mon, or Clans Across the Sea 1927,My 8,29:4
Hartford, Edward
Second Man, The 1927,Ap 12,24:3
Doctor's Dilemma, The 1927,N 22,33:1
Troika 1930,Ap 2,32:6
Unto the Third 1933,Ap 21,24:8
Hartford, Edward (Director)
Intimate Relations 1932,Mr 29,23:2
Hartford, Huntington (Playwright)
Jane Eyre 1958,My 2,31:1
Hartford, Huntington (Producer)
Day by the Sea, A 1955,S 27,42:1
Does a Tiger Wear a Necktie? 1969,F 26,38:1
Hartford, Madelane
Just Beyond 1925,D 2,22:4
Harth, Roger (Lighting Director)
Otage, L' 1959,O 27,42:1
Harth, Roger (Scenic Designer)
Otage, L' 1959,O 27,42:1
Harth, Sidney (Musical Director)
Bacchae, The 1963,Ap 25,39:5
Hartig, Herb (Miscellaneous)
Not While I'm Eating 1961,D 20,37:1
Hartig, Herb (Playwright)
Shoestring '57 1956,N 6,31:1
Hartig, Mary
Time Out for Ginger 1952,N 27,50:4
Hartigan, Brian
Candida 1969,F 3,29:1
Dance of Death, The 1969,My 26,53:1
Lady From Maxim's, The 1970,Je 1,41:1
Hartingsveldt, Will (Composer)
Lotte Goslar's Pantomime Circus-For Humans
Only 1957,D 17,45:1
Hartke, G V (Rev) (Director)
Yankee Doodle Boy 1939,D 19,29:5
Athalie 1942,Mr 18,29:2
Oedipus Rex 1959,Ap 30,36:1
Hartke, G V (Rev) (Miscellaneous)
All Gaul Is Divided 1947,Je 24,27:3
Hartley, Arthur
Here's Howe! 1928,My 2,19:3
Hartley, Carroll
Comes the Revelation 1942,My 27,26:2
Hartley, George
Sign of the Leopard 1928,D 12,34:4
Hartley, Jack
My Girl 1924,N 25,27:2
Room 349 1930,Ap 23,24:5
Her Supporting Cast 1931,My 5,33:3
Dangerous Corner 1933,Jl 18,20:4
Stevedore 1934,Ap 19,33:2
Lady Detained, A 1935,Ja 10,23:3
Journey by Night, A 1935,Ap 17,26:3
Prelude 1935,Je 27,17:4
Beginner's Luck 1935,Jl 23,24:4
Puritan, The 1936,Ja 24,14:3
Snookie 1941,Je 4,26:2
Land Is Bright, The 1941,O 29,26:2
Hope for the Best 1945,F 8,14:4
Buy Me Blue Ribbons 1951,O 18,33:2
Hartley, Mariette
All's Well That Ends Well 1959,Ag 3,20:4
Measure for Measure 1960,Jl 27,33:1
Hartley, Neil (Miscellaneous)
Middle of the Night 1956,F 9,39:1
Jamaica 1957,N 1,32:2
Entertainer, The 1958,F 13,22:2
World of Suzie Wong, The 1958,O 15,47:1
Plume de Ma Tante, La 1958,N 12,42:1
Take Me Along 1959,O 23,22:2
Good Soup, The 1960,Mr 3,26:4
Do Re Mi 1960,D 27,23:2
Carnival! 1961,My 14,22:2
Subways Are for Sleeping 1961,D 28,22:1
I Can Get It for You Wholesale 1962,Mr 23,29:1
Arturo Ui 1963,N 12,49:1
Milk Train Doesn't Stop Here Anymore, The
1964,Ja 2,33:1
Hartley, Patricia
York Nativity Play, The 1956,D 5,49:2
Hartley, Percy
Paolo and Francesca 1924,D 3,24:2
Hartley-Milburn, Julie
Autumn Fire 1926,O 27,25:3

Hartley-Milburn, Mary
Autumn Fire 1926,O 27,25:3
Hartly, Neil (Miscellaneous)
Destry Rides Again 1959,Ap 24,24:1
Hartman, David
Meet Peter Grant 1961,My 11,41:4
Hello, Dolly! 1964,Ja 17,22:1
Yearling, The 1965,D 11,25:1
Hartman, Don (Playwright)
All in Favor 1942,Ja 21,20:6
Hartman, Donald
Much Ado About Nothing 1927,N 19,14:6
Doctor Knock 1928,F 24,15:2
Hartman, E (Lyricist)
Ziegfeld Follies 1934,Ja 5,24:3
Hartman, E (Playwright)
Ziegfeld Follies 1934,Ja 5,24:3
Hartman, Elek
Where People Gather 1967,O 26,56:1
Goa 1968,F 23,46:1
We Bombed in New Haven 1968,O 17,51:1
Hartman, Elizabeth
Our Town 1969,N 28,50:1
Our Town 1969,D 7,II,7:1 ·
Hartman, Ferris
Captain Jinks 1925,S 9,22:1
Treasure Girl 1928,N 9,22:1
Trip to Scarborough, A 1929,Mr 18,31:2
Dragon, The 1929,Mr 26,34:2
Hartman, Grace
Red, Hot and Blue! 1936,O 30,26:3
You Never Know 1938,S 22,26:3
Keep 'Em Laughing 1942,Ap 25,9:2
Angel in the Wings 1947,D 21,II,3:1
Angel in the Wings 1948,Ag 29,II,1:1
All for Love 1949,Ja 24,16:5
Tickets, Please! 1950,Ap 28,25:2
Tickets, Please! 1950,My 7,II,1:1
Hartman, Grace (Playwright)
Angel in the Wings 1947,D 12,36:4
Hartman, Howard C (Playwright)
Pastorale 1936,Mr 5,24:6
Hartman, Jack
Scrapbooks 1953,N 6,24:2
Hartman, Louis (Lighting Director)
Theodora, the Queen 1934,F 1,15:3
Hartman, Margot
View From the Bridge, A 1956,N 9,34:4
Bedtime Story 1957,Ap 1,21:2
Hartman, Marie
If a Body 1935,My 1,25:3
Hartman, Paul
Red, Hot and Blue! 1936,O 30,26:3
You Never Know 1938,S 22,26:3
Keep 'Em Laughing 1942,Ap 25,9:2
Angel in the Wings 1947,D 21,II,3:1
Angel in the Wings 1948,Ag 29,II,1:1
All for Love 1949,Ja 24,16:5
Tickets, Please! 1950,Ap 28,25:2
Tickets, Please! 1950,My 7,II,1:1
ANTA Album 1951,My 7,22:7
Of Thee I Sing 1952,My 6,34:2
Of Thee I Sing 1952,My 11,II,1:1
Show Boat 1956,Je 22,16:1
Pajama Game, The 1957,My 16,27:1
Pajama Game, The 1957,My 26,II,1:1
Drink to Me Only 1958,O 9,47:4
What a Killing 1961,Mr 28,41:1
Hartman, Paul (Playwright)
Angel in the Wings 1947,D 12,36:4
Hartman, Peter
Full Moon in March, A 1960,S 20,48:1
Herne's Egg, The 1960,S 20,48:1
Purgatory 1960,S 20,48:1
Hartman, Sam
Straw Hat, The 1926,O 15,20:2
Big Lake 1927,Ap 9,17:2
Hartman, Stefan
Saved 1970,O 29,57:1
Hartmann, Paul
Midsummer Night's Dream, A 1927,N 18,21:1
Jedermann 1927,D 8,33:2
Dantons Tod 1927,D 21,28:3
Danton's Death 1928,Ja 1,VIII,1:1
Peripherie 1928,Ja 3,29:1
Diener Zweier Herren; Servant of Two Masters,
The 1928,Ja 10,28:3
Kabale und Liebe 1928,Ja 17,22:3
Robbers, The 1928,Ag 10,9:2
Kingdom of God in Bohemia, The
1931,Mr 8,VIII,2:7
Kabale und Liebe 1931,N 1,VIII,4:2
Hartmans, The
Keep 'Em Laughing 1942,My 10,VIII,8:3
Top-Notchers 1942,My 30,8:5
Angel in the Wings 1947,D 12,36:4
Hartmine, Betty
On Baile's Strand 1959,Ap 13,34:4
Hartnett, Jerry
Poupees de Paris, Les 1962,D 13,8:2
Hartryce, Jean
King Can Do No Wrong, The 1927,N 17,28:4

Hartsell, Harold
Passion Flower, The 1920,Ja 14,12:1
Alias Jimmy Valentine 1921,D 9,20:3
Casanova 1923,S 27,10:2
Bride of the Lamb 1926,Mr 31,20:3
Macbeth 1928,N 20,28:3
Hartt, Frederick
Flair-Flair the Idol of Paree 1935,Mr 13,16:1
Hartt, Sherle
'Tis of Thee 1940,O 28,21:3
Hartung, Gustav (Director)
Bonaparte 1927,My 15,VIII,1:3
Stempellbrueder 1929,N 24,X,2:4
Hartung, Gustav (Producer)
Kean 1921,D 11,VI,1:4
Hartung, Robert
Our Town 1944,Ja 11,24:5
Hamlet 1945,D 14,25:2
Twelfth Night 1949,O 4,33:2
She Stoops to Conquer 1949,D 29,21:3
Devil's Disciple, The 1950,Ja 26,23:2
Hartung, Robert (Director)
Pursuit of Happiness, The 1952,Mr 22,9:2
Country Wife, The 1955,Ap 6,35:1
Hartwell, Julie
Naughty-Naught 'OO 1937,Ja 25,23:2
Fireman's Flame, The 1937,O 11,26:2
Hartwick, Walter (Miscellaneous)
Closed Room, The 1934,Jl 24,20:2
Hartwig, Maude (Producer)
Dear Judas 1947,Ag 5,26:1
Hartwig, Walter (Director)
White Gold 1925,N 3,34:5
Lancashire Lass, The 1931,D 31,16:3
Loose Moments 1935,F 5,22:3
Murder With Pen and Ink 1935,Jl 30,17:2
Hartwig, Walter (Mrs) (Producer)
Balloon 1946,Ag 13,30:3
Hartwig, Walter (Producer)
If Booth Had Missed 1932,F 5,24:2
Twelfth Night 1934,Jl 17,24:5
Loose Moments 1935,F 5,22:3
At the Theatre 1937,Ag 4,14:1
Harty, Patricia
Sail Away 1961,O 4,48:5
Harty, Tom
Everybody's Welcome 1931,O 14,26:3
Ballyhoo of 1932 1932,S 7,14:2
Hartz, Fanny (Playwright)
India 1928,Ja 17,23:3
Hartzell, E H
If Booth Had Missed 1931,My 14,27:1
Hartzell, Harold
Joseph 1930,F 13,25:3
Hartzell, Rachel
Cloudy With Showers 1931,Ag 23,VIII,2:5
Cloudy With Showers 1931,S 2,17:5
Truth About Blayds, The 1932,Ap 12,25:2
Honeymoon 1932,D 24,11:2
Love on an Island 1934,Jl 24,20:5
Between Two Worlds 1934,O 26,24:2
Mainly for Lovers 1936,F 11,19:5
Mainly for Lovers 1936,F 22,13:2
American Landscape 1938,D 5,19:2
Harum, Avind
Baker Street 1965,F 17,36:1
West Side Story 1968,Je 25,32:1
Harum, Tim
Sophie 1963,Ap 16,32:1
Harvard Dramatic Club
Ever the Twain 1933,D 17,IX,4:2
Harvards, The
Ice Follies 1969,My 23,38:1
Harvath, Julia
Vagabond King, The 1943,Je 30,24:2
Harven, Jane
Buttrio Square 1952,O 15,40:2
Harvey, Alan
Billy Budd 1955,My 4,35:1
Moondreamers, The 1969,D 9,68:1
Harvey, Arline
Lady Comes Across, The 1942,Ja 10,10:2
Harvey, Basil
Barretts of Wimpole Street, The 1931,F 10,25:1
Harvey, Claire
Bright Honor 1936,S 28,14:1
Harvey, Clarence
Last Waltz, The 1921,My 11,20:3
Mimic World of 1921, The 1921,Ag 18,9:2
Merry Widow, The 1929,D 3,29:1
Wonder Bar, The 1931,Mr 18,23:4
Harvey, Edward
Merry Wives of Windsor, The 1938,Ap 15,22:3
Good Hunting 1938,N 22,26:5
At the Stroke of Eight 1940,My 21,29:2
White Cargo 1941,My 14,24:3
Story of Mary Surratt, The 1947,F 10,25:2
Richard II 1956,O 24,44:1
Romeo and Juliet 1956,O 25,41:1
Macbeth 1956,O 30,42:2
Troilus and Cressida 1956,D 27,21:1
Harvey, Ellison (Playwright)
Thais 1931,Je 19,21:3

Harvey, Elwyn
Shooting Shadows 1924,Je 27,16:5
Eve's Leaves 1925,Mr 27,22:2
Electra 1927,D 2,20:6
Nine Till Six 1930,S 29,17:2
Precedent 1931,Ap 15,24:5
It Never Rains 1931,D 25,29:3
Forty-Four Below 1935,Jl 23,24:3
Puritan, The 1936,Ja 24,14:3
Fresh Fields 1936,F 11,19:2
Fresh Fields 1936,Je 23,27:3
Good, The 1938,O 6,27:2
Romantic Mr Dickens 1940,D 3,33:2
Sherlock Holmes 1953,O 31,11:2
Conversation Piece 1957,N 19,38:2
Harvey, Fletcher
Meanest Man in the World, The 1920,O 13,18:2
Hell's Bells! 1925,Ja 27,14:2
Harvey, Forrester
Havoc 1924,S 2,22:2
Harvey, Frank
Money in the Air 1932,Mr 8,19:3
Bonfire to Glory 1936,Jl 28,23:4
Bright Honor 1936,S 28,14:1
Swing Your Lady 1936,O 19,22:4
Devil Takes a Bride, The 1938,O 8,10:3
Harvey, Frank (Playwright)
Last Enemy, The 1930,Ja 5,VIII,2:2
Cape Forlorn 1930,Ap 20,VIII,2:1
Last Enemy, The 1930,O 31,21:1
Three Men and a Woman 1932,Ja 12,29:2
Saloon Bar 1939,N 26,IX,3:6
Harvey, George
She Lived Next to the Firehouse 1931,F 11,23:1
Harvey, Georgette
Runnin' Wild 1923,O 30,17:3
Porgy 1927,O 11,26:2
Porgy 1929,S 14,17:3
Solid South 1930,O 15,27:1
Five Star Final 1930,D 31,11:1
Savage Rhythm 1931,Ja 1,30:4
Ol' Man Satan 1932,O 4,26:3
Party's Over, The 1933,Mr 28,23:3
Stevedore 1934,Ap 19,33:2
Dance With Your Gods 1934,O 8,14:3
Lady of Letters 1935,Mr 29,26:6
Hook-Up, The 1935,My 9,24:6
Porgy and Bess 1935,O 11,30:2
Pre-Honeymoon 1936,My 1,19:4
Brown Sugar 1937,D 3,29:2
Mamba's Daughters 1939,Ja 4,24:2
Mamba's Daughters 1939,Ja 15,IX,1:1
Pastoral 1939,N 2,26:2
Morning Star 1940,Ap 17,26:4
Porgy and Bess 1942,Ja 23,16:2
Porgy and Bess 1943,S 14,26:2
Porgy and Bess 1944,F 8,13:2
Power of Darkness, The 1948,O 11,28:2
Stevedore 1949,F 23,30:2
Lost in the Stars 1949,O 31,21:2
Harvey, Georgia
Sunshine 1926,Ag 18,15:2
Kingdom of God, The 1928,D 21,30:2
Hundred Years Old, A 1929,O 2,28:2
Lady Beyond the Moon 1931,Ap 1,36:5
It Happened Tomorrow 1933,My 6,11:5
Murder in the Cathedral 1936,Mr 21,13:5
It Can't Happen Here 1936,O 28,30:1
Antony and Cleopatra 1937,N 11,30:2
Dear Octopus 1939,Ja 12,22:2
Ten Little Indians 1944,Je 28,21:2
Chalk Garden, The 1955,O 27,29:1
Separate Tables 1956,O 26,33:1
Harvey, Helen
Jumbo 1935,N 18,20:2
Harvey, Helen (Producer)
Natural Look, The 1967,Mr 13,45:2
Harvey, Howard
Never Say Horses 1951,D 7,34:4
Harvey, J L
Front Page, The 1937,N 12,27:2
Harvey, James
King and I, The 1964,Jl 7,26:1
Harvey, Jane
Bless You All 1950,D 15,42:2
Harvey, Jerry
Lady in the Dark 1952,Mr 8,11:3
Harvey, Joan
Tevya and His Daughters 1957,S 17,38:2
All the King's Men 1959,O 17,27:2
Cry of the Raindrop 1961,Mr 8,38:1
Harvey, John
Johnny 2X4 1942,Mr 17,24:6
Kiss and Tell 1943,Mr 18,22:1
Open House 1947,Je 4,33:4
Harvey, John (Lighting Director)
Kean 1961,N 3,28:2
Passage to India, A 1962,F 1,23:1
Come on Strong 1962,O 5,29:1
Tovarich 1963,Mr 20,5:1
Hot Spot 1963,Ap 20,17:2
110 in the Shade 1963,O 25,37:1
Deputy, The 1964,F 27,26:1

Harvey, John (Lighting Director)—Cont
Mating Dance 1965,N 4,58:1
More Stately Mansions 1967,N 1,40:1
Happiness Is Just a Little Thing Called a Rolls
Royce 1968,My 13,54:5
My Daughter, Your Son 1969,My 14,36:2
Harvey, John L Jr
Wings Over Europe 1936,Mr 4,24:7
Harvey, John Martin (Sir)
Via Crucis 1923,F 11,VII,1:4
Devil's Disciple, The 1930,S 21,IX,2:1
Boy David, The 1936,N 22,VI,7:1
Harvey, John Martin (Sir) (Playwright)
Arthur 1923,Mr 18,VII,1:1
Harvey, Katherine
Porgy and Bess 1950,N 26,II,7:8
Harvey, Kathryn
Beggar Student, The 1942,S 26,11:4
Harvey, Ken
I Loved You Wednesday 1932,O 12,27:1
Top Banana 1951,N 2,19:2
Finian's Rainbow 1953,Mr 7,13:2
Grand Prize, The 1955,Ja 27,17:1
Rumple 1957,N 7,42:2
Harvey, Kenneth
Phoenix '55 1955,Ap 25,20:2
Pipe Dream 1955,D 1,44:1
Harvey, Kenneth (Director)
Dear Nobody 1968,Jl 31,33:1
Projection Room, The 1969,Ja 15,38:2
Harvey, Laurence
Island of Goats 1955,O 5,40:1
Country Wife, The 1957,N 28,56:1
Henry V 1958,D 26,2:7
Camelot 1964,Ag 20,34:1
Harvey, Marion
Let's Face It 1941,O 30,26:2
Harvey, Martin
Oedipus Rex 1923,O 26,14:1
Via Crucis 1923,N 13,25:2
Harvey, Mary Lou (Costume Designer)
Immaculate Misconception, The 1970,O 28,63:3
Harvey, Michael
Caesar and Cleopatra 1949,D 22,28:2
Henry V 1964,My 13,52:1
Harvey, Michael (Producer)
Score 1970,O 29,57:4
Harvey, Michael (Pvt)
Winged Victory 1943,N 22,24:1
Harvey, Morris
9 O'Clock Revue 1923,O 5,22:1
Nine to Eleven, The 1925,Jl 12,VII,1:1
Merry World, The 1926,Je 9,18:3
Merry World, The 1926,Je 13,VII,1:1
Passions of 1926 1926,Ag 3,19:4
Anthony and Anna 1935,N 9,18:2
Anthony and Anna 1935,D 8,X,5:1
Harvey, Morris (Playwright)
9 O'Clock Revue 1923,O 5,22:1
Nine to Eleven, The 1925,Jl 12,VII,1:1
Harvey, Muriel Martin
Respect for Riches, The 1920,My 12,9:1
Happy-Go-Lucky 1920,Ag 25,6:1
Harvey, Paul
Skirt, The 1921,N 8,28:1
Awful Truth, The 1922,S 19,14:3
Schemers 1924,S 16,27:1
Youngest, The 1924,D 23,17:1
Downstream 1926,Ja 12,28:1
Donovan Affair, The 1929,Ag 31,15:2
Humbug, The 1929,N 28,34:5
Dishonored Lady 1930,Ja 26,VIII,2:1
Dishonored Lady 1930,F 5,27:1
Rap, The 1931,Ap 7,31:2
Brief Moment 1931,N 10,28:2
Dinner at Eight 1932,O 24,18:2
Harvey, Peggy
Sacred and Profane Love 1920,F 24,11:1
Young Visitors, The 1920,N 30,14:1
Mr Pim Passes By 1921,Mr 1,18:1
Harvey, Peter (Costume Designer)
Baby Want a Kiss 1964,Ap 20,32:1
All Women Are One 1965,Ja 8,21:1
Sweet Enemy, The 1965,F 16,39:1
All in Good Time 1965,F 19,25:1
Mad Show, The 1966,Ja 10,16:1
Hooray!! It's a Glorious Day. . .And All That
1966,Mr 10,28:1
Witness 1968,N 22,38:1
Sweet Eros 1968,N 22,38:1
Dames at Sea 1968,D 21,46:1
Dames at Sea 1969,Ja 5,II,1:3
Watercolor 1970,Ja 22,30:1
Criss-Crossing 1970,Ja 22,30:1
Rooming House, The 1970,Ja 23,25:1
Dr Galley 1970,Ja 23,25:1
Transfers 1970,Ja 23,25:1
Gloria and Esperanza 1970,F 5,32:1
Park 1970,Ap 23,47:1
Dames at Sea 1970,S 24,60:1
Harvey, Peter (Lighting Director)
Plays for Bleecker Street 1962,Ja 12,28:1
Infancy 1962,Ja 12,28:1
Childhood 1962,Ja 12,28:1

Harvey, Peter (Lighting Director)—Cont
Someone From Assisi 1962,Ja 12,28:1
Harvey, Peter (Miscellaneous)
Traveller Without Luggage 1964,S 18,26:2
Harvey, Peter (Scenic Designer)
Confederates, The 1959,S 29,45:1
Noontide 1961,Je 2,37:1
One Way Pendulum 1961,S 19,38:2
Thracian Horses, The 1961,S 28,58:2
Childhood 1962,Ja 12,28:1
Infancy 1962,Ja 12,28:1
Someone From Assisi 1962,Ja 12,28:1
Plays for Bleecker Street 1962,Ja 12,28:1
PS 193 1962,O 31,33:1
Put It in Writing 1963,My 14,31:1
Immoralist, The 1963,N 8,36:2
Baby Want a Kiss 1964,Ap 20,32:1
Sweet Enemy 1965,F 16,39:1
Exhaustion of Our Son's Love, The 1965,O 19,51:1
Good Day 1965,O 19,51:1
Mad Show, The 1966,Ja 10,16:1
Hooray!! It's a Glorious Day. . .And All That
    1966,Mr 10,28:1
Butter and Egg Man, The 1966,O 18,49:1
Death of the Well-Loved Boy, The
    1967,My 16,48:1
Happiness 1967,N 11,25:2
Walking to Waldheim 1967,N 11,25:2
Boys in the Band, The 1968,Ap 15,48:1
Muzeeka 1968,Ap 29,47:2
Red Cross 1968,Ap 29,47:2
Witness 1968,N 22,38:1
Sweet Eros 1968,N 22,38:1
Dames at Sea 1968,D 21,46:1
Dames at Sea 1969,Ja 5,II,1:3
Criss-Crossing 1970,Ja 22,30:1
Watercolor 1970,Ja 22,30:1
Dr Galley 1970,Ja 23,25:1
Rooming House, The 1970,Ja 23,25:1
Transfers 1970,Ja 23,25:1
Gloria and Esperanza 1970,F 5,32:1
Exchange 1970,F 9,47:2
Park 1970,Ap 23,47:1
Nuns, The 1970,Je 2,35:1
Dames at Sea 1970,S 24,60:1
One Night Stands of a Noisy Passenger; Noisy
    Passenger, The 1970,D 31,8:3
One Night Stands of a Noisy Passenger; Passage,
    Un 1970,D 31,8:3
One Night Stands of a Noisy Passenger; Last
    Stand 1970,D 31,8:3
Harvey, Robert
Conjur 1938,N 1,27:2
Everywhere I Roam 1938,D 30,10:4
John Henry 1940,Ja 11,18:2
Run, Little Chillun 1943,Ag 14,6:1
Harvey, Roslyn
Stepping Sisters 1930,Ap 23,24:2
Young Go First, The 1935,My 29,16:2
Crime, The 1936,Mr 2,12:3
Harvey, Roslyn (Lyricist)
Of V We Sing 1942,F 16,20:3
Harvey, Roslyn (Miscellaneous)
Let Freedom Sing 1942,O 6,18:2
Harvey, Russell
Singing Rabbi, The 1931,S 11,24:4
Harvey, Thelma
Salome 1922,My 23,12:4
Earl Carroll's Vanities 1924,S 11,23:6
Harvey, Walter (Scenic Designer)
It Happened Tomorrow 1933,My 6,11:5
Ship Comes in, A 1934,S 20,21:1
Harvey, William D
Critic, The 1965,Jl 26,15:2
Harwell, George (Composer)
What a Killing 1961,Mr 28,41:1
Harwell, George (Lyricist)
What a Killing 1961,Mr 28,41:1
Harwood, Captain (Playwright)
Man in Possession, The 1930,O 12,VIII,4:1
Harwood, Geoffrey
Young Woodley 1925,N 3,34:1
Sinner 1927,F 8,20:2
Synthetic Sin 1927,O 11,26:2
Divorce a la Carte 1928,Mr 27,30:3
Money Lender, The 1928,Ag 28,27:3
When Crummles Played 1928,O 2,34:3
Sign of the Leopard 1928,D 12,34:4
Merchant of Venice, The 1930,D 3,29:2
Silent Witness, The 1931,Mr 24,31:5
Harwood, H M (Director)
Man in Possession, The 1930,N 3,19:1
Lady Jane 1934,S 11,24:2
Harwood, H M (Playwright)
Pinch Hitter, A 1922,Je 2,20:4
Eileen 1922,Je 18,VI,1:6
Pelican, The 1924,O 26,VIII,1:1
Pelican, The 1925,S 22,23:2
Pelican, The 1925,S 27,VII,1:1
Transit of Venus, The 1927,My 22,VIII,2:1
Golden Calf, The 1927,O 2,VIII,1:3
Excelsior 1928,S 30,IX,1:3
Girl's Best Friend, A 1929,N 10,X,2:1
Man in Possession, The 1930,F 9,VIII,2:1

Cynara 1930,Jl 13,VIII,1:3
Man in Possession, The 1930,N 3,19:1
Kiss of Importance, A 1930,D 2,31:3
Cynara 1931,N 3,31:1
So Far and No Father 1932,F 17,19:4
King, Queen, Knave 1932,F 18,24:4
King, Queen, Knave 1932,Mr 6,VIII,2:4
So Far and No Father 1932,Mr 6,VIII,2:4
Old Folks at Home 1934,Ja 14,IX,1:8
Lady Jane 1934,S 11,24:2
These Mortals 1936,Ja 5,IX,1:1
Promise 1936,D 31,20:4
Innocent Party, The 1938,F 13,X,3:3
Man in Possession, The 1939,S 26,21:4
Pin to See the Peepshow, A 1953,S 18,17:2
Pin to See the Peepshow, A 1953,N 8,II,1:1
Harwood, H M (Translator)
Promise 1936,Mr 22,XI,1:7
Harwood, Harry
Straw, The 1921,N 11,16:2
Harwood, Horbert
Tin Pan Alley 1928,N 2,29:1
Harwood, Jack
Honor Code, The 1931,My 19,25:3
Four O'Clock 1933,F 14,19:6
Creeping Fire 1935,Ja 17,22:3
Tapestry in Gray 1935,D 28,10:2
Lady Luck 1936,Ap 16,21:2
Lend Me Your Ears! 1936,O 6,28:5
Harwood, James
Our Lan' 1947,S 29,16:5
New York Idea, The 1948,Ag 18,29:2
Razzle Dazzle 1951,F 20,21:1
Billy the Kid 1951,Ag 21,23:2
Great Magician, The 1951,N 22,45:1
Edward II 1958,F 12,32:5
Saintliness of Margery Kempe, The 1959,F 3,35:6
Greenwich Village U S A 1960,S 29,30:5
O Marry Me 1961,O 28,13:1
Darker Flower, A 1963,Mr 11,7:2
Leader, The 1965,Mr 8,34:1
Bedlam Galore, for Two or More 1965,Mr 8,34:1
Impromptu, L' 1965,Mr 8,34:1
Foursome 1965,Mr 8,34:1
Harwood, John
Tragedy of Nan, The 1920,F 18,9:1
19th Hole, The 1927,O 12,30:3
For Valor 1935,N 19,27:5
Winners and Losers 1947,F 27,27:2
Deputy of Paris, The 1947,Mr 22,9:5
Our Lan' 1947,Ap 19,11:2
King Lear 1964,My 19,43:2
Comedy of Errors, The 1964,My 21,43:1
Persecution and Assassination of Marat As
    Performed by the Inmates of the Asylum of
    Charenton Under the Direction of the Marquis de
    Sade, The 1965,D 28,35:1
Harwood, John (Director)
Tip-Toes 1925,D 29,20:2
Girl Friend, The 1926,Mr 18,26:5
Ramblers, The 1926,S 21,32:2
Oh, Kay! 1926,N 9,31:3
Rio Rita 1927,F 3,18:3
Five O'Clock Girl, The 1927,O 11,26:3
Polly 1929,Ja 9,28:3
Top Speed 1929,D 26,20:1
Harwood, John (Musical Director)
You Said It 1931,Ja 20,21:3
Harwood, Michael (Scenic Designer)
When Did You Last See My Mother?
    1967,Ja 5,27:5
Harwood, P H
It's the Valet 1933,D 15,25:4
Stags at Bay 1934,D 15,9:2
Harwood, R
Gentlemen, the Queen 1927,Ap 23,14:3
Harz, Claude
Soul Gone Home 1959,O 28,40:7
Much Ado About Nothing 1963,Jl 15,25:2
Hasait, Max (Scenic Designer)
Grand Hotel 1931,S 4,22:7
Grand Hotel 1931,S 27,VIII,1:4
Hascall, Lon
Rose of Stamboul, The 1922,Mr 8,11:2
Keep Kool 1924,My 23,16:4
LeMaire's Affairs 1927,Mr 29,22:4
Allez-Opp! 1927,Ag 3,29:3
Top Speed 1929,D 26,20:1
Hasek, Jaroslav (Miscellaneous)
Schweik in the Second World War 1959,My 23,18:3
Hasek, Jaroslav (Original Author)
Adventures of the Worthy Soldier Schwejk, The
    1928,Mr 4,IX,2:1
Good Soldier Schweik, The 1937,D 22,33:2
Good Soldier Schweik, The 1963,Ap 9,57:1
Hasen, Irwin (Playwright)
Russell Patterson's Sketch-Book 1960,F 8,35:1
Hasenclever, Julian (Original Author)
Man of Wax 1933,Ag 6,X,1:6
Hasenclever, Walter (Original Author)
Her Man of Wax 1933,O 12,32:3
Hasenclever, Walter (Playwright)
Beyond 1925,Ja 27,14:1

Hasenclever, Walter (Playwright)—Cont
Beyond 1925,F 1,VII,1:1
Besserer Herr, Ein 1927,My 29,VII,2:1
Bourgeois Gentilhomme, Le 1929,Mr 24,X,2:3
Ehen Werden im Himmel Geschlossen
    1929,Ap 7,X,4:4
Napoleon Will Make Order 1930,F 23,III,7:2
Napoleon Greift Ein 1930,Je 1,VIII,2:1
Kommt ein Vogel Geflogen 1931,My 10,VIII,1:4
Man of Distinction 1957,Ag 27,33:7
Magnificent Hugo, The 1961,Ap 8,12:2
Hasey, Richard
As You Like It 1936,Ap 24,18:4
Hash, Burl (Lighting Director)
Tarot 1970,D 12,19:1
Hash, Burl (Miscellaneous)
Brass Butterfly, The 1970,Ja 31,34:1
Universal Nigger, The 1970,Mr 21,18:1
Tarot 1970,D 12,19:1
Haskel, Benjamin
Alt Heidelberg 1926,My 31,10:5
Haskell, Amory
What Next 1920,Ja 27,7:2
Haskell, Beatrice
Yellow Jacket, The 1923,Ap 20,20:3
Haskell, Celia
Lady Remembers, The 1932,My 11,15:3
Black Diamond 1933,F 24,12:2
Haskell, Jack
Mr President 1962,O 22,34:2
Haskell, Jack (Choreographer)
Song of the Flame 1925,D 31,10:2
Girl Friend, The 1926,Mr 18,26:5
LeMaire's Affairs 1927,Mr 29,22:4
Five O'Clock Girl, The 1927,O 11,26:3
Chee-Chee 1928,S 26,25:1
Hold Everything 1928,O 11,24:2
Polly 1929,Ja 9,28:3
Vanderbilt Revue, The 1930,N 6,22:6
Through the Years 1932,Ja 29,13:3
Haskell, Jack (Director)
Girl Friend, The 1926,Mr 18,26:5
This Way Out 1929,Ap 28,24:4
Haskell, Judith (Choreographer)
Lend an Ear 1969,O 29,32:1
Haskell, Loney
Friars Club Frolic 1933,My 15,16:4
Haskell, Marjorie
Apothecary, The 1926,Mr 17,28:1
Haskell, Martin
Thomas Paine 1930,Mr 21,30:7
Haskell, Peter
Love Nest, The 1963,Ja 28,7:6
Haskell, William
Out of a Blue Sky 1930,F 10,20:6
Haskin, Douglas
Mystery of the Finding of the Cross, The
    1959,Ja 16,35:2
Haskin, Harold
On Your Toes 1936,Ap 13,14:4
Haskins, Charles
Bootleggers, The 1922,N 28,24:1
Haskins, Finis
Hamlet 1927,Ap 7,23:3
Haskins, Nancy
Christopher's Wonders 1960,S 27,41:1
Haslam, Robert
Thunder in the Air 1929,N 12,34:3
Haslam, William (Playwright)
Cid 1934,O 24,24:2
Hasler, Jack
Don't Look Now! 1936,N 4,41:3
Call Me Ziggy 1937,F 13,9:6
Man From Cairo, The 1938,My 5,26:5
Day in the Sun 1939,My 17,29:2
Haslett, Doris
Wicked Age, The 1927,N 5,16:6
Hasley, Harry (Miscellaneous)
Ice Capades 1964,Ag 27,27:2
Haslup, Marion
Guns 1928,Ag 7,25:2
Hasoutra, Miss
Spice of 1922 1922,Jl 7,12:4
Vaudeville (Palace) 1927,Ja 25,18:3
Hass, Alexander (Composer)
Merchant of Yonkers, The 1938,D 29,14:2
Hassall, Christopher (Lyricist)
Dear Miss Phoebe 1950,O 14,13:8
Hassan, Ris
Marseilles 1930,N 18,28:2
Hassan, Rita (Miscellaneous)
Mamba's Daughters 1939,Ja 4,24:2
Alice in Wonderland 1947,Ap 7,19:2
Hassan, Rita (Producer)
Sky Drift 1945,N 14,25:2
Hassan, Sam
Immoral Isabella 1927,O 28,20:3
Hassberger, John B
Cotton Stockings 1923,D 19,16:2
Hasse, O E
Dear Liar 1959,O 6,44:6
Ides of March, The 1962,N 17,16:4
Hassell, George
Florodora 1920,Ap 6,18:1

Hassell, George—Cont
Passing Show of 1922, The 1922,S 21,18:2
Passing Show of 1923, The 1923,Je 15,24:6
Passing Show of 1924, The 1924,S 4,13:4
Student Prince, The 1924,D 3,25:3
Servant in the House, The 1925,Ap 8,24:2
Countess Maritza 1926,Mr 30,20:3
Countess Maritza 1926,S 20,21:1
Circus Princess, The 1927,Ap 26,32:2
Midsummer Night's Dream, A 1927,Je 27,25:1
Wild Man of Borneo, The 1927,S 14,29:2
Wild Man of Borneo, The 1927,S 25,VIII,1:1
Optimists, The 1928,Ja 31,28:2
Chee-Chee 1928,S 26,25:1
Hello, Daddy! 1928,D 27,26:5
Dear Love 1930,My 18,VIII,3:1
Artists and Models 1930,Je 11,33:2
Student Prince, The 1931,Ja 30,18:1
Hassell, Marie
Way of the World, The 1924,N 18,23:4
Hassell, Virginia
Circus Princess, The 1927,Ap 26,32:2
Hassen, Ben Troupe
Vaudeville (Palace) 1926,Mr 16,22:2
Hassilev, Alex
Handful of Fire 1958,O 2,45:3
Hassilev, Alex (Miscellaneous)
Diary of a Madman 1964,Ap 17,29:2
Hassing, Douglas
Our Town 1940,Je 30,35:5
Soft Shoulders 1940,Jl 18,22:5
Hassler, Jack
Summer Wives 1936,Ap 14,18:1
Hassman, Larry
Three Plays of the Sea 1970,Ag 20,39:1
Hasso, Signe
Dunungen 1939,F 26,IX,2:3
Golden Wings 1941,N 25,33:3
Golden Wings 1941,D 9,46:6
Edwina Black 1950,N 22,20:5
Glad Tidings 1951,O 12,33:2
Uncle Vanya 1956,F 1,25:2
Uncle Vanya 1956,F 12,II,1:1
Apple Cart, The 1956,O 19,23:1
Apple Cart, The 1956,O 28,II,1:1
Hasson, Thomas
West Side Story 1960,Ap 28,31:1
Hey You, Light Man! 1963,Mr 2,5:2
Hasson, William
Catskill Dutch 1924,My 7,18:1
Castles in the Air 1926,S 7,19:2
Hast, E
Parasites 1924,N 20,21:1
Grand Duchess and the Waiter, The
1925,O 14,31:1
Hast, Ferdinand
House of Usshher, The 1926,Ja 14,18:4
Vaudeville (Palace) 1928,Ap 3,32:5
Hast, Walter (Producer)
Clubs Are Trumps 1924,O 15,27:1
Hastings, Adele
Love's Old Sweet Song 1940,My 3,16:3
Hastings, B Macdonald (Playwright)
If Winter Comes 1923,Ap 3,26:1
Hastings, Barbar
Love's Old Sweet Song 1940,My 3,16:3
Hastings, Basil MacDonald (Playwright)
If Winter Comes 1923,F 4,VII,1:4
New Sin, The 1923,My 28,18:3
That Sort 1926,Ap 20,24:6
Hastings, Charlotte (Playwright)
High Ground, The 1951,F 21,31:2
Hastings, Donald
Young Man's Fancy, A 1947,Ap 30,33:2
Summer and Smoke 1948,O 7,33:2
Hastings, Edward
Edward II 1958,F 12,32:5
Hastings, Edward (Director)
Saintliness of Margery Kempe, The 1959,F 3,35:6
Epitaph for George Dillon 1960,D 29,17:1
Our Town 1968,S 29,77:4
Hastings, Edward (Miscellaneous)
Ivanov 1958,O 8,42:1
Hastings, Florence
Cloudy With Showers 1931,S 2,17:5
Hastings, Harold (Composer)
Tickets, Please! 1950,Ap 28,25:2
Hastings, Harold (Musical Director)
Top Banana 1951,N 2,19:2
Carnival in Flanders 1953,S 9,38:2
Pajama Game, The 1954,My 14,20:2
Damn Yankees 1955,My 6,17:1
New Girl in Town 1957,My 15,40:1
Once Upon a Mattress 1959,My 12,40:1
Fiorello! 1959,N 24,45:3
Tenderloin 1960,O 18,47:2
Funny Thing Happened on the Way to the Forum,
A 1962,My 9,49:1
She Loves Me 1963,Ap 24,39:1
Baker Street 1965,F 17,36:1
Flora, the Red Menace 1965,My 12,41:2
Anya 1965,N 30,48:1
It's a Bird . . . It's a Plane . . . It's Superman
1966,Mr 30,34:1

Cabaret 1966,N 21,62:1
Zorba 1968,N 18,58:1
Strada, La 1969,D 15,63:1
Company 1970,Ap 27,40:1
Hastings, Harry (Scenic Designer)
Constant Wife, The 1935,Jl 3,20:2
Stardust 1935,Jl 17,22:4
Hastings, Hugh (Director)
Seagulls Over Sorrento 1952,S 12,18:4
Hastings, Hugh (Playwright)
Seagulls Over Sorrento 1952,S 12,18:4
Seagulls Over Sorrento 1952,S 21,II,1:1
Hastings, Katherine
Foolscap 1933,Ja 12,21:2
Hastings, Kaye
Ringside 1928,Ag 30,13:2
Hastings, Marjorie
Trojan Horse, The 1940,O 31,28:3
Hastings, Michael (Playwright)
Silence of Lee Harvey Oswald, The 1966,N 25,47:1
Lee Harvey Oswald: A Far Mean Streak of
Independence Brought on by Negleck
1968,Ap 19,35:1
Hastings, Milo (Playwright)
Class of '29 1936,My 16,10:3
Hastings, Patrick (Playwright)
Scotch Mist 1926,S 21,32:3
Escort 1942,S 6,VIII,1:8
Bonaventure 1950,Ja 8,II,3:7
Hastings, Patty
Twinkle Twinkle 1926,N 17,22:2
Hastings, Russell T (Costume Designer)
Merry Death, A 1959,N 10,55:3
No Trifling With Love 1959,N 10,55:3
Hastings, Russell T (Scenic Designer)
Merry Death, A 1959,N 10,55:3
No Trifling With Love 1959,N 10,55:3
Hastings, Ruth
Little Poor Man, The 1925,Ag 6,14:1
Hastings, Sparke
Danton's Death 1938,N 3,26:2
Hastings, Sue Marionettes
Peter Rabbit 1928,D 27,26:4
Sinbad the Sailor 1929,D 27,26:5
Vaudeville (Palace) 1930,Mr 24,24:5
Hooray for What! 1937,D 2,32:5
Hastings Sisters
George White's Scandals 1926,Je 15,23:2
Hasty Pudding Club, Harvard (Producer)
Laugh It Off 1925,Ap 25,18:4
Haswell, Mary
Young Visitors, The 1920,N 30,14:1
Haswell, Percy
Light of the World, The 1920,Ja 7,17:1
Bab 1920,O 19,12:1
Some Party 1922,Ap 17,22:1
Scaramouche 1923,O 25,14:2
Complex, The 1925,Mr 4,17:2
Peacock 1932,O 12,27:1
Haswell, Robert
Danton's Death 1965,O 22,46:1
Country Wife, The 1965,D 10,58:2
Condemned of Altona, The 1966,F 4,21:1
Alchemist, The 1966,O 14,48:1
East Wind, The 1967,F 10,30:1
Tiger at the Gates 1968,Mr 1,30:1
Cyrano de Bergerac 1968,Ap 26,30:1
Haswin, Nancy
Strangers at Home 1934,S 15,20:5
Devil of Pei-Ling 1936,F 21,20:4
Hatch, Alene
Twelfth Night 1954,N 10,42:2
Twelfth Night 1954,D 12,II,3:1
Merchant of Venice, The 1955,F 23,23:2
Twelfth Night 1957,Ja 5,12:2
Hatch, Bradford
Hamlet 1934,D 26,19:3
Hatch, Cutler (Playwright)
If Love Were All 1931,N 14,14:5
Hatch, David
Cambridge Circus 1964,O 7,53:1
New Cambridge Circus, The 1965,Ja 15,22:2
Hatch, Dorothy
Utopia, Limited; Flowers of Progress, The
1957,F 27,21:1
Mikado, The 1957,Ap 24,28:2
H M S Pinafore 1957,My 1,42:6
Pirates of Penzance, The 1957,My 8,43:1
Yeomen of the Guard, The 1957,My 22,28:3
Gondoliers, The 1957,My 29,34:2
Hatch, Eric (Playwright)
Little Darling 1942,O 28,26:2
Hatch, Frank
Anna Ascends 1920,S 23,14:1
Appearances 1925,O 15,27:3
Kitty's Kisses 1926,My 7,12:2
Hatch, Frank (Director)
Octoroon, The 1929,Mr 13,28:3
Under the Gaslight 1929,Ap 3,27:1
Hatch, George
Building Blocks 1954,My 8,14:4
Hatch, Harry
Dream Play 1926,Ja 21,18:2

Hatch, Harry—Cont
What Every Woman Knows 1926,Ap 14,20:2
Hatch, James (Composer)
Fly Blackbird 1962,F 6,26:2
Hatch, James (Lyricist)
Fly Blackbird 1962,F 6,26:2
Hatch, James (Playwright)
Fly Blackbird 1962,F 6,26:2
Fly Blackbird 1962,Ap 29,II,1:1
Hatch, Riley
Squaw Man, The 1921,D 27,10:3
Nervous Wreck, The 1923,O 10,16:1
Hatchell, Alice
Murder in the Cathedral 1958,Mr 22,12:4
Hatcher, Mary
Texas Li'l Darlin' 1949,N 26,10:5
Hatcher, Tom
Clearing in the Woods, A 1957,Ja 11,20:2
Clearing in the Woods, A 1959,F 13,32:1
Invitation to a March 1960,O 31,27:2
Hatfield, Byron
Playing the Game 1927,D 20,32:5
Black Crook, The 1929,Mr 12,26:5
Hatfield, Hurd
Possessed, The 1939,O 25,26:2
Twelfth Night 1941,D 3,32:2
Strings, My Lord, Are False, The 1942,My 20,24:2
Ivy Green, The 1949,Ap 6,37:2
Venus Observed 1952,F 14,24:2
Love's Labour's Lost 1953,F 5,20:3
Love's Labour's Lost 1953,F 8,II,1:1
Camino Real 1953,Mr 20,26:1
Camino Real 1953,Mr 29,II,1:1
Bullfight 1954,Ja 13,25:2
Anastasia 1954,D 30,13:1
Anastasia 1955,Ja 16,II,1:1
Julius Caesar 1955,Jl 13,20:1
Tempest, The 1955,Ag 2,18:2
Tempest, The 1955,Ag 7,II,1:1
Lovers 1956,My 11,23:1
Duchess of Malfi, The 1957,Mr 20,33:1
Much Ado About Nothing 1959,S 18,25:2
Much Ado About Nothing 1959,S 27,II,1:1
Devils, The 1963,N 5,25:1
Devils, The 1963,N 17,II,1:1
Hatfield, Lansing
Virginia 1937,S 3,13:2
Show Boat 1938,Je 30,21:1
Devil and Daniel Webster, The 1939,My 19,26:1
Susanna, Don't You Cry 1939,My 23,27:2
Sadie Thompson 1944,N 17,25:2
Sadie Thompson 1944,N 26,II,1:1
Hatfield, Margaret
Raw Meat 1933,Mr 23,13:2
Hathaway, Cynthia
Lady From the Sea, The 1935,D 14,11:3
Hathaway, Dorothy
Sky High 1925,Mr 3,21:4
Hathaway, Gwendolyn
Get Me in the Movies 1928,My 22,18:3
Elmer Gantry 1928,Ag 10,9:4
Hathaway, Joan
Good Earth, The 1932,O 18,23:4
Hathaway, Joan (Director)
Searching for the Sun 1936,F 20,22:6
Mr Shaddy 1936,Jl 15,14:4
Infernal Machine, The 1937,D 13,22:7
Cheapside 1938,F 28,18:2
Comedy of Good and Evil, A 1938,Ap 8,16:3
Hathaway, Joy
Slight Case of Murder, A 1935,S 12,28:5
Women, The 1936,D 28,13:1
Hathaway, Jane
Miracle, The 1924,Ag 19,9:1
Hathway, Donald LaMotte (Producer)
Black Diamond 1933,F 24,12:2
Hatoff, Stanley J (Miscellaneous)
Nuns, The 1970,Je 2,35:1
Hatten, Lennie (Miscellaneous)
Uncle Harry 1942,My 21,24:1
Hatton, Brad
Top Banana 1951,N 2,19:2
Hatton, Bradford
Smiling Faces 1932,Ag 31,12:3
Sailor, Beware! 1933,S 29,24:4
Hatton, Donald
Mother Courage and Her Children 1963,Mr 30,5:5
Hatton, Fanny (Playwright)
Checkerboard, The 1920,Ag 20,7:2
We Girls 1921,N 10,26:3
Treat 'Em Rough 1926,My 23,VIII,1:1
Long Island Love 1926,Ag 1,VII,4:1
Treat 'Em Rough 1926,O 5,26:2
Lombardi, Ltd 1927,Je 7,27:3
Synthetic Sin 1927,O 11,26:2
Fatal Woman, The 1930,N 2,IX,4:7
Love, Honor and Betray 1930,Mr 13,22:2
Dancing Partner 1930,Jl 27,VIII,2:3
Dancing Partner 1930,Ag 6,24:2
Tonight or Never 1930,N 19,19:3
Great Lover, The 1932,O 12,27:3
Night of Love 1941,Ja 8,14:2
Hatton, Fanny (Translator)
His Majesty's Car 1930,O 24,30:1

Hatton, Fanny (Translator)—Cont
Stork Is Dead, The 1932,S 24,18:2
Hatton, Frederic (Playwright)
Checkerboard, The 1920,Ag 20,7:2
We Girls 1921,N 10,26:3
Treat 'Em Rough 1926,My 23,VIII,1:1
Long Island Love 1926,Ag 1,VII,4:1
Treat 'Em Rough 1926,O 5,26:2
Lombardi, Ltd 1927,Je 7,27:3
Synthetic Sin 1927,O 11,26:2
Fatal Woman, The 1930,Mr 2,IX,4:7
Love, Honor and Betray 1930,Mr 13,22:2
Dancing Partner 1930,Jl 27,VIII,2:3
Dancing Partner 1930,Ag 6,24:2
Tonight or Never 1930,N 19,19:3
Great Lover, The 1932,O 12,27:3
Hatton, Frederic (Translator)
His Majesty's Car 1930,O 24,30:1
Stork Is Dead, The 1932,S 24,18:2
Hatton, Joy
Kitchen, The 1966,Je 14,50:1
Hatton, Leon
Backslapper, The 1925,Ap 13,25:2
Hatvany, Lili (Playwright)
First Man, The 1927,O 30,IX,4:1
Love Duel, The 1929,Ap 16,32:3
This Night or Never 1930,My 11,IX,3:1
Tonight or Never 1930,N 9,IX,3:2
Tonight or Never 1930,N 19,19:3
Night of Love 1941,Ja 8,14:2
Hauessermann, E (Director)
Rendezvous in Wien 1956,S 5,23:1
Hauff, Hugo (Translator)
From Vienna 1939,Je 21,26:2
Haufrecht, Marcia
Flies, The 1954,S 10,18:2
Haugan, Judith (Costume Designer)
Contributions; Contribution 1970,Mr 10,53:1
Contributions; Plantation 1970,Mr 10,53:1
Contributions; Shoes 1970,Mr 10,53:1
Haugan, Judith (Scenic Designer)
Man and Superman 1964,D 7,45:2
War and Peace 1965,Ja 12,32:1
Judith 1965,Mr 25,42:2
Haugen, Per Theodor
Othello 1963,Ap 13,10:4
Hauger, George (Translator)
Women at the Tomb, The 1961,Ap 25,41:1
Hop, Signor! 1962,My 8,45:2
Pantagleize 1967,D 1,54:1
Victims, The; Escurial 1968,Mr 6,34:1
Haughton, J A (Translator)
Orpheus in Hades 1930,D 16,30:1
Hauk, Heinrich
Passion Play, The 1929,Ap 30,32:1
Haumert, William
Murder in the Cathedral 1958,Mr 22,12:4
Haupt, Ullrich
Queen Victoria 1923,N 16,15:1
Queen Victoria 1923,N 25,VIII,1:1
Dance of Death, The; Totentanz 1923,D 17,23:3
Marionette Man, The 1924,Ja 27,VII,2:7
Man and the Masses 1924,Ap 15,25:1
Masse Mensch; Man and the Masses 1924,Ap 20,VIII,1:1
Versunkene Glocke, Die 1924,N 3,21:2
Alt Heidelberg 1924,D 8,23:2
Wilhelm Tell 1925,Mr 2,15:1
Taps 1925,Ap 15,16:2
Loves of Lulu, The 1925,My 12,26:1
Bridge of Distances, The 1925,S 29,30:1
Bridge of Distances, The 1925,O 4,IX,1:1
Makropoulos Secret, The 1926,Ja 22,12:4
Thou Desperate Pilot 1927,Mr 8,23:1
One Glorious Hour 1927,Ap 15,27:2
Iphigenie in Tauris 1949,Ap 9,8:1
Saint Joan 1950,Mr 4,10:6
Haupt, Ullrich (Director)
Great Music 1924,O 6,24:1
Versunkene Glocke, Die 1924,N 3,21:2
Wilhelm Tell 1925,Mr 2,15:1
Bridge of Distances, The 1925,S 29,30:1
One Glorious Hour 1927,Ap 15,27:2
Hauptman, Lee
Knight of the Burning Pestle, The 1953,O 24,13:2
Moon in Capricorn 1953,O 28,37:2
Misalliance 1955,F 12,10:6
Hauptmann, Carl (Playwright)
Armseligen Besenbinder, Die 1928,N 19,16:2
Hauptmann, Gerhart (Playwright)
Weavers, The 1921,Jl 24,VI,1:7
Rose Bernd 1922,S 27,17:1
Rose Bernd 1922,O 1,VII,1:6
Rose Bernd 1922,O 1,VII,1:1
Rose Bernd 1922,O 8,VI,1:1
Rose Bernd 1922,O 8,VI,1:1
Assumption of Hannele, The 1924,F 16,16:2
Versunkene Glocke, Die 1924,N 3,21:2
Dorothea Angermann 1926,N 22,28:2
Hamlet 1927,D 9,28:2
Hamlet 1928,Ja 15,VIII,1:8
Dorothea Angermann 1928,F 19,VIII,2:1
Weavers, The 1928,Ap 1,IX,2:4
Before Sunset 1932,F 17,19:3

Vor Sonnenuntergang; Before Sunset 1932,Mr 13,VIII,2:7
Sunken Bell, The 1932,O 9,IX,1:8
Rose Bernd 1932,D 4,IX,1:3
Ratten, Die 1932,D 4,IX,1:5
Gabriel Schillings Flucht 1932,D 4,IX,1:6
Michael Kramer 1932,D 4,IX,1:4
Before Sunset 1933,S 29,10:7
Before Sunset 1933,O 15,IX,1:6
Golden Harp, The 1933,O 16,20:4
Hamlet in Wittenberg 1936,N 15,XI,2:4
Versunkene Glocke, Die 1936,N 20,26:3
Michael Kramer 1938,F 20,XI,2:1
Beaver Coat, The 1956,Mr 29,22:5
Before Sundown 1962,Mr 14,43:1
Iphigenia in Aulis; Agamemnon's Death; Electra; Iphigenia in Delphi 1962,N 11,82:4
Ratten, Die 1966,Ap 13,36:1
Haurigot, Paul (Playwright)
Mediterranee 1926,O 10,29:4
Mediterranee 1926,N 7,VIII,2:7
Hausen, Roy
All in Love 1961,N 11,15:2
In the Penal Colony 1962,My 4,27:2
Come Out, Carlo! 1962,My 4,27:2
Gogo Loves You 1964,O 10,19:2
Hauser, Don (Miscellaneous)
Poupees de Paris, Les 1962,D 13,8:2
Poupees de Paris, Les 1964,My 16,11:1
Hauser, Frank (Director)
Heritage and Its History, A 1965,My 19,42:1
Twelfth Night 1966,Je 23,28:1
Promise, The 1967,N 15,38:1
Hauser, Franklin (Composer)
O'Flynn, The 1934,D 28,24:1
Hauser, Lucille
Eternal Sabbath 1963,O 19,17:2
Hauser, Peter
What a Relief 1935,D 14,10:6
Hausman, Eleanor
Would-Be Gentleman, The 1930,Ap 30,29:2
Autumn Crocus 1932,N 21,20:2
Hausman, Howard L
Nautical but Nice 1931,Ap 19,31:6
Hausner, Jerry
Queer People 1934,F 16,16:2
Hausrath, Alfred H (Mrs)
One Woman's Husband 1920,Mr 23,9:3
Haussermann, Michael
Dreigroschenoper, Die 1965,Mr 12,24:1
Haussmann, John (Playwright)
Woman Kind 1933,S 28,25:2
Haut, Frederick John
Simple Life, A 1964,My 18,36:1
Havania
Vaudeville (Palace) 1930,Jl 7,22:2
Havel, Arthur
Vaudeville (Palace) 1926,Jl 27,15:4
Just a Minute 1928,O 9,34:3
Vaudeville (Palace) 1929,Ja 14,20:3
Night in Venice, A 1929,My 22,30:2
Bravo! 1948,N 12,31:2
Havel, Morton
Vaudeville (Palace) 1926,Jl 27,15:4
Just a Minute 1928,O 9,34:3
Vaudeville (Palace) 1929,Ja 14,20:3
Night in Venice, A 1929,My 22,30:2
Bravo! 1948,N 12,31:2
Havel, Tommy
Just a Minute 1928,O 9,34:3
Havel, Vaclav (Playwright)
Memorandum, The 1968,My 6,55:1
Increased Difficulty of Concentration, The 1969,D 5,48:1
Increased Difficulty of Concentration, The 1969,D 21,II,3:1
Havemeyer, H M (Scenic Designer)
In the Days of the Turbins 1934,Mr 7,22:5
Haven, Jane
Weak Sisters 1925,O 14,31:3
Big Blow 1938,O 3,11:2
Havens, Richard
Bohikee Creek 1966,Ap 29,39:1
Havens, Richie (Miscellaneous)
Peter and the Wolf 1969,N 30,85:5
Havercroft, Lorraine
Paint Your Wagon 1951,N 13,32:2
Me and Juliet 1953,My 29,17:1
Haverhill, Jane
Bitter Oleander 1935,F 12,24:3
Haveron, John
Hans's Crime 1961,F 4,15:1
Havey, Norma
Tendresse, La 1922,S 26,18:1
Man in Evening Clothes, The 1924,D 6,13:4
Grand Duchess and the Waiter, The 1925,O 14,31:1
Embers 1926,F 2,20:3
Havican, Charles
Good Old Days, The 1923,Ag 15,21:2
Haviland, Augusta
Sacred and Profane Love 1920,F 24,11:1
Way Things Happen, The 1924,Ja 29,17:5

Haviland, Augusta—Cont
Hedda Gabler 1924,My 17,18:4
Mrs Partridge Presents 1925,Ja 6,23:3
Lucky Sam McCarver 1925,O 22,22:1
Haviland, Kenneth
Florida Girl 1925,N 3,34:1
Star of Bengal 1929,S 26,27:2
As Good As New 1930,N 4,37:3
Havoc, June
Forbidden Melody 1936,N 3,33:1
Sally, Irene and Mary 1938,Jl 5,13:4
Firefly, The 1938,Jl 12,15:4
Pal Joey 1940,D 26,22:2
Mexican Hayride 1944,Ja 29,9:6
Mexican Hayride 1944,F 6,II,1:1
Sadie Thompson 1944,N 17,25:2
Sadie Thompson 1944,N 26,II,1:1
Ryan Girl, The 1945,S 25,28:2
Ryan Girl, The 1945,S 30,II,1:2
Dunnigan's Daughter 1945,D 27,16:1
Dunnigan's Daughter 1946,Ja 6,II,1:1
Infernal Machine, The 1958,F 4,33:1
Midsummer Night's Dream, A 1958,Je 23,19:1
Beaux' Stratagem, The 1959,F 25,35:4
Beaux' Stratagem, The 1959,Mr 1,II,1:1
Warm Peninsula, The 1959,O 21,46:2
Skin of Our Teeth, The 1961,Mr 6,30:1
Skin of Our Teeth, The 1961,Mr 20,32:6
Skin of Our Teeth, The 1961,Mr 28,40:2
Skin of Our Teeth, The 1961,Ap 1,11:2
Skin of Our Teeth, The 1961,Ap 11,43:5
Skin of Our Teeth, The 1961,Ap 21,29:1
Skin of Our Teeth, The 1961,My 1,35:3
Skin of Our Teeth, The 1961,My 19,22:2
Dinner at Eight 1966,S 28,38:1
Dinner at Eight 1966,O 9,II,1:1
Havoc, June (Director)
Marathon '33 1963,D 23,20:1
Havoc, June (Playwright)
Marathon '33 1963,D 23,20:1
Havrevolds, Olaf
Abraham's Offering 1938,D 18,IX,4:2
Mens Vi Venter 1939,Ap 9,X,2:3
Havrilla, Al
Louie the 14th 1925,Mr 4,17:1
Princess Flavia 1925,N 3,34:3
Hawes, Elizabeth (Costume Designer)
Perfumed Lady, The 1934,Mr 13,27:2
Hawes, Mary Margaret
Bare Facts 1927,Je 30,35:1
Hawes, William
Little Inn, The 1935,Ag 20,25:1
Hawes Sisters
Greenwich Villagers, The 1927,Ag 19,20:2
Hawk, Jeremy
Jane 1947,Ja 30,19:6
Hawke, Andrew (Playwright)
Tinker's Dam 1943,Ja 29,22:2
Hawkes, Jacquetta (Playwright)
Dragon's Mouth 1952,Je 8,II,3:1
Dragon's Mouth 1955,N 17,45:1
Hawkes, Kirby
Princess Turandot 1926,N 13,14:2
Last Torture, The 1927,Ja 13,28:4
Man With Red Hair, A 1928,N 9,22:2
Children of Darkness 1930,Ja 8,25:1
Virtue's Bed 1930,Ap 16,26:5
After All 1931,D 4,28:4
Christopher Comes Across 1932,Je 1,19:2
Hawkes, Kirby (Playwright)
Theodora, the Queen 1934,F 1,15:3
Hawkesworth, Gal
Hamlet 1970,D 28,40:1
Hawkins, Bill
Blue Kitten, The 1922,Ja 14,9:3
Hawkins, Buster (Lighting Director)
Almost Faithful 1948,Je 5,9:2
Hawkins, Charles L
Make Me Know It 1929,N 5,32:5
Hawkins, Doug
Banjo Eyes 1941,D 26,20:2
Hawkins, Elizabeth
Big Blow 1938,O 3,11:2
Hawkins, Erick (Choreographer)
Oedipus Tyrannus 1941,My 10,13:8
Hawkins, George (Playwright)
Here Today, Gone Tomorrow 1940,D 5,32:6
Hawkins, Harris
Oklahoma! 1953,S 1,19:1
Hawkins, Jack
Journey's End 1929,Mr 23,23:1
Journey's End 1929,Jl 14,IX,5:1
Journey's End 1930,Ja 27,24:7
Sunshine Sisters 1933,N 26,IX,3:6
Maitlands, The 1934,Jl 22,IX,1:3
King's Breakfast, The 1937,D 13,22:8
Can We Tell? 1938,O 9,X,3:2
Dear Octopus 1939,Ja 12,22:2
Importance of Being Earnest, The 1939,S 17,X,2:3
King Lear 1940,Ap 28,IX,1:7
Candida 1946,D 4,44:2
Othello 1946,D 4,44:2
Romeo and Juliet 1951,Ja 23,24:8
Romeo and Juliet 1951,Mr 12,21:2

Hawkins, Jack—Cont

Romeo and Juliet 1951,Mr 25,II,1:1

Hawkins, John
Long Gallery, The 1958,Mr 7,17:2
Saintliness of Margery Kempe, The 1959,F 3,35:6

Hawkins, John (Composer)
Canterbury Tales 1968,S 7,23:3
Canterbury Tales; Pilgrims, The 1969,F 4,34:1
Canterbury Tales; Steward's Tale, The 1969,F 4,34:1
Canterbury Tales; Miller's Tale, The 1969,F 4,34:1
Canterbury Tales; Merchant's Tale, The 1969,F 4,34:1
Canterbury Tales; Wife of Bath's Tale, The 1969,F 4,34:1

Hawkins, John T Jr (Costume Designer)
Connecticut Yankee, A 1927,N 4,24:2

Hawkins, John T Jr (Scenic Designer)
Connecticut Yankee, A 1927,N 4,24:2

Hawkins, June
Porgy and Bess 1942,Ja 23,16:2
Carmen Jones 1943,D 3,26:2
Carmen Jones 1945,My 3,26:5
St Louis Woman 1946,Ap 1,22:2

Hawkins, Louis
In Any Language 1952,O 9,40:2

Hawkins, Maxwell (Playwright)
Crime Marches on 1935,O 24,19:1

Hawkins, Melba
Garden of Time 1945,Mr 10,13:7

Hawkins, Michael
Love and Let Love 1968,Ja 4,30:1
Getting Married 1970,Ja 20,46:1

Hawkins, Richard W Jr
In the Days of the Turbins 1934,Mr 7,22:5

Hawkins, Robert
Wait Till We're Married 1921,S 27,14:1

Hawkins, Sid
Sunny Days 1928,F 9,29:1

Hawkins, Tom
Strong Breed, The 1967,N 10,60:1

Hawkins, Virginia
Once in a Lifetime 1930,S 25,22:3

Hawkins, Wood
Provincetown Follies, The 1935,N 4,24:3

Hawkins, Yvette
Amen Corner, The 1965,Ap 16,35:1
Strong Breed, The 1967,N 10,60:1
Trials of Brother Jero, The 1967,N 10,60:1

Hawley, Chaplin
What a Relief 1935,D 14,10:6

Hawley, Dudley
Nightcap, The 1921,Ag 16,18:3
Thin Ice 1922,O 2,20:1
Thumbs Down 1923,Ag 7,20:1
Ladies of the Evening 1924,D 24,11:2
Little Spitfire, The 1926,Ag 17,15:2
Congai 1928,N 28,24:3
Ladies of the Jury 1929,O 22,26:2
Mr Samuel 1930,N 11,28:4
Great Barrington, The 1931,F 20,18:1
Pillars of Society, The 1931,O 15,19:1
Bride the Sun Shines On, The 1931,D 28,20:2
Nona 1932,O 5,26:4
First Apple, The 1933,D 28,25:1
I Want a Policeman! 1936,Ja 15,15:5
Western Union 1937,Ag 10,22:7
Western Waters 1937,D 29,17:1

Hawley, James Rolling
This Mad Whirl 1937,Ja 10,II,4:8

Hawley, Kate
Sourball 1969,Ag 6,29:2

Hawley, Kay
White Eagle, The 1927,D 27,24:4

Hawley, Monte
Bomboola 1929,Je 27,17:3

Hawley, Peter
Naughty Riquette 1926,S 14,25:2
War Song, The 1928,S 25,29:3

Hawley, Robert R
Our Town 1944,Ja 11,24:5

Hawley, Thomas
One More River 1960,Mr 19,12:2
Portrait of the Artist as a Young Man, A 1962,My 29,21:1
Barroom Monks, The 1962,My 29,21:1

Hawley, William
Devil's Disciple, The 1950,Ja 26,23:2
Toys in the Attic 1960,F 26,23:2
Her Master's Voice 1964,D 28,33:2

Hawley, William (Scenic Designer)
Jonica 1930,Ap 8,27:1

Hawley and Lee
Harlem Cavalcade 1942,My 2,11:2

Haworth, Jill
Cabaret 1966,N 21,62:1
Cabaret 1966,D 4,II,5:1
Cabaret 1968,Ja 12,19:1

Haworth, Vinton
Scrap Book 1932,Ag 2,20:3

Haworth, William
Your Uncle Dudley 1929,N 19,26:4

Hawray, Lawrence
Habit 1926,N 4,VIII,4:7

Hawthorne, Ben
Bridge, The 1930,My 6,33:1

Hawthorne, David
Thou Desperate Pilot 1927,Mr 8,23:1
Happy Husband, The 1927,Jl 10,VII,2:3
Fourth Wall, The 1928,Mr 25,IX,1:3

Hawthorne, Gordon
Schoolmaster, The 1928,Mr 21,30:1
Zeppelin 1929,Ja 15,22:3

Hawthorne, Irene
Swing Out, Sweet Land! 1944,N 10,24:6
Sing Out, Sweet Land! 1944,D 28,24:2
Autobiography 1956,O 3,29:2

Hawthorne, Irene (Choreographer)
Autobiography 1956,O 3,29:2

Hawthorne, Irene (Playwright)
Autobiography 1956,O 3,29:2

Hawthorne, Jean
School for Scandal, The 1923,Mr 13,19:2

Hawthorne, Jim
New Moon, The; Desert Song, The 1955,Jl 1,13:1
Merry Widow, The 1957,Ap 11,36:6

Hawthorne, Nathaniel (Original Author)
Scarlet Letter, The 1926,Ja 8,16:5
Poisoned Kiss, The 1937,Ap 22,19:1
My Kinsman, Major Molineux 1964,N 2,62:2
Old Glory, The 1964,N 15,II,1:1

Hawthorne, Ruth (Playwright)
Mrs Partridge Presents 1925,Ja 6,23:3
Queen Bee 1929,N 13,25:1
Mrs Partridge Presents 1936,F 29,10:1

Hawthorne, Virginia
Moon Is a Gong, The 1926,Mr 13,21:3

Hawthorne and Cooke
Earl Carroll's Vanities 1924,S 11,23:6

Hawtrey, Anthony (Director)
Women of Twilight 1952,Mr 4,22:2

Hawtrey, Anthony (Producer)
Love Goes to Press 1946,Je 19,16:2

Hawtrey, Charles (Sir)
Send for Dr O'Grady 1923,Jl 29,VI,1:6

Hawtrey, Kathleen
Faust 1927,Ja 4,20:1

Hawtrey, Marjory
Abdication 1948,S 28,32:5
Women of Twilight 1952,Mr 4,22:2

Hay, Adele
Variations of 1940 1940,Ja 29,12:1

Hay, Brett (Playwright)
Once a Husband 1932,N 20,IX,3:6

Hay, Frank
Pasteur 1923,Mr 13,19:1

Hay, Ian (Director)
Middle Watch, The 1929,O 17,27:1

Hay, Ian (Original Author)
Housemaster 1936,N 14,22:6

Hay, Ian (Playwright)
Happy-Go-Lucky 1920,Ag 25,6:1
Happy-Go-Lucky 1920,Ag 29,VI,1:1
Sport of Kings, The 1928,Ag 26,VII,1:3
Damsel in Distress, A 1928,S 2,VII,2:1
Baa, Baa, Black Sheep 1929,My 12,IX,2:3
Middle Watch, The 1929,S 1,VIII,1:3
Middle Watch, The 1929,O 17,27:1
Song of Sixpence, A 1930,Ap 6,IX,2:1
Present From Margate, The 1933,D 15,28:1
Frog, The 1936,Ap 12,II,8:4
Housemaster 1936,N 14,22:6
Bachelor Born 1938,Ja 26,26:3
On Borrowed Time 1938,O 6,27:5
Little Ladyship 1939,F 26,IX,3:5

Hay, James (Miscellaneous)
Talking to You 1961,O 23,22:5
Across the Board on Tomorrow Morning 1961,O 23,22:5

Hay, Joan
Passing Show of 1923, The 1923,Je 15,24:6

Hay, Julia
Houseparty 1929,S 10,26:5

Hay, Julius (Playwright)
Neue Paradies, Das 1933,Ja 22,IX,1:1

Hay, Mary
Ziegfeld 9 o'clock Follies 1920,Mr 9,18:1
Sally 1920,D 22,16:1
Marjolaine 1922,Ja 25,16:1
Mary Jane McKane 1923,D 26,13:2
Sunny 1925,S 23,22:1
Treasure Girl 1928,N 9,22:1
Vaudeville (Palace) 1929,Ja 21,18:3
Valiant, The 1929,S 22,24:6
Vaudeville (Palace) 1929,S 23,24:6
Greater Love 1931,Mr 3,39:1

Hay, Richard L (Costume Designer)
Resistible Rise of Arturo Ui, The 1968,Ag 8,25:1
Resistible Rise of Arturo Ui, The 1968,D 23,44:1

Hay, Richard L (Lighting Director)
Diary of a Madman 1964,Ap 17,29:2

Hay, Richard L (Scenic Designer)
Diary of a Madman 1964,Ap 17,29:2
Resistible Rise of Arturo Ui, The 1968,Ag 8,25:1
Resistible Rise of Arturo Ui, The 1968,D 23,44:1

Hayakawa, Sessue
Love City, The 1926,Ja 26,18:2

Hayakawa, Sessue—Cont

Vaudeville (Palace) 1926,Jl 27,15:4
Vaudeville (Palace) 1928,Ja 31,29:2
Kataki 1959,Ap 10,24:1
Evening of Rare Pleasures, An 1959,Je 4,26:2

Hayden, Betty
Babes in Toyland 1930,D 22,17:1

Hayden, Bill
Servant of Two Masters, The 1958,F 11,35:2

Hayden, Catherine
Unsophisticates, The 1929,D 31,14:5

Hayden, Christine
White-Headed Boy, The 1921,S 16,20:1
Church Street 1934,My 23,15:5

Hayden, Cissie
Good Times 1920,Ag 10,10:1

Hayden, Eleanor
Philadelphia 1929,S 17,34:5
Your Uncle Dudley 1929,N 19,26:4

Hayden, Gerard
Puritan, The 1936,Ja 24,14:3

Hayden, Harry (Director)
Thirsty Soil 1937,F 4,16:2

Hayden, Harry (Miscellaneous)
Thirsty Soil 1937,F 4,16:2

Hayden, John
Star of Bengal 1929,S 26,27:2
Walk Together Chillun 1936,F 5,15:2

Hayden, John (Director)
Enchanted April, The 1925,Ag 25,12:3
Appearances 1925,O 15,27:3
Mama Loves Papa 1926,F 23,26:2
Proud Woman, A 1926,N 16,24:1
Judy 1927,F 8,20:2
Merry Andrew 1929,Ja 22,22:2
So Was Napoleon 1930,Ja 9,22:2
Sisters of the Chorus 1930,O 21,34:3
Bidding High 1932,S 29,17:2
Lost Horizons 1934,O 16,31:2
Knock on Wood 1935,My 29,16:2
Night of January 16 1935,S 10,26:1
Night of January 16 1935,S 17,26:4
Abide With Me 1935,N 22,19:2
Without Warning 1937,My 3,23:2
Devil Takes a Bride, The 1938,O 8,10:3
Good-Bye to Love 1940,Je 8,18:1

Hayden, John (Miscellaneous)
Between the Devil 1937,D 23,24:5

Hayden, John (Playwright)
Lost Horizons 1934,O 16,31:2
Is This a Zither? 1935,Je 11,24:3

Hayden, Katharine
Cousin Sonia 1925,D 8,28:3
Interference 1928,My 8,25:4

Hayden, Kathlyn (Playwright)
Murder on Account 1936,My 25,23:1
Murder on Account 1936,S 26,11:2

Hayden, Kenneth
Mr Sycamore 1942,N 14,13:2

Hayden, Linda J
Carmilla 1970,D 1,61:2

Hayden, Marna
Don Carlos 1962,F 28,27:5
Storm, The 1962,Mr 31,17:2

Hayden, Mary
Journey of the Fifth Horse, The 1966,Ap 22,36:1

Hayden, Robert
Music in My Heart 1947,O 3,30:2

Hayden, Terese
Days of Our Youth, The 1941,N 29,15:2

Hayden, Terese (Director)
Dinosaur Wharf 1951,N 9,23:2
School for Scandal, The 1953,Je 24,29:2
Inherit the Wind 1955,Ap 22,20:2
Secret Concubine, The 1960,Mr 22,29:2
Five Evenings 1963,My 10,37:3
When Did You Last See My Mother? 1967,Ja 5,27:5
Antigone 1967,Ja 14,18:1

Hayden, Terese (Producer)
Parisienne 1950,Jl 25,24:2
Lady From the Sea, The 1950,Ag 8,23:2
Borned in Texas 1950,Ag 22,30:6
Dinosaur Wharf 1951,N 9,23:2
Maya 1953,Je 10,35:1
Scarecrow, The 1953,Je 17,31:1
School for Scandal, The 1953,Je 24,29:2
Little Clay Cart, The 1953,Jl 1,25:1
Secret Concubine, The 1960,Mr 22,29:2
Five Evenings 1963,My 10,37:3

Haydn, Joseph (Composer)
Apothecary, The 1925,S 5,11:4

Haydn, Joseph (Miscellaneous)
Apothecary, The 1926,Mr 17,28:1

Haydn, Maury
Sweet Miani 1962,S 26,33:2

Haydn, Richard
Set to Music 1939,Ja 19,16:2
Two for the Show 1940,F 9,14:2
Two for the Show 1940,F 18,IX,1:1

Haydon, Catherine
Window Panes 1927,F 22,22:2
Woman of Bronze, The 1927,Je 16,25:4
These Modern Women 1928,F 14,26:2

Haydon, Catherine—Cont
Round Table, The 1930,F 28,20:5
Haydon, Fred
Move On 1926,Ja 19,30:1
Haydon, Julie
Autumn Crocus 1934,Ja 21,X,1:6
Bright Star 1935,O 13,IX,1:6
Bright Star 1935,O 16,26:2
Shadow and Substance 1938,Ja 27,16:2
Shadow and Substance 1938,F 6,X,1:1
Time of Your Life, The 1939,O 26,26:2
Time of Your Life, The 1940,S 24,27:2
Life, Laughter And Tears 1942,F 26,15:2
Hello Out There 1942,S 30,28:2
Magic 1942,S 30,28:2
Patriots, The 1943,D 21,22:5
Glass Menagerie, The 1945,Ja 14,II,2:4
Glass Menagerie, The 1945,Ap 2,15:5
Glass Menagerie, The 1945,Ap 8,II,1:1
Miracle in the Mountains 1947,Ap 26,10:2
Our Lan' 1947,S 29,16:5
Haye, Helen
Skin Game, The 1920,My 23,VI,1:3
Last of Mrs Cheyney, The 1925,N 10,23:5
John Gabriel Borkman 1926,Ja 30,13:1
After All 1929,My 26,IX,1:3
Sex Fable, The 1931,O 21,26:1
After All 1931,D 4,28:4
Moonlight Is Silver 1934,O 7,IX,3:7
Someone to Talk To 1956,Jl 19,30:2
Haye, Sheelagh
Closed Room, The 1934,Jl 24,20:2
Hayeem, Benjamin
Shakuntala 1959,S 10,41:2
Secret Concubine, The 1960,Mr 22,29:2
Brouhaha 1960,Ap 27,31:2
In the Jungle of Cities 1960,D 21,39:1
Mountain Giants, The 1961,Ap 5,32:3
Red Eye of Love 1961,Je 13,28:1
Fortuna 1962,Ja 4,26:1
Man Is Man 1962,S 19,31:1
Dynamite Tonight 1967,Mr 16,52:2
Hayes, Albert
Mr Moneypenny 1928,O 17,26:2
Nice Women 1929,Je 11,27:4
Virtue's Bed 1930,Ap 16,26:5
That's the Woman 1930,S 4,27:2
Merchant of Venice, The 1930,D 3,29:2
Berlin 1931,D 31,16:1
Good Earth, The 1932,O 18,23:4
Be So Kindly 1937,F 9,19:4
Ten Minute Alibi 1937,Jl 20,19:3
Blow Ye Winds 1937,S 24,17:4
Hayes, Alfred
'Tis of Thee 1940,O 28,21:3
Hayes, Alfred (Lyricist)
Hellzapoppin 1938,S 23,34:2
'Tis of Thee 1940,O 28,21:3
Of V We Sing 1942,F 16,20:3
It's Up to You 1943,Ap 1,19:1
Hayes, Alfred (Original Author)
Girl on the Via Flaminia, The 1954,F 10,37:1
Hayes, Alfred (Playwright)
Journeyman 1938,Ja 31,14:2
Of V We Sing 1941,O 26,I,39:1
Girl on the Via Flaminia, The 1954,F 10,37:1
Girl on the Via Flaminia, The 1954,Ap 6,35:5
Girl on the Via Flaminia, The 1954,O 13,26:5
Hayes, Alfred (Translator)
Boris Godunoff 1925,F 27,14:1
Hayes, Barbara
Happy as Larry 1961,Ap 26,36:1
Daughter of Silence 1961,D 1,28:1
Hey You, Light Man! 1963,Mr 2,5:2
Big Man 1966,My 20,41:1
Four Seasons, The 1968,Mr 15,32:1
Papp 1969,My 6,39:1
Hayes, Ben
Bivouac at Lucca 1957,O 30,26:1
Children of Darkness 1958,Mr 1,11:4
Come Share My House 1960,F 19,20:2
White Cargo 1960,D 30,12:1
Much Ado About Nothing 1961,Jl 7,17:1
Richard II 1961,Ag 30,25:1
Jackhammer, The 1962,F 6,26:2
Merchant of Venice, The 1962,Je 22,1:4
Calculated Risk 1962,N 1,35:1
Hayes, Bernadene
Mother Sings 1935,N 13,24:1
Mid-West 1936,Ja 8,22:4
Aries Is Rising 1939,N 22,16:5
Blind Alley 1940,O 16,28:2
School for Brides 1944,Ag 2,19:4
Make Yourself at Home 1945,S 14,21:2
Hayes, Beverly
Perfect Party, The 1969,Mr 21,42:1
Hayes, Bill
Me and Juliet 1953,My 29,17:1
Me and Juliet 1953,Je 7,II,1:1
Brigadoon 1967,D 14,59:2
Hayes, Billie
New Faces of 1956 1956,Je 15,32:1
Hayes, Carmen
Tick-Tack-Toe 1920,F 24,11:2

Hayes, Catherine
Three Musketeers, The 1928,Mr 14,28:1
Hayes, Collington
Harlem 1929,F 21,30:3
Hayes, Donald
Kilpatrick's Old-Time Minstrels 1930,Ap 21,20:2
Hayes, Edward
Music in the Air 1932,N 9,28:2
Hayes, Elnora
Arrow-Maker, The 1956,O 5,20:1
Hayes, Frances
Weep for the Virgins 1935,D 2,18:1
Revolt of the Beavers, The 1937,My 21,19:2
Hayes, Genevieve
Elton Case, The 1921,S 12,16:2
Hayes, George
Paul I 1927,O 23,VIII,4:1
Chauve-Souris; Queen of Spades, The 1931,O 22,27:1
Much Ado About Nothing 1941,Ap 20,IX,3:3
Love for Love 1947,My 27,30:2
Hayes, George R
They Shall Not Die 1934,F 22,24:4
Hayes, Georgia
Paris Qui Charme 1929,Je 16,VIII,2:3
Hayes, Georgie
Hello Paris 1930,N 17,29:3
Hayes, Grace
Bunch and Judy, The 1922,N 29,20:1
Merry World, The 1926,Je 9,18:3
Passions of 1926 1926,Ag 3,19:4
Night in Spain, A 1927,My 4,28:2
Vaudeville (Palace) 1929,Jl 15,25:4
Vaudeville (Palace) 1929,O 7,22:4
Ballyhoo 1930,D 23,24:1
Little Racketeer, The 1932,Ja 19,24:4
Vaudeville (Palace) 1932,My 23,18:7
Hayes, Helen
Bab 1920,O 19,12:1
Wren, The 1921,O 11,22:1
Wren, The 1921,O 16,VI,1:1
Golden Days 1921,N 2,20:1
Golden Days 1921,N 6,VI,1:1
To the Ladies! 1922,F 21,20:1
To the Ladies! 1922,Mr 12,VI,1:1
Lonely Lee 1923,N 11,VIII,2:6
We Moderns 1923,D 30,VII,2:1
We Moderns 1924,Mr 12,17:2
We Moderns 1924,Mr 16,VIII,1:1
She Stoops to Conquer 1924,Je 10,24:3
Dancing Mothers 1924,Ag 12,12:2
Quarantine 1924,N 23,VIII,2:4
Quarantine 1924,D 17,19:7
Caesar and Cleopatra 1925,Ap 14,27:1
Young Blood 1925,N 25,15:1
Young Blood 1925,N 29,VIII,1:1
What Every Woman Knows 1926,Ap 14,20:2
What Every Woman Knows 1926,Ap 18,VIII,1:1
Coquette 1927,O 16,IX,2:4
Coquette 1927,N 9,23:1
Coquette 1927,N 13,IX,1:1
Mr Gilhooley 1930,O 1,26:1
Petticoat Influence 1930,D 16,34:6
Good Fairy, The 1931,N 15,VIII,4:1
Good Fairy, The 1931,N 25,17:1
Mary of Scotland 1933,N 19,IX,2:5
Mary of Scotland 1933,N 28,28:3
Mary of Scotland 1933,D 3,IX,5:1
Caesar and Cleopatra 1935,Ag 22,21:1
Victoria Regina 1935,D 13,30:5
Victoria Regina 1935,D 27,15:2
Victoria Regina 1936,Ja 5,IX,1:1
Victoria Regina 1936,Mr 8,IX,1:1
Victoria Regina 1936,S 1,24:5
Victoria Regina 1937,S 26,XI,3:6
Merchant of Venice, The 1938,Ja 15,18:8
What Every Woman Knows 1938,Ag 30,14:5
Victoria Regina 1938,O 4,20:2
Victoria Regina 1938,O 9,X,1:3
Ladies and Gentlemen 1939,S 24,IX,2:5
Ladies and Gentlemen 1939,O 18,30:2
Ladies and Gentlemen 1939,O 22,IX,1:3
Ladies and Gentlemen 1939,O 29,IX,1:3
Twelfth Night 1940,O 18,26:7
Twelfth Night 1940,O 27,IX,1:5
Twelfth Night 1940,N 20,26:3
Twelfth Night 1940,N 24,IX,1:1
Candle in the Wind 1941,S 16,19:6
Candle in the Wind 1941,O 23,26:2
Candle in the Wind 1941,N 2,IX,1:1
Harriet 1943,Ja 29,22:1
Harriet 1943,Mr 4,24:2
Harriet 1943,Mr 14,V,1:1
Harriet 1944,S 28,26:1
Happy Birthday 1946,N 1,31:2
Happy Birthday 1946,N 10,II,1:1
Glass Menagerie, The 1948,Jl 29,17:2
Good Housekeeping 1949,Ag 17,19:3
Wisteria Trees, The 1950,Mr 30,39:1
Wisteria Trees, The 1950,Ap 9,II,1:1
Mrs McThing 1952,F 21,22:1
Mrs McThing 1952,Mr 2,II,1:1
What Every Woman Knows 1954,S 29,23:4

Hayes, Helen—Cont
What Every Woman Knows 1954,D 23,16:2
Wisteria Trees, The 1955,F 3,20:2
Skin of Our Teeth, The 1955,Je 29,25:3
Skin of Our Teeth, The 1955,Ag 18,16:1
Skin of Our Teeth, The 1955,Ag 28,II,1:1
Lovers, Villains and Fools: A Shakespearean Variety Show 1956,O 24,44:7
Glass Menagerie, The 1956,N 22,50:1
Glass Menagerie, The 1956,D 2,II,1:1
Time Remembered 1957,N 13,41:2
Time Remembered 1957,N 24,II,1:1
Touch of the Poet, A 1958,O 3,23:2
Touch of the Poet, A 1958,O 12,II,1:1
Glass Menagerie, The 1961,Mr 6,30:1
Skin of Our Teeth, The 1961,Mr 6,30:1
Skin of Our Teeth, The 1961,Mr 20,32:6
Skin of Our Teeth, The 1961,Mr 28,40:2
Skin of Our Teeth, The 1961,Ap 1,11:2
Glass Menagerie, The 1961,Ap 11,43:5
Glass Menagerie, The 1961,Ap 21,29:1
Skin of Our Teeth, The 1961,Ap 21,29:1
Glass Menagerie, The 1961,My 1,35:3
Skin of Our Teeth, The 1961,My 1,35:3
Skin of Our Teeth, The 1961,My 19,22:2
Glass Menagerie, The 1961,My 19,22:2
Glass Menagerie, The 1961,My 31,28:1
Glass Menagerie, The 1961,Je 16,27:3
Glass Menagerie, The 1961,Ag 21,20:7
Shakespeare Revisited 1962,Jl 19,19:2
White House, The 1964,My 20,39:1
School for Scandal, The 1966,N 22,33:2
Right You Are (If You Think You Are) 1966,N 23,34:2
Right You Are (If You Think You Are) 1966,D 11,II,3:1
We Comrades Three 1966,D 21,46:1
Show-Off, The 1967,D 6,40:2
Show-Off, The 1967,D 17,II,3:7
Front Page, The 1969,N 2,86:1
Harvey 1970,F 25,41:1
Harvey 1970,Mr 8,II,1:1
Hayes, Helen (Miscellaneous)
Country Wife, The 1936,D 2,34:1
Hayes, Helen (Producer)
Country Wife, The 1936,O 7,32:3
Merchant of Venice, The 1938,Ja 15,18:8
Mary Rose 1951,Mr 5,25:2
Mary Rose 1951,Mr 11,II,1:1
Hayes, Henry R Jr
Assorted Nuts 1940,Ap 7,I,44:6
Hayes, Hubert (Playwright)
Tight Britches 1934,S 12,26:2
Hayes, Irene
Righteous Are Bold, The 1955,D 23,12:1
Hayes, J T
Take a Brace 1923,Ap 20,20:3
Hayes, James
Hamlet 1936,N 11,54:2
Fireman's Flame, The 1937,O 11,26:2
First Stop to Heaven 1941,Ja 6,10:7
Steps Leading Up 1941,Ap 19,20:6
Hayes, Janet
Anyone Can Whistle 1964,Ap 6,36:1
Hayes, Jimmy
Great Goodness of Life (A Coon Show) 1969,Ap 27,92:1
Warning, The-A Theme for Linda 1969,Ap 27,92:1
Hayes, John
Harriet 1944,S 28,26:1
Hayes, Johnson
Darkness at Noon 1951,Ja 15,13:4
Hayes, Joseph (Director)
Happiest Millionaire, The 1956,N 21,21:3
Hayes, Joseph (Original Author)
Desperate Hours, The 1955,F 11,20:2
Hayes, Joseph (Playwright)
Leaf and Bough 1949,Ja 22,10:2
Desperate Hours, The 1955,F 11,20:2
Desperate Hours, The 1955,F 20,II,1:1
Calculated Risk 1962,O 17,33:3
Calculated Risk 1962,N 1,35:1
Hayes, Joseph (Producer)
Desperate Hours, The 1955,F 11,20:2
Happiest Millionaire, The 1956,N 21,21:3
Calculated Risk 1962,N 1,35:1
Hayes, Katherine
Vagabond King, The 1925,S 22,23:3
Hayes, L Ann
Watch-Pit 1969,Ja 30,39:1
Hayes, Langford
Old English 1924,D 24,11:2
Hayes, Laurence
New Moon, The 1944,My 18,16:2
Hayes, Lorraine
Growing Pains 1933,N 24,24:2
Red Cat, The 1934,S 20,21:1
Hayes, Maggie
Fair Game for Lovers 1964,F 11,43:2
Hayes, Margaret
Happily Ever After 1945,Mr 16,21:2
Little Women 1945,D 24,18:2
Step on a Crack 1962,O 18,48:1

Hayes, Margaret (Producer)
Ordinary Man, An 1968,S 10,39:1
Hayes, Mariposa
Spring 3100 1928,F 16,14:2
Hayes, Mark
Take It Away 1936,D 15,30:5
Take It Away 1936,D 22,32:3
Once Over Lightly 1938,D 10,13:4
Hayes, Marsh and Hayes
Vaudeville (Palace) 1926,Je 22,21:3
Hayes, Mary
Comedy of Women, A 1929,S 14,17:4
Hayes, Melvyn
South 1955,My 2,17:4
Hayes, Mimi
Vagabond King, The 1925,S 22,23:3
Hayes, Norma
Desire Under the Elms 1952,Ja 17,23:4
Hayes, Pamela
International Playgirls '64 1964,My 22,40:2
Hayes, Patricia
When We Are Married 1938,O 30,IX,1:2
Hayes, Paul
Piper, The 1920,Mr 20,14:2
Birthright, The 1920,My 25,14:2
Kathleen ni Houlihan 1920,Je 29,9:2
Adding Machine, The 1923,Mr 20,24:1
Hayes, Peter Lind
Winged Victory 1943,N 22,24:1
Heaven on Earth 1948,S 17,29:2
Who Was That Lady I Saw You With?
  1958,Mr 4,33:2
Lovers 1968,N 24,II,9:4
Lovers 1968,N 26,43:1
Hayes, Prudence
Red, Hot and Blue! 1936,O 30,26:3
Hayes, Renick
Three Sisters, The 1930,Ja 9,22:2
Hayes, Rich
Vaudeville (Palace) 1924,F 12,20:2
Hayes, Richard
Nervous Set, The 1959,My 13,43:1
Beast in Me, The 1963,My 17,29:1
Hayes, Robert
Let Freedom Ring 1935,N 7,26:2
Hayes, Sheelagh
Pickwick 1927,S 6,35:2
Silver Box, The 1928,Ja 18,23:1
Divorce a la Carte 1928,Mr 27,30:3
Novice and the Duke, The 1929,D 11,37:2
Country Wife, The 1931,Ap 19,31:5
Way of the World, The 1931,Je 2,34:3
Hayes, Sheila
Enter Madame 1920,Ag 17,11:2
Casanova 1923,S 27,10:2
Hayes, Solen
Truckline Cafe 1946,F 28,19:4
Hayes, T Renick
Antigone 1930,Ap 25,28:4
Boeuf sur le Toit, Le 1930,Ap 25,28:4
Hayes, Thomas
Much Ado About Nothing 1927,N 19,14:6
Doctor Knock 1928,F 24,15:2
Wild Duck, The 1928,N 19,17:1
Judas 1929,Ja 25,20:4
Hayes, Tommy
This Year of Grace 1928,N 8,27:1
Hayes, William
Funzapoppin 1949,Jl 1,16:2
Hayes, William T
Inspector General, The 1923,My 1,24:1
Weak Sisters 1925,O 14,31:3
Hayeson, Jimmy
Black Quartet, A; Great Goodness of Life (A Coon
  Show) 1969,Jl 31,28:1
Black Quartet, A; Warning, The-A Theme for
  Linda 1969,Jl 31,28:1
Black Quartet, A; Great Goodness of Life (A Coon
  Show) 1969,Jl 31,28:1
Hayford, June
Across the Board on Tomorrow Morning
  1942,Ag 18,17:1
Haygarth, Anthony
Lunatic the Secret Sportsman and the Woman
  Next 1968,D 5,58:4
Haygood, Rig
Galileo 1968,D 1,88:4
Hayle, Douglas
Henry IV, Part II 1968,Jl 2,33:1
Romeo and Juliet 1968,Ag 16,19:1
In the Matter of J Robert Oppenheimer
  1969,Mr 7,28:1
Miser, The 1969,My 9,35:1
Trelawny of the 'Wells' 1970,O 12,48:1
Hayman, Carole
Isabel's a Jezebel 1970,D 27,II,3:1
Hayman, Charles (Miscellaneous)
Romeo and Jeanette 1969,D 16,53:1
Nature of the Crime 1970,Mr 24,41:1
Hayman, Clifford (Miscellaneous)
Two's Company 1952,D 16,43:5
Someone Waiting 1956,F 15,26:1

Hayman, Clifford (Producer)
Uncle Harry 1942,My 21,24:1
I'll Take the High Road 1943,N 10,28:3
Round Trip 1945,My 30,16:4
Hayman, Coreania
Carmen Jones 1946,Ap 8,32:2
Hayman, H M (Producer)
First Mortgage 1929,O 11,36:1
Hayman, Lillian
Shinbone Alley 1957,Ap 15,23:2
Free and Easy 1959,D 20,II,3:2
Kwamina 1961,O 24,42:1
Along Came a Spider 1963,My 28,33:1
Porgy and Bess 1964,My 7,32:1
Hallelujah, Baby! 1967,Ap 27,51:1
Hallelujah, Baby! 1967,My 7,II,1:1
Hayman, Richard
Hell'z-A-Splashin' 1959,Je 25,22:2
Hayman, Richard (Composer)
Aqua Carnival 1962,Je 29,15:1
Haymen, Kerry (Miscellaneous)
Conerico Was Here to Stay 1969,Mr 11,39:1
Paradise Gardens East 1969,Mr 11,39:1
Haymer, Johnny
New Faces of 1956 1956,Je 15,32:1
Hayner, Emma
Octoroon, The 1929,Mr 13,28:3
Haynes, Alice
Straw, The 1921,N 11,16:2
Haynes, Betty
Caukey 1944,F 18,15:4
Anna Lucasta 1944,Je 17,10:1
Odds on Mrs Oakley, The 1944,O 3,18:8
Tin Top Valley 1947,Mr 1,11:2
Haynes, Daniel
Androcles and the Lion 1938,D 17,10:5
Haynes, Daniel L
Bottom of the Cup, The 1927,F 1,24:2
Earth 1927,Mr 10,23:1
Green Pastures, The 1930,F 27,26:1
Green Pastures, The 1931,Mr 1,VIII,1:1
Green Pastures, The 1935,F 27,16:2
Haynes, Edward (Scenic Designer)
When We Dead Awaken 1966,Ap 19,37:2
Haynes, Gary
Toilet, The 1964,D 17,51:1
Haynes, Helen
World's My Oyster, The 1956,Ag 10,10:4
Haynes, Hilda
Three's a Family 1943,N 19,24:3
On Strivers' Row 1946,Mr 1,17:2
King of Hearts 1954,Ap 2,23:1
Wisteria Trees, The 1955,F 3,20:2
Trouble in Mind 1955,N 5,23:2
Take a Giant Step 1956,S 26,30:1
Irregular Verb to Love, The 1963,S 19,22:2
Great White Hope, The 1967,D 14,58:1
Great White Hope, The 1967,D 24,II,3:1
Great White Hope, The 1968,O 4,40:1
Haynes, Jayne
Terminal 1970,Ap 15,51:2
Endgame 1970,My 6,47:1
Serpent, The 1970,Je 2,35:1
Haynes, John Emerson
My Princess 1927,O 7,24:2
Haynes, Laurel
Show Boat 1954,My 6,44:1
Haynes, Lawrence
Show Boat 1954,My 6,44:1
Haynes, Marie
Immodest Violet 1920,Ag 25,6:2
Dream Maker, The 1921,N 22,17:1
Mister Pitt 1924,Ja 23,15:3
Judge's Husband, The 1926,S 28,31:1
Gringa, La 1928,F 2,17:1
Crashing Through 1928,O 30,26:5
Dread 1929,O 27,IX,2:1
House Afire 1930,Ap 1,34:7
Haynes, Mary
Vaudeville (Palace) 1926,My 11,25:3
Vaudeville (Palace) 1929,Mr 18,30:5
Haynes, Mel
Trial of Dmitri Karamazov, The 1958,Ja 28,30:1
Born Yesterday 1958,Mr 22,12:6
Legend of Lovers 1959,O 28,40:3
Purple Canary, The 1963,Ap 23,31:1
Diamond Orchid 1965,F 11,44:4
Sunset 1966,My 13,34:1
Haynes, Minna Gale
Outrageous Mrs Palmer, The 1920,O 13,18:1
Tarzan of the Apes 1921,S 8,14:3
Golden Days 1921,N 2,20:1
Haynes, Mitzi
Banjo Eyes 1941,D 26,20:2
Haynes, Roberta
Now I Lay Me Down to Sleep 1949,Jl 23,7:3
Madwoman of Chaillot, The 1950,Je 14,41:2
Haynes, Tiger
New Faces of 1956 1956,Je 15,32:1
Fade Out--Fade In 1964,My 27,45:1
Kiss Me, Kate 1965,My 13,31:1
Finian's Rainbow 1967,Ap 6,44:1

Haynor, Jerome
Four O'Clock 1933,F 14,19:6
Haynsworth, Mary
Possessed, The 1939,O 25,26:2
Twelfth Night 1941,D 3,32:2
Hays, Blanche
Verge, The 1921,N 15,23:2
Hays, David (Costume Designer)
Children of Darkness 1958,Mr 1,11:4
Quare Fellow, The 1958,N 28,34:1
Hays, David (Director)
Blueprints 1969,F 25,36:1
Gianni Schicci 1969,F 25,36:1
Tale of Kasane, The 1969,F 25,36:1
On the Harmfulness of Tobacco 1969,Mr 9,76:5
Hays, David (Lighting Director)
Cradle Song 1955,D 2,32:2
Innkeepers, The 1956,F 3,19:1
Iceman Cometh, The 1956,My 8,38:1
Children of Darkness 1958,Mr 1,11:4
Salad Days 1958,N 11,24:1
Quare Fellow, The 1958,N 28,34:1
Our Town 1959,Mr 24,46:2
Bedtime Story 1959,Ap 16,28:1
On the Harmful Effects of Tobacco
  1959,Ap 16,28:1
Portrait of a Madonna 1959,Ap 16,28:1
Pound on Demand, A 1959,Ap 16,28:1
Macbeth 1959,Ag 1,9:2
Tenth Man, The 1959,N 6,24:2
Roman Candle 1960,F 4,34:2
Balcony, The 1960,Mr 4,21:1
All the Way Home 1960,D 1,42:1
Love and Libel 1960,D 8,44:1
Smiling the Boy Fell Dead 1961,Ap 20,28:1
Look: We've Come Through 1961,O 26,40:1
Sunday in New York 1961,N 10,40:1
Gideon 1961,N 10,38:1
Family Affair, A 1962,Ja 29,17:1
No Strings 1962,Mr 16,24:1
In the Counting House 1962,D 15,5:5
Desire Under the Elms 1963,Ja 11,5:6
Lorenzo 1963,F 16,5:2
Strange Interlude 1963,Mr 13,5:2
Next Time I'll Sing to You 1963,N 28,69:2
Marco Millions 1964,F 21,33:1
Murderer Among Us, A 1964,Mr 26,43:1
Baby Want a Kiss 1964,Ap 20,32:1
Last Analysis, The 1964,O 2,30:1
Changeling, The 1964,O 30,32:2
Hughie 1964,D 23,21:2
Peterpat 1965,Ja 7,27:1
Diamond Orchid 1965,F 11,44:4
Matty and the Moron and Madonna
  1965,Mr 30,53:1
Drat! the Cat! 1965,O 11,54:2
Utbu 1966,Ja 5,24:1
Dinner at Eight 1966,S 28,38:1
We Have Always Lived in the Castle
  1966,O 20,53:1
Yerma 1966,D 9,60:1
Dr Cook's Garden 1967,S 26,52:1
Tenth Man, The 1967,N 9,54:1
Goodbye People, The 1968,D 4,52:1
Hays, David (Miscellaneous)
Songs From Milk Wood 1970,Ja 13,41:1
Hays, David (Scenic Designer)
Cradle Song 1955,D 2,32:2
Innkeepers, The 1956,F 3,19:1
Iceman Cometh, The 1956,My 8,38:1
Long Day's Journey Into Night 1956,N 8,47:2
Career 1957,My 1,42:6
Long Day's Journey Into Night 1957,Jl 3,14:1
Endgame 1958,Ja 29,32:4
Children of Darkness 1958,Mr 1,11:4
Hamlet 1958,Je 21,11:1
Midsummer Night's Dream, A 1958,Je 23,19:1
Winter's Tale, The 1958,Jl 21,17:4
Winter's Tale, The 1958,Jl 27,II,1:1
Salad Days 1958,N 11,24:1
Quare Fellow, The 1958,N 28,34:1
Night Circus, The 1958,D 3,44:1
Rivalry, The 1959,F 9,24:2
Rivalry, The 1959,F 15,II,1:1
Portrait of a Madonna 1959,Ap 16,28:1
On the Harmful Effects of Tobacco
  1959,Ap 16,28:1
Pound on Demand, A 1959,Ap 16,28:1
Bedtime Story 1959,Ap 16,28:1
Romeo and Juliet 1959,Je 15,31:1
Romeo and Juliet 1959,Je 21,II,1:1
Macbeth 1959,Ag 1,9:2
Tenth Man, The 1959,N 6,24:2
Tenth Man, The 1959,N 15,II,1:1
Roman Candle 1960,F 4,34:2
Balcony, The 1960,Mr 4,21:1
All the Way Home 1960,D 1,42:1
Love and Libel 1960,D 8,44:1
Look: We've Come Through 1961,O 26,40:1
Gideon 1961,N 10,38:1
Sunday in New York 1961,N 10,40:1
Family Affair, A 1962,Ja 29,17:1
No Strings 1962,Mr 16,24:1

Hays, David (Scenic Designer)—Cont

In the Counting House 1962,D 15,5:5
Desire Under the Elms 1963,Ja 11,5:6
Lorenzo 1963,F 16,5:2
Strange Interlude 1963,Mr 13,5:2
Next Time I'll Sing to You 1963,N 28,69:2
Marco Millions 1964,F 21,33:1
Murderer Among Us, A 1964,Mr 26,43:1
Last Analysis, The 1964,O 2,30:1
Changeling, The 1964,O 30,32:2
Hughie 1964,D 23,21:2
Peterpat 1965,Ja 7,27:1
Tartuffe 1965,Ja 15,23:1
Diamond Orchid 1965,F 11,44:4
Matty and the Moron and Madonna
  1965,Mr 30,53:1
Mrs Dally 1965,S 25,5:7
Drat! the Cat! 1965,O 11,54:2
Utbu 1966,Ja 5,24:1
Murder in the Cathedral 1966,Je 21,38:1
Dinner at Eight 1966,S 28,38:1
We Have Always Lived in the Castle
  1966,O 20,53:1
Yerma 1966,D 9,60:1
Dr Cook's Garden 1967,S 26,52:1
Tenth Man, The 1967,N 9,54:1
Saint Joan 1968,Ja 5,42:1
Tiger at the Gates 1968,Mr 1,30:1
Cyrano de Bergerac 1968,Ap 26,30:1
Cry of Players, A 1968,N 15,40:1
Goodbye People, The 1968,D 4,52:1
Blueprints 1969,F 25,36:1
Gianni Schicci 1969,F 25,36:1
Tale of Kasane, The 1969,F 25,36:1
Miser, The 1969,My 9,35:1
Songs From Milk Wood 1970,Ja 13,41:1
Two by Two 1970,N 11,37:1
Gingerbread Lady, The 1970,D 14,58:3

Hays, Harvey
Romeo and Juliet 1922,D 28,20:1
Hail and Farewell 1923,F 20,12:1
Thumbs Down 1923,Ag 7,20:1
Macbeth 1924,Mr 17,18:1
Killers 1928,Mr 14,28:3

Hays, Hoffman R (Playwright)
Medicine Show 1940,Ap 13,20:6

Hays, Jerome
Springtime of Youth 1922,O 27,15:1

Hays, Kathryn
Moon Besieged, The 1962,D 6,54:1
Irregular Verb to Love, The 1963,S 19,22:2

Hays, Lenore
Metamorphosis 1957,F 20,38:1
Pale Horse, Pale Rider 1957,O 30,26:1

Hays, Lora
American Tragedy, An 1931,F 21,15:5
I Love an Actress 1931,S 18,29:2

Hays, Marjory
It Happened Tomorrow 1933,My 6,11:5

Hays, William T
Six-Fifty, The 1921,O 25,20:1
Six-Fifty, The 1921,O 30,VI,1:1
Squaw Man, The 1921,D 27,10:3
Six Characters in Search of an Author
  1922,O 31,11:2
Processional 1925,Ja 13,17:1
Gentlemen Prefer Blondes 1926,S 29,23:1
Faust 1928,O 9,34:1
Subway Express 1929,S 25,34:3
Green Grow the Lilacs 1931,Ja 27,21:2

Hayter, James
Composite Man, The 1936,S 27,X,3:5
Romeo and Juliet 1951,Ja 23,24:8
Romeo and Juliet 1951,Mr 12,21:2
Romeo and Juliet 1951,Mr 25,II,1:1
Duel, The 1968,Ap 18,56:1

Haythorne, Joan
Venus Observed 1952,F 14,24:2

Hayward, Brooke
Marching Song 1959,D 29,20:1
Mandingo 1961,My 23,43:6

Hayward, Grace (Playwright)
Her Unborn Child 1928,Mr 7,28:3

Hayward, Ina
Passing Show of 1921, The 1920,D 30,16:2
Fashions of 1924 1923,Jl 19,18:2
Merry Malones, The 1927,S 27,30:2
Billie 1928,O 2,34:2
Scrap Book 1932,Ag 2,20:3

Hayward, Leland (Miscellaneous)
Anne of the Thousand Days 1948,D 9,49:2
South Pacific 1949,Ap 8,30:2
South Pacific 1951,Jl 10,30:5

Hayward, Leland (Producer)
Bell for Adano, A 1944,D 7,21:2
State of the Union 1945,N 15,25:2
State of the Union 1945,N 25,II,1:1
Mister Roberts 1948,F 19,27:2
Rat Race, The 1949,D 23,16:2
Wisteria Trees, The 1950,Mr 30,39:1
Daphne Laureola 1950,S 19,38:6

Call Me Madam 1950,O 13,25:1
Remains to Be Seen 1951,O 4,37:1
Point of No Return 1951,O 31,32:2
Point of No Return 1951,O 14,35:2
Wish You Were Here 1952,Je 26,26:6
Prescott Proposals, The 1953,D 17,53:1
Who Was That Lady I Saw You With?
  1958,Mr 4,33:2
Gypsy 1959,My 22,31:6
Sound of Music, The 1959,N 17,40:2
Goodbye Charlie 1959,D 17,50:1
Shot in the Dark, A 1961,O 19,40:1
Mr President 1962,Ag 29,18:4
Mr President 1962,O 14,II,1:7
Mr President 1962,O 22,34:2
Mother Lover, The 1969,F 3,28:1

Hayward, Lister
Stairs, The 1927,N 8,32:7
Would-Be Gentleman, The 1930,Ap 30,29:2

Hayward, Louis
Mrs Fischer's War 1931,Ag 9,VIII,1:3
Point Valaine 1935,Ja 17,22:2
Point Valaine 1935,F 3,VIII,1:1

Hayward, Marjorie
Mikado, The 1944,F 12,11:3
Gondoliers, The 1944,F 22,26:3
Ruddigore 1944,Mr 3,19:5

Hayward, Robert
Inside Story 1942,O 30,22:2
Tinker's Dam 1943,Ja 29,22:2
Earth Journey 1944,Ap 28,24:2

Hayward, Thomas
Gypsy Baron, The 1944,N 15,20:3
Night in Venice, A 1952,Je 27,18:6
Night in Venice, A 1952,Jl 13,II,1:1
Night in Venice, A 1953,Je 26,15:2

Haywood, Billie
New Faces 1934,Mr 16,24:5
Fools Rush In 1934,D 26,19:2
New Faces of 1936 1936,My 20,24:5
World We Make, The 1939,N 21,19:1

Haywood, Frances
Porgy and Bess 1964,My 7,32:1
Show Boat 1966,Jl 20,48:1

Haywood, Herbert
Octoroon, The 1929,Mr 13,28:3

Haywood, Nancy
Beast in Me, The 1963,My 17,29:1
Morning Sun 1963,O 7,36:2
Too Much Johnson 1964,Ja 16,29:1
Education of H*Y*M*A*N K*A*P*L*A*N, The
  1968,Ap 5,57:1

Hayworth, Vinton
Doughgirls, The 1942,D 31,19:2

Hazard, Joe (Miscellaneous)
Ardele 1958,Ap 9,39:4

Hazard, Lawrence (Original Author)
Ladies' Money 1934,N 2,26:6

Hazard, Lawrence (Playwright)
Manhattan Medley 1932,S 25,IX,1:6

Hazard, T Pierrepont
Little Theatre Tournament; Fancy Free
  1929,My 9,34:3

Hazel, Rupert
Pins and Needles 1922,F 2,20:1

Hazel, Rupert (Lyricist)
Pins and Needles 1922,F 2,20:1

Hazell, Hy
Innocent as Hell 1960,Je 30,2:6
No Strings 1964,Ja 1,17:1

Hazelton, George C (Playwright)
Yellow Jacket, The 1928,N 8,27:3

Hazelton, Robert
King Lear 1968,Je 3,55:4
Adding Machine, The 1970,D 5,40:1

Hazelton, Ruth
Mimic World of 1921, The 1921,Ag 18,9:2

Hazlett, Samuel
Sign of Jonah, The 1957,My 2,27:1

Hazlewood, Margaret (Director)
Holiday 1941,Jl 23,15:2
Drifting Apart: or, The Fisherman's Child
  1941,Ag 20,16:6

Hazzard, Adrienne
Victims of Duty 1960,Ja 20,26:1
Connelly vs Connelly 1961,F 18,11:3
Women at the Tomb, The 1961,Ap 25,41:1

Hazzard, Ann
Lightnin' 1938,S 16,17:2

Hazzard, Cliff
Utopia, Limited 1960,Ap 8,27:2

Hazzard, Jack
Bye Bye, Barbara 1924,Ag 26,6:3
Shoot the Works! 1931,Jl 22,19:5
Great Magoo, The 1932,D 3,20:7

Hazzard, Joe (Miscellaneous)
Hamlet of Stepney Green 1958,N 14,21:1

Hazzard, John E
Night Boat, The 1920,F 3,18:1
Tangerine 1921,Ag 10,8:2
For Goodness Sake 1922,F 22,13:1
Greenwich Village Follies 1922,S 13,18:2
One Kiss 1923,N 28,14:2

Hazzard, John E—Cont

Mama Loves Papa 1926,F 23,26:2
H M S Pinafore 1926,Ap 7,26:3
Good Fellow, The 1926,O 6,22:1
Houseboat on the Styx, The 1928,D 16,IX,2:1
Houseboat on the Styx, The 1928,D 26,14:3
House Afire 1930,Ap 1,34:7
Champagne, Sec 1933,O 16,20:2

Hazzard, John E (Playwright)
Houseboat on the Styx, The 1928,D 26,14:3

Hazzard, Lois
Joseph 1930,F 13,25:3
Just Suppose 1920,N 2,15:1

Head, Cloyd (Playwright)
Arabesque 1925,O 21,20:2

Head, Edith (Costume Designer)
Pleasure of His Company, The 1958,O 23,36:1
Edwin Booth 1958,N 25,37:1

Head, Eugene
Brother Elks 1925,S 15,29:2

Head, Horace
Woman of Destiny, A 1936,Mr 3,25:2

Head, Terry
Ice Capades 1970,Ja 7,35:1

Headley, George L
Cox and Box 1942,F 20,20:2
As You Like It 1945,Jl 4,10:4
Girl From Nantucket, The 1945,N 9,17:2

Headley, J
Horse Eats Hat 1936,S 28,14:2
Doctor Faustus 1937,Ja 9,21:2

Headley, Ray
Wind in the Sails 1940,Ag 1,24:6

Headrick, Ralph (Miscellaneous)
Shoestring '57 1956,N 6,31:1

Headrick, Ronny
Wonderful Town 1967,My 18,50:1

Heagney, William (Composer)
There You Are! 1932,My 17,25:4

Heagney, William (Lyricist)
There You Are! 1932,My 17,25:4

Heagy, Harold
Home Is the Hero 1945,Ja 20,16:4

Heal, Joan
Divorce Me, Darling 1965,F 2,29:6

Heald, Anthony
Prince of Peasantmania 1970,F 22,88:1

Healey, Eunice
Girl Crazy 1930,O 5,IX,4:6
Girl Crazy 1930,O 15,27:1
Laugh Parade, The 1931,N 3,31:2
Casino Varieties 1934,Ap 3,26:4
Thumbs Up! 1934,D 28,24:1
Two for the Show 1940,F 9,14:2
Two for the Show 1940,F 18,IX,2:1
Hold On to Your Hats 1940,S 12,30:3
Beat the Band 1942,O 15,26:1

Healey, Eunice (Miscellaneous)
Gentleman From Athens, The 1947,D 10,42:4

Healey, Eunice (Producer)
Gentleman From Athens, The 1947,N 30,I,78:2
Seeds in the Wind 1948,My 26,29:2

Healey, Joseph X (Miscellaneous)
Man of Destiny, The 1926,My 1,10:1
Hero of Santa Maria, The 1926,My 1,10:1

Healey, Robert C (Playwright)
Shake Hands With the Devil 1949,O 21,30:4

Healy, Arthur V (Playwright)
Rejected Loyalty 1932,F 7,VIII,3:2

Healy, Betty
Earl Carroll's Vanities 1925,Jl 7,24:1
Night in Spain, A 1927,My 4,28:2

Healy, Catherine
Passing Show of 1924, The 1924,S 4,13:4

Healy, Dan
Sweetheart Shop, The 1920,S 1,13:4
Adrienne 1923,My 29,10:4
Plain Jane 1924,My 13,24:2
Passing Show of 1924, The 1924,S 4,13:4
Betsy 1926,D 29,24:3
Ziegfeld Follies 1927,Ag 17,27:3
Good Boy 1928,S 6,23:2

Healy, Dan (Miscellaneous)
Woof, Woof 1929,D 26,20:4

Healy, Daniel Sampson
This Mad Whirl 1937,Ja 10,II,4:8

Healy, Ed
Vaudeville (Palace) 1923,O 30,16:1

Healy, Eileen
Sketch Book 1929,Jl 2,33:5

Healy, Eleanor
Slight Case of Murder, A 1935,S 12,28:5

Healy, Florence (Playwright)
What of It? 1929,Mr 9,24:2

Healy, Gerard
Stephen D 1962,S 25,31:3

Healy, Harold
Six-Fifty, The 1921,O 25,20:1
Rain 1922,N 8,18:2
57 Bowery 1928,Ja 27,14:3
Elmer the Great 1928,S 25,29:1
Vermont 1929,Ja 9,28:1
Gambling 1929,Ag 27,31:2

Healy, Harold—Cont
Tavern, The 1930,My 20,32:1
Just to Remind You 1931,S 8,39:1
Healy, Julia Davis (Playwright)
Anvil, The 1961,Ag 8,32:2
Healy, Mark D (Lighting Director)
Drums in the Night 1967,My 18,54:1
Healy, Mark D (Miscellaneous)
White Devil, The 1965,D 7,56:1
We Bombed in New Haven 1967,D 7,58:1
Henry IV 1968,F 7,40:1
Score 1970,O 29,57:4
Healy, Mary
Count Me In 1942,O 9,24:2
Common Ground 1945,Ap 26,27:2
Around the World 1946,Je 1,9:5
Who Was That Lady I Saw You With?
1958,Mr 4,33:2
Healy, Muriel
Bourgeois Gentilhomme, Le 1929,Mr 17,30:4
Healy, Nicholas
Little Theatre Tournament; House With the Twisty
Windows, The 1929,My 8,34:4
Healy, Robert
Magnificent Yankee, The 1946,Ja 23,21:2
Healy, Ted
Earl Carroll's Vanities 1925,Jl 7,24:1
Night in Spain, A 1927,My 4,28:2
Night in Spain, A 1927,My 22,VIII,1:1
Night in Spain, A 1927,Jl 3,VII,1:1
Night in Venice, A 1929,My 22,30:2
Vaudeville (Palace) 1930,S 15,29:2
Vaudeville (Palace) 1930,S 29,19:1
Vaudeville (Palace) 1930,N 24,26:3
Gang's All Here, The 1931,F 19,21:3
Crazy Quilt 1931,My 20,28:4
Vaudeville (New Amsterdam Theatre)
1931,Je 22,17:3
Vaudeville (Broadway) 1932,D 27,11:4
Healy, Ted and the Healy Racketeers
Vaudeville (Palace) 1930,Mr 3,18:5
Healy and Cross
Vaudeville (Palace) 1927,Je 28,29:2
Vaudeville (Palace) 1930,My 26,25:2
Heap, Wells
Half Moon Inn 1925,Mr 10,14:1
Heap, Yvette
Firebird of Florence 1945,Mr 23,13:4
Heaphy, Thomas
Happy Birthday 1946,N 1,31:2
Hear, Samuel (Mrs)
Clarence 1923,My 14,18:4
Heard, Daphne
Three Sisters, The 1970,F 12,30:1
Heard, H
Gentlemen, the Queen 1927,Ap 23,14:3
Hearn, Frank
Wake Up, Jonathan 1921,Ja 18,14:1
Buccaneer, The 1925,O 3,10:2
Shannons of Broadway, The 1927,S 27,30:4
Mystery Square 1929,Ap 5,28:3
Hearn, Fred
Lady in the Dark 1941,Ja 24,14:2
Hearn, Fred (Miscellaneous)
From A to Z 1960,Ap 21,23:2
Hearn, George
As You Like It 1963,Jl 17,19:2
Time for Singing, A 1966,My 23,48:2
Richard III 1966,Ag 11,26:1
Henry IV, Part I 1968,Je 30,54:7
Henry IV, Part II 1968,Jl 2,33:1
Horseman, Pass By 1969,Ja 16,46:4
Country People 1970,Ja 19,35:1
Hearn, Lew
Century Revue and the Midnight Rounders, The
1920,Jl 13,9:1
Make It Snappy 1922,Ap 14,20:2
Ziegfeld Follies 1923,O 22,17:2
Innocent Eyes 1924,My 21,22:2
Lady Do 1927,Ap 19,24:2
Vaudeville (Palace) 1927,N 8,33:3
Ned Wayburn's Gambols 1929,Ja 16,22:3
Vaudeville (Palace) 1931,Ja 5,20:3
Bet Your Life 1937,Ap 6,20:2
Yokel Boy 1939,Jl 7,12:2
Walking Gentleman, The 1942,My 8,26:2
Hearn, Lew (Playwright)
Ned Wayburn's Gambols 1929,Ja 16,22:3
Hearn, Norman
Hamlet 1922,N 17,14:1
Hearn, Sam
Spice of 1922 1922,Jl 7,12:4
Mercenary Mary 1925,Ap 14,27:3
Greenwich Village Follies 1925,D 25,23:3
Greenwich Village Follies 1926,Mr 16,22:2
Good Boy 1928,S 6,23:2
Hearne, Nan C
Pins and Needles 1922,F 2,20:1
Hearne, Richard
Seeing Stars 1935,N 1,25:5
Swing Along 1936,S 20,IX,1:4
Shephard's Pie 1941,My 18,IX,1:5
Fun and Games 1941,Ag 31,IX,1:4
Panama Hattie 1943,D 5,II,5:1

Hearne, William
Sunny River 1941,D 5,28:2
Rosalinda; Fledermaus, Die 1942,O 29,26:5
Hearsey, Charles
Shunned 1960,D 21,39:1
Heaslip, Elizabeth
Brittle Heaven 1934,N 14,22:5
Heaslip, Georgia
Madre, La 1959,F 12,24:1
Stone Tower, The 1962,Ag 24,14:2
Heater, Claude
Top Banana 1951,N 2,19:2
Heath, Ann
Sally, Irene and Mary 1938,Jl 5,13:4
Heath, Anthony
Hymn to the Rising Sun 1937,My 7,28:2
Heath, Babs
Lady Comes Across, The 1942,Ja 10,10:2
Merry Widow, The 1943,Ag 5,19:2
Merry Widow, The 1944,O 9,17:1
Mr Strauss Goes to Boston 1945,S 7,20:2
Heath, Dody
Tree Grows in Brooklyn, A 1951,Ap 20,24:3
Heath, E P (Playwright)
Sari 1930,Ja 29,27:1
Heath, Fenno (Composer)
John Brown's Body 1960,Je 22,31:1
John Brown's Body 1964,Je 29,33:1
Heath, Frankie
Greenwich Village Follies 1922,S 13,18:2
Vaudeville (Palace) 1923,O 30,16:1
Vaudeville (Palace) 1926,N 9,30:3
Vaudeville (Palace) 1928,O 2,35:1
Heath, Gordon
South Pacific 1943,D 30,11:2
Garden of Time 1945,Mr 10,13:7
Deep Are the Roots 1945,S 27,24:4
Deep Are the Roots 1945,O 7,II,1:1
In White America 1965,F 9,42:5
Oedipus 1970,F 23,30:1
Heath, Gordon (Composer)
Garden of Time 1945,Mr 10,13:7
Lady From Maxim's, The 1970,Je 1,41:1
Heath, Gordon (Director)
In White America 1965,F 9,42:5
After the Fall 1966,F 1,26:1
Lady From Maxim's, The 1970,Je 1,41:1
Heath, Gordon (Lyricist)
Lady From Maxim's, The 1970,Je 1,41:1
Heath, Horton
Lady Who Came to Stay, The 1941,Ja 3,13:2
Heath, John
Boy Who Lived Twice, A 1945,S 12,31:2
Would-Be Gentleman, The 1946,Ja 10,29:2
Palm Tree in a Rose Garden, A 1957,N 27,26:2
Heath, Louise
Warning, The-A Theme for Linda 1969,Ap 27,92:1
Man Better Man 1969,Jl 3,22:1
Black Quartet, A; Warning, The-A Theme for
Linda 1969,Jl 31,28:1
Heath, Mary
Me and Harry 1942,Ap 3,24:6
Heath, Neel
Secret Garden, The 1931,N 8,31:4
Heath, Thomas
Red Pepper 1922,My 30,8:3
Heath, Tony
Battle Hymn 1936,My 23,12:1
Having Wonderful Time 1937,F 22,12:5
Heathen, Boyd
Firebird of Florence 1945,Mr 23,13:4
Heather, Alfred
Noble Rogue, A 1929,Ag 20,31:2
Prince Charlie and Flora 1931,Ag 29,16:5
Heather, Alfred (Producer)
Prince Charlie and Flora 1931,Ag 29,16:5
Heather, Josie
Miss Gulliver Travels 1931,N 26,36:4
Heatherley, Lois
Escape 1927,O 27,33:1
Heatherton, Joey
There Was a Little Girl 1960,Mr 1,28:1
Heatherton, Ray
Babes in Arms 1937,Ap 15,18:4
Heathfield, Mary (Playwright)
Ragged Edge, The 1935,N 26,28:3
Heathman, Josephine
Cradle Will Rock, The 1938,Ja 4,19:3
Heaton, Harold
Guest of Honor, The 1920,S 21,12:1
Fan, The 1921,O 4,10:1
Mozart 1926,N 23,26:2
Crown Prince, The 1927,Mr 24,23:2
Greeks Had a Word for It, The 1930,S 26,16:5
Three Times the Hour 1931,Ag 26,15:5
Happy Landing 1932,Mr 28,10:5
Boy Friend, The 1932,Je 8,22:3
Heaton, Robert Allen (Lighting Director)
We Bombed in New Haven 1967,D 7,58:1
Heaton, Robert Allen (Miscellaneous)
'Tis Pity She's a Whore 1967,O 21,15:2
Heaven Gate Singers, The
Scarlet Sister Mary 1930,N 26,19:2

Heavens, Peggy
Parisiana 1928,F 10,26:3
Heawood, John (Choreographer)
Boy Friend, The 1954,O 1,20:1
Joyce Grenfell Requests the Pleasure
1955,O 11,48:1
Heawood, John (Director)
Beggar's Opera, The 1957,Mr 14,35:1
Hebald, Carol
Jane Eyre 1958,My 2,31:1
Hanjo 1960,N 16,51:4
Love of Two Hours, The 1962,O 27,16:2
Hebard, Alfred
County Chairman, The 1936,My 26,26:5
Hebard, Frances
County Chairman, The 1936,My 26,26:5
Hebbard, Eve
Doctor and the Devils, The 1959,Ja 21,27:8
Hebel, Friedrich (Original Author)
Herod and Mariamne 1938,O 27,27:2
Heber-Percy, Neville
Libel! 1935,D 21,10:5
Heberden, Mary
Shall We Join the Ladies? 1925,Ja 14,19:1
Petticoat Influence 1930,D 16,34:6
Firebird 1932,N 22,25:2
Threepenny Opera, The 1933,Ap 14,22:4
Lake, The 1933,D 27,24:2
Merrily We Roll Along 1934,O 1,14:1
Victoria Regina 1935,D 27,15:2
Come Across 1938,S 15,28:3
Lady in Waiting 1940,Mr 28,19:1
Romantic Mr Dickens 1940,D 3,33:2
Ghost for Sale 1941,S 30,27:4
Hebert, Arthur
Papavert 1931,D 30,25:1
Hebert, Delore
Pigeon, The 1930,O 15,26:2
Hebert, Eve
Top Banana 1951,N 2,19:2
Hebert, Fred (Director)
Caretaker, The 1964,Ja 31,16:1
Hebert, Fred (Miscellaneous)
New Girl in Town 1957,My 15,40:1
Pleasure of His Company, The 1958,O 23,36:1
Gazebo, The 1958,D 13,2:7
Five Finger Exercise 1959,D 3,45:4
Caretaker, The 1961,O 5,42:3
First Love 1961,D 26,20:2
Comedy of Errors, The 1964,My 21,43:1
Beekman Place 1964,O 8,50:1
Alfie 1964,D 18,27:1
Coco 1969,D 19,66:1
Hebert, Fred (Playwright)
What a Killing 1961,Mr 28,41:1
Hebert, Fred (Producer)
Donnybrook! 1961,My 19,23:1
Hecht, Albert
Blue Peter, The 1925,Mr 25,25:3
Engaged! or Cheviot's Choice 1925,Je 19,24:2
Magda 1926,Ja 27,16:2
Medea 1947,O 21,27:2
Medea 1947,O 26,II,1:1
Hecht, Ben (Director)
Lily of the Valley 1942,Ja 27,25:2
Hecht, Ben (Playwright)
Egotist, The 1922,D 27,12:1
Egotist, The 1922,D 31,VII,1:1
Stork, The 1925,Ja 27,14:2
Man-Eating Tiger, The 1927,S 25,VIII,4:8
Front Page, The 1928,Ag 15,19:2
Front Page, The 1928,Ag 26,VIII,1:1
Front Page, The 1929,Ja 6,VIII,4:4
Front Page, The 1929,Jl 14,IX,2:1
Great Magoo, The 1932,D 3,20:7
20th Century 1932,D 30,15:1
Twentieth Century 1933,F 12,IX,1:1
Front Page, The 1935,Jl 9,24:4
Jumbo 1935,N 18,20:2
Jumbo 1935,N 24,IX,1:1
To Quito and Back 1937,S 21,29:1
To Quito and Back 1937,S 26,XI,3:6
To Quito and Back 1937,O 7,30:4
Ladies and Gentlemen 1939,S 24,IX,2:5
Ladies and Gentlemen 1939,O 18,30:2
Ladies and Gentlemen 1939,O 22,IX,1:3
Ladies and Gentlemen 1939,O 29,IX,1:3
Lily of the Valley 1942,Ja 27,25:2
Swan Song 1946,My 16,29:2
Front Page, The 1946,S 5,22:4
Flag Is Born, A 1946,S 7,10:6
Flag Is Born, A 1946,S 15,II,21:1
Front Page, The 1946,S 15,II,21:1
Twentieth Century 1950,D 25,23:6
Hazel Flagg 1953,F 12,22:2
Winkelberg 1958,Ja 15,26:2
Front Page, The 1968,O 20,85:5
Front Page, The 1969,My 12,54:2
Front Page, The 1969,My 25,II,1:1
Front Page, The 1969,N 2,86:1
Hecht, Bess
Shylock and His Daughter 1947,S 30,22:2

Hecht, Harold
Straw Hat, The 1926,O 15,20:2
Big Lake 1927,Ap 9,17:2
Much Ado About Nothing 1927,N 19,14:6
Doctor Knock 1928,F 24,15:2
Wild Duck, The 1928,N 19,17:1
Hecht, Harold (Director)
Sing for Your Supper 1939,Ap 25,18:6
Hecht, Herbert
Four in Hand 1923,S 7,10:2
Hecht, Herbert E (Composer)
Kaleidoscope 1957,Je 14,20:2
Hecht, Herbert E (Musical Director)
Kaleidoscope 1957,Je 14,20:2
Hecht, Ida
Shylock and His Daughter 1947,S 30,22:2
Hecht, Jenny
Mid-Summer 1953,Ja 22,19:1
Plough and the Stars, The 1960,D 7,56:2
Antigone 1968,O 11,36:1
Hecht, Manfred
Lady in the Dark 1941,Ja 24,14:2
Hecht, Marie Armstrong (Playwright)
Such Is Life 1927,S 1,27:3
Three Little Girls 1930,Mr 30,VIII,2:7
Three Little Girls 1930,Ap 15,29:1
Hecht, Mary Ellen (Miscellaneous)
Love Me Little 1958,Ap 15,42:2
U S A 1959,O 29,38:1
Hecht, Paul
Serjeant Musgrave's Dance 1966,Mr 9,44:1
All's Well That Ends Well 1966,Je 17,39:1
Measure for Measure 1966,Jl 14,27:1
Richard III 1966,Ag 11,26:1
MacBird! 1967,F 23,38:1
Volpone 1967,Je 30,29:1
Rosencrantz and Guildenstern Are Dead 1967,O 17,53:1
Rosencrantz and Guildenstern Are Dead 1967,O 29,II,1:1
1776 1969,Mr 17,46:2
1776 1969,Mr 23,II,1:1
Rothschilds, The 1970,O 20,40:1
Rothschilds, The 1970,N 1,II,1:1
Hecht, Theodore
Wonderful Visit, The 1924,F 13,17:3
Dybbuk, The 1926,D 17,27:2
Pinwheel 1927,F 4,16:4
Joan of Arc 1927,Ap 15,26:2
Her Unborn Child 1928,Mr 7,28:3
Cyclone Lover, The 1928,Je 6,23:3
Congai 1928,N 28,24:3
Great Man, The 1931,Ap 8,20:6
Perfectly Scandalous 1931,My 14,27:2
Louder, Please! 1931,N 13,26:4
Winterset 1935,S 26,19:2
Heckart, Eileen
Tinker's Dam 1943,Ja 29,22:2
Moment Musical 1943,Je 1,18:1
Our Town 1944,Ja 11,24:5
Trial Honeymoon 1947,N 4,31:2
Hilda Crane 1950,N 2,38:2
In Any Language 1952,O 9,40:2
Picnic 1953,F 20,14:7
Picnic 1953,Mr 1,II,1:1
Picnic 1953,Ag 30,II,1:1
Bad Seed, The 1954,D 9,42:1
Bad Seed, The 1954,D 19,II,3:1
View From the Bridge, A 1955,S 30,21:1
Memory of Two Mondays, A 1955,S 30,21:1
View From the Bridge, A 1955,O 9,II,1:1
Dark at the Top of the Stairs, The 1957,D 6,38:1
Dark at the Top of the Stairs, The 1957,D 15,II,3:1
Before Breakfast 1958,Mr 12,36:1
Invitation to a March 1960,O 31,27:2
Pal Joey 1961,Je 1,32:1
Everybody Loves Opal 1961,O 12,40:2
Family Affair, A 1962,Ja 29,17:1
Too True to Be Good 1963,Mr 14,8:2
Too True to Be Good 1963,Mr 23,5:6
And Things That Go Bump in the Night 1965,Ap 27,27:5
You Know I Can't Hear You When the Water's Running; I'll Be Home for Christmas 1967,Mr 14,54:1
You Know I Can't Hear You When the Water's Running; Footsteps of Doves, The 1967,Mr 14,54:1
You Know I Can't Hear You When the Water's Running; I'm Herbert 1967,Mr 14,54:1
You Know I Can't Hear You When the Water's Running 1967,Mr 26,II,1:1
Mother Lover, The 1969,F 3,28:1
Butterflies Are Free 1969,O 22,30:1
Butterflies Are Free 1969,N 2,II,1:1
Butterflies Are Free 1970,N 5,60:4
Heckart, Mary
Mr Sycamore 1942,N 14,13:2
Heckel, Bertram (Lighting Director)
H M S Pinafore 1960,Ja 29,14:1
Utopia, Limited 1960,Ap 8,27:2
Heckel, Bertram (Scenic Designer)
H M S Pinafore 1960,Ja 29,14:1

Utopia, Limited 1960,Ap 8,27:2
Heckinger, Cliff
Main Street 1921,O 6,21:1
Marjorie 1924,Ag 12,12:2
Blonde Sinner, The 1926,Jl 15,21:2
Storm Center 1927,D 1,33:2
Houseboat on the Styx, The 1928,D 26,14:3
Count of Luxembourg, The 1930,F 18,28:2
Frankie and Johnny 1930,S 26,16:5
Hamlet 1931,N 6,28:4
Music in the Air 1932,N 9,28:2
Jayhawker 1934,N 6,34:2
Panic 1935,Mr 16,18:4
Mid-West 1936,Ja 8,22:4
Lend Me Your Ears! 1936,O 6,28:5
Merry Wives of Windsor, The 1938,Ap 15,22:3
Heckman, Don (Composer)
Death of the Well-Loved Boy, The 1967,My 16,48:1
Heckroth, H (Costume Designer)
Green Table, The 1942,Ja 22,12:2
Heckscher, August (Miscellaneous)
Golden Streets, The 1970,Ag 14,21:1
Heckscher, Elizabeth
Lorelei 1938,N 30,21:2
Hector
Affaires Son les Affaires, Les 1924,Mr 11,17:1
Avare, L'; Miser, The 1924,Mr 12,17:3
Monsieur Brotonneau 1924,Mr 13,14:1
Blanchette 1924,Mr 19,19:4
Hector, Frank
Happy-Go-Lucky 1920,Ag 25,6:1
9 O'Clock Revue 1923,O 5,22:1
Nine to Eleven, The 1925,Jl 12,VII,1:1
Hector, Louis
Unwritten Chapter, The 1920,O 12,18:1
Rotters, The 1922,My 23,12:4
Romeo and Juliet 1923,Ja 25,16:1
Pelleas and Melisande 1923,D 5,23:2
Antony and Cleopatra 1924,F 20,22:1
Arms and the Man 1926,Ja 21,18:3
Road to Rome, The 1927,F 1,24:2
Three Musketeers, The 1928,Mr 4,IX,2:3
Three Musketeers, The 1928,Mr 14,28:1
Three Musketeers, The 1928,Mr 25,IX,1:1
Red Planet 1932,D 19,19:2
No More Ladies 1934,Ja 24,20:3
Simpleton of the Unexpected Isles, The 1935,F 19,27:5
Country Wife, The 1935,Jl 2,24:2
On Stage 1935,O 30,16:6
Eastwood Ho 1936,Jl 8,14:2
Would-Be Gentleman, The 1936,Ag 4,15:1
Country Wife, The 1936,D 2,34:1
Storm Over Patsy 1937,Mr 9,26:4
Devil Takes a Bride, The 1938,O 8,10:3
Outward Bound 1938,D 23,16:5
Outward Bound 1939,Ja 1,IX,1:1
Johnny Belinda 1940,S 19,26:2
More the Merrier, The 1941,S 16,19:3
Banjo Eyes 1941,N 8,10:6
I Killed the Count 1942,S 4,18:1
R U R 1942,D 4,30:2
Duke in Darkness, The 1944,Ja 25,15:2
Cup of Trembling, The 1948,Ap 21,33:5
Harlequinade 1949,O 13,32:2
Browning Version, The 1949,O 13,32:2
Browning Version, The 1949,O 23,II,1:1
ANTA Album 1950,Ja 30,13:2
Richard II 1951,Ja 25,21:2
Mr Pickwick 1952,S 18,36:3
Mr Pickwick 1952,S 28,II,1:1
Inherit the Wind 1955,Ap 22,20:2
Inherit the Wind 1955,S 25,II,1:1
Hedaya, Danny
Lulu; Earth Spirit 1970,Mr 28,32:1
Hedberg, Alice
Adding Machine, The 1970,D 5,40:1
Hedge, Charlice
Mima 1928,D 13,24:2
Queen Bee 1929,N 13,25:1
Hedge, Martha (Producer)
Cat Screams, The 1942,Je 17,26:5
Hedge, Ray
Scrap Book 1932,Ag 2,20:3
Davy Jones's Locker 1959,Mr 30,25:1
Hedges, Billy
Scotch Mist 1926,S 21,32:3
Hedges, David (Producer)
In the Nick of Time 1967,Je 2,36:1
Hedges, Florence
I'll Say She Is 1924,My 20,15:1
Hedges, Muriel
Sonya's Search for the Christmas Star 1929,D 14,24:6
Hedin, Edna
Everybody's Welcome 1931,O 14,26:3
Hedison, Al
Much Ado About Nothing 1952,My 2,20:1
Month in the Country, A 1956,Ap 4,23:1
Hedley, Charles
Three Little Girls 1930,Mr 30,VIII,2:7
Three Little Girls 1930,Ap 15,29:1

Hedley, Charles—Cont
Three Little Girls 1930,S 28,VIII,2:5
Scrap Book 1932,Ag 2,20:3
Hedlund, Dick
House of Leather, The 1970,Mr 19,56:1
Hedman, Martha
Hole in the Wall, The 1920,Mr 27,11:1
Woman Who Laughed, The 1922,Ag 17,14:3
Persons Unknown 1922,O 26,12:1
First Crocus, The 1942,Ja 3,14:6
Hedman, Martha (Director)
What's the Big Idea? 1926,Mr 24,20:3
Hedman, Martha (Playwright)
What's the Big Idea? 1926,Mr 24,20:3
For Valor 1935,N 12,24:4
For Valor 1935,N 19,27:5
Hedvig, Hulda
Gay Divorce 1932,N 30,23:4
Heed, Helen
Noble Rogue, A 1929,Ag 20,31:2
Heede, Charles (Producer)
Strange Prince, The 1926,D 8,24:2
Heege, Philip
Dagger, The 1925,S 10,28:1
Kept 1926,S 18,13:3
Barker, The 1927,Ja 19,20:6
Sherlock Holmes 1928,F 21,18:4
Within the Law 1928,Mr 6,20:1
Back Here 1928,N 27,36:3
Divided Honors 1929,O 1,28:2
Heekin, Katharine
Lazarus Laughed 1948,Ap 9,27:4
Heeley, Desmond (Costume Designer)
Twelfth Night 1958,D 10,54:2
Much Ado About Nothing 1961,Ap 5,31:1
Country Wife, The 1964,Ag 3,16:1
Richard III 1967,Je 25,II,1:2
Rosencrantz and Guildenstern Are Dead 1967,O 17,53:1
Three Musketeers, The 1968,Jl 24,49:2
Heeley, Desmond (Scenic Designer)
Hamlet 1957,Jl 3,15:2
Much Ado About Nothing 1958,Je 26,22:1
Twelfth Night 1958,D 10,54:2
As You Like It 1959,Jl 1,27:1
As You Like It 1959,Jl 5,II,1:1
Much Ado About Nothing 1961,Ap 5,31:1
Tempest, The 1962,Je 22,14:1
Cyrano de Bergerac 1962,Ag 1,21:1
Troilus and Cressida 1963,Je 19,40:2
Cyrano de Bergerac 1963,Je 20,30:1
Richard II 1964,Je 17,47:1
Country Wife, The 1964,Ag 3,16:1
Henry IV, Part I 1965,Je 30,42:1
Falstaff; Henry IV, Part II 1965,Jl 1,35:1
Henry V 1966,Je 8,38:1
Henry VI 1966,Je 9,55:2
Richard III 1967,Je 14,43:1
Rosencrantz and Guildenstern Are Dead 1967,O 17,53:1
Three Musketeers, The 1968,Jl 24,49:2
Merchant of Venice, The 1970,Je 10,39:1
Heemsath, Marion
Jubilee 1935,O 14,20:1
Heenan, James
Mary Jane McKane 1923,D 26,13:2
Heer and Martin
Will Morrissey's Newcomers 1923,Ag 9,16:2
Heermance, Clayton
Hamlet 1928,Je 2,11:3
Bourgeois Gentilhomme, Le 1929,Mr 17,30:4
Heermance, Clayton J Jr
New Freedom, The 1930,My 15,32:4
New Freedom, The 1930,My 17,21:4
Heffelfinger, Jinx
Dark of the Moon 1945,Mr 15,27:2
Heffernan, John
Judge, The 1958,My 14,36:2
Julius Caesar 1959,Ag 4,30:1
Great God Brown, The 1959,O 7,48:1
Henry IV 1960,Mr 2,42:1
Henry IV 1960,Ap 19,41:1
Henry IV, Part II 1960,Ap 24,II,1:1
Taming of the Shrew, The 1960,Ag 20,17:1
She Stoops to Conquer 1960,N 2,42:5
Plough and the Stars, The 1960,D 7,56:2
Octoroon, The 1961,Ja 28,13:1
Hamlet 1961,Mr 17,17:1
Androcles and the Lion 1961,N 22,24:2
Duchess of Malfi, The 1962,Mr 5,27:1
Tempest, The 1962,Jl 17,18:2
Man's a Man, A 1962,S 20,30:2
As You Like It 1963,Jl 17,19:2
Winter's Tale, The 1963,Ag 16,14:1
Luther 1963,S 26,41:1
Alchemist, The 1964,S 15,33:1
Tiny Alice 1964,D 30,14:2
Tiny Alice 1965,Ja 10,II,1:1
Postmark Zero 1965,N 2,28:1
Malcolm 1966,Ja 12,29:1
Arms and the Man 1967,Ap 23,44:2
Saint Joan 1968,Ja 5,42:1
Memorandum, The 1968,My 6,55:1
Woman Is My Idea 1968,S 26,61:1

Heffernan, John—Cont
Noon 1968,N 29,52:1
Night 1968,N 29,52:1
Morning 1968,N 29,52:1
Invitation to a Beheading 1969,Mr 18,36:1
Invitation to a Beheading 1969,Mr 30,II,1:1
Peer Gynt 1969,Jl 17,56:1
Purlie 1970,Mr 16,53:1

Heffernan, Rita
Seven Mirrors 1945,O 26,17:2

Heffner, Henry D
Every Other Evil 1961,Ja 23,20:2
One Is a Lonely Number 1964,Je 19,37:3

Heffner, Hubert
Job's Kinfolks 1929,N 24,31:1

Heflin, Evan
Mr Moneypenny 1928,O 17,26:2

Heflin, Frances
Walrus and the Carpenter, The 1941,N 10,20:2
All in Favor 1942,Ja 21,20:6
Skin of Our Teeth, The 1942,N 19,29:5
Skin of Our Teeth, The 1942,N 22,VIII,1:1
World's Full of Girls, The 1943,D 7,31:2
Sheppey 1944,Ap 19,27:2
I Remember Mama 1944,O 20,16:2
I Remember Mama 1944,O 29,II,1:1
Tempest, The 1945,Ja 26,17:2
Tempest, The 1945,F 4,II,1:1
Galileo 1947,Ag 1,21:4
Streetcar Named Desire, A 1956,F 16,24:1
Five Evenings 1963,My 10,37:3
Physicists, The 1964,O 14,52:1

Heflin, Katie
Midsummer Night's Dream, A 1967,Je 30,23:1

Heflin, Marta
Life With Father 1967,O 20,53:2
Salvation 1969,Mr 13,53:1
Salvation 1969,S 25,55:1

Heflin, Mary Frances
Charley's Aunt 1940,O 18,24:2

Heflin, Van
Bride of Torozko, The 1934,S 14,24:2
Night Remembers, The 1934,N 28,24:3
Mid-West 1936,Ja 8,22:4
End of Summer 1936,Ja 31,17:1
End of Summer 1936,F 18,26:4
Love for Love 1936,Je 30,15:4
Western Waters 1937,D 29,17:1
Casey Jones 1938,F 21,14:2
Philadelphia Story, The 1939,Mr 29,21:1
View From the Bridge, A 1955,Ag 31,16:8
Memory of Two Mondays, A 1955,S 30,21:1
View From the Bridge, A 1955,S 30,21:1
View From the Bridge, A 1955,O 9,II,1:1
Case of Libel, A 1963,O 11,43:2
Case of Libel, A 1963,O 27,II,1:1

Hefner, Keith
Sable Brush, The 1956,N 28,41:1
Doctor in Spite of Himself, The 1957,F 28,18:4

Hefner, Keith (Miscellaneous)
Doctor in Spite of Himself, The 1957,F 28,18:4

Heft, Robert
June Love 1921,Ap 26,20:1

Hegedus, Lorant
Olympia 1928,Mr 25,IX,4:1
Abie's Irish Rose 1928,Je 10,VIII,2:8
Romance of Ida, The 1929,F 3,VIII,2:1
Good Fairy, The 1930,O 13,31:2

Hegedus, Lorant (Director)
Trial of Mary Dugan, The 1928,S 30,IX,4:4

Hegedus, Lorant (Playwright)
Kossuth 1927,D 4,X,2:3

Hegeman, Alice
Demi-Virgin, The 1921,O 19,22:1

Heggen, Thomas (Original Author)
Mister Roberts 1948,F 19,27:2

Heggen, Thomas (Playwright)
Mister Roberts 1948,F 19,27:2
Mister Roberts 1948,F 29,II,1:1
Mister Roberts 1950,My 21,II,1:1
Mister Roberts 1950,Jl 20,22:4
Mister Roberts 1951,F 9,20:7
Mister Roberts 1956,D 6,46:2
Mister Roberts 1962,O 12,27:2

Heggie, O P
Sophie 1920,Mr 3,12:2
Foot-Loose 1920,My 11,12:1
Happy-Go-Lucky 1920,Ag 25,6:1
Truth About Blayds, The 1922,Mr 15,22:1
Fashions for Men 1922,D 6,22:1
Fashions for Men 1922,D 24,VII,1:1
Cup, The 1923,N 13,25:1
We Moderns 1923,D 30,VII,2:1
We Moderns 1924,Mr 12,17:2
We Moderns 1924,Mr 16,VIII,1:1
Baronet and the Butterfly, The 1924,Je 8,VII,1:8
Minick 1924,S 25,20:1
Bit o' Love, A 1925,My 13,24:2
Trelawney of the 'Wells' 1925,Je 2,16:2
School for Scandal, The 1925,D 7,18:2
School for Scandal, The 1925,D 13,IX,3:1
Sport of Kings, The 1926,My 5,24:2
Sunshine 1926,Ag 18,15:2
This Woman Business 1926,D 8,25:1

Trelawney of the 'Wells' 1927,F 1,24:4
Spellbound 1927,N 15,26:2
Spellbound 1927,N 20,IX,1:1
Out of the Sea 1927,D 6,26:2
She Stoops to Conquer 1928,My 15,17:1
She Stoops to Conquer 1928,My 20,VIII,1:1
Beaux' Stratagem, The 1928,Je 5,20:1
Beaux' Stratagem, The 1928,Je 10,VIII,1:1
They Don't Mean Any Harm 1932,F 24,25:2
Truth About Blayds, The 1932,Ap 12,25:2
Green Bay Tree, The 1933,O 21,11:5
Green Bay Tree, The 1933,O 29,IX,1:1

Heggie, O P (Director)
Spellbound 1927,N 15,26:2

Heghinian, Edward N (Lieut USNR) (Playwright)
Slice It Thin 1945,My 11,22:5

Hegira, Anne
Sundown Beach 1948,S 8,37:1
Peer Gynt 1951,Ja 29,15:2
Victim, The 1952,My 3,17:5
Once Upon a Tailor 1955,My 24,36:2
Shadow of My Enemy, A 1957,D 12,35:4
Color of Darkness: An Evening in the World of
James Purdy; Encore 1963,O 1,34:1
Strada, La 1969,D 15,63:1

Hegner, C F
Caesar and Cleopatra 1927,N 6,IX,2:1

Hegoburu, Loulou
Night in Paris, A 1926,Ja 6,16:3
Tip-Toes 1929,My 19,IX,2:1

Hegt, Beatrice
Hansel and Gretel 1929,D 25,21:1

Hegt, Saskia Noordhoek
Alice in Wonderland 1970,O 9,43:1

Heiberg, Gunnar (Playwright)
Gerts Have 1930,D 28,VIII,3:5

Heide, Robert (Playwright)
West of the Moon 1961,Je 29,26:1

Heidemann, Fred
Every Other Evil 1961,Ja 23,20:2
Magnificent Hugo, The 1961,Ap 8,12:2

Heidemann, Horst (Miscellaneous)
Don Carlos 1964,N 25,40:1

Heidemann, Paul
Zarewitsch, Der 1927,Ap 3,VIII,2:1
Rose Marie 1928,Mr 31,23:2
Rose Marie 1928,Ap 29,IX,2:8
Blaue Hemd von Ithaka, Das 1931,Mr 15,IX,2:4

Heider, Fred (Lyricist)
Russell Patterson's Sketch-Book 1960,F 8,35:1

Heidinger, Norman
Hamlet 1959,Jl 11,21:4

Heidt, Charles (Producer)
On to Fortune 1935,Ja 15,23:2
On to Fortune 1935,F 5,22:2
Leaf and Bough 1949,Ja 22,10:2

Heidt, Horace
Vaudeville (Palace) 1929,S 2,16:3
Vaudeville (Palace) 1929,S 9,30:5
Vaudeville (Palace) 1929,S 16,30:4
Vaudeville (Palace) 1929,S 23,24:6
Vaudeville (Palace) 1930,Ap 21,20:7
Vaudeville (Palace) 1931,Ap 6,24:3

Heidt, Winifred
Carousel 1954,Je 3,32:2

Heigh, Helene
Ramshackle Inn 1944,Ja 6,17:5

Heighley, Bruce
Borstal Boy 1970,Ap 1,38:1

Heigren, Stig
H M S Pinafore 1961,Je 9,29:5

Heijermans, Herman (Playwright)
Devil to Pay, The 1925,D 4,26:2
Devil to Pay, The 1925,D 13,IX,3:1
Good Hope, The 1927,O 19,24:2
Good Hope, The 1927,O 23,VIII,1:1
Rising Sun, The 1929,O 27,IX,2:2

Heijermans-Houwink, Caroline (Translator)
Devil to Pay, The 1925,D 4,26:2
Good Hope, The 1927,O 19,24:2

Heikamph, Helen
Passion Play, The 1929,Ap 30,32:1

Heikin, Nancy
Gertrude 1970,N 13,29:1
Carmilla 1970,D 1,61:2

Heilbron, Adelaide (Playwright)
Something Gay 1935,Ap 30,12:2

Heilmann, Ursula (Miscellaneous)
Wozzeck 1966,Ap 6,34:1
Mitschuldigen, Die 1966,Ap 6,34:1

Heilweil, David
Happy Ending 1942,S 28,13:1

Heilweil, David (Lighting Director)
Respectful Prostitute, The 1948,F 15,II,1:1

Heilweil, David (Playwright)
Show-Off, The 1950,Je 1,24:5

Heilweil, David (Producer)
Julius Caesar 1950,Je 21,30:1
Medium, The 1950,Jl 20,22:5
Telephone, The 1950,Jl 20,22:5
Arms and the Man 1950,O 20,34:2
Razzle Dazzle 1951,F 20,21:1
Dark Legend 1952,Mr 25,24:2

Heilweil, David (Producer)—Cont
Victim, The 1952,My 3,17:5

Heim, Alan (Miscellaneous)
Awakening of Spring, The 1964,My 13,50:1

Heim, Alyn (Composer)
Will the Mail Train Run Tonight? 1964,Ja 10,18:1

Heim, Frances
Baby With a Knife 1969,My 15,41:2

Heimann, Philip (Playwright)
First Episode 1934,S 18,18:1

Heimbach, Larry
Mill Shadows 1932,F 29,20:7

Hein, Donald
Midsummer Night's Dream, A 1956,Ja 14,12:2

Hein, Silvio (Composer)
Look Who's Here 1920,Mr 3,12:2
Some Party 1922,Ap 17,22:1

Hein, Silvio (Playwright)
Lambs Gambol 1925,Ap 27,15:1

Heine, Albert (Director)
Gang zum Weiher, Der 1931,Ap 5,VIII,1:6

Heineman, John
York Nativity Play, The 1956,D 5,49:2
Sign of Jonah, The 1957,My 2,27:1

Heineman, Lori
Miracle Worker, The 1959,O 20,44:1
Proposition, The 1968,Ap 20,25:3

Heinemann, Eda
Immodest Violet 1920,Ag 25,6:2
Chains of Dew 1922,Ap 28,20:2
Sylvia 1923,Ap 26,22:1
Jack in the Pulpit 1925,Ja 7,33:1
Adam Solitaire 1925,N 7,19:2
Love 'Em and Leave 'Em 1926,F 4,20:4
Chicago 1926,D 31,11:1
War Song, The 1928,S 25,29:3
Blow the Man Down 1929,Ag 25,VIII,3:1
Commodore Marries, The 1929,S 5,26:3
Commodore Marries, The 1929,S 15,IX,1:1
Broken Dishes 1929,N 6,28:3
Month in the Country, A 1930,Mr 18,30:5
Stepdaughters of War 1930,O 7,27:1
Man on Stilts, The 1931,S 10,23:2
Distant Drums 1932,Ja 19,24:3
Distant Drums 1932,Ja 31,VIII,1:1
Take My Tip 1932,Ap 12,25:2
Autumn Crocus 1932,N 21,20:2
Ah, Wilderness! 1933,S 26,26:3
Ah, Wilderness! 1933,O 3,28:2
Geraniums in My Window 1934,O 27,20:6
Fresh Fields 1935,Jl 24,20:4
County Chairman, The 1936,My 26,26:5
Dr Knock 1936,Jl 14,22:1
As We Forgive Our Debtors 1936,Ag 11,24:6
And Now Goodbye 1937,F 3,26:4
Miss Quis 1937,Ap 8,20:5
Madame Bovary 1937,N 17,26:2
International Incident, An 1940,Ap 3,18:2
Boyd's Daughter 1940,O 12,20:2
My Sister Eileen 1940,D 27,23:2
Watch on the Rhine 1941,Ap 2,26:2
Doctors Disagree 1943,D 29,15:2
Last Stop 1944,S 6,17:2
Woman Bites Dog 1946,Ap 18,21:2
Doctor Social 1948,F 12,29:5
Goodbye My Fancy 1948,N 18,35:2
Arms and the Girl 1950,F 3,28:2
Cellar and the Well, The 1950,D 11,30:2
Make a Wish 1951,Ap 19,38:1
Potting Shed, The 1957,Ja 30,32:1
Silent Night, Lonely Night 1959,D 4,36:1
Giants, Sons of Giants 1962,Ja 8,26:2
My Mother, My Father and Me 1963,Mr 25,5:5

Heinemann, Gelia
Pimpernel! 1964,Ja 7,26:6

Heiners, John H Jr
That's That 1924,Ap 30,19:2

Heininger, Felix
Eisrevue 1969,O 23,55:1

Heininger, Monique
Eisrevue 1969,O 23,55:1

Heinlein, Mary V
Prunella; Love in a Garden 1926,Je 16,23:3
Blind Mice 1930,O 16,28:2

Heinly, Althea
Ripples 1930,F 12,26:1

Heinrich, Cindy
Six Characters in Search of an Author
1961,My 11,43:1

Heinz, Gerard
Dear Charles 1952,D 21,44:5

Heisdorf, Nicholas P (Playwright)
Schoolmaster, The 1928,Mr 21,30:1

Heisdorf, Nicholas P (Producer)
Schoolmaster, The 1928,Mr 21,30:1

Heisey, Jean
Yours Is My Heart 1946,S 6,16:5

Heisey, Mart E
Dear Me 1921,Ja 18,14:1

Heisler, Jack
Tickle Me 1920,Ag 18,9:1
Jimmie 1920,N 18,15:3

Heiss, Maxine
Courtyard 1960,Mr 1,28:1

Heit, Michael
Party on Greenwich Avenue, The 1967,My 11,52:1
Hamlet 1967,D 27,45:1
Romeo and Juliet 1968,Ag 16,19:1
Heitland, W Emerton (Scenic Designer)
Earth Journey 1944,Ap 28,24:2
Heitmanek, John
Tom Paine 1969,Mr 30,71:2
Heitmanek, Lana
Tom Paine 1969,Mr 30,71:2
Helasz, Emmerich (Lyricist)
Kuss-und Sonst Gar Nichts, Ein 1933,N 19,IX,3:1
Helburn, Theresa
Susannah and the Elders 1938,Ag 2,15:5
Helburn, Theresa (Director)
Chrysalis 1932,N 16,15:2
Mary of Scotland 1933,N 28,28:3
Jane Eyre 1937,Ja 3,X,2:1
Madame Bovary 1937,O 6,28:4
Helburn, Theresa (Miscellaneous)
R U R 1922,O 22,VIII,1:1
Mourning Becomes Electra; Hunted, The
1931,O 27,22:1
Mourning Becomes Electra; Homecoming
1931,O 27,22:1
Mourning Becomes Electra; Haunted, The
1931,O 27,22:1
Reunion in Vienna 1931,N 17,31:1
Too True to Be Good 1932,Ap 5,27:5
Mourning Becomes Electra; Haunted, The
1932,My 10,25:2
Mourning Becomes Electra; Hunted, The
1932,My 10,25:2
Mourning Becomes Electra; Homecoming
1932,My 10,25:2
Chrysalis 1932,N 16,15:2
Biography 1932,D 13,25:3
Both Your Houses 1933,Mr 7,20:3
Mask and the Face, The 1933,My 9,20:2
They Shall Not Die 1934,F 22,24:4
Rain From Heaven 1934,D 25,28:4
And Stars Remain 1936,O 13,32:2
Prelude to Exile 1936,N 22,XI,3:2
But for the Grace of God 1937,Ja 13,21:4
Fifth Column, The 1940,Mr 7,18:2
Somewhere in France 1941,Ap 29,16:8
Ah, Wilderness! 1941,O 3,26:2
Rivals, The 1941,N 18,32:2
Papa Is All 1942,Ja 7,22:2
Rivals, The 1942,Ja 15,24:2
Yesterday's Magic 1942,Ap 15,27:2
Mr Sycamore 1942,N 14,13:2
Innocent Voyage, The 1943,N 16,27:2
Sing Out, Sweet Land! 1944,D 28,24:2
Carousel 1945,Ap 20,24:2
Oklahoma! 1947,My 1,35:3
Allegro 1947,O 11,10:2
Oklahoma! 1951,My 30,15:2
Helburn, Theresa (Playwright)
Other Lives 1921,S 11,VI,1:6
Hero Is Born, A 1937,O 2,18:6
Little Dark Horse 1941,N 17,14:4
Helburn, Theresa (Producer)
Mary of Scotland 1933,N 19,IX,2:5
Valley Forge 1934,D 11,28:3
Prelude to Exile 1936,D 1,31:1
Masque of the Kings, The 1937,F 9,19:4
Storm Over Patsy 1937,Mr 9,26:4
To Quito and Back 1937,O 7,30:4
Madame Bovary 1937,N 17,26:2
Ghost of Yankee Doodle, The 1937,N 23,26:3
Wine of Choice 1938,F 22,18:4
Dame Nature 1938,S 27,24:3
Philadelphia Story, The 1939,Mr 29,21:1
Time of Your Life, The 1939,O 26,26:2
Fifth Column, The 1940,Ja 27,9:1
Time of Your Life, The 1940,S 24,27:2
Twelfth Night 1940,N 20,26:3
Liberty Jones 1941,F 6,24:2
Iceman Cometh, The 1946,O 10,31:3
You Never Can Tell 1948,Mr 17,31:2
Carousel 1949,Ja 26,28:2
As You Like It 1950,Ja 27,27:2
Come Back, Little Sheba 1950,F 16,28:5
Saint Joan 1951,O 5,23:2
Held, Anna Jr (Producer)
Restless Women 1927,D 27,24:1
Quicksand 1928,F 14,26:3
Held, John Jr
Spring Tonic 1936,My 11,16:1
Boy Friend, The 1970,Ap 26,II,5:7
Held, John Jr (Costume Designer)
Follies 1925,Mr 11,19:2
Americana 1928,O 31,28:2
Held, John Jr (Scenic Designer)
Americana 1926,Jl 27,15:3
Americana 1926,D 5,VIII,5:1
Held, Lillian
Yours Is My Heart 1946,S 6,16:5
Heldabrand, John
Tovarich 1952,My 15,39:2
Maya 1953,Je 10,35:1
School for Scandal, The 1953,Je 24,29:2

Immoralist, The 1954,F 9,22:1
Immoralist, The 1954,F 14,II,1:1
Sin of Pat Muldoon, The 1957,Mr 14,35:1
Desert Incident, A 1959,Mr 25,40:1
Glimpse of the Domesticity of Franklyn Barnabas,
A 1960,Mr 7,24:2
Idiot, The 1960,S 26,38:1
Montserrat 1961,Ja 9,30:5
Helena, Justa and Charlie
Vaudeville (Palace) 1930,Ag 4,13:2
Helene, Patrica
Bagels and Yox 1951,S 13,38:2
Helene and Cortez
Will Morrissey's Folies Bergere Revue
1930,Ap 16,26:6
Helfand, Jonathan W
Tableaux 1961,D 18,41:3
Helfend, Dennis
Universal Nigger, The 1970,Mr 21,18:1
Helfer, Felix
Lebende Leichnam, Der, Der; Living Corpse, The
1928,Ja 24,26:2
Helfrich, K H
Why Not? 1922,D 30,13:4
Helga
Ice Capades 1957,S 5,33:2
Ice Capades 1958,S 4,33:2
Ice Capades 1959,S 4,12:1
Helger, Fritz
Passion Play, The 1929,Ap 30,32:1
Helier, Ivy
Words and Music 1932,Ag 26,21:2
Hell, Arthur
Blaue Hemd von Ithaka, Das 1931,Mr 15,IX,2:4
Hell, Peter (Playwright)
Alles Fuer Marion 1931,F 15,VIII,3:1
Hellaire, Vera
Letty Pepper 1922,Ap 11,22:2
Hellberg, Ruth
Raetzel um Beate 1936,N 8,X,2:1
Heller, Barbara
Vintage '60 1960,S 13,41:1
Heller, Bob
Terrible Swift Sword, The 1955,N 16,42:1
Heller, Buck
Riding Hood Revisited 1961,Ja 4,26:1
Golden Boy 1964,O 21,56:1
Heller, Claire (Producer)
End as a Man 1953,S 16,39:1
Heller, Clara
Dream Out of Time, A 1970,N 9,52:1
Heller, Don
Nervous Set, The 1959,My 13,43:1
Heller, Edith
Enemy of the People, An 1958,F 26,24:2
Heller, Eugene
Twisting Road, The; Jewel of the South, The
1957,N 18,36:5
Wicked Cooks, The 1967,Ja 24,42:1
Line of Least Existence, The 1968,Mr 25,53:1
Heller, Franklin
Nowhere Bound 1935,Ja 23,20:2
Strip Girl 1935,O 21,22:6
This Our House 1935,D 12,33:3
Bitter Stream 1936,Mr 31,16:6
You Can't Take It With You 1936,D 15,31:1
Heller, Franklin Marx (Miscellaneous)
Counterattack 1943,F 4,27:2
Heller, George
Critic, The 1925,My 9,12:4
Dybbuk, The 1925,D 16,22:2
Burmese Pwe, A 1926,Mr 17,28:1
Grand Street Follies, The 1926,Je 16,23:2
Lion Tamer, The 1926,O 8,26:1
Pinwheel 1927,F 4,16:4
Grand Street Follies, The 1927,My 20,22:3
If 1927,O 26,26:2
Love Nest, The 1927,D 23,17:1
Maya 1928,F 22,19:1
Grand Street Follies, The 1928,My 29,16:2
Grand Street Follies, The 1928,Je 3,VIII,1:1
Grand Street Follies, The 1929,My 2,20:4
Dark Hours, The 1932,N 15,24:2
Threepenny Opera, The 1933,Ap 14,22:4
Climax, The 1933,Je 14,22:2
Sailor, Beware! 1933,S 29,24:4
Till the Day I Die 1935,Mr 27,24:5
Waiting for Lefty 1935,Mr 27,24:5
Squaring the Circle 1935,O 4,24:6
You Can't Take It With You 1936,D 15,31:1
Heller, George (Producer)
Deep Are the Roots 1945,S 27,24:4
Deep Are the Roots 1945,O 7,II,1:1
Heller, Gerald D (Playwright)
You'll Never Know 1921,Ap 21,9:2
Heller, Gwen
Untitled-Revue 1965,Je 25,38:1
Heller, Jack
Great Shakes 1931,Mr 12,22:2
How Revolting! 1932,Mr 11,14:6
Finis for Oscar Wilde 1964,F 15,15:1
One by One 1964,D 2,60:1

Heller, Jackie
Vaudeville (Palace) 1928,O 2,35:1
Yokel Boy 1939,Jl 7,12:2
Heller, Jayne
Praise Of Folly 1954,F 24,23:2
Pipe Dream 1955,D 1,44:1
Winkelberg 1958,Ja 15,26:2
Fourth Pig, The 1965,Ja 27,24:6
Heller, Joseph (Playwright)
We Bombed in New Haven 1967,D 7,58:1
We Bombed in New Haven 1967,D 17,II,3:7
We Bombed in New Haven 1968,S 26,64:2
We Bombed in New Haven 1968,O 17,51:1
We Bombed in New Haven 1968,O 27,II,1:1
Heller, Paul
Electra 1927,D 2,20:6
Heller, Paul M (Lighting Director)
Frankie and Johnny 1952,O 29,37:2
Heller, Paul M (Scenic Designer)
Frankie and Johnny 1952,O 29,37:2
Heller, Rhodelle
In Good King Charles's Golden Days
1957,Ja 25,16:1
Shewing-Up of Blanco Posnet, The 1959,S 19,26:7
Book of Job, The 1962,F 10,13:1
Heller, Rhodelle (Director)
Widowers' Houses 1959,Mr 3,39:2
Prodigal, The 1960,F 12,23:1
Prodigal, The 1960,F 21,II,1:1
Heller, Trude (Producer)
Playroom, The 1965,D 6,49:1
Hellerman, Fred (Composer)
Midnight Caller, The 1958,Jl 2,25:1
John Turner Davis 1958,Jl 2,25:1
Leonard Sillman's New Faces of 1968
1968,My 3,43:1
Hellerman, Fred (Lyricist)
Leonard Sillman's New Faces of 1968
1968,My 3,43:1
Hellerman, Fred (Musical Director)
Moon Besieged, The 1962,D 6,54:1
Hellerman, Michael (Producer)
Boy Friend, The 1970,Ap 15,54:1
Hellgren, Mari
Show Boat 1932,My 20,22:2
Hellinger, Mark (Composer)
Ziegfeld Follies 1931,Jl 2,30:5
Hellinger, Mark (Miscellaneous)
Hot-Cha! 1932,F 21,VIII,2:1
Hellinger, Mark (Original Author)
Hot-Cha! 1932,Mr 9,17:3
Hellinger, Mark (Playwright)
None Are So Blind 1923,My 9,14:4
Ziegfeld Follies 1931,Jl 2,30:5
Hellinger, Mark (Producer)
Double Dummy 1936,N 12,30:1
Hellinger, William
Fragile Fox 1954,O 13,27:1
Hellman, Betty
Geranium Hat, The 1959,Mr 18,45:1
All's Well That Ends Well 1959,Ag 3,20:4
Diamond Orchid 1965,F 11,44:4
Love's Labour's Lost 1965,Je 16,46:1
Hellman, Lillian (Director)
Another Part of the Forest 1946,N 21,42:2
Montserrat 1949,O 31,21:4
Children's Hour, The 1952,D 19,35:2
Children's Hour, The 1952,D 28,II,1:1
Hellman, Lillian (Lyricist)
Leonard Bernstein's Theater Songs 1965,Je 29,27:2
Hellman, Lillian (Original Author)
Regina 1949,N 13,II,1:1
Hellman, Lillian (Playwright)
Children's Hour, The 1934,N 21,23:2
Children's Hour, The 1934,D 2,X,1:1
Children's Hour, The 1934,N 13,27:3
Days to Come 1936,D 16,35:1
Little Foxes, The 1939,F 16,16:2
Little Foxes, The 1939,F 26,IX,1:1
Watch on the Rhine 1941,Mr 25,26:7
Watch on the Rhine 1941,Ap 2,26:2
Watch on the Rhine 1941,Ap 13,IX,1:1
Watch on the Rhine 1941,Ag 24,IX,1:1
Watch on the Rhine 1942,Ap 24,20:6
Watch on the Rhine 1942,My 3,VIII,1:7
Little Foxes, The 1942,N 1,VIII,2:1
Searching Wind, The 1944,Ap 13,25:2
Searching Wind, The 1944,Ap 23,II,1:1
Another Part of the Forest 1946,N 21,42:2
Another Part of the Forest 1946,D 1,II,1:1
Ladies and Gentlemen; Another Part of the Forest
1949,O 17,19:1
Another Part of the Forest; Ladies and Gentlemen
1949,O 18,34:4
Montserrat 1949,O 31,21:4
Regina 1949,N 1,32:2
Another Part of the Forest; Ladies and Gentlemen
1949,N 13,83:4
Autumn Garden, The 1951,Mr 8,36:2
Autumn Garden, The 1951,Mr 18,II,1:1
Montserrat 1952,My 11,II,3:8
Regina 1952,Je 2,25:4
Children's Hour, The 1952,D 19,35:2

Hellman, Lillian (Playwright)—Cont

Children's Hour, The 1952,D 28,II,1:1
Montserrat 1954,My 26,34:2
Lark, The 1955,N 18,20:1
Lark, The 1955,N 27,II,1:1
Candide 1956,D 3,40:2
Candide 1956,D 9,II,5:1
Toys in the Attic 1960,F 26,23:2
Toys in the Attic 1960,Mr 6,II,1:1
Montserrat 1961,Ja 9,30:5
Little Foxes, The 1962,D 6,56:1
My Mother, My Father and Me 1963,Mr 25,5:5
Little Foxes, The 1967,O 27,53:1
Little Foxes, The 1967,N 5,II,1:1
Little Foxes, The 1968,Ja 6,24:4

Hellman, William H

Joy of Serpents 1930,Ap 4,22:4

Hellsen, Erich

Dantons Tod 1927,D 21,28:3

Hellwell, David (Lighting Director)

Lamp at Midnight 1947,D 22,29:2
Respectful Prostitute, The 1948,F 10,27:2
Church Street 1948,F 10,27:2

Hellwell, David (Miscellaneous)

Church Street 1948,F 10,27:2
Respectful Prostitute, The 1948,F 10,27:2

Hellwell, David (Producer)

To Tell You the Truth 1948,Ap 19,28:6

Hellwig, Judith

Everyman 1941,My 9,19:2

Helm, Alan

Picnic on the Battlefield 1960,My 17,42:2
Sandbox, The 1960,My 17,42:2

Helm, Anne

Clerambard 1957,N 8,22:3
Cloud 7 1958,F 15,15:2
Edwin Booth 1958,N 25,37:1
Power of Darkness, The 1959,S 30,33:1

Helm, Ferdinand

Master of the Revels 1935,Ag 14,16:2

Helm, Frances

Deadly Game, The 1960,F 3,27:2
Pets 1969,My 15,41:2

Helm, Geneva

York Nativity Play, The 1956,D 5,49:2
Sign of Jonah, The 1957,My 2,27:1
Family Reunion, The 1960,D 10,26:1

Helm, Harvey

Trapped 1928,S 12,25:3

Helm, Peter

There Was a Little Girl 1960,Mr 1,28:1

Helman, A Boris

Nautical but Nice 1931,Ap 19,31:6

Helmers, June

Oklahoma! 1969,Je 24,37:1
Hello, Dolly! 1970,Ap 12,II,3:7

Helmond, Katherine

Trip to Bountiful, The 1959,F 27,20:4
Orpheus Descending 1959,O 6,45:2

Helmore, Bertha

Nap Hand 1940,Mr 10,XI,2:6

Helmore, Evelyn

Macbeth 1941,N 12,30:2

Helmore, Tom

Day Before Spring, The 1945,N 23,27:2
Day Before Spring, The 1945,D 2,II,1:1
You Never Can Tell 1948,Mr 17,31:2
Clutterbuck 1949,D 5,29:2
Legend of Sarah 1950,O 12,42:4
High Ground, The 1951,F 21,31:2
Love and Let Love 1951,O 20,11:2
International Set, The 1953,Je 12,19:3
Winner, The 1954,F 18,34:1
One Eye Closed 1954,N 25,45:2
Debut 1956,F 23,32:1
Playroom, The 1965,D 6,49:1
House of Flowers 1968,Ja 29,26:2

Helms, Alan

Yes is for a Very Young Man 1963,Mr 6,7:5

Helmuth, Mimi

Veils 1928,Mr 14,28:5

Helou, Victor

Something More! 1964,N 11,36:1
Kiss Me, Kate 1965,My 13,31:1

Helpmann, Max

Henry V 1956,Je 20,27:2
Hamlet 1957,Jl 3,15:2
Twelfth Night 1957,Jl 4,16:4
Henry IV, Part I 1958,Je 25,23:3
Winter's Tale, The 1958,Jl 23,34:3
As You Like It 1959,Jl 1,27:1
King John 1960,Je 29,26:2
Midsummer Night's Dream, A 1960,Je 30,23:5
Henry VIII 1961,Je 22,22:1
Macbeth 1962,Je 20,41:1
Tempest, The 1962,Je 22,14:1
Cyrano de Bergerac 1962,Ag 1,21:1
Moby Dick 1962,N 29,45:1
Troilus and Cressida 1963,Je 19,40:2
Cyrano de Bergerac 1963,Je 20,30:1
Richard II 1964,Je 17,47:1
King Lear 1964,Je 19,36:1
Henry IV, Part I 1965,Je 30,42:1
Falstaff; Henry IV, Part II 1965,Jl 1,35:1

Julius Caesar 1965,Jl 2,18:1
Henry V 1966,Je 8,38:1
Henry VI 1966,Je 9,55:2
Antony and Cleopatra 1967,Ag 2,25:1
Merry Wives of Windsor, The 1967,Ag 4,18:1
Government Inspector, The 1967,O 28,34:1
Romeo and Juliet 1968,Je 11,55:2
Midsummer Night's Dream, A 1968,Je 13,54:1

Helpmann, Robert

Hamlet 1948,My 9,II,2:5
Caesar and Cleopatra 1951,D 20,43:2
Antony and Cleopatra 1951,D 21,22:2
Millionairess, The 1952,Je 28,12:2
Millionairess, The 1952,O 18,17:2
Midsummer Night's Dream, A 1954,S 1,31:3
Midsummer Night's Dream, A 1954,S 22,33:1
Nekrassou 1957,Ag 20,22:1

Helpmann, Robert (Choreographer)

Midsummer Night's Dream, A 1954,S 22,33:1

Helpmann, Robert (Director)

Murder in the Cathedral 1953,Ap 26,II,1:1
Romeo and Juliet 1956,O 25,41:1
Duel of Angels 1960,Ap 20,42:2
Duel of Angels 1960,My 1,II,1:1

Helpmann, Robert (Producer)

After The Ball 1954,Je 11,19:3
Camelot 1964,Ag 20,34:1

Helsdon, Lester D

John Brown's Body 1953,F 16,17:2

Helsey, Edouard (Playwright)

Terre d'Israel 1930,O 12,VIII,4:2

Helstrom, Haidee

Passing of the Third Floor Back, The
1928,Ja 17,22:7

Helstrom, Hilda

Main Street 1921,O 6,21:1
Hedda Gabler 1926,Ja 27,16:5
Passing of the Third Floor Back, The
1928,F 21,18:2

Heltai, Eugene (Original Author)

Silent Knight, The 1937,N 17,26:4
Silent Knight, The 1937,D 5,XII,5:8

Heltai, Eugene (Translator) '

Abie's Irish Rose 1928,Je 10,VIII,2:8

Helton, Alf

Little Old New York 1920,S 9,9:2
You Can't Beat a Woman 1925,Mr 24,26:5
Bit o' Love, A 1925,My 13,24:2
Port O' London 1926,F 10,20:2
Lady in Love, A 1927,F 22,22:1
Trapped 1928,S 12,25:3
Crashing Through 1928,O 30,26:5
Topaze 1930,F 13,25:3
First Night 1930,N 27,32:3
Great Barrington, The 1931,F 20,18:1
Merchant of Venice, The 1931,N 9,22:2
Back Fire 1932,Je 14,26:3
Hotel Alimony 1934,Ja 30,16:2
Lost Horizons 1934,O 16,31:2
Living Dangerously 1935,Ja 14,10:3
Victoria Regina 1935,D 27,15:2

Helton, Percy

Three Live Ghosts 1920,S 30,12:1
Three Live Ghosts 1920,O 10,VI,1:2
To the Ladies! 1922,F 21,20:1
Texas Nightingale, The 1922,N 21,15:2
Texas Nightingale, The 1922,D 3,VIII,1:1
Go West, Young Man 1923,N 13,25:2
You Can't Beat a Woman 1925,Mr 24,26:5
Poor Nut, The 1925,Ap 28,18:1
Happy 1927,D 6,26:3
Lady for a Night, A 1928,Ap 17,26:4
Who Cares 1930,Jl 9,27:1
Shoot the Works! 1931,Jl 22,19:5
Lambs Gambol 1932,Ap 25,18:2
Page Pygmalion 1932,Ag 4,17:5
One Sunday Afternoon 1933,F 16,23:5
Dream Child 1934,Jl 31,20:2
Any Woman 1934,Ag 28,24:4
On to Fortune 1935,F 5,22:2
Hook-Up, The 1935,My 9,24:6
Ah, Wilderness! 1935,Ag 20,25:1
Good Men and True 1935,O 26,12:4
Naughty-Naught '00 1937,Ja 25,23:2
Robin Landing 1937,N 19,26:4
Fabulous Invalid, The 1938,O 10,15:1
Popsy 1941,F 11,26:2
All the Comforts of Home 1942,My 26,24:5

Helward, Dale

Distant Bell, A 1960,Ja 14,29:1
Galileo 1968,D 1,88:4

Hely-Hutchinson, C V (Composer)

Unknown Warrior, The 1931,O 23,28:4

Hembrow, P B (Scenic Designer)

Laburnum Grove 1935,Ja 15,23:5

Heming, Tom

Nowhere Bound 1935,Ja 23,20:2

Heming, Violet

Sonya 1921,Ag 16,18:3
Rubicon, The 1922,F 22,13:1
Rivals, The 1922,Je 6,18:2
Lucky One, The 1922,N 21,15:2
Rivals, The 1923,My 9,14:2

Heming, Violet—Cont

But for the Grace of God 1923,S 9,VII,2:4
Spring Cleaning 1923,N 10,16:3
Spring Cleaning 1923,N 18,VIII,1:1
Trelawney of the 'Wells' 1925,Je 2,16:2
Chivalry 1925,D 16,22:3
Jest, The 1926,F 5,22:2
Jest, The 1926,F 14,VIII,1:1
Vaudeville (Palace) 1926,Je 1,29:5
Loose Ends 1926,N 2,34:2
Mrs Dane's Defense 1928,F 7,30:1
Within the Law 1928,Mr 6,20:1
This Thing Called Love 1928,S 18,32:7
This Thing Called Love 1929,Ja 27,IX,1:3
Soldiers and Women 1929,Ag 25,VIII,3:1
Soldiers and Women 1929,S 3,25:1
Ladies All 1930,Jl 20,VIII,2:1
Ladies All 1930,Jl 29,25:2
Divorce Me, Dear 1931,O 7,29:2
There's Always Juliet 1932,O 28,23:2
All Rights Reserved 1934,N 7,33:5
De Luxe 1935,Mr 6,22:2
Yes, My Darling Daughter 1937,F 10,19:2
Summer Night 1939,N 3,17:1
Love for Love 1940,Je 4,19:5
Beverly Hills 1940,N 8,24:2
And Be My Love 1945,F 22,30:4
Dear Barbarians 1952,F 22,15:2

Hemingway, Ernest (Original Author)

Farewell to Arms, A 1930,S 23,30:3
Kat 1931,O 4,VIII,4:1
Fifth Column, The 1940,F 4,IX,1:6
Fifth Column, The 1940,M 7,18:2

Hemingway, Ernest (Playwright)

Fifth Column, The 1940,Ja 27,9:1
Fifth Column, The 1940,Mr 17,X,1:1

Hemingway, Frank

Katja 1926,O 19,27:3

Hemingway, Richard

Collision 1932,F 17,19:2

Hemme, E

Topaze 1931,F 17,29:1

Hemmer, Carl

O'Brien Girl, The 1921,O 4,10:2

Hemmer, Carl (Choreographer)

Nightingale, The 1927,Ja 4,20:4

Hemmer, Carl (Director)

Allez-Opp! 1927,Ag 3,29:3

Hemmer, Carl (Producer)

Allez-Opp! 1927,Ag 3,29:3

Hemmer, Edward

Doctor Faustus 1937,Ja 9,21:2
Processional 1937,O 14,23:1

Hemmerde, E G (Playwright)

Butterfly on the Wheel 1935,N 10,IX,3:1

Hemming, Alfred

Wrecker, The 1928,F 28,18:2

Hempstead, David B (Playwright)

Rainbow's End 1928,D 26,14:6

Hemsley, Estelle

Conjur' Man Dies 1936,Mr 12,18:5
Turpentine 1936,Je 27,21:6
Case of Philip Lawrence, The 1937,Je 9,31:1
Tobacco Road 1950,Mr 7,23:2
Take a Giant Step 1953,O 4,II,1:1
Mrs Patterson 1954,D 2,37:1
Too Late the Phalarope 1956,O 12,35:1

Hemsley, Gilbert V Jr (Lighting Director)

Duchess of Malfi, The 1962,Mr 5,27:1
Caesar and Cleopatra 1963,Ag 1,18:2
Alchemist, The 1964,S 15,33:1
Man and Superman 1964,D 7,45:2
War and Peace 1965,Ja 12,32:1
Judith 1965,Mr 25,42:2
Oresteia 1966,Je 30,29:1
Birds, The 1966,Jl 1,40:1
School for Scandal, The 1966,N 22,33:2
We Comrades Three 1966,D 21,46:1
Wild Duck, The 1967,Ja 12,49:1
War and Peace 1967,Mr 22,42:1
In the Matter of J Robert Oppenheimer
1968,Je 7,31:1
Murderous Angels 1970,F 8,70:1

Hemsley, Jeroline (Playwright)

Wade in de Water 1929,S 14,17:2
Promis' Lan', De 1930,My 28,31:2

Hemsley, Sherman

People vs Ranchman, The 1968,O 28,56:1
But Never Jam Today 1969,Ap 24,40:1
Old Judge Mose Is Dead 1969,Ag 29,25:1
Moon on a Rainbow Shawl 1969,Ag 29,25:1
Purlie 1970,Mr 16,53:1

Hemsley, Winston DeWitt

Hallelujah, Baby! 1967,My 7,II,1:1
Hello, Dolly! 1967,N 13,61:1

Hemstreet Singers

Greenwich Village Follies 1925,D 25,23:3
Vaudeville (Palace) 1926,S 14,25:3

Hemus, Percy

Madame X 1927,Jl 7,29:3
Command to Love, The 1927,S 21,27:1

Hench, R W Jr

It's the Valet 1933,D 15,25:4

Henchley, Howard
Martinique 1920,Ap 27,18:2
Henckels, Paul (Director)
Baby Mine 1927,Ap 3,VIII,2:1
Hendel, Helena
Grand Music Hall of Israel, The 1968,F 7,42:1
Henderich, Fred A
Little Theatre Tournament; Poor Old Jim
1929,My 10,32:2
Henderson, A C
Atlas and Eva 1928,F 7,30:2
If Booth Had Missed 1932,F 5,24:2
Henderson, A Horton
Winter Soldiers 1942,N 30,19:2
Henderson, Adolph
Shuffle Along of 1933 1932,D 27,11:3
Henderson, Al
All the King's Men 1950,Jl 19,25:6
Out West of Eighth 1951,S 21,20:3
Andersonville Trial, The 1959,D 30,15:1
Henderson, Albert
King Lear 1940,D 16,27:2
Circle of Chalk, The 1941,Mr 27,28:4
Would-Be Gentleman, The 1946,Ja 10,29:2
Orpheus Descending 1957,Mr 22,28:1
Henderson, Albert C
Penal Law 2010 1930,Ap 19,14:2
Henderson, Anne
Slightly Scandalous 1944,Je 14,16:2
Henderson, Arthur (Master)
H M S Pinafore 1942,Ja 22,12:2
H M S Pinafore 1944,F 15,14:4
Henderson, Bert
Wooden Soldier, The 1931,Je 23,28:4
Henderson, C E
1776 1926,Ap 24,11:2
Gentlemen, the Queen 1927,Ap 23,14:3
Henderson, C E (Composer)
Not Now-Later 1928,Ap 14,25:1
Henderson, C E (Lyricist)
Not Now-Later 1928,Ap 14,25:1
Henderson, C E (Miscellaneous)
1776 1926,Ap 24,11:2
Henderson, Charles
Two Blocks Away 1921,Ag 31,8:3
Ice-Bound 1923,F 12,16:2
Black Boy 1926,O 7,30:2
Bye Bye Bonnie 1927,Ja 14,15:3
Thou Desperate Pilot 1927,Mr 8,23:1
White Eagle, The 1927,D 27,24:4
Furies, The 1928,Mr 8,23:1
Gang War 1928,Ag 21,27:2
Judas 1929,Ja 25,20:4
Game of Love and Death, The 1929,N 26,28:4
Passionate Pilgrim, The 1932,O 20,24:3
Great Magoo, The 1932,D 3,20:7
All Good Americans 1933,D 6,29:2
They Shall Not Die 1934,F 22,24:4
Uncle Tom's Cabin 1934,Jl 6,15:1
Ethan Frome 1936,Ja 22,15:2
I Take Care of My Friends 1936,Jl 21,13:2
My Heart's in the Highlands 1939,Ap 14,29:2
Vagabond King, The 1943,Je 30,24:2
On Strivers' Row 1946,Mr 1,17:2
Henderson, Charles (Composer)
Blackouts of 1949 1949,S 7,39:2
Hear! Hear! 1955,S 28,38:1
Henderson, Charles (Lyricist)
Blackouts of 1949 1949,S 7,39:2
Henderson, Charles (Playwright)
Hear! Hear! 1955,S 28,38:1
Henderson, Charles H
Room 349 1930,Ap 23,24:5
Henderson, Charles N (Composer)
Curate's Play, The 1961,D 18,41:3
Tableaux 1961,D 18,41:3
Henderson, Clarence
Criminal Code, The 1929,O 3,28:2
Henderson, Dick
Vaudeville (Palace) 1928,Jl 3,19:2
Vaudeville (Palace) 1928,N 26,31:2
Henderson, Dickie
Wish You Were Here 1953,O 11,83:5
Teahouse of the August Moon, The
1955,My 10,24:1
Henderson, Don
Kiss Me, Kate 1965,My 13,31:1
Yeomen of the Guard, The 1968,My 9,53:1
Henderson, Douglas
Stalag 17 1951,My 9,41:2
Henderson, Florence
Wish You Were Here 1952,Je 26,26:6
Oklahoma! 1953,S 1,19:1
Fanny 1954,N 5,16:1
Fanny 1954,N 21,II,1:1
Girl Who Came to Supper, The 1963,D 9,49:1
South Pacific 1967,Je 13,56:1
Oh, Johnny: or, Jonny Spielt Auf 1970,Mr 15,88:4
Henderson, Frances
Public Relations 1944,Ap 7,23:3
Laffing Room Only 1944,D 25,15:4
Henderson, Frank
Candida 1925,N 10,23:4

Weak Woman, A 1926,Ja 27,16:3
Royal Box, The 1928,N 21,32:3
Sakura 1928,D 26,14:4
Traitor, The 1930,My 3,23:4
Kiss of Importance, A 1930,D 2,31:3
Heat Wave 1931,F 18,14:6
Merchant of Venice, The 1931,N 9,22:2
Henderson, Grace
Straw, The 1921,N 11,16:2
Alias Jimmy Valentine 1921,D 9,20:3
Lesson in Love, A 1923,S 25,10:1
Henderson, Horton
Days of Our Youth, The 1941,N 29,15:2
Criminals, The 1941,D 22,24:3
Mexican Hayride 1944,Ja 29,9:6
Henderson, Isabel
Gypsy Blonde 1934,Je 26,22:5
Henderson, Jack
Wild Duck, The 1951,D 27,17:1
Henderson, James
Robert E Lee 1923,N 21,23:1
Henderson, Jane
Epitaph for George Dillon 1960,D 29,17:1
Henderson, Jo
Camille 1956,S 19,33:1
Little Boxes; Trevor 1969,D 4,71:2
Little Boxes; Coffee Lace, The 1969,D 4,71:2
Henderson, Katherine
Bottomland 1927,Je 28,29:3
Henderson, Kenneth
Side-Show 1931,My 16,13:1
Henderson, Lucius
Nightingale, The 1927,Ja 4,20:4
Henderson, Luther
Ol' Man Satan 1932,O 4,26:3
Our Lan' 1947,Ap 19,11:2
Henderson, Luther (Miscellaneous)
Flower Drum Song 1958,D 2,44:1
Do Re Mi 1960,D 27,23:2
Bravo Giovanni 1962,My 21,41:2
Hot Spot 1963,Ap 20,17:2
Funny Girl 1964,Mr 27,15:1
I Had a Ball 1964,D 16,50:1
Golden Rainbow 1968,F 5,27:1
Henderson, Luther (Musical Director)
Purlie 1970,Mr 16,53:1
Henderson, Marcia
Peter Pan 1950,Ap 25,27:2
Henderson, Mary
Tempest, The 1955,S 3,8:6
Henderson, Maye
Crucible, The 1958,Mr 17,21:1
Henderson, Melanie
Me Nobody Knows, The 1970,My 19,42:1
Henderson, Mina
Golden Days 1921,N 2,20:1
Roger Bloomer 1923,Mr 2,18:3
Henderson, Randell
Egg in Your Beer 1945,My 13,II,1:3
Henderson, Randell (Playwright)
Egg in Your Beer 1945,My 13,II,1:3
Henderson, Ray
Zany Evening With Elsa Lanchester, A
1960,N 5,27:2
Elsa Lanchester-Herself 1961,F 6,28:1
Henderson, Ray (Composer)
George White's Scandals 1925,Je 23,24:2
George White's Scandals 1926,Je 15,23:2
Good News 1927,S 7,35:4
Manhattan Mary 1927,S 27,30:3
George White's Scandals 1928,Jl 3,19:1
Follow Thru 1929,Ja 10,24:3
Flying High 1930,F 9,VIII,4:2
George White's Scandals 1931,S 15,30:1
Hot-Cha! 1932,F 21,VIII,2:1
Hot-Cha! 1932,Mr 9,17:3
Forward March 1932,O 23,IX,3:5
Strike Me Pink 1933,Mr 6,16:3
Say When 1934,O 28,IX,3:1
Say When 1934,N 9,24:2
George White's Scandals 1935,D 26,20:2
Ziegfeld Follies 1943,Ap 2,16:2
Henderson, Ray (Lyricist)
Manhattan Mary 1927,S 27,30:3
George White's Scandals 1928,Jl 3,19:1
Follow Thru 1929,Ja 10,24:3
Flying High 1930,F 9,VIII,4:2
Flying High 1930,Mr 4,24:4
Hot-Cha! 1932,Mr 9,17:3
Henderson, Ray (Miscellaneous)
Billy Barnes People, The 1961,Je 14,10:3
Henderson, Ray (Musical Director)
Zany Evening With Elsa Lanchester, A
1960,N 5,27:2
Elsa Lanchester-Herself 1961,F 6,28:1
Henderson, Ray (Original Author)
Hot-Cha! 1932,Mr 9,17:3
Henderson, Ray (Playwright)
Manhattan Mary 1927,S 27,30:3
Strike Me Pink 1933,Mr 6,16:3
Henderson, Ray (Producer)
Forward March 1932,O 23,IX,3:5
Strike Me Pink 1933,Mr 6,16:3

Henderson, Ray (Producer)—Cont
Say When 1934,N 9,24:2
Henderson, Robert
Tyrant, The 1930,N 13,33:1
Electra 1931,My 24,VIII,3:5
Electra 1932,Ja 9,21:4
I Loved You Wednesday 1932,O 12,27:1
Strangers at Home 1934,S 15,20:5
Tomorrow's Harvest 1934,D 6,26:5
White Cargo 1941,My 14,24:3
Madwoman of Chaillot, The 1970,Mr 23,48:3
Henderson, Robert (Director)
Merry Wives of Windsor, The 1938,Ap 15,22:3
Importance of Being Earnest, The 1939,Ja 13,16:2
When We Are Married 1939,D 10,X,5:6
When We Are Married 1939,D 26,22:3
First Stop to Heaven 1941,Ja 6,10:7
Me and Harry 1942,Ap 3,24:6
Duke in Darkness, The 1944,Ja 25,15:2
It's A Gift 1945,Mr 13,18:7
Caviar to the General 1947,Ja 14,30:3
Madwoman of Chaillot, The 1970,Mr 23,48:3
Henderson, Robert (Producer)
Electra 1931,My 24,VIII,3:5
Electra 1932,Ja 9,21:4
Merry Wives of Windsor, The 1938,Ap 15,22:3
Wuthering Heights 1939,Ap 28,30:4
When We Are Married 1939,D 26,22:3
Me and Harry 1942,Ap 3,24:6
Henderson, Roman
Stevedore 1949,F 23,30:2
Henderson, Rose
Yeah-Man 1932,My 27,27:3
Henderson, Rosemary
Ice Capades 1954,S 16,37:1
Ice Capades 1955,S 15,38:1
Ice Capades 1956,S 13,41:2
Henderson, Slim
Bottomland 1927,Je 28,29:3
Henderson, Wilma
Crime in the Whistler Room, The 1924,O 10,22:2
Hendl, Walter (Composer)
Dark of the Moon 1945,Mr 15,27:2
Hendler, Chana
Dybbuk, The 1926,D 14,24:2
Eternal Jew, The 1926,D 21,21:2
Jacob's Dream 1927,Ja 4,20:2
Hendler, Grace
Blue Butterfly, The 1929,F 17,29:3
Hendler, Hanale
Dybbuk, The 1948,My 3,26:3
Golem, The 1948,My 17,22:3
Hendler, Hanelle
Each Had Six Wings 1964,Mr 12,39:1
Hendon, George A Jr (Original Author)
Johnny on the Spot 1942,Ja 9,24:2
Hendra, Tony
Love and Let Love 1968,Ja 4,30:1
Hendree, Harold
Triumphant Bachelor, The 1927,S 16,21:1
Hendrick, Beatrice
Jane Brady-Editor 1935,Jl 2,24:3
Curse You, Jack Dalton 1935,Jl 16,24:1
Hendrick, John
Jeremiah 1939,F 4,11:2
Hendricks, Adeline (Playwright)
Night Call, The 1922,Ap 27,12:2
Hendricks, Alonzo (Miscellaneous)
Egg and I, The 1958,S 11,43:4
Hendricks, Arch
Find the Fox 1930,Je 21,20:4
Hendricks, Beatrice
Man From Toronto, The 1926,Je 18,27:2
Passing of the Third Floor Back, The
1928,F 21,18:2
Dinner Is Served 1929,Ag 16,18:4
First Mortgage 1929,O 11,36:1
Schoolgirl 1930,N 21,31:1
Are You Decent? 1934,Ap 20,16:2
Season Changes, The 1935,D 24,10:2
Puritan, The 1936,Ja 24,14:3
Hendricks, Ben
Spanish Love 1920,Ag 18,6:1
Triumph of X, The 1921,Ag 25,8:2
Goldfish, The 1922,Ap 18,15:3
Virtue (?) 1922,N 17,14:1
Wasp, The 1923,Mr 28,14:3
Hello, Lola! 1926,Ja 13,30:1
Fog 1927,F 8,20:1
Hendricks, Delmar (Miscellaneous)
Golden Apple, The 1962,F 13,38:2
Stone Tower, The 1962,Ag 24,14:2
Dream of Swallows, A 1964,Ap 15,46:1
Hendricks, John
Lancelot and Elaine 1921,S 13,12:1
Some Party 1922,Ap 17,22:1
Sue, Dear 1922,Jl 11,16:2
Matrimonial Bed, The 1927,O 13,23:2
Mourning Becomes Electra; Hunted, The
1931,O 27,22:1
House of Remsen 1934,Ap 3,26:4
Gypsy Blonde 1934,Je 26,22:5
Pirates of Penzance, The 1938,Je 3,16:2

ᵻndricks, Louis
Bonehead, The 1920,Ap 13,12:1
Skirt, The 1921,N 8,28:1
ᵻndricks, Marc
Miser, The 1950,Mr 27,19:5
ᵻndricks, Roger
'Tis Pity She's a Whore 1967,O 21,15:2
We Bombed in New Haven 1967,D 7,58:1
ᵻndrickson, George (Lighting Director)
27 Wagons Full of Cotton 1955,Ja 19,23:2
ᵻndrickson, George (Scenic Designer)
27 Wagons Full of Cotton 1955,Ja 19,23:2
ᵻndrickson, Ned (Producer)
Bella 1961,N 17,40:1
Digging for Apples 1962,S 28,29:4
Spots of the Leopard, The 1963,S 25,38:1
ᵻndrickson, Robert S Jr
Time of Their Lives 1937,O 26,19:1
ᵻndrickson, Stephen (Costume Designer)
Lemon Sky 1970,My 18,40:1
Tarot 1970,D 12,19:1
ᵻndrickson, Stephen (Lighting Director)
Fireworks; Fireworks for a Hot Fourth
1969,Je 12,51:1
Fireworks; Football 1969,Je 12,51:1
Fireworks; Report, The 1969,Je 12,51:1
ᵻndrickson, Stephen (Scenic Designer)
Fireworks; Report, The 1969,Je 12,51:1
Fireworks; Fireworks for a Hot Fourth
1969,Je 12,51:1
Fireworks; Football 1969,Je 12,51:1
Lemon Sky 1970,My 18,40:1
Tarot 1970,D 12,19:1
ᵻendrie, Christopher
Critic, The 1965,Jl 26,15:2
Macbeth 1968,N 30,49:3
ᵻendrie, Christopher (Miscellaneous)
Macbeth 1968,N 30,49:3
ᵻendrik, John
Vienna at Night 1945,Ap 30,12:4
ᵻendry, Tiffany
Getting Married 1970,Ja 20,46:1
Brotherhood 1970,Mr 18,39:1
ᵻendryx, Shirl (Playwright)
Jumping Fool, The 1970,F 10,53:1
ᵻendzik, Jan
Auntie Mame 1956,N 1,47:2
ᵻeneker, David (Composer)
Half a Sixpence 1965,Ap 26,38:2
ᵻeneker, David (Lyricist)
Irma la Douce 1960,S 30,31:2
Half a Sixpence 1965,Ap 26,38:2
ᵻeneker, David (Playwright)
Irma la Douce 1960,S 30,31:2
ᵻenger, Casper F
Hamlet 1927,Ap 7,23:3
ᵻengst, Marilyn
Not Now Darling 1970,O 30,33:1
ᵻenie, Sonja
In the Land of the Midnight Sun 1930,Ja 7,27:4
Hollywood Ice Revue 1942,Ja 20,26:4
Hollywood Ice Revue 1943,Ja 24,II,1:1
Hollywood Ice Revue 1950,Ja 21,13:4
ᵻenie, Sonja (Producer)
It Happens on Ice 1940,O 11,24:3
It Happens on Ice 1941,Ap 5,13:2
Stars on Ice 1942,Jl 3,12:2
Hollywood Ice Revue 1943,Ja 24,II,1:1
Stars on Ice (2d Edition) 1943,Je 25,13:2
Hats Off to Ice 1944,Je 23,15:2
Icetime 1946,Je 21,20:5
Icetime 1947,My 29,28:2
Howdy Mr Ice 1948,Je 25,28:5
Howdy, Mr Ice of 1950 1949,My 27,24:2
ᵻenin, Ethel
We Americans 1926,O 13,20:4
ᵻeninburg, Gustav (Miscellaneous)
Believers, The 1968,My 10,57:4
ᵻenkle, Carl (Playwright)
Decision 1929,My 28,37:3
Page Pygmalion 1932,Ag 4,17:5
ᵻenley, Drewe
Hail Scrawdyke! 1966,N 29,50:1
ᵻenley, Joan
Time and the Conways 1938,Ja 4,19:2
ᵻenley, W E (Playwright)
Beau Austin 1929,N 17,IX,2:4
ᵻennagin, Michael (Composer)
World of My America, The 1966,O 4,53:1
ᵻennefeld, Edmund B (Playwright)
Deputy of Paris, The 1947,Mr 22,9:5
G-II 1948,My 28,27:3
ᵻennequin, Maurice (Lyricist)
Passionement; Passionately 1929,Mr 8,31:4
ᵻennequin, Maurice (Original Author)
Oh, Please! 1926,D 22,24:3
ᵻennequin, Maurice (Playwright)
Toto 1921,Mr 22,15:2
Alarm Clock, The 1923,D 25,26:2
Monsieur de Cinq Heures 1924,O 12,VIII,1:6
Kiss in a Taxi, The 1925,Ag 26,14:1
On Ne Roule pas Antoinette 1927,Ap 10,VIII,2:7
Passionement 1928,Ja 15,VIII,2:1

Sunny Days 1928,F 9,29:1
Passionement; Passionately 1929,Mr 8,31:4
Hennesey, Dale (Scenic Designer)
Ice Follies 1963,Ja 10,5:2
Hennessey, Ann
Month in the Country, A 1956,Ap 4,23:1
Hanjo 1960,N 16,51:4
Coming Forth by Day of Osiris Jones, The; Kid,
The 1961,Mr 15,45:2
Crime and Crime 1963,D 17,51:2
Blues for Mister Charlie 1964,Ap 24,24:1
Hennessy, David
Miracle, The 1924,Ja 16,17:1
Hennessy, Robert
Armlet of Jade 1936,Ap 15,25:3
Abdication 1948,S 28,32:5
Hennesy, Dale (Scenic Designer)
Ice Follies 1961,Ja 11,25:2
Ice Follies 1962,Ja 10,24:6
Henniger, Rolf
Don Carlos 1964,N 25,40:1
Plebejer Proben Den Aufstand, Die 1966,Ja 18,32:1
Henning, Edgar
Book of Charm, The 1925,S 4,26:3
Kept 1926,S 18,13:3
Mrs Dane's Defense 1928,F 7,30:1
Sherlock Holmes 1928,F 21,18:4
Within the Law 1928,Mr 6,20:1
Divided Honors 1929,O 1,28:2
Wild Duck, The 1938,Ap 16,16:5
Henning, Edgar (Director)
Charm 1929,N 29,24:5
Henning, Ervin (Composer)
Live Like Pigs 1965,Je 8,48:2
Henning, Leo
Bringing Up Father 1925,Mr 31,16:1
Merry Malones, The 1927,S 27,30:2
Belmont Varieties 1932,S 29,17:2
Henning, Leo (Choreographer)
Half Moon Inn 1923,Mr 21,19:2
Henning, Magnus (Composer)
Pepper Mill 1937,Ja 6,19:4
Henning, Pat
Vaudeville (Palace) 1930,F 10,20:3
Henning, Ted
Moondreamers, The 1969,D 9,68:1
Gloria and Esperanza 1970,F 5,32:1
Hennings, Virginia
Great Gatsby, The 1926,F 3,22:1
Henri, Mr
Trois Jeunes Filles Nues; Three Young Maids From
the Folies Bergere 1929,Mr 5,28:2
Henri, Paul
Royal Family, The 1940,Ag 13,15:3
Henrichs, Helmut (Director)
Ratten, Die 1966,Ap 13,36:1
Henrichs, Helmut (Miscellaneous)
Ratten, Die 1966,Ap 13,36:1
Henried, Paul
Flight to the West 1940,D 15,I,59:5
Flight to the West 1940,D 31,19:1
Flight to the West 1941,Ja 19,IX,1:1
Flight to the West 1941,Mr 7,16:3
Festival 1955,Ja 19,22:1
Henriet, Maurice
Sur le Banc 1923,O 16,18:1
Alcide Pepis 1923,O 30,17:2
Crucifies, Les 1923,O 30,17:2
Catherine Goulden 1923,N 6,22:1
Trois Masques, Les 1923,N 6,22:1
Bonheur, Le 1923,N 20,23:3
Laboratoire des Hallucinations, Le 1923,N 20,23:3
Prenez Ma Dame 1923,N 27,23:5
Griffe, La 1923,N 27,23:5
Sol Hyam's Brocanteur 1923,N 27,23:5
Henriette
Trois Jeunes Filles Nues; Three Young Maids From
the Folies Bergere 1929,Mr 5,28:2
Henriksen, Eve (Costume Designer)
Autumn's Here 1966,O 26,40:1
Skits-Oh-Frantics 1967,Ap 3,39:2
Henriksen, Lance
Three Plays of the Sea 1970,Ag 20,39:1
Henriksen, Lance (Lighting Director)
Three Plays of the Sea 1970,Ag 20,39:1
Henriksen, Lance (Scenic Designer)
Three Plays of the Sea 1970,Ag 20,39:1
Henrikson, Alf (Playwright)
Ljusnande Tid, Den 1939,S 17,X,2:4
Henrikson, Anders
Mourning Becomes Electra 1933,My 7,IX,2:3
Henring, Ben
Seven Against One 1930,My 7,25:1
Henriot, Giorgio (Playwright)
Istruttoria, L'; Judicial Inquiry, The 1933,F 13,11:3
Henriques, Winston George
House of Flowers 1954,D 31,11:2
Henritze, Bette
Story Teller, The 1951,D 15,11:3
Purple Dust 1956,D 28,15:1
Antony and Cleopatra 1959,Ja 14,28:1
She Stoops to Conquer 1960,N 2,42:5
Plough and the Stars, The 1960,D 7,56:2

Henritze, Bette—Cont

Octoroon, The 1961,Ja 28,13:1
Richard II 1961,Ag 30,25:1
Giants, Sons of Giants 1962,Ja 8,26:2
Merchant of Venice, The 1962,Je 22,1:4
King Lear 1962,Ag 14,35:1
Abe Lincoln in Illinois 1963,Ja 23,5:2
Lion in Love, The 1963,Ap 26,28:3
Antony and Cleopatra 1963,Ja 21,33:1
Winter's Tale, The 1963,Ag 16,14:1
Ballad of the Sad Cafe, The 1963,O 31,27:1
White House, The 1964,My 20,39:1
Othello 1964,O 13,48:1
Baal 1965,My 7,33:2
All's Well That Ends Well 1966,Je 17,39:1
Measure for Measure 1966,Jl 14,27:1
Long Christmas Dinner, The 1966,S 7,53:1
Queens of France 1966,S 7,53:1
Displaced Person, The 1966,D 30,15:1
Rimers of Eldritch, The 1967,F 21,53:1
Dr Cook's Garden 1967,S 26,52:1
Here's Where I Belong 1968,Mr 4,32:1
Acquisition, The 1968,D 31,19:1
Crimes of Passion; Erpingham Camp, The
1969,O 27,54:1
Wars of the Roses, The (Part I) 1970,Jl 2,30:1
Wars of the Roses, The (Part II) 1970,Jl 3,15:1
Richard III 1970,Jl 4,11:1
Happiness Cage, The 1970,O 5,56:4
Happiness Cage, The 1970,O 11,II,1:1
Henry, Albert
Wall Street 1927,Ap 21,24:4
Henry, Ann
New Faces of 1956 1956,Je 15,32:1
Henry, Arthur (Playwright)
Time 1923,O 14,VIII,2:4
Time 1923,N 27,23:3
Henry, B McK (Lyricist)
Who's Who 1924,Ap 18,19:2
Not Now-Later 1928,Ap 14,25:1
Henry, Betty Bruce
Kongo 1926,Mr 31,20:5
Henry, Bill & Son
Ice Capades 1959,S 4,12:1
Henry, Buck
Fortress of Glass 1952,S 5,19:2
Untitled-Revue 1961,Je 18,II,1:1
Henry, Charles
Searching for the Sun 1936,F 20,22:6
Merry Wives of Windsor, The 1938,Ap 15,22:3
Henry, Charlotte
Courage 1928,O 9,34:2
Hobo 1931,F 12,24:4
Ah, Wilderness! 1934,My 1,26:3
Henry, Emmaline
Vintage '60 1960,S 13,41:1
Henry, Forrest R
Fifty-Fifty 1937,N 20,21:1
Fifty-Fifty 1937,D 5,II,3:4
Henry, Frank
Buckaroo 1929,Mr 18,31:1
Henry, Grace (Composer)
Earl Carroll's Vanities 1926,Ag 25,19:4
Earl Carroll's Vanities 1927,Ja 5,18:1
Earl Carroll's Vanities 1928,Ag 7,25:2
Henry, Grace (Director)
Riff-Raff 1926,F 9,18:6
Henry, Grace (Lyricist)
Riff-Raff 1926,F 9,18:6
Earl Carroll's Vanities 1926,Ag 25,19:4
Earl Carroll's Vanities 1927,Ja 5,18:1
Earl Carroll's Vanities 1928,Ag 7,25:2
Fioretta 1929,F 6,30:3
Henry, Grace (Playwright)
Riff-Raff 1926,F 9,18:6
Henry, Hank
Kiss Me, Kate 1952,Ja 9,24:6
Henry, Helen
Nut Farm, The 1929,O 15,34:3
Mother, The 1935,N 20,26:3
Henry, Horace
Our Town 1944,Ja 11,24:5
Henry, Hubert
Anna Lucasta 1944,Ag 31,15:1
Henry, James
Street Scene 1947,Ja 10,17:2
Henry, John
Circus Princess, The 1927,Ap 26,32:2
Marco Millions 1928,Ja 10,28:2
Volpone 1928,Ap 10,32:1
Buckaroo 1929,Mr 18,31:1
Marco Millions 1930,Mr 4,24:4
Volpone 1930,Mr 11,24:5
She Lived Next to the Firehouse 1931,F 11,23:1
Sex Fable, The 1931,O 21,26:1
Henry, Joyce
Men in White 1955,F 26,13:2
Venice Preserv'd 1955,D 13,54:4
Henry, Joyce (Producer)
There Is a Play Tonight 1961,F 16,24:2
Henry, Lee
Montserrat 1954,My 26,34:2
Tempest, The 1955,S 3,8:6

Henry, Lee—Cont

Twisting Road, The; Housekeeper, The
1957,N 18,36:5
Twisting Road, The; One Tuesday Morning
1957,N 18,36:5
Edward II 1958,F 12,32:5
Electra 1958,My 10,17:7
Tempest, The 1959,D 28,19:2
Miracle, The 1960,D 5,42:3

Henry, Martha

Macbeth 1962,Je 20,41:1
Tempest, The 1962,Je 22,14:1
Troilus and Cressida 1963,Je 19,40:2
Comedy of Errors, The 1963,Je 21,35:3
Timon of Athens 1963,Jl 31,19:2
Bourgeois Gentilhomme, Le 1964,Je 18,28:2
King Lear 1964,Je 19,36:1
Country Wife, The 1964,Ag 3,16:1
Henry IV, Part I 1965,Je 30,42:1
Falstaff; Henry IV, Part II 1965,Jl 1,35:1
Cherry Orchard, The 1965,Ag 2,17:2
Henry VI 1966,Je 9,55:2
Twelfth Night 1966,Je 10,51:2
Tartuffe 1968,Je 12,39:1
Midsummer Night's Dream, A 1968,Je 13,54:1
Tartuffe 1968,Je 23,II,1:1
Midsummer Night's Dream, A 1968,Je 23,II,1:1
Three Musketeers, The 1968,Jl 24,49:2

Henry, Michael

On the Necessity of Being Polygamous
1964,D 9,61:1

Henry, O (Playwright)

Alias Jimmy Valentine 1921,D 9,20:3

Henry, Patrick (Director)

Tom Paine 1969,Mr 30,71:2

Henry, Raoul

Aiglon, L' 1924,O 21,21:1
Naked 1924,O 28,27:2
Madame Sans-Gene 1924,N 4,30:1
Lost Colony, The 1937,Jl 11,X,2:1
Fifth Column, The 1940,Mr 7,18:2

Henry, S R (Composer)

Little Miss Charity 1920,S 3,6:3

Henry, Sam Haigler

Comforter, The 1964,O 22,42:1
Phedre 1966,F 11,36:1
Butterfly Dream, The 1966,My 20,41:1
Mulatto 1967,N 16,61:4

Henry, Thomas Browne (Director)

Not for Children 1936,Mr 1,IX,2:2

Henry, Victor

Hail Scrawdyke! 1966,N 29,50:1
Total Eclipse 1968,S 13,42:1
Look Back in Anger 1968,N 1,38:1
Friends, The 1970,My 22,41:2

Henry, Vincent

Vagabond King, The 1943,Je 30,24:2
Kismet 1965,Je 23,45:1

Henry, Wilfred

Places, Please 1937,N 13,10:6

Henry, Will

How Beautiful With Shoes 1935,N 29,24:1

Henry, William

Trial of Joan of Arc, The 1921,Mr 28,8:2
Midsummer Night's Dream, A 1934,S 19,15:1

Henry, William A

Bacchae, The 1969,Mr 15,24:1

Henry, Yvon (Costume Designer)

Phedre 1969,Mr 1,20:1

Henry (Playwright)

Prosit Gypsy 1929,Je 2,VIII,2:6

Henry-May, Pamela

Victoria Regina 1938,O 4,20:2

Henry-Thomas, John

Patience 1968,My 16,52:1

Henrys, The

Ice Follies 1957,Ja 16,36:1

Hensel, Otto (Composer)

Bare Facts 1927,Ag 17,27:5

Henshaw, John E

Some Party 1922,Ap 17,22:1
Octoroon, The 1929,Mr 13,28:3
If Love Were All 1931,N 14,14:5

Henshaw, Nancy

Dumbbell People in a Barbell World 1962,F 15,25:1

Henske, Judy

Gogo Loves You 1964,O 10,19:2

Hensley, Edwin

Nice People 1921,Mr 3,11:1
Dancers, The 1923,O 18,17:2

Hensley, Mary

Saint of Bleecker Street, The 1954,D 28,21:1

Henson, Basil

Separate Tables 1955,My 22,II,1:1

Henson, Gladys

Design for Living 1933,Ja 3,19:5
Design for Living 1933,Ja 25,13:2
Point Valaine 1935,Ja 17,22:2
George and Margaret 1937,S 23,32:2
Set to Music 1939,Ja 19,16:2
Morning Star, The 1941,D 28,IX,2:3
Curious Savage, The 1950,O 25,44:3

Henson, Hilary

Twelfth Night 1970,Ja 1,18:1

Henson, John

Most Happy Fella, The 1956,My 4,20:1

Henson, Leslie

Sally 1921,S 11,20:2
Funny Face 1928,N 9,22:3
All-Star Special 1931,Jl 18,16:4
Ladies' Night 1933,N 19,IX,3:7
Lucky Break 1934,O 3,25:3
Lucky Break 1934,O 28,IX,3:4
Seeing Stars 1935,N 1,25:5
Swing Along 1936,S 20,IX,1:4
Going Greek 1937,S 17,28:4

Henson, Leslie (Director)

On Your Toes 1937,F 6,15:2

Henson, Leslie (Miscellaneous)

Living Dangerously 1935,Ja 14,10:3

Henson, Leslie (Producer)

Indoor Fireworks 1934,Mr 30,26:6
Aren't Men Beasts? 1936,My 15,29:1

Henson, Nicky

Camelot 1964,Ag 20,34:1
Canterbury Tales 1968,S 7,23:3
Zoo, Zoo, Widdershings, Zoo 1969,S 5,30:1

Henson, Richard

Little Theatre Tournament; Rain 1929,My 11,22:2

Henson, Robert

Trumpets of the Lord 1969,Ap 30,37:1

Hentel, Nathan (Playwright)

In the Groove 1938,Ap 22,14:5

Hentschel, Irene (Director)

Time and the Conways 1938,Ja 4,19:2

Hentschel, Irene (Producer)

Anthony and Anna 1935,D 8,X,5:1
Candida 1937,F 11,19:3

Hentschke, Heinz (Director)

Lauf ins Glueck 1935,My 19,IX,2:5

Henty, Kirk

Twelfth Night 1930,O 16,28:2

Henzel, Margaret

Pirates of Penzance, The 1936,Ap 21,27:5

Hepburn, Audrey

Gigi 1951,N 26,20:4
Ondine 1954,F 19,23:1
Ondine 1954,F 28,II,1:1

Hepburn, Barton

Dancers, The 1923,O 18,17:2
Claw, The 1927,Ja 13,28:4
Cocktail Impromptu 1927,Ja 13,28:4
Butterflies 1927,F 2,22:4
Casualties 1927,Mr 5,12:2
Prisoners of War 1935,Ja 29,24:1
Sea Dogs 1939,N 7,30:3
Suspect 1940,Ap 10,30:4

Hepburn, James

This Year of Grace 1928,N 8,27:1

Hepburn, Katharine

These Days 1928,N 13,36:2
Art and Mrs Bottle 1930,N 19,19:3
Warrior's Husband, The 1932,Mr 12,19:4
Lake, The 1933,D 19,26:3
Lake, The 1933,D 27,24:2
Lake, The 1934,Ja 7,X,1:1
Jane Eyre 1937,Ja 3,X,2:1
Jane Eyre 1937,F 7,X,1:1
Philadelphia Story, The 1939,F 17,14:2
Philadelphia Story, The 1939,Mr 19,XI,2:6
Philadelphia Story, The 1939,Mr 29,21:1
Philadelphia Story, The 1939,Ap 2,X,1:1
Without Love 1942,Mr 5,20:7
Without Love 1942,Ap 28,17:4
Without Love 1942,N 11,28:1
Without Love 1942,N 29,VIII,1:1
As You Like It 1950,Ja 27,27:2
As You Like It 1950,F 19,II,1:1
Millionairess, The 1952,Je 28,12:2
Millionairess, The 1952,Jl 6,II,1:5
Millionairess, The 1952,O 18,17:2
Millionairess, The 1952,O 26,II,1:1
Merchant of Venice, The 1957,Jl 11,19:5
Much Ado About Nothing 1957,Ag 8,15:2
Merchant of Venice, The 1957,Ag 18,II,1:1
Much Ado About Nothing 1957,Ag 18,II,1:1
Twelfth Night 1960,Je 9,29:4
Antony and Cleopatra 1960,Ag 1,19:1
Coco 1969,D 19,66:1
Coco 1969,D 28,II,1:1

Hepburn, Philip

Regina 1949,N 1,32:2
Regina 1949,N 13,II,1:1
Peter Pan 1950,Ap 25,27:2
Green Pastures, The 1951,Mr 16,35:2
Twilight Walk 1951,S 25,25:4
Moby Dick 1955,Ap 26,25:3
World's My Oyster, The 1956,Ag 10,10:4

Hepburn, Philip (Miscellaneous)

World's My Oyster, The 1956,Ag 10,10:4

Hepburn, Richard

My Name is Aquilon 1949,F 10,38:2

Hepburn, Richard (Playwright)

Sudden End of Anne Cinquefoil, The
1961,Ja 11,25:2

Hepburn, Richard Houghton (Playwright)

Behold Your God 1936,Ap 22,28:3

Hepburn, Robert

Hades, the Ladies 1934,Mr 29,25:3

Hepenstall, W D (Playwright)

Banshee, The 1927,D 6,26:2

Heppenstal, W D

Lady Screams, The 1927,My 3,24:2

Hepple, Jeanne

Inadmissible Evidence 1965,D 1,52:1
Serjeant Musgrave's Dance 1966,Mr 9,44:1
Imaginary Invalid, The 1967,My 2,53:1
Touch of the Poet, A 1967,My 3,38:2
Ways and Means 1967,My 4,34:1
Still Life 1967,My 4,34:1
'Tis Pity She's a Whore 1967,O 21,15:2
Henry IV 1968,O 7,40:1
Three Sisters, The 1968,Mr 18,56:1
Wars of the Roses, The (Part II) 1970,Jl 3,15:1
Richard III 1970,Jl 4,11:1
Early Morning 1970,N 26,57:1

Hepton, Bernard (Lighting Director)

Romeo and Juliet 1956,O 25,41:1

Hepton, Bernard (Miscellaneous)

Macbeth 1956,O 30,42:2
Troilus and Cressida 1956,D 27,21:1

Herald, Heinz (Playwright)

Burning Bush, The 1949,D 17,15:5

Heras and Wills

Vaudeville (Palace) 1923,Ja 30,12:2

Herbault, Michel

Caligula 1950,D 31,II,3:7
Three Musketeers, The 1968,Je 26,43:1

Herbaux, Yvette

Trois Jeunes Filles Nues; Three Young Maids From
the Folies Bergere 1929,Mr 5,28:2
Comte Obligado 1929,Mr 12,26:2
Ta Bouche 1929,Mr 15,28:5
Bon Garcon, Un 1929,Mr 19,36:2
Pas Sur La Bouche; Not on the Lips
1929,Mr 26,34:3

Herbert, A J

We Girls 1921,N 10,26:3
Eve's Leaves 1925,Mr 27,22:2
Made in America 1925,O 15,27:2
Money Business 1926,Ja 21,18:1
Playing the Game 1927,D 20,32:5
Hawk Island 1929,S 17,34:7
Virtue's Bed 1930,Ap 26,25:1
Lambs Gambol 1932,Ap 25,18:2
Broadway Boy 1932,My 4,23:5
First Apple, The 1933,D 28,25:1
Are You Decent? 1934,Ap 20,16:2
Accent on Youth 1935,Jl 2,24:3
Jane's Legacy 1935,Ag 13,20:3
Service for Two 1935,Ag 20,25:1
Private Affair, A 1936,My 15,28:7
Laughing Woman, The 1936,O 14,30:1
Matrimony, PFD 1936,N 6,28:4
Matrimony, PFD 1936,N 13,26:3
Point of Honor, A 1937,F 12,26:2
Yr Obedient Husband 1938,Ja 11,26:5
Empress of Destiny 1938,Mr 10,16:2
Man From Cairo, The 1938,My 5,26:5
Fifth Column, The 1940,Mr 7,18:2
Walking Gentleman, The 1942,My 8,26:2
I Killed the Count 1942,S 4,18:1

Herbert, A P

Savonarola Brown 1930,F 26,22:3

Herbert, A P (Composer)

Sunday Nights at Nine 1934,N 19,12:1

Herbert, A P (Lyricist)

Sunday Nights at Nine 1934,N 19,12:1
Belle Helene, La 1941,Jl 8,14:1
Big Ben 1946,Ag 4,II,1:4
Bless the Bride 1947,My 11,II,3:7
Tough at the Top 1949,Jl 17,58:5
Tough at the Top 1949,Ag 7,II,1:4

Herbert, A P (Miscellaneous)

Paganini 1937,My 21,18:6

Herbert, A P (Original Author)

Flood Tide 1938,Mr 24,20:8

Herbert, A P (Playwright)

Two Gentlemen of Soho, The 1928,N 11,X,4:1
Helen 1932,Ja 31,I,5:2
Fair Helen 1932,Jl 17,IX,1:2
Mother of Pearl 1933,Ap 16,26:5
Streamline 1934,S 29,13:1
Streamline 1934,O 21,IX,1:3
Home and Beauty 1937,F 3,26:2
Bless the Bride 1947,My 11,II,3:7

Herbert, Alan

Hamlet 1956,O 29,34:1

Herbert, Allan (Playwright)

Bless the Bride 1947,My 5,31:2
Elsa Lanchester-Herself 1961,F 6,28:1

Herbert, Bruce

Power of Dreams, A 1958,Mr 11,33:1

Herbert, Bryan

John Bull's Other Island 1948,F 11,33:4
Old Lady Says No, The 1948,F 18,35:1
Sherlock Holmes 1953,O 31,11:2
Witness for the Prosecution 1954,D 17,35:2
Righteous Are Bold, The 1955,D 23,12:1
Quare Fellow, The 1958,N 28,34:1

Herbert, Bryan—Cont
Shadow and Substance 1959,N 4,42:1
Herbert, Charles
Married Woman, The 1921,D 26,21:1
Vaudeville (Palace) 1932,Jl 4,14:5
Herbert, Diana
Number, The 1951,O 31,33:2
Men of Distinction 1953,My 1,18:4
Wayside 1957,Ap 18,34:1
Herbert, Don (Miscellaneous)
Tumbler, The 1960,F 25,32:2
Love and Libel 1960,D 8,44:1
Passage to India, A 1962,F 1,23:1
Child Buyer, The 1964,D 22,35:1
Royal Hunt of the Sun, The 1965,O 27,36:2
Help Stamp Out Marriage 1966,S 30,50:1
Herbert, Don (Producer)
Flowering Cherry 1959,O 22,46:1
Day the Whores Came Out to Play Tennis, The 1965,Mr 16,45:1
Sing to Me Through Open Windows 1965,Mr 16,45:1
Herbert, Ellen
Afternoon Storm 1948,Ap 12,24:2
Herbert, Evelyn
Stepping Stones 1923,N 7,14:3
Love Song, The 1925,Ja 14,19:4
Princess Flavia 1925,N 3,34:3
Merry World, The 1926,Je 9,18:3
My Maryland 1927,S 13,37:2
New Moon, The 1928,S 20,33:1
Prince Charming 1930,O 14,31:1
Melody 1933,F 15,17:4
Bitter Sweet 1934,My 8,28:4
Herbert, F Hugh (Director)
Moon Is Blue, The 1953,Jl 8,24:1
Girl Can Tell, A 1953,O 30,28:2
Herbert, F Hugh (Playwright)
Quiet, Please! 1940,O 20,IX,2:3
Quiet, Please! 1940,N 9,20:3
Kiss and Tell 1943,Mr 18,22:1
Kiss and Tell 1943,Mr 28,II,1:1
For Keeps 1944,Je 15,17:5
For Love or Money 1947,N 5,36:2
Out of This World 1950,D 22,17:3
Moon Is Blue, The 1951,Mr 9,29:2
Moon Is Blue, The 1953,Jl 8,24:1
Moon Is Blue, The 1953,Ag 9,II,1:2
Girl Can Tell, A 1953,O 30,28:2
Best House in Naples, The 1956,O 27,16:2
Moon Is Blue, The 1961,Ag 9,29:1
Herbert, Francis
Romancing 'Round 1927,O 4,32:4
Herbert, Frank
Welcome Stranger 1920,S 14,12:1
Herbert, Fred (Director)
Flip Side, The 1968,O 11,36:1
Herbert, Fred (Miscellaneous)
Milk Train Doesn't Stop Here Anymore, The 1963,Ja 18,7:1
King Lear 1964,My 19,43:2
Herbert, Fritz
Vaudeville (Palace) 1930,N 24,26:3
Herbert, Galwey
We Moderns 1924,Mr 12,17:2
Buccaneer, The 1925,O 3,10:2
Androcles and the Lion 1925,N 24,28:1
Herbert, Hans
Rita Coventry 1923,F 20,12:2
Herbert, Henry
Blue Flame, The 1920,Mr 16,18:1
Lady of the Lamp, The 1920,Ag 18,6:4
Lady of the Lamp, The 1920,Ag 22,VI,1:2
Bavu 1922,F 27,16:1
Uptown West 1923,Ap 4,22:2
Laugh, Clown, Laugh! 1923,N 29,30:1
Strong, The 1924,F 27,15:3
Lady of the Rose 1925,My 20,26:4
Accused 1925,S 30,20:1
Window Panes 1927,F 22,22:2
Inspector Kennedy 1929,D 21,16:3
Red Planet 1932,D 19,19:2
Yoshe Kalb 1933,D 29,27:2
Damaged Goods 1937,My 18,27:2
Arsenic and Old Lace 1941,Ja 11,13:2
Herbert, Henry (Director)
Henry IV, Part I 1926,Je 1,29:1
Old Bill, M P 1926,N 11,22:2
Window Panes 1927,F 22,22:2
Troilus and Cressida 1932,Je 7,22:3
Richard III 1934,D 28,24:3
Othello 1935,S 28,13:2
Macbeth 1935,O 8,26:4
Damaged Goods 1937,My 18,27:2
Herbert, Henry (Miscellaneous)
Troilus and Cressida 1932,Je 7,22:3
Damaged Goods 1937,My 18,27:2
Herbert, Hugh
Polly of Hollywood 1927,F 22,22:3
Oh, Herbert! 1945,Je 20,26:3
Herbert, Jean
Vaudeville (Palace) 1930,N 24,26:3
Herbert, Jean (Composer)
Hot Rhythm 1930,Ag 22,18:5

Herbert, Jean (Lyricist)
Hot Rhythm 1930,Ag 22,18:5
Herbert, Jocelyn (Costume Designer)
Luther 1963,S 26,41:1
Inadmissible Evidence 1965,D 1,52:1
Hamlet 1969,My 2,38:1
Herbert, Jocelyn (Scenic Designer)
Chairs, The 1958,Ja 10,20:3
Exit the King 1963,S 13,19:4
Luther 1963,S 26,41:1
Chips With Everything 1963,O 2,49:1
Othello 1964,Ap 22,56:1
St Joan of the Stockyards 1964,Je 12,45:1
Inadmissible Evidence 1965,D 1,52:1
Hamlet 1969,My 2,38:1
Home 1970,N 18,41:1
Herbert, John
Hot Spot 1963,Ap 20,17:2
Cabaret 1966,N 21,62:1
Herbert, John (Playwright)
Fortune and Men's Eyes 1967,F 24,29:1
Fortune and Men's Eyes 1969,O 23,55:1
Fortune and Men's Eyes 1970,Ja 18,II,1:1
Herbert, Joseph
Deburau 1920,D 24,14:3
Tangerine 1921,Ag 10,8:2
Yes, Yes, Yvette 1927,O 4,32:3
Herbert, Joseph (Playwright)
Honeydew 1920,S 7,20:1
Sue, Dear 1922,Jl 11,16:2
Herbert, Leo
Ringside Seat 1938,N 23,24:5
Earth Journey 1944,Ap 28,24:2
Seven Mirrors 1945,O 26,17:2
Herbert, Lew
Signature 1945,F 15,25:2
Remains to Be Seen 1951,O 4,37:1
Herbert, Manuel D (Producer)
Oscar Wilde 1957,Ap 20,21:3
Herbert, Nina
Montmartre 1922,F 14,20:1
Herbert, Pitt
What Big Ears! 1942,Ap 21,18:5
Yellow Jack 1944,Ap 7,23:3
Miracle in the Mountains 1947,Ap 26,10:2
Point of No Return 1951,D 14,35:2
Herbert, Ralph
Gypsy Baron, The 1942,Je 20,8:5
Gypsy Baron, The 1942,Ag 7,12:4
Beggar Student, The 1942,S 26,11:4
Rosalinda; Fledermaus, Die 1942,O 29,26:5
Arabian Nights 1954,Je 25,15:2
Arabian Nights 1955,Je 24,16:1
Dreigroschenoper, Die 1965,Mr 12,24:1
Herbert, Ralph (Director)
Vie Parisienne, La 1945,Ja 13,14:5
Herbert, Sidney
Macbeth 1921,F 18,16:1
Wandering Jew, The 1921,O 27,22:1
Herbert, Thomas
Florida Girl 1925,N 3,34:1
Herbert, Tim
Follow the Girls 1944,Ap 10,15:2
Follow the Girls 1944,Ap 16,II,1:2
Herbert, Tom
Schoolmaster, The 1928,Mr 21,30:1
Herbert, Victor (Composer)
My Golden Girl 1920,F 3,18:2
Ziegfeld Follies 1920,Je 23,14:1
Girl in the Spotlight, The 1920,Jl 13,9:3
Sally 1920,D 22,16:1
Ziegfeld Follies 1921,Je 22,10:1
Ziegfeld Follies 1922,Je 6,18:2
Orange Blossoms 1922,S 20,18:1
Ziegfeld Follies 1924,Je 25,26:1
Dream Girl, The 1924,Ag 21,12:2
Sweethearts 1923,S 23,25:1
Mlle Modiste 1929,O 8,34:1
Naughty Marietta 1929,O 22,26:2
Fortune Teller, The 1929,N 5,32:3
Babes in Toyland 1929,D 24,15:3
Nine Fifteen Revue, The 1930,F 12,26:2
Serenade, The 1930,Mr 5,26:7
Babes in Toyland 1930,D 22,17:1
Naughty Marietta 1931,N 17,31:2
Only Girl, The 1934,My 22,28:2
Naughty Marietta 1936,S 2,19:5
Mlle Modiste 1937,My 5,28:5
Red Mill, The 1945,O 17,16:2
Red Mill, The 1945,O 28,II,1:1
Gypsy Lady 1946,S 18,25:6
Sweethearts 1947,F 2,II,1:1
Romany Love 1947,Mr 10,25:1
Herbert, Victor (Lyricist)
Ziegfeld Follies 1920,Je 23,14:1
Nine Fifteen Revue, The 1930,F 12,26:2
Herbert, Victor (Playwright)
Ziegfeld Follies 1920,Je 23,14:1
Sweethearts 1947,Ja 22,31:2
Herbert, Victoria
George White's Scandals 1921,Jl 12,14:1
Herbertot (Producer)
Mademoiselle Bourrat 1923,F 4,VII,1:4

Herbertt, Stanley
Hollywood Pinafore 1945,Je 17,II,4:5
Herbinger, Paul
Peripherie 1926,D 19,VII,4:4
Herblin, David
Yours Truly 1927,Ja 26,16:5
Heigh-Ho, Everybody 1932,My 26,31:2
Herbsman, Harold
Journey to the Day 1963,N 12,49:1
Herczeg, Ferenc (Playwright)
Silver Fox, The 1921,S 6,13:1
Dagmar 1923,Ja 23,18:2
Kek Roka; Blue Fox 1957,D 5,47:2
Herczeg, Geza (Original Author)
Wonder Bar, The 1931,Mr 8,VIII,3:5
Wonder Bar, The 1931,Mr 18,23:4
Mr Strauss Goes to Boston 1945,S 7,20:2
Herczeg, Geza (Playwright)
Spiegel, Der 1932,Ja 17,VIII,2:1
Campo di Maggio; Hundred Days 1932,F 7,III,3:7
Burning Bush, The 1949,D 17,15:5
Herd, Richard
Harlequinade 1959,F 14,15:1
Electra 1959,F 14,15:1
Herd, Richard (Miscellaneous)
Coach With the Six Insides, The 1967,My 12,50:1
In the Nick of Time 1967,Je 2,36:1
Herden, Marga
Queer People 1934,F 16,16:2
Hereford, Gail
Priorities of 1942 1942,Mr 13,23:2
Hereford, Kathryn
Three Cheers 1928,O 16,28:1
Ripples 1930,F 2,VIII,2:7
Ripples 1930,F 12,26:1
Smiles 1930,N 19,19:2
Hereford, Philip (Translator)
Holy Night 1936,D 24,20:2
Herendeen, Frederick (Lyricist)
All the King's Horses 1934,Ja 31,21:3
Herendeen, Frederick (Playwright)
Mystery Moon 1930,Je 24,23:4
Web, The 1932,Je 28,24:4
All the King's Horses 1934,Ja 31,21:3
Provincetown Follies, The 1935,N 4,24:3
Home Sweet Home 1936,Jl 1,29:2
Come Home to Roost 1936,O 11,X,3:1
Herendeen, Helene
Last Waltz, The 1921,My 11,20:3
No Foolin' 1926,Je 25,25:1
Herendsen, Fred (Lyricist)
Orchids Preferred 1937,My 12,26:5
Herendsen, Fred (Original Author)
Orchids Preferred 1937,My 12,26:5
Herendsen, Fred (Playwright)
Orchids Preferred 1937,My 12,26:5
Popsy 1941,F 11,26:2
Herford, Beatrice
What's in a Name? 1920,Mr 20,14:2
Two by Two 1925,F 24,17:1
Cock Robin 1928,Ja 13,26:6
See Naples and Die 1929,S 27,30:4
Run Sheep Run 1938,N 4,26:2
Herford, Oliver (Playwright)
Greenwich Village Follies 1921,S 1,18:3
Herg, Erich
Wiener Blut 1964,S 12,14:1
Herget, Bob
Lend an Ear 1948,D 17,38:2
Razzle Dazzle 1951,F 20,21:1
Herget, Bob (Choreographer)
Tall Kentuckian, The 1953,Je 17,30:1
Happy Hunting 1956,D 7,30:1
Pale Horse, Pale Rider 1957,O 30,26:1
Moon Shines on Kylenamoe, The 1962,O 31,33:1
Figuro in the Night 1962,O 31,33:1
Boys From Syracuse, The 1963,Ap 16,31:1
Show Me Where the Good Times Are 1970,Mr 6,32:1
Herget, Bob (Director)
Family Affair, A 1962,Ja 29,17:1
Something More! 1964,N 11,36:1
Just for Love 1968,O 18,40:1
Herget, Bob (Musical Director)
Boys From Syracuse, The 1963,Je 2,II,1:1
Heriat, Philippe (Original Author)
Very Rich Woman, A 1965,O 5,5:8
Herion, Allen Paul
Comic Strip 1958,My 15,26:2
Herk, I H (Miscellaneous)
Back Here 1928,N 27,36:3
Herk, I H (Producer)
Wine, Women and Song 1942,S 29,18:3
Herko, Fred
Eccentricities of Davy Crockett, The 1961,Ja 4,26:1
Home Movies 1964,My 12,32:1
Herlein, Lillian
Man Bites Dog 1933,Ap 26,11:2
Herlick, Edith
Robin Hood 1944,N 8,28:2
Herlick, Jety
Magnificent Hugo, The 1961,Ap 8,12:2
Meet Peter Grant 1961,My 11,41:4

Herlie, Eileen
Azrael; Eagle Has Two Heads, The 1946,S 16,9:7
Medea 1948,S 30,32:4
Second Mrs Tanqueray, The 1950,O 8,II,3:7
Matchmaker, The 1954,Ag 24,18:1
Matchmaker, The 1954,S 5,II,3:7
Matchmaker, The 1954,N 14,II,3:1
Matchmaker, The 1955,My 8,II,1:1
Matchmaker, The 1955,D 6,45:6
Matchmaker, The 1955,D 18,II,3:1
Makropoulos Secret, The 1957,D 4,52:4
Much Ado About Nothing 1958,Je 26,22:1
Winter's Tale, The 1958,Jl 23,34:3
Winter's Tale, The 1958,Jl 27,II,1:1
Epitaph for George Dillon 1958,N 5,44:1
Epitaph for George Dillon 1958,N 16,II,1:1
Take Me Along 1959,O 23,22:2
Take Me Along 1959,N 1,II,1:1
All American 1962,Mr 20,44:1
Photo Finish 1963,F 14,5:2
Hamlet 1964,F 28,17:5
Hamlet 1964,Ap 10,30:1
Halfway up the Tree 1967,N 8,52:1
Halfway up the Tree 1967,N 19,II,1:1
Herlihy, James Leo
Zoo Story, The 1963,Je 11,29:2
Herlihy, James Leo (Playwright)
Moon in Capricorn 1953,O 28,37:2
Blue Denim 1958,F 28,17:1
Blue Denim 1958,Ap 20,II,1:1
Stop, You're Killing Me; Laughs, Etc 1969,Mr 20,53:1
Stop, You're Killing Me; Bad Bad Jo-Jo 1969,Mr 20,53:1
Stop, You're Killing Me; Terrible Jim Fitch 1969,Mr 20,53:1
Herlitschka, Herbert E (Translator)
Alcestiade 1957,Je 29,11:5
Herm, Klaus
Don Carlos 1964,N 25,40:1
Herman, Al
Greenwich Village Follies 1921,S 1,18:3
Vaudeville (Palace) 1923,Ja 16,16:3
Vaudeville (Hippodrome) 1924,S 30,27:5
Herman, Alexander C (Playwright)
Downstream 1926,Ja 12,28:1
Herman, Billy
Pursuit of Happiness, The 1952,Mr 22,9:2
Herman, Chester
Piper, The 1920,Mr 20,14:2
Pleasure Bound 1929,F 19,22:4
Babes in Toyland 1929,D 24,15:3
May Wine 1935,D 6,30:3
Herman, David (Director)
Dybbuk, The 1937,F 24,18:4
Herman, David (Miscellaneous)
In-Laws 1934,O 25,28:2
Herman, George
Better Times 1922,S 4,14:2
Criss Cross 1926,O 13,20:2
Herman, Gilbert
Ring Around Elizabeth 1941,N 18,32:2
Winged Victory 1943,N 22,24:1
Yellow Jack 1944,Ap 7,23:3
Herman, Harold
Hamlet of Stepney Green 1958,N 14,21:1
Play That on Your Old Piano 1965,O 15,49:1
Herman, Helene
Matinee Girl, The 1926,F 2,20:3
Herman, Jack
Big Fight, The 1928,S 19,33:1
Herman, Jeffrey
Dirtiest Show in Town, The 1970,My 2,21:1
Dirtiest Show in Town, The 1970,Je 29,43:2
Herman, Jerry (Composer)
I Feel Wonderful 1954,O 19,22:5
Parade 1960,Ja 21,27:4
Milk and Honey 1961,O 11,52:1
Madame Aphrodite 1961,D 30,13:1
Hello, Dolly! 1964,Ja 17,22:1
Hello, Dolly! 1964,Ja 26,II,1:1
Mame 1966,My 25,41:1
Hello, Dolly! 1967,N 13,61:1
Mame 1968,Ap 20,25:1
Dear World 1969,F 7,33:1
Dear World 1969,F 16,II,1:1
Hello, Dolly! 1970,Mr 30,52:1
Herman, Jerry (Director)
I Feel Wonderful 1954,O 19,22:5
Parade 1960,Ja 21,27:4
Herman, Jerry (Lyricist)
I Feel Wonderful 1954,O 19,22:5
Parade 1960,Ja 21,27:4
Milk and Honey 1961,O 11,52:1
Madame Aphrodite 1961,D 30,13:1
Hello, Dolly! 1964,Ja 17,22:1
Mame 1966,My 25,41:1
Hello, Dolly! 1967,Je 14,38:1
Hello, Dolly! 1967,N 13,61:1
Mame 1968,Ap 20,25:1
Dear World 1969,F 7,33:1
Hello, Dolly! 1970,Mr 30,52:1

Herman, John (Miscellaneous)
Advise and Consent 1960,N 18,25:1
Herman, John (Producer)
Passage to India, A 1962,F 1,23:1
Hot Spot 1963,Ap 20,17:2
Dream of Swallows, A 1964,Ap 15,46:1
Roar Like a Dove 1964,My 22,40:2
Herman, Maxine
Nuns, The 1970,Je 2,35:1
Tarot 1970,D 12,19:1
Herman, Melanie (Miscellaneous)
Candaules, Commissioner 1970,My 29,15:1
Herman, Milton
All in Favor 1942,Ja 21,20:6
Herman, Milton C
We Americans 1926,O 13,20:4
By Request 1928,S 28,30:2
Poppa 1928,D 25,31:1
Crooks' Convention, The 1929,S 19,37:4
This Man's Town 1930,Mr 11,24:4
Herman, Shella
Priorities of 1942 1942,Mr 13,23:2
Herman, Simon P (Producer)
By the Beautiful Sea 1954,Ap 9,20:1
Herman, William (Playwright)
Man Out Loud, Girl Quiet 1962,Ap 4,38:1
Spanish Armada, The 1962,Ap 4,38:1
Herman and Seamon
Allez-Opp! 1927,Ag 3,29:3
Hermann, Chester
Humoresque 1923,F 28,13:2
Hermann, George
Black Crook, The 1929,Mr 12,26:5
Hermann, H R (Composer)
Pudding on the Ritz 1932,Ap 9,18:3
Hermann, H R (Lyricist)
Pudding on the Ritz 1932,Ap 9,18:3
Hermann, Simone
Sur le Banc 1923,O 16,18:1
Court Circuit, Le 1923,O 16,18:1
Horrible Experience, L' 1923,O 23,16:1
Trois Masques, Les 1923,N 6,22:1
Fiole, La 1923,N 20,23:3
Petite Bonnie Serieuse 1923,N 27,23:5
Hermansen, Ruth
War and Peace 1942,My 22,26:3
Pygmalion 1952,F 9,11:2
Hermanson, Hjalmar (Scenic Designer)
Triple-A Plowed Under 1936,Mr 16,21:1
1935 1936,My 13,28:2
Injunction Granted! 1936,Jl 25,16:3
Hermanson, Ruth
Yours, A Lincoln 1942,Jl 10,12:3
Hermant, Abel (Playwright)
Starlight 1925,Mr 4,17:2
Hermantier, Raymond (Producer)
Macbeth 1969,D 14,87:1
Hermany, Garda
Music Man, The 1965,Je 17,26:4
Hermany, Richard
Sophie 1963,Ap 16,32:1
Hermany, Roma
Music Man, The 1965,Je 17,26:4
Hermes, Wolf
Brothers Ashkenazi, The 1955,N 12,24:4
Hermsen, Harry
Enchanted Isle 1927,S 20,33:2
Houseboat on the Styx, The 1928,D 26,14:3
Fortune Teller, The 1929,N 5,32:3
Roadside 1930,S 27,21:1
Mourning Becomes Electra; Homecoming 1932,My 10,25:2
Mourning Becomes Electra; Haunted, The 1932,My 10,25:2
Mourning Becomes Electra; Hunted, The 1932,My 10,25:2
They Shall Not Die 1934,F 22,24:4
Valley Forge 1934,D 11,28:3
Storm Over Patsy 1937,Mr 9,26:4
Blow Ye Winds 1937,S 24,17:4
Hernan, Rafael
Cabalgata 1949,Jl 8,14:2
Hernandez, Eduar (Composer)
Mexicana 1939,Ap 22,14:4
Hernandez, Hen
Mexican Hayride 1944,Ja 29,9:6
Hernandez, Juan
Savage Rhythm 1932,Ja 1,30:4
Marriage of Cana, The 1932,F 3,22:4
Black Souls 1932,Mr 31,25:1
Sailor, Beware! 1935,My 7,28:4
Sweet River 1936,O 29,30:2
Brown Sugar 1937,D 3,29:2
Swingin' the Dream 1939,N 30,24:2
Patriots, The 1943,Ja 30,11:2
Strange Fruit 1945,N 30,18:6
Strange Fruit 1945,N 30,18:6
Set My People Free 1948,N 4,38:2
Set My People Free 1948,N 14,II,1:1
Hernandez Brothers
New Moon, The 1928,S 20,33:1
Hot-Cha! 1932,Mr 9,17:3

Hernandez Brothers—Cont
Revenge With Music 1934,N 29,33:5
Herndon, George
Jubilee 1935,O 14,20:1
Herndon, Janie
J B 1958,Ap 24,37:1
Herndon, Richard (Miscellaneous)
Father, The 1928,My 12,9:4
Herndon, Richard (Producer)
Nancy Ann 1924,Ap 1,18:1
Peg o' My Dreams 1924,My 6,25:3
Catskill Dutch 1924,My 11,VIII,1:1
Applesauce 1925,S 29,31:2
Arabesque 1925,O 21,20:2
Patsy, The 1925,D 24,8:5
What's the Big Idea? 1926,Mr 24,20:3
Americana 1926,Jl 27,15:3
Treat 'Em Rough 1926,O 5,26:2
Up the Line 1926,N 23,26:1
Sinner 1927,F 8,20:2
Fog-Bound 1927,Ap 2,21:2
Merry-Go-Round 1927,Je 1,25:4
Creoles 1927,S 23,33:3
Trigger 1927,D 7,32:1
Breaks, The 1928,Ap 17,26:3
Caravan 1928,Ag 30,13:3
Girl Trouble 1928,O 26,22:3
Gypsy 1929,Ja 15,22:2
Be Your Age 1929,F 5,27:1
Mayfair 1930,Mr 18,30:5
Vikings, The 1930,My 13,27:3
First Night 1930,N 27,32:3
Unexpected Husband 1931,Je 3,29:4
Belmont Varieties 1932,S 29,17:2
Ship Comes in, A 1934,S 20,21:1
Home Sweet Home 1936,Jl 1,29:2
Happy Ending 1936,Jl 15,14:3
Come Home to Roost 1936,O 11,X,3:1
Herndon, Venable (Playwright)
Until the Monkey Comes 1966,Je 21,38:1
Herndon, William
Love of Two Hours, The 1962,O 27,16:2
Thistle in My Bed 1963,N 20,48:1
Herne, Chrystal
Acquittal, The 1920,Ja 6,18:2
Untitled-Benefit 1921,My 2,12:3
Elton Case, The 1921,Jl 5,15:1
Elton Case, The 1921,S 12,16:2
Roseanne 1923,D 31,9:5
Expressing Willie 1924,Ap 17,22:1
Expressing Willie 1924,Ap 27,VIII,1:1
Bit o' Love, A 1925,My 13,24:2
Craig's Wife 1925,O 13,21:2
Craig's Wife 1925,O 18,IX,1:2
Skin Deep 1927,O 18,32:1
These Modern Women 1928,F 14,26:2
Vaudeville (Palace) 1928,My 15,17:1
Grey Fox, The 1928,O 23,32:3
Forcing Bed, The 1929,Ag 4,VIII,1:6
Mayfair 1930,Mr 18,30:5
Ladies of Creation 1931,Ag 30,VIII,1:7
Ladies of Creation 1931,S 9,25:1
Room in Red and White, A 1936,Ja 20,23:3
Herne, James A (Playwright)
Drifting Apart: or, The Fisherman's Child 1941,Ag 20,16:6
Hernes, Ramon
Untitled-Stage Show 1931,Ap 7,31:2
Hero, Maria
South Pacific 1965,Je 3,25:1
Where's Charley? 1966,My 26,57:1
Herold, Don (Playwright)
Crazy With the Heat 1941,Ja 15,18:2
Herold, Knox
Shooting Shadows 1924,Je 27,16:5
Mystery Square 1929,Ap 5,28:3
Phantoms 1930,Ja 14,24:3
Oh, Professor 1930,My 2,19:6
Herom, Paul
Dancing Partner 1930,Ag 6,24:2
Heron, Eddie
Shannons of Broadway, The 1927,S 27,30:4
Heron, Joyce
Love Goes to Press 1946,Je 19,16:2
Love Goes to Press 1947,Ja 2,22:2
Gently Does It 1953,O 29,43:4
Herr, Richard (Miscellaneous)
Bridal Night, The 1966,N 8,45:1
Eternal Triangle 1966,N 8,45:1
Frying Pan, The 1966,N 8,45:1
Herrera, Lorenzo
Barrier, The 1950,N 3,32:2
Herrero, Miguel
Cabalgata 1949,Jl 8,14:2
Herrick, Alfred
Stork Mad 1936,O 1,28:4
House in the Country, A 1937,Ja 12,18:3
Marching Song 1937,F 18,18:2
Herrick, Charles
Borak 1960,D 14,51:1
Herrick, Douglas
Andersonville Trial, The 1959,D 30,15:1
Herrick, Florence
Tell Me Pretty Maiden 1937,D 17,33:5

Herrick, Fred
Light Wines and Beer 1930,N 11,28:6
Left Bank, The 1931,O 6,35:3
Black Sheep 1932,O 14,22:6
We the People 1933,Ja 23,9:5
Peace on Earth 1933,N 30,39:2
They Shall Not Die 1934,F 22,24:4
Bridal Quilt 1934,O 11,28:5
Dance Night 1938,O 15,20:5
American Gothic 1953,N 11,35:6
Inherit the Wind 1955,Ap 22,20:2
Herrick, Howard (Playwright)
Drums of Jeopardy, The 1922,My 30,8:4
Herrick, Julia
Trojan Horse, The 1940,O 31,28:3
Herrick, Landon
Would-Be Gentleman, The 1928,O 2,34:1
Peter Pan; Boy Who Would Not Grow Up, The
1928,N 27,36:3
Liliom 1932,O 27,23:2
Alice in Wonderland 1932,D 12,18:3
Herrick, Landon (Playwright)
Garrick Gaieties 1930,Je 5,29:2
Herrick, Mary
Double Door 1935,Ag 21,22:2
Post Road 1936,Ag 5,15:4
Herrick, Robert (Original Author)
Master of the Inn, The 1925,D 23,22:2
Herriman, George
Untitled-Revue 1923,My 12,15:4
Herring, Reed
Hamlet 1936,O 9,30:2
Herring, William
Half-Caste, The 1926,Mr 30,20:4
Herrington, Keith
Merchant of Venice, The 1955,Ja 8,9:7
Candida 1957,F 9,14:1
Dial 'M' for Murder 1958,F 8,12:2
Epitaph for George Dillon 1960,D 29,17:1
Around the World in 80 Days 1963,Je 24,22:1
Herriot, Margot
Second Man, The 1930,My 2,23:2
Herrman, Brad
Semi-Detached 1960,Mr 11,20:2
Herrman, Robert
Say Darling 1959,F 26,38:2
Herrman, Sam
Earl Carroll's Vanities 1923,Jl 6,8:2
Herrmann, Edward
Arsenic and Old Lace 1970,N 5,59:1
Herrmann, Harry (Playwright)
Tickets, Please! 1950,Ap 28,25:2
Herrmann, Julius E
Broadway 1928,Ap 15,IX,4:7
Herrod, Bro (Director)
Chief Thing, The 1963,Ap 30,27:2
Herrod, Bro (Playwright)
Drunkard, The 1970,Ap 14,54:1
Herrod, Bro (Producer)
Chief Thing, The 1963,Ap 30,27:2
Drunkard, The 1970,Ap 14,54:1
Herrod, Jeff
Great Day in the Morning 1962,Mr 29,29:1
Herrod, Julie
Wait Until Dark 1966,F 3,21:1
Herrold, Knox
Scaramouche 1923,O 25,14:2
Herron, Frederick
Prunella 1929,Ap 10,23:3
Herron, Mark
Lady's Not for Burning, The 1957,F 22,26:2
Herrup, Rosalie
Made in America 1925,O 15,27:2
Herschdorfer, Helen (Translator)
Faraway Princess, The 1922,D 6,3:2
Herscher, Sylvia (Miscellaneous)
Will Success Spoil Rock Hunter? 1955,O 14,22:2
Hersey, David (Lighting Director)
Midsummer Night's Dream, A 1968,D 9,59:1
Hamlet 1970,D 28,40:1
Hersey, Frances Ann (Miscellaneous)
Power and the Glory, The 1958,D 12,2:7
Hersey, John (Original Author)
Bell for Adano, A 1944,N 10,24:6
Bell for Adano, A 1944,D 7,21:2
Bell for Adano, A 1945,S 20,31:1
Wall, The 1960,O 12,44:4
Wall, The 1960,O 23,II,1:1
Wall, The 1961,N 9,40:3
Child Buyer, The 1962,My 14,35:1
Child Buyer, The 1964,D 22,35:1
Hersey, Louise
Betty, Be Good 1920,My 5,14:2
Hershaman, Maria G (Director)
Theophilus 1942,Ja 7,23:2
Hershbein, Peretz (Playwright)
Green Fields 1920,Mr 26,11:2
Hershey, Arlene
Dear Judas 1947,O 6,26:4
Hershey, Burnet (Playwright)
Brown Danube, The 1939,My 18,30:4
Hershey, Don (Miscellaneous)
Time Out for Ginger 1952,N 27,50:4

Hershey, Don (Producer)
Room Service 1953,Ap 7,34:1
Hershey, Hal
Don't, George! 1944,N 4,18:6
Sweet Genevieve 1945,Mr 21,27:3
Hershfield, Harry
Untitled-Revue 1923,My 12,15:4
Vaudeville (New Amsterdam Theatre)
1931,Je 22,17:3
Friars Club Frolic 1933,My 15,16:4
Off the Record; Mayor Answers the Newspapers!
Wow! 1935,Je 19,23:3
Laugh Night 1936,S 14,25:1
Hershkowitz, Dorothy
Greenwillow 1970,D 8,60:1
Hershowbevski, H (Playwright)
Fortune 1920,Ap 22,11:3
Hersome, F B
Kansas City Kitty 1929,S 26,27:4
Herson, Marian
Rain or Shine 1928,F 10,26:3
Hertelle, Buddy
Jubilee 1935,O 14,20:1
Between the Devil 1937,D 23,24:5
Herter, William
Birds, The 1966,Jl 1,40:1
Hair 1967,O 30,55:1
Herts, Ross
Furies, The 1928,Mr 8,23:1
Hertsche, Marjorie
Saint's Parade 1930,N 1,23:4
Hertsens, Marc
Alive and Kicking 1950,Ja 18,25:5
Hertsens, Marc (Choreographer)
High Button Shoes 1955,Mr 12,10:6
Lonesome Train, The 1965,Je 17,25:1
Hard Travelin' 1965,Je 17,25:1
Hertz, David (Playwright)
Miles of Heaven, The 1937,Ag 31,27:4
Hertz, Douglas G (Producer)
Tomorrow's Harvest 1934,D 6,26:5
Hertz, Jennings
Scapegoat, The 1950,Ap 20,36:5
Home Is Tomorrow 1950,Je 2,27:2
Hertz, John
Corn Is Green, The 1954,F 27,10:2
Hertz, Ralph
Guns 1928,Ag 7,25:2
Jonica 1930,Ap 8,27:1
Light Wines and Beer 1930,N 11,28:6
She Lived Next to the Firehouse 1931,F 11,23:1
Creeping Fire 1935,Ja 17,22:3
Happy as Larry 1950,Ja 7,11:2
Collector's Item 1952,F 9,11:2
Grass Harp, The 1952,Mr 28,26:2
Hertz, Ross
Service for Two 1926,Ag 31,15:1
Barker, The 1927,Ja 19,20:6
Eva the Fifth 1928,Ag 29,19:3
One Way Street 1928,D 25,31:2
Town's Woman, The 1929,Mr 12,26:2
Strong Man's House, A 1929,S 17,34:3
After Tomorrow 1931,Ag 27,22:4
Rendezvous 1932,O 13,22:3
20th Century 1932,D 30,15:1
June Moon 1933,My 16,15:5
Sailor, Beware! 1933,S 29,24:4
Petrified Forest, The 1935,Ja 8,26:1
Susannah and the Elders 1940,O 30,28:2
Burlesque 1946,D 26,30:3
Remains to Be Seen 1951,O 4,37:1
Hertz, Ross (Miscellaneous)
Autumn's Here 1966,O 26,40:1
Hertz, William
Hobo 1931,F 12,24:4
Hertzfeld, Herbert (Composer)
Nights of Wrath; Nuits de la Colere, Les
1947,D 1,26:4
Hertzsch, Harry
Wozzeck 1966,Ap 6,34:1
Ratten, Die 1966,Ap 13,36:1
Hervey, Harry (Playwright)
Congai 1928,N 28,24:3
Hervey, Irene
No Way Out 1944,O 31,23:1
Hervey, Wilna
Summer Night 1939,N 3,17:1
Herz, Constance R (Miscellaneous)
Antony and Cleopatra 1959,Ja 14,28:1
Herz, Ralph
Always You 1920,Ja 6,18:2
Herz, William
Shoemaker's Holiday, The 1938,Ja 3,17:2
Danton's Death 1938,N 3,26:2
Herz, William (Producer)
Strangler Fig, The 1940,My 7,31:2
Herz (Playwright)
Musik um Susi 1933,Ja 1,IX,1:1
Herzbrun, David J (Lyricist)
What's Up 1953,O 28,37:2
Herzceg, Geza (Playwright)
Hundert Meter Glueck 1933,F 19,IX,3:1

Herzer, Ludwig (Playwright)
Morphia 1923,Mr 7,20:2
Land des Laechelns, Das 1929,D 8,X,4:4
Schoen ist die Welt 1931,Ja 11,VIII,1:8
Lied der Liebe, Das 1932,F 7,VIII,1:3
Katharina 1932,O 2,IX,3:1
Herzer, Martin (Miscellaneous)
Come Slowly, Eden 1966,D 7,56:1
Funny Kind of Evening With David Kossoff, A
1967,Ja 31,52:1
Willie Doesn't Live Here Anymore 1967,F 8,20:2
Have I Got One for You 1968,Ja 8,32:1
Carving a Statue 1968,My 1,43:1
Dream Out of Time, A 1970,N 9,52:1
Herzig, Sig (Miscellaneous)
Bloomer Girl 1947,Ja 7,33:2
Herzig, Sig (Playwright)
Vanderbilt Revue, The 1930,N 6,22:6
Ballyhoo of 1932 1932,S 7,14:2
Vickie 1942,S 23,28:1
Bloomer Girl 1944,O 6,18:5
Around the World in 80 Days 1963,Je 24,22:1
Around the World in 80 Days 1964,Je 29,33:2
Mardi Gras! 1965,Je 28,33:2
Mardi Gras! 1966,Jl 11,32:2
Herzog, Arthur (Lyricist)
Bad Habits of 1926 1926,My 1,11:1
Herzog, Ci
Billy Budd 1959,F 28,13:3
Purlie Victorious 1961,S 29,29:1
Brownstone Urge, The 1969,D 18,63:1
Herzog, Ci (Miscellaneous)
Megilla of Itzik Manger, The 1969,Ap 21,55:1
Herzog, Edward (Composer)
Passion of Gross, The 1955,Ja 24,20:2
Herzog, Pearl
Mr Sycamore 1942,N 14,13:2
Herzog, Wilhelm (Original Author)
I Accuse 1937,O 26,19:1
Herzog, Wilhelm (Playwright)
Dreyfus Affair, The 1930,Mr 30,VIII,4:1
Herzogs, The
Hilarities 1948,S 10,20:2
Heslop, Charles
Nap Hand 1940,Mr 10,XI,2:6
Hess, Ann
Noye's Fludde 1959,Mr 17,41:2
Hess, Antonia
Noye's Fludde 1959,Mr 17,41:2
Hess, Bob (Miscellaneous)
Pilgrim's Progress 1962,Mr 21,36:2
Hess, Bobby (Master)
American, Very Early 1934,Ja 31,21:2
Hess, Edgar
Make a Million 1958,O 24,39:2
Magnificent Hugo, The 1961,Ap 8,12:2
Hess, Elliott (Playwright)
Fifty-Fifty 1937,D 5,II,3:4
Hess, Frances
Present Arms 1928,Ap 27,16:2
Decision 1929,My 28,37:3
Unsophisticates, The 1929,D 31,14:5
Three Little Girls 1930,Ap 15,29:1
Hess, George E
Red Rhumba 1936,Ap 14,18:1
This Mad Whirl 1937,Ja 10,II,4:8
Fifty-Fifty 1937,N 20,21:1
Fifty-Fifty 1937,D 5,II,3:4
Hess, George E (Lyricist)
Fifty-Fifty 1937,D 5,II,3:4
Hess, George E (Playwright)
This Mad Whirl 1937,Ja 10,II,4:8
Fifty-Fifty 1937,N 20,21:1
Hess, John D (Playwright)
Grey-Eyed People, The 1952,D 18,41:2
Hess, Robert (Miscellaneous)
Leave It to Jane 1959,My 26,30:2
Hess, William
Miss Swan Expects 1939,F 21,15:2
Paul Bunyan 1941,My 6,25:1
Hess, William (Musical Director)
Fashion 1959,Ja 21,27:1
Hesse, Alfred A
Twelve Miles Out 1925,N 17,29:2
Garden of Eden, The 1927,S 28,28:1
Zeppelin 1929,Ja 15,22:3
When in Rome 1929,Je 16,VIII,2:1
Week-end 1929,O 23,26:4
Young Sinners 1929,N 29,24:4
Young Sinners 1931,Ap 21,35:5
Left Bank, The 1931,O 6,35:3
Young Sinners 1933,Mr 7,20:4
Laura Garnett 1934,Jl 17,24:4
Between Two Worlds 1934,O 26,24:2
Gather Ye Rosebuds 1934,N 29,33:2
Prisoners of War 1935,Ja 29,24:1
There's Wisdom in Women 1935,O 31,17:1
Ten Million Ghosts 1936,O 24,23:7
American Landscape 1938,D 5,19:2
Burning Deck, The 1940,Mr 2,9:2
Letters to Lucerne 1941,D 24,14:2
Searching Wind, The 1944,Ap 13,25:2
Stranger, The 1945,F 13,21:2

Hesse, Alfred A—Cont
Sherlock Holmes 1953,O 31,11:2
Reclining Figure 1954,O 8,26:5
Golden Fleecing 1959,O 16,24:5
Hesse, N S
1776 1926,Ap 24,11:2
Hesseltine, Stark (Miscellaneous)
Moby Dick 1955,Ap 26,25:3
Queen After Death 1956,Mr 13,33:2
Hession, Frances
Endecott and the Red Cross 1968,My 7,50:1
Hester, Hal (Composer)
Your Own Thing 1968,Ja 15,33:1
Your Own Thing 1968,Ja 28,II,3:1
Your Own Thing 1969,Mr 29,39:1
Hester, Hal (Lyricist)
Your Own Thing 1968,Ja 15,33:1
Hester, Sally
Goodbye My Fancy 1948,N 18,35:2
Hester, Tom
Kittiwake Island 1960,O 13,43:1
Hesterberg, Trude
Bourgeois Gentilhomme, Le 1929,Mr 24,X,2:3
Three Musketeers 1929,O 13,IX,4:7
Heston, Charlton
Antony and Cleopatra 1947,N 27,49:2
Leaf and Bough 1949,Ja 22,10:2
Cock-A-Doodle-Doo 1949,F 28,16:5
Design For A Stained Glass Window
1950,Ja 24,26:2
Mister Roberts 1956,D 6,46:2
Tumbler, The 1960,F 25,32:2
Hetchti, Evamarie
Autumn Crocus 1932,N 21,20:2
Hetherington, J J
Rose in the Wilderness 1949,Ja 5,21:2
Don't Go Away Mad 1949,My 10,28:2
Hetherington, John
Snookie 1941,Je 4,26:2
Antony and Cleopatra 1959,Ja 14,28:1
Romeo and Juliet 1961,F 24,24:1
Abe Lincoln in Illinois 1963,Ja 23,5:2
Dragon, The 1963,Ap 10,32:1
Corruption in the Palace of Justice 1963,O 9,49:2
Troilus and Cressida 1965,Ag 13,17:1
Hetterick, Frank
If Booth Had Missed 1932,F 5,24:2
Heuck, Lois
Noye's Fludde 1959,Mr 17,41:2
Heughan, William
Scott of Abbotsford 1933,Mr 30,20:2
Heugly, Arch
Gordon Reilly 1952,N 26,20:5
Heurlin, Brita
Penal Law 2010 1930,Ap 19,14:2
Heuser, Kurt (Composer)
Captain of Koepenick, The 1964,D 2,60:1
Heuze, Andre (Playwright)
Epinard Gagne le Grand Steeple 1926,D 19,VII,3:3
Hevesi (Director)
Nem Elhetek Muzsikaszo Nelkul
1928,D 30,VIII,4:4
Hevesi (Producer)
A Nagyasszony 1927,O 30,IX,4:1
Hevia, Harold (Producer)
Climax, The 1933,Je 14,22:2
Hevonpaa, Sulo
Of Thee I Sing 1931,D 28,20:1
Hewer, John
Boy Friend, The 1954,O 1,20:1
Hewes, David
Abe Lincoln in Illinois 1938,O 17,12:2
Hewes, Henry (Director)
Hamlet 1957,Ja 29,27:1
Hewes, Henry (Miscellaneous)
Hamlet 1957,Ja 29,27:1
Hewes, Henry (Translator)
Accounting for Love 1954,D 2,37:6
Hewes, Margaret (Director)
Potter's Field 1934,Ap 22,IX,1:1
Roll Sweet Chariot 1934,O 3,24:3
Hewes, Margaret (Producer)
Nine Pine Street 1933,Ap 28,15:5
Alley Cat 1934,S 18,18:1
Roll Sweet Chariot 1934,O 3,24:3
Roll Sweet Chariot 1934,O 14,X,1:1
Woman Brown, The 1939,D 9,18:5
First Stop to Heaven 1941,Ja 6,10:7
I Only Want an Answer 1968,F 6,36:1
Hewes, Mayben
Shoestring '57 1956,N 6,31:1
Russell Patterson's Sketch-Book 1960,F 8,35:1
Hewes, Oscar
Mystery Man, The 1928,Ja 27,14:2
Hewett, Christopher
My Fair Lady 1956,Mr 16,20:2
Tobias and the Angel 1957,O 21,29:5
First Impressions 1959,Mr 20,28:1
Unsinkable Molly Brown, The 1960,N 4,28:1
Kean 1961,N 3,28:2
Affair, The 1962,S 21,34:2
Sound of Music, The 1967,Ap 27,52:1
King and I, The 1968,My 24,39:1
Hadrian VII 1969,Ja 9,22:1

Show Me Where the Good Times Are
1970,Mr 6,32:1
Sound of Music, The 1970,Jl 3,13:1
Hewett, Christopher (Director)
Shoestring Revue 1955,Mr 1,22:2
Almost Crazy 1955,Je 21,37:1
From A to Z 1960,Ap 21,23:2
Boys From Syracuse, The 1963,Ap 16,31:1
Boys From Syracuse, The 1963,Je 2,II,1:1
Where's Charley? 1966,My 26,57:1
By Jupiter 1967,Ja 20,28:2
Hewett, Christopher (Miscellaneous)
By Jupiter 1967,Ja 20,28:2
Hewett, James (Translator)
Picnic on the Battlefield 1960,My 17,42:2
Hewett, Peggy
Jimmy 1969,O 24,38:1
Hewgill, Roland
Henry V 1956,Je 20,27:2
Hamlet 1957,Jl 3,15:2
Falstaff; Henry IV, Part II 1965,Jl 1,35:1
Julius Caesar 1965,Jl 2,18:1
Waltz Invention, The 1969,Ja 12,II,20:4
Hewitson, Herbert
Prince Charlie and Flora 1931,Ag 29,16:5
Hewitt, Ada
Humoresque 1923,F 28,13:2
Hewitt, Alan
Country Wife, The 1935,Jl 2,24:2
Taming of the Shrew, The 1935,S 22,X,3:2
Taming of the Shrew, The 1935,O 1,27:3
Idiot's Delight 1936,Mr 25,25:2
Love for Love 1936,Je 30,15:4
Golden Journey, The 1936,S 16,28:6
Masque of the Kings, The 1937,F 9,19:4
Petticoat Fever 1937,Jl 6,23:1
At Mrs Beam's 1937,Jl 27,24:2
Virginian, The 1937,Ag 10,22:7
Amphitryon 38 1937,N 2,32:2
Sea Gull, The 1938,Mr 29,19:2
American Way, The 1939,Ja 23,9:2
Taming of the Shrew, The 1940,F 6,17:2
Love's Old Sweet Song 1940,My 3,16:3
Walrus and the Carpenter, The 1941,N 10,20:2
Moon Is Down, The 1942,Ap 8,22:2
Gentleman From Athens, The 1947,D 10,42:4
Death of a Salesman 1949,F 11,27:2
Call Me Madam 1950,D 13,25:1
Call Me Madam 1950,O 22,II,1:1
Ondine 1954,F 19,23:1
Ondine 1954,F 28,II,1:1
Hewitt, Edmund
Cradle Will Rock, The 1947,D 27,11:2
Hewitt, Georgia
Betty, Be Good 1920,My 5,14:2
Hewitt, Georgiana
Fables 1922,F 7,12:2
Hewitt, Henry
School for Scandal, The 1929,D 15,X,4:2
Hamlet 1931,Mr 22,VIII,2:1
Little Stranger 1938,Jl 14,16:2
Hewitt, John O
Breakfast in Bed 1920,F 4,12:1
Swifty 1922,O 17,14:1
Three Doors 1925,Ap 24,16:4
Spider, The 1927,Mr 23,29:1
Mystery Man, The 1928,Ja 27,14:2
Tin Pan Alley 1928,N 2,29:1
Crooks' Convention, The 1929,S 19,37:4
Once in a Lifetime 1930,S 25,22:3
Devil's Little Game, The 1932,Ag 2,20:4
Live Life Again 1945,O 1,14:7
Walk Hard 1946,Mr 28,34:2
Twelfth Night 1954,N 10,42:2
Hewitt, Lorna
Month in the Country, A 1959,Mr 2,32:2
Hewitt, Owen
Jeb 1946,F 22,20:2
Hewitt, Ralph E
Nantucket Follies 1927,Jl 30,13:2
Hewitt, Ralph E (Mrs)
Nantucket Follies 1927,Jl 30,13:2
Hewitt, Raymond (Producer)
Fields Beyond, The 1936,Mr 7,11:2
Hewitt, Robert
Chips With Everything 1963,O 2,49:1
Conduct Unbecoming 1970,O 13,50:1
Hewitt, Roberta
Shake Hands With the Devil 1949,O 21,30:4
Hewitt, Russell
Jane Clegg 1920,F 25,14:1
Hewitt, Vivian
Bronx Express 1922,Ap 27,12:2
Hewitt, W W
Espanola 1921,D 30,13:1
Hewlett, Dorothy (Playwright)
Bright Star 1936,F 17,21:4
Hewlett, J Monroe (Scenic Designer)
Merchant of Venice, The 1931,N 9,22:2
Hewlett, Maurice (Original Author)
Sandro Botticelli 1923,Ap 1,VII,1:1
Hewlett, Roger
Best Foot Forward 1941,O 2,28:2

Hewlett, Stanley
Fair Circassian, The 1921,D 7,22:3
Heyburn, Weldon
Play, A 1925,F 11,19:2
Mystery Man, The 1928,Ja 27,14:2
Troika 1930,Ap 2,32:6
Pagan Lady 1930,S 28,VIII,4:1
Menagerie 1935,Jl 2,24:3
Good Men and True 1935,O 26,12:4
I Want a Policeman! 1936,Ja 15,15:5
Story to Be Whispered 1937,Ag 20,21:4
Heydt, Louis Jean
Trial of Mary Dugan, The 1927,S 20,33:1
Strictly Dishonorable 1929,S 19,37:1
Strictly Dishonorable 1929,S 29,IX,1:1
Nikki 1931,S 30,23:4
When the Bough Breaks 1932,F 17,19:2
Housewarming 1932,Ap 8,25:1
Before Morning 1933,F 10,13:4
Thunder on the Left 1933,N 1,25:2
All Rights Reserved 1934,N 7,33:5
Bright Star 1935,O 16,26:2
Pre-Honeymoon 1936,My 1,19:4
Calico Wedding 1945,Mr 8,18:6
Happy Birthday 1946,N 1,31:2
Heyer, Bill
Phoenix '55 1955,Ap 25,20:2
Dinny and the Witches 1959,D 10,53:3
O, Oysters! 1961,Ja 31,23:1
Heyer, Bill (Director)
Mime and Me, The 1960,Ap 8,27:3
Heyer, Bill (Miscellaneous)
O, Oysters! 1961,Ja 31,23:1
Heyer, Bill (Playwright)
Mime and Me, The 1960,Ap 8,27:3
Heyer, Georgette (Original Author)
Merely Murder 1937,D 4,21:4
Heyer, Grace
Up the Ladder 1922,Mr 7,11:2
Uptown West 1923,Ap 4,22:2
Great Gatsby, The 1926,F 3,22:1
Heyer, Grace (Playwright)
Jehovah Joe 1929,Ag 25,VIII,3:1
Heyer, Rosemarie
By Jupiter 1967,Ja 20,28:2
Happy Hypocrite, The 1968,S 6,38:1
Heyer, Walter (Producer)
Ghost Writer, The 1933,Je 20,22:4
Heyert, Leona (Stavis) (Playwright)
Escape This Night 1938,Ap 23,18:1
Heyes, Herbert
Unknown Lady, The 1923,N 6,22:1
Strange Play, A 1944,Je 2,20:3
Down to Miami 1944,S 12,23:5
Happily Ever After 1945,Mr 16,21:2
State of the Union 1945,N 15,25:2
Heyman, Barton
Milk Train Doesn't Stop Here Anymore, The
1965,Jl 27,25:1
Midsummer Night's Dream, A 1967,Je 30,23:1
Iceman Cometh, The 1968,Ap 1,58:1
Indians 1969,My 27,43:1
Indians 1969,O 14,51:1
Indians 1969,O 19,II,1:1
Heyman, Burt
From the Second City 1969,O 15,34:1
Heyman, Edward (Composer)
Rainbow's End 1928,D 26,14:6
Murder at the Vanities 1933,S 13,22:4
She Loves Me Not 1933,N 21,22:4
Heyman, Edward (Lyricist)
Rainbow's End 1928,D 26,14:6
Here Goes the Bride 1931,N 4,31:2
Smiling Through 1932,Ja 3,VIII,3:1
Through the Years 1932,Ja 29,13:3
Murder at the Vanities 1933,S 13,22:4
Caviar 1934,Je 8,19:2
Pardon Our French 1950,O 6,22:4
Heyman, Henry (Scenic Designer)
Yeomen of the Guard, The 1965,Jl 8,34:1
Pirates of Penzance, The 1966,My 24,54:1
Trial by Jury 1966,Je 8,41:2
H M S Pinafore 1966,Je 8,41:2
Heyman, Martin
Sappho 1960,Ja 12,22:1
Dragon, The 1963,Ap 10,32:1
Heyman, Nicholas C
Grey Heir, The 1926,Ap 6,29:2
Heyman, Nicholas C (Playwright)
Grey Heir, The 1926,Ap 6,29:2
Heyman (Composer)
Florestan Ier, Prince de Monaco 1933,D 31,IX,2:2
Heymann, Henry (Costume Designer)
Crime and Crime 1963,D 17,51:2
Queen and the Rebels, The 1965,F 26,16:1
Heyn, Ernest
Romio and Julietta 1925,Ap 21,19:1
Fratricide Punished 1925,Ap 21,19:1
Heyn, Ernest V (Playwright)
Day in the Sun 1937,Jl 27,24:3
Fight's On, The; Uneasy Virtue; Pardon My Back
1937,Ag 4,14:1
Day in the Sun 1939,My 17,29:2

Heyse, Jochen (Director)
Schloss, Das 1968,N 20,35:3
Heyse, Paul (Playwright)
King Saul 1925,S 18,26:3
Heyward, Donald (Composer)
Africana 1927,Jl 12,29:2
Heyward, Donald (Lyricist)
Africana 1927,Jl 12,29:2
Heyward, Dorothy (Original Author)
Porgy and Bess 1944,F 8,13:2
Porgy and Bess 1954,Jl 15,24:2
Porgy and Bess 1954,D 17,36:7
Porgy and Bess 1964,My 7,32:1
Porgy and Bess 1965,Mr 6,17:1
Heyward, Dorothy (Playwright)
Nancy Ann 1924,Mr 9,VIII,2:3
Nancy Ann 1924,Ap 1,18:1
Nancy Ann 1924,Ap 6,VIII,1:1
Porgy 1927,O 11,26:2
Porgy 1927,O 16,IX,1:1
Porgy 1928,Jl 1,VIII,3:5
Porgy 1929,S 14,17:3
Jonica 1930,Mr 30,VIII,2:7
Cinderelative 1930,S 19,18:4
Porgy and Bess 1935,O 11,30:2
Mamba's Daughters 1939,Ja 4,24:2
Mamba's Daughters 1939,Ja 15,IX,1:1
Mamba's Daughters 1940,Mr 25,10:4
Porgy and Bess 1942,Ja 23,16:2
Porgy and Bess 1943,S 14,26:2
South Pacific 1943,D 30,11:2
Set My People Free 1948,N 4,38:2
Set My People Free 1948,N 14,II,1:1
Porgy and Bess 1953,F 17,21:1
Porgy and Bess 1953,Mr 10,25:5
Mamba's Daughters 1953,Mr 21,12:6
Porgy and Bess 1954,S 23,42:6
Heyward, DuBose (Lyricist)
Porgy and Bess 1935,O 1,27:2
Porgy and Bess 1935,O 11,30:2
Mamba's Daughters 1939,Ja 4,24:2
Mamba's Daughters 1940,Mr 25,10:4
Porgy and Bess 1942,Ja 23,16:2
Porgy and Bess 1942,F 1,IX,1:1
Porgy and Bess 1943,S 14,26:2
Porgy and Bess 1944,F 8,13:2
Porgy and Bess 1950,N 26,II,7:8
Porgy and Bess 1953,F 17,21:1
Porgy and Bess 1953,Mr 10,25:5
Porgy and Bess 1964,My 7,32:1
Porgy and Bess 1965,Mr 6,17:1
Heyward, DuBose (Original Author)
Porgy 1927,O 16,IX,1:1
Mamba's Daughters 1939,Ja 4,24:2
Mamba's Daughters 1940,Mr 25,10:4
Porgy and Bess 1942,Ja 23,16:2
Porgy and Bess 1944,F 8,13:2
Porgy and Bess 1954,Jl 15,24:2
Porgy and Bess 1965,Mr 6,17:1
Porgy and Bess 1965,O 20,53:3
Heyward, DuBose (Playwright)
Porgy 1927,O 11,26:2
Porgy 1927,O 16,IX,1:1
Porgy 1928,Jl 1,VIII,3:5
Porgy 1929,S 14,17:3
Brass Ankle 1931,Ap 24,26:4
Porgy and Bess 1935,O 1,27:2
Porgy and Bess 1935,O 11,30:2
Mamba's Daughters 1939,Ja 4,24:2
Mamba's Daughters 1939,Ja 15,IX,1:1
Mamba's Daughters 1940,Mr 25,10:4
Porgy and Bess 1942,Ja 23,16:2
Porgy and Bess 1942,F 1,IX,1:1
Porgy and Bess 1943,S 14,26:2
Porgy and Bess 1944,F 8,13:2
Porgy and Bess 1953,F 17,21:1
Porgy and Bess 1953,Mr 10,25:5
Mamba's Daughters 1953,Mr 21,12:6
Porgy and Bess 1954,S 23,42:6
Porgy and Bess 1954,D 17,36:7
Porgy and Bess 1955,Ja 13,31:1
Porgy and Bess 1955,Ja 21,19:6
Porgy and Bess 1955,F 8,23:4
Porgy and Bess 1955,F 16,26:4
Porgy and Bess 1955,F 23,23:8
Porgy and Bess 1955,Ap 22,20:6
Porgy and Bess 1955,Jl 9,9:5
Porgy and Bess 1955,Ag 5,14:5
Porgy and Bess 1961,My 18,40:1
Porgy and Bess 1964,My 7,32:1
Heyward, Jenifer
Susannah and the Elders 1959,O 19,37:3
Curate's Play, The 1961,D 18,41:3
Heywood, Benji (Miscellaneous)
Only a Countess May Dance When She's Crazy
(An Almost Historical Camp) 1968,Mr 19,41:1
Last Triangle, The (An Embroidered Camp)
1968,Mr 19,41:1
Heywood, Donald
Ringside 1928,Ag 30,13:2
Heywood, Donald (Composer)
Veils 1928,Mr 14,28:5
Ginger Snaps 1930,Ja 1,30:5

Kilpatrick's Old-Time Minstrels 1930,Ap 21,20:2
Hot Rhythm 1930,Ag 22,18:5
Blackberries of 1932 1932,Ap 5,27:5
Ol' Man Satan 1932,O 4,26:3
Africana 1934,N 27,26:3
Heywood, Donald (Director)
Ginger Snaps 1930,Ja 1,30:5
Black Rhythm 1936,D 21,19:2
Heywood, Donald (Lyricist)
Ginger Snaps 1930,Ja 1,30:5
Hot Rhythm 1930,Ag 22,18:5
Blackberries of 1932 1932,Ap 5,27:5
Heywood, Donald (Playwright)
Ginger Snaps 1930,Ja 1,30:5
Africana 1934,N 27,26:3
Black Rhythm 1936,D 21,19:2
How Come Lawd? 1937,O 1,18:5
Heywood, Dorothy (Playwright)
Jonica 1930,Ap 8,27:1
Heywood, Frances
Johnny Doodle 1942,Mr 19,28:2
Heywood, Herbert
Bad Man, The 1920,Ag 31,7:1
Mad Honeymoon, The 1923,Ag 8,10:1
Lady, The 1923,D 5,23:2
Vaudeville (Palace) 1926,Je 1,29:5
Rope 1928,F 23,18:3
Tin Pan Alley 1928,N 2,29:1
Cross Roads 1929,N 12,34:2
Last Mile, The 1930,F 14,21:2
Little Black Book, The 1932,D 27,11:2
Strange Gods 1933,Ap 17,16:6
Queer People 1934,F 16,16:2
Heywood, John (Playwright)
Three Times Three; Merrye Playe, A
1956,My 24,27:2
Heywood, Peter
Johnny Johnson 1941,My 3,20:2
Heyworth, Robert
Martinique 1920,Ap 27,18:2
Hiatt, Adeline
Billy the Kid 1951,Ag 21,23:2
Hiatt, Shelby
Sweet Enemy, The 1965,F 16,39:1
Hibbard, Adelaide
Ballyhoo 1927,Ja 5,18:1
Nigger Rich 1929,S 21,16:7
Peter Flies High 1931,N 10,28:3
Hibbard, Edna
Bad Man, The 1920,Ag 31,7:1
Poppy God, The 1921,Ag 30,10:1
Poppy God, The 1921,S 4,VI,1:1
French Doll, The 1922,F 21,20:2
Queen O' Hearts 1922,O 11,22:1
Gringo 1922,D 15,26:3
Gringo 1922,D 24,VII,1:1
Crooked Square, The 1923,S 11,10:2
Crooked Square, The 1923,S 16,VII,1:1
Peacocks 1924,Mr 2,VIII,2:7
Ladies of the Evening 1924,D 24,11:2
Gentlemen Prefer Blondes 1926,S 29,23:1
Gentlemen Prefer Blondes 1926,O 3,VIII,1:1
Tenth Avenue 1927,Ag 16,31:1
It Is to Laugh 1927,D 27,24:2
Possession 1928,O 3,35:1
Sisters of the Chorus 1930,My 18,VIII,3:1
Sisters of the Chorus 1930,O 21,34:3
Heigh-Ho, Everybody 1932,My 26,31:2
Anybody's Game 1932,D 22,21:4
Tea for Three 1935,Jl 9,24:4
Hibbard, John
David Garrick 1929,Ag 2,17:5
Gasoline Gypsies 1931,Je 8,21:3
Hibbert, Geoffrey
Boy Friend, The 1954,O 1,20:1
Hichens, Robert (Playwright)
Voice From the Minaret, The 1922,Ja 31,11:2
Voice From the Minaret, The 1922,F 5,VI,1:1
Hick, C Bailey
Romeo and Juliet 1923,Ja 25,16:1
Antony and Cleopatra 1924,F 20,22:1
Easy Virtue 1925,D 8,28:2
Hick, Russell
No Trespassing! 1926,S 8,19:1
Hicken, Tana
Great White Hope, The 1967,D 14,58:1
Iceman Cometh, The 1968,Ap 1,58:1
Prince of Peasantmania 1970,F 22,88:1
Hickerson, Harold (Playwright)
Gods of the Lightning 1928,O 25,27:2
Gods of the Lightning 1931,F 19,21:4
Hickerson, Valerie
Welcome Stranger 1920,S 14,12:1
Intruder, The 1928,Jl 26,25:4
Hickey, Ed
Mimic World of 1921, The 1921,Ag 18,9:2
Vaudeville (Palace) 1924,S 30,27:5
Betsy 1926,D 29,24:3
Hickey, John C
Hamlet 1920,D 28,9:3
Merchant of Venice, The 1920,D 30,16:2
Roger Bloomer 1923,Mr 2,18:3
Unsophisticates, The 1929,D 31,14:5

Hickey, John J (Producer)
Viva O'Brien 1941,O 10,27:2
Hickey, John Jr (Producer)
Keep It Clean 1929,Je 25,35:5
Hickey, Tom
Vaudeville (Palace) 1924,S 30,27:5
Hickey, William
Hamlet 1948,D 4,9:2
Tovarich 1952,My 15,39:2
Amedee: or, How to Disentangle Yourself
1955,N 1,27:3
Don Juan; Feast With the Statue, The
1956,Ja 4,21:4
Miss Lonelyhearts 1957,O 4,26:2
Body Beautiful, The 1958,Ja 24,15:2
Hamlet 1958,Je 21,11:1
Midsummer Night's Dream, A 1958,Je 23,19:1
Winter's Tale, The 1958,Jl 21,17:4
Winter's Tale, The 1958,Jl 27,II,1:1
Make a Million 1958,O 24,39:2
On the Town 1959,Ja 16,36:1
On the Town 1959,Ja 25,II,1:1
Moonbirds 1959,O 10,13:1
Twelfth Night 1960,Je 9,29:4
Tempest, The 1960,Je 20,35:1
Three Times Three; Not Enough Rope
1962,Mr 2,24:1
Step on a Crack 1962,O 18,48:1
Decline and Fall of the Entire World As Seen
Through the Eyes of Cole Porter Revisited, The
1965,Mr 31,24:2
Androcles and the Lion 1968,Je 27,47:1
Love's Labour's Lost 1968,Je 28,36:1
Hamlet 1969,Je 30,33:1
Next 1970,Mr 12,46:1
Happy Birthday, Wanda June 1970,O 8,58:2
Happy Birthday, Wanda June 1970,O 18,II,1:1
Hickey, Peter
Three Times Three; Not Enough Rope
1962,Mr 2,24:1
Diary of a Madman 1964,Ap 17,29:2
Hickey, William (Director)
Do You Know the Milky Way? 1961,O 17,45:1
On the Necessity of Being Polygamous
1964,D 9,61:1
Hickey Brothers, The
Vaudeville (Palace) 1926,N 30,27:2
Hickman, Alfred
Madre 1923,D 31,9:6
Rain 1926,O 12,27:1
Fog-Bound 1927,Ap 2,21:2
Lily, The 1927,Ag 2,19:1
Vaudeville (Palace) 1928,Ap 3,32:5
Hickman, Alfred (Director)
Stronger Than Love 1925,D 29,20:2
Fog-Bound 1927,Ap 2,21:2
Hickman, Charles
Bird in Hand 1929,Ap 5,28:2
Hickman, Charles (Director)
Black Chiffon 1950,S 28,39:2
Black Chiffon 1950,O 15,II,1:1
Hickman, Darryl
Where's Charley? 1966,My 26,57:1
Hickman, Howard
Skirt, The 1921,N 8,28:1
Hickman, Howard (Playwright)
Skirt, The 1921,N 8,28:1
Hickman, James
Young and Beautiful, The 1955,O 3,23:2
Affair of Honor 1956,Ap 7,12:3
Hickman, Leland
Lady's Not for Burning, The 1959,Ja 31,13:2
Shewing-Up of Blanco Posnet, The 1959,S 19,26:7
Hickman, N G
Front Page, The 1937,N 12,27:2
Hickman, Wallace
Spanish Love 1920,Ag 18,6:1
Bulldog Drummond 1921,D 27,10:2
Hickok, Harvey
Blue and the Gray, The; War Is Hell Gray, The
1929,D 27,26:4
Hicks, Ami Mali (Costume Designer)
Immortal Thief, The 1926,O 4,21:1
Hicks, Bert (Pvt)
Winged Victory 1943,N 22,24:1
Hicks, Cliff
Mahogany Hall 1934,Ja 18,18:5
Hicks, David
Porgy and Bess 1964,My 7,32:1
Yeomen of the Guard, The 1968,My 9,53:1
Hicks, Eddie (Composer)
Hawk, The 1968,Ap 18,54:1
Hicks, Eleanor
Crooks' Convention, The 1929,S 19,37:4
Oh, Promise Me 1930,N 25,31:1
Life Begins 1932,Mr 29,23:2
Nine Pine Street 1933,Ap 28,15:5
Pursuit of Happiness, The 1933,O 10,24:4
Pursuit of Happiness, The 1934,Je 24,IX,1:4
Strangers at Home 1934,S 15,20:5
Accent on Youth 1934,D 26,19:1
Hicks, Gordon
Elmer the Great 1928,S 25,29:1

Hicks, Henry
No Other Girl 1924,Ag 14,10:4
Bluffing Bluffers 1924,D 23,17:2
Hicks, Israel (Director)
Harangues, The 1970,Ja 14,42:1
Hicks, John
Bedrock 1934,N 18,II,6:3
Hicks, Leonard
Naughty-Naught '00 1946,O 21,27:5
As You Like It 1955,O 29,12:2
Romeo and Juliet 1955,D 16,36:3
Androcles and the Lion 1958,F 22,8:3
Connection, The 1959,Jl 16,30:2
Victims of Duty 1960,Ja 20,26:1
Marrying Maiden, The 1960,Je 23,18:3
Women of Trachis 1960,Je 23,18:3
Purgatory 1960,S 20,48:1
Philoktetes 1961,Ap 25,41:1
Julius Caesar 1962,F 22,19:6
King Lear 1962,Ag 14,35:1
My Mother, My Father and Me 1963,Mr 25,5:5
Awakening of Spring, The 1964,My 13,50:1
Othello 1964,Jl 15,29:1
Othello 1964,O 13,48:1
Baal 1965,My 7,33:2
Coriolanus 1965,Jl 15,23:1
Troilus and Cressida 1965,Ag 13,17:1
Macbeth 1966,Je 29,38:1
Meeting, The 1967,D 13,55:1
Gloria and Esperanza 1969,Ap 5,30:1
Moondreamers, The 1969,D 9,68:1
Gloria and Esperanza 1970,F 5,32:1
Hicks, Mabel
Tragedy of Nan, The 1920,F 18,9:1
Hicks, Malcolm
Sancho Panza 1923,N 27,23:1
Hicks, Octavia
Little Theatre Tournament; Prison Bars 1928,My 10,31:1
Hicks, Patricia
Edward, My Son 1948,O 1,30:2
Black Chiffon 1950,S 28,39:2
Hicks, Robert M
Buzzard, The 1928,Mr 15,29:1
Adventure 1928,S 26,25:2
Deep Channels 1929,O 19,22:3
Hicks, Russell
Wise-Crackers, The 1925,D 17,26:1
Goin' Home 1928,Ag 24,23:2
Torch Song 1930,Ag 3,VIII,3:4
Torch Song 1930,Ag 28,23:1
Nona 1932,O 5,26:4
Little Black Book, The 1932,D 27,11:2
All the King's Horses 1934,Ja 31,21:3
Time for Elizabeth 1948,S 28,32:3
On Borrowed Time 1953,Jl 11,34:1
Caine Mutiny Court-Martial, The 1953,O 14,35:1
Caine Mutiny Court-Martial, The 1954,Ja 21,27:2
Hicks, Seymour
Mr What's-His-Name 1927,My 29,VII,1:3
Gay Adventure, The 1932,Ja 24,VIII,3:5
It's You I Want 1933,Mr 19,IX,2:2
Vintage Wine 1934,My 30,14:2
Vintage Wine 1934,Je 24,IX,1:4
Miracle Man, The 1935,My 14,17:5
Miracle Man, The 1935,Je 9,IX,1:1
Money Talks 1938,My 29,X,1:2
Hicks, Seymour (Playwright)
Man in Dress Clothes, The 1922,Ap 30,VII,1:8
Mr What's-His-Name 1927,My 29,VII,1:3
Mr What's-His-Name 1927,S 4,VII,2:4
Matrimonial Bed, The 1927,O 13,23:2
Vintage Wine 1934,Je 24,IX,1:4
Miracle Man, The 1935,My 14,17:5
Miracle Man, The 1935,Je 9,IX,1:1
Man in Dress Clothes, The 1937,Ag 24,24:4
Hicks, Seymour (Producer)
Miracle Man, The 1935,My 14,17:5
Hickson, Joan
Joe Egg 1968,F 2,26:1
Joe Egg 1968,F 11,II,1:1
Hickson, Leslie (Playwright)
Clubs Are Trumps 1924,O 15,27:1
Hickton, John
Career Angel 1943,N 19,24:2
Walk Hard 1944,D 1,28:2
Hidey, Hal (Miscellaneous)
Beg, Borrow or Steal 1960,F 11,39:4
Hidey, Hal (Musical Director)
Beg, Borrow or Steal 1960,F 11,39:4
Hiegel, Catherine
Troupe Du Roi, La 1970,F 4,38:1
Don Juan 1970,F 7,24:2
Femmes Savaantes, Les 1970,F 14,12:1
Malade Imaginaire, Le 1970,F 18,40:2
Higashi, Y (Director)
Coney Island Play 1970,O 31,34:2
Higashi, Y (Playwright)
Coney Island Play 1970,O 31,34:2
Higgens, Harriet
Guitar 1959,N 11,42:5
Higginbottom, George
Sing High, Sing Low 1931,N 13,26:4

Higginbottom, Jeffrey (Costume Designer)
Don Juan 1970,My 26,32:1
Higginbottom, Jeffrey (Scenic Designer)
Don Juan 1970,My 26,32:1
Higgins, Billy
Lucky Sambo 1926,My 26,24:2
Brain Sweat 1934,Ap 5,24:4
Higgins, David
Welcome Stranger 1920,S 14,12:1
Mayflowers 1925,N 25,14:2
Scalawag, The 1927,Mr 30,22:3
Scarlet Pages 1929,S 10,26:3
Widow in Green, A 1931,N 21,21:4
Higgins, David (Playwright)
Scalawag, The 1927,Mr 30,22:3
Higgins, Dennis
Greenwillow 1970,D 8,60:1
Higgins, Dick
Originale 1964,S 9,46:1
Higgins, Douglas (Costume Designer)
'Tis Pity She's a Whore 1967,O 21,15:2
Mercy Street 1969,O 28,43:1
Higgins, Douglas (Scenic Designer)
'Tis Pity She's a Whore 1967,O 21,15:2
Mercy Street 1969,O 28,43:1
Brass Butterfly, The 1970,Ja 31,34:1
Higgins, Frances
Sonya's Search for the Christmas Star 1929,D 14,24:6
This Our House 1935,D 12,33:3
Higgins, George
Winners and Losers 1947,F 27,27:2
Deputy of Paris, The 1947,Mr 22,9:5
New York Idea, The 1948,Ag 18,29:2
Higgins, James
King Lear 1963,N 23,22:1
Zulu and the Zayda, The 1965,N 11,59:1
Higgins, James E
Little Theatre Tournament; Rhythm of the City, The 1929,My 7,28:1
Higgins, John
Midsummer Night's Dream, A 1963,Jl 1,19:2
Higgins, Loretta
Constant Nymph, The 1926,D 10,31:1
Higgins, Mary
Blithe Spirit 1946,Je 5,17:3
Higgins, Maude
Silhouettes 1969,S 9,41:1
Higgins, Michael
Antigone 1946,F 19,21:3
Our Lan' 1947,S 29,16:5
Romeo and Juliet 1951,Mr 12,21:2
Billy the Kid 1951,Ag 21,23:2
White Devil, The 1955,Mr 15,32:5
Carefree Tree, The 1955,O 12,37:2
Lark, The 1955,N 18,33:1
View From the Bridge, A 1956,N 9,34:4
Easter 1957,Ja 17,35:2
Crucible, The 1958,Mr 12,36:1
Crucible, The 1958,Je 1,II,1:1
On Baile's Strand 1959,Ap 13,34:4
Diff'rent 1961,O 18,52:1
Long Voyage Home, The 1961,D 5,49:1
Deuces Wild; It's All Yours 1962,Ap 25,31:1
Charlatans; On Circe's Island 1962,Ap 27,26:1
King Lear 1962,Ag 14,35:1
Macbeth 1962,N 17,16:2
Antony and Cleopatra 1963,Je 21,33:1
Life Is a Dream 1964,Mr 20,24:1
Queen and the Rebels, The 1965,F 26,16:1
Medea 1965,N 29,46:1
Tom Paine 1969,Mr 30,71:2
Higgins, Peter
Vaudeville (Palace) 1929,Mr 25,33:2
Vaudeville (Palace) 1930,Ap 21,20:7
Vaudeville (Palace) 1930,My 5,27:5
Vaudeville (Palace) 1931,My 4,15:2
Free for All 1931,S 9,25:1
Vaudeville (Palace) 1932,Ap 4,13:4
Sketch Book 1935,Je 5,22:2
Higgins, Ralph
Hamlet 1948,D 4,9:2
Higgins, Ribert
Glory 1922,D 26,10:1
Higgins, Robert
Auntie Mame 1956,N 1,47:2
Higginson, G
1776 1926,Ap 24,11:2
Gentlemen, the Queen 1927,Ap 23,14:3
Higginson, Girvan G (Lighting Director)
Willow and I, The 1942,D 11,32:2
Higginson, Girvan G (Producer)
Eye on the Sparrow 1938,My 4,26:3
Higgs, Richard
Go Show Me a Dragon 1961,O 28,18:1
Stage Affair, A 1962,Ja 17,30:2
Higgs, Richard (Miscellaneous)
Stage Affair, A 1962,Ja 17,30:2
High, John
Lute Song 1946,F 7,29:2
As You Like It 1955,O 29,12:2
Romeo and Juliet 1955,D 16,36:3
Getting Married 1970,Ja 20,46:1

High, John—Cont
Greenwillow 1970,D 8,60:1
High Kickers Chorus
High Kickers 1941,N 1,21:2
High Willows, The
Grand Music Hall of Israel, The 1968,F 7,42:1
Highley, Richard
Taming of the Shrew, The 1921,My 12,20:2
Merchant of Venice, The 1921,My 14,10:4
Highley, Richard (Producer)
Damaged Goods 1937,My 18,27:2
Hight, Pearl
Oh, Please! 1926,D 22,24:3
Town's Woman, The 1929,Mr 12,26:2
Ripples 1930,F 12,26:1
Torch Song 1930,Ag 28,23:1
Loose Moments 1935,F 5,22:3
American Holiday 1936,F 22,13:3
Highton, Sylvia
Dew Drop Inn 1923,My 18,26:4
Hightower, Lewis
By Jupiter 1942,Je 4,22:1
Hightower, Loren
Peter Pan 1950,Ap 25,27:2
Livin' the Life 1957,Ap 29,20:1
Goldilocks 1958,O 13,33:1
110 in the Shade 1963,O 25,37:1
Kiss Me, Kate 1965,My 13,31:1
Hightower, Robert
By Jupiter 1942,Je 4,22:1
By Jupiter 1942,Ag 16,VIII,2:1
Hightower, William
By Jupiter 1942,Ag 16,VIII,2:1
Hightower and Ross
Blackouts of 1949 1949,S 7,39:2
Higley, Hal
Banco 1922,S 21,18:1
As You Like It 1923,Ap 24,24:1
Higley, Philo (Playwright)
Remember the Day 1935,Jl 9,24:3
Remember the Day 1935,S 26,19:3
Remember the Day 1935,O 13,IX,1:1
Traveler's Track 1936,Jl 21,13:5
Hignett, H R
Unknown, The 1920,Ag 29,VI,1:4
Flirting 1923,My 31,12:5
Old English 1924,N 9,VIII,2:3
Julius Caesar 1932,F 28,VIII,2:4
Hiken, Barbara (Miscellaneous)
Critic, The 1965,Jl 26,15:2
Hiken, George
Uncle Vanya 1956,F 12,II,1:1
Hiken, Gerald
Cretan Woman, The 1954,My 21,17:2
Cherry Orchard, The 1955,O 19,38:1
Uncle Vanya 1956,F 1,25:2
Lovers 1956,My 11,23:1
Sea Gull, The 1956,O 23,38:1
Good Woman of Setzuan, The 1956,D 19,41:2
Good Woman of Setzuan, The 1956,D 30,II,1:1
Cave Dwellers, The 1957,O 21,29:2
Cave Dwellers, The 1957,O 27,II,1:1
Enchanted, The 1958,Ap 23,41:1
Enemy of the People, An 1959,F 5,24:4
Nervous Set, The 1959,My 13,43:1
Three Sisters, The 1959,S 22,46:1
Three Sisters, The 1959,O 4,II,1:1
Fighting Cock, The 1959,D 9,57:3
49th Cousin, The 1960,O 28,22:1
Gallows Humor 1961,Ap 19,35:1
One Way Pendulum 1961,S 19,38:2
Foxy 1964,F 17,26:1
Three Sisters, The 1964,Je 23,24:1
Hiken, Nat (Composer)
Along Fifth Avenue 1949,Ja 14,28:2
Hiken, Nat (Lyricist)
Along Fifth Avenue 1949,Ja 14,28:2
Hiken, Nat (Playwright)
Along Fifth Avenue 1949,Ja 14,28:2
Two on the Aisle 1951,Jl 29,II,1:1
Two's Company 1952,D 16,43:5
Littlest Revue, The 1956,My 23,37:2
Hilary, Jennifer
Rehearsal, The 1963,S 24,45:2
Rehearsal, The 1963,O 20,II,1:1
Ivanov 1966,My 4,50:1
Avanti 1968,F 1,29:1
Hilbrandt, James
Adding Machine, The 1970,D 5,40:1
Hilda, Irene
Time, Place and the Girl, The 1942,O 22,24:3
Can-Can 1954,O 24,II,3:1
Hildebrand, Fred
Cinders 1923,Ap 4,22:1
Hildebrand, Rodney
Elmer the Great 1928,S 25,29:1
Hildegarde
Vaudeville (Palace) 1932,O 3,15:5
Keep 'Em Laughing 1942,Ap 25,9:2
Hilden, Melaine
Career 1943,O 29,22:6
Hildreth, Carleton
We All Do 1927,Mr 1,30:3
Diana 1929,D 10,37:1

Hildreth, Carleton (Playwright)
Congai 1928,N 28,24:3
Hildreth, Marjorie (Director)
Respectfully Yours 1947,My 14,29:4
Major Barbara 1951,F 24,10:2
Merchant of Venice, The 1955,F 23,23:2
Hilgenberg, Katherine
Carousel 1965,Ag 11,39:1
Hill, Abram (Director)
Three's a Family 1943,N 19,24:3
Walk Hard 1944,D 1,28:2
Home Is the Hunter 1945,D 21,25:4
On Strivers' Row 1946,Mr 1,17:2
Tin Top Valley 1947,Mr 1,11:2
Power of Darkness, The 1948,O 11,28:2
Hill, Abram (Playwright)
Anna Lucasta 1944,Je 17,10:1
Walk Hard 1944,D 1,28:2
On Strivers' Row 1946,Mr 1,17:2
Walk Hard 1946,Mr 28,34:2
Power of Darkness, The 1948,O 11,28:2
Hill, Alexander (Composer)
Hummin' Sam 1933,Ap 10,8:8
Hill, Alexander (Lyricist)
Hummin' Sam 1933,Ap 10,8:8
Hill, Alice
Our Town 1944,Ja 11,24:5
Hill, Annabelle
Kiss Me, Kate 1948,D 31,10:3
Hill, Arthur
Good Times 1920,Ag 10,10:1
Matchmaker, The 1954,Ag 24,18:1
Matchmaker, The 1955,D 6,45:6
Matchmaker, The 1955,D 18,II,3:1
Look Homeward, Angel 1957,N 29,33:1
Look Homeward, Angel 1957,D 8,II,5:1
Look Homeward, Angel 1958,Ag 31,II,1:1
Gang's All Here, The 1959,O 2,23:1
Gang's All Here, The 1959,O 11,II,1:1
All the Way Home 1960,D 1,42:1
All the Way Home 1960,D 18,II,3:1
All the Way Home 1960,D 27,26:7
Who's Afraid of Virginia Woolf? 1962,O 15,33:1
Who's Afraid of Virginia Woolf? 1962,O 28,II,1:1
Who's Afraid of Virginia Woolf? 1964,F 8,15:1
Something More! 1964,N 11,36:1
More Stately Mansions 1967,S 14,54:1
More Stately Mansions 1967,N 1,40:1
More Stately Mansions 1967,N 12,II,1:1
Caution: A Love Story 1969,Ap 4,45:1
Hill, Barre
Cotton Stockings 1923,D 19,16:2
Tambourine 1925,D 30,10:2
Scrap Book 1932,Ag 2,20:3
Music Hall Varieties 1932,N 23,15:3
Hill, Bennett
Can-Can 1959,Ag 26,25:4
Hill, Billy (Composer)
Private Affair, A 1936,My 15,28:7
Hill, Billy (Lyricist)
Ziegfeld Follies 1934,Ja 5,24:3
Hill, Billy (Playwright)
Ziegfeld Follies 1934,Ja 5,24:3
Hill, Budd (Costume Designer)
Oedipus Rex 1960,Ap 30,15:2
Policemen, The 1961,N 22,24:2
Merchant of Venice, The 1962,F 3,13:2
Thistle in My Bed 1963,N 20,48:1
Hill, Budd (Miscellaneous)
Caucasian Chalk Circle, The 1961,N 1,35:1
Hill, C Wesley
Runnin' Wild 1923,O 30,17:3
Hill, Carol
Mourners' Bench, The 1950,S 22,35:7
Hill, Chandler
Dark of the Moon 1970,Ap 4,21:2
Hill, Charles
Weather Clear, Track Fast 1927,O 19,24:5
Green Pastures, The 1935,F 27,16:2
Hill, Clay
Sweetheart Shop, The 1920,S 1,13:4
Hill, David
World of Suzie Wong, The 1958,O 15,47:1
Hill, Dorothy
Tree Grows in Brooklyn, A 1951,Ap 20,24:3
Hill, Douglas
Lend an Ear 1969,O 29,32:1
Hill, Drina
Caviar 1934,Je 8,19:2
Dead End 1935,O 29,17:2
Susannah and the Elders 1940,O 30,28:2
Hill, E L
Plain Dealer, The 1929,My 23,27:1
Hill, Ellen Cobb
Wisteria Trees, The 1950,Mr 30,39:1
Death of Cuchulain, The 1959,Ap 13,34:4
Hill, Eloise
Caribbean Carnival 1947,D 6,12:2
Hill, Errol (Playwright)
Man Better Man 1969,Jl 3,22:1
Man Better Man 1969,Jl 13,II,3:6
Hill, Francesca
Judge's Husband, The 1926,S 28,31:1

Scarlet Pages 1929,S 10,26:3
Company's Coming! 1931,Ap 21,35:5
House of Doom, The 1932,Ja 26,20:4
Bulls, Bears and Asses 1932,My 7,11:3
Hill, Francis (Playwright)
Genius and the Crowd 1920,S 7,20:1
Hill, Frank
Dew Drop Inn 1923,My 18,26:4
Hill, George Roy
Hay-Foot, Straw-Foot 1942,O 24,11:6
Creditors 1949,N 22,36:5
Heartbreak House 1950,Mr 22,33:2
Richard II 1951,Ja 25,21:2
Taming of the Shrew, The 1951,Ap 26,35:2
Hill, George Roy (Director)
Look Homeward, Angel 1957,N 29,33:1
Look Homeward, Angel 1957,D 8,II,5:1
Look Homeward, Angel 1958,Ag 31,II,1:1
Gang's All Here, The 1959,O 2,23:1
Gang's All Here, The 1959,O 11,II,1:1
Greenwillow 1960,Mr 9,38:1
Greenwillow 1960,Mr 20,II,1:1
Period of Adjustment 1960,N 11,34:1
Period of Adjustment 1960,N 20,II,1:1
Moon on a Rainbow Shawl 1962,Ja 16,30:1
Henry, Sweet Henry 1967,O 24,51:2
Henry, Sweet Henry 1967,N 5,II,3:1
Hill, Glenn (Miscellaneous)
Don't Shoot Mable It's Your Husband
1968,O 23,34:1
Hill, Glenn (Scenic Designer)
Royal Gambit 1959,Mr 5,34:2
Hill, Glynn
Iolanthe 1952,N 11,26:3
Hill, Gus
Friars Club Frolic 1933,My 15,16:4
Hill, Gwendoline
Many Waters 1929,S 26,27:1
Hill, Harry
Last Warning, The 1927,Ap 3,VIII,2:1
Hill, Holly
Where People Gather 1967,O 26,56:1
Hill, Howard
Shuffle Along of 1933 1932,D 27,11:3
Hill, I
First Man, The 1922,Mr 6,9:2
Hill, Inga
Hansel and Gretel 1929,D 25,21:1
Orpheus in Hades 1930,D 16,30:1
May Wine 1935,D 6,30:3
Hill, Irene
Brown Sugar 1937,D 3,29:2
Hill, Isabel
Cradle Song 1921,Mr 1,18:2
Roger Bloomer 1923,Mr 2,18:3
Juno and the Paycock 1926,Mr 16,22:1
Woman of the Earth, A 1927,F 1,24:6
Joy of Serpents 1930,Ap 4,22:4
Country Wife, The 1931,Ap 19,31:5
Hill, Janet
Hamlet 1936,N 11,54:2
If I Were You 1938,Ja 9,II,3:2
If I Were You 1938,Ja 25,24:2
Hill, Joe
Out of This World 1950,D 22,17:3
Allegro 1952,S 18,36:3
Three by Thurber; Imperturbable Spirit, The
1955,Mr 8,23:2
Three by Thurber; Middle Years, The
1955,Mr 8,23:2
Three by Thurber; Mr Montoe Holds the Fort
1955,Mr 8,23:2
Hill, Joe (Director)
Henri Christophe 1945,Je 7,24:5
Hill, John J
Lion in Love, The 1963,Ap 26,28:3
Hill, Joyce
Cloudy With Showers 1931,S 2,17:5
Rosalinda; Fledermaus, Die 1942,O 29,26:5
Insect Comedy, The 1948,Je 4,26:3
Hill, Ken
Triumph of Robert Emmet, The 1969,My 8,54:1
Hill, Kenneth
Blue Flame, The 1920,Mr 16,18:1
Six-Cylinder Love 1921,Ag 26,8:2
Rubicon, The 1922,F 22,13:1
Matrimonial Bed, The 1927,O 13,23:2
Hill, L Rufus
In Abraham's Bosom 1926,D 31,10:2
In Abraham's Bosom 1927,F 20,VII,1:1
Hot Pan 1928,F 16,14:1
Hill, Laurence S
Without the Walls 1920,Je 7,20:1
Little Town of Bethlehem, The 1920,D 27,11:1
Without the Walls 1921,Mr 28,8:1
Hill, Linda Lee
Achilles Had a Heel 1935,O 14,20:2
Summer Wives 1936,Ap 14,18:1
Happy Ending 1936,Jl 15,14:3
Farewell Summer 1937,Mr 30,20:2
Bat, The 1937,Je 1,27:5
Blow Ye Winds 1937,S 24,17:4

Hill, Lucienne
Lark, The 1955,My 13,21:2
Hill, Lucienne (Playwright)
Thieves' Carnival 1955,F 2,21:1
Waltz of the Toreadors, The 1957,Ja 18,17:2
Waltz of the Toreadors, The 1958,Mr 5,37:1
Ardele 1958,Ap 9,39:4
Fighting Cock, The 1959,D 9,57:3
Second String, A 1960,Ap 14,36:2
Hill, Lucienne (Translator)
Waltz of the Toreadors, The 1957,Ja 27,II,1:1
Fighting Cock, The 1959,D 20,II,3:1
Becket 1960,O 6,50:1
Becket 1961,My 9,44:1
Becket 1961,Jl 12,35:6
Traveller Without Luggage 1964,S 18,26:2
Poor Bitos 1964,N 16,40:2
Hill, Margaret
Out West of Eighth 1951,S 21,20:3
Hill, Minnie Ashe
Please, Mrs. Garibaldi 1939,Mr 17,24:3
Hill, Orrin
Out of This World 1950,D 22,17:3
Hill, Peter Murray
Last Train South 1938,S 4,X,2:2
Hill, Phyllis
Lady Comes Across, The 1942,Ja 10,10:2
Rosalinda; Fledermaus, Die 1942,O 29,26:5
Sons and Soldiers 1943,My 5,22:2
What's Up 1943,N 12,24:6
Helen Goes to Troy 1944,Ap 25,17:2
Cyrano de Bergerac 1946,O 9,33:2
Cyrano de Bergerac 1947,Ja 17,27:2
Volpone 1948,Ja 9,24:6
Angel Street 1948,Ja 23,26:6
Bear, The 1948,F 6,29:2
Tragedian in Spite of Himself, A 1948,F 6,29:2
Wedding, The 1948,F 6,29:2
On the Harmfulness of Tobacco 1948,F 6,29:2
Alchemist, The 1948,My 7,31:4
S S Glencairn; Long Voyage Home, The
1948,My 21,21:2
Insect Comedy, The 1948,Je 4,26:3
Shrike, The 1952,Ja 16,20:2
Fifth Season, The 1953,Ja 24,13:2
Hill, R L (Playwright)
Lady Luck 1936,Ap 16,21:2
Hill, Ralston
Valmouth 1960,O 7,29:1
Young Abe Lincoln 1961,Ap 26,36:1
Streets of New York, The 1963,O 30,47:1
Carousel 1965,Ag 11,39:1
Comedy of Errors, The 1968,F 28,40:2
She Stoops to Conquer 1968,Ap 1,58:3
1776 1969,Mr 17,46:2
Hill, Raymond
Freight 1949,F 4,30:2
Freight 1950,Ap 27,36:2
Hill, Richard (Composer)
Canterbury Tales 1968,S 7,23:3
Canterbury Tales; Wife of Bath's Tale, The
1969,F 4,34:1
Canterbury Tales; Merchant's Tale, The
1969,F 4,34:1
Canterbury Tales; Miller's Tale, The 1969,F 4,34:1
Canterbury Tales; Steward's Tale, The
1969,F 4,34:1
Canterbury Tales; Pilgrims, The 1969,F 4,34:1
Hill, Richard (Costume Designer)
Kiss Me, Kate 1954,Mr 27,13:2
Hill, Robert 2d
Moon on a Rainbow Shawl 1962,Ja 16,30:1
Hill, Robert 2d (Composer)
Nat Turner 1960,N 7,46:3
Hill, Ruby
St Louis Woman 1946,Ap 1,22:2
Hill, Ruth K
Nine Girls 1943,Ja 14,26:2
Skipper Next to God 1948,Ja 5,14:5
Hill, Sinclair (Director)
Quitter, The 1934,F 6,24:4
Hill, Stephanie
Flora, the Red Menace 1965,My 12,41:2
Hill, Steven
Flag Is Born, A 1946,S 7,10:6
Mister Roberts 1948,F 19,27:2
Sundown Beach 1948,S 8,37:1
Lady From the Sea, The 1950,Ag 8,23:2
Country Girl, The 1950,N 11,10:6
Country Girl, The 1950,N 19,II,1:1
Far Country, A 1961,Ap 5,32:1
Far Country, A 1961,Ap 16,II,1:1
Hill, Thomas
Right You Are (If You Think You Are)
1950,Je 29,37:2
All the King's Men 1963,Jl 12,12:1
Firebugs, The 1963,N 22,41:1
King Lear 1963,N 23,22:1
Hill, Tom (Director)
Gordon Reilly 1952,N 26,20:5
Hill, Viola (Miscellaneous)
Swing Mikado, The 1939,Mr 2,18:2

Hill, Violet
Henry-Behave 1926,Ag 24,19:4
Mother Sings 1935,N 13,24:1
Hill, W J
Front Page, The 1937,N 12,27:2
Hill, Walter O
First Mortgage 1929,O 11,36:1
False Dreams, Farewell 1934,Ja 16,18:3
Late Wisdom 1934,Ap 24,27:4
Ceiling Zero 1935,Ap 11,26:2
Our Town 1938,F 5,18:3
Cuckoos on the Hearth 1941,S 17,26:2
Our Town 1944,Ja 11,24:5
Hill, Warren K
Bottom of the Cup, The 1927,F 1,24:2
Hill, Wesley
Porgy 1927,O 11,26:2
Porgy 1929,S 14,17:3
Green Pastures, The 1930,F 27,26:1
Hill-Brown, Mary (Director)
Fashion 1937,Mr 21,II,7:8
Hillaire, Marcel
Silk Stockings 1955,F 25,17:3
Heavenly Twins, The 1955,N 5,23:2
Lulu 1958,S 30,24:1
Hillary, Ann
Be Your Age 1953,Ja 15,24:2
Lark, The 1955,N 18,20:1
Separate Tables 1956,O 26,33:1
Dark of the Moon 1958,F 27,22:2
Hillary, Lee
Tell My Story 1939,Mr 16,26:6
Hillary, Lucy
Merry Widow, The 1944,O 9,17:1
Sally 1948,My 7,31:2
Merry Widow, The 1957,Ap 11,36:6
Hillebrand, Fred
Rose Girl, The 1921,F 12,11:1
Optimists, The 1928,Ja 31,28:2
Pleasure Bound 1929,F 19,22:4
Hillel
Peer Gynt 1951,Ja 29,15:2
Hillel (Composer)
Peer Gynt 1951,Ja 29,15:2
Hiller, Wendy
Love on the Dole 1935,F 17,VIII,3:1
Love on the Dole 1936,F 25,23:3
Love on the Dole 1936,Mr 8,IX,1:1
Saint Joan 1936,Jl 26,II,1:3
First Gentleman, The 1945,Jl 19,18:8
First Gentleman, The 1945,Ag 5,II,1:2
Heiress, The 1947,S 30,22:2
Heiress, The 1947,O 5,II,1:1
Ann Veronica 1949,My 21,9:2
Waters of the Moon 1953,Ap 2,34:3
Night of The Ball, The 1955,Ja 13,31:8
Night of The Ball, The 1955,F 13,II,3:1
Othello 1956,Mr 11,II,3:1
Moon for the Misbegotten, A 1957,My 3,21:2
Moon for the Misbegotten, A 1957,My 12,II,1:1
Flowering Cherry 1959,O 22,46:1
Aspern Papers, The 1962,F 8,26:1
Aspern Papers, The 1962,F 18,II,1:1
Wings of the Dove, The 1963,D 4,53:6
Battle of Shrivings, The 1970,F 7,23:1
Hillerman, John
Twelfth Night 1958,Ag 7,21:4
Great God Brown, The 1959,O 7,48:1
Blue Boy in Black, The 1963,My 1,32:1
White Rose and the Red, The 1964,Mr 17,31:1
Hillery, Lee
Living Corpse, The 1929,D 7,19:1
Romeo and Juliet 1930,Ap 22,33:1
Battle Hymn 1936,My 23,12:1
Hilliam, B C (Playwright)
Princess Virtue 1921,My 5,20:2
Hilliard, Audrey
Master Builder Solness 1950,My 26,19:3
Hilliard, Audrey (Director)
Master Builder Solness 1950,My 26,19:3
Hilliard, Audrey (Producer)
Knight of the Burning Pestle, The 1953,O 24,13:2
Moon in Capricorn 1953,O 28,37:2
Hilliard, Bob (Composer)
Angel in the Wings 1947,D 12,36:4
Michael Todd's Peep Show 1950,Je 29,37:2
Hilliard, Bob (Lyricist)
Angel in the Wings 1947,D 12,36:4
Michael Todd's Peep Show 1950,Je 29,37:2
Hazel Flagg 1953,F 12,22:2
Hilliard, Frank
Mister Romeo 1927,S 6,35:3
Ladies Don't Lie 1929,O 11,36:3
Hilliard, Harry
When Crummles Played 1928,O 2,34:3
Hilliard, Jack
Borscht Capades 1951,S 18,38:3
Hilliard, Mack (Miscellaneous)
Hairpin Harmony 1943,O 2,18:5
Hilliard, Mack (Producer)
Take My Tip 1932,Ap 12,25:2
Sailor, Beware! 1935,My 7,28:4
In the Bag 1936,D 18,30:2

Hilliard, Macurdy (Miscellaneous)
Down to Miami 1944,S 12,23:5
Hilliard, Stafford
Touch Wood 1934,Jl 1,X,1:3
Hillias, Peg
Streetcar Named Desire, A 1947,D 4,42:2
Peter Pan 1950,Ap 25,27:2
Child of the Morning 1951,N 17,9:7
Hillich, Ernst
Why Do I Deserve This? 1966,Ja 19,31:2
Hillie, Verna
Night of January 16 1935,S 17,26:4
Night of January 16 1935,D 16,22:5
Hillier, Gwen
Curley McDimple 1969,N 25,53:1
Hillier, W W (Miscellaneous)
Theatre of Robert Frost, The; Masque of Reason, The; Bonfire, The; Masque of Mercy, The; Generations of Men, The 1962,My 31,23:6
Hilligoss, Candace
Once in a Lifetime 1962,O 30,30:1
Hilliker, Katharine (Original Author)
Little Stranger 1938,Jl 14,16:2
Hilliker, Katharine (Playwright)
Never Trouble Trouble 1937,Ag 18,15:2
Little Stranger 1938,Jl 31,IX,1:3
Hilliman, Lillian
Divina Pastora, La 1931,Mr 4,33:2
Sparkin' 1931,Mr 4,33:2
Psychological Moment, The 1931,Mr 4,33:2
Hillman, George
Curley McDimple 1967,N 23,59:2
Curley McDimple 1969,N 25,53:1
Hillman, Gertrude
Springtime of Youth 1922,O 27,15:1
Hillman, J H 3d
Tiger Smiles, The 1930,D 18,29:1
Hillman, Lillian
Old Maid, The 1949,Ja 27,20:6
Post Road 1949,Ap 28,27:3
This Happy Breed 1952,Ap 4,23:2
Hillman, Michael (Miscellaneous)
Glorious Morning 1938,N 28,10:3
Hillmer, Jerry (Miscellaneous)
Mother Courage and Her Children 1964,My 12,32:2
Hillner, Bert
Gypsy Lady 1946,S 18,25:6
Hills, Trevor
Pirates of Penzance, The 1955,O 7,21:1
Princess Ida 1955,O 14,22:3
H M S Pinafore 1955,O 18,48:1
Trial by Jury 1955,O 18,48:1
Hilmer, Lucien
Hamlet 1928,Je 2,11:3
Hilpert, Heinz (Director)
Neidhardt von Gneisenau 1927,Ja 23,VII,4:5
Trial of Mary Dugan, The 1928,Je 24,VIII,1:4
Front Page, The 1929,Jl 14,IX,2:1
Journey's End 1929,S 22,IX,4:1
Street Scene 1930,Mr 16,IX,4:1
Elisabeth von England 1930,D 14,IX,4:1
Hauptmann von Koeepenick, Der; Captain of Kopenick, The 1931,Ap 26,VIII,1:4
Kat 1931,O 4,VIII,4:1
Antony and Cleopatra 1932,F 7,VIII,1:5
Timon 1932,Mr 6,VIII,2:1
Journalisten, Die 1932,Jl 17,IX,1:1
Oliver Cromwells Sendung 1933,Mr 19,IX,2:2
Much Ado About Nothing 1933,Ap 30,IX,2:2
Maria Stuart 1933,D 10,X,5:1
Lantern, The 1935,O 6,XI,3:7
Hamlet in Wittenberg 1936,N 15,XI,2:4
Dominant Sex, The 1937,O 24,XI,3:2
Hilpert, Heinz (Producer)
Elizabeth of England 1931,O 18,VIII,1:3
Amor Vincit Omnia 1936,N 15,XI,2:4
Hamlet in Wittenberg 1936,N 15,XI,2:4
Hilsenroth, Miriam
Familiar Pattern 1943,S 3,15:6
Hilt, Ferdinand
Magdalena 1948,S 21,31:2
Buttrio Square 1952,O 15,40:2
Can-Can 1953,My 8,28:1
Can-Can 1962,My 17,32:2
Where's Charley? 1966,My 26,57:1
Hilton, Andrew
Hamlet 1970,D 28,40:1
Hilton, Dora
Tick-Tack-Toe 1920,F 24,11:2
Hilton, Frank
Made for Each Other 1924,S 30,27:2
Twelve Miles Out 1925,N 17,29:2
Hilton, Frank (Playwright)
Day of the Prince 1963,My 15,33:4
Hilton, Frank L Jr
Caesar and Cleopatra 1927,N 6,IX,2:1
Hilton, Howard
Enemy of the People, An 1959,F 5,24:4
Hilton, James (Lyricist)
Shangri-La 1956,Je 14,40:1
Hilton, James (Original Author)
And Now Goodbye 1937,Ja 19,29:1
And Now Goodbye 1937,F 3,26:4

Hilton, James (Original Author)—Cont
Shangri-La 1956,Je 14,40:1
Hilton, James (Playwright)
Shangri-La 1956,Je 14,40:1
Hilton, John
Lancashire Lass, The 1931,D 31,16:3
Hilton, Maude
Vaudeville (Palace) 1929,N 18,22:4
Hilton, Percy
Clutching Claw, The 1928,F 15,20:1
Hilton, Philip
Hymn to the Rising Sun 1937,My 7,28:2
Hilton, Ray
Founders, The 1957,My 14,39:1
Hilton, Rosemary
Pigs 1924,S 2,22:5
Himes, Ross
Topsy and Eva 1924,D 24,11:1
Vaudeville (Palace) 1928,F 21,19:2
Here's Howe! 1928,My 2,19:3
Himmelstein, Jacob
Golden Ring, The 1930,F 1,14:7
My Little Girl 1931,F 2,22:4
Jewish Melody, The 1933,Mr 27,12:4
Hinckle, William MacFarlane
Aiglon, L' 1925,O 31,20:3
Hinckley, Alfred
Point of No Return 1957,Mr 23,17:2
Wayside 1957,Ap 18,34:1
Born Yesterday 1958,Mr 22,12:6
Legend of Lizzie, The 1959,F 10,39:1
Cockeyed Kite 1961,S 14,27:1
Long Voyage Home, The 1961,D 5,49:1
Entertain a Ghost 1962,Ap 10,48:1
Night of the Dunce 1966,D 29,21:1
Rimers of Eldritch, The 1967,F 21,53:1
People vs Ranchman, The 1968,O 28,56:1
Steambath 1970,Jl 1,49:1
Hinckley, Darthy
Fly Away Home 1937,Ap 27,18:1
Dance Night 1938,O 15,20:5
Hinckley, Gayle (Producer)
Time of the Cuckoo, The 1958,O 28,40:2
Clearing in the Woods, A 1959,F 13,32:1
Come Share My House 1960,F 19,20:2
Hindemith, Paul (Composer)
Lesson in Consent, A 1969,My 26,55:2
Hindle, Winifred
Under the Counter 1947,O 4,10:2
Hindman, Bill
Salvage 1957,Ap 10,39:2
Hindman, Earl
Winter's Tale, The 1963,Je 29,13:1
Midsummer Night's Dream, A 1963,Jl 1,19:2
Dark of the Moon 1970,Ap 4,21:2
Hindman, William
Richard III 1957,N 26,41:1
As You Like It 1958,Ja 21,33:6
Edward II 1958,F 12,32:5
Othello 1958,Jl 4,16:1
Henry IV 1960,Ap 19,41:1
Hamlet 1961,Mr 17,17:1
Case of Libel, A 1963,O 11,43:2
Hindmarsh, Jean
Gondoliers, The 1962,N 16,25:2
Pirates of Penzance, The 1962,N 21,28:1
H M S Pinafore 1962,N 23,32:4
Hindsley, Charles
Gondoliers, The 1964,Mr 28,14:1
Hindson, Will
Comedian, The 1923,Mr 14,14:1
Hindy, Joseph
Winterset 1966,F 10,32:2
Hine, Jennings
Saint Wench 1933,Ja 3,19:3
Hineck, Daniel (Producer)
Ivanov 1958,O 8,42:1
Hineman, Edwin Sharp
This Mad Whirl 1937,Ja 10,II,4:8
Hines, Altonell
Porgy and Bess 1935,O 11,30:2
Four Saints in Three Acts 1952,Ap 17,35:1
Hines, Babe
Dance Me a Song 1950,Ja 21,10:5
Almost Crazy 1955,Je 21,37:1
Hines, Elizabeth
Love Birds 1921,Mr 16,12:1
O'Brien Girl, The 1921,O 4,10:2
Little Nellie Kelly 1922,N 14,16:1
Marjorie 1924,Ag 12,12:2
June Days 1925,Ag 7,12:5
Hines, Gregory
Girl in Pink Tights, The 1954,Mr 6,13:2
Hines, Harold
Green Pastures, The 1935,F 27,16:2
Hines, J H
Take It Away 1936,D 22,32:3
Hines, Jack
Artists and Models 1924,O 16,33:3
Hines, Jerome
South Pacific 1968,Je 30,54:2
South Pacific 1969,Jl 7,27:1
Hines, Jim
Years Between, The 1942,F 7,13:2

Hines, John Jr
What a Relief 1935,D 14,10:6
Take It Away 1936,D 15,30:5
Hines, Joyce
Madame Aphrodite 1961,D 30,13:1
Hines, Laurene
Lew Leslie's Blackbirds of 1939 1939,F 13,12:2
Hines, Maurice
Girl in Pink Tights, The 1954,Mr 6,13:2
Hines, Patrick
King John 1956,Je 28,33:5
Measure for Measure 1956,Je 29,16:1
Taming of the Shrew, The 1956,Ag 6,20:1
Measure for Measure 1957,Ja 23,24:1
Taming of the Shrew, The 1957,F 21,30:2
Duchess of Malfi, The 1957,Mr 20,33:1
Midsummer Night's Dream, A 1957,Je 27,21:3
Hamlet 1958,Je 21,11:1
Midsummer Night's Dream, A 1958,Je 23,19:1
Winter's Tale, The 1958,Jl 21,17:4
Geranium Hat, The 1959,Mr 18,45:1
Romeo and Juliet 1959,Je 15,31:1
Merry Wives of Windsor, The 1959,Jl 9,23:2
All's Well That Ends Well 1959,Ag 3,20:4
Great God Brown, The 1959,O 7,48:1
Lysistrata 1959,N 25,19:4
Peer Gynt 1960,Ja 13,21:1
Henry IV 1960,Mr 2,42:1
Twelfth Night 1960,Je 9,29:4
Tempest, The 1960,Je 20,35:1
Antony and Cleopatra 1960,Ag 1,19:1
As You Like It 1961,Je 17,13:2
Macbeth 1961,Je 19,31:1
Troilus and Cressida 1961,Jl 24,15:1
Passage to India, A 1962,F 1,23:1
Henry IV, Part I 1962,Je 18,20:4
Richard II 1962,Je 18,20:2
King Lear 1963,Je 10,37:1
Comedy of Errors, The 1963,Je 13,28:1
Henry V 1963,Je 14,37:1
Caesar and Cleopatra 1963,Ag 1,18:2
Much Ado About Nothing 1964,Je 11,26:2
Richard III 1964,Je 12,44:2
Hamlet 1964,Jl 4,9:1
Coriolanus 1965,Je 21,36:1
Romeo and Juliet 1965,Je 21,36:3
King Lear 1965,Je 25,39:1
Devils, The 1965,N 17,51:2
Falstaff 1966,Je 20,27:1
Murder in the Cathedral 1966,Je 21,38:1
Twelfth Night 1966,Je 23,28:1
Julius Caesar 1966,Je 24,29:2
Chronicles of Hell, The 1969,O 19,II,12:1
Wars of the Roses, The (Part I) 1970,Jl 2,30:1
Wars of the Roses, The (Part II) 1970,Jl 3,15:1
Hines, Sam
Where's Your Husband? 1927,Ja 15,10:3
Hines, Samuel E
Shore Leave 1922,Ag 9,20:2
Hines, Theodore
Set My People Free 1948,N 4,38:2
Show Boat 1957,Je 28,30:2
Hines, Theresa
Our Lan' 1947,Ap 19,11:2
Hines, Willamette
Idiot, The 1960,S 26,38:1
Emmanuel 1960,D 5,42:2
Hiney, Francis
Secrets 1922,D 26,11:1
Hingle, Pat
End as a Man 1953,S 16,39:1
Festival 1955,Ja 19,22:1
Cat on a Hot Tin Roof 1955,Mr 25,18:2
Cat on a Hot Tin Roof 1955,Ap 3,II,1:1
Girls of Summer 1956,N 20,45:1
Dark at the Top of the Stairs, The 1957,D 6,38:1
Dark at the Top of the Stairs, The 1957,D 15,II,3:1
J B 1958,D 12,2:7
Deadly Game, The 1960,F 3,27:2
Macbeth 1961,Je 19,31:1
Macbeth 1961,Je 25,II,1:1
Troilus and Cressida 1961,Jl 24,15:1
Strange Interlude 1963,Mr 13,5:2
Strange Interlude 1963,Je 18,34:6
Blues for Mister Charlie 1964,Ap 24,24:1
Blues for Mister Charlie 1964,My 3,II,1:1
Girl Could Get Lucky, A 1964,S 21,36:1
Glass Menagerie, The 1965,My 5,53:2
Glass Menagerie, The 1965,My 16,II,1:1
Johnny No-Trump 1967,O 9,60:2
Price, The 1968,F 8,37:1
Price, The 1968,F 18,II,1:1
Child's Play 1970,F 18,39:1
Child's Play 1970,Mr 1,II,1:4
Hinkle, H N (Costume Designer)
Scarlet Lullaby 1968,Mr 11,48:1
Hinkle, William M
Faun, The 1924,Mr 28,17:2
Galloper, The 1924,D 19,26:2
Out o' Luck 1925,D 19,15:1
Orestes 1926,Je 20,II,3:6
Hinkley, Alonzo
Possessed, The 1939,O 25,26:2

Hinkley, Darthy
London Assurance 1937,F 19,14:5
Flying Gerardos, The 1940,D 30,21:4
Alice in Arms 1945,F 1,18:4
Corn Is Green, The 1950,Ja 12,33:2
First Lady 1952,My 29,18:5
Hinkley, Del
Sherry! 1967,Mr 29,39:1
How to Steal an Election 1968,O 14,56:1
Hinkley, Dorothy
Butter and Egg Man, The 1949,Ap 29,27:1
Hinkley, Eleanor Holmes (Playwright)
Dear Jane 1932,N 15,24:3
Hinnant, Bill
No Time for Sergeants 1955,O 21,32:2
All Kinds of Giants 1961,D 19,40:1
Put It in Writing 1963,My 14,31:1
You're a Good Man, Charlie Brown 1967,Mr 8,51:1
You're a Good Man, Charlie Brown
1967,Ap 9,II,1:1
American Hamburger League, The 1969,S 17,51:1
Hinnant, Skip
You're a Good Man, Charlie Brown 1967,Mr 8,51:1
Hinrich, Hans (Director)
Mississippi 1931,Ja 11,VIII,1:6
Hinsdale, Harriet (Original Author)
Swan Song 1946,My 16,29:2
Hinsdell, Oliver (Director)
El Cristo 1926,My 9,II,1:4
Hinson, Bonnie
Me and Juliet 1970,My 15,42:1
Hinson, Mirra
Can-Can 1959,Ag 26,25:4
Hinte, Frederick
Birds, The 1967,My 7,67:1
Hinton, James Jr (Lyricist)
Bartleby 1961,Ja 25,28:1
Hinton, Jane (Miscellaneous)
Good Fairy, The 1932,N 18,22:3
Hinton, Jane (Playwright)
Sex Fable, The 1931,O 21,26:1
Good Fairy, The 1931,N 25,17:1
Meet a Body 1944,O 17,19:5
Obsession 1946,O 2,39:2
Hinton, Lilian
Mr Sampson 1927,My 8,30:1
Hinton, Margaret
March Hares 1928,Ap 3,32:6
Hinton, Mary
Yes, M'Lord 1949,O 5,35:2
Hinton, Michael
Trumpets of the Lord 1963,D 23,22:3
Hinton, Tom (Director)
Brownstone Urge, The 1969,D 18,63:1
Hinton, West
War 1929,S 19,37:3
Hintze, Carl (Playwright)
Endlose Strasse, Die 1932,Mr 27,VIII,3:1
Hinxmann, Paul
Cock-A-Doodle Dandy 1958,N 13,39:2
Hinz, Werner
Don Karlos 1935,Jl 28,X,1:6
Hiondbiad, B J (Miscellaneous)
Ice Follies 1960,Ja 13,20:1
Hipkins, Helen
Clinging Vine, The 1922,D 25,20:2
Hipp, Mary Little (Lighting Director)
Eastward in Eden 1956,Ap 18,25:4
Hipp, Mary Little (Miscellaneous)
Eastward in Eden 1956,Ap 18,25:4
Hippius, Zinaida (Playwright)
Green Ring, The 1922,Ap 5,22:1
Hirano, M
Dear Old Darling 1936,Mr 3,25:1
Hire, Takapia
Make Me Know It 1929,N 5,32:5
Hirigaray
Girofle-Girofla 1926,N 23,26:3
Cloches de Cornville, Les; Chimes of Normandy,
The 1926,D 14,24:4
Hiro, John
Little Theatre Tournament; House With the Twisty
Windows, The 1929,My 8,34:4
Hiromura, Kikuo
Teahouse of the August Moon, The 1953,O 16,32:1
Hirose, George
If This Be Treason 1935,S 24,28:2
Mikado, The 1936,Ap 11,18:4
See My Lawyer 1939,S 28,29:1
Hirsch, Eleanor
Nautical but Nice 1931,Ap 19,31:6
Hirsch, Emil
Professor Mamlock 1937,Ap 14,30:3
Haiti 1938,Mr 3,16:1
Pinocchio 1939,Ja 3,19:2
Hirsch, Harriet
Nautical but Nice 1931,Ap 19,31:6
Hirsch, Henry (Playwright)
Sur le Banc 1923,O 16,18:1
Hirsch, Hugo (Composer)
Toni 1924,My 18,VII,2:8
Wieder Metropol 1926,D 5,VIII,8:7

Hirsch, Irving
Song Writer, The 1928,Ag 14,15:2
Hirsch, John (Costume Designer)
Curley McDimple 1967,N 23,59:2
Another City, Another Land 1968,O 9,42:1
Tango 1969,Ja 20,33:1
Hirsch, John (Director)
Cherry Orchard, The 1965,Ag 2,17:2
Henry VI 1966,Je 9,55:2
Yerma 1966,D 9,60:1
Galileo 1967,Ap 14,31:1
Galileo 1967,Ap 23,II,1:1
Richard III 1967,Je 14,43:1
Richard III 1967,Je 25,II,1:1
Saint Joan 1968,Ja 5,42:1
Saint Joan 1968,Ja 14,II,1:1
Midsummer Night's Dream, A 1968,Je 13,54:1
Three Musketeers, The 1968,Jl 24,49:2
We Bombed in New Haven 1968,O 17,51:1
We Bombed in New Haven 1968,O 27,II,1:1
Hamlet 1969,Je 11,37:1
Hamlet 1969,Je 22,II,1:7
Time of Your Life, The 1969,N 7,37:1
Time of Your Life, The 1969,N 16,II,1:4
Beggar on Horseback 1970,My 15,47:2
Beggar on Horseback 1970,My 24,II,1:1
Hirsch, John (Miscellaneous)
Henry IV, Part I 1965,Je 30,42:1
Hirsch, John (Producer)
Midsummer Night's Dream, A 1968,Je 23,II,1:1
Hirsch, Judd
Scuba Duba 1967,O 11,36:1
Scuba Duba 1969,Ap 7,51:1
Hirsch, Judd (Miscellaneous)
Diary of a Madman 1964,Ap 17,29:2
On the Necessity of Being Polygamous
1964,D 9,61:1
Hirsch, Katherine
Late Christopher Bean, The 1932,N 1,24:3
Brittle Heaven 1934,N 14,22:5
Jackson White 1935,Ap 22,14:6
Hirsch, Lawrence M
Upon My Soul 1927,Ap 22,19:1
Hirsch, Louis (Composer)
Mary 1920,O 19,12:1
O'Brien Girl, The 1921,O 4,10:2
Ziegfeld Follies 1922,Je 6,18:2
Greenwich Village Follies 1922,S 13,18:2
Greenwich Village Follies 1923,S 21,4:6
Betty Lee 1924,D 26,18:2
Hirsch, Minette (Miscellaneous)
Emperor, The 1963,Ap 17,30:1
Hirsch, Myron
Lightnin' 1938,S 16,17:2
Hirsch, Nathan
Sisters' Tragedy, The 1930,My 6,33:1
Mighty Nimrod, The 1931,My 13,23:1
Hirsch, Paul
Midsummer Night's Dream, A 1932,N 18,22:2
Hirsch, Robert
Fourberies de Scapin, Les 1961,F 22,30:1
Britannicus 1961,Mr 3,17:1
Dindon, Le 1961,Mr 8,38:1
File a la Patte, Il 1962,Jl 8,II,1:1
Soif et la Faim, La 1966,Mr 2,47:5
Amphitryon 1970,F 4,38:1
Troupe Du Roi, La 1970,F 4,38:1
Hirsch, Robert (Costume Designer)
Fourberies de Scapin, Les 1961,F 22,30:1
Hirsch, Robert (Scenic Designer)
Fourberies de Scapin, Les 1961,F 22,30:1
Hirsch, Roland A
Electronic Nigger, The 1968,Mr 9,23:2
Hirschbein, Abraham
Parnosseh 1939,F 20,12:5
Hirschbein, Peretz (Playwright)
One Life for Another 1920,D 18,11:2
Idle Inn, The 1921,D 21,26:2
Smith's Daughters, The 1922,Ja 29,VI,1:3
Child of the World, The 1922,Ap 29,18:3
Pioneers 1932,F 26,22:5
Once Upon a Time 1933,S 22,15:1
Far-Away Corner, A 1939,F 15,15:2
Hirschberg, Herbert (Playwright)
German Tragedy, The; or, Bismarck and William II
1926,D 6,4:2
Hirschberg, Herman
What's the Use? 1926,S 7,19:1
Hirschfeld, Fred
Aquashow 1953,Je 24,29:2
Hirschfeld (Playwright)
Auslandreise 1932,N 20,IX,3:5
Hirschfield, Ludwig (Original Author)
Case of Youth, A 1940,Mr 25,10:3
Hirschma, Herbert
Streets of New York, The 1934,Jl 21,14:5
Hirschman, Herbert
Coquette 1935,Jl 10,24:1
Late Christopher Bean, The 1935,Ag 28,13:1
Menonite 1936,Mr 20,29:6
Hirschman, Herbert (Miscellaneous)
Camille 1935,Jl 31,21:1
Mr Pim Passes By 1935,Ag 7,22:2

Hirschman, Herbert (Miscellaneous)—Cont
Late Christopher Bean, The 1935,Ag 28,13:1
Hirschman, Herbert (Scenic Designer)
Vinegar Tree, The 1935,Ag 14,16:1
Hirsh, Gary
Tarot 1970,D 12,19:1
Hirsh, Nathaniel
Armored Train No 1469 1931,N 28,20:3
Hirsh, Sy
Time of Vengeance 1959,D 11,39:1
Hirshbein, A
Jim Cooperkop 1930,O 18,23:1
Hirsh Lekert 1936,Mr 11,23:2
Hirshbein, Abraham
Clinton Street 1939,O 13,27:2
Hirshburg, Henrietta
Geranium Hat, The 1959,Mr 18,45:1
Hirshhorn, Naomi Caryl
Spoon River Anthology 1963,My 2,40:5
Spoon River Anthology 1963,S 30,23:2
Hirshhorn, Naomi Caryl (Composer)
Spoon River Anthology 1963,S 30,23:2
Promises to Keep 1965,Jl 22,25:1
Hirshman, John J (Col) (Director)
Caribbean Carnival 1947,D 6,12:2
Hirson, Alice
Investigation, The 1966,O 5,40:1
Hirson, Roger O (Playwright)
Journey to the Day 1963,N 12,49:1
Walking Happy 1966,N 28,47:1
World War 2 1/2 1969,Mr 25,40:1
Hirst, Don
Johnny Doodle 1942,Mr 19,28:2
Hirst, George (Composer)
Richard III 1943,Mr 27,8:3
Hirst, George (Musical Director)
Connecticut Yankee, A 1943,N 18,30:2
Hollywood Pinafore 1945,Je 1,20:1
Kiss Me, Kate 1952,Ja 9,24:6
Hirt, Eleonore
Absence of a Cello; Mal de Test, Le 1965,S 9,36:3
Hiss, Bosley
Lancelot and Elaine 1921,S 13,12:1
Hitch, Bill
Story of Mary Surratt, The 1947,F 10,25:2
Hitch, Fred H
Untitled-Passion Play 1926,Mr 30,20:2
Hitch, Mary
Seagull, The 1968,Jl 25,27:2
Alchemist, The 1969,Je 12,51:1
Measure for Measure 1969,Je 13,41:3
Hitch, William
Chalk Dust 1936,Mr 5,24:5
Doctor Faustus 1937,Ja 9,21:2
Audition of the Apprentice Theatre 1939,Je 2,26:2
Man Who Killed Lincoln, The 1940,Ja 18,26:4
Hitchcock, George
Antony and Cleopatra 1963,S 14,12:4
Hitchcock, Mr
Dumb as a Fox 1924,N 30,VIII,2:1
Hitchcock, Pat
Solitaire 1942,Ja 28,22:2
Solitaire 1942,F 8,IX,1:1
Violet 1944,O 25,16:1
Hitchcock, Patricia
High Ground, The 1951,F 21,31:2
Hitchcock, Raymond
Hitchy-Koo, 1920 1920,O 20,11:3
Ziegfeld Follies 1921,Je 22,10:1
Untitled-Benefit 1922,My 8,14:5
Friar's Club Frolic 1922,Je 5,16:1
Pinwheel Revel 1922,Je 16,20:6
Hassard Short's Ritz Revue 1924,S 18,19:1
Sap, The 1924,D 16,28:3
Lambs Gambol 1925,Ap 27,15:1
Just Fancy! 1927,O 12,30:2
Beaux' Stratagem, The 1928,Je 5,20:1
Beaux' Stratagem, The 1928,Je 10,VIII,1:1
Hitchell, Thom (Director)
School for Wives 1957,Je 20,23:4
Hitchell, Thom (Playwright)
School for Wives 1957,Je 20,23:4
Hitchell, Thom (Producer)
School for Wives 1957,Je 20,23:4
Hitchock, Jack (Composer)
Say Nothing 1965,Ja 28,21:2
Hite, Hugh M
Machinal 1928,S 8,10:3
Hite, Solly
O K 1925,My 4,16:1
Hitner, Guy
Swifty 1922,O 17,14:1
Clouds 1925,S 3,32:1
Open House 1925,D 15,28:3
90 Horse Power 1926,Mr 16,22:4
Town Boy 1929,O 5,22:4
Spook House 1930,Je 4,33:3
Hitt, Robert
Revenger's Tragedy, The 1970,D 2,58:1
Hitz, Elsie
Restless Women 1927,D 27,24:1
Hitz, Gertrude
Deep Tangled Wildwood, The 1923,N 6,22:1

One Way Street 1928,D 25,31:2
Hix, Clifford
Mother Sings 1935,N 13,24:1
Hixon, Butler
Creeping Fire 1935,Ja 17,22:3
Play, Genius, Play! 1935,O 31,17:2
Bloomer Girl 1944,O 6,18:5
Hixon, Hal
Century Revue and the Midnight Rounders, The 1920,Jl 13,9:1
Hixson, Opal
Elsie 1923,Ap 3,26:1
Hlavaty, F
Mr Pickwick 1931,Ja 11,VIII,3:5
Ho, Norman
Midsummer Night's Dream, A 1968,D 9,59:1
Ho, Wai Ching
People vs Ranchman, The 1968,O 28,56:1
But Never Jam Today 1969,Ap 24,40:1
Moon on a Rainbow Shawl 1970,D 18,52:1
Hoadley, Nancy
As You Like It 1945,Jl 4,10:4
Hoag, George
Dybbuk, The 1925,D 16,22:2
Romantic Young Lady, The 1926,My 5,24:3
Commedia Dell' Arte 1927,Ap 6,24:3
Love Nest, The 1927,D 23,17:1
Within the Law 1928,Mr 6,20:1
Hoag, Mitzi
Heloise 1958,S 25,28:4
Heloise 1958,O 5,II,1:1
Heartbreak House 1963,Je 8,14:2
Heartbreak House 1963,Je 28,24:1
Hoagland, Ben
Play Without a Name, A 1928,N 26,30:5
Everything's Jake 1930,Ja 17,20:4
Bellamy Trial, The 1931,Ap 23,28:6
Hoagland, Carleton (Producer)
Stick-in-the-Mud 1935,D 2,18:2
Hoagland, Tuppi
Empress of Destiny 1938,Mr 10,16:2
Hoar, Joseph
Love Is No Heaven 1943,Mr 16,15:3
Hoare, J E (Playwright)
Red Planet 1932,D 19,19:2
Hoare, John (Playwright)
Great Experiment, The 1936,Ap 22,28:4
Hoare, Wilfred
Holiday 1930,F 6,21:2
Hoban, Molly
Let Freedom Sing 1942,O 6,18:2
Hoban, Stella
Night Boat, The 1920,F 3,18:1
Helen of Troy, New York 1923,Je 20,22:6
Hobard, Rick (Miscellaneous)
Watering Place, The 1969,Mr 13,51:1
Hobard, Rick (Producer)
I Only Want an Answer 1968,F 6,36:1
People vs Ranchman, The 1968,O 28,56:1
Rondelay 1969,N 6,55:1
Hobart, Doty (Playwright)
Thoroughbred 1933,N 7,29:2
Every Thursday 1934,My 11,25:5
Double Dummy 1936,N 12,30:1
Hobart, George V (Composer)
Ziegfeld Follies 1920,Je 23,14:1
Hobart, George V (Lyricist)
Ziegfeld Follies 1920,Je 23,14:1
Hobart, George V (Playwright)
Blue Flame, The 1920,Mr 16,18:1
Fall and Rise of Susan Lenox, The 1920,Je 11,11:2
Ziegfeld Follies 1920,Je 23,14:1
Kissing Time 1920,O 12,18:2
Sonny 1921,Ag 17,12:2
Irving Berlin's Music Box Revue 1921,S 23,18:2
Letty Pepper 1922,Ap 11,22:2
Greenwich Village Follies 1922,S 13,18:2
Irving Berlin's New Music Box Revue 1922,O 24,18:1
Hobart, Ralph
Rain 1935,Ag 27,23:4
Hobart, Rose
Caesar and Cleopatra 1925,Ap 14,27:1
Lucky Sam McCarver 1925,O 22,22:1
John Gabriel Borkman 1926,Ja 30,13:1
What Every Woman Knows 1926,Ap 14,20:2
Three Sisters, The 1926,O 27,24:1
Puppets of Passion 1927,F 25,24:4
Revelry 1927,S 13,37:1
Fanatics, The 1927,N 8,32:4
Diversion 1928,Ja 12,25:1
Crashing Through 1928,O 30,26:5
Zeppelin 1929,Ja 15,22:3
Primer for Lovers, A 1929,N 19,26:5
Death Takes a Holiday 1929,D 27,26:4
Let Us Divorce; Counsel's Opinion 1932,Ap 17,VIII,2:6
When Ladies Meet 1932,Ag 14,IX,1:7
I Loved You Wednesday 1932,O 12,27:1
Girls in Uniform 1932,D 31,10:3
Our Wife 1933,Mr 3,13:2
Eight Bells 1933,O 30,14:2
Eight Bells 1933,N 5,IX,1:1

Hobart, Rose—Cont
Wind and the Rain, The 1934,F 2,20:6
With All My Heart 1935,Jl 30,17:1
County Chairman, The 1936,My 26,26:5
Siege 1937,D 9,31:4
Dear Octopus 1939,Ja 12,22:2
Hobart, Vail
Girl in the Coffin, The 1920,F 10,10:2
Magnanimous Lover, The 1920,F 10,10:2
Suppressed Desires 1920,F 10,10:2
Hobbes, Halliwell
Swan, The 1923,O 24,15:3
Easy Virtue 1925,D 8,28:2
Slaves All 1926,D 7,24:4
Adventurous Age, The 1927,F 8,20:1
Caste 1927,D 24,8:1
Silver Box, The 1928,Ja 18,23:1
When Crummles Played 1928,O 2,34:3
Be Your Age 1929,F 5,27:1
Romeo and Juliet 1940,My 10,27:1
Ten Little Indians 1944,Je 28,21:2
Hidden Horizon 1946,S 20,42:2
Male Animal, The 1952,My 1,35:1
Male Animal, The 1952,My 18,II,1:1
Swan, The 1954,Ag 17,16:6
Portrait of a Lady 1954,D 22,27:6
Tonight in Samarkand 1955,F 17,22:2
Day by the Sea, A 1955,S 27,42:1
Day by the Sea, A 1955,O 2,II,1:1
Hobbes, Halliwell (Director)
When Crummles Played 1928,O 2,34:3
George Barnwell; London Merchant, The 1928,O 2,34:3
Hobbes, Halliwell Jr
Linden Tree, The 1948,Mr 3,28:2
Hobbes, Nancie
Slaves All 1926,D 7,24:4
Marriage Is for Single People 1945,N 22,38:2
Hobbs, Bertram (Playwright)
Loose Moments 1935,F 5,22:3
Hobbs, Carleton
Anatomist, The 1931,O 25,VIII,2:6
Hobbs, Jack
Belinda 1922,Jl 30,VI,1:7
Rasputin 1929,My 12,IX,2:3
Hobbs, Peter
Days of Our Youth, The 1941,N 29,15:2
Life of Reilly, The 1942,Ap 30,13:2
Comes the Revelation 1942,My 27,26:2
Russian People, The 1942,D 30,17:2
Truckline Cafe 1946,F 28,19:4
Joan of Lorraine 1946,N 19,40:2
Uniform of Flesh 1949,Ja 31,15:2
Sun and I, The 1949,Mr 21,18:4
Hobbs, Robert
Charlot's Revue 1924,Ja 10,18:1
Charlot's Revue 1925,N 11,27:1
Nightingale, The 1927,Ja 4,20:4
Noble Rogue, A 1929,Ag 20,31:2
International Revue 1930,F 26,22:2
Hobbs, William (Director)
Hamlet 1970,D 28,40:1
Hobbs, William (Miscellaneous)
Macbeth 1962,F 7,32:2
Romeo and Juliet 1962,F 14,39:1
Hober, Beal
Prelude to Exile 1936,N 22,XI,3:2
Prelude to Exile 1936,D 1,31:1
Hoberman, Henry D
Laugh It Off 1934,Ap 5,24:2
Hobgood, Burnet
Confederacy, The 1958,Jl 3,20:1
Hobgood, Jane
Confederacy, The 1958,Jl 3,20:1
Hobson, Ann
Little Poor Man, The 1925,Ag 6,14:1
Hobson, I M
Galileo 1968,D 1,88:4
Hobson, James
Most Happy Fella, The 1966,My 12,55:1
Lovely Ladies, Kind Gentlemen 1970,D 29,38:1
Hobson, Marie
Wall Street 1927,Ap 21,24:4
Hobson, Valerie
King and I, The 1953,O 9,33:3
King and I, The 1953,O 18,II,3:1
Hobson, Wilder
Coriolanus 1927,Je 18,8:3
Hoch, Debrah
Ruy Blas 1957,D 14,16:3
Hoch, Emil
Poldekin 1920,S 10,12:1
Alias Jimmy Valentine 1921,D 9,20:3
Roger Bloomer 1923,Mr 2,18:3
Anathema 1923,Ap 11,16:2
Inspector General, The 1923,My 1,24:1
June Moon 1929,O 10,34:5
For Valor 1935,N 19,27:5
Hochfelder, Richard
Grand Duchess 1929,D 17,29:2
Gypsy Baron, The 1930,Ap 22,22:8
Hochhuth, Rolf (Playwright)
Stellvertreter, Der 1963,F 23,7:8
Stellvertreter, Der 1963,S 10,46:1

Hochhuth, Rolf (Playwright)—Cont
Stellvertreter, Der 1963,S 26,41:4
Stellvertreter, Der 1963,S 27,19:3
Deputy, The 1964,F 27,26:1
Deputy, The 1964,Mr 8,II,1:1
Soldiers 1967,O 10,14:3
Soldiers 1967,O 11,37:1
Soldiers 1968,Mr 3,88:2
Soldiers 1968,Mr 10,II,1:1
Soldiers 1968,My 2,58:1
Soldiers 1968,My 12,II,3:1
Soldiers 1968,Jl 7,II,1:1
Soldiers 1968,D 14,62:5
Soldiers 1969,Ja 5,II,3:1
Guerrillas 1970,My 17,91:3
Hochman, Edward (Producer)
Ping-Pong 1959,Ap 17,22:1
Hochman, Mark
Peter and the Wolf 1969,N 30,85:5
Hochstein, Harry
His Wife's Lover 1929,O 21,30:6
My Little Girl 1931,F 2,22:4
Night in the Woods, A 1931,Mr 2,19:3
Stranger, The 1935,N 7,26:2
Hochwalder, Fritz (Original Author)
Strong Are Lonely, The 1953,S 30,38:3
Hock, Robert D (Playwright)
Borak 1960,D 14,51:1
Hocker, David (Producer)
My Daughter, Your Son 1969,My 14,36:2
Jumping Fool, The 1970,F 10,53:1
Hocker, Trew (Scenic Designer)
Mrs Patterson 1957,F 6,20:2
Hockley, Roger
Hamlet 1967,F 17,44:1
Hockridge, Edmund
Can-Can 1954,O 24,II,3:1
Hoctor, Harriet
Topsy and Eva 1924,D 24,11:1
Vaudeville (Palace) 1927,Mr 22,31:1
Vaudeville (Palace) 1927,Ap 5,30:2
Vaudeville (Palace) 1927,My 31,25:1
A la Carte 1927,Ag 18,25:3
Vaudeville (Palace) 1927,O 4,34:3
Vaudeville (Palace) 1927,O 11,27:2
Three Musketeers, The 1928,Mr 14,28:1
Show Girl 1929,Jl 3,19:3
Vaudeville (Palace) 1930,Ag 11,13:3
Vaudeville (Palace) 1930,S 15,29:2
Simple Simon 1931,Mr 10,23:2
Vaudeville (Palace) 1931,My 11,15:5
Vaudeville (Palace) 1931,My 18,21:1
Vaudeville (Palace) 1931,My 25,17:4
Vaudeville (Palace) 1931,S 7,19:2
Vanities 1932,S 18,IX,2:1
Vanities 1932,S 28,22:4
Hold Your Horses 1933,Ag 31,20:4
Ziegfeld Follies 1936,Ja 31,17:2
Hoctor, Harriet (Miscellaneous)
Hold Your Horses 1933,S 26,26:4
Hodapp, Ann
Round With Ring, A 1969,O 30,56:1
House of Leather, The 1970,Mr 19,56:1
Ben Bagley's Shoestring Revues 1970,O 24,22:1
Moon Walk 1970,N 27,52:1
Hodas, Martin (Miscellaneous)
Rondelay 1969,N 6,55:1
Hodder, Clark
Who's Who 1924,Ap 18,19:2
Hodes, Gloria
Gantry 1970,F 16,44:1
Hodes, Stuart
Barrier, The 1950,N 3,32:2
Annie Get Your Gun 1958,F 20,29:2
Sophie 1963,Ap 16,32:1
Hodes, Stuart (Miscellaneous)
To Broadway With Love 1964,Ap 30,28:6
Hodgdon, Ray (Playwright)
Married-And How! 1928,Je 15,30:2
Hodge, Eddie
Merry Andrew 1929,Ja 22,22:2
Sons o' Guns 1929,N 27,30:4
Oh, Promise Me 1930,Mr 25,31:1
They Shall Not Die 1934,F 22,24:4
Swing Your Lady 1936,O 19,22:4
Dance Night 1938,O 15,20:5
Johnny 2X4 1942,Mr 17,24:6
Over Twenty-One 1944,Ja 4,20:2
Million Dollar Baby 1945,D 22,17:2
Look, Ma, I'm Dancin' 1948,Ja 30,20:2
Hodge, Edwin
Appearances 1925,O 15,27:3
Tip-Toes 1925,D 29,20:2
Funny Face 1927,N 23,28:2
Lost Horizons 1934,O 16,31:2
Get Away Old Man 1943,N 25,40:2
Hodge, Jeannette
Exception and the Rule, The 1965,My 21,19:1
Prodigal Son, The 1965,My 21,19:1
Hodge, Martha
On to Fortune 1935,F 5,22:2
Patsy, The 1935,Jl 16,24:1
Post Road 1935,Jl 23,24:3
Remember the Day 1935,S 26,19:3

Spring Dance 1936,Jl 7,22:2
Spring Dance 1936,Ag 26,17:4
Red Harvest 1937,Mr 31,29:2
Two on an Island 1940,Ja 23,17:2
Liberty Jones 1941,F 6,24:2
Nineteenth Hole of Europe, The 1949,Mr 28,16:2
Hodge, Merton (Miscellaneous)
Men in White 1934,Je 29,16:3
Hodge, Merton (Playwright)
Wind and the Rain, The 1933,N 5,IX,1:3
Wind and the Rain, The 1934,F 2,20:6
Grief Goes Over 1935,Je 7,24:5
Wind and the Rain, The 1935,Jl 11,24:2
Grief Goes Over 1935,Jl 28,X,1:1
Orchard Walls 1937,F 4,17:3
Orchard Walls 1937,F 21,X,2:1
Island, The 1938,F 11,27:5
Hodge, Ted
Engaged! or Cheviot's Choice 1965,Ap 24,19:2
Hodge, William
Guest of Honor, The 1920,S 21,12:1
Beware of Dogs 1921,O 4,10:1
For All of Us 1923,O 16,19:4
Judge's Husband, The 1926,S 19,IX,1:3
Judge's Husband, The 1926,S 28,31:1
Straight Thru the Door 1928,O 5,17:2
Inspector Kennedy 1929,D 21,16:3
Old Rascal, The 1930,Mr 25,34:4
Old Rascal, The 1930,N 23,IX,1:3
Hodge, William (Playwright)
Guest of Honor, The 1920,S 21,12:1
Beware of Dogs 1921,O 4,10:1
For All of Us 1923,O 16,19:4
Judge's Husband, The 1926,S 28,31:1
Straight Thru the Door 1928,O 5,17:2
Old Rascal, The 1930,Mr 25,34:4
Hodge, William (Producer)
Straight Thru the Door 1928,O 5,17:2
Inspector Kennedy 1929,D 21,16:3
Old Rascal, The 1930,Mr 25,34:4
Hodgeman, Ted
Richard II 1964,Je 17,47:1
Bourgeois Gentilhomme, Le 1964,Je 18,28:2
Hodges, Amy
Lido Girl, The 1928,Ag 24,23:2
Hodges, Ann
No Strings 1962,Mr 16,24:1
Hodges, Barclay
Day by the Sea, A 1955,S 27,42:1
Hodges, Eddie
Music Man, The 1957,D 20,31:1
Music Man, The 1958,S 28,II,1:1
Critic's Choice 1960,D 15,61:3
Hodges, Elijah
Carmen Jones 1943,D 3,26:2
Carmen Jones 1945,My 3,26:5
Hodges, Fred
Finis for Oscar Wilde 1964,F 15,15:1
Comforter, The 1964,O 22,42:1
Go, Go, Go, God is Dead! 1966,O 12,37:1
Hodges, Horace
Lightnin' 1925,F 1,VII,2:1
After Dark 1926,O 10,VIII,2:1
Enemy, The 1928,Ag 19,VII,1:1
Hundred Years Old, A 1928,D 9,X,2:1
Roof, The 1929,N 6,30:4
Roof, The 1929,N 24,X,1:6
Hodges, James
Bananas 1968,D 5,60:1
Hodges, James (Composer)
Bananas 1968,D 5,60:1
Hodges, James (Lyricist)
Bananas 1968,D 5,60:1
Hodges, John King
Little Father of the Wilderness, The 1930,Je 3,27:1
Hodges, John King (Playwright)
Girl Outside, The 1932,O 25,24:3
Hodges, Joy
I'd Rather Be Right 1937,N 3,28:2
Dream With Music 1944,My 19,15:2
Odds on Mrs Oakley, The 1944,O 3,18:8
Nellie Bly 1946,Ja 22,32:2
Nellie Bly 1946,Ja 27,II,1:1
Jo 1964,F 13,25:1
Hodges, Sally
Wednesday's Child 1934,Ja 17,23:2
Hodges, W C
Silence 1924,N 13,18:2
Hodgetts, Craig (Lighting Director)
Man and Superman 1960,Ag 17,35:3
Hodgetts, Craig (Scenic Designer)
Man and Superman 1960,Ag 17,35:3
Hodgkins, W F
Patience 1934,O 12,32:2
Hodgson, Claire
Dew Drop Inn 1923,My 18,26:4
Hodiak, John
Chase, The 1952,Ap 16,30:2
Caine Mutiny Court-Martial, The 1953,O 14,35:1
Caine Mutiny Court-Martial, The 1953,D 15,52:8
Caine Mutiny Court-Martial, The 1954,Ja 21,27:2
Caine Mutiny Court-Martial, The 1954,Ja 31,II,1:1

Hodshire, Allen (Director)
Greenwich Village U S A 1960,S 29,30:5
Hodshire, Allen (Producer)
Greenwich Village U S A 1960,S 29,30:5
Hodshon, Peter
Heimkehr aus der Fremde, Die; Stranger, The 1949,S 2,14:1
Hodson, J L (Original Author)
Hamp 1964,Ag 18,25:1
Hamp 1967,Mr 10,32:1
Hodson, James Lonsdale (Original Author)
Red Night 1936,Mr 5,25:1
Hodson, James Lonsdale (Playwright)
Red Night 1936,Ap 5,IX,1:2
Hodson, Nellie
Happy-Go-Lucky 1920,Ag 25,6:1
Hoefer, Anita
Dreigroschenoper, Die 1965,Mr 12,24:1
Hoefer, Fritz
Versunkene Glocke, Die 1936,N 20,26:3
Hoefler, Charles E (Miscellaneous)
Jimmy 1969,O 24,38:1
Hoeflich, Lucie
Three Sisters, The 1927,Mr 13,VII,2:4
What Every Woman Knows 1928,D 2,X,4:4
Verbrecher, Die 1928,D 23,VIII,4:1
Kreatur, Die 1930,My 25,IX,1:8
Hoel, Sigurd (Playwright)
Don Juan 1930,D 28,VIII,3:5
Hoeller, Harald A (Producer)
Wiener Blut 1964,S 12,14:1
Hoeny, A Winfield
Moon Vine, The 1943,F 12,22:2
Dark of the Moon 1945,Mr 15,27:2
Design For A Stained Glass Window 1950,Ja 24,26:2
Hoerbiger, Paul
Crime 1928,Je 24,VIII,1:4
Ich Tanze um die Welt mit Dir 1930,Ag 31,VIII,2:1
Im Weissen Roessel 1931,Ja 4,VIII,3:5
Hoeri, Arthur (Playwright)
Few Wild Oats, A 1932,Mr 25,22:6
Hoerrmann, Albert
Italienische Nacht 1931,My 10,VIII,1:5
Hoerth, Franz (Scenic Designer)
Fledermaus, Die 1930,Ap 20,VIII,7:7
Hoervath, Oedon (Playwright)
Geschichten aus dem Wienerwald; Stories From the Vienna Woods 1931,D 27,VIII,1:4
Hoey, Dennis
Hassan 1924,S 23,23:1
Katja 1926,O 19,27:3
Green Waters 1936,N 5,34:4
Jane Eyre 1937,Ja 3,X,2:1
Virginia 1937,S 3,13:2
Empress of Destiny 1938,Mr 10,16:2
Circle, The 1938,Ap 19,24:2
Lorelei 1938,N 30,21:2
Burning Deck, The 1940,Mr 2,9:2
Heart of a City 1942,F 13,24:6
Haven, The 1946,N 14,39:4
Getting Married 1951,My 14,28:5
Hoey, Dennis (Playwright)
Haven, The 1946,N 14,39:4
Hoey, Evelyn
Fifty Million Frenchmen 1929,N 28,34:4
Vanderbilt Revue, The 1930,O 26,VIII,3:5
Vanderbilt Revue, The 1930,N 6,22:6
Walk a Little Faster 1932,D 8,24:4
Hoey, Herbert
Ziegfeld Follies 1921,Je 22,10:1
Hoey, Iris
Red Blinds 1926,O 1,27:1
Actresses Will Happen 1941,Je 15,IX,2:6
Hoey, Joan
Getting Married 1959,Je 5,18:2
Hofer, Johanna
Another Sun 1940,F 24,8:6
Hofer, Vida (Costume Designer)
Cast of Characters 1959,Je 11,37:2
Hoff, Fred (Musical Director)
Student Prince, The 1943,Je 9,16:2
Hoff, Isaac
Topsy-Turvy 1939,F 13,12:3
Hoff, J H
Somebody's Lion 1921,Ap 13,20:1
Hoff, Louise
Phoenix '55 1955,Ap 25,20:2
Cloud 7 1958,F 15,15:2
From A to Z 1960,Ap 21,23:2
Hoff, Marie
Kumquat in the Persimmon Tree, The 1962,Je 19,27:2
Hoff, Vanda
Two Little Girls in Blue 1921,My 4,10:3
Hoffe, Arthur
Danton's Death 1938,N 3,26:2
Hoffe, Arthur (Producer)
Zelda 1969,Mr 6,38:1
Hoffe, Barbara
If Winter Comes 1923,F 11,VII,1:4
Asleep 1927,Je 12,VII,2:1

Hoffe, Monckton (Playwright)
Faithful Heart, The 1921,D 4,VII,1:3
Faithful Heart, The 1922,O 11,22:1
Faithful Heart, The 1922,O 15,VIII,1:1
Lady Cristilinda, The 1922,D 26,11:2
Crooked Friday, The 1925,My 21,26:3
Crooked Friday, The 1925,O 9,27:3
Cristilinda 1925,N 1,VIII,1:3
Many Waters 1928,Ag 5,VII,1:1
Many Waters 1929,S 26,27:1
Many Waters 1929,O 6,IX,1:1
Faithful Heart, The 1932,Ja 17,VIII,2:6
Hoffenstein, Samuel (Composer)
Gay Divorce 1932,N 30,23:4
Hoffenstein, Samuel (Miscellaneous)
Gay Divorce 1960,Ap 4,37:1
Hoffenstein, Samuel (Playwright)
Eskimo, The 1926,Je 20,VII,3:1
Gay Divorce 1932,N 13,IX,1:7
Gay Divorce 1937,Jl 20,19:4
Hoffert, Paul (Composer)
Get Thee to Canterbury 1969,Ja 26,74:1
Hoffert, Paul (Miscellaneous)
Get Thee to Canterbury 1969,Ja 26,74:1
Hoffman, "Think a Drink"
Streets of Paris, The 1939,Je 20,25:2
Top-Notchers 1942,My 30,8:5
Take a Bow 1944,Je 16,15:3
Hoffman, Aaron (Original Author)
All for All 1943,S 30,25:2
Hoffman, Aaron (Playwright)
Welcome Stranger 1920,S 14,12:1
Two Blocks Away 1921,Ag 31,8:3
Welcome Stranger 1921,O 21,18:2
Give and Take 1922,D 10,VIII,1:5
Give and Take 1923,Ja 19,13:1
Good Old Days, The 1923,Ag 15,21:2
Good Old Days, The 1923,Ag 9,VI,1:1
No Other Girl 1924,Ag 14,10:4
Light Wines and Beer 1930,N 11,28:6
Hoffman, Alfred
Visit, The 1958,My 6,40:1
Hoffman, Anna
My Little Girl 1931,F 2,22:4
Traveling Salesman, The 1932,N 1,24:4
Here Runs the Bride 1934,S 20,21:3
Hoffman, Annette
Potash and Perlmutter, Detectives; Poisoned by
Pictures 1926,S 1,27:3
Fifty Million Frenchmen 1929,N 28,34:4
Whatever Goes Up 1935,N 26,28:2
Summer Wives 1936,Ap 14,18:1
Hoffman, Annie
Big Surprise, The 1932,O 17,18:3
One in a Million 1934,N 17,13:2
Hoffman, Armin (Miscellaneous)
Billy Barnes Revue, The 1959,Je 10,42:2
Hoffman, Aura
Stairs, The 1927,N 8,32:7
Hoffman, Avremele
Bronx Express, 1968 1968,N 16,43:3
Hoffman, Barry
Lion in Love, The 1963,Ap 26,28:3
Hoffman, Barry (Lighting Director)
Lovers in the Metro, The 1962,Ja 31,21:1
Keyhole, The 1962,Ja 31,21:1
Information Bureau, The 1962,Ja 31,21:1
Hoffman, Barry (Miscellaneous)
Two for Fun 1961,F 14,45:3
Lion in Love, The 1963,Ap 26,28:3
Hoffman, Barry (Producer)
World of Mrs Solomon, The; Second Mrs Aarons,
The 1969,Je 4,37:1
World of Mrs Solomon, The; Another Chance
1969,Je 4,37:1
Hoffman, Basil
South Pacific 1968,Je 30,54:2
Hoffman, Bern
Nineteenth Hole of Europe, The 1949,Mr 28,16:2
Guys and Dolls 1950,N 25,11:2
Hot Corner, The 1956,Ja 26,25:2
Li'l Abner 1956,N 16,24:2
Hoffman, Bernard
Catherine Was Great 1944,Ag 3,16:1
Hoffman, Betty
Crucible, The 1958,Mr 17,21:1
Hoffman, Bill (Playwright)
Affair of Honor 1956,Ap 7,12:3
Hoffman, Clarence
Hamlet of Stepney Green 1958,N 14,21:1
Hoffman, David
Bitter Stream 1936,Mr 31,16:6
Brother Rat 1936,D 17,34:5
Angel Island 1937,O 21,26:2
See My Lawyer 1939,S 28,29:1
Every Man for Himself 1940,D 10,32:3
Lily of the Valley 1942,Ja 27,25:2
Hoffman, Dean
Out of This World 1955,O 13,35:2
Out of This World 1955,N 10,44:2
Hoffman, Dustin
Journey of the Fifth Horse, The 1966,Ap 22,36:1
Journey of the Fifth Horse, The 1966,My 8,II,1:1

Eh? 1966,O 17,47:1
Eh? 1966,N 6,II,1:1
Jimmy Shine 1968,D 6,52:1
Jimmy Shine 1968,D 22,II,3:1
Hoffman, Ed
Richard III 1949,F 9,33:2
Hoffman, Elsbeth
Inside Story 1942,O 30,22:2
Hoffman, Ferdi
Judgment Day 1934,S 13,26:4
Pride and Prejudice 1935,N 6,32:4
Don't Look Now! 1936,N 4,41:3
Candle in the Wind 1941,O 23,26:2
Firebird of Florence 1945,Mr 23,13:4
Dear Judas 1947,Ag 5,26:1
Dear Judas 1947,O 6,26:4
Seventh Heaven 1955,My 27,16:2
Man Who Never Died, The 1958,N 22,27:2
Becket 1960,O 6,50:1
Becket 1961,My 9,44:1
Take Her, She's Mine 1961,D 22,19:1
And Things That Go Bump in the Night
1965,Ap 27,27:5
Investigation, The 1966,O 5,40:1
Hoffman, George
Cotton Stockings 1923,D 19,16:2
Hoffman, George (1st Lieut)
Winged Victory 1943,N 22,24:1
Hoffman, Gert (Playwright)
Willie Doesn't Live Here Anymore 1967,F 8,20:2
Let Them Down, Gently; On Vacation
1968,Ja 31,28:2
Let Them Down, Gently; Our Man in Madras
1968,Ja 31,28:2
Hoffman, Gertrude (Choreographer)
Student Prince, The 1936,Jl 12,II,5:2
Rose Marie 1936,Jl 22,22:6
Blossom Time 1936,Jl 29,23:1
My Maryland 1936,Ag 12,14:2
Hoffman, Gertrude (Miscellaneous)
Night in Spain, A 1927,My 4,28:2
Hoffman, Gertrude Girls, The
Night in Paris, A 1926,Jl 27,15:4
Hoffman, Guy
Henry V 1956,Je 20,27:2
Hoffman, Guy (Director)
Another City, Another Land 1968,O 9,42:1
Hoffman, Guy (Playwright)
Another City, Another Land 1968,O 9,42:1
Hoffman, H R
Farmer's Wife, The 1924,O 10,22:3
Hoffman, Jane
'Tis of Thee 1940,O 28,21:3
It's About Time 1942,Mr 31,28:3
One Touch of Venus 1943,O 8,14:1
Calico Wedding 1945,Mr 8,18:6
Mermaids Singing, The 1945,N 29,26:6
Temporary Island, A 1948,Mr 15,27:3
Story for Strangers, A 1948,S 22,39:2
Two Blind Mice 1949,Mr 3,32:2
Borned in Texas 1950,Ag 22,30:6
Rose Tattoo, The 1951,F 5,19:2
Crucible, The 1953,Ja 23,15:2
Crucible, The 1953,Jl 2,20:2
Good Woman of Setzuan, The 1956,D 19,41:2
Third Best Sport 1958,D 31,15:3
Sandbox, The 1960,My 17,42:2
Rhinoceros 1961,Ja 10,27:1
American Dream, The 1961,Ja 25,28:1
Mother Courage and Her Children 1963,Mr 30,5:5
American Dream, The 1963,My 29,39:6
Fair Game for Lovers 1964,F 11,43:2
Murderer Among Us, A 1964,Mr 26,43:1
Child Buyer, The 1964,D 22,35:1
Corner of the Bed, A 1969,F 27,35:2
Someone's Comin' Hungry 1969,Ap 1,51:1
American Hamburger League, The 1969,S 17,51:1
Increased Difficulty of Concentration, The
1969,D 5,48:1
Slow Memories 1970,N 18,41:1
Hoffman, Jay K (Director)
Moon Walk 1970,N 27,52:1
Hoffman, Jay K (Producer)
Pierrot's Journey 1964,Ag 5,23:1
Threepenny Opera, The 1966,O 28,33:1
Hoffman, Jerry (Producer)
Servant of Two Masters, The 1960,F 24,42:2
Hoffman, Leon
Kibbetzers, Inc 1935,My 13,18:5
Untitled-Revue 1935,S 23,20:2
We Live and Laugh 1936,My 9,10:3
Hoffman, Llora
Cinderella on Broadway 1920,Je 25,18:1
Dancing Girl, The 1923,Ja 25,16:2
Topics of 1923 1923,N 21,23:2
Artists and Models 1925,Je 25,16:2
Hoffman, Louis (Playwright)
All in Favor 1942,Ja 21,20:6
Hoffman, Max Jr
Queen O' Hearts 1922,O 11,22:1
Captain Jinks 1925,S 9,22:1
Gay Paree 1926,N 10,24:2
Sweet Adeline 1929,S 4,33:1

Hoffman, Max Jr—Cont
Ballyhoo 1930,D 23,24:1
Vaudeville (Palace) 1932,Jl 4,14:5
Shady Lady 1933,Jl 6,26:3
World's My Onion, The 1935,Je 16,X,1:8
Good Night Ladies 1945,Ja 18,16:2
Hoffman, Michael
Most Immoral Lady, A 1928,N 27,36:1
Hoffman, Nettie
Family Reunion, The 1960,D 10,26:1
Hoffman, Pamela
From the Second City 1969,O 15,34:1
Hoffman, Patricia
Anya 1965,N 30,48:1
Hoffman, Pauline
Betsy 1926,D 29,24:3
Happy Family, A 1934,S 24,15:2
Tevye the Dairyman 1935,O 25,25:1
Love for Sale 1936,Ja 24,14:2
Let's Get Married 1937,Ja 11,16:2
Mazel Tov, Rabbi 1938,N 28,10:4
Hoffman, Reba (Costume Designer)
Medea 1960,Jl 26,25:2
Hoffman, Rhoda
Best Foot Forward 1941,O 2,28:2
Hoffman, Ruth
Big Blow 1938,O 3,11:2
Hoffman, Sam
House in Berlin, A (Als der Kreig zu Ende War);
Als der Krieg zu Ende War (A House in Berlin)
1950,D 27,32:3
Hoffman, Sky
Riot 1968,D 20,64:1
Hoffman, Sylvia
We Americans 1926,O 13,20:4
Waltz of the Dogs, The 1928,Ap 26,31:3
Poppa 1928,D 25,31:1
Hoffman, Theodore
Bombo 1921,O 7,20:2
Hoffman, Theodore (Miscellaneous)
Futz 1968,Je 14,39:1
Hoffman, William
Hasty Heart, The 1959,S 15,45:2
Hoffman, William (Playwright)
Thank You, Miss Victoria 1966,Ap 12,43:1
Hoffmann, Guy
Malade Imaginaire, Le; Imaginary Invalid, The
1958,Ap 30,28:2
Mariage Force, Le; Forced Wedding, The
1958,My 7,43:1
Sganarelle; Imaginary Cuckold, The 1958,My 7,43:1
Jalousie du Barbouille, La; Jealousy of the
Barbouille, The 1958,My 7,43:1
Hoffmann, Lillian
Lulu; Earth Spirit 1970,Mr 28,32:1
Hoffmann, Michael
Amphitryon 1970,N 18,40:1
Kleinburgerhochzeit, Die 1970,N 25,25:1
Hoffmann, Paul
Maria Stuart 1968,Mr 27,38:1
Hoffmann, Ralph
Decameron, The 1961,Ap 13,32:1
Hoffmann, Richard (Dr)
County Chairman, The 1936,My 26,26:5
Hoffmann-Harnisch (Director)
All's Well That Ends Well 1928,Ap 1,IX,2:4
Komparserie 1933,Mr 19,IX,2:2
Don Juan's Raincoat 1933,O 22,IX,2:3
Hoffmeisterova, Lucie
Button, Button 1970,O 20,41:1
Hoffstein, David (Translator)
Uriel Acosta 1939,D 31,18:3
Hoffstein, Gertrude
Enemy of the People, An 1959,F 5,24:4
Hoflich, Luzie
Kabale und Liebe 1931,N 1,VIII,4:2
Hoflich, Ursula
Kabale und Liebe 1931,N 1,VIII,4:2
Hofmann, Elsbeth
Sky Drift 1945,N 14,25:2
Hofmann, Henry Frank
This Mad Whirl 1937,Ja 10,II,4:8
Hofmann, Oscar
Beggar Student, The 1921,Ja 8,9:3
Trumpeter of Sakkingen 1921,Ja 15,11:3
Hofmann, William (Scenic Designer)
Failures, The 1959,Ja 6,30:2
Hofmannsthal, Hugo von (Playwright)
Via Crucis 1923,F 11,VII,1:4
Everyman 1926,Ag 9,1:1
Rosenkavalier, Der 1927,Mr 6,VII,4:4
Everyman 1927,Ag 1,4:3
Everyman 1929,Ag 5,25:1
Electra 1930,D 27,16:1
Grosses Welttheater 1933,Ap 16,IX,2:5
Weltheater 1933,Je 25,IX,1:2
Hofstadter, Albert
Alt Heidelberg 1926,My 31,10:5
Hofstaetter, Betty
Passion Play, The 1929,Ap 30,32:1
Hogan, Alyce
Star of Bengal 1929,S 26,27:2

Hogan, C Beecher (Director)
Petrified Forest, The 1942,Ag 19,14:3
Hogan, Dan
Madam Will You Walk 1953,D 2,2:4
Don Juan in the Russian Manner 1954,Ap 23,23:2
Hogan, Dick
Winged Victory 1943,N 22,24:1
Time for Elizabeth 1948,S 28,32:3
Hogan, Dominic
Merry Wives of Windsor, The 1967,Ag 4,18:1
Hogan, Edward
Garrick Gaieties 1925,My 18,12:2
Keating 1927,D 26,26:6
Faust 1928,O 9,34:1
Cinderelative 1930,S 19,18:4
Hogan, Fran
Caucasian Chalk Circle, The 1961,N 1,35:1
Hogan, Frances
Petticoat Fever 1935,Mr 5,22:2
Hogan, James (Playwright)
Barber Had Two Sons, The 1943,F 2,22:2
Hogan, Jean
Conduct Unbecoming 1970,O 13,50:1
Hogan, Jerry
Can-Can 1959,Ag 26,25:4
Hogan, Julia
El Cristo 1926,My 9,II,1:4
Hogan, Larry
Street Singer, The 1929,S 18,35:2
Hogan, Michael
Mary Stuart 1957,O 9,39:1
Mary Stuart 1957,O 20,II,1:1
Hogan, Michael (Translator)
Betrayal 1931,Ja 25,VIII,2:7
Hogan, Richard
Richard II 1964,Je 17,47:1
Bourgeois Gentilhomme, Le 1964,Je 18,28:2
Hogan, Robert
Call Me by My Rightful Name 1961,F 1,31:1
Hogan, Robert (Director)
Love Among the Ruins 1963,My 5,85:6
Hogan, Sheila
Show Boat 1946,Ja 7,17:2
Hoganas, Les
Folies Bergere 1964,Je 3,36:1
Hogarth, Leona
Letter of the Law, The; Robe Rouge, La
1920,F 24,11:1
Meanest Man in the World, The 1920,O 13,18:2
Square Peg, A 1923,Ja 29,10:2
Steadfast 1923,O 31,12:1
Lazybones 1924,S 23,23:1
Mismates 1925,Ap 14,27:2
Holy Terror, A 1925,S 29,31:2
Joker, The 1925,N 17,29:1
Great God Brown, The 1926,Ja 25,26:1
Black Velvet 1927,S 28,28:1
King Can Do No Wrong, The 1927,N 17,28:4
Atlas and Eva 1928,F 7,30:2
Buzzard, The 1928,Mr 15,29:1
American Dream; 1849 1933,F 22,24:5
Far Away Horses 1933,Mr 22,21:6
Growing Pains 1933,N 24,24:2
Spring Freshet 1934,O 5,28:3
Hogarth, Lionel
Letter of the Law, The; Robe Rouge, La
1920,F 24,11:1
Macbeth 1921,F 18,16:1
Voltaire 1922,Mr 21,17:1
Romeo and Juliet 1923,Ja 25,16:1
Antony and Cleopatra 1924,F 20,22:1
Easy Virtue 1925,D 8,28:2
Road to Rome, The 1927,F 1,24:2
Jealous Moon, The 1928,N 21,32:2
Paolo and Francesca 1929,Ap 2,28:2
Merchant of Venice, The 1931,N 9,22:2
Richard of Bordeaux 1934,F 15,16:2
Aiglon, L' 1934,N 5,22:2
Most of the Game 1935,O 2,27:4
Richard II 1937,F 6,14:2
Richard II 1937,F 14,X,1:1
Richard II 1937,S 16,28:2
Hogg, Ian
Persecution and Assassination of Marat As
Performed by the Inmates of the Asylum of
Charenton Under the Direction of the Marquis de
Sade, The 1965,D 28,35:1
Hogo Frey's Troubadours
Blonde Sinner, The 1926,Jl 15,21:2
Hogue, Alexander (Scenic Designer)
El Cristo 1926,My 9,II,1:4
Hogue, Roland
Oh, Henry! 1920,My 6,14:2
Sky High 1925,Mr 3,21:4
Friend Indeed 1926,Ap 27,22:3
Wrecker, The 1928,F 28,18:2
Potiphar's Wife 1928,D 24,10:7
Becky Sharp 1929,Je 4,29:1
Lady Clara 1930,Ap 18,28:7
Insult 1930,S 16,30:2
Venetian, The 1931,N 2,26:1
Monkey 1932,F 12,25:2
Prelude to Exile 1936,D 1,31:1

My Dear Children 1939,Mr 25,19:6
My Dear Children 1940,F 1,16:2
Romantic Mr Dickens 1940,D 3,33:2
Rivals, The 1942,Ja 15,24:2
This Rock 1943,F 19,23:2
Hogue, William
Sunny River 1941,D 5,28:2
Heaven on Earth 1948,S 17,29:2
Happy as Larry 1950,Ja 7,11:2
Hoh, Richard Charles
Student Gypsy, The; Prince of Liederkranz, The
1963,O 1,34:1
Babes in the Wood 1964,D 29,21:2
Hohenwald, Heinz
Night of the Iguana, The 1961,D 29,10:1
Hohenwald, Heinz (Miscellaneous)
Utopia! 1963,My 7,47:4
Gogo Loves You 1964,O 10,19:2
Hohl, Arthur
Power of Darkness, The 1920,Ja 22,22:1
Martinique 1920,Ap 27,18:2
Martinique 1920,My 2,VI,2:2
Eyvind of the Hills 1921,F 2,14:1
Montmartre 1922,F 14,20:1
It Is the Law 1922,N 30,28:2
Blonde Beast, The 1923,Mr 3,9:3
Sam Abramovitch 1927,Ja 20,20:5
Wall Street 1927,Ap 21,24:4
Midsummer Night's Dream, A 1927,Je 27,25:1
Trial of Mary Dugan, The 1927,S 20,33:1
Becky Sharp 1929,Je 4,29:1
Forcing Bed, The 1929,Ag 4,VIII,1:6
Mayfair 1930,Mr 18,30:5
Twelfth Night 1930,S 14,VIII,2:8
Twelfth Night 1930,O 16,28:2
Twelfth Night 1930,N 2,VIII,1:1
Distant Drums 1932,Ja 19,24:3
Distant Drums 1932,Ja 31,VIII,1:1
Hoiby, Lee (Composer)
Duchess of Malfi, The 1957,Mr 20,33:1
Tempest, The 1960,Je 20,35:1
She Stoops to Conquer 1960,N 2,42:5
Octoroon, The 1961,Ja 28,13:1
Under Milk Wood 1961,Mr 30,25:1
Androcles and the Lion 1961,N 22,24:2
White House, The 1964,My 20,39:1
Tartuffe 1965,Ja 15,23:1
Gnadiges Fraulein, The 1966,F 23,42:1
Mutilated, The 1966,F 23,42:1
Hamlet 1968,Je 10,59:1
Hoiby, Lee (Lyricist)
Tempest, The 1960,Je 20,35:1
She Stoops to Conquer 1960,N 2,42:5
Hoiby, Lee (Miscellaneous)
Octoroon, The 1961,Ja 28,13:1
Hoier, Thomas
Merchants of Venus 1920,S 28,14:2
Hoier, Tom
Mr Peebles and Mr Hooker 1946,O 11,29:2
Sleepy Hollow 1948,Je 4,26:3
Story for Strangers, A 1948,S 22,39:2
Hoile, Edward (Playwright)
Quitter, The 1934,F 6,24:4
Hoile, Gordon (Playwright)
Quitter, The 1934,F 6,24:4
Hokanson, Hans (Scenic Designer)
Herne's Egg, The 1960,S 20,48:1
Hokanson, Mary Alan
Trio 1944,D 30,13:4
Hoke, Travis (Weather)
Kibitzer, The 1929,F 19,22:5
Holak, Emil (Scenic Designer)
I Killed the Count 1942,S 4,18:1
Mr Winkle's Holliday 1946,Je 24,27:6
Holberg, Ludwig (Playwright)
Jeppe vom Berge 1932,S 4,IX,2:1
Weathercock, The 1948,Ag 6,22:3
Holbert, Maurine
Doll's House, A 1956,My 8,29:2
Courageous One, The 1958,Ja 21,33:6
Holborn, Alfred
Dancers, The 1923,O 18,17:2
Holbrook, A A
Gentlemen, the Queen 1927,Ap 23,14:3
Holbrook, Billy
Hitchy-Koo, 1920 1920,O 20,11:3
Holbrook, Billy (Choreographer)
Burlesque 1946,D 26,30:3
Holbrook, Hal
Mark Twain Tonight! 1959,Ap 7,40:2
Mark Twain Tonight! 1959,Ap 19,II,1:1
Mark Twain Tonight! 1960,S 2,17:6
Mark Twain Tonight! 1960,N 13,1:2
Do You Know the Milky Way? 1961,O 17,45:1
Henry IV, Part I 1962,Je 18,20:4
Richard II 1962,Je 18,20:2
Henry IV, Part I 1962,Je 24,II,1:1
Richard II 1962,Je 24,II,1:1
Mark Twain Tonight! 1962,O 11,48:4
Abe Lincoln in Illinois 1963,Ja 23,5:2
After the Fall 1964,Ja 24,18:1
Marco Millions 1964,F 21,33:1
Incident at Vichy 1964,D 4,44:1

Holbrook, Hal—Cont
Incident at Vichy 1964,D 20,II,3:1
Tartuffe 1965,Ja 15,23:1
Mark Twain Tonight! 1966,Mr 24,48:2
I Never Sang for My Father 1968,Ja 26,30:1
I Never Sang for My Father 1968,F 4,II,1:1
Does a Tiger Wear a Necktie? 1969,F 26,38:1
Does a Tiger Wear a Necktie? 1969,Mr 9,II,1:1
Does a Tiger Wear a Necktie? 1969,Mr 16,II,4:5
Holbrook, Harry
Holka Polka 1925,O 15,27:2
Just a Minute 1928,O 9,34:3
Sons o' Guns 1929,N 27,30:4
Here Goes the Bride 1931,N 4,31:2
Moral Fabric 1932,N 22,25:3
Holbrook, Ruby
Front Page, The 1968,O 20,85:5
Holbrook, Walter
Richard III 1934,D 28,24:3
Winterset 1935,S 26,19:2
Parnell 1935,N 12,24:2
End of Summer 1936,Ja 31,17:1
Holbrook, Walter (Playwright)
Farewell Summer 1937,Mr 30,20:2
Holbrook, William
Blushing Bride, The 1922,F 7,12:1
Nifties of 1923 1923,S 26,10:1
Sweet Little Devil 1924,Ja 22,15:4
Vaudeville (Palace) 1927,Mr 22,31:1
Vaudeville (Palace) 1927,Ap 5,30:2
Vaudeville (Palace) 1927,My 31,25:1
A la Carte 1927,Ag 18,25:3
Vaudeville (Palace) 1927,O 4,34:3
Vaudeville (Palace) 1928,Ap 10,32:4
Ned Wayburn's Gambols 1929,Ja 16,22:3
Who Cares 1930,Jl 9,27:1
Vaudeville (Palace) 1931,Je 15,23:5
Holbrook, William (Choreographer)
Ripples 1930,F 12,26:1
Everybody's Welcome 1931,O 14,26:3
Lid's Off, The 1936,Ap 4,11:6
Roberta 1937,Je 27,II,6:1
So Proudly We Hail 1938,Ap 9,11:1
Assorted Nuts 1940,Ap 7,I,44:6
Connecticut Yankee, A 1943,N 18,30:2
Holbrook, William (Director)
Who Cares 1930,Jl 9,27:1
Hades, the Ladies 1934,Mr 29,25:3
Holbrooke, Josef (Composer)
Children of the Don, The 1923,Mr 30,14:2
Holchak, Allen V
And People All Around 1968,F 12,46:1
Holcombe, Ernest
Paul Bunyan 1941,My 6,25:1
Holcombe, Harry
Hot Corner, The 1956,Ja 26,25:2
Only in America 1959,N 20,35:1
Holcroft, Thomas (Playwright)
Road to Ruin 1937,F 12,26:2
Holden, Charles
Re-Echo 1934,Ja 12,28:4
Noah 1935,F 14,25:2
How Beautiful With Shoes 1935,N 29,24:1
Masque of the Kings, The 1937,F 9,19:4
Night Before Christmas, The 1941,Ap 11,25:2
Holden, Gloria
Long Frontier, The 1935,Jl 23,24:4
Holden, Hal
Of Thee I Sing 1969,Mr 8,19:1
Holden, James
O'Daniel 1947,F 25,32:2
Command Decision 1947,O 2,30:2
Remarkable Mr Pennypacker, The 1953,D 31,11:2
Holden, John (Director)
Sixth Finger in a Five Finger Glove 1956,O 9,31:4
Holden, Lloyd
Anybody Home 1949,F 26,10:5
Holden, Morgan
Ah, Wilderness! 1953,F 7,10:6
Infernal Machine, The 1954,Mr 22,22:2
Holden, Peter
On Borrowed Time 1938,F 4,16:4
Holden, Phyllis
Stork Is Dead, The 1932,S 24,18:2
Censored 1938,F 28,18:2
Anybody Home 1949,F 26,10:5
Holden, Phyllis (Producer)
Anybody Home 1949,F 26,10:5
Holden, Reginald
Gang War 1928,Ag 21,27:2
Holden, Ruth
Burlesque 1927,S 2,15:3
Buckaroo 1929,Mr 18,31:1
Right of Happiness 1931,Ap 3,34:2
Ah, Wilderness! 1933,O 3,28:2
Weather Permitting 1935,My 24,24:5
Prodigal Father, The 1935,Jl 2,24:2
All Editions 1936,D 23,17:2
Cross-Town 1937,Mr 18,21:5
Aries Is Rising 1939,N 22,16:5
I Killed the Count 1942,S 4,18:1
Ramshackle Inn 1944,Ja 6,17:5
Auntie Mame 1958,Ag 12,33:2

Holden, Ruth (Producer)
Marriage Is for Single People 1945,N 22,38:2
Holden, Steve (Playwright)
Now 1968,Je 6,53:1
Holden, Virginia
To Quito and Back 1937,O 7,30:4
Holden, William
Miss Lulu Bett 1920,D 28,9:1
Dreams for Sale 1922,S 14,24:1
Swifty 1922,O 17,14:1
Dew Drop Inn 1923,My 18,26:4
Nervous Wreck, The 1923,O 10,16:1
Applesauce 1925,S 29,31:2
Lovely Lady 1927,D 30,22:1
Holder, Geoffrey
House of Flowers 1954,D 31,11:2
Show Boat 1956,Je 22,16:1
Waiting for Godot 1957,Ja 22,25:1
Twelfth Night 1959,Jl 11,10:2
Josephine Baker and Her Company 1964,F 5,30:1
Holder, Geoffrey (Choreographer)
Rosalie 1957,Je 26,28:2
Holder, Geoffrey (Miscellaneous)
Brouhaha 1960,Ap 27,31:2
Holder, James
Member of the Wedding, The 1950,Ja 6,26:6
Holder, Owen
Winslow Boy, The 1947,O 30,32:2
Holderlin, Friederich (Translator)
Antigone 1968,O 11,36:1
Holding, Eileen (Costume Designer)
American Mime Theatre 1958,S 25,28:4
Holding, Thomas
Jeweled Tree, The 1926,O 8,26:2
Lady Dedlock 1929,Ja 1,61:2
Mystery Square 1929,Ap 5,28:3
Holdridge, Lee (Miscellaneous)
Joyful Noise, A 1966,D 16,57:1
By Jupiter 1967,Ja 20,28:2
Harold Arlen Songbook, The 1967,Mr 1,48:1
Education of H*Y*M*A*N K*A*P*L*A*N, The 1968,Ap 5,57:1
Hole, John
Peter Flies High 1931,N 10,28:3
Hole, Jonathan
Dr David's Dad 1924,Ag 14,10:3
57 Bowery 1928,Ja 27,14:3
Cinderelative 1930,S 19,18:4
Little Black Book, The 1932,D 27,11:2
Locked Room, The 1933,D 26,18:5
Lost Horizons 1934,O 16,31:2
Three Men on a Horse 1936,Mr 24,26:4
Holer, Tom
Suds in Your Eye 1944,Ja 13,15:5
Survivors, The 1948,Ja 20,27:2
Kiss Me, Kate 1948,D 31,10:3
Holgate, Danny (Musical Director)
Don't Bother Me, I Can't Cope 1970,O 8,60:3
Holgate, Ray
Taming of the Shrew, The 1935,O 1,27:3
Taming of the Shrew, The 1940,F 6,17:2
Holgate, Ronald
Hobo 1961,Ap 11,41:2
Funny Thing Happened on the Way to the Forum, A 1962,My 9,49:1
Hooray!! It's a Glorious Day. . .And All That 1966,Mr 10,28:1
1776 1969,Mr 17,46:2
1776 1969,Mr 23,II,1:1
Holicky, Joseph
Tavern, The 1920,S 28,14:1
Baby Cyclone, The 1927,S 13,37:4
Black Crook, The 1929,Mr 12,26:5
Constant Sinner, The 1931,S 15,30:1
Cradle Snatchers 1932,N 17,23:2
Holiday, Billie
Holiday on Broadway 1948,Ap 28,33:3
Holiday, Bob
Fiorello! 1959,N 24,45:3
It's a Bird . . . It's a Plane . . . It's Superman 1966,Mr 30,34:1
Holiday, Hope
Arabian Nights 1954,Je 25,15:2
Arabian Nights 1955,Je 24,16:1
Holiday, Joy
Arabian Nights 1967,Jl 3,12:1
Holiday, Ron
Arabian Nights 1967,Jl 3,12:1
Holiner, Mann
All Wet 1925,Jl 7,24:1
Holiner, Mann (Composer)
Gay Paree 1926,N 10,24:2
Rhapsody in Black 1931,My 5,33:2
Blackbirds 1933,D 4,22:3
Holiner, Mann (Lyricist)
Gay Paree 1926,N 10,24:2
Angela 1928,D 4,28:2
Boom Boom 1929,Ja 29,26:4
Rhapsody in Black 1931,My 5,33:2
Blackbirds 1933,D 4,22:3
Holiner, Mann (Miscellaneous)
Hey, Nonny, Nonny! 1932,Je 7,22:3

Holiner, Mann (Playwright)
Blackbirds 1933,D 4,22:3
Holl, Friedrich (Director)
Faust 1928,O 9,34:1
Trojaner 1929,My 26,IX,2:3
Holladay, Adele
Adam Solitaire 1925,N 7,19:2
Hollaender, Friedrich (Composer)
Hetaerengespraeche 1927,Ja 9,VII,4:1
Bourgeois Gentilhomme, Le 1929,Mr 24,X,2:3
Nass Oder Trocken? 1929,Jl 7,VIII,2:1
Ich Tanze um die Welt mit Dir 1930,Ag 31,VIII,2:1
Holland, Alexandra
Sweet Enemy, The 1965,F 16,39:1
Holland, Anthony
Amedee: or, How to Disentangle Yourself 1955,N 1,27:3
Venice Preserv'd 1955,D 13,54:4
Duchess of Malfi, The 1957,Mr 20,33:1
Androcles and the Lion 1958,F 22,8:3
Quare Fellow, The 1958,N 28,34:1
My Mother, My Father and Me 1963,Mr 25,5:5
Dynamite Tonight 1964,Mr 16,36:2
Victims of Duty 1964,My 28,40:2
New Tenant, The 1964,My 28,40:2
Day the Whores Came Out to Play Tennis, The 1965,Mr 16,45:1
Nathan Weinstein, Mystic, Connecticut 1966,F 26,15:2
'Tis Pity She's a Whore 1967,O 21,15:2
We Bombed in New Haven 1967,D 7,58:1
Henry IV 1968,F 7,40:1
We Bombed in New Haven 1968,O 17,51:1
White House Murder Case, The 1970,F 19,59:1
Holland, Arthur
Biff, Bing, Bang 1921,My 10,20:1
Reunion 1938,Ap 12,26:4
Out of the Frying Pan 1941,F 12,24:2
Holland, Beth
Duchess of Malfi, The 1946,O 16,35:2
Cat and the Canary, The 1965,Ja 5,26:1
Holland, Betsy
Top Banana 1951,N 2,19:2
Holland, Betty Lou
Goodbye My Fancy 1948,N 18,35:2
Devil's Disciple, The 1950,Ja 26,23:2
Picnic 1953,Ag 30,II,1:1
Six Characters in Search of an Author 1955,D 12,38:1
Six Characters in Search of an Author 1955,D 25,II,3:1
White Rose and the Red, The 1964,Mr 17,31:1
Good Day 1965,O 19,51:1
Holland, Charles
Jeb 1946,F 22,20:2
Wedding in Japan 1957,Mr 12,37:7
Holland, Clinton
Sweet River 1936,O 29,30:2
Holland, Edna
Mandarin, The 1920,N 10,18:2
Warrior's Husband, The 1932,Mr 12,19:4
Moral Fabric 1932,N 22,25:3
Post Road 1934,D 5,28:3
Dear Old Darling 1936,Mr 3,25:1
Fulton of Oak Falls 1937,Ja 2,15:3
Fulton of Oak Falls 1937,F 11,18:2
Lorelei 1938,N 30,21:2
Holland, Edward T
Holy Terror, A 1925,S 29,31:2
Holland, Edwin
Sweet Nell of Old Drury 1923,My 19,16:4
Holland, Gilbert
Rang Tang 1927,Jl 13,20:1
Keep Shufflin' 1928,F 28,18:3
Great Day! 1929,Je 9,VIII,1:2
Holland, Gladys
Sixth Finger in a Five Finger Glove 1956,O 9,31:4
Fools Are Passing Through 1958,Ap 3,24:2
Don Juan in Hell 1960,O 4,47:3
Holland, J Talbot
Macbeth 1955,O 8,12:6
Last Love of Don Juan, The 1955,N 24,40:1
Ponder Heart, The 1956,F 17,14:2
Marvellous History of Saint Bernard, The 1958,F 24,16:3
Blood, Sweat & Stanley Poole 1961,O 6,31:1
Holland, Jack
Vaudeville (Palace) 1929,N 11,20:5
Streamline 1934,O 21,IX,1:3
Laughter Over Broadway 1939,Ja 16,10:3
Holland, James Buchanan
This Mad Whirl 1937,Ja 10,II,4:8
Holland, Joseph
Romeo and Juliet 1934,D 21,30:3
Othello 1935,S 28,13:2
Macbeth 1935,O 8,26:4
Parnell 1935,N 12,24:2
Saint Joan 1936,Mr 10,27:4
Hamlet 1936,O 20,31:3
Hamlet 1936,N 11,54:2
Masque of Kings, The 1937,Ja 31,XI,2:1
Masque of the Kings, The 1937,F 9,19:4
Julius Caesar 1937,N 12,26:6

Holland, Joseph—Cont
Clean Beds 1939,My 26,21:2
Swingin' the Dream 1939,N 30,24:2
White Plume, The 1939,D 27,16:1
Contrast, The 1940,Mr 26,17:2
Elizabeth the Queen 1941,O 17,27:2
Antony and Cleopatra 1947,N 27,49:2
Show-Off, The 1950,Je 1,24:5
Julius Caesar 1950,Je 21,30:1
Coriolanus 1954,Ja 20,34:2
Bad Seed, The 1954,D 9,42:1
Great Sebastians, The 1956,Ja 5,27:1
Small War on Murray Hill 1957,Ja 4,19:1
Small War on Murray Hill 1957,Ja 13,II,1:1
Holland, Lee K (Producer)
Bathsheba 1947,Mr 27,40:2
Holland, Leland
Jotham Valley 1951,F 7,37:2
Holland, Maurice
Love Dreams 1921,O 11,22:2
Marjolaine 1922,Ja 25,16:1
Sue, Dear 1922,Jl 11,16:2
June Days 1925,Ag 7,12:5
Sunny Days 1928,F 9,29:1
White Lilacs 1928,S 11,31:2
Count of Luxembourg, The 1930,F 18,28:2
Holland, Mildred
Tales of Rigo 1927,My 31,25:3
Holland, Norman (Playwright)
Years of the Locusts 1968,Ag 23,32:1
Holland, Paul (Lighting Director)
Americana Pastoral 1968,D 11,51:1
Tango 1969,Ja 20,33:1
Holland, Paul (Miscellaneous)
Adaptation 1969,F 11,27:1
Next 1969,F 11,27:1
And I Met a Man 1970,Ap 11,20:3
Holland, Ralph
Censored 1938,F 28,18:2
Holland, Roy
Horse Play 1937,Ag 28,8:3
Holland, Tom
Billy Budd 1955,My 4,35:1
Typewriter, The 1955,Jl 29,8:3
Lovers, Villains and Fools: A Shakespearean Variety Show 1956,O 24,44:7
Hollander, Anna
All in a Lifetime 1934,Ap 2,12:5
Verdict, The 1934,S 22,12:5
Parnosseh 1935,F 16,8:8
God Man and Devil 1935,Mr 6,22:3
Motke Ganef 1935,Mr 18,15:2
Sappho 1935,Mr 22,26:4
Hollander, Hannah
In-Laws 1934,O 25,28:2
Jealousy 1934,D 20,31:4
Matinee Wife 1936,Ap 25,21:3
Hollander, Isidore
All in a Lifetime 1934,Ap 2,12:5
Verdict, The 1934,S 22,12:5
In-Laws 1934,O 25,28:2
Jealousy 1934,D 20,31:4
60,000 Heroes 1935,Ja 28,11:5
Parnosseh 1935,F 16,8:8
God Man and Devil 1935,Mr 6,22:3
Power That Builds, The 1935,Mr 9,18:4
Hollander, Jack
Have You Heard This One 1953,N 9,23:4
Dybbuk, The 1954,O 27,33:6
Anna Christie 1955,N 22,41:1
Girl of the Golden West, The 1957,N 6,44:1
Journey to the Day 1963,N 12,49:1
Impossible Years, The 1965,O 14,55:1
Comedy of Errors, The 1967,Je 15,58:4
Titus Andronicus 1967,Ag 10,43:2
Ergo 1968,Mr 4,29:1
Man in the Glass Booth, The 1968,S 27,41:1
Inquest 1970,Ap 24,38:1
Hollander, Jean
39 Steps 1938,Mr 12,13:1
Hollander, Owen
Scarlet Lullaby 1968,Mr 11,48:1
Hollander, Victor (Composer)
Hochste Eisenbahn 1932,O 23,IX,3:1
Hollander, Victor (Lyricist)
Hochste Eisenbahn 1932,O 23,IX,3:1
Hollander, Victor (Producer)
Hochste Eisenbahn 1932,O 23,IX,3:1
Hollar, Lloyd
Tiger at the Gates 1968,Mr 1,30:1
Ordinary Man, An 1968,S 10,39:1
Pequod 1969,Je 30,33:1
Holleman, Ed
I Feel Wonderful 1954,O 19,22:5
Hollenbeck, D W
Tiger Smiles, The 1930,D 18,29:1
Hollenbeck, J F
Tiger Smiles, The 1930,D 18,29:1
Hollenbeck, William
Up the Rebels 1941,O 31,21:1
Hollerith, Charles Jr (Producer)
Rape of the Belt, The 1960,N 7,46:1
Amorous Flea, The 1964,F 18,26:1
How's the World Treating You? 1966,O 25,50:1

Holles, Antony
Diplomacy 1928,My 29,16:3
Diplomacy 1928,Je 3,VIII,1:1
Sorry You've Been Troubled 1929,O 13,IX,4:1
Holley, Bertha
Bunch and Judy, The 1922,N 29,20:1
Holley, Jean
Nina Rosa 1930,My 31,19:3
Holley, R E
Birthright 1933,N 22,22:3
Holley, Robert Bruce (Miscellaneous)
Beautiful Dreamer 1960,D 28,22:1
Holley, Robert M (Miscellaneous)
Sound of Silence, A 1965,Mr 9,30:1
Hollicky, James
Nine Pine Street 1933,Ap 28,15:5
Hollicky, Joseph M
Paid 1925,N 26,32:1
Holliday, David
No Strings 1964,Ja 1,17:1
Man of La Mancha 1969,My 3,38:4
Coco 1969,D 19,66:1
Holliday, Harry
Legend of Leonora, The 1927,Mr 30,22:4
Holliday, Judy
Kiss Them for Me 1945,Mr 21,27:2
Kiss Them for Me 1945,Mr 25,II,1:1
Born Yesterday 1946,F 5,18:2
Born Yesterday 1946,F 10,II,1:1
Born Yesterday 1947,My 18,II,1:1
Dream Girl 1951,My 10,39:1
Bells Are Ringing 1956,N 29,43:4
Bells Are Ringing 1956,N 30,18:2
Bells Are Ringing 1956,D 16,II,3:1
Hot Spot 1963,Ap 20,17:2
Holliday, Mark
Athenian Touch, The 1964,Ja 15,25:4
Hollinghead, John (Miscellaneous)
Verdict, The 1958,My 24,19:8
Hollingsworth, Dossie
California 1953,Je 18,38:5
Where There's a Will 1953,Je 18,38:5
Hopalong--Freud 1953,Je 18,38:5
Brandy Is My True Love's Name 1953,Je 18,38:5
Three by Thurber; Middle Years, The
1955,Mr 8,23:2
Hollingsworth, Indus
New Faces of 1936 1936,My 20,24:5
Hollins, Frank
Genius and the Crowd 1920,S 7,20:1
Young Visitors, The 1920,N 30,14:1
Squaw Man, The 1921,D 27,10:3
Madeleine and the Movies 1922,Mr 7,11:1
Masked Woman, The 1922,D 23,14:2
Hollis, Alan
Vortex, The 1925,S 17,20:1
Enchantment 1927,Ap 28,27:3
Hollis, Marjorie
Sophie 1920,Mr 3,12:2
Kiss of Importance, A 1930,D 2,31:3
Wooden Slipper, The 1934,Ja 4,16:3
Hollister, David (Miscellaneous)
Lend an Ear 1959,S 25,20:5
Miss Emily Adam 1960,Mr 30,43:1
Tattooed Countess, The 1961,My 4,40:2
Hollister, J J Jr
Who's Who 1924,Ap 18,19:2
Hollister, Len D
Back Seat Drivers 1928,D 26,14:4
This Man's Town 1930,Mr 11,24:4
Bulls, Bears and Asses 1932,My 7,11:3
Granite 1936,Ja 14,24:6
Return of the Vagabond, The 1940,My 14,27:2
Life of Reilly, The 1942,Ap 30,13:2
Decision 1944,F 3,23:2
Decision 1944,F 13,II,1:1
Sleep No More 1944,S 1,11:5
Violet 1944,O 25,16:1
Hollister, Len D (Director)
Back Seat Drivers 1928,D 26,14:4
Hollister, Len D (Playwright)
Morning After, The 1925,Jl 28,24:2
House Unguarded 1928,D 30,VIII,1:6
House Unguarded 1929,Ja 16,22:2
Hollister, Leona
Come-On Man, The 1929,Ap 23,26:2
Hollister, Louis
Lamp at Midnight 1947,D 22,29:2
Blood Wedding 1949,F 7,16:2
Sun and I, The 1949,Mr 21,18:4
She Stoops to Conquer 1949,D 29,21:3
Corn Is Green, The 1950,Ja 12,33:2
Devil's Disciple, The 1950,Ja 26,23:2
Hollister, Margery
Tonight We Improvise 1959,N 7,27:4
Hollmann, Gene
Maggie 1953,F 19,20:2
Hollmann, Sonya
People vs Ranchman, The 1968,O 28,56:1
Hollo, Anslem (Translator)
Jungle of Cities 1970,Mr 1,75:2
Holloman, Charlotte
Barrier, The 1950,N 3,32:2

Holloway, Baliol
Othello 1925,Ja 12,11:1
Doctor's Dilemma, The 1927,N 22,33:1
Marco Millions 1928,Ja 10,28:2
Devil and the Lady, The 1930,Ag 10,VIII,1:3
Richard III 1930,S 21,IX,2:1
Measure for Measure 1931,Ag 9,VIII,1:3
Julius Caesar 1932,F 9,30:7
Emperor of Make-Believe, The 1936,Mr 17,25:5
Love's Labour's Lost 1949,O 24,18:3
Holloway, Fred
Gold 1921,Je 2,14:2
Seventh Heaven 1922,O 31,11:1
Blue and the Gray, The; War Is Hell Gray, The
1929,D 27,26:4
Holloway, Joan
Shangri-La 1956,Je 14,40:1
Holloway, Julian
Spitting Image 1968,S 11,42:1
Holloway, Robert
Out of This World 1955,N 10,44:2
Holloway, Stanley
All Wave 1936,N 25,18:3
Midsummer Night's Dream, A 1954,S 22,33:1
My Fair Lady 1956,Mr 16,20:2
My Fair Lady 1956,Mr 25,II,1:1
My Fair Lady 1956,Ap 29,II,17:1
My Fair Lady 1956,Je 3,II,1:1
My Fair Lady 1958,My 1,34:5
Laughs and Other Events 1960,O 11,57:1
Holloway, Sterling
Evil Doers of Good, The 1923,Ja 17,22:2
Failures, The 1923,N 23,20:1
Roseanne 1923,D 31,9:5
Fata Morgana 1924,Mr 4,16:3
Garrick Gaieties 1925,My 18,12:2
Garrick Gaieties 1926,My 11,25:2
Get Me in the Movies 1928,My 22,18:3
Shoestring Revue 1929,N 23,19:2
Garrick Gaieties 1930,Je 5,29:2
Garrick Gaieties 1930,O 17,21:2
Midsummer Night's Dream, A 1934,S 19,15:1
Grass Harp, The 1952,Mr 28,26:2
Holloway, Sterling (Director)
Desert Song, The 1946,Ja 9,20:2
Holloway, Sterling (Lyricist)
Garrick Gaieties 1930,Je 5,29:2
Holloway, Sterling (Playwright)
Garrick Gaieties 1930,Je 5,29:2
Holloway, W E
Hamlet 1931,Ap 24,26:4
Holloway Sisters
Hilarities 1948,S 10,20:2
Holly, Charles Vaughn
Vagabond King, The 1925,S 22,23:3
Holly, Ellen
2 for Fun; Anniversary, The 1955,My 26,34:1
2 for Fun; Switch in Time, A 1955,My 26,34:1
Too Late the Phalarope 1956,O 12,35:1
Tevya and His Daughters 1957,S 17,38:2
Othello 1958,Jl 4,16:1
Face of a Hero 1960,O 21,29:5
Moon on a Rainbow Shawl 1962,Ja 16,30:1
Tiger Tiger Burning Bright 1962,D 24,5:2
Antony and Cleopatra 1963,Je 21,33:1
Funnyhouse of a Negro 1964,Ja 15,25:3
Midsummer Night's Dream, A 1964,Je 30,23:2
Henry V 1965,Je 29,27:2
Taming of the Shrew, The 1965,Jl 3,10:5
Macbeth 1966,Je 29,38:1
Macbeth 1966,Jl 14,27:2
Hand Is on the Gate, A 1966,S 22,54:1
John Brown's Body 1968,F 13,49:2
Comedy of Errors, The 1968,F 28,40:2
Holly, Ernest
But Never Jam Today 1969,Ap 24,40:1
Holly, Karl
Knights of Song 1938,O 18,29:2
Devil and Daniel Webster, The 1939,My 19,26:1
Holly, William
Back Here 1928,N 27,36:3
Solitaire 1929,Mr 13,28:3
Hollywood, Daniel (Producer)
Andersonville Trial, The 1959,D 30,15:1
Never Too Late 1962,N 28,42:1
Hollywood, Miss
International Playgirls '64 1964,My 22,40:2
Holm, Cecil
Whirlpool 1929,D 4,37:3
Penal Law 2010 1930,Ap 19,14:2
Bloodstream 1932,Mr 31,25:1
Dangerous Corner 1932,O 28,23:1
Mary of Scotland 1933,N 28,28:3
Holm, Celeste
Mad Morning 1935,Je 25,14:1
Gloriana 1938,N 26,18:4
Time of Your Life, The 1939,O 26,26:2
Another Sun 1940,F 24,8:6
Return of the Vagabond, The 1940,My 14,27:2
Time of Your Life, The 1940,S 24,27:2
Eight O'Clock Tuesday 1941,Ja 7,18:2
My Fair Ladies 1941,Mr 24,12:7
Papa Is All 1942,Ja 7,22:2

Holm, Celeste—Cont
Papa Is All 1942,Ja 18,IX,1:1
All the Comforts of Home 1942,My 26,24:5
Damask Cheek, The 1942,O 23,24:2
Oklahoma! 1943,Ap 1,27:1
Oklahoma! 1943,Ap 11,II,1:1
Bloomer Girl 1944,O 6,18:5
Bloomer Girl 1944,O 8,II,1:1
She Stoops to Conquer 1949,D 29,21:3
Affairs of State 1950,S 26,37:2
Affairs of State 1950,O 1,II,1:1
Oklahoma! 1951,S 13,38:2
Anna Christie 1952,Ja 10,33:1
Anna Christie 1952,Ja 20,II,1:1
His and Hers 1954,Ja 8,18:2
Interlock 1958,F 7,18:1
Third Best Sport 1958,D 31,15:3
Glimpse of the Domesticity of Franklyn Barnabas,
A 1960,Mr 7,24:2
Invitation to a March 1960,O 31,27:2
Month in the Country, A 1963,My 29,39:2
Mame 1967,Ag 15,31:2
Candida 1970,Ap 7,41:1
Holm, Eleanor
Aquacade 1939,My 5,26:2
New Aquacade Revue, The 1940,My 13,20:5
Holm, Gustav (Original Author)
Cissy 1932,D 24,10:5
Holm, Hanya (Choreographer)
Insect Comedy, The 1948,Je 4,26:3
E-MC2 1948,Je 16,36:2
Kiss Me, Kate 1948,D 31,10:3
Kiss Me, Kate 1949,Ja 30,II,6:5
Blood Wedding 1949,F 7,16:2
Out of This World 1950,D 22,17:3
Kiss Me, Kate 1952,Ja 9,24:6
My Darlin' Aida 1952,O 28,36:4
Golden Apple, The 1954,Mr 12,15:2
Golden Apple, The 1954,Mr 21,II,1:1
My Fair Lady 1956,Mr 16,20:2
My Fair Lady 1956,Mr 25,II,1:1
My Fair Lady 1956,Ap 29,II,17:1
Kiss Me, Kate 1956,My 10,27:2
My Fair Lady 1956,Je 3,II,1:1
My Fair Lady 1958,Mr 9,II,1:1
Christine 1960,Ap 29,27:1
Camelot 1960,D 5,42:1
Camelot 1960,D 11,II,5:1
My Fair Lady 1964,My 21,43:2
Kiss Me, Kate 1965,My 13,31:1
Anya 1965,N 30,48:1
My Fair Lady 1968,Je 14,42:1
Holm, Hanya (Miscellaneous)
Liar, The 1950,My 19,30:2
Holm, Ian
Midsummer Night's Dream, A 1962,Ap 18,30:3
Tempest, The 1963,Ap 3,43:1
Richard III 1963,Ag 21,37:5
Homecoming, The 1967,Ja 6,29:1
Friends, The 1970,My 22,41:2
Bequest to the Nation, A 1970,S 25,36:1
Holm, Jan (Costume Designer)
Frankie and Johnny 1952,O 29,37:2
Holm, John Cecil
Joan of Arkansas 1925,Ap 5,16:1
Mighty Man Is He, A 1960,Ja 7,25:2
Midgie Purvis 1961,F 2,25:3
Mr President 1962,O 22,34:2
Advocate, The 1963,O 15,46:7
Her Master's Voice 1964,D 28,33:2
Philadelphia, Here I Come! 1966,F 17,28:1
South Pacific 1968,Je 30,54:2
Forty Carats 1968,D 27,45:1
Forty Carats 1969,Ja 5,II,1:3
Holm, John Cecil (Director)
Three Men on a Horse 1942,O 10,10:2
Holm, John Cecil (Miscellaneous)
Sweethearts 1947,Ja 22,31:2
Holm, John Cecil (Original Author)
Best Foot Forward 1941,O 2,28:2
Banjo Eyes 1941,N 8,10:6
Banjo Eyes 1941,D 26,20:2
Let It Ride 1961,O 13,27:4
Holm, John Cecil (Playwright)
Three Men on a Horse 1935,Ja 22,22:7
Three Men on a Horse 1935,Ja 31,22:3
Best Foot Forward 1941,O 26,IX,1:3
Banjo Eyes 1941,N 8,10:6
Three Men on a Horse 1942,O 10,10:2
Brighten the Corner 1945,D 13,33:2
Gramercy Ghost 1951,Ap 27,20:2
Southwest Corner, The 1955,F 4,18:2
Southwest Corner, The 1955,F 13,II,1:1
Best Foot Forward 1956,Mr 3,16:1
Best Foot Forward 1963,Ap 3,43:1
Three Men on a Horse 1969,O 17,35:1
Holm, Jorg
Ratten, Die 1966,Ap 13,36:1
Holm, Klaus (Lighting Director)
Golden Apple, The 1954,Mr 12,15:2
Girl on the Via Flaminia, The 1954,Ap 6,35:5
Sea Gull, The 1954,My 12,38:1
Sing Me No Lullaby 1954,O 15,17:2
Doctor's Dilemma, The 1955,Ja 12,22:1

Holm, Klaus (Lighting Director)—Cont

Phoenix '55 1955,Ap 25,20:2
Ronde, La 1955,Je 28,24:2
Carefree Tree, The 1955,O 12,37:2
Miss Julie 1956,F 22,23:2
Stronger, The 1956,F 22,23:2
Month in the Country, A 1956,Ap 4,23:1
Littlest Revue, The 1956,My 23,37:2
Saint Joan 1956,S 12,42:1
Diary of a Scoundrel 1956,N 5,41:1
Good Woman of Setzuan, The 1956,D 19,41:2
Livin' the Life 1957,Ap 29,20:1
Power and the Glory, The 1958,D 12,2:7
Semi-Detached 1960,Mr 11,20:2
King and I, The 1960,My 12,40:1
Advise and Consent 1960,N 18,25:1
Once There Was a Russian 1961,F 20,32:2
Donnybrook! 1961,My 19,23:1
Something About a Soldier 1962,Ja 5,36:2
Moby Dick 1962,N 29,45:1
Heroine, The 1963,F 21,5:5
Too Much Johnson 1964,Ja 16,29:1
Wait a Minim! 1966,Mr 8,43:1

Holm, Klaus (Miscellaneous)

Private Ear, The 1963,O 10,51:1
Public Eye, The 1963,O 10,51:1
Oh What a Lovely War 1964,O 1,30:1

Holm, Klaus (Scenic Designer)

Girl on the Via Flaminia, The 1954,Ap 6,35:5
Doctor's Dilemma, The 1955,Ja 12,22:1
Six Characters in Search of an Author
 1955,D 12,38:1
Six Characters in Search of an Author
 1955,D 25,II,3:1
Stronger, The 1956,F 22,23:2
Miss Julie 1956,F 22,23:2
Month in the Country, A 1956,Ap 4,23:1
Month in the Country, A 1956,Ap 15,II,1:1
Littlest Revue, The 1956,My 23,37:2
Saint Joan 1956,S 12,42:1
Diary of a Scoundrel 1956,N 5,41:1

Holman, Byco

Amorous Flea, The 1964,F 18,26:1

Holman, Elizabeth

Sapphire Ring, The 1925,Ap 16,25:2
Garrick Gaieties 1925,My 18,12:2

Holman, Frank

Macbeth 1928,N 20,28:3

Holman, Irene

East of Broadway 1932,Ja 27,19:3

Holman, Libby

Merry-Go-Round 1927,Je 1,25:4
Rainbow 1928,N 22,25:1
Rainbow 1928,D 16,IX,1:1
Ned Wayburn's Gambols 1929,Ja 16,22:3
Little Show, The 1929,My 1,28:5
Three's a Crowd 1930,O 5,IX,4:6
Three's a Crowd 1930,O 16,28:3
Three's a Crowd 1930,O 26,VIII,1:1
Revenge With Music 1934,N 29,33:5
Accent on Youth 1935,Jl 2,24:3
Silver Box, The 1935,Jl 16,24:2
You Never Know 1938,Mr 4,16:3
You Never Know 1938,S 22,26:3
Mexican Mural; Miracle Painting 1942,Ap 27,19:2
Blues, Ballads and Sin-Songs 1954,O 5,23:4

Holman, Lola

But Never Jam Today 1969,Ap 24,40:1

Holman, Martin (Producer)

Pygmalion 1947,F 6,29:4

Holman, Sandra

Rich Full Life, The 1945,N 10,9:2

Holman, Vincent

Havoc 1924,S 2,22:2

Holman, Vinnie

Make Me Disappear 1969,My 14,34:1

Holme, Stanford

Much Ado About Nothing 1929,N 17,30:4

Holme, Thea

Much Ado About Nothing 1929,N 17,30:4
Hassan 1931,Mr 8,VIII,2:6
Those Naughty Nineties 1931,S 13,IX,2:7

Holme, Thea (Playwright)

Roman Holiday 1937,Ap 14,31:5

Holmes, Ben

Gay Paree 1926,N 10,24:2

Holmes, Bertram

Macbeth 1936,Ap 15,25:4
Case of Philip Lawrence, The 1937,Je 9,31:1
Brown Sugar 1937,D 3,29:2
Big White Fog 1940,O 23,26:2

Holmes, Buddy

Anna Lucasta 1944,Je 17,10:1

Holmes, Carleton (Producer)

Free for All 1947,S 18,28:2

Holmes, Denis

Richard II 1956,O 24,44:1
Romeo and Juliet 1956,O 25,41:1
Macbeth 1956,O 30,42:2
Troilus and Cressida 1956,D 27,21:1

Holmes, Derby

All-Star Jamboree 1921,Jl 14,18:1

Holmes, Edward

Richard III 1953,Jl 15,22:2

Measure for Measure 1954,Je 30,23:1
Taming of the Shrew, The 1954,Jl 1,22:2
Merchant of Venice, The 1955,Jl 1,13:1
Henry VIII 1961,Je 22,22:1
Gideon 1961,N 10,38:1
Dinner at Eight 1966,S 28,38:1

Holmes, Frank

Bombo 1921,O 7,20:2

Holmes, George

Sunny River 1941,D 5,28:2

Holmes, Harry

Vaudeville (Palace) 1926,My 11,25:3

Holmes, Helen

That Day 1922,O 4,27:3
Devil Within, The 1925,Mr 17,19:4
Vaudeville (Palace) 1926,S 21,32:5
Dorian Gray 1928,My 22,18:4
Adam's Apple 1929,Je 11,27:5
Love Expert, The 1929,S 24,29:1
Short Cut, The 1930,Ja 28,28:2
This Our House 1935,D 12,33:3

Holmes, J Merrill

What Price Glory 1924,S 6,14:3
First Flight 1925,S 18,26:2
Diamond Lil 1928,Ap 10,32:1

Holmes, Jack (Choreographer)

New Faces of 1962 1962,F 2,25:1

Holmes, Jack (Composer)

From A to Z 1960,Ap 21,23:2
New Faces of 1962 1962,F 2,25:1
Cats' Pajamas, The 1962,Je 1,16:2
O Say Can You See! 1962,O 9,45:1

Holmes, Jack (Lyricist)

New Faces of 1962 1962,F 2,25:1
Cats' Pajamas, The 1962,Je 1,16:2

Holmes, Jack (Miscellaneous)

From A to Z 1960,Ap 21,23:2

Holmes, Jack (Musical Director)

O Say Can You See! 1962,O 9,45:1
Streets of New York, The 1963,O 30,47:1
Dames at Sea 1970,Ja 5,46:3
Whispers on the Wind 1970,Je 4,50:1

Holmes, Jerry

Harold Arlen Songbook, The 1967,Mr 1,48:1

Holmes, John

Hamlet 1931,N 6,28:4

Holmes, John Haynes (Playwright)

If This Be Treason 1935,Jl 30,17:1
If This Be Treason 1935,S 24,28:2
If This Be Treason 1935,S 29,X,1:1

Holmes, Lana

Good Night Ladies 1945,Ja 18,16:2

Holmes, Lois

Cherry Orchard, The 1944,Ja 26,22:1
Autumn Garden, The 1951,Mr 8,36:2
I've Got Sixpence 1952,D 3,44:2
Lark, The 1955,N 18,20:1
Easter 1957,Ja 17,35:2
Winesburg, Ohio 1958,F 6,22:2
Journey With Strangers, A 1958,N 27,53:1
Enemy of the People, An 1959,F 5,24:4
Hedda Gabler 1960,N 10,61:1
Curate's Play, The 1961,D 18,41:3
Hooray!! It's a Glorious Day. . .And All That
 1966,Mr 10,28:1
Penny Wars, The 1969,O 16,52:1

Holmes, Madeleine

Reflected Glory 1936,S 18,19:5
Reflected Glory 1936,S 22,30:2
My Romance 1948,O 20,38:5

Holmes, Mary

Head or Tail 1926,N 10,24:1

Holmes, Mary Elsie

Vagabond King, The 1935,N 29,22:7

Holmes, Maurine

Show Boat 1932,My 20,22:2

Holmes, Maynard

Cradle Will Rock, The 1938,Ja 4,19:3

Holmes, Michael

Rosencrantz and Guildenstern Are Dead
 1967,O 17,53:1

Holmes, Michael (Director)

Make Me Disappear 1969,My 14,34:1

Holmes, Millicent

Change Your Luck 1930,Je 7,10:2
Vagabond King, The 1935,N 29,22:7

Holmes, Mozelle

Conjur' Man Dies 1936,Mr 12,18:5

Holmes, Peggy

Banjo Eyes 1941,D 26,20:2
Dark of the Moon 1945,Mr 15,27:2

Holmes, Peter

Gentlemen Prefer Blondes 1949,D 9,35:3

Holmes, Philip R

Napoleon Passes 1927,D 21,29:2

Holmes, Price

Chalked Out 1937,Mr 26,24:2

Holmes, Ralph

Lady Detained, A 1935,Ja 10,23:3
You Can't Take It With You 1936,D 15,31:1
Thanks for Tomorrow 1938,S 28,28:2
Where Do We Go From Here? 1938,N 16,26:2
Day in the Sun 1939,My 17,29:2

Holmes, Ralph—Cont

Yokel Boy 1939,Jl 7,12:2

Holmes, Ralph (Lighting Director)

General Seeger 1962,Mr 1,26:2

Holmes, Rapley

Charm School, The 1920,Ag 3,12:1
Right Girl, The 1921,Mr 16,12:1
Wait Till We're Married 1921,S 27,14:1
Rose of Stamboul, The 1922,Mr 8,11:2
I Will IF You Will 1922,Ag 30,10:4
Rain 1922,N 8,18:2
Rain 1926,O 12,27:1

Holmes, Robert

Sorry You've Been Troubled 1929,O 13,IX,4:1
Frailties 1931,Ja 30,18:3
Second Shot, The 1937,Ap 20,28:4
Trial of Dr Beck, The 1937,Ag 10,22:2

Holmes, Roy (Lighting Director)

Meet the People 1940,D 26,22:2

Holmes, Steven (Miscellaneous)

Go Fly a Kite! 1969,O 20,60:1

Holmes, Steven (Scenic Designer)

From the Second City 1969,O 15,34:1

Holmes, Taylor

Crooked Gamblers 1920,Ag 2,12:1
Hotel Mouse, The 1922,Mr 14,11:3
Not so Fast 1923,My 23,18:4
Happy-Go-Lucky 1926,O 1,27:2
Vaudeville (Palace) 1926,D 28,12:3
Vaudeville (Palace) 1928,Ja 17,23:3
Great Necker, The 1928,Mr 7,28:2
Joy of Living 1931,Ap 7,31:1
Cold in Sables 1931,D 24,20:7
New York to Cherbourg 1932,F 20,11:4
Lambs Gambol 1932,Ap 25,18:2
That's Gratitude 1932,Je 17,24:3
Riddle Me This! 1933,Mr 15,21:3
Say When 1934,N 9,24:2
It's You I Want 1935,F 6,23:3
I'd Rather Be Right 1937,N 3,28:2
I'd Rather Be Right 1939,F 21,15:4
Day in the Sun 1939,My 17,29:2
First Stop to Heaven 1941,Ja 6,10:7
Boudoir 1941,F 8,18:4
What Big Ears! 1942,Ap 21,18:5
Vickie 1942,S 23,28:1
Marinka 1945,Jl 19,19:2
Woman Bites Dog 1946,Ap 18,21:2

Holmes, Terry

Manhattan Nocturne 1943,O 27,26:2

Holmes, Tracy

Bitter Sweet 1929,N 6,30:2
Man in Possession, The 1930,N 3,19:1

Holmes, Virginia

Here Comes Santa Claus 1962,My 18,34:1

Holmes, Wendell

Respectful Prostitute, The 1948,F 10,27:2
Respectful Prostitute, The 1948,F 15,II,1:1
Bruno and Sidney 1949,My 4,38:2
Mrs Warren's Profession 1950,O 26,39:2

Holmes, Wyman

Kiss the Boys Goodbye 1938,S 29,30:2
Days of Our Youth, The 1941,N 29,15:2
Savonarola 1942,Ap 24,20:2

Holmes-Gore, Dorothy

Little Eyolf 1930,N 2,VIII,2:6

Holmes-Gow, Miss

Apple Cart, The 1929,Ag 20,30:2

Holmroos, Eero

Betrothal, The 1959,F 16,52:2

Holms, John P (Miscellaneous)

Alice in Wonderland 1970,O 9,43:1

Holms, Karl

Mistress of the House, The 1950,Ja 31,19:1

Holmstrom, John (Playwright)

Caucasian Chalk Circle, The 1961,N 1,35:1

Holmstrom, John (Translator)

Caucasian Chalk Circle, The 1962,Mr 30,28:1

Holofcener, Lawrence (Composer)

Mr Wonderful 1956,Mr 23,23:2

Holofcener, Lawrence (Lyricist)

Mr Wonderful 1956,Mr 23,23:2

Holofcener, Lawrence (Playwright)

Before You Go 1968,Ja 12,20:1
Before You Go 1969,Ap 9,51:1
Shepherd of Avenue B, The 1970,My 16,30:1

Hololka, Oskar

Faust 1932,Je 19,IX,1:3

Holse, Glenn (Scenic Designer)

Billy Barnes Revue, The 1959,Je 10,42:2
Eddie Fisher at the Winter Garden 1962,O 3,47:1
Ice Capades 1966,Je 2,50:2
Ice Capades 1967,Je 2,33:1
Holiday on Ice 1967,Ag 31,29:2
Holiday on Ice 1968,Ag 29,44:1
Holiday on Ice 1969,Ag 28,44:1

Holsman, Mary

Devil in the Mind 1931,My 2,23:2
One Sunday Afternoon 1933,F 16,23:5
Night Remembers, The 1934,N 28,24:3
Postman Always Rings Twice, The 1936,F 26,17:2
Lend Me Your Ears! 1936,O 6,28:5

Holst, Gustav (Composer)

Coming of Christ, The 1928,My 29,6:2

Holst, Gustav (Composer)—Cont
  Coming of Christ, The 1957,D 23,29:8
Holsten, Harry
  Long Watch, The 1952,Mr 21,19:5
  Winkelberg 1958,Ja 15,26:2
Holt, Alexander
  Susannah and the Elders 1959,O 19,37:3
Holt, Calvin
  Infernal Machine, The 1954,Mr 22,22:2
  Catch a Star! 1955,S 7,35:2
Holt, Charles
  Antony and Cleopatra 1947,N 27,49:2
  Uniform of Flesh 1949,Ja 31,15:2
Holt, Chifra
  Merry-Go-Rounders, The 1956,N 22,50:1
Holt, Christ
  Veils 1928,Mr 14,28:5
Holt, E
  Vaudeville (Palace) 1926,Je 1,29:5
Holt, Ethelyne
  Red, Hot and Blue! 1936,O 30,26:3
  Merry Widow, The 1943,Ag 5,19:2
Holt, Fritz (Miscellaneous)
  By Jupiter 1967,Ja 20,28:2
Holt, Helen
  Wake Up, Jonathan 1921,Ja 18,14:1
Holt, Henry (Composer)
  As You Like It 1941,O 21,29:2
Holt, Henry (Playwright)
  Ledge, A 1929,N 19,26:3
Holt, Sabina
  Best Foot Forward 1956,Mr 3,16:1
Holt, Stella (Miscellaneous)
  Marcus in the High Grass 1960,N 22,38:6
  Yeomen of the Guard, The 1961,Ap 28,23:1
  Mikado, The 1961,My 5,23:1
  Grand Duke, The 1961,My 12,24:1
  Princess Ida 1961,My 19,23:1
  Iolanthe 1961,My 26,29:6
  H M S Pinafore 1961,Je 9,29:5
  Student Prince, The 1961,Jl 14,14:1
  Chief Thing, The 1963,Ap 30,27:2
  Ox Cart, The 1966,D 20,58:1
Holt, Stella (Producer)
  Simply Heavenly 1957,My 22,28:2
  Long Gallery, The 1958,Mr 7,17:2
  Journey With Strangers, A 1958,N 27,53:1
  Trip to Bountiful, The 1959,F 27,20:4
  Orpheus Descending 1959,O 6,45:2
  Ballad of Jazz Street, The 1959,N 12,28:1
  Donogoo 1961,Ja 19,25:3
  Cave Dwellers, The 1961,O 16,34:2
  All in Love 1961,N 11,15:2
  Red Roses for Me 1961,N 28,41:1
  Jericho-Jim Crow 1964,Ja 13,25:3
  Prodigal Son, The 1965,My 21,19:1
  Exception and the Rule, The 1965,My 21,19:1
  Javelin 1966,N 10,63:1
  Carricknabauna 1967,Mr 31,30:1
Holt, Thelma
  Macbeth 1969,Je 1,II,4:5
Holt, Vivian
  Red Pepper 1922,My 30,8:3
Holt, Will
  Signs Along the Cynic Route 1961,D 15,49:5
  World of Kurt Weill in Song, The 1964,My 13,53:1
Holt, Will (Composer)
  Signs Along the Cynic Route 1961,D 15,49:5
  Return of Second City in "20,000 Frozen
    Grenadiers," The 1966,Ap 22,36:1
Holt, Will (Director)
  World of Kurt Weill in Song, The 1964,My 13,53:1
  Leonard Bernstein's Theater Songs 1965,Je 29,27:2
Holt, Will (Lyricist)
  Signs Along the Cynic Route 1961,D 15,49:5
  Come Summer 1969,Mr 19,43:1
  Me Nobody Knows, The 1970,My 19,42:1
Holt, Will (Miscellaneous)
  Drums in the Night 1967,My 18,54:1
Holt, Will (Musical Director)
  Baal 1965,My 7,33:2
Holt, Will (Playwright)
  Signs Along the Cynic Route 1961,D 15,49:5
  World of Kurt Weill in Song, The 1964,My 13,53:1
  That 5 A.M. Jazz 1964,O 20,42:2
  Come Summer 1969,Mr 19,43:1
  Whores, Wars & Tin Pan Alley 1969,Je 17,37:1
Holtby, Grace
  Hamlet 1948,D 4,9:2
Holtby, Winifred (Playwright)
  Take Back Your Freedom 1940,S 1,IX,2:2
Holter, Bill
  Political Party, A 1963,S 27,17:5
Holton, Bob (Miscellaneous)
  From Here to There; Real Strange One, A
    1958,Ap 24,37:3
Holton, Robert (Composer)
  Hi, Paisano 1961,O 2,36:2
Holtum, Christian
  Clinging Vine, The 1922,D 25,20:2
Holtz, Aaron
  Thousand and One Nights 1959,D 16,53:2
  Life Is a Dream 1962,Ja 15,22:3

Holtz, Jacob
  Eleventh Inheritor, The 1962,N 22,43:5
Holtz, Lou
  Scandals 1920,Je 8,9:1
  George White's Scandals 1921,Jl 12,14:1
  Dancing Girl, The 1923,Ja 25,16:2
  Vaudeville (Palace) 1924,Ja 1,21:1
  Vaudeville (Hippodrome) 1924,F 19,12:1
  Tell Me More 1925,Ap 14,27:3
  Stylish Stouts 1926,S 19,IX,1:3
  Manhattan Mary 1927,S 27,30:3
  Vaudeville (Palace) 1928,Ag 21,27:5
  Vaudeville (Palace) 1929,Ap 8,32:7
  Vaudeville (Palace) 1929,Ag 19,23:1
  Vaudeville (Palace) 1930,Jl 7,22:2
  Vaudeville (Palace) 1930,N 3,19:2
  Vaudeville (Palace) 1930,N 10,17:1
  Vaudeville (Palace) 1930,N 17,21:2
  You Said It 1931,Ja 20,21:3
  Vaudeville (Palace) 1931,Jl 13,13:4
  Vaudeville (Palace) 1931,Jl 20,20:3
  Vaudeville (Palace) 1931,Ag 3,15:7
  Vaudeville (Hollywood) 1932,F 16,24:3
  Vaudeville (Hollywood) 1932,Mr 22,17:5
  Vaudeville (Hollywood) 1932,Ap 19,25:5
  Humpty Dumpty 1932,S 18,IX,2:1
  Friars Club Frolic 1933,My 15,16:4
  Calling All Stars 1934,N 22,26:1
  Calling All Stars 1934,D 14,28:2
  Transatlantic Rhythm 1936,O 2,16:3
  Laughter Over London 1936,D 8,31:3
  Priorities of 1942 1942,Mr 13,23:2
  Priorities of 1942 1942,Mr 29,VIII,1:1
  Star Time 1944,S 13,16:2
  Star Time 1944,S 17,II,1:1
Holtz, Lou (Producer)
  You Said It 1931,Ja 20,21:3
  Vaudeville (Hollywood) 1932,Mr 22,17:5
Holtz, Tenen
  Golem, The 1931,N 6,28:5
  Armored Train No 1469 1931,N 28,20:3
  Divided by Three 1934,O 3,24:2
  Room in Red and White, A 1936,Ja 20,23:3
Holver, Chuck (Lighting Director)
  Chief Thing, The 1963,Ap 30,27:2
Holwerk, S Otis
  Geisha, The 1931,O 6,35:4
Holzer, Hans (Miscellaneous)
  Safari! 1955,My 12,32:6
Holzer, Hans (Playwright)
  Safari! 1955,My 12,32:6
Holzer, Leslie (Scenic Designer)
  Peace 1969,Ja 28,49:1
Holzer, William (Scenic Designer)
  Nether-World 1938,O 22,15:2
Holzman, John J
  Those That Play the Clowns 1966,N 25,48:1
Holzman, William (Producer)
  Walk-Up 1961,F 24,24:1
Holzmayer, Silvia
  Wiener Blut 1964,S 12,14:1
Holzschuh, Lizzi
  Ihr Erster Ball 1930,N 25,30:3
Holzwasser, Florence
  Knight of the Burning Pestle, The 1927,Ap 23,15:1
Homan, Alfred
  Kiss Me, Kate 1952,Ja 9,24:6
Homan, David (Scenic Designer)
  And Be My Love 1934,Ja 19,25:2
Homann, Charlotte
  Here Goes the Bride 1931,N 4,31:2
Homann, Domani
  Great Way, The 1921,N 8,28:2
Homans, Robert E
  Like a King 1921,O 4,10:1
Home, John (Rev) (Playwright)
  Douglas Once 1950,S 10,II,3:1

Home, William
  Chauve-Souris; Queen of Spades, The
    1931,O 22,27:1
Home, William Douglas (Playwright)
  Great Possessions 1937,F 9,18:3
  Now Barabbas 1947,Ap 20,II,3:7
  Chiltern Hundreds, The 1947,S 14,II,3:8
  Ambassador Extraordinary 1948,Jl 11,II,1:2
  Yes, M'Lord 1949,O 5,35:2
  Reluctant Debutante, The 1956,O 11,50:1
  Reluctant Debutante, The 1956,O 21,II,1:1
  Cigarette Girl, The 1962,Je 21,26:2
  Reluctant Peer, The 1964,Ja 16,30:2
  Secretary Bird, The 1968,O 18,40:5
  Secretary Bird, The 1969,S 14,94:4
Homeier, Skippy
  Tomorrow the World 1943,Ap 15,22:2
  Tomorrow the World 1943,Ap 25,II,1:1
Homer, Charles
  Elizabeth the Queen 1930,N 4,37:1
  Passionate Pilgrim, The 1932,O 20,24:3
  O'Flynn, The 1934,D 28,24:1
Homer, Irene
  Last Warning, The 1922,O 25,23:1
  Bluffing Bluffers 1924,D 23,17:2

Homer, Irene—Cont
  Half-Naked Truth, The 1926,Je 8,23:1
  Revelry 1927,S 13,37:1
  Playing the Game 1927,D 20,32:5
  Carry On 1928,Ja 24,26:1
  No More Frontier 1931,O 22,27:1
  Christopher Comes Across 1932,Je 1,19:2
Homer, J
  Green Pastures, The 1935,F 27,16:2
Homer, Randall
  Green Pastures, The 1935,F 27,16:2
Homer, Renah
  Intimate Relations 1932,Mr 29,23:2
Homer, Simmons
  Ginger Snaps 1930,Ja 1,30:5
Homewood, A S
  Mary Rose 1920,D 23,9:2
Hommel, Edward
  Great Music 1924,O 6,24:1
Hommen, Willi (Miscellaneous)
  Before Sundown 1962,Mr 14,43:1
Homolka, Oscar
  Emperor Jones, The 1924,Ja 10,18:2
  Peripherie 1926,D 19,VII,4:4
  Neidhardt von Gneisenau 1927,Ja 23,VII,4:5
  Bonaparte 1927,My 15,VIII,1:3
  Trial of Mary Dugan, The 1928,Je 24,VIII,1:4
  Karl und Anna 1929,Mr 10,X,2:1
  Brest-Litovsk 1930,N 30,IX,2:1
  Timon 1932,Mr 6,VIII,2:1
  Power and Glory 1938,My 1,X,2:5
  Grey Farm 1940,My 4,12:7
  Innocent Voyage, The 1943,N 16,27:2
  I Remember Mama 1944,O 20,16:2
  I Remember Mama 1944,O 29,II,1:1
  Last Dance, The 1948,Ja 28,27:2
  Bravo! 1948,N 12,31:2
  Master Builder, The 1955,Mr 2,23:2
  Master Builder, The 1955,Mr 20,II,1:1
  Rashomon 1959,Ja 28,36:2
  Rashomon 1959,F 8,II,1:1
Homolka, Oscar (Director)
  Master Builder, The 1955,Mr 2,23:2
Homond, Ruth
  Man's House, A 1943,Ap 3,10:4
  And Be My Love 1945,F 22,30:4
Honan, Ethne
  Old English 1924,N 9,VIII,2:3
Hone, Mary
  R U R 1922,O 10,16:1
  Floriani's Wife 1923,O 7,IX,1:1
  Leah Kleschna 1924,Ap 22,19:2
  School for Scandal, The 1925,D 7,18:2
  Becky Sharp 1929,Je 4,29:1
  King Lear 1930,D 26,18:2
  Admirable Crichton, The 1931,Mr 10,23:2
  Romeo and Juliet 1933,F 3,21:5
  Joyous Season, The 1934,Ja 30,16:3
  Lady From the Sea, The 1934,My 2,25:2
  Few Are Chosen 1935,S 18,19:3
  Hallowe'en 1936,F 21,20:3
Hone, Mary (Producer)
  Arms for Venus 1937,Mr 12,18:7
Honegger, Arthur (Composer)
  Maitresse de Roi 1926,D 1,24:1
  Imperatrice aux Rochers, L' 1927,Mr 20,VIII,2:4
  Antigone 1930,Ap 25,28:4
  Roi Pausole, Le 1931,Ja 25,VIII,8:8
  Hamlet 1952,D 2,39:1
  Joan At The Stake 1954,Je 25,15:3
Hones, Nathaniel
  I Had a Ball 1964,D 16,50:1
Hong, Arabella
  Flower Drum Song 1958,D 2,44:1
  Flower Drum Song 1958,D 7,II,5:1
Honig, Gail
  Cyrano de Bergerac 1968,Ap 26,30:1
Honig, Howard
  Comforter, The 1964,O 22,42:1
  Henry V 1965,Je 29,27:2
  Front Page, The 1968,O 20,85:5
  Rothschilds, The 1970,O 20,40:1
Honig, Ida
  World Is a Stage, The 1962,N 5,37:4
  Both Kooney Lemels 1964,O 12,37:2
Honig, Morris
  Wooden Idol, The 1930,My 13,27:2
Honig, Morris (Choreographer)
  Both Kooney Lemels 1964,O 12,37:2
Honigman, Clara
  Radio Girl, The 1929,O 19,22:4
  Jolly Orphan, The 1929,D 23,18:6
  Little Clown, The 1930,Mr 15,23:3
  Little Cantor, The 1930,S 24,26:2
Honigman, Irving
  It Is to Laugh 1927,D 27,24:2
  Love and Politics 1929,O 21,30:7
  One Woman 1931,D 14,16:4
  Wedding Chains 1932,Mr 28,10:5
  Love for Sale 1936,Ja 24,14:2
  Jewish Heart, The 1939,Ja 25,16:6
Honigman, Irving (Director)
  Happy Family, A 1934,S 24,15:2

Honkamp, Helen
Kumquat in the Persimmon Tree, The
1962,Je 19,27:2
Honohan, William
Remote Control 1929,S 11,24:5
Honrath, Donald (Composer)
New Faces 1934,Mr 16,24:5
Hontley, Hugh
Nice People 1921,Mr 3,11:1
Hood, Ann
H M S Pinafore 1964,N 20,40:1
Ruddigore 1964,D 4,44:1
Ruddigore 1966,N 23,28:1
H M S Pinafore 1966,N 24,64:1
Patience 1966,N 30,58:1
Hood, Arthur (Playwright)
Thou Art the Man 1937,Ap 9,18:5
Hood, Basil (Lyricist)
Count of Luxembourg, The 1930,F 18,28:2
Hood, Basil (Playwright)
Rose of Persia 1935,Mr 1,17:4
Hood, Curtis
Pelleas and Melisande 1957,F 20,38:1
Hood, Danny
Strings, My Lord, Are False, The 1942,My 20,24:2
Hood, Marion
Romeo and Juliet 1956,O 25,41:1
Hood, Thomas
It Is the Law 1922,N 30,28:2
Woman on the Jury, The 1923,Ag 16,10:4
Hoogland, Benjamin
John 1927,N 5,16:4
Hook, Lillian
Man of Destiny, The 1926,My 1,10:1
Hook, Walter
Anya 1965,N 30,48:1
Hooker, Brian (Composer)
Engaged! or Cheviot's Choice 1925,Je 19,24:2
Hooker, Brian (Lyricist)
June Love 1921,Ap 26,20:1
Marjolaine 1922,Ja 25,16:1
Our Nell 1922,D 5,24:1
Engaged! or Cheviot's Choice 1925,Je 19,24:2
Vagabond King, The 1925,S 22,23:3
White Eagle, The 1927,D 27,24:4
Falstaff 1928,D 26,14:2
O'Flynn, The 1934,D 28,24:1
Vagabond King, The 1935,N 29,22:7
Vagabond King, The 1943,Je 30,24:2
Hooker, Brian (Original Author)
Through the Years 1932,Ja 29,13:3
Hooker, Brian (Playwright)
Our Nell 1922,D 5,24:1
Vagabond King, The 1925,S 22,23:3
Mozart 1926,N 23,26:2
White Eagle, The 1927,D 27,24:4
Smiling Through 1932,Ja 3,VIII,3:1
O'Flynn, The 1934,D 28,24:1
Vagabond King, The 1935,N 29,22:7
Vagabond King, The 1943,Je 30,24:2
Vagabond King, The 1961,N 24,36:1
Hooker, Brian (Translator)
Cyrano de Bergerac 1923,N 2,14:1
Cyrano de Bergerac 1926,F 19,18:1
Cyrano de Bergerac 1932,D 27,11:2
Ruy Blas 1933,O 10,24:4
Cyrano de Bergerac 1936,Ap 28,17:1
Ruy Blas 1938,Jl 24,IX,2:1
Cyrano de Bergerac 1946,O 9,33:2
Cyrano de Bergerac 1946,N 3,II,1:1
Cyrano de Bergerac 1946,N 3,I,54:6
Cyrano de Bergerac 1953,N 13,24:3
Cyrano de Bergerac 1962,Ag 1,21:1
Cyrano de Bergerac 1963,Je 20,30:1
Hooker, D H
Tiger Smiles, The 1930,D 18,29:1
Hooker, Rea
Sea Gull, The 1956,O 23,38:1
Hooker, West
Winners and Losers 1947,F 27,27:2
Command Decision 1947,O 2,30:2
Hooks, Bill (Choreographer)
Lend an Ear 1959,S 25,20:5
Hooks, Bobby Dean
Tiger Tiger Burning Bright 1962,D 24,5:2
Ballad for Bimshire 1963,O 16,54:1
Milk Train Doesn't Stop Here Anymore, The
1964,Ja 2,33:1
Hooks, David
Coriolanus 1953,Ag 21,9:2
Madam Will You Walk 1953,D 2,2:4
Golden Apple, The 1954,Mr 12,15:2
Sandhog 1954,N 24,17:1
Doctor's Dilemma, The 1955,Ja 12,22:1
Master Builder, The 1955,Mr 2,23:2
Moby Dick 1955,Ap 26,25:3
Macbeth 1955,O 8,12:6
Last Love of Don Juan, The 1955,N 24,40:1
Thesmophoriazusae, The; Goddesses of Athens,
The 1955,D 14,52:4
Tobias and the Angel 1957,O 21,29:5
For the Time Being 1957,D 18,42:7
Ardele 1958,Ap 9,39:4

Moon for the Misbegotten, A 1958,Je 7,10:6
Foenix in Choir 1958,O 28,40:2
Antony and Cleopatra 1959,Ja 14,28:1
Ping-Pong 1959,Ap 17,22:1
Antigone 1959,S 16,46:2
Gideon 1961,N 10,38:1
School for Scandal, The 1962,Mr 19,36:1
Seagull, The 1962,Mr 22,42:1
Tavern, The 1962,Ap 5,29:1
American Dream, The 1963,My 29,39:6
Zoo Story, The 1963,My 29,39:6
Corruption in the Palace of Justice 1963,O 9,49:2
Medea 1965,N 29,46:1
Gantry 1970,F 16,44:1
Wars of the Roses, The (Part I) 1970,Jl 2,30:1
Wars of the Roses, The (Part II) 1970,Jl 3,15:1
Hooks, Ed
Wuziz! 1970,O 2,25:2
Here Be Dragons 1970,D 21,52:1
Hooks, Robert
Dutchman 1964,Mr 25,46:2
Henry V 1965,Je 29,27:2
Happy Ending 1965,N 16,56:1
Day of Absence 1965,N 16,56:1
Where's Daddy? 1966,Mr 3,27:1
Hallelujah, Baby! 1967,Ap 27,51:1
Hallelujah, Baby! 1967,My 7,II,1:1
Kongi's Harvest 1968,Ap 15,49:1
Harangues, The 1970,Ja 14,42:1
Harangues, The 1970,Ja 25,II,1:4
Hooks, Robert (Director)
Day of Absence 1970,Mr 18,39:1
Brotherhood 1970,Mr 18,39:1
Hooks, Robert (Miscellaneous)
Taming of the Shrew, The 1965,Jl 3,10:5
We Real Cool 1965,Jl 3,10:5
Hooks, Robert (Producer)
Song of the Lusitanian Bogey, The 1968,Ja 3,52:1
Walk Together Children 1968,N 12,54:1
Hooks, William (Choreographer)
King and the Duke, The 1955,Je 2,25:2
Hoolihann, Horace
Good Morning 1937,D 4,20:7
Hooper, Bronwyn (Miscellaneous)
Homo 1969,Ap 12,40:2
Queen of Greece, The 1969,Ap 12,40:2
Hooper, Claire
Mama Loves Papa 1926,F 23,26:2
Sunny Days 1928,F 9,29:1
Hello Paris 1930,N 17,29:3
Hooper, Conrad
Coming of Christ, The 1957,D 23,29:8
Hooper, Ewan
Spithead 1969,N 22,46:3
Hooper, Grace
This Fine-Pretty World 1923,D 27,11:1
Hooper, Lee
West Side Story 1968,Je 25,32:1
Zorba 1968,N 18,58:1
Hooper, Lewis (Director)
Florodora 1936,Ag 23,II,8:2
Hooper, Lorenzo
As the Earth Turns 1938,Ag 7,IX,2:1
Hooper and Gachett
Vaudeville (Palace) 1929,Ag 19,23:1
Hoopes, Isabella
Wonderful Town 1953,F 26,22:3
Wonderful Town 1958,Mr 6,32:4
Saratoga 1959,D 8,59:4
Show Boat 1961,Ap 13,32:1
Front Page, The 1968,O 20,85:5
Hoot, Roland
Glass Slipper, The 1925,O 20,29:1
Hoover, Bruce A (Miscellaneous)
Quotations From Chairman Mao Tse-Tung
1968,O 1,39:1
Box 1968,O 1,39:1
Death of Bessie Smith, The 1968,O 3,55:1
American Dream, The 1968,O 3,55:1
Krapp's Last Tape 1968,O 11,41:1
Zoo Story, The 1968,O 11,41:1
Happy Days 1968,O 14,54:1
Gingham Dog, The 1969,Ap 24,41:1
Harvey 1970,F 25,41:1
Hoover, Bruce A (Producer)
Crimes of Passion; Ruffian on the Stair, The
1969,O 27,54:1
Crimes of Passion; Erpingham Camp, The
1969,O 27,54:1
Hoover, Carol (Lighting Director)
Cherry Orchard, The 1955,O 19,38:1
Sea Gull, The 1956,O 23,38:1
Easter 1957,Ja 17,35:2
Easter 1957,F 3,II,1:1
Coach With the Six Insides, The 1967,My 12,50:1
Hoover, Carol (Miscellaneous)
Coach With the Six Insides, The 1967,My 12,50:1
Hoover, Hyram (Scenic Designer)
Devil's Little Game, The 1932,Ag 2,20:4
Hoover, Katherine
Saint's Parade 1930,N 1,23:4

Hoover, Ken
Founders, The 1957,My 14,39:1
Hoover, Mallory
Volpone 1967,Je 30,29:1
Hoover, Paul
Trick for Trick 1932,F 19,14:2
Hoover, Peggy
Hello, Yourself 1928,O 31,28:2
Dance of Death, The 1932,Ja 11,29:5
Vaudeville (Loew's State) 1932,Je 13,19:7
Hoover, Stuart
Winners and Losers 1947,F 27,27:2
Our Lan' 1947,S 29,16:5
Hoover, Vilma
Midsummer Night's Dream, A 1932,N 18,22:2
Hope, Adele Blood
Fly Away Home 1936,Jl 21,13:1
Hope, Adele Blood (Director)
Remember the Day 1936,Je 30,15:1
Hope, Anthony (Playwright)
Princess Flavia 1925,N 3,34:3
Hope, Bob
Ups-A-Daisy 1928,O 9,34:2
Vaudeville (Palace) 1932,My 30,16:7
Ballyhoo of 1932 1932,S 7,14:2
Roberta 1933,N 20,18:4
Say When 1934,O 28,IX,3:1
Say When 1934,N 9,24:2
Ziegfeld Follies 1935,D 31,10:1
Ziegfeld Follies 1936,Ja 5,IX,3:1
Ziegfeld Follies 1936,Ja 31,17:2
Red, Hot and Blue! 1936,O 8,26:1
Red, Hot and Blue! 1936,O 11,X,3:1
Red, Hot and Blue! 1936,O 30,26:3
Hope, Dawn
Remember the Day 1936,Je 30,15:1
Fly Away Home 1936,Jl 21,13:1
Hope, Dorothy
Peter Pan 1924,N 7,16:2
Hope, Edward (Original Author)
She Loves Me Not 1933,N 21,22:4
She Loves Me Not 1933,N 26,IX,1:1
She Loves Me Not 1934,My 2,25:1
Hope, Edward (Playwright)
Garrick Gaieties 1930,O 17,21:2
Hope, Fay
Forbidden Melody 1936,N 3,33:1
Hope, Florence
It's Up to You 1921,Mr 29,20:1
Hope, Gloria
Higher and Higher 1940,Ap 5,24:3
Hope, Jane
Pride 1923,My 3,22:3
Hope, Mariel
No More Blondes 1920,Ja 8,22:1
Hope, Peggy
Vaudeville (Palace) 1926,Ag 3,19:2
Hope, Vida (Director)
Boy Friend, The 1954,O 1,20:1
Boy Friend, The 1954,O 10,II,1:1
Valmouth 1960,O 7,29:1
Hope Twins, The
Vaudeville (Hippodrome) 1924,Ap 1,18:1
Hopeton, Gladys
Spellbound 1927,N 15,26:2
These Days 1928,N 13,36:2
As Good As New 1930,N 4,37:3
Hopkins, Angus
Meet the People 1940,D 26,22:2
Hopkins, Anthony
As You Like It 1967,O 6,33:4
As You Like It 1967,O 15,II,9:3
Hopkins, Anthony (Composer)
Oedipus 1946,My 21,19:2
Romanoff and Juliet 1957,O 11,24:1
Hopkins, Arthur (Director)
Samson and Delilah 1920,N 28,VI,1:1
What Price Glory 1924,S 6,14:3
Second Mrs Tanqueray, The 1924,O 28,27:1
Close Harmony 1924,D 2,23:1
First Flight 1925,S 18,26:2
Buccaneer, The 1925,O 3,10:2
In a Garden 1925,N 17,29:1
Jest, The 1926,F 5,22:2
Deep River 1926,O 5,26:2
Burlesque 1927,S 2,15:3
House of Women, The 1927,O 4,32:2
Paris Bound 1927,D 28,26:3
Paris Bound 1928,Ja 1,VIII,1:1
Paris Bound 1928,Ja 15,VIII,1:1
Salvation 1928,F 1,31:1
Burlesque 1928,Jl 1,VIII,3:5
Paris Bound 1928,Jl 1,VIII,3:5
Machinal 1928,S 8,10:3
These Days 1928,N 13,36:2
Holiday 1928,N 27,36:1
Commodore Marries, The 1929,S 5,26:3
Commodore Marries, The 1929,S 15,IX,1:1
Channel Road, The 1929,O 18,24:2
Family Affairs 1929,D 11,34:6
Half Gods 1929,D 23,18:5
Rebound 1930,F 4,29:1
Torch Song 1930,Ag 28,23:1

Hopkins, Arthur (Director)—Cont
Roadside 1930,S 27,21:1
This Is New York 1930,N 29,21:1
Man on Stilts, The 1931,S 10,23:2
Passing Present, The 1931,D 8,36:2
Rendezvous 1932,O 13,22:3
Conquest 1933,F 20,11:3
Joyous Season, The 1934,Ja 30,16:3
Petrified Forest, The 1934,D 21,31:6
Petrified Forest, The 1935,Ja 8,26:1
Petrified Forest, The 1935,Ja 13,IX,1:1
Paths of Glory 1935,S 27,24:2
Bright Star 1935,O 13,IX,1:6
Bright Star 1935,O 16,26:2
Star Spangled 1936,Mr 11,23:1
Plumes in the Dust 1936,N 7,14:2
Blow Ye Winds 1937,S 24,17:4
Waltz in Goose Step 1938,N 2,26:2
Farm of Three Echoes 1939,N 29,18:3
Broken Journey 1942,Je 24,22:2
Feathers in a Gale 1943,D 22,26:2
Magnificent Yankee, The 1946,Ja 2,23:6
Magnificent Yankee, The 1946,Ja 23,21:2
Hear That Trumpet 1946,O 8,19:2
Burlesque 1946,D 26,30:3
Hopkins, Arthur (Miscellaneous)
Lady Jane 1934,S 11,24:2
Petrified Forest, The 1935,Ja 8,26:1
Farm of Three Echoes 1939,N 29,18:3
Without Love 1942,N 11,28:1
Hopkins, Arthur (Playwright)
Burlesque 1927,S 2,15:3
Conquest 1933,F 20,11:3
Burlesque 1946,D 26,30:3
Burlesque 1947,Ja 5,II,1:1
Hopkins, Arthur (Producer)
Richard III 1920,Mr 21,VI,6:1
Night Lodging 1920,Ap 14,18:2
Night Lodging 1920,Ap 18,VI,2:1
Macbeth 1921,F 20,VI,1:1
Macbeth 1921,F 27,VI,1:1
Daddy's Gone A-Hunting 1921,O 2,VII,1:1
Claw, The 1921,O 2,VII,1:8
Idle Inn, The 1922,Ja 22,VI,1:1
Rose Bernd 1922,O 8,VI,1:2
Hamlet 1922,N 26,VIII,1:1
Hamlet 1923,Ja 14,VII,1:1
Macbeth 1923,F 11,VII,1:1
Anna Christie 1923,Ap 11,16:2
What Price Glory 1924,S 6,14:3
Second Mrs Tanqueray, The 1924,S 28,VII,2:1
Hamlet 1925,Mr 29,VIII,1:1
First Flight 1925,S 18,26:2
Buccaneer, The 1925,O 3,10:2
In a Garden 1925,N 17,29:1
Jest, The 1926,F 5,22:2
Deep River 1926,O 5,26:2
Deep River 1926,O 10,VIII,1:1
Burlesque 1927,S 2,15:3
House of Women, The 1927,S 11,VIII,1:3
Burlesque 1927,S 11,VIII,1:1
House of Women, The 1927,O 4,32:2
Paris Bound 1927,D 28,26:3
Salvation 1928,F 1,31:1
Machinal 1928,S 8,10:3
Machinal 1928,S 16,IX,1:1
These Days 1928,N 4,IX,1:3
These Days 1928,N 13,36:2
Holiday 1928,N 27,36:1
Paris Bound 1929,My 1,28:6
Blow the Man Down 1929,Ag 25,VIII,3:1
Commodore Marries, The 1929,S 5,26:3
Commodore Marries, The 1929,S 15,IX,1:1
Channel Road, The 1929,O 18,24:2
Family Affairs 1929,D 11,34:6
Half Gods 1929,D 23,18:5
Rebound 1930,F 4,29:1
Torch Song 1930,Ag 3,VIII,3:4
Torch Song 1930,Ag 28,23:1
Torch Song 1930,S 7,IX,1:1
Roadside 1930,S 27,21:1
This Is New York 1930,N 29,21:1
Man on Stilts, The 1931,S 10,23:2
Passing Present, The 1931,N 29,VIII,2:2
Passing Present, The 1931,D 8,36:2
Rendezvous 1932,O 13,22:3
Conquest 1933,F 20,11:3
Joyous Season, The 1934,Ja 30,16:3
Petrified Forest, The 1934,D 21,31:6
Paths of Glory 1935,S 19,29:1
Paths of Glory 1935,S 27,24:2
Bright Star 1935,O 16,26:2
Star Spangled 1936,Mr 6,25:4
Star Spangled 1936,Mr 11,23:1
Plumes in the Dust 1936,N 7,14:2
Plumes in the Dust 1936,N 15,XI,1:1
Blow Ye Winds 1937,S 8,20:5
Blow Ye Winds 1937,S 24,17:4
Spring Thaw 1938,Mr 22,18:1
Feathers in a Gale 1943,D 22,26:2
Magnificent Yankee, The 1946,Ja 2,23:6
Magnificent Yankee, The 1946,Ja 23,21:2
Hear That Trumpet 1946,O 8,19:2

Hopkins, Charles (Director)
Makropoulos Secret, The 1926,Ja 22,12:4
Devil in the Cheese, The 1926,D 30,22:4
Ivory Door, The 1927,O 19,24:5
Unknown Warrior, The 1928,O 30,26:6
Perfect Alibi, The 1928,N 28,24:2
Ladies Leave 1929,O 2,28:3
Michael and Mary 1929,D 14,23:3
Mrs Moonlight 1930,S 30,24:3
Give Me Yesterday 1931,Mr 5,32:1
Roof, The 1931,O 31,22:4
They Don't Mean Any Harm 1932,F 24,25:2
Saint Wench 1933,Ja 3,19:3
Strange Orchestra 1933,N 29,23:2
I Myself 1934,My 10,24:6
Noble Prize, The 1935,Jl 9,24:3
No More Peace 1937,Je 4,26:7
Pygmalion 1937,Jl 7,26:3
Coriolanus 1937,O 10,VI,4:7
Diff'rent 1937,N 21,II,10:7
Pygmalion 1938,Ja 27,16:3
Captain Jinks of the Horse Marines 1938,Ja 28,16:2
No More Peace 1938,Ja 29,13:2
Hopkins, Charles (Producer)
Makropoulos Secret, The 1926,Ja 22,12:4
Devil in the Cheese, The 1926,D 30,22:4
Ivory Door, The 1927,O 19,24:5
Unknown Warrior, The 1928,O 30,26:6
Perfect Alibi, The 1928,N 28,24:2
Ladies Leave 1929,O 2,28:3
Michael and Mary 1929,D 14,23:3
Michael and Mary 1929,D 29,VIII,2:4
Michael and Mary 1930,F 2,5:1
Mrs Moonlight 1930,S 30,24:3
Give Me Yesterday 1931,Mr 5,32:1
Roof, The 1931,O 31,22:4
Roof, The 1931,N 8,VIII,1:1
They Don't Mean Any Harm 1932,F 24,25:2
Strange Orchestra 1933,N 29,23:2
Rag Picker of Paris, The: or, Modest Modiste 1935,N 12,23:7
Kind Lady 1935,N 19,27:3
Tulips Are Blooming, The 1935,D 4,27:6
Queen's Husband, The 1936,Je 2,33:2
Mrs Moonlight 1936,Je 16,21:3
Springtime for Henry 1936,Je 23,27:6
Diff'rent 1938,Ja 26,26:4
Coriolanus 1938,F 2,14:5
Hopkins, Charles F Jr
Little Theatre Tournament; Poor Old Jim 1929,My 10,32:2
Hopkins, Claude
Make Me Know It 1929,N 5,32:5
Hopkins, Edwin (Director)
Lingering Past, The 1932,Je 30,26:5
Hopkins, F Richard (Producer)
Ghost Writer, The 1933,Je 20,22:4
Hopkins, Florence (Playwright)
Madame Alias 1927,S 4,VII,2:4
Hopkins, Glenn
Poppy God, The 1921,Ag 30,10:1
Hopkins, H S
Page Miss Glory 1934,N 28,24:2
Hopkins, Hazel
Little Theatre Tournament; Poor Old Jim 1929,My 10,32:2
Hopkins, Irving
Legend 1930,My 7,25:1
Second Comin', The 1931,D 9,32:4
Hopkins, J P
Philadelphia 1929,S 17,34:5
Hopkins, J S
Why Not? 1922,D 30,13:4
Hopkins, Jerry
Serjeant Musgrave's Dance 1966,Mr 9,44:1
Let Them Down, Gently; On Vacation 1968,Ja 31,28:2
Hopkins, John
Julius Caesar 1930,Ap 4,22:3
Master of the Revels 1935,Ag 14,16:2
Hopkins, John (Playwright)
This Story of Yours 1968,D 14,60:4
Hopkins, Joseph
Jazz Singer, The 1925,S 15,29:2
Hopkins, Kenyon (Composer)
Hollywood Ice Revue 1956,Ja 13,17:1
Metamorphosis 1957,F 20,38:1
Hopkins, Lea (Miscellaneous)
Three Plays of the Sea 1970,Ag 20,39:1
Hopkins, Linda
Purlie 1970,Mr 16,53:1
Hopkins, May
Ruined Lady, The 1920,Ja 21,10:2
Montmartre 1922,F 14,20:1
World We Live In, The 1922,N 1,16:1
For Value Received 1923,My 8,22:3
Nancy Ann 1924,Ap 1,18:1
Treat 'Em Rough 1926,O 5,26:2
Barker, The 1927,Ja 19,20:6
Hopkins, Miriam
Little Jessie James 1923,Ag 16,10:4
Puppets 1925,Mr 10,19:1
Lovely Lady 1925,O 15,27:1

Hopkins, Miriam—Cont
American Tragedy, An 1926,O 12,31:2
American Tragedy, An 1926,O 24,VIII,1:1
Thou Desperate Pilot 1927,Mr 8,23:1
Garden of Eden, The 1927,S 28,28:1
Excess Baggage 1927,D 27,24:2
John Ferguson 1928,Ja 18,23:1
Flight 1929,F 10,IX,2:1
Flight 1929,F 19,22:3
Flight 1929,Mr 24,X,1:1
Camel Through the Needle's Eye, The 1929,Ap 16,32:2
Camel Through the Needle's Eye, The 1929,Ap 28,IX,1:1
Bachelor Father, The 1929,O 20,IX,1:4
Ritzy 1930,F 11,30:4
Lysistrata 1930,Ap 29,30:5
Lysistrata 1930,Je 1,VIII,1:1
Lysistrata 1930,Je 6,20:1
His Majesty's Car 1930,O 24,30:1
Anatol 1931,Ja 17,23:3
Jezebel 1933,D 20,26:3
Wine of Choice 1937,D 14,32:3
Battle of Angels 1940,D 31,18:6
Battle of Angels 1941,Ja 5,IX,1:7
Perfect Marriage, The 1944,O 27,17:6
Perfect Marriage, The 1944,N 5,II,1:2
Message for Margaret 1947,Ap 17,34:2
Look Homeward, Angel 1958,Ag 31,II,1:1
Hopkins, Nan
Lady Windermere's Fan 1946,O 15,29:2
Hopkins, Olyve P
Meek Mose 1928,F 7,30:1
Hopkins, Pauline (Playwright)
Mr Whistler 1931,D 6,VIII,2:6
Hopkinson, Elinor
Tide Rising 1937,Ja 26,17:2
Hoppe, Fritz
Consul, The 1951,S 8,9:3
Hoppe, Vera
Caroline 1923,F 1,13:2
Love Song, The 1925,Ja 14,19:4
Hopper, De Wolf
Erminie 1921,Ja 4,11:1
Snapshots of 1921 1921,Je 3,19:2
Some Party 1922,Ap 17,22:1
Lambs Gambol 1925,Ap 27,15:1
White Lilacs 1928,S 11,31:2
When Father Smiles 1931,Mr 22,VIII,4:4
Monster, The 1933,F 11,11:5
Hopper, Dennis
Mandingo 1961,My 23,43:6
Hopper, Hedda
Six-Cylinder Love 1921,Ag 26,8:2
That Day 1922,Jl 9,VI,1:4
That Day 1922,O 4,27:3
Dinner at Eight 1933,Ap 9,IX,1:7
Divided by Three 1934,O 3,24:2
Hopper, Jack
Golden Screw, The 1967,Ja 31,52:1
Hopper, Lawrence
Street Sounds 1970,O 23,32:1
Hopper, Miss
Man Without Money, A 1929,N 3,27:4
Hopper, Molly
Contrast, The 1926,O 1,26:2
Hopper, Richard B
What a Relief 1935,D 14,10:6
Hopper, William
Order Please 1934,O 10,21:2
Romeo and Juliet 1934,D 21,30:3
Hoppin, W W Jr
Galloper, The 1924,D 19,26:2
Hopple, Mary
Fledermaus, Die 1933,My 14,II,3:8
Vagabond King, The 1935,N 29,22:7
Hopwood, Avery (Original Author)
Good Night Ladies 1945,Ja 18,16:2
Ladies Night in a Turkish Bath 1961,Mr 22,38:1
Hopwood, Avery (Playwright)
Ladies' Night 1920,Ag 10,10:1
Spanish Love 1920,Ag 18,6:1
Bat, The 1920,Ag 24,6:1
Bat, The 1920,N 14,VI,1:1
Getting Gertie's Garter 1921,Ag 2,16:2
Demi-Virgin, The 1921,O 19,22:1
Bat, The 1922,Ap 30,VII,1:1
Why Men Leave Home 1922,Jl 30,VI,1:3
Why Men Leave Home 1922,S 13,18:2
Return, The 1923,Jl 22,VI,1:1
Little Miss Bluebeard 1923,Ag 29,12:1
Little Miss Bluebeard 1923,S 9,VII,1:1
Alarm Clock, The 1923,D 25,26:2
Best People, The 1924,Ag 20,8:1
Harem, The 1924,D 3,24:1
Naughty Cinderella 1925,N 10,23:6
Gold Diggers, The 1926,D 19,VII,6:4
Gold Diggers, The 1926,D 26,VII,4:3
Garden of Eden, The 1927,Je 26,VIII,1:3
Garden of Eden, The 1927,Ag 14,VII,2:1
Garden of Eden, The 1927,S 28,28:1
Best People, The 1933,Mr 16,21:5
Ladies' Night 1933,N 19,IX,3:7
Sea Legs 1937,My 19,26:5

Hopwood, Avery (Playwright)—Cont
Bat, The 1937,Je 1,27:5
Bat, The 1953,Ja 21,28:2
Horace, William
Sojourner Truth 1948,Ap 22,35:2
Horacek, Jaroslav
Laterna Magika 1964,Ag 4,21:1
Horak, Buddy
Hold Everything 1928,O 11,24:2
Horam and Myrtill
Untitled-Revue 1928,Ja 15,VIII,2:3
Horan, Bill
Texas Li'l Darlin' 1949,N 26,10:5
Horan, Charles (Playwright)
Devil Within, The 1925,Mr 17,19:4
Horan, Edward A (Composer)
All the King's Horses 1934,Ja 31,21:3
Horan, Harold J T
You'll Never Know 1921,Ap 21,9:2
Horan, John
Gang War 1928,Ag 21,27:2
Horan, Mary
Here's Howe! 1928,My 2,19:3
Sons o' Guns 1929,N 27,30:4
Horbiger, Attila
Sturm im Wasserglas 1930,D 28,VIII,2:4
Horbiger, Paul
Professor Bernhardi 1968,Mr 20,38:1
Horder, Barbara
Romeo and Juliet 1940,My 10,27:1
Hordern, Michael
Moonbirds 1959,O 10,13:1
Flint 1970,Jl 26,49:2
Horen, Bob
Fig Leaf in Her Bonnet, A 1961,Je 15,50:1
Horen, Leah
Celebration 1969,Ja 23,55:2
Horen, Michael (Scenic Designer)
Happy Hypocrite, The 1968,S 6,38:1
Horen, Robert (Miscellaneous)
Fig Leaf in Her Bonnet, A 1961,Je 15,50:1
Horgan, Betty
Embers 1926,F 2,20:3
Horgan, James
Ringside 1928,Ag 30,13:2
Horgan, Patrick
Redhead 1959,F 6,21:1
Heartbreak House 1959,O 19,37:1
Baker Street 1965,F 17,36:1
Horgan, Paul (Playwright)
Yours, A Lincoln 1942,Jl 10,12:3
Horine, Agnew
Sign of the Leopard 1928,D 12,34:4
Kibitzer, The 1929,F 19,22:5
Horine, Alice
Laugh, Clown, Laugh! 1923,N 29,30:1
Horine, Charles (Playwright)
Me and Thee 1965,D 8,58:4
Horison, Rose
Diff'rent 1937,N 21,II,10:7
Horler, Sydney (Playwright)
Midnight Love 1931,S 13,IX,2:5
Horn, Alex (Director)
Puntila 1959,My 15,26:2
Big Man 1966,My 20,41:1
Horn, Arthur
Brigadoon 1947,Mr 14,28:2
Horn, Barbara Lee (Miscellaneous)
Show Me Where the Good Times Are 1970,Mr 6,32:1
Horn, Benjamin
Jazz Singer, The 1925,S 15,29:2
Horn, Charles
Virgin Man, The 1927,Ja 19,20:4
Strong Man's House, A 1929,S 17,34:3
Light Wines and Beer 1930,N 11,28:6
Horn, Christine
Lady in the Dark 1943,Mr 1,14:2
Horn, Edmund
Time Remembered 1957,N 13,41:2
Horn, Eleanor (Producer)
Voice of the Turtle, The 1961,Je 28,41:1
Susan Slept Here 1961,Jl 12,35:2
Little Hut, The 1961,Jl 26,34:2
Moon Is Blue, The 1961,Ag 9,29:1
Tender Trap, The 1961,Ag 26,15:1
Horn, Elie (Producer)
Walk-Up 1961,F 24,24:1
Horn, Frank
Circus Princess, The 1927,Ap 26,32:2
White Lilacs 1928,S 11,31:2
Nina Rosa 1930,My 31,19:3
Nina Rosa 1930,S 22,22:5
Horn, J E (Producer)
Conflict 1929,Mr 7,22:4
Horn, Jack
Captain Brassbound's Conversion 1950,D 28,21:1
Lady in the Dark 1952,Mr 8,11:3
Horn, John
Every Other Evil 1961,Ja 23,20:2
Natural Affection 1963,F 2,5:2
Place for Chance, The 1964,My 15,44:2
Long Christmas Dinner, The 1966,S 7,53:1
Patriot for Me, A 1969,O 6,58:1

Horn, Lew
Telemachus Clay 1963,N 16,17:2
That Hat! 1964,S 24,45:1
Horn, Steve
Case of Philip Lawrence, The 1937,Je 9,31:1
Horn-Griner (Scenic Designer)
Walk-Up 1961,F 24,24:1
Hornaday, Frank
Night of Love 1941,Ja 8,14:2
Student Prince, The 1943,Je 9,16:2
Hornaday, Mr
Tattle Tales 1930,Jl 20,VIII,2:1
Hornady, Ernestine
Schoolgirl 1930,N 21,31:1
Hornady, Julie
It Never Rains 1931,D 25,29:3
Hornblow, Arthur Jr (Playwright)
Madame Pierre 1922,F 16,11:1
Pasteur 1923,Mr 13,19:1
Captive, The 1926,S 30,23:1
Captive, The 1926,O 10,VIII,1:1
Kiss of Importance, A 1930,D 2,31:3
Horne, David
Journey's End 1929,Jl 14,IX,5:1
Insult; Dolle Hans 1930,My 4,XI,1:3
Betrayal 1931,Ja 25,VIII,2:7
Hamlet 1931,N 6,28:4
Dusty Ermine 1936,Mr 7,11:6
Horne, Geoffrey
High Named Today 1954,D 11,11:2
Too Late the Phalarope 1956,O 12,35:1
Jeannette 1960,Mr 25,20:2
Strange Interlude 1963,Mr 13,5:2
Horne, Kenneth (Playwright)
Father of Lies 1935,Ja 27,VIII,3:1
Yes and No 1937,N 14,XI,3:1
Love in a Mist 1941,N 30,IX,3:1
Horne, Lena
Dance With Your Gods 1934,O 8,14:3
Lew Leslie's Blackbirds of 1939 1939,F 13,12:2
Jamaica 1957,N 1,32:2
Jamaica 1957,N 10,II,1:1
Horne, Marvin
Winners and Losers 1947,F 27,27:2
Deputy of Paris, The 1947,Mr 22,9:5
Horne, Mary
Best Years 1932,S 8,16:2
Strange Gods 1933,Ap 17,16:6
Horne, Nat
I'm Solomon 1968,Ap 24,51:1
Zorba 1968,N 18,58:1
Applause 1970,Mr 31,35:1
Horne, Terry
Artists and Models 1930,Je 11,33:2
Horne, Victoria
On the Rocks 1938,Je 16,20:2
Aries Is Rising 1939,N 22,16:5
Horne, William
Sex Fable, The 1931,O 21,26:1
This Is the Army 1942,Jl 5,28:2
Helen Goes to Troy 1944,Ap 25,17:2
Helen Goes to Troy 1944,Ap 30,II,1:1
Gypsy Baron, The 1944,N 15,20:3
Horner, Charles (Playwright)
Hook'n Ladder 1952,Ap 30,31:2
Lyle 1970,Mr 21,16:2
Horner, Ed
Peer Gynt 1951,Ja 29,15:2
Horner, Harry
Iron Men 1936,O 20,30:6
Horner, Harry (Costume Designer)
Jeremiah 1939,F 4,11:2
Family Portrait 1939,Mr 9,18:4
Railroads on Parade 1939,My 14,XI,1:2
Horner, Harry (Director)
Eternal Road, The 1937,Ja 8,14:2
In Time to Come 1941,D 29,20:2
Tovarich 1952,My 15,39:2
Horner, Harry (Lighting Director)
Lily of the Valley 1942,Ja 27,25:2
Christopher Blake 1946,D 2,33:2
Hazel Flagg 1953,F 12,22:2
Horner, Harry (Miscellaneous)
Christopher Blake 1946,D 2,33:2
Horner, Harry (Scenic Designer)
All the Living 1938,Mr 25,14:4
Escape This Night 1938,Ap 23,18:1
Gloriana 1938,N 26,18:4
Jeremiah 1939,F 4,11:2
Family Portrait 1939,Mr 9,18:4
World We Make, The 1939,N 21,19:1
Reunion in New York 1940,F 22,28:4
Burning Deck, The 1940,Mr 2,9:2
Weak Link, The 1940,Mr 5,19:2
Lady in the Dark 1941,Ja 24,14:2
Lady in the Dark 1941,F 2,IX,1:1
Five Alarm Waltz 1941,Mr 14,16:2
Lady in the Dark 1941,S 3,26:6
Let's Face It 1941,O 30,26:2
Banjo Eyes 1941,D 26,20:2
Lily of the Valley 1942,Ja 27,25:2
Heart of a City 1942,F 13,24:6
Kiss for Cinderella, A 1942,Mr 11,22:2

Horner, Harry (Scenic Designer)—Cont
Walking Gentleman, The 1942,My 8,26:2
Star and Garter 1942,Je 25,26:2
Winged Victory 1943,N 22,24:1
Winged Victory 1943,N 28,II,1:1
Me and Molly 1948,F 27,27:2
Me and Molly 1948,Mr 7,II,1:1
Joy to the World 1948,Mr 19,28:2
My L A 1951,D 9,87:1
Tovarich 1952,My 15,39:2
Hazel Flagg 1953,F 12,22:2
How to Make a Man 1961,F 3,16:1
Idiot's Delight 1970,Mr 24,39:1
Horner, Jack
Stairs, The 1927,N 8,32:7
Horner, Jacqueline
Swan Song 1946,My 16,29:2
Horner, Jed (Director)
Cloud 7 1958,F 15,15:2
Masquerade 1959,Mr 17,42:1
Horner, Jed (Miscellaneous)
Fair Game 1957,N 4,39:1
Horner, Matt
Mrs Moonlight 1952,N 21,21:1
Horner, Richard (Producer)
Debut 1956,F 23,32:1
High Spirits 1964,Ag 8,34:1
Queen and the Rebels, The 1965,F 26,16:1
Hadrian VII 1969,Ja 9,22:1
Hornick, Harry
Oh, Promise Me 1930,N 25,31:1
Threepenny Opera, The 1933,Ap 14,22:4
Sailor, Beware! 1933,S 29,24:4
Horniman, Roy (Playwright)
Love in Pawn 1923,Ap 8,VIII,1:7
Money Lender, The 1924,N 23,VIII,2:4
Money Lender, The 1928,Ag 28,27:3
Hornsby, Joe (Composer)
Tall Story 1959,Ja 30,33:2
Hornsby, Nancy
Women of Property 1937,Ag 1,X,1:7
Horovitz, Israel (Lyricist)
Night 1968,N 29,52:1
Noon 1968,N 29,52:1
Morning 1968,N 29,52:1
Honest-to-God Schnozzola, The 1969,Ap 22,40:2
Leader, The 1969,Ap 22,40:2
Horovitz, Israel (Playwright)
Indian Wants the Bronx, The 1968,Ja 18,47:2
It's Called the Sugar Plum 1968,Ja 18,47:2
Collision Course; Rats 1968,My 9,55:2
Rats 1968,Je 30,II,1:1
Indian Wants the Bronx, The 1968,Je 30,II,1:1
Morning 1968,N 29,52:1
Morning 1968,D 8,II,5:4
Leader, The 1969,Ap 22,40:2
Honest-to-God Schnozzola, The 1969,Ap 22,40:2
Horowitz, Hirschel (Composer)
Political Party, A 1963,S 27,17:5
Horowitz, Hirschel (Lyricist)
Political Party, A 1963,S 27,17:5
Horowitz, Hirschel (Playwright)
Political Party, A 1963,S 27,17:5
Horowitz, Norbert
Wall, The 1960,O 12,44:4
Horowitz, Rochelle
Enchanting Melody 1964,N 25,40:1
Horrego, Milagros
Pericas, Las 1969,N 2,86:5
Horrey, Frederick
King Lear 1947,F 19,32:2
As You Like It 1947,F 21,16:2
Merchant of Venice, The 1947,F 24,16:2
Volpone 1947,F 25,32:2
Hamlet 1947,F 27,27:2
Horrigan, Patrick
In the Matter of J Robert Oppenheimer 1969,Mr 7,28:1
Horrigan, Patrick (Miscellaneous)
Place for Chance, The 1964,My 15,44:2
Red Cross 1968,Ap 29,47:2
Muzeeka 1968,Ap 29,47:2
Year Boston Won the Pennant, The 1969,My 23,38:1
Horrocks, Cyril
Escape Me Never! 1935,Ja 22,22:2
Horrocks, Esther
On the Town 1959,Ja 16,36:1
Horsely, Chorcy
Blithe Spirit 1946,Je 5,17:3
Horsford, Anna Maria
Black Quartet, A; Great Goodness of Life (A Coon Show) 1969,Jl 31,28:1
Horst, Louis
Untitled-Dance 1930,F 13,25:2
Horst, Louis (Choreographer)
Noah 1935,F 14,25:2
Horst, Louis (Composer)
Noah 1935,F 14,25:2
Horst, Louis (Miscellaneous)
Mascaiada 1929,D 28,10:6
Horstmann, Del
Damn Yankees 1955,My 6,17:1
Fiorello! 1959,N 24,45:3

Horstmann, Del—Cont

Oklahoma! 1969,Je 24,37:1
Jimmy 1969,O 24,38:1

Horswill, James

Richard III 1965,Je 3,26:1

Hortenstein, Jascha (Lyricist)

Circle of Chalk, The 1941,Mr 27,28:4

Horton, Ann Elizabeth (Scenic Designer)

Caretaker, The 1963,N 25,23:2

Horton, Bert

Slightly Married 1943,O 26,19:2

Horton, Claude

Come Across 1938,S 15,28:3
There Shall Be No Night 1940,Ap 30,25:2
Rebecca 1945,Ja 19,17:2
Constant Wife, The 1951,D 10,34:3
Pin to See the Peepshow, A 1953,S 18,17:2
Witness for the Prosecution 1954,D 17,35:2
Dial 'M' for Murder 1958,F 8,12:2
Three Love Affairs; Still Life 1958,Mr 11,33:1
King and I, The 1960,My 12,40:1
Call on Kuprin, A 1961,My 26,29:3
Importance of Being Earnest, The 1963,F 27,5:2
Not Now Darling 1970,O 30,33:1

Horton, Edward Everett

Among the Married 1929,D 8,X,2:7
Springtime for Henry 1940,F 27,16:3
Springtime for Henry 1951,Mr 15,36:2
Carousel 1965,Ag 11,39:1

Horton, Edward Everett (Producer)

Among the Married 1929,D 8,X,2:7

Horton, Frank

Little Old New York 1920,S 9,9:2
Lady, The 1923,D 5,23:2
Port O' London 1926,F 10,20:2
Triple Crossed 1927,My 6,21:2
Love in the Tropics 1927,O 19,24:3
Excess Baggage 1927,D 27,24:2
Guns 1928,Ag 7,25:2
Carnival 1929,Ap 25,32:5
Crooks' Convention, The 1929,S 19,37:4
Suspense 1930,Ag 13,22:3
Purity 1930,D 26,18:2
Privilege Car 1931,Mr 4,33:1
Adam Had Two Sons 1932,Ja 21,17:1

Horton, Helen

Seven Mirrors 1945,O 26,17:2
Mary of Magdala 1946,Mr 26,24:5

Horton, John

Hamlet 1957,Jl 3,15:2
Twelfth Night 1957,Jl 4,16:4
Henry IV, Part I 1958,Je 25,23:3
Much Ado About Nothing 1958,Je 26,22:1
Winter's Tale, The 1958,Jl 23,34:3
As You Like It 1959,Jl 1,27:1
Othello 1959,Jl 2,17:2
King John 1960,Je 29,26:2
Tempest, The 1962,Je 22,14:1
Cyrano de Bergerac 1962,Ag 1,21:1
Moby Dick 1962,N 29,45:1
Photo Finish 1963,F 14,5:2
Chemmy Circle, The 1968,Ag 10,17:2

Horton, Kate (Playwright)

Harvest 1925,Ap 19,IX,2:1
Harvest 1925,S 21,16:2
Ballyhoo 1927,Ja 5,18:1

Horton, Lloyd

Roll Sweet Chariot 1934,O 3,24:3

Horton, Louis

Wooden Idol, The 1930,My 13,27:2

Horton, Louisa

Happiest Years, The 1949,Ap 26,29:8
Mrs Warren's Profession 1950,O 26,39:2
Grand Tour, The 1951,D 11,45:2
Tall Kentuckian, The 1953,Je 17,30:1
Pony Cart, The 1954,S 15,39:2

Horton, Peter

Achilles Had a Heel 1935,O 14,20:2

Horton, Robert

110 in the Shade 1963,O 25,37:1

Horton, Roy

Hayride 1954,S 14,24:2

Horton, Russell

Displaced Person, The 1966,D 30,15:1
What Did We Do Wrong? 1967,O 23,56:1
Papers 1968,D 3,54:1
Satisfaction Guaranteed 1969,F 12,31:1

Horton, Susan (Miscellaneous)

Confederacy, The 1958,Jl 3,20:1

Horton, Walter

Nightcap, The 1921,Ag 16,18:3
Dagger, The 1925,S 10,28:1
Tia Juana 1927,N 16,28:4
Great Scott! 1929,S 3,25:1

Horvath, Joan (Producer)

And the Wind Blows 1959,Ap 29,28:1

Horvath, Julia

Rosalinda; Fledermaus, Die 1942,O 29,26:5

Horvath, Odeon (Playwright)

Bergbahn 1929,My 26,IX,2:3
Italienische Nacht 1931,My 10,VIII,1:5
Kasimir und Karoline 1932,D 18,X,4:5

Horwin, Jerry (Playwright)

One More Genius 1936,Ag 11,24:6

My Dear Children 1939,Mr 25,19:6
My Dear Children 1940,F 1,16:2

Horwitt, Arnold B (Lyricist)

Are You With It? 1945,N 12,17:3
Plain and Fancy 1955,Ja 28,14:2
Plain and Fancy 1955,F 6,II,1:1
Girls Against the Boys, The 1959,N 3,26:1

Horwitt, Arnold B (Playwright)

It's About Time 1942,Mr 31,28:3
Inside U S A 1948,My 1,19:2
Two's Company 1952,D 16,43:5
Girls Against the Boys, The 1959,N 3,26:1

Horwitz, Aurum

Uriel Acosta 1939,D 31,18:3

Horwitz, Seymour B

Cocktails of 1934 1934,My 5,22:1

Horwood, Robert

Beyond Evil 1926,Je 8,23:2

Hosalla, Hans-Dieter (Composer)

Resistable Ascension of Arturo Ui, The 1960,D 25,II,5:1

Hosford, Maud

Letter of the Law, The; Robe Rouge, La 1920,F 24,11:1

Hosier, Beverly

Red, Hot and Blue! 1936,O 30,26:3
Million Dollar Baby 1945,D 22,17:2
Come of Age 1952,Ja 24,22:2

Hoskins, Fred

Month in the Country, A 1959,Mr 2,32:2
Clandestine on the Morning Line 1959,D 5,18:2
Caucasian Chalk Circle, The 1961,N 1,35:1

Hoskins, Fred (Miscellaneous)

Month in the Country, A 1959,Mr 2,32:2
Burning of the Lepers, The 1962,Ap 5,29:1
Devils, The 1963,N 5,25:1

Hoskins, Grania (Miscellaneous)

Sunday Dinner 1970,N 3,28:1

Hoskins, Roberta

Carry Nation 1932,O 31,18:2

Hoskins, Sheldon B

Carmen Jones 1943,D 3,26:2

Hoskins, Sheldon B (Choreographer)

Carmen Jones 1951,S 22,8:6

Hosler, Beverly

Lend an Ear 1948,D 17,38:2

Hoss, Kurt D

Tableaux 1961,D 18,41:3

Hot Shots, Four

Earl Carroll's Vanities 1940,Ja 15,11:2

Hotchkis, Joan

Alley of the Sunset 1959,D 31,11:1

Hotchkis, John (Composer)

Legend of Lovers 1951,D 27,17:1
Firstborn, The 1957,Ja 7,29:2
Waltz of the Toreadors, The 1958,Mr 5,37:1

Hotchkiss, Elizabeth

Ghost Bereft 1933,F 1,13:5

Hotchkiss, James R (Scenic Designer)

Shylock and His Daughter 1947,S 30,22:2

Hotchkiss, Marlow

Jack Jack 1968,Je 23,74:5

Hotchkiss, Mary

Just Because 1922,Mr 23,11:1

Hotchner, A E (Lyricist)

White House, The 1964,My 20,39:1

Hotchner, A E (Playwright)

White House, The 1964,My 20,39:1

Hotopp, Michael (Scenic Designer)

Patience 1967,O 13,32:1
Iolanthe 1967,O 18,40:1
Mikado, The 1967,O 25,42:2
Gondoliers, The 1967,O 29,83:1
H M S Pinafore 1967,N 1,40:1

Hott, Jordan (Producer)

Dames at Sea 1968,D 21,46:1
Dames at Sea 1970,S 24,60:1

Hotton, Donald

High Named Today 1954,D 11,11:2
Lady From the Sea, The 1956,D 13,49:5
Two Executioners, The 1960,My 17,42:2
This Side of Paradise 1962,F 22,19:6
Crime and Crime 1963,D 17,51:2
Malcolm 1966,Ja 12,29:1

Hou, Philemon

Sponono 1964,Ap 3,28:1

Houck, Ted

Truce of the Bear 1957,O 24,39:1
Dark of the Moon 1958,F 27,22:2

Houck, Thomas

Little Old New York 1920,S 9,9:2

Houdini, Harry

Untitled-Magic Show 1925,D 15,4:6

Hougenot, Harry

Fatal Wedding, The 1924,Je 3,22:3

Hough, Will M (Original Author)

Time, Place and the Girl, The 1942,O 22,24:3

Hough, Will M (Playwright)

Pitter Patter 1920,S 29,12:2

Houghton, Chandler

Spring Fever 1925,Ag 4,14:2

Houghton, Ella

Merry Wives of Windsor, The 1928,Mr 20,20:1

Houghton, Ella—Cont

Under the Gaslight 1929,Ap 3,27:1

Houghton, Genevieve

Broadway Brevities, 1920 1920,S 30,12:2

Houghton, Jane

Masked Woman, The 1922,D 23,14:2

Houghton, Katharine

Front Page, The 1969,My 12,54:2
Scent of Flowers, A 1969,O 21,42:1
Scent of Flowers, A 1969,N 2,II,3:1

Houghton, Norris

Zuider Zee 1928,D 19,24:4
Torch Bearers, The 1929,Mr 22,30:4
Second Man, The 1930,My 2,23:2

Houghton, Norris (Costume Designer)

Coriolanus 1954,Ja 20,34:2
Who'll Save the Plowboy? 1962,Ja 10,24:2

Houghton, Norris (Director)

Macbeth 1948,Ap 1,30:2
Macbeth 1948,Ap 11,II,1:1
Uniform of Flesh 1949,Ja 31,15:2
Clutterbuck 1949,D 5,29:2
Billy Budd 1951,F 12,18:3
Billy Budd 1951,F 18,II,1:1
Tall Kentuckian, The 1953,Je 17,30:1
Sea Gull, The 1954,My 12,38:1
Sea Gull, The 1954,My 23,II,1:1
Mary Stuart 1957,O 9,39:1
World of Cilli Wang, The 1957,O 15,38:4
Makropoulos Secret, The 1957,D 4,52:4
Infernal Machine, The 1958,F 4,33:1
Two Gentlemen of Verona 1958,Mr 19,35:1
Family Reunion, The 1958,O 21,39:1
Power and the Glory, The 1958,D 12,2:7
Taming of the Shrew, The 1963,Mr 8,9:1
Next Time I'll Sing to You 1963,N 28,69:2
Right You Are (If You Think You Are) 1964,Mr 5,37:1
Tavern, The 1964,Mr 6,39:2
Scapin 1964,Mr 10,43:1
Impromptu at Versailles 1964,Mr 10,43:1
Lower Depths, The 1964,Mr 31,30:1
Tragical Historie of Doctor Faustus, The 1964,O 6,34:2

Houghton, Norris (Miscellaneous)

Carry Nation 1932,O 31,18:2
You Can't Take It With You 1965,N 24,32:1

Houghton, Norris (Producer)

Golden Apple, The 1954,Mr 12,15:2
Sandhog 1954,N 24,17:1
Doctor's Dilemma, The 1955,Ja 12,22:1
Master Builder, The 1955,Mr 2,23:2
Phoenix '55 1955,Ap 25,20:2
Carefree Tree, The 1955,O 12,37:2
Anna Christie 1955,N 22,41:1
Six Characters in Search of an Author 1955,D 12,38:1
Venice Preserv'd 1955,D 13,54:4
Stronger, The 1956,F 22,23:2
Miss Julie 1956,F 22,23:2
Queen After Death 1956,Mr 13,33:2
Month in the Country, A 1956,Ap 4,23:1
Littlest Revue, The 1956,My 23,37:2
Saint Joan 1956,S 12,42:1
Diary of a Scoundrel 1956,N 5,41:1
Good Woman of Setzuan, The 1956,D 19,41:2
Measure for Measure 1957,Ja 23,24:1
Duchess of Malfi, The 1957,Mr 20,33:1
Livin' the Life 1957,Ap 29,20:1
Beaux' Stratagem, The 1959,F 25,35:4
Once Upon a Mattress 1959,My 12,40:1
Pirates of Penzance, The 1961,S 7,41:1
Androcles and the Lion 1961,N 22,24:2
Who'll Save the Plowboy? 1962,Ja 10,24:2
Oh Dad, Poor Dad, Mamma's Hung You in the Closet and I'm Feelin' So Sad 1962,F 27,28:1
Abe Lincoln in Illinois 1963,Ja 23,5:2
Dragon, The 1963,Ap 10,32:1
Too Much Johnson 1964,Ja 16,29:1

Houghton, Norris (Scenic Designer)

In Clover 1937,O 14,23:1
Stop-Over 1938,Ja 12,16:5
How to Get Tough About It 1938,F 9,16:2
Whiteoaks 1938,Mr 24,20:2
Dame Nature 1938,S 27,24:3
Waltz in Goose Step 1938,N 2,26:2
Good Hunting 1938,N 22,26:5
Sleeping Prince, The 1956,N 2,31:1
Makropoulos Secret, The 1957,D 4,52:4
Family Reunion, The 1958,O 21,39:1
Family Reunion, The 1958,O 26,II,1:1
Who'll Save the Plowboy? 1962,Ja 10,24:2
Dragon, The 1963,Ap 10,32:1

Houghton, Stanley (Playwright)

Fanny Hawthorn 1922,My 12,22:2
Little Theatre Tournament; Fancy Free 1929,My 9,34:3

Houlene, Joseph

Smyth With a y 1937,Je 30,19:5

Houloos, Jean

Allegro 1947,O 11,10:2
Kiss Me, Kate 1949,Ja 30,II,6:5

Hourigan, Edmund B

Steppe Around 1922,Mr 29,17:4

Hourwich, Ena
Drunkard, The; Fallen Saved, The 1929,D 31,14:6
Hourwich, Ena (Costume Designer)
Drunkard, The; Fallen Saved, The 1929,D 31,14:6
House, Billy
Vaudeville (Palace) 1927,N 1,20:3
Vaudeville (Palace) 1928,Jl 17,15:5
Luckee Girl 1928,S 17,28:6
Murder at the Vanities 1933,Ag 31,20:1
Murder at the Vanities 1933,S 13,22:4
White Horse Inn 1936,O 2,28:5
Show Boat 1948,S 9,33:2
House, Charles A
Beggar on Horseback 1924,F 13,17:2
House, Earl
Blue Flame, The 1920,Mr 16,18:1
Loggerheads 1925,F 10,21:1
Harvest 1925,Ap 19,IX,2:1
My Country 1926,Ag 10,19:1
Set a Thief 1927,F 22,22:1
House, Eric
All's Well That Ends Well 1953,Jl 16,18:2
Measure for Measure 1954,Je 30,23:1
Taming of the Shrew, The 1954,Jl 1,22:2
Oedipus Rex 1954,Jl 17,6:6
Merchant of Venice, The 1955,Jl 1,13:1
Tamburlaine the Great 1956,Ja 20,19:1
Henry V 1956,Je 20,27:2
Merry Wives of Windsor, The 1956,Je 21,34:4
Makropoulos Secret, The 1957,D 4,52:4
Two Gentlemen of Verona 1958,Mr 19,35:1
H M S Pinafore 1960,S 8,41:1
Pirates of Penzance, The 1961,S 7,41:1
Pirates of Penzance, The 1961,S 17,II,1:1
Richard II 1964,Je 17,47:1
Bourgeois Gentilhomme, Le 1964,Je 18,28:2
Country Wife, The 1964,Ag 3,16:1
Soldiers 1968,Mr 3,88:2
Soldiers 1968,My 2,58:1
Vatzlav 1970,Ag 23,II,1:6
House, Florence
Straw Hat, The 1926,O 15,20:2
At the Gate of the Kingdom 1927,D 9,28:5
Doctor Knock 1928,F 24,15:2
Red Rust 1929,D 18,31:1
House, Fred
Plot Thickens, The 1922,S 6,16:1
Six Characters in Search of an Author 1922,O 31,11:2
All Gummed Up 1923,Ja 29,11:2
Loose Ankles 1926,Ag 17,15:1
Spread Eagle 1927,Ap 5,30:2
Mongolia 1927,D 27,24:5
Five Star Final 1930,D 31,11:1
Sing High, Sing Low 1931,N 13,26:4
House, Henry Arthur (Playwright)
What's the Big Idea? 1926,Mr 24,20:3
For Valor 1935,N 12,24:4
For Valor 1935,N 19,27:5
House, Wallace
Outside Looking In 1925,S 8,28:1
Juno and the Paycock 1926,Mr 16,22:1
Humble, The 1926,O 14,22:2
Witch, The 1926,N 19,22:5
As You Like It 1936,Ap 24,18:4
As You Like It 1941,O 21,29:2
Mexican Mural; Vera Cruz Interior 1942,Ap 27,19:2
Mexican Mural; Moonlight Scene 1942,Ap 27,19:2
House, Wallace (Director)
Wall Street Scene 1937,O 19,29:2
House, William
Troika 1930,Ap 2,32:6
Houseman, John (Director)
Lady From the Sea, The 1934,My 2,25:2
Valley Forge 1934,D 11,28:3
Hamlet 1936,N 11,54:2
Tragical Historie of Doctor Faustus, The 1937,Ja 31,XI,1:1
Devil and Daniel Webster, The 1939,My 19,26:1
Devil and Daniel Webster, The 1939,My 21,X,1:1
Liberty Jones 1941,F 6,24:2
Anna Christie 1941,Ag 10,IX,1:8
Lute Song 1946,F 7,29:2
King Lear 1950,D 26,18:1
King Lear 1950,D 31,II,1:1
Coriolanus 1954,Ja 20,34:2
Coriolanus 1954,Ja 24,II,1:1
King John 1956,Je 28,33:5
Measure for Measure 1956,Je 29,16:1
Measure for Measure 1957,Ja 23,24:1
Measure for Measure 1957,F 3,II,1:1
Taming of the Shrew, The 1957,F 21,30:2
Othello 1957,Je 24,19:2
Othello 1957,Je 30,II,1:1
Much Ado About Nothing 1957,Ag 8,15:2
Much Ado About Nothing 1957,Ag 18,II,1:1
Hamlet 1958,Je 21,11:1
Winter's Tale, The 1958,Jl 21,17:4
Winter's Tale, The 1958,Jl 27,II,1:1
Merry Wives of Windsor, The 1959,Jl 9,23:2
All's Well That Ends Well 1959,Ag 3,20:4
King Lear 1964,Jl 28,18:2
Murder in the Cathedral 1966,Je 21,38:1

Macbeth 1967,Jl 31,21:1
Pantagleize 1967,D 1,54:1
Pantagleize 1967,D 17,II,3:7
Chronicles of Hell, The 1969,O 19,II,12:1
Criminals, The 1970,F 26,33:2
Houseman, John (Miscellaneous)
Macbeth 1936,Ap 5,IX,1:4
Duchess of Malfi, The 1957,Mr 20,33:1
Houseman, John (Playwright)
Three and One 1933,O 26,22:6
And Be My Love 1934,Ja 19,25:2
Houseman, John (Producer)
Macbeth 1936,Ap 15,25:4
Julius Caesar 1937,N 28,XI,1:1
Native Son 1941,Mr 25,26:5
Native Son 1941,Ap 6,IX,1:1
Galileo 1947,Ag 1,21:4
Joy to the World 1948,Mr 19,28:2
Taming of the Shrew, The 1956,Ag 6,20:1
Houseman, MacGregor
Pigeon, The 1930,O 15,26:2
Houser, Gretchen
Idiot's Delight 1951,My 24,46:3
Houser, W D
Tiger Smiles, The 1930,D 18,29:1
Housman, Fred
Dream Play 1960,N 23,22:1
Housman, Laurence (Playwright)
Prunella; Love in a Garden 1926,Je 16,23:3
Prunella 1929,Ap 10,23:3
Victoria Regina 1935,D 13,30:5
Victoria Regina 1935,D 27,15:2
Victoria Regina 1936,Ja 5,IX,1:1
Victoria Regina 1936,S 1,24:5
Victoria Regina 1937,Je 22,26:2
Victoria Regina 1937,Jl 11,X,1:7
Victoria Regina 1938,Ap 17,X,2:1
Victoria Regina 1938,O 4,20:2
Victoria Regina 1938,O 9,X,1:3
Jacob 1942,Je 14,VIII,1:7
Houstin, Levin
Drunkard, The; Fallen Saved, The 1929,D 31,14:6
Houston, Alta Virginia
Johannes Kreisler 1922,D 25,20:3
Houston, Bill
Red, Hot and Blue! 1936,O 30,26:3
Houston, Donald
Cocktail Party, The 1949,Ag 23,28:6
Cocktail Party, The 1950,My 7,II,2:5
Under Milk Wood 1957,O 16,42:5
Under Milk Wood 1957,N 10,II,1:1
Houston, Elizabeth
Face the Music 1932,F 18,24:5
Illustrators' Show, The 1936,Ja 23,25:3
Merry Widow, The 1942,Jl 16,22:1
New Moon, The 1944,My 18,16:2
Houston, George
Chee-Chee 1928,S 26,25:1
Fioretta 1929,Ja 6,VIII,4:6
Fioretta 1929,F 6,30:3
Venetian Glass Nephew, The 1931,F 24,26:3
Cyrano de Bergerac 1932,N 13,IX,1:6
Melody 1933,F 15,17:4
Shooting Star 1933,Je 13,22:2
Caviar 1934,Je 8,19:2
O'Flynn, The 1934,D 28,24:1
Faust 1938,Ag 28,IX,2:5
Houston, Gil
Cradle Will Rock, The 1947,D 27,11:2
Houston, Grace (Costume Designer)
Two Mrs Carrolls, The 1943,Ag 4,14:1
Land of Fame 1943,S 22,31:5
What's Up 1943,N 12,24:6
Hats Off to Ice 1944,Je 23,15:2
Men to the Sea 1944,O 4,25:2
Violet 1944,O 25,16:1
Up in Central Park 1945,Ja 29,17:2
Live Life Again 1945,O 1,14:7
Call Me Mister 1946,Ap 19,26:2
Burlesque 1946,D 26,30:3
Up in Central Park 1947,My 20,29:2
Sun and I, The 1949,Mr 21,18:4
Consul, The 1950,Mr 16,41:1
Consul, The 1950,Mr 26,II,1:1
Golden State, The 1950,N 27,29:3
Hollywood Ice Revue 1953,Ja 16,17:2
Hollywood Ice Revue 1954,Ja 15,16:2
Fourposter, The 1955,Ja 6,23:3
Time of Your Life, The 1955,Ja 20,34:1
Wisteria Trees, The 1955,F 3,20:2
Grass Is Always Greener, The 1955,F 16,25:2
Houston, Grace (Miscellaneous)
What Every Woman Knows 1954,D 23,16:2
Houston, James P
First Flight 1925,S 18,26:2
Twelve Miles Out 1925,N 17,29:2
Wild Man of Borneo, The 1927,S 14,29:2
Whoopee 1928,D 5,34:3
Distant Drums 1932,Ja 19,24:3
Nine Pine Street 1933,Ap 28,15:5
Amourette 1933,S 28,25:2
Ladies' Money 1934,N 2,26:6
Jefferson Davis 1936,F 19,17:2

Houston, James P—Cont
Prologue to Glory 1938,Mr 18,22:2
Houston, Jane
Call the Doctor 1920,S 1,14:1
Open House 1925,D 15,28:3
Springboard, The 1927,O 13,23:1
Free Soul, A 1928,Ja 13,26:5
Back Here 1928,N 27,36:3
Houston, Josephine
Life Begins at 8:40 1934,Ag 28,24:2
Russian Bank 1940,My 25,20:2
Houston, Lee
Sun Showers 1923,F 6,14:2
Houston, Levin
Schoolgirl 1930,N 21,31:1
Houston, Noel (Playwright)
One-Act Variety Theatre; According to Law 1940,Mr 20,36:2
According to Law 1944,Je 2,20:3
Houston, Norman
Varying Shore, The 1921,D 6,24:1
Secrets 1922,D 26,11:1
Houston, Norman (Director)
Ghost Train, The 1926,Ag 26,17:2
Houston, Norman (Playwright)
Red Light Annie 1923,Ag 22,10:3
Houston, Paula
King Midas and the Golden Touch 1948,O 25,28:3
Bat, The 1953,Ja 21,28:2
Houston, Philip
Romance 1935,Ag 27,23:4
Houston, Robert E Jr
Coriolanus 1927,Je 18,8:3
Houston, Tom
Three Little Girls 1930,Ap 15,29:1
Houston, William
Illustrators' Show, The 1936,Ja 23,25:3
Houston (Playwright)
Last Christmas, The 1940,Ap 26,24:2
Housum, Robert (Playwright)
Persons Unknown 1922,O 26,12:1
Maid Errant 1926,Ag 8,VII,3:1
Houze, Duke (Miscellaneous)
Kicking the Castle Down 1967,Ja 19,43:1
Hovenden, Peggy
Her Friend the King 1929,O 8,34:5
Lean Harvest 1931,O 14,26:3
Berlin 1931,D 31,16:1
Foolscap 1933,Ja 12,21:2
New Faces 1934,Mr 16,24:5
Fools Rush In 1934,D 26,19:2
Hovenkamp, Henry
Falstaff; Henry IV, Part II 1965,Jl 1,35:1
Julius Caesar 1965,Jl 2,18:1
Hover, Chuck (Lighting Director)
Night of the Auk 1963,My 22,35:2
Hover, Hermie
Half Moon Inn 1925,Mr 10,14:1
Hovey, Ruth
Too True to Be Good 1937,Jl 27,24:2
Hovey, Serge (Composer)
World of Sholom Aleichem, The 1953,S 12,13:2
Tevya and His Daughters 1957,S 17,38:2
Hovhaness, Alan (Composer)
Echmiadzin 1946,O 21,27:3
Flowering Peach, The 1954,D 29,19:2
Flowering Peach, The 1955,Ja 9,II,1:1
Hoving, Lucas
Green Table, The 1942,Ja 22,12:2
Prodigal Son, The 1942,F 18,22:2
Kiss for Cinderella, A 1942,Mr 11,22:2
Rape of Lucretia, The 1948,D 30,24:2
Hovis, Joan
Country Wife, The 1957,N 28,56:1
Love Me Little 1958,Ap 15,42:2
Hovis, Larry
From A to Z 1960,Ap 21,23:2
How, George
Hamlet 1939,Jl 16,IX,2:1
Howalt, Ejnar (Playwright)
I Shall Have a Child; Jeg Skal Ha' et Barn 1939,Ap 2,X,2:4
Howard, Al
Threepenny Opera, The 1955,S 21,38:1
Howard, Alan
Titus Andronicus 1956,D 3,40:2
Garden of Sweets, The 1961,N 1,35:1
King of the Whole Damn World 1962,Ap 16,32:2
Broken Heart, The 1962,Jl 10,28:2
Square in the Eye 1965,My 20,54:1
Playroom, The 1965,D 6,49:1
Falstaff 1966,Je 20,27:1
Julius Caesar 1966,Je 24,29:2
Titus Andronicus 1967,Ag 10,43:2
Certain Young Man, A 1967,D 27,45:1
Much Ado About Nothing 1968,O 16,33:1
Troilus and Cressida 1969,Jl 31,26:1
Much Ado About Nothing 1969,S 1,13:1
Hamlet 1970,My 5,23:1
Hamlet 1970,Ag 3,37:3
Midsummer Night's Dream, A 1970,Ag 28,15:1
Midsummer Night's Dream, A 1970,S 13,II,7:1
Howard, Alison
Androcles and the Lion 1961,N 22,24:2

oward, Alison—Cont
Dark Lady of the Sonnets, The 1961,D 15,48:1
oward, Ann
Kiss Me, Kate 1970,D 26,10:4
oward, Ann (Costume Designer)
Doll's House, A 1956,My 8,29:2
loward, Arthur
Hottentot, The 1920,Mr 2,9:1
loward, Bart (Composer)
John Murray Anderson's Almanac 1953,D 11,42:2
loward, Bart (Lyricist)
John Murray Anderson's Almanac 1953,D 11,42:2
loward, Bart (Playwright)
Play on Love 1970,Ja 16,31:1
loward, Bette
Raisin' Hell in the Son 1962,Jl 3,13:2
In the Wine Time 1968,D 22,II,7:1
Ceremonies in Dark Old Men 1969,O 11,42:1
loward, Bob
Early to Bed 1943,Je 18,16:2
loward, Booth
Torch Bearers, The 1922,Ag 30,10:2
Something to Brag About 1925,Ag 14,14:3
loward, Bruce
Belle Helene, La 1941,Jl 8,14:1
Pirate, The 1942,N 26,39:2
Howard, Celia
Patrick--The First 1965,F 19,25:1
Howard, Charles
Innocent Eyes 1924,My 21,22:2
Fioretta 1929,Ja 6,VIII,4:6
Fioretta 1929,F 6,30:3
Pure in Heart, The 1934,Mr 21,24:3
Tide Rising 1937,Ja 26,17:2
Arsenic and Old Lace 1943,D 13,18:6
Bloomer Girl 1944,O 6,18:5
Howard, Claire
Wingless Victory, The 1936,D 24,20:2
Hamlet 1970,D 28,40:1
Howard, Cy
Storm Operation 1944,Ja 12,28:2
Howard, David S
Hamp 1967,Mr 10,32:1
Howard, Diane
Much Ado About Nothing 1952,My 2,20:1
Howard, Don
Sketch Book 1929,Jl 2,33:5
Howard, Dorothy
Moon Is a Gong, The 1926,Mr 13,21:3
Merry-Go-Round 1932,Ap 23,11:2
Marching Song 1937,F 18,18:2
Howard, E
After Dark: or, Neither Maid, Wife nor Widow
1929,F 10,IX,1:1
Howard, Edna
Little Jessie James 1923,Ag 16,10:4
Two Seconds 1931,O 10,20:6
Howard, Edwin R
Riff-Raff 1926,F 9,18:6
Howard, Eleanor Harris (Playwright)
Mating Dance 1965,N 4,58:1
Howard, Elizabeth
Rat, The 1925,F 11,19:3
Howard, Ernest
Bootleggers, The 1922,N 28,24:1
Sam Abramovitch 1927,Ja 20,20:5
Wall Street 1927,Ap 21,24:4
Little Theatre Tournament; Aristocrat, The
1929,My 8,34:4
Howard, Estelle
Sonny 1921,Ag 17,12:2
Howard, Esther
Sweetheart Shop, The 1920,S 1,13:4
Wildflower 1923,F 8,17:2
Tell Me More 1925,Ap 14,27:3
Sunny 1925,S 23,22:1
Allez-Opp! 1927,Ag 3,29:3
Lady for a Night, A 1928,Ap 17,26:4
New Moon, The 1928,S 20,33:1
Howard, Ethel
Cradle Song 1921,Mr 1,18:2
Howard, Eugene
Passing Show of 1921, The 1920,D 30,16:2
Passing Show of 1922, The 1922,S 21,18:2
Vaudeville (Palace) 1924,O 21,21:2
Vaudeville (Hippodrome) 1926,Ap 20,24:6
George White's Scandals 1926,Je 15,23:2
George White's Scandals 1928,Jl 3,19:1
Vaudeville (Palace) 1929,Jl 15,25:4
George White's Scandals 1929,S 24,29:1
Vaudeville (Palace) 1931,Je 15,23:5
Vaudeville (Palace) 1931,Je 22,17:2
Scandals 1931,Ag 11,28:4
Scandals 1931,Ag 16,VIII,1:1
George White's Scandals 1931,S 15,30:1
Ballyhoo of 1932 1932,S 7,14:2
Music Hall Varieties 1933,Ja 3,19:4
Ziegfeld Follies 1934,Ja 5,24:3
George White's Scandals 1935,D 26,20:2
Show Is On, The 1937,S 20,18:4
Scandals 1939,Ag 20,IX,2:1
Scandals 1939,Ag 29,17:2
Howard, Eunice
Pleased to Meet You 1928,O 30,27:2

Black Crook, The 1929,Mr 12,26:5
Howard, Ezra
Ivanov 1958,O 8,42:1
Howard, Felicia
Live and Learn 1930,Ap 10,24:6
Howard, Frances
Like a King 1921,O 4,10:1
Intimate Strangers, The 1921,N 8,28:1
Swifty 1922,O 17,14:1
Best People, The 1924,Ag 20,8:1
Howard, Frank
Sex 1926,Ap 27,22:4
Falstaff 1928,D 26,14:2
Rockefeller and the Red Indians 1968,O 25,37:1
Howard, Fred
One Thing After Another 1937,D 29,17:2
How to Get Tough About It 1938,F 9,16:2
Howard, Fred (Playwright)
Tempest in a Top Hat, A 1938,Ap 24,II,2:8
Howard, Frederick
For All of Us 1923,O 16,19:4
Mismates 1925,Ap 14,27:2
Hook-Up, The 1935,My 9,24:6
Meet the Prince 1935,Jl 9,24:5
Good Men and True 1935,O 26,12:4
I Take Care of My Friends 1936,Jl 21,13:2
All Editions 1936,D 23,17:2
Aries Is Rising 1939,N 22,16:5
Howard, Garland
Change Your Luck 1930,Je 7,10:2
Howard, Garland (Playwright)
Change Your Luck 1930,Je 7,10:2
Howard, George
Mary the 3d 1923,F 6,14:2
Howard, Grace Virginia
Soliloquy 1938,N 29,26:4
Howard, Gus
Free for All 1931,S 9,25:1
Howard, H C
Student Prince, The 1931,Ja 30,18:1
Howard, Halle
Macbeth 1936,Ap 15,25:4
Howard, Harold
Innocent Idea, An 1920,My 26,9:4
Champion, The 1921,Ja 4,11:1
Howard, Harry (Producer)
Scene of the Crime, The 1940,Mr 29,24:1
Marinka 1945,Jl 19,19:2
Howard, Harvey
Ruddigore 1927,My 21,25:2
Howard, Henry
Kibitzer, The 1929,F 19,22:5
Living Corpse, The 1929,D 7,19:1
Doctor X 1930,Jl 31,12:4
Up Pops the Devil 1930,S 2,19:1
Incubator 1932,N 2,23:3
Man Is Man 1962,S 19,31:1
Brig, The 1963,My 16,40:1
Antigone 1968,O 11,36:1
Howard, Irene
Berkeley Square 1929,N 5,32:4
Howard, Jack
Diamond Lil 1928,Ap 10,32:1
Little Ol' Boy 1933,Ap 25,15:5
Hold Your Horses 1933,S 26,26:4
High Kickers 1941,N 1,21:2
Place of Our Own, A 1945,Ap 3,23:7
Up in Central Park 1947,My 20,29:2
Diamond Lil 1948,N 30,33:2
Diamond Lil 1949,F 7,16:2
Diamond Lil 1951,S 15,8:2
Howard, James
Music Hall Varieties 1932,N 23,15:3
Troilus and Cressida 1965,Ag 13,17:1
Howard, Jan
Bagels and Yox 1951,S 13,38:2
Howard, Jean
Age of Innocence, The 1928,N 28,24:2
Howard, Jennifer
Winter's Tale, The 1946,Ja 16,18:6
Fatal Witness, The 1946,N 20,43:2
Sundown Beach 1948,S 8,37:1
Love Me Long 1949,N 8,34:5
Howard, Jewel
Sextet 1958,N 27,53:1
Howard, Jim
Kiss Me, Kate 1952,Ja 9,24:6
Aunt Caroline's Will 1954,Ag 11,21:1
Howard, Joe E
Time, Place and the Girl, The 1942,O 22,24:3
Howard, Joe E (Composer)
Time, Place and the Girl, The 1942,O 22,24:3
Howard, Joe E (Original Author)
Time, Place and the Girl, The 1942,O 22,24:3
Howard, John
Tired Business Man, The 1929,Je 5,32:5
Hazel Flagg 1953,F 12,22:2
Howard, Jordon
Henry V 1964,My 13,52:1
Howard, Joseph E
Vaudeville (Palace) 1928,Mr 13,23:2
Howard, Katherine
Jubilee 1935,O 14,20:1

Howard, Keble (Playwright)
Sweet William 1921,My 29,VI,1:7
Howard, Ken
We Bombed in New Haven 1967,D 7,58:1
Promises, Promises 1968,D 2,59:3
1776 1969,Mr 17,46:2
1776 1969,Mr 23,II,1:1
Child's Play 1970,F 18,39:1
Child's Play 1970,Mr 1,II,1:4
Howard, Larry
By the Beautiful Sea 1954,Ap 9,20:1
Howard, Leslie
Just Suppose 1920,N 2,15:1
Wren, The 1921,O 11,22:1
Danger 1921,D 23,18:3
Truth About Blayds, The 1922,Mr 15,22:1
Serpent's Tooth, A 1922,Ag 25,8:5
Romantic Age, The 1922,N 15,22:1
Lady Cristilinda, The 1922,D 26,11:2
Anything Might Happen 1923,F 21,22:3
Anything Might Happen 1923,F 25,VII,1:1
Aren't We All? 1923,My 22,14:2
Outward Bound 1924,Ja 8,26:1
Outward Bound 1924,Ja 13,VII,1:1
Werewolf, The 1924,Ag 26,6:1
Shall We Join the Ladies? 1925,Ja 14,19:1
Isabel 1925,Ja 14,19:1
Green Hat, The 1925,S 16,23:2
Her Cardboard Lover 1927,Mr 22,30:5
Murray Hill 1927,Ag 21,VII,1:8
Murray Hill 1927,S 30,29:1
Escape 1927,O 27,33:1
Escape 1927,N 6,IX,1:1
Her Cardboard Lover 1928,S 9,IX,2:7
Berkeley, Square 1929,Mr 24,X,4:5
Candle Light 1929,S 22,IX,2:6
Candle-Light 1929,O 1,28:2
Berkeley Square 1929,N 5,32:4
Berkeley Square 1929,D 1,X,1:1
Animal Kingdom, The 1932,Ja 3,VIII,3:1
Animal Kingdom, The 1932,Ja 13,26:4
Animal Kingdom, The 1932,Ja 24,1:1
This Side Idolatry 1933,O 20,15:4
This Side Idolatry 1933,N 5,IX,1:3
Petrified Forest, The 1934,D 21,31:6
Petrified Forest, The 1934,D 30,IX,1:6
Petrified Forest, The 1935,Ja 8,26:1
Petrified Forest, The 1935,Ja 13,IX,1:1
Hamlet 1936,O 20,31:3
Hamlet 1936,O 25,X,1:5
Hamlet 1936,N 11,54:2
Howard, Leslie (Director)
Murray Hill 1927,S 30,29:1
Berkeley Square 1929,N 5,32:4
Out of a Blue Sky 1930,F 10,20:6
We Are No Longer Children 1932,Ap 1,17:2
Hamlet 1936,O 20,31:3
Hamlet 1936,N 11,54:2
Howard, Leslie (Playwright)
Murray Hill 1927,Ag 21,VII,1:8
Murray Hill 1927,S 30,29:1
Out of a Blue Sky 1930,F 10,20:6
Elizabeth Sleeps Out 1935,Ag 27,23:4
Elizabeth Sleeps Out 1936,Ap 21,27:6
Howard, Leslie (Producer)
Berkeley Square 1929,N 5,32:4
Animal Kingdom, The 1932,Ja 3,VIII,3:1
Animal Kingdom, The 1932,Ja 13,26:4
This Side Idolatry 1933,O 20,15:4
Petrified Forest, The 1934,D 21,31:6
Petrified Forest, The 1935,Ja 8,26:1
Hamlet 1936,O 20,31:3
Hamlet 1936,N 11,54:2
Howard, Lewis
While the Sun Shines 1944,S 20,21:3
While the Sun Shines 1944,S 24,II,1:1
Howard, Lisa
'Tis Pity She's a Whore 1958,D 6,21:1
Howard, Lita
Across the Board on Tomorrow Morning
1942,Mr 21,13:5
Theatre of the Soul 1942,Mr 21,13:5
Howard, Louisa
Porgy and Bess 1935,O 11,30:2
Porgy and Bess 1942,Ja 23,16:2
Howard, Lucy T
Kind Lady 1938,Jl 11,14:2
Howard, Marc
Secret Concubine, The 1960,Mr 22,29:2
Howard, Marcella
I Married an Angel 1938,My 12,26:2
Howard, Marcia
White Cargo 1960,D 30,12:1
Howard, Mary
Hundred Years Old, A 1929,O 2,28:2
This Man's Town 1930,Mr 11,24:4
Unexpected Husband 1931,Je 3,29:4
Howard, Max
Tempest, The 1970,F 15,67:1
Howard, Mel (Producer)
Once There Was a Russian 1961,F 20,32:2
Howard, Melvin
Carmen Jones 1943,D 3,26:2

Howard, Michael
Many Moons 1947,D 15,35:2
Lamp at Midnight 1947,D 22,29:2
Rumpelstiltskin 1948,Mr 15,27:3
King Midas and the Golden Touch 1948,O 25,28:3
Blood Wedding 1949,F 7,16:2
Sun and I, The 1949,Mr 21,18:4
Pied Piper of Hamelin, The 1950,Ap 3,19:2
Hall of Healing 1952,My 8,35:6
Time to Go 1952,My 8,35:6
Victims of Duty 1964,My 28,40:2
New Tenant, The 1964,My 28,40:2
Howard, Michael (Director)
Finian's Rainbow 1953,Mr 7,13:2
Time of Storm 1954,F 26,14:2
Troublemakers, The 1954,D 31,11:3
Land Beyond the River, A 1957,Mr 29,15:7
Third Best Sport 1958,D 31,15:3
I Am a Camera 1961,Jl 10,26:1
O Marry Me 1961,O 28,13:1
King Arthur 1968,N 3,87:1
Howard, Moe
Night in Venice, A 1929,My 22,30:2
Vaudeville (Palace) 1930,Mr 3,18:5
Howard, Nicholas
Escapade 1953,N 19,40:1
Howard, Norah
Words and Music 1932,Ag 26,21:2
Geneva 1940,Ja 31,15:2
Wookey, The 1941,Ag 26,23:2
Wookey, The 1941,S 11,20:5
You Touched Me! 1945,S 26,27:2
Tonight at 8:30; Ways and Means 1948,F 21,8:2
Tonight at 8:30; Family Album 1948,F 21,8:2
Tonight at 8:30; Red Peppers 1948,F 21,8:2
Tonight at 8:30; Hands Across the Sea
  1948,F 24,20:4
Tonight at 8:30; Shadow Play 1948,F 24,20:4
Tonight at 8:30; Fumed Oak 1948,F 24,20:4
Music in the Air 1951,O 9,32:2
Mr Pickwick 1952,S 18,36:3
Dear Charles 1954,S 16,37:2
Someone Waiting 1956,F 15,26:1
Child of Fortune 1956,N 14,41:1
Jane Eyre 1958,My 2,31:1
Howard, Norman
All the King's Men 1950,Jl 19,25:6
Howard, Paul
Follow Thru 1929,Ja 10,24:3
Howard, Peter (Choreographer)
I Can Get It for You Wholesale 1962,Mr 23,29:1
Wonder World 1964,My 18,32:1
Minnie's Boys 1970,Mr 27,27:1
Howard, Peter (Composer)
Desert Incident, A 1959,Mr 25,40:1
Her First Roman 1968,O 21,53:3
Minnie's Boys 1970,Mr 27,27:1
Howard, Peter (Miscellaneous)
Say Darling 1958,Ap 4,17:1
Party With Betty Comden and Adolph Green, A
  1958,D 24,2:7
Carnival! 1961,Ap 14,22:2
Subways Are for Sleeping 1961,D 28,22:1
I Can Get It for You Wholesale 1962,Mr 23,29:1
Here's Love 1963,O 4,28:1
Hello, Dolly! 1964,Ja 17,22:1
Roar of the Greasepaint-the Smell of the Crowd
  1965,My 17,46:2
Hello, Dolly! 1967,N 13,61:1
Strada, La 1969,D 15,63:1
Howard, Peter (Musical Director)
On the Town 1959,Ja 16,36:1
How Now, Dow Jones 1967,D 8,53:1
Carnival! 1968,D 13,58:1
1776 1969,Mr 17,46:2
Howard, Philip (Playwright)
And Now Goodbye 1937,Ja 19,29:1
And Now Goodbye 1937,F 3,26:4
Howard, Rance
Mister Roberts 1956,D 6,46:2
Howard, Richard (Translator)
Ping-Pong 1959,Ap 17,22:1
Two Executioners, The 1960,My 17,42:2
Automobile Graveyard, The 1961,N 14,46:2
Howard, Rita
Keep Kool 1924,My 23,16:4
Howard, Robin
Fall 1957,N 22,19:1
Howard, Robin (Producer)
Fall 1957,N 22,19:1
Howard, Ronald
To Dorothy, A Son 1951,N 20,37:2
Howard, Sally
Sojourner Truth 1948,Ap 22,35:2
Howard, Shemp
Night in Spain, A 1927,My 4,28:2
Night in Venice, A 1929,My 22,30:2
Vaudeville (Palace) 1930,Mr 3,18:5
Howard, Sidney (Director)
Lucky Sam McCarver 1925,O 22,22:1
Ode to Liberty 1934,D 22,20:2
Most Happy Fella, The 1966,My 12,55:1

Howard, Sidney (Miscellaneous)
Morals 1925,D 1,22:2
Howard, Sidney (Original Author)
Most Happy Fella, The 1956,My 4,20:1
Most Happy Fella, The 1956,My 13,II,1:1
Most Happy Fella, The 1956,Je 10,II,7:1
Most Happy Fella, The 1959,F 11,50:2
Howard, Sidney (Playwright)
Swords 1921,S 2,9:3
Casanova 1923,S 27,10:2
Bewitched 1924,O 2,26:3
They Knew What They Wanted 1924,N 25,27:1
They Knew What They Wanted 1924,N 30,VIII,1:2
Lucky Sam McCarver 1925,O 22,22:1
Lucky Sam McCarver 1925,N 1,VIII,1:1
Ned McCobb's Daughter 1926,N 30,26:2
Ned McCobb's Daughter 1926,D 5,VIII,5:1
Silver Cord, The 1926,D 21,21:1
Silver Cord, The 1927,Ja 16,VII,1:1
Silver Cord, The 1927,S 14,29:2
Silver Cord, The 1927,O 2,VIII,1:3
Salvation 1928,F 1,31:1
Salvation 1928,F 12,VIII,1:1
Silver Cord, The 1928,F 19,VIII,2:1
Olympia 1928,O 17,26:1
Half Gods 1929,D 23,18:5
Marseilles 1930,N 18,28:2
Late Christopher Bean, The 1932,N 1,24:3
Alien Corn 1933,F 14,19:5
Alien Corn 1933,F 21,17:2
Alien Corn 1933,F 26,IX,1:1
Dodsworth 1934,F 26,20:4
Yellow Jack 1934,Mr 7,22:6
Yellow Jack 1934,Mr 18,IX,1:1
Dodsworth 1934,Ag 21,12:3
Gather Ye Rosebuds 1934,N 29,33:2
Gather Ye Rosebuds 1934,D 2,X,1:1
Ode to Liberty 1934,D 11,28:2
Ode to Liberty 1934,D 22,20:2
Alien Corn 1935,Ja 20,X,3:8
Ode to Liberty 1935,Jl 9,24:4
Late Christopher Bean, The 1935,Ag 28,13:1
Paths of Glory 1935,S 19,29:1
Paths of Glory 1935,S 27,24:2
They Knew What They Wanted 1936,Jl 7,17:2
They Knew What They Wanted 1936,Jl 8,14:2
They Knew What They Wanted 1936,Jl 21,13:1
They Knew What They Wanted 1936,Jl 28,23:4
Ode to Liberty 1937,Ag 18,15:2
Ghost of Yankee Doodle, The 1937,O 28,28:5
Ghost of Yankee Doodle, The 1937,N 7,XI,2:4
Ghost of Yankee Doodle, The 1937,N 23,26:3
Dodsworth 1938,F 23,26:2
Dodsworth 1938,Mr 13,XI,3:1
Alien Corn 1939,Jl 6,26:8
Alien Corn 1939,Jl 23,IX,2:3
They Knew What They Wanted 1939,O 3,19:1
Madam Will You Walk 1939,N 14,20:3
Yellow Jack 1944,Ap 7,23:3
Yellow Jack 1944,Ap 16,II,1:1
Lute Song 1946,F 7,29:2
Lute Song 1946,F 17,II,1:1
Yellow Jack 1947,F 28,26:2
Lute Song 1948,O 12,32:3
They Knew What They Wanted 1949,F 17,28:2
Lucky Sam McCarver 1950,Ap 15,10:6
Madam Will You Walk 1953,D 2,2:4
Madam Will You Walk 1953,D 20,II,3:1
Lute Song 1959,Mr 13,24:1
Howard, Sidney (Producer)
Abe Lincoln in Illinois 1938,O 17,12:2
Howard, Sidney (Translator)
Casanova 1923,S 16,VII,2:8
Last Night of Don Juan, The 1925,N 10,23:2
Howard, Snub
Deacon, The 1925,N 25,14:3
Howard, Sydney
Ladies' Night 1933,N 19,IX,3:7
Anything Goes 1935,Je 15,20:5
Fun and Games 1941,Ag 31,IX,1:4
Howard, Sydney (Playwright)
One, Two, Three! 1930,S 30,24:2
Howard, Terriann
Cage, The 1961,Mr 6,30:1
Daddy Come Home 1963,Ap 17,33:1
Howard, Theodore
Horse Play 1937,Ag 28,8:3
Howard, Tom
Untitled-Revue 1922,S 16,18:2
Greenwich Village Follies 1923,S 21,4:6
Vaudeville (Hippodrome) 1924,Ap 29,12:2
Greenwich Village Follies 1925,D 25,23:3
Greenwich Village Follies 1926,Ja 10,VII,1:1
Greenwich Village Follies 1926,Mr 16,22:2
Rain or Shine 1928,F 10,26:3
Rain or Shine 1928,F 19,VIII,1:1
Smiles 1930,N 19,19:2
Gang's All Here, The 1931,F 19,21:3
Keep Moving 1934,Ag 24,10:2
Bead-Tangle 1970,Jl 16,38:1
Howard, Tom (Playwright)
Dixie to Broadway 1924,O 30,22:1

Howard, Trevor
Taming of the Shrew, The 1947,D 7,II,7:1
Devil's General, The 1953,O 11,II,3:7
Howard, Velma Swanston (Translator)
Easter 1926,Mr 19,24:3
Howard, Vernon
Sing High, Sing Low 1931,N 13,26:4
Howard, Virginia
Meet the Prince 1935,Ag 6,20:4
Darkness at Noon 1951,Ja 15,13:4
Howard, Warda
Red Light Annie 1923,Ag 22,10:3
Desert Flower, The 1924,N 19,18:2
Jamboree 1932,N 25,18:4
Too Much Party 1934,Mr 6,28:4
Howard, William
Vaudeville (Palace) 1923,Mr 6,26:1
Keep Kool 1924,My 23,16:4
Storm Center 1927,D 1,33:2
Berlin 1931,D 31,16:1
Howard, Willie
Passing Show of 1921, The 1920,D 30,16:2
Passing Show of 1922, The 1922,S 21,18:2
Vaudeville (Palace) 1924,O 21,21:2
Sky High 1925,Mr 3,21:4
Vaudeville (Hippodrome) 1926,Ap 20,24:6
George White's Scandals 1926,Je 15,23:2
Scandals 1927,Jl 3,VII,1:1
George White's Scandals 1928,Jl 3,19:1
Vaudeville (Palace) 1929,Jl 15,25:4
George White's Scandals 1929,S 24,29:1
Girl Crazy 1930,O 5,IX,4:6
Girl Crazy 1930,O 15,27:1
Girl Crazy 1930,D 28,VIII,1:1
Vaudeville (Palace) 1931,Je 15,23:5
Vaudeville (Palace) 1931,Je 22,17:2
Scandals 1931,Ag 11,28:4
Scandals 1931,Ag 16,VIII,1:1
George White's Scandals 1931,S 15,30:1
Ballyhoo of 1932 1932,S 7,14:2
Music Hall Varieties 1933,Ja 3,19:4
Ziegfeld Follies 1934,Ja 5,24:3
Ziegfeld Follies 1934,Ja 21,X,1:1
George White's Scandals 1935,D 26,20:2
Show Is On, The 1937,S 20,18:4
Scandals 1939,Ag 20,IX,2:1
Scandals 1939,Ag 29,17:2
Scandals 1939,S 3,IX,1:1
Crazy With the Heat 1940,D 26,22:1
Crazy With the Heat 1941,Ja 15,18:2
Crazy With the Heat 1941,Ja 31,15:2
Priorities of 1942 1942,Mr 13,23:2
Priorities of 1942 1942,Mr 29,VIII,1:1
My Dear Public 1943,S 10,28:1
Sally 1948,My 7,31:2
Howard, Willie (Original Author)
Money Mad 1937,My 25,32:5
Howard, Willie (Playwright)
Bet Your Life 1937,Ap 6,20:2
Howard-Smith, Trevor
Faithful, The 1935,Ja 20,X,3:8
Howard's Ponies
Vaudeville (Hippodrome) 1926,Ap 27,22:3
Howarth, Donald (Director)
Lily of Little India, A 1966,Ja 22,17:2
Howarth, Donald (Playwright)
Lily of Little India, A 1966,Ja 22,17:2
Three Months Gone 1970,S 10,59:1
Howarth, Michael
Midsummer Night's Dream, A 1968,D 9,59:1
Howarth, Milton (Miscellaneous)
Coach With the Six Insides, The 1962,N 27,44:1
Coach With the Six Insides, The 1967,My 12,50:1
Howarth, Milton (Scenic Designer)
Pygmalion 1947,F 6,29:4
Night Must Fall 1947,F 13,33:6
Howat, Clark
Come Marching Home 1946,My 20,18:6
Wanhope Building, The 1947,F 11,36:5
Howe, Bette
Jenny Kissed Me 1948,D 24,12:2
Howe, Elaine
Glass of Water, A 1930,Mr 6,16:3
Howe, Estelle
Revolt of the Beavers, The 1937,My 21,19:2
Howe, Frederick
Faithful Heart, The 1922,O 11,22:1
Howe, George
Make Me Know It 1929,N 5,32:5
Queen of Scots 1934,Jl 15,X,1:3
Hamlet 1934,D 2,X,3:6
Lady's Not for Burning, The 1950,N 9,42:2
Lady's Not for Burning, The 1950,N 26,II,1:1
Mr Pickwick 1952,S 18,36:3
Mr Pickwick 1952,S 28,II,1:1
Macbeth 1962,F 7,32:2
Saint Joan 1962,F 21,57:4
Howe, Helen
Three Sisters, The 1930,Ja 9,22:2
Characters and Caricatures 1935,F 1,17:2
Sunday Nights at 9 1935,N 11,21:1
Characters and Caricatures 1937,Mr 8,22:1
These People 1938,Ap 5,19:2

Howe, Helen—Cont

Washington-All Change! 1939,N 14,19:2
Howe, Helen (Playwright)
Washington-All Change! 1939,N 14,19:2
Howe, Hilda Heywood
Comedy of Women, A 1929,S 14,17:4
Schoolgirl 1930,N 21,31:1
Social Register, The 1931,N 10,28:2
Howe, Linda
Carousel 1965,Ag 11,39:1
Howe, Martin
Bad Girl 1930,O 3,30:2
I Myself 1934,My 10,24:6
Jayhawker 1934,N 6,34:2
Howe, Prentiss
Patience 1935,S 3,24:4
Howe, Stanley H
Off the Record; Mayor Answers the Newspapers!
Wow! 1935,Je 19,23:3
Howe, Tina (Playwright)
Nest, The 1970,Ap 10,46:1
Howe, Virginia
Banjo Eyes 1941,D 26,20:2
Howe, Walter
Purple Mask, The 1920,Ja 6,18:1
Don Juan 1921,S 8,14:2
Laughing Lady, The 1923,F 13,25:1
Crooked Square, The 1923,S 11,10:2
Royal Fandango, A 1923,N 13,25:1
Second Mrs Tanqueray, The 1924,O 28,27:1
Bridge of Distances, The 1925,S 29,30:1
Master of the Inn, The 1925,D 23,22:2
Howell, Ada
Opportunity 1920,Jl 31,5:1
Howell, Bert
Kilpatrick's Old-Time Minstrels 1930,Ap 21,20:2
Howell, Billy
Around the World 1946,Je 1,9:5
Howell, Bobbie
Merry Widow, The 1943,Ag 5,19:2
Howell, David
All in the Family 1935,Jl 24,20:4
Son, The 1950,Ag 16,24:6
Macbeth 1955,O 8,12:6
Last Love of Don Juan, The 1955,N 24,40:1
Oklahoma! 1958,Mr 8,15:2
Howell, Dean
Son, The 1950,Ag 16,24:6
Howell, Elizabeth
Damn Yankees 1955,My 6,17:1
Sound of Music, The 1959,N 17,40:2
Anya 1965,N 30,48:1
Howell, Erik
Who's Who, Baby? 1968,Ja 30,36:1
Howell, George
To the Ladies! 1922,F 21,20:1
To the Ladies! 1922,Mr 12,VI,1:1
Whispering Wires 1922,Ag 8,26:2
Howell, Harry (Miscellaneous)
Girl From Nantucket, The 1945,N 9,17:2
Howell, Helen
Merry-Go-Round 1927,Je 1,25:4
Howell, Henry
Doughgirls, The 1942,D 31,19:2
Howell, Herman
World's My Oyster, The 1956,Ag 10,10:4
Howell, Herman (Miscellaneous)
But Never Jam Today 1969,Ap 24,40:1
Howell, Hoke
Make a Million 1958,O 24,39:2
Howell, Jane (Director)
Houses by the Green, The 1968,O 4,42:3
Howell, Jane (Producer)
Narrow Road to the Deep North 1968,Je 27,49:2
Howell, John (Producer)
Murder Without Crime 1943,Ag 19,24:6
Once Over Lightly 1955,Mr 16,39:1
Howell, John Daggett (Miscellaneous)
Rape of Lucretia, The 1948,D 30,24:2
Howell, Juliette
Money Mad 1937,My 25,32:5
Howell, Lois (Playwright)
Enemy Within 1931,O 6,35:3
Bidding High 1932,S 29,17:2
Howell, Lottice
Deep River 1926,S 26,VIII,2:7
Deep River 1926,O 5,26:2
Bye Bye Bonnie 1927,Ja 14,15:3
Vaudeville (Palace) 1929,S 9,30:5
Howell, Margaret
Dark of the Moon 1970,Ap 4,21:2
Howell, Martha
Mime and Me, The 1960,Ap 8,27:3
Howell, Mary
Merchants of Venus 1920,S 28,14:2
Howell, Patricia
Bright Honor 1936,S 28,14:1
Howell, Raynor
Sweethearts 1947,Ja 22,31:2
Howell, Rita
Out of This World 1955,N 10,44:2
Hobo 1961,Ap 11,41:2
Macbeth 1962,Je 20,41:1
Comedy of Errors, The 1963,Je 21,35:3

Timon of Athens 1963,Jl 31,19:2
Howell, Virginia
That Awful Mrs Eaton! 1924,S 30,27:1
Hell's Bells! 1925,Ja 27,14:2
Deacon, The 1925,N 25,14:3
Yes, Yes, Yvette 1927,O 4,32:3
Girl Trouble 1928,O 26,22:3
Congratulations 1929,My 1,28:4
This Is New York 1930,N 29,21:1
Sentinels 1931,D 26,15:1
Howell, William
Shoemaker's Holiday, The 1938,Ja 3,17:2
Lady in the Dark 1941,S 3,26:6
Rats of Norway, The 1948,Ap 16,27:6
Howells, Leon
This Way to the Tomb 1961,D 9,21:1
Howells, Reby
To Broadway With Love 1964,Ap 30,28:6
Half a Sixpence 1965,Ap 26,38:2
Maggie Flynn 1968,O 24,52:1
Howells, Ursula
Springtime for Henry 1951,Mr 15,36:2
Howes, Basil
Mr Pickwick 1952,S 18,36:3
Pin to See the Peepshow, A 1953,S 18,17:2
Burning Glass, The 1954,Mr 5,15:2
Howes, Bobby
Big Business 1937,F 19,15:3
Shephard's Pie 1941,My 18,IX,1:5
Let's Face It 1942,N 29,VIII,2:1
Finian's Rainbow 1960,Ap 28,31:1
Howes, John
Place of Our Own, A 1945,Ap 3,23:7
Howes, Mary
Merrily We Roll Along 1934,O 1,14:1
Meet the Prince 1935,Jl 9,24:5
O Evening Star 1936,Ja 9,24:6
Laughing Woman, The 1936,Jl 8,14:7
Laughing Woman, The 1936,O 14,30:1
Now You've Done It 1937,Mr 6,10:4
Save Me the Waltz 1938,Mr 1,19:2
Burning Deck, The 1940,Mr 2,9:2
Trojan Women, The 1941,Ap 9,32:5
Howes, Sally Ann
My Fair Lady 1958,Mr 9,II,1:1
My Fair Lady 1959,Ja 19,24:6
Kwamina 1961,O 24,42:1
Brigadoon 1962,My 31,21:4
Brigadoon 1963,F 1,6:2
What Makes Sammy Run? 1964,F 28,19:1
Howes (Producer)
Wild Waves 1932,Ja 24,VIII,3:3
Howett, Noel
George and Margaret 1937,F 26,25:2
Howitt, Arnold B (Lyricist)
Make Mine Manhattan 1948,Ja 16,26:2
Howitt, Arnold B (Playwright)
Make Mine Manhattan 1948,Ja 16,26:2
Howkins, James
White Lights 1927,O 12,30:4
Nine Fifteen Revue, The 1930,F 12,26:2
Howland, Alice
Gypsy Baron, The 1944,N 15,20:3
Howland, Beth
Darling of the Day 1968,Ja 29,26:2
Company 1970,Ap 27,40:1
Company 1970,My 3,II,1:4
Howland, Frederick
What Big Ears! 1942,Ap 21,18:5
Howland, Jobyna
Texas Nightingale, The 1922,N 21,15:2
Texas Nightingale, The 1922,D 3,VIII,1:1
Kid Boots 1923,D 16,IX,2:4
Kid Boots 1924,Ja 1,21:3
Gold Diggers, The 1926,D 19,VII,6:4
Gold Diggers, The 1926,D 26,VII,4:3
Stepping Out 1929,My 21,29:1
Dinner at Eight 1933,Ap 9,IX,1:7
O Evening Star 1935,D 26,20:1
O Evening Star 1936,Ja 9,24:6
Howland, Kinnaird
William Had the Words! 1964,Mr 30,36:1
Howland, Olin
What's in a Name? 1920,Mr 20,14:2
Two Little Girls in Blue 1921,My 4,10:3
Just Because 1922,Mr 23,11:1
Our Nell 1922,D 5,24:1
Wildflower 1923,F 8,17:2
Nine to Eleven, The 1925,Jl 12,VII,1:1
Vaudeville (Palace) 1926,Jl 13,19:4
Golden Dawn 1927,D 1,32:3
Howland, Olin (Choreographer)
Garrick Gaieties 1930,Je 5,29:2
Howle, Conrad
Contrast, The 1940,Mr 26,17:2
Howles, Paul (Composer)
South Pacific 1943,D 30,11:2
Howlett, Noel
Gioconda Smile, The 1948,Je 20,II,2:3
Howlett, Palmer
Shipwrecked 1924,N 13,18:1

Howlett, Stanley
Rollo's Wild Oat 1920,N 24,14:1
Back to Methuselah (Part II: The Gospel of the
Brothers Barnabas); Gospel of the Brothers
Barnabas, The (Back to Methuselah, Part II)
1922,F 28,17:2
Back to Methuselah (Part III: The Thing Happens);
Thing Happens, The (Back to Methuselah, Part
III) 1922,Mr 7,11:1
Back to Methuselah (Part V: As Far as Thought
Can Reach); As Far as Thought Can Reach (Back
to Methuselah, Part V) 1922,Mr 14,11:2
What the Public Wants 1922,My 2,22:3
Tidings Brought to Mary, The 1922,D 25,20:1
Peer Gynt 1923,F 6,14:1
Scaramouche 1923,O 25,14:2
Fashion 1924,F 5,21:2
Saint, The 1924,O 13,20:3
S S Glencairn 1924,N 4,31:4
Patience 1924,D 30,15:1
Love for Love 1925,Ap 1,21:2
Love for Love 1925,Ap 5,IX,1:2
Love for Love 1925,S 15,29:3
Adam Solitaire 1925,N 7,19:2
Morals 1925,D 1,22:2
Dream Play 1926,Ja 21,18:2
East Lynne 1926,Mr 11,18:4
Beau-Strings 1926,Ap 27,22:2
Immortal Thief, The 1926,O 4,21:1
Caponsacchi 1926,O 27,24:2
Enemy of the People, An 1927,O 4,32:5
Hamlet 1928,Ja 5,33:2
Henry V 1928,Mr 16,26:2
Howlett, Stanley (Director)
Crime in the Whistler Room, The 1924,O 10,22:2
Adam Solitaire 1925,N 7,19:2
East Lynne 1926,Mr 11,18:4
Howlin, Olin
Marie Antoinette in Pennsylvania 1949,My 12,26:2
Howlitt, Stanley
Spook Sonata, The 1924,Ja 7,23:3
Howson, Albert
Cinderella on Broadway 1920,Je 25,18:1
Twelfth Night 1921,N 1,17:1
Merchant of Venice, The 1921,N 22,17:1
Imaginary Invalid, The 1922,Jl 26,26:2
Cymbeline 1923,O 3,12:1
Virgin of Bethulia, The 1925,F 24,17:2
Lord Byron's Cain 1925,Ap 9,20:3
Howson, Albert (Director)
Shall We Join the Ladies? 1929,My 12,28:3
Howson, Frank
Prince and the Pauper, The 1920,N 2,15:1
Twelfth Night 1921,N 1,17:1
Merchant of Venice, The 1921,N 22,17:1
Romeo and Juliet 1922,D 28,20:1
If Winter Comes 1923,Ap 3,26:1
Strawberry Blonde, The 1927,F 8,20:3
Killers 1928,Mr 14,28:3
Fast Life 1928,S 27,35:2
Wild Duck, The 1928,N 19,17:1
Noble Rogue, A 1929,Ag 20,31:2
Merchant of Venice, The 1930,D 3,29:2
Merry-Go-Round 1932,Ap 23,11:2
Green Stick 1934,O 10,21:2
Woman Brown, The 1939,D 9,18:5
Howson, Loretta
Little Theatre Tournament; Shall We Join the
Ladies? 1929,My 9,34:3
Shall We Join the Ladies? 1929,My 12,28:3
Rogues and Vagabonds 1930,My 8,32:5
Hoxie, George
Doodle Dandy of the U S A 1942,O 19,15:2
Captain Brassbound's Conversion 1950,D 28,21:1
Desire Under the Elms 1952,Ja 17,23:4
Hoxie, Richmond
Dracula Sabbat 1970,O 2,28:2
Hoxworth, Duncan
Take a Gander 1956,D 14,36:4
Hoxworth, Mary Ann
Mrs Patterson 1954,D 2,37:1
Hoy, Helen
Good Earth, The 1932,O 18,23:4
Hoye, Gloria
Highest Tree, The 1959,N 5,41:1
Hoyem, Robert
Juno 1959,Mr 10,41:1
Hoyer, Roy
Tip-Top 1920,O 6,13:2
Stepping Stones 1923,N 7,14:3
Criss Cross 1926,O 13,20:2
Angela 1928,D 4,28:2
Pleasure Bound 1929,F 19,22:4
Hoyer, Roy (Choreographer)
Front Page Stuff 1926,D 29,24:4
Hoyer, Roy (Miscellaneous)
Tambourine 1925,D 30,10:2
Hoyland, William
Dance of Death, The 1967,O 20,50:1
Love for Love 1967,O 21,17:1
Hoysradt, John
Galloper, The 1924,D 19,26:2
Aiglon, L' 1925,O 31,20:3
Out o' Luck 1925,D 19,15:1

Hoysradt, John—Cont
Overture 1930,D 8,26:4
Lean Harvest 1931,O 14,26:3
Clear All Wires! 1932,S 15,19:1
Clear All Wires! 1932,S 25,IX,1:1
Valley Forge 1934,D 11,28:3
Barretts of Wimpole Street, The 1935,F 26,16:2
Patience 1935,S 3,24:4
Ziegfeld Follies 1936,Ja 31,17:2
Masque of the Kings, The 1937,F 9,19:4
Storm Over Patsy 1937,Mr 9,26:4
Julius Caesar 1937,N 12,26:6
Cradle Will Rock, The 1937,D 6,19:4
Shoemaker's Holiday, The 1938,Ja 3,17:2
Heartbreak House 1938,Ap 30,18:2
Man Who Came to Dinner, The 1939,O 17,31:1
Fledgling 1940,N 28,29:2
Actors Fund Fete 1942,F 23,24:5
Allah Be Praised! 1944,Ap 21,14:2

Hoyt, Arthur P
Octoroon, The 1929,Mr 13,28:3

Hoyt, Bradford
Moon in Capricorn 1953,O 28,37:2
Song Out of Sorrow 1955,N 1,27:3
Candida 1957,F 9,14:1

Hoyt, C Sherman (Producer)
Eternal Cage 1945,Mr 22,19:7

Hoyt, Charles (Playwright)
Texas Steer, A 1968,N 13,39:1

Hoyt, Charles Bamfield (Playwright)
Move On 1926,Ja 19,30:1

Hoyt, Charles H (Playwright)
Temperance Town, A 1929,Ag 11,VIII,2:1

Hoyt, Dick
Yeomen of the Guard, The 1957,My 22,28:3

Hoyt, George
Gala Night 1930,F 26,22:4

Hoyt, Harriet
Green Pastures, The 1935,F 27,16:2

Hoyt, Howard (Producer)
Ankles Aweigh 1955,Ap 19,27:1

Hoyt, Jacqueline
Midsummer Night's Dream, A 1932,N 18,22:2
Chinese Nightingale, The 1934,O 6,20:4

Hoyt, John
Maggie 1953,F 19,20:2

Hoyt, Julia
Squaw Man, The 1921,D 27,10:3
Rose Briar 1922,D 26,11:3
Virgin of Bethulia, The 1925,F 24,17:2
School for Scandal, The 1925,D 7,18:2
Pearl of Great Price, The 1926,N 2,34:3
Dark, The 1927,F 2,22:5
Mrs Dane's Defense 1928,F 7,30:1
Sherlock Holmes 1928,F 21,18:4
Within the Law 1928,Mr 6,20:1
Serena Blandish 1929,Ja 24,30:3
Rhapsody, The 1930,S 16,30:3
Wiser They Are, The 1931,Ap 7,31:1
Hay Fever 1931,D 30,25:1

Hoyt, Kathleen
Revolt of the Beavers, The 1937,My 21,19:2

Hoyt, Leo
Wonder Bar, The 1931,Mr 18,23:4
One Sunday Afternoon 1933,F 16,23:5
Body Beautiful, The 1935,N 1,24:3

Hoyt, Russell
Texas Town 1941,Ap 30,22:3

Hrosvitha (Playwright)
Abraham; Dulcitus; Callimachus 1926,Mr 29,24:2

Hrzan, Jiri
Whose Turn Next? 1970,Ap 19,74:3

Hsiung, S I (Director)
Lady Precious Stream 1936,Ja 28,15:2

Hsiung, S I (Playwright)
Lady Precious Stream 1936,Ja 28,15:2
Professor From Peking, The 1939,Ag 27,IX,1:5

Hsiung, S I (Translator)
Lady Precious Stream 1934,D 29,11:4
Romance of the Western Chamber 1936,F 23,X,1:1
Western Chamber, The 1936,F 23,X,1:1
Lady Precious Stream 1936,F 23,X,1:1

Hsu, Yung Ying
Family, The 1943,Mr 31,22:4

Huabiel, Charles (Composer)
Passionate Pilgrim, The 1932,O 20,24:3

Huan, A O
What the Doctor Ordered 1927,Ag 19,20:2

Huang, Alice
Business Widow, The 1923,D 11,27:1

Huang, Julia (Choreographer)
Adding Machine, The 1970,D 5,40:1

Huara, Helba
Night in Spain, A 1927,My 4,28:2
Night in Spain, A 1927,My 22,VIII,1:1
Night in Spain, A 1927,Jl 3,VII,1:1

Huban, Eileen
Paddy the Next Best Thing 1920,Ag 28,5:5
Fanny Hawthorn 1922,My 12,22:2
Henry IV, Part I 1926,Je 1,29:1
Window Panes 1927,F 22,22:2
Troilus and Cressida 1932,Je 7,22:3

Hubar, Alex
Dancers, The 1923,O 18,17:2

Hubbard, Alma
Porgy and Bess 1942,Ja 23,16:2
Porgy and Bess 1943,S 14,26:2
Porgy and Bess 1944,F 8,13:2
Green Pastures, The 1951,Mr 16,35:2
Finian's Rainbow 1953,Mr 7,13:2
Simply Heavenly 1957,My 22,28:2
Shadow of My Enemy, A 1957,D 12,35:4
Shakespeare in Harlem 1959,O 28,40:7
God's Trombones 1960,F 10,43:4
Shakespeare in Harlem 1960,F 10,43:4
Shakespeare in Harlem 1960,F 21,II,1:1

Hubbard, Benjamin (Miscellaneous)
Hit the Road 1941,Ap 4,18:3

Hubbard, Benjamin (Producer)
Life Begins in '40 1940,Ap 5,24:2

Hubbard, Chalee
Cradle Song 1927,Ja 25,18:2

Hubbard, Douglas
Counterattack 1943,F 4,27:2

Hubbard, Douglas (Director)
Misalliance 1955,F 12,10:6

Hubbard, Edna
Rain Before Seven 1935,Ag 13,20:3

Hubbard, Elizabeth
Magnificent Hugo, The 1961,Ap 8,12:2
Affair, The 1962,S 21,34:2
Passion of Josef D, The 1964,F 12,29:1
Physicists, The 1964,O 14,52:1
Physicists, The 1964,O 25,II,1:1
Time for Singing, A 1966,My 23,48:2
Joe Egg 1968,F 2,26:1
Joe Egg 1968,F 11,II,1:1
Possibilities 1968,D 5,60:1

Hubbard, Gail (Miscellaneous)
Castro Complex, The 1970,N 19,40:1

Hubbard, Irene
Celebrity 1927,D 27,24:3

Hubbard, Lloyd
Along Came a Spider 1963,My 28,33:1
Of Thee I Sing 1969,Mr 8,19:1

Hubbard, Lulu Mae
Steadfast 1923,O 31,12:1
Easy Mark, The 1924,Ag 27,14:2
Book of Charm, The 1925,S 4,26:3
Square Crooks 1926,Mr 2,23:2
Money Lender, The 1928,Ag 28,27:3
Royal Box, The 1928,N 21,32:3
Sakura 1928,D 26,14:4
American, Very Early 1934,Ja 31,21:2
Order Please 1934,O 10,21:2
Seen But Not Heard 1936,S 18,19:2
Kiss and Tell 1943,Mr 18,22:1
Kiss and Tell 1943,Mr 28,II,1:1
January Thaw 1946,F 5,18:2
Goodbye My Fancy 1948,N 18,35:2
Girl Can Tell, A 1953,O 30,28:2
Bicycle Ride to Nevada 1963,S 25,38:1

Hubbard, Margie
Blackbirds 1928,My 10,31:3

Hubbard, Mary
Launzi 1923,O 11,16:3
Minick 1924,S 25,20:1
Salvation 1928,F 1,31:1
These Days 1928,N 13,36:2
Before You're 25 1929,Ap 17,30:2

Hubbard, Ohalee
Inheritors 1927,Mr 8,23:1
2 + 2 = 5 1927,N 29,30:3

Hubbard, Penelope
Aloma of the South Seas 1925,Ap 21,18:1
Houseparty 1929,S 10,26:5
After Tomorrow 1930,Ag 10,VIII,2:3
London Calling 1930,O 20,29:1

Hubbard, Valeska
Chocolate Soldier, The 1932,F 9,30:3

Hubbard, W C
Take It Away 1936,D 15,30:5
Take It Away 1936,D 22,32:3

Hubbell, Dorrance M
Polly Preferred 1923,Ja 12,13:3

Hubbell, Raymond (Composer)
Good Times 1920,Ag 10,10:1
Sonny 1921,Ag 17,12:2
Some Party 1922,Ap 17,22:1
Better Times 1922,S 4,14:2
Ziegfeld Follies 1924,Je 25,26:1
Lambs Gambol 1925,Ap 27,15:1
Follies 1925,Jl 7,24:3
Yours Truly 1927,Ja 26,16:5
Three Cheers 1928,O 16,28:1

Hubeau, Catherine
Avare, L', L'; Miser, The 1966,F 9,32:1
Fil a la Paite, Un 1966,F 18,25:1

Huber, Alberta
Veronica's Veil 1933,F 20,11:7

Huber, Gusti
Flight Into Egypt 1952,Mr 19,33:2
Flight Into Egypt 1952,Mr 30,II,1:1
Dial 'M' for Murder 1952,O 30,41:2
Diary of Anne Frank, The 1955,O 6,24:2
Diary of Anne Frank, The 1955,O 16,II,1:1

Huber, Harold
Farewell to Arms, A 1930,S 23,30:3
First Night 1930,N 27,32:3
Two Seconds 1931,O 10,20:6
Merry-Go-Round 1932,Ap 23,11:2
Assassin, The 1945,O 18,20:2
Lulu 1958,S 30,24:1

Huber, Paul
Spanish Love 1920,Ag 18,6:1
Hamlet 1922,N 17,14:1
King Lear 1923,Mr 10,9:4
Edgar Allan Poe 1925,O 6,31:1
Wise-Crackers, The 1925,D 17,26:1
Sure Fire! 1926,O 21,23:1
Bye Bye Bonnie 1927,Ja 14,15:3
Black Crook, The 1929,Mr 12,26:5
New Yorkers, The 1930,D 9,31:1
Constant Sinner, The 1931,S 15,30:1
$25 an Hour 1933,My 11,14:4
Sailor, Beware! 1933,S 29,24:4
Crime Marches on 1935,O 24,19:1
I Want a Policeman! 1936,Ja 15,15:5
Everywhere I Roam 1938,D 30,10:4
Johnny on the Spot 1942,Ja 9,24:2
Strip for Action 1942,O 1,26:2
Decision 1944,F 3,23:2
Mr Peebles and Mr Hooker 1946,O 11,29:2
Parlor Story 1947,Mr 5,29:2
Story for Strangers, A 1948,S 22,39:2
Immoralist, The 1954,F 2,18:7
Immoralist, The 1954,F 9,22:1
Immoralist, The 1954,F 14,II,1:1
Deadfall 1955,O 28,20:1
Sixth Finger in a Five Finger Glove 1956,O 9,31:4
One Flew Over the Cuckoo's Nest 1963,N 14,40:2
Never Live Over a Pretzel Factory 1964,Mr 30,37:1

Huberi, Marcie
Immoralist, The 1963,N 8,36:2

Hubert, Ann
Tall Kentuckian, The 1953,Je 17,30:1

Hubert, Frank
Sweeney Todd 1924,Jl 19,10:4
Bombasters Furioso 1924,Jl 19,10:4
Sweeney Todd 1924,Jl 19,10:4
Undercurrent, The 1925,F 4,18:2
His Queen 1925,My 12,26:1
Star and Garter 1942,Je 25,26:2
Matty and the Moron and Madonna 1965,Mr 30,53:1

Hubert, Fritz
Vaudeville (Palace) 1931,Je 29,20:1
Saluta 1934,Ag 29,13:4

Hubert, Irene
Geisha, The 1931,O 6,35:4

Hubert, Jean
Vaudeville (Palace) 1931,Je 29,20:1
Saluta 1934,Ag 29,13:4
Star and Garter 1942,Je 25,26:2

Hubert, Marcie
Noah 1954,O 11,32:2
Curious Savage, The 1956,Mr 17,12:3
9 by Six: A Cry of Players 1956,D 5,49:2
Legend of Lovers 1959,O 28,40:3
Lysistrata 1959,N 25,19:4
Policemen, The 1961,N 22,24:2
Cantilevered Terrace, The 1962,Ja 18,24:1
Coriolanus 1965,Jl 15,23:1
Danton's Death 1965,O 22,46:1
Country Wife, The 1965,D 10,58:2
Rose Tattoo, The 1966,O 21,36:2

Hubert, Rene (Costume Designer)
Merry Widow, The 1964,Ag 18,24:2

Hubert, Rene (Scenic Designer)
Going Greek 1937,S 17,28:4

Hubert, Russell
Iceman Cometh, The 1968,Ap 1,58:1

Huberth, Helen
Mascaiada 1929,D 28,10:6
Carry Nation 1932,O 31,18:2
Spring in Autumn 1933,O 25,22:5
Broomsticks Amen! 1934,F 10,20:4
Wife Insurance 1934,Ap 13,24:5
Brittle Heaven 1934,N 14,22:5

Hubschmid, Paul
My Fair Lady 1961,O 26,40:1
My Fair Lady 1962,Je 14,24:1

Huck, Sade
Would-Be Gentleman, The 1930,Ap 30,29:2

Hudd, Roy
Danny La Rue at the Palace 1970,Ag 31,24:1

Hudd, Walter
Too True to Be Good 1932,Ag 7,I,23:2
On the Rocks 1933,N 26,II,2:8
Three Set Out 1937,Je 23,29:3
Cherry Orchard, The 1941,S 7,IX,2:5
You Never Can Tell 1948,Mr 17,31:2
Love's Labour's Lost 1949,O 24,18:3

Huddle, Elizabeth
Merchant of Venice, The 1964,Jl 23,18:1
Country Wife, The 1965,D 10,58:2
Caucasian Chalk Circle, The 1966,Mr 25,35:1
Alchemist, The 1966,O 14,48:1
Good Woman of Setzuan, The 1970,N 6,51:1

Huddle, Ruth
Hansel and Gretel 1929,D 25,21:1
Huddleston, David
Harry, Noon and Night 1965,My 6,44:1
Woman Is My Idea 1968,S 26,61:1
Huddleston, Floyd (Miscellaneous)
Shuffle Along 1952,My 9,20:5
Hudelson, Douglas
He Who Gets Slapped 1946,Mr 21,31:4
Hudge, Gertrude
Fifty Million Frenchmen 1929,N 28,34:4
Hudgins, Johnny
Lucky Sambo 1925,Je 8,19:4
Hudiakoff, Andre (Scenic Designer)
White Guard, The; Days of the Turbins
1935,Mr 7,27:5
We Live and Laugh 1936,My 9,10:3
Hudnut, Robert
York Nativity Play, The 1956,D 5,49:2
Hudson, Alan
Rogues and Vagabonds 1930,My 8,32:5
Hudson, Charles
Billy Budd 1951,F 12,18:3
Summer of Daisy Miller, The 1963,My 28,33:1
Great Scot! 1965,N 12,56:3
Hudson, Derek (Musical Director)
Three Sisters, The 1970,F 12,30:1
Hudson, Doloris
As You Like It 1941,O 21,29:2
Hudson, Don
Walk in Darkness 1963,O 29,30:2
Hudson, Edward
Wild Duck, The 1928,N 19,17:1
Magnificent Yankee, The 1946,Ja 23,21:2
Hudson, Helen
George White's Scandals 1923,Je 19,22:5
Scandals 1924,Jl 1,16:1
George White's Scandals 1925,Je 23,24:2
Red, Hot and Blue! 1936,O 30,26:3
Between the Devil 1937,D 23,24:5
Banjo Eyes 1941,D 26,20:2
Kittiwake Island 1960,O 13,43:1
Hudson, Jed
White Cargo 1960,D 30,12:1
Hudson, Jed (Playwright)
White Cargo 1960,D 30,12:1
Hudson, John
Junior Miss 1941,N 19,28:2
January Thaw 1946,F 5,18:2
Craig's Wife 1947,F 13,35:2
Men We Marry, The 1948,Ja 17,11:2
Coast of Illyria, The 1949,Ap 5,37:4
Coast of Illyria, The 1949,Ap 13,39:2
Golden State, The 1950,N 27,29:3
Hudson, Ralph
Light Wines and Beer 1930,N 11,28:6
Hudson, Ray
Sketch Book 1935,Je 5,22:2
Hudson, Robert
Bab 1920,O 19,12:1
National Anthem, The 1922,Ja 24,16:3
Sporting Thing to Do, The 1923,F 20,12:2
Close Harmony 1924,D 2,23:1
Jazz Singer, The 1925,S 15,29:2
Donovan Affair, The 1926,Ag 31,15:2
Exceeding Small 1928,O 23,32:2
One Way Street 1928,D 25,31:2
Through the Night 1930,Ag 19,19:1
Mr Samuel 1930,N 11,28:4
Forsaking All Others 1933,Mr 2,21:2
Petrified Forest, The 1935,Ja 8,26:1
Cyrano de Bergerac 1936,Ap 28,17:1
Hudson, Roland
Pleasure Bound 1929,F 19,22:4
Hudson, Sunshine
Sketch Book 1935,Je 5,22:2
Hudson, Teddy
Sweetheart Shop, The 1920,S 1,13:4
Be Yourself! 1924,S 4,13:3
Hudson, Tony
Toilet, The 1964,D 17,51:1
Hudson, Travis
Tattooed Countess, The 1961,My 4,40:2
New Faces of 1962 1962,F 2,25:1
Pousse-Cafe 1966,Mr 19,19:2
Get Thee to Canterbury 1969,Ja 26,74:1
Hudson Wonders, The
Star and Garter 1942,Je 25,26:2
Huebing, Craig
Time of the Cuckoo, The 1958,O 28,40:2
Look After Lulu 1959,Mr 4,35:1
Huebl, Karl
One Glorious Hour 1927,Ap 15,27:2
Huebner, Herbert
Kyrill Reist ins Abendland 1933,Ja 8,IX,2:1
Huebner, Karin
My Fair Lady 1961,O 26,40:1
My Fair Lady 1962,Je 14,24:1
Hueglin, Karl (Lighting Director)
Hostage, The 1961,D 13,55:4
Billy Liar 1965,Mr 18,26:1
Hueglin, Karl (Scenic Designer)
Trouble in July 1949,D 2,36:2

Hostage, The 1961,D 13,55:4
Billy Liar 1965,Mr 18,26:1
Huelle, Walter
Patience 1935,S 3,24:4
Huerta, F
Sirena Varada, La 1937,O 23,15:3
Hues, Peter
Howdy Stranger 1937,Ja 15,17:5
Huett, Richard
This Our House 1935,D 12,33:3
Huey, Richard
In Abraham's Bosom 1926,D 31,10:2
In Abraham's Bosom 1927,F 20,VII,1:1
Porgy 1927,O 11,26:2
Solid South 1930,O 15,27:1
Five Star Final 1930,D 31,11:1
Wild Waves 1932,F 20,11:4
Three Men on a Horse 1935,Ja 31,22:3
Brown Sugar 1937,D 3,29:2
Sunny River 1941,D 5,28:2
Three Men on a Horse 1942,O 10,10:2
Bloomer Girl 1944,O 6,18:5
Bloomer Girl 1944,O 8,II,1:1
Hufeisen, Gene
Buoyant Billions 1959,My 27,32:2
Getting Married 1959,Je 5,18:2
Huff, Betty
Magdalena 1948,S 21,31:2
Huff, Carrie
Sugar Hill 1931,D 26,15:2
Louisiana 1933,F 28,15:5
Huff, Forrest
Bombo 1921,O 7,20:2
White Eagle, The 1927,D 27,24:4
Serenade, The 1930,Mr 5,26:7
Huff, Grace
Praying Curve 1927,Ja 25,18:2
Back Seat Drivers 1928,D 26,14:4
Stepping Sisters 1930,Ap 23,24:2
Huff, Helen
Rain Before Seven 1935,Ag 13,20:3
Huff, Louise
Mary the 3d 1923,F 6,14:2
Mary the 3d 1923,F 11,VII,1:1
New Englander, The 1924,F 8,22:2
Huff, Tess
Mill Shadows 1932,F 29,20:7
Huff, William
Macbeth 1962,Je 20,41:1
Seagull, The 1968,Jl 25,27:2
Huffington, Anita
By Hex 1956,Je 19,25:1
Huffman, Cal
Simpleton of the Unexpected Isles, The
1954,Ja 12,19:1
Huffman, J C (Director)
Student Prince, The 1924,D 3,25:3
Princess Flavia 1925,N 3,34:3
Night in Paris, A 1926,Ja 6,16:3
Great Temptations, The 1926,My 19,29:1
Merry World, The 1926,Je 9,18:3
Night in Paris, A 1926,Jl 27,15:4
Countess Maritza 1926,S 20,21:1
Pearl of Great Price, The 1926,N 2,34:3
Gay Paree 1926,N 10,24:2
Circus Princess, The 1927,Ap 26,32:2
My Maryland 1927,S 13,37:2
Love Call, The 1927,O 25,33:1
Artists and Models 1927,N 16,28:2
Lovely Lady 1927,D 30,22:1
Greenwich Village Follies 1928,Ap 10,32:2
Nina Rosa 1930,S 22,22:5
Huffman, John
Caine Mutiny Court-Martial, The 1954,Ja 21,27:2
Huffman, Robert
Murder in the Cathedral 1958,Mr 22,12:4
Huffman, Rosanna
Half a Sixpence 1965,Ap 26,38:2
Huffmaster, Ellen
Paul Bunyan 1941,My 6,25:1
Hugge, Dan (Costume Designer)
Commedia Dell' Arte 1957,Jl 5,13:2
Huggins, Ellen
Finian's Rainbow 1967,Ap 6,44:1
Hugh, Edwin C
Counsellor-at-Law 1942,N 25,17:2
Come Marching Home 1946,My 20,18:6
Hughes, Adelaide
Vaudeville (Hippodrome) 1926,F 23,26:2
Vaudeville (Palace) 1928,Ap 10,32:4
Hughes, Allan
Sisters of the Chorus 1930,O 21,34:3
Hughes, Anne
Nine Till Six 1936,Mr 14,10:3
Hughes, Annie
Tragedy of Nan, The 1920,F 18,9:1
Tragedy of Nan, The 1920,F 22,III,6:1
Great Adventure, The 1921,F 26,9:2
Hughes, Anthony
Betty Lee 1924,D 26,18:2
Lady Screams, The 1927,My 3,24:2
Simple Simon 1930,F 19,22:1

Hughes, Arthur
King Lear 1923,Mr 10,9:4
Man and the Masses 1924,Ap 15,25:1
Out of Step 1925,Ja 30,12:1
Blue Peter, The 1925,Mr 25,25:3
Rosmersholm 1925,My 6,27:2
Man's Man, A 1925,O 14,31:2
Unchastened Woman, The 1926,F 17,12:1
Easter 1926,Mr 19,24:3
American Tragedy, An 1926,O 12,31:2
Wall Street 1927,Ap 21,24:4
Jacob Slovak 1927,O 6,28:4
Queen's Husband, The 1928,Ja 26,17:2
Harlem 1929,F 21,30:3
Subway Express 1929,S 25,34:3
Elizabeth the Queen 1930,N 4,37:1
Mourning Becomes Electra; Haunted, The
1931,O 27,22:1
Mourning Becomes Electra; Homecoming
1931,O 27,22:1
Noble Prize, The 1933,Jl 4,16:4
Tight Britches 1934,S 12,26:2
If This Be Treason 1935,S 24,28:2
New Faces of 1936 1936,My 20,24:5
Behind the Red Lights 1937,Ja 14,17:4
Censored 1938,F 28,18:2
Wind in the Sails 1940,Ag 1,24:6
Quiet, Please! 1940,N 9,20:3
Cuckoos on the Hearth 1941,S 17,26:2
Winesburg, Ohio 1958,F 6,22:2
Man in the Dog Suit, The 1958,O 31,34:2
How Now, Dow Jones 1967,D 8,53:1
Hughes, Babette (Playwright)
March Heir, The 1932,D 14,27:3
Hughes, Barnard
Please, Mrs. Garibaldi 1939,Mr 17,24:3
Ivy Green, The 1949,Ap 6,37:2
Dinosaur Wharf 1951,N 9,23:2
Teahouse of the August Moon, The 1956,N 9,33:2
Will and the Way, The 1957,D 3,46:5
Majority of One, A 1959,F 17,28:2
Advise and Consent 1960,N 18,25:1
Rosmersholm 1962,Ap 12,42:1
Rosmersholm 1962,Ap 22,II,1:1
Doll's House, A 1963,F 4,5:6
Advocate, The 1963,O 15,46:7
Nobody Loves an Albatross 1963,D 20,20:1
Nobody Loves an Albatross 1964,Ja 5,II,1:1
Hamlet 1964,Ap 10,30:1
I Was Dancing 1964,N 9,40:4
Hogan's Goat 1965,N 12,56:1
How Now, Dow Jones 1967,D 8,53:1
Wrong Way Light Bulb, The 1969,Mr 5,40:1
Sheep on the Runway 1970,F 2,28:3
Sheep on the Runway 1970,F 8,II,5:5
Hughes, Bryan
Macbeth 1928,N 20,28:3
Hughes, C Anthony
Sap Runs High, The 1936,F 5,15:3
Hughes, Carl
Hamlet 1927,Ap 7,23:3
Hughes, Catharine (Playwright)
Madame Lafayette 1960,Mr 4,21:1
Hughes, Charles A
Every Man for Himself 1940,D 10,32:3
Hughes, D M
Hamlet 1969,Je 11,37:1
Alchemist, The 1969,Je 12,51:1
Measure for Measure 1969,Je 13,41:3
Hughes, Dana
Girls in Uniform 1932,D 31,10:3
Hughes, David
Diamond Lil 1928,Ap 10,32:1
Room 349 1930,Ap 23,24:5
Lady With a Lamp, The 1931,N 20,27:2
Papavert 1931,D 30,25:1
Mr Papavert 1932,Ja 23,18:6
Man Who Reclaimed His Head 1932,S 9,17:3
Eight Bells 1933,O 30,14:2
I Myself 1934,My 10,24:6
De Luxe 1935,Mr 6,22:2
Chalked Out 1937,Mr 26,24:2
Hughes, Del
Vickie 1942,S 23,28:1
Open House 1947,Je 4,33:4
Rip Van Winkle 1947,Jl 16,28:2
Crucible, The 1953,Jl 2,20:2
Hughes, Del (Miscellaneous)
Legend of Sarah 1950,O 12,42:4
Wedding Breakfast 1954,N 22,29:2
Taste of Honey, A 1960,O 5,46:1
Complaisant Lover, The 1961,N 2,43:2
Perfect Setup, The 1962,O 25,47:1
Enter Laughing 1963,Mr 15,8:1
One Flew Over the Cuckoo's Nest 1963,N 14,40:2
Traveller Without Luggage 1964,S 18,26:2
Peterpat 1965,Ja 7,27:1
That Summer-That Fall 1967,Mr 17,33:1
Trial of Lee Harvey Oswald, The 1967,N 6,64:1
Price, The 1968,F 8,37:1
Hughes, Donald
Is Zat So? 1925,Ap 25,18:2

Hughes, Donald—Cont
  Enemy, The 1925,O 21,20:1
Hughes, Doris
  Kiss for Cinderella, A 1942,Mr 11,22:2
Hughes, Evelyn
  Trilby 1958,Ja 9,40:3
Hughes, Frank
  Blue Flame, The 1920,Mr 16,18:1
Hughes, Frederick H (Director)
  Arsenic and Old Lace 1942,My 11,18:6
Hughes, Gareth
  Dunce Boy, The 1925,Ap 4,20:2
Hughes, Gene (Mrs)
  What the Doctor Ordered 1927,Ag 19,20:2
Hughes, Glenn (Playwright)
  Bon Voyage 1949,Ap 26,28:2
Hughes, Gwyneth
  Corn Is Green, The 1940,N 27,27:2
  Corn Is Green, The 1943,My 4,18:3
  Minnie and Mr Williams 1948,O 28,37:2
  Corn Is Green, The 1950,Ja 12,33:2
Hughes, Hatcher
  Hell-Bent Fer Heaven 1924,F 10,VII,1:1
Hughes, Hatcher (Director)
  Fields Beyond, The 1933,F 14,19:5
  Lord Blesses the Bishop, The 1934,N 28,24:5
Hughes, Hatcher (Playwright)
  Wake Up, Jonathan 1921,Ja 18,14:1
  Wake Up, Jonathan 1921,Ja 23,VI,1:6
  Wake Up, Jonathan 1921,Ja 23,VI,1:1
  Hell-Bent Fer Heaven 1924,Ja 5,10:1
  Ruint 1925,Ap 8,24:2
  Honeymooning on High 1927,F 27,VII,4:6
  Honeymooning 1927,Mr 18,25:3
  It's a Grand Life 1930,F 2,VIII,2:7
  It's a Grand Life 1930,F 11,30:3
  Lord Blesses the Bishop, The 1934,N 28,24:5
Hughes, Hatcher (Producer)
  Sun and I, The 1933,Ap 4,15:2
Hughes, Hazel
  Way of the World, The 1969,Ag 7,29:1
Hughes, Helen Ann
  Strange Interlude 1928,D 18,37:3
Hughes, Helena
  Where Stars Walk 1948,F 25,27:2
Hughes, Henry M (Composer)
  Once Over Lightly 1938,D 10,13:4
Hughes, Henry M (Lyricist)
  Once Over Lightly 1938,D 10,13:4
Hughes, Henry M Jr
  Many a Slip 1940,N 16,12:7
Hughes, Henry M Jr (Playwright)
  Any Moment Now 1939,N 25,13:6
Hughes, Herbert (Composer)
  Within the Gates 1934,F 8,14:4
  Rivals, The 1935,S 25,19:6
Hughes, J Anthony
  Marry the Man! 1929,Ap 23,26:3
  Wild Birds 1929,Je 23,VIII,2:3
  City Haul 1929,D 31,14:4
  Camels Are Coming, The 1931,O 3,20:4
  Black Tower 1932,Ja 12,29:2
  Lambs Gambol 1932,Ap 25,18:2
  Give Us This Day 1933,O 28,20:6
  Page Miss Glory 1934,N 28,24:2
Hughes, J J (Choreographer)
  Lace Petticoat 1927,Ja 5,18:2
Hughes, Jack
  Five O'Clock Girl, The 1927,O 11,26:3
Hughes, James
  Last Warning, The 1922,O 25,23:1
  Right to Dream, The 1924,My 27,14:2
Hughes, Jane
  Antigone 1956,Ap 3,32:2
  Lower Depths, The 1956,O 3,29:2
Hughes, Johnny
  Whirl of New York, The 1921,Je 14,18:1
Hughes, Julie (Producer)
  Effect of Gamma Rays on Man-in-the-Moon
    Marigolds, The 1970,Ap 8,32:1
Hughes, Karl
  Caesar and Cleopatra 1927,N 6,IX,2:1
Hughes, Kelly
  Galileo 1968,D 1,88:4
Hughes, Langston (Composer)
  Canteen Show, The 1942,S 4,18:1
Hughes, Langston (Lyricist)
  Street Scene 1947,Ja 10,17:2
  Street Scene 1947,Ja 19,II,1:1
  Simply Heavenly 1957,My 22,28:2
  Tambourines to Glory 1963,N 4,47:1
Hughes, Langston (Miscellaneous)
  Year Round, The 1953,My 6,38:7
  Shakespeare in Harlem 1959,O 28,40:7
Hughes, Langston (Original Author)
  Shakespeare in Harlem 1960,F 21,II,1:1
  Tambourines to Glory 1963,N 4,47:1
Hughes, Langston (Playwright)
  Mulatto 1935,Ag 8,13:2
  Mulatto 1935,O 25,25:2
  Barrier, The 1950,N 3,32:2
  Simply Heavenly 1957,My 22,28:2
  Simply Heavenly 1957,Je 2,II,1:1
  Soul Gone Home 1959,O 28,40:7

  Shakespeare in Harlem 1960,F 10,43:4
  Black Nativity 1961,D 12,54:2
  Gospel Glow 1962,O 28,87:5
  Tambourines to Glory 1963,N 4,47:1
  Jericho-Jim Crow 1964,Ja 13,25:3
  Prodigal Son, The 1965,My 21,19:1
  Mulatto 1967,N 16,61:4
  Jericho-Jim Crow 1968,Mr 23,22:2
Hughes, Lloyd
  Gods We Make, The 1934,Ja 4,16:4
Hughes, Mary
  Richard III 1920,Mr 8,7:1
  Macbeth 1921,F 18,16:1
  Billeted 1922,My 10,22:4
Hughes, Mildred
  As the Girls Go 1948,N 15,21:2
  Tickets, Please! 1950,Ap 28,25:2
  Almost Crazy 1955,Je 21,37:1
Hughes, Molly
  Matriarch, The 1930,Mr 19,24:5
Hughes, Phil
  On the Make 1932,My 24,23:2
Hughes, Revella
  Runnin' Wild 1923,O 30,17:3
  Bomboola 1929,Je 27,17:3
  Hot Rhythm 1930,Ag 22,18:5
Hughes, Richard
  Eight Bells 1933,O 30,14:2
  Desert Song, The 1946,Ja 9,20:2
Hughes, Richard (Original Author)
  Innocent Voyage, The 1943,N 16,27:2
Hughes, Richard (Playwright)
  Sisters' Tragedy, The 1930,My 6,33:1
  Comedy of Good and Evil, A 1938,Ap 8,16:3
  Minnie and Mr Williams 1948,O 28,37:2
Hughes, Richard B (Lighting Director)
  Bella 1961,N 17,40:1
Hughes, Richard B (Scenic Designer)
  Ladies Night in a Turkish Bath 1961,Mr 22,38:1
  Bella 1961,N 17,40:1
Hughes, Robert
  Red Mill, The 1945,O 17,16:2
Hughes, Roddy
  Bird in Hand 1929,Ap 5,28:2
Hughes, Rowland
  Lazarus Laughed 1948,Ap 9,27:4
Hughes, Rupert (Playwright)
  Cat-Bird, The 1920,F 17,18:1
  Cat-Bird, The 1920,F 22,III,6:1
Hughes, Stanley
  Wild Justice 1935,Jl 9,24:3
  So Proudly We Hail 1936,S 23,28:4
Hughes, T J Jr
  Marching Song 1937,F 18,18:2
Hughes, T Penry
  Trial by Jury 1936,S 1,24:4
  Trial by Jury 1939,Ja 6,25:1
  Gondoliers, The 1939,Ja 20,14:2
Hughes, Ted (Playwright)
  Oedipus 1968,Ap 2,54:1
  Oedipus 1968,Jl 31,29:1
Hughes, Thomas
  Possessed, The 1939,O 25,26:2
  Out of My House 1942,Ja 8,28:6
Hughes, Tresa
  Electra 1958,My 10,17:7
  Devil's Advocate, The 1961,Mr 10,20:1
  Devil's Advocate, The 1961,Mr 19,II,1:1
  Dumbbell People in a Barbell World 1962,F 15,25:1
  Dear Me, the Sky Is Falling 1963,Mr 4,9:1
  Advocate, The 1963,O 15,46:7
  Last Analysis, The 1964,O 2,30:1
  Hogan's Goat 1965,N 12,56:1
  Fragments 1967,O 3,56:1
  Fragments; Basement, The 1967,O 15,II,3:3
  Spofford 1967,D 15,54:3
  Man in the Glass Booth, The 1968,S 27,41:1
  Passing Through From Exotic Places; Burial of
    Esposito, The 1969,D 8,60:4
  Passing Through From Exotic Places; Sunstroke
    1969,D 8,60:4
  Passing Through From Exotic Places; Son Who
    Hunted Tigers in Jakarta, The 1969,D 8,60:4
  Beggar on Horseback 1970,My 15,47:2
  Early Morning 1970,N 26,57:1
Hughes, William
  Last Stop 1944,S 6,17:2
  Oedipus Rex 1945,D 17,16:7
  Mummers and Men 1962,Mr 27,41:6
  Anvil, The 1962,O 31,33:3
Hughston, Regan
  Sweet Nell of Old Drury 1923,My 19,16:4
Hugnet
  Aiglon, L' 1924,O 21,21:1
Hugo, Larry
  Distant City, The 1941,S 23,27:5
  Mexican Mural; Moonlight Scene 1942,Ap 27,19:2
  I'll Take the High Road 1943,N 10,28:3
  Decision 1944,F 3,23:2
  Decision 1944,F 13,II,1:1
Hugo, Laurence
  Bird Cage, The 1950,F 23,32:2

Hugo, Laurence—Cont
  Stalag 17 1951,My 9,41:2
  Double in Hearts 1956,O 17,41:7
  U S A 1959,O 29,38:1
  U S A 1959,N 8,II,1:1
  King Lear 1961,My 15,34:6
  Touch of the Poet, A 1961,My 15,34:6
Hugo, Victor (Original Author)
  Clair de Lune 1921,Ap 10,VI,1:1
  Clair de Lune 1921,Ap 24,VI,1:1
  Ruy Blas 1933,O 10,24:4
  Miserabili I, 1934,S 24,15:1
Hugo, Victor (Playwright)
  Hernani 1930,Mr 2,II,1:5
  Hernani 1930,Mr 23,IX,2:1
  Ruy Blas 1938,Jl 24,IX,2:1
  Ruy Blas 1957,D 14,16:3
  Marie Tudor 1958,O 22,39:1
Hugo (Musical Director)
  House of Leather, The 1970,Mr 19,56:1
Hugo-Vidal, Victor (Miscellaneous)
  And Be My Love 1945,F 22,30:4
Hugo-Vidal, Victor (Producer)
  Last Stop 1944,S 6,17:2
Huguenot, Harry
  Commodore Marries, The 1929,S 5,26:3
  Mikado, The 1932,Jl 29,18:4
Huguenot, Harry (Director)
  Mikado, The 1932,Jl 29,18:4
Huguette
  Miss France 1930,Ap 13,X,2:7
  Bloomfield 1930,O 12,VIII,4:2
  Cyclone, Le 1931,O 25,VIII,1:6
Huhan, A O
  Marie Antoinette 1921,N 23,16:1
  Rosa Machree 1922,Ja 10,15:2
  Peter Weston 1923,S 20,5:2
  Move On 1926,Ja 19,30:1
  Trouper, The 1926,Mr 9,21:1
  What Every Woman Knows 1926,Ap 14,20:2
  Gentlemen of the Press 1928,Ag 28,27:2
  Now-A-Days 1929,Ag 6,29:3
  Devil in the Mind 1931,My 2,23:2
  All in the Family 1935,Jl 24,20:4
Huhan, A O (Director)
  Decoy, The 1932,Ap 2,13:4
Huhan, A O (Producer)
  Decoy, The 1932,Ap 2,13:4
Hujer, Flower
  By Jupiter 1942,Je 4,22:1
  Jackpot 1944,Ja 14,15:2
Hulas, Emma
  Blue Butterfly, The 1929,F 17,29:3
Hulbert, Jack
  By the Way 1925,D 29,20:3
  By the Way 1926,Ap 4,VIII,1:1
  By the Way 1926,Ap 16,20:3
Hulbert, Jack (Director)
  Under the Counter 1947,O 4,10:2
Hulbert, Jack (Miscellaneous)
  By the Way 1925,D 29,20:3
Hulbert, Jack (Playwright)
  Follow a Star 1930,S 18,28:2
Hulbert, Jack (Producer)
  By the Way 1925,N 22,VIII,1:8
  By the Way 1925,D 29,20:3
  Nightingale, The 1947,Jl 17,16:4
Hulbut, Gladys (Playwright)
  Lovers' Meeting 1937,Je 3,23:1
Hulbut, William (Playwright)
  Hidden 1927,O 5,30:4
Hulett, Otto
  If 1927,O 26,26:2
  Love Nest, The 1927,D 23,17:1
  Maya 1928,F 22,19:1
  Grand Street Follies, The 1928,My 29,16:2
  Grand Street Follies, The 1928,Je 3,VIII,1:1
  Grand Street Follies, The 1929,My 2,20:4
  Grand Street Follies, The 1929,My 12,IX,1:2
  Winter Bound 1929,N 13,24:6
  Garrick Gaieties 1930,Je 5,29:2
  Rock Me, Julie 1931,F 4,21:1
  Her Supporting Cast 1931,My 5,33:3
  Guest Room, The 1931,O 7,29:2
  Thunder on the Left 1933,N 1,25:2
  Whatever Possessed Her 1934,Ja 26,21:2
  Personal Appearance 1934,O 18,26:7
  Ten Million Ghosts 1936,O 24,23:7
  Chalked Out 1937,Mr 26,24:2
  Western Union 1937,Ag 10,22:7
  Tell Me Pretty Maiden 1937,D 17,33:5
  There's Always a Breeze 1938,Mr 3,16:2
  Off to Buffalo! 1939,F 22,18:2
  My Dear Children 1939,Mr 25,19:6
  My Dear Children 1940,F 1,16:2
  My Fair Ladies 1941,Mr 24,12:7
  Mr Sycamore 1942,N 14,13:2
  Born Yesterday 1946,F 5,18:2
  Born Yesterday 1946,F 10,II,1:1
  Born Yesterday 1947,My 18,II,1:1
  Come on Strong 1962,O 5,29:1
Hulicius, Otto
  Little Clay Cart, The 1924,D 6,13:3
  Critic, The 1925,My 9,12:4

Hulicius, Otto—Cont

Grand Street Follies, The 1925,Je 19,24:1
Dybbuk, The 1925,D 16,22:2
Romantic Young Lady, The 1926,My 5,24:3
Grand Street Follies, The 1926,Je 16,23:2
Lion Tamer, The 1926,O 8,26:1
Dybbuk, The 1926,D 17,27:2
Pinwheel 1927,F 4,16:4
Commedia Dell' Arte 1927,Ap 6,24:3
Grand Street Follies, The 1927,My 20,22:3
Lovers and Enemies 1927,S 21,27:1

Huling, Ray

Vaudeville (Palace) 1930,Ag 18,24:3
Vaudeville (Palace) 1930,D 22,16:5

Hull, Arthur Stuart

Jazz Singer, The 1925,S 15,29:2
Spider, The 1927,Mr 23,29:1
Mima 1928,D 13,24:2

Hull, Bryan

Knack With Horses, A 1970,D 21,52:1

Hull, Camilla

Everywhere I Roam 1938,D 30,10:4

Hull, Charles

Certain Young Man, A 1967,D 27,45:1
Another City, Another Land 1968,O 9,42:1

Hull, Harriet

Jonah and the Whale 1940,My 5,II,8:4

Hull, Henry

When We Are Young 1920,N 23,11:1
Everyday 1921,N 17,15:1
Cat and the Canary, The 1922,F 8,13:1
Roger Bloomer 1923,Mr 2,18:3
In Love With Love 1923,Ag 7,20:1
In Love With Love 1923,Ag 12,VI,1:1
Other Rose, The 1923,D 21,15:2
Other Rose, The 1923,D 30,VII,1:1
Vaudeville (Palace) 1924,Mr 18,25:1
God Bless Our Home 1924,N 23,VIII,2:4
Youngest, The 1924,D 23,17:1
Naked Man, The 1925,N 8,VIII,2:1
Lulu Belle 1926,F 10,20:1
Our Little Wife 1927,My 10,25:3
Candida 1927,Ag 31,19:4
Ivory Door, The 1927,O 19,24:5
Grey Fox, The 1928,O 23,32:3
Young Alexander 1929,Mr 13,28:2
Congratulations 1929,My 1,28:4
Ladies Leave 1929,O 2,28:3
Veneer 1929,N 13,24:5
Veneer 1929,N 24,X,1:1
Michael and Mary 1929,D 14,23:3
Michael and Mary 1929,D 29,VIII,2:4
Grand Hotel 1930,N 14,30:4
Grand Hotel 1930,N 23,IX,1:1
Roof, The 1931,O 31,22:4
Roof, The 1931,N 8,VIII,1:1
Bride the Sun Shines On, The 1931,D 28,20:2
Moon in the Yellow River, The 1932,F 21,VIII,2:1
Moon in the Yellow River, The 1932,Mr 1,19:3
Moon in the Yellow River, The 1932,Mr 13,VIII,1:1
Foreign Affairs 1932,Ap 14,25:5
Springtime for Henry 1933,My 2,20:5
Tobacco Road 1933,D 5,31:2
Tobacco Road 1934,Je 20,24:1
Springtime for Henry 1936,Je 23,27:6
Plumes in the Dust 1936,O 26,21:3
Plumes in the Dust 1936,N 7,14:2
Plumes in the Dust 1936,N 15,XI,1:1
Masque of Kings, The 1937,Ja 19,28:3
Masque of Kings, The 1937,Ja 31,XI,2:1
Masque of the Kings, The 1937,F 9,19:4
Attack 1942,S 8,13:4
Foolish Notion 1945,Mr 14,23:2

Hull, Henry (Director)

Places, Please 1937,N 13,10:6

Hull, Henry (Playwright)

Manhattan 1922,Ag 16,7:5

Hull, Henry Jr

Hamlet 1936,O 9,30:2
Masque of the Kings, The 1937,F 9,19:4
Man Who Killed Lincoln, The 1940,Ja 18,26:4

Hull, Iona

One Shot Fired 1927,N 8,32:5

Hull, J W

Love Song, The 1925,Ja 14,19:4

Hull, James

Romeo and Juliet 1922,D 28,20:1

Hull, Josephine

Neighbors 1923,D 27,11:1
Fata Morgana 1924,Mr 4,16:3
Rosmersholm 1925,My 6,27:2
Craig's Wife 1925,O 13,21:2
Daisy Mayme 1926,O 26,24:2
Wild Man of Borneo, The 1927,S 14,29:2
March Hares 1928,Ap 3,32:6
Beaux' Stratagem, The 1928,Je 5,20:1
Hotbed 1928,N 10,20:7
Jonesy 1929,F 24,IX,4:1
Before You're 25 1929,Ap 17,30:2
Those We Love 1930,F 20,22:2
In the Meantime 1930,D 7,IX,1:6
Midnight 1930,D 30,25:1
Unexpected Husband 1931,Je 3,29:4

After Tomorrow 1931,Ag 27,22:4
Thousand Summers, A 1932,My 25,23:4
American Dream; 1650 1933,F 22,24:5
American Dream; 1933 1933,F 22,24:5
Divine Drudge 1933,O 27,22:3
By Your Leave 1934,Ja 25,15:3
Fresh Fields 1934,Jl 15,X,1:1
On to Fortune 1935,F 5,22:2
Seven Keys to Baldpate 1935,My 28,30:2
Night in the House 1935,N 8,19:5
You Can't Take It With You 1936,D 1,30:8
You Can't Take It With You 1936,D 6,XII,6:2
You Can't Take It With You 1936,D 15,31:1
You Can't Take It With You 1936,D 20,XI,3:1
You Can't Take It With You 1937,Ag 29,X,1:1
International Incident, An 1940,Ap 3,18:2
Arsenic and Old Lace 1941,Ja 11,13:2
Arsenic and Old Lace 1941,F 23,IX,1:1
Harvey 1944,N 2,23:2
Harvey 1944,N 12,II,1:1
Harvey 1947,Jl 15,27:3
Minnie and Mr Williams 1948,O 28,37:2
Golden State, The 1950,N 27,29:3
Whistler's Grandmother 1952,D 12,40:2
Solid Gold Cadillac, The 1953,N 6,24:2
Solid Gold Cadillac, The 1953,N 15,II,1:1
Solid Gold Cadillac, The 1954,Ag 16,13:4

Hull, Josephine (Director)

Habitual Husband, The 1924,D 25,27:3

Hull, Mary

Sleep No More 1944,S 1,11:5

Hull, Milfred

Antony and Cleopatra 1947,N 27,49:2

Hull, Shelley

As Husbands Go 1935,Jl 10,24:1
Amateur Hour 1936,Jl 21,13:1
White Cargo 1941,My 14,24:3
Hope for a Harvest 1941,N 27,28:2

Hull, Suzanne

J B 1958,Ap 24,37:1

Hull, Tom

I Dreamt I Dwelt in Bloomingdale's 1970,F 13,26:1

Hull, Tom (Miscellaneous)

Round With Ring, A 1969,O 30,56:1

Hull, Warren

My Maryland 1927,S 13,37:2
Rain or Shine 1928,F 10,26:3

Hull, Weslyn

Merry Widow, The 1921,S 6,13:1

Hulme, George (Playwright)

Lionel Touch, The 1969,N 6,57:2

Hulse, Kay

Frugal Noon 1964,My 23,15:2

Hulswit, Mart

Cradle of Willow, A 1961,D 16,20:2
Merchant of Venice, The 1962,Je 22,1:4
Macbeth 1962,N 17,16:2
Amazing Grace 1967,D 10,82:1

Hult, Gottfried (Translator)

Lady From the Sea, The 1935,D 14,11:3

Hultman, Robert L

Carnival! 1968,D 13,58:1

Hultman, Rune (Sgt)

Winged Victory 1943,N 22,24:1

Human, Walter A (Producer)

One by One 1964,D 2,60:1

Humans, Maria (Costume Designer)

Crazy With the Heat 1941,Ja 31,15:2

Humason, Sally (Playwright)

Garrick Gaieties 1926,Je 13,VII,1:1

Humbert, George

Gentlemen of the Press 1928,Ag 28,27:2
Street Scene 1929,Ja 11,20:4

Humbert, Melville (Composer)

Steppe Around 1922,Mr 29,17:4

Humbert, Melville (Lyricist)

Steppe Around 1922,Mr 29,17:4

Hume, Benita

Symphony in Two Flats 1930,S 17,30:4

Hume, Derex

Serena Blandish 1929,Ja 24,30:3

Hume, Elaine

Show Boat 1948,S 9,33:2

Hume, Kenny

Taste of Honey, A 1960,O 5,46:1

Hume, Rita Joan

Forbidden Melody 1936,N 3,33:1

Hume, Thomas

Blind Alley 1940,O 16,28:2
Brooklyn Biarritz 1941,F 28,16:2
Lady Behave 1943,N 17,30:1
World's Full of Girls, The 1943,D 7,31:2

Hummel, Carolyn

Innocent Voyage, The 1943,N 16,27:2
Our Town 1944,Ja 11,24:5
Chicken Every Sunday 1944,Ap 6,27:2
I Remember Mama 1944,O 20,16:2
I Remember Mama 1944,O 29,II,1:1

Hummel, George F (Playwright)

World Waits, The 1933,O 26,22:5
World Waits, The 1935,S 30,12:5

Hummert, James

Three Plays of the Sea 1970,Ag 20,39:1

Humperdinck, Engelbert (Composer)

Miracle, The 1924,Ja 16,17:1
Miracle, The 1924,Ag 19,9:1
Hansel and Gretel 1929,D 25,21:1

Humphrey, Cavada

Man's House, A 1943,Ap 3,10:4
House in Paris, The 1944,Mr 21,17:1
Song of Bernadette 1946,Mr 27,22:2
What Every Woman Knows 1946,N 9,13:2
Pound on Demand 1946,D 20,29:3
As the Girls Go 1948,N 15,21:2
Devil's Disciple, The 1950,Ja 26,23:2
Richard II 1951,Ja 25,21:2
Love's Labour's Lost 1953,F 5,20:3
Moon in Capricorn 1953,O 28,37:2
Othello 1955,S 8,27:2
Othello 1955,S 18,II,1:1
Henry IV, Part I 1955,S 22,34:2
Girl of the Golden West, The 1957,N 6,44:1
Dear Liar 1962,Mr 19,36:1
We Comrades Three 1962,O 12,26:1
Life Is a Dream 1964,Mr 20,24:1
Colombe 1965,F 24,33:1
King John 1967,Jl 14,19:1
Candida 1970,Ap 7,41:1

Humphrey, David

Child of the Morning 1958,Ap 22,40:2

Humphrey, Dick

Silk Stockings 1955,F 25,17:3

Humphrey, Doris

White Peacock, The 1929,Ap 27,16:4
Americana 1932,O 6,19:3
Dream of Sganarelle, The 1933,O 17,26:5
School for Husbands, The 1933,O 17,26:5
School for Husbands, The 1933,D 3,IX,6:5

Humphrey, Doris (Choreographer)

Lysistrata 1930,Ap 29,30:5
Lysistrata 1930,Je 6,20:1
Americana 1932,O 16,IX,11:2
Run, Little Chillun! 1933,Mr 12,IX,7:1
School for Husbands, The 1933,O 17,26:5
Dream of Sganarelle, The 1933,O 17,26:5
School for Husbands, The 1933,D 3,IX,6:5
Sing Out, Sweet Land! 1944,D 28,24:2
Rose in the Wilderness 1949,Ja 5,21:2
Barrier, The 1950,N 3,32:2

Humphrey, Doris (Director)

Barrier, The 1950,N 3,32:2

Humphrey, Doris (Playwright)

Merry-Go-Rounders, The 1956,N 22,50:1

Humphrey, Doris Dance Group

Americana 1932,O 6,19:3

Humphrey, Ellen

Miser, The 1950,Mr 27,19:5

Humphrey, Harry E

Dream Maker, The 1921,N 22,17:1
Jolly Roger, The 1923,Ag 31,10:4
Cyrano de Bergerac 1923,N 2,14:1

Humphrey, Harry E (Playwright)

Skull, The 1928,Ap 24,28:3

Humphrey, John

2 Girls Wanted 1926,S 10,25:3

Humphrey, Martha Rosalie

Sonya's Search for the Christmas Star 1929,D 14,24:6

Humphrey, Mr

Man Without Money, A 1929,N 3,27:4

Humphrey, Philip C

Contrast, The 1926,O 1,26:2

Humphrey, Robin

Eastward in Eden 1947,N 19,33:2
Pied Piper of Hamelin, The 1950,Ap 3,19:2

Humphrey, William

Julius Caesar 1926,S 19,28:5

Humphreys, Carolyn

Honeymooning 1927,Mr 18,25:3

Humphreys, Cecil

Parasites 1924,N 20,21:1
Tovarich 1936,O 16,31:4
Tovarich 1936,O 25,X,1:1
Merchant of Venice, The 1938,Ja 15,18:8
Circle, The 1938,Ap 19,24:2
Woman Brown, The 1939,D 9,18:5
Passenger to Bali, A 1940,Mr 15,26:2
International Incident, An 1940,Ap 3,18:2
Eight O'Clock Tuesday 1941,Ja 7,18:2
Doctor's Dilemma, The 1941,F 18,26:6
Doctor's Dilemma, The 1941,Mr 12,18:2
Hedda Gabler 1942,Ja 30,22:2
Kiss for Cinderella, A 1942,Mr 11,22:2
Morning Star, The 1942,S 19,8:4
Morning Star, The 1942,S 20,VIII,1:1
Patriots, The 1943,Ja 30,11:2
Patriots, The 1943,F 7,II,1:1
Patriots, The 1943,D 21,22:5
Pygmalion 1945,D 27,16:1

Humphreys, Cecil (Director)

Late One Evening 1933,Ja 10,27:3

Humphreys, Dick

Jerry Lewis' Variety Show 1957,F 8,18:5

Humphreys, Dorothy

Bye Bye Bonnie 1927,Ja 14,15:3
Houseboat on the Styx, The 1928,D 26,14:3

Humphreys, Gillian
Iolanthe 1964,N 18,52:1
Mikado, The 1964,N 27,43:1
Humphreys, Gloria
Maid in the Ozarks 1946,Jl 16,20:3
Humphreys, Haroldine
You and I 1925,O 20,29:1
Importance of Being Earnest, The 1926,My 4,30:1
Becky Sharp 1929,Je 4,29:1
Humphreys, Kalita
Black Eye, The 1938,Mr 8,22:4
Everywhere I Roam 1938,D 30,10:4
Let's Face It 1941,O 30,26:2
Cock-A-Doodle-Doo 1949,F 28,16:5
Humphreys, Kalita (Director)
Bedrock 1934,N 18,II,6:3
Humphreys, Norbert
One, Two, Three! 1930,S 30,24:2
Humphreys, Richard
Coquette 1935,Jl 10,24:1
Humphries, Ada
Merry Wives of Windsor, The 1938,Ap 15,22:3
Humphries, Barry
Oliver 1963,Ja 8,5:5
Humphries, Carolyn
Camels Are Coming, The 1931,O 3,20:4
Beauty and the Beast 1932,Ja 10,I,29:2
Humphries, Collette
At Your Service 1937,Ag 17,23:1
Humphries, Joe
Big Fight, The 1928,S 19,33:1
Humphries, Julie
Allegro 1947,O 11,10:2
Humphry, John
Twelfth Night 1958,D 10,54:2
Hamlet 1958,D 17,2:7
Henry V 1958,D 26,2:7
Hundley, Clark
Squealer, The 1928,N 13,36:3
Richelieu 1929,D 26,20:3
Hundley, John
Merry Merry 1925,S 25,24:3
Girl Friend, The 1926,Mr 18,26:5
Just Fancy! 1927,O 12,30:2
Just a Minute 1928,O 9,34:3
Polly 1929,Ja 9,28:3
Spring Is Here 1929,Mr 12,26:1
Heads Up! 1929,N 12,34:1
Walk a Little Faster 1932,D 8,24:4
Hundley, Roger
Arrest That Woman 1936,S 19,20:4
Lightnin' 1938,S 16,17:2
Hung, Peng Chun (Playwright)
Mu Lan 1921,F 25,16:2
Hung-Yen, Hu (Director)
Butterfly Dream, The 1966,My 20,41:1
Hungerford, Edward (Producer)
Railroads on Parade 1939,My 14,XI,1:2
Hungerford, Mona
Man From Toronto, The 1926,Je 18,27:2
Hunnewell, Clyde
Extra 1923,Ja 24,22:3
Helen of Troy, New York 1923,Je 20,22:6
Hunnicutt, Arthur
Love's Old Sweet Song 1940,Ap 14,IX,3:3
Love's Old Sweet Song 1940,My 3,16:3
Time of Your Life, The 1940,S 24,27:2
Lower North 1944,Ag 26,15:4
Dark Hammock 1944,D 12,27:8
Too Hot for Maneuvers 1945,My 3,26:5
Beggars Are Comming to Town 1945,O 29,16:2
Apple of His Eye 1946,F 6,18:2
Mr Peebles and Mr Hooker 1946,O 11,29:2
Hunt, Althea (Miscellaneous)
Common Glory, The 1947,Jl 19,11:2
Common Glory, The 1947,Jl 27,II,1:1
Hunt, Annette
9 by Six: A Cry of Players 1956,D 5,49:2
Anatomist, The 1957,F 27,21:5
Legitimate Steal, The 1958,Ap 1,35:1
Cherry Orchard, The 1960,Je 4,17:2
Taming of the Shrew, The 1963,Mr 8,9:1
Medea 1965,N 29,46:1
Hunt, Bill
Hickory Stick 1944,My 9,15:6
Men to the Sea 1944,O 4,25:2
Stone Tower, The 1962,Ag 24,14:2
Hunt, Bradford
Clinging Vine, The 1922,D 25,20:2
School for Scandal, The 1923,Mr 13,19:2
Rust 1924,F 1,12:1
First Lady 1935,N 27,17:4
Public Relations 1944,Ap 7,23:3
Thorntons, The 1956,F 15,26:1
Hunt, Carl (Director)
Silent House, The 1928,F 8,28:5
Boy Friend, The 1932,Je 8,22:3
Silent House, The 1932,N 9,28:3
Young Sinners 1933,Mr 7,20:4
Springtime for Henry 1933,My 2,20:5
June Moon 1933,My 16,15:5
Kick Back, The 1936,Je 23,27:3
Howdy Stranger 1937,Ja 15,17:5

Hunt, Carl (Producer)
Boy Friend, The 1932,Je 8,22:3
Hunt, Charlotte
Tin Pan Alley 1928,N 2,29:1
Hunt, Derek (Lighting Director)
John Brown's Body 1960,Je 22,31:1
Critic, The 1965,Jl 26,15:2
Hunt, Doug
Most Happy Fella, The 1966,My 12,55:1
Hunt, Edward
Lifeline 1942,D 1,20:3
Say Darling 1959,F 26,38:2
Hunt, Elizabeth
Earth Journey 1944,Ap 28,24:2
Hunt, Estelle
Nic-Nax of 1926 1926,Ag 5,19:1
Hunt, Estelle (Playwright)
Woof, Woof 1929,D 26,20:4
Hunt, Eugene (Miscellaneous)
Crystal Heart, The 1960,F 16,31:2
Hunt, Eugenie
Fourth Avenue North 1961,S 28,50:2
Hunt, Eunice
Lombardi, Ltd 1927,Je 7,27:3
Waterloo Bridge 1930,Ja 7,29:2
Blind Mice 1930,O 16,28:2
Hunt, Frances
Victoria Regina 1938,O 4,20:2
Hunt, George
Headquarters 1929,D 5,32:4
Hunt, Gordon (Director)
Whistling Wizard and the Sultan of Tuffet 1970,F 1,70:1
Ali Baba and the Forty Thieves 1970,D 29,40:1
Hunt, Grady (Costume Designer)
Billy Barnes People, The 1961,Je 14,10:3
Hunt, Hugh (Director)
White Steed, The 1939,Ja 11,16:2
Love's Labour's Lost 1949,O 24,18:3
Twelfth Night 1950,D 3,II,3:1
Living Room, The 1954,N 18,41:1
Living Room, The 1954,N 28,II,1:1
Well of the Saints, The 1970,Ag 10,34:1
Hunt, Hugh (Playwright)
In the Train 1937,N 22,14:5
Hunt, Hugh (Producer)
Village Wooing 1935,O 27,IX,2:5
Candida 1935,O 27,IX,2:5
Noah 1935,D 1,XI,6:4
Romeo and Juliet 1952,S 17,34:6
Shaughraun, The 1968,My 22,54:1
Hunt, Ida Brooks
Robin Hood 1929,N 20,26:5
Hunt, J H
Bulldog Drummond 1921,D 27,10:2
Hunt, June
Eugenia 1957,Ja 31,20:1
Damask Drum, The 1961,F 4,15:1
Wives, The 1965,My 18,35:4
Hunt, Leslie
I Will IF You Will 1922,Ag 30,10:4
Roseanne 1923,D 31,9:5
Downstream 1926,Ja 12,28:1
Lily Sue 1926,N 17,22:2
Jacob Slovak 1927,O 6,28:4
Rope 1928,F 23,18:3
Commodore Marries, The 1929,S 5,26:3
He 1931,S 22,33:1
Miss Gulliver Travels 1931,N 26,36:4
Tree, The 1932,Ap 13,23:5
Battle Hymn 1936,My 23,12:1
Processional 1937,O 14,23:1
Big Blow 1938,O 3,11:2
Visit, The 1958,My 6,40:1
Hunt, Lois
Buttrio Square 1952,O 15,40:2
Hunt, Marguerite
Phedre 1966,F 11,36:1
Hunt, Marie
Ladies of the Jury 1929,O 22,26:2
With Privileges 1930,S 16,30:2
Wonder Bar, The 1931,Mr 18,23:4
Inside Story, The 1932,F 23,23:2
Man Who Reclaimed His Head 1932,S 9,17:3
Symphony 1935,Ap 27,20:3
Weep for the Virgins 1935,D 2,18:1
Puritan, The 1936,Ja 24,14:3
Hunt, Marsha
Joy to the World 1948,Mr 19,28:2
Joy to the World 1948,Mr 28,II,1:1
Devil's Disciple, The 1950,Ja 26,23:2
Devil's Disciple, The 1950,F 5,II,1:1
Borned in Texas 1950,Ag 22,30:6
Legend of Sarah 1950,O 12,42:4
Heartbreak House 1963,Je 8,14:2
Heartbreak House 1963,Je 28,24:1
Paisley Convertible, The 1967,F 13,42:1
Hunt, Martita
King Lear 1927,Mr 13,VII,1:4
Rasputin 1929,My 12,IX,2:3
Autumn Crocus 1931,Ap 26,VIII,2:4
Distaff Side, The 1933,S 24,X,1:6
Not for Children 1935,N 25,23:8

Hunt, Martita—Cont
Great Expectations 1939,D 17,IX,4:5
Madwoman of Chaillot, The 1949,Ja 9,II,1:1
Madwoman of Chaillot, The 1949,S 11,II,1:1
Madwoman of Chaillot, The 1950,Je 14,41:2
Madwoman of Chaillot, The 1951,Mr 4,II,3:7
Sleeping Prince, The 1953,N 6,24:4
Sleeping Prince, The 1953,D 20,II,4:2
Hunt, Maurice
Many Mansions 1937,O 28,28:6
Hunt, Morris
Henry IV, Part I 1955,S 22,34:2
Hunt, Neil
And People All Around 1968,F 12,46:1
Hunt, Pamela
Lend an Ear 1969,O 29,32:1
Hunt, Peter (Director)
1776 1969,Mr 17,46:2
Georgy 1970,F 27,26:1
Hunt, Peter (Lighting Director)
Sap of Life, The 1961,O 3,44:1
Color of Darkness: An Evening in the World of James Purdy; Cracks 1963,O 1,24:1
Color of Darkness: An Evening in the World of James Purdy; You Reach for Your Hat 1963,O 1,34:1
Color of Darkness: An Evening in the World of James Purdy; Sermon 1963,O 1,34:1
Color of Darkness: An Evening in the World of James Purdy; Everything Under the Sun 1963,O 1,34:1
Color of Darkness: An Evening in the World of James Purdy; Encore 1963,O 1,34:1
Color of Darkness: An Evening in the World of James Purdy; Don't Call Me By My Right Name 1963,O 1,34:1
Tambourines to Glory 1963,N 4,47:1
Dynamite Tonight 1964,Mr 16,36:2
Kismet 1965,Je 23,45:1
Carousel 1965,Ag 11,39:1
Wayward Stork, The 1966,Ja 20,27:1
Annie Get Your Gun 1966,Je 1,42:2
Have I Got One for You 1968,Ja 8,32:1
West Side Story 1968,Je 25,32:1
Firebugs, The 1968,Jl 2,36:1
Hunt, Peter (Producer)
1776 1970,Je 18,54:4
Hunt, Phoebe
Night Lodging 1920,Ap 14,18:2
Hunt, Phyllis
Ol' Man Satan 1932,O 4,26:3
Hunt, Ray
Manhattan Mary 1927,S 27,30:3
Hunt, Roger
Man Who Came to Dinner, The 1940,F 10,19:5
Hunt, Roy
Martinique 1920,Ap 27,18:2
Hunt, William (Director)
Black Monday 1962,Mr 7,29:1
Say Nothing 1965,Ja 28,21:2
Ludlow Fair 1966,Mr 23,42:1
Madness of Lady Bright, The 1966,Mr 23,42:1
Eternal Triangle 1966,N 8,45:1
Frying Pan, The 1966,N 8,45:1
Bridal Night, The 1966,N 8,45:1
Autograph Hound 1968,D 14,60:1
Lemonade 1968,D 14,60:1
Three by Ferlinghetti; Three Thousand Red Ants 1970,S 23,43:1
Three by Ferlinghetti; Alligation, The 1970,S 23,43:1
Three by Ferlinghetti; Victims of Amnesia, The 1970,S 23,43:1
Hunt, William (Producer)
Black Monday 1962,Mr 7,29:1
Hunt, William Morris
At Your Service 1937,Ag 17,23:1
Hunt, William Morris (Miscellaneous)
Henry IV, Part I 1955,S 22,34:2
Henry V 1956,Jl 7,11:2
Saint Joan 1956,S 12,42:1
Hunt, William Morris (Producer)
Twelfth Night 1959,Jl 11,10:2
Macbeth 1959,Ag 1,9:2
Hunt (Commander) (Playwright)
Below the Surface 1932,Ja 31,VIII,2:1
Hunter, Alberta
Change Your Luck 1930,Je 7,10:2
Cherry Lane Follies, The 1930,Je 30,22:4
Mamba's Daughters 1939,Ja 4,24:2
Mamba's Daughters 1940,Mr 25,10:4
Debut 1956,F 23,32:1
Hunter, Alison McLellan (Costume Designer)
Everybody's Welcome 1931,O 14,26:3
Hunter, Anne
Women, The 1936,D 28,13:1
Girl From Wyoming, The 1938,O 31,12:1
Passion, Poison and Petrifaction 1959,Ag 21,13:1
Hunter, Barbara
Girls in Uniform 1932,D 31,10:3
Naughty-Naught '00 1937,Ja 25,23:2
Hunter, Bush
2 for Fun; Anniversary, The 1955,My 26,34:1

Hunter, Carla
Great Man, The 1931,Ap 8,20:6
Hunter, Chic
High Flyers 1927,Je 26,VIII,1:1
Hunter, Colin
Old Bill, M P 1926,N 11,22:2
Interference 1927,O 19,24:3
Interference 1928,My 8,25:4
Sign of the Leopard 1928,D 12,34:4
One, Two, Three! 1930,S 30,24:2
Marseilles 1930,N 18,28:2
Lancashire Lass, The 1931,D 31,16:3
Firebird 1932,N 22,25:2
Yellow Jack 1934,Mr 7,22:6
Ode to Liberty 1934,D 22,20:2
Libel! 1935,D 21,10:5
Oscar Wilde 1938,O 11,20:2
Anne of England 1941,O 8,26:2
Hunter, Diana
Sophie 1963,Ap 16,32:1
Hunter, Douglas
Potters, The 1923,D 10,21:4
Hunter, Eddie
How Come? 1923,Ap 17,26:1
My Magnolia 1926,Jl 13,19:2
Blackbirds 1933,D 4,22:3
Hunter, Eddie (Director)
My Magnolia 1926,Jl 13,19:2
Hunter, Eddie (Playwright)
My Magnolia 1926,Jl 13,19:2
Hunter, Ernest
Man About Town, A 1921,Mr 22,15:1
Play Without a Name, A 1928,N 26,30:5
20th Century 1932,D 30,15:1
Hunter, Evaline
First Crocus, The 1942,Ja 3,14:6
Hunter, Evan (Playwright)
Easter Man, The 1964,Jl 1,39:1
Race of Hairy Men!, A 1965,Ap 30,42:1
Hunter, Florence
Present Arms 1928,Ap 27,16:2
Hunter, Frank
Folly Town 1920,My 18,9:2
Hunter, Frank (Lyricist)
Jazz a La Carte 1922,Je 3,8:3
Hunter, Fred
Kiss for Cinderella, A 1942,Mr 11,22:2
Hunter, George
Caviar 1934,Je 8,19:2
Hunter, Glenn
Intimate Strangers, The 1921,N 8,28:1
Merton of the Movies 1922,N 14,16:2
Merton of the Movies 1922,N 19,VII,1:1
Young Woodley 1925,O 11,VIII,2:6
Young Woodley 1925,N 3,34:1
Young Woodley 1925,N 8,VIII,1:1
Behold This Dreamer 1927,O 16,IX,2:4
Behold This Dreamer 1927,N 1,20:4
She Stoops to Conquer 1928,My 15,17:1
She Stoops to Conquer 1928,My 20,VIII,1:1
Spring Is Here 1929,Mr 12,26:1
Vaudeville (Palace) 1929,Je 24,27:4
Waterloo Bridge 1929,D 1,X,4:7
Waterloo Bridge 1930,Ja 7,29:2
Regular Guy, A; Man's Man, A 1931,Je 5,27:1
Way Out, The 1932,D 14,27:3
Wind and the Rain, The 1935,Jl 11,24:2
Petrified Forest, The 1935,N 24,II,9:3
Petrified Forest, The 1935,D 8,X,5:8
Empress of Destiny 1938,Mr 10,16:2
Journey's End 1939,S 19,29:2
Journey's End 1939,S 24,IX,1:1
Hunter, Glenn (Playwright)
Peter Flies High 1931,S 20,VIII,3:1
Hunter, Greg
Trouble in July 1949,D 2,36:2
Hunter, Hal
Are You With It? 1945,N 12,17:3
Hunter, Harrison
Bat, The 1920,Ag 24,6:1
Hunter, Herbert L
Betty Behave 1927,Mr 9,28:4
Hunter, Ian
School for Scandal, The 1925,D 7,18:2
High Road, The 1927,S 25,VIII,2:1
Olympia 1928,O 17,26:1
Business With America 1933,Ja 1,IX,1:3
Acropolis 1933,D 10,X,3:6
Without Witness 1933,D 28,25:1
Spring, 1600 1934,F 1,14:1
Touch Wood 1934,Jl 1,X,1:3
Edward, My Son 1948,O 1,30:2
Edward My Son 1948,O 10,II,1:1
Hunter, Ian McLellan (Playwright)
Foxy 1962,Jl 4,12:2
Foxy 1964,F 17,26:1
Hunter, J G
Why Not? 1922,D 30,13:4
Hunter, Jacquelyn
Daffy Dill 1922,Ag 23,14:5
Hunter, James
French Doll, The 1922,F 21,20:2
Loot 1968,Mr 19,40:2

Hunter, Jay
Jubilee 1935,O 14,20:1
Hunter, Judith
Trojan Women, The 1957,Mr 19,42:7
Hunter, Kenneth
Bat, The 1920,Ag 24,6:1
Endless Chain, The 1922,S 5,21:2
Romeo and Juliet 1922,D 28,20:1
Laughing Lady, The 1923,F 13,25:1
Hamlet 1923,N 27,23:6
Outsider, The 1924,Mr 4,16:4
Izzy 1924,S 17,16:2
Red Falcon, The 1924,O 8,22:1
Little Minister, The 1925,Mr 24,21:1
Hamlet 1925,O 12,19:2
Merchant of Venice, The 1925,D 28,12:1
Off Key 1927,F 9,16:2
Julius Caesar 1927,Je 7,27:2
Lady of the Orchids, The 1928,D 14,37:3
Let Us Be Gay 1929,F 22,19:1
Fatal Alibi, The 1932,F 10,26:6
Living Dangerously 1935,Ja 14,10:3
Othello 1935,S 13,19:2
Othello 1935,S 28,13:2
Macbeth 1935,O 8,26:4
Hunter, Kenneth (Composer)
Pink Slips on Parade 1937,F 1,14:4
Hunter, Kermit (Playwright)
Forever This Land 1951,Jl 29,II,1:1
Forever This Land 1952,Je 30,14:6
Forever This Land 1952,Jl 6,II,1:1
Eleventh Hour, The 1956,Jl 10,26:7
Thy Kingdom Come 1957,Je 25,24:6
Hunter, Kim
Streetcar Named Desire, A 1947,D 4,42:2
Streetcar Named Desire, A 1947,D 14,II,3:1
Darkness at Noon 1951,Ja 15,13:4
Darkness at Noon 1951,Ja 21,II,1:1
Chase, The 1952,Ap 16,30:2
Children's Hour, The 1952,D 19,35:2
Children's Hour, The 1952,D 28,II,1:1
Tender Trap, The 1954,O 14,37:2
As You Like It 1961,Je 17,13:2
Macbeth 1961,Je 19,31:1
As You Like It 1961,Je 25,II,1:1
Troilus and Cressida 1961,Jl 24,15:1
Write Me a Murder 1961,O 27,28:2
Come Slowly, Eden 1966,D 7,56:1
Weekend 1968,Mr 14,50:2
Weekend 1968,Mr 31,II,1:1
Hello and Goodbye 1968,N 13,36:2
Penny Wars, The 1969,O 16,52:1
Hunter, Leslye
Christine 1960,Ap 29,27:1
Garden of Sweets, The 1961,N 1,35:1
Gift of Time, A 1962,F 23,34:1
Nobody Loves an Albatross 1963,D 20,20:1
Nobody Loves an Albatross 1964,Ja 5,II,1:1
Hunter, Loraine
Lulu Belle 1926,F 10,20:1
Hunter, Louise
Golden Dawn 1927,O 2,VIII,4:6
Golden Dawn 1927,D 1,32:3
Hunter, Margaret
Patience 1929,D 16,34:5
Hunter, Mark
Stop the World-I Want to Get Off 1962,O 4,45:4
Hunter, Mary
Out of My House 1942,Ja 8,28:6
Hunter, Mary (Director)
Trojan Women, The 1938,Ja 25,24:2
Texas Town 1941,Ap 30,22:3
American Legend 1941,My 12,13:2
Out of My House 1942,Ja 8,28:6
Only the Heart 1942,D 7,22:3
Only the Heart 1944,Ap 5,17:2
Carib Song 1945,S 28,17:2
Respectful Prostitute, The 1948,F 10,27:2
Respectful Prostitute, The 1948,F 15,II,1:1
Happy Journey to Trenton and Camden, The 1948,Mr 21,II,1:1
Respectful Prostitute, The 1948,Mr 21,II,1:1
Victors, The 1948,D 27,17:2
Great to Be Alive! 1950,Mr 24,28:2
Hunter, Mary (Miscellaneous)
Peter Pan 1954,O 21,30:2
Othello 1970,S 15,51:1
Hunter, N C (Playwright)
Little Stranger 1938,Jl 14,16:2
Waters of the Moon 1953,Ap 2,34:3
Day by the Sea, A 1953,N 27,22:3
Day by the Sea, A 1953,D 20,II,4:2
Day by the Sea, A 1955,S 27,42:1
Day by the Sea, A 1955,O 2,II,1:1
Tulip Tree, The 1962,N 30,25:5
Hunter, Norman (Playwright)
Ladies and Gentlemen 1937,My 19,26:6
Hunter, Oliver
Antony and Cleopatra 1951,D 21,22:2
Hunter, Paget
In the Night Watch 1921,Ja 31,10:1
Hunter, Patricia
Commedia Dell' Arte 1957,Jl 5,13:2

Hunter, Rachel
Dove, The 1925,F 12,17:3
Hunter, Raymond
Lady Butterfly 1923,Ja 23,18:1
Untitled-Recital 1932,F 8,21:1
Hunter, Richard
Searching for the Sun 1936,F 20,22:6
Places, Please 1937,N 13,10:6
Hunter, Robert
Much Ado About Nothing 1963,Jl 15,25:2
Hunter, Robert (Musical Director)
Show Girl 1961,Ja 13,37:1
Hunter, Ron
All the King's Men 1963,Jl 12,12:1
Hunter, Ruth
Veneer 1929,N 13,24:5
Up and Up, The 1930,S 9,25:2
Tobacco Road 1933,D 5,31:2
Hunter, T Hayes (Miscellaneous)
Heart of a City 1942,F 13,24:6
Hunter, Tab
Milk Train Doesn't Stop Here Anymore, The 1964,Ja 2,33:1
Hunter, Tookie
Love in My Fashion 1937,D 4,21:4
Hunter, Walt
Annie Get Your Gun 1966,Je 1,42:2
Hunter, William
Let Freedom Ring 1935,N 7,26:2
Bury the Dead 1936,Ap 20,17:4
Prelude 1936,Ap 20,17:4
Clean Beds 1939,My 26,21:2
Huntingdon, B
In the Night Watch 1921,Ja 31,10:1
Huntingford, Nora
Little Theatre Tournament; Old Lady Shows Her Medals, The 1928,My 11,28:1
Huntington, Berkley
Fair Circassian, The 1921,D 7,22:3
Huntington, Gale
Dream Child 1934,Jl 31,20:2
Dream Child 1934,S 28,26:2
Huntington, John
Ceiling Zero 1935,Ap 11,26:2
Marching Song 1937,F 18,18:2
Too Many Heroes 1937,N 16,26:2
Washington Jitters 1938,My 3,19:1
Tinker's Dam 1943,Ja 29,22:2
Huntington, John (Miscellaneous)
Dark of the Moon 1945,Mr 15,27:2
Second Best Bed 1946,Je 4,20:2
Huntington, John (Playwright)
Lawrence of Arabia 1954,D 10,35:3
Huntington, John (Producer)
Southwest Corner, The 1955,F 4,18:2
Huntington, Lois
Good-Bye Please 1934,O 25,26:6
Huntington, Louise
Nut Farm, The 1929,O 15,34:3
Pygmalion 1938,Ja 27,16:3
Captain Jinks of the Horse Marines 1938,Ja 28,16:2
World We Make, The 1939,N 21,19:1
Huntington, Rex (Costume Designer)
This Was Burlesque 1970,F 12,31:1
Huntington, W P
Tiger Smiles, The 1930,D 18,29:1
Huntley, Bruce
Gentlemen Prefer Blondes 1926,S 29,23:1
Huntley, Florence
Garden of Weeds 1924,Ap 29,12:3
Huntley, G P
Hitchy-Koo, 1920 1920,O 20,11:3
Peg o' My Dreams 1924,My 6,25:3
Be Yourself! 1924,S 4,13:3
Second Mrs Tanqueray, The 1924,O 28,27:1
Gentlemen Prefer Blondes 1926,S 29,23:1
Huntley, G P Jr
This Year of Grace 1928,N 8,27:1
Soldiers and Women 1929,S 3,25:1
Journey's End 1930,Ag 5,26:4
Stepdaughters of War 1930,O 7,27:1
Art and Mrs Bottle 1930,N 19,19:3
Divorce Me, Dear 1931,O 7,29:2
Berlin 1931,D 31,16:1
Experience Unnecessary 1932,Mr 28,10:2
Gay Divorce 1932,N 30,23:4
Othello 1936,N 27,26:5
Othello 1937,Ja 7,16:4
Huntley, Hugh
Paddy the Next Best Thing 1920,Ag 28,5:5
Persons Unknown 1922,O 26,12:1
Enchanted April, The 1925,Ag 25,12:3
Witch, The 1926,N 19,22:5
Sinner 1927,F 8,20:2
Arabian, The 1927,N 1,20:5
Song Writer, The 1928,Ag 14,15:2
Royal Box, The 1928,N 21,32:3
Sakura 1928,D 26,14:4
All the King's Men 1929,F 5,27:1
Dinner Is Served 1929,Ag 16,18:4
Huntley, Jack
Summer Wives 1936,Ap 14,18:1

Huntley, Jobe (Composer)
Tambourines to Glory 1963,N 4,47:1
Huntley, Marian
May Wine 1935,D 6,30:3
Huntley, Raymond
Venetian Glass Nephew, The 1931,F 24,26:3
Young Madame Conti 1937,Ap 1,18:4
Susannah and the Elders 1937,N 21,XI,3:6
Rhondda Roundabout 1939,Je 18,IX,1:7
They Came to a City 1943,Je 6,II,1:6
Black Chiffon 1950,S 28,39:2
Black Chiffon 1950,O 15,II,1:1
Huot, Denise
How's the World Treating You? 1966,O 25,50:1
Carricknabauna 1967,Mr 31,30:1
Prime of Miss Jean Brodie, The 1968,Ja 17,39:1
Richard II 1968,Je 24,42:3
Love's Labour's Lost 1968,Je 28,36:1
Huot, Victor
Mikado, The 1924,Jl 29,9:1
Hupfeld, Herman (Composer)
Merry World, The 1926,Je 9,18:3
A la Carte 1927,Ag 18,25:3
Americana 1932,O 6,19:3
Music Hall Varieties 1932,N 23,15:3
Show Is On, The 1936,D 26,14:2
Dance Me a Song 1950,Ja 21,10:5
Hupfeld, Herman (Lyricist)
A la Carte 1927,Ag 18,25:3
Music Hall Varieties 1932,N 23,15:3
Show Is On, The 1936,D 26,14:2
Show Is On, The 1937,S 20,18:4
Hupfeld, Herman (Miscellaneous)
Hey, Nonny, Nonny! 1932,Je 7,22:3
Hupp, Rosalind
Sound of Music, The 1970,Jl 3,13:1
Hura, Helba
Nina Rosa 1930,My 31,19:3
Hurd, Alex
Stars on Ice 1942,Jl 3,12:2
Hurd, George
O'Brien Girl, The 1921,O 4,10:2
Hurd, Hugh
Finian's Rainbow 1953,Mr 7,13:2
Detective Story 1954,F 13,11:2
That Thing at the Cherry Lane 1965,My 19,42:1
Skin of Our Teeth, The 1966,Je 2,51:1
As You Like It 1966,Je 4,19:1
Hurd, James
Point of Honor, A 1937,F 12,26:2
Hurd, Malcolm
No Place to Be Somebody 1969,My 5,53:3
No Place to Be Somebody 1969,D 31,17:1
Hurdle, James
Merchant of Venice, The 1970,Je 10,39:1
School for Scandal, The 1970,Je 11,51:1
Hurdle, John
Doodle Dandy of the U S A 1942,O 19,15:2
Hurdle, L M
They Shall Not Die 1934,F 22,24:4
Hurdle, Lawrence
He 1931,S 22,33:1
If This Be Treason 1935,Jl 30,17:1
If This Be Treason 1935,S 24,28:2
Puritan, The 1936,Ja 24,14:3
Hurdle, Lawrence (Director)
New Faces of 1943 1942,D 23,22:2
Hurlbert, Jackie
Hassard Short's Ritz Revue 1924,S 18,19:1
Sunny 1925,S 23,22:1
Vaudeville (Palace) 1925,O 6,31:3
Boom Boom 1929,Ja 29,26:4
Hurlbut, Gladys
Mrs Jimmie Thompson 1920,Mr 30,9:1
Merchant of Venice, The 1921,Ap 2,14:2
Dragon, The 1922,D 27,12:1
Cat Comes Back, The 1923,Ja 29,11:2
Ashes 1924,O 21,21:2
Caught 1925,O 6,31:2
For Better or Worse 1927,F 1,24:3
Just to Remind You 1931,S 8,39:1
Life With Mother 1948,O 21,32:2
Hurlbut, Gladys (Playwright)
By Your Leave 1934,Ja 25,15:3
Mad Morning 1935,Je 25,14:1
Ring Two 1939,N 14,20:3
Ring Two 1939,N 23,38:2
Higher and Higher 1940,Mr 17,X,2:5
Higher and Higher 1940,Ap 5,24:3
Yankee Point 1942,N 24,28:2
Hurlbut, William (Playwright)
Trimmed in Scarlet 1920,F 3,18:1
Lilies of the Field 1921,O 5,20:1
On the Stairs 1922,S 26,18:2
Hail and Farewell 1923,F 20,12:1
Writing on the Wall, The 1923,Jl 3,25:2
Writing on the Wall, The 1923,Jl 8,VI,1:1
Cup, The 1923,N 13,25:1
Chivalry 1925,D 16,22:3
Bride of the Lamb 1926,Mr 31,20:3
Bride of the Lamb 1926,Ap 4,VIII,1:1
Hidden 1927,S 25,VIII,4:8
Paradise 1927,D 26,26:4

Primer for Lovers, A 1929,N 19,26:5
Bride of the Lamb 1934,Mr 29,26:1
Story to Be Whispered 1937,Ag 20,21:4
Hurley, Arthur
Deluge, The 1922,Ja 28,14:2
Hurley, Arthur (Director)
Firebrand, The 1924,O 16,33:1
Don Q Jr 1926,Ja 28,16:3
Desert Song, The 1926,D 1,24:2
Night Hawk 1926,D 27,21:3
Fog 1927,F 8,20:1
Menace 1927,Mr 15,28:2
Julie 1927,My 10,24:4
Playing the Game 1927,D 20,32:5
Brothers 1928,D 26,14:3
Lid's Off, The 1936,Ap 4,11:6
Hurley, Arthur (Miscellaneous)
Heigh-Ho, Everybody 1932,My 26,31:2
Hurley, Edward (Playwright)
Hot Rhythm 1930,Ag 22,18:5
Hurley, Irma
Absalom 1956,My 17,37:2
Eugenia 1957,Ja 31,20:1
Charlatans; Summer Ghost, A 1962,Ap 27,26:1
God, Man & You, Baby! 1963,O 30,47:1
Hurley, J Albert (Musical Director)
Trial by Jury 1934,Ap 17,27:2
H M S Pinafore 1934,Ap 17,27:2
Iolanthe 1934,My 1,26:4
Hurley, J R (Mrs)
Two Orphans, The 1926,Ap 6,26:2
Hurley, John
Badges 1924,D 4,25:1
Hurley, Laurel
Night in Venice, A 1952,Je 27,18:6
Night in Venice, A 1952,Jl 13,II,1:1
Show Boat 1954,My 6,44:1
Show Boat 1954,O 29,28:4
Hurley, Maureen
Monique 1957,O 23,38:1
Passage to India, A 1962,F 1,23:1
Importance of Being Earnest, The 1963,F 27,5:2
Hurney, Kate
Beautiful Dreamer 1960,D 28,22:1
Galileo 1967,Ap 14,31:1
Iolanthe 1967,O 18,40:1
Mikado, The 1967,O 25,42:2
Gondoliers, The 1967,O 29,83:1
Hurok, S (Miscellaneous)
Blue Bird, The 1932,Ap 22,23:2
Poverty Is No Crime 1935,F 21,22:5
Strange Child 1935,F 26,16:1
White Guard, The; Days of the Turbins
1935,Mr 7,27:5
Enemies 1935,Mr 19,24:7
Deluge, The 1935,Mr 26,23:7
Untitled-Reading 1952,Ja 30,20:2
Occupe-Toi d'Amelie; Keep Your Eyes on Amelie
1952,N 25,35:2
Repetition, La; Rehearsal, The 1952,N 28,22:2
Hamlet 1952,D 2,39:1
Bleak House 1953,Ap 21,33:2
Midsummer Night's Dream, A 1954,S 22,33:1
Bourgeois Gentilhomme, Le 1955,O 26,26:1
Arlequin Poli par l'Amour 1955,N 9,40:1
Jeu de l'Amour et du Hasard, Le 1955,N 16,42:4
Caprice, Un 1955,N 16,42:4
Romeo and Juliet 1956,O 25,41:1
Troilus and Cressida 1956,D 27,21:1
Volpone 1957,F 5,27:2
Misanthrope, Le 1957,F 8,19:1
Nuits de La Colere, Les; Nights of Fury
1957,F 12,31:1
Feu la Mere de Madame; Dear Departed
Mother-in-Law 1957,F 12,31:1
Intermezzo 1957,F 15,20:4
Chien du Jardinier, Le; Gardener's Dog, The
1957,F 19,36:1
Adieux, Les 1957,F 19,36:1
Lorenzaccio 1958,O 15,44:2
Triomphe de l'Amour, Le 1958,O 17,32:1
Don Juan 1958,O 29,29:1
Cid, Le 1958,O 31,35:2
Twelfth Night 1958,D 10,54:2
Dear Liar 1960,Mr 18,19:2
Britannicus 1961,Mr 3,17:1
Macbeth 1962,F 7,32:2
Romeo and Juliet 1962,F 14,39:1
Saint Joan 1962,F 21,57:4
Iolanthe 1962,N 18,52:1
Trial by Jury 1964,N 20,40:1
H M S Pinafore 1964,N 20,40:1
Mikado, The 1964,N 27,43:1
Pirates of Penzance, The 1964,N 27,43:1
Ruddigore 1964,D 4,44:1
Hurok, S (Producer)
Revisor; Inspector General, The 1935,F 18,19:6
Cabalgata 1949,Jl 8,14:2
Emlyn Williams 1952,F 5,25:2
Fausses Confidences, Les 1952,N 13,34:2
Baptiste 1952,N 13,34:2
Proces, Le; Trial, The 1952,N 18,36:2
Fourberies de Scapin, Les 1952,N 21,21:2

Hurok, S (Producer)—Cont
Amphitryon 1952,N 21,21:2
Richard II 1956,O 24,44:1
Macbeth 1956,O 30,42:2
Christophe Colomb 1957,Ja 31,20:5
Boy Growing Up, A 1957,O 8,41:1
Hamlet 1958,D 17,2:7
Henry V 1958,D 26,2:7
Lovely Light, A 1960,F 9,27:4
Duel of Angels 1960,Ap 20,42:2
Impromptu de Versailles, L' 1961,F 22,30:1
Fourberies de Scapin, Les 1961,F 22,30:1
Tartuffe 1961,Mr 1,28:1
Dindon, Le 1961,Mr 8,38:1
Importance of Being Oscar, The 1961,Mr 15,45:2
Mikado, The 1962,N 14,43:1
Gondoliers, The 1962,N 16,25:2
Pirates of Penzance, The 1962,N 21,28:1
H M S Pinafore 1962,N 23,32:4
Trial by Jury 1962,N 23,32:4
Iolanthe 1962,N 28,42:1
Obratsov Russian Pupper Theater in an Unusual
Concert 1963,O 3,28:1
Phedre 1963,O 21,39:1
Aladdin and His Wonderful Lamp 1963,O 21,39:1
Berenice 1963,O 30,46:1
Mariage de Figaro, Le 1964,F 26,41:2
Andromaque 1964,F 29,13:1
Pieton de L'Air, Le 1964,Mr 4,33:2
Vie Parisienne, La 1964,Mr 11,34:2
Cambridge Circus 1964,O 7,53:1
Post Office, The 1965,Ja 6,32:1
Labyrinth, The 1965,Ja 6,32:1
Nightmare, The 1965,Ja 6,32:1
Jaselka 1965,Ja 6,32:1
Woman, The 1965,Ja 6,32:1
Kernel and the Shell, The 1965,Ja 6,32:1
Book, The 1965,Ja 6,32:1
Jacob and the Angel 1965,Ja 6,32:1
Dead Souls 1965,F 5,34:1
Cherry Orchard, The 1965,F 10,46:1
Three Sisters, The 1965,F 12,15:1
Kremlin Chimes 1965,F 25,23:1
Fil a la Paite, Un; How to Cut the Thread That
Ties You to Your Mistress 1966,F 9,32:1
Cid, Le 1966,F 9,32:1
Avare, L', L'; Miser, The 1966,F 9,32:1
Reine Morte, La; Dead Queen, The 1966,F 9,32:1
Cid, Le 1966,F 12,17:1
Reine Morte, La 1966,F 16,52:1
Fil a la Paite, Un 1966,F 18,25:1
Pirates of Penzance, The 1966,N 16,54:1
Mikado, The 1966,N 18,36:1
Ruddigore 1966,N 23,28:1
H M S Pinafore 1966,N 24,64:1
Patience 1966,N 30,58:1
Measure for Measure 1967,F 15,37:1
Hamlet 1967,F 17,44:1
Romeo and Juliet 1967,F 22,18:1
H M S Pinafore 1968,O 30,35:1
Mikado, The 1968,N 2,29:4
Pirates of Penzance, The 1968,N 7,54:1
Iolanthe 1968,N 9,37:3
Don Juan 1970,F 7,24:2
Femmes Savaantes, Les 1970,F 14,12:1
Malade Imaginaire, Le 1970,F 21,57:4
Emlyn Williams as Charles Dickens 1970,N 4,41:1
Hurren, Bonnie
Cherry Orchard, The 1970,My 7,63:2
Hurry, Leslie (Costume Designer)
Tamburlaine the Great 1956,Ja 20,19:1
Richard II 1956,O 24,44:1
Henry VI (Part III) 1957,O 18,19:5
Saint Joan 1962,F 21,57:4
Beggar's Opera, The 1963,Jl 17,20:1
Hurry, Leslie (Scenic Designer)
Living Room, The 1953,Ap 17,29:5
Tamburlaine the Great 1956,Ja 20,19:1
Richard II 1956,O 24,44:1
Hamlet 1961,Ap 12,46:1
Saint Joan 1962,F 21,57:4
King Lear 1964,Je 19,36:1
Julius Caesar 1965,Jl 2,18:1
Government Inspector, The 1967,Je 15,55:1
Government Inspector, The 1967,O 28,34:1
Midsummer Night's Dream, A 1968,Je 13,54:1
School for Scandal, The 1970,Je 11,51:1
Hurst, Brandon
Lady of the Lamp, The 1920,Ag 18,6:4
Montmartre 1922,F 14,20:1
Night Call, The 1922,Ap 27,12:2
Hurst, David
Jack 1958,Je 4,39:2
Bald Soprano, The 1958,Je 4,39:2
Look After Lulu 1959,Mr 4,35:1
Under the Sycamore Tree 1960,Mr 8,37:2
Brouhaha 1960,Ap 27,31:2
Camelot 1960,D 5,42:1
Caucasian Chalk Circle, The 1961,N 1,35:1
Burning of the Lepers, The 1961,Ap 5,29:1
Fun Couple, The 1962,O 27,15:2
Month in the Country, A 1963,My 29,39:2
Dynamite Tonight 1964,Mr 16,36:2
Electra 1964,Ag 12,42:1

Hurst, David—Cont
Prometheus Bound 1967,My 11,52:1
Hurst, Deirdre
Panic 1935,Mr 16,18:4
Possessed, The 1939,O 25,26:2
Happy Ending 1942,S 28,13:1
Hurst, Dorothy
By the Way 1925,D 29,20:3
Hurst, Emil
If Love Were All 1931,N 14,14:5
Hurst, Fannie (Playwright)
Back Pay 1921,Ag 21,VI,1:8
Back Pay 1921,Ag 31,8:2
Humoresque 1923,F 28,13:2
Humoresque 1923,Mr 4,VII,1:1
It Is to Laugh 1927,D 27,24:2
Hurst, Frank
Mimic World of 1921, The 1921,Ag 18,9:2
Hurst, Hawthorne (Playwright)
Christopher Comes Across 1932,Je 1,19:2
Hurst, James
Oklahoma! 1958,Mr 8,15:2
Sail Away 1961,O 4,48:5
Arabian Nights 1967,Jl 3,12:1
Ballad for a Firing Squad 1968,D 12,64:2
Hurst, Liane (Costume Designer)
39 Steps 1938,Mr 12,13:1
Simpleton of the Unexpected Isles, The
1954,Ja 12,19:1
Hurst, Lou
Are You With It? 1945,N 12,17:3
Hurst, Vera
Wandering Jew, The 1927,F 2,22:4
Congai 1928,N 28,24:3
Cape Cod Follies 1929,S 19,37:2
Virtue's Bed 1930,Ap 16,26:5
As You Desire Me 1931,Ja 29,21:2
Dinner at Eight 1932,O 24,18:2
Divided by Three 1934,O 3,24:2
Night Remembers, The 1934,N 28,24:3
Play, Genius, Play! 1935,O 31,17:2
O Evening Star 1936,Ja 9,24:6
Dorian Gray 1936,Jl 21,13:3
Hurst and Vogt
Vaudeville (Palace) 1929,O 14,20:4
Hurt, Jo
Cradle Will Rock, The 1947,D 27,11:2
Pal Joey 1949,Mr 7,17:2
Babes in Arms 1951,Mr 10,7:3
Single Man at a Party 1959,Ap 22,30:4
Hurt, John
Hamp 1964,Ag 18,25:1
Hurtado's Marimba Band
Vaudeville (Palace) 1926,Je 1,29:5
Hurtig, Jules (Producer)
Virgin, The 1926,F 23,26:1
Hurtubise, Marjorie
Song of Bernadette 1946,Mr 27,22:2
Hurwitz, Richard (Miscellaneous)
Up Eden 1968,N 27,42:1
Husby, Herman (Scenic Designer)
Ali Baba 1951,Mr 27,34:2
Husing, Ted
Double Dummy 1936,N 12,30:1
Husmann, Ron
Guys and Dolls 1959,Jl 22,22:2
Tenderloin 1960,O 18,47:2
All American 1962,Mr 20,44:1
Lovely Ladies, Kind Gentlemen 1970,D 29,38:1
Hussenot, Olivier
Lettre Morte 1970,Ap 16,55:1
Architruc 1970,Ap 16,55:1
Oh, Les Beaux Jours 1970,Ap 25,32:3
Hussenot, Olivier (Director)
Architruc 1970,Ap 16,55:1
Hussey, Ed
Injury Sustained 1940,O 24,30:3
When Differences Disappear 1941,Je 3,17:4
Hussey, Ed (Producer)
When Differences Disappear 1941,Je 3,17:4
Hussey, Jimmy
Mimic World of 1921, The 1921,Ag 18,9:2
Spice of 1922 1922,Jl 7,12:4
Fashions of 1924 1923,Jl 19,18:2
Izzy 1924,S 17,16:2
Puzzles of 1925 1925,F 3,25:3
Vaudeville (Palace) 1926,Ag 31,15:3
Betsy 1926,D 29,24:3
Vaudeville (Palace) 1927,My 24,23:1
Hussey, Jimmy (Lyricist)
Mimic World of 1921, The 1921,Ag 18,9:2
Hussey, Jimmy (Playwright)
Mimic World of 1921, The 1921,Ag 18,9:2
Hussey, John
Persecution and Assassination of Marat As
Performed by the Inmates of the Asylum of
Charenton Under the Direction of the Marquis de
Sade, The 1965,D 28,35:1
Hussey, Ruth
State of the Union 1945,N 7,21:3
State of the Union 1945,N 15,25:2
State of the Union 1945,N 25,II,1:1
State of the Union 1946,S 8,II,1:1
Royal Family, The 1951,Ja 11,28:2

Hussig, William
Crucible, The 1953,Jl 2,20:2
Hussman, Lothar (Dr) (Producer)
Tempest, The 1959,D 28,19:2
Husson, Albert (Original Author)
My 3 Angels 1953,Mr 12,23:2
Husson, Albert (Playwright)
Heavenly Twins, The 1955,N 5,23:2
My 3 Angels 1956,F 4,24:2
Absence of a Cello; Mal de Test, Le 1965,S 9,36:3
Hussung, Will
Simon's Wife 1945,Mr 9,16:4
First Lady 1952,My 29,18:5
Ankles Aweigh 1955,Ap 19,27:1
Girls in 509, The 1958,O 16,47:1
Becket 1961,My 9,44:1
Investigation, The 1966,O 5,40:1
Inherit the Wind 1967,Je 23,50:1
Golden Rainbow 1968,F 5,27:1
Brightower 1970,Ja 29,32:1
Husting, Lucille
Stronger Than Love 1925,D 29,20:2
Huston, Anjelica
Hamlet 1969,My 2,38:1
Huston, Carla
As You Like It 1961,Je 17,13:2
Macbeth 1961,Je 19,31:1
Huston, Eric
Gondoliers, The 1948,Ja 27,31:2
Huston, Gaye Ellen
Cockeyed Kite 1961,S 14,27:1
Huston, Grace (Costume Designer)
Howdy, Mr Ice of 1950 1949,My 27,24:2
Huston, John
Triumph of the Egg, The 1925,F 11,19:3
Ruint 1925,Ap 8,24:2
Adam Solitaire 1925,N 7,19:2
Vaudeville (Palace) 1927,D 20,33:4
Huston, John (Director)
Passenger to Bali, A 1940,Mr 15,26:2
No Exit 1946,N 27,21:1
Huston, John (Playwright)
Storm Child 1935,Jl 16,24:1
In Time to Come 1941,D 29,20:2
In Time to Come 1942,Ja 4,IX,1:1
Frankie and Johnny 1952,O 29,37:2
Huston, Josephine
Vanities 1932,S 18,IX,2:1
Vanities 1932,S 28,22:4
Pardon My English 1933,Ja 21,11:4
Threepenny Opera, The 1933,Ap 14,22:4
Huston, Margaret
Othello 1934,Jl 22,23:4
Huston, Martin
Only in America 1959,N 20,35:1
Take Her, She's Mine 1961,D 22,19:1
Race of Hairy Men!, A 1965,Ap 30,42:1
Harold 1967,My 10,39:1
Norman, Is That You? 1970,F 20,30:1
Huston, Philip
Whatever Possessed Her 1934,Ja 26,21:2
Western Union 1937,Ag 10,22:7
Damn Deborah 1937,Ag 17,23:1
Girl From Wyoming, The 1938,O 31,12:1
Window Shopping 1938,D 24,13:2
Journey's End 1939,S 19,29:2
They Knew What They Wanted 1939,O 3,19:1
Twelfth Night 1940,N 20,26:3
Macbeth 1941,N 12,30:2
Othello 1943,O 20,18:1
Catherine Was Great 1944,Ag 3,16:1
Tempest, The 1945,Ja 26,17:2
Othello 1945,My 23,25:4
Make Yourself at Home 1945,S 14,21:2
Winter's Tale, The 1946,Ja 16,18:6
Father, The 1949,N 17,36:2
With a Silk Thread 1950,Ap 13,34:3
Tower Beyond Tragedy, The 1950,N 27,29:1
Shrike, The 1952,Ja 16,20:2
Cyrano de Bergerac 1953,N 13,24:3
Shrike, The 1953,N 26,51:2
Richard III 1953,D 10,65:2
Cave at Machpelah, The 1959,Jl 1,25:1
Mandingo 1961,My 23,43:6
Huston, Walter
Mister Pitt 1924,Ja 6,VII,1:4
Mister Pitt 1924,Ja 23,15:3
Easy Mark, The 1924,Ag 27,14:2
Desire Under the Elms 1924,N 12,20:7
Desire Under the Elms 1924,D 7,VIII,5:1
Fountain, The 1925,D 11,26:1
Kongo 1926,Mr 31,20:5
Barker, The 1927,Ja 19,20:6
Barker, The 1927,Ja 23,VII,1:1
Elmer the Great 1928,S 25,29:1
Elmer the Great 1928,S 30,IX,1:1
Blow the Man Down 1929,Ag 25,VIII,3:1
Commodore Marries, The 1929,S 5,26:3
Commodore Marries, The 1929,S 15,IX,1:1
Dodsworth 1934,F 26,20:4
Othello 1934,Jl 22,23:4
Othello 1934,Jl 29,IX,1:3
Dodsworth 1934,Ag 21,12:3

Huston, Walter—Cont
Othello 1936,N 27,26:5
Othello 1936,D 6,XII,6:1
Othello 1937,Ja 7,16:4
Miles of Heaven, The 1937,Ag 31,27:4
Knickerbocker Holiday 1938,O 2,IX,3:3
Knickerbocker Holiday 1938,O 16,I,3:3
Knickerbocker Holiday 1938,O 20,26:2
Knickerbocker Holiday 1938,N 20,IX,1:1
Passenger to Bali, A 1940,Mr 15,26:2
Love's Old Sweet Song 1940,Ap 7,I,44:6
Love's Old Sweet Song 1940,Ap 14,IX,3:3
Love's Old Sweet Song 1940,My 3,16:3
Apple of His Eye 1946,F 6,18:2
Huston, Walter (Miscellaneous)
Apple of His Eye 1946,F 6,18:2
Huston, Walter (Producer)
Othello 1936,D 6,XII,6:1
Huszagh, Jane
Snark Was a Boojum, The 1943,S 2,14:4
Huszar, Karl
Street Scene 1930,Mr 16,IX,4:1
Hutaine, Ione
Lady Beyond the Moon 1931,Ap 1,36:5
Hutcherson, Le Vern
Carmen Jones 1945,My 3,26:5
Carmen Jones 1946,Ap 8,32:2
Carmen Jones 1951,S 22,8:6
Porgy and Bess 1953,F 17,21:1
Porgy and Bess 1953,Mr 10,25:5
Porgy and Bess 1954,D 17,36:7
Porgy and Bess 1955,Jl 9,9:5
Porgy and Bess 1955,O 13,37:4
Hutcheson, David
Sons o' Guns 1929,N 27,30:4
Free for All 1931,S 9,25:1
Doctor's Dilemma, The 1969,Je 24,37:1
Hutcheson, Elinor
Piper, The 1920,Mr 20,14:2
Hutchins, Andrew F
Bloodstream 1932,Mr 31,25:1
Hutchins, Brice
Ziegfeld Follies 1934,Ja 5,24:3
Hutchins, Harriet
Keep Moving 1934,Ag 24,10:2
Hutchins, Margaret
Scrambled Wives 1920,Ag 6,16:1
Carnaval 1924,D 30,15:1
Hutchins, Marion
Main Street 1921,O 6,21:1
Virtue (?) 1922,N 17,14:1
Lesson in Love, A 1923,S 25,10:1
Hutchins, Traver
Wild Duck, The 1938,Ap 16,16:5
Hutchinson, A S M (Original Author)
If Winter Comes 1923,F 4,VII,1:4
If Winter Comes 1923,Ap 3,26:1
Hutchinson, A S M (Playwright)
If Winter Comes 1923,Ap 3,26:1
Hutchinson, Ann
Everyman 1941,My 9,19:2
It's About Time 1942,Mr 31,28:3
Hutchinson, Arthur (Producer)
Every Man for Himself 1940,D 10,32:3
Hutchinson, Dave
Five Star Saint 1970,F 11,41:2
Hutchinson, David
Meet the Wife 1927,Jl 3,VII,1:4
Hutchinson, Ernest (Playwright)
Right to Strike, The 1920,O 31,VI,1:4
Right to Strike, The 1921,O 25,20:1
Hutchinson, Harold (Playwright)
Out of the Night 1927,O 18,32:3
Hutchinson, Harry
White-Headed Boy, The 1921,S 16,20:1
Plough and the Stars, The 1927,N 29,30:2
Juno and the Paycock 1927,D 20,32:2
Anatomist, The 1931,O 25,VIII,2:6
Hutchinson, J K
Dear Me 1921,Ja 18,14:1
Magnolia 1923,Ag 28,12:3
Blue Bird, The 1923,D 26,13:3
Thoroughbreds 1924,S 9,12:1
Hutchinson, James P (Mrs) (Hare, Amory)
/(Playwright)
Return of Hannibal, The 1937,F 2,21:1
Hutchinson, Josephine
Bird Cage, The 1925,Je 3,26:2
Man's Man, A 1925,O 14,31:2
Man's Man, A 1925,O 25,VIII,1:1
Unchastened Woman, The 1926,F 17,12:1
One Day More 1926,Mr 19,24:3
Twelfth Night 1926,D 21,21:4
Cradle Song 1927,Ja 25,18:2
Inheritors 1927,Mr 8,23:1
Good Hope, The 1927,O 19,24:2
2 + 2 = 5 1927,N 29,30:3
First Stone, The 1928,Ja 14,12:2
Improvisations in June 1928,F 27,16:5
Hedda Gabler 1928,Mr 27,30:2
Cherry Orchard, The 1928,O 16,28:5
Cherry Orchard, The 1928,N 18,IX,1:2
Peter Pan; Boy Who Would Not Grow Up, The
1928,N 27,36:3

Hutchinson, Josephine—Cont
Sea Gull, The 1929,S 17,34:1
Mademoiselle Bourrat 1929,O 8,34:3
Living Corpse, The 1929,D 7,19:1
Women Have Their Way, The 1930,Ja 28,28:1
Alison's House 1930,D 2,31:2
Lady of the Camellias, The 1931,Ja 27,21:2
Camille 1932,O 28,23:2
Dear Jane 1932,N 15,24:3
Alice in Wonderland 1932,D 12,18:3
Alice in Wonderland 1932,D 25,IX,1:1
Alice in Wonderland 1933,F 2,21:2
Cherry Orchard, The 1933,Mr 7,20:3
Shining Hour, The 1936,Ag 12,15:3
Hutchinson, Kay
Enemy of the People, An 1958,F 26,24:2
Hutchinson, Laurie
Up Eden 1968,N 27,42:1
Greenwillow 1970,D 8,60:1
Hutchinson, Mary
Castles in the Air 1926,S 7,19:2
Yellow Jacket, The 1928,N 8,27:3
Town's Woman, The 1929,Mr 12,26:2
Rip Van Winkle 1935,Ag 7,22:2
Master of the Revels 1935,Ag 14,16:2
In Heaven and Earth 1936,Mr 27,24:8
Kick Back, The 1936,Je 23,27:3
Moroni 1936,Ag 19,19:1
Hutchinson, Mitch
Everything's Jake 1930,Ja 17,20:4
Hutchinson, R C (Playwright)
Last Train South 1938,S 4,X,2:2
Hutchinson Sisters
Petticoat Fever 1935,Je 25,14:5
Hutchison, Eleanor
All Soul's Eve 1920,My 13,9:1
Macbeth 1921,F 18,16:1
Hairy Ape, The 1922,Mr 10,18:2
Hail and Farewell 1923,F 20,12:1
Hutchison, Jim
Pajama Game, The 1954,My 14,20:2
Hutchison, Muriel
Hamlet 1931,Ap 24,26:4
Sap Runs High, The 1936,F 5,15:3
Amazing Dr. Clitterhouse, The 1937,Mr 3,26:4
Merely Murder 1937,D 4,21:4
Lightnin' 1938,S 16,17:2
Shakespeare's Merchant 1939 1939,Ja 10,16:3
Astonished Heart, The; Tonight at Eight
  1940,Ag 6,15:3
Land Is Bright, The 1941,O 29,26:2
Proof Thro' the Night 1942,D 26,14:2
Vigil, The 1948,My 22,8:6
Huth, Edward
One Woman's Husband 1920,Mr 23,9:3
Huth, Harold
Dishonored Lady 1930,My 25,IX,2:4
Years Between, The 1931,My 10,VIII,2:1
Little Catherine 1931,N 19,27:2
Hutt, Jack (Miscellaneous)
As You Like It 1959,Jl 1,27:1
Love and Libel 1960,D 8,44:1
Troilus and Cressida 1963,Je 19,40:2
Cyrano de Bergerac 1963,Je 20,30:1
Comedy of Errors, The 1963,Je 21,35:3
Hutt, Larry
Let Freedom Ring 1935,N 7,26:2
Hutt, Lynn
Hungerers, The 1955,D 22,19:1
Floydada to Matador 1955,D 22,19:1
Hutt, Walter
Doctor Faustus 1961,Ag 22,23:1
Hutt, William
Richard III 1953,Jl 15,22:2
Measure for Measure 1954,Je 30,23:1
Taming of the Shrew, The 1954,Jl 1,22:2
Oedipus Rex 1954,Jl 17,6:6
Merchant of Venice, The 1955,Jl 1,13:1
Tamburlaine the Great 1956,Ja 20,19:1
Henry V 1956,Je 20,27:2
Merry Wives of Windsor, The 1956,Je 21,34:4
Hamlet 1957,Jl 3,15:2
Mary Stuart 1957,O 9,39:1
Mary Stuart 1957,O 20,II,1:1
Makropoulos Secret, The 1957,D 4,52:4
Henry IV, Part I 1958,Je 25,23:3
Much Ado About Nothing 1958,Je 26,22:1
As You Like It 1959,Jl 1,27:1
Othello 1959,Jl 2,17:2
As You Like It 1959,Jl 5,II,1:1
Othello 1959,Jl 5,II,1:1
Tempest, The 1962,Je 22,14:1
Cyrano de Bergerac 1962,Ag 1,21:1
Troilus and Cressida 1963,Je 19,40:2
Cyrano de Bergerac 1963,Je 20,30:1
Timon of Athens 1963,Jl 31,19:2
Richard II 1964,Je 17,47:1
Bourgeois Gentilhomme, Le 1964,Je 18,28:2
Country Wife, The 1964,Ag 3,16:1
Tiny Alice 1964,D 30,14:2
Tiny Alice 1965,Ja 10,II,1:1
Falstaff; Henry IV, Part II 1965,Jl 1,35:1
Julius Caesar 1965,Jl 2,18:1
Cherry Orchard, The 1965,Ag 2,17:2

Henry V 1966,Je 8,38:1
Henry VI 1966,Je 9,55:2
Richard III 1967,Je 14,43:1
Government Inspector, The 1967,Je 15,55:1
Government Inspector, The 1967,Je 25,II,1:2
Antony and Cleopatra 1967,Ag 2,25:1
Antony and Cleopatra 1967,S 17,II,1:1
Government Inspector, The 1967,O 28,34:1
Antony and Cleopatra 1967,O 29,83:4
Saint Joan 1968,Ja 5,42:1
Tartuffe 1968,Je 12,39:1
Tartuffe 1968,Je 23,II,1:1
Edward II 1969,Ja 19,II,30:5
Alchemist, The 1969,Je 12,51:1
Measure for Measure 1969,Je 13,41:3
Alchemist, The 1969,Je 22,II,1:7
Measure for Measure 1969,Je 22,II,1:7
Alchemist, The 1970,Ag 26,36:1
Hutto, Jack (Miscellaneous)
Lesson, The 1956,O 3,29:2
Escurial 1956,O 3,29:2
Hutton, Betty
Two for the Show 1940,F 9,14:2
Two for the Show 1940,F 18,IX,1:1
Panama Hattie 1940,O 4,28:4
Panama Hattie 1940,O 31,28:2
Vaudeville (Palace) 1952,Ap 14,23:2
Vaudeville (Palace) 1952,Ap 27,II,1:1
Vaudeville (Palace) 1953,O 15,42:1
Hutton, Michael Clayton (Playwright)
Power Without Glory 1948,Ja 14,30:2
Hutty, Leigh (Playwright)
House of Shadows, The 1927,Ap 22,18:4
Huxley, Aldous (Original Author)
This Way to Paradise 1930,Ja 31,24:2
This Way to Paradise 1930,F 16,IX,2:1
Genius and the Goddess, The 1957,D 11,41:1
Devils, The 1961,F 21,41:1
Devils, The 1963,N 17,II,1:1
Devils, The 1965,N 17,51:2
Devils, The 1965,N 28,II,1:1
Huxley, Aldous (Playwright)
World of Light, The 1931,Mr 31,25:6
World of Light, The 1931,Ap 19,VIII,3:1
World of Light, The 1931,Ap 27,24:5
Gioconda Smile, The 1948,Je 20,II,2:3
Gioconda Smile, The 1950,O 9,21:2
Gioconda Smile, The 1950,O 15,II,1:1
Genius and the Goddess, The 1957,D 11,41:1
Huxley, Carroll (Miscellaneous)
Once Upon a Mattress 1959,My 12,40:1
Huxley, David
Tempest, The 1950,S 17,II,3:7
Huxley, W P
Tiger Smiles, The 1930,D 18,29:1
Huyler, Frank
Montmartre 1922,F 14,20:1
Scrap Book 1932,Ag 2,20:3
Hyams, Barry
Empress of Destiny 1938,Mr 10,16:2
Hyams, Barry (Miscellaneous)
Endgame 1958,Ja 29,32:4
41 in a Sack 1960,Mr 26,15:2
Hyams, Nicholas
Moonbirds 1959,O 10,13:1
Hyams, Nicholas (Producer)
Journey to the Day 1963,N 12,49:1
Hyans, Eddie
Sister Oakes 1949,Ap 25,19:4
Rose Tattoo, The 1951,F 5,19:2
Hyatt, Dave
French Touch, The 1945,D 10,18:2
Hyatt, Gordon (Miscellaneous)
House of Breath, The 1957,Ap 15,23:2
Hyatt, Thaddeus
Here's Howe 1923,Ap 26,19:3
Hyde, Albert
Thank You 1921,O 4,10:2
Bootleggers, The 1922,N 28,24:1
My Aunt From Ypsilanti 1923,My 2,22:6
Barker, The 1927,Ja 19,20:6
Wasp's Nest, The 1927,O 26,26:3
Hyde, Bruce
Girl in the Freudian Slip, The 1967,My 19,34:3
Canterbury Tales; Miller's Tale, The 1969,F 4,34:1
Canterbury Tales; Steward's Tale, The
  1969,F 4,34:1
Canterbury Tales; Pilgrims, The 1969,F 4,34:1
Canterbury Tales; Wife of Bath's Tale, The
  1969,F 4,34:1
Hyde, Cynthia
Secrets 1922,D 26,11:1
Nerves 1924,S 2,22:2
Hyde, Frances
They Knew What They Wanted 1924,N 25,27:1
Moon Is a Gong, The 1926,Mr 13,21:3
Hyde, J C
Great Way, The 1921,N 8,28:2
Hyde, Mariette
Teaser, The 1921,Jl 28,8:3
What the Public Wants 1922,My 2,22:3
Malvaloca 1922,O 3,22:1
Man and the Masses 1924,Ap 15,25:1

Hyde, Simeon Jr (Scenic Designer)
Once Over Lightly 1938,D 10,13:4
Hyde and Burrill
Vaudeville (Palace) 1927,S 27,31:3
Hyder, Donald
Bourgeois Gentilhomme, Le 1964,Je 18,28:2
Hyer, June
Madame Aphrodite 1961,D 30,13:1
Hyers, Frank
Panama Hattie 1940,O 31,28:2
Panama Hattie 1940,N 10,IX,1:1
Hykin, Mark
Macbeth 1955,O 20,42:2
Legitimate Steal, The 1958,Ap 1,35:1
Hylan, Donald
Anniversary Waltz 1954,Ap 8,34:1
Laughwind 1966,Mr 3,27:1
Hyland, Diana
Sweet Bird of Youth 1959,Mr 11,39:2
Sweet Bird of Youth 1959,Mr 22,II,1:1
Hyland, Frances
Measure for Measure 1954,Je 30,23:1
Taming of the Shrew, The 1954,Jl 1,22:2
Measure for Measure 1954,Jl 4,II,1:1
Merchant of Venice, The 1955,Jl 1,13:1
Hamlet 1957,Jl 3,15:2
Twelfth Night 1957,Jl 4,16:4
Twelfth Night 1957,Jl 7,II,1:1
Hamlet 1957,Jl 7,II,1:1
Look Homeward, Angel 1957,N 29,33:1
Look Homeward, Angel 1957,D 8,II,5:1
Winter's Tale, The 1958,Jl 23,34:3
As You Like It 1959,Jl 1,27:1
Othello 1959,Jl 2,17:2
Othello 1959,Jl 5,II,1:1
Moby Dick 1962,N 29,45:1
Bourgeois Gentilhomme, Le 1964,Je 18,28:2
King Lear 1964,Je 19,36:1
Country Wife, The 1964,Ag 3,16:1
Falstaff; Henry IV, Part II 1965,Jl 1,35:1
Julius Caesar 1965,Jl 2,18:1
Cherry Orchard, The 1965,Ag 2,17:2
Henry VI 1966,Je 9,55:2
Richard III 1967,Je 14,43:1
Merry Wives of Windsor, The 1967,Ag 4,18:1
Heartbreak House 1968,Je 6,9:1
Chemmy Circle, The 1968,Ag 10,17:2
Hyland, J J
Alias Jimmy Valentine 1921,D 9,20:3
To the Ladies! 1922,F 21,20:1
Behold This Dreamer 1927,N 1,20:4
Sweet Land of Liberty 1929,S 24,29:2
Hyland, Joe
Adventure 1928,S 26,25:2
Hyland, John
Vaudeville (Palace) 1927,Ap 19,24:3
Hyland, Lily (Composer)
Grand Street Follies, The 1925,Je 19,24:1
Grand Street Follies, The 1926,Je 16,23:2
Grand Street Follies, The 1928,My 29,16:2
Hyland, Patricia
Sunset 1966,My 13,34:1
Hyland, Peggy
Little Bit of Fluff, A 1923,F 25,VII,1:7
Hylands, Scott
Billy Liar 1965,Mr 18,26:1
Hamlet 1968,Je 10,59:1
Hyldoft, Joan
Icetime 1946,Je 21,20:5
Icetime 1947,My 29,28:2
Hyle, Therese
Merry Widow, The 1931,S 8,39:1
Hyler, Timmie
New Life, A 1943,S 16,26:6
Hylton, Jack
Night of January 16 1936,S 30,29:3
Hylton, Jack (Miscellaneous)
Plume de Ma Tante, La 1958,N 12,42:1
Hylton, Jack (Producer)
Rocket to the Moon 1948,Mr 23,30:4
Women of Twilight 1952,Mr 4,22:2
Call Me Madam 1952,Mr 16,84:3
Pal Joey 1954,Ap 1,40:5
King Kong 1961,F 24,24:1
Rugantino 1964,F 2,II,1:4
Rugantino 1964,F 7,34:1
Hylton, Richard
Visitor, The 1944,O 18,24:5
Medea 1947,O 21,27:2
Last Dance, The 1948,Ja 28,27:2
Play's the Thing, The 1948,Ap 29,19:2
Hylton Sisters
Streets of Paris, The 1939,Je 20,25:2
Hym, Richard
End as a Man 1953,S 16,39:1
Hyman, Earle
Anna Lucasta 1944,Je 17,10:1
Anna Lucasta 1944,Ag 31,15:1
Anna Lucasta 1944,S 10,II,1:1
Anna Lucasta 1947,O 30,31:3
Sister Oakes 1949,Ap 25,19:4
Hamlet 1951,Jl 20,13:6
Climate of Eden, The 1952,N 7,20:2

Hyman, Earle—Cont

Merchant of Venice, The 1953,Mr 5,20:2
Othello 1953,O 30,28:2
Merchant of Venice, The 1955,F 23,23:2
Julius Caesar 1955,Jl 13,20:1
Tempest, The 1955,Ag 2,18:2
No Time for Sergeants 1955,O 21,32:2
Mister Johnson 1956,Mr 30,11:1
Mister Johnson 1956,Ap 8,II,1:1
King John 1956,Je 28,33:5
Saint Joan 1956,S 12,42:1
Waiting for Godot 1957,Ja 22,25:1
Hamlet 1957,Ja 29,27:1
Duchess of Malfi, The 1957,Mr 20,33:1
Othello 1957,Je 24,19:2
Othello 1957,Je 30,II,1:1
Merchant of Venice, The 1957,Jl 11,19:5
Everyman Today 1958,Ja 16,32:4
Infernal Machine, The 1958,F 4,33:1
Hamlet 1958,Je 21,11:1
Midsummer Night's Dream, A 1958,Je 23,19:1
Winter's Tale, The 1958,Jl 21,17:4
Winter's Tale, The 1958,Jl 27,II,1:1
Raisin in the Sun, A 1959,Ag 5,32:3
Tempest, The 1960,Je 20,35:1
Tempest, The 1960,Je 26,II,1:1
Antony and Cleopatra 1960,Ag 1,19:1
Mister Roberts 1962,O 12,27:2
Othello 1963,Ap 13,10:4
Worlds of Shakespeare, The 1963,D 5,58:1
White Rose and the Red, The 1964,Mr 17,31:1
Jonah! 1966,F 16,52:1
Saint Joan 1968,Ja 5,42:1
Blancs, Les 1970,N 16,48:4
Blancs, Les 1970,N 29,II,3:5
Blancs, Les 1970,N 29,II,3:1
Life and Times of J Walter Smintheus, The
    1970,D 10,59:1
Hyman, Elaine
Passion of Gross, The 1955,Ja 24,20:2
Javelin 1966,N 10,63:1
Night of the Dunce 1966,D 29,21:1
What the Butler Saw 1970,O 14,38:1
Hyman, Jack (Composer)
Life Is Like That 1930,D 23,24:3
Hyman, Jack (Playwright)
It Never Rains 1931,D 25,29:3
Hyman, Jack (Producer)
Let and Sub-Let 1930,My 20,32:2
Cinderelative 1930,S 19,18:4
Hyman, Johnny
Vaudeville (Palace) 1926,Je 15,23:3
Hyman, Joseph M (Miscellaneous)
Christopher Blake 1946,D 2,33:2
Hyman, Joseph M (Producer)
There's Always a Breeze 1938,Mr 3,16:2
????? 1939,Ja 2,28:2
Dear Ruth 1944,D 14,29:2
Secret Room, The 1945,N 8,16:2
Mr Peebles and Mr Hooker 1946,O 11,29:2
Make Mine Manhattan 1948,Ja 16,26:2
Light Up the Sky 1948,N 19,34:2
Climate of Eden, The 1952,N 7,20:2
Anniversary Waltz 1954,Ap 8,34:1
Fair Game 1957,N 4,39:1
Hyman, Lionel A (Director)
Chameleon, The 1932,Jl 19,20:4
Hyman, Lionel A (Playwright)
It Never Rains 1931,D 25,29:3
Hyman, Lionel A (Producer)
Let and Sub-Let 1930,My 20,32:2
Cinderelative 1930,S 19,18:4
Chameleon, The 1932,Jl 19,20:4
Hyman, Louis
My Little Girl 1931,F 2,22:4
Jacques Bergson 1936,O 31,24:6
Hyman, Mac (Original Author)
No Time for Sergeants 1955,O 21,32:2
No Time for Sergeants 1955,N 6,II,1:1
No Time for Sergeants 1956,F 26,II,1:1
Hyman, Myron
Five Little Peppers, The 1952,My 19,13:1
Hyman, Robert
Exciters, The 1922,S 23,10:4
Ink 1927,N 2,24:2
Caravan 1928,Ag 30,13:3
Hyman, Sarah Ellis (Playwright)
Seventh Heart, The 1927,My 3,24:4
Hyman, Selma
Shylock and His Daughter 1947,S 30,22:2
Hyman, Walter A (Producer)
Impossible Years, The 1965,O 14,55:1
Lion in Winter, The 1966,Mr 4,23:1
Something Different 1967,N 29,52:1
Hymer, John B
Vaudeville (Palace) 1924,Ja 15,17:3
Hymer, John B (Playwright)
Aloma of the South Seas 1925,Ap 21,18:1
Deacon, The 1925,N 25,14:3
Crime Wave, The 1927,F 13,VII,1:4
Crime 1927,F 23,27:3
Crime 1927,O 19,24:2
Crime 1928,My 13,IX,2:2
Crime 1928,My 19,7:4

Fast Life 1928,S 27,35:2
Scarlet Pages 1929,S 1,VIII,1:1
Scarlet Pages 1929,S 10,26:3
Scarlet Pages 1929,S 22,IX,1:1
Zoom 1932,Ja 31,VIII,1:8
Happy Landing 1932,Mr 28,10:5
Lady Detained, A 1935,Ja 10,23:3
Little Inn, The 1935,Ag 20,25:1
Hymer, Warren
Patriarch, The 1926,D 11,15:1
Grey Fox, The 1928,O 23,32:3
Hymes, Phil
Son, The 1950,Ag 16,24:6
Hymes, Philip (Lighting Director)
Trial of Dmitri Karamazov, The 1958,Ja 28,30:1
Hymes, Steve
Instructions for the Running of Trains, etc on the
    Erie Railway to Go Into Effect January 1,1862
    1970,Ja 7,36:2
Hynd, Gene
Unsophisticates, The 1929,D 31,14:5
Hynds, Theresa
Shelter 1926,Ja 26,18:2
Hynes, Katherine
Lovers and Friends 1943,N 30,23:2
Point of No Return 1951,D 14,35:2
Cretan Woman, The 1954,Jl 8,18:2
Red Roses for Me 1955,D 29,15:2
Apple Cart, The 1956,O 19,23:1
Hyrt, Nell
Reunion in New York 1940,F 22,28:4
Hyser, Ray
Sacco-Vanzetti 1969,F 9,78:1
Hyslop, Alfred
Shop at Sly Corner, The 1949,Ja 19,35:2
Hyslop, Alfred (Director)
Magistrate, The 1959,My 14,30:6
Hyslop, Alfred (Producer)
Magistrate, The 1959,My 14,30:6
Hyslop, Stephen
Cup of Trembling, The 1959,My 1,33:5
Hyson, Carl
Lassie 1920,Ap 7,9:2
Snapshots of 1921 1921,Je 3,19:2
Hyson, Dorothy
Touch Wood 1934,Jl 1,X,1:3
Ringmaster, The 1935,Mr 12,24:5
Most of the Game 1935,O 2,27:4
To Have and to Hold 1937,Je 27,X,1:3
Hyson, Ray
Wish You Were Here 1952,Je 26,26:6
By the Beautiful Sea 1954,Ap 9,20:1
Plain and Fancy 1955,Ja 28,14:2
Young Abe Lincoln 1961,Ap 26,36:1
Hyun, Peter (Director)
Revolt of the Beavers, The 1937,My 21,19:2

I

i, Andrew
Evening With the Times Square Two, An
    1967,My 21,83:6
Iakland, Vivian
Yankee Princess, The 1922,O 3,22:1
Iams, Samuel H Jr
Tiger Smiles, The 1930,D 18,29:1
Ianni, Richard
Athenian Touch, The 1964,Ja 15,25:4
Iannicelli, Tom (Miscellaneous)
Suburban Tragedy 1966,Mr 7,22:1
Make Like a Dog 1966,Mr 7,22:1
Princess Rebecca Birnbaum 1966,Mr 7,22:1
Young Marrieds Play Monopoly 1966,Mr 7,22:1
Iannucci, Michael P (Producer)
This Was Burlesque 1962,Mr 7,29:1
This Was Burlesque 1965,Mr 17,55:3
Ianuzzi, Jimmy
Aquashow 1953,Je 24,29:2
Iavorsky, Valerian
Cricket on the Hearth, The 1925,My 29,20:2
Ibanez, Blasco (Original Author)
Blood and Sand 1921,S 21,16:2
Ibanez, Blasco (Playwright)
Blood and Sand 1921,S 25,VI,1:4
Ibberson, Alfred
Via Crucis 1923,N 13,25:2
Burgomaster of Stilemonde, The 1923,N 16,15:3
Hamlet 1923,N 20,23:3
Iben, Conrad (Father) (Director)
Veronica's Veil 1936,Mr 2,4:3
Iben, Conrad (Father) (Playwright)
Veronica's Veil 1936,Mr 2,4:3
Ibert, Jacques (Composer)
Italian Straw Hat, The 1957,O 1,37:2
Ibn-Zahav, Ari (Miscellaneous)
Shylock and His Daughter 1947,S 30,22:2
Ibn-Zahav, Ari (Original Author)
Shylock and His Daughter 1947,N 30,II,1:1
Ibn-Zahav, Ari (Playwright)
Shylock and His Daughter 1947,S 30,22:2

Ibrahim, Mohammid
Wonder Bar, The 1931,Mr 18,23:4
Ibsen, Henrik (Original Author)
Ghosts 1927,Ja 11,36:3
Ghosts 1933,My 24,24:5
Fantasmi 1937,Mr 22,26:5
Enemy of the People, An 1950,D 29,14:1
Enemy of the People, An 1959,F 5,24:4
Meet Peter Grant 1961,My 11,41:4
Ibsen, Henrik (Playwright)
Enemy of the People, An 1920,S 7,19:3
Hedda Gabler 1920,O 5,12:2
Ghosts 1922,F 7,12:1
Peer Gynt 1923,F 6,14:1
Donna Del Mare, La; Lady From the Sea, The
    1923,O 30,17:1
Lady of the Sea 1923,N 3,8:2
Lady of the Sea 1923,N 4,VIII,1:2
Spretti; Ghosts 1923,N 7,14:1
Enemy of the People, An 1923,D 4,25:1
Rosmersholm 1924,F 8,22:3
Hedda Gabler 1924,My 17,18:4
Wild Duck, The 1925,F 25,16:4
Wild Duck, The 1925,Mr 1,VII,1:1
Rosmersholm 1925,My 6,27:2
Master Builder, The 1925,N 11,27:1
Master Builder, The 1925,N 15,VIII,1:1
Hedda Gabler 1926,Ja 27,16:5
John Gabriel Borkman 1926,Ja 30,13:1
Master Builder, The; Hedda Gabler; John Gabriel
    Borkman; Little Eyolf 1926,Ja 31,VII,1:1
Little Eyolf 1926,F 3,22:1
Hedda Gabler 1926,F 21,VII,1:2
Ghosts 1926,Mr 17,28:2
When We Dead Awaken 1926,My 18,29:3
Ghosts 1927,Ja 16,VII,1:1
Enemy of the People, An 1927,O 4,32:5
Baumeister Solness 1927,O 30,IX,4:1
Lady Inger of Ostrat 1927,N 27,IX,4:1
Gespenster, Die; Ghosts 1928,F 8,28:6
Wild Duck, The 1928,F 19,VIII,2:1
League of Youth 1928,Mr 17,9:1
Peer Gynt 1928,Mr 24,4:6
Hedda Gabler 1928,Mr 27,30:2
Peer Gynt 1928,Ap 1,IX,2:4
Doll's House, A; Enemy of the People, An
    1928,Ap 22,IX,2:7
Master Builder, The 1928,O 21,IX,1:3
Enemy of the People, An 1928,N 6,34:3
Wild Duck, The 1928,N 19,17:1
Peer Gynt 1928,D 2,X,2:1
Hedda Gabler 1929,F 4,20:3
Ghosts; Gespenster 1929,F 6,30:3
Ghosts 1929,F 17,IX,1:1
Hedda Gabler 1929,F 17,IX,1:1
Lady From the Sea, The 1929,Mr 19,36:1
Vikings, The 1930,My 13,27:3
Little Eyolf 1930,N 2,VIII,2:6
Gli Spettri 1930,D 22,16:4
Pillars of Society, The 1931,O 15,19:1
Lady From the Sea, The 1934,My 2,25:2
Hedda Gabler 1934,D 4,22:5
Peer Gynt 1935,S 24,28:2
Peer Gynt 1935,O 20,XI,3:7
Rosmersholm 1935,D 3,32:5
Ghosts 1935,D 13,30:6
Lady From the Sea, The 1935,D 14,11:3
Catiline 1936,Ja 28,14:6
Doll's House, A 1936,Mr 3,25:2
Ghosts 1936,My 12,26:8
Hedda Gabler 1936,N 17,34:4
Enemy of the People, An 1937,F 16,19:1
Peer Gynt 1937,Mr 14,II,7:8
Doll's House, A 1937,Jl 18,II,6:8
Doll's House, A 1937,Jl 25,X,2:3
Ghosts 1937,N 28,XI,2:1
Doll's House, A 1937,D 28,28:6
Hedda Gabler 1942,Ja 30,22:2
Peer Gynt 1944,O 1,II,1:3
Lady of the Sea 1945,S 9,II,1:5
John Gabriel Borkman 1946,N 13,33:2
Rosmersholm 1946,N 23,11:5
Ghosts 1948,F 17,31:2
Hedda Gabler 1948,F 25,27:2
Master Builder Solness 1950,My 26,19:3
Lady From the Sea, The 1950,Ag 8,23:2
Enemy of the People, An 1951,Ja 7,II,1:1
Peer Gynt 1951,Ja 29,15:2
Peer Gynt 1951,F 4,II,1:1
Wild Duck, The 1951,D 27,17:1
Hedda Gabler 1954,O 24,II,3:3
Doll's House, A 1954,N 15,32:2
Master Builder, The 1955,Mr 2,23:2
Master Builder, The 1955,Mr 20,II,1:1
Wild Duck, The 1956,Ja 8,II,3:1
Doll's House, A 1956,My 8,29:2
Lady From the Sea, The 1956,D 13,49:5
Master Builder, The 1957,D 18,42:7
Enemy of the People, An 1958,F 26,24:2
John Gabriel Borkman 1959,N 26,57:4
Peer Gynt 1960,Ja 13,21:1
Peer Gynt 1960,Ja 24,II,1:1
Hedda Gabler 1960,N 25,24:3

Ibsen, Henrik (Playwright)—Cont
Ghosts 1961,S 22,29:1
Ghosts 1961,O 1,II,1:1
Rosmersholm 1962,Ap 12,42:1
Rosmersholm 1962,Ap 22,II,1:1
Peer Gynt 1962,S 27,33:7
Hedda Gabler 1962,D 13,8:5
Doll's House, A 1963,F 4,5:6
Little Eyolf 1964,Mr 17,31:1
Master Builder, The 1964,Je 10,50:2
When We Dead Awaken 1966,Ap 19,37:2
Wild Duck, The 1967,Ja 12,49:1
Wild Duck, The 1967,Ja 22,II,1:1
Hedda Gabler 1968,Je 5,39:1
Master Builder, The 1968,Je 22,26:1
Peer Gynt 1969,Jl 17,56:1
Hedda Gabler 1970,Ja 18,78:1
Hedda Gabler 1970,Je 12,28:1
Hedda Gabler 1970,Je 21,II,1:1
Hedda Gabler 1970,Jl 18,12:1
Peer Gynt 1970,D 23,12:5

Ibsen, Lillebil
Peer Gynt 1923,F 6,14:1

Ice Age Quartet
It Happens on Ice 1940,O 11,24:3

Ice Follies Boys
Ice Follies 1970,My 23,27:1

Ice Folliettes, The
Ice Follies 1963,Ja 10,5:2
Ice Follies 1970,My 23,27:1

Ichikawa, Somegoro
Fiddler on the Roof 1967,S 7,50:1

Ide, Knox
Little Theatre Tournament; End of the Dance, The 1929,My 11,22:2

Ide, Leonard
Exile, The 1923,Ap 10,24:2
Loves of Lulu, The 1925,My 12,26:1
Old Bill, M P 1926,N 11,22:2

Ide, Leonard (Playwright)
These Few Ashes 1928,O 31,28:1
Marriage Has Been Disarranged, A 1930,D 10,28:2
Peacock 1932,O 12,27:1
Ringside Seat 1938,N 23,24:5

Ide, Richard
Livin' the Life 1957,Ap 29,20:1

Ideal, Amalie
Caviar 1934,Je 8,19:2

Iden, Rosalind
Hamlet 1947,Ja 8,26:2
King Lear 1947,F 19,32:2
As You Like It 1947,F 21,16:2
Merchant of Venice, The 1947,F 24,16:2
Volpone 1947,F 25,32:2
Hamlet 1947,F 27,27:2

Idlet, Charles
Amedee: or, How to Disentangle Yourself 1955,N 1,27:3

Idlet, Charles (Miscellaneous)
Amedee: or, How to Disentangle Yourself 1955,N 1,27:3

Idoine, Christopher (Scenic Designer)
Fire! 1968,My 12,II,7:1

Ifo, Michio (Choreographer)
Mikado, The; Town of Titipu, The 1927,S 19,30:1

Iglesias, Franco
Fiesta in Madrid 1969,My 29,49:1

Igo, Harold (Playwright)
Steel 1939,D 20,30:2

Iitropodi, Josie
Diana 1929,D 10,37:1

Ilaky, Josef (Scenic Designer)
Light, Lively and Yiddish 1970,O 28,58:1

Ilan and Ilanit
Grand Music Hall of Israel, The 1968,F 7,42:1

Iles, Bruce
Nativity Play, The 1937,D 21,29:1

Ilges, F Walter (Playwright)
Lantern, The 1935,O 6,XI,3:7

Ilka, Marie
Bless You, Sister 1927,D 27,24:5

Ilma, Alfred
Naughty Cinderella 1925,N 10,23:6
Gather Ye Rosebuds 1934,N 29,33:2

Ilma, Viola
Cloudy With Showers 1931,S 2,17:5

Ilnn, Leon M (Director)
Fanatics, The 1927,N 8,32:4

Ilyinsky, Igor
Last Defensive, The 1931,S 27,VIII,3:2

Imai, Masahiko (Miscellaneous)
General's Daughter, The 1966,Mr 16,50:1
Fishing for Wives 1966,Mr 16,50:1
Greengrocer's Daughter, The 1966,Mr 16,50:1

Imbrie, McCrea (Playwright)
Someone's Comin' Hungry 1969,Ap 1,51:1

Imerion, Matt
Madmen and Specialists 1970,Ag 3,38:1

Imeson, A B I
Escape 1927,O 27,33:1

Imhof, Peter
Vaudeville (Palace) 1924,O 21,21:2

Imhof, Roger
Jack and Jill 1923,Mr 23,17:2

Vaudeville (Palace) 1926,N 23,27:3
Vaudeville (Palace) 1929,Mr 25,33:2

Immella, Alessandro
My Wife Is Different 1931,Ap 27,24:4

Immerman, G (Producer)
Hot Chocolates 1929,Je 21,17:4

Imperato, Arthur
Anything Goes 1934,N 22,26:1

Imperial Russian Entertainers
Vaudeville (Palace) 1923,O 23,18:2

Impressionaires, The
Aquashow 1953,Je 24,29:2

Impromptu Players
Untitled-Play 1931,Ap 6,24:4

Inaba, M (Lighting Director)
Coney Island Play 1970,O 31,34:2

Inarticulate
Ingeborg 1933,D 11,23:3

Ince, Alexander (Producer)
Egg, The 1962,Ja 9,23:2

Ince, Lionel
King Lear 1930,D 26,18:2
Merchant of Venice, The 1931,N 17,31:1
Julius Caesar 1931,N 18,26:3
Hamlet 1931,N 19,26:6
Near to the Stars 1932,F 23,23:2
Singapore 1932,N 15,24:2
Richard II 1937,F 6,14:2
Ten Minute Alibi 1937,Jl 20,19:3
Empress of Destiny 1938,Mr 10,16:2
Coggerers, The 1939,Ja 21,18:4
Red Velvet Goat, The 1939,Ja 21,18:4
Mr Banks of Birmingham 1939,Ja 21,18:4
Woman Brown, The 1939,D 9,18:5
My Fair Ladies 1941,Mr 24,12:7
Winter's Tale, The 1946,Ja 16,18:6
Kiss Me, Kate 1952,Ja 9,24:6

Inches, Howard
King Lear 1930,D 26,18:2

Inches, Howard (Director)
Passionate Pilgrim, The 1932,O 20,24:3

Inches, Howard (Producer)
Passionate Pilgrim, The 1932,O 20,24:3

Indian Joe
Bad Man, The 1920,Ag 31,7:1

Indig, Otto (Playwright)
Braut von Torozko, Die 1932,Je 19,IX,1:6
Man Under the Bridge, The 1933,N 5,IX,2:2
Bride of Torozko, The 1934,Jl 10,24:7
Bride of Torozko, The 1934,S 14,24:2

Ines, Denis d'
Passion, La 1930,My 11,IX,2:4

Inescort, Frieda
Truth About Blayds, The 1922,Mr 15,22:1
You and I 1923,F 20,12:1
Woman on the Jury, The 1923,Ag 16,10:4
Windows 1923,O 9,17:2
Fake, The 1924,O 7,26:3
Ariadne 1925,F 24,17:1
Hay Fever 1925,O 5,25:1
Love in a Mist 1926,Ap 13,28:3
Mozart 1926,N 23,26:2
Trelawney of the 'Wells' 1927,F 1,24:4
Escape 1927,O 27,33:1
Escape 1927,N 6,IX,1:1
Napi 1931,Mr 12,22:5
Company's Coming! 1931,Ap 21,35:5
Springtime for Henry 1931,D 10,29:2
When Ladies Meet 1932,O 7,19:1
When Ladies Meet 1932,O 16,IX,1:1
False Dreams, Farewell 1934,Ja 16,18:3
Lady Jane 1934,S 11,24:2
We Were Dancing; Tonight at Eight 1940,Ag 6,15:3
Tonight at 8:30 1940,Ag 11,IX,11:2
Soldier's Wife 1944,O 5,18:6
Mermaids Singing, The 1945,N 29,26:6
You Never Can Tell 1948,Mr 17,31:2

Infante, Tomas E
Handful of Fire 1958,O 2,45:3

Ing, Alvin
Tenth of an Inch Makes the Difference, A 1962,N 13,44:1

Ingalls, Albert Jr (Producer)
Dream Child 1934,S 28,26:2
Searching for the Sun 1936,F 20,22:6

Ingalls, Frances
Ah, Wilderness! 1953,F 7,10:6
Scrapbooks 1953,N 6,24:2
Pony Cart, The 1954,S 15,39:2
Thunder Rock 1956,F 27,18:1
Enchanted, The 1958,Ap 23,41:1
Henry V 1960,Je 30,23:1
Embers 1960,O 26,44:1
Misalliance 1961,S 26,32:2

Ingalls, Phil (Composer)
Tickets, Please! 1950,Ap 28,25:2

Ingalls, Phil (Musical Director)
Angel in the Wings 1947,D 12,36:4

Inge, Benson
Dybbuk, The 1925,D 16,22:2
Burmese Pwe, A 1926,Mr 17,28:1

Inge, Benson (Playwright)
Blue Monday 1932,Je 3,23:2

Inge, Benson (Translator)
It Can't Happen Here 1936,O 28,30:1

Inge, William (Playwright)
Farther Off From Heaven 1947,Je 4,33:3
Come Back, Little Sheba 1950,F 16,28:5
Come Back, Little Sheba 1950,F 26,II,1:1
Come Back, Little Sheba 1950,My 14,II,1:1
Picnic 1953,F 20,14:7
Picnic 1953,Mr 1,II,1:1
Picnic 1953,Ag 30,II,1:1
Bus Stop 1955,Mr 3,23:2
Bus Stop 1955,Mr 13,II,1:1
Picnic 1957,F 21,32:1
Dark at the Top of the Stairs, The 1957,D 6,38:1
Dark at the Top of the Stairs, The 1957,D 15,II,3:1
Loss of Roses, A 1959,N 30,27:1
Loss of Roses, A 1959,D 6,II,5:1
Glory in the Flower 1959,D 9,57:5
Natural Affection 1963,F 2,5:2
Where's Daddy? 1966,Mr 3,27:1
Last Pad, The 1970,D 8,61:1

Ingenues, The
Vaudeville (Palace) 1927,Je 14,33:3
Vaudeville (Palace) 1930,My 5,27:5
Vaudeville (Palace) 1931,My 4,15:2
Vaudeville (Palace) 1932,Jl 11,11:6

Inger, Manfred
Professor Bernhardi 1968,Mr 20,38:1

Ingerlid, Joseph Jay (Playwright)
Devil's Little Game, The 1932,Ag 2,20:4

Ingersoll, Harriet
Lucrece 1932,D 21,22:2

Ingersoll, William
Ouija Board, The 1920,Mr 30,9:1
Half-Moon, The 1920,N 2,15:2
Alias Jimmy Valentine 1921,D 9,20:3
Charlatan, The 1922,Ap 25,14:2
Lights Out 1922,Ag 18,8:4
It Is the Law 1922,N 30,28:2
Thumbs Down 1923,Ag 7,20:1
Queen Victoria 1923,N 16,15:1
Fata Morgana 1924,Mr 4,16:3
Devil Within, The 1925,Mr 17,19:4
Goat Song 1926,Ja 26,18:1
Half-Caste, The 1926,Mr 30,20:4
Trapped 1928,S 12,25:3
Hotbed 1928,N 10,20:7
Brothers 1928,D 26,14:3
Fata Morgana 1931,D 26,15:3
Angeline Moves In 1932,Ap 20,27:5
Web, The 1932,Je 28,24:4
We the People 1933,Ja 23,9:5
Nine Pine Street 1933,Ap 28,15:5
Church Mouse, A 1933,Je 27,13:7
Divine Moment, A 1934,Ja 8,21:8
First Legion, The 1934,O 2,18:2

Ingham, Barrie
Much Ado About Nothing 1959,S 18,25:2
Indians 1968,Jl 9,30:2
Winter's Tale, The 1969,Je 1,II,4:5
Winter's Tale, The 1969,S 1,13:1
Twelfth Night 1969,S 1,13:1
London Assurance 1970,Ag 7,26:1

Ingham, George
Hamlet 1936,N 11,54:2

Ingham, Robert E
Simple Life, A 1964,My 18,36:1

Ingham, Robert E (Playwright)
Simple Life, A 1964,My 18,36:1

Ingham, Tom
'Toinette 1961,N 21,46:1

Inghram, Rose
By Jupiter 1942,Je 4,22:1
Helen Goes to Troy 1944,Ap 25,17:2
Polonaise 1945,O 8,20:2
Three to Make Ready 1946,Mr 8,16:2
Where's Charley? 1951,Ja 30,21:7

Ingig, Joyce
Seven Mirrors 1945,O 26,17:2

Inglefield, Violet
Buzzin' Around 1920,Jl 7,14:1

Inglehart, Wendy
Variations of 1940 1940,Ja 29,12:1

Inglesi, Ricky
Ice Follies 1969,My 23,38:1
Ice Follies 1970,My 23,27:1

Ingleson, Liz
Lion in Love, The 1963,Ap 26,28:3
On the Necessity of Being Polygamous 1964,D 9,61:1

Inglis, Liza
Anne of England 1941,O 8,26:2

Inglis, William
Beggar's Opera, The 1957,Mr 14,35:1

Inglis, William (Miscellaneous)
Hamp 1967,Mr 10,32:1

Inglise, Elizabeth
Billy Draws a Horse 1939,D 22,14:5
Storm Operation 1944,Ja 12,28:2
Mrs Kimball Presents 1944,Mr 1,17:3

Ingot, John Memorial Troupe
Plant in the Sun 1937,D 13,22:8

Ingram, George L
How Come Lawd? 1937,O 1,18:5

Ingram, Georgia
Oh! Oh! Nurse 1925,D 8,28:4
Americana 1926,Jl 27,15:3
Merry-Go-Round 1927,Je 1,25:4
Vaudeville (Palace) 1928,F 14,26:2

Ingram, Harry D
How Come Lawd? 1937,O 1,18:5

Ingram, Marguerite
Sancho Panza 1923,N 27,23:1

Ingram, Michael
Men in Shadow 1943,Mr 11,16:2
House in Paris, The 1944,Mr 21,17:1

Ingram, Milroy
Green Pastures, The 1951,Mr 16,35:2
Big Deal, The 1953,Mr 7,13:6

Ingram, Rex
Theodora, the Queen 1934,F 1,15:3
Stevedore 1934,Ap 19,33:2
Dance With Your Gods 1934,O 8,14:3
Caesar and Cleopatra 1935,Ag 22,21:1
Stick-in-the-Mud 1935,D 2,18:2
Emperor Jones, The 1936,Ag 11,24:6
Marching Song 1937,F 18,18:2
How Come Lawd? 1937,O 1,18:5
Haiti 1938,Mr 3,16:1
Sing Out the News 1938,S 26,12:5
Cabin in the Sky 1940,O 26,19:2
Cabin in the Sky 1940,N 3,IX,1:1
St Louis Woman 1946,Ap 1,22:2
Lysistrata 1946,O 18,27:5
Waiting for Godot 1957,Ja 22,25:1
Kwamina 1961,O 24,42:1

Ingram, Richard (Playwright)
Mrs Wilson's Diary 1967,O 8,II,13:5

Ingram, Roland T (Playwright)
Tiara, The 1932,D 12,18:3

Ingrand, Max (Costume Designer)
Christophe Colomb 1957,Ja 31,20:5

Ingrand, Max (Scenic Designer)
Christophe Colomb 1957,Ja 31,20:5

Ingre, Tonia
Vanderbilt Revue, The 1930,O 26,VIII,3:5

Inky Dinky the Bear
Ice Follies 1966,Ja 12,27:6
Ice Follies 1970,My 23,27:1

Inlender, Avraham (Playwright)
On an Open Roof 1963,Ja 30,7:3

Inman, C Clay
Topics of 1923 1923,N 21,23:2

Inman, James
Cock-A-Doodle Dandy 1955,N 4,26:5
J B 1958,Ap 24,37:1
Geranium Hat, The 1959,Mr 18,45:1
Wilde Evening with Shaw, A 1963,Mr 7,8:2

Innes, George
Chips With Everything 1963,O 2,49:1

Inness, Jean
Not for Children 1936,Mr 1,IX,2:2

Innez, John (Director)
Acid Wine 1964,My 23,15:2
Frugal Noon 1964,My 23,15:2

Innez, John (Playwright)
Acid Wine 1964,My 23,15:2
Frugal Noon 1964,My 23,15:2

Innis, Albert
Ziegfeld Follies 1921,Je 22,10:1

Innis, Frank
Ziegfeld Follies 1921,Je 22,10:1
Fine and Dandy 1930,S 24,26:1

Innocent, Harold
Hamlet 1958,D 17,2:7

Inouye, James
Fuente Ovejuna; Sheep Well, The 1936,My 3,II,4:1

Insardi, Nicholas J
Vie Parisienne, La 1945,Ja 13,14:5

Insull, Mrs
School for Scandal, The 1925,O 24,19:1
Runaway Road, The 1926,N 14,VIII,5:1

International Street Singers
Kibbetzers, Inc 1935,My 13,18:5

Interrante, Florence
Mary of Magdala 1946,Mr 26,24:5

Intorcia, John
Lazarus Laughed 1948,Ap 9,27:4

Intropidi, Ethel
Guilty One, The 1923,Mr 21,19:1
Bride Retires, The 1925,My 18,12:3
Edgar Allan Poe 1925,O 6,31:1
Madcap, The 1928,F 1,31:2
Commodore Marries, The 1929,S 5,26:3
Commodore Marries, The 1929,S 15,IX,1:1
Apron Strings 1930,F 18,28:2
Made in France 1930,N 12,21:1
Dinner at Eight 1932,O 24,18:2
Peace on Earth 1933,N 30,39:2
Judgment Day 1934,S 13,26:4
Rain 1935,F 13,24:1
Good Men and True 1935,O 26,12:4
O Evening Star 1936,Ja 9,24:6
Babes in Arms 1937,Ap 15,18:4
Ghost of Yankee Doodle, The 1937,N 23,26:3

American Landscape 1938,D 5,19:2
Young Couple Wanted 1940,Ja 25,16:2
Doctors Disagree 1943,D 29,15:2

Intropidi, Josie
Betty, Be Good 1920,My 5,14:2
Letty Pepper 1922,Ap 11,22:2
Sally, Irene and Mary 1922,S 5,21:2
Honeymoon Lane 1926,S 21,32:3
Apron Strings 1930,F 18,28:2
O Evening Star 1936,Ja 9,24:6

Inventar, Isaac
Voice of Israel, The 1948,O 26,40:2
Hershel, The Jester 1948,D 14,39:2

Inverso, Paul (Lighting Director)
Scarlet Lullaby 1968,Mr 11,48:1

Inze, Lionel
Fly Away Home 1937,Jl 27,24:3

Iolas
Variations of 1940 1940,Ja 29,12:1

Iolas, Alexander
Tinguely Machine Mystery, or the Love Suicide at
Kaluka, The 1965,D 24,15:5

Ionesco, Eugene (Playwright)
Amedee: or, How to Disentangle Yourself
1955,N 1,27:3
Lesson, The 1956,O 3,29:2
Chairs, The 1958,Ja 10,20:3
Lesson, The 1958,Ja 10,20:3
Chairs, The; Lesson, The 1958,F 16,II,1:1
Bald Soprano, The 1958,Je 4,39:2
Jack 1958,Je 4,39:2
Rhinoceros 1959,N 2,41:1
Victims of Duty 1960,Ja 20,26:1
Killer, The 1960,Mr 23,33:1
Killer, The 1960,Ap 3,II,1:1
Rhinoceros 1960,Ap 30,15:3
Shepherd's Chameleon, The 1960,N 30,41:1
Rhinoceros 1961,Ja 10,27:1
Rhinoceros 1961,Ja 22,II,1:1
Cantatrice Chauve, La 1962,Ja 16,30:1
Tableau, Le 1963,S 4,34:3
Exit the King 1963,S 13,19:4
Bald Soprano, The 1963,S 18,35:4
Lesson, The 1963,S 18,35:4
Pieton de L'Air, Le 1964,Mr 4,33:2
New Tenant, The 1964,My 28,40:2
Victims of Duty 1964,My 28,40:2
Hunger and Durst 1965,Ja 19,28:6
Impromptu, L' 1965,Mr 8,34:1
Bedlam Galore, for Two or More 1965,Mr 8,34:1
Leader, The 1965,Mr 8,34:1
Foursome 1965,Mr 8,34:1
Soif et la Faim, La 1966,Mr 2,47:5
Exit the King 1968,Ja 10,48:1
Exit the King 1968,Ja 21,II,1:2
Victims, The; Victims of Duty 1968,Mr 6,34:1
Jeune Fille a Marier, La 1970,My 6,49:1
Chaises, Les 1970,My 6,49:1
Lacune, La 1970,My 6,49:1

Ireland, Anthony
To Account Rendered 1931,F 15,VIII,2:5
Nelson Touch, The 1931,S 20,VIII,2:6
Sex Fable, The 1931,O 21,26:1
Flashing Stream, The 1938,S 2,21:4
Flashing Stream, The 1939,Ap 11,19:2
Light of Heart, The 1940,Mr 3,X,3:4
Black Chiffon 1950,S 28,39:2

Ireland, Bernard
How Revolting! 1932,Mr 11,14:6

Ireland, John
Fiddler's House, The 1941,Mr 28,27:5
Not in Our Stars 1941,Ap 26,20:5
Macbeth 1941,N 12,30:2
Native Son 1942,O 24,10:6
Counterattack 1943,F 4,27:2
Richard III 1943,Mr 27,8:3
New Life, A 1943,S 16,26:6
Doctors Disagree 1943,D 29,15:2
Highland Fling, A 1944,Ap 29,13:2
Rats of Norway, The 1948,Ap 16,27:6
Summer and Smoke 1950,O 29,II,3:7
Deadfall 1955,O 28,20:1

Ireland, Lawrence
Many Waters 1929,S 26,27:1

Ireland, Peter
Critic, The 1965,Jl 26,15:2

Ireland, Richard (Scenic Designer)
An Evening With G B S; Press Cuttings
1957,F 19,35:7
Evening With G B S, An; O'Flaherty, V C
1957,F 19,35:7

Ireya, John
Heart of a City 1942,F 13,24:6
Othello 1943,O 20,18:1

Irgens, Henning
Pal Joey 1940,D 26,22:2

Irion, Elizabeth
Variations of 1940 1940,Ja 29,12:1

Irion, Yolanda Mero (Producer)
Merry Widow, The 1943,Ag 22,II,5:1
Vie Parisienne, La 1945,Ja 13,14:5

Irish, Nathaniel (Playwright)
Near to the Stars 1932,F 23,23:2

Irish Players
Plough and the Stars, The 1927,D 4,X,1:1

Irish Repertory Players
Riders to the Sea 1937,F 15,13:2
Workhouse Ward, The 1937,F 15,13:2
Rising of the Moon, The 1937,F 15,13:2

Irizarry, Julia
Does a Tiger Wear a Necktie? 1967,F 4,17:1

Irle, Hans
Faust, Part I; Play, The 1961,F 5,27:2

Irmanette
Vaudeville (Palace) 1926,Mr 16,22:2
Vaudeville (Palace) 1926,Ag 24,19:3

Irmanette and Violette
Vaudeville (Palace) 1924,O 21,21:2

Irolli, Vincent
Mother Sings 1935,N 13,24:1

Ironside, Christopher (Costume Designer)
Midsummer Night's Dream, A 1954,S 22,33:1

Ironside, Christopher (Scenic Designer)
Midsummer Night's Dream, A 1954,S 22,33:1

Ironside, Robin (Costume Designer)
Midsummer Night's Dream, A 1954,S 22,33:1

Ironside, Robin (Scenic Designer)
Midsummer Night's Dream, A 1954,S 22,33:1

Irvin, Billie
Blue Butterfly, The 1929,F 17,29:3

Irvine, Harry
George Washington 1920,Mr 2,9:1
Hamlet 1920,Mr 17,14:2
Taming of the Shrew, The 1921,My 12,20:2
Merchant of Venice, The 1921,My 14,10:4
Clouds of the Sun 1922,My 6,11:2
This Our House 1935,D 12,33:3
Murder in the Cathedral 1936,Mr 21,13:5
Class of '29 1936,My 16,10:3
Daughters of Atreus 1936,O 15,33:1
On the Rocks 1938,Je 16,20:2
Millionairess, The 1938,Ag 16,22:5
Dame Nature 1938,S 27,24:3
Jeremiah 1939,F 4,11:2
Delicate Story 1940,D 5,32:2
Macbeth 1941,N 12,30:2
Bird in Hand 1942,O 20,24:2
Richard III 1943,Mr 27,8:3
Trio 1944,D 30,13:4
Mermaids Singing, The 1945,N 29,26:6
Oedipus Rex 1945,D 17,16:7
Joan of Lorraine 1946,N 19,40:2
Dear Judas 1947,Ag 5,26:1
Dear Judas 1947,O 6,26:4
Skipper Next to God 1948,Ja 5,14:5
Anne of the Thousand Days 1948,D 9,49:2
Caesar and Cleopatra 1949,D 22,28:2

Irvine, Harry (Director)
Hamlet 1928,Je 2,11:3

Irvine, St John (Playwright)
First Mrs Fraser, The 1929,O 20,10:1

Irving, Ben
Lamp at Midnight 1947,D 22,29:2
Blood Wedding 1949,F 7,16:2
Sun and I, The 1949,Mr 21,18:4

Irving, Clayton
Lysistrata 1930,Je 6,20:1

Irving, David
Waiting for Godot 1958,Ag 6,22:1

Irving, Dorothy
Sweetheart Shop, The 1920,S 1,13:4
Love Letter, The 1921,O 5,20:1
Puzzles of 1925 1925,F 3,25:3

Irving, Elizabeth
Mystery Ship, The 1927,Mr 15,28:2

Irving, Ellis
Marigold 1930,O 9,23:1
Twelfth Night 1940,N 20,26:3
Plan M 1942,F 21,15:2

Irving, Ernest (Composer)
Yellow Sands 1927,S 12,29:3

Irving, Fiddlin'
Hayride 1954,S 14,24:2

Irving, Franklin
If Booth Had Missed 1931,My 14,27:1

Irving, George S
Oklahoma! 1943,Ap 1,27:1
Call Me Mister 1946,Ap 19,26:2
Along Fifth Avenue 1949,Ja 14,28:2
Gentlemen Prefer Blondes 1949,D 9,35:3
Two's Company 1952,D 16,43:5
Me and Juliet 1953,My 29,17:1
Me and Juliet 1953,Je 7,II,1:1
Bells Are Ringing 1956,N 29,43:4
Bells Are Ringing 1956,N 30,18:2
Beggar's Opera, The 1957,Mr 14,35:1
Shinbone Alley 1957,Ap 15,23:2
Shinbone Alley 1957,Ap 28,II,1:1
Good Soup, The 1960,Mr 3,26:4
Irma la Douce 1960,S 30,31:2
Romulus 1962,Ja 11,27:1
Bravo Giovanni 1962,My 21,41:2
Bravo Giovanni 1962,My 27,II,1:1
Tovarich 1963,Mr 20,5:1
Murderer Among Us, A 1964,Mr 26,43:1
Alfie 1964,D 18,27:1

Irving, George S—Cont
Dreigroschenoper, Die 1965,Mr 12,24:1
Anya 1965,N 30,48:1
Galileo 1967,Ap 14,31:1
Happy Time, The 1968,Ja 19,32:2
Up Eden 1968,N 27,42:1
Promenade 1969,Je 5,56:1

Irving, Harry R
Broken Branches 1922,Mr 7,11:1
Deep Tangled Wildwood, The 1923,N 6,22:1
Fool's Bells 1925,D 24,8:3
Nightstick 1927,N 11,20:4

Irving, Harry R (Producer)
Aries Is Rising 1939,N 22,16:5

Irving, Hollis
Men of Distinction 1953,My 1,18:4

Irving, Irma
Sweetheart Shop, The 1920,S 1,13:4
Love Letter, The 1921,O 5,20:1
One Kiss 1923,N 28,14:2
Puzzles of 1925 1925,F 3,25:3
Oh, Please! 1926,D 22,24:3

Irving, Isabel
Bachelor's Night, A 1921,O 18,20:1
To the Ladies! 1922,F 21,20:1
To the Ladies! 1922,Mr 12,VI,1:1
We Moderns 1924,Mr 12,17:2
Bride, The 1924,My 6,25:1
Lady's Virtue, A 1925,N 24,28:2
Gringa, La 1928,F 2,17:1
Age of Innocence, The 1928,N 28,24:2
Uncle Vanya 1930,S 23,30:3
Three Wise Fools 1936,Mr 2,12:2

Irving, Jack (Producer)
Fun City 1968,Mr 7,53:2

Irving, Jane
Lady in the Dark 1943,Mr 1,14:2

Irving, John
Edward II 1958,F 12,32:5
Ernest in Love 1960,My 5,39:4
Mousetrap, The 1960,N 7,46:1
Write Me a Murder 1961,O 27,28:2
Day the Whores Came Out to Play Tennis, The 1965,Mr 16,45:1

Irving, Jules
Gift of Fury, A 1958,Mr 24,21:4
Waiting for Godot 1958,Ag 6,22:1

Irving, Jules (Director)
Caretaker, The 1963,N 25,23:2
House of Bernarda Alba, The 1963,N 25,23:2
Danton's Death 1965,O 22,46:1
Caucasian Chalk Circle, The 1966,Mr 25,35:1
Alchemist, The 1966,O 14,48:1
Yerma 1966,D 9,60:1
East Wind, The 1967,F 10,30:1
Galileo 1967,Ap 14,31:1
Little Foxes, The 1967,O 27,53:1
Saint Joan 1968,Ja 5,42:1
Tiger at the Gates 1968,Mr 1,30:1
Cyrano de Bergerac 1968,Ap 26,30:1
King Lear 1968,N 8,43:1
Cry of Players, A 1968,N 15,40:1
In the Matter of J Robert Oppenheimer 1969,Mr 7,28:1
Inner Journey, The 1969,Mr 21,42:1
Time of Your Life, The 1969,N 7,37:1
Operation Sidewinder 1970,Mr 13,33:1

Irving, Jules (Producer)
Danton's Death 1965,O 31,II,1:1

Irving, Laurence (Playwright)
Humble, The 1926,O 14,22:2

Irving, Laurence (Scenic Designer)
There's Always Juliet 1932,F 16,24:2
Punchinello 1932,Mr 27,VIII,2:1
There's Always Juliet 1932,O 28,23:2
Evensong 1933,F 1,13:4
Sun Never Sets, The 1938,Je 26,IX,2:1
I Have Been Here Before 1938,O 14,26:2

Irving, Lester Trio
Vaudeville (Palace) 1929,Mr 11,22:5

Irving, Margaret
Irving Berlin's New Music Box Revue 1922,O 24,18:1
Mercenary Mary 1925,Ap 14,27:3
Desert Song, The 1926,D 1,24:2
Animal Crackers 1928,O 24,26:2
Where There's a Will 1939,Ja 18,16:6
Streets of Paris, The 1939,Je 20,25:2
Hold On to Your Hats 1940,S 12,30:3
Hairpin Harmony 1943,O 2,18:5
Happy Birthday 1946,N 1,31:2

Irving, Paul
Unwritten Chapter, The 1920,O 12,18:1
Afgar 1920,N 9,13:2
World We Live In, The 1922,N 1,16:1

Irving, Richard
Cinderelative 1930,S 19,18:4
Audition of the Apprentice Theatre 1939,Je 2,26:2
They Should Have Stood in Bed 1942,F 14,18:5

Irving, Richard (Director)
Live and Learn 1930,Ap 10,24:6

Irving, Robert (Composer)
As You Like It 1950,Ja 27,27:2

Irving, Robert (Miscellaneous)
Mikado, The 1959,O 2,24:1
Pirates of Penzance, The 1960,O 7,29:1

Irving, Robert (Musical Director)
As You Like It 1950,F 19,II,1:1
Mikado, The 1961,Ja 18,26:1
H M S Pinafore 1961,F 2,26:6

Irving, Roland (Composer)
Malinda 1929,D 4,37:2

Irving, Roland (Lyricist)
Malinda 1929,D 4,37:2

Irving, Roy
John Bull's Other Island 1948,F 11,33:4
Where Stars Walk 1948,F 25,27:2
Lo and Behold! 1951,D 13,45:2

Irving, Stephen
Salvation 1928,F 1,31:1
Bonds of Interest, The 1929,O 15,34:2
Richelieu 1929,D 26,20:3
Grand Hotel 1930,N 14,30:4

Irving, Washington (Original Author)
Half Moon Inn 1923,Mr 21,19:2
Headless Horseman, The 1937,Mr 6,10:4
Sleepy Hollow 1948,Je 4,26:3
Autumn's Here 1966,O 26,40:1
Rip Van Wrinkle 1967,D 23,28:1

Irving Aaronson's Orchestra
Paris 1928,O 9,34:3

Irvings, Harry R
What's the Use? 1926,S 7,19:1

Irwin, Boyd
Under Glass 1933,O 31,24:3
Yoshe Kalb 1933,D 29,27:2
Hat, a Coat, a Glove, A 1934,F 1,15:2
Man Who Came to Dinner, The 1940,F 10,19:5

Irwin, Carlotta
Egotist, The 1922,D 27,12:1
Stork, The 1925,Ja 27,14:2
Weak Sisters 1925,O 14,31:3
Trouper, The 1926,Mr 9,21:1
Loose Ankles 1926,Ag 17,15:1
Say It With Flowers 1926,D 6,29:1
Gentlemen of the Press 1928,Ag 28,27:2

Irwin, Charles
Find Daddy 1926,Mr 9,21:3
Ned Wayburn's Gambols 1929,Ja 16,22:3
Up in Central Park 1945,Ja 29,17:2

Irwin, Deedy
Fiorello! 1959,N 24,45:3

Irwin, Edward
Eden End 1935,O 22,17:1

Irwin, Felix
Autumn Fire 1926,O 27,25:3

Irwin, Flo
Glory 1922,D 26,10:1

Irwin, Jack
Broadway Boy 1932,My 4,23:5
Cross-Town 1937,Mr 18,21:5
Arsenic and Old Lace 1943,D 13,18:6
Best Foot Forward 1963,Ap 3,43:1

Irwin, John
Cup, The 1923,N 13,25:1
Haunted House, The 1924,S 3,12:1
Easy Come, Easy Go 1925,O 27,20:2
Barker, The 1927,Ja 19,20:6
Goin' Home 1928,Ag 24,23:2
Goin' Home 1928,S 2,VII,1:1
School for Wives 1934,N 14,22:2
Siege 1937,D 9,31:4

Irwin, May
49ers 1922,N 7,14:1
Vaudeville (Palace) 1925,O 20,29:2

Irwin, Richard
Partition 1948,O 29,31:2

Irwin, Robert
Night of January 16 1935,D 16,22:5
Fireworks on the James 1940,My 15,30:2

Irwin, Smiley W
Sancho Panza 1923,N 27,23:1

Irwin, Thomas
Play, A 1925,F 11,19:2
For Better or Worse 1927,F 1,24:3
Fast Life 1928,S 27,35:2

Irwin, Will (Composer)
Grand Street Follies, The 1929,My 2,20:4
Shoestring Revue 1929,N 23,19:2
Garrick Gaieties 1930,Je 5,29:2
Fools Rush In 1934,D 26,19:2
All in Fun 1940,D 28,11:2
Star and Garter 1942,Je 25,26:2
Angel in the Pawnshop 1951,Ja 19,20:3
Portofino 1958,F 22,8:3
Stage Affair, A 1962,Ja 17,30:2

Irwin, Will (Lyricist)
Shoestring Revue 1929,N 23,19:2
Fools Rush In 1934,D 26,19:2
Show Is On, The 1937,S 20,18:4
All in Fun 1940,D 28,11:2
Star and Garter 1942,Je 25,26:2

Irwin, Will (Miscellaneous)
Hey, Nonny, Nonny! 1932,Je 7,22:3
Men to the Sea 1944,O 4,25:2

Irwin, Will (Musical Director)
What's Up 1943,N 12,24:6
If the Shoe Fits 1946,D 6,29:4
Texas Li'l Darlin' 1949,N 26,10:5
Littlest Revue, The 1956,My 23,37:2
Portofino 1958,F 22,8:3
Nativity, The 1965,D 3,44:2

Irwin, Will (Playwright)
Lute Song 1946,F 7,29:2
Lute Song 1946,F 17,II,1:1
Lute Song 1948,O 12,32:3
Lute Song 1959,Mr 13,24:1

Irwin, William
Polly 1925,O 12,19:1

Isaacs, Bryna Rachel
Gods Are Wise, The 1930,My 6,33:1

Isaacs, Ken (Miscellaneous)
Inquest 1970,Ap 24,38:1

Isaacs, Rael
Don Juan in the Russian Manner 1954,Ap 23,23:2

Isaburo, Toyozawa
Kumagai Jinya 1969,S 18,64:1

Iscove, Robert
Henry, Sweet Henry 1967,O 24,51:2

Isenberg, Charles (Producer)
Zelda 1969,Mr 6,38:1

Isenman, Don (Composer)
Follies of 1910, The 1960,Ja 15,37:3

Isenman, Don (Musical Director)
Follies of 1910, The 1960,Ja 15,37:3

Ish, Kathryn
Committee, The 1964,S 17,53:1

Isham, Frederic (Original Author)
Three Live Ghosts 1920,S 30,12:1
Yes, Yes, Yvette 1927,O 4,32:3
Tell Her the Truth 1932,O 29,18:2

Isham, Frederic (Playwright)
Three Live Ghosts 1920,S 30,12:1
Three Live Ghosts 1920,O 10,VI,1:2
Jack and Jill 1923,Mr 23,17:2
One Shot Fired 1927,N 8,32:5
Kidding Kidders 1928,Ap 24,28:3

Isham, Gyles
And So to Bed 1927,N 10,23:1
Queen's Husband, The 1928,Ja 26,17:2
Cherry Orchard, The 1928,Mr 6,20:1
Bride of the Lamb 1934,Mr 29,26:1
Family Affairs 1934,S 16,X,2:1
Dog Beneath the Skin, The 1936,F 23,X,1:3
Stubble Before Swords 1936,Mr 24,26:8
My Son's My Son 1936,My 27,26:4

Isham, Virginia (Playwright)
And Life Burns On 1938,Jl 31,IX,1:4

Isherwood, Christopher (Original Author)
I Am a Camera 1951,D 9,II,5:1
I Am a Camera 1954,Mr 13,11:1
I Am a Camera 1954,Ap 11,II,2:1
Cabaret 1966,D 4,II,5:1
Cabaret 1968,Ja 12,19:1

Isherwood, Christopher (Playwright)
Dog Beneath the Skin, The 1936,F 23,X,1:3
Ascent of F 6, The 1937,Mr 28,XI,2:1
I Am a Camera 1951,N 29,39:6
I Am a Camera 1956,O 10,47:2
Cabaret 1966,N 21,62:1
Adventures of the Black Girl in Her Search for God, The 1969,Mr 22,24:4

Ishikawa
Diamond Lil 1948,N 30,33:2

Ishikawa, Kame
Teahouse of the August Moon, The 1953,O 16,32:1

Ishil, Kanna
Majority of One, A 1959,F 17,28:2

Ishimoto, Dale
Kataki 1959,D 16,55:1

Isiburo, Toyozawa
Chushingura; Treasury of Loyal Retainers, The 1969,S 11,53:1

Iskin, A E (Producer)
Bells, The 1926,Ap 14,20:3

Iskin, R R (Producer)
Bells, The 1926,Ap 14,20:3

Isler, Lloyd (Miscellaneous)
Collector's Item 1952,F 9,11:2

Ismaeloff, Sergei
Polonaise 1945,O 8,20:2

Ismailoff, Bettilu
Lady Comes Across, The 1942,Ja 10,10:2

Isom, Brunette (Costume Designer)
Raisin' Hell in the Son 1962,Jl 3,13:2

Isquith, Louis (Director)
Messin' Around 1929,Ap 23,26:3

Isquith, Louis (Playwright)
Messin' Around 1929,Ap 23,26:3

Isquith, Louis (Producer)
Messin' Around 1929,Ap 23,26:3
Dora Mobridge 1930,Ap 21,20:2

Israel, Ann (Miscellaneous)
Kitchen, The 1966,Je 14,50:1

Israel, Bruce
Richard II 1968,Je 24,42:3
Androcles and the Lion 1968,Je 27,47:1
Greenwillow 1970,D 8,60:1

Israel, Irving
Having Wonderful Time 1937,F 22,12:5
Israel, Laurie
Milk Train Doesn't Stop Here Anymore, The 1965,Jl 27,25:1
Israel, Neil (Director)
Conerico Was Here to Stay 1969,Mr 11,39:1
Paradise Gardens East 1969,Mr 11,39:1
Israel, Steven Ben
Brig, The 1963,My 16,40:1
Antigone 1968,O 11,36:1
Israelev, G (Playwright)
Oh What a Wedding! 1969,O 20,60:1
Istomina, Anna
Vie Parisienne, La 1945,Ja 13,14:5
Istria, Evelyne
On Ne Badine Pas Avec l'Amour; No Trifling With Love 1968,Mr 5,35:1
Italiano, Joseph
They Knew What They Wanted 1949,F 17,28:2
Italie, Jean-Claude van (Playwright)
America Hurrah 1966,N 27,II,1:1
Itamar
Sing Israel Sing 1967,My 12,50:1
Itkin, D
Dybbuk, The 1926,D 14,24:2
Eternal Jew, The 1926,D 21,21:2
Jacob's Dream 1927,Ja 4,20:2
Deluge, The 1927,Ja 11,36:2
Itkin, David (Director)
Moon Besieged, The 1950,N 4,13:1
Itkin, Iza (Director)
Infernal Machine, The 1954,Mr 22,22:2
Doll's House, A 1954,N 15,32:2
Merchant of Venice, The 1955,Ja 8,9:7
Ito, Gail (Costume Designer)
Coach With the Six Insides, The 1967,My 12,50:1
Ito, Gerald
Tom Sawyer - Ballad of the Mississippi 1947,D 27,11:3
All the King's Men 1950,Jl 19,25:6
Ito, Kisaku (Scenic Designer)
Azuma Kabuki Dancers and Musicians 1954,Mr 10,29:4
Ito, Michio (Choreographer)
Cherry Blossoms 1927,Mr 29,22:3
Turandot 1929,Ja 12,14:4
Ito, Michio (Director)
Kage-No-Chikara; Shadow Man, The 1930,Mr 5,26:7
Matsuri; Festival 1930,Mr 5,26:7
Koi No Yozakura; Romance in Cherry Blossom Lane 1930,Mr 5,26:7
Ito, Michio (Playwright)
Koi No Yozakura; Romance in Cherry Blossom Lane 1930,Mr 5,26:7
Kage-No-Chikara; Shadow Man, The 1930,Mr 5,26:7
Matsuri; Festival 1930,Mr 5,26:7
Ito, Robert
Our Town 1968,D 14,62:1
Ito, Teiji
Sotoba Komachi 1961,F 1,15:1
Damask Drum, The 1961,F 4,15:1
Hans's Crime 1961,F 4,15:1
Mountain Giants, The 1961,Ap 5,32:3
Caucasian Chalk Circle, The 1961,N 1,35:1
Ito, Teiji (Composer)
Absalom 1956,My 17,37:2
In the Jungle of Cities 1960,D 21,39:1
Sotoba Komachi 1961,F 1,15:1
Hans's Crime 1961,F 4,15:1
Damask Drum, The 1961,F 4,15:1
Mountain Giants, The 1961,Ap 5,32:3
Caucasian Chalk Circle, The 1961,N 1,35:1
Coach With the Six Insides, The 1962,N 27,44:1
Fitz 1966,My 17,51:2
Biscuit 1966,My 17,51:2
Coach With the Six Insides, The 1967,My 12,50:1
Bench, The 1968,Mr 5,35:2
Ito, Teiji (Miscellaneous)
One Flew Over the Cuckoo's Nest 1963,N 14,40:2
Fitz 1966,My 17,51:2
Biscuit 1966,My 17,51:2
Exercise, The 1968,Ap 25,54:1
Itow, Michio
Pinwheel Revel 1922,Je 16,20:6
Pinwheel Revel 1922,Ag 1,14:2
Itsuro, Shimoda (Composer)
Golden Bat 1970,Je 27,18:2
Itter, Margaret
Seven Mirrors 1945,O 26,17:2
Ittner, Alice
Knight of the Burning Pestle, The 1927,Ap 23,15:1
Itts, Jules (Producer)
Pets 1969,My 15,41:2
Baby With a Knife 1969,My 15,41:2
Silver Grey Toy Poodle 1969,My 15,41:2
Ivan, Charles
Green Pastures, The 1935,F 27,16:2
Ivan, Rosalind
Richard III 1920,Mr 8,7:1
Life Line, The 1930,D 29,19:3

Lake, The 1933,D 27,24:2
Once Is Enough 1938,F 16,16:2
Knights of Song 1938,O 18,29:2
Don't Throw Glass Houses 1938,D 28,24:4
Corn Is Green, The 1940,N 27,27:2
Ivan, Rosalind (Translator)
Brothers Karamazov, The 1927,Ja 4,20:1
Ivancovich, John
Lady Dedlock 1929,Ja 1,61:2
Mystery Square 1929,Ap 5,28:3
Ivanoff, Sonia
Kid Boots 1924,Ja 1,21:3
Ivanoff, Vsevolod (Playwright)
Armored Train No 1469 1931,N 28,20:3
Ivanova, Olga
Cricket on the Hearth, The 1925,My 29,20:2
Ivanovic, Olga
Progress of Bora, The Tailor, The 1968,Je 27,49:2
Ivanovic, Predrag
Progress of Bora, The Tailor, The 1968,Je 27,49:2
Ivans, Elaine
Mrs Partridge Presents 1925,Ja 6,23:3
Just Life 1926,S 15,33:3
Padre, The 1926,D 28,16:3
Headquarters 1929,D 5,32:4
Crime Marches on 1935,O 24,19:1
Ivans, Perry
This Fine-Pretty World 1923,D 27,11:1
Ivantzoff, Ivan
Variations of 1940 1940,Ja 29,12:1
Ivarson, Ivar
Broken Hearts of Broadway 1944,Je 13,16:2
Iverclyde, June (Lady)
Fanfare 1932,Je 24,15:2
Iveria, Miki (Translator)
Three Sisters, The 1965,F 12,15:1
Kremlin Chimes 1965,F 25,23:1
Ivernel, Daniel
Piano Dans l'Herbe, Un 1970,S 17,56:1
Iversen, Marya
Firebird of Florence 1945,Mr 23,13:4
Iversen, William
Smell the Sweet Savor 1940,F 3,8:4
Ives, Agnes
Journeyman 1938,Ja 31,14:2
Ives, Anne
Sister Oakes 1949,Ap 25,19:4
Crucible, The 1958,Mr 12,36:1
Crucible, The 1958,Je 1,II,1:1
Masquerade 1959,Mr 17,42:1
Her Master's Voice 1964,D 28,33:2
Hedda Gabler 1970,Je 12,28:1
Hedda Gabler 1970,Je 21,II,1:1
Good Woman of Setzuan, The 1970,N 6,51:1
Ives, Burl
Boys From Syracuse, The 1938,N 24,36:1
Heavenly Express 1940,Ap 19,24:2
This Is the Army 1942,Jl 5,28:2
Sing Out, Sweet Land! 1944,Ja 7,II,1:1
Swing Out, Sweet Land! 1944,N 10,24:6
Sing Out, Sweet Land! 1944,D 28,24:2
She Stoops to Conquer 1949,D 29,21:3
Show Boat 1954,My 6,44:1
Cat on a Hot Tin Roof 1955,Mr 25,18:2
Cat on a Hot Tin Roof 1955,Ap 3,II,1:1
Dr Cook's Garden 1967,S 26,52:1
Ives, C M
Faun, The 1924,Mr 28,17:2
Ives, Charlotte
She Had to Know 1925,F 3,25:3
Ives, Chauncey B
Orestes 1926,Je 20,II,3:6
Coriolanus 1927,Je 18,8:3
Ives, George
Alice in Arms 1945,F 1,18:4
Mr Barry's Etchings 1950,F 1,26:2
Season in the Sun 1950,S 29,31:2
Seven Year Itch, The 1952,N 21,21:2
Happy Town 1959,O 8,49:2
Alley of the Sunset 1959,D 31,11:1
Ives, Gerard M
Faun, The 1924,F 6,19:2
Galloper, The 1924,D 19,26:2
Ives, Jeremy
Song of Norway 1959,Je 26,16:2
Ivies, William
Thumbs Down 1923,Ag 7,20:1
Ivins, Perry
Julius Caesar 1923,F 9,10:4
Fashion 1924,F 5,21:2
Crime in the Whistler Room, The 1924,O 10,22:2
Desire Under the Elms 1924,N 12,20:7
Diff'rent 1925,F 11,19:3
Love for Love 1925,Ap 1,21:2
Fountain, The 1925,D 11,26:1
Juarez and Maximilian 1926,O 12,31:1
Paths of Glory 1935,S 27,24:2
Boy Meets Girl 1935,N 28,38:2
Ivins, Perry (Director)
Half Moon Inn 1923,Mr 21,19:2
Half Moon Inn 1925,Mr 10,14:1
Ivins, Perry (Playwright)
Half Moon Inn 1923,Mr 21,19:2

Ivins, Perry (Playwright)—Cont
Half Moon Inn 1925,Mr 10,14:1
Ivleps, Egron
It Happened Tomorrow 1933,My 6,11:5
Ivo, Alexander
Flare Path 1942,D 24,20:2
While the Sun Shines 1944,S 20,21:3
Nineteenth Hole of Europe, The 1949,Mr 28,16:2
Iwamoto, Kajiko
Azuma Kabuki Dancers and Musicians 1955,D 27,31:4
Iza Volpin's Ensemble
Continental Varieties 1935,D 27,15:3
Izard, Winifred
Wandering Jew, The 1927,F 2,22:4
Izzo, Rex
House in Berlin, A (Als der Krieg zu Ende War); Als der Krieg zu Ende War (A House in Berlin) 1950,D 27,32:3

J

Jaap, Herbert
Macbeth 1921,F 18,16:1
Jaap, Nelan
Robert E Lee 1923,N 21,23:1
Busybody, The 1924,S 30,27:5
Craig's Wife 1925,O 13,21:2
Black Velvet 1927,S 28,28:1
Great Power, The 1928,S 12,25:1
Kibitzer, The 1929,F 19,22:5
Jabala, Matilde Perez
Logia a la Natividad de Nuestro Senor Jesucristo, El 1937,D 14,33:4
Jabara, Paul
Hair 1967,O 30,55:1
Hair 1968,Ap 30,40:2
Hair 1969,F 5,36:1
Jablonski, Carl
Laundry, The 1963,F 19,5:2
Jacchia, Paul
Romantic Age, The 1922,N 15,22:1
Sandro Botticelli 1923,Mr 27,24:2
Sweet Nell of Old Drury 1923,My 19,16:4
Is Zat So? 1925,Ap 25,18:2
Move On 1926,Ja 19,30:1
Order Please 1934,O 10,21:2
American Holiday 1936,F 22,13:3
Jack, Bill
Ice Follies 1959,Ja 14,30:1
Ice Follies 1961,Ja 11,25:2
Ice Follies 1966,Ja 12,27:6
Jack, Charlotte-Ann
Mamba's Daughters 1940,Mr 25,10:4
Jack, Richard
Vikings, The 1930,My 13,27:3
Pillars of Society, The 1931,O 15,19:1
Saturday Night 1933,Mr 1,13:2
Saturday Night 1933,Mr 19,IX,1:1
Wednesday's Child 1934,Ja 17,23:2
Eldest, The 1935,F 12,24:3
Love in My Fashion 1937,D 4,21:4
Jack, William
Chicago 1926,D 31,11:1
Jacker, Corinne (Director)
Pale Horse, Pale Rider 1957,O 30,26:1
Jacker, Corinne (Lighting Director)
Edward II 1958,F 12,32:5
Aria Da Capo 1958,My 21,40:1
Guests of the Nation 1958,My 21,40:1
Song of Songs 1958,O 29,31:1
Maidens and Mistresses at Home at the Zoo 1958,O 29,31:1
Jacker, Corinne (Playwright)
Pale Horse, Pale Rider 1957,O 30,26:1
Jackie and Billie
Vaudeville (Palace) 1924,O 21,21:2
Jackin, Henry
Rosalie 1928,Ja 11,26:3
Jacklow, Ben
Dew Drop Inn 1923,My 18,26:4
Jackman, Helena
Wonderful World of Burlesque, The 1965,Ap 29,38:1
Jackman, Hope
Oliver 1963,Ja 8,5:5
Jacko
Better Times 1922,S 4,14:2
Jackpots, The
Ice Follies 1969,My 23,38:1
Jacks, Bill
Ice Follies 1963,Ja 10,5:2
Jackson, Alfred (Playwright)
Hush Money 1926,Mr 16,22:3
Piggy 1927,Ja 12,22:2
Jackson, Anita
Jezebel 1933,D 20,26:3
Jackson, Anna
Set to Music 1939,Ja 19,16:2
Pirate, The 1942,N 26,39:2
Jackson, Anne
Signature 1945,F 15,25:2
John Gabriel Borkman 1946,N 13,33:2

Jackson, Anne—Cont

Yellow Jack 1947,F 28,26:2
Last Dance, The 1948,Ja 28,27:2
Summer and Smoke 1948,O 7,33:2
Summer and Smoke 1948,O 17,II,1:1
Magnolia Alley 1949,Ap 19,29:2
Love Me Long 1949,N 8,34:5
Lady From the Sea, The 1950,Ag 8,23:2
Arms and the Man 1950,O 20,34:2
Never Say Never 1951,N 21,21:2
Bedtime Story 1952,My 8,35:6
Scarecrow, The 1953,Je 17,31:1
Oh, Men! Oh, Women! 1953,D 18,37:2
Middle of the Night 1956,F 9,39:1
Middle of the Night 1956,F 19,II,1:1
Rhinoceros 1961,Ja 10,27:1
Rhinoceros 1961,Ja 22,II,1:1
Brecht on Brecht 1961,N 15,52:2
Brecht on Brecht 1962,Ja 4,26:1
Brecht on Brecht 1962,Ja 14,II,1:1
Tiger, The 1963,F 6,5:2
Typists, The 1963,F 6,5:2
Luv 1964,N 12,43:1
Luv 1964,N 22,II,1:1
Exercise, The 1968,Ap 25,54:1
Exercise, The 1968,My 12,II,1:1
Front Page, The 1968,O 20,85:5
Inquest 1970,Ap 24,38:1
Inquest 1970,My 3,II,3:1

Jackson, Arthur (Lyricist)

Scandals 1920,Je 8,9:1
George White's Scandals 1921,Jl 12,14:1
For Goodness Sake 1922,F 22,13:1

Jackson, Barry

Vivat! Vivat Regina! 1970,Jl 20,21:2

Jackson, Barry (Sir) (Director)

Taming of the Shrew, The 1928,My 27,VIII,1:8
Barretts of Wimpole Street, The 1930,Ag 21,13:4
Too True to Be Good 1932,Ag 28,IX,1:1
Romeo and Juliet 1947,Ap 7,18:5
Hamlet 1948,My 9,II,2:5

Jackson, Barry (Sir) (Miscellaneous)

Henry IV 1955,My 15,II,1:1

Jackson, Barry (Sir) (Producer)

Hamlet 1925,Ag 26,19:4
All's Well That Ends Well 1927,Ap 17,17:6
Yellow Sands 1927,S 12,29:3
Harold 1928,Ap 29,IX,1:3
Six Characters in Search of an Author
1928,Je 24,VIII,4:2
White Assegai, The 1930,Ja 22,21:1
Caravan 1932,My 1,VIII,2:2
Evensong 1933,F 1,13:4
Sleeping Clergyman, A 1933,S 21,24:2
Marriage Is No Joke 1934,F 7,16:2
Counsellor-at-Law 1934,My 6,IX,2:5
Jane Eyre 1936,F 28,19:2

Jackson, Barry (Sir) (Translator)

Marvellous History of Saint Bernard, The
1958,F 24,16:3

Jackson, Bee

Carnival 1929,Ap 25,32:5

Jackson, Betty

What Next 1920,Ja 27,7:2

Jackson, Blois

Jezebel 1933,D 20,26:3

Jackson, Brady

Blackbirds 1933,D 4,22:3

Jackson, Brian (Costume Designer)

Henry VIII 1961,Jl 2,II,1:1

Jackson, Brian (Scenic Designer)

Midsummer Night's Dream, A 1960,Je 30,23:5
H M S Pinafore 1960,S 8,41:1
Henry VIII 1961,Je 22,22:1
Pirates of Penzance, The 1961,S 7,41:1
Macbeth 1962,Je 20,41:1
Timon of Athens 1963,Jl 31,19:2
Cherry Orchard, The 1965,Ag 2,17:2
Twelfth Night 1966,Je 10,51:2
Merry Wives of Windsor, The 1967,Ag 4,18:1
Seagull, The 1968,Jl 25,27:2

Jackson, Bruce

Christmas in the Market Place 1960,D 10,26:1

Jackson, C (Composer)

Fly Blackbird 1962,F 6,26:2

Jackson, C (Lyricist)

Fly Blackbird 1962,F 6,26:2

Jackson, C (Playwright)

Fly Blackbird 1962,F 6,26:2
Fly Blackbird 1962,Ap 29,II,1:1

Jackson, C Bernard (Director)

Our Town 1968,D 14,62:1

Jackson, Clifford

Paul Bunyan 1941,My 6,25:1

Jackson, Columbus

Deep Harlem 1929,Ja 8,35:2
How Come Lawd? 1937,O 1,18:5

Jackson, Craig

Billy Budd 1959,F 28,13:3
Caucasian Chalk Circle, The 1961,N 1,35:1

Jackson, Delmar (Original Author)

Cut of the Axe 1960,F 2,38:2

Jackson, Donald

Ice Follies 1963,Ja 10,5:2

Ice Follies 1964,Ja 8,41:2
Ice Follies 1965,Ja 13,35:1
Ice Follies 1966,Ja 12,27:6
Ice Follies 1967,Ja 11,51:1
Ice Follies 1969,My 23,38:1

Jackson, Donald (Miscellaneous)

Many Loves 1959,Ja 14,28:1
Don Carlos 1962,F 28,27:5
Storm, The 1962,Mr 31,17:2

Jackson, Dorothea

Red, Hot and Blue! 1936,O 30,26:3
Right This Way 1938,Ja 6,22:3
Portrait in Black 1947,My 15,30:2

Jackson, E B

Gentlemen, the Queen 1927,Ap 23,14:3

Jackson, Eddie

Show Girl 1929,Jl 3,19:3
New Yorkers, The 1930,D 9,31:1
New Yorkers, The 1930,D 28,VIII,1:1
Vaudeville (Palace) 1931,My 11,15:5

Jackson, Emmett

X Has No Value 1970,F 17,35:1

Jackson, Ernest

Bonds of Interest, The 1951,D 1,7:2
Yerma 1952,F 8,18:4

Jackson, Ethel

Masked Woman, The 1922,D 23,14:2
Blue Bird, The 1923,D 26,13:3
Lady Killer, The 1924,Mr 13,14:2
One for All 1927,My 14,25:5
Brown Buddies 1930,O 8,29:1
Girls in Uniform 1932,D 31,10:3
Her Tin Soldier 1933,Ap 7,22:6
Dodsworth 1934,F 26,20:4
So Proudly We Hail 1936,S 23,28:4
Women, The 1936,D 28,13:1
I Must Love Someone 1939,F 8,18:7
Key Largo 1939,N 28,30:2

Jackson, Euliebel

Come Angel Band 1936,F 19,17:1

Jackson, Frank

Swing It 1937,Jl 23,17:2

Jackson, Fred

Plot Against the Chase Manhattan Bank, The
1963,N 27,29:1
Will the Mail Train Run Tonight? 1964,Ja 10,18:1

Jackson, Frederick (Director)

Slightly Scandalous 1944,Je 14,16:2

Jackson, Frederick (Miscellaneous)

By Appointment 1934,O 13,10:4

Jackson, Frederick (Original Author)

Dear Charles 1952,D 21,44:5
Dear Charles 1953,Ap 20,22:4
Dear Charles 1954,S 26,II,1:1

Jackson, Frederick (Playwright)

Hole in the Wall, The 1920,Mr 27,11:1
Two Little Girls in Blue 1921,My 4,10:3
For Goodness Sake 1922,F 22,13:1
Cold Feet 1923,My 22,14:2
Cold Feet 1923,My 22,14:3
Her Past 1929,F 10,IX,4:7
Wife Insurance 1934,Ap 13,24:5
Bishop Misbehaves, The 1935,F 21,22:4
Prelude 1935,Je 27,17:4
Naked Man, The 1935,Jl 2,24:3
Beginner's Luck 1935,Jl 23,24:4
Murder With Pen and Ink 1935,Jl 30,17:2
Carrida 1935,Ag 2,22:2
King's Messenger, The 1935,Ag 14,16:3
Murder With Pen and Ink 1935,Ag 20,25:1
Bishop Misbehaves, The 1935,Ag 27,23:4
Ascending Dragon, The 1935,O 1,27:6
Slightly Scandalous 1944,Je 14,16:2
Dear Charles 1954,S 16,37:2

Jackson, Frederick (Producer)

Road to Paradise, The 1935,Jl 16,24:2
Beginner's Luck 1935,Jl 23,24:4

Jackson, Frederick C

Macbeth 1967,Jl 31,21:1

Jackson, George

Salome 1923,My 8,22:2
Merrily We Roll Along 1934,O 1,14:1

Jackson, Gerald (Costume Designer)

Mrs Warren's Profession 1963,Ap 25,39:1
Picture of Dorian Gray, The 1963,Ag 29,37:4

Jackson, Gerald (Lighting Director)

Picture of Dorian Gray, The 1963,Ag 29,37:4

Jackson, Gerald (Scenic Designer)

Mrs Warren's Profession 1963,Ap 25,39:1
Picture of Dorian Gray, The 1963,Ag 29,37:4

Jackson, Glenda

Persecution and Assassination of Marat As
Performed by the Inmates of the Asylum of
Charenton Under the Direction of the Marquis de
Sade, The 1964,Ag 21,14:2
Hamlet 1965,Ag 20,18:2
Persecution and Assassination of Marat As
Performed by the Inmates of the Asylum of
Charenton Under the Direction of the Marquis de
Sade, The 1965,D 28,35:1

Jackson, Glenda—Cont

Persecution and Assassination of Marat As
Performed by the Inmates of the Asylum of
Charenton Under the Direction of the Marquis de
Sade, The 1966,Ja 9,II,1:1
US 1966,N 6,II,1:5

Jackson, Gordon

This Story of Yours 1968,D 14,60:4
Hamlet 1969,My 2,38:1
Hedda Gabler 1970,Je 12,28:1
Hedda Gabler 1970,Je 21,II,1:1

Jackson, H B

1776 1926,Ap 24,11:2

Jackson, Harriett

Porgy and Bess 1935,O 11,30:2
Sweet River 1936,O 29,30:2
Porgy and Bess 1942,Ja 23,16:2
Sons and Soldiers 1943,My 5,22:2
Porgy and Bess 1943,S 14,26:2
Porgy and Bess 1944,F 8,13:2
Memphis Bound 1945,My 25,23:2
Carib Song 1945,S 28,17:2

Jackson, Harry

Would-Be Gentleman, The 1930,Ap 30,29:2
Honor Code, The 1931,My 19,25:3
Jumbo 1935,N 18,20:2
Whatever Goes Up 1935,N 26,28:2
Too Many Girls 1939,O 19,26:2
Teahouse of the August Moon, The 1953,O 16,32:1

Jackson, Harry Jr

Jumbo 1935,N 18,20:2

Jackson, Helen

Dice of the Gods, The 1923,Ap 6,20:2
Madre 1923,D 31,9:6

Jackson, Helen Girls

Vanities 1932,S 28,22:4

Jackson, Horace (Playwright)

Yr Obedient Husband 1937,N 27,21:2
Yr Obedient Husband 1938,Ja 11,26:5

Jackson, Howard (Composer)

Tattle Tales 1933,Je 2,22:6

Jackson, Howard (Lyricist)

Tattle Tales 1933,Je 2,22:6

Jackson, Irving

Good Morning, Dearie 1921,N 2,20:2
Gambling 1929,Ag 27,31:2

Jackson, J B (Playwright)

Pudding on the Ritz 1932,Ap 9,18:3

Jackson, J G Jr

Tiger Smiles, The 1930,D 18,29:1

Jackson, James

Lulu Belle 1926,F 10,20:1
Big Fight, The 1928,S 19,33:1
Challenge of Youth 1930,Ja 21,28:5
Natural Man 1941,My 8,20:4
Tin Top Valley 1947,Mr 1,11:2

Jackson, Joe

Good Times 1920,Ag 10,10:1
Vaudeville (Palace) 1921,My 17,20:3
Vaudeville (Palladium) 1935,O 30,16:8
American Jubilee 1940,My 13,20:5

Jackson, Joe Jr

Icetime 1947,My 29,28:2
Red White and Blue 1950,O 8,64:5
Ice Capades 1966,Je 2,50:2

Jackson, Joseph (Playwright)

Cold in Sables 1931,D 24,20:7

Jackson, Josephine (Composer)

Believers, The 1968,My 10,57:4

Jackson, Josephine (Lyricist)

Believers, The 1968,My 10,57:4

Jackson, Josephine (Playwright)

Believers, The 1968,My 10,57:4

Jackson, Julia

House of Women, The 1927,O 4,32:2

Jackson, Larry

Ice Capades 1953,S 11,25:1
Ice Capades 1954,S 16,37:1
Ice Capades 1955,S 15,38:1

Jackson, Laura Mae (Lighting Director)

Henry IV 1968,F 7,40:1

Jackson, Leonard

Coriolanus 1965,Jl 15,23:1

Jackson, Lonny

On the Town 1944,D 29,11:4

Jackson, Lorna Doone

Serenade, The 1930,Mr 5,26:7

Jackson, Louis

Alt Heidelberg 1926,My 31,10:5

Jackson, Louise

Big White Fog 1940,O 23,26:2

Jackson, Margie

Let Freedom Sing 1942,O 6,18:2
Allah Be Praised! 1944,Ap 21,14:2

Jackson, Mary

Jumbo 1935,N 18,20:2
Eastward in Eden 1947,N 19,33:2

Jackson, Mike

Ol' Man Satan 1932,O 4,26:3
Courageous One, The 1958,Ja 21,33:6

Jackson, Montgomery (Producer)

Constant Wife, The 1935,Jl 3,20:2
Stardust 1935,Jl 17,22:4

Jackson, Myrtis
  Knights of Song 1938,O 18,29:2
Jackson, N Hart (Translator)
  Two Orphans, The 1926,Ap 6,26:2
Jackson, Nagle (Director)
  Hamlet 1968,Je 10,59:1
Jackson, Nora
  Buds of 1927 1927,F 22,22:5
Jackson, Patty Ann
  Me and Juliet 1953,My 29,17:1
  Me and Juliet 1953,Je 7,II,1:1
  Chic 1959,My 19,28:2
Jackson, Percival
  Beau Gallant 1926,Ap 6,26:3
Jackson, Peter
  Seagull, The 1968,Jl 25,27:2
Jackson, Philip
  Merry-Go-Rounders, The 1956,N 22,50:1
Jackson, Richard (Lighting Director)
  Dybbuk, The 1954,O 27,33:6
  Take a Giant Step 1956,S 26,30:1
  Three Sisters, The 1959,S 22,46:1
  Deadly Game, The 1966,F 14,34:1
Jackson, Richard (Scenic Designer)
  Ice Capades 1952,S 12,18:1
  Three Sisters, The 1955,F 26,13:2
  Three Sisters, The 1955,Mr 20,II,1:1
  Take a Giant Step 1956,S 26,30:1
  Three Sisters, The 1959,S 22,46:1
  Deadly Game, The 1966,F 14,34:1
  Curley McDimple 1967,N 23,59:2
Jackson, Robert
  Hang Down Your Head and Die 1964,O 19,38:1
  Skin of Our Teeth, The 1966,Je 2,51:1
  Dance of Death, The 1966,Je 3,31:1
  As You Like It 1966,Je 4,19:1
  House of Flowers 1968,Ja 29,26:2
  Henry V 1969,N 11,43:1
  X Has No Value 1970,F 17,35:1
  Ododo 1970,N 25,26:1
Jackson, Sam
  Smile of the World, The 1949,Ja 13,26:5
  Springtime Folly 1951,F 27,23:4
Jackson, Scott (Miscellaneous)
  Cue for Passion 1958,N 26,25:2
Jackson, Sheila (Costume Designer)
  Merchant of Venice, The 1947,F 24,16:2
Jackson, Shirley (Original Author)
  We Have Always Lived in the Castle
    1966,O 20,53:1
Jackson, Shirley (Playwright)
  When I Was a Child 1960,D 9,38:1
Jackson, Susan
  Iolanthe 1968,N 9,37:3
Jackson, Suzanne
  Immortal Thief, The 1926,O 4,21:1
  Little Accident 1928,O 10,32:3
  Hot Money 1931,N 9,22:2
  Order Please 1934,O 10,21:2
  Eldest, The 1935,F 12,24:3
  And Stars Remain 1936,O 13,32:2
  Farewell Summer 1937,Mr 30,20:2
  Many Mansions 1937,O 28,28:6
  Flying Gerardos, The 1940,D 30,21:4
  Pillar to Post 1943,D 11,11:2
  Public Relations 1944,Ap 7,23:3
  Make Yourself at Home 1945,S 14,21:2
Jackson, Thomas
  Her Salary Man 1921,N 29,20:1
  Madeleine and the Movies 1922,Mr 7,11:1
  Shore Leave 1922,Ag 9,20:2
  Vagabond, The 1923,D 28,13:4
  Shipwrecked 1924,N 13,18:1
  Broadway 1926,S 17,19:3
  Broadway 1926,S 26,VIII,1:1
Jackson, Thomas (Director)
  Ten Per Cent 1927,S 14,29:3
Jackson, Thomas (Producer)
  Ten Per Cent 1927,S 14,29:3
  Gentlemen of the Press 1928,Ag 28,27:2
Jackson, Thurman
  Turpentine 1936,Je 27,21:6
  One-Act Plays of the Sea; Long Voyage Home,
    The 1937,O 30,23:2
  One-Act Plays of the Sea; Bound East for Cardiff
    1937,O 30,23:2
  Big Blow 1938,O 3,11:2
  Homecoming 1942,N 17,28:5
Jackson, Tod (Choreographer)
  Mandragola 1958,My 29,23:2
Jackson, Van
  Change Your Luck 1930,Je 7,10:2
Jackson, W C (Playwright)
  It's Only Natural 1922,Ap 21,13:2
Jackson, Wallace
  Letter of the Law, The; Robe Rouge, La
    1920,F 24,11:1
  Will Shakespeare 1923,Ja 2,14:1
Jackson, Warren
  Laugh Time 1943,S 9,35:2
Jackson, William
  Birthright 1933,N 22,22:3
  Mary of Scotland 1933,N 28,28:3

Stardust 1935,Jl 17,22:4
Play's the Thing, The 1935,Jl 24,20:4
Ode to Liberty 1935,Ag 6,20:3
Bride the Sun Shines On, The 1936,Jl 1,29:2
Plumes in the Dust 1936,N 7,14:2
Miser, The 1950,Mr 27,19:5
Misalliance 1955,F 12,10:6
Apple Cart, The 1956,O 19,23:1
Bride in the Morning, A 1960,My 26,38:2
Man and Superman 1960,Ag 17,35:3
Jackson, William (Producer)
  Constant Wife, The 1935,Jl 3,20:2
  Stardust 1935,Jl 17,22:4
Jackson, Yolande
  Josef Suss 1930,Ja 21,28:5
Jackson, Zaidee
  Rang Tang 1927,Jl 13,20:1
Jackson & Lynam
  Ice Capades 1952,S 12,18:1
Jacob, Angela
  Head or Tail 1926,N 10,24:1
Jacob, Ben
  World Is a Stage, The 1962,N 5,37:4
Jacob, Bill (Composer)
  Jimmy 1969,O 24,38:1
Jacob, Bill (Lyricist)
  Jimmy 1969,O 24,38:1
Jacob, Gordon (Composer)
  Twelfth Night 1958,D 10,54:2
  Hamlet 1958,D 17,2:7
Jacob, Gordon (Miscellaneous)
  Midsummer Night's Dream, A 1954,S 22,33:1
Jacob, Norman
  High John De Conquer 1969,Ap 23,39:1
  X Has No Value 1970,F 17,35:1
  Touch 1970,N 9,52:1
Jacob, Patti (Composer)
  Jimmy 1969,O 24,38:1
Jacob, Patti (Lyricist)
  Jimmy 1969,O 24,38:1
Jacob, Peter
  Troilus and Cressida 1965,Ag 13,17:1
  White Devil, The 1965,D 7,56:1
  Volpone 1967,Je 30,29:1
Jacobi, Derek
  As You Like It 1968,Jl 6,9:1
  Most Unwarrantable Intrusion, A 1968,Jl 9,30:2
  Love's Labour's Lost 1968,D 22,54:3
  Beaux' Stratagem, The 1970,F 10,50:2
  Three Sisters, The 1970,F 12,30:1
  Idiot, The 1970,Jl 17,18:1
  Idiot, The 1970,Jl 30,39:1
Jacobi, Lou
  Diary of Anne Frank, The 1955,O 6,24:2
  Tenth Man, The 1959,N 6,24:2
  Tenth Man, The 1959,N 15,II,1:1
  Come Blow Your Horn 1961,F 23,31:3
  Come Blow Your Horn 1961,Mr 5,II,1:1
  Fade Out--Fade In 1964,My 27,45:1
  Fade Out--Fade In 1965,F 16,40:2
  Don't Drink the Water 1966,N 18,37:1
  Don't Drink the Water 1966,D 25,II,1:1
  Norman, Is That You? 1970,F 20,30:1
  Norman, Is That You? 1970,Mr 1,II,1:4
Jacobi, Victor (Composer)
  Half-Moon, The 1920,N 2,15:2
  Love Letter, The 1921,O 5,20:1
Jacobowitz, Anna
  Hello Charlie 1965,O 25,47:2
Jacobs, Albert
  Mother's Sabbath Days 1960,N 21,33:2
Jacobs, Angela
  Uptown West 1923,Ap 4,22:2
  Strong, The 1924,F 27,15:3
  Comedienne 1924,O 22,18:1
  Napoleon's Barber 1927,F 2,22:4
  Butterflies 1927,F 2,22:4
  We're All in the Gutter 1927,Mr 5,12:2
  Merry Malones, The 1927,S 27,30:2
  Broken Chain, The 1929,F 21,30:4
  Bad Girl 1930,O 3,30:2
  Counsellor-at-Law 1931,N 7,17:2
  Spring Song 1934,O 2,18:2
  Be So Kindly 1937,F 9,19:4
  Take It As It Comes 1944,F 11,17:2
  Streetcar Named Desire, A 1950,My 24,36:1
Jacobs, Arthur (Playwright)
  In the Groove 1938,Ap 22,14:5
Jacobs, Betty
  Golden Ring, The 1930,F 1,14:7
  Motke From Slobodke 1930,Ap 12,23:3
  Hello Grandpa! 1931,Ja 2,25:3
  Jolly World, A 1931,Ja 24,15:3
  Sins of Mothers 1937,Mr 30,20:2
Jacobs, Carl
  Troilus and Cressida 1953,Ag 19,25:2
  Coriolanus 1953,Ag 21,9:2
  White Rose and the Red, The 1964,Mr 17,31:1
  Rosencrantz and Guildenstern Are Dead
    1967,O 17,53:1
Jacobs, Carl M Jr
  Wings Over Europe 1936,Mr 4,24:7

Jacobs, Christine
  Fiddler on the Roof 1970,F 28,20:1
Jacobs, Clarence
  Porgy and Bess 1935,O 11,30:2
Jacobs, Danny
  Wonderful World of Burlesque, The
    1965,Ap 29,38:1
Jacobs, Elias A (Producer)
  Dr Willy Nilly 1959,Je 5,18:2
Jacobs, Irving L (Producer)
  Silk Hat Harry 1943,Ag 22,II,1:6
  Sound of Hunting, A 1945,N 21,16:6
  Clutterbuck 1949,D 5,29:2
  Bernardine 1952,O 17,33:4
Jacobs, Jacob
  Soul of a Woman, The 1930,F 22,13:1
  Motke From Slobodke 1930,Ap 12,23:3
  Eretz Israel 1930,N 27,32:3
  Hello Grandpa! 1931,Ja 2,25:3
  Jolly World, A 1931,Ja 24,15:3
  Women of New York 1931,Mr 23,24:3
  Sins of Mothers 1937,Mr 30,20:2
  Farblondjete Honeymoon 1955,S 27,42:1
  Family Mishmash, A 1958,O 20,36:1
  Bei Mir Bistu Schoen 1961,O 23,22:2
  Cowboy in Israel, A 1962,O 29,36:2
  My Wife With Conditions 1963,O 21,39:1
  Good Luck 1964,O 19,38:3
  Hello Charlie 1965,O 25,47:2
  Bride Got Farblondjet, The 1967,N 6,61:6
  It's Never Too Late for Happiness 1968,O 21,59:3
  Oh What a Wedding! 1969,O 20,60:1
  President's Daughter, The 1970,N 4,41:2
Jacobs, Jacob (Director)
  President's Daughter, The 1970,N 4,41:2
Jacobs, Jacob (Lyricist)
  Motke From Slobodke 1930,Ap 12,23:3
  Berdichever Bridegroom, The 1930,S 24,26:2
  Second Marriage 1953,O 12,30:1
  Wish Me Luck! 1954,N 1,37:2
  Farblondjete Honeymoon 1955,S 27,42:1
  It Could Happen to You 1957,O 28,30:5
  Family Mishmash, A 1958,O 20,36:1
  Bei Mir Bistu Schoen 1961,O 23,22:2
  Cowboy in Israel, A 1962,O 29,36:2
  My Wife With Conditions 1963,O 21,39:1
  Good Luck 1964,O 19,38:3
  Hello Charlie 1965,O 25,47:2
  Bride Got Farblondjet, The 1967,N 6,61:6
  It's Never Too Late for Happiness 1968,O 21,59:3
  Oh What a Wedding! 1969,O 20,60:1
  President's Daughter, The 1970,N 4,41:2
Jacobs, Jacob (Miscellaneous)
  It's Never Too Late for Happiness 1968,O 21,59:3
Jacobs, Jacob (Playwright)
  Bride Got Farblondjet, The 1967,N 6,61:6
Jacobs, Jacob (Producer)
  Farblondjete Honeymoon 1955,S 27,42:1
  Family Mishmash, A 1958,O 20,36:1
  Bei Mir Bistu Schoen 1961,O 23,22:2
  Cowboy in Israel, A 1962,O 29,36:2
  My Wife With Conditions 1963,O 21,39:1
  Good Luck 1964,O 19,38:3
  Hello Charlie 1965,O 25,47:2
  Poor Millionaire, The 1966,O 24,48:2
  Bride Got Farblondjet, The 1967,N 6,61:6
  It's Never Too Late for Happiness 1968,O 21,59:3
  Oh What a Wedding! 1969,O 20,60:1
  President's Daughter, The 1970,N 4,41:2
Jacobs, Jesse
  Barrier, The 1950,N 3,32:2
  Beaux' Stratagem, The 1959,F 25,35:4
  Cast of Characters 1959,Je 11,37:2
  Dinny and the Witches 1959,D 10,53:3
Jacobs, Jesse (Costume Designer)
  World of My America, The 1966,O 4,53:1
Jacobs, John (Lyricist)
  Hello Grandpa! 1931,Ja 2,25:3
Jacobs, Joseph
  This Side of Paradise 1962,F 22,19:6
Jacobs, Milton
  Nautical but Nice 1931,Ap 19,31:6
Jacobs, Morris (Producer)
  Avanti 1968,F 1,29:1
Jacobs, Naomi
  Nutmeg Tree 1941,O 19,IX,2:5
Jacobs, Noah (Miscellaneous)
  Take a Giant Step 1956,S 26,30:1
Jacobs, Sally (Costume Designer)
  Persecution and Assassination of Marat As
    Performed by the Inmates of the Asylum of
    Charenton Under the Direction of the Marquis de
    Sade, The 1966,Ja 9,II,1:1
Jacobs, Sally (Director)
  Persecution and Assassination of Marat As
    Performed by the Inmates of the Asylum of
    Charenton Under the Direction of the Marquis de
    Sade, The 1965,D 28,35:1
Jacobs, Sally (Scenic Designer)
  Persecution and Assassination of Marat As
    Performed by the Inmates of the Asylum of
    Charenton Under the Direction of the Marquis de
    Sade, The 1966,Ja 9,II,1:1

Jacobs, Sally (Scenic Designer)—Cont
Midsummer Night's Dream, A 1970,Ag 28,15:1
Midsummer Night's Dream, A 1970,S 13,II,7:1
Jacobs, Steven
Walking Happy 1966,N 28,47:1
Jacobs, Terrell
Circus-Madison Square Garden 1939,Ap 6,23:5
Jacobs, W W (Original Author)
Monkey's Paw, The 1923,My 12,15:4
Sol Hyam's Brocanteur 1923,N 27,23:5
Jacobs, W W (Playwright)
Little Theatre Tournament; Monkey's Paw, The
1929,My 10,32:2
Jacobsen, Ciri
J B 1958,D 12,2:7
Jacobsen, John (Lighting Director)
In 3 Zones 1970,N 3,28:1
Jacobsen, John (Scenic Designer)
Coriolanus 1968,My 26,II,7:1
In 3 Zones 1970,N 3,28:1
Jacobsen, Russell Allen (Miscellaneous)
Kill the One-Eyed Man 1965,O 21,56:1
Jacobson, Arthur
Prunella; Love in a Garden 1926,Je 16,23:3
Twelfth Night 1926,D 21,21:4
Jacobson, Dan (Original Author)
Zulu and the Zayda, The 1965,N 11,59:1
Jacobson, Helen (Miscellaneous)
See the Jaguar 1952,D 4,46:2
Jacobson, Helen (Producer)
Fly Blackbird 1962,F 6,26:2
Abraham Cochrane 1964,F 18,26:1
After the Rain 1967,O 10,54:1
Jacobson, Henrietta
Two Hearts 1935,My 6,22:2
Abi Gezunt 1949,O 10,19:4
Sadie Is a Lady 1950,Ja 28,9:2
It's a Funny World 1956,O 22,24:1
It Could Happen to You 1957,O 28,30:5
Nice People 1958,O 20,36:1
Kosher Widow, The 1959,N 2,40:2
My Son and I 1960,O 24,24:2
Go Fight City Hall 1961,N 3,28:5
Bride Got Farblondjet, The 1967,N 6,61:6
World of Mrs Solomon, The; Another Chance
1969,Je 4,37:1
Jacobson, Henrietta (Choreographer)
My Son and I 1960,O 24,24:2
Go Fight City Hall 1961,N 3,28:5
President's Daughter, The 1970,N 4,41:2
Jacobson, Henrietta (Producer)
Stone for Danny Fisher, A 1954,O 22,24:2
Jacobson, Henrietta (Scenic Designer)
My Son and I 1960,O 24,24:2
Go Fight City Hall 1961,N 3,28:5
Jacobson, Hy (Composer)
Bagels and Yox 1951,S 13,38:2
Jacobson, Hymie
Souls for Sale 1936,S 21,27:6
Of One Mother 1937,Ja 18,21:3
Jacobson, Irving
Golden Ring, The 1930,F 1,14:7
Soul of a Woman, The 1930,F 22,13:1
Twice 100,000 1931,N 22,VIII,3:1
Topsy-Turvy 1939,F 13,12:3
Parnosseh 1939,F 20,12:5
Abi Gezunt 1949,O 10,19:4
Sadie Is a Lady 1950,Ja 28,9:2
Mazel Tov, Molly 1950,O 2,18:1
Take It Easy 1950,D 25,23:6
Second Marriage 1953,O 12,30:1
Wish Me Luck! 1954,N 1,37:2
Wedding March, The 1955,O 17,33:1
It's a Funny World 1956,O 22,24:1
It Could Happen to You 1957,O 28,30:5
Nice People 1958,O 20,36:1
Kosher Widow, The 1959,N 2,40:2
My Son and I 1960,O 24,24:2
Go Fight City Hall 1961,N 3,28:5
Enter Laughing 1963,Mr 15,8:1
Man of La Mancha 1965,N 23,52:1
Man of La Mancha 1967,N 24,61:1
Jacobson, Irving (Producer)
Second Marriage 1953,O 12,30:1
Wish Me Luck! 1954,N 1,37:2
Wedding March, The 1955,O 17,33:1
It's a Funny World 1956,O 22,24:1
It Could Happen to You 1957,O 28,30:5
Nice People 1958,O 20,36:1
Kosher Widow, The 1959,N 2,40:2
Go Fight City Hall 1961,N 3,28:5
Jacobson, Janet
High Button Shoes 1955,Mr 12,10:6
Jacobson, John (Scenic Designer)
Prayer Meeting: or, The First Militant Minister
1969,Ap 27,92:1
Warning, The-A Theme for Linda 1969,Ap 27,92:1
Great Goodness of Life (A Coon Show)
1969,Ap 27,92:1
Gentleman Caller, The 1969,Ap 27,92:1
Black Quartet, A; Prayer Meeting or The First
Militant Minister 1969,Jl 31,28:1
Black Quartet, A; Warning, The-A Theme for
Linda 1969,Jl 31,28:1

Jacobson, Kenneth (Composer)
Judge, The 1958,My 14,36:2
Show Me Where the Good Times Are
1970,Mr 6,32:1
Jacobson, Leonard
Thomas Paine 1930,Mr 21,30:7
Jacobson, Leopold (Lyricist)
Chocolate Soldier, The 1921,D 13,24:2
Jacobson, Leopold (Miscellaneous)
Chocolate Soldier, The 1947,Mr 13,34:2
Jacobson, Leopold (Playwright)
Chocolate Soldier, The 1942,Je 24,22:2
Jacobson, Lou
Goodbye Again 1937,S 1,15:1
Jacobson, Louis
Elizabeth the Queen 1937,Ag 25,24:3
Jacobson, Milton
Merchant of Venice, The 1955,F 23,23:2
Macbeth 1955,O 20,42:2
Midsummer Night's Dream, A 1956,Ja 14,12:2
Romeo and Juliet 1956,F 24,20:4
Twelfth Night 1957,Ja 5,12:2
Jacobson, Oscar
First American Dictator 1939,Mr 15,18:2
Jacobson, Paul (Producer)
What Did We Do Wrong? 1967,O 23,56:1
Jacobson, Rachel
Hair 1970,Ja 13,39:1
Jacobson, Vernon
Rain or Shine 1928,F 10,26:3
Jacobson, William
My Kinsman, Major Molineux 1964,N 2,62:2
Jacobson (Playwright)
Chocolate Soldier, The 1931,S 22,33:3
Chocolate Soldier, The 1934,My 3,15:3
Jacobus, J (Playwright)
Little Angel, The 1924,S 29,10:3
Jacobus, Phil
Ivanov 1958,O 8,42:1
Jacoby, Andree
Ice Follies 1961,Ja 11,25:2
Ice Follies 1962,Ja 10,24:6
Ice Follies 1963,Ja 10,5:2
Jacoby, Coleman (Playwright)
Ziegfeld Follies 1957,Mr 2,19:2
Jacoby, Donald
Ice Follies 1962,Ja 10,24:6
Ice Follies 1963,Ja 10,5:2
Jacoby, Elliot (Composer)
Edna His Wife 1937,D 8,30:3
Hilarities 1948,S 10,20:2
Jacoby, Frank
Bright Boy 1944,Mr 3,19:5
Jacoby, Ronnie
Day Will Come, The 1944,S 8,17:2
Young Man's Fancy, A 1947,Ap 30,33:2
Jacoby, Scott
Golden Rainbow 1968,F 5,27:1
Time of Your Life, The 1969,N 7,37:1
Summertree 1969,D 10,60:1
Cry for Us All 1970,Ap 9,48:2
Jacobys, Donald
Ice Follies 1961,Ja 11,25:2
Jacobys, The
Ice Follies 1960,Ja 13,20:1
Jacons, Benny
Clinton Street 1939,O 13,27:2
Jacoven, Felix (Director)
Village Green 1941,Je 17,24:7
Jacoves, Felix
Garrick Gaieties 1926,My 11,25:2
Centuries, The 1927,N 30,23:1
International, The 1928,Ja 16,24:4
Jacoves, Felix (Director)
Ragged Army 1934,F 27,16:5
Your Young Men 1935,Ag 8,13:2
Let Us Be Gay 1937,Je 29,18:3
Kind Lady 1937,Jl 6,23:1
Naughty-Naught ('00) 1937,Jl 13,22:3
Night of January 16 1937,Jl 20,19:3
Pride and Prejudice 1937,Ag 3,20:5
Idiot's Delight 1937,Ag 10,22:7
Fumed Oak 1937,Ag 24,24:5
Hands Across the Sea 1937,Ag 24,24:5
Still Life 1937,Ag 24,24:5
Two Weeks With Pay 1940,Je 25,28:3
Kind Lady 1940,S 4,28:3
Village Green 1941,S 4,24:4
Jacoves, Felix (Producer)
Village Green 1941,S 4,24:4
Jacquemont, M (Scenic Designer)
Barbier de Seville, Le 1939,Mr 7,19:2
Jacquemont, Maurice
Voyage de Monsieur Perrichon, Le 1937,N 2,32:3
Knock 1937,N 17,26:3
Roi Cerf, Le 1937,N 30,26:3
Jean de la Lune 1937,D 14,33:3
Nationale 6 1938,Ja 11,26:6
Y'Avait un Prisonnier 1938,Ja 25,24:3
Fantasio 1938,F 8,17:2
Bal des Voleurs, Le 1938,N 29,26:4
Precieuses Ridicules, Les 1938,D 13,30:3
Fourberies de Scapin, Les 1938,D 13,30:3

Jacquemont, Maurice—Cont
Faiseur, Le; Promoter, The 1938,D 27,12:3
Occasion, L' 1939,Ja 10,16:4
Paquebot Tenacity, Le 1939,Ja 10,16:4
Chacun Sa Verite 1939,Ja 24,17:1
37 Sous de M Montaudoin, Les 1939,F 7,17:2
Enterrement, L' 1939,F 7,17:2
37 Sous de M Montaudoin, Les 1939,F 7,17:2
Siegfried 1939,F 21,15:2
Barbier de Seville, Le 1939,Mr 7,19:2
Jacquemont, Maurice (Director)
Jalousie du Barbouille, La 1937,D 28,28:7
Jacquemont, Ray
Louisiana Lady 1947,Je 3,35:2
Jacques
Lacune, La 1970,My 6,49:1
Jacques, Annie Laurie
House Beautiful, The 1931,Mr 13,20:4
Jacques, Laurie
Five Star Final 1930,D 31,11:1
Jacques, Le Petit
Topaze 1931,F 17,29:1
Jacques, Nita
Tell Me More 1925,Ap 14,27:3
Ramblers, The 1926,S 21,32:2
Jacques, Ted
See the Jaguar 1952,D 4,46:2
Jacques-Charles (Playwright)
Ca. . . C'Est Paris 1927,F 6,VII,4:1
Jacquet, Frank
Man Who Came to Dinner, The 1940,F 10,19:5
Jacquet, H Maurice (Composer)
Spanish Love 1920,Ag 18,6:1
Silver Swan, The 1929,N 3,IX,1:7
Silver Swan, The 1929,N 28,34:5
Well of Romance, The 1930,N 8,21:2
Jacquillard, Joseph R
Fiesta 1933,D 16,12:2
Jacquin, Robert
Bullfight 1954,Ja 13,25:2
Lovers 1956,My 11,23:1
Jacubowitz, Anna
Going to America 1961,O 30,33:7
Jaeckle, Charles E
Betty Behave 1927,Mr 9,28:4
Jaeger, C P (Producer)
Cup of Trembling, The 1948,Ap 21,33:5
Jaeger, Clarence
Lady Comes Across, The 1942,Ja 10,10:2
This Is the Army 1942,Jl 5,28:2
Jaeger, Hanns Ernst
Schweik in the Second World War 1959,My 23,18:3
Jaffe, Arnold
Paul Bunyan 1941,My 6,25:1
Jaffe, Henry (Producer)
Tea Party 1968,O 16,40:1
Basement, The 1968,O 16,40:1
In the Bar of a Tokyo Hotel 1969,My 12,54:1
Jaffe, Joan
Rich Man, Poor Man 1950,F 13,15:4
Jaffe, Moe (Composer)
Red Rhumba 1936,Ap 14,18:1
Jaffe, Moe (Lyricist)
Night in Venice, A 1929,My 22,30:2
Broadway Nights 1929,Jl 16,23:2
Red Rhumba 1936,Ap 14,18:1
This Mad Whirl 1937,Ja 10,II,4:8
Jaffe, Sam
Samson and Delilah 1920,N 18,18:1
Idle Inn, The 1921,D 21,26:2
God of Vengeance, The 1922,D 20,22:5
Main Line, The 1924,Mr 26,19:4
Izzy 1924,S 17,16:2
Ruint 1925,Ap 8,24:2
Jazz Singer, The 1925,S 15,29:2
Grand Hotel 1930,N 14,30:4
Grand Hotel 1930,N 23,IX,1:1
Divine Drudge 1933,Jl 4,16:4
Bride of Torozko, The 1934,Jl 10,24:7
Bride of Torozko, The 1934,S 14,24:2
Eternal Road, The 1937,Ja 8,14:2
Doll's House, A 1937,Jl 18,II,6:8
Doll's House, A 1937,Jl 25,X,2:3
Doll's House, A 1937,D 28,28:6
Gentle People, The 1939,Ja 6,25:1
Sarah Adler Testimonial 1939,Mr 15,18:2
King Lear 1940,D 16,27:2
King's Maid, The 1941,Ag 27,15:3
Cafe Crown 1942,Ja 24,12:5
Thank You Svoboda 1944,Mr 2,13:2
This Time Tomorrow 1947,N 4,31:2
Mademoiselle Colombe 1954,Ja 7,26:1
Sea Gull, The 1954,My 12,38:1
Saint Joan 1954,S 18,12:1
Adding Machine, The 1956,F 10,17:1
Idiot's Delight 1970,Mr 24,39:1
Jaffee, Charles (Musical Director)
West Side Story 1964,Ap 9,24:2
Jaffin, Nicki
Zaporogetz Za Dunayem 1937,My 9,II,5:3
Jaffrey, Madhur
Shakuntala 1959,S 10,41:2
Brouhaha 1960,Ap 27,31:2
King of the Dark Chamber 1961,F 10,21:1

affrey, Madhur—Cont
Tenth of an Inch Makes the Difference, A 1962,N 13,44:1
Guide, The 1968,Mr 7,50:1
Conduct Unbecoming 1970,O 13,50:1

affrey, Saeed
Passage to India, A 1962,F 1,23:1
Passage to India, A 1962,F 11,II,1:1
Tenth of an Inch Makes the Difference, A 1962,N 13,44:1
Nathan Weinstein, Mystic, Connecticut 1966,F 26,15:2

affry, Joan
Simpleton of the Unexpected Isles, The 1954,Ja 12,19:1

afin, Sylvia
What of It? 1929,Mr 9,24:2

agemann, Walter (Scenic Designer)
George White's Scandals 1935,D 26,20:2
Yokel Boy 1939,Jl 7,12:2
Swingin' the Dream 1939,N 30,24:2

agger, Dean
Tobacco Road 1933,D 5,31:2
They Shall Not Die 1934,F 22,24:4
Missouri Legend 1938,S 20,27:2
Missouri Legend 1938,S 25,IX,1:1
Everywhere I Roam 1938,D 30,10:4
Everywhere I Roam 1939,Ja 8,IX,1:1
Brown Danube, The 1939,My 18,30:4
Farm of Three Echoes 1939,N 29,18:3
Unconquered, The 1940,F 14,25:2
Doctor Social 1948,F 12,29:5

Jaglom, Henry
Uncommon Denominator, The 1963,My 8,35:2

Jaglom, Henry (Director)
Uncommon Denominator, The 1963,My 8,35:2

Jaglom, Henry (Lyricist)
Uncommon Denominator, The 1963,My 8,35:2

Jaglom, Henry (Producer)
Mime Theatre of Etienne Decroux, The 1959,D 24,15:1

Jago, June
Summer of the Seventeenth Doll 1958,Ja 23,23:2
Little Boxes; Coffee Lace, The; Trevor 1968,Jl 5,20:1

Jahn, Daniel (Composer)
Cradle of Willow, A 1961,D 16,20:2

Jahoda, Joan A
Guimpes and Saddles 1967,O 11,36:3

Jaholkowski, Antoni
Constant Prince, The 1969,O 18,36:1
Acropolis 1969,N 5,40:1
Apocalypsis cum Figuris 1969,N 20,60:2

Jahrbeck, Gustav
Bajadere, Die 1925,O 2,26:2
Anneliese von Dessau 1926,F 26,24:3

Jahre, J I (Producer)
Sign in Sidney Brustein's Window, The 1964,O 16,32:1

Jaillet, Lorraine
Would-Be Gentleman, The 1930,Ap 30,29:2
Smiles 1930,N 19,19:2
Saint Wench 1933,Ja 3,19:3

Jaimes, Raymond (Miscellaneous)
Let It Ride 1961,O 13,27:4

Jaine, Ellen
Redemptor, The 1959,My 5,40:1
What Did You Say "What" For? 1959,My 5,40:1

Jakeman, Clint (Miscellaneous)
Awake and Sing! 1970,My 28,35:1
Foreplay 1970,D 11,58:2

Jakobi, Anita
Hold On to Your Hats 1940,S 12,30:3

Jakobi, Muniera
Jack Jack 1968,Je 23,74:5

Jakobowski, E (Composer)
Erminie 1921,Ja 4,11:1

Jakobs, Ned (Producer)
Money Lender, The 1928,Ag 28,27:3
Houseboat on the Styx, The 1928,D 26,14:3
Mimie Scheller 1936,O 1,28:4

Jakovits, Ivan (Miscellaneous)
Wizard of Oz, The 1968,N 28,69:2

Jaks, Leopold (Lyricist)
Chocolate Soldier, The 1930,Ja 28,28:1

Jamerson, Pauline (Playwright)
Feathers in a Gale 1943,D 22,26:2
Oh, Mr Meadowbrook! 1948,D 27,17:2

James, Agnes Hamilton (Playwright)
Straw Hat, The 1926,O 15,20:2

James, Alan
Oscar Wilde 1957,Ap 20,21:3
Marvellous History of Saint Bernard, The 1958,F 24,16:3
Potting Shed, The 1958,N 3,49:2
Susannah and the Elders 1959,O 19,37:3

James, Alan (Director)
Simpleton of the Unexpected Isles, The 1954,Ja 12,19:1

James, Alan (Miscellaneous)
Tobias and the Angel 1957,O 21,29:5

James, Alfred P
Sally 1920,D 22,16:1

Louie the 14th 1925,Mr 4,17:1
Rio Rita 1927,F 3,18:3
Simple Simon 1930,F 19,22:1

James, Alnah
Antigone 1923,My 4,18:4
Antigone 1923,My 25,28:1

James, Aphie
Torch Song 1930,Ag 28,23:1
Great Waltz, The 1934,S 24,14:4

James, Barry
Love for Love 1967,O 21,17:1

James, Bert
Suds in Your Eye 1944,Ja 13,15:5

James, Betty
King and the Duke, The 1955,Je 2,25:2
Cradle Song 1955,D 2,32:2

James, Billy
Devil's Disciple, The 1950,Ja 26,23:2
Four Twelves Are 48 1951,Ja 18,30:2
Male Animal, The 1952,My 1,35:1
Bernardine 1952,O 17,33:4
This Property Is Condemned 1956,O 29,34:1

James, Bob (Composer)
Pantagleize 1967,D 1,54:1
Cock-A-Doodle Dandy 1969,Ja 21,40:1

James, C L R (Playwright)
Toussaint L'Ouverture 1936,Mr 16,21:6

James, Carl
Henry IV, Part I 1946,My 7,25:2

James, Clarence
Achilles Had a Heel 1935,O 14,20:2

James, Cliff (Producer)
Laughwind 1966,Mr 3,27:1

James, Clifton
Time of Your Life, The 1955,Ja 20,34:1
Career 1957,My 1,42:6
Cave Dwellers, The 1957,O 21,29:2
Cave Dwellers, The 1957,O 27,II,1:1
J B 1958,D 12,2:7
Sweet Confession 1959,Ap 15,30:1
All the King's Men 1959,O 17,27:2
All the King's Men 1959,O 25,II,1:1
Long Dream, The 1960,F 18,36:2
Twelfth Night 1960,Je 9,29:4
Tempest, The 1960,Je 20,35:1
Antony and Cleopatra 1960,Ag 1,19:1
All the Way Home 1960,D 1,42:1
Great Day in the Morning 1962,Mr 29,29:1
Man's a Man, A 1962,S 20,30:2
Andorra 1963,F 11,5:5
Burning, The 1963,D 4,57:1
Midsummer Night's Dream, A 1964,Je 30,23:2
And Things That Go Bump in the Night 1965,Ap 27,27:5
Coop, The 1966,Mr 2,48:1
Trial of Lee Harvey Oswald, The 1967,N 6,64:1

James, Curtis
Caribbean Carnival 1947,D 6,12:2

James, Dan
Marching Song 1937,F 18,18:2

James, Dan (Original Author)
Bloomer Girl 1944,O 6,18:5

James, Dan (Playwright)
Winter Soldiers 1942,N 30,19:2

James, Dorothea
Piper, The 1920,Mr 20,14:2
Harry Delmar's Revels 1927,N 29,30:2
Vaudeville (Palace) 1930,Mr 31,24:2
Prince Charming 1930,O 14,31:1
Free for All 1931,S 9,25:1

James, Dorothy
Measure for Measure 1960,Jl 27,33:1

James, Eddie
Ethan Frome 1936,Ja 22,15:2
Foxy 1964,F 17,26:1
Kismet 1965,Je 23,45:1

James, Edna
Pigeon, The 1922,F 3,13:1
East Lynne 1926,Mr 11,18:4
Camille 1932,N 2,23:3
Come of Age 1934,Ja 13,16:6
Trojan Women, The 1941,Ap 9,32:5

James, Edward
Othello 1937,Ja 7,16:4

James, Ellen
Summer and Smoke 1948,O 7,33:2

James, Elmore
Moon on a Rainbow Shawl 1970,D 18,52:1

James, Emrys
Twelfth Night 1969,S 1,13:1
Plebeians Rehearse the Uprising, The 1970,Jl 23,26:1

James, Eric
Mother Courage and Her Children 1964,My 12,32:2

James, Farley J
Teahouse of the August Moon, The 1955,Ag 7,60:3

James, Finlay (Scenic Designer)
Conduct Unbecoming 1970,O 13,50:1

James, Florence
To Tell You the Truth 1948,Ap 19,28:6

James, Frances
Prince Charlie and Flora 1931,Ag 29,16:5

James, Francis
Misanthrope, The 1937,F 24,18:6

James, Frank
Unexpected Husband 1931,Je 3,29:4

James, Frankie
Will Morrissey's Newcomers 1923,Ag 9,16:2
Big Boy 1925,Ja 8,28:2

James, Gardner
Advertising of Kate, The 1922,My 9,22:2

James, Gee Gee
Michael Drops In 1938,D 28,24:3
No Time for Comedy 1939,Ap 18,26:4
Three's a Family 1943,My 6,24:2
Streetcar Named Desire, A 1947,D 4,42:2

James, Georg (Scenic Designer)
Firebugs, The 1963,N 22,41:1
King Lear 1963,N 23,22:1

James, Gerald
Romeo and Juliet 1962,F 14,39:1
Saint Joan 1962,F 21,57:4
Most Unwarrantable Intrusion, A 1968,Jl 9,30:2
Beaux' Stratagem, The 1970,F 10,50:2
Three Sisters, The 1970,F 12,30:1

James, Gilmore
Hitch Your Wagon! 1937,Ap 9,18:2

James, Gladys
Mimic World of 1921, The 1921,Ag 18,9:2

James, Hal
Weep for the Virgins 1935,D 2,18:1

James, Hal (Producer)
Man of La Mancha 1965,N 23,52:1
Hallelujah, Baby! 1967,Ap 27,51:1
Portrait of a Queen 1968,F 29,29:1
Come Summer 1969,Mr 19,43:1

James, Henry (Original Author)
Berkeley Square 1926,O 24,VIII,2:1
Tragic Muse, The 1928,Jl 22,VII,1:3
Berkeley, Square 1929,Mr 24,X,4:5
Berkeley Square 1929,N 5,32:4
Turn of the Screw 1946,O 28,19:2
Heiress, The 1947,S 30,22:2
Heiress, The 1947,O 5,II,1:1
Heiress, The 1949,F 3,26:2
Innocents, The 1950,F 2,30:2
Heiress, The 1950,F 9,34:2
Innocents, The 1950,F 12,II,1:1
Heiress, The 1950,F 12,II,1:1
Innocents, The 1952,Jl 4,9:7
Letter From Paris 1952,O 11,17:8
Letter From Paris 1952,N 9,II,3:1
Portrait of a Lady 1954,D 22,27:6
Child of Fortune 1956,N 14,41:1
Eugenia 1957,Ja 31,20:1
Innocents, The 1959,Ap 21,41:2
Aspern Papers, The 1959,Ag 13,21:5
Aspern Papers, The 1962,F 8,26:1
Aspern Papers, The 1962,F 18,II,1:1
Summer of Daisy Miller, The 1963,My 28,33:1
Wings of the Dove, The 1963,D 4,53:6
Boston Story, A 1968,S 21,26:2

James, Hibbard
An Evening With G B S; Press Cuttings 1957,F 19,35:7

James, Horace
Sonny 1921,Ag 17,12:2
Fan, The 1921,O 4,10:1

James, Ida
New Meet the People, The 1943,Ag 22,II,1:6
Laffing Room Only 1944,D 25,15:4
Memphis Bound 1945,My 25,23:2
How Long Till Summer 1949,D 28,30:3

James, J Campbell
Power of Darkness, The 1948,O 11,28:2

James, Jessie
Boy Friend, The 1932,Je 8,22:3

James, Joe
Porgy and Bess 1965,Mr 6,17:1

James, John
Where Do We Go From Here? 1938,N 16,26:2
Mr Adam 1949,My 26,34:6

James, John M
Queen's Husband, The 1928,Ja 26,17:2
Bottled 1928,Ap 11,25:1
Zeppelin 1929,Ja 15,22:3
Hot Water 1929,Ja 22,22:3
Crime Marches on 1935,O 24,19:1
Chalked Out 1937,Mr 26,24:2

James, Joseph
Porgy and Bess 1935,O 11,30:2
Henry IV, Part I 1946,My 7,25:2
Henry IV, Part II 1946,My 8,33:4
Oedipus; Critic, The 1946,My 21,19:2
Long Way From Home, A 1948,F 9,25:2
Lost in the Stars 1949,O 31,21:2
Regina 1952,Je 2,25:4
Porgy and Bess 1953,Mr 10,25:5
Carmen Jones 1956,Je 1,28:2

James, Ken
Falstaff; Henry IV, Part II 1965,Jl 1,35:1
Julius Caesar 1965,Jl 2,18:1

James, LeRoy
Babes in Arms 1937,Ap 15,18:4

James, Lester
Parade 1960,Ja 21,27:4
That 5 A.M. Jazz 1964,O 20,42:2
James, Lilith (Original Author)
Bloomer Girl 1944,O 6,18:5
James, Luther
Fortunato 1956,Mr 24,15:2
Mary and the Fairy 1956,Mr 24,15:2
James, Luther (Director)
Fortunato 1956,Mr 24,15:2
Mary and the Fairy 1956,Mr 24,15:2
James, Luther (Producer)
Fortunato 1956,Mr 24,15:2
Mary and the Fairy 1956,Mr 24,15:2
James, M (Miscellaneous)
Anything Goes 1962,My 16,35:1
James, Marcia
Sweethearts 1947,Ja 22,31:2
James, Marguerite
Red, Hot and Blue! 1936,O 30,26:3
James, Mary
Apple of His Eye 1946,F 6,18:2
Crime and Punishment 1947,D 23,29:3
Mid-Summer 1953,Ja 22,19:1
Country Wife, The 1955,Ap 6,35:1
Career 1957,My 1,42:6
Career 1957,My 19,II,1:1
John Turner Davis 1958,Jl 2,25:1
Midnight Caller, The 1958,Jl 2,25:1
James, Michael
Jubilee 1935,O 14,20:1
James, Millie
Robert E Lee 1923,N 21,23:1
June Days 1925,Ag 7,12:5
James, Morgan
Dame Nature 1938,S 27,24:3
James, Morgan (Lighting Director)
Buoyant Billions 1959,My 27,32:2
Overruled 1959,My 27,32:2
Getting Married 1959,Je 5,18:2
James, Morgan (Miscellaneous)
River Line, The 1957,Ja 3,29:2
Lady's Not for Burning, The 1957,F 22,26:2
Buoyant Billions 1959,My 27,32:2
Overruled 1959,My 27,32:2
Getting Married 1959,Je 5,18:2
James, Murphy
It's a Bird . . . It's a Plane . . . It's Superman
1966,Mr 30,34:1
James, Nancy
Johnny Summit 1957,S 25,23:4
James, Olga
Mr Wonderful 1956,Mr 23,23:2
Our Town 1968,D 14,62:1
James, Orland
Lightnin' 1938,S 16,17:2
James, Paul (Composer)
Nine Fifteen Revue, The 1930,F 12,26:2
James, Paul (Lyricist)
Nine Fifteen Revue, The 1930,F 12,26:2
Garrick Gaieties 1930,Je 5,29:2
Fine and Dandy 1930,S 24,26:1
James, Paulette
Twelfth Night 1968,Je 15,40:1
Merton of the Movies 1968,S 26,62:1
James, Philip (Composer)
Arms for Venus 1937,Mr 12,18:7
James, Polly
Half a Sixpence 1965,Ap 26,38:2
Anne of Green Gables 1969,Ag 25,41:1
James, Ralph
Paradise 1931,My 12,29:2
James, Ray
Little Mary Sunshine 1959,N 19,49:3
Little Mary Sunshine 1959,N 29,II,1:1
James, Ray (Choreographer)
Ladies Night in a Turkish Bath 1961,Mr 22,38:1
Hobo 1961,Ap 11,41:2
James, Spencer
Mexican Mural; Moonlight Scene 1942,Ap 27,19:2
Mexican Mural; Miracle Painting 1942,Ap 27,19:2
Around the World 1946,Je 1,9:5
Summer and Smoke 1948,O 7,33:2
Red Rainbow, A 1953,S 15,37:4
James, Stanley
Babies a La Carte 1927,Ag 16,31:1
James, T Jr (Playwright)
That Thing at the Cherry Lane 1965,My 19,42:1
James, Vanessa (Costume Designer)
Whistle in the Dark, A 1969,O 9,55:1
James, Vincent
Ladies of the Jury 1929,O 22,26:2
James, Vonnie
Caroline 1923,F 1,13:2
James, Walter
Monster, The 1922,Ag 10,20:3
Faustina 1952,My 26,19:5
Angelic Doctor 1953,Ap 14,30:2
Grass Harp, The 1953,Ap 28,32:2
Susannah 1955,F 25,18:4
James, William
My Fair Lady 1968,Je 14,42:1
Maggie Flynn 1968,O 24,52:1

James, William S
Live and Learn 1930,Ap 10,24:6
James-Moore, Jonathan
Midsummer Night's Dream, A 1968,D 9,59:1
Twelfth Night 1970,Ja 1,18:1
Hamlet 1970,D 28,40:1
Jameson, Frank
Devils 1926,Mr 18,26:4
Jameson, House
Taming of the Shrew, The 1925,D 19,14:1
Goat Song 1926,Ja 26,18:1
Chief Thing, The 1926,Mr 23,24:2
American Tragedy, An 1926,O 12,31:2
Dark Hours, The 1932,N 15,24:2
We the People 1933,Ja 23,9:5
Judgment Day 1934,S 13,26:4
In Time to Come 1941,D 29,20:2
Patriots, The 1943,Ja 30,11:2
Patriots, The 1943,F 7,II,1:1
Requiem for a Nun 1959,Ja 31,13:2
Never Too Late 1962,N 28,42:1
Great Indoors, The 1966,F 2,23:1
Don't Drink the Water 1966,N 18,37:1
Jameson, James (Miscellaneous)
Brigadoon 1963,F 1,6:2
Jameson, Jo Anne
Kicking the Castle Down 1967,Ja 19,43:1
Jameson, Joyce
Billy Barnes Revue, The 1959,Je 10,42:2
Billy Barnes People, The 1961,Je 14,10:3
Venus at Large 1962,Ap 13,30:1
Jameson, Lois
Romeo and Juliet 1934,D 21,30:3
This Is Today 1935,Jl 30,17:2
Romeo and Juliet 1935,D 24,10:2
Wingless Victory, The 1936,D 24,20:2
Black Eye, The 1938,Mr 8,22:4
Family Portrait 1939,Mr 9,18:4
Jameson, Pauline
Merry Wives of Windsor, The 1956,Je 21,34:4
King Lear 1964,My 19,43:2
Comedy of Errors, The 1964,My 21,43:1
Jameson, Ralph
Eternal Road, The 1937,Ja 8,14:2
Jameson, Storm (Original Author)
Hidden River, The 1957,Ja 24,32:1
Hidden River, The 1959,Ap 14,41:2
Jamiaque, Yves (Original Author)
Murderer Among Us, A 1964,Mr 26,43:1
Jamieson, Henry
Sign of the Leopard 1928,D 12,34:4
Jamieson, Isabel
Little Theatre Tournament; Old Lady Shows Her
Medals, The 1928,My 11,28:1
Jamieson, James
Brigadoon 1950,My 3,36:2
Jamieson, James (Miscellaneous)
Brigadoon 1957,Mr 28,37:1
Brigadoon 1962,My 31,21:4
Brigadoon 1964,D 24,9:1
Jamieson, Marsha (Scenic Designer)
Merry Wives of Windsor, The 1956,Je 21,34:4
Jamieson, Raymond (Translator)
Pelican, The 1929,N 14,25:1
Jamison, Frank E
Pot-Luck 1921,S 30,10:1
Jeweled Tree, The 1926,O 8,26:2
War 1929,S 19,37:3
Jamison, Marshall
Cure for Matrimony 1939,O 26,26:3
Naughty-Naught '00 1946,O 21,27:5
Mister Roberts 1948,F 19,27:2
Jamison, Marshall (Director)
On Borrowed Time 1953,F 11,34:1
Kind Sir 1953,N 5,41:2
By the Beautiful Sea 1954,Ap 9,20:1
By the Beautiful Sea 1954,Ap 18,II,1:1
Young and Beautiful, The 1955,O 3,23:2
Jamison, Marshall (Miscellaneous)
Kind Sir 1953,N 5,41:2
Jamison, Priscilla
Cure for Matrimony 1939,O 26,26:3
Steel 1939,D 20,30:2
Jamison, Seymour
Sweet Nell of Old Drury 1923,My 19,16:4
Jamois, Marguerite
Amour Magicien, L' 1926,D 26,VII,2:1
Dybbuk, The 1928,F 26,VIII,4:1
Departs 1928,D 23,VIII,2:1
Karl und Anna 1929,My 5,IX,2:4
Bifur 1932,F 28,VIII,1:1
Prosper 1935,Ja 13,IX,2:1
Madame Bovary 1936,N 8,X,3:6
Britannicus 1958,N 29,17:2
Jampolis, Neil Peter (Lighting Director)
Displaced Person, The 1966,D 30,15:1
Not a Way of Life 1967,Mr 23,28:1
Tea Party 1968,O 16,40:1
Basement, The 1968,O 16,40:1
People vs Ranchman, The 1968,O 28,56:1
Little Murders 1969,Ja 6,38:1
In the Bar of a Tokyo Hotel 1969,My 12,54:1
Arf 1969,My 28,36:1

Jampolis, Neil Peter (Lighting Director)—Cont
Great Airplane Snatch, The 1969,My 28,36:1
Rondelay 1969,N 6,55:1
Show Me Where the Good Times Are
1970,Mr 6,32:1
Borstal Boy 1970,Ap 1,38:1
Blancs, Les 1970,N 16,48:4
Jampolis, Neil Peter (Scenic Designer)
War Games 1969,Ap 18,37:1
In the Bar of a Tokyo Hotel 1969,My 12,54:1
Borstal Boy 1970,Ap 1,38:1
Jamrog, Joe
Nobody Hears A Broken Drum 1970,Mr 20,55:1
Jan (Costume Designer)
Fortune and Men's Eyes 1967,F 24,29:1
Jana
Ice Capades 1967,Je 2,33:1
Janaver, Richard
Hamlet 1938,O 13,28:1
Henry IV, Part I 1939,Ja 31,17:2
Janaver, Richard (Miscellaneous)
Machinal 1960,Ap 8,27:1
Jane, Marjorie
Family Upstairs, The 1933,O 28,20:6
Jane, Mary
Jimmie 1920,N 18,15:3
City Chap, The 1925,O 27,21:1
Merry Malones, The 1927,S 27,30:2
Whoopee 1928,D 5,34:3
Sign of the Leopard 1928,D 12,34:4
Jane, Sara
Laugh Parade, The 1931,S 20,VIII,3:1
Laugh Parade, The 1931,N 3,31:2
Take a Chance 1932,N 28,11:2
Janes, Billy
Corn Is Green, The 1950,Ja 12,33:2
Janet Sisters
Broadway Whirl, The 1921,Je 9,10:4
Janezic, Barbara
Crystal Heart, The 1960,F 16,31:2
Jani, Bob (Producer)
Disney on Parade 1970,S 24,63:1
Janice, Dorothy
Passing Show of 1924, The 1924,S 4,13:4
Janice, Kaye
Dear Judas 1947,O 6,26:4
Janick and Arnaut
Arabian Nights 1954,Je 25,15:2
Arabian Nights 1955,Je 24,16:1
Janik, Nina
Carnival! 1968,D 13,58:1
Janis, Beverly
Mikado, The 1949,O 5,35:2
Pirates of Penzance, The 1949,O 11,41:2
H M S Pinafore 1949,O 18,34:2
Janis, Conrad
Dark of the Moon 1945,Mr 15,27:2
Next Half Hour, The 1945,O 30,14:6
Next Half Hour, The 1945,N 4,II,1:1
Brass Ring, The 1952,Ap 11,19:2
Time Out for Ginger 1952,N 27,50:4
Terrible Swift Sword, The 1955,N 16,42:1
Visit to a Small Planet 1957,F 8,18:1
Make a Million 1958,O 24,39:2
Sunday in New York 1961,N 10,40:1
Marathon '33 1963,D 23,20:1
Front Page, The 1969,My 12,54:2
Front Page, The 1969,My 25,II,1:1
Front Page, The 1969,N 2,86:1
Janis, Ed and Girls
Vaudeville (Palace) 1926,S 7,24:6
Janis, Elsie
Elsie Janis and Her Gang 1922,Ja 17,13:2
Puzzles of 1925 1925,F 3,25:3
Vaudeville (Palace) 1925,D 29,21:2
Vaudeville (Hippodrome) 1926,Mr 23,24:3
Vaudeville (Hippodrome) 1926,Mr 30,20:4
Vaudeville (Palace) 1927,Mr 22,31:1
Vaudeville (Palace) 1927,Mr 29,22:6
Vaudeville (Palace) 1927,My 17,27:4
Vaudeville (Palace) 1927,Je 7,27:3
Vaudeville (Palace) 1928,Ja 3,29:3
Vaudeville (Palace) 1928,Ja 10,28:5
Untitled-Revue 1929,F 24,IX,1:8
????? 1939,Ja 2,28:2
Frank Fay's Vaudeville 1939,Mr 3,20:4
Janis, Elsie (Director)
New Faces 1934,Mr 16,24:5
Janis, Elsie (Miscellaneous)
New Faces 1934,Ap 1,X,1:1
Janis, Elsie (Playwright)
Elsie Janis and Her Gang 1922,Ja 17,13:2
Janis, Vivian
Vaudeville (Palace) 1932,Je 6,18:2
Ziegfeld Follies 1934,Ja 5,24:3
Janisch, Michael
Professor Bernhardi 1968,Mr 20,38:1
Jux Will Er Sich Machen, Einen 1968,Ap 3,41:1
Janiss, Vivi
Miracle in the Mountains 1947,Ap 26,10:2
Jankelowitz, Marion
Mascaiada 1929,D 28,10:6
Jankuhn, Walter
Merry Widow, The 1929,F 17,IX,2:3

Jannett, James
Idiot's Delight 1957,F 23,14:2
Jannette, Gertrude
Moon on a Rainbow Shawl 1962,Ja 16,30:1
Janney, Ben
Julius Caesar 1955,Jl 13,20:1
Affair of Honor 1956,Ap 7,12:3
Janney, Ben (Director)
Sponono 1964,Ap 3,28:1
Janney, Ben (Miscellaneous)
Irma la Douce 1960,S 30,31:2
Giants, Sons of Giants 1962,Ja 8,26:2
Photo Finish 1963,F 14,5:2
Irregular Verb to Love, The 1963,S 19,22:2
And Things That Go Bump in the Night
  1965,Ap 27,27:5
Love in E Flat 1967,F 14,38:1
After the Rain 1967,O 10,54:1
Joe Egg 1968,F 2,26:1
Flip Side, The 1968,O 11,36:1
Hadrian VII 1969,Ja 9,22:1
Gantry 1970,F 16,44:1
Not Now Darling 1970,O 30,33:1
Janney, Billy
Merton of the Movies 1922,N 14,16:2
Janney, Leon
Vaudeville (Palace) 1932,Jl 11,11:6
Every Thursday 1934,My 11,25:5
Simpleton of the Unexpected Isles, The
  1935,F 19,27:5
Parade 1935,My 21,22:2
Ah, Wilderness! 1935,Ag 20,25:1
Jazz Age 1937,Jl 20,19:3
Bough Breaks, The 1937,N 20,21:4
Foreigners 1939,D 6,30:2
Ghost for Sale 1941,S 30,27:4
Days of Our Youth, The 1941,N 29,15:2
Lamp at Midnight 1947,D 22,29:2
Victors, The 1948,D 27,17:2
School for Scandal, The 1953,Je 24,29:2
Madam Will You Walk 1953,D 2,2:4
Madam Will You Walk 1953,D 20,II,3:1
Flowering Peach, The 1954,D 29,19:2
Flowering Peach, The 1955,Ja 9,II,1:1
Threepenny Opera, The 1956,Mr 11,II,1:1
Measure for Measure 1957,Ja 23,24:1
Country Wife, The 1957,Je 27,22:1
Shadow of My Enemy, A 1957,D 12,35:4
Gazebo, The 1958,D 13,2:7
Summer of the Seventeenth Doll 1959,O 14,52:1
Call on Kuprin, A 1961,My 26,29:3
Policemen, The 1961,N 22,24:2
Venus at Large 1962,Ap 13,30:1
Nobody Loves an Albatross 1963,D 20,20:1
Nobody Loves an Albatross 1964,Ja 5,II,1:1
Last Analysis, The 1964,O 2,30:1
Kelly 1965,F 8,28:2
Three Men on a Horse 1969,O 17,35:1
Janney, Russell (Lyricist)
O'Flynn, The 1934,D 28,24:1
Vagabond King, The 1943,Je 30,24:2
Janney, Russell (Playwright)
O'Flynn, The 1934,D 28,24:1
Vagabond King, The 1943,Je 30,24:2
Janney, Russell (Producer)
Vagabond King, The 1925,S 22,23:3
Ballyhoo 1927,Ja 5,18:1
White Eagle, The 1927,D 27,24:4
O'Flynn, The 1934,D 28,24:1
Vagabond King, The 1943,Je 30,24:2
Janney, Sam
Lights Out 1922,Ag 18,8:4
Ever Green Lady, The 1922,O 12,25:2
Deep Tangled Wildwood, The 1923,N 6,22:1
Janney, Sam (Playwright)
Loose Ankles 1926,Ag 17,15:1
Loose Ankles 1926,Ag 29,VII,1:1
Very Wise Virgin, A 1927,Je 3,25:3
Monkey 1932,F 12,25:2
Janney, Sam (Producer)
Very Wise Virgin, A 1927,Je 3,25:3
Janney, William
Great Music 1924,O 6,24:1
Bridge of Distances, The 1925,S 29,30:1
Tommy 1927,Ja 11,36:4
Take My Tip 1932,Ap 12,25:2
Four O'Clock 1933,F 14,19:6
Ah, Wilderness! 1934,My 1,26:3
Never Trouble Trouble 1937,Ag 18,15:2
Jannings, Emil
Minister-Praesident, Der 1936,Je 28,IX,2:1
Jannings, Orin
Circle of Chalk, The 1941,Mr 27,28:4
Winter Soldiers 1942,N 30,19:2
Counterattack 1943,F 4,27:2
Innocent Voyage, The 1943,N 16,27:2
Jannings, Orin (Miscellaneous)
Men to the Sea 1944,O 4,25:2
Jannings, Orin (Playwright)
Hear That Trumpet 1946,O 8,19:2
Jans, Harry
Luana 1930,S 18,28:1

Jans and Whalen
Padlocks of 1927 1927,Jl 6,23:4
Greenwich Village Follies 1928,Ap 10,32:2
Vaudeville (Palace) 1929,S 9,30:5
International Revue 1930,F 26,22:2
Vaudeville (Palace) 1931,Je 29,20:1
Friars Club Frolic 1933,My 15,16:4
Jansen, Neil (Playwright)
Fun Couple, The 1962,O 27,15:2
Jansleys, The
Ziegfeld Follies 1943,Ap 2,16:2
Janssen, Bernard
Red, Hot and Blue! 1936,O 30,26:3
Janssen, Walter
Constant Nymph, The 1927,Ap 24,VII,2:1
Janssen, Werner
Follies 1925,Mr 11,19:2
Janssen, Werner (Composer)
Love Dreams 1921,O 11,22:2
Letty Pepper 1922,Ap 11,22:2
Lady Butterfly 1923,Ja 23,18:1
Nic-Nax of 1926 1926,Ag 5,19:1
Sam Abramovitch 1927,Ja 20,20:5
Boom Boom 1929,Ja 29,26:4
Janssen, Werner (Miscellaneous)
Neighborhood Playhouse Program 1930,F 21,23:1
Janszen, Jack
Little Theatre Tournament; Yellow Triangle, The
  1929,My 10,32:2
January, Lois
Yokel Boy 1939,Jl 7,12:2
High Kickers 1941,N 1,21:2
Janus, Lester
Paradise Island 1961,Je 24,11:1
Janus, Stanley
Paradise Island 1961,Je 24,11:1
Janusz, Tom (Musical Director)
Exchange 1970,F 9,47:2
Me and Juliet 1970,My 15,42:1
Janvier, Emma
Two Little Girls in Blue 1921,My 4,10:3
Molly Darling 1922,S 2,10:2
Poppy 1923,S 4,14:2
Janvier, Janie
I Feel Wonderful 1954,O 19,22:5
Damn Yankees 1955,My 6,17:1
Jaowez, Lisa (Scenic Designer)
Drifting Apart: or, The Fisherman's Child
  1941,Ag 20,16:6
Japley, Rose
Zombie 1932,F 11,17:2
Jaques, Annie-Laurie
Charm 1929,N 29,24:5
Penny Arcade 1930,Mr 11,24:5
Jaquet, Frank
When in Rome 1934,F 28,22:6
Alley Cat 1934,S 18,18:1
Ladies' Money 1934,N 2,26:6
Battleship Gertie 1935,Ja 19,9:2
Potash and Perlmutter 1935,Ap 6,11:3
Then Came the Dawn 1935,Ag 29,25:4
Mulatto 1935,O 25,25:2
Iron Men 1936,O 20,30:6
Chalked Out 1937,Mr 26,24:2
Red Mill, The 1945,O 17,16:2
Jara, Victor (Composer)
Remolienda, La; Bawdy Party 1968,F 3,20:1
Jara, Victor (Director)
Remolienda, La; Bawdy Party 1968,F 3,20:1
Jarahal
Kilpatrick's Old-Time Minstrels 1930,Ap 21,20:2
Hot Rhythm 1930,Ag 22,18:5
Yeah-Man 1932,My 27,27:3
Jaray, Hans
Great Love, The 1935,D 24,11:5
Another Sun 1940,F 24,8:6
Jarbeau, Maryland
Noose, The 1926,O 21,23:3
Bachelor Father, The 1928,F 29,28:2
Jardine, Betty
Night Must Fall 1936,S 29,34:1
Jardinere, Pearl
Ladies' Night 1920,Ag 10,10:1
Jardon, Dorothy
Vaudeville (Hippodrome) 1924,Ap 29,12:2
Jarecki, Marjorie
Take My Tip 1932,Ap 12,25:2
I Loved You Wednesday 1932,O 12,27:1
Sophisticrats, The 1933,F 14,19:5
Enemy of the People, An 1937,F 16,19:1
Jarkowsky, Andrew
Javelin 1966,N 10,63:1
Jarlot, Gerard (Playwright)
Miracle Worker, The 1961,O 8,II,3:4
Jarman, John J Jr
Hippolytus 1935,Je 15,20:4
Jarman, Reginald
Hamlet 1931,Ap 24,26:4
John Bull's Other Island 1948,F 11,33:4
Old Lady Says No, The 1948,F 18,35:1
Abdication 1948,S 28,32:5
Jarmann, Sunshine
Hassard Short's Ritz Revue 1924,S 18,19:1

Jarmann, Sunshine—Cont
Artists and Models 1925,Je 25,16:2
Americana 1926,Jl 27,15:3
Jarnac, Dorothy
Heaven on Earth 1948,S 17,29:2
Tickets, Please! 1950,Ap 28,25:2
Tickets, Please! 1950,My 7,II,1:1
Littlest Revue, The 1956,My 23,37:2
Jarnach, Wolfgang
Before Sundown 1962,Mr 14,43:1
Jarnigan, Jerry
Vaudeville (Palace) 1925,O 6,31:3
Vaudeville (Palace) 1926,My 8,29:2
Sweet Adeline 1929,S 4,33:1
Vaudeville (Palace) 1930,Mr 7,21:2
Jaroff, J
Blue Bird, The 1932,Ap 22,23:2
Jaroslow, Ruth
Cage, The 1961,Mr 6,30:1
Women at the Tomb, The 1961,Ap 25,41:1
That 5 A.M. Jazz 1964,O 20,42:2
Jonah! 1966,F 16,52:1
Jarratt, Howard
My Darlin' Aida 1952,O 28,36:4
Jarre, Maurice (Composer)
Lorenzaccio 1958,O 15,44:2
Triomphe de l'Amour, Le 1958,O 17,32:1
Marie Tudor 1958,O 22,39:1
Don Juan 1958,O 29,29:1
Jarrel, Stig
Autumn Manoeuvers 1938,N 27,IX,3:6
Jarrell, Randall (Playwright)
Three Sisters, The 1964,Je 23,24:1
Jarrell, Randall (Translator)
Three Sisters, The 1964,Jl 5,II,1:1
Jarrett, Arthur
K Guy, The 1928,O 16,28:4
Keeping Expenses Down 1932,O 21,25:2
Three After Three 1939,N 25,13:5
Walk With Music 1940,Je 5,33:2
Gentleman From Athens, The 1947,D 10,42:4
All the King's Men 1950,Jl 19,25:6
Shrike, The 1952,Ja 16,20:2
Madam Will You Walk 1953,D 2,2:4
Time of Your Life, The 1955,Ja 20,34:1
Time of Your Life, The 1955,Ja 30,II,1:1
Jarrett, Arthur (Playwright)
My Fair Ladies 1941,Mr 24,12:7
Jarrett, Bella
Cicero 1961,F 9,37:2
Devils, The 1963,N 5,25:1
Pequod 1969,Je 30,33:1
Jarrett, Dan
Riddle Me This! 1932,F 26,22:5
Jarrett, Dan (Director)
London Calling 1930,O 20,29:1
Keeping Expenses Down 1932,O 21,25:2
Big Hearted Herbert 1934,Ja 2,17:3
Jarrett, Dan (Playwright)
Salt Water 1929,N 27,30:3
Keeping Expenses Down 1932,O 21,25:2
Jarrett, Dorothy
Lovely Lady 1927,D 30,22:1
Jarrett, Jan
Clearing in the Woods, A 1959,F 13,32:1
Jarrett, Jerry
At War With the Army 1949,Mr 9,32:2
Me, Candido! 1956,O 16,36:2
That 5 A.M. Jazz 1964,O 20,42:2
Fiddler on the Roof 1969,Je 26,47:1
Jarrett, Renne
Loud Red Patrick, The 1956,O 4,28:1
Rope Dancers, The 1959,Mr 14,26:1
Giants, Sons of Giants 1962,Ja 8,26:2
Jarrett, Stephen (Miscellaneous)
Line of Least Existence, The 1968,Mr 25,53:1
In Circles 1968,Je 28,36:1
Ordinary Man, An 1968,S 10,39:1
Conerico Was Here to Stay 1969,Mr 11,39:1
Paradise Gardens East 1969,Mr 11,39:1
Rose 1969,O 29,30:1
Jarry, Alfred (Playwright)
Ubu Roi 1968,Je 29,20:1
Ubu Roi 1968,Jl 14,II,1:1
Ubu Roi 1970,F 17,33:1
Jarry, Philippe
On Ne Badine Pas Avec l'Amour; No Trifling With
  Love 1968,Mr 5,35:1
Jarvis, Bill
Hamlet 1969,My 2,38:1
Jarvis, Bud (Miscellaneous)
Harold Arlen Songbook, The 1967,Mr 1,48:1
Jarvis, Frank
Merry World, The 1926,Je 9,18:3
Jarvis, Fred
Boo Hoo! East Lynne 1959,S 9,50:4
Jarvis, Fred (Director)
Boo Hoo! East Lynne 1959,S 9,50:4
Jarvis, Fred (Playwright)
Boo Hoo! East Lynne 1959,S 9,50:4
Jarvis, Graham
Egghead, The 1957,O 10,39:1
Best Man, The 1960,Ap 1,39:1
Cherry Orchard, The 1960,Je 4,17:2

Jarvis, Graham—Cont
Hi, Paisano 1961,O 2,36:2
Romulus 1962,Ja 11,27:1
Marco Millions 1964,F 21,33:1
Incident at Vichy 1964,D 4,44:1
Arms and the Man 1965,Je 24,32:5
Investigation, The 1966,O 5,40:1
Halfway up the Tree 1967,N 8,52:1
Adaptation 1969,F 11,27:1

Jarvis, John (Playwright)
Vacant Possession 1933,O 22,IX,2:2

Jarvis, Lilian
Soldier's Tale, A 1955,Jl 13,21:2

Jarvis, Louise
Early to Bed 1943,Je 18,16:2
Allah Be Praised! 1944,Ap 21,14:2
Good Night Ladies 1945,Ja 18,16:2

Jarvis, Robert C (Director)
Carmen Jones 1951,S 22,8:6
Allegro 1952,S 18,36:3

Jarvis, Scott
Here's Where I Belong 1968,Mr 4,32:1
1776 1969,Mr 17,46:2

Jaschke, Arthur
Before Sundown 1962,Mr 14,43:1

Jason, Astrid
Town's Woman, The 1929,Mr 12,26:2

Jason, Harvey
Cicero 1961,F 9,37:2
Saving Grace, The 1963,Ap 19,28:1
Hostile Witness 1966,F 18,26:1

Jason, Larry
Fifty Million Frenchmen 1929,N 28,34:4

Jason, Mitchell
House Remembered, A 1957,F 7,20:2
Androcles and the Lion 1958,F 22,8:3
On the Town 1959,Ja 16,36:1
On the Town 1959,Ja 25,II,1:1
Gideon 1961,N 10,38:1
Seidman and Son 1962,O 16,32:2
Fade Out--Fade In 1964,My 27,45:1
View From the Bridge, A 1965,Ja 29,24:1
Darling of the Day 1968,Ja 29,26:2
License, The 1969,Ap 23,42:1
Jar, The 1969,Ap 23,42:1
Show Me Where the Good Times Are
    1970,Mr 6,32:1
Steambath 1970,Jl 1,49:1

Jason, Mitchell (Director)
Hamlet 1956,O 29,34:1

Jason, Rick
Now I Lay Me Down to Sleep 1950,Mr 3,21:2

Jasono, Mitchell
Telemachus Clay 1963,N 16,17:2

Jasper, Zina
Saturday Night 1968,F 26,43:1
Moondreamers, The 1969,D 9,68:1
Paris Is Out! 1970,F 3,35:1
Dream Out of Time, A 1970,N 9,52:1

Javits, Joan (Lyricist)
Young Abe Lincoln 1961,Ap 26,36:1
Hotel Passionato 1965,O 23,16:1

Javits, Marion (Producer)
Hang Down Your Head and Die 1964,O 19,38:1

Javne, Haidee
Kreutzer Sonata, The 1924,My 15,22:3

Jaxson, Frankie
Policy Kings 1938,D 31,6:2

Jay, Bill
Daddy Goodness 1968,Je 5,37:1

Jay, Ernest
Good Companions, The 1931,O 2,31:1
Amazing Dr. Clitterhouse, The 1937,Mr 3,26:4
Gentle People, The 1939,Jl 30,IX,1:3
Daphne Laureola 1950,S 19,38:6

Jay, Lester
Dead End 1936,S 20,IX,3:7

Jay, Leticia (Miscellaneous)
Hoofers, The 1969,Jl 30,23:4

Jay, Stanley
Hamlet 1948,D 4,9:2
Othello 1955,S 8,27:2
Henry IV, Part I 1955,S 22,34:2
Country Wife, The 1957,Je 27,22:1
Fashion 1959,Ja 21,27:1

Jay, William
Song of the Lusitanian Bogey, The 1968,Ja 3,52:1
Summer of the Seventeenth Doll 1968,F 21,59:1
Kongi's Harvest 1968,Ap 15,49:1
God Is a (Guess What?) 1968,D 18,56:1
Ceremonies in Dark Old Men 1969,F 6,33:1
Man Better Man 1969,Jl 3,22:1
Harangues, The 1970,Ja 14,42:1
Day of Absence 1970,Mr 18,39:1
Brotherhood 1970,Mr 18,39:1

Jay, William (Playwright)
Golden Wings 1941,N 25,33:3
Golden Wings 1941,D 9,46:6

Jay and Lucille
Revels of 1936 1935,S 30,12:4

Jaye, Angela
Round Trip 1945,My 30,16:4

Jaye, L Errol
Who's Got His Own 1966,O 13,52:1
Great White Hope, The 1967,D 14,58:1
Clara's Ole Man 1968,Mr 9,23:2
Electronic Nigger, The 1968,Mr 9,23:2
Prayer Meeting: or, The First Militant Minister
    1969,Ap 27,92:1
Warning, The-A Theme for Linda 1969,Ap 27,92:1
Great Goodness of Life (A Coon Show)
    1969,Ap 27,92:1
Great Goodness of Life (A Coon Show)
    1969,My 4,II,1:5
Black Quartet, A; Warning, The-A Theme for
    Linda 1969,Jl 31,28:1
Black Quartet, A; Great Goodness of Life (A Coon
    Show) 1969,Jl 31,28:1
Black Quartet, A; Prayer Meeting or The First
    Militant Minister 1969,Jl 31,28:1
Five on the Black Hand Side 1970,Ja 2,32:2
Moon on a Rainbow Shawl 1970,D 18,52:1

Jayne, Dwight
Touch 1970,N 9,52:1

Jayne, Estelle
Kidding Kidders 1928,Ap 24,28:3
George White's Scandals 1935,D 26,20:2

Jayne, Horace H F (Lyricist)
Wetward Ho 1921,Ap 22,13:2

Jayne Sisters
Greenwich Villagers, The 1927,Ag 19,20:2

Jayson, Vernon
Face the Music 1932,F 18,24:5

Jeakins, Dorothy (Costume Designer)
King Lear 1950,D 26,18:1
King Lear 1950,D 31,II,1:1
Taming of the Shrew, The 1956,Ag 6,20:1
Too Late the Phalarope 1956,O 12,35:1
Major Barbara 1956,O 31,27:1
Taming of the Shrew, The 1957,F 21,30:2
Winesburg, Ohio 1958,F 6,22:2
Winter's Tale, The 1958,Jl 21,17:4
Winter's Tale, The 1958,Jl 27,II,1:1
World of Suzie Wong, The 1958,O 15,47:1
Cue for Passion 1958,N 26,25:2
Romeo and Juliet 1959,Je 15,31:1
All's Well That Ends Well 1959,Ag 3,20:4
Taste of Honey, A 1960,O 5,46:1
My Mother, My Father and Me 1963,Mr 25,5:5

Jean, Albert (Playwright)
Je Serai Seule Apres Minuit 1927,O 23,VIII,2:2

Jean, Martha
Young American, A 1946,Ja 18,14:5

Jeane, Ira
Natja 1925,F 17,19:2

Jeanette, Gertrude
417 1961,Mr 6,30:1

Jeanmaire, Zizi
Girl in Pink Tights, The 1954,Mr 6,13:2
Zizi 1964,N 23,51:1

Jeanmarie, Redvera
Street Sounds 1970,O 23,32:1

Jeanne and Gower
Streets of Paris, The 1939,Je 20,25:2

Jeannette, Gertrude
Lost in the Stars 1949,O 31,21:2
Long Dream, The 1960,F 18,36:2
Deep Are the Roots 1960,O 4,47:1
Nobody Loves an Albatross 1963,D 20,20:1
Nobody Loves an Albatross 1964,Ja 5,II,1:1
Amen Corner, The 1965,Ap 16,35:1
To Be Young Gifted and Black; World of Lorraine
    Hansberry, The 1969,Ja 3,15:1

Jeannotte, Jean-Paul
Malade Imaginaire, Le; Imaginary Invalid, The
    1958,Ap 30,28:2
Mariage Force, Le; Forced Wedding, The
    1958,My 7,43:1

Jeans, Desmond
Bitter Sweet 1929,O 27,IX,2:1
Bitter Sweet 1929,N 6,30:2

Jeans, Isabel
Cobra 1925,Ag 23,VII,1:8
Road to Rome, The 1928,Je 10,VIII,1:3
Garey Divorce Case, The 1929,My 12,IX,2:3
Man in Possession, The 1930,F 9,VIII,2:1
Man in Possession, The 1930,O 12,VIII,4:1
Man in Possession, The 1930,N 3,19:1
Counsel's Opinion 1931,S 13,IX,2:5
Spring, 1600 1934,F 1,14:1
Full House 1935,Ag 22,20:3
Full House 1935,S 22,X,3:3
Happy Hypocrite, The 1936,Ap 9,21:6
Make Way for Lucia 1948,D 23,23:5
Importance of Being Earnest, The 1968,Jl 6,9:1

Jeans, Jean
Young and Beautiful, The 1955,O 3,23:2

Jeans, Ronald (Lyricist)
Garrick Gaieties 1930,Je 5,29:2

Jeans, Ronald (Miscellaneous)
Earl Carroll's Vanities 1927,Ja 5,18:1

Jeans, Ronald (Playwright)
By the Way 1925,D 29,20:3
Earl Carroll's Vanities 1927,Ja 5,18:1

Jeans, Ronald (Playwright)—Cont
Lean Harvest 1931,My 8,20:2
Lean Harvest 1931,O 4,VIII,2:2
Lean Harvest 1931,O 14,26:3
Can the Leopard...? 1932,Ja 3,VIII,2:1
Streamline 1934,S 29,13:1
Streamline 1934,O 21,IX,1:3
Composite Man, The 1936,S 9,32:2
Composite Man, The 1936,S 27,X,3:5
Ghost for Sale 1941,S 30,27:4

Jeans, Ursula
Second Man, The 1928,F 12,VIII,2:1
Play's the Thing, The 1928,D 23,VIII,4:7
Grand Hotel 1931,S 4,22:7
Grand Hotel 1931,S 27,VIII,1:4
Late One Evening 1933,Ja 10,27:3
Short Story 1935,D 1,XI,5:3
Children's Hour, The 1936,N 29,XII,2:1
They Came by Night 1937,O 25,X,1:3
Cocktail Party, The 1949,Ag 23,28:6
Twelfth Night 1950,D 3,II,3:1
Escapade 1953,N 19,40:1
Escapade 1953,N 29,II,1:1

Jeanson, Henri (Playwright)
Amis Comme Avant 1930,Ja 26,VIII,2:1

Jeaves, Allan
Spook Sonata, The 1927,Jl 10,VII,2:3
Letter, The 1927,S 27,30:1

Jebob
Porgy and Bess 1953,Mr 10,25:5

Jedd, Gerry
Midsummer Night's Dream, A 1950,Je 22,33:2
Come of Age 1952,Ja 24,22:2
Wise Have Not Spoken, The 1954,F 11,35:2
Macbeth 1955,O 8,12:6
Last Love of Don Juan, The 1955,N 24,40:1
Thesmophoriazusae, The; Goddesses of Athens,
    The 1955,D 14,52:4
Riders to the Sea 1957,Mr 7,24:1
In the Shadow of the Glen 1957,Mr 7,24:1
Riders to the Sea 1957,Mr 17,II,1:1
Tobias and the Angel 1957,O 21,29:5
Bivouac at Lucca 1957,O 30,26:1
Blood Wedding 1958,Ap 1,35:1
Othello 1958,Jl 4,16:1
Twelfth Night 1958,Ag 7,21:4
Great God Brown, The 1959,O 7,48:1
Great God Brown, The 1959,O 18,II,1:1
Lysistrata 1959,N 25,19:4
Pictures in the Hallway 1959,D 28,19:1
Peer Gynt 1960,Ja 13,21:1
Henry IV 1960,Mr 2,42:1
Henry IV 1960,Mr 13,II,1:1
Henry IV 1960,Ap 19,41:1
She Stoops to Conquer 1960,N 2,42:5
She Stoops to Conquer 1960,N 13,II,1:1
She Stoops to Conquer 1960,N 15,36:3
Plough and the Stars, The 1960,D 7,56:2
Octoroon, The 1961,Ja 28,13:1
Seagull, The 1962,Mr 22,42:1
Tavern, The 1962,Ap 5,29:1

Jedlicka, Milan (Miscellaneous)
Pierrot's Journey 1964,Ag 5,23:1

Jeeter, Bert
Boy Meets Girl 1943,Je 23,15:5

Jeffcott, Lucy
Variations of 1940 1940,Ja 29,12:1

Jeffers, Robinson (Original Author)
Dear Judas 1947,Ag 5,26:1
Dear Judas 1947,O 6,26:4

Jeffers, Robinson (Playwright)
Medea 1947,O 21,27:2
Medea 1947,O 26,II,1:1
Medea 1948,S 30,32:4
Medea 1949,My 3,31:2
Tower Beyond Tragedy, The 1950,N 27,29:1
Tower Beyond Tragedy, The 1950,D 10,II,5:1
Medea 1951,S 14,22:5
Cretan Woman, The 1954,My 21,17:2
Cretan Woman, The 1954,Jl 8,18:2
Cretan Woman, The 1954,S 5,II,1:1
Medea 1955,Je 16,35:4
Medea 1960,Jl 26,25:2
Medea 1965,N 29,46:1

Jefferson, Herbert Jr
Electra 1969,Ag 8,14:1
Murderous Angels 1970,F 8,70:1

Jefferson, James
I Will IF You Will 1922,Ag 30,10:4
Wild Oats Lane 1922,S 7,12:1

Jefferson, Joe (Miscellaneous)
Rivals, The 1922,Je 6,18:2

Jefferson, Joe (Playwright)
Rip Van Winkle 1947,Jl 16,28:2

Jefferson, Lauretta (Choreographer)
Beat the Band 1942,O 15,26:1
My Dear Public 1943,S 10,28:1
Artists and Models 1943,N 6,16:6
Jackpot 1944,Ja 14,15:2

Jefferson, Margo
Riot 1968,D 20,64:1

Jefferson, Norman
Three Showers 1920,Ap 6,18:1

Jefferson, William Winter
Three Showers 1920,Ap 6,18:1
Jeffery, Clare (Costume Designer)
Salad Days 1958,N 11,24:1
Jeffery, Mary
Beyond the Horizon 1920,F 4,12:1
Up the Ladder 1922,Mr 7,11:2
Carry Nation 1932,O 31,18:2
American Dream; 1933 1933,F 22,24:5
White Man 1936,O 19,22:4
Jeffery, Richard W
Betty Behave 1927,Mr 9,28:4
Jeffery, Thomas
Romio and Julietta 1925,Ap 21,19:1
Jeffery, William
Man Who Killed Lincoln, The 1940,Ja 18,26:4
Jefford, Barbara
Measure for Measure 1950,Mr 10,33:5
Tiger at the Gates 1955,O 4,40:1
Henry VI (Part III) 1957,O 18,19:5
Twelfth Night 1958,Ag 27,32:1
Twelfth Night 1958,D 10,54:2
Hamlet 1958,D 17,2:7
Macbeth 1961,Ja 10,28:1
Mourning Becomes Electra 1961,N 22,24:3
Macbeth 1962,F 7,32:2
Saint Joan 1962,F 21,57:4
Jeffrey, Clare (Costume Designer)
Entertainer, The 1958,F 13,22:2
Jeffrey, Ellis
No More Ladies 1934,O 7,IX,3:7
Jeffrey, Howard (Choreographer)
Georgy 1970,F 27,26:1
Jeffrey, J Wesley
Runnin' Wild 1923,O 30,17:3
Jeffrey, Michael
On Borrowed Time 1953,F 11,34:1
Jeffrey, Peter
Taming of the Shrew, The 1962,Ap 24,33:3
Macbeth 1962,Je 6,35:2
Jeffrey, William
Tavern, The 1920,S 28,14:1
Such Is Life 1927,S 1,27:3
Squealer, The 1928,N 13,36:3
Cortez 1929,N 5,32:2
Leaf and Bough 1949,Ja 22,10:2
Jeffreys, Alan (Playwright)
Ziegfeld Follies 1957,Mr 2,19:2
Vintage '60 1960,S 13,41:1
Jeffreys, Anne
Street Scene 1947,Ja 10,17:2
Street Scene 1947,Ja 19,II,1:1
My Romance 1948,O 20,38:5
ANTA Album 1951,My 7,22:7
Three Wishes for Jamie 1952,Mr 22,9:2
Kismet 1965,Je 23,45:1
Jeffreys, Ellis
On Approval 1927,My 15,VIII,2:6
Avalanche 1932,F 14,VIII,1:8
Fresh Fields 1933,F 5,IX,3:5
Jeffreys, Jane
Our Town 1940,Je 30,35:5
Across the Board on Tomorrow Morning
1942,Ag 18,17:1
Jeffreys, Lisa
High Button Shoes 1955,Mr 12,10:6
Jeffri, Joan
Inner Journey, The 1969,Mr 21,42:1
Year Boston Won the Pennant, The
1969,My 23,38:1
Jeffries, Billy
Mid-Summer 1953,Ja 22,19:1
Jeffries, Don
Coming of Christ, The 1957,D 23,29:8
Jeffries, Douglas
Within the Gates 1934,F 25,IX,3:7
Jeffries, Jay (Miscellaneous)
Fun City 1968,Mr 7,53:2
Jeffry, J (Onion)
Meek Mose 1928,F 7,30:1
Jeffry, William
Sure Fire! 1926,O 21,23:1
Jelin, Max J (Miscellaneous)
Lysistrata 1946,O 18,27:5
Jelin, Max J (Producer)
Lower North 1944,Ag 26,15:4
Jelinek, Maria
Ice Capades 1962,Ag 30,34:1
Ice Capades 1963,Ag 29,37:2
Ice Capades 1964,Ag 27,27:2
Ice Capades 1966,Je 2,50:2
Ice Capades 1967,Je 2,33:1
Jelinek, Otto
Ice Capades 1962,Ag 30,34:1
Ice Capades 1963,Ag 29,37:2
Ice Capades 1964,Ag 27,27:2
Ice Capades 1966,Je 2,50:2
Ice Capades 1967,Je 2,33:1
Jelley, Herbert
Turpentine 1936,Je 27,21:6
Jellicoe, Ann (Playwright)
Knack, The 1964,My 28,42:2
Knack, The 1964,Je 7,II,1:1

Jemima, Aunt
George White's Scandals 1921,Jl 12,14:1
Vaudeville (Palace) 1923,Ja 16,16:3
Show Boat 1927,D 28,26:1
Show Boat 1932,My 20,22:2
Jemma, Jean-Louis
Bourgeois Gentilhomme, Le 1955,O 26,26:1
Arlequin Poli par l'Amour 1955,N 9,40:1
Jeu de l'Amour et du Hasard, Le 1955,N 16,42:4
Avare, L', L'; Miser, The 1966,F 9,32:1
Cid, Le 1966,F 12,17:1
Reine Morte, La 1966,F 16,52:1
Fil a la Paite, Un 1966,F 18,25:1
Troupe Du Roi, La 1970,F 4,38:1
Don Juan 1970,F 7,24:2
Femmes Savaantes, Les 1970,F 14,12:1
Jenckes, Betty
Petticoat Fever 1935,Jl 2,24:4
Richard II 1937,F 6,14:2
Merely Murder 1937,D 4,21:4
Escape This Night 1938,Ap 23,18:1
Jencks, Frederick
Countess Maritza 1936,Ag 19,18:2
Jendell, Gary
Annie Get Your Gun 1966,Je 1,42:2
Jenke, Dietrich
Midsummer Night's Dream, A 1927,N 18,21:1
Redemption: Lebende Leichnam, Der; Living
Corpse, The 1928,N 20,28:2
Jenkin, Alfred
Hobo 1931,F 12,24:4
Dark Hours, The 1932,N 15,24:2
Raw Meat 1933,Mr 23,13:2
It Happened Tomorrow 1933,My 6,11:5
Abe Lincoln in Illinois 1938,O 17,12:2
Stop Press 1939,Mr 20,13:2
Jenkins, Allen
Florodora 1920,Ap 6,18:1
Secrets 1922,D 26,11:1
Glory Hallelujah 1926,Ap 7,26:2
Potash and Perlmutter, Detectives; Poisoned by
Pictures 1926,S 1,27:3
Front Page, The 1928,Ag 15,19:2
Five Star Final 1930,D 31,11:1
Wonder Boy 1931,O 24,20:1
Blessed Event 1932,F 13,23:2
Blessed Event 1932,F 21,VIII,1:1
Something for the Boys 1943,Ja 17,VIII,1:1
My L A 1951,D 9,87:1
Jenkins, Bunker (Director)
Come Out, Carlo! 1962,My 4,27:2
Jenkins, Bunker (Miscellaneous)
Mark Twain Tonight! 1959,Ap 7,40:2
In the Penal Colony 1962,My 4,27:2
Jenkins, Bunker (Playwright)
Come Out, Carlo! 1962,My 4,27:2
Jenkins, Bunker (Producer)
Shadow of Heroes 1961,D 6,59:1
Jenkins, Carol Mayo
Three Sisters, The 1969,O 10,38:1
Jenkins, Carolyn
Adding Machine, The 1956,F 10,17:1
Jenkins, Curtis
Joseph 1930,F 13,25:3
Jenkins, D Atwood (Lighting Director)
Room Service 1970,My 13,49:1
Jenkins, D Atwood (Scenic Designer)
Room Service 1970,My 13,49:1
Jenkins, David (Lighting Director)
Cherry Orchard, The 1960,Je 4,17:2
Jenkins, David (Scenic Designer)
Cherry Orchard, The 1960,Je 4,17:2
Jenkins, Dorothy (Costume Designer)
Affairs of State 1950,S 26,37:2
Jenkins, Gene
Hayride 1954,S 14,24:2
Jenkins, Geoffrey (Original Author)
Twist of Sand, A 1969,F 22,36:1
Jenkins, George
Policy Kings 1938,D 31,6:2
Jenkins, George (Lighting Director)
Allah Be Praised! 1944,Ap 21,14:2
I Remember Mama 1944,O 20,16:2
Dark of the Moon 1945,Mr 15,27:2
Memphis Bound 1945,My 25,23:2
Are You With It? 1945,N 12,17:3
Strange Fruit 1945,N 30,18:6
French Touch, The 1945,D 10,18:2
Touchstone 1953,F 4,33:2
Gently Does It 1953,O 29,43:4
Bad Seed, The 1954,D 9,42:1
Ankles Aweigh 1955,Ap 19,27:1
Desk Set, The 1955,O 25,36:7
Too Late the Phalarope 1956,O 12,35:1
Happiest Millionaire, The 1956,N 21,21:3
Rumple 1957,N 7,42:2
Two for the Seesaw 1958,Ja 17,15:1
Song of Norway 1958,Je 23,19:2
Once More With Feeling 1958,O 22,39:1
Cue for Passion 1958,N 26,25:2
Tall Story 1959,Ja 30,33:2
Song of Norway 1959,Je 26,16:2
Miracle Worker, The 1959,O 20,44:1

Jenkins, George (Lighting Director)—Cont
One More River 1960,Mr 19,12:2
Hit the Deck 1960,Je 24,32:1
13 Daughters 1961,Mr 3,17:2
Thousand Clowns, A 1962,Ap 6,31:2
Step on a Crack 1962,O 18,48:1
Catch Me if You Can 1965,Mr 10,50:1
Mardi Gras! 1965,Je 28,33:2
Wait Until Dark 1966,F 3,21:1
Mardi Gras! 1966,Jl 11,32:2
Jenkins, George (Miscellaneous)
Royal Hunt of the Sun, The 1965,O 27,36:2
Jenkins, George (Scenic Designer)
Early to Bed 1943,Je 18,16:2
Mexican Hayride 1944,Ja 29,9:6
Allah Be Praised! 1944,Ap 21,14:2
I Remember Mama 1944,O 20,16:2
Dark of the Moon 1945,Mr 15,27:2
Memphis Bound 1945,My 25,23:2
Are You With It? 1945,N 12,17:3
Strange Fruit 1945,N 30,18:6
French Touch, The 1945,D 10,18:2
Tonight at 8:30; Red Peppers 1948,F 21,8:2
Tonight at 8:30; Ways and Means 1948,F 21,8:2
Tomight at 8:30; Family Album 1948,F 21,8:2
Tonight at 8:30; Shadow Play 1948,F 24,20:4
Tonight at 8:30; Hands Across the Sea
1948,F 24,20:4
Tonight at 8:30; Fumed Oak 1948,F 24,20:4
Time for Elizabeth 1948,S 28,32:3
Lost in the Stars 1949,O 31,21:2
On Trial 1949,D 9,35:5
Curious Savage, The 1950,O 25,44:3
Bell, Book and Candle 1950,N 15,37:4
Three Wishes for Jamie 1952,Mr 22,9:2
Touchstone 1953,F 4,33:2
Gently Does It 1953,O 29,43:4
Immoralist, The 1954,F 2,18:7
Immoralist, The 1954,F 9,22:1
Immoralist, The 1954,F 14,II,1:1
Bad Seed, The 1954,D 9,42:1
Ankles Aweigh 1955,Ap 19,27:1
Desk Set, The 1955,O 25,36:7
Too Late the Phalarope 1956,O 12,35:1
Happiest Millionaire, The 1956,N 21,21:3
Merry Widow, The 1957,Ap 11,36:6
Rumple 1957,N 7,42:2
Two for the Seesaw 1958,Ja 17,15:1
Two for the Seesaw 1958,Ja 26,II,1:1
Annie Get Your Gun 1958,F 20,29:2
Song of Norway 1958,Je 23,19:2
Once More With Feeling 1958,O 22,39:1
Cue for Passion 1958,N 26,25:2
Tall Story 1959,Ja 30,33:2
Song of Norway 1959,Je 26,16:2
Ice Capades 1959,S 4,12:1
Miracle Worker, The 1959,O 20,44:1
Jolly's Progress 1959,D 7,42:2
One More River 1960,Mr 19,12:2
Hit the Deck 1960,Je 24,32:1
Ice Capades 1960,S 1,30:1
Critic's Choice 1960,D 15,61:3
13 Daughters 1961,Mr 3,17:2
Paradise Island 1961,Je 24,11:1
Thousand Clowns, A 1962,Ap 6,31:2
Paradise Island 1962,Je 28,22:1
Step on a Crack 1962,O 18,48:1
Around the World in 80 Days 1963,Je 24,22:1
Jennie 1963,O 18,35:2
Around the World in 80 Days 1964,Je 29,33:2
Catch Me if You Can 1965,Mr 10,50:1
Mardi Gras! 1965,Je 28,33:2
Wait Until Dark 1966,F 3,21:1
Mardi Gras! 1966,Jl 11,32:2
Only Game in Town, The 1968,My 21,42:1
Jenkins, Gordon (Composer)
Along Fifth Avenue 1949,Ja 14,28:2
Eddie Fisher at the Winter Garden 1962,O 3,47:1
Jenkins, Gordon (Lyricist)
Eddie Fisher at the Winter Garden 1962,O 3,47:1
Jenkins, Gordon (Miscellaneous)
Eddie Fisher at the Winter Garden 1962,O 3,47:1
Jenkins, Gordon (Musical Director)
Judy Garland 1959,My 12,40:1
Jenkins, Gordon (Playwright)
California 1953,Je 18,38:5
Jenkins, Harry
White Lights 1927,O 12,30:4
Buzzard, The 1928,Mr 15,29:1
One Way Street 1928,D 25,31:2
Jehovah Joe 1929,Ag 25,VIII,3:1
Privilege Car 1931,Mr 4,33:1
Pygmalion 1938,Ja 27,16:3
Captain Jinks of the Horse Marines 1938,Ja 28,16:2
Coriolanus 1938,F 2,14:5
Threepenny Opera, The 1955,S 21,38:1
Jenkins, Ian
Walk in Darkness 1963,O 29,30:2
Tragical Historie of Doctor Faustus, The
1964,O 6,34:2
Room, The 1964,D 10,62:1
Measure for Measure 1966,Jl 14,27:1
Richard III 1966,Ag 11,26:1

Jenkins, Joseph
This Mad Whirl 1937,Ja 10,II,4:8
Fifty-Fifty 1937,N 20,21:1
Jenkins, Ken
Merchant of Venice, The 1962,Je 22,1:4
Lion in Love, The 1963,Ap 26,28:3
Jenkins, Leroy
Horse Play 1937,Ag 28,8:3
Jenkins, Louise
Diamond Lil 1948,N 30,33:2
Diamond Lil 1949,F 7,16:2
Jenkins, Lucille
Veronica's Veil 1934,F 19,20:7
Jenkins, Mark
Carricknabauna 1967,Mr 31,30:1
King John 1967,Jl 14,19:1
Jenkins, Megs
Wind of Heaven, The 1945,Ap 22,II,2:3
Day by the Sea, A 1953,D 20,II,4:2
Day by the Sea, A 1955,S 27,42:1
Day by the Sea, A 1955,O 2,II,1:1
View From the Bridge, A 1956,O 12,35:3
Jenkins, Patricia
Auntie Mame 1956,N 1,47:2
Diamond Orchid 1965,F 11,44:4
Jenkins, Sally
Lady From the Sea, The 1935,D 14,11:3
Jenkins, Trent
Galileo 1968,D 1,88:4
Jenkins, Virginia
Don't Go Away Mad 1949,My 10,28:2
When the Bough Breaks 1950,Mr 9,25:5
Gods of the Mountain, The 1950,My 25,36:2
Jenkins (Costume Designer)
Anything Goes 1934,N 22,26:1
Jenkins Gowns (Costume Designer)
Come Play With Me 1959,My 1,33:5
Jenks, Dean
Let Freedom Ring 1935,N 7,26:2
Jenks, Hart
Hamlet 1925,O 12,19:2
Merchant of Venice, The 1925,D 28,12:1
Cyrano de Bergerac 1926,F 19,18:1
Immortal Thief, The 1926,O 4,21:1
Caponsacchi 1926,O 27,24:2
Hamlet 1928,Ja 5,33:2
Julius Caesar 1929,N 19,26:5
Hamlet 1930,Mr 25,34:4
Macbeth 1930,Mr 26,24:6
Merchant of Venice, The 1930,Mr 27,24:7
Twelfth Night 1930,Mr 27,24:7
Taming of the Shrew, The 1930,Mr 28,22:8
Richard III 1930,Mr 31,24:1
King Lear 1930,Ap 1,34:6
As You Like It 1930,Ap 3,32:5
Julius Caesar 1930,Ap 4,22:3
King Lear 1930,D 26,18:2
Merchant of Venice, The 1931,N 17,31:1
Julius Caesar 1931,N 18,26:3
Hamlet 1931,N 19,26:6
Master of the Revels 1935,Ag 14,16:2
Jenn, Myvanwy
Oh What a Lovely War 1964,O 1,30:1
Jennery, Trixie
Ed Wynn's Carnival 1920,Ap 6,18:2
Jennings, Darin
Loco 1946,O 17,29:2
Jennings, DeWitt C
Blue Flame, The 1920,Mr 16,18:1
Jennings, Donald (Miscellaneous)
What a Killing 1961,Mr 28,41:1
Jennings, Dorothy
Bedrock 1934,N 18,II,6:3
Jennings, Fred
Chocolate Dandies, The 1924,S 2,22:2
Jennings, Gertrude (Playwright)
Love Among the Paint Pots 1921,My 29,VI,1:7
Isabel, Edward and Anne 1923,Ap 8,VIII,1:7
Family Affairs 1934,Ag 23,13:3
Family Affairs 1934,S 16,X,2:1
Jennings, James (Miscellaneous)
Rondelay 1969,N 6,55:1
Jennings, John
Elton Case, The 1921,S 12,16:2
Jennings, John (Composer)
Riverwind 1962,D 14,5:5
Jennings, John (Lyricist)
Riverwind 1962,D 14,5:5
Jennings, Mary
Yeomen of the Guard, The 1964,Mr 19,29:2
Gondoliers, The 1964,Mr 28,14:1
Saint of Bleecker Street, The 1965,Mr 19,28:1
Mikado, The 1965,Ap 17,11:3
Yeomen of the Guard, The 1965,Ap 22,26:1
Jennings, Rebecca (Lighting Director)
Respectfully Yours 1947,My 14,29:4
Jennings, Robert
By the Beautiful Sea 1954,Ap 9,20:1
Jennings, Stanley
As You Like It 1945,Jl 4,10:4
Jennings, Talbot (Playwright)
No More Frontier 1931,O 22,27:1
This Side Idolatry 1933,O 20,15:4

This Side Idolatry 1933,N 5,IX,1:3
Jennings, Wardell
Paths of Glory 1935,S 27,24:2
Jenny, Bernard (Director)
Hostage, The; Crusts 1962,N 30,28:1
Jens, Arnette
Devils, The 1963,N 5,25:1
Jens, Salome
Sixth Finger in a Five Finger Glove 1956,O 9,31:4
Bald Soprano, The 1958,Je 4,39:2
Jack 1958,Je 4,39:2
Disenchanted, The 1958,D 4,53:4
Deirdre of the Sorrows 1959,O 15,46:1
Balcony, The 1960,Mr 4,21:1
Far Country, A 1961,Ap 5,32:1
Shadow of Heroes 1961,D 6,59:1
Night Life 1962,O 24,44:1
Winter's Tale, The 1963,Ag 16,14:1
After the Fall 1964,Ja 24,18:1
But for Whom Charlie 1964,Mr 13,42:2
Tartuffe 1965,Ja 15,23:1
First One Asleep, Whistle 1966,F 28,19:1
Meeting, The 1967,D 13,55:1
I'm Solomon 1968,Ap 24,51:1
Moon for the Misbegotten, A 1968,Je 13,55:2
Moon for the Misbegotten, A 1968,Je 30,II,1:1
Patriot for Me, A 1969,O 6,58:1
Patriot for Me, A 1969,O 12,II,1:1
Jensby, Wes (Miscellaneous)
Moondreamers, The 1969,D 9,68:1
Jensen, Betty
Good Morning 1937,D 4,20:7
Jensen, Carol-Leigh
My Wife and I 1966,O 11,53:2
Jensen, Christopher
Peter and the Wolf 1969,N 30,85:5
Jensen, Don (Costume Designer)
Winkelberg 1958,Ja 15,26:2
Cock-A-Doodle Dandy 1958,N 13,39:2
Jensen, Don (Lighting Director)
Anything Goes 1962,My 16,35:1
Jensen, Don (Scenic Designer)
In the Shadow of the Glen 1957,Mr 7,24:1
Riders to the Sea 1957,Mr 7,24:1
Tinker's Wedding, The 1957,Mr 7,24:1
Guitar 1959,N 11,42:5
Oh, Kay! 1960,Ap 18,37:2
Anything Goes 1962,My 16,35:1
Sunday Man, The 1964,My 14,41:3
Jensen, Elida
Sweet Miani 1962,S 26,33:2
Jensen, Martha
Flamingo Road 1946,Mr 20,18:2
Jensen, Shirley
Anatomist, The 1957,F 27,21:5
Jensen, Sterling
Desk Set, The 1955,O 25,36:7
Mime Theatre of Etienne Decroux, The 1959,D 24,15:1
King Lear 1968,Je 3,55:4
Dance of Death, The 1969,My 26,53:1
Trumpets and Drums 1969,O 13,52:1
Macbeth 1969,D 23,25:1
Oedipus 1970,F 23,30:1
Lady From Maxim's, The 1970,Je 1,41:1
Hamlet 1970,O 19,51:1
Jensen, Thit (Playwright)
Stork, The 1930,N 2,VIII,3:2
Jensick, Jerry (Miscellaneous)
Poupees de Paris, Les 1964,My 16,11:1
Jeoffrie, Fleurette
Vaudeville (Palace) 1928,Je 5,21:3
Jephson, Edward
Pigeon, The 1922,F 3,13:1
So This Is London 1922,Ag 31,18:2
Sweeney Todd 1924,Jl 19,10:4
Lady Be Good 1924,D 2,23:4
Service for Two 1926,Ag 31,15:1
Pickwick 1927,S 6,35:2
Spring 3100 1928,F 16,14:2
This Our House 1935,D 12,33:3
O Evening Star 1936,Ja 9,24:6
Jepp, Marie
Fall and Rise of Susan Lenox, The 1920,Je 11,11:2
Jeppson, Edward
Henrietta the Eighth 1935,Je 25,15:4
Jepson, Robert
Never Live Over a Pretzel Factory 1964,Mr 30,37:1
Jereaux, Gene
Madame Lafayette 1960,Mr 4,21:1
Jerecki, Marjorie
Accent on Youth 1935,Jl 11,24:3
Jergan, Louise (Playwright)
Miser, The 1955,Mr 18,34:2
Jergens, Adele
Banjo Eyes 1941,D 26,20:2
Jerger, Alfred
Three Musketeers 1929,O 13,IX,4:7
Jerit, Ron (Scenic Designer)
Cross and the Sword, The 1965,Je 28,32:6
Jeritza, Maria
Annina 1934,Mr 12,21:6

Jerold, Mary
Sacred Flame, The 1928,N 20,28:2
Jerome
Malinda 1929,D 4,37:2
Jerome, Adele
Summer Night 1939,N 3,17:1
Of V We Sing 1942,F 16,20:3
Jerome, Ben (Composer)
Yes, Yes, Yvette 1927,O 4,32:3
Jerome, Charles
Princess Virtue 1921,My 5,20:2
Jerome, Edwin
Aiglon, L' 1927,D 27,24:3
War Song, The 1928,S 25,29:3
Roberta 1933,N 20,18:4
Eastward in Eden 1947,N 19,33:2
Town House 1948,S 24,31:2
Grand Tour, The 1951,D 11,45:2
Madam Will You Walk 1953,D 2,2:4
Jerome, Elmer
Soliloquy 1938,N 29,26:4
Jerome, Helen (Playwright)
Pride and Prejudice 1935,O 23,19:2
Pride and Prejudice 1935,N 3,X,1:5
Pride and Prejudice 1935,N 6,32:4
Pride and Prejudice 1935,N 10,IX,2:5
Pride and Prejudice 1935,N 17,IX,1:1
Pride and Prejudice 1936,F 28,19:2
Jane Eyre 1936,F 28,19:2
Pride and Prejudice 1936,Mr 29,IX,1:2
Limelight 1936,O 13,32:3
Jane Eyre 1936,O 14,31:3
Jane Eyre 1936,N 8,X,3:4
Jane Eyre 1937,Ja 3,X,2:1
Jane Eyre 1937,F 7,X,1:1
Pride and Prejudice 1937,Ag 3,20:5
All the Comforts of Home 1942,My 26,24:5
First Impressions 1959,Mr 20,28:1
Jerome, Jerome K (Playwright)
Passing of the Third Floor Back, The 1924,F 8,19:4
Man or Devil 1925,My 22,22:4
Passing of the Third Floor Back, The 1928,Ja 17,22:7
Passing of the Third Floor Back, The 1928,F 21,18:2
Celebrity, The 1928,Ag 26,VII,2:5
Passing of the Third Floor Back, The 1937,Ag 3,20:6
Jerome, Leonard
Two Seconds 1931,O 10,20:6
Jerome, Margaret Neff
Sleeping Prince, The 1956,N 2,31:1
Jerome, Nat S
Beyond Evil 1926,Je 8,23:2
Merry Malones, The 1927,S 27,30:2
Jerome, Peter
Faith of Our Fathers 1950,Ag 6,72:2
Jerome, Timothy
Rothschilds, The 1970,O 20,40:1
Jerome and Gray
Vaudeville (Palace) 1928,O 2,35:1
Jerome and Herbert
Ziegfeld Follies 1920,Je 23,14:1
Jerrems, Jeanne
Mademoiselle Colombe 1954,Ja 7,26:1
Macbeth 1955,O 20,42:2
God Slept Here, A 1957,F 20,38:1
Jerris, Jeanne
Tempest, The 1955,S 3,8:6
Jerrold, Gene
All the Comforts of Home 1942,My 26,24:5
Jerrold, Mary
Constant Wife, The 1927,My 1,VIII,2:7
Sacred Flame, The 1929,Mr 3,VIII,2:5
Laburnum Grove 1933,D 17,IX,4:2
Arsenic and Old Lace 1943,Ja 1,26:5
Arsenic And Old Lace 1943,Ja 10,VIII,1:6
Living Room, The 1953,Ap 17,29:5
Jerry and Her Baby Grands
Vaudeville (Hippodrome) 1924,Ap 29,12:2
Vaudeville (Palace) 1926,My 8,29:2
Vaudeville (Palace) 1927,N 1,20:3
Jersey, Tom (Miscellaneous)
Here Be Dragons 1970,D 21,52:1
Knack With Horses, A 1970,D 21,52:1
Jesse, F Tennyson (Original Author)
Pin to See the Peepshow, A 1953,S 18,17:2
Jesse, F Tennyson (Playwright)
Pelican, The 1924,O 26,VIII,1:1
Quarantine 1924,D 17,19:7
Pelican, The 1925,S 22,23:2
Pelican, The 1925,S 27,VII,1:1
Pin to See the Peepshow, A 1953,S 18,17:2
Pin to See the Peepshow, A 1953,N 8,II,1:1
Jessel, George
Passing Show of 1923, The 1923,Je 15,24:6
Vaudeville (Hippodrome) 1924,O 21,21:2
Jazz Singer, The 1925,S 15,29:2
Vaudeville (Palace) 1928,Jl 17,15:5
Vaudeville (Palace) 1928,Jl 24,13:4
War Song, The 1928,S 25,29:3
Even in Egypt 1930,Ja 19,VIII,2:6
Joseph 1930,F 13,25:3

Jessel, George—Cont
Vaudeville (Palace) 1930,Ag 11,13:3
Sweet and Low 1930,N 18,28:5
Vaudeville (Palace) 1931,Je 8,21:2
Vaudeville (Palace) 1931,N 2,26:2
Casino Varieties 1934,Ap 3,26:4
Lost Paradise 1934,D 14,28:3
High Kickers 1941,N 1,21:2
Actors Fund Fete 1942,F 23,24:5
Show Time 1942,S 17,20:2
Show Time 1942,O 4,VIII,1:1
Red White and Blue 1950,O 8,64:5
Jessel, George (Miscellaneous)
Schoolhouse on the Lot 1938,Mr 23,18:4
Spring Meeting 1938,D 9,30:4
Vigil, The 1948,My 22,8:6
Jessel, George (Playwright)
War Song, The 1928,S 25,29:3
High Kickers 1941,O 12,I,54:3
High Kickers 1941,N 1,21:2
Jessel, George (Producer)
This Man's Town 1930,Mr 2,IX,4:7
This Man's Town 1930,Mr 11,24:4
Millions 1930,O 3,30:4
Glory for All 1937,F 9,18:2
High Kickers 1941,N 1,21:2
Run, Little Chillun 1943,Ag 14,6:1
Jessel, Patricia
Witness for the Prosecution 1954,D 17,35:2
Witness for the Prosecution 1954,D 26,II,1:1
Monique 1957,O 23,38:1
Jessel, Ralph
Teahouse of the August Moon, The
1955,My 10,24:1
Jessel, Raymond (Composer)
Baker Street 1965,F 17,36:1
Jessel, Raymond (Lyricist)
Baker Street 1965,F 17,36:1
Jessic, Miroslav (Composer)
Eastward in Eden 1956,Ap 18,25:4
Jessic, Miroslav (Miscellaneous)
Eastward in Eden 1956,Ap 18,25:4
Jessner, Leopold (Director)
Amphitryon 1926,O 24,VIII,2:1
Hamlet 1927,F 13,VII,2:3
Weavers, The 1928,Ap 1,IX,2:4
King John 1929,Je 23,VIII,2:1
Othello 1932,Mr 6,VIII,2:1
Rosse 1933,My 7,IX,2:5
Jessner, Leopold (Producer)
Glueck im Winkel 1921,Jl 24,VI,1:7
Egmont 1929,Mr 24,X,2:3
Oedipus on Colonos 1929,Mr 24,X,2:3
Oedipus Rex 1929,Mr 24,X,2:3
Will Hill Be Pardoned; Wird Hill Amnestiert?
1930,Je 1,VIII,2:1
Kabale und Liebe 1933,O 18,24:3
Jesson, Lois
Diamond Lil 1928,Ap 10,32:1
Squealer, The 1928,N 13,36:3
Live and Learn 1930,Ap 10,24:6
Schoolgirl 1930,N 21,31:1
She Lived Next to the Firehouse 1931,F 11,23:1
Magnanimous Lover, The 1933,F 1,13:5
Ghost Bereft 1933,F 1,13:5
One Day More 1933,F 1,13:5
Mountain, The 1933,S 12,28:6
Jessop, Wilfred
Ashes of Love 1926,Mr 23,24:3
Journey's End 1930,Ag 5,26:4
Party, A 1933,Ag 24,18:4
Night Remembers, The 1934,N 28,24:3
Jessor, Howard
All the King's Men 1948,Ja 19,19:2
Jessup, Richard
House in Berlin, A (Als der Kreig zu Ende War);
Als der Krieg zu Ende War (A House in Berlin)
1950,D 27,32:3
Jessup, Sally
Grey-Eyed People, The 1952,D 18,41:2
Tall Story 1959,Ja 30,33:2
Jessup, Stanley
Two Little Girls in Blue 1921,My 4,10:3
Madame Pierre 1922,F 16,11:1
Shore Leave 1922,Ag 9,20:2
Woman on the Jury, The 1923,Ag 16,10:4
Bluffing Bluffers 1924,D 23,17:2
Starlight 1925,Mr 4,17:2
Cradle Snatchers 1925,S 8,28:2
Sandalwood 1926,S 23,23:1
Love Call, The 1927,O 25,33:1
Nina Rosa 1930,S 22,22:5
Ode to Liberty 1934,D 22,20:2
Ten Million Ghosts 1936,O 24,23:7
Sea Dogs 1939,N 7,30:3
Mr and Mrs North 1941,Ja 13,11:2
Candle in the Wind 1941,O 23,26:2
Jessup, Wilfred
Fog 1927,F 8,20:1
Jessye, Eva
Porgy and Bess 1935,O 11,30:2
Jessye, Eva (Miscellaneous)
Memphis Bound 1945,My 25,23:2
Porgy and Bess 1953,Mr 10,25:5

Jessye, Eva (Musical Director)
Porgy and Bess 1944,F 8,13:2
Jessye, Eva Choir
Porgy and Bess 1942,Ja 23,16:2
ANTA Album 1951,My 7,22:7
Jester, May Callas (Lighting Director)
Pony Cart, The 1954,S 15,39:2
Jester, May Callas (Scenic Designer)
Pony Cart, The 1954,S 15,39:2
Jeter, Bert
Milky Way, The 1943,Je 10,17:2
Rats of Norway, The 1948,Ap 16,27:6
Jeter, Jim
Three Love Affairs; Still Life 1958,Mr 11,33:1
Sweet Bird of Youth 1959,Mr 11,39:2
Long Dream, The 1960,F 18,36:2
Friends and Lovers; In the Zone; Bound East for
Cardiff 1961,My 11,43:1
Jeter, Jim (Lighting Director)
Six Characters in Search of an Author
1961,My 11,43:1
Jette, Mlle
Bourgeois Gentilhomme, Le 1955,O 26,26:1
Jetter, Tom
Hangman's Whip 1933,F 25,20:2
Jeudis, Les Quat'
Show Girl 1961,Ja 13,37:1
Jewel, Izetta
Victoria Regina 1938,O 4,20:2
Richard II 1940,Ap 2,31:2
Elizabeth the Queen 1941,O 17,27:2
Jewell, Bruce
Devil's Disciple, The 1950,Ja 26,23:2
Jewell, Cliffman
God Loves Us 1926,O 20,22:2
Jewell, F Cliff
20th Century 1932,D 30,15:1
Drums Begin, The 1933,N 25,10:5
Jewell, Isabel
Blessed Event 1932,F 13,23:2
Johnny 2X4 1942,Mr 17,24:6
Jewell, James
Razzle Dazzle 1951,F 20,21:1
Allegro 1952,S 18,36:3
John Murray Anderson's Almanac 1953,D 11,42:2
Jewell, Martin
Kismet 1965,Je 23,45:1
Jewett, Eric
Dunce Boy, The 1925,Ap 4,20:2
Lucky Sam McCarver 1925,O 22,22:1
Jewett, Marilyn
Shoemaker and the Peddler, The 1960,O 15,27:4
Patience 1967,O 13,32:1
Iolanthe 1967,O 18,40:1
Mikado, The 1967,O 25,42:2
Gondoliers, The 1967,O 29,83:1
H M S Pinafore 1967,N 1,40:1
Jewett, Tom (Costume Designer)
Vagrant, The 1962,F 16,35:2
Witch, The 1962,F 16,35:2
Music Shop, The 1962,F 16,35:2
Jewett, Tom (Lighting Director)
Music Shop, The 1962,F 16,35:2
Vagrant, The 1962,F 16,35:2
Witch, The 1962,F 16,35:2
Jewett, Tom (Scenic Designer)
Hole in the Head, A 1958,N 26,25:2
Witch, The 1962,F 16,35:2
Vagrant, The 1962,F 16,35:2
Music Shop, The 1962,F 16,35:2
Jewish Art Quartet
Untitled-Benefit 1933,Ja 25,13:3
Jezek (Composer)
Golem, The 1931,D 13,VIII,3:4
Jiboye, Titus
Madmen and Specialists 1970,Ag 3,38:1
Jilinsky, A
White Guard, The; Days of the Turbins
1935,Mr 7,27:5
Marriage 1935,Mr 12,24:8
Enemies 1935,Mr 19,24:7
Deluge, The 1935,Mr 26,23:7
Jilinsky, A (Director)
Deluge, The 1935,Mr 26,23:7
Bridal Crown, The 1938,F 7,11:2
Jillson, Joyce
Route 1 1964,N 18,52:3
Roar of the Greasepaint-the Smell of the Crowd
1965,My 17,46:2
Grosse Valise, La 1965,D 15,52:1
Jim, Marion
King and I, The 1960,My 12,40:1
Apple, The 1961,D 8,44:1
Jim, Sonny
In the Wine Time 1968,D 22,II,7:1
Jimsohn, A N (Producer)
Man Out Loud, Girl Quiet 1962,Ap 4,38:1
Spanish Armada, The 1962,Ap 4,38:1
Jines, Henry
Swing It 1937,Jl 23,17:2
Jinguji, Sakura
Scarlett 1970,Ja 3,19:1

Jinnette, Bettina
Sweeney Todd 1957,Ag 28,21:4
Joachimsohn, Felix (Miscellaneous)
Journalisten, Die 1932,Jl 17,IX,1:1
Joachimsohn, Felix (Playwright)
Five From the Jazz Band; Fuenf von der Jazzband
1927,N 20,IX,4:7
Wie Werde Ich Reich und Gluecklich?
1930,Ag 31,VIII,2:1
Haessliche Maedchen, Das 1930,N 2,VIII,3:1
Haus Dazwischen, Das 1933,F 19,IX,3:1
Joannidou, Th
Electra 1952,N 20,38:2
Job, Thomas (Playwright)
Barchester Towers 1937,N 19,26:6
Barchester Towers 1937,D 1,27:1
Immortality, Ltd 1938,Mr 6,II,2:3
Uncle Harry 1942,My 21,24:1
Uncle Harry 1944,Ap 30,II,1:4
Therese 1945,O 10,24:2
Therese 1945,O 28,II,1:1
Land's End 1946,D 12,37:5
Job, William
Glass Cage, The 1957,Mr 11,21:2
Jobin, Andre
Misanthrope, Le 1957,F 8,19:1
Adieux, Les 1957,F 19,36:1
Chien du Jardinier, Le; Gardener's Dog, The
1957,F 19,36:1
Jobin, Peter
Antony and Cleopatra 1967,Ag 2,25:1
Hadrian VII 1969,Ja 9,22:1
Jocabson, John (Scenic Designer)
Black Quartet, A; Gentleman Caller, The
1969,Jl 31,28:1
Black Quartet, A; Great Goodness of Life (A Coon
Show) 1969,Jl 31,28:1
Jocelyn, Fanny (Playwright)
Come Out to Play 1937,F 10,18:5
Jocelyn, Mildred
Rhapsody 1944,N 23,37:2
Are You With It? 1945,N 12,17:3
Jocelyn (Costume Designer)
Out West of Eighth 1951,S 21,20:3
Number, The 1951,O 31,33:2
Jochim, Andrew
Passing Show of 1923, The 1923,Je 15,24:6
Passing Show of 1924, The 1924,S 4,13:4
Artists and Models 1925,Je 25,16:2
Jochim, Anthony
Treasure, The 1920,O 5,13:1
Passing Show of 1921, The 1920,D 30,16:2
Years Between, The 1942,F 7,13:2
Theatre of the Soul 1942,Mr 21,13:5
Across the Board on Tomorrow Morning
1942,Mr 21,13:5
Jochlin, Anthony
Cyrano de Bergerac 1923,N 2,14:1
Jockers, Ernest (Dr) (Director)
Alt Heidelberg 1926,My 31,10:5
Jockin, Henry
Half a Widow 1927,S 13,37:3
Jocko (Crow)
Get Together 1921,S 11,VI,1:6
Joe, Jeanne
Our Town 1968,D 14,62:1
Joel, Clara
Light of the World, The 1920,Ja 7,17:1
Near Santa Barbara 1921,F 1,14:1
Sporting Thing to Do, The 1923,F 20,12:2
Mismates 1925,Ap 14,27:2
Joel, Dennis
Auntie Mame 1958,Je 8,II,1:1
Joel, Lynn
Private Life of the Master Race, The
1956,Ja 31,33:3
Joels, Merrill E
Sun and I, The 1949,Mr 21,18:4
Joelson, Lynn
Pal Joey 1952,Ja 4,17:6
Joeres, Charlotte
Don Carlos 1964,N 25,40:1
Captain of Koepenick, The 1964,D 2,60:1
Joffe, Charles (Miscellaneous)
Don't Drink the Water 1966,N 18,37:1
Play It Again, Sam 1969,F 13,52:3
Joffe, Max
Vaudeville (Hippodrome) 1926,Mr 16,22:2
Joffrey, Marisa
Richard III 1964,Je 12,44:2
Joffrey, Robert (Choreographer)
Johnny Johnson 1956,O 22,24:1
Joglar, Frank
Christopher's Wonders 1960,S 27,41:1
Joh, Paula
Revolt of the Beavers, The 1937,My 21,19:2
Johan, Carl
Perfumed Lady, The 1934,Mr 13,27:2
Johann, John
Autumn's Here 1966,O 26,40:1
My Fair Lady 1968,Je 14,42:1
Me and Juliet 1970,My 15,42:1

Johann, Zita
Man and the Masses 1924,Ap 15,25:1
Dawn 1924,N 25,27:1
Drift 1925,N 25,15:3
Goat Song 1926,Ja 26,18:1
Machinal 1928,S 8,10:3
Machinal 1928,S 16,IX,1:1
Troika 1930,Ap 2,32:6
Uncle Vanya 1930,S 23,30:3
Tomorrow and Tomorrow 1931,Ja 14,26:3
Tomorrow and Tomorrow 1931,Ja 25,VIII,1:1
Tomorrow and Tomorrow 1931,F 1,VIII,2:1
Panic 1935,Mr 16,18:4
Seven Keys to Baldpate 1935,My 28,30:2
Flight Into China 1939,S 12,28:1
Burning Deck, The 1940,Mr 2,9:2
Broken Journey 1942,Je 24,22:2
Johannsen, Ebba
Gang zum Weiher, Der 1931,Ap 5,VIII,1:6
Kyrill Reist ins Abendland 1933,Ja 8,IX,2:1
Johannsen, Sigurd (Playwright)
White Lilacs 1928,S 11,31:2
Johannson, Rhoda
Make Mine Manhattan 1948,Ja 16,26:2
Johansen, Agnete
Romeo and Juliet 1934,D 21,30:3
Johansson, Ronny
White Peacock, The 1929,Ap 27,16:4
Johf, Earl
Plan M 1942,F 21,15:2
Johl, Peter
Pousse-Cafe 1966,Mr 19,19:2
John, Alice
Madame Pierre 1922,F 16,11:1
Banco 1922,S 21,18:1
Romeo and Juliet 1922,D 28,20:1
Laughing Lady, The 1923,F 13,25:1
Swan, The 1923,O 24,15:3
Assumption of Hannele, The 1924,F 16,16:2
Far Cry, The 1924,O 1,24:1
Youngest, The 1924,D 23,17:1
Call of Life, The 1925,O 10,10:1
Master Builder, The 1925,N 11,27:1
Master Builder, The 1925,N 15,VIII,1:1
Morals 1925,D 1,22:2
Port O' London 1926,F 10,20:2
Love in a Mist 1926,Ap 13,28:3
Serena Blandish 1929,Ja 24,30:3
Berkeley Square 1929,N 5,32:4
Peter Ibbetson 1931,Ap 9,30:3
Tom Sawyer 1931,D 26,15:3
We the People 1933,Ja 23,9:5
Sleeping Clergyman, A 1934,O 9,16:1
Portrait of Gilbert 1934,D 29,11:5
Romeo and Juliet 1935,D 24,10:2
Happy Ending 1936,Jl 15,14:3
Green Waters 1936,N 5,34:4
Young Mr Disraeli 1937,N 10,30:5
All the Living 1938,Mr 25,14:4
Madame Capet 1938,O 26,26:2
Gloriana 1938,N 26,18:4
Brown Danube, The 1939,My 18,30:4
Crime and Punishment 1947,D 23,29:3
John, Anthony (Director)
Party, A 1933,Ag 24,18:4
John, Augustus (Scenic Designer)
Silver Tassie, The 1929,N 3,IX,4:1
Boy David, The 1936,N 22,VI,7:1
John, Brooks and His Oklahoma Orchestra
Vaudeville (Palace) 1925,D 8,28:6
John, Errol
South 1955,My 2,17:4
John, Errol (Playwright)
Moon on a Rainbow Shawl 1962,Ja 16,30:1
Moon on a Rainbow Shawl 1962,Ja 28,II,1:1
Moon on a Rainbow Shawl 1969,Ag 29,25:1
Moon on a Rainbow Shawl 1970,D 18,52:1
John, Evan (Producer)
Life I Gave You, The 1931,My 12,29:3
John, Florence
Child of Manhattan 1932,Mr 2,15:1
John, Graham (Costume Designer)
Seeing Stars 1935,N 1,25:5
John, Graham (Lyricist)
By the Way 1925,D 29,20:3
Street Singer, The 1929,Jl 28,VIII,1:6
Street Singer, The 1929,S 18,35:2
Ripples 1930,F 2,VIII,2:7
Ripples 1930,F 12,26:1
John, Karl
Iphigenia in Aulis; Agamemnon's Death; Electra;
Iphigenia in Delphi 1962,N 11,82:4
John, Mary W (Miscellaneous)
Colette 1970,O 15,58:1
John, Miriam (Translator)
Jeannette 1960,Mr 25,20:2
John, Stephen
Tomorrow's a Holiday! 1935,D 31,10:2
John, Tom (Scenic Designer)
George M! 1968,Ap 11,48:1
Show Me Where the Good Times Are
1970,Mr 6,32:1

John, Walter
Annie Get Your Gun 1946,My 17,14:2
John, Wesley
Twelfth Night 1926,D 21,21:4
Inheritors 1927,Mr 8,23:1
John Brothers, The Original
Vaudeville (Palace) 1926,Mr 23,24:3
John Robinson's Elephants
Vaudeville (Hippodrome) 1925,D 8,28:6
Vaudeville (Hippodrome) 1926,My 4,31:2
Vaudeville (Hippodrome) 1926,My 11,25:3
John Teller Girls, The
Yours Truly 1927,Ja 26,16:5
Johnnie Dunn Vodeny's Plantation Orchestra
Dixie to Broadway 1924,O 30,22:1
Johnny Mann Singers
Danny Kaye Show 1963,Ap 11,28:2
Johns, Andrew
Unknown Soldier and His Wife, The 1967,Jl 7,22:1
Johns, Andrew (Scenic Designer)
Tempest, The 1959,D 28,19:2
Johns, Brooke
Jack and Jill 1923,Mr 23,17:2
Ziegfeld Follies 1923,O 22,17:2
Comic Supplement, The 1925,Ja 25,VII,1:4
Piggy 1927,Ja 12,22:2
Johns, Clay
Cast of Characters 1959,Je 11,37:2
Drunkard, The 1970,Ap 14,54:1
Johns, Eric
Makropoulos Secret, The 1926,Ja 22,12:4
Johns, Evan
Two Kingdoms 1934,N 20,24:2
Johns, Evan (Playwright)
Two Kingdoms 1934,N 20,24:2
Johns, Florence
Mary Stuart 1921,Mr 22,15:1
Charlatan, The 1922,Ap 25,14:2
Children of the Moon 1923,Ag 18,10:3
Children of the Moon 1923,Ag 26,VI,1:1
Children of the Moon 1923,S 9,VII,1:1
Children of the Moon 1923,S 16,VII,1:1
Best People, The 1924,Ag 20,8:1
Love 'Em and Leave 'Em 1926,F 4,20:4
Love 'Em and Leave 'Em 1926,F 14,VIII,1:1
Up the Line 1926,N 23,26:1
Father, The 1928,My 12,9:4
Headquarters 1929,D 5,32:4
American, Very Early 1934,Ja 31,21:2
Johns, Florence (Playwright)
American, Very Early 1934,Ja 31,21:2
Johns, Glynis
Way Things Go, The 1950,Mr 3,19:8
Gertie 1952,Ja 31,23:1
Major Barbara 1956,O 31,27:1
Too True to Be Good 1963,Mr 14,8:2
Too True to Be Good 1963,Mr 23,5:6
King's Mare, The 1966,Jl 21,23:1
Come as You Are 1970,Ag 12,32:1
Johns, John
Espanola 1921,D 30,13:1
Johns, Kenneth (Playwright)
Gypsy Blonde 1934,Je 26,22:5
Johns, Larry
Town Boy 1929,O 5,22:4
Dark Hours, The 1932,N 15,24:2
Bridal Quilt 1934,O 11,28:5
Libel! 1935,D 21,10:5
Tide Rising 1937,Ja 26,17:2
Greatness Comes to the Maronies 1937,Ag 18,15:2
Story of Mary Surratt, The 1947,F 10,25:2
Johns, Lawrence
Much Ado About Nothing 1929,N 17,30:4
Johns, Mary
S S Glencairn 1924,N 4,31:4
S S Glencairn 1929,Ja 10,24:5
Johns, Mervyn
Saloon Bar 1939,N 26,IX,3:6
Johns, Pierce (Playwright)
Sky's the Limit, The 1934,D 18,25:5
Johns, Romaine
Shuffle Along of 1933 1932,D 27,11:3
Jezebel 1933,D 20,26:3
Johns, Romaine (Composer)
Jezebel 1933,D 20,26:3
Johns, Vere E
Promis' Lan', De 1930,My 28,31:2
Johnsen, Carol
Everyman 1941,My 9,19:2
Johnsen, Jeannie
Of Thee I Sing 1969,Mr 8,19:1
Johnson, Alan
West Side Story 1960,Ap 28,31:1
Anyone Can Whistle 1964,Ap 6,36:1
Johnson, Alan (Choreographer)
Ballad for a Firing Squad 1968,D 12,64:2
Johnson, Albert (Lighting Director)
Americana 1932,O 6,19:3
Crazy With the Heat 1941,Ja 31,15:2
Girl From Nantucket, The 1945,N 9,17:2
Dear Judas 1947,O 6,26:4
Fancy Meeting You Again 1952,Ja 15,23:2
Chase, The 1952,Ap 16,30:2

Johnson, Albert (Lighting Director)—Cont
Stockade 1954,F 5,14:2
Show Boat 1956,Je 22,16:1
Show Boat 1957,Je 28,30:2
Cloud 7 1958,F 15,15:2
Night Life 1962,O 24,44:1
Johnson, Albert (Miscellaneous)
American Jubilee 1940,My 13,20:5
Johnson, Albert (Producer)
American Jubilee 1940,My 13,20:5
Johnson, Albert (Scenic Designer)
Criminal Code, The 1929,O 3,28:2
Half Gods 1929,D 23,18:5
Three's a Crowd 1930,O 5,IX,4:6
Three's a Crowd 1930,O 16,28:3
Band Wagon, The 1931,My 17,VIII,3:2
Band Wagon, The 1931,Je 4,31:3
Band Wagon, The 1931,Je 14,VIII,1:1
Face the Music 1932,F 18,24:5
Foreign Affairs 1932,Ap 14,25:5
Americana 1932,O 6,19:3
Mad Hopes, The 1932,D 2,26:3
As Thousands Cheer 1933,O 2,22:1
Let 'Em Eat Cake 1933,O 3,26:5
As Thousands Cheer 1933,O 15,IX,1:1
Let 'Em Eat Cake 1933,O 23,18:1
Let 'Em Eat Cake 1933,N 12,IX,1:1
Follies 1933,N 19,IX,2:5
Ziegfeld Follies 1934,Ja 5,24:3
Life Begins at 8:40 1934,Ag 7,20:7
Life Begins at 8:40 1934,Ag-12,IX,1:1
Life Begins at 8:40 1934,Ag 28,24:2
Life Begins at 8:40 1934,S 2,IX,1:1
Great Waltz, The 1934,S 24,14:4
Great Waltz, The 1934,S 30,IX,1:1
Revenge With Music 1934,N 29,33:5
Jumbo 1935,N 18,20:2
Jumbo 1935,N 24,IX,1:1
Between the Devil 1937,D 23,24:5
You Never Know 1938,S 22,26:3
Leave It to Me! 1938,N 10,32:2
Great Lady 1938,D 2,26:6
Aquacade 1939,My 5,26:2
Scandals 1939,Ag 29,17:2
John Henry 1939,D 17,IX,5:6
John Henry 1940,Ja 11,18:2
Crazy With the Heat 1941,Ja 15,18:2
Crazy With the Heat 1941,Ja 31,15:2
Skin of Our Teeth, The 1942,N 19,29:5
Proof Thro' the Night 1942,D 26,14:2
My Dear Public 1943,S 10,28:1
Sing Out, Sweet Land! 1944,Ja 7,II,1:1
Swing Out, Sweet Land! 1944,N 10,24:6
Sing Out, Sweet Land! 1944,D 28,24:2
Live Life Again 1945,O 1,14:7
Girl From Nantucket, The 1945,N 9,17:2
Dear Judas 1947,Ag 5,26:1
Dear Judas 1947,O 6,26:4
Two Blind Mice 1949,Mr 3,32:2
Pardon Our French 1950,O 6,22:4
Fancy Meeting You Again 1952,Ja 15,23:2
Chase, The 1952,Ap 16,30:2
Of Thee I Sing 1952,My 6,34:2
Shuffle Along 1952,My 9,20:5
Stockade 1954,F 5,14:2
Aquashow 1954,Je 23,20:4
Elliott Murphy's Aquashow 1956,Je 20,26:2
Show Boat 1956,Je 22,16:1
Show Boat 1957,Je 28,30:2
Cloud 7 1958,F 15,15:2
Night Life 1962,O 24,44:1
What Did We Do Wrong? 1967,O 23,56:1
Johnson, Alice
Thank You 1921,O 4,10:2
Johnson, Alvin
Rhapsody 1944,N 23,37:2
Johnson, Ames (Composer)
Runnin' Wild 1923,O 30,17:3
Johnson, Ames (Lyricist)
Runnin' Wild 1923,O 30,17:3
Johnson, Andrea
All the King's Men 1948,Ja 19,19:2
Johnson, Ann
Ghost Parade, The 1929,O 31,28:4
Chimes of Normandy, The 1931,N 3,31:3
Naughty Marietta 1931,N 17,31:2
Johnson, Anthony
We Bombed in New Haven 1967,D 7,58:1
Bacchae, The 1969,Mr 15,24:1
Adding Machine, The 1970,D 5,40:1
Johnson, Arch
Detective Story 1954,F 13,11:2
Terrible Swift Sword, The 1955,N 16,42:1
Saint Joan 1956,S 12,42:1
West Side Story 1957,S 27,14:4
Johnson, Arnold
Vaudeville (Palace) 1927,D 13,33:5
Johnson, Arnold (Producer)
So Was Napoleon 1930,Ja 9,22:2
Johnson, Arnold and His Orchestra
Vaudeville (Palace) 1927,S 20,33:3
Vaudeville (Palace) 1929,O 7,22:4
Johnson, Arte
Shoestring Revue 1955,Mr 1,22:2

Johnson, Barbara
Beautiful Changes, The 1956,Mr 24,15:2
Johnson, Bayn
Curley McDimple 1967,N 23,59:2
Johnson, Ben
Welcome Stranger 1920,S 14,12:1
Whispering Wires 1922,Ag 8,26:2
Tiger Cats 1924,O 22,18:1
Aloma of the South Seas 1925,Ap 21,18:1
Home Towners, The 1926,Ag 24,19:3
Tommy 1927,Ja 11,36:4
Anna 1928,My 17,25:2
Johnson, Bernard
Cabin in the Sky 1964,Ja 22,32:1
On a Clear Day You Can See Forever
1965,O 18,44:1
Johnson, Bernard (Costume Designer)
Song of the Lusitanian Bogey, The 1968,Ja 3,52:1
God Is a (Guess What?) 1968,D 18,56:1
Perfect Party, The 1969,Mr 21,42:1
Man Better Man 1969,Jl 3,22:1
Johnson, Bill
All in Fun 1940,D 28,11:2
Banjo Eyes 1941,D 26,20:2
Yours, A Lincoln 1942,Jl 10,12:3
Day Before Spring, The 1945,N 23,27:2
Annie Get Your Gun 1947,Je 8,I,63:2
Kiss Me, Kate 1951,Mr 9,30:5
Hostage, The 1961,D 13,55:4
Johnson, Bob
Harlem Cavalcade 1942,My 2,11:2
Here's Josephine Premice 1966,Ap 26,54:4
Hair 1967,O 30,55:1
Johnson, Bobby
Kiss Me, Kate 1952,Ja 9,24:6
Johnson, Buck
How Beautiful With Shoes 1935,N 29,24:1
Johnson, Carl
Stop Press 1939,Mr 20,13:2
Johnson, Catherine
Laffing Room Only 1944,D 25,15:4
Johnson, Cecil
Cranmer of Canterbury 1959,D 4,36:1
Johnson, Celia
Debonair 1930,Ap 24,29:2
Cynara 1930,Jl 13,VIII,1:3
Hamlet 1931,O 25,VIII,2:2
Hamlet 1931,N 6,28:4
Hamlet 1931,N 15,VIII,1:1
Vinegar Tree, The 1932,Je 9,27:7
Tomorrow Will Be Friday 1932,S 18,IX,1:1
Key, The 1933,S 7,17:5
Wind and the Rain, The 1933,N 5,IX,1:3
Pride and Prejudice 1936,Mr 29,IX,1:2
Pride and Prejudice 1936,Ag 30,IX,1:1
Old Music 1937,Ag 19,22:2
Old Music 1937,S 5,X,2:1
Rebecca 1940,Ap 14,IX,1:6
Saint Joan 1948,Ja 11,II,3:7
Tulip Tree 1962,N 30,25:5
Master Builder, The 1964,Je 10,50:2
Johnson, Charles
Elmer the Great 1928,S 25,29:1
Gambling 1929,Ag 27,31:2
Johnson, Charles G
Murder at the Vanities 1933,S 13,22:4
Hat, a Coat, a Glove, A 1934,F 1,15:2
Johnson, Chic
Vaudeville (Palace) 1923,My 15,22:2
Vaudeville (Palace) 1926,Je 15,23:3
Betty Behave 1927,Mr 9,28:4
Hot Pan 1928,F 16,14:1
Vaudeville (Palace) 1928,N 12,18:7
Sons o' Fun 1941,D 2,28:2
Laffing Room Only 1944,D 25,15:4
Funzapoppin 1949,Jl 1,16:2
Pardon Our French 1950,O 6,22:4
Hell'z-A-Splashin' 1959,Je 25,22:2
Johnson, Chic (Composer)
Funzapoppin 1949,Jl 1,16:2
Johnson, Chic (Lyricist)
Funzapoppin 1949,Jl 1,16:2
Pardon Our French 1950,O 6,22:4
Johnson, Chic (Miscellaneous)
Count Me In 1942,O 9,24:2
Johnson, Chic (Playwright)
Hellzapoppin 1938,O 2,IX,1:1
New Hellzapoppin, The 1939,D 12,36:4
Sons o' Fun 1941,D 2,28:2
Laffing Room Only 1944,D 25,15:4
Pardon Our French 1950,O 6,22:4
Johnson, Chic (Producer)
Hellzapoppin 1938,S 23,34:2
Streets of Paris, The 1939,Je 20,25:2
New Hellzapoppin, The 1939,D 12,36:4
Snookie 1941,Je 4,26:2
Sons o' Fun 1941,N 1,20:1
Ice Follies 1941,D 2,32:2
Laffing Room Only 1944,D 25,15:4
Johnson, Choo Choo
Early to Bed 1943,Je 18,16:2
Goose for the Gander, A 1945,Ja 24,16:4

Johnson, Christine
Carousel 1945,Ap 20,24:2
Carousel 1945,Ap 29,II,1:1
Carousel 1949,Ja 26,28:2
Carousel 1949,F 6,II,1:1
Johnson, Daisy
Devil in the Mind 1931,My 2,23:2
Johnson, Dale
Family Reunion, The 1960,D 10,26:1
This Way to the Tomb 1961,D 9,21:1
Johnson, Dale (Miscellaneous)
Family Reunion, The 1960,D 10,26:1
Johnson, Dan
South Pacific 1943,D 30,11:2
Johnson, Danny (Scenic Designer)
Babes in Arms 1951,Mr 10,7:3
I Am a Camera 1956,O 10,47:2
Johnson, Dawn
Sound of Music, The 1970,Jl 3,13:1
Johnson, De Loyle
Clair de Lune 1921,Ap 19,15:1
Johnson, Della
Sporting Thing to Do, The 1923,F 20,12:2
Johnson, Dennis
Man Who Washed His Hands, The 1967,F 16,33:1
Johnson, Dorothy
Venetian Glass Nephew, The 1931,F 24,26:3
Music in the Air 1932,N 9,28:2
Music in the Air 1932,N 20,IX,1:1
Come of Age 1934,Ja 13,16:6
Knights of Song 1938,O 18,29:2
Mr Winkle's Holliday 1946,Je 24,27:6
Beggar's Holiday 1946,D 27,13:3
Devil's Disciple, The 1950,Ja 26,23:2
Johnson, Dorothy (Costume Designer)
Ronde, La 1955,Je 28,24:2
Johnson, Dots
Rain 1948,F 2,15:2
Almost Faithful 1948,Je 5,9:2
Freight 1949,F 4,30:2
Freight 1950,Ap 27,36:2
Johnson, Eddie
Meet the People 1940,D 26,22:2
Meet the People 1941,Ja 12,IX,1:1
Johnson, Edward (Miscellaneous)
Meet Peter Grant 1961,My 11,41:4
Johnson, Ellen
Squaring the Circle 1936,Ag 12,15:3
Johnson, Elsa
It's A Gift 1945,Mr 13,18:7
Johnson, Fiona
Three Love Affairs; Still Life 1958,Mr 11,33:1
Johnson, Frances
Deep Channels 1929,O 19,22:3
Johnson, Francis E
Hades, the Ladies 1934,Mr 29,25:3
Foemen of the Yard 1935,Ap 6,10:4
Johnson, Francis E (Composer)
Foemen of the Yard 1935,Ap 6,10:4
Johnson, Francis E (Lyricist)
Foemen of the Yard 1935,Ap 6,10:4
Johnson, Frank
Better Times 1922,S 4,14:2
Elmer Gantry 1928,Ag 10,9:4
Challenge of Youth 1930,Ja 21,28:5
Johnson, Fred
Gallant Cassian 1934,N 14,22:2
Six Characters in Search of an Author
1934,D 5,29:1
Marks and Mabel 1945,S 9,II,1:4
Playboy of the Western World, The 1946,O 28,18:3
Johnson, Freddie (Director)
Lucky Sambo 1925,Je 8,19:4
Johnson, Gary
Ice Follies 1959,Ja 14,30:1
Ice Follies 1961,Ja 11,25:2
Ice Follies 1966,Ja 12,27:6
Ice Follies 1969,My 23,38:1
Johnson, Geoffrey (Producer)
People vs Ranchman, The 1968,O 28,56:1
Johnson, Georgann
Room Service 1953,Ap 7,34:1
Reclining Figure 1954,O 8,26:5
Drink to Me Only 1958,O 9,47:4
Critic's Choice 1960,D 15,61:3
Johnson, George
West Side Story 1960,Ap 28,31:1
Johnson, Georgina
Murder in the Cathedral 1935,D 21,11:3
Johnson, Georgina (Director)
Culbin Sands 1935,Mr 23,10:3
Johnson, Georgina (Producer)
Culbin Sands 1935,Mr 23,10:3
Johnson, Gil
Hairpin Harmony 1943,O 2,18:5
Johnson, Grace
Free for All 1931,Ag 16,VIII,1:1
Free for All 1931,S 9,25:1
Johnson, Greer (Lyricist)
Mrs Patterson 1954,D 2,37:1
Johnson, Greer (Miscellaneous)
Razzle Dazzle 1951,F 20,21:1

Johnson, Greer (Playwright)
Mrs Patterson 1954,D 2,37:1
Mrs Patterson 1957,F 6,20:2
Whisper to Me 1960,N 22,38:6
Johnson, Gustave
Does a Tiger Wear a Necktie? 1967,F 4,17:1
Johnson, Hal
Simple Life, A 1964,My 18,36:1
Johnson, Hall (Composer)
Earth 1927,Mr 10,23:1
Run, Little Chillun! 1933,Mr 2,21:3
Run, Little Chillun 1943,Ag 14,6:1
Johnson, Hall (Musical Director)
Blue Holiday 1945,My 22,13:3
Green Pastures, The 1951,Mr 16,35:2
Johnson, Hall (Playwright)
Run, Little Chillun! 1933,Mr 2,21:3
Run, Little Chillun! 1933,Mr 12,IX,7:1
Run, Little Chillun! 1939,Ap 30,XI,2:1
Run, Little Chillun 1943,Ag 14,6:1
Johnson, Hall Choir
Blue Holiday 1945,My 22,13:3
Johnson, Harry
Killers 1928,Mr 14,28:3
Johnson, Haven
Brown Sugar 1937,D 3,29:2
Johnson, Haven (Composer)
Brown Sugar 1937,D 3,29:2
Johnson, Helen
Girl From Wyoming, The 1938,O 31,12:1
Johnson, Herbert
Circle of Chalk, The 1950,D 2,8:3
Johnson, Howard
Hamlet 1968,Jl 4,15:1
Johnson, Howard (Lyricist)
Tangerine 1921,Ag 10,8:2
Paradise Alley 1924,Ap 2,17:3
Lace Petticoat 1927,Ja 5,18:2
Johnson, Hugh
Helen Goes to Troy 1944,Ap 25,17:2
Johnson, Ida
Four Saints in Three Acts 1952,Ap 17,35:1
Johnson, Ira
Brown Sugar 1937,D 3,29:2
Johnson, J Andrew
Peer Gynt 1923,F 6,14:1
Johnson, J B
Macbeth 1936,Ap 15,25:4
Johnson, J C (Composer)
Change Your Luck 1930,Je 7,10:2
Brown Buddies 1930,O 8,29:1
Year Round, The 1953,My 6,38:7
Johnson, J C (Lyricist)
Change Your Luck 1930,Je 7,10:2
Year Round, The 1953,My 6,38:7
Johnson, J Louis
Lulu Belle 1926,F 10,20:1
Goat Alley 1927,Ap 21,24:3
Show Boat 1927,D 28,26:1
Kilpatrick's Old-Time Minstrels 1930,Ap 21,20:2
Sugar Hill 1931,D 26,15:2
Show Boat 1932,My 20,22:2
Come Angel Band 1936,F 19,17:1
Macbeth 1936,Ap 15,25:4
Case of Philip Lawrence, The 1937,Je 9,31:1
Haiti 1938,Mr 3,16:1
Androcles and the Lion 1938,D 17,10:5
Susanna, Don't You Cry 1939,My 23,27:2
Fireworks on the James 1940,My 15,30:2
Cabin in the Sky 1940,O 26,19:2
Johnson, J Rosamond
Vaudeville (Palace) 1923,Mr 13,19:2
Americana 1928,O 31,28:2
Untitled-Revue 1928,N 19,16:2
Friars Club Frolic 1933,My 15,16:4
Porgy and Bess 1935,O 11,30:2
Mamba's Daughters 1939,Ja 4,24:2
Mamba's Daughters 1940,Mr 25,10:4
Cabin in the Sky 1940,O 26,19:2
Porgy and Bess 1942,Ja 23,16:2
Johnson, J Rosamond (Composer)
Brown Buddies 1930,O 8,29:1
Lew Leslie's Blackbirds of 1939 1939,F 13,12:2
Johnson, J Rosamond (Miscellaneous)
Lew Leslie's Blackbirds of 1930 1930,O 23,34:5
Johnson, J S
Arms and the Man 1964,Ap 28,41:1
Johnson, Jack
Country Scandal, A 1960,My 6,21:8
Wedding, The 1961,Ap 21,26:2
Johnson, James P (Composer)
Policy Kings 1938,D 31,6:2
Johnson, James Weldon (Original Author)
God's Trombones 1960,F 21,II,1:1
Trumpets of the Lord 1969,Ap 30,37:1
Johnson, James Weldon (Playwright)
God's Trombones 1960,F 10,43:4
Trumpets of the Lord 1963,D 23,22:3
Trumpets of the Lord 1967,Je 1,51:3
Johnson, Jay
Merchant of Venice, The 1962,F 3,13:2
Johnson, Jerimantha
Child of the Morning 1958,Ap 22,40:2

Johnson, Jimmy (Composer)
Keep Shufflin' 1928,F 28,18:3
Messin' Around 1929,Ap 23,26:3
Sugar Hill 1931,D 26,15:2
Johnson, Joe
Pick-Up Girl 1944,My 4,25:2
Joy Forever, A 1946,Ja 8,20:2
Johnson, John B
One-Act Plays of the Sea; Long Voyage Home,
The 1937,O 30,23:2
Johnson, Joseph
What the Doctor Ordered 1927,Ag 19,20:2
Lady Comes Across, The 1942,Ja 10,10:2
Johnson, Josi
Johnny 2X4 1942,Mr 17,24:6
Johnson, Joyce
Jubilee 1935,O 14,20:1
Johnson, Judy
Gay Divorce 1960,Ap 4,37:1
Johnson, Jules
Pirate, The 1942,N 26,39:2
Johnson, Julia
Shoot the Works! 1931,Jl 22,19:5
Johnson, Julius
Wheel, The 1921,Ag 30,10:1
Johnson, June
Funzapoppin 1949,Jl 1,16:2
Pardon Our French 1950,O 6,22:4
Hell'z-A-Splashin' 1959,Je 25,22:2
Johnson, Karen
Fourth Pig, The 1965,Ja 27,24:6
You're a Good Man, Charlie Brown 1967,Mr 8,51:1
You're a Good Man, Charlie Brown 1969,N 14,39:1
Johnson, Katharine
Shakespeare's Merchant 1939 1939,Ja 10,16:3
Johnson, Katie
Escape Me Never! 1935,Ja 22,22:2
Johnson, Kay
Go West, Young Man 1923,N 13,25:2
Beggar on Horseback 1924,F 13,17:2
Morning After, The 1925,Jl 28,24:2
All Dressed Up 1925,S 10,28:1
One of the Family 1925,D 23,22:3
No Trespassing! 1926,S 8,19:1
Crime 1927,F 23,27:3
Free Soul, A 1928,Ja 13,26:5
State of the Union 1945,N 15,25:2
State of the Union 1945,N 25,II,1:1
Johnson, Ken (Scenic Designer)
Ice Capades 1970,Ja 7,35:1
Johnson, Kilmer
Betty Behave 1927,Mr 9,28:4
Johnson, Lamont
Pony Cart, The 1954,S 15,39:2
Johnson, Lamont (Director)
Yes is for a Very Young Man 1949,Je 7,27:2
Before Breakfast 1958,Mr 12,36:1
Egg, The 1962,Ja 9,23:2
Perfect Setup, The 1962,O 25,47:1
Johnson, Larry
Boo Hoo! East Lynne 1959,S 9,50:4
Johnson, Larry E (Playwright)
Brother Elks 1925,S 15,29:2
What Ann Brought Home 1927,F 22,22:2
High Gear 1927,O 7,24:3
Back Seat Drivers 1928,D 26,14:4
It's a Wise Child 1929,Jl 28,VIII,1:6
It's a Wise Child 1929,Ag 7,29:1
It's a Wise Child 1929,Ag 25,VIII,1:1
It's a Wise Child 1933,My 17,15:2
Sea Legs 1937,My 19,26:5
Johnson, Lawson
Yeomen of the Guard, The 1955,O 4,39:2
Johnson, Louis (Choreographer)
World's My Oyster, The 1956,Ag 10,10:4
Darwin's Theories 1960,O 19,53:2
Black Nativity 1961,D 12,54:2
Kongi's Harvest 1968,Ap 15,49:1
God Is a (Guess What?) 1968,D 18,56:1
Electra 1969,Ag 8,14:1
Purlie 1970,Mr 16,53:1
Johnson, Louis (Miscellaneous)
Junebug Graduates Tonight! 1967,F 27,35:1
Song of the Lusitanian Bogey, The 1968,Ja 3,52:1
Believers, The 1968,My 10,57:4
Electra 1969,Ag 8,14:1
Blancs, Les 1970,N 16,48:4
Johnson, Lucille
Red, Hot and Blue! 1936,O 30,26:3
Johnson, Lydia
Revue des Femmes Nouvelles, La 1926,D 5,VIII,6:1
Johnson, M S (Playwright)
Nautical Knot, A 1927,F 27,30:2
Johnson, Margaret
He and She 1920,F 13,16:3
Johnson, Marian (Playwright)
Mother Said No 1951,Ap 17,34:2
Johnson, Marion
Centuries, The 1927,N 30,23:1
Johnson, Martha
Straw Hat, The 1926,O 15,20:2
Much Ado About Nothing 1927,N 19,14:6

Johnson, Mary Kate
Confederacy, The 1958,Jl 3,20:1
Johnson, Mason
Great Magician, The 1951,N 22,45:1
Johnson, Matthew Bernard Jr
Five on the Black Hand Side 1970,Ja 2,32:2
Johnson, Molly
Havoc 1924,S 2,22:2
Old English 1924,D 24,11:2
Johnson, Momodu (Director)
Bassa Moona 1936,D 9,35:4
Johnson, Momodu (Playwright)
Bassa Moona 1936,D 9,35:4
Johnson, Myra
Vaudeville Marches On 1938,D 30,11:1
John Henry 1939,D 17,IX,5:6
John Henry 1940,Ja 11,18:2
Johnson, Naomi
Three Musketeers, The 1928,Mr 14,28:1
Earl Carroll's Vanities 1928,Ag 7,25:2
Me for You 1929,S 22,IX,2:6
Artists and Models 1930,Je 11,33:2
Johnson, Nora (Original Author)
Henry, Sweet Henry 1967,O 24,51:2
Johnson, Nuggie
Bottomland 1927,Je 28,29:3
Johnson, Nunnally (Original Author)
Park Avenue 1946,N 5,31:2
Johnson, Nunnally (Playwright)
Shoot the Works! 1931,Jl 26,VIII,2:1
World's Full of Girls, The 1943,D 7,31:2
Park Avenue 1946,N 5,31:2
Breakfast at Tiffany's 1966,D 15,60:1
Henry, Sweet Henry 1967,O 24,51:2
Henry, Sweet Henry 1967,N 5,II,3:1
Johnson, O-Lan
Hawk, The 1968,Ap 18,54:1
Johnson, Orrin
Love Dreams 1921,O 11,22:2
Ostriches 1925,Mr 31,16:1
Johnson, Oscar
Ice Follies 1937,D 22,29:1
Ice Follies 1941,D 2,32:2
Johnson, Oscar (Producer)
Ice Follies 1957,Ja 16,36:1
Ice Follies 1958,Ja 15,26:2
Ice Follies 1959,Ja 14,30:1
Ice Follies 1960,Ja 13,20:1
Ice Follies 1961,Ja 11,25:2
Ice Follies 1962,Ja 10,24:6
Ice Follies 1963,Ja 10,5:2
Ice Follies 1964,Ja 8,41:2
Ice Follies 1965,Ja 13,35:1
Ice Follies 1966,Ja 12,27:6
Ice Follies 1967,Ja 11,51:1
Ice Follies 1969,My 23,38:1
Ice Follies 1970,My 23,27:1
Johnson, Page
Rumpelstiltskin 1948,Mr 15,27:3
Indian Captive, The 1949,Ja 31,15:2
Romeo and Juliet 1951,Mr 12,21:2
Camino Real 1953,Mr 20,26:1
In April Once 1955,Mr 14,29:3
Red Roses for Me 1955,D 29,15:2
Metamorphosis 1957,F 20,38:1
Enchanted, The 1958,Ap 23,41:1
Guitar 1959,N 11,42:5
Two Executioners, The 1960,My 17,42:2
Picnic on the Battlefield 1960,My 17,42:2
Chip, The 1960,My 17,42:2
School for Scandal, The 1962,Mr 19,36:1
Seagull, The 1962,Mr 22,42:1
Tavern, The 1962,Ap 5,29:1
Boys in the Band, The 1970,Ap 18,34:1
Johnson, Pamela Hansford (Playwright)
Rehearsal, The 1963,S 24,45:2
Rehearsal, The 1963,O 20,II,1:1
Johnson, Patricia
Oklahoma! 1951,My 30,15:2
Oklahoma! 1951,S 13,38:2
Johnson, Paul
Louisiana 1933,F 28,15:5
Sailor, Beware! 1935,My 7,28:4
Conjur' Man Dies 1936,Mr 12,18:5
Sweet River 1936,O 29,30:2
One-Act Plays of the Sea; Bound East for Cardiff
1937,O 30,23:2
One-Act Plays of the Sea; In the Zone
1937,O 30,23:2
Brown Sugar 1937,D 3,29:2
Androcles and the Lion 1938,D 17,10:5
Johnson, Peter
Midsummer Night's Dream, A 1954,S 22,33:1
Candida 1969,F 3,29:1
Johnson, Philander (Lyricist)
Kissing Time 1920,O 12,18:2
Johnson, Philip (Playwright)
Legend 1930,My 7,25:1
Queer Cattle 1932,My 19,24:2
Mainly for Lovers 1936,F 22,13:2
New School for Scandal 1937,My 5,28:2
Johnson, Ray
Ripples 1930,F 12,26:1

Johnson, Ray—Cont
Girl Crazy 1930,O 15,27:1
Anything Goes 1934,N 22,26:1
Banjo Eyes 1941,D 26,20:2
High Named Today 1954,D 11,11:2
No Time for Sergeants 1955,O 21,32:2
Johnson, Ray M (Lighting Director)
Magistrate, The 1959,My 14,30:6
Johnson, Raymond
Country Wife, The 1936,D 2,34:1
Merchant of Venice, The 1938,Ja 15,18:8
Victoria Regina 1938,O 4,20:2
As You Like It 1939,My 9,28:4
As You Like It; Midsummer Night's Dream, A;
Comedy of Errors, The; Taming of the Shrew,
The 1939,My 9,28:4
Hamlet 1939,D 5,35:2
Romeo and Juliet 1940,My 10,27:1
Twelfth Night 1940,N 20,26:3
Anne of England 1941,O 8,26:2
Rivals, The 1942,Ja 15,24:2
Wild Duck, The 1951,D 27,17:1
Merchant of Venice, The 1953,Mr 5,20:2
Knight of the Burning Pestle, The 1953,O 24,13:2
Hamlet 1954,Ap 24,15:2
Way of the World, The 1954,S 30,38:2
Thieves' Carnival 1955,F 2,21:1
Well of the Saints, The 1959,Ap 11,15:4
Workhouse Ward, The 1959,Ap 11,15:4
This Island Is Mine 1959,Jl 1,26:4
Johnson, Raymond (Director)
Pygmalion 1952,F 9,11:2
Johnson, Raymond Edward
Patriots, The 1943,Ja 30,11:2
Patriots, The 1943,F 7,II,1:1
To Tell You the Truth 1948,Ap 19,28:6
Johnson, Reggie
Sambo 1970,Jl 23,24:1
Johnson, Renee
Innocent Idea, An 1920,My 26,9:4
Johnson, Richard
Lark, The 1955,My 13,21:2
Much Ado About Nothing 1958,Ag 27,34:6
Complaisant Lover, The 1961,N 2,43:2
Elizabethans, The 1962,Ja 22,19:1
Flower of Cities All 1962,Jl 12,21:2
Twist of Sand, A 1969,F 22,36:1
Johnson, Richard (Playwright)
Elizabethans, The 1962,Ja 22,19:1
Golden Age, The 1963,N 19,49:2
Johnson, Rita
If This Be Treason 1935,S 24,28:2
Fulton of Oak Falls 1937,Ja 2,15:3
Fulton of Oak Falls 1937,F 11,18:2
Johnson, Robert
Black Scandals 1928,O 27,23:2
Weep for the Virgins 1935,D 2,18:1
New Faces of 1936 1936,My 20,24:5
Johnson, Roger Jr (Lighting Director)
Play That on Your Old Piano 1965,O 15,49:1
Johnson, Roger Jr (Miscellaneous)
Cuban Thing, The 1968,S 25,36:2
Johnson, Roy
Let Freedom Ring 1935,N 7,26:2
This Our House 1935,D 12,33:3
Sweet River 1936,O 29,30:2
Trojan Women, The 1941,Ap 9,32:5
Snookie 1941,Je 4,26:2
Merry Widow, The 1942,Jl 16,22:1
I Know My Love 1949,N 3,36:1
Legend of Lovers 1951,D 27,17:1
Hotel Paradiso 1957,Ap 12,22:2
Oklahoma! 1958,Mr 8,15:2
Johnson, Ruth
Blackbirds 1928,My 10,31:3
Mrs Moonlight 1952,N 21,21:1
Johnson, S D
It's the Valet 1933,D 15,25:4
Johnson, Scarlett
Hawk, The 1968,Ap 18,54:1
Johnson, Selene
Title, The 1921,N 15,23:3
Drifting 1922,Ja 3,20:3
Golden Age, The 1928,Ap 25,31:3
Johnson, Shelley
Dream Play 1960,N 23,22:1
Johnson, Sidney D
Fiesta 1933,D 16,12:2
Stags at Bay 1934,D 15,9:2
Johnson, Sondra
Tobacco Road 1942,S 7,34:2
Johnson, Sterling (Miscellaneous)
Murderous Angels 1970,F 8,70:1
Johnson, Stretch
New Faces of 1936 1936,My 20,24:5
Johnson, Susan
Brigadoon 1950,My 3,36:2
Buttrio Square 1952,O 15,40:2
Most Happy Fella, The 1956,My 4,20:1
Most Happy Fella, The 1956,My 13,II,1:1
Oh Captain! 1958,F 5,21:2
Whoop-Up 1958,D 23,2:7
Donnybrook! 1961,My 19,23:1
Donnybrook! 1961,My 28,II,1:1

ohnson, Suzzanne
This Rock 1943,F 19,23:2

ohnson, Tabby
Hair 1970,Ja 13,39:1

ohnson, Thomas (Musical Director)
Renard 1970,Mr 25,36:4
Only Jealousy of Emer, The 1970,Mr 25,36:4

ohnson, Van
New Faces of 1936 1936,My 20,24:5
Too Many Girls 1939,O 19,26:2
Pal Joey 1940,D 26,22:2
Music Man, The 1961,Mr 18,17:3
Come on Strong 1962,O 5,29:1
Mating Dance 1965,N 4,58:1
Forty Carats 1970,Ja 6,48:1

ohnson, Viola
Gypsy Baron, The 1944,Je 15,17:3

ohnson, Virgil (Costume Designer)
Tom Paine 1969,Mr 30,71:2

ohnson, Virginia
Vaudeville (Palace) 1930,S 29,19:1

ohnson, Walter
Sky High 1925,Mr 3,21:4
Artists and Models 1927,N 16,28:2
Street Singer, The 1929,S 18,35:2
Little Racketeer, The 1932,Ja 19,24:4
Student Prince, The 1943,Je 9,16:2
Blossom Time 1943,S 6,21:2

ohnson, Warren
Veronica's Veil 1950,F 12,II,1:5

ohnson, Wille Lee
Sojourner Truth 1948,Ap 22,35:2

ohnson, William
Shipwrecked 1924,N 13,18:1
Caukey 1944,F 18,15:4
Carousel 1953,My 6,38:1
Pipe Dream 1955,D 1,44:1
Pipe Dream 1955,D 11,II,5:1

ohnson, Wini
New Faces of 1936 1936,My 20,24:5
Harlem Cavalcade 1942,My 2,11:2
South Pacific 1943,D 30,11:2

ohnson & Manning
Ice Follies 1960,Ja 13,20:1

ohnson and Baker
Vaudeville (Palace) 1924,Ap 1,18:1

ohnson and Olsen
Hellzapoppin 1938,S 23,34:2

ohnson-Shepard, O-lan
Forensic and the Navigators 1970,Ap 2,43:1

ohnsons, The
Night in Venice, A 1929,My 22,30:2

Johnsrud, Harold
Prisoner, The 1927,D 30,22:2
Hot Pan 1928,F 16,14:1
Waltz of the Dogs, The 1928,Ap 26,31:3
Uncle Vanya 1930,Ap 16,26:5
Inspector General, The 1930,D 24,19:2
Devil in the Mind 1931,My 2,23:2
Jewel Robbery 1932,Ja 14,17:2
Sailors of Cattaro 1934,D 11,28:4
Panic 1935,Mr 16,18:4
Black Pit 1935,Mr 21,26:6
Winterset 1935,S 26,19:2
Eternal Road, The 1937,Ja 8,14:2
Doll's House, A 1937,D 28,28:6
Roosty 1938,F 15,21:2
Waltz in Goose Step 1938,N 2,26:2
Key Largo 1939,O 31,26:6
Key Largo 1939,N 28,30:2

Johnsrud, Harold (Director)
Americana 1932,O 6,19:3

Johnsrud, R C
Channel Road, The 1929,O 18,24:2

Johnston, Agnes Christine (Playwright)
Sweet Stranger 1930,O 22,23:3

Johnston, Alfred Cheney (Lighting Director)
Sea Legs 1937,My 19,26:5

Johnston, Arthur (Composer)
Dixie to Broadway 1924,O 30,22:1

Johnston, Audre
Half-Past Wednesday 1962,Ap 7,16:2

Johnston, Barney
My Fair Lady 1964,My 21,43:2

Johnston, Ben (Composer)
Gertrude 1970,N 13,29:1
Carmilla 1970,D 1,61:2

Johnston, David (Lighting Director)
There Is a Play Tonight 1961,F 16,24:2

Johnston, David (Scenic Designer)
There Is a Play Tonight 1961,F 16,24:2
Creditors 1962,Ja 26,19:1
Man Out Loud, Girl Quiet 1962,Ap 4,38:1
Spanish Armada, The 1962,Ap 4,38:1

Johnston, Denis
Armlet of Jade 1936,Ap 15,25:3

Johnston, Denis (Playwright)
Moon in the Yellow River, The 1932,F 21,VIII,2:1
Moon in the Yellow River, The 1932,Mr 1,19:3
Moon in the Yellow River, The
1932,Mr 13,VIII,1:1
Old Lady Says No, The 1935,Jl 28,X,1:1
Storm Song 1936,Jl 7,22:1

Bride for the Unicorn, A 1936,Jl 26,IX,1:3
Old Lady Says No, The 1948,F 18,35:1
Old Lady Says No, The 1948,F 22,II,1:1
Blind Man's Buff 1953,N 15,II,3:1
Dreaming Dust, The 1955,D 8,46:5
Moon in the Yellow River, The 1961,F 7,40:2
Moon in the Yellow River, The 1961,Mr 19,II,1:1

Johnston, Donald E
His Majesty the Queen 1926,Mr 9,8:1

Johnston, Edmund
Montserrat 1954,My 26,34:2
No Time for Sergeants 1955,O 21,32:2

Johnston, Elizabeth (Lighting Director)
Great Big Doorstep, The 1950,Mr 18,8:6

Johnston, Ernestine
Long Gallery, The 1958,Mr 7,17:2

Johnston, Gail
Streets of New York, The 1963,O 30,47:1
Mardi Gras! 1965,Je 28,33:2
Mardi Gras! 1966,Jl 11,32:2
Shoemaker's Holiday, The 1967,Mr 3,25:1

Johnston, Jane A
Greenwich Village U S A 1960,S 29,30:5

Johnston, Joan
Red Mill, The 1945,O 17,16:2

Johnston, Johnny
Tree Grows in Brooklyn, A 1951,Ap 20,24:3
Tree Grows in Brooklyn, A 1951,Ap 29,II,1:1

Johnston, Julia
Great Lover, The 1932,O 12,27:3
Mrs Moonlight 1936,Je 16,21:3
30 Days Hath September 1938,O 1,10:5
Look Homeward, Angel 1957,N 29,33:1

Johnston, Justine
Polly Preferred 1924,Ap 13,VIII,1:3
How He Lied to Her Husband 1924,S 30,27:5
Vaudeville (Palace) 1924,S 30,27:5
Vaudeville (Palace) 1925,D 8,28:6
Hush Money 1926,Mr 16,22:3
Love in Our Time 1952,O 4,14:3
Man and Superman 1953,F 21,11:2
Time of Your Life, The 1955,Ja 20,34:1
Dark of the Moon 1958,F 27,22:2
Time of the Cuckoo, The 1958,O 28,40:2
Harlequinade 1959,F 14,15:1
Smiling the Boy Fell Dead 1961,Ap 20,28:1
How to Succeed in Business Without Really Trying
1966,Ap 21,45:1

Johnston, Mabel (Costume Designer)
Woof, Woof 1929,D 26,20:4

Johnston, Margaret
Summer and Smoke 1952,Ja 25,13:5
Summer and Smoke 1952,F 10,II,2:3
Second Threshold 1952,O 12,II,3:7
Dark Is Light Enough, The 1954,My 1,12:4

Johnston, Marionne
Measure for Measure 1954,Je 30,23:1
Taming of the Shrew, The 1954,Jl 1,22:2
Oedipus Rex 1954,Jl 17,6:6

Johnston, Moffat
Back to Methuselah (Part II: The Gospel of the
Brothers Barnabas); Gospel of the Brothers
Barnabas, The (Back to Methuselah, Part II)
1922,F 28,19:2
Back to Methuselah (Part III: The Thing Happens);
Thing Happens, The (Back to Methuselah, Part
III) 1922,Mr 7,11:1
Back to Methuselah (Part V: As Far as Thought
Can Reach); As Far as Thought Can Reach (Back
to Methuselah, Part V) 1922,Mr 14,11:2
What the Public Wants 1922,My 2,22:3
R U R 1922,O 10,16:1
Six Characters in Search of an Author
1922,O 31,11:2
All Gummed Up 1923,Ja 29,11:2
King Lear 1923,Mr 10,9:4
March Hares 1923,Mr 13,19:5
Devil's Disciple, The 1923,Ap 24,24:1
Devil's Disciple, The 1923,My 6,VII,1:1
Windows 1923,O 9,17:2
Hamlet 1923,N 27,23:6
Macbeth 1924,Mr 17,18:1
Little Angel, The 1924,S 29,10:3
Wild Duck, The 1925,F 25,16:4
Accused 1925,S 30,20:1
What Never Dies 1926,D 29,24:2
Legend of Leonora, The 1927,Mr 30,22:4
Cock Robin 1928,Ja 13,26:6
Tonight at 12 1928,N 16,28:1
Meet the Prince 1929,F 26,30:5
Becky Sharp 1929,Je 4,29:1
Jehovah Joe 1929,Ag 25,VIII,3:1
Richelieu 1929,D 26,20:3
Solid South 1930,O 15,27:1
Affair of State, An 1930,N 20,30:3
Way of the World, The 1931,Je 2,34:3
Streets of New York, The 1931,O 7,29:1
Pillars of Society, The 1931,O 15,19:1
Berlin 1931,D 31,16:1
Fatal Alibi, The 1932,F 10,26:6
Camille 1932,N 2,23:3
20th Century 1932,D 30,15:1
Twentieth Century 1933,F 12,IX,1:1

Johnston, Moffat—Cont
Move on, Sister 1933,O 25,22:4
Drums Begin, The 1933,N 25,10:5
Joyous Season, The 1934,Ja 30,16:3
Shatter'd Lamp, The 1934,Mr 22,26:3
Lady From the Sea, The 1934,My 2,25:2
All Paris Knows 1934,Jl 24,20:1
Within the Gates 1934,O 23,23:1
Times Have Changed 1935,F 26,16:1
Flowers of the Forest 1935,Ap 9,25:2
Stag at Bay, The 1935,Jl 30,17:1

Johnston, Moffat (Director)
Julius Caesar 1923,F 9,10:4
Affair of State, An 1930,N 20,30:3

Johnston, Moffat (Playwright)
Stag at Bay, The 1935,Jl 30,17:1

Johnston, Muriel
Escape Me Never! 1935,Ja 22,22:2

Johnston, Peter
Remember the Day 1935,S 26,19:3
Cyrano de Bergerac 1936,Ap 28,17:1
So Proudly We Hail 1936,S 23,28:4
Trojan Horse, The 1940,O 31,28:3

Johnston, Romain (Costume Designer)
I Feel Wonderful 1954,O 19,22:5

Johnston, Romain (Scenic Designer)
I Feel Wonderful 1954,O 19,22:5
Kittiwake Island 1960,O 13,43:1

Johnston, Ronald
Hi, Paisano 1961,O 2,36:2
Troilus and Cressida 1965,Ag 13,17:1
Does a Tiger Wear a Necktie? 1967,F 4,17:1

Johnston, Thomas
Twelfth Night 1958,D 10,54:2
Hamlet 1958,D 17,2:7
Henry V 1958,D 26,2:7
Mystery of the Finding of the Cross, The
1959,Ja 16,35:2

Johnston, Winifred
King Lear 1923,Mr 10,9:4
Streets of New York, The 1931,O 7,29:1
Tomorrow's a Holiday! 1935,D 31,10:2

Johnstone, Alyce
Honeymoon Lane 1926,S 21,32:3

Johnstone, Anna Hill (Costume Designer)
Temper the Wind 1946,D 28,10:2
For Love or Money 1947,N 5,36:2
Lost in the Stars 1949,O 31,21:2
Curious Savage, The 1950,O 25,44:3
Country Girl, The 1950,N 11,10:6
Bell, Book and Candle 1950,N 15,37:4
Autumn Garden, The 1951,Mr 8,36:2
Flight Into Egypt 1952,Mr 19,33:2
Children's Hour, The 1952,D 19,35:2
Tea and Sympathy 1953,O 1,35:1
All Summer Long 1954,S 24,26:2
Tender Trap, The 1954,O 14,37:2
Hidden River, The 1957,Ja 24,32:1
Sin of Pat Muldoon, The 1957,Mr 14,35:1
Egghead, The 1957,O 10,39:1
Man in the Dog Suit, The 1958,O 31,34:2
Whoop-Up 1958,D 23,2:7
Sweet Bird of Youth 1959,Mr 11,39:2
Bedtime Story 1959,Ap 16,28:1
Portrait of a Madonna 1959,Ap 16,28:1
On the Harmful Effects of Tobacco
1959,Ap 16,28:1
Pound on Demand, A 1959,Ap 16,28:1
One More River 1960,Mr 19,12:2
After the Fall 1964,Ja 24,18:1
Investigation, The 1966,O 5,40:1
Warm Body, A 1967,Ap 17,44:2

Johnstone, Anna Hill (Miscellaneous)
Pygmalion 1952,F 9,11:2

Johnstone, E M
Squealer, The 1928,N 13,36:3
Claire Adams 1929,N 20,26:3

Johnstone, Elizabeth
Madam Will You Walk 1953,D 2,2:4

Johnstone, Florence
Great Music 1924,O 6,24:1

Johnstone, Gordon
Mrs Jimmie Thompson 1920,Mr 30,9:1

Johnstone, Jane
Let Freedom Sing 1942,O 6,18:2

Johnstone, Johnnie (Costume Designer)
That Old Devil 1944,Je 6,14:2

Johnstone, Pinkie
School for Scandal, The 1963,Ja 26,5:2

Johnstone, Russell
Broken Branches 1922,Mr 7,11:1
Sap, The 1924,D 16,28:3

Johnstone, Thomas A (Composer)
Snookie 1941,Je 4,26:2

Johnstone, Thomas A (Playwright)
Snookie 1941,Je 4,26:2

Johnstone, Tom (Composer)
Frivolities of 1920 1920,Ja 9,22:2
Up in the Clouds 1922,Ja 3,20:3
Molly Darling 1922,S 2,10:2
Plain Jane 1924,My 13,24:2
I'll Say She Is 1924,My 20,15:1
When You Smile 1925,O 6,31:2

Johnstone, Tom (Lyricist)
Frivolities of 1920 1920,Ja 9,22:2
Johnstone, Tom (Playwright)
When You Smile 1925,O 6,31:2
Johnstone, Will B (Composer)
Nine Fifteen Revue, The 1930,F 12,26:2
Johnstone, Will B (Lyricist)
I'll Say She Is 1924,My 20,15:1
Nine Fifteen Revue, The 1930,F 12,26:2
Johnstone, Will B (Playwright)
Up in the Clouds 1922,Ja 3,20:3
I'll Say She Is 1924,My 20,15:1
Johnstone, William
Garrick Gaieties 1926,My 11,25:2
Fog-Bound 1927,Ap 2,21:2
Manhatters, The 1927,Jl 19,27:3
Manhatters, The 1927,Ag 4,25:4
Him 1928,Ap 19,23:3
These Days 1928,N 13,36:2
Confederates, The 1959,S 29,45:1
Johst, Hanns (Playwright)
Thomas Paine 1927,Ap 10,II,9:4
Thomas Paine 1930,Mr 21,30:7
Schlageter 1933,My 28,IX,1:3
Schlageter 1933,Je 25,IX,1:2
Johst, Mr (Playwright)
Thomas Paine 1938,S 20,27:1
Joken, Karl
Veilchen von Montmartre 1931,Mr 29,VIII,3:1
Jolie, Marilyn
Yr Obedient Husband 1938,Ja 11,26:5
Jolivet, Andre (Composer)
Antigone 1960,D 14,52:1
Jolivet, Marc
Pique-Nique en Campagne 1969,My 1,50:1
Guernica 1969,My 1,50:1
Jolle, James
Point of No Return 1951,D 14,35:2
Jolle, Marilyn
Farewell Summer 1937,Mr 30,20:2
Jolley, James
Fata Morgana 1924,Mr 4,16:3
Old Bill, M P 1926,N 11,22:2
Piggy 1927,Ja 12,22:2
Merry-Go-Round 1927,Je 1,25:4
Sign of the Leopard 1928,D 12,34:4
Fata Morgana 1931,D 26,15:3
School for Husbands, The 1933,O 17,26:5
Within the Gates 1934,O 23,23:1
Bishop Misbehaves, The 1935,F 21,22:4
Pride and Prejudice 1935,N 6,32:4
Jolley, Stanford
Sweet Seventeen 1924,Mr 18,24:2
Jollie, June
Come of Age 1952,Ja 24,22:2
Jolliffe, Dorothy
Crucible, The 1953,Ja 23,15:2
Crucible, The 1953,Jl 2,20:2
Jolliver, Simone (Miscellaneous)
Faiseur, Le; Promoter, The 1938,D 27,12:3
Jolly, James
Farmer's Wife, The 1924,O 10,22:3
Good Companions, The 1931,O 2,31:1
Jolson, Al
Bombo 1921,O 7,20:2
Bombo 1923,My 15,22:2
Big Boy 1925,Ja 8,28:2
Lambs Gambol 1925,Ap 27,15:1
Big Boy 1925,Ag 25,12:2
Big Boy 1925,S 6,VII,1:1
Artists and Models 1926,Mr 22,16:2
Artists and Models 1926,Ap 4,VIII,1:1
Wonder Bar, The 1931,Mr 6,26:6
Wonder Bar, The 1931,Mr 18,23:4
Hold On to Your Hats 1940,Jl 17,25:3
Hold On to Your Hats 1940,S 12,30:3
Hold On to Your Hats 1940,S 29,IX,1:1
Jolson, Al (Producer)
Hold On to Your Hats 1940,Jl 17,25:3
Hold On to Your Hats 1940,S 12,30:3
Jon, Paula
Revolt of the Beavers, The 1937,My 21,19:2
Jonah, Dolly
Iceman Cometh, The 1956,My 8,38:1
Jackknife 1958,S 23,36:2
Signs Along the Cynic Route 1961,D 15,49:5
That 5 A.M. Jazz 1964,O 20,42:2
Jonah, Dolly (Playwright)
Signs Along the Cynic Route 1961,D 15,49:5
Jonap, Amy
As You Desire Me 1931,Ja 29,21:2
Jonas, Everett
Steel 1931,N 19,26:5
Jonas, Nita (Lyricist)
Half-Past Wednesday 1962,Ap 7,16:2
Jonay, Roberta
Save Me the Waltz 1938,Mr 1,19:2
Allegro 1947,O 11,10:2
Allegro 1952,S 18,36:3
Three by Thurber; Imperturbable Spirit, The
1955,Mr 8,23:2
Three by Thurber; Mr Montoe Holds the Fort
1955,Mr 8,23:2

Three by Thurber; Middle Years, The
1955,Mr 8,23:2
Jones, A Berney Jr (Miscellaneous)
Sap of Life, The 1961,O 3,44:1
Jones, A L (Miscellaneous)
Fountain, The 1925,D 11,26:1
Jones, A L (Producer)
Love for Love 1925,S 15,29:3
Squall, The 1926,N 12,20:1
That French Lady 1927,Mr 16,29:3
Love Is Like That 1927,Ap 19,24:1
People Don't Do Such Things 1927,N 24,28:3
Rain or Shine 1928,F 10,26:3
Remote Control 1929,S 11,24:5
Boundry Line, The 1930,F 6,21:1
Louder, Please! 1931,N 13,26:4
After Such Pleasures 1934,F 8,15:2
Without Warning 1937,My 3,23:2
Jones, Alexander (Costume Designer)
Swing It 1937,Jl 23,17:2
Life and Death of an American 1939,My 20,11:2
Morning Star 1940,Ap 17,26:4
Jones, Allan
Bitter Sweet 1934,My 8,28:4
Chocolate Soldier, The 1942,Je 24,22:2
Jackpot 1944,Ja 14,15:2
Jones, Altomay
Lulu Belle 1926,F 10,20:1
Jones, Anne
Once Upon a Mattress 1959,My 12,40:1
Jones, Archie
No More Peace 1937,F 27,9:1
Jones, Arthur (Composer)
Provincetown Follies, The 1935,N 4,24:3
Nine O'Clock Revue 1936,Jl 8,14:3
Buttrio Square 1952,O 15,40:2
Jones, Arthur (Lyricist)
Foemen of the Yard 1935,Ap 6,10:4
Nine O'Clock Revue 1936,Jl 8,14:3
Jones, Arthur M (Composer)
Foemen of the Yard 1935,Ap 6,10:4
Jones, Arthur M (Playwright)
Foemen of the Yard 1935,Ap 6,10:4
Jones, Arthur Tupper (Miscellaneous)
Love Expert, The 1929,S 24,29:1
Jones, Bambi
String 1969,Ap 2,37:1
Jones, Barry
Man and the Masses 1924,Ap 15,25:1
Bully, The 1924,D 26,18:1
Constant Nymph, The 1926,D 10,31:1
Road to Rome, The 1927,F 1,24:2
Queen's Husband, The 1931,N 15,VIII,2:1
Woman Kind 1933,S 28,25:2
And Be My Love 1934,Ja 19,25:2
Moonlight Is Silver 1934,S 20,21:1
Moonlight Is Silver 1934,O 7,IX,3:7
Glamorous Night 1935,My 3,23:6
Charles the King 1936,O 10,20:6
Geneva 1940,Ja 31,15:2
Love for Love 1940,Je 4,19:5
Barefoot in Athens 1951,N 1,35:2
Barefoot in Athens 1951,N 11,II,1:1
Misalliance 1953,F 19,20:1
Misalliance 1953,Mr 22,II,1:1
Cave Dwellers, The 1957,O 21,29:2
Cave Dwellers, The 1957,O 27,II,1:1
Jones, Barry (Miscellaneous)
Geneva 1940,Ja 31,15:2
Jones, Barry (Producer)
Queen's Husband, The 1931,N 15,VIII,2:1
Woman Kind 1933,S 28,25:2
And Be My Love 1934,Ja 19,25:2
Jones, Bill
Jackpot 1944,Ja 14,15:2
Jones, Bob
Easy Street 1924,Ag 15,16:4
Jones, Bobby (Scenic Designer)
Hairy Ape, The 1922,Ap 16,VI,1:1
Jones, Bonnie
Once for the Asking 1963,N 21,42:2
Jones, Broadway
Lew Leslie's Blackbirds of 1930 1930,O 23,34:5
Sugar Hill 1931,D 26,15:2
Jones, Brooks
Spree de Corps 1955,D 9,33:8
Jones, Brooks (Composer)
Spree de Corps 1955,D 9,33:8
Jones, Brooks (Lyricist)
Spree de Corps 1955,D 9,33:8
Jones, Byron
Keep Shufflin' 1928,F 28,18:3
Jones, Candy
Polonaise 1945,O 8,20:2
Jones, Carl
Memphis Bound 1945,My 25,23:2
Jones, Carol
Saint of Bleecker Street, The 1954,D 28,21:1
Jones, Carolyn
Homecoming, The 1967,O 5,47:3
Jones, Catherine
Passing of the Third Floor Back, The
1928,Ja 17,22:7

Jones, Ceinwen
Gondoliers, The 1951,F 13,27:2
Jones, Chailendra
Desert Incident, A 1959,Mr 25,40:1
Jones, Charles (Director)
Ruddigore 1927,My 21,25:2
Jones, Charlotte
Buttrio Square 1952,O 15,40:2
Camino Real 1960,My 17,42:2
Sign of Jonah, The 1960,S 9,35:1
Tattooed Countess, The 1961,My 4,40:2
Red Roses for Me 1961,N 28,41:1
Infancy 1962,Ja 12,28:1
Night Is Black Bottles, The 1962,D 5,56:1
Dream of Swallows, A 1964,Ap 15,46:1
Pigeons 1965,Mr 4,37:1
Great Scot! 1965,N 12,56:3
Serjeant Musgrave's Dance 1966,Mr 9,44:1
Mame 1966,My 25,41:1
How Now, Dow Jones 1967,D 8,53:1
Papers 1968,D 3,54:1
Jones, Christopher
Night of the Iguana, The 1961,D 29,10:1
Jones, Claude
Hamlet 1957,O 29,34:2
Jones, Clifford
She Lived Next to the Firehouse 1931,F 11,23:1
Friendship 1931,S 1,30:2
Monkey 1932,F 12,25:2
Bulls, Bears and Asses 1932,My 7,11:3
Jones, Dale
Just a Minute 1928,O 9,34:3
Music Man, The 1965,Je 17,26:4
Jones, Dave
Earl Carroll's Vanities 1925,Jl 7,24:1
Second Little Show, The 1930,Ag 17,VIII,2:2
Second Little Show, The 1930,S 3,36:1
On Your Toes 1936,Ap 13,14:4
On Your Toes 1937,Ag 3,21:2
I Married an Angel 1938,My 12,26:2
Oliver 1963,Ja 8,5:5
Jones, David (Director)
Silver Tassle, The 1969,S 12,35:2
Plebeians Rehearse the Uprising, The
1970,Jl 23,26:1
Jones, David C
Career Angel 1943,N 19,24:2
Beaux' Stratagem, The 1959,F 25,35:4
King of the Whole Damn World 1962,Ap 16,32:2
Amorous Flea, The 1964,F 18,26:1
Midsummer Night's Dream, A 1964,Je 30,23:2
Wilson in the Promise Land 1970,Ja 11,78:1
Wilson in the Promise Land 1970,My 27,41:1
Jones, Dean
There Was a Little Girl 1960,Mr 1,28:1
Under the Yum-Yum Tree 1960,N 17,45:1
Company 1970,Ap 27,40:1
Company 1970,My 3,II,1:4
Jones, Dennis
Coriolanus 1965,Je 21,36:1
Romeo and Juliet 1965,Je 21,36:3
Coriolanus 1965,Je 21,36:1
King Lear 1965,Je 25,39:1
Falstaff 1966,Je 20,27:1
Twelfth Night 1966,Je 23,28:1
Julius Caesar 1966,Je 24,29:2
Richard II 1968,Je 24,42:3
Jones, Disley (Scenic Designer)
Mikado, The 1964,N 27,43:1
Jones, Doris
Frankie and Johnny 1952,O 29,37:2
Jones, Douglas
Lower North 1944,Ag 26,15:4
Kiss Them for Me 1945,MR 21,27:2
Million Dollar Baby 1945,D 22,17:2
Jones, Duane
Lulu; Earth Spirit 1970,Mr 28,32:1
Jones, Dudley
Twelfth Night 1958,D 10,54:2
Hamlet 1958,D 17,2:7
Henry V 1958,D 26,2:7
Jones, E Boyd (Lyricist)
Florodora 1920,Ap 6,18:1
Florodora 1936,Ag 23,II,8:2
Jones, Earl
Hasty Heart, The 1945,Ja 4,14:2
Strange Fruit 1945,N 30,18:6
Volpone 1948,Ja 9,24:6
Set My People Free 1948,N 4,38:2
Fancy Meeting You Again 1952,Ja 15,23:2
Mister Johnson 1956,Mr 30,11:1
Eagle Has Two Heads, The 1956,D 14,37:2
Jones, Edward
Madame X 1927,Jl 7,29:3
Inside Story, The 1932,F 23,23:2
Victoria Regina 1935,D 27,15:2
Victoria Regina 1938,O 4,20:2
Jones, Edwin
Trial of Mary Dugan, The 1927,S 20,33:1
Mountain Fury 1929,S 26,27:2
Jones, Egbert
These Two 1934,My 8,28:3

Jones, Eleanor
  Bloomer Girl 1944,O 6,18:5
Jones, Elinor (Playwright)
  Colette 1970,My 7,60:1
  Colette 1970,My 17,II,1:1
  Colette 1970,O 15,58:1
Jones, Elizabeth A
  Storm Over Patsy 1937,Mr 9,26:4
Jones, Ellis O (Playwright)
  Vanderbilt Revue, The 1930,N 6,22:6
Jones, Ellsworth
  Whole Town's Talking, The 1923,Ag 30,8:2
  Easy Terms 1925,S 23,22:2
  Great God Brown, The 1926,Ja 25,26:1
  God Loves Us 1926,O 20,22:2
  Street Scene 1929,Ja 11,20:4
  Company's Coming! 1931,Ap 21,35:5
Jones, Enos F
  Evil Doers of Good, The 1923,Ja 17,22:2
Jones, Eugene D
  Hasty Heart, The 1954,Mr 13,10:1
Jones, Evan
  Conversation Piece 1934,O 24,24:1
Jones, Florence
  Rita Coventry 1923,F 20,12:2
Jones, Floyd
  Hassard Short's Ritz Revue 1924,S 18,19:1
Jones, Frank
  Pleasure Bound 1929,F 19,22:4
Jones, Frank (Playwright)
  Drums in the Night 1967,My 18,54:1
Jones, Fred
  Saint of Bleecker Street, The 1954,D 28,21:1
Jones, Freddie
  Persecution and Assassination of Marat As
    Performed by the Inmates of the Asylum of
    Charenton Under the Direction of the Marquis de
    Sade, The 1965,D 28,35:1
Jones, Frederick (Scenic Designer)
  Starlight 1925,Mr 4,17:2
  Caesar and Cleopatra 1925,Ap 14,27:1
  Captain Jinks 1925,S 9,22:1
  Hamlet 1925,N 10,23:1
  Shanghai Gesture, The 1926,F 2,20:2
  Unknown Warrior, The 1928,O 30,26:6
Jones, Gail
  Valmouth 1960,O 7,29:1
Jones, Gattison
  Jim Jam Jems 1920,O 5,13:2
  Spice of 1922 1922,Jl 7,12:4
  Angela 1928,D 4,28:2
Jones, Gemma
  There'll Be Some Changes Made 1969,O 2,56:2
Jones, Gene (Costume Designer)
  Corn Is Green, The 1954,F 27,10:2
Jones, Gene (Miscellaneous)
  Career 1957,My 1,42:6
Jones, Geoffrey (Producer)
  Cantilevered Terrace, The 1962,Ja 18,24:1
Jones, Geoffrey M T
  Jim Dandy 1941,N 8,10:5
Jones, George
  Right to Dream, The 1924,My 27,14:2
Jones, George Jr
  Shuffle Along of 1933 1932,D 27,11:3
  John Henry 1940,Ja 11,18:2
Jones, George W
  To Damascus 1961,F 15,40:2
Jones, George W (Miscellaneous)
  To Damascus 1961,F 15,40:2
Jones, Gloria
  Diary of Anne Frank, The 1955,O 6,24:2
Jones, Gordon
  Quiet, Please! 1940,O 20,IX,2:3
  Quiet, Please! 1940,N 9,20:3
  My Sister Eileen 1940,D 27,23:2
Jones, Griffith
  Escape Me Never! 1935,Ja 22,22:2
  Women of Property 1937,Ag 1,X,1:7
  Operette 1938,Ap 3,XI,1:8
  Quadrille 1953,Ap 5,II,1:1
  Innocent as Hell 1960,Je 30,2:6
Jones, Gwen
  Song of Norway 1944,Ag 22,20:2
Jones, H Oakes (Capt) (Costume Designer)
  Marigold 1930,O 9,23:1
Jones, Hank
  Copper and Brass 1957,O 18,19:2
Jones, Hazel
  Pygmalion 1945,D 27,16:1
  First Mrs Fraser, The 1947,N 6,36:2
  Gayden 1949,My 11,34:4
  Living Room, The 1954,N 18,41:1
  Potting Shed, The 1958,N 3,49:2
  Major Barbara 1965,My 18,33:1
  Tea Party 1968,O 16,40:1
Jones, Henry
  She Lived Next to the Firehouse 1931,F 11,23:1
  Kit Marlowe 1936,My 24,35:1
  Hamlet 1938,O 13,28:1
  Henry IV, Part I 1939,Ja 31,17:2
  Circle, The 1939,Jl 12,17:2
  What a Life 1939,Ag 2,17:5

  White Steed, The 1939,Ag 16,21:3
  Blind Alley 1939,Ag 23,18:8
  Good Fairy, The 1939,Ag 30,15:5
  Hamlet 1939,D 5,35:2
  Time of Your Life, The 1940,S 24,27:2
  Village Green 1941,S 4,24:4
  Village Green 1941,S 14,IX,1:1
  January Thaw 1946,F 5,18:2
  Alice in Wonderland 1947,Ap 7,19:2
  How I Wonder 1947,O 1,34:2
  Kathleen 1948,F 4,26:2
  Town House 1948,S 24,31:2
  Metropole 1949,D 7,43:2
  Story for a Sunday Evening, A 1950,N 18,10:5
  Solid Gold Cadillac, The 1953,N 6,24:2
  Bad Seed, The 1954,D 9,42:1
  Bad Seed, The 1954,D 19,II,3:1
  Sunrise at Campobello 1958,Ja 31,25:1
  Sunrise at Campobello 1958,F 9,II,1:1
  Advise and Consent 1960,N 18,25:1
  Child Buyer, The 1962,My 14,35:1
Jones, Henry Arthur (Playwright)
  Lie, The 1923,O 21,VIII,2:2
  Mrs Dane's Defense 1928,F 7,30:1
Jones, Henry Burk
  They Knew What They Wanted 1949,F 17,28:2
Jones, Herman
  Blessed Event 1932,F 13,23:2
Jones, Houghton
  Machinal 1960,Ap 8,27:1
  Rendezvous at Senlis 1961,F 28,39:2
Jones, Howard
  Side-Show 1931,My 16,13:1
Jones, Ifor (Musical Director)
  York Nativity Play, The 1956,D 5,49:2
Jones, Isobel
  Near to the Stars 1932,F 23,23:2
Jones, J Franklin
  Janie 1942,S 11,24:2
Jones, J Glenwood (Mrs) (Director)
  Wooden Idol, The 1930,My 13,27:2
Jones, J Richard
  Searching for the Sun 1936,F 20,22:6
  Young Couple Wanted 1940,Ja 25,16:2
  Medicine Show 1940,Ap 13,20:6
  Charley's Aunt 1940,O 18,24:2
Jones, Jack (Playwright)
  Rhondda Roundabout 1939,Je 18,IX,1:7
Jones, Jackie
  He Who Gets Slapped 1946,Mr 21,31:4
Jones, James (Original Author)
  Stockade 1954,F 5,14:2
Jones, James C
  Without the Walls 1920,Je 7,20:1
  Without the Walls 1921,Mr 28,8:1
Jones, James Earl
  Wedding in Japan 1957,Mr 12,37:7
  Sunrise at Campobello 1958,Ja 31,25:1
  Pretender, The 1960,My 25,42:1
  Henry V 1960,Je 30,23:1
  Romeo and Juliet 1961,F 24,24:1
  Blacks, The 1961,My 5,23:1
  Midsummer Night's Dream, A 1961,Ag 3,13:1
  Richard II 1961,Ag 30,25:1
  Clandestine on the Morning Line 1961,O 31,28:1
  Apple, The 1961,D 8,44:1
  Moon on a Rainbow Shawl 1962,Ja 16,30:1
  Merchant of Venice, The 1962,Je 22,1:4
  Tempest, The 1962,Jl 17,18:2
  PS 193 1962,O 31,33:1
  Love Nest, The 1963,Ja 28,7:6
  Winter's Tale, The 1963,Ag 16,14:1
  Next Time I'll Sing to You 1963,N 28,69:2
  Blood Knot, The 1964,Mr 3,30:2
  Othello 1964,Jl 15,29:1
  Emperor Jones, The 1964,Ag 6,20:4
  Emperor Jones, The 1964,Ag 16,II,5:1
  Othello 1964,O 13,48:1
  Baal 1965,My 7,33:2
  Coriolanus 1965,Jl 15,23:1
  Troilus and Cressida 1965,Ag 13,17:1
  Danton's Death 1965,O 22,46:1
  Bohikee Creek 1966,Ap 29,39:1
  Macbeth 1966,Je 29,38:1
  Macbeth 1966,Jl 14,27:2
  Hand Is on the Gate, A 1966,S 22,54:1
  Great White Hope, The 1967,D 14,58:1
  Great White Hope, The 1967,D 24,II,3:1
  Great White Hope, The 1968,O 4,40:1
  Great White Hope, The 1968,O 13,II,1:1
  Boesman and Lena 1970,Je 23,35:1
  Boesman and Lena 1970,Jl 5,II,1:3
  Blancs, Les 1970,N 16,48:4
  Blancs, Les 1970,N 29,II,3:5
  Blancs, Les 1970,N 29,II,3:1
Jones, Jean
  Heartbreak House 1950,Mr 22,33:2
Jones, Jen
  Diff'rent 1961,O 18,52:1
  Long Voyage Home, The 1961,D 5,49:1
  Grab Bag, The 1968,N 5,53:2
  Subscriber, The 1968,N 5,53:2
  Susie Is a Good Girl 1968,N 5,53:2

Jones, Jen—Cont
  But, Seriously... 1969,F 28,29:1
Jones, Jennie Rothman (Choreographer)
  Washington Square College Varsity Show
    1931,Ap 19,31:6
Jones, Jennifer
  Portrait of a Lady 1954,D 22,27:6
  Country Girl, The 1966,S 30,55:1
Jones, Jeremy
  Elizabeth the Queen 1966,N 4,30:1
Jones, Jim
  Contributions; Shoes 1970,Mr 10,53:1
Jones, Jo (Miscellaneous)
  Mime and Me, The 1960,Ap 8,27:3
Jones, John
  Sh! The Octopus 1928,F 22,19:2
Jones, John Bill
  Trip to Bountiful, The 1959,F 27,20:4
Jones, John E
  What a Relief 1935,D 14,10:6
Jones, John Price
  Good Morning, Dearie 1921,N 2,20:2
  One Kiss 1923,N 28,14:2
  Oh! Oh! Nurse 1925,D 8,28:4
  LeMaire's Affairs 1927,Mr 29,22:4
  Good News 1927,Ag 14,VII,2:1
  Good News 1927,S 7,35:4
  Lady Fingers 1929,F 1,22:4
Jones, John Randolph
  Zulu and the Zayda, The 1965,N 11,59:1
  Dinner at Eight 1966,S 28,38:1
  Pequod 1969,Je 30,33:1
Jones, Johnnie (Scenic Designer)
  In Circles 1968,Je 28,36:1
Jones, Jonatha
  Girls in Uniform 1932,D 31,10:3
  Wooden Slipper, The 1934,Ja 4,16:3
Jones, Joseph Pope
  One-Act Plays of the Sea; Moon of the Caribbees
    1937,O 30,23:2
  One-Act Plays of the Sea; In the Zone
    1937,O 30,23:2
Jones, Judd
  Not While I'm Eating 1961,D 20,37:1
  Royal Hunt of the Sun, The 1965,O 27,36:2
  South Pacific 1967,Je 13,56:1
  Take One Step 1968,Jl 5,17:1
Jones, Jumel
  Big Deal, The 1953,Mr 7,13:6
Jones, Katherine
  Passing of the Third Floor Back, The
    1928,F 21,18:2
  Me and Harry 1942,Ap 3,24:6
Jones, Ken
  Lily of Little India, A 1966,Ja 22,17:2
Jones, Kit (Playwright)
  Watch-Pit 1969,Ja 30,39:1
Jones, Lauren
  Ben Franklin in Paris 1964,O 28,52:1
  Trials of Brother Jero, The 1967,N 10,60:1
  Does a Tiger Wear a Necktie? 1969,F 26,38:1
  Does a Tiger Wear a Necktie? 1969,Mr 9,II,1:1
  Does a Tiger Wear a Necktie? 1969,Mr 16,II,4:5
Jones, LeRoi (Playwright)
  Dutchman 1964,Mr 25,46:2
  Toilet, The 1964,D 17,51:1
  Slave, The 1964,D 17,51:1
  Dutchman; Slave, The 1965,N 17,53:7
  Home on the Range 1968,My 21,42:1
  Great Goodness of Life (A Coon Show)
    1969,Ap 27,92:1
  Great Goodness of Life (A Coon Show)
    1969,My 4,II,1:5
  Black Quartet, A; Great Goodness of Life (A Coon
    Show) 1969,Jl 31,28:1
  Great Goodness of Life (A Coon Show)
    1969,Ag 3,II,1:4
  Great Goodness of Life (A Coon Show)
    1969,S 22,36:1
  Black Quartet, A 1969,S 22,36:1
  Slave Ship 1969,N 22,46:1
  Slave Ship 1969,N 23,II,3:1
  Slave Ship 1969,N 23,II,1:1
  Slave Ship 1970,S 13,II,1:1
Jones, Leslie
  Walk Hard 1946,Mr 28,34:2
Jones, Lewis
  Dance of Death, The 1967,O 20,50:1
  Love for Love 1967,O 21,17:1
Jones, Linda
  Carmilla 1970,D 1,61:2
Jones, Liz Ellsworth
  Resounding Tinkle, The 1961,Ap 4,42:2
Jones, Louise
  Vigil, The 1948,My 22,8:6
Jones, Mamie
  Evening With Shaw, An; Excerpts From Shaw
    1955,Ag 13,6:6
  Shadow Years, The 1957,Ja 9,26:2
Jones, Mamie (Choreographer)
  Kumquat in the Persimmon Tree, The
    1962,Je 19,27:2
Jones, Margo (Director)
  You Touched Me! 1943,O 17,II,2:4

Jones, Margo (Director)—Cont
Glass Menagerie, The 1945,Ap 2,15:5
On Whitman Avenue 1946,My 9,28:2
Joan of Lorraine 1946,N 19,40:2
Farther Off From Heaven 1947,Je 4,33:3
Summer and Smoke 1947,Jl 9,18:5
Throng o' Scarlet 1947,D 2,37:2
Summer and Smoke 1948,O 7,33:2
Coast of Illyria, The 1949,Ap 5,37:4
Coast of Illyria, The 1949,Ap 13,39:2
Southern Exposure 1950,S 27,36:3
Heel, The 1954,My 27,33:2
Purification, The 1954,My 29,12:1
Apollo of Bellac, The 1954,My 29,12:1
Apollo of Bellac, The 1954,Je 6,II,1:1
Purification, The 1954,Je 6,II,1:1
Inherit the Wind 1955,Ja 12,24:1
Jones, Margo (Miscellaneous)
Summer and Smoke 1947,Ag 10,II,1:1
Inherit the Wind 1955,Ap 22,20:2
Inherit the Wind 1955,S 25,II,1:1
Jones, Margo (Producer)
Summer and Smoke 1948,O 7,33:2
Cock-A-Doodle Dandy 1950,F 1,26:2
Southern Exposure 1950,S 27,36:3
Rising Heifer, The 1952,D 24,12:4
Jones, Marguerite E
Faraway Princess, The 1922,D 6,3:2
Jones, Mark
Persecution and Assassination of Marat As
Performed by the Inmates of the Asylum of
Charenton Under the Direction of the Marquis de
Sade, The 1965,D 28,35:1
Jones, Marlowe
Paul Bunyan 1941,My 6,25:1
Jones, Marryverne (Director)
Near to the Stars 1932,F 23,23:2
Jones, Martha
Pirate, The 1942,N 26,39:2
Harriet 1944,S 28,26:1
Jones, Martin (Director)
Mulatto 1935,Ag 8,13:2
Mulatto 1935,O 25,25:2
Jones, Martin (Producer)
Greater Love 1931,Mr 3,39:1
Then Came the Dawn 1935,Ag 29,25:4
Mulatto 1935,O 25,25:2
Satyr 1937,Je 17,18:5
Untitled-One Woman Show 1938,O 31,12:2
Jones, Mary
Time and the Conways 1938,Ja 4,19:2
Swan Song 1946,My 16,29:2
Vigil, The 1948,My 22,8:6
Jones, Mary Berne (Director)
Sea Shells 1935,Jl 16,24:2
Jones, Mary Kay
Strange Bedfellows 1948,Ja 15,27:3
Jones, Mary Sue (Scenic Designer)
Macbeth 1968,N 30,49:3
Jones, Mary Tupper
Four O'Clock 1933,F 14,19:6
Jones, Maryverne (Director)
News Item 1935,Ag 6,20:3
Swan, The 1936,Je 30,15:1
Jones, Maryverne (Playwright)
Across the Blue 1937,Je 1,27:1
Jones, Maryverne (Producer)
Man in Dress Clothes, The 1937,Ag 24,24:4
Jones, Maxine (Costume Designer)
Swing It 1937,Jl 23,17:2
Jones, Maxwell
Legal Murder 1934,F 16,16:2
Jones, Mr
Something Different 1967,N 29,52:1
Jones, Neil F
Lady or the Tiger?, The 1966,O 19,53:1
Passionella 1966,O 19,53:1
Jones, Olive
Champagne, Sec 1933,O 16,20:2
Jones, Oliver (Ali Abdou) (Choreographer)
Slave Ship 1969,N 22,46:1
Jones, Paul
Say It With Flowers 1926,D 6,29:1
Courage 1928,O 9,34:2
Winter Soldiers 1942,N 30,19:2
Proposition, The 1968,Ap 20,25:3
Conduct Unbecoming 1969,Jl 26,14:1
Conduct Unbecoming 1970,O 13,50:1
Jones, Peggy Ann
Mikado, The 1962,N 14,43:1
Gondoliers, The 1962,N 16,25:2
Pirates of Penzance, The 1962,N 21,28:1
Mikado, The 1964,N 27,43:1
Pirates of Penzance, The 1964,N 27,43:1
Ruddigore 1964,D 4,44:1
Pirates of Penzance, The 1966,N 16,54:1
Mikado, The 1966,N 18,36:1
Ruddigore 1966,N 23,28:1
Patience 1966,N 30,58:1
Patience 1968,N 1,34:1
Mikado, The 1968,N 2,29:4
Pirates of Penzance, The 1968,N 7,54:1
Iolanthe 1968,N 9,37:3

Jones, Phil
Let Freedom Ring 1935,N 7,26:2
Jones, Philip
Fountain, The 1925,D 11,26:1
Garrick Gaieties 1926,My 11,25:2
American Tragedy, An 1926,O 12,31:2
Nowhere Bound 1935,Ja 23,20:2
Sunny River 1941,D 5,28:2
Jones, Philip Cary
Infinite Shoeblack, The 1930,F 18,28:1
Peter Ibbetson 1931,Ap 9,30:3
Best Sellers 1933,My 4,20:2
Catherine Was Great 1944,Ag 3,16:1
Jones, Preston
Latent Heterosexual, The 1968,Mr 22,52:1
Macbeth 1968,N 30,49:3
Jones, Preston (Director)
Days Between, The 1965,Je 4,39:1
Jones, Quincy (Musical Director)
Free and Easy 1959,D 20,II,3:2
Jones, Ralph
Blue Blood 1924,Ap 3,21:2
Jones, Ramon
Year Boston Won the Pennant, The
1969,My 23,38:1
Jones, Raymond
Theodora, the Queen 1934,F 1,15:3
Jones, Richard
What a Life 1939,Ag 2,17:5
Jones, Robert Earl
Caesar and Cleopatra 1949,D 22,28:2
Winkelberg 1958,Ja 15,26:2
Moon on a Rainbow Shawl 1962,Ja 16,30:1
Room, The 1964,D 10,62:1
Displaced Person, The 1966,D 30,15:1
Jones, Robert Edmond (Costume Designer)
Living Mask, The 1924,Ja 22,15:1
Buccaneer, The 1925,S 20,VIII,2:4
Fountain, The 1925,D 11,26:1
Ladder, The 1927,O 7,24:2
Becky Sharp 1929,Je 4,29:1
Children of Darkness 1930,Ja 8,25:1
Mourning Becomes Electra; Haunted, The
1931,O 27,22:1
Mourning Becomes Electra; Hunted, The
1931,O 27,22:1
Mourning Becomes Electra; Homecoming
1931,O 27,22:1
Night Over Taos 1932,Mr 10,25:3
Mourning Becomes Electra; Hunted, The
1932,My 10,25:2
Mourning Becomes Electra; Homecoming
1932,My 10,25:2
Mourning Becomes Electra; Haunted, The
1932,My 10,25:2
Lucrece 1932,N 30,22:8
Lucrece 1932,D 21,22:2
Alien Corn 1933,F 26,IX,1:1
Nine Pine Street 1933,Ap 28,15:5
Mary of Scotland 1933,N 28,28:3
Othello 1934,Jl 29,IX,1:3
Othello 1937,Ja 7,16:4
Sea Gull, The 1938,Mr 29,19:2
Devil and Daniel Webster, The 1939,My 21,X,1:1
Lute Song 1946,F 7,29:2
Lute Song 1959,Mr 13,24:1
Jones, Robert Edmond (Director)
Patience 1924,D 30,15:1
Fountain, The 1925,D 11,26:1
Great God Brown, The 1926,Ja 25,26:1
Camille 1932,N 2,23:3
Merry Widow, The 1933,Ag 13,IX,1:3
Othello 1934,Jl 22,23:4
Othello 1934,Jl 29,IX,1:3
Othello 1937,Ja 7,16:4
Ruy Blas 1938,Jl 24,IX,2:1
Kindred 1939,D 27,17:2
Love for Love 1940,Je 4,19:5
Jones, Robert Edmond (Lighting Director)
Fountain, The 1925,D 20,VII,3:1
Green Pastures, The 1930,Mr 9,IX,1:1
Alien Corn 1933,F 26,IX,1:1
Philadelphia Story, The 1939,Mr 29,21:1
Susanna, Don't You Cry 1939,My 23,27:2
Summer Night 1939,N 3,17:1
Romeo and Juliet 1940,My 10,27:1
Without Love 1942,N 11,28:1
Othello 1943,O 20,18:1
Helen Goes to Troy 1944,Ap 25,17:2
Othello 1945,My 23,25:4
Lute Song 1946,F 7,29:2
Iceman Cometh, The 1946,O 10,31:3
Lute Song 1959,Mr 13,24:1
Jones, Robert Edmond (Miscellaneous)
Love for Love 1925,S IX,1:2
Love for Love 1925,S 15,29:3
Camille 1932,N 2,23:3
Juno and the Paycock 1940,Ja 17,24:2
Enchanted, The 1950,Ja 19,34:2
Jones, Robert Edmond (Producer)
Fountain, The 1925,D 11,26:1
Othello 1936,N 27,26:5

Jones, Robert Edmond (Scenic Designer)
Richard III 1920,Mr 21,VI,6:1
Samson and Delilah 1920,N 28,VI,1:1
Macbeth 1921,F 20,VI,1:1
Macbeth 1921,F 27,VI,1:1
Daddy's Gone A-Hunting 1921,O 2,VII,1:1
Hamlet 1922,N 26,VIII,1:1
Hamlet 1922,D 17,VII,1:1
Hamlet 1923,Ja 14,VII,1:1
Macbeth 1923,F 11,VII,1:1
Hamlet 1923,Ap 22,VII,1:1
Hamlet 1923,N 25,VIII,1:1
Spook Sonata, The 1924,Ja 13,VII,1:1
Living Mask, The 1924,Ja 22,15:1
Welded 1924,Mr 18,24:1
Ancient Mariner, The 1924,Ap 7,15:5
Ancient Mariner, The 1924,Ap 13,VIII,1:1
Saint, The 1924,O 13,20:3
Patience 1924,D 30,15:1
Hamlet 1925,Mr 29,VIII,1:1
Trelawney of the 'Wells' 1925,Je 2,16:2
Buccaneer, The 1925,S 20,VIII,2:4
Buccaneer, The 1925,O 3,10:2
In a Garden 1925,N 17,29:1
Fountain, The 1925,D 11,26:1
Fountain, The 1925,D 20,VII,3:1
Great God Brown, The 1926,Ja 25,26:1
Jest, The 1926,F 5,22:2
House of Women, The 1927,O 4,32:2
Ladder, The 1927,O 7,24:2
Paris Bound 1927,D 28,26:3
Salvation 1928,F 1,31:1
Martine 1928,Ap 5,19:3
Machinal 1928,S 8,10:3
Machinal 1928,S 16,IX,1:1
Mr Moneypenny 1928,O 17,26:2
These Days 1928,N 13,36:2
Holiday 1928,N 27,36:1
Serena Blandish 1929,Ja 24,30:3
Serena Blandish 1929,F 3,VIII,1:1
Becky Sharp 1929,Je 4,29:1
Commodore Marries, The 1929,S 5,26:3
Commodore Marries, The 1929,S 15,IX,1:1
See Naples and Die 1929,S 27,30:4
Ladies Leave 1929,O 2,28:3
Channel Road, The 1929,O 18,24:2
Week-end 1929,O 23,26:4
Cross Roads 1929,N 12,34:2
Children of Darkness 1930,Ja 8,25:1
Rebound 1930,F 4,29:1
Green Pastures, The 1930,F 27,26:1
Green Pastures, The 1930,Mr 9,IX,1:1
Roadside 1930,S 27,21:1
Mourning Becomes Electra; Hunted, The
1931,O 27,22:1
Mourning Becomes Electra; Haunted, The
1931,O 27,22:1
Mourning Becomes Electra; Homecoming
1931,O 27,22:1
Mourning Becomes Electra 1931,N 1,VIII,1:1
Lady With a Lamp, The 1931,N 20,27:2
Passing Present, The 1931,D 8,36:2
Night Over Taos 1932,Mr 10,25:3
Mourning Becomes Electra 1932,Ap 10,VIII,1:1
Mourning Becomes Electra; Hunted, The
1932,My 10,25:2
Mourning Becomes Electra; Homecoming
1932,My 10,25:2
Mourning Becomes Electra; Haunted, The
1932,My 10,25:2
Camille 1932,N 2,23:3
Lucrece 1932,N 30,22:8
Lucrece 1932,D 4,IX,3:3
Lucrece 1932,D 21,22:2
Lucrece 1933,Ja 1,IX,1:1
Alien Corn 1933,F 26,IX,1:1
Nine Pine Street 1933,Ap 28,15:5
Ah, Wilderness! 1933,O 3,28:2
Green Bay Tree, The 1933,O 21,11:5
Green Bay Tree, The 1933,O 29,IX,1:1
Mary of Scotland 1933,N 28,28:3
Mary of Scotland 1933,D 3,IX,5:1
Joyous Season, The 1934,Ja 30,16:3
Othello 1934,Jl 29,IX,1:3
Dark Victory 1934,N 10,18:2
Green Pastures, The 1935,F 27,16:2
Othello 1936,N 27,26:5
Othello 1936,D 6,XII,6:1
Othello 1937,Ja 7,16:4
Sea Gull, The 1938,Mr 29,19:2
Ruy Blas 1938,Jl 24,IX,2:1
Everywhere I Roam 1938,D 30,10:4
Everywhere I Roam 1939,Ja 8,IX,1:1
Philadelphia Story, The 1939,Mr 29,21:1
Devil and Daniel Webster, The 1939,My 19,26:1
Devil and Daniel Webster, The 1939,My 21,X,1:1
Susanna, Don't You Cry 1939,My 23,27:2
Summer Night 1939,N 3,17:1
Kindred 1939,D 27,17:2
Juno and the Paycock 1940,Ja 17,24:2
Love for Love 1940,Je 4,19:5
Astonished Heart, The; Tonight at Eight
1940,Ag 6,15:3

Jones, Robert Edmond (Scenic Designer)—Cont
We Were Dancing; Tonight at Eight 1940,Ag 6,15:3
Red Peppers; Tonight at Eight 1940,Ag 6,15:3
Without Love 1942,N 11,28:1
Othello 1943,O 20,18:1
Jackpot 1944,Ja 14,15:2
Helen Goes to Troy 1944,Ap 25,17:2
Helen Goes to Troy 1944,Ap 30,II,1:1
Othello 1945,My 23,25:4
Lute Song 1946,F 7,29:2
Lute Song 1946,F 17,II,1:1
Iceman Cometh, The 1946,O 10,31:3
Iceman Cometh, The 1946,O 20,II,1:1
Green Pastures, The 1951,Mr 16,35:2
Lute Song 1959,Mr 13,24:1
Jones, Roland
Green Pastures, The 1935,F 27,16:2
Jones, Ronnie
Riot 1968,D 20,64:1
Jones, S O H
Plain Dealer, The 1929,My 23,27:1
Jones, Sam
Brown Buddies 1930,O 8,29:1
Jones, Sandra (Costume Designer)
Futz 1968,Je 14,39:1
Jones, Shirley
Oklahoma! 1955,Je 21,37:7
Oklahoma! 1955,Jl 11,19:7
Beggar's Opera, The 1957,Mr 14,35:1
Maggie Flynn 1968,O 24,52:1
Maggie Flynn 1968,N 3,II,1:1
Jones, Sidney (Composer)
Geisha, The 1931,O 6,35:4
Jones, Starr
Garrick Gaieties 1925,Je 28,VIII,1:1
Circus Princess, The 1927,Ap 26,32:2
Girl Crazy 1930,O 15,27:1
Near to the Stars 1932,F 23,23:2
Tapestry in Gray 1935,D 28,10:2
Jones, Stephen (Composer)
Poppy 1923,S 4,14:2
Marjorie 1924,Ag 12,12:2
Captain Jinks 1925,S 9,22:1
Talk About Girls 1927,Je 15,31:3
Jones, Stewart O H
Coriolanus 1927,Je 18,8:3
Jones, Strappy
Florida Girl 1925,N 3,34:1
Jones, Sue
Home Away From, A 1969,Ap 29,40:3
Jones, Suzanna (Costume Designer)
Narrow Road to the Deep North 1969,D 2,64:1
Jungle of Cities 1970,Mr 1,75:2
Jones, T C
New Faces of 1956 1956,Je 15,32:1
Mask and Gown 1957,S 11,29:1
Jones, Teddy
Royal Fandango, A 1923,N 13,25:1
Blue Bird, The 1923,D 26,13:3
Assumption of Hannele, The 1924,F 16,16:2
Macbeth 1924,Mr 17,18:1
Caesar and Cleopatra 1925,Ap 14,27:1
Say It With Flowers 1926,D 6,29:1
Taming of the Shrew, The 1927,O 26,26:4
Courage 1928,O 9,34:2
News Item 1935,Ag 6,20:3
In the Bag 1936,D 18,30:2
Jones, Thelma
Golem, The 1959,F 26,38:2
Jones, Thomas B
Faith of Our Fathers 1950,Ag 6,72:2
Jones, Todd
Cry for Us All 1970,Ap 9,48:2
Jones, Tom (Director)
Celebration 1969,Ja 23,55:2
Jones, Tom (Lyricist)
Fantasticks, The 1960,My 4,55:2
110 in the Shade 1963,O 25,37:1
I Do! I Do! 1966,D 6,58:1
Celebration 1969,Ja 23,55:2
Colette 1970,O 15,58:1
Jones, Tom (Playwright)
Shoestring '57 1956,N 6,31:1
Fantasticks, The 1960,My 4,55:2
I Do! I Do! 1966,D 6,58:1
I Do! I Do! 1967,N 28,54:1
Celebration 1969,F 2,II,3:1
Jones, Tom Lee
Patriot for Me, A 1969,O 6,58:1
Jones, Trevor (Composer)
Provincetown Follies, The 1935,N 4,24:3
Jones, Valerie
Man in Evening Clothes, The 1924,D 6,13:4
You Can't Beat a Woman 1925,Mr 24,26:5
Jones, Venezuela
Savage Rhythm 1932,Ja 1,30:4
Jones, Verman
Blessed Event 1932,F 13,23:2
Jones, Vernon
Would-Be Gentleman, The 1928,O 2,34:1
Invitation au Voyage, L' 1928,O 5,17:1
Peter Pan; Boy Who Would Not Grow Up, The 1928,N 27,36:3
Would-Be Gentleman, The 1930,Ap 30,29:2

Jones, Vi
Marriage of Cana, The 1932,F 3,22:4
Jones, Violet
Little Theatre Tournament; Sightseers 1929,My 8,34:4
Jones, W
Hamlet 1923,N 20,23:3
Jones, W Boardman
Importance of Being Earnest, The 1936,O 22,31:2
Jones, W Boardman Jr (Producer)
Take It Away 1936,D 15,30:5
Jones, W E
It's the Valet 1933,D 15,25:4
Jones, W Wallace
Devil Within, The 1925,Mr 17,19:4
Jones, Walter
Getting Gertie's Garter 1921,Ag 2,16:2
Gingham Girl, The 1922,Ag 29,15:5
New Sin, The 1923,My 28,18:3
She Couldn't Say No! 1926,S 1,27:3
Lady in Love, A 1927,F 22,22:1
Married-And How! 1928,Je 15,30:2
Stork Mad 1936,O 1,28:4
Yr Obedient Husband 1938,Ja 11,26:5
Toilet, The 1964,D 17,51:1
No Place to Be Somebody 1969,My 5,53:3
No Place to Be Somebody 1969,D 31,17:1
Life and Times of J Walter Smintheus, The 1970,D 10,59:1
Jones, Walter (Director)
X Has No Value 1970,F 17,35:1
Jones, Walter Tupper
Nancy Ann 1924,Ap 1,18:1
Good Hope, The 1927,O 19,24:2
2 + 2 = 5 1927,N 29,30:3
First Stone, The 1928,Ja 14,12:2
Improvisations in June 1928,F 27,16:5
Jones, William
Creoles 1927,S 23,33:3
Carmen Jones 1943,D 3,26:2
Jones, William H
Play Without a Name, A 1928,N 26,30:5
Jones & Allen
Hummin' Sam 1933,Ap 10,8:8
Jones-Crane, Maudean
Twelfth Disciple, The 1930,My 17,21:4
Jones-Henry, Nancy
When I Was a Child 1960,D 9,38:1
Jonic, Bettina
Musical World of Bertolt Brecht, The 1968,My 14,39:1
Jonns, Birl
Carousel 1965,Ag 11,39:1
Jons, Joelle
'Toinette 1961,N 21,46:1
Banker's Daughter, The 1962,Ja 23,37:1
Jonsen, Tommy (Choreographer)
Sambo 1969,D 22,42:1
Sambo 1970,Ja 11,II,1:1
Sambo 1970,Jl 23,24:1
Jonson, Ben (Original Author)
Volpone 1957,Ja 13,II,10:1
Foxy 1962,Jl 4,12:2
Foxy 1964,F 17,26:1
Jonson, Ben (Playwright)
Volpone 1928,Ap 10,32:1
Volpone 1928,Ap 22,IX,1:1
Volpone 1928,D 9,X,2:7
Volpone 1930,Mr 11,24:5
Alchemist, The 1931,Je 5,27:1
Alchemist, The 1932,Ag 28,IX,1:1
Every Man in His Humour 1937,Ag 7,7:3
Volpone 1937,N 16,26:4
Volpone 1947,F 25,32:2
Volpone 1948,Ja 9,24:6
Alchemist, The 1948,My 7,31:4
Volpone 1957,Ja 8,27:1
Volpone 1957,F 5,27:2
Alchemist, The 1962,N 29,44:1
Volpone 1964,Jl 20,18:3
Alchemist, The 1964,S 15,33:1
Triumph of Delight 1965,My 1,19:1
Alchemist, The 1966,O 14,48:1
Alchemist, The 1966,O 30,II,1:1
Volpone 1967,Je 30,29:1
Alchemist, The 1969,Je 12,51:1
Alchemist, The 1969,Je 22,II,1:7
Alchemist, The 1970,Ag 26,36:1
Jonson, Bill (Musical Director)
Courtin' Time 1951,Je 14,30:2
Jonson, Jane
Regular Guy, A; Man's Man, A 1931,Je 5,27:1
Hot Money 1931,N 9,22:2
Girls in Uniform 1932,D 31,10:3
Jonson, Joe
Three to Make Ready 1946,Mr 8,16:2
Jonson, William (Miscellaneous)
Four Saints in Three Acts 1952,Ap 17,35:1
Mikado, The 1959,O 2,24:1
Pirates of Penzance, The 1960,O 7,29:1
Gondoliers, The 1961,Ja 26,33:2
Show Boat 1961,Ap 13,32:1
Porgy and Bess 1961,My 18,40:1

Jonson, William (Miscellaneous)—Cont
Porgy and Bess 1964,My 7,32:1
Brigadoon 1964,D 24,9:1
Dreigroschenoper, Die 1965,Mr 12,24:1
Jonsson, Judyann
Song of the Lusitanian Bogey, The 1968,Ja 3,52:1
Kongi's Harvest 1968,Ap 15,49:1
Daddy Goodness 1968,Je 5,37:1
God Is a (Guess What?) 1968,D 18,56:1
Ceremonies in Dark Old Men 1969,F 6,33:1
Jooss, Kurt (Choreographer)
Green Table, The 1942,Ja 22,12:2
Green Table, The 1942,F 1,IX,2:2
Prodigal Son, The 1942,F 18,22:2
Jooss, Kurt (Miscellaneous)
Green Table, The 1942,Ja 22,12:2
Jooss Ballet Dance Theatre
Actors Fund Fete 1942,F 23,24:5
Joplin, Carol
South Pacific 1965,Je 3,25:1
Jopling, M
Foemen of the Yard 1935,Ap 6,10:4
Joray, Peter
Sunday Nights at Nine 1934,Mr 5,18:5
Joray, Willard
Antony and Cleopatra 1924,F 20,22:1
Road to Rome, The 1927,F 1,24:2
Jordan, Al (Director)
Parasite, The 1965,D 17,43:2
Jordan, Al (Producer)
Parasite, The 1965,D 17,43:2
Jordan, Albert
Star of Bengal 1929,S 26,27:2
Jordan, Anders (Playwright)
Chinese Lily, A 1925,Mr 24,26:5
Jordan, Ann
Getting Even 1929,Ag 20,31:1
Jordan, Anthony
Cyrano de Bergerac 1946,O 9,33:2
Cyrano de Bergerac 1947,Ja 17,27:2
Jordan, Bert
Tip-Top 1920,O 6,13:2
Stepping Stones 1923,N 7,14:3
Jordan, Betty
Jarnegan 1928,S 25,29:2
Jordan, Billy
Sacco-Vanzetti 1969,F 9,78:1
Jordan, Bobby
Would-Be Gentleman, The 1930,Ap 30,29:2
Dead End 1935,O 29,17:2
Jordan, Charles
Let Freedom Ring 1935,N 7,26:2
Bitter Stream 1936,Mr 31,16:6
200 Were Chosen 1936,N 21,21:1
Tide Rising 1937,Ja 26,17:2
Chalked Out 1937,Mr 26,24:2
Come Across 1938,S 15,28:3
Fifth Column, The 1940,Mr 7,18:2
Jupiter Laughs 1940,S 10,27:1
Jordan, Charles A
Happy Landing 1932,Mr 28,10:5
Jordan, Charles E
Old Bill, M P 1926,N 11,22:2
Jordan, Charlie
Vaudeville (Palace) 1932,My 9,19:3
Jordan, Claudia
Bloomer Girl 1944,O 6,18:5
Jordan, David S
That Old Devil 1944,Je 6,14:2
Jordan, Doris
Year of Pilar, The 1952,Ja 7,14:3
Jordan, Dorothy
Garrick Gaieties 1926,My 11,25:2
Funny Face 1927,N 23,28:2
Treasure Girl 1928,N 9,22:1
Jordan, Dulcy
Men of Distinction 1953,My 1,18:4
Jordan, Earl
Patience 1928,Je 26,29:3
Jordan, Edith
Dead End 1935,O 29,17:2
Jordan, Elena
Love Is No Heaven 1943,Mr 16,15:3
Jordan, Frederick
Evensong 1933,F 1,13:4
Jordan, G Adam (Director)
Another Evening With Harry Stoones 1961,O 23,22:2
Jordan, Gaye
Mr Barry's Etchings 1950,F 1,26:2
Collector's Item 1952,F 9,11:2
Ondine 1954,F 19,23:1
Happiest Millionaire, The 1956,N 21,21:3
Jordan, Glenn (Director)
Fledermaus, Die 1954,My 20,38:5
Jordan, Hal (Composer)
Rondelay 1969,N 6,55:1
Jordan, Henrietta
Dice of the Gods, The 1923,Ap 6,20:2
Jordan, Irene
Sing Out, Sweet Land! 1944,D 28,24:2
Jordan, Jack
Sunup to Sundown 1938,F 2,14:3

Jordan, Jack Jr
Best Foot Forward 1941,O 2,28:2
Jordan, Jackie
Hilda Cassidy 1933,My 5,18:3
Remember the Day 1935,Jl 9,24:3
Green Waters 1936,N 5,34:4
Jordan, Jackson
Lady Says Yes, A 1945,Ja 11,18:5
Hollywood Pinafore 1945,Je 1,20:1
Jordan, Jean
Jenny Kissed Me 1948,D 24,12:2
First Lady 1952,My 29,18:5
Jordan, Jerome
Baby Mine 1927,Je 10,21:2
Mongolia 1927,D 27,24:5
Mima 1928,D 13,24:2
Jordan, Joe (Composer)
Deep Harlem 1929,Ja 8,35:2
Brown Buddies 1930,O 8,29:1
Jordan, John
Wanhope Building, The 1947,F 11,36:5
Mister Roberts 1948,F 19,27:2
Kean 1961,N 3,28:2
Jordan, Judy
Rose 1969,O 29,30:1
Jordan, Jules
Melody Man, The 1924,My 14,14:2
Jordan, Justine (Lady)
Happy Landing 1932,Mr 28,10:5
Jordan, Kate (Playwright)
Masked Woman, The 1922,D 23,14:2
Jordan, Kathryn
Riff-Raff 1926,F 9,18:6
Jordan, Marc
Yeomen of the Guard, The 1957,My 22,28:3
Gondoliers, The 1957,My 29,34:2
Can-Can 1959,Ag 26,25:4
Funny Girl 1964,Mr 27,15:1
Passionella 1966,O 19,53:1
Lady or the Tiger?, The 1966,O 19,53:1
Darling of the Day 1968,Ja 29,26:2
Her First Roman 1968,O 21,53:3
Get Thee to Canterbury 1969,Ja 26,74:1
Jordan, Marie
Mummers and Men 1962,Mr 27,41:6
Jordan, Mary (Producer)
Noontide 1961,Je 2,37:1
Jordan, Miriam
Cynara 1931,N 3,31:1
Michael Drops In 1938,D 28,24:3
Jordan, Owen
Audition of the Apprentice Theatre 1939,Je 2,26:2
Mexican Mural; Moonlight Scene 1942,Ap 27,19:2
Jordan, Paul
Kean 1961,N 3,28:2
Jordan, Richard
Romeo and Juliet 1961,F 24,24:1
Midsummer Night's Dream, A 1961,Ag 3,13:1
Richard II 1961,Ag 30,25:1
Take Her, She's Mine 1961,D 22,19:1
Merchant of Venice, The 1962,Je 22,1:4
Tempest, The 1962,Jl 17,18:2
As You Like It 1963,Jl 17,19:2
Bicycle Ride to Nevada 1963,S 25,38:1
War and Peace 1965,Ja 12,32:1
Judith 1965,Mr 25,42:2
Love's Labour's Lost 1965,Je 16,46:1
Troilus and Cressida 1965,Ag 13,17:1
Generation 1965,O 8,5:6
All's Well That Ends Well 1966,Je 17,39:1
'Tis Pity She's a Whore 1967,O 21,15:2
We Bombed in New Haven 1967,D 7,58:1
Henry IV 1968,F 7,40:1
Three Sisters, The 1968,Mr 18,56:1
Possibilities 1968,D 5,60:1
Patriot for Me, A 1969,O 6,58:1
Jordan, Robert (Miscellaneous)
Behind the Wall 1960,N 1,47:1
Jordan, Robert (Playwright)
Stubble Before Swords 1936,Mr 24,26:8
Jordan, Robert A Jr
Laugh It Off 1925,Ap 25,18:4
Jordan, Ted
Stockade 1954,F 5,14:2
Jordan, Thomas
One Way Street 1928,D 25,31:2
Love's Old Sweet Song 1940,My 3,16:3
Jordan, Thomas G
East Lynne Goes West 1931,My 3,I,26:5
Jordan, Tom
Cafe Crown 1942,Ja 24,12:5
Jordan, Tom (Lighting Director)
Misalliance 1955,F 12,10:6
High Button Shoes 1955,Mr 12,10:6
Jordan, William
Oh, Ernest! 1927,My 10,24:3
Wait Until Dark 1966,F 3,21:1
Displaced Person, The 1966,D 30,15:1
Jorden, Jeanne
Joy to the World 1948,Mr 19,28:2
Jordon, Charles
Iron Flowers 1933,Je 13,22:2

Jordon, Shirley
Singin' the Blues 1931,S 17,21:3
Jordon, T Gihon
Hoot Mon, or Clans Across the Sea 1927,My 8,29:4
Jordon and Jordon
Singin' the Blues 1931,S 17,21:3
Jorgensen, C Theodore
Upon My Soul 1927,Ap 22,19:1
Jorgensen, Ted
Oh, Hector! 1929,Mr 6,33:2
Jorgulesco, Jonel (Costume Designer)
Too True to Be Good 1932,Mr 1,19:2
Too True to Be Good 1932,Ap 5,27:5
Jorgulesco, Jonel (Scenic Designer)
Chair, The 1930,O 4,15:4
Too True to Be Good 1932,Mr 1,19:2
Child of Manhattan 1932,Mr 2,15:1
Too True to Be Good 1932,Ap 5,27:5
Joris, Victor (Costume Designer)
War Games 1969,Ap 18,37:1
Jory, Jon
Doctor Faustus 1961,Ap 26,36:1
Simple Life, A 1964,My 18,36:1
Jory, Victor
Lazarus Laughed 1928,Ap 10,33:1
Two Mrs Carrolls, The 1943,Ag 4,14:1
Two Mrs Carrolls, The 1943,Ag 8,II,1:1
Perfect Marriage, The 1944,O 27,17:6
Perfect Marriage, The 1944,N 5,II,1:2
Therese 1945,O 10,24:2
Therese 1945,O 28,II,1:1
Henry VIII 1946,N 7,42:2
John Gabriel Borkman 1946,N 13,33:2
Androcles and the Lion 1946,D 20,29:2
Yellow Jack 1947,F 28,26:2
Devil's Disciple, The 1950,Ja 26,23:2
Devil's Disciple, The 1950,F 5,II,1:1
Jory, Victor (Miscellaneous)
Androcles and the Lion 1946,D 20,29:2
Jose, Jay (Scenic Designer)
Mummers and Men 1962,Mr 27,41:6
Jose, Mr
Trois Jeunes Filles Nues; Three Young Maids From the Folies Bergere 1929,Mr 5,28:2
Josef, Carl
Made in America 1925,O 15,27:2
Joselow, I B (Miscellaneous)
Uncle Willie 1956,D 21,17:1
Joselow, I B (Producer)
Pony Cart, The 1954,S 15,39:2
Joseph, Allen
Winners and Losers 1947,F 27,27:2
All Summer Long 1953,Ja 29,23:1
Cretan Woman, The 1954,My 21,17:2
View From the Bridge, A 1956,N 9,34:4
Bedtime Story 1957,Ap 1,21:2
Portrait of a Madonna 1957,Ap 1,21:2
Apollo of Bellac, The 1958,Mr 7,17:2
Time of Vengeance 1959,D 11,39:1
Time of Vengeance 1959,D 27,II,1:1
Taming of the Shrew, The 1960,Ag 20,17:1
Mousetrap, The 1960,N 7,46:1
Buskers, The 1961,O 31,28:1
Joseph, Carl
Patriot for Me, A 1969,O 6,58:1
Joseph, Edmund (Miscellaneous)
Seperate Rooms 1940,Mr 25,10:3
Joseph, Edmund (Playwright)
Polly of Hollywood 1927,F 22,22:3
Joseph, George
Sundown Beach 1948,S 8,37:1
Joseph, Irving (Composer)
Luv 1964,N 12,43:1
Joseph, Irving (Musical Director)
Jimmy Shine 1968,D 6,52:1
Joseph, Jackie
Billy Barnes Revue, The 1959,Je 10,42:2
Billy Barnes People, The 1961,Je 14,10:3
Joseph, Lionel
Seventh Heaven 1922,O 31,11:1
Joseph, Marilyn
Patriot for Me, A 1969,O 6,58:1
Joseph, Peter (Costume Designer)
Banker's Daughter, The 1962,Ja 23,37:1
Catch Me if You Can 1965,Mr 10,50:1
Joyful Noise, A 1966,D 16,57:1
Joseph, Robert
Young Madame Conti 1937,Ap 1,18:4
Joseph, Robert L (Miscellaneous)
King Lear 1950,D 26,18:1
Joseph, Robert L (Playwright)
Face of a Hero 1960,O 21,29:5
Isle of Children 1962,Mr 17,16:2
Joseph, Robert L (Producer)
Father, The 1949,N 17,36:2
My Darlin' Aida 1952,O 28,36:4
Mademoiselle Colombe 1954,Ja 7,26:1
Tiger at the Gates 1955,O 4,40:1
Major Barbara 1956,O 31,27:1
Heartbreak House 1959,O 19,37:1
Joseph, Robert L (Translator)
Father, The 1949,N 17,36:2

Joseph, Ruth
Between the Devil 1937,D 23,24:5
Joseph, Stanley A
Seven Against One 1930,My 7,25:1
Joseph, Stephen M (Miscellaneous)
Me Nobody Knows, The 1970,My 19,42:1
Me Nobody Knows, The 1970,My 31,II,1:6
Josephine, Lois
June Love 1921,Ap 26,20:1
Josephs, Conrad
Power of Dreams, A 1958,Mr 11,33:1
Deirdre of the Sorrows 1959,O 15,46:1
Josephson, Ragnar (Playwright)
Nyckelromanen 1931,Mr 1,VIII,3:1
Josephson, Sam
Love for Sale 1936,Ja 24,14:2
Street Singers 1938,D 12,25:6
Josey, Vilma
Sons o' Fun 1941,D 2,28:2
Joslin, Howard
Pardon Our French 1950,O 6,22:4
Joslyn, Allyn
Johannes Kreisler 1922,D 25,20:3
Sandro Botticelli 1923,Mr 27,24:2
Scaramouche 1923,O 25,14:2
Man and the Masses 1924,Ap 15,25:1
Firebrand, The 1924,O 16,33:1
Taming of the Shrew, The 1925,D 19,14:1
Moon Is a Gong, The 1926,Mr 13,21:3
Head or Tail 1926,N 10,24:1
Lady in Love, A 1927,F 22,22:1
One for All 1927,My 14,25:5
Mystery Man, The 1928,Ja 27,14:2
Vermont 1929,Ja 9,28:1
Troilus and Cressida 1932,Je 7,22:3
Boy Meets Girl 1935,N 19,27:2
Boy Meets Girl 1935,N 28,38:2
All That Glitters 1938,Ja 20,18:2
Arsenic and Old Lace 1941,Ja 11,13:2
Collector's Item 1952,F 9,11:2
Jospey, Louis
Subway Express 1929,S 25,34:3
Joss, Benjamin
Folly Town 1920,My 18,9:2
Josset, Andre (Playwright)
Elizabeth, la Femme Sans Hommes 1935,N 24,IX,3:7
Borgia, Les 1938,Je 12,X,2:3
Jostyn, Jay
Deadfall 1955,O 28,20:1
Joudry, Patricia (Playwright)
Country Wife, The 1955,Ap 6,35:1
Semi-Detached 1960,Mr 11,20:2
Joue, Simone
Felix 1926,O 10,VIII,2:1
Joullot, Eugene (Playwright)
Court Circuit, Le 1923,O 16,18:1
Jourdan, Louis
Immoralist, The 1954,F 2,18:7
Immoralist, The 1954,F 9,22:1
Immoralist, The 1954,F 14,II,1:1
Tonight in Samarkand 1955,F 17,22:2
Jourist
Chauve-Souris 1922,Je 6,17:4
Journet, Marcel
If This Be Treason 1935,S 24,28:2
Atout... Coeur 1936,Mr 27,25:4
Martine 1936,N 26,38:2
Homme Que J'Ai Tue, L'; Man Whom I Have Killed, The 1936,D 10,34:3
Bichon; Little Dear 1936,D 31,20:5
Sexe Fort, Le; Strong Sex, The 1937,Ja 14,17:4
Si Je Voulais; If I Wished to 1937,Ja 28,22:5
Dans Le Noir; In the Dark 1937,F 11,18:3
Good Hunting 1938,N 22,26:5
New Moon, The 1942,Ag 19,14:2
Journet, Marcel Jr
Social Register, The 1931,N 10,28:2
Mad Hopes, The 1932,D 2,26:3
Jouvet, Louis
Outward Bound 1927,Ja 30,VII,2:4
Revisor 1927,My 1,VIII,2:4
Leopold le Bien-Aime 1927,O 30,IX,4:7
Suzanne 1929,F 17,IX,4:2
Jean de la Lune 1929,My 12,IX,5:3
Amphitryon 38 1929,D 1,X,4:1
Prof' d'Anglais, Le 1930,My 25,IX,2:8
Eau Fraiche, L' 1931,Je 7,VIII,3:5
Taciturne, Un 1931,N 22,VIII,1:6
Margrave, La 1932,D 18,X,3:6
Intermezzo 1933,Mr 26,IX,2:1
Tessa 1935,Ja 6,IX,2:1
Folle de Chaillot, La 1945,D 20,17:4
Ecole des Femmes, L'; School for Wives 1951,Mr 19,22:1
Jouvet, Louis (Director)
Amphitryon 38 1929,D 1,X,4:1
Tessa 1935,Ja 6,IX,2:1
Folle de Chaillot, La 1945,D 20,17:4
Ecole des Femmes, L'; School for Wives 1951,Mr 19,22:1
Diable et le Bon Dieu, Le 1951,Ag 19,II,1:6
Fourberies de Scapin, Les 1952,N 21,21:2

Jouvet, Louis (Lighting Director)
Outward Bound 1927,Ja 30,VII,2:4
Amphitryon 38 1929,D 1,X,4:1

Jouvet, Louis (Producer)
Deux Paires d'Amis 1926,O 3,VIII,2:1
Revisor 1927,My 1,VIII,2:4
Coup du Deux-Decembre, Le 1928,Ap 15,IX,2:2
Siegfried 1928,My 20,VIII,1:3
Suzanne 1929,F 17,IX,4:2
Jean de la Lune 1929,My 12,IX,5:3
Prof' d'Anglais, Le 1930,My 25,IX,2:8
Donogoo 1930,N 16,VIII,2:6
Eau Fraiche, L' 1931,Je 7,VIII,3:5
Taciturne, Un 1931,N 22,VIII,1:6
Domino 1932,F 28,VIII,1:1
Petrus 1933,D 31,IX,2:2
Machine Infernale, La 1934,My 13,IX,2:2
Ecole des Femmes, L' 1936,Je 21,IX,2:4

Jouvet, Louis (Scenic Designer)
Outward Bound 1927,Ja 30,VII,2:4
Folle de Chaillot, La 1945,D 20,17:4

Jovanowitsch, Rani
They All Come to Moscow 1933,My 12,20:6

Jowitt, Deborah
Getting Married 1970,Ja 20,46:1

Jowitt, Deborah (Choreographer)
Greenwillow 1970,D 8,60:1

Jowsey, Nancy (Scenic Designer)
American Hamburger League, The 1969,S 17,51:1
Chicago 70 1970,My 26,33:1

Joy, Alice
Vaudeville (Palace) 1932,My 2,13:2

Joy, Bernie (Costume Designer)
Capacity for Wings 1957,Ja 10,25:2
Romeo and Juliet 1957,Je 28,30:2
Two Gentlemen of Verona 1957,Jl 23,21:5
Macbeth 1957,Ag 16,11:2
Pink String and Sealing Wax 1957,S 6,13:1
Richard III 1957,N 26,41:1
Bald Soprano, The 1958,Je 4,39:2
Jack 1958,Je 4,39:2
She Shall Have Music 1959,Ja 23,18:4

Joy, Bernie (Lighting Director)
Arms and the Man 1956,O 2,39:4

Joy, Bernie (Scenic Designer)
Titus Andronicus 1956,D 3,40:2
Romeo and Juliet 1957,Je 28,30:2
Two Gentlemen of Verona 1957,Jl 23,21:5
Macbeth 1957,Ag 16,11:2
Richard III 1957,N 26,41:1

Joy, Bernie (Translator)
Arms and the Man 1956,O 2,39:4

Joy, Carol
Carmen Jones 1956,Je 1,28:2
Egg and I, The 1958,S 11,43:4

Joy, Edward (Producer)
Mighty Man Is He, A 1960,Ja 7,25:2

Joy, Helen
Strawberry Blonde, The 1927,F 8,20:3
Nice Women 1929,Je 11,27:4
Hawk Island 1929,S 17,34:7

Joy, John
Guys and Dolls 1959,Jl 22,22:2
How Now, Dow Jones 1967,D 8,53:1
Fig Leaves Are Falling, The 1969,Ja 3,19:1

Joy, Leatrice
Vaudeville (Palace) 1929,Ap 22,22:6

Joy, Louis Mount
We've Got to Have Money 1923,Ag 21,12:1

Joy, Nicholas
Carnaval 1924,D 30,15:1
Embers 1926,F 2,20:3
No Trespassing! 1926,S 8,19:1
Nightingale, The 1927,Ja 4,20:4
Wings Over Europe 1928,D 11,35:1
Topaze 1930,F 13,25:3
Modern Virgin, A 1931,My 21,33:4
Bride the Sun Shines On, The 1931,D 28,20:2
Music in the Air 1932,N 9,28:2
Ode to Liberty 1934,D 22,20:2
Rain 1935,F 13,24:1
Journey by Night 1935,Ap 7,IX,2:1
Journey by Night, A 1935,Ap 17,26:3
Knock on Wood 1935,My 29,16:2
Ode to Liberty 1935,Jl 2,24:3
Ode to Liberty 1935,Jl 9,24:4
Ode to Liberty 1935,Ag 6,20:3
Ragged Edge, The 1935,N 26,28:3
Season Changes, The 1935,D 24,10:2
Julie the Great 1936,Ja 15,15:3
Alice Takat 1936,F 11,19:2
Sweet Aloes 1936,Mr 5,24:5
Difficulty of Getting Married, The 1936,Jl 7,22:1
Yes, My Darling Daughter 1937,F 10,19:2
Good Hunting 1938,N 22,26:5
Philadelphia Story, The 1939,Mr 29,21:1
Walrus and the Carpenter, The 1941,N 10,20:2
All the Comforts of Home 1942,My 26,24:5
Morning Star, The 1942,S 15,18:4
Morning Star, The 1942,S 20,VIII,1:1
Bird in Hand 1942,O 20,24:2
This Rock 1943,F 19,23:2
Mrs January & Mr Ex 1944,Ap 1,10:2

Ten Little Indians 1944,Je 28,21:2
Joy Forever, A 1946,Ja 8,20:2
Iceman Cometh, The 1946,O 10,31:3
Caesar and Cleopatra 1949,D 22,28:2
Dear Barbarians 1952,F 22,15:2
Small War on Murray Hill 1957,Ja 4,19:1
Small War on Murray Hill 1957,Ja 13,II,1:1
Family Reunion, The 1958,O 21,39:1

Joyce, Andrea
Trumpets and Drums 1969,O 13,52:1
Macbeth 1969,D 23,25:1

Joyce, Baby
Tobacco Road 1950,Mr 7,23:2

Joyce, Barbara
Tobacco Road 1943,S 6,21:3
Petrified Forest, The 1943,N 2,30:6
Calico Wedding 1945,Mr 8,18:6
Hidden Horizon 1946,S 20,42:2
Church Street 1948,F 10,27:2
Stone for Danny Fisher, A 1954,O 22,24:2
Lovers, Villains and Fools: A Shakespearean
  Variety Show 1956,O 24,44:7
Golden Six, The 1958,O 27,31:2

Joyce, Burton
As You Like It 1936,Ap 24,18:4

Joyce, Carol
When You Smile 1925,O 6,31:2
Bunk of 1926 1926,F 17,12:3

Joyce, Cherilyn
Finian's Rainbow 1953,Mr 7,13:2

Joyce, Denise
Deputy, The 1964,F 27,26:1

Joyce, Edna
Paradise 1931,My 12,29:2

Joyce, Edward
Doughgirls, The 1942,D 31,19:2

Joyce, Jack
Vaudeville (Palace) 1925,D 29,21:2

Joyce, James (Original Author)
Ulysses in Nighttown 1958,Je 6,30:1
Ulysses in Nighttown 1958,Je 15,II,1:1
Portrait of the Artist as a Young Man, A
  1962,My 29,21:1
Stephen D 1962,S 25,31:3
Stephen D 1962,D 21,7:2
Stephen D 1963,F 14,5:2

Joyce, James (Playwright)
Exiles 1925,F 20,20:2
Exiles 1957,Mr 13,27:1
Coach With the Six Insides, The 1962,N 27,44:1
Stephen D 1966,Ag 5,17:1
Coach With the Six Insides, The 1967,My 12,50:1
Stephen D 1967,S 25,58:1
Exiles 1970,N 19,42:4

Joyce, Janice
Dream of Sganarelle, The 1933,O 17,26:5
School for Husbands, The 1933,O 17,26:5
Jubilee 1935,O 14,20:1
Let's Face It 1941,O 30,26:2

Joyce, Lee
Allah Be Praised! 1944,Ap 21,14:2

Joyce, Louise
Yankee Princess, The 1922,O 3,22:1
Well of Romance, The 1930,N 8,21:2

Joyce, Mara
Enchanted, The 1958,Ap 23,41:1

Joyce, Marjorie
Summer Wives 1936,Ap 14,18:1

Joyce, Martha
Answered the Flute 1960,Mr 10,37:4

Joyce, Michael
Winter's Tale, The 1963,Je 29,13:1
Midsummer Night's Dream, A 1963,Jl 1,19:2

Joyce, Paul
Silver Swan, The 1929,N 28,34:5

Joyce, Peggy
So This Is Love 1928,D 2,X,4:2

Joyce, Peggy Hopkins
Earl Carroll's Vanities 1923,Jl 6,8:2
Lady of the Orchids, The 1928,D 14,37:3
Vaudeville (Palace) 1931,Ap 20,16:2

Joyce, Phyllis
9 O'Clock Revue 1923,O 5,22:1
Exiles 1925,F 20,20:2
Hay Fever 1925,O 5,25:1
Behavior of Mrs Crane, The 1928,Mr 21,30:1
Jade God, The 1929,My 14,28:3
Country Wife, The 1931,Ap 19,31:5
Tiara, The 1932,D 12,18:3
Bishop Misbehaves, The 1935,F 21,22:4
Season Changes, The 1935,D 24,10:2
Middle Man 1936,S 8,23:1
Heartbreak House 1938,Ap 30,18:2
Dear Octopus 1939,Ja 12,22:2
School for Scandal, The 1940,Je 18,29:5
Blithe Spirit 1941,N 6,26:2

Joyce, Regis
If This Be Treason 1935,S 24,28:2
O Evening Star 1936,Ja 9,24:6
Sun Field, The 1942,D 10,33:2

Joyce, Stephen
Teahouse of the August Moon, The
  1954,Ap 23,23:6

Joyce, Stephen—Cont
Tinker's Wedding, The 1957,Mr 7,24:1
Riders to the Sea 1957,Mr 7,24:1
Riders to the Sea 1957,Mr 17,II,1:1
Romeo and Juliet 1957,Je 28,30:2
Legend of Lizzie, The 1959,F 10,39:1
Caucasian Chalk Circle, The 1961,N 1,35:1
Burning of the Lepers, The 1962,Ap 5,29:1
Winter's Tale, The 1963,Je 29,13:1
Midsummer Night's Dream, A 1963,Jl 1,19:2
King Lear 1963,N 23,22:1
King Lear 1964,Jl 28,18:2
King Lear 1965,Je 25,39:1
Falstaff 1966,Je 20,27:1
Murder in the Cathedral 1966,Je 21,38:1
Julius Caesar 1966,Je 24,29:2
Those That Play the Clowns 1966,N 25,48:1
Galileo 1967,Ap 14,31:1
Stephen D 1967,S 25,58:1
Stephen D 1967,O 8,II,1:6
Saint Joan 1968,Ja 5,42:1
Exercise, The 1968,Ap 25,54:1
Exercise, The 1968,My 12,II,1:1
Fireworks; Report, The 1969,Je 12,51:1
Fireworks; Football 1969,Je 12,51:1
Fireworks; Fireworks for a Hot Fourth
  1969,Je 12,51:1

Joyce, Thomas
Shannons of Broadway, The 1927,S 27,30:4

Joyce, Van (Producer)
King of the Dark Chamber 1961,F 10,21:1

Joyce, Vernon
People vs Ranchman, The 1968,O 28,56:1

Joyce, Vivian
Best Foot Forward 1956,Mr 3,16:1

Joyceburg
Back to Methuselah 1923,O 14,VIII,1:8

Joyner, Frank
Common Sin, The 1928,O 16,28:2
Short Cut, The 1930,Ja 28,28:2

Joyner, Harry
Ashes of Love 1926,Mr 23,24:3
Our Betters 1928,F 21,18:2
Mr Samuel 1930,N 11,28:4
Admirable Crichton, The 1931,Mr 10,23:2
Midsummer Night's Dream, A 1932,N 18,22:2
Twelfth Night 1932,N 19,20:5
Comedy of Errors, The 1932,N 22,25:3
Merchant of Venice, The 1932,N 24,34:5
Romeo and Juliet 1933,F 3,21:5
Sleeping Clergyman, A 1934,O 9,16:1

Joyner, Hendrick
Love Kills 1934,My 2,25:3

Joynes, Alane
Child of the Morning 1958,Ap 22,40:2

Jscherey and Hully
Artists and Models 1927,N 16,28:2

Juanita
White Lilacs 1928,S 11,31:2

Juarez, Juanita
Beat the Band 1942,O 15,26:1

Jubelirer, Perry
Best Foot Forward 1941,O 2,28:2

Jubilee Singers
So This Is Paris 1930,Ap 27,IX,2:3

Juda, Walter (Miscellaneous)
Creditors 1962,Ja 26,19:1

Judah, Catherine
Gondoliers, The 1940,O 1,29:2
Mikado, The 1944,F 12,11:3
H M S Pinafore 1944,F 15,14:4
Pirates of Penzance, The 1944,F 18,15:5
Gondoliers, The 1944,F 22,26:3
Iolanthe 1944,F 23,17:1
Patience 1944,F 26,11:4
Ruddigore 1944,Mr 3,19:5
Yeomen of the Guard, The 1944,Mr 5,34:3
Pirates of Penzance, The 1946,My 17,14:6

Judals, May (Director)
Howdy, Mr Ice of 1950 1949,My 27,24:2

Judd, Carl
Whirl of New York, The 1921,Je 14,18:1
Five O'Clock Girl, The 1927,O 11,26:3
Privilege Car 1931,Mr 4,33:1
Christopher Blake 1946,D 2,33:2
Temporary Island, A 1948,Mr 15,27:3
Small Hours, The 1951,F 16,22:1
Solid Gold Cadillac, The 1953,N 6,24:2

Judd, Carl (Miscellaneous)
Goodbye Again 1956,Ap 25,38:1

Judd, J R Jr
Wings Over Europe 1936,Mr 4,24:7
Front Page, The 1937,N 12,27:2

Judd, Rex (Playwright)
Suspect 1937,Mr 7,XI,2:1

Judd, Terry
Romeo and Juliet 1968,Je 11,55:2

Judd, Valerie (Costume Designer)
E-MC2 1948,Je 16,36:2
New York Idea, The 1948,Ag 18,29:2
Peg o' My Heart 1948,Ag 25,29:2

Judelevitch, Tmima
Dybbuk, The 1948,My 3,26:3
Golem, The 1948,My 17,22:3

Judelewitch, T
Eternal Jew, The 1926,D 21,21:2
Judels, Charles
Mary 1920,O 19,12:1
For Goodness Sake 1922,F 22,13:1
Wildflower 1923,F 8,17:2
Louisiana Lady 1947,Je 3,35:2
Judels, Charles (Director)
My Country 1926,Ag 10,19:1
Gay Paree 1926,N 10,24:2
Night in Spain, A 1927,My 4,28:2
Judels, May
Stars on Ice (2d Edition) 1943,Je 25,13:2
Judels, May (Director)
Stars on Ice (2d Edition) 1943,Je 25,13:2
Judels, May (Miscellaneous)
Hats Off to Ice 1944,Je 23,15:2
Icetime 1946,Je 21,20:5
Icetime 1947,My 29,28:2
Howdy Mr Ice 1948,Je 25,28:5
Judge, Curley
Squaw Man, The 1921,D 27,10:3
Judge, Don (Miscellaneous)
Arms and the Man 1967,Je 23,44:2
Judge, Elsie
Wandering Jew, The 1927,F 2,22:4
Judge, James P (Playwright)
Square Crooks 1926,Mr 2,23:2
Judge, Jane
Mis-Guided Tour 1959,O 13,44:7
Judge, Robert E (Director)
Sniper, The 1959,O 28,40:4
Judge, Robert E (Miscellaneous)
Sniper, The 1959,O 28,40:4
Abortion 1959,O 28,40:4
Movie Man 1959,O 28,40:4
Dance of Death, The 1960,S 14,51:1
Judge, Robert E (Producer)
Every Other Evil 1961,Ja 23,20:2
Judson, Helen
Thank You 1921,O 4,10:2
Arabesque 1925,O 21,20:2
Judson, James
Up in Central Park 1947,My 20,29:2
Judson, Lester (Lyricist)
Chic 1959,My 19,28:2
Judson, Lester (Playwright)
Chic 1959,My 19,28:2
Judson-Stiles, Pamela (Miscellaneous)
Enemy of the People, An 1959,F 5,24:4
Judy, Edwin
Little Theatre Tournament; Trifles 1928,My 11,28:1
Juergens, Robert
Here Comes Santa Claus 1962,My 18,34:1
Juillard, Jean
Baptiste 1952,N 13,34:2
Proces, Le; Trial, The 1952,N 18,36:2
Amphitryon 1952,N 21,21:2
Fourberies de Scapin, Les 1952,N 21,21:2
Occupe-Toi d'Amelie; Keep Your Eyes on Amelie
1952,N 25,35:2
Hamlet 1952,D 2,39:1
Volpone 1957,F 5,27:2
Misanthrope, Le 1957,F 8,19:1
Nuits de La Colere, Les; Nights of Fury
1957,F 12,31:1
Intermezzo 1957,F 15,20:4
Chien du Jardinier, Le; Gardener's Dog, The
1957,F 19,36:1
Adieux, Les 1957,F 19,36:1
Jukes, Bernard
Dracula 1927,O 6,29:1
Sari 1930,Ja 29,27:1
Smiles 1930,N 19,19:2
Lancashire Lass, The 1931,D 31,16:3
Saint Wench 1933,Ja 3,19:3
Yellow Jack 1934,Mr 7,22:6
Julein, Edward (Miscellaneous)
Night Circus, The 1958,D 3,44:1
Jules, Mr
Trois Jeunes Filles Nues; Three Young Maids From
the Folies Bergere 1929,Mr 5,28:2
Julia, Raul
Vida es Sueno, La 1964,Mr 18,49:1
Marriage Proposal, The 1966,Je 28,51:1
Macbeth 1966,Ag 29,23:4
Ox Cart, The 1966,D 20,58:1
Titus Andronicus 1967,Ag 10,43:2
No Exit 1967,O 31,38:2
Memorandum, The 1968,My 6,55:1
Cuban Thing, The 1968,S 25,36:2
Paradise Gardens East 1969,Mr 11,39:1
Conerico Was Here to Stay 1969,Mr 11,39:1
Indians 1969,My 27,43:1
Indians 1969,O 14,51:1
Persians, The 1970,Ap 16,53:1
Castro Complex, The 1970,N 19,40:1
Julian, Don
Untitled-Revue 1930,Ap 22,33:2
Julian, Donald
Land Beyond the River, A 1957,Mr 29,15:7
Julian, Joseph
Judgment Day 1934,S 13,26:4

Walk Into My Parlor 1941,N 20,38:2
War and Peace 1942,My 22,26:3
Rope Dancers, The 1957,N 21,39:1
Case of Libel, A 1963,O 11,43:2
Julian, Paul
Romeo and Juliet 1934,D 21,30:3
Juliana
Mystery Moon 1930,Je 24,23:4
Juliani, J C
Bourgeois Gentilhomme, Le 1964,Je 18,28:2
King Lear 1964,Je 19,36:1
Henry IV, Part I 1965,Je 30,42:1
Falstaff; Henry IV, Part II 1965,Jl 1,35:1
Julius Caesar 1965,Jl 2,18:1
Juliano, John
King and I, The 1951,Mr 30,26:2
King and I, The 1951,Ap 8,II,1:1
Julien
Perichole, La 1926,D 29,24:4
Julien, Charlotte
Dead End 1935,O 29,17:2
Julien, Edward
Mademoiselle Colombe 1954,Ja 7,26:1
Julien, Edward (Miscellaneous)
Fun Couple, The 1962,O 27,15:2
Joyful Noise, A 1966,D 16,57:1
Spofford 1967,D 15,54:3
Julien, Jay (Miscellaneous)
Cambridge Circus 1964,O 7,53:1
Julien, Jay (Producer)
Mademoiselle Colombe 1954,Ja 7,26:1
Hatful of Rain, A 1955,N 10,44:1
Night Circus, The 1958,D 3,44:1
Fun Couple, The 1962,O 27,15:2
Hostile Witness 1966,F 18,26:1
Juliet, Miss
Vaudeville (Palace) 1924,Ap 29,12:2
Vaudeville (Palace) 1928,My 29,17:4
Julius, Carl
It Never Rains 1929,N 20,26:4
It Never Rains 1931,D 25,29:3
Julius, Oscar Art Quartet
Organ Grinder, The 1934,Ja 1,28:3
Jun, Arakawa
Golden Bat 1970,Je 27,18:2
Junaluska
Strong Are Lonely, The 1953,S 30,38:3
Arrow-Maker, The 1956,O 5,20:1
Shakuntala 1959,S 10,41:2
Junaluska (Director)
Arrow-Maker, The 1956,O 5,20:1
Junaluska (Producer)
Arrow-Maker, The 1956,O 5,20:1
June
Polly 1928,D 23,VIII,4:1
Polly 1929,Ja 9,28:3
Cinderella 1935,Ja 13,IX,3:1
June, Milly
Queer People 1934,F 16,16:2
Junes, Teddy
Sea Shells 1935,Jl 16,24:2
Junger, Esther
Parade 1935,My 21,22:2
'Tis of Thee 1940,O 28,21:3
Junger, Esther (Choreographer)
'Tis of Thee 1940,O 28,21:3
Dark of the Moon 1945,Mr 15,27:2
Dear Judas 1947,O 6,26:4
Jungwirth, Manfred
Porgy and Bess 1950,N 26,II,7:8
Junion, Nancy
Meet Peter Grant 1961,My 11,41:4
I Want You 1961,S 15,29:1
Junior, George
Marilyn's Affairs 1933,Mr 16,21:5
Junior, Herbert
Decision 1944,F 3,23:2
Strange Fruit 1945,N 30,18:6
Junior, John
Good Old Days, The 1923,Ag 15,21:2
Among the Married 1929,O 4,24:3
Ritzy 1930,F 11,30:4
Torch Song 1930,Ag 28,23:1
Adam Had Two Sons 1932,Ja 21,17:1
Experience Unnecessary 1932,Mr 28,10:2
American Holiday 1936,F 22,13:3
Night Before Christmas, The 1941,Ap 11,25:2
Junius, Charlotte
Conjur 1938,N 1,27:2
Junker, Kurt
Neidhardt von Gneisenau 1927,Ja 23,VII,4:5
Junod, Don
Trial by Jury 1966,Je 8,41:2
Jupp, Kenneth (Playwright)
Buskers, The 1961,O 31,28:1
Jurado, Katy
Best House in Naples, The 1956,O 27,16:2
Jurgens, Adele
Jubilee 1935,O 14,20:1
Jurgens, Curt
Great Indoors, The 1966,F 2,23:1
Jurgens, Klaus
Dreigroschenoper, Die 1965,Mr 12,24:1

Jurist, Edward
First Stop to Heaven 1941,Ja 6,10:7
Jurist, Irma (Choreographer)
Hold It! 1948,My 6,31:5
Jurist, Irma (Composer)
Caesar and Cleopatra 1949,D 22,28:2
Alive and Kicking 1950,Ja 18,25:5
Razzle Dazzle 1951,F 20,21:1
Witches' Sabbath 1962,Ap 20,22:2
Portrait of the Artist as a Young Man, A
1962,My 29,21:1
Barroom Monks, The 1962,My 29,21:1
Bless the Child 1968,My 5,II,16:1
Jurist, Irma (Miscellaneous)
Antigone 1967,Ja 14,18:1
Juriste, Stephen
Surgeon, The 1932,O 28,23:1
Jurmann, Walter (Composer)
Rally 'Round The Girls 1942,Mr 29,VIII,2:2
Just, Emy St
Dear Judas 1947,O 6,26:4
Justice, Barry
Man and Boy 1963,N 13,34:1
Young Visitors, The 1968,D 26,48:1
Justice, Clare
Grand Tour, The 1951,D 11,45:2
Big Knife, The 1959,N 13,25:1
Hobo 1961,Ap 11,41:2
Justice, George Lewis
This Mad Whirl 1937,Ja 10,II,4:8
Justice, June
With Privileges 1930,S 16,30:2
House of Doom, The 1932,Ja 26,20:4
Justice, Katherine
Lonesome Train, The 1965,Je 17,25:1
Hard Travelin' 1965,Je 17,25:1
Justin, George
O Evening Star 1936,Ja 9,24:6
Justin, George (Miscellaneous)
Moonbirds 1959,O 10,13:1
Justin, John
Someone to Talk To 1956,Jl 19,30:2
Little Moon of Alban 1960,D 2,34:1
Justin, Mark (Director)
Solo 1962,Ap 27,26:1
Night Is Black Bottles, The 1962,D 5,56:1
Justin, Mark (Playwright)
Solo 1962,Ap 27,26:1
Justin, Mark (Scenic Designer)
Solo 1962,Ap 27,26:1
Justin, Norma
Drunkard, The; Fallen Saved, The 1959,Je 24,37:2
Idiot, The 1960,S 26,38:1
Man and Superman 1960,N 7,46:2
Emmanuel 1960,D 5,42:2
Justus, William
Country Wife, The 1936,D 2,34:1
Jutkevigch, Sergei (Director)
It Happened One Night; On the Road to New
York 1944,Je 21,23:4
Jutte, William B (Playwright)
Bad Manners 1933,Ja 31,15:5
Jutzi, Al (Lighting Director)
Midsummer Night's Dream, A 1967,Je 30,23:1
Juville, Emil (Rev) (Director)
Untitled-Passion Play 1925,Mr 2,5:6

K

Kaalund, Raymond
Hoofers, The 1969,Jl 30,23:4
Kabatchnik, Amnon
Hamlet of Stepney Green 1958,N 14,21:1
Kabatchnik, Amnon (Director)
Vincent 1959,O 1,40:1
Vincent 1959,O 11,II,1:1
Country Scandal, A 1960,My 6,21:8
Bride in the Morning, A 1960,My 26,38:2
Behind the Wall 1960,N 1,47:1
On the High Road 1961,Ap 21,26:2
Anniversary, The 1961,Ap 21,26:2
Wedding, The 1961,Ap 21,26:2
Buskers, The 1961,O 31,28:1
Call It Virtue 1963,Mr 28,8:2
Cat and the Canary, The 1965,Ja 5,26:1
Winterset 1966,F 10,32:2
Javelin 1966,N 10,63:1
Kabatchnik, Amnon (Miscellaneous)
Winterset 1966,F 10,32:2
Megilla of Itzik Manger, The 1968,O 10,60:1
Megilla of Itzik Manger, The 1969,Ap 21,55:1
Kabatchnik, Amnon (Producer)
Vincent 1959,O 1,40:1
Country Scandal, A 1960,My 6,21:8
Behind the Wall 1960,N 1,47:1
Buskers, The 1961,O 31,28:1
Kaber, Grace
Ladies' Night 1920,Ag 10,10:1
Kaburagi, Kiyokata (Costume Designer)
Azuma Kabuki Dancers and Musicians
1954,Mr 10,29:4

Kachaloff
Scenes From the Lives of the Romanoffs 1927,F 16,4:6
Kachanova, Larissa
Cherry Orchard, The 1965,F 10,46:1
Kremlin Chimes 1965,F 25,23:1
Kacsoh (Composer)
Dorottya 1929,F 3,VIII,2:1
Kadari, Benjamin
Oedipus Rex 1948,My 24,23:2
Kadelburg (Original Author)
Im Weissen Roessel 1931,Ja 4,VIII,3:5
Kader, Zahra
Ladies Night in a Turkish Bath 1961,Mr 22,38:1
Kadishov, Roxanne (Lighting Director)
Mira 1970,Je 3,51:1
Golden Bat 1970,Je 27,18:2
Kadison, Harry
Arsenic and Old Lace 1944,Jl 3,7:3
Signature 1945,F 15,25:2
Beggars Are Comming to Town 1945,O 29,16:2
Diamond Lil 1951,S 15,8:2
Kadison, Leib
Back Streets 1933,My 18,17:4
Germany Aflame 1933,O 28,20:5
Verdict, The 1934,S 22,12:5
Jealousy 1934,D 20,31:4
Motke Ganef 1935,Mr 18,15:2
Topsy-Turvy 1939,F 13,12:3
Parnosseh 1939,F 20,12:5
Song of Dnieper 1946,O 26,10:5
Kadison, Leib (Director)
Once Upon a Time 1933,S 22,15:1
Power That Builds, The 1935,Mr 9,18:4
Topsy-Turvy 1939,F 13,12:3
Kadison, Leib (Scenic Designer)
Once Upon a Time 1933,S 22,15:1
Germany Aflame 1933,O 28,20:5
Heroic Years 1934,Ja 12,28:4
Kadison, Leon
60,000 Heroes 1935,Ja 28,11:5
Warson at Night 1938,Ja 31,14:3
Kadison, Luba
Witch of Castile, The 1930,O 25,21:1
Man With the Portfolio, The 1931,F 12,24:6
Kibitzer, The 1931,N 7,17:3
Under One Roof 1932,F 8,21:2
New Man, The 1932,Ap 22,23:2
Back Streets 1933,My 18,17:4
Once Upon a Time 1933,S 22,15:1
Germany Aflame 1933,O 28,20:5
Little Giants 1933,D 2,9:5
Organ Grinder, The 1934,Ja 1,28:3
Verdict, The 1934,S 22,12:5
Treasure, The 1934,D 18,25:5
Jealousy 1934,D 20,31:4
60,000 Heroes 1935,Ja 28,11:5
Power That Builds, The 1935,Mr 9,18:4
Motke Ganef 1935,Mr 18,15:2
Kibbetzers, Inc 1935,My 13,18:5
Three Cities 1938,O 11,20:3
Untitled-Revue 1939,Ja 16,11:3
Yoshe Kalb 1939,F 6,9:2
Far-Away Corner, A 1939,F 15,15:2
Day of Judgement, The 1941,O 9,27:3
Doctor Herzl 1945,D 21,25:4
Song of Dnieper 1946,O 26,10:5
Wish Me Luck! 1954,N 1,37:2
Wedding March, The 1955,O 17,33:1
Kadison, Luba (Director)
Parnosseh 1935,F 16,8:8
Kadison, Luba (Miscellaneous)
Brothers Ashkenazi, The 1970,N 17,53:2
Kadison, Luba (Playwright)
Vagrant, The 1962,F 16,35:2
Witch, The 1962,F 16,35:2
Music Shop, The 1962,F 16,35:2
Brothers Ashkenazi, The 1970,N 17,53:2
Kadison, Paula (Miscellaneous)
Devil's Game, A 1959,N 9,35:6
Kadison, Philip (Composer)
Assorted Nuts 1940,Ap 7,I,44:6
One on the House 1941,Mr 30,I,47:3
Kaelred, Katherine
Mamma's Affair 1920,Ja 20,10:1
Kaetner, Hannes
Wozzeck 1966,Ap 6,34:1
Kafka, Franz (Original Author)
Trial, The 1947,N 2,II,3:7
On Trial 1949,D 9,35:5
Trial, The 1950,Ap 13,34:3
Scapegoat, The 1950,Ap 20,36:5
Proces, Le; Trial, The 1952,N 18,36:2
Trial, The 1955,Je 15,35:2
Metamorphosis 1957,F 20,38:1
Metamorphosis 1957,Mr 17,II,8:5
In the Penal Colony 1962,My 4,27:2
Schloss, Das 1968,N 20,35:3
Kafkalis, Nikos
School for Scandal, The 1966,N 22,33:2
Kafkalis, Nikos (Miscellaneous)
Cocktail Party, The 1968,O 8,42:1
Misanthrope, The 1968,O 10,59:1

All's Well That Ends Well 1970,Je 16,53:1
Othello 1970,Je 22,43:1
Kaftan, Jiri
Pierrot's Journey 1964,Ag 5,23:1
Button, Button 1970,O 20,41:1
Kagan, Diane
Chinese Prime Minister, The 1964,Ja 3,14:1
Death of the Well-Loved Boy, The 1967,My 16,48:1
Tiger at the Gates 1968,Mr 1,30:1
Kagan, Maria (Choreographer)
Dutchman's Farm, A 1941,My 11,I,43:3
Kagan, Richard (Producer)
World's a Stage, The 1969,My 13,42:1
Kagar, Lurie
Armored Train No 1469 1931,N 28,20:3
Kagar, Uri
60,000 Heroes 1935,Ja 28,11:5
Kage, Ivar
Dream Play 1935,D 8,X,4:5
Kagen, Abraham (Playwright)
Oliver Twist 1937,F 21,II,4:4
Kaghan, Leonora (Playwright)
All Bow Down 1935,Ag 6,20:4
Touch of Brimstone, A 1935,S 23,20:1
Kahal, Irving (Composer)
Right This Way 1938,Ja 6,22:3
Boys and Girls Together 1940,O 2,19:2
Kahal, Irving (Lyricist)
Everybody's Welcome 1931,O 14,26:3
Kahan, Mathew (Composer)
Pigeon, The 1957,My 17,19:2
Kahane, Eric (Playwright)
Philosophy in the Boudoir 1969,My 22,55:2
Kahl, Elsa
Green Table, The 1942,Ja 22,12:2
Prodigal Son, The 1942,F 18,22:2
Kahl, Howard
Beautiful Dreamer 1960,D 28,22:1
Hot Spot 1963,Ap 20,17:2
Anya 1965,N 30,48:1
Cabaret 1966,N 21,62:1
Applause 1970,Mr 31,35:1
Kahler, Edward
What a Relief 1935,D 14,10:6
Kahler, Kingsley
Caesar and Cleopatra 1927,N 6,IX,2:1
Kahn, Arthur C (Playwright)
Bad Habits of 1925 1925,F 9,17:1
Kahn, Florence
Life I Gave You, The 1931,My 12,29:3
Peer Gynt 1935,S 24,28:2
Kahn, George (Director)
Passing of Chow-Chow, The 1929,O 4,24:4
Kahn, Gus (Lyricist)
Holka Polka 1925,O 15,27:2
Kitty's Kisses 1926,My 7,12:2
Whoopee 1928,D 5,34:3
Show Girl 1929,Jl 3,19:3
Whoopee 1929,Ag 6,29:4
Kahn, Harold
Summer Wives 1936,Ap 14,18:1
Kahn, Leon
As You Like It 1936,Ap 24,18:4
Face, The 1941,N 29,15:3
Doodle Dandy of the U S A 1942,O 19,15:2
Kahn, Lucille
Laugh, Clown, Laugh! 1923,N 29,30:1
Kahn, Madeline
Leonard Sillman's New Faces of 1968 1968,My 3,43:1
New Faces of 1968 1968,My 12,II,7:1
Promenade 1969,Je 5,56:1
Promenade 1969,Je 15,II,1:1
Two by Two 1970,N 11,37:1
Two by Two 1970,N 22,II,1:1
Kahn, Margaret
What Next 1920,Ja 27,7:2
Kahn, Maud
What Next 1920,Ja 27,7:2
Kahn, Michael (Director)
Love Nest, The 1963,Ja 28,7:6
Funnyhouse of a Negro 1964,Ja 15,25:3
Victims of Duty 1964,My 28,40:2
New Tenant, The 1964,My 28,40:2
That 5 A.M. Jazz 1964,O 20,42:2
Helen 1964,D 11,55:4
Measure for Measure 1966,Jl 14,27:1
Long Christmas Dinner, The 1966,S 7,53:1
Happy Journey to Trenton and Camden, The 1966,S 7,53:1
Queens of France 1966,S 7,53:1
Rimers of Eldritch, The 1967,F 21,53:1
Merchant of Venice, The 1967,Je 22,46:2
Here's Where I Belong 1968,Mr 4,32:1
Richard II 1968,Je 24,42:3
Love's Labour's Lost 1968,Je 28,36:1
Death of Bessie Smith, The 1968,O 3,55:1
Henry V 1969,Je 9,57:1
Henry V 1969,Je 15,II,3:1
Three Sisters, The 1969,Ag 4,29:1
Three Sisters, The 1969,Ag 10,II,3:1

Kahn, Michael (Director)—Cont
Crimes of Passion; Ruffian on the Stair, The 1969,O 27,54:1
Crimes of Passion; Erpingham Camp, The 1969,O 27,54:1
Henry V 1969,N 11,43:1
All's Well That Ends Well 1970,Je 16,53:1
Othello 1970,Je 22,43:1
Othello 1970,Je 28,II,1:1
Othello 1970,S 15,51:1
Kahn, Morton
These Are the Times 1950,My 11,37:2
Kahn, Norman (Composer)
Com Zaa 1945,Ja 10,28:2
Kahn, Norman (Lyricist)
Com Zaa 1945,Ja 10,28:2
Kahn, Olive Evans
Constant Wife, The 1935,Jl 3,20:2
Kahn, Regina
Bitter Stream 1936,Mr 31,16:6
Happy Valley, Limited 1936,Je 30,15:1
Kahn, Roger Wolfe
Vaudeville (Palace) 1926,O 19,27:5
Kahn, Roger Wolfe (Composer)
Here's Howe! 1928,My 2,19:3
Americana 1928,O 31,28:2
New Americana 1928,N 30,32:4
Nine Fifteen Revue, The 1930,F 12,26:2
Kahn, Roger Wolfe (Lyricist)
Nine Fifteen Revue, The 1930,F 12,26:2
Kahn, Roger Wolfe and His Orchestra
Vaudeville (Palace) 1929,F 11,26:2
Kahn, Stan
Glory in the Flower 1959,D 9,57:5
Purification, The 1959,D 9,57:5
Kahn, Stanley (Director)
Ice Follies 1957,Ja 16,36:1
Ice Follies 1961,Ja 11,25:2
Ice Follies 1962,Ja 10,24:6
Ice Follies 1963,Ja 10,5:2
Ice Follies 1967,Ja 11,51:1
Ice Follies 1970,My 23,27:1
Kahn, Stanley (Miscellaneous)
Ice Follies 1965,Ja 13,35:1
Ice Follies 1966,Ja 12,27:6
Ice Follies 1967,Ja 11,51:1
Kahn, Tamara (Playwright)
Grass Is Always Greener, The 1955,F 16,25:2
Kahn, Theodore (Scenic Designer)
K Guy, The 1928,O 16,28:4
Sugar Hill 1931,D 26,15:2
Barrister, The 1932,N 22,25:2
Good-Bye Please 1934,O 25,26:6
Kahn, Vicki (Costume Designer)
House of Bernarda Alba, The 1963,N 25,23:2
Kahne, Harry
Vaudeville (Palace) 1926,Ag 24,19:3
Kahrum
Vaudeville (Palace) 1926,D 21,20:5
Kaifin, Robert (Director)
Tarot 1970,D 12,19:1
Kain, Frances
Hawk Island 1929,S 17,34:7
Kainer, Ludwig (Costume Designer)
Broadway 1928,Ap 15,IX,4:7
Fledermaus, Die 1929,Jl 14,IX,2:1
Kainer, Ludwig (Scenic Designer)
An und Aus 1926,D 5,VIII,8:7
Fledermaus, Die 1929,Jl 14,IX,2:1
Kaiser, Ardyth
Parasite, The 1965,D 17,43:2
Not Now Darling 1970,O 30,33:1
Kaiser, Burton C (Producer)
Borstal Boy 1970,Ap 1,38:1
Kaiser, Georg (Original Author)
From Morn to Midnight 1931,S 22,30:4
Kaiser, Georg (Playwright)
From Morn to Midnight 1922,My 22,17:2
Morn to Midnight 1922,Je 27,16:4
Nebeneinander 1924,Mr 2,VII,2:1
Zweimal Oliver 1926,N 7,VIII,4:3
Zar Laesst Sich Photographieren, Der 1928,Ap 22,IX,6:7
Phantom Lover, The 1928,S 25:1
Oktobertag 1928,D 2,X,4:4
Two Neck-Ties 1929,O 13,IX,4:7
Fire in the Opera House 1930,Ap 6,IX,2:1
Wedding Night 1930,N 2,VIII,3:2
Mississippi 1931,Ja 11,VIII,1:6
Hellseherei 1931,Je 7,VIII,2:5
From Morn to Midnight 1931,S 26,25:5
From Morn Till Midnight 1948,D 7,41:6
Kaiser, Jo
Androcles and the Lion 1958,F 22,8:3
Kaiser, Lee
Nights of Wrath; Nuits de la Colere, Les 1947,D 1,26:4
Kaiser, Norma
Call Me Madam 1950,O 13,25:1
Guys and Dolls 1955,Ap 21,32:2
Kaiser, Russ (Producer)
Day the Whores Came Out to Play Tennis, The 1965,Mr 16,45:1

Kaiser, Russ (Producer)—Cont
Sing to Me Through Open Windows
1965,Mr 16,45:1
Kaiserlian, Harry
Tobacco Road 1960,My 11,44:2
Kaiserman, Ken (Producer)
Steal the Old Man's Bundle 1970,My 16,30:1
Shepherd of Avenue B, The 1970,My 16,30:1
Kaisha
Bare Facts 1927,Ag 17,27:5
Kakatsakis, Charles
'Toinette 1961,N 21,46:1
Kakitsu, Ichimura
Kagotsurube; Courtesan, The 1960,Je 3,26:1
Migawari Zazen; Substitute, The 1960,Je 10,37:1
Chushingura; Forty-Seven Ronin, The
1960,Je 16,33:2
Takatsuki; Clog Dance, The 1960,Je 17,35:4
Chushingura; Forty-Seven Ronin, The
1960,Je 17,35:4
Kakos, Kenneth
Frogs of Spring, The 1953,O 21,36:2
Sunrise at Campobello 1958,Ja 31,25:1
Kalan, Charles
Zorba 1968,N 18,58:1
Kalan, Sy
Pigeon, The 1957,My 17,19:2
Kalbfuss, F (Original Author)
Little Racketeer, The 1931,O 11,VIII,4:7
Kalbfuss, F (Translator)
Little Racketeer, The 1932,Ja 19,24:4
Kalcheim, Lee (Playwright)
Party for Divorce, A 1966,O 12,37:1
Match-Play 1966,O 12,37:1
Kaldenberg, Keith
Saint of Bleecker Street, The 1954,D 28,21:1
Most Happy Fella, The 1956,My 4,20:1
Most Happy Fella, The 1959,F 11,50:2
Kale, Hathaway
Jeannie 1940,N 13,29:2
Kalegi, Sylvia (Costume Designer)
Plot Against the Chase Manhattan Bank, The
1963,N 27,29:1
Phedre 1966,F 11,36:1
Kaler, Mlle
Cloches de Cornville, Les; Chimes of Normandy,
The 1926,D 14,24:4
Kaley, Charles
Earl Carroll's Vanities 1927,Ja 5,18:1
Kalfayan, Chris
Mercy Street 1969,O 28,43:1
Kalff, Marie
Amour Magicien, L' 1926,D 26,VII,2:1
Prosper 1935,Ja 13,IX,2:1
Kalfin, Robert
Cock-A-Doodle Dandy 1955,N 4,26:5
Kalfin, Robert (Director)
Golem, The 1959,F 26,38:2
Good Soldier Schweik, The 1963,Ap 9,57:1
Junebug Graduates Tonight! 1967,F 27,35:1
Slave Ship 1969,N 22,46:1
Brass Butterfly, The 1970,Ja 31,34:1
Universal Nigger, The 1970,Mr 21,18:1
Saved 1970,O 29,57:1
Kalfin, Robert (Miscellaneous)
Junebug Graduates Tonight! 1967,F 27,35:1
Kalfin, Robert (Playwright)
Good Soldier Schweik, The 1963,Ap 9,57:1
Kalfin, Robert (Producer)
Golem, The 1959,F 26,38:2
Evening of European Theatre, An 1960,Ap 26,41:1
Kalgarin, T S
Shuffle Along 1952,My 9,20:5
Kaliban, Bob
Conquering Hero, The 1961,Ja 17,40:2
Ben Franklin in Paris 1964,O 28,52:1
Kalich, Bertha
One of the Many 1921,O 4,10:3
Child of the World, The 1922,Ap 29,18:3
Jitta's Atonement 1923,Ja 18,16:3
Kreutzer Sonata, The 1924,My 15,22:3
Magda 1925,D 22,18:4
Magda 1926,Ja 27,16:2
Soul of a Woman, The 1930,F 22,13:1
Sacrifice of Isaac, The 1933,N 22,22:4
Sappho 1935,Mr 22,26:4
Kalich, Jacob
Bublitchki 1938,Ja 17,11:2
Oy, Is Dus a Leben!; Oh, What a Life!
1942,O 13,19:2
Abi Gezunt 1949,O 10,19:4
Sadie Is a Lady 1950,Ja 28,9:2
Farblondjete Honeymoon 1955,S 27,42:1
Kosher Widow, The 1959,N 2,40:2
Kalich, Jacob (Director)
Some Girl 1927,D 24,8:2
Circus Girl, The 1928,O 21,IX,1:1
Radio Girl, The 1929,O 19,22:4
Jolly Orphan, The 1929,D 23,18:6
Little Clown, The 1930,Mr 15,23:3
Here Runs the Bride 1934,S 20,21:3
Here Runs the Bride 1934,N 4,IX,2:1
One in a Million 1934,N 17,13:2
Motel Peissi, The Contor's Kid 1934,N 29,33:3

My Malkele 1937,S 20,18:6
Oy, Is Dus a Leben!; Oh, What a Life!
1942,O 13,19:2
Abi Gezunt 1949,O 10,19:4
Sadie Is a Lady 1950,Ja 28,9:2
Mazel Tov, Molly 1950,O 2,18:1
Take It Easy 1950,D 25,23:6
Farblondjete Honeymoon 1955,S 27,42:1
Kosher Widow, The 1959,N 2,40:2
Kalich, Jacob (Playwright)
Girl of Yesterday, The 1930,S 27,21:2
Oy, Is Dus a Leben!; Oh, What a Life!
1942,O 13,19:2
Abi Gezunt 1949,O 10,19:4
Sadie Is a Lady 1950,Ja 28,9:2
Mazel Tov, Molly 1950,O 2,18:1
Farblondjete Honeymoon 1955,S 27,42:1
Kosher Widow, The 1959,N 2,40:2
Kalich, Jacob (Producer)
Kid Mother 1927,Mr 6,VII,1:6
Radio Girl, The 1929,O 19,22:4
Little Clown, The 1930,Mr 15,23:3
Love Thief, The 1931,Ja 19,24:5
Kalidasa (Playwright)
Shakuntala 1959,S 10,41:2
Kalil-Ogly
Nina Rosa 1930,S 22,22:5
Kalin, Katy (Costume Designer)
Trial of Dmitri Karamazov, The 1958,Ja 28,30:1
Kalina, Vladimir (Playwright)
Matter of Days, A 1969,My 20,40:1
Kaline, Robert
On Borrowed Time 1953,F 11,34:1
Kalinova, Dora
Shepherd King, The 1955,O 13,36:2
Kalinovskaya, Galina
Dead Souls 1965,F 5,34:1
Kalioujny, Alexandre
Girl in Pink Tights, The 1954,Mr 6,13:2
Kalish, Mitzi
Dover Road, The 1924,D 20,18:2
Kaliz, Armand
Vaudeville (Palace) 1921,Jl 5,15:1
Spice of 1922 1922,Jl 7,12:4
Kalkanis, Harry
Illya Darling 1967,Ap 12,37:1
Kalkhurst, Eric
Restless Women 1927,D 27,24:1
Paris 1928,O 9,34:3
Mourning Becomes Electra; Haunted, The
1932,My 10,25:2
Mourning Becomes Electra; Homecoming
1932,My 10,25:2
Mourning Becomes Electra; Hunted, The
1932,My 10,25:2
World Waits, The 1933,O 26,22:5
False Dreams, Farewell 1934,Ja 16,18:3
Late Wisdom 1934,Ap 24,27:4
Katy Did So What? 1935,N 6,32:3
Storm Child 1936,Ap 18,18:4
Bat, The 1937,Je 1,27:5
Cat and the Canary, The 1937,Je 15,26:3
At Your Service 1937,Ag 17,23:1
Good, The 1938,O 6,27:2
Kalkhurst, Stanley
As You Like It 1923,Ap 24,24:1
Swan, The 1923,O 24,15:3
Assumption of Hannele, The 1924,F 16,16:2
Red Falcon, The 1924,O 8,22:1
In the Near Future 1925,Mr 11,19:1
Call of Life, The 1925,O 10,10:1
Kalkman, Adelaide
Right of Possession 1930,My 9,20:5
Twelfth Disciple, The 1930,My 17,21:4
Kalkstein, Ruth (Miscellaneous)
Empire Builders, The 1968,O 2,34:1
Perfect Party, The 1969,Mr 21,42:1
Kalkstein, Ruth (Producer)
Love and Maple Syrup 1970,Ja 8,47:1
Slow Dance on the Killing Ground
1970,My 14,43:1
Kalkut, Noah (Lighting Director)
Summer and Smoke 1952,My 4,II,1:1
Grass Harp, The 1953,Ap 28,32:2
Girl on the Via Flaminia, The 1954,F 10,37:1
Sound of Hunting, A 1954,Ap 7,41:1
Kall, Willie
Ice Capades 1953,S 11,25:1
Ice Capades 1954,S 16,37:1
Kallen, Lucille (Composer)
Tickets, Please! 1950,Ap 28,25:2
Kallen, Lucille (Lyricist)
Tickets, Please! 1950,Ap 28,25:2
Kallen, Lucille (Playwright)
Maybe Tuesday 1958,Ja 30,18:3
Kallender, Ken
Young and Beautiful, The 1959,My 29,13:1
Kallesser, Michael (Playwright)
One Man's Woman 1926,My 26,25:1
Trial Marriage 1927,F 1,24:3
Marriage on Approval 1928,Mr 2,28:2
He Understood Women 1928,Ag 16,25:1
Rockbound 1929,Ap 20,23:2

Kallesser, Michael (Playwright)—Cont
Brother Cain 1941,S 13,21:5
Babes Don't Cry Anymore 1968,F 21,55:1
Kallesser, Michael (Producer)
Trial Marriage 1927,F 1,24:3
Marriage on Approval 1928,Mr 2,28:2
He Understood Women 1928,Ag 16,25:1
Live and Learn 1930,Ap 10,24:6
Kallini, Joseph
There's Wisdom in Women 1935,O 31,17:1
Tapestry in Gray 1935,D 28,10:2
Leave It to Me! 1938,N 10,32:2
My Sister Eileen 1940,D 27,23:2
Jacobowsky and the Colonel 1944,Mr 15,17:2
Song of Norway 1958,Je 23,19:2
Song of Norway 1959,Je 26,16:2
Kallman, Dick
Seventeen 1951,Je 22,16:6
Fifth Season, The 1953,Ja 24,13:2
Kalman, Emmerich (Composer)
Yankee Princess, The 1922,O 3,22:1
Bajadere, Die 1925,O 2,26:2
Circus Princess, The 1926,Mr 28,23:5
Countess Maritza 1926,Mr 30,20:3
Countess Maritza 1926,S 20,21:1
Parisian Love 1927,Ja 28,15:5
Countess Maritza 1927,Ja 30,VII,4:3
Circus Princess, The 1927,Ap 26,32:2
Golden Dawn 1927,O 2,VIII,4:6
Golden Dawn 1927,D 1,32:3
Duchess of Chicago, The 1928,Ap 15,II,2:4
Herzogin von Chicago, Die 1929,F 17,IX,2:3
Duchess of Chicago, The 1929,N 17,IX,4:1
Sari 1930,Ja 29,27:1
Veilchen von Montmartre 1931,Mr 29,VIII,3:1
Circus Princess, The 1937,Ag 31,26:6
Marinka 1945,Jl 19,19:2
Kalmanoff, Martin (Playwright)
Brandy Is My True Love's Name 1953,Je 18,38:5
Kalmanov, H (Playwright)
President's Daughter, The 1970,N 4,41:2
Kalmanowich, H (Lyricist)
Some Girl 1927,D 24,8:2
Kalmanowich, H (Original Author)
Hello Charlie 1965,O 25,47:2
Kalmanowich, H (Playwright)
Some Girl 1927,D 24,8:2
Soul of a Woman, The 1930,F 22,13:1
Motke From Slobodke 1930,Ap 12,23:3
Girl of Yesterday, The 1930,S 27,21:2
Hello Grandpa! 1931,Ja 2,25:3
Women of New York 1931,Mr 23,24:3
In a Tenement House 1932,Ja 25,20:4
Wedding Chains 1932,Mr 28,10:5
Love for Sale 1932,D 5,21:4
Little Giants 1933,D 2,9:5
All in a Lifetime 1934,Ap 2,12:5
Oh, You Girls! 1935,D 2,19:5
Love for Sale 1936,Ja 24,14:2
Freidel Becomes a Bride 1936,F 10,14:3
Schlemihl 1936,S 19,20:4
Semele's Bar Mitzvah 1938,Ja 17,11:2
Life Marches On 1940,Ja 4,18:2
Mazel Tov, Molly 1950,O 2,18:1
Farblondjete Honeymoon 1955,S 27,42:1
It Could Happen to You 1957,O 28,30:5
Go Fight City Hall 1961,N 3,28:5
Don't Worry Brother! 1963,O 14,35:2
Kalmar, Bert (Composer)
Helen of Troy, New York 1923,Je 20,22:6
No Other Girl 1924,Ag 14,10:4
Ramblers, The 1926,S 21,32:2
Twinkle Twinkle 1926,N 17,22:2
Five O'Clock Girl, The 1927,O 11,26:3
Good Boy 1928,S 6,23:2
Animal Crackers 1928,O 24,26:2
High Kickers 1941,N 1,21:2
Kalmar, Bert (Lyricist)
Helen of Troy, New York 1923,Je 20,22:6
No Other Girl 1924,Ag 14,10:4
By the Way 1925,D 29,20:3
Ramblers, The 1926,S 21,32:2
Twinkle Twinkle 1926,N 17,22:2
Lucky 1927,Mr 23,28:3
Five O'Clock Girl, The 1927,O 11,26:3
Good Boy 1928,S 6,23:2
Animal Crackers 1928,O 24,26:2
High Kickers 1941,N 1,21:2
Kalmar, Bert (Playwright)
Broadway Brevities, 1920 1920,S 30,12:2
Holka Polka 1925,O 15,27:2
Ramblers, The 1926,S 21,32:2
Twinkle Twinkle 1926,N 17,22:2
Lucky 1927,Mr 23,28:3
She's My Baby 1928,Ja 4,22:2
Top Speed 1929,N 17,IX,4:1
Top Speed 1929,D 26,20:1
High Kickers 1941,N 1,21:2
Kalmar, Bert Jr
Corn Is Green, The 1943,My 4,18:3
Kalmykow, Andrew
Betty Behave 1927,Mr 9,28:4
Kalser, Erwin
Another Sun 1940,F 24,8:6

Kaltman, Marilyn
Little Theatre Tournament; Father Returns, The 1929,My 7,28:1

Kalus, Jack
In the Groove 1938,Ap 22,14:5

Kalworth, Lincoln (Playwright)
Live and Learn 1930,Ap 10,24:6

Kaly, Chandra (Choreographer)
Ice Capades 1960,S 1,30:1

Kamada, Eisuke (Miscellaneous)
Greengrocer's Daughter, The 1966,Mr 16,50:1
General's Daughter, The 1966,Mr 16,50:1
Fishing for Wives 1966,Mr 16,50:1

Kamarova, Natalie (Choreographer)
Artists and Models 1943,N 6,16:6
Lady Says Yes, A 1945,Ja 11,18:5

Kamen, Milt
Safari! 1955,My 12,32:6
Across the Board on Tomorrow Morning 1961,O 23,22:5
Passion of Josef D, The 1964,F 12,29:1

Kamen, Milt (Playwright)
Safari! 1955,My 12,32:6

Kamerny (Producer)
Bagrovyostrov 1928,D 16,III,3:5

Kamhi, Morris
Twilight Walk 1951,S 25,25:4

Kamineff, Mr (Original Author)
Absconders, The; Defraudanten, Die 1931,Ja 25,VIII,4:1

Kamins, Estelle
Broken Chain, The 1929,F 21,30:4
If I Were You 1931,S 24,21:1

Kamins, Jeanette (Miscellaneous)
Visit to a Small Planet 1957,F 8,18:1
Desert Incident, A 1959,Mr 25,40:1

Kaminska, Ida
Mirele Efros 1967,O 20,55:1
Mother Courage 1967,N 17,55:1
Trees Die Standing, The 1969,O 13,52:1
Mirele Efros 1969,D 26,41:1

Kaminska, Ida (Director)
Mirele Efros 1967,O 20,55:1
Mother Courage 1967,N 17,55:1
Trees Die Standing, The 1969,O 13,52:1
Mirele Efros 1969,D 26,41:1

Kaminska, Ida (Playwright)
Mirele Efros 1967,O 20,55:1
Mother Courage 1967,N 17,55:1
Trees Die Standing, The 1969,O 13,52:1
Mirele Efros 1969,D 26,41:1

Kaminska, Ruth
Mirele Efros 1967,O 20,55:1
Mother Courage 1967,N 17,55:1
Mirele Efros 1969,D 26,41:1

Kaminska-Turkow, Ruth
Trees Die Standing, The 1969,O 13,52:1

Kaminski, Thomas 2d
Kittiwake Island 1960,O 13,43:1

Kaminsky, Helen (Composer)
Life Is Like That 1930,D 23,24:3

Kaminsky, J (Composer)
Brothers Ashkenazi, The 1970,N 17,53:2

Kaminsky (M) (Producer)
Ma Femme 1927,D 18,IX,4:4

Kamitses, Zoe
Comedy of Errors, The 1967,Je 15,58:4
Titus Andronicus 1967,Ag 10,43:2
Richard II 1968,Je 24,42:3
As You Like It 1968,Je 24,42:3
Love's Labour's Lost 1968,Je 28,36:1
Crimes of Passion; Erpingham Camp, The 1969,O 27,54:1

Kamlot, Robert
Deirdre of the Sorrows 1949,D 15,51:2
Venice Preserv'd 1955,D 13,54:4

Kamlot, Robert (Director)
Once Around the Block 1956,O 29,34:1

Kamlot, Robert (Playwright)
Willie Doesn't Live Here Anymore 1967,F 8,20:2

Kamlot, Robert (Producer)
Ernest in Love 1960,My 5,39:4

Kamm, Joseph
Walk Hard 1944,D 1,28:2
Walk Hard 1946,Mr 28,34:2

Kamnitzer, Ernst (Playwright)
London Prodigal, The 1928,D 23,VIII,4:1

Kamp, Irene (Playwright)
Great Indoors, The 1966,F 2,23:1

Kamp, Rhoda Rammel
Beware of the Bull 1933,My 30,13:7

Kamp, Tana
Show Boat 1927,D 28,26:1
Show Boat 1932,My 20,22:2

Kampers, Fritz
Italienische Nacht 1931,My 10,VIII,1:5

Kamsler, B F
Loud Speaker 1927,Mr 3,27:2
Out of a Blue Sky 1930,F 10,20:6

Kamsler, B F (Director)
Farewell Summer 1937,Mr 30,20:2
Bat, The 1937,Je 1,27:5
Cat and the Canary, The 1937,Je 15,26:3

Kamsler, B F (Producer)
Foreign Affairs 1932,Ap 14,25:5
Farewell Summer 1937,Mr 30,20:2

Kanakis, Basil
Oedipus Tyrannus 1952,N 25,35:2

Kanaley, John
Minute's Wait, A 1920,Je 22,9:1

Kanaley, John (Playwright)
Little Theatre Tournament; Another Room for Rent 1929,My 7,28:1

Kanapielka, Helen
Steel 1939,D 20,30:2

Kanbar, Maury (Miscellaneous)
Lovers and Other Strangers 1968,S 19,63:1

Kanbar, Maury (Producer)
Moondreamers, The 1969,D 9,68:1

Kanca, Steve
Wedding in Japan 1957,Mr 12,37:7

Kandel, Aben (Playwright)
Wonder Bar, The 1931,Mr 18,23:4
Hot Money 1931,N 9,22:2

Kandel, Judith (Playwright)
Play, Genius, Play! 1935,O 31,17:2

Kander, John (Composer)
Family Affair, A 1962,Ja 29,17:1
Never Too Late 1962,N 28,42:1
Flora, the Red Menace 1965,My 12,41:2
Cabaret 1966,N 21,62:1
Cabaret 1966,D 4,II,5:1
Cabaret 1968,Ja 12,19:1
Happy Time, The 1968,Ja 19,32:2
Happy Time, The 1968,Ja 28,II,3:1
Cabaret 1968,Mr 1,32:1
Zorba 1968,N 18,58:1
Zorba 1968,N 24,II,1:1

Kander, John (Lyricist)
Family Affair, A 1962,Ja 29,17:1
Cabaret 1969,F 2,74:2

Kander, John (Miscellaneous)
Gypsy 1959,My 22,31:6
Irma la Douce 1960,S 30,31:2

Kander, John (Musical Director)
Conversation Piece 1957,N 19,38:2

Kander, John (Playwright)
Mister Mayor! 1967,Ap 4,36:3

Kane, Allegro
Simply Heavenly 1957,My 22,28:2
Androcles and the Lion 1958,F 22,8:3
Egg and I, The 1958,S 11,43:4

Kane, Charlie
Safari! 1955,My 12,32:6

Kane, Don
Broadway Boy 1932,My 4,23:5

Kane, Dorothy
Wonderful Night, A; Fledermaus, Die 1929,N 1,23:3
Babes in Toyland 1930,D 22,17:1

Kane, Eddie
Excess Baggage 1928,Ja 29,VIII,1:1

Kane, Edward
Eternal Road, The 1937,Ja 8,14:2
Rape of Lucretia, The 1948,D 30,24:2

Kane, Eugene
Getting Even 1929,Ag 20,31:1

Kane, Francis (Luther Adler) (Director)
Stone for Danny Fisher, A 1954,O 22,24:2

Kane, Frank (Sgt)
Winged Victory 1943,N 22,24:1

Kane, Gail
Come Seven 1920,Jl 20,10:1
Lawful Larceny 1922,Ja 3,20:2
Breaking Point, The 1923,Ag 17,8:4
Alarm Clock, The 1923,D 25,26:2
Two Strangers From Nowhere 1924,Ap 8,22:2
Artistic Temperament 1924,D 10,20:2
Loggerheads 1925,F 10,21:1
Paid 1925,N 26,32:1

Kane, Gregg (Scenic Designer)
Shake Hands With the Devil 1949,O 21,30:4

Kane, Helen
Night in Spain, A 1927,My 4,28:2
Night in Spain, A 1927,My 22,VIII,1:1
Good Boy 1928,S 6,23:2
Vaudeville (Palace) 1929,Je 3,27:4
Vaudeville (Palace) 1929,Je 10,22:6
Vaudeville (Palace) 1929,N 4,29:1
Vaudeville (Palace) 1929,N 11,20:5
Vaudeville (Palace) 1930,D 8,27:2
Shady Lady 1933,Jl 6,26:3

Kane, Howard (Miscellaneous)
Steal the Old Man's Bundle 1970,My 16,30:1
Shepherd of Avenue B, The 1970,My 16,30:1

Kane, Irene
Threepenny Opera, The 1955,S 21,38:1
Mrs Patterson 1957,F 6,20:2
Tenderloin 1960,O 18,47:2

Kane, Jeanne
Hotel Passionato 1965,O 23,16:1

Kane, John
Half-Naked Truth, The 1926,Je 8,23:1
Happy-Go-Lucky 1926,O 1,27:2
Happy 1927,D 6,26:3
Veneer 1929,N 13,24:5

Kane, John—Cont
Prince Charming 1930,O 14,31:1
Sky's the Limit, The 1934,D 18,25:5
Sleep No More 1944,S 1,11:5
In Bed We Cry 1944,N 15,20:2
Calico Wedding 1945,Mr 8,18:6
Hold It! 1948,My 6,31:5
Visit, The 1958,My 6,40:1
Visit, The 1960,Mr 9,38:3
Hooray!! It's a Glorious Day. . .And All That 1966,Mr 10,28:1
Midsummer Night's Dream, A 1970,Ag 28,15:1

Kane, Lida
Crooked Square, The 1923,S 11,10:2
Judy Drops In 1924,O 6,24:2
Service for Two 1926,Ag 31,15:1
Judy 1927,F 8,20:2
Kidding Kidders 1928,Ap 24,28:3
Commodore Marries, The 1929,S 5,26:3
Room 349 1930,Ap 23,24:5
Mother Lode 1934,D 24,16:5
Few Are Chosen 1935,S 18,19:3
Lend Me Your Ears! 1936,O 6,28:5
Talley Method, The 1941,F 25,26:3

Kane, Lucille
Hotel Passionato 1965,O 23,16:1

Kane, Mary
Sandhog 1954,N 24,17:1

Kane, Maureen
Hotel Passionato 1965,O 23,16:1

Kane, Michael
Exiles 1957,Mr 13,27:1
Notes From the Underground 1960,Ja 20,26:1
Devil's Advocate, The 1961,Mr 10,20:1
Devil's Advocate, The 1961,Mr 19,II,1:1
Portrait of the Artist as a Young Man, A 1962,My 29,21:1
Barroom Monks, The 1962,My 29,21:1

Kane, Michael (Playwright)
Notes From the Underground 1960,Ja 20,26:1

Kane, Michael J (Director)
Happy Birthday, Wanda June 1970,O 8,58:2

Kane, Mickey
Pinocchio 1939,Ja 3,19:2

Kane, Mikel
Mister Roberts 1948,F 19,27:2

Kane, Pat
Crooks' Convention, The 1929,S 19,37:4

Kane, Patricia
This Is Edwin Booth 1958,Ag 27,32:7

Kane, Richard
Miss Gulliver Travels 1931,N 26,36:4
Proposal, The 1970,Ag 26,36:1

Kane, Rick
Dream of a Blacklisted Actor 1969,D 18,64:1

Kane, Rita
Trial of Mary Dugan, The 1927,S 20,33:1

Kane, Royce
Madre, La 1959,F 12,24:1

Kane, Sherman
Rat Race, The 1949,D 23,16:2

Kane, Stephen
Ruddigore 1965,Ag 27,16:1

Kane, Tida
Forty-Four Below 1935,Jl 23,24:3

Kane, Timothy
Cornered 1920,D 9,18:2

Kane, Viola
Marilyn's Affairs 1933,Mr 16,21:5

Kane, Whitford
Mob, The 1920,O 11,18:1
Whispering Well, The 1920,D 6,19:1
Cradle Song 1921,Mr 1,18:2
Harlequinade 1921,My 11,20:3
Madras House, The 1921,O 31,18:2
Idle Inn, The 1921,D 21,26:2
Pigeon, The 1922,F 3,13:1
Fanny Hawthorn 1922,My 12,22:2
Dolly Jordan 1922,O 4,26:1
Hamlet 1922,N 17,14:1
Children of the Moon 1923,Ag 18,10:3
Hamlet 1923,N 27,23:6
Outsider, The 1924,Mr 4,16:4
Loggerheads 1925,F 10,21:1
Critic, The 1925,My 9,12:4
Grand Street Follies, The 1925,Je 19,24:1
Devil to Pay, The 1925,D 4,26:2
One Day More 1926,Mr 19,24:3
Wild Duck, The 1928,F 19,VIII,2:1
Midsummer Night's Dream, A 1931,Ag 19,19:
Merchant of Venice, The 1931,N 17,31:1
Julius Caesar 1931,N 18,26:3
Hamlet 1931,N 19,26:6
Cyrano de Bergerac 1932,D 27,11:2
Is Life Worth Living? 1933,N 10,24:6
Yellow Jack 1934,Mr 7,22:6
First Legion, The 1934,O 2,18:2
Searching for the Sun 1936,F 20,22:6
Parnell 1936,My 5,26:2
St Helena 1936,S 29,35:1
St Helena 1936,O 7,32:1
Richard II 1937,F 6,14:2
Excursion 1937,Ap 10,11:4
Excursion 1937,Ap 18,XI,1:1

Kane, Whitford—Cont

Excursion 1937,Jl 27,24:3
Robin Landing 1937,N 19,26:4
Shoemaker's Holiday, The 1938,Ja 3,17:2
Shoemaker's Holiday, The 1938,Ja 9,X,1:1
Hamlet 1938,O 13,28:1
Hamlet 1938,O 30,IX,1:1
Man Who Killed Lincoln, The 1939,D 30,9:1
Man Who Killed Lincoln, The 1940,Ja 18,26:4
Boyd's Daughter 1940,O 12,20:2
Doctor's Dilemma, The 1941,F 18,26:6
Doctor's Dilemma, The 1941,Mr 12,18:2
Elizabeth the Queen 1941,O 17,27:2
Moon Is Down, The 1942,Ap 8,22:2
Lifeline 1942,D 1,20:3
Land of Fame 1943,S 22,31:5
Thank You Svoboda 1944,Mr 2,13:2
Career Angel 1944,My 24,23:7
Meet a Body 1944,O 17,19:5
It's A Gift 1945,Mr 13,18:7
Winter's Tale, The 1946,Ja 16,18:6
Winter's Tale, The 1946,Ja 20,II,1:1
Kathleen 1948,F 4,26:2
As You Like It 1950,Ja 27,27:2
Merchant of Venice, The 1955,Ja 8,9:7
Red Roses for Me 1955,D 29,15:2
Red Roses for Me 1956,Ja 8,II,1:1
King John 1956,Je 28,33:5
Measure for Measure 1956,Je 29,16:1
Taming of the Shrew, The 1956,Ag 6,20:1
Kane, Whitford (Director)
Midsummer Night's Dream, A 1931,Ag 19,19:3
Kane, Whitford (Producer)
Midsummer Night's Dream, A 1931,Ag 19,19:3
Kane, William R
Midnight 1930,D 30,25:1
Kane, Wyman
Richard III 1934,D 28,24:3
Enemy of the People, An 1937,F 16,19:1
Oscar Wilde 1938,O 11,20:2
Wild Duck, The 1951,D 27,17:1
Hamlet 1954,Ap 24,15:2
Capacity for Wings 1957,Ja 10,25:2
Conversation Piece 1957,N 19,38:2
Kane, Wyman (Costume Designer)
Hamlet 1954,Ap 24,15:2
Kane, Wyman (Scenic Designer)
Pygmalion 1952,F 9,11:2
Kanel, Francoise
Avare, L', L'; Miser, The 1966,F 9,32:1
Cid, Le 1966,F 12,17:1
Fil a la Paite, Un 1966,F 18,25:1
Kanellis, Thanos
Iphigenia in Aulis 1968,N 13,40:1
Hippolytus 1968,N 20,38:3
Kaner, Ruth
House Remembered, A 1957,F 7,20:2
Beautiful Jailer, The 1957,My 17,19:2
Tevya and His Daughters 1957,S 17,38:2
Legitimate Steal, The 1958,Ap 1,35:1
Sextet 1958,N 27,53:1
Come Share My House 1960,F 19,20:2
Secret Concubine, The 1960,Mr 22,29:2
Seven at Dawn, The 1961,Ap 18,43:1
Kaner, Ruth (Miscellaneous)
House Remembered, A 1957,F 7,20:2
Creditors 1962,Ja 26,19:1
Kaner, Ruth (Producer)
Diff'rent 1961,O 18,52:1
Long Voyage Home, The 1961,D 5,49:1
Kanfer, Stefan (Composer)
I Want You 1961,S 15,29:1
Kanfer, Stefan (Lyricist)
I Want You 1961,S 15,29:1
Kanfer, Stefan (Playwright)
I Want You 1961,S 15,29:1
Kanin, Fay (Playwright)
Goodbye My Fancy 1948,N 18,35:2
Goodbye My Fancy 1948,N 28,II,1:1
His and Hers 1954,Ja 8,18:2
Rashomon 1959,Ja 28,36:2
Rashomon 1959,F 8,II,1:1
Gay Life, The 1961,N 20,38:1
Kanin, Garson
Little Ol' Boy 1933,Ap 25,15:5
Spring Song 1934,O 2,18:2
Ladies' Money 1934,N 2,26:6
Three Men on a Horse 1935,Ja 31,22:3
Body Beautiful, The 1935,N 1,24:3
Boy Meets Girl 1935,N 28,38:2
Star Spangled 1936,Mr 11,23:1
Kanin, Garson (Director)
Hitch Your Wagon! 1937,Ap 9,18:2
Too Many Heroes 1937,N 16,26:2
Rugged Path, The 1945,N 12,17:2
Rugged Path, The 1945,N 18,II,1:1
Born Yesterday 1946,F 5,18:2
Years Ago 1946,D 4,44:2
Born Yesterday 1947,My 18,II,1:1
How I Wonder 1947,O 1,34:2
Leading Lady 1948,O 19,33:1
Smile of the World, The 1949,Ja 13,26:5
Rat Race, The 1949,D 23,16:2
Live Wire, The 1950,Jl 19,26:2

Live Wire, The 1950,Ag 18,16:2
Into Thin Air 1955,My 25,39:1
Diary of Anne Frank, The 1955,O 6,24:2
Diary of Anne Frank, The 1955,O 16,II,1:1
Small War on Murray Hill 1957,Ja 4,19:1
Small War on Murray Hill 1957,Ja 13,II,1:1
Hole in the Head, A 1957,Mr 1,15:1
Hole in the Head, A 1957,Mr 10,II,1:1
Good Soup, The 1960,Mr 3,26:4
Do Re Mi 1960,D 27,23:2
Do Re Mi 1961,Ja 8,II,1:1
Sunday in New York 1961,N 10,40:1
Gift of Time, A 1962,F 23,34:1
Come on Strong 1962,O 5,29:1
Funny Girl 1964,Mr 27,15:1
I Was Dancing 1964,N 9,40:4
Very Rich Woman, A 1965,O 5,5:8
We Have Always Lived in the Castle
  1966,O 20,53:1
Idiot's Delight 1970,Mr 24,39:1
Kanin, Garson (Playwright)
Born Yesterday 1946,F 5,18:2
Born Yesterday 1946,F 10,II,1:1
Born Yesterday 1947,My 18,II,1:1
Born Yesterday 1948,Ap 9,26:3
Smile of the World, The 1949,Ja 13,26:5
Rat Race, The 1949,D 23,16:2
Live Wire, The 1950,Jl 19,26:2
Live Wire, The 1950,Ag 18,16:2
Live Wire, The 1950,Ag 27,II,1:1
Born Yesterday 1954,Ja 1,16:6
Born Yesterday 1958,Mr 22,12:6
Good Soup, The 1960,Mr 3,26:4
Do Re Mi 1960,D 27,23:2
Do Re Mi 1961,Ja 8,II,1:1
Gift of Time, A 1962,F 23,34:1
Gift of Time, A 1962,Mr 4,II,1:1
Come on Strong 1962,O 5,29:1
Kanin, Garson (Producer)
How I Wonder 1947,O 1,34:2
Kanin, Michael (Playwright)
His and Hers 1954,Ja 8,18:2
Rashomon 1959,Ja 28,36:2
Rashomon 1959,F 8,II,1:1
Gay Life, The 1961,N 20,38:1
Kanin, Michael (Producer)
Goodbye My Fancy 1948,N 18,35:2
Seidman and Son 1962,O 16,32:2
Kanin, Myer (Scenic Designer)
Blackberries of 1932 1932,Ap 5,27:5
Kanka, Screemati
Ramayana 1931,Ja 13,35:4
Kanluk, Paul
Emerald Slippers, The 1970,S 2,31:2
Kann, Lily
Awake and Sing! 1942,My 31,VIII,2:3
Kanner, Alexis
King John 1960,Je 29,26:2
Kanter, David (Miscellaneous)
Will Success Spoil Rock Hunter? 1955,O 14,22:2
Once More With Feeling 1958,O 22,39:1
Tenth Man, The 1959,N 6,24:2
Kanter, David (Producer)
Enchanted, The 1958,Ap 23,41:1
Kanter, Nathan
Song of Dnieper 1946,O 26,10:5
Kanter, Phil (Playwright)
Them's the Reporters 1935,My 30,21:4
Kantor, Leonard (Playwright)
Dead Pigeon 1953,D 24,10:2
Stone for Danny Fisher, A 1954,O 22,24:2
Kantor, Pepa
Seven Mirrors 1945,O 26,17:2
Time of the Cuckoo, The 1958,O 28,40:2
Deputy, The 1964,F 27,26:1
Kantor, Selma
Here Runs the Bride 1934,N 4,IX,2:1
What Girls Do 1935,Ja 14,10:4
Kantosky, Walter
Utopia, Limited; Flowers of Progress, The
  1957,F 27,21:1
Yeomen of the Guard, The 1957,My 22,28:3
Gondoliers, The 1957,My 29,34:2
Kantrowitz, Rivka
Chair, The 1930,O 4,15:4
Kanty, Manya
California 1953,Je 18,38:5
Hopalong--Freud 1953,Je 18,38:5
Where There's a Will 1953,Je 18,38:5
Brandy Is My True Love's Name 1953,Je 18,38:5
Kanzaburo, Nakamura XVII
Tsubosaka Reigenki; Miracle at Tsubosaka Temple,
  The 1960,Je 3,26:1
Kanjincho; Subscription List, The 1960,Je 3,26:1
Kagotsurube; Courtesan, The 1960,Je 3,26:1
Migawari Zazen; Substitute, The 1960,Je 10,37:1
Chushingura; Forty-Seven Ronin, The
  1960,Je 10,37:1
Takatsuki; Clog Dance, The 1960,Je 17,35:4
Chushingura; Forty-Seven Ronin, The
  1960,Je 17,35:4
Kanzleiter, Maurice (Rev) (Director)
Veronica's Veil 1933,F 20,11:7

Kanzleiter, Maurice (Rev) (Playwright)
Joan of Arc-The Warrior Maid 1931,N 9,21:6
Kaoge, Ivar
Fiesco 1930,Jl 13,VIII,2:1
Kapek, Michael
Where People Gather 1967,O 26,56:1
Homo 1969,Ap 12,40:2
Kapen, Ben
Man in the Glass Booth, The 1968,S 27,41:1
Penny Wars, The 1969,O 16,52:1
Kaper, Bronislaw (Composer)
Polonaise 1945,O 8,20:2
Kaper, Bronislaw (Playwright)
Polonaise 1945,O 8,20:2
Kapfer, Joseph
Afternoon Storm 1948,Ap 12,24:2
Child and the Dragon, The 1966,Je 24,30:2
Kapfer, Joseph (Miscellaneous)
Auntie Mame 1958,Ag 12,33:2
French Way, The; Edward and Agrippina
  1962,Mr 21,36:2
French Way, The; Grand Vizier, The
  1962,Mr 21,36:2
French Way, The; Deceased, The 1962,Mr 21,36:2
Zoo Story, The 1963,My 29,39:6
American Dream, The 1963,My 29,39:6
Kaplan, David
Seven Mirrors 1945,O 26,17:2
Kaplan, Donald
Ruddigore 1965,Ag 27,16:1
Kaplan, Elliot (Composer)
Talking to You 1961,O 23,22:5
Across the Board on Tomorrow Morning
  1961,O 23,22:5
Go Show Me a Dragon 1961,O 28,18:1
Immoralist, The 1963,N 8,36:2
Kaplan, Elliott (Composer)
Cicero 1961,F 9,37:2
Kaplan, Harry
Seven Against One 1930,My 7,25:1
Kaplan, Henry (Director)
Glass Cage, The 1957,Mr 11,21:2
Any Wednesday 1964,F 19,34:1
White House, The 1964,My 20,39:1
P S I Love You 1964,N 20,40:1
Minor Adjustment, A 1967,O 7,33:3
Kaplan, Jeanne
View From the Bridge, A 1965,Ja 29,24:1
Electronic Nigger, The 1968,Mr 9,23:2
Cuban Thing, The 1968,S 25,36:2
Kaplan, L
Man With the Portfolio, The 1931,F 12,24:6
Kaplan, Lionel (Producer)
Breaking Wall, The 1960,Ja 26,27:5
Kaplan, Marvin
Uncle Vanya 1969,Ag 31,II,4:1
Kaplan, Nicki
Adding Machine, The 1970,D 5,40:1
Kaplan, Philip
Where E'er We Go 1943,Je 15,16:1
Kaplan, Sam
Don Juan in the Russian Manner 1954,Ap 23,23:2
Kaplan, Shirley (Miscellaneous)
Decline and Fall of the Entire World As Seen
  Through the Eyes of Cole Porter Revisited, The
  1965,Mr 31,24:2
Ben Bagley's New Cole Porter Revue
  1965,D 23,20:1
Kaplan, Sidney
American Gothic 1953,N 11,35:6
Kaplan, Sol (Composer)
Tonight in Samarkand 1955,F 17,22:2
Once Upon a Tailor 1955,My 24,36:2
Uncle Willie 1956,D 21,17:1
Masquerade 1959,Mr 17,42:1
Dear Liar 1960,Mr 18,19:2
Secret Concubine, The 1960,Mr 22,29:2
Rape of the Belt, The 1960,N 7,46:1
Banker's Daughter, The 1962,Ja 23,37:1
Kaplan, Zelda
In-Laws 1960,O 17,32:4
Cowboy in Israel, A 1962,O 29,36:2
My Wife With Conditions 1963,O 21,39:1
Kaplen, Arthur (Composer)
Every Other Evil 1961,Ja 23,20:2
Kapp, David (Producer)
Donnybrook! 1961,My 19,23:1
Kapp, Walter
Abe Lincoln in Illinois 1938,O 17,12:2
Journey to Jerusalem 1940,O 7,21:2
Pygmalion 1945,D 27,16:1
Kappeler, Alfred
Thank You 1921,O 4,10:2
Seventh Heaven 1922,O 31,11:1
China Rose 1925,Ja 20,18:1
Lambs Gambol 1925,Ap 27,15:1
Honest Liars 1926,Jl 20,17:2
Howdy King 1926,D 14,24:4
Restless Women 1927,D 27,24:1
Furies, The 1928,Mr 8,23:1
Modern Virgin, A 1931,My 21,33:4
Heigh-Ho, Everybody 1932,My 26,31:2
Peacock 1932,O 12,27:1

Kappeler, Alfred—Cont
Eight Bells 1933,O 30,14:2
Eight Bells 1933,N 5,IX,1:1
Woman of the Soil, A 1935,Mr 26,23:6
Achilles Had a Heel 1935,O 14,20:2
Meet the Wife 1937,Jl 6,23:1
Three Waltzes 1937,D 27,10:2
Good Hunting 1938,N 22,26:5
Kappell, Fred
John Brown 1950,My 4,32:7
Kapper, Jimmy
Melody Man, The 1924,My 14,14:2
Kappes, Burdette
Dolly Jordan 1922,O 4,26:1
Kapral, Janet
Trelawny of the 'Wells' 1970,O 12,48:1
Kaprow, Allen
Originale 1964,S 9,46:1
Kaprow, Allen (Director)
Originale 1964,S 9,46:1
Kaprow, Allen (Miscellaneous)
Killer, The 1960,Mr 23,33:1
Kapur, Jagga (Miscellaneous)
Ubu Roi 1970,F 17,33:1
Arden of Faversham 1970,F 17,33:1
Kara and Sek
Good Times 1920,Ag 10,10:1
Karabanova
Chauve-Souris 1922,Je 6,17:4
Chauve-Souris 1925,Ja 15,25:1
Chauve-Souris 1929,Ja 23,20:2
Karakaian, Ed
Full Moon in March, A 1960,S 20,48:1
Purgatory 1960,S 20,48:1
Herne's Egg, The 1960,S 20,48:1
Karakas, Leslie
People vs Ranchman, The 1968,O 28,56:1
Karam, Elena
Men in White 1933,S 27,24:2
Revolt of the Beavers, The 1937,My 21,19:2
Haiti 1938,Mr 3,16:1
Russian Bank 1940,My 25,20:2
Homecoming 1942,N 17,28:5
In Bed We Cry 1944,N 15,20:2
Assassin, The 1945,O 18,20:2
Bravo! 1948,N 12,31:2
Cherry Orchard, The 1960,Je 4,17:2
That Summer-That Fall 1967,Mr 17,33:1
Karanikas, Anna
John Brown 1950,My 4,32:7
Karant, Bryna
Obbligato 1958,F 19,22:2
Karasevich, Joan
Henry IV, Part I 1965,Je 30,42:1
Karaty, Tommy
Cindy 1964,Mr 20,24:1
Pousse-Cafe 1966,Mr 19,19:2
Karavaeff, Simeon
Ziegfeld Follies 1922,Je 6,18:2
Vaudeville (Palace) 1924,S 30,27:5
Vaudeville (Palace) 1927,O 4,34:3
Take the Air 1927,N 23,28:2
Chauve-Souris of 1943 1943,Ag 13,13:2
Karczag (Producer)
Schon Ist die Welt; Endlich Allein
1932,Ja 17,VIII,2:1
Kardeman, Harry (Lighting Director)
Curious Savage, The 1956,Mr 17,12:3
Kardeman, Harry (Scenic Designer)
Curious Savage, The 1956,Mr 17,12:3
Kardon, Helen
New Faces of 1962 1962,F 2,25:1
Karel, Charles
Dear World 1969,F 7,33:1
Kareman, Fred
Time of Your Life, The 1955,Ja 20,34:1
Skin of Our Teeth, The 1955,Ag 18,16:1
Salvage 1957,Ap 10,39:2
Taming of the Shrew, The 1960,Ag 20,17:1
Sudden and Accidental Re-education of Horse
Johnson, The 1968,D 19,63:1
Karen, Anna
Red Gloves 1948,D 6,28:2
Karen, James
Rumpelstiltskin 1948,Mr 15,27:3
Celebration 1948,Ap 12,24:2
Indian Captive, The 1949,Ja 31,15:2
Madame Is Served 1949,F 15,28:1
Major Barbara 1951,F 24,10:2
Time of Storm 1954,F 26,14:2
Third Best Sport 1958,D 31,15:3
Deep Are the Roots 1960,O 4,47:1
Coming Forth by Day of Osiris Jones, The; Kid,
The 1961,Mr 15,45:2
Jackhammer, The 1962,F 6,26:2
Matter of Like Life and Death, A 1963,O 3,28:2
Engagement Baby, The 1970,My 22,40:1
Karens, Mr
Hannibal Ante Portas 1929,Jl 7,VIII,2:4
Karettas, G
Screwball, The 1957,My 25,24:7
Karew, Nan
Good Old Days, The 1923,Ag 15,21:2

Kari, Magda
Streets of Paris, The 1939,Je 20,25:2
Karin, Fia
Parade 1960,Ja 21,27:4
Karin, Rita
Call on Kuprin, A 1961,My 26,29:3
Pocket Watch, The 1966,Ja 6,18:1
Scuba Duba 1967,O 11,36:1
Scuba Duba 1969,Ap 7,51:1
Penny Wars, The 1969,O 16,52:1
Karina, Elena
These Are the Times 1950,My 11,37:2
Karinthy, Fred (Playwright)
Comedy of Crooks, A 1936,Je 8,22:3
Kariofylli, A
Electra 1961,S 20,23:4
Karl, Robert
Guys and Dolls 1955,Ap 21,32:2
Karl-Gerhard
Autumn Manoeuvers 1938,N 27,IX,3:6
Karl-Gerhard (Playwright)
Autumn Manoeuvers 1938,N 27,IX,3:6
Karl-Gerhard (Producer)
Autumn Manoeuvers 1938,N 27,IX,3:6
Karlan, Michael
Lady Akane, The 1960,N 16,51:4
Karlan, Richard
Brother Cain 1941,S 13,21:5
Johnny on the Spot 1942,Ja 9,24:2
Comes the Revelation 1942,My 27,26:2
Song of Bernadette 1946,Mr 27,22:2
Magic Touch, The 1947,S 4,30:1
Karlan, Richard (Producer)
Comes the Revelation 1942,My 27,26:2
Karle, George
Vagabond King, The 1943,Je 30,24:2
Karle, Theodore
Fioretta 1929,Ja 6,VIII,4:6
Fioretta 1929,F 6,30:3
Karlen, John
Golden Six, The 1958,O 27,31:2
Clearing in the Woods, A 1959,F 13,32:1
Season of Choice 1959,Ap 14,40:1
Twelfth Night 1959,Jl 11,10:2
All in Good Time 1965,F 19,25:1
Postmark Zero 1965,N 2,28:1
Suburban Tragedy 1966,Mr 7,22:1
Young Marrieds Play Monopoly 1966,Mr 7,22:1
'Tis Pity She's a Whore 1967,O 21,15:2
Karli, A Francis
Good Earth, The 1932,O 18,23:4
Karlin, Elsie
Heigh-Ho, Everybody 1932,My 26,31:2
Karlin, Fred (Miscellaneous)
Morning Sun 1963,O 7,36:2
Karlin, George (Composer)
To Tell You the Truth 1948,Ap 19,28:6
Karlin, Miriam
Women of Twilight 1952,Mr 4,22:2
All Kinds of Men 1957,S 20,20:3
Fiddler on the Roof 1967,F 17,50:1
Karlling, Dagmar
Fireworks on the James 1940,My 15,30:2
Karloff, Boris
Arsenic and Old Lace 1941,Ja 11,13:2
Arsenic and Old Lace 1941,F 23,IX,1:1
Linden Tree, The 1948,Mr 3,28:2
Shop at Sly Corner, The 1949,Ja 19,35:2
Peter Pan 1950,Ap 25,27:2
Peter Pan 1950,Ap 30,II,1:1
Lark, The 1955,N 18,20:1
Lark, The 1955,N 27,II,1:1
Karlov, Sonia
Sisters of the Chorus 1930,O 21,34:3
Karlton, Sylvia
Allegro 1947,O 11,10:2
Karlweis, Ninon Tallon (Miscellaneous)
Constant Prince, The 1969,O 18,36:1
Acropolis 1969,N 5,40:1
Apocalypsis cum Figuris 1969,N 20,60:2
Karlweis, Ninon Tallon (Producer)
World of Gunter Grass, The 1966,Ap 27,38:1
Diary of a Madman 1967,Mr 24,25:1
Tango 1969,Ja 20,33:1
Karlweis, Oscar
Baby Mine 1927,Ap 3,VIII,2:1
Fledermaus, Die 1929,Jl 14,IX,2:1
Menschen im Hotel 1930,Mr 16,IX,4:1
Cocktail 1931,F 15,VIII,3:2
Cue for Passion 1940,D 20,33:4
Rosalinda; Fledermaus, Die 1942,O 29,26:5
Rosalinda 1943,F 14,II,1:4
Jacobowsky and the Colonel 1944,Mr 15,17:2
Jacobowsky and the Colonel 1944,Mr 19,II,1:1
Jacobowsky and the Colonel 1944,My 21,II,1:1
I Like It Here 1946,Mr 23,8:6
Ist Geraldine ein Engel? 1946,N 4,33:4
Topaze 1947,D 29,21:5
Harvey 1949,Mr 24,34:1
Cry of the Peacock 1950,Ap 12,33:2
Ring Around the Moon 1950,N 24,30:1
Teahouse of the August Moon, The 1954,S 18,13:4
Once Upon a Tailor 1955,My 24,36:2

Karlweis, Oscar (Translator)
Teahouse of the August Moon, The
1954,My 20,37:1
Karm, Beata
King Lear 1923,Mr 10,9:4
Karm, Mickey
South Pacific 1965,Je 3,25:1
South Pacific 1967,Je 13,56:1
Two by Two 1970,N 11,37:1
Karman, Werner
Wiener Blut 1964,S 12,14:1
Karmany, Sheila (Playwright)
Psychological Moment, The 1931,Mr 4,33:2
Karmon, Jonathan (Choreographer)
Grand Music Hall of Israel, The 1968,F 7,42:1
Karmon, Jonathan (Director)
Grand Music Hall of Israel, The 1968,F 7,42:1
Karmon Dancers
New Music Hall of Israel, The 1969,O 3,40:1
Karmon Histadruth Ballet, The
Grand Music Hall of Israel, The 1968,F 7,42:1
Karner, Christine
Sing Out, Sweet Land! 1944,D 28,24:2
Talent '49 1949,Ap 13,39:4
Razzle Dazzle 1951,F 20,21:1
Karnilova, Maria
Call Me Mister 1946,Ap 19,26:2
Miss Liberty 1949,Jl 16,6:5
Miss Liberty 1949,Ag 7,II,6:4
Two's Company 1952,D 16,43:5
Two's Company 1952,D 21,II,3:1
Beggar's Opera, The 1957,Mr 14,35:1
Kaleidoscope 1957,Je 14,20:2
Gypsy 1959,My 22,31:6
Bravo Giovanni 1962,My 21,41:2
Bravo Giovanni 1962,My 27,II,1:1
Fiddler on the Roof 1964,S 23,56:2
Fiddler on the Roof 1967,S 28,59:2
Zorba 1968,N 18,58:1
Zorba 1968,N 24,II,1:1
Karnilova, Maria (Choreographer)
Triumph of Delight 1965,My 1,19:1
Karnot, Greta
Professor Mamlock 1937,Ap 14,30:3
Karnot, Stephen
Young Go First, The 1935,My 29,16:2
Karns, Ad
Steel 1939,D 20,30:2
Russian People, The 1942,D 30,17:2
Playboy of Newark, The 1943,Mr 20,11:2
Karns, Ad (Director)
Cure for Matrimony 1939,O 26,26:3
Steel 1939,D 20,30:2
Karns, Ad (Miscellaneous)
Double in Hearts 1956,O 17,41:7
Karns, Ad (Producer;
Double in Hearts 1956,O 17,41:7
Karns, Margaret (Costume Designer)
Steel 1939,D 20,30:2
Karns, Roscoe
School for Brides 1944,Ag 2,19:4
Karoku
Kagami-Jishi; Mirror Lion Dance, The
1969,S 11,53:1
Kumagai Jinya 1969,S 18,64:1
Karoku, Onoe
Kagotsurube; Courtesan, The 1960,Je 3,26:1
Musume Dojoji; Maiden at the Dojo Temple, The
1960,Je 10,37:1
Musume Dojoji; Maiden at the Dojo Temple, The
1960,Je 17,35:4
Karol, Hana
Days of Our Youth, The 1941,N 29,15:2
Karol, Milton
Brooklyn Biarritz 1941,F 28,16:2
All Men Are Alike 1941,O 7,27:2
First Crocus, The 1942,Ja 3,14:6
Karolou, Haritini
Electra 1964,S 8,33:1
Karolya
Love City, The 1926,Ja 26,18:2
Karp, Abe
Brownsville Grandfather, The 1935,Ap 19,24:6
Karp, Ed
Wedding, The 1961,Ap 21,26:2
Karp, Richard (Producer)
Enemy of the People, An 1959,F 5,24:4
Come Share My House 1960,F 19,20:2
Machinal 1960,Ap 8,27:1
Karpe, Curtis
Rita Coventry 1923,F 20,12:2
White Cargo 1923,N 6,22:2
Humble, The 1926,O 14,22:2
Tin Pan Alley 1928,N 2,29:1
Damn Your Honor 1929,D 31,14:3
Mystery Moon 1930,Je 24,23:4
Rhapsody, The 1930,S 16,30:3
Berlin 1931,D 31,16:1
Web, The 1932,Je 28,24:4
Great Lover, The 1932,O 12,27:3
Whistling in the Dark 1932,N 4,25:2
Monster, The 1933,F 11,11:5
Her Tin Soldier 1933,Ap 7,22:6

Karpe, Curtis—Cont

Yoshe Kalb 1933,D 29,27:2
Sweet Mystery of Life 1935,O 12,13:3
Fabulous Invalid, The 1938,O 10,15:1
White Cargo 1941,My 14,24:3
Arsenic and Old Lace 1944,Jl 3,7:3
Front Page, The 1946,S 5,22:4

Karr, David
Way of the World, The 1965,Je 2,40:1
Merton of the Movies 1968,S 26,62:1

Karr, David (Miscellaneous)
Playroom, The 1965,D 6,49:1

Karr, David (Producer)
Xmas in Las Vegas 1965,N 5,31:1

Karr, Frederick
Hottentot, The 1920,Mr 2,9:1
Mountain Man, The 1921,D 13,24:2
Exciters, The 1922,S 23,10:4

Karr, Harold (Composer)
New Faces of 1956 1956,Je 15,32:1
Happy Hunting 1956,D 7,30:1
Happy Hunting 1956,D 16,II,3:1

Karr, Harold (Lyricist)
New Faces of 1956 1956,Je 15,32:1

Karr, James
Ponder Heart, The 1956,F 17,14:2
Loud Red Patrick, The 1956,O 4,28:1
Say Darling 1959,F 26,38:2

Karr, James (Miscellaneous)
Lady Akane, The 1960,N 16,51:4
Hanjo 1960,N 16,51:4

Karr, Joan
Allez-Opp! 1927,Ag 3,29:3

Karr, Kathleen
Boy Friend, The 1932,Je 8,22:3

Karr, Patti
New Faces of 1962 1962,F 2,25:1
To Broadway With Love 1964,Ap 30,28:6
Skits-Oh-Frantics 1967,Ap 3,39:2
Month of Sundays 1968,S 17,50:1
Up Eden 1968,N 27,42:1
Look to the Lilies 1970,Mr 30,59:1

Karrakis, S
Treasure, The 1920,O 5,13:1

Karras, Athan
Son, The 1950,Ag 16,24:6
Pelleas and Melisande 1957,F 20,38:1
Oedipus Rex 1960,Ap 30,15:2

Karreys, The Four
Vaudeville (Palace) 1929,Ag 19,23:1

Karrol, Dorothy
Yours Is My Heart 1946,S 6,16:5

Karson, Nat (Costume Designer)
Macbeth 1936,Ap 15,25:4
Horse Eats Hat 1936,S 28,14:2
Hot Mikado, The 1939,Mr 24,26:2
Hot Mikado, The 1939,Ap 2,X,1:3
Hot Mikado, The 1939,Je 23,23:4
Liliom 1940,Mr 26,17:2
Keep Off the Grass 1940,My 24,22:6
Connecticut Yankee, A 1943,N 18,30:2
Nellie Bly 1946,Ja 22,32:2

Karson, Nat (Lighting Director)
Liliom 1940,Mr 26,17:2
Connecticut Yankee, A 1943,N 18,30:2
Nellie Bly 1946,Ja 22,32:2

Karson, Nat (Miscellaneous)
High Kickers 1941,N 1,21:2

Karson, Nat (Producer)
Nellie Bly 1946,Ja 22,32:2
Long Way From Home, A 1948,F 9,25:2
Hamlet 1949,Je 18,9:6

Karson, Nat (Scenic Designer)
Calling All Stars 1934,D 14,28:2
Hook-Up, The 1935,My 9,24:6
Macbeth 1936,Ap 15,25:4
Horse Eats Hat 1936,S 28,14:2
White Man 1936,O 19,22:4
Arms for Venus 1937,Mr 12,18:7
Without Warning 1937,My 3,23:2
Right This Way 1938,Ja 6,22:3
Journeyman 1938,Ja 31,14:2
Roosty 1938,F 15,21:2
Hot Mikado, The 1939,Mr 24,26:2
Liliom 1940,Mr 26,17:2
Keep Off the Grass 1940,My 24,22:6
High Kickers 1941,N 1,21:2
Connecticut Yankee, A 1943,N 18,30:2
Nellie Bly 1946,Ja 22,32:2
Front Page, The 1946,S 5,22:4

Kartalian, Buck
Romeo and Juliet 1951,Mr 12,21:2
Detective Story 1954,F 13,11:2
Adding Machine, The 1956,F 10,17:1
Golden Fleecing 1959,O 16,24:5
One More River 1960,Mr 19,12:2

Kartavin, Leon
Natja 1925,F 17,19:2

Karter, Richard
Rose in the Wilderness 1949,Ja 5,21:2

Karthaz, Dick
Kiss Me, Kate 1954,Mr 27,13:2

Karvelis, Al
He Who Gets Slapped 1956,F 2,18:1

Karyle, Ann
Sons o' Guns 1929,N 27,30:4

Kasakoff, Sam
Porgy and Bess 1953,Mr 10,25:5

Kasdan, Michael
Hamlet 1958,Je 21,11:1
Winter's Tale, The 1958,Jl 21,17:4

Kasdan, Michael (Miscellaneous)
Lovey 1965,Mr 26,27:1
Do Not Pass Go 1965,Ap 20,44:1
Match-Play 1966,O 12,37:1
Party for Divorce, A 1966,O 12,37:1
Night of the Dunce 1966,D 29,21:1
Rimers of Eldritch, The 1967,F 21,53:1
Party on Greenwich Avenue, The 1967,My 11,52:1
Box 1968,O 1,39:1
Quotations From Chairman Mao Tse-Tung 1968,O 1,39:1
Death of Bessie Smith, The 1968,O 3,55:1
American Dream, The 1968,O 3,55:1
Krapp's Last Tape 1968,O 11,41:1
Zoo Story, The 1968,O 11,41:1
Happy Days 1968,O 14,54:1

Kasdan, Michael (Producer)
What the Butler Saw 1970,My 5,56:1

Kasha, Charles (Producer)
Hadrian VII 1969,Ja 9,22:1

Kasha, Lawrence (Director)
Anything Goes 1962,My 16,35:1
Bajour 1964,N 24,42:1
Show Boat 1966,Jl 20,48:1
Lovely Ladies, Kind Gentlemen 1970,D 29,38:1

Kasha, Lawrence (Miscellaneous)
Happy Town 1959,O 8,49:2
She Loves Me 1963,Ap 24,39:1
Funny Girl 1964,Mr 27,15:1

Kasha, Lawrence (Producer)
Parade 1960,Ja 21,27:4
Hadrian VII 1969,Ja 9,22:1
Applause 1970,Mr 31,35:1

Kasher, Charles (Producer)
Crystal Heart, The 1960,F 16,31:2
Staircase 1968,Ja 11,41:2

Kashins, Beulah
Sisters' Tragedy, The 1930,My 6,33:1
Dole Brothers 1932,Mr 26,17:7

Kashinsky, Dora
What's the Use? 1926,S 7,19:1

Kashioff, Joseph
Farewell to Arms, A 1930,S 23,30:3

Kashman, Betty
Honor Code, The 1931,My 19,25:3
Moon Over Mulberry Street 1935,S 5,24:6

Kashman, Betty (Director)
God Strikes Back 1943,F 27,11:2

Kashner, David
Vamp, The 1955,N 11,30:1

Kasia (Costume Designer)
Blue Holiday 1945,My 22,13:3

Kaskal, Arthur
Berlin 1931,D 31,16:1

Kaskas, Anna
Yeomen of the Guard, The 1939,Jl 23,IX,2:1

Kasket, Harold
Caesar and Cleopatra 1951,D 20,43:2
Antony and Cleopatra 1951,D 21,22:2

Kaslik, Vaclav (Director)
Laterna Magika 1964,Ag 4,21:1

Kaslik, Vaclav (Musical Director)
Laterna Magika 1964,Ag 4,21:1

Kason, Corrine
Unfair to Goliath 1970,Ja 26,27:1

Kaspar, Eddie
Tired Business Man, The 1929,Je 5,32:5

Kasparian, Robert (Director)
Agatha Sue, I Love You 1966,D 15,61:1

Kasper, Edwin
Green Ring, The 1922,Ap 5,22:1
Women Go on Forever 1927,S 8,25:1

Kasper, Edwin H
Makers of Light 1922,My 24,22:3

Kasper, John
Howdy, Mr Ice of 1950 1949,My 27,24:2

Kass, Alan
Guitar 1959,N 11,42:5
Golden Rainbow 1968,F 5,27:1

Kass, Aysa
Flame of Love 1924,Ap 22,19:2
Fool's Bells 1925,D 24,8:3
White Eagle, The 1927,D 27,24:4

Kass, Jerome (Playwright)
Princess Rebecca Birnbaum 1966,Mr 7,22:1
Make Like a Dog 1966,Mr 7,22:1
Young Marrieds Play Monopoly 1966,Mr 7,22:1
Suburban Tragedy 1966,Mr 7,22:1
Saturday Night 1968,F 26,43:1

Kass, Joanne (Miscellaneous)
Breaking Wall, The 1960,Ja 26,27:5

Kass, Peter
Innocent Voyage, The 1943,N 16,27:2
Jacobowsky and the Colonel 1944,Mr 15,17:2
No Exit 1946,N 27,21:1
Skipper Next to God 1948,Ja 5,14:5

Kass, Peter—Cont

Country Girl, The 1950,N 11,10:6

Kass, Peter (Director)
Night Music 1951,Ap 9,29:6
Judge, The 1958,My 14,36:2
Marching Song 1959,D 29,20:1
Sign in Sidney Brustein's Window, The 1964,O 16,32:1
All Women Are One 1965,Ja 8,21:1
Postmark Zero 1965,N 2,28:1
Nathan Weinstein, Mystic, Connecticut 1966,F 26,15:2

Kass, Peter (Producer)
Marching Song 1959,D 29,20:1

Kassabian, Jack
Experiment, The 1967,My 9,54:2

Kassapian, Serene
Echmiadzin 1946,O 21,27:3

Kassapian, Serene (Director)
Echmiadzin 1946,O 21,27:3

Kassapian, Serene (Playwright)
Echmiadzin 1946,O 21,27:3

Kassul, Art
Legitimate Steal, The 1958,Ap 1,35:1
Darker Flower, A 1963,Mr 11,7:2
Fourth Pig, The 1965,Ja 27,24:6
Fisherman, The 1965,Ja 27,24:6

Kasten, Rae
Squealer, The 1928,N 13,36:3

Kasten, Sam
Radio Girl, The 1929,O 19,22:4
Jolly Orphan, The 1929,D 23,18:6
Little Clown, The 1930,Mr 15,23:3
Love Thief, The 1931,Ja 19,24:5
Longing for Home 1933,S 22,15:1
Slaves of the Public 1934,Mr 10,18:6
Here Runs the Bride 1934,N 4,IX,2:1
Lost Paradise 1934,D 14,28:3
What Girls Do 1935,Ja 14,10:4
Holiday in Town, A 1935,S 30,12:3
Secret of Love, The 1936,F 24,15:2
Yossel and His Wives 1937,S 19,II,8:3
Warson at Night 1938,Ja 31,14:3
Should a Mother Tell? 1938,N 25,18:3
Street Singers 1938,D 12,25:6
Queen Mother 1938,D 26,29:4
Schwartse Mamme 1939,Ja 16,11:3
Oy, Is Dus a Leben!; Oh, What a Life! 1942,O 13,19:2

Kastl, Paul
Best Foot Forward 1963,Ap 3,43:1

Kastle, Leonard (Musical Director)
Lady in the Dark 1952,Mr 8,11:3

Kastner, Martin (Translator)
Trumpets and Drums 1969,O 13,52:1

Kastner, Peter
Playroom, The 1965,D 6,49:1

Kastner, Rose (Translator)
Trumpets and Drums 1969,O 13,52:1

Kaszas, Joan
Macbeth 1969,D 23,25:1

Kasznar, Kurt
Eternal Road, The 1937,Ja 8,14:2
Joy to the World 1948,Mr 19,28:2
Make Way for Lucia 1948,D 23,23:5
Nineteenth Hole of Europe, The 1949,Mr 28,16:2
Montserrat 1949,O 31,21:4
Happy Time, The 1950,Ja 25,24:1
Seventh Heaven 1955,My 27,16:2
Six Characters in Search of an Author 1955,D 12,38:1
Six Characters in Search of an Author 1955,D 25,II,3:1
Waiting for Godot 1956,Ap 20,21:2
Waiting for Godot 1956,Ap 29,II,1:2
Look After Lulu 1959,Mr 4,35:1
Sound of Music, The 1959,N 17,40:2
Barefoot in the Park 1963,O 24,36:2
Dreigroschenoper, Die 1965,Mr 12,24:1

Kasznar, Kurt (Director)
Crazy With the Heat 1941,Ja 15,18:2

Kasznar, Kurt (Playwright)
First Cousins 1943,Je 15,16:1

Kasznar, Kurt (Producer)
Crazy With the Heat 1940,D 26,22:1
Crazy With the Heat 1941,Ja 15,18:2
Crazy With the Heat 1941,Ja 31,15:2

Katayev, Valentin (Original Author)
Squaring the Circle 1931,Ap 27,24:4

Katayev, Valentin (Playwright)
Quadrature of the Circle; Squaring the Circle 1931,D 13,VIII,3:1
Squaring the Circle 1935,S 22,X,3:2
Squaring the Circle 1935,O 4,24:6
Million Torments, A 1936,Ja 16,24:5
Squaring the Circle 1936,Ag 12,15:3
Path of Flowers, The 1936,S 18,19:3
Squaring the Circle 1941,S 7,IX,2:5

Katch, Kurt
Brothers Ashkenazi, The 1937,S 21,28:6
One Sabbath Afternoon 1939,Ja 17,27:5
Topsy-Turvy 1939,F 13,12:3
Parnosseh 1939,F 20,12:5

Katchaloff, Vassily
Tsar Fyodor Ivanovitch 1923,Ja 11,25:1
Lower Depths, The 1923,Ja 16,16:1
Three Sisters, The 1923,Ja 30,12:2
Brothers Karamazov, The 1923,F 27,14:2
Brothers Karamazov, The 1923,Mr 4,VII,1:1
Brothers Karamazov, The 1923,N 20,23:4
Ivanoff 1923,N 27,23:2
In the Claws of Life 1923,N 30,23:4
Enemy of the People, An 1923,D 4,25:1
Enough Stupidity in Every Wise Man
   1923,D 6,23:1
Brothers Karamazov, The 1924,My 6,25:2
Moscow Art Theatre 1924,My 13,25:2
Resurrection 1930,Je 8,IX,3:1
Kate and Wiley
Vaudeville (Palace) 1929,D 16,34:4
Kates, Barney
Play With a Tiger 1964,D 31,14:2
Kates, Bernard
Jack and the Beanstalk 1947,N 3,28:2
At War With the Army 1949,Mr 9,32:2
Naked 1950,S 7,39:2
Billy Budd 1951,F 12,18:3
Troublemakers, The 1954,D 31,11:3
Disenchanted, The 1958,D 4,53:4
Heartbreak House 1963,Je 28,24:1
Have I Got a Girl for You! 1963,D 3,53:2
Devils, The 1965,N 17,51:2
Kates, Viola
Mexican Mural; Patio With Flamingo
   1942,Ap 27,19:2
Mexican Mural; Moonlight Scene 1942,Ap 27,19:2
Kathryne
Geisha, The 1931,O 6,35:4
Kato, Sakae
Coney Island Play 1970,O 31,34:2
Katsanos, Constantine
View From the Bridge, A 1965,Ja 29,24:1
Cannibals, The 1968,N 4,60:1
Katscher, Robert (Composer)
You Never Know 1938,S 22,26:3
Vaudeville Marches On 1938,D 30,11:1
Katscher, Robert (Musical Director)
Wonder Bar, The 1931,Mr 18,23:4
Katscher, Robert (Original Author)
Wonder Bar, The 1931,Mr 8,VIII,3:5
You Never Know 1938,S 22,26:3
Katselas, Milton (Director)
Zoo Story, The 1960,Ja 15,37:2
Zoo Story, The 1960,Ja 31,II,1:1
Call Me by My Rightful Name 1961,F 1,31:1
Garden of Sweets, The 1961,N 1,35:1
On an Open Roof 1963,Ja 30,7:3
Journey to the Day 1963,N 12,49:1
Rose Tattoo, The 1966,O 21,36:2
Butterflies Are Free 1969,O 22,30:1
Butterflies Are Free 1969,N 2,II,1:1
Camino Real 1970,Ja 9,42:1
Katselas, Milton (Producer)
On an Open Roof 1963,Ja 30,7:3
Katsileris, Evangelos
Cute Gata.....Oute Zhmia; Neither Cat . . . Nor
   Damage 1957,D 20,31:1
Katz, Alex (Costume Designer)
Three Times Three; George Washington Crossing
   the Delaware 1962,Mr 2,24:1
Katz, Alex (Scenic Designer)
Three Times Three; George Washington Crossing
   the Delaware 1962,Mr 2,24:1
Katz, Arthur Joel (Producer)
Infantry, The 1966,N 15,51:1
Katz, Ben Zion
Gardener's Dog, The 1927,O 21,27:1
Roaming Stars 1930,Ja 25,12:2
Chains 1930,F 23,29:2
Witch of Castile, The 1930,O 25,21:1
Far-Away Corner, A 1939,F 15,15:2
Katz, Emil
Dole Brothers 1932,Mr 26,17:7
Katz, Estelle
Blue Butterfly, The 1929,F 17,29:3
Katz, Harriet
Othello 1929,F 4,21:2
Katz, Joel
Cyanamide 1954,Mr 26,17:6
Katz, Leandro (Lighting Director)
Bluebeard 1970,My 5,58:1
Katz, Leon (Playwright)
Dracula Sabbat 1970,O 2,28:2
Katz, Lillian
Shylock and His Daughter 1947,S 30,22:2
Katz, M (Playwright)
Kreutzer Sonata, The 1920,O 3,VI,1:7
Katz, Mickey
Borscht Capades 1951,S 18,38:3
Hello Solly! 1967,Ap 6,44:3
Katz, Mickey (Director)
Borscht Capades 1951,S 18,38:3
Katz, Peter S (Miscellaneous)
Evening With Mike Nichols and Elaine May, An
   1960,O 10,37:1
Child Buyer, The 1962,My 14,35:1

Katz, Peter S (Producer)
Any Wednesday 1964,F 19,34:1
Peterpat 1965,Ja 7,27:1
Katz, Ruth
Cyanamide 1954,Mr 26,17:6
Katz, Vera
Moroni 1936,Ag 19,19:1
Katz, Zisy
World Trembles, The 1939,F 28,17:3
Katzakian, Marsha
Lady From Maxim's, The 1970,Je 1,41:1
Katzell, William R (Miscellaneous)
Home of the Brave 1945,D 28,13:2
Katzell, William R (Producer)
Joy to the World 1948,Mr 19,28:2
Lend an Ear 1948,D 17,38:2
Alive and Kicking 1950,Ja 18,25:5
Katzin, Olga
Pickwick 1927,Mr 13,VII,1:1
Pickwick 1927,S 6,35:2
Katzin, Olga (Director)
Novice and the Duke, The 1929,D 11,37:2
Country Wife, The 1931,Ap 19,31:5
Alchemist, The 1931,Je 5,27:1
Katzin, Olga (Playwright)
Novice and the Duke, The 1929,D 11,37:2
One Chaste Man 1930,Je 11,33:5
Country Wife, The 1931,Ap 19,31:5
Katzin, Winifred (Translator)
Failures, The 1923,N 23,20:1
Time Is a Dream 1924,Ap 23,24:2
Failures, The 1959,Ja 6,30:2
Katzka, Emil (Miscellaneous)
Pal Joey 1952,Ja 4,17:6
Katzka, Gabriel (Miscellaneous)
Beyond the Fringe 1962,O 29,36:1
School for Scandal, The 1963,Ja 26,5:2
Man and Boy 1963,N 13,34:1
Hamlet 1964,Ap 10,30:1
Baker Street 1965,F 17,36:1
Katzka, Gabriel (Producer)
Hide and Seek 1957,Ap 3,26:1
Katzman, Jacob
Kreutzer Sonata, The 1924,My 15,22:3
Kibitzer, The 1929,F 19,22:5
Kibitzer, The 1931,N 7,17:3
Katzman, Louis (Musical Director)
Time, Place and the Girl, The 1942,O 22,24:3
Kauffer, McKnight (Scenic Designer)
Queen of Scots 1934,Jl 15,X,1:3
Kauffman, Cindy
Ice Follies 1970,My 23,27:1
Kauffman, Ron
Ice Follies 1970,My 23,27:1
Kauffmann, Stanley
As You Like It 1936,Ap 24,18:4
Kauffmann, Stanley (Playwright)
Bobino 1944,Ap 7,23:4
Kauflin, Jack
Best Foot Forward 1956,Mr 3,16:1
Annie Get Your Gun 1957,Mr 9,15:5
Fallout 1959,My 21,36:2
Kaufman, Allan (Director)
Cyanamide 1954,Mr 26,17:6
Kaufman, Alvin (Composer)
Belmont Varieties 1932,S 29,17:2
Kaufman, Alvin (Lyricist)
Belmont Varieties 1932,S 29,17:2
Kaufman, Anna
Twelfth Night 1954,N 10,42:2
Kaufman, Artie
Set a Thief 1927,F 22,22:1
Kaufman, Beatrice (Playwright)
Divided by Three 1934,S 28,26:3
White Haired Boy, The 1940,O 29,32:6
Kaufman, Brian (Miscellaneous)
In 3 Zones 1970,N 3,28:1
Kaufman, Charles K (Director)
Diamond Lil 1949,F 7,16:2
Kaufman, David (Miscellaneous)
Have I Got a Girl for You! 1963,D 3,53:2
Kaufman, Don
Montserrat 1954,My 26,34:2
Kaufman, Ed
Afternoon Storm 1948,Ap 12,24:2
Kaufman, Esther (Playwright)
Worm in Horseradish, A 1961,Mr 14,32:3
Kaufman, Eugene
Brouhaha 1960,Ap 27,31:2
Kaufman, Frederick
Cherry Blossoms 1927,Mr 29,22:3
Love Call, The 1927,O 25,33:1
Amourette 1933,S 28,25:2
Kill That Story 1934,Ag 30,22:2
Nowhere Bound 1935,Ja 23,20:2
Lend Me Your Ears! 1936,O 6,28:5
Chalked Out 1937,Mr 26,24:2
Good, The 1938,O 6,27:2
Kaufman, George S
Once in a Lifetime 1930,S 7,IX,2:4
Once in a Lifetime 1930,S 25,22:3
Spring Tonic 1936,My 11,16:1
Man Who Came to Dinner, The 1941,Jl 29,13:5

Kaufman, George S (Director)
Good Fellow, The 1926,O 6,22:1
Front Page, The 1928,Ag 15,19:2
Front Page, The 1928,Ag 26,VII,1:1
June Moon 1929,O 10,34:5
Joseph 1930,F 13,25:3
Once in a Lifetime 1930,S 25,22:3
Of Thee I Sing 1931,D 28,20:1
Face the Music 1932,F 4,25:4
Face the Music 1932,F 18,24:5
Here Today 1932,S 7,14:2
Dinner at Eight 1932,O 24,18:2
Dinner at Eight 1933,Ja 7,11:5
Dinner at Eight 1933,Ap 9,IX,1:7
Let 'Em Eat Cake 1933,O 23,18:1
Dark Tower, The 1933,N 27,20:3
Merrily We Roll Along 1934,O 1,14:1
Merrily We Roll Along 1934,O 7,IX,1:1
First Lady 1935,N 27,17:4
Stage Door 1936,S 29,35:1
Stage Door 1936,O 23,26:3
Stage Door 1936,N 1,X,1:1
You Can't Take It With You 1936,D 6,XII,6:2
You Can't Take It With You 1936,D 15,31:1
Of Mice and Men 1937,N 24,20:5
Of Mice and Men 1937,D 12,XI,3:1
Of Mice and Men 1938,Ja 23,XI,1:6
Fabulous Invalid, The 1938,O 10,15:1
American Way, The 1939,Ja 23,9:2
Man Who Came to Dinner, The 1939,O 17,31:1
Man Who Came to Dinner, The 1940,F 10,19:5
Man Who Came to Dinner, The 1940,F 18,IX,3:6
George Washington Slept Here 1940,O 19,20:3
My Sister Eileen 1940,D 27,23:2
My Sister Eileen 1941,Ja 5,IX,1:1
Mr Big 1941,S 14,IX,2:5
Mr Big 1941,O 1,24:2
Land Is Bright, The 1941,O 21,28:5
Land Is Bright, The 1941,O 29,26:2
Doughgirls, The 1942,D 31,19:2
Doughgirls, The 1943,Ja 10,VIII,1:1
Naked Genius, The 1943,O 22,20:5
Naked Genius, The 1943,O 31,II,1:1
Naked Genius, The 1943,N 7,II,1:6
Over Twenty-One 1944,Ja 4,20:2
While the Sun Shines 1944,S 20,21:3
While the Sun Shines 1944,S 24,II,1:1
Late George Apley, The 1944,N 22,26:2
Late George Apley, The 1944,D 3,II,1:1
Hollywood Pinafore 1945,Je 1,20:1
Next Half Hour, The 1945,O 30,14:6
Park Avenue 1946,N 5,31:2
Town House 1948,S 24,31:2
Bravo! 1948,N 12,31:2
Metropole 1949,D 7,43:2
Enchanted, The 1950,Ja 19,34:2
Guys and Dolls 1950,D 3,II,1:1
Small Hours, The 1951,F 16,22:1
Guys and Dolls 1951,O 7,II,1:1
Fancy Meeting You Again 1952,Ja 15,23:2
Of Thee I Sing 1952,My 6,34:2
Solid Gold Cadillac, The 1953,N 6,24:2
Romanoff and Juliet 1957,O 11,24:1
Kaufman, George S (Lyricist)
Hollywood Pinafore 1945,Je 1,20:1
Hollywood Pinafore 1945,Je 10,II,1:1
Kaufman, George S (Miscellaneous)
Strike Up the Band 1930,Ja 15,29:1
Here Today 1932,S 18,IX,1:1
I'd Rather Be Right 1937,N 3,28:2
Sing Out the News 1938,S 26,12:5
Kaufman, George S (Original Author)
Inside U S A 1948,Ag 29,II,1:1
Sherry! 1967,Ap 9,II,1:1
Kaufman, George S (Playwright)
Dulcy 1921,Ag 15,14:1
Dulcy 1921,Ag 21,VI,1:1
To the Ladies! 1922,F 21,20:1
To the Ladies! 1922,Mr 12,VI,1:1
49ers, The 1922,N 7,14:1
49ers, The 1922,N 12,VIII,1:1
Merton of the Movies 1922,N 14,16:2
Helen of Troy, New York 1923,Je 20,22:6
Deep Tangled Wildwood, The 1923,N 6,22:1
Beggar on Horseback 1924,F 13,17:2
Beggar on Horseback 1924,F 17,VII,1:1
Be Yourself! 1924,Ag 24,VII,1:8
Old Man Minick 1924,Ag 24,VII,1:8
Be Yourself! 1924,S 4,13:3
Minick 1924,S 25,20:1
Butter and Egg Man, The 1925,S 24,28:1
Cocoanuts, The 1925,D 9,30:1
Cocoanuts, The 1925,D 13,IX,3:1
Cocoanuts, The 1926,Ap 18,VIII,1:1
Cocoanuts, The 1926,Je 11,25:2
Good Fellow, The 1926,Je 27,VII,3:1
Good Fellow, The 1926,O 6,22:1
Butter and Egg Man, The 1927,Ag 31,19:3
Royal Family, The 1927,D 29,26:4
Royal Family, The 1928,Ja 8,VIII,1:1
Royal Family, The 1928,Jl 1,VIII,3:5
Animal Crackers 1928,O 24,26:2
Little Show, The 1929,My 12,IX,1:2

Kaufman, George S (Playwright)—Cont

June Moon 1929,Ag 4,VIII,1:6
June Moon 1929,O 10,34:5
Channel Road, The 1929,O 18,24:2
Channel Road, The 1929,O 27,IX,1:1
Once in a Lifetime 1930,S 7,IX,2:4
Once in a Lifetime 1930,S 25,22:3
Once in a Lifetime 1930,D 7,IX,1:1
Once in a Lifetime 1931,F 1,VIII,1:3
Royal Family, The 1931,Ap 12,IX,1:3
Band Wagon, The 1931,My 17,VIII,3:2
Band Wagon, The 1931,Je 4,31:3
Band Wagon, The 1931,Je 14,VIII,1:1
Eldorado 1931,O 25,VIII,2:5
Of Thee I Sing 1931,D 13,VIII,2:4
Of Thee I Sing 1931,D 28,20:1
Of Thee I Sing 1932,Mr 20,VIII,1:1
Of Thee I Sing 1932,My 8,VIII,1:1
Dinner at Eight 1932,O 24,18:2
Dinner at Eight 1932,N 6,IX,1:1
Dinner at Eight 1933,Ja 7,11:5
Dinner at Eight 1933,Ja 29,IX,1:3
Once in a Lifetime 1933,F 24,13:1
Once in a Lifetime 1933,Mr 19,IX,2:2
Dinner at Eight 1933,Ap 9,IX,1:7
June Moon 1933,My 16,15:5
Let 'Em Eat Cake 1933,O 3,26:5
Dinner at Eight 1933,O 17,26:2
Let 'Em Eat Cake 1933,O 23,18:1
Let 'Em Eat Cake 1933,N 12,IX,1:1
Dark Tower, The 1933,N 27,20:3
Dark Tower, The 1934,Je 10,IX,1:1
Merrily We Roll Along 1934,O 1,14:1
Merrily We Roll Along 1934,O 7,IX,1:1
Bring on the Girls 1934,O 23,23:2
Theatre Royal 1934,N 11,IX,1:1
First Lady 1935,N 11,21:3
First Lady 1935,N 27,17:4
First Lady 1935,D 8,X,3:1
Merrily We Roll Along 1936,Je 30,15:1
Royal Family, The 1936,Jl 16,15:4
Royal Family, The 1936,Ag 12,15:1
Stage Door 1936,S 29,35:1
Stage Door 1936,O 4,IX,2:1
Stage Door 1936,O 23,26:3
Stage Door 1936,N 1,X,1:1
You Can't Take It With You 1936,D 1,30:8
You Can't Take It With You 1936,D 6,XII,6:2
You Can't Take It With You 1936,D 15,31:1
You Can't Take It With You 1936,D 20,XI,3:1
Of Thee I Sing 1937,Ag 10,22:3
You Can't Take It With You 1937,Ag 29,X,1:1
First Lady 1937,O 9,17:2
I'd Rather Be Right 1937,O 12,27:6
I'd Rather Be Right 1937,O 17,XI,2:1
I'd Rather Be Right 1937,N 3,28:2
I'd Rather Be Right 1937,N 14,XI,1:1
You Can't Take It With You 1937,D 23,25:5
You Can't Take It With You 1938,Ja 9,X,1:7
You Can't Take It With You 1938,Ja 16,X,1:6
Sing Out the News 1938,S 26,12:5
Fabulous Invalid, The 1938,O 10,15:1
American Way, The 1939,Ja 23,9:2
American Way, The 1939,Ja 29,IX,1:1
Man Who Came to Dinner, The 1939,S 26,21:3
Man Who Came to Dinner, The 1939,O 1,IX,2:5
Man Who Came to Dinner, The 1939,O 17,31:1
Man Who Came to Dinner, The 1939,O 22,IX,1:1
Man Who Came to Dinner, The 1940,F 10,19:5
Man Who Came to Dinner, The 1940,F 18,IX,3:6
Royal Family, The 1940,Ag 13,15:3
George Washington Slept Here 1940,S 24,27:3
George Washington Slept Here 1940,O 19,20:3
George Washington Slept Here 1940,O 27,IX,1:1
Man Who Came to Dinner, The 1941,Jl 29,13:5
Land Is Bright, The 1941,O 21,28:5
Land Is Bright, The 1941,O 29,26:2
Land Is Bright, The 1941,N 9,IX,1:1
Man Who Came to Dinner, The 1941,D 14,IX,4:3
Lunchtime Follies, The 1942,Je 23,22:3
Late George Apley, The 1944,O 20,16:4
Late George Apley, The 1944,N 22,26:2
Late George Apley, The 1944,D 3,II,1:1
Seven Lively Arts 1944,D 8,26:6
Seven Lively Arts 1944,D 17,II,3:1
You Can't Take It With You 1945,Mr 27,23:7
Hollywood Pinafore 1945,Je 1,20:1
Hollywood Pinafore 1945,Je 10,II,1:1
Park Avenue 1946,N 5,31:2
Bravo! 1948,N 12,31:2
Butter and Egg Man, The 1949,Ap 29,27:1
Royal Family, The 1951,Ja 11,28:2
Small Hours, The 1951,F 16,22:1
You Can't Take It With You 1951,Ap 7,8:6
Fancy Meeting You Again 1952,Ja 15,23:2
Of Thee I Sing 1952,My 6,34:2
Of Thee I Sing 1952,My 11,II,1:1
First Lady 1952,My 29,18:5
Solid Gold Cadillac, The 1953,N 6,24:2
Solid Gold Cadillac, The 1953,N 15,II,1:1
Solid Gold Cadillac, The 1954,Ag 16,13:4
Silk Stockings 1955,F 25,17:3
Silk Stockings 1955,Mr 27,II,1:1
Once in a Lifetime 1962,O 30,30:1

Once in a Lifetime 1964,Ja 29,20:1
You Can't Take It With You 1965,N 24,32:1
You Can't Take It With You 1965,D 5,II,5:1
Dinner at Eight 1966,S 28,38:1
Dinner at Eight 1966,O 9,II,1:1
Butter and Egg Man, The 1966,O 18,49:1
Sherry! 1967,Mr 29,39:1
Merton of the Movies 1968,S 26,62:1
Of Thee I Sing 1969,Mr 8,19:1
Beggar on Horseback 1970,My 15,47:2
Beggar on Horseback 1970,My 24,II,1:1

Kaufman, George S (Producer)
Of Thee I Sing 1931,D 13,VIII,2:4
Mr Big 1941,S 7,I,51:3
Mr Big 1941,S 14,IX,2:5
Mr Big 1941,O 1,24:2

Kaufman, Harry (Miscellaneous)
Hooray for What! 1937,D 2,32:5
Between the Devil 1937,D 23,24:5
Hellzapoppin 1938,S 23,34:2
Streets of Paris, The 1939,Je 20,25:2
New Hellzapoppin, The 1939,D 12,36:4
Sons o' Fun 1941,D 2,28:2
Count Me In 1942,O 9,24:2
Laffing Room Only 1944,D 25,15:4

Kaufman, Harry (Producer)
Ziegfeld Follies 1936,S 15,37:1
Keep Off the Grass 1940,My 24,22:6
Ziegfeld Follies 1943,Ap 2,16:2

Kaufman, Hunter
Kibitzer, The 1929,F 19,22:5

Kaufman, Irving
Street Scene 1947,Ja 10,17:2

Kaufman, Madeleine
Passion Play 1938,Mr 7,11:2
Veronica's Veil 1950,F 12,II,1:5

Kaufman, Margie Ann
Woman's a Fool-To Be Clever, A 1938,O 19,18:6

Kaufman, Mildred (Composer)
Belmont Varieties 1932,S 29,17:2

Kaufman, Mildred (Lyricist)
Belmont Varieties 1932,S 29,17:2

Kaufman, Norma
Bursting the Barriers 1930,My 7,25:1

Kaufman, Ola
Blood Wedding 1958,Ap 1,35:1

Kaufman, Rita
Way of the World, The 1950,Ap 9,73:5

Kaufman, S Jay (Miscellaneous)
Streets of Paris, The 1939,Je 20,25:2

Kaufman, S Jay (Playwright)
Keep Off the Grass 1940,My 24,22:6

Kaufman, S Jay (Producer)
Lottery, The 1930,N 23,IX,3:5

Kaufman, William I (Producer)
Pink Elephant, The 1953,Ap 23,37:2

Kaufman, Willie
Processional 1937,O 14,23:1
Trojan Incident 1938,Ap 22,15:2

Kaunas, Joseph
Failures, The 1959,Ja 6,30:2

Kaup, Edith
Susannah 1955,F 25,18:4

Kaurin, Birger
House in Berlin, A (Als der Kreig zu Ende War);
Als der Krieg zu Ende War (A House in Berlin)
1950,D 27,32:3
Along Came a Spider 1963,My 28,33:1

Kauser, Benjamin
Red Geranium, The 1922,My 9,22:3
Crowns 1922,N 10,20:3
Sylvia 1923,Ap 26,22:1
Brook 1923,Ag 20,14:3

Kautman, Hyacinthe
Fuente Ovejuna; Sheep Well, The 1936,My 3,II,4:1

Kautsky, Robert (Scenic Designer)
Consul, The 1951,S 8,9:3

Kavanagh, J A (Producer)
If Five Years Pass 1964,My 11,37:1
One-Woman Show, A 1962,My 22,31:1

Kavanagh, Stan
Vaudeville (Hippodrome) 1926,Ap 27,22:3
Vaudeville (Palace) 1926,Jl 20,17:4
Ziegfeld Follies 1936,Ja 31,17:2
Ziegfeld Follies 1936,S 15,37:1

Kavanaugh, Dorrie
Saved 1970,O 29,57:1
Saved 1970,N 1,II,10:1

Kavanaugh, Ray (Miscellaneous)
Take a Bow 1944,Je 16,15:3

Kavanaugh, Ray (Musical Director)
Two for the Show 1940,F 18,IX,1:1
Dark of the Moon 1945,Mr 15,27:2
Three to Make Ready 1946,Mr 8,16:2

Kavanaugh, Ray Orchestra
Vaudeville (Palace) 1928,Ja 10,28:5
Vanities 1932,S 28,22:4

Kavanaugh, Richard
Wilson in the Promise Land 1970,Ja 11,78:1
Wilson in the Promise Land 1970,My 27,41:1

Kavenaugh, Clarence
Snow Maiden, The 1960,Ap 5,43:3

Kawakita, Kiyomasa (Director)
Marie Vison, La 1970,Jl 15,29:1

Kawamura, Miyako (Costume Designer)
Marie Vison, La 1970,Jl 15,29:1

Kawamura, Miyako (Miscellaneous)
Marie Vison, La 1970,Jl 15,29:1

Kawata, Sizuo
Mystery Man, The 1928,Ja 27,14:2

Kawate, Nelson
Family, The 1943,Mr 31,22:4

Kay, Arthur
Hooray for What! 1937,D 2,32:5

Kay, Arthur (Miscellaneous)
Song of Norway 1944,Ag 22,20:2
Gypsy Lady 1946,S 18,25:6
Kismet 1953,D 4,2:4
Kismet 1965,Je 23,45:1

Kay, Arthur (Musical Director)
Song of Norway 1944,Ag 22,20:2
Gypsy Lady 1946,S 18,25:6
Magdalena 1948,S 21,31:2

Kay, Barbara
Flowering Peach, The 1954,D 29,19:2
Safari! 1955,My 12,32:6

Kay, Beatrice
Secrets 1922,D 26,11:1
Jarnegan 1928,S 25,29:2
Provincetown Follies, The 1935,N 4,24:3
Behind the Red Lights 1937,Ja 14,17:4
Tell Me Pretty Maiden 1937,D 17,33:5

Kay, Bernard
Cat and the Canary, The 1935,Ag 13,20:3

Kay, Bill
Pardon Our French 1950,O 6,22:4

Kay, Charles
As You Like It 1967,O 15,II,9:3
As You Like It 1968,Jl 6,9:1
Beaux' Stratagem, The 1970,F 10,50:2
Three Sisters, The 1970,F 12,30:1
Three Sisters, The 1970,F 22,II,1:1

Kay, David (Producer)
For Heaven's Sake Mother 1948,N 17,33:4

Kay, Edward
Cortez 1929,N 5,32:2

Kay, Frances
Escape This Night 1938,Ap 23,18:1

Kay, Geraldine
Escape 1927,O 27,33:1
Good Earth, The 1932,O 18,23:4
Fly Away Home 1935,Ja 16,20:4
Man From Cairo, The 1938,My 5,26:5

Kay, Hershy (Miscellaneous)
Peter Pan 1950,Ap 25,27:2
Peter Pan 1950,Ap 30,II,1:1
Sandhog 1954,N 24,17:1
Candide 1956,D 3,40:2
Livin' the Life 1957,Ap 29,20:1
Juno 1959,Mr 10,41:1
Once Upon a Mattress 1959,My 12,40:1
Happiest Girl in the World, The 1961,Ap 4,42:1
Milk and Honey 1961,O 11,52:1
110 in the Shade 1963,O 25,37:1
Kelly 1965,F 8,28:2
Drat! the Cat! 1965,O 11,54:2
I'm Solomon 1968,Ap 24,51:1
Coco 1969,D 19,66:1

Kay, James (Musical Director)
Lend an Ear 1969,O 29,32:1

Kay, Lisan
Lute Song 1946,F 7,29:2

Kay, Marlene
South Pacific 1965,Je 3,25:1

Kay, Mary
Oh, Professor 1930,My 2,19:6

Kay, Meegan
Exchange 1970,F 9,47:2

Kay, Merle
Candida 1925,D 19,14:2

Kay, Mildred
Blossom Time 1921,S 30,10:1

Kay, Richard
As You Like It 1967,O 6,33:4
As You Like It 1967,O 15,II,9:3
Beaux' Stratagem, The 1970,F 10,50:2
Three Sisters, The 1970,F 12,30:1

Kay, Roger (Director)
Maya 1953,Je 10,35:1

Kay, Roger (Translator)
Maya 1953,Je 10,35:1

Kay, Roslyn
Summer Wives 1936,Ap 14,18:1

Kay, Sidney
Golden Boy 1952,Mr 13,24:3
Flowering Peach, The 1954,D 29,19:2
Man With the Golden Arm, The 1956,My 22,28:1
Cock-A-Doodle Dandy 1958,N 13,39:2
Big Knife, The 1959,N 13,25:1

Kay, Susan
Mrs Patterson 1957,F 6,20:2

Kayden, Mildred (Composer)
Conerico Was Here to Stay 1969,Mr 11,39:1
Paradise Gardens East 1969,Mr 11,39:1
Exhibition 1969,My 16,41:1

Kayden, Mildred (Composer)—Cont

Pequod 1969,Je 30,33:1
Kayden, Mildred (Lyricist)
Pequod 1969,Je 30,33:1
Kayden, Mildred (Miscellaneous)
Pequod 1969,Je 30,33:1
Kaydison, Bernard
Stop Press 1939,Mr 20,13:2
Kaye, A P
Champion, The 1921,Ja 4,11:1
Back to Methuselah (Part II: The Gospel of the
  Brothers Barnabas); Gospel of the Brothers
  Barnabas, The (Back to Methuselah, Part II)
  1922,F 28,17:2
Back to Methuselah (Part IV: The Tragedy of an
  Elderly Gentleman); Tragedy of an Elderly
  Gentleman, The (Back to Methuselah, Part IV)
  1922,Mr 7,11:1
Back to Methuselah (Part III: The Thing Happens);
  Thing Happens, The (Back to Methuselah, Part
  III) 1922,Mr 7,11:1
Back to Methuselah (Part V: As Far as Thought
  Can Reach); As Far as Thought Can Reach (Back
  to Methuselah, Part V) 1922,Mr 14,11:2
Lady Cristilinda, The 1922,D 26,11:2
Comedian, The 1923,Mr 14,14:1
Mary, Mary, Quite Contrary 1923,S 12,14:1
Strong, The 1924,F 27,15:3
Man and the Masses 1924,Ap 15,25:1
Quarantine 1924,D 17,19:7
Shall We Join the Ladies? 1925,Ja 14,19:1
Isabel 1925,Ja 14,19:1
Green Hat, The 1925,S 16,23:2
Enchantment 1927,Ap 28,27:3
Ivory Door, The 1927,O 19,24:5
Major Barbara 1928,N 20,28:4
Wings Over Europe 1928,D 11,35:1
Whispering Gallery, The 1929,F 12,22:2
Scotland Yard 1929,S 28,16:6
Novice and the Duke, The 1929,D 11,37:2
Lost Sheep 1930,My 6,33:2
Violet, The 1930,S 30,24:2
Streets of New York, The 1931,O 7,29:1
Cynara 1931,N 3,31:1
Peace Palace 1933,Je 6,30:2
Chimes of Corneville, The 1934,Je 29,16:2
Musical Chairs 1934,Jl 31,20:7
Sleeping Clergyman, A 1934,O 9,16:1
Living Dangerously 1935,Ja 14,10:3
Bishop Misbehaves, The 1935,F 21,22:4
Jumbo 1935,N 18,20:2
Black Limelight 1936,N 10,31:1
Othello 1937,Ja 7,16:4
Candida 1937,Mr 11,20:2
You Can't Take It With You 1938,Ja 16,X,1:6
Come Across 1938,S 15,28:3
Where There's a Will 1939,Ja 18,16:6
Gas Light 1939,Ag 30,20:8
Journey's End 1939,S 19,29:2
When We Are Married 1939,N 21,19:5
When We Are Married 1939,D 26,22:3
They Walk Alone 1941,Mr 13,24:2
All Men Are Alike 1941,O 7,27:2
Plan M 1942,F 21,15:2
Uncle Harry 1942,My 21,24:1
Kaye, Alma
Swing Out, Sweet Land! 1944,N 10,24:6
Sing Out, Sweet Land! 1944,D 28,24:2
Kaye, Anne
Now Is the Time for all Good Men 1967,S 27,42:1
Have I Got One for You 1968,Ja 8,32:1
Kaye, Benjamin M (Playwright)
She Couldn't Say No! 1926,S 1,27:3
What a Question 1930,F 23,VIII,2:5
I Want My Wife 1930,Mr 21,30:7
Garrick Gaieties 1930,Je 5,29:2
Curtain Rises, The 1933,O 20,15:2
On Stage 1935,Jl 23,24:4
On Stage 1935,O 30,16:6
Kaye, Beryl
Joyce Grenfell Requests the Pleasure
  1955,O 11,48:1
Kaye, Beryl (Choreographer)
Joyce Grenfell Requests the Pleasure
  1955,O 11,48:1
Kaye, Buddy (Composer)
Hilarities 1948,S 10,20:2
Kaye, Buddy (Lyricist)
Hilarities 1948,S 10,20:2
Kaye, Charles
As You Like It 1967,O 6,33:4
Kaye, Charlie
Strip for Action 1942,O 1,26:2
Kaye, Danny
Straw Hat, The 1939,S 30,10:6
Lady in the Dark 1941,Ja 5,IX,1:7
Lady in the Dark 1941,Ja 24,14:2
Let's Face It 1941,O 10,27:1
Let's Face It 1941,O 30,26:2
Actors Fund Fete 1942,F 23,24:5
Untitled-One Man Show 1949,Ap 26,30:4
Untitled-One Man Show 1949,My 4,38:2
Danny Kaye's International Show 1953,Ja 19,20:2
Danny Kaye's International Show 1953,Ja 25,II,1:1

Untitled-One Man Show 1955,My 25,39:1
Danny Kaye Show 1963,Ap 11,28:2
Two by Two 1970,N 11,37:1
Two by Two 1970,N 22,II,1:1
Kaye, Gina
King and I, The 1964,Jl 7,26:1
Kaye, Gloria
Conversation Piece 1957,N 19,38:2
Who's Who, Baby? 1968,Ja 30,36:1
Kaye, Henrietta
Torch Song 1930,Ag 28,23:1
Horse Eats Hat 1936,S 28,14:2
Having Wonderful Time 1937,F 22,12:5
Kaye, Irene
Blackouts of 1949 1949,S 7,39:2
Kaye, John (Miscellaneous)
Peace 1969,Ja 28,49:1
Kaye, Lindy
Pigeon, The 1957,My 17,19:2
Kaye, Lionel
Sons o' Fun 1941,D 2,28:2
Kaye, Lucy
Revolt of the Beavers, The 1937,My 21,19:2
Kaye, Muriel
Vaudeville (Palace) 1928,Jl 24,13:4
Kaye, Nora
Two's Company 1952,D 16,43:5
Two's Company 1952,D 21,II,3:1
Kaye, Nora (Miscellaneous)
Gay Life, The 1961,N 20,38:1
Kaye, Paul (Pvt)
Winged Victory 1943,N 22,24:1
Kaye, Paula
Show Boat 1946,Ja 7,17:2
Kaye, Robert
Wonderful Town 1963,F 15,10:2
Flora, the Red Menace 1965,My 12,41:2
By Jupiter 1967,Ja 20,28:2
Maggie Flynn 1968,O 24,52:1
Mame 1969,Je 20,36:1
Kaye, Sonya
Ice Capades 1952,S 12,18:1
Ice Capades 1953,S 11,25:1
Kaye, Sparky
Kiss Me, Kate 1952,Ja 9,24:6
Kaye, Stubby
Guys and Dolls 1950,N 25,11:2
Guys and Dolls 1950,D 3,II,1:1
Guys and Dolls 1951,O 7,II,1:1
Guys and Dolls 1953,My 29,17:5
Li'l Abner 1956,N 16,24:2
Li'l Abner 1956,N 25,II,1:1
Everybody Loves Opal 1961,O 12,40:2
Kaye, V Ann
Show Boat 1932,My 20,22:2
Kaye, Virginia
Ah, Wilderness! 1941,O 3,26:2
In Bed We Cry 1944,N 15,20:2
Kiss Them for Me 1945,MR 21,27:2
After the Fall 1964,Ja 24,18:1
Marco Millions 1964,F 21,33:1
Kaye, William (Lyricist)
Pimpernel! 1964,Ja 7,26:6
Kaye, William (Playwright)
Pimpernel! 1964,Ja 7,26:6
Kayes, Gordon
Doctor Faustus 1957,F 19,35:7
Kayne, A P
Rosalie 1928,Ja 11,26:3
Kayne, Gregory (Director)
My Fair Lady 1962,Ag 23,24:6
Kayne, Gregory (Scenic Designer)
Armor of Light 1950,F 24,26:4
Kayne, Richard (Playwright)
Single Man at a Party 1959,Ap 22,30:4
Kayser, Judith (Miscellaneous)
Haunted Host, The 1969,O 28,43:1
Kayser, Martha (Martha Cabanne) (Original Author)
Way, The 1940,O 12,20:3
Kayser, Martha (Martha Cabanne) (Playwright)
Way, The 1940,O 12,20:3
Kayssler, Friedrich
Journey's End 1929,S 15,IX,2:6
Journey's End 1929,S 22,IX,4:1
Brest-Litovsk 1930,N 30,IX,2:1
Timon 1932,Mr 6,VIII,2:1
Kayworth, Leo
Out of This World 1950,D 22,17:3
Kaz, Fred (Composer)
From the Second City 1969,O 15,34:1
Kaz, Fred (Musical Director)
From the Second City 1969,O 15,34:1
Kazakavich, I
King Oedipus 1933,Ja 16,12:4
Kazan, Elia
Chrysalis 1932,N 16,15:2
Men in White 1933,S 27,24:2
Waiting for Lefty 1935,F 11,14:5
Till the Day I Die 1935,Mr 27,24:5
Waiting for Lefty 1935,Mr 27,24:5
Till the Day I Die 1935,Mr 27,24:5
Paradise Lost 1935,D 10,31:5
Case of Clyde Griffiths 1936,Mr 14,10:4

Kazan, Elia—Cont

Johnny Johnson 1936,N 20,26:3
Golden Boy 1937,N 5,18:5
Gentle People, The 1939,Ja 6,25:1
Night Music 1940,F 23,18:2
Night Music 1940,Mr 3,X,1:1
Liliom 1940,Mr 26,17:2
Five Alarm Waltz 1941,Mr 14,16:2
Kazan, Elia (Director)
Young Go First, The 1935,My 29,16:2
Casey Jones 1938,F 21,14:2
Thunder Rock 1939,N 15,18:1
Cafe Crown 1942,Ja 24,12:5
Strings, My Lord, Are False, The 1942,My 20,24:2
Skin of Our Teeth, The 1942,N 19,29:5
Harriet 1943,Mr 4,24:2
It's Up to You 1943,Ap 1,19:1
One Touch of Venus 1943,O 8,14:1
One Touch of Venus 1943,O 17,II,1:1
Jacobowsky and the Colonel 1944,Mr 15,17:2
Jacobowsky and the Colonel 1944,Mr 19,II,1:1
Harriet 1944,S 28,26:1
Deep Are the Roots 1945,S 27,24:4
Deep Are the Roots 1945,O 7,II,1:1
Dunnigan's Daughter 1945,D 27,16:1
All My Sons 1947,Ja 30,21:2
All My Sons 1947,F 9,II,1:1
Streetcar Named Desire, A 1947,D 4,42:2
Streetcar Named Desire, A 1947,D 14,II,3:1
Sundown Beach 1948,S 8,37:1
Sundown Beach 1948,S 12,II,1:1
Love Life 1948,O 8,31:2
Death of a Salesman 1949,F 11,27:2
Death of a Salesman 1949,F 20,II,1:1
Streetcar Named Desire, A 1949,Je 12,II,1:1
Death of a Salesman 1949,Jl 29,12:5
Death of a Salesman 1950,Mr 12,II,1:1
Streetcar Named Desire, A 1950,My 24,36:1
Death of a Salesman 1950,S 21,20:5
Point of No Return 1951,D 23,II,3:1
Flight Into Egypt 1952,Mr 19,33:2
Flight Into Egypt 1952,Mr 30,II,1:1
Camino Real 1953,Mr 20,26:1
Camino Real 1953,Mr 29,II,1:1
Tea and Sympathy 1953,O 1,35:1
Tea and Sympathy 1953,O 11,II,1:1
Tea and Sympathy 1954,Ag 15,II,1:1
Cat on a Hot Tin Roof 1955,Mr 25,18:2
Cat on a Hot Tin Roof 1955,Ap 3,II,1:1
Dark at the Top of the Stairs, The 1957,D 6,38:1
Dark at the Top of the Stairs, The 1957,D 15,II,3:1
J B 1958,D 12,2:7
Sweet Bird of Youth 1959,Mr 11,39:2
Sweet Bird of Youth 1959,Mr 22,II,1:1
J B 1959,My 10,II,1:1
After the Fall 1964,Ja 24,18:1
After the Fall 1964,F 2,II,1:1
Marco Millions 1964,F 21,33:1
But for Whom Charlie 1964,Mr 13,42:2
Changeling, The 1964,O 30,32:2
Incident at Vichy 1964,D 4,44:1
Kazan, Elia (Playwright)
Group Theatre Sketches 1935,F 11,14:5
Kazan, Elia (Producer)
Truckline Cafe 1946,F 28,19:4
All My Sons 1947,Ja 30,21:2
Death of a Salesman 1950,S 21,20:5
Dark at the Top of the Stairs, The 1957,D 6,38:1
Kazan, Lainie
Kittiwake Island 1960,O 13,43:1
Happiest Girl in the World, The 1961,Ap 4,42:1
Kazan, Michel (Miscellaneous)
Do Re Mi 1960,D 27,23:2
Carnival! 1961,Ap 14,22:2
Sail Away 1961,O 4,48:5
Come on Strong 1962,O 5,29:1
Dear Me, the Sky Is Falling 1963,Mr 4,9:1
110 in the Shade 1963,O 25,37:1
One Flew Over the Cuckoo's Nest 1963,N 14,40:2
Milk Train Doesn't Stop Here Anymore, The
  1964,Ja 2,33:1
Kazan, Molly (Playwright)
Egghead, The 1957,O 10,39:1
Alligators, The 1960,N 15,47:1
Rosemary 1960,N 15,47:1
Kazan, Sandra
Time of Storm 1954,F 26,14:2
Kazanoff, Ted
Stevedore 1949,F 23,30:2
Kazanova, Ulla
First Lady 1935,N 27,17:4
You Can't Take It With You 1945,Mr 27,23:7
First Lady 1952,My 29,18:5
Shadow of My Enemy, A 1957,D 12,35:4
Kazantzakis, Nikos (Original Author)
Zorba 1968,N 24,II,1:1
Kazantzakis, Nikos (Playwright)
Burn Me to Ashes 1963,N 20,48:1
Zorba 1968,N 18,58:1
Kazda, Patrick
Icetime 1946,Je 21,20:5
Kazounoff, Berenece (Composer)
Illustrators' Show, The 1936,Ja 23,25:3
Reunion in New York 1940,F 22,28:4

Kazze, Jacob (Musical Director)
Zaporogetz Za Dunayem 1937,My 9,II,5:3
Keable, Robert (Original Author)
Simon Called Peter 1924,My 4,VIII,2:1
Simon Called Peter 1924,N 11,20:2
Keach, Stacy
Hamlet 1964,Je 17,49:1
Country Wife, The 1965,D 10,58:2
MacBird! 1967,F 23,38:1
MacBird! 1967,Mr 12,II,1:1
Niggerlovers, The; Demonstration, The
1967,O 2,54:2
Niggerlovers, The; Man and Dog 1967,O 2,54:2
We Bombed in New Haven 1967,D 7,58:1
We Bombed in New Haven 1967,D 17,II,3:7
Henry IV 1968,F 7,40:1
Three Sisters, The 1968,Mr 18,56:1
Coriolanus 1968,My 26,II,7:1
Henry IV, Part I 1968,Je 30,54:7
Henry IV, Part II 1968,Jl 2,33:1
Henry IV, Part II 1968,Jl 14,II,1:1
King Lear 1968,N 8,43:1
King Lear 1968,N 17,II,1:3
Indians 1969,My 18,II,3:5
Indians 1969,My 27,43:1
Peer Gynt 1969,Jl 17,56:1
Indians 1969,O 14,51:1
Indians 1969,O 19,II,1:1
Keach, Stacy (Composer)
Three Sisters, The 1968,Mr 18,56:1
Keady, Emily
Untitled-Revue 1926,O 26,18:3
Keady, Florence
Three Sisters, The 1930,Ja 9,22:2
Antigone 1930,Ap 25,28:4
Keagy, Grace
Shoemaker's Holiday, The 1967,Je 3,19:1
Harpers Ferry 1967,Je 6,52:2
Visit, The 1967,S 13,41:1
Keal, Anita
Private Life of the Master Race, The
1956,Ja 31,33:3
Witches' Sabbath 1962,Ap 20,22:2
Kealeigh, Brandon
Sea Dogs 1939,N 7,30:3
Kealy, Kenny
Conquering Hero, The 1961,Ja 17,40:2
Something More! 1964,N 11,36:1
Kean, Betty
Music Hall Varieties 1932,N 23,15:3
Crazy With the Heat 1941,Ja 15,18:2
Crazy With the Heat 1941,Ja 31,15:2
Sun Field, The 1942,D 10,33:2
Ankles Aweigh 1955,Ap 19,27:1
Kean, Gerald
Russian Bank 1940,My 25,20:2
Any Day Now 1941,Je 10,28:2
Kean, Gordon (Playwright)
Hindu, The 1922,Mr 22,13:3
Arabian, The 1927,N 1,20:5
Kean, Jane
It's All Yours 1942,Mr 26,26:2
Early to Bed 1943,Je 18,16:2
Girl From Nantucket, The 1945,N 9,17:2
Ankles Aweigh 1955,Ap 19,27:1
Ankles Aweigh 1955,Ap 24,II,1:1
Pajama Game, The 1957,My 16,27:1
Pajama Game, The 1957,My 26,II,1:1
Hit the Deck 1960,Je 24,32:1
Show Boat 1961,Ap 13,32:1
Kean, Malcolm (Producer)
Always Afternoon 1929,F 24,IX,4:3
Kean, Marie
Juno and the Paycock 1966,Ag 3,40:1
Kean, Norman (Miscellaneous)
Johnny Johnson 1956,O 22,24:1
Pantagleize 1967,D 1,54:1
Show-Off, The 1967,D 6,40:2
Cocktail Party, The 1968,O 8,42:1
Misanthrope, The 1968,O 10,59:1
Hamlet 1969,Mr 4,34:1
Kean, Norman (Producer)
Worlds of Shakespeare, The 1963,D 5,58:1
Woman and the Blues, A 1966,Mr 29,35:2
Opium 1970,O 6,58:1
Kean, Richard
Keep Kool 1924,My 23,16:4
Keane, Arthur
Long Gallery, The 1958,Mr 7,17:2
Keane, Charles
Within the Gates 1934,O 23,23:1
Crime Marches on 1935,O 24,19:1
On Location 1937,S 28,19:1
Siege 1937,D 9,31:4
Man Who Killed Lincoln, The 1940,Ja 18,26:4
Signature 1945,F 15,25:2
Keane, Charlotte
Tempest, The 1945,Ja 26,17:2
Deep Mrs Sykes, The 1945,Mr 20,22:6
Strange Fruit 1945,N 30,18:6
Keane, Doris
Romance 1921,Mr 1,18:2
Romance 1921,Mr 6,VI,1:2

Untitled-Benefit 1921,My 2,12:3
Czarina, The 1922,F 1,22:1
Untitled-Benefit 1922,My 8,14:5
Welded 1924,Mr 18,24:1
Welded 1924,Mr 23,VIII,1:1
Starlight 1924,O 5,VIII,1:3
Starlight 1925,Mr 4,17:2
Starlight 1925,Mr 8,VII,1:1
Romance 1926,N 4,VIII,4:7
Pirate, The 1929,Ap 21,IX,1:4
Keane, Edward
Busybody, The 1924,S 30,27:5
Appearances 1925,O 15,27:3
So That's That 1925,D 15,28:3
Weak Woman, A 1926,Ja 27,16:3
Four Walls 1927,S 20,33:1
Town's Woman, The 1929,Mr 12,26:2
Nut Farm, The 1929,O 15,34:3
House of Doom, The 1932,Ja 26,20:4
Inside Story, The 1932,F 23,23:2
Keane, George
Black Eye, The 1938,Mr 8,22:4
Hamlet 1938,O 13,28:1
Henry IV, Part I 1939,Ja 31,17:2
Hamlet 1939,D 5,35:2
Richard II 1940,Ap 2,31:2
Twelfth Night 1940,N 20,26:3
Elizabeth the Queen 1941,O 17,27:2
Moon Is Down, The 1942,Ap 8,22:2
Lifeline 1942,D 1,20:3
Brigadoon 1947,Mr 14,28:2
Love Me Long 1949,N 8,34:5
Seven Year Itch, The 1952,N 21,21:2
Keane, James
Dove, The 1925,F 12,17:3
Sweet Land of Liberty 1929,S 24,29:2
Keane, John (Playwright)
No More in Dust 1961,S 14,26:8
Keane, John B (Playwright)
Sive 1959,S 6,II,1:3
Sharon's Grave 1961,N 9,39:2
Keane, Lew
Plantation Revue, The 1922,Jl 18,18:4
Keane, Richard
Too Many Heroes 1937,N 16,26:2
Keane, Robert (Mrs) (Miscellaneous)
Spring Meeting 1938,D 9,30:4
Keane, Robert Edward
Buds of 1927 1927,F 22,22:5
Keane, Robert Emmett
Innocent Idea, An 1920,My 26,9:4
Across the Street 1924,Mr 25,24:1
Vaudeville (Palace) 1924,S 16,26:5
Mama Loves Papa 1926,F 23,26:2
Sweet Adeline 1929,S 4,33:1
Vaudeville (Palace) 1930,F 17,18:4
Page Pygmalion 1932,Ag 4,17:5
Hotel Alimony 1934,Ja 30,16:2
Broadway Interlude 1934,Ap 20,16:3
Only Girl, The 1934,My 22,28:2
Keane, Ronda
Hyde Park Corner 1934,O 6,20:1
Jeannie 1940,N 13,29:2
Keane, Rose
Tale of the Wolf, The 1925,O 8,31:2
Monkey Talks, The 1925,D 29,20:1
Celebrity 1927,D 27,24:3
Command Performance, The 1928,O 4,27:1
Uncle Vanya 1929,My 25,17:1
Lady From the Sea, The 1934,My 2,25:2
Bride of Torozko, The 1934,Jl 10,24:7
Bride of Torozko, The 1934,S 14,24:2
Let Freedom Ring 1935,N 7,26:2
Bury the Dead 1936,Ap 20,17:4
Prelude 1936,Ap 20,17:4
200 Were Chosen 1936,N 21,21:1
Washington Jitters 1938,My 3,19:1
Keane, Ryder
Unwritten Chapter, The 1920,O 12,18:1
Rosa Machree 1922,Ja 10,15:2
Cat and the Canary, The 1922,F 8,13:1
Synthetic Sin 1927,O 11,26:2
March Hares 1928,Ap 3,32:6
K Guy, The 1928,O 16,28:4
Solitaire 1929,Mr 13,28:3
Judgment Day 1934,S 13,26:4
Touch of Brimstone, A 1935,S 23,20:1
Censored 1938,F 28,18:2
Keane, Teresa
Swing Your Lady 1936,O 19,22:4
What a Life 1938,Ap 14,26:2
Keane, Teri
Vagabond King, The 1943,Je 30,24:2
Hairpin Harmony 1943,O 2,18:5
Keane, Vega
Bathsheba 1947,Mr 27,40:2
Kearney, Jack
Be Yourself! 1924,S 4,13:3
Kearney, James
Bab 1920,O 19,12:1
Your Woman and Mine 1922,F 28,17:2
Pigs 1924,S 2,22:5

Kearney, James—Cont
New Brooms 1924,N 18,23:5
Betty Lee 1924,D 26,18:2
Sour Grapes 1926,S 7,19:1
Man Bites Dog 1933,Ap 26,11:2
Simon's Wife 1945,Mr 9,16:4
Kearney, John
Adrienne 1923,My 29,10:4
Be Yourself! 1924,S 4,13:3
Matinee Girl, The 1926,F 2,20:3
Yours Truly 1927,Ja 26,16:5
Night Hostess 1928,S 13,31:2
Great Man, The 1931,Ap 8,20:6
Whistling in the Dark 1932,Ja 20,16:6
Her Tin Soldier 1933,Ap 7,22:6
They Shall Not Die 1934,F 22,24:4
If This Be Treason 1935,Jl 30,17:1
Mother Sings 1935,N 13,24:1
Postman Always Rings Twice, The 1936,F 26,17:2
Behind the Red Lights 1937,Ja 14,17:4
Excursion 1937,Ap 10,11:4
Places, Please 1937,N 13,10:6
Shadow and Substance 1938,Ja 27,16:2
Man Who Killed Lincoln, The 1940,Ja 18,26:4
Horse Fever 1940,N 25,21:2
Counsellor-at-Law 1942,N 25,17:2
Jackpot 1944,Ja 14,15:2
Kearney, John R (Pvt)
Winged Victory 1943,N 22,24:1
Kearney, Michael
Family Way, The 1965,Ja 14,44:5
Tea Party 1968,O 16,40:1
Kearney, Patrick (Director)
Regular Guy, A; Man's Man, A 1931,Je 5,27:1
Kearney, Patrick (Playwright)
Man's Man, A 1925,O 14,31:2
Man's Man, A 1925,O 25,VIII,1:1
American Tragedy, An 1926,O 12,31:2
American Tragedy, An 1926,O 24,VIII,1:1
Elmer Gantry 1928,Ag 10,9:4
American Tragedy, An 1931,F 21,15:5
Old Man Murphy 1931,My 19,25:2
Regular Guy, A; Man's Man, A 1931,Je 5,27:1
Kearney, Tyrone
On Your Toes 1936,Ap 13,14:4
Canteen Show, The 1942,S 4,18:1
Sleepy Hollow 1948,Je 4,26:3
Kearns, Allen
What's in a Name? 1920,Mr 20,14:2
Tickle Me 1920,Ag 18,9:1
Lady Butterfly 1923,Ja 23,18:1
Little Jessie James 1923,Ag 16,10:4
Mercenary Mary 1925,Ap 14,27:3
Tip-Toes 1925,D 29,20:2
Tip-Toes 1926,S 1,27:4
Betsy 1926,D 29,24:3
Funny Face 1927,N 23,28:2
Here's Howe! 1928,My 2,19:3
Hello, Daddy! 1928,D 27,26:5
Girl Crazy 1930,O 5,IX,4:6
Girl Crazy 1930,O 15,27:1
Girl Crazy 1930,D 28,VIII,1:1
Divine Moment, A 1934,Ja 8,21:8
Nine O'Clock Revue 1936,Jl 8,14:3
Odds on Mrs Oakley, The 1944,O 3,18:8
Kearns, Elsie Herndon
George Washington 1920,Mr 2,9:1
Hamlet 1920,Mr 17,14:2
Cyrano de Bergerac 1920,Mr 20,14:3
Servant in the House, The 1921,My 3,20:1
Taming of the Shrew, The 1921,My 12,20:2
Merchant of Venice, The 1921,My 14,10:4
Cyrano de Bergerac 1923,N 2,14:1
Othello 1925,Ja 12,11:1
Little Poor Man, The 1925,Ag 6,14:1
Kearns, Jack
Bombo 1921,O 7,20:2
Kearns, James
Slight Case of Murder, A 1935,S 12,28:5
Kearns, Jil
School for Wives 1957,Je 20,23:4
Kearns, John
Cinderella on Broadway 1920,Je 25,18:1
Kearse, Timothy Lynn
Slight Case of Murder, A 1935,S 12,28:5
Life With Father 1939,N 9,26:2
Othello 1943,O 20,18:1
Joan of Lorraine 1946,N 19,40:2
Keary, Thomas (Scenic Designer)
Simon's Wife 1945,Mr 9,16:4
Keast, Raymond
Allegro 1947,O 11,10:2
Keath, Donna
Playboy of Newark, The 1943,Mr 20,11:2
Sophie 1944,D 26,22:7
Keathley, George (Director)
Square Root of Wonderful, The 1957,O 31,40:1
Immoralist, The 1963,N 8,36:2
Glass Menagerie, The 1965,My 5,53:2
Better Luck Next Time 1966,Ja 28,21:1
Walk in Dark Places, A 1966,Ja 28,21:1
Keating
Keating 1927,D 26,26:6

Keating, Alice B
Nica 1926,Ja 26,19:1
Abraham; Dulcitus; Callimachus 1926,Mr 29,24:2
Trip to Scarborough, A 1929,Mr 18,31:2
Dragon, The 1929,Mr 26,34:2
Keating, Aurel (Director)
Commedia Dell' Arte 1957,Jl 5,13:2
Master Builder, The 1957,D 18,42:7
Keating, Aurel (Playwright)
Commedia Dell' Arte 1957,Jl 5,13:2
Keating, B J
Out of This World 1950,D 22,17:3
Keating, Charles
Twelfth Night 1968,Je 15,40:1
Serjeant Musgrave's Dance 1968,Je 16,52:4
Resistible Rise of Arturo Ui, The 1968,Ag 8,25:1
House of Atreus, The 1968,D 18,55:1
Resistible Rise of Arturo Ui, The 1968,D 23,44:1
Keating, David
Silver Tassie, The 1929,O 25,26:1
Keating, F Serano
Young Visitors, The 1920,N 30,14:1
Keating, Frances (Scenic Designer)
Dragon, The 1929,Mr 26,34:2
Keating, Fred
Murray Anderson's Almanac 1929,Ag 4,VIII,1:6
Murray Anderson's Almanac 1929,Ag 15,20:3
Vaudeville (Palace) 1929,N 4,29:1
Magic and Mimicry 1929,D 23,18:6
Nine Fifteen Revue, The 1930,F 12,26:2
Vaudeville (Palace) 1930,S 8,17:3
Vaudeville (Palace) 1931,Mr 9,25:7
Vaudeville (Palace) 1932,Jl 11,11:6
Forsaking All Others 1933,Mr 2,21:2
All Good Americans 1933,D 6,29:2
Yours Is My Heart 1946,S 6,16:5
Dear Charles 1954,S 16,37:2
Dear Charles 1954,S 26,II,1:1
Characters and Chicanery 1956,Ja 24,26:2
Fun and Magic 1957,D 30,19:4
Keating, Joseph
My Heart's in the Highlands 1950,F 18,8:4
Barefoot in the Park 1963,O 24,36:2
Keating, Joseph (Miscellaneous)
Do You Know the Milky Way? 1961,O 17,45:1
Keating, Lawrence
Locked Room, The 1933,D 26,18:5
Queer People 1934,F 16,16:2
Keating, Lucille
Romancing 'Round 1927,O 4,32:4
Keating, Micheline
Laugh, Clown, Laugh! 1923,N 29,30:1
Keating, Mr
Tattle Tales 1930,Jl 20,VIII,2:1
Keating, Thomas
Betty Behave 1927,Mr 9,28:4
Oh, Hector! 1929,Mr 6,33:2
Keaton, Diane
Hair 1968,Ap 30,40:2
Play It Again, Sam 1969,F 13,52:3
Play It Again, Sam 1969,F 23,II,1:1
Play It Again, Sam 1969,Jl 13,II,1:1
Keaton, Douglas
Inside Story 1942,O 30,22:2
Pick-Up Girl 1944,My 4,25:2
Keats, H L Jr
Tiger Smiles, The 1930,D 18,29:1
Keats, Harry
Tiger Smiles, The 1930,D 18,29:1
Keats, Mildred
Pitter Patter 1920,S 29,12:2
Bombo 1921,O 7,20:2
Battling Buttler 1923,O 9,17:2
Bye Bye, Barbara 1924,Ag 26,6:3
Kitty's Kisses 1926,My 7,12:2
Keats, Norman
Stockade 1954,F 5,14:2
Keats, Viola
All's Over, Then? 1934,Je 10,IX,1:1
Distaff Side, The 1934,S 26,17:2
Gentle Rain 1936,S 20,IX,1:4
Once Is Enough 1938,F 16,16:2
Macbeth 1941,N 12,30:2
Murder Without Crime 1943,Ag 19,24:6
Linden Tree, The 1948,Mr 3,28:2
Anne of the Thousand Days 1948,D 9,49:2
Keays, Ethelyn E (Playwright)
Thousand Generations and One, A 1923,My 9,14:4
Keck, Gladys
Take the Air 1927,N 23,28:2
Keddy, Sheila
Playboy of the Western World, The 1946,O 28,18:3
Climate of Eden, The 1953,N 21,11:2
Kedney, Robert
As You Like It 1936,Ap 24,18:4
Kedrov, Mikhail
Dead Souls 1965,F 5,34:1
Kedrova, Anna
Dead Souls 1965,F 5,34:1
Kedrova, Elizabeth
Poverty Is No Crime 1935,F 21,22:5
Strange Child 1935,F 26,16:1
Enemies 1935,Mr 19,24:7

Deluge, The 1935,Mr 26,23:7
Kedrova, Lila
Guardsman, The 1969,Ag 17,II,5:1
Kee, Hoi Poi
What Do We Know 1927,D 24,8:1
Kee, Juan
Ballad of Jazz Street, The 1959,N 12,28:1
Kee, William
Admirable Bashville, The 1956,F 21,38:1
Keedwell, Norval
Checkerboard, The 1920,Ag 20,7:2
Checkerboard, The 1920,Ag 29,VI,1:2
Meanest Man in the World, The 1920,O 13,18:2
Main Street 1921,O 6,21:1
Why Men Leave Home 1922,S 13,18:2
Out of the Seven Seas 1923,N 20,23:3
Two Strangers From Nowhere 1924,Ap 8,22:2
Sap, The 1924,D 16,28:3
Laff That Off 1925,N 3,34:2
Square Crooks 1926,Mr 2,23:2
Gossipy Sex, The 1927,Ap 20,28:3
Keefe, Adam
Nature of the Crime 1970,Mr 24,41:1
Keefe, Cornelius
Poor Nut, The 1925,Ap 28,18:1
Keefe, Esther
Carnival 1929,Ap 25,32:5
Keefe, John
Spite Corner 1922,S 26,18:1
Within Four Walls 1923,Ap 18,24:1
Keefe, Katherine
Lady of the Lamp, The 1920,Ag 18,6:4
Keefe, Willard (Playwright)
Celebrity 1927,D 27,24:3
Privilege Car 1931,Mr 4,33:1
Keefer, Don
As You Like It 1939,My 9,28:4
Adventures of Marco Polo, The 1941,D 28,I,31:7
Othello 1945,My 23,25:4
Death of a Salesman 1949,F 11,27:2
Flight Into Egypt 1952,Mr 19,33:2
Child Buyer, The 1962,My 14,35:1
Keefer, Leona
Six Characters in Search of an Author
1922,O 31,11:2
Keegan, Arthur
Sky Drift 1945,N 14,25:2
Henry VIII 1946,N 7,42:2
What Every Woman Knows 1946,N 9,13:2
Androcles and the Lion 1946,D 20,29:2
Yellow Jack 1947,F 28,26:2
Alice in Wonderland 1947,Ap 7,19:2
No Time for Sergeants 1955,O 21,32:2
Keegan, Fran
Men of Distinction 1953,My 1,18:4
Keegan, Robert
Don Juan; Feast With the Statue, The
1956,Ja 4,21:4
Persecution and Assassination of Marat As
Performed by the Inmates of the Asylum of
Charenton Under the Direction of the Marquis de
Sade, The 1967,Ja 4,34:1
Keegan, Robert (Miscellaneous)
Alley of the Sunset 1959,D 31,11:1
Death of Satan, The 1960,Ap 6,49:1
Keehan, John
Magic 1929,D 17,28:5
Seven Keys to Baldpate 1930,Ja 8,25:2
Keehn, Harriet
Hot Water 1929,Ja 22,22:3
Keel, Howard
Oklahoma! 1947,My 1,35:3
Carousel 1957,S 12,38:2
Saratoga 1959,D 8,59:4
Keeler, Eloise
Four Walls 1927,S 20,33:1
Bless You, Sister 1927,D 27,24:5
Revolt 1928,N 1,25:3
Jonesy 1929,Ap 10,32:2
Keeler, Eloise (Playwright)
Wrong Number 1934,Mr 14,23:6
Keeler, Marion
Cherry Blossoms 1927,Mr 29,22:3
White Eagle, The 1927,D 27,24:4
Keeler, Ruby
Lucky 1927,Mr 23,28:3
Sidewalks of New York 1927,O 4,33:1
Show Girl 1929,Jl 3,19:3
Hold On to Your Hats 1940,Jl 17,25:3
Keeler, S E
Front Page, The 1937,N 12,27:2
Keeler, Samuel Clark
This Mad Whirl 1937,Ja 10,II,4:8
Keeler, Stephen
Whispering Gallery, The 1935,D 1,II,12:6
Keeler, Willard
Shannons of Broadway, The 1927,S 27,30:4
Keeley, Christopher J
Guimpes and Saddles 1967,O 11,36:3
Keeley, Duke
Gambling 1929,Ag 27,31:2
Keeley, Francis
Decision 1929,My 28,37:3

Keeling, Lucyle
Sweethearts 1929,S 23,25:1
Mlle Modiste 1929,O 8,34:1
Keely, Ann (Costume Designer)
Penny Change 1963,O 25,37:1
Keen, Elizabeth (Miscellaneous)
Hamlet 1969,Je 30,33:1
Keen, Geoffrey
Follow Your Saint 1936,S 25,20:3
Follow Your Saint 1936,O 11,X,3:1
Ross 1961,D 27,20:2
Man and Boy 1963,N 13,34:1
Keen, Harriet
Song and Dance Man, The 1930,Je 17,25:5
Keen, Joseph
At War With the Army 1949,Mr 9,32:2
Keen, M L (Costume Designer)
Tom Sawyer 1931,D 26,15:3
Keen, Malcolm
Squall, The 1927,D 4,X,1:3
Making of an Immortal, The 1928,Ap 29,IX,1:3
Paris Bound 1929,My 19,IX,1:8
Josef Suss 1930,Ja 21,28:5
Hamlet 1931,Mr 22,VIII,2:1
Caesar and Cleopatra 1932,O 16,IX,3:7
Hamlet 1936,O 1,28:3
Hamlet 1936,O 9,30:2
Love for Love 1947,My 27,30:2
Man and Superman 1947,O 9,31:2
Man and Superman 1947,O 19,II,1:1
Man and Superman 1949,My 17,28:6
Enchanted, The 1950,Ja 19,34:2
Romeo and Juliet 1951,Mr 12,21:2
Romeo and Juliet 1951,Mr 25,II,1:1
Three Wishes for Jamie 1952,Mr 22,9:2
Much Ado About Nothing 1959,S 18,25:2
School for Scandal, The 1963,Ja 26,5:2
Keen, Noah
Crucible, The 1958,Mr 12,36:1
Crucible, The 1958,Je 1,II,1:1
Keen, William L
Tom Sawyer 1931,D 26,15:3
Keena, Tom
Family Portrait 1959,My 6,48:2
Poker Session, The 1967,S 20,42:2
Ordinary Man, An 1968,S 10,39:1
David Show, The 1968,N 1,34:2
Keenan, Charles
Juno and the Paycock 1940,Ja 17,24:2
Keenan, Frank
Peter Weston 1923,S 20,5:2
Peter Weston 1923,S 30,II,1:1
Sherlock Holmes 1928,F 21,18:4
Keenan, Frank (Director)
Praying Curve 1927,Ja 25,18:2
Keenan, Geneva
Every Man for Himself 1940,D 10,32:3
Keenan, Harry G
My Girl 1924,N 25,27:2
Keenan, Joan
Carousel 1945,Ap 20,24:2
Arms and the Girl 1950,F 3,28:2
Keenan, Marjorie
Untitled-Nativity Play 1946,D 25,46:1
Keenan, Norman
Belafonte at the Palace 1959,D 16,55:1
Keenan, Peggy
Father, The 1928,My 12,9:4
Keenan, Thomas
Good Times 1920,Ag 10,10:1
Little Theatre Tournament; Father Returns, The
1929,My 7,28:1
No Mother to Guide Her 1933,D 26,18:5
Keenan, Walter F Jr (Choreographer)
Great Guns 1939,N 18,23:4
Keene, Christopher (Musical Director)
Amahl and the Night Visitors 1970,D 24,10:2
Help! Help! the Globolinks 1970,D 24,10:2
Keene, Dick
Sidewalks of New York 1927,O 4,33:1
Spring Is Here 1929,Mr 12,26:1
Keene, Donald (Translator)
Hanjo 1960,N 16,51:4
Lady Akane, The 1960,N 16,51:4
Sotoba Komachi 1961,F 1,15:1
Damask Drum, The 1961,F 4,15:1
Keene, Elsie
Becky Sharp 1929,Je 4,29:1
Ladies of the Jury 1929,O 22,26:2
It's a Grand Life 1930,F 11,30:3
Keene, Jay B (Lighting Director)
Fig Leaf in Her Bonnet, A 1961,Je 15,50:1
Keene, Jay B (Scenic Designer)
Fig Leaf in Her Bonnet, A 1961,Je 15,50:1
Keene, Josephine
Barrier, The 1950,N 3,32:2
Keene, Madelyn
Mandragola 1956,Mr 1,36:4
Keene, Madora
Seperate Rooms 1940,Mr 25,10:3
Keene, Mattie
Blue Bonnet 1920,Ag 30,12:1
Spite Corner 1922,S 26,18:1

Keene, Mattie—Cont
Caroline 1923,F 1,13:2
Alloy 1924,O 28,27:1
Naked 1926,N 9,31:2
My Maryland 1927,S 13,37:2
Keene, Michael
Burlesque 1946,D 26,30:3
Diamond Lil 1948,N 30,33:2
Diamond Lil 1949,F 7,16:2
Sixth Finger in a Five Finger Glove 1956,O 9,31:4
Keene, Paul
As You Like It 1936,Ap 24,18:4
Keene, Richard
Irving Berlin's Music Box Revue 1921,S 23,18:2
Hello, Lola! 1926,Ja 13,30:1
Only Girl, The 1934,My 22,28:2
Mrs O'Brien Entertains 1939,F 9,16:3
Keene, William
Many Things 1940,F 3,8:4
Keene Twins
Ziegfeld Follies 1921,Je 22,10:1
Mary Jane McKane 1923,D 26,13:2
Greenwich Village Follies 1924,N 25,26:2
Keener, Stephen
Tempest, The 1970,F 15,67:1
Keener, Suzanne
Peg o' My Dreams 1924,My 6,25:3
Keenhold, Ron
Aquarama 1960 1960,Jl 1,14:6
Keeny, Marie
Commuting Distance 1936,Je 30,15:1
Keep, Stephen
Jungle of Cities 1970,Mr 1,75:2
Kees, Weldon
Poet's Follies of 1955 1955,My 15,II,3:1
Kees, Weldon (Producer)
Poet's Follies of 1955 1955,My 15,II,3:1
Keese, Des
Dooley Cashes In 1935,Ag 17,18:6
Keeshon, Grace
Cinderella on Broadway 1920,Je 25,18:1
Passing Show of 1921, The 1920,D 30,16:2
Bombo 1921,O 7,20:2
Keesler, Robert
Henry IV, Part I 1968,Je 30,54:7
Henry IV, Part II 1968,Jl 2,33:1
Romeo and Juliet 1968,Ag 16,19:1
Time of Your Life, The 1969,N 7,37:1
Camino Real 1970,Ja 9,42:1
Keesmiak, Eugene (Miscellaneous)
Peer Gynt 1951,Ja 29,15:2
Keezel, Florence
Mikado, The 1942,F 4,22:2
Pirates of Penzance, The 1942,F 18,22:2
Iolanthe 1942,F 24,26:4
Gondoliers, The 1942,Mr 4,22:3
Gondoliers, The 1944,F 22,26:3
Kegley, Kermit
Moon Is Down, The 1942,Ap 8,22:2
Doughgirls, The 1942,D 31,19:2
Christopher Blake 1946,D 2,33:2
Miracle in the Mountains 1947,Ap 26,10:2
One Bright Day 1952,Mr 20,37:2
Oklahoma! 1963,My 16,40:1
Kegley, Kermit (Miscellaneous)
South Pacific 1957,Ap 25,35:1
Gang's All Here, The 1959,O 2,23:1
Fighting Cock, The 1959,D 9,57:3
Toys in the Attic 1960,F 26,23:2
Wall, The 1960,O 12,44:4
Gay Life, The 1961,N 20,38:1
Nowhere to Go But Up 1962,N 12,36:2
My Mother, My Father and Me 1963,Mr 25,5:5
Milk Train Doesn't Stop Here Anymore, The 1964,Ja 2,33:1
Kehler, Emma Lou
Hay-Foot, Straw-Foot 1942,O 24,11:6
Kehlmann, Michael (Director)
10th Man, The 1966,Ap 23,15:6
Kehoe, Jack
Drums in the Night 1967,My 18,54:1
Moon for the Misbegotten, A 1968,Je 13,55:2
Kehr, Hollyn
Fine and Dandy 1930,S 24,26:1
Kehrig, Diana
Pirates of Penzance, The 1968,Ap 26,32:1
Keighley, William
Richard III 1920,Mr 8,7:1
Just Suppose 1920,N 2,15:1
Listening In 1922,D 5,24:1
Romeo and Juliet 1922,D 28,20:1
Keighley, William (Director)
Perfect Alibi, The 1928,N 28,24:2
Town Boy 1929,O 5,22:4
Penny Arcade 1930,Mr 11,24:5
Keighley, William (Producer)
Penny Arcade 1930,Mr 11,24:5
Keightley, Cyril
He and She 1920,F 13,16:3
All Soul's Eve 1920,My 13,9:1
Green Goddess, The 1921,Ja 19,14:1
Tyranny of Love, The 1921,Mr 2,7:3
Texas Nightingale, The 1922,N 21,15:2
Texas Nightingale, The 1922,D 3,VIII,1:1

Laughing Lady, The 1923,F 13,25:1
Forbidden 1923,O 2,10:2
Royal Fandango, A 1923,N 13,25:1
Vaudeville (Palace) 1924,Mr 18,25:1
Comedienne 1924,O 22,18:1
Just Beyond 1925,D 2,22:4
Shanghai Gesture, The 1926,F 2,20:2
Comic, The 1927,Ap 20,28:2
Trial of Mary Dugan, The 1927,S 20,33:1
Keightley, Isabel
Forest Ring, The 1930,Ap 26,11:2
Little Princess, The 1931,F 7,11:3
Racketty Packetty House 1931,N 7,16:1
Late One Evening 1933,Ja 10,27:3
Revolt of the Beavers, The 1937,My 21,19:2
Prologue to Glory 1938,Mr 18,22:2
Keil-Moller, Carlo (Director)
Dear Octopus 1939,N 12,IX,2:5
Keila, Maya
Black Crook, The 1929,Mr 17,X,8:1
Keim, Betty Lou
Strange Fruit 1945,N 30,18:6
Crime and Punishment 1947,D 23,29:3
Texas Li'l Darlin' 1949,N 26,10:5
Child of the Morning 1951,N 17,9:7
Remarkable Mr Pennypacker, The 1953,D 31,11:2
Roomful of Roses, A 1955,O 18,48:1
Keim, Chauncey (Director)
Few Wild Oats, A 1932,Mr 25,22:6
Keim, Chauncey (Scenic Designer)
Roof, The 1931,O 31,22:4
Keir, David
Man in Possession, The 1930,N 3,19:1
Keiser, Joan (Miscellaneous)
Killer, The 1960,Mr 23,33:1
Keiser, Kris
Clara's Ole Man 1968,Mr 9,23:2
Keiser, Lee
Tom Sawyer - Ballad of the Mississippi 1947,D 27,11:3
Keiser, Russ
Shewing-Up of Blanco Posnet, The 1959,S 19,26:7
Keitel, Harvey
Up to Thursday 1965,F 11,45:1
Keith, Alan
Matriarch, The 1930,Mr 19,24:5
Keith, Betty Jane
Mistress of the House, The 1950,Ja 31,19:1
Keith, Bob Jr
Mister Roberts 1948,F 19,27:2
Keith, Clare
Pirate, The 1942,N 26,39:2
Keith, Dennis
Mrs Snow 1970,Ja 6,48:3
Keith, Diane
Carousel 1949,Ja 26,28:2
Carousel 1949,F 6,II,1:1
Keith, Edward (Mrs) (Miscellaneous)
Merchant of Venice, The 1950,My 3,37:2
Keith, Eugene
Stork, The 1925,Ja 27,14:2
Devils 1926,Mr 18,26:4
Petrified Forest, The 1935,Ja 8,26:1
Mid-West 1936,Ja 8,22:4
Swing Your Lady 1936,O 19,22:4
Lily of the Valley 1942,Ja 27,25:2
Keith, Ian
Silver Fox, The 1921,S 6,13:1
Czarina, The 1922,F 1,22:1
As You Like It 1923,Ap 24,24:1
Laugh, Clown, Laugh! 1923,N 29,30:1
Master of the Inn, The 1925,D 23,22:2
Command Performance, The 1928,O 4,27:1
Queen Bee 1929,N 13,25:1
Firebird 1932,N 22,25:2
Hangman's Whip 1933,F 25,20:2
Best Sellers 1933,My 4,20:2
Moon and Sixpence, The 1933,D 17,IX,4:3
Richard II 1937,F 6,14:2
Richard II 1937,F 14,X,1:1
Robin Landing 1937,N 19,26:4
Woman's a Fool-To Be Clever, A 1938,O 19,18:6
Leading Lady 1948,O 19,33:1
Touchstone 1953,F 4,33:2
International Set, The 1953,Je 12,19:3
Henry V 1956,Jl 7,11:2
Saint Joan 1956,S 12,42:1
Edwin Booth 1958,N 25,37:1
Andersonville Trial, The 1959,D 30,15:1
Keith, Isham
Naughty-Naught '00 1937,Ja 25,23:2
Fireman's Flame, The 1937,O 11,26:2
Keith, Ivy
It Never Rains 1931,D 25,29:3
Keith, Jane
If This Be Treason 1935,S 24,28:2
Keith, Kermit (Scenic Designer)
Hamlet 1951,Jl 20,13:6
Keith, Lawrence
High Spirits 1964,Ap 8,34:1
Keith, Leonard
Cue for Passion 1940,D 20,33:4

Keith, R (Miscellaneous)
Have I Got a Girl for You! 1963,D 3,53:2
Keith, Richard
Cortez 1929,N 5,32:2
Room 349 1930,Ap 23,24:5
Great Lover, The 1932,O 12,27:3
Assassin, The 1945,O 18,20:2
Keith, Robert
Triumph of X, The 1921,Ag 25,8:2
New Brooms 1924,N 18,23:5
Great God Brown, The 1926,Ja 25,26:1
Gentle Grafters 1926,O 28,23:1
Beyond the Horizon 1926,D 1,24:2
Fog 1927,F 8,20:1
Under Glass 1933,O 31,24:3
Peace on Earth 1933,N 30,39:2
Yellow Jack 1934,Mr 7,22:6
Good-Bye Please 1934,O 25,26:6
Children's Hour, The 1934,N 21,23:2
All Desirable Young Men 1936,Jl 22,22:5
Othello 1936,N 27,26:5
Othello 1936,D 6,XII,6:1
Work Is for Horses 1937,N 22,14:6
Tortilla Flat 1938,Ja 13,16:2
Good, The 1938,O 6,27:2
Ladies and Gentlemen 1939,O 18,30:2
Romantic Mr Dickens 1940,D 3,33:2
Spring Again 1941,N 11,28:2
Kiss and Tell 1943,Mr 18,22:1
Kiss and Tell 1943,Mr 28,II,1:1
No Way Out 1944,O 31,23:1
Place of Our Own, A 1945,Ap 3,23:7
January Thaw 1946,F 5,18:2
Mister Roberts 1948,F 19,27:2
Mister Roberts 1948,F 29,II,1:1
Keith, Robert (Director)
No Way Out 1944,O 31,23:1
Keith, Robert (Playwright)
Tightwad, The 1927,Ap 18,18:2
Singapore 1932,N 15,24:2
Keith, Robert (Producer)
No Way Out 1944,O 31,23:1
Keith, Robert Jr
Darkness at Noon 1951,Ja 15,13:4
Out West of Eighth 1951,S 21,20:3
Keith, Roberta
Funny Thing Happened on the Way to the Forum, A 1962,My 9,49:1
Keith, Sally
New Priorities of 1943 1942,S 16,28:2
Keith, Wendell
Waiting for Lefty 1935,Mr 27,24:5
Keith-Johnston, Colin
Rates, Les; Might-Have-Beens, The 1927,Je 19,VII,2:3
Journey's End 1929,Mr 23,23:1
Journey's End 1929,Jl 14,IX,5:1
Journey's End 1930,Ja 27,24:7
Hamlet 1931,N 6,28:4
Hamlet 1931,N 15,VIII,1:1
Warrior's Husband, The 1932,Mr 12,19:4
Dangerous Corner 1932,O 28,23:1
Magnolia Street 1934,Mr 9,22:6
Pride and Prejudice 1935,O 23,19:2
Pride and Prejudice 1935,N 3,X,1:5
Pride and Prejudice 1935,N 6,32:4
Pride and Prejudice 1935,N 10,IX,2:5
Pride and Prejudice 1935,N 17,IX,1:1
Pride and Prejudice 1936,Ag 30,IX,1:1
Flood Tide 1938,Mr 24,20:8
Journey's End 1939,S 19,29:2
Journey's End 1939,S 24,IX,1:1
Woman Brown, The 1939,D 9,18:5
Passenger to Bali, A 1940,Mr 15,26:2
Doctor's Dilemma, The 1941,F 18,26:6
Doctor's Dilemma, The 1941,Mr 12,18:2
Strings, My Lord, Are False, The 1942,My 20,24:2
Lifeline 1942,D 1,20:3
Winter's Tale, The 1946,Ja 16,18:6
Winter's Tale, The 1946,Ja 20,II,1:1
Dancer, The 1946,Je 6,16:5
Rats of Norway, The 1948,Ap 16,27:6
Autumn Garden, The 1951,Mr 8,36:2
Autumn Garden, The 1951,Mr 18,II,1:1
Point of No Return 1951,O 31,32:2
Point of No Return 1951,D 14,35:2
Major Barbara 1956,O 31,27:1
Kekauoha, Joe
Paradise Island 1961,Je 24,11:1
Kelder, Howard
Othello 1937,Ja 7,16:4
Kelety, Julia
Two Little Girls in Blue 1921,My 4,10:3
Half a Widow 1927,S 13,37:3
Kelety, Julie
Music in the Air 1951,O 9,32:2
Kelham, Bruce
Samarkand 1926,D 22,24:4
Hamlet 1927,Ap 7,23:3
Zuider Zee 1928,D 19,24:4
Kelk, Jackie
Bridal Wise 1932,My 31,15:5
Perfect Marriage, The 1932,N 17,23:2

Kelk, Jackie—Cont
Goodbye Again 1932,D 29,16:4
Jubilee 1935,O 14,20:1
County Chairman, The 1936,My 26,26:5
Tenting Tonight 1947,Ap 3,32:2
Me and Juliet 1953,My 29,17:1
Me and Juliet 1953,Je 7,II,1:1
Kellam, Alan (Composer)
How's the World Treating You? 1966,O 25,50:1
Kellam, Ian (Composer)
Young Visitors, The 1968,D 26,48:1
Kellam, William (Mrs) (Director)
Grey Heir, The 1926,Ap 6,29:2
Kellar, Andrew
There You Are! 1932,My 17,25:4
Kellar, Arthur
White Eagle, The 1927,D 27,24:4
Kellard, John E
Trelawney of the 'Wells' 1927,F 1,24:4
Kellard, Ralph
Light of the World, The 1920,Ja 7,17:1
It Is the Law 1922,N 30,28:2
Easy Street 1924,Ag 15,16:4
She Couldn't Say No! 1926,S 1,27:3
Skin of Our Teeth, The 1942,N 19,29:5
Kellard, Robert
Mother Lode 1934,D 24,16:5
Hitch Your Wagon! 1937,Ap 9,18:2
Kellaway, Cecil
Greenwillow 1960,Mr 9,38:1
Greenwillow 1960,Mr 20,II,1:1
Kelleen, Christian
Eurydice 1948,O 17,I,67:4
Kelleher, Charles
Anything Goes 1937,Ag 17,23:4
Kelleher, George Carl
This Mad Whirl 1937,Ja 10,II,4:8
Kelleher, Jerry
Savonarola 1942,Ap 24,20:2
Kelleher, William
Deirdre of the Sorrows 1949,D 15,51:2
Once Around the Block 1950,My 25,36:2
Kellems, Vivien
Carolinian, The 1925,N 3,34:2
Kellenberger, Arnold (Miscellaneous)
Veronica's Veil 1950,F 12,II,1:5
Kellenberger, Arnold Jr
Veronica's Veil 1950,F 12,II,1:5
Keller, Anthony (Director)
Philoctetes 1964,Ag 19,29:1
Keller, Ben
Another Evening With Harry Stoones 1961,O 23,22:2
Open Season at Second City 1964,Ja 23,25:1
Keller, David
Plough and the Stars, The 1956,Ap 6,14:1
Keller, Dorothy
Follow the Girls 1944,Ap 10,15:2
Heaven on Earth 1948,S 17,29:2
Keller, Elisabeth
Touch of the Poet, A 1961,My 15,34:6
King Lear 1961,My 15,34:6
Keller, Evelyn
God Loves Us 1926,O 20,22:2
Medium, The 1947,My 2,28:2
Medium, The 1947,My 11,II,1:1
Medium, The 1948,D 8,41:6
Medium, The 1950,Jl 20,22:5
Keller, Gertrude
Contrast, The 1926,O 1,26:2
Keller, Helen
Vaudeville (Palace) 1923,Ja 16,16:3
Night of January 16 1935,D 16,22:5
Keller, John
Shoemaker's Holiday, The 1967,Mr 3,25:1
Keller, Judith
Show Boat 1966,Jl 20,48:1
Keller, Kerry
Remolienda, La; Bawdy Party 1968,F 3,20:1
Keller, Kurt
All the Living 1938,Mr 25,14:4
Keller, Marcelle
Vaudeville (Palace) 1928,F 14,26:2
Keller, Miss
Man Without Money, A 1929,N 3,27:4
Keller, Sue
As Husbands Go 1933,Ja 20,20:5
Keller Sisters
Vaudeville (Palace) 1927,Ag 2,19:1
Vaudeville (Palace) 1931,Je 22,17:2
Keller Sisters and Lynch
Vaudeville (Hippodrome) 1925,S 1,18:3
Kellerman, Odette
Farmer's Wife, The 1924,O 10,22:3
Kellermann, Susan
Three...With Women in Mind; Jeff Chandler 1970,N 28,22:1
Three...With Women in Mind; How a Nice Girl Named Janet Contracted Syphilis 1970,N 28,22:1
Three...With Women in Mind; I Hear It Kissing Me Ladies 1970,N 28,22:1
Kellert, Jack
Dead End 1935,O 29,17:2

Kellesser, Michael (Producer)
Rockbound 1929,Ap 20,23:2
Kelley, Barry
Within the Gates 1934,O 23,23:1
Parnell 1935,N 12,24:2
Saint Joan 1936,Mr 10,27:4
Hamlet 1936,O 9,30:2
Wingless Victory, The 1936,D 24,20:2
Star-Wagon, The 1937,S 30,18:5
Mamba's Daughters 1940,Mr 25,10:4
Strip for Action 1942,O 1,26:2
Oklahoma! 1943,Ap 1,27:1
Loco 1946,O 17,29:2
Wonderful Journey 1946,D 26,30:2
Portrait in Black 1947,My 15,30:2
Kelley, Betty
Counsellor-at-Law 1942,N 25,17:2
I'll Take the High Road 1943,N 10,28:3
Devils Galore 1945,S 13,27:2
Kelley, Bunty
Brigadoon 1947,Mr 14,28:2
Rape of Lucretia, The 1948,D 30,24:2
Kelley, Charles
Everyman 1941,My 9,19:2
Kelley, Desmond
Cock Robin 1928,Ja 13,26:6
Little Accident 1928,O 10,32:3
Kelley, Irene
Ups-A-Daisy 1928,O 9,34:2
Kelley, Louise
Snapshots of 1921 1921,Je 3,19:2
Melody Man, The 1924,My 14,14:2
My Girl Friday! 1929,F 13,20:2
Broken Hearts of Broadway 1944,Je 13,16:2
French Touch, The 1945,D 10,18:2
Kelley, Martin J
Chief Thing, The 1963,Ap 30,27:2
Kelley, Norman
Consul, The 1952,O 30,41:2
Consul, The 1957,S 4,40:3
Maria Golovin 1958,N 6,43:1
Mikado, The 1959,O 2,24:1
Mikado, The 1961,Ja 18,26:1
Gondoliers, The 1961,Ja 26,33:2
Iolanthe 1962,Ap 12,42:4
Gondoliers, The 1962,Ap 19,34:2
Yeoman of the Guard, The 1964,Mr 19,29:2
Gondoliers, The 1964,Mr 28,14:1
H M S Pinafore 1965,Ap 15,39:1
Mikado, The 1965,Ap 17,11:3
Yeomen of the Guard, The 1965,Ap 22,26:1
Kelley, Peter
Two's Company 1952,D 16,43:5
Kelley, Vivian
Vagabond King, The 1925,S 22,23:3
Kelley, Walter E (Composer)
Half Moon Inn 1925,Mr 10,14:1
Kellin, Mike
At War With the Army 1949,Mr 9,32:2
Bird Cage, The 1950,F 23,32:2
Emperor's Clothes, The 1953,F 10,24:2
Time of Storm 1954,F 26,14:2
Time of Your Life, The 1955,Ja 20,34:1
Time of Your Life, The 1955,Ja 30,II,1:1
Ankles Aweigh 1955,Ap 19,27:1
Pipe Dream 1955,D 1,44:1
Taming of the Shrew, The 1956,Ag 6,20:1
Diary of a Scoundrel 1956,N 5,41:1
Purple Dust 1956,D 28,15:1
Taming of the Shrew, The 1957,F 21,30:2
Tevya and His Daughters 1957,S 17,38:2
Tevya and His Daughters 1957,S 29,II,1:1
Winkelberg 1958,Ja 15,26:2
God and Kate Murphy 1959,F 27,21:2
Rhinoceros 1961,Ja 10,27:1
Rhinoceros 1961,Ja 22,II,1:1
Mother Courage and Her Children 1963,Mr 30,5:5
King Lear 1964,Jl 28,18:2
Kellin, Mike (Director)
Widowers' Houses 1952,S 21,II,1:1
Kellino, Pamela
Bathsheba 1947,Mr 27,40:2
Kellner, Peggy (Costume Designer)
Winter's Tale, The 1963,Je 29,13:1
Midsummer Night's Dream, A 1963,Jl 1,19:2
Kellner, Peggy (Scenic Designer)
Winter's Tale, The 1963,Je 29,13:1
Midsummer Night's Dream, A 1963,Jl 1,19:2
Kellog, Caroline (Lyricist)
Drunkard, The; Fallen Saved, The 1959,Je 24,37:2
Kellogg, Abigail
Seven at Dawn, The 1961,Ap 18,43:1
Kellogg, Donald
City Haul 1929,D 31,14:4
Kellogg, Giles
Escape This Night 1938,Ap 23,18:1
Kellogg, John
Salvation on a String; Chair Endowed 1954,Jl 7,23:1
Kellogg, Lynn
Hair 1968,Ap 30,40:2
Kellogg, Marjorie (Scenic Designer)
Sambo 1969,D 22,42:1
Happiness Cage, The 1970,O 5,56:4

Kellogg, Robert (Lighting Director)
X Has No Value 1970,F 17,35:1
Kellogg, Shirley
Rainbow Revue, The 1924,F 24,VII,1:4
Kellogg, Virginia
Sonya's Search for the Christmas Star 1929,D 14,24:6
Kelly, Al
My Dear Public 1943,S 10,28:1
Hilarities 1948,S 10,20:2
Kelly, Allan
Immodest Violet 1920,Ag 25,6:2
Kelly, Andrew Jackson
This Mad Whirl 1937,Ja 10,II,4:8
Kelly, Barbara
Anniversary Waltz 1955,D 2,31:3
Spoon River Anthology 1964,F 15,14:7
Kelly, Billy
Top Hole 1924,S 2,22:3
Kelly, Blanche
Sweet Bird of Youth 1956,Ap 17,27:2
Kelly, Christopher
Tiger at the Gates 1968,Mr 1,30:1
Kelly, Christopher (Miscellaneous)
Blitzstein! 1966,D 1,58:2
Sondra 1967,My 10,39:1
Harold 1967,My 10,39:1
Bananas 1968,D 5,60:1
Inner Journey, The 1969,Mr 21,42:1
Time of Your Life, The 1969,N 7,37:1
Kelly, Clyde
Bitter Sweet 1934,My 8,28:4
Kelly, Constance
Lovers in the Metro, The 1962,Ja 31,21:1
Good Soldier Schweik, The 1963,Ap 9,57:1
Kelly, Craig
Heiress, The 1947,S 30,22:2
Kelly, Daniel
Up the Line 1926,N 23,26:1
Sinner 1927,F 8,20:2
Banshee, The 1927,D 6,26:2
Big Fight, The 1928,S 19,33:1
Kelly, David
Career Angel 1943,N 19,24:2
Career Angel 1944,My 24,23:7
Kelly, Don
To Quito and Back 1937,O 7,30:4
Kelly, Doris
Crooked Gamblers 1920,Ag 2,12:1
Lady Killer, The 1924,Mr 13,14:2
Kelly, Eamon
Philadelphia, Here I Come! 1966,F 17,28:1
Well of the Saints, The 1970,Ag 10,34:1
Kelly, Edward H
Petticoat Fever 1937,Mr 21,II,7:3
Kelly, Emmet
Keep Off the Grass 1940,My 24,22:6
Kelly, Eric
Hi, Paisano 1961,O 2,36:2
Kelly, Evelyn
Red, Hot and Blue! 1936,O 30,26:3
Kelly, Francis J (Miscellaneous)
Red Rhumba 1936,Ap 14,18:1
Kelly, Frank
Bystander 1937,S 15,27:1
Kelly, Fred
Time of Your Life, The 1940,S 24,27:2
Kelly, Fred (Director)
This Is the Army 1942,Jl 5,28:2
Kelly, Frederic N (Choreographer)
My Romance 1948,O 20,38:5
Kelly, Gene
One for the Money 1939,F 6,9:2
Time of Your Life, The 1939,O 26,26:2
Time of Your Life, The 1939,N 5,IX,1:1
Pal Joey 1940,D 26,22:2
Kelly, Gene (Choreographer)
Two Weeks With Pay 1940,Je 25,28:3
Best Foot Forward 1941,O 2,28:2
Best Foot Forward 1941,O 26,IX,1:3
Kelly, Gene (Director)
Flower Drum Song 1958,D 2,44:1
Flower Drum Song 1958,D 7,II,5:1
Kelly, George
Johnny 2X4 1942,Mr 17,24:6
Kelly, George (Director)
Craig's Wife 1925,O 13,21:2
Daisy Mayme 1926,O 26,24:2
Behold the Bridegroom 1927,D 27,24:1
Maggie, the Magnificent 1929,O 22,26:1
Maggie, The Magnificent 1929,N 3,IX,1:1
Philip Goes Forth 1931,Ja 4,VIII,2:2
Philip Goes Forth 1931,Ja 13,35:4
Philip Goes Forth 1931,Ja 18,VIII,1:1
Reflected Glory 1936,S 22,30:2
Deep Mrs Sykes, The 1945,Mr 20,22:6
Fatal Witness, The 1946,N 20,43:2
Craig's Wife 1947,F 13,35:2
Craig's Wife 1947,Mr 30,II,1:1
Kelly, George (Original Author)
Philip Goes Forth 1931,Ja 13,35:4
Kelly, George (Playwright)
Torch Bearers, The 1922,Ag 30,10:2

Kelly, George (Playwright)—Cont

Torch Bearers, The 1922,S 3,VI,1:1
Show-Off, The 1924,Ja 20,VII,2:8
Show-Off, The 1924,F 6,16:2
Show-Off, The 1924,F 17,VII,1:1
Show-Off, The 1924,O 21,21:1
Show-Off, The 1925,F 15,VII,1:1
Craig's Wife 1925,O 4,IX,2:1
Craig's Wife 1925,O 13,21:2
Craig's Wife 1925,O 18,IX,1:2
Daisy Mayme 1926,O 17,VIII,2:4
Daisy Mayme 1926,O 26,24:2
Daisy Mayme 1926,O 31,VIII,1:4
A la Carte 1927,Ag 18,25:3
Behold the Bridegroom 1927,D 27,24:1
Behold the Bridegroom 1928,Ja 1,VIII,1:1
Smarty's Party 1928,S 25,29:4
Torch Bearers, The 1929,Mr 22,30:4
Maggie, the Magnificent 1929,O 22,26:1
Maggie, The Magnificent 1929,N 3,IX,1:1
Philip Goes Forth 1931,Ja 4,VIII,2:2
Philip Goes Forth 1931,Ja 18,VIII,1:1
Show-Off, The 1932,D 13,25:4
Reflected Glory 1936,Jl 22,23:1
Reflected Glory 1936,S 18,19:5
Reflected Glory 1936,S 22,30:2
Deep Mrs Sykes, The 1945,Mr 20,22:6
Deep Mrs Sykes, The 1945,Mr 25,II,1:1
Fatal Witness, The 1946,N 20,43:2
Craig's Wife 1947,F 13,35:2
Craig's Wife 1947,Mr 30,II,1:1
Show-Off, The 1950,Je 1,24:5
Show-Off, The 1950,Je 11,II,1:1
Show-Off, The 1967,D 6,40:2
Show-Off, The 1967,D 17,II,3:7

Kelly, Gloria
Constant Nymph, The 1926,D 10,31:1
Macbeth 1928,N 20,28:3

Kelly, Grace
Father, The 1949,N 17,36:2
To Be Continued 1952,Ap 24,37:2

Kelly, Gregory
Dulcy 1921,Ag 15,14:1
Tweedles 1923,Ag 14,10:1
Tweedles 1923,Ag 19,VI,1:1
King for a Day, A 1923,D 2,VIII,2:1
Badges 1924,D 4,25:1
Butter and Egg Man, The 1925,S 24,28:1
Vaudeville (Palace) 1926,Ag 17,21:2

Kelly, Harry
Century Revue and the Midnight Rounders, The
   1920,Jl 13,9:1
Friars Club Frolic 1921,Je 13,16:2
Springtime of Youth 1922,O 27,15:1
Artists and Models 1923,Ag 21,12:2
Sweetheart Time 1926,Ja 20,23:2
Yours Truly 1927,Ja 26,16:5
Sh! The Octopus 1928,F 22,19:2

Kelly, Helen Steele (Musical Director)
Clouds of the Sun 1922,My 6,11:2

Kelly, Hugh
Yes, M'Lord 1949,O 5,35:2

Kelly, J Gordon
Adventure 1928,S 26,25:2
Two Seconds 1931,O 10,20:6

Kelly, Jack
Street Singer, The 1929,S 18,35:2
St Helena 1936,O 7,32:1
Ghost of Yankee Doodle, The 1937,N 23,26:3
Schoolhouse on the Lot 1938,Mr 23,18:4
Night Life 1962,O 24,44:1
Family Way, The 1965,Ja 14,44:5

Kelly, James
Stairs, The 1927,N 8,32:7
Hot Pan 1928,F 16,14:1
Ship, The 1929,N 21,24:7
Seven Keys to Baldpate 1930,Ja 8,25:2
Round Table, The 1930,F 28,20:5
Unexpected Husband 1931,Je 3,29:4
Processional 1937,O 14,23:1

Kelly, James C
Red Roses for Me 1955,D 29,15:2

Kelly, Jeanne
Name Your Poison 1936,Ja 21,27:4

Kelly, Jim
Quare Fellow, The 1958,N 28,34:1

Kelly, Jimmy
Hollywood Ice Revue 1950,Ja 21,13:4

Kelly, John
Spider, The 1927,Mr 23,29:1
Big Fight, The 1928,S 19,33:1

Kelly, John J (Producer)
Adam's Apple 1929,Je 11,27:5

Kelly, John Walter (Playwright)
Out From Under 1940,My 6,13:2

Kelly, Judy
It Happened to Adam 1934,N 10,18:6
Women Aren't Angels 1941,Ap 27,IX,1:6

Kelly, Kendal
Doll's House, A 1954,N 15,32:2

Kelly, Kendal (Miscellaneous)
Man's a Man, A 1962,S 20,30:2

Kelly, Kitty
Whirl of New York, The 1921,Je 14,18:1

Mary Jane McKane 1923,D 26,13:2
Tame Cat, The 1926,Ja 10,VII,1:3
Oh, Please! 1926,D 22,24:3
19th Hole, The 1927,O 12,30:3
Back Here 1928,N 27,36:3
Little Orchard Annie 1930,Ap 22,33:1
Mystery Moon 1930,Je 24,23:4

Kelly, Louise
Nativity Play, The 1937,D 21,29:1

Kelly, M A
Toto 1921,Mr 22,15:2
Face Value 1921,D 27,10:2
Egotist, The 1922,D 27,12:1
Great Lover, The 1932,O 12,27:3

Kelly, Mal
Racket, The 1927,N 23,28:3

Kelly, Margot
Florodora 1920,Ap 6,18:1
Deburau 1920,D 24,14:3
Second Mrs Tanqueray, The 1924,O 28,27:1
Loves of Lulu, The 1925,My 12,26:1
Pearl of Great Price, The 1926,N 2,34:3

Kelly, Mary Kevin
Inherit the Wind 1955,Ap 22,20:2

Kelly, Maurice
Between the Devil 1937,D 23,24:5

Kelly, May
Pygmalion 1938,Ja 27,16:3
Captain Jinks of the Horse Marines 1938,Ja 28,16:2
No More Peace 1938,Ja 29,13:2

Kelly, Michael
Low Bridge 1933,F 10,13:4

Kelly, Mimi
Babes in Arms 1951,Mr 10,7:3

Kelly, Nancy
Give Me Yesterday 1931,Mr 5,32:1
Susan and God 1937,Ap 11,II,12:3
Susan and God 1937,Ap 25,X,2:6
Susan and God 1937,O 8,26:4
Flare Path 1942,D 24,20:2
Big Knife, The 1949,F 25,27:5
Big Knife, The 1949,Mr 6,II,1:1
Season in the Sun 1950,S 29,31:2
Season in the Sun 1950,O 8,II,1:1
Twilight Walk 1951,S 25,25:4
Bad Seed, The 1954,D 9,42:1
Bad Seed, The 1954,D 19,II,3:1
Genius and the Goddess, The 1957,D 11,41:1
Rivalry, The 1959,F 9,24:2
Rivalry, The 1959,F 15,II,1:1
Mighty Man Is He, A 1960,Ja 7,25:2
Giants, Sons of Giants 1962,Ja 8,26:2
Quotations From Chairman Mao Tse-Tung
   1968,O 1,39:1
Quotations From Chairman Mao Tse-Tung
   1968,O 13,II,5:1
Remote Asylum 1970,D 13,II,3:1

Kelly, Nell
Ups-A-Daisy 1928,O 9,34:2
Boom Boom 1929,Ja 29,26:4
Street Singer, The 1929,S 18,35:2
Variety Anthology 1932,Mr 21,19:4

Kelly, Orry (Costume Designer)
Kingdom of God, The 1928,D 21,30:2
Wonderful Night, A; Fledermaus, Die
   1929,N 1,23:3
Nina Rosa 1930,My 31,19:3
Nina Rosa 1930,S 22,22:5
Scarlet Sister Mary 1930,N 26,19:2

Kelly, P J
O'Flaherty, V C 1920,Je 22,9:1
Rising of the Moon, The 1920,Je 22,9:1
Minute's Wait, A 1920,Je 22,9:1
Taming of the Shrew, The 1921,My 12,20:2
Merchant of Venice, The 1921,My 14,10:4
Jolly Roger, The 1923,Ag 31,10:4
Cyrano de Bergerac 1923,N 2,14:1
Othello 1925,Ja 12,11:1
Hamlet 1925,O 12,19:2
Merchant of Venice, The 1925,D 28,12:1
Cyrano de Bergerac 1926,F 19,18:1
Joan of Arc 1926,Ap 24,21:2
Immortal Thief, The 1926,O 4,21:1
Caponsacchi 1926,O 27,24:2
Hamlet 1928,Ja 5,33:2
Henry V 1928,Mr 16,26:2
Milestones 1930,Je 3,27:1
Mr Gilhooley 1930,O 1,26:1
Five Star Final 1930,D 31,11:1
Miss Gulliver Travels 1931,N 26,36:4
Well of the Saints, The 1932,Ja 22,15:2
Troilus and Cressida 1932,Je 7,22:3
Mikado, The 1932,Jl 29,18:4
Cyrano de Bergerac 1932,D 27,11:2
John Ferguson 1933,Jl 11,15:7
Richelieu 1934,My 22,28:1
Hamlet 1934,D 26,19:3
Richard III 1934,D 28,24:3
News Item 1935,Ag 6,20:3
Name Your Poison 1936,Ja 21,27:4
You Can't Take It With You 1951,Ap 7,8:6
Child of the Morning 1951,N 17,9:7
Righteous Are Bold, The 1955,D 23,12:1

Kelly, P J—Cont

Saint Joan 1956,S 12,42:1
Purple Dust 1956,D 28,15:1
Endgame 1958,Ja 29,32:4
Endgame 1958,F 16,II,1:1
Whoop-Up 1958,D 23,2:7

Kelly, Pamela
Murder in the Cathedral 1938,F 17,16:2

Kelly, Patricia
Unsinkable Molly Brown, The 1960,N 4,28:1
Here's Where I Belong 1968,Mr 4,32:1

Kelly, Patrick J
Finian's Rainbow 1947,O 22,38:4
Finian's Rainbow 1947,N 9,II,3:7

Kelly, Patsy
Harry Delmar's Revels 1927,N 29,30:2
Three Cheers 1928,O 16,28:1
Sketch Book 1929,Jl 2,33:5
Earl Carroll's Vanities 1930,Jl 2,28:3
Wonder Bar, The 1931,Mr 18,23:4
Vaudeville (Palace) 1932,Ap 25,18:3
Flying Colors 1932,S 16,24:2
Flying Colors 1932,O 9,IX,1:1

Kelly, Paul
Honors Are Even 1921,Ag 11,8:2
Up the Ladder 1922,Mr 7,11:2
Whispering Wires 1922,Ag 8,26:2
Chains 1923,S 20,5:2
Lady Killer, The 1924,Mr 13,14:2
Nerves 1924,S 2,22:2
Houses of Sand 1925,F 18,17:1
Sea Woman, The 1925,Ag 25,12:2
Find Daddy 1926,Mr 9,21:3
Nine Fifteen Revue, The 1930,F 12,26:2
Long Road, The 1930,Jl 20,VIII,2:1
Bad Girl 1930,O 3,30:2
Hobo 1931,F 12,24:4
Just to Remind You 1931,S 8,39:1
Adam Had Two Sons 1932,Ja 17,VIII,3:5
Adam Had Two Sons 1932,Ja 21,17:1
Great Magoo, The 1932,D 3,20:7
Beggars Are Comming to Town 1945,O 29,16:2
Command Decision 1947,S 21,I,59:7
Command Decision 1947,O 2,30:2
Command Decision 1947,O 12,II,1:1
Country Girl, The 1950,N 11,10:6
Country Girl, The 1950,N 19,II,1:1

Kelly, Paula
Dozens, The 1969,Mr 14,51:1

Kelly, Phil
It Never Rains 1929,N 20,26:4

Kelly, Red
Taste of Honey, A 1960,O 5,46:1

Kelly, Renee
Joy Will Come Back 1937,Mr 22,27:3

Kelly, Richard
Goodbye in the Night 1940,Mr 19,31:2
Greatest Man Alive!, The 1957,My 9,37:2

Kelly, Robert
Beyond the Horizon 1920,Mr 10,9:2
Merchants of Venus 1920,S 28,14:2
Easiest Way, The 1921,S 7,14:1
Rain 1922,N 8,18:2
Carry On 1928,Ja 24,26:1
Street Scene 1929,Ja 11,20:4
Cherry Orchard, The 1955,O 19,38:1

Kelly, Robert (Miscellaneous)
Asmodee 1958,Mr 26,42:2

Kelly, Robert (Producer)
Asmodee 1958,Mr 26,42:2
Sign of Winter 1958,My 8,35:1

Kelly, Robert (Scenic Designer)
Egg, The 1962,Ja 9,23:2

Kelly, Roger
Macbeth 1969,D 23,25:1

Kelly, Terry
Best Foot Forward 1941,O 2,28:2
Follow the Girls 1944,Ap 10,15:2

Kelly, Therese
Twinkle Twinkle 1926,N 17,22:2

Kelly, Thomas
Gods of the Lightning 1928,O 25,27:2

Kelly, Thomas (Lyricist)
Blitzstein! 1966,D 1,58:2

Kelly, Thomas A
Riff-Raff 1926,F 9,18:6

Kelly, Tim (Playwright)
Darker Flower, A 1963,Mr 11,7:2

Kelly, Tresha
Cabaret 1966,N 21,62:1

Kelly, Verner E
On the Level 1937,Mr 26,24:4

Kelly, Walter
Boyd's Daughter 1940,O 12,20:2
This Rock 1943,F 19,23:2
Tomorrow the World 1943,Ap 15,22:2
Cyrano de Bergerac 1946,O 9,33:2
Cyrano de Bergerac 1947,Ja 17,27:2

Kelly, Walter C
Vaudeville (Palace) 1925,O 6,31:3
Great Day! 1929,O 18,24:3
Both Your Houses 1933,Mr 7,20:3
Both Your Houses 1933,My 23,22:2
Jayhawker 1934,N 6,34:2

Kelly, Walter C—Cont
Lend Me Your Ears! 1936,O 6,28:5
Kelly, William J
Brothers 1928,D 26,14:3
Room Service 1935,N 17,II,7:7
You Can't Take It With You 1936,D 15,31:1
Beverly Hills 1940,N 8,24:2
Doughgirls, The 1942,D 31,19:2
Leading Lady 1948,O 19,33:1
Biggest Thief in Town 1949,Mr 31,31:2
Kelm, Kathy (Costume Designer)
Homo 1969,Ap 12,40:2
Queen of Greece, The 1969,Ap 12,40:2
Kelo Brothers
Great Temptations, The 1926,My 19,29:1
Kelpe, Henry
Master of the Revels 1935,Ag 14,16:2
Kelsey, Carlton (Composer)
Sky High 1925,Mr 3,21:4
Kelsey, Harry
Streetcar Named Desire, A 1950,My 24,36:1
Kelsey, Pat
From Morn Till Midnight 1948,D 7,41:6
Butter and Egg Man, The 1949,Ap 29,27:1
Kelsey, William
Immaculate Misconception, The 1970,O 28,63:3
Kelso, James
Keep Kool 1924,My 23,16:4
It Never Rains 1931,D 25,29:3
Off to Buffalo! 1939,F 22,18:2
Panama Hattie 1940,O 31,28:2
Kelso, Lee
Dew Drop Inn 1923,My 18,26:4
Kelso, Vernon
Twelfth Night 1921,N 1,17:1
Merchant of Venice, The 1921,N 22,17:1
Dolly Jordan 1922,O 4,26:1
Romeo and Juliet 1923,Ja 25,16:1
Pelleas and Melisande 1923,D 5,23:2
Antony and Cleopatra 1924,F 20,22:1
Depths, The 1925,Ja 28,15:3
Easy Virtue 1925,D 8,28:2
My Princess 1927,O 7,24:2
Outsider, The 1928,Ap 10,32:2
Stripped 1929,O 13,IX,5:1
Stripped 1929,O 22,26:1
Michael and Mary 1929,D 14,23:3
Mrs Moonlight 1930,S 30,24:3
Roof, The 1931,O 31,22:4
They Don't Mean Any Harm 1932,F 24,25:2
Kelton, Dorrit
Montmartre 1922,F 14,20:1
Personal Appearance 1934,O 18,26:7
Moroni 1936,Ag 19,19:1
More the Merrier, The 1941,S 16,19:3
Days of Our Youth, The 1941,N 29,15:2
Autumn Hill 1942,Ap 14,17:4
First Million, The 1943,Ap 29,27:4
Visitor, The 1944,O 18,24:5
Rose Tattoo, The 1951,F 5,19:2
Madam Will You Walk 1953,D 2,2:4
Morning's at Seven 1955,Je 23,25:1
Streetcar Named Desire, A 1956,F 16,24:1
Season of Choice 1959,Ap 14,40:1
All the Way Home 1960,D 1,42:1
Calculated Risk 1962,N 1,35:1
Kelton, Eric
Bitter Oleander 1935,F 12,24:3
Kelton, Gene
Applause 1970,Mr 31,35:1
Kelton, Pert
Sunny 1925,S 23,22:1
Sunny 1925,S 27,VII,1:6
Five O'Clock Girl, The 1927,O 11,26:3
Du Barry 1932,N 13,IX,1:8
Du Barry 1932,N 23,15:2
All in Fun 1940,N 22,26:2
All in Fun 1940,D 28,11:2
Any Day Now 1941,Je 10,28:2
Guest in the House 1942,F 25,25:2
Lady Behave 1943,N 17,30:1
Music Man, The 1957,D 20,31:1
Music Man, The 1958,S 28,II,1:1
Greenwillow 1960,Mr 9,38:1
Greenwillow 1960,Mr 20,II,1:1
Come Blow Your Horn 1961,F 23,31:3
I Was Dancing 1964,N 9,40:4
Spofford 1967,D 15,54:3
Spofford 1967,D 24,II,3:2
Kelton, Stan
Truce of the Bear 1957,O 24,39:1
Kelvin, Alec
Strings, My Lord, Are False, The 1942,My 20,24:2
Kelvin, Walter
Wonderful Town 1953,F 26,22:3
Silk Stockings 1955,F 25,17:3
Kemball, Colin
Oh What a Lovely War 1964,O 1,30:1
Kemble, Christopher
Whistling Wizard and the Sultan of Tuffet 1970,F 1,70:1
Kemble, Diana
Duchess of Malfi, The 1946,O 16,35:2

Kemble, Doris
Silence 1924,N 13,18:2
Kemble, Enid Sikevin
Malice Domestic 1942,Jl 21,22:1
Kemble, Lillian
Fool, The 1922,O 24,18:1
What Do We Know 1927,D 24,8:1
Kemble, Robert
Romio and Julietta 1925,Ap 21,19:1
Samarkand 1926,D 22,24:4
Kemble-Cooper, Anthony
His Majesty's Car 1930,O 24,30:1
Hay Fever 1931,D 6,VIII,2:8
Hay Fever 1931,D 30,25:1
Mary of Scotland 1933,N 28,28:3
Sheppey 1944,Ap 19,27:2
Sweethearts 1947,Ja 22,31:2
Much Ado About Nothing 1955,Ag 20,20:4
Kemble-Cooper, Lillian
All Dressed Up 1925,S 10,28:1
Kemble-Cooper, Lily
I Know My Love 1949,N 3,36:1
Kemble-Cooper, Violet
School for Scandal, The 1923,Je 5,24:3
Unchastened Woman, The 1926,F 17,12:1
Mackerel Skies 1934,Ja 24,20:4
Kemii
Love in the Tropics 1927,O 19,24:3
Kemmerling, Warren
Pipe Dream 1955,D 1,44:1
Orpheus Descending 1957,Mr 22,28:1
Kemmet, Ralph G
Trial of Joan of Arc, The 1921,Mr 28,8:2
Kemo, Jeremy
Twist of Sand, A 1969,F 22,36:1
Kemp, Billie
Queer People 1934,F 16,16:2
Kemp, Catherine
Dead End 1935,O 29,17:2
Kemp, Frederick
Carry Nation 1932,O 31,18:2
Kemp, Harry (Playwright)
Boccacco's Untold Tale 1923,My 8,22:3
Kemp, Isabel (Playwright)
Courage 1927,Ja 20,20:1
Kemp, Louise
Trouble in Mind 1955,N 5,23:2
Kemp, Paul
Menschen im Hotel 1930,Mr 16,IX,4:1
Kemp, Roger
Rosencrantz and Guildenstern Are Dead 1967,O 17,53:1
Kemp, Sally
Thorntons, The 1956,F 15,26:1
I Am a Camera 1956,O 10,47:2
Advise and Consent 1960,N 18,25:1
Milk Train Doesn't Stop Here Anymore, The 1965,Jl 27,25:1
Kemp, Stewart
Young Visitors, The 1920,N 30,14:1
We've Got to Have Money 1923,Ag 21,12:1
Kemp, William
Red Rainbow, A 1953,S 15,37:4
Kemper, Charles
Showboat Revue 1935,Ag 18,13:2
Anything Goes 1937,Ag 26,24:3
You Never Know 1938,Mr 4,16:3
You Never Know 1938,S 22,26:3
What Price Glory 1949,Mr 3,33:2
Kemper, Colin (Director)
Lovely Lady 1925,O 15,27:1
Joker, The 1925,N 17,29:1
Kemper, Doris
Fall of Eve, The 1925,S 1,18:1
Kemper, Peggy
Fuente Ovejuna; Sheep Well, The 1936,My 3,II,4:1
Kemper, Peggy (Director)
Nine Till Six 1936,Mr 14,10:3
Kempner, Brenda
Persecution and Assassination of Marat As Performed by the Inmates of the Asylum of Charenton Under the Direction of the Marquis de Sade, The 1965,D 28,35:1
Kempner, Dolores
Carnival in Flanders 1953,S 9,38:2
Kempner, Nicholas (Composer)
Street Singer, The 1929,Jl 28,VIII,1:6
Street Singer, The 1929,S 18,35:2
Kempson, Rachel
Jacobowsky and the Colonel 1945,Je 24,II,1:3
Kempson, Voight
Dames at Sea 1970,S 24,60:1
Kendal, Madge (Dame)
Caste 1929,F 24,IX,4:3
Kendal, Myra
David Garrick 1929,Ag 2,17:5
Kendal, Stephen
Play's the Thing, The 1926,N 4,25:1
Kendall, Adelaide
City Haul 1929,D 31,14:4
Kendall, Cyrus W
Around the Corner 1936,D 29,17:2

Kendall, Daphne
Scalawag, The 1927,Mr 30,22:3
Kendall, Elizabeth
John Brown 1934,Ja 23,22:3
Journey by Night, A 1935,Ap 17,26:3
Kendall, Harry
Buccaneer, The 1925,O 3,10:2
Just Fancy! 1927,O 12,30:2
Kendall, Henry
Naughty Cinderella 1925,N 10,23:6
This Woman Business 1926,D 8,25:1
Baa, Baa, Black Sheep 1929,My 12,IX,2:3
Kendall, Jo
Cambridge Circus 1964,O 7,53:1
Kendall, Kuy
Honeydew 1920,S 7,20:1
Kendall, Kuy (Choreographer)
Katja 1926,O 19,27:3
Kendall, Messmore (Producer)
Letter, The 1927,S 27,30:1
Our Betters 1928,F 21,18:2
Sacred Flame, The 1928,N 20,28:2
Sandy Hooker, The 1929,N 10,X,4:8
Breadwinner, The 1931,S 23,19:4
Kendall, Pat
Great Temptations, The 1926,My 19,29:1
Schoen und Schick 1928,Ag 26,II,1:2
Kendall, Richard
Gianni Schicci 1969,F 25,36:1
Songs From Milk Wood 1970,Ja 13,41:1
Sganarelle 1970,Ja 13,41:1
Kendall, Robin
People Is the Thing That the World Is Fullest Of 1967,F 21,53:1
Kendall, Seth
Man Who Died Twice, The 1925,D 14,19:1
Great God Brown, The 1926,Ja 25,26:1
God Loves Us 1926,O 20,22:2
Damn the Tears 1927,Ja 22,11:1
Loud Speaker 1927,Mr 3,27:2
Wall Street 1927,Ap 21,24:4
Kendall, Terry
Great Temptations, The 1926,My 19,29:1
Schoen und Schick 1928,Ag 26,II,1:2
Kendall, William
Between the Devil 1937,D 23,24:5
Kendrick, Beatrice
Noble Prize, The 1935,Jl 9,24:3
Kendrick, John
Let Them Down, Gently; On Vacation 1968,Ja 31,28:2
Kendrick, Rexford
Sonya 1921,Ag 16,18:3
Marie Antoinette 1921,N 23,16:1
World We Live In, The 1922,N 1,16:1
Steadfast 1923,O 31,12:1
You Can't Beat a Woman 1925,Mr 24,26:5
So's Your Old Antique 1930,My 8,32:5
Kendrick, Richard
Double Door 1933,S 22,15:5
Personal Appearance 1934,O 18,26:7
Room in Red and White, A 1936,Ja 20,23:3
Spring Dance 1936,Jl 7,22:2
Spring Dance 1936,Ag 26,17:4
Stage Door 1936,S 29,35:1
Stage Door 1936,O 23,26:3
Excursion 1937,Ap 10,11:4
Case of Youth, A 1940,Mr 25,10:3
Two Blind Mice 1949,Mr 3,32:2
Golden Fleecing 1959,O 16,24:5
Kenealy, William
Last Man In, The 1930,My 8,32:5
Keneman, Albert Lord Jr
This Mad Whirl 1937,Ja 10,II,4:8
Keneven, Richard
Gypsy Baron, The 1944,Je 15,17:3
Kenick, Althea
Canteen Show, The 1942,S 4,18:1
Kenin, Jean
George White's Scandals 1926,Je 15,23:2
Kenin, Maya
Marathon '33 1963,D 23,20:1
Duet for Three 1966,My 20,41:1
Kenkichi, Sato
Golden Bat 1970,Je 27,18:2
Kenkichi, Sato (Scenic Designer)
Golden Bat 1970,Je 27,18:2
Kenley, John
Pimpernel! 1964,Ja 7,26:6
Kenmore, Octavia
Blood and Sand 1921,S 21,16:2
Accused 1925,S 30,20:1
Out of the Sea 1927,D 6,26:2
Hundred Years Old, A 1929,O 2,28:2
Is Life Worth Living? 1933,N 10,24:6
Musical Chairs 1934,Jl 31,20:7
Hedda Gabler 1942,Ja 30,22:2
Song of Bernadette 1946,Mr 27,22:2
Wanhope Building, The 1947,F 11,36:5
Kenna, Tom
Zelda 1969,Mr 6,38:1
Kennan, Frances
Pot-Luck 1921,S 30,10:1

Kennan, Frances—Cont
Babbling Brookes 1927,F 26,13:2
White Flame 1929,N 5,32:7
Kennard, Grace
Love Child, The 1922,N 15,22:1
Kenneally, Jerri (Miscellaneous)
Delightful Season, A 1960,S 29,30:1
Kenneally, Philip
Shake Hands With the Devil 1949,O 21,30:4
Macbeth 1955,O 8,12:6
Desert Incident, A 1959,Mr 25,40:1
Burning Bright 1959,O 17,27:2
Much Ado About Nothing 1961,Jl 7,17:1
Midsummer Night's Dream, A 1961,Ag 3,13:1
Richard II 1961,Ag 30,25:1
Kenneally, Robert
Captains and the Kings, The 1962,Ja 3,25:2
Kennedy
Anna Christie 1921,N 3,22:1
Kennedy, Adam
Riot Act, The 1963,Mr 9,5:2
Kennedy, Adrienne (Playwright)
Funnyhouse of a Negro 1964,Ja 15,25:3
In His Own Write 1968,Je 20,50:5
In His Own Write 1968,Jl 9,30:2
In His Own Write 1968,Jl 14,II,4:5
Cities in Bezique; Owl Answers, The
  1969,Ja 13,26:1
Cities in Bezique; Beast's Story, A 1969,Ja 13,26:1
Cities in Bezique 1969,Ja 19,II,3:5
Rat's Mass, A 1969,N 1,39:1
Kennedy, Alfred C (Playwright)
Crooked Square, The 1923,S 11,10:2
Kennedy, Arthur
Life and Death of an American 1939,My 20,11:2
International Incident, An 1940,Ap 3,18:2
All My Sons 1947,Ja 30,21:2
All My Sons 1947,F 9,II,1:1
Death of a Salesman 1949,F 11,27:2
Death of a Salesman 1949,F 20,II,1:1
Death of a Salesman 1950,Mr 12,II,1:1
See the Jaguar 1952,D 4,46:2
Crucible, The 1953,Ja 23,15:2
Crucible, The 1953,F 1,II,1:1
Time Limit! 1956,Ja 25,27:2
Time Limit! 1956,F 5,II,1:1
Loud Red Patrick, The 1956,O 4,28:1
Loud Red Patrick, The 1956,O 14,II,1:1
Becket 1961,My 9,44:1
Price, The 1968,F 8,37:1
Price, The 1968,F 18,II,1:1
Kennedy, Aubrey (Playwright)
Seeing Things 1920,Je 18,19:2
Behold This Dreamer 1927,N 1,20:4
Kennedy, Bill
Kiss Me, Kate 1965,My 13,31:1
Kennedy, Bob
Girl From Nantucket, The 1945,N 9,17:2
Kennedy, Bryce
Bootleggers, The 1922,N 28,24:1
Kennedy, Caroline
Immoral Support 1935,S 3,24:3
Kennedy, Charles
Little Old New York 1920,S 9,9:2
Claw, The 1921,O 18,20:1
Sweet Little Devil 1924,Ja 22,15:4
Blue Bandanna, The 1924,Je 24,18:4
Tantrum, The 1924,S 5,20:2
They Knew What They Wanted 1924,N 25,27:1
Gentle Grafters 1926,O 28,23:1
Hangman's House 1926,D 17,27:2
Nightstick 1927,N 11,20:4
Machinal 1928,S 8,10:3
Adam's Apple 1929,Je 11,27:5
Everything's Jake 1930,Ja 17,20:4
Mr Gilhooley 1930,O 1,26:1
Rendezvous 1932,O 13,22:3
Lone Valley 1933,Mr 11,18:6
Too Many Boats 1934,S 12,26:3
Plumes in the Dust 1936,N 7,14:2
Journeyman 1938,Ja 31,14:2
They Knew What They Wanted 1939,O 3,19:1
Kindred 1939,D 27,17:2
They Knew What They Wanted 1949,F 17,28:2
Kennedy, Charles O'Brien (Director)
Mighty Nimrod, The 1931,My 13,23:1
Kennedy, Charles O'Brien (Playwright)
Mighty Nimrod, The 1931,My 13,23:1
Kennedy, Charles Rann
Chastening, The 1923,F 17,9:2
Antigone 1923,My 4,18:4
Antigone 1923,My 25,28:1
Admiral, The 1924,Ap 25,20:2
Admiral, The 1924,My 4,VIII,1:1
Kennedy, Charles Rann (Director)
Servant in the House, The 1925,Ap 8,24:2
Seventh Trumpet, The 1941,N 22,10:6
Kennedy, Charles Rann (Playwright)
Servant in the House, The 1921,My 3,20:1
Chastening, The 1923,F 17,9:2
Admiral, The 1924,Ap 25,20:2
Servant in the House, The 1925,Ap 8,24:2
Servant in the House, The 1925,Ap 12,VIII,1:1
Servant in the House, The 1926,My 4,30:1

Admiral, The 1929,Ja 23,21:1
Terrible Meek, The 1930,My 4,XI,3:1
Seventh Trumpet, The 1941,N 22,10:6
Kennedy, Charles Rann (Producer)
Admiral, The 1924,My 4,VIII,1:1
Admiral, The 1929,Ja 23,21:1
Kennedy, Dick
Lovely Lady 1927,D 30,22:1
Kennedy, Don
Magnolia Alley 1949,Ap 19,29:2
Great to Be Alive! 1950,Mr 24,28:2
Kennedy, Don (Director)
Up in Central Park 1945,Ja 29,17:2
Kennedy, E J
Erminie 1921,Ja 4,11:1
Plough and the Stars, The 1927,N 29,30:2
Juno and the Paycock 1927,D 20,32:2
Kennedy, E J (Director)
First Million, The 1943,Ap 29,27:4
Kennedy, Elizabeth
Merrily We Roll Along 1934,O 1,14:1
Laughing Woman, The 1936,Jl 8,14:7
Kennedy, Ellenor
Whole Town's Talking, The 1923,Ag 30,8:2
Wisdom Tooth, The 1926,F 16,22:2
Kennedy, Harold
Moon Is a Gong, The 1926,Mr 13,21:3
Adventure 1928,S 26,25:2
Tired Business Man, The 1929,Je 5,32:5
Phantoms 1930,Ja 14,24:3
Man on Stilts, The 1931,S 10,23:2
Hot Money 1931,N 9,22:2
Locked Room, The 1933,D 26,18:5
Kennedy, Harold J
In Time to Come 1941,D 29,20:2
Goose for the Gander, A 1945,Ja 24,16:4
Front Page, The 1968,O 20,85:5
Front Page, The 1969,My 12,54:2
Front Page, The 1969,My 25,II,1:1
Front Page, The 1969,N 2,86:1
Kennedy, Harold J (Director)
Front Page, The 1969,My 12,54:2
Front Page, The 1969,My 25,II,1:1
Front Page, The 1969,N 2,86:1
Kennedy, Harold J (Playwright)
Goose for the Gander, A 1945,Ja 24,16:4
Kennedy, Harold J (Producer)
Treat Her Gently 1941,Mr 30,I,48:1
Kennedy, Helen
Nine Till Six 1936,Mr 14,10:3
Kennedy, Henry M
Tiger Smiles, The 1930,D 18,29:1
Kennedy, J E
Kid Himself, The 1925,D 25,23:2
Kennedy, Jack
Sun Showers 1923,F 6,14:2
Good News 1927,S 7,35:4
Kennedy, James
Sign of the Leopard 1928,D 12,34:4
Kennedy, James E (Producer)
Menace 1927,Mr 15,28:2
Kennedy, James H (Playwright)
Take It Away 1936,D 15,30:5
Take It Away 1936,D 22,32:3
Kennedy, Jay Richard (Producer)
Your Loving Son 1941,Ap 5,13:2
Kennedy, Jerome
We Americans 1926,O 13,20:4
Town's Woman, The 1929,Mr 12,26:2
Unsophisticates, The 1929,D 31,14:5
Kennedy, John
Alias Jimmy Valentine 1921,D 9,20:3
To the Ladies! 1922,F 21,20:1
Woof, Woof 1929,D 26,20:4
Merrily We Roll Along 1934,O 1,14:1
Everywhere I Roam 1938,D 30,10:4
Henry IV, Part I 1939,Ja 31,17:2
Antigone 1959,S 16,46:2
Kennedy, John (Director)
Artists and Models 1943,N 6,16:6
Mexican Hayride 1944,Ja 29,9:6
Would-Be Gentleman, The 1946,Ja 10,29:2
Sweethearts 1947,Ja 22,31:2
Angel in the Wings 1947,D 12,36:4
Ziegfeld Follies 1957,Mr 2,19:2
Oklahoma! 1969,Je 24,37:1
Kennedy, John (Miscellaneous)
Show Boat 1956,Je 22,16:1
Show Boat 1957,Je 28,30:2
Kennedy, John (Playwright)
Up in Central Park 1947,My 20,29:2
Kennedy, Joseph
Paid 1925,N 26,32:1
Free Soul, A 1928,Ja 13,26:5
Billie 1928,O 2,34:2
Gray Shadow 1931,Mr 11,23:4
Kennedy, Joseph P Jr
On the Level 1937,Mr 26,24:4
Kennedy, Joyce
Winding Journey, The 1934,My 8,28:6
Kennedy, Kathryne
Rain 1922,N 8,18:2

Kennedy, Leo
Goat Alley 1921,Je 21,20:2
All-Star Jamboree 1921,Jl 14,18:1
Spring Fever 1925,Ag 4,14:2
Deacon, The 1925,N 25,14:3
Ink 1927,N 2,24:2
Caravan 1928,Ag 30,13:3
Adventure 1928,S 26,25:2
When in Rome 1929,Je 16,VIII,2:1
June Moon 1929,O 10,34:5
Scarlet Sister Mary 1930,N 26,19:2
Hot Money 1931,N 9,22:2
Angels Don't Kiss 1932,Ap 6,22:5
Great Lover, The 1932,O 12,27:3
Whistling in the Dark 1932,N 4,25:2
June Moon 1933,My 16,15:5
Undesirable Lady, An 1933,O 10,24:4
Merrily We Roll Along 1934,O 1,14:1
Night of January 16 1935,S 17,26:4
Chalked Out 1937,Mr 26,24:2
Empress of Destiny 1938,Mr 10,16:2
Run Sheep Run 1938,N 4,26:2
Kennedy, Lizbeth
Game of Love and Death, The 1929,N 26,28:4
Kennedy, Mack
Lady Billy 1920,D 15,18:2
Kennedy, Madge
Cornered 1920,D 9,18:2
Spite Corner 1922,S 26,18:1
Poppy 1923,S 4,14:2
Beware of Widows 1925,N 8,VIII,2:1
Beware of Widows 1925,D 2,22:3
Love in a Mist 1926,Ap 13,28:3
Springboard, The 1927,O 13,23:1
Paris Bound 1927,D 28,26:3
Paris Bound 1928,Ja 15,VIII,1:1
Paris Bound 1929,Jl 20,8:3
Prima Donna 1929,S 22,IX,2:6
Vaudeville (Palace) 1929,D 16,34:4
Private Lives 1931,My 12,29:3
Bridal Wise 1932,My 31,15:5
Very Rich Woman, A 1965,O 5,5:8
Kennedy, Margaret (Original Author)
Constant Nymph, The 1926,D 10,31:1
Constant Nymph, The 1927,Mr 6,VIII,1:4
Tessa 1935,Ja 6,IX,2:1
Kennedy, Margaret (Playwright)
Constant Nymph, The 1926,O 3,VIII,2:1
Constant Nymph, The 1926,D 10,31:1
Constant Nymph, The 1926,D 19,VII,3:1
Come With Me 1928,My 20,VIII,2:3
Escape Me Not 1933,D 9,18:6
Escape Me Never! 1934,Ja 7,X,3:5
Escape Me Never! 1935,Ja 22,22:2
Escape Me Never! 1935,F 10,VIII,1:1
Escape Me Never! 1936,Je 21,IX,2:4
Happy With Either 1948,Ap 23,28:1
Kennedy, Mary
Not So Long Ago 1920,My 5,14:1
Love Habit, The 1923,Mr 15,17:1
In the Next Room 1923,N 28,14:1
Blue Peter, The 1925,Mr 25,25:3
Mariners 1927,Mr 29,22:2
19th Hole, The 1927,O 12,30:3
Man With Red Hair, A 1928,N 9,22:2
Camel Through the Needle's Eye, The
  1929,Ap 16,32:2
Joyous Season, The 1934,Ja 30,16:3
Kennedy, Mary (Playwright)
Mrs Partridge Presents 1925,Ja 6,23:3
Mrs Partridge Presents 1936,F 29,10:1
Kennedy, Matt (Playwright)
Nic-Nax of 1926 1926,Ag 5,19:1
Kennedy, Michael
Merchant of Venice, The 1957,Jl 11,19:5
Hamlet 1958,Je 21,11:1
Hair 1970,Ja 13,39:1
Kennedy, Pat
Vaudeville (Palace) 1932,Je 13,19:7
Kennedy, Patricia
Where Stars Walk 1948,F 25,27:2
Kennedy, R G
Kid Himself, The 1925,D 25,23:2
Kennedy, Raleigh
Remote Control 1929,S 11,24:5
Kennedy, Richard
Season of the Beast 1958,Mr 14,29:2
Kennedy, Robert
Mikado, The 1939,Mr 11,15:6
Kennedy, S
Gentlemen, the Queen 1927,Ap 23,14:3
Kennedy, Sandy
King and I, The 1951,Mr 30,26:2
Midsummer Night Scream, A 1960,D 16,45:1
Kennedy, Scott
As You Like It 1945,Jl 4,10:4
Kennedy, Sheelagh
Jamboree 1932,N 25,18:4
Kennedy, Thomas C
Coriolanus 1927,Je 18,8:3
Kennedy, Thomas Conger (Playwright)
Song of the Bridge 1942,Ap 7,27:5

Kennedy, Tom
Rope Dancers, The 1959,Mr 14,26:1
Kennedy, Violet J
Hickory Stick 1944,My 9,15:6
Kennedy, William (Playwright)
House in Berlin, A (Als der Kreig zu Ende War);
Als der Krieg zu Ende War (A House in Berlin)
1950,D 27,32:3
Kennedy, Zona
Autumn's Here 1966,O 26,40:1
Kennedy-Fox, Dorothy
Fools Rush In 1934,D 26,19:2
Kennel, Louis (Costume Designer)
Twelfth Night 1949,O 4,33:2
Twelfth Night 1949,O 9,II,1:1
Difficult Woman, The 1962,Ap 26,22:7
Kennel, Louis (Lighting Director)
Anybody Home 1949,F 26,10:5
Difficult Woman, The 1962,Ap 26,22:7
Kennel, Louis (Scenic Designer)
House of Ussher, The 1926,Ja 14,18:4
Apron Strings 1930,F 18,28:2
Plutocrat, The 1930,F 21,23:3
Little Black Book, The 1932,D 27,11:2
Re-Echo 1934,Ja 12,28:4
Moor Born 1934,Ap 4,26:4
Order Please 1934,O 10,21:2
Moon Over Mulberry Street 1935,S 5,24:6
Black Widow 1936,F 13,24:3
Hallowe'en 1936,F 21,20:3
London Assurance 1937,F 19,14:5
Don't Throw Glass Houses 1938,D 28,24:4
Day in the Sun 1939,My 17,29:2
Horse Fever 1940,N 25,21:2
First Stop to Heaven 1941,Ja 6,10:7
Brother Cain 1941,S 13,21:5
Anybody Home 1949,F 26,10:5
Twelfth Night 1949,O 4,33:2
Twelfth Night 1949,O 9,II,1:1
Springtime Folly 1951,F 27,23:4
Red Rainbow, A 1953,S 15,37:4
Waiting for Godot 1956,Ap 20,21:2
Waiting for Godot 1957,Ja 22,25:1
Difficult Woman, The 1962,Ap 26,22:7
Kennell, Louis (Scenic Designer)
Hangman's House 1926,D 17,27:2
Magic Touch, The 1947,S 4,30:1
Kennell, Murray
Merchant of Venice, The 1928,Ja 17,22:2
Kennell, Ruth (Playwright)
They All Come to Moscow 1933,My 12,20:6
Kennelly, Francis
Silver Tassie, The 1929,O 25,26:1
Playboy of the Western World, The 1930,Ja 3,20:4
General John Regan 1930,Ja 30,16:5
Threepenny Opera, The 1933,Ap 14,22:4
Kennelly, Norman (Playwright)
Undercover Man 1966,Je 3,30:2
Kenneth, Leroy
Pride 1923,My 3,22:3
Kenneths, Louis
Thomas Paine 1930,Mr 21,30:7
Kennett, David
Wilson in the Promise Land 1970,Ja 11,78:1
Wilson in the Promise Land 1970,My 27,41:1
Kennett, Luther (Director)
Burning Glass, The 1954,Mr 5,15:2
Kennett, Luther M
Art and Mrs Bottle 1936,S 2,18:1
Kennett, Rebekah
Rapid Transit 1927,Ap 8,21:2
Kenney, Ed
Shangri-La 1956,Je 14,40:1
Flower Drum Song 1958,D 2,44:1
Flower Drum Song 1958,D 7,II,5:1
13 Daughters 1961,Mr 3,17:2
Kenney, Ethel
Respectfully Yours 1947,My 14,29:4
Kenney, James E (Producer)
Forbidden Roads 1928,Ap 17,26:4
White Flame 1929,N 5,32:7
Absent Father 1932,O 18,23:5
Kenney, Kay (Playwright)
Gypsy Love; Moon Rises, The 1934,Ap 16,21:6
Kenney, Laurie
Crime and Crime 1963,D 17,51:2
Kenney, Marie
Jamboree 1932,N 25,18:4
Suds in Your Eye 1944,Ja 13,15:5
Kennington, Alan (Playwright)
Time and the Hour 1936,O 5,24:1
Kennon-Wilson, James
Mardi Gras! 1965,Je 28,33:2
Hello, Dolly! 1967,N 13,61:1
Kenny, Charles (Composer)
Belmont Varieties 1932,S 29,17:2
Kenny, Charles (Lyricist)
Belmont Varieties 1932,S 29,17:2
Kenny, James
Purple Dust 1956,D 28,15:1
Drums Under the Windows 1960,O 14,26:1
Friends and Lovers; In the Zone; Bound East for
Cardiff 1961,My 11,43:1

Six Characters in Search of an Author
1961,My 11,43:1
One Way Pendulum 1961,S 19,38:2
Figuro in the Night 1962,O 31,33:1
Moon Shines on Kylenamoe, The 1962,O 31,33:1
Abe Lincoln in Illinois 1963,Ja 23,5:2
Hard Travelin' 1965,Je 17,25:1
Lonesome Train, The 1965,Je 17,25:1
Great White Hope, The 1967,D 14,58:1
Iceman Cometh, The 1968,Ap 1,58:1
Kenny, Patricia
War Song, The 1928,S 25,29:3
Kenny, Richard
Seeds in the Wind 1948,Ap 26,27:2
Seeds in the Wind 1948,My 26,29:2
Kenny, Sean (Costume Designer)
Hamlet 1963,O 23,37:2
Kenny, Sean (Lighting Director)
Stop the World-I Want to Get Off 1962,O 4,45:4
Roar of the Greasepaint-the Smell of the Crowd
1965,My 17,46:2
Kenny, Sean (Scenic Designer)
Romeo and Juliet 1961,Ag 16,36:3
Stop the World-I Want to Get Off 1962,O 4,45:4
Stop the World-I Want to Get Off 1962,O 14,II,1:1
Oliver 1963,Ja 8,5:5
Pickwick 1963,Jl 5,13:2
Beggar's Opera, The 1963,Jl 17,20:1
Hamlet 1963,O 23,37:2
Roar of the Greasepaint-the Smell of the Crowd
1965,My 17,46:2
Pickwick 1965,O 6,5:3
Oliver 1966,F 5,32:2
Kenny, Sharon
Mamba's Daughters 1953,Mr 21,12:6
Kenny, Thomas
Seven Lively Arts 1944,D 8,26:6
Kenny, Walter
Sandro Botticelli 1923,Mr 27,24:2
Good Bad Woman, A 1925,F 10,21:1
Hangman's House 1926,D 17,27:2
Keno, Joe
Whirl of New York, The 1921,Je 14,18:1
Keno and Green
Vaudeville (Hippodrome) 1926,My 8,29:2
Vaudeville (Palace) 1928,D 31,9:3
Kenrick, Marie
Open House 1925,D 15,28:3
Kensington, K K
Men of Distinction 1953,My 1,18:4
Kent, Alice
Age and Grace 1956,F 21,38:2
Kent, Allegra
Shinbone Alley 1957,Ap 15,23:2
Shinbone Alley 1957,Ap 28,II,1:1
Kent, Anthony
Ghost for Sale 1941,S 30,27:4
Food for Midas 1942,Ja 31,12:7
Kent, Arthur
I Married an Angel 1938,My 12,26:2
Kent, Bally
Camelot 1964,Ag 20,34:1
Kent, Barbara
Happy Days 1941,My 14,24:2
Foolish Notion 1945,Mr 14,23:2
Foolish Notion 1945,Mr 18,II,1:1
Kent, Bertha
Sacred and Profane Love 1920,F 24,11:1
Kent, Carl (Costume Designer)
As We Forgive Our Debtors 1947,Mr 11,37:2
Kent, Carl (Director)
Love, Honor and Oh Baby 1940,Mr 29,25:2
Kent, Carl (Lighting Director)
Peepshow 1944,F 4,12:2
Rip Van Winkle 1947,Jl 16,28:2
Kent, Carl (Miscellaneous)
Peepshow 1944,F 4,12:2
Kent, Carl (Scenic Designer)
'Tis of Thee 1940,O 28,21:3
Career Angel 1944,My 24,23:7
As We Forgive Our Debtors 1947,Mr 11,37:2
Rip Van Winkle 1947,Jl 16,28:2
Leaf and Bough 1949,Ja 22,10:2
Kent, Charlotte
Big Mogul, The Big Mogul, The 1925,My 12,26:3
Kent, Charlotte (Composer)
Illustrators' Show, The 1936,Ja 23,25:3
Kent, Charlotte (Playwright)
Sing for Your Supper 1939,Ap 25,18:6
Kent, Craufurd
Charlatan, The 1922,Ap 25,14:2
Kent, Doris
Banjo Eyes 1941,D 26,20:2
Kent, Edgar
John Hawthorne 1921,Ja 24,16:1
Great Adventure, The 1921,F 26,9:2
Pinch Hitter, A 1922,Je 2,20:4
If Winter Comes 1923,Ap 3,26:1
Madame Pompadour 1924,N 12,20:6
Grand Street Follies, The 1925,Je 19,24:1
Dybbuk, The 1925,D 16,22:2
Dybbuk, The 1926,D 17,27:2
Julius Caesar 1927,Je 7,27:2

Kent, Edgar—Cont
Escape 1927,O 27,33:1
Major Barbara 1928,N 20,28:4
Major Barbara 1928,D 2,X,1:1
Dynamo 1929,F 12,22:1
R U R 1930,F 18,28:1
Volpone 1930,Mr 11,24:5
Alchemist, The 1931,Je 5,27:1
Lady With a Lamp, The 1931,N 20,27:2
Firebird 1932,N 22,25:2
Distant Shore, The 1935,F 22,26:2
If This Be Treason 1935,S 24,28:2
Mainly for Lovers 1936,F 22,13:2
And Stars Remain 1936,O 13,32:2
And Now Goodbye 1937,F 3,26:4
Young Mr Disraeli 1937,N 10,30:5
Trojan Women, The 1941,Ap 9,32:5
White Cargo 1941,My 14,24:3
I Killed the Count 1942,S 4,18:1
Innocent Voyage, The 1943,N 16,27:2
Rebecca 1945,Ja 19,17:2
Dancer, The 1946,Je 6,16:5
Where's Charley? 1948,O 12,33:2
Merchant of Venice, The 1955,Ja 8,9:7
Kent, Edward
Wandering Jew, The 1921,O 27,22:1
Kent, Elaine
Scene of the Crime, The 1940,Mr 29,24:1
Kent, Elsie
Little Inn, The 1935,Ag 20,25:1
Kent, Enid
Our Town 1969,N 28,50:1
Kent, Gerald
Brass Buttons 1927,D 6,26:3
That's Gratitude 1930,S 12,28:1
That's Gratitude 1930,S 21,IX,1:1
New York to Cherbourg 1932,F 20,11:4
Angeline Moves In 1932,Ap 20,27:5
That's Gratitude 1932,Je 17,24:3
Divine Drudge 1933,Jl 4,16:4
Divine Drudge 1933,O 27,22:3
Arrest That Woman 1936,S 19,20:4
Iron Men 1936,O 20,30:6
Kent, Gordon
Life Begins in '40 1940,Ap 5,24:2
Kent, Guy (Costume Designer)
Magnolia Alley 1949,Ap 19,29:2
Pink Elephant, The 1953,Ap 23,37:2
Innkeepers, The 1956,F 3,19:1
Wake Up, Darling 1956,My 3,34:2
Uncle Willie 1956,D 21,17:1
Midgie Purvis 1961,F 2,25:3
Let It Ride 1961,O 13,27:4
Boys From Syracuse, The 1963,Ap 16,31:1
Kent, Howard
This Our House 1935,D 12,33:3
Kent, James
Everyman 1941,My 9,19:2
Kent, Kenneth
St Helena 1936,F 5,15:8
St Helena 1936,Mr 8,IX,1:1
Muted Strings 1936,N 11,54:4
To Have and to Hold 1937,Je 9,31:2
To Have and to Hold 1937,Je 27,X,1:3
Kent, Lennie
Hairpin Harmony 1943,O 2,18:5
Kent, Lucille
Girl in the Spotlight, The 1920,Jl 13,9:3
Kent, Madalyn
Pietro 1920,Ja 20,10:2
Kent, Margaret
Rut, The 1923,My 8,22:3
Kent, Mildred
Flossie 1924,Je 4,25:2
Seventh Heart, The 1927,My 3,24:4
Girl From Wyoming, The 1938,O 31,12:1
Kent, Peter (Producer)
Leave It to Jane 1959,My 26,30:2
Kent, Rikel
Exile, The 1923,Ap 10,24:2
Nigger Rich 1929,S 21,16:7
Kent, S Miller
Tomorrow's a Holiday! 1935,D 31,10:2
Kent, Sandra
Zulu and the Zayda, The 1965,N 11,59:1
Kent, Stanley
No Trifling With Love 1959,N 10,55:3
Kent, Stapleton
Marry the Poor Girl 1920,S 27,18:3
Danger 1921,D 23,18:3
Out of the Seven Seas 1923,N 20,23:3
Blue Bird, The 1923,D 26,13:3
Garden of Eden, The 1927,S 28,28:1
Behavior of Mrs Crane, The 1928,Mr 21,30:1
Scotland Yard 1929,S 28,16:6
Mayfair 1930,Mr 18,30:5
Melo 1931,Ap 17,26:6
Melo 1931,O 20,29:3
Barrister, The 1932,N 22,25:2
Whatever Possessed Her 1934,Ja 26,21:2
Play, Genius, Play! 1935,O 31,17:2
Damaged Goods 1937,My 18,27:2
She Gave Him All She Had 1939,D 2,20:7
All Men Are Alike 1941,O 7,27:2

Kent, Stapleton—Cont
Plan M 1942,F 21,15:2
Boy Who Lived Twice, A 1945,S 12,31:2
Trial Honeymoon 1947,N 4,31:2
Kent, Stephen
One Thing After Another 1937,D 29,17:2
Kent, Walter (Composer)
Seventeen 1951,Je 22,16:6
Seventeen 1951,Jl 1,II,1:1
Kent, Walter (Miscellaneous)
Let Freedom Sing 1942,O 6,18:2
Kent, William
Pitter Patter 1920,S 29,12:2
Good Morning, Dearie 1921,N 2,20:2
Battling Buttler 1923,O 9,17:2
Rose Marie 1924,S 3,12:2
Love Spell, The 1925,N 25,14:2
Lady Be Good 1926,Ap 15,25:1
Funny Face 1927,N 23,28:2
Ups-A-Daisy 1928,O 9,34:2
Girl Crazy 1930,O 15,27:1
Girl Crazy 1930,D 28,VIII,1:1
Little Racketeer, The 1932,Ja 19,24:4
Kenter, Else
Tanzgraefin, Die 1925,S 18,26:3
Kenter, Heinz (Director)
Dreyfus Affair, The 1930,Mr 30,VIII,4:1
Kenter, Heinz (Producer)
Marguerite Divided by Three 1930,S 28,VIII,4:4
Kentish, David
Henry IV, Part I 1946,My 7,25:2
Henry IV, Part II 1946,My 8,33:4
Kentish, Elizabeth
Caesar and Cleopatra 1951,D 20,43:2
Antony and Cleopatra 1951,D 21,22:2
Kenton, Barry
Saint, The 1924,O 13,20:3
Rat, The 1925,F 11,19:3
Kenton, Godfrey
Time and the Conways 1938,Ja 4,19:2
Edward, My Son 1948,O 1,30:2
Kentucky Beau Brummel Orchestra
Vaudeville (Hippodrome) 1924,Ap 1,18:1
Kenward, Allan R (Director)
Proof Thro' the Night 1942,D 26,14:2
Kenward, Allan R (Playwright)
Cry Havoc 1942,N 8,VIII,1:7
Proof Thro' the Night 1942,D 26,14:2
Kenwith, Herbert
I Remember Mama 1944,O 20,16:2
Kenwith, Herbert (Director)
Friday Night; River, The 1965,F 9,42:5
Friday Night; Passport 1965,F 9,42:5
Friday Night; Mary Agnes Is Thirty-Five 1965,F 9,42:5
Kenwith, Herbert (Producer)
Me and Molly 1948,F 27,27:2
Kenworthy, Patricia
Egoists, The 1959,O 14,52:2
Kenyon, Bernice
Order Please 1934,O 10,21:2
Kenyon, Charles (Playwright)
Top O' the Hill 1929,N 27,30:4
Kenyon, Doris
White Villa, The 1921,F 15,7:1
Up the Ladder 1922,Mr 7,11:2
Gift, The 1924,Ja 23,15:4
Bride, The 1924,F 24,VII,2:5
Royal Exchange 1935,D 7,22:3
Kenyon, Ethel
Strike Up the Band 1930,Ja 15,29:1
Kenyon, Fred
Wedding in Japan 1957,Mr 12,37:7
Breaking Wall, The 1960,Ja 26,27:5
Kenyon, Joan
Holiday 1930,F 6,21:2
Guest Room, The 1931,O 7,29:2
Kenyon, Joel
Government Inspector, The 1967,Je 15,55:1
Antony and Cleopatra 1967,Ag 2,25:1
Government Inspector, The 1967,O 28,34:1
Romeo and Juliet 1968,Je 11,55:2
Midsummer Night's Dream, A 1968,Je 13,54:1
Seagull, The 1968,Jl 25,27:2
Hamlet 1969,Je 11,37:1
Alchemist, The 1969,Je 12,51:1
Measure for Measure 1969,Je 13,41:3
Merchant of Venice, The 1970,Je 10,39:1
School for Scandal, The 1970,Je 11,51:1
Kenyon, Larry (Lighting Director)
Poupees de Paris, Les 1962,D 13,8:2
Kenyon, Nancy
Show Boat 1946,Ja 7,17:2
Kenyon, Neal
Boy Friend, The 1958,Ja 27,24:4
Kenyon, Neal (Choreographer)
Streets of New York, The 1963,O 30,47:1
Dames at Sea 1968,D 21,46:1
Dames at Sea 1969,Ag 29,24:3
Dames at Sea 1970,Ja 5,46:3
Dames at Sea 1970,S 24,60:1
Kenyon, Neal (Director)
Dames at Sea 1968,D 21,46:1
Dames at Sea 1969,Ag 29,24:3

Dames at Sea 1970,Ja 5,46:3
Dames at Sea 1970,S 24,60:1
Kenyon, Sandy
Purple Dust 1956,D 28,15:1
Pale Horse, Pale Rider 1957,O 30,26:1
Conversation at Midnight 1964,N 13,27:1
Promises to Keep 1965,Jl 22,25:1
Kenyon, Taldo
Those That Play the Clowns 1966,N 25,48:1
Kenzel, F L (Rev) (Playwright)
Pilate's Daughter 1927,Mr 7,17:2
Kenzie, Alfred P (Composer)
Lost Child's Fireflies, A 1954,Jl 16,11:4
Keo, Taki and Yoki
Vaudeville (Palace) 1926,Je 15,23:3
Keo, Tom
Butterfly Dream, The 1966,My 20,41:1
Keogan, James
Jubilee 1935,O 14,20:1
So Proudly We Hail 1936,S 23,28:4
Keogh, Frank
Wheel, The 1921,Ag 30,10:1
Keogh, J Augustus
Juno and the Paycock 1926,Mr 16,22:1
This Woman Business 1926,D 8,25:1
Sherlock Holmes 1929,N 26,28:3
King Lear 1930,D 26,18:2
Inside Story 1942,O 30,22:2
Keogh, J Augustus (Director)
General John Regan 1930,Ja 30,16:5
Mr Jiggins of Jigginstown 1936,D 18,30:2
Riders to the Sea 1937,F 15,13:2
Workhouse Ward, The 1937,F 15,13:2
Rising of the Moon, The 1937,F 15,13:2
Fiddler's House, The 1941,Mr 28,27:5
Keogh, Thomas J
Roger Bloomer 1923,Mr 2,18:3
Keohane, Norma
Seven Mirrors 1945,O 26,17:2
Kepros, Nicholas
Golden Six, The 1958,O 27,31:2
What Did You Say "What" For? 1959,My 5,40:1
Redemptor, The 1959,My 5,40:1
Julius Caesar 1959,Ag 4,30:1
Henry IV 1960,Mr 2,42:1
She Stoops to Conquer 1960,N 2,42:5
Hamlet 1961,Mr 17,17:1
Androcles and the Lion 1961,N 22,24:2
Taming of the Shrew, The 1963,Mr 8,9:1
Winter's Tale, The 1963,Je 29,13:1
Midsummer Night's Dream, A 1963,Jl 1,19:2
White Rose and the Red, The 1964,Mr 17,31:1
Measure for Measure 1964,Jl 27,22:3
Saint Joan 1968,Ja 5,42:1
Endecott and the Red Cross 1968,My 7,50:1
Millionairess, The 1969,Mr 3,28:1
Narrow Road to the Deep North 1969,D 2,64:1
Jungle of Cities 1970,Mr 1,75:2
Wars of the Roses, The (Part I) 1970,Jl 2,30:1
Wars of the Roses, The (Part II) 1970,Jl 3,15:1
Richard III 1970,Jl 4,11:1
Henry VI, Parts I, II, III 1970,Jl 5,II,3:1
In 3 Zones 1970,N 3,28:1
Ker, Paul
Blossom Time 1921,S 30,10:1
Nica 1926,Ja 26,19:1
Half-Naked Truth, The 1926,Je 8,23:1
Constant Nymph, The 1926,D 10,31:1
Get Me in the Movies 1928,My 22,18:3
War Song, The 1928,S 25,29:3
Ker, William
Fatal Wedding, The 1924,Je 3,22:3
Ker-Appleby, Stephen
Bachelor Born 1938,Ja 26,26:3
Ker-Shaw, James (Miscellaneous)
Tiger at the Gates 1968,Mr 1,30:1
Kerans, James (Director)
Sourball 1969,Ag 6,29:2
Kerbler, Eva
Konzert, Das 1968,Mr 25,52:1
Kerby, Frederick
Dope 1926,Ja 4,16:3
Kerby, Marion
Easiest Way, The 1921,S 7,14:1
Seventh Heaven 1922,O 31,11:1
Pearl of Great Price, The 1926,N 2,34:3
Honeymooning 1927,Mr 18,25:3
Banshee, The 1927,D 6,26:2
John Ferguson 1928,Ja 18,23:1
Kerby, Marion (Director)
Honeymooning 1927,Mr 18,25:3
Kerby, Paul (Lyricist)
Rosalinda; Fledermaus, Die 1942,O 29,26:5
Kercheval, Judith
Dream of a Blacklisted Actor 1969,D 18,64:1
Kercheval, Ken
Glory in the Flower 1959,D 9,57:5
Purification, The 1959,D 9,57:5
Young Abe Lincoln 1961,Ap 26,36:1
Something About a Soldier 1962,Ja 5,36:2
Black Monday 1962,Mr 7,29:1
Man's a Man, A 1962,S 20,30:2
Happily Never After 1966,Mr 11,37:1

Kercheval, Ken—Cont
Father Uxbridge Wants to Marry 1967,O 30,57:1
Here's Where I Belong 1968,Mr 4,32:1
Who's Happy Now? 1969,N 18,39:1
Kerekjarto, Duci de
Vaudeville (Palace) 1927,D 13,33:5
Kerff, Arnold
In Time to Come 1941,D 29,20:2
Kerker, Gustave (Composer)
Belle of New York, The 1948,D 2,36:6
Kerker, Gustave (Miscellaneous)
Some Party 1922,Ap 17,22:1
Kerker, Gustave (Playwright)
Whirl of New York, The 1921,Je 14,18:1
Kerman, David
Vegetable, The, or From President to Postman 1929,Ap 11,32:3
Sea Gull, The 1929,S 17,34:1
Living Corpse, The 1929,D 7,19:1
Lady of the Camellias, The 1931,Ja 27,21:2
Dark Hours, The 1932,N 15,24:2
Peace on Earth 1933,N 30,39:2
Sailors of Cattaro 1934,D 11,28:4
Young Go First, The 1935,My 29,16:2
Steps Leading Up 1941,Ap 19,20:6
Lily of the Valley 1942,Ja 27,25:2
Strip for Action 1942,O 1,26:2
Sappho 1960,Ja 12,22:1
Too Close for Comfort 1960,F 3,27:2
Love Your Crooked Neighbor 1969,D 30,40:1
Kerman, Sheppard
Prescott Proposals, The 1953,D 17,53:1
Tonight in Samarkand 1955,F 17,22:2
Great Sebastians, The 1956,Ja 5,27:1
Two Gentlemen of Verona 1957,Jl 23,21:5
Richard III 1957,N 26,41:1
As You Like It 1958,Ja 21,33:6
Oklahoma! 1958,Mr 20,32:3
Fools Are Passing Through 1958,Ap 3,24:2
Projection Room, The 1969,Ja 15,38:2
Kerman, Sheppard (Director)
Mr Simian 1963,O 22,44:1
Kerman, Sheppard (Playwright)
Cut of the Axe 1960,F 2,38:2
Mr Simian 1963,O 22,44:1
Kermond, Eric
Ice Follies 1959,Ja 14,30:1
Ice Follies 1961,Ja 11,25:2
Ice Follies 1962,Ja 10,24:6
Ice Follies 1963,Ja 10,5:2
Kermond, Norman
Ice Follies 1961,Ja 11,25:2
Ice Follies 1962,Ja 10,24:6
Ice Follies 1963,Ja 10,5:2
Kermond Brothers
Ice Follies 1957,Ja 16,36:1
Ice Follies 1958,Ja 15,26:2
Ice Follies 1959,Ja 14,30:1
Ice Follies 1960,Ja 13,20:1
Ice Follies 1965,Ja 13,35:1
Kermoyan, Michael
Sandhog 1954,N 24,17:1
Oklahoma! 1958,Mr 8,15:2
Whoop-Up 1958,D 23,2:7
Happy Town 1959,O 8,49:2
Camelot 1960,D 5,42:1
Happiest Girl in the World, The 1961,Ap 4,42:1
Fly Blackbird 1962,F 6,26:2
Angels of Anadarko 1962,O 11,47:1
Tovarich 1963,Mr 20,5:1
King and I, The 1964,Jl 7,26:1
Something More! 1964,N 11,36:1
Anya 1965,N 30,48:1
Carousel 1966,D 16,56:2
Guide, The 1968,Mr 7,50:1
King and I, The 1968,My 24,39:1
Kern, Adele
Fledermaus, Die 1929,Jl 14,IX,2:1
Schon Ist die Welt; Endlich Allein 1932,Ja 17,VIII,2:1
Kern, Cecil
Something to Brag About 1925,Ag 14,14:3
Morals 1925,D 1,22:2
Gringa, La 1928,F 2,17:1
Kern, Grace
9th Street Guest, The 1930,Ag 26,24:3
Kern, Jerome (Composer)
Night Boat, The 1920,F 3,18:1
Charm School, The 1920,Ag 3,12:1
Hitchy-Koo, 1920 1920,O 20,11:3
Sally 1920,D 22,16:1
Good Morning, Dearie 1921,N 2,20:2
Good Morning, Dearie 1921,N 6,VI,1:1
Good Morning, Dearie 1921,N 27,VI,1:1
Bunch and Judy, The 1922,N 12,VIII,1:6
Bunch and Judy, The 1922,N 29,20:1
Stepping Stones 1923,N 7,14:3
Sitting Pretty 1924,Mr 30,VIII,2:7
Dear Sir 1924,S 24,21:3
Sunny 1925,S 23,22:1
City Chap, The 1925,O 27,21:1
Criss Cross 1926,O 13,20:2
Lucky 1927,Mr 23,28:3
Show Boat 1927,D 28,26:1

Kern, Jerome (Composer)—Cont

Show Boat 1928,Ja 8,VIII,1:1
Pleased to Meet You 1928,O 30,27:2
Sweet Adeline 1929,Ag 25,VIII,3:1
Sweet Adeline 1929,S 4,33:1
Sweet Adeline 1929,S 15,IX,1:8
Cat and the Fiddle, The 1931,S 27,VIII,3:1
Cat and the Fiddle, The 1931,O 16,26:4
Show Boat 1932,My 20,22:2
Show Boat 1932,My 29,VIII,5:6
Music in the Air 1932,O 23,IX,3:3
Music in the Air 1932,N 9,28:2
Music in the Air 1932,N 20,IX,1:1
Roberta 1933,N 20,18:4
Roberta 1935,Ag 18,II,3:2
Roberta 1937,Je 27,II,6:1
Roberta 1937,S 7,16:4
Gentlemen Unafraid 1938,Je 5,II,6:8
Mamba's Daughters 1939,Ja 4,24:2
Mamba's Daughters 1939,Ja 15,IX,1:1
Very Warm for May 1939,N 12,IX,2:3
Hay-Foot, Straw-Foot 1942,O 24,11:6
Show Boat 1946,Ja 13,II,1:1
Sally 1948,My 7,31:2
Show Boat 1948,S 19,II,1:1
Music in the Air 1951,O 9,32:2
Music in the Air 1951,O 21,II,1:1
Show Boat 1954,My 6,44:1
Show Boat 1956,Je 22,16:1
Leave It to Jane 1959,My 26,30:2
Round With Ring, A 1969,O 30,56:1

Kern, Jerome (Director)

Music in the Air 1932,N 9,28:2

Kern, Jerome (Lyricist)

Show Boat 1932,My 29,VIII,5:6
Mamba's Daughters 1939,Ja 15,IX,1:1
Mamba's Daughters 1940,Mr 25,10:4

Kern, Jerome (Miscellaneous)

Show Boat 1946,Ja 7,17:2

Kern, Jerome (Playwright)

Sitting Pretty 1924,Ap 9,24:2
Show Boat 1938,Je 30,21:1
Very Warm for May 1939,N 18,23:2
Show Boat 1946,Ja 7,17:2
Show Boat 1948,S 9,33:2
Show Boat 1957,Je 28,30:2
Show Boat 1961,Ap 13,32:1
Show Boat 1966,Jl 20,48:1

Kern, Mabel

Under the Gaslight 1929,Ap 3,27:1

Kern, Malcolm

Great Experiment, The 1936,Ap 22,28:4

Kern, Mina

Mother's Sabbath Days 1960,N 21,33:2
Backlane Center 1961,N 23,51:1
Eleventh Inheritor, The 1962,N 22,43:5
Sage of Rottenburg, The 1963,N 20,48:1
Enchanting Melody 1964,N 25,40:1
Fifth Commandment, The 1965,N 15,48:4
Wandering Stars 1966,N 14,52:2
Brothers Ashkenazi, The 1970,N 17,53:2

Kern, Minnie

Prince Reuvaini 1967,N 19,83:1

Kernan, David

God Strikes Back 1943,F 27,11:2

Kernell, John

Measure for Measure 1960,Jl 27,33:1

Kernell, William B (Composer)

Hello, Lola! 1926,Ja 13,30:1

Kerner, Ben (Playwright)

All Women Are One 1965,Ja 8,21:1

Kerner, Mlle

Bourgeois Gentilhomme, Le 1955,O 26,26:1

Kerns, Rhoda

Shoestring Revue 1955,Mr 1,22:2

Kerns, Robert

Mikado, The 1959,O 2,24:1

Kerns, Stuart

High Button Shoes 1955,Mr 12,10:6

Kerr, Allan (Lighting Director)

Egoists, The 1959,O 14,52:2
Madame Lafayette 1960,Mr 4,21:1

Kerr, Allan (Scenic Designer)

Egoists, The 1959,O 14,52:2
Madame Lafayette 1960,Mr 4,21:1

Kerr, Alvin

Lolly 1929,O 17,26:2
Novice and the Duke, The 1929,D 11,37:2
Everything's Jake 1930,Ja 17,20:4
Five Star Final 1930,D 31,11:1
Babes in Arms 1937,Ap 15,18:4

Kerr, Alvin (Playwright)

Plum Hollow 1935,Je 16,II,6:7

Kerr, Berilla

God Innis 1937,Ag 25,24:3

Kerr, Betty

May Wine 1935,D 6,30:3
Forbidden Melody 1936,N 3,33:1

Kerr, Constance

Adam Had Two Sons 1932,Ja 21,17:1

Kerr, Deborah

Tea and Sympathy 1953,O 1,35:1
Tea and Sympathy 1953,O 11,II,1:1

Kerr, Donald

Poor Little Ritz Girl 1920,Jl 29,7:1
All-Star Jamboree 1921,Jl 14,18:1
Talk About Girls 1927,Je 15,31:3

Kerr, Elaine

Trojan Women, The 1963,D 24,7:6

Kerr, Elizabeth

Angel in the Pawnshop 1951,Ja 19,20:3
Conquering Hero, The 1961,Ja 17,40:2
Her Master's Voice 1964,D 28,33:2

Kerr, Fred

Just Suppose 1920,N 7,VII,1:1
Pelican, The 1925,S 22,23:2
High Road, The 1927,S 25,VIII,2:1
Middle Watch, The 1929,O 17,27:1

Kerr, Frederick

Czarina, The 1922,F 1,22:1
Kiss of Importance, A 1930,D 2,31:3

Kerr, Frederick (Director)

Pelican, The 1925,S 22,23:2

Kerr, Garland

Noble Experiment, The 1930,O 28,21:4
Man on Stilts, The 1931,S 10,23:2
When in Rome 1934,F 28,22:6

Kerr, Geoffrey

Just Suppose 1920,N 2,15:1
Just Suppose 1920,N 7,VII,1:1
East of Suez 1922,S 22,16:3
You and I 1923,F 20,12:1
Changelings, The 1923,S 18,16:3
Changelings, The 1923,S 30,II,1:1
In His Arms 1924,O 14,23:1
Stork, The 1925,Ja 27,14:2
Vaudeville (Palace) 1926,Ag 10,19:4
First Love 1926,N 9,31:2
Our Little Wife 1927,My 10,25:3
Manhattan Mary 1927,S 27,30:3
Bachelor Father, The 1928,F 29,28:2
London Calling 1930,O 20,29:1
This Is New York 1930,N 29,21:1
Collision 1932,F 17,19:2
We Are No Longer Children 1932,Ap 1,17:2
Domino 1932,Ag 7,IX,1:1
Domino 1932,Ag 17,13:2
Foolscap 1933,Ja 12,21:2
Yellow Jack 1934,Mr 7,22:6
I Know My Love 1949,F 24,29:2
I Know My Love 1949,N 3,36:1

Kerr, Geoffrey (Director)

Ada Beats the Drum 1930,My 9,20:4
Foolscap 1933,Ja 12,21:2

Kerr, Geoffrey (Miscellaneous)

Lake, The 1933,D 27,24:2

Kerr, Geoffrey (Playwright)

Nine Fifteen Revue, The 1930,F 12,26:2
London Calling 1930,S 28,VIII,4:1
London Calling 1930,O 20,29:1
Sunday Nights at Nine 1934,N 19,12:1
Till the Cows Come Home 1936,O 28,30:6
Till the Cows Come Home 1936,N 15,XI,3:2
Black Swans 1938,Mr 6,XI,3:6
Cottage to Let 1940,Ag 11,IX,2:5
Cottage to Let 1941,My 18,IX,1:5

Kerr, Jarvis

Ghosts 1927,Ja 11,36:3
Salvation 1928,F 1,31:1

Kerr, Jean (Lyricist)

Touch and Go 1949,O 14,34:2
Goldilocks 1958,O 13,33:1

Kerr, Jean (Playwright)

Song of Bernadette 1944,Jl 27,15:3
Song of Bernadette 1946,Mr 27,22:2
Jenny Kissed Me 1948,D 24,12:2
Touch and Go 1949,O 14,34:2
Touch and Go 1949,O 30,II,1:1
John Murray Anderson's Almanac 1953,D 11,42:2
Almanac 1954,Ja 3,II,1:1
King of Hearts 1954,Ap 2,23:1
King of Hearts 1954,Ap 11,II,1:1
Goldilocks 1958,O 13,33:1
Goldilocks 1958,O 19,II,1:1
Mary, Mary 1961,Mr 9,24:2
Poor Richard 1964,D 3,59:1

Kerr, John

Mamba's Daughters 1940,Mr 25,10:4
Bernardine 1952,O 17,33:4
Bernardine 1952,N 9,II,1:1
Tea and Sympathy 1953,O 1,35:1
Tea and Sympathy 1953,O 11,II,1:1
All Summer Long 1954,S 24,26:2
All Summer Long 1954,O 3,II,1:1
Infernal Machine, The 1958,F 4,33:1
Cue for Passion 1958,N 26,25:2
Cue for Passion 1958,D 7,II,5:1
Tenth Man, The 1967,N 9,54:1

Kerr, John H

Second Man, The 1930,My 2,23:2

Kerr, Kathleen

You Can't Take It With You 1951,Ap 7,8:6
Pygmalion 1952,F 9,11:2

Kerr, Leo (Lighting Director)

For Heaven's Sake Mother 1948,N 17,33:4

Kerr, Leo (Scenic Designer)

For Heaven's Sake Mother 1948,N 17,33:4

Kerr, Lily

Courage 1927,Ja 20,20:1
Escape 1927,O 27,33:1

Kerr, Molly

Vortex, The 1925,S 17,20:1
Escape 1926,S 12,VIII,2:1
Loose Ends 1926,N 2,34:2

Kerr, Nancy

Romeo and Juliet 1968,Je 11,55:2

Kerr, Peter

Tiger at the Gates 1955,O 4,40:1

Kerr, Philip

New York Idea, The 1963,Jl 13,12:2
Skin of Our Teeth, The 1966,Je 2,51:1
Dance of Death, The 1966,Je 3,31:1
As You Like It 1966,Je 4,19:1
Shoemaker's Holiday, The 1967,Je 3,19:1
Thieves' Carnival 1967,Je 5,52:1
Harpers Ferry 1967,Je 6,52:2
House of Atreus, The; Furies, The 1967,Jl 24,23:1
House of Atreus, The; Bringers of Offerings, The 1967,Jl 24,23:1
Hamlet 1968,Je 10,59:1
Tiny Alice 1969,S 30,42:1
Flea in Her Ear, A 1969,O 4,25:1
Three Sisters, The 1969,O 10,38:1

Kerr, Robert

Reunion of Sorts 1969,O 15,40:1

Kerr, Sophie (Playwright)

Big Hearted Herbert 1934,Ja 2,17:3

Kerr, Walter (Director)

Sing Out, Sweet Land! 1944,D 28,24:2
Song of Bernadette 1946,Mr 27,22:2
All Gaul Is Divided 1947,Je 24,27:3
Touch and Go 1949,O 14,34:2
Touch and Go 1949,O 30,II,1:1
King of Hearts 1954,Ap 2,23:1
Goldilocks 1958,O 13,33:1
Goldilocks 1958,O 19,II,1:1

Kerr, Walter (Lyricist)

Touch and Go 1949,O 14,34:2
Goldilocks 1958,O 13,33:1

Kerr, Walter (Miscellaneous)

King of Hearts 1954,Ap 11,II,1:1

Kerr, Walter (Playwright)

Yankee Doodle Boy 1939,D 19,29:5
Count Me In 1942,O 9,24:2
Sing Out, Sweet Land! 1944,Ja 7,II,1:1
Song of Bernadette 1944,Jl 27,15:3
Swing Out, Sweet Land! 1944,N 10,24:6
Sing Out, Sweet Land! 1944,D 28,24:2
Song of Bernadette 1946,Mr 27,22:2
Touch and Go 1949,O 14,34:2
Touch and Go 1949,O 30,II,1:1
Goldilocks 1958,O 13,33:1
Goldilocks 1958,O 19,II,1:1
Birds, The 1967,My 7,67:1

Kerr, William A

Grey Heir, The 1926,Ap 6,29:2

Kerras, Zito

Displaced Person, The 1966,D 30,15:1

Kerridge, Philip M Jr

Little Theatre Tournament; White Peacock, The 1928,My 11,28:1

Kerrigan, J M

Rollo's Wild Oat 1920,N 24,14:1
John Ferguson 1921,Je 21,20:2
Broken Branches 1922,Mr 7,11:1
Shadow, The 1922,Ap 25,14:2
Pinch Hitter, A 1922,Je 2,20:4
Ever Green Lady, The 1922,O 12,25:2
Romantic Age, The 1922,N 15,22:1
Rivals, The 1923,My 9,14:2
Scaramouche 1923,O 25,14:2
Outward Bound 1924,Ja 8,26:1
She Stoops to Conquer 1924,Je 10,24:3
Little Minister, The 1925,Mr 24,21:1
Rosmersholm 1925,My 6,27:2
Engaged! or Cheviot's Choice 1925,Je 19,24:2
Gypsy Fires 1925,D 8,28:3
Ghosts 1926,Mr 17,28:2
Bells, The 1926,Ap 14,20:3
Henry IV, Part I 1926,Je 1,29:1
White Wings 1926,O 16,15:1
Trelawney of the 'Wells' 1927,F 1,24:4
Grey Fox, The 1928,O 23,32:3
Meet the Prince 1929,F 26,30:5
Meet the Prince 1929,Mr 10,X,1:1
Barchester Towers 1937,D 1,27:1
Playboy of the Western World, The 1946,O 28,18:3
Moon for the Misbegotten, A 1947,F 21,16:2

Kerrigan, Kathleen

Laugh, Clown, Laugh! 1923,N 29,30:1

Kerrigan, Kevin

Beautiful Changes, The 1956,Mr 24,15:2

Kerry, Anita

New Brooms 1924,N 18,23:5
Fanatics, The 1927,N 8,32:4
Security 1929,Mr 29,20:1
Criminal Code, The 1929,O 3,28:2
Elizabeth the Queen 1930,N 4,37:1

Kerry, Anita—Cont
Springtime for Henry 1936,Je 30,15:1
Kerry, Joyce
O Say Can You See! 1962,O 9,45:1
Kerry, Lee
Louisiana Lady 1947,Je 3,35:2
Kerry, Otto
Professor Bernhardi 1968,Mr 20,38:1
Kerry, Richard (Costume Designer)
Does a Tiger Wear a Necktie? 1967,F 4,17:1
Kerry, Richard (Lighting Director)
Winter Journey 1968,Mr 13,39:1
Kerry, Richard (Scenic Designer)
Winter Journey 1968,Mr 13,39:1
Kerschell, William
Three Cheers 1928,O 16,28:1
Ripples 1930,F 12,26:1
Kersey, Mary Jane
Cyrano de Bergerac 1946,O 9,33:2
Cyrano de Bergerac 1947,Ja 17,27:2
Kershaw, Craig
Ballyhoo 1930,D 23,24:1
Kershaw, James (Miscellaneous)
Country Wife, The 1965,D 10,58:2
Caucasian Chalk Circle, The 1966,Mr 25,35:1
Alchemist, The 1966,O 14,48:1
East Wind, The 1967,F 10,30:1
Galileo 1967,Ap 14,31:1
Happiness 1967,N 11,25:2
Walking to Waldheim 1967,N 11,25:2
Kershaw, Wilette
Woman to Woman 1921,S 10,12:3
Decameron Nights 1922,Ap 21,14:5
Reno 1937,Ag 10,22:7
Kershaw, William
Havoc 1924,S 2,22:2
Marquise, The 1927,N 15,26:4
Three Musketeers, The 1928,Mr 14,28:1
His Majesty's Car 1930,O 24,30:1
School for Scandal, The 1931,N 11,26:4
Kert, Larry
Tickets, Please! 1950,Ap 28,25:2
West Side Story 1957,S 27,14:4
West Side Story 1957,O 6,II,1:1
West Side Story 1960,Ap 28,31:1
Family Affair, A 1962,Ja 29,17:1
Cabaret 1969,F 2,74:2
Strada, La 1969,D 15,63:1
Company 1970,Jl 29,31:1
Kerwin, David
Me, Candido! 1956,O 16,36:2
Kerz, Leo (Costume Designer)
Bobino 1944,Ap 7,23:4
Flamingo Road 1946,Mr 20,18:2
Open House 1947,Je 4,33:4
Kerz, Leo (Director)
Moonbirds 1959,O 10,13:1
Kerz, Leo (Lighting Director)
Strange Play, A 1944,Je 2,20:3
According to Law 1944,Je 2,20:3
Private Life of the Master Race, The
 1945,Je 13,28:3
Christopher Blake 1946,D 2,33:2
Little A 1947,Ja 16,31:2
Heads or Tails 1947,My 3,10:6
Louisiana Lady 1947,Je 3,35:2
Open House 1947,Je 4,33:4
Long Way From Home, A 1948,F 9,25:2
Me and Molly 1948,F 27,27:2
Ti-Coq 1951,F 10,10:2
Sacred Flame, The 1952,O 8,35:2
Whistler's Grandmother 1952,D 12,40:2
Hit the Trail 1954,D 3,31:2
Clerambard 1957,N 8,22:3
Rhinoceros 1961,Ja 10,27:1
Hidden Stranger 1963,Ja 10,5:5
Damn You, Scarlett O'Hara 1964,F 5,30:1
All My Pretty Little Ones 1964,F 5,30:1
Kerz, Leo (Lyricist)
Biggest Thief in Town 1949,Mr 31,31:2
Kerz, Leo (Miscellaneous)
Sage of Rottenburg, The 1963,N 20,48:1
Kerz, Leo (Producer)
Clerambard 1957,N 8,22:3
Rhinoceros 1961,Ja 10,27:1
Kerz, Leo (Scenic Designer)
Savonarola 1942,Ap 24,20:2
Doodle Dandy of the U S A 1942,O 19,15:2
Bobino 1944,Ap 7,23:4
Private Life of the Master Race, The
 1945,Je 13,28:3
Open House 1947,Je 4,33:4
Antony and Cleopatra 1947,N 27,49:2
Antony and Cleopatra 1947,D 7,II,5:1
Long Way From Home, A 1948,F 9,25:2
Voice of Israel, The 1948,O 26,40:2
Bravo! 1948,N 12,31:2
Biggest Thief in Town 1949,Mr 31,31:2
Edwina Black 1950,N 22,20:5
Sacred Flame, The 1952,O 8,35:2
Whistler's Grandmother 1952,D 12,40:2
Hit the Trail 1954,D 3,31:2
Clerambard 1957,N 8,22:3
Moonbirds 1959,O 10,13:1

Rhinoceros 1961,Ja 10,27:1
Rhinoceros 1961,Ja 22,II,1:1
Hidden Stranger 1963,Ja 10,5:5
Burn Me to Ashes 1963,N 20,48:1
Damn You, Scarlett O'Hara 1964,F 5,30:1
All My Pretty Little Ones 1964,F 5,30:1
Kesdekian, Mesrop (Director)
Best Foot Forward 1956,Mr 3,16:1
Apollo of Bellac, The 1958,Mr 7,17:2
Browning Version, The 1958,Mr 7,17:2
Skin of Our Teeth, The 1960,O 14,24:1
Kesdekian, Mesrop (Lighting Director)
Best Foot Forward 1956,Mr 3,16:1
Annie Get Your Gun 1957,Mr 9,15:5
Kesdekian, Mesrop (Miscellaneous)
Absalom 1956,My 17,37:2
Kesdekian, Mesrop (Scenic Designer)
Apollo of Bellac, The 1958,Mr 7,17:2
Month in the Country, A 1959,Mr 2,32:2
Summer of the Seventeenth Doll 1959,O 14,52:1
Kesey, Ken (Original Author)
One Flew Over the Cuckoo's Nest 1963,N 14,40:2
Kesler, Lew (Composer)
Gypsy Lady 1946,S 18,25:6
Kesler, Lew (Director)
Almost Crazy 1955,Je 21,37:1
Kessel, Joseph (Original Author)
Equipage, L' 1930,Ap 13,X,2:7
Kesselring, Joseph (Playwright)
There's Wisdom in Women 1935,Jl 16,24:1
There's Wisdom in Women 1935,O 31,17:1
Cross-Town 1937,Mr 18,21:5
Arsenic and Old Lace 1941,Ja 11,13:2
Arsenic and Old Lace 1943,Ja 1,26:5
Arsenic And Old Lace 1943,Ja 10,VIII,1:6
Arsenic and Old Lace 1943,D 13,18:6
Four Twelves Are 48 1951,Ja 18,30:2
Arsenic and Old Lace 1970,N 5,59:1
Kessler, Beatrice
Wandering Stars 1946,D 14,18:2
Kessler, Jan (Director)
Anna Kleiber 1965,Ja 20,33:1
Masks of Angels 1965,Ja 20,33:1
Kessler, Jeni
Bride Got Farblondjet, The 1967,N 6,61:6
Kessler, Lew (Composer)
Ned Wayburn's Gambols 1929,Ja 16,22:3
Littlest Crown, The 1968,Ap 15,41:1
Kessler, Lyle (Director)
Viewing, The 1967,Ja 11,51:1
Kessler, Lyle (Playwright)
Viewing, The 1967,Ja 11,51:1
Watering Place, The 1969,Mr 13,51:1
Kessler, Mitch (Miscellaneous)
Limb of Snow 1967,D 13,55:1
Meeting, The 1967,D 13,55:1
Kessler, Natalie
Squealer, The 1928,N 13,36:3
Kessler, Philip (Costume Designer)
Trial Honeymoon 1947,N 4,31:2
Kessler, Philip (Scenic Designer)
Trial Honeymoon 1947,N 4,31:2
Kessler, R W
Tiger Smiles, The 1930,D 18,29:1
Kessler, Richard (Playwright)
Kiss Me! 1927,Jl 22,17:1
Kessler, Robert (Composer)
Fallout 1959,My 21,36:2
O Marry Me 1961,O 28,13:1
Kessler, Robert (Lyricist)
Fallout 1959,My 21,36:2
Kessler, Robyn
Light, Lively and Yiddish 1970,O 28,58:1
Kessler, Thelma
Hansel and Gretel 1929,D 25,21:1
Kessler, Zale
Nervous Set, The 1959,My 13,43:1
O, Oysters! 1961,Ja 31,23:1
Dear World 1969,F 7,33:1
Gantry 1970,F 16,44:1
Kessler (Playwright)
Liselott 1932,My 22,VIII,2:3
Kessner, Rose
Flossie 1924,Je 4,25:2
Kestelman, Sara
Midsummer Night's Dream, A 1970,Ag 28,15:1
Kesten, Herrmann (Lyricist)
Bourgeois Gentilhomme, Le 1929,Mr 24,X,2:3
Kestenbaum, Alex
Mighty Nimrod, The 1931,My 13,23:1
Dole Brothers 1932,Mr 26,17:7
Kester, Hermann (Playwright)
Miracle in America 1934,O 2,18:4
Kester, Paul (Playwright)
Woman of Bronze, The 1920,S 8,9:2
Sweet Nell of Old Drury 1923,My 19,16:4
Woman of Bronze, The 1927,Je 16,25:4
Lady Dedlock 1929,Ja 1,61:2
Tom Sawyer 1931,D 26,15:3
Tom Sawyer - Ballad of the Mississippi
 1947,D 27,11:3
Kester, William
Ninth Month Midnight 1949,F 17,28:2

Kester, William—Cont
Girl Can Tell, A 1953,O 30,28:2
Ketchum, Dave
Billy Barnes People, The 1961,Je 14,10:3
Ketchum, Edith
Passing of the Third Floor Back, The
 1937,Ag 3,20:6
Ketchum, Walter (Scenic Designer)
It's About Time 1942,Mr 31,28:3
Kettering, Ralph Thomas (Playwright)
Easy Street 1924,Ag 15,16:4
Clutching Claw, The 1928,F 15,20:1
Kettle, Audrey
Midsummer Night's Dream, A 1932,N 18,22:2
Keusch, Betty Hamilton (Mrs)
Volpone 1937,N 16,26:4
Keutgen, David C (Lyricist)
Hit the Road 1941,Ap 4,18:3
Keval, Mara
Poppa 1928,D 25,31:1
Wooden Soldier, The 1931,Je 23,28:4
Lingering Past, The 1932,Je 30,26:5
Kevan, Walter
Queer People 1934,F 16,16:2
Kevelers, The
Zizi 1964,N 23,51:1
Keveson, Peter (Playwright)
How Much, How Much? 1970,Ap 21,49:1
Kevin, Ilsa
New Faces of 1943 1942,D 23,22:2
Kevin, Lynn
Banquet for the Moon, A 1961,Ja 20,24:2
Effect of Gamma Rays on Man-in-the-Moon
 Marigolds, The 1965,Je 7,48:1
Key, Harold Eustace (Musical Director)
Prince Charlie and Flora 1931,Ag 29,16:5
Key, Leonard (Producer)
Pal Joey 1952,Ja 4,17:6
Once There Was a Russian 1961,F 20,32:2
Key, Mary
Alexander Hamilton 1949,Mr 30,29:2
Keyer, T Hall 3d (Miscellaneous)
Who Is Leslie? 1941,My 20,15:5
Keyes, Arthur H Jr (Scenic Designer)
Once Over Lightly 1938,D 10,13:4
Keyes, Betty
Singing Rabbi, The 1931,S 11,24:4
Keyes, Daniel
From Morn Till Midnight 1948,D 7,41:6
Butter and Egg Man, The 1949,Ap 29,27:1
Man Who Never Died, The 1958,N 22,27:2
Our Town 1959,Mr 24,46:2
Only in America 1959,N 20,35:1
Christine 1960,Ap 29,27:1
Epitaph for George Dillon 1960,D 29,17:1
Baker Street 1965,F 17,36:1
Hooray!! It's a Glorious Day. . .And All That
 1966,Mr 10,28:1
Dinner at Eight 1966,S 28,38:1
Arms and the Man 1967,Je 23,44:2
I Never Sang for My Father 1968,Ja 26,30:1
Wrong Way Light Bulb, The 1969,Mr 5,40:1
Place for Polly, A 1970,Ap 20,45:1
Keyes, Donald
Straw Hat, The 1926,O 15,20:2
Manhattan Nocturne 1943,O 27,26:2
Our Town 1944,Ja 11,24:5
Thank You Svoboda 1944,Mr 2,13:2
You Can't Take It With You 1945,Mr 27,23:7
Henry VIII 1946,N 7,42:2
Yellow Jack 1947,F 28,26:2
Alice in Wonderland 1947,Ap 7,19:2
Small Hours, The 1951,F 16,22:1
Mummers and Men 1962,Mr 27,41:6
Keyes, Edwrey
Little Poor Man, The 1925,Ag 6,14:1
Keyes, Evelyn
Keep Shufflin' 1928,F 28,18:3
Keyes, Frances
Louisiana Lady 1947,Je 3,35:2
Keyes, Gordon
Shadow and Substance 1956,Mr 14,38:1
Hamlet 1956,O 29,34:1
Parade at the Devil's Bridge 1957,F 19,35:7
Julius Caesar 1957,O 24,39:1
Keyes, Lloyd
Kid Boots 1924,Ja 1,21:3
Keyes, Peter
Lady Windermere's Fan 1946,O 15,29:2
Keys, Kathryn
Transplanting Jean 1921,Ja 4,11:2
Ghost Between, The 1921,Mr 23,11:2
Little Inn, The 1935,Ag 20,25:1
Prodigal Father, The 1937,Ag 17,23:1
Slightly Married 1943,O 26,19:2
Keys, Nelson
Charlot's Revue 1924,Ap 15,25:2
Spread It Abroad 1936,Ap 2,29:5
Spread It Abroad 1936,My 3,X,1:2
Home and Beauty 1937,F 3,26:2
Keysar, Franklin (Miscellaneous)
Wilson in the Promise Land 1970,My 27,41:1
Keyse, Connie
Empire Builders, The 1968,O 2,34:1

Keywan, Helene
Good Morning 1937,D 4,20:7
Kezer, Glenn
Walk in Darkness 1963,O 29,30:2
Trial of Lee Harvey Oswald, The 1967,N 6,64:1
Other Man, The 1968,F 9,50:1
Oh, Say Can You See L A 1968,F 9,50:1
Firebugs, The 1968,Jl 2,36:1
David Show, The 1968,N 1,34:2
Promenade 1969,Je 5,56:1
Kharklin, Hortense
Lady Comes Across, The 1942,Ja 10,10:2
Khemiri, Tahar el (Dr) (Translator)
Othello 1964,Ag 3,16:6
Khessin, A (Musical Director)
Porgy and Bess 1945,Je 17,II,4:3
Kholopova, Galina
Moscow Circus on Ice 1970,D 9,63:1
Kiamos, Eleni
Garden of Sweets, The 1961,N 1,35:1
Mike Downstairs 1968,Ap 19,35:1
Kibbe, S
Front Page, The 1937,N 12,27:2
Kibbee, Guy
Torch Song 1930,Ag 28,23:1
Torch Song 1930,S 7,IX,1:1
Marseilles 1930,N 18,28:2
Joy Forever, A 1946,Ja 8,20:2
Kibbee, Lois
As You Like It 1961,Je 17,13:2
Arms and the Man 1965,Je 24,32:5
Kibbee, Robert
Martyr Without Tears 1942,N 23,19:2
Kibbee, Roland
Achilles Had a Heel 1935,O 14,20:2
Kibrig, Joan
Conversation Piece 1957,N 19,38:2
Young Abe Lincoln 1961,Ap 26,36:1
Kibrig, Jordan
Macbeth 1955,O 20,42:2
Kichijuro, Nakamura
Kagotsurube; Courtesan, The 1960,Je 3,26:1
Chushingura; Forty-Seven Ronin, The 1960,Je 10,37:1
Musume Dojoji; Maiden at the Dojo Temple, The 1960,Je 10,37:1
Chushingura; Forty-Seven Ronin, The 1960,Je 17,35:4
Takatsuki; Clog Dance, The 1960,Je 17,35:4
Musume Dojoji; Maiden at the Dojo Temple, The 1960,Je 17,35:4
Kickey, John C
Dark Hours, The 1932,N 15,24:2
Kid, Baby
Legal Murder 1934,F 16,16:2
Kidd, John
Importance of Being Earnest, The 1947,Mr 4,30:2
Love for Love 1947,My 27,30:2
Kidd, Kathleen
Grand Street Follies, The 1929,My 2,20:4
Kidd, Michael (Choreographer)
Finian's Rainbow 1947,Ja 11,23:2
Hold It! 1948,My 6,31:5
Love Life 1948,O 8,31:2
Arms and the Girl 1950,F 3,28:2
Guys and Dolls 1950,N 25,11:2
Guys and Dolls 1950,D 3,II,1:1
Guys and Dolls 1951,O 7,II,1:1
Can-Can 1953,My 8,28:1
Can-Can 1953,My 17,II,1:1
Guys and Dolls 1955,Ap 21,32:2
Finian's Rainbow 1955,My 19,25:1
Li'l Abner 1956,N 16,24:2
Li'l Abner 1956,N 25,II,1:1
Destry Rides Again 1959,Ap 24,24:1
Destry Rides Again 1959,My 3,II,1:1
Subways Are for Sleeping 1961,D 28,22:1
Here's Love 1963,O 4,28:1
Wonder World 1964,My 18,32:1
Ben Franklin in Paris 1964,O 28,52:1
Skyscraper 1965,N 15,48:1
Breakfast at Tiffany's 1966,D 15,60:1
Rothschilds, The 1970,O 20,40:1
Rothschilds, The 1970,N 1,II,1:1
Kidd, Michael (Director)
Li'l Abner 1956,N 16,24:2
Destry Rides Again 1959,Ap 24,24:1
Destry Rides Again 1959,My 3,II,1:1
Wildcat 1960,D 17,20:2
Subways Are for Sleeping 1961,D 28,22:1
Ben Franklin in Paris 1964,O 28,52:1
Rothschilds, The 1970,O 20,40:1
Rothschilds, The 1970,N 1,II,1:1
Kidd, Michael (Miscellaneous)
Guys and Dolls 1950,N 25,11:2
Wonder World 1964,My 18,32:1
Kidd, Michael (Producer)
Li'l Abner 1956,N 16,24:2
Wildcat 1960,D 17,20:2
Kidd, Robert
Everyman 1953,O 12,30:2
Picture of Dorian Gray, The 1956,Ag 18,15:5
Doctor Faustus 1957,F 19,35:7

Edward II 1958,F 12,32:5
Tempest, The 1959,D 28,19:2
Henry V 1960,Je 30,23:1
Merchant of Venice, The 1962,Je 22,1:4
Kidd, Robert (Playwright)
Edward II 1958,F 12,32:5
Kidder, Hugh
Michel Auclair 1925,Mr 5,23:1
Love for Love 1925,Ap 1,21:2
Adam Solitaire 1925,N 7,19:2
Man Who Died Twice, The 1925,D 14,19:1
Great God Brown, The 1926,Ja 25,26:1
Squall, The 1926,N 12,20:1
Damn the Tears 1927,Ja 22,11:1
Polly of Hollywood 1927,F 22,22:3
Tales of Rigo 1927,My 31,25:3
Kidder, Kathleen
Remember the Day 1935,Jl 9,24:3
Remember the Day 1935,S 26,19:3
Kiddon, George
Paese dei Campanelli, Il; Land of Bells, The 1935,My 10,25:4
Kidner, Frances
Storm Over Patsy 1937,Mr 9,26:4
Kidwell, Gene
You're a Good Man, Charlie Brown 1969,N 14,39:1
Kiehl, William
Memorandum, The 1968,My 6,55:1
Romeo and Juliet 1968,Ag 16,19:1
Kielland, Casper
Merry Wives of Windsor, The 1954,F 17,27:1
Kiendl, Agnes
Little Theatre Tournament; Shall We Join the Ladies? 1929,My 9,34:3
Shall We Join the Ladies? 1929,My 12,28:3
Rogues and Vagabonds 1930,My 8,32:5
Kiendl, Frederick
Little Theatre Tournament; Shall We Join the Ladies? 1929,My 9,34:3
Shall We Join the Ladies? 1929,My 12,28:3
Rogues and Vagabonds 1930,My 8,32:5
Kienitz, Bea (Miscellaneous)
Poupees de Paris, Les 1962,D 13,8:2
Kiepfer
Faust 1932,Je 19,IX,1:3
Kiepura, Jan
Merry Widow, The 1943,Ag 5,19:2
Merry Widow, The 1943,Ag 22,II,5:1
Merry Widow, The 1943,S 26,II,1:5
Merry Widow, The 1944,O 9,17:1
Polonaise 1945,O 8,20:2
Polonaise 1945,O 14,II,1:1
Merry Widow, The 1957,Ap 11,36:6
Kier, Aaron
Jacques Bergson 1936,O 31,24:6
Kier, Harvey
Yours Is My Heart 1946,S 6,16:5
Kierman, Frank
Gondoliers, The 1940,O 1,29:2
Kiernan, Chris (Composer)
Lazarus Laughed 1948,Ap 9,27:4
Kiernan, DeWitt
Lady of the Camellias, The 1931,Ja 27,21:2
Kiernan, Jack
Last Pad, The 1970,D 8,61:1
Kiernan, Robert (Miscellaneous)
Hair 1968,Ap 30,40:2
Kiesler, Frederick (Lighting Director)
No Exit 1946,N 27,21:1
Kiesler, Frederick (Scenic Designer)
No Exit 1946,N 27,21:1
Tempest, The 1955,S 3,8:6
Kieva, Maria
Night in Paris, A 1926,Ja 6,16:3
Kight, Esmond
Emperor's Clothes, The 1953,F 10,24:2
Kightley, Cyril
Fools Errant 1922,Ag 22,12:3
Kikel, Frank
No Mother to Guide Her 1933,D 26,18:5
Kikiritake, Monya (Miscellaneous)
General's Daughter, The 1966,Mr 16,50:1
Fishing for Wives 1966,Mr 16,50:1
Greengrocer's Daughter, The 1966,Mr 16,50:1
Kikuchi, Lynn
King and I, The 1956,Ap 19,35:4
King and I, The 1960,My 12,40:1
Kikunosuke
Kagami-Jishi; Mirror Lion Dance, The 1969,S 11,53:1
Chushingura; Treasury of Loyal Retainers, The 1969,S 11,53:1
Kumagai Jinya 1969,S 18,64:1
Kikuta, Kazuo (Producer)
My Fair Lady 1963,S 2,19:4
How to Succeed in Business Without Really Trying 1964,Jl 18,10:1
Kiss Me, Kate 1966,F 5,32:1
Scarlett 1970,Ja 3,19:1
Kikutas, The
Vaudeville (Palace) 1924,Ja 15,17:3
Vaudeville (Palace) 1930,F 10,20:3

Kikuzo
Kagami-Jishi; Mirror Lion Dance, The 1969,S 11,53:1
Chushingura; Treasury of Loyal Retainers, The 1969,S 11,53:1
Momiji-Gari 1969,S 18,64:1
Kumagai Jinya 1969,S 18,64:1
Kilborn, Michael
Polly 1925,O 12,19:1
Kilbourne, Fanny (Original Author)
Connie Goes Home 1923,Jl 1,VI,1:4
Kilbourne, Fanny (Playwright)
Connie Goes Home 1923,S 7,10:1
Kilbride, Percy
Buzzard, The 1928,Mr 15,29:1
Adam's Apple 1929,Je 11,27:5
Getting Even 1929,Ag 20,31:1
Those We Love 1930,F 20,22:2
Up and Up, The 1930,S 9,25:2
Louder, Please! 1931,N 13,26:4
Lilly Turner 1932,S 20,26:1
Great Magoo, The 1932,D 3,20:7
Whatever Possessed Her 1934,Ja 26,21:2
Good-Bye Please 1934,O 25,26:6
Post Road 1934,D 5,28:3
Ragged Edge, The 1935,N 26,28:3
Name Your Poison 1936,Ja 21,27:4
Please Do Not Disturb 1936,Je 23,27:1
Stork Mad 1936,O 1,28:4
Post Road 1937,Ap 21,18:2
Day in the Sun 1937,Jl 27,24:3
Western Union 1937,Ag 10,22:7
Sunup to Sundown 1938,F 2,14:3
Censored 1938,F 28,18:2
Flying Ginzburgs, The 1938,N 13,IX,2:1
When We Are Married 1939,N 21,19:5
When We Are Married 1939,D 10,X,5:6
George Washington Slept Here 1940,O 19,20:3
Two Story House 1941,S 2,20:3
Cuckoos on the Hearth 1941,S 17,26:2
Little Brown Jug 1946,Mr 7,32:2
Kilburn, Terence
Candida 1952,Ap 23,23:6
Sherlock Holmes 1953,O 31,11:2
Charley's Aunt 1953,D 23,22:2
Hasty Heart, The 1954,Mr 13,10:1
Kilburn, Terence (Director)
Heartbreak House 1963,Je 8,14:2
Heartbreak House 1963,Je 28,24:1
Kilburn, Theresa
Merchant of Venice, The 1924,N 18,23:2
Window Panes 1927,F 22,22:2
Kilcullen, Edward
Embezzled Heaven 1944,N 1,20:2
Kilcullen, William (Director)
Bright Rebel 1938,D 28,24:2
Kilcullen, William (Producer)
Bright Rebel 1938,D 28,24:2
Kildare, Harrison G (Playwright)
Joan of Arkansas 1925,Ap 5,16:1
Kildare, Owen (Mrs)
One Woman's Husband 1920,Mr 23,9:3
Kiley, Richard
Sun and I, The 1949,Mr 21,18:4
Misalliance 1953,F 19,20:1
Kismet 1953,D 4,2:4
Sing Me No Lullaby 1954,O 15,17:2
Sing Me No Lullaby 1954,O 24,II,1:1
Time Limit! 1956,Ja 25,27:2
Time Limit! 1956,F 5,II,1:1
Moon for the Misbegotten, A 1958,Je 7,10:6
Redhead 1959,F 6,21:1
Redhead 1959,F 15,II,1:1
Advise and Consent 1960,N 18,25:1
No Strings 1962,Mr 16,24:1
No Strings 1962,Mr 25,II,1:1
I Had a Ball 1964,D 16,50:1
Man of La Mancha 1965,N 23,52:1
Her First Roman 1968,O 21,53:3
Her First Roman 1968,N 3,II,1:1
Kilfeather, Jack
Sex Fable, The 1931,O 21,26:1
Kilgallen, Dorothy (Playwright)
Dream With Music 1944,My 19,15:2
Kilgour, Adam
Kumquat in the Persimmon Tree, The 1962,Je 19,27:2
Poupees de Paris, Les 1964,My 16,11:1
Kilgour, Joseph
Easiest Way, The 1921,S 7,14:1
It's a Boy! 1922,S 20,18:3
Spring Fever 1925,Ag 4,14:2
If I Was Rich 1926,S 3,15:2
Hangman's House 1926,D 17,27:2
Lady Alone 1927,Ja 21,12:5
One Glorious Hour 1927,Ap 15,27:2
Julius Caesar 1927,Je 7,27:2
Spring 3100 1928,F 16,14:2
Wings Over Europe 1928,D 11,35:1
Camel Through the Needle's Eye, The 1929,Ap 16,32:2
Little Father of the Wilderness, The 1930,Je 3,27:1

Kilgren, Cheryl
Love Nest, The 1963,Ja 28,7:6
Kilhenny, Thomas T (Producer)
Not a Way of Life 1967,Mr 23,28:1
Kilian, Victor
Good Fellow, The 1926,O 6,22:1
Beyond the Horizon 1926,D 1,24:2
Rapid Transit 1927,Ap 8,21:2
Triple Crossed 1927,My 6,21:2
What the Doctor Ordered 1927,Ag 19,20:2
Nightstick 1927,N 11,20:4
Big Fight, The 1928,S 19,33:1
Black Crook, The 1929,Mr 12,26:5
At the Bottom 1930,Ja 10,24:3
This One Man 1930,O 22,32:3
Hobo 1931,F 12,24:4
Cloudy With Showers 1931,S 2,17:5
Adams' Wife 1931,D 29,27:1
Collision 1932,F 17,19:2
Great Magoo, The 1932,D 3,20:7
Man Bites Dog 1933,Ap 26,11:2
Heat Lightning 1933,S 16,9:6
Divine Drudge 1933,O 27,22:3
Peace on Earth 1933,N 30,39:2
Broomsticks Amen! 1934,F 10,20:4
Bride of Torozko, The 1934,S 14,24:2
Valley Forge 1934,N 27,26:4
Valley Forge 1934,D 11,28:3
Solitaire 1942,Ja 28,22:2
Solitaire 1942,F 8,IX,1:1
Miracle in the Mountains 1947,Ap 26,10:2
Look Homeward, Angel 1957,N 29,33:1
Look Homeward, Angel 1957,D 8,II,5:1
Look Homeward, Angel 1958,Ag 31,II,1:1
Gang's All Here, The 1959,O 2,23:1
Gideon 1961,N 10,38:1
Killa, John
Mother Courage and Her Children 1964,My 12,32:2
Killalea, Madeleine
Little Theatre Tournament; House With the Twisty Windows, The 1929,My 8,34:4
Killcoyne, Kathleen
Gondoliers, The 1940,O 1,29:2
Killeen, Madelyn
Earl Carroll's Vanities 1925,D 29,20:3
Talk About Girls 1927,Je 15,31:3
Killiam, Paul (Miscellaneous)
Naughty-Naught '00 1946,O 21,27:5
Killian, Michael
Roosty 1938,F 15,21:2
Killmer, Nancy
Coco 1969,D 19,66:1
Killmurray, Patti
Enemy of the People, An 1958,F 26,24:2
Kilmartin, Thomas
Hoboken Blues 1928,F 18,10:1
Pleased to Meet You 1928,O 30,27:2
Kilmer, Dorene
On Your Toes 1954,O 12,24:4
Kilne, John M
In Time to Come 1941,D 29,20:2
Kilpack, Bennett
Hot Pan 1928,F 16,14:1
Untitled-Recital 1932,F 8,21:1
Kilpatrick, Bennett
Man Who Died Twice, The 1925,D 14,19:1
Kilpatrick, James
Sonny 1921,Ag 17,12:2
Kilpatrick, Lincoln
Deep Are the Roots 1960,O 4,47:1
One Flew Over the Cuckoo's Nest 1963,N 14,40:2
Blues for Mister Charlie 1964,Ap 24,24:1
Kilpatrick, Thomas (Producer)
Hawk Island 1929,S 17,34:7
Kilpatrick's Old-Time Minstrels 1930,Ap 21,20:2
In The Best of Families 1931,F 3,29:1
Other One, The 1932,O 4,26:3
Young Sinners 1933,Mr 7,20:4
Springtime for Henry 1933,My 2,20:5
June Moon 1933,My 16,15:5
Broomsticks Amen! 1934,F 10,20:4
Black Widow 1936,F 13,24:3
Window Shopping 1938,D 24,13:2
Kilroe, Frank
Betty Behave 1927,Mr 9,28:4
Kilroy, Thomas (Playwright)
Death and Resurrection of Mr Roche, The 1968,O 11,44:4
Kilty, Jack
It Happens on Ice 1940,O 11,24:3
Make Mine Manhattan 1948,Ja 16,26:2
Kilty, Jerome
Relapse, The 1950,N 23,54:2
Love's Labour's Lost 1953,F 5,20:3
Misalliance 1953,F 19,20:1
Misalliance 1953,Mr 22,II,1:1
Pin to See the Peepshow, A 1953,S 18,17:2
Frogs of Spring, The 1953,O 21,36:2
Qudrille 1954,N 4,39:2
Quadrille 1954,N 14,II,1:1
Othello 1955,S 8,27:2
Othello 1955,S 18,II,1:1
Henry IV, Part I 1955,S 22,34:2

Dear Liar 1962,Mr 19,36:1
Falstaff 1966,Je 20,27:1
Rivals, The 1969,O 18,37:1
Kilty, Jerome (Director)
Moby Dick 1955,Ap 26,25:3
Henry IV, Part I 1955,S 22,34:2
Girl of the Golden West, The 1957,N 6,44:1
Dear Liar 1960,Mr 18,19:2
Dear Liar 1960,Mr 27,II,1:1
Dear Liar 1962,Mr 19,36:1
Antigone 1967,Je 19,43:1
Don't Shoot Mable It's Your Husband 1968,O 23,34:1
Possibilities 1968,D 5,60:1
Kilty, Jerome (Playwright)
Dear Liar 1959,O 6,44:6
Dear Liar 1960,Mr 18,19:2
Dear Liar 1960,Mr 27,II,1:1
Dear Liar 1962,Mr 19,36:1
Ides of March, The 1962,N 17,16:4
Ides of March, The 1963,Ag 9,12:1
Don't Shoot Mable It's Your Husband 1968,O 23,34:1
Kim
Yellow Jack 1934,Mr 7,22:6
Kim, Helen
Congai 1928,N 28,24:3
Farewell to Arms, A 1930,S 23,30:3
Lady Precious Stream 1936,Ja 28,15:2
Kim, Jane
Divided Honors 1929,O 1,28:2
People on the Hill 1931,S 26,25:5
Locked Room, The 1933,D 26,18:5
Kim, June
Family, The 1943,Mr 31,22:4
Kim, Mara
Happy as Larry 1950,Ja 7,11:2
Teahouse of the August Moon, The 1953,O 16,32:1
Tenth of an Inch Makes the Difference, A 1962,N 13,44:1
Kim, Meayon You
Man With Red Hair, A 1928,N 9,22:2
Kim, Sam
Dove, The 1925,F 12,17:3
Letter, The 1927,S 27,30:1
My Girl Friday! 1929,F 13,20:2
Kim, Willa (Costume Designer)
Are You With It? 1945,N 12,17:3
Duchess Misbehaves, The 1946,F 14,32:2
Red Eye of Love 1961,Je 13,28:1
Fortuna 1962,Ja 4,26:1
Saving Grace, The 1963,Ap 19,28:1
Have I Got a Girl for You! 1963,D 3,53:2
Funnyhouse of a Negro 1964,Ja 15,25:3
Midsummer Night's Dream, A 1964,Je 30,23:2
Benito Cereno 1964,N 2,62:2
My Kinsman, Major Molineux 1964,N 2,62:2
Helen 1964,D 11,55:4
Sing to Me Through Open Windows 1965,Mr 16,45:1
Day the Whores Came Out to Play Tennis, The 1965,Mr 16,45:1
Malcolm 1966,Ja 12,29:1
Hail Scrawdyke! 1966,N 29,50:1
Scuba Duba 1967,O 11,36:1
Ceremony of Innocence, The 1968,Ja 2,33:1
Papp 1969,My 6,39:1
Promenade 1969,Je 5,56:1
Operation Sidewinder 1970,Mr 13,33:1
Sunday Dinner 1970,N 3,28:1
Kim, Willa (Scenic Designer)
Dynamite Tonight 1964,Mr 16,36:2
Kim, William
Man With Red Hair, A 1928,N 9,22:2
Kim, Yen Soo
Teahouse of the August Moon, The 1956,N 9,33:2
Kim-Loos, The
Scandals 1939,Ag 20,IX,2:1
Scandals 1939,Ag 29,17:2
Kimball, Dolly
What Next 1920,Ja 27,7:2
Kimball, Dorothy
Seven Mirrors 1945,O 26,17:2
Kimball, Elizabeth
Beware of the Bull 1933,My 30,13:7
Vinegar Tree, The 1935,Ag 14,16:1
Art and Mrs Bottle 1936,S 2,18:1
Kimball, Elizabeth (Director)
Hay Fever 1935,Jl 24,20:4
Mr Pim Passes By 1935,Ag 7,22:2
Post Road 1936,Ag 5,15:4
Kimball, F M
Balcony, The 1960,Mr 4,21:1
Kimball, Fred
Othello 1955,S 8,27:2
Kimball, Gladys
Mr Jiggins of Jigginstown 1936,D 18,30:2
Kimball, John Talbot
So's Your Old Antique 1930,My 8,32:5
Kimball, Kitty
What Next 1920,Ja 27,7:2
Kimball, Louis
Daddy Dumplins 1920,N 23,11:1

Kimball, Louis—Cont
Getting Gertie's Garter 1921,Ag 2,16:2
Partners Again 1922,My 2,22:2
For Value Received 1923,My 8,22:3
Green Beetle, The 1924,S 3,12:3
Head First 1926,Ja 7,22:4
Find Daddy 1926,Mr 9,21:3
Little Spitfire, The 1926,Ag 17,15:2
Shelf, The 1926,S 28,31:1
Crime 1927,O 19,24:2
Gang War 1928,Ag 21,27:2
Indiscretion 1929,Mr 5,28:1
Nut Farm, The 1929,O 15,34:3
Kimball, Richard (Composer)
Geese 1969,Ja 13,26:6
Parents and Children 1969,Ja 13,26:6
Kimball, Ward (Playwright)
Disney on Parade 1970,S 24,63:1
Kimbell, Spencer
Red Rust 1929,D 18,31:1
Penal Law 2010 1930,Ap 19,14:2
First Night 1930,N 27,32:3
Sing High, Sing Low 1931,N 13,26:4
Call Me Ziggy 1937,F 13,9:6
Kimber, Kathryn
Two for the Show 1940,F 9,14:2
Kimber, Kay
By Jupiter 1942,Je 4,22:1
Kimber, Mary
Linden Tree, The 1948,Mr 3,28:2
Kimberly, Nancy
Hamlet 1938,N 8,26:1
Kimberly, Robert
Louisiana Lady 1947,Je 3,35:2
Kimbrell, Marketa
Wall, The 1960,O 12,44:4
Alchemist, The 1966,O 14,48:1
Yerma 1966,D 9,60:1
East Wind, The 1967,F 10,30:1
Kimbro, John M
Every Other Evil 1961,Ja 23,20:2
Lovers in the Metro, The 1962,Ja 31,21:1
Information Bureau, The 1962,Ja 31,21:1
Kimbrough, Charles
All in Love 1961,N 11,15:2
Home Fires 1969,Ap 8,42:1
Company 1970,Ap 27,40:1
Company 1970,My 3,II,1:4
Kimbrough, Clinton
Mister Roberts 1956,D 6,46:2
Our Town 1959,Mr 24,46:2
Our Town 1959,Ap 5,II,1:1
Camino Real 1960,My 17,42:2
Look: We've Come Through 1961,O 26,40:1
After the Fall 1964,Ja 24,18:1
But for Whom Charlie 1964,Mr 13,42:2
Changeling, The 1964,O 30,32:2
Incident at Vichy 1964,D 4,44:1
Kimbrough, Fred
Boys From Syracuse, The 1963,Ap 16,31:1
Kimbrough, Mary Jane
Prince of Peasantmania 1970,F 22,88:1
Kimes, Bruce
Vincent 1959,O 1,40:1
Alley of the Sunset 1959,D 31,11:1
Country Scandal, A 1960,My 6,21:8
Romeo and Juliet 1961,F 24,24:1
Anniversary, The 1961,Ap 21,26:2
On the High Road 1961,Ap 21,26:2
Wedding, The 1961,Ap 21,26:2
Buskers, The 1961,O 31,28:1
If Five Years Pass 1962,My 11,37:1
Yes is for a Very Young Man 1963,Mr 6,7:5
Good Soldier Schweik, The 1963,Ap 9,57:1
Passion of Josef D, The 1964,F 12,29:1
Cat and the Canary, The 1965,Ja 5,26:1
Kimm, Helen
Roar China! 1930,O 28,23:1
Play, Genius, Play! 1935,O 31,17:2
Kimmel, Alan (Costume Designer)
Cabin in the Sky 1964,Ja 22,32:1
You're a Good Man, Charlie Brown 1967,Mr 8,51:1
Who's Who, Baby? 1968,Ja 30,36:1
Fortune and Men's Eyes 1969,O 23,55:1
Kimmel, Alan (Scenic Designer)
Sweeney Todd 1957,Ag 28,21:4
Birthday Party, The 1961,My 15,34:6
Cabin in the Sky 1964,Ja 22,32:1
Princess Rebecca Birnbaum 1966,Mr 7,22:1
Suburban Tragedy 1966,Mr 7,22:1
Make Like a Dog 1966,Mr 7,22:1
Young Marrieds Play Monopoly 1966,Mr 7,22:1
You're a Good Man, Charlie Brown 1967,Mr 8,51:1
Who's Who, Baby? 1968,Ja 30,36:1
Fortune and Men's Eyes 1969,O 23,55:1
Kimmel, Jess (Director)
Dinny and the Witches 1959,D 10,53:3
Kimmel, Jess (Miscellaneous)
Cyrano de Bergerac 1954,Ja 17,27:2
Cyrano de Bergerac 1953,N 13,24:3
Charley's Aunt 1953,D 23,22:2
Kimmel, Jess (Producer)
Dinny and the Witches 1959,D 10,53:3

Kimmel, Stanley (Playwright)
Black Diamond 1933,F 24,12:2
Kimmins, Anthony (Composer)
While Parents Sleep 1934,Je 5,28:2
Kimmins, Anthony (Playwright)
While Parents Sleep 1934,Je 5,28:2
Chase theAce 1935,Mr 26,23:3
Chase the Ace 1935,Ap 21,IX,2:2
Kimmins, Arthur (Playwright)
Night Club Queen 1933,D 3,IX,7:6
Kimmins, Kenneth
Stephen D 1966,Ag 5,17:1
Fig Leaves Are Falling, The 1969,Ja 3,19:1
Kimouli, Ritsa
Hippolytus 1968,N 20,38:3
Kimris
Jumbo 1935,N 18,20:2
Kincade, Claire
Merry Death, A 1959,N 10,55:3
Kincade, Claire (Choreographer)
Merry Death, A 1959,N 10,55:3
No Trifling With Love 1959,N 10,55:3
Kincaid, Tim
Dracula Sabbat 1970,O 2,28:2
Kinch, Myra (Choreographer)
Anatomist, The 1957,F 27,21:5
Founders, The 1957,My 14,39:1
Kinder, George (Playwright)
What a Relief 1935,D 14,10:6
Kindl, Charles
Lover, The 1964,Ja 6,35:1
Two Executioners, The 1964,Mr 25,46:2
Conerico Was Here to Stay 1965,Mr 4,37:1
Inquest 1970,Ap 24,38:1
Kindl, Charles (Miscellaneous)
Kittiwake Island 1960,O 13,43:1
Difficult Woman, The 1962,Ap 26,22:7
Conerico Was Here to Stay 1965,Mr 4,37:1
Pigeons 1965,Mr 4,37:1
Do Not Pass Go 1965,Ap 20,44:1
That Thing at the Cherry Lane 1965,My 19,42:1
Butter and Egg Man, The 1966,O 18,49:1
Night of the Dunce 1966,D 29,21:1
House of Flowers 1968,Ja 29,26:2
Boys in the Band, The 1968,Ap 15,48:1
Kindler, Jan
Watched Pot, The 1947,O 29,31:4
Topaze 1947,D 29,21:5
Kindy, Christopher
Jungle of Cities 1970,Mr 1,75:2
Kinego, Joe
Little Clay Cart, The 1953,Jl 1,25:1
Kineya, Katsusaburo (Composer)
Azuma Kabuki Dancers and Musicians 1955,D 27,31:4
Kineya, Katsusaburo (Musical Director)
Azuma Kabuki Dancers and Musicians 1956,Ja 8,II,3:1
Kineya, Katsutoji
Azuma Kabuki Dancers and Musicians 1954,F 19,22:3
King, (Miss) (Costume Designer)
Kai Khosru 1925,Ap 27,14:2
King, (Miss) (Scenic Designer)
Kai Khosru 1925,Ap 27,14:2
King, Ada
Mary Rose 1920,D 23,9:2
Bill of Divorcement, A 1921,O 11,22:2
Sirocco 1927,D 18,IX,4:1
King, Alan
Judy Garland's New Variety Show 1956,S 27,43:2
Judy Garland 1959,My 12,40:1
Guys and Dolls 1965,Ap 29,39:1
Impossible Years, The 1965,O 14,55:1
Applause 1970,Mr 31,35:1
King, Alan (Producer)
Lion in Winter, The 1966,Mr 4,23:1
Dinner at Eight 1966,S 28,38:1
Investigation, The 1966,O 5,40:1
Something Different 1967,N 29,52:1
King, Aldine
Electra 1969,Ag 8,14:1
King, Alexander (Playwright)
Profound Bow to Memory 1939,S 25,16:2
Night Watch In Syria 1943,Ja 5,15:5
King, Allan
Bishop Misbehaves, The 1935,Ag 27,23:4
King, Allan (Playwright)
White Assegai, The 1930,Ja 22,21:1
King, Allyn
Ladies' Night 1920,Ag 10,10:1
Sun Showers 1923,F 6,14:2
Moonlight 1924,Ja 31,13:7
Florida Girl 1925,N 3,34:1
90 Horse Power 1926,Mr 16,22:4
King, Alta
Sally 1920,D 22,16:1
Orange Blossoms 1922,S 20,18:1
King, Anne
Familiar Pattern 1943,S 3,15:6
Career 1943,O 29,22:6
King, Archer (Producer)
Miracle in the Mountains 1947,Ap 26,10:2

Two Blind Mice 1949,Mr 3,32:2
King, Archie
Stop Press 1939,Mr 20,13:2
Summer Night 1939,N 3,17:1
King, Arthur
Love Is No Heaven 1943,Mr 16,15:3
King, Bernard (Producer)
Inquest 1970,Ap 24,38:1
King, Betty (Producer)
Will and the Way, The 1957,D 3,46:5
King, Beulah (Playwright)
Sea Legs 1937,My 19,26:5
King, Bob
Pillar to Post 1943,D 11,11:2
King, Cameron
No More Frontier 1931,O 22,27:1
Mourning Becomes Electra; Hunted, The 1932,My 10,25:2
Mourning Becomes Electra; Haunted, The 1932,My 10,25:2
King, Carol
Artists and Models 1943,N 6,16:6
King, Carolyn
Children's Hour, The 1952,D 19,35:2
King, Charles
It's Up to You 1921,Mr 29,20:1
George White's Scandals 1921,Jl 12,14:1
Little Nellie Kelly 1922,N 14,16:1
Vaudeville (Palace) 1924,F 12,20:2
Keep Kool 1924,My 23,16:4
Vaudeville (Palace) 1926,My 4,31:2
No Foolin' 1926,Je 25,25:1
Hit the Deck! 1927,Ap 26,32:1
Present Arms 1928,Ap 27,16:2
Vaudeville (Palace) 1929,N 25,22:4
New Yorkers, The 1930,N 16,VIII,3:1
New Yorkers, The 1930,D 9,31:1
Vaudeville (Palace) 1931,My 11,15:5
Vaudeville (New Amsterdam Theatre) 1931,Je 22,17:3
Lambs Gambol 1933,Ap 24,10:1
Sea Legs 1937,My 19,26:5
Fabulous Invalid, The 1938,O 10,15:1
King, Charles (Playwright)
Great American Family, The 1939,D 10,X,5:6
King, Charmion
Henry IV, Part I 1958,Je 25,23:3
Winter's Tale, The 1958,Jl 23,34:3
Love and Libel 1960,D 8,44:1
King, Claude
Fair Circassian, The 1921,D 7,22:3
Back to Methuselah (Part II: The Gospel of the Brothers Barnabas); Gospel of the Brothers Barnabas, The (Back to Methuselah, Part II) 1922,F 28,17:2
Back to Methuselah (Part IV: The Tragedy of an Elderly Gentleman); Tragedy of an Elderly Gentleman, The (Back to Methuselah, Part IV) 1922,Mr 7,11:1
Back to Methuselah (Part III: The Thing Happens); Thing Happens, The (Back to Methuselah, Part III) 1922,Mr 7,11:1
Back to Methuselah (Part V: As Far as Thought Can Reach); As Far as Thought Can Reach (Back to Methuselah, Part V) 1922,Mr 14,11:2
What the Public Wants 1922,My 2,22:3
Crooked Square, The 1923,S 11,10:2
In the Next Room 1923,N 28,14:1
Far Cry, The 1924,S 28,VII,2:1
Far Cry, The 1924,O 1,24:1
Paolo and Francesca 1924,D 3,24:2
Trelawney of the 'Wells' 1925,Je 2,16:2
Fall of Eve, The 1925,S 1,18:1
Mad Hopes, The 1932,My 29,VIII,2:2
King, Clinton (Director)
E-MC2 1948,Je 16,36:2
King, Constance
School for Brides 1944,Ag 2,19:4
King, Dean
Lower North 1944,Ag 26,15:4
King, Dennis
Clair de Lune 1921,Ap 19,15:1
Fair Circassian, The 1921,D 7,22:3
Back to Methuselah (Part I: In the Beginning); In the Beginning (Back to Methuselah, Part I) 1922,F 28,17:2
Back to Methuselah (Part IV: The Tragedy of an Elderly Gentleman); Tragedy of an Elderly Gentleman, The (Back to Methuselah, Part IV) 1922,Mr 7,11:1
Back to Methuselah (Part V: As Far as Thought Can Reach); As Far as Thought Can Reach (Back to Methuselah, Part V) 1922,Mr 14,11:2
Lucky One, The 1922,N 21,15:2
Romeo and Juliet 1923,Ja 25,16:1
Antony and Cleopatra 1924,F 20,22:1
Rose Marie 1924,S 3,12:2
Vagabond King, The 1925,S 22,23:3
Three Musketeers, The 1928,Mr 4,IX,2:3
Three Musketeers, The 1928,Mr 14,28:1
Three Musketeers, The 1928,Mr 25,IX,1:1
Peter Ibbetson 1931,Ap 9,30:3
Vaudeville (Palace) 1931,Je 29,20:1

King, Dennis—Cont
Show Boat 1932,My 20,22:2
Show Boat 1932,My 29,VIII,5:6
Command Performance 1933,O 18,24:3
Richard of Bordeaux 1934,F 4,IX,2:2
Richard of Bordeaux 1934,F 15,16:2
Richard of Bordeaux 1934,F 25,IX,1:1
Petticoat Fever 1935,Mr 5,22:2
Love Is Not So Simple 1935,N 5,33:1
Love Is Not So Simple 1935,N 10,IX,1:6
Parnell 1936,My 5,26:2
Love for Love 1936,Je 30,15:4
Frederika 1937,F 5,16:5
Doll's House, A 1937,Jl 25,X,2:3
Doll's House, A 1937,D 28,28:6
I Married an Angel 1938,My 12,26:2
I Married an Angel 1938,My 22,XI,1:1
Three Sisters, The 1942,D 22,31:2
Three Sisters, The 1942,D 27,VIII,1:1
Searching Wind, The 1944,Ap 13,25:2
Searching Wind, The 1944,Ap 23,II,1:1
Dunnigan's Daughter 1945,D 27,16:1
Dunnigan's Daughter 1946,Ja 6,II,1:1
He Who Gets Slapped 1946,Mr 21,31:4
He Who Gets Slapped 1946,Mr 31,II,1:1
Pygmalion 1947,F 6,29:4
Devil's Disciple, The 1950,Ja 26,23:2
Devil's Disciple, The 1950,F 5,II,1:1
Getting Married 1950,Je 14,41:2
Billy Budd 1951,F 12,18:3
Billy Budd 1951,F 18,II,1:1
ANTA Album 1951,My 7,22:7
Music in the Air 1951,O 9,32:2
Music in the Air 1951,O 21,II,1:1
Strong Are Lonely, The 1953,S 30,38:3
Lunatics and Lovers 1954,D 14,44:2
Day by the Sea, A 1955,S 27,42:1
Day by the Sea, A 1955,O 2,II,1:1
Affair of Honor 1956,Ap 7,12:3
Shangri-La 1956,Je 14,40:1
Hidden River, The 1957,Ja 24,32:1
Greatest Man Alive!, The 1957,My 9,37:2
Goodwill Ambassador 1959,Mr 3,39:2
Love and Libel 1960,D 8,44:1
Photo Finish 1963,F 14,5:2
Minor Miracle 1965,O 8,4:3
Loves of Cass McGuire, The 1966,O 7,36:1
Portrait of a Queen 1968,F 29,29:1
Patriot for Me, A 1969,O 6,58:1
Patriot for Me, A 1969,O 12,II,1:1
King, Dennis (Producer)
Richard of Bordeaux 1934,F 15,16:2
Lorelei 1938,N 30,21:2
King, Dennis Jr
Trojan Horse, The 1940,O 31,28:3
Kiss Them for Me 1945,MR 21,27:2
Kiss Them for Me 1945,Mr 25,II,1:1
Playboy of the Western World, The 1946,O 28,18:3
Parlor Story 1947,Mr 5,29:2
Cradle Will Rock, The 1947,D 27,11:2
Vigil, The 1948,My 22,8:6
King, Dorothy
Jenny Kissed Me 1948,D 24,12:2
King, Edith
Bab 1920,O 19,12:1
Thank You 1921,O 4,10:2
Good Bad Woman, A 1925,F 10,21:1
Right to Love, The 1925,Je 9,16:4
White Flame 1929,N 5,32:7
Going Gay 1933,Ag 4,18:5
Cross Ruff 1935,F 20,23:3
Hallowe'en 1936,F 21,20:3
Frederika 1937,F 5,16:5
Amphitryon 38 1937,N 2,32:2
Sea Gull, The 1938,Mr 29,19:2
Taming of the Shrew, The 1940,F 6,17:2
Burning Deck, The 1940,Mr 2,9:2
Popsy 1941,F 11,26:2
Beggar's Opera, The 1941,Ag 12,14:6
Hope for a Harvest 1941,N 27,28:2
Kiss for Cinderella, A 1942,Mr 11,22:2
Othello 1943,O 20,18:1
Othello 1945,My 23,25:4
Would-Be Gentleman, The 1946,Ja 10,29:2
Eurydice 1948,O 17,I,67:4
Legend of Lovers 1951,D 27,17:1
Ondine 1954,F 19,23:1
Ondine 1954,F 28,II,1:1
Affair of Honor 1956,Ap 7,12:3
Miss Isobel 1957,D 27,22:1
Cheri 1959,O 13,44:1
Saratoga 1959,D 8,59:4
Wildcat 1960,D 17,20:2
Murderer Among Us, A 1964,Mr 26,43:1
King, Edith (Costume Designer)
Aucassin and Nicolette 1947,Ap 28,26:2
King, Edith (Miscellaneous)
Aucassin and Nicolette 1921,Ap 17,VI,1:1
King, Edith (Scenic Designer)
Aucassin and Nicolette 1947,Ap 28,26:2
King, Eleanor
After Tomorrow 1931,Ag 27,22:4
Whistling in the Dark 1932,N 4,25:2
Blue Widow, The 1933,Ag 31,20:2

King, Eleanor—Cont
Dream of Sganarelle, The 1933,O 17,26:5
I Myself 1934,My 10,24:6
King, Elizabeth
Lingering Past, The 1932,Je 30,26:5
King, Eugene W
O'Flynn, The 1934,D 28,24:1
King, Everett
Lysistrata 1959,My 20,40:2
King, Frank
Love Call, The 1927,O 25,33:1
Rainbow 1928,N 22,25:1
King, Geoffrey
Chauve-Souris; Queen of Spades, The
 1931,O 22,27:1
King, Gilbert
Reunion 1938,Ap 12,26:4
King, Gladys
Paradise 1931,My 12,29:2
King, Harrison (Playwright)
Decoy, The 1932,Ap 2,13:4
King, J
Springtime of Youth 1922,O 27,15:1
King, Jack (Scenic Designer)
School for Scandal, The 1970,Je 11,51:1
King, Jane
Letty Pepper 1922,Ap 11,22:2
Little Theatre Tournament; Tale Retold, A
 1928,My 10,31:1
King, Joan
Midsummer Night's Dream, A 1954,S 22,33:1
King, Joe
Tantrum, The 1924,S 5,20:2
King, John C
Is Zat So? 1925,Ja 6,23:4
Merry Andrew 1929,Ja 22,22:2
Little Father of the Wilderness, The 1930,Je 3,27:1
Uncle Tom's Cabin 1933,My 30,13:4
Anything Goes 1934,N 22,26:1
County Chairman, The 1936,My 26,26:5
Life With Father 1939,N 9,26:2
King, John L
Love Call, The 1927,O 25,33:1
King, John M
Music in the Air 1951,O 9,32:2
King, John Michael
My Fair Lady 1956,Mr 16,20:2
Anya 1965,N 30,48:1
Oresteia 1966,Je 30,29:1
Have I Got One for You 1968,Ja 8,32:1
Sound of Music, The 1970,Jl 3,13:1
King, John P
Little Theatre Tournament; Rhythm of the City,
 The 1929,My 7,28:1
King, Joseph
Lady's Virtue, A 1925,N 24,28:2
Royal Family, The 1927,D 29,26:4
Caught Wet 1931,N 5,29:1
Wild Waves 1932,F 20,11:4
Midsummer Night's Dream, A 1932,Jl 13,15:1
As Husbands Go 1933,Ja 20,20:5
World Waits, The 1933,O 26,22:5
No Questions Asked 1934,F 6,24:3
Small Miracle 1934,S 27,24:3
King, Joyce
Crucible, The 1958,Mr 17,21:1
King, Kenneth
Zaporogetz Za Dunayem 1937,My 9,II,5:3
King, King and King
Broadway Nights 1929,Jl 16,23:2
Vaudeville (Palace) 1929,S 23,24:6
King, Lamar
Tobacco Road 1933,D 5,31:2
Sweet River 1936,O 29,30:2
On Location 1937,S 28,19:1
King, Larry
Airways, Inc 1929,F 21,30:5
King, Lawrence Station (Costume Designer)
Rivals, The 1969,O 18,37:1
King, Lawrence Station (Scenic Designer)
Rivals, The 1969,O 18,37:1
King, Leslie
Rust 1924,F 1,12:1
Dagger, The 1925,S 10,28:1
Oh! Oh! Nurse 1925,D 8,28:4
Right to Kill, The 1926,F 16,22:2
Beau Gallant 1926,Ap 6,26:3
Jeweled Tree, The 1926,O 8,26:2
Jade God, The 1929,My 14,28:3
Blue Ghost, The 1930,Mr 11,24:5
Incubator 1932,N 2,23:3
Divine Drudge 1933,Jl 4,16:4
Her Man of Wax 1933,O 12,32:3
Creeping Fire 1935,Ja 17,22:3
Lady of Letters 1935,Mr 29,26:6
Lady Luck 1936,Ap 16,21:2
Point of Honor, A 1937,F 12,26:2
Money Mad 1937,My 25,32:5
Eye on the Sparrow 1938,My 4,26:3
Delicate Story 1940,D 5,32:2
King, Linda
Diamond Lil 1951,S 15,8:2
King, Louise
Stage Affair, A 1962,Ja 17,30:2

King, Lucille
Trumpets and Drums 1969,O 13,52:1
King, Lulu
Run, Little Chillun! 1933,Mr 2,21:3
Sailor, Beware! 1935,My 7,28:4
Trial of Dr Beck, The 1937,Ag 10,22:2
Haiti 1938,Mr 3,16:1
Run, Little Chillun 1943,Ag 14,6:1
Mamba's Daughters 1953,Mr 21,12:6
Roomful of Roses, A 1955,O 18,48:1
King, Mabel
Hello, Dolly! 1967,N 13,61:1
King, Madeleine
Prince and the Pauper, The 1920,N 2,15:1
Proud Woman, A 1926,N 16,24:1
Stairs, The 1927,N 8,32:7
Mima 1928,D 13,24:2
Those We Love 1930,F 20,22:2
Man on Stilts, The 1931,S 10,23:2
State of the Union 1945,N 15,25:2
Hilda Crane 1950,N 2,38:2
Point of No Return 1951,D 14,35:2
Madam Will You Walk 1953,D 2,2:4
King, Marjorie
Gondoliers, The 1940,O 1,29:2
King, Martha
Lady Says Yes, A 1945,Ja 11,18:5
King, Mary
Letty Pepper 1922,Ap 11,22:2
King, Matt
Maya 1953,Je 10,35:1
King, Maxine
Strangers at Home 1934,S 15,20:5
King, Michael
Tobacco Road 1943,S 6,21:3
Wallflower 1944,Ja 27,14:2
Devils Galore 1945,S 13,27:2
Me and Juliet 1953,My 29,17:1
King, Mina Jo
Death of the Well-Loved Boy, The
 1967,My 16,48:1
Gondoliers, The 1967,O 29,83:1
King, Mollie
Blue Eyes 1921,F 22,11:2
King, Naida
Porgy and Bess 1935,O 11,30:2
King, Nancy
Girl in Pink Tights, The 1954,Mr 6,13:2
King, Pamela
Doctor in Spite of Himself, The 1957,F 28,18:4
Candida 1962,N 12,35:5
King, Patsi
On the Town 1959,Ja 16,36:1
On the Town 1959,Ja 25,II,1:1
Sophie 1963,Ap 16,32:1
King, Paul
Telephone, The 1948,D 8,41:6
Medium, The 1948,D 8,41:6
Medium, The 1950,Jl 20,22:5
Telephone, The 1950,Jl 20,22:5
Medium, The 1950,S 3,II,1:1
King, Phil
Vaudeville (Palace) 1929,D 30,16:3
King, Phil (Miscellaneous)
This Was Burlesque 1962,Mr 7,29:1
King, Philip
Crazy With the Heat 1941,Ja 15,18:2
Around the World 1946,Je 1,9:5
King, Philip (Playwright)
Sailor, Beware! 1955,Mr 6,II,3:1
King, Phoebe Hart
Silks and Satins 1920,Jl 16,19:1
King, Queenie
Minskey the Magnificent 1936,D 26,14:3
King, Ray
Broadway Nights 1929,Jl 16,23:2
King, Rex
Bell for Adano, A 1944,D 7,21:2
Born Yesterday 1946,F 5,18:2
King, Rosalie
Porgy and Bess 1935,O 11,30:2
Porgy and Bess 1942,Ja 23,16:2
Jericho-Jim Crow 1964,Ja 13,25:3
King, Rose
Vaudeville (Hippodrome) 1924,Ja 22,15:6
Vaudeville (Palace) 1926,N 16,24:3
A la Carte 1927,Ag 18,25:3
Take the Air 1927,N 23,28:2
Vaudeville (Palace) 1930,My 26,25:2
Vaudeville (Palace) 1931,Je 8,21:2
Thumbs Up! 1934,D 28,24:1
Show Is On, The 1937,S 20,18:4
High Kickers 1941,N 1,21:2
King, Rose Mary
Torch Bearers, The 1922,Ag 30,10:2
Conscience 1924,S 12,19:3
Wasp's Nest, The 1927,O 26,26:3
Brothers 1928,D 26,14:3
Queen at Home 1930,D 30,25:2
Camels Are Coming, The 1931,O 3,20:4
King, Rufus (Playwright)
Murder at the Vanities 1933,S 13,22:4

King, Rufus (Playwright)—Cont
Invitation to a Murder 1934,My 18,26:3
I Want a Policeman! 1936,Ja 15,15:5
King, Ruth
Honor Be Damned! 1927,Ja 27,13:1
King, Shirley
Back to Methuselah (Part IV: The Tragedy of an
 Elderly Gentleman); Tragedy of an Elderly
 Gentleman, The (Back to Methuselah, Part IV)
 1922,Mr 7,11:1
What the Public Wants 1922,My 2,22:3
Rain 1922,N 8,18:2
King, Stuart (Musical Director)
Orphee 1935,Mr 23,10:3
King, T J
Shrike, The 1953,N 26,51:2
King, Tedd
Have I Got a Girl for You! 1963,D 3,53:2
King, Teddy
Lady, The 1923,D 5,23:2
King, Teresa (Lighting Director)
Line of Least Existence, The 1968,Mr 25,53:1
King, Thomas J
Story for a Sunday Evening, A 1950,N 18,10:5
King, Vivian
Miracle in the Mountains 1947,Ap 26,10:2
King, Wallace
Room 349 1930,Ap 23,24:5
King, Walter G (Composer)
Half Moon Inn 1925,Mr 10,14:1
King, Walter G (Lyricist)
Steppe Around 1922,Mr 29,17:4
King, Walter Woolf
May Wine 1935,D 6,30:3
King, Wanza
Set My People Free 1948,N 4,38:2
Porgy and Bess 1964,My 7,32:1
King, William (Miscellaneous)
Major Barbara 1965,My 18,33:1
King, Woodie
Boy; Job, The; Study in Color 1964,Ag 1,13:1
Displaced Person, The 1966,D 30,15:1
Perfect Party, The 1969,Mr 21,42:1
King, Woodie (Director)
Warning, The-A Theme for Linda 1969,Ap 27,92:1
Black Quartet, A; Warning, The-A Theme for
 Linda 1969,Jl 31,28:1
King, Woodie (Miscellaneous)
Gentleman Caller, The 1969,Ap 27,92:1
Great Goodness of Life (A Coon Show)
 1969,Ap 27,92:1
Prayer Meeting: or, The First Militant Minister
 1969,Ap 27,92:1
Warning, The-A Theme for Linda 1969,Ap 27,92:1
Slave Ship 1969,N 22,46:1
King, Woodie (Producer)
Black Quartet, A; Warning, The-A Theme for
 Linda 1969,Jl 31,28:1
Black Quartet, A; Prayer Meeting or The First
 Militant Minister 1969,Jl 31,28:1
Black Quartet, A; Gentleman Caller, The
 1969,Jl 31,28:1
Black Quartet, A; Great Goodness of Life (A Coon
 Show) 1969,Jl 31,28:1
King, Wright
Bird Cage, The 1950,F 23,32:2
Streetcar Named Desire, A 1950,My 24,36:1
Borned in Texas 1950,Ag 22,30:6
Salvation on a String; No Count Boy, The
 1954,Jl 7,23:1
King, Zola
Macbeth 1936,Ap 15,25:4
Case of Philip Lawrence, The 1937,Je 9,31:1
Haiti 1938,Mr 3,16:1
King and King
Artists and Models 1927,N 16,28:2
Vaudeville (Palace) 1928,Ag 14,15:5
King Brothers and Cully
Vaudeville (Palace) 1932,My 16,19:2
King-Hall, Stephen (Playwright)
Middle Watch, The 1929,S 1,VIII,1:3
Middle Watch, The 1929,O 17,27:1
B J One 1930,Ap 11,24:6
B J One 1930,Ap 27,IX,1:8
B J One 1931,My 7,21:3
King-Reavis, Hattie
On Strivers' Row 1946,Mr 1,17:2
King-Wood, David
Hidden River, The 1957,Ja 24,32:1
Beaux' Stratagem, The 1959,F 25,35:4
Much Ado About Nothing 1959,S 18,25:2
Kingdon, Edith
Hidden Horizon 1946,S 20,42:2
Kingdon, Frank
Letter of the Law, The; Robe Rouge, La
 1920,F 24,11:1
Americans in France, The 1920,Ag 4,14:1
Unwritten Chapter, The 1920,O 12,18:1
Sally 1920,D 22,16:1
Trial of Joan of Arc, The 1921,Mr 28,8:2
Annie Dear 1924,N 5,25:3
Mercenary Mary 1925,Ap 14,27:3
Blonde Sinner, The 1926,Jl 15,21:2
Yellow 1926,S 22,30:1

Kingdon, Frank—Cont
Honeymooning 1927,Mr 18,25:3
Sidewalks of New York 1927,O 4,33:1
Follow Thru 1929,Ja 10,24:3
Reunion in Vienna 1931,N 17,31:1
Murder at the Vanities 1933,S 13,22:4
Sleeping Clergyman, A 1934,O 9,16:1
Living Dangerously 1935,Ja 14,10:3
Kingdon, Leslie
Jubilee 1935,O 14,20:1
Kingdon, Marcella
Good Old Days, The 1951,Jl 18,21:2
Kingdon, Patrick
Barefoot Boy With Cheek 1947,Ap 4,20:2
Kingman, Dan
Yeomen of the Guard, The 1965,Jl 8,34:1
Kingman, Flavia Hsu
World of Suzie Wong, The 1958,O 15,47:1
Kingsberry, J H
Dodsworth 1934,F 26,20:4
Men in White 1955,F 26,13:2
Kingsberry, Jack (Director)
Guns 1928,Ag 7,25:2
Kingsberry, Jack (Producer)
Guns 1928,Ag 7,25:2
Kingsberry, Jacob
Samson and Delilah 1920,N 18,18:1
Kreutzer Sonata, The 1924,My 15,22:3
Izzy 1924,S 17,16:2
Arabesque 1925,O 21,20:2
Jest, The 1926,F 5,22:2
Good Fellow, The 1926,O 6,22:1
Kingsbury, Lillian
Liliom 1921,Ap 21,18:1
Forbidden 1923,O 2,10:2
Firebrand, The 1924,O 16,33:1
Kingsford, Guy
Once Is Enough 1938,F 16,16:2
Kingsford, Walter
Tragedy of Nan, The 1920,F 18,9:1
Cyrano de Bergerac 1920,Mr 20,14:3
All Soul's Eve 1920,My 13,9:1
Mob, The 1920,O 11,18:1
S S Glencairn 1924,N 4,31:4
Bachelor's Brides 1925,My 29,20:2
Hamlet 1925,N 10,23:1
Port O' London 1926,F 10,20:2
Sport of Kings, The 1926,My 5,24:2
Henry IV, Part I 1926,Je 1,29:1
Constant Wife, The 1926,N 30,26:3
Candida 1927,Ag 31,19:4
If 1927,O 26,26:2
So Am I 1928,Ja 28,9:1
Twelve Thousand 1928,Mr 13,23:1
Twelve Thousand 1928,Mr 18,IX,1:1
Criminal Code, The 1929,O 3,28:2
Children of Darkness 1930,Ja 8,25:1
Children of Darkness 1930,Ja 19,VIII,1:1
Twelfth Night 1930,S 14,VIII,2:8
Twelfth Night 1930,O 16,28:2
Twelfth Night 1930,N 2,VIII,1:1
Art and Mrs Bottle 1930,N 19,19:3
If Love Were All 1931,N 14,14:5
After All 1931,D 4,28:4
Black Tower 1932,Ja 12,29:2
Christopher Comes Across 1932,Je 1,19:2
Domino 1932,Ag 7,IX,1:1
Domino 1932,Ag 17,13:2
Criminal at Large 1932,O 11,26:3
For Services Rendered 1933,Ap 13,15:5
Going Gay 1933,Ag 4,18:5
Song of Norway 1944,Ag 22,20:2
Kingsland, Evelyn
Evil Doers of Good, The 1923,Ja 17,22:2
Kingsley, Charles
Pirates of Penzance, The 1942,F 20,20:2
Kingsley, Eleanore
Kismet 1965,Je 23,45:1
Kingsley, Evelyn
Megilla of Itzik Manger, The 1969,Ap 21,55:1
To Be or Not to Be-What Kind of a Question Is
That? 1970,O 20,39:1
Kingsley, Gershon
Cradle Will Rock, The 1964,N 9,40:4
Kingsley, Gershon (Composer)
But Never Jam Today 1969,Ap 24,40:1
Kingsley, Gershon (Miscellaneous)
Ernest in Love 1960,My 5,39:4
King of the Whole Damn World 1962,Ap 16,32:2
Put It in Writing 1963,My 14,31:1
Great Scot! 1965,N 12,56:3
Hooray!! It's a Glorious Day. . .And All That
1966,Mr 10,28:1
Kingsley, Gershon (Musical Director)
Entertainer, The 1958,F 13,22:2
Plume de Ma Tante, La 1958,N 12,42:1
Vintage '60 1960,S 13,41:1
Fly Blackbird 1962,F 6,26:2
Josephine Baker and Her Company 1964,F 5,30:1
Cafe Crown 1964,Ap 18,32:1
Cradle Will Rock, The 1964,N 9,40:4
Hotel Passionato 1965,O 23,16:1
I'm Solomon 1968,Ap 24,51:1

Kingsley, Guy
Danton's Death 1938,N 3,26:2
Male Animal, The 1941,Jl 9,24:6
Holiday 1941,Jl 23,15:2
Kingsley, Hal
Eternal Road, The 1937,Ja 8,14:2
Kingsley, Helen
Barrister, The 1932,N 22,25:2
Them's the Reporters 1935,My 30,21:4
Kingsley, Herbert
Mum's the Word 1940,D 6,28:5
Kingsley, Herbert (Composer)
Taming of the Shrew, The 1940,F 6,17:2
Pirate, The 1942,N 26,39:2
Mr Winkle's Holliday 1946,Je 24,27:6
Kingsley, Herbert (Lyricist)
Mr Winkle's Holliday 1946,Je 24,27:6
Kingsley, Herbert (Miscellaneous)
Belle Helene, La 1941,Jl 8,14:1
Kingsley, Lionel
Queen After Death 1956,Mr 13,33:2
Kingsley, Martin
Antony and Cleopatra 1947,N 27,49:2
Red Gloves 1948,D 6,28:2
Richard III 1953,D 10,65:2
Kingsley, Michael
Winslow Boy, The 1947,O 30,32:2
Out of This World 1950,D 22,17:3
Kingsley, Mona
Humming Bird, The 1923,Ja 16,16:2
Love Scandal, A 1923,N 7,14:1
Dr David's Dad 1924,Ag 14,10:3
White Collars 1925,F 24,17:2
What Women Do? 1925,Jl 21,26:4
Wise-Crackers, The 1925,D 17,26:1
Still Waters 1926,Mr 2,23:1
Lost 1927,Mr 29,22:2
Thief, The 1927,Ap 23,15:2
Triumphant Bachelor, The 1927,S 16,21:1
Kingsley, Pamela
Tenth Man, The 1967,N 9,54:1
Kingsley, Patti
Louisiana Lady 1947,Je 3,35:2
Kingsley, Sidney (Director)
Dead End 1935,O 29,17:2
Ten Million Ghosts 1936,O 24,23:7
World We Make, The 1939,N 21,19:1
Detective Story 1949,Mr 24,34:2
Detective Story 1949,Ap 3,II,1:1
Darkness at Noon 1951,Ja 15,13:4
Darkness at Noon 1951,Ja 21,II,1:1
Lunatics and Lovers 1954,D 14,44:2
Night Life 1962,O 2,45:2
Night Life 1962,O 24,44:1
Kingsley, Sidney (Playwright)
Men in White 1933,S 27,24:2
Men in White 1933,O 1,IX,1:1
Men in White 1934,Je 29,16:3
Dead End 1935,O 29,17:2
Dead End 1935,N 3,X,1:1
Ten Million Ghosts 1936,O 24,23:7
Dead End 1937,Je 29,18:3
Dead End 1937,Ag 17,23:1
World We Make, The 1939,N 21,19:1
World We Make, The 1939,N 26,IX,1:3
World We Make, The 1939,D 3,IX,5:1
Patriots, The 1943,Ja 30,11:2
Patriots, The 1943,Ja 31,V,16:1
Patriots, The 1943,F 7,II,1:1
Patriots, The 1943,My 9,II,1:1
Patriots, The 1943,D 21,22:5
Detective Story 1949,Mr 24,34:2
Detective Story 1949,Ap 3,II,1:1
Detective Story 1950,Mr 27,18:2
Darkness at Noon 1951,Ja 15,13:4
Darkness at Noon 1951,Ja 21,II,1:1
Detective Story 1954,F 13,11:2
Lunatics and Lovers 1954,D 14,44:2
Men in White 1955,F 26,13:2
Night Life 1962,O 2,45:2
Night Life 1962,O 24,44:1
Kingsley, Sidney (Producer)
Ten Million Ghosts 1936,O 24,23:7
World We Make, The 1939,N 21,19:1
Night Life 1962,O 24,44:1
Kingstead, Helen
Lally 1927,F 9,16:3
Greeks Had a Word for It, The 1930,S 26,16:5
Chauve-Souris; Queen of Spades, The
1931,O 22,27:1
New Life, A 1943,S 16,26:6
Kingston, Gaylord B
Squealer, The 1928,N 13,36:3
Crooks' Convention, The 1929,S 19,37:4
Charm 1929,N 29,24:5
Othello 1937,Ja 7,16:4
Kingston, Gertrude
Red Blinds 1926,O 1,27:1
Kingston, Harry
Happy Birthday 1946,N 1,31:2
Kingston, Kay
As You Like It 1955,O 29,12:2
Midsummer Night's Dream, A 1956,Ja 14,12:2

Kingston, Kay—Cont
Call It Virtue 1963,Mr 28,8:2
Victims, The; Victims of Duty 1968,Mr 6,34:1
Kingston, Leonard (Playwright)
Travelling Light 1965,Ap 9,18:1
Kingston, Rose
Sherlock Holmes 1929,N 26,28:3
Kingston, Winifred
Matrimonial Bed, The 1927,O 13,23:2
Caste 1927,D 24,8:1
Kingwill, Andie Wilson (Lighting Director)
Tonight in Living Color; Golden Fleece, The
1969,Je 11,43:1
Tonight in Living Color; David Show, The
1969,Je 11,43:1
Kinigstein, Jonah (Scenic Designer)
Eagle Has Two Heads, The 1956,D 14,37:2
Kinkead, Cleves (Playwright)
Your Woman and Mine 1922,F 28,17:2
Kinne, Roger
This Is the Army 1942,Jl 5,28:2
Kinnear, Roy
Travails of Sancho Panza, The 1969,D 20,35:1
Kinnell, Gertrude
As You Like It 1945,Jl 4,10:4
Song of Bernadette 1946,Mr 27,22:2
Knight of the Burning Pestle, The 1953,O 24,13:2
Moon in Capricorn 1953,O 28,37:2
Corn Is Green, The 1954,F 27,10:2
Romeo and Juliet 1956,F 24,20:4
Measure for Measure 1957,Ja 23,24:1
Visit, The 1958,My 6,40:1
Sudden End of Anne Cinquefoil, The
1961,Ja 11,25:2
Kinnell, Murray
Cymbeline 1923,O 3,12:1
Twelfth Night 1923,O 23,17:1
Hassan 1924,S 23,23:1
Way of the World, The 1924,N 18,23:4
Sign of the Leopard 1928,D 12,34:4
Elizabeth and Essex 1930,Mr 2,IX,4:7
Royal Virgin, The 1930,Mr 18,30:5
Kinnell, Peter
Escape This Night 1938,Ap 23,18:1
Kinney, James
World We Live In, The 1922,N 1,16:1
Kinney, Joseph
Blue Blood 1924,Ap 3,21:2
Kinney, Ray
Hellzapoppin 1938,S 23,34:2
Kinney, William
It's A Gift 1945,Mr 13,18:7
Kinnon, Roberta
Love and Libel 1960,D 8,44:1
Kinoy, Ernest (Playwright)
Something About a Soldier 1962,Ja 5,36:2
Bajour 1964,N 24,42:1
Golden Rainbow 1968,F 5,27:1
Kinsberry, Jacob
Letter of the Law, The; Robe Rouge, La
1920,F 24,11:1
Casanova 1923,S 27,10:2
Kinsella, Walter
Road to Rome, The 1927,F 1,24:2
Ladies of the Jury 1929,O 22,26:2
It's a Grand Life 1930,F 11,30:3
Blessed Event 1932,F 13,23:2
Arrest That Woman 1936,S 19,20:4
Mrs O'Brien Entertains 1939,F 9,16:3
Seven Scenes for Yeni 1963,My 13,36:2
Kinsolving, Lee
Winesburg, Ohio 1958,F 6,22:2
Kinsolving, William
Irregular Verb to Love, The 1963,S 19,22:2
Roar Like a Dove 1964,My 22,40:2
Kinston, Frank Weir
Tea for Three 1935,Jl 9,24:4
Kinter, Richard
Merry Death, A 1959,N 10,55:3
No Trifling With Love 1959,N 10,55:3
White Cargo 1960,D 30,12:1
Kinyard, Peggy
Can-Can 1959,Ag 26,25:4
Kinz, Franziska
Peripherie 1926,D 19,VII,4:4
Kinzer, William E (Director)
Immaculate Misconception, The 1970,O 28,63:3
Kinzer, William E (Scenic Designer)
Immaculate Misconception, The 1970,O 28,63:3
Kipen, Elsa
Audition of the Apprentice Theatre 1939,Je 2,26:2
Kiper, Miriam
Medea 1920,Mr 23,12:2
Kipfer, Victor
Nautical but Nice 1931,Ap 19,31:6
Kipling, Kenneth
Blood and Sand 1921,S 21,16:2
Kipness, Joseph (Miscellaneous)
Conscience 1952,My 16,17:6
Kipness, Joseph (Producer)
Brights Lights of 1944 1943,S 17,27:4
Duke in Darkness, The 1944,Ja 25,15:2
Star Spangled Family 1945,Ap 11,18:6
High Button Shoes 1947,O 10,32:2

Kipness, Joseph (Producer)—Cont
All You Need Is One Good Break 1950,F 10,20:3
Women of Twilight 1952,Mr 4,22:2
Be Your Age 1953,Ja 15,24:2
Plume de Ma Tante, La 1958,N 12,42:1
Have I Got a Girl for You! 1963,D 3,53:2
I Had a Ball 1964,D 16,50:1
Grosse Valise, La 1965,D 15,52:1
But, Seriously... 1969,F 28,29:1
Applause 1970,Mr 31,35:1
Kipnis, Claude (Playwright)
Men and Dreams 1966,S 7,51:2
Kipnis, Dinah (Costume Designer)
Men and Dreams 1966,S 7,51:2
Kipnis, Leonid (Miscellaneous)
Dinner at Eight 1966,S 28,38:1
Kipnis, Leonid (Translator)
Three Sisters, The 1963,Jl 22,19:2
Cherry Orchard, The 1965,Ag 2,17:2
Three Sisters, The 1968,Mr 18,56:1
Kippen, Manart
Poldekin 1920,S 10,12:1
Samson and Delilah 1920,N 18,18:1
Daddy's Gone A-Hunting 1921,S 1,18:3
Johannes Kreisler 1922,D 25,20:3
Kreutzer Sonata, The 1924,My 15,22:3
Puppets of Passion 1927,F 25,24:4
Royal Box, The 1928,N 21,32:3
Sakura 1928,D 26,14:4
Fifty Million Frenchmen 1929,N 28,34:4
Mr Samuel 1930,N 11,28:4
Wolves 1932,Ja 7,26:3
American Dream; 1933 1933,F 22,24:5
Mask and the Face, The 1933,My 9,20:2
Yoshe Kalb 1933,D 29,27:2
All the King's Horses 1934,Ja 31,21:3
Ship Comes in, A 1934,S 20,21:1
For Valor 1935,N 19,27:5
Bitter Stream 1936,Mr 31,16:6
Marching Song 1937,F 18,18:2
To Quito and Back 1937,O 7,30:4
Miracle in the Mountains 1947,Ap 26,10:2
Kipphardt, Heinar (Original Author)
Oppenheimer File, The 1964,D 15,56:1
Kipphardt, Heinar (Playwright)
In der Sache J Robert Oppenheimer 1964,N 3,27:2
In the Matter of J Robert Oppenheimer
  1968,My 27,55:1
In the Matter of J Robert Oppenheimer
  1968,Je 7,31:1
In the Matter of J Robert Oppenheimer
  1968,Je 9,II,1:1
In the Matter of J Robert Oppenheimer
  1969,Mr 7,28:1
In the Matter of J Robert Oppenheimer
  1969,Mr 16,II,1:3
Kirby, Ann
Coquette 1935,My 22,23:4
Kirby, Annette
????? 1939,Ja 2,28:2
Kirby, Bruce
King and the Duke, The 1955,Je 2,25:2
Diamond Orchid 1965,F 11,44:4
Kirby, Durward
Me and Thee 1965,D 8,58:4
Kirby, George
Cotton Club Revue of 1957 1957,Jl 10,23:4
Kirby, John
Tip-Toes 1926,S 1,27:4
Kirby, John and his Orchestra
Brights Lights of 1944 1943,S 17,27:4
Kirby, Keith
Wisteria Trees, The 1955,F 3,20:2
Best Foot Forward 1956,Mr 3,16:1
School for Wives 1957,Je 20,23:4
Hamlet 1970,D 28,40:1
Kirby, Lorraine
Truckline Cafe 1946,F 28,19:4
Kirby, Max
Bitter Sweet 1929,N 6,30:2
Good Companions, The 1931,O 2,31:1
Kirby, Michael
Hollywood Ice Revue 1950,Ja 21,13:4
Hollywood Ice Revue 1953,Ja 16,17:2
Kirby, Michael (Director)
Beautiful Jailer, The 1957,My 17,19:2
Kirby, Michael (Scenic Designer)
Dionysus in 69 1968,Je 7,35:3
Dionysus in 69 1968,N 19,52:1
Kirby, Nan (Playwright)
Career 1943,O 29,22:6
Kirby, Randy
Me and Thee 1965,D 8,58:4
Mame 1966,My 25,41:1
Kirby, Richard
Finian's Rainbow 1953,Mr 7,13:2
Kirby, Thom (Miscellaneous)
This Was Burlesque 1970,F 12,31:1
Kirchnak, John
Richard II 1951,Ja 25,21:2
Kirchner, R G
Pursuit of Happiness, The 1933,O 10,24:4
Kirchner, Ray
By the Beautiful Sea 1954,Ap 9,20:1

Kirchon, V (Playwright)
Red Rust 1929,D 18,31:1
Kirillin, Tamara
Clear All Wires! 1932,S 15,19:1
Kiriloff, Fred (Miscellaneous)
Otage, L' 1959,O 27,42:1
Kiritake, Icho (Miscellaneous)
Greengrocer's Daughter, The 1966,Mr 16,50:1
General's Daughter, The 1966,Mr 16,50:1
Fishing for Wives 1966,Mr 16,50:1
Kiritake, Kamematsu (Miscellaneous)
Greengrocer's Daughter, The 1966,Mr 16,50:1
General's Daughter, The 1966,Mr 16,50:1
Fishing for Wives 1966,Mr 16,50:1
Kiritake, Kanjuro (Miscellaneous)
General's Daughter, The 1966,Mr 16,50:1
Greengrocer's Daughter, The 1966,Mr 16,50:1
Fishing for Wives 1966,Mr 16,50:1
Kiritake, Monju (Miscellaneous)
General's Daughter, The 1966,Mr 16,50:1
Greengrocer's Daughter, The 1966,Mr 16,50:1
Fishing for Wives 1966,Mr 16,50:1
Kiritake, Monjuro (Miscellaneous)
General's Daughter, The 1966,Mr 16,50:1
Greengrocer's Daughter, The 1966,Mr 16,50:1
Fishing for Wives 1966,Mr 16,50:1
Kirk, Al
Great White Hope, The 1967,D 14,58:1
Kirk, Alan
Song of Norway 1959,Je 26,16:2
Kirk, Alexander
King of Nowhere, The 1938,Ap 3,XI,1:8
Kirk, Frank J
Triumph of X, The 1921,Ag 25,8:2
Intimate Strangers, The 1921,N 8,28:1
Listening In 1922,D 5,24:1
Kirk, George
Nina Rosa 1930,My 31,19:3
Nina Rosa 1930,S 22,22:5
Cat and the Fiddle, The 1931,O 16,26:4
Let 'Em Eat Cake 1933,O 23,18:1
Revenge With Music 1934,N 29,33:5
Kirk, J F
Body Beautiful, The 1935,N 1,24:3
Happy Valley, Limited 1936,Je 30,15:1
Lend Me Your Ears! 1936,O 6,28:5
On Location 1937,S 28,19:1
Run Sheep Run 1938,N 4,26:2
Susanna, Don't You Cry 1939,My 23,27:2
Snookie 1941,Je 4,26:2
Sweet Charity 1942,N 29,26:4
Harvey 1944,N 2,23:2
Kirk, J F (Director)
Regular Guy, A; Man's Man, A 1931,Je 5,27:1
Kirk, Jimmy
Mimic World of 1921, The 1921,Ag 18,9:2
Kirk, Lawrence (Playwright)
Innocent Party, The 1938,F 13,X,3:3
Kirk, Lisa
Good Night Ladies 1945,Ja 18,16:2
Allegro 1947,O 11,10:2
Kiss Me, Kate 1948,D 31,10:3
Kiss Me, Kate 1949,Ja 16,II,1:1
Kirk, Patrick
Magdalena 1948,S 21,31:2
Kirk, Phyllis
My Name is Aquilon 1949,F 10,38:2
Point of No Return 1951,O 31,32:2
Kirk, Richard (Costume Designer)
Comrades 1956,Je 6,38:1
Kirk, Richard (Scenic Designer)
He Who Gets Slapped 1956,F 2,18:1
Comrades 1956,Je 6,38:1
Long Voyage Home, The 1961,D 5,49:1
Kirk, Tommy
Ah, Wilderness! 1954,Ag 21,20:4
Kirk, Van
'Tis of Thee 1940,O 28,21:3
Kirkbride, Bradford
Princess Virtue 1921,My 5,20:2
Sue, Dear 1922,Jl 11,16:2
Escape This Night 1938,Ap 23,18:1
Kirke, Donald
Gang War 1928,Ag 21,27:2
Remote Control 1929,S 11,24:5
Old Rascal, The 1930,Mr 25,34:4
Woman Denied, A 1931,F 26,21:1
Constant Sinner, The 1931,S 15,30:1
Kirkham, Sam
Cyrano de Bergerac 1946,O 9,33:2
Cyrano de Bergerac 1947,Ja 17,27:2
South Pacific 1957,Ap 25,35:1
Pajama Game, The 1957,My 16,27:1
Carousel 1957,S 12,38:2
King and I, The 1960,My 12,40:1
King and I, The 1963,Je 13,30:2
South Pacific 1965,Je 3,25:1
Persecution and Assassination of Marat As
  Performed by the Inmates of the Asylum of
  Charenton Under the Direction of the Marquis de
  Sade, The 1967,Ja 4,34:1
King and I, The 1968,My 24,39:1
Oklahoma! 1969,Je 24,37:1

Kirkland, Alexander
Devil to Pay, The 1925,D 4,26:2
Right Age to Marry, The 1926,F 16,22:3
Yellow Jacket, The 1928,N 8,27:3
Wings Over Europe 1928,D 11,35:1
Month in the Country, A 1930,Mr 18,30:5
Marseilles; Marius 1930,N 9,IX,3:2
Marseilles 1930,N 18,28:2
Men Must Fight 1931,Ap 12,IX,2:1
Men in White 1933,S 27,24:2
Men in White 1933,O 1,IX,1:1
Gold Eagle Guy 1934,N 29,33:4
Gold Eagle Guy 1934,D 9,X,1:1
Till the Day I Die 1935,Mr 27,24:5
Berkeley Square 1935,Ag 20,25:1
Weep for the Virgins 1935,D 2,18:1
Case of Clyde Griffiths 1936,Mr 14,10:4
County Chairman, The 1936,My 26,26:5
Black Limelight 1936,N 10,31:1
Many Mansions 1937,Ag 3,20:5
Many Mansions 1937,O 28,28:6
Outward Bound 1938,D 23,16:5
Junior Miss 1941,N 19,28:2
Lady in Danger 1945,Mr 30,18:6
Kirkland, Alexander (Director)
Shadow Play 1939,Ag 15,14:5
Out of the Frying Pan 1941,F 12,24:2
Snark Was a Boojum, The 1943,S 2,14:4
Family Affair, A 1946,N 28,41:2
Kirkland, Alexander (Miscellaneous)
Strings, My Lord, Are False, The 1942,My 20,24:2
Kirkland, Alexander (Playwright)
Lady in Danger 1945,Mr 30,18:6
Kirkland, Alexander (Producer)
Out of the Frying Pan 1941,F 12,24:2
Kirkland, Frances
Petticoat Fever 1935,Jl 2,24:4
Kirkland, Hardee
Man Higher Up, The 1926,N 23,27:3
Vaudeville (Palace) 1926,N 23,27:3
Kirkland, Jack (Director)
Tortilla Flat 1938,Ja 13,16:2
Suds in Your Eye 1944,Ja 13,15:5
Mr Adam 1949,My 26,34:6
Kirkland, Jack (Playwright)
Tobacco Road 1933,D 5,31:2
Tortilla Flat 1938,Ja 13,16:2
I Must Love Someone 1939,F 8,18:7
Tobacco Road 1940,D 5,32:3
Tobacco Road 1942,S 7,34:2
Tobacco Road 1943,S 6,21:3
Suds in Your Eye 1944,Ja 13,15:5
Mr Adam 1949,My 26,34:6
Tobacco Road 1949,Ag 11,27:5
Tobacco Road 1950,Mr 7,23:2
Man With the Golden Arm, The 1956,My 22,28:1
Tobacco Road 1960,My 11,44:2
Mandingo 1961,My 23,43:6
Kirkland, Jack (Producer)
Bright Honor 1936,S 28,14:1
Forbidden Melody 1936,O 13,30:3
Forbidden Melody 1936,N 3,33:1
Tortilla Flat 1938,Ja 13,16:2
I Must Love Someone 1939,F 8,18:7
Susannah and the Elders 1940,O 30,28:2
Tanyard Street 1941,F 5,16:2
They Can't Get You Down 1941,N 2,IX,3:5
Tobacco Road 1942,S 7,34:2
Moon Vine, The 1943,F 12,22:2
Tobacco Road 1943,S 6,21:3
Mr Adam 1949,My 26,34:6
Kirkland, James
Betty Behave 1927,Mr 9,28:4
Kirkland, John M (Playwright)
Frankie and Johnny 1930,S 26,16:5
Kirkland, John M (Producer)
Frankie and Johnny 1930,S 26,16:5
Kirkland, Muriel
School for Scandal, The 1923,Mr 13,19:2
Brass Buttons 1927,D 6,26:3
Cock Robin 1928,Ja 13,26:6
Strictly Dishonorable 1929,S 19,37:1
Strictly Dishonorable 1929,S 29,IX,1:1
Greeks Had a Word for It, The 1930,S 26,16:5
I Love an Actress 1931,S 18,29:2
Fast Service 1931,N 18,26:3
Sailor, Beware! 1934,Ja 21,X,1:6
Lady of Letters 1935,Mr 29,26:6
Bride the Sun Shines On, The 1936,Jl 1,29:2
Suddenly a Stranger 1936,Ag 4,15:2
Stop-Over 1938,Ja 12,16:5
Abe Lincoln in Illinois 1938,O 4,20:1
Abe Lincoln in Illinois 1938,O 17,12:2
Inherit the Wind 1955,Ap 22,20:2
Legend of Lizzie, The 1959,F 10,39:1
Tango 1969,Ja 20,33:1
Kirkland, Patricia
For Keeps 1944,Je 15,17:5
Snafu 1944,O 26,19:5
Round Trip 1945,My 30,16:4
Years Ago 1946,D 4,44:2
Years Ago 1946,D 15,II,3:1
You Never Can Tell 1948,Mr 17,31:2

Kirkland, Patricia—Cont
Young and Fair, The 1948,N 23,35:2
Wonderful Town 1955,My 17,33:4
Kirkland, Paul
Vaudeville (Palace) 1926,Je 29,21:3
Kirkland, Sally
Love Nest, The 1963,Ja 28,7:6
Fitz 1966,My 17,51:2
Tom Paine 1968,Mr 26,38:1
Futz 1968,Je 14,39:1
Sweet Eros 1968,N 22,38:1
Witness 1968,N 22,38:1
One Night Stands of a Noisy Passenger; Noisy
    Passenger, The 1970,D 31,8:3
Kirkland, William
Sandro Botticelli 1923,Mr 27,24:2
Time 1923,N 27,23:3
Tyrants 1924,Mr 5,14:1
Kirkley, Donald
Patience 1928,Je 26,29:3
Kirkley, Donald (Playwright)
Happily Ever After 1945,Mr 16,21:2
Kirkman, Sam
Alive and Kicking 1950,Ja 18,25:5
Kirkpatrick, Hubbard
Sophie 1920,Mr 3,12:2
Pasteur 1923,Mr 13,19:1
Moon-Flower, The 1924,F 26,15:1
Man in Evening Clothes, The 1924,D 6,13:4
Kirkpatrick, John (Musical Director)
Romio and Julietta 1925,Ap 21,19:1
Fratricide Punished 1925,Ap 21,19:1
Kirkpatrick, John (Playwright)
Book of Charm, The 1925,S 4,26:3
Book of Charm, The 1925,S 13,VIII,1:1
When in Rome 1929,Je 16,VIII,2:1
Love Expert, The 1929,S 24,29:1
Charm 1929,N 29,24:5
Ada Beats the Drum 1930,My 9,20:4
Kirkpatrick, Mary (Producer)
Thou Desperate Pilot 1927,Mr 8,23:1
Kirkpatrick, Mary H (Playwright)
Fatal Wedding, The 1924,Je 3,22:3
Kirkpatrick, Peggy
Trials of Brother Jero, The 1967,N 10,60:1
Strong Breed, The 1967,N 10,60:1
Kirkpatrick, Sam (Scenic Designer)
Hamlet 1969,Je 11,37:1
Kirkpatrick, Sidney
Chip Woman's Fortune, The 1923,My 8,22:2
Salome 1923,My 8,22:2
Comedy of Errors, The 1923,My 16,22:5
Salome 1923,My 20,VII,1:1
Chip Woman's Fortune, The 1923,My 20,VII,1:1
Meek Mose 1928,F 7,30:1
Kirksey, Kirk
Big Time Buck White 1968,D 9,58:1
Five on the Black Hand Side 1970,Ja 2,32:2
Kirksey, Van
Big Time Buck White 1968,D 9,58:1
Kirkup, James (Playwright)
Physicists, The 1964,O 14,52:1
Kirkwood, James
Fool, The 1922,O 24,18:1
Ladies of the Evening 1924,D 24,11:2
Lambs Gambol 1925,Ap 27,15:1
Edgar Allan Poe 1925,O 6,31:1
Edgar Allan Poe 1925,O 11,VIII,1:1
House of Remsen 1934,Ap 3,26:4
Seven Keys to Baldpate 1935,My 28,30:2
Noble Prize, The 1935,Jl 9,24:3
Three Wise Fools 1936,Ja 14,25:2
Three Wise Fools 1936,Mr 2,12:2
County Chairman, The 1936,My 26,26:5
Kirkwood, James Jr
Dance Me a Song 1950,Ja 21,10:5
Wonderful Town 1963,F 15,10:2
Kirkwood, James Jr (Playwright)
Dance Me a Song 1950,Ja 21,10:5
Utbu 1966,Ja 5,24:1
Kirkwood, Joe
Vaudeville (Palace) 1929,My 13,26:3
Kirkwood, John (Playwright)
13 Belgrave Square 1931,Je 14,VIII,2:2
Kirkwood, Kathleen
Ten Nights in a Barroom 1928,Mr 28,31:2
Kirkwood, Kathleen (Director)
Malinda 1929,D 4,37:2
Bare Facts of Today 1930,Ap 17,24:4
Kirkwood, Kathleen (Lyricist)
Bare Facts of Today 1930,Ap 17,24:4
Kirkwood, Kathleen (Producer)
Bare Facts 1926,Jl 19,13:3
Bare Facts 1927,Ag 17,27:5
Ten Nights in a Barroom 1928,Mr 28,31:2
Malinda 1929,D 4,37:2
Kirkwood, Pat
Ace of Clubs 1950,Jl 8,7:2
Wonderful Town 1955,Mr 6,II,3:1
Kirland, Robert W
Rhapsody 1944,N 23,37:2
Kirle, Bruce (Composer)
Caution: A Love Story 1969,Ap 4,45:1

Kirov, Ivan
Sons o' Fun 1941,D 2,28:2
Kirov, Yaroslav
Lady in the Dark 1941,Ja 24,14:2
Kirsch, Carolyn
Coco 1969,D 19,66:1
Kirsch, M
Aristocrats 1935,My 2,16:2
Kirschner, Don (Miscellaneous)
Golden Rainbow 1968,F 5,27:1
Kirschner, Richard (Director)
Oresteia 1966,Je 30,29:1
Birds, The 1966,Jl 1,40:1
Kirschner, Theodore
Fifty-Fifty 1937,N 20,21:1
Fifty-Fifty 1937,D 5,II,3:4
Kirshner, May (Miscellaneous)
Darkness at Noon 1951,Ja 15,13:4
Night Life 1962,O 24,44:1
Kirshner, May (Producer)
Lunatics and Lovers 1954,D 14,44:2
Kirstein, Lincoln (Choreographer)
Would-Be Gentleman, The 1936,Ag 4,15:1
Kirstein, Lincoln (Director)
Julius Caesar 1955,Jl 13,20:1
Kirstein, Lincoln (Miscellaneous)
Much Ado About Nothing 1955,Ag 20,20:4
Play of Daniel, The 1960,D 27,23:6
Play of Daniel, The 1961,D 28,22:6
Kirstein, Lincoln (Playwright)
White House Happening 1967,Ag 27,II,4:8
Kirstein, Lincoln (Producer)
Saint of Bleecker Street, The 1954,D 28,21:1
Play of Daniel, The 1958,Ja 3,15:3
Play of Daniel, The 1958,Ja 26,II,1:1
Play of Daniel, The 1959,Ja 6,30:2
Play of Herod, The 1963,D 10,55:2
Kirsten, Dorothy
New Moon, The 1944,My 18,16:2
Kirsten, Robert
Minstrel Boy, The 1948,O 15,28:2
Kirtland, Louise
Night Hostess 1928,S 13,31:2
Getting Even 1929,Ag 20,31:1
Light Wines and Beer 1930,N 11,28:6
Church Mouse, A 1931,O 13,26:4
Tell Her the Truth 1932,O 29,18:2
Melody 1933,F 15,17:4
Shady Lady 1933,Jl 6,26:3
Her Man of Wax 1933,O 12,32:3
Only Girl, The 1934,My 22,28:2
Few Are Chosen 1935,S 18,19:3
In Heaven and Earth 1936,Mr 27,24:8
Love in My Fashion 1937,D 4,21:4
Along Fifth Avenue 1949,Ja 14,28:2
Alive and Kicking 1950,Ja 18,25:5
Waltz of the Toreadors, The 1957,Ja 18,17:2
Waltz of the Toreadors, The 1957,Ja 27,II,1:1
Winkelberg 1958,Ja 15,26:2
Tovarich 1963,Mr 20,5:1
Kirujuro
Kagami-Jishi; Mirror Lion Dance, The
    1969,S 11,53:1
Kirwin, Kathleen
Gondoliers, The 1957,My 29,34:2
Kis, Irena (Choreographer)
Progress of Bora, The Tailor, The 1968,Je 27,49:2
Kisch, Flora
Trojan Women, The 1923,My 27,10:2
Kiser, Franklin
Valmouth 1960,O 7,29:1
Ben Franklin in Paris 1964,O 28,52:1
Kiser, Jane
Helen Goes to Troy 1944,Ap 25,17:2
Kiser, Terry
Night of the Dunce 1966,D 29,21:1
Fortune and Men's Eyes 1967,F 24,29:1
Horseman, Pass By 1969,Ja 16,46:4
Conerico Was Here to Stay 1969,Mr 11,39:1
Paradise Gardens East 1969,Mr 11,39:1
Ofay Watcher, The 1969,S 16,40:1
Ofay Watcher, The 1969,S 21,II,1:2
Paris Is Out! 1970,F 3,35:1
Paris Is Out! 1970,F 15,II,1:1
Paris Is Out! 1970,F 22,II,5:5
Castro Complex, The 1970,N 19,40:1
Kiser, Virginia
Mummers and Men 1962,Mr 27,41:6
Chocolates 1967,Ap 11,51:1
Perfect Party, The 1969,Mr 21,42:1
Kish, Stephen
Mother Courage and Her Children 1964,My 12,32:2
Kishida, Kyoko
Taming of the Shrew, The 1966,F 5,32:1
Kishon, Ephraim (Director)
Unfair to Goliath 1970,Ja 26,27:1
Kishon, Ephraim (Playwright)
Unfair to Goliath 1970,Ja 26,27:1
Kisner, Bernard
Paths of Glory 1935,S 27,24:2
Paradise Lost 1935,D 10,31:5
Plumes in the Dust 1936,N 7,14:2

Kiss
Postmistress, The 1928,Ja 15,VIII,2:1
Olympia 1928,Mr 25,IX,4:1
Kiss, Edmund (Playwright)
Wittekind 1935,F 24,VIII,2:1
Kiss, Ferencz
Death of Danton, The 1928,O 28,IX,2:1
Kissel, Jac
Nobody Hears A Broken Drum 1970,Mr 20,55:1
Kissell, Irene
What Next 1920,Ja 27,7:2
Kissman, Lee
Up to Thursday 1965,F 11,45:1
Hawk, The 1968,Ap 18,54:1
Unseen Hand, The 1970,Ap 2,43:1
Kistenmaeckers, Henry (Playwright)
Woman of Bronze, The 1920,S 8,9:2
Plein aux As 1926,O 31,VIII,2:4
Woman of Bronze, The 1927,Je 16,25:4
Deodat 1931,Ap 19,VIII,2:8
Kistner, Marlene
Ice Follies 1959,Ja 14,30:1
Kistner & Clark
Ice Follies 1960,Ja 13,20:1
Kitaros, The
Vaudeville (Palace) 1924,Mr 18,25:1
Vaudeville (Palace) 1926,Ag 24,19:3
Kitch, Kenneth
Galileo 1963,Ja 5,5:2
Milk Train Doesn't Stop Here Anymore, The
    1965,Jl 27,25:1
Kitch, Kenneth (Director)
Cage, The 1970,Je 19,25:1
Kitch, Kenneth (Miscellaneous)
Midsummer Night's Dream, A 1967,Je 30,23:1
Kitchell, Iva
That Girl at the Bijou 1956,N 10,15:4
That Girl at the Bijou 1956,N 18,II,11:2
Kitchen, David
World of Suzie Wong, The 1958,O 15,47:1
Kitchen, Mary Cory
Plain Jane 1924,My 13,24:2
Kitoaji, Kinya
Scarlett 1970,Ja 3,19:1
Kitson, Barbara
Nerves 1924,S 2,22:2
She Had to Know 1925,F 3,25:3
Kitson, Rett
Rats of Norway, The 1948,Ap 16,27:6
Kitt, Eartha
New Faces of 1952 1952,My 17,23:2
New Faces of 1952 1952,My 25,II,1:1
Mrs Patterson 1954,D 2,37:1
Shinbone Alley 1957,Ap 15,23:2
Shinbone Alley 1957,Ap 28,II,1:1
Jolly's Progress 1959,D 7,42:2
Kitto, H D F (Translator)
Electra 1964,Ag 12,42:1
Electra 1969,Ag 8,14:1
Kittredge, Dorothy
Good Morning 1937,D 4,20:7
Kittredge, Harry
Prince and the Pauper, The 1920,N 2,15:1
Kittredge, Helen Gholson (Director)
Doing Nicely 1940,D 4,34:3
Man-Hunt 1940,D 4,34:3
Kittredge, Helen Gholson (Playwright)
Doing Nicely 1940,D 4,34:3
Reaper 1940,D 4,34:3
Man-Hunt 1940,D 4,34:3
Time to Burn 1940,D 4,34:3
Kivi, Aleksis (Playwright)
Betrothal, The 1959,F 16,52:2
Kiviette (Costume Designer)
Here's Howe! 1928,My 2,19:3
Treasure Girl 1928,N 9,22:1
Heads Up! 1929,N 12,34:1
You Said It 1931,Ja 20,21:3
Band Wagon, The 1931,Je 4,31:3
Shoot the Works! 1931,Jl 22,19:5
Free for All 1931,S 9,25:1
Singin' the Blues 1931,S 17,21:3
Here Goes the Bride 1931,N 4,31:2
Strike Me Pink 1933,Mr 6,16:3
Roberta 1933,N 20,18:4
Ziegfeld Follies 1934,Ja 5,24:3
Between the Devil 1937,D 23,24:5
Light Up the Sky 1948,N 19,34:2
Kiyoko, Chiba (Costume Designer)
Golden Bat 1970,Je 27,18:2
Kjeldsen, Ingeborg
Kismet 1965,Je 23,45:1
Kjellstrom, Axel (Original Author)
Scandal in Assyria 1939,My 28,X,2:5
Kjems, Constant
Audition of the Apprentice Theatre 1939,Je 2,26:2
Klabund (Original Author)
Chalk Circle, The 1933,Ag 22,20:5
Klabund (Playwright)
Cromwell 1926,N 7,VIII,4:3
Chalk Circle, The 1928,Ja 15,VIII,2:1
Circle of Chalk, The 1929,Mr 31,VIII,2:6
X Y Z 1929,Ap 7,X,4:4

Klabund (Playwright)—Cont
Circle of Chalk, The 1941,Mr 27,28:4
Circle of Chalk, The 1950,D 2,8:3
Klabund (Translator)
Love in the Country 1930,S 28,VIII,4:4
Klachkin, Raphael
Dybbuk, The 1964,F 4,30:2
Children of the Shadows 1964,F 27,26:1
Klaer, Adele
Wandering Jew, The 1921,O 27,22:1
Up the Ladder 1922,Mr 7,11:2
Untitled-Revue 1923,My 12,15:4
Artists and Models 1923,Ag 21,12:2
Critic, The 1925,My 9,12:4
Strange Prince 1926,D 8,24:2
Revelry 1927,S 13,37:1
Elmer Gantry 1928,Ag 10,9:4
Let Us Be Gay 1929,F 22,19:1
Gala Night 1930,F 26,22:4
Klages, Raymond (Lyricist)
Sally, Irene and Mary 1922,S 5,21:2
Klaif, Sharon
Pequod 1969,Je 30,33:1
Klanfer, Francois Regis
Chicago 70 1970,My 26,33:1
Klarich, Mark
Tom Paine 1969,Mr 30,71:2
Klarmann, Adolph (Translator)
Thomas Paine 1930,Mr 21,30:7
Klarsfeld, Sylvia
Boutique Fantasque, La 1929,D 28,10:6
Master of the Revels 1935,Ag 14,16:2
Klatzkin, Raphael
Dybbuk, The 1948,My 3,26:3
David's Crown 1948,My 10,26:2
Golem, The 1948,My 17,22:3
Oedipus Rex 1948,My 24,23:2
Klauber, Adolph (Producer)
Emperor Jones, The 1920,D 28,9:1
Charlatan, The 1922,Ap 30,VII,1:1
Diversion 1928,Ja 12,25:1
Klauber, Marcel (Playwright)
My Fair Ladies 1941,Mr 24,12:7
Klaus, Lili
Vielgeliebte, Die 1935,My 19,IX,2:5
Klaveness, Harda
Harriet 1943,Mr 4,24:2
Klavun, Walter
Journey by Night, A 1935,Ap 17,26:3
Arms for Venus 1937,Mr 12,18:7
Lysistrata 1937,Jl 20,19:3
Twelfth Night 1949,O 4,33:2
Dream Girl 1951,My 10,39:1
Grey-Eyed People, The 1952,D 18,41:2
Morning's at Seven 1955,Je 23,25:1
Dandy Dick 1956,Ja 11,37:2
Auntie Mame 1956,N 1,47:2
Say Darling 1958,Ap 4,17:1
Say Darling 1958,Ap 13,II,1:1
Desert Incident, A 1959,Mr 25,40:1
What Makes Sammy Run? 1964,F 28,19:1
Klawans, Barney (Producer)
Young Madame Conti 1937,Ap 1,18:4
Klawans, Bernard (Miscellaneous)
Alley Cat 1934,S 18,18:1
Roll Sweet Chariot 1934,O 3,24:3
Klawans, Bernard (Producer)
Man Bites Dog 1933,Ap 26,11:2
Wise Tomorrow 1937,O 16,22:5
Happily Ever After 1945,Mr 16,21:2
Therese 1945,O 10,24:2
Klechot, Rajmund
Post Office, The 1965,Ja 6,32:1
Labyrinth, The 1965,Ja 6,32:1
Woman, The 1965,Ja 6,32:1
Jaselka 1965,Ja 6,32:1
Book, The 1965,Ja 6,32:1
Jacob and the Angel 1965,Ja 6,32:1
Nightmare, The 1965,Ja 6,32:1
Kernel and the Shell, The 1965,Ja 6,32:1
Kleema, Joseph
Double Dummy 1936,N 12,30:1
Howdy Stranger 1937,Ja 15,17:5
Kleeman, Paul
Peg o' My Dreams 1924,My 6,25:3
Passing Show of 1924, The 1924,S 4,13:4
Student Prince, The 1924,D 3,25:3
Kleibacker, Fred (Playwright)
King's Coat, The 1933,Ja 12,21:4
Kleide, Paula
Motke From Slobodke 1930,Ap 12,23:3
Schlemihl 1936,S 19,20:4
Kleima, Joseph
Red Rust 1929,D 18,31:1
Kleiman, Harlan P (Producer)
Have I Got One for You 1968,Ja 8,32:1
Futz 1968,Je 14,39:1
Tonight in Living Color; Golden Fleece, The 1969,Je 11,43:1
Tonight in Living Color; David Show, The 1969,Je 11,43:1
Ofay Watcher, The 1969,S 16,40:1
Klein, A M (Playwright)
Conscience 1952,My 16,17:6

Klein, Adelaide
Double Dummy 1936,N 12,30:1
Brooklyn, U S A 1941,D 22,24:2
Brooklyn, U S A 1941,D 28,IX,1:1
Uncle Harry 1942,My 21,24:1
Collector's Item 1952,F 9,11:2
Immoralist, The 1954,F 9,22:1
Immoralist, The 1954,F 14,II,1:1
Once Upon a Tailor 1955,My 24,36:2
Anna Christie 1955,N 22,41:1
Jane Eyre 1958,My 2,31:1
Secret Concubine, The 1960,Mr 22,29:2
Poppa Is Home 1961,D 20,37:1
Klein, Al
Lady Says Yes, A 1945,Ja 11,18:5
Klein, Alan Edward (Lighting Director)
Lady of Mexico 1962,O 20,13:2
Klein, Alan Edward (Scenic Designer)
Lady of Mexico 1962,O 20,13:2
Klein, Allen Edward (Lighting Director)
My Beginning 1962,Ja 31,21:1
Daddy Come Home 1963,Ap 17,33:1
Finis for Oscar Wilde 1964,F 15,15:1
Comforter, The 1964,O 22,42:1
Patrick--The First 1965,F 19,25:1
Go, Go, Go, God is Dead! 1966,O 12,37:1
Man Who Washed His Hands, The 1967,F 16,33:1
Ballad of John Ogilvie, The 1968,O 9,42:4
Klein, Allen Edward (Scenic Designer)
Connelly vs Connelly 1961,F 18,11:3
My Beginning 1962,Ja 31,21:1
Daddy Come Home 1963,Ap 17,33:1
Finis for Oscar Wilde 1964,F 15,15:1
Comforter, The 1964,O 22,42:1
Patrick--The First 1965,F 19,25:1
Man Who Washed His Hands, The 1967,F 16,33:1
Ballad of John Ogilvie, The 1968,O 9,42:4
Klein, Arthur
French Leave 1920,N 9,13:1
Klein, Arthur (Director)
Anna Russell and Her Little Show 1953,S 8,27:2
Klein, Arthur (Producer)
Tidbits of 1946 1946,Jl 9,17:2
Tickets, Please! 1950,Ap 28,25:2
Anna Russell and Her Little Show 1953,S 8,27:2
Klein, Billy
Little Poor Man, The 1925,Ag 6,14:1
Klein, Bob
Return of Second City in "20,000 Frozen Grenadiers," The 1966,Ap 22,36:1
Klein, Charles (Playwright)
Music Master, The 1927,S 7,34:4
Music Master, The 1927,S 25,VIII,2:1
Potash and Perlmutter 1935,Ap 6,11:3
Klein, Charlotte
Ponder Heart, The 1956,F 17,14:2
Klein, E (Playwright)
Potasch und Perlmutter 1921,Je 5,VI,1:3
Klein, Evlyn
Nina Rosa 1930,S 22,22:5
Klein, Frank
Right You Are (If You Think You Are) 1950,Je 29,37:2
Klein, Franklin
This Our House 1935,D 12,33:3
Tell My Story 1939,Mr 16,26:6
Janie 1942,S 11,24:2
Night Is Black Bottles, The 1962,D 5,56:1
Klein, Franklin (Producer)
Solo 1962,Ap 27,26:1
Klein, Frederick
For Valor 1935,N 19,27:5
Klein, I W
Sweet Charity 1966,Ja 31,22:1
Klein, I W (Composer)
Merry Death, A 1959,N 10,55:3
No Trifling With Love 1959,N 10,55:3
Klein, I W (Lyricist)
No Trifling With Love 1959,N 10,55:3
Merry Death, A 1959,N 10,55:3
Klein, James (Playwright)
Love Song, The 1925,Ja 14,19:4
Klein, James (Producer)
Alles Nackt 1927,D 18,IX,1:8
Klein, Jeanette
Professor Mamlock 1937,Ap 14,30:3
Klein, John
Charlotte Corday 1936,O 27,31:1
Charlotte Corday 1936,N 15,XI,3:2
Klein, Johnny
Seven Year Itch, The 1952,N 21,21:2
Ponder Heart, The 1956,F 17,14:2
Klein, Lawrence
Hamlet 1956,O 29,34:1
Klein, Leonard
Othello 1945,My 23,25:4
Klein, Leslie
But for the Grace of God 1937,Ja 13,21:4
Enemy of the People, An 1937,F 16,19:1
Klein, Manuel (Composer)
It's Up to You 1921,Mr 29,20:1
Klein, Maxine (Director)
Approaching Simone 1970,Mr 9,43:1

Klein, Morris
Dole Brothers 1932,Mr 26,17:7
Klein, Patsy
Diamond Lil 1928,Ap 10,32:1
Collision 1932,F 17,19:2
Jamboree 1932,N 25,18:4
Klein, Paul (Composer)
From A to Z 1960,Ap 21,23:2
Morning Sun 1963,O 7,36:2
Klein, Reid
Kittiwake Island 1960,O 13,43:1
Half a Sixpence 1965,Ap 26,38:2
Sound of Music, The 1967,Ap 27,52:1
Darling of the Day 1968,Ja 29,26:2
Klein, Reid (Miscellaneous)
Sound of Music, The 1967,Ap 27,52:1
Klein, Richard
Ponder Heart, The 1956,F 17,14:2
Klein, Robert
Passionella 1966,O 19,53:1
Lady or the Tiger?, The 1966,O 19,53:1
Leonard Sillman's New Faces of 1968 1968,My 3,43:1
New Faces of 1968 1968,My 12,II,7:1
Night 1968,N 29,52:1
Morning 1968,N 29,52:1
Noon 1968,N 29,52:1
Klein, Robert (Director)
Any Day Now 1941,Je 10,28:2
Klein, Robert (Playwright)
Leonard Sillman's New Faces of 1968 1968,My 3,43:1
Klein, Robert (Producer)
Two Neck-Ties 1929,O 13,IX,4:7
Street Scene 1930,Mr 16,IX,4:1
Strictly Dishonorable 1931,Ap 12,IX,1:3
Frau Die Weiss Was Sie Will, Eine 1932,O 9,IX,3:7
Klein, Ruth
Occasion, L' 1939,Ja 10,16:4
Klein, Stephanie (Costume Designer)
It's About Time 1942,Mr 31,28:3
Kleine, Grace
Sweet Genevieve 1945,Mr 21,27:3
Kleiner, Arthur
Laterna Magika 1964,Ag 4,21:1
Kleiner, Arthur (Miscellaneous)
Too Much Johnson 1964,Ja 16,29:1
Merton of the Movies 1968,S 26,62:1
Kleiner, Harry (Playwright)
Sky Drift 1945,N 14,25:2
Kleinhesselink, Pauline
Paul Bunyan 1941,My 6,25:1
Kleinman, Marlene
Iolanthe 1962,Ap 12,42:4
Gondoliers, The 1962,Ap 19,34:2
H M S Pinafore 1964,Mr 21,13:4
Patience 1964,Mr 26,42:1
Gondoliers, The 1964,Mr 28,14:1
H M S Pinafore 1965,Ap 15,39:1
Mikado, The 1965,Ap 17,11:3
Kleinman, Sy (Producer)
Catch a Star! 1955,S 7,35:2
Kleinpeter, Charles
Shoemaker's Prodigious Wife, The 1949,Je 15,38:2
Kleinsinger, George (Composer)
Of V We Sing 1942,F 16,20:3
Bil and Cora Baird's Marionette Theater 1955,D 27,29:2
Bil and Cora Baird's Marionette Theater; Ali Baba and the Forty Thieves 1956,S 3,10:1
Shinbone Alley 1957,Ap 15,23:2
Shinbone Alley 1957,Ap 28,II,1:1
Ali Baba and the Forty Thieves 1970,D 29,40:1
Kleinsinger, George (Miscellaneous)
Shinbone Alley 1957,Ap 15,23:2
Kleist, Heinrich von (Playwright)
Amphitryon 1926,O 24,VIII,2:1
Klemmer, Vincent
Mother Said No 1951,Ap 17,34:2
Klemperer, Otto Jr
Trojan Horse, The 1940,O 31,28:3
Klemperer, Werner
Heads or Tails 1947,My 3,10:6
Lucky Sam McCarver 1950,Ap 15,10:6
Twentieth Century 1950,D 25,23:6
Dear Charles 1954,S 16,37:2
Dear Charles 1954,S 26,II,1:1
Klenburg, Jana
Romeo y Julieta 1965,Ag 28,13:3
Deadly Game, The 1966,F 14,34:1
Make Me Disappear 1969,My 14,34:1
Klendon, Jack
Kidding Kidders 1928,Ap 24,28:3
Up Pops the Devil 1930,S 2,19:1
Papavert 1931,D 30,25:1
Mr Papavert 1932,Ja 23,18:6
Marathon 1933,Ja 28,8:8
Klendon, John
Ramblers, The 1926,S 21,32:2
Klenosky, William (Composer)
Utopia! 1963,My 7,47:4
Klenosky, William (Lyricist)
Utopia! 1963,My 7,47:4

Klenosky, William (Playwright)
Utopia! 1963,My 7,47:4
Kleppel, Bernice (Miscellaneous)
Frying Pan, The 1966,N 8,45:1
Bridal Night, The 1966,N 8,45:1
Eternal Triangle 1966,N 8,45:1
Klewer, Emil
Joan of Arc 1927,Ap 15,26:2
Kley, Lyn
Ladies Night in a Turkish Bath 1961,Mr 22,38:1
Kliban, Ken
Bacchants, The 1967,F 25,14:1
And Puppy Dog Tails 1969,O 20,60:1
Klick, Mary
Hayride 1954,S 14,24:2
Klicks, Lee
Vaudeville (Palace) 1924,Ja 15,17:3
Klida, Paula
Great Miracle, The 1931,D 12,23:5
Rich Paupers 1932,Mr 14,13:4
Big Surprise, The 1932,O 17,18:3
Honeymoon for Three, A 1933,Ja 30,9:6
Jewish Melody, The 1933,Mr 27,12:4
Straw Hero, The 1936,N 24,35:1
Give Me Back My Heart 1937,O 4,17:6
Klien, Franklin
Black Rhythm 1936,D 21,19:2
Klietsch, Erwin
Versailles 1931,Ja 25,I,14:2
Klimoska, Donna
Sound of Music, The 1970,Jl 3,13:1
Klimowski, Joseph
Bacchae, The 1963,Ap 25,39:5
As You Like It 1966,Je 4,19:1
Thieves' Carnival 1967,Je 5,52:1
Harpers Ferry 1967,Je 6,52:2
Visit, The 1967,S 13,41:1
She Stoops to Conquer 1968,Ja 1,11:1
Kline, A A (Playwright)
Out of Step 1925,Ja 30,12:1
Kline, Devra
Silk Stockings 1955,F 25,17:3
Kline, Henry
Merry Wives of Windsor, The 1938,Ap 15,22:3
Kline, J H
Three Musketeers, The 1921,My 20,18:5
Kline, John M
Inspector General, The 1923,My 1,24:1
Brother Elks 1925,S 15,29:2
Barefoot 1925,O 20,29:2
Padre, The 1926,D 28,16:3
Heaven-Tappers, The 1927,Mr 9,28:3
Three Musketeers, The 1928,Mr 14,28:1
On the Spot 1930,O 30,33:3
Budget, The 1932,S 21,26:4
She Loves Me Not 1933,N 21,22:4
Lady Detained, A 1935,Ja 10,23:3
Slight Case of Murder, A 1935,S 12,28:5
Tapestry in Gray 1935,D 28,10:2
High Tor 1937,Ja 11,15:2
Sweet Charity 1942,D 29,26:4
Kline, Marvin
See Naples and Die 1929,S 27,30:4
Forest Ring, The 1930,Ap 26,11:2
Counsellor-at-Law 1931,N 7,17:2
Picnic 1934,My 3,15:2
Kline, Norman (Playwright)
Leonard Sillman's New Faces of 1968
1968,My 3,43:1
American Hamburger League, The 1969,S 17,51:1
Kline, Stephanie (Costume Designer)
Story Theater 1970,O 27,54:1
Kline, Tiny
Jumbo 1935,N 18,20:2
Kline, William
Electra 1932,Ja 9,21:4
Kline, William (Scenic Designer)
People on the Hill 1931,S 26,25:5
Kline, William J
Will Shakespeare 1923,Ja 2,14:1
In the Next Room 1923,N 28,14:1
Chivalry 1925,D 16,22:3
Kling, Candace (Lighting Director)
Candida 1969,F 3,29:1
Score 1970,O 29,57:4
Kling, Helen
Chiffon Girl, The 1924,F 20,23:2
Kling, Irene
Miss Julie 1965,N 11,59:1
Stronger, The 1965,N 11,59:1
Kling, Saxon
Shavings 1920,F 17,18:1
Cave Girl, The 1920,Ag 19,12:2
Kiki 1921,N 30,13:1
Launzi 1923,O 11,16:3
Haunted House, The 1924,S 3,12:1
Trelawney of the 'Wells' 1925,Je 2,16:2
Dagger, The 1925,S 10,28:1
Dark, The 1927,F 2,22:5
Kling, Saxon (Director)
Lady Refuses, The 1933,Mr 8,18:6
Kling, Saxon (Playwright)
Crashing Through 1928,O 30,26:5

Tomorrow 1928,D 29,20:2
Lady Refuses, The 1933,Mr 8,18:6
Klinge, Johanna (Costume Designer)
Candida 1942,Ap 28,24:4
Klingeman, Clara (Producer)
Dream Out of Time, A 1970,N 9,52:1
Klingeman, Harvey (Producer)
Dream Out of Time, A 1970,N 9,52:1
Klingmann, Carl (Playwright)
Heimkehr aus der Fremde, Die; Stranger, The
1949,S 2,14:1
Klint, Harry
Adam Had Two Sons 1932,Ja 21,17:1
Klock, Polly
Merry Wives of Windsor, The 1938,Ap 15,22:3
Klok, Daniel
View From the Bridge, A 1956,N 9,34:4
Klopfer, Eugene
Rain 1925,N 25,23:5
Kabale und Liebe 1931,N 1,VIII,4:2
Oliver Cromwells Sendung 1933,Mr 19,IX,2:2
Klopfer, Ludwig (Producer)
Spread Eagle 1929,N 10,X,4:8
Klopping, Monica
Howdy Stranger 1937,Ja 15,17:5
Kloten, Edgar L (Miscellaneous)
Lazarus Laughed 1948,Ap 9,27:4
Kloth, Stanley (Scenic Designer)
Ping-Pong 1959,Ap 17,22:1
Klotz, Florence (Costume Designer)
Call on Kuprin, A 1961,My 26,29:3
Take Her, She's Mine 1961,D 22,19:1
Never Too Late 1962,N 28,42:1
Nobody Loves an Albatross 1963,D 20,20:1
Owl and the Pussycat, The 1964,N 19,48:1
One by One 1964,D 2,60:1
Mating Dance 1965,N 4,58:1
Best Laid Plans, The 1966,Mr 26,15:2
It's a Bird . . . It's a Plane . . . It's Superman
1966,Mr 30,34:1
Paris Is Out! 1970,F 3,35:1
Norman, Is That You? 1970,F 20,30:1
Klotz, Florence (Miscellaneous)
Carousel 1957,S 12,38:2
Annie Get Your Gun 1958,F 20,29:2
Oklahoma! 1958,Mr 20,32:3
Klouder, Charles
Weak Woman, A 1926,Ja 27,16:3
Kluenter, Beatrice (Composer)
Electra 1958,My 10,17:7
Kluge, Kurt (Playwright)
Ewiges Volk 1933,Ap 30,IX,2:2
Ewiges Volk 1933,Je 25,IX,1:2
Klugherz, Daniel (Director)
Step a Little Closer 1948,My 28,26:6
Klugherz, Daniel (Playwright)
Step a Little Closer 1948,My 28,26:6
Klugman, Jack
Stevedore 1949,F 23,30:2
Golden Boy 1952,Mr 13,24:3
Coriolanus 1954,Ja 20,34:2
Very Special Baby, A 1956,N 15,43:2
Gypsy 1959,My 22,31:6
Gypsy 1959,My 31,II,1:1
Sudden and Accidental Re-education of Horse
Johnson, The 1968,D 19,63:1
Klummer, Clare (Composer)
Amourette 1933,S 28,25:2
Klump, Will
Absalom 1956,My 17,37:2
Twelfth Night 1957,Ja 5,12:2
Klunis, Tom
Man Who Never Died, The 1958,N 22,27:2
Measure for Measure 1960,Jl 27,33:1
Immoralist, The 1963,N 8,36:2
Hamlet 1964,Je 17,49:1
Arms and the Man 1965,Je 24,32:5
Devils, The 1965,N 17,51:2
Iphigenia in Aulis 1967,N 22,40:2
Hamlet 1969,Je 30,33:1
Three Sisters, The 1969,Ag 4,29:1
Henry V 1969,N 11,43:1
Kluver, Olga
Originale 1964,S 9,46:1
Knabe, Birgit (Costume Designer)
Frankenstein 1968,O 3,54:1
Knabenshue, Harry
Babes in Toyland 1930,D 22,17:1
Knaggs, Skelton
Heart of a City 1942,F 13,24:6
Hand in Glove 1944,D 5,19:1
Hand in Glove 1944,D 10,II,5:1
Knaiz, Judy
Shoemaker's Holiday, The 1967,Mr 3,25:1
Arabian Nights 1967,Jl 3,12:1
Knapp, Bobby
Aquashow 1952,Je 25,25:1
Aquashow 1953,Je 24,29:2
Aquashow 1954,Je 23,20:4
Elliott Murphy's Aquashow 1955,Je 23,25:1
Elliott Murphy's Aquashow 1956,Je 20,26:2
Aquacircus 1958,Je 30,24:6
Aquarama 1960 1960,Jl 1,14:6

Knapp, Bobby (Choreographer)
Aquashow 1952,Je 25,25:1
Mermaid's Holiday 1961,Jl 1,8:1
Knapp, Bobby (Miscellaneous)
Mermaid's Holiday 1961,Jl 1,8:1
Knapp, Bridget
Show Boat 1961,Ap 13,32:1
Knapp, Dorothy
Follies 1925,Jl 7,24:3
Earl Carroll's Vanities 1925,D 29,20:3
Earl Carroll's Vanities 1926,Ag 25,19:4
Fioretta 1929,Ja 6,VIII,4:6
Fioretta 1929,F 6,30:3
Free for All 1931,S 9,25:1
Broadway Interlude 1934,Ap 20,16:3
Knapp, Harry
Six-Fifty, The 1921,O 25,20:1
Man on Stilts, The 1931,S 10,23:2
Knapp, J Merrill
Hippolytus 1935,Je 15,20:4
Wings Over Europe 1936,Mr 4,24:7
Knapp, Jacques
Thomas Paine 1930,Mr 21,30:7
Knapp, John (Lighting Director)
Doctor X 1930,Jl 31,12:4
Knapp, Kenneth
Carousel 1949,Ja 26,28:2
Knapp, Lawrence W Jr
Fiesta 1933,D 16,12:2
Knapp, Marcia
Song of Norway 1959,Je 26,16:2
Knapp, Marjorie
Star and Garter 1942,Je 25,26:2
Knapp, Nicholas
Alt Heidelberg 1926,My 31,10:5
Knapp, Rue
H M S Pinafore 1949,Jl 29,13:2
Mikado, The 1954,Mr 24,31:1
Pirates of Penzance, The 1954,Mr 31,32:5
Patience 1954,Ap 7,41:1
Gondoliers, The 1954,Ap 14,24:3
Ruddigore 1954,Ap 21,36:4
Iolanthe 1954,Ap 28,36:8
Yeomen of the Guard, The 1954,My 5,36:2
H M S Pinafore 1954,My 19,36:8
Sorcerer, The 1954,My 26,34:3
Knapp, Sally
H M S Pinafore 1949,Jl 29,13:2
Mikado, The 1954,Mr 24,31:1
Pirates of Penzance, The 1954,Mr 31,32:5
Gondoliers, The 1954,Ap 14,24:3
Ruddigore 1954,Ap 21,36:4
Iolanthe 1954,Ap 28,36:8
Yeomen of the Guard, The 1954,My 5,36:2
H M S Pinafore 1954,My 19,36:8
Sorcerer, The 1954,My 26,34:3
Utopia, Limited; Flowers of Progress, The
1957,F 27,21:1
Knapp, Varney
Effect of Gamma Rays on Man-in-the-Moon
Marigolds, The 1965,Je 7,48:1
Knapp, Walter
Antony and Cleopatra 1924,F 20,22:1
Knaster, Ira
Blue and the Gray, The; War Is Hell Gray, The
1929,D 27,26:4
Kneale, Beatrice
Patience 1927,My 24,23:2
Knebel, M O (Director)
Kremlin Chimes 1965,F 25,23:1
Kneebone, Tom
Salad Days 1958,N 11,24:1
Noel Coward's Sweet Potato 1968,S 30,59:1
Noel Coward's Sweet Potato 1968,O 13,II,5:1
Kneeland, Frank
Student Prince, The 1924,D 3,25:3
Kneeland, Richard
All the King's Men 1959,O 17,27:2
Years of the Locusts 1968,Ag 23,32:1
Brother to Dragons 1968,D 8,86:1
Kneerim, Arthur
Pleased to Meet You 1928,O 30,27:2
Knego, Peter
Fifth Column, The 1940,Mr 7,18:2
My Sister Eileen 1940,D 27,23:2
Men in Shadow 1943,Mr 11,16:2
Knell, Dane
See the Jaguar 1952,D 4,46:2
Knell, Grace
Power of Darkness, The 1920,Ja 22,22:1
Knepler, Paul (Composer)
Du Barry 1932,N 23,15:2
Knepler, Paul (Original Author)
Three Waltzes 1937,D 27,10:2
Knepler, Paul (Playwright)
Paganini 1925,N 22,VIII,1:8
Toni aus Wien, Die 1931,Ag 30,VIII,2:2
Du Barry 1931,S 20,VIII,2:7
Du Barry 1932,My 8,VIII,1:6
Giuditta 1934,Ja 21,30:1
Knepper, Virginia
Letter to the Times, A 1966,D 5,63:1

Kniepert, Ernie (Costume Designer)
Konzert, Das 1968,Mr 25,52:1
Jux Will Er Sich Machen, Einen 1968,Ap 3,41:1
Kniffen, O
It's the Valet 1933,D 15,25:4
Kniffen, O (Composer)
It's the Valet 1933,D 15,25:4
Kniffen, O (Lyricist)
It's the Valet 1933,D 15,25:4
Knight, Atherton
Sourball 1969,Ag 6,29:2
Knight, Charles
Try and Get It 1943,Ag 3,13:2
Knight, Charlott
Minstrel Boy, The 1948,O 15,28:2
Knight, Charlott (Director)
Late Arrival 1953,O 20,35:5
Knight, Darwin
Russell Patterson's Sketch-Book 1960,F 8,35:1
Knight, Darwin (Director)
My Wife and I 1966,O 11,53:2
Get Thee to Canterbury 1969,Ja 26,74:1
Round With Ring, A 1969,O 30,56:1
Knight, David
Simon's Wife 1945,Mr 9,16:4
Caine Mutiny Court-Martial, The 1956,Je 14,40:1
Knight, Edward
Sidewalks and the Sound of Crying 1956,O 29,34:1
Measure for Measure 1964,Jl 27,22:3
Knight, Emory
Finian's Rainbow 1955,My 19,25:1
Knight, Eric W (Musical Director)
Cabin in the Sky 1964,Ja 22,32:1
Knight, Etheridge
Madmen and Specialists 1970,Ag 3,38:1
Knight, Felix
It Happens on Ice 1940,O 11,24:3
Merry Widow, The 1942,Jl 16,22:1
Once Over Lightly 1942,N 20,26:2
Knight, Flora
Lower North 1944,Ag 26,15:4
Knight, Francis
House Divided, The 1923,N 12,14:1
Knight, Frank
Nancy Ann 1924,Ap 1,18:1
Fatal Wedding, The 1924,Je 3,22:3
House Unguarded 1929,Ja 16,22:2
Farmer Takes a Wife, The 1934,O 9,17:2
Farmer Takes a Wife, The 1934,O 31,17:1
Knight, Fred
Window Panes 1927,F 22,22:2
Trick for Trick 1932,F 19,14:2
Hilda Cassidy 1933,My 5,18:3
Joy Forever, A 1946,Ja 8,20:2
Knight, Fuzzy
Here's Howe! 1928,My 2,19:3
Vaudeville (Palace) 1928,O 2,35:1
Ned Wayburn's Gambols 1929,Ja 16,22:3
Knight, George
Life Begins in '40 1940,Ap 5,24:2
Knight, Gillian
Mikado, The 1962,N 14,43:1
Gondoliers, The 1962,N 16,25:2
Pirates of Penzance, The 1962,N 21,28:1
H M S Pinafore 1962,N 23,32:4
Iolanthe 1962,N 28,42:1
Iolanthe 1964,N 18,52:1
H M S Pinafore 1964,N 20,40:1
Pirates of Penzance, The 1964,N 27,43:1
Mikado, The 1964,N 27,43:1
Ruddigore 1964,D 4,44:1
Knight, Harlan E
Bottom of the Cup, The 1927,F 1,24:2
Knight, Hilda
New Yorkers, The 1930,D 9,31:1
Music Hall Varieties 1932,N 23,15:3
Orchids Preferred 1937,Ap 29,16:6
Orchids Preferred 1937,My 12,26:5
Knight, Jack
Wonderful Town 1967,My 18,50:1
South Pacific 1967,Je 13,56:1
Steambath 1970,Jl 1,49:1
Knight, Jacqueline (Costume Designer)
Manhatters, The 1927,Jl 19,27:3
Knight, Jacqueline (Scenic Designer)
Manhatters, The 1927,Jl 19,27:3
Knight, James
Jolly's Progress 1959,D 7,42:2
Knight, John
Starlight 1925,Mr 4,17:2
Uncle Tom's Cabin 1933,My 30,13:4
Knight, Joseph
Babes in Toyland 1930,D 22,17:1
Knight, Judith
Seven Keys to Baldpate 1930,Ja 8,25:2
Knight, June
Hot-Cha! 1932,F 21,VIII,2:1
Hot-Cha! 1932,Mr 9,17:3
Take a Chance 1932,N 28,11:2
Jubilee 1935,S 23,20:3
Jubilee 1935,S 29,X,1:1
Jubilee 1935,O 14,20:1
Jubilee 1935,N 24,IX,8:1

Going Places 1936,O 9,30:5
Going Places 1936,O 25,X,2:4
And On We Go 1937,Ap 22,19:5
Would-Be Gentleman, The 1946,Ja 10,29:2
Sweethearts 1947,Ja 22,31:2
Knight, Kemble
Venetian, The 1931,N 2,26:1
Fata Morgana 1931,D 26,15:3
Knight, Larry
Aquashow 1953,Je 24,29:2
Knight, Laura (Dame) (Scenic Designer)
Caravan 1932,My 1,VIII,2:2
Knight, Leonard
Lark, The 1955,N 18,20:1
Knight, Lloyd
Long Watch, The 1952,Mr 21,19:5
Knight, Margaret
Triumph of X, The 1921,Ag 25,8:2
Mad Dog, The 1921,N 9,20:1
Knight, Martha (Miscellaneous)
Just for Love 1968,O 18,40:1
Get Thee to Canterbury 1969,Ja 26,74:1
Khaki Blue 1969,Mr 27,54:2
Lime Green 1969,Mr 27,54:2
Ofay Watcher, The 1969,S 16,40:1
Passing Through From Exotic Places; Sunstroke 1969,D 8,60:4
Passing Through From Exotic Places; Burial of Esposito, The 1969,D 8,60:4
Passing Through From Exotic Places; Son Who Hunted Tigers in Jakarta, The 1969,D 8,60:4
Lyle 1970,Mr 21,16:2
Me Nobody Knows, The 1970,My 19,42:1
Knight, Michael
Exchange 1970,F 9,47:2
Knight, Michael (Composer)
Exchange 1970,F 9,47:2
Knight, Michael (Lyricist)
Exchange 1970,F 9,47:2
Knight, Michael (Scenic Designer)
Kiss Me, Kate 1970,D 26,10:4
Knight, Patricia
Sea Legs 1937,My 19,26:5
Western Wind 1949,Ag 9,20:6
Knight, Percival
Thin Ice 1922,O 2,20:1
Knight, Percival (Playwright)
Thin Ice 1922,O 2,20:1
Knight, Raymond (Playwright)
At Home Abroad 1935,S 20,17:4
Run Sheep Run 1938,N 4,26:2
Knight, Rosalind
As You Like It 1961,Jl 5,30:1
Knight, Shirley
Journey to the Day 1963,N 12,49:1
Three Sisters, The 1964,Je 23,24:1
Three Sisters, The 1964,Jl 5,II,1:1
Walk in Dark Places, A 1966,Ja 28,21:1
Better Luck Next Time 1966,Ja 28,21:1
We Have Always Lived in the Castle 1966,O 20,53:1
Watering Place, The 1969,Mr 13,51:1
Knight, Sisters
Scandals 1939,Ag 29,17:2
Knight, Tanya
Viva O'Brien 1941,O 10,27:2
Knight, Tom
She Gave Him All She Had 1939,D 2,20:7
Criminals, The 1941,D 22,24:3
R U R 1942,D 4,30:2
Knighton, Willis (Costume Designer)
Shop at Sly Corner, The 1949,Ja 19,35:2
Knighton, Willis (Miscellaneous)
All the King's Men 1948,Ja 19,19:2
Knighton, Willis (Scenic Designer)
Meet a Body 1944,O 17,19:5
Brighten the Corner 1945,D 13,33:2
Song of Bernadette 1946,Mr 27,22:2
Nights of Wrath; Nuits de la Colere, Les 1947,D 1,26:4
All the King's Men 1948,Ja 19,19:2
Shop at Sly Corner, The 1949,Ja 19,35:2
Gayden 1949,My 11,34:4
All the King's Men 1950,Jl 19,25:6
Merchant of Venice, The 1955,F 23,23:2
Macbeth 1955,O 20,42:2
Midsummer Night's Dream, A 1956,Ja 14,12:2
Romeo and Juliet 1956,F 24,20:4
Knights, Rob (Miscellaneous)
Romeo and Juliet 1967,F 22,18:1
Knights of the Orient
Vaudeville (Belmont) 1931,Ja 6,24:1
Knill, Emma
Toto 1921,Mr 22,15:2
Knilling, Anthony
Canary Dutch 1925,S 9,22:1
Lulu Belle 1926,F 10,20:1
Hit the Deck! 1927,Ap 26,32:1
Present Arms 1928,Ap 27,16:2
Knipper-Tchekhova, Olga
Tsar Fyodor Ivanovitch 1923,Ja 9,26:1
Lower Depths, The 1923,Ja 16,16:1
Cherry Orchard, The 1923,Ja 23,18:1

Knipper-Tchekhova, Olga—Cont
Cherry Orchard, The 1923,Ja 28,VII,1:1
Three Sisters, The 1923,Ja 30,12:2
Lady From the Provinces, The 1923,F 27,14:2
Mistress of the Inn, The; Locandiera, La 1923,N 22,16:1
Ivanoff 1923,N 27,23:2
In the Claws of Life 1923,N 30,23:4
Enough Stupidity in Every Wise Man 1923,D 6,23:1
Death of Pazukhin, The 1924,F 12,20:1
Moscow Art Theatre 1924,My 13,25:2
Knittel, John (Playwright)
Torch, The 1922,O 8,VI,1:7
Knittel, Wolfgang (Miscellaneous)
Jacques Brel Is Alive and Well and Living in Paris 1968,Ja 23,25:2
Conerico Was Here to Stay 1969,Mr 11,39:1
Paradise Gardens East 1969,Mr 11,39:1
Knoblock, Edward (Original Author)
Kismet 1953,D 4,2:4
Kismet 1965,Je 23,45:1
Knoblock, Edward (Playwright)
One 1920,S 15,12:2
Lullaby, The 1923,S 9,VII,2:4
Lullaby, The 1923,O 7,IX,1:1
Lullaby, The 1923,D 16,IX,1:1
Faun, The 1924,F 6,19:2
Faun, The 1924,Mr 28,17:2
Simon Called Peter 1924,My 4,VIII,2:1
Simon Called Peter 1924,N 11,20:2
Speakeasy 1927,S 27,30:1
Mulberry Bush, The 1927,O 27,33:1
Mr Prohack 1927,D 4,X,1:3
Mr Prohack 1928,Ja 1,VIII,1:3
Mulberry Bush, The 1930,My 18,VIII,2:6
Milestones 1930,Je 3,27:1
Good Companions, The 1931,My 15,20:8
Good Companions, The 1931,My 31,VIII,2:6
Grand Hotel 1931,S 4,22:7
Good Companions, The 1931,O 2,31:1
Good Companions, The 1931,O 11,VIII,1:1
Evensong 1932,Jl 1,19:6
Evensong 1932,Jl 24,IX,2:1
Evensong 1933,F 1,13:4
If a Body 1935,Ap 21,II,8:3
If a Body 1935,My 1,25:3
Edwardians, The 1937,Ap 20,28:4
Edwardians, The 1937,My 9,XI,1:4
Knoche, Bradley
Elsie Janis and Her Gang 1922,Ja 17,13:2
Knockey, Cay
Cretan Woman, The 1954,My 21,17:2
Knopf, Edwin H
Treasure, The 1920,O 5,13:1
Knopf, Edwin H (Director)
Garden of Eden, The 1927,S 28,28:1
Big Pond, The 1928,Ag 22,25:1
Knopf, Edwin H (Producer)
Garden of Eden, The 1927,Ag 14,VII,2:1
Big Pond, The 1928,Ag 22,25:1
Knopf, Joseph
Idiot's Delight 1936,Mr 25,25:2
Knopf, Mildred (Playwright)
Long Frontier, The 1935,Jl 23,24:4
Knopp, K
Passion Play, The 1929,Ap 30,32:1
Knopper, Heinrich
Passion Play, The 1929,Ap 30,32:1
Knott, Frederick (Playwright)
Dial 'M' for Murder 1952,O 14,41:5
Dial 'M' for Murder 1952,O 30,41:2
Dial 'M' for Murder 1952,N 30,II,1:1
Dial 'M' for Murder 1953,N 8,II,1:1
Dial 'M' for Murder 1957,Ja 9,27:4
Dial 'M' for Murder 1958,F 8,12:2
Mr Fox of Venice 1959,Ap 16,28:1
Write Me a Murder 1961,O 27,28:2
Wait Until Dark 1966,F 3,21:1
Knotts, Don
No Time for Sergeants 1955,O 21,32:2
Knowland, Alice
Edgar Allan Poe 1925,O 6,31:1
Knowles, Allen
Miss Liberty 1949,Jl 16,6:5
Bye Bye Birdie 1960,Ap 15,13:4
Knowles, Eleanor (Costume Designer)
Mrs Warren's Profession 1958,Je 26,22:1
Death of Cuchulain, The 1959,Ap 13,34:4
On Baile's Strand 1959,Ap 13,34:4
Knowles, Patrick
Good-Bye to Love 1940,Je 8,18:1
Knowles, Priscilla
Milgrim's Progress 1924,D 23,17:1
Aloma of the South Seas 1925,Ap 21,18:1
Half-Naked Truth, The 1926,Je 8,23:1
Spider, The 1927,Mr 23,29:1
Zeppelin 1929,Ja 15,22:3
Coastwise 1931,D 1,23:1
Scrap Book 1932,Ag 2,20:3
Knowlton, Alice
Dancing Girl, The 1923,Ja 25,16:2

Knox, Alexander
In Good King Charles's Golden Days 1939,Ag 13,28:1
Romeo and Juliet 1940,My 10,27:1
Jupiter Laughs 1940,S 10,27:1
Somewhere in France 1941,Ap 29,16:8
Jason 1942,Ja 22,12:2
Three Sisters, The 1942,D 22,31:2
Three Sisters, The 1942,D 27,VIII,1:1
Closing Door, The 1949,D 2,36:2
Return to Tyassi 1950,D 1,31:4
Knox, Alexander (Playwright)
Closing Door, The 1949,D 2,36:2
Knox, Andrew
No Foolin' 1926,Je 25,25:1
Knox, Arthur Jr
Caesar and Cleopatra 1927,N 6,IX,2:1
Knox, Carrie
Little Theatre Tournament; End of the Dance, The 1929,My 11,22:2
Knox, Dorothy
Girl From Wyoming, The 1938,O 31,12:1
Knox, Elizabeth L
Saint's Parade 1930,N 1,23:4
Knox, Emma
Eastward in Eden 1947,N 19,33:2
Knox, Harvey G
Our Town 1959,Mr 24,46:2
Knox, Harvey G (Miscellaneous)
Happy as Larry 1961,Ap 26,36:1
Knox, Howard
Pins and Needles 1922,F 2,20:1
Knox, Julia
Corn Is Green, The 1943,My 4,18:3
Knox, Mickey
Deer Park, The 1967,F 1,27:2
Knox, Richard
Tom Sawyer - Ballad of the Mississippi 1947,D 27,11:3
Peter Pan 1950,Ap 25,27:2
Knudsen, Betsy
Way, The 1940,O 12,20:3
Knudsen, Eveta
Opportunity 1920,Jl 31,5:1
Knudsen, Gene
Return of Ulysses, The 1943,Ja 28,22:2
Return of Ulysses, The 1943,F 7,II,1:6
Knuth, Gustav
Alcestiade 1957,Je 29,11:5
Kobart, Ruth
Heimkehr aus der Fremde, Die; Stranger, The 1949,S 2,14:1
Maria Golovin 1958,N 6,43:1
Pirates of Penzance, The 1960,O 7,29:1
Mikado, The 1961,Ja 18,26:1
How to Succeed in Business Without Really Trying 1961,O 16,34:1
Funny Thing Happened on the Way to the Forum, A 1962,My 9,49:1
Mardi Gras! 1965,Je 28,33:2
Oklahoma! 1965,D 16,62:1
Mardi Gras! 1966,Jl 11,32:2
Flea in Her Ear, A 1969,O 4,25:1
Three Sisters, The 1969,O 10,38:1
Kobayashi, Tsuruko
Majority of One, A 1959,F 17,28:2
Kobbe, Philip
Passing of the Third Floor Back, The 1924,F 8,19:4
Kobe, Gail
Promises to Keep 1965,Jl 22,25:1
Kobeless, Constantin
Cinderella on Broadway 1920,Je 25,18:1
Kober, Arthur (Playwright)
Having Wonderful Time 1937,F 22,12:5
Having Wonderful Time 1937,F 28,XI,1:1
Wish You Were Here 1952,Je 26,26:6
Wish You Were Here 1952,Ag 31,II,1:1
Mighty Man Is He, A 1960,Ja 7,25:2
Kober, Arthur (Producer)
Me 1925,N 24,28:1
Kober, William M
How Revolting! 1932,Mr 11,14:6
Kobi, Michi
Teahouse of the August Moon, The 1956,N 9,33:2
One Flew Over the Cuckoo's Nest 1963,N 14,40:2
Koblentz, Eugene (Miscellaneous)
All the King's Men 1959,O 17,27:2
Kobler, Jay
All the King's Men 1959,O 17,27:2
Koblitz, Albert (Playwright)
Steadfast 1923,O 31,12:1
Kobrin, Leon (Playwright)
Riverside Drive 1931,Ja 6,24:2
Lost Paradise 1934,D 14,28:3
Golden Stream, The 1936,F 13,25:1
Country Boy, The 1963,O 28,20:1
Kocers, Lydia
Green Table, The 1942,Ja 22,12:2
Prodigal Son, The 1942,F 18,22:2
Koch, Albert H
Grey Heir, The 1926,Ap 6,29:2
Koch, Celia
Inspector General, The 1923,My 1,24:1

Koch, Elaine
Beyond the Horizon 1926,D 1,24:2
These Days 1928,N 13,36:2
Koch, Frederick H (Director)
Job's Kinfolks 1929,N 24,31:1
Enchanted Maze, The 1935,D 14,10:4
Lost Colony, The 1937,Jl 11,X,2:1
Koch, Georg August
Rothschild Siegt bei Waterloo 1937,Ja 3,X,2:5
Koch, Howard (Playwright)
Great Scott! 1929,S 3,25:1
Give Us This Day 1933,O 28,20:6
In Time to Come 1941,D 29,20:2
In Time to Come 1942,Ja 4,IX,1:1
Koch, John
Candida 1925,D 19,14:2
Passing of Chow-Chow, The 1929,O 4,24:4
Ship, The 1929,N 21,24:7
Magic 1929,D 17,28:5
Round Table, The 1930,F 28,20:5
Koch, Kenneth (Playwright)
Bertha 1962,F 12,27:1
Three Times Three; George Washington Crossing the Delaware 1962,Mr 2,24:1
Tinguely Machine Mystery, or the Love Suicide at Kaluka, The 1965,D 24,15:5
Koch, Philip
Power of Darkness, The 1959,S 30,33:1
Koch, Richard
Nina Rosa 1930,S 22,22:5
Koch, Richard H (Scenic Designer)
Hamlet 1938,N 8,26:1
Kochera, Angela
Guimpes and Saddles 1967,O 11,36:3
Kochetov, Vsevolod (Original Author)
Yershov Brothers, The 1959,Je 2,6:4
Kock, John
Seven Keys to Baldpate 1930,Ja 8,25:2
Kock, Joseph
Veronica's Veil 1927,Mr 7,17:2
Kodama, T
Dear Me 1921,Ja 18,14:1
Koeber, Betty
Kittiwake Island 1960,O 13,43:1
Koefoed, Bjorn
Zeppelin 1929,Ja 15,22:3
Channel Road, The 1929,O 18,24:2
Overture 1930,D 8,26:4
Reunion in Vienna 1931,N 17,31:1
Jezebel 1933,D 20,26:3
Ship Comes in, A 1934,S 20,21:1
Too Many Heroes 1937,N 16,26:2
Asmodee 1958,Mr 26,42:2
Death of Satan, The 1960,Ap 6,49:1
Top Secret 1960,S 6,40:1
Koehler, D W (Miscellaneous)
Johnny No-Trump 1967,O 9,60:2
Henry IV, Part I 1968,Je 30,54:7
Henry IV, Part II 1968,Jl 2,33:1
Romeo and Juliet 1968,Ag 16,19:1
My Daughter, Your Son 1969,My 14,36:2
Love and Maple Syrup 1970,Ja 8,47:1
Postcards 1970,Mr 17,36:1
Grin and Bare It 1970,Mr 17,36:1
Place for Polly, A 1970,Ap 20,45:1
Koehler, Florence
Puppets 1925,Mr 10,19:1
Koehler, Hattie
East of Broadway 1932,Ja 27,19:3
Koehler, Ted (Composer)
Nine Fifteen Revue, The 1930,F 12,26:2
Earl Carroll's Vanities 1930,Jl 2,28:3
Vanities 1932,S 28,22:4
Koehler, Ted (Lyricist)
Nine Fifteen Revue, The 1930,F 12,26:2
Earl Carroll's Vanities 1930,Jl 2,28:3
Vanities 1932,S 28,22:4
Say When 1934,N 9,24:2
Harold Arlen Songbook, The 1967,Mr 1,48:1
Koeller, Rudolf (Playwright)
Vielgeliebte, Die 1935,My 19,IX,2:5
Koelsch, Beulah
Technique 1931,My 15,21:1
Koenig, Barbara (Costume Designer)
Don Juan in the Russian Manner 1954,Ap 23,23:2
Koenig, Charles Joseph Jr
This Mad Whirl 1937,Ja 10,II,4:8
Koenig, John (Costume Designer)
Charley's Aunt 1940,O 18,24:2
Pal Joey 1940,D 26,22:2
In Time to Come 1941,D 29,20:2
Koenig, John (Scenic Designer)
Orphee 1935,Mr 23,10:3
Front Page, The 1935,Jl 9,24:4
Post Road 1935,Jl 23,24:3
Caste 1935,Ag 13,20:3
Patience 1935,S 3,24:4
Many Mansions 1937,O 28,28:6
Heartbreak House 1938,Ap 30,18:2
Missouri Legend 1938,S 20,27:2
Glorious Morning 1938,N 28,10:3
Here Come the Clowns 1938,D 8,36:2
Charley's Aunt 1940,O 18,24:2

Koenig, John (Scenic Designer)—Cont
Little Dark Horse 1941,N 17,14:4
What Every Woman Knows 1954,D 23,16:2
Koenig, Laird (Playwright)
Dozens, The 1969,Mr 14,51:1
Koenigsberg, Joseph (Miscellaneous)
Cocktails of 1934 1934,My 5,22:1
Koeppke, Frau
Hannibal Ante Portas 1929,Ap 15,22:2
Koeppke, Margarethe
Troilus and Cressida 1927,N 20,IX,4:7
Koerber, Hilde
Heilige Crispin, Der 1933,Je 25,IX,1:2
Koerner, Hermine
Richard III 1937,My 30,X,2:2
Koerpel, Geraldine
Mariners 1927,Mr 29,22:2
Koesis, Robert
Recruiting Officer, The 1958,F 8,12:2
Koester, Frederick (Scenic Designer)
Well of the Saints, The 1959,Ap 11,15:4
Workhouse Ward, The 1959,Ap 11,15:4
Koester, Willi
Versunkene Glocke, Die 1936,N 20,26:3
Koestler, Arthur (Original Author)
Darkness at Noon 1951,Ja 15,13:4
Darkness at Noon 1951,Ja 21,II,1:1
Koestner, Emma
No Mother to Guide Her 1933,D 26,18:5
Koestner, Mitzi
No Mother to Guide Her 1933,D 26,18:5
Koestner, William
No Mother to Guide Her 1933,D 26,18:5
Kogan, Boris
Woman Bites Dog 1946,Ap 18,21:2
Kogan, Charlotte
Seven Mirrors 1945,O 26,17:2
Kogan, Edward
Weep for the Virgins 1935,D 2,18:1
Kogan, Jack
Girl Friend, The 1926,Mr 18,26:5
Kogan, Marlene
Mother Courage and Her Children 1964,My 12,32:2
Kogan, Maurice
Silk Stockings 1955,F 25,17:3
Kogan, Ramona
Carnival 1929,Ap 25,32:5
Kogan, Sergio (Producer)
Carnival 1962,Je 6,37:1
Kogan, Zinovy (Composer)
Russian Bank 1940,My 25,20:2
Kogel, George (Producer)
Camino Real 1960,My 17,42:2
Smiling the Boy Fell Dead 1961,Ap 20,28:1
Kogelnik, Kiki
Tinguely Machine Mystery, or the Love Suicide at Kaluka, The 1965,D 24,15:5
Koger, Allen F
Little Theatre Tournament; Man Who Died at Twelve O'Clock, The 1929,My 11,22:2
Kohan, Lynn-Rose
Finian's Rainbow 1955,My 19,25:1
Kohana
Golden Dawn 1927,D 1,32:3
Pinocchio 1939,Ja 3,19:2
Kohl, Arthur
That Ferguson Family 1928,D 24,10:7
Kohl, Eva
Inspector Kennedy 1929,D 21,16:3
Kohler, Albert A
Flair-Flair the Idol of Paree 1935,Mr 13,16:1
Kohler, Donald
Overtons, The 1945,F 7,16:6
Kohler, Estelle
Measure for Measure 1970,Ap 5,71:1
Kohler, Katharine
Her Friend the King 1929,O 8,34:5
Kohler, Kathryn
Wall Street 1927,Ap 21,24:4
Temperance Town, A 1929,Ag 11,VIII,2:1
Kohler, Marion
On the Town 1944,D 29,11:4
Kohler, Ott
Armseligen Besenbinder, Die 1928,N 19,16:2
Kohler, Roslyn
Mikado, The 1935,Ag 24,17:5
Kohler, Walter
Russian People, The 1942,D 30,17:2
Storm Operation 1944,Ja 12,28:2
Searching Wind, The 1944,Ap 13,25:2
Kohler, Willi (Lighting Director)
Don Carlos 1964,N 25,40:1
Captain of Koepenick, The 1964,D 2,60:1
Kohlman, Michelle
Picture of Dorian Gray, The 1956,Ag 18,15:5
Kohlman, Michelle (Producer)
Picture of Dorian Gray, The 1956,Ag 18,15:5
Kohlmar, Lee
Partners Again 1922,My 2,22:2
Tangletoes 1925,F 18,17:1
June Days 1925,Ag 7,12:5
My Country 1926,Ag 10,19:1
Sam Abramovitch 1927,Ja 20,20:5
Brass Buttons 1927,D 6,26:3

Kohlmar, Lee—Cont
She Means Business 1931,Ja 27,21:2
Kohn, Koby (Playwright)
Solitaire 1929,Mr 13,28:3
Kohn, Rose Simon (Playwright)
Pillar to Post 1943,D 11,11:2
Kohne, Wayne
Americana 1926,Jl 27,15:3
Kohner, Frederick (Playwright)
Bees and the Flowers, The 1946,S 27,19:3
Kohner, Susan
Love Me Little 1958,Ap 15,42:2
Pullman Car Hiawatha 1962,D 4,46:2
Kohout, Jara
Wicked Cooks, The 1967,Ja 24,42:1
Kohrs, Karl
Crime Marches on 1935,O 24,19:1
Red, Hot and Blue! 1936,O 30,26:3
Tell Me Pretty Maiden 1937,D 17,33:5
Kohutek, Walter
Wozzeck 1966,Ap 6,34:1
Ratten, Die 1966,Ap 13,36:1
Kokic, Kazimir
Rape of Lucretia, The 1948,D 30,24:2
Miss Liberty 1949,Jl 16,6:5
Gentlemen Prefer Blondes 1949,D 9,35:3
Kola, Horace
Parisiana 1928,F 10,26:3
Kola and Sylvia
Vaudeville (Palace) 1927,N 1,20:3
Kolb, Mina
From the Second City 1961,S 27,32:1
Hooray!! It's a Glorious Day. . .And All That
1966,Mr 10,28:1
Kolb, Sandra
This Property Is Condemned 1956,O 29,34:1
Koler, Harry
I Must Love Someone 1939,F 8,18:7
Too Hot for Maneuvers 1945,My 3,26:5
Koler, Manning
So That's That 1925,D 15,28:3
Kolik, Al
Antony and Cleopatra 1967,O 29,83:4
Kolitz, Zvi (Miscellaneous)
I'm Solomon 1968,Ap 24,51:1
Tango 1969,Ja 20,33:1
Slow Dance on the Killing Ground
1970,My 14,43:1
Kolitz, Zvi (Producer)
Deputy, The 1964,F 27,26:1
I'm Solomon 1968,Ap 24,51:1
Megilla of Itzik Manger, The 1968,O 10,60:1
Megilla of Itzik Manger, The 1969,Ap 21,55:1
Kolk, Scott
Take the Air 1927,N 23,28:2
Baby Pompadour 1934,D 28,24:2
Personal Appearance 1936,Jl 9,17:4
Koll, Don
Rehearsal, The 1952,My 27,30:5
Idiot's Delight 1957,F 23,14:2
Kolleane
Vaudeville (Hippodrome) 1924,S 30,27:5
Koller, Dagmar
Wiener Blut 1964,S 12,14:1
Kollhammer, Eveline
Wiener Blut 1964,S 12,14:1
Kollmar, Richard
Knickerbocker Holiday 1938,O 20,26:2
Too Many Girls 1939,O 19,26:2
Crazy With the Heat 1940,D 26,22:1
Crazy With the Heat 1941,Ja 15,18:2
Early to Bed 1943,Je 18,16:2
Kollmar, Richard (Director)
Dream With Music 1944,My 19,15:2
Kollmar, Richard (Miscellaneous)
By Jupiter 1942,Je 4,22:1
Kollmar, Richard (Producer)
Early to Bed 1943,Je 18,16:2
Dream With Music 1944,My 19,15:2
Are You With It? 1945,N 12,17:3
Plain and Fancy 1955,Ja 28,14:2
Body Beautiful, The 1958,Ja 24,15:2
Kollo, Walter (Composer)
Phoebe of Quality Street 1921,My 10,20:1
An und Aus 1926,D 5,VIII,8:7
Three Little Girls 1930,Mr 30,VIII,2:7
Three Little Girls 1930,Ap 15,29:1
Kolmar, Hanns
Winter Soldiers 1942,N 30,19:2
Kolmar, Klaus
Private Life of the Master Race, The
1945,Je 13,28:3
Kolon, Myriame
Bamboo Cross 1955,F 22,17:2
Kolonel Keds
Wonder World 1964,My 18,32:1
Koltai, Ralph (Costume Designer)
Back to Methuselah 1969,Ag 31,46:3
Koltai, Ralph (Scenic Designer)
Merchant of Venice, The 1965,Ap 17,9:1
Jew of Malta, The 1965,Ap 17,9:1
As You Like It 1967,O 6,33:4
As You Like It 1967,O 15,II,9:3
Soldiers 1968,Mr 3,88:2

Soldiers 1968,My 2,58:1
As You Like It 1968,Jl 6,9:1
Back to Methuselah 1969,Ag 31,46:3
Koltz, George (Costume Designer)
Herne's Egg, The 1960,S 20,48:1
Komack, Jimmie
Damn Yankees 1955,My 6,17:1
Sixth Finger in a Five Finger Glove 1956,O 9,31:4
Komar, Arthur (Miscellaneous)
From Here to There; Slow Dusk 1958,Ap 24,37:3
From Here to There; Real Strange One, A
1958,Ap 24,37:3
From Here to There; Otherwise Engaged
1958,Ap 24,37:3
Komar, Arthur (Musical Director)
H M S Pinafore; Trial by Jury 1957,Jl 29,16:1
Komisarjevsky, Theodore
Chauve-Souris 1922,Je 6,17:4
Chauve-Souris 1925,Ja 15,25:1
Chauve-Souris 1929,Ja 23,20:2
Chauve-Souris; Romantic Adventure of an Italian
Ballerina and a Marquis, A 1931,O 22,27:1
Komisarjevsky, Theodore (Composer)
Russian Bank 1940,My 25,20:2
Komisarjevsky, Theodore (Director)
Maitresse de Roi 1926,D 1,24:1
Liliom 1927,Ja 9,VII,2:1
Fourteenth of July, The 1928,Mr 11,VIII,1:3
Escape Me Not 1933,D 9,18:6
Magnolia Street 1934,Mr 9,22:6
Magnolia Street 1934,Ap 1,X,1:7
Revenge With Music 1934,N 29,33:5
Escape Me Never! 1935,Ja 22,22:2
King Lear 1936,Ap 21,27:4
Seagull, The 1936,My 21,19:2
Antony and Cleopatra 1936,N 1,X,3:7
Russian Bank 1940,My 25,20:2
Crime and Punishment 1947,D 23,29:3
Crime and Punishment 1948,Ja 4,II,1:1
Komisarjevsky, Theodore (Lighting Director)
Antony and Cleopatra 1936,N 1,X,3:7
Komisarjevsky, Theodore (Playwright)
Brass Paperweight, The 1928,N 4,IX,2:4
Fraeulein Elsa 1932,D 18,X,5:8
Russian Bank 1940,My 25,20:2
Komisarjevsky, Theodore (Producer)
Peer Gynt 1923,F 11,VII,1:1
Cherry Orchard, The 1926,O 17,VIII,2:1
King Lear 1927,Mr 13,VII,1:4
Brass Paperweight, The 1928,N 4,IX,2:4
Seagull, The 1928,Ag 30,IX,1:1
Antony and Cleopatra 1936,N 1,X,3:7
Taming of the Shrew, The 1939,Ap 23,X,2:4
Russian Bank 1940,My 25,20:2
Komisarjevsky, Theodore (Scenic Designer)
Brass Paperweight, The 1928,N 4,IX,2:4
Escape Me Not 1933,D 9,18:6
Magnolia Street 1934,Mr 9,22:6
Escape Me Never! 1935,Ja 22,22:2
Seagull, The 1936,My 21,19:2
Seagull, The 1936,Je 21,IX,1:5
Antony and Cleopatra 1936,N 1,X,3:7
Komissarov, Alexander
Cherry Orchard, The 1965,F 10,46:1
Kremlin Chimes 1965,F 25,23:1
Kommissarov, A M
Pikvikski Klub; Pickwick Club, The 1936,O 4,IX,1:8
Komptish, Amelia
Blue Monday 1932,Je 3,23:2
Kon, Henech (Composer)
Mother's Sabbath Days 1960,N 21,33:2
Sage of Rottenburg, The 1963,N 20,48:1
Enchanting Melody 1964,N 25,40:1
Kondo, Naoe
Mary, Mary, Quite Contrary 1923,S 12,14:1
Houses of Sand 1925,F 18,17:1
Arabesque 1925,O 21,20:2
Petticoat Fever 1935,Mr 5,22:2
If This Be Treason 1935,S 24,28:2
First Lady 1935,N 27,17:4
Teahouse of the August Moon, The 1953,O 16,32:1
Teahouse of the August Moon, The 1956,N 9,33:2
Kondolf, George (Producer)
Hangman's Whip 1933,F 25,20:2
Wind and the Rain, The 1934,F 2,20:6
Hell Freezes Over 1935,D 30,14:2
Room in Red and White, A 1936,Ja 20,23:3
Morning Star 1940,Ap 17,26:4
Fifth Season, The 1953,Ja 24,13:2
49th Cousin, The 1960,O 28,22:1
Kondratev, Nikita
Kremlin Chimes 1965,F 25,23:1
Konesni, Pauline
Holy Night 1941,D 22,23:3
Konig, Leib
Shylock and His Daughter 1947,S 30,22:2
Konniver, Lillian
Mikado, The 1942,F 4,22:2
Pirates of Penzance, The 1942,F 18,22:2
Iolanthe 1942,F 24,26:4
Gondoliers, The 1942,Mr 4,22:3
Konopka, Kenneth
Porgy and Bess 1943,S 14,26:2

Konopka, Kenneth—Cont
Porgy and Bess 1944,F 8,13:2
Konrad, Alan
Ice Capades 1952,S 12,18:1
Ice Capades 1953,S 11,25:1
Ice Capades 1954,S 16,37:1
Ice Capades 1955,S 15,38:1
Ice Capades 1960,S 1,30:1
Ice Capades 1961,Ag 31,24:4
Ice Capades 1962,Ag 30,34:1
Ice Capades 1963,Ag 29,37:2
Konradi, Inge
Jux Will Er Sich Machen, Einen 1968,Ap 3,41:1
Konsky, Grigory
Dead Souls 1965,F 5,34:1
Cherry Orchard, The 1965,F 10,46:1
Kremlin Chimes 1965,F 25,23:1
Konstam, Phyllis
Murder on the Second Floor 1929,S 12,35:1
Magnolia Street 1934,Mr 9,22:6
Jotham Valley 1951,F 7,37:2
Konstantin
Feast of Panthers 1961,Mr 21,32:1
Konstantin, Leopoldine
Ballerina des Koenigs, Die 1921,Jl 24,VI,1:7
Ballerina des Koenigs, Die 1921,D 11,VI,1:4
Ballerina des Koenigs, Die 1922,Jl 23,VI,1:1
Constant Wife, The 1928,My 20,VIII,2:1
Iphigenie in Tauris 1949,O 22,11:2
Konyots, The
Pardon Our French 1950,O 6,22:4
Kooiman, Dirk
Guitar 1959,N 11,42:5
Not a Way of Life 1967,Mr 23,28:1
Kookwalter, DeVeren
Androcles and the Lion 1968,Je 27,47:1
Koon, Helene
Ghost of Elsinore, The 1949,Ap 16,10:2
Serpent in the Orchard, The 1949,Ap 24,II,1:1
Koonen, Alice
Saint Joan 1925,Ja 11,VII,2:7
Kootz, Samuel (Playwright)
Home Is the Hunter 1945,D 21,25:4
Kopel, Harold (Costume Designer)
Fuente Ovejuna; Sheep Well, The 1936,My 3,II,4:1
Kopel, Harold (Scenic Designer)
Fuente Ovejuna; Sheep Well, The 1936,My 3,II,4:1
Kopernak, Galina
Montmartre 1922,F 14,20:1
Wasp, The 1923,Mr 28,14:3
Four in Hand 1923,S 7,10:2
Pierrot the Prodigal; Enfant Prodigue, L'
1925,Mr 7,8:1
Love's Call 1925,S 11,20:1
What the Doctor Ordered 1927,Ag 19,20:2
She Got What She Wanted 1929,Mr 5,28:1
Kopiloff, William
Woman of Bronze, The 1920,S 8,9:2
Kopin, Sergei (Composer)
If I Were You 1931,S 24,21:1
Kopit, Arthur (Playwright)
Oh Dad, Poor Dad, Mamma's Hung You in the
Closet and I'm Feelin' So Sad 1961,Jl 6,19:2
Oh Dad, Poor Dad, Mamma's Hung You in the
Closet and I'm Feelin' So Sad 1962,F 27,28:1
Oh Dad, Poor Dad, Mamma's Hung You in the
Closet and I'm Feelin' So Sad 1962,Mr 11,II,1:1
Oh Dad, Poor Dad, Mamma's Hung You in the
Closet and I'm Feelin' So Sad 1962,Ap 29,II,3:1
Oh Dad, Poor Dad, Mamma's Hung You in the
Closet and I'm Feelin' So Sad 1963,Ag 28,28:2
Day the Whores Came Out to Play Tennis, The
1965,Mr 16,45:1
Sing to Me Through Open Windows
1965,Mr 16,45:1
Indians 1968,Jl 9,30:2
Indians 1968,Jl 21,II,12:1
Indians 1969,My 18,II,3:5
Indians 1969,My 27,43:1
Indians 1969,O 14,51:1
Indians 1969,O 19,II,1:1
Koplin, Merton Y (Producer)
Bring Me a Warm Body 1962,Ap 17,29:3
Kopp, Marian
Johnny Doodle 1942,Mr 19,28:2
Koppel, Holger (Translator)
2 + 2 = 5 1927,N 29,30:3
Koppenhoefer, Maria
Richard III 1937,My 30,X,2:2
Kops, Bernard (Playwright)
Hamlet of Stepney Green 1958,N 14,21:1
Dream of Peter Mann, The 1960,S 6,40:1
Kops, Josephine
Bursting the Barriers 1930,My 7,25:1
Korber, Hilde
Strictly Dishonorable 1931,Ap 12,IX,1:3
Korchmar, David
Waiting for Lefty 1935,F 11,14:5
Korchunov, Viktor (Director)
Colleagues, The 1962,Je 21,26:1
Korda, Alexander (Director)
Josephine 1934,S 26,17:5
Korda, Alexander (Producer)
Mary Read 1934,N 22,26:7

Kordel, John
Athenian Touch, The 1964,Ja 15,25:4
Kordt, Fritz
Lulu 1927,Ja 30,VII,4:3
Koreff, Nora
Blue Butterfly, The 1929,F 17,29:3
Korene, Vera
Circe 1929,Mr 31,VIII,2:7
Korenieva, Lydia
Tsar Fyodor Ivanovitch 1923,Ja 9,26:1
Three Sisters, The 1923,Ja 30,12:2
Brothers Karamazov, The 1923,F 27,14:2
Brothers Karamazov, The 1923,Mr 4,VII,1:1
Brothers Karamazov, The 1923,N 20,23:4
Enemy of the People, An 1923,D 4,25:1
Uncle Vanya 1924,Ja 29,16:2
Brothers Karamazov, The 1924,My 6,25:2
Koretz, Sheldon
Judge, The 1958,My 14,36:2
Koretzky, Viera (Mme)
Homme Qui Assassina, L' 1924,N 11,20:1
Homme et Ses Fantomes, L' 1924,N 14,16:1
Merchant of Venice, The 1924,N 18,23:2
Bourgeois Gentilhomme, Le 1924,N 20,21:2
Taming of the Shrew, The 1924,N 25,27:3
Korff, Anni
Dantons Tod 1927,D 21,28:3
Lebende Leichnam, Der, Der; Living Corpse, The 1928,Ja 24,26:2
Korff, Arnold
Living Mask, The 1924,Ja 22,15:1
Leah Kleschna 1924,Ap 22,19:2
Leah Kleschna 1924,Ap 27,VIII,1:1
White Cargo 1925,O 25,30:3
White Cargo 1925,N 22,VIII,1:8
Midsummer Night's Dream, A 1927,N 18,21:1
Jedermann 1927,D 8,33:2
Dantons Tod 1927,D 21,28:3
Danton's Death 1928,Ja 1,VIII,1:1
Peripherie 1928,Ja 3,29:1
Kabale und Liebe 1928,Ja 17,22:3
Lebende Leichnam, Der, Der; Living Corpse, The 1928,Ja 24,26:2
Olympia 1928,O 17,26:1
Age of Innocence, The 1928,N 28,24:2
Biography 1932,D 13,25:3
Biography 1934,F 6,24:4
Love Is Not So Simple 1935,N 5,33:1
Love Is Not So Simple 1935,N 10,IX,1:6
Tapestry in Gray 1935,D 28,10:2
Alice Takat 1936,F 11,19:2
White Horse Inn 1936,O 2,28:5
Save Me the Waltz 1938,Mr 1,19:2
Escape This Night 1938,Ap 23,18:1
Lorelei 1938,N 30,21:2
My Dear Children 1939,Mr 25,19:6
My Dear Children 1940,F 1,16:2
Another Sun 1940,F 24,8:6
Liliom 1940,Mr 26,17:2
Delicate Story 1940,D 5,32:2
Family, The 1943,Mr 31,22:4
Thank You Svoboda 1944,Mr 2,13:2
Searching Wind, The 1944,Ap 13,25:2
Searching Wind, The 1944,Ap 23,II,1:1
Korff, Arnold (Director)
White Cargo 1925,N 22,VIII,1:8
Korff, Arnold (Producer)
White Cargo 1925,O 25,30:3
Korff, William
Henri Christophe 1945,Je 7,24:5
John Brown 1950,My 4,32:7
Korkes, Jon
Little Murders 1969,Ja 6,38:1
Penny Wars, The 1969,O 16,52:1
Carpenters, The 1970,D 22,40:1
Korlin, Boris
Red Rust 1929,D 18,31:1
Country Wife, The 1931,Ap 19,31:5
Her Man of Wax 1933,O 12,32:3
Ship Comes in, A 1934,S 20,21:1
Woman of Destiny, A 1936,Mr 3,25:2
Korman, Harvey
Captain Brassbound's Conversion 1950,D 28,21:1
Korman, Jess J (Composer)
I Want You 1961,S 15,29:1
Korman, Jess J (Lyricist)
I Want You 1961,S 15,29:1
Korman, Jess J (Playwright)
I Want You 1961,S 15,29:1
Korn, Mina
Melody Lingers On, The 1969,N 17,55:1
Korn, William
Fly Away Home 1937,Ap 27,18:1
Kornblum, I B (Composer)
Blue Eyes 1921,F 22,11:2
Kornbluth, Bruce M
Hamlet 1970,O 19,51:1
Korneichuk, Alexander (Playwright)
Front, The 1942,N 7,8:3
Mr Perkins' Mission to the Land of the Bolsheviks 1944,D 17,I,7:2
Kornelia, Irma
Man in Evening Clothes, The 1924,D 6,13:4

Kornfeld, Barry
Place for Chance, The 1964,My 15,44:2
Kornfeld, Barry (Musical Director)
Place for Chance, The 1964,My 15,44:2
Kornfeld, Lawrence
Many Loves 1959,Ja 14,28:1
Kornfeld, Lawrence (Director)
Full Moon in March, A 1960,S 20,48:1
Purgatory 1960,S 20,48:1
Billygoat Eddie 1964,Ap 21,43:2
Home Movies 1964,My 12,32:1
Softly, and Consider the Nearness 1964,My 12,32:1
Jonah! 1966,F 16,52:1
Gorilla Queen 1967,Mr 26,II,1:2
In Circles 1967,O 14,12:1
In Circles 1967,N 5,II,1:7
Line of Least Existence, The 1968,Mr 25,53:1
In Circles 1968,Je 28,36:1
Peace 1968,N 10,87:1
Peace 1969,Ja 28,49:1
Promenade 1969,Je 5,56:1
Dracula Sabbat 1970,O 2,28:2
Kornfeld, Lawrence (Miscellaneous)
Many Loves 1959,Ja 14,28:1
Cave at Machpelah, The 1959,Jl 1,25:1
Man Is Man 1962,S 19,31:1
Kornfeld, Paul (Playwright)
Jud Suess 1930,N 30,IX,2:1
Kornfeld, Robert (Playwright)
Kicking the Castle Down 1967,Ja 19,43:1
Korngold, Erich Wolfgang (Composer)
Rose of Florida, The 1929,F 23,17:1
Lied der Liebe, Das 1932,F 7,VIII,1:3
Fair Helen 1932,Jl 17,IX,1:2
Korngold, Erich Wolfgang (Miscellaneous)
Rosalinda; Fledermaus, Die 1942,O 29,26:5
Korngold, Erich Wolfgang (Musical Director)
Fair Helen 1931,Ag 30,VIII,2:1
Lied der Liebe, Das 1932,F 7,VIII,1:3
Helen Goes to Troy 1944,Ap 30,II,1:1
Korngold, Erich Wolfgang (Playwright)
Helen Goes to Troy 1944,Ap 25,17:2
Kornman, Mary
Vaudeville (Palace) 1929,Je 17,29:3
Kornstein, Malka
Counsellor-at-Law 1931,N 7,17:2
Counsellor-at-Law 1932,S 13,17:2
Spring Song 1934,O 2,18:2
Kornyechuk, Alexander (Playwright)
Platon Krechet 1936,O 4,IX,1:8
Kornzweig, Susan
Tarot 1970,D 12,19:1
Korsak, E
Revisor; Inspector General, The 1935,F 18,19:6
Poverty Is No Crime 1935,F 21,22:5
Strange Child 1935,F 26,16:1
Marriage 1935,Mr 12,24:8
Enemies 1935,Mr 19,24:7
Korshner, M (Composer)
Both Kooney Lemels 1964,O 12,37:2
Korshner, M (Playwright)
Both Kooney Lemels 1964,O 12,37:2
Kortchmar, David
Yoshe Kalb 1933,D 29,27:2
Till the Day I Die 1935,Mr 27,24:5
As You Like It 1936,Ap 24,18:4
Korth, Charles
Comedian, The 1956,O 18,36:4
Korthaze, Richard
Skyscraper 1965,N 15,48:1
Kortlucke, Sheila (Miscellaneous)
Cave Dwellers, The 1961,O 16,34:2
Kortner, Franz
Herod and Mariamne 1938,O 27,27:2
Kortner, Fritz
Hamlet 1927,F 13,VII,2:3
Merchant of Venice, The 1928,Ap 1,IX,2:4
Rote General, Der 1928,D 23,VIII,4:1
Oedipus Rex 1929,Mr 24,X,2:3
What Price Glory 1929,Ap 28,IX,1:4
Kortner, Fritz (Director)
Another Sun 1940,F 24,8:6
Kortner, Fritz (Playwright)
Another Sun 1940,F 24,8:6
Somewhere in France 1941,Ap 29,16:8
Korvin, Ada
Dream of Sganarelle, The 1933,O 17,26:5
Korvin, Geza
Winter Soldiers 1942,N 30,19:2
Dark Eyes 1943,Ja 15,20:2
Kos, Stasia
He Who Gets Slapped 1956,F 2,18:1
Kosak, Michael
Trojan Women, The 1941,Ap 9,32:5
Kosanza, Nakamura
Kanjincho; Subscription List, The 1960,Je 3,26:1
Kagotsurube; Courtesan, The 1960,Je 3,26:1
Musume Dojoji; Maiden at the Dojo Temple, The 1960,Je 10,37:1
Musume Dojoji; Maiden at the Dojo Temple, The 1960,Je 17,35:4
Kosarin, Oscar (Miscellaneous)
Mr Wonderful 1956,Mr 23,23:2

To Broadway With Love 1964,Ap 30,28:6
Kosarin, Oscar (Musical Director)
Carmen Jones 1951,S 22,8:6
Allegro 1952,S 18,36:3
Something More! 1964,N 11,36:1
Arabian Nights 1967,Jl 3,12:1
Happy Time, The 1968,Ja 19,32:2
Park 1970,Ap 23,47:1
Sound of Music, The 1970,Jl 3,13:1
Kosek, Francis Malcolm
This Mad Whirl 1937,Ja 10,II,4:8
Koser, David
Yours, A Lincoln 1942,Jl 10,12:3
Russian People, The 1942,D 30,17:2
Othello 1943,O 20,18:1
Koshiji, Fubuki
Fiddler on the Roof 1967,S 7,50:1
Kosicsky, Karl
Jumbo 1935,N 18,20:2
Koski, Fraun
Jeweled Tree, The 1926,O 8,26:2
Koski, Irja
Dole Brothers 1932,Mr 26,17:7
Slight Case of Murder, A 1935,S 12,28:5
Koski, Yon (Miscellaneous)
Only a Countess May Dance When She's Crazy (An Almost Historical Camp) 1968,Mr 19,41:1
Last Triangle, The (An Embroidered Camp) 1968,Mr 19,41:1
Kosleck, Martin
Miles of Heaven, The 1937,Ag 31,27:4
Shakespeare's Merchant 1939 1939,Ja 10,16:3
Madwoman of Chaillot, The 1950,Je 14,41:2
'Tis Pity She's a Whore 1958,D 6,21:1
Kosleck, Martin (Scenic Designer)
Shakespeare's Merchant 1939 1939,Ja 10,16:3
Kosloff, Alexis
Broadway Brevities, 1920 1920,S 30,12:2
Koslow, Esther
Slow Memories 1970,N 18,41:1
Kosma (Composer)
Baptiste 1952,N 13,34:2
Kosmaiska, Wieslawa
Jaselka 1965,Ja 6,32:1
Woman, The 1965,Ja 6,32:1
Labyrinth, The 1965,Ja 6,32:1
Nightmare, The 1965,Ja 6,32:1
Jacob and the Angel 1965,Ja 6,32:1
Kernel and the Shell, The 1965,Ja 6,32:1
Book, The 1965,Ja 6,32:1
Post Office, The 1965,Ja 6,32:1
Kosmowskaja, L
Blue Bird, The 1932,Ap 22,23:2
Kosofsky, Milton
Candida 1925,D 19,14:2
Kossi, Estanislao
Song of Norway 1959,Je 26,16:2
Kossmayer, Karl
Holiday on Ice 1965,S 2,38:4
Kossmayer's Mules
Holiday on Ice 1969,Ag 28,44:1
Kossoff, David
Funny Kind of Evening With David Kossoff, A 1967,Ja 31,52:1
Kossoff, David (Playwright)
Funny Kind of Evening With David Kossoff, A 1967,Ja 31,52:1
Kossoff, George
Red Velvet Goat, The 1939,Ja 21,18:4
Mr Banks of Birmingham 1939,Ja 21,18:4
Kosta, Hilda
Threepenny Opera, The 1933,Ap 14,22:4
Kosta, Tessa
Lassie 1920,Ap 7,9:2
Princess Virtue 1921,My 5,20:2
Chocolate Soldier, The 1921,D 13,24:2
Rose of Stamboul, The 1922,Mr 8,11:2
Caroline 1923,F 1,13:2
Vaudeville (Palace) 1924,Ap 1,18:1
Princess April 1924,D 2,23:2
Princess Ida 1925,Ap 14,27:2
Song of the Flame 1925,D 11,26:4
Song of the Flame 1925,D 31,10:2
Fioretta 1929,Ja 6,VIII,4:6
Fortune Teller, The 1929,N 5,32:3
Kostal, Irwin (Miscellaneous)
Shinbone Alley 1957,Ap 15,23:2
West Side Story 1957,S 27,14:4
West Side Story 1957,O 13,II,9:1
Fiorello! 1959,N 24,45:3
West Side Story 1960,Ap 28,31:1
Tenderloin 1960,O 18,47:2
Sail Away 1961,O 4,48:5
Kwamina 1961,O 24,42:1
Funny Thing Happened on the Way to the Forum, A 1962,My 9,49:1
West Side Story 1968,Je 25,32:1
Kostant, Anna
Howdy King 1926,D 14,24:4
Baby Mine 1927,Je 10,21:2
Trial of Mary Dugan, The 1927,S 20,33:1
Faust 1928,O 9,34:1
Street Scene 1929,Ja 11,20:4

Kostant, Anna—Cont
Counsellor-at-Law 1931,N 7,17:2
Koster, Lewis Willem
Pirates of Penzance, The 1942,F 20,20:2
Kostic, Vojislav (Composer)
Progress of Bora, The Tailor, The 1968,Je 27,49:2
Ubu Roi 1968,Je 29,20:1
Kostner, Sondra
Curtain Call 1937,Ap 23,24:7
Kostner, Stanley S (Miscellaneous)
Frankie and Johnny 1952,O 29,37:2
Kotanyi, Gustave (Producer)
Gypsy Baron, The 1942,Je 20,8:5
Gypsy Baron, The 1942,Ag 7,12:4
Beggar Student, The 1942,S 26,11:4
Kotchetovsky
Chauve-Souris 1922,Je 6,17:4
Kotchetovsky, Mme
Chauve-Souris 1922,Je 6,17:4
Kotek, Fred
Sancho Panza 1923,N 27,23:1
Koterbska, Maria
Visit With the Family, A 1957,O 17,42:5
Kothe, Ken
Crime and Crime 1963,D 17,51:2
Kothe, Ken (Lighting Director)
Crime and Crime 1963,D 17,51:2
Kotliar, Sonia
Riverside Drive 1931,Ja 6,24:2
Man With the Portfolio, The 1931,F 12,24:6
Kott, Jan (Director)
Orestes 1968,F 17,32:5
Kott, Jan (Miscellaneous)
As You Like It 1967,O 6,33:4
As You Like It 1967,O 15,II,9:3
Kottler, Joseph
Inherit the Wind 1967,Je 23,50:1
Kotto, Yaphet
Great Western Union, The 1965,F 10,45:1
Zulu and the Zayda, The 1965,N 11,59:1
Great White Hope, The 1969,S 27,26:1
Kottow, Hans (Playwright)
Stork Is Dead, The 1932,S 24,18:2
Kouchitachvili (Scenic Designer)
Grandee Penitence, La 1926,N 14,VIII,2:1
Chagrins d'Amour 1926,N 14,VIII,2:1
Kouchta, Vassili (Scenic Designer)
Grand Duchess 1929,D 17,29:2
Koud, Billy
Strip for Action 1942,O 1,26:2
Strip for Action 1942,O 11,VIII,1:1
Koudriatzeff, Nicholas de (Producer)
Marius 1956,F 6,27:4
Koun, Karolos (Director)
Frogs, The 1966,Jl 25,22:5
Kouns, Nellie
Frivolities of 1920 1920,Ja 9,22:2
Vaudeville (Hippodrome) 1924,F 12,20:2
Vaudeville (Palace) 1927,O 4,34:3
Vaudeville (Palace) 1928,N 12,18:7
Kouns, Sara
Frivolities of 1920 1920,Ja 9,22:2
Vaudeville (Hippodrome) 1924,F 12,20:2
Vaudeville (Palace) 1927,O 4,34:3
Vaudeville (Palace) 1928,N 12,18:7
Kouns Sisters
Vaudeville (Hippodrome) 1924,F 19,12:1
Vaudeville (Palace) 1927,O 11,27:2
Koupal, T Morse
Salome 1922,My 23,12:4
Devil Within, The 1925,Mr 17,19:4
Kourkoulos, Nikos
Illya Darling 1967,Ap 12,37:1
Illya Darling 1967,N 2,58:1
Kousnezoff, Mme
Russian Isba 1920,F 17,19:2
Revue Russe, The 1922,O 6,28:1
Koutoukas, H M
Doll's House, A 1956,My 8,29:2
Koutoukas, H M (Director)
Last Triangle, The (An Embroidered Camp)
1968,Mr 19,41:1
Only a Countess May Dance When She's Crazy
(An Almost Historical Camp) 1968,Mr 19,41:1
Koutoukas, H M (Playwright)
Only a Countess May Dance When She's Crazy
(An Almost Historical Camp) 1968,Mr 19,41:1
Last Triangle, The (An Embroidered Camp)
1968,Mr 19,41:1
Koutsoukos, Thom
Escurial 1960,Jl 22,13:1
Calvary 1960,Jl 22,13:1
Valmouth 1960,O 7,29:1
How to Steal an Election 1968,O 14,56:1
Koutzen, Leo (Composer)
Wise Men of Chelm, The 1933,O 18,24:4
Yoshe Kalb 1933,D 29,27:2
Kovac, Jan
Out of This World 1950,D 22,17:3
Kiss Me, Kate 1952,Ja 9,24:6
Kovach, Edward
No More Peace 1937,F 27,9:1
Kovach, Nora
Judy Garland's New Variety Show 1956,S 27,43:2

From A to Z 1960,Ap 21,23:2
Kovacs, Coloman (Playwright)
Dream Queen 1930,F 23,III,7:2
Kovacs, Gabo
Untitled-Passion Play 1922,Je 15,4:5
Koval
J'Aime 1927,Ja 23,VII,2:1
Kovarova, Ludmila
Pierrot's Journey 1964,Ag 5,23:1
Button, Button 1970,O 20,41:1
Kovarova, Mirka (Costume Designer)
Pierrot's Journey 1964,Ag 5,23:1
Kovarsky, Anatole (Miscellaneous)
Owl and the Pussycat, The 1964,N 19,48:1
Kove, Martin
Man and Superman 1970,F 24,48:1
Koven, Miss
East of Suez 1922,S 22,16:3
Koven, Stanley (Playwright)
Dark Corners 1964,My 6,43:1
Mr Grossman 1964,My 6,43:1
Kovens, Edward
Two Times One; Last Straw, The 1970,Ap 5,76:4
Kovensky, I (Playwright)
New Man, The 1932,Ap 22,23:2
Kovner, Rose (Miscellaneous)
Milk and Honey 1961,O 11,52:1
Kovon, Lenore
Miss Julie 1954,Mr 29,24:3
Kovy, Mary (Pfc)
Swing Sister Wac Swing 1944,Ja 4,20:4
Kowa, Maria
Wiener Blut 1964,S 12,14:1
Kowa, Victor de
Frau Die Weiss Was Sie Will, Eine 1932,O 9,IX,3:7
Kowal, Mitchell
Horse Fever 1940,N 25,21:2
Gramercy Ghost 1951,Ap 27,20:2
Collector's Item 1952,F 9,11:2
Kowalska, Ruth
Mirele Efros 1967,O 20,55:1
Mother Courage 1967,N 17,55:1
Kowalski, Matus
Dybbuk, The 1924,Ja 29,17:7
Kowit, Billie
Wooden Idol, The 1930,My 13,27:2
Koycan, Barbara
Fifth Horseman, The 1949,Je 14,26:6
Koyke, Hizi
Mikado, The; Town of Titipu, The 1931,My 5,33:2
Mikado, The 1931,Ag 25,17:7
Geisha, The 1931,O 6,35:4
Mikado, The 1933,Ap 18,13:4
Mikado, The 1934,Ap 3,26:3
Mikado, The 1934,Ap 24,27:5
Kozelka, Paul (Dr) (Director)
Weathercock, The 1948,Ag 6,22:3
Kozintzev, G (Producer)
Hamlet 1954,My 31,9:1
Kozlenko, William (Playwright)
One-Act Variety Theatre; Devil Is a Good Man,
The 1940,Mr 20,36:2
This Earth Is Ours 1940,Ap 26,24:2
Kozlik, Al
Taming of the Shrew, The 1962,Je 21,25:1
Tempest, The 1962,Je 22,14:1
Timon of Athens 1963,Jl 31,19:2
Richard II 1964,Je 17,47:1
Bourgeois Gentilhomme, Le 1964,Je 18,28:2
Henry IV, Part I 1965,Je 30,42:1
Falstaff; Henry IV, Part II 1965,Jl 1,35:1
Julius Caesar 1965,Jl 2,18:1
Cherry Orchard, The 1965,Ag 2,17:2
Henry V 1966,Je 8,38:1
Henry VI 1966,Je 9,55:2
Antony and Cleopatra 1967,Ag 2,25:1
Merry Wives of Windsor, The 1967,Ag 4,18:1
Government Inspector, The 1967,O 28,34:1
Kozlowski, Jerzy
Labyrinth, The 1965,Ja 6,32:1
Nightmare, The 1965,Ja 6,32:1
Jaselka 1965,Ja 6,32:1
Book, The 1965,Ja 6,32:1
Woman, The 1965,Ja 6,32:1
Jacob and the Angel 1965,Ja 6,32:1
Kernel and the Shell, The 1965,Ja 6,32:1
Post Office, The 1965,Ja 6,32:1
Kozlowski, Julius
Uncle Vanya 1960,F 13,13:4
Kozma, Tibor (Musical Director)
Alice in Wonderland 1947,Ap 7,19:2
Alice in Wonderland 1947,Ap 13,II,1:1
Kraal, Elli
Lauf ins Glueck 1935,My 19,IX,2:5
Kraber, Gerrit
House of Connelly, The 1931,S 29,22:4
1931 1931,D 11,34:3
Night Over Taos 1932,Mr 10,25:3
Men in White 1933,S 27,24:2
Waiting for Lefty 1935,F 11,14:5
Panic 1935,Mr 16,18:4
Till the Day I Die 1935,Mr 27,24:5
Waiting for Lefty 1935,Mr 27,24:5

Kraber, Gerrit—Cont
Till the Day I Die 1935,Mr 27,24:5
Case of Clyde Griffiths 1936,Mr 14,10:4
Kraber, Karl F
Saint Joan 1950,Mr 4,10:6
Kraber, Tony
Weep for the Virgins 1935,D 2,18:1
Johnny Johnson 1936,N 20,26:3
Having Wonderful Time 1937,F 22,12:5
Girl From Wyoming, The 1938,O 31,12:1
Everywhere I Roam 1938,D 30,10:4
Stop Press 1939,Mr 20,13:2
Summer Night 1939,N 3,17:1
Night Music 1940,F 23,18:2
Golden Boy 1952,Mr 13,24:3
See the Jaguar 1952,D 4,46:2
Ponder Heart, The 1956,F 17,14:2
Of Mice and Men 1958,D 5,38:1
Twelfth Night 1959,Jl 11,10:2
Macbeth 1959,Ag 1,9:2
Roman Candle 1960,F 4,34:2
Banker's Daughter, The 1962,Ja 23,37:1
Foxy 1964,F 17,26:1
Kraber, Tony (Playwright)
Group Theatre Sketches 1935,F 11,14:5
Krach, Bill
Come of Age 1952,Ja 24,22:2
Krach, William
Gentlemen Prefer Blondes 1949,D 9,35:3
My Fair Lady 1964,My 21,43:2
Krachmalnick, Samuel (Miscellaneous)
Happy Town 1959,O 8,49:2
Krachmalnick, Samuel (Musical Director)
Saint of Bleecker Street, The 1954,D 28,21:1
Candide 1956,D 3,40:2
Candide 1956,D 9,II,5:1
Carmen Jones 1959,Ag 18,25:1
Happy Town 1959,O 8,49:2
Kracht, Joseph C
His Majesty the Queen 1926,Mr 9,8:1
Kracke, Frederick J H
Off the Record; Mayor Answers the Newspapers!
Wow! 1935,Je 19,23:3
Kradoska, Charles
Three Sisters, The 1930,Ja 9,22:2
Glass of Water, A 1930,Mr 6,16:3
Boeuf sur le Toit, Le 1930,Ap 25,28:4
Antigone 1930,Ap 25,28:4
Kraemer, Florence
Broadway Whirl, The 1921,Je 9,10:4
Kraemer, Jean
Can-Can 1953,My 8,28:1
Kraemer, Valentina
Cricket on the Hearth, The 1925,My 29,20:2
Kraff, Lillian
Mlle Modiste 1937,My 5,28:5
Krafft, Paul (Playwright)
Deep Channels 1929,O 19,22:3
Kraft, Beatrice
Allah Be Praised! 1944,Ap 21,14:2
Sadie Thompson 1944,N 17,25:2
Kismet 1953,D 4,2:4
Kismet 1965,Je 23,45:1
Kraft, Beatrice (Choreographer)
Doctor Faustus 1957,F 19,35:7
Parade at the Devil's Bridge 1957,F 19,35:7
Kraft, Charles
Early to Bed 1943,Je 18,16:2
Kraft, Evelyne
Allah Be Praised! 1944,Ap 21,14:2
Kraft, H S (Director)
Mr Papavert 1932,Ja 23,18:6
Thank You Svoboda 1944,Mr 2,13:2
Kraft, H S (Original Author)
Hot-Cha! 1932,Mr 9,17:3
Kraft, H S (Playwright)
Mr Papavert 1932,Ja 23,18:6
Cue for Passion 1940,D 20,33:4
Cafe Crown 1942,Ja 24,12:5
Thank You Svoboda 1944,Mr 2,13:2
Top Banana 1951,N 2,19:2
Cafe Crown 1964,Ap 18,32:1
Kraft, H S (Producer)
Ten Per Cent 1927,S 14,29:3
Gentlemen of the Press 1928,Ag 28,27:2
Poppa 1928,D 25,31:1
Kraft, Irma (Miscellaneous)
Bridge of Distances, The 1925,O 4,IX,1:1
Kraft, Irma (Playwright)
Bridge of Distances, The 1925,S 29,30:1
Kraft, Irma (Producer)
Uncle Vanya 1929,My 25,17:1
Kraft, Jack
Buzzin' Around 1920,Jl 7,14:1
Kraft, Jill
Cyrano de Bergerac 1953,N 13,24:3
Dear Me, the Sky Is Falling 1963,Mr 4,9:1
Kraft, Martin
Three to Make Ready 1946,Mr 8,16:2
Kraft, Myron
Seven Against One 1930,My 7,25:1
Kraft, Richard
Walk Hard 1946,Mr 28,34:2

raft, Victor
Weep for the Virgins 1935,D 2,18:1
rahl, Hilde
Maria Stuart 1968,Mr 27,38:1
rahn, Meta
All for Love 1938,Ap 5,19:4
Straw Hat, The 1939,S 30,10:6
rainis, Abraham
S S Glencairn 1924,N 4,31:4
rakeur, Jacques (Composer)
Sunday Nights at Nine 1934,N 19,12:1
rakeur, Jacques (Lyricist)
Sunday Nights at Nine 1934,N 19,12:1
rakeur, Richard W (Miscellaneous)
Count Me In 1942,O 9,24:2
Young and Fair, The 1948,N 23,35:2
rakeur, Richard W (Producer)
This One Man 1930,O 22,32:3
Mainly for Lovers 1936,F 22,13:2
Kiss for Cinderella, A 1942,Mr 11,22:2
Sleep, My Pretty One 1944,N 3,26:8
This, Too, Shall Pass 1946,My 1,32:4
Father, The 1949,N 17,36:2
Affairs of State 1950,S 26,37:2
Twilight Walk 1951,S 25,25:4
Faithfully Yours 1951,O 19,22:5
On Borrowed Time 1953,Ja 1,19:1
On Borrowed Time 1953,F 11,34:1
Loud Red Patrick, The 1956,O 4,28:1
Masquerade 1959,Mr 17,42:1
Have I Got a Girl for You! 1963,D 3,53:2
rakovska, Ruth
As You Like It 1941,O 21,29:2
rall, Heidi
Dance Me a Song 1950,Ja 21,10:5
raly, Hans (Playwright)
Quiet, Please! 1940,O 20,IX,2:3
Quiet, Please! 1940,N 9,20:3
ram, Hall
Here Come the Clowns 1960,S 20,48:1
ramarr, Elena
Vie Parisienne, La 1945,Ja 13,14:5
ramberg, Hal
Comrades 1956,Je 6,38:1
Kramer, Allen (Miscellaneous)
Billy Barnes Revue, The 1959,Je 10,42:2
Billy Barnes People, The 1961,Je 14,10:3
Kramer, Clair
Free for All 1931,S 9,25:1
Devil and Daniel Webster, The 1939,My 19,26:1
Hairpin Harmony 1943,O 2,18:5
Kramer, Clark
Forbidden Melody 1936,N 3,33:1
Kramer, Dave (Director)
You'll See Stars 1943,Ja 1,26:6
Kramer, Dave (Producer)
You'll See Stars 1943,Ja 1,26:6
Kramer, H O (Director)
Gypsy Baron, The 1944,Je 15,17:3
Kramer, Helen
Kiss for Cinderella, A 1942,Mr 11,22:2
Kramer, Herbert (Director)
Hamlet 1954,Ap 24,15:2
Kramer, John
Troilus and Cressida 1932,Je 7,22:3
Uncle Tom's Cabin 1933,My 30,13:4
Kitchen, The 1966,Je 14,50:1
Patriot for Me, A 1969,O 6,58:1
Kramer, Jonathan
Hair 1968,Ap 30,40:2
Kramer, Les (Lyricist)
Russell Patterson's Sketch-Book 1960,F 8,35:1
Kramer, Les (Playwright)
Russell Patterson's Sketch-Book 1960,F 8,35:1
Kramer, Lloyd
Child's Play 1970,F 18,39:1
Kramer, Mark
Love Life 1948,O 8,31:2
Kramer, Rebecca (Choreographer)
Red Roses for Me 1961,N 28,41:1
Kramer, Sam
Witness for the Prosecution 1954,D 17,35:2
Kramer, Sam (Miscellaneous)
Beauty Part, The 1962,D 28,5:2
Kramer, Stephen
Richard III 1965,Je 3,26:1
Kramer, Wright
Light of the World, The 1920,Ja 7,17:1
Genius and the Crowd 1920,S 7,20:1
Varying Shore, The 1921,D 6,24:1
Exciters, The 1922,S 23,10:4
In the Next Room 1923,N 28,14:1
Poor Nut, The 1925,Ap 28,18:1
Taming of the Shrew, The 1925,D 19,14:1
Cock Robin 1928,Ja 13,26:6
Becky Sharp 1929,Je 4,29:1
Holiday 1930,F 6,21:2
Little Father of the Wilderness, The 1930,Je 3,27:1
Monkey 1932,F 12,25:2
Uncle Tom's Cabin 1933,My 30,13:4
Kramer and Boyle
Vaudeville (Palace) 1926,Jl 27,15:4
Vaudeville (Palace) 1926,N 23,27:3

Vaudeville (Palace) 1929,S 30,22:3
Kramm, Joseph
Living Corpse, The 1929,D 7,19:1
Romeo and Juliet 1930,Ap 22,33:1
Siegfried 1930,O 21,34:1
Lady of the Camellias, The 1931,Ja 27,21:2
Two Seconds 1931,O 10,20:6
Liliom 1932,O 27,23:2
Camille 1932,O 28,23:2
Dear Jane 1932,N 15,24:3
Alice in Wonderland 1932,D 12,18:3
Aiglon, L' 1934,N 5,22:2
Prelude 1936,Ap 20,17:4
Bury the Dead 1936,Ap 20,17:4
Processional 1937,O 14,23:1
Trojan Incident 1938,Ap 22,15:2
Man Who Killed Lincoln, The 1940,Ja 18,26:4
Liliom 1940,Mr 26,17:2
Journey to Jerusalem 1940,O 7,21:2
Afternoon Storm 1948,Ap 12,24:2
Kramm, Joseph (Director)
Hope Is the Thing With Feathers 1948,Ap 12,24:2
Gone Tomorrow; Hope's the Thing
  1948,My 12,34:6
Hope Is the Thing With Feathers; Hope's the
  Thing 1948,My 12,34:6
Home Life of a Buffalo; Hope's the Thing
  1948,My 12,34:6
Me, The Sleeper 1949,My 16,18:6
Gods of the Mountain, The 1950,My 25,36:2
Once Around the Block 1950,My 25,36:2
Aria Da Capo 1950,My 25,36:2
Shrike, The 1953,N 26,51:2
Giants, Sons of Giants 1962,Ja 8,26:2
Kramm, Joseph (Playwright)
Shrike, The 1952,Ja 16,20:2
Shrike, The 1952,Ja 27,II,1:1
Shrike, The 1953,N 26,51:2
Giants, Sons of Giants 1962,Ja 8,26:2
Kranendonk, Leonard
Hear! Hear! 1955,S 28,38:1
Krantzor, Douglas
Singing Jailbirds 1928,D 5,34:4
Broken Chain, The 1929,F 21,30:4
Mr Papavert 1932,Ja 23,18:6
Kranz, Ben D
Reunion in Vienna 1931,N 17,31:1
O Evening Star 1936,Ja 9,24:6
Having Wonderful Time 1937,F 22,12:5
Kranz, Ben D (Miscellaneous)
Inadmissible Evidence 1965,D 1,52:1
Only Game in Town, The 1968,My 21,42:1
Wrong Way Light Bulb, The 1969,Mr 5,40:1
Kranz, Heinrich B (Playwright)
Waterloo Bridge 1931,N 29,VIII,4:1
Krasko, Annette
Eternal Sabbath 1963,O 19,17:2
Krasna, Norman (Director)
Man With Blonde Hair, The 1941,N 5,30:2
Time for Elizabeth 1948,S 28,32:3
Krasna, Norman (Playwright)
Louder, Please! 1931,N 13,26:4
Small Miracle 1934,S 27,24:3
Man With Blonde Hair, The 1941,N 5,30:2
Dear Ruth 1944,D 14,29:2
Dear Ruth 1944,D 31,II,1:1
Dear Ruth 1946,Mr 1,17:3
John Loves Mary 1947,F 5,29:2
Time for Elizabeth 1948,S 28,32:3
Kind Sir 1953,S 28,21:2
Kind Sir 1953,N 5,41:2
Kind Sir 1953,N 15,II,1:1
Who Was That Lady I Saw You With?
  1958,Mr 4,33:2
Sunday in New York 1961,N 10,40:1
Love in E Flat 1967,F 14,38:1
Krasnoff, Syuleen
Well of Romance, The 1930,N 8,21:2
Krasnopolsky, Urey
All in One; Trouble in Tahiti 1955,Ap 20,40:3
Krasny, Diana (Producer)
Anyone Can Whistle 1964,Ap 6,36:1
Krassner, Alan M (Director)
Shadow Years, The 1957,Ja 9,26:2
Krassner, Alan M (Producer)
Shadow Years, The 1957,Ja 9,26:2
Krassner, Paul (Producer)
Information Bureau, The 1962,Ja 31,21:1
Keyhole, The 1962,Ja 31,21:1
Lovers in the Metro, The 1962,Ja 31,21:1
Krassner, Sol
Mighty Nimrod, The 1931,My 13,23:1
Kratochvil, Frantisek
Apparition Theater of Prague, The 1966,N 17,56:2
Kratochvilova, Zdenka
Pierrot's Journey 1964,Ag 5,23:1
Button, Button 1970,O 20,41:1
Kratz, William C (Composer)
Cotton Stockings 1923,D 19,16:2
Kratz, William C (Lyricist)
Cotton Stockings 1923,D 19,16:2
Kratz, William C (Playwright)
Cotton Stockings 1923,D 19,16:2

Kratzinger, Ernest (Musical Director)
Ice Follies 1937,D 22,29:1
Kraus, Charles
Martinique 1920,Ap 27,18:2
Mad Dog, The 1921,N 9,20:1
Airways, Inc 1929,F 21,30:5
Month in the Country, A 1930,Mr 18,30:5
Kraus, Clifford (Playwright)
Salvage 1957,Ap 10,39:2
Kraus, Clifford (Producer)
Story Teller, The 1951,D 15,11:3
Kraus, John (Composer)
Macbeth 1969,D 23,25:1
Kraus, Lewis
By Hex 1956,Je 19,25:1
Krause, Gertrude
Jolly World, A 1931,Ja 24,15:3
Women of New York 1931,Mr 23,24:3
Krause, Jay (Scenic Designer)
Day by the Sea, A 1955,S 27,42:1
Day by the Sea, A 1955,O 2,II,1:1
Krause, Margaret
Engaged! or Cheviot's Choice 1965,Ap 24,19:2
Krause, Ralph
Seven Against One 1930,My 7,25:1
Krause, Richard
From Here to There; Otherwise Engaged
  1958,Ap 24,37:3
From Here to There; Slow Dusk 1958,Ap 24,37:3
Iolanthe 1962,Ap 12,42:4
Yeomen of the Guard, The 1964,Mr 19,29:2
Patience 1964,Mr 26,42:1
Patience 1965,Ap 16,34:1
Yeomen of the Guard, The 1965,Ap 22,26:1
Krause, Sol
Sonitchka 1930,Mr 8,21:3
Wise Men of Chelm, The 1933,O 18,24:4
Song of Dnieper 1946,O 26,10:5
Wandering Stars 1946,D 14,18:2
Shylock and His Daughter 1947,S 30,22:2
Voice of Israel, The 1948,O 26,40:2
Hershel, The Jester 1948,D 14,39:2
Yosele the Nightingale 1949,O 21,30:4
Kraushaar, Janice
Hansel and Gretel 1929,D 25,21:1
Krausneck, Arthur
All's Well That Ends Well 1928,Ap 1,IX,2:4
Krauss, Marvin A (Miscellaneous)
Sherry! 1967,Mr 29,39:1
Krauss, Paul
Come Back, Little Sheba 1950,F 16,28:5
Krauss, Werner
Miracle, The 1924,Ja 16,17:1
Miracle, The 1924,F 3,VII,1:1
Neidhardt von Gneisenau 1927,Ja 23,VII,4:5
Bonaparte 1927,My 15,VIII,1:3
Dorothea Angermann 1928,F 19,VIII,2:1
Peer Gynt 1928,Ap 1,IX,2:4
Merry Wives of Windsor 1929,Mr 24,X,2:3
Apple Cart, The 1930,Mr 9,IX,4:3
Napoleon Greift Ein 1930,Je 1,VIII,2:1
Elisabeth von England 1930,D 14,IX,4:1
Hauptmann von Koeepenick, Der; Captain of
  Kopenick, The 1931,Ap 26,VIII,1:4
Before Sunset 1932,F 17,19:3
Rauhnacht 1932,F 21,VIII,2:1
Othello 1932,Mr 6,VIII,2:1
Vor Sonnenuntergang; Before Sunset
  1932,Mr 13,VIII,2:7
Wilhelm Tell 1932,N 20,IX,3:5
Before Sunset 1933,S 29,10:7
Before Sunset 1933,S 30,18:2
Before Sunset 1933,O 15,IX,1:6
Hundred Days 1934,Ap 29,IX,2:3
Richard III 1937,My 30,X,2:2
Michael Kramer 1938,F 20,XI,2:1
Krausz, Michael (Composer)
Alt Heidelberg; Student Prince, The
  1932,N 20,IX,3:3
Kraut, Elaine
Iolanthe 1965,My 19,42:1
Krautter, Emil
Passion Play, The 1929,Ap 30,32:1
Krauze, Solomon
Jacques Bergson 1936,O 31,24:6
Kravitt, Harold
Cherry Blossoms 1927,Mr 29,22:3
Krawford, Gary
Love's Labour's Lost 1961,Je 23,19:1
Macbeth 1962,Je 20,41:1
Pousse-Cafe 1966,Mr 19,19:2
Education of H*Y*M*A*N K*A*P*L*A*N, The
  1968,Ap 5,57:1
Kray, Antoinette
Chief Thing, The 1963,Ap 30,27:2
Kray, Michael (Director)
Madame Lafayette 1960,Mr 4,21:1
Connelly vs Connelly 1961,F 18,11:3
Anthony on Overtime 1961,O 21,13:2
Krebill, Dorothy
Saint of Bleecker Street, The 1954,D 28,21:1
Krebs, Beatrice
Pirates of Penzance, The 1961,Ja 20,24:5

Krebs, Beatrice—Cont

H M S Pinafore 1961,F 2,26:6
Sound of Music, The 1970,Jl 3,13:1

Krebs, Blanche

Bye Bye Bonnie 1927,Ja 14,15:3

Krebs, Cela

Cyrano de Bergerac 1936,Ap 28,17:1
Orchids Preferred 1937,My 12,26:5

Krebs, Max

What a Relief 1935,D 14,10:6

Krech, Warren

Mrs Jimmie Thompson 1920,Mr 30,9:1
John Hawthorne 1921,Ja 24,16:1
We Girls 1921,N 10,26:3

Kreegan, Gilda

Flame of Love 1924,Ap 22,19:2
Love in the Tropics 1927,O 19,24:3

Krehan, Hermann (Scenic Designer)

Wieder Metropol 1926,D 5,VIII,8:7
Alt Heidelberg; Student Prince, The
1932,N 20,IX,3:3

Kreig, Frank

What's Up 1943,N 12,24:6
Follow the Girls 1944,Ap 10,15:2

Kreigenhofer, Frank Jr

Night Before Christmas, The 1941,Ap 11,25:2

Kreiling, Edward

Too Many Heroes 1937,N 16,26:2

Krein, Alexander (Composer)

Eternal Jew, The 1926,D 21,21:2

Kreis, John

Crime Marches on 1935,O 24,19:1

Kreis, Robert (Miscellaneous)

King of the Dark Chamber 1961,F 10,21:1

Kreisel, Joseph (Lighting Director)

Will the Mail Train Run Tonight? 1964,Ja 10,18:1

Kreisler, Edward

Jacobowsky and the Colonel 1944,Mr 15,17:2
You Can't Take It With You 1945,Mr 27,23:7
As You Like It 1945,Jl 4,10:4
Walk Hard 1946,Mr 28,34:2

Kreisler, Fritz (Composer)

Cissy 1932,D 24,10:5
Sissy the Rose of Bavaria 1933,Ja 15,IX,8:6
Rhapsody 1944,N 23,37:2

Kreitel, Herbert

Young Madame Conti 1937,Ap 1,18:4

Kreitzberg, Yasha (Composer)

Farblondjete Honeymoon 1955,S 27,42:1

Krejca, Otomar (Director)

Hamlet 1965,Ja 23,15:4

Krell, Frances

Pal Joey 1940,D 26,22:2
Pal Joey 1952,Ja 4,17:6

Krellberg, Sherman S (Miscellaneous)

Julia, Jake, and Uncle Joe 1961,Ja 30,19:1

Krellberg, Sherman S (Producer)

Live Life Again 1945,O 1,14:7
Starcross Story, The 1954,Ja 14,25:2
Josephine Baker and Her Company 1964,F 5,30:1

Krembs, Felix

Crooked Gamblers 1920,Ag 2,12:1
Man's Name, The 1921,N 16,22:1
Lawful Larceny 1922,Ja 3,20:2
Lights Out 1922,Ag 18,8:4
Thin Ice 1922,O 2,20:1
Changelings, The 1923,Ag 26,VI,2:1
Changelings, The 1923,S 18,16:3
Changelings, The 1923,S 30,II,1:1
Badges 1924,D 4,25:1
It All Depends 1925,Ag 11,16:4
Stolen Fruit 1925,O 8,31:4
Night Duel, The 1926,F 16,22:3
Glory Hallelujah 1926,Ap 7,26:2
Spread Eagle 1927,Ap 5,30:2
Jimmie's Women 1927,S 27,30:3
King Can Do No Wrong, The 1927,N 17,28:4
Distant Drum, A 1928,Ja 21,13:1
Trapped 1928,S 12,25:3
Congai 1928,N 28,24:3
Biarritz 1929,Ag 11,VIII,2:1

Kremenetzky, B

Revisor; Inspector General, The 1935,F 18,19:6
Strange Child 1935,F 26,16:1
White Guard, The; Days of the Turbins
1935,Mr 7,27:5
Marriage 1935,Mr 12,24:8
I Forgot 1935,Mr 12,24:8
Enemies 1935,Mr 19,24:7
Deluge, The 1935,Mr 26,23:7

Kremer, Isa

Vaudeville (Palace) 1927,S 27,31:3
Vaudeville (Palace) 1927,O 18,32:4
Vaudeville (Palace) 1928,Ag 14,15:5
Blue Bird, The 1932,Ap 22,23:2
Song of the Ghetto, The 1932,O 3,15:5

Kremer, Theodore (Playwright)

Fatal Wedding, The 1924,Je 3,22:3

Kremolina

Vaudeville (Palace) 1926,My 11,25:3
Vaudeville (Palace) 1929,N 11,20:5

Kremoyan, Kalem

Girl in Pink Tights, The 1954,Mr 6,13:2

Krenek (Composer)

Johnny Spielt Auf 1928,Ap 15,IX,4:1
Beloved Augustine, The 1931,Ap 26,VIII,2:6

Kresge, Karen

Ice Follies 1969,My 23,38:1
Ice Follies 1970,My 23,27:1

Kress, Rose Irene

Vaudeville (Palace) 1926,N 23,27:3

Kressen, Sam

Across the Board on Tomorrow Morning
1961,O 23,22:5
Golden Rainbow 1968,F 5,27:1

Kressyn, Miriam

Souls for Sale 1936,S 21,27:6
Of One Mother 1937,Ja 18,21:3
My Baby's Wedding 1938,O 10,15:3
Long Live America 1939,Ja 2,28:3
Polish Rabbi, The 1939,Mr 20,13:3
If I Were Rothschild 1940,Ja 1,28:7
Second Marriage 1953,O 12,30:1
Shepherd King, The 1955,O 13,36:2
Brothers Ashkenazi, The 1955,N 12,24:4
It's a Funny World 1956,O 22,24:1
It Could Happen to You 1957,O 28,30:5
Bei Mir Bistu Schoen 1961,O 23,22:2
Cowboy in Israel, A 1962,O 29,36:2
My Wife With Conditions 1963,O 21,39:1
Good Luck 1964,O 19,38:3
Hello Charlie 1965,O 25,47:2
Bride Got Farblondjet, The 1967,N 6,61:6
It's Never Too Late for Happiness 1968,O 21,59:3
From Israel With Laughter 1969,O 17,34:1
Light, Lively and Yiddish 1970,O 28,58:1

Kreste, Mary

Pirates of Penzance, The 1946,S 21,19:2
Consul, The 1952,O 30,41:2

Kreth, Charles Jr

Trojan Horse, The 1940,O 31,28:3

Kretzmer, Herbert (Composer)

Our Man Crichton 1964,D 23,21:1

Kretzmer, Herbert (Playwright)

Our Man Crichton 1964,D 23,21:1

Kreuger, Knud

Candle in the Wind 1941,O 23,26:2

Kreuger, Lorna (Scenic Designer)

Puntila 1959,My 15,26:2

Kreuger, Miles (Producer)

Mime Theatre of Etienne Decroux, The
1959,D 24,15:1

Kreutz, Arthur (Composer)

Wanhope Building, The 1947,F 11,36:5
E-MC2 1948,Je 16,36:2
Outside the Door 1949,Mr 2,33:2

Kreutzberg, Harald

Miracle, The 1927,Ap 15,27:1
Midsummer Night's Dream, A 1927,N 18,21:1
Midsummer Night's Dream, A 1927,D 4,X,6:1
Jedermann 1927,D 8,33:2
Jedermann 1927,D 18,IX,6:1
Dantons Tod 1927,D 21,28:3
Dantons Tod 1928,Ja 1,VIII,3:1
Peripherie 1928,Ja 3,29:1
Servant of Two Masters, The 1928,Ja 22,VIII,6:1

Kreuzberg, Richard

Saint Joan 1940,Mr 11,10:6

Krevoff, Samuel

Sweet and Low 1930,N 18,28:5
Marching By 1932,Mr 4,17:1

Krewe, Daniel

Bright Rebel 1938,D 28,24:2

Kreymborg, Alfred (Director)

Dance of Death, The 1936,My 20,24:5

Kreymborg, Alfred (Lyricist)

Tom Sawyer - Ballad of the Mississippi
1947,D 27,11:3

Kreymborg, Alfred (Playwright)

Manikin and Minikin 1927,My 4,29:1

Krichbaum, Tom

Winterset 1966,F 10,32:2

Kricker, Sandy Struth (Miscellaneous)

Place Without Doors, A 1970,D 1,60:1

Krieger, Lee

Mister Roberts 1948,F 19,27:2
Along Fifth Avenue 1949,Ja 14,28:2
All You Need Is One Good Break 1950,F 10,20:3
Pink Elephant, The 1953,Ap 23,37:2
Redhead 1959,F 6,21:1
Viva Madison Avenue 1960,Ap 7,42:1

Kriese, Gladys

Gondoliers, The 1961,Ja 26,33:2

Krifstofer, Lou (Director)

Penny Friend, The 1966,D 27,46:1

Krijanovskaya, M

Revisor; Inspector General, The 1935,F 18,19:6
Poverty Is No Crime 1935,F 21,22:5
Marriage 1935,Mr 12,24:8

Krikoff, John

Saint Wench 1933,Ja 3,19:3

Krimbelbine, Allen

Sun-Up 1930,My 10,25:1

Krims, Milton

Don Q Jr 1926,Ja 28,16:3
Zeppelin 1929,Ja 15,22:3

Krimsky, Jerrold (Miscellaneous)

Girl From Wyoming, The 1938,O 31,12:1

Krimsky, Jerrold (Producer)

Naughty-Naught '00 1937,Ja 25,23:2
In Clover 1937,S 21,29:1
Fireman's Flame, The 1937,O 11,26:2
In Clover 1937,O 14,23:1
Girl From Wyoming, The 1938,O 31,12:1

Krimsky, Jerrold (Translator)

Threepenny Opera, The 1933,Ap 14,22:4

Krimsky, John (Miscellaneous)

Yes, M'Lord 1949,O 5,35:2

Krimsky, John (Producer)

Threepenny Opera, The 1933,Ap 14,22:4
Naughty-Naught '00 1937,Ja 25,23:2
In Clover 1937,S 21,29:1
Fireman's Flame, The 1937,O 11,26:2
In Clover 1937,O 14,23:1
Girl From Wyoming, The 1938,O 31,12:1
Cranks 1956,N 27,32:1

Krisch, Pepi

How to Make a Man 1961,F 3,16:1

Kristen, Eric

Firebird of Florence 1945,Mr 23,13:4
Look, Ma, I'm Dancin' 1948,F 8,II,2:1
Out of This World 1950,D 22,17:3

Kristen, Eric (Miscellaneous)

Pajama Game, The 1957,My 16,27:1

Kristen, Robert

Bajour 1964,N 24,42:1

Kristin, Karen (Choreographer)

Plot Against the Chase Manhattan Bank, The
1963,N 27,29:1

Kristofer, Louis

Taming of the Shrew, The 1960,Ag 20,17:1

Kristopher, Andrei

Hats Off to Ice 1944,Je 23,15:2

Kristy, Gloria

Funny Thing Happened on the Way to the Forum,
A 1962,My 9,49:1

Kritas, Theodore (Producer)

Screwball, The 1957,My 25,24:7
Electra 1961,S 20,23:4
Choephori 1961,S 27,32:4
Eumenides 1961,S 27,32:4

Krivitt, Harry

Vaudeville (Palace) 1930,Mr 10,24:4

Krob, Lillian Wood (Composer)

Burning Deck, The 1940,Mr 2,9:2

Kroeger, Berry

Tempest, The 1945,Ja 26,17:2
Therese 1945,O 10,24:2
Joan of Lorraine 1946,N 19,40:2
Julius Caesar 1950,Je 21,30:1
Reclining Figure 1954,O 8,26:5
Shangri-La 1956,Je 14,40:1

Kroel, Heinz

Holiday on Ice 1967,Ag 31,29:2

Kroener, Helen

As You Were 1920,Ja 28,22:3

Krofft, Marty (Director)

Poupees de Paris, Les 1962,D 13,8:2
Poupees de Paris, Les 1964,My 16,11:1

Krofft, Marty (Playwright)

Poupees de Paris, Les 1962,D 13,8:2
Poupees de Paris, Les 1964,My 16,11:1

Krofft, Marty (Producer)

Poupees de Paris, Les 1962,D 13,8:2
Poupees de Paris, Les 1964,My 16,11:1

Krofft, Sid

Howdy, Mr Ice of 1950 1949,My 27,24:2

Krofft, Sid (Director)

Poupees de Paris, Les 1962,D 13,8:2
Poupees de Paris, Les 1964,My 16,11:1

Krofft, Sid (Playwright)

Poupees de Paris, Les 1962,D 13,8:2
Poupees de Paris, Les 1964,My 16,11:1

Krofft, Sid (Producer)

Poupees de Paris, Les 1962,D 13,8:2
Poupees de Paris, Les 1964,My 16,11:1

Krog, Helge (Miscellaneous)

Don Juan 1930,D 28,VIII,3:5

Krohner, Maurice

It Can't Happen Here 1936,O 28,30:4
Devil's Game, A 1959,N 9,35:6

Krohner, Morris

Song of Dnieper 1946,O 26,10:5
Wandering Stars 1946,D 14,18:2
Voice of Israel, The 1948,O 26,40:2
Hershel, The Jester 1948,D 14,39:2
Yosele the Nightingale 1949,O 21,30:4

Krohner, Sarah

In a Jewish Grocery 1939,O 2,15:2
Me and Molly 1948,F 27,27:2

Kroll, Bernice (Composer)

Razzle Dazzle 1951,F 20,21:1

Kroll, Louis (Musical Director)

Iolanthe 1942,F 24,26:4
Gondoliers, The 1942,Mr 4,22:3
Mikado, The 1944,F 12,11:3

Kroll, Mark (Producer)

Ziegfeld Follies 1957,Mr 2,19:2

Kroll, Nathan (Composer)
  Mary Rose 1951,Mr 5,25:2
Kroll, William (Musical Director)
  Jazz a La Carte 1922,Je 3,8:3
Krolow, Olga
  High Gear 1927,O 7,24:3
  Back Seat Drivers 1928,D 26,14:4
  It's a Wise Child 1929,Ag 7,29:1
  They All Come to Moscow 1933,My 12,20:6
Kroman, Mabel
  Puppy Love 1926,Ja 28,16:3
  We Never Learn 1928,Ja 24,26:1
  Saint Wench 1933,Ja 3,19:3
  Halfway to Hell 1934,Ja 3,22:3
  When in Rome 1934,F 28,22:6
  Jig Saw 1934,My 1,26:3
  Farmer Takes a Wife, The 1934,O 31,17:1
Kronberg, Virginia (Producer)
  Marriage Is for Single People 1945,N 22,38:2
Krone, Gerald (Director)
  No Trifling With Love 1959,N 10,55:3
  Merry Death, A 1959,N 10,55:3
  Worm in Horseradish, A 1961,Mr 14,32:3
  Brotherhood 1970,Mr 18,39:1
  Day of Absence 1970,Mr 18,39:1
Krone, Gerald (Producer)
  Merry Death, A 1959,N 10,55:3
  No Trifling With Love 1959,N 10,55:3
  Worm in Horseradish, A 1961,Mr 14,32:3
  Golden Apple, The 1962,F 13,38:2
  Lion in Love, The 1963,Ap 26,28:3
  Pimpernel! 1964,Ja 7,26:6
  Song of the Lusitanian Bogey, The 1968,Ja 3,52:1
Kronenberger, Arthur (Composer)
  Love, Honor and Oh Baby 1940,Mr 29,25:2
Kronenberger, Louis (Playwright)
  International Set, The 1953,Je 12,19:3
Kronenberger, Louis (Translator)
  Mademoiselle Colombe 1954,Ja 7,26:1
  Mademoiselle Colombe 1954,Ja 17,II,1:1
Kronenfeld, Judith
  Dybbuk, The 1964,F 4,30:2
  Each Had Six Wings 1964,Mr 12,39:1
Kroner, Morris
  Shylock and His Daughter 1947,S 30,22:2
Kronman, Florence (Costume Designer)
  Playboy of the Western World, The 1930,Ja 3,20:4
Kronold, Richard
  Bridal Crown, The 1938,F 7,11:2
  Trial, The 1955,Je 15,35:2
  Spring's Awakening 1955,O 10,30:2
  Certain Young Man, A 1967,D 27,45:1
  Pequod 1969,Je 30,33:1
Krooks, Dorothy
  Matty and the Moron and Madonna
    1965,Mr 30,53:1
Kroonder, Hans
  Zizi 1964,N 23,51:1
Kroopf, Milton R
  Steppe Around 1922,Mr 29,17:4
Kroopf, Milton R (Producer)
  Sap Runs High, The 1936,F 1,9:4
  Sap Runs High, The 1936,F 5,15:3
Krop, Hildo (Costume Designer)
  Fighting the Waves 1929,S 22,IX,4:1
Krop, Hildo (Director)
  Fighting the Waves 1929,Ag 14,15:6
Kropf, Milton R
  You'll Never Know 1921,Ap 21,9:2
Kroschell, Joan
  Utopia, Limited 1960,Ap 8,27:2
  Parasite, The 1965,D 17,43:2
  Hooray!! It's a Glorious Day. . .And All That
    1966,Mr 10,28:1
  Happy Hypocrite, The 1968,S 6,38:1
Kross, Ronald
  1776 1969,Mr 17,46:2
Krot, William
  Grass Is Always Greener, The 1955,F 16,25:2
Krot, William (Miscellaneous)
  Persecution and Assassination of Marat As
    Performed by the Inmates of the Asylum of
    Charenton Under the Direction of the Marquis de
    Sade, The 1967,Ja 4,34:1
  How to Be a Jewish Mother 1967,D 29,18:1
  Mike Downstairs 1968,Ap 19,35:1
  Jimmy Shine 1968,D 6,52:1
Krotchman, David
  Legal Murder 1934,F 16,16:2
Krowetz, Andrew
  Venice Preserv'd 1955,D 13,54:4
Krstic, Ljiljana
  Who's Afraid of Virginia Woolf? 1968,Jl 4,13:1
Krueger, James
  Young and Beautiful, The 1959,My 29,13:1
Krueger, Robert
  Man and Superman 1960,Ag 17,35:3
  Cradle of Willow, A 1961,D 16,20:2
Kruener, Viola (Scenic Designer)
  Don't, George! 1944,N 4,18:6
Krug, Alicia
  Maggie 1953,F 19,20:2

Krug, Katherine
  Wild Duck, The 1928,F 19,VIII,2:1
Krug, Vera
  Merchant of Venice, The 1930,D 3,29:2
  Social Register, The 1931,N 10,28:2
Kruger, Alma
  Twelfth Night 1921,N 1,17:1
  Merchant of Venice, The 1921,N 22,17:1
  Salome 1922,My 23,12:4
  Daisy Mayme 1926,O 26,24:2
  Good Hope, The 1927,O 19,24:2
  2 + 2 = 5 1927,N 29,30:3
  First Stone, The 1928,Ja 14,12:2
  Hedda Gabler 1928,Mr 27,30:2
  Would-Be Gentleman, The 1928,O 2,34:1
  Lady From Alfaqueque, The; Consuela, La
    1929,Ja 15,22:3
  Katerina 1929,F 26,30:3
  Mademoiselle Bourrat 1929,O 8,34:3
  Living Corpse, The 1929,D 7,19:1
  Alison's House 1930,D 2,31:2
  Lady of the Camellias, The 1931,Ja 27,21:2
  Electra 1932,Ja 9,21:4
  Moon in the Yellow River, The 1932,F 21,VIII,2:1
  Moon in the Yellow River, The 1932,Mr 1,19:3
  Men Must Fight 1932,O 15,13:4
  Six Miracle Plays; Miraculous Birth and the
    Midwives, The; Lamentation of the Virgin Mary,
    The; Magdalen, The; Trois Rois, Les; Trois
    Maries, Les; Nativite, La 1933,F 12,IX,2:1
  John Brown 1934,Ja 23,22:3
  Field of Ermine 1935,F 9,10:4
  Few Are Chosen 1935,S 18,19:3
  Pride and Prejudice 1935,O 23,19:2
  Pride and Prejudice 1935,N 3,X,1:5
  Pride and Prejudice 1935,N 6,32:4
  Pride and Prejudice 1935,N 17,IX,1:1
Kruger, Alma (Director)
  Would-Be Gentleman, The 1930,Ap 30,29:2
Kruger, Hardy
  Postmark Zero 1965,N 2,28:1
Kruger, Jess
  Trojan Horse, The 1940,O 31,28:3
Kruger, Joan
  Out of This World 1950,D 22,17:3
Kruger, Marc (Miscellaneous)
  Adding Machine, The 1970,D 5,40:1
Kruger, Nathaniel
  House on Grand Street, A 1953,O 10,12:6
Kruger, Norman
  Thousand and One Nights 1959,D 16,53:2
  Mother's Sabbath Days 1960,N 21,33:2
  Brothers Ashkenazi, The 1970,N 17,53:2
Kruger, Olga
  Johnny Doodle 1942,Mr 19,28:2
Kruger, Ottilie
  I Remember Mama 1944,O 20,16:2
  Joy Forever, A 1946,Ja 8,20:2
  Naughty-Naught '00 1946,O 21,27:5
  Little A 1947,Ja 16,31:2
  Time for Elizabeth 1948,S 28,32:3
Kruger, Otto
  Nobody's Money 1921,My 22,VI,1:6
  Sonya 1921,Ag 16,18:3
  Straw, The 1921,N 11,16:2
  Alias Jimmy Valentine 1921,D 9,20:3
  To the Ladies! 1922,F 21,20:1
  To the Ladies! 1922,Mr 12,VI,1:1
  Will Shakespeare 1923,Ja 2,14:1
  Wasp, The 1923,Mr 28,14:3
  Nervous Wreck, The 1923,O 10,16:1
  Nervous Wreck, The 1923,O 21,VIII,1:1
  Easy Come, Easy Go 1925,O 27,20:2
  Trelawney of the 'Wells' 1927,F 1,24:4
  Royal Family, The 1927,D 29,26:4
  Royal Family, The 1928,Ja 8,VIII,1:1
  Karl and Anna 1929,O 8,34:1
  Game of Love and Death, The 1929,N 26,28:4
  Boundry Line, The 1930,F 6,21:1
  They Never Grow Up 1930,Ap 8,27:1
  Long Road, The 1930,Jl 20,VIII,2:1
  Long Road, The 1930,S 10,30:2
  As Good as new 1930,O 19,IX,3:4
  As Good As New 1930,N 4,37:3
  Great Barrington, The 1931,F 20,18:1
  Private Lives 1931,My 12,29:3
  Counsellor-at-Law 1932,S 13,17:2
  Moon Is Down, The 1942,Ap 8,22:2
  Little A 1947,Ja 16,31:2
  Laura 1947,Je 27,16:1
  Time for Elizabeth 1948,S 28,32:3
  Smile of the World, The 1949,Ja 13,26:5
Kruger, Stubby
  New Aquacade Revue, The 1940,My 13,20:5
Krugman, Louis
  Yoshe Kalb 1933,D 29,27:2
  Twelfth Night 1934,Jl 17,24:5
Krull, Gertrud (Miscellaneous)
  Marriage of Mr Mississippi, The 1969,N 20,60:5
Krumschmidt, E A
  Russian People, The 1942,D 30,17:2
  Big Two, The 1947,Ja 9,21:2
  Miracle in the Mountains 1947,Ap 26,10:2

Krumschmidt, E A—Cont
  I Gotta Get Out 1947,S 26,27:2
  Crime and Punishment 1947,D 23,29:3
  Call Me Madam 1950,O 13,25:1
Krumschmidt, Liselotte
  Sweet Charity 1942,D 29,26:4
Krupa, Anatol
  Post Office, The 1965,Ja 6,32:1
  Kernel and the Shell, The 1965,Ja 6,32:1
  Nightmare, The 1965,Ja 6,32:1
  Jacob and the Angel 1965,Ja 6,32:1
  Woman, The 1965,Ja 6,32:1
  Jaselka 1965,Ja 6,32:1
  Book, The 1965,Ja 6,32:1
  Labyrinth, The 1965,Ja 6,32:1
Krupska, Dania
  Chauve-Souris of 1943 1943,Ag 13,13:2
  Oklahoma! 1943,N 14,II,1:1
  Can-Can 1953,My 8,28:1
  Girl in Pink Tights, The 1954,Mr 6,13:2
Krupska, Dania (Choreographer)
  Seventeen 1951,Je 22,16:6
  Seventeen 1951,Jl 1,II,9:5
  Shoestring Revue 1955,Mr 1,22:2
  Most Happy Fella, The 1956,My 4,20:1
  Oh, Kay! 1960,Ap 18,37:2
  Happiest Girl in the World, The 1961,Ap 4,42:1
  Rugantino 1964,F 7,34:1
  That Hat! 1964,S 24,45:1
Krupska, Dania (Director)
  Most Happy Fella, The 1959,F 11,50:2
  Show Boat 1961,Ap 13,32:1
  Fiorello! 1962,Je 14,24:1
  That Hat! 1964,S 24,45:1
  Her First Roman 1968,O 21,53:3
Krupska, Dania (Miscellaneous)
  Most Happy Fella, The 1959,F 11,50:2
Kruschen, Jack
  I Can Get It for You Wholesale 1962,Mr 23,29:1
Kruse, Werner (Composer)
  Pepper Mill 1937,Ja 6,19:4
  Why Do I Deserve This? 1966,Ja 19,31:2
Kruvi, Hovav (Costume Designer)
  Grand Music Hall of Israel, The 1968,F 7,42:1
Krygar, Ruth
  Bomboola 1929,Je 27,17:3
Krygier, Waldemar (Costume Designer)
  Constant Prince, The 1969,O 18,36:1
  Apocalypsis cum Figuris 1969,N 20,60:2
Kubansky, Abraham
  Tenth Commandment, The 1926,N 18,27:1
  Major Noah 1929,F 23,17:2
Kubansky, Joseph
  Anathema 1923,Ap 11,16:2
Kubiak, Gordon
  Hamlet 1970,O 27,54:2
Kubiak, Thomas
  End of All Things Natural, The 1969,S 12,38:1
Kubly, Herbert (Miscellaneous)
  E-MC2 1948,Je 16,36:2
Kubly, Herbert (Playwright)
  Men to the Sea 1944,O 4,25:2
Kuch, Richard
  Camelot 1960,D 5,42:1
Kuchiki, Sashi
  Ice Capades 1962,Ag 30,34:1
  Ice Capades 1963,Ag 29,37:2
  Ice Capades 1964,Ag 27,27:2
  Ice Capades 1966,Je 2,50:2
  Ice Capades 1967,Je 2,33:1
Kucta, Stanley
  Year Boston Won the Pennant, The
    1969,My 23,38:1
Kudo, Dainl
  Zizi 1964,N 23,51:1
Kuebler, John
  Peace 1969,Ja 28,49:1
Kuehl, Craig
  Peace 1969,Ja 28,49:1
Kuehl, Kaethe
  Threepenny Opera, The 1928,D 2,X,4:4
Kuehn, Robert
  Golden Age, The 1963,N 19,49:2
Kuehne, Friedrich
  Neidhardt von Gneisenau 1927,Ja 23,VII,4:5
Kuehne, Wolfgang
  Don Carlos 1964,N 25,40:1
Kuersteiner, Karl (Dr) (Musical Director)
  Susannah 1955,F 25,18:4
Kuerti
  Letter, The 1927,O 30,IX,4:1
Kuestner, Charles
  Show Boat 1954,My 6,44:1
  Show Boat 1954,O 29,28:4
Kuffler, June
  39 Steps 1938,Mr 12,13:1
Kugel, Bernard
  Dybbuk, The 1925,D 16,22:2
Kugel, Lee (Miscellaneous)
  Six-Fifty, The 1921,O 30,VI,1:1
Kugel, Lee (Producer)
  Six-Fifty, The 1921,O 2,VII,1:8

Kugell, Joan
Country Wife, The 1957,Je 27,22:1
Ivanov 1958,O 8,42:1
Kuhlen, Giraud
Fuente Ovejuna; Sheep Well, The 1936,My 3,II,4:1
Kuhlman, Donald
Merry Wives of Windsor, The 1954,F 17,27:1
Cock-A-Doodle Dandy 1955,N 4,26:5
Kuhlmann, Rosemary
Courtin' Time 1951,Je 14,30:2
Consul, The 1952,O 30,41:2
Kuhn, Casper
Ringside Seat 1938,N 23,24:5
Kuhn, Charles
Chicago 1926,D 31,11:1
Singing Jailbirds 1928,D 5,34:4
Airways, Inc 1929,F 21,30:5
Distant Drums 1932,Ja 19,24:3
Let Freedom Ring 1935,N 7,26:2
Marching Song 1937,F 18,18:2
Land of Fame 1943,S 22,31:5
Signature 1945,F 15,25:2
Silver Whistle, The 1948,N 25,49:2
Kuhn, J L Jr
Front Page, The 1937,N 12,27:2
Kuhn, John
Maria Golovin 1958,N 6,43:1
Kuhn, Katherine (Costume Designer)
Artists and Models 1943,N 6,16:6
Hollywood Pinafore 1945,Je 1,20:1
If the Shoe Fits 1946,D 6,29:4
Icetime 1947,My 29,28:2
Howdy Mr Ice 1948,Je 25,28:5
Howdy, Mr Ice of 1950 1949,My 27,24:2
Kuhn, Victoria (Playwright)
If in the Green Wood 1947,Ja 17,27:6
Kuhn, Walt (Choreographer)
Pinwheel Revel 1922,Ag 1,14:2
Kuhn, Walt (Miscellaneous)
Merry-Go-Round 1927,Je 1,25:4
Kuhn, Walt (Playwright)
49ers, The 1922,N 12,VIII,1:1
Kuhne, Friedrich
Redemption: Lebende Leichnam, Der; Living
Corpse, The 1928,N 20,28:2
Ghosts; Gespenster 1929,F 6,30:3
Kuhner, John
Your Own Thing 1968,Ja 15,33:1
House of Leather, The 1970,Mr 19,56:1
Tarot 1970,D 12,19:1
Kuhnert, Hans (Producer)
Prosit Gypsy 1929,Je 2,VIII,2:6
Kuhnly, Fred
Time, Place and the Girl, The 1942,O 22,24:3
Kuhns, John
Good Old Days, The 1923,Ag 15,21:2
Kukoff, Ben
That Thing at the Cherry Lane 1965,My 19,42:1
Kukoff, Bernard
Cock-A-Doodle Dandy 1955,N 4,26:5
Glory in the Flower 1959,D 9,57:5
Kulagin, O L
In the Heat of the Night 1969,F 6,12:3
Kulback, M (Playwright)
Outlaw, The 1937,O 6,28:1
Outlaw, The 1937,N 8,18:2
Kulle, Jarl
Long Day's Journey Into Night 1956,F 19,II,1:6
My Fair Lady 1959,F 16,24:1
Long Day's Journey Into Night 1962,My 16,35:4
Kuller, Doris (Miscellaneous)
Happy Ending 1965,N 16,56:1
Day of Absence 1965,N 16,56:1
Something Different 1967,N 29,52:1
Kuller, Doris (Producer)
Paradise Gardens East 1969,Mr 11,39:1
Conerico Was Here to Stay 1969,Mr 11,39:1
Kuller, Sid (Composer)
Meet the People 1940,O 20,IX,3:3
Alive and Kicking 1950,Ja 18,25:5
Ice Capades 1966,Je 2,50:2
Kuller, Sid (Lyricist)
Alive and Kicking 1950,Ja 18,25:5
Ice Capades 1966,Je 2,50:2
Kuller, Sid (Miscellaneous)
Ziegfeld Follies 1943,Ap 2,16:2
Ice Capades 1966,Je 2,50:2
Kullers, John
Devils Galore 1945,S 13,27:2
Mister Roberts 1948,F 19,27:2
Fifth Season, The 1953,Ja 24,13:2
Kullmann, Charles
Yeomen of the Guard, The 1939,Jl 16,30:4
Yeomen of the Guard, The 1939,Jl 23,IX,2:1
Kulolia, James
Half-Caste, The 1926,Mr 30,20:4
Kuluva, Will
Steel 1939,D 20,30:2
Hold On to Your Hats 1940,S 12,30:3
Steps Leading Up 1941,Ap 19,20:6
Wanhope Building, The 1947,F 11,36:5
Open House 1947,Je 4,33:4
Tragedian in Spite of Himself, A 1948,F 6,29:2

Wedding, The 1948,F 6,29:2
Bear, The 1948,F 6,29:2
On the Harmfulness of Tobacco 1948,F 6,29:2
Alchemist, The 1948,My 7,31:4
Richard III 1949,F 9,33:2
That Lady 1949,N 23,18:4
Gods of the Mountain, The 1950,My 25,36:2
Arms and the Man 1950,O 20,34:2
Darkness at Noon 1951,Ja 15,13:4
Shrike, The 1952,Ja 16,20:2
My 3 Angels 1953,Mr 12,23:2
Doctor's Dilemma, The 1955,Ja 12,22:1
Doctor's Dilemma, The 1955,Ja 23,II,1:1
Very Special Baby, A 1956,N 15,43:2
Clerambard 1957,N 8,22:3
Clerambard 1957,N 17,II,1:1
Buffalo Skinner, The 1959,F 20,18:1
Confederates, The 1959,S 29,45:1
Kulz, Sandra
Ice Follies 1960,Ja 13,20:1
Ice Follies 1961,Ja 11,25:2
Kuma, K T
Vaudeville (Palace) 1925,D 29,21:2
Vaudeville (Palace) 1927,Je 7,27:3
Kumari, Kamala
Shakuntala 1959,S 10,41:2
Kumari, Surya
King of the Dark Chamber 1961,F 10,21:1
King of the Dark Chamber 1961,Ap 9,II,1:1
Kumihara, T
Cortez 1929,N 5,32:2
Kumme, Walter
Adam Solitaire 1925,N 7,19:2
Dream Play 1926,Ja 21,18:2
Kummer, Clare (Composer)
Annie 1924,O 12,VIII,2:1
Annie Dear 1924,N 5,25:3
Her Master's Voice 1933,O 24,24:3
Kummer, Clare (Lyricist)
Annie Dear 1924,N 5,25:3
Jewel Robbery 1932,F 10,27:1
Three Waltzes 1937,N 15,15:6
Three Waltzes 1937,D 27,10:2
Kummer, Clare (Playwright)
Rollo's Wild Oat 1920,N 24,14:1
Rollo's Wild Oat 1921,Ja 23,VI,1:1
Robbery, The 1921,Mr 1,18:1
Choir Rehearsal, The; Four One-Act Plays
1921,Mr 1,18:1
Chinese Love 1921,Mr 1,18:1
Four One-Act Plays 1921,Mr 6,VI,1:2
Successful Calamity, A 1921,Mr 19,11:2
Mountain Man, The 1921,D 13,24:2
Banco 1922,S 21,18:1
One Kiss 1923,N 28,14:2
Annie 1924,O 12,VIII,2:1
Madame Pompadour 1924,N 2,VII,2:3
Annie Dear 1924,N 5,25:3
Madame Pompadour 1924,N 12,20:6
Pomeroy's Past 1926,Ap 20,24:4
Pomeroy's Past 1926,My 2,VIII,1:2
So's Your Old Antique 1930,My 8,32:5
Amourette 1933,S 28,25:2
Her Master's Voice 1933,O 24,24:3
Her Master's Voice 1933,D 10,X,3:1
Pomeroy's Past 1936,Ag 4,15:2
Three Waltzes 1937,N 15,15:6
Three Waltzes 1937,D 27,10:2
Spring Thaw 1938,Mr 22,18:1
Many Happy Returns 1945,Ja 6,15:5
Her Master's Voice 1964,D 28,33:2
Kummer, Frederic Arnold (Lyricist)
My Golden Girl 1920,F 3,18:2
Kummer, Frederic Arnold (Playwright)
My Golden Girl 1920,F 3,18:2
Bonehead, The 1920,Ap 13,12:1
Bonehead, The 1920,Ap 18,VI,2:4
Fatal Lady, The 1936,Mr 19,23:7
Kummer, Marjorie
Rollo's Wild Oat 1920,N 24,14:1
Mountain Man, The 1921,D 13,24:2
Pomeroy's Past 1926,Ap 20,24:4
Kuner, Mildred C (Playwright)
Capacity for Wings 1957,Ja 10,25:2
Kuney, Jack (Director)
Gay Apprentice, The 1960,F 3,27:2
Too Close for Comfort 1960,F 3,27:2
Kunihari, J
Squealer, The 1928,N 13,36:3
Kunkle, George T C
Joan of Arkansas 1925,Ap 5,16:1
Kunneke, Edward (Composer)
Caroline 1923,F 1,13:2
Love Song, The 1925,Ja 14,19:4
Mayflowers 1925,N 25,14:2
Liselott 1932,My 22,VIII,2:3
Glueckliche Reise 1933,Ja 1,IX,1:1
Kuntz, John B (Lyricist)
Whispers on the Wind 1970,Je 4,50:1
Kuntz, John B (Playwright)
Now 1968,Je 6,53:1
Whispers on the Wind 1970,Je 4,50:1

Kunz, Alfred
Rosalinda; Fledermaus, Die 1942,O 29,26:5
Kunz, Gerald
Idiot's Delight 1936,Mr 25,25:2
Kunz-Baker, Bertha
Eternal Road, The 1937,Ja 8,14:2
Kunzig, Robert L
Red Rhumba 1936,Ap 14,18:1
This Mad Whirl 1937,Ja 10,II,4:8
Fifty-Fifty 1937,D 5,II,3:4
Kupferman, Meyer (Composer)
Jonah! 1966,F 16,52:1
Kupferman, Meyer (Miscellaneous)
Zulu and the Zayda, The 1965,N 11,59:1
Kupferman, Sydney
Great Shakes 1931,Mr 12,22:2
How Revolting! 1932,Mr 11,14:6
Kupperman, Alvin
Minnie's Boys 1970,Mr 27,27:1
Minnie's Boys 1970,Ap 5,II,3:1
Kurahashi, Takeshi (Prof) (Translator)
My Fair Lady 1963,S 2,19:4
Kuras, Leonard
Brig, The 1963,My 16,40:1
Kurasaki, H
Pearl of Great Price, The 1926,N 2,34:3
Kurasaki, S
Merchants of Venus 1920,S 28,14:2
Kurer, Vilma
Reunion in New York 1940,F 22,28:4
Wallflower 1944,Ja 27,14:2
Private Life of the Master Race, The
1945,Je 13,28:3
Temper the Wind 1946,D 28,10:2
Faust 1947,N 29,9:2
Winner, The 1954,F 18,34:1
Kurian, David
Show Boat 1957,Je 28,30:2
Kurilla, Dorothy
Italian Straw Hat, The 1957,O 1,37:2
Kurlan, Arthur (Director)
Prodigal Father, The 1935,Jl 2,24:2
Kurlan, David
Eternal Road, The 1937,Ja 8,14:2
Peter Pan 1950,Ap 25,27:2
Night in Venice, A 1952,Je 27,18:6
Buttrio Square 1952,O 15,40:2
Show Boat 1956,Je 22,16:1
Show Boat 1957,Je 28,30:2
Song of Norway 1959,Je 26,16:2
49th Cousin, The 1960,O 28,22:1
Kurland, Jerry
Hit the Deck 1960,Je 24,32:1
Kurnitz, Harry (Playwright)
Reclining Figure 1954,O 8,26:5
Once More With Feeling 1958,O 22,39:1
Once More With Feeling 1959,Jl 10,30:1
Shot in the Dark, A 1961,O 19,40:1
Girl Who Came to Supper, The 1963,D 9,49:1
Kurnitz, Julie
In Circles 1968,Je 28,36:1
Peace 1968,N 10,87:1
Peace 1969,Ja 28,49:1
Minnie's Boys 1970,Mr 27,27:1
Kuroemon
Kagotsurube; Courtesan, The 1960,Je 3,26:1
Chushingura; Forty-Seven Ronin, The
1960,Je 10,37:1
Chushingura; Forty-Seven Ronin, The
1960,Je 17,35:4
Chushingura; Treasury of Loyal Retainers, The
1969,S 11,53:1
Kumagai Jinya 1969,S 18,64:1
Momiji-Gari 1969,S 18,64:1
Kurtagh, Emeric (Composer)
Dutchman's Farm, A 1941,My 11,I,43:3
Kurth, Henry (Lighting Director)
Heloise 1958,S 25,28:4
Darker Flower, A 1963,Mr 11,7:2
Kurth, Henry (Scenic Designer)
Heloise 1958,S 25,28:4
Heloise 1958,O 5,II,1:1
Darker Flower, A 1963,Mr 11,7:2
Kurthy, Peter
Kek Roka; Blue Fox 1957,D 5,47:2
Egerfogo; Mousetrap, The 1958,Ja 30,18:6
Kurton, Peggy
Good Morning, Dearie 1921,N 2,20:2
Kurty, Hella
Roulette 1935,Je 16,X,1:1
Kurty, Lee
Absence of a Cello 1964,S 22,45:1
Kurtz, Leda
Brothers Ashkenazi, The 1970,N 17,53:2
Kurtz, Marcia Jean
Jonah! 1966,F 16,52:1
Viet Rock 1966,N 11,38:1
America Hurrah; Interview; TV; Motel
1967,O 10,55:2
Red Cross 1968,Ap 29,47:2
Muzeeka 1968,Ap 29,47:2
Yes, Yes, No No 1969,Ja 1,16:1

urtz, Marcia Jean—Cont
Year Boston Won the Pennant, The
1969,My 23,38:1
Chinese, The 1970,Mr 11,42:2
Kurtz, Maurice (Playwright)
War and Peace 1942,My 22,26:3
Kurtz, Swoosie
Firebugs, The 1968,Jl 2,36:1
Effect of Gamma Rays on Man-in-the-Moon
Marigolds, The 1970,Ap 8,32:1
Kurz, C
Passion Play, The 1929,Ap 30,32:1
Kurz, Gerhard
Wiener Blut 1964,S 12,14:1
Kurz, Leo (Lighting Director)
Victim, The 1952,My 3,17:5
Kurz, Wilbur
Jubilee 1935,O 14,20:1
Kusabue, Mitsuko
How to Succeed in Business Without Really Trying
1964,Jl 18,10:1
Kusama (Costume Designer)
Republic, The 1970,Ap 28,49:1
Kusell, Daniel (Playwright)
Gingham Girl, The 1922,Ag 29,15:5
Piggy 1927,Ja 12,22:2
Cross My Heart 1928,S 18,32:7
Party's Over, The 1933,Mr 28,23:3
Kusell, Daniel (Producer)
Party's Over, The 1933,Mr 28,23:3
Kushner, Gordon (Miscellaneous)
Salad Days 1958,N 11,24:1
Kushner, Gordon (Musical Director)
Salad Days 1958,N 11,24:1
Kushnirov, A (Playwright)
Hirsh Lekert 1936,Mr 11,23:2
Kusmiak, Eugene (Miscellaneous)
Mikado, The 1952,O 21,35:2
H M S Pinafore 1952,N 4,32:2
Trial by Jury 1952,N 4,32:2
Iolanthe 1952,N 11,26:3
H M S Pinafore 1960,S 8,41:1
Kusmiak, Eugene (Musical Director)
Lute Song 1946,F 7,29:2
H M S Pinafore 1952,N 4,32:2
Kusov, Vladimir
Aladdin and His Wonderful Lamp 1963,O 21,39:1
Kuss, Richard
Mother Said No 1951,Ap 17,34:2
Men in White 1955,F 26,13:2
Mummers and Men 1962,Mr 27,41:6
Witches' Sabbath 1962,Ap 20,22:2
Firebugs, The 1963,F 13,7:2
Life Is a Dream 1964,Mr 20,24:1
John Brown's Body 1964,Je 29,33:1
Philoctetes 1964,Ag 19,29:1
Romeo and Juliet 1965,Je 21,36:3
Coriolanus 1965,Je 21,36:1
Romeo and Juliet 1965,Je 21,36:3
King Lear 1965,Je 25,39:1
Wait Until Dark 1966,F 3,21:1
Beyond Desire 1967,O 11,36:1
Kuss, Richard (Director)
Masque of Reason, The 1959,N 25,19:4
Texas Steer, A 1968,N 13,39:1
Kussel, Maurice L (Choreographer)
Calling All Stars 1934,D 14,28:2
Kussell, Daniel (Director)
Talk About Girls 1927,Je 15,31:3
Kussell, Daniel (Playwright)
Talk About Girls 1927,Je 15,31:3
Kuster, Carol
Hollywood Ice Revue 1953,Ja 16,17:2
Kuster, Hans
Hollywood Ice Revue 1953,Ja 16,17:2
Kuster, Sam
Processional 1937,O 14,23:1
Kutal, Ari
Jacob's Dream 1927,N 14,21:1
Turandot 1929,Ja 12,14:4
At the Bottom 1930,Ja 10,24:3
Clear All Wires! 1932,S 15,19:1
Golem, The 1948,My 17,22:3
Oedipus Rex 1948,My 24,23:2
Dybbuk, The 1964,F 4,30:2
Children of the Shadows 1964,F 27,26:1
Kutler, Jane L
Coney Island Play 1970,O 31,34:2
Kutsukian, Hilda
Sing High, Sing Low 1931,N 13,26:4
Kuttner, Michael (Musical Director)
Merry Widow, The 1957,Ap 11,36:6
Kutz, Karina
Consul, The 1951,S 8,9:3
Kutzen, Leo (Composer)
Yoshe Kalb 1932,N 6,IX,2:1
Kuzmany, Elfriede
Ratten, Die 1966,Ap 13,36:1
Kuznetzoff, Adia
Vaudeville (Palace) 1929,My 13,26:3
Symphony 1935,Ap 27,20:3
Kvares, Donald (Lyricist)
Wuzisi! 1970,O 2,25:2

Kvares, Donald (Playwright)
Modern Statuary 1968,My 28,41:1
Wuzisi! 1970,O 2,25:2
Kwan, Kikuchi (Playwright)
Little Theatre Tournament; Father Returns, The
1929,My 7,28:1
Kwartin, Clara
Everyman 1941,My 9,19:2
Kwartin, Paul
No for an Answer 1941,Ja 6,10:6
Kwartz, Berta (Costume Designer)
Grand Music Hall of Israel, The 1968,F 7,42:1
Kwitkor, John
Three Plays of the Sea 1970,Ag 20,39:1
Kya-Hill, Robert
Winterset 1966,F 10,32:2
Kyd, Joanna
Bacchae, The 1969,Mr 15,24:1
Kydoniatis, K (Composer)
Electra 1961,S 20,23:4
Eumenides 1961,S 27,32:4
Choephori 1961,S 27,32:4
Medea 1964,S 1,31:1
Electra 1964,S 8,33:1
Iphigenia in Aulis 1968,N 13,40:1
Kyle, Alastair
This Rock 1943,F 19,23:2
House in Paris, The 1944,Mr 21,17:1
Too Hot for Maneuvers 1945,My 3,26:5
Kyle, Anthony
Hamlet 1967,F 17,44:1
Romeo and Juliet 1967,F 22,18:1
Kyle, Billy (Composer)
Alive and Kicking 1950,Ja 18,25:5
Kyle, Billy (Lyricist)
Alive and Kicking 1950,Ja 18,25:5
Kyle, Frances
Kiki 1921,N 30,13:1
Kyle, Howard
Maker of Dreams, The 1920,Ap 28,9:3
Untitled-Benefit 1920,My 2,VI,2:2
Trial of Joan of Arc, The 1921,Mr 28,8:2
Tarzan of the Apes 1921,S 8,14:3
Imaginary Invalid, The 1922,Jl 26,26:2
Pasteur 1923,Mr 13,19:1
If Booth Had Missed 1932,F 5,24:2
Troilus and Cressida 1932,Je 7,22:3
Midsummer Night's Dream, A 1932,Jl 13,15:1
Little Black Book, The 1932,D 27,11:2
Kyle, Joe
Leonard Sillman's New Faces of 1968
1968,My 3,43:1
Kyoichi, Nagakura
Golden Bat 1970,Je 27,18:2
Kyra
Whirl of New York, The 1921,Je 14,18:1
Artists and Models 1923,Ag 21,12:2
Kyveli-Theohari
Screwball, The 1957,My 25,24:7

L

La Belle, Rupert
Peacock 1932,O 12,27:1
La Bernicia, Mlle
Untitled-Revue 1924,F 19,12:1
La Bey, Louis
Respect for Riches, The 1920,My 12,9:1
Mountebank, The 1923,My 8,22:2
Man in Evening Clothes, The 1924,D 6,13:4
Shelter 1926,Ja 26,18:2
Black Velvet 1927,S 28,28:1
Kibitzer, The 1929,F 19,22:5
Passing Present, The 1931,D 8,36:2
Judgment Day 1934,S 13,26:4
La Cata, Minta
Nine O'Clock Revue 1936,Jl 8,14:3
La Centra, Peg
Canteen Show, The 1942,S 4,18:1
Patriots, The 1943,Ja 30,11:2
La Crosse, Bob
Yearling, The 1965,D 11,25:1
Show Boat 1966,Jl 20,48:1
La Curto, James
No More Women 1926,Ag 4,17:2
New York Exchange 1926,D 31,11:2
Plutocrat, The 1930,F 21,23:3
Noble Experiment, The 1930,O 28,21:4
Company's Coming! 1931,Ap 21,35:5
Slight Case of Murder, A 1935,S 12,28:5
Tomorrow's a Holiday! 1935,D 31,10:2
County Chairman, The 1936,My 26,26:5
Fulton of Oak Falls 1937,Ja 2,15:3
Fulton of Oak Falls 1937,F 11,18:2
Brooklyn Biarritz 1941,F 28,16:2
Land Is Bright, The 1941,O 29,26:2
Johnny 2X4 1942,Mr 17,24:6
La Della, Pete
Simple Simon 1931,Mr 10,23:2
La Farge, C
Here's Howe 1923,Ap 26,19:3

La Farge, John (Lyricist)
Foemen of the Yard 1935,Ap 6,10:4
La Farge, Peter
King Lear 1959,Ja 3,11:2
La Faye, Georges and Company
International Soiree 1958,Mr 13,25:1
La Ferla, James
Glorious Ruler, The 1969,Jl 1,31:1
la Fleur, Arthur
Jumbo 1935,N 18,20:2
La Follette, Robert
Jazz a La Carte 1922,Je 3,8:3
La Forge, Eleanor
Hobo 1961,Ap 11,41:2
La Forge, Joy (Miscellaneous)
Born Yesterday 1958,Mr 22,12:6
Lady's Not for Burning, The 1959,Ja 31,13:2
La Franconi, Terry
Viva O'Brien 1941,O 10,27:2
La Granna, Louis
Hello Paris 1930,N 17,29:3
La Guardia, Mayor
Off the Record; Mayor Answers the Newspapers!
Wow! 1935,Je 19,23:3
La Guardia, Mayor (Director)
Off the Record; Mayor Answers the Newspapers!
Wow! 1935,Je 19,23:3
La Guardia, Mayor (Playwright)
Off the Record; Mayor Answers the Newspapers!
Wow! 1935,Je 19,23:3
La Guardia, Mayor (Producer)
Off the Record; Mayor Answers the Newspapers!
Wow! 1935,Je 19,23:3
La Gue, Jeanne
Glass Slipper, The 1925,O 20,29:1
La Gue, Mildred
Passing Show of 1921, The 1920,D 30,16:2
La Joie, Ramon
This Fine-Pretty World 1923,D 27,11:1
Bare Facts 1927,Je 30,35:1
La Mance, Eleanor
Robin Hood 1932,Ja 28,25:4
La Mar, Marge
Vaudeville (Palace) 1927,F 8,20:3
La Marche, Marie
What Next 1920,Ja 27,7:2
La Mon, Janet (Choreographer)
Oklahoma! 1958,Mr 8,15:2
La Mont, Leslie
Madre, La 1959,F 12,24:1
La Monte, Lestra
Vaudeville (Palace) 1930,Ap 21,20:7
La Moree, Jules
Caravan 1928,Ag 30,13:3
La Mori, Leonardo
Way, The 1940,O 12,20:3
La Motta, Johnny
I'm Solomon 1968,Ap 24,51:1
Zorba 1968,N 18,58:1
La Motte, Jeanne
That French Lady 1927,Mr 16,29:3
La Mure, Pierre (Original Author)
Beyond Desire 1967,O 11,36:1
La Nier, Vanita
Dove, The 1925,F 12,17:3
Betsy 1926,D 29,24:3
La Paugh, Roy (Scenic Designer)
Mountain, The 1933,S 12,28:6
La Penna, Giuseppe
Ora di Diana, L' 1937,My 17,22:3
La Penna, James (Producer)
White Lights 1927,O 12,30:4
La Pointe, Floy
Baby Mine 1927,Je 10,21:2
La Pue, Maurice
Earl Carroll's Vanities 1928,Ag 7,25:2
Hello Paris 1930,N 17,29:3
La Redd, Cora
Say When 1928,Je 27,29:3
Messin' Around 1929,Ap 23,26:3
Vaudeville (Palace) 1930,My 26,25:2
Change Your Luck 1930,Je 7,10:2
Vaudeville (Palace) 1930,S 8,17:3
Minskey the Magnificent 1936,D 26,14:3
La Reux, Leah
Great Music 1924,O 6,24:1
La Riviere, Lucien
Greenwich Villagers, The 1927,Ag 19,20:2
Belmont Varieties 1932,S 29,17:2
La Rocco, Jody
Most Happy Fella, The 1966,My 12,55:1
La Roche, Edouard
Lady, The 1923,D 5,23:2
Great Music 1924,O 6,24:1
Age of Innocence, The 1928,N 28,24:2
Rebound 1930,F 4,29:1
Cafe 1930,Ag 29,11:1
Miracle at Verdun 1931,Mr 17,34:6
Roof, The 1931,O 31,22:4
Roof, The 1931,N 8,VIII,1:1
Adam Had Two Sons 1932,Ja 21,17:1
Foreign Affairs 1932,Ap 14,25:5
I Loved You Wednesday 1932,O 12,27:1

519

La Roche, Edouard—Cont
20th Century 1932,D 30,15:1
La Roche, Mary
Girl From Wyoming, The 1938,O 31,12:1
La Rocque, Rod
Anna Ascends 1920,S 23,14:1
Cherries Are Ripe 1930,O 19,IX,3:4
Domino 1932,Ag 7,IX,1:1
Domino 1932,Ag 17,13:2
La Rol, Arthur
Little Clay Cart, The 1953,Jl 1,25:1
La Rosa, Julius
Kiss Mama 1964,O 2,30:1
La Rose, Melba Jr
Glamour, Glory and Gold 1967,O 4,43:1
La Rubia, Marga
Back Here 1928,N 27,36:3
Scotland Yard 1929,S 28,16:6
La Rue, Danny
Danny La Rue at the Palace 1970,Ag 31,24:1
La Rue, Eugene
So That's That 1925,D 15,28:3
La Rue, Grace
Dear Me 1921,Ja 18,14:1
Dear Me 1921,Ja 30,VI,1:1
Irving Berlin's New Music Box Revue
1922,O 24,18:1
Vaudeville (Palace) 1924,Ja 22,15:6
Vaudeville (Palace) 1924,O 21,21:2
Vaudeville (Palace) 1927,Ag 23,29:3
Greenwich Village Follies 1928,Ap 10,32:2
Stepping Out 1929,My 21,29:1
La Rue, Jack
Diamond Lil 1928,Ap 10,32:1
Fiesta 1929,S 18,35:1
Farewell to Arms, A 1930,S 23,30:3
La Rue, John
Kilpatrick's Old-Time Minstrels 1930,Ap 21,20:2
La Rue, Roy
Eyvind of the Hills 1921,F 2,14:1
la Salle, Victor
Marie Antoinette 1921,N 23,16:1
La Selva, Vincent
Saint of Bleecker Street, The 1965,Mr 19,28:1
La Tana, Teresita (Choreographer)
Blood Wedding 1958,Ap 1,35:1
La Tier, Harry
Forever This Land 1951,Jl 29,II,1:1
La Torre, Charles
We Never Learn 1928,Ja 24,26:1
Gala Night 1930,F 26,22:4
Papavert 1931,D 30,25:1
Mr Papavert 1932,Ja 23,18:6
Hot-Cha! 1932,Mr 9,17:3
We the People 1933,Ja 23,9:5
Mahogany Hall 1934,Ja 18,18:5
Hipper's Holiday 1934,O 19,26:2
Drums Professor, The 1935,Jl 30,17:2
In the Bag 1936,D 18,30:2
Streets of Paris, The 1939,Je 20,25:2
Aries Is Rising 1939,N 22,16:5
Two on an Island 1940,Ja 23,17:2
Louisiana Purchase 1940,My 29,19:2
La Touche, Treville (Composer)
Flair-Flair the Idol of Paree 1935,Mr 13,16:1
La Touche, Treville (Lyricist)
Flair-Flair the Idol of Paree 1935,Mr 13,16:1
La Touche, Treville (Playwright)
Flair-Flair the Idol of Paree 1935,Mr 13,16:1
La Tour, Charles
Flame of Love 1924,Ap 22,19:2
La Tour, Evelyn
Garrick Gaieties 1930,Je 5,29:2
La Tourneaux, Robert
Illya Darling 1967,Ap 12,37:1
Boys in the Band, The 1968,Ap 15,48:1
Sambo 1969,D 22,42:1
La Vallee, Bill
Ben Bagley's Shoestring Revues 1970,O 24,22:1
La Varre, Madelon
Century Revue and the Midnight Rounders, The
1920,Jl 13,9:1
La Varre, Myrtland
R U R 1922,O 10,16:1
Frankie and Johnny 1930,S 26,16:5
La Varre Brothers
Boys and Girls Together 1940,O 2,19:2
Untitled-Revue 1941,My 18,IX,1:1
La Vere, Paul
Vaudeville (Palace) 1926,O 26,24:2
La Verne, Grace
Sun-Up 1929,F 19,22:6
La Verne, Lucille
Come Seven 1920,Jl 20,10:1
Back Pay 1921,Ag 31,8:2
Goldfish, The 1922,Ap 18,15:3
Sun-Up 1925,My 5,25:1
Sun-Up 1925,Ag 14,13:4
Vaudeville (Palace) 1928,S 18,34:6
Sun-Up 1928,S 18,34:6
Sun-Up 1928,O 23,33:1
Merchant of Venice, The 1929,S 24,28:4
Black Widow 1936,F 13,24:3

La Verne, Lucille (Producer)
Sun-Up 1928,O 23,33:1
Sun-Up 1929,F 19,22:6
La Verni, Marie
Noble Rogue, A 1929,Ag 20,31:2
La Vigne, Gary W
Days Between, The 1965,Je 4,39:1
La Violette, Bijoute
Lawful Larceny 1922,Ja 3,20:2
La Von, Boo
Strip for Action 1942,O 1,26:2
La Vonne, Helen
George White's Scandals 1922,Ag 29,10:1
Fashions of 1924 1923,Jl 19,18:2
Battling Buttler 1923,O 9,17:2
Labaudt, Lucien (Costume Designer)
Lady Dedlock 1929,Ja 1,61:2
Laberer, Freddie
Guns 1928,Ag 7,25:2
Labey, Louis
Soliloquy 1938,N 29,26:4
Labiche, Eugene (Original Author)
Horse Eats Hat 1936,S 28,14:2
That Hat! 1964,S 24,45:1
Labiche, Eugene (Playwright)
Straw Hat, The 1926,O 15,20:2
Voyage de Monsieur Perrichon, Le 1937,N 2,32:3
37 Sous de M Montaudoin, Les 1939,F 7,17:2
Italian Straw Hat, The 1957,O 1,37:2
Labisse, Felix (Scenic Designer)
Proces, Le; Trial, The 1952,N 18,36:2
Occupe-Toi d'Amelie; Keep Your Eyes on Amelie
1952,N 25,35:2
Nuits de La Colere, Les; Nights of Fury
1957,F 12,31:1
Labisse, Georges (Costume Designer)
Teahouse of the August Moon, The 1955,F 17,22:1
Labisse, Georges (Scenic Designer)
Teahouse of the August Moon, The 1955,F 17,22:1
LaBossiere, Paul
And the Wind Blows 1959,Ap 29,28:1
Labourdette, Elina
Baptiste 1952,N 13,34:2
Proces, Le; Trial, The 1952,N 18,36:2
Amphitryon 1952,N 21,21:2
Occupe-Toi d'Amelie; Keep Your Eyes on Amelie
1952,N 25,35:2
Repetition, La; Rehearsal, The 1952,N 28,22:2
LaBow, Myrna
Eternal Sabbath 1963,O 19,17:2
Those That Play the Clowns 1966,N 25,48:1
Labreche, Gaetan
Malade Imaginaire, Le; Imaginary Invalid, The
1958,Ap 30,28:2
Sganarelle; Imaginary Cuckold, The 1958,My 7,43:1
Jalousie du Barbouille, La; Jealousy of the
Barbouille, The 1958,My 7,43:1
Mariage Force, Le; Forced Wedding, The
1958,My 7,43:1
Henry VI 1966,Je 9,55:2
Labrecque, John
Ice Capades 1956,S 13,41:2
Ice Capades 1957,S 5,33:2
Ice Capades 1960,S 1,30:1
Ice Capades 1961,Ag 31,24:4
Ice Capades 1962,Ag 30,34:1
Ice Capades 1963,Ag 29,37:2
Ice Capades 1964,Ag 27,27:2
Ice Capades 1969,Ja 8,42:1
Labrecque & Gray
Ice Capades 1958,S 4,33:2
Labrecque and Bussey
Ice Capades 1966,Je 2,50:2
Labriola, Tony
Vaudeville (Palace) 1931,Jl 6,24:6
Viva O'Brien 1941,O 10,27:2
Labzina, Olga
Kremlin Chimes 1965,F 25,23:1
Laceby, E W
Right to Strike, The 1921,O 25,20:1
Lacey, Catherine
Venetian, The 1931,N 2,26:1
Happy and Glorious 1931,N 21,21:4
Maitlands, The 1934,Jl 22,IX,1:3
Antony and Cleopatra 1935,Ap 16,26:7
Waste 1936,D 20,XI,3:3
Ame en Peine, L'; Unquiet Spirit, The
1937,N 14,XI,3:1
Marco Millions 1939,Ja 15,IX,3:1
All's Well That Ends Well 1940,O 13,IX,1:5
Tiger at the Gates 1955,O 4,40:1
Mary Stuart 1958,S 3,38:1
Hidden River, The 1959,Ap 14,41:2
Lacey, Catherine (Producer)
Happy and Glorious 1931,N 21,21:4
Lacey, Franklin (Original Author)
Music Man, The 1957,D 20,31:1
Music Man, The 1965,Je 17,26:4
Lacey, John Milton
Androcles and the Lion 1938,D 17,10:5
Lacey, Madge
Gala Night 1930,F 26,22:4

Lacey, Milton
Case of Philip Lawrence, The 1937,Je 9,31:1
Lacey, Ronald
Chips With Everything 1963,O 2,49:1
Fourth of June, The 1964,F 1,12:1
Lachamp, Adrienne
Roar China! 1930,O 28,23:1
Lacirignola, James
Six Characters in Search of an Author
1955,D 12,38:1
Queen After Death 1956,Mr 13,33:2
Lack, Andrew
United States vs Julius and Ethel Rosenberg, The
1969,Ap 20,II,3:1
Lackaye, Bob
Lower North 1944,Ag 26,15:4
Lackaye, Helene
Crooked Gamblers 1920,Ag 2,12:1
Captain Applejack 1921,D 31,14:2
Izzy 1924,S 17,16:2
90 Horse Power 1926,Mr 16,22:4
Gentle Grafters 1926,O 28,23:1
Revolt 1928,N 1,25:3
Lackaye, William Jr
Merton of the Movies 1922,N 14,16:2
Lackaye, Wilton
Trilby 1921,D 24,7:2
Goldfish, The 1922,Ap 18,15:3
Monster, The 1922,Ag 10,20:3
High Stakes 1924,S 10,21:3
Lambs Gambol 1925,Ap 27,15:1
Monkey Talks, The 1925,D 29,20:1
Two Orphans, The 1926,Ap 6,26:2
Two Orphans, The 1926,Ap 11,VIII,1:1
Trelawney of the 'Wells' 1927,F 1,24:4
Trelawney of the 'Wells' 1927,F 6,VII,1:1
Ladies of the Jury 1929,O 6,IX,1:4
Ladies of the Jury 1929,O 22,26:2
Fatal Woman 1930,Mr 2,IX,4:7
Love, Honor and Betray 1930,Mr 13,22:2
Lackaye, Wilton (Playwright)
Oh! Mama 1925,Ag 20,22:2
Oh! Mama 1925,Ag 30,VII,1:1
Lackaye, Wilton Jr
Spring Fever 1925,Ag 4,14:2
Appearances 1925,O 15,27:3
Two Orphans, The 1926,Ap 6,26:2
Sweet Land of Liberty 1929,S 24,29:2
Lackaye, Wilton Jr (Director)
American, Very Early 1934,Ja 31,21:2
Lackaye, Wilton Jr (Playwright)
American, Very Early 1934,Ja 31,21:2
Lackaye, Wilton Jr (Producer)
American, Very Early 1934,Ja 31,21:2
Lackey, R B (Playwright)
Angels Don't Kiss 1932,Ap 6,22:5
Lackland, Ben
Prunella; Love in a Garden 1926,Je 16,23:3
White Wings 1926,O 16,15:1
Road to Rome, The 1927,F 1,24:2
Jealous Moon, The 1928,N 21,32:2
Paolo and Francesca 1929,Ap 2,28:2
Jenny 1929,O 9,34:4
Wiser They Are, The 1931,Ap 7,31:1
Way of the World, The 1931,Je 2,34:3
Three Times the Hour 1931,Ag 26,15:5
Sing High, Sing Low 1931,N 13,26:4
Bridal Wise 1932,My 31,15:5
Sophisticrats, The 1933,F 14,19:5
Three-Cornered Moon 1933,Mr 17,20:6
Uncle Tom's Cabin 1933,My 30,13:4
Murder at the Vanities 1933,S 13,22:4
Perfumed Lady, The 1934,Mr 13,27:2
But Not for Love 1934,N 27,26:2
Seven Keys to Baldpate 1935,My 28,30:2
Remember the Day 1935,Jl 9,24:3
Stag at Bay, The 1935,Jl 30,17:1
Little Inn, The 1935,Ag 20,25:1
Rain 1935,Ag 27,23:4
Dear Old Darling 1936,Mr 3,25:1
County Chairman, The 1936,My 26,26:5
Feather in the Breeze 1936,Jl 14,22:2
Two Time Mary 1937,Ag 3,20:5
Reno 1937,Ag 10,22:7
Something for Nothing 1937,D 10,33:5
Sea Dogs 1939,N 7,30:3
International Incident, An 1940,Ap 3,18:2
Spring Again 1941,N 11,28:2
Snark Was a Boojum, The 1943,S 2,14:4
Jackpot 1944,Ja 14,15:2
Velvet Glove, The 1949,D 27,26:2
Golden State, The 1950,N 27,29:3
Last Love of Don Juan, The 1955,N 24,40:1
King and I, The 1956,Ap 19,35:4
Kiss Me, Kate 1956,My 10,27:2
Lackman, Michael
To Quito and Back 1937,O 7,30:4
Lacy, Gordon
Great Magician, The 1951,N 22,45:1
Lacy, Jerry
Play It Again, Sam 1969,F 13,52:3
Play It Again, Sam 1969,F 23,II,1:1
Play It Again, Sam 1970,F 7,25:2

Lacy, Tom
Fourth Pig, The 1965,Ja 27,24:6
Shoemaker's Holiday, The 1967,Mr 3,25:1
Midsummer Night's Dream, A 1967,Je 19,42:1
Merchant of Venice, The 1967,Je 22,46:2
Love and Let Love 1968,Ja 4,30:1
Millionairess, The 1969,Mr 3,28:1
Crimes of Passion; Erpingham Camp, The 1969,O 27,54:1

Ladd, Diane
Orpheus Descending 1959,O 6,45:2
Carry Me Back to Morningside Heights 1968,F 28,41:1
One Night Stands of a Noisy Passenger; Last Stand 1970,D 31,8:3

Ladd, Eleanor
Just Married 1921,Ap 27,21:1
Dr David's Dad 1924,Ag 14,10:3

Ladd, Eric
Career Angel 1943,N 19,24:2

Ladd, Hank
New Priorities of 1943 1942,S 16,28:2
Angel in the Wings 1947,D 12,36:4
Angel in the Wings 1947,D 21,II,3:1
Angel in the Wings 1948,Ag 29,II,1:1
Along Fifth Avenue 1949,Ja 14,28:2
Skits-Oh-Frantics 1967,Ap 3,39:2

Ladd, Hank (Director)
Skits-Oh-Frantics 1967,Ap 3,39:2

Ladd, Hank (Playwright)
Angel in the Wings 1947,D 12,36:4
Skits-Oh-Frantics 1967,Ap 3,39:2

Ladd, Ivanelle
Sun-Kist 1921,My 24,20:2

Ladd, John
Maid in the Ozarks 1946,Jl 16,20:3

Ladd, Margaret
Great Indoors, The 1966,F 2,23:1
Experiment, The 1967,My 9,54:2
Sheep on the Runway 1970,F 2,28:3

Ladd, Schuyler
Yellow Jacket, The 1921,Ja 5,11:1
Shore Leave 1922,Ag 9,20:2
Sweet Nell of Old Drury 1923,My 19,16:4
Miracle, The 1924,Ja 16,17:1
Miracle, The 1924,Ag 19,9:1
Caesar and Cleopatra 1925,Ap 14,27:1
Miracle, The 1926,D 28,16:2
Miracle, The 1927,F 1,24:5
Yellow Jacket, The 1928,N 8,27:3
Yellow Jacket, The 1929,Ja 11,21:1
Yellow Jacket, The 1934,F 25,IX,2:6
Moroni 1936,Ag 19,19:1

Ladd, Tom
Girl From Nantucket, The 1945,N 9,17:2

Ladd, William
Peg o' My Dreams 1924,My 6,25:3
Hassard Short's Ritz Revue 1924,S 18,19:1
Sunny 1925,S 23,22:1
Greenwich Village Follies 1925,D 25,23:3

Laderman, Ezra (Composer)
Machinal 1960,Ap 8,27:1
Machinal 1960,Ap 17,II,1:1
Entertain a Ghost 1962,Ap 10,48:1

Ladimer, Lou
Paradise 1931,My 12,29:2

Ladimer, Pamela
Noye's Fludde 1959,Mr 17,41:2

Ladoux, Emile
East Wind 1931,O 28,19:1

LaDuc, Marvin
Side-Show 1931,My 16,13:1

Ladue, John
Holiday on Ice 1965,S 2,38:4
Holiday on Ice 1967,Ag 31,29:2
Holiday on Ice 1969,Ag 28,44:1

Laemmle, Carl (Producer)
Parson's Bride, The 1929,Ja 22,22:3

Laencina, Juan de (Playwright)
Logia a la Natividad de Nuestro Senor Jesucristo, El 1937,D 14,33:4

Laerum, Ursula (Miscellaneous)
Ratten, Die 1966,Ap 13,36:1

Laesch, Noble
Little Theatre Tournament; Thirst 1929,My 10,32:2

Lafaur, Andre
Triplepatte 1926,N 14,VIII,2:1

Lafaurie, Charles (Playwright)
Parce Que Je T'Aime 1928,S 30,IX,2:1
Bloomfield 1930,O 12,VIII,4:2

Laffan, Kevin
Zoo, Zoo, Widdershins, Zoo 1969,S 5,30:1

Laffey, Bruce
Kiss Me, Kate 1952,Ja 9,24:6
Ziegfeld Follies 1957,Mr 2,19:2

Laffey, Bruce (Miscellaneous)
Make a Million 1958,O 24,39:2

Laffin, Charles
Wallflower 1944,Ja 27,14:2
Joy Forever, A 1946,Ja 8,20:2

Lafflin, L E Jr (Composer)
Drake's Drum 1923,D 26,17:7

Laffon, Yolande
Tessa 1935,Ja 6,IX,2:1

Lafham, Louis A
Roof, The 1930,Je 14,9:2

Lafleur, Joy
Hamlet 1957,Jl 3,15:2

Laflin, Louis E
Man From Earth, The 1923,Ja 3,6:2

Laflin, Louis E (Playwright)
Man From Earth, The 1923,Ja 3,6:2

Lafollette, Sherry
Tall Story 1959,Ja 30,33:2

LaFontaine, Gerald De
Case of Philip Lawrence, The 1937,Je 9,31:1

Lagarovici, Josef
Fiesta 1929,S 18,35:1

Lagerkvist, Per (Playwright)
Moment Difficile, Le 1926,D 26,VII,2:1
Hangman, The 1935,O 23,18:6

Lagerlof, Selma (Original Author)
Gosta Berling's Saga 1936,Je 28,IX,1:6

Lagerlof, Selma (Playwright)
Gosta Berling's Saga 1936,Je 28,IX,1:6
Dunungen 1939,F 26,IX,2:3

LaGioia, John
Lovers in the Metro, The 1962,Ja 31,21:1
Keyhole, The 1962,Ja 31,21:1
Cherry Orchard, The 1962,N 15,46:2
Titus Andronicus 1967,Ag 10,43:2
Richard II 1968,Je 24,42:3
Henry V 1969,N 11,43:1

Lagodmas, Poppy (Costume Designer)
Playboy of the Western World, The 1958,My 9,19:2

Lagodmos, Poppy (Miscellaneous)
Ivanov 1958,O 8,42:1
Under Milk Wood 1961,Mr 30,25:1

LaGoff, Natalynne
Schoolhouse on the Lot 1938,Mr 23,18:4

Lagos, Poppy
Out of This World 1955,N 10,44:2

LaHarte, Rose
Matinee Girl, The 1926,F 2,20:3

Lahiri, Amalandu
Ramayana 1931,Ja 13,35:4

Lahiri, Sarat
Little Clay Cart, The 1924,D 6,13:3
Soldiers and Women 1929,S 3,25:1
Virtue's Bed 1930,Ap 16,26:5
Theodora, the Queen 1934,F 1,15:3

Lahiri, Sarat (Composer)
Virtue's Bed 1930,Ap 16,26:5

Lahman, Alfred (Costume Designer)
Gogo Loves You 1964,O 10,19:2

Lahr, Bert
Folly Town 1920,My 18,9:2
Harry Delmar's Revels 1927,N 29,30:2
Hold Everything 1928,O 11,24:2
Flying High 1930,F 9,VIII,4:2
Flying High 1930,Mr 4,24:4
Vaudeville (Palace) 1931,Ap 13,17:2
Vaudeville (Palace) 1931,O 26,22:3
Hot-Cha! 1932,F 21,VIII,2:1
Hot-Cha! 1932,Mr 9,17:3
Hot-Cha! 1932,Mr 20,VIII,1:1
Music Hall Varieties 1932,N 23,15:3
Music Hall Varieties 1933,Ja 3,19:4
Friars Club Frolic 1933,My 15,16:4
Life Begins at 8:40 1934,Ag 7,20:7
Life Begins at 8:40 1934,Ag 12,IX,1:1
Life Begins at 8:40 1934,Ag 28,24:2
Life Begins at 8:40 1934,S 2,IX,1:1
Scandals 1935,O 30,17:1
George White's Scandals 1935,D 26,20:2
Show Is On, The 1936,N 9,22:2
Show Is On, The 1936,N 15,XI,2:1
Show Is On, The 1936,D 26,14:2
Show Is On, The 1937,Ja 10,X,1:1
Du Barry 1939,N 19,X,3:4
Du Barry Was a Lady 1939,D 7,34:2
Du Barry 1939,D 24,IX,1:1
Seven Lively Arts 1944,D 8,26:6
Seven Lively Arts 1944,D 17,II,3:1
Burlesque 1946,D 26,30:3
Burlesque 1947,Ja 5,II,1:1
Two on the Aisle 1951,Jl 20,13:6
Two on the Aisle 1951,Jl 29,II,1:1
Waiting for Godot 1956,Ap 20,21:2
Waiting for Godot 1956,Ap 29,II,1:2
Hotel Paradiso 1957,Ap 12,22:2
Hotel Paradiso 1957,Ap 21,II,1:1
Girls Against the Boys, The 1959,N 3,26:1
Girls Against the Boys, The 1959,N 8,II,1:1
Foxy 1962,Jl 4,12:2
Beauty Part, The 1962,D 28,5:2
Beauty Part, The 1963,Ja 5,5:1
Foxy 1964,F 17,26:1
Foxy 1964,Mr 20,30:1
Birds, The 1966,Jl 1,40:1

Lahr, Bert and Mercedes
Vaudeville (Palace) 1926,Mr 30,20:4

Lahr, John (Lyricist)
Beggar on Horseback 1970,My 15,47:2
Beggar on Horseback 1970,My 24,II,1:1

Laidlaw, Alan
Zuider Zee 1928,D 19,24:4

Laidlaw, Betty (Playwright)
Wise Girl 1932,Mr 20,VIII,2:5

Laidley, Alice
Small Timers, The 1925,Ja 28,15:3

Laik, Bernard
Mariage de Figaro, Le 1964,F 26,41:2

Lailique, Suzanne (Costume Designer)
Amphitryon 1970,F 4,38:1

Lailique, Suzanne (Scenic Designer)
Amphitryon 1970,F 4,38:1

Laimbeer, Fifi
Fifty Million Frenchmen 1929,N 28,34:4

Laine, Ray (Miscellaneous)
Rose Tattoo, The 1966,O 21,36:2

Laing, Amos
Texas Town 1941,Ap 30,22:3

Laing, Curtis
Tobias and the Angel 1937,Ap 29,16:5

Laing, Hugh
Day Before Spring, The 1945,N 23,27:2

Laing, Hugh (Costume Designer)
American Legend 1941,My 12,13:2

Laing, Malcolm
Touch of Brimstone, A 1935,S 23,20:1
Lightnin' 1938,S 16,17:2

Laing, Ralph
Tobias and the Angel 1937,Ap 29,16:5

Laird, Effie
Mr Adam 1949,My 26,34:6

Laird, George
Parisiana 1928,F 10,26:3

Laird, Gladys
Garrick Gaieties 1926,My 11,25:2

Laird, Helen
Lonesome West, The 1936,Je 30,15:1

Laird, Jenny
Cherry Orchard, The 1970,My 7,63:2

Laird, John
Where Do We Go From Here? 1938,N 16,26:2

Laird, Kenneth
My Fair Lady 1959,Ja 27,26:1

Laird, Marvin (Composer)
Georgy 1970,F 27,26:1

Laird, Marvin (Miscellaneous)
Skyscraper 1965,N 15,48:1
Where's Charley? 1966,My 26,57:1
Happy Time, The 1968,Ja 19,32:2

Laire, Judson
Technique 1931,My 15,21:1
Nude in Washington Square, The 1934,Ag 7,20:1
Constant Wife, The 1935,Jl 3,20:2
Stardust 1935,Jl 17,22:4
Play's the Thing, The 1935,Jl 24,20:4
First Lady 1935,N 27,17:4
All That Glitters 1938,Ja 20,18:2
Mr Big 1941,S 7,I,51:3
Mr Big 1941,O 1,24:2
Patriots, The 1943,Ja 30,11:2
Doctors Disagree 1943,D 29,15:2
Signature 1945,F 15,25:2
Candida 1957,Mr 29,18:5
Third Best Sport 1958,D 31,15:3
Advise and Consent 1960,N 18,25:1

Lait, Jack (Playwright)
Spice of 1922 1922,Jl 7,12:4
Hook-Up, The 1935,My 9,24:6

Laite, Charles
Wheel, The 1921,My 8,VI,1:1
Wheel, The 1921,Ag 30,10:1
Dream Maker, The 1921,N 22,17:1
Polly Preferred 1923,Ja 12,13:3
Wild Westcotts, The 1923,D 25,26:2
Wisdom Tooth, The 1926,F 16,22:2
2 Girls Wanted 1926,S 10,25:3
Night Hostess 1928,S 13,31:2
Primer for Lovers, A 1929,N 19,26:5
House Afire 1930,Ap 1,34:7
Sisters of the Chorus 1930,O 21,34:3
Louder, Please! 1931,N 13,26:4
Riddle Me This! 1932,F 26,22:5
Lost Horizons 1934,O 16,31:2
Bishop Misbehaves, The 1935,F 21,22:4
For Valor 1935,N 19,27:5
Feather in the Breeze 1936,Jl 14,22:2

Lajarrige, Bernard
Ecole des Femmes, L' 1961,Ap 28,23:1

Lakatos, Laszlo (Playwright)
Sapphire Ring, The 1925,Ap 16,25:2
Head or Tail 1926,N 10,24:1
Pajtashazassag 1928,D 30,VIII,4:4
Our Eighteen-Year-Olds 1929,N 17,IX,4:7

Lake, Harriette
America's Sweetheart 1931,Ja 25,VIII,2:4
America's Sweetheart 1931,F 11,23:1
Everybody's Welcome 1931,S 20,VIII,3:2
Everybody's Welcome 1931,O 14,26:3

Lake, Loral
Innocent Idea, An 1920,My 26,9:4

Lakewood Players
Harbor Light, The 1932,Ag 7,IX,2:2

Laklan, Carli (Director)
Legal Grounds 1940,D 2,18:4
Lalaew, Antonina
Rosalie 1928,Ja 11,26:3
LaLage
Folies Bergere 1939,D 25,28:2
Lalic, Ivan (Miscellaneous)
Ubu Roi 1968,Je 29,20:1
Laliche (Original Author)
Passage de Venus, Le 1928,Mr 18,IX,2:1
Lalicki, Vladislav (Costume Designer)
Ubu Roi 1968,Je 29,20:1
Lalicki, Vladislav (Scenic Designer)
Ubu Roi 1968,Je 29,20:1
Lalique (Costume Designer)
Bourgeois Gentilhomme, Le 1955,O 26,26:1
Bourgeois Gentilhomme, Le 1955,O 30,II,1:1
Jeu de l'Amour et du Hasard, Le 1955,N 16,42:4
Impromptu de Versailles, L' 1961,F 22,30:1
Dindon, Le 1961,Mr 8,38:1
Femmes Savaantes, Les 1970,F 14,12:1
Lalique, Suzanne (Scenic Designer)
Bourgeois Gentilhomme, Le 1955,O 26,26:1
Bourgeois Gentilhomme, Le 1955,O 30,II,1:1
Barbier de Seville, Le 1955,N 9,40:1
Arlequin Poli par l'Amour 1955,N 9,40:1
Impromptu de Versailles, L' 1961,F 22,30:1
Dindon, Le 1961,Mr 8,38:1
Femmes Savaantes, Les 1970,F 14,12:1
Lalli, Franco (Playwright)
Signori, Il Figlio E' Nato 1935,Je 8,13:7
Lally, Helen
Veronica's Veil 1933,F 20,11:7
Lally, Janet
Great Big Doorstep, The 1950,Mr 18,8:6
Lally, Joanne
Great Big Doorstep, The 1950,Mr 18,8:6
Lally, Lorraine
Henry-Behave 1926,Ag 24,19:4
Adam's Apple 1929,Je 11,27:5
Lalor, Frank
Suzette 1921,N 25,18:3
Luckee Girl 1928,S 17,28:6
Street Singer, The 1929,S 18,35:2
Robin Hood 1932,Ja 28,25:4
Lamar, George
Great Barrington, The 1931,F 20,18:1
Mother Lode 1934,D 24,16:5
Tapestry in Gray 1935,D 28,10:2
LaMarr, Henry
Jumbo 1935,N 18,20:2
LaMarr, Moses
Porgy and Bess 1953,Mr 10,25:5
World's My Oyster, The 1956,Ag 10,10:4
Shinbone Alley 1957,Ap 15,23:2
Free and Easy 1959,D 15,51:4
Free and Easy 1959,D 20,II,3:2
Lamarre, Ginger
Story Teller, The 1951,D 15,11:3
Lamarre, Priscilla
Story Teller, The 1951,D 15,11:3
Lamas, Fernando
Happy Hunting 1956,D 7,30:1
Lamb, A J (Playwright)
Flesh 1925,My 8,22:3
Lamb, Don
Wedding in Japan 1957,Mr 12,37:7
Othello 1958,Jl 4,16:1
Entertain a Ghost 1962,Ap 10,48:1
Lamb, Don (Miscellaneous)
Blood Wedding 1958,Ap 1,35:1
Power of Darkness, The 1959,S 30,33:1
Shoemaker and the Peddler, The 1960,O 15,27:4
Eccentricities of Davy Crockett, The 1961,Ja 4,26:1
Willie the Weeper 1961,Ja 4,26:1
Riding Hood Revisited 1961,Ja 4,26:1
Entertain a Ghost 1962,Ap 10,48:1
Dames at Sea 1970,S 24,60:1
Lamb, George
Old Bill, M P 1926,N 11,22:2
Lamb, Gil
Show Is On, The 1936,N 9,22:2
Show Is On, The 1936,N 15,XI,2:1
Folies Bergere 1939,D 25,28:2
Hold On to Your Hats 1940,Jl 17,25:3
Hold On to Your Hats 1940,S 12,30:3
Sleepy Hollow 1948,Je 4,26:3
Lamb, Myrna (Lyricist)
Mod Donna 1970,My 4,48:1
Lamb, Myrna (Playwright)
Mod Donna 1970,My 4,48:1
Mod Donna 1970,My 10,II,1:1
Lamb, Paul C
Clarence 1923,My 14,18:4
Lamb, Sybil
Wish You Were Here 1952,Je 26,26:6
Maybe Tuesday 1958,Ja 30,18:3
Lamb, Wayne (Choreographer)
Midsummer Night's Dream, A 1956,Ja 14,12:2
Twelfth Night 1957,Ja 5,12:2
Lambart, Ernest
Snapshots of 1921 1921,Je 3,19:2
Alarm Clock, The 1923,D 25,26:2

Keep Moving 1934,Ag 24,10:2
Lambart, Richard
Mima 1928,D 13,24:2
Peter Ibbetson 1931,Ap 9,30:3
Great Waltz, The 1934,S 24,14:4
Lambelet, Kathlyn
Bitter Sweet 1929,N 6,30:2
Lamberson, Ralph
Paradise 1931,My 12,29:2
Lambert, Adrian
Coriolanus 1927,Je 18,8:3
Lambert, Albert
Aventuriere, L' 1922,N 14,16:1
Dame aux Camelias, La 1922,N 16,22:2
Duel, Le 1922,N 16,22:2
Tartuffe 1922,N 23,21:3
Oedipe a Colone 1924,S 7,III,12:4
Lambert, Andree
Chief Thing, The 1963,Ap 30,27:2
Lambert, David
Are You With It? 1945,N 12,17:3
Lambert, Deatra
Slave Ship 1969,N 22,46:1
Tarot 1970,D 12,19:1
Lambert, Dorothy
Inside Story 1942,O 30,22:2
Mrs January & Mr Ex 1944,Ap 1,10:2
Dark of the Moon 1945,Mr 15,27:2
Lambert, Doug
Mighty Man Is He, A 1960,Ja 7,25:2
Lambert, Edward J
Vaudeville (Palace) 1927,D 20,33:4
Saluta 1934,Ag 29,13:4
Smile at Me 1935,Ag 24,18:4
Mr Strauss Goes to Boston 1945,S 7,20:2
If the Shoe Fits 1946,D 6,29:4
Lambert, Edward J (Composer)
Smile at Me 1935,Ag 24,18:4
Lambert, Edward J (Lyricist)
Smile at Me 1935,Ag 24,18:4
Lambert, Edward J (Playwright)
Smile at Me 1935,Ag 24,18:4
Lambert, Ernest
Rain or Shine 1928,F 10,26:3
Lambert, Frank
Dearest Enemy 1925,S 19,9:2
Criss Cross 1926,O 13,20:2
Lambert, George
Small Miracle 1934,S 27,24:3
O Evening Star 1936,Ja 9,24:6
Empress of Destiny 1938,Mr 10,16:2
New Life, A 1943,S 16,26:6
Lambert, Gloria
Illya Darling 1967,Ap 12,37:1
Lambert, Happy
Better Times 1922,S 4,14:2
Lambert, Harry (Producer)
Little A 1947,Ja 16,31:2
Lambert, Helen
Right You Are (If You Think You Are)
1957,Mr 5,37:1
Lambert, Henry
Sherlock Holmes 1929,N 26,28:3
Lambert, Hugh
Vamp, The 1955,N 11,30:1
Lambert, Hugh (Choreographer)
How to Succeed in Business Without Really Trying
1961,O 16,34:1
Lambert, Jack
Little Theatre Tournament; Old Lady Shows Her
Medals, The 1928,My 11,28:1
Heavenly Express 1940,Ap 19,24:2
Blind Alley 1940,O 16,28:2
Brother Cain 1941,S 13,21:5
Johnny 2X4 1942,Mr 17,24:6
Lambert, Jane
Delightful Season, A 1960,S 29,30:1
Lambert, John
Stepping Stones 1923,N 7,14:3
Criss Cross 1926,O 13,20:2
Three Cheers 1928,O 16,28:1
Lambert, John (Composer)
Saint Joan 1962,F 21,57:4
Lambert, Lucia
Plain and Fancy 1955,F 6,II,6:6
Lambert, Madeleine
Traite d'Auteuil, Le 1921,Jl 17,VI,1:8
As You Like It 1934,N 11,IX,3:6
Lambert, Marie
Bunk of 1926 1926,Ap 23,25:2
Lambert, Mary
Patience 1929,D 16,34:5
Lambert, Patricia
Music Man, The 1961,Mr 18,17:3
Lambert, Paul
Night Music 1951,Ap 9,29:6
Detective Story 1954,F 13,11:2
Lambert, Richard
Candida 1925,D 19,14:2
Ballyhoo 1930,D 23,24:1
If Booth Had Missed 1931,My 14,27:1
Lambert, Sammy (Miscellaneous)
Up in Central Park 1947,My 20,29:2

Lambert, Sammy (Miscellaneous)—Cont
Show Boat 1956,Je 22,16:1
To Broadway With Love 1964,Ap 30,28:6
Oklahoma! 1969,Je 24,37:1
Lambert, Sammy (Producer)
Hold It! 1948,My 6,31:5
All for Love 1949,Ja 24,16:5
Seventeen 1951,Je 22,16:6
Lambert, Sherry
Miss Emily Adam 1960,Mr 30,43:1
Lambert, William
Dice of the Gods, The 1923,Ap 6,20:2
Vagabond, The 1923,D 28,13:4
Lambert (M)
Demi-Monde, Le 1922,N 15,22:3
Megere Apprivoisee, La 1922,N 20,21:2
Misanthrope, Le 1922,N 22,18:2
Lamberti (Professor)
Star and Garter 1942,Je 25,26:2
Star and Garter 1942,S 13,VIII,1:1
Lamberts, Heath
Richard II 1964,Je 17,47:1
Bourgeois Gentilhomme, Le 1964,Je 18,28:2
Country Wife, The 1964,Ag 3,16:1
Henry IV, Part I 1965,Je 30,42:1
Falstaff; Henry IV, Part II 1965,Jl 1,35:1
Julius Caesar 1965,Jl 2,18:1
Henry V 1966,Je 8,38:1
Henry VI 1966,Je 9,55:2
Twelfth Night 1966,Je 10,51:2
Lambrecht, Heinz (Musical Director)
Kiss Me, Kate 1959,Ag 10,24:1
Lambrinos, Ted
Eccentricities of Davy Crockett, The 1961,Ja 4,26:1
Bible Salesman, The 1961,F 21,40:1
Lambrinos, Vassili (Choreographer)
Bacchants, The 1967,F 25,14:1
Lambrinos, Vassili (Director)
Hi, Paisano 1961,O 2,36:2
Bacchants, The 1967,F 25,14:1
Lambrinos, Vassili (Miscellaneous)
Zorba 1968,N 18,58:1
Lambrose, George
R U R 1942,D 4,30:2
Music in My Heart 1947,O 3,30:2
Lambs' Club
Vaudeville (Palace) 1929,F 11,26:2
Lambton, Doris (Miscellaneous)
Feast of Panthers 1961,Mr 21,32:1
Lamdan, I (Translator)
David's Crown 1948,My 10,26:2
Lamdon, Adella
Roaming Stars 1930,Ja 25,12:2
Lamendola, Ronald
Long Gallery, The 1958,Mr 7,17:2
Lamers, Patsy
Conquest of the Universe 1967,N 27,60:1
Laming, Dorothy
Coriolanus 1953,Ag 21,9:2
Romeo and Juliet 1961,F 24,24:1
Lamison, Nora
Opportunity 1920,Jl 31,5:1
Lamkin, Speed (Playwright)
Comes a Day 1958,N 7,22:1
Lamm, Earl
Life Begins in '40 1940,Ap 5,24:2
Lammers, Paul (Director)
Mandragola 1956,Mr 1,36:4
Littlest Revue, The 1956,My 23,37:2
Shoestring '57 1956,N 6,31:1
Lamon, Isabel
Advertising of Kate, The 1922,My 9,22:2
Vaudeville (Palace) 1926,Ag 17,21:2
Lamont, Adele
Out of This World 1955,N 10,44:2
He Who Gets Slapped 1956,F 2,18:1
Blood Wedding 1958,Ap 1,35:1
Lamont, Adele (Choreographer)
Out of This World 1955,N 10,44:2
Lamont, Florence (Costume Designer)
Lazarus Laughed 1948,Ap 9,27:4
Lamont, Jean
Man in Evening Clothes, The 1924,D 6,13:4
Abie's Irish Rose 1954,N 19,19:1
Lamont, Jennie
Guest of Honor, The 1920,S 21,12:1
Straw, The 1921,N 11,16:2
Lamont, Michael
Do I Hear a Waltz? 1965,Mr 19,28:1
Royal Hunt of the Sun, The 1965,O 27,36:2
Lamont, Miki
King and I, The 1960,My 12,40:1
Lamont, Owen
Brooklyn Biarritz 1941,F 28,16:2
Golden Wings 1941,N 25,33:3
What Big Ears! 1942,Ap 21,18:5
Lamont, Robert
Kismet 1965,Je 23,45:1
Lamont, Syl
Johnny 2X4 1942,Mr 17,24:6
Afternoon Storm 1948,Ap 12,24:2
Lamonte, Paul
Private Affair, A 1936,My 15,28:7

LaMotta, Jake
Guys and Dolls 1959,Jl 22,22:2
Guys and Dolls 1965,Ap 29,39:1
Lamoureaux, Robert
Turlututu 1962,S 29,14:2
Lampee, Robert
Master of the Revels 1935,Ag 14,16:2
Lampel, Peter Martin (Playwright)
Poison Gas Over Berlin 1929,Mr 6,12:3
Revolte in Erziehungshaus 1929,Mr 10,X,2:1
Lampell, Millard (Playwright)
Wall, The 1960,O 12,44:4
Wall, The 1960,O 23,II,1:1
Wall, The 1961,N 9,40:3
Hard Travelin' 1965,Je 17,25:1
Lonesome Train, The 1965,Je 17,25:1
Hard Travelin' 1965,Je 27,II,1:1
Lonesome Train, The 1965,Je 27,II,1:1
Lampert, Rachel
West Side Story 1968,Je 25,32:1
Lampert, Zohra
Maybe Tuesday 1958,Ja 30,18:3
Look: We've Come Through 1961,O 26,40:1
First Love 1961,D 26,20:2
Mother Courage and Her Children 1963,Mr 30,5:5
After the Fall 1964,Ja 24,18:1
Marco Millions 1964,F 21,33:1
Nathan Weinstein, Mystic, Connecticut 1966,F 26,15:2
Natural Look, The 1967,Mr 13,45:2
Lovers and Other Strangers 1968,S 19,63:1
Lampi, Carl (Composer)
Hilarities 1948,S 10,20:2
Lampi, Carl (Lyricist)
Hilarities 1948,S 10,20:2
Lamson, Peggy (Playwright)
Respectfully Yours 1947,My 14,29:4
Lamson, Roy Jr
Gentlemen, the Queen 1927,Ap 23,14:3
Lamys, The
Vaudeville (Hippodrome) 1925,D 29,21:2
Lan-Fang, Mei
Untitled-Recital 1930,Mr 10,24:4
Lan-Fang, Mei (Costume Designer)
Lady Precious Stream 1936,Ja 28,15:2
Lancaster, Betty
Gentlemen of the Press 1928,Ag 28,27:2
Indiscretion 1929,Mr 5,28:1
Shoestring Revue 1929,N 23,19:2
Forest Ring, The 1930,Ap 26,11:2
Let and Sub-Let 1930,My 20,32:2
Little Princess, The 1931,F 7,11:3
Racketty Packetty House 1931,N 7,16:1
Reluctant Dragon, The 1931,D 12,23:5
Uncle Tom's Cabin 1933,O 10,24:3
Big Hearted Herbert 1934,Ja 2,17:3
Lost Horizons 1934,O 16,31:2
Sap Runs High, The 1936,F 5,15:3
Lancaster, Burt
Sound of Hunting, A 1945,N 21,16:6
Lancaster, Dick
Harry Delmar's Revels 1927,N 29,30:2
Lancaster, Joyce
Milk Train Doesn't Stop Here Anymore, The 1965,Jl 27,25:1
Lancaster, Lucie
Heads or Tails 1947,My 3,10:6
Mr Pickwick 1952,S 18,36:3
Girl Who Came to Supper, The 1963,D 9,49:1
Bajour 1964,N 24,42:1
How Now, Dow Jones 1967,D 8,53:1
Little Boxes; Coffee Lace, The 1969,D 4,71:2
Lancaster, Maurice
Twelfth Night 1934,Jl 17,24:5
Lancaster, Osbert (Costume Designer)
Hotel Paradiso 1957,Ap 12,22:2
Hotel Paradiso 1957,Ap 21,II,1:1
Lancaster, Osbert (Scenic Designer)
Hotel Paradiso 1957,Ap 12,22:2
Hotel Paradiso 1957,Ap 21,II,1:1
Candide 1959,My 1,35:4
Lancaster, Stuart
All the Comforts of Home 1942,My 26,24:5
Lance, Robert
Any Woman 1934,Ag 28,24:4
Patriots, The 1943,Ja 30,11:2
Lance, Robert G
Winter Soldiers 1942,N 30,19:2
Lance, Robert J
Mystery Ship, The 1927,Mr 15,28:2
Reunion 1938,Ap 12,26:4
Legal Grounds 1940,D 2,18:4
Petrified Forest, The 1943,N 2,30:6
Lancelot, Jean
Intermezzo 1957,F 15,20:4
Chien du Jardinier, Le; Gardener's Dog, The 1957,F 19,36:1
Adieux, Les 1957,F 19,36:1
Lancer, John (Playwright)
White Hell 1935,Ag 13,20:3
Lancet, Robert
Caukey 1944,F 18,15:4

Lanchester, Elsa
Payment Deferred 1931,O 1,24:2
Tempest, The 1934,F 4,IX,3:4
They Walk Alone 1941,Mr 13,24:2
No Strings 1942,Je 14,VIII,2:1
Party, The 1958,My 30,13:1
Zany Evening With Elsa Lanchester, A 1960,N 5,27:2
Elsa Lanchester-Herself 1961,F 6,28:1
Lanchester, Robert
She Stoops to Conquer 1968,Ja 1,11:1
Flea in Her Ear, A 1969,O 4,25:1
Three Sisters, The 1969,O 10,38:1
Greenwillow 1970,D 8,60:1
Lanchester, Robert (Director)
Twelfth Night 1968,Je 15,40:1
Lancourt, Saul (Director)
Doodle Dandy of the U S A 1942,O 19,15:2
Lancourt, Saul (Playwright)
Adventures of Marco Polo, The 1941,D 28,I,31:7
Doodle Dandy of the U S A 1942,O 19,15:2
Land, Lucy
This Our House 1935,D 12,33:3
Trojan Women, The 1938,Ja 25,24:2
Land, Robert E
Me and Juliet 1970,My 15,42:1
Landa, Walter
Night Music 1951,Ap 9,29:6
Landau
Ragged Edge, The 1927,F 13,VII,1:4
Landau, Beverly (Miscellaneous)
Firebugs, The 1963,F 13,7:2
Landau, Beverly (Producer)
Red Roses for Me 1961,N 28,41:1
Exception and the Rule, The 1965,My 21,19:1
Prodigal Son, The 1965,My 21,19:1
Yes, Yes, No No 1969,Ja 1,16:1
Landau, Daniel
World of Illusion 1964,Je 25,26:2
Bead-Tangle 1970,Jl 16,38:1
Landau, David
Robert E Lee 1923,N 21,23:1
Catskill Dutch 1924,My 7,18:1
Play, A 1925,F 11,19:2
Ruint 1925,Ap 8,24:2
Mud Turtle, The 1925,Ag 21,8:2
Devils 1926,Mr 18,26:4
Humble, The 1926,O 14,22:2
Witch, The 1926,N 19,22:5
Women Go on Forever 1927,S 8,25:1
Golden Age, The 1928,Ap 25,31:3
Octoroon, The 1929,Mr 13,28:3
Street Scene 1930,S 28,VIII,2:4
Landau, Jack (Costume Designer)
Phoenix Too Frequent, A 1950,Ap 27,36:2
Freight 1950,Ap 27,36:2
Buy Me Blue Ribbons 1951,O 18,33:2
Dear Barbarians 1952,F 22,15:2
Landau, Jack (Director)
Clandestine Marriage, The 1954,O 4,23:2
White Devil, The 1955,Mr 15,32:5
Carefree Tree, The 1955,O 12,37:2
King John 1956,Je 28,33:5
Measure for Measure 1956,Je 29,16:1
Measure for Measure 1957,Ja 23,24:1
Measure for Measure 1957,F 3,II,1:1
Duchess of Malfi, The 1957,Mr 20,33:1
Merchant of Venice, The 1957,Jl 11,19:5
Much Ado About Nothing 1957,Ag 8,15:2
Merchant of Venice, The 1957,Ag 18,II,1:1
Midsummer Night's Dream, A 1958,Je 23,19:1
Winter's Tale, The 1958,Jl 21,17:4
Winter's Tale, The 1958,Jl 27,II,1:1
Romeo and Juliet 1959,Je 15,31:1
Romeo and Juliet 1959,Je 21,II,1:1
Merry Wives of Windsor, The 1959,Jl 9,23:2
Twelfth Night 1960,Je 9,29:4
Antony and Cleopatra 1960,Ag 1,19:1
Macbeth 1961,Je 19,31:1
Macbeth 1961,Je 25,II,1:1
Troilus and Cressida 1961,Jl 24,15:1
Riot Act, The 1963,Mr 9,5:2
White Devil, The 1965,D 7,56:1
Landau, Jack (Scenic Designer)
Phoenix Too Frequent, A 1950,Ap 27,36:2
Freight 1950,Ap 27,36:2
Mary Rose 1951,Mr 5,25:2
Buy Me Blue Ribbons 1951,O 18,33:2
Dear Barbarians 1952,F 22,15:2
Carefree Tree, The 1955,O 12,37:2
Duchess of Malfi, The 1957,Mr 20,33:1
Landau, Leonora
Desire Under the Elms 1963,Ja 11,5:6
Matty and the Moron and Madonna 1965,Mr 30,53:1
Landau, Leonora (Choreographer)
Desire Under the Elms 1963,Ja 11,5:6
Landau, Lucy
Cheri 1959,O 13,44:1
Ernest in Love 1960,My 5,39:4
Night of the Iguana, The 1961,D 29,10:1
Penny Change 1963,O 25,37:1

Landauer, Barrie (Miscellaneous)
Antigone 1967,Ja 14,18:1
Lande, Irving (Producer)
Carnival 1929,Ap 25,32:5
Crooks' Convention, The 1929,S 19,37:4
Two Seconds 1931,O 10,20:6
Landek, Violetta
Boys From Syracuse, The 1963,Ap 16,31:1
Where's Charley? 1966,My 26,57:1
Macbeth 1966,Ag 29,23:4
Landen, Hope
Girls in Uniform 1932,D 31,10:3
Landen, Rick (Miscellaneous)
Streetcar Named Desire, A 1955,Mr 4,18:2
Lander, Frank
School for Wives 1957,Je 20,23:4
Lander, Robert
Mexican Mural; Vera Cruz Interior 1942,Ap 27,19:2
Mexican Mural; Moonlight Scene 1942,Ap 27,19:2
Landers, Richard
Harlem 1929,F 21,30:3
Landers, Scott
All the King's Men 1948,Ja 19,19:2
Landes, Marie
Overcoat, The 1960,S 7,45:1
Landes, Nathalie
Pirates of Penzance, The 1942,F 20,20:2
Landesman, Fran (Lyricist)
Nervous Set, The 1959,My 13,43:1
Landesman, Jay (Original Author)
Nervous Set, The 1959,My 13,43:1
Landesman, Jay (Playwright)
Nervous Set, The 1959,My 13,43:1
Landey, Dora
Bonds of Interest, The 1958,My 7,43:1
Landey, Miriam (Costume Designer)
Lucky Sam McCarver 1950,Ap 15,10:6
Landford, Elsie
Interference 1927,O 19,24:3
Landi, Elissa
Farewell to Arms, A 1930,S 23,30:3
Tapestry in Gray 1935,D 28,10:2
Lady Has a Heart, The 1937,S 27,24:1
Empress of Destiny 1938,Mr 10,16:2
Apology 1943,Mr 23,14:2
Dark Hammock 1944,D 12,27:8
Landi, Gino (Director)
Festa Italiana 1966,S 30,55:1
Landi, Mara
New Girl in Town 1957,My 15,40:1
Fiorello! 1959,N 24,45:3
How to Succeed in Business Without Really Trying 1961,O 16,34:1
It's a Bird . . . It's a Plane . . . It's Superman 1966,Mr 30,34:1
Cabaret 1966,N 21,62:1
Fig Leaves Are Falling, The 1969,Ja 3,19:1
Landi, Michael (Costume Designer)
Fun City 1968,Mr 7,53:2
Landi, Ugo
Romanticismo 1933,My 1,10:5
Landin, Hope
Stepping Sisters 1930,Ap 23,24:2
Old Maid, The 1935,Ja 8,26:1
Season Changes, The 1935,D 24,10:2
Happy Valley, Limited 1936,Je 30,15:1
Landin, Nils
Merry Widow, The 1944,O 9,17:1
Landis, Arthur
Come Angel Band 1936,F 19,17:1
Landis, Carole
Lady Says Yes, A 1945,Ja 11,18:5
Landis, Courteen
Let Them Down, Gently; On Vacation 1968,Ja 31,28:2
Landis, Cullen
Chippies 1929,My 30,23:3
Biarritz 1929,Ag 11,VIII,2:1
Landis, Elizabeth (Costume Designer)
Fools Are Passing Through 1958,Ap 3,24:2
Philanderer, The 1958,My 13,26:2
You Never Can Tell 1958,Je 17,25:1
Widowers' Houses 1959,Mr 3,39:2
Shewing-Up of Blanco Posnet, The 1959,S 19,26:7
Prodigal, The 1960,F 12,23:1
Man and Superman 1960,Ag 17,35:3
Landis, Elizabeth (Producer)
Arms and the Man 1956,O 2,39:4
In Good King Charles's Golden Days 1957,Ja 25,16:1
Beaux' Stratagem, The 1957,Jl 9,25:4
Landis, Helen
Treat 'Em Rough 1926,O 5,26:2
Landis, Jeanette
Persecution and Assassination of Marat As Performed by the Inmates of the Asylum of Charenton Under the Direction of the Marquis de Sade, The 1965,D 28,35:1
Landis, Jessie Royce
Honor of the Family, The 1926,D 27,21:1
Command Performance, The 1928,O 4,27:1
Young Alexander 1929,Mr 13,28:2
Stripped 1929,Je 9,VIII,1:2

Landis, Jessie Royce—Cont
Stripped 1929,O 13,IX,5:1
Stripped 1929,O 22,26:1
Damn Your Honor 1929,D 31,14:3
Solid South 1930,My 11,IX,2:6
Solid South 1930,O 15,27:1
Colonel Satan 1931,Ja 12,24:1
Peter Ibbetson 1931,Ap 9,30:3
Marriage for Three 1931,N 12,30:5
Little Women 1931,D 8,36:2
Domino 1932,Ag 17,13:2
Before Morning 1933,F 10,13:4
Merrily We Roll Along 1934,O 1,14:1
Merrily We Roll Along 1934,O 7,IX,1:1
Ugly Runts, The 1935,Je 11,24:4
Prelude 1935,Je 27,17:4
Substitute for Murder 1935,O 23,18:6
Her Week-End 1936,Mr 20,28:5
Pre-Honeymoon 1936,My 1,19:4
Traveler's Track 1936,Jl 21,13:5
Love From a Stranger 1936,S 22,31:5
Love From a Stranger 1936,S 30,28:1
Miss Quis 1937,Ap 8,20:5
Millionairess, The 1938,Ag 16,22:5
Dame Nature 1938,S 27,24:3
Where There's a Will 1939,Ja 18,16:6
Brown Danube, The 1939,My 18,30:4
Love's Old Sweet Song 1940,Ap 7,I,44:6
Love's Old Sweet Song 1940,Ap 14,IX,3:3
Love's Old Sweet Song 1940,My 3,16:3
Your Loving Son 1941,Ap 5,13:2
Papa Is All 1942,Ja 7,22:2
Papa Is All 1942,Ja 18,IX,1:1
Kiss and Tell 1943,Mr 18,22:1
Kiss and Tell 1943,Mr 28,II,1:1
Winter's Tale, The 1946,Ja 16,18:6
Winter's Tale, The 1946,Ja 20,II,1:1
Little A 1947,Ja 16,31:2
Last Dance, The 1948,Ja 28,27:2
Magnolia Alley 1949,Ap 19,29:2
Larger Than Life 1950,F 8,33:2
Larger Than Life 1950,Mr 12,II,3:7
Richard III 1953,D 10,65:2
Sing Me No Lullaby 1954,O 15,17:2
Sing Me No Lullaby 1954,O 24,II,1:1
Someone Waiting 1956,F 15,26:1
Roar Like a Dove 1964,My 22,40:2
I Knock at the Door 1964,N 26,53:2
Club Bedroom, The 1967,D 6,41:1
Landis, Jessie Royce (Director)
Little Women 1944,D 13,29:2
Lovely Me 1946,D 26,30:4
Landis, Kenesaw M 2d
Betty Behave 1927,Mr 9,28:4
Landis, William
Othello 1953,O 30,28:2
Othello 1955,S 8,27:2
In Good King Charles's Golden Days
1957,Ja 25,16:1
Philanderer, The 1958,My 13,26:2
You Never Can Tell 1958,Je 17,25:1
Widowers' Houses 1959,Mr 3,39:2
Prodigal, The 1960,F 12,23:1
Prodigal, The 1960,F 21,II,1:1
Landis, William (Director)
Beaux' Stratagem, The 1957,Jl 9,25:4
Landis, William (Miscellaneous)
Man of Destiny, The 1956,Ap 26,38:1
On the Harmfulness of Tobacco 1956,Ap 26,38:1
Landis, William (Producer)
Arms and the Man 1956,O 2,39:4
In Good King Charles's Golden Days
1957,Ja 25,16:1
Beaux' Stratagem, The 1957,Jl 9,25:4
Boy Friend, The 1958,Ja 27,24:4
Philanderer, The 1958,My 13,26:2
You Never Can Tell 1958,Je 17,25:1
Widowers' Houses 1959,Mr 3,39:2
Prodigal, The 1960,F 12,23:1
Landolf, George
Time Remembered 1957,N 13,41:2
Landon, B
Letter, The 1927,S 27,30:1
Landon, Elliot
One Way Pendulum 1961,S 19,38:2
Landon, Harold
Walrus and the Carpenter, The 1941,N 10,20:2
Landon, Lois
Cross-Town 1937,Mr 18,21:5
Landon, Margaret (Original Author)
King and I, The 1951,Mr 30,26:2
King and I, The 1951,Ap 8,II,1:1
King and I, The 1956,Ap 19,35:4
King and I, The 1960,My 12,40:1
King and I, The 1963,Je 13,30:2
King and I, The 1964,Jl 7,26:1
King and I, The 1968,My 24,39:1
Landor, Alison
Wisteria Trees, The 1955,F 3,20:2
Landor, Neville
Blossom Time 1938,D 27,12:2
Landou, Anna
Hippolytus 1968,N 20,38:3

Landowska, Wanda
Retablo de Maese Pedro, El 1925,D 30,10:1
Landowski, Marcel (Composer)
Cid, Le 1966,F 12,17:1
Landres, Simm
Night of the Auk 1963,My 22,35:2
Passion of Josef D, The 1964,F 12,29:1
Serjeant Musgrave's Dance 1966,Mr 9,44:1
Let Them Down, Gently; On Vacation
1968,Ja 31,28:2
Let Them Down, Gently; Our Man in Madras
1968,Ja 31,28:2
Billy 1969,Mr 24,56:1
Landron, Jack
Ododo 1970,N 25,26:1
Landrum, Michael
No Place to Be Somebody 1969,D 31,17:1
Landrum, Richard Pablo
Kongi's Harvest 1968,Ap 15,49:1
Landry, Art and His Orchestra
Vaudeville (Palace) 1929,D 30,16:3
Landry, Cy
Spring Is Here 1929,Mr 12,26:1
Me for You 1929,S 22,IX,2:6
Sweet and Low 1930,N 18,28:5
Landsbergis, Algirdas (Playwright)
Five Posts in the Market Place 1961,Mr 6,30:1
Landsman, Bill
Me, Candido! 1956,O 16,36:2
Truce of the Bear 1957,O 24,39:1
Landsman, Dick
Little Darling 1942,O 28,26:2
Landsman, Wolf
Hamlet 1959,S 11,21:4
Man and Superman 1960,N 7,46:2
Worm in Horseradish, A 1961,Mr 14,32:3
Landsteiner, Carl (Composer)
Untitled-Passion Play 1927,Jl 31,VII,1:6
Landstone, Charles
Front of the House 1936,S 21,26:3
Landstone, Charles (Playwright)
Front of the House 1936,S 21,26:3
Behind Your Back 1937,F 14,X,3:1
Landt Trio and White
Vaudeville (Palace) 1932,Mr 7,13:4
Landy, Doris
June Love 1921,Ap 26,20:1
Landy, Robert
King Lear 1968,Je 3,55:4
Lane, Abbe
Oh Captain! 1958,F 5,21:2
Lane, Arthur
Jazz Singer, The 1925,S 15,29:2
Lane, Barbara
Private Life of the Master Race, The
1956,Ja 31,33:3
Lane, Beverley
Priorities of 1942 1942,Mr 13,23:2
Lane, Bobby
Babes in Arms 1937,Ap 15,18:4
Mexican Hayride 1944,Ja 29,9:6
Lane, Bradley F
Love Call, The 1927,O 25,33:1
Lane, Burt (Director)
Chiaroscuro; Judges, The 1963,Je 6,40:8
Chiaroscuro; Kitty, I Hardly Knew You
1963,Je 6,40:8
Chiaroscuro; Maggie French Understands
1963,Je 6,40:8
Lane, Burton (Composer)
Earl Carroll's Vanities 1931,Ag 28,18:7
Hold On to Your Hats 1940,S 12,30:3
Laffing Room Only 1944,D 25,15:4
Finian's Rainbow 1947,Ja 11,23:2
Finian's Rainbow 1948,Ag 29,II,1:1
Jollyanna; Flahooley 1952,Ag 13,17:7
Finian's Rainbow 1953,Mr 7,13:2
Finian's Rainbow 1955,My 19,25:1
Finian's Rainbow 1960,Ap 28,31:1
On a Clear Day You Can See Forever
1965,O 18,44:1
Finian's Rainbow 1967,Ap 6,44:1
Lane, Burton (Lyricist)
Earl Carroll's Vanities 1931,Ag 28,18:7
Lane, Byron
Haiti 1938,Mr 3,16:1
Lane, C Michael (Miscellaneous)
Local Stigmatic, The; That's All 1969,N 4,55:2
Local Stigmatic, The; That's Your Trouble
1969,N 4,55:2
Local Stigmatic, The; Trouble in the Works
1969,N 4,55:2
Local Stigmatic, The; Applicant 1969,N 4,55:2
Local Stigmatic, The; Request Stop 1969,N 4,55:2
Local Stigmatic, The; Interview 1969,N 4,55:2
Local Stigmatic, The; Last to Go 1969,N 4,55:2
Local Stigmatic, The 1969,N 4,55:2
Lane, Charles
Love in E Flat 1967,F 14,38:1
Lane, Charles A (Scenic Designer)
B J One 1931,My 7,21:3
Lane, Constance
Follow Thru 1929,Ja 10,24:3

Lane, Doreen
Sleepy Hollow 1948,Je 4,26:3
Lane, Dorothy
Carmen Jones 1959,Ag 18,25:1
Lane, Dorothy (Original Author)
Happy End 1929,O 27,IX,4:1
Lane, Edith
Siegfried 1930,O 21,34:1
My Romance 1948,O 20,38:5
South Pacific 1955,My 5,39:5
Lane, Elissa (Miscellaneous)
Front Page, The 1968,O 20,85:5
Front Page, The 1969,My 12,54:2
Unseen Hand, The 1970,Ap 2,43:1
Forensic and the Navigators 1970,Ap 2,43:1
Nuns, The 1970,Je 2,35:1
Charley's Aunt 1970,Jl 6,38:1
My House Is Your House 1970,O 16,53:2
Lane, Elmira
Rose of Stamboul, The 1922,Mr 8,11:2
Desert Song, The 1926,D 1,24:2
Lane, Fred
Student Prince, The 1943,Je 9,16:2
Lane, George
Up in Central Park 1945,Ja 29,17:2
Up in Central Park 1947,My 20,29:2
Lane, Gloria
Consul, The 1950,Mr 2,32:3
Consul, The 1950,Mr 16,41:1
Consul, The 1950,Mr 26,II,1:1
Consul, The 1952,O 30,41:2
Saint of Bleecker Street, The 1954,D 28,21:1
Saint of Bleecker Street, The 1955,Ja 2,II,1:1
Consul, The 1957,S 4,40:3
Lane, Grace
If Winter Comes 1923,F 11,VII,1:4
Queen's Husband, The 1931,N 15,VIII,2:1
Lane, Herbert
Pied Piper of Hamelin, The 1950,Ap 3,19:2
Lane, Howard
Thou Desperate Pilot 1927,Mr 8,23:1
Fast Service 1931,N 18,26:3
Scene of the Crime, The 1940,Mr 29,24:1
Lane, Isa
Music Hath Charms 1934,D 31,8:2
Lane, Ivan (Miscellaneous)
Ice Capades 1966,Je 2,50:2
Holiday on Ice 1969,Ag 28,44:1
Lane, James
2 Girls Wanted 1926,S 10,25:3
Four Walls 1927,S 20,33:1
Ringside 1928,Ag 30,13:2
Let Us Be Gay 1929,F 22,19:1
Salt Water 1929,N 27,30:3
That's Gratitude 1930,S 12,28:1
Caught Wet 1931,N 5,29:1
Riddle Me This! 1932,F 26,22:5
Divine Drudge 1933,O 27,22:3
John Brown 1934,Ja 23,22:3
Kill That Story 1934,Ag 30,22:2
Small Miracle 1934,S 27,24:3
Three Men on a Horse 1935,Ja 31,22:3
Mrs O'Brien Entertains 1939,F 9,16:3
Pal Joey 1940,D 26,22:2
Beat the Band 1942,O 15,26:1
Kiss and Tell 1943,Mr 18,22:1
Kiss and Tell 1943,Mr 28,II,1:1
Highland Fling, A 1944,Ap 29,13:2
Barefoot Boy With Cheek 1947,Ap 4,20:2
Look, Ma, I'm Dancin' 1948,Ja 30,20:2
Where's Charley? 1948,O 12,33:2
Lane, Jody
South Pacific 1965,Je 3,25:1
Lane, Joe (Miscellaneous)
Ben Bagley's Shoestring Revues 1970,O 24,22:1
Lane, Joel
On the Town 1959,F 14,15:1
Lane, John
Chips With Everything 1963,O 2,49:1
Lane, Josephine
Live Like Pigs 1965,Je 8,48:2
Lane, Julia
Peg o' My Dreams 1924,My 6,25:3
Music in May 1929,Ap 2,29:1
Lane, Katherine
Hamlet 1934,D 26,19:3
Richard III 1934,D 28,24:3
Lane, Kenneth
Adam's Apple 1929,Je 11,27:5
Most Happy Fella, The 1959,F 11,50:2
Lane, Kent (Producer)
Tenth of an Inch Makes the Difference, A
1962,N 13,44:1
Lane, Lenita
Flame of Love 1924,Ap 22,19:2
Kept 1926,S 18,13:3
Howdy King 1926,D 14,24:4
Congratulations 1929,My 1,28:4
Penny Arcade 1930,Mr 11,24:5
Cradle Call 1930,N 23,IX,1:3
Border-Land 1932,Mr 30,15:5
Blood on the Moon 1934,S 30,IX,3:1
Timber House 1936,S 21,27:5

ne, Leopold
Macbeth 1928,N 20,28:3
ne, Leotabel
Babes in Toyland 1929,D 24,15:3
ne, Lillian
Madcap, The 1928,F 1,31:2
Three Little Girls 1930,Ap 15,29:1
ne, Lola
War Song, The 1928,S 25,29:3
ne, Lupino
Afgar 1920,N 9,13:2
Afgar 1920,N 14,VI,1:1
Ziegfeld Follies 1924,Je 25,26:1
Mikado, The 1925,Ap 13,25:1
Vaudeville (Palace) 1928,Ap 3,32:5
Hollywood Music Box Revue, The
1929,Ja 6,VIII,4:4
Please 1933,N 17,22:2
Please 1933,D 3,IX,7:6
Twenty to One 1935,N 13,24:3
ane, Lupino (Producer)
Twenty to One 1935,N 13,24:3
ane, Margaret
Priorities of 1942 1942,Mr 13,23:2
ane, Margy
Blonde Sinner, The 1926,Jl 15,21:2
ane, Marjorie
Little Nellie Kelly 1922,N 14,16:1
Rise of Rosie O'Reilly, The 1923,D 26,13:4
Merry Malones, The 1927,S 27,30:2
Billie 1928,O 2,34:2
ane, Monica
Tenth of an Inch Makes the Difference, A
1962,N 13,44:1
ane, Ned
Silver Tassie, The 1929,O 25,26:1
ane, Owen
Goat Alley 1921,Je 21,20:2
ane, Peter
Mime and Me, The 1960,Ap 8,27:3
Critic, The 1965,Jl 26,15:2
Lane, Richard
Present Arms 1928,Ap 27,16:2
Vanderbilt Revue, The 1930,N 6,22:6
George White's Scandals 1935,D 26,20:2
Lane, Robert M (Playwright)
Foreplay 1970,D 11,58:2
Lane, Robin
World of Mrs Solomon, The; Second Mrs Aarons,
The 1969,Je 4,37:1
How Much, How Much? 1970,Ap 21,49:1
Lane, Ronald
Mary Stuart 1956,Ap 28,10:2
Lane, Rosemary
Best Foot Forward 1941,S 12,24:4
Best Foot Forward 1941,O 2,28:2
Best Foot Forward 1941,O 26,IX,1:3
Lane, Rusty
Decision 1944,F 3,23:2
Decision 1944,F 13,II,1:1
Lower North 1944,Ag 26,15:4
Bathsheba 1947,Mr 27,40:2
Galileo 1947,D 8,34:2
Mister Roberts 1948,F 19,27:2
Stockade 1954,F 5,14:2
Desperate Hours, The 1955,F 11,20:2
Lane, Ruth (Miscellaneous)
Orphee 1935,Mr 23,10:3
Lane, Sylvia
Bees and the Flowers, The 1946,S 27,19:3
Sleepy Hollow 1948,Je 4,26:3
Lane, Walter
Mecca 1920,O 5,12:2
Lane, William S
Fuente Ovejuna; Sheep Well, The 1936,My 3,II,4:1
Lane and Clare
Mr Winkle's Holliday 1946,Je 24,27:6
Lane Sisters
Greenwich Village Follies 1926,Mr 16,22:2
Vaudeville (Palace) 1927,D 6,26:3
Lanese, Lillian
Rosalinda; Fledermaus, Die 1942,O 29,26:5
Laney, Ben
Annie Get Your Gun 1966,Je 1,42:2
Wonderful Town 1967,My 18,50:1
Look to the Lilies 1970,Mr 30,59:1
Laney, Flora
May Wine 1935,D 6,30:3
Lang, Alois
Untitled-Passion Play 1930,My 9,9:1
Untitled-Passion Play 1930,My 12,1:5
Untitled-Passion Play 1934,My 18,12:1
Untitled-Passion Play 1950,My 19,29:6
Passion of Christ, The 1960,My 18,46:1
Lang, Andrew (Original Author)
Hero Is Born, A 1937,O 2,18:6
Lang, Andrew (Playwright)
Aucassin and Nicolette 1921,Ap 9,9:3
Diable 1926,O 31,VIII,2:4
Charmante Fille, Une 1927,O 2,VIII,2:4
Fragile 1929,F 10,IX,4:6
Trios Henry, Les 1930,Ap 13,X,2:7
Aucassin and Nicolette 1937,F 14,II,3:6

Lang, Anton
Untitled-Passion Play 1922,My 10,21:3
Untitled-Passion Play 1930,My 9,9:1
Untitled-Passion Play 1930,My 12,1:5
Lang, Barbara
Anything Goes 1962,My 16,35:1
Lady or the Tiger?, The 1966,O 19,53:1
Passionella 1966,O 19,53:1
Rondelay 1969,N 6,55:1
Lang, Charles
Pastoral 1939,N 2,26:2
World's Full of Girls, The 1943,D 7,31:2
Down to Miami 1944,S 12,23:5
Overtons, The 1945,F 7,16:6
Lang, Clifford (Composer)
Life Is Like That 1930,D 23,24:3
Lang, Doreen
Make Way for Lucia 1948,D 23,23:5
I Know My Love 1949,N 3,36:1
Season in the Sun 1950,S 29,31:2
Faithfully Yours 1951,O 19,22:5
Lang, Edna
Lady of the Lamp, The 1920,Ag 18,6:4
Lang, Eva
Main Street 1921,O 6,21:1
Lang, Georg Johann (Director)
Passion of Christ, The 1960,My 18,46:1
Lang, Gertrude
Passing Show of 1922, The 1922,S 21,18:2
Blossom Time 1923,My 22,14:3
Blossom Time 1923,Je 1,22:2
Half a Widow 1927,S 13,37:3
Music in May 1929,Ap 2,29:1
Lang, Harold
Mr Strauss Goes to Boston 1945,S 7,20:2
Three to Make Ready 1946,Mr 8,16:2
Look, Ma, I'm Dancin' 1948,Ja 30,20:2
Look, Ma, I'm Dancin' 1948,F 8,II,2:1
Kiss Me, Kate 1948,D 31,10:3
Kiss Me, Kate 1949,Ja 16,II,1:1
Kiss Me, Kate 1949,Ja 30,II,6:5
Kiss Me, Kate 1951,Mr 9,30:5
Make a Wish 1951,Ap 19,38:1
Pal Joey 1952,Ja 4,17:6
Pal Joey 1952,Ja 13,II,1:1
Pal Joey 1952,F 17,II,13:5
Pal Joey 1954,Ap 1,40:5
Pal Joey 1954,Ap 11,II,2:1
Time of Your Life, The 1955,Ja 20,34:1
Time of Your Life, The 1955,Ja 30,II,1:1
Shangri-La 1956,Je 14,40:1
Ziegfeld Follies 1957,Mr 2,19:2
On the Town 1959,Ja 16,36:1
On the Town 1959,Ja 25,II,1:1
I Can Get It for You Wholesale 1962,Mr 23,29:1
Decline and Fall of the Entire World As Seen
Through the Eyes of Cole Porter Revisited, The
1965,Mr 31,24:2
Lang, Harry
Lady Billy 1920,D 15,18:2
Lang, Harry (Producer)
Tin Pan Alley 1928,N 2,29:1
Lang, Howard
Ouija Board, The 1920,Mr 30,9:1
Unwritten Chapter, The 1920,O 12,18:1
Wake Up, Jonathan 1921,My 14,14:1
Wandering Jew, The 1921,O 27,22:1
Abie's Irish Rose 1922,My 24,22:4
East of Suez 1922,S 22,16:3
Thumbs Down 1923,Ag 7,20:1
Dawn 1924,N 25,27:1
Lady of the Rose 1925,My 20,26:4
Jazz Singer, The 1925,S 15,29:2
Silent House, The 1928,F 8,28:5
Strong Man's House, A 1929,S 17,34:3
Doctor X 1931,F 10,25:1
Border-Land 1932,Mr 30,15:5
Silent House, The 1932,N 9,28:3
Lang, Howard (Producer)
Sun Field, The 1942,D 10,33:2
School for Brides 1944,Ag 2,19:4
Good Night Ladies 1945,Ja 18,16:2
Lang, Jeanie
Ballyhoo 1930,D 23,24:1
Lang, Kim
Jimmy Shine 1968,D 6,52:1
Lang, Lester E (Director)
No More Peace 1937,F 27,9:1
Lang, Louis
Goat Alley 1921,Je 21,20:2
Lang, Mark
Hotel Paradiso 1957,Ap 12,22:2
Lang, Matheson
Bad Man, The 1923,F 25,VII,1:7
Bad Man, The 1923,Mr 11,VIII,2:4
Wandering Jew, The 1927,F 2,22:4
Such Men Are Dangerous 1928,O 7,IX,2:7
Chinese Bungalow, The 1929,F 3,VIII,2:1
Jew Suess 1929,O 6,IX,1:1
Elizabeth of England 1931,O 18,VIII,1:3
For the Defense 1935,F 27,17:3
For the Defense; There Go All of Us
1935,Mr 24,VIII,2:3

Lang, Matheson (Director)
Wandering Jew, The 1927,F 2,22:4
Lang, Matheson (Playwright)
Purple Mask, The 1920,Ja 6,18:1
Lang, Matheson (Producer)
Wandering Jew, The 1927,F 2,22:4
Lang, Monica
Anne of the Thousand Days 1948,D 9,49:2
Day After Tomorrow 1950,O 27,25:2
Lang, Morton
Tom Sawyer - Ballad of the Mississippi
1947,D 27,11:3
Lang, Nancy
Pelleas and Melisande 1957,F 20,38:1
Lang, Pearl
Carousel 1945,Ap 20,24:2
Touch and Go 1949,O 14,34:2
Touch and Go 1949,O 30,II,1:1
Peer Gynt 1951,Ja 29,15:2
Lang, Pearl (Choreographer)
Murder in the Cathedral 1966,Je 21,38:1
Lang, Peggy
Buskers, The 1961,O 31,28:1
Giants, Sons of Giants 1962,Ja 8,26:2
Lang, Peter
It's a Boy! 1922,S 20,18:3
Glory 1922,D 26,10:1
Mongrel, The 1924,D 16,28:2
Play, A 1925,F 11,19:2
One Man's Woman 1926,My 26,25:1
Michael and Mary 1929,D 14,23:3
Free for All 1931,S 9,25:1
Lang, Philip J (Composer)
Where's Charley? 1948,O 12,33:2
To Broadway With Love 1964,Ap 30,28:6
Roar of the Greasepaint-the Smell of the Crowd
1965,My 17,46:2
Lang, Philip J (Miscellaneous)
Let Freedom Sing 1942,O 6,18:2
High Button Shoes 1947,O 10,32:2
Arms and the Girl 1950,F 3,28:2
Make a Wish 1951,Ap 19,38:1
Two on the Aisle 1951,Jl 20,13:6
My Fair Lady 1956,Mr 16,20:2
Shangri-La 1956,Je 14,40:1
Li'l Abner 1956,N 16,24:2
New Girl in Town 1957,My 15,40:1
Jamaica 1957,N 1,32:2
Portofino 1958,F 22,8:3
Goldilocks 1958,O 13,33:1
Whoop-Up 1958,D 23,2:7
Redhead 1959,F 6,21:1
Destry Rides Again 1959,Ap 24,24:1
Take Me Along 1959,O 23,22:2
Saratoga 1959,D 8,59:4
Christine 1960,Ap 29,27:1
Hit the Deck 1960,Je 24,32:1
Camelot 1960,D 5,42:1
Carnival! 1961,Ap 14,22:2
Kean 1961,N 3,28:2
Subways Are for Sleeping 1961,D 28,22:1
Mr President 1962,O 22,34:2
Tovarich 1963,Mr 20,5:1
Around the World in 80 Days 1963,Je 24,22:1
Jennie 1963,O 18,35:2
Hello, Dolly! 1964,Ja 17,22:1
My Fair Lady 1964,My 21,43:2
Around the World in 80 Days 1964,Je 29,33:2
Ben Franklin in Paris 1964,O 28,52:1
I Had a Ball 1964,D 16,50:1
Mardi Gras! 1965,Je 28,33:2
Mame 1966,My 25,41:1
Mardi Gras! 1966,Jl 11,32:2
I Do! I Do! 1966,D 6,58:1
Hello, Dolly! 1967,N 13,61:1
How Now, Dow Jones 1967,D 8,53:1
George M! 1968,Ap 11,48:1
My Fair Lady 1968,Je 14,42:1
Maggie Flynn 1968,O 24,52:1
Carnival! 1968,D 13,58:1
Dear World 1969,F 7,33:1
Rondelay 1969,N 6,55:1
Lang, Philip J (Musical Director)
Barefoot Boy With Cheek 1947,Ap 4,20:2
Fanny 1954,N 5,16:1
Fanny 1954,N 21,II,1:1
Plain and Fancy 1955,Ja 28,14:2
Destry Rides Again 1959,My 3,II,1:1
Show Me Where the Good Times Are
1970,Mr 6,32:1
Applause 1970,Mr 31,35:1
Lovely Ladies, Kind Gentlemen 1970,D 29,38:
Lang, Plant
Goat Alley 1921,Je 21,20:2
Lang, Robert
Crucible, The 1965,Ja 20,35:1
Dance of Death, The 1967,O 20,50:1
Love for Love 1967,O 21,17:1
Dance of Death 1967,O 29,II,5:1
Flea in Her Ear, A 1967,O 30,59:1
Love for Love 1967,O 30,59:1
H 1969,F 14,34:2
Way of the World, The 1969,Ag 7,29:1

Lang, Sandy
Vaudeville (Palace) 1931,Ap 6,24:3
Langan, Glenn
Glamour Preferred 1940,N 16,13:2
Kiss for Cinderella, A 1942,Mr 11,22:2
Fancy Meeting You Again 1952,Ja 15,23:2
Langan, Vincent
Holka Polka 1925,O 15,27:2
Oh! Oh! Nurse 1925,D 8,28:4
Langan, William
Patience 1927,My 24,23:2
Langbord, Eva
Panic 1935,Mr 16,18:4
Winterset 1935,S 26,19:2
Winterset 1936,Je 2,35:2
Be So Kindly 1937,F 9,19:4
Two on an Island 1940,Ja 23,17:2
Langdon, Dick
Yokel Boy 1939,Jl 7,12:2
Langdon, Dory (Lyricist)
Harold Arlen Songbook, The 1967,Mr 1,48:1
Langdon, Gwynn (Playwright)
Provincetown Follies, The 1935,N 4,24:3
Langdon, Harry
Jim Jam Jems 1920,O 5,13:2
Vaudeville (Palace) 1929,Mr 18,30:5
Langdon, J Jewett
Merry Wives of Windsor, The 1954,F 17,27:1
Langdon, Laurence
Hamlet 1920,Mr 17,14:2
Langdon, Rose
Jim Jam Jems 1920,O 5,13:2
Langdon, Sue Anne
Apple Tree, The 1967,N 10,61:1
Langdon, Virginia
Lady, The 1923,D 5,23:2
Lange, Bobbi
Something More! 1964,N 11,36:1
Lange, Gordon
Saint's Parade 1930,N 1,23:4
Post Road 1936,Ag 5,15:4
Lange, Hope
Patriots, The 1943,Ja 30,11:2
Lange, Illah
Case of Clyde Griffiths 1936,Mr 14,10:4
Lange, Joy
House of Remsen 1934,Ap 3,26:4
Lange, M
Shadow, The 1923,D 15,16:2
Lange, Minelda
Laughing Woman, The 1936,O 14,30:1
Lange, Stanley
Double Door 1935,Ag 21,22:2
Lange, Sven (Original Author)
Samson and Delilah 1920,D 5,VII,1:1
Lange, Sven (Playwright)
Samson and Delilah 1920,N 18,18:1
Langella, Frank
Immoralist, The 1963,N 8,36:2
Benito Cereno 1964,N 2,62:2
Exhaustion of Our Son's Love, The 1965,O 19,51:1
White Devil, The 1965,D 7,56:1
Yerma 1966,D 9,60:1
Cry of Players, A 1968,N 15,40:1
Langen, Inge
Iphigenia in Aulis; Agamemnon's Death; Electra;
Iphigenia in Delphi 1962,N 11,82:4
Langenbein, Marei
Holiday on Ice 1968,Ag 29,44:1
Holiday on Ice 1969,Ag 28,44:1
Langer, Arthur (Producer)
Passion of Gross, The 1955,Ja 24,20:2
Langer, Francis (Playwright)
Ragged Edge, The 1927,F 13,VII,1:4
Langer, Frantisek (Playwright)
Periphery 1926,O 2,40:6
Peripherie 1926,D 19,VII,4:4
Peripherie 1928,Ja 3,29:1
Camel Through the Needle's Eye, The
1929,Ap 16,32:2
Camel Through the Needle's Eye, The
1929,Ap 28,IX,1:1
Mr Pickwick 1931,Ja 11,VIII,3:5
Engel Unter Uns 1933,Ja 22,IX,1:1
Langer, Joseph
Passion Play, The 1929,Ap 30,32:1
Langer, P (Playwright)
Back Streets 1933,My 18,17:4
Langer, Siegfried
Geisha, The 1931,O 6,35:4
Firefly, The 1931,D 1,23:2
Pirates of Penzance, The 1936,Ap 21,27:5
Langford, Frances
Here Goes the Bride 1931,N 4,31:2
Pure in Heart, The 1934,Mr 21,24:3
Langford, William
Private Lives 1948,O 5,30:2
Private Lives 1948,N 7,II,1:1
Langham, Michael (Director)
Julius Caesar 1955,Je 29,23:3
Henry V 1956,Je 20,27:2
Merry Wives of Windsor, The 1956,Je 21,34:4
Henry V 1956,Je 24,II,1:1

Henry V 1956,Ag 29,25:3
Hamlet 1957,Jl 3,15:2
Two Gentlemen of Verona 1958,Mr 19,35:1
Broken Jug, The 1958,Ap 2,36:1
Henry IV, Part I 1958,Je 25,23:3
Much Ado About Nothing 1958,Je 26,22:1
Merchant of Venice, The 1960,Ap 13,46:5
Romeo and Juliet 1960,Jl 1,14:1
Much Ado About Nothing 1961,Ap 5,31:1
Coriolanus 1961,Je 21,31:2
Love's Labour's Lost 1961,Je 23,19:1
Love's Labour's Lost 1961,Jl 2,II,1:1
Coriolanus 1961,Jl 5,30:1
Taming of the Shrew, The 1962,Je 21,25:1
Cyrano de Bergerac 1962,Ag 1,21:1
Andorra 1963,F 11,5:5
Troilus and Cressida 1963,Je 19,40:2
Cyrano de Bergerac 1963,Je 20,30:1
Timon of Athens 1963,Jl 31,19:2
King Lear 1964,Je 19,36:1
Country Wife, The 1964,Ag 3,16:1
Henry V 1966,Je 8,38:1
Government Inspector, The 1967,Je 15,55:1
Government Inspector, The 1967,Je 25,II,1:2
Antony and Cleopatra 1967,Ag 2,25:1
Antony and Cleopatra 1967,S 17,II,1:1
Government Inspector, The 1967,O 28,34:1
Antony and Cleopatra 1967,O 29,83:4
Prime of Miss Jean Brodie, The 1968,Ja 17,39:1
Prime of Miss Jean Brodie, The 1968,Ja 28,II,1:1
Way of the World, The 1969,Ag 7,29:1
School for Scandal, The 1970,Je 11,51:1
School for Scandal, The 1970,Je 21,II,1:1
Play by Aleksandr Solzhenitsyn, A 1970,O 18,94:1
Play by Aleksandr Solzhenitsyn, A 1970,O 25,II,1:3
Langham, Michael (Playwright)
Cyrano de Bergerac 1962,Ag 1,21:1
Cyrano de Bergerac 1963,Je 20,30:1
Langham, Michael (Producer)
Julius Caesar 1955,Je 29,23:3
Hamlet 1956,Ap 11,28:1
Henry V 1956,Je 24,II,1:1
Hamlet 1957,Jl 7,II,1:1
Langhoff, Wolfgang (Director)
Russian Question, The 1947,My 4,I,54:3
Langhoff, Wolfgang (Producer)
Family Portrait; Familie, Eine 1946,N 11,44:1
Langhoper, Viadanka
Zizi 1964,N 23,51:1
Langhorne, John
Fortuno 1925,D 23,22:1
Langier, Lawrence (Producer)
Fifth Column, The 1940,Ja 27,9:1
Langill, Judson
Blue Eyes 1921,F 22,11:2
Poppy God, The 1921,Ag 30,10:1
White Peacock, The 1921,D 27,10:2
My Girl Friday! 1929,F 13,20:2
Penal Law 2010 1930,Ap 19,14:2
Life and Death of an American 1939,My 20,11:2
Naked Genius, The 1943,O 22,20:5
Langille, Elizabeth
Devil of Pei-Ling 1936,F 21,20:4
Langlen, Paula
Iolanthe 1926,Ap 20,24:2
Pirates of Penzance, The; Slave of Duty, The
1926,D 7,25:1
Mikado, The; Town of Titipu, The 1927,S 19,30:1
Langley, A N (Playwright)
Walrus and the Carpenter, The 1941,N 10,20:2
Langley, Edward
Anne of England 1941,O 8,26:2
Heart of a City 1942,F 13,24:6
Langley, Hubert
Hamlet 1927,Mr 27,VII,2:6
Langley, Margaret
Young Man's Fancy, A 1947,Ap 30,33:2
Langley, Noel (Original Author)
Cage Me a Peacock 1948,Jl 11,II,1:2
Langley, Noel (Playwright)
Forever 1934,N 27,27:2
Farm of Three Echoes 1935,D 2,19:4
Farm of Three Echoes 1939,N 29,18:3
Farm of Three Echoes 1939,D 3,IX,5:4
Cage Me a Peacock 1948,Jl 11,II,1:2
Edward, My Son 1948,O 1,30:2
Edward My Son 1948,O 10,II,1:1
Burning Bush, The 1949,D 17,15:5
Langley, Stuart
Best Foot Forward 1941,O 2,28:2
Langman, Richard
Thesmophoriazusae, The; Goddesses of Athens,
The 1955,D 14,52:4
Langner, Ilse (Playwright)
Heilige aus U.S.A., Die; Saint From USA, The
1931,D 13,VIII,3:5
Langner, Lawrence (Director)
Streets of New York, The 1931,O 7,29:1
Bride the Sun Shines On, The 1931,D 28,20:2
School for Husbands, The 1933,O 17,26:5
Dream of Sganarelle, The 1933,O 17,26:5
Chimes of Corneville, The 1934,Je 29,16:2
Country Wife, The 1935,Jl 2,24:2

Langner, Lawrence (Director)—Cont
Jane Eyre 1937,Ja 3,X,2:1
Madame Bovary 1937,O 6,28:4
Julius Caesar 1955,Jl 13,20:1
Langner, Lawrence (Miscellaneous)
Reunion in Vienna 1931,N 17,31:1
Moon in the Yellow River, The 1932,Mr 1,19:3
Good Earth, The 1932,O 18,23:4
Chrysalis 1932,N 16,15:2
Biography 1932,D 13,25:3
Mary of Scotland 1933,N 28,28:3
Dream Child 1934,S 28,26:2
Sleeping Clergyman, A 1934,O 9,16:1
Long Frontier, The 1935,Jl 23,24:4
And Stars Remain 1936,O 13,32:2
Prelude to Exile 1936,N 22,XI,3:2
But for the Grace of God 1937,Ja 13,21:4
Fifth Column, The 1940,Mr 7,18:2
Somewhere in France 1941,Ap 29,16:8
Ah, Wilderness! 1941,O 3,26:2
Rivals, The 1941,N 18,32:2
Papa Is All 1942,Ja 7,22:2
Rivals, The 1942,Ja 15,24:2
Yesterday's Magic 1942,Ap 15,27:2
Mr Sycamore 1942,N 14,13:2
Innocent Voyage, The 1943,N 16,27:2
Sing Out, Sweet Land! 1944,D 28,24:2
Carousel 1945,Ap 20,24:2
Oklahoma! 1947,My 1,35:3
Allegro 1947,O 11,10:2
Oklahoma! 1951,My 30,15:2
Langner, Lawrence (Mrs) (Playwright)
Pursuit of Happiness, The 1933,O 10,24:4
Susannah and the Elders 1938,Ag 2,15:5
Langner, Lawrence (Original Author)
Arms and the Girl 1950,F 3,28:2
Langner, Lawrence (Playwright)
Matinata 1920,N 14,VI,1:4
Don Juan 1921,S 8,14:2
Another Way Out 1923,My 12,15:4
Another Way Out 1923,My 26,8:4
Henry-Behave 1926,Ag 24,19:4
These Modern Women 1928,F 14,26:2
Family Exit, The 1932,D 14,27:3
Pursuit of Happiness, The 1933,O 10,24:4
Champagne, Sec 1933,O 16,20:2
School for Husbands, The 1933,O 17,26:5
Dream of Sganarelle, The 1933,O 17,26:5
Pursuit of Happiness, The 1934,Je 24,IX,1:4
On to Fortune 1935,Ja 15,23:2
On to Fortune 1935,F 5,22:2
Dr Knock 1936,Jl 14,22:1
Princess Turandot 1937,Ag 3,20:5
Susannah and the Elders 1938,Ag 2,15:5
Susannah and the Elders 1940,O 13,47:7
Susannah and the Elders 1940,O 30,28:2
Winter's Tale, The 1946,Ja 16,18:6
Importance of Wearing Clothes, The
1951,D 11,44:7
Pursuit of Happiness, The 1952,Mr 22,9:2
Langner, Lawrence (Producer)
Noble Prize, The 1933,Jl 4,16:4
Days Without End 1934,Ja 9,19:1
Bride of Torozko, The 1934,Jl 10,24:7
Love on an Island 1934,Jl 24,20:5
Dream Child 1934,Jl 31,20:2
Hide and Seek 1934,Ag 7,20:2
Valley Forge 1934,D 11,28:3
Simpleton of the Unexpected Isles, The
1935,F 19,27:5
Country Wife, The 1935,Jl 2,24:2
Ode to Liberty 1935,Jl 9,24:4
Love for Love 1936,Je 30,15:4
Prelude to Exile 1936,D 1,31:1
Masque of the Kings, The 1937,F 9,19:4
Storm Over Patsy 1937,Mr 9,26:4
To Quito and Back 1937,O 7,30:4
Madame Bovary 1937,N 17,26:2
Ghost of Yankee Doodle, The 1937,N 23,26:3
Wine of Choice 1938,F 22,18:4
Millionairess, The 1938,Ag 16,22:5
Dame Nature 1938,S 27,24:3
Philadelphia Story, The 1939,Mr 29,21:1
Time of Your Life, The 1939,O 26,26:2
Time of Your Life, The 1940,S 24,27:2
Twelfth Night 1940,N 20,26:3
Liberty Jones 1941,F 6,24:2
Iceman Cometh, The 1946,O 10,31:3
You Never Can Tell 1948,Mr 17,31:2
Carousel 1949,Ja 26,28:2
As You Like It 1950,Ja 27,27:2
Come Back, Little Sheba 1950,F 16,28:5
Saint Joan 1951,O 5,23:2
Julius Caesar 1955,Jl 17,II,1:1
Tempest, The 1955,Ag 7,II,1:1
Skin of Our Teeth, The 1961,Mr 6,30:1
Glass Menagerie, The 1961,Mr 6,30:1
Langner, Philip (Miscellaneous)
Tunnel of Love, The 1957,F 14,31:4
Majority of One, A 1959,F 17,28:2
Langner, Philip (Producer)
Seagulls Over Sorrento 1952,S 12,18:4
Langner, Phyllis
Love on an Island 1934,Jl 24,20:5

Langner, Phyllis—Cont
Country Wife, The 1935,Jl 2,24:2
Love for Love 1936,Je 30,15:4
Russet Mantle 1936,Ag 18,15:2
Storm Over Patsy 1937,Mr 9,26:4
Red Harvest 1937,Mr 31,29:2
Petticoat Fever 1937,Jl 6,23:1
Lysistrata 1937,Jl 20,19:3
Princess Turandot 1937,Ag 3,20:5
Romance 1937,Ag 17,23:1

Langner, Ruth (Playwright)
Bride of Torozko, The 1934,Jl 10,24:7

Langner, Ruth (Translator)
Goat Song 1926,Ja 26,18:1
Juarez and Maximilian 1926,O 12,31:1
Volpone 1928,Ap 10,32:1
Karl and Anna 1929,O 8,34:1
Volpone 1930,Mr 11,24:5
Roar China! 1930,O 28,23:1
Bride of Torozko, The 1934,S 14,24:2
Volpone 1957,Ja 8,27:1

Langnese, Rolf (Composer)
Alcestiade 1957,Je 29,11:5

Langs, The
Vaudeville (Palace) 1951,O 17,36:6

Langsley, Stuart (Pvt)
Winged Victory 1943,N 22,24:1

Langsner, Clara
We Americans 1926,O 13,20:4
Four Walls 1927,S 20,33:1
Four Walls 1927,O 2,VIII,1:1
War Song, The 1928,S 25,29:3
God's Thieves 1930,O 27,17:4
Town Lunatics 1933,F 6,11:4
Brooklyn Biarritz 1941,F 28,16:2
Counsellor-at-Law 1942,N 25,17:2

Langstaff, John
Toy Box 1955,D 18,95:3

Langston, Eugene
Possessed, The 1939,O 25,26:2

Langton, Basil
Awake and Sing! 1938,F 21,15:1
Macbeth 1955,O 8,12:6
On Baile's Strand 1959,Ap 13,34:4
This Island Is Mine 1959,Jl 1,26:4
Soldiers 1968,My 2,58:1

Langton, Basil (Director)
Sing Till Tomorrow 1953,D 29,17:2
Cretan Woman, The 1954,My 21,17:2
Cretan Woman, The 1954,S 5,II,1:1
Midsummer Night's Dream, A 1956,Jl 20,9:5
This Island Is Mine 1959,Jl 1,26:4
Fig Leaf in Her Bonnet, A 1961,Je 15,50:1

Langton, Basil (Producer)
Tempest, The 1955,S 3,8:6

Langton, Paul
Harbor Lights 1956,O 5,20:1

Langton, Virginia
Rose Bernd 1922,S 27,17:1

Lanier, Camille
Congai 1928,N 28,24:3

Lanier, Sidney (Miscellaneous)
Jonah! 1966,F 16,52:1
Gnadiges Fraulein, The 1966,F 23,42:1
Mutilated, The 1966,F 23,42:1
Who's Got His Own 1966,O 13,52:1
At the Drop of Another Hat 1966,D 28,30:2
Black Comedy; White Lies 1967,F 13,42:1
Black Comedy 1967,F 13,42:1
Little Murders 1967,Ap 26,38:1

Lanier, Sterling
Betty Behave 1927,Mr 9,28:4

Lanigon, Joe
Three Doors 1925,Ap 24,16:4

Lanin, George (Director)
Kumquat in the Persimmon Tree, The 1962,Je 19,27:2

Lanin, George (Producer)
Kumquat in the Persimmon Tree, The 1962,Je 19,27:2

Lanin, Jay
Henry IV, Part I 1955,S 22,34:2
Montserrat 1961,Ja 9,30:5

Lanin, Lester (Miscellaneous)
Hotel Paradiso 1957,Ap 12,22:2

Lanin, Marilyn
Power of Darkness, The 1959,S 30,33:1

Lanin, Paul (Composer)
Two Little Girls in Blue 1921,My 4,10:3
For Goodness Sake 1922,F 22,13:1
A la Carte 1927,Ag 18,25:3

Lanin, Paul (Lyricist)
A la Carte 1927,Ag 18,25:3

Lanin, Sam and His Roseland Orchestra
Vaudeville (Hippodrome) 1924,Ap 29,12:2

Laning, Eleanor
Faust 1927,Ja 4,20:1
Babbling Brookes 1927,F 26,13:2

Laning, Robert (Director)
Knight of the Burning Pestle, The 1953,O 24,13:2
Men in White 1955,F 26,13:2

Lankston, John
Pal Joey 1961,Je 1,32:1
Funny Girl 1964,Mr 27,15:1

Mikado, The 1968,My 2,59:1
Yeomen of the Guard, The 1968,My 9,53:1
Patience 1968,My 16,52:1

Lanmark, Hildur
Weep for the Virgins 1935,D 2,18:1

Lanner, Susi
Good Hunting 1938,N 22,26:5

Lanning, Don
Who Cares 1930,Jl 9,27:1

Lanning, Jerry
Mame 1966,My 25,41:1
Mame 1967,Ag 15,31:2

Lannon, David
So Proudly We Hail 1938,Ap 9,11:1

Lannon, David (Composer)
So Proudly We Hail 1938,Ap 9,11:1

Lannucci, Michael P (Producer)
This Was Burlesque 1970,F 12,31:1

Lanphier, James
Dark of the Moon 1945,Mr 15,27:2
Scrapbooks 1953,N 6,24:2
Ondine 1954,F 19,23:1

Lansbury, Angela
Hotel Paradiso 1957,Ap 12,22:2
Hotel Paradiso 1957,Ap 21,II,1:1
Taste of Honey, A 1960,O 5,46:1
Taste of Honey, A 1960,N 6,II,1:1
Anyone Can Whistle 1964,Ap 6,36:1
Mame 1966,My 25,41:1
Dear World 1969,F 7,33:1
Dear World 1969,F 16,II,1:1

Lansbury, Bruce (Producer)
First One Asleep, Whistle 1966,F 28,19:1

Lansbury, Edgar (Miscellaneous)
Jackhammer, The 1962,F 6,26:2

Lansbury, Edgar (Producer)
Subject Was Roses, The 1964,My 26,45:1
Alchemist, The 1964,S 15,33:1
First One Asleep, Whistle 1966,F 28,19:1
That Summer-That Fall 1967,Mr 17,33:1
Arms and the Man 1967,Je 23,44:2
Basement, The 1967,O 3,56:1
Fragments 1967,O 3,56:1
Only Game in Town, The 1968,My 21,42:1
To Be Young Gifted and Black; World of Lorraine Hansberry, The 1969,Ja 3,15:1
Millionairess, The 1969,Mr 3,28:1
Promenade 1969,Je 5,56:1
Look to the Lilies 1970,Mr 30,59:1
Engagement Baby, The 1970,My 22,40:1

Lansbury, Edgar (Scenic Designer)
Wise Have Not Spoken, The 1954,F 11,35:2
Sound of Hunting, A 1954,Ap 7,41:1
Misalliance 1955,F 12,10:6
Jackhammer, The 1962,F 6,26:2
Five Evenings 1963,My 10,37:3
Subject Was Roses, The 1964,My 26,45:1

Lanser, Howard
Merry Wives of Windsor, The 1954,F 17,27:1

Lansing, Charlotte
East Wind 1931,O 28,19:1
East Wind 1931,D 11,VIII,4:3
Robin Hood 1932,Ja 28,25:4
Blossom Time 1938,D 27,12:2

Lansing, Eleanor
Vienna at Night 1945,Ap 30,12:4

Lansing, Robert
Trelawney of the 'Wells' 1927,F 1,24:4
Richard III 1953,D 10,65:2
Charley's Aunt 1953,D 23,22:2
Lovers 1956,My 11,23:1
House of Breath, The 1957,Ap 15,23:2
Garden District; Suddenly Last Summer 1958,Ja 8,23:4
Garden District; Suddenly Last Summer 1958,Ja 19,II,1:1
Cue for Passion 1958,N 26,25:2
Cue for Passion 1958,D 7,II,5:1
Great God Brown, The 1959,O 7,48:1
Great God Brown, The 1959,O 18,II,1:1
Cut of the Axe 1960,F 2,38:2
Brightower 1970,Ja 29,32:1

Lansing, Sally
Volpone 1967,Je 30,29:1

Lanteau, William
At War With the Army 1949,Mr 9,32:2
Mrs McThing 1952,F 21,22:1
Remarkable Mr Pennypacker, The 1953,D 31,11:2
What Every Woman Knows 1954,D 23,16:2
Matchmaker, The 1955,D 6,45:6
Li'l Abner 1956,N 16,24:2

Lanti, Al
Damn Yankees 1955,My 6,17:1
Wildcat 1960,D 17,20:2
Bravo Giovanni 1962,My 21,41:2
Drat! the Cat! 1965,O 11,54:2
Walking Happy 1966,N 28,47:1

Lanti, Al (Choreographer)
Out of This World 1955,N 10,44:2

Lantz, Lou (Playwright)
Revolt of the Beavers, The 1937,My 21,19:2

Lantz, Robert (Miscellaneous)
Macbeth 1969,N 21,51:1

Lantz, Robert (Producer)
Nervous Set, The 1959,My 13,43:1
Kean 1961,N 3,28:2

Lanvin, Helen
H M S Pinafore 1942,Ja 22,12:2
Mikado, The 1942,F 4,22:2
Pirates of Penzance, The 1942,F 18,22:2
Iolanthe 1942,F 24,26:4
Gondoliers, The 1942,Mr 4,22:3

Lanvin, Ida
Othello 1929,F 4,21:2

Lanyon, Wilma
Patience 1928,Je 26,29:3
Gang War 1928,Ag 21,27:2

Lanz, Fritz (Director)
Johnny Johnson 1941,My 3,20:2

Lanza, Robert (Costume Designer)
Laura 1947,Je 27,16:1

Lanzarini, Bruno
Servant of Two Masters, The 1960,F 24,42:2

Lanzaroni, Bhen (Miscellaneous)
How to Steal an Election 1968,O 14,56:1

Lanzaroni, Bhen (Musical Director)
How to Steal an Election 1968,O 14,56:1

Lanzi, Dina
Serata D'Inverno; Winter Evening, A 1929,Ap 8,32:5
Strana Avventura, Una; Queer Adventure, A 1930,O 27,17:6
In Fondo Al Cuore; Depths of the Heart, The 1930,D 8,27:1
Cardinale, Il; Cardinal, The 1931,Ja 12,24:2
Delitto e Castigo; Crime and Punishment 1931,Ja 26,20:5
Sansone; Samson 1931,F 9,25:1
Marchese di Priola, Il 1931,Mr 2,19:3
Berretto a Songali, Il; Cap With Bells, The 1931,N 30,16:3
Piccolo Santo, Il; Little Saint, The 1931,D 14,16:4
Park Avenue, Ltd 1932,Mr 4,17:1

Lanzillotti, Leonore
Sound of Music, The 1970,Jl 3,13:1

Lanzmann, Jacques (Lyricist)
Hair 1969,S 13,30:1

Lanzmann, Jacques (Playwright)
Hair 1969,Je 2,53:1

Lapara, Leo
Ecole des Femmes, L'; School for Wives 1951,Mr 19,22:1

Laparcerie, Cora
Black Divan 1921,Ap 10,VI,1:1

Laparcerie, Cora (Producer)
Vive l'Empereur 1926,N 21,VIII,2:1
Notre Dame du Cinema 1936,Ja 19,IX,3:4

Laparcerie, Miarka
Notre Dame du Cinema 1936,Ja 19,IX,3:4

LaPell, Minnie
Jumbo 1935,N 18,20:2

LaPenna, J Anthony
Face, The 1941,N 29,15:3
Common Ground 1945,Ap 26,27:2
Red Gloves 1948,D 6,28:2

Lapham, Harry H
William Had the Words! 1964,Mr 30,36:1

Lapica, Ray (Playwright)
Underground 1952,F 13,33:2

Lapin, David
Diamond Lil 1949,F 7,16:2

Lapointe, Mlle
Bourgeois Gentilhomme, Le 1955,O 26,26:1

Laporte, John H
What a Relief 1935,D 14,10:6

Lappart, Angela
Dear Judas 1947,O 6,26:4

Lappner, Hilda
Rat, The 1925,F 11,19:3

LaPrade, Jan
Hello, Dolly! 1964,Ja 17,22:1

LaPrade, Malcolm (Playwright)
Flame of Love 1924,Ap 22,19:2

LaPrade, Malcolm L (Lyricist)
Will the Mail Train Run Tonight? 1964,Ja 10,18:1

LaPrade, Malcolm L (Playwright)
Will the Mail Train Run Tonight? 1964,Ja 10,18:1

Lapram, Lewis A
Racket, The 1930,N 20,30:6

Lapsien, Ingeborg
Schloss, Das 1968,N 20,35:3

Lapsley, Frances
Ever Green Lady, The 1922,O 12,25:2

Lapsley, Jimmie
Ever Green Lady, The 1922,O 12,25:2

Lapson, Dvorah
Motel Peissi, The Contor's Kid 1934,N 29,33:3

Lapteff, Alexander
Clear All Wires! 1932,S 15,19:1
Clear All Wires! 1932,S 15,19:1

Lapue, Maurice
Strike Up the Band 1930,Ja 15,29:1
New Yorkers, The 1930,D 9,31:1

Larabee, Louise
Angel Island 1937,O 21,26:2
One Thing After Another 1937,D 29,17:2

Larabee, Louise—Cont
Ringside Seat 1938,N 23,24:5
Land Is Bright, The 1941,O 29,26:2
First Million, The 1943,Ap 29,27:4
Sleep No More 1944,S 1,11:5
Carousel 1949,Ja 26,28:2
Carousel 1949,F 6,II,1:1
Miser, The 1950,Mr 27,19:5
Number, The 1951,O 31,33:2
Date With April, A 1953,Ap 16,36:2
Legend of Lovers 1959,O 28,40:3
Farewell, Farewell Eugene 1960,S 28,35:1
Smiling the Boy Fell Dead 1961,Ap 20,28:1
Right Honourable Gentleman, The 1965,O 20,50:2
Carousel 1966,D 16,56:2
Larayne, Sybil
Carnival 1929,Ap 25,32:5
Larchet, J F (Dr) (Composer)
Spell, The 1930,Mr 23,4:3
Cat and the Moon, The 1931,N 8,VIII,4:3
Larcy, Lillian (Pfc)
Swing Sister Wac Swing 1944,Ja 4,20:4
Lardner, Ring (Composer)
June Moon 1929,O 10,34:5
June Moon 1933,My 16,15:5
Lardner, Ring (Lyricist)
June Moon 1929,O 10,34:5
Smiles 1930,N 19,19:2
Lardner, Ring (Original Author)
Love Nest, The 1927,D 23,17:1
Love Nest, The 1928,My 27,VIII,1:1
June Moon 1929,Ag 4,VIII,1:6
Round With Ring, A 1969,O 30,56:1
Lardner, Ring (Playwright)
Ziegfeld Follies 1922,Je 6,18:2
49ers, The 1922,N 7,14:1
49ers, The 1922,N 12,VIII,1:1
Elmer the Great 1928,S 25,29:1
Elmer the Great 1928,S 30,IX,1:1
June Moon 1929,Ag 4,VIII,1:6
June Moon 1929,O 10,34:5
Nine Fifteen Revue, The 1930,F 12,26:2
June Moon 1933,My 16,15:5
Elmer the Great 1940,N 1,32:2
Lardner, Ring Jr (Playwright)
Foxy 1962,Jl 4,12:2
Foxy 1964,F 17,26:1
Laredd, Cora
Vaudeville (Palace) 1931,Je 15,23:5
Largay, Raymond
Mr Sycamore 1942,N 14,13:2
But Not Goodbye 1944,Ap 12,19:2
Large, Mary
Lady From the Sea, The 1935,D 14,11:3
Lari and Conchita
Priorities of 1942 1942,Mr 13,23:2
Larimer, Freddy
Congratulations 1929,My 1,28:4
Larimer, Robert (Composer)
King of the Whole Damn World 1962,Ap 16,32:2
Larimer, Robert (Lyricist)
King of the Whole Damn World 1962,Ap 16,32:2
Larimore, Earle
Made in America 1925,O 15,27:2
Love City, The 1926,Ja 26,18:2
Nirvana 1926,Mr 4,19:1
Juarez and Maximilian 1926,O 12,31:1
Ned McCobb's Daughter 1926,N 30,26:2
Silver Cord, The 1926,D 21,21:1
Second Man, The 1927,Ap 12,24:3
Doctor's Dilemma, The 1927,N 22,33:1
Strange Interlude 1928,Ja 31,28:1
Strange Interlude 1928,F 5,VIII,1:1
Man's Estate 1929,Ap 2,28:2
Man's Estate 1929,Ap 28,IX,1:1
R U R 1930,F 18,28:1
Marco Millions 1930,Mr 4,24:4
Volpone 1930,Mr 11,24:5
Hotel Universe 1930,Ap 15,29:1
Month in the Country, A 1930,N 23,IX,1:3
Melo 1931,Ap 17,26:6
Mourning Becomes Electra; Hunted, The 1931,O 27,22:1
Mourning Becomes Electra; Haunted, The 1931,O 27,22:1
Mourning Becomes Electra 1931,N 1,VIII,1:1
Biography 1932,D 13,25:3
Days Without End 1933,D 31,IX,2:2
Days Without End 1934,Ja 14,IX,1:1
Too Many Boats 1934,S 12,26:3
Dark Victory 1934,N 10,18:2
It's You I Want 1935,F 6,23:3
To See Ourselves 1935,My 1,25:2
Meet the Prince 1935,Jl 9,24:5
Meet the Prince 1935,Ag 6,20:4
Abide With Me 1935,N 22,19:2
Ethan Frome 1936,N 15,XI,2:1
Larimore, Louis
Playing the Game 1927,D 20,32:5
Lark, Tobi
Hair 1970,Ja 13,39:1
Larkcom, Harry
Passing of the Third Floor Back, The 1924,F 8,19:4

Larkey, Joan (Lighting Director)
J B 1958,Ap 24,37:1
Brouhaha 1960,Ap 27,31:2
She Stoops to Conquer 1960,N 2,42:5
Plough and the Stars, The 1960,D 7,56:2
Octoroon, The 1961,Ja 28,13:1
Hamlet 1961,Mr 17,17:1
Policemen, The 1961,N 22,24:2
Androcles and the Lion 1961,N 22,24:2
Dark Lady of the Sonnets, The 1961,D 15,48:1
Man With a Load of Mischief, The 1966,N 7,65:1
To Clothe the Naked 1967,Ap 28,30:1
Month of Sundays 1968,S 17,50:1
Don't Shoot Mable It's Your Husband 1968,O 23,34:1
Larkey, Joan (Miscellaneous)
Hidden Stranger 1963,Ja 10,5:5
Larkey, Joan (Scenic Designer)
Dark Lady of the Sonnets, The 1961,D 15,48:1
Man With a Load of Mischief, The 1966,N 7,65:1
To Clothe the Naked 1967,Ap 28,30:1
Salvation 1969,S 25,55:1
Larkin, George
Trapped 1928,S 12,25:3
Larkin, John
Victors, The 1948,D 27,17:2
Larkin, John Jr (Playwright)
Society Girl 1931,D 31,16:1
Larkin, Margaret (Composer)
Round-Up, The 1932,Mr 8,19:4
Larkin, Margaret (Playwright)
Little Theatre Tournament; El Cristo 1926,My 8,21:2
El Cristo 1926,My 9,II,1:4
Larkin, Peter (Costume Designer)
Protective Custody 1956,D 29,8:7
Larkin, Peter (Lighting Director)
Dial 'M' for Murder 1952,O 30,41:2
Teahouse of the August Moon, The 1953,O 16,32:1
Teahouse of the August Moon, The 1956,N 9,33:2
Larkin, Peter (Scenic Designer)
Wild Duck, The 1951,D 27,17:1
First Lady 1952,My 29,18:5
Dial 'M' for Murder 1952,O 30,41:2
Teahouse of the August Moon, The 1953,O 16,32:1
Teahouse of the August Moon, The 1953,O 25,II,1:1
Ondine 1954,F 19,23:1
Ondine 1954,F 28,II,1:1
Teahouse of the August Moon, The 1954,Ap 23,23:5
Peter Pan 1954,Jl 20,15:3
Teahouse of the August Moon, The 1954,S 12,II,1:1
Peter Pan 1954,O 21,30:2
Peter Pan 1954,O 31,II,1:1
Inherit the Wind 1955,Ap 22,20:2
Teahouse of the August Moon, The 1955,My 10,24:1
Inherit the Wind 1955,S 25,II,1:1
No Time for Sergeants 1955,O 21,32:2
No Time for Sergeants 1955,N 6,II,1:1
Shangri-La 1956,Je 14,40:1
New Faces of 1956 1956,Je 15,32:1
Teahouse of the August Moon, The 1956,N 9,33:2
Protective Custody 1956,D 29,8:7
Good as Gold 1957,Mr 8,22:2
Compulsion 1957,O 25,21:1
Miss Isobel 1957,D 27,22:1
Blue Denim 1958,F 28,17:1
Goldilocks 1958,O 13,33:1
Goldilocks 1958,O 19,II,1:1
Shadow of a Gunman, The 1958,N 21,26:1
Shadow of a Gunman, The 1958,N 30,II,1:1
First Impressions 1959,Mr 20,28:1
Only in America 1959,N 20,35:1
Greenwillow 1960,Mr 9,38:1
Wildcat 1960,D 17,20:2
Giants, Sons of Giants 1962,Ja 8,26:2
Nowhere to Go But Up 1962,N 12,36:2
Marathon '33 1963,D 23,20:1
Seagull, The 1964,Ap 6,36:1
Crucible, The 1964,Ap 7,30:2
Great Indoors, The 1966,F 2,23:1
Happily Never After 1966,Mr 11,37:1
Hail Scrawdyke! 1966,N 29,50:1
Scuba Duba 1967,O 11,36:1
Sheep on the Runway 1970,F 2,28:3
Blancs, Les 1970,N 16,48:4
Larking, Lambert
And Be My Love 1934,Ja 19,25:2
Larkins, Ellis
Pousse-Cafe 1966,Mr 19,19:2
Larkins, Grady (Lighting Director)
Galileo 1968,D 1,88:4
Larkins, Grady (Scenic Designer)
Galileo 1968,D 1,88:4
Larl Becham Trio, The
Josephine Baker and Her Company 1964,F 5,30:1
Larmon, Leila (Costume Designer)
My House Is Your House 1970,O 16,53:2
Larmore, James
Russet Mantle 1936,Ja 17,15:5
Daughters of Atreus 1936,O 15,33:1

Larmore, James—Cont
Good Hunting 1938,N 22,26:5
Larned, Ellen
Peer Gynt 1923,F 6,14:1
Within the Gates 1934,O 23,23:1
Larned, Mel
Shoestring Revue 1955,Mr 1,22:2
Larnen, Brendan (Playwright)
Angelic Doctor 1953,Ap 14,30:2
Connelly vs Connelly 1961,F 18,11:3
My Beginning 1962,Ja 31,21:1
Patrick--The First 1965,F 19,25:1
Larner, Elizabeth
Wish You Were Here 1953,O 11,83:5
Camelot 1964,Ag 20,34:1
Larnie, Thomas Mac
Treat 'Em Rough 1926,O 5,26:2
LaRoche, Mark
We're Civilized? 1962,N 9,30:1
International Playgirls '64 1964,My 22,40:2
Larocque, Joseph
It's Only Natural 1922,Ap 21,13:2
Larocque, Theodora
Charm School, The 1920,Ag 3,12:1
LaRouge, Wilbur
Free Soul, A 1928,Ja 13,26:5
Larrabeiti, Mariana
Road to Happiness, The 1927,My 3,24:1
Girl and the Cat, The 1927,My 6,21:2
Blind Heart, The 1927,My 8,30:2
Cradle Song 1927,My 10,24:4
Pygmalion 1927,My 12,25:2
Larranaga, Carmen
Cape Cod Follies 1929,S 19,37:2
Larric, Jack (Playwright)
Easy Mark, The 1924,Ag 27,14:2
Made in France 1930,O 19,IX,3:4
Made in France 1930,N 12,21:1
Larrimore, Francine
Nice People 1921,Mr 3,11:1
Nice People 1921,Mr 6,VI,1:2
Nobody's Business 1923,O 23,17:1
Nobody's Business 1923,O 28,VIII,1:1
Nancy Ann 1924,Mr 9,VIII,2:3
Nancy Ann 1924,Ap 1,18:1
Nancy Ann 1924,Ap 6,VIII,1:1
Parasites 1924,N 20,21:1
Parasites 1924,N 23,VIII,1:1
His Queen 1925,My 12,26:1
Arms and the Man 1925,O 4,IX,1:1
This Was a Man 1926,N 24,27:1
Chicago 1926,D 31,11:1
Let Us Be Gay 1929,F 22,19:1
Brief Moment 1931,O 25,VIII,2:1
Brief Moment 1931,N 10,28:2
Shooting Star 1933,Je 13,22:2
Spring Song 1934,O 2,18:2
ANTA Album 1950,Ja 30,13:2
Larrimore, Martha
South Pacific 1968,Je 30,54:2
South Pacific 1969,Jl 7,27:1
Larrimore, Stella
Samson and Delilah 1920,N 18,18:1
Don Juan 1921,S 8,14:2
House Divided, The 1923,N 12,14:1
Arms and the Man 1925,S 15,28:1
Phantom Ship, The 1926,Je 27,VII,3:1
Larsen, Bjorn (Director)
Tivoli Pantomine 1968,S 9,57:2
Larsen, Carl (Playwright)
Plot Against the Chase Manhattan Bank, The 1963,N 27,29:1
Larsen, Johannes (Lighting Director)
Boyd's Daughter 1940,O 12,20:2
Larsen, Johannes (Miscellaneous)
Twelfth Night 1941,D 3,32:2
Larsen, Johannes (Scenic Designer)
Culbin Sands 1935,Mr 23,10:3
Three Sisters, The 1939,O 16,23:1
Boyd's Daughter 1940,O 12,20:2
Return Engagement 1940,N 2,19:2
First Crocus, The 1942,Ja 3,14:6
Larsen, Pierre (Costume Designer)
Misanthrope, Le 1960,Mr 9,38:3
Larsen, Sven (Choreographer)
Autumn Manoeuvers 1938,N 27,IX,3:6
Larsen, Sven Aage (Director)
My Fair Lady 1962,Je 14,24:1
Larsen, Thomas
Immodest Violet 1920,Ag 25,6:2
Larsen, William
Midsummer Night's Dream, A 1957,Je 27,21:3
Crucible, The 1958,Mr 12,36:1
Legend of Lovers 1959,O 28,40:3
Fantasticks, The 1960,My 4,55:2
As You Like It 1961,Je 17,13:2
Macbeth 1961,Je 19,31:1
School for Scandal, The 1962,Mr 19,36:1
Seagull, The 1962,Mr 22,42:1
Tavern, The 1962,Ap 5,29:1
Pimpernel! 1964,Ja 7,26:6
Tavern, The 1964,Mr 6,39:2
Lower Depths, The 1964,Mr 31,30:1

Larsen, William—Cont

Tragical Historie of Doctor Faustus, The
  1964,O 6,34:2
Half a Sixpence 1965,Ap 26,38:2
Halfway up the Tree 1967,N 8,52:1
Dear World 1969,F 7,33:1
Larson, Brent (Playwright)
Chicago 70 1970,My 26,33:1
Larson, Carolyn
Sold to the Movies; Life Size 1970,Je 18,54:2
Larson, Eileen
I Gotta Get Out 1947,S 26,27:2
Larson, Harry
Side-Show 1931,My 16,13:1
Larson, J H (Mrs)
One Woman's Husband 1920,Mr 23,9:3
Larson, Jack (Playwright)
Collision Course; Chuck 1968,My 9,55:2
Chuck 1968,My 19,II,1:1
Larson, John
Fatal Witness, The 1946,N 20,43:2
Larson, John (Director)
Angel in the Pawnshop 1951,Ja 19,20:3
Long Watch, The 1952,Mr 21,19:5
Larson, Pat
Frankie and Johnny 1952,O 29,37:2
Larson, Paul
Father, The 1949,N 17,36:2
Dylan 1964,Ja 20,18:1
Investigation, The 1966,O 5,40:1
Larson, Stig
Ice Capades 1953,S 11,25:1
Ice Capades 1954,S 16,37:1
Ice Capades 1955,S 15,38:1
Ice Capades 1956,S 13,41:2
Ice Capades 1957,S 5,33:2
Larson, Yngve (Scenic Designer)
Miss Julie 1962,My 17,31:1
Larsson, Karl (Scenic Designer)
Sonya's Search for the Christmas Star
  1929,D 14,24:6
LaRue, Bartell
Night Circus, The 1958,D 3,44:1
LaRue, Charles
Dead End 1935,O 29,17:2
First Lady 1935,N 27,17:4
Larue, Esco
Ice Capades 1952,S 12,18:1
LaRue, Eugene
Right to Love, The 1925,Je 9,16:4
LaRue, Jack
Crooked Square, The 1923,S 11,10:2
Crime 1927,F 23,27:3
Los Angeles 1927,D 20,32:3
Midnight 1930,D 30,25:1
LaRue, Roy
What Price Glory 1924,S 6,14:3
Lary, Betty June
Latent Heterosexual, The 1968,Mr 22,52:1
Macbeth 1968,N 30,49:3
LaSalle, Richard
Rust 1924,F 1,12:1
Lascano, Vincent
Passenger to Bali, A 1940,Mr 15,26:2
Lascarides, Sp
Oedipus Tyrannus 1952,N 25,35:2
Lascelles, Ernita
Madras House, The 1921,O 31,18:2
Back to Methuselah (Part I: In the Beginning); In
  the Beginning (Back to Methuselah, Part I)
  1922,F 28,17:2
Back to Methuselah (Part IV: The Tragedy of an
  Elderly Gentleman); Tragedy of an Elderly
  Gentleman, The (Back to Methuselah, Part IV)
  1922,Mr 7,11:1
Back to Methuselah (Part V: As Far as Thought
  Can Reach); As Far as Thought Can Reach (Back
  to Methuselah, Part V) 1922,Mr 14,11:2
From Morn to Midnight 1922,My 22,17:2
Dice of the Gods, The 1923,Ap 6,20:2
Living Mask, The 1924,Ja 22,15:1
Mongrel, The 1924,D 16,28:2
Adam Solitaire 1925,N 7,19:2
One Wife or Another 1933,F 7,23:6
Service for Two 1935,Ag 20,25:1
Lascelles, Kendrew
Wait a Minim! 1966,Mr 8,43:1
Lascelles, Kendrew (Choreographer)
Wait a Minim! 1966,Mr 8,43:1
Lascoe, Henry
Journey to Jerusalem 1940,O 7,21:2
Brooklyn, U S A 1941,D 22,24:2
Rugged Path, The 1945,N 12,17:2
Tenting Tonight 1947,Ap 3,32:2
Magic Touch, The 1947,S 4,30:1
Me and Molly 1948,F 27,27:2
Talent '49 1949,Ap 13,39:4
Now I Lay Me Down to Sleep 1950,Mr 3,21:2
Call Me Madam 1950,O 13,25:1
Wonderful Town 1953,F 26,22:3
Wonderful Town 1954,My 7,II,1:1
Silk Stockings 1955,F 25,17:3
Romanoff and Juliet 1957,O 11,24:1
Carnival! 1961,Ap 14,22:2

Arturo Ui 1963,N 12,49:1
Lase, Henry
These Days 1928,N 13,36:2
False Dreams, Farewell 1934,Ja 16,18:3
Libel! 1935,D 21,10:5
Cyrano de Bergerac 1936,Ap 28,17:1
Lasell, Fen (Costume Designer)
Puntila 1959,My 15,26:2
Lasell, John
Golden Six, The 1958,O 27,31:2
Doctor and the Devils, The 1959,Ja 21,27:8
Puntila 1959,My 15,26:2
Big Knife, The 1959,N 13,25:1
Roman Candle 1960,F 4,34:2
Laselle, Verneda
On Strivers' Row 1946,Mr 1,17:2
Laseur, Cees
They Came by Night 1937,Jl 25,X,1:3
Lash, Isidor (Playwright)
Russian Love 1930,N 27,32:3
His Jewish Girl 1936,D 9,34:1
Three Men and a Girl 1939,F 6,9:3
Lasher, Albert C (Producer)
Bible Salesman, The 1961,F 21,40:1
Oldest Trick in the World, The 1961,F 21,40:1
Lashin, Orrie (Playwright)
Class of '29 1936,My 16,10:3
Lashley, Donald
Cape Smoke 1925,F 17,19:1
Lashly, James
Tom Paine 1969,Mr 30,71:2
Laska, Howard (Playwright)
We've Got to Have Money 1923,Ag 21,12:1
Laska, Lucia
Jimmie's Women 1927,S 27,30:3
Triumph 1935,O 15,18:5
Laskaris, Ion C (Miscellaneous)
York Nativity Play, The 1956,D 5,49:2
Laskawy, Harris
Man and Superman 1970,F 24,48:1
Moby Dick 1970,Je 3,52:1
Hamlet 1970,O 27,54:2
Rosencrantz and Guildenstern Are Dead
  1970,N 19,39:3
Laskawy, Harris (Miscellaneous)
Hamlet 1970,O 27,54:2
Laske, Gene (Miscellaneous)
Evening With Mike Nichols and Elaine May, An
  1960,O 10,37:1
Lasker, Harvey (Director)
Old Bucks and New Wings 1962,N 6,39:4
Lasker, Harvey (Lyricist)
Old Bucks and New Wings 1962,N 6,39:4
Lasker, Harvey (Playwright)
Old Bucks and New Wings 1962,N 6,39:4
Lasker, Harvey (Producer)
Old Bucks and New Wings 1962,N 6,39:4
Laskey, Charles
I Married an Angel 1938,My 12,26:2
Louisiana Purchase 1940,My 29,19:2
Oklahoma! 1943,N 14,II,1:1
Lasko, Gene (Director)
Gianni Schicci 1969,F 25,36:1
Blueprints 1969,F 25,36:1
Tale of Kasane, The 1969,F 25,36:1
Laskofsky, Philip (Composer)
Little Bandit 1935,Ap 19,24:2
Souls for Sale 1936,S 21,27:6
Lasky, Jesse L (Producer)
Quiet, Please! 1940,O 20,IX,2:3
Quiet, Please! 1940,N 9,20:3
Lasley, Blythe
Passion of Christ, The 1960,My 18,46:1
Laslo, Mary
Born Yesterday 1946,F 5,18:2
Treatment, The 1968,My 10,54:7
Lasons, Fothringham
Money Lender, The 1928,Ag 28,27:3
Lasser, Louise
Third Ear, The 1964,My 29,16:1
Henry, Sweet Henry 1967,O 24,51:2
Lime Green 1969,Mr 27,54:2
Chinese, The 1970,Mr 11,42:2
Lassiter, Mildred
Sweet River 1936,O 29,30:2
Lassner, Margot
Hidden River, The 1957,Ja 24,32:1
Blood Wedding 1958,Ap 1,35:1
Cheri 1959,O 13,44:1
Lasswell, Mary (Original Author)
Suds in Your Eye 1944,Ja 13,15:5
LaSusa, Don (Miscellaneous)
Country Wife, The 1957,N 28,56:1
Laszlo, Miklos (Playwright)
She Loves Me 1963,Ap 24,39:1
Latchford, George
Red Eye of Love 1961,Je 13,28:1
Lateiner, Joseph (Original Author)
Jewish Heart, The 1939,Ja 25,16:6
Lateiner, Joseph (Playwright)
Little Clown, The 1930,Mr 15,23:3
Lateiner, S (Miss)
Love and Politics 1929,O 21,30:7

Latell, Alfred
Untitled-Revue 1926,O 26,18:3
Count Me In 1942,O 9,24:2
Latell, Blanche
Mad Honeymoon, The 1923,Ag 8,10:1
Go West, Young Man 1923,N 13,25:2
Oh, Please! 1926,D 22,24:3
Latessa, Dick
Miss Emily Adam 1960,Mr 30,43:1
Pimpernel! 1964,Ja 7,26:6
Education of H*Y*M*A*N K*A*P*L*A*N, The
  1968,Ap 5,57:1
Honor and Offer 1968,D 1,II,3:1
Latham, Cynthia
Right to Strike, The 1921,O 25,20:1
Pelican, The 1925,S 22,23:2
Foolscap 1933,Ja 12,21:2
Flare Path 1942,D 24,20:2
Suds in Your Eye 1944,Ja 13,15:5
Ring Around the Moon 1950,N 24,30:1
Buy Me Blue Ribbons 1951,O 18,33:2
Boy With a Cart, The 1954,Ap 5,19:2
Country Wife, The 1957,N 28,56:1
Redhead 1959,F 6,21:1
Living Room, The 1962,N 22,43:5
Photo Finish 1963,F 14,5:2
Georgy 1970,F 27,26:1
Arsenic and Old Lace 1970,N 5,59:1
Latham, Eric
Searching Wind, The 1944,Ap 13,25:2
Latham, Fred G (Director)
Happy-Go-Lucky 1926,O 1,27:2
Latham, Joseph
Jolly Roger, The 1923,Ag 31,10:4
Cyrano de Bergerac 1923,N 2,14:1
Henry V 1928,Mr 16,26:2
War Song, The 1928,S 25,29:3
Remains to Be Seen 1951,O 4,37:1
Latham, Lorraine
Lady Comes Across, The 1942,Ja 10,10:2
Latham, Louise
Major Barbara 1956,O 31,27:1
Month in the Country, A 1959,Mr 2,32:2
Summer of the Seventeenth Doll 1959,O 14,52:1
Isle of Children 1962,Mr 17,16:2
Latham, S L (Producer)
Lady Detained, A 1935,Ja 10,23:3
Lathbury, Stanley
Hamlet 1936,N 11,54:2
Lathom, Lord (Playwright)
Red Blinds 1926,O 1,27:1
Lathrop, Dorothy (Scenic Designer)
Without the Walls 1921,Mr 28,8:1
Lathrop, Jack
Between the Devil 1937,D 23,24:5
Lathrop, Julia
All the Living 1938,Mr 25,14:4
Lathrop, Marian (Costume Designer)
Lend an Ear 1959,S 25,20:5
Courtyard 1960,Mr 1,28:1
Roots 1961,Mr 7,40:2
Mr Simian 1963,O 22,44:1
Latimer, Ed
Sleep No More 1944,S 1,11:5
Gentleman From Athens, The 1947,D 10,42:4
Latimer, Edward B
Devil's Little Game, The 1932,Ag 2,20:4
Latimer, Ken
Days Between, The 1965,Je 4,39:1
Latent Heterosexual, The 1968,Mr 22,52:1
Macbeth 1968,N 30,49:3
Latimer, Lenore (Choreographer)
Feast of Panthers 1961,Mr 21,32:1
Latimer, Louise
When in Rome 1934,F 28,22:6
Scene of the Crime, The 1940,Mr 29,24:1
LaTouche, John
Pepper Mill 1937,Ja 6,19:4
LaTouche, John (Composer)
Banjo Eyes 1941,N 8,10:6
Lady Comes Across, The 1942,Ja 10,10:2
Littlest Revue, The 1956,My 23,37:2
LaTouche, John (Lyricist)
Cabin in the Sky 1940,O 26,19:2
Cabin in the Sky 1940,N 3,IX,1:1
Banjo Eyes 1941,N 8,10:6
Banjo Eyes 1941,D 26,20:2
Lady Comes Across, The 1942,Ja 10,10:2
Rhapsody 1944,N 23,37:2
Polonaise 1945,O 8,20:2
Beggar's Holiday 1946,D 27,13:3
Beggar's Holiday 1947,Ja 26,II,1:1
Golden Apple, The 1954,Mr 12,15:2
Golden Apple, The 1954,Mr 21,II,1:1
Vamp, The 1955,N 11,30:1
Littlest Revue, The 1956,My 23,37:2
Candide 1956,D 3,40:2
Candide 1956,D 9,II,5:1
Cabin in the Sky 1964,Ja 22,32:1
LaTouche, John (Original Author)
Beggar's Holiday 1946,D 27,13:3
LaTouche, John (Playwright)
Pins and Needles 1939,Ap 21,26:2

LaTouche, John (Playwright)—Cont
Sing for Your Supper 1939,Ap 25,18:6
Beggar's Holiday 1947,Ja 26,II,1:1
Golden Apple, The 1954,Mr 12,15:2
Golden Apple, The 1954,Mr 21,II,1:1
Vamp, The 1955,N 11,30:1
Riding Hood Revisited 1961,Ja 4,26:1
Willie the Weeper 1961,Ja 4,26:1
Eccentricities of Davy Crockett, The 1961,Ja 4,26:1
Golden Apple, The 1962,F 13,38:2
LaTouche, John (Translator)
Pepper Mill 1937,Ja 6,19:4
From Vienna 1939,Je 21,26:2
Latour, Clement
Ti-Coq 1951,F 10,10:2
Latowicz, Karol
Mirele Efros 1967,O 20,55:1
Mother Courage 1967,N 17,55:1
Trees Die Standing, The 1969,O 13,52:1
Mirele Efros 1969,D 26,41:1
Latronica, Patrick (Miscellaneous)
Hello and Goodbye 1968,N 13,36:2
Hello and Goodbye 1969,S 19,54:1
Latson, Claude
Merchant of Venice, The 1955,F 23,23:2
Latta, Robert
New York Idea, The 1948,Ag 18,29:2
Peg o' My Heart 1948,Ag 25,29:2
Devil's Disciple, The 1950,Ja 26,23:2
Master Builder, The 1955,D 18,42:7
Lattes, Marcel (Composer)
Diable a Paris, Le 1927,N 13,IX,4:2
Lattimer, Armithine
In Abraham's Bosom 1926,D 31,10:2
Lattimore, Richmond (Translator)
Trojan Women, The 1957,Mr 19,42:7
Oresteia 1966,Je 30,29:1
Lattuca, Vincent
Trumpets and Drums 1969,O 13,52:1
Latvala, William
Electra 1958,My 10,17:7
Latzell, William R (Producer)
Finian's Rainbow 1947,Ja 11,23:2
Latzer, Louis
Vegetable, The, or From President to Postman
1929,Ap 11,32:3
Latzer, Louis G
Paradise Lost 1935,D 10,31:5
Latzer, Louis John
Rutherford and Son 1927,Ap 13,29:2
Subway, The 1929,Ja 26,15:1
At the Bottom 1930,Ja 10,24:3
They Shall Not Die 1934,F 22,24:4
Power of the Press 1936,Ap 6,19:2
Don't Throw Glass Houses 1938,D 28,24:4
Laubenthal, Hannsgeorg
Don Karlos 1935,Jl 28,X,1:6
Laubert, Arthur
Peripherie 1928,Ja 3,29:1
Lebende Leichnam, Der, Der; Living Corpse, The
1928,Ja 24,26:2
Laudati, Anthony (Producer)
How Beautiful With Shoes 1935,N 29,24:1
Lauder, Harry (Sir)
Vaudeville (Lexington) 1921,O 18,20:2
Untitled-Revue 1922,O 3,22:4
Untitled-Revue 1924,F 19,12:1
Untitled-Revue 1926,O 26,18:3
Vaudeville (Knickerbocker) 1928,F 19,VIII,1:1
Untitled-Revue 1930,Ap 22,33:2
Laudicina, Dino
King of the Dark Chamber 1961,F 10,21:1
Rosencrantz and Guildenstern Are Dead
1967,O 17,53:1
Laufer, Murray (Scenic Designer)
Salad Days 1958,N 11,24:1
Laufkoetter, Hilda
It's A Gift 1945,Mr 13,18:7
Laughlin, Ben
Booster, The 1929,O 25,26:2
Geraniums in My Window 1934,O 27,20:6
Sun Kissed 1937,Mr 11,20:2
One Thing After Another 1937,D 29,17:2
Pie in the Sky 1941,D 23,26:5
I'll Take the High Road 1943,N 10,28:3
Odds on Mrs Oakley, The 1944,O 3,18:8
Quare Fellow, The 1958,N 28,34:1
Laughlin, Catheryn
Stage Door 1936,O 23,26:3
My Heart's in the Highlands 1939,Ap 14,29:2
Swingin' the Dream 1939,N 30,24:2
Laughlin, Edgar
Orpheus in Hades 1930,D 16,30:1
King Oedipus 1933,Ja 16,12:4
Laughlin, Henry A
Clarence 1923,My 14,18:4
Laughlin, Jane
Around the World in 80 Days 1963,Je 24,22:1
Around the World in 80 Days 1964,Je 29,33:2
Walking Happy 1966,N 28,47:1
Laughlin, Kay
Case of Clyde Griffiths 1936,Mr 14,10:4
Laughlin, Sharon
If Five Years Pass 1962,My 11,37:1

One by One 1964,D 2,60:1
Henry IV, Part I 1968,Je 30,54:7
Henry IV, Part II 1968,Jl 2,33:1
Huui, Huui 1968,N 25,58:1
Mod Donna 1970,My 4,48:1
Mod Donna 1970,My 10,II,1:1
Laughlin (Scenic Designer)
Nativite, La; Miraculous Birth and the Midwives,
The; Trois Rois, Les; Trois Maries, Les;
Lamentation of the Virgin Mary, The; Magdalen,
The; Six Miracle Plays 1933,F 6,11:3
Laughton, Charles
Happy Husband, The 1927,Jl 10,VII,2:3
Paul I 1927,O 23,VIII,4:1
Man With Red Hair, A 1928,Mr 25,IX,1:3
Making of an Immortal, The 1928,Ap 29,IX,1:3
Alibi 1928,Je 10,VIII,1:3
On the Spot 1930,Ap 20,VIII,2:1
Payment Deferred 1931,O 1,24:2
Fatal Alibi, The 1932,F 10,26:6
Tempest, The 1934,F 4,IX,3:4
Macbeth 1934,Ap 3,26:4
Galileo 1947,Ag 1,21:4
Galileo 1947,D 8,34:2
Don Juan in Hell 1951,O 23,34:4
Don Juan in Hell 1951,N 4,II,1:1
Major Barbara 1956,O 31,27:1
Party, The 1958,My 30,13:1
Midsummer Night's Dream, A 1959,Je 3,30:1
King Lear 1959,Ag 19,34:7
Laughton, Charles (Director)
Fatal Alibi, The 1932,F 10,26:6
Don Juan in Hell 1951,O 23,34:4
Don Juan in Hell 1951,N 4,II,1:1
John Brown's Body 1952,N 3,25:8
John Brown's Body 1952,D 16,43:5
John Brown's Body 1953,F 16,17:2
Caine Mutiny Court-Martial, The 1954,Ja 21,27:2
Caine Mutiny Court-Martial, The 1954,Ja 31,II,1:1
Major Barbara 1956,O 31,27:1
Elsa Lanchester-Herself 1961,F 6,28:1
Laughton, Charles (Miscellaneous)
John Brown's Body 1953,F 22,II,1:1
Hamlet 1956,My 8,28:5
Laughton, Charles (Playwright)
John Brown's Body 1952,N 3,25:8
John Brown's Body 1952,D 16,43:5
John Brown's Body 1953,F 16,17:2
John Brown's Body 1960,Je 22,31:1
Galileo 1967,Ap 14,31:1
Laughton, Charles (Producer)
Don Juan 1934,F 27,16:5
Party, The 1958,My 30,13:1
Laughton, Charles (Translator)
Galileo 1947,Ag 1,21:4
Galileo 1947,D 8,34:2
Galileo 1968,D 1,88:4
Laumann, M (Playwright)
Catherine Goulden 1923,N 6,22:1
Laumer, Edith
Lady Comes Across, The 1942,Ja 10,10:2
My Dear Public 1943,S 10,28:1
Laun, Louis (Miscellaneous)
Small Wonder 1948,S 16,33:5
Launt, Judith
Well of the Saints, The 1959,Ap 11,15:4
Lauray, Doris
Fata Morgana 1931,D 26,15:3
Laure, Katherine (Playwright)
Don't, George! 1944,N 4,18:6
Laureche, Gaejan
Henry V 1946,Je 8,38:1
Laurell, Kay
Agent 666, L' 1923,My 30,10:5
Quarantine 1924,D 17,19:7
Nocturne 1925,F 17,19:1
Lauren, Barbara
Phaedra 1967,My 22,50:2
Lauren, Charles
Untitled-Nativity Play 1941,D 25,28:5
Lauren, Jane
Black Eye, The 1938,Mr 8,22:4
Suspect 1940,Ap 10,30:4
Lauren, S K (Playwright)
Those We Love 1930,F 20,22:2
Those We Love 1930,Mr 2,IX,1:1
Lottery, The 1930,N 23,IX,3:5
Men Must Fight 1932,O 15,13:4
Laurence, Ann
Dumbbell People in a Barbell World 1962,F 15,25:1
Laurence, Harry
Two on the Aisle 1951,Jl 20,13:6
Laurence, James Howard
Moths, The 1970,My 12,46:1
Laurence, Larry
Around the World 1946,Je 1,9:5
Night in Venice, A 1952,Je 27,18:6
By the Beautiful Sea 1954,Ap 9,20:1
Laurence, Lester
Diamond Lil 1948,N 30,33:2
Diamond Lil 1949,F 7,16:2
Diamond Lil 1951,S 15,8:2

Laurence, Lester (Miscellaneous)
Ziegfeld Follies 1943,Ap 2,16:2
Laurence, Marc
Thomas Paine 1930,Mr 21,30:7
Tree, The 1932,Ap 13,23:5
Survivors, The 1948,Ja 20,27:2
Laurence, Mark
Any Moment Now 1939,N 25,13:6
Laurence, Mark (Composer)
Any Moment Now 1939,N 25,13:6
Laurence, Mark (Lyricist)
Any Moment Now 1939,N 25,13:6
Laurence, Michael Clarke
Red Roses for Me 1955,D 29,15:2
Laurence, Neil
Trip to Bountiful, The 1953,N 4,30:3
Noah 1954,O 11,32:2
Hotel Paradiso 1957,Ap 12,22:2
Handful of Fire 1958,O 2,45:3
Laurence, Paula
Horse Eats Hat 1936,S 28,14:2
Doctor Faustus 1937,Ja 9,21:2
Sing for Your Supper 1939,Ap 25,18:6
Junior Miss 1941,N 19,28:2
Actors Fund Fete 1942,F 23,24:5
Something for the Boys 1943,Ja 17,VIII,1:1
One Touch of Venus 1943,O 8,14:1
Duchess Misbehaves, The 1946,F 14,32:2
Cyrano de Bergerac 1946,O 9,33:2
Cyrano de Bergerac 1947,Ja 17,27:2
Volpone 1948,Ja 9,24:6
On the Harmfulness of Tobacco 1948,F 6,29:2
Tragedian in Spite of Himself, A 1948,F 6,29:2
Bear, The 1948,F 6,29:2
Wedding, The 1948,F 6,29:2
Insect Comedy, The 1948,Je 4,26:3
Liar, The 1950,My 19,30:2
Season in the Sun 1950,S 29,31:2
Season in the Sun 1950,O 8,II,1:1
Tovarich 1952,My 15,39:2
Cyrano de Bergerac 1953,N 13,24:3
Coriolanus 1954,Ja 20,34:2
Time of Your Life, The 1955,Ja 20,34:1
Time of Your Life, The 1955,Ja 30,II,1:1
Beggar's Opera, The 1957,Mr 14,35:1
Have I Got a Girl for You! 1963,D 3,53:2
Ivanov 1966,My 4,50:1
Seven Days of Mourning 1969,D 17,64:1
Seven Days of Mourning 1970,Ja 4,II,5:1
Laurence, Wanda
Mirage, The 1920,O 1,14:1
Fool, The 1922,O 24,18:1
Laurence, William L (Playwright)
Thieves 1926,Je 8,23:1
At the Bottom 1930,Ja 10,24:3
Devil in the Mind 1931,My 2,23:2
Laurents, Arthur (Director)
Invitation to a March 1960,O 31,27:2
I Can Get It for You Wholesale 1962,Mr 23,29:1
Anyone Can Whistle 1964,Ap 6,36:1
Laurents, Arthur (Playwright)
Home of the Brave 1945,D 28,13:2
Home of the Brave 1946,Ja 6,II,1:1
Way Back, The 1949,Ja 29,9:5
Bird Cage, The 1950,F 23,32:2
Time of the Cuckoo, The 1952,O 16,37:4
Time of the Cuckoo, The 1952,N 2,II,1:1
Time of the Cuckoo, The 1953,Ja 4,II,1:1
Clearing in the Woods, A 1957,Ja 11,20:2
Clearing in the Woods, A 1957,Ja 20,II,1:1
West Side Story 1957,S 27,14:4
West Side Story 1957,O 6,II,1:1
Time of the Cuckoo, The 1958,O 28,40:2
Clearing in the Woods, A 1959,F 13,32:1
Gypsy 1959,My 22,31:6
Gypsy 1959,My 31,II,1:1
West Side Story 1960,Ap 28,31:1
West Side Story 1960,My 8,II,1:1
Invitation to a March 1960,O 31,27:2
West Side Story 1961,Mr 31,22:3
Anyone Can Whistle 1964,Ap 6,36:1
West Side Story 1964,Ap 9,24:2
Do I Hear a Waltz? 1965,Mr 19,28:1
Do I Hear a Waltz? 1965,Mr 28,II,1:1
West Side Story 1965,Je 25,37:2
Hallelujah, Baby! 1967,Ap 27,51:1
Hallelujah, Baby! 1967,My 7,II,1:1
West Side Story 1968,Je 25,32:1
Laurents, Jules (Scenic Designer)
To My Husband 1936,Je 2,35:2
30 Days Hath September 1938,O 1,10:5
Laurentz, Maria Christina
Projimos, Los 1966,Je 29,38:5
Laurenzi, Richard (Scenic Designer)
Pirates of Penzance, The 1970,D 6,84:6
Laurenzo, Lucien
Trois Jeunes Filles Nues; Three Young Maids From
the Folies Bergere 1929,Mr 5,28:2
Passionement; Passionately 1929,Mr 8,31:4
Bon Garcon, Un 1929,Mr 19,36:2
Lauret, Armand
Seventh Heart, The 1927,My 3,24:4

_auret, Laryssa
Julia, Jake, and Uncle Joe 1961,Ja 30,19:1
Night of the Iguana, The 1961,D 29,10:1
Paris Is Out! 1970,F 3,35:1
_aurey, Doris
All Good Americans 1933,D 6,29:2
_auri, St John
Conversation Piece 1934,O 24,24:1
_auria, John B (Producer)
Kiss Mama 1964,O 2,30:1
_auria, Larri
Macbeth 1936,Ap 15,25:4
Cradle Will Rock, The 1937,D 6,19:4
Cradle Will Rock, The 1938,Ja 4,19:3
Two on an Island 1940,Ja 23,17:2
Stevedore 1949,F 23,30:2
_aurie, Joe Jr
Plain Jane 1924,My 13,24:2
If I Was Rich 1926,S 3,15:2
Vaudeville (Palace) 1927,Ja 18,23:2
Weather Clear, Track Fast 1927,O 19,24:5
Vaudeville (Palace) 1928,Mr 13,23:2
Vaudeville (New Amsterdam Theatre)
1931,Je 22,17:3
Vaudeville (Palace) 1932,My 16,19:2
Swing Your Lady 1936,O 19,22:4
_aurie, Joe Jr (Director)
Friars Club Frolic 1933,My 15,16:4
_aurie, John
Passing of the Essenes, The 1930,O 19,IX,4:1
Son of Man 1933,O 22,IX,2:2
Tudor Wench, The 1933,N 12,IX,3:6
Tiger at the Gates 1955,O 4,40:1
King Lear 1964,My 19,43:2
_aurie, Kimetha
Loud Red Patrick, The 1956,O 4,28:1
Infernal Machine, The 1958,F 4,33:1
Mighty Man Is He, A 1960,Ja 7,25:2
Laurie, Piper
Rosemary 1960,N 15,47:1
Alligators, The 1960,N 15,47:1
Glass Menagerie, The 1965,My 5,53:2
Glass Menagerie, The 1965,My 16,II,1:1
Laurie, Ronald
Bourgeois Gentilhomme, Le 1964,Je 18,28:2
Laurier, Jay
Taming of the Shrew, The 1939,Ap 23,X,2:4
As You Like It 1939,Ap 23,X,2:5
Much Ado About Nothing 1941,Ap 20,IX,3:3
Midsummer Night's Dream, A 1942,Ap 12,VIII,1:7
Laurier, Richard
Nobody's Child 1956,Ag 23,25:2
Laurini, Peter (Miscellaneous)
Oklahoma! 1951,My 30,15:2
Oklahoma! 1953,S 1,19:1
Lauriston, John
Marigold 1930,O 9,23:1
Lautner, Joe
New Faces of 1952 1952,My 17,23:2
Me and Juliet 1953,My 29,17:1
Me and Juliet 1953,Je 7,II,1:1
Once Over Lightly 1955,Mr 16,39:1
Kittiwake Island 1960,O 13,43:1
Lautner, Joseph
Angel in the Pawnshop 1951,Ja 19,20:3
Laval, Marie
Cherry Blossoms 1927,Mr 29,22:3
Lavall, Kathryn
Brown Sugar 1937,D 3,29:2
Conjur 1938,N 1,27:2
LaValle, Babe
International Revue 1930,F 26,22:2
Lavalliere, Eve
Roi, Le 1931,Ap 5,VIII,3:1
Lavandero, L S (Playwright)
Marriage Proposal, The 1966,Je 28,51:1
Lavandero, S L
Sirena Varada, La 1937,O 23,15:3
Lavando, Pincus
Girl From Warsaw, The 1931,S 14,15:5
Lavaree, M (Mme)
Homme et Ses Fantomes, L' 1924,N 14,16:1
Lavedan, Henri (Playwright)
Duel, Le 1922,N 16,22:2
Marchese di Priola, Il 1931,Mr 2,19:3
Lavella, Gertrude
Bringing Up Father 1925,Mr 31,16:1
LaVelle, Miriam
Sunny River 1941,D 5,28:2
Lavelle, Pat
My 3 Angels 1956,F 4,24:2
Lavelli, Jorge (Director)
Cosmonaute Agricole, Le 1970,Ap 8,38:3
Grand Vizir, Le 1970,Ap 8,38:3
Lavenziano, Joe (Producer)
I Got Shoes 1963,Ja 25,12:2
Laver, James (Original Author)
Nymph Errant 1933,O 7,18:2
Laver, James (Playwright)
Nymph Errant 1933,O 29,IX,1:6
Heart Was Not Burned, The 1938,D 11,X,5:3
Streets of Paris, The 1939,Je 20,25:2

Laver, James (Translator)
Circle of Chalk, The 1929,Mr 31,VIII,2:6
Circle of Chalk, The 1941,Mr 27,28:4
Circle of Chalk, The 1950,D 2,8:3
Lavergne, Antenin (Playwright)
Spanish Love 1920,Ag 18,6:1
Laverty, Johnny
Allegro 1952,S 18,36:3
New Faces of 1956 1956,Je 15,32:1
Lavery, Emmet (Miscellaneous)
Seven Mirrors 1945,O 26,17:2
Lavery, Emmet (Playwright)
First Legion, The 1934,O 2,18:2
First Legion, The 1937,Je 8,30:7
First Legion, The 1937,Ag 15,X,2:3
Magnificent Yankee, The 1946,Ja 2,23:6
Magnificent Yankee, The 1946,Ja 23,21:2
Magnificent Yankee, The 1946,F 3,II,1:2
Gentleman From Athens, The 1947,N 30,I,78:2
Gentleman From Athens, The 1947,D 10,42:4
Dawn's Early Light 1959,Ag 9,76:4
Lavery, James
Something More! 1964,N 11,36:1
Lavetta, Gertrude
Folly Town 1920,My 18,9:2
Lavezzo, Marie
Electra 1932,Ja 9,21:4
Lavialle
Aiglon, L' 1924,O 21,21:1
Madame Sans-Gene 1924,N 4,30:1
Lavie, Aric
Irma la Douce 1960,S 30,31:2
Lavigne, Maurice
Bohemian Girl, The 1933,Jl 28,18:5
Plumes in the Dust 1936,N 7,14:2
LaVigne, Robert (Costume Designer)
Endecott and the Red Cross 1968,My 7,50:1
LaVigne, Robert (Scenic Designer)
Midsummer Night's Dream, A 1967,Je 30,23:1
Lavin, Linda
Oh, Kay! 1960,Ap 18,37:2
Fourth Avenue North 1961,S 28,50:2
Riot Act, The 1963,Mr 9,5:2
Wet Paint 1965,Ap 13,33:1
Hotel Passionato 1965,O 23,16:1
Mad Show, The 1966,Ja 10,16:1
It's a Bird . . . It's a Plane . . . It's Superman
1966,Mr 30,34:1
Something Different 1967,N 29,52:1
Little Murders 1969,Ja 6,38:1
Little Murders 1969,Ja 26,II,1:1
Cop-Out 1969,Ap 8,42:1
Cop-Out 1969,Ap 20,II,11:4
Last of the Red Hot Lovers 1969,D 29,37:1
Last of the Red Hot Lovers 1970,Ja 4,II,1:1
Oh, Johnny: or, Jonny Spielt Auf 1970,Mr 15,88:4
Lavin, Ric
Knight of the Burning Pestle, The 1953,O 24,13:2
Absalom 1956,My 17,37:2
LaVine, W Robert (Costume Designer)
Joan of Arkansas 1925,Ap 5,16:1
Maggie Flynn 1968,O 24,52:1
Jimmy 1969,O 24,38:1
Lavino, Edwin M (Costume Designer)
Here's Howe 1923,Ap 26,19:3
Lavino, Edwin M (Playwright)
Don Quixote, Esquire 1920,My 7,12:6
Somebody's Lion 1921,Ap 13,20:1
That's That 1924,Ap 30,19:2
Lavis, Janet
Pal Joey 1940,D 26,22:2
Lavrenoff, B (Playwright)
Enemies 1935,Mr 19,24:7
Lavrova, Vera
Innocent Eyes 1924,My 21,22:2
Law, Alyse
Garrick Gaieties 1926,My 11,25:2
Law, Evelyn
Two Little Girls in Blue 1921,My 4,10:3
Ziegfeld Follies 1922,Je 6,18:2
Ziegfeld Follies 1924,Je 25,26:1
Louie the 14th 1925,Mr 4,17:1
Betsy 1926,D 29,24:3
Greenwich Village Follies 1928,Ap 10,32:2
Law, Jenny Lou
Lend an Ear 1948,D 17,38:2
Maggie 1953,F 19,20:2
Beggar's Opera, The 1957,Mr 14,35:1
Lend an Ear 1959,S 25,20:5
Law, Jenny Lou (Director)
Lend an Ear 1959,S 25,20:5
Law, Jenny Lou (Producer)
Lend an Ear 1959,S 25,20:5
Law, John Phillip
After the Fall 1964,Ja 24,18:1
Marco Millions 1964,F 21,33:1
Changeling, The 1964,O 30,32:2
Tartuffe 1965,Ja 15,23:1
Law, Lindsay (Miscellaneous)
De Sade Illustrated 1969,My 13,42:4
Contributions; Shoes 1970,Mr 10,53:1
Contributions; Contribution 1970,Mr 10,53:1
Contributions; Plantation 1970,Mr 10,53:1

Law, Mary
Cyrano de Bergerac 1926,F 19,18:1
Wall Street 1927,Ap 21,24:4
Women Go on Forever 1927,S 8,25:1
Law, Mildred
Too Many Girls 1939,O 19,26:2
Artists and Models 1943,N 6,16:6
Law, Mouzon (Producer)
Crucible, The 1958,Mr 12,36:1
Law, Robert
R U R 1942,D 4,30:2
Law, Walter
Shipwrecked 1924,N 13,18:1
Good Bad Woman, A 1925,F 10,21:1
Devil Within, The 1925,Mr 17,19:4
Solid Ivory 1925,N 17,29:3
Law, Winifred
Hotel Alimony 1934,Ja 30,16:2
Reno 1937,Ag 10,22:7
Lawbaugh, Vera
Royal Family, The 1940,Ag 13,15:3
Lawber, Hope
Ceiling Zero 1935,Ag 17,18:4
Lawde, George
Maker of Images, The 1927,Mr 5,12:2
Lawder, Donald Jr
Fashion 1937,Mr 21,II,7:8
All the Living 1938,Mr 25,14:4
Lawder, H M
Monkey's Paw, The 1922,D 30,13:4
Lawder, Hope
Ceiling Zero 1935,Ap 11,26:2
Little Inn, The 1935,Ag 20,25:1
Lawder, Hope (Producer)
Be So Kindly 1937,F 9,19:4
Lawder, Wallace
Danton's Death 1938,N 3,26:2
Lawder, Walter
Fashion 1937,Mr 21,II,7:8
Lawery, Harry
Macbeth 1955,O 20,42:2
Lawes, Ellie
Lady in the Dark 1941,Ja 24,14:2
Lawes, Joan
Lady in the Dark 1941,Ja 24,14:2
Lawes, Lewis E (Warden) (Playwright)
Chalked Out 1937,Mr 26,24:2
Lawford, Betty
Midsummer Night's Dream, A 1927,Je 27,25:1
Lady Lies, The 1928,N 27,36:2
Bon Voyage 1929,D 29,VIII,4:3
Heat Wave 1931,F 18,14:6
Penny Wise 1935,Jl 2,24:2
With All My Heart 1935,Jl 30,17:1
There's Wisdom in Women 1935,O 31,17:1
Women, The 1936,D 8,30:6
Women, The 1936,D 28,13:1
Walk With Music 1940,Je 5,33:2
Glamour Preferred 1940,N 16,13:2
Voice of the Turtle, The 1944,D 10,II,6:4
Lawford, Ernest
New Morality, The 1921,Ja 31,10:1
Circle, The 1921,S 13,12:1
As You Like It 1923,Ap 24,24:1
School for Scandal, The 1923,Je 5,24:3
Meet the Wife 1923,N 27,23:4
O Nightingale 1925,Ap 16,25:2
Trelawney of the 'Wells' 1925,Je 2,16:2
Hamlet 1925,N 10,23:1
Hamlet 1925,N 22,VIII,1:1
Stronger Than Love 1925,D 29,20:2
Iolanthe 1926,Ap 20,24:2
Pirates of Penzance, The; Slave of Duty, The
1926,D 7,25:1
Ivory Door, The 1927,O 19,24:5
White Lilacs 1928,S 11,31:2
Wings Over Europe 1928,D 11,35:1
They Don't Mean Any Harm 1932,F 24,25:2
Truth About Blayds, The 1932,Ap 12,25:2
Christopher Comes Across 1932,Je 1,19:2
Late Christopher Bean, The 1932,N 1,24:3
Mary of Scotland 1933,N 28,28:3
Accent on Youth 1934,D 26,19:1
Libel! 1935,D 8,X,5:8
Libel! 1935,D 21,10:5
Tovarich 1936,O 16,31:4
Fabulous Invalid, The 1938,O 10,15:1
Brown Danube, The 1939,My 18,30:4
Lawder, Anderson
Her First Affaire 1927,Ag 23,29:2
Caste 1927,D 24,8:1
Forsaking All Others 1933,Mr 2,21:2
It's the Valet 1933,D 15,25:4
O Evening Star 1936,Ja 9,24:6
Lawler, Anderson (Miscellaneous)
Great to Be Alive! 1950,Mr 24,28:2
Oh, Men! Oh, Women! 1953,D 18,37:2
Copper and Brass 1957,O 18,19:2
Lawler, Anderson (Producer)
Protective Custody 1956,D 29,8:7
Lawler, Jerome
Romeo and Juliet 1922,D 28,20:1
As You Like It 1923,Ap 24,24:1

Lawler, Jerome—Cont
Little Poor Man, The 1925,Ag 6,14:1
Me 1925,N 24,28:1
Crown Prince, The 1927,Mr 24,23:2
Diana 1929,D 10,37:1
Little Father of the Wilderness, The 1930,Je 3,27:1
Silent Witness, The 1931,Mr 24,31:5
Merchant of Venice, The 1931,N 9,22:2
Troilus and Cressida 1932,Je 7,22:3
Is Life Worth Living? 1933,N 10,24:6
Joyous Season, The 1934,Ja 30,16:3
Othello 1935,S 28,13:2
Macbeth 1935,O 8,26:4
Return of Hannibal, The 1937,F 2,21:1
Lawler, Marvin
Ziegfeld Follies 1936,S 15,37:1
Lawler, Mary
Annie Dear 1924,N 5,25:3
Lawler, Ray
Summer of the Seventeenth Doll 1958,Ja 23,23:2
Lawler, Ray (Playwright)
Summer of the Seventeenth Doll 1958,Ja 23,23:2
Summer of the Seventeenth Doll 1959,O 14,52:1
Unshaven Cheek, The 1963,Ag 20,38:2
Summer of the Seventeenth Doll 1968,F 21,59:1
Summer of the Seventeenth Doll 1968,Mr 3,II,3:1
Lawler, Robert
Enemy of the People, An 1920,S 7,19:3
World We Live In, The 1922,N 1,16:1
Macbeth 1924,Mr 17,18:1
Wisdom Tooth, The 1926,F 16,22:2
Lawless, James
Way of the World, The 1965,Je 2,40:1
Richard III 1965,Je 3,26:1
Skin of Our Teeth, The 1966,Je 2,51:1
As You Like It 1966,Je 4,19:1
Shoemaker's Holiday, The 1967,Je 3,19:1
Harpers Ferry 1967,Je 6,52:2
Visit, The 1967,S 13,41:1
She Stoops to Conquer 1968,Ja 1,11:1
Twelfth Night 1968,Je 15,40:1
Master Builder, The 1968,Je 22,26:1
Resistible Rise of Arturo Ui, The 1968,Ag 8,25:1
House of Atreus, The 1968,D 18,55:1
Resistible Rise of Arturo Ui, The 1968,D 23,44:1
Lawless, Sue
Shoemaker's Holiday, The 1967,Mr 3,25:1
In the Nick of Time 1967,Je 2,36:1
Now 1968,Je 6,53:1
Don't Shoot Mable It's Your Husband 1968,O 23,34:1
Pastry Shop, The 1970,Je 12,28:1
Lawless, Sue (Director)
Lend an Ear 1969,O 29,32:1
Lawless, Sue (Playwright)
In the Nick of Time 1967,Je 2,36:1
Now 1968,Je 6,53:1
Lawley, Cooper
Love Song, The 1925,Ja 14,19:4
Vaudeville (Palace) 1929,S 9,30:5
Lawlor, Andrew Jr
Three Showers 1920,Ap 6,18:1
Daddy Dumplins 1920,N 23,11:1
Blue Lagoon, The 1921,S 15,16:1
Alias Jimmy Valentine 1921,D 9,20:3
Ice-Bound 1923,F 12,16:2
Other Rose, The 1923,D 21,15:2
Dearest Enemy 1925,S 19,9:2
Little Spitfire, The 1926,Ag 17,15:2
Coquette 1927,N 9,23:1
Coquette 1927,N 13,IX,1:1
It's a Grand Life 1930,F 11,30:3
Lawlor, David (Producer)
To Bury a Cousin 1967,My 17,38:3
Lawlor, James Reed (Composer)
Razzle Dazzle 1951,F 20,21:1
Fun City 1968,Mr 7,53:2
Lawlor, James Reed (Musical Director)
Razzle Dazzle 1951,F 20,21:1
My Wife and I 1966,O 11,53:2
Fun City 1968,Mr 7,53:2
Lawlor, John
Muzeeka 1968,Ap 29,47:2
Lawlor, Mary
Passing Show of 1922, The 1922,S 21,18:2
Rise of Rosie O'Reilly, The 1923,D 26,13:4
No, No, Nanette 1925,S 17,20:2
Queen High 1926,S 9,21:2
Good News 1927,Ag 14,VII,2:1
Good News 1927,S 7,35:4
Cross My Heart 1928,S 18,32:7
Hello, Daddy! 1928,D 27,26:5
Vaudeville (Palace) 1929,Mr 11,22:5
You Said It 1931,Ja 20,21:3
Budget, The 1932,S 21,26:4
Lawlor, Nora (Playwright)
Few Are Chosen 1935,S 18,19:3
Lawlor, Nora (Producer)
Few Are Chosen 1935,S 18,19:3
Lawlor, Sam
Headquarters 1929,D 5,32:4
Lawlor, Terry
Show Is On, The 1937,S 20,18:4

Lawlor, Thomas
Mikado, The 1966,N 18,36:1
H M S Pinafore 1968,O 30,35:1
Mikado, The 1968,N 2,29:4
Iolanthe 1968,N 9,37:3
Lawnor, Mort
Big Deal, The 1953,Mr 7,13:6
Lawrance, Joan
Greenwich Villagers, The 1927,Ag 19,20:2
Lawren, Joseph (Producer)
Manhatters, The 1927,Jl 19,27:3
Lawren, Jules (Producer)
Intimate Relations 1932,Mr 29,23:2
Lawrence, Albert
Plan M 1942,F 21,15:2
Lawrence, Andrew
Liliom 1956,F 18,12:5
Lawrence, Bea (Miscellaneous)
Crime and Punishment 1947,D 23,29:3
Paint Your Wagon 1951,N 13,32:2
Lawrence, Bea (Producer)
Kathleen 1948,F 4,26:2
Lawrence, Bert (Composer)
Meet the People 1940,D 26,22:2
Lawrence, Bert (Lyricist)
Meet the People 1940,D 26,22:2
Lawrence, Bert (Playwright)
Meet the People 1940,D 26,22:2
Lawrence, Betty
Where's Your Husband? 1927,Ja 15,10:3
Madame X 1927,Jl 7,29:3
Storm Center 1927,D 1,33:2
Lady for a Night, A 1928,Ap 17,26:4
Houseparty 1929,S 10,26:5
Little Orchard Annie 1930,Ap 22,33:1
Christopher Comes Across 1932,Je 1,19:2
Lawrence, Beverly
Bernardine 1952,O 17,33:4
Lawrence, Bob
Jumbo 1935,N 18,20:2
Boys From Syracuse, The 1938,N 24,36:1
Sunny River 1941,D 5,28:2
Lawrence, Boyle (Playwright)
Decameron Nights 1922,Ap 21,14:5
Lawrence, Brian
Vie Parisienne, La 1945,Ja 13,14:5
Lawrence, Bruce
Iolanthe 1965,My 19,42:1
Yeomen of the Guard, The 1965,Jl 8,34:1
Ruddigore 1965,Ag 27,16:1
Lawrence, Carol
New Faces of 1952 1952,My 17,23:2
South Pacific 1955,My 5,39:5
Shangri-La 1956,Je 14,40:1
Ziegfeld Follies 1957,Mr 2,19:2
West Side Story 1957,S 27,14:4
West Side Story 1957,O 6,II,1:1
Saratoga 1959,D 8,59:4
West Side Story 1960,Ap 28,31:1
Subways Are for Sleeping 1961,D 28,22:1
Night Life 1962,O 24,44:1
I Do! I Do! 1967,N 28,54:1
Lawrence, Catherine
Masque of the Kings, The 1937,F 9,19:4
Haiti 1938,Mr 3,16:1
Mr and Mrs North 1941,Ja 13,11:2
Lawrence, Charles
Half-Moon, The 1920,N 2,15:2
Love Letter, The 1921,O 5,20:1
Elsie Janis and Her Gang 1922,Ja 17,13:2
It's a Boy! 1922,S 20,18:3
Extra 1923,Ja 24,22:3
Helen of Troy, New York 1923,Je 20,22:6
Nervous Wreck, The 1924,O 19,VIII,2:1
Half-Caste, The 1926,Mr 30,20:4
Kiss Me! 1927,Jl 22,17:1
Love Call, The 1927,O 25,33:1
Music in May 1929,Ap 2,29:1
Nine Fifteen Revue, The 1930,F 12,26:2
Mystery Moon 1930,Je 24,23:4
London Calling 1930,O 20,29:1
Once in a Lifetime 1931,F 1,VIII,1:3
Face the Music 1933,F 1,13:4
No Questions Asked 1934,F 6,24:3
Portrait of Gilbert 1934,D 29,11:5
Eldest, The 1935,F 12,24:3
One Thing After Another 1937,D 29,17:2
Sing Out the News 1938,S 26,12:5
Lawrence, D H (Original Author)
You Touched Me! 1943,O 17,II,2:4
You Touched Me! 1945,S 26,27:2
You Touched Me! 1945,S 30,II,1:1
Lawrence, D H (Playwright)
My Son's My Son 1936,My 27,26:4
Lawrence, David
Let 'Em Eat Cake 1933,O 23,18:1
Parade 1935,My 21,22:2
Lawrence, Eddie
Threepenny Opera, The 1955,S 21,38:1
Bells Are Ringing 1956,N 29,43:4
Bells Are Ringing 1956,N 30,18:2
Sherry! 1967,Mr 29,39:1

Lawrence, Eddie (Lyricist)
Kelly 1965,F 8,28:2
Lawrence, Eddie (Playwright)
Beautiful Mariposa, The 1952,Jl 2,22:8
Kelly 1965,F 8,28:2
Lawrence, Edwin
Merry World, The 1926,Je 9,18:3
Lawrence, Elizabeth
Hasty Heart, The 1954,Mr 13,10:1
Joan of Lorraine 1955,Mr 26,12:2
Look Homeward, Angel 1957,N 29,33:1
Moon Besieged, The 1962,D 6,54:1
Devils, The 1963,N 5,25:1
Francesca da Rimini 1967,S 12,54:1
Certain Young Man, A 1967,D 27,45:1
Lawrence, Elliot (Musical Director)
Bye Bye Birdie 1960,Ap 15,13:4
How to Succeed in Business Without Really Trying 1961,O 16,34:1
Here's Love 1963,O 4,28:1
Golden Boy 1964,O 21,56:1
Diary of Adam and Eve, The 1966,O 19,53:1
Lady or the Tiger?, The 1966,O 19,53:1
Passionella 1966,O 19,53:1
Golden Rainbow 1968,F 5,27:1
Georgy 1970,F 27,26:1
Lawrence, Emily
Barretts of Wimpole Street, The 1945,Mr 27,23:6
First Mrs Fraser, The 1947,N 6,36:2
Julius Caesar 1950,Je 21,30:1
Gioconda Smile, The 1950,O 9,21:2
Prescott Proposals, The 1953,D 17,53:1
Lawrence, Ernice
Devil and Daniel Webster, The 1939,My 19,26:1
Lawrence, Ethel
Music Hall Varieties 1932,N 23,15:3
Lawrence, Francis
So Proudly We Hail 1938,Ap 9,11:1
Lawrence, Frank
False Dreams, Farewell 1934,Ja 16,18:3
Lawrence, Fred
For Charity 1937,Ag 25,24:3
Everywhere I Roam 1938,D 30,10:4
Lawrence, George
Sonny 1921,Ag 17,12:2
Red Poppy, The 1922,D 21,18:2
Lingering Past, The 1932,Je 30,26:5
Tonight at 8:30; Hands Across the Sea 1948,F 24,20:4
Oklahoma! 1953,S 1,19:1
Lawrence, Gerald
Monsieur Beaucaire 1924,Mr 2,VIII,2:7
Lawrence, Gertrude
Charlot's Revue 1924,Ja 10,18:1
Charlot's Revue 1924,Ap 6,VIII,1:1
Charlot's Revue 1924,Ap 15,25:2
Charlot's Revue 1925,N 11,27:1
Charlot's Revue 1925,N 15,VIII,1:1
Charlot's's Revue 1925,D 27,VII,1:1
Oh, Kay! 1926,N 9,31:3
Oh, Kay! 1927,Jl 3,VII,1:1
Oh, Kay! 1927,S 22,33:3
Treasure Girl 1928,O 21,IX,2:1
Treasure Girl 1928,N 9,22:1
Candle Light 1929,S 22,IX,2:6
Candle-Light 1929,O 1,28:2
International Revue 1930,F 9,VIII,4:2
International Revue 1930,F 26,22:2
Private Lives 1930,S 25,14:2
Private Lives 1930,O 12,VIII,1:8
Private Lives 1931,Ja 28,24:1
Take Two From One 1931,O 4,VIII,2:6
Can the Leopard...? 1932,Ja 3,VIII,2:1
Behold We Live 1932,Ag 17,13:2
Behold We Live 1932,S 11,IX,1:1
This Inconstancy 1933,Mr 25,13:6
This Inconstancy 1933,Ap 16,IX,1:3
Nymph Errant 1933,O 7,18:2
Nymph Errant 1933,O 29,IX,1:6
Winding Journey, The 1934,My 8,28:6
Here Lies Truth 1934,Ag 28,24:6
Moonlight Is Silver 1934,S 20,21:1
Moonlight Is Silver 1934,O 7,IX,3:7
Hervey House 1935,My 18,21:2
Players' Masque for Marie Tempest, The 1935,Je 23,IX,1:3
Tonight at Seven-Thirty; We Were Dancing; Astonished Heart, The; Red Peppers 1935,O 17,28:3
Tonight at Seven-Thirty; Hands Across the Sea; Fumed Oak; Shadow Play 1935,O 22,16:5
Family Album 1936,Ja 10,16:1
Astonished Heart, The 1936,Ja 10,16:1
Tonight at 8:30 1936,Ja 10,16:1
Red Peppers 1936,Ja 10,16:1
Tonight at ;:O/ 1936,Ja 11,9:4
Shadow Play 1936,Ja 14,25:1
Hands Across the Sea 1936,Ja 14,25:1
Fumed Oak 1936,Ja 14,25:1
Astonished Heart, The 1936,F 2,IX,3:4
Hands Across the Sea 1936,F 16,IX,3:1
Tonight at 8:30; Hands Across the Sea; Astonished Heart, The; Red Peppers 1936,O 27,30:7

awrence, Gertrude—Cont

Hands Across the Sea 1936,N 25,17:2
Astonished Heart, The 1936,N 25,17:2
Red Peppers 1936,N 25,17:2
Shadow Play 1936,N 28,13:1
We Were Dancing 1936,N 28,13:1
Fumed Oak 1936,N 28,13:1
Ways and Means 1936,D 1,31:1
Still Life 1936,D 1,31:1
Family Album 1936,D 1,31:1
Tonight at 8:30; Astonished Heart, The; Hands
   Across the Sea; Red Peppers; We Were Dancing;
   Fumed Oak; Shadow Play 1936,D 6,XII,5:1
Susan and God 1937,Ap 11,II,12:3
Susan and God 1937,Ap 25,X,2:6
Susan and God 1937,O 8,26:4
Susan and God 1937,O 17,XI,1:1
Susan and God 1938,Ja 23,XI,1:6
Skylark 1939,Mr 19,XI,2:5
Skylark 1939,O 12,32:2
Skylark 1939,O 22,IX,1:3
Lady in the Dark 1940,D 31,18:6
Lady in the Dark 1941,Ja 5,IX,1:7
Lady in the Dark 1941,Ja 24,14:2
Lady in the Dark 1941,F 2,IX,1:1
Lady in the Dark 1941,S 3,26:6
Lady in the Dark 1941,S 7,IX,1:1
Actors Fund Fete 1942,F 23,24:5
Lady in the Dark 1943,Mr 1,14:2
Susan and God 1943,D 14,30:2
Pygmalion 1945,D 27,16:1
Pygmalion 1946,Ja 6,II,1:1
Pygmalion 1947,F 6,29:4
Lady Maria, The 1947,Ag 5,26:1
Tomight at 8:30; Family Album 1948,F 21,8:2
Tonight at 8:30; Ways and Means 1948,F 21,8:2
Tonight at 8:30; Red Peppers 1948,F 21,8:2
Tonight at 8:30; Shadow Play 1948,F 24,20:4
Tonight at 8:30; Fumed Oak 1948,F 24,20:4
September Tide 1948,D 16,39:5
September Tide 1949,Ja 9,II,3:7
King and I, The 1951,Mr 30,26:2
King and I, The 1951,Ap 8,II,1:1
King and I, The 1952,Ap 14,23:1
Lawrence, Harold E (Director)
Ladies Night in a Turkish Bath 1961,Mr 22,38:1
Lawrence, Henry
Night Hostess 1928,S 13,31:2
Salt Water 1929,N 27,30:3
Show Boat 1956,Je 22,16:1
Show Boat 1957,Je 28,30:2
Sail Away 1961,O 4,48:5
My Fair Lady 1964,My 21,43:2
How to Succeed in Business Without Really Trying
   1966,Ap 21,45:1
Wonderful Town 1967,My 18,50:1
Brigadoon 1967,D 14,59:2
Jimmy 1969,O 24,38:1
Lawrence, Jack (Composer)
Courtin' Time 1951,Je 14,30:2
Ziegfeld Follies 1957,Mr 2,19:2
I Had a Ball 1964,D 16,50:1
Lawrence, Jack (Lyricist)
Courtin' Time 1951,Jl 1,II,1:1
Ziegfeld Follies 1957,Mr 2,19:2
I Had a Ball 1964,D 16,50:1
Lawrence, Jack (Producer)
Maybe Tuesday 1958,Ja 30,18:3
Lawrence, Jane
Oklahoma! 1943,Ap 1,27:1
Inside U S A 1948,My 1,19:2
Where's Charley? 1948,O 12,33:2
Lawrence, Jean
Way, The 1940,O 12,20:3
Pirates of Penzance, The 1942,F 20,20:2
Lawrence, Jerome (Lyricist)
Shangri-La 1956,Je 14,40:1
Lawrence, Jerome (Original Author)
Look, Ma, I'm Dancin' 1948,Ja 30,20:2
Lawrence, Jerome (Playwright)
Inherit the Wind 1955,Ja 12,24:1
Inherit the Wind 1955,Ap 22,20:2
Inherit the Wind 1955,S 25,II,1:1
Shangri-La 1956,Je 14,40:1
Auntie Mame 1956,N 1,47:2
Auntie Mame 1956,N 11,II,1:1
Auntie Mame 1958,Je 8,II,1:1
Gang's All Here, The 1959,O 2,23:1
Gang's All Here, The 1959,O 11,II,1:1
Only in America 1959,N 20,35:1
Call on Kuprin, A 1961,My 26,29:3
Call on Kuprin, A 1961,Je 4,II,1:1
Diamond Orchid 1965,F 11,44:4
Mame 1966,My 25,41:1
Inherit the Wind 1967,Je 23,50:1
Mame 1968,Ap 20,25:1
Dear World 1969,F 7,33:1
Night Thoreau Spent in Jail, The 1970,N 2,66:1
Lawrence, Jerome (Producer)
Auntie Mame 1958,Ag 12,33:2
Lawrence, Jim
Chicago 70 1970,My 26,33:1
Chicago 70 1970,Je 7,II,3:1

Lawrence, Joan
Young Man's Fancy, A 1947,Ap 30,33:2
Lawrence, John
Children of Darkness 1958,Mr 1,11:4
Hamlet 1970,O 27,54:2
Rosencrantz and Guildenstern Are Dead
   1970,N 19,39:3
Lawrence, John (Playwright)
Wall Street Scene 1937,O 19,29:2
Lawrence, Joseph
Mongolia 1927,D 27,24:5
Lady Beyond the Moon 1931,Ap 1,36:5
Lawrence, Judith
Midsummer Night's Dream, A 1932,N 18,22:2
Lawrence, Judy
Ice Follies 1959,Ja 14,30:1
Lawrence, Julie
Paradise Lost 1935,D 10,31:5
Excursion 1937,Ap 10,11:4
Bonds of Interest, The 1951,D 1,7:2
Lawrence, Kay
School for Brides 1944,Ag 2,19:4
Lawrence, Lela
Will the Mail Train Run Tonight? 1964,Ja 10,18:1
Lawrence, Leon
Mlle Modiste 1937,My 5,28:5
Lawrence, Lorna
American Born 1925,O 6,31:3
Scotch Mist 1926,S 21,32:3
Lawrence, Marcia
Mourners' Bench, The 1950,S 22,35:7
Lawrence, Margaret
Transplanting Jean 1921,Ja 4,11:2
Transplanting Jean 1921,Ja 9,VI,1:1
Lawful Larceny 1922,Ja 3,20:2
Endless Chain, The 1922,S 5,21:2
Secrets 1922,D 26,11:1
Secrets 1922,D 31,VII,1:1
In His Arms 1924,O 14,23:1
Isabel 1925,Ja 14,19:1
Shall We Join the Ladies? 1925,Ja 14,19:1
Pelican, The 1925,S 22,23:2
Pelican, The 1925,S 27,VII,1:1
Long Island Love 1926,Ag 1,VII,4:1
Heaven-Tappers, The 1927,Mr 9,28:3
Mixed Doubles 1927,Ap 27,22:3
Behavior of Mrs Crane, The 1928,Mr 21,30:1
Possession 1928,O 3,35:1
Lawrence, Marion
Finian's Rainbow 1953,Mr 7,13:2
Lawrence, Mark (Composer)
Once Over Lightly 1938,D 10,13:4
Owl and the Pussycat, The 1964,N 19,48:1
Dinner at Eight 1966,S 28,38:1
Lawrence, Mark (Lyricist)
Once Over Lightly 1938,D 10,13:4
Lawrence, Mark (Producer)
Passion of Josef D, The 1964,F 12,29:1
Lawrence, Mary
Merrily We Roll Along 1936,Je 30,15:1
Overtons, The 1945,F 7,16:6
Lawrence, Morton
Church Street 1948,F 10,27:2
Lawrence, Myrtle
Springtime of Youth 1922,O 27,15:1
Lawrence, Norman
Earl Carroll's Vanities 1940,Ja 15,11:2
Meet the People 1940,D 26,22:2
Sadie Thompson 1944,N 17,25:2
Lawrence, Pam
Ethan Frome 1936,Ja 22,15:2
Lawrence, Paul
All the King's Men 1963,Jl 12,12:1
Lawrence, Pegeen
Fair Game for Lovers 1964,F 11,43:2
Wives, The 1965,My 18,35:4
Lawrence, Peter
Mr Big 1941,O 1,24:2
Lawrence, Peter (Miscellaneous)
Hall of Healing 1952,My 8,35:6
Time to Go 1952,My 8,35:6
Bedtime Story 1952,My 8,35:6
Lawrence, Peter (Playwright)
Peter Pan 1950,Ap 25,27:2
Let's Make an Opera 1950,D 14,50:2
Lawrence, Peter (Producer)
Shinbone Alley 1957,Ap 15,23:2
Lawrence, Philip
Twelfth Night 1954,N 10,42:2
Twelfth Night 1954,D 12,II,3:1
Merchant of Venice, The 1955,F 23,23:2
Macbeth 1955,O 20,42:2
Midsummer Night's Dream, A 1956,Ja 14,12:2
Romeo and Juliet 1956,F 24,20:4
Hamlet 1956,O 29,34:1
Twelfth Night 1957,Ja 5,12:2
Go Show Me a Dragon 1961,O 28,18:1
Lawrence, Philip (Director)
Twelfth Night 1957,Ja 5,12:2
Julius Caesar 1957,O 24,39:1
King Lear 1959,Ja 3,11:2
Royal Gambit 1959,Mr 5,34:2
Royal Gambit 1959,Mr 15,II,1:1

Lawrence, Philip (Director)—Cont

Jackass, The 1960,Mr 24,39:2
Electra 1962,Mr 22,42:1
Lawrence, R Webb
Lost 1927,Mr 29,22:2
Lawrence, Reginald (Director)
Burning Deck, The 1940,Mr 2,9:2
Lawrence, Reginald (Miscellaneous)
Out of This World 1955,O 13,35:2
Lawrence, Reginald (Playwright)
Men Must Fight 1931,Ap 12,IX,2:1
Men Must Fight 1932,O 15,13:4
Hervey House 1935,My 18,21:2
If This Be Treason 1935,Jl 30,17:1
If This Be Treason 1935,S 24,28:2
If This Be Treason 1935,S 29,X,1:1
Feathers in a Gale 1943,D 22,26:2
Out of This World 1950,D 22,17:3
Out of This World 1955,N 10,44:2
Legend of Lizzie, The 1959,F 10,39:1
Lawrence, Robert
They Shall Not Die 1934,F 22,24:4
It Can't Happen Here 1936,O 28,30:1
Lawrence, Robert (Composer)
Flair-Flair the Idol of Paree 1935,Mr 13,16:1
Lawrence, Robert (Lyricist)
Flair-Flair the Idol of Paree 1935,Mr 13,16:1
Lawrence, Robert (Musical Director)
Flair-Flair the Idol of Paree 1935,Mr 13,16:1
Lawrence, Robert Webb
Open House 1925,D 15,28:3
90 Horse Power 1926,Mr 16,22:4
Pyramids 1926,Jl 20,17:2
High Hatters, The 1928,My 11,28:2
Come-On Man, The 1929,Ap 23,26:2
Lawrence, Robert Webb (Director)
Perfectly Scandalous 1931,My 14,27:2
Lawrence, Sardis
Right to Dream, The 1924,My 27,14:2
Ladies of the Jury 1929,O 22,26:2
As Good As New 1930,N 4,37:3
Lawrence, Smith
Room Service 1970,My 13,49:1
Lawrence, Smith (Miscellaneous)
Penny Friend, The 1966,D 27,46:1
Bill Noname 1970,Mr 3,37:1
Lawrence, Stephen
Montserrat 1949,O 31,21:4
Lawrence, Stephen (Miscellaneous)
Great Scot! 1965,N 12,56:3
Now Is the Time for all Good Men 1967,S 27,42:1
Lawrence, Stephen (Musical Director)
Utopia! 1963,My 7,47:4
Now Is the Time for all Good Men 1967,S 27,42:1
Lawrence, Steve
What Makes Sammy Run? 1964,F 28,19:1
Golden Rainbow 1968,F 5,27:1
Golden Rainbow 1968,Mr 3,II,3:1
Lawrence, Stradella
Finian's Rainbow 1953,Mr 7,13:2
Kiss Me, Kate 1954,Mr 27,13:2
Lawrence, Suzanne
Old Bill, M P 1926,N 11,22:2
She Stoops to Conquer 1928,My 15,17:1
Lawrence, Tessie
Blue Flame, The 1920,Mr 16,18:1
Lawrence, Thelma
Diamond Lil 1928,Ap 10,32:1
Lawrence, Vincent (Playwright)
Ghost Between, The 1921,Mr 23,11:2
Two Fellows and a Girl 1923,Jl 20,8:2
In Love With Love 1923,Ag 7,20:1
In Love With Love 1923,Ag 12,VI,1:1
Kelly's Vacation 1924,Mr 16,VIII,2:1
Two Married Men 1925,Ja 14,19:1
Spring Fever 1925,Ag 4,14:2
Sour Grapes 1926,Jl 4,VII,3:2
Sour Grapes 1926,S 7,19:1
Sour Grapes 1926,S 12,VIII,1:1
Happy 1927,D 6,26:3
Distant Drum, A 1928,Ja 21,13:1
Treasure Girl 1928,N 9,22:1
Conflict, The 1929,F 11,26:2
Among the Married 1929,O 4,24:3
Among the Married 1929,D 8,X,2:7
Washington Heights 1931,S 30,23:4
Silk Hat Harry 1943,Ag 22,II,1:6
Overtons, The 1945,F 7,16:6
Lawrence, Vivian
War and Peace 1942,My 22,26:3
Lawrence, Walter
Lancelot and Elaine 1921,S 13,12:1
Bootleggers, The 1922,N 28,24:1
Within Four Walls 1923,Ap 18,24:1
No Trespassing! 1926,S 8,19:1
Sleeping Clergyman, A 1934,O 9,16:1
American Holiday 1936,F 22,13:3
Lawrence, Warren F (Director)
Restless Women 1927,D 27,24:1
Quicksand 1928,F 14,26:3
Lawrence, Warren F (Playwright)
Quicksand 1928,F 14,26:3
Scars 1929,F 10,IX,2:1
Conflict 1929,Mr 7,22:4

Lawrence, Warren F (Playwright)—Cont

Conflict 1929,Mr 24,X,1:1

Lawrence, William
Solid Ivory 1925,N 17,29:3
Beau Gallant 1926,Ap 6,26:3

Lawrenson, John
Hollow Crown, The 1963,Ja 31,5:1

Lawrie, Ted
Beautiful Dreamer 1960,D 28,22:1

Laws, Jerry
Porgy and Bess 1942,Ja 23,16:2
Porgy and Bess 1943,S 14,26:2
Porgy and Bess 1944,F 8,13:2
Carmen Jones 1951,S 22,8:6
Porgy and Bess 1953,Mr 10,25:5
Porgy and Bess 1961,My 18,40:1
Porgy and Bess 1965,Mr 6,17:1
Finian's Rainbow 1967,Ap 6,44:1

Laws, Jerry (Director)
Along Came a Spider 1963,My 28,33:1

Laws, Maury (Composer)
Month of Sundays 1968,S 17,50:1

Laws, Richard (Miscellaneous)
Gertrude 1970,N 13,29:1
Carmilla 1970,D 1,61:2

Laws, Sam
Cabin in the Sky 1964,Ja 22,32:1
Who's Got His Own 1966,O 13,52:1
Murderous Angels 1970,F 8,70:1

Lawshe, Freddie
Personality 1921,Ag 29,14:3

Lawshe, Winifred
Drifting 1922,Ja 3,20:3
Comedienne 1924,O 22,18:1

Lawson, Ailsa
We Americans 1926,O 13,20:4

Lawson, Alan
Caesar and Cleopatra 1935,Ag 22,21:1

Lawson, Arthur Del
Stevedore 1949,F 23,30:2

Lawson, Christyne
Jamaica 1957,N 1,32:2

Lawson, Claude
My Magnolia 1926,Jl 13,19:2
Bomboola 1929,Je 27,17:3

Lawson, Dorothy
It Never Rains 1931,D 25,29:3

Lawson, Edwin
Macbeth 1928,N 20,28:3

Lawson, Eleanor
Time for Elizabeth 1948,S 28,32:3

Lawson, Elsie
Dancing Mothers 1924,Ag 12,12:2
Triumphant Bachelor, The 1927,S 16,21:1
People Don't Do Such Things 1927,N 24,28:3
Whispering Friends 1928,F 21,18:3
Room of Dreams 1930,N 6,22:4

Lawson, Joan
Time and the Hour 1936,O 5,24:1

Lawson, John Howard (Director)
International, The 1928,Ja 16,24:4

Lawson, John Howard (Miscellaneous)
Processional 1937,O 14,23:1

Lawson, John Howard (Playwright)
Roger Bloomer 1923,Mr 2,18:3
Roger Bloomer 1923,Mr 11,VIII,1:3
Processional 1925,Ja 13,17:1
Processional 1925,Ja 18,VII,1:1
Processional 1925,Ja 25,VII,1:1
Nirvana 1926,Mr 4,19:1
Nirvana 1926,Ap 11,VIII,1:1
Loud Speaker 1927,Mr 3,27:2
Loud Speaker 1927,Mr 20,VIII,1:1
International, The 1928,Ja 16,24:4
Success Story 1932,S 27,24:4
Success Story 1932,O 2,IX,1:1
Pure in Heart, The 1932,O 9,IX,3:7
Success Story 1934,Ja 2,17:4
Pure in Heart, The 1934,Mr 21,24:3
Gentlewoman 1934,Mr 23,28:4
Marching Song 1937,F 18,18:2
Processional 1937,O 14,23:1
Processional 1937,O 24,XI,1:1

Lawson, Kate Drain
Chief Thing, The 1926,Mr 23,24:2
Garrick Gaieties 1930,Je 5,29:2

Lawson, Kate Drain (Costume Designer)
R U R 1930,F 18,28:1
Garrick Gaieties 1930,Je 5,29:2
Point of Honor, A 1937,F 12,26:2
Knights of Song 1938,O 18,29:2
Meet the People 1940,D 26,22:2

Lawson, Kate Drain (Scenic Designer)
Mr Pim Passes By 1927,Ap 19,24:1
Garrick Gaieties 1930,Je 5,29:2
Valley Forge 1934,D 11,28:3
To See Ourselves 1935,My 1,25:2
Caesar and Cleopatra 1935,Ag 22,21:1
Slight Case of Murder, A 1935,S 12,28:5
Eden End 1935,O 22,17:1
Love From a Stranger 1936,S 30,28:1
Holmeses of Baker Street, The 1936,D 10,34:3
Point of Honor, A 1937,F 12,26:2
Anna Christie 1941,Ag 10,IX,1:8

Lawson, Lee
Firebugs, The 1963,F 13,7:2
Agatha Sue, I Love You 1966,D 15,61:1
My Daughter, Your Son 1969,My 14,36:2

Lawson, Robert
Weekend 1968,Mr 14,50:2

Lawson, Roger
Hello, Dolly! 1967,N 13,61:1
Bill Noname 1970,Mr 3,37:1

Lawson, Sid
Polonaise 1945,O 8,20:2
Miss Liberty 1949,Jl 16,6:5
Diamond Lil 1951,S 15,8:2

Lawson, Wilfrid
Antony and Cleopatra 1934,S 18,18:2
Hurricane 1934,D 23,IX,1:8
Libel! 1935,D 8,X,5:8
Libel! 1935,D 21,10:5
Prelude to Exile 1936,N 17,34:6
Prelude to Exile 1936,N 22,XI,3:2
Prelude to Exile 1936,D 1,31:1
Point of Honor, A 1937,Ja 31,II,10:4
Point of Honor, A 1937,F 12,26:2
King's Pirate, The 1937,Je 11,26:1
I Have Been Here Before 1937,S 23,32:3
I Have Been Here Before 1938,O 14,26:2
Bridge, The 1939,My 28,X,1:3
Wooden Dish, The 1954,Jl 30,9:4
Rainmaker, The 1956,Je 1,26:7
All Kinds of Men 1957,S 20,20:3
Peer Gynt 1962,S 27,33:7

Lawson, William
Distant Drums 1932,Ja 19,24:3
Late Christopher Bean, The 1932,N 1,24:3
Bitter Oleander 1935,F 12,24:3

Lawson-Johnston, Andrew (Director)
Audition, The 1968,Jl 8,45:1

Lawton, Frank
Young Woodley 1928,Mr 11,VIII,1:3
Michael and Mary 1930,F 23,VIII,2:1
Lucky Dip 1930,N 16,VIII,4:1
London Wall 1931,My 24,VIII,1:6
Somebody Knows 1932,My 29,VIII,1:1
Wind and the Rain, The 1934,F 2,20:6
Promise 1936,D 31,20:4
French Without Tears 1937,S 26,II,4:3
French Without Tears 1937,S 29,19:1
I Am My Youth 1938,Mr 8,22:4
Waiting For Gillian 1954,Ap 22,36:2

Lawton, Gardner
Daddy Dumplins 1920,N 23,11:1

Lawton, Janet
Electra 1932,Ja 9,21:4

Lawton, Kenneth
In the Night Watch 1921,Ja 31,10:1
He Who Gets Slapped 1922,Ja 10,15:1
School for Scandal, The 1923,Mr 13,19:2
Blue Bandanna, The 1924,Je 24,18:4
Carnaval 1924,D 30,15:1
Loose Ankles 1926,Ag 17,15:1
Legend of Leonora, The 1927,Mr 30,22:4
Behold the Bridegroom 1927,D 27,24:1
Common Sin, The 1928,O 16,28:2
Sign of the Leopard 1928,D 12,34:4
Mystery Square 1929,Ap 5,28:3

Lawton, Martin (Playwright)
Locked Door, The 1924,Je 20,17:2

Lawton, Mary
Back to Methuselah (Part III: The Thing Happens); Thing Happens, The (Back to Methuselah, Part III) 1922,Mr 7,11:1
Back to Methuselah (Part V: As Far as Thought Can Reach); As Far as Thought Can Reach (Back to Methuselah, Part V) 1922,Mr 14,11:2

Lawton, Thais
Blue Flame, The 1920,Mr 16,18:1
Wandering Jew, The 1921,O 27,22:1
Exciters, The 1922,S 23,10:4
Jitta's Atonement 1923,Ja 18,16:3
Thumbs Down 1923,Ag 7,20:1
Blue Bird, The 1923,D 26,13:3
Two Strangers From Nowhere 1924,Ap 8,22:2
Red Falcon, The 1924,O 8,22:1
Lord Byron's Cain 1925,Ap 9,20:3
Castles in the Air 1926,S 7,19:2
Midsummer Night's Dream, A 1927,Je 27,25:1
Mister Romeo 1927,S 6,35:3
Napoleon 1928,Mr 9,21:1
Novice and the Duke, The 1929,D 11,37:2
Elizabeth and Essex 1930,Mr 2,IX,4:7
Royal Virgin, The 1930,Mr 18,30:5
9th Street Guest, The 1930,Ag 26,24:3
Philip Goes Forth 1931,Ja 4,VIII,2:1
Philip Goes Forth 1931,Ja 13,35:4
Philip Goes Forth 1931,Ja 18,VIII,1:1
Going Gay 1933,Ag 4,18:5
Birthright 1933,N 22,22:3
Times Have Changed 1935,F 26,16:1
Love in My Fashion 1937,D 4,21:4
Romantic Mr Dickens 1940,D 3,33:2

Lawton, Tonia
In the Bag 1936,D 18,30:2
Howdy Stranger 1937,Ja 15,17:5

Lax, Abe
Little Bandit 1935,Ap 19,24:2
Souls for Sale 1936,S 21,27:6
Stepsisters 1936,O 13,32:3
Of One Mother 1937,Ja 18,21:3
If I Were Rothschild 1940,Ja 1,28:7

Lax, Francis
Huis Clos 1962,Ja 16,30:1
Cantatrice Chauve, La 1962,Ja 16,30:1

Lax, Miriam
Merry World, The 1926,Je 9,18:3

Laxton, Ann
George White's Scandals 1935,D 26,20:2

Lay, Ann
Louisiana Lady 1947,Je 3,35:2

Lay, Dilys
Boy Friend, The 1954,O 1,20:1

Layden, William
Man on Stilts, The 1931,S 10,23:2

Laye, Evelyn
Bitter Sweet 1929,O 27,IX,2:1
Bitter Sweet 1929,N 6,30:2
Bitter Sweet 1930,N 4,37:3
Helen 1932,Ja 31,I,5:2
Sweet Aloes 1936,F 25,23:5
Sweet Aloes 1936,Mr 5,24:5
Paganini 1937,My 21,18:6
Paganini 1937,Je 6,XI,1:2
Between the Devil 1937,O 15,19:1
Between the Devil 1937,O 24,XI,2:1
Between the Devil 1937,D 23,24:5
Lights Up 1940,F 18,IX,2:5
Belle of New York, The 1942,O 4,VIII,2:3
Wedding in Paris 1954,Ap 6,35:2

Laye, Gabrielle
Love for Love 1967,O 21,17:1
Love for Love 1967,O 30,59:1

Layman, Si
Chiffon Girl, The 1924,F 20,23:2

Layne, Barbara
Whatever Goes Up 1935,N 26,28:2

Layne-Smith, Donald
Hamlet 1931,Ap 24,26:4

Laynee, Fifie
One, Two, Three! 1930,S 30,24:2

Layton, Frank
This Is New York 1930,N 29,21:1
Man on Stilts, The 1931,S 10,23:2
Merry-Go-Round 1932,Ap 23,11:2
Chrysalis 1932,N 16,15:2

Layton, George
Chips With Everything 1963,O 2,49:1

Layton, Joe (Choreographer)
On the Town 1959,Ja 16,36:1
On the Town 1959,Ja 25,II,1:1
Once Upon a Mattress 1959,My 12,40:1
Once Upon a Mattress 1959,My 17,II,1:1
Sound of Music, The 1959,N 17,40:2
Greenwillow 1960,Mr 9,38:1
Greenwillow 1960,Mr 20,II,1:1
Tenderloin 1960,O 18,47:2
Sail Away 1961,O 4,48:5
No Strings 1962,Mr 16,24:1
Drat! the Cat! 1965,O 11,54:2
George M! 1968,Ap 11,48:1
George M! 1968,Ap 21,II,1:5
Dear World 1969,F 7,33:1
Scarlett 1970,Ja 3,19:1

Layton, Joe (Director)
No Strings 1962,Mr 16,24:1
On the Town 1963,My 31,30:7
Girl Who Came to Supper, The 1963,D 9,49:1
Peterpat 1965,Ja 7,27:1
Drat! the Cat! 1965,O 11,54:2
Sherry! 1967,Mr 29,39:1
South Pacific 1967,Je 13,56:1
George M! 1968,Ap 11,48:1
George M! 1968,Ap 21,II,1:5
Dear World 1969,F 7,33:1
Tale of Kasane, The 1969,F 25,36:1
Blueprints 1969,F 25,36:1
Gianni Schicci 1969,F 25,36:1
Critic, The 1969,Mr 9,76:5
Scarlett 1970,Ja 3,19:1
Two by Two 1970,N 11,37:1
Two by Two 1970,N 22,II,1:1

Layton, Mary Lynn
One Is a Lonely Number 1964,Je 19,37:3

Layton, Philip
Hear That Trumpet 1946,O 8,19:2

Layton, Robert
Petrified Forest, The 1942,Ag 19,14:3

Layton, William
Audition of the Apprentice Theatre 1939,Je 2,26:2
Mr Big 1941,O 1,24:2
Duchess of Malfi, The 1946,O 16,35:2
Command Decision 1947,O 2,30:2
Summer and Smoke 1948,O 7,33:2

Layton, William (Playwright)
Song of the Grasshopper 1967,S 29,52:2

Layton (Playwright)
Strut Miss Lizzie 1922,Je 20,22:6

Layuna, Verna
Zunguru 1938,Ag 7,IX,8:2

Lazar, Zelda
Major Noah 1929,F 23,17:2

Lazar (Producer)
Mercenary Mary 1927,D 4,X,2:3

Lazare, Sam
Processional 1937,O 14,23:1

Lazareff, Elsa
At the Bottom 1930,Ja 10,24:3

Lazareff, Elsa (Mrs Harry Moses) (Director)
Dangerous Corner 1932,O 28,23:1

Lazareff, Ivan
Pierrot the Prodigal; Enfant Prodigue, L'
  1925,Mr 7,8:1
Cricket on the Hearth, The 1925,My 29,20:2

Lazarev, Vladimir
Chauve-Souris of 1943 1943,Ag 13,13:2

Lazarieff, Ivan
Tsar Fyodor Ivanovitch 1923,Ja 9,26:1
Cherry Orchard, The 1923,Ja 23,18:1

Lazarin, Louis
Americana 1926,Jl 27,15:3

Lazaron, Harold
Yours Is My Heart 1946,S 6,16:5

Lazarous, Bill
R U R 1942,D 4,30:2

Lazarovici, Joseph
Broken Dishes 1929,N 6,28:3
Inspector General, The 1930,D 24,19:2
Lancashire Lass, The 1931,D 31,16:3
Little Ol' Boy 1933,Ap 25,15:5

Lazarow, Victor
Man and Superman 1970,F 24,48:1
Moby Dick 1970,Je 3,52:1

Lazarowitz, Murray
Hershel, The Jester 1948,D 14,39:2

LaZarre, Jerry
Pipe Dream 1955,D 1,44:1

Lazarus, Bill
Skipper Next to God 1948,Ja 5,14:5
Mummers and Men 1962,Mr 27,41:6

Lazarus, Maurice
Professor Mamlock 1937,Ap 14,30:3

Lazarus, Milton (Miscellaneous)
Red Mill, The 1945,O 17,16:2

Lazarus, Milton (Playwright)
Whatever Goes Up 1935,N 26,28:2
I Want a Policeman! 1936,Ja 15,15:5
Every Man for Himself 1940,D 10,32:3
Sun Field, The 1942,D 10,33:2
Song of Norway 1944,Ag 22,20:2
Song of Norway 1944,Ag 27,II,1:1
Song of Norway 1958,Je 23,19:2
Song of Norway 1959,Je 26,16:2
Merry Widow, The 1964,Ag 18,24:2

Lazarus, Roy
Most Happy Fella, The 1956,My 4,20:1

Lazarus, Sherman
Marriage Is for Single People 1945,N 22,38:2

Lazarus, Sidney (Playwright)
Dixie to Broadway 1924,O 30,22:1

Lazell, Kathryn
Sing Out the News 1938,S 26,12:5

Lazelle, Kay
Walk a Little Faster 1932,D 8,24:4

Lazer, Joan
Me and Molly 1948,F 27,27:2

Lazer, Peter
Hide and Seek 1957,Ap 3,26:1
Miss Isobel 1957,D 27,22:1
Watercolor 1970,Ja 22,30:1

Lazowski, Yurek (Choreographer)
Arabian Nights 1954,Je 25,15:2
Arabian Nights 1967,Jl 3,12:1

Lazowski, Yurek (Director)
Arabian Nights 1967,Jl 3,12:1

Lazowski, Yurek Ballet
Arabian Nights 1967,Jl 3,12:1

Lazzarini, Giulia
Servant of Two Masters, The 1960,F 24,42:2

Le Baron, William (Lyricist)
Half-Moon, The 1920,N 2,15:2
Love Letter, The 1921,O 5,20:1

Le Baron, William (Playwright)
Half-Moon, The 1920,N 2,15:2
Nobody's Money 1921,My 22,VI,1:6
Nobody's Money 1921,Ag 18,9:3
Scarlet Man, The 1921,Ag 23,10:3
Love Letter, The 1921,O 5,20:1
Yankee Princess, The 1922,O 3,22:1
Moonlight 1924,Ja 31,13:7
Something to Brag About 1925,Jl 12,VII,1:8
Something to Brag About 1925,Ag 14,14:3

Le Bay, Louis
Tendresse, La 1922,S 26,18:1

Le Beau, Madeleine
French Touch, The 1945,D 10,18:2

Le Berthon, Helene
Student Prince, The 1943,Je 9,16:2
Blossom Time 1943,S 6,21:2
Lady Says Yes, A 1945,Ja 11,18:5

Le Blanc, Whitney J (Scenic Designer)
Ceremonies in Dark Old Men 1969,O 11,42:1

Le Bret, Andre (Playwright)
Homme Qui Jouait du Banjo, L' 1926,O 24,VIII,2:1

Le Breton, Flora
Lass O' Laughter 1924,N 16,VIII,2:8
Lass O' Laughter 1925,Ja 9,13:2
Optimists, The 1928,Ja 31,28:2
Present Arms 1928,Ap 27,16:2
Singing Rabbi, The 1931,S 11,24:4
Cat and the Fiddle, The 1931,O 16,26:4
School for Husbands 1933,O 17,26:5
Chinese Nightingale, The 1934,O 6,20:4

Le Brett, Andre (Playwright)
Prisons de Femmes 1931,O 4,VIII,2:4

Le Clair, Blanche
Great Day! 1929,O 18,24:3

Le Compte, Jo Ann
Obbligato 1958,F 19,22:2
Living Premise, The 1963,Je 14,34:1

Le Comte, Edmond
First American Dictator 1939,Mr 15,18:2
Aries Is Rising 1939,N 22,16:5
Plan M 1942,F 21,15:2
Wanhope Building, The 1947,F 11,36:5

Le Couey, Catherine
Lorenzaccio 1958,O 15,44:2
Triomphe de l'Amour, Le 1958,O 17,32:1
Don Juan 1958,O 29,29:1

Le Count, Muriel
George White's Scandals 1926,Je 15,23:2

Le Duc, Bob
Ice Follies 1963,Ja 10,5:2

Le Duc, Edward
Johannes Kreisler 1922,D 25,20:3

Le Febvre, Edouard
Good Morning, Dearie 1921,N 2,20:2

Le Fevre, Jean
Plume de Ma Tante, La 1958,N 12,42:1
Plume de Ma Tante, La 1959,S 13,II,1:1

Le Gallienne, Eva
Not So Long Ago 1920,My 5,14:1
Not So Long Ago 1920,Ag 29,VI,1:3
Liliom 1921,Ap 21,18:1
Liliom 1921,My 1,VII,1:1
Liliom 1921,N 27,VI,1:1
Aglavaine and Selysette 1922,Ja 4,11:1
Sandro Botticelli 1923,Mr 27,24:2
Sandro Botticelli 1923,Ap 1,VII,1:1
Rivals, The 1923,My 9,14:2
Agent 666, L' 1923,My 30,10:5
Swan, The 1923,O 14,VIII,2:4
Swan, The 1923,O 24,15:3
Swan, The 1923,O 28,VIII,1:1
Assumption of Hannele, The 1924,F 16,16:2
Vierge Folle, La; Foolish Virgin, The
  1924,Mr 22,12:2
Jehanne d'Arc 1925,Je 13,10:1
Joan of Arc 1925,Je 21,VIII,1:2
Jehanne d'Arc 1925,Jl 12,VII,1:1
Call of Life, The 1925,O 10,10:1
Master Builder, The 1925,N 11,27:1
Master Builder, The 1925,N 15,VIII,1:1
John Gabriel Borkman 1926,Ja 30,13:1
Saturday Night 1926,O 26,25:1
Three Sisters, The 1926,O 27,24:1
Locandiera, La; Mistress of the Inn, The
  1926,N 23,26:1
Twelfth Night 1926,D 21,21:4
Cradle Song 1927,Ja 25,18:2
Inheritors 1927,Mr 8,23:1
Good Hope, The 1927,O 19,24:2
First Stone, The 1928,Ja 14,12:2
Improvisations in June 1928,F 27,16:5
Hedda Gabler 1928,Mr 27,30:2
Vaudeville (Palace) 1928,Je 26,29:4
Open Door, The 1928,Je 26,29:4
Vaudeville (Palace) 1928,Jl 3,19:2
Invitation au Voyage, L' 1928,O 5,17:1
Cherry Orchard, The 1928,O 16,28:5
Cherry Orchard, The 1928,N 18,IX,1:2
Peter Pan; Boy Who Would Not Grow Up, The
  1928,N 27,36:3
Sea Gull, The 1929,S 17,34:1
Living Corpse, The 1929,D 7,19:1
Open Door, The 1930,Ja 28,28:1
Women Have Their Way, The 1930,Ja 28,28:1
Romeo and Juliet 1930,Ap 22,33:1
Siegfried 1930,O 21,34:1
Alison's House 1930,D 2,31:2
Lady of the Camellias, The 1931,Ja 27,21:2
Camille 1931,F 15,VIII,1:1
Alison's House 1931,My 12,29:2
Liliom 1932,O 27,23:2
Camille 1932,O 28,23:2
Dear Jane 1932,N 15,24:3
Alice in Wonderland 1932,D 12,18:3
Alice in Wonderland 1932,D 25,IX,1:1
Cherry Orchard, The 1933,Mr 7,20:3
Aiglon, L' 1934,N 5,22:2
Hedda Gabler 1934,D 4,22:5
Cradle Song 1934,D 11,28:4
Rosmersholm 1935,D 3,32:5

Le Gallienne, Eva—Cont
Love for Love 1936,Je 30,15:4
Prelude to Exile 1936,N 17,34:6
Prelude to Exile 1936,N 22,XI,3:2
Prelude to Exile 1936,D 1,31:1
Mistress of the Inn, The 1937,Je 22,26:3
Hamlet 1937,Ag 24,24:4
Madame Capet 1938,O 26,26:2
Frank Fay's Vaudeville 1939,Mr 3,20:4
Uncle Harry 1942,My 21,24:1
Cherry Orchard, The 1944,Ja 26,22:1
Cherry Orchard, The 1944,F 6,II,1:1
Therese 1945,O 10,24:2
Therese 1945,O 28,II,1:1
Henry VIII 1946,N 7,42:2
What Every Woman Knows 1946,N 9,13:2
John Gabriel Borkman 1946,N 13,33:2
Alice in Wonderland 1947,Ap 7,19:2
Ghosts 1948,F 17,31:2
Hedda Gabler 1948,F 25,27:2
Corn Is Green, The 1950,Ja 12,33:2
ANTA Album 1951,My 7,22:7
Evening With Will Shakespeare, An 1952,D 7,86:5
Starcross Story, The 1954,Ja 14,25:2
Southwest Corner, The 1955,F 4,18:2
Southwest Corner, The 1955,F 13,II,1:1
Untitled-Reading 1957,Ja 23,24:6
Mary Stuart 1957,O 9,39:1
Mary Stuart 1957,O 20,II,1:1
Mary Stuart 1959,Jl 30,21:3
Seagull, The 1964,Ap 6,36:1
Exit the King 1968,Ja 10,48:1
Exit the King 1968,Ja 21,II,1:2
All's Well That Ends Well 1970,Je 16,53:1
All's Well That Ends Well 1970,Je 21,II,3:2

Le Gallienne, Eva (Director)
Saturday Night 1926,O 26,25:1
Three Sisters, The 1926,N 7,VIII,1:1
Saturday Night 1926,N 7,VIII,1:1
Twelfth Night 1926,D 21,21:4
Cradle Song 1927,Ja 25,18:2
Inheritors 1927,Mr 8,23:1
Inheritors 1927,Mr 20,VIII,1:1
Good Hope, The 1927,O 23,VIII,1:1
Would-Be Gentleman, The 1928,O 2,34:1
Invitation au Voyage, L' 1928,O 5,17:1
Bourgeois Gentilhomme, Le 1928,O 7,IX,1:1
Cherry Orchard, The 1928,O 16,28:5
Peter Pan; Boy Who Would Not Grow Up, The
  1928,N 27,36:3
Cherry Orchard, The 1929,Je 2,VIII,1:1
Mademoiselle Bourrat 1929,O 8,34:3
Cradle Song, The 1929,O 22,26:4
Romeo and Juliet 1930,Ap 22,33:1
Dear Jane 1932,N 15,24:3
Alice in Wonderland 1932,D 12,18:3
Alice in Wonderland 1932,D 25,IX,1:1
Alice in Wonderland 1933,F 2,21:2
Cherry Orchard, The 1933,Mr 7,20:3
Aiglon, L' 1934,N 5,22:2
Hedda Gabler 1934,D 4,22:5
Rosmersholm 1935,D 3,32:5
Hamlet 1937,Ag 24,24:4
Ah, Wilderness! 1941,O 3,26:2
Rivals, The 1941,N 18,32:2
Rivals, The 1942,Ja 15,24:2
Cherry Orchard, The 1944,Ja 26,22:1
Cherry Orchard, The 1944,F 6,II,1:1
John Gabriel Borkman 1946,N 13,33:2
Alice in Wonderland 1947,Ap 7,19:2
Alice in Wonderland 1947,Ap 13,II,1:1
Hedda Gabler 1948,F 25,27:2
Seagull, The 1964,Ap 6,36:1
Cherry Orchard, The 1968,Mr 20,41:1

Le Gallienne, Eva (Miscellaneous)
Ah, Wilderness! 1941,O 3,26:2
Tempest, The 1945,Ja 26,17:2

Le Gallienne, Eva (Original Author)
Cherry Orchard, The 1968,Ap 7,II,3:7

Le Gallienne, Eva (Playwright)
Alice in Wonderland 1932,D 12,18:3
Alice in Wonderland 1947,Ap 7,19:2
Alice in Wonderland 1947,Ap 13,II,1:1
Strong Are Lonely, The 1953,S 30,38:3

Le Gallienne, Eva (Producer)
Sea Gull, The 1930,My 4,XI,1:1
Cherry Orchard, The 1933,Mr 7,20:3
Hedda Gabler 1934,D 4,22:5
Rosmersholm 1935,D 3,32:5
John Gabriel Borkman 1946,N 13,33:2

Le Gallienne, Eva (Translator)
Rosmersholm 1935,D 3,32:5
John Gabriel Borkman 1946,N 13,33:2
Ghosts 1948,F 17,31:2
Hedda Gabler 1948,F 25,27:2
Strong Are Lonely, The 1956,F 5,II,3:1
Cherry Orchard, The 1960,Je 4,17:2
Seagull, The 1964,Ap 6,36:1
Wild Duck, The 1967,Ja 12,49:1
Wild Duck, The 1967,Ja 22,II,1:1
Cherry Orchard, The 1968,Mr 20,41:1

Le Gallienne, Julie (Translator)
Hedda Gabler 1928,Mr 27,30:2
Hedda Gabler 1934,D 4,22:5

Le Gallo
Attachee, L' 1929,My 19,IX,2:1
Le Gant, Omar
Little Poor Man, The 1925,Ag 6,14:1
Such Is Life 1927,S 1,27:3
Light of Asia, The 1928,O 10,32:2
Le Gant, Rose
Hamlet 1934,D 26,19:3
Cyrano de Bergerac 1936,Ap 28,17:1
Le Gon, Jeni
Black Rhythm 1936,D 21,19:2
Early to Bed 1943,Je 18,16:2
Le Gouriadec, Roger
Mr Papavert 1932,Ja 23,18:6
Le Grand, John M
Getting Married 1970,Ja 20,46:1
Le Grand, Phyllis
Orange Blossoms 1922,S 20,18:1
Le Grant, David
Oklahoma! 1953,S 1,19:1
Le Guere, George
Mamma's Affair 1920,Ja 20,10:1
Survival of the Fittest 1921,Mr 15,14:1
Up the Ladder 1922,Mr 7,11:2
Voltaire 1922,Mr 21,17:1
Old Soak, The 1922,Ag 23,14:5
Right to Kill, The 1926,F 16,22:2
Black Cockatoo, The 1926,D 31,11:1
Married-And How! 1928,Je 15,30:2
Le Hay, Edward
Rose Bernd 1922,S 27,17:1
Casanova 1923,S 27,10:2
Le Kids, The
Vaudeville (Palace) 1928,Ap 3,32:5
Le Leon, Bobby
Ginger Snaps 1930,Ja 1,30:5
Le Lorde, Andre (Playwright)
Sur la Dalle 1923,O 30,17:2
Le Mac, Joe (Miscellaneous)
Holiday on Ice 1965,S 2,38:4
Le Maire, Charles (Costume Designer)
Cocoanuts, The 1925,D 9,30:1
Greenwich Village Follies 1925,D 25,23:3
Twinkle Twinkle 1926,N 17,22:2
LeMaire's Affairs 1927,Mr 29,22:4
New Moon, The 1928,S 20,33:1
Hello, Yourself 1928,O 31,28:2
Hello, Daddy! 1928,D 27,26:5
Fioretta 1929,F 6,30:3
Sweet Adeline 1929,S 4,33:1
Sons o' Guns 1929,N 27,30:4
Ripples 1930,F 12,26:1
Flying High 1930,Mr 4,24:4
Earl Carroll's Vanities 1930,Jl 2,28:3
Luana 1930,S 18,28:1
Fine and Dandy 1930,S 24,26:1
Prince Charming 1930,O 14,31:1
Ballyhoo 1930,D 23,24:1
America's Sweetheart 1931,F 11,23:1
Shoot the Works! 1931,Jl 22,19:5
George White's Scandals 1931,S 15,30:1
East Wind 1931,O 28,19:1
Hot-Cha! 1932,Mr 9,17:3
Forward March 1932,O 23,IX,3:5
Music Hall Varieties 1932,N 23,15:3
Take a Chance 1932,N 28,11:2
Melody 1933,F 15,17:4
Strike Me Pink 1933,Mr 6,16:3
Blackbirds 1933,D 4,22:3
Ziegfeld Follies 1934,Ja 5,24:3
Say When 1934,O 28,IX,3:1
Say When 1934,N 9,24:2
George White's Scandals 1935,D 26,20:2
Le Maire, George
Broadway Brevities, 1920 1920,S 30,12:2
Friars Club Frolic 1921,Je 13,16:2
George White's Scandals 1921,Jl 12,14:1
Dream Girl, The 1924,Ag 21,12:2
Gay Paree 1925,Ag 19,14:3
Sweetheart Time 1926,Ja 20,23:2
Vaudeville (Palace) 1926,O 26,24:2
Le Maire, George (Playwright)
Broadway Brevities, 1920 1920,S 30,12:2
Le Maire, Ken
Henry IV, Part I 1958,Je 25,23:3
Le Maire, Kiviette (Costume Designer)
Forward March 1932,O 23,IX,3:5
Le Mans, Marcel
Lady, The 1923,D 5,23:2
Taming of the Shrew, The 1924,N 25,27:3
Le Marchand, Louis
Lorenzaccio 1958,O 15,44:2
Le Marchand, Louis (Playwright)
Vent de Folie, Un 1926,D 5,VIII,6:1
Vent de Folie, Un 1927,Ap 24,VII,2:2
Le Marchand, Lucienne
Cid, Le 1958,O 31,35:2
Tartuffe 1968,Jl 3,28:2
Phedre 1969,Mr 1,20:1
Le Massena, William
Taming of the Shrew, The 1940,F 6,17:2
There Shall Be No Night 1940,Ap 30,25:2
Mexican Mural; Moonlight Scene 1942,Ap 27,19:2

Tragedian in Spite of Himself, A 1948,F 6,29:2
On the Harmfulness of Tobacco 1948,F 6,29:2
Bear, The 1948,F 6,29:2
Wedding, The 1948,F 6,29:2
Inside U S A 1948,My 1,19:2
I Know My Love 1949,N 3,36:1
Dream Girl 1951,My 10,39:1
Nina 1951,D 6,44:3
Ondine 1954,F 19,23:1
Thieves' Carnival 1955,F 2,21:1
Fallen Angels 1956,Ja 18,27:1
Annie Get Your Gun 1958,F 20,29:2
Ardele 1958,Ap 9,39:4
Redhead 1959,F 6,21:1
Susannah and the Elders 1959,O 19,37:3
Conquering Hero, The 1961,Ja 17,40:2
Romulus 1962,Ja 11,27:1
Beauty Part, The 1962,D 28,5:2
Coop, The 1966,Mr 2,48:1
Life With Father 1967,O 20,53:2
Brigadoon 1967,D 14,59:2
Come Summer 1969,Mr 19,43:1
Grin and Bare It 1970,Mr 17,36:1
Le May, Annette
Slight Case of Murder, A 1935,S 12,28:5
Le May, Roy
Up and Up, The 1930,S 9,25:2
Hot Money 1931,N 9,22:2
Little Ol' Boy 1933,Ap 25,15:5
Uncle Tom's Cabin 1933,My 30,13:4
Portrait of Gilbert 1934,D 29,11:5
Distant Shore, The 1935,F 22,26:2
Slight Case of Murder, A 1935,S 12,28:5
Bright Honor 1936,S 28,14:1
Marching Song 1937,F 18,18:2
Le Meau, Ann
Up She Goes 1922,N 7,14:2
Le Noir, Lelya
New York Exchange 1926,D 31,11:2
One for All 1927,My 14,25:5
Le Noir, Pass
Sweet Mystery of Life 1935,O 12,13:3
Pre-Honeymoon 1936,My 1,19:4
Empress of Destiny 1938,Mr 10,16:2
Ringside Seat 1938,N 23,24:5
Le Noire, Rosetta
Hot Mikado, The 1939,Mr 24,26:2
Belle Helene, La 1941,Jl 8,14:1
Canteen Show, The 1942,S 4,18:1
Anna Lucasta 1944,Ag 31,15:1
Four Twelves Are 48 1951,Ja 18,30:2
Salvation on a String; Supper for the Dead
  1954,Jl 7,23:1
White Devil, The 1955,Mr 15,32:5
Finian's Rainbow 1955,My 19,25:1
Mister Johnson 1956,Mr 30,11:1
Take a Giant Step 1956,S 26,30:1
Destry Rides Again 1959,Ap 24,24:1
Bible Salesman, The 1960,F 22,12:2
Oldest Trick in the World, The 1961,F 21,40:1
Bible Salesman, The 1961,F 21,40:1
South Pacific 1961,Ap 27,26:3
Clandestine on the Morning Line 1961,O 31,28:1
Sophie 1963,Ap 16,32:1
Tambourines to Glory 1963,N 4,47:1
Cabin in the Sky 1964,Ja 22,32:1
Blues for Mister Charlie 1964,Ap 24,24:1
Blues for Mister Charlie 1964,My 3,II,1:1
I Had a Ball 1964,D 16,50:1
Great Indoors, The 1966,F 2,23:1
Show Boat 1966,Jl 20,48:1
Cry of Players, A 1968,N 15,40:1
Le Page, R
Hot Money 1931,N 9,22:2
Le Pey, Mortimer
Nut Farm, The 1929,O 15,34:3
Amorous Antic, The 1929,D 3,29:2
Le Poulain, Jean
Otage, L' 1959,O 27,42:1
Le Quinlan, Leach Trio
Vaudeville (Palace) 1929,Mr 18,30:5
Le Roux, Leah
Laugh, Clown, Laugh! 1923,N 29,30:1
Le Roux, Madeleine
Homo 1969,Ap 12,40:2
Dirtiest Show in Town, The 1970,My 2,21:1
Dirtiest Show in Town, The 1970,Je 29,43:2
Le Roy, Hal
Vaudeville (Palace) 1930,S 22,23:2
Gang's All Here, The 1931,F 19,21:3
Ziegfeld Follies 1931,Jl 2,30:5
Vaudeville (Hollywood) 1932,Mr 22,17:5
Strike Me Pink 1933,Mr 6,16:3
Friars Club Frolic 1933,My 15,16:4
Thumbs Up! 1934,D 28,24:1
Too Many Girls 1939,O 19,26:2
Count Me In 1942,O 9,24:2
Show Boat 1952,Je 6,19:5
Show Boat 1956,Je 22,16:1
Le Roy, Hal (Choreographer)
Autumn's Here 1966,O 26,40:1

Le Roy, Hal (Director)
Autumn's Here 1966,O 26,40:1
Le Roy, Jesse
Kidding Kidders 1928,Ap 24,28:3
Deep Channels 1929,O 19,22:3
Le Roy, June
Red, Hot and Blue! 1936,O 30,26:3
Pal Joey 1940,D 26,22:2
Le Roy, Ken
Morning Star 1940,Ap 17,26:4
Anne of England 1941,O 8,26:2
West Side Story 1957,S 27,14:4
I Can Get It for You Wholesale 1962,Mr 23,29:1
King and I, The 1963,Je 13,30:2
Le Roy, Kenneth
Land of Fame 1943,S 22,31:5
Firebird of Florence 1945,Mr 23,13:4
Le Roy, Martin
Cross My Heart 1928,S 18,32:7
Of Thee I Sing 1931,D 28,20:1
Le Roy, Mickey
Just a Minute 1928,O 9,34:3
Le Roy, Milton
Grand Hotel 1930,N 14,30:4
Experience Unnecessary 1931,D 31,16:2
Experience Unnecessary 1932,Mr 28,10:2
Melody 1933,F 15,17:4
Le Roy, Odette
Please, Mrs. Garibaldi 1939,Mr 17,24:3
Le Roy, Sam
Subway Express 1929,S 25,34:3
Le Rumeur, Pierre
Three Musketeers, The 1968,Je 26,43:1
Le Sage (Playwright)
Turcaret 1928,Mr 4,IX,4:5
Le Saint, E J
Big Fight, The 1928,S 19,33:1
Houseparty 1929,S 10,26:5
Le Sand, Leola
Yes is for a Very Young Man 1949,Je 7,27:2
Le Seuer, Louis
Scaramouche 1923,O 25,14:2
Le Seyeux, Jean (Costume Designer)
Earl Carroll's Vanities 1940,Ja 15,11:2
Le Seyeux, Jean (Director)
New Priorities of 1943 1942,S 16,28:2
Le Seyeux, Jean (Miscellaneous)
Streets of Paris, The 1939,Je 20,25:2
Le Seyeux, Jean (Scenic Designer)
Earl Carroll's Vanities 1940,Ja 15,11:2
Le Soir, George
Mirage, The 1920,O 1,14:1
Blue Kitten, The 1922,Ja 14,9:3
Fool, The 1922,O 24,18:1
Anything Might Happen 1923,F 21,22:3
Half-Naked Truth, The 1926,Je 8,23:1
New York Exchange 1926,D 31,11:2
Merry Wives of Windsor, The 1928,Mr 20,20:1
Subway Express 1929,S 25,34:3
They Never Grow Up 1930,Ag 8,27:1
Paging Danger 1931,F 27,19:2
Country Wife, The 1931,Ap 19,31:5
Devil's Host, The 1931,N 20,27:2
Few Wild Oats, A 1932,Mr 25,22:6
Murder in the Cathedral 1936,Mr 21,13:5
Help Yourself! 1936,Jl 15,15:1
Hero Is Born, A 1937,O 2,18:6
On the Rocks 1938,Je 16,20:2
Swingin' the Dream 1939,N 30,24:2
Le Sueur, Robert
This Fine-Pretty World 1923,D 27,11:1
Wonderful Visit, The 1924,F 13,17:3
Father, The 1928,My 12,9:4
Married-And How! 1928,Je 15,30:2
What's Your Number? 1929,Ag 16,18:3
He 1931,S 22,33:1
Troilus and Cressida 1932,Je 7,22:3
Camille 1932,N 2,23:3
Brittle Heaven 1934,N 14,22:5
De Luxe 1935,Mr 6,22:2
Strip Girl 1935,O 21,22:6
Libel! 1935,D 21,10:5
Woman Bites Dog 1946,Ap 18,21:2
Le Tang, Henry (Choreographer)
My Dear Public 1943,S 10,28:1
Dream With Music 1944,My 19,15:2
Shuffle Along 1952,My 9,20:5
Le Veille, Fayn
By Jupiter 1967,Ja 20,28:2
Le Velle, Miriam
Keep 'Em Laughing 1942,Ap 25,9:2
Le Vere, Florrie
Vaudeville (Palace) 1926,N 16,24:3
Le Verne, Lucille
Sun-Up 1923,My 25,28:1
Hot Water 1929,Ja 22,22:3
Le Vigan, Gretillat
Great Catherine, The 1927,Ap 3,VIII,4:7
Le Voy, George
Lady of the Lamp, The 1920,Ag 18,6:4
Lea, Barbary
Painted Days, The 1961,Ap 7,24:1

Lea, Emilie
Love Birds 1921,Mr 16,12:1
Lea, Fanny Heaslip (Playwright)
Lolly 1929,O 17,26:2
Lea, Flora
Topics of 1923 1923,N 21,23:2
Artists and Models 1924,O 16,33:3
Lea, Maida
Did I Say No? 1931,S 23,19:4
Lea, Mark
Steps Leading Up 1941,Ap 19,20:6
Leabo, Lou
Oklahoma! 1965,D 16,62:1
Leach, Archie
Golden Dawn 1927,D 1,32:3
Boom Boom 1929,Ja 29,26:4
Wonderful Night, A; Fledermaus, Die
1929,N 1,23:3
Nikki 1931,S 30,23:4
Leach, Charles
Turpentine 1936,Je 27,21:6
Leach, Dan
Autumn's Here 1966,O 26,40:1
Leach, Edward
Girl With Carmine Lips, The 1920,Ag 11,6:1
Leach, George
Front Page, The 1928,Ag 15,19:2
Remote Control 1929,S 11,24:5
Last Mile, The 1930,F 14,21:2
Name Your Poison 1936,Ja 21,27:4
You Can't Take It With You 1936,D 15,31:1
Return of the Vagabond, The 1940,My 14,27:2
Comes the Revelation 1942,My 27,26:2
Leach, Jack
Anne of England 1941,O 8,26:2
Leach, Marian
Dance Night 1938,O 15,20:5
Leach, Marjorie
Innocent Eyes 1924,My 21,22:2
Music in May 1929,Ap 2,29:1
Mexican Hayride 1944,Ja 29,9:6
As the Girls Go 1948,N 15,21:2
Leach, Muriel
Fatal Lady, The 1936,Mr 19,23:7
Leach, Nellie
Love 'Em and Leave 'Em 1926,F 4,20:4
Leach, Viola
Genius and the Crowd 1920,S 7,20:1
Tantrum, The 1924,S 5,20:2
Edgar Allan Poe 1925,O 6,31:1
Leach, Wilford (Director)
Renard 1970,Mr 25,36:4
Only Jealousy of Emer, The 1970,Mr 25,36:4
Only Jealousy of Emer, The 1970,Ap 26,II,1:3
Carmilla 1970,D 1,61:2
Leach, Wilford (Playwright)
In 3 Zones 1970,N 3,28:1
Gertrude 1970,N 13,29:1
Carmilla 1970,D 1,61:2
Leach, William
Trial of Lee Harvey Oswald, The 1967,N 6,64:1
Leachman, Cloris
Sundown Beach 1948,S 8,37:1
As You Like It 1950,Ja 27,27:2
Story for a Sunday Evening, A 1950,N 18,10:5
Lo and Behold! 1951,D 13,45:2
Dear Barbarians 1952,F 22,15:2
Sunday Breakfast 1952,My 30,12:2
King of Hearts 1954,Ap 2,23:1
King of Hearts 1954,Ap 11,II,1:1
Masquerade 1959,Mr 17,42:1
Leacock, Bubblesette
Virginia 1937,S 3,13:2
Leaf, Allen
King's Darling, The 1951,Jl 25,17:2
Bed Time 1958,Ap 11,20:2
Devil's Advocate, The 1961,Mr 10,20:1
Leaf, Mildred
Jazz Singer, The 1925,S 15,29:2
Leaf, Paul (Miscellaneous)
Measure for Measure 1957,Ja 23,24:1
Elizabethans, The 1962,Ja 22,19:1
Lorenzo 1963,F 16,5:2
Subject Was Roses, The 1964,My 26,45:1
Leafer, Woodrow
Oedipus 1970,F 23,30:1
League, Janet
Tiger at the Gates 1968,Mr 1,30:1
Cyrano de Bergerac 1968,Ap 26,30:1
To Be Young Gifted and Black; World of Lorraine
Hansberry, The 1969,Ja 3,15:1
Mrs Snow 1970,Ja 6,48:3
League, Raymond A (Producer)
Sound of Silence, A 1965,Mr 9,30:1
Leahy, Christopher
Brass Butterfly, The 1970,Ja 31,34:1
Early Morning 1970,N 26,57:1
Leahy, Eugene
Dizzy 1932,O 30,IX,2:2
Leahy, Robert
Take a Gander 1956,D 14,36:4
Leal, M
Road to Happiness, The 1927,My 3,24:1

Romantic Young Lady, The 1927,My 5,30:2
Girl and the Cat, The 1927,My 6,21:2
Blind Heart, The 1927,My 8,30:2
Cradle Song 1927,My 10,24:4
Fragila Rosina 1927,My 10,24:4
Leaming, Chet
Entertain a Ghost 1962,Ap 10,48:1
Leaming, Chet (Miscellaneous)
Misanthrope, The 1968,O 10,59:1
Leaming, Helen
Weak Sisters 1925,O 14,31:3
Lean, Cecil
Look Who's Here 1920,Mr 3,12:2
Blushing Bride, The 1922,F 7,12:1
Innocent Eyes 1924,My 21,22:2
Everybody's Welcome 1931,O 14,26:3
Lean, Cecil (Playwright)
Look Who's Here 1920,Mr 3,12:2
Lean, Leonard
Man and the Masses 1924,Ap 15,25:1
Lean, Roberta
Go Fight City Hall 1961,N 3,28:5
Leander, Zarah
Stockholm Is Stockholm 1930,N 2,VIII,3:2
Leap, Tommy
King and I, The 1963,Je 13,30:2
Lear, Edward (Original Author)
How Pleasant to Know Mr Lear 1968,S 2,14:2
Lear, Eileen
Skin of Our Teeth, The 1955,Ag 18,16:1
Lear, Fay Evelyn
What Next 1920,Ja 27,7:2
Lear, Howard
Finian's Rainbow 1955,My 19,25:1
Lear, Joyce
Small Hours, The 1951,F 16,22:1
Tonight in Samarkand 1955,F 17,22:2
Auntie Mame 1956,N 1,47:2
Learned, Michael
God Slept Here, A 1957,F 20,38:1
Coriolanus 1961,Je 21,31:2
Love's Labour's Lost 1961,Je 23,19:1
Three Sisters, The 1969,O 10,38:1
Learsi, Rufus (Playwright)
Little Theatre Tournament; His Children
1926,My 4,30:2
Learson, Mary (Miscellaneous)
Virtuous Island, The 1957,Ap 10,39:1
Apollo of Bellac, The 1957,Ap 10,39:1
Leary, Bayard
Merry Wives of Windsor, The 1954,F 17,27:1
Leary, Gilda
Danger 1921,D 23,18:3
Fanny Hawthorn 1922,My 12,22:2
Woman Who Laughed, The 1922,Ag 17,14:3
Thin Ice 1922,O 2,20:1
Dancing Girl, The 1923,Ja 25,16:2
Lesson in Love, A 1923,S 25,10:1
We Moderns 1924,Mr 12,17:2
Shipwrecked 1924,N 13,18:1
Naked Man, The 1925,N 8,VIII,2:1
Sandalwood 1926,S 23,23:1
Puppets of Passion 1927,F 25,24:4
Leary, Helen (Playwright)
Belmont Varieties 1932,S 29,17:2
Leary, Marie
What Next 1920,Ja 27,7:2
Leary, Nolan
Happy Landing 1932,Mr 28,10:5
Rendezvous 1932,O 13,22:3
Dodsworth 1934,F 26,20:4
Leary, Nolan (Playwright)
Belmont Varieties 1932,S 29,17:2
Leary, Thomas
Mecca 1920,O 5,12:2
Leary, Timothy (Dr)
Reincarnation of Christ Show, The 1966,D 4,II,5:1
Leath, Ron
My Wife and I 1966,O 11,53:2
Leatherbee, Charles
Fiesta 1928,D 13,25:2
Karl and Anna 1929,O 8,34:1
Pure in Heart, The 1934,Mr 21,24:3
Leatherbee, Charles (Director)
Fiesta 1928,D 13,25:2
Leavelle, Katharin
Bacchae, The 1969,Mr 15,24:1
Leavens, George
Our Betters 1937,Jl 22,16:2
Leaver, Philip
Young Madame Conti 1937,Ap 1,18:4
Royal Highness 1949,Ap 14,29:3
Leaver, Philip (Playwright)
Tomorrow Will Be Friday 1932,S 18,IX,1:1
Way to the Stars, The 1932,O 2,IX,2:5
Winding Journey, The 1934,My 8,28:6
Causes Unknown 1936,O 5,24:1
Three Set Out 1937,Je 23,29:3
Leavin, Paul
Mercy Street 1969,O 28,43:1
Leavitt, Douglas
It's Up to You 1921,Mr 29,20:1
Gay Paree 1926,N 10,24:2

Leavitt, Douglas—Cont
Student Prince, The 1936,Jl 12,II,5:2
Rose Marie 1936,Jl 22,22:6
Blossom Time 1936,Jl 29,23:1
My Maryland 1936,Ag 12,14:2
Countess Maritza 1936,Ag 19,18:2
Florodora 1936,Ag 23,II,8:2
Blossom Time 1936,Ag 30,II,5:8
Maytime 1937,Jl 6,23:4
Wonderful Night, A; Fledermaus, Die
1937,Jl 14,17:1
Gay Divorce 1937,Jl 20,19:4
On Your Toes 1937,Ag 3,21:2
Nina Rosa 1937,Ag 26,24:3
Circus Princess, The 1937,Ag 31,26:6
Blossom Time 1938,D 27,12:2
White Plume, The 1939,D 27,16:1
Blossom Time 1943,S 6,21:2
Leavitt, Douglas (Director)
Student Prince, The 1937,Jl 28,15:1
Leavitt, Douglas (Playwright)
It's Up to You 1921,Mr 29,20:1
Leavitt, Max
Moon Is a Gong, The 1926,Mr 13,21:3
Centuries, The 1927,N 30,23:1
Family Portrait 1939,Mr 9,18:4
Winter Soldiers 1942,N 30,19:2
Milky Way, The 1943,Je 10,17:2
Broken Hearts of Broadway 1944,Je 13,16:2
Lute Song 1946,F 7,29:2
Leavitt, Norman
How Beautiful With Shoes 1935,N 29,24:1
Leavitt, Philip B
Bad Habits of 1925 1925,F 9,17:1
Leavitt, Theodore
Where Do We Go From Here? 1938,N 16,26:2
Patriots, The 1943,D 21,22:5
Rugged Path, The 1945,N 12,17:2
Leavitt and Lockwood
Vaudeville (Palace) 1929,S 30,22:3
Lebaire, Dorothy
City Haul 1929,D 31,14:4
LeBargy
Moloch 1929,Ja 27,IX,2:8
Lebau, Arthur
Untitled-Passion Play 1925,Ag 17,8:1
Lebaudy, Jacques
Floriani's Wife 1923,O 1,10:1
Lebedeff, Aaron
Motke From Slobodke 1930,Ap 12,23:3
Village Wedding, A 1930,S 24,26:2
Russian Love 1930,N 27,32:3
Night in the Woods, A 1931,Mr 2,19:3
Lucky Night, The 1931,S 14,15:5
Great Miracle, The 1931,D 12,23:5
Rich Paupers 1932,Mr 14,13:4
Big Surprise, The 1932,O 17,18:3
Love for Sale 1932,D 5,21:4
Untitled-Benefit 1933,Ja 25,13:3
Honeymoon for Three, A 1933,Ja 30,9:6
Jewish Melody, The 1933,Mr 27,12:4
Happy Family, A 1934,S 24,15:2
Game of Love, A 1934,O 25,26:6
East Side Wedding, An 1935,Ja 21,18:2
Lovka Maladetz 1935,Mr 27,25:5
Heaven on Earth 1935,O 8,26:2
Oh, You Girls! 1935,D 2,19:5
Love for Sale 1936,Ja 24,14:2
My Malkele 1937,S 20,18:6
Bublitchki 1938,Ja 17,11:2
Lebedeff, Aaron (Director)
Big Surprise, The 1932,O 17,18:3
Happy Family, A 1934,S 24,15:2
Lebedeff, Aaron (Playwright)
Lovka Maladetz 1935,Mr 27,25:5
Lebedeff, Aaron (Producer)
Motke From Slobodke 1930,Ap 12,23:3
Night in the Woods, A 1931,Mr 2,19:3
Lebedeff, Paula
Motke From Slobodke 1930,Ap 12,23:3
Lebedeva
Moscow Circus on Ice 1970,D 9,63:1
Leberfeld, Alfred
At War With the Army 1949,Mr 9,32:2
49th Cousin, The 1960,O 28,22:1
Dumbbell People in a Barbell World 1962,F 15,25:1
Seidman and Son 1962,O 16,32:2
Volpone 1967,Je 30,29:1
Leberman, Joseph
Emperor Jones, The 1945,Ja 17,18:4
Twilight Walk 1951,S 25,25:4
Brass Ring, The 1952,Ap 11,19:2
Visit, The 1958,My 6,40:1
Visit, The 1960,Mr 9,38:3
Leberman, Joseph (Director)
Climate of Eden, The 1953,N 21,11:2
Leberman, Joseph (Miscellaneous)
Madness of Lady Bright, The 1966,Mr 23,42:1
Ludlow Fair 1966,Mr 23,42:1
Lebhar, Neil F
Fiesta 1933,D 16,12:2
Leblanc, Diana
Henry V 1966,Je 8,38:1
Heartbreak House 1968,Jl 6,9:1

Leblang, Joe (Mrs) (Miscellaneous)
Shoot the Works! 1931,Jl 26,VIII,2:1
Leblang, Tillie (Producer)
Tell Her the Truth 1932,O 29,18:2
Du Barry 1932,N 23,15:2
Lebok, Edith
J B 1958,Ap 24,37:1
Antigone 1959,S 16,46:2
LeBouvier, Jean
Streetcar Named Desire, A 1955,Mr 4,18:2
Plough and the Stars, The 1956,Ap 6,14:1
Caucasian Chalk Circle, The 1961,N 1,35:1
Mrs Warren's Profession 1963,Ap 25,39:1
Burning, The 1963,D 4,57:1
Lebowitz, Joan (Miscellaneous)
Where People Gather 1967,O 26,56:1
Brass Butterfly, The 1970,Ja 31,34:1
Lebowsky, Stanley (Composer)
Gantry 1970,F 16,44:1
Lebowsky, Stanley (Miscellaneous)
Irma la Douce 1960,S 30,31:2
Lebowsky, Stanley (Musical Director)
Irma la Douce 1960,S 30,31:2
Family Affair, A 1962,Ja 29,17:1
Tovarich 1963,Mr 20,5:1
Wonder World 1964,My 18,32:1
Half a Sixpence 1965,Ap 26,38:2
Lebrocq, E L
Marjolaine 1922,Ja 25,16:1
Lebrun, Daniele
Huis Clos 1962,Ja 16,30:1
Cantatrice Chauve, La 1962,Ja 16,30:1
George Dandin 1968,Je 28,36:1
Lebuc, Bob
Ice Follies 1959,Ja 14,30:1
Lecat, Annette
Voyage de Monsieur Perrichon, Le 1937,N 2,32:3
Knock 1937,N 17,26:3
Roi Cerf, Le 1937,N 30,26:3
Jean de la Lune 1937,D 14,33:3
Medecin Malgre Lui, Le 1937,D 28,28:7
Fantasio 1938,F 8,17:2
Caprice, Un 1938,F 8,17:2
Lechay, James
Joy of Serpents 1930,Ap 4,22:4
Lecke, Katherine
Clash by Night 1941,D 29,20:2
Leckel, Jack
Titus Andronicus 1956,D 3,40:2
Leckstroem, Eva
Green Table, The 1942,Ja 22,12:2
LeClair, Henry
Flora, the Red Menace 1965,My 12,41:2
Wonderful Town 1967,My 18,50:1
1776 1969,Mr 17,46:2
Leclerc, J
Deburau 1926,D 28,16:1
Mozart 1926,D 28,16:1
Illusioniste, L' 1927,Ja 11,36:5
Lecocq, Charles (Composer)
Girofle-Girofla 1926,N 23,26:3
1860: or, Aris; 1860, or an Interrupted Festival 1931,O 22,27:1
Lecocq, Charles (Playwright)
Girofle-Girofla 1926,N 24,26:2
Lecompte, Jo Ann
Mrs Patterson 1957,F 6,20:2
Lecourtois
Trois et Une 1933,Ja 1,IX,3:4
L'Ecuyer, Guy
Henry V 1966,Je 8,38:1
Henry VI 1966,Je 9,55:2
Twelfth Night 1966,Je 10,51:2
Ledbetter, William
H M S Pinafore 1965,Ap 15,39:1
Pirates of Penzance, The 1965,Ap 21,50:6
Yeomen of the Guard, The 1965,Ap 22,26:1
Pirates of Penzance, The 1968,Ap 26,32:1
Mikado, The 1968,My 2,59:1
Leder, Robert (Producer)
Daphne in Cottage D 1967,O 16,56:1
Lederer, Charles (Playwright)
Kismet 1953,D 4,2:4
Kismet 1965,Je 23,45:1
Lederer, Charles (Producer)
Kismet 1953,D 4,2:4
Lederer, Francis
Autumn Crocus 1931,Ap 26,VIII,2:4
Autumn Crocus 1932,N 21,20:2
Autumn Crocus 1934,Ja 21,X,1:6
Parisienne 1950,Jl 25,24:2
Arms and the Man 1950,O 20,34:2
Lederer, George W (Miscellaneous)
Joy of Living 1931,Ap 7,31:1
Lederer, George W (Producer)
Pajama Lady, The 1930,O 12,VIII,4:1
Lederer, Peppi
Nine Fifteen Revue, The 1930,F 12,26:2
Lederer, Richard
Lucky Sam McCarver 1950,Ap 15,10:6
Lederer, Virginia
Flowers of Virtue, The 1942,F 6,22:2

Lederman, D W (Miscellaneous)
Piper Paid 1934,D 26,19:1
Lederman, David (Producer)
Errant Lady 1934,S 18,18:2
Ledig, Howard
Pal Joey 1940,D 26,22:2
Ledl, Lotte
Konzert, Das 1968,Mr 25,52:1
Jux Will Er Sich Machen, Einen 1968,Ap 3,41:1
Ledner, Sam
Manhattan Mary 1927,S 27,30:3
Ledoux, Francoise
Feu la Mere de Madame; Dear Departed Mother-in-Law 1957,F 12,31:1
Intermezzo 1957,F 15,20:4
Chien du Jardinier, Le; Gardener's Dog, The 1957,F 19,36:1
Adieux, Les 1957,F 19,36:1
Ledova
Vaudeville (Palace) 1927,Ja 4,21:2
Vaudeville (Palace) 1928,Mr 6,20:5
Vaudeville (Palace) 1929,N 4,29:1
LeDuc, Bob
Ice Follies 1961,Ja 11,25:2
Ice Follies 1966,Ja 12,27:6
Ledyard, F H
Don Quixote, Esquire 1920,My 7,12:6
Somebody's Lion 1921,Ap 13,20:1
Lee
Gang's All Here, The 1931,F 19,21:3
Lee, Adele
Nativity Play, The 1937,D 21,29:1
Lee, Alan
Hook'n Ladder 1952,Ap 30,31:2
Lee, Allen
Cock o' the Roost 1924,O 14,23:1
Town Boy 1929,O 5,22:4
Nowhere Bound 1935,Ja 23,20:2
Sketch Book 1935,Je 5,22:2
Lee, Ann
Lady in the Dark 1941,Ja 24,14:2
Lady in the Dark 1941,S 3,26:6
Canteen Show, The 1942,S 4,18:1
Lady in the Dark 1943,Mr 1,14:2
O Mistress Mine 1946,Ja 24,25:2
Lee, Anne Marie
Faith and Prudence 1952,O 15,40:2
Lee, Arthur
Storm Center 1927,D 1,33:2
Lee, Auriol
Way of the World, The 1924,N 18,23:4
Dark Angel, The 1925,F 11,19:2
Vortex, The 1925,S 17,20:1
This Was a Man 1926,N 24,27:1
Lady Alone 1927,Ja 21,12:5
Nine Till Six 1930,S 29,17:2
Lee, Auriol (Director)
Nine Till Six 1930,S 29,17:2
There's Always Juliet 1931,O 13,26:5
After All 1931,D 4,28:4
There's Always Juliet 1932,F 16,24:2
Oliver Oliver 1934,Ja 6,18:5
Family Affairs 1934,Ag 23,13:3
Distaff Side, The 1934,S 26,17:2
Times Have Changed 1935,F 26,16:1
Flowers of the Forest 1935,Ap 9,25:2
Most of the Game 1935,O 2,27:4
Eden End 1935,O 22,17:1
Love From a Stranger 1936,S 30,28:1
I Know What I Like 1939,N 25,13:5
Leave Her to Heaven 1940,F 28,16:2
Old Acquaintance 1940,D 24,18:3
Lee, Auriol (Producer)
Distaff Side, The 1934,S 26,17:2
Flowers of the Forest 1934,N 21,23:2
Most of the Game 1935,O 2,27:4
Lee, Baayork
King and I, The 1951,Mr 30,26:2
Promises, Promises 1968,D 2,59:3
Lee, Beatrice
No, No, Nanette 1925,S 17,20:2
Speakeasy 1927,S 27,30:1
Lee, Bernard
If I Were You 1938,Ja 9,II,3:2
If I Were You 1938,Ja 25,24:2
Desperate Hours, The 1955,My 1,II,3:1
Lee, Bernice
Everybody's Welcome 1931,O 14,26:3
Walk a Little Faster 1932,D 8,24:4
Lee, Bert (Lyricist)
Tell Her the Truth 1932,O 29,18:2
Lee, Bert (Playwright)
Tell Her the Truth 1932,O 29,18:2
Lee, Betts
Dear Judas 1947,O 6,26:4
Lee, Big
Lovely Ladies, Kind Gentlemen 1970,D 29,38:1
Lee, Bob
Runnin' Wild 1923,O 30,17:3
Lee, Bryarly
Spring's Awakening 1955,O 10,30:2
Sea Gull, The 1956,O 23,38:1
Romeo and Juliet 1957,Je 28,30:2

Lee, Bryarly—Cont
Power of Dreams, A 1958,Mr 11,33:1
Summer of Daisy Miller, The 1963,My 28,33:1
Twelfth Night 1963,O 9,47:1
Lee, C Y (Original Author)
Flower Drum Song 1958,D 2,44:1
Flower Drum Song 1958,D 7,II,5:1
Lee, Canada
Stevedore 1934,O 2,18:2
Sailor, Beware! 1935,My 7,28:4
Macbeth 1936,Ap 15,25:4
One-Act Plays of the Sea; Bound East for Cardiff 1937,O 30,23:2
One-Act Plays of the Sea; Moon of the Caribbees 1937,O 30,23:2
Brown Sugar 1937,D 3,29:2
Haiti 1938,Mr 3,16:1
Mamba's Daughters 1939,Ja 4,24:2
Mamba's Daughters 1940,Mr 25,10:4
Big White Fog 1940,O 23,26:2
Native Son 1941,Mr 25,26:5
Native Son 1941,Ap 6,IX,1:1
Across the Board on Tomorrow Morning 1942,Ag 18,17:1
Talking to You 1942,Ag 18,17:1
Native Son 1942,O 24,10:6
Native Son 1942,N 1,VIII,1:1
South Pacific 1943,D 30,11:2
Anna Lucasta 1944,Ag 31,15:1
Anna Lucasta 1944,S 10,II,1:1
Tempest, The 1945,Ja 26,17:2
Tempest, The 1945,F 4,II,1:1
Tempest, The 1945,N 13,24:6
On Whitman Avenue 1946,My 9,28:2
Duchess of Malfi, The 1946,S 26,33:4
Duchess of Malfi, The 1946,O 16,35:2
Set My People Free 1948,N 4,38:2
Set My People Free 1948,N 14,II,1:1
Lee, Canada (Producer)
On Whitman Avenue 1946,My 9,28:2
Lee, Carl
Connection, The 1959,Jl 16,30:2
Shakespeare in Harlem 1959,O 28,40:7
Connection, The 1960,F 7,II,1:1
Marrying Maiden, The 1960,Je 23,18:3
Hamlet 1968,Jl 4,15:1
Ceremonies in Dark Old Men 1969,O 11,42:1
Lee, Cecile
Her Family Tree 1920,D 28,9:2
Lee, Charles (Playwright)
Mr Sampson 1927,My 6,20:3
Mr Sampson 1927,My 8,30:1
Lee, Dai-Keong (Composer)
Teahouse of the August Moon, The 1953,O 16,32:1
Teahouse of the August Moon, The 1956,N 9,33:2
Lee, Danny
Goodbye Again 1956,Ap 25,38:1
Lee, David (Composer)
Our Man Crichton 1964,D 23,21:1
Lee, David (Lyricist)
Our Man Crichton 1964,D 23,21:1
Lee, Dedette
What the Doctor Ordered 1927,Ag 19,20:2
Lee, Donald
Princess Flavia 1925,N 3,34:3
John 1927,N 5,16:4
Devil and Daniel Webster, The 1939,My 19,26:1
Innocent Voyage, The 1943,N 16,27:2
Jacobowsky and the Colonel 1944,Mr 15,17:2
Teahouse of the August Moon, The 1955,My 10,24:1
Lee, Dora
Allez-Opp! 1927,Ag 3,29:3
Lee, Dorothy
Hello, Yourself 1928,O 31,28:2
Vaudeville (Palace) 1929,D 2,28:6
Lee, Earle
Princess Flavia 1925,N 3,34:3
Lee, Eugene (Scenic Designer)
Fitz 1966,My 17,51:2
Biscuit 1966,My 17,51:2
Brother to Dragons 1968,D 8,86:1
World War 2 1/2 1969,Mr 25,40:1
Slave Ship 1969,N 22,46:1
Wilson in the Promise Land 1970,Ja 11,78:1
Universal Nigger, The 1970,Mr 21,18:1
Wilson in the Promise Land 1970,My 27,41:1
Alice in Wonderland 1970,O 9,43:1
Saved 1970,O 29,57:1
Lee, Eunice
Kiss for Cinderella, A 1942,Mr 11,22:2
Lee, Evelyn
Cherry Lane Follies, The 1930,Je 30,22:4
Finian's Rainbow 1953,Mr 7,13:2
Lee, Florence
Kiki 1921,N 30,13:1
Make Me Know It 1929,N 5,32:5
Ol' Man Satan 1932,O 4,26:3
Four O'Clock 1933,F 14,19:6
Sailor, Beware! 1935,My 7,28:4
Lee, Fran
Simon's Wife 1945,Mr 9,16:4
Lee, Frances
Hassard Short's Ritz Revue 1924,S 18,19:1

Lee, Gene
Medea 1947,O 21,27:2
Lee, George
Tom Sawyer 1931,D 26,15:3
Baker Street 1965,F 17,36:1
Lee, George W 4th
Hair 1970,Ja 13,39:1
Lee, Gypsy Rose
Spring Tonic 1936,My 11,16:1
Ziegfeld Follies 1936,S 15,37:1
Star and Garter 1942,Je 25,26:2
Star and Garter 1942,S 13,VIII,1:1
Curious Evening With Gypsy Rose Lee, A
  1961,My 10,53:1
Lee, Gypsy Rose (Director)
Curious Evening With Gypsy Rose Lee, A
  1961,My 10,53:1
Lee, Gypsy Rose (Miscellaneous)
Gypsy 1959,My 22,31:6
Gypsy 1959,My 31,II,1:1
Curious Evening With Gypsy Rose Lee, A
  1961,My 10,53:1
Lee, Gypsy Rose (Playwright)
Naked Genius, The 1943,O 22,20:5
Naked Genius, The 1943,O 31,II,1:1
Naked Genius, The 1943,N 7,II,1:6
Lee, Gypsy Rose (Producer)
Curious Evening With Gypsy Rose Lee, A
  1961,My 10,53:1
Lee, Harriette
Sun Showers 1923,F 6,14:2
Lee, Harry (Playwright)
Little Poor Man, The 1925,Ag 6,14:1
Little Poor Man, The 1925,Ag 23,VII,1:1
Lee, Helen
Pirates of Penzance, The 1942,F 20,20:2
Lee, Hermione
Midsummer Night's Dream, A 1968,D 9,59:1
Lee, Howard
Boom Boom 1929,Ja 29,26:4
Cock-A-Doodle Dandy 1958,N 13,39:2
Lee, Ira
Young Madame Conti 1937,Ap 1,18:4
Lee, Irene
Bulls, Bears and Asses 1932,My 7,11:3
Lee, J R
Jolly Roger, The 1923,Ag 31,10:4
Lee, Jack
Subway Express 1929,S 25,34:3
Marching By 1932,Mr 4,17:1
This Thing Called Love 1935,Jl 2,24:4
Holmeses of Baker Street, The 1936,D 10,34:3
Lost Colony, The 1937,Jl 11,X,2:1
Too Many Heroes 1937,N 16,26:2
Abortion 1959,O 28,40:4
Lee, Jack (Miscellaneous)
Best Foot Forward 1956,Mr 3,16:1
Valmouth 1960,O 7,29:1
Fig Leaves Are Falling, The 1969,Ja 3,19:1
Lee, Jack (Musical Director)
Best Foot Forward 1956,Mr 3,16:1
Fortuna 1962,Ja 4,26:1
Up Eden 1968,N 27,42:1
Billy 1969,Mr 24,56:1
Sensations 1970,O 26,48:2
Lee, Jackie
Song of Norway 1944,Ag 22,20:2
Lee, James (Miscellaneous)
Trial of Dmitri Karamazov, The 1958,Ja 28,30:1
Lee, James (Playwright)
Career 1957,My 1,42:6
Career 1957,My 19,II,1:1
Lee, Jane
Laugh Parade, The 1931,S 20,VIII,3:1
Dance of Death, The 1932,Ja 11,29:5
Lee, Jane and Katherine
Vaudeville (Palace) 1932,Je 13,19:7
Lee, Janie C (Miscellaneous)
Thistle in My Bed 1963,N 20,48:1
Lee, Jay (Director)
Annie Get Your Gun 1957,Mr 9,15:5
Lee, Jesica (Playwright)
Empress of Destiny 1938,Mr 10,16:2
Lee, Joan
Ice Capades 1958,S 4,33:2
Lee, John
Ginger Snaps 1930,Ja 1,30:5
Hummin' Sam 1933,Ap 10,8:8
Bamboo Cross 1955,F 22,17:2
Flower Drum Song 1958,D 2,44:1
In the Bar of a Tokyo Hotel 1969,My 12,54:1
Lee, John (Costume Designer)
Buoyant Billions 1959,My 27,32:2
Overruled 1959,My 27,32:2
Getting Married 1959,Je 5,18:2
Lee, Joseph
Back Here 1928,N 27,36:3
Street Scene 1929,Ja 11,20:4
Lee, Joshua (Composer)
Set My People Free 1948,N 4,38:2
Lee, Joshua (Miscellaneous)
Our Lan' 1947,Ap 19,11:2
Our Lan' 1947,S 29,16:5

Sojourner Truth 1948,Ap 22,35:2
Lee, Joshua (Musical Director)
Our Lan' 1947,S 29,16:5
Set My People Free 1948,N 4,38:2
Lee, Joyce
Winterset 1966,F 10,32:2
Lee, Katherine
Jean le Mauranc 1927,Ja 2,VII,2:1
Laugh Parade, The 1931,S 20,VIII,3:1
Dance of Death, The 1932,Ja 11,29:5
Lee, Kathryn
Helen Goes to Troy 1944,Ap 25,17:2
Laffing Room Only 1944,D 25,15:4
Allegro 1947,O 11,10:2
Allegro 1948,Ja 18,II,3:5
As the Girls Go 1948,N 15,21:2
Maggie 1953,F 19,20:2
Lee, Kenneth
Nature's Nobleman 1921,N 15,23:2
Lee, Kimo
Arrow-Maker, The 1956,O 5,20:1
Lee, Laura
Greenwich Village Follies 1928,Ap 10,32:2
Broadway Nights 1929,Je 23,VIII,2:4
Broadway Nights 1929,Jl 16,23:2
Auntie Mame 1958,Ag 12,33:2
Lee, Lawrence
Lady Billy 1920,D 15,18:2
Lee, Leonard (Playwright)
Deadfall 1955,O 28,20:1
Lee, Lester (Composer)
Harry Delmar's Revels 1927,N 29,30:2
Keep It Clean 1929,Je 25,35:5
Star and Garter 1942,Je 25,26:2
New Priorities of 1943 1942,S 16,28:2
All for Love 1949,Ja 24,16:5
Lee, Lester (Lyricist)
Keep It Clean 1929,Je 25,35:5
Star and Garter 1942,Je 25,26:2
New Priorities of 1943 1942,S 16,28:2
All for Love 1949,Ja 24,16:5
Lee, Lester (Miscellaneous)
Ziegfeld Follies 1943,Ap 2,16:2
Lee, Lila
Bride Retires, The 1925,My 18,12:3
Edgar Allan Poe 1925,O 6,31:1
Edgar Allan Poe 1925,O 11,VIII,1:1
Lady Jane 1934,S 11,24:2
Blind Alley 1940,O 16,28:2
Milky Way, The 1943,Je 10,17:2
Lee, Lillian
Cinders 1923,Ap 4,22:1
Lee, Linda
Between the Devil 1937,D 23,24:5
Medicine Show 1940,Ap 13,20:6
It's About Time 1942,Mr 31,28:3
Seven Mirrors 1945,O 26,17:2
Women of Twilight 1952,Mr 4,22:2
Lee, Lois
High Button Shoes 1947,O 10,32:2
Lee, Lorelei
Diary of a Scoundrel 1956,N 5,41:1
Lee, Lovey
Peg o' My Dreams 1924,My 6,25:3
Magnolia Lady, The 1924,N 26,17:2
Tip-Toes 1925,D 29,20:2
Tip-Toes 1926,S 1,27:4
Lee, Mabel
Shuffle Along 1952,My 9,20:5
Hoofers, The 1969,Jl 30,23:4
Lee, Madeline
Embezzled Heaven 1944,N 1,20:2
Lee, Madeline (Miscellaneous)
Portrait of the Artist as a Young Man, A
  1962,My 29,21:1
Barroom Monks, The 1962,My 29,21:1
Lee, Margaret
Dr David's Dad 1924,Ag 14,10:3
Beware of Widows 1925,D 2,22:3
Keep Shufflin' 1928,F 28,18:3
Follow Thru 1929,Ja 10,24:3
June Moon 1929,O 10,34:5
Three's a Crowd 1930,O 5,IX,4:6
Three's a Crowd 1930,O 16,28:3
Sugar Hill 1931,D 26,15:2
Face the Music 1932,F 18,24:5
Face the Music 1933,F 1,13:4
Revenge With Music 1934,N 29,33:5
Lee, Margie
Hollywood Ice Revue 1956,Ja 13,17:1
Lee, Marie
Finian's Rainbow 1953,Mr 7,13:2
Lee, Marie (Musical Director)
Finian's Rainbow 1953,Mr 7,13:2
Lee, Marion
These Days 1928,N 13,36:2
Flight 1929,F 19,22:3
Lee, Marsha
Fun With Music 1946,N 25,38:5
Lee, Martin (Producer)
Slight Ache, A 1964,D 10,62:1
Room, The 1964,D 10,62:1
Boeing-Boeing 1965,F 3,30:1

Lee, Martin (Producer)—Cont
Wayward Stork, The 1966,Ja 20,27:1
Lee, Mary
Vaudeville (Palace) 1928,S 4,21:3
Lee, Mercedes
Martinique 1920,Ap 27,18:2
Lee, Michael
Finian's Rainbow 1953,Mr 7,13:2
Lee, Michele
Vintage '60 1960,S 13,41:1
Bravo Giovanni 1962,My 21,41:2
Bravo Giovanni 1962,My 27,II,1:1
Lee, Mickey
Marcus in the High Grass 1960,N 22,38:6
Lee, Mildred
Complex, The 1925,Mr 4,17:2
Lee, Ming Cho (Lighting Director)
Crucible, The 1958,Mr 12,36:1
Merchant of Venice, The 1962,Je 22,1:4
Tempest, The 1962,Jl 17,18:2
King Lear 1962,Ag 14,35:1
Macbeth 1962,N 17,16:2
Moon Besieged, The 1962,D 6,54:1
Antony and Cleopatra 1963,Je 21,33:1
As You Like It 1963,Jl 17,19:2
Walk in Darkness 1963,O 29,30:2
Hamlet 1964,Je 17,49:1
Lee, Ming Cho (Scenic Designer)
Infernal Machine, The 1958,F 4,33:1
Evening With Ethel Waters, An 1959,Ap 9,36:1
Merchant of Venice, The 1962,Je 22,1:4
Tempest, The 1962,Jl 17,18:2
King Lear 1962,Ag 14,35:1
Macbeth 1962,N 17,16:2
Mother Courage and Her Children 1963,Mr 30,5:5
Antony and Cleopatra 1963,Je 21,33:1
As You Like It 1963,Jl 17,19:2
Winter's Tale, The 1963,Ag 16,14:1
Walk in Darkness 1963,O 29,30:2
Hamlet 1964,Je 17,49:1
Othello 1964,Jl 15,29:1
Electra 1964,Ag 12,42:1
Othello 1964,O 13,48:1
Love's Labour's Lost 1965,Je 16,46:1
Henry V 1965,Je 29,27:2
Taming of the Shrew, The 1965,Jl 3,10:5
Coriolanus 1965,Jl 15,23:1
Troilus and Cressida 1965,Ag 13,17:1
Gnadiges Fraulein, The 1966,F 23,42:1
Mutilated, The 1966,F 23,42:1
Time for Singing, A 1966,My 23,48:2
All's Well That Ends Well 1966,Je 17,39:1
Measure for Measure 1966,Jl 14,27:1
Richard III 1966,Ag 11,26:1
Little Murders 1967,Ap 26,38:1
Comedy of Errors, The 1967,Je 15,58:4
Titus Andronicus 1967,Ag 10,43:2
Hair 1967,O 30,55:1
Ergo 1968,Mr 4,29:1
Here's Where I Belong 1968,Mr 4,32:1
Iceman Cometh, The 1968,Ap 1,58:1
Henry IV, Part I 1968,Je 30,54:7
Henry IV, Part II 1968,Jl 2,33:1
Romeo and Juliet 1968,Ag 16,19:1
King Lear 1968,N 8,43:1
Cities in Bezique; Owl Answers, The
  1969,Ja 13,26:1
Cities in Bezique; Beast's Story, A 1969,Ja 13,26:1
Invitation to a Beheading 1969,Mr 18,36:1
Billy 1969,Mr 24,56:1
Peer Gynt 1969,Jl 17,56:1
Electra 1969,Ag 8,14:1
Strada, La 1969,D 15,63:1
Sambo 1969,D 22,42:1
Wars of the Roses, The (Part I) 1970,Jl 2,30:1
Wars of the Roses, The (Part II) 1970,Jl 3,15:1
Richard III 1970,Jl 4,11:1
Sambo 1970,Jl 23,24:1
Gandhi 1970,O 21,37:1
Night Thoreau Spent in Jail, The 1970,N 2,66:1
Jack MacGowran in the Works of Samuel Beckett
  1970,N 20,32:1
Jack MacGowran in the Works of Samuel Beckett
  1970,N 27,46:1
Lee, Morris
Man With Red Hair, A 1928,N 9,22:2
Skyrocket, The 1929,Ja 12,14:7
Lee, Nancy
Within Four Walls 1923,Ap 18,24:1
Red, Hot and Blue! 1936,O 30,26:3
Lee, Norma
Dulcy 1921,Ag 15,14:1
Wild Westcotts, The 1923,D 25,26:2
Poor Nut, The 1925,Ap 19,IX,2:1
Poor Nut, The 1925,Ap 28,18:1
1776 1926,Ap 24,11:2
Kempy 1927,My 12,25:2
By Request 1928,Ag 26,VII,2:1
By Request 1928,S 28,30:2
Lee, Olga
Transplanting Jean 1921,Ja 4,11:2
Out of the Seven Seas 1923,N 20,23:3
Cheaper to Marry 1924,Ap 16,26:1

Lee, Olga—Cont
Great Music 1924,O 6,24:1
Grand Duchess and the Waiter, The 1925,O 14,31:1
Mouthpiece, The 1929,Je 16,VIII,2:1
Hawk Island 1929,S 17,34:7
Macbeth 1930,Mr 26,24:6
Lee, Paula
Flossie 1924,Je 4,25:2
Lee, Phoebe
George White's Scandals 1921,Jl 12,14:1
Lee, Pinky
Wine, Women and Song 1942,S 29,18:3
Lee, Ralph
King Lear 1963,N 23,22:1
Terminal 1970,Ap 15,51:2
Serpent, The 1970,Je 2,35:1
Lee, Ralph (Miscellaneous)
Tragical Historie of Doctor Faustus, The 1964,O 6,34:2
Galileo 1967,Ap 14,31:1
Dracula Sabbat 1970,O 2,28:2
Lee, Richard
Passing Show of 1924, The 1924,S 4,13:4
See My Lawyer 1939,S 28,29:1
Richard III 1966,Ag 11,26:1
Lee, Robert E
Blue Flame, The 1920,Mr 16,18:1
Lady in the Dark 1941,Ja 24,14:2
Yours, A Lincoln 1942,Jl 10,12:3
Career Angel 1944,My 24,23:7
Lee, Robert E (Lyricist)
Shangri-La 1956,Je 14,40:1
Lee, Robert E (Original Author)
Look, Ma, I'm Dancin' 1948,Ja 30,20:2
Lee, Robert E (Playwright)
Inherit the Wind 1955,Ja 12,24:1
Inherit the Wind 1955,Ap 22,20:2
Inherit the Wind 1955,S 25,II,1:1
Shangri-La 1956,Je 14,40:1
Auntie Mame 1956,N 1,47:2
Auntie Mame 1956,N 11,II,1:1
Auntie Mame 1958,Je 8,II,1:1
Auntie Mame 1958,Ag 12,33:2
Gang's All Here, The 1959,O 2,23:1
Gang's All Here, The 1959,O 11,II,1:1
Only in America 1959,N 20,35:1
Call on Kuprin, A 1961,My 26,29:3
Call on Kuprin, A 1961,Je 4,II,1:1
Diamond Orchid 1965,F 11,44:4
Mame 1966,My 25,41:1
Inherit the Wind 1967,Je 23,50:1
Mame 1968,Ap 20,25:1
Dear World 1969,F 7,33:1
Night Thoreau Spent in Jail, The 1970,N 2,66:1
Lee, Robert E (Scenic Designer)
Beaux' Stratagem, The 1957,Jl 9,25:4
Pink String and Sealing Wax 1957,S 6,13:1
Magistrate, The 1959,My 14,30:6
Lee, Robert Tyler (Scenic Designer)
Summer and Smoke 1950,O 29,II,3:7
Lee, Ronie
West Side Story 1957,S 27,14:4
Lee, Ronnie (Miscellaneous)
Volpone 1957,Ja 8,27:1
Lee, Rosa
Happy 1927,D 6,26:3
Lee, Ruth
Yankee Princess, The 1922,O 3,22:1
Hush Money 1926,Mr 16,22:3
Sunshine 1926,Ag 18,15:2
We Americans 1926,O 13,20:4
June Moon 1929,Ag 4,VIII,1:6
Queer People 1934,F 16,16:2
Lost Horizons 1934,O 16,31:2
In the Bag 1936,D 18,30:2
Case History 1938,O 22,15:2
Window Shopping 1938,D 24,13:2
Your Loving Son 1941,Ap 5,13:2
Lee, Saja
International Playgirls '64 1964,My 22,40:2
Lee, Sally
Nowhere to Go But Up 1962,N 12,36:2
Half a Sixpence 1965,Ap 26,38:2
Lee, Sammy
Five O'Clock Girl, The 1927,O 11,26:3
Scarlet Fox, The 1928,Mr 28,31:1
Pleasure Bound 1929,F 19,22:4
Vaudeville (Palace) 1930,Ag 18,24:3
Vaudeville (Palace) 1931,S 28,17:5
Lee, Sammy (Choreographer)
Oh, Kay! 1926,N 9,31:3
Talk About Girls 1927,Je 15,31:3
Ziegfeld Follies 1927,Ag 17,27:3
Show Boat 1927,D 28,26:1
Here's Howe! 1928,My 2,19:3
Lady Fingers 1929,F 1,22:4
Crazy Quilt 1931,My 20,28:4
Singin' the Blues 1931,S 17,21:3
Lee, Sammy (Director)
Cocoanuts, The 1925,D 9,30:1
Tip-Toes 1925,D 29,20:2
Queen High 1926,S 9,21:2
Betsy 1926,D 29,24:3

Follies 1927,Ag 28,VII,1:1
Yes, Yes, Yvette 1927,O 4,32:3
Cross My Heart 1928,S 18,32:7
Lee, Sammy (Miscellaneous)
Ramblers, The 1926,S 21,32:2
Lee, Sammy (Producer)
Cross My Heart 1928,S 18,32:7
Going Gay 1933,Ag 4,18:5
Hold Your Horses 1933,S 26,26:4
Green Waters 1936,N 5,34:4
Day After Tomorrow 1950,O 27,25:2
Lee, Samuel S
Fanny 1926,S 22,30:1
Lee, Sandra
Sunday in New York 1961,N 10,40:1
Lee, Selina
Ice Capades 1958,S 4,33:2
Lee, Sharon
High Button Shoes 1955,Mr 12,10:6
Lee, Sidney
Long Gallery, The 1958,Mr 7,17:2
John Turner Davis 1958,Jl 2,25:1
Trip to Bountiful, The 1959,F 27,20:4
Lee, Sondra
High Button Shoes 1947,O 10,32:2
Peter Pan 1954,O 21,30:2
Peter Pan 1954,O 31,II,1:1
Hotel Paradiso 1957,Ap 12,22:2
Hotel Paradiso 1957,Ap 21,II,1:1
Winkelberg 1958,Ja 15,26:2
Hello, Dolly! 1964,Ja 17,22:1
Hello, Dolly! 1965,Ag 10,17:2
Lee, Sondra (Director)
Exchange 1970,F 9,47:2
Lee, Sylvan
Naughty Riquette 1926,S 14,25:2
Lee, Sylvia
Will, The 1930,My 6,33:1
Tree, The 1932,Ap 13,23:5
Lee, Thelma
Sing Out the News 1938,S 26,12:5
Lee, Theophane (Playwright)
Bamboo Cross 1955,F 22,17:2
Lee, Tom
It Happens on Ice 1941,Ap 5,13:2
Lee, Tom (Costume Designer)
Louisiana Purchase 1940,My 29,19:2
Walk With Music 1940,Je 5,33:2
Lee, Tom (Playwright)
Variations of 1940 1940,Ja 29,12:1
Lee, Tom (Scenic Designer)
Louisiana Purchase 1940,My 29,19:2
Lee, Tong Wi
Finian's Rainbow 1953,Mr 7,13:2
Lee, Valerie
Here's Love 1963,O 4,28:1
Glorious Ruler, The 1969,Jl 1,31:1
Lee, Vanessa
After The Ball 1954,Je 11,19:3
Lee, Virginia
Silks and Satins 1920,Jl 16,19:1
Red White and Blue 1950,O 8,64:5
Lee, Wendy (Lighting Director)
Kaleidoscope 1957,Je 14,20:2
Power of Dreams, A 1958,Mr 11,33:1
Lee, Wendy (Scenic Designer)
Power of Dreams, A 1958,Mr 11,33:1
Lee, Will
Grab Bag, The 1924,O 7,26:2
Young Go First, The 1935,My 29,16:2
Family Portrait 1939,Mr 9,18:4
Time of Your Life, The 1939,O 26,26:2
Night Music 1940,F 23,18:2
Heavenly Express 1940,Ap 19,24:2
Lily of the Valley 1942,Ja 27,25:2
Strings, My Lord, Are False, The 1942,My 20,24:2
Mexican Hayride 1944,Ja 29,9:6
Dream Girl 1945,D 15,13:2
As We Forgive Our Debtors 1947,Mr 11,37:2
Strange Bedfellows 1948,Ja 15,27:3
Jenny Kissed Me 1948,D 24,12:2
Dream Girl 1951,My 10,39:1
Grand Tour, The 1951,D 11,45:2
Shrike, The 1952,Ja 16,20:2
World of Sholom Aleichem, The 1953,S 12,13:2
World of Sholom Aleichem, The 1953,S 20,II,1:1
Carnival! 1961,Ap 14,22:2
Last Analysis, The 1964,O 2,30:1
Incident at Vichy 1964,D 4,44:1
Incident at Vichy 1964,D 20,II,3:1
Deer Park, The 1967,F 1,27:2
Deer Park, The 1967,F 12,II,1:4
Lee, Winston
Airways, Inc 1929,F 21,30:5
Lee, Young
Egotist, The 1922,D 27,12:1
Lee Trio
Mexicana 1939,Ap 22,14:4
Leebove, Isaiah (Producer)
New York 1927,N 15,26:2
Leech, George
Round-Up, The 1932,Mr 8,19:4

Leech, Johnny
Holiday on Ice 1967,Ag 31,29:2
Holiday on Ice 1969,Ag 28,44:1
Leech, Lloyd Thomas
Fledermaus, Die 1954,My 20,38:5
Leech, Margaret (Playwright)
Divided by Three 1934,S 28,26:3
Divided by Three 1934,O 3,24:2
Leech, Richard
Lady's Not for Burning, The 1950,N 9,42:2
Leedom, Edna
Vaudeville (Palace) 1923,F 13,25:1
Ziegfeld Follies 1923,O 22,17:2
Follies 1925,Jl 7,24:3
No Foolin' 1926,Je 25,25:1
Lovely Lady 1927,D 30,22:1
Leeds, Barbara
Children's Hour, The 1934,N 21,23:2
Boy Meets Girl 1937,Jl 6,23:1
Virginia Reel 1947,Ap 15,28:2
Leeds, Dorothy
Florodora 1920,Ap 6,18:1
Leeds, Felice
Beggarman, Thief 1935,Jl 16,24:1
Leeds, Jo-Anne
Stop the World-I Want to Get Off 1962,O 4,45:4
Leeds, Lyda Sue
Show Is On, The 1937,S 20,18:4
Leeds, Myra
Uncle Sam in Israel 1952,D 8,38:5
Leeds, Nancy (Lyricist)
Great Scot! 1965,N 12,56:3
Leeds, Peter
Press Time 1938,N 28,10:4
My Heart's in the Highlands 1939,Ap 14,29:2
As You Like It 1939,My 9,28:4
Summer Night 1939,N 3,17:1
Leeds, Phil
Of V We Sing 1941,O 26,I,39:1
Of V We Sing 1942,F 16,20:3
Let Freedom Sing 1942,O 6,18:2
Make a Wish 1951,Ap 19,38:1
Can-Can 1953,My 8,28:1
Matchmaker, The 1955,D 6,45:6
Matchmaker, The 1955,D 18,II,3:1
Romanoff and Juliet 1957,O 11,24:1
Christine 1960,Ap 29,27:1
Smiling the Boy Fell Dead 1961,Ap 20,28:1
Banker's Daughter, The 1962,Ja 23,37:1
Nowhere to Go But Up 1962,N 12,36:2
Wonderful Town 1963,F 15,10:2
Sophie 1963,Ap 16,32:1
Nobody Loves an Albatross 1963,D 20,20:1
Mardi Gras! 1965,Je 28,33:2
Hotel Passionato 1965,O 23,16:1
Mardi Gras! 1966,Jl 11,32:2
Dinner at Eight 1966,S 28,38:1
Dinner at Eight 1966,O 9,II,1:1
Little Murders 1967,Ap 26,38:1
Inquest 1970,Ap 24,38:1
Leeds, Sandy
Royal Hunt of the Sun, The 1965,O 27,36:2
Leeds, Strelsa
Boy Who Lived Twice, A 1945,S 12,31:2
Leeds, Tom
Privilege Car 1931,Mr 4,33:1
Leeman, Joanne
Follies of 1910, The 1960,Ja 15,37:3
Leemans, Fernand
Eisrevue 1969,O 23,55:1
Leeming, Esther
Petrified Forest, The 1935,Ja 8,26:1
Straw Hat, The 1937,D 31,8:2
Lees, Bob
Hobo 1961,Ap 11,41:2
Lees, C Lowell (Director)
Promised Valley 1947,Jl 23,18:3
Lees, C Lowell (Miscellaneous)
Macbeth 1947,My 30,25:1
Lees, Justin
Man in the Making, The 1921,S 21,16:2
Golden Days 1921,N 2,20:1
Leet, Marjorie
Criss Cross 1926,O 13,20:2
Leewah, Eva
Mu Lan 1921,F 25,16:2
LeFaun, J V (Original Author)
Carmilla 1970,D 1,61:2
Lefaur, Andre
Miracle, Un 1927,D 25,VIII,4:3
Maud et Son Banquier 1928,Ap 1,IX,4:7
Topaze 1928,N 4,IX,4:4
Homme, la Bete et la Vertu, L'; Say It With Flowers 1931,D 13,VIII,2:2
Onzieme Commandement 1932,My 15,VIII,2:2
Monsieur le Comte 1933,F 12,IX,3:4
Tovarich 1933,D 3,IX,7:7
Lefeaux, Charles
These Mortals 1936,Ja 5,IX,1:1
LeFevre, George
Marion Show, The 1923,My 8,22:3
LeFevre, May
Marion Show, The 1923,My 8,22:3

Leffingwell, Dolores
Iolanthe 1965,My 19,42:1
Yeomen of the Guard, The 1965,Jl 8,34:1
Leffler, George (Producer)
One Way Street 1928,D 25,31:2
Leffler, John (Producer)
Octoroon, The 1929,Mr 13,28:3
Leffler, Martha
Pride 1923,My 3,22:3
Lefkowitz, John
Boy on the Straight-Back Chair 1969,Mr 18,36:1
Lefrancq, Germaine (Playwright)
Aurelie 1932,D 18,X,3:6
Leftwich, Alexander
Silver Swan, The 1929,N 28,34:5
Bellamy Trial, The 1931,Ap 23,28:6
Leftwich, Alexander (Director)
Set a Thief 1927,F 22,22:1
Hit the Deck! 1927,Ap 26,32:1
Connecticut Yankee, A 1927,N 4,24:2
Take the Air 1927,N 23,28:2
Rain or Shine 1928,F 10,26:3
Present Arms 1928,Ap 27,16:2
Song Writer, The 1928,Ag 14,15:2
Chee-Chee 1928,S 26,25:1
Hello, Daddy! 1928,D 27,26:5
Spring Is Here 1929,Mr 12,26:1
Strike Up the Band 1930,Ja 15,29:1
Girl Crazy 1930,O 15,27:1
Sweet and Low 1930,N 18,28:5
Third Little Show, The 1931,Je 2,34:3
Hey, Nonny, Nonny! 1932,Je 7,22:3
Orchids Preferred 1937,Ap 29,16:6
Orchids Preferred 1937,My 12,26:5
Leftwich, Alexander (Miscellaneous)
Eternal Road, The 1937,Ap 25,X,1:6
Leftwich, Alexander (Producer)
Tattle Tales 1930,Jl 20,VIII,2:1
Leftwich, Helen
Orchids Preferred 1937,My 12,26:5
Legal, Ernst (Director)
Goetz von Berlichingen 1930,D 14,IX,4:1
Legant, Dan (Miscellaneous)
Doll's House, A 1956,My 8,29:2
Legate, Tommy
Hippolytus 1948,N 22,25:5
Legendre, Micheline (Director)
Toy Box 1955,D 18,95:3
Leger, Gilles
Good Woman of Setzuan, The 1960,D 25,II,5:1
Legg, Harris
Ice Follies 1937,D 22,29:1
Ice Follies 1939,D 5,38:2
Legg, Lodema
Sunny River 1941,D 5,28:2
Leggatt, Alison
Fanatics, The 1927,Ap 10,VIII,1:3
March Hares 1928,Ja 1,VIII,1:3
Astonished Heart, The 1936,Ja 10,16:1
Astonished Heart, The 1936,F 2,IX,3:4
Epitaph for George Dillon 1958,N 5,44:1
Leggatt, Alison Joy
Big House, The 1934,Mr 18,IX,2:3
Legge, Tressie
Ol' Man Satan 1932,O 4,26:3
Leggett, Gene
Macbeth 1968,N 30,49:3
Leggett, John Ward (Translator)
Frogs, The 1941,N 14,25:3
Leggi, James
Conduct Unbecoming 1970,O 13,50:1
Legionaire, Robert
Ah, Wilderness! 1969,N 9,86:1
Legrand, Michel (Composer)
Of Love Remembered 1967,F 20,46:5
Legras, Jacques
Plume de Ma Tante, La 1958,N 12,42:1
Cantatrice Chauve, La 1962,Ja 16,30:1
LeGuardia, Robert
Don Juan in the Russian Manner 1954,Ap 23,23:2
Lehak, Ned
You Can't Sleep Here 1941,My 11,I,42:6
Lehak, Ned (Composer)
Nine Fifteen Revue, The 1930,F 12,26:2
Garrick Gaieties 1930,Je 5,29:2
Let's Play Fair 1938,Ja 19,26:4
Of V We Sing 1942,F 16,20:3
Lehak, Ned (Lyricist)
Nine Fifteen Revue, The 1930,F 12,26:2
Lehak, Ned (Miscellaneous)
Sing for Your Supper 1939,Ap 25,18:6
Lehar, Franz (Composer)
Blaue Mazur, Der 1921,My 15,VI,1:6
Merry Widow, The 1921,S 6,13:1
Yellow Jacket, The 1923,F 9,10:6
Three Graces, The 1924,F 3,VII,1:4
Frasquita 1924,Mr 2,VIII,2:1
Frasquita 1925,My 3,VIII,2:1
Paganini 1925,N 22,VIII,1:8
Love Spell, The 1925,N 25,14:2
Zarewitsch, Der 1927,Ap 3,VIII,2:1
Friederike 1929,F 17,IX,2:3
Merry Widow, The 1929,D 3,29:1

Land des Laechelns, Das 1929,D 8,X,4:4
Count of Luxembourg, The 1930,F 18,28:2
Prince Chu Chang 1930,O 12,VIII,4:1
Schoen ist die Welt 1931,Ja 11,VIII,1:8
Land of Smiles 1931,My 9,15:2
Merry Widow, The 1931,S 8,39:1
Schon Ist die Welt; Endlich Allein
1932,Ja 17,VIII,2:1
Merry Widow, The 1932,F 21,VIII,23:3
Merry Widow, The 1932,N 27,IX,1:2
Merry Widow, The 1933,Ag 13,IX,1:3
Giuditta 1934,Ja 21,30:1
Gypsy Love; Moon Rises, The 1934,Ap 16,21:6
Moon Rises, The 1934,Ap 22,IX,1:1
Chanson du Bonheur, La 1935,N 24,IX,6:4
Frederika 1937,F 5,16:5
Paganini 1937,My 21,18:6
Paganini 1937,Je 6,XI,1:2
Frederika 1937,Jl 28,15:2
Merry Widow, The 1942,Jl 16,22:1
Merry Widow, The 1943,Ag 22,II,5:1
Merry Widow, The 1943,S 26,II,1:5
Yours Is My Heart 1946,S 6,16:5
Merry Widow, The 1957,Ap 11,36:6
Lehar, Franz (Musical Director)
Giuditta 1934,Ja 21,30:1
Lehar, Franz (Original Author)
Merry Widow, The 1961,O 27,28:2
Lehar, Franz (Playwright)
Merry Widow, The 1964,Ag 18,24:2
Lehman, Al (Costume Designer)
Cherry Orchard, The 1955,O 19,38:1
Antigone 1956,Ap 3,32:2
Leave It to Jane 1959,My 26,30:2
Kittiwake Island 1960,O 13,43:1
Secret Life of Walter Mitty, The 1964,O 27,44:5
Lehman, Alexander (Director)
Hamlet 1938,N 8,26:1
Lehman, Alexander (Playwright)
Once Over Lightly 1938,D 10,13:4
Once Over Lightly 1938,D 17,10:8
Lehman, Leo (Playwright)
East Wind, The 1967,F 10,30:1
Lehman, Orin (Miscellaneous)
Little Murders 1969,Ja 6,38:1
Lehman, Orin (Producer)
Sudden and Accidental Re-education of Horse
Johnson, The 1968,D 19,63:1
Tonight in Living Color; David Show, The
1969,Je 11,43:1
Tonight in Living Color; Golden Fleece, The
1969,Je 11,43:1
American Hamburger League, The 1969,S 17,51:1
White House Murder Case, The 1970,F 19,59:1
Effect of Gamma Rays on Man-in-the-Moon
Marigolds, The 1970,Ap 8,32:1
Lehman, Paul (Producer)
Oldest Trick in the World, The 1961,F 21,40:1
Bible Salesman, The 1961,F 21,40:1
Lehman, Robert
Another City, Another Land 1968,O 9,42:1
Lehman, Susan
Secret Life of Walter Mitty, The 1964,O 27,44:5
Ben Bagley's Shoestring Revues 1970,O 24,22:1
Lehmann, Beatrix
Tudor Wench, The 1933,N 12,IX,3:6
Various Heavens 1936,Mr 8,IX,1:1
Charlotte Corday 1936,O 27,31:1
Charlotte Corday 1936,N 15,XI,3:2
Mourning Becomes Electra 1937,D 12,XI,3:8
They Walk Alone 1939,F 5,IX,3:2
Close Quarters 1941,Ag 17,IX,1:8
Jam Today 1942,Mr 1,VIII,1:3
Uncle Harry 1944,Ap 30,II,1:4
Garden District 1958,S 17,44:2
Lehmann, Fritz
Professor Bernhardi 1968,Mr 20,38:1
Lehmann, Helen (Playwright)
Locandiera, La; Mistress of the Inn, The
1926,N 23,26:1
Lehmann, Helen (Translator)
Locandiera, La; Mistress of the Inn, The
1926,N 23,26:1
Lehmann, Herman (Capt)
War Song, The 1928,S 25,29:3
Lehmann, Mimi
Remote Control 1929,S 11,24:5
Lehmann-Haupt, Miriam
Cabaret 1966,N 21,62:1
Moths, The 1970,My 12,46:1
Lehmeyer, John (Costume Designer)
Brother to Dragons 1968,D 8,86:1
Wilson in the Promise Land 1970,Ja 11,78:1
Wilson in the Promise Land 1970,My 27,41:1
Lehn, Norma
Best Foot Forward 1941,O 2,28:2
January Thaw 1946,F 5,18:2
Lehne, John
Ah, Wilderness! 1953,F 7,10:6
Ah, Wilderness! 1953,F 15,II,1:1
Lehne, John (Director)
Beast in Me, The 1963,My 17,29:1

Lehnerts, Mary Frances
Poisoned Kiss, The 1937,Ap 22,19:1
Lehr, Elmer
Harriet 1944,S 28,26:1
Sundown Beach 1948,S 8,37:1
Sister Oakes 1949,Ap 25,19:4
Lehr, Wilson (Miscellaneous)
Spiro Who? 1969,My 19,55:1
Lehr, Wilson (Playwright)
Of Mice and Men 1958,D 5,38:1
Lehrain, George C
Mayflowers 1925,N 25,14:2
Lehren, Samuel
Gardener's Dog, The 1927,O 21,27:1
Lehrer, Albert
Pirates of Penzance, The 1942,F 20,20:2
Lehrer, Albert (Scenic Designer)
Dole Brothers 1932,Mr 26,17:7
Lehrer, Samuel
If I Were You 1931,S 24,21:1
Jacques Bergson 1936,O 31,24:6
Lehrian, George C
Mikado, The; Town of Titipu, The 1927,S 19,30:1
Lehrman, Elizabeth (Scenic Designer)
New York Idea, The 1948,Ag 18,29:2
Lehrman, Lewis E (Producer)
Memory Bank, The 1970,Ja 12,24:3
Leib, Mani
We Live and Laugh 1936,My 9,10:3
Leib, Manyeh
All God's Chillum Got Shoes 1932,Ap 23,11:3
Leibelt, Hans
Broadway 1928,Ap 15,IX,4:7
Heilige Crispin, Der 1933,Je 25,IX,1:2
Leiber, Fritz
Hamlet 1920,D 28,9:3
Merchant of Venice, The 1920,D 30,16:2
Macbeth 1921,D 27,10:3
Two Strangers From Nowhere 1924,Ap 8,22:2
Hedda Gabler 1924,My 17,18:4
Field God, The 1927,Ap 22,18:2
Julius Caesar 1929,N 19,26:5
Hamlet 1930,Mr 25,34:4
Macbeth 1930,Mr 26,24:6
Merchant of Venice, The 1930,Mr 27,24:7
Twelfth Night 1930,Mr 27,24:7
Taming of the Shrew, The 1930,Mr 28,22:8
Richard III 1930,Mr 31,24:1
King Lear 1930,Ap 1,34:6
As You Like It 1930,Ap 3,32:5
Julius Caesar 1930,Ap 4,22:3
King Lear 1930,D 26,18:2
Merchant of Venice, The 1931,N 17,31:1
Julius Caesar 1931,N 18,26:3
Hamlet 1931,N 19,26:6
Yoshe Kalb 1933,D 29,27:2
Leiber, Fritz (Director)
Julius Caesar 1929,N 19,26:5
Leiber, Jerry (Miscellaneous)
Hail Scrawdyke! 1966,N 29,50:1
Leibler, Allen (Playwright)
Try It With Alice 1924,Je 24,18:4
Leibman, Ron
Legend of Lovers 1959,O 28,40:3
Dear Me, the Sky Is Falling 1963,Mr 4,9:1
Bicycle Ride to Nevada 1963,S 25,38:1
Deputy, The 1964,F 27,26:1
Prometheus Bound 1967,My 11,52:1
Poker Session, The 1967,S 20,42:2
We Bombed in New Haven 1967,D 7,58:1
We Bombed in New Haven 1967,D 17,II,3:7
Three Sisters, The 1968,Mr 18,56:1
We Bombed in New Haven 1968,O 17,51:1
We Bombed in New Haven 1968,O 27,II,1:1
Cop-Out 1969,Ap 8,42:1
Cop-Out 1969,Ap 20,II,11:4
Dr Galley 1970,Ja 23,25:1
Transfers 1970,Ja 23,25:1
Rooming House, The 1970,Ja 23,25:1
Transfers 1970,F 1,II,7:2
Room Service 1970,My 13,49:1
Room Service 1970,My 24,II,1:1
Leibowitz, Max J
You'll Never Know 1921,Ap 21,9:2
Leicester, William
Return Engagement 1940,N 2,19:2
Leicht, Allan (Director)
Brass Butterfly, The 1970,Ja 31,34:1
Leichtling, Selma (Miscellaneous)
Ninety Day Mistress, The 1967,N 7,49:1
Leidal, Marie
Cradle Will Rock, The 1947,D 27,11:2
Leider, Jerry (Miscellaneous)
Shinbone Alley 1957,Ap 15,23:2
Portofino 1958,F 22,8:3
Leider, Jerry (Producer)
Ages of Man 1958,D 29,21:1
Leidol, Marie
Cradle Will Rock, The 1947,N 25,38:3
Leif, Lou
Brooklyn, U S A 1941,D 22,24:2
Leigh, Andrew
Gooseberry Fool 1929,N 2,14:8

Deep Are the Roots 1945,S 27,24:4
Leigh, Andrew (Director)
Twelfth Night 1930,S 14,VIII,2:8
Twelfth Night 1930,O 16,28:2
Twelfth Night 1930,O 19,IX,4:5
Twelfth Night 1930,N 2,VIII,1:1
Merchant of Venice, The 1930,D 3,29:2
Leigh, Andrew (Original Author)
Merchant of Venice, The 1930,N 16,VIII,3:1
Leigh, Barbara
Mrs Mouse Are You Within? 1968,Jl 8,45:1
Leigh, Brad
Tartuffe 1965,Ja 15,23:1
Leigh, Carolyn
By the Beautiful Sea 1954,Ap 9,20:1
Leigh, Carolyn (Composer)
Ziegfeld Follies 1957,Mr 2,19:2
Leigh, Carolyn (Lyricist)
Peter Pan 1954,Jl 20,15:3
Peter Pan 1954,O 21,30:2
Shoestring '57 1956,N 6,31:1
Ziegfeld Follies 1957,Mr 2,19:2
Wildcat 1960,D 17,20:2
Little Me 1962,N 19,41:3
Little Me 1962,D 2,II,1:1
How Now, Dow Jones 1967,D 8,53:1
Leigh, Dorian
Fifth Season, The 1953,Ja 24,13:2
Leigh, Freya
We Are No Longer Children 1932,Ap 1,17:2
Leigh, Gilbert
Winter Soldiers 1942,N 30,19:2
Leigh, Howland (Miscellaneous)
Earl Carroll's Vanities 1927,Ja 5,18:1
Leigh, Jack
High Button Shoes 1955,Mr 12,10:6
Leigh, Jack (Miscellaneous)
Sudden and Accidental Re-education of Horse
Johnson, The 1968,D 19,63:1
Leigh, Jenny
Iphigenia in Aulis 1967,N 22,40:2
Iphigenia in Aulis 1967,D 3,II,1:1
Iphigenia in Aulis 1968,Ap 6,43:1
Leigh, Julian (Translator)
Miracle at Verdun 1931,Mr 17,34:6
Leigh, Kelly
Say Darling 1959,F 26,38:2
Leigh, Lisle
Rust 1924,F 1,12:1
Busybody, The 1924,S 30,27:5
Leigh, Mitch (Composer)
Too True to Be Good 1963,Mr 14,8:2
Never Live Over a Pretzel Factory 1964,Mr 30,37:1
Man of La Mancha 1965,N 23,52:1
Man of La Mancha 1969,My 3,38:4
Cry for Us All 1970,Ap 9,48:2
Leigh, Mitch (Producer)
Man of La Mancha 1966,O 5,42:5
Cry for Us All 1970,Ap 9,48:2
Leigh, Nelson
Hamlet 1945,D 14,25:2
Leigh, Philip
He Who Gets Slapped 1922,Ja 10,15:1
Tidings Brought to Mary, The 1922,D 25,20:1
Peer Gynt 1923,F 6,14:1
Sandro Botticelli 1923,Mr 27,24:2
Saint Joan 1923,D 29,8:4
Wild Duck, The 1925,F 25,16:4
Bit o' Love, A 1925,My 13,24:2
Lucky Sam McCarver 1925,O 22,22:1
Androcles and the Lion 1925,N 24,28:1
Schweiger 1926,Mr 24,20:4
Juarez and Maximilian 1926,O 12,31:1
Ned McCobb's Daughter 1926,N 30,26:2
Brothers Karamazov, The 1927,Ja 4,20:1
Right You Are (If You Think You Are)
1927,F 24,27:1
Doctor's Dilemma, The 1927,N 22,33:1
Marco Millions 1928,Ja 10,28:2
Strange Interlude 1928,Ja 31,28:1
Volpone 1928,Ap 10,32:1
Volpone 1928,Ap 22,IX,1:1
Karl and Anna 1929,O 8,34:1
Troika 1930,Ap 2,32:6
Cafe 1930,Ag 29,11:1
As You Desire Me 1931,Ja 29,21:2
After All 1931,D 4,28:4
Troilus and Cressida 1932,Je 7,22:3
Peacock 1932,O 12,27:1
Mary of Scotland 1933,N 28,28:3
Judgment Day 1934,S 13,26:4
Leigh, Richard (Playwright)
Sweeney Todd 1957,Ag 28,21:4
Leigh, Roma
Canteen Show, The 1942,S 4,18:1
Leigh, Rowland (Composer)
Man in Dress Clothes, The 1937,Ag 24,24:4
Leigh, Rowland (Director)
Du Barry 1932,N 23,15:2
Divine Moment, A 1934,Ja 8,21:8
You Never Know 1938,S 22,26:3
Return Engagement 1940,N 2,19:2
My Romance 1948,O 20,38:5

Leigh, Rowland (Lyricist)
Du Barry 1932,N 23,15:2
Music Hath Charms 1934,D 31,8:2
Man in Dress Clothes, The 1937,Ag 24,24:4
You Never Know 1938,S 22,26:3
Night of Love 1941,Ja 8,14:2
My Romance 1948,O 20,38:5
Leigh, Rowland (Original Author)
My Romance 1948,O 20,38:5
Leigh, Rowland (Playwright)
Music Hath Charms 1934,D 31,8:2
Three Waltzes 1937,D 27,10:2
You Never Know 1938,S 22,26:3
Night of Love 1941,Ja 8,14:2
Leigh, Rowland (Producer)
Walk With Music 1940,Je 5,33:2
Gabrielle 1941,Mr 26,26:2
Leigh, Rowland (Translator)
Rates, Les; Might-Have-Beens, The
1927,Je 19,VII,2:3
Du Barry 1932,N 23,15:2
Leigh, Sanford (Miscellaneous)
Ages of Man 1958,D 29,21:1
Leigh, Sylvia
Potash and Perlmutter 1935,Ap 6,11:3
Few Are Chosen 1935,S 18,19:3
Greater Lust, The 1936,Jl 14,22:4
Excursion 1937,Ap 10,11:4
Straw Hat, The 1937,D 31,8:2
Salvation on a String; Chair Endowed 1954,Jl 7,23:1
Solo 1962,Ap 27,26:1
Leigh, Sylvia (Playwright)
Dark Halo 1959,Ap 15,28:4
Solo 1962,Ap 27,26:1
Leigh, Vivien
Mask of Virtue, The 1935,My 16,20:1
Mask of Virtue, The 1935,Je 9,IX,1:1
Happy Hypocrite, The 1936,My 9,21:6
Hamlet 1937,Je 4,26:6
Romeo and Juliet 1940,My 10,27:1
Doctor's Dilemma, The 1942,Mr 15,VIII,1:1
Skin of Our Teeth, The 1945,Mr 20,22:8
Skin of Our Teeth, The 1945,My 27,II,1:3
School for Scandal, The 1949,Ja 21,24:5
Streetcar Named Desire, A 1949,S 29,38:1
Streetcar Named Desire, A 1949,O 13,33:6
Streetcar Named Desire, A 1949,D 11,II,3:1
Caesar and Cleopatra 1951,My 11,32:8
Caesar and Cleopatra 1951,D 20,43:2
Antony and Cleopatra 1951,D 21,22:2
Antony and Cleopatra 1951,D 30,II,1:1
Caesar and Cleopatra 1951,D 30,II,1:1
Sleeping Prince, The 1953,S 29,25:1
Sleeping Prince, The 1953,N 6,24:4
Sleeping Prince, The 1953,D 20,II,4:2
Sleeping Prince, The 1954,F 9,22:8
Twelfth Night 1955,My 1,II,3:1
Twelfth Night 1955,Je 7,37:4
Macbeth 1955,Je 19,II,1:1
South Sea Bubble 1956,Ap 26,37:6
South Sea Bubble 1956,My 13,II,3:1
Titus Andronicus 1957,Jl 2,33:8
Look After Lulu 1959,Jl 30,20:1
Duel of Angels 1960,Ap 20,42:2
Duel of Angels 1960,My 1,II,1:1
Tovarich 1963,Ja 23,5:6
Tovarich 1963,Mr 20,5:1
Tovarich 1963,Mr 21,8:3
Ivanov 1966,My 4,50:1
Leigh, Walter (Composer)
Jolly Roger 1933,Mr 26,IX,1:1
Victoria Regina 1935,D 27,15:2
Leigh-Hunt, Barbara
Measure for Measure 1967,F 15,37:1
Hamlet 1967,F 17,44:1
Mrs Mouse Are You Within? 1968,Ap 5,51:4
Mrs Mouse Are You Within? 1968,Je 2,II,3:6
Leight, David
Ten Million Ghosts 1936,O 24,23:7
Leight, Selma
Commedia Dell' Arte 1927,Ap 6,24:3
Leighton, Betty
Richard III 1953,Jl 15,22:2
One Way Pendulum 1961,S 19,38:2
Leighton, Edith
Treasure, The 1920,O 5,13:1
Leighton, G R
1776 1926,Ap 24,11:2
Leighton, G R (Lyricist)
1776 1926,Ap 24,11:2
Leighton, G R (Playwright)
1776 1926,Ap 24,11:2
Leighton, Harry
New Brooms 1924,N 18,23:5
Leighton, Isabel
Deburau 1920,D 24,14:3
Why Men Leave Home 1922,S 13,18:2
Anathema 1923,Ap 11,16:2
What's Your Wife Doing? 1923,O 2,10:3
Sweet Seventeen 1924,Mr 18,24:2
Haunted House, The 1924,S 3,12:1
Dagger, The 1925,S 10,28:1

Leighton, Isabel (Playwright)
Mercenary Mary 1925,Ap 14,27:3
Sapphire Ring, The 1925,Ap 16,25:2
Spring Again 1941,O 28,28:3
Spring Again 1941,N 11,28:2
Leighton, Jan
Home Is Tomorrow 1950,Je 2,27:2
Sound of Hunting, A 1954,Ap 7,41:1
Russell Patterson's Sketch-Book 1960,F 8,35:1
Leighton, John
In Splendid Error 1954,O 27,33:6
Juno and the Paycock 1955,F 24,20:4
Private Life of the Master Race, The
1956,Ja 31,33:3
Brothers Karamazov, The 1957,D 9,39:4
Mrs Warren's Profession 1958,Je 26,22:1
Quare Fellow, The 1958,N 28,34:1
Montserrat 1961,Ja 9,30:5
Merchant of Venice, The 1962,F 3,13:2
Beyond the Horizon 1962,O 26,27:2
Leighton, Julia
Alternate Current 1939,D 23,8:3
Leighton, Margaret
Henry IV, Part I 1946,My 7,25:2
Henry IV, Part II 1946,My 8,33:4
Uncle Vanya 1946,My 14,18:2
Uncle Vanya 1946,My 19,II,1:1
Oedipus; Critic, The 1946,My 21,19:2
Oedipus 1946,My 21,19:2
King Lear 1946,O 13,II,2:3
Cyrano de Bergerac 1946,N 3,I,54:6
Cocktail Party, The 1950,My 7,II,2:5
Apple Cart, The 1953,My 8,29:3
Confidential Clerk, The 1953,O 11,II,3:7
Separate Tables 1954,S 23,42:1
Separate Tables 1955,My 22,II,1:1
Separate Tables 1956,O 26,33:1
Separate Tables 1956,N 4,II,1:1
Variations on a Theme 1958,My 9,16:5
Much Ado About Nothing 1959,S 18,25:2
Much Ado About Nothing 1959,S 27,II,1:1
Night of the Iguana, The 1961,D 29,10:1
Night of the Iguana, The 1962,Ja 7,II,1:1
Tchin-Tchin 1962,O 9,37:3
Tchin-Tchin 1962,O 26,26:2
Tchin-Tchin 1962,N 25,II,1:1
Chinese Prime Minister, The 1964,Ja 3,14:1
Chinese Prime Minister, The 1964,Ja 12,II,1:1
Homage to Shakespeare 1964,Mr 16,36:2
Gnadiges Fraulein, The 1966,F 23,42:1
Mutilated, The 1966,F 23,42:1
Little Foxes, The 1967,O 27,53:1
Little Foxes, The 1967,N 5,II,1:1
Little Foxes, The 1968,Ja 6,24:4
Antony and Cleopatra 1969,Ag 30,10:3
Girlfriend 1970,F 19,59:1
Leighton, Nancy
To Broadway With Love 1964,Ap 30,28:6
Leighton, Sonya
Blossom Time 1922,O 24,18:2
Leighton, Winslow
Solid Ivory 1925,N 17,29:3
Coriolanus 1927,Je 18,8:3
Leimkuehler, F Ray (Scenic Designer)
Twelfth Disciple, The 1930,My 17,21:4
Leindorf, Monroe
Sound of Hunting, A 1954,Ap 7,41:1
Anna Christie 1955,N 22,41:1
Leinwand, Shirley
Song of Norway 1958,Je 23,19:2
Song of Norway 1959,Je 26,16:2
Leipart, Charles
Take One Step 1968,Jl 5,17:1
Lend an Ear 1969,O 29,32:1
Leipzig, Nate
All-Star Idlers of 1921, The 1921,Ag 9,16:3
Leischman, John L
Trial of Dr Beck, The 1937,Ag 10,22:2
Leiser, Henri (Producer)
Once Over Lightly 1942,N 20,26:2
Bobino 1944,Ap 7,23:4
Leisner, Evelyn
Rich Man, Poor Man 1950,F 13,15:4
Leister, Frederick
Scarlet Lady, The 1926,O 17,VIII,2:1
Meet the Wife 1927,Jl 3,VII,1:4
Lady-in-Law, The 1927,O 23,VIII,4:1
Evensong 1933,F 1,13:4
Viceroy Sarah 1934,Je 24,IX,1:4
Dark Victory 1934,N 10,18:2
Libel! 1935,D 8,X,5:8
Libel! 1935,D 21,10:5
Bachelor Born 1938,Ja 26,26:3
Cousin Muriel 1940,Mr 17,X,1:6
Leister, Frederick (Director)
Bachelor Born 1938,Ja 26,26:3
Leister, John P
Star of Bengal 1929,S 26,27:2
Leister, John P (Playwright)
Rap, The 1931,Ap 7,31:2
Leiter, Edward
War Song, The 1928,S 25,29:3
Precious 1929,Ja 15,22:5

Leiter, Edward—Cont

Among the Married 1929,O 4,24:3
Whirlpool 1929,D 4,37:3
London Calling 1930,O 20,29:1
Affair of State, An 1930,N 20,30:3
If I Were You 1931,S 24,21:1
Papavert 1931,D 30,25:1
Mr Papavert 1932,Ja 23,18:6
Boy Friend, The 1932,Je 8,22:3
Saint Wench 1933,Ja 3,19:3
Undesirable Lady, An 1933,O 10,24:4

Leiter, Hans
Ice Capades 1962,Ag 30,34:1
Ice Capades 1963,Ag 29,37:2
Ice Capades 1964,Ag 27,27:2
Ice Capades 1966,Je 2,50:2
Ice Capades 1967,Je 2,33:1
Ice Capades 1970,Ja 7,35:1

Leith, Tom
Becket 1960,O 6,50:1

Leith, William
Oh! Mama 1925,Ag 20,22:2
Great Gatsby, The 1926,F 3,22:1
Lady Alone 1927,Ja 21,12:5
Thief, The 1927,Ap 23,15:2

Leitner, Edith
Puppets of Passion 1927,F 25,24:4

Leitzbach, Adeline (Playwright)
Dora Mobridge 1930,Ap 21,20:2

Leitzel, Lillian
Ziegfeld Midnight Frolic 1920,Mr 17,14:2
Vaudeville (Hippodrome) 1925,D 29,21:2

Leivick, H (Miscellaneous)
Untitled-Poetry Reading 1967,Jl 18,29:1

Leivick, H (Playwright)
Rags 1922,Ja 29,VI,1:3
Andersh; New Worlds 1922,S 26,18:2
Chains 1930,F 23,29:2
Golem, The 1931,N 6,28:5
Heroic Years 1934,Ja 12,28:4
Chains 1937,Ja 22,25:1
Who Is Who? 1938,D 24,13:3
Golem, The 1959,F 26,38:2
Sage of Rottenburg, The 1963,N 20,48:1

Lekstroem, Eva
Prodigal Son, The 1942,F 18,22:2

Leland, Austin
Samarkand 1926,D 22,24:4

Leland, Austin (Playwright)
Samarkand 1926,D 22,24:4

Leland, David
Frankie and Johnny 1952,O 29,37:2
Ponder Heart, The 1956,F 17,14:2

Leland, Elizabeth
Kiss for Cinderella, A 1942,Mr 11,22:2

Leland, Elliott
Hamlet 1934,D 26,19:3

Leland, Frederick
Chinese Nightingale, The 1934,O 6,20:4

Leland, Gordon M (Producer)
Box Seats 1928,Ap 20,27:2

Leland, Janet
Field of Ermine 1935,F 9,10:4
Personal Appearance 1936,Jl 9,17:4

Leland, Robert
Dinny and the Witches 1959,D 10,53:3

Lelar, Jas L
Solid Ivory 1925,N 17,29:3

Lelinska, Helen
Yoshe Kalb 1932,O 3,15:5

Lely, Betty
Courting 1925,S 14,17:1

Lely, Madeleine
Notre Amour 1926,O 31,VIII,2:4

Lemac, Tony
Aquashow 1954,Je 23,20:4

LeMaine and Van
Vaudeville (Palace) 1928,Ja 3,29:3

Lemaire, J
Illusioniste, L' 1927,Ja 11,36:5

LeMaire, Rufus (Producer)
LeMaire's Affairs 1927,Mr 29,22:4

Lemans, Marcel
O Nightingale 1925,Ap 16,25:2

LeMaster, Marie
Three Love Affairs; Bedtime Story 1958,Mr 11,33:1

Lemaster, Marie (Costume Designer)
Six Characters in Search of an Author
1961,My 11,43:1
Long Day's Journey Into Night 1963,Je 27,25:1

Lembeck, Harvey
Mister Roberts 1948,F 19,27:2
Stalag 17 1951,My 9,41:2
Wedding Breakfast 1954,N 22,29:2
Wedding Breakfast 1954,D 5,II,5:1
Phoenix '55 1955,Ap 25,20:2
South Pacific 1957,Ap 25,35:1
Oklahoma! 1958,Mr 20,32:3

Lemcke, Norman
Merry Wives of Windsor, The 1954,F 17,27:1

Lemin, Stanley
Potting Shed, The 1957,Ja 30,32:1

Lemley, John
Fourth Pig, The 1965,Ja 27,24:6

Lemmo, Josephine
Susie Is a Good Girl 1968,N 5,53:2
Grab Bag, The 1968,N 5,53:2
Subscriber, The 1968,N 5,53:2

Lemmon, Frank D (Scenic Designer)
Alice Adams 1947,Ag 5,26:1

Lemmon, Gertrude
Earl Carroll's Vanities 1923,Jl 6,8:2
Florida Girl 1925,N 3,34:1
Just Fancy! 1927,O 12,30:2

Lemmon, Jack
Room Service 1953,Ap 7,34:1
Face of a Hero 1960,O 21,29:5
Idiot's Delight 1970,Mr 24,39:1

LeMonds, Sandra (Costume Designer)
Hedda Gabler 1970,Ja 18,78:1

Lemos, Adamantios
Cute Gata.....Oute Zhmia; Neither Cat . . . Nor
Damage 1957,D 20,31:1

Lemos, Adamantios (Director)
Cute Gata.....Oute Zhmia; Neither Cat . . . Nor
Damage 1957,D 20,31:1

Lemos, Mary
Cute Gata.....Oute Zhmia; Neither Cat . . . Nor
Damage 1957,D 20,31:1

Lemp, Germaine
Myself and I 1929,Ag 31,13:6

Lemuels, William
Nigger Rich 1929,S 21,16:7
Oh, Professor 1930,My 2,19:6

Lenahan, Peter
Billy Budd 1959,F 28,13:3

Lenahan, Peter (Miscellaneous)
Come Out, Carlo! 1962,My 4,27:2
In the Penal Colony 1962,My 4,27:2

Lenard, Mark
Hasty Heart, The 1954,Mr 13,10:1
Exiles 1957,Mr 13,27:1
Clearing in the Woods, A 1959,F 13,32:1
Country Scandal, A 1960,My 6,21:8
Country Scandal, A 1960,My 15,II,1:1
Measure for Measure 1960,Jl 27,33:1
Hedda Gabler 1960,N 10,61:1
Gideon 1961,N 10,38:1
Little Eyolf 1964,Mr 17,31:1

Lenard, Mark (Miscellaneous)
Third Person 1955,D 30,13:4

Lenchner, George (Composer)
In the Groove 1938,Ap 22,14:5

Lenchner, George (Lyricist)
In the Groove 1938,Ap 22,14:5

Lender, Marcelle
Roi, Le 1931,Ap 5,VIII,3:1

Lenert, Marguerite
House of Breath, The 1957,Ap 15,23:2
Long Gallery, The 1958,Mr 7,17:2
Trip to Bountiful, The 1959,F 27,20:4
Red Roses for Me 1961,N 28,41:1
Brother to Dragons 1968,D 8,86:1
Wilson in the Promise Land 1970,Ja 11,78:1
Wilson in the Promise Land 1970,My 27,41:1

Lenfant, P
Vacances de Paques, Les 1927,Ja 2,VII,2:1

Leng, Jerome
Journey by Night, A 1935,Ap 17,26:3

Lengel, Frank
Mima 1928,D 13,24:2
Philadelphia 1929,S 17,34:5

L'Engle, Tracy
Fools Errant 1922,Ag 22,12:3
Fool, The 1922,O 24,18:1
Roseanne 1923,D 31,9:5
Cock o' the Roost 1924,O 14,23:1

Lengsfelder, H J (Playwright)
Heads or Tails 1947,My 3,10:6

Lengyel, Melchior (Director)
Antonia 1925,O 21,20:1

Lengyel, Melchior (Original Author)
Silk Stockings 1955,Mr 27,II,1:1

Lengyel, Melchior (Playwright)
Czarina, The 1922,F 1,22:1
Sancho Panza 1923,N 27,23:1
Sancho Panza 1923,D 2,VIII,1:1
Antonia 1925,O 11,VIII,2:6
Antonia 1925,O 21,20:1
Postmistress, The 1928,Ja 15,VIII,2:1
Angel 1933,D 8,31:1
Angel 1933,D 24,IX,2:2
Comedy of Crooks, A 1936,Je 8,22:3
Silk Stockings 1955,F 25,17:3

Lenhardt, Mary
Winged Victory 1943,N 22,24:1

Lenhart, James B
Bad Man, The 1920,Ag 31,7:1

Lenhart, Richard
H M S Pinafore 1949,Jl 29,13:2

Leni, Jules
Talking to You 1942,Ag 18,17:1
Jacobowsky and the Colonel 1944,Mr 15,17:2

Lenihan, Cecilia
Pillars of Society, The 1931,O 15,19:1

Lenihan, Deirdre
Ardele 1958,Ap 9,39:4

Lenihan, Liam
Hall of Healing 1952,My 8,35:6
Trouble in Mind 1955,N 5,23:2
Playboy of the Western World, The 1958,My 9,19:2
Juno 1959,Mr 10,41:1
Painted Days, The 1961,Ap 7,24:1

Lenihan, Vera (Director)
Blind Mice 1930,O 16,28:2

Lenihan, Winifred
Survival of the Fittest 1921,Mr 15,14:1
Dover Road, The 1921,D 24,7:2
Will Shakespeare 1923,Ja 2,14:1
Failures, The 1923,N 23,20:1
Failures, The 1923,D 2,VIII,1:1
Saint Joan 1923,D 29,8:4
Saint Joan 1924,Ja 6,VII,1:1
Nerves 1924,S 2,22:2
Nerves 1924,S 7,VII,1:1
White Wings 1926,O 16,15:1
Major Barbara 1928,N 20,28:4
Boundry Line, The 1930,F 6,21:1
Difficulty of Getting Married, The 1936,Jl 7,22:1
Black Limelight 1936,N 10,31:1

Lenihan, Winifred (Director)
Mongrel, The 1924,D 16,28:2
Blind Mice 1930,S 7,IX,2:4
Pillars of Society, The 1931,O 15,19:1

Lenihan, Winifred (Playwright)
Blind Mice 1930,S 7,IX,2:4
Blind Mice 1930,O 16,28:2

Lening, Albert Lewis
This Mad Whirl 1937,Ja 10,II,4:8

Lenn, Francesca
Fulton of Oak Falls 1937,Ja 2,15:3

Lenn, Robert
Hopalong--Freud 1953,Je 18,38:5
Where There's a Will 1953,Je 18,38:5
Brandy Is My True Love's Name 1953,Je 18,38:5
California 1953,Je 18,38:5
King and I, The 1968,My 24,39:1

Lenn, Robert (Miscellaneous)
Judy Garland 1959,My 12,40:1
Paradise Island 1962,Je 28,22:1

Lenn, Robert (Musical Director)
Idiot's Delight 1957,F 23,14:2
Sweet Miani 1962,S 26,33:2

Lenn, Robert (Producer)
Brandy Is My True Love's Name 1953,Je 18,38:5
Hopalong--Freud 1953,Je 18,38:5
California 1953,Je 18,38:5
Where There's a Will 1953,Je 18,38:5

Lennard, Beatrice
All's Well That Ends Well 1953,Jl 16,18:2

Lennard, Maria
Millionairess, The 1969,Mr 3,28:1

Lennard, William (Choreographer)
Yerma 1952,F 8,18:4

Lennart, Isobel (Playwright)
Funny Girl 1964,Mr 27,15:1

Lennartz, Elisabeth
Broadway 1928,Ap 15,IX,4:7

Lenni, Francesca
Fulton of Oak Falls 1937,F 11,18:2
Eye on the Sparrow 1938,My 4,26:3

Lennikova, Tatiana
Cherry Orchard, The 1965,F 10,46:1
Kremlin Chimes 1965,F 25,23:1

Lennon, Fritz
Latent Heterosexual, The 1968,Mr 22,52:1
Macbeth 1968,N 30,49:3

Lennon, Fritz (Miscellaneous)
Macbeth 1968,N 30,49:3

Lennon, John (Miscellaneous)
Oh! Calcutta! 1969,Je 18,33:1

Lennon, John (Original Author)
In His Own Write 1968,Je 20,50:5
In His Own Write 1968,Jl 9,30:2
In His Own Write 1968,Jl 14,II,4:5

Lennon, John (Playwright)
In His Own Write 1968,Jl 9,30:2
In His Own Write 1968,Jl 14,II,4:5
Oh! Calcutta! 1969,Je 29,II,1:7

Lennon, Percival
Welcome Stranger 1920,S 14,12:1
Common Sin, The 1928,O 16,28:2
Home Sweet Home 1936,Jl 1,29:2

Lennon, Percival (Playwright)
Short Cut, The 1930,Ja 28,28:2

Lennox, Cosmo Gordon (Playwright)
Van Dyck, The 1921,O 12,18:2

Lennox, Fred
One Kiss 1923,N 28,14:2
Peter Pan 1924,N 7,16:2
City Chap, The 1925,O 27,21:1
As Good As New 1930,N 4,37:3

Lennox, Gilbert (Playwright)
Mrs Nobby Clark 1935,F 28,16:2
Close Quarters 1937,Ap 18,II,3:5
Close Quarters 1939,Mr 7,19:2
Third Party Risk 1939,My 28,X,2:5

Lennox, Vera
Anne-One Hundred 1927,Je 26,VIII,1:3
Good Morning, Bill! 1927,D 25,VIII,1:4

Lennox, Vera—Cont
Good Companions, The 1931,O 2,31:1
Good Companions, The 1931,O 11,VIII,1:1
Lennox, William
Scrambled Wives 1920,Ag 6,16:1
We Girls 1921,N 10,26:3
Lenny, Jack
Merry-Go-Round 1927,Je 1,25:4
Lenormand, H R (Original Author)
In Theatre Street 1937,Ap 29,17:5
In Theatre Street 1937,My 16,X,2:2
Lenormand, H R (Playwright)
Failures, The 1923,N 23,20:1
Failures, The 1923,D 2,VIII,1:1
Time Is a Dream 1924,Ap 23,24:2
Homme et Ses Fantomes, L' 1924,Je 29,VII,1:8
Homme et Ses Fantomes, L' 1924,N 14,16:1
Amour Magicien, L' 1926,D 26,VII,2:1
Rates, Les; Might-Have-Beens, The
   1927,Je 19,VII,2:3
Mixture 1927,N 20,IX,4:4
Innocente, L' 1928,Jl 1,VIII,1:8
Vie Secrete, Une 1929,Mr 24,X,2:1
Mixture 1929,N 10,X,4:1
Trois Chambres, Les 1931,Mr 15,IX,1:6
Asie 1932,Ja 10,VIII,3:1
Sortileges 1932,N 13,IX,2:5
Coward, The 1935,Jl 16,24:1
Folle du Ciel, La 1936,My 31,X,2:1
Pacifique 1937,N 14,XI,2:1
Failures, The 1959,Ja 6,30:2
Lenrow, Bernard
Final Balance, The 1928,O 31,28:3
Ten Million Ghosts 1936,O 24,23:7
Lorelei 1938,N 30,21:2
Man With Blonde Hair, The 1941,N 5,30:2
Julius Caesar 1955,Jl 13,20:1
Compulsion 1957,O 25,21:1
Gang's All Here, The 1959,O 2,23:1
Lens, Patricia
Celebration 1969,Ja 23,55:2
Lensky, Leib
Winterset 1966,F 10,32:2
Lent, Connie
Othello 1935,S 28,13:2
Macbeth 1935,O 8,26:4
Having Wonderful Time 1937,F 22,12:5
Lenters, Howard
Million Dollar Baby 1945,D 22,17:2
High Button Shoes 1947,O 10,32:2
Lenthier, John Troupe
Still Life 1937,D 13,22:8
Freedom of the Press 1937,D 13,22:8
Lentin, Louis (Director)
Kreutzer Sonata, The 1961,F 16,24:2
Lento, Juanita
Emerald Slippers, The 1970,S 2,31:2
Lentz, Serge (Miscellaneous)
Fig Leaf in Her Bonnet, A 1961,Je 15,50:1
Lentz, William
Kitty's Kisses 1926,My 7,12:2
Lenville, Mr
George Barnwell; London Merchant, The
   1928,O 2,34:3
Lenwood, Steve
Adding Machine, The 1956,F 10,17:1
Lenya, Lotte
Eternal Road, The 1937,Ja 8,14:2
Candle in the Wind 1941,O 23,26:2
Firebird of Florence 1945,Mr 23,13:4
Barefoot in Athens 1951,N 1,35:2
Threepenny Opera, The 1954,Mr 11,26:5
Threepenny Opera, The 1954,Mr 21,II,1:1
Threepenny Opera, The 1954,Ap 4,II,7:1
Threepenny Opera, The 1955,S 21,38:1
Threepenny Opera, The 1956,Mr 11,II,1:1
Brecht on Brecht 1961,N 15,52:2
Brecht on Brecht 1962,Ja 4,26:1
Brecht on Brecht 1962,Ja 14,II,1:1
Cabaret 1966,N 21,62:1
Cabaret 1966,D 4,II,5:1
Cabaret 1968,Ja 12,19:1
Cabaret 1969,F 2,74:2
Lenya, Lotte (Miscellaneous)
Brecht on Brecht 1962,Ja 4,26:1
Lenz, A Francis
Mad Honeymoon, The 1923,Ag 8,10:1
One Shot Fired 1927,N 8,32:5
Lenz, George
Shangri-La 1956,Je 14,40:1
Lenz, H R (Playwright)
Doctor Herzl 1945,D 21,25:4
Lenz, Jacob Michael Reinhold (Playwright)
Amor Vincit Omnia 1936,N 15,XI,2:4
Lenz, Leo (Playwright)
Trio 1930,N 2,VIII,3:2
Profumo di Mia Moglie, Il; My Wife's Perfume
   1932,Ja 11,29:5
Trio 1932,F 8,21:1
Mann mit den Grauen Schlafen, Der; Man Who Is
   Getting Gray, The 1932,F 21,VIII,2:3
Fabian, Der Elephant 1933,Ap 30,IX,2:2
Terzett zu Viert 1933,O 22,IX,2:3

Lenz, Rick
Mating Dance 1965,N 4,58:1
Infantry, The 1966,N 15,51:1
Calling in Crazy 1969,O 7,42:2
Lenze Duo, The
Jumbo 1935,N 18,20:2
Lenzer, Hugo
Turandot 1929,Ja 12,14:4
Leo, Carl (Playwright)
Never Say Never 1951,N 21,21:2
Leo, Frank
High Named Today 1954,D 11,11:2
Leo, Richard
Love Call, The 1927,O 25,33:1
Leo, Roger
Asmodee 1958,Mr 26,42:2
Leo (Lighting Director)
Beclch 1968,D 17,59:1
Leogrande, Ernest (Playwright)
Plot Against the Chase Manhattan Bank, The
   1963,N 27,29:1
Leon, Arthur
Roar China! 1930,O 28,23:1
Leon, Bruce
Clutching Claw, The 1928,F 15,20:1
Leon, Elsa
Great Lover, The 1932,O 12,27:3
Leon, Felix (Playwright)
Zulu and the Zayda, The 1965,N 11,59:1
Leon, James (Miscellaneous)
Wonderful Town 1963,F 15,10:2
To Broadway With Love 1964,Ap 30,28:6
Leon, James (Musical Director)
American Dream, The 1961,Ja 25,28:1
Bartleby 1961,Ja 25,28:1
Can-Can 1962,My 17,32:2
Leon, Joseph
Right Next to Broadway 1944,F 22,26:2
War President 1944,Ap 25,17:3
Pipe Dream 1955,D 1,44:1
Fair Game 1957,N 4,39:1
Come Share My House 1960,F 19,20:2
Hit the Deck 1960,Je 24,32:1
Julia, Jake, and Uncle Joe 1961,Ja 30,19:1
Beauty Part, The 1962,D 28,5:2
Mr Grossman 1964,My 6,43:1
Merry Widow, The 1964,Ag 18,24:2
Bench, The 1968,Mr 5,35:2
Leon, Monsieur (Miscellaneous)
Not Now Darling 1970,O 30,33:1
Leon, Victor (Lyricist)
Wiener Blut 1964,S 12,14:1
Leon, Victor (Original Author)
Merry Widow, The 1964,Ag 18,24:2
Leon, Victor (Playwright)
Merry Widow, The 1929,D 3,29:1
Land des Laechelns, Das 1929,D 8,X,4:4
Merry Widow, The 1931,S 8,39:1
Merry Widow, The 1932,F 21,VIII,23:3
Wiener Blut 1932,S 4,IX,2:2
Merry Widow, The 1942,Jl 16,22:1
Merry Widow, The 1961,O 27,28:2
Leonard, Anna
Rehearsal, The 1952,My 27,30:5
Leonard, Arthur
Exceeding Small 1928,O 23,32:2
Wild Duck, The 1928,N 19,17:1
Headquarters 1929,D 5,32:4
Leonard, Benny
Dancing Girl, The 1923,Ja 25,16:2
Leonard, Billie
You Said It 1931,Ja 20,21:3
Caviar 1934,Je 8,19:2
Leonard, Charles (Producer)
Slightly Scandalous 1944,Je 14,16:2
Leonard, Clair (Composer)
Dance of Death, The 1936,My 20,24:5
Leonard, Craig
Racket, The 1930,N 20,30:6
Leonard, David
Green Goddess, The 1921,Ja 19,14:1
Taboo 1922,Ap 5,22:1
Burgomaster of Stilemonde, The 1923,N 16,15:3
Lord Byron's Cain 1925,Ap 9,20:3
Outside Looking In 1925,S 8,28:1
Howdy King 1926,D 14,24:4
Tales of Rigo 1927,My 31,25:3
Merchant of Venice, The 1928,Ja 17,22:2
I Love an Actress 1931,S 18,29:2
Blessed Event 1933,N 22,22:3
We the People 1933,Ja 23,9:5
Birthright 1933,N 22,22:3
False Dreams, Farewell 1934,Ja 16,18:3
Field of Ermine 1935,F 9,10:4
Paths of Glory 1935,S 27,24:2
Eternal Road, The 1937,Ja 8,14:2
Passing of the Third Floor Back, The
   1937,Ag 3,20:6
Siege 1937,D 9,31:4
Fabulous Invalid, The 1938,O 10,15:1
Fifth Column, The 1940,Mr 7,18:2
Journey to Jerusalem 1940,O 7,21:2
As You Like It 1941,O 21,29:2

Leonard, David—Cont
Brights Lights of 1944 1943,S 17,27:4
Hairpin Harmony 1943,O 2,18:5
Mexican Hayride 1944,Ja 29,9:6
Leonard, Dorman
God Strikes Back 1943,F 27,11:2
Duke in Darkness, The 1944,Ja 25,15:2
Leonard, Eddie
Vaudeville (Palace) 1924,Mr 18,25:1
Vaudeville (Palace) 1926,N 16,24:3
Vaudeville (Palace) 1927,O 25,33:2
Vaudeville (Palace) 1932,Ap 25,18:3
Leonard, Edmund
Patience 1928,Je 26,29:3
Leonard, Elliot
Cape Cod Follies 1929,S 19,37:2
Leonard, George E
Just a Minute 1928,O 9,34:3
New Moon, The 1942,Ag 19,14:2
Leonard, George E (Miscellaneous)
Flair-Flair the Idol of Paree 1935,Mr 13,16:1
Leonard, Harold
Wolf! Wolf! 1925,O 30,21:1
Vaudeville (Palace) 1928,Ag 28,27:3
Leonard, Helen
Little Town of Bethlehem, The 1922,D 26,15:4
Leonard, Henry
Squaring the Circle 1936,Ag 12,15:3
Hamlet 1936,N 11,54:2
Leonard, Hugh (Playwright)
Stephen D 1962,S 25,31:3
Stephen D 1962,D 21,7:2
Stephen D 1963,F 14,5:2
Poker Session, The 1964,F 12,30:4
Stephen D 1966,Ag 5,17:1
Poker Session, The 1967,S 20,42:2
Stephen D 1967,S 25,58:1
Stephen D 1967,O 8,II,1:6
Leonard, J Elliott
Say When 1934,N 9,24:2
Parade 1935,My 21,22:2
Leonard, Lawrence (Musical Director)
Yeomen of the Guard, The 1962,Jl 11,28:1
Leonard, Leo
Lancelot and Elaine 1921,S 13,12:1
Leonard, Lizzie
Dead End 1935,O 29,17:2
Leonard, Lu
Happiest Girl in the World, The 1961,Ap 4,42:1
Gay Life, The 1961,N 20,38:1
Bravo Giovanni 1962,My 21,41:2
Drat! the Cat! 1965,O 11,54:2
Leonard, Mark
Venice Preserv'd 1955,D 13,54:4
My Mother, My Father and Me 1963,Mr 25,5:5
Leonard, Martia (Playwright)
Immortal Beloved, The 1927,My 5,30:1
Little Theatre Tournament; Tale Retold, A
   1928,My 10,31:1
Leonard, Martin
Take It As It Comes 1944,F 11,17:2
Leonard, Michael (Composer)
Yearling, The 1965,D 11,25:1
How to Be a Jewish Mother 1967,D 29,18:1
Leonard, Michael (Musical Director)
We're Civilized? 1962,N 9,30:1
Leonard, Mickey (Miscellaneous)
Desert Incident, A 1959,Mr 25,40:1
Leonard, Murray
Strip for Action 1942,O 1,26:2
Leonard, Nancy Evans
Galileo 1968,D 1,88:4
Leonard, Orel
Faith of Our Fathers 1950,Ag 6,72:2
Leonard, Patrick A
Tangerine 1921,Ag 10,8:2
Leonard, Patrick A (Producer)
Caviar 1934,Je 8,19:2
Leonard, Queenie
Haven, The 1946,N 14,39:4
Leonard, Ralph
Witness for the Prosecution 1954,D 17,35:2
Leonard, Richard J (Musical Director)
Happy Hypocrite, The 1968,S 6,38:1
Dames at Sea 1968,D 21,46:1
Leonard, Robert
Partners Again 1923,Mr 1,10:3
Izzy 1924,S 17,16:2
Kosher Kitty Kelly 1925,Je 16,24:2
Potash and Perlmutter, Detectives; Poisoned by
   Pictures 1926,S 1,27:3
Potash and Perlmutter, Detectives 1926,S 5,VII,1:1
Ten Per Cent 1927,S 14,29:3
Fifty Million Frenchmen 1929,N 28,34:4
Vaudeville (Palace) 1931,Ja 5,20:3
Wooden Soldier, The 1931,Je 23,28:4
Wonder Boy 1931,O 24,20:1
Geraniums in My Window 1934,O 27,20:6
Potash and Perlmutter 1935,Ap 6,11:3
Menagerie 1935,Jl 2,24:3
Sap Runs High, The 1936,F 5,15:3
Red, Hot and Blue! 1936,O 30,26:3
Cafe Crown 1942,Ja 24,12:5
Down to Miami 1944,S 12,23:5

Leonard, Robert (Director)
Potash and Perlmutter 1935,Ap 6,11:3
Leonard, Sheldon
Hotel Alimony 1934,Ja 30,16:2
Night Remembers, The 1934,N 28,24:3
Fly Away Home 1935,Ja 16,20:4
Having Wonderful Time 1937,F 22,12:5
Siege 1937,D 9,31:4
Kiss the Boys Goodbye 1938,S 29,30:2
Leonard, Warren
Black Crook, The 1929,Mr 12,26:5
Black Crook, The 1929,Mr 17,X,8:1
Untitled-Dance 1930,F 13,25:2
Leonard, William
Love Set, The 1923,Mr 20,24:2
Forbidden 1923,O 2,10:2
Busybody, The 1924,S 30,27:5
Ruint 1925,Ap 8,24:2
Captain Brassbound's Conversion 1950,D 28,21:1
Lord Byron's Love Letter 1955,Ja 19,23:2
Leonard-Boyne, Eva
Laughing Lady, The 1923,F 13,25:1
Little Miss Bluebeard 1923,Ag 29,12:1
Letter, The 1927,S 27,30:1
Apple Cart, The 1930,F 25,30:1
Experience Unnecessary 1932,Mr 28,10:2
Late One Evening 1933,Ja 10,27:3
Lake, The 1933,D 27,24:2
Victoria Regina 1938,O 4,20:2
Corn Is Green, The 1943,My 4,18:3
Stranger, The 1945,F 13,21:2
Hidden Horizon 1946,S 20,42:2
Corn Is Green, The 1950,Ja 12,33:2
Day After Tomorrow 1950,O 27,25:2
Twentieth Century 1950,D 25,23:6
Constant Wife, The 1951,D 10,34:3
Chalk Garden, The 1955,O 27,29:1
Leonardi, Leon (Musical Director)
Bloomer Girl 1944,O 6,18:5
St Louis Woman 1946,Ap 1,22:2
Marie Antoinette in Pennsylvania 1949,My 12,26:2
Leonardos, Urylee
Natural Man 1941,My 8,20:4
Carmen Jones 1943,D 3,26:2
Carmen Jones 1946,Ap 8,32:2
Set My People Free 1948,N 4,38:2
Shuffle Along 1952,My 9,20:5
Porgy and Bess 1953,F 17,21:1
Porgy and Bess 1953,Mr 10,25:5
Sophie 1963,Ap 16,32:1
Bill Noname 1970,Mr 3,37:1
Leone, Danny
Hickory Stick 1944,My 9,15:6
They Knew What They Wanted 1949,F 17,28:2
Leone, Denny
Bad Place to Get Your Head, A 1970,Jl 16,38:1
Leone, Denny (Director)
Bead-Tangle 1970,Jl 16,38:1
Bad Place to Get Your Head, A 1970,Jl 16,38:1
Leone, Joseph F (Producer)
Courtesan 1930,Ap 30,29:3
Leone, Leo
Great Lover, The 1932,O 12,27:3
Leone, Richard
Young Man's Fancy, A 1947,Ap 30,33:2
Galileo 1947,D 8,34:2
Anne of the Thousand Days 1948,D 9,49:2
Leong, Terry (Costume Designer)
To Bury a Cousin 1967,My 17,38:3
Geese 1969,Ja 13,26:6
Parents and Children 1969,Ja 13,26:6
Leoni, Ettore
Signora Dalle Camelie, La; Camille 1934,O 22,13:2
Leonidoff, Leon (Choreographer)
Nine Fifteen Revue, The 1930,F 12,26:2
Well of Romance, The 1930,N 8,21:2
Leonidoff, Leon (Director)
Virginia 1937,S 3,13:2
American Jubilee 1940,My 13,20:5
It Happens on Ice 1940,O 11,24:3
Swing Out, Sweet Land! 1944,N 10,24:6
Sing Out, Sweet Land! 1944,D 28,24:2
Arabian Nights 1955,Je 24,16:1
Wonder World 1964,My 18,32:1
Leonidoff, Leon (Miscellaneous)
It Happens on Ice 1940,O 11,24:3
Leonidoff, Leon (Playwright)
Wonder World 1964,My 18,32:1
Leonidoff, Leon (Producer)
Wonder World 1964,My 18,32:1
Leonidoff, Leon (Scenic Designer)
Nativity, The 1965,D 3,44:2
Leonidoff, Leonid M
Tsar Fyodor Ivanovitch 1923,Ja 9,26:1
Cherry Orchard, The 1923,Ja 23,18:1
Cherry Orchard, The 1923,Ja 28,VII,1:1
Three Sisters, The 1923,Ja 30,12:2
Brothers Karamazov, The 1923,N 20,23:4
Ivanoff 1923,N 27,23:2
Enough Stupidity in Every Wise Man 1923,D 6,23:1
Death of Pazukhin, The 1924,F 12,20:1
Brothers Karamazov, The 1924,My 6,25:2

Leonidov, Leonid (Director)
Kremlin Chimes 1965,F 25,23:1
Leonidov, Yuri
Cherry Orchard, The 1965,F 10,46:1
Three Sisters, The 1965,F 12,15:1
Kremlin Chimes 1965,F 25,23:1
Leonowens, Anna (Original Author)
King and I, The 1951,Ap 8,II,1:1
Leontov, Tania (Costume Designer)
Motel 1966,N 7,66:1
Interview 1966,N 7,66:1
TV 1966,N 7,66:1
Leontov, Eugenie
Revue Russe, The 1922,O 6,28:1
Grand Hotel 1930,N 14,30:4
Grand Hotel 1930,N 23,IX,1:1
20th Century 1932,D 30,15:1
Twentieth Century 1933,F 12,IX,1:1
Bitter Oleander 1935,F 12,24:3
Tovarich 1935,Ap 25,19:8
Tovarich 1935,My 19,IX,1:1
Antony and Cleopatra 1936,O 15,32:8
Antony and Cleopatra 1936,N 1,X,3:7
Tovarich 1937,Ap 25,X,2:4
Romance 1937,Ag 17,23:1
Dark Eyes 1943,Ja 15,20:2
Dark Eyes 1943,Ja 31,II,1:1
Obsession 1946,O 2,39:2
Caviar to the General 1947,Ja 14,30:3
Anastasia 1954,D 30,13:1
Anastasia 1955,Ja 16,II,1:1
Cave Dwellers, The 1957,O 21,29:2
Cave Dwellers, The 1957,O 27,II,1:1
Call on Kuprin, A 1961,My 26,29:3
Call on Kuprin, A 1961,Je 4,II,1:1
Mother Courage and Her Children 1964,My 12,32:2
Leontovich, Eugenie (Miscellaneous)
Dark Eyes 1948,Mr 25,34:4
Leontovich, Eugenie (Playwright)
Cafe de Danse 1929,Ja 16,22:2
Dark Eyes 1943,Ja 15,20:2
Dark Eyes 1943,Ja 31,II,1:1
Caviar to the General 1947,Ja 14,30:3
Leontovich, Eugenie (Producer)
Marie Antoinette in Pennsylvania 1949,My 12,26:2
Leopold, David
Dracula Sabbat 1970,O 2,28:2
Leopold, Tom
Saved 1970,O 29,57:1
Leopoldi, Herman
Vienna at Night 1945,Ap 30,12:4
Leplat, Ted
Young Master Dante, The 1968,D 31,19:1
Steal the Old Man's Bundle 1970,My 16,30:1
Lepooldi, Herman
Day Before Spring, The 1945,N 23,27:2
Leporsky, Zoya
New Moon, The 1944,My 18,16:2
Babes in Arms 1951,Mr 10,7:3
Leppard, Raymond (Composer)
Tempest, The 1963,Ap 3,43:1
Leprevost, Andre (Playwright)
Peter, the Liar 1931,Mr 22,VIII,3:1
Leproux, Pierre
Pique-Nique en Campagne 1969,My 1,50:1
Guernica 1969,My 1,50:1
Leps, Gary
Month in the Country, A 1959,Mr 2,32:2
Lercher, Herman
Mother Courage 1967,N 17,55:1
Lerer, Shifrah
Uncle Sam in Israel 1952,D 8,38:5
Oh What a Wedding! 1969,O 20,60:1
Lerit, Sharon
Bye Bye Birdie 1960,Ap 15,13:4
Lerman, F
Aristocrats 1935,My 2,16:2
Lerman, Omar K (Miscellaneous)
Beaux' Stratagem, The 1959,F 25,35:4
H M S Pinafore 1960,S 8,41:1
Firebugs, The 1963,F 13,7:2
Lerman, Oscar (Producer)
Vamp, The 1955,N 11,30:1
Christine 1960,Ap 29,27:1
Lerner
Merry Wives of Windsor, The 1929,O 27,IX,2:4
Lerner, Alan Jay (Composer)
So Proudly We Hail 1938,Ap 9,11:1
Lerner, Alan Jay (Lyricist)
What's Up 1943,N 12,24:6
Day Before Spring, The 1945,N 23,27:2
Brigadoon 1947,Mr 14,28:2
Love Life 1948,O 8,31:2
Brigadoon 1950,My 3,36:2
Paint Your Wagon 1951,N 13,32:2
My Fair Lady 1956,Mr 16,20:2
My Fair Lady 1956,Mr 25,II,1:1
My Fair Lady 1956,Ap 29,II,17:1
My Fair Lady 1956,Ag 12,II,1:1
My Fair Lady 1956,O 28,II,1:1
Brigadoon 1957,Mr 28,37:1
My Fair Lady 1959,Ja 27,26:1
My Fair Lady 1959,F 21,25:6

Lerner, Alan Jay (Lyricist)—Cont
My Fair Lady 1959,Ap 4,12:5
Camelot 1960,O 3,35:1
Camelot 1960,D 5,42:1
Camelot 1960,D 11,II,5:1
Brigadoon 1962,My 31,21:4
My Fair Lady 1964,F 20,24:4
My Fair Lady 1964,My 21,43:2
Brigadoon 1964,D 24,9:1
My Fair Lady 1964,D 29,22:1
On a Clear Day You Can See Forever 1965,O 18,44:1
Brigadoon 1967,D 14,59:2
My Fair Lady 1968,Je 14,42:1
Whores, Wars & Tin Pan Alley 1969,Je 17,37:1
Coco 1969,D 19,66:1
Coco 1969,D 28,II,1:1
Coco 1970,Ag 7,28:1
Lerner, Alan Jay (Original Author)
Brigadoon 1947,Mr 14,28:2
Love Life 1948,O 8,31:2
Lerner, Alan Jay (Playwright)
What's Up 1943,N 12,24:6
Day Before Spring, The 1945,N 23,27:2
Brigadoon 1947,Mr 23,II,1:1
Brigadoon 1950,My 3,36:2
Paint Your Wagon 1951,N 13,32:2
Paint Your Wagon 1951,N 18,II,1:1
My Fair Lady 1956,Mr 16,20:2
My Fair Lady 1956,Mr 25,II,1:1
My Fair Lady 1956,Ap 29,II,17:1
My Fair Lady 1956,Je 3,II,1:1
My Fair Lady 1956,Je 10,II,7:1
My Fair Lady 1956,Ag 12,II,1:1
My Fair Lady 1956,O 28,II,1:1
Brigadoon 1957,Mr 28,37:1
My Fair Lady 1958,Mr 9,II,1:1
My Fair Lady 1958,My 1,34:5
My Fair Lady 1959,Ja 27,26:1
My Fair Lady 1959,F 21,25:6
Camelot 1960,O 3,35:1
Camelot 1960,D 5,42:1
Brigadoon 1962,My 31,21:4
Brigadoon 1963,F 1,6:2
My Fair Lady 1964,F 20,24:4
My Fair Lady 1964,My 21,43:2
Brigadoon 1964,D 24,9:1
On a Clear Day You Can See Forever 1965,O 18,44:1
Brigadoon 1967,D 14,59:2
My Fair Lady 1968,Je 14,42:1
Coco 1969,D 19,66:1
Coco 1969,D 28,II,1:1
Lerner, Alan Jay (Producer)
Camelot 1960,D 5,42:1
On a Clear Day You Can See Forever 1965,O 18,44:1
Lerner, Carl
Revolt of the Beavers, The 1937,My 21,19:2
Lerner, Diki
Shoestring '57 1956,N 6,31:1
Lerner, Jacques
Monkey Talks, The 1925,D 29,20:1
Monkey Talks, The 1926,Ja 3,VII,1:1
Lerner, Joseph
Young Go First, The 1935,My 29,16:2
Lerner, Judith
West Side Story 1968,Je 25,32:1
Lerner, Max K (Miscellaneous)
Machinal 1960,Ap 8,27:1
Lerner, Renee
Time to Go 1960,Mr 23,33:1
Lerner, Richard (Producer)
Other Man, The 1968,F 9,50:1
Oh, Say Can You See L A 1968,F 9,50:1
Lerner, Robert (Producer)
My Fair Lady 1959,F 21,25:6
Funny Thing Happened on the Way to the Forum, A 1962,O 14,83:4
Lerner, Rose
Left Bank, The 1931,O 6,35:3
Lerner, Sam (Composer)
My Dear Public 1943,S 10,28:1
Lerner, Sam (Lyricist)
Hold It! 1948,My 6,31:5
Lerner, Selma
Trial of Dr Beck, The 1937,Ag 10,22:2
Lerner, Yafa
Ivanov 1958,O 8,42:1
Sappho 1960,Ja 12,22:1
Seidman and Son 1962,O 16,32:2
Lerner, Zelda
Clinton Street 1939,O 13,27:2
Untitled-Poetry Reading 1967,Jl 18,29:1
Lernet-Holenia (Playwright)
Ollapotrida 1927,My 1,VIII,1:3
Leroy, Adele
Genius and the Crowd 1920,S 7,20:1
Lombardi, Ltd 1927,Je 7,27:3
LeRoy, Alan
Two on the Aisle 1951,Jl 20,13:6
Leroy, Dickie
Son, The 1950,Ap 1,12:4

LeRoy, Gloria
Bella 1961,N 17,40:1
Boy on the Straight-Back Chair 1969,Mr 18,36:1
Show Me Where the Good Times Are
1970,Mr 6,32:1
Leroy, Mary (Mrs)
Sharlee 1923,N 23,20:1
LeRoy, Myrtle
Twinkle Twinkle 1926,N 17,22:2
Leroy, Nat (Playwright)
Bringing Up Father 1925,Mr 31,16:1
Leroy, Pamela
Pins and Needles 1922,F 2,20:1
LeRoy, Peggy
Golden Apple, The 1962,F 13,38:2
LeRoy, Warner (Director)
Golden Six, The 1958,O 27,31:2
Between Two Thieves 1960,F 12,23:1
Shadow of Heroes 1961,D 6,59:1
LeRoy, Warner (Miscellaneous)
Waiting for Godot 1958,Ag 6,22:1
LeRoy, Warner (Playwright)
Between Two Thieves 1960,F 12,23:1
LeRoy, Warner (Producer)
Garden District; Something Unspoken
1958,Ja 8,23:4
Garden District; Suddenly Last Summer
1958,Ja 8,23:4
Golden Six, The 1958,O 27,31:2
Shadow of Heroes 1961,D 6,59:1
Lertora, Joseph
Sweetheart Shop, The 1920,S 1,13:4
Helen of Troy, New York 1923,Je 20,22:6
Louie the 14th 1925,Mr 4,17:1
Hush Money 1926,Mr 16,22:3
Twinkle Twinkle 1926,N 17,22:2
Lady Do 1927,Ap 19,24:2
Music in May 1929,Ap 2,29:1
Wonderful Night, A; Fledermaus, Die
1929,N 1,23:3
Blossom Time 1931,Mr 5,32:1
There You Are! 1932,My 17,25:4
Lesage, Rene
Waiting for Godot 1968,Ap 23,38:1
Lesage, Rene (Director)
Waiting for Godot 1968,Ap 23,38:1
Lesan, David
Peace on Earth 1933,N 30,39:2
Parade 1935,My 21,22:2
Whatever Goes Up 1935,N 26,28:2
Lesan, David (Playwright)
Parade 1935,My 7,26:1
Parade 1935,My 12,X,2:5
Parade 1935,My 21,22:2
Illustrators' Show, The 1936,Ja 23,25:3
Sing for Your Supper 1939,Ap 25,18:6
LeSauvage, George Ross
This Mad Whirl 1937,Ja 10,II,4:8
Lesberg, Sandy (Director)
Before I Wake 1968,O 14,56:1
Lescoulie, Jack
Tapestry in Gray 1935,D 28,10:2
Leser, Arthur (Producer)
Maurice Chevalier 1947,Mr 11,37:2
Leser, Robert
Othello 1945,My 23,25:4
Leser, Tina (Costume Designer)
Park Avenue 1946,N 5,31:2
Leseuer, Robert
You and I 1925,O 20,29:1
Lesh, Rebecca
Gold Diggers, The 1927,D 3,19:2
Alexander Pushkin 1928,Ja 27,14:2
Lesinski, Frank
Sniper, The 1959,O 28,40:4
Leskin, Betty Jayne
My Son and I 1960,O 24,24:2
Lesko, Andrew (Musical Director)
What a Killing 1961,Mr 28,41:1
Lesko, Andrew Orestes
In the Nick of Time 1967,Je 2,36:1
Lesko, John (Miscellaneous)
Come Play With Me 1959,My 1,33:5
What a Killing 1961,Mr 28,41:1
Lesko, John (Musical Director)
Come Play With Me 1959,My 1,33:5
Jennie 1963,O 18,35:2
Skyscraper 1965,N 15,48:1
I Do! I Do! 1966,D 6,58:1
South Pacific 1968,Je 30,54:2
Maggie Flynn 1968,O 24,52:1
Lesley, Brenda
Burn Me to Ashes 1963,N 20,48:1
Medea 1965,N 29,46:1
To Clothe the Naked 1967,Ap 28,30:1
Halfway up the Tree 1967,N 8,52:1
Lesley, Leonard (Playwright)
Victim, The 1952,My 3,17:5
Lesley, Leonard (Producer)
Clerambard 1957,N 8,22:3
Leslie, Aleen (Playwright)
Slightly Married 1943,O 26,19:2

Leslie, Alfred (Scenic Designer)
Dybbuk, The 1954,O 27,33:6
Leslie, Anne
Cretan Woman, The 1954,My 21,17:2
Leslie, Bethel
Snafu 1944,O 26,19:5
Dancer, The 1946,Je 6,16:5
Years Ago 1946,D 4,44:2
How I Wonder 1947,O 1,34:2
Goodbye My Fancy 1948,N 18,35:2
Goodbye My Fancy 1948,N 28,II,1:1
Wisteria Trees, The 1950,Mr 30,39:1
Mary Rose 1951,Mr 5,25:2
Mary Rose 1951,Mr 11,II,1:1
Pygmalion 1952,F 9,11:2
Brass Ring, The 1952,Ap 11,19:2
Inherit the Wind 1955,Ap 22,20:2
Catch Me if You Can 1965,Mr 10,50:1
But, Seriously... 1969,F 28,29:1
Leslie, Bob
Mr Wonderful 1956,Mr 23,23:2
Ziegfeld Follies 1957,Mr 2,19:2
Leslie, Doree
Manhattan Mary 1927,S 27,30:3
Simple Simon 1930,F 19,22:1
Leslie, Dudley (Playwright)
Between Us Two 1935,Ja 31,22:4
Between Us Two 1935,F 17,VIII,3:1
Leslie, Earl
Innocent Eyes 1924,My 21,22:2
Leslie, Earl (Producer)
Ca. . . C'Est Paris 1927,F 6,VII,4:1
Leslie, Eddie
Earl Carroll's Vanities 1924,S 11,23:6
Belmont Varieties 1932,S 29,17:2
Leslie, Edgar (Composer)
Howdy Stranger 1937,Ja 15,17:5
Leslie, Edith
Window Shopping 1938,D 24,13:2
Too Hot for Maneuvers 1945,My 3,26:5
Leslie, Edna
Girl With Carmine Lips, The 1920,Ag 11,6:1
For Better or Worse 1927,F 1,24:3
Leslie, Frank
Earl Carroll's Vanities 1924,S 11,23:6
White Lights 1927,O 12,30:4
Star of Bengal 1929,S 26,27:2
Winter's Tale, The 1946,Ja 16,18:6
Candida 1952,Ap 23,23:6
Leslie, Fred
Charlot's Revue 1924,Ja 10,18:1
Sweetheart Time 1926,Ja 20,23:2
Silent House, The 1932,N 9,28:3
One Wife or Another 1933,F 7,23:6
Picnic 1934,My 3,15:2
Bridal Quilt 1934,O 11,28:5
Point Valaine 1935,Ja 17,22:2
This Our House 1935,D 12,33:3
Laughing Woman, The 1936,O 14,30:1
Aged 26 1936,D 22,32:1
Anything Goes 1937,Ag 26,24:3
Susan and God 1937,O 8,26:4
Leslie, Henrietta (Original Author)
Mrs Fischer's War 1931,Ag 9,VIII,1:3
Leslie, Henrietta (Playwright)
Mrs Fischer's War 1931,Ag 9,VIII,1:3
Leslie, J Frank
Earl Carroll's Vanities 1923,Jl 6,8:2
Leslie, Jack
What Do We Know 1927,D 24,8:1
Wrecker, The 1928,F 28,18:2
Great Power, The 1928,S 12,25:1
Gambling 1929,Ag 27,31:2
Tavern, The 1930,My 20,32:1
Song and Dance Man, The 1930,Je 17,25:5
Counsellor-at-Law 1931,N 7,17:2
Marching By 1932,Mr 4,17:1
Between Two Worlds 1934,O 26,24:2
Forbidden Melody 1936,N 3,33:1
Mr Big 1941,O 1,24:2
Marinka 1945,Jl 19,19:2
Leslie, Jean
Have You Heard This One 1953,N 9,23:4
Leslie, John
Tomorrow's a Holiday! 1935,D 31,10:2
Lady in the Dark 1943,Mr 1,14:2
Prescott Proposals, The 1953,D 17,53:1
Happy Hunting 1956,D 7,30:1
Disenchanted, The 1958,D 4,53:4
General Seeger 1962,Mr 1,26:2
Leslie, June
Garden of Eden, The 1927,S 28,28:1
Tapestry in Gray 1935,D 28,10:2
Leslie, Katherine
Rebound 1930,F 4,29:1
Leslie, Kenny
Hollywood Ice Revue 1955 1955,Ja 14,16:1
Leslie, Larry
Mr Wonderful 1956,Mr 23,23:2
Ziegfeld Follies 1957,Mr 2,19:2
Leslie, Lawrence
Shelf, The 1926,S 28,31:1
John 1927,N 5,16:4

Leslie, Lawrence—Cont
Marriage on Approval 1928,Mr 2,28:2
Box Seats 1928,Ap 20,27:2
Gentlemen of the Press 1928,Ag 28,27:2
Remote Control 1929,S 11,24:5
Remote Control 1929,S 22,IX,1:1
Meteor 1929,D 24,15:1
Leslie, Lew (Director)
Dixie to Broadway 1924,O 30,22:1
International Revue 1930,F 26,22:2
Lew Leslie's Blackbirds of 1930 1930,O 23,34:5
Blackbirds 1933,D 4,22:3
Lew Leslie's Blackbirds of 1939 1939,F 13,12:2
Leslie, Lew (Playwright)
Plantation Revue, The 1922,Jl 18,18:4
Dixie to Broadway 1924,O 30,22:1
International Revue 1930,F 26,22:2
Blackbirds 1933,D 4,22:3
Blackbirds 1936,Jl 10,15:1
Blackbirds 1938,N 13,IX,2:1
Leslie, Lew (Producer)
White Birds 1927,Je 26,VIII,1:3
Blackbirds 1928,My 10,31:3
International Revue 1930,F 9,VIII,4:2
International Revue 1930,F 26,22:2
Lew Leslie's Blackbirds of 1930 1930,O 23,34:5
Blackbirds 1933,D 4,22:3
Blackbirds 1934,Ag 26,II,6:5
Lew Leslie's Blackbirds of 1939 1939,F 13,12:2
Leslie, May (Choreographer)
Riff-Raff 1926,F 9,18:6
Leslie, Noel
Power of Darkness, The 1920,Ja 22,22:1
Ambush 1921,O 11,22:1
Shadow, The 1922,Ap 25,14:2
Salome 1922,My 23,12:4
Guilty One, The 1923,Mr 21,19:1
Druid Circle, The 1947,O 23,29:5
Linden Tree, The 1948,Mr 3,28:2
I Know My Love 1949,N 3,36:1
Day After Tomorrow 1950,O 27,25:2
Captain Brassbound's Conversion 1950,D 28,21:1
Sacred Flame, The 1952,O 8,35:2
Tempest, The 1955,S 3,8:6
Apple Cart, The 1956,O 19,23:1
World of Suzie Wong, The 1958,O 15,47:1
Leslie, Norma
Bootleggers, The 1922,N 28,24:1
Leslie, Paul
Have You Heard This One 1953,N 9,23:4
Leslie, Paul (Playwright)
Satyr 1937,Je 17,18:5
Satyr 1937,Jl 4,X,1:4
Have You Heard This One 1953,N 9,23:4
Leslie, Robert
Barrister, The 1932,N 22,25:2
Don't Look Now! 1936,N 4,41:3
Leslie, S J
Night Remembers, The 1934,N 28,24:3
Leslie, Sylvia
Bitter Sweet 1929,O 27,IX,2:1
Bitter Sweet 1929,N 6,30:2
Conversation Piece 1934,O 24,24:1
Leslie and Simone
Arabian Nights 1967,Jl 3,12:1
Lesold, Helmuth (Miscellaneous)
Gentleman Caller, The 1969,Ap 27,92:1
Warning, The-A Theme for Linda 1969,Ap 27,92:1
Great Goodness of Life (A Coon Show)
1969,Ap 27,92:1
Prayer Meeting: or, The First Militant Minister
1969,Ap 27,92:1
Less, Max
Tobias and the Angel 1937,Ap 29,16:5
Less, Robert
I'd Rather Be Right 1937,N 3,28:2
Lessane, Leroy
Gandhi 1970,O 21,37:1
Lessard, Connie
Richard III 1949,F 9,33:2
Lesser, Arthur (Producer)
Along Fifth Avenue 1949,Ja 14,28:2
Two on the Aisle 1951,Jl 20,13:6
International Soiree 1958,Mr 13,25:1
Folies Bergere 1964,Je 3,36:1
Grosse Valise, La 1965,D 15,52:1
Lesser, Eugene (Director)
Passing Through From Exotic Places; Sunstroke
1969,D 8,60:4
Passing Through From Exotic Places; Son Who
Hunted Tigers in Jakarta, The 1969,D 8,60:4
Passing Through From Exotic Places; Burial of
Esposito, The 1969,D 8,60:4
Prince of Peasantmania 1970,F 22,88:1
Carpenters, The 1970,D 22,40:1
Lesser, Len
House in Berlin, A (Als der Kreig zu Ende War);
Als der Krieg zu Ende War (A House in Berlin)
1950,D 27,32:3
Lesser, Lou
O'Brien Girl, The 1921,O 4,10:2
Lessey, George
Bless You, Sister 1927,D 27,24:5
Mystery Man, The 1928,Ja 27,14:2

Lessey, George—Cont

Remote Control 1929,S 11,24:5
Seven 1929,D 28,10:5
Gala Night 1930,F 26,22:4
Monkey 1932,F 12,25:2
Cradle Snatchers 1932,N 17,23:2
Forsaking All Others 1933,Mr 2,21:2
Her Man of Wax 1933,O 12,32:3
Big Hearted Herbert 1934,Ja 2,17:3
Battleship Gertie 1935,Ja 19,9:2
Sketch Book 1935,Je 5,22:2
Porgy and Bess 1935,O 11,30:2
Arrest That Woman 1936,S 19,20:4
Now You've Done It 1937,Mr 6,10:4
Many Mansions 1937,O 28,28:6
Susanna, Don't You Cry 1939,My 23,27:2
Man Who Came to Dinner, The 1939,O 17,31:1
Signature 1945,F 15,25:2
State of the Union 1945,N 15,25:2

Lessin, Harry
Young Go First, The 1935,My 29,16:2
Professor Mamlock 1937,Ap 14,30:3
Medicine Show 1940,Ap 13,20:6

Lessing, Doris (Playwright)
Play With a Tiger 1964,D 31,14:2

Lessing, Florence
Kismet 1953,D 4,2:4

Lessing, Gotthold Ephraim (Original Author)
Nathan the Wise 1942,Ap 4,18:4

Lessing, Gotthold Ephraim (Playwright)
Nathan the Wise 1942,Mr 12,25:4
Nathan the Wise 1962,Mr 7,29:1
Nathan the Wise 1962,Mr 23,29:1
Nathan der Weise 1966,D 10,45:2
Minna von Barnhelm 1968,N 13,37:1

Lessing, Gotthold Ephraim (Translator)
Nathan the Wise 1944,F 22,26:3

Lessing, Madge
Erminie 1921,Ja 4,11:1

Lessner, George (Composer)
Sleepy Hollow 1948,Je 4,26:3

Lessner, George (Musical Director)
Sleepy Hollow 1948,Je 4,26:3

Lessy, Ben
All in Fun 1940,N 22,26:2

Lester, Barbara
Queen After Death 1956,Mr 13,33:2
Protective Custody 1956,D 29,8:7
Macbeth 1962,N 17,16:2
Johnny No-Trump 1967,O 9,60:2
Grin and Bare It 1970,Mr 17,36:1

Lester, Dottie
Carnival! 1968,D 13,58:1

Lester, Edward
Wonderful Thing, The 1920,F 18,9:1
Fedora 1922,F 11,18:1
Plot Thickens, The 1922,S 6,16:1
Lady Butterfly 1923,Ja 23,18:1
Carolinian, The 1925,N 3,34:2
Wings Over Europe 1928,D 11,35:1
Three Little Girls 1930,Ap 15,29:1
New York to Cherbourg 1932,F 20,11:4
Ragged Edge, The 1935,N 26,28:3
Processional 1937,O 14,23:1
All That Glitters 1938,Ja 20,18:2
Empress of Destiny 1938,Mr 10,16:2
Woman Brown, The 1939,D 9,18:5

Lester, Edwin (Director)
Carousel 1953,My 6,38:1

Lester, Edwin (Miscellaneous)
Magdalena 1948,Jl 28,27:2

Lester, Edwin (Playwright)
Merry Widow, The 1964,Ag 18,24:2

Lester, Edwin (Producer)
Song of Norway 1944,Ag 22,20:2
Song of Norway 1944,Ag 27,II,1:1
Gypsy Lady 1946,S 18,25:6
Magdalena 1948,S 21,31:2
Peter Pan 1954,Jl 20,15:3
Peter Pan 1954,O 21,30:2
Annie Get Your Gun 1957,Ag 31,18:2

Lester, Elliott (Playwright)
Mud Turtle, The 1925,Ag 21,8:2
Mud Turtle, The 1925,S 6,VII,1:1
Medicine Man, The 1927,O 16,IX,2:4
Take My Advice 1927,N 2,24:3
Two Seconds 1931,O 10,20:6

Lester, Hugh
Free Soul, A 1928,Ja 13,26:5

Lester, Hugh (Miscellaneous)
White Cargo 1960,D 30,12:1
Indians 1969,My 27,43:1
Night Thoreau Spent in Jail, The 1970,N 2,66:1

Lester, Jerry
Earl Carroll's Vanities 1940,Ja 15,11:2
All in Fun 1940,N 22,26:2
Beat the Band 1942,O 15,26:1
Jackpot 1944,Ja 14,15:2
South Pacific 1969,Jl 7,27:1

Lester, Ketty
Cabin in the Sky 1964,Ja 22,32:1

Lester, Lorraine (Producer)
Sleepy Hollow 1948,Je 4,26:3

Lester, Margot
His Queen 1925,My 12,26:1
Hay Fever 1925,O 5,25:1
Ashes of Love 1926,Mr 23,24:3
If 1927,O 26,26:2

Lester, Marguerite
Hansel and Gretel 1929,D 25,21:1

Lester, Nancy
God and Kate Murphy 1959,F 27,21:2

Lester, Paul
Lady in Love, A 1927,F 22,22:1

Lester, Sue
Cyanamide 1954,Mr 26,17:6

Lester, William
Patience 1928,Je 26,29:3

Lestina, Welba
At the Bottom 1930,Ja 10,24:3

Lestora, Joseph
Chiffon Girl, The 1924,F 20,23:2

L'Estrange, David (Playwright)
Rat, The 1925,F 11,19:3

LeStrange, Philip
Stephen D 1966,Ag 5,17:1
Getting Married 1970,Ja 20,46:1

Leszczynska, Homorata
Women's House, The 1930,Ap 27,IX,3:1

Letchworth, Eileen
Say Darling 1958,Ap 4,17:1
Cactus Flower 1965,D 9,60:2

Leticia
Star and Garter 1942,Je 25,26:2

Letondal, Ginette
Henry V 1956,Je 20,27:2
Henry V 1956,Je 24,II,1:1

Letora, Joseph
Say When 1928,Je 27,29:3

Letra, Hans von (Playwright)
Glueck in Haus 1933,My 7,IX,2:5

Letrax, Jean de (Playwright)
Fessee, La 1937,Ja 24,X,2:1

Letrie, Walter
You Said It 1931,Ja 20,21:3

Lettengarver, Johnny
Ice Capades 1954,S 16,37:1

Lettice, Michael
Let Freedom Ring 1935,N 7,26:2
How Beautiful With Shoes 1935,N 29,24:1

Letton, Francis
Othello 1945,My 23,25:4
Strange Fruit 1945,N 30,18:6
Cyrano de Bergerac 1946,O 9,33:2
Cyrano de Bergerac 1947,Ja 17,27:2
On the Harmfulness of Tobacco 1948,F 6,29:2
Wedding, The 1948,F 6,29:2
Bear, The 1948,F 6,29:2
Tragedian in Spite of Himself, A 1948,F 6,29:2
Troublemakers, The 1954,D 31,11:3

Letton, Francis (Playwright)
Young Elizabeth, The 1952,Ap 3,45:1
Young Elizabeth, The 1952,Ap 13,II,3:8

Lettor, Elaine
Virgin of Bethulia, The 1925,F 24,17:2

Leuffgen, Joseph
Passion Play 1934,F 12,15:1
Veronica's Veil 1936,F 10,19:6
Passion Play 1940,F 12,2:7

Leupolt, Heide
Faust, Part I; Play, The 1961,F 5,27:2

Lev, G Israel (Composer)
Honeymoon in Israel, A 1962,O 15,33:5

Levando, Pincus
Matinee Wife 1936,Ap 25,21:3
Let's Get Married 1937,Ja 11,16:2

Levansaler, Atwood
Single Man at a Party 1959,Ap 22,30:4

Levant, Harry (Musical Director)
My Dear Public 1943,S 10,28:1

Levant, Marcia
Tender Trap, The 1961,Ag 26,15:1
Egg, The 1962,Ja 9,23:2

Levant, Oscar
Burlesque 1927,S 2,15:3

Levant, Oscar (Composer)
Ripples 1930,F 2,VIII,2:7
Ripples 1930,F 12,26:1
American Way, The 1939,Ja 23,9:2

Levanthal, Harold (Producer)
Mother Courage 1967,N 17,55:1

Levasseur, Andre (Costume Designer)
Avare, L', L'; Miser, The 1966,F 9,32:1
Fil a la Paite, Un 1966,F 18,25:1

Levasseur, Andre (Scenic Designer)
Avare, L', L'; Miser, The 1966,F 9,32:1
Fil a la Paite, Un 1966,F 18,25:1
Flea in Her Ear, A 1967,O 30,59:1

Leve, Samuel (Costume Designer)
Revolt of the Beavers, The 1937,My 21,19:2
Beat the Band 1942,O 15,26:1

Leve, Samuel (Lighting Director)
Medicine Show 1940,Ap 13,20:6
Apology 1943,Mr 23,14:2
Madwoman of Chaillot, The 1950,Je 14,41:2
Highway Robbery 1955,N 8,36:1

Leve, Samuel (Lighting Director)—Cont

Double in Hearts 1956,O 17,41:7
Comes a Day 1958,N 7,22:1
Mother's Sabbath Days 1960,N 21,33:2
Jack Benny 1963,Mr 1,10:5
Have I Got a Girl for You! 1963,D 3,53:2
Cafe Crown 1964,Ap 18,32:1

Leve, Samuel (Scenic Designer)
Tobias and the Angel 1937,Ap 29,16:5
Revolt of the Beavers, The 1937,My 21,19:2
Julius Caesar 1937,N 12,26:6
Wild Duck, The 1938,Ap 16,16:5
Big Blow 1938,O 3,11:2
Who Is Who? 1938,D 24,13:3
Medicine Show 1940,Ap 13,20:6
Beautiful People, The 1941,Ap 22,27:2
Distant City, The 1941,S 23,27:5
Macbeth 1941,N 12,30:2
They Should Have Stood in Bed 1942,F 14,18:5
Life of Reilly, The 1942,Ap 30,13:2
Beat the Band 1942,O 15,26:1
Mr Sycamore 1942,N 14,13:2
Apology 1943,Mr 23,14:2
Wallflower 1944,Ja 27,14:2
Thank You Svoboda 1944,Mr 2,13:2
Last Stop 1944,S 6,17:2
Hand in Glove 1944,D 5,19:1
Dark Hammock 1944,D 12,27:8
Sophie 1944,D 26,22:7
Round Trip 1945,My 30,16:4
Oh, Herbert! 1945,Je 20,26:3
Sound of Hunting, A 1945,N 21,16:6
Song of Dnieper 1946,O 26,10:5
Family Affair, A 1946,N 28,41:2
Story of Mary Surratt, The 1947,F 10,25:2
Clutterbuck 1949,D 5,29:2
All You Need Is One Good Break 1950,F 10,20:3
Lace on Her Petticoat 1951,S 5,40:3
Dinosaur Wharf 1951,N 9,23:2
Fifth Season, The 1953,Ja 24,13:2
Grass Is Always Greener, The 1955,F 16,25:2
Miser, The 1955,Mr 18,34:2
Hear! Hear! 1955,S 28,38:1
Highway Robbery 1955,N 8,36:1
Goodbye Again 1956,Ap 25,38:1
Double in Hearts 1956,O 17,41:7
Comes a Day 1958,N 7,22:1
Mother's Sabbath Days 1960,N 21,33:2
Jack Benny 1963,Mr 1,10:5
Have I Got a Girl for You! 1963,D 3,53:2
Cafe Crown 1964,Ap 18,32:1

Leveen, Raymond (Composer)
Viva O'Brien 1941,O 10,27:2

Leveen, Raymond (Lyricist)
Viva O'Brien 1941,O 10,27:2

Leveiliee, Claude (Composer)
Gogo Loves You 1964,O 10,19:2

Levelle, Fatelle
Artists and Models 1923,Ag 21,12:2

Leven, Jeremy (Director)
Proposition, The 1968,Ap 20,25:3

Leven, Jeremy (Playwright)
Proposition, The 1968,Ap 20,25:3

Levenda, Leo
Silver Tassie, The 1949,Jl 22,16:5

Levene, Sam
Headquarters 1929,D 5,32:4
Three Times the Hour 1931,Ag 26,15:5
Wonder Boy 1931,O 24,20:1
Dinner at Eight 1932,O 24,18:2
Yellow Jack 1934,Mr 7,22:6
Spring Song 1934,O 2,18:2
Three Men on a Horse 1935,Ja 22,22:7
Three Men on a Horse 1935,Ja 31,22:3
Room Service 1937,My 20,16:1
Room Service 1937,My 30,X,1:1
Margin for Error 1939,O 15,48:7
Margin for Error 1939,N 4,11:3
Margin for Error 1939,N 12,IX,1:1
Sound of Hunting, A 1945,N 21,16:6
Sound of Hunting, A 1945,D 2,II,1:1
Light Up the Sky 1948,N 19,34:2
Light Up the Sky 1948,D 5,II,5:1
Guys and Dolls 1950,N 25,11:2
Guys and Dolls 1950,D 3,II,1:1
Guys and Dolls 1951,O 7,II,1:1
Guys and Dolls 1953,Je 7,II,1:3
Matchmaker, The 1954,Ag 24,18:1
Matchmaker, The 1954,S 5,II,3:7
Matchmaker, The 1955,My 8,II,1:1
Hot Corner, The 1956,Ja 26,25:2
Fair Game 1957,N 4,39:1
Make a Million 1958,O 24,39:2
Heartbreak House 1959,O 19,37:1
Heartbreak House 1959,O 25,II,1:1
Good Soup, The 1960,Mr 3,26:4
Devil's Advocate, The 1961,Mr 10,20:1
Devil's Advocate, The 1961,Mr 19,II,1:1
Let It Ride 1961,O 13,27:4
Seidman and Son 1962,O 16,32:2
Cafe Crown 1964,Ap 18,32:1
Last Analysis, The 1964,O 2,30:1
Last Analysis, The 1964,O 11,II,1:1

Levene, Sam—Cont

Nathan Weinstein, Mystic, Connecticut 1966,F 26,15:2
Three Men on a Horse 1969,O 26,II,1:1
Paris Is Out! 1970,F 3,35:1
Paris Is Out! 1970,F 22,II,5:5
Dream Out of Time, A 1970,N 9,52:1

Levene, Sam (Director)
Hot Corner, The 1956,Ja 26,25:2

Levenhagen, Joan (Costume Designer)
Long Moment, The 1950,My 22,16:6

Levensaler, Atwood
Firstborn, The 1957,Ja 7,29:2

Levension, Sara
Song of Bernadette 1944,Jl 27,15:3

Levenson, David
Let's Get Married 1937,Ja 11,16:2
Warson at Night 1938,Ja 31,14:3

Levenson, Gabriel (Miscellaneous)
Walk Down Mah Street! 1968,Je 13,54:1

Levenson, Lew (Director)
East of Broadway 1932,Ja 27,19:3

Levenson, Robert
Threepenny Opera, The 1955,S 21,38:1

Leventhal, A Marc (Miscellaneous)
Confederates, The 1959,S 29,45:1

Leventhal, Harold (Producer)
King of the Dark Chamber 1961,F 10,21:1
Mirele Efros 1967,O 20,55:1
We Bombed in New Haven 1968,O 17,51:1
But, Seriously... 1969,F 28,29:1

Leventhal, J J (Playwright)
Dangerous Corner 1933,Jl 18,20:4

Leventhal, J J (Producer)
On Call 1928,N 10,20:7
Lady Dedlock 1929,Ja 1,61:2
Great Lover, The 1932,O 12,27:3
Whistling in the Dark 1932,N 4,25:2
Good Fairy, The 1932,N 18,22:3
Show-Off, The 1932,D 13,25:4
As Husbands Go 1933,Ja 20,20:5
Monster, The 1933,F 11,11:5
Riddle Me This! 1933,Mr 15,21:3
Best People, The 1933,Mr 16,21:5
It's a Wise Child 1933,My 17,15:2
John Ferguson 1933,Jl 11,15:7
Perfumed Lady, The 1934,Mr 13,27:2
Every Thursday 1934,My 11,25:5
Nowhere Bound 1935,Ja 23,20:2
Dead End 1937,Ag 17,23:1
When We Are Married 1939,D 26,22:3
Strangler Fig, The 1940,My 7,31:2
Goose for the Gander, A 1945,Ja 24,16:4
Marinka 1945,Jl 19,19:2
Flag Is Born, A 1946,S 7,10:6

Leventhal, Peter
Originale 1964,S 9,46:1

Leveque, Claude
On Ne Badine Pas Avec l'Amour; No Trifling With Love 1968,Mr 5,35:1

Leverage, Henry (Original Author)
Whispering Wires 1922,Ag 8,26:2

Leverett, Lewis
Moon Is a Gong, The 1926,Mr 13,21:3
Spring Song 1927,D 22,26:3
Would-Be Gentleman, The 1928,O 2,34:1
Peter Pan; Boy Who Would Not Grow Up, The 1928,N 27,36:3
On the High Road 1929,Ja 15,22:3
Playing With Love 1929,F 27,16:4
Sea Gull, The 1929,Ap 10,32:2
At the Bottom 1930,Ja 10,24:3
Sea Gull, The 1930,F 26,22:2
Life Line, The 1930,D 29,19:3
1931 1931,D 11,34:3
Night Over Taos 1932,Mr 10,25:3
Big Night 1933,Ja 18,16:2
Black Diamond 1933,F 24,12:2
Men in White 1933,S 27,24:2
Gentlewoman 1934,Mr 23,28:4
Gold Eagle Guy 1934,N 29,33:4
Waiting for Lefty 1935,F 11,14:5
Till the Day I Die 1935,Mr 27,24:5
Waiting for Lefty 1935,Mr 27,24:5
Paradise Lost 1935,D 10,31:5
Case of Clyde Griffiths 1936,Mr 14,10:4

Leverett, Lewis (Director)
Revolt of the Beavers, The 1937,My 21,19:2

Leveridge, Lynn Ann
Saved 1970,O 29,57:1

Levering, Nancy
Jayhawker 1934,N 6,34:2

Levering, Nancy (Producer)
Song of the Grasshopper 1967,S 29,52:2

LeVerne
It Happens on Ice 1940,O 11,24:3

Levers, James
Queer People 1934,F 16,16:2

Leversee, Loretta
House in Berlin, A (Als der Kreig zu Ende War); Als der Krieg zu Ende War (A House in Berlin) 1950,D 27,32:3
Bullfight 1954,Ja 13,25:2
Home Is the Hero 1954,S 23,42:2

Good as Gold 1957,Mr 8,22:2
Deep Are the Roots 1960,O 4,47:1
Entertain a Ghost 1962,Ap 10,48:1

Levertoff, Paul P (Translator)
Paul Among the Jews 1928,Ag 5,VII,1:1

Leverton, Garrett H (Miscellaneous)
Gloriana 1938,N 26,18:4

Leveson, Rita
As You Like It 1936,Ap 24,18:4

Levey, Bernard (Producer)
Bedfellows 1929,Jl 3,19:2

Levey, Ed
Man and Superman 1964,D 7,45:2

Levey, Ethel
Vaudeville (Palace) 1921,Ja 25,14:2
Go Easy Mabel 1922,My 9,22:2
Sunny River 1941,D 5,28:2
Marinka 1945,Jl 19,19:2

Levey, Harold (Composer)
Lady Billy 1920,D 15,18:2
Magic Ring, The 1923,O 2,10:1
Magnolia Lady, The 1924,N 26,17:2
Broke 1925,My 3,VIII,2:1
Lucky Break 1925,Ag 12,16:2
Greenwich Village Follies 1925,D 25,23:3
Rainbow Rose 1926,Mr 17,28:2
Lovely Lady 1927,D 30,22:1

Levey, Harold (Lyricist)
Broke 1925,My 3,VIII,2:1
Greenwich Village Follies 1925,D 25,23:3

Levey, J H (Producer)
Black Rhythm 1936,D 21,19:2

Levey, Ted
Slight Case of Murder, A 1935,S 12,28:5

Levi, Gavri (Miscellaneous)
Grand Music Hall of Israel, The 1968,F 7,42:1

Levi, Stephen (Playwright)
Daphne in Cottage D 1967,O 16,56:1
Daphne in Cottage D 1967,N 5,II,3:1

Levian, Frances
Slight Case of Murder, A 1935,S 12,28:5

Levian, Harry
Gentlemen of the Press 1928,Ag 28,27:2
Birthright 1933,N 22,22:3
Slight Case of Murder, A 1935,S 12,28:5
Bitter Stream 1936,Mr 31,16:6
But for the Grace of God 1937,Ja 13,21:4
Abe Lincoln in Illinois 1938,O 17,12:2

Levick, R J (Choreographer)
On the Necessity of Being Polygamous 1964,D 9,61:1

Levien, Francis J
Half Moon Inn 1925,Mr 10,14:1
Betty Behave 1927,Mr 9,28:4

LeVien, Nicole
Intermezzo 1957,F 15,20:4

Levien, Ruth
Canteen Show, The 1942,S 4,18:1

Levik, H (Playwright)
Golem, The 1948,My 17,22:3

Levin, Bob (Lighting Director)
Thorntons, The 1956,F 15,26:1

Levin, Dan (Director)
Stevedore 1949,F 23,30:2
Miser, The 1950,Mr 27,19:5
Julius Caesar 1950,Je 21,30:1
Wayward Stork, The 1966,Ja 20,27:1

Levin, David
Diary of Anne Frank, The 1955,O 6,24:2

Levin, Donald (Playwright)
Awakening of Spring, The 1964,My 13,50:1

Levin, Gertrude (Pvt)
Swing Sister Wac Swing 1944,Ja 4,20:4

Levin, Hefman (Producer)
Bless You All 1950,D 15,42:2

Levin, Henry
Prelude to Exile 1936,D 1,31:1
Crime at Blossoms, The 1937,Jl 17,12:8
To Quito and Back 1937,O 7,30:4
Fifth Column, The 1940,Mr 7,18:2
Glamour Preferred 1940,N 16,13:2
Cuckoos on the Hearth 1941,S 17,26:2

Levin, Herbert
Let Freedom Ring 1935,N 7,26:2

Levin, Herman (Producer)
Call Me Mister 1946,Ap 19,26:2
Call Me Mister 1946,Ap 28,II,1:1
No Exit 1946,N 27,21:1
Richard III 1949,F 9,33:2
Gentlemen Prefer Blondes 1949,D 9,35:3
My Fair Lady 1956,Mr 16,20:2
My Fair Lady 1957,F 5,27:2
My Fair Lady 1958,My 1,34:5
My Fair Lady 1959,Ja 19,24:6
Girl Who Came to Supper, The 1963,D 9,49:1
Great White Hope, The 1968,O 4,40:1
Lovely Ladies, Kind Gentlemen 1970,D 29,38:1

Levin, Ira (Director)
Dr Cook's Garden 1967,S 26,52:1

Levin, Ira (Lyricist)
Drat! the Cat! 1965,O 11,54:2

Levin, Ira (Playwright)
No Time for Sergeants 1955,O 21,32:2

Levin, Ira (Playwright)—Cont

No Time for Sergeants 1955,N 6,II,1:1
No Time for Sergeants 1956,F 26,II,1:1
No Time for Sergeants 1956,Ag 24,15:8
Interlock 1958,F 7,18:1
Critic's Choice 1960,D 15,61:3
Critic's Choice 1961,D 7,53:2
General Seeger 1962,Mr 1,26:2
Drat! the Cat! 1965,O 11,54:2
Dr Cook's Garden 1967,S 26,52:1

Levin, Jack (Playwright)
Good Neighbor 1941,O 22,26:2

Levin, Jane
Hair 1967,O 30,55:1

Levin, John (Playwright)
House of Atreus, The 1968,D 18,55:1

Levin, Lucy
Radio Girl, The 1929,O 19,22:4
Jolly Orphan, The 1929,D 23,18:6
Little Clown, The 1930,Mr 15,23:3
Love Thief, The 1931,Ja 19,24:5
Great Miracle, The 1931,D 12,23:5
Rich Paupers 1932,Mr 14,13:4
Big Surprise, The 1932,O 17,18:3
Jewish Melody, The 1933,Mr 27,12:4
Happy Family, A 1934,S 24,15:2
Game of Love, A 1934,O 25,26:6
East Side Wedding, An 1935,Ja 21,18:2
Lovka Maladetz 1935,Mr 27,25:5
Heaven on Earth 1935,O 8,26:2
Oh, You Girls! 1935,D 2,19:5
Love for Sale 1936,Ja 24,14:2
Pinye of Pinchev 1936,S 21,27:5
Night in Budapest, A 1936,N 3,33:2
His Jewish Girl 1936,D 9,34:1
Let's Get Married 1937,Ja 11,16:2

Levin, M J (Composer)
Laugh It Off 1934,Ap 5,24:2

Levin, Meyer
If I Were You 1931,S 24,21:1

Levin, Meyer (Director)
Good Old Days, The 1951,Jl 18,21:2

Levin, Meyer (Original Author)
Compulsion 1957,N 3,II,1:1

Levin, Meyer (Playwright)
Good Old Days, The 1951,Jl 18,21:2
Compulsion 1957,O 25,21:1
Diary, The 1966,N 27,159:3

Levin, Meyer (Producer)
Good Old Days, The 1951,Jl 18,21:2

Levin, Michael
Hamlet 1963,My 9,41:1
Death of a Salesman 1963,Jl 20,11:2
Henry V 1964,My 13,52:1
Saint Joan 1964,My 14,41:1
Royal Hunt of the Sun, The 1965,O 27,36:2
End of All Things Natural, The 1969,S 12,38:1
Camino Real 1970,Ja 9,42:1
Operation Sidewinder 1970,Mr 13,33:1
Good Woman of Setzuan, The 1970,N 6,51:1

Levin, Mildred
To Quito and Back 1937,O 7,30:4

Levin, Robert
Merchant of Venice, The 1955,Ja 8,9:7

Levin, S
Dostigayev 1935,Ja 14,10:5

Levin, Sam
Love Thief, The 1931,Ja 19,24:5

Levin, Sidney
Last Enemy, The 1934,Jl 13,14:4

Levin, Stuart
United States vs Julius and Ethel Rosenberg, The 1969,Ap 20,II,3:1
United States vs Julius and Ethel Rosenberg, The 1969,Ap 27,92:1

Levin, Sylvan (Composer)
Wayward Saint, The 1955,F 18,17:1
Three by Thurber; Imperturbable Spirit, The 1955,Mr 8,23:2
Three by Thurber; Mr Montoe Holds the Fort 1955,Mr 8,23:2
Three by Thurber; Middle Years, The 1955,Mr 8,23:2

Levin, Sylvan (Miscellaneous)
Girl in Pink Tights, The 1954,Mr 6,13:2

Levin, Sylvan (Musical Director)
Lute Song 1959,Mr 13,24:1

Levine, Anna
Stepsisters 1936,O 13,32:3

Levine, Bruce
Street Sounds 1970,O 23,32:1

Levine, Elliot
On the High Road 1961,Ap 21,26:2
Pilgrim's Progress 1962,Mr 21,36:2
Finian's Rainbow 1967,Ap 6,44:1
To Bury a Cousin 1967,My 17,38:3

Levine, Harry (Playwright)
Warson at Night 1938,Ja 31,14:3

Levine, Howard
Winners and Losers 1947,F 27,27:2

Levine, Irving (Producer)
Mystery of Theodosia Burr, The 1947,Mr 10,24:7

Levine, Isaac Don (Miscellaneous)
Devil in the Mind 1931,My 2,23:2

Levine, Isaac Don (Playwright)
Princess Turandot 1926,N 13,14:2
Levine, Jeff (Lighting Director)
Night Is Black Bottles, The 1962,D 5,56:1
Levine, Johnna (Producer)
Bob and Ray-The Two and Only 1970,S 25,36:1
Levine, Joseph E (Director)
Square in the Eye 1965,My 20,54:1
Princess Rebecca Birnbaum 1966,Mr 7,22:1
Young Marrieds Play Monopoly 1966,Mr 7,22:1
Make Like a Dog 1966,Mr 7,22:1
Suburban Tragedy 1966,Mr 7,22:1
Serjeant Musgrave's Dance 1966,Mr 9,44:1
Hand Is on the Gate, A 1966,S 22,54:1
Levine, Joseph E (Miscellaneous)
Kelly 1965,F 8,28:2
Mother Lover, The 1969,F 3,28:1
Levine, Joseph E (Producer)
Photo Finish 1963,F 14,5:2
Hughie 1964,D 23,21:2
All Women Are One 1965,Ja 8,21:1
View From the Bridge, A 1965,Ja 29,24:1
All in Good Time 1965,F 19,25:1
And Things That Go Bump in the Night
1965,Ap 27,27:5
Levine, Joseph I (Miscellaneous)
Goldilocks 1958,O 13,33:1
J B 1958,D 12,2:7
At the Drop of a Hat 1959,O 9,22:2
Big Fish, Little Fish 1961,Mr 16,42:2
Levine, Joseph I (Producer)
Bob and Ray-The Two and Only 1970,S 25,36:1
Levine, Maurice (Composer)
Lost in the Stars 1949,O 31,21:2
Levine, Maurice (Miscellaneous)
Flahooley 1951,My 15,39:1
Regina 1952,Je 2,25:4
Levine, Maurice (Musical Director)
Flahooley 1951,My 15,39:1
Music in the Air 1951,O 9,32:2
Of Thee I Sing 1952,My 6,34:2
Of Thee I Sing 1952,My 11,II,1:1
Buttrio Square 1952,O 15,40:2
Maggie 1953,F 19,20:2
Shinbone Alley 1957,Ap 15,23:2
Copper and Brass 1957,O 18,19:2
Levine, Rhoda
Follies of 1910, The 1960,Ja 15,37:3
Valmouth 1960,O 7,29:1
Levine, Rhoda (Choreographer)
Fashion 1959,Ja 21,27:1
Young Abe Lincoln 1961,Ap 26,36:1
Cradle Will Rock, The 1964,N 9,40:4
Serjeant Musgrave's Dance 1966,Mr 9,44:1
Levine, Rhoda (Miscellaneous)
Valmouth 1960,O 7,29:1
I Want You 1961,S 15,29:1
O Marry Me 1961,O 28,13:1
Mr Simian 1963,O 22,44:1
Thistle in My Bed 1963,N 20,48:1
Mad Show, The 1966,Ja 10,16:1
Carricknabauna 1967,Mr 31,30:1
Love and Let Love 1968,Ja 4,30:1
Levine, Richard (Playwright)
Naughty-Naught '00 1946,O 21,27:5
Levine, Robert
Mary Stuart 1956,Ap 28,10:2
Opening of a Window, The 1961,S 26,32:2
Cyrano de Bergerac 1968,Ap 26,30:1
Inner Journey, The 1969,Mr 21,42:1
Miser, The 1969,My 9,35:1
Time of Your Life, The 1969,N 7,37:1
Good Woman of Setzuan, The 1970,N 6,51:1
Levine, Roy (Director)
MacBird! 1967,F 23,38:1
MacBird! 1967,Mr 12,II,1:1
MacBird! 1967,Ap 16,II,3:6
Candaules, Commissioner 1970,My 29,15:1
Levine, Sam
Wall Street 1927,Ap 21,24:4
Solitaire 1929,Mr 13,28:3
Yegor Bulevitch 1934,Ja 8,21:7
Outlaw, The 1937,O 6,28:1
Oy, Is Dus a Leben!; Oh, What a Life!
1942,O 13,19:2
Three Men on a Horse 1969,O 17,35:1
Levine, Sam (Producer)
I Dreamt I Dwelt in Bloomingdale's 1970,F 13,26:1
Levine, Wally (Musical Director)
I Feel Wonderful 1954,O 19,22:5
Levine, Wendy (Miscellaneous)
Conerico Was Here to Stay 1969,Mr 11,39:1
Paradise Gardens East 1969,Mr 11,39:1
Levinge, Gloria
Marching Song 1937,F 18,18:2
Levinson, Ben
Injury Sustained 1940,O 24,30:3
Levinson, Ben (Director)
Injury Sustained 1940,O 24,30:3
Story Teller, The 1951,D 15,11:3
Young Provincials, The 1958,S 19,22:4
Levinson, Ben (Playwright)
Injury Sustained 1940,O 24,30:3

Story Teller, The 1951,D 15,11:3
Young Provincials, The 1958,S 19,22:4
Levinson, Ben (Producer)
Injury Sustained 1940,O 24,30:3
Levinson, Borrah
Sweet Adeline 1929,S 4,33:1
Levinson, George
Dead End 1936,S 20,IX,3:7
Levinson, J J (Producer)
Katy Did 1927,My 10,24:3
Kiss Me! 1927,Jl 22,17:1
Levinson, Leonard (Playwright)
Rhapsody 1944,N 23,37:2
Mr Strauss Goes to Boston 1945,S 7,20:2
Levinson, Mark (Composer)
Metamorphoses 1969,D 12,69:1
Levinthal, Sylvia
Whiteheaded Boy, The 1937,Ag 11,27:3
Levinthal, Sylvia (Director)
Party Line, The 1937,Ag 30,25:4
Levister, Alonzo (Composer)
This Music Crept by Me Upon the Waters
1959,N 25,19:4
Leonard Sillman's New Faces of 1968
1968,My 3,43:1
Yes, Yes, No No 1969,Ja 1,16:1
Levister, Alonzo (Lyricist)
Leonard Sillman's New Faces of 1968
1968,My 3,43:1
Levitch, Sula
Get Away Old Man 1943,N 25,40:2
Levitina, Sophia (Playwright)
Verdict, The 1934,S 22,12:5
Levitt, Amy
Hamlet 1968,Jl 21,II,21:2
Hamlet 1969,Mr 4,34:1
Effect of Gamma Rays on Man-in-the-Moon
Marigolds, The 1970,Ap 8,32:1
Levitt, Bill
Hamlet 1945,D 14,25:2
Levitt, Dan
Big Deal, The 1953,Mr 7,13:6
Levitt, Harold (Playwright)
Passion of Gross, The 1955,Ja 24,20:2
Levitt, John
Chips With Everything 1963,O 2,49:1
Levitt, Joseph (Producer)
Absent Father 1932,O 18,23:5
Levitt, Mortimer (Producer)
Concept, The 1968,My 7,51:1
Levitt, Paul
Family Carnovsky, The 1943,O 19,16:7
Throng o' Scarlet 1950,F 6,20:5
Pied Piper of Hamelin, The 1950,Ap 3,19:2
Levitt, Saul (Playwright)
Andersonville Trial, The 1959,D 30,15:1
Andersonville Trial, The 1960,Ja 10,II,1:1
Andersonville Trial, The 1960,N 25,33:3
Levoir and Lane
Vaudeville (Hippodrome) 1924,F 19,12:1
Levy, Benn (Director)
Devil Passes, The 1932,Ja 5,20:3
Accent on Youth 1934,D 26,19:1
Young Madame Conti 1937,Ap 1,18:4
Madame Bovary 1937,O 6,28:4
Madame Bovary 1937,N 17,26:2
If I Were You 1938,Ja 9,II,3:2
If I Were You 1938,Ja 25,24:2
Legend of Sarah 1950,O 12,42:4
Levy, Benn (Playwright)
This Woman Business 1926,D 8,25:1
Man With Red Hair, A 1928,Mr 25,IX,1:3
Man With Red Hair, A 1928,Je 17,VIII,1:6
Man With Red Hair, A 1928,N 9,22:2
Mrs Moonlight 1928,D 23,VIII,4:7
Art and Mrs Bottle 1929,N 13,25:2
Art and Mrs Bottle 1929,D 8,X,2:5
Devil, The 1930,F 2,VIII,2:4
Topaze 1930,F 13,25:3
Mrs Moonlight 1930,S 30,24:3
Evergreen 1930,O 14,31:2
Art and Mrs Bottle 1930,N 19,19:3
Evergreen 1930,D 4,30:4
Church Mouse, A 1931,My 3,VIII,2:1
Hollywood Holiday 1931,N 8,VIII,4:1
Springtime for Henry 1931,D 10,29:2
Devil Passes, The 1932,Ja 5,20:3
Devil Passes, The 1932,Ja 10,VIII,1:1
Springtime for Henry 1932,Ja 10,VIII,1:1
Springtime for Henry 1932,D 4,IX,3:8
Springtime for Henry 1933,My 2,20:5
Art and Mrs Bottle 1936,S 2,18:1
Young Madame Conti 1936,D 6,XII,7:6
Young Madame Conti 1937,Ap 1,18:4
Madame Bovary 1937,O 6,28:4
Madame Bovary 1937,N 17,26:2
If I Were You 1938,Ja 9,II,3:2
If I Were You 1938,Ja 25,24:2
Springtime for Henry 1938,Ag 31,12:5
Jealous God, The 1939,Mr 26,X,3:1
Topaze 1947,D 29,21:7
Clutterbuck 1949,D 5,29:2
Return to Tyassi 1950,D 1,31:4

Levy, Benn (Playwright)—Cont
Springtime for Henry 1951,Mr 15,36:2
Mrs Moonlight 1952,N 21,21:1
Tumbler, The 1960,F 25,32:2
Rape of the Belt, The 1960,N 7,46:1
Levy, Benn (Producer)
Hollywood Holiday 1931,N 8,VIII,4:1
Madame Bovary 1937,N 17,26:2
Levy, Bert
Get Together 1921,S 5,12:2
Levy, C Leonard
Vita Nuova; Life Begins Again 1935,F 26,16:2
Levy, Charles (Lighting Director)
Camille 1956,S 19,33:1
Trojan Women, The 1957,Mr 19,42:7
Smokeweaver's Daughter, The 1959,Ap 15,30:1
Gay Divorce 1960,Ap 4,37:1
Three Times Three; George Washington Crossing
the Delaware 1962,Mr 2,24:1
Three Times Three; Not Enough Rope
1962,Mr 2,24:1
Three Times Three; Twenty-Five Cent White Cap,
The 1962,Mr 2,24:1
Levy, Dorothy
Junebug Graduates Tonight! 1967,F 27,35:1
Levy, Eric (Playwright)
Exchange 1970,F 9,47:2
Levy, Estelle
Second Hurricane 1937,Ap 22,18:4
Levy, Florence L
Little Theatre Tournement; Where The Cross Is
Made 1928,My 10,31:1
Levy, Harold (Composer)
Clinging Vine, The 1922,D 25,20:2
Levy, Harold (Musical Director)
Three Waltzes 1938,Je 26,II,7:5
Sally, Irene and Mary 1938,Jl 5,13:4
Firefly, The 1938,Jl 12,15:4
Levy, Harry R
Half Moon Inn 1925,Mr 10,14:1
Levy, Jacqueline
City of Kings 1949,F 18,27:2
Levy, Jacques (Director)
Interview 1966,N 7,66:1
Motel 1966,N 7,66:1
TV 1966,N 7,66:1
America Hurrah; Interview; TV; Motel
1967,O 10,55:2
Scuba Duba 1967,O 11,36:1
Scuba Duba 1967,O 22,II,3:7
Red Cross 1968,Ap 29,47:2
Oh! Calcutta! 1969,Je 18,33:1
Levy, Jacques (Miscellaneous)
Oh! Calcutta! 1969,Je 18,33:1
Levy, Jacques (Playwright)
Oh! Calcutta! 1969,Je 18,33:1
Levy, Joan
Nautical but Nice 1931,Ap 19,31:6
Levy, Jose G (Playwright)
Pile ou Face 1936,Jl 5,IX,1:8
Levy, Kay
On the Town 1959,F 14,15:1
Levy, Leo A (Playwright)
It Happened Tomorrow 1933,My 6,11:5
Levy, Leo A (Producer)
It Happened Tomorrow 1933,My 6,11:5
Levy, Marvin David (Composer)
Iphigenia in Aulis 1967,N 22,40:2
Levy, Maxine (Costume Designer)
Saint's Parade 1930,N 1,23:4
People on the Hill 1931,S 26,25:5
Levy, Melvin (Playwright)
Gold Eagle Guy 1934,N 18,IX,1:7
Gold Eagle Guy 1934,N 29,33:4
Gold Eagle Guy 1934,D 9,X,1:1
House in the Country, A 1937,Ja 12,18:3
Levy, Michel (Betove) (Composer)
Pom' Pom' ! 1928,Ap 1,IX,4:7
Levy, Michel-Maurice (Composer)
Clotture, Le 1927,Ja 23,VII,2:1
Levy, Muriel
Mascaiada 1929,D 28,10:6
Levy, Murray
Picture of Dorian Gray, The 1956,Ag 18,15:5
Great God Brown, The 1959,O 7,48:1
Something About a Soldier 1962,Ja 5,36:2
PS 193 1962,O 31,33:1
Levy, Newman (Playwright)
Garrick Gaieties 1926,Je 13,VII,1:1
Little Show, The 1929,My 12,IX,1:2
Garrick Gaieties 1930,Je 5,29:2
Three's a Crowd 1930,O 5,IX,4:6
Garrick Gaieties 1930,O 17,21:2
Keep Moving 1934,Ag 24,10:2
Levy, Parke (Playwright)
Three After Three 1939,N 25,13:5
Keep Off the Grass 1940,My 24,22:6
Walk With Music 1940,Je 5,33:2
Off the Record 1940,D 1,63:5
Johnny on the Spot 1942,Ja 9,24:2
Levy, Parks (Lyricist)
Right This Way 1938,Ja 6,22:3
Levy, Rita
Miracle Worker, The 1959,O 20,44:1

Levy, Sam (Producer)
Hedda Gabler 1936,N 17,34:4
Levzzi, Lea
Roberta 1937,Je 27,II,6:1
Lewellyn, Harry
Sancho Panza 1923,N 27,23:1
Where's Your Husband? 1927,Ja 15,10:3
19th Hole, The 1927,O 12,30:3
Lewenstein, Oscar (Miscellaneous)
Luther 1963,S 26,41:1
Philadelphia, Here I Come! 1966,F 17,28:1
Loot 1968,Mr 19,40:2
Lovers; Winners 1968,Jl 26,21:4
Lovers; Losers 1968,Jl 26,21:4
Spitting Image 1969,Mr 3,28:1
Lewes, Miriam
Wandering Jew, The 1921,O 27,22:1
Oedipus Rex 1923,O 26,14:1
Via Crucis 1923,N 13,25:2
Lewin, B N
Three Musketeers, The 1921,My 20,18:5
Casanova 1923,S 27,10:2
Great Music 1924,O 6,24:1
Lewin, Bernard S
Betty Behave 1927,Mr 9,28:4
Lewin, Jaime
Trees Die Standing, The 1969,O 13,52:1
President's Daughter, The 1970,N 4,41:2
Lewin, John
Death of a Salesman 1963,Jl 20,11:2
Henry V 1964,My 13,52:1
Saint Joan 1964,My 14,41:1
Richard III 1965,Je 3,26:1
As You Like It 1966,Je 4,19:1
Harpers Ferry 1967,Je 6,52:2
Visit, The 1967,S 13,41:1
Lewin, John (Lyricist)
Blood Red Roses 1970,Mr 23,48:1
Good Woman of Setzuan, The 1970,N 6,51:1
Lewin, John (Playwright)
House of Atreus, The; Agamemnon 1967,Jl 24,23:1
House of Atreus, The; Bringers of Offerings, The 1967,Jl 24,23:1
Tango 1968,Ja 1,11:1
Blood Red Roses 1970,Mr 23,48:1
Persians, The 1970,Ap 16,53:1
Persians, The 1970,Ap 26,II,1:3
Lewin, Michael
Wonderful Journey 1946,D 26,30:2
Tenting Tonight 1947,Ap 3,32:2
Skipper Next to God 1948,Ja 5,14:5
Sundown Beach 1948,S 8,37:1
Night Music 1951,Ap 9,29:6
Golden Boy 1952,Mr 13,24:3
Hall of Healing 1952,My 8,35:6
Sands of the Negev 1954,O 20,32:1
Troublemakers, The 1954,D 31,11:3
Plough and the Stars, The 1956,Ap 6,14:1
Lewine, Richard (Composer)
Fools Rush In 1934,D 26,19:2
Naughty-Naught '00 1937,Ja 25,23:2
Fireman's Flame, The 1937,O 11,26:2
Girl From Wyoming, The 1938,O 31,12:1
It's All Yours 1942,Mr 26,26:2
Make Mine Manhattan 1948,Ja 16,26:2
Girls Against the Boys, The 1959,N 3,26:1
Lewine, Richard (Lyricist)
Fools Rush In 1934,D 26,19:2
It's All Yours 1942,Mr 26,26:2
Lewine, Richard (Miscellaneous)
'Tis of Thee 1940,O 28,21:3
It's All Yours 1942,Mr 26,26:2
Lewine, Richard (Musical Director)
It's All Yours 1942,Mr 26,26:2
Naughty-Naught '00 1946,O 21,27:5
Lewine, Richard (Producer)
Two Weeks With Pay 1940,Je 25,28:3
Look to the Lilies 1970,Mr 30,59:1
Lewins, Jaime
Mirele Efros 1969,D 26,41:1
Lewis, Abby
Macbeth 1941,N 12,30:2
Howie 1958,S 18,35:2
Fig Leaf in Her Bonnet, A 1961,Je 15,50:1
Life With Father 1967,O 20,53:2
Lewis, Ada
Night Boat, The 1920,F 3,18:1
Good Morning, Dearie 1921,N 2,20:2
One Kiss 1923,N 28,14:2
Busybody, The 1924,S 30,27:5
Lewis, Albert
Panic 1935,Mr 16,18:4
Iceman Cometh, The 1956,My 8,38:1
Night Circus, The 1958,D 3,44:1
One More River 1960,Mr 19,12:2
Do Re Mi 1960,D 27,23:2
Lewis, Albert (Director)
Jazz Singer, The 1925,S 15,29:2
Donovan Affair, The 1926,Ag 31,15:2
Spider, The 1927,F 13,VII,1:4
Spider, The 1927,Mr 23,29:1
Mirrors 1928,Ja 19,17:1
War Song, The 1928,S 25,29:3

Roosty 1938,F 15,21:2
My Fair Ladies 1941,Mr 24,12:7
Banjo Eyes 1941,D 26,20:2
Chameleon, The 1949,F 7,16:2
Lewis, Albert (Miscellaneous)
Cabin in the Sky 1940,O 26,19:2
Lewis, Albert (Producer)
Nervous Wreck, The 1924,O 19,VIII,2:1
Donovan Affair, The 1926,Ag 31,15:2
Spider, The 1927,Mr 23,29:1
Mirrors 1928,Ja 19,17:1
Big Fight, The 1928,S 19,33:1
War Song, The 1928,S 25,29:3
Roosty 1938,F 15,21:2
Off to Buffalo! 1939,F 22,18:2
Cabin in the Sky 1940,O 26,19:2
My Fair Ladies 1941,Mr 24,12:7
Banjo Eyes 1941,N 8,10:6
Banjo Eyes 1941,D 26,20:2
Walking Gentleman, The 1942,My 8,26:2
Uncle Willie 1956,D 21,17:1
Lewis, Albon
Hamlet 1934,D 26,19:3
Richard III 1934,D 28,24:3
Cyrano de Bergerac 1936,Ap 28,17:1
Lewis, Alexander
Present Arms 1928,Ap 27,16:2
Street Scene 1929,Ja 11,20:4
Drums Begin, The 1933,N 25,10:5
Within the Gates 1934,O 23,23:1
Lewis, Alfred
Juarez and Maximilian 1926,O 12,31:1
Lewis, Allen
Porgy and Bess 1935,O 11,30:2
Sweet River 1936,O 29,30:2
Lewis, Allen Jack (Playwright)
Corner of the Bed, A 1969,F 27,35:2
Lewis, Andy (Director)
Infantry, The 1966,N 15,51:1
Lewis, Andy (Playwright)
Infantry, The 1966,N 15,51:1
Lewis, Arthur
Camel's Back, The 1923,N 4,19:2
Two by Two 1925,F 24,17:1
Servant in the House, The 1925,Ap 8,24:2
School for Scandal, The 1925,D 7,18:2
Captive, The 1926,S 30,23:1
Her Cardboard Lover 1927,Mr 22,30:5
Interference 1927,O 19,24:3
Potiphar's Wife 1928,D 24,10:7
Hundred Years Old, A 1929,O 2,28:2
Adding Machine, The 1948,N 18,35:2
Hamlet 1948,D 4,9:2
Butter and Egg Man, The 1949,Ap 29,27:1
Lewis, Arthur (Producer)
Rockefeller and the Red Indians 1968,O 25,37:1
Lewis, Artis
Iolanthe 1965,My 19,42:1
Yeomen of the Guard, The 1965,Jl 8,34:1
Ruddigore 1965,Ag 27,16:1
Lewis, Ben
Murder at the Vanities 1933,S 13,22:4
Lewis, Bob
Men in White 1933,S 27,24:2
Gold Eagle Guy 1934,N 29,33:4
Waiting for Lefty 1935,F 11,14:5
Till the Day I Die 1935,Mr 27,24:5
Waiting for Lefty 1935,Mr 27,24:5
Paradise Lost 1935,D 10,31:5
Case of Clyde Griffiths 1936,Mr 14,10:4
Johnny Johnson 1936,N 20,26:3
Kaleidoscope 1957,Je 14,20:2
Lewis, Bob (Director)
My Heart's in the Highlands 1939,My 7,X,1:1
Time of Your Life, The 1939,N 5,IX,1:1
Heavenly Express 1940,Ap 28,IX,1:1
Brigadoon 1947,Mr 23,II,1:1
Teahouse of the August Moon, The 1953,O 25,II,1:1
Teahouse of the August Moon, The 1954,S 12,II,1:1
Lewis, Bob (Playwright)
Group Theatre Sketches 1935,F 11,14:5
Lewis, Brayton
Shadow of My Enemy, A 1957,D 12,35:4
Play of Daniel, The 1958,Ja 3,15:3
Play of Daniel, The 1959,Je 6,30:2
Play of Daniel, The 1959,D 28,17:6
Play of Daniel, The 1960,D 27,23:6
Play of Daniel, The 1961,D 28,22:6
Play of Daniel, The 1966,Ja 2,64:4
Lewis, Brenda
Rape of Lucretia, The 1948,D 30,24:2
Regina 1949,N 1,32:2
Regina 1952,Je 2,25:4
Girl in Pink Tights, The 1954,Mr 6,13:2
New Moon, The; Desert Song, The 1955,Jl 1,13:1
Song of Norway 1958,Je 23,19:2
Song of Norway 1959,Je 26,16:2
Cafe Crown 1964,Ap 18,32:1
Lewis, Burton
Off to Buffalo! 1939,F 22,18:2
Metropole 1949,D 7,43:2

Lewis, Carmen
Cross-Town 1937,Mr 18,21:5
In Clover 1937,O 14,23:1
Lewis, Carmen (Miscellaneous)
Arsenic and Old Lace 1941,Ja 11,13:2
Lewis, Carole Ann
This Side of Paradise 1962,F 22,19:6
Parasite, The 1965,D 17,43:2
Butter and Egg Man, The 1966,O 18,49:1
Spofford 1967,D 15,54:3
Lewis, Carrington
Stevedore 1934,Ap 19,33:2
Sailor, Beware! 1935,My 7,28:4
Merrily We Roll Along 1936,Je 30,15:1
All Editions 1936,D 23,17:2
Sun Kissed 1937,Mr 11,20:2
St Louis Woman 1946,Ap 1,22:2
Porgy and Bess 1965,Mr 6,17:1
Lewis, Cecil (Playwright)
Improvisations in June 1928,F 27,16:5
Unknown Warrior, The 1928,Mr 4,IX,4:7
Unknown Warrior, The 1928,O 30,26:6
Unknown Warrior, The 1931,O 23,28:4
Only the Young 1932,S 22,25:2
Iron Flowers 1933,Je 13,22:2
Lewis, Charles
Vaudeville (Palace) 1926,Je 8,23:1
Thieves 1926,Je 8,23:1
Arabian Nightmare, The 1927,Ja 11,36:3
Scalawag, The 1927,Mr 30,22:3
New York 1927,N 15,26:2
Free Soul, A 1928,Ja 13,26:5
Gang War 1928,Ag 21,27:2
Lewis, Charles (Lighting Director)
Touch 1970,N 9,52:1
Lewis, Clarence T
Through the Night 1930,Ag 19,19:1
Lewis, Connie (Miscellaneous)
Last Pad, The 1970,D 8,61:1
Lewis, Curigwen
Jane Eyre 1936,O 14,31:3
Jane Eyre 1936,N 8,X,3:4
Othello 1938,F 27,X,1:4
Lewis, David
Dybbuk, The 1926,D 17,27:2
Wall Street 1927,Ap 21,24:4
Goodbye Again 1943,N 10,28:4
Take It As It Comes 1944,F 11,17:2
Little Women 1944,D 13,29:2
Little Women 1945,D 24,18:2
Taming of the Shrew, The 1951,Ap 26,35:2
Wild Duck, The 1951,D 27,17:1
King of Hearts 1954,Ap 2,23:1
King of Hearts 1954,Ap 11,II,1:1
Bead-Tangle 1970,Jl 16,38:1
Lewis, David (Playwright)
Infantry, The 1966,N 15,51:1
Lewis, Denham
Wandering Jew, The 1927,F 2,22:4
Lewis, Dolly
Gingham Girl, The 1922,Ag 29,15:5
Lewis, Don
Tableaux 1961,D 18,41:3
Lewis, Dorothy
Pleased to Meet You 1928,O 30,27:2
Lewis, Edward
Porgy and Bess 1942,Ja 23,16:2
Lewis, Edward (Playwright)
Precious Bane 1932,Ap 24,VIII,1:1
Lewis, Edward (Producer)
One Flew Over the Cuckoo's Nest 1963,N 14,40:2
Lewis, Edwin
Dance of Death, The 1969,My 26,53:1
Macbeth 1969,D 23,25:1
Oedipus 1970,F 23,30:1
Lady From Maxim's, The 1970,Je 1,41:1
Lewis, Edwin (Miscellaneous)
Dance of Death, The 1969,My 26,53:1
Lewis, Flo
Tick-Tack-Toe 1920,F 24,11:2
Big Boy 1925,Ja 8,28:2
Vaudeville (Palace) 1926,Ag 31,15:3
Twinkle Twinkle 1926,N 17,22:2
Vaudeville (Palace) 1930,Mr 24,24:5
Lewis, Frank
Unexpected Husband 1931,Je 3,29:4
First Lady 1937,O 9,17:2
Lewis, Frank (Producer)
Another Love 1934,Mr 20,26:3
Lewis, Fred G
Lambs Gambol 1925,Ap 27,15:1
Lewis, Fred Irving
Connie Goes Home 1923,S 7,10:1
Nobody's Business 1923,O 23,17:1
Wild Westcotts, The 1923,D 25,26:2
Izzy 1924,S 17,16:2
O Nightingale 1925,Ap 16,25:2
If I Was Rich 1926,S 3,15:2
Racket, The 1927,N 23,28:3
Tomorrow 1928,D 29,20:2
Modern Virgin, A 1931,My 21,33:4
Inside Story, The 1932,F 23,23:2
I Loved You Wednesday 1932,O 12,27:1

Lewis, Fred Irving—Cont

June Moon 1933,My 16,15:5
Save Me the Waltz 1938,Mr 1,19:2
Let's Face It 1941,O 30,26:2
Another Love Story 1943,O 13,29:2
Wallflower 1944,Ja 27,14:2
Harvey 1944,N 2,23:2
Collector's Item 1952,F 9,11:2
Brass Ring, The 1952,Ap 11,19:2
Red Rainbow, A 1953,S 15,37:4

Lewis, Frederick
Twelfth Night 1921,N 1,17:1
Merchant of Venice, The 1921,N 22,17:1
Hamlet 1922,N 17,14:1
Pasteur 1923,Mr 13,19:1
Cymbeline 1923,O 3,12:1
Twelfth Night 1923,O 23,17:1
Hamlet 1923,O 31,12:1
Madame Pompadour 1924,N 12,20:6
School for Scandal, The 1925,O 24,19:1
Little Father of the Wilderness, The 1930,Je 3,27:1
In Times Square 1931,N 24,29:3
Heart of His Mystery, The 1933,Ap 24,10:1
Ghost Writer, The 1933,Je 20,22:4
Come of Age 1934,Ja 13,16:6

Lewis, Frederick (Playwright)
Heart of His Mystery, The 1933,Ap 24,10:1

Lewis, Frederick Jr (Miscellaneous)
Oh, Kay! 1960,Ap 18,37:2

Lewis, Garrett
Vintage '60 1960,S 13,41:1

Lewis, Geoffrey
Black Monday 1962,Mr 7,29:1

Lewis, George
Reunion in Vienna 1931,N 17,31:1
For Valor 1935,N 19,27:5
Behind the Red Lights 1937,Ja 14,17:4
To Quito and Back 1937,O 7,30:4
One Flight Down 1937,D 14,32:4
How to Get Tough About It 1938,F 9,16:2
Natural Man 1941,My 8,20:4

Lewis, George (Lighting Director)
Sojourner Truth 1948,Ap 22,35:2
Almost Faithful 1948,Je 5,9:2
Riders to the Sea 1949,F 4,30:2
Freight 1949,F 4,30:2

Lewis, George (Producer)
First American Dictator 1939,Mr 15,18:2

Lewis, Gerard
Brother Rat 1936,D 17,34:5

Lewis, Gilbert
Transfers 1970,Ja 23,25:1

Lewis, Gwendolyn
Sonya's Search for the Christmas Star 1929,D 14,24:6

Lewis, Harry (Pvt)
Winged Victory 1943,N 22,24:1

Lewis, Helen
Tick-Tack-Toe 1920,F 24,11:2

Lewis, Henry
Frivolities of 1920 1920,Ja 9,22:2

Lewis, Henry Jr
Matriarch, The 1930,Mr 19,24:5

Lewis, Herbert C (Playwright)
Name Your Poison 1936,Ja 21,27:4

Lewis, Ira
Cave at Machpelah, The 1959,Jl 1,25:1
Connection, The 1959,Jl 16,30:2
Women of Trachis 1960,Je 23,18:3
Romeo and Juliet 1961,F 24,24:1
Shoemaker's Prodigious Wife, The 1962,S 2,44:4
Antigone 1962,D 29,5:5
Awakening of Spring, The 1964,My 13,50:1
Alchemist, The 1964,S 15,33:1
Incident at Vichy 1964,D 4,44:1
David Show, The 1968,N 1,34:2

Lewis, Ivan
Hymn to the Rising Sun 1937,My 7,28:2

Lewis, James
Bronx Express 1922,Ap 27,12:2
It's the Valet 1933,D 15,25:4
Strip Girl 1935,O 21,22:6

Lewis, Janet
Murder in the Cathedral 1938,F 17,16:2

Lewis, Jean
Harriet 1944,S 28,26:1

Lewis, Jeffreys
Americans in France, The 1920,Ag 4,14:1
Easy Terms 1925,S 23,22:2

Lewis, Jerry
Jerry Lewis' Variety Show 1957,F 8,18:5

Lewis, Jessie
Girl in the Spotlight, The 1920,Jl 13,9:3

Lewis, Joe E
Second Little Show, The 1930,Ag 17,VIII,2:2
Right This Way 1938,Ja 6,22:3
Lady Comes Across, The 1942,Ja 10,10:2
Actors Fund Fete 1942,F 23,24:5

Lewis, John
Henry's Harem 1926,S 14,25:2
Scarlet Lily, The 1927,Ja 31,12:3
Judy Garland's New Variety Show 1956,S 27,43:2

Lewis, John (Composer)
Natural Affection 1963,F 2,5:2

Lewis, John (Playwright)
House of Atreus, The; Furies, The 1967,Jl 24,23:1

Lewis, Joseph
All in One; Trouble in Tahiti 1955,Ap 20,40:3

Lewis, Joseph (Costume Designer)
Oedipus Rex 1959,Ap 30,36:1
Ticket-of-Leave Man, The 1961,D 23,15:1

Lewis, Joseph (Musical Director)
West Side Story 1960,Ap 28,31:1
West Side Story 1960,My 8,II,1:1

Lewis, Josephine
This Thing Called Love 1928,S 18,32:7

Lewis, Ken
Madame Aphrodite 1961,D 30,13:1

Lewis, Ken (Costume Designer)
Brownstone Urge, The 1969,D 18,63:1

Lewis, Ken (Scenic Designer)
Brownstone Urge, The 1969,D 18,63:1

Lewis, Laura May
Unfair to Goliath 1970,Ja 26,27:1

Lewis, Leopold (Playwright)
Bells, The 1926,Ap 14,20:3

Lewis, Little Ferdie
Brown Buddies 1930,O 8,29:1

Lewis, Lloyd (Playwright)
Jayhawker 1934,O 16,31:4
Jayhawker 1934,N 6,34:2

Lewis, Loney
Gypsy 1959,My 22,31:6

Lewis, Lorette
Afgar 1920,N 9,13:2

Lewis, Lorna
Luther 1963,S 26,41:1
And People All Around 1968,F 12,46:1

Lewis, Lynn (Miscellaneous)
Man Out Loud, Girl Quiet 1962,Ap 4,38:1
Spanish Armada, The 1962,Ap 4,38:1

Lewis, Mabel Terry
Easy Virtue 1925,D 8,28:2
Hundred Years Old, A 1928,D 9,X,2:1
Battle Royal 1934,Ap 19,33:4
They Came to a City 1943,Je 6,II,1:6

Lewis, Mable Sanford
Carib Song 1945,S 28,17:2

Lewis, Marcia
Who's Who, Baby? 1968,Ja 30,36:1
Time of Your Life, The 1969,N 7,37:1

Lewis, Marguerite
House in Paris, The 1944,Mr 21,17:1
Marriage Is for Single People 1945,N 22,38:2
Now I Lay Me Down to Sleep 1950,Mr 3,21:2

Lewis, Martin
One 1920,S 15,12:2
Polonaise 1945,O 8,20:2

Lewis, Mary
Greenwich Village Follies 1920,Ag 31,7:3
Ziegfeld Follies 1921,Je 22,10:1
Ziegfeld Follies 1922,Je 6,18:2
Vaudeville (Palace) 1930,N 24,26:3
Best People, The 1933,Mr 16,21:5
Carib Song 1945,S 28,17:2
Our Lan' 1947,S 29,16:5

Lewis, Mary Jane (Director)
Ice Follies 1957,Ja 16,36:1
Ice Follies 1960,Ja 13,20:1

Lewis, Mary Jane (Miscellaneous)
Ice Follies 1959,Ja 15,26:2
Ice Follies 1959,Ja 14,30:1

Lewis, Matthew
Watch-Pit 1969,Ja 30,39:1

Lewis, Maxine
Vaudeville (Palace) 1930,F 17,18:4

Lewis, Michael
Time of Storm 1954,F 26,14:2
Qudrille 1954,N 4,39:2
Macbeth 1955,O 8,12:6
Small War on Murray Hill 1957,Ja 4,19:1
Winkelberg 1958,Ja 15,26:2
Born Yesterday 1958,Mr 22,12:6
Philanderer, The 1958,My 13,26:2
Guests of the Nation 1958,My 21,40:1
Widowers' Houses 1959,Mr 3,39:2
Visit, The 1960,Mr 9,38:3
Once There Was a Russian 1961,F 20,32:2
Hidden Stranger 1963,Ja 10,5:5
Man for All Seasons, A 1964,Ja 28,24:2
On a Clear Day You Can See Forever 1965,O 18,44:1
Darling of the Day 1968,Ja 29,26:2
Soldiers 1968,My 2,58:1

Lewis, Michael (Director)
Philanderer, The 1958,My 13,26:2

Lewis, Mildred
Marching Song 1937,F 18,18:2

Lewis, Milton (Playwright)
Dancer, The 1946,Je 6,16:5

Lewis, Miriam
Saint's Parade 1930,N 1,23:4
Borrowed Life, The 1931,Ja 4,VIII,2:6

Lewis, Mona
Centuries, The 1927,N 30,23:1
Hoboken Blues 1928,F 18,10:1

Lewis, Monica
Johnny 2X4 1942,Mr 17,24:6

Lewis, Morgan (Choreographer)
Idiot's Delight 1936,Mr 25,25:2
Take It Away 1936,D 15,30:5

Lewis, Morgan (Composer)
New Faces 1934,Mr 16,24:5
One for the Money 1939,F 6,9:2
Two for the Show 1940,F 9,14:2
Two for the Show 1940,F 18,IX,1:1
It's All Yours 1942,Mr 26,26:2
Three to Make Ready 1946,Mr 8,16:2

Lewis, Morgan (Lyricist)
It's All Yours 1942,Mr 26,26:2

Lewis, Morgan (Miscellaneous)
What a Relief 1935,D 14,10:6

Lewis, Morgan (Musical Director)
Fireman's Flame, The 1937,O 11,26:2
It's All Yours 1942,Mr 26,26:2

Lewis, Mort (Playwright)
Keep Off the Grass 1940,My 24,22:6

Lewis, Nadine
Sound of Music, The 1967,Ap 27,52:1

Lewis, Nick
Rate of Exchange 1968,Ap 2,50:1
No Place to Be Somebody 1969,My 5,53:3
No Place to Be Somebody 1969,D 31,17:1

Lewis, Norman
Trial of Dr Beck, The 1937,Ag 10,22:2

Lewis, Oretta
Genius and the Crowd 1920,S 7,20:1

Lewis, Pamela (Scenic Designer)
Sponono 1964,Ap 3,28:1

Lewis, Philip
Fifth Column, The 1940,Mr 7,18:2

Lewis, Philip (Playwright)
Fledgling 1940,N 28,29:2

Lewis, Ralph
As You Like It 1936,Ap 24,18:4
Face, The 1941,N 29,15:3
New Faces of 1943 1942,D 23,22:2
Naked Genius, The 1943,O 22,20:5

Lewis, Rhoda
Pony Cart, The 1954,S 15,39:2

Lewis, Rhode (Costume Designer)
Lysistrata 1968,N 15,42:1

Lewis, Richard Glen
Measure for Measure 1967,F 15,37:1
Hamlet 1967,F 17,44:1
Romeo and Juliet 1967,F 22,18:1

Lewis, Robert
Living Corpse, The 1929,D 7,19:1
Romeo and Juliet 1930,Ap 22,33:1
Gods of the Lightning 1931,F 19,21:4
House of Connelly, The 1931,S 29,22:4
1931 1931,D 11,34:3
Night Over Taos 1932,Mr 10,25:3
Jubilee 1935,O 14,20:1
Golden Boy 1937,N 5,18:5
Thunder Rock 1939,N 15,18:1

Lewis, Robert (Director)
My Heart's in the Highlands 1939,Ap 14,29:2
Heavenly Express 1940,Ap 19,24:2
Five Alarm Waltz 1941,Mr 14,16:2
Mexican Mural; Miracle Painting 1942,Ap 27,19:2
Mexican Mural; Vera Cruz Interior 1942,Ap 27,19:2
Mexican Mural; Moonlight Scene 1942,Ap 27,19:2
Mexican Mural; Patio With Flamingo 1942,Ap 27,19:2
Land's End 1946,D 12,37:5
Brigadoon 1947,Mr 14,28:2
Regina 1949,N 1,32:2
Regina 1949,N 13,II,1:1
Happy Time, The 1950,Ja 25,24:1
Brigadoon 1950,My 3,36:2
Enemy of the People, An 1950,D 29,14:1
Enemy of the People, An 1951,Ja 7,II,1:1
Grass Harp, The 1952,Mr 28,26:2
Grass Harp, The 1952,Ap 6,II,1:1
Teahouse of the August Moon, The 1953,O 16,32:1
Teahouse of the August Moon, The 1954,Ap 23,23:5
Teahouse of the August Moon, The 1954,My 2,II,3:1
Witness for the Prosecution 1954,D 17,35:2
Witness for the Prosecution 1954,D 26,II,1:1
Teahouse of the August Moon, The 1955,My 10,24:1
Mister Johnson 1956,Mr 30,11:1
Mister Johnson 1956,Ap 8,II,1:1
Hidden River, The 1957,Ja 24,32:1
Jamaica 1957,N 1,32:2
Jamaica 1957,N 10,II,1:1
Handful of Fire 1958,O 2,45:3
Cheri 1959,O 13,44:1
Kwamina 1961,O 24,42:1
Foxy 1964,F 17,26:1
Traveller Without Luggage 1964,S 18,26:2
On a Clear Day You Can See Forever 1965,O 18,44:1
Crimes and Crimes 1970,Ja 19,35:1

Lewis, Robert (Producer)
Mexican Mural; Patio With Flamingo
1942,Ap 27,19:2
Mexican Mural; Moonlight Scene 1942,Ap 27,19:2
Mexican Mural; Miracle Painting 1942,Ap 27,19:2
Mexican Mural; Vera Cruz Interior 1942,Ap 27,19:2
Brigadoon 1949,Ap 16,11:1
Mister Johnson 1956,Mr 30,11:1
Cheri 1959,O 13,44:1
Lewis, Ronald
South Sea Bubble 1956,My 13,II,3:1
Oresteia 1961,N 8,43:5
Square Root of Wonderful, The 1970,Mr 12,47:1
Lewis, Ruby
Girl in the Spotlight, The 1920,Jl 13,9:3
Lewis, Russell
Othello 1934,Jl 22,23:4
Lewis, Russell (Miscellaneous)
Obsession 1946,O 2,39:2
Lady Windermere's Fan 1946,O 15,29:2
Tonight at 8:30; Ways and Means 1948,F 21,8:2
Tonight at 8:30; Family Album 1948,F 21,8:2
Tonight at 8:30; Red Peppers 1948,F 21,8:2
Tonight at 8:30; Fumed Oak 1948,F 24,20:4
Tonight at 8:30; Shadow Play 1948,F 24,20:4
Tonight at 8:30; Hands Across the Sea
1948,F 24,20:4
Lewis, Russell (Playwright)
Curious Savage, The 1950,O 25,44:3
Lewis, Russell (Producer)
Story of Mary Surratt, The 1947,F 10,25:2
Time for Elizabeth 1948,S 28,32:3
Lewis, Sam
Big Blow 1938,O 3,11:2
Pinocchio 1939,Ja 3,19:2
Lewis, Sam M (Lyricist)
Lady Do 1927,Ap 19,24:2
Lewis, Seaman (Director)
Lawyers' Dilemma, The 1928,Jl 10,17:2
Lewis, Seaman (Playwright)
Babies a La Carte 1927,Ag 16,31:1
Lawyers' Dilemma, The 1928,Jl 10,17:2
Lewis, Selma
Tinker's Dam 1943,Ja 29,22:2
Lewis, Sheila
Lower Depths, The 1956,O 3,29:2
Lewis, Sheldon
Pierre of the Plains 1929,Ja 6,VIII,4:4
Lewis, Shelton
Pal Joey 1949,Mr 7,17:2
Gentlemen Prefer Blondes 1949,D 9,35:3
Lewis, Sinclair
It Can't Happen Here 1938,Jl 26,22:2
Angela Is Twenty-Two 1938,D 31,6:3
My Dear Children 1941,Jl 22,22:6
Lewis, Sinclair (Director)
Good Neighbor 1941,O 22,26:2
Lewis, Sinclair (Original Author)
Main Street 1921,Jl 24,VI,1:1
Main Street 1921,O 6,21:1
Elmer Gantry 1928,Ag 10,9:4
Dodsworth 1934,F 26,20:4
Dodsworth 1934,Ag 21,12:3
It Can't Happen Here 1936,O 28,30:3
It Can't Happen Here 1936,O 28,30:1
It Can't Happen Here 1936,N 8,X,1:1
It Can't Happen Here 1936,N 29,XII,3:3
Dodsworth 1938,F 23,26:2
Dodsworth 1938,Mr 13,XI,3:1
It Can't Happen Here 1938,Jl 26,22:2
Gantry 1970,F 16,44:1
Gantry 1970,S 6,II,1:1
Lewis, Sinclair (Playwright)
Jayhawker 1934,O 16,31:4
Jayhawker 1934,N 6,34:2
It Can't Happen Here 1936,O 28,30:1
It Can't Happen Here 1936,O 28,30:3
It Can't Happen Here 1936,O 28,30:1
It Can't Happen Here 1936,N 8,X,1:1
It Can't Happen Here 1936,N 29,XII,3:3
It Can't Happen Here 1938,Jl 26,22:2
Angela Is Twenty-Two 1938,D 31,6:3
Lewis, Sully (Playwright)
Freedom of the Press 1937,D 13,22:8
Lewis, Sylvia
Vintage '60 1960,S 13,41:1
Lewis, Ted
Greenwich Village Follies 1921,S 1,18:3
Friar's Club Frolic 1922,Je 5,16:1
Rufus Le Maire's Affairs 1926,Jl 18,VII,1:7
LeMaire's Affairs 1927,Mr 29,22:4
Rufus Le Maire's Affairs 1927,Ap 10,VIII,1:1
Artists and Models 1927,N 16,28:2
Vaudeville (Palace) 1928,Jl 10,17:3
Vaudeville (Palace) 1928,N 26,31:2
Vaudeville (Palace) 1928,D 3,30:6
Vaudeville (Palace) 1929,D 16,34:4
Vaudeville (Palace) 1929,D 23,19:1
Friars Club Frolic 1933,My 15,16:4
Lewis, Ted (Lyricist)
Artists and Models 1927,N 16,28:2
Lewis, Thomas
Joseph 1930,F 13,25:3

Lewis, Tim
Last Pad, The 1970,D 8,61:1
Lewis, Tom
All-Star Idlers of 1921, The 1921,Jl 16,5:2
All-Star Idlers of 1921, The 1921,Ag 9,16:3
Blushing Bride, The 1922,F 7,12:1
Helen of Troy, New York 1923,Je 20,22:6
Ziegfeld Follies 1924,Je 25,26:1
Follies 1925,Mr 11,19:2
Lambs Gambol 1925,Ap 27,15:1
Midnight 1930,D 30,25:1
Mrs Gibsons' Boys 1949,My 5,35:2
Lewis, Tommy
Ah, Wilderness! 1941,O 3,26:2
All in Favor 1942,Ja 21,20:6
Kiss and Tell 1943,Mr 18,22:1
Kiss and Tell 1943,Mr 28,II,1:1
Lewis, Walter
Hole in the Wall, The 1920,Mr 27,11:1
Jumbo 1935,N 18,20:2
Lewis, Well (Playwright)
Who Is Leslie? 1941,My 20,15:5
Lewis, William
Front Page Stuff 1926,D 29,24:4
Lewis, William (Composer)
Rainbow's End 1928,D 26,14:6
Lewis, William (Lyricist)
Front Page Stuff 1926,D 29,24:4
Rainbow's End 1928,D 26,14:6
Lewis, Willie
Angel in the Pawnshop 1951,Ja 19,20:3
Lewis, Wilmarth (Playwright)
Tadpole, The 1931,D 6,VIII,2:7
Lewis, Windsor (Director)
Time Limit! 1956,Ja 25,27:2
Time Limit! 1956,F 5,II,1:1
One More River 1960,Mr 19,12:2
Living Room, The 1962,N 22,43:5
Lewis & Van
Murder at the Vanities 1933,S 13,22:4
Lewis and Dody
Vaudeville (Palace) 1923,Ap 3,26:4
Lewishon, Alice (Director)
Dybbuk, The 1925,D 20,VII,3:1
Lewisohn, Alice
Great Adventure, The 1921,F 26,9:2
Lewisohn, Alice (Director)
Dybbuk, The 1926,D 17,27:2
Pinwheel 1927,F 4,16:4
Lewisohn, Alice (Miscellaneous)
Dybbuk, The 1925,D 16,22:2
Lewisohn, Irene
Little Clay Cart, The 1924,D 6,13:3
Grand Street Follies, The 1925,Je 19,24:1
Dybbuk, The 1925,D 16,22:2
Grand Street Follies, The 1926,Je 16,23:2
Lewisohn, Irene (Choreographer)
Tone Pictures and the White Peacock
1927,Ap 6,24:3
Lewisohn, Irene (Director)
Little Clay Cart, The 1924,D 6,13:3
Heldenleben, Ein 1929,Ap 27,16:4
Neighborhood Playhouse Program 1930,F 21,23:1
Bitter Oleander 1935,F 12,24:3
Lewisohn, Irene (Playwright)
Burmese Pwe, A 1926,Mr 17,28:1
Ritornell 1927,Ap 6,24:3
Lewisohn, Ludwig (Playwright)
Rose Bernd 1922,S 27,17:1
Lewisohn, Ludwig (Translator)
Rose Bernd 1922,O 1,VII,1:1
Eternal Road, The 1937,Ja 8,14:2
Beaver Coat, The 1956,Mr 29,22:5
Lewitin, Margot
Peace 1969,Ja 28,49:1
Lewsen, Charles
Puntila 1959,My 15,26:2
How Pleasant to Know Mr Lear 1968,S 2,14:2
Lewson, Charles
Stiffkey Scandals of 1932, The 1969,Je 14,24:3
Ley, Benton (Playwright)
Little Miss Door-Step 1924,Ap 1,18:1
Ley, Marie
Divin Mensonge 1926,N 14,VIII,2:1
Ley, Violet
Matriarch, The 1930,Mr 19,24:5
Ley-Piscator, Maria (Director)
Tom Sawyer - Ballad of the Mississippi
1947,D 27,11:3
Ley-Piscator, Maria (Playwright)
Nights of Wrath; Nuits de la Colere, Les
1947,D 1,26:4
Leyba, Claire
Natural Man 1941,My 8,20:4
Caukey 1944,F 18,15:4
Anna Lucasta 1947,O 30,31:3
Hamlet 1951,Jl 20,13:6
Mamba's Daughters 1953,Mr 21,12:6
Balls 1965,F 11,45:1
Leyden, Leo
Love and Libel 1960,D 8,44:1
Darling of the Day 1968,Ja 29,26:2
Seagull, The 1968,Jl 25,27:2

Mundy Scheme, The 1969,D 12,75:1
Rothschilds, The 1970,O 20,40:1
Leyden, Norman (M/Sgt) (Composer)
Yellow Jack 1944,Ap 7,23:3
Leyhausen, Wilhelm (Director)
Persians, The 1927,F 27,VII,2:3
Leyland, Norma
Nina Rosa 1930,My 31,19:3
Leyman, Randolph
Warrior's Husband, The 1932,Mr 12,19:4
Rendezvous 1932,O 13,22:3
Leyssac, Paul
Hail and Farewell 1923,F 20,12:1
Cyrano de Bergerac 1923,N 2,14:1
Assumption of Hannele, The 1924,F 16,16:2
Saturday Night 1926,O 26,25:1
Three Sisters, The 1926,O 27,24:1
Locandiera, La; Mistress of the Inn, The
1926,N 23,26:1
2 + 2 = 5 1927,N 29,30:3
Improvisations in June 1928,F 27,16:5
Hedda Gabler 1928,Mr 27,30:2
Would-Be Gentleman, The 1928,O 2,34:1
Cherry Orchard, The 1928,O 16,28:5
Cherry Orchard, The 1928,N 18,IX,1:2
Lady From Alfaqueque, The; Consulesa, La
1929,Ja 15,22:3
Sea Gull, The 1929,S 17,34:1
Mademoiselle Bourrat 1929,O 8,34:3
Living Corpse, The 1929,D 7,19:1
Siegfried 1930,O 21,34:1
Lady of the Camellias, The 1931,Ja 27,21:2
Liliom 1932,O 27,23:2
Camille 1932,O 28,23:2
Dear Jane 1932,N 15,24:3
Six Miracle Plays; Miraculous Birth and the
Midwives, The; Lamentation of the Virgin Mary,
The; Magdalen, The; Trois Rois, Les; Trois
Maries, Les; Nativite, La 1933,F 12,IX,2:1
Cherry Orchard, The 1933,Mr 7,20:3
Aiglon, L' 1934,N 5,22:2
Hedda Gabler 1934,D 4,22:5
Tempest, The 1945,Ja 26,17:2
Leyssac, Paul (Translator)
Hedda Gabler 1928,Mr 27,30:2
Hedda Gabler 1934,D 4,22:5
Leyton, Drue
Red Harvest 1937,Mr 31,29:2
Hero Is Born, A 1937,O 2,18:6
Li, Chao
Flower Drum Song 1958,D 2,44:1
Li, Lydia
Redemption: Lebende Leichnam, Der; Living
Corpse, The 1928,N 20,28:2
Li, Mona
Insult 1930,S 16,30:2
Liandre, Lil
Dark of the Moon 1945,Mr 15,27:2
Libaire, Dorothy
Wall Street 1927,Ap 21,24:4
Triumphant Bachelor, The 1927,S 16,21:1
Solitaire 1929,Mr 13,28:3
As Good As New 1930,N 4,37:3
When the Bough Breaks 1932,F 17,19:2
Howdy Stranger 1937,Ja 15,17:5
I Must Love Someone 1939,F 8,18:7
Brooklyn Biarritz 1941,F 28,16:2
Libassi, Alfredo
Aria del Continente, L' 1927,O 5,30:2
Libassi, Giuseppe
Aria del Continente, L' 1927,O 5,30:2
Libassi, Pia
Aria del Continente, L' 1927,O 5,30:2
Libby, Dennis
House of Leather, The 1970,Mr 19,56:1
Libby, James
Well of Romance, The 1930,N 8,21:2
Libby and Sparrow
Passing Show of 1923, The 1923,Je 15,24:6
Liberace
Liberace's Variety Bill 1957,Ap 22,29:5
Liberace (Director)
Liberace's Variety Bill 1957,Ap 22,29:5
Liberace (Miscellaneous)
Liberace's Variety Bill 1957,Ap 22,29:5
Liberace (Producer)
Liberace's Variety Bill 1957,Ap 22,29:5
Libertini, Richard
Stewed Prunes 1960,N 15,47:1
Infancy 1962,Ja 12,28:1
Three Times Three; Twenty-Five Cent White Cap,
The 1962,Mr 2,24:1
Three Times Three; George Washington Crossing
the Delaware 1962,Mr 2,24:1
Cats' Pajamas, The 1962,Je 1,16:2
Mad Show, The 1966,Ja 10,16:1
Don't Drink the Water 1966,N 18,37:1
White House Murder Case, The 1970,F 19,59:1
Story Theater 1970,O 27,54:1
Libertini, Richard (Playwright)
Stewed Prunes 1960,N 15,47:1
Cats' Pajamas, The 1962,Je 1,16:2

Liberto, Don
It's All Yours 1942,Mr 26,26:2
By Jupiter 1942,Je 4,22:1
Look, Ma, I'm Dancin' 1948,Ja 30,20:2
Russell Patterson's Sketch-Book 1960,F 8,35:1
Kittiwake Island 1960,O 13,43:1
Beautiful Dreamer 1960,D 28,22:1
To Broadway With Love 1964,Ap 30,28:6
Major Barbara 1965,My 18,33:1
Liberto, Don (Choreographer)
If the Shoe Fits 1946,D 6,29:4
Libgold, Leon
Bei Mir Bistu Schoen 1961,O 23,22:2
Cowboy in Israel, A 1962,O 29,36:2
Libidins, D
Blue Bird, The 1932,Ap 22,23:2
Libin, Paul (Director)
Iphigenia in Aulis 1967,N 22,40:2
Moon for the Misbegotten, A 1968,Je 13,55:2
Morning 1968,N 29,52:1
Noon 1968,N 29,52:1
Night 1968,N 29,52:1
Trumpets of the Lord 1969,Ap 30,37:1
Ah, Wilderness! 1969,N 9,86:1
Arsenic and Old Lace 1970,N 5,59:1
Libin, Paul (Miscellaneous)
Thank You, Miss Victoria 1966,Ap 12,43:1
Birdbath 1966,Ap 12,43:1
This Is the Rill Speaking 1966,Ap 12,43:1
War 1966,Ap 13,36:1
Recluse, The 1966,Ap 13,36:1
Chicago 1966,Ap 13,36:1
Libin, Paul (Producer)
Crucible, The 1958,Mr 12,36:1
Time of Vengeance 1959,D 11,39:1
Between Two Thieves 1960,F 12,23:1
Shadow of Heroes 1961,D 6,59:1
Banker's Daughter, The 1962,Ja 23,37:1
Barroom Monks, The 1962,My 29,21:1
Portrait of the Artist as a Young Man, A
  1962,My 29,21:1
Othello 1964,O 13,48:1
Baal 1965,My 7,33:2
Medea 1965,N 29,46:1
Dynamite Tonight 1967,Mr 16,52:2
Midsummer Night's Dream, A 1967,Je 30,23:1
White House Murder Case, The 1970,F 19,59:1
Chicago 70 1970,My 26,33:1
Boesman and Lena 1970,Je 23,35:1
Libman, Yisrol
Bitter Oleander 1935,F 12,24:3
Panic 1935,Mr 16,18:4
Libott, Robert Yale (Playwright)
Too Late the Phalarope 1956,O 12,35:1
Librandi, Geraldine
Approaching Simone 1970,Mr 9,43:1
Libuse, Frank
Sons o' Fun 1941,D 2,28:2
Laffing Room Only 1944,D 25,15:4
Licata, Judith
Enchanted, The 1950,Ja 19,34:2
Lichine, David (Choreographer)
Beat the Band 1942,O 15,26:1
Polonaise 1945,O 8,20:2
Polonaise 1945,O 14,II,1:1
Lichine, David (Director)
Rhapsody 1944,N 23,37:2
Licht, David (Director)
Song of Dnieper 1946,O 26,10:5
King And the Cobbler, The 1954,D 13,33:6
Lonesome Ship, The 1956,D 7,32:6
Father Holds Court 1957,D 12,35:3
Mother's Sabbath Days 1960,N 21,33:2
Backlane Center 1961,N 23,51:1
Eleventh Inheritor, The 1962,N 22,43:5
Sage of Rottenburg, The 1963,N 20,48:1
Enchanting Melody 1964,N 25,40:1
Fifth Commandment, The 1965,N 15,48:4
Prince Reuvaini 1967,N 19,83:1
Bronx Express, 1968 1968,N 16,43:3
Melody Lingers On, The 1969,N 17,55:1
Licht, David (Miscellaneous)
Thousand and One Nights 1959,D 16,53:2
Licht, David (Playwright)
Song of Dnieper 1946,O 26,10:5
Thousand and One Nights 1959,D 16,53:2
Mother's Sabbath Days 1960,N 21,33:2
Melody Lingers On, The 1969,N 17,55:1
Licht, David (Producer)
Eleventh Inheritor, The 1962,N 22,43:5
Lichtenstein, Eduard
Morgen Wieder Lustig 1921,Je 5,VI,1:3
Lichter, Morton
He Who Gets Slapped 1956,F 2,18:1
Lichterman, Marvin
Simple Life, A 1964,My 18,36:1
Saturday Night 1968,F 26,43:1
Happiness Is Just a Little Thing Called a Rolls
  Royce 1968,My 13,54:5
Lovers and Other Strangers 1968,S 19,63:1
Dr Fish 1970,Mr 11,42:2
Steambath 1970,Jl 1,49:1

Lichtman, Nat (Director)
'Tis of Thee 1940,O 28,21:3
Lichtman, Nat (Miscellaneous)
'Tis of Thee 1940,O 28,21:3
Lichtman, Nat (Producer)
'Tis of Thee 1940,O 28,21:3
Liddell, Hilary
Power Without Glory 1948,Ja 14,30:2
Liddle, James (Producer)
These Two 1934,My 8,28:3
Fresh Fields 1934,Jl 15,X,1:1
Liddy, James R
Artists and Models 1923,Ag 21,12:2
Sky High 1925,Mr 3,21:4
Lide, Miller
Sotoba Komachi 1961,F 1,15:1
Hans's Crime 1961,F 4,15:1
Comedy of Errors, The 1963,Je 13,28:1
Henry V 1963,Je 14,37:1
Caesar and Cleopatra 1963,Ag 1,18:2
Lidell, Alvar
Practical Cats 1954,Ag 27,11:5
Liden, Robert (Miscellaneous)
Shangri-La 1956,Je 14,40:1
Lidkey, Jim
Ruy Blas 1957,D 14,16:3
Lidkey, Jim
Ruy Blas 1957,D 14,16:3
Lidwell, Wauna
Passionate Pilgrim, The 1932,O 20,24:3
Girls in Uniform 1932,D 31,10:3
Lieb, Arthur (Miscellaneous)
Richard II 1956,O 24,44:1
Lieb, Francis
Erminie 1921,Ja 4,11:1
Lieb, Hermann
Call of Life, The 1925,O 10,10:1
Dope 1926,Ja 4,16:3
Wooden Kimono 1926,D 28,16:2
Sweet Land of Liberty 1929,S 24,29:2
Old Rascal, The 1930,Mr 25,34:4
Order Please 1934,O 10,21:2
So Many Paths 1934,D 7,26:5
Bat, The 1937,Je 1,27:5
Cat and the Canary, The 1937,Je 15,26:3
Quiet, Please! 1940,N 9,20:3
Lieb, Hermann (Playwright)
Dope 1926,Ja 4,16:3
Lieb, Robert P
O'Daniel 1947,F 25,32:2
Great Campaign, The 1947,Ap 1,33:2
Two Blind Mice 1949,Mr 3,32:2
Inherit the Wind 1955,Ap 22,20:2
Liebeneines, Wolfgang (Director)
Lauter Luegen 1937,O 24,XI,3:1
Lieberman, Al (Producer)
Orpheus Descending 1959,O 6,45:2
Lieberman, Henry
Laugh It Off 1934,Ap 5,24:2
Flair-Flair the Idol of Paree 1935,Mr 13,16:1
Oy, Is Dus a Leben!; Oh, What a Life!
  1942,O 13,19:2
Lieberman, Herbert (Playwright)
Matty and the Moron and Madonna
  1965,Mr 30,53:1
Lieberman, Lawrence
Rosalinda; Fledermaus, Die 1942,O 29,26:5
Lieberman, Leo (Playwright)
Captains and the Kings, The 1962,Ja 3,25:2
Lieberman, Maxine
Rivals, The 1969,O 18,37:1
Metamorphoses 1969,D 12,69:1
Three Philip Roth Stories; Epstein 1970,Jl 31,14:1
Three Philip Roth Stories; Defender of the Faith
  1970,Jl 31,14:1
Cops and Horrors; Fly Paper 1970,Ag 11,27:1
Cops and Horrors; Dracula 1970,Ag 11,27:1
Story Theater Repertory; Gimpel the Food
  1970,O 21,40:1
Story Theater Repertory; Saint Julian the
  Hospitaler 1970,O 21,40:1
Lieberman, Michael (Lighting Director)
Children of the Shadows 1964,F 27,26:1
Lieberson, Martin R (Playwright)
Springtime Folly 1951,F 27,23:4
Lieberson, William H (Playwright)
Springtime Folly 1951,F 27,23:4
Lieberstein, Danny (Composer)
Lysistrata 1968,N 15,42:1
Liebert, Sam
Honor Code, The 1931,My 19,25:3
Thumbs Up! 1934,D 28,24:1
Liebeskind, Abraham
Chair, The 1930,O 4,15:4
Liebgold, Leon
Mazel Tov, Molly 1950,O 2,18:1
Take It Easy 1950,D 25,23:6
Wedding March, The 1955,O 17,33:1
Family Mishmash, A 1958,O 20,36:1
My Son and I 1960,O 24,24:2
Hello Charlie 1965,O 25,47:2
Bride Got Farblondjet, The 1967,N 6,61:6
It's Never Too Late for Happiness 1968,O 21,59:3
From Israel With Laughter 1969,O 17,34:1
Light, Lively and Yiddish 1970,O 28,58:1

Lieblich, Nathan
Bronx Express, 1968 1968,N 16,43:3
Liebling, Howard (Director)
Beautiful Changes, The 1956,Mr 24,15:2
Liebling, Howard (Playwright)
Beautiful Changes, The 1956,Mr 24,15:2
Liebling, Joseph (Composer)
Stevedore 1949,F 23,30:2
Scarecrow, The 1953,Je 17,31:1
Knight of the Burning Pestle, The 1953,O 24,13:2
Moon in Capricorn 1953,O 28,37:2
Liebling, William (Producer)
Stop-Over 1938,Ja 12,16:5
Liebman, August
Victory 1937,N 14,XI,2:5
Liebman, Herr
Journey's End 1930,Mr 30,VIII,3:4
Liebman, Jay (Costume Designer)
Me and Juliet 1970,My 15,42:1
Liebman, Joseph (Composer)
Follies of 1910, The 1960,Ja 15,37:3
Liebman, Max (Composer)
It's All Yours 1942,Mr 26,26:2
Liebman, Max (Director)
Straw Hat, The 1939,S 30,10:6
Tars and Spars 1944,Ap 7,23:1
Liebman, Max (Lyricist)
It's All Yours 1942,Mr 26,26:2
Liebman, Max (Miscellaneous)
Make Mine Manhattan 1948,Ja 16,26:2
Liebman, Max (Playwright)
Illustrators' Show, The 1936,Ja 23,25:3
Flying Ginzburgs, The 1938,N 13,IX,2:2
Off to Buffalo! 1939,F 22,18:2
Straw Hat, The 1939,S 30,10:6
Crazy With the Heat 1941,Ja 15,18:2
Liebman, Max (Producer)
Autumn Hill 1942,Ap 14,17:4
Wine, Women and Song 1942,S 29,18:3
From the Second City 1961,S 27,32:1
Liebovitz, David (Playwright)
John Hawthorne 1921,Ja 24,16:1
Liebowitz, Max J
Steppe Around 1922,Mr 29,17:4
Lieck, Peter
Minna von Barnhelm 1968,N 13,37:1
Schloss, Das 1968,N 20,35:3
Lieder, Rose
Girls in Uniform 1932,D 31,10:3
Bitter Oleander 1935,F 12,24:3
Fireman's Flame, The 1937,O 11,26:2
Lief, Arthur (Miscellaneous)
Romeo and Juliet 1956,O 25,41:1
Macbeth 1956,O 30,42:2
Troilus and Cressida 1956,D 27,21:1
Obratsov Russian Puppet Theater in an Unusual
  Concert 1963,O 3,28:1
Lief, Arthur (Musical Director)
Cox and Box 1942,F 20,20:2
Midsummer Night's Dream, A 1954,S 22,33:1
Rosalie 1957,Je 26,28:2
Banker's Daughter, The 1962,Ja 23,37:1
Lief, Max (Composer)
Say When 1928,Je 27,29:3
Hey, Nonny, Nonny! 1932,Je 7,22:3
Illustrators' Show, The 1936,Ja 23,25:3
Lief, Max (Lyricist)
Greenwich Village Follies 1928,Ap 10,32:2
Say When 1928,Je 27,29:3
Luckee Girl 1928,S 17,28:6
Pleasure Bound 1929,F 19,22:4
Hey, Nonny, Nonny! 1932,Je 7,22:3
Lief, Nat (Composer)
Illustrators' Show, The 1936,Ja 23,25:3
Lief, Nathaniel (Composer)
Say When 1928,Je 27,29:3
Hey, Nonny, Nonny! 1932,Je 7,22:3
Lief, Nathaniel (Lyricist)
Greenwich Village Follies 1928,Ap 10,32:2
Say When 1928,Je 27,29:3
Luckee Girl 1928,S 17,28:6
Pleasure Bound 1929,F 19,22:4
Hey, Nonny, Nonny! 1932,Je 7,22:3
Lieferant, Henry (Playwright)
Hilda Cassidy 1933,My 5,18:3
Lieferant, Sylvia (Playwright)
Hilda Cassidy 1933,My 5,18:3
Lien, Evanna
Sound of Music, The 1959,N 17,40:2
Lien, Juanita
Mystery of the Finding of the Cross, The
  1959,Ja 16,35:2
Lienaweaver, Richard
Enemy of the People, An 1958,F 26,24:2
Liepolt, Werner (Playwright)
Young Master Dante, The 1968,D 31,19:1
Young Master Dante, The 1969,Ja 12,II,1:1
Lier, Frank
Headless Horseman, The 1937,Mr 6,10:4
Lieske, Trude
Rose Marie 1928,Ap 29,IX,2:8
Lietzau, Hans (Director)
Mitschuldigen, Die 1966,Ap 6,34:1

Lietzau, Hans (Director)—Cont
Wozzeck 1966,Ap 6,34:1
Liewehr, Fred
Professor Bernhardi 1968,Mr 20,38:1
Jux Will Er Sich Machen, Einen 1968,Ap 3,41:1
Life, Larry
Pins and Needles 1967,Je 9,51:2
Life, Larry (Choreographer)
Pins and Needles 1967,Je 9,51:2
Liff, Samuel (Director)
Night in Venice, A 1953,Je 26,15:2
My Fair Lady 1964,F 20,24:4
My Fair Lady 1964,My 21,43:2
My Fair Lady 1968,Je 14,42:1
Liff, Samuel (Miscellaneous)
Matchmaker, The 1955,D 6,45:6
My Fair Lady 1956,Mr 16,20:2
Bravo Giovanni 1962,My 21,41:2
Lady of the Camellias, The 1963,Mr 22,7:1
Severed Head, A 1964,O 29,40:1
I Was Dancing 1964,N 9,40:4
Roar of the Greasepaint-the Smell of the Crowd
  1965,My 17,46:2
Inadmissible Evidence 1965,D 1,52:1
Cactus Flower 1965,D 9,60:2
Philadelphia, Here I Come! 1966,F 17,28:1
Loves of Cass McGuire, The 1966,O 7,36:1
We Have Always Lived in the Castle
  1966,O 20,53:1
Don't Drink the Water 1966,N 18,37:1
Astrakhan Coat, The 1967,Ja 13,18:1
Keep It in the Family 1967,S 28,59:1
Rosencrantz and Guildenstern Are Dead
  1967,O 17,53:1
How Now, Dow Jones 1967,D 8,53:1
Seven Descents of Myrtle, The 1968,Mr 28,54:1
Rockefeller and the Red Indians 1968,O 25,37:1
Promises, Promises 1968,D 2,59:3
Forty Carats 1968,D 27,45:1
Play It Again, Sam 1969,F 13,52:3
Patriot for Me, A 1969,O 6,58:1
Penny Wars, The 1969,O 16,52:1
Liff, Samuel (Producer)
My Fair Lady 1959,Ja 27,26:1
Moby Dick 1962,N 29,45:1
Child's Play 1970,F 18,39:1
Lifschutz, Adele
Mascaiada 1929,D 28,10:6
Lifson, David (Playwright)
Mummers and Men 1962,Mr 27,41:6
Lifson, David S
Steel 1931,N 19,26:5
Lifson, David S (Playwright)
Familiar Pattern 1943,S 3,15:6
Lifter, Cecile
Centuries, The 1927,N 30,23:1
Liftin, Robert (Miscellaneous)
Oh! Calcutta! 1969,Je 18,33:1
Look to the Lilies 1970,Mr 30,59:1
Lifton, Betty Jean (Miscellaneous)
Moon Walk 1970,N 27,52:1
Lifton, Betty Jean (Playwright)
Moon Walk 1970,N 27,52:1
Lifton, Harold (Miscellaneous)
Flahooley 1951,My 15,39:1
Ligeri, Bruno
Cyanamide 1954,Mr 26,17:6
Liggins, Donna
In Splendid Error 1954,O 27,33:6
Lighstone, Marilyn
Government Inspector, The 1967,Je 15,55:1
Light, Doris
Jack in the Box 1960,My 19,43:3
Light, James
Last Masks 1920,Ap 4,VI,6:1
Light, James (Costume Designer)
Ancient Mariner, The 1924,Ap 7,15:5
Ancient Mariner, The 1924,Ap 13,VIII,1:1
Light, James (Director)
All God's Chillun Got Wings 1924,My 16,22:3
All God's Chillun Got Wings 1924,Ag 19,9:1
S S Glencairn 1924,N 4,31:4
Hamlet 1925,N 10,23:1
Dream Play 1926,Ja 21,18:2
East Lynne 1926,Mr 11,18:4
Beyond the Horizon 1926,D 1,24:2
Rapid Transit 1927,Ap 8,21:2
Jacob Slovak 1927,O 6,28:4
Stairs, The 1927,N 8,32:7
Prisoner, The 1927,D 30,22:2
Hot Pan 1928,F 16,14:1
Final Balance, The 1928,O 31,28:3
Before Breakfast 1929,Mr 6,33:1
Earth Between, The 1929,Mr 6,33:1
Fiesta 1929,S 18,35:1
Star of Bengal 1929,S 26,27:2
Winter Bound 1929,N 13,24:6
Emperor Jones, The 1930,Ap 1,10:1
Rock Me, Julie 1931,F 4,21:1
Hairy Ape, The 1931,My 12,29:4
Lost Boy 1932,Ja 6,24:4
Black Souls 1932,Mr 31,25:1
Panic 1935,Mr 16,18:4
This Our House 1935,D 12,33:3

Chalk Dust 1936,Mr 5,24:5
Native Ground 1937,Mr 24,28:4
Circle of Chalk, The 1941,Mr 27,28:4
Days of Our Youth, The 1941,N 29,15:2
Nathan the Wise 1942,Mr 12,25:4
Nathan the Wise 1942,Ap 4,18:4
Nathan the Wise 1944,F 22,26:3
Oedipus Rex 1945,D 17,16:7
Mayor of Zalamea, The 1946,Ja 28,15:5
Lysistrata 1946,O 18,27:5
Circle of Chalk, The 1950,D 2,8:3
Light, James (Miscellaneous)
Lysistrata 1946,O 18,27:5
Three Sisters, The 1955,F 26,13:2
Light, James (Producer)
Emperor Jones, The 1930,Ap 1,10:1
Emperor Jones, The 1930,My 25,IX,1:8
Oedipus Rex 1945,D 17,16:7
Mayor of Zalamea, The 1946,Ja 28,15:5
Light, Karl
Romeo and Juliet 1951,Mr 12,21:2
Barefoot in Athens 1951,N 1,35:2
Sea Gull, The 1954,My 12,38:1
Inherit the Wind 1955,Ap 22,20:2
Firstborn, The 1957,Ja 7,29:2
Edward II 1958,F 12,32:5
Arms and the Man 1967,Je 23,44:2
Light, Robert
Fulton of Oak Falls 1937,Ja 2,15:3
Fulton of Oak Falls 1937,F 11,18:2
Lightdale, Joan
Passion of Gross, The 1955,Ja 24,20:2
Lighter, Fred
Off to Buffalo! 1939,F 22,18:2
Lightfoot, James
Porgy and Bess 1935,O 11,30:2
Sweet River 1936,O 29,30:2
Miss Quis 1937,Ap 8,20:5
John Henry 1940,Ja 11,18:2
Natural Man 1941,My 8,20:4
Lightfoot, James E
$25 an Hour 1933,My 11,14:4
Lightner, Frances (Playwright)
Puppets 1925,Mr 10,19:1
Lightner, Fred
Night in Venice, A 1953,Je 26,15:2
Hit the Trail 1954,D 3,31:2
Lightner, Theodore
George White's Scandals 1923,Je 19,22:5
Scandals 1924,Jl 1,16:1
Lightner, William
Arms and the Man 1956,O 2,39:4
Beaux' Stratagem, The 1957,Jl 9,25:4
Lightner, Winnie
George White's Scandals 1923,Je 19,22:5
Scandals 1924,Jl 1,16:1
Gay Paree 1925,Ag 19,14:3
Gay Paree 1926,N 10,24:2
Vaudeville (Palace) 1927,Je 14,33:3
Harry Delmar's Revels 1927,N 29,30:2
Lightner Sisters and Alexander, The
George White's Scandals 1922,Ag 29,10:1
Lightstone, Marilyn
Antony and Cleopatra 1967,Ag 2,25:1
Government Inspector, The 1967,O 28,34:1
Midsummer Night's Dream, A 1968,Je 13,54:1
Seagull, The 1968,Jl 25,27:2
King Lear 1968,N 8,43:1
Ligliaccio, Cau E
Sirena 1931,S 22,33:4
Ligon, Tom
Have I Got a Girl for You! 1963,D 3,53:2
Hard Travelin' 1965,Je 17,25:1
Your Own Thing 1969,Mr 29,39:1
Angela 1969,O 31,33:1
Love Is a Time of Day 1969,D 23,21:3
Lihamba, Amandina
Akokawe 1970,Je 5,21:1
Likely, Pat
Let's Face It 1941,O 30,26:2
Lilburn, Douglas (Composer)
Macbeth 1946,D 1,II,3:7
Lilenthal, Charles
Our Lan' 1947,Ap 19,11:2
Liles, Mary
My Heart's in the Highlands 1939,Ap 14,29:2
Lilford, Harry
Sitting Pretty 1924,Ap 9,24:2
Green Hat, The 1925,S 16,23:2
Potiphar's Wife 1928,D 24,10:7
Liliana, Lily
Untitled-Revue 1939,Ap 5,31:2
Wedding March, The 1955,O 17,33:1
My Son and I 1960,O 24,24:2
Hut a Yid a Landele 1968,O 19,28:1
From Israel With Laughter 1969,O 17,34:1
Light, Lively and Yiddish 1970,O 28,58:1
Lilienthal, Charles
Machine Wreckers, The 1937,Ap 12,14:2
Winners and Losers 1947,F 27,27:2
Our Lan' 1947,S 29,16:5
Lilienthal, Ruth
Winners and Losers 1947,F 27,27:2

Lilienthal, Ruth—Cont
G-II 1948,My 28,27:3
Liliputians, The
Follies 1924,O 31,19:3
Liljencrantz, Torvald (Playwright)
People on the Hill 1931,S 26,25:5
Liljenquist, Don C (Director)
Woman Is My Idea 1968,S 26,61:1
Liljenquist, Don C (Playwright)
Woman Is My Idea 1968,S 26,61:1
Lillard, James A
Brown Buddies 1930,O 8,29:1
Hot Mikado, The 1939,Mr 24,26:2
Lillard, Mildred
If I Was Rich 1926,S 3,15:2
Lillard, Robert (Playwright)
White Flame 1929,N 5,32:7
Lillard, Tom
Brig, The 1963,My 16,40:1
Lilley, Edward Clarke (Director)
Me 1925,N 24,28:1
Money Lender, The 1928,Ag 28,27:3
Conflict 1929,Mr 7,22:4
Congratulations 1929,My 1,28:4
International Revue 1930,F 26,22:2
Flying High 1930,Mr 4,24:4
Who Cares 1930,Jl 9,27:1
Prince Charming 1930,O 14,31:1
Here Goes the Bride 1931,N 4,31:2
Our Wife 1933,Mr 3,13:2
Thumbs Up! 1934,D 28,24:1
Dominant Sex, The 1935,Ap 2,24:5
Sketch Book 1935,Je 5,22:2
Crime Marches on 1935,O 24,19:1
Ziegfeld Follies 1936,S 15,37:1
Show Is On, The 1936,D 26,14:2
So Proudly We Hail 1938,Ap 9,11:1
Come Across 1938,S 15,28:3
One for the Money 1939,F 6,9:2
Crazy With the Heat 1941,Ja 15,18:2
Sun Field, The 1942,D 10,33:2
Good Night Ladies 1945,Ja 18,16:2
Girl From Nantucket, The 1945,N 9,17:2
Ankles Aweigh 1955,Ap 19,27:1
Lilley, Edward Clarke (Miscellaneous)
Ziegfeld Follies 1931,Jl 2,30:5
Ziegfeld Follies 1934,Ja 5,24:3
Ziegfeld Follies 1936,Ja 31,17:2
Virginia 1937,S 3,13:2
All in Fun 1940,D 28,11:2
Lilley, Edward Clarke (Playwright)
Who Cares 1930,Jl 9,27:1
Show Is On, The 1937,S 20,18:4
Lilley, Joseph (Musical Director)
Nellie Bly 1946,Ja 22,32:2
Lilley, William D
This Way Out 1929,Ap 28,24:4
Lillford, Harry
Seeing Things 1920,Je 18,19:2
Dulcy 1921,Ag 15,14:1
Charley's Aunt 1925,Je 2,16:2
Murray Hill 1927,S 30,29:1
Marquise, The 1927,N 15,26:4
Our Betters 1928,F 21,18:2
Lady Lies, The 1928,N 27,36:2
Gambling 1929,Ag 27,31:2
Song and Dance Man, The 1930,Je 17,25:5
Lillian, Isidor (Composer)
Queen Mother 1938,D 26,29:4
Lillian, Isidor (Lyricist)
Queen Mother 1938,D 26,29:4
Lillian, Kurt
An und Aus 1926,D 5,VIII,8:7
Lilliard, James A
Bottomland 1927,Je 28,29:3
Lillie, Beatrice
Charlot's Revue 1924,Ja 10,18:1
Charlot's Revue 1924,Ap 6,VIII,1:1
Charlot's Revue 1924,Ap 15,25:2
Charlot's Revue 1925,N 11,27:1
Charlot's Revue 1925,N 15,VIII,1:1
Charlot's's Revue 1927,VII,1:1
Oh, Please! 1926,D 22,24:3
She's My Baby 1928,Ja 4,22:2
This Year of Grace 1928,N 8,27:1
This Year of Grace 1928,N 25,X,1:1
This Year of Grace 1929,Ap 21,IX,1:6
Vaudeville (Palace) 1929,S 23,24:6
Vaudeville (Palace) 1929,S 30,22:3
Vaudeville (Palace) 1929,N 25,22:4
Charlot's Masquerade 1930,S 5,30:7
Vaudeville (Palace) 1931,F 16,16:3
Third Little Show, The 1931,My 10,VIII,2:4
Third Little Show, The 1931,Je 2,34:3
Third Little Show, The 1931,Je 14,VIII,1:2
Too True to Be Good 1932,Mr 1,19:2
Too True to Be Good 1932,Mr 6,VIII,1:1
Too True to Be Good 1932,Ap 5,27:5
Music in the Air 1932,N 20,IX,1:1
Walk a Little Faster 1932,D 8,24:4
Please 1933,N 17,22:2
Please 1933,D 3,IX,7:6
At Home Abroad 1935,S 4,22:3
At Home Abroad 1935,S 8,IX,1:1

Lillie, Beatrice—Cont
At Home Abroad 1935,S 20,17:4
At Home Abroad 1935,O 27,IX,8:1
At Home Abroad 1935,O 27,IX,1:1
Show Is On, The 1936,N 9,22:2
Show Is On, The 1936,N 15,XI,2:1
Show Is On, The 1936,D 26,14:2
Show Is On, The 1937,Ja 10,X,1:1
Happy Returns 1938,My 20,16:6
Set to Music 1939,Ja 19,16:2
Big Top 1942,My 9,11:1
Big Top 1942,My 17,VIII,1:3
Seven Lively Arts 1944,D 8,26:6
Seven Lively Arts 1944,D 17,II,3:1
Inside U S A 1948,Mr 30,27:3
Inside U S A 1948,My 1,19:2
Inside U S A 1948,My 23,II,1:1
Inside U S A 1948,Je 13,II,6:6
Inside U S A 1948,Ag 29,II,1:1
Evening With Beatrice Lillie, An 1952,O 3,17:2
Evening With Beatrice Lillie, An 1952,O 12,II,1:1
Evening With Beatrice Lillie, An 1954,N 26,26:7
Evening With Beatrice Lillie, An 1954,D 12,II,5:1
Ziegfeld Follies 1957,Mr 2,19:2
Auntie Mame 1958,Je 8,II,1:1
High Spirits 1964,Ap 8,34:1
Lilliford, Harry
What's Your Wife Doing? 1923,O 2,10:3
Lillig, Jane
Fighting Cock, The 1959,D 9,57:3
Pimpernel! 1964,Ja 7,26:6
Lilling, Bill
Kiss Me, Kate 1948,D 31,10:3
Lilling, William
Johannes Kreisler 1922,D 25,20:3
Pardon My English 1933,Ja 21,11:4
Music Hath Charms 1934,D 31,8:2
Let's Face It 1941,O 30,26:2
Lilliput (Original Author)
Sins of Mothers 1937,Mr 30,20:2
Lillite, William
Florodora 1920,Ap 6,18:1
Lillith, Ola
Girl From Warsaw, The 1931,S 14,15:5
Pleasure 1931,D 28,20:2
Perfect Fishel, The 1935,S 30,12:4
David and Esther 1938,O 12,34:3
Lillo, George (Original Author)
When Crummles Played 1928,S 23,IX,2:2
Lillo, George (Playwright)
George Barnwell; London Merchant, The 1928,O 2,34:3
When Crummles Played 1928,O 2,34:3
Lilly, Ada
Drunkard, The 1936,S 20,IX,3:4
Lilly, Harry (Mrs)
One Woman's Husband 1920,Mr 23,9:3
Lilly, Paul
Twentieth Century 1950,D 25,23:6
Marvellous History of Saint Bernard, The 1958,F 24,16:3
Potting Shed, The 1958,N 3,49:2
Lilly, Paul (Producer)
Country Wife, The 1955,Ap 6,35:1
Lilo
Can-Can 1953,My 8,28:1
Can-Can 1953,My 17,II,1:1
Pousse-Cafe 1966,Mr 19,19:2
Lim, Peter
York Nativity Play, The 1956,D 5,49:2
Lima, Alberto
Sirena Varada, La 1937,O 23,15:3
Limber, Charles F
Once Over Lightly 1938,D 10,13:4
Limberg, Edward A Jr
What a Relief 1935,D 14,10:6
Take It Away 1936,D 15,30:5
Take It Away 1936,D 22,32:3
Limburg, Olga
Unentbehrliche, Der 1937,O 24,XI,3:1
Lime, Yvonne
Ah, Wilderness! 1954,Ag 21,20:4
Lime Trio, The
Vaudeville (Palace) 1929,D 9,33:2
Folies Bergere 1939,D 25,28:2
Limon, Jose
Keep Off the Grass 1940,My 5,X,1:6
Keep Off the Grass 1940,My 24,22:6
Rosalinda; Fledermaus, Die 1942,O 29,26:5
Limon, Jose (Choreographer)
Roberta 1933,N 20,18:4
Limozin, Jean (Playwright)
Philippine 1937,N 14,XI,7:5
Limpy
Christmas Eve 1939,D 28,17:2
Lin, Hui Mei (Scenic Designer)
Baby With a Knife 1969,My 15,41:2
Pets 1969,My 15,41:2
Silver Grey Toy Poodle 1969,My 15,41:2
Lina Trio
Mexicana 1939,My 7,X,3:1
Linaker, Kay
Yesterday's Orchids 1934,O 6,20:4
Every Man for Himself 1940,D 10,32:3

Linbermann, Jan
Father, The 1931,O 9,21:1
Linch, Johanna
Puntila 1959,My 15,26:2
Linchart, James
Sh! The Octopus 1928,F 22,19:2
Lincoln, Abbey
Cotton Club Revue of 1957 1957,Jl 10,23:4
Lincoln, Alpheus
Four in Hand 1923,S 7,10:2
Lincoln, Ann
Foxhole in the Parlor 1945,My 24,15:4
Lincoln, Arthur
Polonaise 1945,O 8,20:2
Lincoln, Dan
Girl From Samos, The 1954,N 24,17:1
Lincoln, Eugene
Diff'rent 1925,F 11,19:3
Lincoln, Glen
Madre, La 1959,F 12,24:1
Lincoln, Joseph C (Original Author)
Shavings 1920,F 22,III,6:1
Lincoln, Joseph C (Playwright)
Shavings 1920,F 17,18:1
Lincoln, Lorna
Better Times 1922,S 4,14:2
Lincoln, Stoddard (Composer)
Anatomist, The 1957,F 27,21:5
Lincovsky, Cipe
Projimos, Los 1966,Je 29,38:5
Lind, Betty
Make Mine Manhattan 1948,Ja 16,26:2
Lind, Betty (Choreographer)
Finian's Rainbow 1953,Mr 7,13:2
Lind, Christina
Sing Out the News 1938,S 26,12:5
Hi-Ya Gentlemen 1940,D 4,34:2
It's All Yours 1942,Mr 26,26:2
Lind, Della
Streets of Paris, The 1939,Je 20,25:2
Music in My Heart 1947,O 3,30:2
Lady From Paris, The 1950,S 27,36:1
Lind, Geoffrey
Slight Case of Murder, A 1935,S 12,28:5
Stick-in-the-Mud 1935,D 2,18:2
Cyrano de Bergerac 1936,Ap 28,17:1
Lind, Gillian
Habit 1926,N 4,VIII,4:7
Clive of India 1934,F 18,IX,3:7
Man of Yesterday 1935,Mr 17,VIII,1:4
Lind, Gloria
Sweethearts 1947,Ja 22,31:2
Fledermaus, Die 1954,My 20,38:5
Lind, Jakov (Original Author)
Ergo 1968,Mr 4,29:1
Lind, Jakov (Playwright)
Ergo 1968,Mr 4,29:1
Lind, Lillian
Heiress, The 1949,F 3,26:2
Lind, Norman
Illustrators' Show, The 1936,Ja 23,25:3
Red, Hot and Blue! 1936,O 30,26:3
Trumpets and Drums 1969,O 13,52:1
Lady From Maxim's, The 1970,Je 1,41:1
Lind, Paula
White Eagle, The 1927,D 27,24:4
O'Flynn, The 1934,D 28,24:1
Lind, Stefan
Carmen Jones 1956,Je 1,28:2
Linda
Sidewalks of New York 1927,O 4,33:1
Lindahl, Stanley
Bewitched 1924,O 2,26:3
Processional 1925,Ja 13,17:1
Headquarters 1929,D 5,32:4
Lindau, Carl (Playwright)
Vienna at Night 1945,Ap 30,12:4
Lindavist, Jan-Erik
Father, The 1962,My 15,49:1
Lindberg, Lucille (Costume Designer)
Mikado, The 1935,Ag 24,17:5
Lindberg, Paul
Reunion in New York 1940,F 22,28:4
Lindberg, Per (Producer)
To Damascus 1933,N 12,IX,1:1
Lindburg, Per (Director)
Merry Widow, The 1931,O 11,VIII,4:4
Hangman, The 1935,O 23,18:6
Linde, Iris
Three to Make Ready 1946,Mr 8,16:2
Lindeau, Max (Original Author)
Procureur Hallers, Le 1924,N 13,18:1
Lindeberg, Linda
White Christmas 1936,Jl 7,22:2
Lindemann, Mitchell
Love, Honor and Oh Baby 1940,Mr 29,25:2
Linden, Anne
Yeomen of the Guard, The 1964,Ag 3,16:1
Linden, Eeta
Seeds in the Wind 1948,Ap 26,27:2
Seeds in the Wind 1948,My 26,29:2
Linden, Eric
Faust 1928,O 9,34:1

Linden, Eric—Cont
Ladies' Money 1934,N 2,26:6
Linden, Florence
Merrily We Roll Along 1936,Je 30,15:1
All That Glitters 1938,Ja 20,18:2
Linden, Hal
Anything Goes 1962,My 16,35:1
Something More! 1964,N 11,36:1
Illya Darling 1967,Ap 12,37:1
Apple Tree, The 1967,N 10,61:1
Education of H*Y*M*A*N K*A*P*L*A*N, The 1968,Ap 5,57:1
Three Men on a Horse 1969,O 17,35:1
Rothschilds, The 1970,O 20,40:1
Rothschilds, The 1970,N 1,II,1:1
Linden, Joyce
Daphne Laureola 1950,S 19,38:6
Linden, Margaret
Madras House, The 1921,O 31,18:2
Listening In 1922,D 5,24:1
Little Miss Bluebeard 1923,Ag 29,12:1
Saint Wench 1933,Ja 3,19:3
Dead End 1935,O 29,17:2
Linden, Maria (Costume Designer)
Present Laughter 1946,O 30,31:2
Linden, Marie
Via Crucis 1923,N 13,25:2
Hamlet 1923,N 20,23:3
Linden, Marta
Present Laughter 1946,O 30,31:2
Men We Marry, The 1948,Ja 17,11:2
Cry of the Peacock 1950,Ap 12,33:2
Curious Savage, The 1950,O 25,44:3
Starcross Story, The 1954,Ja 14,25:2
Linden, Robert
Mrs Dane's Defense 1928,F 7,30:1
Sherlock Holmes 1928,F 21,18:4
Within the Law 1928,Mr 6,20:1
Linden, Robert (Choreographer)
It Happens on Ice 1940,O 11,24:3
Linden, Robert (Miscellaneous)
Desk Set, The 1955,O 25,36:7
Auntie Mame 1956,N 1,47:2
Redhead 1959,F 6,21:1
There Was a Little Girl 1960,Mr 1,28:1
Advise and Consent 1960,N 18,25:1
Passage to India, A 1962,F 1,23:1
Hot Spot 1963,Ap 20,17:2
Double Dublin 1963,D 27,16:2
Roar Like a Dove 1964,My 22,40:2
Cambridge Circus 1964,O 7,53:1
Sweet Charity 1966,Ja 31,22:1
Linden, Van Der
Chacun Sa Verite 1939,Ja 24,17:1
Lindenberg, Paul
Shakespeare's Merchant 1939 1939,Ja 10,16:3
From Vienna 1939,Je 21,26:2
Linder, Alfred
Winter Soldiers 1942,N 30,19:2
Bobino 1944,Ap 7,23:4
Beggars Are Comming to Town 1945,O 29,16:2
Flies, The; Mouches, Les 1947,Ap 18,26:3
Linder, Cec
In the Matter of J Robert Oppenheimer 1969,Mr 7,28:1
Linder, Charles (Producer)
Honor Code, The 1931,My 19,25:3
Linder, Jack (Producer)
Diamond Lil 1928,Ap 10,32:1
Squealer, The 1928,N 13,36:3
Cortez 1929,N 5,32:2
Honor Code, The 1931,My 19,25:3
Summer Wives 1936,Ap 14,18:1
Linder, Lloyd
Two Misers, The 1943,D 9,30:5
Linder, Mark
Diamond Lil 1928,Ap 10,32:1
On Location 1937,S 28,19:1
Linder, Mark (Director)
Honor Code, The 1931,My 19,25:3
Linder, Mark (Playwright)
Diamond Lil 1928,Ap 10,32:1
Squealer, The 1928,N 13,36:3
Room 349 1930,Ap 23,24:5
Honor Code, The 1931,My 19,25:3
Triplets 1932,S 22,25:2
Summer Wives 1936,Ap 14,18:1
Linder, Mark (Producer)
Triplets 1932,S 22,25:2
Linder, Seymour
Summer Wives 1936,Ap 14,18:1
Linder, Virginia
Seventeen 1926,My 1,10:1
Lindermann, Jan
Henry V 1928,Mr 16,26:2
Light of Asia, The 1928,O 10,32:2
Purity 1930,D 26,18:2
Lindfors, Viveca
Eurydice 1948,O 17,I,67:4
I've Got Sixpence 1952,D 3,44:2
I've Got Sixpence 1952,D 7,II,5:1
Anastasia 1954,D 30,13:1
Anastasia 1955,Ja 16,II,1:1
King Lear 1956,Ja 13,17:1

Lindfors, Viveca—Cont

Miss Julie 1956,F 22,23:2
Stronger, The 1956,F 22,23:2
Miss Julie 1956,Mr 4,II,1:1
Golden Six, The 1958,O 27,31:2
I Rise in Flame, Cried the Phoenix 1959,Ap 15,30:1
Mary Stuart 1959,Jl 30,21:3
Glimpse of the Domesticity of Franklyn Barnabas, A 1960,Mr 7,24:2
Brouhaha 1960,Ap 27,31:2
Miss Julie 1961,Jl 10,26:1
I Am a Camera 1961,Jl 10,26:1
Jewish Wife 1961,N 15,52:2
Brecht on Brecht 1961,N 15,52:2
Brecht on Brecht 1962,Ja 4,26:1
Brecht on Brecht 1962,Ja 14,II,1:1
Pal Joey 1963,My 30,21:1
Postmark Zero 1965,N 2,28:1
Niggerlovers, The; Demonstration, The 1967,O 2,54:2
Niggerlovers, The; Man and Dog 1967,O 2,54:2
Guns of Carrar, The 1968,D 10,53:1
Cuba Si 1968,D 10,53:1

Lindgard, Gerald
Macbeth 1928,N 20,28:3

Lindgren, Karen
Temporary Island, A 1948,Mr 15,27:3
Liar, The 1950,My 19,30:2

Lindgren, Robert
Plain and Fancy 1955,F 6,II,6:6

Lindhard, Leo
Brother Elks 1925,S 15,29:2
Shannons of Broadway, The 1927,S 27,30:4

Lindholm, Herbert
Quicksand 1928,F 14,26:3
Street Scene 1929,Ja 11,20:4

Lindig, Jillian
Brownstone Urge, The 1969,D 18,63:1

Lindinger, Hugo
Wiener Blut 1964,S 12,14:1

Lindley, Audra
Comes the Revelation 1942,My 27,26:2
Hear That Trumpet 1946,O 8,19:2
Heads or Tails 1947,My 3,10:6
Cockeyed Kite 1961,S 14,27:1
Spofford 1967,D 15,54:3
Spofford 1967,D 24,II,3:2
Fire! 1969,Ja 29,26:1

Lindner, Barbara
Show Boat 1966,Jl 20,48:1

Lindo, Olga
Rain 1925,My 13,24:2
Untitled-Play 1928,Je 10,VIII,1:3
Rings on Her Fingers 1932,My 22,VIII,1:3
Laying the Devil 1933,Jl 23,IX,1:3
Viceroy Sarah 1935,Mr 10,VIII,2:1
Miss Smith 1936,Jl 5,IX,1:8

Lindorm, Erik (Playwright)
Krasch 1930,N 2,VIII,3:2

Lindsay, Bob
All the King's Men 1948,Ja 19,19:2

Lindsay, Christine
Evensong 1933,F 1,13:4

Lindsay, Claudia
Porgy and Bess 1965,Mr 6,17:1

Lindsay, David
Measure for Measure 1969,Je 13,41:3

Lindsay, Earl (Choreographer)
Great Temptations, The 1926,My 19,29:1
Bye Bye Bonnie 1927,Ja 14,15:3
Artists and Models 1927,N 16,28:2
Ups-A-Daisy 1928,O 9,34:2
Luana 1930,S 18,28:1
Ballyhoo 1930,D 23,24:1

Lindsay, Earl (Director)
Tip-Toes 1925,D 29,20:2

Lindsay, Earl (Miscellaneous)
Love Call, The 1927,O 25,33:1

Lindsay, Frank
Whatever Goes Up 1935,N 26,28:2
Chalked Out 1937,Mr 26,24:2
Peter Pan 1954,O 21,30:2

Lindsay, Fred
Vaudeville (Palace) 1928,Ja 24,26:4

Lindsay, George (Director)
Carmilla 1970,D 1,61:2

Lindsay, Howard
Dulcy 1921,Ag 15,14:1
49ers, The 1922,N 7,14:1
Sweet Nell of Old Drury 1923,My 19,16:4
Two by Two 1925,F 24,17:1
By Your Leave 1934,Ja 25,15:3
Life With Father 1939,Ag 15,14:4
Life With Father 1939,N 9,26:2
Life With Father 1939,N 19,X,1:1
Life With Mother 1948,Je 9,36:3
Life With Mother 1948,O 21,32:2
Life With Mother 1948,O 31,II,1:1
Life With Mother 1949,Mr 27,II,1:1
Remains to Be Seen 1951,O 4,37:1
One Bright Day 1952,Mr 20,37:2

Lindsay, Howard (Director)
Good Fellow, The 1926,O 6,22:1
Tommy 1927,Ja 11,36:4

Beaux' Stratagem, The 1928,Je 5,20:1
This Thing Called Love 1928,S 18,32:7
Your Uncle Dudley 1929,N 19,26:4
Up and Up, The 1930,S 9,25:2
Oh, Promise Me 1930,N 25,31:1
Child of Manhattan 1932,Mr 2,15:1
Gay Divorce 1932,N 30,23:4
Party's Over, The 1933,Mr 28,23:3
She Loves Me Not 1933,N 21,22:4
She Loves Me Not 1933,N 26,IX,1:1
Anything Goes 1934,N 22,26:1
Distant Shore, The 1935,F 22,26:2
Slight Case of Murder, A 1935,S 12,28:5
Red, Hot and Blue! 1936,O 30,26:3
Prescott Proposals, The 1953,D 17,53:1
Prescott Proposals, The 1953,D 27,II,3:1
Lovely Light, A 1960,F 9,27:4
Lovely Light, A 1964,Ja 21,24:2

Lindsay, Howard (Original Author)
Hooray for What! 1937,D 2,32:5

Lindsay, Howard (Playwright)
Apartment to Let 1924,Ap 1,18:1
Tommy 1927,Ja 11,36:4
Tommy 1927,Mr 27,VII,1:1
Your Uncle Dudley 1929,N 19,26:4
Oh, Promise Me 1930,N 25,31:1
Tommy 1933,Ag 8,22:5
She Loves Me Not 1933,N 21,22:4
She Loves Me Not 1933,N 26,IX,1:1
She Loves Me Not 1934,My 2,25:1
Anything Goes 1934,N 18,IX,1:7
Anything Goes 1934,N 22,26:1
Slight Case of Murder, A 1935,S 12,28:5
Anything Goes 1935,S 15,IX,1:1
Slight Case of Murder, A 1935,S 22,X,1:1
Achilles Had a Heel 1935,O 14,20:2
Red, Hot and Blue! 1936,O 8,26:1
Red, Hot and Blue! 1936,O 11,X,3:1
Red, Hot and Blue! 1936,O 30,26:3
Anything Goes 1937,Ag 26,24:3
Hooray for What! 1937,N 7,XI,2:4
Great Lady 1938,D 2,26:6
Life With Father 1939,Ag 15,14:4
Life With Father 1939,N 9,26:2
Life With Father 1939,N 19,X,1:1
Life With Father 1940,Mr 3,X,2:5
Life With Father 1940,Ag 18,IX,1:1
Arsenic and Old Lace 1941,Mr 25,26:7
Strip for Action 1942,O 1,26:2
Strip for Action 1942,O 11,VIII,1:1
State of the Union 1945,N 7,21:3
State of the Union 1945,N 15,25:2
State of the Union 1945,N 25,II,1:1
State of the Union 1946,S 8,II,1:1
State of the Union 1947,Jl 15,26:2
Life With Mother 1948,Je 9,36:3
Life With Mother 1948,O 21,32:2
Life With Mother 1948,O 31,II,1:1
Life With Mother 1949,Mr 27,II,1:1
Call Me Madam 1950,O 13,25:1
Call Me Madam 1950,O 22,II,1:1
Remains to Be Seen 1951,O 4,37:1
Call Me Madam 1952,Mr 16,84:3
Remains to Be Seen 1952,D 17,44:4
Remains to Be Seen 1953,Ja 25,II,3:1
Prescott Proposals, The 1953,D 17,53:1
Prescott Proposals, The 1953,D 27,II,3:1
Great Sebastians, The 1956,Ja 5,27:1
Great Sebastians, The 1956,Ja 15,II,1:1
Happy Hunting 1956,D 7,30:1
Happy Hunting 1956,D 16,II,3:1
Tall Story 1959,Ja 30,33:2
Sound of Music, The 1959,N 17,40:2
Anything Goes 1962,My 16,35:1
Mr President 1962,Ag 29,18:4
Mr President 1962,S 26,36:1
Mr President 1962,O 14,II,1:7
Mr President 1962,O 22,34:2
Sound of Music, The 1967,Ap 27,52:1
Life With Father 1967,O 20,53:2
Sound of Music, The 1970,Jl 3,13:1

Lindsay, Howard (Producer)
Slight Case of Murder, A 1935,S 12,28:5
Arsenic and Old Lace 1941,Ja 11,13:2
Arsenic and Old Lace 1942,My 11,18:6
Strip for Action 1942,O 1,26:2
Hasty Heart, The 1945,Ja 4,14:2
Hasty Heart, The 1945,Ja 14,II,1:1
Detective Story 1949,Mr 24,34:2
One Bright Day 1952,Mr 20,37:2
Great Sebastians, The 1956,Ja 5,27:1

Lindsay, Ian
King Lear 1964,My 19,43:2
Comedy of Errors, The 1964,My 21,43:1

Lindsay, Ian (Director)
Experiment, The 1967,My 9,54:2

Lindsay, Jack (Scenic Designer)
Umbrella, The 1965,My 27,31:1

Lindsay, Jack Martin (Costume Designer)
My Sweet Charlie 1966,D 7,56:1

Lindsay, James
Lancashire Lass, The 1931,D 31,16:3
Green Pastures, The 1935,F 27,16:2

Lindsay, John V
Mister Mayor! 1967,Ap 4,36:3
Oh, Johnny: or, Jonny Spielt Auf 1970,Mr 15,88:4

Lindsay, Kevin
Me Nobody Knows, The 1970,My 19,42:1

Lindsay, Lex
Lost Horizons 1934,O 16,31:2
Chalked Out 1937,Mr 26,24:2
Fly Away Home 1937,Ap 27,18:1
Kiss the Boys Goodbye 1938,S 29,30:2
Glamour Preferred 1940,N 16,13:2
Mr and Mrs North 1941,Ja 13,11:2
Moon for the Misbegotten, A 1947,F 21,16:2

Lindsay, Margaret
Another Love Story 1943,O 13,29:2

Lindsay, Mort (Miscellaneous)
Judy Garland 1961,Ap 24,36:1
Bajour 1964,N 24,42:1

Lindsay, Phillip
Mamba's Daughters 1953,Mr 21,12:6
Clandestine on the Morning Line 1961,O 31,28:1

Lindsay, Powell
Tobacco Road 1950,Mr 7,23:2
Born Yesterday 1954,Ja 1,16:6

Lindsay, Powell (Director)
Big White Fog 1940,O 23,26:2

Lindsay, Powell (Producer)
Born Yesterday 1954,Ja 1,16:6

Lindsay, Walter O (Miscellaneous)
Pluma en el Viento; Feather in the Wind 1932,Ap 2,13:4

Lindsay-Hogg, Michael
Taming of the Shrew, The 1957,F 21,30:2

Lindsay-Hogg, Michael (Director)
Cave Dwellers, The 1961,O 16,34:2

Lindsey, Anita
Brother Cain 1941,S 13,21:5

Lindsey, Gene
Gogo Loves You 1964,O 10,19:2
Deer Park, The 1967,F 1,27:2
My Daughter, Your Son 1969,My 14,36:2

Lindsey, Jay
Four Walls 1927,S 20,33:1

Lindsey, Lee
Nervous Set, The 1959,My 13,43:1

Lindsey, Nina
Macbeth 1921,F 18,16:1

Lindsey, Robert
Devil Takes a Bride, The 1938,O 8,10:3
Lorelei 1938,N 30,21:2
Brown Danube, The 1939,My 18,30:4
Not in Our Stars 1941,Ap 26,20:5

Lindsey, Walter O (Director)
Cuando Los Hijos De Eva No Son Los Hijos De Adan; When Eve's Children Are Not Adam's 1932,Ap 23,11:2
De Muy Buena Familia; Of Very Good Family 1932,Ap 29,13:3

Lindsey, Walter O (Miscellaneous)
Tambor y Cascabel; Drum and Bell 1932,Ap 21,25:4

Lindsey, Walter O (Producer)
Forbidden Roads 1928,Ap 17,26:4

Lindsey, Watson
Restless Flame, The 1952,Ap 15,30:6

Lindsley, Murray
Pygmalion 1938,Ja 27,16:3
Captain Jinks of the Horse Marines 1938,Ja 28,16:2

Lindstrom, Eric
Streetcar Named Desire, A 1955,Mr 4,18:2

Lindstrom, Erik
Hamlet 1947,Jl 13,I,47:2

Lindtberg, Leopold (Producer)
Alcestiade 1957,Je 29,11:5

Lindup, David (Miscellaneous)
Stop the World-I Want to Get Off 1962,O 4,45:4

Lindy, Hoppers
Singin' the Blues 1931,S 17,21:3

Lineberger, James
Henry V 1964,My 13,52:1
Way of the World, The 1965,Je 2,40:1

Linehan, Fergus (Lyricist)
Fursey 1962,O 3,47:2

Linehan, Fergus (Playwright)
Fursey 1962,O 3,47:2

Linehan, Joseph
In White America 1965,F 9,42:5

Linenthal, Michael
Lucky Sam McCarver 1950,Ap 15,10:6

Lines, Jack
Yeomen of the Guard, The 1965,Jl 8,34:1
Ruddigore 1965,Ag 27,16:1

Ling, Barbara (Playwright)
Dark Saint, The; Envers d'une Sainte, L' 1932,F 21,VIII,1:6

Ling, Richie
Ed Wynn's Carnival 1920,Ap 6,18:2
Sonny 1921,Ag 17,12:2
National Anthem, The 1922,Ja 24,16:3
Rose Briar 1922,D 26,11:3
Sweet Nell of Old Drury 1923,My 19,16:4
Swan, The 1923,O 24,15:3
Candida 1925,N 10,23:4

Ling, Richie—Cont

Vaudeville (Palace) 1926,D 28,12:3
Road to Rome, The 1927,F 1,24:2
Olympia 1928,O 17,26:1
Perfect Alibi, The 1928,N 28,24:2
Divorce Me, Dear 1931,O 7,29:2
They Don't Mean Any Harm 1932,F 24,25:2
For Services Rendered 1933,Ap 13,15:5
Yellow Jack 1934,Mr 7,22:6
Great Waltz, The 1934,S 24,14:4
Jubilee 1935,O 14,20:1
And Now Goodbye 1937,F 3,26:4

Lingeman, Jean Anne (Composer)
Political Party, A 1963,S 27,17:5

Lingeman, Jean Anne (Lyricist)
Political Party, A 1963,S 27,17:5

Lingeman, Jean Anne (Playwright)
Political Party, A 1963,S 27,17:5

Lingeman, Richard (Composer)
Political Party, A 1963,S 27,17:5

Lingeman, Richard (Lyricist)
Political Party, A 1963,S 27,17:5

Lingeman, Richard (Playwright)
Political Party, A 1963,S 27,17:5

Lingen, Theo
Alt Heidelberg; Student Prince, The
1932,N 20,IX,3:3

Lingenstein, Perry (Miscellaneous)
Macbeth 1968,N 30,49:3

Lingren, Robert
On Your Toes 1954,O 12,24:4

Linhart, James
It Is the Law 1922,N 30,28:2

Linieris, George
Infantry, The 1966,N 15,51:1
Cannibals, The 1968,N 4,60:1

Link, Adolph
Sophie 1920,Mr 3,12:2
Enemy of the People, An 1920,S 7,19:3
Youth 1920,O 27,14:3
Student Prince, The 1924,D 3,25:3
Student Prince, The 1931,Ja 30,18:1

Link, Peter
Salvation 1969,S 25,55:1

Link, Peter (Composer)
Salvation 1969,Mr 13,53:1
Salvation 1969,S 25,55:1

Link, Peter (Director)
Salvation 1969,Mr 13,53:1

Link, Peter (Lyricist)
Salvation 1969,S 25,55:1

Link, Peter (Miscellaneous)
Salvation 1969,Mr 13,53:1

Link, Peter (Playwright)
Salvation 1969,Mr 13,53:1
Salvation 1969,S 25,55:1
Salvation 1969,O 5,II,1:1

Link, Ron (Director)
Glamour, Glory and Gold 1967,O 4,43:1

Linker, Thomas A
Gentlemen of the Press 1928,Ag 28,27:2

Linkey, Harry
Good Old Days, The 1923,Ag 15,21:2

Linklater, Eric (Playwright)
Crisis in Heaven 1944,Je 25,II,1:4
Love in Albania 1949,Jl 17,II,1:6
Atom Doctor, The 1950,S 10,II,3:1
Breakspear on Gascony 1959,Ag 26,25:3

Linkroum, Richard
Hippolytus 1935,Je 15,20:4
Whispering Gallery, The 1935,D 1,II,12:6

Linley, Betty
Six-Cylinder Love 1921,Ag 26,8:2
Great Broxopp, The 1921,N 16,22:1
That Day 1922,O 4,27:3
Pilgrimage, The; Pelerin, Le 1925,N 10,23:2
Merchants of Glory 1925,D 15,28:3
Port O' London 1926,F 10,20:2
Sport of Kings, The 1926,My 5,24:2
Dybbuk, The 1926,D 17,27:2
Fog-Bound 1927,Ap 2,21:2
Taming of the Shrew, The 1927,O 26,26:4
So Am I 1928,Ja 28,9:1
Rivals, The 1930,Mr 14,24:4
Rivals, The 1930,Mr 23,IX,1:1
Breadwinner, The 1931,S 23,19:4
Hay Fever 1931,D 6,VIII,2:8
Hay Fever 1931,D 30,25:1
Party, A 1933,Ag 24,18:4
Private Affair, A 1936,My 15,28:7
Heiress, The 1947,S 30,22:2
Heiress, The 1950,F 9,34:2

Linn, Bambi
Oklahoma! 1943,Ap 1,27:1
Carousel 1945,Ap 20,24:2
Carousel 1945,Ap 29,II,1:1
Alice in Wonderland 1947,Ap 7,19:2
Sally 1948,My 7,31:2
Great to Be Alive! 1950,Mr 24,28:2
Carousel 1950,Je 8,37:2
Carousel 1954,Je 3,32:2
Carousel 1957,S 12,38:2
I Can Get It for You Wholesale 1962,Mr 23,29:1

Linn, Ben
Caroline 1923,F 1,13:2

Linn, Catherine
Boy Meets Girl 1943,Je 23,15:5

Linn, James
Family Reunion, The 1947,N 29,9:2

Linn, Libby
French Touch, The 1945,D 10,18:2

Linn, Margaret
Pale Horse, Pale Rider 1957,O 30,26:1
Room, The 1964,D 10,62:1
Billy Liar 1965,Mr 18,26:1
Love's Labour's Lost 1965,Je 16,46:1
How's the World Treating You? 1966,O 25,50:1
Halfway up the Tree 1967,N 8,52:1
Huui, Huui 1968,N 25,58:1
Disintegration of James Cherry, The
1970,Ja 30,33:3

Linn, Ralph
Carousel 1945,Ap 20,24:2
Me and Juliet 1953,My 29,17:1
Li'l Abner 1956,N 16,24:2

Linn, Ray Jr (Miscellaneous)
Ice Follies 1969,My 23,38:1

Linnane, Joseph
Juno and the Paycock 1937,D 7,32:5
Drama at Inish 1937,D 14,33:2

Linnetz, Edward H
Joy of Serpents 1930,Ap 4,22:4

Linney, Romulus
Merry Wives of Windsor, The 1954,F 17,27:1

Linney, Romulus (Playwright)
Sorrow of Frederick, The 1967,Jl 8,14:2

Linsalata, Joseph
We Bombed in New Haven 1967,D 7,58:1

Linse, Margaret
Seven Mirrors 1945,O 26,17:2

Linsenmann, George (Composer)
Chief Thing, The 1963,Ap 30,27:2

Linsk, Lester (Miscellaneous)
Walking Happy 1966,N 28,47:1

Linskie, Margaret
Broken Hearts of Broadway 1944,Je 13,16:2

Linsley, Ann
If in the Green Wood 1947,Ja 17,27:6

Linthicum, Lotta
Blue Eyes 1921,F 22,11:2
Ice-Bound 1923,F 12,16:2
Shelf, The 1926,S 28,31:1
Piggy 1927,Ja 12,22:2
Wild Man of Borneo, The 1927,S 14,29:2
Atlas and Eva 1928,F 7,30:2
Skyrocket, The 1929,Ja 12,14:7
Nice Women 1929,Je 11,27:4
She Lived Next to the Firehouse 1931,F 11,23:1
Papavert 1931,D 30,25:1

Linton, Betty Hyatt
Wonderful Town 1963,F 15,10:2
Pal Joey 1963,My 30,21:1
How to Succeed in Business Without Really Trying
1966,Ap 21,45:1
Wonderful Town 1967,My 18,50:1
Maggie Flynn 1968,O 24,52:1

Linton, Betty Hyatt (Choreographer)
Finian's Rainbow 1967,Ap 6,44:1

Linton, Betty Hyatt (Miscellaneous)
Music Man, The 1965,Je 17,26:4

Linton, William
Rogues and Vagabonds 1930,My 8,32:5
Song of Norway 1958,Je 23,19:2
Song of Norway 1959,Je 26,16:2
Wildcat 1960,D 17,20:2
Family Affair, A 1962,Ja 29,17:1

Lintz, Horace
Joan of Arc 1927,Ap 15,26:2

Linville, Albert
Tree Grows in Brooklyn, A 1951,Ap 20,24:3
Wonderful Town 1953,F 26,22:3
Damn Yankees 1955,My 6,17:1
Let It Ride 1961,O 13,27:4

Linville, Joanne
Daughter of Silence 1961,D 1,28:1

Linville, Lawrence
More Stately Mansions 1967,N 1,40:1
In the Matter of J Robert Oppenheimer
1968,Je 7,31:1

Linwood, Anne
Infinite Shoeblack, The 1930,F 18,28:1

Linwood, Robert
Old Maid, The 1949,Ja 27,20:6
Post Road 1949,Ap 28,27:3

Lion, Eugene (Director)
Women at the Tomb, The 1961,Ap 25,41:1

Lion, Eva
Dybbuk, The 1964,F 4,30:2
Each Had Six Wings 1964,Mr 12,39:1

Lion, Leon M
Count X 1921,My 29,VI,1:7
Listeners 1928,Mr 11,VIII,1:3
This Way to Paradise 1930,Ja 31,24:2
Money! Money! 1931,Mr 15,IX,2:8

Lion, Leon M (Director)
Many Waters 1929,S 26,27:1

Lion, Leon M (Miscellaneous)
Many Waters 1929,S 26,27:1
While Parents Sleep 1934,Je 5,28:2

Lion, Leon M (Producer)
Count X 1921,My 29,VI,1:7
In the Snare 1924,Jl 13,VII,1:6
Cristilinda 1925,N 1,VIII,1:3
Untitled-Play 1927,O 2,II,7:2
Night Club Queen 1933,D 3,IX,7:6

Lion, Margo
Hetaerengespraeche 1927,Ja 9,VII,4:1
Es Liegt in der Luft 1928,S 23,IX,2:2
Ich Tanze um die Welt mit Dir 1930,Ag 31,VIII,2:1
Alles Schwindel 1931,Je 7,VIII,2:5
Roulette 1932,Mr 27,VIII,3:1

Lionel, Alain
Phedre 1963,O 21,39:1
Berenice 1963,O 30,46:1

Lionello, Alberto
Venetian Twins, The 1968,My 29,23:1

Liotta, Jerome (Lighting Director)
Moon Is Blue, The 1961,Ag 9,29:1
I Want You 1961,S 15,29:1

Liotta, Jerome (Miscellaneous)
I Want You 1961,S 15,29:1

Liotta, Jerome (Scenic Designer)
Jack in the Box 1960,My 19,43:3
Little Hut, The 1961,Jl 26,34:2
Moon Is Blue, The 1961,Ag 9,29:1
Tender Trap, The 1961,Ag 26,15:1

LiPari, Victor
Thank You, Miss Victoria 1966,Ap 12,43:1
This Is the Rill Speaking 1966,Ap 12,43:1
Chicago 1966,Ap 13,36:1
Tom Paine 1968,Mr 26,38:1
Futz 1968,Je 14,39:1

Lipari Trio
Cortez 1929,N 5,32:2

Lipinskaja, Dela
Schoen und Schick 1928,Ag 26,II,1:2

Lipinsky, Isaac
Little Tailor, The 1938,Mr 21,18:2
In-Laws 1960,O 17,32:4

Lipinsky, Isaac (Producer)
In-Laws 1960,O 17,32:4

Lipinsky, Isidore
World Is a Stage, The 1962,N 5,37:4
Country Boy, The 1963,O 28,20:1
Both Kooney Lemels 1964,O 12,37:2

Lipinsky, Isidore (Producer)
World Is a Stage, The 1962,N 5,37:4
Both Kooney Lemels 1964,O 12,37:2

Lipkowsk, Lydia
Merry Widow, The 1921,S 6,13:1

Lipman, Clara
That French Lady 1927,Mr 16,29:3

Lipman, Clara (Playwright)
Nature's Nobleman 1921,N 15,23:2

Lippa, Louis A
Aria Da Capo 1958,My 21,40:1
Aria Da Capo 1958,Je 27,18:5

Lippa, Louis A (Director)
House Remembered, A 1957,F 7,20:2

Lippa, Louis A (Playwright)
House Remembered, A 1957,F 7,20:2
Breaking Wall, The 1960,Ja 26,27:5
Seven at Dawn, The 1961,Ap 18,43:1

Lipper, Arthur Jr (R A Reppil) (Producer)
Saluta 1934,Ag 29,13:4

Lippich, Angelo
Bajadere, Die 1925,O 2,26:2

Lippit, Margaret
Antigone 1923,My 4,18:4

Lippman, Mortiber
Revolt of the Beavers, The 1937,My 21,19:2

Lippman, Sidney (Composer)
Barefoot Boy With Cheek 1947,Ap 4,20:2

Lippold, Tiana
Tom Paine 1969,Mr 30,71:2

Lippy, Carl
Pimpernel! 1964,Ja 7,26:6

Lipscomb, W P (Playwright)
Clive of India 1934,F 18,IX,3:7
Thank You, Mr Pepys; Ninety Sail 1937,D 1,27:2
Lady Maria, The 1947,Ag 5,26:1

Lipscott, Alan (Lyricist)
Right This Way 1938,Ja 6,22:3

Lipscott, Alan (Playwright)
Three After Three 1939,N 25,13:5
Keep Off the Grass 1940,My 24,22:6
Walk With Music 1940,Je 5,33:2
Off the Record 1940,D 1,63:5
Johnny on the Spot 1942,Ja 9,24:2

Lipsett, Richard (Director)
Epitaph for George Dillon 1960,D 29,17:1

Lipshitz, M (Playwright)
From Morn to Midnight 1931,S 22,30:4

Lipsky, David (Miscellaneous)
Jackass, The 1960,Mr 24,39:2
Yeomen of the Guard, The 1961,Ap 28,23:1
Mikado, The 1961,My 5,23:1
Grand Duke, The 1961,My 12,24:1
Princess Ida 1961,My 19,23:1

Lipsky, David (Miscellaneous)—Cont
  Iolanthe 1961,My 26,29:6
  H M S Pinafore 1961,Je 9,29:5
  Student Prince, The 1961,Jl 14,14:1
Lipsky, David (Producer)
  Merry Widow, The 1961,O 27,28:2
  Vagabond King, The 1961,N 24,36:1
  Gondoliers, The 1961,D 8,44:1
Lipson, Arthur
  Dear Sir 1924,S 24,21:3
  Oh! Oh! Nurse 1925,D 8,28:4
  Americana 1926,Jl 27,15:3
  Animal Crackers 1928,O 24,26:2
Lipson, Kalman (Playwright)
  It's Never Too Late for Happiness 1968,O 21,59:3
Lipson, Paul
  Criminals, The 1941,D 22,24:3
  Lily of the Valley 1942,Ja 27,25:2
  Heads or Tails 1947,My 3,10:6
  Remains to Be Seen 1951,O 4,37:1
  I've Got Sixpence 1952,D 3,44:2
  Carnival in Flanders 1953,S 9,38:2
  Vamp, The 1955,N 11,30:1
  Fiorello! 1962,Je 14,24:1
  Fiddler on the Roof 1964,S 23,56:2
  Fiddler on the Roof 1970,F 28,20:1
Lipstiz, Hilary (Producer)
  Bonds of Interest, The 1958,My 7,43:1
  Under the Sycamore Tree 1960,Mr 8,37:2
Lipston, Marcia
  Noye's Fludde 1959,Mr 17,41:2
Lipton, Albert
  Revolt of the Beavers, The 1937,My 21,19:2
  Strings, My Lord, Are False, The 1942,My 20,24:2
Lipton, Ann
  Vie Parisienne, La 1941,N 6,20:3
Lipton, Bill
  Family, The 1943,Mr 31,22:4
Lipton, Celia
  Maggie 1953,F 19,20:2
  John Murray Anderson's Almanac 1953,D 11,42:2
Lipton, George
  Robin Hood 1944,N 8,28:2
  Annie Get Your Gun 1946,My 17,14:2
  Regina 1949,N 1,32:2
  Merry Widow, The 1957,Ap 11,36:6
  13 Daughters 1961,Mr 3,17:2
Lipton, George (Director)
  Lady in the Dark 1952,Mr 8,11:3
Lipton, James
  Autumn Garden, The 1951,Mr 8,36:2
  Autumn Garden, The 1951,Mr 18,II,1:1
  Dark Legend 1952,Mr 25,24:2
Lipton, James (Lyricist)
  Miss Emily Adam 1960,Mr 30,43:1
  Nowhere to Go But Up 1962,N 12,36:2
  Sherry! 1967,Mr 29,39:1
Lipton, James (Playwright)
  Miss Emily Adam 1960,Mr 30,43:1
  Nowhere to Go But Up 1962,N 12,36:2
  Sherry! 1967,Mr 29,39:1
Lipton, Lynne
  Along Came a Spider 1963,My 28,33:1
  Awakening of Spring, The 1964,My 13,50:1
  Drums in the Night 1967,My 18,54:1
Lipton, Michael
  Sing Me No Lullaby 1954,O 15,17:2
  Rendezvous at Senlis 1961,F 28,39:2
  Lover, The 1964,Ja 6,35:1
  Play 1964,Ja 6,35:1
  Long Christmas Dinner, The 1966,S 7,53:1
  Hamp 1967,Mr 10,32:1
  Inquest 1970,Ap 24,38:1
Lipton, Michel
  Trigon, The 1965,O 11,62:2
Lipton, Miriam
  Legend of Leonora, The 1926,My 1,10:1
  Knight of the Burning Pestle, The 1927,Ap 23,15:1
Lipton, Richard
  Triumph of Robert Emmet, The 1969,My 8,54:1
Lipton, Richard (Miscellaneous)
  Dracula Sabbat 1970,O 2,28:2
Lipton, Susan
  Journey of the Fifth Horse, The 1966,Ap 22,36:1
Liquigli, Michael
  Macbeth 1967,Jl 31,21:1
Lisa, Luba
  Carnival! 1961,Ap 14,22:2
  West Side Story 1964,Ap 9,24:2
  I Had a Ball 1964,D 16,50:1
Lisanby, Charles (Lighting Director)
  Little Glass Clock, The 1956,Mr 27,40:2
  All in Love 1961,N 11,15:2
Lisanby, Charles (Miscellaneous)
  Hotel Paradiso 1957,Ap 12,22:2
Lisanby, Charles (Scenic Designer)
  All in Love 1961,N 11,15:2
Lisbona
  Bitter Sweet 1929,N 6,30:2
Lisby, Maurice
  Walk Hard 1944,D 1,28:2
  Henri Christophe 1945,Je 7,24:5
  Walk Hard 1946,Mr 28,34:2

Lischner, Rose
  Milk and Honey 1961,O 11,52:1
Liscinsky, Michael
  Tempest, The 1970,F 15,67:1
Lisetskaya, Anna
  Lysistrata 1925,D 15,28:2
Lishchiner, Leon
  Vie Parisienne, La 1941,N 6,20:3
Lishner, Leon
  Consul, The 1950,Mr 2,32:3
  Consul, The 1950,Mr 16,41:1
  Consul, The 1950,Mr 26,II,1:1
  Threepenny Opera, The 1954,Mr 11,26:5
  Threepenny Opera, The 1954,Mr 21,II,1:1
  Saint of Bleecker Street, The 1954,D 28,21:1
  Saint of Bleecker Street, The 1955,Ja 2,II,1:1
Lisle, Lucille
  Stepdaughters of War 1930,O 7,27:1
  Merchant of Venice, The 1930,D 3,29:2
  Widow in Green, A 1931,N 21,21:4
  Alice Sit-By-The-Fire 1932,Mr 8,19:3
Lison, David (Choreographer)
  Shylock and His Daughter 1947,S 30,22:2
Liss, Judith (Miscellaneous)
  Hot Feet 1970,D 22,38:1
Liss, Ronny
  Journey to Jerusalem 1940,O 7,21:2
Lissek, Leon
  Persecution and Assassination of Marat As
    Performed by the Inmates of the Asylum of
    Charenton Under the Direction of the Marquis de
    Sade, The 1965,D 28,35:1
Lissim, Simon (Scenic Designer)
  Annonce Faite a Marie, L'; Tidings Brought to
    Mary, The 1942,My 21,24:1
Lissman, Edward
  Crime Marches on 1935,O 24,19:1
List, Shelley (Miscellaneous)
  Entertain a Ghost 1962,Ap 10,48:1
Liste, Margaret
  Lovely Lady 1927,D 30,22:1
Lister, Dorothy
  Here's Where I Belong 1968,Mr 4,32:1
  Of Thee I Sing 1969,Mr 8,19:1
Lister, Eve
  King and I, The 1955,My 17,33:4
Lister, Francis
  Mary, Mary, Quite Contrary 1923,S 12,14:1
  Dishonored Lady 1930,Ja 26,VIII,2:1
  Dishonored Lady 1930,F 5,27:1
  Richard of Bordeaux 1934,F 4,IX,2:2
  Richard of Bordeaux 1934,F 15,16:2
  Red Cat, The 1934,S 20,21:1
  Substitute for Murder 1935,O 23,18:6
  Follow Your Saint 1936,O 11,X,3:1
  Macbeth 1942,Jl 26,VIII,1:7
  Indifferent Shepherd, The 1948,Mr 14,II,2:4
Lister, Lance
  Wake Up and Dream 1929,D 31,14:3
Lister, Laurier
  Flashing Stream, The 1938,S 2,21:4
  Flashing Stream, The 1939,Ap 11,19:2
Lister, Laurier (Director)
  Joyce Grenfell Requests the Pleasure
    1955,O 11,48:1
Lister, Laurier (Playwright)
  Soldier and the Gentlewoman, The
    1933,My 7,IX,1:4
  She, Too, Was Young 1938,S 4,X,2:1
Lister, Laurier (Producer)
  Joyce Grenfell 1958,Ap 8,32:1
Lister, Moira
  Don't Listen, Ladies 1948,D 29,16:2
Lister, Walter (Playwright)
  Spread Eagle 1927,Ap 5,30:2
  Spread Eagle 1927,Ap 10,VIII,1:1
  Spread Eagle 1929,Jl 22,VII,1:3
  Spread Eagle 1929,N 10,X,4:8
  Spread Eagle 1935,N 5,33:6
Listerino, Herman
  Keep Shufflin' 1928,F 28,18:3
Listman, Ryan
  Saint Joan 1968,Ja 5,42:1
  Tiger at the Gates 1968,Mr 1,30:1
  Spiro Who? 1969,My 19,55:1
  Spiro Who? 1969,Je 15,II,3:6
Litel, John
  Thoroughbreds 1924,S 9,12:1
  Beaten Track, The 1926,F 9,23:2
  Sherlock Holmes 1928,F 21,18:4
  Adventure 1928,S 26,25:2
  Back Seat Drivers 1928,D 26,14:4
  Ladies of Creation 1931,Ag 30,VIII,1:7
  Ladies of Creation 1931,S 9,25:1
  Lilly Turner 1932,S 20,26:1
  Before Morning 1933,F 10,13:4
  Strange Gods 1933,Ap 17,16:6
  Lambs Gambol 1933,Ap 24,10:1
  First Legion, The 1934,O 2,18:2
  Ceiling Zero 1935,Ap 2,24:3
  Ceiling Zero 1935,Ap 11,26:2
  Life's Too Short 1935,S 21,18:5
  Room Service 1935,N 17,II,7:7

Litel, John—Cont
  Hell Freezes Over 1935,D 30,14:2
  Sweet Aloes 1936,Mr 5,24:5
Lithgow, Arthur
  Audition of the Apprentice Theatre 1939,Je 2,26:2
  Cure for Matrimony 1939,O 26,26:3
  Steel 1939,D 20,30:2
  Macbeth 1955,O 8,12:6
Lithgow, Arthur (Director)
  Troilus and Cressida 1953,Ag 19,25:2
  Thesmophoriazusae, The; Goddesses of Athens,
    The 1955,D 14,52:4
  Village, The: A Party 1968,N 13,39:1
Lithgow, John
  White House Happening 1967,Ag 27,II,4:8
  Knack With Horses, A 1970,D 21,52:1
Lithgow, Minnie
  Unto Such Glory 1937,My 7,28:2
Litke, Carmen
  Hair 1970,Ja 13,39:1
Litomy, Leslie
  Naughty-Naught '00 1937,Ja 25,23:2
  Sing Out the News 1938,S 26,12:5
  Sweet Charity 1942,D 29,26:4
  Violet 1944,O 25,16:1
  Cradle Will Rock, The 1947,D 27,11:2
  Joy to the World 1948,Mr 19,28:2
  Liar, The 1950,My 19,30:2
  Those That Play the Clowns 1966,N 25,48:1
Litonius, Marian
  Venetian, The 1931,N 2,26:1
Littau, Joseph
  Carmen Jones 1943,D 3,26:2
Littau, Joseph (Miscellaneous)
  Three Wishes for Jamie 1952,Mr 22,9:2
Littau, Joseph (Musical Director)
  Carmen Jones 1943,D 19,II,9:1
  Carousel 1945,Ap 20,24:2
  Love Life 1948,O 8,31:2
Littell, Robert (Playwright)
  Gather Ye Rosebuds 1934,N 29,33:2
  Gather Ye Rosebuds 1934,D 2,X,1:1
Little, Alfred
  Phoebe of Quality Street 1921,My 10,20:1
  Humoresque 1923,F 28,13:2
  Sandro Botticelli 1923,Mr 27,24:2
  Blue Bird, The 1923,D 26,13:3
  Bit o' Love, A 1925,My 13,24:2
  Clouds 1925,S 3,32:1
  Androcles and the Lion 1925,N 24,28:1
Little, B K
  Take a Brace 1923,Ap 20,20:3
Little, Betty Greene
  On Whitman Avenue 1946,My 9,28:2
  Farther Off From Heaven 1947,Je 4,33:3
  Summer and Smoke 1947,Jl 9,18:5
  Summer and Smoke 1948,O 7,33:2
  Summer and Smoke 1948,O 17,II,1:1
  Southern Exposure 1950,S 27,36:3
Little, Bill
  Snapshots of 1921 1921,Je 3,19:2
Little, Cleavon
  MacBird! 1967,F 23,38:1
  Scuba Duba 1967,O 11,36:1
  Hamlet 1968,Jl 4,15:1
  Jimmy Shine 1968,D 6,52:1
  Someone's Comin' Hungry 1969,Ap 1,51:1
  Ofay Watcher, The 1969,S 16,40:1
  Ofay Watcher, The 1969,S 21,II,1:2
  Purlie 1970,Mr 16,53:1
  Purlie Victorious 1970,Mr 22,II,3:1
Little, D Muir
  Hamlet 1923,N 20,23:3
Little, David
  Falstaff 1966,Je 20,27:1
  Murder in the Cathedral 1966,Je 21,38:1
  Twelfth Night 1966,Je 23,28:1
  Julius Caesar 1966,Je 24,29:2
Little, Florence
  Babes in Toyland 1930,D 22,17:1
Little, George A (Composer)
  Brown Buddies 1930,O 8,29:1
Little, Holmer (Playwright)
  Raw Meat 1933,Mr 23,13:2
Little, James
  Sons o' Fun 1941,D 2,28:2
Little, Jimmy
  Bruno and Sidney 1949,My 4,38:2
Little, Lillian
  Playboy of Newark, The 1943,Mr 20,11:2
  Queen After Death 1956,Mr 13,33:2
Little, Little Jack
  Vaudeville (Palace) 1932,My 30,16:7
Little, Lucille (Costume Designer)
  Oh, Mr Meadowbrook! 1948,D 27,17:2
  Big Knife, The 1949,F 25,27:5
  Come Back, Little Sheba 1950,F 16,28:5
Little, Muir
  Via Crucis 1923,N 13,25:2
Little, Roger
  Cinderella on Broadway 1920,Je 25,18:1
  George White's Scandals 1922,Ag 29,10:1
Little, Susan
  Hair 1970,Ja 13,39:1

Little, Sylvia
Mob, The 1920,O 11,18:1
Lady, The 1923,D 5,23:2
Little, Terence (Miscellaneous)
Li'l Abner 1956,N 16,24:2
Greenwillow 1960,Mr 9,38:1
Let It Ride 1961,O 13,27:4
Here's Love 1963,O 4,28:1
Folies Bergere 1964,Je 3,36:1
Half a Sixpence 1965,Ap 26,38:2
Mame 1966,My 25,41:1
Golden Rainbow 1968,F 5,27:1
Maggie Flynn 1968,O 24,52:1
Fig Leaves Are Falling, The 1969,Ja 3,19:1
Strada, La 1969,D 15,63:1
Applause 1970,Mr 31,35:1
Little, Terry
Streets Are Guarded, The 1944,N 21,19:7
Anniversary Waltz 1954,Ap 8,34:1
Little Billy
Mamma's Affair 1920,Ja 20,10:1
A la Carte 1927,Ag 18,25:3
Little Fred, and his Football Dogs
Folies Bergere 1939,D 25,28:2
Littlefield, Bancroft Jr
William Had the Words! 1964,Mr 30,36:1
Littlefield, Carl (Choreographer)
Funzapoppin 1949,Jl 1,16:2
Hollywood Ice Revue 1953,Ja 16,17:2
Hollywood Ice Revue 1954,Ja 15,16:2
Littlefield, Carl (Director)
Funzapoppin 1949,Jl 1,16:2
Hollywood Ice Revue 1953,Ja 16,17:2
Hollywood Ice Revue 1954,Ja 15,16:2
Littlefield, Catherine (Choreographer)
American Jubilee 1940,My 13,20:5
Hold On to Your Hats 1940,S 12,30:3
It Happens on Ice 1940,O 11,24:3
Crazy With the Heat 1941,Ja 15,18:2
Crazy With the Heat 1941,Ja 31,15:2
Kiss for Cinderella, A 1942,Mr 11,22:2
Stars on Ice 1942,Jl 3,12:2
Stars on Ice (2d Edition) 1943,Je 25,13:2
Follow the Girls 1944,Ap 10,15:2
Hats Off to Ice 1944,Je 23,15:2
Firebird of Florence 1945,Mr 23,13:4
Icetime 1946,Je 21,20:5
Icetime 1947,My 29,28:2
Howdy Mr Ice 1948,Je 25,28:5
Howdy, Mr Ice of 1950 1949,My 27,24:2
Funzapoppin 1949,Jl 1,16:2
Littlefield, Catherine (Director)
Stars on Ice 1942,Jl 3,12:2
Stars on Ice (2d Edition) 1943,Je 25,13:2
Hats Off to Ice 1944,Je 23,15:2
Icetime 1946,Je 21,20:5
Icetime 1947,My 29,28:2
Howdy Mr Ice 1948,Je 25,28:5
Funzapoppin 1949,Jl 1,16:2
Littlefield, Catherine (Miscellaneous)
Sweethearts 1947,Ja 22,31:2
Littlefield, Dorothie
Vagabond King, The 1943,Je 30,24:2
Littlefield, Dorothie (Choreographer)
Hats Off to Ice 1944,Je 23,15:2
Icetime 1946,Je 21,20:5
Icetime 1947,My 29,28:2
Hollywood Ice Revue 1953,Ja 16,17:2
Littlefield, Dorothie (Director)
Hollywood Ice Revue 1953,Ja 16,17:2
Littlefield, James (Composer)
Hats Off to Ice 1944,Je 23,15:2
Icetime 1946,Je 21,20:5
Icetime 1947,My 29,28:2
Littlefield, Nick
Kismet 1965,Je 23,45:1
Littlejohn, Dorothy
Escape This Night 1938,Ap 23,18:1
Ah, Wilderness! 1941,O 3,26:2
Littlejohn, Peggy
Let's Face It 1941,O 30,26:2
Littler, Emile
Michael and Mary 1929,D 14,23:3
His Majesty's Car 1930,O 24,30:1
Littler, Emile (Playwright)
All in Marriage 1936,O 29,31:3
Littler, Emile (Producer)
Affairs of State 1952,Ag 22,12:2
Littler, Prince (Producer)
Teahouse of the August Moon, The
1955,My 10,24:1
Littlewood, Joan (Director)
Taste of Honey, A 1959,Mr 15,II,3:1
Hostage, The 1960,S 21,42:1
Oh What a Lovely War 1964,O 1,30:1
Oh What a Lovely War 1964,O 11,II,1:1
MacBird! 1967,Ap 11,54:5
MacBird! 1967,Ap 16,II,3:6
Mrs Wilson's Diary 1967,O 8,II,13:5
Littlewood, Joan (Producer)
Taste of Honey, A 1959,Mr 15,II,3:1
Hostage, The 1960,O 2,II,1:1

Litvack, Barry (Playwright)
Slow Memories 1970,N 18,41:1
Litvak, Zelda
Riverside Drive 1931,Ja 6,24:2
Litvinas, Zita
De Sade Illustrated 1969,My 13,42:4
Litvinoff, Olga
Maitresse de Roi 1926,D 1,24:1
Litvinoff, Seymour (Producer)
Girl of the Golden West, The 1957,N 6,44:1
Cry of the Raindrop 1961,Mr 8,38:1
Leonard Bernstein's Theater Songs 1965,Je 29,27:2
Litwack, Ned C (Miscellaneous)
Heaven on Earth 1948,S 17,29:2
Litwin, Wallace (Miscellaneous)
Decline and Fall of the Entire World As Seen
Through the Eyes of Cole Porter Revisited, The
1965,Mr 31,24:2
Ben Bagley's New Cole Porter Revue
1965,D 23,20:1
Litwyn, Alyce
Censored 1938,F 28,18:2
Litz, Katherine
Crystal Heart, The 1960,F 16,31:2
Line of Least Existence, The 1968,Mr 25,53:1
Soap Opera 1968,My 10,54:7
Litz, Tommy
Ice Capades 1964,Ag 27,27:2
Ice Capades 1966,Je 2,50:2
Ice Capades 1967,Je 2,33:1
Ice Capades 1969,Ja 8,42:1
Ice Capades 1970,Ja 7,35:1
Liu, Frank
Gandhi 1970,O 21,37:1
Liuzzi, Fernando (Composer)
Oedipus Rex 1937,My 9,XI,7:5
Livadas, M
Screwball, The 1957,My 25,24:7
Livanov, Boris
Dead Souls 1965,F 5,34:1
Kremlin Chimes 1965,F 25,23:1
Lively, Bob
Sunny Days 1928,F 9,29:1
Flying High 1930,Mr 4,24:4
Lively, Robert (Director)
Scrap Book 1932,Ag 2,20:3
Church Mouse, A 1933,Je 27,13:7
Liveright, Horace (Producer)
Hamlet 1925,N 10,23:1
Black Boy 1926,S 26,VIII,2:7
Black Boy 1926,O 7,30:2
American Tragedy, An 1926,O 12,31:2
Dracula 1927,O 6,29:1
Liverman, Phyllis
Me and Molly 1948,F 27,27:2
Livesay, Barrie
Barbara's Wedding 1931,O 9,21:1
Father, The 1931,O 9,21:1
Livesay, Jack
Yellow Sands 1927,S 12,29:3
Time and the Hour 1936,O 5,24:1
Apple Cart, The 1956,O 19,23:1
Look Back in Anger 1957,O 2,28:2
Livesey, Roger
Country Wife, The 1936,D 2,34:1
Storm Over Patsy 1937,Mr 2,16:4
Storm Over Patsy 1937,Mr 9,26:4
Twelfth Night 1950,D 3,II,3:1
Hamlet 1969,Mr 2,II,3:1
Hamlet 1969,My 2,38:1
Livesey, Sam
Bulldog Drummond 1921,D 27,10:2
Runaways, The 1928,D 2,X,4:1
Father of Lies 1935,Ja 27,VIII,3:1
Livikou, Ilya
Screwball, The 1957,My 25,24:7
Livings, Henry (Playwright)
Eh? 1966,O 17,47:1
Eh? 1966,N 6,II,1:1
Honor and Offer 1968,D 1,II,3:1
Honor and Offer 1969,My 14,36:1
Livingston, Arthur (Translator)
Living Mask, The 1924,Ja 22,15:1
Naked 1926,N 9,31:2
Livingston, Billy (Costume Designer)
Calling All Stars 1934,D 14,28:2
Who's Who 1938,Mr 2,16:2
Naked Genius, The 1943,O 22,20:5
Laffing Room Only 1944,D 25,15:4
Good Night Ladies 1945,Ja 18,16:2
Icetime 1946,Je 21,20:5
Icetime 1947,My 29,28:2
Howdy Mr Ice 1948,Je 25,28:5
All for Love 1949,Ja 24,16:5
Howdy, Mr Ice of 1950 1949,My 27,24:2
Ice Capades 1952,S 12,18:1
Ice Capades 1953,S 11,25:1
Ice Capades 1954,S 16,37:1
Ice Capades 1955,S 15,38:1
Ice Capades 1956,S 13,41:2
Ice Capades 1957,S 5,33:2
Ice Capades 1958,S 4,33:2
Ice Capades 1959,S 4,12:1

Livingston, Billy (Costume Designer)—Cont
Ice Capades 1960,S 1,30:1
Ice Capades 1961,Ag 31,24:4
Ice Capades 1962,Ag 30,34:1
Ice Capades 1963,Ag 29,37:2
Ice Capades 1966,Je 2,50:2
Livingston, Charles D
Cotton Stockings 1923,D 19,16:2
Livingston, Donald C (Miscellaneous)
Who Is Leslie? 1941,My 20,15:5
Livingston, Eleanor
Lady Billy 1920,D 15,18:2
Clinging Vine, The 1922,D 25,20:2
Mister Romeo 1927,S 6,35:3
Livingston, Evelyn
Mismates 1925,Ap 14,27:2
Livingston, Henrietta
Pleasure Bound 1929,F 19,22:4
Livingston, J H (Producer)
Recruiting Officer, The 1958,F 8,12:2
Livingston, Jack
Deputy, The 1964,F 27,26:1
Livingston, James
Happy Birthday 1946,N 1,31:2
Livingston, Jay (Composer)
Oh Captain! 1958,F 5,21:2
Let It Ride 1961,O 13,27:4
Livingston, Jay (Lyricist)
Oh Captain! 1958,F 5,21:2
Let It Ride 1961,O 13,27:4
Livingston, Jerry (Composer)
Brights Lights of 1944 1943,S 17,27:4
Livingston, Jock
Recruiting Officer, The 1958,F 8,12:2
Antigone 1959,S 16,46:2
Balcony, The 1960,Mr 4,21:1
Livingston, John
Richard III 1967,Je 14,43:1
Merry Wives of Windsor, The 1967,Ag 4,18:1
Livingston, Patricia
Play of Daniel, The 1960,D 27,23:6
Livingston, Ray
Lady From the Sea, The 1935,D 14,11:3
Livingston, Raymond
Fuente Ovejuna; Sheep Well, The 1936,My 3,II,4:1
Livingston, Robert
Revolt of the Beavers, The 1937,My 21,19:2
Livingston, Robert (Director)
Match-Play 1966,O 12,37:1
Party for Divorce, A 1966,O 12,37:1
How to Steal an Election 1968,O 14,56:1
Me Nobody Knows, The 1970,My 19,42:1
Me Nobody Knows, The 1970,My 31,II,1:6
Livingston, Robert (Miscellaneous)
Next President, The 1958,Ap 10,34:3
Saturday Night Kid, The 1958,My 16,22:1
Livingston, Robert L (Miscellaneous)
Kelly 1965,F 8,28:2
All in Good Time 1965,F 19,25:1
Livingston, Robert L (Producer)
Chaparral 1958,S 10,38:2
Dr Galley 1970,Ja 23,25:1
Transfers 1970,Ja 23,25:1
Rooming House, The 1970,Ja 23,25:1
Livingston, Ruth
Young and Beautiful, The 1959,My 29,13:1
Delightful Season, A 1960,S 29,30:1
Livingstone, Charles
If I Were You 1931,S 24,21:1
Bloody Laughter 1931,D 5,20:6
Wolves 1932,Ja 7,26:3
Livshitz, Moshe (Playwright)
Hershel, The Jester 1948,D 14,39:2
Lix, Germaine
Revue des Femmes Nouvelles, La 1926,D 5,VIII,6:1
Lizaso, Antonio (Musical Director)
Triumph of Delight 1965,My 1,19:1
Lizt, Herbert
Wooden Idol, The 1930,My 13,27:2
Lizzio, Sara
Barbara 1929,N 18,24:5
Ljungberg, Goeta
Three Musketeers 1929,O 13,IX,4:7
Tales of Hoffmann 1932,Ja 10,VIII,1:6
Llech, Richard
All My Sons 1948,My 12,33:3
Llelan, Everett
Vaudeville (Palace) 1929,Mr 25,33:2
Llewellyn, Dorothy
Cape Cod Follies 1929,S 19,37:2
Llewellyn, Richard (Original Author)
Time for Singing, A 1966,My 23,48:2
Llewellyn, Richard (Playwright)
Poison Pen 1937,Ag 10,22:3
Lloyd, Alice
Vaudeville (Palace) 1925,S 29,31:2
Vaudeville (Hippodrome) 1926,My 8,29:2
Lloyd, Alma
Simpleton of the Unexpected Isles, The
1935,F 19,27:5
Story to Be Whispered 1937,Ag 20,21:4
Lloyd, Ann
Show Boat 1948,S 9,33:2

Lloyd, Anzonetta
Desert Sands 1922,F 14,20:1
Vagabond, The 1923,D 28,13:4
Lloyd, Bernard
Much Ado About Nothing 1968,O 16,33:1
Square Root of Wonderful, The 1970,Mr 12,47:1
Lloyd, Bob E
Scarlet Lullaby 1968,Mr 11,48:1
Lloyd, Christopher
Red, White and Maddox 1969,Ja 27,27:1
Lloyd, Doris
Cinderella on Broadway 1920,Je 25,18:1
Inspector Calls, An 1947,O 22,38:2
Lloyd, Frank
Black Scandals 1928,O 27,23:2
Lloyd, Frederick
Makers of Light 1922,My 24,22:3
Avalanche 1932,F 14,VIII,1:8
Napoleon: The Hundred Days 1932,Ap 19,25:2
Seagull, The 1936,Je 21,IX,1:5
Merchant of Venice, The 1938,My 15,X,1:5
Lloyd, George
Shoemaker's Holiday, The 1938,Ja 3,17:2
One for the Money 1939,F 6,9:2
Burning Deck, The 1940,Mr 2,9:2
'Tis of Thee 1940,O 28,21:3
Rally 'Round The Girls 1942,Mr 29,VIII,2:2
Hand in Glove 1944,D 5,19:1
Hand in Glove 1944,D 10,II,5:1
Saint Joan 1954,S 18,12:1
Colombe 1965,F 24,33:1
Lloyd, Gladys
Applesauce 1925,S 29,31:2
Henry-Behave 1926,Ag 24,19:4
Young Alexander 1929,Mr 13,28:2
I Want My Wife 1930,Mr 21,30:7
Mr Samuel 1930,N 11,28:4
Lloyd, Henry (Composer)
Belmont Varieties 1932,S 29,17:2
Lloyd, Henry (Lyricist)
Belmont Varieties 1932,S 29,17:2
Lloyd, Irving
Food for Midas 1942,Ja 31,12:7
Lloyd, Jack
Winter Soldiers 1942,N 30,19:2
Patriots, The 1943,Ja 30,11:2
Lloyd, Jefferson
Bride, The 1924,My 6,25:1
Wisdom Tooth, The 1926,F 16,22:2
Marseilles 1930,N 18,28:2
Lloyd, John Robert
Lute Song 1946,F 7,29:2
Lloyd, John Robert (Costume Designer)
Mrs Gibsons' Boys 1949,My 5,35:2
Lloyd, John Robert (Lighting Director)
Stalag 17 1951,My 9,41:2
Bernardine 1952,O 17,33:4
Almost Crazy 1955,Je 21,37:1
Holiday for Lovers 1957,F 15,20:1
Drink to Me Only 1958,O 9,47:4
Man Who Never Died, The 1958,N 22,27:2
Laughs and Other Events 1960,O 11,57:1
Lloyd, John Robert (Miscellaneous)
Drink to Me Only 1958,O 9,47:4
Lloyd, John Robert (Scenic Designer)
Touch and Go 1949,O 14,34:2
Stalag 17 1951,My 9,41:2
Bernardine 1952,O 17,33:4
Almost Crazy 1955,Je 21,37:1
Holiday for Lovers 1957,F 15,20:1
Monique 1957,O 23,38:1
Drink to Me Only 1958,O 9,47:4
Man Who Never Died, The 1958,N 22,27:2
Dinny and the Witches 1959,D 10,53:3
Laughs and Other Events 1960,O 11,57:1
Lloyd, Ken
Kumquat in the Persimmon Tree, The
1962,Je 19,27:2
Lloyd, Lewis (Producer)
Sap of Life, The 1961,O 3,44:1
Lloyd, Lorayne
Priorities of 1942 1942,Mr 13,23:2
Lloyd, Michael
Tin Top Valley 1947,Mr 1,11:2
Lloyd, Nolan
Madam Will You Walk 1953,D 20,II,3:1
Lloyd, Norman
Noah 1935,F 14,25:2
Crime, The 1936,Mr 2,12:3
Power of the Press 1936,Ap 6,19:2
Julius Caesar 1937,N 12,26:6
Shoemaker's Holiday, The 1938,Ja 3,17:2
Everywhere I Roam 1938,D 30,10:4
Everywhere I Roam 1939,Ja 8,IX,1:1
Medicine Show 1940,Ap 13,20:6
Village Green 1941,S 4,24:4
Ask My Friend Sandy 1943,F 5,16:2
King Lear 1950,D 26,18:1
King Lear 1950,D 31,II,1:1
Madam Will You Walk 1953,D 2,2:4
Measure for Measure 1956,Je 29,16:1
Measure for Measure 1957,Ja 23,24:1
Measure for Measure 1957,F 3,II,1:1

Lloyd, Norman (Director)
Madam Will You Walk 1953,D 2,2:4
Madam Will You Walk 1953,D 20,II,3:1
Golden Apple, The 1954,Mr 12,15:2
Taming of the Shrew, The 1956,Ag 6,20:1
Taming of the Shrew, The 1957,F 21,30:2
Lloyd, Paula
Merry Widow, The 1957,Ap 11,36:6
Lloyd, Richard
Grand Hotel 1930,N 14,30:4
Lloyd, Robert
Persecution and Assassination of Marat As
Performed by the Inmates of the Asylum of
Charenton Under the Direction of the Marquis de
Sade, The 1965,D 28,35:1
Lloyd, Robin
Henry IV, Part I 1946,My 7,25:2
Henry IV, Part II 1946,My 8,33:4
Oedipus; Critic, The 1946,My 21,19:2
Daphne Laureola 1950,S 19,38:6
Lloyd, Rollo
Chains of Dew 1922,Ap 28,20:2
Fool, The 1922,O 24,18:1
New Sin, The 1923,My 28,18:3
Bluffing Bluffers 1924,D 23,17:2
Bells, The 1926,Ap 14,20:3
Lady in Love, A 1927,F 22,22:1
Lloyd, Rollo (Director)
Stolen Fruit 1925,O 8,31:4
Bells, The 1926,Ap 14,20:3
She Couldn't Say No! 1926,S 1,27:3
Sure Fire! 1926,O 21,23:1
Bye Bye Bonnie 1927,Ja 14,15:3
Off Key 1927,F 9,16:2
Lady in Love, A 1927,F 22,22:1
Lost 1927,Mr 29,22:2
Tenth Avenue 1927,Ag 16,31:1
Arabian, The 1927,N 1,20:5
It Is to Laugh 1927,D 27,24:2
Clutching Claw, The 1928,F 15,20:1
Caravan 1928,Ag 30,13:3
Adventure 1928,S 26,25:2
Carnival 1929,Ap 25,32:5
Lloyd, Roy
Broadway 1926,S 17,19:3
Broadway 1927,Ja 9,VII,2:1
Lloyd, Sam
Long Moment, The 1950,My 22,16:6
Philoctetes 1959,Ja 14,28:1
Saintliness of Margery Kempe, The 1959,F 3,35:6
Shakuntala 1959,S 10,41:2
Under the Sycamore Tree 1960,Mr 8,37:2
Magnificent Hugo, The 1961,Ap 8,12:2
Lloyd, Sherman
Uniform of Flesh 1949,Ja 31,15:2
Corn Is Green, The 1950,Ja 12,33:2
Enemy of the People, An 1958,F 26,24:2
Twelfth Night 1958,Ag 7,21:4
Billy Budd 1959,F 28,13:3
Lloyd, Stephen
Beautiful Dreamer 1960,D 28,22:1
Lloyd, Susan
Taming of the Shrew, The 1956,Ag 6,20:1
Taming of the Shrew, The 1957,F 21,30:2
Lloyd, Virginia
Mayflowers 1925,N 25,14:2
Young Sinners 1933,Mr 7,20:4
June Moon 1933,My 16,15:5
Dragon, The 1963,Ap 10,32:1
Lloyd, Vivian
Hello Solly! 1967,Ap 6,44:3
Lloyd-Jones, Jane
Shop at Sly Corner, The 1949,Ja 19,35:2
Grey-Eyed People, The 1952,D 18,41:2
Llyn, Lola
Praise Of Folly 1954,F 24,23:2
Merchant of Venice, The 1955,Ja 8,9:7
Lo Bianco, Tony
Answered the Flute 1960,Mr 10,37:4
Oh Dad, Poor Dad, Mamma's Hung You in the
Closet and I'm Feelin' So Sad 1962,F 27,28:1
Journey to the Day 1963,N 12,49:1
Incident at Vichy 1964,D 4,44:1
Ninety Day Mistress, The 1967,N 7,49:1
Goodbye People, The 1968,D 4,52:1
Nature of the Crime 1970,Mr 24,41:1
Lo Gerfo, Michael
Make Me Disappear 1969,My 14,34:1
Lo Savio, Frank
Roberta 1937,Je 27,II,6:1
Loadwick, Frederick
Gondoliers, The 1940,O 1,29:2
Loan, Leonard
Caesar and Cleopatra 1925,Ap 14,27:1
This Was a Man 1926,N 24,27:1
Caprice 1929,Ja 1,61:1
Meteor 1929,D 24,15:1
Loane, Kenneth
Vaudeville (Palace) 1926,Je 1,29:5
Out of the Night 1927,O 18,32:3
Loane, Mary
Cradle Snatchers 1925,S 8,28:2
That French Lady 1927,Mr 16,29:3

Loane, Mary—Cont
Out of the Night 1927,O 18,32:3
Tomorrow 1928,D 29,20:2
Peter Flies High 1931,N 10,28:3
Affair of Honor 1956,Ap 7,12:3
Sherry! 1967,Mr 29,39:1
Lobb, J
Plain Dealer, The 1929,My 23,27:1
Lobe, Claudia
Kleinburgerhochzeit, Die 1970,N 25,25:1
Lobell, Marc
Grand Street Follies, The 1925,Je 19,24:1
Lobell, William
Broadway Boy 1932,My 4,23:5
Lober, David
Touch and Go 1949,O 14,34:2
Wonderful Town 1953,F 26,22:3
Lober, Greb
Touch and Go 1949,O 14,34:2
LoBianco, Bob
Lysistrata 1968,N 15,42:1
Loblov, Bela
May Wine 1935,D 6,30:3
Lobo, Edu (Composer)
Arena Conta Zumbi 1969,Ag 19,31:1
Lobo (Dog)
Vaudeville (Palace) 1929,S 9,30:5
Locante, Sam
Beaver Coat, The 1956,Mr 29,22:5
Hidden Stranger 1963,Ja 10,5:5
Loch, Sydney (Playwright)
Forty-Seven 1930,F 4,29:1
Lochbiler, Don (Playwright)
Man Bites Dog 1933,Ap 26,11:2
Locher, Loretta
Side-Show 1931,My 16,13:1
Locher, Robert E (Costume Designer)
Greenwich Village Follies 1921,S 1,18:3
Engaged! or Cheviot's Choice 1925,Je 19,24:2
Locher, Robert E (Scenic Designer)
Engaged! or Cheviot's Choice 1925,Je 19,24:2
Lochner, Don
Tenth of an Inch Makes the Difference, A
1962,N 13,44:1
Rainy Day in Newark, A 1963,O 23,35:1
Pequod 1969,Je 30,33:1
Lochy, Claude
Three Musketeers, The 1968,Je 26,43:1
George Dandin 1968,Je 28,36:1
Tartuffe 1968,Jl 3,28:2
Lochy, Claude (Composer)
Three Musketeers, The 1968,Je 26,43:1
George Dandin 1968,Je 28,36:1
Tartuffe 1968,Jl 3,28:2
Locke, Caroline
Ruined Lady, The 1920,Ja 21,10:2
Locke, Charles O (Lyricist)
So This Is Paris 1930,Ap 27,IX,2:3
Hello Paris 1930,N 17,29:3
White Plume, The 1939,D 27,16:1
Locke, Charles O (Playwright)
Please Do Not Disturb 1936,Je 23,27:1
White Plume, The 1939,D 27,16:1
Locke, Edward
Beggarman, Thief 1935,Jl 16,24:1
Our Town 1938,F 5,18:3
Locke, Edward (Director)
Climax, The 1926,My 18,29:3
Locke, Edward (Playwright)
Woman Who Laughed, The 1922,Ag 17,14:3
Mike Angelo 1923,Ja 9,26:2
Mountebank, The 1923,My 13,VIII,1:1
Swanee River 1923,Jl 15,VI,1:2
Sweet Peggy Clive 1924,F 12,20:2
Climax, The 1926,My 18,29:3
Bonita 1927,S 4,VII,2:4
Love Call, The 1927,O 25,33:1
57 Bowery 1928,Ja 27,14:3
Climax, The 1933,Je 14,22:2
Locke, Harry
Hold Everything 1928,O 11,24:2
Locke, Irving
Tide Rising 1937,Ja 26,17:2
Locke, Katherine
Joy of Serpents 1930,Ap 4,22:4
Firebird 1932,N 22,25:2
Halfway to Hell 1934,Ja 3,22:3
Crime and Punishment 1935,Ja 23,20:3
If a Body 1935,My 1,25:3
Having Wonderful Time 1937,F 22,12:5
Having Wonderful Time 1937,F 28,XI,1:1
How to Get Tough About It 1938,F 9,16:2
Hamlet 1938,O 13,28:1
Hamlet 1938,O 30,IX,1:1
Hamlet 1939,D 5,35:2
Christmas Eve 1939,D 28,17:2
Fifth Column, The 1940,Ja 27,9:1
Fifth Column, The 1940,F 4,IX,1:6
Fifth Column, The 1940,Mr 7,18:2
Fifth Column, The 1940,Mr 17,X,1:1
Proof Thro' the Night 1942,D 26,14:2
Locke, Mary Susan
Desert Incident, A 1959,Mr 25,40:1

ocke, Mary Susan—Cont

Sound of Music, The 1959,N 17,40:2

ocke, Philip
Midsummer Night's Dream, A 1954,S 22,33:1

ocke, Ralph
Plain Jane 1924,My 13,24:2
Izzy 1924,S 17,16:2
Puppets 1925,Mr 10,19:1
American Born 1925,O 6,31:3
Noose, The 1926,O 21,23:3
Trapped 1928,S 12,25:3
These Few Ashes 1928,O 31,28:1
Sign of the Leopard 1928,D 12,34:4
Pleasure Bound 1929,F 19,22:4
Sing High, Sing Low 1931,N 13,26:4
Blessed Event 1932,F 13,23:2
Americana 1932,O 6,19:3
Her Tin Soldier 1933,Ap 7,22:6
Best Sellers 1933,My 4,20:2
Blue Widow, The 1933,Ag 31,20:2
She Loves Me Not 1933,N 21,22:4
Baby Pompadour 1934,D 28,24:2
Stage Door 1936,O 23,26:3
Cue for Passion 1940,D 20,33:4

Locke, Sam (Director)
Tidbits of 1946 1946,Jl 9,17:2

Locke, Sam (Playwright)
'Tis of Thee 1940,O 28,21:3
Of V We Sing 1942,F 16,20:3
It's About Time 1942,Mr 31,28:3
Let Freedom Sing 1942,O 6,18:2
Tidbits of 1946 1946,Jl 9,17:2
Vamp, The 1955,N 11,30:1
Fair Game 1957,N 4,39:1

Locke, Shamus
Red Roses for Me 1955,D 29,15:2

Locke, W J (Original Author)
Mountebank, The 1923,My 8,22:2

Locke, W J (Playwright)
Mountebank, The 1923,My 8,22:2
Light on the Mountain, The 1926,Ag 22,VII,1:2
Light on the Mountain, The 1926,S 2,15:4

Locke Elliott, Sumner (Playwright)
Almanac 1954,Ja 3,II,1:1

Locker, E M Bowles
Bedrock 1934,N 18,II,6:3

Locker, Em Bowles
Fuente Ovejuna; Sheep Well, The 1936,My 3,II,4:1

Locker, Judy
Certain Young Man, A 1967,D 27,45:1
Goa 1968,F 23,46:1

Lockett, Lou
Vaudeville (Palace) 1928,N 12,18:7

Lockford, Naro
Rose of Stamboul, The 1922,Mr 8,11:2
Vaudeville (Palace) 1926,S 21,32:5

Lockford, Zita
Rose of Stamboul, The 1922,Mr 8,11:2
Vaudeville (Palace) 1926,S 21,32:5

Lockfords, The
Passing Show of 1924, The 1924,S 4,13:4
Vaudeville (Palace) 1927,D 13,33:5

Lockhart, Araby
Hamlet 1957,Jl 3,15:2
Twelfth Night 1957,Jl 4,16:4

Lockhart, Beverly
Master Builder, The 1968,Je 22,26:1

Lockhart, Calvin
Cool World, The 1960,F 23,38:2
Pretender, The 1960,My 25,42:1

Lockhart, Gene
Skylark 1921,Jl 26,10:6
Sun-Up 1923,My 25,28:1
Handy Man, The 1925,Mr 10,19:2
Bunk of 1926 1926,F 17,12:3
Bunk of 1926 1926,Ap 23,25:2
Sure Fire! 1926,O 21,23:1
Faust 1927,Ja 4,20:1
Untitled-Revue 1928,N 19,16:2
Little Father of the Wilderness, The 1930,Je 3,27:1
Way of the World, The 1931,Je 2,34:3
Uncle Tom's Cabin 1933,My 30,13:4
Ah, Wilderness! 1933,S 26,26:3
Ah, Wilderness! 1933,O 3,28:2
Sweet Mystery of Life 1935,O 12,13:3
Virginia 1937,S 3,13:2
Happily Ever After 1945,Mr 16,21:2
Death of a Salesman 1950,Mr 12,II,1:1

Lockhart, Gene (Composer)
Bunk of 1926 1926,F 17,12:3
Bunk of 1926 1926,Ap 23,25:2

Lockhart, Gene (Director)
Bunk of 1926 1926,F 17,12:3

Lockhart, Gene (Lyricist)
Bunk of 1926 1926,F 17,12:3

Lockhart, Gene (Playwright)
Bunk of 1926 1926,F 17,12:3
Bunk of 1926 1926,Ap 23,25:2

Lockhart, Helen
Just a Minute 1928,O 9,34:3

Lockhart, June
For Love or Money 1947,N 5,36:2
Grand Prize, The 1955,Ja 27,17:1

Lockhart, Kathleen
Little Father of the Wilderness, The 1930,Je 3,27:1
Way of the World, The 1931,Je 2,34:3
Happily Ever After 1945,Mr 16,21:2

Lockhart, Ronald
Medea 1960,Jl 26,25:2

Lockhart, Travis
Harpers Ferry 1967,Je 6,52:2

Lockin, Danny
Morning Sun 1963,O 7,36:2

Lockman, Lycurgus
Porgy and Bess 1935,O 11,30:2

Lockridge, Frances (Original Author)
Mr and Mrs North 1941,Ja 13,11:2
Mr and Mrs North 1941,F 23,IX,1:1

Lockridge, Richard (Original Author)
Mr and Mrs North 1941,Ja 13,11:2
Mr and Mrs North 1941,F 23,IX,1:1

Lockwood, Alexander
Soliloquy 1938,N 29,26:4
Hamlet 1945,D 14,25:2
Biggest Thief in Town 1949,Mr 31,31:2
Remains to Be Seen 1951,O 4,37:1

Lockwood, Carole
Dark of the Moon 1970,Ap 4,21:2

Lockwood, Gary
There Was a Little Girl 1960,Mr 1,28:1

Lockwood, Gordon
Blue Blood 1924,Ap 3,21:2

Lockwood, Helen
Hansel and Gretel 1929,D 25,21:1

Lockwood, John P (Miscellaneous)
Who Is Leslie? 1941,My 20,15:5

Lockwood, Lansing
Fuente Ovejuna; Sheep Well, The 1936,My 3,II,4:1

Lockwood, Lee (Miscellaneous)
Cuban Thing, The 1968,S 25,36:2

Lockwood, Margaret
Subway in the Sky 1957,F 28,19:1
Lady Frederick 1970,S 17,57:1

Lockwood, Rhodes
Who's Who 1924,Ap 18,19:2

Lockwood, Ruth
Blossom Time 1938,D 27,12:2

Lockwood, Ruth Mary
It's Up to You 1921,Mr 29,20:1

Lockwood, T Renaud
Geneva 1940,Ja 31,15:2

Lockwood, Vera
Yerma 1966,D 9,60:1
Corner of the Bed, A 1969,F 27,35:2
Exhibition 1969,My 16,41:1

Locky, Leif
Continental Varieties 1935,D 27,15:3

Locky, Paal
Continental Varieties 1935,D 27,15:3

Locock, C D (Translator)
Dance of Death, The 1967,O 20,50:1

Locust Sisters
Hit the Deck! 1927,Ap 26,32:1

Loday, Vera
Bare Facts 1927,Je 30,35:1
Bare Facts 1927,Ag 17,27:5
Schoolmaster, The 1928,Mr 21,30:1
Under the Gaslight 1929,Ap 3,27:1

Loden, Barbara
Out of This World 1955,N 10,44:2
Compulsion 1957,O 25,21:1
Look After Lulu 1959,Mr 4,35:1
Long Dream, The 1960,F 18,36:2
41 in a Sack 1960,Mr 26,15:2
After the Fall 1964,Ja 24,18:1
After the Fall 1964,F 2,II,1:1
Changeling, The 1964,O 30,32:2
Winter Journey 1968,Mr 13,39:1

Loder, Anthony
Warm Body, A 1967,Ap 17,44:2
Groove Tube 1969,O 12,88:3

Loder, Friedrich (Playwright)
Konjunktur 1933,D 10,X,5:1

Loder, John
For Love or Money 1947,N 5,36:2
Mrs Warren's Profession 1950,O 26,39:2

Loder, Kathryn
As You Like It 1961,Je 17,13:2
Macbeth 1961,Je 19,31:1
Merchant of Venice, The 1962,F 3,13:2
Night Is Black Bottles, The 1962,D 5,56:1
Arms and the Man 1964,Ap 28,41:1

Loder, Lotti
Smiling Faces 1931,D 13,VIII,2:5

Loder, Roxanne
Groove Tube 1969,O 12,88:3

Loder, Theo
Vaudeville (Palace) 1926,Ap 13,28:3

Lodge, Elizabeth
Vagabond King, The 1935,N 29,22:7

Lodge, John
Night of Love 1940,O 29,32:6
Night of Love 1941,Ja 8,14:2
Watch on the Rhine 1941,Ap 2,26:2

Lodge, John D
Who's Who 1924,Ap 18,19:2

Lodge, Lily
Wisteria Trees, The 1955,F 3,20:2

Lodge, Marguerite
What a Life 1938,Ap 14,26:2

Lodge, Muriel
Florodora 1920,Ap 6,18:1

Lodge, Ruth
Measure for Measure 1946,Ag 24,6:8

Lodge, Thomas (Original Author)
As You Like It 1923,Ap 29,VII,1:1

Lods, Sabine
Mariage de Figaro, Le 1964,F 26,41:2
Pieton de L'Air, Le 1964,Mr 4,33:2
Salut a Moliere 1964,Mr 4,33:2

Loeb, Aillene
Silence 1924,N 13,18:2
Three Doors 1925,Ap 24,16:4

Loeb, Annie
Spring Song 1934,O 2,18:2

Loeb, Arthur (Miscellaneous)
Cave Dwellers, The 1961,O 16,34:2

Loeb, Arthur Lehman (Producer)
Last Minstrel, The 1963,My 9,40:2
Save Me a Place at Forest Lawn 1963,My 9,40:2

Loeb, Harold (Director)
Sidewalks and the Sound of Crying 1956,O 29,34:1

Loeb, Harold (Miscellaneous)
Carry Me Back to Morningside Heights
1968,F 28,41:1

Loeb, Jacob (Miscellaneous)
Arabian Nights 1967,Jl 3,12:1

Loeb, John Jacob (Composer)
Arabian Nights 1954,Je 25,15:2
Arabian Nights 1955,Je 24,16:1
Paradise Island 1961,Je 24,11:1
Paradise Island 1962,Je 28,22:1
Mardi Gras! 1965,Je 28,33:2
Mardi Gras! 1966,Jl 11,32:2
Arabian Nights 1967,Jl 3,12:1

Loeb, John Jacob (Lyricist)
Arabian Nights 1954,Je 25,15:2
Arabian Nights 1955,Je 24,16:1
Paradise Island 1961,Je 24,11:1
Paradise Island 1962,Je 28,22:1
Mardi Gras! 1965,Je 28,33:2
Mardi Gras! 1966,Jl 11,32:2
Arabian Nights 1967,Jl 3,12:1

Loeb, John Jacob (Playwright)
Paradise Island 1961,Je 24,11:1
Paradise Island 1962,Je 28,22:1

Loeb, Lee (Playwright)
Sleep No More 1944,S 1,11:5
My House Is Your House 1970,O 16,53:2

Loeb, Leo
Ice Capades 1954,S 16,37:1

Loeb, Philip
Wife With a Smile, The 1921,N 29,20:1
Boubouroche 1921,N 29,20:1
He Who Gets Slapped 1922,Ja 10,15:1
Failures, The 1923,N 23,20:1
Guardsman, The 1924,O 14,23:1
Processional 1925,Ja 13,17:1
Garrick Gaieties 1925,My 18,12:2
Merchants of Glory 1925,D 15,28:3
Merchants of Glory 1925,D 27,VII,1:1
Goat Song 1926,Ja 26,18:1
Garrick Gaieties 1926,My 11,25:2
Juarez and Maximilian 1926,O 12,31:1
Ned McCobb's Daughter 1926,N 30,26:2
Brothers Karamazov, The 1927,Ja 4,20:1
Right You Are (If You Think You Are)
1927,F 24,27:1
Merry-Go-Round 1927,Je 1,25:4
Chee-Chee 1928,S 26,25:1
June Moon 1929,Ag 4,VIII,1:6
June Moon 1929,O 10,34:5
Garrick Gaieties 1930,Je 5,29:2
Garrick Gaieties 1930,O 17,21:2
Band Wagon, The 1931,Je 4,31:3
Band Wagon, The 1931,Je 14,VIII,1:1
Flying Colors 1932,S 16,24:2
Flying Colors 1932,O 9,IX,1:1
Let 'Em Eat Cake 1933,O 23,18:1
Room Service 1935,N 17,II,7:7
Room Service 1937,My 20,16:1
Room Service 1937,My 30,X,1:1
Sing Out the News 1938,S 26,12:5
Sing Out the News 1938,O 2,IX,1:1
My Heart's in the Highlands 1939,Ap 14,29:2
My Heart's in the Highlands 1939,My 7,X,1:1
Night Music 1940,F 23,18:2
Heavenly Express 1940,Ap 19,24:2
Heavenly Express 1940,Ap 28,IX,1:1
Sweet Charity 1942,D 29,26:4
Over Twenty-One 1944,Ja 4,20:2
Common Ground 1945,Ap 26,27:2
Common Ground 1945,My 6,II,1:1
Wonderful Journey 1946,D 26,30:2
Me and Molly 1948,F 27,27:2
Me and Molly 1948,Mr 7,II,1:1
Wild Duck, The 1951,D 27,17:1
Time Out for Ginger 1952,N 27,50:4
Three Sisters, The 1955,F 26,13:2

Loeb, Philip—Cont

Loeb, Philip (Director)
Three Sisters, The 1955,Mr 20,II,1:1
Garrick Gaieties 1926,My 11,25:2
Garrick Gaieties 1930,Je 5,29:2
Life Begins at 8:40 1934,Ag 28,24:2
Parade 1935,My 21,22:2
Would-Be Gentleman, The 1936,Ag 4,15:1
Seven Lively Arts 1944,D 8,26:6
Bruno and Sidney 1949,My 4,38:2

Loeb, Philip (Playwright)
Swingin' the Dream 1939,N 30,24:2

Loebell, Marc
Little Clay Cart, The 1924,D 6,13:3
Critic, The 1925,My 9,12:4
Dybbuk, The 1925,D 16,22:2
Romantic Young Lady, The 1926,My 5,24:3
Grand Street Follies, The 1926,Je 16,23:2
Lion Tamer, The 1926,O 8,26:1
Dybbuk, The 1926,D 17,27:2
Commedia Dell' Arte 1927,Ap 6,24:3
Grand Street Follies, The 1927,My 20,22:3
Lovers and Enemies 1927,S 21,27:1
If 1927,O 26,26:2
Love Nest, The 1927,D 23,17:1
Maya 1928,F 22,19:1
Grand Street Follies, The 1928,My 29,16:2
Grand Street Follies, The 1929,My 2,20:4
Grand Street Follies, The 1929,My 12,IX,1:2
Grand Street Follies, The 1929,Je 19,34:3
Once in a Lifetime 1930,S 25,22:3
If Love Were All 1931,N 14,14:5
Dark Hours, The 1932,N 15,24:2
Four O'Clock 1933,F 14,19:6
Hilda Cassidy 1933,My 5,18:3
St Helena 1936,O 7,32:1

Loebell, Mary
Pinwheel 1927,F 4,16:4

Loeffel, Evelyn (Costume Designer)
Mummers and Men 1962,Mr 27,41:6

Loeffler, Edward H
Bells, The 1926,Ap 14,20:3
Carry On 1928,Ja 24,26:1
Breaks, The 1928,Ap 17,26:3
Turpentine 1936,Je 27,21:6

Loeffler, Peter (Director)
Wilhelm Tell 1964,Ja 19,II,5:1

Loehner, Don
Jackass, The 1960,Mr 24,39:2

Loehner, Fritz (Playwright)
Land des Laechelns, Das 1929,D 8,X,4:4
Giuditta 1934,Ja 21,30:1

Loehner-Beda (Playwright)
Ball at the Savoy 1933,F 19,IX,3:1

Loehr (Director)
Abraham Lincoln 1928,N 13,31:2

Loesberg, Nat
Revolt of the Beavers, The 1937,My 21,19:2
Life and Death of an American 1939,My 20,11:2

Loesser, Frank (Composer)
Illustrators' Show, The 1936,Ja 23,25:3
Where's Charley? 1948,O 12,33:2
Where's Charley? 1950,Ag 20,II,1:1
Guys and Dolls 1950,N 25,11:2
Guys and Dolls 1950,D 3,II,1:1
Guys and Dolls 1951,O 7,II,1:1
Guys and Dolls 1953,My 29,17:5
Guys and Dolls 1955,Ap 21,32:2
Most Happy Fella, The 1956,My 4,20:1
Most Happy Fella, The 1956,My 13,II,1:1
Most Happy Fella, The 1956,Je 10,II,7:1
Guys and Dolls 1959,Jl 22,22:2
Greenwillow 1960,Mr 9,38:1
Greenwillow 1960,Mr 20,II,1:1
Most Happy Fella, The 1960,Ap 22,25:3
How to Succeed in Business Without Really Trying 1961,O 16,34:1
Guys and Dolls 1965,Ap 29,39:1
How to Succeed in Business Without Really Trying 1966,Ap 21,45:1
Most Happy Fella, The 1966,My 12,55:1
Where's Charley? 1966,My 26,57:1
Guys and Dolls 1966,Je 9,55:2
Greenwillow 1970,D 8,60:1

Loesser, Frank (Lyricist)
Guys and Dolls 1950,N 25,11:2
Guys and Dolls 1950,D 3,II,1:1
Guys and Dolls 1953,My 29,17:5
Guys and Dolls 1955,Ap 21,32:2
Most Happy Fella, The 1956,My 4,20:1
Most Happy Fella, The 1956,My 13,II,1:1
Most Happy Fella, The 1956,Je 10,II,7:1
Guys and Dolls 1959,Jl 22,22:2
Greenwillow 1960,Mr 9,38:1
Greenwillow 1960,Mr 20,II,1:1
How to Succeed in Business Without Really Trying 1961,O 16,34:1
Guys and Dolls 1965,Ap 29,39:1
How to Succeed in Business Without Really Trying 1966,Ap 21,45:1
Most Happy Fella, The 1966,My 12,55:1
Where's Charley? 1966,My 26,57:1
Guys and Dolls 1966,Je 9,55:2
Greenwillow 1970,D 8,60:1

Loesser, Frank (Playwright)
Most Happy Fella, The 1956,My 4,20:1
Most Happy Fella, The 1956,My 13,II,1:1
Most Happy Fella, The 1956,Je 10,II,7:1
Most Happy Fella, The 1959,F 11,50:2
Greenwillow 1960,Mr 9,38:1
Greenwillow 1960,Mr 20,II,1:1
Most Happy Fella, The 1966,My 12,55:1
Guys and Dolls 1966,Je 9,55:2
Greenwillow 1970,D 8,60:1

Loesser, Lynn (Producer)
Most Happy Fella, The 1956,My 4,20:1
Chocolates 1967,Ap 11,51:1

Loessin, Ed (Miscellaneous)
Lend an Ear 1959,S 25,20:5

Loeffler, Charles Martin (Miscellaneous)
Neighborhood Playhouse Program 1930,F 21,23:1

Loew, Arthur (Producer)
Jolly's Progress 1959,D 7,42:2

Loew, E M (Producer)
Artists and Models 1943,N 6,16:6

Loewe, Frederick (Composer)
Illustrators' Show, The 1936,Ja 23,25:3
Salute to Spring 1937,Jl 14,16:2
Great Lady 1938,D 2,26:6
What's Up 1943,N 12,24:6
Day Before Spring, The 1945,N 23,27:2
Day Before Spring, The 1945,D 2,II,1:1
Brigadoon 1947,Mr 14,28:2
Brigadoon 1950,My 3,36:2
Paint Your Wagon 1951,N 13,32:2
Paint Your Wagon 1951,N 18,II,1:1
My Fair Lady 1956,Mr 16,20:2
My Fair Lady 1956,Mr 25,II,1:1
My Fair Lady 1956,Ap 29,II,17:1
My Fair Lady 1956,Je 3,II,1:1
My Fair Lady 1956,Je 10,II,7:1
My Fair Lady 1956,Ag 12,II,1:1
My Fair Lady 1956,O 28,II,1:1
Brigadoon 1957,Mr 28,37:1
My Fair Lady 1958,Mr 9,II,1:1
My Fair Lady 1958,My 1,34:5
My Fair Lady 1959,Ja 27,26:1
My Fair Lady 1959,Ap 4,12:5
Camelot 1960,O 3,35:1
Camelot 1960,D 5,42:1
Camelot 1960,D 11,II,5:1
Brigadoon 1962,My 31,21:4
My Fair Lady 1962,S 7,34:1
My Fair Lady 1963,S 21,13:1
My Fair Lady 1964,F 20,24:4
My Fair Lady 1964,My 21,43:2
Brigadoon 1964,D 24,9:1
My Fair Lady 1964,D 29,22:1
Brigadoon 1967,D 14,59:2
My Fair Lady 1968,Je 14,42:1

Loewe, Frederick (Miscellaneous)
Day Before Spring, The 1945,N 23,27:2
Brigadoon 1950,My 3,36:2

Loewe, Frederick (Playwright)
Brigadoon 1947,Mr 23,II,1:1
Brigadoon 1963,F 1,6:2

Loewe, Frederick (Producer)
Camelot 1960,D 5,42:1

Loewenfeldt, Dushanne Von
Gift of Fury, A 1958,Mr 24,21:4

Loewi, Joseph F (Miscellaneous)
Your Loving Son 1941,Ap 5,13:2

Loff, Jeannette
Free for All 1931,S 9,25:1

Loft, Betty
Crooked Square, The 1923,S 11,10:2
Schemers 1924,S 16,27:1

Loft, Phyllis
Earl Carroll's Vanities 1927,Ja 5,18:1

Loftin, Dixie
Spooks 1925,Je 2,16:4
Tragic 18 1926,O 11,18:2

Loftis, Linda
Oh What a Lovely War 1964,O 1,30:1

Loftness, Alma
York Nativity Play, The 1956,D 5,49:2
Sign of Jonah, The 1957,My 2,27:1

Loftus, Alexander
Prince and the Pauper, The 1920,N 2,15:1

Loftus, Cecilia
Untitled-Recital 1923,D 29,8:2
Venus 1927,D 26,26:5
Diplomacy 1928,My 29,16:3
Diplomacy 1928,Je 3,VIII,1:1
Becky Sharp 1929,Je 4,29:1
Recapture 1930,Ja 30,16:4
Lost Sheep 1930,My 6,33:2
Widow in Green, A 1931,N 21,21:4
Devil Passes, The 1932,Ja 5,20:3
Devil Passes, The 1932,Ja 10,VIII,1:1
Three-Cornered Moon 1933,Mr 17,20:6
Uncle Tom's Cabin 1933,My 30,13:4
Party, A 1933,Ag 24,18:4
Strange Orchestra 1933,N 29,23:2
Wooden Slipper, The 1934,Ja 4,16:3
Merrily We Roll Along 1934,O 1,14:1
Times Have Changed 1935,F 26,16:1

Loftus, Cecilia—Cont
Abide With Me 1935,N 22,19:2
Holmeses of Baker Street, The 1936,D 10,34:3
Glory for All 1937,F 9,18:2
There's Always a Breeze 1938,Mr 3,16:2
Evening With Cecilia Loftus, An 1938,Mr 28,19:2
Untitled-One Woman Show 1938,O 31,12:2
Little Dark Horse 1941,N 17,14:4

Loftus, Cissie
Vaudeville (Palace) 1923,N 13,24:2
Vaudeville (Palace) 1925,Ap 21,18:1
Vaudeville (Palace) 1926,N 2,35:2
Patriarch, The 1929,N 26,28:5
Party, A 1933,S 3,IX,1:1

Logan, Barbara
Nine Till Six 1936,Mr 14,10:3

Logan, Danny
Salad of the Mad Cafe, The 1964,Ap 1,43:1

Logan, Danny (Director)
Salad of the Mad Cafe, The 1964,Ap 1,43:1

Logan, Danny (Playwright)
Salad of the Mad Cafe, The 1964,Ap 1,43:1

Logan, Ella
Calling All Stars 1934,D 14,28:2
Scandals 1939,Ag 29,17:2
Scandals 1939,S 3,IX,1:1
Hi-Ya Gentlemen 1940,D 4,34:2
Sons o' Fun 1941,D 2,28:2
Actors Fund Fete 1942,F 23,24:5
Show Time 1942,S 17,20:2
Show Time 1942,O 4,VIII,1:1
Finian's Rainbow 1947,Ja 11,23:2
ANTA Album 1951,My 7,22:7

Logan, Grant Clifford (Miscellaneous)
Adding Machine, The 1970,D 5,40:1

Logan, Jacqueline
Two Strange Women 1933,Ja 11,23:3
Merrily We Roll Along 1934,O 1,14:1

Logan, Joshua L
Zuider Zee 1928,D 19,24:4
Golden Dog, The 1929,D 25,21:2
Tiger Smiles, The 1930,D 18,29:1
Carry Nation 1932,O 31,18:2
I Was Waiting for You 1933,N 14,23:3
Caesar and Cleopatra 1935,Ag 22,21:1
Most of the Game 1935,O 2,27:4
Room in Red and White, A 1936,Ja 20,23:3

Logan, Joshua L (Choreographer)
Wish You Were Here 1952,Je 26,26:6

Logan, Joshua L (Director)
Torch Bearers, The 1929,Mr 22,30:4
Stags at Bay 1934,D 15,9:2
It's You I Want 1935,F 6,23:3
To See Ourselves 1935,My 1,25:2
What a Relief 1935,D 14,10:6
Hell Freezes Over 1935,D 30,14:2
Emperor Jones, The 1936,Ag 11,24:6
Middle Man 1936,S 8,23:1
On Borrowed Time 1938,F 4,16:4
I Married an Angel 1938,My 12,26:2
Knickerbocker Holiday 1938,O 20,26:2
Stars in Your Eyes 1939,F 10,18:2
Morning's at Seven 1939,N 7,30:2
Morning's at Seven 1939,N 12,IX,2:3
Morning's at Seven 1939,N 26,26:2
Two for the Show 1940,F 9,14:2
Higher and Higher 1940,Ap 5,24:3
Charley's Aunt 1940,O 18,24:2
By Jupiter 1942,Je 4,22:1
Annie Get Your Gun 1946,My 17,14:2
Annie Get Your Gun 1946,My 26,II,1:1
Happy Birthday 1946,N 1,31:2
Happy Birthday 1946,N 10,II,1:1
John Loves Mary 1947,F 5,29:2
Mister Roberts 1948,F 19,27:2
South Pacific 1949,Ap 8,30:2
South Pacific 1949,Ap 17,II,1:1
Wisteria Trees, The 1950,Mr 30,39:1
Mister Roberts 1950,My 21,II,1:1
South Pacific 1951,S 2,II,1:1
Wish You Were Here 1952,Je 26,26:6
Wish You Were Here 1952,Ag 31,II,1:1
Picnic 1953,F 20,14:7
Picnic 1953,Mr 1,II,1:1
Picnic 1953,Ag 30,II,1:1
Kind Sir 1953,N 5,41:2
Kind Sir 1953,N 15,II,1:1
Fanny 1954,N 5,16:1
Middle of the Night 1956,F 9,39:1
Middle of the Night 1956,F 19,II,1:1
Blue Denim 1958,F 28,17:1
Blue Denim 1958,Ap 20,II,1:1
World of Suzie Wong, The 1958,O 15,47:1
World of Suzie Wong, The 1958,O 19,II,1:1
There Was a Little Girl 1960,Mr 1,28:1
All American 1962,Mr 20,44:1
Mr President 1962,S 26,36:1
Mr President 1962,O 14,II,1:7
Mr President 1962,O 22,34:2
Tiger Tiger Burning Bright 1962,D 24,5:2
Ready When You Are, C. B.! 1964,D 8,55:1
Look to the Lilies 1970,Mr 30,59:1
Look to the Lilies 1970,Ap 12,II,3:7

Logan, Joshua L (Lyricist)
Tiger Smiles, The 1930,D 18,29:1
Logan, Joshua L (Miscellaneous)
John Loves Mary 1947,F 5,29:2
South Pacific 1949,Ap 8,30:2
South Pacific 1950,Ap 26,36:5
South Pacific 1951,Jl 10,30:5
Logan, Joshua L (Playwright)
Tiger Smiles, The 1930,D 18,29:1
Higher and Higher 1940,Mr 17,X,2:5
Higher and Higher 1940,Ap 5,24:3
Mister Roberts 1948,F 19,27:2
Mister Roberts 1948,F 29,II,1:1
South Pacific 1949,Ap 8,30:2
Wisteria Trees, The 1950,Mr 30,39:1
Wisteria Trees, The 1950,Ap 9,II,1:1
Mister Roberts 1950,My 21,II,1:1
Mister Roberts 1950,Jl 20,22:4
Mister Roberts 1950,Jl 23,II,1:6
Mister Roberts 1951,F 9,20:7
South Pacific 1951,S 2,II,1:1
Wish You Were Here 1952,Je 26,26:6
Wish You Were Here 1952,Ag 31,II,1:1
Fanny 1954,N 5,16:1
Fanny 1954,N 21,II,1:1
Wisteria Trees, The 1955,F 3,20:2
South Pacific 1955,My 5,39:5
Mister Roberts 1956,D 6,46:2
South Pacific 1957,Ap 25,35:1
South Pacific 1961,Ap 27,26:3
Mister Roberts 1962,O 12,27:2
South Pacific 1965,Je 3,25:1
South Pacific 1967,Je 13,56:1
South Pacific 1968,Je 30,54:2
South Pacific 1969,Jl 7,27:1
Logan, Joshua L (Producer)
To See Ourselves 1935,My 1,25:2
Wisteria Trees, The 1950,Mr 30,39:1
Wish You Were Here 1952,Je 26,26:6
Picnic 1953,F 20,14:7
Kind Sir 1953,S 28,21:2
Kind Sir 1953,N 5,41:2
Fanny 1954,N 5,16:1
Middle of the Night 1956,F 9,39:1
Middle of the Night 1956,F 19,II,1:1
Epitaph for George Dillon 1958,N 5,44:1
Logan, Lyn
Pie in the Sky 1941,D 23,26:5
Down to Miami 1944,S 12,23:5
Logan, Lyn (Producer)
Pie in the Sky 1941,D 23,26:5
Logan, Mary Lee
Spring Dance 1936,Ag 26,17:4
Hamlet 1936,O 9,30:2
Kind Lady 1937,Jl 6,23:1
Logan, Stanley
Little Miss Bluebeard 1923,Ag 29,12:1
Carnaval 1924,D 30,15:1
Dark Angel, The 1925,F 11,19:2
Last Night of Don Juan, The 1925,N 10,23:2
Loose Ends 1926,N 2,34:2
Padre, The 1926,D 28,16:3
Dark, The 1927,F 2,22:5
Her Cardboard Lover 1927,Mr 22,30:5
Her First Affaire 1927,Ag 23,29:2
People Don't Do Such Things 1927,N 24,28:3
Mrs Dane's Defense 1928,F 7,30:1
Sherlock Holmes 1928,F 21,18:4
Within the Law 1928,Mr 6,20:1
Sacred Flame, The 1928,N 20,28:2
Logan, Stanley (Director)
Padre, The 1926,D 28,16:3
Red Robe, The 1928,D 26,15:1
Security 1929,Mr 29,20:1
Music in May 1929,Ap 2,29:1
Broadway Nights 1929,Jl 16,23:2
Young Sinners 1929,N 29,24:4
Topaze 1930,F 13,25:3
Lady Clara 1930,Ap 18,28:7
His Majesty's Car 1930,O 24,30:1
Purity 1930,D 26,18:2
Colonel Satan 1931,Ja 12,24:1
Modern Virgin, A 1931,My 21,33:4
Marriage for Three 1931,N 12,30:5
Society Girl 1931,D 31,16:1
Alice Sit-By-The-Fire 1932,Mr 8,19:3
Old Lady Shows Her Medals, The 1932,Mr 8,19:3
Domino 1932,Ag 17,13:2
Marriage Is for Single People 1945,N 22,38:2
Logan, Stanley (Playwright)
Padre, The 1926,D 28,16:3
Logan, Terrence
Impossible Years, The 1965,O 14,55:1
Logan, Warren
World of Sholom Aleichem, The 1953,S 12,13:2
Loggia, Robert
Man With the Golden Arm, The 1956,My 22,28:1
Three Sisters, The 1964,Je 23,24:1
World War 2 1/2 1969,Mr 25,40:1
Passing Through From Exotic Places; Son Who
Hunted Tigers in Jakarta, The 1969,D 8,60:4
Passing Through From Exotic Places; Sunstroke
1969,D 8,60:4

Passing Through From Exotic Places; Burial of
Esposito, The 1969,D 8,60:4
Passing Through From Exotic Places
1969,D 21,II,3:1
Loghe, Alex
Veils 1928,Mr 14,28:5
Logothetidis, Basil
Screwball, The 1957,My 25,24:7
Logothetidis, Basil (Director)
Screwball, The 1957,My 25,24:7
Logothetis, Richard (Miscellaneous)
Golden Streets, The 1970,Ag 14,21:1
Logue, Elizabeth
Brigadoon 1950,My 3,36:2
Flahooley 1951,My 15,39:1
Loguen, William H
Natural Man 1941,My 8,20:4
Logvinova, Mami
Oklahoma! 1958,Mr 8,15:2
Lohae and Sterling
Vaudeville (Palace) 1925,D 29,21:2
Lohde, Sigurd
200,000 1966,F 15,33:5
Lohman, Mary
Elmer the Great 1928,S 25,29:1
Lohmann, Otto
Hasty Heart, The 1959,S 15,45:2
Sappho 1960,Ja 12,22:1
Hobo 1961,Ap 11,41:2
Lohmuller, Bernard (Producer)
Woof, Woof 1929,D 26,20:4
Lohner-Beda, Fritz (Playwright)
Schoen ist die Welt 1931,Ja 11,VIII,1:8
Ball at the Savoy 1933,S 9,9:7
Lohr, Marie
Voice From the Minaret, The 1922,Ja 31,11:2
Voice From the Minaret, The 1922,F 5,VI,1:1
Fedora 1922,F 11,18:1
Aren't We All? 1923,Ap 15,VII,2:4
Girl's Best Friend, A 1929,N 10,X,2:1
Breadwinner, The 1931,S 23,19:4
And On We Go 1937,Ap 22,19:5
Crest of the Wave 1937,S 19,XI,3:1
Waiting in the Wings 1960,Ag 9,31:4
Waiting in the Wings 1960,S 8,40:3
Lohse, Ron
All's Well That Ends Well 1970,Je 16,53:1
Loines, Margot
Panic 1935,Mr 16,18:4
Loiseau, Mayo
Wilde Evening with Shaw, A 1963,Mr 7,8:2
Loiseau, Mayo (Playwright)
Wilde Evening with Shaw, A 1963,Mr 7,8:2
Lojekova, Flora
Wiener Blut 1964,S 12,14:1
Lokos, Allan
H M S Pinafore 1960,Ja 29,14:1
Utopia, Limited 1960,Ap 8,27:2
Autumn's Here 1966,O 26,40:1
Lokos, Allan (Director)
Sacco-Vanzetti 1969,F 9,78:1
Lola, Raine
Night in Spain, A 1927,My 4,28:2
Lollos, John (Director)
Love and Let Love 1968,Ja 4,30:1
Lollos, John (Lyricist)
Love and Let Love 1968,Ja 4,30:1
Lollos, John (Playwright)
Love and Let Love 1968,Ja 4,30:1
Lom, Herbert
King and I, The 1953,O 9,33:3
King and I, The 1953,O 18,II,3:1
Lomaki, Sigurd
Me, Candido! 1956,O 16,36:2
Lomaki, Sigurd (Scenic Designer)
Journey With Strangers, A 1958,N 27,53:1
Lomakin, Victor
Moscow Circus on Ice 1970,D 9,63:1
Lomakina
Chauve-Souris 1922,Je 6,17:4
Loman, Hal
Make Mine Manhattan 1948,Ja 16,26:2
Top Banana 1951,N 2,19:2
Mr Wonderful 1956,Mr 23,23:2
Lomas, Herbert
Skin Game, The 1920,O 21,11:1
Skin Game, The 1920,O 31,VI,1:2
Fanny Hawthorn 1922,My 12,22:2
Bird in Hand 1929,Ap 5,28:2
Inquest 1931,Jl 19,VIII,1:8
In Good King Charles's Golden Days
1939,Ag 13,28:1
Wind of Heaven, The 1945,Ap 22,II,2:3
Summer Day's Dream 1949,S 9,28:5
Summer Day's Dream 1949,O 9,II,3:7
Lomas, Tom
Jumbo 1935,N 18,20:2
Lomas, Virginia
Pursuit of Happiness, The 1936,Jl 15,14:1
Post Road 1936,Ag 5,15:4
Royal Family, The 1936,Ag 12,15:1
Truth About Blayds, The 1936,Ag 19,18:5
Art and Mrs Bottle 1936,S 2,18:1

Lomas, Virginia—Cont
Private Lives 1937,Jl 14,17:4
Kind Lady 1937,Jl 21,19:3
Fly Away Home 1937,Jl 28,15:1
Candida 1937,Ag 4,14:5
Whiteheaded Boy, The 1937,Ag 11,27:3
Father Malachy's Miracle 1937,N 18,26:4
White Steed, The 1939,Ag 16,21:3
Blind Alley 1939,Ag 23,18:8
Lomas Troupe
Jumbo 1935,N 18,20:2
Lomasney, D A
Gentlemen, the Queen 1927,Ap 23,14:3
Lomax, Lawrence
Swing It 1937,Jl 23,17:2
Lomax, Perry
Oliver 1963,Ja 8,5:5
Lomax, Rosemary
Set to Music 1939,Ja 19,16:2
Lomax, Terry
All in Good Time 1965,F 19,25:1
Serjeant Musgrave's Dance 1966,Mr 9,44:1
Borstal Boy 1970,Ap 1,38:1
Lombard, Leda
Scrap Book 1932,Ag 2,20:3
Lombard, Michael
Merchant of Venice, The 1962,Je 22,1:4
Poor Bitos 1964,N 16,40:2
Devils, The 1965,N 17,51:2
Elizabeth the Queen 1966,N 4,30:1
'Tis Pity She's a Whore 1967,O 21,15:2
We Bombed in New Haven 1967,D 7,58:1
Henry IV 1968,F 7,40:1
Three Sisters, The 1968,Mr 18,56:1
Bacchae, The 1969,Mr 15,24:1
Room Service 1970,My 13,49:1
Room Service 1970,My 24,II,1:1
Gingerbread Lady, The 1970,D 14,58:3
Gingerbread Lady, The 1970,D 20,II,3:7
Lombard, Peter
Conquering Hero, The 1961,Ja 17,40:2
Will the Mail Train Run Tonight? 1964,Ja 10,18:1
Cat and the Canary, The 1965,Ja 5,26:1
Lombard, Rebecca
Much Ado About Nothing 1955,Ag 20,20:4
Lombard, Robert
Mariage de Figaro, Le 1964,F 26,41:2
Salut a Moliere 1964,Mr 4,33:2
Pieton de L'Air, Le 1964,Mr 4,33:2
Vie Parisienne, La 1964,Mr 11,34:2
Lombardi, Jo (Miscellaneous)
Danny Kaye's International Show 1953,Ja 19,20:2
Lombardi, Ralph
When the Bough Breaks 1950,Mr 9,25:5
Once Around the Block 1950,My 25,36:2
Lombardo, C (Playwright)
Paese dei Campanelli, Il; Land of Bells, The
1935,My 10,25:4
Lombardo, Carmen (Composer)
Music Hall Varieties 1932,N 23,15:3
Arabian Nights 1954,Je 25,15:2
Arabian Nights 1955,Je 24,16:1
Paradise Island 1961,Je 24,11:1
Paradise Island 1962,Je 28,22:1
Mardi Gras! 1965,Je 28,33:2
Mardi Gras! 1966,Jl 11,32:2
Arabian Nights 1967,Jl 3,12:1
Lombardo, Carmen (Lyricist)
Music Hall Varieties 1932,N 23,15:3
Arabian Nights 1954,Je 25,15:2
Arabian Nights 1955,Je 24,16:1
Paradise Island 1961,Je 24,11:1
Paradise Island 1962,Je 28,22:1
Mardi Gras! 1965,Je 28,33:2
Mardi Gras! 1966,Jl 11,32:2
Arabian Nights 1967,Jl 3,12:1
Lombardo, Carmen (Playwright)
Paradise Island 1961,Je 24,11:1
Paradise Island 1962,Je 28,22:1
Lombardo, Carmen (Producer)
Arabian Nights 1967,Jl 3,12:1
Lombardo, Guy
Mardi Gras! 1966,Jl 11,32:2
Lombardo, Guy (Miscellaneous)
Arabian Nights 1954,Je 25,15:2
Lombardo, Guy (Producer)
Arabian Nights 1955,Je 24,16:1
Show Boat 1956,Je 22,16:1
Show Boat 1957,Je 28,30:2
Song of Norway 1958,Je 23,19:2
Song of Norway 1959,Je 26,16:2
Hit the Deck 1960,Je 24,32:1
Paradise Island 1961,Je 24,11:1
Paradise Island 1962,Je 28,22:1
Around the World in 80 Days 1963,Je 24,22:1
Around the World in 80 Days 1964,Je 29,33:2
Mardi Gras! 1965,Je 28,33:2
Mardi Gras! 1966,Jl 11,32:2
South Pacific 1968,Je 30,54:2
South Pacific 1969,Jl 7,27:1
Sound of Music, The 1970,Jl 3,13:1
Lombardo, Guy and His Royal Canadians
Paradise Island 1961,Je 24,11:1
Paradise Island 1962,Je 28,22:1

Lombardo, Guy and His Royal Canadians—Cont
Around the World in 80 Days 1963,Je 24,22:1
Lombardo, Josephine
Career 1943,O 29,22:6
Spring Production 1944,My 20,12:4
Lombardo, Lebert (Miscellaneous)
Arabian Nights 1954,Je 25,15:2
Arabian Nights 1955,Je 24,16:1
Lombardo, Robert (Composer)
Tempest, The 1970,F 15,67:1
Lombardo, Robert (Miscellaneous)
Tempest, The 1970,F 15,67:1
Lombardo, Sal
Bajour 1964,N 24,42:1
Londin, A Joseph (Lighting Director)
Farther Off From Heaven 1947,Je 4,33:3
Summer and Smoke 1947,Ag 10,II,1:1
Londin, Joseph
Caesar and Cleopatra 1935,Ag 22,21:1
London, Charles
57 Bowery 1928,Ja 27,14:3
London, Charlotte
Temper the Wind 1946,D 28,10:2
London, Chet
Shoemaker and the Peddler, The 1960,O 15,27:4
Romeo and Juliet 1961,F 24,24:1
Hamlet 1964,Je 17,49:1
Deadly Game, The 1966,F 14,34:1
London, David
Merry Malones, The 1927,S 27,30:2
Billie 1928,O 2,34:2
Cape Cod Follies 1929,S 19,37:2
Fiorello! 1959,N 24,45:3
London, Frank R
Lido Girl, The 1928,Ag 24,23:2
London, Howard
Trip to Bountiful, The 1959,F 27,20:4
London, Howard (Miscellaneous)
Long Gallery, The 1958,Mr 7,17:2
Journey With Strangers, A 1958,N 27,53:1
Mousetrap, The 1960,N 7,46:1
London, Marc
Secret Life of Walter Mitty, The 1964,O 27,44:5
London, Roy
Princess Rebecca Birnbaum 1966,Mr 7,22:1
Viet Rock 1966,N 11,38:1
America Hurrah; Interview; TV; Motel 1967,O 10,55:2
Gingham Dog, The 1969,Ap 24,41:1
London, William
Is Zat So? 1925,Ja 6,23:4
Londres, Albert (Original Author)
Au Bagne 1929,Jl 21,VIII,2:1
Lone, Robert
Sappho 1960,Ja 12,22:1
Vintage '60 1960,S 13,41:1
Leonard Sillman's New Faces of 1968 1968,My 3,43:1
Lonegan, Lester 3d
Wednesday's Child 1934,Ja 17,23:2
Lonergan, John (Choreographer)
Cape Cod Follies 1929,S 19,37:2
Vanderbilt Revue, The 1930,N 6,22:6
Caviar 1934,Je 8,19:2
Lonergan, John (Miscellaneous)
Tattle Tales 1933,Je 2,22:6
Lonergan, John E (Director)
Flair-Flair the Idol of Paree 1935,Mr 13,16:1
Lonergan, Lenore
Mother Lode 1934,D 24,16:5
Crime Marches on 1935,O 24,19:1
Fields Beyond, The 1936,Mr 7,11:2
Philadelphia Story, The 1939,Mr 29,21:1
Junior Miss 1941,N 19,28:2
Junior Miss 1941,N 30,IX,1:1
Dear Ruth 1944,D 14,29:2
Dear Ruth 1944,D 31,II,1:1
Brighten the Corner 1945,D 13,33:2
Young Man's Fancy, A 1947,Ap 30,33:2
Alive and Kicking 1950,Ja 18,25:5
Of Thee I Sing 1952,My 6,34:2
Of Thee I Sing 1952,My 11,II,1:1
Lonergan, Lester
Deluge, The 1922,Ja 28,14:2
Outsider, The 1924,Mr 4,16:4
Accused 1925,S 20,VIII,2:4
Accused 1925,S 30,20:1
Noose, The 1926,O 21,23:3
Stairs, The 1927,N 8,32:7
Free Soul, A 1928,Ja 13,26:5
House Unguarded 1929,Ja 16,22:2
Brass Ankle 1931,Ap 24,26:4
Mother Lode 1934,D 24,16:5
Crime Marches on 1935,O 24,19:1
I'll Take the High Road 1943,N 10,28:3
Lonergan, Lester (Director)
Road to Rome, The 1927,F 1,24:2
Command to Love, The 1927,S 21,27:1
Golden Age, The 1928,Ap 25,31:3
Tin Pan Alley 1928,N 2,29:1
This Man's Town 1930,Mr 11,24:4
Love, Honor and Betray 1930,Mr 13,22:2
That's the Woman 1930,S 4,27:2

Lonergan, Lester (Playwright)
Golden Age, The 1928,Ap 25,31:3
House Unguarded 1928,D 30,VIII,1:6
House Unguarded 1929,Ja 16,22:2
Lonergan, Lester Jr
Chinese Nightingale, The 1934,O 6,20:4
Mother, The 1935,N 20,26:3
Marching Song 1937,F 18,18:2
Johnny 2X4 1942,Mr 17,24:6
Live Life Again 1945,O 1,14:7
Bruno and Sidney 1949,My 4,38:2
Lonergan, Lester 3d
Between Two Worlds 1934,O 26,24:2
Mother Lode 1934,D 24,16:5
Come Angel Band 1936,F 19,17:1
But for the Grace of God 1937,Ja 13,21:4
Marching Song 1937,F 18,18:2
Bachelor Born 1938,Ja 26,26:3
Lonergan, Ray (Miscellaneous)
Coach With the Six Insides, The 1962,N 27,44:1
Long, Audrey
Sons and Soldiers 1943,My 5,22:2
Long, Avon
Black Rhythm 1936,D 21,19:2
Belle Helene, La 1941,Jl 8,14:1
Porgy and Bess 1942,Ja 23,16:2
Porgy and Bess 1943,S 14,26:2
Porgy and Bess 1944,F 8,13:2
Memphis Bound 1945,My 25,23:2
Carib Song 1945,S 28,17:2
Beggar's Holiday 1946,D 27,13:3
Beggar's Holiday 1947,Ja 26,II,1:1
Green Pastures, The 1951,Mr 16,35:2
Shuffle Along 1952,My 9,20:5
Mrs Patterson 1954,D 2,37:1
Ballad of Jazz Street, The 1959,N 12,28:1
Fly Blackbird 1962,F 6,26:2
Fly Blackbird 1962,Ap 29,II,1:1
Porgy and Bess 1965,Mr 6,17:1
Long, Barbara
Watched Pot, The 1947,O 29,31:4
Family Reunion, The 1947,N 29,9:2
Long, Bethell
She Stoops to Conquer 1949,D 29,21:3
Long, Bob
Nina Rosa 1930,My 31,19:3
On Your Toes 1936,Ap 13,14:4
Long, Brenda
Saratoga 1959,D 8,59:4
Long, David
Billy Budd 1951,F 12,18:3
Long, David (Director)
Junebug Graduates Tonight! 1967,F 27,35:1
Long, David (Lighting Director)
Me, Candido! 1956,O 16,36:2
Long, David (Miscellaneous)
Golem, The 1959,F 26,38:2
Long, David (Producer)
Sweeney Todd 1957,Ag 28,21:4
Power of Dreams, A 1958,Mr 11,33:1
Long, Dillard (Playwright)
Good Woman, Poor Thing, A 1932,D 11,IX,5:1
Good Woman, Poor Thing, A 1933,Ja 10,27:3
Long, Dillard (Producer)
Trojan Incident 1938,Ap 22,15:2
Long, Ellen
Salvation on a String; Supper for the Dead 1954,Jl 7,23:1
Long, Fay
Orchids Preferred 1937,My 12,26:5
Long, Gary (Lighting Director)
Trumpets and Drums 1969,O 13,52:1
Lady From Maxim's, The 1970,Je 1,41:1
Long, Gretchen
Salvation on a String; Supper for the Dead 1954,Jl 7,23:1
Long, Harry
Yours Truly 1927,Ja 26,16:5
Long, Hubert
Democratic Body, A 1942,F 13,24:7
Catherine Was Great 1944,Ag 3,16:1
Long, Janice
Salvation on a String; Supper for the Dead 1954,Jl 7,23:1
Long, Jesse (Producer)
Family Affair, A 1946,N 28,41:2
Long, Jodi Kim
Nowhere to Go But Up 1962,N 12,36:2
Long, John Luther (Playwright)
Crowns 1922,N 10,20:3
Long, Johnny
Hot Rhythm 1930,Ag 22,18:5
Blackberries of 1932 1932,Ap 5,27:5
Long, Joseph
Caviar 1934,Je 8,19:2
Long, Ken
Touch 1970,N 9,52:1
Long, Kenn (Composer)
Touch 1970,N 9,52:1
Long, Kenn (Lyricist)
Touch 1970,N 9,52:1
Long, Kenn (Playwright)
Touch 1970,N 9,52:1

Long, Lily
Merry World, The 1926,Je 9,18:3
Long, Loretta
Pins and Needles 1967,Je 9,51:2
Long, Mang
Squealer, The 1928,N 13,36:3
Long, Natalie
Hot Rhythm 1930,Ag 22,18:5
Long, Nick
Shore Leave 1922,Ag 9,20:2
Merchant of Venice, The 1922,D 22,13:1
Agent 666, L' 1923,My 30,10:5
Laugh, Clown, Laugh! 1923,N 29,30:1
Lollipop 1924,Ja 22,15:3
Still Waters 1926,Mr 2,23:1
Kitty's Kisses 1926,My 7,12:2
Oh, Please! 1926,D 22,24:3
She's My Baby 1928,Ja 4,22:2
Street Singer, The 1929,S 18,35:2
Through the Years 1932,Ja 29,13:3
Say When 1934,O 28,IX,3:1
Say When 1934,N 9,24:2
Louisiana Purchase 1940,My 29,19:2
Artists and Models 1943,N 6,16:6
Long, Philip J (Miscellaneous)
Can-Can 1953,My 8,28:1
Long, Ray
Ziegfeld Follies 1943,Ap 2,16:2
Texas Li'l Darlin' 1949,N 26,10:5
Long, Ray (Lighting Director)
Stop, You're Killing Me; Laughs, Etc 1969,Mr 20,53:1
Stop, You're Killing Me; Terrible Jim Fitch 1969,Mr 20,53:1
Stop, You're Killing Me; Bad Bad Jo-Jo 1969,Mr 20,53:1
Long, Reginald (Playwright)
Almost in Confidence 1936,F 18,26:7
Long, Robert
Possession 1928,O 3,35:1
Music Hath Charms 1934,D 31,8:2
Story to Be Whispered 1937,Ag 20,21:4
Long, Robert C
Her Man of Wax 1933,O 12,32:3
Long, Robert W
Bare Facts 1927,Ag 17,27:5
Long, Ronald
Pin to See the Peepshow, A 1953,S 18,17:2
Nature's Way 1957,O 17,42:2
Brouhaha 1960,Ap 27,31:2
Long, Sadie
Creditors 1949,N 22,36:5
Long, Sally
George White's Scandals 1922,Ag 29,10:1
Long, Shorty
Most Happy Fella, The 1956,My 4,20:1
Most Happy Fella, The 1956,My 13,II,1:1
Long, Stewart
Cyrano de Bergerac 1946,O 9,33:2
Cyrano de Bergerac 1947,Ja 17,27:2
Long, Sumner Arthur (Playwright)
Never Too Late 1962,N 28,42:1
Angela 1969,O 31,33:1
Long, Sydney
Bellamy Trial, The 1928,Ag 20,21:1
Long, Tamara
Dames at Sea 1968,D 21,46:1
Long, Thomas
Wandering Jew, The 1927,F 2,22:4
Long, Verna
George White's Scandals 1935,D 26,20:2
Orchids Preferred 1937,My 12,26:5
Long, Walter
Very Warm for May 1939,N 18,23:2
Boys and Girls Together 1940,O 2,19:2
Follow the Girls 1944,Ap 10,15:2
Toplitzky of Notre Dame 1946,D 27,13:4
Long, William Jr
Career 1957,My 1,42:6
Long, Zola
You Can't Take It With You 1951,Ap 7,8:6
Detective Story 1954,F 13,11:2
Joan of Lorraine 1955,Mr 26,12:2
My 3 Angels 1956,F 4,24:2
Persecution and Assassination of Marat As Performed by the Inmates of the Asylum of Charenton Under the Direction of the Marquis de Sade, The 1967,Ja 4,34:1
Long Track Sam
Better Times 1922,S 4,14:2
Vaudeville (Palace) 1927,My 3,25:2
Longden, John
Delilah 1930,O 12,VIII,1:8
Longdon, Terence
Midsummer Night's Dream, A 1954,S 22,33:1
Longe, Jeffrey (Miscellaneous)
Land Beyond the River, A 1957,Mr 29,15:7
Oh, Kay! 1960,Ap 18,37:2
Longford, Christine Lady (Playwright)
Mr Jiggins of Jigginstown 1936,D 18,30:2
Longford, Gordon (Miscellaneous)
Stop the World-I Want to Get Off 1962,O 4,45:4

Longford, Lord (Director)
Youth's the Season 1937,O 24,XI,3:3
Longford, Lord (Miscellaneous)
Ascendancy 1935,Ja 31,22:3
Longford, Lord (Playwright)
Melians, The 1931,O 11,VIII,4:8
Yahoo 1935,Jl 28,X,1:1
Armlet of Jade 1936,Ap 15,25:3
Longford, Lord (Producer)
Ah, Wilderness! 1936,My 5,26:1
Lady of the Sea 1945,S 9,II,1:5
Longley, Ralph
Lucky Sam McCarver 1950,Ap 15,10:6
Small Hours, The 1951,F 16,22:1
Longman, Richard
Qudrille 1954,N 4,39:2
Last Love of Don Juan, The 1955,N 24,40:1
Little Glass Clock, The 1956,Mr 27,40:2
Potting Shed, The 1957,Ja 30,32:1
Under Milk Wood 1957,O 16,42:5
Browning Version, The 1958,Mr 7,17:2
You Never Can Tell 1958,Je 17,25:1
Longmire, Adele
Abe Lincoln in Illinois 1938,O 4,20:1
Abe Lincoln in Illinois 1938,O 17,12:2
Two on an Island 1940,Ja 23,17:2
Old Acquaintance 1940,D 24,18:3
Nine Girls 1943,Ja 14,26:2
Outrageous Fortune 1943,N 4,28:5
Longmire, William
John Brown's Body 1953,F 16,17:2
Longo, Marietta
Aria del Continente, L' 1927,O 5,30:2
Longo, Stella
Enemy of the People, An 1959,F 5,24:4
Longpre, Guy
Holiday on Ice 1965,S 2,38:4
Longson, Lila (Playwright)
What Women Do? 1925,Jl 21,26:4
Longstreet, David (Director)
Year of Pilar, The 1952,Ja 7,14:3
Longstreet, David (Producer)
Year of Pilar, The 1952,Ja 7,14:3
Longstreet, David (Scenic Designer)
Year of Pilar, The 1952,Ja 7,14:3
Longstreet, Stephen (Original Author)
High Button Shoes 1947,O 10,32:2
High Button Shoes 1955,Mr 12,10:6
Longstreet, Stephen (Playwright)
High Button Shoes 1947,O 10,32:2
High Button Shoes 1955,Mr 12,10:6
Longstreth, Edward
Don Quixote, Esquire 1920,My 7,12:6
Longstreth, Joseph
Devil's Disciple, The 1950,Ja 26,23:2
Longuet, Paul
Payment Deferred 1931,O 1,24:2
Longwell, Dennis
Duchess of Malfi, The 1962,Mr 5,27:1
Longwell, Nancy
Ballad of John Ogilvie, The 1968,O 9,42:4
Lonner, Ernst (Producer)
Singing Jailbirds 1928,My 20,VIII,2:1
Lonsdale, Frederick (Director)
High Road, The 1928,S 11,31:1
Another Love Story 1943,O 13,29:2
Lonsdale, Frederick (Playwright)
Lady in Ermine, The 1922,O 3,22:2
Aren't We All? 1923,Ap 15,VII,2:4
Aren't We All? 1923,My 22,14:2
Aren't We All? 1923,My 27,VII,1:1
But for the Grace of God 1923,S 9,VII,2:4
Spring Cleaning 1923,N 10,16:3
Spring Cleaning 1923,N 18,VIII,1:1
Fake, The 1924,Mr 23,VIII,1:3
Fake, The 1924,O 7,26:3
Last of Mrs Cheyney, The 1925,N 1,VIII,2:4
Last of Mrs Cheyney, The 1925,N 10,23:5
Katja 1926,O 19,27:3
On Approval 1926,O 19,27:1
On Approval 1927,My 15,VIII,2:6
High Road, The 1927,S 25,VIII,2:1
High Road, The 1928,S 11,31:1
Canaries Sometimes Sing 1929,O 22,26:3
Canaries Sometimes Sing 1929,N 10,X,2:1
Canaries Sometimes Sing 1930,O 21,34:2
Never Come Back 1932,O 29,18:6
Once Is Enough 1938,Ja 28,17:2
Once Is Enough 1938,F 16,16:2
Foreigners 1939,D 6,30:2
On Approval 1942,Mr 1,VIII,1:5
Another Love Story 1943,O 13,29:2
But for the Grace of God 1946,S 4,27:2
But for the Grace of God 1946,S 17,5:5
Way Things Go, The 1950,My 3,19:8
Way Things Go, The 1950,Mr 12,II,3:7
Day After Tomorrow 1950,O 27,25:2
Loo, Richard Kuen
Who Was That Lady I Saw You With?
1958,Mr 4,33:2
Loo-Ylang, Bol
Outrageous Mrs Palmer, The 1920,O 13,18:1

Look, Allan
Prunella 1929,Ap 10,23:3
Loomis, Amy
Electra 1931,My 24,VIII,3:5
Loomis, Clarence (Playwright)
Susanna, Don't You Cry 1939,My 23,27:2
Loomis, Harrison
Hamlet 1931,Ap 24,26:4
Loomis, Joe
Swing It 1937,Jl 23,17:2
Loomis, Judith
Night Circus, The 1958,D 3,44:1
Loomis, Sheldon
Secret Garden, The 1931,N 8,31:4
Loomis, William F
Hades, the Ladies 1934,Mr 29,25:3
Loomis Sisters
Scandals 1931,Ag 11,28:4
George White's Scandals 1931,S 15,30:1
Music Hall Varieties 1932,N 23,15:3
Music Hall Varieties 1933,Ja 3,19:4
Loos, Anita (Director)
Social Register, The 1931,N 10,28:2
Loos, Anita (Original Author)
Gentlemen Prefer Blondes 1926,S 29,23:1
Gentlemen Prefer Blondes 1949,D 9,35:3
Gentlemen Prefer Blondes 1949,D 18,II,3:1
Loos, Anita (Playwright)
Whole Town's Talking, The 1923,Ag 30,8:2
Whole Town's Talking, The 1923,S 9,VII,1:1
Fall of Eve, The 1925,S 1,18:1
Fall of Eve, The 1925,S 6,VII,1:1
Gentlemen Prefer Blondes 1926,Ap 25,VIII,1:8
Whole Town's Talking, The 1926,S 8,19:3
Gentlemen Prefer Blondes 1926,S 29,23:1
Gentlemen Prefer Blondes 1926,O 3,VIII,1:1
Gentlemen Prefer Blondes 1928,Ap 3,32:3
Nine Fifteen Revue, The 1930,F 12,26:2
Social Register, The 1931,O 4,VIII,2:3
Social Register, The 1931,N 10,28:2
Happy Birthday 1946,N 1,31:2
Happy Birthday 1946,N 10,II,1:1
Gentlemen Prefer Blondes 1949,D 9,35:3
Gentlemen Prefer Blondes 1949,D 18,II,3:1
Gigi 1951,N 26,20:4
Cheri 1959,O 13,44:1
Gogo Loves You 1964,O 10,19:2
King's Mare, The 1966,Jl 21,23:1
Loos, Theodor
Constant Wife, The 1928,My 20,VIII,2:1
Loose, Anne-Marie
Persians, The 1927,F 27,VII,2:3
Loose, John
Ticket-of-Leave Man, The 1961,D 23,15:1
Lope, Lita
Belmont Varieties 1932,S 29,17:2
Loper, Don
One for the Money 1939,F 6,9:2
Very Warm for May 1939,N 18,23:2
All in Fun 1940,D 28,11:2
Loper, Robert (Director)
Twelfth Night 1964,Jl 23,18:1
Lopes, Victor
Marie Vison, La 1970,Jl 15,29:1
Lopez, Aimee
Variations of 1940 1940,Ja 29,12:1
Lopez, Alexandro
Riot Act, The 1963,Mr 9,5:2
Lopez, Carlos
Vanderbilt Revue, The 1930,O 26,VIII,3:5
Lopez, Lita
Love's Call 1925,S 11,20:1
Sex Fable, The 1931,O 21,26:1
Lopez, Maria Luisa
Mexicana 1939,Ap 22,14:4
Viva O'Brien 1941,O 10,27:2
Lopez, Pedro
Louisiana 1933,F 28,15:5
Lopez, Pilar
Top-Notchers 1942,My 30,8:5
Lopez, Priscilla
Your Own Thing 1969,Mr 29,39:1
Lopez, Radames
Vida es Sueno, La 1964,Mr 18,49:1
Lopez, Ronald
Bullfight 1954,Ja 13,25:2
Lopez, Sabatino (Playwright)
Face Value 1921,D 27,10:2
Lopez, Vincent
Love Birds 1921,Mr 16,12:1
Vaudeville (Hippodrome) 1924,Ja 22,15:6
Vaudeville (Hippodrome) 1924,F 12,20:2
Lopez, Vincent (Musical Director)
Vaudeville (Hollywood) 1932,F 16,24:3
Aquarama 1960 1960,Jl 1,14:6
Lopez, Vincent and His Orchestra
Vaudeville (Palace) 1923,Ja 23,18:2
Vaudeville (Palace) 1923,Ja 30,12:2
Untitled-Revue 1928,N 19,16:2
Vaudeville (Palace) 1929,Mr 25,33:2
Aquarama 1960 1960,Jl 1,14:6
Lopokova, Lydia
Tale of the Soldier, The 1927,Ag 14,VII,1:7

Lopokova, Lydia—Cont
Doll's House, A 1936,Mr 3,25:2
Misanthrope, The 1937,F 24,18:6
Lopoukin, Peter
Clear All Wires! 1932,S 15,19:1
Loprete, Lee
Priorities of 1942 1942,Mr 13,23:2
Lopus, Michael
Babes in Arms 1951,Mr 10,7:3
Loquasto, Santo (Costume Designer)
Bacchae, The 1969,Mr 15,24:1
Three Philip Roth Stories; Conversion of the Jews
1970,Jl 31,14:1
Three Philip Roth Stories; Epstein 1970,Jl 31,14:1
Three Philip Roth Stories; Defender of the Faith
1970,Jl 31,14:1
Cops and Horrors; Fly Paper 1970,Ag 11,27:1
Cops and Horrors; Dracula 1970,Ag 11,27:1
Story Theater Repertory; Saint Julian the
Hospitaler 1970,O 21,40:1
Story Theater Repertory; Gimpel the Food
1970,O 21,40:1
Loquasto, Santo (Scenic Designer)
Bacchae, The 1969,Mr 15,24:1
Narrow Road to the Deep North 1969,D 2,64:1
Forensic and the Navigators 1970,Ap 2,43:1
Unseen Hand, The 1970,Ap 2,43:1
Three Philip Roth Stories; Epstein 1970,Jl 31,14:1
Three Philip Roth Stories; Defender of the Faith
1970,Jl 31,14:1
Three Philip Roth Stories; Conversion of the Jews
1970,Jl 31,14:1
Cops and Horrors; Fly Paper 1970,Ag 11,27:1
Cops and Horrors; Dracula 1970,Ag 11,27:1
Story Theater Repertory; Saint Julian the
Hospitaler 1970,O 21,40:1
Story Theater Repertory; Gimpel the Food
1970,O 21,40:1
Revenger's Tragedy, The 1970,D 2,58:1
Loquasto, Santo (Translator)
Bacchae, The 1969,Mr 23,II,11:1
Lor, Denise
To Be or Not to Be-What Kind of a Question Is
That? 1970,O 20,39:1
Loraine, Emily
Kiss for Cinderella, A 1942,Mr 11,22:2
Loraine, Karol
Day Before Spring, The 1945,N 23,27:2
Loraine, Robert
Tiger Cats 1924,O 19,VIII,2:6
Tiger Cats 1924,O 22,18:1
Man With a Load of Mischief, The 1925,O 27,20:1
Man With a Load of Mischief, The
1925,N 1,VIII,1:1
Master of the Inn, The 1925,D 23,22:2
Two Orphans, The 1926,Ap 6,26:2
Two Orphans, The 1926,Ap 11,VIII,1:1
Romeo and Juliet 1927,Ja 2,VII,2:5
Father, The 1927,S 4,VII,2:1
Cyrano de Bergerac 1927,N 27,IX,4:1
Dance of Death, The 1928,F 5,VIII,4:7
Art and Mrs Bottle 1929,D 8,X,2:5
Canaries Sometimes Sing 1930,O 21,34:2
Barbara's Wedding 1931,O 9,21:1
Father, The 1931,O 9,21:1
Devil Passes, The 1932,Ja 5,20:3
Devil Passes, The 1932,Ja 10,VIII,1:1
Domino 1932,Ag 7,IX,1:1
Domino 1932,Ag 17,13:2
Lucrece 1932,N 30,22:8
Lucrece 1932,D 4,IX,3:3
Lucrece 1932,D 21,22:2
Lucrece 1933,Ja 1,IX,1:1
Days Without End 1934,Ja 9,19:1
Times Have Changed 1935,F 26,16:1
Loraine, Robert (Director)
Father, The 1931,O 9,21:1
Barbara's Wedding 1931,O 9,21:1
Loraine, Violet
Clara Gibbings 1928,D 9,X,2:1
Fanfare 1932,Je 24,15:2
Bing Boys Are Here, The 1934,D 19,26:6
Loraine, Wauna
Why Men Leave Home 1922,Jl 30,VI,1:3
Why Men Leave Home 1922,S 13,18:2
Lorance, Milton
New Yorkers, The 1927,Mr 11,24:3
Lorber, Martha
Mecca 1920,O 5,12:2
Ziegfeld Follies 1922,Je 6,18:2
Ziegfeld Follies 1924,Je 25,26:1
Mozart 1926,N 23,26:2
Three Little Girls 1930,Mr 30,VIII,2:7
Three Little Girls 1930,Ap 15,29:1
Lorca, Federico Garcia (Composer)
Autobiography 1956,O 3,29:2
Lorca, Federico Garcia (Miscellaneous)
Dama Boba, La; Villano En Su Rincon, El;
Fuenteovejuna 1935,S 22,X,2:5
Lorca, Federico Garcia (Original Author)
Wind Remains, The 1943,Mr 31,16:6
Esta Noche... Teatro 1968,O 15,40:1
Lorca, Federico Garcia (Playwright)
Bitter Oleander 1935,F 12,24:3

Lorca, Federico Garcia (Playwright)—Cont
Blood Wedding 1949,F 7,16:2
Blood Wedding 1949,F 13,II,1:1
Shoemaker's Prodigious Wife, The 1949,Je 15,38:2
House of Bernarda Alba, The 1951,Ja 8,14:6
Yerma 1952,F 8,18:4
Love of Don Perlimplin and Belisa in the Garden,
    The 1953,N 4,30:5
Blood Wedding 1958,Ap 1,35:1
Tragicomedy of Don Cristobita and Dona Rosita,
    The 1958,My 30,12:2
If Five Years Pass 1962,My 11,37:1
Shoemaker's Prodigious Wife, The 1962,S 2,44:4
House of Bernarda Alba, The 1963,N 25,23:2
Retabilillo de Don Cristobal, El; Puppet Theater of
    Don Cristobal, The; Zapatera Prodigiosa, La;
    Shoemaker's Prodigious Wife, The 1964,S 3,23:2
Yerma 1966,D 9,60:1
Lorca, Mario
Remolienda, La; Bawdy Party 1968,F 3,20:1
Lorca, Peter
Criminals, The 1941,D 22,24:3
Lord, Alex
Dybbuk, The 1954,O 27,33:6
Three Sisters, The 1955,F 26,13:2
Lord, Barbara
Taming of the Shrew, The 1956,Ag 6,20:1
Taming of the Shrew, The 1957,F 21,30:2
Duchess of Malfi, The 1957,Mr 20,33:1
Clearing in the Woods, A 1959,F 13,32:1
Lord, Beman
Doodle Dandy of the U S A 1942,O 19,15:2
Bright Boy 1944,Mr 3,19:5
Lord, Bob
Oklahoma! 1953,S 1,19:1
Lord, Catita
Does a Tiger Wear a Necktie? 1969,F 26,38:1
Lord, Dorothy
Cold in Sables 1931,D 24,20:7
Lord, Ed
Vaudeville (Palace) 1923,O 23,18:2
Lord, Ellen
Prunella 1929,Ap 10,23:3
Lord, Frances
Mary Stuart 1956,Ap 28,10:2
Lord, Jack
Traveling Lady 1954,O 28,45:2
Lord, Leonard
Babies a La Carte 1927,Ag 16,31:1
Who Cares 1930,Jl 9,27:1
Tragedy of the Ages, The 1933,Ap 7,22:7
Queer People 1934,F 16,16:2
First Lady 1952,My 29,18:5
Lord, Louis
Dead End 1935,O 29,17:2
Lord, Marion
Red Geranium, The 1922,My 9,22:3
Last Warning, The 1922,O 25,23:1
Last Warning, The 1922,O 29,VII,1:1
Tarnish 1923,O 2,10:1
Lord, Marjorie
Springtime for Henry 1940,F 27,16:3
Signature 1945,F 15,25:2
Little Brown Jug 1946,Mr 7,32:2
Girl in the Freudian Slip, The 1967,My 19,34:3
Lord, Mindret (Playwright)
New Faces of 1936 1936,My 20,24:5
Lord, Pauline
Big Game 1920,Ja 22,23:1
Big Game 1920,Ja 25,VIII,2:2
Samson and Delilah 1920,N 18,18:1
Samson and Delilah 1920,N 28,VI,1:1
Anna Christie 1921,N 3,22:1
Anna Christie 1921,N 6,VI,1:1
Anna Christie 1921,N 13,VI,1:1
Anna Christie 1922,Ja 15,III,3:1
Anna Christie 1923,Ap 11,16:2
Anna Christie 1923,Ap 15,VII,2:4
Launzi 1923,O 11,16:3
She Stoops to Conquer 1924,Je 10,24:3
They Knew What They Wanted 1924,N 25,27:1
They Knew What They Wanted 1924,N 30,VIII,1:2
Sandalwood 1926,S 23,23:1
Sandalwood 1926,O 3,VIII,1:1
Trelawney of the 'Wells' 1927,F 1,24:4
Mariners 1927,Mr 29,22:2
Mariners 1927,Ap 3,VIII,1:1
Candida 1927,Ag 31,19:4
Surmise 1927,O 23,VIII,1:3
Spellbound 1927,N 15,26:2
Spellbound 1927,N 20,IX,1:1
Salvation 1928,F 1,31:1
Salvation 1928,F 12,VIII,1:1
She Stoops to Conquer 1928,My 20,VIII,1:1
Strange Interlude 1928,D 18,37:3
Ann Vroome 1930,Jl 27,VIII,2:3
Distant Drums 1932,Ja 19,24:3
Distant Drums 1932,Ja 31,VIII,1:1
Truth About Blayds, The 1932,Ap 12,25:2
Late Christopher Bean, The 1932,N 1,24:3
Ethan Frome 1936,Ja 7,24:7
Ethan Frome 1936,Ja 22,15:2
Ethan Frome 1936,F 2,IX,1:1
Ethan Frome 1936,N 15,XI,2:1

Suspect 1940,Ap 10,30:4
Eight O'Clock Tuesday 1941,Ja 7,18:2
Walrus and the Carpenter, The 1941,N 10,20:2
Sleep, My Pretty One 1944,N 3,26:8
Lord, Pauline (Miscellaneous)
She Stoops to Conquer 1928,My 15,17:1
Lord, Philip
Fall and Rise of Susan Lenox, The 1920,Je 11,11:2
Nobody's Money 1921,Ag 18,9:3
Lights Out 1922,Ag 18,8:4
Persons Unknown 1922,O 26,12:1
Silence 1924,N 13,18:2
When You Smile 1925,O 6,31:2
Square Crooks 1926,Mr 2,23:2
Free for All 1931,S 9,25:1
Here Goes the Bride 1931,N 4,31:2
Untitled-Recital 1932,F 8,21:1
Marching By 1932,Mr 4,17:1
Saint Wench 1933,Ja 3,19:3
Lord, Philip (Director)
Untitled-Recital 1932,F 8,21:1
Lord, Sophie
Any Woman 1934,Ag 28,24:4
Lord, Sylvia
New Faces of 1962 1962,F 2,25:1
Cats' Pajamas, The 1962,Je 1,16:2
Lorde, Andre de (Playwright)
System du Docteur Goudron et du Professeur
    Plume, Le 1923,N 13,24:2
Untitled-Play 1924,F 3,VII,1:4
Untitled-Play 1929,Mr 3,VIII,4:8
Old Women, The 1935,Jl 12,15:3
Lorde, Athena
Bruno and Sidney 1949,My 4,38:2
Loredo, Armando (Composer)
Pinocchio 1939,Ja 3,19:2
Lorendain, Marie
Abisso 1920,O 10,VI,1:8
Lorentz, Anne
Breakfast in Bed 1920,F 4,12:1
Lorentz, Kay
Why Do I Deserve This? 1966,Ja 19,31:2
Lorentz, Kay (Playwright)
Why Do I Deserve This? 1966,Ja 19,31:2
Lorentz, Lore
Why Do I Deserve This? 1966,Ja 19,31:2
Lorentz, Lore (Director)
Why Do I Deserve This? 1966,Ja 19,31:2
Lorentz, Lore (Playwright)
Why Do I Deserve This? 1966,Ja 19,31:2
Lorentz, Lyle
Trumpets and Drums 1969,O 13,52:1
Macbeth 1969,D 23,25:1
Hamlet 1970,O 19,51:1
Lorenz, Elsie
Miracle, The 1924,Ja 16,17:1
Lorenz, Fred
From Vienna 1939,Je 21,26:2
Reunion in New York 1940,F 22,28:4
Winter Soldiers 1942,N 30,19:2
Big Two, The 1947,Ja 9,21:2
Lorenz, Guy
Courage 1927,Ja 20,20:1
Romancing 'Round 1927,O 4,32:4
Lorenz, Hans (Playwright)
Raetzel um Beate 1936,N 8,X,2:1
Lorenz, Herbert Richard (Playwright)
Henky 1924,Ap 27,VIII,2:3
Melody Man, The 1924,My 14,14:2
Lorenz, John
Spook House 1930,Je 4,33:3
Fabulous Invalid, The 1938,O 10,15:1
American Way, The 1939,Ja 23,9:2
Strangler Fig, The 1940,My 7,31:2
As You Like It 1941,O 21,29:2
Ramshackle Inn 1944,Ja 6,17:5
Lorenz, Robert
On the Town 1944,D 29,11:4
Lorenz, William
Blood and Sand 1921,S 21,16:2
Comedian, The 1923,Mr 14,14:1
Man in Evening Clothes, The 1924,D 6,13:4
Behold This Dreamer 1927,N 1,20:4
She Stoops to Conquer 1928,My 15,17:1
Mrs Bumpstead-Leigh 1929,Ap 2,28:3
Ladies of the Jury 1929,O 22,26:2
It's a Grand Life 1930,F 11,30:3
Lorenz-Inger, Fred
Ist Geraldine ein Engel? 1946,N 4,33:4
Faust 1947,N 29,9:2
Loretta, Dee
Jimmie 1920,N 18,15:3
Loreze, Henriette
Affaires Son les Affaires, Les 1924,Mr 11,17:1
Avare, L'; Miser, The 1924,Mr 12,17:3
Monsieur Brotonneau 1924,Mr 13,14:1
Blanchette 1924,Mr 19,19:4
Lorimer, Katherine
Hearts Are Trumps! 1927,Ap 8,21:1
Lady Dedlock 1929,Ja 1,61:2
Lorimer, Louise
East Lynne 1926,Mr 11,18:4
Witch, The 1926,N 19,22:5

Lorimer, Louise—Cont
Rapid Transit 1927,Ap 8,21:2
Maya 1928,F 22,19:1
Feathers in a Gale 1943,D 22,26:2
Take It As It Comes 1944,F 11,17:2
I Remember Mama 1944,O 20,16:2
Lorimer, Robert (Composer)
But Never Jam Today 1969,Ap 24,40:1
Lorimer, Robert (Lyricist)
But Never Jam Today 1969,Ap 24,40:1
Lorin, Will (Composer)
It's About Time 1942,Mr 31,28:3
Send Me No Flowers 1960,D 6,54:1
Loring, Ann
Bright Rebel 1938,D 28,24:2
Brooklyn Biarritz 1941,F 28,16:2
Loring, August
Geisha, The 1931,O 6,35:4
Pirates of Penzance, The 1936,Ap 21,27:5
Mikado, The 1944,F 12,11:3
Ruddigore 1944,Mr 3,19:5
Loring, Beatrice
Henry's Harem 1926,S 14,25:2
Cyclone Lover, The 1928,Je 6,23:3
Loring, Claire
Lady Comes Across, The 1942,Ja 10,10:2
Loring, Estelle
Day Before Spring, The 1945,N 23,27:2
Cradle Will Rock, The 1947,N 25,38:3
Cradle Will Rock, The 1947,D 27,11:2
Inside U S A 1948,Mr 30,27:3
Inside U S A 1948,My 1,19:2
Loring, Eugene
Beautiful People, The 1941,Ap 22,27:2
Loring, Eugene (Choreographer)
Carmen Jones 1943,D 3,26:2
Carmen Jones 1943,D 12,II,3:1
Carmen Jones 1945,My 3,26:5
Carmen Jones 1946,Ap 8,32:2
Buttrio Square 1952,O 15,40:2
Ice Capades 1958,S 4,33:2
Ice Capades 1966,Je 2,50:2
Loring, Eugene (Director)
Buttrio Square 1952,O 15,40:2
Silk Stockings 1955,F 25,17:3
Loring, Gregory
Fools Errant 1922,Ag 22,12:3
Loring, Gus
Yeomen of the Guard, The 1944,Mr 5,34:3
Loring, Kay
Having Wonderful Time 1937,F 22,12:5
What a Life 1938,Ap 14,26:2
Horse Fever 1940,N 25,21:2
Three Men on a Horse 1942,O 10,10:2
Ask My Friend Sandy 1943,F 5,16:2
Rugged Path, The 1945,N 12,17:2
Christopher Blake 1946,D 2,33:2
Great Campaign, The 1947,Ap 1,33:2
Loring, Marcia
Republic, The 1970,Ap 28,49:1
Loring, Marie
Deacon, The 1925,N 25,14:3
Loring, Michael
Who's Who 1938,Mr 2,16:2
Sing Out the News 1938,S 26,12:5
Loring, Norman (Director)
Mozart 1926,N 23,26:2
Loring, Teris
Shore Leave 1922,Ag 9,20:2
Lorino, Lynn Gay
Oh, Kay! 1960,Ap 18,37:2
Lormer, Jon
American Holiday 1936,F 22,13:3
Murder in the Cathedral 1936,Mr 21,13:5
Class of '29 1936,My 16,10:3
Sun and I, The 1937,F 27,9:5
Treasure Island 1938,My 15,II,2:3
Fireworks on the James 1940,My 15,30:2
Hippolytus 1948,N 22,25:5
Lorne, Marion
Pansy's Arabian Night 1924,Ag 24,VII,1:3
Sorry You've Been Troubled 1929,O 13,IX,4:1
Road House 1932,O 30,IX,2:3
Hyde Park Corner 1934,O 28,IX,3:4
Espionage 1935,N 10,IX,3:1
Fugitive, The 1936,Je 28,IX,1:8
London After Dark 1937,Ap 8,21:2
Dance Me a Song 1950,Ja 21,10:5
Loros, George
Nighthawks 1967,D 30,14:2
Happiness Cage, The 1970,O 5,56:4
Lorrain, Jon
Moby Dick 1970,Je 3,52:1
Lorraine, Dorothy
Genius and the Crowd 1920,S 7,20:1
Lorraine, Emily
Paddy the Next Best Thing 1920,Ag 28,5:5
Title, The 1921,N 15,23:3
Squaw Man, The 1921,D 27,10:3
Mister Pitt 1924,Ja 23,15:3
Mourning Becomes Electra; Homecoming
    1931,O 27,22:1
Romantic Mr Dickens 1940,D 3,33:2
Strings, My Lord, Are False, The 1942,My 20,24:2

Lorraine, Emily—Cont
Skin of Our Teeth, The 1942,N 19,29:5
Lorraine, Harriett
Lady Do 1927,Ap 19,24:2
Bachelor Father, The 1928,F 29,28:2
Lorraine, Irene
Frankie and Johnny 1930,S 26,16:5
Lorraine, Jeanne
Laughter Over Broadway 1939,Ja 16,10:3
Lorraine, Lillian
Ziegfeld 9 o'clock Follies 1920,Mr 9,18:1
Ziegfeld Midnight Frolic 1920,Mr 17,14:2
Blue Kitten, The 1922,Ja 14,9:3
Lorraine, Marjorie
Marriage of Cana, The 1932,F 3,22:4
Lorraine, Oscar
Earl Carroll's Vanities 1925,Jl 7,24:1
Lorraine, Paulette
Dejeuner d'Amoureax, Un; Lovers Breakfast, A
   1936,N 26,38:2
Martine 1936,N 26,38:2
Lorraine, Robert
Mary Rose 1920,Ag 8,VI,1:1
Master of the Inn, The 1925,D 23,22:2
Lorraine, Ted
Century Revue and the Midnight Rounders, The
   1920,Jl 13,9:1
Last Waltz, The 1921,My 11,20:3
Lorraine Sisters
Vaudeville (Hippodrome) 1926,My 11,25:3
Wann und Wo 1927,D 18,IX,1:8
Lorrin, Joe
Simpleton of the Unexpected Isles, The
   1954,Ja 12,19:1
Lorring, Joan
Come Back, Little Sheba 1950,F 16,28:5
Autumn Garden, The 1951,Mr 8,36:2
Autumn Garden, The 1951,Mr 18,II,1:1
Dead Pigeon 1953,D 24,10:2
Clearing in the Woods, A 1957,Ja 11,20:2
Awake and Sing! 1970,My 28,35:1
Awake and Sing! 1970,Je 7,II,1:1
Lortel, Lucille
One Man's Woman 1926,My 26,25:1
Vaudeville (Palace) 1928,Ja 31,29:2
Man Who Reclaimed His Head 1932,S 9,17:3
Lortel, Lucille (Director)
Hamlet 1957,Ja 29,27:1
Metamorphosis 1957,F 20,38:1
Pelleas and Melisande 1957,F 20,38:1
Pale Horse, Pale Rider 1957,O 30,26:1
Maidens and Mistresses at Home at the Zoo
   1958,O 29,31:1
Song of Songs 1958,O 29,31:1
Soul Gone Home 1959,O 28,40:7
Shakespeare in Harlem 1959,O 28,40:7
Purification, The 1959,D 9,57:5
Glory in the Flower 1959,D 9,57:5
Victims of Duty 1960,Ja 20,26:1
Notes From the Underground 1960,Ja 20,26:1
Too Close for Comfort 1960,F 3,27:2
Gay Apprentice, The 1960,F 3,27:2
Time to Go 1960,Mr 23,33:1
Coggerers, The 1960,Mr 23,33:1
Embers 1960,O 26,44:1
Nekros 1960,O 26,44:1
Fam and Yam 1960,O 26,44:1
Hanjo 1960,N 16,51:4
Lady Akane, The 1960,N 16,51:4
Shepherd's Chameleon, The 1960,N 30,41:1
Coming Forth by Day of Osiris Jones, The; Kid,
   The 1961,Mr 15,45:2
Brecht on Brecht 1961,N 15,52:2
Cayenne Pepper 1961,D 13,55:5
Grand Vizier, The 1961,D 13,55:5
Brecht on Brecht 1962,Ja 4,26:1
Moon Shines on Kylenamoe, The 1962,O 31,33:1
Figuro in the Night 1962,O 31,33:1
Come Slowly, Eden 1966,D 7,56:1
Willie Doesn't Live Here Anymore 1967,F 8,20:2
Club Bedroom, The 1967,D 6,41:1
Postcards 1967,D 6,41:1
Limb of Snow 1967,D 13,55:1
Meeting, The 1967,D 13,55:1
Let Them Down, Gently; On Vacation
   1968,Ja 31,28:2
Let Them Down, Gently; Our Man in Madras
   1968,Ja 31,28:2
Madrigal of Shakespeare, A 1968,F 14,56:2
Mr and Mrs Lyman 1968,Mr 6,35:1
Hello and Goodbye 1968,N 13,36:2
Guns of Carrar, The 1968,D 10,53:1
Cuba Si 1968,D 10,53:1
Projection Room, The 1969,Ja 15,38:2
Neighbors 1969,Ja 15,38:2
Round With Ring, A 1969,O 30,56:1
Oh, Pioneers 1969,N 12,41:1
Dream of a Blacklisted Actor 1969,D 18,64:1
Perfect Match, The 1970,N 18,41:1
Slow Memories 1970,N 18,41:1
Life and Times of J Walter Smintheus, The
   1970,D 10,59:1
Lortel, Lucille (Miscellaneous)
Threepenny Opera, The 1955,S 21,38:1

Aria Da Capo 1958,My 21,40:1
Guests of the Nation 1958,My 21,40:1
Philoctetes 1959,Ja 14,28:1
I Rise in Flame, Cried the Phoenix 1959,Ap 15,30:1
Sweet Confession 1959,Ap 15,30:1
Masque of Reason, The 1959,N 25,19:4
This Music Crept by Me Upon the Waters
   1959,N 25,19:4
Conditioned Reflex 1967,Ja 11,51:1
Viewing, The 1967,Ja 11,51:1
Midsummer Night's Dream, A 1967,Je 30,23:1
Cruising Speed 600 MPH 1970,Ja 6,48:3
Lortel, Lucille (Producer)
River Line, The 1957,Ja 3,29:2
I Know at the Door 1957,S 30,27:2
Cock-A-Doodle Dandy 1958,N 13,39:2
Balcony, The 1960,Mr 4,21:1
Happy as Larry 1961,Ap 26,36:1
Funny Kind of Evening With David Kossoff, A
   1967,Ja 31,52:1
Let Them Down, Gently; On Vacation
   1968,Ja 31,28:2
Let Them Down, Gently; Our Man in Madras
   1968,Ja 31,28:2
Lortz, Richard (Playwright)
Journey With Strangers, A 1958,N 27,53:1
Lory, Jane
Vilaine Femme, Une 1933,Ja 1,IX,3:4
Lorys, Daniel
Topaze 1931,F 17,29:1
Losch, Tilly
Midsummer Night's Dream, A 1927,Ag 8,6:1
Midsummer Night's Dream, A 1927,N 18,21:1
Midsummer Night's Dream, A 1927,D 4,X,6:1
Jedermann 1927,D 18,IX,6:1
Dantons Tod 1927,D 21,28:3
Dantons Tod 1928,Ja 1,VIII,3:1
Servant of Two Masters, The 1928,Ja 22,VIII,6:1
Wake Up and Dream 1929,Ap 14,X,1:8
Wake Up and Dream 1929,D 31,14:3
Wake Up and Dream 1930,Ja 12,9:1
Wake Up and Dream 1930,Ja 12,VIII,1:1
Band Wagon, The 1931,My 17,VIII,3:2
Band Wagon, The 1931,Je 4,31:3
Band Wagon, The 1931,Je 14,VIII,1:1
Miracle, The 1932,Ap 10,I,18:1
Miracle, The 1932,My 8,VIII,2:2
Streamline 1934,O 21,IX,1:3
Topaze 1947,D 29,21:5
Losch, Tilly (Choreographer)
This Year of Grace 1928,N 8,27:1
Bitter Sweet 1929,N 6,30:2
Wake Up and Dream 1929,D 31,14:3
Wake Up and Dream 1930,Ja 12,9:1
Loscht, Mildred
Bridal Crown, The 1938,F 7,11:2
Losee, Frank
For All of Us 1923,O 16,19:4
Is Zat So? 1925,Ap 25,18:2
Losee, Harry (Choreographer)
Keep Moving 1934,Ag 24,10:2
At Home Abroad 1935,S 20,17:4
At Home Abroad 1935,O 27,IX,8:1
Very Warm for May 1939,N 18,23:2
Losey, Joe (Director)
Little Ol' Boy 1933,Ap 25,15:5
Jayhawker 1934,N 6,34:2
Hymn to the Rising Sun 1936,Ja 13,14:4
Conjur' Man Dies 1936,Mr 12,18:5
Triple-A Plowed Under 1936,Mr 16,21:1
Injunction Granted! 1936,Jl 25,16:3
Who Fights This Battle? 1936,S 21,26:3
Sunup to Sundown 1938,F 2,14:3
Great Campaign, The 1947,Ap 1,33:2
Galileo 1947,Ag 1,21:4
Galileo 1947,D 8,34:2
Lossen, Lina
Anatol 1922,F 5,VI,1:7
Three Sisters, The 1927,Mr 13,VII,2:4
Lota, Remo
Soldiers and Women 1929,S 3,25:1
Street Scene 1947,Ja 10,17:2
Lota (Composer)
Virtue's Bed 1930,Ap 16,26:5
Lotas, John (Miscellaneous)
Mark Twain Tonight! 1966,Mr 24,48:2
Lotas, John (Producer)
Mark Twain Tonight! 1959,Ap 7,40:2
Moby Dick 1961,Ap 11,41:2
Lothar, Corinna
No Strings 1942,Je 14,VIII,2:1
Simpleton of the Unexpected Isles, The
   1954,Ja 12,19:1
Lothar, Ernst (Producer)
Death of a Salesman 1950,Mr 4,10:7
Lothar, Mark (Composer)
Faust, Part I; Prologue in Heaven 1961,F 5,27:2
Faust, Part I; Play, The 1961,F 5,27:2
Faust, Part I; Prelude in the Theater 1961,F 5,27:2
Mitschuldigen, Die 1966,Ap 6,34:1
Lothar, Rudolph (Original Author)
Command to Love, The 1927,S 21,27:1

Lothar, Rudolph (Playwright)
Werewolf, The 1924,Je 8,VII,1:8
Werewolf, The 1924,Ag 26,6:1
Werewolf, The 1924,Ag 31,VII,1:1
Phantom Ship, The 1926,Je 27,VII,3:1
Vive l'Empereur 1926,N 21,VIII,2:1
Anna 1928,My 17,25:2
Joy of Living 1931,Ap 7,31:1
Red Cat, The 1934,S 20,21:1
Lothar, Rudolph (Translator)
Collision 1932,F 17,19:2
Lothar and the Hand People (Miscellaneous)
Forensic and the Navigators 1970,Ap 2,43:1
Unseen Hand, The 1970,Ap 2,43:1
Lothian, Joseph
Merton of the Movies 1922,N 14,16:2
Lothigius, Ingrid
Marie Vison, La 1970,Jl 15,29:1
Loti, Elisa
Come Share My House 1960,F 19,20:2
Laundry, The 1963,F 19,5:2
Lotito, Louis (Miscellaneous)
Visit, The 1958,My 6,40:1
Lotito, Louis (Producer)
Another Love Story 1943,O 13,29:2
Goldilocks 1958,O 13,33:1
Cold Wind and the Warm, The 1958,D 9,55:1
Much Ado About Nothing 1959,S 18,25:2
Lott, John
Great Music 1924,O 6,24:1
Traitor, The 1930,My 3,23:4
Lott, Ruth
Return Engagement 1940,N 2,19:2
Lott, Walter
Country Girl, The 1966,S 30,55:1
Lotterhand, J C
New Freedom, The 1930,My 15,32:4
New Freedom, The 1930,My 17,21:4
Loty, Maud
Mademoiselle Flute 1927,Je 12,VII,2:1
Miracle, Un 1927,D 25,VIII,4:3
Maud et Son Banquier 1928,Ap 1,IX,4:7
Loubet, Jean
Creoles 1927,S 23,33:3
Loubier, Charles (Miscellaneous)
Spots of the Leopard, The 1963,S 25,38:1
Loud, Edward
Once in a Lifetime 1930,S 25,22:3
Caviar 1934,Je 8,19:2
Merrily We Roll Along 1934,O 1,14:1
Louden, Dorothy
Noel Coward's Sweet Potato 1968,O 13,II,5:1
Louden, Francis
Little Minister, The 1925,Mr 24,21:1
Louden, Thomas
Lady Cristilinda, The 1922,D 26,11:2
Living Mask, The 1924,Ja 22,15:1
Command to Love, The 1927,S 21,27:1
Man Who Changed His Name, The 1932,My 3,25:3
Red Planet 1932,D 19,19:2
Lost Horizons 1934,O 16,31:2
Timber House 1936,S 21,27:5
Lady Windermere's Fan 1946,O 15,29:2
Louden, Thomas (Playwright)
Champion, The 1921,Ja 4,11:1
Champion, The 1921,Ja 9,VI,1:1
Love Set, The 1923,Mr 20,24:2
Louderback, Darragh
Take a Brace 1923,Ap 20,20:3
Loudon, Dorothy
Nowhere to Go But Up 1962,N 12,36:2
Noel Coward's Sweet Potato 1968,S 30,59:1
Fig Leaves Are Falling, The 1969,Ja 19:1
Three Men on a Horse 1969,O 17,35:1
Loudon, Isabelle (Mrs Lawrence Langer) (Playwright)
Pursuit of Happiness, The 1933,O 10,24:4
Loudon, Joseph
Poor Nut, The 1925,Ap 28,18:1
Loughlin, Ben
Open House 1947,Je 4,33:4
Small Hours, The 1951,F 16,22:1
Loughlin, Kay
Case of Clyde Griffiths 1936,Mr 14,10:4
Loughlin, Lisa
Ladies Night in a Turkish Bath 1961,Mr 22,38:1
Loughrane, Basil
Kosher Kitty Kelly 1925,Je 16,24:2
Louika (Choreographer)
Medea 1964,S 1,31:1
Louis, Jean (Costume Designer)
Love and Let Love 1951,O 20,11:2
Louis, Louise
Peter Ibbetson 1926,Mr 26,24:7
Louis, Miriam
Singapore 1932,N 15,24:2
Louis-Raymond
Merchant of Venice, The 1924,N 18,23:2
Louise, Carol
Mother Sings 1935,N 13,24:1
Louise, Helene
Jubilee 1935,O 14,20:1
Louise, Mary
Carmen Jones 1959,Ag 18,25:1

Louise, Mary—Cont
Fly Blackbird 1962,F 6,26:2
Fly Blackbird 1962,Ap 29,II,1:1
Lady or the Tiger?, The 1966,O 19,53:1
Passionella 1966,O 19,53:1
Louise, Merle
That Hat! 1964,S 24,45:1
Company 1970,Ap 27,40:1
Company 1970,My 3,II,1:4
Louise, Rose
Hot-Cha! 1932,Mr 9,17:3
Melody 1933,F 15,17:4
Louise, Sara
Lend an Ear 1969,O 29,32:1
Louise, Tina
Will Success Spoil Rock Hunter? 1955,O 14,22:2
Li'l Abner 1956,N 16,24:2
Fade Out--Fade In 1964,My 27,45:1
Louiseville Loons, The
Vaudeville (Palace) 1930,Ag 11,13:3
Louka
Arms and the Man 1926,Ja 21,18:3
Loukia (Choreographer)
Electra 1961,S 20,23:4
Choephori 1961,S 27,32:4
Eumenides 1961,S 27,32:4
Electra 1964,S 8,33:1
Iphigenia in Aulis 1968,N 13,40:1
Hippolytus 1968,N 20,38:3
Lounsbery, Dan
Innocent Voyage, The 1943,N 16,27:2
Lounsbery, David
Days of Our Youth, The 1941,N 29,15:2
Lounsbery, James
Scrambled Wives 1920,Ag 6,16:1
Lourie, Don
Espanola 1921,D 30,13:1
Louvain, Marguerite
Printemps 1929,Ap 21,X,2:7
Louvigny
Nuit, Une 1935,Je 16,X,1:1
Louw, Allan
Time of the Key, A 1963,S 12,33:3
Yearling, The 1965,D 11,25:1
Persecution and Assassination of Marat As
  Performed by the Inmates of the Asylum of
  Charenton Under the Direction of the Marquis de
  Sade, The 1967,Ja 4,34:1
Loux, Constance (Playwright)
Beyond Desire 1967,O 11,36:1
Love, Agnes
Watched Pot, The 1933,My 5,13:7
Love, Andy
Between the Devil 1937,D 23,24:5
Love, Bessie
South 1955,My 2,17:4
Homecoming, The 1958,Ap 22,38:6
Love, Bessie (Playwright)
Homecoming, The 1958,Ap 22,38:6
Love, C R Jr
Galloper, The 1924,D 19,26:2
Love, Charles (Playwright)
Take Me to Bed 1969,Je 14,24:1
Time for Bed 1969,Je 14,24:1
Love, Cornelius Ruxton
Faun, The 1924,Mr 28,17:2
Love, Dorothea
Fly Away Home 1937,Ap 27,18:1
First Lady 1937,O 9,17:2
Misalliance 1955,F 12,10:6
Love, Dorothy (Producer)
Your Own Thing 1968,Ja 15,33:1
Love, Edmund G (Original Author)
Subways Are for Sleeping 1961,D 28,22:1
Love, Elizabeth
Sentinels 1931,D 26,15:1
Noble Prize, The 1933,Jl 4,16:4
By Your Leave 1934,Ja 25,15:3
Loose Moments 1935,F 5,22:3
Three Wise Fools 1936,Mr 2,12:2
Red Harvest 1937,Mr 31,29:2
Lysistrata 1937,Jl 20,19:3
Off to Buffalo! 1939,F 22,18:2
Love, Ellen
Cape Cod Follies 1929,S 19,37:2
London Assurance 1937,F 19,14:5
Farewell Summer 1937,Mr 30,20:2
Tell Me Pretty Maiden 1937,D 17,33:5
Cue for Passion 1940,D 20,33:4
Oklahoma! 1943,Ap 1,27:1
Swing Out, Sweet Land! 1944,N 10,24:6
Sing Out, Sweet Land! 1944,D 28,24:2
Love, James (Miscellaneous)
By Jupiter 1967,Ja 20,28:2
Love, James K
Kilpatrick's Old-Time Minstrels 1930,Ap 21,20:2
Love, Kermit
Naughty-Naught '00 1937,Ja 25,23:2
Love, Kermit (Costume Designer)
Wind Remains, The 1943,Mr 31,16:6
One Touch of Venus 1943,O 8,14:1
Suds in Your Eye 1944,Ja 13,15:5
Dark Hammock 1944,D 12,27:8

Love, Kermit (Lighting Director)
Naughty-Naught '00 1946,O 21,27:5
Love, Kermit (Miscellaneous)
Naughty-Naught '00 1946,O 21,27:5
Love, Leona
Constant Sinner, The 1931,S 15,30:1
Love, Margaret
Antigone 1923,My 4,18:4
Antigone 1923,My 25,28:1
Diff'rent 1925,F 11,19:3
Blue Peter, The 1925,Mr 25,25:3
Engaged! or Cheviot's Choice 1925,Je 19,24:2
Man's Man, A 1925,O 14,31:2
Cradle Song 1927,Ja 25,18:2
Good Hope, The 1927,O 19,24:2
2 + 2 = 5 1927,N 29,30:3
First Stone, The 1928,Ja 14,12:2
On the High Road 1929,Ja 15,22:3
Liliom 1932,O 27,23:2
Dear Jane 1932,N 15,24:3
Love, Mary
Jack and the Beanstalk 1947,N 3,28:2
Many Moons 1947,D 15,35:2
Love, Montagu
Survival of the Fittest 1921,Mr 15,14:1
Kiss of Importance, A 1930,D 2,31:3
Firebird 1932,N 22,25:2
Hangman's Whip 1933,F 25,20:2
Peace Palace 1933,Je 6,30:2
Iron Flowers 1933,Je 13,22:2
Birthright 1933,N 22,22:3
Wooden Slipper, The 1934,Ja 4,16:3
Richard of Bordeaux 1934,F 15,16:2
Love, Phyllis
Country Girl, The 1950,N 11,10:6
Rose Tattoo, The 1951,F 5,19:2
Rose Tattoo, The 1951,F 11,II,1:1
Remarkable Mr Pennypacker, The 1953,D 31,11:2
Bus Stop 1955,Mr 3,23:2
Bus Stop 1955,Mr 13,II,1:1
Easter 1957,Ja 17,35:2
Easter 1957,F 3,II,1:1
Egghead, The 1957,O 10,39:1
Flowering Cherry 1959,O 22,46:1
Distant Bell, A 1960,Ja 14,29:1
Love, Ruxton Jr
Aiglon, L' 1925,O 31,20:3
Love, Samuel (Scenic Designer)
All in Favor 1942,Ja 21,20:6
Lovejoy, Albert R
Midsummer Night's Dream, A 1931,Ag 19,19:3
Lovejoy, Albert R (Miscellaneous)
Midsummer Night's Dream, A 1931,Ag 19,19:3
Lovejoy, Alex
Change Your Luck 1930,Je 7,10:2
Sweet Chariot 1930,O 24,30:2
Black Rhythm 1936,D 21,19:2
How Come Lawd? 1937,O 1,18:5
Lovejoy, Frank
Judgment Day 1934,S 13,26:4
Chalked Out 1937,Mr 26,24:2
Greatest Show on Earth, The 1938,Ja 6,22:2
Censored 1938,F 28,18:2
Snark Was a Boojum, The 1943,S 2,14:4
Sound of Hunting, A 1945,N 21,16:6
Woman Bites Dog 1946,Ap 18,21:2
Best Man, The 1960,Ap 1,39:1
Best Man, The 1960,Ap 10,II,1:1
Lovejoy, William
Gringa, La 1928,F 2,17:1
Trip to Scarborough, A 1929,Mr 18,31:2
Dragon, The 1929,Mr 26,34:2
Love Expert, The 1929,S 24,29:1
Challenge of Youth 1930,Ja 21,28:5
If Booth Had Missed 1931,My 14,27:1
Tom Sawyer 1931,D 26,15:3
Mask and the Face, The 1933,My 9,20:2
Mountain, The 1933,S 12,28:6
Lovel, Leigh
Zeno 1923,Ag 27,14:2
Accused 1925,S 30,20:1
King Can Do No Wrong, The 1927,N 17,28:4
Hotbed 1928,N 10,20:7
Lovelace, Catherine
Censored 1938,F 28,18:2
Lovelace, Henrietta
John Henry 1940,Ja 11,18:2
Mexican Mural; Miracle Painting 1942,Ap 27,19:2
Lovelace, Jean
Mary of Magdala 1946,Mr 26,24:5
Come Marching Home 1946,My 20,18:6
Lovelady, Bruce (Miscellaneous)
Don't Shoot Mable It's Your Husband
  1968,O 23,34:1
Lovelady, John
Killer, The 1960,Mr 23,33:1
Loveless, David (Costume Designer)
Time for Bed 1969,Je 14,24:1
Take Me to Bed 1969,Je 14,24:1
Loveless, David (Scenic Designer)
Take Me to Bed 1969,Je 14,24:1
Time for Bed 1969,Je 14,24:1

Lovell, Leigh
Piper, The 1920,Mr 20,14:2
Lovell, Raymond
Queen Who Kept Her Head, The 1934,F 21,23:4
King's Breakfast, The 1937,D 13,22:8
Cry of the Peacock 1950,Ap 12,33:2
Lovell, Roderick
Kreutzer Sonata, The 1961,F 16,24:2
Lovell, Roderick (Playwright)
Kreutzer Sonata, The 1961,F 16,24:2
Lovell, Susan
Me and Juliet 1953,My 29,17:1
Lovelle, Louise
Hummin' Sam 1933,Ap 10,8:8
Lovely Girls
Nine Fifteen Revue, The 1930,F 12,26:2
Loverde, Frank
Idiot's Delight 1957,F 23,14:2
Lovesee, Geo
Banjo Eyes 1941,D 26,20:2
Lovett, Benjamin
Great Music 1924,O 6,24:1
Lovett, Beresford
Stronger Than Love 1925,D 29,20:2
Henry-Behave 1926,Ag 24,19:4
Piggy 1927,Ja 12,22:2
One for All 1927,My 14,25:5
Lombardi, Ltd 1927,Je 7,27:3
Taming of the Shrew, The 1927,O 26,26:4
Napoleon 1928,Mr 9,21:1
Outsider, The 1928,Ap 10,32:2
Lovett, Helen
Genius and the Crowd 1920,S 7,20:1
Lovett, Monica
Crime and Crime 1963,D 17,51:2
Macbeth 1966,Jl 14,27:2
Lovey, Raymond (Costume Designer)
Saint Joan 1923,D 29,8:4
Lovey, Raymond (Scenic Designer)
Saint Joan 1923,D 29,8:4
Loville, Aljan
Dans Le Noir; In the Dark 1937,F 11,18:3
Christian 1937,F 25,18:6
Lovinger, Rudolph
Waltz of the Dogs, The 1928,Ap 26,31:3
Low, Betty
Antony and Cleopatra 1947,N 27,49:2
Insect Comedy, The 1948,Je 4,26:3
Great to Be Alive! 1950,Mr 24,28:2
Juno 1959,Mr 10,41:1
Miss Emily Adam 1960,Mr 30,43:1
Shout From the Rooftops 1964,O 29,40:1
Low, Carl
Love Me Long 1949,N 8,34:5
Desire Under the Elms 1951,N 22,45:1
Touchstone 1953,F 4,33:2
King of Hearts 1954,Ap 2,23:1
Anastasia 1954,D 30,13:1
Last Love of Don Juan, The 1955,N 24,40:1
Very Special Baby, A 1956,N 15,43:2
Fools Are Passing Through 1958,Ap 3,24:2
Viva Madison Avenue 1960,Ap 7,42:1
Don Juan in Hell 1960,O 4,47:3
Deputy, The 1964,F 27,26:1
Low, Clara (Director)
Torches, The 1923,My 11,20:3
Low, Colin (Scenic Designer)
Do You Know the Milky Way? 1961,O 17,45:1
Low, Fred
Betty Behave 1927,Mr 9,28:4
Yegor Bulevitch 1934,Ja 8,21:7
Aristocrats 1935,My 2,16:2
Low, Louis
Bivouac at Lucca 1957,O 30,26:1
Low, Lucille
Schoolhouse on the Lot 1938,Mr 23,18:4
Low, Rosa
Vaudeville (Palace) 1927,Jl 19,27:6
Low, Virginia
What Every Woman Knows 1954,D 23,16:2
Lowande, Oscar
Circus Princess, The 1927,Ap 26,32:2
Lowden, Charles
Great Adventure, The 1926,D 23,23:1
Lowden, Isabel (Playwright)
In the Land of the Midnight Sun 1930,Ja 7,27:4
Lowe, Alan
Chee-Chee 1928,S 26,25:1
Broken Chain, The 1929,F 21,30:4
Pressing Business 1930,N 18,28:5
Lowe, Arthur
Inadmissible Evidence 1964,S 10,31:1
Lowe, Carrie
Come Seven 1920,Jl 20,10:1
Four in Hand 1923,S 7,10:2
Gertie 1926,N 16,24:2
Farewell to Arms, A 1930,S 23,30:3
Lowe, Charles (Producer)
Show Girl 1961,Ja 13,37:1
Lowe, David
Trojan Horse, The 1940,O 31,28:3
Lowe, David (Director)
Trojan Horse, The 1940,O 31,28:3

Lowe, David (Miscellaneous)
Sally 1948,My 7,31:2
Lowe, David (Producer)
Trojan Horse, The 1940,O 31,28:3
South Pacific 1943,D 30,11:2
Lovely Me 1946,D 26,30:4
Portrait in Black 1947,My 15,30:2
Enchanted, The 1950,Ja 19,34:2
Lowe, Edmond
In the Night Watch 1921,Ja 31,10:1
Right to Strike, The 1921,O 25,20:1
Desert Sands 1922,F 14,20:1
I Will IF You Will 1922,Ag 30,10:4
War Song, The 1928,S 25,29:3
Channel Road, The 1929,O 18,24:2
Tonight or Never 1930,N 19,19:3
Ryan Girl, The 1945,S 25,28:2
Ryan Girl, The 1945,S 30,II,1:2
Lowe, Elizabeth
Dead End 1935,O 29,17:2
Lowe, Ellen
Broken Dishes 1929,N 6,28:3
Stepdaughters of War 1930,O 7,27:1
House Beautiful, The 1931,Mr 13,20:4
I Love an Actress 1931,S 18,29:2
Life Begins 1932,Mr 29,23:2
House of Remsen 1934,Ap 3,26:4
Love on an Island 1934,Jl 24,20:5
Soliloquy 1938,N 29,26:4
Cradle Song 1955,D 2,32:2
There Is a Play Tonight 1961,F 16,24:2
Lowe, Florence (Playwright)
49th Cousin, The 1960,O 28,22:1
Lowe, Gene
Thunder on the Left 1933,N 1,25:2
Dead End 1935,O 29,17:2
But for the Grace of God 1937,Ja 13,21:4
Lowe, Grace
Dover Road, The 1926,Ap 29,20:3
Hamlet 1927,Ap 7,23:3
Lowe, Harry Shaw
Passenger to Bali, A 1940,Mr 15,26:2
Remains to Be Seen 1951,O 4,37:1
Bat, The 1953,Ja 21,28:2
Festival 1955,Ja 19,22:1
Four Winds 1957,S 26,21:2
Flower Drum Song 1958,D 2,44:1
Lowe, Isabelle
Marry the Poor Girl 1920,S 27,18:3
Izzy 1924,S 17,16:2
Mister Romeo 1927,S 6,35:3
Lowe, Joan
Family Affair, A 1962,Ja 29,17:1
Lowe, John V
Century Revue and the Midnight Rounders, The
1920,Jl 13,9:1
Last Waltz, The 1921,My 11,20:3
Rose of Stamboul, The 1922,Mr 8,11:2
Fashions of 1924 1923,Jl 19,18:2
Vogues of 1924 1924,Mr 28,14:3
Lowe, K Elmo
Broomsticks Amen! 1934,F 10,20:4
Lowe, K Elmo (Director)
Picnic 1934,My 3,15:2
Lowe, Marilyn
Diamond Lil 1948,N 30,33:2
Diamond Lil 1949,F 7,16:2
Lowe, Milton (Lighting Director)
Yours Is My Heart 1946,S 6,16:5
Lowe, Ralph
Arabian Nights 1954,Je 25,15:2
Russell Patterson's Sketch-Book 1960,F 8,35:1
Lowe, Ralph (Producer)
Ruy Blas 1957,D 14,16:3
Lowe, Robert
Dear Me 1921,Ja 18,14:1
Serpent's Tooth, A 1922,Ag 25,8:5
Babies a La Carte 1927,Ag 16,31:1
Jealous Moon, The 1928,N 21,32:2
Paolo and Francesca 1929,Ap 2,28:2
Jenny 1929,O 9,34:4
Twelfth Night 1930,O 16,28:2
Pillars of Society, The 1931,O 15,19:1
Rendezvous 1932,O 13,22:3
Baby Pompadour 1934,D 28,24:2
If This Be Treason 1935,S 24,28:2
Life and Death of an American 1939,My 20,11:2
Lowe, Roslynd
South Pacific 1949,Ap 8,30:2
Wish You Were Here 1952,Je 26,26:6
Lowe, Stanja
Midsummer Night's Dream, A 1950,Je 22,33:2
Lowe, Van
Earl Carroll's Vanities 1925,Jl 7,24:1
Earl Carroll's Vanities 1925,D 29,20:3
Shooting Star 1933,Je 13,22:2
Halfway to Hell 1934,Ja 3,22:3
Lowe, William
Buckaroo 1929,Mr 18,31:1
Lowe-Porter, H T (Mrs) (Playwright)
Abdication 1948,S 28,32:5
Lowell, Allan
Mikado, The 1942,F 4,22:2

Pirates of Penzance, The 1942,F 18,22:2
Gondoliers, The 1942,Mr 4,22:3
Music in My Heart 1947,O 3,30:2
Lowell, Helen
Blue Bonnet 1920,Ag 30,12:1
Nobody's Money 1921,Ag 18,9:3
Nature's Nobleman 1921,N 15,23:2
Montmartre 1922,F 14,20:1
Night Call, The 1922,Ap 27,12:2
Torch Bearers, The 1922,Ag 30,10:2
Show-Off, The 1924,F 6,16:2
God Loves Us 1926,O 20,22:2
Arabian Nightmare, The 1927,Ja 11,36:3
A la Carte 1927,Ag 18,25:3
Atlas and Eva 1928,F 7,30:2
Lady for a Night, A 1928,Ap 17,26:4
It's a Wise Child 1929,Ag 7,29:1
Guest Room, The 1931,O 7,29:2
Take My Tip 1932,Ap 12,25:2
Come Easy 1933,Ag 30,22:5
Lowell, James Russell (Playwright)
Half Horse, Half Alligator 1966,Mr 14,37:2
Lowell, Joan
Port O' London 1926,F 10,20:2
Star of Bengal 1929,S 26,27:2
Lowell, Larry
Shadow Years, The 1957,Ja 9,26:2
Lowell, Mary
Madame Lafayette 1960,Mr 4,21:1
Lowell, Robert (Playwright)
Benito Cereno 1964,N 2,62:2
My Kinsman, Major Molineux 1964,N 2,62:2
Old Glory, The 1964,N 15,II,1:1
Prometheus Bound 1967,My 11,52:1
Phaedra 1967,My 22,50:2
Prometheus Bound 1967,Je 11,II,1:1
Phaedra 1967,Je 11,II,1:1
Endecott and the Red Cross 1968,My 7,50:1
Lowenadler, Holger
Dream Play 1970,Ap 17,45:1
Lowens, Curt
Stalag 17 1951,My 9,41:2
Merry-Go-Rounders, The 1956,N 22,50:1
Golem, The 1959,F 26,38:2
Dreigroschenoper, Die 1965,Mr 12,24:1
Postmark Zero 1965,N 2,28:1
Lowenstein, Henry (Lighting Director)
Cock-A-Doodle Dandy 1955,N 4,26:5
Lowenstein, Henry (Scenic Designer)
Cock-A-Doodle Dandy 1955,N 4,26:5
Lowenstein, Sonia (Costume Designer)
Time of Vengeance 1959,D 11,39:1
Time of Vengeance 1959,D 27,II,1:1
Between Two Thieves 1960,F 12,23:1
Under the Sycamore Tree 1960,Mr 8,37:2
Idiot, The 1960,S 26,38:1
Emmanuel 1960,D 5,42:2
Montserrat 1961,Ja 9,30:5
Five Posts in the Market Place 1961,Mr 6,30:1
Painted Days, The 1961,Ap 7,24:1
O Marry Me 1961,O 28,13:1
We're Civilized? 1962,N 9,30:1
Pimpernel! 1964,Ja 7,26:6
Henry V 1965,Je 29,27:2
Taming of the Shrew, The 1965,Jl 3,10:5
Peddler, The 1967,D 9,62:1
Dodo Bird, The 1967,D 9,62:1
Lowenstein, Sonia (Scenic Designer)
Juno and the Paycock 1955,F 24,20:4
2 for Fun; Anniversary, The 1955,My 26,34:1
2 for Fun; Switch in Time, A 1955,My 26,34:1
Me, Candido! 1956,O 16,36:2
Hobo 1961,Ap 11,41:2
Lowenthal, Jean (Playwright)
Sing Till Tomorrow 1953,D 29,17:2
Lowenthal, Karl
Empress of Destiny 1938,Mr 10,16:2
Lowenworth, Ann
We Americans 1926,O 13,20:4
Lower, Edward S Jr
Sale and a Sailor, A, or Glory! What Price!
1926,Ap 25,30:4
Lowery, Marcella
Americana Pastoral 1968,D 11,51:1
Lowery, Robert J (Composer)
Exchange 1970,F 9,47:2
Lowery, Robert J (Lyricist)
Exchange 1970,F 9,47:2
Lowes, Robert
Gala Night 1930,F 26,22:4
Caught Wet 1931,N 5,29:1
Riddle Me This! 1932,F 26,22:5
When Ladies Meet 1932,O 7,19:1
Laura Garnett 1934,Jl 17,24:4
Menagerie 1935,Jl 2,24:3
Lightnin' 1938,S 16,17:2
Lowing, Robert
Business Widow, The 1923,D 11,27:1
Bedfellows 1929,Jl 3,19:2
Doctor X 1931,F 10,25:1
Hamlet 1931,N 6,28:4
Border-Land 1932,Mr 30,15:5

Lowndes, Belloc (Mrs) (Playwright)
Her Last Adventure 1936,Mr 31,17:1
Lowrance, Dee
Tide Rising 1937,Ja 26,17:2
Lowrie, Renee
Topsy and Eva 1924,D 24,11:1
Lowry, Agatha
Veils 1928,Mr 14,28:5
Lowry, Ed
Vaudeville (Palace) 1924,S 16,26:5
Broadway Sho-Window 1936,Ap 13,14:5
Lowry, Elizabeth
United States vs Julius and Ethel Rosenberg, The
1969,Ap 20,II,3:1
United States vs Julius and Ethel Rosenberg, The
1969,Ap 27,92:1
Lowry, Emily
Gone Hollywood 1930,D 28,VIII,2:1
Man Who Reclaimed His Head 1932,S 9,17:3
Anybody's Game 1932,D 22,21:4
Her Tin Soldier 1933,Ap 7,22:6
June Moon 1933,My 16,15:5
Heat Lightning 1933,S 16,9:6
Ragged Army 1934,F 27,16:5
Milky Way, The 1934,My 9,23:2
Kill That Story 1934,Ag 30,22:2
Lowry, Jane
Hole, The 1961,Ap 4,42:2
This Side of Paradise 1962,F 22,19:6
Poor Bitos 1964,N 16,40:2
Lowry, Judith
Crime in the Whistler Room, The 1924,O 10,22:2
Goat Song 1926,Ja 26,18:1
Easter 1926,Mr 19,24:3
Beyond the Horizon 1926,D 1,24:2
Nightstick 1927,N 11,20:4
Light of Asia, The 1928,O 10,32:2
Fall 1957,N 22,19:1
J B 1958,D 12,2:7
Effect of Gamma Rays on Man-in-the-Moon
Marigolds, The 1970,Ap 8,32:1
Lowry, Kathleen
Elton Case, The 1921,S 12,16:2
Night Hawk 1925,F 25,16:4
Honest Liars 1926,Jl 20,17:2
Scarlet Lily, The 1927,Ja 31,12:3
Divorce a la Carte 1928,Mr 27,30:3
Exceeding Small 1928,O 23,32:2
Exceeding Small 1928,N 4,IX,1:1
Silent Witness, The 1931,Mr 24,31:5
Masks and Faces 1933,Mr 20,18:5
Kultur 1933,S 27,24:3
Noble Prize, The 1935,Jl 9,24:3
Lowry, Roswell
Young Visitors, The 1920,N 30,14:1
Lowry, Rudd
Iphigenie in Tauris 1949,O 22,11:2
Restless Flame, The 1952,Ap 15,30:6
Fall 1957,N 22,19:1
Many Loves 1959,Ja 14,28:1
Lowry, Scooter
Vaudeville (Palace) 1929,Je 17,29:3
Loy, Myrna
Button Your Lip 1943,Je 15,16:1
Loy, Robert
Life Begins in '40 1940,Ap 5,24:2
Loyal, Alf
Vaudeville (Hippodrome) 1923,D 18,16:1
Loyal's Dogs
Vaudeville (Palace) 1924,F 12,20:2
Vaudeville (Palace) 1924,F 19,12:1
Vaudeville (Palace) 1926,Ag 17,21:2
Vaudeville (Palace) 1928,F 28,18:7
Loyd, Rollo (Director)
Find Daddy 1926,Mr 9,21:3
Lozano, Roy
Rosencrantz and Guildenstern Are Dead
1967,O 17,53:1
Lozito, Alfred
Emerald Slippers, The 1970,S 2,31:2
Luaks, William T Jr
Faun, The 1924,Mr 28,17:2
Luban, Milton
Shatter'd Lamp, The 1934,Mr 22,26:3
Lubar, Bernard (Producer)
Passion of Gross, The 1955,Ja 24,20:2
Lubbock, Ian
Don't Listen, Ladies 1948,D 29,16:2
Lubell, Lily
Harlequinade 1921,My 11,20:3
Green Ring, The 1922,Ap 5,22:1
This Fine-Pretty World 1923,D 27,11:1
Little Clay Cart, The 1924,D 6,13:3
Grand Street Follies, The 1925,Je 19,24:1
Dybbuk, The 1925,D 16,22:2
Grand Street Follies, The 1926,Je 16,23:2
Lion Tamer, The 1926,O 8,26:1
Dybbuk, The 1926,D 17,27:2
Pinwheel 1927,F 4,16:4
Grand Street Follies, The 1927,My 20,22:3
Lovers and Enemies 1927,S 21,27:1
If 1927,O 26,26:2
Love Nest, The 1927,D 23,17:1

Lubell, Lily—Cont
Grand Street Follies, The 1928,My 29,16:2
Grand Street Follies, The 1928,Je 3,VIII,1:1
Lubelska, Paula
Sins of Mothers 1937,Mr 30,20:2
Luber, Helen
Wild Birds 1929,Je 23,VIII,2:3
Lubimov, Yuri
Sea Gull, The 1954,Jl 7,22:1
Lubin, Arthur
Anything Might Happen 1923,F 21,22:3
Back to Methuselah 1923,O 14,VIII,1:8
Lubin, Arthur (Director)
When the Bough Breaks 1932,F 17,19:2
Her Man of Wax 1933,O 12,32:3
Growing Pains 1933,N 24,24:2
Lubin, Arthur (Producer)
This One Man 1930,O 22,32:3
When the Bough Breaks 1932,F 17,19:2
Growing Pains 1933,N 24,24:2
Lubin, Harry (Composer)
Singing Rabbi, The 1931,S 11,24:4
Lubin, Lou
Horse Fever 1940,N 25,21:2
Snookie 1941,Je 4,26:2
Lubitsch, F
Dybbuk, The 1926,D 14,24:2
Lubitsch, Nicola
Good Soup, The 1960,Mr 3,26:4
Lublov, Bela
Reunion in Vienna 1931,N 17,31:1
Forbidden Melody 1936,N 3,33:1
Luboff, Norman (Miscellaneous)
Jerry Lewis' Variety Show 1957,F 8,18:5
Luboff, Vera
Night in the Woods, A 1931,Mr 2,19:3
Traveling Salesman, The 1932,N 1,24:4
Heaven on Earth 1935,O 8,26:2
Tevye the Dairyman 1935,O 25,25:1
Lubosq, Lucien
Merchant of Venice, The 1924,N 18,23:2
Lubotsky, Jacob
Dybbuk, The 1924,Ja 29,17:7
Lubov, Vera
My Little Girl 1931,F 2,22:4
Honeymoon for Three, A 1933,Ja 30,9:6
Jewish Melody, The 1933,Mr 27,12:4
Happy Family, A 1934,S 24,15:2
East Side Wedding, An 1935,Ja 21,18:2
Lubow, Anna
Little Poor Man, The 1925,Ag 6,14:1
Light of Asia, The 1928,O 10,32:2
Channel Road, The 1929,O 18,24:2
Rebound 1930,F 4,29:1
Noble Experiment, The 1930,O 28,21:4
I Loved You Wednesday 1932,O 12,27:1
Ship Comes in, A 1934,S 20,21:1
You Can't Take It With You 1936,D 15,31:1
Lubritsky, Dave
Eretz Israel 1930,N 27,32:3
Jolly World, A 1931,Ja 24,15:3
Longing for Home 1933,S 22,15:1
Here Runs the Bride 1934,S 20,21:3
Here Runs the Bride 1934,N 4,IX,2:1
One in a Million 1934,N 17,13:2
Motel Peissi, The Contor's Kid 1934,N 29,33:3
What Girls Do 1935,Ja 14,10:4
Holiday in Town, A 1935,S 30,12:3
Secret of Love, The 1936,F 24,15:2
Oy, Is Dus a Leben!; Oh, What a Life!
1942,O 13,19:2
Mazel Tov, Molly 1950,O 2,18:1
Take It Easy 1950,D 25,23:6
Lubritsky, Dave (Choreographer)
Oy, Is Dus a Leben!; Oh, What a Life!
1942,O 13,19:2
Lubritsky, Fanny
His Wife's Lover 1929,O 21,30:6
Once Upon a Time 1933,S 22,15:1
Three in Love 1933,N 8,32:5
Organ Grinder, The 1934,Ja 1,28:3
Happy Days 1934,Ap 2,12:5
One Sabbath Afternoon 1939,Ja 17,27:5
Parnosseh 1939,F 20,12:5
Lubritsky, Goldie
Three Little Business Men, The 1923,S 4,12:1
Love and Politics 1929,O 21,30:7
Slaves of Luxury 1930,F 8,13:3
Hello Grandpa! 1931,Ja 2,25:3
Jolly World, A 1931,Ja 24,15:3
One Woman 1931,D 14,16:4
Wedding Chains 1932,Mr 28,10:5
Longing for Home 1933,S 22,15:1
Slaves of the Public 1934,Mr 10,18:6
Holiday in Town, A 1935,S 30,12:3
Secret of Love, The 1936,F 24,15:2
Souls for Sale 1936,S 21,27:6
Of One Mother 1937,Ja 18,21:3
Chaver, Nachman 1939,O 2,15:2
Luc, Jean-Bernard (Original Author)
Happy Marriage, The 1952,Ag 8,9:2
Luc-Durtain (Playwright)
Mari Singulier, Le 1937,Jl 4,X,2:2

Lucas, Daisy
Kreutzer Sonata, The 1924,My 15,22:3
Lucas, David
Grass Harp, The 1953,Ap 28,32:2
Lower Depths, The 1956,O 3,29:2
Lucas, David (Musical Director)
Golden Screw, The 1967,Ja 31,52:1
Lucas, Elizabeth
Cradle of Willow, A 1961,D 16,20:2
Lucas, Frank
Man's House, A 1943,Ap 3,10:4
Lucas, Frank (Miscellaneous)
Sign of Winter 1958,My 8,35:1
Lucas, George
Land Beyond the River, A 1957,Mr 29,15:7
Lucas, Graham
Guest of Honor, The 1920,S 21,12:1
Hero, The 1921,Mr 15,14:1
Kreutzer Sonata, The 1924,My 15,22:3
Lucas, J
Hamlet 1928,Je 2,11:3
Lucas, J Frank
Long Gallery, The 1958,Mr 7,17:2
Trip to Bountiful, The 1959,F 27,20:4
Orpheus Descending 1959,O 6,45:2
Guitar 1959,N 11,42:5
Coggerers, The 1960,Mr 23,33:1
Time to Go 1960,Mr 23,33:1
Chocolates 1967,Ap 11,51:1
To Bury a Cousin 1967,My 17,38:3
Lucas, James S Jr (Miscellaneous)
God Is a (Guess What?) 1968,D 18,56:1
Ceremonies in Dark Old Men 1969,F 6,33:1
String 1969,Ap 2,37:1
Contribution 1969,Ap 2,37:1
Malcochon 1969,Ap 2,37:1
Harangues, The 1970,Ja 14,42:1
Day of Absence 1970,Mr 18,39:1
Brotherhood 1970,Mr 18,39:1
Akokawe 1970,Je 5,21:1
Lucas, John
Shall We Join the Ladies? 1929,Mr 17,30:4
Mahogany Hall 1934,Ja 18,18:5
Lucas, Jonathan
Small Wonder 1948,S 16,33:5
Me, The Sleeper 1949,My 16,18:6
Touch and Go 1949,O 14,34:2
Of Thee I Sing 1952,My 6,34:2
Golden Apple, The 1954,Mr 12,15:2
Golden Apple, The 1954,Mr 21,II,1:1
Lucas, Jonathan (Choreographer)
First Impressions 1959,Mr 20,28:1
Vintage '60 1960,S 13,41:1
Lucas, Jonathan (Director)
Vintage '60 1960,S 13,41:1
Lucas, Kirke
Six Characters in Search of an Author
1931,Ap 16,29:2
Jackson White 1935,Ap 22,14:6
Tobias and the Angel 1937,Ap 29,16:5
Lucas, Loyal
Men in White 1955,F 26,13:2
Lucas, Mary
Cinders 1923,Ap 4,22:1
Judy 1927,F 8,20:2
Lucas, Morton
Diversion 1928,Ja 12,25:1
Lucas, Nick
Vaudeville (Palace) 1929,S 2,16:3
Vaudeville (Palace) 1930,D 8,27:2
Vaudeville (Palace) 1931,O 26,22:3
Blackouts of 1949 1949,S 7,39:2
Lucas, Peter
Madwoman of Chaillot, The 1970,Mr 23,48:3
Lucas, Philip
Guys and Dolls 1965,Ap 29,39:1
South Pacific 1965,Je 3,25:1
Lucas, Rupert
Rainbow 1928,N 22,25:1
Lucas, Theron
You and I 1925,O 20,29:1
Lucas, Wilfred
Noose, The 1926,O 21,23:3
Madame X 1927,Jl 7,29:3
Restless Women 1927,D 27,24:1
Lucaz and Inez
Vaudeville (Palace) 1925,Ap 21,18:1
Luce, Alethea (Playwright)
Gift, The 1924,Ja 23,15:4
K Guy, The 1928,O 16,28:4
Luce, Alexis
Princess April 1924,D 2,23:2
Luce, Clair
Dear Sir 1924,S 24,21:3
Luce, Claire
Music Box Revue 1924,D 2,23:3
No Foolin' 1926,Je 25,25:1
Ziegfeld Follies 1927,Ag 17,27:3
Scarlet Pages 1929,S 10,26:3
Society Girl 1931,D 31,16:1
Gay Divorce 1932,N 13,IX,1:7
Gay Divorce 1932,N 30,23:4
Gay Divorce 1933,N 19,IX,3:7

Luce, Claire—Cont
Vintage Wine 1934,Je 24,IX,1:4
Love and Let Love 1935,Mr 26,23:4
Follow the Sun 1935,D 24,10:3
Follow the Sun 1936,F 5,15:8
Of Mice and Men 1937,N 24,20:5
Of Mice and Men 1939,Ap 30,XI,3:5
Taming of the Shrew, The 1941,Ag 17,IX,1:8
Antony and Cleopatra 1945,Ap 25,26:5
Vanity Fair 1946,N 3,I,54:6
Vanity Fair 1946,N 10,II,3:1
Portrait in Black 1947,My 15,30:2
With a Silk Thread 1950,Ap 13,34:3
Taming of the Shrew, The 1951,Ap 26,35:2
Much Ado About Nothing 1952,My 2,20:1
These Are My Loves 1960,Ap 19,41:2
Feast of Panthers 1961,Mr 21,32:1
Seven Scenes for Yeni 1963,My 13,36:2
Milk Train Doesn't Stop Here Anymore, The
1963,S 18,32:1
Luce, Edna
Love Birds 1921,Mr 16,12:1
Luce, John
Stephen D 1967,S 25,58:1
Luce, Lex
Tempest, The 1959,D 28,19:2
Luce, Ted (Playwright)
Angel in the Wings 1947,D 12,36:4
Tickets, Please! 1950,Ap 28,25:2
Luce, Tom
Geranium Hat, The 1959,Mr 18,45:1
Antony and Cleopatra 1963,S 14,12:4
Lucha, A M (Miscellaneous)
Fisherman, The 1965,Ja 27,24:6
Fourth Pig, The 1965,Ja 27,24:6
Luchan, Milton
King of the Dark Chamber 1961,F 10,21:1
Lucienne
Boys and Girls Together 1940,S 5,28:6
Lucienne and Ashour
Boys and Girls Together 1940,O 2,19:2
Laugh Time 1943,S 9,35:2
Lucier, Alvin
Originale 1964,S 9,46:1
Lucier, Alvin (Miscellaneous)
Fire! 1969,Ja 29,26:1
Henry V 1969,Je 9,57:1
Henry V 1969,N 11,43:1
Lucille
Vaudeville (Palace) 1924,S 30,27:5
Lucior, Luce
Trois Jeunes Filles Nues; Three Young Maids From
the Folies Bergere 1929,Mr 5,28:2
Luck, James
Chips With Everything 1963,O 2,49:1
Lucke, Lydia
Babes in Toyland 1930,D 22,17:1
Luckenbach, Edgar F (Producer)
Portrait in Black 1947,My 15,30:2
Men We Marry, The 1948,Ja 17,11:2
Lucker, Leo
Twilight Walk 1951,S 25,25:4
School for Scandal, The 1953,Je 24,29:2
Little Clay Cart, The 1953,Jl 1,25:1
Absalom 1956,My 17,37:2
Carousel 1957,S 12,38:2
Annie Get Your Gun 1958,F 20,29:2
Auntie Mame 1958,Ag 12,33:2
Season of Choice 1959,Ap 14,40:1
Susannah and the Elders 1959,O 19,37:3
Damask Drum, The 1961,F 4,15:1
Hans's Crime 1961,F 4,15:1
French Way, The; Grand Vizier, The
1962,Mr 21,36:2
French Way, The; Edward and Agrippina
1962,Mr 21,36:2
Wives, The 1965,My 18,35:4
Luckett, Edith
Right to Kill, The 1926,F 16,22:2
Elmer the Great 1928,S 25,29:1
Luckey, R G (Playwright)
Bulls and Belles 1931,Ap 18,17:2
Luckey, Susan
Take Me Along 1959,O 23,22:2
Take Me Along 1959,N 1,II,1:1
Luckham, Cyril
All's Well That Ends Well 1959,Ap 22,30:3
Luckinbill, Laurence
Oedipus Rex 1959,Ap 30,36:1
There Is a Play Tonight 1961,F 16,24:2
Man for All Seasons, A 1964,Ja 28,24:2
Beekman Place 1964,O 8,50:1
Tartuffe 1965,Ja 15,23:1
Arms and the Man 1965,Je 24,32:5
Boys in the Band, The 1968,Ap 15,48:1
Boys in the Band, The 1968,Ap 28,II,1:6
Horseman, Pass By 1969,Ja 16,46:4
Memory Bank, The 1970,Ja 12,24:3
Memory Bank, The 1970,Ja 25,II,1:4
What the Butler Saw 1970,My 5,56:1
What the Butler Saw 1970,My 17,II,1:1
Lucking, Laviah
Family Reunion, The 1947,N 29,9:2

ucking, William
  In the Matter of J Robert Oppenheimer 1968,Je 7,31:1
  Murderous Angels 1970,F 8,70:1
uckman, Arthur
  Near to the Stars 1932,F 23,23:2
uckman, Milton
  Would-Be Gentleman, The 1930,Ap 30,29:2
  Near to the Stars 1932,F 23,23:2
uckman, Stanley
  Near to the Stars 1932,F 23,23:2
ucks, June
  Adding Machine, The 1970,D 5,40:1
uckstone, Alice
  Blonde Beast, The 1923,Mr 3,9:3
ucky Latinos, The
  Wonder World 1964,My 18,32:1
ucot, Sandra
  Displaced Person, The 1966,D 30,15:1
ucy, Arnold
  Light of the World, The 1920,Ja 7,17:1
  Bill of Divorcement, A 1921,O 11,22:2
  As You Like It 1923,Ap 24,24:1
  Hassan 1924,S 23,23:1
  American Born 1925,O 6,31:3
  Yes, Yes, Yvette 1927,O 4,32:3
  Venus 1927,D 26,26:5
ucy, Michael
  Hot Pan 1928,F 16,14:1
ucyk, Michael (Costume Designer)
  Sweethearts 1947,Ja 22,31:2
ucyor, Luce
  Bon Garcon, Un 1929,Mr 19,36:2
  Pas Sur La Bouche; Not on the Lips 1929,Mr 26,34:3
Luders, Gustav (Composer)
  Prince of Pilsen, The 1930,Ja 14,24:3
Ludgin, Chester
  Saint of Bleecker Street, The 1954,D 28,21:1
Ludig, Edwin (Composer)
  Mima 1928,D 13,24:2
Ludington, N S
  Galloper, The 1924,D 19,26:2
Ludium, Edward (Director)
  My Heart's in the Highlands 1949,N 22,36:7
Ludlam, Charles
  Bluebeard 1970,My 5,58:1
Ludlam, Charles (Director)
  Bluebeard 1970,My 5,58:1
Ludlam, Charles (Playwright)
  Conquest of the Universe 1967,N 27,60:1
  Bluebeard 1970,My 5,58:1
Ludlow, Ben Jr (Miscellaneous)
  Liar, The 1950,My 19,30:2
Ludlow, John Price Crozer
  This Mad Whirl 1937,Ja 10,II,4:8
Ludlow, Patrick
  Bitter Sweet 1929,N 6,30:2
  Geneva 1940,Ja 31,15:2
Ludlum, Edward (Director)
  Trial Honeymoon 1947,N 4,31:2
  Sister Oakes 1949,Ap 25,19:4
  My Heart's in the Highlands 1950,F 18,8:4
  Long Days, The 1951,Ap 21,10:5
  Desire Under the Elms 1951,N 22,45:1
  27 Wagons Full of Cotton 1955,Ja 19,23:2
  Eastward in Eden 1956,Ap 18,25:4
Ludlum, John Plumer (Scenic Designer)
  Provincetown Follies, The 1935,N 4,24:3
Ludlum, Robert
  Richard III 1953,D 10,65:2
  Admirable Bashville, The 1956,F 21,38:1
Ludmila, Anna
  Tip-Top 1920,O 6,13:2
  Greenwich Village Follies 1924,S 17,16:1
Ludvig, Herman (Composer)
  King And the Cobbler, The 1954,D 13,33:6
Ludwig, Arthur
  Anathema 1923,Ap 11,16:2
  Inspector General, The 1923,My 1,24:1
  Rose Marie 1924,S 3,12:2
Ludwig, Emil (Original Author)
  Peace Palace 1933,Je 6,30:2
Ludwig, Emil (Playwright)
  Dismissal, The 1923,Ap 24,10:3
  Versailles 1931,Ja 25,I,14:2
  Versailles 1932,O 20,19:5
  Return of Ulysses, The 1943,Ja 28,22:2
  Return of Ulysses, The 1943,F 7,II,1:6
Ludwig, George
  Music in the Air 1932,N 9,28:2
Ludwig, Gordon
  Return of Ulysses, The 1943,Ja 28,22:2
  Return of Ulysses, The 1943,F 7,II,1:6
Ludwig, Jack (Playwright)
  Alchemist, The 1969,Je 12,51:1
Ludwig, Karen
  Trojan Women, The 1963,D 24,7:6
  Devils, The 1965,N 17,51:2
  Oresteia 1966,Je 30,29:1
  Huui, Huui 1968,N 25,58:1
Ludwig, Nathan
  Nautical but Nice 1931,Ap 19,31:6

Ludwig, Otto
  Passion Play, The 1929,Ap 30,32:1
Ludwig, Salem
  Miracle in the Mountains 1947,Ap 26,10:2
  Sun and I, The 1949,Mr 21,18:4
  Bruno and Sidney 1949,My 4,38:2
  All You Need Is One Good Break 1950,F 10,20:3
  Missouri Legend 1951,F 10,10:4
  Victim, The 1952,My 3,17:5
  Camino Real 1953,Mr 20,26:1
  Maya 1953,Je 10,35:1
  Trip to Bountiful, The 1953,N 4,30:3
  Troublemakers, The 1954,D 31,11:3
  Inherit the Wind 1955,Ap 22,20:2
  Disenchanted, The 1958,D 4,53:4
  Witches' Sabbath 1962,Ap 20,22:2
  Three Sisters, The 1964,Je 23,24:1
  Night of the Dunce 1966,D 29,21:1
  Corner of the Bed, A 1969,F 27,35:2
  Honest-to-God Schnozzola, The 1969,Ap 22,40:2
  Leader, The 1969,Ap 22,40:2
  Awake and Sing! 1970,My 28,35:1
  Awake and Sing! 1970,Je 7,II,1:1
  Friends, The 1970,Jl 24,17:2
  Friends, The 1970,Ag 30,II,1:1
Ludwig, Salem (Director)
  In Splendid Error 1954,O 27,33:6
  Mrs Warren's Profession 1958,Je 26,22:1
Ludwig, William (Playwright)
  How Revolting! 1932,Mr 11,14:6
Lueck, David
  Jack Jack 1968,Je 23,74:5
Luedke, Hermann (Playwright)
  Abraham Lincoln 1928,N 13,31:2
Luening, Otto (Miscellaneous)
  King Lear 1956,Ja 13,17:1
  Back to Methuselah 1958,Mr 27,41:5
Luersen, Margaret
  Within the Law 1928,Mr 6,20:1
Luetzkendorf, Felix (Playwright)
  Dallas-November 22d 1965,N 12,54:1
Luft, Joey
  At Home at the Palace 1967,Ag 1,23:1
  Untitled-Judy Garland 1967,D 26,45:1
Luft, Lorna
  At Home at the Palace 1967,Ag 1,23:1
  Untitled-Judy Garland 1967,D 26,45:1
Luft, Sidney (Miscellaneous)
  Judy Garland's New Variety Show 1956,S 27,43:2
Luft, Sidney (Producer)
  Judy Garland 1959,My 12,40:1
  At Home at the Palace 1967,Ag 1,23:1
Luft, Uriel
  Camino Real 1960,My 17,42:2
  Shepherd's Chameleon, The 1960,N 30,41:1
Lugne-Poe
  Deux Amis, Les 1927,Je 12,VII,2:1
  Miss Ba; Barretts of Wimpole Street, The 1934,N 11,IX,3:6
Lugne-Poe (Producer)
  Deux Amis, Les 1927,Je 12,VII,2:1
  Bourgeoise, La 1927,O 2,VIII,2:4
  Bourgeoise, La 1927,O 16,IX,4:7
  Jules, Juliette et Julien, ou L'Ecole du Sentiment 1929,Je 9,VIII,2:4
  Papavert 1931,O 11,VIII,2:1
  Miss Ba; Barretts of Wimpole Street, The 1934,N 11,IX,3:6
Lugo, Ricarda
  Ice Capades 1958,S 4,33:2
Lugosi, Bela
  Red Poppy, The 1922,D 21,18:2
  Arabesque 1925,O 21,20:2
  Open House 1925,D 15,28:3
  Devil in the Cheese, The 1926,D 30,22:4
  Dracula 1927,O 6,29:1
  Murder at the Vanities 1933,S 13,22:4
  Tovarich 1937,Ap 25,X,2:4
Luguet, Andre
  Trois Jeunes Filles Nues; Three Young Maids From the Folies Bergere 1929,Mr 5,28:2
  Trio 1929,Mr 17,X,2:7
  Trois et Une 1933,Ja 1,IX,3:4
  Quand Jouons-Nous La Comedie? 1935,O 27,IX,2:1
  Trois, Six, Neuf 1936,Je 21,IX,2:4
  Mes Amours 1940,My 3,16:5
Luhr, Peter
  Alcestiade 1957,Je 29,11:5
  In der Sache J Robert Oppenheimer 1964,N 3,27:2
  Nathan der Weise 1966,D 10,45:2
  Schloss, Das 1968,N 20,35:3
Lui, Harold
  Five Alarm Waltz 1941,Mr 14,16:2
Luisi, James
  Courtyard 1960,Mr 1,28:1
  Alfie 1964,D 18,27:1
  Sweet Charity 1966,Ja 31,22:1
  Soldiers 1968,My 2,58:1
  Zorba 1968,N 18,58:1
Lujan, James Graham (Translator)
  House of Bernarda Alba, The 1951,Ja 8,14:6
  If Five Years Pass 1962,My 11,37:1

Luk, Wong
  Teahouse of the August Moon, The 1955,My 10,24:1
Lukan, Sylvia
  Konzert, Das 1968,Mr 25,52:1
  Maria Stuart 1968,Mr 27,38:1
  Jux Will Er Sich Machen, Einen 1968,Ap 3,41:1
Lukas, Karl
  Mister Roberts 1948,F 19,27:2
  Remains to Be Seen 1951,O 4,37:1
  Volpone 1957,Ja 8,27:1
Lukas, Paul
  Doll's House, A 1937,D 28,28:6
  Watch on the Rhine 1941,Mr 25,26:7
  Watch on the Rhine 1941,Ap 2,26:2
  Watch on the Rhine 1941,Ap 13,IX,1:1
  Watch on the Rhine 1941,Ag 24,IX,1:1
  Call Me Madam 1950,O 13,25:1
  Call Me Madam 1950,O 22,II,1:1
  Flight Into Egypt 1952,Mr 19,33:2
  Flight Into Egypt 1952,Mr 30,II,1:1
  Wayward Saint, The 1955,F 18,17:1
Luke, Keye
  Flower Drum Song 1958,D 2,44:1
Luke, Lewis
  Searching for the Sun 1936,F 20,22:6
Luke, Peter (Playwright)
  Hadrian VII 1968,Jl 4,14:1
  Hadrian VII 1969,Ja 9,22:1
  Hadrian VII 1969,Ja 19,II,1:2
  Hadrian VII 1969,S 20,20:1
Lukeman, Gerald
  'Tis Pity She's a Whore 1958,D 6,21:1
Lukes, Ivan
  Pierrot's Journey 1964,Ag 5,23:1
  Button, Button 1970,O 20,41:1
Lukins, Richard (Miscellaneous)
  Ping-Pong 1959,Ap 17,22:1
Lukschy, Wolfgang
  Nathan the Wise 1962,Mr 7,29:1
  Before Sundown 1962,Mr 14,43:1
  My Fair Lady 1962,S 7,34:1
Lull, Dorothy
  Earl Carroll's Vanities 1928,Ag 7,25:2
Lulling, Marian
  Lady Comes Across, The 1942,Ja 10,10:2
Lullo, Georgio de (Director)
  Diary of Anne Frank, The 1963,Ap 12,33:1
Lully, Jean-Baptiste (Composer)
  Would-Be Gentleman, The 1946,Ja 10,29:2
  Bourgeois Gentilhomme, Le 1955,O 26,26:1
  Bourgeois Gentilhomme, Le 1955,O 30,II,1:1
  Jalousie du Barbouille, La; Jealousy of the Barbouille, The 1958,My 7,43:1
  Sganarelle; Imaginary Cuckold, The 1958,My 7,43:1
  Mariage Force, Le; Forced Wedding, The 1958,My 7,43:1
  Troupe Du Roi, La 1970,F 4,38:1
Lulu
  Circus-Madison Square Garden 1939,Ap 6,23:5
Lum, Alvin
  Lovely Ladies, Kind Gentlemen 1970,D 29,38:1
Lum, Harry
  Carefree Tree, The 1955,O 12,37:2
Lumatt, Boruch
  Tenth Commandment, The 1926,N 18,27:1
  Witch of Castile, The 1930,O 25,21:1
  Man With the Portfolio, The 1931,F 12,24:6
  Chinese Nightingale, The 1934,O 6,20:4
Lumatt, Boruch (Playwright)
  Once Upon a Tailor 1955,My 24,36:2
Lumb, Geoffrey
  Harriet 1943,Mr 4,24:2
  For Keeps 1944,Je 15,17:5
  Summer and Smoke 1947,Jl 9,18:5
  Temporary Island, A 1948,Mr 15,27:3
  E-MC2 1948,Je 16,36:2
  Minnie and Mr Williams 1948,O 28,37:2
  Two Blind Mice 1949,Mr 3,32:2
  Call Me Madam 1950,O 13,25:1
  Solid Gold Cadillac, The 1953,N 6,24:2
  Fighting Cock, The 1959,D 9,57:3
  Miracle Worker, The 1961,F 7,40:2
  Daughter of Silence 1961,D 1,28:1
  Oliver 1963,Ja 8,5:5
Lumb, Geoffrey (Director)
  Democratic Body, A 1942,F 13,24:7
Lumb, Geoffrey (Playwright)
  Democratic Body, A 1942,F 13,24:7
Lumb, Mary (Playwright)
  Democratic Body, A 1942,F 13,24:7
Lumbard, Agnes
  Cherry Pie 1926,Ap 15,24:4
  Loud Speaker 1927,Mr 3,27:2
Lumet, Baruch
  Brownsville Grandfather, The 1935,Ap 19,24:6
Lumet, Sidney
  Brownsville Grandfather, The 1935,Ap 19,24:6
  Dead End 1935,O 29,17:2
  It Can't Happen Here 1936,O 28,30:1
  Eternal Road, The 1937,Ja 8,14:2
  Sunup to Sundown 1938,F 2,14:3
  Schoolhouse on the Lot 1938,Mr 23,18:4

Lumet, Sidney—Cont

My Heart's in the Highlands 1939,Ap 14,29:2
My Heart's in the Highlands 1939,My 7,X,1:1
Christmas Eve 1939,D 28,17:2
Morning Star 1940,Ap 17,26:4
Journey to Jerusalem 1940,O 7,21:2
Brooklyn, U S A 1941,D 22,24:2
Seeds in the Wind 1948,My 26,29:2

Lumet, Sidney (Director)

Bourgeois Gentleman, The 1949,Ag 31,27:2
Doctor's Dilemma, The 1955,Ja 12,22:1
Night of the Auk 1956,D 4,50:2
Caligula 1960,F 17,31:1
Caligula 1960,F 28,II,1:1
Nowhere to Go But Up 1962,N 12,36:2

Lumish, Robert

Man and Superman 1964,D 7,45:2
War and Peace 1965,Ja 12,32:1
Judith 1965,Mr 25,42:2
Richard II 1968,Je 24,42:3
As You Like It 1968,Je 24,42:3

Lumley, Terry

Does a Tiger Wear a Necktie? 1967,F 4,17:1

Lummis, Dayton

Moment Musical 1943,Je 1,18:1
Peepshow 1944,F 4,12:2
According to Law 1944,Je 2,20:3
Catherine Was Great 1944,Ag 3,16:1
Miracle in the Mountains 1947,Ap 26,10:2
Antony and Cleopatra 1947,N 27,49:2
Edward, My Son 1948,O 1,30:2
As You Like It 1950,Ja 27,27:2

Lumpkin, Grace (Original Author)

Let Freedom Ring 1935,N 7,26:2

Lumsden, E W H

Upon My Soul 1927,Ap 22,19:1

Lumsden, Geoffrey

Affair, The 1962,S 21,34:2
Hostile Witness 1966,F 18,26:1

Luna, Barbara

West Side Story 1968,Je 25,32:1

Luna (Maestro) (Composer)

Picara Molinera, La 1929,Ja 3,25:2

Lund, Alan (Choreographer)

Salad Days 1958,N 11,24:1
Henry VIII 1961,Je 22,22:1
Tempest, The 1962,Je 22,14:1
Gondoliers, The 1962,Jl 7,9:4
Bourgeois Gentilhomme, Le 1964,Je 18,28:2

Lund, Alan (Director)

Anne of Green Gables 1969,Ag 25,41:1

Lund, Art

Most Happy Fella, The 1956,My 4,20:1
Most Happy Fella, The 1956,My 13,II,1:1
Of Mice and Men 1958,D 5,38:1
Most Happy Fella, The 1959,F 11,50:2
Donnybrook! 1961,My 19,23:1
Donnybrook! 1961,My 28,II,1:1
Fiorello! 1962,Je 14,24:1
Sophie 1963,Ap 16,32:1
No Strings 1964,Ja 1,17:1
Wayward Stork, The 1966,Ja 20,27:1
Most Happy Fella, The 1966,My 12,55:1

Lund, Blanche (Choreographer)

Salad Days 1958,N 11,24:1
Henry VIII 1961,Je 22,22:1
Tempest, The 1962,Je 22,14:1

Lund, Herb

Ballyhoo 1930,D 23,24:1

Lund, John

As You Like It 1941,O 21,29:2
Early to Bed 1943,Je 18,16:2
Hasty Heart, The 1945,Ja 4,14:2
Hasty Heart, The 1945,Ja 14,II,1:1

Lund, John (Lyricist)

New Faces of 1943 1942,D 23,22:2

Lund, John (Playwright)

New Faces of 1943 1942,D 23,22:2

Lund, Karen

Song of Norway 1944,Ag 22,20:2
Cave Dwellers, The 1961,O 16,34:2

Lund, Lee

West Side Story 1968,Je 25,32:1

Lund, Ruth

Aquashow 1954,Je 23,20:4
Elliott Murphy's Aquashow 1956,Je 20,26:2

Lund, Walter

Many Things 1940,F 3,8:4

Lund-Schiller, Zoe (Translator)

Outside the Door 1949,Mr 2,33:2

Lundblad, B J (Miscellaneous)

Ice Follies 1959,Ja 14,30:1
Ice Follies 1961,Ja 11,25:2
Ice Follies 1962,Ja 10,24:6
Ice Follies 1963,Ja 10,5:2

Lundborg, Arne (Scenic Designer)

Big Pond, The 1928,Ag 22,25:1
Nut Farm, The 1929,O 15,34:3
World Waits, The 1933,O 26,22:5
False Dreams, Farewell 1934,Ja 16,18:3
Page Miss Glory 1934,N 28,24:2
Boy Meets Girl 1935,N 19,27:2
Boy Meets Girl 1935,N 28,38:2
Illustrators' Show, The 1936,Ja 23,25:3

Schoolhouse on the Lot 1938,Mr 23,18:4

Lundee, Burnel

Hamlet 1922,N 17,14:1
Hamlet 1923,N 27,23:6

Lundegard, Gerald

Adding Machine, The 1923,Mr 20,24:1

Lundell, Kert (Costume Designer)

Hogan's Goat 1965,N 12,56:1
Journey of the Fifth Horse, The 1966,Ap 22,36:1
Who's Got His Own 1966,O 13,52:1
Under the Weather 1966,O 28,35:1
Displaced Person, The 1966,D 30,15:1
Two Times One; Last Straw, The 1970,Ap 5,76:4
Two Times One; Duet for Solo Voice 1970,Ap 5,76:4

Lundell, Kert (Director)

Orange Souffle; Wen, The; Out From Under 1966,Jl 16,14:6

Lundell, Kert (Lighting Director)

Hogan's Goat 1965,N 12,56:1
Perfect Party, The 1969,Mr 21,42:1

Lundell, Kert (Scenic Designer)

Gogo Loves You 1964,O 10,19:2
Hogan's Goat 1965,N 12,56:1
Journey of the Fifth Horse, The 1966,Ap 22,36:1
Journey of the Fifth Horse, The 1966,My 8,II,1:1
Investigation, The 1966,O 5,40:1
Who's Got His Own 1966,O 13,52:1
Under the Weather 1966,O 28,35:1
Displaced Person, The 1966,D 30,15:1
Not a Way of Life 1967,Mr 23,28:1
Basement, The 1967,O 3,56:1
Fragments 1967,O 3,56:1
Ceremony of Innocence, The 1968,Ja 2,33:1
House of Flowers 1968,Ja 29,26:2
Carry Me Back to Morningside Heights 1968,F 28,41:1
People vs Ranchman, The 1968,O 28,56:1
Walk Together Children 1968,N 12,54:1
Perfect Party, The 1969,Mr 21,42:1
Papp 1969,My 6,39:1
Indians 1969,My 27,43:1
Calling in Crazy 1969,O 7,42:2
Whistle in the Dark, A 1969,O 9,55:1
Two Times One; Duet for Solo Voice 1970,Ap 5,76:4
Two Times One; Last Straw, The 1970,Ap 5,76:4
Sunday Dinner 1970,N 3,28:1
Castro Complex, The 1970,N 19,40:1
Carpenters, The 1970,D 22,40:1

Lunden, Joseph

Republic, The 1970,Ap 28,49:1

Lundigan, William

What Price Glory 1949,Mr 3,33:2

London, Mary

Mikado, The 1942,F 4,22:2
Pirates of Penzance, The 1942,F 18,22:2
Iolanthe 1942,F 24,26:4
Gondoliers, The 1942,Mr 4,22:3
Pirates of Penzance, The 1944,F 18,15:5
Gondoliers, The 1944,F 22,26:3
Iolanthe 1944,F 23,17:1
Patience 1944,F 26,11:4
Ruddigore 1944,Mr 3,19:5

Lundt, Ernest C

Grey Heir, The 1926,Ap 6,29:2

Lundy, Ben (Producer)

Bat, The 1937,Je 1,27:5
Cat and the Canary, The 1937,Je 15,26:3

Lundy, William

Are You With It? 1945,N 12,17:3

Luneau, Sylvie (Playwright)

Diary of a Madman 1964,Ap 17,29:2
Diary of a Madman 1967,Mr 24,25:1

Lungreen, Margo

Thurber Carnival, A 1960,F 27,13:2

Lunney, David (Miscellaneous)

Tartuffe 1967,S 18,60:1

Lunney, Mildred

George White's Scandals 1922,Ag 29,10:1

Lunning, Everette Jr

Prometheus Bound 1967,My 11,52:1
Bacchae, The 1969,Mr 15,24:1

Lunritzky, Dave

Slaves of the Public 1934,Mr 10,18:6

Lunsford, Beverly

Rope Dancers, The 1957,N 21,39:1
Rope Dancers, The 1957,D 1,II,1:1

Lunt, Alfred

Intimate Strangers, The 1921,N 8,28:1
Banco 1922,S 21,18:1
Sweet Nell of Old Drury 1923,My 19,16:4
Robert E Lee 1923,N 21,23:1
Outward Bound 1924,Ja 8,26:1
Outward Bound 1924,Ja 13,VII,1:1
Guardsman, The 1924,O 14,23:1
Arms and the Man 1925,S 15,28:1
Arms and the Man 1925,O 4,IX,1:1
Goat Song 1926,Ja 26,18:1
At Mrs Beam's 1926,Ap 26,24:3
At Mrs Beam's 1926,My 2,VIII,1:1
Juarez and Maximilian 1926,O 12,31:1
Juarez and Maximilian 1926,O 17,VIII,1:1

Lunt, Alfred—Cont

Ned McCobb's Daughter 1926,N 30,26:2
Ned McCobb's Daughter 1926,D 5,VIII,5:1
Brothers Karamazov, The 1927,Ja 4,20:1
Second Man, The 1927,Ap 12,24:3
Doctor's Dilemma, The 1927,N 22,33:1
Marco Millions 1928,Ja 10,28:2
Volpone 1928,Ap 10,32:1
Volpone 1928,Ap 22,IX,1:1
Caprice 1928,D 23,VIII,4:1
Caprice 1929,Ja 1,61:1
Caprice 1929,Ja 13,VIII,1:1
Caprice 1929,Je 23,VIII,1:3
Meteor 1929,D 8,X,2:1
Meteor 1929,D 24,15:1
Elizabeth the Queen 1930,O 5,IX,4:6
Elizabeth the Queen 1930,N 4,37:1
Reunion in Vienna 1931,O 11,VIII,4:6
Reunion in Vienna 1931,N 17,31:1
Reunion in Vienna 1931,N 29,VIII,1:1
Design for Living 1933,Ja 3,19:5
Design for Living 1933,Ja 8,IX,3:2
Design for Living 1933,Ja 25,13:2
Design for Living 1933,Ja 29,IX,1:1
Reunion in Vienna 1934,Ja 4,17:1
Reunion in Vienna 1934,Ja 28,IX,3:4
Point Valaine 1934,D 30,IX,1:6
Point Valaine 1935,Ja 17,22:2
Point Valaine 1935,F 3,VIII,1:1
Taming of the Shrew, The 1935,Ap 23,24:1
Taming of the Shrew, The 1935,S 22,X,3:2
Taming of the Shrew, The 1935,S 29,X,3:1
Taming of the Shrew, The 1935,O 1,27:3
Taming of the Shrew, The 1935,O 20,X,1:1
Idiot's Delight 1936,Mr 10,26:7
Idiot's Delight 1936,Mr 25,25:2
Idiot's Delight 1936,Ap 12,IX,1:1
Idiot's Delight 1936,S 1,24:5
Amphitryon 38 1937,Je 24,30:2
Amphitryon 38 1937,N 2,32:2
Amphitryon 38 1937,N 7,XI,1:1
Amphitryon 1938,Ja 23,XI,1:6
Sea Gull, The 1938,Mr 17,16:5
Sea Gull, The 1938,Mr 29,19:2
Sea Gull, The 1938,Ap 3,XI,1:1
Amphitryon 38 1938,My 18,17:2
Amphitryon 38 1938,Je 5,IX,2:6
Taming of the Shrew, The 1940,F 6,17:2
There Shall Be No Night 1940,Mr 30,11:2
There Shall Be No Night 1940,Ap 30,25:2
There Shall Be No Night 1940,My 5,X,1:1
There Shall Be No Night 1940,S 10,27:3
There Shall Be No Night 1940,S 22,IX,1:1
Pirate, The 1942,S 15,18:6
Pirate, The 1942,N 26,39:2
Pirate, The 1942,D 6,VIII,1:1
There Shall Be No Night 1943,D 16,34:5
There Shall Be No Night 1944,Ja 2,II,1:5
Love in Idleness 1944,D 22,13:2
Love in Idleness 1945,Ja 7,II,2:3
O Mistress Mine 1946,Ja 24,25:2
O Mistress Mine 1946,F 3,II,1:1
O Mistress Mine 1946,S 1,II,1:1
I Know My Love 1949,F 24,29:2
I Know My Love 1949,Ap 23,10:2
I Know My Love 1949,N 3,36:1
I Know My Love 1949,N 20,II,1:1
Quadrille 1952,Jl 17,20:4
Quadrille 1952,S 13,10:7
Quadrille 1952,O 12,II,3:7
Quadrille 1953,Ap 5,II,1:1
Qudrille 1954,N 4,39:2
Quadrille 1954,N 14,II,1:1
Great Sebastians, The 1956,Ja 5,27:1
Great Sebastians, The 1956,Ja 15,II,1:1
Visit, The 1958,My 6,40:1
Visit, The 1958,My 18,II,1:1
Visit, The 1958,S 7,II,1:1
Visit, The 1958,N 16,II,1:1
Visit, The 1960,Mr 9,38:3
Visit, The 1960,Je 25,13:5

Lunt, Alfred (Director)

There Shall Be No Night 1940,Ap 30,25:2
Candle in the Wind 1941,S 16,19:6
Candle in the Wind 1941,O 23,26:2
Candle in the Wind 1941,N 2,IX,1:1
Pirate, The 1942,N 26,39:2
O Mistress Mine 1946,Ja 24,25:2
I Know My Love 1949,N 3,36:1
Ondine 1954,F 19,23:1
Ondine 1954,F 28,II,1:1
Qudrille 1954,N 4,39:2
First Love 1961,D 26,20:2

Lunt, Alfred (Miscellaneous)

Idiot's Delight 1936,Mr 10,26:7
Amphitryon 38 1937,N 2,32:2

Lunt, Alfred (Playwright)

Taming of the Shrew, The 1935,O 1,27:3
Taming of the Shrew, The 1940,F 6,17:2

Lunt, Alfred (Producer)

Point Valaine 1935,Ja 17,22:2
Idiot's Delight 1936,Mr 25,25:2
Amphitryon 38 1937,Je 24,30:2
Amphitryon 38 1937,N 2,32:2

Lunt, Clinton E
Side-Show 1931,My 16,13:1
Lunts (Miscellaneous)
George and Margaret 1937,S 23,32:2
Luongo, Alba
Arzigogolo, L'; Whim, The 1931,Ap 27,24:4
Alba, Il Gioro, La Notte, L'; Dawn, the Day, the
Night, The 1931,My 18,21:4
Giuochi di Prestigio 1931,N 2,26:1
Incendio Doloso, L'; False Flame, The
1931,N 16,22:4
Berretto a Songali, Il; Cap With Bells, The
1931,N 30,16:3
Piccolo Santo, Il; Little Saint, The 1931,D 14,16:4
Profumo di Mia Moglie, Il; My Wife's Perfume
1932,Ja 11,29:5
Civil Death, The 1932,Ja 25,20:3
Trio 1932,F 8,21:1
T'Amo E Sarai Mia; I Love You and You'll Be
Mine 1932,Mr 21,19:4
Casa di Tutti, La; Everybody's Home 1932,D 5,21:4
Cardinale, Il 1933,Ja 9,24:2
Zia Morta, La; Dead Aunt, The 1933,F 13,11:3
Curioso Accidente, Un 1933,Mr 6,16:3
Liane, Le (Ties That Bind) 1933,Je 12,20:3
Ingeborg 1933,O 11,23:3
Conte di Monte Cristo, Il 1934,Ja 22,13:2
Padrone Delle Ferriere, Il 1934,Mr 19,13:5
Colonello Bridall, L' 1934,Ap 16,20:3
Miserabili I, 1934,S 24,15:1
Miserabili I, 1934,O 1,14:2
Signora Dalle Camelie, La; Camille 1934,O 22,13:2
Processo dei Veleni, Il; Case of Poisons, The
1935,Ja 21,18:2
Romanzo di un Giovane Povero, Il 1935,F 25,12:3
Conte di Monte Cristo, Il 1935,Ap 1,17:6
Signo Della Croce, Il 1935,O 7,11:1
Three Guardsmen, The 1936,F 17,21:3
Testamento della Zia d'America, Il; American
Aunt's Will, The 1936,Mr 23,22:4
Due Orfanelle, Le; Two Orphans, The
1936,O 5,24:4
Tombola, La; Lottery, The 1936,N 9,23:4
Morte Civile, La; Civic Death 1936,N 9,23:4
Sansone; Samson 1936,N 30,25:2
Asino di Buridano, L' 1936,N 30,25:2
Feudalismo Oppure La Terra Bassa; Feudalism or
the Lowland 1937,Mr 8,22:2
Lucrezia Borgia 1937,Mr 8,22:2
Sposa e la Cavalla, La 1937,Mr 22,26:5
Medico Delle Pazze, Il; Physician of Mad Woman,
The 1937,S 27,24:2
Signora Dalle Camelie, La; Dame aux Camelias, La
1937,O 9,16:3
Lupas, Sylvia
Stage Door 1936,O 23,26:3
Lupino, Barry
Love Call, The 1927,O 25,33:1
Red Robe, The 1928,D 26,15:1
Babes in Toyland 1929,D 24,15:3
Prince Chu Chang 1930,O 12,VIII,4:1
Lupino, Pandora Bronson
Conduct Unbecoming 1970,O 13,50:1
Lupino, Richard
Major Barbara 1956,O 31,27:1
Othello 1957,Je 24,19:2
Merchant of Venice, The 1957,Jl 11,19:5
Much Ado About Nothing 1957,Ag 8,15:2
Conduct Unbecoming 1970,O 13,50:1
Lupino, Stanley
Naughty Riquette 1926,S 14,25:2
Naughty Riquette 1926,S 19,IX,1:1
Nightingale, The 1927,Ja 4,20:4
Over She Goes 1936,S 24,28:7
Lupino, Stanley (Director)
Lady Behave 1941,Ag 3,IX,2:2
Lupino, Stanley (Playwright)
Over She Goes 1936,S 24,28:7
Lady Behave 1941,Ag 3,IX,2:2
Lupino, Stanley (Producer)
Over She Goes 1936,S 24,28:7
Lupo, Frances
Arsenic and Old Lace 1942,My 11,18:6
LuPone, Robert
West Side Story 1968,Je 25,32:1
Lupton, La Verne
Too Many Girls 1939,O 19,26:2
Lupton, LaVerne
Star and Garter 1942,Je 25,26:2
Lupue, Maurice
Take the Air 1927,N 23,28:2
Luria, Lajos (Playwright)
Comic, The 1927,Ap 20,28:2
Luriea, Florence
Blood Wedding 1949,F 7,16:2
Sun and I, The 1949,Mr 21,18:4
House of Bernarda Alba, The 1951,Ja 8,14:6
Lurio, Don
Peter Pan 1954,O 21,30:2
Lusby, Constance
Six Characters in Search of an Author
1922,O 31,11:2

Lusby, Vernon
110 in the Shade 1963,O 25,37:1
Lusby, Vernon (Choreographer)
Music Man, The 1965,Je 17,26:4
Oh, Say Can You See L A 1968,F 9,50:1
Other Man, The 1968,F 9,50:1
Celebration 1969,Ja 23,55:2
Lusby, Vernon (Director)
Celebration 1969,Ja 23,55:2
Lusby, Vernon (Miscellaneous)
Decline and Fall of the Entire World As Seen
Through the Eyes of Cole Porter Revisited, The
1965,Mr 31,24:2
Come Summer 1969,Mr 19,43:1
Luscombe, George (Director)
American Hamburger League, The 1969,S 17,51:1
Chicago 70 1970,My 26,33:1
Lush, S Beryl (Producer)
House Remembered, A 1957,F 7,20:2
Lusk, Julia (Costume Designer)
Sarah and the Sax 1964,My 5,53:1
Dirty Old Man, The 1964,My 5,53:1
Lusk, Milton (Composer)
Within the Gates 1934,O 23,23:1
Many Mansions 1937,O 28,28:6
Lusk, Stanley
Lady of the Lamp, The 1920,Ag 18,6:4
Lusk, William T
Successful Calamity, A 1921,Mr 19,11:2
Lussier, Laura
French Doll, The 1922,F 21,20:2
Lussier, R Robert (Lighting Director)
Believers, The 1968,My 10,57:4
Lussier, R Robert (Miscellaneous)
Shoemaker's Holiday, The 1967,Mr 3,25:1
Lust, Geraldine (Producer)
Death of Satan, The 1960,Ap 6,49:1
Lust, Geraldine (Director)
Death of Satan, The 1960,Ap 6,49:1
Herne's Egg, The 1960,S 20,48:1
Mountain Giants, The 1961,Ap 5,32:3
Lust, Geraldine (Miscellaneous)
Blacks, The 1961,My 5,23:1
Lust, William Thompson
Faun, The 1924,F 6,19:2
Lustberg, Arch
Political Party, A 1963,S 27,17:5
Lustberg, Arch (Director)
Political Party, A 1963,S 27,17:5
Lustberg, Arch (Producer)
Political Party, A 1963,S 27,17:5
Luster, Betty
Wayward Saint, The 1955,F 18,17:1
Luster, Betty (Miscellaneous)
Wayward Saint, The 1955,F 18,17:1
Luster, Robert
Measure for Measure 1964,Jl 27,22:3
Luster Brothers
Vaudeville (Palace) 1923,Ap 3,26:4
Lustik, Marlena
Pousse-Cafe 1966,Mr 19,19:2
Lutes, Richard H
Front Page Stuff 1926,D 29,24:4
Luther, Doug
As the Girls Go 1948,N 15,21:2
Top Banana 1951,N 2,19:2
Luther, Frank (Composer)
Tom Sawyer 1958,Jl 15,21:8
Luther, Frank (Lyricist)
Tom Sawyer 1958,Jl 15,21:8
Luther, Frank (Miscellaneous)
Artists and Models 1943,N 6,16:6
Lutsky, Daniel
Cave at Machpelah, The 1959,Jl 1,25:1
Lutton, Eleanor
Allegro 1952,S 18,36:3
Lutyens, Edith (Costume Designer)
Shrike, The 1952,Ja 16,20:2
Crucible, The 1953,Ja 23,15:2
Crucible, The 1953,Jl 2,20:2
Girl Can Tell, A 1953,O 30,28:2
Wedding Breakfast 1954,N 22,29:2
Lutyens, Edith (Miscellaneous)
Telephone, The 1947,My 2,28:2
Medium, The 1947,My 2,28:2
Telephone, The 1948,D 8,41:6
Medium, The 1948,D 8,41:6
Lutyens, Elizabeth (Composer)
Bacchae, The 1963,Ap 25,39:5
Lutyens, R A, Edward (Sir) (Scenic Designer)
Berkeley Square 1929,N 5,32:4
Lutz, Carl Frederick
Petticoat Fever 1937,Mr 21,II,7:3
Lutz, Charles
Victims, The; Victims of Duty 1968,Mr 6,34:1
Victims, The; Escurial 1968,Mr 6,34:1
Lutz, Douglas (Producer)
Three Times Three; How He Lied to Her Husband
1956,My 24,27:2
Three Times Three; Box and Cox 1956,My 24,27:2
Three Times Three; Merrye Playe, A
1956,My 24,27:2

Lutz, H B (Miscellaneous)
Krapp's Last Tape 1960,Ja 15,37:2
Zoo Story, The 1960,Ja 15,37:2
Killer, The 1960,Mr 23,33:1
Lutz, H B (Playwright)
Chip, The 1960,My 17,42:2
Lutz, Herbert Barr (Producer)
Siegfried 1939,F 21,15:2
Lutz, M (Producer)
Barbier de Seville, Le 1939,Mr 7,19:2
Luvadis, Jerry
Big Fight, The 1928,S 19,33:1
Lux, Lillian
Hole in the Head, A 1958,N 26,25:2
Megilla of Itzik Manger, The 1968,O 10,60:1
Megilla of Itzik Manger, The 1969,Ap 21,55:1
Lux, Michael
Sage of Rottenburg, The 1963,N 20,48:1
Fifth Commandment, The 1965,N 15,48:4
Luxembourg, Ella
Moondreamers, The 1969,D 9,68:1
Luxembourg, Ella (Costume Designer)
Gloria and Esperanza 1970,F 5,32:1
Luzhsky, Vassily
Tsar Fyodor Ivanovitch 1923,Ja 9,26:1
Lower Depths, The 1923,Ja 16,16:1
Cherry Orchard, The 1923,Ja 23,18:1
Cherry Orchard, The 1923,Ja 28,VII,1:1
Three Sisters, The 1923,Ja 30,12:2
Brothers Karamazov, The 1923,N 20,23:4
Ivanoff 1923,N 27,23:2
In the Claws of Life 1923,N 30,23:4
Enemy of the People, An 1923,D 4,25:1
Enough Stupidity in Every Wise Man
1923,D 6,23:1
Uncle Vanya 1924,Ja 29,16:2
Death of Pazukhin, The 1924,F 12,20:1
Brothers Karamazov, The 1924,My 6,25:2
Luzzatto, Danielle
Macbeth 1955,O 8,12:6
Lybel, Jai (Miscellaneous)
Kumquat in the Persimmon Tree, The
1962,Je 19,27:2
Lycan, Bryan
Lady Be Good 1924,D 2,23:4
Vagabond King, The 1925,S 22,23:3
Silent House, The 1928,F 8,28:5
Back Here 1928,N 27,36:3
Lyday, Paul
Out of This World 1950,D 22,17:3
Lyde, Fanny
Spring's Awakening 1955,O 10,30:2
Lydecker, George
Book of Charm, The 1925,S 4,26:3
Charm 1929,N 29,24:5
Lydiard, Bob
Round With Ring, A 1969,O 30,56:1
Lydiate, Maude
Love Dreams 1921,O 11,22:2
Lydman, Jak
As You Like It 1937,N 1,25:2
Lydon, Hal (Staff Sgt)
Swing Sister Wac Swing 1944,Ja 4,20:4
Lydon, Jimmy
Western Waters 1937,D 29,17:1
Sunup to Sundown 1938,F 2,14:3
Prologue to Glory 1938,Mr 18,22:2
Sing Out the News 1938,S 26,12:5
Happiest Days, The 1939,Ap 12,26:2
Lydon, Ormond
Sunup to Sundown 1938,F 2,14:3
Everywhere I Roam 1938,D 30,10:4
Lyel, Viola
Murder on the Second Floor 1929,S 12,35:1
Nine Till Six 1930,S 29,17:2
Lyev, Ziskind (Playwright)
Reapers, The 1935,O 7,11:4
Lykomitros, Nikos
Medea 1964,S 1,31:1
Electra 1964,S 8,33:1
Iphigenia in Aulis 1968,N 13,40:1
Hippolytus 1968,N 20,38:3
Lykomitrou, Gianna
Hippolytus 1968,N 20,38:3
Lykoudis, George (Miscellaneous)
Electra 1952,N 20,38:2
Oedipus Tyrannus 1952,N 25,35:2
Lylak, Ola
Spring Production 1944,My 20,12:4
Lyle, Henry
Circus Princess, The 1927,Ap 26,32:2
Lyle, Herbert
Circus Princess, The 1927,Ap 26,32:2
Lyle, Jocelyn
Ups-A-Daisy 1928,O 9,34:2
Lyle, Richard
Kiss Me, Kate 1965,My 13,31:1
Lyles, Aubrey
Shuffle Along 1921,My 23,16:2
Runnin' Wild 1923,O 30,17:3
Keep Shufflin' 1928,F 28,18:3
Sugar Hill 1931,D 26,15:2

Lyles, Aubrey (Playwright)
Shuffle Along 1921,My 23,16:2
Runnin' Wild 1923,O 30,17:3
Keep Shufflin' 1928,F 28,18:3
Lyles, Shirley
Born Yesterday 1954,Ja 1,16:6
Lyles, Tracee
Perfect Party, The 1969,Mr 21,42:1
Lyman, Abe
Vaudeville (Palace) 1931,S 7,19:2
Revels of 1936 1935,S 30,12:4
Lyman, Abe and His Band
Friars Club Frolic 1933,My 15,16:4
Lyman, Debra
By Jupiter 1967,Ja 20,28:2
Lyman, Dorothy
America Hurrah; Interview; TV; Motel
1967,O 10,55:2
Pequod 1969,Je 30,33:1
American Hamburger League, The 1969,S 17,51:1
Lyman, Francis
Music in May 1929,Ap 2,29:1
Lyman, George
Crooked Gamblers 1920,Ag 2,12:1
Lyman, Henry
Foemen of the Yard 1935,Ap 6,10:4
Lyman, Jimmie
Street Singer, The 1929,S 18,35:2
Lyman, John (Playwright)
Incubator 1932,N 2,23:3
Lymmborn, A
Judas 1929,Ja 25,20:4
Lyn, Bea
Paese dei Campanelli, Il; Land of Bells, The
1935,My 10,25:4
Lynam, Bernie
Ice Capades 1953,S 11,25:1
Ice Capades 1954,S 16,37:1
Ice Capades 1955,S 15,38:1
Lynch, Alfred
Hostage, The 1960,S 21,42:1
Hostage, The 1960,O 2,II,1:1
Lynch, Brid
Bugle in the Blood, The 1949,Mr 15,34:5
Bridal Night, The 1966,N 8,45:1
Carricknabauna 1967,Mr 31,30:1
Lynch, Brother
Vaudeville (Palace) 1927,Ag 2,19:1
Lynch, Doreen
By the Way 1925,D 29,20:3
Lynch, Eddie
Blessed Event 1932,F 13,23:2
Lynch, Edward
Two Gentlemen of Verona 1957,Jl 23,21:5
Macbeth 1957,Ag 16,11:2
Recruiting Officer, The 1958,F 8,12:2
Lynch, Frances
Love 'Em and Leave 'Em 1926,F 4,20:4
Lynch, Frances (Playwright)
He Understood Women 1928,Ag 16,25:1
Lynch, George
Whispering Wires 1922,Ag 8,26:2
Bye Bye, Barbara 1924,Ag 26,6:3
Malinda 1929,D 4,37:2
Lynch, Grace
Blue Butterfly, The 1929,F 17,29:3
Blue Butterfly, The 1929,My 4,17:2
Lynch, Hal
Spoon River Anthology 1963,S 30,23:2
Lynch, Hal (Miscellaneous)
Promises to Keep 1965,Jl 22,25:1
Lynch, Jerry
Man's Man, A 1925,O 14,31:2
Decoy, The 1932,Ap 2,13:4
Lynch, Joanna
Doctor and the Devils, The 1959,Ja 21,27:8
Lynch, Kenneth Jr
Hobo 1961,Ap 11,41:2
Lynch, Lola
Egg, The 1962,Ja 9,23:2
Lynch, Louise
New Faces 1934,Mr 16,24:5
Lynch, Marjorie
Patience 1929,D 16,34:5
Lynch, Paul
Shake Hands With the Devil 1949,O 21,30:4
Lynch, Raymond
In the Matter of J Robert Oppenheimer
1968,Je 7,31:1
Lynch, Richard
Devils, The 1965,N 17,51:2
One Night Stands of a Noisy Passenger; Noisy
Passenger, The 1970,D 31,8:3
Lynch, Rose (Producer)
Ruy Blas 1957,D 14,16:3
Old Tune, The 1961,Mr 24,37:1
Square, The 1961,Mr 24,37:1
Dock Brief, The 1961,N 22,24:2
What Shall We Tell Caroline? 1961,N 22,24:2
Lynch, Teddy
Fools Rush In 1934,D 26,19:2
Lynch, Theodore
Marie Antoinette in Pennsylvania 1949,My 12,26:2

Lynch and the Six Lido Ladies
Vaudeville (Palace) 1931,Je 22,17:2
Lynd, Helen
Rain or Shine 1928,F 10,26:3
Rainbow 1928,N 22,25:1
Little Show, The 1929,My 1,28:5
Vanities 1931,Ag 11,28:4
Vanities 1931,Ag 16,VIII,1:1
Earl Carroll's Vanities 1931,Ag 28,18:7
Ladies' Money 1934,N 2,26:6
Battleship Gertie 1935,Ja 19,9:2
Hook-Up, The 1935,My 9,24:6
Illustrators' Show, The 1936,Ja 23,25:3
Lynd, Helene
Yes, Yes, Yvette 1927,O 4,32:3
Lyndall, Barry
Mikado, The 1944,F 12,11:3
Lynde, Paul
New Faces of 1952 1952,My 17,23:2
Bye Bye Birdie 1960,Ap 15,13:4
Lynde, Paul (Director)
New Faces of 1956 1956,Je 15,32:1
Lynde, Paul (Playwright)
New Faces of 1956 1956,Je 15,32:1
New Faces of 1962 1962,F 2,25:1
Lyndeck, Edmund
Billy Budd 1959,F 28,13:3
Around the World in 80 Days 1963,Je 24,22:1
Around the World in 80 Days 1964,Je 29,33:2
South Pacific 1968,Je 30,54:2
1776 1969,Mr 17,46:2
Lyndon, Barre (Playwright)
Hell for Leather 1936,N 27,27:2
Amazing Dr. Clitterhouse, The 1937,Mr 3,26:4
They Came by Night 1937,Jl 8,21:1
They Came by Night 1937,Jl 25,X,1:3
Man in Half Moon Street, The 1939,Ap 9,X,1:8
Lyndon, Lilian
Night Hostess 1928,S 13,31:2
Lyndon, Nicolas Wolff (Lighting Director)
Carmilla 1970,D 1,61:2
Lyndon, Nicolas Wolff (Miscellaneous)
Carmilla 1970,D 1,61:2
Lynds, Jack
Good Fairy, The 1931,N 25,17:1
Johnny Belinda 1940,S 19,26:2
Ghost for Sale 1941,S 30,27:4
Cherry Orchard, The 1944,Ja 26,22:1
Lynds, John
Long Road, The 1930,S 10,30:2
Good Fairy, The 1932,N 18,22:3
Thoroughbred 1933,N 7,29:2
On the Rocks 1938,Je 16,20:2
Boy Meets Girl 1943,Je 23,15:5
Where's Charley? 1948,O 12,33:2
Lynley, Carol
Potting Shed, The 1957,Ja 30,32:1
Blue Denim 1958,F 28,17:1
Blue Denim 1958,Ap 20,II,1:1
Answered the Flute 1960,Mr 10,37:4
Lynn, Amy (Producer)
Lord Pengo 1962,N 20,41:2
Right Honourable Gentleman, The 1965,O 20,50:2
Lynn, Anne
Beyond the Horizon 1962,O 26,27:2
Lynn, Bambi
Oklahoma! 1943,My 9,II,6:4
Lynn, Basil
Vaudeville (Palace) 1926,Ag 3,19:2
Lynn, Bert
Sketch Book 1935,Je 5,22:2
Lynn, Billy
Girl From Nantucket, The 1945,N 9,17:2
Lynn, Bob Jr
Tall Story 1959,Ja 30,33:2
Lynn, Carr
Vaudeville (Palace) 1927,Ja 25,18:3
Lynn, Catherine (Miscellaneous)
Show-Off, The 1950,Je 1,24:5
Lynn, David (Director)
From the Second City 1969,O 15,34:1
Lynn, Diana
Wild Duck, The 1951,D 27,17:1
Horses in Midstream 1953,Ap 3,18:7
Moon Is Blue, The 1953,Jl 8,24:1
Moon Is Blue, The 1953,Ag 9,II,1:2
Lynn, Elaine
Plain and Fancy 1955,Ja 28,14:2
Uncle Willie 1956,D 21,17:1
Annie Get Your Gun 1958,F 20,29:2
Lynn, Eleanor
Bridal Quilt 1934,O 11,28:5
Come Angel Band 1936,F 19,17:1
Golden Journey, The 1936,S 16,28:6
Rocket to the Moon 1938,N 25,18:2
Sarah Adler Testimonial 1939,Mr 15,18:2
Swingin' the Dream 1939,N 30,24:2
Gabrielle 1941,Mr 26,26:2
Man With Blonde Hair, The 1941,N 5,30:2
Strip for Action 1942,O 1,26:2
Strip for Action 1942,O 11,VIII,1:1
Bird Cage, The 1950,F 23,32:2
Viewing, The 1967,Ja 11,51:1

Lynn, Elizabeth
Nathan the Wise 1944,F 22,26:3
Lynn, Emmett
Gasoline Gypsies 1931,Je 8,21:3
Lynn, Eve
Little Theatre Tournament; Man in the Stalls, The
1929,My 8,34:4
Alive and Kicking 1950,Ja 18,25:5
Lynn, Grace
Window Panes 1927,F 22,22:2
Lynn, Iola
Song Out of Sorrow 1955,N 1,27:3
Doctor Faustus 1957,F 19,35:7
Ever Since Paradise 1957,Jl 12,18:4
Nude With Violin 1957,N 15,36:1
Jane Eyre 1958,My 2,31:1
Lynn, Jeffrey
Philadelphia Story, The 1949,Je 28,32:4
Long Days, The 1951,Ap 21,10:5
Lo and Behold! 1951,D 13,45:2
Call on Kuprin, A 1961,My 26,29:3
Call on Kuprin, A 1961,Je 4,II,1:1
Dinner at Eight 1966,S 28,38:1
Dinner at Eight 1966,O 9,II,1:1
Lynn, Jim
Annie Get Your Gun 1966,Je 1,42:2
Lynn, Johnny
Once Upon a Time 1939,D 21,28:2
Lynn, Jonathan
Cambridge Circus 1964,O 7,53:1
Blue Comedy 1968,O 23,36:1
Lynn, Joyce
Jo 1964,F 13,25:1
Autumn's Here 1966,O 26,40:1
Lynn, Judy
Top Banana 1951,N 2,19:2
What a Killing 1961,Mr 28,41:1
Lynn, Kerrie
Square in the Eye 1965,My 20,54:1
Lynn, Kitty
This Was Burlesque 1965,Mr 17,55:3
Lynn, Leni
All for Love 1949,Ja 24,16:5
Lynn, Lorna
Trojan Women, The 1941,Ap 9,32:5
This Rock 1943,F 19,23:2
Arsenic and Old Lace 1943,D 13,18:6
January Thaw 1946,F 5,18:2
Lynn, Lysbeth
King Lear 1940,D 16,27:2
Lynn, Mara
Body Beautiful, The 1958,Ja 24,15:2
This Was Burlesque 1962,Mr 7,29:1
Can-Can 1962,My 17,32:2
Deer Park, The 1967,F 1,27:2
Lynn, Marion
Lovely Lady 1927,D 30,22:1
Lynn, Mary
Love for Love 1947,My 27,30:2
Happy Journey to Trenton and Camden, The
1948,Mr 21,II,1:1
Lynn, Ralph
Thark 1927,Jl 24,VII,1:7
Plunder 1928,Jl 22,VII,1:3
Night Like This, A 1930,Mr 9,IX,4:1
Ladies' Night 1933,N 19,IX,3:7
Hello Again 1934,Je 14,28:4
Inside Stand, The 1935,N 22,18:1
Nap Hand 1940,Mr 10,XI,2:6
Rookery Nook 1942,My 31,VIII,2:3
Is Your Honeymoon Really Necessary?
1944,S 10,II,2:6
Lynn, Regina
Autumn's Here 1966,O 26,40:1
Now Is the Time for all Good Men 1967,S 27,42:1
Lynn, Robert
Right to Love, The 1925,Je 9,16:4
Adam Solitaire 1925,N 7,19:2
Man Who Died Twice, The 1925,D 14,19:1
Dream Play 1926,Ja 21,18:2
White Lights 1927,O 12,30:4
Buzzard, The 1928,Mr 15,29:1
Sweet Land of Liberty 1929,S 24,29:2
Keeper of the Keys 1933,O 19,23:2
Broadway Interlude 1934,Ap 20,16:3
Sun Field, The 1942,D 10,33:2
Kiss and Tell 1943,Mr 18,22:1
Lynn, Timothy
As You Like It 1939,My 9,28:4
Lynn, Vicki
Marie Vison, La 1970,Jl 15,29:1
Lynn, William
Stepping Sisters 1930,Ap 23,24:2
Sing High, Sing Low 1931,N 13,26:4
Humpty Dumpty 1932,S 18,IX,2:1
Tragedy of the Ages, The 1933,Ap 7,22:7
Little Ol' Boy 1933,Ap 25,15:5
Peace Palace 1933,Je 6,30:2
Amourette 1933,S 28,25:2
They Shall Not Die 1934,F 22,24:4
Dream Child 1934,Jl 31,20:2
Kill That Story 1934,Ag 30,22:2
Three Men on a Horse 1935,Ja 22,22:7

ynn, William—Cont

Three Men on a Horse 1935,Ja 31,22:3
There's Always a Breeze 1938,Mr 3,16:2
Ladies and Gentlemen 1939,O 18,30:2
Liberty Jones 1941,F 6,24:2
Three Men on a Horse 1942,O 10,10:2
Something for the Boys 1943,Ja 17,VIII,1:1
Front Page, The 1946,S 5,22:4
Silver Whistle, The 1948,N 25,49:2
Twentieth Century 1950,D 25,23:6

Lynn-Thomas, Derrick
Nathan the Wise 1944,F 22,26:3
Broken Hearts of Broadway 1944,Je 13,16:2

Lynn-Thomas, Derrick (Miscellaneous)
Telephone, The 1950,Jl 20,22:5

Lynn-Thomas, Derrick (Playwright)
Show-Off, The 1950,Je 1,24:5

Lynn-Thomas, Derrick (Producer)
Julius Caesar 1950,Je 21,30:1
Medium, The 1950,Jl 20,22:5
Arms and the Man 1950,O 20,34:2
Razzle Dazzle 1951,F 20,21:1

Lynne, Ada
Hold It! 1948,My 6,31:5

Lynne, Betty
Grand Hotel 1931,S 27,VIII,1:4
Animal Kingdom, The 1932,Ja 13,26:4

Lynne, Carol
Stars on Ice 1942,Jl 3,12:2
Stars on Ice (2d Edition) 1943,Je 25,13:2
Hats Off to Ice 1944,Je 23,15:2
Hollywood Ice Revue 1953,Ja 16,17:2

Lynne, Ethel
Sweethearts 1929,S 23,25:1
Merry Widow, The 1929,D 3,29:1
Babes in Toyland 1929,D 24,15:3
Babes in Toyland 1930,D 22,17:1

Lynne, Gillian
Can-Can 1954,O 24,II,3:1

Lynne, Gillian (Choreographer)
Roar of the Greasepaint-the Smell of the Crowd 1965,My 17,46:2
Pickwick 1965,O 6,5:3
How Now, Dow Jones 1967,D 8,53:1

Lynne, Herbert Ritter
Summer Wives 1936,Ap 14,18:1

Lynne, James Broom (Playwright)
Trigon, The 1965,O 11,62:2

Lynne, Mimi
Brights Lights of 1944 1943,S 17,27:4

Lynne, Phyllis
Toplitzky of Notre Dame 1946,D 27,13:4

Lynne, Terry
When Differences Disappear 1941,Je 3,17:4

Lynne, Vincent
Best Foot Forward 1956,Mr 3,16:1

Lynne, Vincent (Miscellaneous)
Best Laid Plans, The 1966,Mr 26,15:2
Four Seasons, The 1968,Mr 15,32:1

Lyns, Warren (Producer)
Muzeeka 1968,Ap 29,47:2
Red Cross 1968,Ap 29,47:2

Lynwood, Ann
Lady With a Lamp, The 1931,N 20,27:2
Electra 1932,Ja 9,21:4

Lynwood, Stia
Dark of the Moon 1958,F 27,22:2

Lyo, Sacha
Untitled-Revue 1930,N 30,IX,3:3

Lyon, Annabelle
Great Lady 1938,D 2,26:6
Carousel 1945,Ap 20,24:2
Insect Comedy, The 1948,Je 4,26:3

Lyon, Ben
Mary the 3d 1923,F 6,14:2

Lyon, C T F B
1776 1926,Ap 24,11:2

Lyon, Camilla
Charm School, The 1920,Ag 3,12:1
Wild Oats Lane 1922,S 7,12:1

Lyon, Esther
Not So Long Ago 1920,My 5,14:1
Romance 1921,Mr 1,18:2
Starlight 1925,Mr 4,17:2
Holka Polka 1925,O 15,27:2

Lyon, Frank
Squaw Man, The 1921,D 27,10:3
Loose Ankles 1926,Ag 17,15:1
Weather Clear, Track Fast 1927,O 19,24:5
Mermaids Singing, The 1945,N 29,26:6
Family Affair, A 1946,N 28,41:2

Lyon, Fred
Say When 1934,N 9,24:2

Lyon, Jane
Wild Duck, The 1938,Ap 16,16:5

Lyon, Josephine
Without the Walls 1920,Je 7,20:1
Without the Walls 1922,Ap 17,17:1

Lyon, Milton
Show Boat 1954,My 6,44:1
Show Boat 1954,O 29,28:4

Lyon, Milton (Director)
Kiss Me, Kate 1954,Mr 27,13:2
Spree de Corps 1955,D 9,33:8

Take a Gander 1956,D 14,36:4
Our Town 1961,N 4,14:7

Lyon, Miss
Ragged Edge, The 1927,F 13,VII,1:4

Lyon, Nyla (Director)
Three Plays of the Sea 1970,Ag 20,39:1

Lyon, Robert
We Never Learn 1928,Ja 24,26:1
Bloomer Girl 1944,O 6,18:5

Lyon, Theresa
Time for Elizabeth 1948,S 28,32:3

Lyon, Wanda
Mike Angelo 1923,Ja 9,26:2
In Love With Love 1923,Ag 7,20:1
Madame Pompadour 1924,N 12,20:6
Close Harmony 1924,D 2,23:1
Stork, The 1925,Ja 27,14:2
Just Beyond 1925,D 2,22:4
Piggy 1927,Ja 12,22:2
Rock Me, Julie 1931,Ja 4,VIII,2:3
Rock Me, Julie 1931,F 4,21:1
Wonder Bar, The 1931,Mr 18,23:4
I'll Take the High Road 1943,N 10,28:3

Lyons, Adolph
Singing Rabbi, The 1931,S 11,24:4

Lyons, Albert S
Nautical but Nice 1931,Ap 19,31:6

Lyons, Camilla
Mirage, The 1920,O 1,14:1

Lyons, Carl E
Schoolmaster, The 1928,Mr 21,30:1

Lyons, Cecil
Laugh It Off 1925,Ap 25,18:4

Lyons, Charlotte
Aunt Caroline's Will 1954,Ag 11,21:1

Lyons, Collette
Scandals 1939,Ag 29,17:2
Vickie 1942,S 23,28:1
Artists and Models 1943,N 6,16:6
Show Boat 1946,Ja 7,17:2

Lyons, Donald F
Front Page Stuff 1926,D 29,24:4

Lyons, Dorothy
Humbug, The 1929,N 28,34:5

Lyons, Esther
Anathema 1923,Ap 11,16:2

Lyons, Eugene (Playwright)
Squaring the Circle 1935,S 22,X,3:2
Squaring the Circle 1935,O 4,24:6

Lyons, Eugene (Translator)
In the Days of the Turbins 1934,Mr 7,22:5
Squaring the Circle 1935,O 4,24:6

Lyons, Gene
Inside Story 1942,O 30,22:2
This Rock 1943,F 19,23:2
Moment Musical 1943,Je 1,18:1
Troublemakers, The 1952,N 9,II,3:2
Tall Kentuckian, The 1953,Je 17,30:1
Trip to Bountiful, The 1953,N 4,30:3
Witness for the Prosecution 1954,D 17,35:2
Witness for the Prosecution 1954,D 26,II,1:1
River Line, The 1957,Ja 3,29:2
Clearing in the Woods, A 1959,F 13,32:1
Masquerade 1959,Mr 17,42:1

Lyons, George
Untitled-Revue 1926,O 26,18:3
You'll See Stars 1943,Ja 1,26:6
Front Page, The 1946,S 5,22:4

Lyons, Harry
Money Business 1926,Ja 21,18:1
What's the Big Idea? 1926,Mr 24,20:3

Lyons, Helen
Rose Girl, The 1921,F 12,11:1
Music Box Revue 1923,S 24,5:3
Music Box Revue 1924,D 2,23:3
Face the Music 1932,F 18,24:5

Lyons, Henry
Fall and Rise of Susan Lenox, The 1920,Je 11,11:2

Lyons, J Warren
Kingdom of God, The 1928,D 21,30:2
Woman of Destiny, A 1936,Mr 3,25:2
Lady Behave 1943,N 17,30:1

Lyons, James
Vie Parisienne, La 1945,Ja 13,14:5

Lyons, Joan
June Days 1925,Ag 7,12:5

Lyons, Joe
Greenwich Village Follies 1923,S 21,4:6
Vaudeville (Hippodrome) 1924,Ap 29,12:2
Rain or Shine 1928,F 10,26:3
Smiles 1930,N 19,19:2
Star and Garter 1942,Je 25,26:2

Lyons, John
Bootleggers, The 1922,N 28,24:1
Magic Ring, The 1923,O 2,10:1
Silence 1924,N 13,18:2
Humbug, The 1929,N 28,34:5
Tyrant, The 1930,N 13,33:1

Lyons, Katharine
Ladies Leave 1929,O 2,28:3

Lyons, Lynne
Twilight Walk 1951,S 25,25:4
Killer, The 1960,Mr 23,33:1

Lyons, Robert F
Andorra 1963,F 11,5:5
Up to Thursday 1965,F 11,45:1

Lyons, Rolla
Treasure, The 1920,O 5,13:1

Lyons, Ruth
Backslapper, The 1925,Ap 13,25:2
Judge's Husband, The 1926,S 28,31:1
Matrimonial Bed, The 1927,O 13,23:2
Mulberry Bush, The 1927,O 27,33:1
Night Hostess 1928,S 13,31:2

Lyons, Stuart
American Gothic 1953,N 11,35:6

Lyons, Thomas
Corn Is Green, The 1940,N 27,27:2

Lyons, Warren
Neighbors 1923,D 27,11:1
That Old Devil 1944,Je 6,14:2
P S I Love You 1964,N 20,40:1

Lyses, Charlotte
Cocktail 1928,F 5,VIII,2:1
Coucou 1930,Je 1,VIII,2:1
Banque Nemo, La 1931,D 13,VIII,2:2

Lyses, Charlotte (Playwright)
Coucou 1930,Je 1,VIII,2:1

Lyson, Fred
George White's Scandals 1926,Je 15,23:2

Lysons, A Fothringham
Padre, The 1926,D 28,16:3
Taming of the Shrew, The 1927,O 26,26:4
Marseilles 1930,N 18,28:2
Lean Harvest 1931,O 14,26:3
Fatal Alibi, The 1932,F 10,26:6
Evensong 1933,F 1,13:4
Double Door 1933,S 22,15:5
Order Please 1934,O 10,21:2
Victoria Regina 1935,D 27,15:2
Victoria Regina 1938,O 4,20:2

Lysons, Samuel
Rope's End 1929,S 20,34:5

Lyston, Richard
Ruy Blas 1957,D 14,16:3

Lyte, Ray
Vaudeville (Palace) 1929,O 21,31:2

Lyte, Ray (Mrs)
Vaudeville (Palace) 1929,O 21,31:2

Lytell, Bert
Valiant, The 1927,F 22,22:5
Untitled-Play 1928,N 18,IX,2:6
Brothers 1928,D 26,14:3
Valiant, The 1929,S 22,24:6
Vaudeville (Palace) 1929,S 23,24:6
Church Mouse, A 1931,O 13,26:4
Bad Manners 1933,Ja 31,15:5
First Legion, The 1934,O 2,18:2
Susan and God 1937,Ap 11,II,12:3
Margin for Error 1939,O 15,48:7
Margin for Error 1939,N 4,11:3
Return Engagement 1940,N 2,19:2
Lady in the Dark 1941,Ja 5,IX,1:7
Lady in the Dark 1941,Ja 24,14:2
Wind Is Ninety, The 1945,Je 22,12:2
I Like It Here 1946,Mr 23,8:6

Lytell, Bert (Producer)
First Legion, The 1934,O 2,18:2

Lytell, Billy
Vaudeville (Palace) 1923,My 15,22:2

Lytell, Blanche
All the King's Horses 1934,Ja 31,21:3
Forty-Four Below 1935,Jl 23,24:3
Front Page, The 1946,S 5,22:4

Lytell, Jessie
Rust 1924,F 1,12:1

Lytell, Marjorie
Straight Thru the Door 1928,O 5,17:2
It Never Rains 1929,N 20,26:4
As Husbands Go 1931,Mr 6,26:5
Best Years 1932,S 8,16:2
As Husbands Go 1933,Ja 20,20:5
Boy Meets Girl 1935,N 28,38:2
Star Spangled 1936,Mr 11,23:1
Behind the Red Lights 1937,Ja 14,17:4

Lytell, Wilfred
Goldfish, The 1922,Ap 18,15:3
Peter Weston 1923,S 20,5:2
Sisters 1927,D 26,26:5
Spook House 1930,Je 4,33:3

Lytell and Fant
Spider, The 1927,Mr 23,29:1

Lytle, Andrew
Patriarch, The 1926,D 11,15:1
Grey Fox, The 1928,O 23,32:3

Lytle, Marjorie
Keating 1927,D 26,26:6

Lytton, Edward Bulwer (Sir) (Playwright)
Richelieu 1929,D 26,20:3

Lytton, Henry Jr
Earl Carroll's Vanities 1927,Ja 5,18:1

Lytton, Louis
Six Characters in Search of an Author 1931,Ap 16,29:2
Merry Wives of Windsor, The 1938,Ap 15,22:3
Othello 1945,My 23,25:4

Lytton, Louis—Cont
Devil's Disciple, The 1950,Ja 26,23:2
Parade at the Devil's Bridge 1957,F 19,35:7
Doctor Faustus 1957,F 19,35:7
As You Like It 1958,Ja 21,33:6
Othello 1958,Jl 4,16:1
Lytton, Peggy
Why Men Leave Home 1922,S 13,18:2
Lyubimov, Yuri (Producer)
Save Your Face 1970,My 28,28:1

M

Ma-Belle
Blushing Bride, The 1922,F 7,12:1
Maas, Stephen (Miscellaneous)
Nobody's Child 1956,Ag 23,25:2
Maascolo, Joseph
Operation Sidewinder 1970,Mr 13,33:1
Maasen, Linda
Republic, The 1970,Ap 28,49:1
Mabaso, Lemmy
King Kong 1961,F 24,24:1
Mabie, Dorothea
Oh, Ernest! 1927,My 10,24:3
Mabie, E C (Miscellaneous)
Tread the Green Grass 1932,Jl 24,IX,1:3
Mabley, Edward (Director)
Peer Gynt 1937,Mr 14,II,7:8
Mabley, Edward (Playwright)
Temper the Wind 1946,D 28,10:2
Temper the Wind 1947,Ja 12,II,1:1
Glad Tidings 1951,O 12,33:2
Mabley, Edward (Producer)
Pan Pipes and Donkeys' Ears 1929,D 27,26:5
Mabley, Jackie
Blackberries of 1932 1932,Ap 5,27:5
Swingin' the Dream 1939,N 30,24:2
Mac, Jenny
Merrily We Roll Along 1934,O 1,14:1
O Evening Star 1936,Ja 9,24:6
MacAaron, James
Visit, The 1958,My 6,40:1
MacAdam, William
Antigone 1967,Je 19,43:1
Macbeth 1967,Jl 31,21:1
Loot 1968,Mr 19,40:2
Early Morning 1970,N 26,57:1
McAdams, Stacy
Up Eden 1968,N 27,42:1
McAdoo, Eva
Passing of the Third Floor Back, The 1924,F 8,19:4
McAfee, Diane
Flora, the Red Menace 1965,My 12,41:2
West Side Story 1968,Je 25,32:1
McAfee, Don (Composer)
Great Scot! 1965,N 12,56:3
McAfee, Jocelyn
Comedian, The 1956,O 18,36:4
McAfer, Robert
Right of Happiness 1931,Ap 3,34:2
McAherney, J M
Tiger Smiles, The 1930,D 18,29:1
Macaleese, Richard
Houseboat on the Styx, The 1928,D 26,14:3
Heads Up! 1929,N 12,34:1
McAliece, F J (Lighting Director)
Chic 1959,My 19,28:2
McAlinney, Patrick
Matchmaker, The 1955,D 6,45:6
Matchmaker, The 1955,D 18,II,3:1
McAllister, Alexander
Life Begins in '40 1940,Ap 5,24:2
McAllister, Blue
Blackbirds 1928,My 10,31:3
Lew Leslie's Blackbirds of 1930 1930,O 23,34:5
Rhapsody in Black 1931,My 5,33:2
Blackbirds 1933,D 4,22:3
McAllister, Paul
Don Juan 1921,S 8,14:2
She Stoops to Conquer 1924,Je 10,24:3
Grand Duchess and the Waiter, The 1925,O 14,31:1
McAllister, Shorty
High Flyers 1927,Je 26,VIII,1:1
McAllister, Ward
Jeweled Tree, The 1926,O 8,26:2
McAloney, Michael (Producer)
Borstal Boy 1970,Ap 1,38:1
McAnally, David
Earthlight Theater 1970,N 4,38:2
MacAndrew, James F
Man of Destiny, The 1926,My 1,10:1
McAndrew, Pat
When We Dead Awaken 1966,Ap 19,37:2
McAndrews, Mary
Treasure, The 1920,O 5,13:1
MacAneny, H
Monkey's Paw, The 1922,D 30,13:4
McAneny, Patricia
Winterset 1966,F 10,32:2
Rosencrantz and Guildenstern Are Dead 1967,O 17,53:1

Borstal Boy 1970,Ap 1,38:1
McAnistan, John
Poupees de Paris, Les 1964,My 16,11:1
MacAnna, Tomas (Director)
Playboy of the Western World, The 1968,S 4,40:1
Borstal Boy 1970,Ap 1,38:1
MacAnna, Tomas (Scenic Designer)
Borstal Boy 1970,Ap 1,38:1
McAnney, Jill (Miscellaneous)
Idiot's Delight 1957,F 23,14:2
Dial 'M' for Murder 1958,F 8,12:2
McAoney, Michael
Witness for the Prosecution 1954,D 17,35:2
McArdle, Cliff
Ice Capades 1969,Ja 8,42:1
McArdle, Frank
Our Lan' 1947,Ap 19,11:2
McArdle, James Francis
Medea 1949,My 3,31:2
McArdle, Joseph (Scenic Designer)
Satisfaction Guaranteed 1969,F 12,31:1
Open 24 Hours 1969,F 12,31:1
McArdle, Kip
Detective Story 1954,F 13,11:2
Face of a Hero 1960,O 21,29:5
Midgie Purvis 1961,F 2,25:3
McArt, Don
Pajama Tops 1963,Je 1,15:1
McArt, Jan
Golden Apple, The 1962,F 13,38:2
Around the World in 80 Days 1964,Je 29,33:2
Macart, Mr (Playwright)
Peace Harbor 1925,My 3,VIII,2:1
MacArthur, Arthur
Mima 1928,D 13,24:2
MacArthur, Charles (Director)
Ladies and Gentlemen 1939,O 18,30:2
Johnny on the Spot 1942,Ja 9,24:2
Front Page, The 1946,S 5,22:4
Front Page, The 1946,S 15,II,21:1
MacArthur, Charles (Playwright)
Lulu Belle 1926,F 10,20:1
Lulu Belle 1926,F 14,VIII,1:1
Salvation 1928,F 1,31:1
Salvation 1928,F 12,VIII,1:1
Front Page, The 1928,Ag 15,19:2
Front Page, The 1928,Ag 26,VII,1:1
Front Page, The 1929,Ja 6,VIII,4:4
Front Page, The 1929,Jl 14,IX,2:1
20th Century 1932,D 30,15:1
Twentieth Century 1933,F 12,IX,1:1
Front Page, The 1935,Jl 9,24:4
Jumbo 1935,N 18,20:2
Jumbo 1935,N 24,IX,1:1
Ladies and Gentlemen 1939,S 24,IX,2:5
Ladies and Gentlemen 1939,O 18,30:2
Ladies and Gentlemen 1939,O 22,IX,1:3
Ladies and Gentlemen 1939,O 29,IX,1:3
Johnny on the Spot 1942,Ja 9,24:2
Swan Song 1946,My 16,29:2
Front Page, The 1946,S 5,22:4
Front Page, The 1946,S 15,II,21:1
Twentieth Century 1950,D 25,23:6
Front Page, The 1968,O 20,85:5
Front Page, The 1969,My 12,54:2
Front Page, The 1969,My 25,II,1:1
Front Page, The 1969,N 2,86:1
MacArthur, Chester
On the Level 1937,Mr 26,24:4
MacArthur, Claude (Musical Director)
Fountania 1926,Ja 17,II,8:8
McArthur, Edwin (Musical Director)
Sweethearts 1947,Ja 22,31:2
MacArthur, James
Invitation to a March 1960,O 31,27:2
McArthur, Jane
Quick Years, The 1953,N 26,51:2
Noah 1954,O 11,32:2
Country Wife, The 1955,Ap 6,35:1
Young and Beautiful, The 1955,O 3,23:2
Box of Watercolors, A 1957,F 18,22:2
Point of No Return 1957,Mr 23,17:2
Will and the Way, The 1957,D 3,46:5
Marvellous History of Saint Bernard, The 1958,F 24,16:3
Our Town 1959,Mr 24,46:2
Our Town 1959,Ap 5,II,1:1
Our Town 1961,N 4,14:7
Hostage, The 1961,D 13,55:4
Merchant of Venice, The 1962,Je 22,1:4
Right You Are (If You Think You Are) 1964,Mr 5,37:1
Tavern, The 1964,Mr 6,39:2
Scapin 1964,Mr 10,43:1
Impromptu at Versailles 1964,Mr 10,43:1
Lower Depths, The 1964,Mr 31,30:1
MacArthur, John D (Producer)
Child of the Morning 1951,N 17,9:7
MacArthur, Mary
Good Housekeeping 1949,Ag 17,19:3
McArthur, Molly (Scenic Designer)
Love's Labour's Lost 1932,Ag 7,IX,1:7

McArthur, Susan
Romeo and Juliet 1968,Ag 16,19:1
Invitation to a Beheading 1969,Mr 18,36:1
Richard III 1970,Jl 4,11:1
McAtamney, Ann
Lazarus Laughed 1948,Ap 9,27:4
Macateer, Alan
Piper, The 1920,Mr 20,14:2
Kathleen ni Houlihan 1920,Je 29,9:2
Youth 1920,O 27,14:3
Pigeon, The 1922,F 3,13:1
Devil's Disciple, The 1923,Ap 24,24:1
Chalk Dust 1936,Mr 5,24:5
Battle Hymn 1936,My 23,12:1
Path of Flowers, The 1936,S 18,19:3
Native Ground 1937,Mr 24,28:4
Any Day Now 1941,Je 10,28:2
Days of Our Youth, The 1941,N 29,15:2
Virginia Reel 1947,Ap 15,28:2
Scarecrow, The 1953,Je 17,31:1
Little Clay Cart, The 1953,Jl 1,25:1
Painted Days, The 1961,Ap 7,24:1
Macaulay, Anne Marie
Listen Professor! 1943,D 23,22:1
Macaulay, Charles
Dark Is Light Enough, The 1955,F 24,20:1
Duchess of Malfi, The 1957,Mr 20,33:1
Buoyant Billions 1959,My 27,32:2
Overruled 1959,My 27,32:2
Getting Married 1959,Je 5,18:2
Passion, Poison and Petrifaction 1959,Ag 21,13:1
Overruled 1959,Ag 21,13:1
Dark Lady of the Sonnets, The 1959,Ag 21,13:1
Much Ado About Nothing 1964,Jl 24,15:2
Much Ado About Nothing 1964,Jl 27,22:3
Macbeth 1964,Jl 27,22:3
Macaulay, J Harper
Passion Flower, The 1920,Ja 14,12:1
Macaulay, Joseph
Sonya 1921,Ag 16,18:3
Dice of the Gods, The 1923,Ap 6,20:2
Magic Ring, The 1923,O 2,10:1
Saint Joan 1923,D 29,8:4
Saint Joan 1924,Ja 6,VII,1:1
Music Box Revue 1924,D 2,23:3
Don't Bother Mother 1925,F 4,18:2
Bit o' Love, A 1925,My 13,24:2
Wild Rose, The 1926,O 21,23:1
Rapid Transit 1927,Ap 8,21:2
Patience 1927,My 24,23:2
Kiss Me! 1927,Jl 22,17:1
Love Call, The 1927,O 25,33:1
Three Musketeers, The 1928,Mr 4,IX,2:3
Three Musketeers, The 1928,Mr 14,28:1
Three Musketeers, The 1928,Mr 25,IX,1:1
Show Girl 1929,Jl 3,19:3
Luana 1930,S 18,28:1
H M S Pinafore 1931,My 19,25:2
Gondoliers, The 1931,Je 2,34:4
Patience 1931,Je 16,30:4
Iolanthe 1931,Jl 14,21:5
Trial by Jury 1931,Jl 28,17:6
H M S Pinafore 1931,Jl 28,17:6
Face the Music 1932,F 18,24:5
Champagne, Sec 1933,O 16,20:2
Revenge With Music 1934,N 29,33:5
St Helena 1936,S 29,35:1
St Helena 1936,O 7,32:1
Eternal Road, The 1937,Ja 8,14:2
I'd Rather Be Right 1937,N 3,28:2
Great Lady 1938,D 2,26:6
Sea Dogs 1939,N 7,30:3
Liliom 1940,Mr 26,17:2
Let's Face It 1941,O 30,26:2
Gypsy Lady 1946,S 18,25:5
Mikado, The 1949,O 5,35:2
Pirates of Penzance, The 1949,O 11,41:2
H M S Pinafore 1949,O 18,34:2
Much Ado About Nothing 1952,My 2,20:1
Mikado, The 1952,O 21,35:2
Pirates of Penzance, The 1952,O 28,36:4
H M S Pinafore 1952,N 4,32:2
Iolanthe 1952,N 11,26:3
Coriolanus 1954,Ja 20,34:2
Coming of Christ, The 1957,D 23,29:8
Smiling the Boy Fell Dead 1961,Ap 20,28:1
King of the Whole Damn World 1962,Ap 16,32:2
Funny Girl 1964,Mr 27,15:1
Macaulay, Pauline (Playwright)
Creeper, The 1965,Jl 15,21:1
Astrakhan Coat, The 1967,Ja 13,18:1
Macaulay, Richard (Playwright)
Hide and Seek 1934,Ag 7,20:2
Macaulay, Tom
Yes, M'Lord 1949,O 5,35:2
Macauley, Thurston
Man Who Ate the Popomack, The 1924,Mr 25,24:1
McAuliffe, Jere
Little Miss Charity 1920,S 3,6:3
Honeymoon Lane 1926,S 21,32:3
Stepping Out 1929,My 21,29:1
McAvity, Helen (Playwright)
Mating Dance 1965,N 4,58:1

McAvoy, John
Honeymoon Lane 1926,S 21,32:3
MacBane, Ralph
Robert E Lee 1923,N 21,23:1
Living Mask, The 1924,Ja 22,15:1
Glass Slipper, The 1925,O 20,29:1
Bride of the Lamb 1926,Mr 31,20:3
Co-Respondent Unknown 1936,F 12,24:4
Cradle Will Rock, The 1938,Ja 4,19:3
MacBane, Ralph (Director)
Only the Young 1932,S 22,25:2
Black Diamond 1933,F 24,12:2
McBee, Johnny
Macbeth 1968,N 30,49:3
Macbeth, Allan
Earl Carroll's Vanities 1927,Ja 5,18:1
Macbeth, Allan (Mrs)
Earl Carroll's Vanities 1927,Ja 5,18:1
Macbeth, George O
Shunned 1960,D 21,39:1
Macbeth, Robert
Merchant of Venice, The 1962,F 3,13:2
Tiger Tiger Burning Bright 1962,D 24,5:2
Who's Got His Own 1967,O 14,13:3
Macbeth, Robert (Director)
Who's Got His Own 1967,O 14,13:3
Son, Come Home, A 1968,Mr 9,23:2
Clara's Ole Man 1968,Mr 9,23:2
Electronic Nigger, The 1968,Mr 9,23:2
In the Wine Time 1968,D 22,II,7:1
McBride, Charles
Jazz a La Carte 1922,Je 3,8:3
MacBride, Donald
Glory for All 1937,F 9,18:2
Room Service 1937,My 20,16:1
McBride, Edith
Peter Ibbetson 1926,Mr 26,24:7
McBride, Irene
Thumbs Up! 1934,D 28,24:1
McBride, Jemison
Cure for Matrimony 1939,O 26,26:3
McBride, Louise
Mr Sycamore 1942,N 14,13:2
McBride, Mary Lucille
Our Lan' 1947,S 29,16:5
McBride, Mildred
Yellow Jacket, The 1923,Ap 20,20:3
McBrown, Gertrude
Sweet River 1936,O 29,30:2
MacBryde, Jack
Girl Trouble 1928,O 26,22:3
McCabe, Bernice
Glory 1922,D 26,10:1
McCabe, Eileen
Light, Lively and Yiddish 1970,O 28,58:1
McCabe, Frances
Pillar to Post 1943,D 11,11:2
McCabe, Julia
Dove, The 1925,F 12,17:3
McCabe, Leo
Empress of Destiny 1938,Mr 10,16:2
McCabe, May
If I Was Rich 1926,S 3,15:2
In Times Square 1931,N 24,29:3
McCahill, Angela
Kathleen ni Houlihan 1920,Je 29,9:2
Mixed Marriage 1920,D 15,18:2
Cradle Song 1921,Mr 1,18:2
John Ferguson 1921,My 24,20:1
John Ferguson 1921,Je 21,20:2
Detour, The 1921,Ag 24,12:2
Malvaloca 1922,O 3,22:1
McCain, Lee
Lemon Sky 1970,My 18,40:1
McCall, Don
House in Berlin, A (Als der Kreig zu Ende War);
  Als der Krieg zu Ende War (A House in Berlin)
  1950,D 27,32:3
McCall, George Henry (Playwright)
Gods We Make, The 1934,Ja 4,16:4
McCall, Helen
Hopalong--Freud 1953,Je 18,38:5
Brandy Is My True Love's Name 1953,Je 18,38:5
California 1953,Je 18,38:5
Where There's a Will 1953,Je 18,38:5
McCall, John
Race of Hairy Men!, A 1965,Ap 30,42:1
McCall, Lizzie
Texas Nightingale, The 1922,N 21,15:2
Honor Be Damned! 1927,Ja 27,13:1
Carry On 1928,Ja 24,26:1
Under the Gaslight 1929,Ap 3,27:1
City Haul 1929,D 31,14:4
McCall, Sabina
Blue Butterfly, The 1929,F 17,29:3
Blue Butterfly, The 1929,My 4,17:2
McCall, Teresa
Blue Butterfly, The 1929,My 4,17:2
McCallie, Elizabeth
Little Theatre Tournament; Pink and Patches
  1928,My 11,28:1
McCallin, Clement
Gentle People, The 1939,Jl 30,IX,1:3

McCallin, Clement (Miscellaneous)
Caesar and Cleopatra 1951,D 20,43:2
Antony and Cleopatra 1951,D 21,22:2
McCallion, James
Yours Truly 1927,Ja 26,16:5
Would-Be Gentleman, The 1930,Ap 30,29:2
Lysistrata 1930,Je 6,20:1
But for the Grace of God 1937,Ja 13,21:4
Roosty 1938,F 15,21:2
Sea Dogs 1939,N 7,30:3
Kathleen 1948,F 4,26:2
McCallion, Joseph
Peg o' My Dreams 1924,My 6,25:3
Bunk of 1926 1926,Ap 23,25:2
Family Affairs 1929,D 11,34:6
Intimate Relations 1932,Mr 29,23:2
Trial of Dr Beck, The 1937,Ag 10,22:2
McCallion, Margaret
Great Campaign, The 1947,Ap 1,33:2
McCallum, Charles R (Director)
Prince of Peasantmania 1970,F 22,88:1
McCallum, Charles Ray (Miscellaneous)
At War With the Army 1949,Mr 9,32:2
McCallum, David
Flip Side, The 1968,O 11,36:1
McCallum, John
Waiting For Gillian 1954,Ap 22,36:2
McCallum, Kim
Richard III 1965,Je 3,26:1
McCallum, Mabel
Derryowen 1946,O 29,34:2
McCallum, Neil
Period of Adjustment 1962,Je 4,24:2
McCallum, Sandy
Henry V 1964,My 13,52:1
Saint Joan 1964,My 14,41:1
Cherry Orchard, The 1965,Ag 2,17:2
Skin of Our Teeth, The 1966,Je 2,51:1
As You Like It 1966,Je 4,19:1
Red, White and Maddox 1969,Ja 27,27:1
McCambridge, Mercedes
Place of Our Own, A 1945,Ap 3,23:7
Woman Bites Dog 1946,Ap 18,21:2
Young and Fair, The 1948,Je 23,35:2
Child Buyer, The 1962,My 14,35:1
McCandless, J H (Producer)
Coriolanus 1927,Je 18,8:3
McCandless, Peter
Here Comes Santa Claus 1962,My 18,34:1
McCandless, Stanley (Lighting Director)
King's Coat, The 1933,Ja 12,21:4
Lady Has a Heart, The 1937,S 27,24:1
Many Mansions 1937,O 28,28:6
Rhapsody 1944,N 23,37:2
McCann, Donal
Shaughraun, The 1968,My 22,54:1
McCann, Frances
Rosalinda; Fledermaus, Die 1942,O 29,26:5
Vagabond King, The 1943,Je 30,24:2
Chocolate Soldier, The 1947,Mr 13,34:2
McCann, James R
Be Yourself! 1924,S 4,13:3
McCann, John M
Hippolytus 1935,Je 15,20:4
Front Page, The 1937,N 12,27:2
McCann, Thomas
Oedipus 1970,F 23,30:1
Hamlet 1970,O 19,51:1
McCann, William J (Mrs)
Little Town of Bethlehem, The 1920,D 27,11:1
McCann Sisters
International Revue 1930,F 26,22:2
McCardell, Roy (Playwright)
Bare Facts of Today 1930,Ap 17,24:4
McCarrick, Martin
Lower Depths, The 1956,O 3,29:2
Orpheus Descending 1959,O 6,45:2
McCarten, Joan
Christmas in the Market Place 1960,D 10,26:1
McCarther, Avis
Penny Wars, The 1969,O 16,52:1
McCarthey, Arthur
Gypsy Baron, The 1944,Je 15,17:3
McCarthy, Agnes
Chains of Dew 1922,Ap 28,20:2
Sandro Botticelli 1923,Mr 27,24:2
Laugh, Clown, Laugh! 1923,N 29,30:1
Assumption of Hannele, The 1924,F 16,16:2
Dream Play 1926,Ja 21,18:2
On the High Road 1929,Ja 15,22:3
Katerina 1929,Mr 26,30:3
Mademoiselle Bourrat 1929,O 8,34:3
Siegfried 1930,O 21,34:1
Cherry Orchard, The 1933,Mr 7,20:3
McCarthy, Alicia
Look Who's Here 1920,Mr 3,12:2
McCarthy, Bill
Billy Budd 1955,My 4,35:1
McCarthy, Charles
Paddy the Next Best Thing 1920,Ag 28,5:5
Firebrand, The 1924,O 16,33:1
Canary Dutch 1925,S 9,22:1
Vaudeville (Palace) 1926,S 21,32:5

McCarthy, Charles—Cont
Judge's Husband, The 1926,S 28,31:1
Baby Cyclone, The 1927,S 13,37:4
Good Hope, The 1927,O 19,24:2
2 + 2 = 5 1927,N 29,30:3
First Stone, The 1928,Ja 14,12:2
Peter Pan; Boy Who Would Not Grow Up, The
  1928,N 27,36:3
On the High Road 1929,Ja 15,22:3
Congratulations 1929,My 1,28:4
Fiesta 1929,S 18,35:1
Richelieu 1929,D 26,20:3
Way of the World, The 1931,Je 2,34:3
Is Life Worth Living? 1933,N 10,24:6
McCarthy, Colleen
Ice Follies 1959,Ja 14,30:1
McCarthy, Dan
Conscience 1924,S 12,19:3
McCarthy, Dennis
Medea 1947,O 21,27:2
Silver Tassie, The 1949,Jl 22,16:5
McCarthy, Dorothy
Lady Fingers 1929,F 1,22:4
McCarthy, E A
Tiger Smiles, The 1930,D 18,29:1
McCarthy, Elizabeth
Gondoliers, The 1963,Je 5,33:2
McCarthy, Frank
Passion Play 1934,F 12,15:1
Veronica's Veil 1936,F 10,19:6
McCarthy, Gerald
Scotland Yard 1929,S 28,16:6
Truth Game, The 1930,D 29,19:1
McCarthy, Helen
Her Family Tree 1920,D 28,9:2
McCarthy, J Barry (Playwright)
Joy of Serpents 1930,Ap 4,22:4
McCarthy, J Bernard (Playwright)
Crusaders, The 1929,Mr 3,VIII,2:1
McCarthy, J J (Lyricist)
Ziegfeld Follies 1924,Je 25,26:1
MacCarthy, Joan
Don't Throw Glass Houses 1938,D 28,24:4
McCarthy, Joan
Ziegfeld Follies 1920,Je 23,14:1
Rio Rita 1927,F 3,18:3
John Murray Anderson's Almanac 1953,D 11,42:2
McCarthy, Joseph (Lyricist)
Ziegfeld Follies 1920,Je 23,14:1
Up She Goes 1922,N 7,14:2
Glory 1922,D 26,10:1
Kid Boots 1924,Ja 1,21:3
Rio Rita 1927,F 3,18:3
Cross My Heart 1928,S 18,32:7
New Aquacade Revue, The 1940,My 13,20:5
John Murray Anderson's Almanac 1953,D 11,42:2
McCarthy, Joseph (Playwright)
Ziegfeld Follies 1920,Je 23,14:1
McCarthy, Justin Huntly (Original Author)
O'Flynn, The 1934,D 28,24:1
McCarthy, Justin Huntly (Playwright)
Vagabond King, The 1925,S 22,23:3
Vagabond King, The 1943,Je 30,24:2
McCarthy, Kevin
Abe Lincoln in Illinois 1938,O 17,12:2
Flight to the West 1940,D 31,19:1
Mexican Mural; Moonlight Scene 1942,Ap 27,19:2
Winged Victory 1943,N 22,24:1
Truckline Cafe 1946,F 28,19:4
Joan of Lorraine 1946,N 19,40:2
Survivors, The 1948,Ja 20,27:2
Bravo! 1948,N 12,31:2
Death of a Salesman 1949,Jl 29,12:5
Red Roses for Me 1951,Ap 26,35:8
Anna Christie 1952,Ja 10,33:1
Anna Christie 1952,Ja 20,II,1:1
Love's Labour's Lost 1953,F 5,20:3
Sea Gull, The 1954,My 12,38:1
Sea Gull, The 1954,My 23,II,1:1
Red Roses for Me 1955,D 29,15:2
Red Roses for Me 1956,Ja 8,II,1:1
Day the Money Stopped, The 1958,F 21,19:4
Marching Song 1959,D 29,20:1
Glimpse of the Domesticity of Franklyn Barnabas,
  A 1960,Mr 7,24:2
Advise and Consent 1960,N 18,25:1
Something About a Soldier 1962,Ja 5,36:2
Three Sisters, The 1964,Ja 23,24:1
Warm Body, A 1967,Ap 17,44:2
Happy Birthday, Wanda June 1970,O 8,58:2
Happy Birthday, Wanda June 1970,O 18,II,1:1
McCarthy, Kevin (Playwright)
Sea Gull, The 1954,My 12,38:1
McCarthy, Lillah
Iphigenie in Tauris 1915,Je 1,15:5
McCarthy, Lin
Chase, The 1952,Ap 16,30:2
Clearing in the Woods, A 1957,Ja 11,20:2
McCarthy, Margaret
Lady Fingers 1929,F 1,22:4
Fiddler's House, The 1941,Mr 28,27:5
McCarthy, Mary
Look Who's Here 1920,Mr 3,12:2

McCarthy, Mary (Playwright)
Please, Mrs. Garibaldi 1939,Mr 17,24:3
McCarthy, Michael
Man and Superman 1964,D 7,45:2
Judith 1965,Mr 25,42:2
McCarthy, Molly
Go Show Me a Dragon 1961,O 28,18:1
McCarthy, Nancy
Big Knife, The 1959,N 13,25:1
McCarthy, Patricia
Much Ado About Nothing 1952,My 2,20:1
McCarthy, Robert
Henry's Harem 1926,S 14,25:2
McCarthy, William J
Twinkle Twinkle 1926,N 17,22:2
She's My Baby 1928,Ja 4,22:2
Sweethearts 1929,S 23,25:1
Mlle Modiste 1929,O 8,34:1
Naughty Marietta 1929,O 22,26:2
Fortune Teller, The 1929,N 5,32:3
Robin Hood 1929,N 20,26:5
Merry Widow, The 1929,D 3,29:1
Babes in Toyland 1929,D 24,15:3
Good Woman, Poor Thing, A 1933,Ja 10,27:3
Champagne, Sec 1933,O 16,20:2
Jumbo 1935,N 18,20:2
Arms and the Girl 1950,F 3,28:2
McCarthy Sisters
Irving Berlin's New Music Box Revue
1922,O 24,18:1
George White's Scandals 1925,Je 23,24:2
George White's Scandals 1926,Je 15,23:2
Manhattan Mary 1927,S 27,30:3
Vaudeville (Palace) 1928,Ag 28,27:3
McCarty, Eddie
Last Triangle, The (An Embroidered Camp)
1968,Mr 19,41:1
McCarty, Ernest (Composer)
I Dreamt I Dwelt in Bloomingdale's 1970,F 13,26:1
McCarty, Ernest (Lyricist)
I Dreamt I Dwelt in Bloomingdale's 1970,F 13,26:1
McCarty, Ernest (Miscellaneous)
I Dreamt I Dwelt in Bloomingdale's 1970,F 13,26:1
McCarty, Mary
Sleepy Hollow 1948,Je 4,26:3
Small Wonder 1948,S 16,33:5
Small Wonder 1948,S 26,II,1:1
Miss Liberty 1949,Je 14,26:6
Miss Liberty 1949,Jl 16,6:5
Miss Liberty 1949,Jl 24,II,1:1
Miss Liberty 1949,Ag 7,II,6:4
Bless You All 1950,D 15,42:2
Rainy Day in Newark, A 1963,O 23,35:1
McCarty, Paul
Jim Jam Jems 1920,O 5,13:2
McCary, Albert
Show Boat 1948,S 9,33:2
McCauley, Jack
Gang's All Here, The 1931,F 19,21:3
Hey, Nonny, Nonny! 1932,Je 7,22:3
Show Is On, The 1936,D 26,14:2
Johnny on the Spot 1942,Ja 9,24:2
Ziegfeld Follies 1943,Ap 2,16:2
Sing Out, Sweet Land! 1944,D 28,24:2
High Button Shoes 1947,O 10,32:2
Gentlemen Prefer Blondes 1949,D 9,35:3
Gentlemen Prefer Blondes 1949,D 18,II,3:1
McCauley, Jerry
High Flyers 1927,Je 26,VIII,1:1
McCauley, John
Nerves 1924,S 2,22:2
Hit the Deck! 1927,Ap 26,32:1
Little Show, The 1929,My 1,28:5
Please Do Not Disturb 1936,Je 23,27:1
Show Is On, The 1937,S 20,18:4
Streets of Paris, The 1939,Je 20,25:2
Keep Off the Grass 1940,My 24,22:6
Snookie 1941,Je 4,26:2
Count Me In 1942,O 9,24:2
McCauley, Joseph
Life With Father 1939,Ag 15,14:4
McCauley, Judith
Jo 1964,F 13,25:1
Oklahoma! 1969,Je 24,37:1
McCauley, Margaret
Diana 1929,D 10,37:1
MacCauley, Mark
Crimes of Passion; Erpingham Camp, The
1969,O 27,54:1
McCauley, Miriam
Guest of Honor, The 1920,S 21,12:1
McCauley, Robbie
Neighbors 1966,N 15,51:4
Cities in Bezique; Beast's Story, A 1969,Ja 13,26:1
Electra 1969,Ag 8,14:1
McCauley, Sanford
Constant Wife, The 1935,Jl 3,20:2
New Life, A 1943,S 16,26:6
Born Yesterday 1958,Mr 22,12:6
McCauliffe, Anthony
Big Fight, The 1928,S 19,33:1
MacCausland, Kay
Genius and the Crowd 1920,S 7,20:1

Snapshots of 1921 1921,Je 3,19:2
McCawley, Charles H
Sacred Flame, The 1952,O 8,35:2
McCawley, Jerome
Spring's Awakening 1955,O 10,30:2
McCay, Mary
Firefly, The 1938,Jl 12,15:4
McCay, Peggy
Cock-A-Doodle Dandy 1950,F 1,26:2
King of Friday's Men, The 1951,F 22,26:2
Uncle Vanya 1956,F 1,25:2
Uncle Vanya 1956,F 12,II,1:1
Easter 1957,Ja 17,35:2
Failures, The 1959,Ja 6,30:2
U S A 1959,O 29,38:1
U S A 1959,N 8,II,1:1
McCay, Peggy Ann
Seven Mirrors 1945,O 26,17:2
McCay, Winsor
Untitled-Revue 1923,My 12,15:4
McCeady, Tom
Hamlet 1967,D 27,45:1
McChesney, Ernest
Prince Charming 1930,O 14,31:1
Chocolate Soldier, The 1947,Mr 13,34:2
McClain, John J
Caukey 1944,F 18,15:4
McClain, Tana
Midsummer Night's Dream, A 1964,Je 30,23:2
McClanahan, Rue
Secret Life of Walter Mitty, The 1964,O 27,44:5
Big Man 1966,My 20,41:1
MacBird! 1967,F 23,38:1
Jimmy Shine 1968,D 6,52:1
Tonight in Living Color; Golden Fleece, The
1969,Je 11,43:1
Who's Happy Now? 1969,N 18,39:1
Who's Happy Now? 1970,F 15,II,1:1
Dark of the Moon 1970,Ap 4,21:2
McClaney, Howard
Minute's Wait, A 1920,Je 22,9:1
McClarney, Pat
Girl From Nantucket, The 1945,N 9,17:2
Front Page, The 1946,S 5,22:4
McClave, Roland (Composer)
Flair-Flair the Idol of Paree 1935,Mr 13,16:1
McClave, Roland (Lyricist)
Flair-Flair the Idol of Paree 1935,Mr 13,16:1
McClay, Gary
Moby Dick 1970,Je 3,52:1
Hamlet 1970,O 27,54:2
Rosencrantz and Guildenstern Are Dead
1970,N 19,39:3
McCleary, William (Scenic Designer)
Romeo and Juliet 1949,O 17,19:2
McCleery, Albert
Romeo and Juliet 1934,D 21,30:3
McCleery, Albert (Director)
Trial by Fire 1947,D 5,31:5
Lazarus Laughed 1948,Ap 9,27:4
McCleery, William (Playwright)
Hope for the Best 1945,F 8,14:4
Hope for the Best 1945,F 18,II,1:1
Parlor Story 1947,Mr 5,29:2
Good Housekeeping 1949,Ag 17,19:3
McClellan, Clark (Miscellaneous)
Who's Who, Baby? 1968,Ja 30,36:1
Bill Noname 1970,Mr 3,37:1
McClellan, Clark (Musical Director)
Cindy 1964,Mr 20,24:1
Bill Noname 1970,Mr 3,37:1
McClellan, Ellis
Mystery Ship, The 1927,Mr 15,28:2
McClellan, Jack (Playwright)
Half-Caste, The 1926,Mr 30,20:4
Lady Do 1927,Ap 19,24:2
McClellan, Kenneth
Murder in the Cathedral 1958,Mr 22,12:4
McClellan, Robert
Good Times 1920,Ag 10,10:1
Better Times 1922,S 4,14:2
McClellan, Walter (Playwright)
Delta Wife, The 1927,My 6,20:3
McClelland, Charles
Meteor 1929,D 24,15:1
Whistling in the Dark 1932,Ja 20,16:6
Whistling in the Dark 1932,N 4,25:2
John Brown 1934,Ja 23,22:3
Prisoners of War 1935,Ja 29,24:1
Boy Meets Girl 1935,N 19,27:2
Boy Meets Girl 1935,N 28,38:2
Too Many Heroes 1937,N 16,26:2
Quiet, Please! 1940,N 9,20:3
Land Is Bright, The 1941,O 29,26:2
Dark Hammock 1944,D 12,27:8
Faith of Our Fathers 1950,Ag 6,72:2
Jolly's Progress 1959,D 7,42:2
McClelland, Charles (Director)
Whistling in the Dark 1932,N 4,25:2
McClelland, Dona
Return of the Vagabond, The 1940,My 14,27:2
McClelland, Donald
Sylvia 1923,Ap 26,22:1

McClelland, Donald—Cont
White Collars 1925,F 24,17:2
Fast Life 1928,S 27,35:2
Back Here 1928,N 27,36:3
Scarlet Pages 1929,S 10,26:3
Lady Beyond the Moon 1931,Ap 1,36:5
Mask and the Face, The 1933,My 9,20:2
Ah, Wilderness! 1933,O 3,28:2
Too Many Boats 1934,S 12,26:3
To My Husband 1936,Je 2,35:2
Treasure Island 1938,My 15,II,2:3
Night Before Christmas, The 1941,Ap 11,25:2
Yankee Point 1942,N 24,28:2
Make Yourself at Home 1945,S 14,21:2
Light Up the Sky 1948,N 19,34:2
Miss Liberty 1949,Jl 16,6:5
Small Hours, The 1951,F 16,22:1
Out West of Eighth 1951,S 21,20:3
Child of the Morning 1951,N 17,9:7
Hook'n Ladder 1952,Ap 30,31:2
McClelland, Keith (Miscellaneous)
Curley McDimple 1967,N 23,59:2
MacClelland, Kenneth (Scenic Designer)
Adventures of Marco Polo, The 1941,D 28,I,31:7
McClelland, Reed
Marathon 1933,Ja 28,8:8
Too Much Party 1934,Mr 6,28:4
In the Bag 1936,D 18,30:2
McClendon, Ernestine
Twisting Road, The; One Tuesday Morning
1957,N 18,36:5
Alley of the Sunset 1959,D 31,11:1
Goose, The 1960,Mr 16,44:1
McClendon, Jack (Miscellaneous)
Judy Garland 1959,My 12,40:1
McClendon, Rose
Roseanne 1924,Mr 11,16:3
Deep River 1926,O 5,26:2
In Abraham's Bosom 1926,D 31,10:2
In Abraham's Bosom 1927,F 20,VII,1:1
Porgy 1927,O 11,26:2
Porgy 1929,S 14,17:3
House of Connelly, The 1931,S 29,22:4
Never No More 1932,Ja 8,27:1
Black Souls 1932,Mr 31,25:1
Brain Sweat 1934,Ap 5,24:4
Roll Sweet Chariot 1934,O 3,24:3
Roll Sweet Chariot 1934,O 14,X,1:1
Panic 1935,Mr 16,18:4
Mulatto 1935,O 25,25:2
McClennon, George
O K 1925,My 4,16:1
Shuffle Along of 1933 1932,D 27,11:3
McClintic, Guthrie
Brief Moment 1931,O 25,VIII,2:1
High Tor 1937,Ja 17,X,1:1
Barretts of Wimpole Street, The 1944,S 17,II,1:3
McClintic, Guthrie (Director)
Lazybones 1924,S 23,23:1
In His Arms 1924,O 14,23:1
All Dressed Up 1925,S 10,28:1
Green Hat, The 1925,S 16,23:2
Shanghai Gesture, The 1926,F 2,20:2
Glory Hallelujah 1926,Ap 7,26:2
God Loves Us 1926,O 20,22:2
Saturday's Children 1927,Ja 27,13:1
Mariners 1927,Mr 29,22:2
Mariners 1927,Ap 3,VIII,1:1
Letter, The 1927,S 27,30:1
John 1927,N 5,16:4
Fallen Angels 1927,D 2,20:4
Cock Robin 1928,Ja 13,26:6
Jealousy 1928,O 23,32:2
Age of Innocence, The 1928,N 28,24:2
Skyrocket, The 1929,Ja 12,14:7
Cross Roads 1929,N 12,34:2
Dishonored Lady 1930,F 5,27:1
Barretts of Wimpole Street, The 1931,F 10,25:1
Barretts of Wimpole Street, The 1931,F 22,VIII,1:1
Brief Moment 1931,N 10,28:2
Distant Drums 1932,Ja 19,24:3
Distant Drums 1932,Ja 31,VIII,1:1
Truth About Blayds, The 1932,Ap 12,25:2
Criminal at Large 1932,O 11,26:3
Lucrece 1932,N 30,22:8
Lucrece 1932,D 21,22:2
Lucrece 1933,Ja 1,IX,1:1
Alien Corn 1933,F 21,17:2
Alien Corn 1933,F 26,IX,1:1
Jezebel 1933,D 20,26:3
Yellow Jack 1934,Mr 7,22:6
Yellow Jack 1934,Mr 18,IX,1:1
Divided by Three 1934,O 3,24:2
Romeo and Juliet 1934,D 21,30:3
Romeo and Juliet 1934,D 30,IX,1:1
Old Maid, The 1935,Ja 8,26:1
Barretts of Wimpole Street, The 1935,F 26,16:2
Flowers of the Forest 1935,Ap 9,25:2
Winterset 1935,S 26,19:2
Parnell 1935,N 12,24:2
Romeo and Juliet 1935,D 24,10:2
Ethan Frome 1936,Ja 7,24:7
Ethan Frome 1936,Ja 22,15:2
Ethan Frome 1936,F 2,IX,1:1

McClintic, Guthrie (Director)—Cont

Saint Joan 1936,Mr 10,27:4
Saint Joan 1936,Mr 15,X,1:1
Anteroom, The 1936,Ag 15,6:7
Anteroom, The 1936,S 6,IX,1:1
Hamlet 1936,O 9,30:2
Wingless Victory, The 1936,D 24,20:2
High Tor 1937,Ja 11,15:2
High Tor 1937,Ja 17,X,1:1
Candida 1937,Mr 11,20:2
Star-Wagon, The 1937,S 30,18:5
Star-Wagon, The 1937,O 10,XI,1:1
Barchester Towers 1937,D 1,27:1
How to Get Tough About It 1938,F 9,16:2
Missouri Legend 1938,S 20,27:2
Missouri Legend 1938,S 25,IX,1:1
Mamba's Daughters 1939,Ja 4,24:2
No Time for Comedy 1939,Ap 18,26:4
No Time for Comedy 1939,Ap 30,XI,1:1
Key Largo 1939,N 28,30:2
Christmas Eve 1939,D 28,17:2
Mamba's Daughters 1940,Mr 25,10:4
International Incident, An 1940,Ap 3,18:2
Lady Who Came to Stay, The 1941,Ja 3,13:2
Doctor's Dilemma, The 1941,F 18,26:6
Doctor's Dilemma, The 1941,Mr 12,18:2
Doctor's Dilemma, The 1941,Mr 30,IX,1:1
Spring Again 1941,O 28,28:3
Spring Again 1941,N 11,28:2
Rose Burke 1942,Ja 25,IX,2:5
Candida 1942,Ap 28,24:4
Morning Star, The 1942,S 15,18:4
Morning Star, The 1942,S 20,VIII,1:1
Three Sisters, The 1942,D 22,31:2
Three Sisters, The 1942,D 27,VIII,1:1
Lovers and Friends 1943,N 30,23:2
Barretts of Wimpole Street, The 1944,S 17,II,1:3
Barretts of Wimpole Street, The 1945,Mr 27,23:6
You Touched Me! 1945,S 26,27:2
You Touched Me! 1945,S 30,II,1:1
Antigone 1946,F 19,21:3
Antigone 1946,F 24,II,1:1
Candida 1946,Ap 4,33:2
Playboy of the Western World, The 1946,O 28,18:3
Antony and Cleopatra 1947,N 27,49:2
Antony and Cleopatra 1947,D 7,II,5:1
Life With Mother 1948,Je 9,36:3
Life With Mother 1948,O 21,32:2
Life With Mother 1948,O 31,II,1:1
Medea 1949,My 3,31:2
That Lady 1949,N 23,18:4
That Lady 1949,D 4,II,5:1
Velvet Glove, The 1949,D 27,26:2
Burning Bright 1950,O 19,40:2
Burning Bright 1950,O 29,II,1:1
Medea 1951,S 14,22:5
Medea 1951,S 23,II,3:1
Constant Wife, The 1951,D 10,34:3
Constant Wife, The 1951,D 16,II,6:1
Come of Age 1952,Ja 24,22:2
To Be Continued 1952,Ap 24,37:2
Bernardine 1952,O 17,33:4
Bernardine 1952,N 9,II,1:1
Mrs Patterson 1954,D 2,37:1
Dark Is Light Enough, The 1955,F 24,20:1
Roomful of Roses, A 1955,O 18,48:1
Four Winds 1957,S 26,21:2

McClintic, Guthrie (Miscellaneous)

Skyrocket, The 1929,Ja 12,14:7
Dishonored Lady 1930,F 5,27:1
Truth About Blayds, The 1932,Ap 12,25:2
Parnell 1936,My 5,26:2
Mamba's Daughters 1940,Mr 25,10:4
Electra 1952,N 20,38:2
Oedipus Tyrannus 1952,N 25,35:2

McClintic, Guthrie (Producer)

Way Things Happen, The 1924,Ja 29,17:5
Mrs Partridge Presents 1925,Ja 11,VII,1:2
Glory Hallelujah 1926,Ap 7,26:2
Cock Robin 1928,Ja 13,26:6
Brief Moment 1931,N 10,28:2
Distant Drums 1932,Ja 19,24:3
Criminal at Large 1932,O 11,26:3
Jezebel 1933,D 20,26:3
Yellow Jack 1934,Mr 7,22:6
Yellow Jack 1934,Mr 18,IX,1:1
Divided by Three 1934,O 3,24:2
Winterset 1935,S 26,19:2
Hamlet 1936,O 1,28:3
High Tor 1937,Ja 11,15:2
Star-Wagon, The 1937,S 30,18:5
Barchester Towers 1937,N 19,26:6
Barchester Towers 1937,D 1,27:1
How to Get Tough About It 1938,F 9,16:2
Missouri Legend 1938,S 20,27:2
Mamba's Daughters 1939,Ja 4,24:2
Christmas Eve 1939,D 28,17:2
International Incident, An 1940,Mr 21,30:3
International Incident, An 1940,Ap 3,18:2
Lady Who Came to Stay, The 1941,Ja 3,13:2
Spring Again 1941,O 28,28:3
Spring Again 1941,N 11,28:2
Morning Star, The 1942,S 15,18:4
You Touched Me! 1945,S 26,27:2

Medea 1949,My 3,31:2
Velvet Glove, The 1949,D 27,26:2
To Be Continued 1952,Ap 24,37:2
Dark Is Light Enough, The 1955,Mr 6,II,1:1
Medea 1955,Je 16,35:4
Roomful of Roses, A 1955,O 18,48:1
Dear Liar 1960,Mr 18,19:2

McClintock, Ernie

Henry V 1965,Je 29,27:2

McClintock, Ernie (Director)

Hajj Malik, El 1970,O 4,II,5:1

McClintock, Jean

Take Her, She's Mine 1961,D 22,19:1

McClintock, Marshall

Blue Blood 1924,Ap 3,21:2

McClintock, Mignon

Hindu, The 1922,Mr 22,13:3

McClintock, Poley

Hear! Hear! 1955,S 28,38:1

McClintock, Susan

Tristram 1962,O 29,36:1

McClish, Douglas

Quick Years, The 1953,N 26,51:2

McClory, Sean

King of Friday's Men, The 1951,F 22,26:2

McCloskey, John

Nona 1932,O 5,26:4

McCloskey, Kevin

Respectfully Yours 1947,My 14,29:4

McCloud, Leslie

Naughty Marietta 1931,N 17,31:2
Firefly, The 1931,D 1,23:2

McCloud, Wesley

Naughty Marietta 1929,O 22,26:2

MacCloy, June

Hot-Cha! 1932,Mr 9,17:3

McClung, Bob

Find the Fox 1930,Je 21,20:4

McClung, Robert M

Once Over Lightly 1938,D 10,13:4

McClung, Robert M (Playwright)

Once Over Lightly 1938,D 10,13:4
Once Over Lightly 1938,D 17,10:8

McClure, Bob

Hot Spot 1963,Ap 20,17:2

McClure, Don

London Assurance 1937,F 19,14:5
In Clover 1937,O 14,23:1

McClure, Don (Director)

Commuting Distance 1936,Je 30,15:1
Miss Temple Is Willing 1936,Jl 21,13:1

McClure, Laura

Home Is the Hero 1945,Ja 20,16:4

McClure, Michael (Playwright)

Beard, The 1967,O 25,40:1
Beard, The 1967,N 5,II,3:1

McClure, Olive

Night in Paris, A 1926,Ja 6,16:3
Night in Paris, A 1926,Jl 27,15:4
Americana 1928,O 31,28:2
Ned Wayburn's Gambols 1929,Ja 16,22:3

McClure, William J

Little Old New York 1920,S 9,9:2
Launzi 1923,O 11,16:3

McClusky, Jack

Fine and Dandy 1930,S 24,26:1

McCob, Kate

Morning's at Seven 1939,N 7,30:2

MacColl, James

At Home Abroad 1935,S 4,22:3
At Home Abroad 1935,S 20,17:4
Boy Meets Girl 1935,N 28,38:2
Miss Swan Expects 1939,F 21,15:2
Too Many Girls 1939,O 19,26:2
This Is the Army 1942,Jl 5,28:2
Polonaise 1945,O 8,20:2
Duchess Misbehaves, The 1946,F 14,32:2
Leading Lady 1948,O 19,33:1

McCollum, Barry

Up the Line 1926,N 23,26:1
Parnell 1936,My 5,26:2

McCollum, H H

Sancho Panza 1923,N 27,23:1
Vagabond King, The 1925,S 22,23:3
Marco Millions 1928,Ja 10,28:2
Jade God, The 1929,My 14,28:3
They Never Grow Up 1930,Ap 8,27:1
Insult 1930,S 16,30:2
Alchemist, The 1931,Je 5,27:1
Hamlet 1931,N 6,28:4
Mahogany Hall 1934,Ja 18,18:5
O'Flynn, The 1934,D 28,24:1
Whatever Goes Up 1935,N 26,28:2

McCollum, Warren

Dark, The 1927,F 2,22:5
Mongolia 1927,D 27,24:5
Nice Women 1929,Je 11,27:4
White Flame 1929,N 5,32:7
Incubator 1932,N 2,23:3
Saturday Night 1933,Mr 1,13:2

McComas, Carroll

Merchants of Venus 1920,S 28,14:2
Miss Lulu Bett 1920,D 28,9:1

McComas, Carroll—Cont

School for Scandal, The 1923,Je 5,24:3
Jolly Roger, The 1923,Ag 31,10:4
Cyrano de Bergerac 1923,N 2,14:1
New Gallantry, The 1925,S 25,24:2
You Can't Win 1926,F 17,12:1
Pyramids 1926,Jl 20,17:2
Night Hawk 1926,D 27,21:3
Madame X 1927,Jl 7,29:3
Ladder, The 1927,O 7,24:2
Design For A Stained Glass Window 1950,Ja 24,26:2
Innocents, The 1959,Ap 21,41:2

McComb, Kate

March Hares 1923,Mr 13,19:5
Juno and the Paycock 1926,Mr 16,22:1
Lally 1927,F 9,16:3
Blood Money 1927,Ag 23,29:2
Mongolia 1927,D 27,24:5
Whirlpool 1929,D 4,37:3
After Tomorrow 1930,Ag 10,VIII,2:3
Riddle Me This! 1932,F 26,22:5
Ghost Bereft 1933,F 1,13:5
Magnanimous Lover, The 1933,F 1,13:5
Black Diamond 1933,F 24,12:2
No Questions Asked 1934,F 6,24:3
Morning's at Seven 1939,D 1,26:2
Moon Vine, The 1943,F 12,22:2

McComb, Malcolm

Zuleika 1928,Mr 7,28:7

McComb, Malcolm (Lyricist)

Garrick Gaieties 1930,Je 5,29:2

McComb, Malcolm (Miscellaneous)

Hey, Nonny, Nonny! 1932,Je 7,22:3

McComb, Marilyn

H M S Pinafore 1960,Ja 29,14:1

McCombs, Carroll

Jolly Roger, The 1923,S 9,VII,1:1

Maccone, Ronald

Nobody's Child 1956,Ag 23,25:2

McConkey, Joel

Texas Li'l Darlin' 1949,N 26,10:5

McConnachie, Morton

Kid Boots 1924,Ja 1,21:3
Tell Me More 1925,Ap 14,27:3

McConnell, Frederic (Director)

Daughters of Atreus 1936,O 15,33:1
Romeo and Juliet 1949,O 17,19:2
Long Moment, The 1950,My 22,16:6

McConnell, Frederic (Scenic Designer)

Romeo and Juliet 1949,O 17,19:2

McConnell, Lulu

Poor Little Ritz Girl 1920,Jl 29,7:1
Snapshots of 1921 1921,Je 3,19:2
Passing Show of 1924, The 1924,S 4,13:4
Artists and Models 1925,Je 25,16:2
Vaudeville (Palace) 1926,S 28,30:4
Peggy-Ann 1926,D 28,16:3
Cross My Heart 1928,S 18,32:7
Vaudeville (Palace) 1929,Jl 15,25:4
Me for You 1929,S 22,IX,2:6
Vaudeville (Palace) 1929,D 2,28:6
Vanderbilt Revue, The 1930,O 26,VIII,3:5
Vanderbilt Revue, The 1930,N 6,22:6
Vaudeville (Palace) 1930,D 8,27:2
Vaudeville (Palace) 1932,Jl 4,14:5
Ballyhoo of 1932 1932,S 7,14:2
Bet Your Life 1937,Ap 6,20:2
Something for Nothing 1937,D 10,33:5

McConnell, Ty

Dear World 1969,F 7,33:1
Promenade 1969,Je 5,56:1

McConnie, Marilyn

Man Better Man 1969,Jl 3,22:1

McConnor, Vincent (Playwright)

Joy Forever, A 1946,Ja 8,20:2

McCooey, Everett D

Lady of Mexico 1962,O 20,13:2

McCool, Jean

Bet Your Life 1937,Ap 6,20:2

McCoon, Frances

Riff-Raff 1926,F 9,18:6

McCord, D T W (Lyricist)

It's Only Natural 1922,Ap 21,13:2

McCord, J C

Inside U S A 1948,Je 13,II,6:6
Small Wonder 1948,S 16,33:5
Great to Be Alive! 1950,Mr 24,28:2
Two on the Aisle 1951,Jl 20,13:6
Beggar's Opera, The 1957,Mr 14,35:1

McCord, J C (Choreographer)

This Side of Paradise 1962,F 22,19:6

McCord, John

Banjo Eyes 1941,D 26,20:2

McCord, Joseph Jr (Scenic Designer)

Greater Lust, The 1936,Jl 14,22:4
Amateur Hour 1936,Jl 21,13:1

McCord, Mary

Phoebe of Quality Street 1921,My 10,20:1

McCord, Nancy

Beau Brummell 1933,Ag 9,20:6
All the King's Horses 1934,Ja 31,21:3
May Wine 1935,D 6,30:3
Devil and Daniel Webster, The 1939,My 19,26:1

McCormack, Frank
Thank You 1921,O 4,10:2
Monster, The 1922,Ag 10,20:3
Chicken Feed 1923,S 25,10:2
Gorilla, The 1925,Ap 29,24:2
Sancho's Master 1927,Ap 10,VIII,4:7
Wasp's Nest, The 1927,O 26,26:3
Cartney and Kevney 1928,Ja 1,VIII,2:8
Ziegfeld Follies 1931,Jl 2,30:5
Bridgehead 1934,Je 20,24:1
Jackson White 1935,Ap 22,14:6
Bridgehead 1935,Ag 7,22:3
Silver Tassie, The 1935,Ag 14,16:1
Good Men and True 1935,O 26,12:4
Name Your Poison 1936,Ja 21,27:4
In the Bag 1936,D 18,30:2
Tide Rising 1937,Ja 26,17:2
I Must Love Someone 1939,F 8,18:7
Day in the Sun 1939,My 17,29:2
Man Who Killed Lincoln, The 1940,Ja 18,26:4
Case of Youth, A 1940,Mr 25,10:3
McCormack, Frank (Director)
Wasp's Nest, The 1927,O 26,26:3
Kidding Kidders 1928,Ap 24,28:3
Border-Land 1932,Mr 30,15:5
Web, The 1932,Je 28,24:4
Monster, The 1933,F 11,11:5
In the Bag 1936,D 18,30:2
McCormack, Herbert P (Playwright)
Love and Babies 1933,Ag 23,21:4
McCormack, James (Playwright)
Merry Wives of West Point, The 1932,Mr 20,II,7:7
McCormack, John
Chocolate Soldier, The 1921,D 13,24:2
Untitled-Recital 1923,D 29,8:2
Shoestring Revue 1929,N 23,19:2
Mr Jiggins of Jigginstown 1936,D 18,30:2
Big Blow 1938,O 3,11:2
McCormack, Laverta
George White's Scandals 1926,Je 15,23:2
McCormack, Mary
Cross-Town 1937,Mr 18,21:5
Madame Bovary 1937,N 17,26:2
Bright Rebel 1938,D 28,24:2
Nine Girls 1943,Ja 14,26:2
McCormack, Patty
Touchstone 1953,F 4,33:2
Bad Seed, The 1954,D 9,42:1
Bad Seed, The 1954,D 19,II,3:1
McCormack, Pearl
Deep Harlem 1929,Ja 8,35:2
Pansy 1929,My 15,36:3
MacCormick, Cara Duff
Love Your Crooked Neighbor 1969,D 30,40:1
McCormick, Elizabeth
Fireworks on the James 1940,My 15,30:2
McCormick, Elizabeth (Director)
Billy the Kid 1951,Ag 21,23:2
McCormick, Elizabeth (Miscellaneous)
Fireworks on the James 1940,My 15,30:2
McCormick, Elizabeth (Producer)
Billy the Kid 1951,Ag 21,23:2
McCormick, F J
Things That Are Caesar's, The 1932,O 18,23:4
Far-Off Hills, The 1932,O 19,22:4
Juno and the Paycock 1932,O 20,24:3
Rising of the Moon, The 1932,O 21,25:1
Playboy of the Western World, The 1932,O 21,25:1
New Gossoon, The 1932,O 22,18:2
Words Upon the Window Pane, The 1932,O 29,18:2
Shadow of a Gunman, The 1932,O 31,18:1
Shadow of the Glen, The 1932,N 4,25:1
Big House, The 1933,Ja 5,19:3
King Oedipus 1933,Ja 16,12:4
Days Without End 1934,Ap 24,26:7
On the Rocks 1934,Jl 11,20:4
Plough and the Stars, The 1934,N 13,22:2
Drama at Inish 1934,N 15,24:2
Look at the Heffernans 1934,N 17,13:2
Church Street 1934,N 20,24:5
Resurrection 1934,N 20,24:5
Coiner, The 1934,N 22,26:2
Well of the Saints, The 1934,N 22,26:2
Village Wooing 1935,O 27,IX,2:5
Saint in a Hurry, A 1935,D 29,IX,2:1
Please Do Not Disturb 1936,Je 23,27:1
Katie Roche 1937,O 4,17:4
Far-Off Hills, The 1937,O 12,30:4
Playboy of the Western World, The 1937,N 22,14:5
In the Train 1937,N 22,14:5
New Gossoon, The 1937,N 30,26:2
Juno and the Paycock 1937,D 7,32:5
Drama at Inish 1937,D 14,33:2
Marks and Mabel 1945,S 9,II,1:4
McCormick, H F (Composer)
They Never Come Back 1920,D 19,I,22:3
McCormick, Langdon (Miscellaneous)
Ghost Train, The 1926,Ag 26,17:2
McCormick, Langdon (Playwright)
Shipwrecked 1924,N 2,VII,2:3
Shipwrecked 1924,N 13,18:1

McCormick, Myron
Tiger Smiles, The 1930,D 18,29:1
Carry Nation 1932,O 31,18:2
Goodbye Again 1932,D 29,16:4
I Was Waiting for You 1933,N 14,23:3
Yellow Jack 1934,Mr 7,22:6
Small Miracle 1934,S 27,24:3
On to Fortune 1935,F 5,22:2
Ode to Liberty 1935,Jl 2,24:3
Front Page, The 1935,Jl 9,24:4
Post Road 1935,Jl 23,24:3
Silent House, The 1935,Ag 7,22:2
Caste 1935,Ag 13,20:3
Paths of Glory 1935,S 19,29:1
Paths of Glory 1935,S 27,24:2
Substitute for Murder 1935,O 23,18:6
How Beautiful With Shoes 1935,N 29,24:1
Hell Freezes Over 1935,D 30,14:2
Winterset 1936,Je 2,35:2
Wingless Victory, The 1936,N 25,17:5
Wingless Victory, The 1936,D 24,20:2
Lysistrata 1937,Jl 20,19:3
In Clover 1937,O 14,23:1
How to Get Tough About It 1938,F 9,16:2
Thunder Rock 1939,N 15,18:1
Cream in the Well, The 1941,Ja 21,19:2
Lily of the Valley 1942,Ja 27,25:2
Damask Cheek, The 1942,O 23,24:2
Storm Operation 1944,Ja 12,28:2
Soldier's Wife 1944,O 5,18:6
Soldier's Wife 1944,O 15,II,1:1
State of the Union 1945,N 7,21:3
State of the Union 1945,N 15,25:2
State of the Union 1945,N 25,II,1:1
State of the Union 1946,S 8,II,1:1
Joy to the World 1948,Mr 19,28:2
South Pacific 1949,Ap 8,30:2
South Pacific 1949,Ap 17,II,1:1
South Pacific 1949,Je 5,II,1:1
South Pacific 1951,Jl 10,30:5
South Pacific 1951,S 2,II,1:1
Time of Your Life, The 1955,Ja 20,34:1
Time of Your Life, The 1955,Ja 30,II,1:1
All in One; 27 Wagons Full of Cotton 1955,Ap 20,40:3
No Time for Sergeants 1955,O 21,32:2
No Time for Sergeants 1955,N 6,II,1:1
McCormick, Nancy
Boy on the Straight-Back Chair 1969,Mr 18,36:1
McCormick, Oliver T
Wildcat, The 1921,N 28,16:2
Johannes Kreisler 1922,D 25,20:3
McCormick, Parker
Tender Trap, The 1954,O 14,37:2
One Eye Closed 1954,N 25,45:2
Third Best Sport 1958,D 31,15:3
Dr Willy Nilly 1959,Je 5,18:2
Play That on Your Old Piano 1965,O 15,49:1
McCourt, Malachy
Playboy of the Western World, The 1958,My 9,19:2
Shadow and Substance 1959,N 4,42:1
McCowan, Alec
Antony and Cleopatra 1951,D 21,22:2
Escapade 1953,Ap 8,37:2
Comedy of Errors, The 1962,S 12,34:2
King Lear 1964,My 19,43:2
Comedy of Errors, The 1964,My 21,43:1
After the Rain 1966,S 3,13:5
After the Rain 1967,O 10,54:1
After the Rain 1967,O 22,II,3:7
Hadrian VII 1968,Jl 4,14:1
Hadrian VII 1969,Ja 9,22:1
Hadrian VII 1969,Ja 19,II,1:2
Philanthropist, The 1970,Ag 5,20:1
Philanthropist, The 1970,S 10,59:1
McCowan, George
Hamlet 1957,Jl 3,15:2
Twelfth Night 1957,Jl 4,16:4
Two Gentlemen of Verona 1958,Mr 19,35:1
Broken Jug, The 1958,Ap 2,36:1
Henry IV, Part I 1958,Je 25,23:3
Much Ado About Nothing 1958,Je 26,22:1
Winter's Tale, The 1958,Jl 23,34:3
McCowan, George (Director)
Othello 1959,Jl 2,17:2
Othello 1959,Jl 5,II,1:1
Henry VIII 1961,Je 22,22:1
Henry VIII 1961,Jl 2,II,1:1
Tempest, The 1962,Je 22,14:1
McCowan, George (Miscellaneous)
Henry IV, Part I 1958,Je 25,23:3
McCown, Ellen
Seventeen 1951,Je 22,16:6
Boy Friend, The 1958,Ja 27,24:4
Greenwillow 1960,Mr 9,38:1
Greenwillow 1960,Mr 20,II,1:1
McCoy, Albert
Macbeth 1936,Ap 15,25:4
McCoy, Frank
Rose Briar 1922,D 26,11:3
McCoy, Frank (Director)
On Call 1928,N 10,20:7
Fine and Dandy 1930,S 24,26:1

McCoy, Frank (Director)—Cont
Gang's All Here, The 1931,F 19,21:3
Love and Babies 1933,Ag 23,21:4
Candida 1935,Ag 20,25:1
You Can't Take It With You 1945,Mr 27,23:7
Little Women 1945,D 24,18:2
McCoy, Frank (Producer)
Love and Babies 1933,Ag 23,21:4
Curtain Rises, The 1933,O 20,15:2
Lambent Flame, The 1935,Jl 16,24:2
Kind Lady 1935,Jl 23,24:4
Drums Professor, The 1935,Jl 30,17:2
Meet the Prince 1935,Ag 6,20:4
White Hell 1935,Ag 13,20:3
Goose for the Gander, A 1945,Ja 24,16:4
You Can't Take It With You 1945,Mr 27,23:7
Little Women 1945,D 24,18:2
Song of Bernadette 1946,Mr 27,22:2
McCoy, Harry
Racket, The 1927,N 23,28:3
McCoy, Jean
Howdy Stranger 1937,Ja 15,17:5
Winged Victory 1943,N 22,24:1
McCoy, Joseph
Web, The 1932,Je 28,24:4
McCoy, Leo
Joan of Arc-The Warrior Maid 1931,N 9,21:6
McCoy, Mary
Wonderful Night, A; Fledermaus, Die 1929,N 1,23:3
Way of the World, The 1931,Je 2,34:3
Wonderful Night, A; Fledermaus, Die 1937,Jl 14,17:1
Blossom Time 1938,D 27,12:2
McCoy, Mildred
Man Who Died Twice, The 1925,D 14,19:1
Dream Play 1926,Ja 21,18:2
Juno and the Paycock 1926,Mr 16,22:1
Bottled 1928,Ap 11,25:1
These Days 1928,N 13,36:2
Before You're 25 1929,Ap 17,30:2
It's a Wise Child 1929,Jl 28,VIII,1:6
It's a Wise Child 1929,Ag 7,29:1
It's a Wise Child 1929,Ag 25,VIII,1:1
Her Supporting Cast 1931,My 5,33:3
McCoy, Noel
Instructions for the Running of Trains, etc on the Erie Railway to Go Into Effect January 1,1862 1970,Ja 7,36:2
McCracken, Esther (Playwright)
Quiet Wedding 1938,N 6,IX,3:5
Quiet Weekend 1941,Ag 3,IX;1:8
No Medals 1944,N 19,II,2:4
McCracken, Gordon
Aiglon, L' 1927,D 27,24:3
Great Man, The 1931,Ap 8,20:6
Two Seconds 1931,O 10,20:6
Mimie Scheller 1936,O 1,28:4
McCracken, James
Buttrio Square 1952,O 15,40:2
Arabian Nights 1955,Je 24,16:1
McCracken, Joan
Oklahoma! 1943,Ap 1,27:1
Oklahoma! 1943,My 9,II,6:4
Bloomer Girl 1944,O 6,18:5
Bloomer Girl 1944,O 8,II,1:1
Million Dollar Baby 1945,D 22,17:2
Billion Dollar Baby 1945,D 30,II,1:1
Galileo 1947,D 8,34:2
Big Knife, The 1949,F 25,27:5
Big Knife, The 1949,Mr 6,II,1:1
Dance Me a Song 1950,Ja 21,10:5
Angel in the Pawnshop 1951,Ja 19,20:3
Me and Juliet 1953,My 29,17:1
Me and Juliet 1953,Je 7,II,1:1
Infernal Machine, The 1958,F 4,33:1
McCracken, Joan (Miscellaneous)
Galileo 1947,D 8,34:2
McCracken, Richard
Haiti 1938,Mr 3,16:1
Dear Ruth 1944,D 14,29:2
McCrae, Maurice
Strong, The 1924,F 27,15:3
McCrary, Marc
Bella 1961,N 17,40:1
McCrary, Risa
Mundy Scheme, The 1969,D 12,75:1
McCrary, Robert
Lady From Maxim's, The 1970,Je 1,41:1
McCraw, Charles
Brigadoon 1964,D 24,9:1
McCrea, Marion
Medea 1920,Mr 23,12:2
Clouds of the Sun 1922,My 6,11:2
McCready, Tom
Stephen D 1967,S 25,58:1
Hamlet 1968,Jl 4,15:1
McCreary, William (Scenic Designer)
Long Moment, The 1950,My 22,16:6
McCreery, Bud
Shoestring '57 1956,N 6,31:1
McCreery, Bud (Lyricist)
Shoestring Revue 1955,Mr 1,22:2

McCreery, Bud (Miscellaneous)
Decline and Fall of the Entire World As Seen Through the Eyes of Cole Porter Revisited, The 1965,Mr 31,24:2
Ben Bagley's New Cole Porter Revue 1965,D 23,20:1
McCreery, Bud (Playwright)
Littlest Revue, The 1956,My 23,37:2
Shoestring '57 1956,N 6,31:1
McCreery, Harold
American Tragedy, An 1926,O 12,31:2
McCrey, Maxine
Homo 1969,Ap 12,40:2
McCrory, Muriel
Turpentine 1936,Je 27,21:6
McCrum, Betty
Legend 1930,My 7,25:1
McCue, Frank (Composer)
Star and Garter 1942,Je 25,26:2
McCue, Frank (Lyricist)
Star and Garter 1942,Je 25,26:2
McCullagh, Jack (Scenic Designer)
Perfect Setup, The 1962,O 25,47:1
McCullers, Carson (Original Author)
Member of the Wedding, The 1950,My 14,II,1:1
Ballad of the Sad Cafe, The 1963,O 31,27:1
Ballad of the Sad Cafe, The 1963,N 10,II,1:1
McCullers, Carson (Playwright)
Member of the Wedding, The 1950,Ja 6,26:6
Member of the Wedding, The 1950,Ja 15,II,1:1
Member of the Wedding, The 1950,My 14,II,1:1
Member of the Wedding, The 1950,S 17,II,1:1
Member of the Wedding, The 1957,F 6,20:7
Square Root of Wonderful, The 1957,O 31,40:1
Square Root of Wonderful, The 1970,Mr 12,47:1
McCulley, Howard
Lingering Past, The 1932,Je 30,26:5
McCulloch, Ian
Tempest, The 1963,Ap 3,43:1
McCullom, Warren
Golden Age, The 1928,Ap 25,31:3
McCullough, Carl
Vaudeville (Palace) 1926,Je 8,23:1
Vaudeville (Palace) 1926,Ag 31,15:3
McCullough, Pat
Case of Philip Lawrence, The 1937,Je 9,31:1
Horse Play 1937,Ag 28,8:3
McCullough, Patrick
Happy Faculty, The 1967,Ap 19,50:1
McCullough, Paul
Ramblers, The 1926,S 21,32:2
Ramblers, The 1926,N 28,VIII,1:1
Strike Up the Band 1930,Ja 15,29:1
Vaudeville (Pavilion) 1931,Mr 20,29:3
Here Goes the Bride 1931,N 4,31:2
Vaudeville (Hollywood) 1932,F 16,24:3
Thumbs Up! 1934,D 28,24:1
McCullum, H H
Joseph 1930,F 13,25:3
McCullum, Warren
Topaze 1930,F 13,25:3
McCully, Gary
Bachelor Born 1938,Ja 26,26:3
McCully, William
Allegro 1947,O 11,10:2
MacCully, William
Saint of Bleecker Street, The 1954,D 28,21:1
McCune, Bettie
Nine Till Six 1936,Mr 14,10:3
McCuntic, Guthrie (Director)
Candida 1942,My 3,VIII,1:1
McCurdy, Jane
Flossie 1924,Je 4,25:2
McCurry, John
Porgy and Bess 1952,O 10,21:4
Porgy and Bess 1953,Mr 10,25:5
Porgy and Bess 1953,Mr 15,II,1:1
Porgy and Bess 1954,D 22,30:2
Porgy and Bess 1955,Jl 9,9:5
Porgy and Bess 1955,O 13,37:4
Connection, The 1959,Jl 16,30:2
Shakespeare in Harlem 1959,O 28,40:7
Connection, The 1960,F 7,II,1:1
Shakespeare in Harlem 1960,F 10,43:4
God's Trombones 1960,F 10,43:4
Shakespeare in Harlem 1960,F 21,II,1:1
Death of Bessie Smith, The 1961,Mr 2,19:1
Come Out, Carlo! 1962,My 4,27:2
Marco Millions 1964,F 21,33:1
Blues for Mister Charlie 1964,Ap 24,24:1
Big Man 1966,My 20,41:1
Finian's Rainbow 1967,Ap 6,44:1
Volpone 1967,Je 30,29:1
We Bombed in New Haven 1967,D 7,58:1
Wrong Way Light Bulb, The 1969,Mr 5,40:1
McCutcheon, Bill
Out West of Eighth 1951,S 21,20:3
New Faces of 1956 1956,Je 15,32:1
Wet Paint 1965,Ap 13,33:1
West Side Story 1968,Je 25,32:1
How to Steal an Election 1968,O 14,56:1
My Daughter, Your Son 1969,My 14,36:2

McCutcheon, George Barr (Playwright)
Daddy Dumplins 1920,N 23,11:1
McCutcheon, Ray (Lighting Director)
Three by Ferlinghetti; Alligation, The 1970,S 23,43:1
Three by Ferlinghetti; Victims of Amnesia, The 1970,S 23,43:1
Three by Ferlinghetti; Three Thousand Red Ants 1970,S 23,43:1
Adding Machine, The 1970,D 5,40:1
McCutcheon, Sherry
Seventeen 1951,Je 22,16:6
I Feel Wonderful 1954,O 19,22:5
Oklahoma! 1958,Mr 8,15:2
Lend an Ear 1959,S 25,20:5
McCutcheon, Wallace
Rat, The 1925,F 11,19:3
Earl Carroll's Vanities 1925,Jl 7,24:1
Earl Carroll's Vanities 1925,D 29,20:3
McCutcheons, The
Holiday on Ice 1966,S 1,30:1
McDaniel, Charles
Debut 1956,F 23,32:1
Wayside 1957,Ap 18,34:1
Howie 1958,S 18,35:2
Sweet Bird of Youth 1959,Mr 11,39:2
Long Dream, The 1960,F 18,36:2
Period of Adjustment 1960,N 11,34:1
McDaniel, David
Red Roses for Me 1955,D 29,15:2
McDaniel, Diane
Annie Get Your Gun 1957,Mr 9,15:5
McDaniel, Donna
John Brown's Body 1953,F 16,17:2
McDaniel, Junius
Porgy and Bess 1935,O 11,30:2
MacDaniel, Margery
Pullman Car Hiawatha 1962,D 4,46:2
McDaniel, William
Porgy and Bess 1942,Ja 23,16:2
Set My People Free 1948,N 4,38:2
Green Pastures, The 1951,Mr 16,35:2
Shuffle Along 1952,My 9,20:5
MacDennell, Kyle
Make Mine Manhattan 1948,Ja 16,26:2
McDermid, Del
Philadelphia 1929,S 17,34:5
McDermid, Dorothy
Side-Show 1931,My 16,13:1
MacDermot, Galt (Composer)
Hair 1967,O 30,55:1
Hair 1967,N 14,50:1
Hamlet 1967,D 27,45:1
Hair 1968,Ap 30,40:2
Hamlet 1968,Jl 4,15:1
Hair 1969,F 5,36:1
Twelfth Night 1969,Ag 14,29:2
Hair 1969,S 13,30:1
Hair 1970,Ja 13,39:1
Hair 1970,S 27,II,1:2
Isabel's a Jezebel 1970,D 27,II,3:1
MacDermot, Galt (Musical Director)
Hair 1968,Ap 30,40:2
MacDermot, Robert (Lyricist)
Your Number's Up 1936,D 24,22:2
MacDermot, Robert (Playwright)
Your Number's Up 1936,D 24,22:2
Bats in the Belfry 1937,Mr 16,12:1
Bats in the Belfry 1937,Ap 4,X,2:4
McDermott, Aline
Go West, Young Man 1923,N 13,25:2
Bachelor's Brides 1925,My 29,20:2
American Born 1925,S 27,VII,2:1
American Born 1925,O 6,31:3
Rhapsody, The 1930,S 16,30:3
Page Pygmalion 1932,Ag 4,17:5
Strangers at Home 1934,S 15,20:5
Children's Hour, The 1934,N 21,23:2
Our Town 1938,F 5,18:3
Blind Alley 1940,O 16,28:2
State of the Union 1945,N 15,25:2
Life With Mother 1948,Je 9,36:3
McDermott, Cyril L
Dover Road, The 1924,D 20,18:2
Champion, The 1925,Ap 24,16:4
McDermott, Hugh
But for the Grace of God 1946,S 4,27:2
McDermott, John (Playwright)
Adam Had Two Sons 1932,Ja 17,VIII,3:5
Adam Had Two Sons 1932,Ja 21,17:1
MacDermott, Norman (Producer)
Within the Gates 1934,F 8,14:4
Within the Gates 1934,F 25,IX,3:7
McDermott, Patrick
Dionysus in 69 1968,Je 7,35:3
McDermott, Patrick (Producer)
Only Jealousy of Emer, The 1970,Mr 25,36:4
Renard 1970,Mr 25,36:4
McDermott, Tom
Yours, A Lincoln 1942,Jl 10,12:3
Three Sisters, The 1942,D 22,31:2
Blithe Spirit 1946,Je 5,17:3

McDermott, Tom—Cont
Uniform of Flesh 1949,Ja 31,15:2
Billy Budd 1955,My 4,35:1
Tiger at the Gates 1955,O 4,40:1
Comedian, The 1956,O 18,36:4
Jane Eyre 1958,My 2,31:1
Best Man, The 1960,Ap 1,39:1
Love of Two Hours, The 1962,O 27,16:2
Emperor Jones, The 1964,Ag 6,20:4
My Kinsman, Major Molineux 1964,N 2,62:2
Child and the Dragon, The 1966,Je 24,30:2
Pin Up 1966,Je 24,30:2
McDermott, Tom (Miscellaneous)
Jane Eyre 1958,My 2,31:1
McDermott, William (Composer)
Medium, The 1948,D 8,41:6
Telephone, The 1948,D 8,41:6
McDermott, William (Musical Director)
Medium, The 1950,Jl 20,22:5
Telephone, The 1950,Jl 20,22:5
McDevitt, Ruth
Straw Hat, The 1937,D 31,8:2
Young Couple Wanted 1940,Ja 25,16:2
Goodbye in the Night 1940,Mr 19,31:2
Not in Our Stars 1941,Ap 26,20:5
Mr Big 1941,O 1,24:2
Meet a Body 1944,O 17,19:5
Sleepy Hollow 1948,Je 4,26:3
High Ground, The 1951,F 21,31:2
Fancy Meeting You Again 1952,Ja 15,23:2
Male Animal, The 1952,My 1,35:1
Male Animal, The 1952,My 18,II,1:1
First Lady 1952,My 29,18:5
Picnic 1953,F 20,14:7
Picnic 1953,Mr 1,II,1:1
Diary of a Scoundrel 1956,N 5,41:1
Rosalie 1957,Je 26,28:2
Clerambard 1957,N 8,22:3
Clerambard 1957,N 17,II,1:1
Best Man, The 1960,Ap 1,39:1
Save Me a Place at Forest Lawn 1963,My 9,40:2
Absence of a Cello 1964,S 22,45:1
Uncle Vanya 1969,Ag 31,II,4:1
McDonagh, Deidre
Jitta's Atonement 1935,Ja 31,22:3
MacDonagh, Donagh (Playwright)
Fading Mansion 1949,S 1,25:4
Happy as Larry 1950,Ja 7,11:2
Happy as Larry 1961,Ap 26,36:1
MacDonagh, John (Playwright)
Remains, The 1928,Jl 15,VIII,2:1
MacDonagh, John (Producer)
Remains, The 1928,Jl 15,VIII,2:1
MacDonald, Adams
Darkness at Noon 1951,Ja 15,13:4
MacDonald, Alberta
Gang's All Here, The 1959,O 2,23:1
McDonald, Alexander
Cabin in the Sky 1940,O 26,19:2
MacDonald, Ann
Purple Mask, The 1920,Ja 6,18:1
MacDonald, Ann (Playwright)
Apothecary, The 1926,Mr 17,28:1
Commedia Dell' Arte 1927,Ap 6,24:3
Mcdonald, Anne Sprague (Translator)
Room of Dreams 1930,N 6,22:4
MacDonald, Ballard (Lyricist)
Midnight Frolic 1920,Ag 4,7:1
Love Birds 1921,Mr 16,12:1
George White's Scandals 1923,Je 19,22:5
Battling Buttler 1923,O 9,17:2
Sweetheart Time 1926,Ja 20,23:2
LeMaire's Affairs 1927,Mr 29,22:4
Harry Delmar's Revels 1927,N 29,30:2
Ziegfeld Follies 1934,Ja 5,24:3
Thumbs Up! 1934,D 28,24:1
MacDonald, Ballard (Playwright)
Battling Buttler 1923,O 9,17:2
LeMaire's Affairs 1927,Mr 29,22:4
Padlocks of 1927 1927,Jl 6,23:4
Greenwich Villagers, The 1927,Ag 19,20:2
Hot Rhythm 1930,Ag 22,18:5
Ziegfeld Follies 1934,Ja 5,24:3
MacDonald, Barbara
Strike Me Pink 1933,Mr 6,16:3
MacDonald, Betty
Mascaiada 1929,D 28,10:6
MacDonald, Betty (Original Author)
Egg and I, The 1958,S 11,43:4
McDonald, Bill
On the Town 1959,F 14,15:1
Take Me Along 1959,O 23,22:2
Conquering Hero, The 1961,Ja 17,40:2
Family Affair, A 1962,Ja 29,17:1
MacDonald, Blossom
After Such Pleasures 1934,F 8,15:2
Dead End 1935,O 29,17:2
MacDonald, Bob
Penny Change 1963,O 25,37:1
MacDonald, Bob (Miscellaneous)
Passage to E M Forster, A 1970,O 28,62:1
Perfect Match, The 1970,N 18,41:1
Slow Memories 1970,N 18,41:1

MacDonald, Bob (Miscellaneous)—Cont

Life and Times of J Walter Smintheus, The 1970,D 10,59:1
MacDonald, Brian
Earl Carroll's Vanities 1928,Ag 7,25:2
MacDonald, Brian (Choreographer)
Maggie Flynn 1968,O 24,52:1
MacDonald, Charles
New Brooms 1924,N 18,23:5
19th Hole, The 1927,O 12,30:3
Hot Water 1929,Ja 22,22:3
Sun-Up 1929,F 19,22:6
McDonald, Cherie
Touch 1970,N 9,52:1
MacDonald, Christie
Florodora 1920,Ap 6,18:1
MacDonald, Cordelia
Hole in the Wall, The 1920,Mr 27,11:1
We Girls 1921,N 10,26:3
Lady Lies, The 1928,N 27,36:2
McDonald, Dallard (Lyricist)
Pins and Needles 1922,F 2,20:1
MacDonald, Dan
Macbeth 1962,F 7,32:2
Falstaff; Henry IV, Part II 1965,Jl 1,35:1
Julius Caesar 1965,Jl 2,18:1
Cherry Orchard, The 1965,Ag 2,17:2
McDonald, Dennis
Caukey 1944,F 18,15:4
Earth Journey 1944,Ap 28,24:2
McDonald, Dennis (Miscellaneous)
Redhead 1959,F 6,21:1
MacDonald, Donald
Checkerboard, The 1920,Ag 20,7:2
Getting Gertie's Garter 1921,Ag 2,16:2
Jack and Jill 1923,Mr 23,17:2
Processional 1925,Ja 13,17:1
Beware of Widows 1925,N 8,VIII,2:1
Beware of Widows 1925,D 2,22:3
Love 'Em and Leave 'Em 1926,F 4,20:4
Love 'Em and Leave 'Em 1926,F 14,VIII,1:1
White Wings 1926,O 16,15:1
Paris Bound 1927,D 28,26:3
Paris Bound 1928,Ja 15,VIII,1:1
Strange Interlude 1928,D 18,37:3
Up and Up, The 1930,S 9,25:2
Strange Interlude 1931,F 22,VIII,1:3
Left Bank, The 1931,O 6,35:3
Left Bank, The 1931,O 18,VIII,1:1
Here Today 1932,S 7,14:2
Here Today 1932,S 18,IX,1:1
Black Sheep 1932,O 14,22:6
Forsaking All Others 1933,Mr 2,21:2
Sing and Whistle 1934,F 12,18:3
Little Shot 1935,Ja 18,28:4
World's My Onion, The 1935,Je 16,X,1:8
On Stage 1935,O 30,16:6
Reunion 1938,Ap 12,26:4
Girl From Wyoming, The 1938,O 31,12:1
McDonald, Earl
Prunella; Love in a Garden 1926,Je 16,23:3
White Wings 1926,O 16,15:1
Devil in the Cheese, The 1926,D 30,22:4
Ivory Door, The 1927,O 19,24:5
Love Expert, The 1929,S 24,29:1
Claire Adams 1929,N 20,26:3
Brittle Heaven 1934,N 14,22:5
Tea for Three 1935,Jl 9,24:4
Immoral Support 1935,S 3,24:3
Merrily We Roll Along 1936,Je 30,15:1
I Take Care of My Friends 1936,Jl 21,13:2
One More Genius 1936,Ag 11,24:6
Frederika 1937,F 5,16:5
Three Waltzes 1937,D 27,10:2
Two on an Island 1940,Ja 23,17:2
Three's a Family 1943,My 6,24:2
Susan and God 1943,D 14,30:2
Lady Says Yes, A 1945,Ja 11,18:5
Brigadoon 1964,D 24,9:1
Brigadoon 1967,D 14,59:2
MacDonald, Edmund
Getting Even 1929,Ag 20,31:1
Web, The 1932,Je 28,24:4
Her Tin Soldier 1933,Ap 7,22:6
I Myself 1934,My 10,24:6
Noble Prize, The 1935,Jl 9,24:3
She Cried for the Moon 1935,Jl 23,24:3
MacDonald, Edwin
Wall Street 1927,Ap 21,24:4
MacDonald, Eva
Idle Inn, The 1921,D 21,26:2
McDonald, Frank
Puppets 1925,Mr 10,19:1
K Guy, The 1928,O 16,28:4
Just to Remind You 1931,S 8,39:1
Bulls, Bears and Asses 1932,My 7,11:3
McDonald, Gertrude
One Kiss 1923,N 28,14:2
Tip-Toes 1925,D 29,20:2
Oh, Please! 1926,D 22,24:3
Funny Face 1927,N 23,28:2
Treasure Girl 1928,N 9,22:1
Lady Fingers 1929,F 1,22:4
Third Little Show, The 1931,My 10,VIII,2:4

Third Little Show, The 1931,Je 2,34:3
Vaudeville (Palace) 1932,F 15,13:3
McDonald, Glen
Man Who Never Died, The 1958,N 22,27:2
McDonald, Gordon
Wind Is Ninety, The 1945,Je 22,12:2
McDonald, Grace
Babes in Arms 1937,Ap 15,18:4
One for the Money 1939,F 6,9:2
Very Warm for May 1939,N 18,23:2
More the Merrier, The 1941,S 16,19:3
MacDonald, Hector
Plan M 1942,F 21,15:2
MacDonald, Hugh (Composer)
Cambridge Circus 1964,O 7,53:1
MacDonald, James
Laugh It Off 1925,Ap 25,18:4
Silent House, The 1928,F 8,28:5
Machinal 1928,S 8,10:3
Commodore Marries, The 1929,S 5,26:3
Man on Stilts, The 1931,S 10,23:2
Silent House, The 1932,N 9,28:3
Peace on Earth 1933,N 30,39:2
Sailors of Cattaro 1934,D 11,28:4
Distant Shore, The 1935,F 22,26:2
Mother, The 1935,N 20,26:3
Marching Song 1937,F 18,18:2
Mr Big 1941,S 7,I,51:3
Mr Big 1941,O 1,24:2
Doughgirls, The 1942,D 31,19:2
Man Who Had All the Luck, The 1944,N 24,18:5
Point of No Return 1951,D 14,35:2
MacDonald, Jan
Vigil, The 1948,My 22,8:6
MacDonald, Jeannette
Magic Ring, The 1923,O 2,10:1
Tip-Toes 1925,D 29,20:2
Yes, Yes, Yvette 1927,O 4,32:3
Sunny Days 1928,F 9,29:1
Angela 1928,D 4,28:2
Boom Boom 1929,Ja 29,26:4
MacDonald, Jet
Beggar's Holiday 1946,D 27,13:3
Beggar's Holiday 1947,Ja 26,II,1:1
Promised Valley 1947,Jl 23,18:3
Hold It! 1948,My 6,31:5
Razzle Dazzle 1951,F 20,21:1
McDonald, Jon Renn
Henry V 1965,Je 29,27:2
McDonald, Joyce
Show Boat 1966,Jl 20,48:1
MacDonald, Julian L (Playwright)
Marriage of Cana, The 1932,F 3,22:4
MacDonald, Julian L (Producer)
Marriage of Cana, The 1932,F 3,22:4
MacDonald, Kathryn
Bootleggers, The 1922,N 28,24:1
McDonald, Kay
Live Life Again 1945,O 1,14:7
Song of Bernadette 1946,Mr 27,22:2
Laura 1947,Je 27,16:1
McDonald, Laetitia (Playwright)
Lady Alone 1927,Ja 16,VII,2:4
Lady Alone 1927,Ja 21,12:5
MacDonald, Margery
Tobias and the Angel 1957,O 21,29:5
McDonald, Mary
Sally 1920,D 22,16:1
Houseboat on the Styx, The 1928,D 26,14:3
MacDonald, Maxine
Happy-Go-Lucky 1920,Ag 25,6:1
Circle, The 1921,S 13,12:1
Spring Cleaning 1923,N 10,16:3
McDonald, Michael Allen
School for Scandal, The 1966,N 22,33:2
McDonald, Michael Allen (Lighting Director)
Undercover Man 1966,Je 3,30:2
MacDonald, Murray (Playwright)
Lake, The 1933,Mr 26,IX,1:1
Lake, The 1933,D 19,26:3
Lake, The 1933,D 27,24:2
Lake, The 1934,Ja 7,X,1:1
Mrs Nobby Clark 1935,F 28,16:2
Daphne Laureola 1950,S 19,38:6
Dear Charles 1953,Ap 20,22:4
MacDonald, Norman
Sign of the Leopard 1928,D 12,34:4
Hamlet 1964,Je 17,49:1
Henry V 1965,Je 29,27:2
MacDonald, Patricia
Trip to Bountiful, The 1953,N 4,30:3
McDonald, Peter (Miscellaneous)
Love of Two Hours, The 1962,O 27,16:2
MacDonald, Pirie
Under Milk Wood 1957,O 16,42:5
Romeo and Juliet 1959,Je 15,31:1
Merry Wives of Windsor, The 1959,Jl 9,23:2
Henry IV 1960,Ap 19,41:1
MacDonald, Pirie (Producer)
Deirdre of the Sorrows 1959,O 15,46:1
McDonald, Ralph
Trumpets of the Lord 1963,D 23,22:3

McDonald, Ray
Babes in Arms 1937,Ap 15,18:4
Winged Victory 1943,N 22,24:1
Park Avenue 1946,N 5,31:2
McDonald, Robert A Jr
Henry IV 1968,F 7,40:1
MacDonald, Robert David (Playwright)
War and Peace 1965,Ja 12,32:1
War and Peace 1967,Mr 22,42:1
MacDonald, Robert David (Translator)
War and Peace 1965,Ja 31,II,1:1
Soldiers 1968,Mr 3,88:1
Soldiers 1968,My 2,58:1
MacDonald, Roberta
Mis-Guided Tour 1959,O 13,44:7
Golden Apple, The 1962,F 13,38:2
MacDonald, Rose
Captain Jinks of the Horse Marines 1938,Ja 28,16:2
McDonald, Rosemary
Purgatory 1960,S 20,48:1
MacDonald, Ruth
Three Waltzes 1937,D 27,10:2
MacDonald, Ryan
Big Knife, The 1959,N 13,25:1
Once There Was a Russian 1961,F 20,32:2
Not a Way of Life 1967,Mr 23,28:1
MacDonald, Sandra
Tragicomedy of Don Cristobita and Dona Rosita, The 1958,My 30,12:2
Someone From Assisi 1962,Ja 12,28:1
Romeo and Juliet 1962,Ap 3,42:1
McDonald, Scott
Happy Faculty, The 1967,Ap 19,50:1
MacDonald, T Stewart
Marshall 1930,My 10,25:1
McDonald, Tanny
Utopia, Limited 1960,Ap 8,27:2
Carricknabauna 1967,Mr 31,30:1
MacDonald-Rouse, Heather (Costume Designer)
Wait a Minim! 1966,Mr 8,43:1
MacDonell, Kathlene
Hero, The 1921,Mr 15,14:1
Danger 1921,D 23,18:3
Deluge, The 1922,Ja 18,14:2
R U R 1922,O 10,16:1
Dancers, The 1923,O 18,17:2
Episode 1925,F 5,23:2
On Approval 1926,O 19,27:1
Interference 1927,O 19,24:3
McDonnell, Austine
Two for the Show 1940,F 9,14:2
McDonnell, Ed (Scenic Designer)
Wonderful World of Burlesque, The 1965,Ap 29,38:1
MacDonnell, Kyle
Touch and Go 1949,O 14,34:2
MacDonnell, Lulu
Ziegfeld Follies 1922,Je 6,18:2
McDonnell, Maggi
Abie's Irish Rose 1954,N 19,19:1
McDonnell, Mary
Allah Be Praised! 1944,Ap 21,14:2
Three to Make Ready 1946,Mr 8,16:2
MacDonnell, Ray
Midsummer Night's Dream, A 1957,Je 27,21:3
Philoctetes 1959,Ja 14,28:1
Deirdre of the Sorrows 1959,O 15,46:1
McDonough, Dorothy
Guys and Dolls 1959,Jl 22,22:2
MacDonough, Glen (Lyricist)
Hitchy-Koo, 1920 1920,O 20,11:3
Babes in Toyland 1930,D 22,17:1
MacDonough, Glen (Playwright)
As You Were 1920,Ja 28,22:3
Hitchy-Koo, 1920 1920,O 20,11:3
Within Four Walls 1923,Ap 18,24:1
Her Dearest Friend 1923,My 15,22:2
Babes in Toyland 1929,D 24,15:3
Count of Luxembourg, The 1930,F 18,28:2
McDonough, James
Paradise 1931,My 12,29:2
McDonough, Justin
Hallelujah, Baby! 1967,Ap 27,51:1
South Pacific 1967,Je 13,56:1
McDonough, Leonore
Gift, The 1924,Ja 23,15:4
MacDonough, Ward
Spooks 1925,Je 2,16:4
McDougall, Florence
Pins and Needles 1922,F 2,20:1
McDougall, Gordon (Miscellaneous)
Would You Look At Them Smashing All the Lovely Windows! 1969,S 5,30:1
MacDougall, Ina Brown
So's Your Old Antique 1930,My 8,32:5
MacDougall, Roger (Playwright)
To Dorothy, A Son 1951,N 20,37:2
Escapade 1953,F 15,II,2:1
Escapade 1953,Ap 8,37:2
Escapade 1953,N 19,40:1
Escapade 1953,N 29,II,1:1
Hide and Seek 1957,Ap 3,26:1

MacDougall, William
Dandy Dick 1956,Ja 11,37:2
McDowall, Betty
Period of Adjustment 1962,Je 4,24:2
McDowall, Roddy
Misalliance 1953,F 19,20:1
Misalliance 1953,Mr 22,II,1:1
Escapade 1953,N 19,40:1
Homeward Look, The 1954,Je 4,26:2
Doctor's Dilemma, The 1955,Ja 12,22:1
Doctor's Dilemma, The 1955,Ja 23,II,1:1
Julius Caesar 1955,Jl 13,20:1
Tempest, The 1955,Ag 2,18:2
Tempest, The 1955,Ag 7,II,1:1
No Time for Sergeants 1955,O 21,32:2
No Time for Sergeants 1955,N 6,II,1:1
Diary of a Scoundrel 1956,N 5,41:1
Good as Gold 1957,Mr 8,22:2
Compulsion 1957,O 25,21:1
Compulsion 1957,N 3,II,1:1
Handful of Fire 1958,O 2,45:3
Look After Lulu 1959,Mr 4,35:1
Fighting Cock, The 1959,D 9,57:3
Camelot 1960,D 5,42:1
Astrakhan Coat, The 1967,Ja 13,18:1
McDowell, Alice Dudley
Pipe in the Fields, The 1931,Mr 14,23:4
McDowell, Jack
Frankie and Johnny 1930,S 26,16:5
McDowell, John
Artists and Models 1927,N 16,28:2
McDowell, John Herbert (Composer)
East Wind, The 1967,F 10,30:1
Dracula Sabbat 1970,O 2,28:2
In 3 Zones 1970,N 3,28:1
MacDowell, Louise Irving
Time of Their Lives 1937,O 26,19:1
McDowell, Violet
Run, Little Chillun 1943,Ag 14,6:1
McDuff, Richard
Time to Go 1960,Mr 23,33:1
Coggerers, The 1960,Mr 23,33:1
McDuffie, Tom
Carousel 1945,Ap 20,24:2
MacDwyer, Jane
Bridal Crown, The 1938,F 7,11:2
Mace, Alyce
Show Boat 1946,Ja 7,17:2
Show Boat 1948,S 9,33:2
Mace, Jed (Costume Designer)
Porgy and Bess 1953,Mr 10,25:5
Mace, Mary
Legend of Lizzie, The 1959,F 10,39:1
Mace, Paul
Semi-Detached 1960,Mr 11,20:2
Midgie Purvis 1961,F 2,25:3
Me Nobody Knows, The 1970,My 19,42:1
Mace, Roy
Venetian Glass Nephew, The 1931,F 24,26:3
Mace, Sterling
Dooley Cashes In 1935,Ag 17,18:6
Democratic Body, A 1942,F 13,24:7
Across the Board on Tomorrow Morning
  1942,Mr 21,13:5
Theatre of the Soul 1942,Mr 21,13:5
What Big Ears! 1942,Ap 21,18:5
Winter Soldiers 1942,N 30,19:2
Day Will Come, The 1944,S 8,17:2
Mace, Sterling (Miscellaneous)
Greatest Man Alive!, The 1957,My 9,37:2
Fair Game 1957,N 4,39:1
McEachin, Douglas
Story of Mary Surratt, The 1947,F 10,25:2
McElhaney, Jan
My House Is Your House 1970,O 16,53:2
McElhany, Thomas
House of Ussher, The 1926,Ja 14,18:4
Friend Indeed 1926,Ap 27,22:3
One Shot Fired 1927,N 8,32:5
McElhany, Tom
Kidding Kidders 1928,Ap 24,28:3
Manhattan Nocturne 1943,O 27,26:2
Suds in Your Eye 1944,Ja 13,15:5
Alice in Arms 1945,F 1,18:4
Deep Mrs Sykes, The 1945,Mr 20,22:6
Finian's Rainbow 1947,Ja 11,23:2
Leaf and Bough 1949,Ja 22,10:2
Finian's Rainbow 1960,Ap 28,31:1
McElhone, A Lawton (Producer)
Jackson White 1935,Ap 22,14:6
McElhone, Charles
Little Theatre Tournament; Rachel Cowan
  1929,My 9,34:3
McElhone, Dorothy
Five Star Final 1930,D 31,11:1
Macellari, John
Beautiful Changes, The 1956,Mr 24,15:2
McElroy, Evie
Way of the World, The 1965,Je 2,40:1
Skin of Our Teeth, The 1966,Je 2,51:1
As You Like It 1966,Je 4,19:1
McElroy, Jack
Rust 1924,F 1,12:1

McElroy, Yvonne
Henry V 1964,My 13,52:1
Saint Joan 1964,My 14,41:1
McElwee, William (Playwright)
Time and the Hour 1936,O 5,24:1
McEnaney, William
Three Plays of the Sea 1970,Ag 20,39:1
McEndree, Maurice
Nobody's Child 1956,Ag 23,25:2
McEnery, Peter
Hamlet 1961,Ap 12,46:1
Afore Night Come 1964,Je 26,34:1
McEnnis, Pat
How to Succeed in Business Without Really Trying
  1966,Ap 21,45:1
McEnroe, Robert E (Playwright)
Silver Whistle, The 1948,N 25,49:2
Donnybrook! 1961,My 19,23:1
Donnybrook! 1961,My 28,II,1:1
MacEntee, George
Meek Mose 1928,F 7,30:1
Wanted 1928,Jl 3,19:2
Gala Night 1930,F 26,22:4
Stepping Sisters 1930,Ap 23,24:2
American Holiday 1936,F 22,13:3
MacEntee, George (Director)
Meek Mose 1928,F 7,30:1
MacEntee, George (Playwright)
Case of Philip Lawrence, The 1937,Je 9,31:1
Macero, Teo (Composer)
Bugs 1965,N 19,31:1
Veronica 1965,N 19,31:1
McEvilly, Burton
Letter, The 1927,S 27,30:1
Truth Game, The 1930,D 29,19:1
Hamlet 1931,N 6,28:4
Porgy and Bess 1935,O 11,30:2
McEvoy, Charles (Playwright)
Three Barrows, The 1926,N 28,VIII,1:4
McEvoy, J P (Director)
Americana 1928,O 31,28:2
McEvoy, J P (Lyricist)
Americana 1928,O 31,28:2
McEvoy, J P (Original Author)
Show Girl 1929,Jl 3,19:3
Stars in Your Eyes 1939,F 10,18:2
McEvoy, J P (Playwright)
Potters, The 1923,O 28,VIII,2:1
Potters, The 1923,D 10,21:4
Potters, The 1923,D 16,IX,1:1
Comic Supplement, The 1925,Ja 25,VII,1:4
No Foolin' 1926,Je 25,25:1
Americana 1926,Jl 27,15:3
God Loves Us 1926,O 20,22:2
God Loves Us 1926,O 31,VIII,1:4
Americana 1926,D 5,VIII,5:1
Allez-Opp! 1927,Ag 3,29:3
Americana 1928,O 31,28:2
New Americana 1928,N 30,32:4
Americana 1932,O 6,19:3
McEvoy, J P (Producer)
Americana 1928,O 14,X,1:6
Americana 1932,S 25,IX,1:6
McEvoy, L J
Somebody's Lion 1921,Ap 13,20:1
McEvoy, Rennie
Stars in Your Eyes 1939,F 10,18:2
McEvoy, Robert
Quick Years, The 1953,N 26,51:2
McEwan, Geraldine
Member of the Wedding, The 1957,F 6,20:7
Much Ado About Nothing 1961,Ap 5,31:1
Hamlet 1961,Ap 12,46:1
School for Scandal, The 1963,Ja 26,5:2
Public Eye, The 1963,O 10,51:1
Private Ear, The 1963,O 10,51:1
Semi-Detached 1963,O 20,II,1:1
Dance of Death, The 1967,O 20,50:1
Love for Love 1967,O 21,17:1
Dance of Death 1967,O 29,II,5:1
Flea in Her Ear, A 1967,O 30,59:1
Love for Love 1967,O 30,59:1
Way of the World, The 1969,Ag 7,29:1
White Devil, The 1969,N 14,38:2
McEwen, Caryl (Lyricist)
Commedia Dell' Arte 1957,Jl 5,13:2
McEwen, James (Producer)
Guitar 1959,N 11,42:5
MacEwen, Molly (Costume Designer)
Old Lady Says No, The 1948,F 18,35:1
MacEwen, Molly (Scenic Designer)
John Bull's Other Island 1948,F 11,33:4
Where Stars Walk 1948,F 25,27:2
McEwen, Odette
Difficult Woman, The 1962,Ap 26,22:7
McEwen, Walter
Rubicon, The 1922,F 22,13:1
Macey, Shirley
Case of Philip Lawrence, The 1937,Je 9,31:1
Macey, Wanda
Case of Philip Lawrence, The 1937,Je 9,31:1
McFadden, Beverly
Salvage 1957,Ap 10,39:2

McFadden, Beverly—Cont
Death of Satan, The 1960,Ap 6,49:1
McFadden, Blair (Miscellaneous)
Shout From the Rooftops 1964,O 29,40:1
McFadden, Elizabeth (Playwright)
Double Door 1933,S 22,15:5
Nineties; Double Door 1934,Mr 22,24:6
Double Door 1934,Ap 15,X,2:2
Beggarman, Thief 1935,Jl 16,24:1
Signature 1945,F 15,25:2
McFadden, Grania (Composer)
Deirdre of the Sorrows 1949,D 15,51:2
MacFadden, Hamilton
Floriani's Wife 1923,O 1,10:1
Beggar on Horseback 1924,F 13,17:2
McFadden, Hamilton (Director)
Importance of Being Earnest, The 1925,Jl 28,24:2
MacFadden, Hamilton (Director)
Carolinian, The 1925,N 3,34:2
Gringa, La 1928,F 2,17:1
Gods of the Lightning 1928,O 25,27:2
One Way Street 1928,D 25,31:2
Buckaroo 1929,Mr 18,31:1
MacFadden, Hamilton (Producer)
Gringa, La 1928,F 2,17:1
Gods of the Lightning 1928,O 25,27:2
Buckaroo 1929,Mr 18,31:1
McFadden, James
Highland Fling, A 1944,Ap 29,13:2
Brigadoon 1947,Mr 14,28:2
Brigadoon 1950,My 3,36:2
MacFadden, R P
1776 1926,Ap 24,11:2
McFadden, William
Booster, The 1929,O 25,26:2
House Afire 1930,Ap 1,34:7
Once in a Lifetime 1930,S 25,22:3
East of Broadway 1932,Ja 27,19:3
Life Begins 1932,Mr 29,23:2
Heigh-Ho, Everybody 1932,My 26,31:2
Dinner at Eight 1932,O 24,18:2
Dark Tower, The 1933,N 27,20:3
Merrily We Roll Along 1934,O 1,14:1
MacFadyen, Virginia
God of Vengeance, The 1922,D 20,22:5
Wonderful Visit, The 1924,F 13,17:3
McFarland, Ada
Macbeth 1941,N 12,30:2
McFarland, Beulah
Two Little Girls in Blue 1921,My 4,10:3
MacFarland, Bruce
Odds on Mrs Oakley, The 1944,O 3,18:8
MacFarland, Dorothea
As We Forgive Our Debtors 1947,Mr 11,37:2
Mrs Patterson 1957,F 6,20:2
MacFarland, Dorothea (Costume Designer)
Mrs Patterson 1957,F 6,20:2
McFarland, Frank
Story of Mary Surratt, The 1947,F 10,25:2
MacFarland, Lewis
Elizabeth the Queen 1937,Ag 25,24:3
MacFarland, Lewis (Scenic Designer)
Mr Pim Passes By 1935,Ag 7,22:2
Double Door 1935,Ag 21,22:2
Late Christopher Bean, The 1935,Ag 28,13:1
Post Road 1936,Ag 5,15:4
Art and Mrs Bottle 1936,S 2,18:1
Private Lives 1937,Jl 14,17:4
Whiteheaded Boy, The 1937,Ag 11,27:3
Goodbye Again 1937,S 1,15:1
McFarland, Nan
Othello 1945,My 23,25:4
Hamlet 1945,D 14,25:2
Cyrano de Bergerac 1946,O 9,33:2
Cyrano de Bergerac 1947,Ja 17,27:2
Angel Street 1948,Ja 23,26:6
Alchemist, The 1948,My 7,31:4
S S Glencairn; Long Voyage Home, The
  1948,My 21,21:2
Insect Comedy, The 1948,Je 4,26:3
Man and Superman 1949,My 17,28:6
Wild Duck, The 1951,D 27,17:1
Chase, The 1952,Ap 16,30:2
My 3 Angels 1953,Mr 12,23:2
Country Wife, The 1955,Ap 6,35:1
Hot Corner, The 1956,Ja 26,25:2
Auntie Mame 1956,N 1,47:2
Sound of Music, The 1959,N 17,40:2
McFarland, Owen
Black Eye, The 1938,Mr 8,22:4
McFarland, William
Green Pastures, The 1935,F 27,16:2
MacFarlane, Bruce
Last Mile, The 1930,F 14,21:2
Twelfth Disciple, The 1930,My 17,21:4
Five Star Final 1930,D 31,11:1
Wild Waves 1932,F 20,11:4
Intimate Relations 1932,Mr 29,23:2
Far Away Horses 1933,Mr 22,21:6
Sailor, Beware! 1933,S 29,24:4
Geraniums in My Window 1934,O 27,20:6
Page Miss Glory 1934,N 28,24:2
Knock on Wood 1935,My 29,16:2
White Hell 1935,Ag 13,20:3

MacFarlane, Bruce—Cont
Stick-in-the-Mud 1935,D 2,18:2
Happy Valley, Limited 1936,Je 30,15:1
Timber 1936,Jl 29,11:5
Behind the Red Lights 1937,Ja 14,17:4
Quiet, Please! 1940,O 20,IX,2:3
Quiet, Please! 1940,N 9,20:3
My Sister Eileen 1940,D 27,23:2
Bell for Adano, A 1944,D 7,21:2
Bell for Adano, A 1944,D 17,II,3:2
Front Page, The 1946,S 5,22:4

MacFarlane, Carol
Bloomer Girl 1944,O 6,18:5

MacFarlane, George
Springtime of Youth 1922,O 27,15:1
Broke 1925,My 3,VIII,2:1
Lucky Break 1925,Ag 12,16:2
Revelry 1927,S 13,37:1
Salvation 1928,F 1,31:1

MacFarlane, George (Producer)
Honest Liars 1926,Jl 20,17:2
We All Do 1927,Mr 1,30:3

McFarlane, John
We Girls 1921,N 10,26:3
Why Men Leave Home 1922,Jl 30,VI,1:3
Why Men Leave Home 1922,S 13,18:2
Cymbeline 1923,O 3,12:1
Penal Law 2010 1930,Ap 19,14:2

MacFarlane, Lewis
Camille 1935,Jl 31,21:1

McFarlane, Peter
Easy Virtue 1925,D 8,28:2

MacFayden, Harry
Other Rose, The 1923,D 21,15:2

MacFayden, Harry (Director)
Nut Farm, The 1929,O 15,34:3

McFee, Neil
Passing Present, The 1931,D 8,36:2
Wild Waves 1932,F 20,11:4
World Waits, The 1933,O 26,22:5
False Dreams, Farewell 1934,Ja 16,18:3

McFerrin, Robert
Green Pastures, The 1951,Mr 16,35:2

McGahey, Robert
Last Enemy, The 1934,Jl 13,14:4

McGann, Jack
Claire Adams 1929,N 20,26:3

McGarraghy, Jeanne
Recruiting Officer, The 1958,F 8,12:2

McGarrity, Joseph
Little Ol' Boy 1933,Ap 25,15:5

MacGaskill, Duncan
Brigadoon 1957,Mr 28,37:1

McGavin, Darren
Cock-A-Doodle-Doo 1949,F 28,16:5
My 3 Angels 1953,Mr 12,23:2
Rainmaker, The 1954,O 29,28:1
Rainmaker, The 1954,N 7,II,1:1
Anna Christie 1955,N 22,41:1
Innkeepers, The 1956,F 3,19:1
Lovers 1956,My 11,23:1
Tunnel of Love, The 1957,F 14,31:4
Blood, Sweat & Stanley Poole 1961,O 6,31:1
King and I, The 1964,Jl 7,26:1
Dinner at Eight 1966,S 28,38:1
Dinner at Eight 1966,O 9,II,1:1

McGavin, Darren (Producer)
Dark Legend 1952,Mr 25,24:2

McGaw, Baldwin
Winter's Tale, The 1946,Ja 16,18:6

McGeary, John
Half Moon Inn 1923,Mr 21,19:2

McGee, Ann
House With the Twisty Windows, The 1930,My 8,32:5

McGee, Arthur (Costume Designer)
Walk Together Children 1968,N 12,54:1

McGee, Edward
House With the Twisty Windows, The 1930,My 8,32:5

McGee, Florence
Back Here 1928,N 27,36:3
Marry the Man! 1929,Ap 23,26:3
Girls in Uniform 1932,D 31,10:3
Mahogany Hall 1934,Ja 18,18:5
Children's Hour, The 1934,N 21,23:2
Children's Hour, The 1934,D 2,X,1:1
Sunup to Sundown 1938,F 2,14:3
Importance of Being Earnest, The 1939,Ja 13,16:2

McGee, Frances
David Garrick 1929,Ag 2,17:5

McGee, Frank
Jotham Valley 1951,F 7,37:2

McGee, Harold
Mr Faust 1922,Ja 31,11:2
Hairy Ape, The 1922,Mr 10,18:2
Taboo 1922,Ap 5,22:1
World We Live In, The 1922,N 1,16:1
Fashion 1924,F 5,21:2
S S Glencairn 1924,N 4,31:4
Love for Love 1925,Ap 1,21:2
Adam Solitaire 1925,N 7,19:2
Man Who Died Twice, The 1925,D 14,19:1
Dream Play 1926,Ja 21,18:2

Princess Turandot 1926,N 13,14:2
Rapid Transit 1927,Ap 8,21:2
Hot Pan 1928,F 16,14:1
S S Glencairn 1929,Ja 10,24:5
Uncle Tom's Cabin 1933,My 30,13:4
Panic 1935,Mr 16,18:4
This Our House 1935,D 12,33:3
County Chairman, The 1936,My 26,26:5
But Not Goodbye 1944,Ap 12,19:2
Live Life Again 1945,O 1,14:7
Anne of the Thousand Days 1948,D 9,49:2

McGee, James Vincent (Playwright)
Danny Larkin 1948,My 10,26:3

McGee, John
Last Enemy, The 1934,Jl 13,14:4

McGee, John (Director)
Last Enemy, The 1934,Jl 13,14:4

McGee, John (Playwright)
Jefferson Davis 1936,F 19,17:2

McGee, Maury (Producer)
Picnic 1957,F 21,32:1

McGee, Randall
As You Like It 1966,Je 4,19:1

McGee, Truly (Choreographer)
Hot Mikado, The 1939,Mr 24,26:2
New Priorities of 1943 1942,S 16,28:2
Brights Lights of 1944 1943,S 17,27:4

McGee, Truly (Director)
Wine, Women and Song 1942,S 29,18:3

McGehee, Gloria
Stone for Danny Fisher, A 1954,O 22,24:2

McGehee, Helen (Choreographer)
Oresteia 1966,Je 30,29:1

McGeorge, Nancy
South Pacific 1965,Je 3,25:1

McGerr, Joe
Riders to the Sea 1957,Mr 7,24:1

McGhan, Julia
Surgeon, The 1932,O 28,23:1

McGhee, Brownie
Cat on a Hot Tin Roof 1955,Mr 25,18:2

MacGibbon, Harriet
Howdy King 1926,D 14,24:4
Ringside 1928,Ag 30,13:2
Marriage Bed, The 1929,Ja 8,35:1
Houseparty 1929,S 10,26:5
Midnight 1930,D 30,25:1
Inside Story, The 1932,F 23,23:2
Shooting Star 1933,Ja 13,22:2
Our Betters 1937,Jl 22,16:2
Lightnin' 1938,S 16,17:2
Two on an Island 1940,Ja 23,17:2
Ladies of the Corridor, The 1953,O 22,33:5
Cloud 7 1958,F 15,15:2

McGill, Aline
Blue Eyes 1921,F 22,11:2
Perfect Fool, The 1921,N 8,28:2
Lady Butterfly 1923,Ja 23,18:1
Lollipop 1924,Ja 22,15:3

McGill, Earl (Director)
Menagerie 1935,Jl 2,24:3

McGill, Harvey
Porgy and Bess 1942,Ja 23,16:2

MacGill, Moyna
Interference 1927,F 27,VII,1:3
Boy Friend, The 1954,O 1,20:1
Heartbreak House 1963,Je 28,24:1

MacGill, Patrick (Playwright)
Suspense 1930,Ap 10,24:5
Suspense 1930,Ap 27,IX,1:8
Suspense 1930,Ag 13,22:3

McGill, Sadie
Porgy and Bess 1935,O 11,30:2
John Henry 1940,Ja 11,18:2
Porgy and Bess 1942,Ja 23,16:2

McGill, Shawn
Sound of Music, The 1970,Jl 3,13:1

McGillian, Eugene
Easy Street 1924,Ag 15,16:4

McGillicuddy, James
Sin of Pat Muldoon, The 1957,Mr 14,35:1

McGinley, Phyllis (Lyricist)
Small Wonder 1948,S 16,33:5
Small Wonder 1948,S 26,II,1:1

McGinn, Walter
Willie Doesn't Live Here Anymore 1967,F 8,20:2
Here's Where I Belong 1968,Mr 4,32:1
Spitting Image 1969,Mr 3,28:1

McGinnes, Mac
Ladies Night in a Turkish Bath 1961,Mr 22,38:1

McGinnis, Donald
Rapid Transit 1927,Ap 8,21:2
New Yorkers, The 1930,D 9,31:1

MacGinnis, Niall
Of Mice and Men 1939,Ap 30,XI,3:5
Caesar and Cleopatra 1951,D 20,43:2
Antony and Cleopatra 1951,D 21,22:2

McGinty, Artiebell
Loose Moments 1935,F 5,22:3
Plumes in the Dust 1936,N 7,14:2
Janie 1942,S 11,24:2
Laffing Room Only 1944,D 25,15:4

McGiveney, Owen
Vaudeville (Palace) 1927,Je 28,29:2
Blackouts of 1949 1949,S 7,39:2

McGiver, John
All Gaul Is Divided 1947,Je 24,27:3
Little Glass Clock, The 1956,Mr 27,40:2
Cloud 7 1958,F 15,15:2
Drink to Me Only 1958,O 9,47:4
God and Kate Murphy 1959,F 27,21:2
Thurber Carnival, A 1960,F 27,13:2
Thurber Carnival, A 1960,Mr 6,II,1:1
Cook for Mr General, A 1961,O 20,39:1
Happiness Is Just a Little Thing Called a Rolls Royce 1968,My 13,54:5
Our Town 1968,S 29,77:4
Front Page, The 1968,O 20,85:5
Front Page, The 1969,My 12,54:2
Front Page, The 1969,My 25,II,1:1
Front Page, The 1969,N 2,86:1

McGiver, John (Playwright)
All Gaul Is Divided 1947,Je 24,27:3

McGiver, Ruth Shmigelsky (Mrs) (Scenic Designer)
All Gaul Is Divided 1947,Je 24,27:3

McGiveran, Ben S
Here's Howe 1923,Ap 26,19:3

McGivern, Tom J
Story of Mary Surratt, The 1947,F 10,25:2

MacGlashan, Don (Scenic Designer)
God, Man & You, Baby! 1963,O 30,47:1

McGlynn, Frank
Abraham Lincoln 1920,Mr 14,V,5:1
Steadfast 1923,O 31,12:1
Catskill Dutch 1924,My 7,18:1
That Awful Mrs Eaton! 1924,S 30,27:1
Free Soul, A 1928,Ja 13,26:5
Broken Chain, The 1929,F 21,30:4
Abraham Lincoln 1929,O 22,26:3
Frankie and Johnny 1930,S 26,16:5

McGlynn, Frank (Mrs)
Tragedy of the Ages, The 1933,Ap 7,22:7

McGlynn, Grace
Tragedy of the Ages, The 1933,Ap 7,22:7

McGlynn, Mary Rose
Nancy Ann 1924,Ap 1,18:1

McGlynn, Thomas (Rev) (Playwright)
Caukey 1944,F 18,15:4

McGoldrick, A J (Producer)
Among Those Sailing 1936,F 12,24:4

McGonagill, Gerald E
Good Woman of Setzuan, The 1956,D 19,41:2
Death of Satan, The 1960,Ap 6,49:1
Much Ado About Nothing 1961,Jl 7,17:1
Richard II 1961,Ag 30,25:1
Julius Caesar 1962,F 22,19:6
Merchant of Venice, The 1962,Je 22,1:4
King Lear 1962,Ag 14,35:1
Antony and Cleopatra 1963,Je 21,33:1
Bald Soprano, The 1963,S 18,35:4
Telemachus Clay 1963,N 16,17:2
Deputy, The 1964,F 27,26:1
Love's Labour's Lost 1965,Je 16,46:1
Troilus and Cressida 1965,Ag 13,17:1
Richard III 1966,Ag 11,26:1

McGonigal, Maurice (Scenic Designer)
Silver Tassie, The 1935,Ag 14,16:1

McGough, Dorin
Adding Machine, The 1970,D 5,40:1

McGovern, Don
Nobody's Child 1956,Ag 23,25:2

McGovern, Don (Miscellaneous)
She Shall Have Music 1959,Ja 23,18:4

McGovern, Don (Scenic Designer)
Nobody's Child 1956,Ag 23,25:2

McGovern, John
Green Ring, The 1922,Ap 5,22:1
Man and the Masses 1924,Ap 15,25:1
Glass Slipper, The 1925,O 20,29:1
Nirvana 1926,Mr 4,19:1
Garrick Gaieties 1926,My 11,25:2
Wall Street 1927,Ap 21,24:4
Taming of the Shrew, The 1927,O 26,26:4
Twelve Thousand 1928,Mr 13,23:1
Double Dummy 1936,N 12,30:1
Retreat to Pleasure 1940,D 18,32:2
Gabrielle 1941,Mr 26,26:2
Uncle Harry 1942,My 21,24:1
I'll Take the High Road 1943,N 10,28:3
Thank You Svoboda 1944,Mr 2,13:2
Sophie 1944,D 26,22:7
Kiss Them for Me 1945,Mr 21,27:2
January Thaw 1946,F 5,18:2
All My Sons 1947,Ja 30,21:2
Story for Strangers, A 1948,S 22,39:2
Tea and Sympathy 1953,O 1,35:1
Ponder Heart, The 1956,F 17,14:2
Shadow of My Enemy, A 1957,D 12,35:4
Man in the Dog Suit, The 1958,O 31,34:2

McGovern, Milton
Trigger 1927,D 7,32:1

McGowan, Adair
Anya 1965,N 30,48:1

McGowan, Jack
Mary 1920,O 19,12:1

McGowan, Jack—Cont
Rose of Stamboul, The 1922,Mr 8,11:2
George White's Scandals 1922,Ag 29,10:1
Rise of Rosie O'Reilly, The 1923,D 26,13:4
McGowan, Jack (Director)
Heigh-Ho, Everybody 1932,My 26,31:2
Strike Me Pink 1933,Mr 6,16:3
McGowan, Jack (Playwright)
Mama Loves Papa 1926,F 23,26:2
Hold Everything 1928,S 2,VII,4:4
Parade 1929,S 1,VIII,1:1
Flying High 1930,F 9,VIII,4:2
Flying High 1930,Mr 4,24:4
Heigh-Ho, Everybody 1932,My 26,31:2
Vanities 1932,S 28,22:4
Say When 1934,O 28,IX,3:1
Say When 1934,N 9,24:2
McGowan, Jack (Producer)
Say When 1934,N 9,24:2
McGowan, John (Director)
Nigger Rich 1929,S 21,16:7
Pardon My English 1933,Ja 21,11:4
McGowan, John (Playwright)
Tenth Avenue 1927,Ag 16,31:1
Excess Baggage 1927,D 27,24:2
Excess Baggage 1928,Ja 29,VIII,1:1
Hold Everything 1928,O 11,24:2
Murray Anderson's Almanac 1929,Ag 15,20:3
Nigger Rich 1929,S 21,16:7
Heads Up! 1929,N 12,34:1
Girl Crazy 1930,O 5,IX,4:6
Girl Crazy 1930,O 15,27:1
Singin' the Blues 1931,Ap 12,IX,2:1
Singin' the Blues 1931,S 17,21:3
Lambs Gambol 1932,Ap 25,18:2
McGowan, John (Producer)
Lady Lies, The 1928,N 27,36:2
MacGowan, Kenneth (Costume Designer)
Spook Sonata, The 1924,Ja 13,VII,1:1
MacGowan, Kenneth (Director)
God Loves Us 1926,O 31,VIII,1:4
MacGowan, Kenneth (Miscellaneous)
Love for Love 1925,S 15,29:3
St Joan 1949,Ap 23,10:2
Sea Gull, The 1949,Ap 23,10:2
MacGowan, Kenneth (Producer)
Marquise, The 1927,N 15,26:4
These Modern Women 1928,F 14,26:2
Young Love 1928,O 31,28:1
Children of Darkness 1930,Ja 8,25:1
Fall of Berg-Op-Zoom, The 1930,Je 8,IX,2:7
Twelfth Night 1930,S 14,VIII,2:8
When Hell Froze 1930,O 5,IX,4:6
Twelfth Night 1930,O 16,28:2
Art and Mrs Bottle 1930,N 19,19:3
Lean Harvest 1931,O 4,VIII,2:2
Lean Harvest 1931,O 14,26:3
Lady With a Lamp, The 1931,N 20,27:2
Springtime for Henry 1931,D 10,29:2
McGowan, Oliver
In the Matter of J Robert Oppenheimer 1968,Je 7,31:1
MacGowan, Robert (Director)
Route 1 1964,N 18,52:3
MacGowran, Jack
Juno 1959,Mr 10,41:1
In the Zone; Before Breakfast 1963,Je 11,29:4
Endgame 1964,F 21,32:1
Juno and the Paycock 1966,Ag 3,40:1
Beginning to End 1970,Ap 25,32:3
Gandhi 1970,O 21,37:1
Jack MacGowran in the Works of Samuel Beckett 1970,N 20,32:1
Jack MacGowran in the Works of Samuel Beckett 1970,N 27,46:1
Jack MacGowran in the Works of Samuel Beckett 1970,N 29,II,1:1
MacGowran, Jack (Playwright)
Jack MacGowran in the Works of Samuel Beckett 1970,N 20,32:1
McGrail, Agnes
Pipe in the Fields, The 1931,Mr 14,23:4
Well of the Saints, The 1932,Ja 22,15:2
McGrail, Walter
Poet's Follies of 1955 1955,My 15,II,3:1
McGranary, Al
Behold Your God 1936,Ap 22,28:3
Iceman Cometh, The 1946,O 10,31:3
Solid Gold Cadillac, The 1953,N 6,24:2
McGrane, Paul (Composer)
Who's Who 1938,Mr 2,16:2
Stars on Ice 1942,Jl 3,12:2
Icetime 1947,My 29,28:2
McGrane, William
Would-Be Gentleman, The 1930,Ap 30,29:2
McGrath, Anthony
Grass Harp, The 1952,Mr 28,26:2
McGrath, Byron
Steel 1931,N 19,26:5
Carry Nation 1932,O 31,18:2
Amourette 1933,S 28,25:2
Broomsticks Amen! 1934,F 10,20:4
Within the Gates 1934,O 23,23:1
Granite 1936,Ja 14,24:6

Middle Man 1936,S 8,23:1
High Tor 1937,Ja 11,15:2
Night of January 16 1937,Jl 20,19:3
Jeremiah 1939,F 4,11:2
As You Like It 1939,My 9,28:4
As You Like It; Midsummer Night's Dream, A; Comedy of Errors, The; Taming of the Shrew, The 1939,My 9,28:4
Taming of the Shrew, The 1940,F 6,17:2
Journey to Jerusalem 1940,O 7,21:2
Gabrielle 1941,Mr 26,26:2
Elizabeth the Queen 1941,O 17,27:2
Brooklyn, U S A 1941,D 22,24:2
Rip Van Winkle 1947,Jl 16,28:2
How I Wonder 1947,O 1,34:2
McGrath, Frances
Two Strangers From Nowhere 1924,Ap 8,22:2
Tired Business Man, The 1929,Je 5,32:5
McGrath, Frank (Playwright)
Carry Nation 1932,O 31,18:2
McGrath, George
Titus Andronicus 1967,Ag 10,43:2
In Circles 1967,O 14,12:1
In Circles 1968,Je 28,36:1
Peace 1968,N 10,87:1
Peace 1969,Ja 28,49:1
MacGrath, Harold (Original Author)
Drums of Jeopardy, The 1922,My 30,8:4
MacGrath, Harold (Playwright)
Drums of Jeopardy, The 1922,My 30,8:4
McGrath, Joe
Most Happy Fella, The 1966,My 12,55:1
How Now, Dow Jones 1967,D 8,53:1
Fig Leaves Are Falling, The 1969,Ja 3,19:1
McGrath, John
Don Q Jr 1926,Ja 28,16:3
McGrath, Joseph
Jimmy 1969,O 24,38:1
McGrath, Katherine
Comedy of Errors, The 1968,F 28,40:2
She Stoops to Conquer 1968,Ap 1,58:3
McGrath, Kevin
William Had the Words! 1964,Mr 30,36:1
MacGrath, Leueen
King's Breakfast, The 1937,D 13,22:8
Edward, My Son 1948,O 1,30:2
Edward My Son 1948,O 10,II,1:1
Enchanted, The 1950,Ja 19,34:2
High Ground, The 1951,F 21,31:2
Fancy Meeting You Again 1952,Ja 15,23:2
Evening With Will Shakespeare, An 1952,D 7,86:5
Love of Four Colonels, The 1953,Ja 16,17:2
Tiger at the Gates 1955,O 4,40:1
Tiger at the Gates 1955,O 23,II,1:1
Potting Shed, The 1957,Ja 30,32:1
Potting Shed, The 1957,F 10,II,1:1
Maidens and Mistresses at Home at the Zoo 1958,O 29,31:1
Lute Song 1959,Mr 13,24:1
Farewell, Farewell Eugene 1960,S 28,35:1
Ghosts 1961,S 22,29:1
Love Nest, The 1963,Ja 28,7:6
MacGrath, Leueen (Playwright)
Small Hours, The 1951,F 16,22:1
Fancy Meeting You Again 1952,Ja 15,23:2
Silk Stockings 1955,F 25,17:3
Silk Stockings 1955,Mr 27,II,1:1
McGrath, Paul
In the Near Future 1925,Mr 11,19:1
Made in America 1925,O 15,27:2
Arabian, The 1927,N 1,20:5
Good Fairy, The 1931,N 25,17:1
Here Today 1932,S 7,14:2
Here Today 1932,S 18,IX,1:1
Pigeons and People 1933,Ja 17,22:3
Three and One 1933,O 26,22:6
Lady Jane 1934,S 11,24:2
Ode to Liberty 1934,D 22,20:2
Ode to Liberty 1935,Jl 9,24:4
Ode to Liberty 1935,Ag 6,20:3
Room Service 1935,N 17,II,7:7
Mrs Moonlight 1936,Je 16,21:3
Seen But Not Heard 1936,S 18,19:2
Susan and God 1937,Ap 11,II,12:3
Susan and God 1937,Ap 25,X,2:3
Inconstant Moon, The 1937,Ag 18,15:2
Susan and God 1937,O 8,26:4
Ring Two 1939,N 14,20:3
Ring Two 1939,N 23,38:2
Lady in the Dark 1941,S 3,26:6
In Bed We Cry 1944,N 15,20:2
Common Ground 1945,Ap 26,27:2
Common Ground 1945,My 6,II,1:1
Candida 1945,Ag 7,25:3
Command Decision 1947,S 21,I,59:7
Command Decision 1947,O 2,30:2
Big Knife, The 1949,F 25,27:5
Small Hours, The 1951,F 16,22:1
Love and Let Love 1951,O 20,11:2
Touchstone 1953,F 4,33:2
Girl Can Tell, A 1953,O 30,28:2
Gang's All Here, The 1959,O 2,23:1
Giants, Sons of Giants 1962,Ja 8,26:2

McGrath, Paul—Cont
Bicycle Ride to Nevada 1963,S 25,38:1
Child Buyer, The 1964,D 22,35:1
Brightower 1970,Ja 29,32:1
McGrath, Raymond
You and I 1925,O 20,29:1
McGrath, Russell (Miscellaneous)
King Lear 1962,Ag 14,35:1
Antony and Cleopatra 1963,Je 21,33:1
Hamlet 1964,Je 17,49:1
Electra 1964,Ag 12,42:1
Hard Travelin' 1965,Je 17,25:1
Lonesome Train, The 1965,Je 17,25:1
Troilus and Cressida 1965,Ag 13,17:1
MacBird! 1967,F 23,38:1
Comedy of Errors, The 1967,Je 15,58:4
Hair 1967,O 30,55:1
Hamlet 1967,D 27,45:1
McGrath, Russell (Playwright)
Invitation to a Beheading 1969,Mr 18,36:1
Invitation to a Beheading 1969,Mr 30,II,1:1
McGrath, Rusty (Miscellaneous)
White Rose and the Red, The 1964,Mr 17,31:1
McGrath, Tony
Cherry Orchard, The 1955,O 19,38:1
McGrattan, Alice
From Morn Till Midnight 1948,D 7,41:6
McGraw, Bill
Angel in the Wings 1947,D 12,36:4
McGraw, Jock
What Price Glory 1924,S 6,14:3
Hangman's House 1926,D 17,27:2
Road to Rome, The 1927,F 1,24:2
White Eagle, The 1927,D 27,24:4
John Ferguson 1928,Ja 18,23:1
Present Arms 1928,Ap 27,16:2
Solitaire 1929,Mr 13,28:3
Anatomist, The 1932,O 25,24:3
Mary of Scotland 1933,N 28,28:3
Valley Forge 1934,D 11,28:3
Love on the Dole 1936,F 25,23:3
Red Roses for Me 1955,D 29,15:2
MacGraw, Martha
Zeno 1923,Ag 27,14:2
Jest, The 1926,F 5,22:2
Macgregor, Ann
Nine Till Six 1930,S 29,17:2
MacGregor, Barry
Lark, The 1955,My 13,21:2
Comedy of Errors, The 1962,S 12,34:2
King Lear 1964,My 19,43:2
Comedy of Errors, The 1964,My 21,43:1
Yeomen of the Guard, The 1964,Ag 3,16:1
Henry V 1966,Je 8,38:1
Henry VI 1966,Je 9,55:2
Richard III 1967,Je 14,43:1
Government Inspector, The 1967,Je 15,55:1
Antony and Cleopatra 1967,Ag 2,25:1
Government Inspector, The 1967,O 28,34:1
Don't Shoot Mable It's Your Husband 1968,O 23,34:1
Flea in Her Ear, A 1969,O 4,25:1
Merchant of Venice, The 1970,Je 10,39:1
School for Scandal, The 1970,Je 11,51:1
McGregor, Dion (Lyricist)
Who's Happy Now? 1969,N 18,39:1
MacGregor, Edgar (Director)
Four Flusher, The 1925,Ap 5,IX,2:4
Captain Jinks 1925,S 9,22:1
Magda 1926,Ja 27,16:2
No More Women 1926,Ag 4,17:2
Queen High 1926,S 9,21:2
Honeymoon Lane 1926,S 21,32:3
Black Cockatoo, The 1926,D 31,11:1
Lady Do 1927,Ap 19,24:2
Good News 1927,S 7,35:4
Sidewalks of New York 1927,O 4,33:1
Anna 1928,My 17,25:2
Earl Carroll's Vanities 1928,Ag 7,25:2
Ups-A-Daisy 1928,O 9,34:2
Follow Thru 1929,Ja 10,24:3
Stepping Out 1929,My 21,29:1
Sketch Book 1929,Jl 2,33:5
Laugh Parade, The 1931,N 3,31:2
Through the Years 1932,Ja 29,13:3
Hot-Cha! 1932,Mr 9,17:3
Take a Chance 1932,N 28,11:2
Story to Be Whispered 1937,Ag 20,21:4
Du Barry Was a Lady 1939,D 7,34:2
Seperate Rooms 1940,Mr 25,10:3
Let's Face It 1941,O 30,26:2
Pie in the Sky 1941,D 23,26:5
Time, Place and the Girl, The 1942,O 22,24:3
My Dear Public 1943,S 10,28:1
Louisiana Lady 1947,Je 3,35:2
MacGregor, Edgar (Miscellaneous)
Stepping Out 1929,My 21,29:1
Vanities 1932,S 28,22:4
Nellie Bly 1946,Ja 22,32:2
MacGregor, Edgar (Playwright)
Night Duel, The 1926,F 16,22:3
Earl Carroll's Vanities 1931,Ag 28,18:7
Louisiana Purchase 1940,My 29,19:2
Hold On to Your Hats 1940,S 12,30:3

MacGregor, Edgar (Playwright)—Cont
Panama Hattie 1940,O 31,28:2
MacGregor, Edgar (Producer)
Story to Be Whispered 1937,Ag 20,21:4
Pie in the Sky 1941,D 23,26:5
Down to Miami 1944,S 12,23:5
McGregor, Edward (Director)
Lady Fingers 1929,F 1,22:4
MacGregor, Eugene
Within Four Walls 1923,Ap 18,24:1
Battling Buttler 1923,O 9,17:2
Four Flusher, The 1925,Ap 14,27:4
McGregor, G W (Producer)
Well of Romance, The 1930,N 8,21:2
MacGregor, Harmon
Dawn of Ireland, The 1920,O 1,14:2
Mixed Marriage 1920,D 15,18:2
Mixed Marriage 1920,D 26,VI,3:3
Cradle Song 1921,Mr 1,18:2
Mask of Hamlet, The 1921,Ag 23,10:3
Chains of Dew 1922,Ap 28,20:2
MacGregor, Hector
Royal Highness 1949,Ap 14,29:3
MacGregor, Jock
Lace on Her Petticoat 1951,S 5,40:3
Legend of Lizzie, The 1959,F 10,39:1
McGregor, Katherine
Tom Sawyer - Ballad of the Mississippi 1947,D 27,11:3
McGregor, Mary
Immaculate Misconception, The 1970,O 28,63:3
MacGregor, Nancy
Cradle Snatchers 1932,N 17,23:2
MacGregor, Rae
Time, Place and the Girl, The 1942,O 22,24:3
Follow the Girls 1944,Ap 10,15:2
MacGregor, Scottie
Handful of Fire 1958,O 2,45:3
'Toinette 1961,N 21,46:1
Telemachus Clay 1963,N 16,17:2
My Kinsman, Major Molineux 1964,N 2,62:2
MacGregor, Sherman
Strings, My Lord, Are False, The 1942,My 20,24:2
Yours, A Lincoln 1942,Jl 10,12:3
McGrew, James
Sound of Hunting, A 1945,N 21,16:6
McGrew, Janet
Strings, My Lord, Are False, The 1942,My 20,24:2
McGrew, John (Playwright)
Nights of Wrath; Nuits de la Colere, Les 1947,D 1,26:4
McGrew, Mr
Merry Wives of West Point, The 1932,Mr 20,II,7:7
McGroarty, John Steven (Playwright)
Mission Play, The 1925,F 1,IV,20:3
McGroder, Jack (Costume Designer)
Moon Walk 1970,N 27,52:1
McGroder, Jack (Scenic Designer)
Moon Walk 1970,N 27,52:1
McGroder, John A (Scenic Designer)
Sold to the Movies; Crossing the Gap 1970,Je 18,54:2
Sold to the Movies; Life Size 1970,Je 18,54:2
Sold to the Movies; Type 424 Meet Type Oh-Oh, No! 1970,Je 18,54:2
MacGuffin, Schuyler
Mima 1928,D 13,24:2
Silver Tassie, The 1929,O 25,26:1
Black Diamond 1933,F 24,12:2
McGuigan, William
Conversation Piece 1934,O 24,24:1
McGuinness, Lillian
Talking to You 1942,Ag 18,17:1
Across the Board on Tomorrow Morning 1942,Ag 18,17:1
McGuire, Barry
Girl Can Tell, A 1953,O 30,28:2
Young and Beautiful, The 1955,O 3,23:2
Hair 1969,F 5,36:1
McGuire, Betty
Oh Captain! 1958,F 5,21:2
McGuire, Biff
Make Mine Manhattan 1948,Ja 16,26:2
South Pacific 1949,Ap 8,30:2
Dance Me a Song 1950,Ja 21,10:5
Moon Is Blue, The 1953,Jl 8,24:1
Moon Is Blue, The 1953,Ag 9,II,1:2
Time of Your Life, The 1955,Ja 20,34:1
Time of Your Life, The 1955,Ja 30,21:1
Memory of Two Mondays, A 1955,S 30,21:1
Greatest Man Alive!, The 1957,My 9,37:2
Egghead, The 1957,O 10,39:1
Portrait of a Madonna 1959,Ap 16,28:1
Bedtime Story 1959,Ap 16,28:1
Pound on Demand, A 1959,Ap 16,28:1
Portrait of a Madonna 1959,Ap 26,II,1:1
Happy Town 1959,O 8,49:2
Beg, Borrow or Steal 1960,F 11,39:4
Finian's Rainbow 1960,Ap 28,31:1
Time of Your Life, The 1969,N 7,37:1
Time of Your Life, The 1969,N 16,II,1:4
McGuire, Dorothy
My Dear Children 1939,Mr 25,19:6
Swingin' the Dream 1939,N 30,24:2

Medicine Show 1940,Ap 13,20:6
Kind Lady 1940,S 4,28:3
Claudia 1941,F 13,24:2
Claudia 1941,Mr 9,IX,1:1
Claudia 1942,My 25,11:3
Summer and Smoke 1950,O 29,II,3:7
Legend of Lovers 1951,D 27,17:1
Winesburg, Ohio 1958,F 6,22:2
McGuire, Florence
Charm School, The 1920,Ag 3,12:1
Clinging Vine, The 1922,D 25,20:2
McGuire, James
Topaze 1930,F 13,25:3
Bright Rebel 1938,D 28,24:2
McGuire, John (Playwright)
Praise Of Folly 1954,F 24,23:2
McGuire, Ken (Playwright)
Grin and Bare It 1970,Mr 17,36:1
McGuire, Lou
That Old Devil 1944,Je 6,14:2
McGuire, Lu
If I Was Rich 1926,S 3,15:2
McGuire, Maeve
Cyrano de Bergerac 1968,Ap 26,30:1
Miser, The 1969,My 9,35:1
McGuire, Maggie
Give My Regards to Off Off Broadway 1966,D 9,57:1
McGuire, Michael
Legitimate Steal, The 1958,Ap 1,35:1
Doctor Faustus 1961,Ap 26,36:1
Along Came a Spider 1963,My 28,33:1
Burning, The 1963,D 4,57:1
Passion of Josef D, The 1964,F 12,29:1
Sound of Silence, A 1965,Mr 9,30:1
Coriolanus 1965,Jl 15,23:1
Troilus and Cressida 1965,Ag 13,17:1
Macbeth 1966,Je 29,38:1
King John 1967,Jl 14,19:1
Cannibals, The 1968,N 4,60:1
Guns of Carrar, The 1968,D 10,53:1
Henry V 1969,Je 9,57:1
Much Ado About Nothing 1969,Je 16,57:1
Three Sisters, The 1969,Ag 4,29:1
Three Sisters, The 1969,Ag 10,II,3:1
Whistle in the Dark, A 1969,O 9,55:1
Whistle in the Dark, A 1969,N 9,II,3:1
Child's Play 1970,F 18,39:1
Hay Fever 1970,N 10,55:1
Hay Fever 1970,N 22,II,18:6
McGuire, Michael (Director)
Candida 1961,Ap 27,26:1
McGuire, Mitchell
Go, Go, Go, God is Dead! 1966,O 12,37:1
McGuire, Paul C (Costume Designer)
Southwest Corner, The 1955,F 4,18:2
McGuire, Paul C (Lighting Director)
Oklahoma! 1969,Je 24,37:1
McGuire, Paul C (Miscellaneous)
Evening With Beatrice Lillie, An 1952,O 3,17:2
McGuire, Paul C (Scenic Designer)
King and I, The 1964,Jl 7,26:1
Carousel 1965,Ag 11,39:1
Annie Get Your Gun 1966,Je 1,42:2
Carousel 1966,D 16,56:2
Oklahoma! 1969,Je 24,37:1
McGuire, Tucker
Mackerel Skies 1934,Ja 24,20:4
Every Thursday 1934,My 11,25:5
Substitute for Murder 1935,O 23,18:6
Roosty 1938,F 15,21:2
McGuire, William
Bright Boy 1944,Mr 3,19:5
Comforter, The 1964,O 22,42:1
McGuire, William Anthony (Director)
Twelve Miles Out 1925,N 17,29:2
Whoopee 1928,D 5,34:3
Ripples 1930,F 12,26:1
Smiles 1930,N 19,19:2
McGuire, William Anthony (Playwright)
It's a Boy! 1922,S 20,18:3
Kid Boots 1924,Ja 1,21:3
Follies 1924,Je 19,25:7
Ziegfeld Follies 1924,Je 25,26:1
Twelve Miles Out 1925,N 17,29:2
If I Was Rich 1926,S 3,15:2
12 Miles Out 1927,F 20,VII,1:4
Rosalie 1928,Ja 11,26:3
Three Musketeers, The 1928,Mr 4,IX,2:3
Three Musketeers, The 1928,Mr 14,28:1
Whoopee 1928,D 5,34:3
Show Girl 1929,Jl 3,19:3
Whoopee 1929,Ag 6,29:4
Ripples 1930,F 2,VIII,2:7
Ripples 1930,F 12,26:1
Smiles 1930,N 19,19:2
Bad Penny, A 1931,Ag 23,VIII,2:4
Rosalie 1957,Je 26,28:2
McGuire, William Anthony (Producer)
Twelve Miles Out 1925,N 17,29:2
McGuirk, Fred
Bells, The 1926,Ap 14,20:3
Deep River 1926,O 5,26:2

McGuirk, Fred—Cont
Quicksand 1928,F 14,26:3
MacGunigle, Robert (Playwright)
Walk a Little Faster 1932,D 8,24:4
McGunigle, Rupert B
Out o' Luck 1925,D 19,15:1
McGurn, Ned
Rainbow 1928,N 22,25:1
McGurn, Ned (Choreographer)
Vanities 1932,S 28,22:4
Murder at the Vanities 1933,S 13,22:4
Let 'Em Eat Cake 1933,O 23,18:1
New Faces of 1936 1936,My 20,24:5
I'd Rather Be Right 1937,N 3,28:2
Sing Out the News 1938,S 26,12:5
Sing for Your Supper 1939,Ap 25,18:6
McGushion, Dorothy
Luckee Girl 1928,S 17,28:6
McGushion, Gertrude
Luckee Girl 1928,S 17,28:6
Mach, Milan
Matter of Days, A 1969,My 20,40:1
Machada y Ruis, Antonio (Playwright)
Juan de Manara 1927,Ag 28,VII,2:1
Machada y Ruis, Manuel (Playwright)
Juan de Manara 1927,Ag 28,VII,2:1
Machado, Cathy
Ice Capades 1956,S 13,41:2
Ice Capades 1957,S 5,33:2
Ice Capades 1958,S 4,33:2
Ice Capades 1959,S 4,12:1
Ice Capades 1961,Ag 31,24:4
Ice Capades 1962,Ag 30,34:1
Ice Capades 1963,Ag 29,37:2
McHale, Duke
Prince Charming 1930,O 14,31:1
Ziegfeld Follies 1936,Ja 31,17:2
Babes in Arms 1937,Ap 15,18:4
Are You With It? 1945,N 12,17:3
Machan, Ben (Composer)
Safari! 1955,My 12,32:6
Machard, Alfred (Playwright)
Folle Jeunesse 1927,O 9,VIII,2:4
Machard, Ernest
Nuit au Bouge, Une 1923,O 16,18:1
MacHardy, Eileen (Costume Designer)
Jonah! 1967,S 22,52:2
Machat, Sydney
S S Glencairn 1924,N 4,31:4
Outside Looking In 1925,S 8,28:1
Saturday Night 1926,O 26,25:1
Three Sisters, The 1926,O 27,24:1
McHattie, Stephen
Henry IV, Part I 1968,Je 30,54:7
Henry IV, Part II 1968,Jl 2,33:1
American Dream, The 1968,O 3,55:1
Hamlet 1969,Je 11,37:1
Measure for Measure 1969,Je 13,41:3
Persians, The 1970,Ap 16,53:1
Persians, The 1970,Ap 26,II,1:3
McHatton, Adele
Hassard Short's Ritz Revue 1924,S 18,19:1
McHenry, Don
Black Eye, The 1938,Mr 8,22:4
Don't Throw Glass Houses 1938,D 28,24:4
Elizabeth the Queen 1941,O 17,27:2
Medea 1947,O 21,27:2
Medea 1949,My 3,31:2
Tower Beyond Tragedy, The 1950,N 27,29:1
Crucible, The 1953,Ja 23,15:2
Crucible, The 1953,Jl 2,20:2
Fanny 1954,N 5,16:1
In April Once 1955,Mr 14,29:3
Hour Glass, The 1955,O 17,33:1
Thunder Rock 1956,F 27,18:1
Tobias and the Angel 1957,O 21,29:5
Destry Rides Again 1959,Ap 24,24:1
Cantilevered Terrace, The 1962,Ja 18,24:1
Elizabeth the Queen 1966,N 4,30:1
King Lear 1968,N 8,43:1
Cry of Players, A 1968,N 15,40:1
McHenry, Jean
Bamboo Cross 1955,F 22,17:2
McHenry, Paul
Twelfth Night 1969,Ag 14,29:2
Machet, Sydney
Master Builder, The 1925,N 11,27:1
Machiavelli, Niccolo (Playwright)
Mandragola 1930,F 2,VIII,4:1
Clizia 1939,Jl 23,IX,6:3
Mandragola 1949,Ja 25,26:6
Mandragola 1956,Mr 1,36:4
Mandragola 1958,My 29,23:2
Mandragola 1970,Ap 19,74:3
Machiz, Herbert (Director)
Love of Don Perlimplin and Belisa in the Garden, The 1953,N 4,30:5
Immortal Husband, The 1955,F 15,32:2
Streetcar Named Desire, A 1956,F 16,24:1
Absalom 1956,My 17,37:2
Eugenia 1957,Ja 31,20:1
Garden District; Something Unspoken 1958,Ja 8,23:4

Machiz, Herbert (Director)—Cont
Garden District; Suddenly Last Summer 1958,Ja 8,23:4
Garden District; Suddenly Last Summer 1958,Ja 19,II,1:1
Pretender, The 1960,My 25,42:1
Sotoba Komachi 1961,F 1,15:1
Hans's Crime 1961,F 4,15:1
Damask Drum, The 1961,F 4,15:1
Automobile Graveyard, The 1961,N 14,46:2
Deuces Wild; Thus 1962,Ap 25,31:1
Deuces Wild; It's All Yours 1962,Ap 25,31:1
Charlatans; Summer Ghost, A 1962,Ap 27,26:1
Charlatans; On Circe's Island 1962,Ap 27,26:1
Milk Train Doesn't Stop Here Anymore, The 1963,Ja 18,7:1
Wives, The 1965,My 18,35:4
Elizabeth the Queen 1966,N 4,30:1
In the Bar of a Tokyo Hotel 1969,My 12,54:1
Gertrude Stein's First Reader 1969,D 16,56:1
Machiz, Herbert (Miscellaneous)
Gertrude Stein's First Reader 1969,D 16,56:1
Machiz, Herbert (Playwright)
Hans's Crime 1961,F 4,15:1
Macho, Carole
Philanderer, The 1958,My 13,26:2
You Never Can Tell 1958,Je 17,25:1
Prodigal, The 1960,F 12,23:1
Prodigal, The 1960,F 21,II,1:1
Yes is for a Very Young Man 1963,Mr 6,7:5
Alchemist, The 1964,S 15,33:1
Machon, J Harold
Tyrant, The 1930,N 13,33:1
McHone, William (Costume Designer)
Forty Carats 1968,D 27,45:1
Macht, Stephen
Much Ado About Nothing 1963,Jl 15,25:2
MacHugh, Augustin (Original Author)
Meanest Man in the World, The 1920,O 8,14:4
MacHugh, Augustin (Playwright)
Meanest Man in the World, The 1920,O 13,18:2
It's Up to You 1921,Mr 29,20:1
True to Form 1921,S 13,12:1
McHugh, Burke
Derryowen 1946,O 29,34:2
Magic Touch, The 1947,S 4,30:1
Greenwich Village U S A 1960,S 29,30:5
McHugh, Burke (Director)
Greenwich Village U S A 1960,S 29,30:5
McHugh, Edward (Director)
Corn Is Green, The 1950,Ja 12,33:2
McHugh, Edward (Miscellaneous)
Wooden Dish, The 1955,O 7,20:1
McHugh, Florence
Master Builder, The 1928,O 21,IX,1:3
McHugh, Frances
Precious 1929,Ja 15,22:5
That's Gratitude 1932,Je 17,24:3
Show-Off, The 1932,D 13,25:4
Fulton of Oak Falls 1937,Ja 2,15:3
Fulton of Oak Falls 1937,F 11,18:2
Time of Your Life, The 1940,S 24,27:2
McHugh, Frank
Fog 1927,F 8,20:1
Tenth Avenue 1927,Ag 16,31:1
Excess Baggage 1927,D 27,24:2
Conflict 1929,Mr 7,22:4
Show Girl 1929,Jl 3,19:3
Finian's Rainbow 1967,Ap 6,44:1
McHugh, Jimmy (Composer)
Blackbirds 1928,My 10,31:3
Hello, Daddy! 1928,D 27,26:5
International Revue 1930,F 26,22:2
Singin' the Blues 1931,Ap 12,IX,2:1
Rhapsody in Black 1931,My 5,33:2
Singin' the Blues 1931,S 17,21:3
Streets of Paris, The 1939,Je 20,25:2
Keep Off the Grass 1940,My 24,22:6
As the Girls Go 1948,N 15,21:2
McHugh, Jimmy (Lyricist)
International Revue 1930,F 26,22:2
Rhapsody in Black 1931,My 5,33:2
McHugh, John (Costume Designer)
Maidens and Mistresses at Home at the Zoo 1958,O 29,31:1
Song of Songs 1958,O 29,31:1
McHugh, Katherine
Two Seconds 1931,O 10,20:6
McHugh, Martin (Playwright)
Minute's Wait, A 1920,Je 22,9:1
McHugh, Mary Anna
Vagabond King, The 1935,N 29,22:7
McHugh, Mary Frances
Best People, The 1933,Mr 16,21:5
McHugh, Matt
Swing Your Lady 1936,O 19,22:4
McHugh, Matthew
Street Scene 1929,Ja 11,20:4
McHugh, Nancy
Priest in the Cellar, The 1969,F 19,39:1
McHugh, Raymond
Under Milk Wood 1957,O 16,42:5
McHugh, Vincent
Poet's Follies of 1955 1955,My 15,II,3:1

Macias, Ernest
Nobody's Child 1956,Ag 23,25:2
Macieay, Eide
As You Like It 1936,Ap 24,18:4
McIlrath, Patricia (Dr) (Director)
Electra 1959,F 14,15:1
McIlvaine, D H
It's the Valet 1933,D 15,25:4
MacIlwinen, William (Director)
Forever This Land 1952,Je 30,14:6
McInerney, Bernard Jr
Caucasian Chalk Circle, The 1961,N 1,35:1
McInerney, Joseph
First Flight 1925,S 18,26:2
God Loves Us 1926,O 20,22:2
Beyond the Horizon 1926,D 1,24:2
Journey by Night, A 1935,Ap 17,26:3
Wild Justice 1935,Jl 9,24:3
If This Be Treason 1935,Jl 30,17:1
Good Men and True 1935,O 26,12:4
McIntire, Janet
Cherry Orchard, The 1970,My 7,63:2
McIntire, Robb
King Lear 1968,Je 3,55:4
MacIntosh, Agnes (Gordon Daviot) (Playwright)
Richard of Bordeaux 1934,F 25,IX,1:1
MacIntosh, Alice
Tomorrow and Tomorrow 1931,Ja 14,26:3
McIntosh, Ann (Miscellaneous)
Exercise, The 1968,Ap 25,54:1
McIntosh, Ann (Producer)
Coop, The 1966,Mr 2,48:1
Nest, The 1970,Ap 10,46:1
McIntosh, Blaine
Phoebe of Quality Street 1921,My 10,20:1
McIntosh, Burr
Squaw Man, The 1921,D 27,10:3
Robert E Lee 1923,N 21,23:1
McIntosh, Frank L
Hasty Heart, The 1954,Mr 13,10:1
McIntosh, George
Strings, My Lord, Are False, The 1942,My 20,24:2
MacIntosh, James
Scarlet Coat, The 1924,D 24,11:1
MacIntosh, Joan
Dionysus in 69 1968,Je 7,35:3
Macbeth 1969,N 21,51:1
MacIntosh, Kenneth
Three Sisters, The 1970,F 12,30:1
McIntosh, Lois
What of It? 1929,Mr 9,24:2
MacIntosh, Louise
Crooked Gamblers 1920,Ag 2,12:1
Diana 1929,D 10,37:1
MacIntosh, Randolph
Zunguru 1938,Ag 7,IX,8:2
McIntosh, Stuart
Dinosaur Wharf 1951,N 9,23:2
MacIntyre, Anna
Daddy Dumplins 1920,N 23,11:1
McIntyre, Dennis (Playwright)
Children in the Rain 1970,O 3,14:1
MacIntyre, Don
Twelfth Night 1970,Ja 1,18:1
McIntyre, Frank
Seeing Things 1920,Je 18,19:2
Vaudeville (Palace) 1922,F 14,21:1
Sitting Pretty 1924,Ap 9,24:2
Greenwich Village Follies 1925,D 25,23:3
Queen High 1926,S 9,21:2
Sunny Days 1928,F 9,29:1
Boom Boom 1929,Ja 29,26:4
McIntyre, H C
Vaudeville (Palace) 1923,O 30,16:1
McIntyre, James
Red Pepper 1922,My 30,8:3
MacIntyre, Jean
Rag Picker of Paris, The: or, Modest Modiste 1935,N 12,23:7
Tulips Are Blooming, The 1935,D 4,27:6
Idiot's Delight 1936,Mr 25,25:2
McIntyre, John T (Playwright)
Genius and the Crowd 1920,S 7,20:1
McIntyre, Molly
Expressing Willie 1924,Ap 17,22:1
Infinite Shoeblack, The 1930,F 18,28:1
McIntyre, Tom
Dead End 1935,O 29,17:2
McIntyre and Heath
Vaudeville (Palace) 1924,S 30,27:5
McIver, Ray (Playwright)
God Is a (Guess What?) 1968,D 18,56:1
God Is a (Guess What?) 1968,D 19,63:6
God Is a (Guess What?) 1968,D 29,II,1:1
God Is a (Guess What?) 1969,My 13,41:1
McIver, William
Love's Labour's Lost 1953,F 5,20:3
Mack, Adrian (Composer)
Soliloquy 1938,N 29,26:4
Mack, Agnes
Good Times 1920,Ag 10,10:1
Mack, Andrew
Friar's Club Frolic 1922,Je 5,16:1

Mack, Andrew—Cont
Humming Bird, The 1923,Ja 16,16:2
Lambs Gambol 1925,Ap 27,15:1
Woof, Woof 1929,D 26,20:4
Rivals, The 1930,Mr 14,24:4
Pressing Business 1930,N 18,28:5
Mack, Arthur
Desire Under the Elms 1924,N 12,20:7
Second Mate, The 1930,Mr 25,34:5
Regular Guy, A; Man's Man, A 1931,Je 5,27:1
That's Gratitude 1932,Je 17,24:3
As Husbands Go 1933,Ja 20,20:5
John Ferguson 1933,Jl 11,15:7
Othello 1937,Ja 7,16:4
Mack, Bertha
Summer Wives 1936,Ap 14,18:1
Mack, Betty
Love Birds 1921,Mr 16,12:1
Mack, Bobbye
Wonderful World of Burlesque, The 1965,Ap 29,38:1
Mack, Cecil (Composer)
Runnin' Wild 1923,O 30,17:3
Rhapsody in Black 1931,My 5,33:2
Mack, Cecil (Director)
Swing It 1937,Jl 23,17:2
Mack, Cecil (Lyricist)
Runnin' Wild 1923,O 30,17:3
Rhapsody in Black 1931,My 5,33:2
Mack, Cecil (Playwright)
Swing It 1937,Jl 23,17:2
Mack, Charles
Dancing Girl, The 1923,Ja 25,16:2
Earl Carroll's Vanities 1927,Ja 5,18:1
Mack, Clifford
Crucible 1933,S 5,22:4
Second Hurricane 1937,Ap 22,18:4
Processional 1937,O 14,23:1
Mack, Delores
Tobacco Road 1950,Mr 7,23:2
Mack, Dorothy
London, Paris and New York 1926,Je 8,23:1
Vaudeville (Palace) 1926,Je 8,23:1
Mack, Ernie
He Loved the Ladies 1927,My 11,29:2
Mack, Florence
Nest, The 1922,F 2,20:1
Mack, George C
Squealer, The 1928,N 13,36:3
Mack, George E
Barnum Was Right 1923,Mr 13,19:3
Sitting Pretty 1924,Ap 9,24:2
China Rose 1925,Ja 20,18:1
Holka Polka 1925,O 15,27:2
Hush Money 1926,Mr 16,22:3
Enchanted Isle 1927,S 20,33:2
Of Thee I Sing 1931,D 28,20:1
Let 'Em Eat Cake 1933,O 23,18:1
Anything Goes 1934,N 22,26:1
Babes in Arms 1937,Ap 15,18:4
Mack, Georgie
Look Who's Here 1920,Mr 3,12:2
Mack, Gilbert
Bell for Adano, A 1944,D 7,21:2
Springtime Folly 1951,F 27,23:4
Comic Strip 1958,My 15,26:2
Mack, Harry
Let Freedom Sing 1942,O 6,18:2
Mack, Helen
Dybbuk, The 1925,D 16,22:2
Mack, James
Tattle Tales 1933,Je 2,22:6
Mack, James C
Anna Christie 1921,N 3,22:1
Mack, Joe
Ginger 1923,O 17,14:1
Mack, Johnny
Beat the Band 1942,O 15,26:1
Take a Bow 1944,Je 16,15:3
Mack, Leo
Rainbow 1928,N 22,25:1
Mack, Lester
Period of Adjustment 1960,N 11,34:1
Mack, Nila
Eva the Fifth 1928,Ag 29,19:3
Buckaroo 1929,Mr 18,31:1
Mack, Ollie
Bringing Up Father 1925,Mr 31,16:1
Mack, Robert
Imaginary Invalid, The 1922,Jl 26,26:2
Mack, Ron
Moon on a Rainbow Shawl 1962,Ja 16,30:1
Two Executioners, The 1964,Mr 25,46:2
Mack, Russell
Always You 1920,Ja 6,18:2
Girl From Home, The 1920,My 4,9:2
Bombo 1921,O 7,20:2
Go Easy Mabel 1922,My 9,22:2
Gingham Girl, The 1922,Ag 29,15:5
My Girl 1924,N 25,27:2
Four Flusher, The 1925,Ap 5,IX,2:4
Four Flusher, The 1925,Ap 14,27:4
Square Crooks 1926,Mr 2,23:2
Little Spitfire, The 1926,Ag 17,15:2

Mack, Russell—Cont

Talk About Girls 1927,Je 15,31:3
Storm Center 1927,D 1,33:2
Mack, Russell (Director)
Uninvited Guest, The 1927,S 28,28:2
Mack, Sweety
Conjur 1938,N 1,27:2
Mack, Tony
Troika 1930,Ap 2,32:6
Mack, Willard
Near Santa Barbara 1921,F 1,14:1
Smooth as Silk 1921,F 23,18:3
Gold 1921,Je 2,14:2
Canary Dutch 1925,S 9,22:1
All the Way From Texas 1926,Ag 8,VII,3:1
Vaudeville (Palace) 1926,S 21,32:5
Lily Sue 1926,N 17,22:2
Lily Sue 1926,N 28,VIII,1:1
Honor Be Damned! 1927,Ja 27,13:1
Scarlet Fox, The 1928,Mr 28,31:1
Vaudeville (Palace) 1929,F 4,21:4
Mack, Willard (Director)
Noose, The 1926,O 21,23:3
Honor Be Damned! 1927,Ja 27,13:1
Weather Clear, Track Fast 1927,O 19,24:5
Scarlet Fox, The 1928,Mr 28,31:1
Gang War 1928,Ag 21,27:2
Common Sin, The 1928,O 16,28:2
Mack, Willard (Playwright)
Breakfast in Bed 1920,F 4,12:1
Near Santa Barbara 1921,F 1,14:1
Smooth as Silk 1921,F 23,18:3
Ziegfeld Follies 1921,Je 22,10:1
High Stakes 1924,S 10,21:3
Dove, The 1925,F 12,17:3
Canary Dutch 1925,S 9,22:1
All the Way From Texas 1926,Ag 8,VII,3:1
Fanny 1926,S 22,30:1
Noose, The 1926,O 21,23:3
Lily Sue 1926,N 17,22:2
Lily Sue 1926,N 28,VIII,1:1
Hangman's House 1926,D 17,27:2
Trial Divorce 1927,Ja 9,30:2
Trial Divorce 1927,Ja 16,VII,2:4
Honor Be Damned! 1927,Ja 27,13:1
Wolf's Cub, The 1927,Ag 30,21:2
Weather Clear-Track Fast 1927,O 2,VIII,4:6
Weather Clear, Track Fast 1927,O 19,24:5
Free Soul, A 1928,Ja 13,26:5
Spring 3100 1928,F 16,14:2
Scarlet Fox, The 1928,Mr 28,31:1
Paid Off 1928,Jl 8,VII,1:2
Gang War 1928,Ag 12,VII,1:2
Gang War 1928,Ag 21,27:2
Common Sin, The 1928,O 16,28:2
Mack, Willard (Producer)
Gang War 1928,Ag 21,27:2
Common Sin, The 1928,O 16,28:2
Mack, William B
Crooked Gamblers 1920,Ag 2,12:1
All-Star Idlers of 1921, The 1921,Jl 16,5:2
Man in the Making, The 1921,S 21,16:2
Some Party 1922,Ap 17,22:1
Rose Bernd 1922,S 27,17:1
Rose Bernd 1922,O 8,VI,1:2
Square Peg, A 1923,Ja 29,10:2
Zeno 1923,Ag 27,14:2
Cobra 1924,Ap 23,24:1
Cobra 1924,Ap 27,VIII,1:1
Makropoulos Secret, The 1926,Ja 22,12:4
Adorable Liar, The 1926,Ag 31,15:2
Praying Curve 1927,Ja 25,18:2
Savages Under the Skin 1927,Mr 25,25:2
Revelry 1927,S 13,37:1
Kingdom of God, The 1928,D 21,30:2
Damn Your Honor 1929,D 31,14:3
House Afire 1930,Ap 1,34:7
Scarlet Sister Mary 1930,N 26,19:2
Mack and La Rue
Spider, The 1927,Mr 23,29:1
Mack Cecil Choir
Lew Leslie's Blackbirds of 1930 1930,O 23,34:5
Mack Triplets
Mr Winkle's Holliday 1946,Je 24,27:6
Mackaben, Theo (Musical Director)
Du Barry 1932,N 23,15:2
McKaig, Alexander (Producer)
Damn the Tears 1927,Ja 22,11:1
Racket, The 1927,N 23,28:3
Solid South 1930,O 15,27:1
Whistling in the Dark 1932,Ja 20,16:6
Dark Victory 1934,N 10,18:2
McKaig, James M
Fiesta 1933,D 16,12:2
McKail, David
Vivat! Vivat Regina! 1970,Jl 20,21:2
Mackaill, Dorothy
Personal Appearance 1936,Jl 9,17:4
Mackall, Lawton (Playwright)
Buy, Buy Baby 1926,O 8,26:2
Mackay, Alfred (Director)
Schoolmaster, The 1928,Mr 21,30:1
Mackay, Anne (Lighting Director)
Edge of the Sword, The 1949,N 10,40:3

Building 222 1950,F 3,28:2
Aria Da Capo 1950,My 25,36:2
Gods of the Mountain, The 1950,My 25,36:2
Once Around the Block 1950,My 25,36:2
Mackay, Barbara
Bacchae, The 1969,Mr 15,24:1
MacKay, Bruce
Shinbone Alley 1957,Ap 15,23:2
Copper and Brass 1957,O 18,19:2
Most Happy Fella, The 1959,F 11,50:2
Happy Town 1959,O 8,49:2
Greenwillow 1960,Mr 9,38:1
Greenwillow 1960,Mr 20,II,1:1
Bartleby 1961,Ja 25,28:1
Donnybrook! 1961,My 19,23:1
Her First Roman 1968,O 21,53:3
1776 1969,Mr 17,46:2
MacKay, C C
Faun, The 1924,Mr 28,17:2
McKay, Constance
Gertie 1926,N 16,24:2
Women Go on Forever 1927,S 8,25:1
Celebrity 1927,D 27,24:3
K Guy, The 1928,O 16,28:4
Tin Pan Alley 1928,N 2,29:1
This One Man 1930,O 22,32:3
Washington Heights 1931,S 30,23:4
Counsellor-at-Law 1931,N 7,17:2
Whatever Possessed Her 1934,Ja 26,21:2
Between Two Worlds 1934,O 26,24:2
Good Men and True 1935,O 26,12:4
Tell Me Pretty Maiden 1937,D 17,33:5
Flight to the West 1940,D 15,I,59:5
Flight to the West 1940,D 31,19:1
McKay, David
Chicken Every Sunday 1944,Ap 6,27:2
Late George Apley, The 1944,N 22,26:2
Late George Apley, The 1944,D 3,II,1:1
McKay, Don
West Side Story 1964,Ap 9,24:2
McKay, Donald
Late George Apley, The 1944,O 20,16:4
Mackay, Edward
Swords 1921,S 2,9:3
Tendresse, La 1922,S 26,18:1
Pasteur 1923,Mr 13,19:1
Mackay, Elsie
Poldekin 1920,S 10,12:1
Deburau 1920,D 24,14:3
Comedian, The 1923,Mr 14,14:1
Comedian, The 1923,Ap 8,VIII,1:1
New Gallantry, The 1925,S 25,24:2
McKay, Frank
Legal Grounds 1940,D 2,18:4
Mackay, Gayer (Playwright)
Paddy the Next Best Thing 1920,Ag 28,5:5
McKay, George
Honey Girl 1920,My 4,9:1
Snapshots of 1921 1921,Je 3,19:2
Rat, The 1925,F 11,19:3
Merrily We Roll Along 1934,O 1,14:1
Mackay, George E
Babes in Arms 1937,Ap 15,18:4
McKay, Gilbert
Jezebel 1933,D 20,26:3
Victoria Regina 1935,D 27,15:2
McKay, Glen
Legal Murder 1934,F 16,16:2
Mackay, Helene Marion
County Chairman, The 1936,My 26,26:5
McKay, James
Simple Simon 1931,Mr 10,23:2
McKay, Jocelyn
Fig Leaves Are Falling, The 1969,Ja 3,19:1
Sound of Music, The 1970,Jl 3,13:1
MacKay, John
Playboy of the Western World, The 1958,My 9,19:2
Under the Yum-Yum Tree 1960,N 17,45:1
Gift of Time, A 1962,F 23,34:1
Henry V 1964,My 13,52:1
Saint Joan 1964,My 14,41:1
Richard III 1965,Je 3,26:1
Borstal Boy 1970,Ap 1,38:1
McKay, Kay
Starlight 1925,Mr 4,17:2
Arabesque 1925,O 21,20:2
One Man's Woman 1926,My 26,25:1
Artists and Models 1930,Je 11,33:2
Meet My Sister 1931,N 11:1
McKay, Kay (Producer)
Jefferson Davis 1936,F 19,17:2
Mackay, Marianne (Miscellaneous)
Riot Act, The 1963,Mr 9,5:2
McKay, Morris
Main Street 1921,O 6,21:1
Monster, The 1922,Ag 10,20:3
Rose Bernd 1922,S 27,17:1
Rose Bernd 1922,O 8,VI,1:2
Romeo and Juliet 1922,D 28,20:1
Laughing Lady, The 1923,F 13,25:1
Rivals, The 1923,My 9,14:2
School for Scandal, The 1923,Je 5,24:3
Breaking Point, The 1923,Ag 17,8:4

McKay, Morris—Cont

Red Hawk, The 1923,D 2,VIII,2:1
Red Falcon, The 1924,O 8,22:1
Virgin of Bethulia, The 1925,F 24,17:2
Taps 1925,Ap 15,16:2
Man or Devil 1925,My 22,22:4
Shanghai Gesture, The 1926,F 2,20:2
Chief Thing, The 1926,Mr 23,24:2
Off Key 1927,F 9,16:2
Volpone 1928,Ap 10,32:1
Kingdom of God, The 1928,D 21,30:2
Third Day, The 1929,Ag 13,23:4
Prima Donna 1929,S 22,IX,2:6
Road to Rome, The 1929,N 23,19:1
Road to Rome, The 1929,D 29,VIII,2:6
Colonel Satan 1931,Ja 12,24:1
Woman Denied, A 1931,F 26,21:1
School for Scandal, The 1931,N 11,26:4
Before Morning 1933,F 10,13:4
Simpleton of the Unexpected Isles, The
  1935,F 19,27:5
Country Wife, The 1935,Jl 2,24:2
Coward, The 1935,Jl 16,24:1
If This Be Treason 1935,Jl 30,17:1
Romance 1935,Ag 27,23:4
If This Be Treason 1935,S 24,28:2
Ghosts 1935,D 13,30:6
Ghosts 1936,My 12,26:8
Hedda Gabler 1936,N 17,34:4
Retreat From Folly 1937,Je 29,18:3
Princess Turandot 1937,Ag 3,20:5
Romance 1937,Ag 17,23:1
Merchant of Venice, The 1938,Ja 15,18:8
Herod and Marianne 1938,O 27,27:2
American Way, The 1939,Ja 23,9:2
Farm of Three Echoes 1939,N 29,18:3
Another Sun 1940,F 24,8:6
Return of the Vagabond, The 1940,My 14,27:2
Wind in the Sails 1940,Ag 1,24:6
Eight O'Clock Tuesday 1941,Ja 7,18:2
Ring Around Elizabeth 1941,N 18,32:2
Three Sisters, The 1942,D 22,31:2
Three Sisters, The 1942,D 27,VIII,1:1
Barretts of Wimpole Street, The 1945,Mr 27,23:6
Barretts of Wimpole Street, The 1945,Ap 1,II,1:1
Lute Song 1946,F 7,29:2
MacKay, Norman
Boy Meets Girl 1943,Je 23,15:5
Feathers in a Gale 1943,D 22,26:2
Diamond Lil 1948,N 30,33:2
Mackay, Phoebe
Live Life Again 1945,O 1,14:7
Man and Superman 1947,O 9,31:2
Man and Superman 1949,My 17,28:6
Come of Age 1952,Ja 24,22:2
In the Summer House 1953,D 30,17:1
Boy Friend, The 1954,O 1,20:1
Boy Friend, The 1958,Ja 27,24:4
Mackay, Richard
Coquette 1935,Jl 10,24:1
Hay Fever 1935,Jl 24,20:4
Camille 1935,Jl 31,21:1
Mr Pim Passes By 1935,Ag 7,22:2
Vinegar Tree, The 1935,Ag 14,16:1
Double Door 1935,Ag 21,22:2
Late Christopher Bean, The 1935,Ag 28,13:1
Pursuit of Happiness, The 1936,Jl 15,14:1
Kind Lady 1937,Jl 21,19:3
Fly Away Home 1937,Jl 28,15:1
Candida 1937,Ag 4,14:5
Whiteheaded Boy, The 1937,Ag 11,27:3
Ode to Liberty 1937,Ag 18,15:2
Goodbye Again 1937,S 1,15:1
Audition of the Apprentice Theatre 1939,Je 2,26:2
Liliom 1940,Mr 26,17:2
Jeannie 1940,N 13,29:2
Flying Gerardos, The 1940,D 30,21:4
McKay, Scott
Swan Song 1946,My 16,29:2
Another Part of the Forest 1946,N 21,42:2
Mr Barry's Etchings 1950,F 1,26:2
Live Wire, The 1950,Ag 18,16:2
Bell, Book and Candle 1950,N 15,37:4
Bell, Book and Candle 1950,D 17,II,3:1
First Lady 1952,My 29,18:5
Sabrina Fair 1953,N 12,37:1
Brigadoon 1957,Mr 28,37:1
Nature's Way 1957,O 17,42:2
Requiem for a Nun 1959,Ja 31,13:2
Once for the Asking 1963,N 21,42:2
Brigadoon 1964,D 24,9:1
Little Foxes, The 1968,Ja 6,24:4
McKay, Tony
Man Better Man 1969,Jl 3,22:1
McKay (Producer)
Paging Danger 1931,F 27,19:2
Mackaye, Dorothy
Seeing Things 1920,Je 18,19:2
Getting Gertie's Garter 1921,Ag 2,16:2
It's a Boy! 1922,Jl 23,VI,1:6
It's a Boy! 1922,S 20,18:3
Mike Angelo 1923,Ja 9,26:2
What's Your Wife Doing? 1923,O 2,10:3
Rose Marie 1924,S 3,12:2
Song of the Flame 1925,D 31,10:2

Mackaye, Dorothy—Cont
Ladies of Creation 1931,S 9,25:1
Cold in Sables 1931,D 24,20:7
Mackaye, Elsie
Dark Angel, The 1925,F 11,19:2
MacKaye, Percy
Nantucket Follies 1927,Jl 30,13:2
MacKaye, Percy (Playwright)
George Washington 1920,Mr 2,9:1
Jeanne d'Arc 1922,Ap 22,9:3
This Fine-Pretty World 1923,D 27,11:1
Ghost of Elsinore, The 1949,Ap 16,10:2
Serpent in the Orchard, The 1949,Ap 24,II,1:1
Scarecrow, The 1953,Je 17,31:1
McKayle, Donald (Choreographer)
Tempest, The 1962,Jl 17,18:2
As You Like It 1963,Jl 17,19:2
Golden Boy 1964,O 21,56:1
Golden Boy 1964,N 1,II,1:1
Time for Singing, A 1966,My 23,48:2
McKayle, Donald (Director)
Free and Easy 1959,D 15,51:4
Free and Easy 1959,D 20,II,3:2
Trumpets of the Lord 1963,D 23,22:3
I'm Solomon 1968,Ap 24,51:1
McKayle, Donald (Miscellaneous)
Redhead 1959,F 6,21:1
McKayle, Donny
Talent '54 1954,Ap 13,40:1
Macke, Bob
Go, Go, Go, God is Dead! 1966,O 12,37:1
McKean, Harry
Saint Wench 1933,Ja 3,19:3
McKean, Thomas (Playwright)
Main Line, The 1924,Mr 26,19:4
Main Line, The 1924,Mr 30,VIII,1:1
Mackeben, Theo (Composer)
Journalisten, Die 1932,Jl 17,IX,1:1
Mackeben, Theo (Musical Director)
Du Barry 1931,S 20,VIII,2:7
MacKechnie, Donald (Miscellaneous)
Back to Methuselah 1969,Ag 31,46:3
MacKechnie, Donald (Producer)
Travails of Sancho Panza, The 1969,D 20,35:1
McKechnie, Donna
Education of H*Y*M*A*N K*A*P*L*A*N, The 1968,Ap 5,57:1
Promises, Promises 1968,D 2,59:3
Company 1970,Ap 27,40:1
Company 1970,My 3,II,1:4
McKee, Blanchard
El Cristo 1926,My 9,II,1:4
McKee, Donald
White Wings 1926,O 16,15:1
Before You're 25 1929,Ap 17,30:2
Brigadoon 1950,My 3,36:2
Ladies of the Corridor, The 1953,O 22,33:5
His and Hers 1954,Ja 8,18:2
Grand Prize, The 1955,Ja 27,17:1
McKee, Georgette
Growing Pains 1933,N 24,24:2
Fly Away Home 1935,Ja 16,20:4
McKee, Harry
Springtime of Youth 1922,O 27,15:1
Connie Goes Home 1923,S 7,10:1
Piker, The 1925,Ja 16,14:1
Jefferson Davis 1936,F 19,17:2
Horse Eats Hat 1936,S 28,14:2
Doctor Faustus 1937,Ja 9,21:2
McKee, Jack
Spring 3100 1928,F 16,14:2
Back Here 1928,N 27,36:3
Town's Woman, The 1929,Mr 12,26:2
Greater Love 1931,Mr 3,39:1
Constant Sinner, The 1931,S 15,30:1
Rain· 1935,F 13,24:1
McKee, Jack (Director)
Kansas City Kitty 1929,S 26,27:4
McKee, Jack (Producer)
Kansas City Kitty 1929,S 26,27:4
McKee, Jeanelle (Producer)
Kaleidoscope 1957,Je 14,20:2
McKee, John
Hotel. Alimony 1934,Ja 30,16:2
Whatever Goes Up 1935,N 26,28:2
Three Wise Fools 1936,Mr 2,12:2
All the Living 1938,Mr 25,14:4
Gloriana 1938,N 26,18:4
Jeremiah 1939,F 4,11:2
Brown Danube, The 1939,My 18,30:4
Woman Brown, The 1939,D 9,18:5
Popsy 1941,F 11,26:2
More the Merrier, The 1941,S 16,19:3
Strings, My Lord, Are False, The 1942,My 20,24:2
Magic 1942,S 30,28:2
Moon Vine, The 1943,F 12,22:2
Embezzled Heaven 1944,N 1,20:2
Signature 1945,F 15,25:2
Second Best Bed 1946,Je 4,20:2
Miracle in the Mountains 1947,Ap 26,10:2
Hallams, The 1948,Mr 5,18:2
Big Knife, The 1949,F 25,27:5

Design For A Stained Glass Window 1950,Ja 24,26:2
Romeo and Juliet 1951,Mr 12,21:2
McKee, Lillian
Goat Alley 1921,Je 21,20:2
McKee, Margaret
Vaudeville (Lexington) 1921,O 18,20:2
Irving Berlin's New Music Box Revue 1922,O 24,18:1
Vaudeville (Hippodrome) 1924,F 19,12:1
Untitled-Revue 1924,F 19,12:1
McKee, Wesley (Director)
Good Fairy, The 1939,Ag 30,15:5
Our Town 1944,Ja 11,24:5
McKee & Kramer
Laffing Room Only 1944,D 25,15:4
McKeehan, Gary
Chemmy Circle, The 1968,Ag 10,17:2
McKeen, Hale (Director)
Touchstone 1953,F 4,33:2
McKeen, John
Star of Bengal 1929,S 26,27:2
McKeever, Jacqueline
Oh Captain! 1958,F 5,21:2
Wonderful Town 1963,F 15,10:2
MacKellar, Helen
Beyond the Horizon 1920,F 4,12:1
Beyond the Horizon 1920,F 8,VIII,2:1
Back Pay 1921,Ag 21,VI,1:8
Back Pay 1921,Ag 31,8:2
Bought and Paid For 1921,D 8,17:5
Shadow, The 1922,Ap 25,14:2
Shadow, The 1922,Ap 30,VII,1:1
Masked Woman, The 1922,D 23,14:2
Desert Flower, The 1924,N 19,18:2
Good Bad Woman, A 1925,F 10,21:1
Mud Turtle, The 1925,Ag 21,8:2
Mud Turtle, The 1925,S 6,VII,1:1
Open House 1925,N 1,VIII,2:4
Open House 1925,D 15,28:3
Romancing 'Round 1927,O 4,32:4
Lovebound 1929,My 19,IX,2:1
Through the Night 1930,Ag 19,19:1
Bloody Laughter 1931,D 5,20:6
Return of Hannibal, The 1937,F 2,21:1
McKellen, Ian
Lily of Little India, A 1966,Ja 22,17:2
Promise, The 1967,N 15,38:1
Promise, The 1967,N 26,II,1:1
Richard II 1969,S 4,50:1
Edward II 1969,S 4,50:1
McKellen Brothers
Ice Follies 1941,D 2,32:2
Macken, Walter
King of Friday's Men, The 1951,F 22,26:2
Home Is the Hero 1954,S 23,42:2
Macken, Walter (Playwright)
Home Is the Hero 1954,S 23,42:2
Mackendrick, Alexander (Director)
Face of a Hero 1960,O 21,29:5
McKendrick, Blaine
Hot Water 1929,Ja 22,22:3
McKenna, Boots
Bunk of 1926 1926,F 17,12:3
Bunk of 1926 1926,Ap 23,25:2
McKenna, Boots (Choreographer)
Gang's All Here, The 1931,F 19,21:3
Saluta 1934,Ag 29,13:4
Sketch Book 1935,Je 5,22:2
Student Prince, The 1937,Jl 28,15:1
Anything Goes 1937,Ag 26,24:3
Lady Says Yes, A 1945,Ja 11,18:5
McKenna, Boots (Miscellaneous)
Lady Says Yes, A 1945,Ja 11,18:5
McKenna, Edwin
Tobias and the Angel 1937,Ap 29,16:5
McKenna, Harry
Adding Machine, The 1923,Mr 20,24:1
McKenna, James (Playwright)
Scatterin', The 1960,S 15,44:2
MacKenna, Kenneth
Opportunity 1920,Jl 31,5:1
Immodest Violet 1920,Ag 25,6:2
Nest, The 1922,F 2,20:1
Endless Chain, The 1922,S 5,21:2
World We Live In, The 1922,N 1,16:1
Mad Honeymoon, The 1923,Ag 8,10:1
Crooked Square, The 1923,S 11,10:2
Windows 1923,O 9,17:2
Dumb-Bell 1923,N 27,23:2
We Moderns 1924,Mr 12,17:2
Catskill Dutch 1924,My 7,18:1
Nerves 1924,S 2,22:2
Nerves 1924,S 7,VII,1:1
Far Cry, The 1924,O 1,24:1
Sapphire Ring, The 1925,Ap 16,25:2
Oh! Mama 1925,Ag 20,22:2
Masque of Venice, The 1926,Mr 3,27:3
What Every Woman Knows 1926,Ap 14,20:2
Big Pond, The 1928,Ag 22,25:1
Play Without a Name, A 1928,N 26,30:5
By Your Leave 1934,Ja 25,15:3
Wife Insurance 1934,Ap 13,24:5

MacKenna, Kenneth—Cont
Othello 1934,Jl 22,23:4
Othello 1934,Jl 29,IX,1:3
Merrily We Roll Along 1934,O 1,14:1
Merrily We Roll Along 1934,O 7,IX,1:1
Othello 1935,S 22,X,2:5
Othello 1935,S 28,13:2
Macbeth 1935,O 8,26:4
Aged 26 1936,D 22,32:1
Penny Wise 1937,Ap 20,28:6
Highest Tree, The 1959,N 5,41:1
MacKenna, Kenneth (Director)
Co-Respondent Unknown 1936,F 12,24:4
Be So Kindly 1937,F 9,19:4
MacKenna, Kenneth (Producer)
Co-Respondent Unknown 1936,F 12,24:4
McKenna, Margaret
Earth Journey 1944,Ap 28,24:2
McKenna, Marilyn
Midsummer Night's Dream, A 1967,Je 19,42:1
McKenna, Michael
Bead-Tangle 1970,Jl 16,38:1
McKenna, Philip C (Miscellaneous)
She Loves Me 1963,Ap 24,39:1
McKenna, Siobhan
Saint Joan 1955,F 13,II,3:1
Saint Joan 1955,My 29,II,1:1
Chalk Garden, The 1955,O 27,29:1
Chalk Garden, The 1955,N 13,II,1:1
Saint Joan 1956,S 12,42:1
Saint Joan 1956,S 16,II,1:1
Hamlet 1957,Ja 29,27:1
Twelfth Night 1957,Jl 4,16:4
Twelfth Night 1957,Jl 7,II,1:1
Rope Dancers, The 1957,N 21,39:1
Rope Dancers, The 1957,D 1,II,1:1
Twelfth Night 1959,Jl 11,10:2
Macbeth 1959,Ag 1,9:2
St Joan of the Stockyards 1964,Je 12,45:1
Juno and the Paycock 1966,Ag 3,40:1
Best of Friends 1970,F 21,22:1
McKenna, T P
Contractor, The 1970,Ag 17,32:1
McKenna, Thomas
Trial of Dr Beck, The 1937,Ag 10,22:2
McKennan, Arnett
Foemen of the Yard 1935,Ap 6,10:4
McKennan, Arnett (Playwright)
Come Across 1937,Ap 10,10:7
McKenney, Chick
Change Your Luck 1930,Je 7,10:2
McKenney, Morris
Never No More 1932,Ja 8,27:1
If Booth Had Missed 1932,F 5,24:2
Black Souls 1932,Mr 31,25:1
Louisiana 1933,F 28,15:5
Green Pastures, The 1935,F 27,16:2
Mulatto 1935,O 25,25:2
Conjur 1938,N 1,27:2
Signature 1945,F 15,25:2
Jeb 1946,F 22,20:2
McKenney, Ruth (Original Author)
My Sister Eileen 1940,D 27,23:2
My Sister Eileen 1941,Ja 5,IX,1:1
Wonderful Town 1953,Mr 8,II,1:1
Wonderful Town 1954,My 7,II,1:1
Loud Red Patrick, The 1956,O 4,28:1
Wonderful Town 1958,Mr 6,32:4
McKenney, Ruth (Playwright)
Wonderful Town 1953,F 26,22:3
Wonderful Town 1963,F 15,10:2
Mackenroth, Steven
Macbeth 1968,N 30,49:3
MacKenzie, Alice
Some Party 1922,Ap 17,22:1
Judy 1927,F 8,20:2
Houseboat on the Styx, The 1928,D 26,14:3
Silver Swan, The 1929,N 28,34:5
Chocolate Soldier, The 1930,Ja 28,28:1
Menagerie 1935,Jl 2,24:3
Strings, My Lord, Are False, The 1942,My 20,24:2
MacKenzie, Compton (Original Author)
Babes in the Zoo 1930,F 26,22:3
MacKenzie, Compton (Playwright)
Babes in the Zoo 1930,F 26,22:3
MacKenzie, Donald
Spider, The 1927,Mr 23,29:1
If This Be Treason 1935,S 24,28:2
First Lady 1935,N 27,17:4
Love in My Fashion 1937,D 4,21:4
Window Shopping 1938,D 24,13:2
Ladies and Gentlemen 1939,O 18,30:2
McKenzie, Fay
Meet the People 1940,D 26,22:2
Mackenzie, Ian Lloyd (Scenic Designer)
Marigold 1930,O 9,23:1
McKenzie, J M
Bunch and Judy, The 1922,N 29,20:1
Mackenzie, Jack
Checkerboard, The 1920,Ag 20,7:2
McKenzie, James B (Producer)
Major Barbara 1965,My 18,33:1
Girl in the Freudian Slip, The 1967,My 19,34:3

MacKenzie, Jan
Me and Juliet 1970,My 15,42:1
McKenzie, Jane
Farewell to Arms, A 1930,S 23,30:3
Music Hath Charms 1934,D 31,8:2
MacKenzie, Kenneth
Carousel 1949,Ja 26,28:2
Carousel 1949,F 6,II,1:1
McKenzie, Louis
Cave at Machpelah, The 1959,Jl 1,25:1
Connection, The 1959,Jl 16,30:2
Marrying Maiden, The 1960,Je 23,18:3
MacKenzie, Margaret (Playwright)
Young Visitors, The 1920,N 30,14:1
Mackenzie, Michael
Via Crucis 1923,N 13,25:2
Hamlet 1923,N 20,23:3
McKenzie, Neil (Director)
Guests of the Nation 1958,My 21,40:1
Aria Da Capo 1958,My 21,40:1
Aria Da Capo 1958,Je 27,18:5
Guests of the Nation 1958,Je 27,18:5
Cockeyed Kite 1961,S 14,27:1
McKenzie, Neil (Playwright)
Guests of the Nation 1958,My 21,40:1
Guests of the Nation 1958,Je 27,18:5
Guests of the Nation 1958,Ag 31,II,1:1
McKenzie, Richard
9 by Six: A Cry of Players 1956,D 5,49:2
Lonesome Train, The 1965,Je 17,25:1
Hard Travelin' 1965,Je 17,25:1
Great White Hope, The 1967,D 14,58:1
Iceman Cometh, The 1968,Ap 1,58:1
Indians 1969,O 14,51:1
Nobody Hears A Broken Drum 1970,Mr 20,55:1
McKenzie, Ronald (Playwright)
Musical Chairs 1931,D 6,VIII,2:7
Maitlands, The 1934,Jl 22,IX,1:3
Musical Chairs 1934,Jl 31,20:7
Mackenzie, Scobie (Playwright)
Jolly Roger 1933,Mr 26,IX,1:1
Mackenzie, Thomas
No More Peace 1937,F 27,9:1
MacKenzie, Will
Put It in Writing 1963,My 14,31:1
Morning Sun 1963,O 7,36:2
Brigadoon 1964,D 24,9:1
Half a Sixpence 1965,Ap 26,38:2
Hello, Dolly! 1965,Ag 10,17:2
Sheep on the Runway 1970,F 2,28:3
McKeon, Joey
Hold Your Horses 1933,S 26,26:4
McKeown, Charles
Measure for Measure 1967,F 15,37:1
Romeo and Juliet 1967,F 22,18:1
MacKeown, M J J (Playwright)
Real McCoy, The 1928,Jl 15,VIII,2:1
McKereghan, William
Prince of Peasantmania 1970,F 22,88:1
McKern, Leo
Lark, The 1955,My 13,21:2
Cat on a Hot Tin Roof 1958,Ja 31,24:2
Man for All Seasons, A 1961,N 23,51:1
Man for All Seasons, A 1961,D 3,II,1:1
Peer Gynt 1962,S 27,33:7
McKernan, Suzanne
White-Headed Boy, The 1921,S 16,20:1
McKesson, Mary
Riff-Raff 1926,F 9,18:6
Mackesy, John
Well of the Saints, The 1932,Ja 22,15:2
Is Life Worth Living? 1933,N 10,24:6
MacKeuar, Helen
Maggie 1924,N 2,VII,2:3
Mackey, Bill
High John De Conquer 1969,Ap 23,39:1
Mackey, George
Coquette 1935,My 22,23:4
Mackey, Keith
Candida 1970,Ap 7,41:1
Mackey, Robert (Costume Designer)
Man and Superman 1960,N 7,46:2
Mackey, William Wellington (Playwright)
Bill Noname 1970,Mr 3,37:1
Mackiammoir, Michael
Ever the Twain 1929,O 20,III,3:5
McKible, Joel
Mary Stuart 1956,Ap 28,10:2
Mackie, Elsie
Kind Lady 1937,Jl 6,23:1
Ghost for Sale 1941,S 30,27:4
Mackie, Robert
Lonesome Train, The 1965,Je 17,25:1
Mackie, Robert (Costume Designer)
Heartbreak House 1963,Je 28,24:1
Mackie & Lavallie
Murder at the Vanities 1933,S 13,22:4
McKim, Josephine
Dance Night 1938,O 15,20:5
Family Portrait 1939,Mr 9,18:4
McKim, Lois
Visit, The 1958,My 6,40:1

Potting Shed, The 1958,N 3,49:2
Mackin, Clara
Face Value 1921,D 27,10:2
Loves of Lulu, The 1925,My 12,26:1
McKinley, Andrew
Consul, The 1950,Mr 2,32:3
Consul, The 1950,Mr 16,41:1
Consul, The 1950,Mr 26,II,1:1
McKinley, Mary (Costume Designer)
Courageous One, The 1958,Ja 21,33:6
Smokeweaver's Daughter, The 1959,Ap 15,30:1
Calculated Risk 1962,N 1,35:1
Heroine, The 1963,F 21,5:5
Holiday on Ice 1965,S 2,38:4
Keep It in the Family 1967,S 28,59:1
McKinley, Roy
Green Pastures, The 1935,F 27,16:2
McKinley, Violet
Chalk Dust 1936,Mr 5,24:5
Path of Flowers, The 1936,S 18,19:3
McKinnel, Norman
Family Man, A 1921,Je 26,VI,1:1
Truth About Blayds, The 1922,Ja 15,VI,1:7
Old English 1924,O 26,VIII,1:1
Old English 1924,N 9,VIII,2:3
Habit 1926,N 4,VIII,4:7
Hen Upon a Steeple 1927,Ap 24,VII,2:3
Devil, The 1930,F 2,VIII,2:4
To Account Rendered 1931,F 15,VIII,2:5
McKinney, Duane
Walk Into My Parlor 1941,N 20,38:2
McKinney, Duane (Director)
Sea Gull, The 1954,My 12,38:1
McKinney, Duane (Miscellaneous)
Can-Can 1959,Ag 26,25:4
McKinney, James (Miscellaneous)
Immoralist, The 1963,N 8,36:2
McKinney, Morris
Born Yesterday 1954,Ja 1,16:6
McKinney, Nina Mae
Ballyhoo of 1932 1932,S 7,14:2
McKinnon, Andrea
Aloma of the South Seas 1925,Ap 21,18:1
MacKinnon, Cecil
Alice in Wonderland 1970,O 9,43:1
MacKinnon, Georgia
Once in a Lifetime 1930,S 25,22:3
McKinnon, Rik
Ice Follies 1966,Ja 12,27:6
MacKinnon, Sterling A
Awhile to Work 1937,Mr 20,23:1
McKinsey, Beverlee
PS 193 1962,O 31,33:1
Love Nest, The 1963,Ja 28,7:6
All the King's Men 1963,Jl 12,12:1
Who's Afraid of Virginia Woolf? 1964,F 8,15:1
Mackintosh, Agnes (Gordon Daviot) (Playwright)
Laughing Woman, The 1934,Ap 8,33:6
Mackintosh, Kenneth
Beaux' Stratagem, The 1970,F 10,50:2
Three Sisters, The 1970,F 22,II,1:1
Mackintosh, Louise
Some Party 1922,Ap 17,22:1
Awful Truth, The 1922,S 19,14:3
Lost 1927,Mr 29,22:2
Playing the Game 1927,D 20,32:5
Silver Box, The 1928,Ja 18,23:1
Phantom Lover, The 1928,S 25,25:1
Houseparty 1929,S 10,26:5
Mackintosh, Robert (Costume Designer)
Wish You Were Here 1952,Je 26,26:6
Gambler, The 1952,O 14,40:1
At Home With Ethel Waters 1953,S 23,36:1
Anniversary Waltz 1954,Ap 8,34:1
Boy Friend, The 1954,O 1,20:1
Silk Stockings 1955,F 25,17:3
Mr Wonderful 1956,Mr 23,23:2
Fair Game 1957,N 4,39:1
Interlock 1958,F 7,18:1
Third Best Sport 1958,D 31,15:3
Masquerade 1959,Mr 17,42:1
Second String, A 1960,Ap 14,36:2
Hotel Passionato 1965,O 23,16:1
Mame 1966,My 25,41:1
Sherry! 1967,Mr 29,39:1
How Now, Dow Jones 1967,D 8,53:1
Fig Leaves Are Falling, The 1969,Ja 3,19:1
Butterflies Are Free 1969,O 22,30:1
McKissick, Stanford
Kilpatrick's Old-Time Minstrels 1930,Ap 21,20:2
Mackle, Jane
Yours Is My Heart 1946,S 6,16:5
Mackley, John
Veils 1928,Mr 14,28:5
Macklin, Frederick
Gift, The 1924,Ja 23,15:4
Taps 1925,Ap 15,16:2
Thieves 1926,Je 8,23:1
Vaudeville (Palace) 1926,Je 8,23:1
McKnight, John
Elliott Murphy's Aquashow 1955,Je 23,25:1
Elliott Murphy's Aquashow 1956,Je 20,26:2

McKnight, John (Director)
Aquarama 1960 1960,Jl 1,14:6
Mermaid's Holiday 1961,Jl 1,8:1
McKnight, John (Producer)
Mermaid's Holiday 1961,Jl 1,8:1
McKnight, Theodore
But for the Grace of God 1937,Ja 13,21:4
McKnight, Thomas H
Thumbs Down 1923,Ag 7,20:1
McKnight, Thomas H (Playwright)
Blue Blood 1924,Ap 3,21:2
Double Dummy 1936,N 12,30:1
Streets of Paris, The 1939,Je 20,25:2
McKool, Yolanda
These Are the Times 1950,My 11,37:2
Macks, Helen
Neighbors 1923,D 27,11:1
Yellow 1926,S 22,30:1
Mackus, Dalia
Mother Courage and Her Children 1964,My 12,32:2
McKusick, Hal
Sandbox, The 1960,My 17,42:2
Two Executioners, The 1960,My 17,42:2
MacLachlan, Janet
Raisin' Hell in the Son 1962,Jl 3,13:2
Tiger Tiger Burning Bright 1962,D 24,5:2
Death of a Salesman 1963,Jl 20,11:2
McLaglen, Clifford
Affair of State, An 1930,N 20,30:3
McLain, George
You Can't Take It With You 1945,Mr 27,23:7
McLain, George (Miscellaneous)
On Whitman Avenue 1946,My 9,28:2
McLain, John (Lighting Director)
View From the Bridge, A 1965,Ja 29,24:1
Hamlet 1968,Je 10,59:1
Tiny Alice 1969,S 30,42:1
Flea in Her Ear, A 1969,O 4,25:1
Three Sisters, The 1969,O 10,38:1
McLain, Minor
Florodora 1920,Ap 6,18:1
McLallen, Jack
Vaudeville (Palace) 1924,Ja 22,15:6
Vaudeville (Palace) 1928,O 9,35:2
Vaudeville (Palace) 1931,Jl 6,24:6
McLallen, Jack and Sarah
Vaudeville (Palace) 1926,S 14,25:3
MacLane, Barton
Trial of Mary Dugan, The 1927,S 20,33:1
Gods of the Lightning 1928,O 25,27:2
Subway Express 1929,S 25,34:3
Steel 1931,N 19,26:5
Tree, The 1932,Ap 13,23:5
Rendezvous 1932,O 13,22:3
Hangman's Whip 1933,F 25,20:2
Yellow Jack 1934,Mr 7,22:6
Hide and Seek 1934,Ag 7,20:2
MacLane, Barton (Playwright)
Rendezvous 1932,O 13,22:3
MacLane, Gretchen
Jonah! 1966,F 16,52:1
McLane, Wood (Scenic Designer)
Awake and Sing! 1938,D 23,16:6
McLaren, Charlene
Ice Capades 1969,Ja 8,42:1
Maclaren, Ian
Iphigenie in Tauris 1915,Je 1,15:5
Mob, The 1920,O 11,18:1
Whispering Well, The 1920,D 6,19:1
Great Adventure, The 1921,F 26,9:2
Harlequinade 1921,My 11,20:3
Fan, The 1921,O 4,10:1
Hindu, The 1922,Mr 22,13:3
Green Ring, The 1922,Ap 5,22:1
Makers of Light 1922,My 24,22:3
Merchant of Venice, The 1922,D 22,13:1
Saint Joan 1923,D 29,8:4
Saint Joan 1924,Ja 6,VII,1:1
Green Beetle, The 1924,S 3,12:3
Little Clay Cart, The 1924,D 6,13:3
Exiles 1925,F 20,20:2
Critic, The 1925,My 9,12:4
Grand Street Follies, The 1925,Je 19,24:1
Dybbuk, The 1925,D 16,22:2
Apothecary, The 1926,Mr 17,28:1
Romantic Young Lady, The 1926,My 5,24:3
Grand Street Follies, The 1926,Je 16,23:2
Lion Tamer, The 1926,O 8,26:1
Dybbuk, The 1926,D 17,27:2
Commedia Dell' Arte 1927,Ap 6,24:3
Ladder, The 1927,O 7,24:2
Electra 1927,D 2,20:6
Furies, The 1928,Mr 8,23:1
Merry-Go-Round 1932,Ap 23,11:2
Midsummer Night's Dream, A 1932,N 18,22:2
Twelfth Night 1932,N 20,20:5
Comedy of Errors, The 1932,N 22,25:3
Merchant of Venice, The 1932,N 24,34:5
This Our House 1935,D 12,33:3
Truly Valiant 1936,Ja 10,17:3
Hallowe'en 1936,F 21,20:3
Seventh Trumpet, The 1941,N 22,10:6
Earth Journey 1944,Ap 28,24:2

McLaren, Jack
Biff, Bing, Bang 1921,My 10,20:1

MacLaren, June
Lady in the Dark 1941,Ja 24,14:2

MacLaren, Margaret
Knickerbocker Holiday 1938,O 20,26:2

Maclaren, Pauline
This Our House 1935,D 12,33:3

MacLarnie, Thomas
Rising Son, The 1924,O 28,27:2
Stork, The 1925,Ja 27,14:2
Wild Birds 1925,Ap 10,16:1
Cyclone Lover, The 1928,Je 6,23:3

McLaughlin, Alexander
Bridal Crown, The 1938,F 7,11:2

McLaughlin, Andra
Hollywood Ice Revue 1953,Ja 16,17:2
Hollywood Ice Revue 1955 1955,Ja 14,16:1
Elliott Murphy's Aquashow 1955,Je 23,25:1
Hollywood Ice Revue 1956,Ja 13,17:1
Ice Follies 1957,Ja 16,36:1
Ice Follies 1958,Ja 15,26:2

McLaughlin, Cele
Far Away Horses 1933,Mr 22,21:6
Thunder on the Left 1933,N 1,25:2
Wednesday's Child 1934,Ja 17,23:2
Lonesome West, The 1936,Je 30,15:1
Too True to Be Good 1937,Jl 27,24:2
Cloud 7 1958,F 15,15:2

McLaughlin, Constance
Charm School, The 1920,Ag 3,12:1

MacLaughlin, Don
Fifth Column, The 1940,Mr 7,18:2
Virginia Reel 1947,Ap 15,28:2
Happy Journey to Trenton and Camden, The
1948,Mr 21,II,1:1

McLaughlin, Dorothy
Streets of New York, The 1934,Jl 21,14:5
Oliver Twist 1934,Ag 11,16:5

McLaughlin, Frances
Charm School, The 1920,Ag 3,12:1

McLaughlin, Gerard
Career Angel 1943,N 19,24:2

McLaughlin, J S
Playboy of the Western World, The 1930,Ja 3,20:4
Sing High, Sing Low 1931,N 13,26:4
Devil's Little Game, The 1932,Ag 2,20:4
Triplets 1932,S 22,25:2

McLaughlin, James
House of Fear, The 1929,O 8,34:2

McLaughlin, Jane (Choreographer)
South Pacific 1968,Je 30,54:2
South Pacific 1969,Jl 7,27:1

McLaughlin, Jean
Nine Till Six 1936,Mr 14,10:3

McLaughlin, Kathryn
Vaudeville (Palace) 1924,Ap 29,12:2

McLaughlin, Marian
Legal Murder 1934,F 16,16:2

McLaughlin, Mignon (Playwright)
Gayden 1949,My 11,34:4

McLaughlin, Millicent
Antigone 1923,My 4,18:4

McLaughlin, Rita
Warm Body, A 1967,Ap 17,44:2

McLaughlin, Robert (Playwright)
Decameron Nights 1922,Ap 21,14:5
Pearl of Great Price, The 1926,N 2,34:3
Fires of Spring 1929,O 13,IX,5:1
Gayden 1949,My 11,34:4

McLaughlin, Vic
Spring 3100 1928,F 16,14:2

McLaughlin and Evans
Vaudeville (Palace) 1927,O 25,33:2

McLaurin, Billy
Messin' Around 1929,Ap 23,26:3

McLaurin, Kate L (Playwright)
When We Are Young 1920,N 23,11:1
Six-Fifty, The 1921,O 2,VII,1:8
Six-Fifty, The 1921,O 25,20:1
Six-Fifty, The 1921,O 30,VI,1:1
Whispering Wires 1922,Ag 8,26:2
It All Depends 1925,Ag 11,16:4
Caught 1925,O 6,31:2

McLean, Alan
Savonarola 1942,Ap 24,20:2

McLean, Arthur
Ol' Man Satan 1932,O 4,26:3
Porgy and Bess 1935,O 11,30:2
Porgy and Bess 1942,Ja 23,16:2

MacLean, Barbara Barondess
Faithfully Yours 1951,O 19,22:5

McLean, Betty
Three Doors 1925,Ap 24,16:4
Brother Elks 1925,S 15,29:2
Hearts Are Trumps! 1927,Ap 8,21:1

McLean, Beverley
Ice Follies 1961,Ja 11,25:2

McLean, Bob and Orchestra
Vaudeville (Palace) 1923,Ja 16,16:3

McLean, Bobby
Vaudeville (Hippodrome) 1926,Mr 30,20:4
Vaudeville (Hippodrome) 1926,My 4,31:2

McLean, Carolyne
Myrtie 1924,F 5,21:2
All Wet 1925,Jl 7,24:1
Head First 1926,Ja 7,22:4
Katy Did 1927,My 10,24:3
Betty, Be Careful 1931,My 5,33:3

McLean, Charles
Biff, Bing, Bang 1921,My 10,20:1

McLean, Doreen
Bell for Adano, A 1944,D 7,21:2
Copper and Brass 1957,O 18,19:2

Maclean, Dorothy
Bureau-Crazy 1935,Ag 29,25:4

McLean, Douglas
Saint's Parade 1930,N 1,23:4
Case of Libel, A 1963,O 11,43:2

MacLean, Douglas (Producer)
Suspect 1940,Ap 10,30:4

McLean, Fred
Red Light Annie 1923,Ag 22,10:3

MacLean, Hector
Darker Flower, A 1963,Mr 11,7:2

McLean, Ian
Storm Over Patsy 1937,Mr 2,16:4
Storm Over Patsy 1937,Mr.9,26:4

McLean, Jackie
Connection, The 1959,Jl 16,30:2

McLean, Jane and Group
Tinker's Dam 1943,Ja 29,22:2

Maclean, Joan
Skin Game, The 1920,O 21,11:1
Camel's Back, The 1923,N 4,19:2
Dark Angel, The 1925,F 11,19:2
American Born 1925,S 27,VII,2:1
American Born 1925,O 6,31:3
Beau-Strings 1926,Ap 27,22:2
Beau-Strings 1926,My 2,VIII,1:1
Fanatics, The 1927,N 8,32:4

McLean, Jordie
Johnny 2X4 1942,Mr 17,24:6
All the Comforts of Home 1942,My 26,24:5

McLean, Ken
Cicero 1961,F 9,37:2

McLean, LeRoy
Pirates of Penzance, The 1936,Ap 21,27:5

McLean, Lorna
Goat Song 1926,Ja 26,18:1

McLean, Pat (Miscellaneous)
Look After Lulu 1959,Mr 4,35:1

MacLean, Paula
Chivalry 1925,D 16,22:3
Menace 1927,Mr 15,28:2
Heigh-Ho, Everybody 1932,My 26,31:2
Saint Wench 1933,Ja 3,19:3
Strangler Fig, The 1940,My 7,31:2

MacLean, Peter
Does a Tiger Wear a Necktie? 1967,F 4,17:1
Fire! 1968,My 12,II,7:1
Fire! 1969,Ja 29,26:1
Indians 1969,My 27,43:1
Indians 1969,O 14,51:1
Child's Play 1970,F 18,39:1

MacLean, R D
Julius Caesar 1926,S 19,28:5

McLean, Rae
Take Me Along 1959,O 23,22:2

MacLean, Ross
George White's Scandals 1931,S 15,30:1

MacLean, Ted
Funny Face 1927,N 23,28:2

McLean, Willard
Blackbirds 1928,My 10,31:3

McLeay, Janet
Fool's Bells 1925,D 24,8:3
Shelter 1926,Ja 26,18:2
American Tragedy, An 1926,O 12,31:2
Weather Clear, Track Fast 1927,O 19,24:5
Trapped 1928,S 12,25:3
Diana 1929,D 10,37:1
Penal Law 2010 1930,Ap 19,14:2
Up Pops the Devil 1930,S 2,19:1
Take My Tip 1932,Ap 12,25:2
Tommy 1933,Ag 8,22:5
All Good Americans 1933,D 6,29:2
Too Much Party 1934,Mr 6,28:4

McLee, Svetlana
Me and Juliet 1953,My 29,17:1
Me and Juliet 1953,Je 7,II,1:1

MacLeish, Archibald (Playwright)
Panic 1935,Mr 16,18:4
This Music Crept by Me Upon the Waters
1953,O 23,20:8
J B 1958,Ap 24,37:1
J B 1958,My 4,II,1:1
J B 1958,D 12,2:7
J B 1959,My 10,II,1:1
This Music Crept by Me Upon the Waters
1959,N 25,19:4
J B 1964,N 11,38:6
Play of Herod, The 1968,D 27,40:1

McLellan, C M S (Playwright)
Leah Kleschna 1924,Ap 22,19:2
Leah Kleschna 1924,Ap 27,VIII,1:1

MacLellan, Elizabeth
Little Boxes; Coffee Lace, The; Trevor
1968,Jl 5,20:1

McLellan, George B (Producer)
Werewolf, The 1924,Ag 26,6:1

MacLellan, Lilias
Up in Central Park 1947,My 20,29:2

McLellan, Robert (Playwright)
Flouers O' Edinburgh, The 1957,Ag 22,22:8
Young Auchinleck 1962,Ag 23,24:4

McLellan, W
Bunch and Judy, The 1922,N 29,20:1

Maclennan, Jack
Mirrors 1928,Ja 19,17:1

MacLennan, Leslie
Saint of Bleecker Street, The 1954,D 28,21:1

MacLennan, Michael
Saint of Bleecker Street, The 1954,D 28,21:1

McLennan, Oliver
Rosalie 1927,D 18,IX,2:3
Rosalie 1928,Ja 11,26:3

McLennan, Rodney
Ziegfeld Follies 1936,Ja 31,17:2
Johnny 2X4 1942,Mr 17,24:6
What's Up 1943,N 12,24:6
Lady in Danger 1945,Mr 30,18:6
My Fair Lady 1956,Mr 16,20:2

McLeod, A (Playwright)
So English! 1938,N 27,IX,1:7

McLeod, Alex
Clutching Claw, The 1928,F 15,20:1

MacLeod, Angus
Breadwinner, The 1931,S 23,19:4

MacLeod, Archie
Fly Away Home 1937,Jl 28,15:1
Elizabeth the Queen 1937,Ag 25,24:3

MacLeod, Beatrice Beach (Director)
Yes, My Darling Daughter 1938,Jl 13,19:2
Animal Kingdom, The 1938,Jl 27,14:5
Biography 1938,Ag 3,14:7
Bachelor Born 1938,Ag 17,23:1
Springtime for Henry 1938,Ag 31,12:5
Male Animal, The 1941,Jl 9,24:6

MacLeod, Gavin
Captains and the Kings, The 1962,Ja 3,25:2

McLeod, Gordon
Oedipus Rex 1923,O 26,14:1
Via Crucis 1923,N 13,25:2
Burgomaster of Stilemonde, The 1923,N 16,15:3
Hamlet 1923,N 20,23:3

McLeod, Jane (Playwright)
Johnny Doodle 1942,Mr 19,28:2

McLeod, John
We're Civilized? 1962,N 9,30:1
Twelfth Night 1969,Ag 14,29:2

McLeod, Lane
Elsie Janis and Her Gang 1922,Ja 17,13:2

McLeod, Leslie
Fortune Teller, The 1929,N 5,32:3
Merry Widow, The 1929,D 3,29:1
I'll Take the High Road 1943,N 10,28:3

McLeod, Mac
King of Friday's Men, The 1951,F 22,26:2
Collector's Item 1952,F 9,11:2

McLeod, Marsh
Great Campaign, The 1947,Ap 1,33:2

MacLeod, Mary
Shop at Sly Corner, The 1949,Ja 19,35:2
With a Silk Thread 1950,Ap 13,34:3

McLeod, Mercer
Green Bay Tree, The 1951,F 2,18:2
Deadfall 1955,O 28,20:1
Apple Cart, The 1956,O 19,23:1
Pink String and Sealing Wax 1957,S 6,13:1
Half a Sixpence 1965,Ap 26,38:2

MacLeod, Mildred
Mary the 3d 1923,F 6,14:2
Tarnish 1923,O 2,10:1
Little Angel, The 1924,S 29,10:3
Tangletoes 1925,F 18,17:1
Wild Birds 1925,Ap 10,16:1
Book of Charm, The 1925,S 4,26:3
Book of Charm, The 1925,S 13,VIII,1:1
No More Women 1926,Ag 4,17:2
If I Was Rich 1926,S 3,15:2
Triumphant Bachelor, The 1927,S 16,21:1
Bless You, Sister 1927,D 27,24:5
Undertow 1929,N 10,X,4:8
Claire Adams 1929,N 20,26:3
Blind Mice 1930,O 16,28:2

McLeod, Tex
Vaudeville (Palace) 1928,F 7,30:5
Vaudeville (Palace) 1928,O 30,27:3

McLeod, William
Black Widow 1936,F 13,24:3

McLerie, Allyn
Where's Charley? 1948,O 12,33:2
Where's Charley? 1948,O 24,II,1:1
Miss Liberty 1949,Je 14,26:6
Miss Liberty 1949,Jl 16,6:5
Miss Liberty 1949,Jl 24,II,1:1
Miss Liberty 1949,Ag 7,II,6:4
Where's Charley? 1951,Ja 30,21:7

McLerie, Allyn—Cont
Time Limit! 1956,Ja 25,27:2
West Side Story 1960,Ap 28,31:1
South Pacific 1961,Ap 27,26:3
Beast in Me, The 1963,My 17,29:1
Show Boat 1966,Jl 20,48:1
Dynamite Tonight 1967,Mr 16,52:2

McLiam, John
Nights of Wrath; Nuits de la Colere, Les 1947,D 1,26:4
Barefoot in Athens 1951,N 1,35:2
Desire Under the Elms 1952,Ja 17,23:4
Hall of Healing 1952,My 8,35:6
Bedtime Story 1952,My 8,35:6
Time to Go 1952,My 8,35:6
Macbeth 1957,Ag 16,11:2
Antony and Cleopatra 1959,Ja 14,28:1
Shadow and Substance 1959,N 4,42:1
One More River 1960,Mr 19,12:2
Promises to Keep 1965,Jl 22,25:1

McLiam, John (Director)
Promises to Keep 1965,Jl 22,25:1

McLiam, John (Playwright)
Sin of Pat Muldoon, The 1957,Mr 14,35:1

MacLiammoir, Michael
Diarmuid and Grainne 1928,D 16,IX,4:6
Julius Caesar 1934,O 24,25:2
Old Lady Says No, The 1935,Jl 28,X,1:1
Marriage of St Francis, The 1935,D 1,XI,6:4
John Bull's Other Island 1948,F 11,33:4
Old Lady Says No, The 1948,F 18,35:1
Where Stars Walk 1948,F 25,27:2
Abdication 1948,S 28,32:5
Hamlet 1957,O 29,34:2
Much Ado About Nothing 1959,S 18,25:2
Importance of Being Oscar, The 1961,Mr 15,45:2
Othello 1962,S 28,27:1
Roses Are Real, The 1964,Ja 23,27:1
I Must Be Talking to My Friends 1967,N 17,59:1

MacLiammoir, Michael (Costume Designer)
Old Lady Says No, The 1948,F 18,35:1

MacLiammoir, Michael (Director)
Diarmuid and Grainne 1928,D 16,IX,4:6
Abdication 1948,S 28,32:5

MacLiammoir, Michael (Playwright)
Diarmuid and Grainne 1928,D 16,IX,4:6
Where Stars Walk 1948,F 25,27:2

MacLiammoir, Michael (Producer)
Julius Caesar 1934,O 24,25:2
Skin of Our Teeth, The 1945,N 18,II,2:5

MacLiammoir, Michael (Scenic Designer)
Peer Gynt 1928,D 2,X,2:1
Diarmuid and Grainne 1928,D 16,IX,4:6
Old Lady Says No, The 1948,F 18,35:1

Maclome, John
Adventure 1928,S 26,25:2

Macloon, Louis (Playwright)
It Pays to Sin 1933,N 4,18:6

Macloon, Louis (Producer)
It Pays to Sin 1933,N 4,18:6
Blood on the Moon 1934,S 30,IX,3:1

McLoughlin, Cele
Playboy of the Western World, The 1930,Ja 3,20:4

McLoughlin, Charles
I'd Rather Be Right 1937,N 3,28:2

MacLow, Jackson
Originale 1964,S 9,46:1

MacLow, Jackson (Playwright)
Marrying Maiden, The 1960,Je 23,18:3

McLucas, Marjorie
Virgin of Bethulia, The 1925,F 24,17:2

MacMackin, David (Miscellaneous)
Year Round, The 1953,My 6,38:7

MacMahan, Julia
Becky Sharp 1929,Je 4,29:1

MacMahn, Patrick J
Lady Dedlock 1929,Ja 1,61:2

MacMahon, Aline
Madras House, The 1921,O 31,18:2
Green Ring, The 1922,Ap 5,22:1
Exciters, The 1922,S 23,10:4
This Fine-Pretty World 1923,D 27,11:1
Time Is a Dream 1924,Ap 23,24:2
Artists and Models 1925,Je 16,16:2
Beyond the Horizon 1926,D 1,24:2
Spread Eagle 1927,Ap 5,30:2
Midsummer Night's Dream, A 1927,Je 27,25:1
Her First Affaire 1927,Ag 23,29:2
Maya 1928,F 22,19:1
Arms and the Man 1929,Ag 13,23:4
Winter Bound 1929,N 13,24:6
Once in a Lifetime 1931,F 1,VIII,1:3
If Love Were All 1931,N 14,14:5
Kindred 1939,D 27,17:2
Heavenly Express 1940,Ap 19,24:2
Heavenly Express 1940,Ap 28,IX,1:1
Eve of St Mark, The 1942,O 8,30:2
Confidential Clerk, The 1954,F 12,22:1
Confidential Clerk, The 1954,F 21,II,1:1
Day by the Sea, A 1955,S 27,42:1
Day by the Sea, A 1955,O 2,II,1:1
I Knock at the Door 1956,Mr 19,27:5
Pictures in the Hallway 1956,My 28,23:1
Pictures in the Hallway 1956,S 17,23:2

Pictures in the Hallway 1956,S 23,II,1:1
I Know at the Door 1957,S 30,27:2
Romeo and Juliet 1959,Je 15,31:1
Romeo and Juliet 1959,Je 21,II,1:1
All's Well That Ends Well 1959,Ag 3,20:4
All the Way Home 1960,D 1,42:1
All the Way Home 1960,D 18,II,3:1
All the Way Home 1960,D 27,26:7
Coriolanus 1965,Je 21,36:1
Alchemist, The 1966,O 14,48:1
Yerma 1966,D 9,60:1
East Wind, The 1967,F 10,30:1
Galileo 1967,Ap 14,31:1
Walking to Waldheim 1967,N 11,25:2
Walking to Waldheim 1967,N 19,II,1:1
Tiger at the Gates 1968,Mr 1,30:1
Inner Journey, The 1969,Mr 21,42:1

McMahon, Arlina
Connie Goes Home 1923,S 7,10:1

MacMahon, B H
Wall Street 1927,Ap 21,24:4

MacMahon, Bryan (Playwright)
Bugle in the Blood, The 1949,Mr 15,34:5

McMahon, Cowal
Porgy and Bess 1943,S 14,26:2
Porgy and Bess 1944,F 8,13:2

McMahon, Edward (Pfc)
Winged Victory 1943,N 22,24:1

McMahon, Frank (Playwright)
Borstal Boy 1967,O 11,39:2
Borstal Boy 1967,O 12,55:2
Borstal Boy 1970,Ap 1,38:1

McMahon, Frazer
Music in May 1929,Ap 2,29:1

McMahon, Horace
Wild Waves 1932,F 20,11:4
Far Away Horses 1933,Mr 22,21:6
Man Bites Dog 1933,Ap 26,11:2
Sailor, Beware! 1933,S 29,24:4
Battleship Gertie 1935,Ja 19,9:2
Knock on Wood 1935,My 29,16:2
White Hell 1935,Ag 13,20:3
Name Your Poison 1936,Ja 21,27:4
Three Men on a Horse 1942,O 10,10:2
Red Gloves 1948,D 6,28:2
Detective Story 1949,Mr 24,34:2
Say Darling 1958,Ap 4,17:1
Say Darling 1958,Ap 13,II,1:1
Mundy Scheme, The 1969,D 12,75:1

McMahon, James
Wallflower 1944,Ja 27,14:2
Major Barbara 1954,Je 30,23:2
Juno and the Paycock 1955,F 24,20:4
Trouble in Mind 1955,N 5,23:2
Doll's House, A 1956,My 8,29:2
Mrs Warren's Profession 1958,Je 26,22:1
Madwoman of Chaillot, The 1970,Mr 23,48:3

McMahon, James (Director)
Twisting Road, The; Jewel of the South, The 1957,N 18,36:5
Twisting Road, The; Housekeeper, The 1957,N 18,36:5
Twisting Road, The; One Tuesday Morning 1957,N 18,36:5

McMahon, Jere
Brights Lights of 1944 1943,S 17,27:4
Connecticut Yankee, A 1943,N 18,30:2
Seven Lively Arts 1944,D 8,26:6

McMahon, John
John Brown's Body 1953,F 16,17:2

MacMahon, Julia
No More Frontier 1931,O 22,27:1
Spring Freshet 1934,O 5,28:3

McMahon, Vincent
Kiss Me, Kate 1956,My 10,27:2

McMahon, Virginia
Abie's Irish Rose 1954,N 19,19:1
Johnny Johnson 1956,O 22,24:1

MacManamy, Sue
True to Form 1921,S 13,12:1
Nature's Nobleman 1921,N 15,23:2
Thumbs Down 1923,Ag 7,20:1
High Stakes 1924,S 10,21:3
Four Flusher, The 1925,Ap 14,27:4
Human Nature 1925,S 25,24:3
Ink 1927,N 2,24:2
Angels Don't Kiss 1932,Ap 6,22:5

McManus, George (Playwright)
Bringing Up Father 1925,Mr 31,16:1

McManus, Jo
Antigone 1959,S 16,46:2

McManus, John (Miscellaneous)
Count Me In 1942,O 9,24:2

McManus, John L (Composer)
It's Up to You 1921,Mr 29,20:1

McManus, Lawrence
Little Theatre Tournament; Another Room for Rent 1929,My 7,28:1

McManus, Loyal
Come Angel Band 1936,F 19,17:1

McManus, Maureen
Mrs O'Brien Entertains 1939,F 9,16:3

McManus, Walter J
Marion Show, The 1923,My 8,22:3

McMartin, John
Little Mary Sunshine 1959,N 19,49:3
Little Mary Sunshine 1959,N 29,II,1:1
Conquering Hero, The 1961,Ja 17,40:2
Blood, Sweat & Stanley Poole 1961,O 6,31:1
Children From Their Games 1963,Ap 12,33:1
Rainy Day in Newark, A 1963,O 23,35:1
Too Much Johnson 1964,Ja 16,29:1
Sweet Charity 1966,Ja 31,22:1

MacMartin, Lorraine
Manhattan Nocturne 1943,O 27,26:2
According to Law 1944,Je 2,20:3
Solid Gold Cadillac, The 1953,N 6,24:2

MacMaster, Charles (Producer)
Song for a Certain Midnight 1959,S 17,49:1

McMaster, Rachel
Cherry Pie 1926,Ap 15,24:4

McMasters, William (Playwright)
Undercurrent, The 1925,Ja 18,VII,2:8
Undercurrent, The 1925,F 4,18:2

MacMichael, Florence
Sarah Simple 1940,N 18,22:5
Out of the Frying Pan 1941,F 12,24:2
Proof Thro' the Night 1942,D 26,14:2
Snark Was a Boojum, The 1943,S 2,14:4
On the Town 1944,D 29,11:4

McMichael, Lewis
This Fine-Pretty World 1923,D 27,11:1
Dybbuk, The 1925,D 16,22:2
Burmese Pwe, A 1926,Mr 17,28:1
Wall Street 1927,Ap 21,24:4
If Love Were All 1931,N 14,14:5
American Holiday 1936,F 22,13:3

McMichael, Myrtle
What's Your Number? 1929,Ag 16,18:3

McMillan, David
Tiger Smiles, The 1930,D 18,29:1
Mystery of the Finding of the Cross, The 1959,Ja 16,35:2

MacMillan, Donald
Ashes 1924,O 21,21:2
They All Want Something 1926,O 13,20:2
One, Two, Three! 1930,S 30,24:2
Miss Gulliver Travels 1931,N 26,36:4
Good Earth, The 1932,O 18,23:4
Tomorrow's a Holiday! 1935,D 31,10:2
Kick Back, The 1936,Je 23,27:3

McMillan, Elizabeth
Walk-Up 1961,F 24,24:1

McMillan, J
Carmen Jones 1956,Je 1,28:2

Macmillan, Jacqueline
Lady in the Dark 1941,Ja 24,14:2

McMillan, James
Killer, The 1960,Mr 23,33:1

McMillan, James (Lighting Director)
Gift of Fury, A 1958,Mr 24,21:4
Birthday Party, The 1961,My 15,34:6

McMillan, Jeanne
Watched Pot, The 1933,My 5,13:7

McMillan, Jim
South Pacific 1957,Ap 25,35:1
Finian's Rainbow 1967,Ap 6,44:1

McMillan, Kenneth
Out of This World 1955,N 10,44:2
King of the Whole Damn World 1962,Ap 16,32:2
Babes in the Wood 1964,D 29,21:2
Borstal Boy 1970,Ap 1,38:1

MacMillan, Lida
Elmer the Great 1928,S 25,29:1
Tavern, The 1930,My 20,32:1
Other One, The 1932,O 4,26:3
Two Strange Women 1933,Ja 11,23:3
Halfway to Hell 1934,Ja 3,22:3
Chalk Dust 1936,Mr 5,24:5
Battle Hymn 1936,My 23,12:1

MacMillan, Louis (Director)
Man With the Golden Arm, The 1956,My 22,28:1
Obbligato 1958,F 19,22:2
She Shall Have Music 1959,Ja 23,18:4
Guitar 1959,N 11,42:5
Mandingo 1961,My 23,43:6
Sweet Miani 1962,S 26,33:2

MacMillan, Louis (Miscellaneous)
Man With the Golden Arm, The 1956,My 22,28:1

MacMillan, Lydia
Gambling 1929,Ag 27,31:2

MacMillan, Thomas
Pleasure Bound 1929,F 19,22:4

McMillen, Don
Great Magician, The 1951,N 22,45:1

McMillen, William
Signature 1945,F 15,25:2

MacMillian, Donald
Horse Eats Hat 1936,S 28,14:2

McMullan, Frank (Director)
Measure for Measure 1946,Ag 24,6:8
First in Heart, The 1947,N 14,29:2
Merry Wives of Windsor, The 1954,F 17,27:1
Cock-A-Doodle Dandy 1955,N 4,26:5

MacMullan, Hugh (Director)
Wise Tomorrow 1937,O 16,22:5
McMullen, Charles R
Thou Desperate Pilot 1927,Mr 8,23:1
McMullen, Douglas
Jayhawker 1934,N 6,34:2
Mrs Moonlight 1936,Je 16,21:3
Pygmalion 1937,Jl 7,26:3
30 Days Hath September 1938,O 1,10:5
MacMullen, Ruth
Three Doors 1925,Ap 24,16:4
Henry's Harem 1926,S 14,25:2
McMullen, Susan
No Exit 1967,O 31,38:2
Little Private World of Arthur Morton Fenwick,
The 1967,O 31,38:2
McMunn, Frank
Tenth Man, The 1929,Mr 21,29:2
McMurray, Richard
Volpone 1948,Ja 9,24:6
Wedding, The 1948,F 6,29:2
On the Harmfulness of Tobacco 1948,F 6,29:2
Tragedian in Spite of Himself, A 1948,F 6,29:2
Bear, The 1948,F 6,29:2
Story for Strangers, A 1948,S 22,39:2
Hilda Crane 1950,N 2,38:2
Passion of Gross, The 1955,Ja 24,20:2
Night Circus, The 1958,D 3,44:1
Send Me No Flowers 1960,D 6,54:1
Case of Libel, A 1963,O 11,43:2
One by One 1964,D 2,60:1
McMurrow, Sally
Springtime for Henry 1940,F 27,16:3
McMurtry, John
Midsummer Night's Dream, A 1963,Jl 1,19:2
McMyers, Richard
Sweet River 1936,O 29,30:2
Brown Sugar 1937,D 3,29:2
McNab, Dorothy Cumming (Director)
Woman Brown, The 1939,D 9,18:5
McNab, Dorothy Cumming (Playwright)
Woman Brown, The 1939,D 9,18:5
McNab, R Duncan (Playwright)
Morphia 1923,Mr 7,20:2
McNabb, Maureen
Show Boat 1966,Jl 20,48:1
McNabb, Theodore H (Miscellaneous)
Bring Me a Warm Body 1962,Ap 17,29:3
McNair, Barbara
Body Beautiful, The 1958,Ja 24,15:2
McNair, Claude
Battleship Gertie 1935,Ja 19,9:2
McNair, Emily
Criminals, The 1941,D 22,24:3
Hedda Gabler 1948,F 25,27:2
McNair, Marjorie (Choreographer)
Winter's Tale, The 1963,Je 29,13:1
Midsummer Night's Dream, A 1963,Jl 1,19:2
McNall, Theda (Corp)
Swing Sister Wac Swing 1944,Ja 4,20:4
McNalley, Maureen
Mis-Guided Tour 1959,O 13,44:7
Rendezvous at Senlis 1961,F 28,39:2
McNally, Edward
What Makes Sammy Run? 1964,F 28,19:1
McNally, Gerald
Chips With Everything 1963,O 2,49:1
McNally, Horace
Johnny Belinda 1940,S 19,26:2
Wookey, The 1941,Ag 26,23:2
Wookey, The 1941,S 11,20:5
McNally, Jeanne
Heart of a City 1942,F 13,24:6
McNally, Terrence (Playwright)
Lady of the Camellias, The 1963,Mr 22,7:1
And Things That Go Bump in the Night
1965,Ap 27,27:5
And Things That Go Bump in the Night
1965,My 9,II,1:2
Collision Course; Tour 1968,My 9,55:2
Witness 1968,N 22,38:1
Sweet Eros 1968,N 22,38:1
Noon 1968,N 29,52:1
Noon 1968,D 8,II,5:4
Cuba Si 1968,D 10,53:1
Next 1969,F 11,27:1
Next 1969,F 23,II,1:1
Next 1970,Mr 12,46:1
McNally, Vincent
Before I Wake 1968,O 14,56:1
McNally, Walter
Vaudeville (Palace) 1927,Jl 26,16:5
McNally, William (Playwright)
Good Bad Woman, A 1925,F 10,21:1
Prelude to Exile 1936,N 17,34:6
Prelude to Exile 1936,N 22,XI,3:2
Prelude to Exile 1936,D 1,31:1
McNamara, Betty
Decameron, The 1961,Ap 13,32:1
MacNamara, Brinsley (Playwright)
Master, The 1928,Ap 1,IX,2:1
Look at the Heffernans 1934,N 17,13:2
Marks and Mabel 1945,S 9,II,1:4

McNamara, Brooks (Miscellaneous)
Macbeth 1969,N 21,51:1
McNamara, Dermot
Wise Have Not Spoken, The 1954,F 11,35:2
Shadow and Substance 1956,Mr 14,38:1
No Exit 1956,Ag 15,23:1
In the Shadow of the Glen 1957,Mr 7,24:1
Playboy of the Western World, The 1958,My 9,19:2
Shadow and Substance 1959,N 4,42:1
Happy as Larry 1961,Ap 26,36:1
Sharon's Grave 1961,N 9,39:2
Three Times Three; George Washington Crossing
the Delaware 1962,Mr 2,24:1
Taming of the Shrew, The 1963,Mr. 8,9:1
Philadelphia, Here I Come! 1966,F 17,28:1
Stephen D 1967,S 25,58:1
Whistle in the Dark, A 1968,F 17,32:2
Crossroads 1969,Ag 7,28:1
Whistle in the Dark, A 1969,O 9,55:1
McNamara, Edward J
Becky Sharp 1929,Je 4,29:1
Strictly Dishonorable 1929,S 19,37:1
Shoot the Works! 1931,Jl 22,19:5
Monkey 1932,F 12,25:2
Uncle Tom's Cabin 1933,My 30,13:4
Hold Your Horses 1933,S 26,26:4
Laura Garnett 1934,Jl 17,24:4
Jayhawker 1934,O 16,31:4
Jayhawker 1934,N 6,34:2
On to Fortune 1935,F 5,22:2
Seven Keys to Baldpate 1935,My 28,30:2
Parnell 1935,N 12,24:2
Margin for Error 1939,N 4,11:3
Margin for Error 1939,N 12,IX,1:1
Return of the Vagabond, The 1940,My 14,27:2
McNamara, Maggie
King of Friday's Men, The 1951,F 22,26:2
Step on a Crack 1962,O 18,48:1
McNamara, Patrick
Red Roses for Me 1961,N 28,41:1
Triumph of Robert Emmet, The 1969,My 8,54:1
Crossroads 1969,Ag 7,28:1
Nobody Hears A Broken Drum 1970,Mr 20,55:1
McNamara, Patrick (Miscellaneous)
Ofay Watcher, The 1969,S 16,40:1
McNamara, Rosemary
Most Happy Fella, The 1966,My 12,55:1
Carricknabauna 1967,Mr 31,30:1
McNamara, Teddy
Up She Goes 1922,N 7,14:2
Glory 1922,D 26,10:1
Battling Buttler 1923,O 9,17:2
McNamee, Mary
Heiress, The 1950,F 9,34:2
MacNamee, R D (Miscellaneous)
It's the Valet 1933,D 15,25:4
MacNanamy, Sue
Long Road, The 1930,Jl 20,VIII,2:1
MacNaughtan, Alan
Fighting Cock, The 1959,D 9,57:3
Duel of Angels 1960,Ap 20,42:2
After the Rain 1967,O 10,54:1
Hadrian VII 1968,Jl 4,14:1
McNaughton, Charles
Three Live Ghosts 1920,S 30,12:1
Plain Jane 1924,My 13,24:2
Right Age to Marry, The 1926,F 16,22:3
Old Bill, M P 1926,N 11,22:2
Pickwick 1927,Mr 13,VII,1:1
Pickwick 1927,S 6,35:2
Pickwick 1927,S 11,VIII,1:1
Silent House, The 1928,F 8,28:5
McNaughton, Glen N W (Producer)
Lord Blesses the Bishop, The 1934,N 28,24:5
Creeping Fire 1935,Ja 17,22:3
McNaughton, Harry
French Leave 1920,N 9,13:1
Rotters, The 1922,My 23,12:4
Topics of 1923 1923,N 21,23:2
Flossie 1924,Je 4,25:2
Passing Show of 1924, The 1924,S 4,13:4
American Born 1925,S 27,VII,2:1
American Born 1925,O 6,31:3
Kongo 1926,Mr 31,20:5
Number 7 1926,S 9,21:3
Piggy 1927,Ja 12,22:2
Oh, Ernest! 1927,My 10,24:3
Ziegfeld Follies 1927,Ag 17,27:3
By Request 1928,S 28,30:2
Whispering Gallery, The 1929,F 12,22:2
Nine Fifteen Revue, The 1930,F 12,26:2
Lost Sheep 1930,My 6,33:2
Vaudeville (Palace) 1931,Ap 13,17:2
Air-Minded 1932,F 11,17:3
Calling All Stars 1934,D 14,28:2
MacNaughton, Virginia
Is Zat So? 1925,Ap 25,18:2
Macnee, Patrick
Midsummer Night's Dream, A 1954,S 22,33:1
McNeel, P J
It's the Valet 1933,D 15,25:4
McNeil, Angela
Miss Emily Adam 1960,Mr 30,43:1

McNeil, Claudia
Simply Heavenly 1957,My 22,28:2
Winesburg, Ohio 1958,F 6,22:2
Raisin in the Sun, A 1959,Mr 12,27:1
Raisin in the Sun, A 1959,Mr 29,II,1:1
Tiger Tiger Burning Bright 1962,D 24,5:2
Amen Corner, The 1965,Je 13,82:4
Amen Corner, The 1965,Ag 9,19:5
Something Different 1967,N 29,52:1
Something Different 1967,D 10,II,15:6
Her First Roman 1968,O 21,53:3
Her First Roman 1968,N 3,II,1:1
Wrong Way Light Bulb, The 1969,Mr 5,40:1
Contributions; Plantation 1970,Mr 10,53:1
Contributions; Contribution 1970,Mr 10,53:1
Contributions 1970,Mr 29,II,1:1
MacNeil, Cornell
Sweethearts 1947,Ja 22,31:2
Consul, The 1950,Mr 2,32:3
Consul, The 1950,Mr 16,41:1
Consul, The 1950,Mr 26,II,1:1
Consul, The 1950,Mr 26,II,1:1
MacNeil, Dorothy
Song of Norway 1951,Ja 11,28:5
Mikado, The 1952,O 21,35:2
Pirates of Penzance, The 1952,O 28,36:4
McNeil, Kathleen
Talking to You 1961,O 23,22:5
Across the Board on Tomorrow Morning
1961,O 23,22:5
McNeil, Neil
Don't Tell 1920,S 29,12:1
McNeil, Philip
Peter Pan 1924,N 7,16:2
McNeil, Ron
Single Man at a Party 1959,Ap 22,30:4
McNeill, Cyril (Lieut Col) (Sapper) (Playwright)
Bulldog Drummond Hits Out 1937,D 22,33:2
McNeill, William W
Bulldog Drummond 1921,D 27,10:2
MacNeille, M
Plain Dealer, The 1929,My 23,27:1
McNelis, Neil
Kismet 1965,Je 23,45:1
Show Boat 1966,Jl 20,48:1
McNellis, Frank
Five O'Clock Girl, The 1927,O 11,26:3
Round-Up, The 1932,Mr 8,19:4
Drums Professor, The 1935,Jl 30,17:2
Strip Girl 1935,O 21,22:6
Wallflower 1944,Ja 27,14:2
Flamingo Road 1946,Mr 20,18:2
Command Decision 1947,O 2,30:2
Man, The 1950,Ja 20,28:2
MacNicol, Josephine
High Hatters, The 1928,My 11,28:2
McNight, John
Aquashow 1953,Je 24,29:2
Aquashow 1954,Je 23,20:4
McNulty, Dorothy
Great Temptations, The 1926,My 19,29:1
Hey, Nonny, Nonny! 1932,Je 7,22:3
Walk a Little Faster 1932,D 8,24:4
McNulty, Henry P
What a Relief 1935,D 14,10:6
McNulty, J Archibald
One Woman's Husband 1920,Mr 23,9:3
McNulty, J Archibald (Mrs)
One Woman's Husband 1920,Mr 23,9:3
McNulty, John
Road to Rome, The 1927,F 1,24:2
Did I Say No? 1931,S 23,19:4
Jamboree 1932,N 25,18:4
McNulty, Marguerite
High Hatters, The 1928,My 11,28:2
McNulty, Terry
Pirates of Penzance, The 1970,Jl 26,49:5
McNutt, Patterson
Trelawney of the 'Wells' 1925,Je 2,16:2
McNutt, Patterson (Director)
Kibitzer, The 1929,F 19,22:5
McNutt, Patterson (Playwright)
Pigs 1924,Je 8,VII,1:8
Pigs 1924,S 2,22:5
Hay Fever 1931,D 30,25:1
McNutt, Patterson (Producer)
Ghosts 1927,Ja 11,36:3
This Thing Called Love 1928,S 18,32:7
Kibitzer, The 1929,F 19,22:5
Cloudy With Showers 1931,S 2,17:5
Hay Fever 1931,D 6,VIII,2:8
Macollum, Barry
Mandarin, The 1920,N 10,18:2
Mixed Marriage 1920,D 15,18:2
John Ferguson 1921,Je 21,20:2
Shadow, The 1922,Ap 25,14:2
Romeo and Juliet 1922,D 28,20:1
Macbeth 1924,Mr 17,18:1
Loggerheads 1925,F 10,21:1
Outside Looking In 1925,S 8,28:1
Taming of the Shrew, The 1925,D 19,14:1
Shelter 1926,Ja 26,18:2
Juno and the Paycock 1926,Mr 16,22:1

Macollum, Barry—Cont
Banshee, The 1927,D 6,26:2
John Ferguson 1928,Ja 18,23:1
Caravan 1928,Ag 30,13:3
Mountain Fury 1929,S 26,27:2
Mr Gilhooley 1930,O 1,26:1
Elizabeth the Queen 1930,N 4,37:1
Doctor X 1931,F 10,25:1
In Times Square 1931,N 24,29:3
Moon in the Yellow River, The 1932,F 21,VIII,2:1
Moon in the Yellow River, The 1932,Mr 1,19:3
Moon in the Yellow River, The
  1932,Mr 13,VIII,1:1
Jamboree 1932,N 25,18:4
Far Away Horses 1933,Mr 22,21:6
John Ferguson 1933,Jl 11,15:7
Joyous Season, The 1934,Ja 30,16:3
Within the Gates 1934,O 23,23:1
Parnell 1935,N 12,24:2
Love on the Dole 1936,F 25,23:3
Slightly Scandalous 1944,Je 14,16:2
Happily Ever After 1945,Mr 16,21:2
Playboy of the Western World, The 1946,O 28,18:3
Hope Is the Thing With Feathers; Hope's the
  Thing 1948,My 12,34:6
Gone Tomorrow; Hope's the Thing
  1948,My 12,34:6
Home Life of a Buffalo; Hope's the Thing
  1948,My 12,34:6
Much Ado About Nothing 1952,My 2,20:1
Red Roses for Me 1955,D 29,15:2
In the Shadow of the Glen 1957,Mr 7,24:1
Quare Fellow, The 1958,N 28,34:1
Macbeth 1959,Ag 1,9:2
Much Ado About Nothing 1959,S 18,25:2
Painted Days, The 1961,Ap 7,24:1
More Stately Mansions 1967,N 1,40:1
Macollum, Barry (Producer)
Shelter 1926,Ja 26,18:2
In Times Square 1931,N 24,29:3
Macomb, Alexander
That Awful Mrs Eaton! 1924,S 30,27:1
Macomber, Constance (Producer)
Thistle in My Bed 1963,N 20,48:1
Macomber, David
My Sister Eileen 1940,D 27,23:2
Macomber, Joan
All Paris Knows 1934,Jl 24,20:1
Nude in Washington Square, The 1934,Ag 7,20:1
In Clover 1937,O 14,23:1
Macomber, Ken (Composer)
Rhapsody in Black 1931,My 5,33:2
Yeah-Man 1932,My 27,27:3
Macomber, Ken (Lyricist)
Rhapsody in Black 1931,My 5,33:2
Yeah-Man 1932,My 27,27:3
Macomber, Ken (Miscellaneous)
Caribbean Carnival 1947,D 6,12:2
Macon, Norman
Tall Kentuckian, The 1953,Je 17,30:1
Macon, Sara
What's Up 1943,N 12,24:6
MacOwan, Michael (Director)
Summer Day's Dream 1949,S 9,28:5
Sleep of Prisoners, A 1951,My 16,46:6
Sleep of Prisoners, A 1951,O 17,36:2
MacOwan, Michael (Producer)
Hamlet 1937,Ag 8,X,1:7
MacOwan, Norman
Infinite Shoeblack, The 1930,F 18,28:1
MacOwan, Norman (Director)
Infinite Shoeblack, The 1930,F 18,28:1
MacOwan, Norman (Playwright)
Blue Lagoon, The 1921,S 15,16:1
Infinite Shoeblack, The 1929,My 5,IX,1:3
Infinite Shoeblack, The 1929,D 1,X,4:7
Infinite Shoeblack, The 1930,F 18,28:1
Infinite Shoeblack, The 1930,Mr 2,IX,1:1
Glorious Morning 1938,Je 12,X,2:4
Glorious Morning 1938,N 28,10:3
McOwen, Bernard J
Elton Case, The 1921,S 12,16:2
Ladies of the Evening 1924,D 24,11:2
Woman Disputed, A 1926,S 29,23:2
Talk About Girls 1927,Je 15,31:3
Sh! The Octopus 1928,F 22,19:2
Blue Ghost, The 1930,Mr 11,24:5
McOwen, Bernard J (Miscellaneous)
Slightly Delirious 1935,Ja 1,25:3
McOwen, Bernard J (Playwright)
Dust Heap, The 1924,F 24,VII,2:5
Dust Heap, The 1924,Ap 25,20:2
Uninvited Guest, The 1927,S 28,28:2
Skull, The 1928,Ap 24,28:3
Blue Ghost, The 1930,Mr 11,24:5
Paid Companions 1931,Je 23,28:4
Scorpion, The 1933,N 28,28:4
Slightly Delirious 1935,Ja 1,25:3
McPhail, Addie
Vaudeville (Loew's State) 1932,O 3,15:5
McPheeters, James
Ol' Man Satan 1932,O 4,26:3
McPheeters, W L
Tiger Smiles, The 1930,D 18,29:1

MacPherson, Douglas
Shavings 1920,F 17,18:1
Cousin Sonia 1925,D 8,28:3
Howdy King 1926,D 14,24:4
Gambling 1929,Ag 27,31:2
Tavern, The 1930,My 20,32:1
Life Begins 1932,Mr 29,23:2
Little Black Book, The 1932,D 27,11:2
McPherson, Fred
Better Times 1922,S 4,14:2
Macpherson, L du Rocher (Playwright)
Henrietta the Eighth 1935,Je 25,15:4
McPhillips, Edward
Stephen D 1966,Ag 5,17:1
Stephen D 1967,S 25,58:1
Victims, The; Victims of Duty 1968,Mr 6,34:1
Victims, The; Escurial 1968,Mr 6,34:1
Happy Hypocrite, The 1968,S 6,38:1
McPhillips, Edward (Choreographer)
Stephen D 1966,Ag 5,17:1
McQuade, Anton
Naked Genius, The 1943,O 22,20:5
McQuade, Arlene
Summer and Smoke 1948,O 7,33:2
McQuade, Fuzzy
Violet 1944,O 25,16:1
Secret Room, The 1945,N 8,16:2
McQuade, Garth J (Pfc)
Swing Sister Wac Swing 1944,Ja 4,20:4
McQuade, John
Hamlet 1939,D 5,35:2
Richard II 1940,Ap 2,31:2
Trojan Women, The 1941,Ap 9,32:5
Elizabeth the Queen 1941,O 17,27:2
Counsellor-at-Law 1942,N 25,17:2
Petrified Forest, The 1943,N 2,30:6
Highland Fling, A 1944,Ap 29,13:2
Arsenic and Old Lace 1944,Jl 3,7:3
Meet a Body 1944,O 17,19:5
Ghosts 1961,S 22,29:1
Calculated Risk 1962,N 1,35:1
McQuade, Mary
Near to the Stars 1932,F 23,23:2
Music in the Air 1932,N 9,28:2
Thunder on the Left 1933,N 1,25:2
Farmer Takes a Wife, The 1934,O 31,17:1
Remember the Day 1935,Jl 9,24:3
Remember the Day 1935,S 26,19:3
As We Forgive Our Debtors 1936,Ag 11,24:6
Stork Mad 1936,O 1,28:4
McQuade, Robert
No Time for Sergeants 1955,O 21,32:2
MacQuarrie, Benedict
Triumph of X, The 1921,Ag 25,8:2
Mad Honeymoon, The 1923,Ag 8,10:1
Launzi 1923,O 11,16:3
Go West, Young Man 1923,N 13,25:2
Try It With Alice 1924,Je 24,18:4
Eve's Leaves 1925,Mr 27,22:2
Lally 1927,F 9,16:3
Love in the Tropics 1927,O 19,24:3
Aiglon, L' 1927,D 27,24:3
Queen's Husband, The 1928,Ja 26,17:2
Brothers 1928,D 26,14:3
As Husbands Go 1933,Ja 20,20:5
Mahogany Hall 1934,Ja 18,18:5
Aiglon, L' 1934,N 5,22:2
Paths of Glory 1935,S 27,24:2
This Our House 1935,D 12,33:3
Father Malachy's Miracle 1937,N 18,26:4
Gloriana 1938,N 26,18:4
Jeremiah 1939,F 4,11:2
Candle in the Wind 1941,O 23,26:2
Harriet 1943,Mr 4,24:2
Harriet 1944,S 28,26:1
Cyrano de Bergerac 1946,O 9,33:2
Cyrano de Bergerac 1947,Ja 27,27:2
Hall of Healing 1952,My 8,35:6
Cyrano de Bergerac 1953,N 13,24:3
Richard III 1953,D 10,65:2
Pony Cart, The 1954,S 15,39:2
MacQuarrie, George
Poppy God, The 1921,Ag 30,10:1
That Day 1922,O 4,27:3
Virtue (?) 1922,N 17,14:1
My Son 1924,S 18,18:2
Canary Dutch 1925,S 9,22:1
New York 1927,N 15,26:2
Phantom Lover, The 1928,S 5,25:1
These Days 1928,N 13,36:2
Flight 1929,F 19,22:3
Come-On Man, The 1929,Ap 23,26:2
White Flame 1929,N 5,32:7
Rebound 1930,F 4,29:1
Through the Night 1930,Ag 19,19:1
First Night 1930,N 27,32:3
Enemy Within 1931,O 6,35:3
Air-Minded 1932,F 11,17:3
McQueen, Butterfly
Brown Sugar 1937,D 3,29:2
What a Life 1938,Ap 14,26:2
Swingin' the Dream 1939,N 30,24:2
World's My Oyster, The 1956,Ag 10,10:4

McQueen, Butterfly—Cont
School for Wives 1957,Je 20,23:4
Athenian Touch, The 1964,Ja 15,25:4
Three Men on a Horse 1969,O 17,35:1
McQueen, Simon
Boy Friend, The 1970,Ap 15,54:1
McQueeney, Robert
Uniform of Flesh 1949,Ja 31,15:2
Billy Budd 1951,F 12,18:3
Climate of Eden, The 1953,N 21,11:2
Fragile Fox 1954,O 13,27:1
Lovers, Villains and Fools: A Shakespearean
  Variety Show 1956,O 24,44:7
McQuiggan, Jack (Miscellaneous)
Seagull, The 1962,Mr 22,42:1
McQuiggan, John A (Producer)
Horseman, Pass By 1969,Ja 16,46:4
McQuillan, Thomas
Noble Experiment, The 1930,O 28,21:4
Camels Are Coming, The 1931,O 3,20:4
Coastwise 1931,D 1,23:1
McQuillan, Thomas (Miscellaneous)
Slightly Scandalous 1944,Je 14,16:2
McQuillen, Claire
Growing Pains 1933,N 24,24:2
George White's Scandals 1935,D 26,20:2
Macrae, Arthur
George and Margaret 1937,S 23,32:2
Sugar Plum 1939,Ap 2,X,1:7
South Sea Bubble 1956,My 13,II,3:1
Macrae, Arthur (Playwright)
Flat to Let 1931,D 20,VIII,3:6
Indoor Fireworks 1934,Mr 30,26:6
Sugar Plum 1939,Ap 2,X,1:7
Under the Counter 1947,O 4,10:2
John Murray Anderson's Almanac 1953,D 11,42:2
Both Ends Meet 1954,Jl 18,II,1:7
Shoestring '57 1956,N 6,31:1
McRae, Bruce
Awful Truth, The 1922,S 19,14:3
Little Miss Bluebeard 1923,Ag 29,12:1
Little Miss Bluebeard 1923,S 2,VI,1:1
Alarm Clock, The 1923,D 25,26:2
Grounds for Divorce 1924,Mr 2,VIII,2:7
Steam Roller, The 1924,O 26,VIII,2:1
Steam Roller, The 1924,N 11,20:2
She Had to Know 1925,F 3,25:3
Lovely Lady 1925,S 20,VIII,2:4
Lovely Lady 1925,S 27,25:7:1
First Love 1926,S 19,IX,1:3
First Love 1926,N 9,31:2
Legend of Leonora, The 1927,Mr 30,22:4
McRae, Charles
Set My People Free 1948,N 4,38:2
Mister Johnson 1956,Mr 30,11:1
Simply Heavenly 1957,My 22,28:2
Toys in the Attic 1960,F 26,23:2
MacRae, Elizabeth
Gay Apprentice, The 1960,F 3,27:2
McRae, Ellen
Fair Game 1957,N 4,39:1
McRae, Gordon
John 1927,N 5,16:4
Our Betters 1928,F 21,18:2
Exceeding Small 1928,O 23,32:2
Trojan Horse, The 1940,O 31,28:3
Three to Make Ready 1946,Mr 8,16:2
I Do! I Do! 1967,N 28,54:1
MacRae, Heather
Here's Where I Belong 1968,Mr 4,32:1
Hair 1969,F 5,36:1
McRae, Maurice
Man and the Masses 1924,Ap 15,25:1
Arms and the Man 1925,S 15,28:1
Juarez and Maximilian 1926,O 12,31:1
Ned McCobb's Daughter 1926,N 30,26:2
Right You Are (If You Think You Are)
  1927,F 24,27:1
Porgy 1927,O 11,26:2
Distant Drums 1932,Ja 19,24:3
McRae, Maurice (Director)
Back Fire 1932,Je 14,26:3
MacRae, Sheila
Guys and Dolls 1965,Ap 29,39:1
MacRae, Susan
Daddy Come Home 1963,Ap 17,33:1
Macready, George
Scarlet Letter, The 1926,Ja 8,16:5
Trumpet Shall Sound, The 1926,D 11,15:2
Granite 1927,F 12,13:1
Much Ado About Nothing 1927,N 19,14:6
Martine 1928,Ap 5,19:3
Macbeth 1928,N 20,28:3
Passionate Pilgrim, The 1932,O 20,24:3
Lucrece 1932,D 21,22:2
Lucrece 1933,Ja 1,IX,1:1
School for Husbands, The 1933,O 17,26:5
Romeo and Juliet 1934,D 21,30:3
Victoria Regina 1935,D 27,15:2
Fresh Fields 1936,Je 23,27:3
Pomeroy's Past 1936,Ag 4,15:2
Merely Murder 1937,D 4,21:4
Save Me the Waltz 1938,Mr 1,19:2
American Landscape 1938,D 5,19:2

Macready, George—Cont
Brown Danube, The 1939,My 18,30:4
Foreigners 1939,D 6,30:2
Royal Family, The 1940,Ag 13,15:3
Saint Joan 1954,S 18,12:1
Waltz of the Toreadors, The 1958,Mr 5,37:1
Macready, Michael
Christmas Eve 1939,D 28,17:2
Macready, Renee
Escape 1927,O 27,33:1
Victoria Regina 1935,D 27,15:2
McRoberts, Eva
Don't Tell 1920,S 29,12:1
If Winter Comes 1923,Ap 3,26:1
McRobie, William
If Booth Had Missed 1932,F 5,24:2
MacRostie, James
Walk-Up 1961,F 24,24:1
MacRostie, James (Lighting Director)
Walk-Up 1961,F 24,24:1
MacRostie, James (Miscellaneous)
Walk-Up 1961,F 24,24:1
McShane, Doreen
Blue Butterfly, The 1929,F 17,29:3
McShane, Ian
Promise, The 1967,N 15,38:1
Promise, The 1967,N 26,II,1:1
MacSunday, Con
Dantons Tod 1927,D 21,28:3
Inspector General, The 1930,D 24,19:2
Miracle at Verdun 1931,Mr 17,34:6
Sing High, Sing Low 1931,N 13,26:4
I Want a Policeman! 1936,Ja 15,15:5
Empress of Destiny 1938,Mr 10,16:2
American Landscape 1938,D 5,19:2
McSweeney, George
Pygmalion 1938,Ja 27,16:3
No More Peace 1938,Ja 29,13:2
Coriolanus 1938,F 2,14:5
McSweeney, Joan
Solitaire 1942,Ja 28,22:2
Broken Journey 1942,Je 24,22:2
Sons and Soldiers 1943,My 5,22:2
McTarnahan, Grace
First Lady 1937,O 9,17:2
All the Comforts of Home 1942,My 26,24:5
Jeb 1946,F 22,20:2
Oh, Mr Meadowbrook! 1948,D 27,17:2
McTigue, Cecelia
King Oedipus 1933,Ja 16,12:4
McTigue, Roseleen
King Oedipus 1933,Ja 16,12:4
MacUeice, Louis (Translator)
Agamemnon 1936,N 2,25:6
Macunovich, John Allan
Man and Superman 1964,D 7,45:2
War and Peace 1965,Ja 12,32:1
Judith 1965,Mr 25,42:2
Macurdy, John
H M S Pinafore 1961,F 2,26:6
MacVae, Cynthia
Oh, Please! 1926,D 22,24:3
McVeagh, Eve
Snafu 1944,O 26,19:5
Too Hot for Maneuvers 1945,My 3,26:5
MacVeigh, Earle
May Wine 1935,D 6,30:3
On Your Toes 1936,Ap 13,14:4
Would-Be Gentleman, The 1946,Ja 10,29:2
Up in Central Park 1947,My 20,29:2
Mikado, The 1949,O 5,35:2
Pirates of Penzance, The 1949,O 11,41:2
H M S Pinafore 1949,O 18,34:2
Trial by Jury 1949,O 18,34:2
Kismet 1953,D 4,2:4
Kismet 1965,Je 23,45:1
McVey, Patrick
Hold It! 1948,My 6,31:5
Detective Story 1949,Mr 24,34:2
Bus Stop 1955,Mr 3,23:2
Catch Me if You Can 1965,Mr 10,50:1
Let Them Down, Gently; On Vacation
  1968,Ja 31,28:2
Transgressor Rides Again, The 1969,My 21,42:1
Sourball 1969,Ag 6,29:2
Time of Your Life, The 1969,N 7,37:1
Camino Real 1970,Ja 9,42:1
Sunday Dinner 1970,N 3,28:1
McVey, Paul
Slightly Scandalous 1944,Je 14,16:2
McVicker, Julius
School for Scandal, The 1923,Mr 13,19:2
Ladder, The 1926,O 23,15:1
Immoral Isabella 1927,O 28,20:3
McVicker, Laurie
Passing of the Third Floor Back, The
  1928,F 21,18:2
Crucible 1933,S 5,22:4
Last Stop 1944,S 6,17:2
McVine, Jas J
Solid Ivory 1925,N 17,29:3
McVitty, Edward
Trojan Horse, The 1940,O 31,28:3

McWade, Robert
Crooked Gamblers 1920,Ag 2,12:1
Deluge, The 1922,Ja 28,14:2
Old Soak, The 1922,Ag 23,14:5
We've Got to Have Money 1923,Ag 21,12:1
Deep Tangled Wildwood, The 1923,N 6,22:1
New Toys 1924,F 19,12:1
She Stoops to Conquer 1924,Je 10,24:3
New Brooms 1924,N 18,23:5
Home Towners, The 1926,Ag 24,19:3
Home Towners, The 1926,Ag 29,VII,1:1
Home Towners, The 1926,S 5,VII,1:1
Devil in the Cheese, The 1926,D 30,22:4
McWaith, A
Young Alexander 1929,Mr 13,28:2
MacWatters, Virginia
Rosalinda; Fledermaus, Die 1942,O 29,26:5
Mr Strauss Goes to Boston 1945,S 7,20:2
Pirates of Penzance, The 1946,My 17,14:6
Pirates of Penzance, The 1946,S 21,19:2
McWatters, W O
Whatever Goes Up 1935,N 26,28:2
Pygmalion 1938,Ja 27,16:3
Captain Jinks of the Horse Marines 1938,Ja 28,16:2
No More Peace 1938,Ja 29,13:2
Coriolanus 1938,F 2,14:5
Hill Between, The 1938,Mr 12,12:5
Janie 1942,S 11,24:2
Boy Who Lived Twice, A 1945,S 12,31:2
Macwey, The
Passing Show of 1922, The 1922,S 21,18:2
McWherter, Joe
Deer Park, The 1967,F 1,27:2
McWhinney, Michael (Composer)
Leonard Sillman's New Faces of 1968
  1968,My 3,43:1
McWhinney, Michael (Lyricist)
Leonard Sillman's New Faces of 1968
  1968,My 3,43:1
McWhinney, Michael (Playwright)
That Thing at the Cherry Lane 1965,My 19,42:1
McWhinnie, Donald (Director)
Caretaker, The 1961,O 5,42:3
Caretaker, The 1961,O 15,II,1:1
Passage to India, A 1962,F 1,23:1
Macbeth 1962,Je 6,35:2
Rattle of a Simple Man 1963,Ap 18,39:1
All in Good Time 1965,F 19,25:1
Creeper, The 1965,Jl 15,21:1
Astrakhan Coat, The 1967,Ja 13,18:1
McWhorter, George
Show Boat 1966,Jl 20,48:1
McWilliams, Al
Ten Nights in a Barroom 1927,Ja 16,VII,1:1
Ten Nights in a Barroom 1928,Mr 28,31:2
McWilliams, Albert
Strip Girl 1935,O 21,22:6
Big Blow 1938,O 3,11:2
McWilliams, Caroline
Ordinary Man, An 1968,S 10,39:1
McWilliams, Ernest Leslie
This Mad Whirl 1937,Ja 10,II,4:8
McWilliams, Jim
Vaudeville (Palace) 1927,Ja 4,21:2
Vaudeville (Palace) 1928,F 14,26:2
Vaudeville (Palace) 1929,D 16,34:4
Vaudeville (Palace) 1930,Ap 21,20:7
Vaudeville (Palace) 1932,Je 6,18:2
Macy, Anne Sullivan
Vaudeville (Palace) 1923,Ja 16,16:3
Macy, Bill
Interview 1966,N 7,66:1
TV 1966,N 7,66:1
Guns of Carrar, The 1968,D 10,53:1
Oh! Calcutta! 1969,Je 18,33:1
Awake and Sing! 1970,My 28,35:1
Awake and Sing! 1970,Je 7,II,1:1
Macy, Carleton
Trouper, The 1926,Mr 9,21:1
Up the Line 1926,N 23,26:1
Scarlet Lily, The 1927,Ja 31,12:3
Scalawag, The 1927,Mr 30,22:3
Skidding 1928,My 22,18:5
Temperance Town, A 1929,Ag 11,VIII,2:1
Mountain Fury 1929,S 26,27:2
Bidding High 1932,S 29,17:2
Jamboree 1932,N 25,18:4
Halfway to Hell 1934,Ja 3,22:3
Woman of Destiny, A 1936,Mr 3,25:2
Stork Mad 1936,O 1,28:4
Don't Look Now! 1936,N 4,41:3
Macy, Frederick
Firebird 1932,N 22,25:2
Macy, Gertrude (Producer)
One for the Money 1939,F 6,9:2
Two for the Show 1940,F 9,14:2
Happiest Years, The 1949,Ap 26,29:8
I Am a Camera 1951,N 29,39:6
I've Got Sixpence 1952,D 3,44:2
Macy, Sydney
Beyond the Horizon 1920,Mr 10,9:2
Neighbors 1923,D 27,11:1

Macy, Wanda
Macbeth 1936,Ap 15,25:4
Macy, William
Machinal 1960,Ap 8,27:1
Cannibals, The 1968,N 4,60:1
MaDan, Chester
Mikado, The 1944,F 12,11:3
Ruddigore 1944,Mr 3,19:5
Yeomen of the Guard, The 1944,Mr 5,34:3
Madcap Comediennes, The
Aquashow 1953,Je 24,29:2
Madd, Pierrette
Ma Femme 1927,D 18,IX,4:4
Maddala, Suddha
Mahabharata 1970,N 28,22:1
Madden, Cecil (Translator)
Max and Mr Max 1932,Ja 24,VIII,3:5
Madden, Donald
First Impressions 1959,Mr 20,28:1
Julius Caesar 1959,Ag 4,30:1
Julius Caesar 1959,Ag 16,II,1:1
Lysistrata 1959,N 25,19:4
Pictures in the Hallway 1959,D 28,19:1
Henry IV 1960,Mr 2,42:1
Henry IV 1960,Mr 13,II,1:1
She Stoops to Conquer 1960,N 2,42:5
She Stoops to Conquer 1960,N 13,II,1:1
She Stoops to Conquer 1960,N 15,36:3
Plough and the Stars, The 1960,D 7,56:2
Hamlet 1961,Mr 17,17:1
Hamlet 1961,Mr 26,II,1:1
Hamlet 1961,Ap 30,II,1:1
Step on a Crack 1962,O 18,48:1
Milk Train Doesn't Stop Here Anymore, The
  1963,S 18,32:1
One by One 1964,D 2,60:1
Black Comedy; White Lies 1967,F 13,42:1
Black Comedy 1967,F 13,42:1
Black Comedy 1967,O 19,58:1
Ceremony of Innocence, The 1968,Ja 2,33:1
Richard II 1968,Je 24,42:3
In the Bar of a Tokyo Hotel 1969,My 12,54:1
In the Bar of a Tokyo Hotel 1969,My 25,II,5:4
Wars of the Roses, The (Part II) 1970,Jl 3,15:1
Richard III 1970,Jl 4,11:1
Henry VI, Parts I, II, III 1970,Jl 5,II,3:1
Madden, Edward (Lyricist)
Buzzin' Around 1920,Jl 7,14:1
Madden, Edward (Playwright)
Buzzin' Around 1920,Jl 7,14:1
Madden, Harry Timothy (Playwright)
Kill That Story 1934,Ag 30,22:2
Mrs O'Brien Entertains 1939,F 9,16:3
Madden, J C (Playwright)
Parted 1927,Je 5,VII,2:3
Madden, Jeanne
Knickerbocker Holiday 1938,O 20,26:2
Madden, Johanna
All the King's Men 1963,Jl 12,12:1
Madden, John
Twelfth Night 1970,Ja 1,18:1
Hamlet 1970,D 28,40:1
Madden, Peggy
As Husbands Go 1935,Jl 10,24:1
Maddern, Marie
Sandro Botticelli 1923,Mr 27,24:2
Expressing Willie 1924,Ap 17,22:1
Romeo and Juliet 1930,Ap 22,33:1
Maddern, Merle
Nice People 1921,Mr 3,11:1
In the Next Room 1923,N 28,14:1
Assumption of Hannele, The 1924,F 16,16:2
Expressing Willie 1924,Ap 27,VIII,1:1
Enchanted April, The 1925,Ag 25,12:3
Sinner 1927,F 8,20:2
Trial of Mary Dugan, The 1927,S 20,33:1
Sea Gull, The 1929,S 17,34:1
Women Have Their Way, The 1930,Ja 28,28:1
Five Star Final 1930,D 31,11:1
Left Bank, The 1931,O 6,35:3
O Evening Star 1935,D 26,20:1
O Evening Star 1936,Ja 9,24:6
Fields Beyond, The 1936,Mr 7,11:2
Around the Corner 1936,D 29,17:2
Madame Capet 1938,O 26,26:2
Susanna, Don't You Cry 1939,My 23,27:2
Distant City, The 1941,S 23,27:5
Apology 1943,Mr 23,14:2
New Life, A 1943,S 16,26:6
Decision 1944,F 3,23:2
Decision 1944,F 13,II,1:1
Down to Miami 1944,S 12,23:5
Antigone 1946,F 19,21:3
Land's End 1946,D 12,37:5
Druid Circle, The 1947,O 23,29:5
Hedda Gabler 1948,F 25,27:2
Maddern, Victor
Heartbreak House 1963,Je 28,24:1
Maddock, Mary
Is Life Worth Living? 1933,N 10,24:6
Maddocks Tricks
Vaudeville (Palace) 1928,Jl 3,19:2

Maddox, Alvie
Littlest Circus, The 1959,D 26,5:6
Maddox, Diana
Henry IV, Part I 1946,My 7,25:2
Oedipus; Critic, The 1946,My 21,19:2
Under Milk Wood 1957,O 16,42:5
Under Milk Wood 1957,N 10,II,1:1
Two Gentlemen of Verona 1958,Mr 19,35:1
Broken Jug, The 1958,Ap 2,36:1
Henry IV, Part I 1958,Je 25,23:3
Much Ado About Nothing 1958,Je 26,22:1
Troilus and Cressida 1963,Je 19,40:2
Cyrano de Bergerac 1963,Je 20,30:1
Bourgeois Gentilhomme, Le 1964,Je 18,28:2
King Lear 1964,Je 19,36:1
Maddox, Douglas (Miscellaneous)
Does a Tiger Wear a Necktie? 1967,F 4,17:1
Maddox, Frances
With All My Heart 1935,Jl 30,17:1
Maddox, Gloria
Tarot 1970,D 12,19:1
Maddox, John (Lighting Director)
Pullman Car Hiawatha 1962,D 4,46:2
Maddox, Lou
My Romance 1948,O 20,38:5
Maddox, Mulford
Shooting Shadows 1924,Je 27,16:5
Maddux, Frances
Hey, Nonny, Nonny! 1932,Je 7,22:3
There's Wisdom in Women 1935,O 31,17:1
Maddux, James
Founders, The 1957,My 14,39:1
Hatfields & McCoys 1970,Je 23,34:1
Madeira, Louis C
This Mad Whirl 1937,Ja 10,II,4:8
Madeira, Louis C (Playwright)
Red Rhumba 1936,Ap 14,18:1
This Mad Whirl 1937,Ja 10,II,4:8
Fifty-Fifty 1937,N 20,21:1
Fifty-Fifty 1937,D 5,II,3:4
Madie and Ray
Vaudeville (Palace) 1930,Ag 4,13:2
Vaudeville (Palace) 1931,Ap 6,24:3
Madigan, Maisie
Juno and the Paycock 1966,Ag 3,40:1
Madigan, Virginia
Minute's Wait, A 1920,Je 22,9:1
Madis, Alex (Playwright)
Divin Mensonge 1926,N 14,VIII,2:1
Madison, Connie
Merrily We Roll Along 1934,O 1,14:1
Madison, Constance
June Love 1921,Ap 26,20:1
Madison, Ella
Porgy 1927,O 11,26:2
Madison, Ellen
Gay Apprentice, The 1960,F 3,27:2
Milk and Honey 1961,O 11,52:1
Moon Besieged, The 1962,D 6,54:1
Madison, Ellen (Miscellaneous)
Power of Darkness, The 1959,S 30,33:1
Madison, James
Rehearsal, The 1952,My 27,30:5
Madison, Jean
In the Near Future 1925,Mr 11,19:1
Madison, Joan
Skidding 1928,My 22,18:5
With Privileges 1930,S 16,30:2
Young Go First, The 1935,My 29,16:2
Paradise Lost 1935,D 10,31:5
Madison, Louise
Blackbirds 1933,D 4,22:3
Madison, Martha
Connie Goes Home 1923,S 7,10:1
My Son 1924,S 18,18:2
Broadway 1926,S 17,19:3
Set a Thief 1927,F 22,22:1
Madison, Martha (Playwright)
Subway Express 1929,S 25,34:3
Up and Up, The 1930,S 9,25:2
Up and Up, The 1930,S 14,VIII,1:1
Night Remembers, The 1934,N 28,24:3
Madison, Robert
Gospel Glow 1962,O 28,87:5
Madison, Ronnie
Cherry Blossoms 1927,Mr 29,22:3
Furnished Rooms 1934,My 30,14:6
Madison, Rosalind
Vagabond King, The 1943,Je 30,24:2
Madjette, Claire
Castles in the Air 1926,S 7,19:2
Madsen, Ethel
Topaze 1947,D 29,21:5
Show Boat 1957,Je 28,30:2
Madsen, Harold
Just a Minute 1928,O 9,34:3
Madson, Ronnee
First Night 1930,N 27,32:3
Mady-Berry
Eunuque, L' 1927,Ap 3,VIII,4:7
Mae, Billie
Wooden Soldier, The 1931,Je 23,28:4

Mae, Lida
Mayflowers 1925,N 25,14:2
Mae-Martin, Winnie
Jenny Kissed Me 1948,D 24,12:2
Mae-Phillips, Barbara (Miscellaneous)
In the Matter of J Robert Oppenheimer
1969,Mr 7,28:1
Maeda, Seison (Costume Designer)
Azuma Kabuki Dancers and Musicians
1954,Mr 10,29:4
Maedchen, Yvonne
Almost Faithful 1948,Je 5,9:2
Maere, Gene
Mistress of the House, The 1950,Ja 31,19:1
Maestro, Lorna Del
Almost Crazy 1955,Je 21,37:1
Maeterlinck, Maurice (Playwright)
Aglavaine and Selysette 1922,Ja 4,11:1
Burgomaster of Stilemonde, The 1923,N 16,15:3
Pelleas and Melisande 1923,D 5,23:2
Blue Bird, The 1923,D 26,13:3
Blue Bird, The 1923,D 30,VII,1:1
Princesse Isabelle 1935,N 10,IX,1:1
Pelleas et Melisande 1939,Ap 2,X,7:4
Pelleas and Melisande 1957,F 20,38:1
Maeterlinck, Maurice (Translator)
Macbeth 1969,D 14,87:1
Maeterlinck, Renee
Pelleas et Melisande 1939,Ap 2,X,7:4
Mafata, Ferdinand
Sponono 1964,Ap 3,28:1
Magallanes, Nicholas
Music in My Heart 1947,O 3,30:2
Maganini, Margaretta (Costume Designer)
Anatomist, The 1957,F 27,21:5
Fashion 1959,Ja 21,27:1
Colombe 1965,F 24,33:1
Magdalany, Philip
In the Summer House 1964,Mr 26,43:1
Magdalany, Philip (Miscellaneous)
Possibilities 1968,D 5,60:1
Magdalany, Philip (Playwright)
Criss-Crossing 1970,Ja 22,30:1
Watercolor 1970,Ja 22,30:1
Mage and Karr
Vaudeville (Palace) 1949,My 20,32:4
Magee, D S
Front Page, The 1937,N 12,27:2
Magee, Edwin C
Sale and a Sailor, A, or Glory! What Price!
1926,Ap 25,30:4
Magee, Joe (Miscellaneous)
Little Blue Light, The 1951,Ap 30,17:2
Magee, Judith
Fiddler's House, The 1941,Mr 28,27:5
Magee, Patrick
Endgame 1964,F 21,32:1
Afore Night Come 1964,Je 26,34:1
Persecution and Assassination of Marat As
Performed by the Inmates of the Asylum of
Charenton Under the Direction of the Marquis de
Sade, The 1964,Ag 21,14:2
Hamlet 1965,Ag 20,18:2
Persecution and Assassination of Marat As
Performed by the Inmates of the Asylum of
Charenton Under the Direction of the Marquis de
Sade, The 1965,D 28,35:1
Persecution and Assassination of Marat As
Performed by the Inmates of the Asylum of
Charenton Under the Direction of the Marquis de
Sade, The 1966,Ja 9,II,1:1
Keep It in the Family 1967,S 28,59:1
Keep It in the Family 1967,O 8,II,1:6
Battle of Shrivings, The 1970,F 7,23:1
Mageean, J R
Castlereagh 1935,F 20,22:4
Magelssen, Ralph
Great Waltz, The 1934,S 24,14:4
Frederika 1937,F 5,16:5
Roberta 1937,Je 27,II,6:1
Wonderful Night, A; Fledermaus, Die
1937,Jl 14,17:1
Three Waltzes 1937,D 27,10:2
Vie Parisienne, La 1941,N 6,20:3
Song of Norway 1951,Ja 11,28:5
Magennis, Margaret
Diamond Lil 1949,F 7,16:2
Maggart, Brandon
Sing Muse 1961,D 7,52:1
Put It in Writing 1963,My 14,31:1
Kelly 1965,F 8,28:2
Leonard Sillman's New Faces of 1968
1968,My 3,43:1
New Faces of 1968 1968,My 12,II,7:1
Applause 1970,Mr 31,35:1
Applause 1970,Ap 5,II,1:1
Maggart, Brandon (Miscellaneous)
Hay Fever 1970,N 10,55:1
Maggi, Anthony
Sunup to Sundown 1938,F 2,14:3
Maggio, Glenn E
Anvil, The 1962,O 31,33:3

Maggioni, Ettore
Pinocchio 1939,Ja 3,19:2
Maggiore, Charles
Spofford 1967,D 15,54:3
Gloria and Esperanza 1969,Ap 5,30:1
Magid, Marion
House on Grand Street, A 1953,O 10,12:6
Magidson, Herb (Composer)
Music Hall Varieties 1932,N 23,15:3
Michael Todd's Peep Show 1950,Je 29,37:2
Magidson, Herb (Lyricist)
Music Hall Varieties 1932,N 23,15:3
Michael Todd's Peep Show 1950,Je 29,37:2
Magidson, Herman
Student Prince, The 1943,Je 9,16:2
Magidson, Herman (Miscellaneous)
What Did We Do Wrong? 1967,O 23,56:1
Magill, Gertrude
Young Madame Conti 1937,Ap 1,18:4
Magill, Urwin
Birthright 1933,N 22,22:3
Maginnis, Helen
Mirage, The 1920,O 1,14:1
Magis, George
Rainbow 1928,N 22,25:1
Sweet Adeline 1929,S 4,33:1
Miracle at Verdun 1931,Mr 17,34:6
Cat and the Fiddle, The 1931,O 16,26:4
Forbidden Melody 1936,N 3,33:1
Magis, Oscar
Fifty Million Frenchmen 1929,N 28,34:4
Magnani, Anna
Lupa, La 1965,N 12,57:1
Medea 1966,D 21,42:1
Lupa, La 1969,Je 5,54:1
Magni, Eava
Long Day's Journey Into Night 1956,O 17,40:1
Magni, Gioacchino
Mother Martyr 1935,Ja 28,10:3
Magnier, Claude (Playwright)
3 Bags Full 1966,Mr 7,22:1
Magnin, Jerome (Director)
Marco Millions 1938,N 24,36:2
Magnin, Jerome (Scenic Designer)
Marco Millions 1938,N 24,36:2
Magnin, Michelle
Priorities of 1942 1942,Mr 13,23:2
Magnus, Elva
Elsie Janis and Her Gang 1922,Ja 17,13:2
Magnus, Gene
Spellbound 1927,N 15,26:2
Trip to Scarborough, A 1929,Mr 18,31:2
Dragon, The 1929,Mr 26,34:2
Magnus, Klar
Chippies 1929,My 30,23:3
Magnusson, Georg (Scenic Designer)
Long Day's Journey Into Night 1962,My 16,35:4
Magoon, Eaton Jr (Composer)
13 Daughters 1961,Mr 3,17:2
Magoon, Eaton Jr (Lyricist)
13 Daughters 1961,Mr 3,17:2
Magoon, Eaton Jr (Playwright)
13 Daughters 1961,Mr 3,17:2
Magpiong, Richard
Sacco-Vanzetti 1969,F 9,78:1
Magrane, Thais
Merchants of Venus 1920,S 28,14:2
Apache, The 1923,My 9,14:3
Steam Roller, The 1924,N 11,20:2
Magre, Maurice (Playwright)
Beux Billes de Cadix, Les 1923,Ja 21,VII,1:3
Maguire, Fenella
Summer of the Seventeenth Doll 1958,Ja 23,23:2
Maguire, Frank
Many Loves 1959,Ja 14,28:1
Cave at Machpelah, The 1959,Jl 1,25:1
Maguire, Joan
Guys and Dolls 1968,S 2,14:2
Maguire, Kathleen
Sundown Beach 1948,S 8,37:1
Greatest Man Alive!, The 1957,My 9,37:2
Miss Isobel 1957,D 27,22:1
Time of the Cuckoo, The 1958,O 28,40:2
Best Man, The 1960,Ap 1,39:1
Sudden and Accidental Re-education of Horse
Johnson, The 1968,D 19,63:1
Maguire, M A (Playwright)
Trial Divorce 1927,Ja 16,VII,2:4
Maguire, Maureen
Paddy the Next Best Thing 1920,Ag 28,5:5
Maguire, Tucker
Between Two Worlds 1934,O 26,24:2
Maguire, William Anthony (Director)
Betsy 1926,D 29,24:3
Maguire, William Anthony (Playwright)
Frivolities of 1920 1920,Ja 9,22:2
Six-Cylinder Love 1921,Jl 24,VI,1:1
Six-Cylinder Love 1921,Ag 26,8:2
It's a Boy! 1922,Jl 23,VI,1:6
Magureanu, Corina
Ox Cart, The 1966,D 20,58:1
Mahaffie, Ray
Seven Mirrors 1945,O 26,17:2

Mahan, Chris (Miscellaneous)
Clerambard 1957,N 8,22:3
Queen and the Rebels, The 1965,F 26,16:1
Mahan, Frances
Music Box Revue 1923,S 24,5:3
Mahar, Ellen
For Keeps 1944,Je 15,17:5
I Remember Mama 1944,O 20,16:2
Sundown Beach 1948,S 8,37:1
Flight Into Egypt 1952,Mr 19,33:2
Maharis, George
Deathwatch 1958,O 10,34:2
Saintliness of Margery Kempe, The 1959,F 3,35:6
Zoo Story, The 1960,Ja 15,37:2
Zoo Story, The 1960,Ja 31,II,1:1
Maher, Antoinette
Jack Jack 1968,Je 23,74:5
Maher, Bernard
Yeomen of the Guard, The 1936,S 15,37:2
Maher, James N
Gantry 1970,F 16,44:1
Maher, Jan (Producer)
Glorious Ruler, The 1969,Jl 1,31:1
Maher, John
Devil's Disciple, The 1970,Je 30,48:1
Maher, Joseph
Live Like Pigs 1965,Je 8,48:2
Eh? 1966,O 17,47:1
Prime of Miss Jean Brodie, The 1968,Ja 17,39:1
Prime of Miss Jean Brodie, The 1968,Ja 28,II,1:1
Henry V 1969,Je 9,57:1
Much Ado About Nothing 1969,Je 16,57:1
Hamlet 1969,Je 30,33:1
Three Sisters, The 1969,Ag 4,29:1
Local Stigmatic, The; Request Stop 1969,N 4,55:2
Local Stigmatic, The; Applicant 1969,N 4,55:2
Local Stigmatic, The; Trouble in the Works
 1969,N 4,55:2
Local Stigmatic, The; Interview 1969,N 4,55:2
Local Stigmatic, The; Last to Go 1969,N 4,55:2
Local Stigmatic, The 1969,N 4,55:2
Henry V 1969,N 11,43:1
All's Well That Ends Well 1970,Je 16,53:1
All's Well That Ends Well 1970,Je 21,II,3:2
Maher, Paul
Last Man In, The 1930,My 8,32:5
Maher, Phil
Find the Fox 1930,Je 21,20:4
Maher, Symonds Jack
Bright Honor 1936,S 28,14:1
Maher, Wally
Every Man for Himself 1940,D 10,32:3
Mahieu, Charles
Proces, Le; Trial, The 1952,N 18,36:2
Fourberies de Scapin, Les 1952,N 21,21:2
Occupe-Toi d'Amelie; Keep Your Eyes on Amelie
 1952,N 25,35:2
Hamlet 1952,D 2,39:1
Mahieu (Costume Designer)
Sugar Hill 1931,D 26,15:2
Mahin, John
Bad Habits of 1926 1926,My 1,11:1
Plan M 1942,F 21,15:2
Mahler, Albert
White Horse Inn 1936,O 2,28:5
Mahler, Eugene W
Hit the Road 1941,Ap 4,18:3
Mahler, Fritz
Rhapsody 1944,N 23,37:2
Mahlon, Leslie
If 1927,O 26,26:2
Mahon, John
Pequod 1969,Je 30,33:1
Nobody Hears A Broken Drum 1970,Mr 20,55:1
Mahoney, Arthur
Vienna at Night 1945,Ap 30,12:4
Mahoney, Bill (Composer)
My Wife and I 1966,O 11,53:2
Mahoney, Bill (Lyricist)
My Wife and I 1966,O 11,53:2
Mahoney, Bill (Playwright)
My Wife and I 1966,O 11,53:2
Mahoney, F X
Murder at the Vanities 1933,S 13,22:4
Mahoney, Francis
Show Boat 1946,Ja 7,17:2
Mahoney, Francis X
Passing Show of 1921, The 1920,D 30,16:2
Passing Show of 1923, The 1923,Je 15,24:6
Show Boat 1927,D 28,26:1
Show Boat 1932,My 20,22:2
Mahoney, Kathleen
O'Brien Girl, The 1921,O 4,10:2
Mahoney, Tommy (Choreographer)
Ice Capades 1959,S 4,12:1
Ice Capades 1960,S 1,30:1
Mahoney, Will
Scandals 1924,Jl 1,16:1
Vaudeville (Palace) 1925,D 29,21:2
Vaudeville (Hippodrome) 1926,Mr 30,20:4
Vaudeville (Palace) 1926,Ag 24,19:3
Vaudeville (Palace) 1927,My 24,23:1
Take the Air 1927,N 23,28:2

Vaudeville (Palace) 1928,My 29,17:4
Vaudeville (Palace) 1928,Je 5,21:3
Vaudeville (Palace) 1929,Ap 8,32:7
Sketch Book 1929,Jl 2,33:5
Vanities 1931,Ag 11,28:4
Vanities 1931,Ag 16,VIII,1:1
Earl Carroll's Vanities 1931,Ag 28,18:7
Vaudeville (Palace) 1932,Ap 18,19:5
Vaudeville (Palace) 1933,Ja 16,13:2
Veronica's Veil 1933,F 20,11:7
Vaudeville (Palladium) 1935,O 30,16:8
ANTA Album 1950,Ja 30,13:2
Finian's Rainbow 1955,My 19,25:1
Man Who Never Died, The 1958,N 22,27:2
Mahool, Barry
Lucrece 1932,D 21,22:2
Shooting Star 1933,Je 13,22:2
Dance of Death, The 1936,My 20,24:5
Cross-Town 1937,Mr 18,21:5
Adventures of Marco Polo, The 1941,D 28,I,31:7
Mahr, Clara
Bellamy Trial, The 1931,Ap 23,28:6
Amourette 1933,S 28,25:2
Allure 1934,O 30,22:6
Nowhere Bound 1935,Ja 23,20:2
Squaring the Circle 1935,O 4,24:6
Daughters of Atreus 1936,O 15,33:1
Mai, Antoine
Femmes Savantes, Les 1967,F 7,34:2
Maibaum, Richard
Romeo and Juliet 1933,F 3,21:5
Maibaum, Richard (Playwright)
Tree, The 1932,Ap 13,23:5
Birthright 1933,N 22,22:3
Sweet Mystery of Life 1935,O 12,13:3
See My Lawyer 1939,S 28,29:1
Maidman, Edith (Miscellaneous)
Month in the Country, A 1963,My 29,39:2
Maier, Kenneth
Ah, Wilderness! 1953,F 7,10:6
Mail, Leone (Miscellaneous)
Bourgeois Gentilhomme, Le 1955,O 26,26:1
Mailer, Adele
Parents and Children 1969,Ja 13,26:6
Mailer, Norman (Original Author)
Deer Park, The 1967,F 12,II,1:4
Mailer, Norman (Playwright)
Deer Park, The 1967,F 1,27:2
Deer Park, The 1967,F 12,II,1:4
Mailey, Frederick E (Producer)
Reprise 1935,My 2,16:2
Mailliard, Charles
I Was Waiting for You 1933,N 14,23:3
Maillat, Serge
Avare, L', L'; Miser, The 1966,F 9,32:1
Mailo, Chris
Son, The 1950,Ag 16,24:6
Main, Claude
We Never Learn 1928,Ja 24,26:1
Main, Ian (Playwright)
Subway in the Sky 1957,F 28,19:1
Main, John
Merchant of Venice, The 1955,F 23,23:2
Main, John (Miscellaneous)
Ivory Branch, The 1956,My 25,27:1
Main, Laurie
First Impressions 1959,Mr 20,28:1
Jolly's Progress 1959,D 7,42:2
Lord Pengo 1962,N 20,41:2
Main, Marjorie
House Divided, The 1923,N 12,14:1
Salvation 1928,F 1,31:1
Scarlet Sister Mary 1930,N 26,19:2
Ebb Tide 1931,Je 9,33:6
Music in the Air 1932,N 9,28:2
Jackson White 1935,Ap 22,14:6
Dead End 1935,O 29,17:2
Women, The 1936,D 28,13:1
Main, Sam
Brooklyn Biarritz 1941,F 28,16:2
Mainbocher (Costume Designer)
Foolish Notion 1945,Mr 14,23:2
Dream Girl 1945,D 15,13:2
Leading Lady 1948,S 15,38:1
Leading Lady 1948,O 19,33:1
Great Sebastians, The 1956,Ja 15,II,1:1
Tiny Alice 1964,D 30,14:2
Maine, Bruno (Lighting Director)
Bagels and Yox 1951,S 13,38:2
Maine, Bruno (Scenic Designer)
Stars on Ice 1942,Jl 3,12:2
Stars on Ice (2d Edition) 1943,Je 25,13:2
Hats Off to Ice 1944,Je 23,15:2
Icetime 1947,My 29,28:2
Howdy Mr Ice 1948,Je 25,28:5
Howdy, Mr Ice of 1950 1949,My 27,24:2
Mainionis, Anthony
Yerma 1966,D 9,60:1
Antigone 1967,Je 19,43:1
Macbeth 1967,Jl 31,21:1
As You Like It 1968,Je 24,42:3
Androcles and the Lion 1968,Je 27,47:1
Love's Labour's Lost 1968,Je 28,36:1

Mainland, Louise
Caravan 1928,Ag 30,13:3
Maiokano, Robert Joseph
Trojan Women, The 1957,Mr 19,42:7
Maiori, Anthony
Honor Code, The 1931,My 19,25:3
Passion Play 1937,Mr 22,26:6
Maiori, Renato
Due Orfanelle, Le; Two Orphans, The
 1936,O 5,24:4
Tombola, La; Lottery, The 1936,N 9,23:4
Morte Civile, La; Civic Death 1936,N 9,23:4
Feudalismo Oppure La Terra Bassa; Feudalism or
 the Lowland 1937,Mr 8,22:2
Medico Delle Pazze, Il; Physician of Mad Woman,
 The 1937,S 27,24:2
Signora Dalle Camelie, La; Dame aux Camelias, La
 1937,O 9,16:3
Maire, Fred
Schloss, Das 1968,N 20,35:3
Mairich, Max
Nathan the Wise 1962,Mr 7,29:1
Wozzeck 1966,Ap 6,34:1
Mitschuldigen, Die 1966,Ap 6,34:1
Ratten, Die 1966,Ap 13,36:1
Mais, Suzette
As You Like It 1934,N 11,IX,3:6
Maisel, George
Enemy of the People, An 1958,F 26,24:2
Maismith, Laurence
School for Scandal, The 1962,Ap 6,31:3
Maison, Alice
Princess Virtue 1921,My 5,20:2
Maison, Bernice
Naked Genius, The 1943,O 22,20:5
Maison, Edith
Pirates of Penzance, The 1936,Ap 21,27:5
Mikado, The 1942,F 4,22:2
Pirates of Penzance, The 1942,F 18,22:2
Iolanthe 1942,F 24,26:4
Gondoliers, The 1942,Mr 4,22:3
Maison, Gil
Star and Garter 1942,Je 25,26:2
Naked Genius, The 1943,O 22,20:5
Naked Genius, The 1943,N 7,II,1:6
Maisonet, Luis A (Scenic Designer)
Soles Truncos, Los; House on Cristo Street, The
 1959,Ag 31,15:2
Maisonet, Victoria Espinosa de (Director)
Soles Truncos, Los; House on Cristo Street, The
 1959,Ag 31,15:2
Maissel, Alexander
Partition 1948,O 29,31:2
Maissel, Alexander (Composer)
What's It to You? 1931,Mr 18,25:4
Rip Van Wrinkle 1967,D 23,28:1
Maissel, Alexander (Lyricist)
Rip Van Wrinkle 1967,D 23,28:1
Maissel, Alexander (Miscellaneous)
Take Me to Bed 1969,Je 14,24:1
Time for Bed 1969,Je 14,24:1
Maissel, Alexander (Scenic Designer)
Wrong Number 1934,Mr 14,23:6
Maissel, Sarah N (Playwright)
Rip Van Wrinkle 1967,D 23,28:1
Maistre, Francois (Director)
Brigitta, La 1962,S 25,30:1
Maitland, Dexter
This Was Burlesque 1965,Mr 17,55:3
Maitland, Emma
Messin' Around 1929,Ap 23,26:3
Maitland, Gertrude
Marry the Poor Girl 1920,S 27,18:3
Lady Butterfly 1923,Ja 23,18:1
Kingdom of God, The 1928,D 21,30:2
Love Duel, The 1929,Ap 16,32:3
His Majesty's Car 1930,O 24,30:1
Boy Friend, The 1932,Je 8,22:3
Living Dangerously 1935,Ja 14,10:3
Few Are Chosen 1935,S 18,19:3
Maitland, Gloria
Solid Gold Cadillac, The 1953,N 6,24:2
Maitland, Michael
Mame 1966,My 25,41:1
Rothschilds, The 1970,O 20,40:1
Maitland, Richard
Li'l Abner 1956,N 16,24:2
Maitland, Ruth
Double-Or Quit 1922,O 8,VI,1:7
Johnny 2X4 1942,Mr 17,24:6
Majeroni, Giorgio
Claw, The 1921,O 18,20:1
Listening In 1922,D 5,24:1
Laugh, Clown, Laugh! 1923,N 29,30:1
Majeroni, Mario
Mandarin, The 1920,N 10,18:2
Casanova 1923,S 27,10:2
Kongo 1926,Mr 31,20:5
Stripped 1929,O 22,26:1
Cynara 1931,N 3,31:1
Major, Aime
Henry V 1956,Je 20,27:2

Major, Austin J (Director)
When in Rome 1934,F 28,22:6
Major, Austin J (Playwright)
When in Rome 1934,F 28,22:6
Major, Clare Tree
Secret Garden, The 1931,N 8,31:4
Major, Clare Tree (Director)
Beauty and the Beast 1932,Ja 10,I,29:2
Major, Clare Tree (Playwright)
Under the Lilacs 1934,N 19,13:3
Major, Clare Tree (Producer)
Under the Lilacs 1934,N 19,13:3
Major, Dorothy
Little Poor Man, The 1925,Ag 6,14:1
Courage 1927,Ja 20,20:1
Major, Gerri (Miscellaneous)
Year Round, The 1953,My 6,38:7
Major, Henry
Padre, The 1926,D 28,16:3
Major, John (Mrs)
Miracle, The 1924,Ja 16,17:1
Major, Leon (Director)
Gondoliers, The 1962,Jl 7,9:4
Patience 1968,My 16,52:1
Major, William
Rosmersholm 1946,N 23,11:5
American Gothic 1953,N 11,35:6
As You Like It 1955,O 29,12:2
Romeo and Juliet 1955,O 16,36:3
Changeling, The 1956,My 4,20:3
Taming of the Shrew, The 1956,Ag 11,11:2
Camille 1956,S 19,33:1
Sleeping Prince, The 1956,N 2,31:1
In Good King Charles's Golden Days
1957,Ja 25,16:1
Beaux' Stratagem, The 1957,Jl 9,25:4
Widowers' Houses 1959,Mr 3,39:2
Taming of the Shrew, The 1960,Ag 20,17:1
King Lear 1961,My 15,34:6
Makarenko, Daniel
Relations 1928,Ag 21,27:3
Puppet Show 1930,O 29,26:5
Overture 1930,D 8,26:4
Saluta 1934,Ag 29,13:4
Summer Wives 1936,Ap 14,18:1
Makarov, Yuri
Moscow Circus on Ice 1970,D 9,63:1
Make, Maya Angelou
Blacks, The 1961,My 5,23:1
Makeham, Eliot
Lady's Not for Burning, The 1950,N 9,42:2
Lady's Not for Burning, The 1950,N 26,II,1:1
Midsummer Night's Dream, A 1954,S 22,33:1
Makem, Tom
Guests of the Nation 1958,My 21,40:1
Maker, Jessie
Keep Kool 1924,My 23,16:4
Makgoba, Paul
Sponono 1964,Ap 3,28:1
Akokawe 1970,Je 5,21:1
Maki, Kotaro (Scenic Designer)
Fiddler on the Roof 1967,S 7,50:1
Makinson, George
Bright Honor 1936,S 28,14:1
Thirsty Soil 1937,F 4,16:2
Maklary
Letter, The 1927,O 30,IX,4:1
Makman, Michael
Frere Jacques 1968,Je 8,23:2
Mako
Banquet for the Moon, A 1961,Ja 20,24:2
Maksimov, Vladimir (Playwright)
Man Alive 1965,My 23,13:1
Maksimova, Raissa
Three Sisters, The 1965,F 12,15:1
Kremlin Chimes 1965,F 25,23:1
Malaby, Richard (Composer)
Electra 1932,Ja 9,21:4
Malach, L (Playwright)
With Open Eyes 1938,O 27,27:2
Malaidy, James
Flame of Love 1924,Ap 22,19:2
Stairs, The 1927,N 8,32:7
Papavert 1931,D 30,25:1
Cyrano de Bergerac 1936,Ap 28,17:1
Enemy of the People, An 1937,F 16,19:1
Malaidy, James C
Piker, The 1925,Ja 16,14:1
Witch, The 1926,N 19,22:5
Malakoff
Chauve-Souris 1922,Je 6,17:4
Malamuth, Charles (Playwright)
Squaring the Circle 1935,S 22,X,3:2
Squaring the Circle 1935,O 4,24:6
Malamuth, Charles (Translator)
Squaring the Circle 1935,O 4,24:6
Million Torments, A 1936,Ja 16,24:5
Malarkey, Jack
Great White Hope, The 1967,D 14,58:1
Indians 1969,My 27,43:1
Malarkey, John Edward
Iceman Cometh, The 1968,Ap 1,58:1

Malas, Spiro
Oklahoma! 1969,Je 24,37:1
Oklahoma! 1969,Jl 6,II,1:1
Malatzky, Ann Berger
Rose Tattoo, The 1966,O 21,36:2
Malatzky, Joanna Sandra
Rose Tattoo, The 1966,O 21,36:2
Malatzky, Susan Carol
Rose Tattoo, The 1966,O 21,36:2
Malbin, Elaine
Mikado, The 1949,O 5,35:2
Pirates of Penzance, The 1949,O 11,41:2
Trial by Jury 1949,O 18,34:2
My Darlin' Aida 1952,O 28,36:4
Paradise Island 1961,Je 24,11:1
Around the World in 80 Days 1963,Je 24,22:1
Malbourne, Lee
Story of Mary Surratt, The 1947,F 10,25:2
Malchien, Richard
Erminie 1921,Ja 4,11:1
Wheel, The 1921,Ag 30,10:1
Czarina, The 1922,F 1,22:1
Polly Preferred 1923,Ja 12,13:3
Malcia
Folies Bergere 1939,D 25,28:2
Malcies, Jean-Dennis (Costume Designer)
Occupe-Toi d'Amelie; Keep Your Eyes on Amelie
1952,N 25,35:2
Repetition, La; Rehearsal, The 1952,N 28,22:2
Lark, The 1955,My 13,21:2
Chien du Jardinier, Le; Gardener's Dog, The
1957,F 19,36:1
Adieux, Les 1957,F 19,36:1
Vie Parisienne, La 1964,Mr 11,34:2
Malcies, Jean-Dennis (Scenic Designer)
Repetition, La; Rehearsal, The 1952,N 28,22:2
Lark, The 1955,My 13,21:2
Adieux, Les 1957,F 19,36:1
Chien du Jardinier, Le; Gardener's Dog, The
1957,F 19,36:1
Romanoff and Juliet 1957,O 11,24:1
Malcolm, Eleanor
Places, Please 1937,N 13,10:6
Malcolm, Frederick
Thank You 1921,O 4,10:2
Holy Terror, A 1925,S 29,31:2
Privilege Car 1931,Mr 4,33:1
Strangers at Home 1934,S 15,20:5
Strip Girl 1935,O 21,22:6
Malcolm, George
Abe Lincoln in Illinois 1938,O 17,12:2
Malcolm, George Horace (Playwright)
Bachelor's Brides 1925,My 29,20:2
Malcolm, James
This Way to the Tomb 1961,D 9,21:1
Malcolm, John
Jane Eyre 1958,My 2,31:1
Time for Singing, A 1966,My 23,48:2
Malcolm, Maude
Possession 1928,O 3,35:1
Malcolm, Nellie
House of Usssher, The 1926,Ja 14,18:4
Legend of Leonora, The 1927,Mr 30,22:4
Fanatics, The 1927,N 8,32:4
These Days 1928,N 13,36:2
Lady With a Lamp, The 1931,N 20,27:2
Evensong 1933,F 1,13:4
Party, A 1933,Ag 24,18:4
Between Two Worlds 1934,O 26,24:2
Private Affair, A 1936,My 15,28:7
Love From a Stranger 1936,S 22,31:5
Doctor Social 1948,F 12,29:5
Malcolm, Reginald
Lally 1927,F 9,16:3
Simpleton of the Unexpected Isles, The
1935,F 19,27:5
Petticoat Fever 1935,Jl 2,24:4
As Husbands Go 1935,Jl 10,24:1
Oscar Wilde 1938,O 11,20:2
Malcolm (Composer)
Republic, The 1970,Ap 28,49:1
Malcolm (Miscellaneous)
Republic, The 1970,Ap 28,49:1
Malcolm (Musical Director)
Republic, The 1970,Ap 28,49:1
Malcolm-Smith, George (Original Author)
Are You With It? 1945,N 12,17:3
Malcom, David
Return of Peter Grimm, The 1921,S 22,12:2
Malcom, Fred
Pigs 1924,S 2,22:5
Malden, Karl
Golden Boy 1937,N 5,18:5
How to Get Tough About It 1938,F 9,16:2
Missouri Legend 1938,S 20,27:2
Gentle People, The 1939,Ja 6,25:1
Key Largo 1939,N 28,30:2
Journey to Jerusalem 1940,O 7,21:2
Flight to the West 1940,D 31,19:1
Uncle Harry 1942,My 21,24:1
Sun Field, The 1942,D 10,33:2
Counterattack 1943,F 4,27:2
Sons and Soldiers 1943,My 5,22:2

Malden, Karl—Cont
Winged Victory 1943,N 22,24:1
Assassin, The 1945,O 18,20:2
Truckline Cafe 1946,F 28,19:4
All My Sons 1947,Ja 30,21:2
All My Sons 1947,F 9,II,1:1
Streetcar Named Desire, A 1947,D 4,42:2
Streetcar Named Desire, A 1947,D 14,II,3:1
Peer Gynt 1951,Ja 29,15:2
Desire Under the Elms 1952,Ja 17,23:4
Desire Under the Elms 1952,Ja 20,II,1:1
Desperate Hours, The 1955,F 11,20:2
Desperate Hours, The 1955,F 20,II,1:1
Egghead, The 1957,O 10,39:1
Maldener, Fritz (Composer)
Why Do I Deserve This? 1966,Ja 19,31:2
Maldonado, George
Merry Widow, The 1961,O 27,28:2
Maldone, Solly
Rust 1924,F 1,12:1
Male, Gordon
Vagabond King, The 1935,N 29,22:7
Maleczech, Ruth
Red Horse Animation, The 1970,N 20,32:1
Malek, Bernard
Headless Horseman, The 1937,Mr 6,10:4
Malek, Frances (Costume Designer)
School for Scandal, The 1953,Je 24,29:2
Malek, Richard
Montserrat 1949,O 31,21:4
King Lear 1950,D 26,18:1
Malekos, Nick
Maggie Flynn 1968,O 24,52:1
Malet, Arthur
Othello 1955,S 8,27:2
Henry IV, Part I 1955,S 22,34:2
Henry V 1956,Jl 7,11:2
Misanthrope, The 1956,N 13,44:1
Volpone 1957,Ja 8,27:1
Volpone 1957,Ja 13,II,10:1
Apollo of Bellac, The 1957,Ap 10,39:1
Virtuous Island, The 1957,Ap 10,39:1
Country Wife, The 1957,Je 27,22:1
Children of Darkness 1958,Mr 1,11:4
Shadow of a Gunman, The 1958,N 21,26:1
Shadow of a Gunman, The 1958,N 30,II,1:1
Look After Lulu 1959,Mr 4,35:1
Moonbirds 1959,O 10,13:1
Balcony, The 1960,Mr 4,21:1
Henry V 1960,Je 30,23:1
Measure for Measure 1960,Jl 27,33:1
Heartbreak House 1963,Je 28,24:1
Maley, Denman
Lady Bug 1922,Ap 18,15:3
49ers, The 1922,N 7,14:1
Barnum Was Right 1923,Mr 13,19:3
Greenwich Village Follies 1923,S 21,4:6
Deep Tangled Wildwood, The 1923,N 6,22:1
Haunted House, The 1924,S 3,12:1
Butter and Egg Man, The 1925,S 24,28:1
Maley, Peggy
I Gotta Get Out 1947,S 26,27:2
Joy to the World 1948,Mr 19,28:2
Maley, Stephen
Spite Corner 1921,Jl 17,VI,1:1
Spite Corner 1922,S 26,18:1
Breaking Point, The 1923,Ag 17,8:4
Gorilla, The 1925,Ap 29,24:2
Sure Fire! 1926,O 21,23:1
Chalked Out 1937,Mr 26,24:2
Mali, Derek (Producer)
Call It Virtue 1963,Mr 28,8:2
Malin, Barbara
Walk-Up 1961,F 24,24:1
Malin, Jean
Sisters of the Chorus 1930,O 21,34:3
Malina, Judith
Many Loves 1959,Ja 14,28:1
Cave at Machpelah, The 1959,Jl 1,25:1
Tonight We Improvise 1959,N 7,27:4
Women of Trachis 1960,Je 23,18:3
Mountain Giants, The 1961,Ap 5,32:3
Man Is Man 1962,S 19,31:1
Antigone 1968,O 11,36:1
Malina, Judith (Director)
Cave at Machpelah, The 1959,Jl 1,25:1
Connection, The 1959,Jl 16,30:2
Connection, The 1960,F 7,II,1:1
Marrying Maiden, The 1960,Je 23,18:3
In the Jungle of Cities 1960,D 21,39:1
Connection, The 1961,Je 16,29:1
Apple, The 1961,D 8,44:1
Apple, The 1962,Ap 20,22:1
Brig, The 1963,My 16,40:1
Mysteries and Smaller Pieces 1966,F 26,14:1
Frankenstein 1968,O 3,54:1
Antigone 1968,O 11,36:1
Paradise Now 1969,Je 10,52:3
Malina, Judith (Translator)
Antigone 1968,O 11,36:1
Malina, Luba
Cradle Snatchers 1932,N 17,23:2
Revels of 1936 1935,S 30,12:4
Firefly, The 1937,Ag 4,14:1

Malina, Luba—Cont

Nina Rosa 1937,Ag 26,24:3
Mexican Hayride 1944,Ja 29,9:6
Marinka 1945,Jl 19,19:2
Lovely Me 1946,D 26,30:4
Festival 1955,Ja 19,22:1
Nude With Violin 1957,N 15,36:1

Malina, Racquel
Florodora 1936,Ag 23,II,8:2

Malinowitz, Rebecca
Mikado, The 1935,Ag 24,17:5

Malipiero, Francesco (Composer)
Citta Morta, La 1935,S 22,X,7:7

Malis, Claire
Jar, The 1969,Ap 23,42:1
License, The 1969,Ap 23,42:1

Malis, Fran
Montserrat 1954,My 26,34:2
Romeo and Juliet 1955,D 16,36:3
Admirable Bashville, The 1956,F 21,38:1
Toy for the Clowns, A 1962,S 13,31:2
Laundry, The 1963,F 19,5:2
Lesson, The 1963,S 18,35:4
Bald Soprano, The 1963,S 18,35:4
Shout From the Rooftops 1964,O 29,40:1
Impromptu, L' 1965,Mr 8,34:1
Leader, The 1965,Mr 8,34:1
Bedlam Galore, for Two or More 1965,Mr 8,34:1

Malis, Fran (Director)
Opening of a Window, The 1961,S 26,32:2

Malkin, Richard P (Lyricist)
Step a Little Closer 1948,My 28,26:6

Malkin, William
Ame en Peine, L' 1950,My 31,25:2

Mall, Paul
Great Temptations, The 1926,My 19,29:1

Mallah, Vivian
Marriage Is for Single People 1945,N 22,38:2

Mallen, Dave
Padlocks of 1927 1927,Jl 6,23:4
Arrest That Woman 1936,S 19,20:4
Censored 1938,F 28,18:2
Ringside Seat 1938,N 23,24:5
Oklahoma! 1951,My 30,15:2

Malleson, Miles
Henry IV, Part I 1946,My 7,25:2
Henry IV, Part II 1946,My 8,33:4
Henry IV 1946,My 12,II,1:1
Oedipus; Critic, The 1946,My 21,19:2
Oedipus 1946,My 21,19:2
Love's Labour's Lost 1949,O 24,18:3

Malleson, Miles (Director)
Ace, The 1933,Ag 25,12:4
Mother, The 1939,Ap 26,26:2
Oedipus; Critic, The 1946,My 21,19:2

Malleson, Miles (Miscellaneous)
Scrapped 1927,O 16,IX,2:7
Night Must Fall 1936,S 29,34:1

Malleson, Miles (Playwright)
Merrileon Wise 1926,D 19,VII,6:4
Fanatics, The 1927,Ap 10,VIII,1:3
Love at Second Sight 1927,S 11,VIII,2:4
Fanatics, The 1927,N 8,32:4
Ace, The 1933,Ag 25,12:4
Ace, The 1933,S 17,X,1:6
Mother, The 1939,Mr 19,XI,3:3
Mother, The 1939,Ap 26,26:2
Tartuffe 1957,O 9,39:1

Malleson, Miles (Producer)
Mother, The 1939,Mr 19,XI,3:3

Malleson, Miles (Translator)
Imaginary Invalid, The 1967,My 2,53:1

Mallett, Chuck (Miscellaneous)
Three Sisters, The 1970,F 12,30:1

Malley, Dann (Director)
Paid Companions 1931,Je 23,28:4

Malley, Martin
High Gear 1927,O 7,24:3

Malley, William
American Mime Theatre 1958,S 25,28:4

Mallier, Julien
Three Musketeers, The 1968,Je 26,43:1
George Dandin 1968,Je 28,36:1

Mallina, Trudy
Count of Luxembourg, The 1930,F 18,28:2

Mallinson, Hiram R
Wings Over Europe 1936,Mr 4,24:7

Mallinson, Patricia
Why We Misbehave 1935,Jl 25,14:8
Mulatto 1935,Ag 8,13:2
Then Came the Dawn 1935,Ag 29,25:4

Malloch, Elizabeth
Country Wife, The 1936,D 2,34:1
Contrast, The 1940,Mr 26,17:2

Mallon, James
Son, The 1950,Ag 16,24:6

Mallon, Marie
Dodsworth 1934,F 26,20:4

Mallon, Paul
Veronica's Veil 1933,F 20,11:7
Veronica's Veil 1936,Mr 2,4:3
Passion Play 1938,Mr 7,11:2

Mallonee, George (Director)
Legend of Lovers 1959,O 28,40:3

Dumbbell People in a Barbell World 1962,F 15,25:1

Mallonee, George (Miscellaneous)
Iceman Cometh, The 1968,Ap 1,58:1

Mallory, Burton
Dorian Gray 1928,My 22,18:4
Once in a Lifetime 1930,S 25,22:3
Mr Papavert 1932,Ja 23,18:6
Intimate Relations 1932,Mr 29,23:2
Blue Monday 1932,Je 3,23:2
Romeo and Juliet 1933,F 3,21:5
Merrily We Roll Along 1934,O 1,14:1
Big Blow 1938,O 3,11:2
Fireworks on the James 1940,My 15,30:2
Johnny on the Spot 1942,Ja 9,24:2
Victory Belles 1943,O 27,26:3
According to Law 1944,Je 2,20:3
Silver Whistle, The 1948,N 25,49:2
As You Like It 1950,Ja 27,27:2
Twentieth Century 1950,D 25,23:6
Goodbye Again 1956,Ap 25,38:1
Will and the Way, The 1957,D 3,46:5
Crucible, The 1958,Mr 12,36:1
Crucible, The 1958,Je 1,II,1:1
Who'll Save the Plowboy? 1962,Ja 10,24:2
Anvil, The 1962,O 31,33:3

Mallory, Francetta
Spring Fever 1925,Ag 4,14:2

Mallory, Jay (Playwright)
Sweet Aloes 1934,N 1,24:1
Sweet Aloes 1936,F 25,23:5
Sweet Aloes 1936,Mr 5,24:5

Mallory, Kay
Crooks' Convention, The 1929,S 19,37:4

Mallory, Martin
Sweet Chariot 1930,O 24,30:2
Overture 1930,D 8,26:4

Mallory, Victoria
West Side Story 1968,Je 25,32:1
Carnival! 1968,D 13,58:1

Mallory, Vincent
Love 'Em and Leave 'Em 1926,F 4,20:4
If 1927,O 26,26:2
Love Nest, The 1927,D 23,17:1

Mallory, Vincent (Producer)
Green Stick 1934,O 10,21:2

Mallory, Wilfred
Hamlet 1930,Mr 25,34:4
Macbeth 1930,Mr 26,24:6
Twelfth Night 1930,Mr 27,24:7
Taming of the Shrew, The 1930,Mr 28,22:8
Richard III 1930,Mr 31,24:1
King Lear 1930,Ap 1,34:6
As You Like It 1930,Ap 3,32:5
Julius Caesar 1930,Ap 4,22:3

Mallow, Paul
Veronica's Veil 1931,F 23,36:2

Malloy, Dann
Rivals, The 1930,Mr 14,24:4
Monkey 1932,F 12,25:2
Slight Case of Murder, A 1935,S 12,28:5
No More Peace 1938,Ja 29,13:2
Coriolanus 1938,F 2,14:5
Meet a Body 1944,O 17,19:5

Malloy, Francetta
America's Sweetheart 1931,F 11,23:1
Americana 1932,S 25,IX,1:6
Americana 1932,O 6,19:3
Howdy Stranger 1937,Ja 15,17:5
New Priorities of 1943 1942,S 16,28:2

Malloy, Francis X
His Queen 1925,My 12,26:1

Malloy, Martin
Blue Flame, The 1920,Mr 16,18:1
Madeleine and the Movies 1922,Mr 7,11:1
Square Peg, A 1923,Ja 29,10:2
Yellow 1926,S 22,30:1
Wanted 1928,Jl 3,19:2
Poppa 1928,D 25,31:1
Penny Arcade 1930,Mr 11,24:5

Malloy, Neil
Big Fight, The 1928,S 19,33:1
Would-Be Gentleman, The 1930,Ap 30,29:2
Incubator 1932,N 2,23:3

Malloy, Thomas (Playwright)
Paradise 1931,My 12,29:2

Malmud, Helen
Morgue, The 1927,F 2,22:4
Butterflies 1927,F 2,22:4
Florentine Tragedy, A 1927,F 2,22:4

Malneck, Matty Orchestra
Very Warm for May 1939,N 18,23:2

Malnick, Michael
King Lear 1950,Ag 30,26:2

Malo, Gina
Gang's All Here, The 1931,F 19,21:3
On Your Toes 1937,F 6,15:2
Gentle People, The 1939,Jl 30,IX,1:3

Malon, Allen
Shoemaker's Prodigious Wife, The 1949,Je 15,38:2

Malon, David
Coney Island Play 1970,O 31,34:2

Malon, Ray
Shoemaker's Prodigious Wife, The 1949,Je 15,38:2

Malon, Ray—Cont

Pied Piper of Hamelin, The 1950,Ap 3,19:2
Bonds of Interest, The 1951,D 1,7:2

Malone, Bettye
Red, White and Maddox 1969,Ja 27,27:1

Malone, Dale
Guys and Dolls 1966,Je 9,55:2

Malone, Danny
Church Street 1934,N 20,24:5

Malone, Elizabeth
Clouds of the Sun 1922,My 6,11:2
Mountain, The 1933,S 12,28:6
Doctor Faustus 1937,Ja 9,21:2
Big Blow 1938,O 3,11:2
White Steed, The 1939,Ja 11,16:2
Annie Get Your Gun 1946,My 17,14:2

Malone, Florence
Respect for Riches, The 1920,My 12,9:1

Malone, J A E (Producer)
Sally 1921,S 11,20:2

Malone, Kay
Catch a Star! 1955,S 7,35:2

Malone, Kitty
Doctor Faustus 1957,F 19,35:7

Malone, Lynn
Banjo Eyes 1941,D 26,20:2

Malone, Mark
Salad of the Mad Cafe, The 1964,Ap 1,43:1

Malone, Mary
Peg o' My Heart 1948,Ag 25,29:2
Goodbye My Fancy 1948,N 18,35:2
Good Housekeeping 1949,Ag 17,19:3

Malone, Nancy
Time Out for Ginger 1952,N 27,50:4
Major Barbara 1956,O 31,27:1
Makropoulos Secret, The 1957,D 4,52:4

Malone, Pat
She Stoops to Conquer 1949,D 29,21:3
Pin to See the Peepshow, A 1953,S 18,17:2
Montserrat 1954,My 26,34:2
Cherry Orchard, The 1955,O 19,38:1
Mrs Warren's Profession 1956,Je 7,35:2
Quare Fellow, The 1958,N 28,34:1
Macbeth 1959,Ag 1,9:2
Deadly Game, The 1960,F 3,27:2
Camino Real 1960,My 17,42:2

Malone, Penny
Adding Machine, The 1956,F 10,17:1
Kaleidoscope 1957,Je 14,20:2

Malone, Rayford
Banjo Eyes 1941,D 26,20:2

Malone, William
Native Son 1941,Mr 25,26:5
Native Son 1942,O 24,10:6
Catherine Was Great 1944,Ag 3,16:1

Malone, William H
Joy of Serpents 1930,Ap 4,22:4
Let Freedom Ring 1935,N 7,26:2
Excursion 1937,Ap 10,11:4
Father Malachy's Miracle 1937,N 18,26:4

Maloney, James
Detective Story 1949,Mr 24,34:2
Inherit the Wind 1955,Ap 22,20:2

Maloney, Peter
Fisherman, The 1965,Ja 27,24:6
Fourth Pig, The 1965,Ja 27,24:6
Experiment, The 1967,My 9,54:2
Forensic and the Navigators 1970,Ap 2,43:1
Terminal 1970,Ap 15,51:2
Endgame 1970,My 6,47:1
Serpent, The 1970,Je 2,35:1

Maloney, Peter (Miscellaneous)
Telemachus Clay 1963,N 16,17:2
Dirty Old Man, The 1964,My 5,53:1
Sarah and the Sax 1964,My 5,53:1

Maloney, Russell (Lyricist)
Sleepy Hollow 1948,Je 4,26:3

Maloney, Russell (Playwright)
Sleepy Hollow 1948,Je 4,26:3

Maloney, Seamus
Derryowen 1946,O 29,34:2

Maloney, Thomas
Sweetheart Shop, The 1920,S 1,13:4

Maloney, William J
King Lear 1930,D 26,18:2

Malongo
Hangman's Whip 1933,F 25,20:2

Malory, Kenneth
Almost Faithful 1948,Je 5,9:2

Maloy, Richard
You Can't Take It With You 1945,Mr 27,23:7

Malstrom, Gustava
Student Prince, The 1931,Ja 30,18:1

Maltby, H F (Lyricist)
Jack o' Diamonds 1935,F 26,17:3

Maltby, H F (Playwright)
Such a Nice Young Man 1920,Jl 11,VI,1:6
Rotters, The 1922,My 23,12:4
Right Age to Marry, The 1926,F 16,22:3
Virgin Man, The 1927,Ja 19,20:4
Dear Old England 1930,Ja 19,VIII,2:6
Dear Old England 1930,Mr 26,24:6
Red Light 1931,D 6,VIII,2:7
Rings on Her Fingers 1932,My 22,VIII,1:3

Maltby, H F (Playwright)—Cont

Jack o' Diamonds 1935,F 26,17:3
Shadow, The 1936,Ap 26,II,12:6

Maltby, Richard Jr (Composer)

Leonard Sillman's New Faces of 1968
1968,My 3,43:1

Maltby, Richard Jr (Lyricist)

Sap of Life, The 1961,O 3,44:1
Leonard Sillman's New Faces of 1968
1968,My 3,43:1

Maltby, Richard Jr (Playwright)

Sap of Life, The 1961,O 3,44:1

Malten, William

Candle in the Wind 1941,O 23,26:2
Thank You Svoboda 1944,Mr 2,13:2
Private Life of the Master Race, The
1945,Je 13,28:3
Assassin, The 1945,O 18,20:2
French Touch, The 1945,D 10,18:2

Maltin, Bernard (Composer)

Bomboola 1929,Je 27,17:3

Maltin, Bernard (Lyricist)

Bomboola 1929,Je 27,17:3

Maltz, Albert (Playwright)

Merry-Go-Round 1932,Ap 23,11:2
Merry-Go-Round 1932,My 1,VIII,1:1
Peace on Earth 1933,N 30,39:2
Black Pit 1935,Mr 21,26:6
Private Hicks 1936,Ja 13,14:4

Maltz, Albert J

Betty Behave 1927,Mr 9,28:4

Maltz, Maxwell (Playwright)

Hidden Stranger 1963,Ja 10,5:5
Hidden Stranger 1963,Ja 15,8:5

Maltz, Philip

Jolly Orphan, The 1929,D 23,18:6

Malville, William

Woman of Destiny, A 1936,Mr 3,25:2

Malvin, Joseph

Banjo Eyes 1941,D 26,20:2

Maly

Uri Muri 1928,Ap 15,IX,4:1

Malzkuhn, Eric

Arsenic and Old Lace 1942,My 11,18:6

Malzkuhn, Eric (Playwright)

Critic, The 1969,Mr 9,76:5
Sganarelle 1970,Ja 13,41:1

Mamakas, Andreas

Triumph of Robert Emmet, The 1969,My 8,54:1

Mamales, George

Decameron, The 1961,Ap 13,32:1

Mamel, Ruth

Knickerbocker Holiday 1938,O 20,26:2

Mameluch, Robert

Flossie 1924,Je 4,25:2

Mamet, Liane

My Girl 1924,N 25,27:2

Mamlet, Alexander (Choreographer)

Pinocchio 1939,Ja 3,19:2

Mammen, Edward

Contrast, The 1926,O 1,26:2
Zuleika 1928,Mr 7,28:7
Man Without Money, A 1929,N 3,27:4

Mamorsky, Morris (Composer)

Jonah! 1967,S 22,52:2

Mamorsky, Morris (Miscellaneous)

Family Portrait 1959,My 6,48:2

Mamoulian, Rouben (Director)

Porgy 1927,O 11,26:2
Marco Millions 1928,Ja 10,28:2
These Modern Women 1928,F 14,26:2
Porgy 1928,Jl 1,VIII,3:5
Congai 1928,N 28,24:3
Wings Over Europe 1928,D 11,35:1
Game of Love and Death, The 1929,N 26,28:4
R U R 1930,F 18,28:1
Month in the Country, A 1930,Mr 18,30:5
Solid South 1930,My 11,IX,2:6
Farewell to Arms, A 1930,S 23,30:3
Solid South 1930,O 15,27:1
Porgy and Bess 1935,O 1,27:2
Porgy and Bess 1935,O 11,30:2
Oklahoma! 1943,Ap 1,27:1
Oklahoma! 1943,Ap 11,II,1:1
Sadie Thompson 1944,N 17,25:2
Sadie Thompson 1944,N 26,II,1:1
Carousel 1945,Ap 20,24:2
Carousel 1945,Ap 29,II,1:1
St Louis Woman 1946,Ap 1,22:2
Leaf and Bough 1949,Ja 22,10:2
Carousel 1949,Ja 26,28:2
Carousel 1949,F 6,II,1:1
Lost in the Stars 1949,O 31,21:2
Lost in the Stars 1949,N 6,II,1:1
Arms and the Girl 1950,F 3,28:2
Oklahoma! 1951,My 30,15:2
Oklahoma! 1953,S 1,19:1
Oklahoma! 1958,Mr 20,32:3

Mamoulian, Rouben (Lighting Director)

Porgy and Bess 1935,O 1,27:2
Leaf and Bough 1949,Ja 22,10:2

Mamoulian, Rouben (Original Author)

Oklahoma! 1951,S 23,II,3:1

Mamoulian, Rouben (Playwright)

Sadie Thompson 1944,N 17,25:2
Arms and the Girl 1950,F 3,28:2

Mamoulian, Rouben (Producer)

Porgy 1929,Ap 28,IX,1:4

Man, Christopher

Trojan Women, The 1963,D 24,7:6
Family Way, The 1965,Ja 14,44:5

Manabozho

All Soul's Eve 1920,My 13,9:1

Manacher, Alfred T (Miscellaneous)

Blacks, The 1961,My 5,23:1
Deuces Wild; It's All Yours 1962,Ap 25,31:1
Deuces Wild; Thus 1962,Ap 25,31:1
Charlatans; On Circe's Island 1962,Ap 27,26:1
Charlatans; Summer Ghost, A 1962,Ap 27,26:1

Manager, Itzik (Miscellaneous)

Untitled-Poetry Reading 1967,Jl 18,29:1

Manahan, Anna

Lovers; Losers 1968,Jl 26,21:4

Manaku, David

Half-Caste, The 1926,Mr 30,20:4

Manasse, George (Miscellaneous)

Mr Simian 1963,O 22,44:1

Manatis, Janine

Evening With Shaw, An; Village Wooing
1955,Ag 13,6:6
Too Late the Phalarope 1956,O 12,35:1
Trial of Dmitri Karamazov, The 1958,Ja 28,30:1

Manatis, Janine (Miscellaneous)

Cantilevered Terrace, The 1962,Ja 18,24:1

Manatt, Fred

Her Way Out 1924,Je 24,18:3
Yes, Yes, Yvette 1927,O 4,32:3
Box Seats 1928,Ap 20,27:2
Chinese O'Neill 1929,My 23,27:1
Mountain Fury 1929,S 26,27:2
Flying High 1930,Mr 4,24:4
George White's Scandals 1931,S 15,30:1
Say When 1934,N 9,24:2
Thanks for Tomorrow 1938,S 28,28:2
Scandals 1939,Ag 29,17:2

Manche, Hugo

Agent 666, L' 1923,My 30,10:5

Manchester, Joe (Playwright)

Secret Life of Walter Mitty, The 1964,O 27,44:5

Manchester, Joe (Producer)

Deadly Game, The 1960,F 3,27:2
Secret Life of Walter Mitty, The 1964,O 27,44:5

Manchester, Mary

Gondoliers, The 1963,Je 5,33:2
Show Boat 1966,Jl 20,48:1

Mancini, Al

Davy Jones's Locker 1959,Mr 30,25:1
What a Killing 1961,Mr 28,41:1
Red Eye of Love 1961,Je 13,28:1
I Want You 1961,S 15,29:1

Manciotti, Silvio

Adventurer, The 1935,N 11,21:1

Mancuso, Philip

Awakening of Spring, The 1964,My 13,50:1

Mandal Brothers

Ziegfeld Follies 1921,Je 22,10:1

Mandan, Robert

No Exit 1956,Ag 15,23:1
Speaking of Murder 1956,D 20,37:1
Trojan Women, The 1957,Mr 19,42:7
Julius Caesar 1957,O 24,39:1
King Lear 1959,Ja 3,11:2
Death of Satan, The 1960,Ap 6,49:1
Here Come the Clowns 1960,S 20,48:1
Trojan Women, The 1963,D 24,7:6
Maggie Flynn 1968,O 24,52:1
But, Seriously... 1969,F 28,29:1
Applause 1970,Mr 31,35:1
Applause 1970,Ap 5,II,1:1

Mandas, Catherine

Ruy Blas 1957,D 14,16:3

Mandel, Alice (Playwright)

Lady Killer, The 1924,F 24,VII,2:5
Lady Killer, The 1924,Mr 13,14:2

Mandel, Evan William (Miscellaneous)

Up Eden 1968,N 27,42:1

Mandel, Frank (Director)

Vickie 1942,S 23,28:1

Mandel, Frank (Lyricist)

Tickle Me 1920,Ag 18,9:1
Mary 1920,O 19,12:1
Jimmie 1920,N 18,15:3
O'Brien Girl, The 1921,O 4,10:2
Desert Song, The 1946,Ja 9,20:2

Mandel, Frank (Original Author)

Only Girl, The 1934,My 22,28:2
Desert Song, The 1946,Ja 9,20:2

Mandel, Frank (Playwright)

Look Who's Here 1920,Mr 3,12:2
Tickle Me 1920,Ag 18,9:1
Jimmie 1920,N 18,15:3
O'Brien Girl, The 1921,O 4,10:2
Queen O' Hearts 1922,O 11,22:1
Nobody's Business 1923,O 23,17:1
Nobody's Business 1923,O 28,VIII,1:1
Sweet Little Devil 1924,Ja 22,15:4

Mandel, Frank (Playwright)—Cont

Lady Killer, The 1924,F 24,VII,2:5
Lady Killer, The 1924,Mr 13,14:2
Captain Jinks 1925,S 9,22:1
No, No, Nanette 1925,S 17,20:2
Desert Song, The 1926,D 11,24:2
New Moon, The 1928,S 20,33:1
East Wind 1931,O 28,19:1
East Wind 1931,D 11,VIII,4:3
May Wine 1935,N 23,23:1
May Wine 1935,D 6,30:3
New Moon, The 1942,Ag 19,14:2
New Moon, The 1944,My 18,16:2

Mandel, Frank (Producer)

Captain Jinks 1925,S 9,22:1
Desert Song, The 1926,D 1,24:2
Good News 1927,S 7,35:4
Follow Thru 1929,Ja 10,24:3
America's Sweetheart 1931,Ja 25,VIII,2:4
America's Sweetheart 1931,F 11,23:1
Free for All 1931,Ag 16,VIII,1:1
East Wind 1931,O 28,19:1
East Wind 1931,D 11,VIII,4:3
Vickie 1942,S 23,28:1

Mandel, Israel (Miscellaneous)

Father and Son 1956,O 20,17:4

Mandel, Joe

Greenwich Village Follies 1923,S 21,4:6
Vaudeville (Palace) 1926,My 8,29:2
Vaudeville (Palace) 1927,Je 28,29:2
Vaudeville (Palace) 1929,Ag 19,23:1

Mandel, Loring (Playwright)

Advise and Consent 1960,O 19,57:3
Advise and Consent 1960,N 18,25:1
Advise and Consent 1960,N 27,II,1:1

Mandel, William

Greenwich Village Follies 1923,S 21,4:6
Vaudeville (Palace) 1926,My 8,29:2
Vaudeville (Palace) 1927,Je 28,29:2
Vaudeville (Palace) 1929,Ag 19,23:1

Mandel Brothers, The

Vaudeville (Hippodrome) 1925,S 1,18:3
Vaudeville (Palace) 1928,My 29,17:4

Mandelker, Philip (Miscellaneous)

Daphne in Cottage D 1967,O 16,56:1

Mandell, Alan

Gift of Fury, A 1958,Mr 24,21:4

Mandell, M S (Translator)

Month in the Country, A 1930,Mr 18,30:5

Mandell, Rick (Miscellaneous)

How to Be a Jewish Mother 1967,D 29,18:1
Blood Red Roses 1970,Mr 23,48:1

Mandell, Rick (Producer)

War Games 1969,Ap 18,37:1

Mandels, The

Vaudeville (Hippodrome) 1924,Ap 29,12:2

Manderino, Ned

Prometheus Bound 1957,Ag 9,11:6

Mandeville, Butler

Passing of the Third Floor Back, The
1928,F 21,18:2
Tenth Man, The 1929,Mr 21,29:2
David Garrick 1929,Ag 2,17:5

Mandeville, Ernest W (Miscellaneous)

Truly Valiant 1936,Ja 10,17:3

Mandia, John

Killer, The 1960,Mr 23,33:1

Mandis, Renos

Tarot 1970,D 12,19:1

Mandley, Percy G (Playwright)

Eight Bells 1933,O 30,14:2
Eight Bells 1933,N 5,IX,1:1

Mandola, John

Son, The 1950,Ag 16,24:6

Mandolidou, Vasso

Joan of Lorraine 1947,N 14,29:1

Mandolin Art Ensemble

Motel Peissi, The Contor's Kid 1934,N 29,33:3

Mandruzzato, Maria

Giuochi di Prestigio 1931,N 2,26:1
Berretto a Songali, Il; Cap With Bells, The
1931,N 30,16:3
Ladro, Il; Thief, The 1932,F 22,23:4

Mane, Doura

Macbeth 1969,D 14,87:1

Manelli, T

Piacere Dell 'Onesta, Il 1929,Mr 25,33:1

Maner, William

Conerico Was Here to Stay 1965,Mr 4,37:1

Manessier, Jean Baptiste (Scenic Designer)

Architect and the Emperor of Assyria, The
1970,Jl 24,17:2

Manet, Eduardo (Playwright)

Nuns, The 1970,Je 2,35:1

Manetto, Corinna

Conversation Piece 1957,N 19,38:2

Manfred, Gertrude

Four Walls 1927,S 20,33:1

Manfred, Paul

Man in the Glass Booth, The 1968,S 27,41:1

Manfredi, Don (Scenic Designer)
Obbligato 1958,F 19,22:2
Opening Night 1963,O 3,28:2
Matter of Like Life and Death, A 1963,O 3,28:2
Maids, The 1963,N 15,29:1
Manfredi, Nino
Rugantino 1964,F 2,II,1:4
Rugantino 1964,F 7,34:1
Manfro, Anthony
Aria Da Capo 1950,My 25,36:2
Mangan, Buddy
Her Tin Soldier 1933,Ap 7,22:6
Second Hurricane 1937,Ap 22,18:4
Mangan, Frank
Miss Emily Adam 1960,Mr 30,43:1
Manger, Itsik (Playwright)
Enchanting Melody 1964,N 25,40:1
Let's Sing Yiddish 1966,N 10,63:1
Mangione, Jasper
Spanish Love 1920,Ag 18,6:1
Plot Thickens, The 1922,S 6,16:1
Trial of Mary Dugan, The 1927,S 20,33:1
Sunup to Sundown 1938,F 2,14:3
Mango, Angelo
Leave It to Jane 1959,My 26,30:2
Angela 1969,O 31,33:1
Mango, Angelo (Miscellaneous)
Point of No Return 1957,Mr 23,17:2
Mangoode, Richard
Oresteia 1966,Je 30,29:1
Mangus, Gene
Beauty and the Beast 1932,Ja 10,I,29:2
Manheim, Leonard F
You'll Never Know 1921,Ap 21,9:2
Man Who Married a Dumb Wife, The
1923,My 10,22:3
Manheim, Leonard F (Director)
Man Who Married a Dumb Wife, The
1923,My 10,22:3
Manheim, Ralph (Translator)
Diary of a Madman 1967,Mr 24,25:1
Ergo 1968,Mr 4,29:1
Tango 1969,Ja 20,33:1
Amphitryon 1970,My 29,13:1
Good Woman of Setzuan, The 1970,N 6,51:1
Manheimer, Wallace A (Playwright)
Mister Romeo 1927,S 6,35:3
Kith and Kin 1930,My 14,31:1
Broadway Boy 1932,My 4,23:5
Manhoff, Bill (Playwright)
My L A 1951,D 9,87:1
Owl and the Pussycat, The 1964,N 19,48:1
Maniccia, Pat
Jar, The 1969,Ap 23,42:1
Manigault, Kenneth
Natural Man 1941,My 8,20:4
Freight 1949,F 4,30:2
Freight 1950,Ap 27,36:2
Hall of Healing 1952,My 8,35:6
Major Barbara 1954,Je 30,23:2
In Splendid Error 1954,O 27,33:6
417 1961,Mr 6,30:1
Manillow, Barry (Composer)
Drunkard, The 1970,Ap 14,54:1
Manillow, Barry (Lyricist)
Drunkard, The 1970,Ap 14,54:1
Manilow, Barry (Musical Director)
Now 1968,Je 6,53:1
Manilow, Lewis (Producer)
Purple Dust 1956,D 28,15:1
Manings, Allan (Playwright)
Littlest Revue, The 1956,My 23,37:2
Manings, Muriel
Sandhog 1954,N 24,17:1
Manino, Tony
Playboy of Newark, The 1943,Mr 20,11:2
Manion, Kenneth
Mating Season, The 1927,Jl 19,27:6
King Can Do No Wrong, The 1927,N 17,28:4
Manion, Lucille
Betty, Be Good 1920,My 5,14:2
Manis, James
Fourth Wall, The 1968,S 5,53:1
Manisoff, M
If Booth Had Missed 1931,My 14,27:1
Manisoff, M (Director)
Unto Such Glory 1937,My 7,28:2
Manker, Tamzon
Gypsy Fires 1925,D 8,28:3
Mankiewicz, Herman J (Playwright)
Good Fellow, The 1926,Je 27,VII,3:1
Good Fellow, The 1926,O 6,22:1
Wild Man of Borneo, The 1927,S 14,29:2
Wild Man of Borneo, The 1927,S 25,VIII,1:1
Mankiewicz, Joseph (Original Author)
Applause 1970,Ap 5,II,1:1
Mankiewicz, Tom (Playwright)
Georgy 1970,F 27,26:1
Mankin, Robert S (Miscellaneous)
Dames at Sea 1968,D 21,46:1
Dames at Sea 1970,S 24,60:1
Mankoff, Allan H (Miscellaneous)
Wet Paint 1965,Ap 13,33:1

Mankowitz, L
How Revolting! 1932,Mr 11,14:6
Mankowitz, Wolf (Playwright)
Pickwick 1963,Jl 5,13:2
Pickwick 1965,O 6,5:3
Manley, Beatrice
Eve of St Mark, The 1942,O 8,30:2
Cherry Orchard, The 1944,Ja 26,22:1
Eastward in Eden 1947,N 19,33:2
Gift of Fury, A 1958,Mr 24,21:4
King Lear 1961,My 15,34:6
House of Bernarda Alba, The 1963,N 25,23:2
Country Wife, The 1965,D 10,58:2
Caucasian Chalk Circle, The 1966,Mr 25,35:1
Alchemist, The 1966,O 14,48:1
Yerma 1966,D 9,60:1
Manley, David
Room 349 1930,Ap 23,24:5
Bulls, Bears and Asses 1932,My 7,11:3
Manley, Dorothy (Playwright)
Stigma 1927,F 11,19:1
Manley, Iris
Show Boat 1946,Ja 7,17:2
Manley, J
Veils 1928,Mr 14,28:5
Manley, Linda
Americana Pastoral 1968,D 11,51:1
Manley, Marian Warring
Genius and the Crowd 1920,S 7,20:1
Anybody's Game 1932,D 22,21:4
Manley, Miti
Sharlee 1923,N 23,20:1
China Rose 1925,Ja 20,18:1
Manley, William (Playwright)
Crow's Nest, The 1923,My 10,22:3
Shooting Shadows 1924,Je 27,16:5
Wild Waves 1932,Ja 24,VIII,3:3
Wild Waves 1932,F 20,11:4
Mann, Allan
Americana 1932,O 6,19:3
Earthlight Theater 1970,N 4,38:2
Mann, Allan (Director)
Earthlight Theater 1970,N 4,38:2
Mann, Andrea
Sally 1948,My 7,31:2
Mann, Bertha
That Day 1922,Jl 9,VI,1:4
Whispering Wires 1922,Ag 8,26:2
Man With a Load of Mischief, The 1925,O 27,20:1
Virgin, The 1926,F 23,26:1
Mann, Beverly
Fantasticks, The 1960,My 4,55:2
Mann, Budd
Pimpernel! 1964,Ja 7,26:6
Mann, Charlton (Playwright)
Blue Lagoon, The 1921,S 15,16:1
Beau Geste 1929,F 17,IX,2:1
Mann, Chris
Something More! 1964,N 11,36:1
Mann, Daniel (Director)
Come Back, Little Sheba 1950,F 16,28:5
Rose Tattoo, The 1951,F 5,19:2
Rose Tattoo, The 1951,F 11,II,1:1
Paint Your Wagon 1951,N 13,32:2
Immoralist, The 1954,F 2,18:7
Immoralist, The 1954,F 9,22:1
Immoralist, The 1954,F 14,II,1:1
Loss of Roses, A 1959,N 30,27:1
Loss of Roses, A 1959,D 6,II,5:1
Mann, Daniel (Miscellaneous)
Golden State, The 1950,N 27,29:3
Flahooley 1951,My 15,39:1
Mann, David
Conflict 1929,Mr 7,22:4
Mann, David (Composer)
Angel in the Wings 1947,D 12,36:4
Mann, Delbert (Director)
Speaking of Murder 1956,D 20,37:1
Zelda 1969,Mr 6,38:1
Mann, Dolores
Thieves' Carnival 1955,F 2,21:1
Aria Da Capo 1958,My 21,40:1
Mann, Dulce
Hamlet 1959,S 11,21:4
Mann, Edward
Spider, The 1927,Mr 23,29:1
Big Fight, The 1928,S 19,33:1
Under the Gaslight 1929,Ap 3,27:1
Getting Even 1929,Ag 20,31:1
Judgment Day 1934,S 13,26:4
Sailors of Cattaro 1934,D 11,28:4
Crime and Punishment 1935,Ja 23,20:3
Panic 1935,Mr 16,18:4
Young Go First, The 1935,My 29,16:2
Bitter Stream 1936,Mr 31,16:6
200 Were Chosen 1936,N 21,21:1
Having Wonderful Time 1937,F 22,12:5
Mann, Edward (Director)
Bonds of Interest, The 1951,D 1,7:2
Mann, Edwin
Dance Night 1938,O 15,20:5
Mann, Erich
Dantons Tod 1927,D 21,28:3

Mann, Erika
Pepper Mill 1937,Ja 6,19:4
Mann, Erika (Lyricist)
Pepper Mill 1937,Ja 6,19:4
Mann, Erika (Playwright)
Pepper Mill 1937,Ja 6,19:4
Mann, Ethel
Sing Out, Sweet Land! 1944,D 28,24:2
Mann, Florence
Rutherford and Son 1927,Ap 13,29:2
Mann, Frances
Marry the Poor Girl 1920,S 27,18:3
Mann, Friederike
Wiener Blut 1964,S 12,14:1
Mann, Gertrude
Advertising of Kate, The 1922,My 9,22:2
Mann, Gloria
All in Favor 1942,Ja 21,20:6
Right Next to Broadway 1944,F 22,26:2
Blood Wedding 1949,F 7,16:2
Mann, Gubi
Morning's at Seven 1955,Je 23,25:1
Adding Machine, The 1956,F 10,17:1
Diversions 1958,N 8,14:4
On the Town 1959,Ja 16,36:1
Mann, Gwen
Sunny River 1941,D 5,28:2
Mann, Herbie (Composer)
Banquet for the Moon, A 1961,Ja 20,24:2
Mann, Howard
Trial of Dmitri Karamazov, The 1958,Ja 28,30:1
Golden Rainbow 1968,F 5,27:1
Mann, Irene
Girl From Wyoming, The 1938,O 31,12:1
Mann, Iris
Galileo 1947,D 8,34:2
Cup of Trembling, The 1948,Ap 21,33:5
Innocents, The 1950,F 2,30:2
Innocents, The 1950,F 12,II,1:1
Children's Hour, The 1952,D 19,35:2
Children's Hour, The 1952,D 28,II,1:1
Mann, Jack
High Kickers 1941,N 1,21:2
Mann, Jean
Poor Nut, The 1925,Ap 28,18:1
Fast Service 1931,N 18,26:3
Home Sweet Home 1936,Jl 1,29:2
Tell Me Pretty Maiden 1937,D 17,33:5
Window Shopping 1938,D 24,13:2
Pillar to Post 1943,D 11,11:2
Song of Bernadette 1946,Mr 27,22:2
Mann, Jerome
Vaudeville (Palace) 1926,S 14,25:3
Mann, Jerry
Oklahoma! 1951,My 30,15:2
Mann, Joan
Million Dollar Baby 1945,D 22,17:2
Park Avenue 1946,N 5,31:2
Inside U S A 1948,My 1,19:2
Small Wonder 1948,S 16,33:5
Of Thee I Sing 1952,My 6,34:2
Mann, Joan (Choreographer)
Tickets, Please! 1950,Ap 28,25:2
Gay Divorce 1960,Ap 4,37:1
Mann, Johnny (Musical Director)
Danny Kaye Show 1963,Ap 11,28:2
Mann, Joseph R
Plot Thickens, The 1922,S 6,16:1
Mann, Jules
Jubilee 1935,O 14,20:1
Mann, June
Scandals 1939,Ag 29,17:2
Mann, Klaus (Lyricist)
Pepper Mill 1937,Ja 6,19:4
Mann, Klaus (Playwright)
Pepper Mill 1937,Ja 6,19:4
Mann, Lew
Harry Delmar's Revels 1927,N 29,30:2
Mann, Lili
Winter's Tale, The 1946,Ja 16,18:6
Mann, Louis
Unwritten Chapter, The 1920,O 12,18:1
Whirl of New York, The 1921,Je 14,18:1
Nature's Nobleman 1921,N 15,23:2
Give and Take 1923,Ja 19,13:1
Milgrim's Progress 1924,N 30,VIII,2:1
Milgrim's Progress 1924,D 23,17:1
Vaudeville (Palace) 1926,Ap 23,24:3
Vaudeville (Hippodrome) 1926,Ap 13,28:2
That French Lady 1927,Mr 16,29:3
Mann, Louis (Director)
That French Lady 1927,Mr 16,29:3
Mann, Martin
Up She Goes 1922,N 7,14:2
Mann, Michael
Helen Goes to Troy 1944,Ap 25,17:2
Chocolate Soldier, The 1947,Mr 13,34:2
High Button Shoes 1955,Mr 12,10:6
Lulu 1958,S 30,24:1
Mann, N D
1776 1926,Ap 24,11:2
Mann, Nancy
Helen Goes to Troy 1944,Ap 25,17:2

Mann, Pat
Smiles 1930,N 19,19:2
Show Boat 1932,My 20,22:2
Mann, Paul
Bitter Oleander 1935,F 12,24:3
Flight to the West 1940,D 31,19:1
Criminals, The 1941,D 22,24:3
It's About Time 1942,Mr 31,28:3
War and Peace 1942,My 22,26:3
Lamp at Midnight 1947,D 22,29:2
Bruno and Sidney 1949,My 4,38:2
Flight Into Egypt 1952,Mr 19,33:2
Too Late the Phalarope 1956,O 12,35:1
Golden Six, The 1958,O 27,31:2
After the Fall 1964,Ja 24,18:1
Changeling, The 1964,O 30,32:2
Incident at Vichy 1964,D 4,44:1
Danton's Death 1965,O 22,46:1
'Tis Pity She's a Whore 1967,O 21,15:2
Three Sisters, The 1968,Mr 18,56:1
Mann, Paul (Lyricist)
Hellzapoppin 1938,S 23,34:2
Mann, Peanuts
Michael Todd's Peep Show 1950,Je 29,37:2
Peep Show 1950,Jl 9,II,1:1
Mann, Philip
Green Ring, The 1922,Ap 5,22:1
Little Clay Cart, The 1924,D 6,13:3
Critic, The 1925,My 9,12:4
Jubilee 1935,O 14,20:1
Mann, Ronald De (Miscellaneous)
Look to the Lilies 1970,Mr 30,59:1
Mann, Ruth
Girl From Wyoming, The 1938,O 31,12:1
Mann, Sam
We Americans 1926,O 13,20:4
Of Thee I Sing 1931,D 28,20:1
Spring Song 1934,O 2,18:2
Mann, Seymour
Jubilee 1935,O 14,20:1
Mann, Stanley (Miscellaneous)
You're a Good Man, Charlie Brown 1967,Mr 8,51:1
Mann, Stanley (Playwright)
Hide and Seek 1957,Ap 3,26:1
Walk in Dark Places, A 1966,Ja 28,21:1
Better Luck Next Time 1966,Ja 28,21:1
Mann, Stuart
King and I, The 1964,Jl 7,26:1
Guys and Dolls 1965,Ap 29,39:1
Mann, Sylvia
Magnificent Hugo, The 1961,Ap 8,12:2
Dear Me, the Sky Is Falling 1963,Mr 4,9:1
Cindy 1964,Mr 20,24:1
Sunset 1966,My 13,34:1
Mann, Theodore (Director)
Drums in the Night 1967,My 18,54:1
Iphigenia in Aulis 1967,N 22,40:2
Moon for the Misbegotten, A 1968,Je 13,55:2
Moon for the Misbegotten, A 1968,Je 30,II,1:1
Morning 1968,N 29,52:1
Night 1968,N 29,52:1
Noon 1968,N 29,52:1
Night 1968,N 29,52:1
Morning 1968,N 29,52:1
Noon 1968,N 29,52:1
Little Murders 1969,Ja 6,38:1
Trumpets of the Lord 1969,Ap 30,37:1
Ah, Wilderness! 1969,N 9,86:1
Seven Days of Mourning 1969,D 17,64:1
Seven Days of Mourning 1970,Ja 4,II,5:1
Arsenic and Old Lace 1970,N 5,59:1
Mann, Theodore (Miscellaneous)
Innkeepers, The 1956,F 3,19:1
Iceman Cometh, The 1956,My 8,38:1
Camino Real 1960,My 17,42:2
Smiling the Boy Fell Dead 1961,Ap 20,28:1
Thank You, Miss Victoria 1966,Ap 12,43:1
Birdbath 1966,Ap 12,43:1
This Is the Rill Speaking 1966,Ap 12,43:1
Chicago 1966,Ap 13,36:1
Recluse, The 1966,Ap 13,36:1
War 1966,Ap 13,36:1
Mann, Theodore (Producer)
Cradle Song 1955,D 2,32:2
Long Day's Journey Into Night 1956,N 8,47:2
House of Breath, The 1957,Ap 15,23:2
Children of Darkness 1958,Mr 1,11:4
Quare Fellow, The 1958,N 28,34:1
Our Town 1959,Mr 24,46:2
Smiling the Boy Fell Dead 1961,Ap 20,28:1
Someone From Assisi 1962,Ja 12,28:1
Childhood 1962,Ja 12,28:1
Infancy 1962,Ja 12,28:1
Plays for Bleecker Street 1962,Ja 12,28:1
General Seeger 1962,Mr 1,26:2
Great Day in the Morning 1962,Mr 29,29:1
Pullman Car Hiawatha 1962,D 4,46:2
Desire Under the Elms 1963,Ja 11,5:6
Six Characters in Search of an Author 1963,Mr 11,7:2
Trumpets of the Lord 1963,D 23,22:3
Trojan Women, The 1963,D 24,7:6
Othello 1964,O 13,48:1

Hughie 1964,D 23,21:2
And Things That Go Bump in the Night 1965,Ap 27,27:5
Baal 1965,My 7,33:2
Live Like Pigs 1965,Je 8,48:2
Royal Hunt of the Sun, The 1965,O 27,36:2
Zulu and the Zayda, The 1965,N 11,59:1
White Devil, The 1965,D 7,56:1
Eh? 1966,O 17,47:1
Drums in the Night 1967,My 18,54:1
Midsummer Night's Dream, A 1967,Je 30,23:1
Noon 1968,D 8,II,5:4
Morning 1968,D 8,II,5:4
Night 1968,D 8,II,5:4
Chicago 70 1970,My 26,33:1
Boesman and Lena 1970,Je 23,35:1
Mann, Thomas (Original Author)
Gabrielle 1941,Mr 26,26:2
Mann, Winifred
Gift of Fury, A 1958,Mr 24,21:4
Birthday Party, The 1961,My 15,34:6
House of Bernarda Alba, The 1963,N 25,23:2
Milk Train Doesn't Stop Here Anymore, The 1965,Jl 27,25:1
King John 1967,Jl 14,19:1
Cyrano de Bergerac 1968,Ap 26,30:1
Mann, Yvonne
Old Maid, The 1935,Ja 8,26:1
Mann and Barto
Hellzapoppin 1938,S 23,34:2
Manna, Charlie
Shoestring '57 1956,N 6,31:1
Mannadiar, Chandra
Mahabharata 1970,N 28,22:1
Mannat, Fred
Ziegfeld Follies 1934,Ja 5,24:3
Manne, Betsy
Littlest Circus, The 1959,D 26,5:6
Mannering, Jay
Russian Bank 1940,My 25,20:2
Manners, Bernice
Whoopee 1928,D 5,34:3
Manners, David
Truckline Cafe 1946,F 28,19:4
Hidden Horizon 1946,S 20,42:2
Manners, Diana (Lady)
Miracle, The 1924,Ja 16,17:1
Miracle, The 1924,Ja 26,10:1
Miracle, The 1924,F 17,4:3
Miracle, The 1924,My 22,14:3
Miracle, The 1925,Ag 17,10:4
Miracle, The 1925,S 29,31:6
Miracle, The 1925,O 29,29:1
Miracle, The 1926,D 28,16:2
Miracle, The 1927,F 1,24:5
Miracle, The 1927,Ap 15,27:1
Miracle, The 1927,My 29,II,2:5
Miracle, The 1927,Je 8,23:2
Miracle, The 1932,Ap 10,I,18:1
Miracle, The 1932,My 8,VIII,2:2
Manners, Ginger
Sing Out the News 1938,S 26,12:5
Manners, Harry (Director)
Brother Elks 1925,S 15,29:2
Manners, Hilda
Loud Speaker 1927,Mr 3,27:2
Tired Business Man, The 1929,Je 5,32:5
Manners, J Hartley
Don't Tell George 1928,Jl 22,VII,1:1
Manners, J Hartley (Playwright)
One Night in Rome 1920,Ap 30,1:2
Peg o' My Heart 1921,F 15,7:1
National Anthem, The 1922,Ja 24,16:3
National Anthem, The 1922,F 5,VI,1:1
Peg o' My Dreams 1924,My 6,25:3
Gay Divorce 1932,N 30,23:4
Peg o' My Heart 1948,Ag 25,29:2
Manners, Jane
Merry Malones, The 1927,S 27,30:2
Angela 1928,D 4,28:2
Manners, Jayne
By Jupiter 1942,Je 4,22:1
Brights Lights of 1944 1943,S 17,27:4
Allah Be Praised! 1944,Ap 21,14:2
Manners, John
Steel 1939,D 20,30:2
Manners, Loraine
Vaudeville (Hollywood) 1932,F 16,24:3
Blossom Time 1943,S 6,21:2
Manners, Margaret
George White's Scandals 1926,Je 15,23:2
Manners, Marlene
Russell Patterson's Sketch-Book 1960,F 8,35:1
Manners, Martha Lee
Wise-Crackers, The 1925,D 17,26:1
Dream Play 1926,Ja 21,18:2
American Tragedy, An 1926,O 12,31:2
Los Angeles 1927,D 20,32:3
Manners, Millicent
Pre-Honeymoon 1936,My 1,19:4
Manners, Sylvia
Queer People 1934,F 16,16:2
Spring Song 1934,O 2,18:2

Manners, Zeke (Sgt)
Winged Victory 1943,N 22,24:1
Mannes, Marya (Playwright)
Cafe 1930,Ag 29,11:1
Dance Me a Song 1950,Ja 21,10:5
She Stoops to Conquer 1968,Ap 1,58:3
Manney, Sara
Sisters' Tragedy, The 1930,My 6,33:1
Mighty Nimrod, The 1931,My 13,23:1
Mannheim, Lucie
Three Sisters, The 1927,Mr 13,VII,2:4
Trial of Mary Dugan, The 1928,Je 24,VIII,1:4
Nass Oder Trocken? 1929,Jl 7,VIII,2:1
Will Hill Be Pardoned; Wird Hill Amnestiert? 1930,Je 1,VIII,2:1
Love in the Country 1930,S 28,VIII,4:4
Marriage 1931,N 1,VIII,4:3
Nina 1935,S 18,19:6
Nina 1935,O 13,IX,3:1
Girl Unknown 1936,S 17,18:2
Girl Unknown 1936,O 4,IX,3:7
Mannheimer, Albert (Director)
Bees and the Flowers, The 1946,S 27,19:3
Mannheimer, Albert (Playwright)
Bees and the Flowers, The 1946,S 27,19:3
Mannigault, Kenneth
Rain 1948,F 2,15:2
Manning, Alice
Vogues of 1924 1924,Mr 28,14:3
Artists and Models 1924,O 16,33:3
Vaudeville (Palace) 1930,Mr 3,18:5
Vaudeville (Palace) 1930,D 1,19:1
Manning, Ambrose
Great Waltz, The 1934,S 24,14:4
Manning, Bruce (Original Author)
9th Street Guest, The 1930,Ag 26,24:3
Manning, Conne
Canteen Show, The 1942,S 4,18:1
Manning, D M
Caesar and Cleopatra 1927,N 6,IX,2:1
Manning, David
Lawyers' Dilemma, The 1928,Jl 10,17:2
Tin Pan Alley 1928,N 2,29:1
Pinocchio 1939,Ja 3,19:2
Flag Is Born, A 1946,S 7,10:6
H M S Pinafore 1960,Ja 29,14:1
Annie Get Your Gun 1966,Je 1,42:2
Manning, De Witt M
Hamlet 1927,Ap 7,23:3
Manning, Don
Ice Follies 1959,Ja 14,30:1
Utopia, Limited 1960,Ap 8,27:2
Manning, Ellis III
Stephen D 1966,Ag 5,17:1
Manning, Frances
Roseanne 1923,D 31,9:5
Manning, Frank
Humoresque 1923,F 28,13:2
With Privileges 1930,S 16,30:2
Dinner at Eight 1932,O 24,18:2
Ship Comes in, A 1934,S 20,21:1
Creeping Fire 1935,Ja 17,22:3
Manning, Hallie
Broadway Whirl, The 1921,Je 9,10:4
Paradise Alley 1924,Ap 2,17:3
Prunella; Love in a Garden 1926,Je 16,23:3
Ladies of the Jury 1929,O 22,26:2
Blind Mice 1930,O 16,28:2
Society Girl 1931,D 31,16:1
Manning, Hope
Susanna, Don't You Cry 1939,My 23,27:2
All in Fun 1940,N 22,26:2
Manning, Hugh
Saint Joan 1962,F 21,57:4
Manning, Irene
Day Before Spring, The 1945,N 23,27:2
Day Before Spring, The 1945,D 2,II,1:1
Tattooed Countess, The 1961,My 4,40:2
Manning, Jack
Junior Miss 1941,N 19,28:2
Great Big Doorstep, The 1942,N 27,26:2
Harriet 1943,Mr 4,24:2
Othello 1943,O 20,18:1
Streets Are Guarded, The 1944,N 21,19:7
Mermaids Singing, The 1945,N 29,26:6
Mayor of Zalamea, The 1946,Ja 28,15:5
O'Daniel 1947,F 25,32:2
Alice in Wonderland 1947,Ap 7,19:2
Rip Van Winkle 1947,Jl 16,28:2
Man and Superman 1947,O 9,31:2
Sun and I, The 1949,Mr 21,18:4
Good Housekeeping 1949,Ag 17,19:3
Mrs Warren's Profession 1950,O 26,39:2
Billy Budd 1951,F 12,18:3
Tender Trap, The 1954,O 14,37:2
Lovers, Villains and Fools: A Shakespearean Variety Show 1956,O 24,44:7
Say Darling 1958,Ap 4,17:1
Do I Hear a Waltz? 1965,Mr 19,28:1
Manning, Jack (Director)
Lovers, Villains and Fools: A Shakespearean Variety Show 1956,O 24,44:7

Manning, James
Treat 'Em Rough 1926,O 5,26:2
Manning, Jane
Ben Bagley's New Cole Porter Revue 1965,D 23,20:1
Manning, Jeff
Mamba's Daughters 1953,Mr 21,12:6
Manning, John
When Differences Disappear 1941,Je 3,17:4
Manning, Marcia
Tin Pan Alley 1928,N 2,29:1
Manning, Margo
Democratic Body, A 1942,F 13,24:7
Manning, Mary (Playwright)
Youth's the Season 1937,O 24,XI,3:3
Castle Irish 1938,Mr 21,20:1
Manning, Mildred
Du Barry 1932,N 23,15:2
Manning, Monroe
Yours Is My Heart 1946,S 6,16:5
Manning, Monroe (Miscellaneous)
Yours Is My Heart 1946,S 6,16:5
Manning, Natalie
Cornered 1920,D 9,18:2
Manning, Paula
Oedipus Rex 1960,Ap 30,15:2
Manning, Peter
Stephen D 1966,Ag 5,17:1
Manning, Phelps (Miscellaneous)
Johnny Summit 1957,S 25,23:4
Manning, Philip
Lady Windermere's Fan 1927,F 27,VII,2:3
Manning, Rena
Last Waltz, The 1921,My 11,20:3
Some Party 1922,Ap 17,22:1
Manning, Richard
Schoolhouse on the Lot 1938,Mr 23,18:4
Manning, Ruth
Face, The 1941,N 29,15:3
Sweet Genevieve 1945,Mr 21,27:3
Tower Beyond Tragedy, The 1950,N 27,29:1
Come Out, Carlo! 1962,My 4,27:2
Mr Simian 1963,O 22,44:1
Rose Tattoo, The 1966,O 21,36:2
Yerma 1966,D 9,60:1
Rimers of Eldritch, The 1967,F 21,53:1
Dream Out of Time, A 1970,N 9,52:1
Manning, Samuel D
Processional 1925,Ja 13,17:1
Manning, Samuel L
Caribbean Carnival 1947,D 6,12:2
Manning, Samuel L (Composer)
Caribbean Carnival 1947,D 6,12:2
Manning, Samuel L (Director)
Caribbean Carnival 1947,D 6,12:2
Manning, Samuel L (Lyricist)
Caribbean Carnival 1947,D 6,12:2
Manning, Sylvia (Choreographer)
Revolt of the Beavers, The 1937,My 21,19:2
Manning, Thomas H
High Hatters, The 1928,My 11,28:2
Macbeth 1928,N 20,28:3
Street Scene 1929,Ja 11,20:4
Counsellor-at-Law 1931,N 7,17:2
Between Two Worlds 1934,O 26,24:2
Manning and Glass
Vaudeville (Palace) 1925,D 8,28:6
Mannini, Elena (Costume Designer)
Orlando Furioso 1970,N 5,59:1
Mannino, Anthony
Flowers of Virtue, The 1942,F 6,22:2
All You Need Is One Good Break 1950,F 10,20:3
Manny, Alice
Veils 1928,Mr 14,28:5
Manoff, Arnold (Playwright)
All You Need Is One Good Break 1950,F 10,20:3
Manon, Yvonne
What's the Use? 1926,S 7,19:1
Manor, John
Rope Dancers, The 1959,Mr 14,26:1
Manors, Jane
Bonds of Interest, The 1951,D 1,7:2
Yerma 1952,F 8,18:4
Manos, Chris
Here Come the Clowns 1954,My 5,36:2
Manos, George (Musical Director)
Lonesome Train, The 1965,Je 17,25:1
Hard Travelin' 1965,Je 17,25:1
Manosalvas, Alfonso
Romeo y Julieta 1965,Ag 28,13:3
Fiesta in Madrid 1969,My 29,49:1
Manoussi, Jean (Original Author)
Purple Mask, The 1920,Ja 6,18:1
Manoussi (Playwright)
Petite Bonnie Serieuse 1923,N 27,23:5
Manrique, Luis
Road to Happiness, The 1927,My 3,24:1
Romantic Young Lady, The 1927,My 5,30:2
Girl and the Cat, The 1927,My 6,21:2
Blind Heart, The 1927,My 8,30:2
Mansell, William
American Primitive 1937,Ag 13,12:5

Manser, James
Measure for Measure 1954,Je 30,23:1
Mansfield, Charles
Yoshe Kalb 1933,D 29,27:2
Mansfield, Eric
Too Many Boats 1934,S 12,26:3
Distant Shore, The 1935,F 22,26:2
Hamlet 1936,N 11,54:2
Mansfield, Gail
Perfect Match, The 1970,N 18,41:1
Mansfield, J Barry (Scenic Designer)
Song of the Bridge 1942,Ap 7,27:5
Mansfield, Jayne
Will Success Spoil Rock Hunter? 1955,O 14,22:2
Mansfield, Katherine (Original Author)
Daughters of the Late Colonel, The 1951,O 15,21:2
Mansfield, Lawrence (Scenic Designer)
Springtime Folly 1951,F 27,23:4
Mansfield, Mr
Something Different 1967,N 29,52:1
Mansfield, Rankin
Maggie, the Magnificent 1929,O 22,26:1
One Sunday Afternoon 1933,F 16,23:5
Mansfield, Rankin (Director)
Day in the Sun 1937,Jl 27,24:3
Mansfield, Richard
Up to Thursday 1965,F 11,45:1
Mansfield, Richard (Mrs)
You and I 1925,O 20,29:1
Mansfield, S
Under the Gaslight 1929,Ap 3,27:1
Mansfield, Sidney Little
Marco Millions 1930,Mr 4,24:4
Mansfield, Walda
Weather Clear, Track Fast 1927,O 19,24:5
Manship, Helen
Tidings Brought to Mary, The 1922,D 25,20:1
Manship, Ruth
Tidings Brought to Mary, The 1922,D 25,20:1
Manson, Alan
Journey to Jerusalem 1940,O 7,21:2
This Is the Army 1942,Jl 5,28:2
Call Me Mister 1946,Ap 19,26:2
Great Campaign, The 1947,Ap 1,33:2
Southern Exposure 1950,S 27,36:3
Angels Kiss Me 1951,Ap 18,37:6
Ponder Heart, The 1956,F 17,14:2
Tenth Man, The 1959,N 6,24:2
Gideon 1961,N 10,38:1
Midsummer Night's Dream, A 1967,Je 30,23:1
Other Man, The 1968,F 9,50:1
Oh, Say Can You See L A 1968,F 9,50:1
Place for Polly, A 1970,Ap 20,45:1
Manson, Charlotte
As You Like It 1936,Ap 24,18:4
Manson, Day
Dawn 1924,N 25,27:1
Manson, Eddy
Tidbits of 1946 1946,Jl 9,17:2
Manson, Florence
Great Big Doorstep, The 1950,Mr 18,8:6
Manson, Mary
Broadway Nights 1929,Jl 16,23:2
Lady Refuses, The 1933,Mr 8,18:6
Manson, Maurice
They All Come to Moscow 1933,My 12,20:6
Mary of Scotland 1933,N 28,28:3
Baby Pompadour 1934,D 28,24:2
Othello 1935,S 28,13:2
Macbeth 1935,O 8,26:4
No More Peace 1937,F 27,9:1
Madame Bovary 1937,N 17,26:2
Waltz in Goose Step 1938,N 2,26:2
Bright Rebel 1938,D 28,24:2
Three Sisters, The 1939,O 16,23:1
Janie 1942,S 11,24:2
Made in Heaven 1946,O 25,28:2
Traitor, The 1949,Ap 1,30:2
Mansour, Salem G
Upon My Soul 1927,Ap 22,19:1
Mansuelle
Gosseline 1921,Je 19,VI,1:8
Mantas, Algis
Dream Play 1960,N 23,22:1
Thracian Horses, The 1961,S 28,58:2
Mantel, Joseph
Alternate Current 1939,D 23,8:3
Mantell, George C
Jamboree 1932,N 25,18:4
Mantell, Joe
Buttrio Square 1952,O 15,40:2
Mantell, Robert
School for Scandal, The 1923,Je 5,24:3
Hamlet 1925,O 24,18:3
Manthey, Kurt
Bruder Straubinger 1921,N 16,22:3
Bajadere, Die 1925,O 2,26:2
Mantilla, Rosita
Cup, The 1923,N 13,25:1
Manton, Kevitt
Dolly Jordan 1922,O 4,26:1
Dancers, The 1923,O 18,17:2
Main Line, The 1924,Mr 26,19:4

Manton, Kevitt—Cont
Shooting Shadows 1924,Je 27,16:5
Valley of Content, The 1925,Ja 14,19:2
Matinee Girl, The 1926,F 2,20:3
Manton, Maria
Foolish Notion 1945,Mr 14,23:2
Manton, Stephen
Hollow Crown, The 1963,Ja 31,5:1
Manuel, J S
Plain Dealer, The 1929,My 23,27:1
Manuel, R A
Front Page, The 1937,N 12,27:2
Manuel, Richard
Immoralist, The 1963,N 8,36:2
Manuel, Robert
Bourgeois Gentilhomme, Le 1955,O 26,26:1
King of the Dark Chamber 1961,F 10,21:1
Man of La Mancha 1968,D 12,61:1
Manuel, Robert (Playwright)
Fiddler on the Roof 1969,N 16,82:6
Manuel, Vida
Merry-Go-Round 1927,Je 1,25:4
Manuel, W S
Plain Dealer, The 1929,My 23,27:1
Manuelian, Ethel
Tonight We Improvise 1959,N 7,27:4
Marrying Maiden, The 1960,Je 23,18:3
In the Jungle of Cities 1960,D 21,39:1
Mountain Giants, The 1961,Ap 5,32:3
Manulis, Martin
Laugh It Off 1934,Ap 5,24:2
Flair-Flair the Idol of Paree 1935,Mr 13,16:1
They Walk Alone 1941,Mr 13,24:2
Manulis, Martin (Director)
Duchess Misbehaves, The 1946,F 14,32:2
Made in Heaven 1946,O 25,28:2
Men We Marry, The 1948,Ja 17,11:2
Private Lives 1948,O 5,30:2
Show-Off, The 1950,Je 1,24:5
Pride's Crossing 1950,N 21,37:5
Manulis, Martin (Miscellaneous)
Little Blue Light, The 1951,Ap 30,17:2
Manville, Lorraine
Blue Kitten, The 1922,Ja 14,9:3
Plain Jane 1924,My 13,24:2
Manz, Vincent
Othello 1937,Ja 7,16:4
Manzer, Chester (Lighting Director)
Trial Honeymoon 1947,N 4,31:2
Manzi, Tony
Best Foot Forward 1963,Ap 3,43:1
Manzi, Tony (Miscellaneous)
Founders, The 1957,My 14,39:1
All My Pretty Little Ones 1964,F 5,30:1
Damn You, Scarlett O'Hara 1964,F 5,30:1
Bajour 1964,N 24,42:1
Hello, Dolly! 1967,N 13,61:1
Manzini, Mario (Producer)
We'd Rather Switch 1969,D 20,35:1
Manzoni (Original Author)
Promessi Sposi I,; Betrothed, The 1934,O 22,13:2
Mapes, Bruce
International Ice Frolics, The 1938,My 7,18:3
Ice Follies 1939,D 5,38:2
Ice Follies 1941,D 2,32:2
Mapes, H Pierson (Miscellaneous)
Russell Patterson's Sketch-Book 1960,F 8,35:1
Mapes, Jerry
Aquashow 1953,Je 24,29:2
Hollywood Ice Revue 1954,Ja 15,16:2
Mapes, Kenneth Lloyd (Lighting Director)
Beautiful Changes, The 1956,Mr 24,15:2
Mapes, Kenneth Lloyd (Scenic Designer)
Beautiful Changes, The 1956,Mr 24,15:2
Mapes, Victor (Playwright)
Hottentot, The 1920,Mr 2,9:1
Maphis, Cousin Joe and Rose
Hayride 1954,S 14,24:2
Maple, Audrey
Princess April 1924,D 2,23:2
Naughty Riquette 1926,S 14,25:2
My Princess 1927,O 7,24:2
Sunny Days 1928,F 9,29:1
Angela 1928,D 4,28:2
Street Singer, The 1929,S 18,35:2
Maple, Ian
Victoria Regina 1938,O 4,20:2
Mara, Alma
Lassie 1920,Ap 7,9:2
Mara, Thalia
Vienna at Night 1945,Ap 30,12:4
Maracci, A
Tutto Per Bene; All's Well That Ends Well 1929,Je 3,27:1
Marais, Josef
Tidbits of 1946 1946,Jl 9,17:2
Marais, Josef (Composer)
Too Late the Phalarope 1956,O 12,35:1
Maran, George
Hold On to Your Hats 1940,S 12,30:3
Marand, Patricia
Wish You Were Here 1952,Je 26,26:6
It's a Bird . . . It's a Plane . . . It's Superman 1966,Mr 30,34:1

Marans, Dona
Lady Akane, The 1960,N 16,51:4
Magnificent Hugo, The 1961,Ap 8,12:2
Marantz, Michael
Much Ado About Nothing 1963,Jl 15,25:2
Marantz, Samuel J
Little Theatre Tournement; Where The Cross Is Made 1928,My 10,31:1
Marasco, Robert (Playwright)
Child's Play 1970,F 18,39:1
Child's Play 1970,Mr 1,II,1:4
Marasek, Jan
Bonds of Interest, The 1951,D 1,7:2
Marasek, Jan (Lighting Director)
King and the Duke, The 1955,Je 2,25:2
Maravilla, Gloria
Schoen und Schick 1928,Ag 26,II,1:2
Marbe, Fay
Hotel Mouse, The 1922,Mr 14,11:3
Topics of 1923 1923,N 21,23:2
Marble, Dan
Bye Bye, Barbara 1924,Ag 26,6:3
Marble, Mary
Love in a Mist 1926,Ap 13,28:3
Springboard, The 1927,O 13,23:1
Merry Andrew 1929,Ja 22,22:2
Marble, William
Octoroon, The 1929,Mr 13,28:3
Marburger, Dorothy
Joy of Serpents 1930,Ap 4,22:4
Marburgh, Bertram
Lancelot and Elaine 1921,S 13,12:1
Squaw Man, The 1921,D 27,10:3
Your Woman and Mine 1922,F 28,17:2
Wild Waves 1932,F 20,11:4
Marbury, Elisabeth (Miscellaneous)
Electra 1930,D 27,16:1
Ramayana 1931,Ja 13,35:4
Marbury, Elisabeth (Producer)
Say When 1928,Je 27,29:3
Marbury, Jane
Wonderful Thing, The 1920,F 18,9:1
Paid 1925,N 26,32:1
Come-On Man, The 1929,Ap 23,26:2
Bedfellows 1929,Jl 3,19:2
Kick Back, The 1936,Je 23,27:3
Jacobowsky and the Colonel 1944,Mr 15,17:2
Silver Whistle, The 1948,N 25,49:2
Marc, Agnes
Crooked Square, The 1923,S 11,10:2
Edgar Allan Poe 1925,O 6,31:1
This Our House 1935,D 12,33:3
Marc-Michel (Playwright)
Italian Straw Hat, The 1957,O 1,37:2
Marcato, Robert
Red Harvest 1937,Mr 31,29:2
Marceau, Felicien (Playwright)
Good Soup, The 1960,Mr 3,26:4
Etouffe Chretien, L' 1960,N 5,28:1
Egg, The 1962,Ja 9,23:2
Marceau, Marcel
Soldier's Tale, A 1955,Jl 13,21:2
Evening of Pantomime, An 1955,S 21,38:1
Marcel Marceau 1956,F 2,18:1
Untitled-Pantomime 1958,Ja 22,23:1
Overcoat, The 1960,S 7,45:1
Marcel Marceau 1963,Ja 3,5:7
Untitled-One Man Show 1963,Ja 12,5:2
Marcel Marceau 1970,Ap 8,38:3
Marceau, Marcel (Director)
Overcoat, The 1960,S 7,45:1
Marceau, Marcel (Playwright)
Overcoat, The 1960,S 7,45:1
Marceau, William
Petrified Forest, The 1943,N 2,30:6
War President 1944,Ap 25,17:3
Assassin, The 1945,O 18,20:2
Marcel, Andre
Maitresse de Roi 1926,D 1,24:1
Marcel, Jerry (Costume Designer)
Dracula Sabbat 1970,O 2,28:2
Marcel, Joyce (Costume Designer)
Dracula Sabbat 1970,O 2,28:2
Marcel, Melba
There You Are! 1932,My 17,25:4
Marcel, Ted
Will Morrissey's Folies Bergere Revue 1930,Ap 16,26:6
Marcel-Andre
As-tu du Coeur? 1926,O 31,VIII,2:4
Marcelie, Sonia
Rosa Machree 1922,Ja 10,15:2
Marceline
Good Times 1920,Ag 10,10:1
Better Times 1922,S 4,14:2
Marceline and Moron
Get Together 1921,S 5,12:2
Marcella, Joyce
End of All Things Natural, The 1969,S 12,38:1
Marcelle
Vaudeville (Hippodrome) 1924,F 12,20:2
Vaudeville (Hippodrome) 1924,F 19,12:1
Vaudeville (Hippodrome) 1924,Mr 18,25:1

Marcelle, Melba
Noble Rogue, A 1929,Ag 20,31:2
March, Alexander
Look, Ma, I'm Dancin' 1948,Ja 30,20:2
Nineteenth Hole of Europe, The 1949,Mr 28,16:2
March, C L
Why Not? 1922,D 30,13:4
March, Carol
Love Duel, The 1929,Ap 16,32:3
Young Sinners 1929,N 29,24:4
March, Charles (Playwright)
Symphony 1935,Ap 27,20:3
March, Ellen
Pins and Needles 1967,Je 9,51:2
March, Elspeth
Tinker's Wedding, The 1957,Mr 7,24:1
Riders to the Sea 1957,Mr 7,24:1
Riders to the Sea 1957,Mr 17,II,1:1
Playboy of the Western World, The 1958,My 9,19:2
March, Eve
Home Sweet Home 1936,Jl 1,29:2
Here Come the Clowns 1938,D 8,36:2
World We Make, The 1939,N 21,19:1
Coco 1969,D 19,66:1
March, Fredric
Melody Man, The 1924,My 14,14:2
Puppets 1925,Mr 10,19:1
Harvest 1925,S 21,16:2
Half-Caste, The 1926,Mr 30,20:4
Devil in the Cheese, The 1926,D 30,22:4
Yr Obedient Husband 1937,N 27,21:2
Yr Obedient Husband 1938,Ja 11,26:5
American Way, The 1939,Ja 23,9:2
American Way, The 1939,Ja 29,IX,1:1
Hope for a Harvest 1941,Ap 5,18:4
Hope for a Harvest 1941,N 27,28:2
Hope for a Harvest 1941,D 7,X,5:1
Skin of Our Teeth, The 1942,N 19,29:5
Skin of Our Teeth, The 1942,N 22,VIII,1:1
Bell for Adano, A 1944,N 10,24:6
Bell for Adano, A 1944,D 7,21:2
Bell for Adano, A 1944,D 17,II,3:2
Years Ago 1946,D 4,44:2
Years Ago 1946,D 15,II,3:1
Now I Lay Me Down to Sleep 1950,Mr 3,21:2
Now I Lay Me Down to Sleep 1950,Mr 19,II,1:1
Enemy of the People, An 1950,D 29,14:1
Enemy of the People, An 1951,Ja 7,II,1:1
Autumn Garden, The 1951,Mr 8,36:2
Autumn Garden, The 1951,Mr 18,II,1:1
Long Day's Journey Into Night 1956,O 17,40:1
Long Day's Journey Into Night 1956,N 8,47:2
Long Day's Journey Into Night 1956,N 18,II,1:1
Long Day's Journey Into Night 1957,Jl 3,14:1
Gideon 1961,N 10,38:1
Gideon 1961,N 19,II,1:1
March, Fredric (Producer)
Yr Obedient Husband 1938,Ja 11,26:5
March, Hal
Come Blow Your Horn 1961,F 23,31:3
March, Howard
Show Boat 1928,Ja 8,VIII,1:1
March, JoAnna
Miss Lonelyhearts 1957,O 4,26:2
Marcus in the High Grass 1960,N 22,38:6
March, June
Truckline Cafe 1946,F 28,19:4
March, Kathryn
They Never Grow Up 1930,Ap 8,27:1
Great Barrington, The 1931,F 20,18:1
Move on, Sister 1933,O 25,22:4
Sweet Mystery of Life 1935,O 12,13:3
Sweet River 1936,O 29,30:2
March, Kendall
Autograph Hound, The 1968,D 14,60:1
Front Page, The 1969,N 2,86:1
March, Liska (Miscellaneous)
School for Scandal, The 1953,Je 24,29:2
Little Clay Cart, The 1953,Jl 1,25:1
Genius and the Goddess, The 1957,D 11,41:1
Shadow of a Gunman, The 1958,N 21,26:1
March, Liska (Producer)
Brouhaha 1960,Ap 27,31:2
March, Lori
All the King's Men 1950,Jl 19,25:6
House in Berlin, A (Als der Kreig zu Ende War); Als der Krieg zu Ende War (A House in Berlin) 1950,D 27,32:3
Cyrano de Bergerac 1953,N 13,24:3
Charley's Aunt 1953,D 23,22:2
Coriolanus 1954,Ja 20,34:2
Measure for Measure 1960,Jl 27,33:1
Hedda Gabler 1960,N 10,61:1
Giants, Sons of Giants 1962,Ja 8,26:2
Candida 1962,N 12,35:5
March, Marvin (Lighting Director)
After the Angels 1961,F 11,27:5
Caretaker, The 1964,Ja 31,16:1
March, Marvin (Scenic Designer)
After the Angels 1961,F 11,27:5
March, Pauline
Creoles 1927,S 23,33:3

March, Ruth
Romeo and Juliet 1934,D 21,30:3
Romeo and Juliet 1935,D 24,10:2
Saint Joan 1936,Mr 10,27:4
Hamlet 1936,O 9,30:2
How to Get Tough About It 1938,F 9,16:2
Key Largo 1939,N 28,30:2
March, Sandra
Children's Hour, The 1952,D 19,35:2
March, William (Original Author)
Bad Seed, The 1954,D 9,42:1
Bad Seed, The 1954,D 19,II,3:1
Marchado, Cathy
Ice Capades 1960,S 1,30:1
Marchaix, Jacques
Untitled-Revue 1968,O 21,55:4
Cabaret Rive Gauche 1969,S 5,30:1
Marchand, Colette
Two on the Aisle 1951,Jl 20,13:6
Two on the Aisle 1951,Jl 29,II,1:1
Marchand, Frances
Merry Merry 1925,S 25,24:3
Marchand, Leopold (Original Author)
Cheri 1930,N 16,VIII,4:1
Money Talks 1938,My 29,X,1:2
Marchand, Leopold (Playwright)
Cheri 1921,D 25,VI,1:8
Nous ne Sommes Plus des Enfants 1927,My 29,VII,2:7
J'ai tue 1928,O 28,IX,2:7
Durand, Bijoutier 1930,F 2,VIII,4:1
We Are No Longer Children 1932,Ap 1,17:2
Mes Amours 1940,My 3,16:5
Marchand, Nancy
Throng o' Scarlet 1950,F 6,20:5
Taming of the Shrew, The 1951,Ap 26,35:2
Love's Labour's Lost 1953,F 5,20:3
Merchant of Venice, The 1953,Mr 5,20:2
Country Wife, The 1955,Ap 6,35:1
Antigone 1956,Ap 3,32:2
Good Woman of Setzuan, The 1956,D 19,41:2
Good Woman of Setzuan, The 1956,D 30,II,1:1
Miss Isobel 1957,D 27,22:1
Winter's Tale, The 1958,Jl 21,17:4
Merry Wives of Windsor, The 1959,Jl 9,23:2
Much Ado About Nothing 1959,S 18,25:2
Balcony, The 1960,Mr 4,21:1
School for Scandal, The 1962,Mr 19,36:1
Seagull, The 1962,Mr 22,42:1
Right You Are (If You Think You Are) 1964,Mr 5,37:1
Tavern, The 1964,Mr 6,39:2
Lower Depths, The 1964,Mr 31,30:1
Man and Superman 1964,D 7,45:2
Man and Superman 1965,Ja 31,II,1:1
Judith 1965,Mr 25,42:2
Exhaustion of Our Son's Love, The 1965,O 19,51:1
3 Bags Full 1966,Mr 7,22:1
Murder in the Cathedral 1966,Je 21,38:1
Alchemist, The 1966,O 14,48:1
Yerma 1966,D 9,60:1
Sorrow of Frederick, The 1967,Jl 8,14:2
After the Rain 1967,O 10,54:1
Cyrano de Bergerac 1968,Ap 26,30:1
Forty Carats 1968,D 27,45:1
Forty Carats 1969,Ja 5,II,1:3
Marchand, Robert
King and the Duke, The 1955,Je 2,25:2
Marchant, Claude
Show Boat 1946,Ja 7,17:2
Caribbean Carnival 1947,D 6,12:2
Marchant, Claude (Choreographer)
Caribbean Carnival 1947,D 6,12:2
Marchant, William (Playwright)
To Be Continued 1952,Ap 24,37:2
Desk Set, The 1955,O 25,36:7
Marchante, Marion
Nina Rosa 1930,My 31,19:3
Nina Rosa 1930,S 22,22:5
Marchette, Gerard (Director)
Summer Pygmies, The 1960,D 13,24:6
Marchette, Gerard (Playwright)
Summer Pygmies, The 1960,D 13,24:6
Sold to the Movies; Type 424 Meet Type Oh-Oh, No! 1970,Je 18,54:2
Sold to the Movies; Life Size 1970,Je 18,54:2
Sold to the Movies; Crossing the Gap 1970,Je 18,54:2
Marchetti, Henry
Bruder Straubinger 1921,N 16,22:3
Marchiabelli, Princess (Maria Carmi)
Miracle, The 1924,Ja 26,10:1
Marcil, Isidore
Richard III 1920,Mr 8,7:1
Daddy Dumplins 1920,N 23,11:1
Flame of Love 1924,Ap 22,19:2
Little Poor Man, The 1925,Ag 6,14:1
Silver Box, The 1928,Ja 18,23:1
Major Barbara 1928,N 20,28:4
One, Two, Three! 1930,S 30,24:2
New York to Cherbourg 1932,F 20,11:4
Hired Husband 1932,Je 4,9:5
Late One Evening 1933,Ja 10,27:3

Marcin, Max (Director)
Trapped 1928,S 12,25:3
Humbug, The 1929,N 28,34:5
Censored 1938,F 28,18:2
Marcin, Max (Miscellaneous)
Los Angeles 1927,D 20,32:3
Marcin, Max (Playwright)
Nightcap, The 1921,Ag 16,18:3
Silence 1924,F 17,VII,2:8
Silence 1924,N 13,18:2
Badges 1924,D 4,25:1
Los Angeles 1927,D 20,32:3
Trapped 1928,Ag 26,VII,2:1
Big Fight, The 1928,Ag 31,23:1
Trapped 1928,S 12,25:3
Big Fight, The 1928,S 19,33:1
Big Fight, The 1928,S 23,IX,1:1
Humbug, The 1929,N 28,34:5
Censored 1938,F 28,18:2
Marcin, Max (Producer)
Trapped 1928,S 12,25:3
Marciona, Anthony
Zorba 1968,N 18,58:1
Marciona, Susan
Zorba 1968,N 18,58:1
Marco, Mr
Sun-Kist 1921,My 24,20:2
Marco, Pepita
Cabalgata 1949,Jl 8,14:2
Marco, Raoul
Waiting for Godot 1968,Ap 23,38:1
Marco, Sano
Gondoliers, The 1931,Je 2,34:4
Pirates of Penzance, The; Slave of Duty, The 1931,Je 30,23:6
Ruddigore 1931,Ag 11,28:3
Merry Widow, The 1931,S 8,39:1
Geisha, The 1931,O 6,35:4
Marco (Composer)
Sun-Kist 1921,My 24,20:2
Marco (Lyricist)
Sun-Kist 1921,My 24,20:2
Marcum, James (Scenic Designer)
Woman of Destiny, A 1936,Mr 3,25:2
Marcus, Carol
Jim Dandy 1941,N 8,10:5
Across the Board on Tomorrow Morning 1942,Ag 18,17:1
Marcus, D Frank (Composer)
Bomboola 1929,Je 27,17:3
Marcus, D Frank (Director)
Bomboola 1929,Je 27,17:3
Make Me Know It 1929,N 5,32:5
It Happened Tomorrow 1933,My 6,11:5
Marcus, D Frank (Lyricist)
Bomboola 1929,Je 27,17:3
Marcus, D Frank (Playwright)
Bomboola 1929,Je 27,17:3
Make Me Know It 1929,N 5,32:5
It Happened Tomorrow 1933,My 6,11:5
Marcus, D Frank (Producer)
It Happened Tomorrow 1933,My 6,11:5
Marcus, Frank (Playwright)
Killing of Sister George, The 1965,Je 18,28:5
Killing of Sister George, The 1966,O 6,57:1
Killing of Sister George, The 1966,O 16,II,1:1
Mrs Mouse Are You Within? 1968,Ap 5,51:4
Mrs Mouse Are You Within? 1968,Je 2,II,3:6
Mrs Mouse Are You Within? 1968,Jl 8,45:1
Marcus, Frank (Translator)
Guardsman, The 1969,Ag 17,II,5:1
Marcus, Jack
If I Were You 1931,S 24,21:1
Marcus, Jacob
Riverside Drive 1931,Ja 6,24:2
Marcus, Jesse (Director)
Love, Honor and Oh Baby 1940,Mr 29,25:2
Marcus, Joe
Mister Roberts 1956,D 6,46:2
Marcus, Lyone
Girl in Pink Tights, The 1954,Mr 6,13:2
Marcus, Marian
Rotters, The 1922,My 23,12:4
Marcus, Mitchell Padraic
Rutherford and Son 1927,Ap 13,29:2
Vegetable, The, or From President to Postman 1929,Ap 11,32:3
Marcus, R F
Front Page, The 1937,N 12,27:2
Marcus, Ruth
Shoemaker's Prodigious Wife, The 1949,Je 15,38:2
Marcus, Theodore (Director)
Cretan Woman, The 1954,Jl 8,18:2
Marcus, Vickie
Jack Benny 1963,Mr 1,10:5
Marcus, Vickie
Two Hearts 1935,My 6,22:2
Marcuse, Theodore
Antony and Cleopatra 1947,N 27,49:2
Medea 1949,My 3,31:2
Richard II 1951,Ja 25,21:2
Dragon's Mouth 1955,N 17,45:1

Marcy, Eileen
Untitled-Revue 1926,O 26,18:3
Marcy, Everett (Playwright)
New Faces of 1936 1936,My 20,24:5
Who's Who 1938,Mr 2,16:2
All in Fun 1940,D 28,11:2
Marcy, George
Kiss Me, Kate 1954,Mr 27,13:2
Damn Yankees 1955,My 6,17:1
Littlest Revue, The 1956,My 23,37:2
Shoestring '57 1956,N 6,31:1
West Side Story 1957,S 27,14:4
West Side Story 1960,Ap 28,31:1
Carnival! 1961,Ap 14,22:2
Hang Down Your Head and Die 1964,O 19,38:1
Wonderful Town 1967,My 18,50:1
Ballad for a Firing Squad 1968,D 12,64:2
Billy 1969,Mr 24,56:1
Marcy, Helen
In Bed We Cry 1944,N 15,20:2
Dream Girl 1945,D 15,13:2
Afternoon Storm 1948,Ap 12,24:2
Twelfth Night 1949,O 4,33:2
Love and Let Love 1951,O 20,11:2
Marcy, Joe (Sherman, Nathan) (Playwright)
First American Dictator 1939,Mr 15,18:2
Marcy, M (Composer)
Ecole des Femmes, L' 1961,Ap 28,23:1
Marcy, Robert (Director)
Ecole des Femmes, L' 1961,Ap 28,23:1
Marden, Adrienne
Merrily We Roll Along 1934,O 1,14:1
Women, The 1936,D 28,13:1
American Way, The 1939,Ja 23,9:2
Hickory Stick 1944,My 9,15:6
Marden, Grant
Macbeth 1969,D 23,25:1
Marden, Mabel
Nut Farm, The 1929,O 15,34:3
Unsophisticates, The 1929,D 31,14:5
Mardenn, Bennes
Our Town 1944,Ja 11,24:5
Tonight We Improvise 1959,N 7,27:4
Marrying Maiden, The 1960,Je 23,18:3
In the Jungle of Cities 1960,D 21,39:1
Mountain Giants, The 1961,Ap 5,32:3
Mardirosian, Florence (Musical Director)
Echmiadzin 1946,O 21,27:3
Mardo, Al
Blackouts of 1949 1949,S 7,39:2
Mardy, Jim
Jumbo 1935,N 18,20:2
Marechal, Judith Rutherford (Producer)
Days and Nights of Beebee Fenstermaker, The 1962,S 18,33:1
Cages; Snowangel; Epiphany 1963,Je 14,36:1
In White America 1963,N 1,26:1
Marechal, Kelsey (Miscellaneous)
Ulysses in Nighttown 1958,Je 6,30:1
Marechal, Kelsey (Producer)
Cry of the Raindrop 1961,Mr 8,38:1
Marek, Keith
Yanqui and the Senorita, The 1952,Ag 8,8:7
Marel, William
Knickerbocker Holiday 1938,O 20,26:2
Lady in the Dark 1941,Ja 24,14:2
Maren, Greta
All Paris Knows 1934,Jl 24,20:1
Journey by Night 1935,Ap 7,IX,2:1
Journey by Night, A 1935,Ap 17,26:3
Marenko, Daniel
Adam Had Two Sons 1932,Ja 21,17:1
Maresca, Lina
Mother Martyr 1935,Ja 28,10:3
Maresch, Harald (Producer)
My L A 1951,D 9,87:1
Maresti, Carlo (Miscellaneous)
Rugantino 1964,F 7,34:1
Maret, Joyce
By Jupiter 1967,Ja 20,28:2
Maretskaya, Vera
Orpheus Descending 1961,Ag 28,21:2
Marewa, M
Blue Bird, The 1932,Ap 22,23:2
Marfield, Dwight
Audition of the Apprentice Theatre 1939,Je 2,26:2
Gabrielle 1941,Mr 26,26:2
Texas Town 1941,Ap 30,22:3
Playboy of Newark, The 1943,Mr 20,11:2
Private Life of the Master Race, The 1945,Je 13,28:3
Day Before Spring, The 1945,N 23,27:2
Galileo 1947,D 8,34:2
Gordon Reilly 1952,N 26,20:5
American Gothic 1953,N 11,35:6
Ponder Heart, The 1956,F 17,14:2
Look Homeward, Angel 1957,N 29,33:1
Margetson, Arthur
Passing Show of 1922, The 1922,S 21,18:2
Dancing Girl, The 1923,Ja 25,16:2
Paris 1928,O 9,34:3
Painted Veil, The 1931,O 11,VIII,2:4
Nona 1932,O 5,26:4

Margetson, Arthur—Cont
Good Woman, Poor Thing, A 1933,Ja 10,27:3
Saturday Night 1933,Mr 1,13:2
No More Ladies 1934,O 7,IX,3:7
Mainly for Lovers 1936,F 11,19:5
Mainly for Lovers 1936,F 22,13:2
Billy Draws a Horse 1939,D 22,14:5
Case of Youth, A 1940,Mr 25,10:3
Charley's Aunt 1940,O 18,24:2
Theatre 1941,O 26,IX,2:3
Theatre 1941,N 13,34:2
Flare Path 1942,D 24,20:2
Another Love Story 1943,O 13,29:2
Mrs Kimball Presents 1944,Mr 1,17:3
Little Brown Jug 1946,Mr 7,32:2
Around the World 1946,Je 1,9:5
Around the World 1946,Je 9,II,1:1
Park Avenue 1946,N 5,31:2
Play's the Thing, The 1948,Ap 29,19:2
Play's the Thing, The 1948,My 9,II,1:1
Clutterbuck 1949,D 5,29:2
Margetson, Arthur (Composer)
Good Woman, Poor Thing, A 1933,Ja 10,27:3
Margo
Sunday Nights at Nine 1934,Mr 5,18:5
Winterset 1935,S 26,19:2
Masque of Kings, The 1937,Ja 19,28:3
Masque of Kings, The 1937,Ja 31,XI,2:1
Masque of the Kings, The 1937,F 9,19:4
Faust 1938,Ag 28,IX,2:5
World We Make, The 1939,N 21,19:1
World We Make, The 1939,N 26,IX,1:3
World We Make, The 1939,D 3,IX,5:1
Tanyard Street 1941,F 5,16:2
Bell for Adano, A 1944,N 10,24:6
Bell for Adano, A 1944,D 7,21:2
Bell for Adano, A 1944,D 17,II,3:2
ANTA Album 1950,Ja 30,13:2
Margo and Beth
Vaudeville (Palace) 1928,F 28,18:7
Margolese, E M
Orthee 1962,D 29,5:5
Antigone 1962,D 29,5:5
Margolies, Abe (Producer)
Mike Downstairs 1968,Ap 19,35:1
I'm Solomon 1968,Ap 24,51:1
Mahagonny 1970,Ap 29,51:1
Margolies, Albert (Producer)
Violet 1944,O 25,16:1
Margolies, Annette
Scorpion, The 1933,N 28,28:4
Margolin, Arnold
Floydada to Matador 1955,D 22,19:1
Opera Opera 1955,D 22,19:1
Hungerers, The 1955,D 22,19:1
Margolin, Arnold (Miscellaneous)
Shangri-La 1956,Je 14,40:1
Margolin, Janet
Daughter of Silence 1961,D 1,28:1
Margolis, George
Goose for the Gander, A 1945,Ja 24,16:4
Margolis, Henry M (Miscellaneous)
Tiger at the Gates 1955,O 4,40:1
King Lear 1956,Ja 13,17:1
Margolis, Henry M (Producer)
Reclining Figure 1954,O 8,26:5
Hidden River, The 1957,Ja 24,32:1
Once More With Feeling 1958,O 22,39:1
Margolis, Ken (Lighting Director)
Milk Train Doesn't Stop Here Anymore, The 1965,Jl 27,25:1
Margolis, Mel
Beaux' Stratagem, The 1957,Jl 9,25:4
Margolis, Zora
Don't Shoot Mable It's Your Husband 1968,O 23,34:1
Mod Donna 1970,My 4,48:1
Margot and Diane
Ice Capades 1970,Ja 7,35:1
Marguerite, Mlle
Honeydew 1920,S 7,20:1
Irving Berlin's Music Box Revue 1921,S 23,18:2
Just Fancy! 1927,O 12,30:2
Femme Dans un Lit, Une 1928,Ja 15,VIII,2:3
Marguerite and Gill
Vaudeville (Palace) 1927,Ja 18,23:2
Margueritte, Victor (Playwright)
Mother, The 1937,Ag 29,X,1:3
Margulies, Annette
White Cargo 1923,N 6,22:2
Margulies, David
Golden Six, The 1958,O 27,31:2
'Tis Pity She's a Whore 1958,D 6,21:1
Thistle in My Bed 1963,N 20,48:1
Life Is a Dream 1964,Mr 20,24:1
Tragical Historie of Doctor Faustus, The 1964,O 6,34:2
Measure for Measure 1966,Jl 14,27:1
Tango 1969,Ja 20,33:1
Seven Days of Mourning 1969,D 17,64:1
Margulies, David (Miscellaneous)
Under Milk Wood 1961,Mr 30,25:1
Margulies, Robert (Producer)
Hostage, The 1961,D 13,55:4

Margulies, Robert (Producer)—Cont
Billy Liar 1965,Mr 18,26:1
Margullies, Henry
Will, The 1930,My 6,33:1
Mari, Ella
Religione e Patria 1936,Mr 23,22:4
Due Orfanelle, Le; Two Orphans, The
1936,O 5,24:4
Medico Delle Pazze, Il; Physician of Mad Woman,
The 1937,S 27,24:2
Signora Dalle Camelie, La; Dame aux Camelias, La
1937,O 9,16:3
Maria, Lisa
Memorandum, The 1968,My 6,55:1
Marian, Paul
Bitter Stream 1936,Mr 31,16:6
Marian Williams and the Stars of Faith
Black Nativity 1961,D 12,54:2
Mariano, Patti
George M! 1968,Ap 11,48:1
Me and Juliet 1970,My 15,42:1
Maricle, Leona
Trial of Mary Dugan, The 1927,S 20,33:1
First Mortgage 1929,O 11,36:1
Little Orchard Annie 1930,Ap 22,33:1
Once in a Lifetime 1930,S 7,IX,2:4
Once in a Lifetime 1930,S 25,22:3
Sex Fable, The 1931,O 21,26:1
Bad Manners 1933,Ja 31,15:5
Under Glass 1933,O 31,24:3
Dark Tower, The 1933,N 27,20:3
First Episode 1934,S 18,18:1
It's You I Want 1935,F 6,23:3
Slightly Married 1943,O 26,19:2
Harvest of Years 1948,Ja 13,29:2
Small Hours, The 1951,F 16,22:1
Never Too Late 1962,N 28,42:1
Little Boxes; Trevor 1969,D 4,71:2
Little Boxes; Coffee Lace, The 1969,D 4,71:2
Maricle, Marijane
Paint Your Wagon 1951,N 13,32:2
Cyrano de Bergerac 1953,N 13,24:3
Bye Bye Birdie 1960,Ap 15,13:4
Hair 1967,O 30,55:1
Marie, Dainty
Vaudeville (Palace) 1923,N 20,23:4
Marie, Julienne
Whoop-Up 1958,D 23,2:7
Boys From Syracuse, The 1963,Ap 16,31:1
Boys From Syracuse, The 1963,Je 2,II,1:1
Foxy 1964,F 17,26:1
Othello 1964,Jl 15,29:1
Othello 1964,O 13,48:1
Do I Hear a Waltz? 1965,Mr 19,28:1
Comedy of Errors, The 1967,Je 15,58:4
Marie, Rose
Top Banana 1951,N 2,19:2
Marie, Shirley
Ice Capades 1964,Ag 27,27:2
Marietta
George White's Scandals 1929,S 24,29:1
Marievsky, (Messr)
Chauve-Souris 1922,Je 6,17:4
Chauve-Souris 1925,Ja 15,25:1
Marillier, Jacques (Costume Designer)
Malade Imaginaire, Le 1970,F 18,40:2
Marillier, Jacques (Scenic Designer)
Malade Imaginaire, Le 1970,F 18,40:2
Marin, Paul
Montserrat 1954,My 26,34:2
He Who Gets Slapped 1956,F 2,18:1
Fair Game 1957,N 4,39:1
Rope Dancers, The 1959,Mr 14,26:1
Tenth Man, The 1959,N 6,24:2
Gideon 1961,N 10,38:1
Marinaccio, Robert
Hamlet 1970,O 19,51:1
Marinaro, Francesca
Paese dei Campanelli, Il; Land of Bells, The
1935,My 10,25:4
Marine, Joe
Hear! Hear! 1955,S 28,38:1
Marini, Giorgio
Tombola, La; Lottery, The 1936,N 9,23:4
Marinker, Peter
Edward II 1969,Ja 19,II,30:5
Marinno, Sunbo
Madmen and Specialists 1970,Ag 3,38:1
Marino, Frank
Honor Code, The 1931,My 19,25:3
Her Man of Wax 1933,O 12,32:3
Saluta 1934,Ag 29,13:4
Between Two Worlds 1934,O 26,24:2
Creeping Fire 1935,Ja 17,22:3
If a Body 1935,My 1,25:3
Marino, Joseph
Ghosts 1961,S 22,29:1
Marino, Quinn
Listen to the Quiet 1958,O 28,40:2
Marino and Martin
Vaudeville (Palace) 1924,Ja 15,17:3
Marinoff, Fania
Call the Doctor 1920,S 1,14:1
Hero, The 1921,S 6,13:2

Fables 1922,F 7,12:2
Charlatan, The 1922,Ap 25,14:2
Love Habit, The 1923,Mr 15,17:1
Tarnish 1923,O 2,10:1
Streets of New York, The 1931,O 7,29:1
Pillars of Society, The 1931,O 15,19:1
Bride the Sun Shines On, The 1931,D 28,20:2
Christopher Comes Across 1932,Je 1,19:2
Judgment Day 1934,S 13,26:4
Judgment Day 1934,S 23,X,1:1
Times Have Changed 1935,F 26,16:1
Love for Love 1936,Je 30,15:4
Laugh Night 1936,S 14,25:1
Antony and Cleopatra 1937,N 11,30:2
Marinoff, Jacob
Laugh Night 1936,S 14,25:1
Mario, Al
Just a Minute 1928,O 9,34:3
Mario, Maria
Saint of Bleecker Street, The 1955,Ja 2,II,1:1
Mario, Paul
Mr Strauss Goes to Boston 1945,S 7,20:2
Mario, Pierre
Carolinian, The 1925,N 3,34:2
Cafe de Danse 1929,Ja 16,22:2
Three Times the Hour 1931,Ag 26,15:5
Giuochi di Prestigio 1931,N 2,26:1
Incendio Doloso, L'; False Flame, The
1931,N 16,22:4
Piccolo Santo, Il; Little Saint, The 1931,D 14,16:4
Profumo di Mia Moglie, Il; My Wife's Perfume
1932,Ja 11,29:5
Happy Landing 1932,Mr 28,10:5
Canto Della Vita, Il; Song of Life, The
1932,Ap 4,13:3
Casa di Tutti, La; Everybody's Home 1932,D 5,21:4
Cardinale, Il 1933,Ja 9,24:2
Istruttoria, L'; Judicial Inquiry, The 1933,F 13,11:3
Curioso Accidente, Un 1933,Mr 6,16:3
Romanticismo 1933,My 1,10:5
Liane, Le (Ties That Bind) 1933,Je 12,20:3
Marion, Ben
Springtime of Youth 1922,O 27,15:1
Marion, Dave
Marion Show, The 1923,My 8,22:3
Marion, Dave (Playwright)
Marion Show, The 1923,My 8,22:3
Marion, Else
Bajadere, Die 1925,O 2,26:2
Anneliese von Dessau 1926,F 26,24:3
Marion, Floyd
Talk About Girls 1927,Je 15,31:3
Marion, Frances (Playwright)
Happy Ending 1936,Jl 15,14:3
Marion, George Jr
George Washington 1920,Mr 2,9:1
When We Are Young 1920,N 23,11:1
Gold 1921,Je 2,14:2
Anna Christie 1921,N 3,22:1
Anna Christie 1923,Ap 11,16:2
Anna Christie 1923,Ap 15,VII,2:4
Out of the Seven Seas 1923,N 20,23:3
Horse-Thief, The 1924,Ap 27,VIII,2:3
Thoroughbreds 1924,S 9,12:1
Lambs Gambol 1925,Ap 27,15:1
First Love 1926,S 19,IX,1:3
First Love 1926,N 9,31:2
Aiglon, L' 1927,D 27,24:3
Atlas and Eva 1928,F 7,30:2
Golden Age, The 1928,Ap 25,31:3
Marion, George Jr (Director)
First Love 1926,N 9,31:2
White Lilacs 1928,S 11,31:2
Angela 1928,D 4,28:2
Boom Boom 1929,Ja 29,26:4
Marion, George Jr (Lyricist)
Early to Bed 1943,Je 18,16:2
Allah Be Praised! 1944,Ap 21,14:2
Marinka 1945,Jl 19,19:2
Toplitzky of Notre Dame 1946,D 27,13:4
Marion, George Jr (Original Author)
Too Many Girls 1939,O 19,26:2
Toplitzky of Notre Dame 1946,D 27,13:4
Arabian Nights 1954,Je 25,15:2
Marion, George Jr (Playwright)
Too Many Girls 1939,O 29,IX,1:6
Early to Bed 1943,Je 18,16:2
Allah Be Praised! 1944,Ap 21,14:2
Marinka 1945,Jl 19,19:2
Arabian Nights 1955,Je 24,16:1
Arabian Nights 1967,Jl 3,12:1
Marion, Ira (Producer)
Tree, The 1932,Ap 13,23:5
Marion, Joan
Mask and the Face, The 1933,My 9,20:2
Man Proposes 1933,D 24,IX,2:2
Men in White 1934,Je 29,16:3
Delusion 1935,Mr 29,26:4
Libel! 1935,D 8,X,5:8
Libel! 1935,D 21,10:5
Marion, Madeleine
Phedre 1969,Mr 1,20:1

Marion, Marie
Vaudeville (Palace) 1932,Jl 4,14:5
White Horse Inn 1936,O 2,28:5
Marion, Mlle
Spice of 1922 1922,Jl 7,12:4
Marion, Mr
Anna Christie 1922,Ja 15,III,3:1
Marion, Paul
Soliloquy 1938,N 29,26:4
Quiet, Please! 1940,N 9,20:3
My Sister Eileen 1940,D 27,23:2
Marion, Ruth
Yellow Jacket, The 1928,N 8,27:3
Falstaff 1928,D 26,14:2
Lady's Not for Burning, The 1957,F 22,26:2
Marion, Sidney
Vaudeville (Palace) 1928,Ag 14,15:5
Vaudeville (Palace) 1929,O 14,20:4
**Marionette Players From the Teatro dei Piccoli of
/Rome**
Untitled-Marionettes 1923,S 11,10:2
Marionette Studio
Hairy Ape, The 1931,Ap 15,24:4
Marionette Theatre of Braunschweig
Untitled-Marionettes 1957,D 24,11:6
Marionette Workshop (Scenic Designer)
Oliver Twist 1937,F 21,II,4:4
Marionnettes de Montreal, Les
Toy Box 1955,D 18,95:3
Marionno, M
Mozart 1926,D 28,16:1
Illusioniste, L' 1927,Ja 11,36:5
Mariott-Watson, Nan
If 1927,O 26,26:2
Mariotte, Harriett
Easy Come, Easy Go 1925,O 27,20:2
Mariotti, Ralph (Director)
Cherry Orchard, The 1955,O 19,38:1
Maris, Dorothy
Right This Way 1938,Ja 6,22:3
Red Velvet Goat, The 1939,Ja 21,18:4
Mr Banks of Birmingham 1939,Ja 21,18:4
Marischka, Ernst (Original Author)
Great Waltz, The 1934,S 24,14:4
Marischka, Hubert
Circus Princess, The 1926,Mr 28,23:5
Goldne Meisterin 1927,O 25,33:4
Rose of Florida, The 1929,F 23,17:1
Farmer General, The 1931,Mr 31,24:8
Mariscka (Producer)
Schon Ist die Welt; Endlich Allein
1932,Ja 17,VIII,2:1
Marius, Robert
Virtuous Island, The 1957,Ap 10,39:1
Marivaux (Playwright)
Fausses Confidences, Les 1948,S 11,13:3
Fausses Confidences, Les 1952,N 13,34:2
Arlequin Poli par l'Amour 1955,N 9,40:1
Jeu de l'Amour et du Hasard, Le 1955,N 16,42:4
Arlequin Poli par l'Amour 1955,N 20,II,1:1
Triomphe de l'Amour, Le 1958,O 17,32:1
Marjo, Maria
Saint of Bleecker Street, The 1954,D 28,21:1
Mark, Alfred
Young Visitors, The 1968,D 26,48:1
Mark, Donald
Me and Juliet 1970,My 15,42:1
Mark, Flip
Annie Get Your Gun 1958,F 20,29:2
Mark, Frederick
R U R 1922,O 10,16:1
Mark, Gina (Miscellaneous)
Home Is Tomorrow 1950,Je 2,27:2
Mark, Joe E
Peter Pan 1954,O 31,II,1:1
Mark, John
Tobacco Road 1950,Mr 7,23:2
Born Yesterday 1954,Ja 1,16:6
Markah, Lisa
Armseligen Besenbinder, Die 1928,N 19,16:2
Marching Song 1937,F 18,18:2
Seven at Dawn, The 1961,Ap 18,43:1
Markam, Genevieve
Daffy Dill 1922,Ag 23,14:5
Markarian, Alicia Helen
Zorba 1968,N 18,58:1
Marke, Edmund B
Mourners' Bench, The 1950,S 22,35:7
Markee, Del
Guys and Dolls 1959,Jl 22,22:2
Markel's Orchestra
Vaudeville (Palace) 1926,My 11,25:3
Marker, Neil
Dream of a Blacklisted Actor 1969,D 18,64:1
Marker, Preshy
Funny Thing Happened on the Way to the Forum,
A 1962,My 9,49:1
Markert, Russell (Choreographer)
Just a Minute 1928,O 9,34:3
Americana 1928,O 31,28:2
New Americana 1928,N 30,32:4
Keep It Clean 1929,Je 25,35:5
Here Goes the Bride 1931,N 4,31:2

Markert, Russell (Choreographer)—Cont

George White's Scandals 1935,D 26,20:2

Markert, Russell (Director)
Music Hall Varieties 1932,N 23,15:3
Say When 1934,N 9,24:2

Markert, Russell (Miscellaneous)
Great to Be Alive! 1950,Mr 24,28:2

Markert Dancers
Vaudeville (Palace) 1928,D 31,9:3

Market, Russell (Choreographer)
George White's Scandals 1928,Jl 3,19:1
Animal Crackers 1928,O 24,26:2

Markey, Alexander (Director)
Vigil, The 1948,My 22,8:6

Markey, Alexander (Producer)
Vigil, The 1948,My 22,8:6

Markey, Enid
Exciters, The 1922,S 23,10:4
Barnum Was Right 1923,Mr 13,19:3
Bluffing Bluffers 1924,D 23,17:2
Something to Brag About 1925,Ag 14,14:3
Find Daddy 1926,Mr 9,21:3
Blonde Sinner, The 1926,Jl 15,21:2
Sisters of the Chorus 1930,My 18,VIII,3:1
Sisters of the Chorus 1930,O 21,34:3
After Such Pleasures 1934,Ja 6,18:6
After Such Pleasures 1934,F 8,15:2
Good Girl, The 1934,Je 26,22:5
Two Bouquets, The 1938,Je 1,19:2
Run Sheep Run 1938,N 4,26:2
Man in Possession, The 1939,S 26,21:4
Morning's at Seven 1939,N 7,30:2
Morning's at Seven 1939,D 1,26:2
Beverly Hills 1940,N 8,24:2
Ah, Wilderness! 1941,O 3,26:2
Pie in the Sky 1941,D 23,26:5
Mr Sycamore 1942,N 14,13:2
Sweet Charity 1942,D 29,26:4
Last Stop 1944,S 6,17:2
Snafu 1944,O 26,19:5
Happy Birthday 1946,N 1,31:2
Buy Me Blue Ribbons 1951,O 18,33:2
Mrs McThing 1952,F 21,22:1
Mrs Patterson 1954,D 2,37:1
Southwest Corner, The 1955,F 4,18:2
Southwest Corner, The 1955,F 13,II,1:1
Fashion 1959,Ja 21,27:1
Only in America 1959,N 20,35:1
Ballad of the Sad Cafe, The 1963,O 31,27:1
What Did We Do Wrong? 1967,O 23,56:1

Markey, Frances
Sons o' Guns 1929,N 27,30:4
Prince Charming 1930,O 14,31:1

Markey, Gene (Playwright)
Eskimo, The 1926,Je 20,VII,3:1

Markey, Melinda
On Borrowed Time 1953,F 11,34:1

Markham, Daisy
Faithful Heart, The 1922,O 11,22:1

Markham, David
Astonished Ostrich, The 1937,Ja 17,X,2:1
Fourth of June, The 1964,F 1,12:1

Markham, Dewey
Hot Rhythm 1930,Ag 22,18:5
Blackberries of 1932 1932,Ap 5,27:5
Lew Leslie's Blackbirds of 1939 1939,F 13,12:2

Markham, Iris (Costume Designer)
Don Juan; Feast With the Statue, The
1956,Ja 4,21:4

Markham, Jewel Marie
Forbidden Melody 1936,N 3,33:1

Markham, Kirah
Red Geranium, The 1922,My 9,22:3
King Lear 1923,Mr 10,9:4
Emperor Jones, The 1924,My 7,18:1

Markham, Kyra (Scenic Designer)
Forest Ring, The 1930,Ap 26,11:2

Markham, Marcella
Vickie 1942,S 23,28:1
Flamingo Road 1946,Mr 20,18:2
Iceman Cometh, The 1946,O 10,31:3
Threepenny Opera, The 1954,Mr 11,26:5

Markham, Michael
Sex 1926,Ap 27,22:4
Crime 1927,F 23,27:3
Romancing 'Round 1927,O 4,32:4
Remote Control 1929,S 11,24:5
Joseph 1930,F 13,25:3

Markhus, Orrin
Ice Capades 1954,S 16,37:1
Ice Capades 1955,S 15,38:1
Ice Capades 1961,Ag 31,24:4

Markim, Alfred
Outside the Door 1949,Mr 2,33:2
Burning Bush, The 1949,D 17,15:5
Hasty Heart, The 1954,Mr 13,10:1
Ronde, La 1955,Je 28,24:2

Markle, Lois
Camino Real 1960,My 17,42:2
Buskers, The 1961,O 31,28:1
Calculated Risk 1962,N 1,35:1
Sound of Silence, A 1965,Mr 9,30:1
Warm Body, A 1967,Ap 17,44:2
Cuba Si 1968,D 10,53:1

Nest, The 1970,Ap 10,46:1

Markle, Stephen
Hamlet 1969,Je 11,37:1
Merchant of Venice, The 1970,Je 10,39:1
School for Scandal, The 1970,Je 11,51:1

Marko, Peter (Miscellaneous)
Conversation at Midnight 1964,N 13,27:1

Markoe, Francis Hartman (Director)
Arms for Venus 1937,Mr 12,18:7

Markoff, Alexander
Clear All Wires! 1932,S 15,19:1

Markoff, M
Revue Russe, The 1922,O 6,28:1

Markov, Vasily
Kremlin Chimes 1965,F 25,23:1

Markov, Vasily (Director)
Kremlin Chimes 1965,F 25,23:1

Markova, Alicia
Seven Lively Arts 1944,D 8,26:6
Seven Lively Arts 1944,D 17,II,3:1

Markovic, Ivanka (Translator)
Ubu Roi 1968,Je 29,20:1

Markow, Marvin
Hamlet 1938,D 4,9:2

Markowski, Andrzei (Musical Director)
Nightmare, The 1965,Ja 6,32:1
Labyrinth, The 1965,Ja 6,32:1
Jaselka 1965,Ja 6,32:1
Kernel and the Shell, The 1965,Ja 6,32:1
Book, The 1965,Ja 6,32:1
Jacob and the Angel 1965,Ja 6,32:1
Post Office, The 1965,Ja 6,32:1
Woman, The 1965,Ja 6,32:1

Marks, Alfred
Unshaven Cheek, The 1963,Ag 20,38:2

Marks, Ben
Summer Wives 1936,Ap 14,18:1

Marks, Bill (Staff Sgt)
Swing Sister Wac Swing 1944,Ja 4,20:4

Marks, Claude (Scenic Designer)
Playboy of the Western World, The 1958,My 9,19:2
Shadow and Substance 1959,N 4,42:1
Romeo and Juliet 1961,F 24,24:1

Marks, David
Alice in Wonderland 1932,D 12,18:3
Browning Version, The 1958,Mr 7,17:2

Marks, Dorothy
Sweet River 1936,O 29,30:2

Marks, Duke (Playwright)
Angels of Anadarko 1962,O 11,47:1

Marks, Eduard
Faust, Part I; Play, The 1961,F 5,27:2

Marks, Gerald (Composer)
My Dear Public 1943,S 10,28:1
Hold It! 1948,My 6,31:5

Marks, Gerald (Miscellaneous)
All the King's Men 1959,O 17,27:2

Marks, Harry
Subway, The 1929,Ja 26,15:1
Vegetable, The, or From President to Postman
1929,Ap 11,32:3

Marks, Harvey
Anna Kleiber 1965,Ja 20,33:1
Masks of Angels 1965,Ja 20,33:1

Marks, Jennifer
Iolanthe 1964,N 18,52:1
Ruddigore 1964,D 4,44:1
Pirates of Penzance, The 1966,N 16,54:1
Ruddigore 1966,N 23,28:1
Patience 1966,N 30,58:1

Marks, Joe E
First Stop to Heaven 1941,Ja 6,10:7
High Kickers 1941,N 1,21:2
Count Me In 1942,O 9,24:2
Bloomer Girl 1944,O 6,18:5
Topaze 1947,D 29,21:5
Vigil, The 1948,My 22,8:6
Enchanted, The 1950,Ja 19,34:2
Peter Pan 1950,Ap 25,27:2
Peter Pan 1954,O 21,30:2
Li'l Abner 1956,N 16,24:2
Li'l Abner 1956,N 25,II,1:1
Harold 1962,N 30,27:1
My Mother, My Father and Me 1963,Mr 25,5:5
Flora, the Red Menace 1965,My 12,41:2
Illya Darling 1967,Ap 12,37:1

Marks, John
Iphigenia in Aulis 1967,N 22,40:2

Marks, Jonathan
Crimes and Crimes 1970,Ja 19,35:1

Marks, Larry (Playwright)
My L A 1951,D 9,87:1

Marks, Lawrence
Tarzan of the Apes 1921,S 8,14:3

Marks, Loretta
Earl Carroll's Vanities 1923,Jl 6,8:2

Marks, Maurice (Playwright)
Stylish Stouts 1926,S 19,IX,1:3
History as Was 1927,My 5,30:1
Rain or Shine 1928,F 10,26:3
Saluta 1934,Ag 29,13:4
King's Breakfast, The 1937,D 13,22:8

Marks, Richard Lee (Producer)
Basement, The 1968,O 16,40:1
Tea Party 1968,O 16,40:1
In the Bar of a Tokyo Hotel 1969,My 12,54:1

Marks, Sandi (Scenic Designer)
Getting Married 1970,Ja 20,46:1
Three by Ferlinghetti; Victims of Amnesia, The
1970,S 23,43:1
Three by Ferlinghetti; Three Thousand Red Ants
1970,S 23,43:1
Three by Ferlinghetti; Alligation, The
1970,S 23,43:1

Marks, Sylvia
Cocktails of 1934 1934,My 5,22:1

Marks, Walter (Composer)
Bajour 1964,N 24,42:1
Peterpat 1965,Ja 7,27:1
Golden Rainbow 1968,F 5,27:1

Marks, Walter (Lyricist)
Bajour 1964,N 24,42:1
Golden Rainbow 1968,F 5,27:1

Markson, Greta
I Am a Camera 1956,O 10,47:2
Picnic on the Battlefield 1967,S 9,25:2
People vs Ranchman, The 1968,O 28,56:1

Markus, Elisabeth
Rendezvous in Wien 1956,S 5,23:1

Markus, Orrin
Ice Capades 1957,S 5,33:2

Markus, Thomas B
Gandhi 1970,O 21,37:1

Markussen, Arne
Willie the Weeper 1961,Ja 4,26:1

Marlatt, Donald
Birds, The 1966,Jl 1,40:1
Elizabeth the Queen 1966,N 4,30:1

Marle, Arnold
Tenth Man, The 1959,N 6,24:2
Tenth Man, The 1959,N 15,II,1:1

Marleau, Louise
Romeo and Juliet 1968,Je 11,55:2
Romeo and Juliet 1968,Je 23,II,1:1
Seagull, The 1968,Jl 25,27:2

Marlene, Beautiful
This Was Burlesque 1970,F 12,31:1

Marley, Helen
Surgeon, The 1932,O 28,23:1

Marley, James
Shinbone Alley 1957,Ap 15,23:2

Marley, John
Johnny Doodle 1942,Mr 19,28:2
Skipper Next to God 1948,Ja 5,14:5
Gramercy Ghost 1951,Ap 27,20:2
Dinosaur Wharf 1951,N 9,23:2
Strong Are Lonely, The 1953,S 30,38:3
Sing Till Tomorrow 1953,D 29,17:2
Sing Me No Lullaby 1954,O 15,17:2
Compulsion 1957,O 25,21:1
Enemy of the People, An 1959,F 5,24:4

Marlieb, John
Stop Press 1939,Mr 20,13:2

Marlin, Max (Composer)
Madam Will You Walk 1953,D 2,2:4
Sea Gull, The 1954,My 12,38:1
What Every Woman Knows 1954,D 23,16:2
Wisteria Trees, The 1955,F 3,20:2
Beyond Desire 1967,O 11,36:1

Marlin, Max (Musical Director)
Taming of the Shrew, The 1951,Ap 26,35:2
Dream Girl 1951,My 10,39:1

Marlin, Paul
Round Trip 1945,My 30,16:4
Lovely Me 1946,D 26,30:4

Marlin-Jones, Davey (Director)
Gingham Dog, The 1968,O 13,II,18:6

Marlin-Jones, Davy (Miscellaneous)
Ping-Pong 1959,Ap 17,22:1

Marlo, Elinor
Bruder Straubinger 1921,N 16,22:3

Marlo, Maria
Consul, The 1950,Mr 16,41:1
Consul, The 1950,Mr 26,II,1:1
Consul, The 1952,O 30,41:2
Consul, The 1957,S 4,40:3

Marlo, Mary
Oklahoma! 1951,My 30,15:2
Oklahoma! 1951,S 13,38:2
Oklahoma! 1953,S 1,19:1

Marlo, Micki
Ziegfeld Follies 1957,Mr 2,19:2

Marlon, Joan
Zeppelin 1929,Ja 15,22:3

Marlow, Brian (Playwright)
New Gallantry, The 1925,S 25,24:2
Command to Love, The 1927,S 21,27:1
Anna 1928,My 17,25:2
Bad Girl 1930,O 3,30:2
Napi 1931,Mr 12,22:5
Good Men and True 1935,O 26,12:4

Marlow, Fred
Tom Paine 1969,Mr 30,71:2
Tempest, The 1970,F 15,67:1

Marlow, Robin
High Kickers 1941,N 1,21:2
Marlowe, Aida
Walk Hard 1944,D 1,28:2
Marlowe, Alan
Macbeth 1961,Je 19,31:1
Marlowe, Alan (Musical Director)
Have I Got One for You 1968,Ja 8,32:1
Marlowe, Arthur
Tyrant, The 1930,N 13,33:1
Man on Stilts, The 1931,S 10,23:2
There You Are! 1932,My 17,25:4
Rendezvous 1932,O 13,22:3
Marathon 1933,Ja 28,8:8
Paths of Glory 1935,S 27,24:2
Holmeses of Baker Street, The 1936,D 10,34:3
Brooklyn Biarritz 1941,F 28,16:2
Johnny on the Spot 1942,Ja 9,24:2
Escapade 1953,N 19,40:1
Hostile Witness 1966,F 18,26:1
Marlowe, Christopher (Original Author)
Edward II 1958,F 12,32:5
Marlowe, Christopher (Playwright)
Dr Faustus 1926,O 27,25:5
Doctor Faustus 1937,Ja 9,21:2
Tragical Historie of Doctor Faustus, The 1937,Ja 31,XI,1:1
Tamburlaine the Great 1951,O 14,II,3:7
Tamburlaine the Great 1956,Ja 20,19:1
Tamburlaine the Great 1956,Ja 29,II,1:1
Doctor Faustus 1957,F 19,35:7
Doctor Faustus 1961,Ap 26,36:1
Doctor Faustus 1961,Ag 22,23:1
Tragical Historie of Doctor Faustus, The 1964,O 6,34:2
Jew of Malta, The 1965,Ap 17,9:1
Dr Faustus 1966,F 16,49:1
Dr Faustus 1968,Je 29,20:1
Edward II 1969,Ja 19,II,30:5
Edward II 1969,S 4,50:1
Marlowe, Dan
Busybody, The 1924,S 30,27:5
Marlowe, Frank
Heaven-Tappers, The 1927,Mr 9,28:3
Toplitzky of Notre Dame 1946,D 27,13:4
Marlowe, Frank E
Mermaid's Holiday 1961,Jl 1,8:1
Marlowe, Geneva
Pins and Needles 1922,F 2,20:1
Marlowe, Gloria
In Any Language 1952,O 9,40:2
Plain and Fancy 1955,Ja 28,14:2
Plain and Fancy 1955,F 6,II,1:1
View From the Bridge, A 1955,Ag 31,16:8
View From the Bridge, A 1955,S 30,21:1
Memory of Two Mondays, A 1955,S 30,21:1
Marlowe, Harvey
War President 1944,Ap 25,17:3
According to Law 1944,Je 2,20:3
Marlowe, Hugh
Arrest That Woman 1936,S 19,20:4
Millionairess, The 1938,Ag 16,22:5
Kiss the Boys Goodbye 1938,S 29,30:2
Young Couple Wanted 1940,Ja 25,16:2
Flight to the West 1940,D 15,I,59:5
Flight to the West 1940,D 31,19:1
Land Is Bright, The 1941,O 21,28:5
Land Is Bright, The 1941,O 29,26:2
Land Is Bright, The 1941,N 9,IX,1:1
Lady in the Dark 1943,Mr 1,14:2
Voice of the Turtle, The 1944,D 10,II,6:4
It Takes Two 1947,F 4,33:4
Laura 1947,Je 27,16:1
Duet for Two Hands 1947,O 8,28:3
Deer Park, The 1967,F 1,27:2
Postcards 1967,D 6,41:1
Woman Is My Idea 1968,S 26,61:1
Marlowe, James C
Mary 1920,O 19,12:1
Go Easy Mabel 1922,My 9,22:2
Clinging Vine, The 1922,D 25,20:2
Marlowe, Jeanne
Iron Men 1936,O 20,30:6
Marlowe, Joan
Mr and Mrs North 1941,Ja 13,11:2
Marlowe, Joanthan
As the Girls Go 1948,N 15,21:2
Marlowe, Jodie
How Beautiful With Shoes 1935,N 29,24:1
Marlowe, Julia
Twelfth Night 1921,N 1,17:1
Twelfth Night 1921,N 6,VI,1:1
Merchant of Venice, The 1921,N 22,17:1
Cymbeline 1923,O 3,12:1
Cymbeline 1923,O 14,VIII,1:1
Taming of the Shrew, The 1923,O 16,19:3
Twelfth Night 1923,O 23,17:1
Hamlet 1923,O 31,12:1
Merchant of Venice, The 1923,N 6,22:2
Romeo and Juliet 1923,N 13,25:2
Marlowe, Julia (Producer)
Taming of the Shrew, The 1923,O 16,19:3
Twelfth Night 1923,O 23,17:1

Hamlet 1923,O 31,12:1
Merchant of Venice, The 1923,N 6,22:2
Romeo and Juliet 1923,N 13,25:2
Marlowe, Julie
Carnival in Flanders 1953,S 9,38:2
Marlowe, Marion
Artists and Models 1924,O 16,33:3
Sound of Music, The 1959,N 17,40:2
Athenian Touch, The 1964,Ja 15,25:4
Marlowe, Mary
Bringing Up Father 1925,Mr 31,16:1
Naughty Riquette 1926,S 14,25:2
Marlowe, Maxine
O Evening Star 1936,Ja 9,24:6
Marlowe, Norma
As the Girls Go 1948,N 15,21:2
Marlowe, Peggy
Order Please 1934,O 10,21:2
Marlowe, Queen
Parson's Bride, The 1929,Ja 22,22:3
Marlowe, Ray
Walk Hard 1944,D 1,28:2
Henri Christophe 1945,Je 7,24:5
Marlowe, Raymond
Student Prince, The 1924,D 3,25:3
Marlowe, Stanley
Triplets 1932,S 22,25:2
Marilyn's Affairs 1933,Mr 16,21:5
Marlowe, Vivian
Love Song, The 1925,Ja 14,19:4
Merry Merry 1925,S 25,24:3
Oh, Ernest! 1927,My 10,24:3
Marmel, Joan
Enemy of the People, An 1958,F 26,24:2
Marmon, James
Colombe 1965,F 24,33:1
Marmont, Patricia
Inspector Calls, An 1947,O 22,38:2
Black Chiffon 1950,S 28,39:2
Marmont, Percy
Years Between, The 1931,My 10,VIII,2:1
Marmy, Mae
Have You Heard This One 1953,N 9,23:4
Man for All Seasons, A 1964,Ja 28,24:2
Marnac, Jane
Montmartre 1924,Je 15,VII,1:4
Rain 1927,Mr 3,23:2
Rain 1927,Mr 27,VII,4:8
Untitled-Revue 1928,Mr 18,III,3:1
1928 1928,Ap 8,VIII,4:1
Marnac, Jane (Playwright)
Women, The 1938,N 5,14:1
Marnac, Jane (Producer)
Ghost Train, The 1929,Je 9,VIII,2:4
Marnay, Carol E
Silver Grey Toy Poodle 1969,My 15,41:2
Marne, Lily
Scarlet Pages 1929,S 10,26:3
Girls in Uniform 1932,D 31,10:3
Marner, Gene
Marvellous History of Saint Bernard, The 1958,F 24,16:3
Marner, Gene (Miscellaneous)
Marvellous History of Saint Bernard, The 1958,F 24,16:3
Marner, Jordan
Sound of Hunting, A 1954,Ap 7,41:1
Marnett, Vivian
Once Around the Block 1950,My 25,36:2
Marnik, Burt (Playwright)
Cyanamide 1954,Mr 26,17:6
Twisting Road, The; Housekeeper, The 1957,N 18,36:5
Twisting Road, The; One Tuesday Morning 1957,N 18,36:5
Twisting Road, The; Jewel of the South, The 1957,N 18,36:5
Marno, Marc
Majority of One, A 1959,F 17,28:2
Never Live Over a Pretzel Factory 1964,Mr 30,37:1
Marofschick, Esther
Kith and Kin 1930,My 14,31:1
Marofschick, Esther (Choreographer)
Kith and Kin 1930,My 14,31:1
Marone, George
Golden Bat 1970,Je 27,18:2
Marone, Terry
My Fair Lady 1964,My 21,43:2
Maronek, James (Scenic Designer)
Mother Courage and Her Children 1964,My 12,32:2
Tempest, The 1970,F 15,67:1
Maroney, John
Demi-Virgin, The 1921,O 19,22:1
Rust 1924,F 1,12:1
Carolinian, The 1925,N 3,34:2
Junk 1927,Ja 6,25:1
Springboard, The 1927,O 13,23:1
If Booth Had Missed 1932,F 5,24:2
Wine of Choice 1938,F 22,18:4
Run Sheep Run 1938,N 4,26:2
Shakespeare's Merchant 1939 1939,Ja 10,16:3
Maross, Joe
Innkeepers, The 1956,F 3,19:i

Marouani, Felix (Miscellaneous)
Gilbert Becaud Sings Love 1968,O 7,53:5
Marowitz, Charles (Director)
Blue Comedy 1968,O 23,36:1
Macbeth 1969,Je 1,II,4:5
Marowitz, Charles (Miscellaneous)
King Lear 1964,My 19,43:2
Marowitz, Charles (Producer)
Chicago/Conspiracy 1970,Ag 26,35:1
Marquand, Jan
Melo 1931,Ap 17,26:6
Marquand, John
Cyrano de Bergerac 1932,D 27,11:2
Marquand, John P
Late George Apley, The 1944,N 22,26:2
Late George Apley, The 1944,D 3,II,1:1
Point of No Return 1951,O 31,32:2
Point of No Return 1951,D 14,35:2
Point of No Return 1951,D 23,II,3:1
Point of No Return 1957,Mr 23,17:2
Marquand, John P (Playwright)
Late George Apley, The 1944,O 20,16:4
Late George Apley, The 1944,N 22,26:2
Late George Apley, The 1944,D 3,II,1:1
Marquand, Nancy
No Way Out 1944,O 31,23:1
Marquardt, Robert (Miscellaneous)
Blood Wedding 1958,Ap 1,35:1
Marquardt, Siegrid
Rendezvous in Wien 1956,S 5,23:1
Marques, Jose (Miscellaneous)
Blood Wedding 1958,Ap 1,35:1
Marques, Rene (Playwright)
Soles Truncos, Los; House on Cristo Street, The 1959,Ag 31,15:2
Ox Cart, The 1966,D 20,58:1
Marquet, Mary
Paquebot Tenacity, Le 1930,Mr 9,IX,2:7
Madame Quinze 1935,Ap 21,IX,2:1
Marquette, Doris
Poppy God, The 1921,Ag 30,10:1
We've Got to Have Money 1923,Ag 21,12:1
Marquina, Eduardo (Playwright)
Dono Maria la Brava 1926,My 18,29:1
Road to Happiness, The 1927,My 3,24:1
Marquis, Dixie
Trojan Women, The 1963,D 24,7:6
Square in the Eye 1965,My 20,54:1
Displaced Person, The 1966,D 30,15:1
Acquisition, The 1968,D 31,19:1
Marquis, Don
Untitled-Revue 1928,N 19,16:2
Marquis, Don (Original Author)
Shinbone Alley 1957,Ap 28,II,1:1
Marquis, Don (Playwright)
Old Soak, The 1922,Ag 23,14:5
Old Soak, The 1922,S 3,VI,1:1
Out of the Sea 1927,D 6,26:2
Everything's Jake 1930,Ja 17,20:4
Dark Hours, The 1932,N 15,24:2
Master of the Revels 1935,Ag 14,16:2
Shinbone Alley 1957,Ap 15,23:2
Marquis, Frank
Vaudeville (Palace) 1952,Ap 27,II,1:1
Marquis, Marjorie
Aiglon, L' 1927,D 27,24:3
Falstaff 1928,D 26,14:2
Apple Cart, The 1930,F 25,30:1
Ah, Wilderness! 1933,S 26,26:3
Ah, Wilderness! 1933,O 3,28:2
Marquis, Marjorie (Director)
Dark Hours, The 1932,N 15,24:2
Dark Hours, The 1932,N 15,24:2
Marquis, Walter
Saint Joan 1936,Mr 10,27:4
Marquis Family
Danny Kaye's International Show 1953,Ja 19,20:2
Danny Kaye Show 1963,Ap 11,28:2
Marquise, Mercer
Lew Leslie's Blackbirds of 1930 1930,O 23,34:5
Marquiss, Walter (Playwright)
Whirlpool 1929,D 4,37:3
Marquita
Vaudeville (Hippodrome) 1924,O 21,21:2
Marqusee, John (Miscellaneous)
Winterset 1966,F 10,32:2
Marr, Edward
Camels Are Coming, The 1931,O 3,20:4
Moon Over Mulberry Street 1935,S 5,24:6
Timber House 1936,S 21,27:5
Don't Look Now! 1936,N 4,41:3
Tide Rising 1937,Ja 26,17:2
Marr, James
John Ferguson 1921,My 24,20:1
Gray Shadow 1931,Mr 11,23:4
Two Seconds 1931,O 10,20:6
Marr, Joe
Iceman Cometh, The 1946,O 10,31:3
Mister Roberts 1948,F 19,27:2
Iceman Cometh, The 1956,My 8,38:1
Marr, Richard
Passion of Gross, The 1955,Ja 24,20:2
Sappho 1960,Ja 12,22:1

Marr, Richard—Cont
Pilgrim's Progress 1962,Mr 21,36:2
Pimpernel! 1964,Ja 7,26:6
How to Succeed in Business Without Really Trying 1966,Ap 21,45:1
Witness 1968,N 22,38:1
Make Me Disappear 1969,My 14,34:1
Coco 1969,D 19,66:1
Marr, William
Casanova 1923,S 27,10:2
Marra, Joseph
If Booth Had Missed 1931,My 14,27:1
Marracci, Livia
International Revue 1930,F 26,22:2
Marre, Albert
Relapse, The 1950,N 23,54:2
Marre, Albert (Director)
Little Blue Light, The 1951,Ap 30,17:2
Love's Labour's Lost 1953,F 5,20:3
Love's Labour's Lost 1953,F 8,II,1:1
Misalliance 1953,F 19,20:1
Merchant of Venice, The 1953,Mr 5,20:2
Kismet 1953,D 4,2:4
Festival 1955,Ja 19,22:1
Chalk Garden, The 1955,O 27,29:1
Chalk Garden, The 1955,N 13,II,1:1
Shangri-La 1956,Je 14,40:1
Saint Joan 1956,S 12,42:1
Good as Gold 1957,Mr 8,22:2
Time Remembered 1957,N 13,41:2
Time Remembered 1957,N 24,II,1:1
Love Doctor, The 1959,O 14,52:4
Rape of the Belt, The 1960,N 7,46:1
Milk and Honey 1961,O 11,52:1
Too True to Be Good 1963,Mr 14,8:2
Too True to Be Good 1963,Mr 23,5:6
Rainy Day in Newark, A 1963,O 23,35:1
Never Live Over a Pretzel Factory 1964,Mr 30,37:1
Man of La Mancha 1965,N 23,52:1
Sorrow of Frederick, The 1967,Jl 8,14:2
Man of La Mancha 1967,N 24,61:1
Man of La Mancha 1969,My 3,38:4
Cry for Us All 1970,Ap 9,48:2
Marre, Albert (Miscellaneous)
Relapse, The 1950,N 23,54:2
Marre, Albert (Playwright)
Love's Labour's Lost 1953,F 5,20:3
Cry for Us All 1970,Ap 9,48:2
Marre, Albert (Producer)
Never Live Over a Pretzel Factory 1964,Mr 30,37:1
Marriott, Crittenden (Original Author)
Black Tower 1932,Ja 12,29:2
Marriott, James
Flying Gerardos, The 1940,D 30,21:4
Steps Leading Up 1941,Ap 19,20:6
Marriott, Jennifer
Happy Apple, The 1970,Jl 26,49:2
Marriott, John
Too Many Boats 1934,S 12,26:3
Sweet River 1936,O 29,30:2
Chalked Out 1937,Mr 26,24:2
Little Foxes, The 1939,F 16,16:2
Janie 1942,S 11,24:2
No Way Out 1944,O 31,23:1
Iceman Cometh, The 1946,O 10,31:3
How I Wonder 1947,O 1,34:2
Respectful Prostitute, The 1948,F 10,27:2
Respectful Prostitute, The 1948,F 15,II,1:1
Small Hours, The 1951,F 16,22:1
Green Pastures, The 1951,Mr 16,35:2
Dinosaur Wharf 1951,N 9,23:2
Ponder Heart, The 1956,F 17,14:2
Orpheus Descending 1957,Mr 22,28:1
Interlock 1958,F 7,18:1
Of Mice and Men 1958,D 5,38:1
Season of Choice 1959,Ap 14,40:1
Miracle Worker, The 1959,O 20,44:1
Bicycle Ride to Nevada 1963,S 25,38:1
Death of the Well-Loved Boy, The 1967,My 16,48:1
More Stately Mansions 1967,N 1,40:1
Weekend 1968,Mr 14,50:2
Marriott-Watson, Nan
Diversion 1928,Ja 12,25:1
Marrow, Macklin
Desire Under the Elms 1924,N 12,20:7
Come of Age 1952,Ja 24,22:2
Marrow, Macklin (Composer)
Saint, The 1924,O 13,20:3
Twelfth Night 1930,O 16,28:2
Camille 1932,N 2,23:3
Love for Love 1940,Je 4,19:5
Marrow, Macklin (Lyricist)
Rivals, The 1942,Ja 15,24:2
Marrow, Macklin (Musical Director)
Patience 1925,F 1,VII,1:1
Finta Giardiniera, La 1927,Ja 19,20:5
Merry Widow, The 1933,Ag 13,IX,1:3
Come of Age 1934,Ja 13,16:6
Mars, Janice
Message for Margaret 1947,Ap 17,34:2
Orpheus Descending 1957,Mr 22,28:1
Midgie Purvis 1961,F 2,25:3
Three Sisters, The 1964,Je 23,24:1

Mars, Kenneth
On the Town 1959,F 14,15:1
Anything Goes 1962,My 16,35:1
Affair, The 1962,S 21,34:2
Best Laid Plans, The 1966,Mr 26,15:2
Mars, Lucien
Zizi 1964,N 23,51:1
Mars, Marjorie
Silver Cord, The 1927,O 2,VIII,1:3
Last Enemy, The 1930,Ja 5,VIII,2:2
Insult; Dolle Hans 1930,My 4,XI,1:3
Barretts of Wimpole Street, The 1930,S 7,IX,2:1
Within the Gates 1934,F 8,14:4
Within the Gates 1934,F 25,IX,3:7
Marsala, Marty
Hear That Trumpet 1946,O 8,19:2
Marsans, Mme
Misanthrope, Le 1922,N 22,18:2
Marschante, Marion
Piggy 1927,Ja 12,22:2
White Lights 1927,O 12,30:4
Marschka, Ernst (Playwright)
Cissy 1932,D 24,10:5
Marschka, Hubert (Playwright)
Cissy 1932,D 24,10:5
Marsden, Betty
On the Brighter Side 1961,Je 25,II,3:5
Thurber Carnival, A 1962,Ap 12,42:1
Marsden, Vickie
Small Hours, The 1951,F 16,22:1
Marsh, Albert
Transplanting Jean 1921,Ja 4,11:2
Exciters, The 1922,S 23,10:4
Dancing Mothers 1924,Ag 12,12:2
Marsh, Audrey
Vaudeville (Palace) 1932,Jl 4,14:5
Marsh, Bernard
Kongi's Harvest 1968,Ap 15,49:1
Marsh, C Leland
Tick-Tack-Toe 1920,F 24,11:2
Marsh, Calden
God's Trombones 1960,F 10,43:4
Shakespeare in Harlem 1960,F 10,43:4
Shakespeare in Harlem 1960,F 21,II,1:1
Marsh, Caren
Heaven on Earth 1948,S 17,29:2
Marsh, Clara
Processional 1937,O 14,23:1
Prologue to Glory 1938,Mr 18,22:2
Marsh, Donald (Choreographer)
Power of Dreams, A 1958,Mr 11,33:1
O, Oysters! 1961,Ja 31,23:1
Marsh, Donald (Composer)
Power of Dreams, A 1958,Mr 11,33:1
Mystery of the Finding of the Cross, The 1959,Ja 16,35:2
Golem, The 1959,F 26,38:2
Cup of Trembling, The 1959,My 1,33:5
Marsh, Donald (Musical Director)
Way of the Cross, The 1959,Ja 16,35:2
Marsh, Edward
Mikado, The 1942,F 4,22:2
Pirates of Penzance, The 1942,F 18,22:2
Iolanthe 1942,F 24,26:4
Gondoliers, The 1942,Mr 4,22:3
Marsh, Edward Owen (Translator)
Rendezvous at Senlis 1961,F 28,39:2
Marsh, Edwin
Mikado, The 1944,F 12,11:3
Gondoliers, The 1944,F 22,26:3
Ruddigore 1944,Mr 3,19:5
Marsh, Emily
Pirates of Penzance, The 1936,Ap 21,27:5
Marsh, Garry
Dear Charles 1952,D 21,44:5
Dear Charles 1953,Ap 20,22:4
Marsh, George
Sweet Shadow 1935,Ag 7,22:2
Cyrano de Bergerac 1936,Ap 28,17:1
Marsh, Howard
Greenwich Village Follies 1920,Ag 31,7:3
Blossom Time 1921,S 30,10:1
Student Prince, The 1924,D 3,25:3
Cherry Blossoms 1927,Mr 29,22:3
Show Boat 1927,D 28,26:1
Well of Romance, The 1930,N 8,21:2
Mikado, The; Town of Titipu, The 1931,My 5,33:2
H M S Pinafore 1931,My 19,25:2
Gondoliers, The 1931,Je 2,34:4
Patience 1931,Je 16,30:4
Pirates of Penzance, The; Slave of Duty, The 1931,Je 30,23:6
Iolanthe 1931,Jl 14,21:5
Trial by Jury 1931,Jl 28,17:6
H M S Pinafore 1931,Jl 28,17:6
Mikado, The 1931,Ag 25,17:7
Iolanthe 1932,Ja 5,20:2
Gondoliers, The 1932,Ja 12,29:1
Robin Hood 1932,Ja 28,25:4
Mikado, The 1935,Jl 16,24:4
Pirates of Penzance, The 1935,Jl 23,24:2
Yeomen of the Guard, The 1935,Jl 30,16:4
Gondoliers, The 1935,Ag 6,20:5

Marsh, Howard—Cont
Trial by Jury 1935,Ag 13,20:6
H M S Pinafore 1935,Ag 13,20:6
Marsh, Jane
Midsummer Night's Dream, A 1932,N 18,22:2
Marsh, Jean
Much Ado About Nothing 1959,S 18,25:2
Marsh, Linda
Breaking Wall, The 1960,Ja 26,27:5
Poppa Is Home 1961,D 20,37:1
Laundry, The 1963,F 19,5:2
Hamlet 1964,Ap 10,30:1
Marsh, Louis
Sea Shells 1935,Jl 16,24:2
Marsh, Lucille
You Can't Take It With You 1945,Mr 27,23:7
Marsh, Marian (Lighting Director)
Anatomist, The 1957,F 27,21:5
Marsh, Mary
Small Timers, The 1925,Ja 28,15:3
Right to Kill, The 1926,F 16,22:2
Manhatters, The 1927,Jl 19,27:3
Marsh, Myrna
Story to Be Whispered 1937,Ag 20,21:4
Marsh, Ngaio (Producer)
Macbeth 1946,D 1,II,3:7
Marsh, Ray
Spring's Awakening 1955,O 10,30:2
Marsh, Ray (Director)
Salvage 1957,Ap 10,39:2
Marsh, Sy
Egg in Your Beer 1945,My 13,II,1:3
Marsh, T L
It's the Valet 1933,D 15,25:4
Marsh, Thelma
Spook House 1930,Je 4,33:3
That's Gratitude 1930,S 12,28:1
Bridal Wise 1932,My 31,15:5
Marsh, Vera
Vaudeville (Palace) 1929,Je 3,27:4
America's Sweetheart 1931,F 11,23:1
Free for All 1931,S 9,25:1
East Wind 1931,O 28,19:1
Marsh, Will
Sam Abramovitch 1927,Ja 20,20:5
Dorian Gray 1928,My 22,18:4
Crooks' Convention, The 1929,S 19,37:4
Marshak, Alma
Have I Got One for You 1968,Ja 8,32:1
Marshal, Alan
Foolscap 1933,Ja 12,21:2
While Parents Sleep 1934,Je 5,28:2
Lady Jane 1934,S 11,24:2
Bishop Misbehaves, The 1935,F 21,22:4
Devil's Disciple, The 1941,S 11,20:6
Marshal, Irby
Warrior's Husband, The 1932,Mr 12,19:4
Marshal, May
Crime Marches on 1935,O 24,19:1
Marshall, Alan
Best Sellers 1933,My 4,20:2
Going Gay 1933,Ag 4,18:5
On Stage 1935,O 30,16:6
Marshall, Arlein
Fly by Night 1933,Je 3,16:2
Kultur 1933,S 27,24:3
Marshall, Armina
Tidings Brought to Mary, The 1922,D 25,20:1
Peer Gynt 1923,F 6,14:1
Race With the Shadow, The 1924,Ja 21,20:5
Fata Morgana 1924,Mr 4,16:3
Ariadne 1925,F 24,17:1
Glass Slipper, The 1925,O 20,29:1
Glass Slipper, The 1925,O 25,VIII,1:1
Merchants of Glory 1925,D 15,28:3
Right You Are (If You Think You Are) 1927,F 24,27:1
Mr Pim Passes By 1927,Ap 19,24:1
Man's Estate 1929,Ap 2,28:2
Those We Love 1930,F 20,22:2
Pillars of Society, The 1931,O 15,19:1
Bride the Sun Shines On, The 1931,D 28,20:2
Noble Prize, The 1933,Jl 4,16:4
If This Be Treason 1935,Jl 30,17:1
If This Be Treason 1935,S 24,28:2
Marshall, Armina (Miscellaneous)
Audition of the Apprentice Theatre 1939,Je 2,26:2
Foolish Notion 1945,Mr 14,23:2
Iceman Cometh, The 1946,O 10,31:3
Marshall, Armina (Original Author)
Arms and the Girl 1950,F 3,28:2
Marshall, Armina (Playwright)
Pursuit of Happiness, The 1934,Je 24,IX,1:4
On to Fortune 1935,Ja 15,23:2
On to Fortune 1935,F 5,22:2
Dr Knock 1936,Jl 14,22:1
Susannah and the Elders 1940,O 13,47:7
Susannah and the Elders 1940,O 30,28:2
Pursuit of Happiness, The 1952,Mr 22,9:2
Marshall, Armina (Producer)
Millionairess, The 1938,Ag 16,22:5
Marshall, Assotta
Porgy and Bess 1935,O 11,30:2
Sweet River 1936,O 29,30:2

Marshall, Assotta—Cont

Porgy and Bess 1942,Ja 23,16:2
Show Boat 1946,Ja 7,17:2
Show Boat 1948,S 9,33:2
Marshall, Austin
Red Rhumba 1936,Ap 14,18:1
I'd Rather Be Right 1937,N 3,28:2
Marshall, Bernice
One Woman's Husband 1920,Mr 23,9:3
Marshall, Betty
Scandals 1920,Je 8,9:1
Jimmie 1920,N 18,15:3
Marshall, Boyd
Lady Billy 1920,D 15,18:2
Magic Ring, The 1923,O 2,10:1
Just Life 1926,S 15,33:3
Excess Baggage 1927,D 27,24:2
Hot Water 1929,Ja 22,22:3
Sari 1930,Ja 29,27:1
Marshall, Bruce (Original Author)
Father Malachy's Miracle 1937,N 18,26:4
Father Malachy's Miracle 1937,D 5,XII,5:1
Marshall, Bruce (Playwright)
Father Malachy's Miracle 1938,Ja 23,XI,1:6
Marshall, Captain (Playwright)
His Excellency the Governor 1930,My 18,VIII,2:6
Marshall, Carmen
Harlem 1929,F 21,30:3
Marshall, Charles Cyrus (Mrs) (Director)
One Woman's Husband 1920,Mr 23,9:3
Marshall, Clark
Weather Clear, Track Fast 1927,O 19,24:5
Scarlet Fox, The 1928,Mr 28,31:1
Marshall, Don
Firebird of Florence 1945,Mr 23,13:4
Marshall, E G
Big Blow 1938,O 3,11:2
Jason 1942,Ja 22,12:2
Skin of Our Teeth, The 1942,N 19,29:5
Petrified Forest, The 1943,N 2,30:6
Jacobowsky and the Colonel 1944,Mr 15,17:2
Beggars Are Comming to Town 1945,O 29,16:2
Woman Bites Dog 1946,Ap 18,21:2
Iceman Cometh, The 1946,O 10,31:3
Dear Judas 1947,Ag 5,26:1
Survivors, The 1948,Ja 20,27:2
Hope Is the Thing With Feathers 1948,Ap 12,24:2
Gone Tomorrow; Hope's the Thing 1948,My 12,34:6
Hope Is the Thing With Feathers; Hope's the Thing 1948,My 12,34:6
Home Life of a Buffalo; Hope's the Thing 1948,My 12,34:6
E-MC2 1948,Je 16,36:2
Gambler, The 1952,O 14,40:1
Crucible, The 1953,Ja 23,15:2
Crucible, The 1953,Jl 2,20:2
Red Roses for Me 1955,D 29,15:2
Red Roses for Me 1956,Ja 8,II,1:1
Queen After Death 1956,Mr 13,33:2
Waiting for Godot 1956,Ap 20,21:2
Waiting for Godot 1956,Ap 29,II,1:2
Gang's All Here, The 1959,O 2,23:1
Little Foxes, The 1967,O 27,53:1
Little Foxes, The 1967,N 5,II,1:1
Little Foxes, The 1968,Ja 6,24:4
Plaza Suite 1968,D 14,61:2
Marshall, Edward
Red Robe, The 1928,D 26,15:1
Devil and Daniel Webster, The 1939,My 19,26:1
Marshall, Eleanor
Easy Terms 1925,S 23,22:2
Marshall, Everett
Scandals 1931,Ag 11,28:4
Scandals 1931,Ag 16,VIII,1:1
George White's Scandals 1931,S 15,30:1
Scandals 1931,S 27,VIII,3:7
Melody 1933,F 15,17:4
Lambs Gambol 1933,Ap 24,10:1
Ziegfeld Follies 1934,Ja 5,24:3
Calling All Stars 1934,N 22,26:1
Calling All Stars 1934,D 14,28:2
Three Waltzes 1938,Je 26,II,7:5
Blossom Time 1938,D 27,12:2
New Aquacade Revue, The 1940,My 13,20:5
Student Prince, The 1943,Je 9,16:2
Marshall, Frank
Bare Facts 1927,Je 30,35:1
Ten Nights in a Barroom 1928,Mr 28,31:2
Mystery Moon 1930,Je 24,23:4
Lingering Past, The 1932,Je 30,26:5
Marshall, Frederick (Composer)
Troilus and Cressida 1956,D 27,21:1
Henry V 1958,D 26,2:7
Marshall, Fredye
Pirate, The 1942,N 26,39:2
Run, Little Chillun 1943,Ag 14,6:1
Carmen Jones 1943,D 3,26:2
Carmen Jones 1946,Ap 8,32:2
Set My People Free 1948,N 4,38:2
Mamba's Daughters 1953,Mr 21,12:6
Marshall, George
Little Racketeer, The 1932,Ja 19,24:4

Marshall, Glesco
Peter Pan; Boy Who Would Not Grow Up, The 1928,N 27,36:3
Katerina 1929,F 26,30:3
Marshall, Harriott
Romeo and Juliet 1935,D 24,10:2
Marshall, Helen
Beggar's Opera, The 1934,Jl 17,24:5
Sunny River 1941,D 5,28:2
Two Misers, The 1943,D 9,30:5
Marshall, Herbert
Voice From the Minaret, The 1922,Ja 31,11:2
Fedora 1922,F 11,18:1
Pelican, The 1925,S 22,23:2
These Charming People 1925,O 7,31:2
Interference 1927,F 27,VII,1:3
High Road, The 1928,S 11,31:1
Paris Bound 1929,My 19,IX,1:8
Michael and Mary 1930,F 2,5:1
Michael and Mary 1930,F 23,VIII,2:1
Swan, The 1930,Jl 27,VIII,1:8
Tomorrow and Tomorrow 1931,Ja 14,26:3
Tomorrow and Tomorrow 1931,Ja 25,VIII,1:1
Tomorrow and Tomorrow 1931,F 1,VIII,2:1
There's Always Juliet 1931,O 13,26:5
There's Always Juliet 1932,F 16,24:2
There's Always Juliet 1932,F 28,VIII,1:1
Another Language 1932,D 25,IX,1:6
Marshall, Irby
Merchant of Venice, The 1920,D 30,16:2
Lady, The 1923,D 5,23:2
Old English 1924,D 24,11:2
Death Takes a Holiday 1931,F 17,29:1
Getting Married 1931,Mr 31,25:5
Ragged Army 1934,F 27,16:5
Romeo and Juliet 1934,D 4,23:2
Romeo and Juliet 1934,D 21,30:3
Kind Lady 1935,Ap 24,24:5
Marshall, James
Suzette 1921,N 25,18:3
Chiffon Girl, The 1924,F 20,23:2
Princess Flavia 1925,N 3,34:3
Cherry Blossoms 1927,Mr 29,22:3
Marshall, James (Scenic Designer)
Egg and I, The 1958,S 11,43:4
Marshall, Janet
As You Like It 1937,N 1,25:2
Marshall, Jay
Love Life 1948,O 8,31:2
Great to Be Alive! 1950,Mr 24,28:2
Ziegfeld Follies 1957,Mr 2,19:2
Marshall, Joe
Ice Capades 1961,Ag 31,24:4
Marshall, John
Sunny River 1941,D 5,28:2
Marshall, Junior
Ponder Heart, The 1956,F 17,14:2
Marshall, Letitia
Technique 1931,My 15,21:1
Marshall, Lisa
Enemy of the People, An 1958,F 26,24:2
Angels of Anadarko 1962,O 11,47:1
Marshall, Lucy
Rosalinda; Fledermaus, Die 1942,O 29,26:5
Marshall, Madeleine
Cave Girl, The 1920,Ag 19,12:2
Star of Bengal 1929,S 26,27:2
Five Star Final 1930,D 31,11:1
Marshall, Maithe
Carmen Jones 1945,My 3,26:5
Marshall, Marianne
Abie's Irish Rose 1954,N 19,19:1
Marshall, Marilyn
This Was Burlesque 1965,Mr 17,55:3
Marshall, Marion
As You Like It 1947,F 21,16:2
Hamlet 1947,F 27,27:2
Marshall, May
Mademoiselle 1932,O 19,22:4
Raw Meat 1933,Mr 23,13:2
Party, A 1933,Ag 24,18:4
While Parents Sleep 1934,Je 5,28:2
Matrimony, PFD 1936,N 6,28:4
Matrimony, PFD 1936,N 13,26:3
Circle, The 1938,Ap 19,24:2
Come Across 1938,S 15,28:3
Marshall, Mort
Frogs, The 1941,N 14,25:3
Small Wonder 1948,S 16,33:5
Gentlemen Prefer Blondes 1949,D 9,35:3
Of Thee I Sing 1952,My 6,34:2
Men of Distinction 1953,My 1,18:4
Best House in Naples, The 1956,O 27,16:2
Gypsy 1959,My 22,31:6
All American 1962,Mr 20,44:1
Little Me 1962,N 19,41:3
Where's Charley? 1966,My 26,57:1
Minnie's Boys 1970,Mr 27,27:1
Marshall, Norman (Director)
Karl and Anna 1935,O 13,IX,3:1
Children's Hour, The 1936,N 29,XII,2:1
Oscar Wilde 1938,O 11,20:2
Indifferent Shepherd, The 1948,Mr 14,II,2:4

Marshall, Norman (Producer)
Miracle in America 1934,O 2,18:4
Various Heavens 1936,Mr 8,IX,1:1
Parnell 1936,My 24,IX,1:7
Out of Sight 1937,Mr 28,XI,2:2
Mr Gladstone 1937,O 17,XI,3:5
Ame en Peine, L'; Unquiet Spirit, The 1937,N 14,XI,3:1
Oscar Wilde 1938,O 11,20:2
First Gentleman, The 1945,Jl 19,18:8
Marshall, Norman Thomas
Boy on the Straight-Back Chair 1969,Mr 18,36:1
Marshall, Oswald
Ghost Parade, The 1929,O 31,28:4
Infinite Shoeblack, The 1930,F 18,28:1
Barretts of Wimpole Street, The 1931,F 10,25:1
Victoria Regina 1935,D 27,15:2
Victoria Regina 1938,O 4,20:2
Woman Brown, The 1939,D 9,18:5
Anne of England 1941,O 8,26:2
Sheppey 1944,Ap 19,27:2
I Remember Mama 1944,O 20,16:2
Nineteenth Hole of Europe, The 1949,Mr 28,16:2
Marshall, Pat
What's Up 1943,N 12,24:6
Hats Off to Ice 1944,Je 23,15:2
Day Before Spring, The 1945,N 23,27:2
Day Before Spring, The 1945,D 2,II,1:1
Mr Wonderful 1956,Mr 23,23:2
Marshall, Peggy
Touch of the Poet, A 1962,S 30,85:8
Marshall, Penelope
Twelfth Night 1941,D 3,32:2
Marshall, Pete
How to Make a Man 1961,F 3,16:1
Skyscraper 1965,N 15,48:1
Marshall, Red
All in Fun 1940,N 22,26:2
All in Fun 1940,D 28,11:2
Time, Place and the Girl, The 1942,O 22,24:3
Michael Todd's Peep Show 1950,Je 29,37:2
Peep Show 1950,Jl 9,II,1:1
Marshall, Richard
Henry V 1965,Je 29,27:2
Taming of the Shrew, The 1965,Jl 3,10:5
By Jupiter 1967,Ja 20,28:2
Marshall, Rita
Arrow-Maker, The 1956,O 5,20:1
Marshall, Robert
Tidbits of 1946 1946,Jl 9,17:2
Marshall, Robert (Playwright)
Angela 1928,D 4,28:2
Marshall, Robin
Romeo and Juliet 1968,Je 11,55:2
Tartuffe 1968,Je 12,39:1
Midsummer Night's Dream, A 1968,Je 13,54:1
Hamlet 1969,Je 11,37:1
Alchemist, The 1969,Je 12,51:1
Measure for Measure 1969,Je 13,41:3
Merchant of Venice, The 1970,Je 10,39:1
School for Scandal, The 1970,Je 11,51:1
Marshall, Roy
Lady Comes Across, The 1942,Ja 10,10:2
Marshall, Sarah
Dream Girl 1951,My 10,39:1
Idiot's Delight 1951,My 24,46:3
Jane 1952,F 2,10:2
Mr Pickwick 1952,S 18,36:3
Charley's Aunt 1953,D 23,22:2
Sea Gull, The 1954,My 12,38:1
Ponder Heart, The 1956,F 17,14:2
Ponder Heart, The 1956,F 26,II,1:1
Visit to a Small Planet 1957,F 8,18:1
Visit to a Small Planet 1957,F 24,II,1:1
World of Suzie Wong, The 1958,O 15,47:1
Goodbye Charlie 1959,D 17,50:1
Come Blow Your Horn 1961,F 23,31:3
Marshall, Sid
Sambo 1969,D 22,42:1
Marshall, Ted (Miscellaneous)
Emperor, The 1963,Ap 17,30:1
Marshall, Tina
Green Pastures, The 1951,Mr 16,35:2
Marshall, Walter
Climax, The 1926,My 18,29:3
Marshall, William
Winged Victory 1943,N 22,24:1
Our Lan' 1947,S 29,16:5
Long Way From Home, A 1948,F 9,25:2
Set My People Free 1948,N 4,38:2
Lost in the Stars 1949,O 31,21:2
Peter Pan 1950,Ap 25,27:2
Green Pastures, The 1951,Mr 16,35:2
Green Pastures, The 1951,Ap 1,II,1:1
Time to Go 1952,My 8,35:6
In Splendid Error 1954,O 27,33:6
Othello 1955,S 8,27:2
Othello 1955,S 18,II,1:1
Virtuous Island, The 1957,Ap 10,39:1
Othello 1958,Jl 4,16:1
Othello 1962,S 28,27:1
Javelin 1966,N 10,63:1
Knack With Horses, A 1970,D 21,52:1

Marshall, William (Lighting Director)
Of Thee I Sing 1969,Mr 8,19:1
Marshalov, Boris
This One Man 1930,O 22,32:3
Doctor X 1931,F 10,25:1
Brief Moment 1931,N 10,28:2
They All Come to Moscow 1933,My 12,20:6
Tight Britches 1934,S 12,26:2
Coward, The 1935,Jl 16,24:1
Libel! 1935,D 8,X,5:8
Libel! 1935,D 21,10:5
Eastwood Ho 1936,Jl 8,14:2
Flight to the West 1940,D 31,19:1
Winter Soldiers 1942,N 30,19:2
Innocent Voyage, The 1943,N 16,27:2
Smile of the World, The 1949,Ja 13,26:5
Julia, Jake, and Uncle Joe 1961,Ja 30,19:1
First Love 1961,D 26,20:2
Marshe, Vera
Ballyhoo of 1932 1932,S 7,14:2
She Loves Me Not 1934,My 27,X,2:5
Parade 1935,My 21,22:2
Good Men and True 1935,O 26,12:4
Marsland, James
Patience 1966,N 30,58:1
Marsland, Nancie B
Swan, The 1923,O 24,15:3
Easy Virtue 1925,D 8,28:2
Caste 1927,D 24,8:1
When Crummles Played 1928,O 2,34:3
Marsolais, Kenneth
Gandhi 1970,O 21,37:1
Marston, Anna
Up the Ladder 1922,Mr 7,11:2
Marston, Joel
.Wallflower 1944,Ja 27,14:2
Good Morning, Corporal 1944,Ag 9,13:7
Streets Are Guarded, The 1944,N 21,19:7
Marriage Is for Single People 1945,N 22,38:2
Family Affair, A 1946,N 28,41:2
Marston, John
Thumbs Down 1923,Ag 7,20:1
Robert E Lee 1923,N 21,23:1
Goose Hangs High, The 1924,Ja 30,16:1
White Collars 1925,F 24,17:2
Human Nature 1925,S 25,24:3
Night Duel, The 1926,F 16,22:3
No More Women 1926,Ag 4,17:2
Proud Woman, A 1926,N 16,24:1
Behold the Bridegroom 1927,D 27,24:1
Behavior of Mrs Crane, The 1928,Mr 21,30:1
House Unguarded 1929,Ja 16,22:2
Up Pops the Devil 1930,S 2,19:1
Ladies of Creation 1931,Ag 30,VIII,1:7
Piper Paid 1934,D 26,19:1
Marston, Lawrence (Director)
Money Business 1926,Ja 21,18:1
Jeweled Tree, The 1926,O 8,26:2
Crown Prince, The 1927,Mr 24,23:2
Half a Widow 1927,S 13,37:3
Death Takes a Holiday 1929,D 27,26:4
Round-Up, The 1932,Mr 8,19:4
Happy Landing 1932,Mr 28,10:5
Martal, Blanche
Aiglon, L' 1924,O 21,21:1
Naked 1924,O 28,27:2
Madame Sans-Gene 1924,N 4,30:1
Caprice, Un 1924,N 25,26:2
Amoureuse 1924,N 28,13:1
Martan, Nita
When You Smile 1925,O 6,31:2
Martel
Kreutzer Sonata, The 1924,My 15,22:3
Martel, Fred
Howdy, Mr Ice of 1950 1949,My 27,24:2
Martel, Gene
At Home Abroad 1935,O 27,IX,8:1
Martel, Jane
Pieton de L'Air, Le 1964,Mr 4,33:2
Salut a Moliere 1964,Mr 4,33:2
Martel, Joseph
Johnny 2X4 1942,Mr 17,24:6
Martel, June
Perfumed Lady, The 1934,Mr 13,27:2
Hide and Seek 1934,Ag 7,20:2
Martel, Michel
Wait a Minim! 1966,Mr 8,43:1
Martel, Remi Remont
Red Rhumba 1936,Ap 14,18:1
This Mad Whirl 1937,Ja 10,II,4:8
Banjo Eyes 1941,D 26,20:2
Let Freedom Sing 1942,O 6,18:2
Heaven on Earth 1948,S 17,29:2
Martel, Rose
Strange Prince, The 1926,D 8,24:2
Martel, William
Mamba's Daughters 1953,Mr 21,12:6
Red Rainbow, A 1953,S 15,37:4
As You Like It 1955,O 29,12:2
Romeo and Juliet 1955,D 16,36:3
Athenian Touch, The 1964,Ja 15,25:4
Of Thee I Sing 1969,Mr 8,19:1

Martell, Fred
Howdy Mr Ice 1948,Je 25,28:5
Martell, Fred J
Pride 1923,My 3,22:3
Martell, Gene (Choreographer)
Chimes of Corneville, The 1934,Je 29,16:2
Martell, Gillian
Hedda Gabler 1970,Je 12,28:1
Martell, Joseph
Steps Leading Up 1941,Ap 19,20:6
Martell, Karl-Heinz
Nathan the Wise 1962,Mr 7,29:1
Before Sundown 1962,Mr 14,43:1
Martell, Morty
Pick-Up Girl 1944,My 4,25:2
Martell, Saul Z
Twelve Miles Out 1925,N 17,29:2
57 Bowery 1928,Ja 27,14:3
Chippies 1929,My 30,23:3
With Privileges 1930,S 16,30:2
Ebb Tide 1931,Je 9,33:6
Allure 1934,O 30,22:6
Hook-Up, The 1935,My 9,24:6
Martell Brothers
Off to Buffalo! 1939,F 22,18:2
Martens, Clara
Prince of Pilsen, The 1930,Ja 14,24:3
Martens, G M (Playwright)
Hoboes in Heaven 1947,O 29,31:4
Martens, Rica
Shrike, The 1953,N 26,51:2
Martens, Valerie von
Perlenkomoedie 1929,Ap 7,X,4:4
Circus Aimee 1932,My 22,VIII,2:2
Marthouret, Francois
On Ne Badine Pas Avec l'Amour; No Trifling With
Love 1968,Mr 5,35:1
Martier, Raymond (Costume Designer)
This Was Burlesque 1970,F 12,31:1
Martin, A (Playwright)
Smilin' Through 1920,Ja 4,IX,2:1
Martin, Al
Whirl of New York, The 1921,Je 14,18:1
Martin, Alice
Diamond Lil 1951,S 15,8:2
Martin, Allen
Patriots, The 1943,D 21,22:5
I Know My Love 1949,N 3,36:1
Martin, Ambrose
Honors Are Even 1921,Ag 11,8:2
Martin, Angela
George M! 1968,Ap 11,48:1
Martin, Ann
World We Live In, The 1922,N 1,16:1
Red Light Annie 1923,Ag 22,10:3
Mama Loves Papa 1926,F 23,26:2
Night Remembers, The 1934,N 28,24:3
Martin, Barney
What a Killing 1961,Mr 28,41:1
All American 1962,Mr 20,44:1
Around the World in 80 Days 1964,Je 29,33:2
Skits-Oh-Frantics 1967,Ap 3,39:2
South Pacific 1968,Je 30,54:2
Tonight in Living Color; David Show, The
1969,Je 11,43:1
Martin, Barry
Gods of the Mountain, The 1950,My 25,36:2
Martin, Barry C
Grosse Valise, La 1965,D 15,52:1
Martin, Bennett
Ring Around the Moon 1950,N 24,30:1
Martin, Beth
What Next 1920,Ja 27,7:2
George Washington 1920,Mr 2,9:1
Not So Long Ago 1920,My 5,14:1
Cold Feet 1923,My 22,14:2
Martin, Bob (Composer)
High Button Shoes 1947,O 10,32:2
Martin, Buzzy
Peter Pan 1950,Ap 25,27:2
Martin, Charles
Show-Off, The 1932,D 13,25:4
Living Dangerously 1935,Ja 14,10:3
Tomorrow's a Holiday! 1935,D 31,10:2
Martin, Charles (Choreographer)
Egg and I, The 1958,S 11,43:4
Martin, Charles (Playwright)
White Haired Boy, The 1940,O 29,32:6
Martin, Charles G
My Sister Eileen 1940,D 27,23:2
Burlesque 1946,D 26,30:3
Diamond Lil 1948,N 30,33:2
Diamond Lil 1949,F 7,16:2
Diamond Lil 1951,S 15,8:2
Hook'n Ladder 1952,Ap 30,31:2
Hit the Trail 1954,D 3,31:2
Martin, Charles H
Still Waters 1926,Mr 2,23:1
Mima 1928,D 13,24:2
Martin, Christopher
Month in the Country, A 1963,My 29,39:2
Man and Superman 1970,F 24,48:1
Moby Dick 1970,Je 3,52:1

Martin, Christopher—Cont
Hamlet 1970,O 27,54:2
Rosencrantz and Guildenstern Are Dead
1970,N 19,39:3
Martin, Christopher (Director)
Man and Superman 1970,F 24,48:1
Moby Dick 1970,Je 3,52:1
Martin, Christopher (Lighting Director)
Hamlet 1970,O 27,54:2
Rosencrantz and Guildenstern Are Dead
1970,N 19,39:3
Martin, Christopher (Playwright)
Moby Dick 1970,Je 3,52:1
Martin, Christopher (Producer)
Hamlet 1970,O 27,54:2
Martin, Claude
Britannicus 1958,N 29,17:2
Martin, Constance
Devil's Little Game, The 1932,Ag 2,20:4
Martin, David
My Heart's in the Highlands 1950,F 18,8:4
Time of Your Life, The 1955,Ja 20,34:1
Martin, David (Composer)
Simply Heavenly 1957,My 22,28:2
Martin, Delores
Shuffle Along 1952,My 9,20:5
Kiss Me, Kate 1956,My 10,27:2
Carmen Jones 1956,Je 1,28:2
Martin, Dolphe (Composer)
Roll Sweet Chariot 1934,O 3,24:3
Roll Sweet Chariot 1934,O 14,X,1:1
I Only Want an Answer 1968,F 6,36:1
Martin, Don (Miscellaneous)
Woman and the Blues, A 1966,Mr 29,35:2
Martin, Donald (Director)
In the Nick of Time 1967,Je 2,36:1
Martin, Dorothy
Twinkle Twinkle 1926,N 17,22:2
Merchant of Venice, The 1931,N 17,31:1
Julius Caesar 1931,N 18,26:3
Martin, D'Urville
Toilet, The 1964,D 17,51:1
Martin, Edgar
How Come Lawd? 1937,O 1,18:5
Martin, Edith
Cross My Heart 1928,S 18,32:7
Martin, Edouard (Playwright)
37 Sous de M Montaudoin, Les 1939,F 7,17:2
Martin, Edward
High Road, The 1928,S 11,31:1
Decision 1929,My 28,37:3
Victoria Regina 1935,D 27,15:2
Martin, Eleanor
Crooked Square, The 1923,S 11,10:2
Great Power, The 1928,S 12,25:1
Martin, Elizabeth (Choreographer)
Riot 1968,D 20,64:1
Martin, Elizabeth (Miscellaneous)
Riot 1968,D 20,64:1
Martin, Elliot (Director)
Beaux' Stratagem, The 1970,F 10,50:2
Three Sisters, The 1970,F 12,30:1
Martin, Elliot (Miscellaneous)
Innkeepers, The 1956,F 3,19:1
Little Glass Clock, The 1956,Mr 27,40:2
Long Day's Journey Into Night 1956,N 8,47:2
Majority of One, A 1959,F 17,28:2
Unsinkable Molly Brown, The 1960,N 4,28:1
Captains and the Kings, The 1962,Ja 3,25:2
Great Day in the Morning 1962,Mr 29,29:1
Murderous Angels 1970,F 8,70:1
Martin, Elliot (Producer)
Painted Days, The 1961,Ap 7,24:1
Never Too Late 1962,N 28,42:1
Nobody Loves an Albatross 1963,D 20,20:1
Mating Dance 1965,N 4,58:1
Dinner at Eight 1966,S 28,38:1
More Stately Mansions 1967,N 1,40:1
Wrong Way Light Bulb, The 1969,Mr 5,40:1
Martin, Emmy
Spooks 1925,Je 2,16:4
Martin, Erik
Little Darling 1942,O 28,26:2
Barretts of Wimpole Street, The 1945,Mr 27,23:6
Martin, Erin
Kaleidoscope 1957,Je 14,20:2
New Faces of 1962 1962,F 2,25:1
Trojan Women, The 1963,D 24,7:6
West Side Story 1964,Ap 9,24:2
Devils, The 1965,N 17,51:2
Titus Andronicus 1967,Ag 10,43:2
Iphigenia in Aulis 1967,N 22,40:2
Iphigenia in Aulis 1968,Ap 6,43:1
Martin, Erin (Miscellaneous)
Trojan Women, The 1963,D 24,7:6
Martin, Ernest H (Playwright)
Whoop-Up 1958,D 23,2:7
Martin, Ernest H (Producer)
Where's Charley? 1948,O 12,33:2
Guys and Dolls 1950,N 25,11:2
Where's Charley? 1951,Ja 30,21:7
Can-Can 1953,My 8,28:1
Silk Stockings 1955,F 25,17:3
Whoop-Up 1958,D 23,2:7

Martin, Ernest H (Producer)—Cont
How to Succeed in Business Without Really Trying 1961,O 16,34:1
Little Me 1962,N 19,41:3
Skyscraper 1965,N 15,48:1
Goodbye People, The 1968,D 4,52:1
Martin, Ernest W (Playwright)
Possibilities 1927,F 19,13:3
Martin, Ethel
Man Who Ate the Popomack, The 1924,Mr 25,24:1
Magnolia Lady, The 1924,N 26,17:2
So That's That 1925,D 15,28:3
Man From Toronto, The 1926,Je 18,27:2
Loose Ankles 1926,Ag 17,15:1
Say It With Flowers 1926,D 6,29:1
Very Wise Virgin, A 1927,Je 3,25:3
Mating Season, The 1927,Jl 19,27:6
Such Is Life 1927,S 1,27:3
Martin, Ethel (Choreographer)
Pal Joey 1963,My 30,21:1
Hamlet 1968,Jl 4,15:1
Martin, Evelyn
Mimic World of 1921, The 1921,Ag 18,9:2
Paradise Alley 1924,Ap 2,17:3
Barefoot 1925,O 20,29:2
Martin, Faye
As Good As New 1930,N 4,37:3
Martin, Florence
Topsy and Eva 1924,D 24,11:1
Martin, Frederic
Hope Is the Thing With Feathers 1948,Ap 12,24:2
Hope Is the Thing With Feathers; Hope's the Thing 1948,My 12,34:6
Home Life of a Buffalo; Hope's the Thing 1948,My 12,34:6
Gone Tomorrow; Hope's the Thing 1948,My 12,34:6
2 for Fun; Anniversary, The 1955,My 26,34:1
2 for Fun; Switch in Time, A 1955,My 26,34:1
Beaver Coat, The 1956,Mr 29,22:5
Martin, George
Pal Joey 1952,Ja 4,17:6
Carnival in Flanders 1953,S 9,38:2
Rumple 1957,N 7,42:2
Donogoo 1961,Ja 19,25:3
Red Roses for Me 1961,N 28,41:1
Wilson in the Promise Land 1970,Ja 11,78:1
Wilson in the Promise Land 1970,My 27,41:1
Martin, George (Choreographer)
Pal Joey 1963,My 30,21:1
Hamlet 1968,Jl 4,15:1
Martin, George (Miscellaneous)
Wet Paint 1965,Ap 13,33:1
Martin, George (Producer)
Intimate Relations 1932,Mr 29,23:2
Moths, The 1970,My 12,46:1
Martin, Georges Andre
Continental Varieties 1935,D 27,15:3
Edith Piaf 1947,O 30,30:2
Martin, Gerard
Sleep No More 1944,S 1,11:5
Martin, Gloria (Costume Designer)
Street Sounds 1970,O 23,32:1
Martin, Gould B (Playwright)
Dooley Cashes In 1935,Ag 17,18:6
Martin, Gregory (Lighting Director)
No Exit 1967,O 31,38:2
Little Private World of Arthur Morton Fenwick, The 1967,O 31,38:2
Martin, Gregory (Scenic Designer)
No Exit 1967,O 31,38:2
Little Private World of Arthur Morton Fenwick, The 1967,O 31,38:2
Martin, Guy (Choreographer)
Wonderful World of Burlesque, The 1965,Ap 29,38:1
Martin, Hal (Miscellaneous)
Vintage '60 1960,S 13,41:1
Egg, The 1962,Ja 9,23:2
Martin, Hall (Playwright)
Escape Into Glory 1941,Mr 20,24:2
Martin, Harold
Firebird 1932,N 22,25:2
Jezebel 1933,D 20,26:3
Winterset 1935,S 26,19:2
Martin, Helen
Native Son 1941,Mr 25,26:5
Native Son 1942,O 24,10:6
Deep Are the Roots 1945,S 27,24:4
Stevedore 1949,F 23,30:2
Major Barbara 1954,Je 30,23:2
Juno and the Paycock 1955,F 24,20:4
Land Beyond the River, A 1957,Mr 29,15:7
Ballad of Jazz Street, The 1959,N 12,28:1
Long Dream, The 1960,F 18,36:2
Period of Adjustment 1960,N 11,34:1
Blacks, The 1961,My 5,23:1
Purlie Victorious 1961,S 29,29:1
My Mother, My Father and Me 1963,Mr 25,5:5
One Is a Lonely Number 1964,Je 19,37:3
Cat and the Canary, The 1965,Ja 5,26:1
Amen Corner, The 1965,Ap 16,35:1
Amen Corner, The 1965,Je 13,82:4
Purlie 1970,Mr 16,53:1

Martin, Henry
Saint Joan 1950,Mr 4,10:6
Martin, Henry (Lighting Director)
Madame Is Served 1949,F 15,28:1
Martin, Henry (Scenic Designer)
Madame Is Served 1949,F 15,28:1
Martin, Herbert (Lyricist)
Yearling, The 1965,D 11,25:1
How to Be a Jewish Mother 1967,D 29,18:1
Martin, Herbert (Playwright)
Yearling, The 1965,D 11,25:1
Martin, Herschel
Victoria Regina 1935,D 27,15:2
Victoria Regina 1938,O 4,20:2
Martin, Howard
Tree Grows in Brooklyn, A 1951,Ap 20,24:3
Martin, Hugh
Louisiana Purchase 1940,My 29,19:2
Martin, Hugh (Composer)
Best Foot Forward 1941,O 2,28:2
Best Foot Forward 1941,O 26,IX,1:3
Barefoot Boy With Cheek 1947,Ap 4,20:2
Look, Ma, I'm Dancin' 1948,Ja 30,20:2
Heaven on Earth 1948,S 17,29:2
Make a Wish 1951,Ap 19,38:1
Best Foot Forward 1956,Mr 3,16:1
High Spirits 1964,Ap 8,34:1
Martin, Hugh (Lyricist)
Best Foot Forward 1941,O 2,28:2
Best Foot Forward 1941,O 26,IX,1:3
Look, Ma, I'm Dancin' 1948,Ja 30,20:2
Make a Wish 1951,Ap 19,38:1
Best Foot Forward 1956,Mr 3,16:1
High Spirits 1964,Ap 8,34:1
Martin, Hugh (Miscellaneous)
Heaven on Earth 1948,S 17,29:2
Make a Wish 1951,Ap 19,38:1
Top Banana 1951,N 2,19:2
Hazel Flagg 1953,F 12,22:2
High Spirits 1964,Ap 8,34:1
Martin, Hugh (Musical Director)
As the Girls Go 1948,N 15,21:2
Gentlemen Prefer Blondes 1949,D 9,35:3
Martin, Hugh (Playwright)
Best Foot Forward 1963,Ap 3,43:1
High Spirits 1964,Ap 8,34:1
High Spirits 1964,N 4,46:4
Martin, Ian
B J One 1931,My 7,21:3
Midsummer Night's Dream, A 1931,Ag 19,19:3
What Every Woman Knows 1938,Ag 30,14:5
All Men Are Alike 1941,O 7,27:2
Devil's Disciple, The 1950,Ja 26,23:2
Devil's Disciple, The 1950,F 5,II,1:1
Captain Brassbound's Conversion 1950,D 28,21:1
King of Friday's Men, The 1951,F 22,26:2
Cock-A-Doodle Dandy 1958,N 13,39:2
Cock-A-Doodle Dandy 1958,N 23,II,1:1
Spofford 1967,D 15,54:3
Martin, Irwin
Bolls of Cotton 1925,D 22,18:3
Martin, Isadora
Welcome Stranger 1920,S 14,12:1
Martin, J S
Man From Earth, The 1923,Ja 3,6:2
Martin, J S (Lyricist)
Espanola 1921,D 30,13:1
Martin, J S (Playwright)
Possibilities 1927,F 19,13:3
Martin, Jack (Miscellaneous)
Kittiwake Island 1960,O 13,43:1
Martin, Jacqueline
Conjur' Man Dies 1936,Mr 12,18:5
One-Act Plays of the Sea; Moon of the Caribbees 1937,O 30,23:2
One-Act Plays of the Sea; Long Voyage Home, The 1937,O 30,23:2
Haiti 1938,Mr 3,16:1
Martin, Jacques (Mrs)
Triumph of X, The 1921,Ag 25,8:2
Shore Leave 1922,Ag 9,20:2
Tarnish 1923,O 2,10:1
Bride Retires, The 1925,My 18,12:3
Gentlemen Prefer Blondes 1926,S 29,23:1
All the King's Men 1929,F 5,27:1
Your Uncle Dudley 1929,N 19,26:4
Angeline Moves In 1932,Ap 20,27:5
Martin, James
Emperor Jones, The 1924,My 7,18:1
All God's Chillun Got Wings 1924,My 16,22:3
All God's Chillun Got Wings 1924,Ag 19,9:1
All God's Chillun Got Wings 1924,Ag 24,VII,1:1
Outside Looking In 1925,S 8,28:1
Dream Play 1926,Ja 21,18:2
Damn the Tears 1927,Ja 22,11:1
Rapid Transit 1927,Ap 8,21:2
Hot Pan 1928,F 16,14:1
Martin, Jared
Hamlet 1967,D 27,45:1
Martin, Jay
Ziegfeld Follies 1943,Ap 2,16:2
Mr Strauss Goes to Boston 1945,S 7,20:2
Icetime 1946,Je 21,20:5

Martin, John
Old Rascal, The 1930,Mr 25,34:4
Rose in the Wilderness 1949,Ja 5,21:2
Martin, John (Director)
Good Girl, The 1934,Je 26,22:5
Martin, John J
Show Boat 1961,Ap 13,32:1
Martin, John S (Playwright)
Man From Earth, The 1923,Ja 3,6:2
Martin, Josef
Vaudeville (Hippodrome) 1924,Mr 18,25:1
Martin, Joseph
Doughgirls, The 1942,D 31,19:2
Martin, Joy
Experiment, The 1967,My 9,54:2
Martin, Judith
Dandelion 1969,D 24,12:1
Hot Feet 1970,D 22,38:1
Martin, Judith (Director)
Hot Feet 1970,D 22,38:1
Martin, Judith (Playwright)
Hot Feet 1970,D 22,38:1
Martin, Judith (Scenic Designer)
Hot Feet 1970,D 22,38:1
Martin, Karlheinz (Director)
Weavers, The 1921,Jl 24,VI,1:7
Franziska 1927,Ja 30,VII,4:3
Death of Danton, The 1928,O 28,IX,2:1
Ewiges Volk 1933,Ap 30,IX,2:2
Martin, Karlheinz (Producer)
Miracle at Verdun 1932,O 9,IX,3:8
Martin, Larry
Mexican Hayride 1944,Ja 29,9:6
Martin, Lee
Till the Day I Die 1935,Mr 27,24:5
Martin, Leila
Wish You Were Here 1952,Je 26,26:6
Guys and Dolls 1955,Ap 21,32:2
Best House in Naples, The 1956,O 27,16:2
Ernest in Love 1960,My 5,39:4
Wall, The 1960,O 12,44:4
Automobile Graveyard, The 1961,N 14,46:2
Pimpernel! 1964,Ja 7,26:6
Rothschilds, The 1970,O 20,40:1
Rothschilds, The 1970,N 1,II,1:1
Martin, Lewis
Lucky Sam McCarver 1925,O 22,22:1
Juno and the Paycock 1926,Mr 16,22:1
Road to Rome, The 1927,F 1,24:2
Paolo and Francesca 1929,Ap 2,28:2
Jenny 1929,O 9,34:4
Twelfth Night 1930,O 16,28:2
Art and Mrs Bottle 1930,N 19,19:3
Life Begins 1932,Mr 29,23:2
Camille 1932,N 2,23:3
Sophisticrats, The 1933,F 14,19:5
School for Husbands, The 1933,O 17,26:5
Dream of Sganarelle, The 1933,O 17,26:5
Farmer Takes a Wife, The 1934,O 31,17:1
Cat and the Canary, The 1935,Jl 9,24:4
Trelawney of the 'Wells' 1935,Jl 16,24:1
All This While 1935,Jl 30,17:2
Declassee 1935,Ag 6,20:3
Accent on Youth 1935,Ag 13,20:3
They Knew What They Wanted 1936,Jl 7,17:2
Shining Hour, The 1936,Ag 12,15:3
Octoroon, The 1936,S 1,24:2
Point of Honor, A 1937,F 12,26:2
Many Mansions 1937,Ag 3,20:5
Abe Lincoln in Illinois 1938,O 4,20:1
Abe Lincoln in Illinois 1938,O 17,12:2
Mr and Mrs North 1941,Ja 13,11:2
First Crocus, The 1942,Ja 3,14:6
Joan of Lorraine 1946,N 19,40:2
Command Decision 1947,O 2,30:2
Martin, Lillian
Squealer, The 1928,N 13,36:3
Martin, Linda
Trojan Women, The 1963,D 24,7:6
Martin, Louise
Comedy of Good and Evil, A 1938,Ap 8,16:3
Martin, Lucy
Happy as Larry 1961,Ap 26,36:1
Martin, Lynn
Shoemaker's Holiday, The 1967,Mr 3,25:1
Martin, Madge
Adding Machine, The 1956,F 10,17:1
Martin, Marguerite
Cynara 1931,N 3,31:1
Martin, Marion
Lombardi, Ltd 1927,Je 7,27:3
Shady Lady 1933,Jl 6,26:3
New Faces of 1936 1936,My 20,24:5
Martin, Marjorie (Miscellaneous)
More Stately Mansions 1967,N 1,40:1
Martin, Marjorie-May
Hello, Daddy! 1928,D 27,26:5
Martin, Mary
Doctor Knock 1928,F 24,15:2
Diamond Lil 1928,Ap 10,32:1
Achilles Had a Heel 1935,O 14,20:2
Young Madame Conti 1937,Ap 1,18:4
Empress of Destiny 1938,Mr 10,16:2

Martin, Mary—Cont

Leave It to Me! 1938,N 10,32:2
Leave It to Me! 1938,N 20,IX,1:1
Johnny 2X4 1942,Mr 17,24:6
One Touch of Venus 1943,O 8,14:1
One Touch of Venus 1943,O 17,II,1:1
Our Town 1944,Ja 11,24:5
Lute Song 1946,F 7,29:2
Lute Song 1946,F 17,II,1:1
Pacific 1860 1946,D 20,30:4
Pacific 1860 1947,Ja 12,II,3:6
South Pacific 1949,Ap 8,30:2
South Pacific 1949,Ap 17,II,1:1
South Pacific 1949,Je 5,II,1:1
South Pacific 1951,N 2,19:1
South Pacific 1951,N 11,II,3:1
Kind Sir 1953,S 28,21:2
Kind Sir 1953,N 5,41:2
Kind Sir 1953,N 15,II,1:1
Peter Pan 1954,Jl 20,15:3
Peter Pan 1954,O 21,30:2
Peter Pan 1954,O 31,II,1:1
Skin of Our Teeth, The 1955,Je 29,25:3
Skin of Our Teeth, The 1955,Ag 18,16:1
Skin of Our Teeth, The 1955,Ag 28,II,1:1
Annie Get Your Gun 1957,Ag 31,18:2
Sound of Music, The 1959,N 17,40:2
Sound of Music, The 1959,N 22,II,1:1
Jennie 1963,O 18,35:2
Hello, Dolly! 1965,S 11,17:1
Hello, Dolly! 1965,O 10,3:3
Hello, Dolly! 1965,D 3,43:1
I Do! I Do! 1966,D 6,58:1
I Do! I Do! 1966,D 18,II,3:1
Martin, Mary Agnes
Song and Dance Man, The 1924,Ja 1,21:2
Martin, Mary Joan
Red, Hot and Blue! 1936,O 30,26:3
Martin, Mary Steichen
Martine 1928,Ap 5,19:3
Martin, Merry
J B 1958,D 12,2:7
Martin, Michael
Annie Get Your Gun 1957,Mr 9,15:5
Hamlet 1969,My 2,38:1
Martin, Michel
Avare, L'; L', Miser, The 1966,F 9,32:1
Reine Morte, La 1966,F 16,52:1
Fil a la Paite, Un 1966,F 18,25:1
Martin, Millicent
Boy Friend, The 1954,O 1,20:1
Our Man Crichton 1964,D 23,21:1
Skin of Our Teeth, The 1968,S 12,55:1
Martin, Nan
Story for a Sunday Evening, A 1950,N 18,10:5
Constant Wife, The 1951,D 10,34:3
Saturday Night Kid, The 1958,My 16,22:1
J B 1958,D 12,2:7
I Rise in Flame, Cried the Phoenix 1959,Ap 15,30:1
Great God Brown, The 1959,O 7,48:1
Great God Brown, The 1959,O 18,II,1:1
Lysistrata 1959,N 25,19:4
Henry IV 1960,Mr 2,42:1
Henry IV 1960,Mr 13,II,1:1
Camino Real 1960,My 17,42:2
Camino Real 1960,My 29,II,1:1
Under the Yum-Yum Tree 1960,N 17,45:1
Coming Forth by Day of Osiris Jones, The; Kid,
  The 1961,Mr 15,45:2
Much Ado About Nothing 1961,Jl 7,17:1
Merchant of Venice, The 1962,Je 22,1:4
Taming of the Shrew, The 1963,Mr 8,9:1
In the Zone; Before Breakfast 1963,Je 11,29:4
Hamlet 1964,Je 17,49:1
Hamlet 1964,Je 18,28:1
Slave, The 1964,D 17,51:1
Richard III 1966,Ag 11,26:1
Come Live With Me 1967,Ja 27,29:1
Martin, Neil
Charm School, The 1920,Ag 3,12:1
Only 38 1921,S 14,22:2
Romantic Age, The 1922,N 15,22:1
Barnum Was Right 1923,Mr 13,19:3
School for Scandal, The 1925,D 7,18:2
Tragic 18 1926,O 11,18:2
Just Suppose 1935,Jl 2,24:3
Martin, Nicholas
School for Scandal, The 1962,Mr 19,36:1
Tavern, The 1962,Ap 5,29:1
King Lear 1963,Je 10,37:1
Henry V 1963,Je 14,37:1
Caesar and Cleopatra 1963,Ag 1,18:2
Much Ado About Nothing 1964,Je 11,26:2
Richard III 1964,Je 12,44:2
Hamlet 1964,Jl 4,9:1
School for Scandal, The 1966,N 22,33:2
Wild Duck, The 1967,Ja 12,49:1
Pantagleize 1967,D 1,54:1
Millionairess, The 1969,Mr 3,28:1
Martin, Norman (Composer)
Put It in Writing 1963,My 14,31:1
Martin, Norman (Miscellaneous)
Fun City 1968,Mr 7,53:2

Martin, Norman (Playwright)
Put It in Writing 1963,My 14,31:1
Martin, Olivia
Bless You, Sister 1927,D 27,24:5
Chocolate Soldier, The 1934,My 3,15:3
Martin, Owen
Spring 3100 1928,F 16,14:2
Big Fight, The 1928,S 19,33:1
As Good As New 1930,N 4,37:3
Cloudy With Showers 1931,S 2,17:5
Man Bites Dog 1933,Ap 26,11:2 ·
Pure in Heart, The 1934,Mr 21,24:3
Small Miracle 1934,S 27,24:3
Come Across 1938,S 15,28:3
Boys From Syracuse, The 1938,N 24,36:1
Goodbye in the Night 1940,Mr 19,31:2
Night Before Christmas, The 1941,Ap 11,25:2
Man With Blonde Hair, The 1941,N 5,30:2
What Big Ears! 1942,Ap 21,18:5
Strip for Action 1942,O 1,26:2
Oklahoma! 1943,Ap 1,27:1
Oklahoma! 1951,My 30,15:2
Oklahoma! 1953,S 1,19:1
Oklahoma! 1958,Mr 20,32:3
Martin, Patricia
Wrong Number 1934,Mr 14,23:6
Jubilee 1935,O 14,20:1
Martin, Patricia (Miscellaneous)
Kiss Mama 1964,O 2,30:1
Martin, Paul
Carolinian, The 1925,N 3,34:2
Decision 1929,My 28,37:3
Martin, Paul (Composer)
What Did We Do Wrong? 1967,O 23,56:1
Martin, Paul (Director)
It Never Rains 1929,N 20,26:4
Martin, Paul E
Fata Morgana 1924,Mr 4,16:3
Puppets of Passion 1927,F 25,24:4
Martin, Paul E (Director)
Let and Sub-Let 1930,My 20,32:2
Life Is Like That 1930,D 23,24:3
New York to Cherbourg 1932,F 20,11:4
Masks and Faces 1933,Mr 20,18:5
Martin, Paul E (Producer)
New York to Cherbourg 1932,F 20,11:4
Masks and Faces 1933,Mr 20,18:5
Martin, Perry (Composer)
Funzapoppin 1949,Jl 1,16:2
Martin, Perry (Lyricist)
Funzapoppin 1949,Jl 1,16:2
Martin, Peter
Park Avenue, Ltd 1932,Mr 4,17:1
Martin, Peter (Playwright)
Young Go First, The 1935,My 29,16:2
Martin, Philip
Make Me Know It 1929,N 5,32:5
Martin, R (Director)
On the Necessity of Being Polygamous
  1964,D 9,61:1
Martin, Rea
Call the Doctor 1920,S 1,14:1
Her Salary Man 1921,N 29,20:1
Fool, The 1922,O 24,18:1
Tiger Cats 1924,O 22,18:1
White Collars 1925,F 24,17:2
Sea Woman, The 1925,Ag 25,12:2
Two Seconds 1931,O 10,20:6
For Valor 1935,N 19,27:5
Martin, Richard
Izzy 1924,S 17,16:2
Deep Mrs Sykes, The 1945,Mr 20,22:6
Cry of the Peacock 1950,Ap 12,33:2
Martin, Robert Dale (Playwright)
Bring Me a Warm Body 1962,Ap 17,29:3
Martin, Ron
Child's Play 1970,F 18,39:1
Sensations 1970,O 26,48:2
Martin, Ross
Hazel Flagg 1953,F 12,22:2
Shinbone Alley 1957,Ap 15,23:2
Martin, Ruth
Sweet Bird of Youth 1956,Ap 17,27:2
Martin, Ruth (Lyricist)
Night in Venice, A 1952,Je 27,18:6
Night in Venice, A 1953,Je 26,15:2
Fledermaus, Die 1954,My 20,38:5
Martin, Ruth (Playwright)
Night in Venice, A 1952,Je 27,18:6
Night in Venice, A 1952,Jl 13,II,1:1
Night in Venice, A 1953,Je 26,15:2
Fledermaus, Die 1954,My 20,38:5
Martin, Sam
Dark Hours, The 1932,N 15,24:2
Martin, Sana
Bitter Oleander 1935,F 12,24:3
Martin, Sara
Bottomland 1927,Je 28,29:3
Martin, Skip (Miscellaneous)
Judy Garland 1959,My 12,40:1
Martin, Stanley
Seeds in the Wind 1948,Ap 26,27:2
Seeds in the Wind 1948,My 26,29:2

Martin, Stanley—Cont

Season in the Sun 1950,S 29,31:2
Martin, Susie
Ronde, La 1960,My 10,44:2
Best Foot Forward 1963,Ap 3,43:1
Martin, Ted
Red, White and Maddox 1969,Ja 27,27:1
Martin, Thomas (Lyricist)
Night in Venice, A 1952,Je 27,18:6
Night in Venice, A 1953,Je 26,15:2
Fledermaus, Die 1954,My 20,38:5
Martin, Thomas (Miscellaneous)
Night in Venice, A 1952,Je 27,18:6
Night in Venice, A 1953,Je 26,15:2
Martin, Thomas (Musical Director)
Night in Venice, A 1952,Jl 13,II,1:1
Fledermaus, Die 1954,My 20,38:5
Martin, Thomas (Playwright)
Night in Venice, A 1952,Je 27,18:6
Night in Venice, A 1952,Jl 13,II,1:1
Night in Venice, A 1953,Je 26,15:2
Fledermaus, Die 1954,My 20,38:5
Martin, Thomas O
Henry IV 1968,F 7,40:1
Martin, Thomas P (Miscellaneous)
H M S Pinafore 1968,Ap 29,47:2
Martin, Tom
Good Boy 1928,S 6,23:2
River Line, The 1957,Ja 3,29:2
All That Fall 1957,O 8,41:2
Resounding Tinkle, The 1961,Ap 4,42:2
Martin, Townsend (Director)
Most Immoral Lady, A 1928,N 27,36:1
Martin, Townsend (Playwright)
Most Immoral Lady, A 1928,N 11,X,2:4
Most Immoral Lady, A 1928,N 27,36:1
Martin, Virginia
New Faces of 1956 1956,Je 15,32:1
How to Succeed in Business Without Really Trying
  1961,O 16,34:1
Little Me 1962,N 19,41:3
Little Me 1962,D 2,II,1:1
Martin, Vivian
Just Married 1921,Ap 27,21:1
Wild Westcotts, The 1923,D 25,26:2
Puppy Love 1926,Ja 28,16:3
Hearts Are Trumps! 1927,Ap 8,21:1
Half a Widow 1927,S 13,37:3
Caste 1927,D 24,8:1
Mrs Dane's Defense 1928,F 7,30:1
Sherlock Holmes 1928,F 21,18:4
Marry the Man! 1929,Ap 23,26:3
Martin, Vivienne
Sunday Man, The 1964,My 14,41:3
Martin, Walter
From Vienna 1939,Je 21,26:2
Reunion in New York 1940,F 22,28:4
Any Day Now 1941,Je 10,28:2
Martin, Wendy
Oklahoma! 1958,Mr 8,15:2
Martin, Wilhelmina Murray
Asmodee 1958,Mr 26,42:2
Martin, William
Fiesta 1929,S 18,35:1
Martin, William (Scenic Designer)
It's About Time 1942,Mr 31,28:3
Martin, Winifred
Social Register, The 1931,N 10,28:2
Martin, Winnie Mae
It's A Gift 1945,Mr 13,18:7
Temporary Island, A 1948,Mr 15,27:3
Seeds in the Wind 1948,Ap 26,27:2
Seeds in the Wind 1948,My 26,29:2
Martin, Ysobel
Aiglon, L' 1934,N 5,22:2
Martin-Barbaz
Three Musketeers, The 1968,Je 26,43:1
Martin Brothers
Carnival! 1961,Ap 14,22:2
Martin D'Urville
Cabin in the Sky 1964,Ja 22,32:1
Martin-Harvey, John (Sir)
Burgomaster of Stilemonde, The 1923,N 16,15:3
Hamlet 1923,N 20,23:3
Bells, The 1933,O 22,IX,2:2
Convict, The 1935,F 5,23:2
Oedipus Rex 1936,O 18,X,3:8
Martin-Harvey, John (Sir) (Producer)
Hamlet 1923,N 20,23:3
Martin-Harvey, Michael (Lyricist)
Nightingale, The 1947,Jl 17,16:4
Martin-Harvey, Muriel
Champ-Blays, The 1936,O 9,30:4
Martindale, James
Carousel 1954,Je 3,32:2
Martindale, Jim
Front Page, The 1968,O 20,85:5
Martindale, Joseph
Pirates of Penzance, The 1942,F 20,20:2
Martindale, Thomas
This Mad Whirl 1937,Ja 10,II,4:8
Martine, Lina
Heure du Berger, L'; Propitious Moment, The
  1936,N 12,30:1

Martine, Lina—Cont
Martine 1936,N 26,38:2
Dejeuner d'Amoureax, Un; Lovers Breakfast, A 1936,N 26,38:2
Bichon; Little Dear 1936,D 31,20:5
Sexe Fort, Le; Strong Sex, The 1937,Ja 14,17:4
Si Je Voulais; If I Wished to 1937,Ja 28,22:5
Christian 1937,F 25,18:6
Martineau, Stanley (Producer)
Member of the Wedding, The 1950,Ja 6,26:6
Martinelli, Charles (Costume Designer)
Yerma 1952,F 8,18:4
Cradle Song 1955,D 2,32:2
Martinet, Eugene
Blossom Time 1921,S 30,10:1
Martinetti, Ignacio
Lady in Ermine, The 1922,O 3,22:2
Hearts Are Trumps! 1927,Ap 8,21:1
Garden of Eden, The 1927,S 28,28:1
Sh! The Octopus 1928,F 22,19:2
Fifty Million Frenchmen 1929,N 28,34:4
Martinez, Chico
Winterset 1968,Jl 23,28:2
Martinez, Diego
Todo un Hombre 1937,Ap 28,19:2
Cuando Los Hijos De Eva No Son Los Hijos De Adan 1937,My 1,17:4
Tierra Baja 1937,My 8,22:4
Martinez, Jocelyn
World's My Oyster, The 1956,Ag 10,10:4
Martinez, Luis
First Lady 1952,My 29,18:5
Martinez, Luis (Director)
Othello 1953,O 30,28:2
Idiot's Delight 1957,F 23,14:2
And the Wind Blows 1959,Ap 29,28:1
And the Wind Blows 1959,My 17,II,1:1
Martinez, Luis (Producer)
And the Wind Blows 1959,Ap 29,28:1
Martinez, Raquel
Amor 1937,Ap 22,18:6
Tierra Baja 1937,My 8,22:4
Martinez, Tony
Jamaica 1957,N 1,32:2
Man of La Mancha 1970,Ja 25,70:6
Martinez, Vaughan
Walk Down Mah Street! 1968,Je 13,54:1
Martinez-Sierra (Playwright)
Romantic Young Lady, The 1926,My 5,24:3
Cradle Song 1927,Ja 30,VII,1:1
Spring in Autumn 1937,Ag 17,23:1
Martini, Fausto (Playwright)
Laugh, Clown, Laugh! 1923,N 29,30:1
Martini, Jean
Maitresse de Roi 1926,D 1,24:1
Martini, Mortimer
Unwritten Chapter, The 1920,O 12,18:1
Martino, Fernando
Rugantino 1964,F 7,34:1
Martinova, B
Revisor; Inspector General, The 1935,F 18,19:6
Martins, Frank
Montmartre 1922,F 14,20:1
Open House 1925,D 15,28:3
Martins, Frank (Playwright)
Find the Fox 1930,Je 21,20:4
Martins, Frank (Producer)
Black Cockatoo, The 1926,D 31,11:1
Martins, The
Lady Comes Across, The 1942,Ja 10,10:2
Martiny, J
Under the Gaslight 1929,Ap 3,27:1
Martoff, Sid
Sky Drift 1945,N 14,25:2
Martoglio, Nino (Playwright)
Aria del Continente, L' 1927,O 5,30:2
Marton, Charles
Quiet, Please! 1940,N 9,20:3
Marton, George Jr (Lyricist)
Beat the Band 1942,O 15,26:1
Marton, George Jr (Playwright)
Beat the Band 1942,O 15,26:1
Martone, John
Cock-A-Doodle-Doo 1949,F 28,16:5
Grey-Eyed People, The 1952,D 18,41:2
Martos, Franz (Original Author)
Prince Charming 1930,O 14,31:1
Martos (Playwright)
Countess Eva 1928,Mr 4,IX,2:7
Martyn, Edward
O'Flynn, The 1934,D 28,24:1
Victoria Regina 1938,O 4,20:2
Martyn, Fay
Young Sinners 1929,N 29,24:4
Boy Friend, The 1932,Je 8,22:3
Summer Wives 1936,Ap 14,18:1
Martyn, Kathlene
Dear Sir 1924,S 24,21:3
Lady Be Good 1924,D 2,23:4
Martyn, Marjorie
Sweet Aloes 1936,Mr 5,24:5
Martyn, May
Times Have Changed 1935,F 26,16:1

Martyn, Peter
Harlequinade 1949,O 13,32:2
Martyn, Willis
Man Who Married a Dumb Wife, The 1930,My 9,20:5
Marucci, (Mr)
Three Guardsmen, The 1936,F 17,21:3
Marucci, Angelo
Promessi Sposi I,; Betrothed, The 1934,O 22,13:2
Marucci, Giovanni
Signo Della Croce, Il 1935,O 7,11:1
Marunas, P Raymond
Kitchen, The 1966,Je 14,50:1
Glorious Ruler, The 1969,Jl 1,31:1
Marvel, Chryst (Producer)
Stockade 1954,F 5,14:2
Marvel, Frank
Cradle Will Rock, The 1937,D 6,19:4
Cradle Will Rock, The 1938,Ja 4,19:3
Marvel, Pauline
Nighthawks 1967,D 30,14:2
Marvellos, The
Vaudeville (Palace) 1949,My 20,32:4
Marvenga, Ilse
Follies 1923,Je 26,14:5
Student Prince, The 1924,D 3,25:3
Naughty Marietta 1929,O 22,26:2
Naughty Marietta 1931,N 17,31:2
Firefly, The 1931,D 1,23:2
There You Are! 1932,My 17,25:4
Great Lover, The 1932,O 12,27:3
Student Prince, The 1936,Jl 12,II,5:2
Naughty Marietta 1936,S 2,19:5
Marver, John
Tall Kentuckian, The 1953,Je 17,30:1
Marvey, Eugene
Orpheus in Hades 1930,D 16,30:1
Marvey, Gene
American Jubilee 1940,My 13,20:5
Marvin, Anthony
Fencing Master, The 1936,Ap 1,29:1
Marvin, Blanche
Hamlet of Stepney Green 1958,N 14,21:1
Marvin, Charles S
What a Relief 1935,D 14,10:6
Marvin, Charles S (Composer)
What a Relief 1935,D 14,10:6
What a Relief 1935,D 19,34:4
Take It Away 1936,D 15,30:5
Take It Away 1936,D 22,32:3
Marvin, Charles S (Lyricist)
What a Relief 1935,D 14,10:6
What a Relief 1935,D 19,34:4
Take It Away 1936,D 15,30:5
Take It Away 1936,D 22,32:3
Marvin, Christopher
Magnificent Yankee, The 1946,Ja 23,21:2
Marvin, Ira (Miscellaneous)
Banker's Daughter, The 1962,Ja 23,37:1
Marvin, Jack
Rap, The 1931,Ap 7,31:2
Marvin, John
Honeymoon Lane 1926,S 21,32:3
Marvin, Lee
Uniform of Flesh 1949,Ja 31,15:2
Nineteenth Hole of Europe, The 1949,Mr 28,16:2
Billy Budd 1951,F 12,18:3
Marvin, Mark (Producer)
On Whitman Avenue 1946,My 9,28:2
Hide and Seek 1957,Ap 3,26:1
Marvin, Mel (Composer)
Shoemaker's Holiday, The 1967,Mr 3,25:1
Marvin, Mel (Musical Director)
Applause 1970,Mr 31,35:1
Marvin, Roy
Clinging Vine, The 1922,D 25,20:2
Marvin, Tony
Aquacircus 1958,Je 30,24:6
Marvin, Virginia
Imaginary Invalid, The 1922,Jl 26,26:2
School for Husbands, The 1933,O 17,26:5
Marwick, Dudley
Princess Flavia 1925,N 3,34:3
Patience 1927,My 24,23:2
Marwick, Irma
Jim Jam Jems 1920,O 5,13:2
Elsie 1923,Ap 3,26:1
Marwick, John Stuart (Miscellaneous)
Long and the Short and the Tall, The 1962,Mr 30,28:2
Marx, Arthur (Playwright)
Impossible Years, The 1965,O 14,55:1
Minnie's Boys 1970,Mr 27,27:1
Marx, Chico
Cocoanuts, The 1925,D 9,30:1
Cocoanuts, The 1926,Ap 18,VIII,1:1
Animal Crackers 1928,O 24,26:2
Shoot the Works! 1931,Ag 21,20:2
Take a Bow 1944,Je 16,15:3
Marx, Claude Roger (Playwright)
Half a Loaf 1926,N 28,VIII,1:4
Marx, Felix
Bruder Straubinger 1921,N 16,22:3

Marx, Fred (Pfc) (Composer)
Swing Sister Wac Swing 1944,Ja 4,20:4
Marx, Groucho
Cocoanuts, The 1925,D 9,30:1
Cocoanuts, The 1926,Ap 18,VIII,1:1
Animal Crackers 1928,O 24,26:2
Shoot the Works! 1931,Ag 21,20:2
Marx, Groucho (Miscellaneous)
Minnie's Boys 1970,Mr 27,27:1
Marx, Groucho (Playwright)
Three's a Crowd 1930,O 5,IX,4:6
Time for Elizabeth 1948,S 28,32:3
Marx, Harpo
Cocoanuts, The 1925,D 9,30:1
Cocoanuts, The 1926,Ap 18,VIII,1:1
Animal Crackers 1928,O 24,26:2
Shoot the Works! 1931,Ag 21,20:2
Untitled-Revue 1933,D 19,26:3
Man Who Came to Dinner, The 1941,Jl 29,13:5
Marx, Henry M
Caesar and Cleopatra 1927,N 6,IX,2:1
Marx, Paul
Everyman 1941,My 9,19:2
Winter Soldiers 1942,N 30,19:2
Marx, Peter (Miscellaneous)
Power of Darkness, The 1959,S 30,33:1
Marx, Zeppo
Cocoanuts, The 1925,D 9,30:1
Animal Crackers 1928,O 24,26:2
Marx Brothers, The
I'll Say She Is 1924,My 20,15:1
Cocoanuts, The 1925,D 13,IX,3:1
Cocoanuts, The 1926,Je 11,25:2
Vaudeville (Palace) 1929,Ap 22,22:6
Vaudeville (Palace) 1930,O 13,31:3
Vaudeville (Palace) 1930,O 20,29:1
Vaudeville (Palace Theatre London) 1931,Ja 6,24:6
Vaudeville (Palace) 1932,Ja 4,27:4
Mary Alice
Strong Breed, The 1967,N 10,60:1
Trials of Brother Jero, The 1967,N 10,60:1
Rat's Mass, A 1969,N 1,39:1
Street Sounds 1970,O 23,32:1
Maryan, Charles (Director)
Let Them Down, Gently; On Vacation 1968,Ja 31,28:2
Let Them Down, Gently; Our Man in Madras 1968,Ja 31,28:2
Mercy Street 1969,O 28,43:1
Maryan, Charles (Miscellaneous)
Days and Nights of Beebee Fenstermaker, The 1962,S 18,33:1
Tiger, The 1963,F 6,5:2
Typists, The 1963,F 6,5:2
Cages; Snowangel; Epiphany 1963,Je 14,36:1
In White America 1963,N 1,26:1
Mariage de Figaro, Le 1964,F 26,41:2
Andromaque 1964,F 29,13:2
Vie Parisienne, La 1964,Mr 11,34:2
Absence of a Cello 1964,S 22,45:1
Catch Me if You Can 1965,Mr 10,50:1
Medea 1965,N 29,46:1
Serjeant Musgrave's Dance 1966,Mr 9,44:1
Hand Is on the Gate, A 1966,S 22,54:1
Marye, Donald
Rapid Transit 1927,Ap 8,21:2
Doctor Faustus Lights the Lights 1951,D 3,23:4
Crucible, The 1953,Ja 23,15:2
Crucible, The 1953,Jl 2,20:2
Detective Story 1954,F 13,11:2
Camille 1956,S 19,33:1
Lady From the Sea, The 1956,D 13,49:5
Make a Million 1958,O 24,39:2
White Cargo 1960,D 30,12:1
Crime and Crime 1963,D 17,51:2
Philadelphia, Here I Come! 1966,F 17,28:1
Marzano, Robert
Robin Landing 1937,N 19,26:4
Mas, Marula
Vida es Sueno, La 1964,Mr 18,49:1
Masamba
Hangman's Whip 1933,F 25,20:2
Masarachia, Felix
Here Come the Clowns 1954,My 5,36:2
Mascagno, Eva
White Lilacs 1928,S 11,31:2
Mascher, Mary
Caviar 1934,Je 8,19:2
Maschwitz, Eric (Lyricist)
Balalaika 1936,D 23,17:4
Maschwitz, Eric (Playwright)
Balalaika 1936,D 23,17:4
Masciarelli, Silvio (Composer)
Two for Fun 1961,F 14,45:3
Mascolo, Joseph
Penny Change 1963,O 25,37:1
Dinner at Eight 1966,S 28,38:1
To Clothe the Naked 1967,Ap 28,30:1
West Side Story 1968,Je 25,32:1
Time of Your Life, The 1969,N 7,37:1
Camino Real 1970,Ja 9,42:1
Good Woman of Setzuan, The 1970,N 6,51:1

Masefield, John
Hamlet 1927,Mr 12,13:1
Hamlet 1927,Mr 27,VII,2:6
Masefield, John (Playwright)
Tragedy of Nan, The 1920,F 18,9:1
Tragedy of Nan, The 1920,F 22,III,6:1
Witch, The 1926,N 19,22:5
Tristan and Isolt 1927,Mr 30,VIII,2:7
Coming of Christ, The 1928,My 29,6:2
Trial of Jesus, The 1932,Ap 17,VIII,3:1
Untitled-Play 1934,Mr 18,IX,2:3
Good Friday 1934,Ap 22,IX,1:6
Faithful, The 1935,Ja 20,X,3:8
Coming of Christ, The 1957,D 23,29:8
Masefield, John (Producer)
Hamlet 1927,Mr 27,VII,2:6
Masefield, Norman
Hamlet 1959,S 11,21:4
Masenia
Sharlee 1923,N 23,20:1
Masi, Frank (Lighting Director)
And People All Around 1968
Masi, Frank (Scenic Designer)
And People All Around 19
Masi, Rossana
As You Like It 1938,Jl ?
Masiell, Joe
Cindy 1964,Mr 20,24:
Dear World 1969,F 7
Sensations 1970,O ?
Maskin, Marc
Royal Hunt of the
Maslova, Lisa
Lute Song 1946
Maslova, Vlaste
Vaudeville (P
Maslow, Soph
Boutique F
Maslow, So
Sandhog
Machin
Shoen
Maslov
Sou
Mas
St
M

M
Grea
Mason, En
Lake, The L
Sweet Aloes 195
Mason, Eric
It's a Bird . . . It's a Pla
1966,Mr 30,34:1
Mason, Ethel
Comedy of Women, A 1929,S 14,1
Mason, Evelyn
Appearances 1925,O 15,27:3
Mason, F Van W
Who's Who 1924,Ap 18,19:2

1,26:2

,O 30,47:1
20,27:1

8,15:3
20:2

,O 3,24:3

36:1

t 1961,F 16,24:2

,8:2
16,40:1
Plane . . . It's Superman

nes 1967,D 8,53:1
ones 1967,D 24,II,3:2
lling, The 1969,Ja 3,19:1

967,F 1,27:2
ugar Plum 1968,Ja 18,47:2
Wanda June 1970,O 8,58:2
Wanda June 1970,O 18,II,1:1
W (Director)
964,Mr 17,31:1
965,F 11,45:1

, The 1923,Ja 25,16:2
d, The 1926,Je 9,18:3
O 19,27:3
e Years 1932,Ja 29,13:3

y
Limit, The 1934,D 18,25:5
rmine 1935,F 9,10:4
Day 1936,Ja 29,15:2

ont
936,D 17,34:5
on the Lot 1938,Mr 23,18:4
ng 1939,N 22,16:5
the Night 1940,Mr 19,31:2
unt 1940,O 18,24:2
an 1941,My 8,20:4
n 1942,Ja 24,12:5
ry-Linn
n Her Bonnet, A 1961,Je 15,50:1
lissa
orse Inn 1936,O 2,28:5
Love 1941,Ja 8,14:2
Yours 1942,Mr 26,26:2
out Time 1942,Mr 31,28:3
Me In 1942,O 9,24:2
Michael
of Least Existence, The 1968,Mr 25,53:1
Norma
Cod Follies 1929,S 19,37:2
n, Pansy
son's Bride, The 1929,Ja 22,22:3
n, Pauline
uie the 14th 1925,Mr 4,17:1
neymoon Lane 1926,S 21,32:3
son, Ralph
I M S Pinafore 1968,O 30,35:1
Iolanthe 1968,N 9,37:3
Mason, Ray
Carnival in Flanders 1953,S 9,38:2
Girl in Pink Tights, The 1954,Mr 6,13:2
Ankles Aweigh 1955,Ap 19,27:1
Destry Rides Again 1959,Ap 24,24:1
Wildcat 1960,D 17,20:2
How to Succeed in Business Without Really Trying
1961,O 16,34:1
Mason, Reginald
Mirage, The 1920,O 1,14:1
Dover Road, The 1921,D 24,7:2
You and I 1923,F 20,12:1
Changelings, The 1923,S 18,16:3
Changelings, The 1923,S 30,II,1:1
Locked Door, The 1924,Je 20,17:2
Tiger Cats 1924,O 22,18:1
Man in Evening Clothes, The 1924,D 6,13:4
Dark Angel, The 1925,F 11,19:2
Fall of Eve, The 1925,S 1,18:1
Creaking Chair, The 1926,F 23,26:1
Pygmalion 1926,N 16,24:1
Right You Are (If You Think You Are)
1927,F 24,27:1
Immoral Isabella 1927,O 28,20:3
Caste 1927,D 24,8:1
Heavy Traffic 1928,S 6,23:3
Security 1929,Mr 29,20:1
One, Two, Three! 1930,S 30,24:2
Violet, The 1930,S 30,24:2
Getting Married 1931,Mr 31,25:5
Divorce Me, Dear 1931,O 7,29:2
In Times Square 1931,N 24,29:3
Firebird 1932,N 22,25:2
Lady Jane 1934,S 11,24:2
Valley Forge 1934,N 27,26:4
Valley Forge 1934,D 11,28:3
To See Ourselves 1935,My 1,25:2
St Helena 1936,S 29,35:1
St Helena 1936,O 7,32:1
Dear Octopus 1939,Ja 12,22:2
Journey's End 1939,S 19,29:2
Journey's End 1939,S 24,IX,1:1
To What Red Hell 1940,My 5,I,54:8
At the Stroke of Eight 1940,My 21,29:2
Jupiter Laughs 1940,S 10,27:1
Anne of England 1941,O 8,26:2
R U R 1942,D 4,30:2
Rebecca 1945,Ja 19,17:2
First Mrs Fraser, The 1947,N 6,36:2
Shop at Sly Corner, The 1949,Ja 19,35:2
Love of Four Colonels, The 1953,Ja 16,17:2
Mason, Richard
Kongi's Harvest 1968,Ap 15,49:1
Daddy Goodness 1968,Je 5,37:1
Mason, Richard (Costume Designer)
Uncle Vanya 1956,F 1,25:2
Uncle Vanya 1956,F 12,II,1:1
Sea Gull, The 1956,O 23,38:1
Antony and Cleopatra 1963,S 14,12:4
Mason, Richard (Original Author)
World of Suzie Wong, The 1958,O 15,47:1
World of Suzie Wong, The 1958,O 19,II,1:1
World of Suzie Wong, The 1959,N 18,49:6
Mason, Richard (Playwright)
Italian Straw Hat, The 1957,O 1,37:2
Mason, Richard (Scenic Designer)
Mourners' Bench, The 1950,S 22,35:7
Antigone 1956,Ap 3,32:2
Easter 1957,Ja 17,35:2
Easter 1957,F 3,II,1:1
Italian Straw Hat, The 1957,O 1,37:2
Fools Are Passing Through 1958,Ap 3,24:2
Antony and Cleopatra 1963,S 14,12:4
Mason, Ricky
Long Gallery, The 1958,Mr 7,17:2

Mason, Robert
Policy Kings 1938,D 31,6:2
Mason, Roger (Composer)
Electra 1962,Mr 22,42:1
Mason, Ruth
You and I 1925,O 20,29:1
Field God, The 1927,Ap 22,18:2
New York 1927,N 15,26:2
Wine, Women and Song 1942,S 29,18:3
Mason, Serena
Black Souls 1932,Mr 31,25:1
Mason, Slim
Trial of Dr Beck, The 1937,Ag 10,22:2
Mason, Snippy
Liza 1922,N 28,24:1
Mason, Sydney
Cat-Bird, The 1920,F 17,18:1
Ebb Tide 1931,Je 9,33:6
Lady Detained, A 1935,Ja 10,23:3
Bitter Stream 1936,Mr 31,16:6
Mason, T E (Scenic Designer)
Dirtiest Show in Town, The 1970,Je 29,43:2
Score 1970,O 29,57:4
Mason, Tom
For Charity 1937,Ag 25,24:3
Mason, Virginia
Hang Down Your Head and Die 1964,O 19,38:1
Mason, Virginia (Choreographer)
Stop the World-I Want to Get Off 1962,O 4,45:4
Orthee 1962,D 29,5:5
Antigone 1962,D 29,5:5
Mason, Virginia (Director)
Orthee 1962,D 29,5:5
Antigone 1962,D 29,5:5
Mason, Walter
Long Dream, The 1960,F 18,36:2
Mason, Walter (Miscellaneous)
Ox Cart, The 1966,D 20,58:1
Mason, William V 3d (Scenic Designer)
Dooley Cashes In 1935,Ag 17,18:6
Mason and Keeler
Vaudeville (Palace) 1928,Ja 17,23:3
Mason and Shaw
Will Morrissey's Newcomers 1923,Ag 9,16:2
Mason Elliot
Follow Me 1932,D 11,IX,5:3
Masotti, Marc A (Translator)
Apollo of Bellac, The 1954,My 29,12:1
Purification, The 1954,My 29,12:1
Apollo of Bellac, The 1954,Je 6,II,1:1
Massager, Andre (Composer)
Deburau 1926,D 28,16:1
Massalsky, Pavel
Cherry Orchard, The 1965,F 10,46:1
Three Sisters, The 1965,F 12,15:1
Kremlin Chimes 1965,F 25,23:1
Massart, Armant (Playwright)
Alcide Pepis 1923,O 30,17:2
Massary, Fritzi
Spanische Nachtigall, Die 1920,D 12,VI,1:4
Prinzessin Olala 1921,D 11,VI,1:4
Merry Widow, The 1929,F 17,IX,2:3
First Mrs Fraser, The 1929,O 20,10:1
First Mrs Fraser, The 1930,Mr 9,IX,4:3
Nina 1932,Ja 24,VIII,1:3
Frau Die Weiss Was Sie Will, Eine 1932,O 9,IX,3:7
Operette 1938,Mr 17,17:4
Operette 1938,Ap 3,XI,1:8
Masse, Mike (Costume Designer)
End of All Things Natural, The 1969,S 12,38:1
Massee, Judith
Gondoliers, The 1963,Je 5,33:2
Massey, Anna
Reluctant Debutante, The 1956,O 11,50:1
Reluctant Debutante, The 1956,O 21,II,1:1
Elder Statesman, The 1958,Ag 26,35:1
Elder Statesman, The 1958,Ag 31,II,3:1
Miracle Worker, The 1961,Mr 10,19:4
School for Scandal, The 1962,Ap 6,31:3
Massey, Daniel
Small War on Murray Hill 1957,Ja 4,19:1
Small War on Murray Hill 1957,Ja 3,II,1:1
Happiest Millionaire, The 1957,N 16,16:5
School for Scandal, The 1962,Ap 6,31:3
She Loves Me 1963,Ap 24,39:1
She Loves Me 1963,My 5,II,1:1
Importance of Being Earnest, The 1968,Jl 6,9:1
Massey, David
Much Ado About Nothing 1952,My 2,20:1
Massey, Edward (Director)
Moon Is a Gong, The 1926,Mr 13,21:3
Beyond Evil 1926,Je 8,23:2
Taming of the Shrew, The 1927,My 4,29:1
Belt, The 1927,O 20,33:1
Hoboken Blues 1928,F 18,10:1
Box Seats 1928,Ap 20,27:2
Airways, Inc 1929,F 21,30:5
Pure in Heart, The 1934,Mr 21,24:3
Michael Drops In 1938,D 28,24:3
Massey, Edward (Playwright)
Box Seats 1928,Ap 20,27:2
Massey, Edward (Producer)
Michael Drops In 1938,D 28,24:3

Massey, Emily
Without Love 1942,N 11,28:1
Massey, Ilona
Ziegfeld Follies 1943,Ap 2,16:2
Ziegfeld Follies 1943,Ap 11,II,1:1
Massey, James Stewardson
This Mad Whirl 1937,Ja 10,II,4:8
Massey, Raymond
Transit of Venus, The 1927,My 22,VIII,2:1
Golden Calf, The 1927,O 2,VIII,1:3
Second Man, The 1928,F 12,VIII,2:1
Black Ace, The 1929,Je 2,VIII,2:7
Man in Possession, The 1930,F 9,VIII,2:1
In the Zone 1930,F 9,VIII,2:1
Late Night Final 1931,Je 26,26:3
All-Star Special 1931,Jl 18,16:4
Five-Star Final 1931,Jl 18,16:4
Hamlet 1931,O 25,VIII,2:2
Hamlet 1931,N 6,28:4
Hamlet 1931,N 15,VIII,1:1
Never Come Back 1932,O 29,18:6
Rats of Norway, The 1933,Ap 30,IX,1:7
Ace, The 1933,Ag 25,12:4
Ace, The 1933,S 17,X,1:6
Acropolis 1933,N 24,25:8
Acropolis 1933,D 10,X,3:6
Shining Hour, The 1934,F 14,22:6
Shining Hour, The 1934,F 25,IX,1:1
Shining Hour, The 1934,S 23,X,3:6
Ethan Frome 1936,Ja 7,24:7
Ethan Frome 1936,Ja 22,15:2
Ethan Frome 1936,F 2,IX,1:1
Night of January 16 1936,S 30,29:3
Idiot's Delight 1938,Mr 23,19:3
Idiot's Delight 1938,Ap 10,X,2:1
Abe Lincoln in Illinois 1938,O 4,20:1
Abe Lincoln in Illinois 1938,O 17,12:2
Abe Lincoln in Illinois 1938,O 23,IX,1:1
Abe Lincoln in Illinois 1939,Ap 23,X,1:1
Abe Lincoln in Illinois 1939,Jl 30,IX,1:1
Doctor's Dilemma, The 1941,F 18,26:6
Doctor's Dilemma, The 1941,Mr 18,22:3
Doctor's Dilemma, The 1941,Mr 30,IX,1:1
Candida 1942,Ap 28,24:4
Candida 1942,My 3,VIII,1:1
Lovers and Friends 1943,N 30,23:2
Lovers and Friends 1943,D 5,II,5:1
Pygmalion 1945,D 27,16:1
Pygmalion 1946,Ja 6,II,1:1
How I Wonder 1947,O 1,34:2
Father, The 1949,N 17,36:2
Father, The 1949,N 27,II,1:1
ANTA Album 1950,Ja 30,13:2
John Brown's Body 1952,N 3,25:8
John Brown's Body 1952,D 16,43:5
John Brown's Body 1953,F 16,17:2
John Brown's Body 1953,F 22,II,1:1
Julius Caesar 1955,Jl 13,20:1
Tempest, The 1955,Ag 2,18:2
Tempest, The 1955,Ag 7,II,1:1
J B 1958,D 12,2:7
Massey, Raymond (Director)
Silver Tassie, The 1929,N 3,IX,4:1
Silver Tassie, The 1929,N 10,X,1:1
Symphony in Two Flats 1930,S 17,30:4
Late Night Final 1931,Je 26,26:3
Shining Hour, The 1934,F 14,22:6
Ringmaster, The 1935,Mr 12,24:5
Father, The 1949,N 17,36:2
Massey, Raymond (Playwright)
Hanging Judge 1952,S 24,40:4
Hanging Judge 1952,O 12,II,3:8
Massey, Raymond (Producer)
In the Zone 1930,F 9,VIII,2:1
Man in Possession, The 1930,F 9,VIII,2:1
Five-Star Final 1931,Jl 18,16:4
Grand Hotel 1931,S 4,22:7
Grand Hotel 1931,S 27,VIII,1:4
Ringmaster, The 1935,Ap 7,IX,1:6
Massey, Sarah Cabell (Costume Designer)
Apollo of Bellac, The 1954,My 29,12:1
Purification, The 1954,My 29,12:1
Massey, Sarah Cabell (Scenic Designer)
Purification, The 1954,My 29,12:1
Apollo of Bellac, The 1954,My 29,12:1
Massey, Valgene (Director)
Chaparral 1958,S 10,38:2
Massey, Valgene (Playwright)
Chaparral 1958,S 10,38:2
Massey, Walter
Joan of Lorraine 1955,Mr 26,12:2
Mister Roberts 1956,D 6,46:2
As You Like It 1959,Jl 1,27:1
Massi, Bernice
Beg, Borrow or Steal 1960,F 11,39:4
No Strings 1962,Mr 16,24:1
No Strings 1962,Mr 25,II,1:1
What Makes Sammy Run? 1964,F 28,19:1
Man of La Mancha 1967,N 24,61:1
Man of La Mancha 1969,My 3,38:4
Massie, Paul
Cat on a Hot Tin Roof 1958,Ja 31,24:2
Henry IV, Part I 1965,Je 30,42:1

Massie, Paul—Cont
Falstaff; Henry IV, Part II 1965,Jl 1,35:1
Julius Caesar 1965,Jl 2,18:1
John Brown's Body 1968,F 13,49:2
Comedy of Errors, The 1968,F 28,40:2
She Stoops to Conquer 1968,Ap 1,58:3
Massimo, Gene
Fortuna 1962,Ja 4,26:1
Massine, Leonide
Miracle, The 1932,My 8,VIII,2:2
Massine, Leonide (Choreographer)
Miracle, The 1932,My 8,VIII,2:2
Helen Goes to Troy 1944,Ap 25,17:2
Helen Goes to Troy 1944,Ap 30,II,1:1
Vie Parisienne, La 1945,Ja 13,14:5
Massine, Leonide (Miscellaneous)
Woof, Woof 1929,D 26,20:4
Miracle, The 1932,Ap 10,I,18:1
Massinger, Charles
Artists and Models 1924,O 16,33:3
Sweethearts 1929,S 23,25:1
Show Boat 1956,Je 22,16:1
Show Boat 1957,Je 28,30:2
Massingham, Dorothy (Playwright)
Not in Our Stars 1924,F 10,VII,2:4
Lake, The 1933,Mr 26,IX,1:1
Soldier and the Gentlewoman, The 1933,My 7,IX,1:4
Lake, The 1933,D 19,26:3
Lake, The 1933,D 27,24:2
Lake, The 1934,Ja 7,X,1:1
Masso, Lenore
Bootleggers, The 1922,N 28,24:1
Masson, Andre (Costume Designer)
Hamlet 1952,D 2,39:1
Masson, Andre (Scenic Designer)
Hamlet 1952,D 2,39:1
Masson, Louis (Musical Director)
Clotture, Le 1927,Ja 23,VII,2:1
Masson, Luis
Mariage de Figaro, Le 1964,F 26,41:2
Salut a Moliere 1964,Mr 4,33:2
Pieton de L'Air, Le 1964,Mr 4,33:2
Masson, William C
Right Age to Marry, The 1926,F 16,22:3
Ghosts 1927,Ja 11,36:3
Merry Wives of Windsor, The 1928,Mr 20,20:1
Mast, Charles
Tip-Top 1920,O 6,13:2
Louie the 14th 1925,Mr 4,17:1
Ripples 1930,F 12,26:1
Mast, Jane (Playwright)
Sex 1926,Ap 27,22:4
Drag, The 1927,F 1,3:6
Mastayer, Harry
Mamba's Daughters 1939,Ja 4,24:2
Masten, Stewart
Good Fellow, The 1926,O 6,22:1
Masteroff, Joe
Prescott Proposals, The 1953,D 17,53:1
Masteroff, Joe (Playwright)
Warm Peninsula, The 1959,O 21,46:2
She Loves Me 1963,Ap 24,39:1
She Loves Me 1963,My 5,II,1:1
Cabaret 1966,N 21,62:1
Cabaret 1969,F 2,74:2
Masters, Alan
Hamlet 1945,D 14,25:2
Masters, Edgar Lee (Original Author)
Spoon River Anthology 1963,My 2,40:5
Spoon River Anthology 1963,O 8,40:5
Spoon River Anthology 1964,F 15,14:7
Spoon River Anthology 1964,Je 27,15:2
Masters, Edgar Lee (Playwright)
Beaux' Stratagem, The 1928,Je 5,20:1
Moroni 1936,Ag 19,19:1
Spoon River Anthology 1950,Ja 16,18:5
Spoon River Anthology 1963,S 30,23:2
Masters, Frank
Mimic World of 1921, The 1921,Ag 18,9:2
Dream Girl, The 1924,Ag 21,12:2
Merry Malones, The 1927,S 27,30:2
Masters, George W
Othello 1937,Ja 7,16:4
Masters, Harry
Buzzin' Around 1920,Jl 7,14:1
Masters, Johnny
Priorities of 1942 1942,Mr 13,23:2
Masters, Lynn
Afternoon Storm 1948,Ap 12,24:2
Masters, Marie
Acid Wine 1964,My 23,15:2
Sound of Silence, A 1965,Mr 9,30:1
Masters, Ruth
Pygmalion 1938,Ja 27,16:3
Masters and Kraft
Fashions of 1924 1923,Jl 19,18:2
Masters and Lamonthe
Will Morrissey's Newcomers 1923,Ag 9,16:2
Masterson, Carroll (Producer)
God and Kate Murphy 1959,F 27,21:2
Villa of Madame Vidac, The 1959,O 1,40:1
Beg, Borrow or Steal 1960,F 11,39:4
Second String, A 1960,Ap 14,36:2

Masterson, Carroll (Producer)—Cont
From A to Z 1960,Ap 21,23:2
New Faces of 1962 1962,F 2,25:1
Lady of the Camellias, The 1963,Mr 22,7:1
Traveller Without Luggage 1964,S 18,26:2
Apparition Theater of Prague, The 1966,N 17,56:2
Masterson, Harris (Producer)
God and Kate Murphy 1959,F 27,21:2
Villa of Madame Vidac, The 1959,O 1,40:1
Beg, Borrow or Steal 1960,F 11,39:4
Second String, A 1960,Ap 14,36:2
From A to Z 1960,Ap 21,23:2
New Faces of 1962 1962,F 2,25:1
Lady of the Camellias, The 1963,Mr 22,7:1
Traveller Without Luggage 1964,S 18,26:2
Bajour 1964,N 24,42:1
Apparition Theater of Prague, The 1966,N 17,56:2
Masterson, Pete
Villa of Madame Vidac, The 1959,O 1,40:1
Masterson, Peter
Trial of Lee Harvey Oswald, The 1967,N 6,64:1
Great White Hope, The 1968,O 4,40:1
Masterson, Peter (Director)
Lime Green 1969,Mr 27,54:2
Khaki Blue 1969,Mr 27,54:2
Masterson, Valerie
Iolanthe 1964,N 18,52:1
Pirates of Penzance, The 1964,N 27,43:1
Pirates of Penzance, The 1966,N 16,54:1
Mikado, The 1966,N 18,36:1
H M S Pinafore 1968,O 30,35:1
Mikado, The 1968,N 2,29:4
Pirates of Penzance, The 1968,N 7,54:1
Mastin, Will
Mr Wonderful 1956,Mr 23,23:2
Mastroianni, Marcello
Ciao, Rudy 1966,Ja 8,15:3
Mastroianni, Marcello (Producer)
Ciao, Rudy 1966,Ja 8,15:3
Masuda, Keaton
How to Succeed in Business Without Really Trying
1964,Jl 18,10:1
Masullo, Maggie
Light, Lively and Yiddish 1970,O 28,58:1
Masullo, Tony
Let's Sing Yiddish 1966,N 10,63:1
Light, Lively and Yiddish 1970,O 28,58:1
Masur, Harold Quincey
Nautical but Nice 1931,Ap 19,31:6
Masur, Richard D
Revenger's Tragedy, The 1970,D 2,58:1
Masury, Ruth Hoffman
Confederacy, The 1958,Jl 3,20:1
Mata, Ruth
Two for Fun 1961,F 14,45:3
Mata, Ruth (Director)
Two for Fun 1961,F 14,45:3
Mata and Hari
Two Weeks With Pay 1940,Je 25,28:3
Laffing Room Only 1944,D 25,15:4
Matachena, Oreste
Subscriber, The 1968,N 5,53:2
Susie Is a Good Girl 1968,N 5,53:2
Grab Bag, The 1968,N 5,53:2
Matagoro, Nakamura
Kagotsurube; Courtesan, The 1960,Je 3,26:1
Chushingura; Forty-Seven Ronin, The
1960,Je 10,37:1
Migawari Zazen; Substitute, The 1960,Je 10,37:1
Takatsuki; Clog Dance, The 1960,Je 17,35:4
Chushingura; Forty-Seven Ronin, The
1960,Je 17,35:4
Matalon, Vivian
Maya 1953,Je 10,35:1
School for Scandal, The 1953,Je 24,29:2
Little Clay Cart, The 1953,Jl 1,25:1
Knight of the Burning Pestle, The 1953,O 24,13:2
Moon in Capricorn 1953,O 28,37:2
Matalon, Vivian (Director)
Song at Twilight, A 1966,Ap 17,86:5
After the Rain 1966,S 3,13:5
After the Rain 1967,O 10,54:1
Square Root of Wonderful, The 1970,Mr 12,47:1
Matalon, Vivian (Producer)
Two Cities 1969,Mr 1,22:1
Matalon, Zack
Irma la Douce 1960,S 30,31:2
Look: We've Come Through 1961,O 26,40:1
Diary of a Madman 1964,Ap 17,29:2
Matao, Nakamura
Kagotsurube; Courtesan, The 1960,Je 3,26:1
Matarrasso, Sam
Walk-Up 1961,F 24,24:1
Susan Slept Here 1961,Jl 12,35:2
Matarrese, Antony (Composer)
Political Party, A 1963,S 27,17:5
Matarrese, Antony (Lyricist)
Political Party, A 1963,S 27,17:5
Matarrese, Antony (Playwright)
Political Party, A 1963,S 27,17:5
Matas, Tony (Miscellaneous)
Liberace's Variety Bill 1957,Ap 22,29:5
Matchabelli, Princess
Creoles 1927,S 23,33:3

Passion Play, The 1929,Ap 30,32:1
Matchet, Sidney
Love for Love 1925,Ap 1,21:2
Mate, Jeno
Burning, The 1963,D 4,57:1
Matera, Pat
West Side Story 1968,Je 25,32:1
Mather, Aubrey
Hamlet 1936,O 20,31:3
Hamlet 1936,N 11,54:2
Bachelor Born 1938,Ja 26,26:3
Good Hunting 1938,N 22,26:5
Hand in Glove 1944,D 5,19:1
Hand in Glove 1944,D 10,II,5:1
Foolish Notion 1945,Mr 14,23:2
Foolish Notion 1945,Mr 18,II,1:1
Candida 1945,Ag 7,25:3
As You Like It 1950,Ja 27,27:2
Separate Tables 1955,My 22,II,1:1
Mather, Charles
Crooked Gamblers 1920,Ag 2,12:1
Demi-Virgin, The 1921,O 19,22:1
Good Old Days, The 1923,Ag 15,21:2
Kiss in a Taxi, The 1925,Ag 26,14:1
Buy, Buy Baby 1926,O 8,26:2
Crime 1927,F 23,27:3
Mather, Charles (Playwright)
Old Timer 1929,Ap 30,33:4
Mather, Denzil
Courting 1925,S 14,17:1
Courting 1925,S 20,VIII,1:1
Mather, Sidney
Woman of Bronze, The 1920,S 8,9:2
Trial of Joan of Arc, The 1921,Mr 28,8:2
Iphigenia in Aulis 1921,Ap 8,18:2
Twelfth Night 1921,N 1,17:1
Merchant of Venice, The 1921,N 22,17:1
Hamlet 1922,N 17,14:1
Hamlet 1923,N 27,23:6
Mathes, Allan
Beauty and the Beast 1932,Ja 10,I,29:2
Matheson, Murray
Relapse, The 1950,N 23,54:2
Escapade 1953,N 19,40:1
Third Person 1955,D 30,13:4
Harlequinade 1959,F 14,15:1
Electra 1959,F 14,15:1
Oh, Kay! 1960,Ap 18,37:2
Mathews, A E
But for the Grace of God 1923,S 9,VII,2:4
Spring Cleaning 1923,N 10,16:3
Spring Cleaning 1923,N 18,VIII,1:1
Mathews, Adelaide (Playwright)
Just Married 1921,Ap 27,21:1
Mathews, Alice L
Lottie Gathers No Moss 1931,F 24,26:4
Mathews, Billy (Director)
Teahouse of the August Moon, The 1956,N 9,33:2
Mathews, Billy (Miscellaneous)
Eddie Fisher at the Winter Garden 1962,O 3,47:1
Mathews, Cameron
Trial of Joan of Arc, The 1921,Mr 28,8:2
Big Mogul, The 1925,My 12,26:3
Jerry for Short 1929,Ag 13,23:4
Mathews, Carmen
Hamlet 1938,O 13,28:1
Henry IV, Part I 1939,Ja 31,17:2
Richard II 1940,Ap 2,31:2
Seventh Trumpet, The 1941,N 22,10:6
Harriet 1943,Mr 4,24:2
Assassin, The 1945,O 18,20:2
Made in Heaven 1946,O 25,28:2
Man and Superman 1947,O 9,31:2
Ivy Green, The 1949,Ap 6,37:2
She Stoops to Conquer 1949,D 29,21:3
Corn Is Green, The 1950,Ja 12,33:2
Show-Off, The 1950,Je 1,24:5
Show-Off, The 1950,Je 11,II,1:1
Courtin' Time 1951,Je 14,30:2
My 3 Angels 1953,Mr 12,23:2
Holiday for Lovers 1957,F 15,20:1
Man in the Dog Suit, The 1958,O 31,34:2
Night Life 1962,O 24,44:1
Lorenzo 1963,F 16,5:2
Yearling, The 1965,D 11,25:1
Delicate Balance, A 1966,S 23,44:1
I'm Solomon 1968,Ap 24,51:1
Dear World 1969,F 7,33:1
Dear World 1969,F 16,II,1:1
Mathews, Carole
With a Silk Thread 1950,Ap 13,34:3
Mathews, Christine
King and I, The 1956,Ap 19,35:4
Mathews, Diana (Miscellaneous)
Indian Wants the Bronx, The 1968,Ja 18,47:2
It's Called the Sugar Plum 1968,Ja 18,47:2
Mathews, Dolly (Wac Pvt)
Swing Sister Wac Swing 1944,Ja 4,20:4
Mathews, Dorothy
Schoolgirl 1930,N 21,31:1
Barretts of Wimpole Street, The 1931,F 10,25:1
I Love an Actress 1931,S 18,29:2
After All 1931,D 4,28:4

Mathews, Dorothy—Cont
Clear All Wires! 1932,S 15,19:1
Sing and Whistle 1934,F 12,18:3
Musical Chairs 1934,Jl 31,20:7
Taming of the Shrew, The 1935,S 22,X,3:2
Taming of the Shrew, The 1935,O 1,27:3
Ethan Frome 1936,N 15,XI,2:1
Three Sisters, The 1939,O 16,23:1
Mathews, George
Processional 1937,O 14,23:1
Escape This Night 1938,Ap 23,18:1
Big Blow 1938,O 3,11:2
Retreat to Pleasure 1940,D 18,32:2
Out of the Frying Pan 1941,F 12,24:2
Night Before Christmas, The 1941,Mr 30,I,48:2
Night Before Christmas, The 1941,Ap 11,25:2
Cuckoos on the Hearth 1941,S 17,26:2
They Should Have Stood in Bed 1942,F 14,18:5
Life of Reilly, The 1942,Ap 30,13:2
Eve of St Mark, The 1942,O 8,30:2
Streets Are Guarded, The 1944,N 21,19:7
Kiss Them for Me 1945,MR 21,27:2
Beggars Are Coming to Town 1945,O 29,16:2
Antigone 1946,F 19,21:3
Temper the Wind 1946,D 28,10:2
Hope Is the Thing with Feathers 1948,Ap 12,24:2
Gone Tomorrow; Hope's the Thing
1948,My 12,34:6
Hope Is the Thing With Feathers; Hope's the
Thing 1948,My 12,34:6
Home Life of a Buffalo; Hope's the Thing
1948,My 12,34:6
S S Glencairn; Moon of the Caribbees
1948,My 21,21:2
S S Glencairn; In the Zone 1948,My 21,21:2
S S Glencairn; Bound East for Cardiff
1948,My 21,21:2
S S Glencairn; Long Voyage Home, The
1948,My 21,21:2
S S Glencairn; Long Voyage Home, The; Moon of
the Caribbees; In the Zone; Bound East for
Cardiff 1948,My 30,II,1:1
Silver Whistle, The 1948,N 25,49:2
Streetcar Named Desire, A 1950,My 24,36:1
Mister Roberts 1950,Jl 23,II,1:6
Barefoot in Athens 1951,N 1,35:2
One Eye Closed 1954,N 25,45:2
Desperate Hours, The 1955,F 11,20:2
Holiday for Lovers 1957,F 15,20:1
Prometheus Bound 1957,Ag 9,11:6
Shadow of a Gunman, The 1958,N 21,26:1
Shadow of a Gunman, The 1958,N 30,II,1:1
Pound on Demand, A 1959,Ap 16,28:1
Portrait of a Madonna 1959,Ap 16,28:1
Portrait of a Madonna 1959,Ap 26,II,1:1
Twelfth Night 1959,Jl 11,10:2
Macbeth 1959,Ag 1,9:2
Do Re Mi 1960,D 27,23:2
Catch Me if You Can 1965,Mr 10,50:1
Time for Singing, A 1966,My 23,48:2
Joyful Noise, A 1966,D 16,57:1
Great White Hope, The 1967,D 14,58:1
Great White Hope, The 1968,O 4,40:1
Mathews, J Cleneay
Lilies of the Field 1921,O 5,20:1
Mathews, Jackson (Translator)
Philoctetes 1959,Ja 14,28:1
Mathews, Junius
Fedora 1922,F 11,18:1
Mathews, Kevin
It's A Gift 1945,Mr 13,18:7
Wind Is Ninety, The 1945,Je 22,12:2
Topaze 1947,D 29,21:5
Home Life of a Buffalo; Hope's the Thing
1948,My 12,34:6
Gone Tomorrow; Hope's the Thing
1948,My 12,34:6
Hope Is the Thing With Feathers; Hope's the
Thing 1948,My 12,34:6
Mathews, Mark
Greenwillow 1970,D 8,60:1
Mathews, Mary
Gay Divorce 1932,N 30,23:4
Let 'Em Eat Cake 1933,O 23,18:1
Blackbirds 1933,D 4,22:3
Women of Twilight 1952,Mr 4,22:2
Mathews, Matt (Composer)
Climate of Eden, The 1953,N 21,11:2
Mathews, Norman
Celebration 1969,Ja 23,55:2
Mathews, Richard
King Lear 1959,Ja 3,11:2
Jackass, The 1960,Mr 24,39:2
Comedy of Errors, The 1963,Je 13,28:1
Richard III 1964,Je 12,44:2
Hamlet 1964,Jl 4,9:1
Coriolanus 1965,Je 21,36:1
Romeo and Juliet 1965,Je 21,36:3
King Lear 1965,Je 25,39:1
Falstaff 1966,Je 20,27:1
Murder in the Cathedral 1966,Je 21,38:1
Twelfth Night 1966,Je 23,28:1
Julius Caesar 1966,Je 24,29:2
Merchant of Venice, The 1967,Je 22,46:2

Mathews, Richard—Cont
Macbeth 1967,Jl 31,21:1
Richard II 1968,Je 24,42:3
As You Like It 1968,Je 24,42:3
Androcles and the Lion 1968,Je 27,47:1
Mathews, Robert (Miscellaneous)
Clandestine on the Morning Line 1961,O 31,28:1
Mathews, Rose
Hoboken Blues 1928,F 18,10:1
Mathews, Vera (Playwright)
Make Yourself at Home 1945,S 14,21:2
Mathews, Walter
Julius Caesar 1955,Jl 13,20:1
King Lear 1956,Ja 13,17:1
Mister Roberts 1956,D 6,46:2
Julius Caesar 1957,O 24,39:1
As You Like It 1959,Jl 1,27:1
Nekros 1960,O 26,44:1
Mathias, Philip (Director)
Guys and Dolls 1955,Ap 21,32:2
Mathias, Philip (Miscellaneous)
Ponder Heart, The 1956,F 17,14:2
Murderous Angels 1970,F 8,70:1
Mathias, Philip (Producer)
Stephen D 1967,S 25,58:1
Mathiesen, Jack
Maid in the Ozarks 1946,Jl 16,20:3
Mathieu, Carl
County Chairman, The 1936,My 26,26:5
Mathieu, Rosalie
Fan, The 1921,O 4,10:1
Mathieu, William (Composer)
From the Second City 1961,S 27,32:1
Return of Second City in "20,000 Frozen
Grenadiers," The 1966,Ap 22,36:1
Mathieu, William (Musical Director)
Return of Second City in "20,000 Frozen
Grenadiers," The 1966,Ap 22,36:1
Mathis, Bonnie
Hello, Dolly! 1964,Ja 17,22:1
Mathis, Claude
This Was Burlesque 1970,F 12,31:1
Mathues, Craig
Scandals 1939,Ag 29,17:2
Mati, Rita (Translator)
Beyond 1925,Ja 27,14:1
Matias (Scenic Designer)
Happy Days 1965,S 14,45:2
Matil, Simone
Proces, Le; Trial, The 1952,N 18,36:2
Occupe-Toi d'Amelie; Keep Your Eyes on Amelie
1952,N 25,35:2
Matin, Elliot (Miscellaneous)
Seidman and Son 1962,O 16,32:2
Matin-Harvey, Lady
Hamlet 1923,N 20,23:3
Matine, Herve
Hair 1969,S 13,30:1
Matlock, Harry
Up in Central Park 1945,Ja 29,17:2
Matlock, Norman
Americana Pastoral 1968,D 11,51:1
Engagement Baby, The 1970,My 22,40:1
Matlock, Ruth
Lace Petticoat 1927,Ja 5,18:2
Matlovsky, Samuel (Miscellaneous)
Porgy and Bess 1953,Mr 10,25:5
Brigadoon 1957,Mr 28,37:1
Carousel 1957,S 12,38:2
Matlovsky, Samuel (Musical Director)
Threepenny Opera, The 1954,Mr 11,26:5
Threepenny Opera, The 1954,Ap 4,II,7:1
Once Over Lightly 1955,Mr 16,39:1
Threepenny Opera, The 1955,S 21,38:1
Johnny Johnson 1956,O 22,24:1
Of Mice and Men 1958,D 5,38:1
Guys and Dolls 1959,Jl 22,22:2
Mother Courage and Her Children 1963,Mr 30,5:5
Kelly 1965,F 8,28:2
Mahagonny 1970,Ap 29,51:1
Matlowsky, Samuel
Threepenny Opera, The 1955,S 21,38:1
Matlowsky, Samuel (Composer)
Month in the Country, A 1956,Ap 4,23:1
Matray, Ernst
Midsummer Night's Dream, A 1927,N 18,21:1
Midsummer Night's Dream, A 1927,D 4,X,6:1
Jedermann 1927,D 8,33:2
Jedermann 1927,D 18,IX,6:1
Dantons Tod 1927,D 21,28:3
Dantons Tod 1928,Ja 1,VIII,3:1
Servant of Two Masters, The 1928,Ja 22,VIII,6:1
Lebende Leichnam, Der, Der; Living Corpse, The
1928,Ja 24,26:2
Matray, Ernst (Choreographer)
Romeo and Juliet 1940,My 10,27:1
Pardon Our French 1950,O 6,22:4
Matray, Ernst (Musical Director)
Pardon Our French 1950,O 6,22:4
Matray, Maria (Choreographer)
Romeo and Juliet 1940,My 10,27:1
Pardon Our French 1950,O 6,22:4
Matray, Maria (Musical Director)
Pardon Our French 1950,O 6,22:4

Matshikiza, Todd (Composer)
Mkhumbhane 1960,Mr 31,29:2
Matsios, Christine
Magdalena 1948,S 21,31:2
Guys and Dolls 1950,N 25,11:2
Matson, David
Summer of Daisy Miller, The 1963,My 28,33:1
Matson, Norman (Playwright)
Comic Artist, The 1928,Jl 22,VII,1:3
Comic Artist, The 1929,N 23,19:3
Comic Artist, The 1933,Ap 20,20:3
Matson, Ralph (Director)
Broken Hearts of Broadway 1944,Je 13,16:2
Matson, Ralph (Playwright)
Broken Hearts of Broadway 1944,Je 13,16:2
Matsuda, Wackichi (Playwright)
Greengrocer's Daughter, The 1966,Mr 16,50:1
Matsumoto, Koshiro
Othello 1960,S 11,II,7:1
Matsushima, Shozaburo
Azuma Kabuki Dancers and Musicians
1954,F 19,22:3
Matsuura, Takeo (Director)
How to Succeed in Business Without Really Trying
1964,Jl 18,10:1
Who's Afraid of Virginia Woolf? 1964,N 26,52:1
Matta, Betty (Scenic Designer)
As You Like It 1958,Ja 21,33:6
Mattaei, Konrad
Don Carlos 1962,F 28,27:5
Mattei, Frank
Marvellous History of Saint Bernard, The
1958,F 24,16:3
Matteini, Aurelio (Scenic Designer)
Medea 1960,Jl 26,25:2
Matter, Franz
Marriage of Mr Mississippi, The 1969,N 20,60:5
Firebugs, The 1969,N 27,52:1
Philipp Hotz 1969,N 27,52:1
Mattern, Kitty
From Vienna 1939,Je 21,26:2
Reunion in New York 1940,F 22,28:4
Keep 'Em Laughing 1942,Ap 25,9:2
Jacobowsky and the Colonel 1944,Mr 15,17:2
Ist Geraldine ein Engel? 1946,N 4,33:4
Mattes, Barbara
Step on a Crack 1962,O 18,48:1
Andorra 1963,F 11,5:5
Matteson, Francis
No More Peace 1937,F 27,9:1
Matteson, Ruth
Geraniums in My Window 1934,O 27,20:6
Symphony 1935,Ap 27,20:3
Triumph 1935,O 15,18:5
Parnell 1935,N 12,24:2
Spring Dance 1936,Jl 7,22:2
Spring Dance 1936,Ag 26,17:4
Wingless Victory, The 1936,N 25,17:5
Wingless Victory, The 1936,D 24,20:2
Barchester Towers 1937,D 1,27:1
What a Life 1938,Ap 14,26:2
One for the Money 1939,F 6,9:2
Male Animal, The 1940,Ja 10,17:2
Male Animal, The 1940,Ja 21,IX,1:1
Merry Widow, The 1943,Ag 5,19:2
Merry Widow, The 1943,Ag 22,II,5:1
In Bed We Cry 1944,N 15,20:2
Mr Strauss Goes to Boston 1945,S 7,20:2
Antigone 1946,F 19,21:3
Park Avenue 1946,N 5,31:2
Clutterbuck 1949,D 5,29:2
Relapse, The 1950,N 23,54:2
Dragon's Mouth 1955,N 17,45:1
Happiest Millionaire, The 1956,N 21,21:3
There Was a Little Girl 1960,Mr 1,28:1
Matthaei, Gay (Miscellaneous)
Don Carlos 1962,F 28,27:5
Matthaei, Konrad
Man's a Man, A 1962,S 20,30:2
Milk Train Doesn't Stop Here Anymore, The
1964,Ja 2,33:1
Place for Polly, A 1970,Ap 20,45:1
Matthaei, Konrad (Miscellaneous)
Don Carlos 1962,F 28,27:5
Matthaei, Konrad (Producer)
Evening's Frost, An 1965,O 12,56:1
George M! 1968,Ap 11,48:1
Blancs, Les 1970,N 16,48:4
Matthau, Walter
Twilight Walk 1951,S 25,25:4
Fancy Meeting You Again 1952,Ja 15,23:2
One Bright Day 1952,Mr 20,37:2
In Any Language 1952,O 9,40:2
Grey-Eyed People, The 1952,D 18,41:2
Ladies of the Corridor, The 1953,O 22,33:5
Ladies of the Corridor, The 1953,N 1,II,1:1
Burning Glass, The 1954,Mr 5,15:2
Burning Glass, The 1954,Mr 14,II,1:1
Wisteria Trees, The 1955,F 3,20:2
Guys and Dolls 1955,Ap 21,32:2
Will Success Spoil Rock Hunter? 1955,O 14,22:2
Once More With Feeling 1958,O 22,39:1
Once There Was a Russian 1961,F 20,32:2

Matthau, Walter—Cont
Shot in the Dark, A 1961,O 19,40:1
My Mother, My Father and Me 1963,Mr 25,5:5
Odd Couple, The 1965,Mr 11,36:1
Odd Couple, The 1965,Mr 21,II,1:1
Matthew, Ross
Infernal Machine, The 1937,D 13,22:7
Red Velvet Goat, The 1939,Ja 21,18:4
Coggerers, The 1939,Ja 21,18:4
King Lear 1940,D 16,27:2
Any Day Now 1941,Je 10,28:2
As You Like It 1941,O 21,29:2
Criminals, The 1941,D 22,24:3
Nathan the Wise 1942,Mr 12,25:4
Nathan the Wise 1942,Ap 4,18:4
Winter Soldiers 1942,N 30,19:2
Patriots, The 1943,Ja 30,11:2
Patriots, The 1943,D 21,22:5
Hickory Stick 1944,My 9,15:6
Love on Leave 1944,Je 21,23:4
Dark of the Moon 1945,Mr 15,27:2
Matthews, A E
Peg o' My Heart 1921,F 15,7:1
Bulldog Drummond 1921,D 27,10:2
Last of Mrs Cheyney, The 1925,N 10,23:5
This Was a Man 1926,N 24,27:1
Happy Husband, The 1927,Jl 10,VII,2:3
Interference 1927,O 19,24:3
Happy Husband, The 1928,My 8,25:2
Happy Husband, The 1928,My 27,VIII,1:1
Heavy Traffic 1928,S 6,23:3
Serena Blandish 1929,Ja 13,VIII,2:4
Serena Blandish 1929,Ja 24,30:3
First Mrs Fraser, The 1929,D 30,16:2
Breadwinner, The 1931,S 23,19:4
Mademoiselle 1932,O 9,IX,3:6
Mademoiselle 1932,O 19,22:4
Hat, a Coat, a Glove, A 1934,F 1,15:2
These Two 1934,My 8,28:3
Dominant Sex, The 1935,Ap 2,24:5
Short Story 1935,N 5,33:2
Short Story 1935,D 1,XI,5:3
Matrimony, PFD 1936,N 6,28:4
Matrimony, PFD 1936,N 13,26:3
Satyr 1937,Jl 4,X,1:4
Spring Meeting 1938,D 9,30:4
They Came to a City 1943,Je 6,II,1:6
But for the Grace of God 1946,S 4,27:2
Yes, M'Lord 1949,O 5,35:2
Gay Invalid, The 1951,F 11,II,3:1
Matthews, A E (Director)
Happy Husband, The 1928,My 8,25:2
Breadwinner, The 1931,S 23,19:4
These Two 1934,My 8,28:3
Matthews, Adelaide (Playwright)
Scrambled Wives 1920,Ag 6,16:1
Teaser, The 1921,Jl 28,8:3
Courting 1925,S 14,17:1
Puppy Love 1925,O 4,IX,2:1
Puppy Love 1926,Ja 28,16:3
Wasp's Nest, The 1927,O 26,26:3
Nearly Married 1929,S 22,IX,4:1
Matthews, Arthur
Utopia, Limited; Flowers of Progress, The
1957,F 27,21:1
Mikado, The 1957,Ap 24,28:2
H M S Pinafore 1957,My 1,42:6
Pirates of Penzance, The 1957,My 8,43:1
Yeomen of the Guard, The 1957,My 22,28:3
Gondoliers, The 1957,My 29,34:2
Leave It to Jane 1959,My 26,30:2
Ben Franklin in Paris 1964,O 28,52:1
Mame 1966,My 25,41:1
Matthews, Babe
Black Rhythm 1936,D 21,19:2
Matthews, Bert
Animal Crackers 1928,O 24,26:2
Jonica 1930,Ap 8,27:1
Babes in Toyland 1930,D 22,17:1
Paint Your Wagon 1951,N 13,32:2
Matthews, Billy (Director)
Guys and Dolls 1959,Jl 22,22:2
Can-Can 1959,Ag 26,25:4
Beg, Borrow or Steal 1960,F 11,39:4
13 Daughters 1961,Mr 3,17:2
Kiss Me, Kate 1965,My 13,31:1
Matthews, Billy (Miscellaneous)
Good as Gold 1957,Mr 8,22:2
13 Daughters 1961,Mr 3,17:2
Sail Away 1961,O 4,48:5
Matthews, Charles
Here Come the Clowns 1960,S 20,48:1
Matthews, Christine
Pal Joey 1961,Je 1,32:1
Matthews, Dan
Flies, The; Mouches, Les 1947,Ap 18,26:3
All the King's Men 1948,Ja 19,19:2
All the King's Men 1950,Jl 19,25:6
Diamond Lil 1951,S 15,8:2
Matthews, Doro
That Ferguson Family 1928,D 24,10:7
Matthews, Douglas
Faithful, The 1935,Ja 20,X,3:8
Alien Corn 1935,Ja 20,X,3:8

Matthews, Edward
Porgy and Bess 1935,O 11,30:2
White Man 1936,O 19,22:4
Black Rhythm 1936,D 21,19:2
Porgy and Bess 1942,Ja 23,16:2
Porgy and Bess 1943,S 14,26:2
Porgy and Bess 1944,F 8,13:2
Four Saints in Three Acts 1952,Ap 17,35:1
Matthews, Emmet
Pirate, The 1942,N 26,39:2
Matthews, F T
School for Scandal, The 1923,Mr 13,19:2
Matthews, Francis
Help Stamp Out Marriage 1966,S 30,50:1
Matthews, Gerald
Love's Old Sweet Song 1940,My 3,16:3
Great Big Doorstep, The 1942,N 27,26:2
This Rock 1943,F 19,23:2
Goodbye Again 1943,N 10,28:4
Career Angel 1944,My 24,23:7
Admirable Bashville, The 1956,F 21,38:1
On a Clear Day You Can See Forever
    1965,O 18,44:1
Nathan Weinstein, Mystic, Connecticut
    1966,F 26,15:2
Don't Drink the Water 1966,N 18,37:1
Matthews, Gordon
Hamlet 1954,Ap 24,15:2
Matthews, Grace
Dame Nature 1938,S 27,24:3
Audition of the Apprentice Theatre 1939,Je 2,26:2
Matthews, Hale (Producer)
Niggerlovers, The; Demonstration, The
    1967,O 2,54:2
Niggerlovers, The; Man and Dog 1967,O 2,54:2
Collision Course; Stars and Stripes 1968,My 9,55:2
Collision Course; Skywriting 1968,My 9,55:2
Collision Course; Chuck 1968,My 9,55:2
Collision Course; Thoughts on the Instant of
    Greeting a Friend on the Street 1968,My 9,55:2
Collision Course; Jew! 1968,My 9,55:2
Collision Course; Metaphors 1968,My 9,55:2
Collision Course; Unexpurgated Memoirs of
    Bernard Mergendeiler, The 1968,My 9,55:2
Collision Course; Wandering 1968,My 9,55:2
Collision Course; Tour 1968,My 9,55:2
Collision Course; Rats 1968,My 9,55:2
Collision Course and Camera Obscura 1968,My 9,55:2
Dozens, The 1969,Mr 14,51:1
Matthews, Inez
Pirate, The 1942,N 26,39:2
Run, Little Chillun 1943,Ag 14,6:1
Carmen Jones 1945,My 3,26:5
Lost in the Stars 1949,O 31,21:2
Lost in the Stars 1949,N 6,II,1:1
Four Saints in Three Acts 1952,Ap 17,35:1
Matthews, Irene
Fall and Rise of Susan Lenox, The 1920,Je 11,11:2
Matthews, Jack
Chivalry 1925,D 16,22:3
Matthews, Jessie
Earl Carroll's Vanities 1927,Ja 5,18:1
Wake Up and Dream 1929,Ap 14,X,1:8
Wake Up and Dream 1929,D 31,14:3
Wake Up and Dream 1930,Ja 12,9:1
Evergreen 1930,O 14,31:2
Evergreen 1930,D 4,30:4
Evergreen 1930,D 21,VIII,1:6
Matthews, John F (Playwright)
Scapegoat, The 1950,Ap 20,36:5
Matthews, Joseph
Trial of Joan of Arc, The 1921,Mr 28,8:2
Matthews, Joyce
Hold On to Your Hats 1940,S 12,30:3
High Kickers 1941,N 1,21:2
Get Away Old Man 1943,N 25,40:2
Men to the Sea 1944,O 4,25:2
Burlesque 1946,D 26,30:3
Open House 1947,Je 4,33:4
Along Fifth Avenue 1949,Ja 14,28:2
Matthews, Junius
Pot-Luck 1921,S 30,10:1
Green Ring, The 1922,Ap 5,22:1
Makers of Light 1922,My 24,22:3
Little Clay Cart, The 1924,D 6,13:3
Critic, The 1925,My 9,12:4
Grand Street Follies, The 1925,Je 19,24:1
Dybbuk, The 1925,D 16,22:2
Grand Street Follies, The 1926,Je 16,23:2
Humble, The 1926,O 14,22:2
Grand Street Follies, The 1927,My 20,22:3
Taming of the Shrew, The 1927,O 26,26:4
Grand Street Follies, The 1929,My 2,20:4
Matthews, Lester
Yellow Sands 1927,S 12,29:3
Dinner Is Served 1930,F 8,13:4
Story to Be Whispered 1937,Ag 20,21:4
Desert Song, The 1946,Ja 9,20:2
Matthews, Marlene
Clearing in the Woods, A 1959,F 13,32:1
Matthews, Patrice
Ice Capades 1954,S 16,37:1

Matthews, Philip
These Are the Times 1950,My 11,37:2
In Good King Charles's Golden Days
    1957,Ja 25,16:1
Matthews, Ross
Belt, The 1927,O 20,33:1
International, The 1928,Ja 16,24:4
Airways, Inc 1929,F 21,30:5
Matthews, Sally
Courage 1927,Ja 20,20:1
Matthews, Tony
By Jupiter 1942,Je 4,22:1
Matthews, William C
Any Moment Now 1939,N 25,13:6
Matthews, William Henry (Costume Designer)
Fioretta 1929,F 6,30:3
Hamlet 1930,Mr 25,34:4
Macbeth 1930,Mr 26,24:6
Twelfth Night 1930,Mr 27,24:7
Merchant of Venice, The 1930,Mr 27,24:7
Richard III 1930,Mr 31,24:1
Matthias, Harry
Nativity Play, The 1937,D 21,29:1
Matthias, Rita
Sign of the Leopard 1928,D 24,17:7
Matthias, Rita (Playwright)
Cradle Snatchers 1927,Ap 15,27:2
Matthias, Rita (Translator)
All God's Chillun Got Wings 1932,Mr 27,VIII,3:3
Criminals, The 1941,D 22,24:3
Matthiessen, Joan
Port-Royal 1960,Ap 26,41:1
Matthison, Edith Wynne
Chastening, The 1923,F 17,9:2
Antigone 1923,My 4,18:4
Antigone 1923,My 25,28:1
Admiral, The 1924,Ap 25,20:2
Admiral, The 1924,My 4,VIII,1:1
Matthison, Edith Wynne (Producer)
Admiral, The 1929,Ja 23,21:1
Mattice, Wallace
My Maryland 1927,S 13,37:2
Mattina, Vincenzo
Paese dei Campanelli, Il; Land of Bells, The
    1935,My 10,25:4
Mattingly, Hedley
King John 1960,Je 29,26:2
Midsummer Night's Dream, A 1960,Je 30,23:5
Romeo and Juliet 1960,Jl 1,14:1
Mattingly, Hendricks
Pansy 1929,My 15,36:3
Hot Rhythm 1930,Ag 22,18:5
Mattioli, Ulisse
See Naples and Die 1929,S 27,30:4
Mattis, Virginia
Othello 1945,My 23,25:4
Hamlet 1956,O 29,34:1
Richard III 1957,N 26,41:1
Mattison, Johnny (Choreographer)
Sea Legs 1937,My 19,26:5
Mattox, Harold
Park Avenue 1946,N 5,31:2
Mattox, Jean
Say Darling 1959,F 26,38:2
Mattox, Matt
Magdalena 1948,S 21,31:2
Carnival in Flanders 1953,S 9,38:2
Vamp, The 1955,N 11,30:1
Brigadoon 1957,Mr 28,37:1
Say Darling 1958,Ap 4,17:1
Say Darling 1959,F 26,38:2
Once Upon a Mattress 1959,My 12,40:1
Mattox, Matt (Choreographer)
Annie Get Your Gun 1957,Mr 9,15:5
Say Darling 1958,Ap 4,17:1
Say Darling 1959,F 26,38:2
Much Ado About Nothing 1961,Jl 7,17:1
Midsummer Night's Dream, A 1961,Ag 3,13:1
Jennie 1963,O 18,35:2
What Makes Sammy Run? 1964,F 28,19:1
Mattson, Eric
White Plume, The 1939,D 27,16:1
Carousel 1945,Ap 20,24:2
Carousel 1949,Ja 26,28:2
Carousel 1949,F 6,II,1:1
Cellar and the Well, The 1950,D 11,30:2
Mattson, Eric (Director)
Oklahoma! 1958,Mr 8,15:2
Mature, Victor
Lady in the Dark 1941,Ja 5,IX,1:7
Lady in the Dark 1941,Ja 24,14:2
Tars and Spars 1944,Ap 7,23:1
Maturin, Eric
Present From Margate, The 1933,D 15,28:1
Matus, Jean
Pirates of Penzance, The 1936,Ap 21,27:5
Matus, John (Scenic Designer)
My Heart's in the Highlands 1950,F 18,8:4
Great Big Doorstep, The 1950,Mr 18,8:6
Matz, Johanna
Konzert, Das 1968,Mr 25,52:1
Matz, Peter (Composer)
Mike Downstairs 1968,Ap 19,35:1

Matz, Peter (Miscellaneous)
Jamaica 1957,N 1,32:2
Conversation Piece 1957,N 19,38:2
Whoop-Up 1958,D 23,2:7
Beg, Borrow or Steal 1960,F 11,39:4
Sail Away 1961,O 4,48:5
No Strings 1962,Mr 16,24:1
Boys From Syracuse, The 1963,Ap 16,31:1
Matz, Peter (Musical Director)
Once Over Lightly 1955,Mr 16,39:1
Sail Away 1961,O 4,48:5
No Strings 1962,Mr 16,24:1
Matzenauer, Adrienne
Life Begins at 8:40 1934,Ag 28,24:2
Symphony 1935,Ap 27,20:3
Matzenauer, Margaret (Mme)
Vickie 1942,S 23,28:1
Mauban, Maria
Andromaque 1964,F 29,13:2
Mauclair, Ann
Coward, The 1935,Jl 16,24:1
Thy People 1935,Ag 13,20:3
Mauclair, Jacques
Eternal Husband, The 1962,O 18,46:4
Chaises, Les 1970,My 6,49:1
Mauclair, Jacques (Director)
Eternal Husband, The 1962,O 18,46:4
Jeune Fille a Marier, La 1970,My 6,49:1
Lacune, La 1970,My 6,49:1
Chaises, Les 1970,My 6,49:1
Mauclair, Jacques (Playwright)
Eternal Husband, The 1962,O 18,46:4
Maud, Caroline
Comedy of Errors, The 1964,My 21,43:1
Maud, Gladys
Wonderful Thing, The 1920,F 18,9:1
Maude, Arthur
Queen Victoria 1923,N 16,15:1
Maude, Aylmer (Miscellaneous)
Kreutzer Sonata, The 1920,O 3,VI,1:7
Maude, Aylmer (Translator)
Kreutzer Sonata, The 1961,F 16,24:2
Maude, Beatrice
George Washington 1920,Mr 2,9:1
Hamlet 1920,Mr 17,14:2
Married Woman, The 1921,D 26,21:1
World We Live In, The 1922,N 1,16:1
Try It With Alice 1924,Je 24,18:4
Buccaneer, The 1925,O 3,10:2
Tragic 18 1926,O 11,18:2
Light of Asia, The 1928,O 10,32:2
Novice and the Duke, The 1929,D 11,37:2
Mourning Becomes Electra; Hunted, The
    1932,My 10,25:2
Mourning Becomes Electra; Homecoming
    1932,My 10,25:2
Show-Off, The 1932,D 13,25:4
Dodsworth 1934,F 26,20:4
Maude, Cyril
If Winter Comes 1923,Ap 3,26:1
If Winter Comes 1923,Ap 8,VIII,1:1
Aren't We All? 1923,My 22,14:2
Aren't We All? 1923,My 27,VII,1:1
These Charming People 1925,O 7,31:2
These Charming People 1925,O 11,VIII,1:1
Wicked Earl, The 1927,Mr 20,VIII,2:7
Once a Husband 1932,N 20,IX,3:6
Cabbages and Kings 1933,N 22,22:3
Maude, Gillian
Mile Away Murder 1937,Ap 18,XI,1:4
Maude, Joan
Old English 1924,N 9,VIII,2:3
King and Mistress Shore, The 1936,N 6,28:5
King and Mistress Shore, The 1936,N 22,XI,1:3
Maude, Margery
Rivals, The 1930,Mr 14,24:4
Romeo and Juliet 1933,F 3,21:5
Old Foolishness, The 1940,D 21,20:2
Anne of England 1941,O 8,26:2
Plan M 1942,F 21,15:2
Walking Gentleman, The 1942,My 8,26:2
Two Mrs Carrolls, The 1943,Ag 4,14:1
O Mistress Mine 1946,Ja 24,25:2
High Ground, The 1951,F 21,31:2
First Lady 1952,My 29,18:5
Escapade 1953,N 19,40:1
My Fair Lady 1964,My 21,43:2
Diamond Orchid 1965,F 11,44:4
My Fair Lady 1968,Je 14,42:1
Maude, Rosemary
Shoemaker's Prodigious Wife, The 1962,S 2,44:4
Maude-Roxby, Roddy
Knack, The 1964,My 28,42:2
Knack, The 1964,Je 7,II,1:1
Help Stamp Out Marriage 1966,S 30,50:1
Maugery, Claudine
Miracle Worker, The 1961,O 8,II,3:4
Maugham, Robin (Playwright)
Rising Heifer, The 1952,D 24,12:4
Odd Man In 1957,Jl 17,21:3
Enemy 1969,D 19,65:6
Maugham, Somerset (Original Author)
Rain 1922,O 15,VIII,1:8

Maugham, Somerset (Original Author)—Cont
Rain 1922,N 8,18:2
Rain 1922,N 12,VIII,1:1
Rain 1926,O 12,27:1
Painted Veil, The 1931,O 11,VIII,2:4
For Services Rendered 1933,Ap 13,15:5
Moon and Sixpence, The 1933,D 17,IX,4:3
Rain 1935,F 13,24:1
Rain 1935,F 17,VIII,1:1
Theatre 1941,N 13,34:2
Sadie Thompson 1944,N 17,25:2
Jane 1947,Ja 30,19:6
Jane 1947,F 9,II,3:7
Rain 1948,F 2,15:2
Larger Than Life 1950,F 8,33:2
Jane 1952,F 2,10:2
Jane 1952,F 10,II,1:1
Adorable Julia 1954,N 28,II,3:1
Maugham, Somerset (Playwright)
Unknown, The 1920,Ag 10,17:7
Unknown, The 1920,Ag 29,VI,1:4
Circle, The 1921,S 13,12:1
Circle, The 1921,S 18,VI,1:1
East of Suez 1922,S 22,16:3
Our Betters 1923,S 14,22:2
Camel's Back, The 1923,N 4,19:2
Camel's Back, The 1923,N 11,VIII,2:6
Camel's Back, The 1923,N 18,VIII,1:1
Camel's Back, The 1924,F 10,VII,2:4
Constant Wife, The 1926,N 14,VIII,5:1
Constant Wife, The 1926,N 30,26:3
Constant Wife, The 1926,D 12,VIII,3:1
Rain 1927,F 13,VII,4:1
Rain 1927,Mr 3,23:2
Letter, The 1927,Mr 6,VII,4:5
Letter, The 1927,Mr 27,VII,2:6
Constant Wife, The 1927,My 1,VIII,2:7
Letter, The 1927,S 27,30:1
Letter, The 1927,O 2,VIII,1:1
Letter, The 1927,O 30,IX,4:1
Our Betters 1928,F 21,18:2
Our Betters 1928,Mr 4,IX,1:1
Constant Wife, The 1928,My 20,VIII,2:1
Sacred Flame, The 1928,N 20,28:2
Constant Wife, The 1928,D 30,VIII,4:4
Sacred Flame, The 1929,Mr 3,VIII,2:5
Tenth Man, The 1929,Mr 21,29:2
Letter, The 1929,N 17,IX,2:6
Breadwinner, The 1930,O 1,26:3
Breadwinner, The 1930,O 19,IX,4:1
Breadwinner, The 1931,S 23,19:4
Cyclone, Le 1931,O 25,VIII,1:6
For Services Rendered 1932,N 2,23:5
For Services Rendered 1932,N 27,IX,1:3
Mask and the Face, The 1933,My 9,20:2
Sheppey 1933,S 15,22:2
Sheppey 1933,O 1,IX,2:2
Constant Wife, The 1935,Jl 3,20:2
Constant Wife, The 1937,Je 6,XI,1:5
Our Betters 1937,Jl 22,16:2
Circle, The 1938,Ap 19,24:2
Circle, The 1939,Jl 12,17:2
Theatre 1941,O 26,IX,2:3
Theatre 1941,N 13,34:2
Sheppey 1944,Ap 19,27:2
Circle, The 1944,N 19,II,2:4
Circle, The 1946,Mr 17,II,1:3
Our Betters 1946,N 10,II,3:1
Constant Wife, The 1951,D 10,34:3
Constant Wife, The 1951,D 16,II,6:1
Sacred Flame, The 1952,O 8,35:2
Lady Frederick 1970,S 17,57:1
Maughan, Dora
Vaudeville (Palace) 1926,Ag 17,21:2
Vaudeville (Palace) 1928,My 8,25:2
Fine and Dandy 1930,S 7,IX,2:4
Fine and Dandy 1930,S 24,26:1
Vaudeville (Palace) 1931,F 2,23:3
Maughan, Dora (Director)
Hairpin Harmony 1943,O 2,18:5
Maule, Annabel
Gertie Maude 1937,Ag 18,14:5
Maule, Donovan
Havoc 1924,S 2,22:2
Maule, Michael
Merry Widow, The 1957,Ap 11,36:6
Maull, Connie
First Crocus, The 1942,Ja 3,14:6
Maull, Harry
First Crocus, The 1942,Ja 3,14:6
Maulner, Thierry (Playwright)
Maison de la Nuit, La 1953,N 29,II,3:1
Mauloy
Famille Lavolette, La 1926,O 10,VIII,2:1
Trouble, Le 1928,Ap 29,IX,2:3
Nuit, Une 1935,Je 16,X,1:1
Maumaw, Barton
Golden Apple, The 1954,Mr 12,15:2
Maunsell, Charles
Bird in Hand 1929,Ap 5,28:2
Maupassant (Miscellaneous)
Channel Road, The 1929,O 18,24:2

Maupassant, Guy de (Original Author)
Channel Road, The 1929,O 27,IX,1:1
Madame Is Served 1949,F 15,28:1
String 1969,Ap 13,II,1:1
Maupassant, Guy de (Playwright)
Chauve-Souris 1922,O 11,22:2
Mauree, Leta
Polonaise 1945,O 8,20:2
Maurel, Barbara
Mikado, The 1925,Ap 13,25:1
Maurelli, Edward
Deburau 1920,D 24,14:3
Sidewalks of New York 1927,O 4,33:1
See Naples and Die 1929,S 27,30:4
Maurer, Emil (Lighting Director)
Poupees de Paris, Les 1964,My 16,11:1
Maurer, Friedrich
Wozzeck 1966,Ap 6,34:1
Ratten, Die 1966,Ap 13,36:1
Maurer, Peggy
Three Sisters, The 1955,F 26,13:2
Three Sisters, The 1955,Mr 20,II,1:1
Loud Red Patrick, The 1956,O 4,28:1
Maurer, Ralph
White Devil, The 1965,D 7,56:1
Sunset 1966,My 13,34:1
Maurette, Marcelle (Original Author)
Anya 1965,N 30,48:1
Maurette, Marcelle (Playwright)
Anastasia 1954,D 30,13:1
Anastasia 1955,Ja 16,II,1:1
Maurette, Marcelle (Translator)
Madame Capet 1938,O 26,26:2
Maurey, Max (Director)
Mademoiselle Flute 1927,Je 12,VII,2:1
Maurey, Max (Playwright)
Fiole, La 1923,N 20,23:3
Untitled-Play 1928,F 5,VIII,2:1
Ami d'Argentine, Un 1930,N 30,IX,3:3
Maurey, Max (Producer)
Onzieme Commandement 1932,My 15,VIII,2:2
Mauri, Gianfranco
Servant of Two Masters, The 1960,F 24,42:2
Mauri, Glauco
Long Day's Journey Into Night 1956,O 17,40:1
Mauriac, Francois (Original Author)
Egoists, The 1959,O 14,52:2
Mauriac, Francois (Playwright)
Asmodee 1938,Je 12,X,2:3
Asmodee 1939,Mr 12,XI,3:5
Asmodee 1939,My 28,X,1:6
Feu sur la Terre, Le 1950,D 31,II,3:7
Asmodee 1958,Mr 26,42:2
Egoists, The 1959,O 14,52:2
Maurice, Jane
Legend of Leonora, The 1927,Mr 30,22:4
Maurice, Michael (Original Author)
Not in Our Stars 1924,F 10,VII,2:4
Maurice, Rolland
Untitled-Passion Play 1925,Ag 17,8:1
Maurice (Rev Father) (Director)
Veronica's Veil 1931,F 23,36:2
Maurice and Hughes
Good Morning, Dearie 1921,N 2,20:2
Mauricet
Untitled-Revue 1926,N 21,VIII,2:1
Par le Temps Qui Court 1930,O 5,IX,4:3
Maurier, Daphne du (Original Author)
Rebecca 1940,Ap 14,IX,1:6
Maurier, Daphne du (Playwright)
Rebecca 1940,Ap 14,IX,1:6
Maurier, James
Tyrant, The 1930,N 13,33:1
Maurin, Gertrude
Dream Play 1926,Ja 21,18:2
Friend Indeed 1926,Ap 27,22:3
Maurin, Yves-Marie
Pique-Nique en Campagne 1969,My 1,50:1
Maurine and Norva
Houseboat on the Styx, The 1928,D 26,14:3
Mauro, David
Titus Andronicus 1956,D 3,40:2
Beaux' Stratagem, The 1957,Jl 9,25:4
Maurstad, Toralv
Of Love Remembered 1967,F 20,46:5
Maurus, Gerda
Nathan the Wise 1962,Mr 7,29:1
Before Sundown 1962,Mr 14,43:1
Maury, Ludlow
Anne of the Thousand Days 1948,D 9,49:2
Maury, Richard (Original Author)
New Faces of 1962 1962,F 2,25:1
Maury, Richard (Playwright)
Shoestring Revue 1955,Mr 1,22:2
New Faces of 1956 1956,Je 15,32:1
New Faces of 1962 1962,F 2,25:1
Mauser, Susanna (Musical Director)
Sacco-Vanzetti 1969,F 9,78:1
Maverick, Honeyboy
Lid's Off, The 1936,Ap 4,11:6
Mavroyenis, J
Oedipus Tyrannus 1952,N 25,35:2

Mawdesley, Robert
Middle Watch, The 1929,O 17,27:1
Mawson, Elizabeth
H M S Pinafore 1960,S 8,41:1
Mawson, Howard
H M S Pinafore 1960,S 8,41:1
Max, Alan M (Lyricist)
His Majesty the Queen 1926,Mr 9,8:1
Max, Alan M (Playwright)
His Majesty the Queen 1926,Mr 9,8:1
Max, Bernard
Kingdom of God, The 1928,D 21,30:2
Max, Jacqueline
Rebecca 1945,Ja 19,17:2
Max, Jean
Cyclone, Le 1931,O 25,VIII,1:6
Max, Jerome (Playwright)
Exhaustion of Our Son's Love, The 1965,O 19,51:1
Maxey, Billy
Hot Chocolates 1929,Je 21,17:4
Maxey, Ed
Cook for Mr General, A 1961,O 20,39:1
Maxfield, George
Caesar and Cleopatra 1935,Ag 22,21:1
Maxfield, John
Merry Duchess, The 1943,Je 24,25:1
Maxfield, Richard (Miscellaneous)
Marrying Maiden, The 1960,Je 23,18:3
Maxim, John
Grosse Valise, La 1965,D 15,52:1
Maximoff, Patten
Family Portrait 1959,My 6,48:2
Maximowna, Ita (Scenic Designer)
Before Sundown 1962,Mr 14,43:1
Maxine, Lauretta
Loco 1946,O 17,29:2
Maxmen, Mimi (Costume Designer)
Dance of Death, The 1969,My 26,53:1
Macbeth 1969,D 23,25:1
Lady From Maxim's, The 1970,Je 1,41:1
Hamlet 1970,O 19,51:1
Maxon, Eric
Purple Mask, The 1920,Ja 6,18:1
Skylark 1921,Jl 26,10:6
King Lear 1947,F 19,32:2
Merchant of Venice, The 1947,F 24,16:2
Volpone 1947,F 25,32:2
Hamlet 1947,F 27,27:2
Maxon, Norman (Costume Designer)
Trumpets of the Lord 1963,D 23,22:3
Maxon, Richard
My Fair Lady 1968,Je 14,42:1
Maxson, Bobby
Ice Follies 1937,D 22,29:1
Ice Follies 1941,D 2,32:2
Ice Capades 1952,S 12,18:1
Ice Capades 1953,S 11,25:1
Ice Capades 1954,S 16,37:1
Ice Capades 1955,S 15,38:1
Ice Capades 1956,S 13,41:2
Ice Capades 1957,S 5,33:2
Maxson, Dianne
Ice Capades 1957,S 5,33:2
Maxson, Ray
Broadway Whirl, The 1921,Je 9,10:4
Maxson, Ruby
Ice Follies 1937,D 22,29:1
Ice Follies 1941,D 2,32:2
Ice Capades 1952,S 12,18:1
Ice Capades 1953,S 11,25:1
Maxtone-Graham, John (Miscellaneous)
Square Root of Wonderful, The 1957,O 31,40:1
Duel of Angels 1960,Ap 20,42:2
Big Fish, Little Fish 1961,Mr 16,42:2
Night of the Iguana, The 1961,D 29,10:1
Ballad of the Sad Cafe, The 1963,O 31,27:1
Brigadoon 1964,D 24,9:1
Maxwell, Arthur
Ziegfeld Follies 1943,Ap 2,16:2
Lady Says Yes, A 1945,Ja 11,18:5
Lend an Ear 1948,D 17,38:2
Me and Juliet 1953,My 29,17:1
Me and Juliet 1953,Je 7,II,1:1
Maxwell, Bob
Hell'z-A-Splashin' 1959,Je 25,22:2
What Makes Sammy Run? 1964,F 28,19:1
Maxwell, Bob (Director)
Aqua Carnival 1962,Je 29,15:1
Maxwell, Bob (Miscellaneous)
Hell'z-A-Splashin' 1959,Je 25,22:2
Wonder World 1964,My 18,32:1
Maxwell, Carolyn (Costume Designer)
Softly, and Consider the Nearness 1964,My 12,32:1
Maxwell, Charles E
Rose, The 1922,D 30,13:4
They Knew What They Wanted 1939,O 3,19:1
Maxwell, Edwin
Lady of the Lamp, The 1920,Ag 18,6:4
Merton of the Movies 1922,N 14,16:2
Kreutzer Sonata, The 1924,My 15,22:3
Dr David's Dad 1924,Ag 14,10:3
Taps 1925,Ap 15,16:2
Lady of the Rose 1925,My 20,26:4

Maxwell, Edwin—Cont
Easy Come, Easy Go 1925,O 27,20:2
Donovan Affair, The 1926,Ag 31,15:2
Cherry Orchard, The 1928,Mr 6,20:1
Maxwell, Edwin (Director)
Trouper, The 1926,Mr 9,21:1
Maxwell, Elsa
De Luxe 1935,F 24,VIII,3:4
De Luxe 1935,Mr 6,22:2
Maxwell, Elsa (Producer)
Who's Who 1938,Mr 2,16:2
Maxwell, Frank
Dance Night 1938,O 15,20:5
Stop Press 1939,Mr 20,13:2
To What Red Hell 1940,My 5,I,54:8
At the Stroke of Eight 1940,My 21,29:2
First Stop to Heaven 1941,Ja 6,10:7
Stalag 17 1951,My 9,41:2
Maggie 1953,F 19,20:2
South Pacific 1955,My 5,39:5
Wonderful Town 1958,Mr 6,32:4
Maxwell, Gary
Tragical Historie of Doctor Faustus, The
1964,O 6,34:2
Young Master Dante, The 1968,D 31,19:1
Maxwell, James (Playwright)
Daniel Deronda 1969,Ja 11,22:2
Maxwell, Jerry
Student Prince, The 1931,Ja 30,18:1
Maxwell, John
Bunk of 1926 1926,F 17,12:3
Bunk of 1926 1926,Ap 23,25:2
Maxwell, Joseph
Jezebel 1933,D 20,26:3
Maxwell, Kenneth H
Good Woman of Setzuan, The 1970,N 6,51:1
Maxwell, Lester
Child Buyer, The 1962,My 14,35:1
Maxwell, Lou
Ice Capades 1955,S 15,38:1
Maxwell, Marguerite
Lawbreaker, The 1922,F 7,12:1
Manhattan 1922,Ag 16,7:5
Maxwell, Marty
Ice Capades 1955,S 15,38:1
Maxwell, Norma (Miscellaneous)
Wonder World 1964,My 18,32:1
Maxwell, Norma Dean (Choreographer)
Hell'z-A-Splashin' 1959,Je 25,22:2
Maxwell, Pauline
Love Dreams 1921,O 11,22:2
Maxwell, Raymond
Clean Beds 1939,My 26,21:2
Maxwell, Roberta
Allegro 1952,S 18,36:3
Two Gentlemen of Verona 1958,Mr 19,35:1
Much Ado About Nothing 1958,Je 26,22:1
Most Happy Fella, The 1966,My 12,55:1
Twelfth Night 1966,Je 10,51:2
Government Inspector, The 1967,Je 15,55:1
Government Inspector, The 1967,O 28,34:1
Serjeant Musgrave's Dance 1968,Je 16,52:4
Resistible Rise of Arturo Ui, The 1968,Ag 8,25:1
Merton of the Movies 1968,S 26,62:1
Resistible Rise of Arturo Ui, The 1968,D 23,44:1
Henry V 1969,Je 9,57:1
Henry V 1969,Je 15,II,3:1
Much Ado About Nothing 1969,Je 16,57:1
Three Sisters, The 1969,Ag 4,29:1
Three Sisters, The 1969,Ag 10,II,3:1
Whistle in the Dark, A 1969,O 9,55:1
Whistle in the Dark, A 1969,N 9,II,3:1
Henry V 1969,N 11,43:1
All's Well That Ends Well 1970,Je 16,53:1
All's Well That Ends Well 1970,Je 21,II,3:2
Othello 1970,Je 22,43:1
Othello 1970,Je 28,II,1:1
Othello 1970,S 15,51:1
Hay Fever 1970,N 10,55:1
Hay Fever 1970,N 22,II,18:6
Maxwell, Roger
Flashing Stream, The 1939,Ap 11,19:2
Maxwell, Rosalie
Kwamina 1961,O 24,42:1
Maxwell, Sanders
What a Relief 1935,D 14,10:6
Maxwell, Sanders (Composer)
Take It Away 1936,D 15,30:5
Once Over Lightly 1938,D 10,13:4
Once Over Lightly 1938,D 17,10:8
Maxwell, Sanders (Lyricist)
Take It Away 1936,D 15,30:5
Once Over Lightly 1938,D 10,13:4
Once Over Lightly 1938,D 17,10:8
Maxwell, Vera
Triple Crossed 1927,My 6,21:2
Maxwell, W B (Playwright)
Little Theatre Tournament; Last Man In, The
1926,My 6,23:3
Last Man In, The 1930,My 8,32:5
Maxwell, Wayne
Titus Andronicus 1956,D 3,40:2
Kataki 1959,D 16,55:1
Gay Apprentice, The 1960,F 3,27:2

Too Close for Comfort 1960,F 3,27:2
Long Voyage Home, The 1961,D 5,49:1
Whitman Portrait, A 1966,O 12,37:1
Maxwell, William
Blue Monday 1932,Je 3,23:2
Rendezvous 1932,O 13,22:3
Hate Planters 1933,My 26,24:5
Maxwell, Zoe
Merry Wives of Windsor, The 1967,Ag 4,18:1
Maxwell-Conover, Teresa
Social Register, The 1931,N 10,28:2
Maxwells, The
Ice Capades 1952,S 12,18:1
Holiday on Ice 1967,Ag 31,29:2
May, Ada
Lollipop 1924,Ja 22,15:3
Rio Rita 1927,Jl 3,VII,1:1
Cochran's 1930 Revue 1930,Mr 28,22:7
Cochran's 1930 Revue 1930,Ap 13,X,1:6
Vaudeville (Pavilion) 1931,Mr 20,29:3
May, Anthony (Director)
Duet for Three 1966,My 20,41:1
May, Bert
Judy Garland's New Variety Show 1956,S 27,43:2
May, Charles
Happy Town 1959,O 8,49:2
May, Donald
Throng o' Scarlet 1950,F 6,20:5
My 3 Angels 1956,F 4,24:2
May, Dorothy
Babes in Toyland 1930,D 22,17:1
May, Elaine
Evening With Mike Nichols and Elaine May, An
1960,O 10,37:1
May, Elaine (Director)
Third Ear, The 1964,My 29,16:1
Next 1969,F 11,27:1
Adaptation 1969,F 11,27:1
May, Elaine (Playwright)
Evening With Mike Nichols and Elaine May, An
1960,O 10,37:1
Adaptation 1969,F 11,27:1
Adaptation 1969,F 23,II,1:1
Adaptation 1970,Mr 12,46:1
May, Henry
Jezebel 1933,D 20,26:3
Porgy and Bess 1935,O 11,30:2
May, Henry (Miscellaneous)
Page From a Diary 1936,Ja 17,14:6
May, Henry (Producer)
At War With the Army 1949,Mr 9,32:2
May, Henry (Scenic Designer)
Moby Dick 1955,Ap 26,25:3
May, Jack
King Lear 1950,Ag 30,26:2
May, James
Carmen Jones 1946,Ap 8,32:2
Let's Sing Yiddish 1966,N 10,63:1
May, Jean
Tragedy of Nan, The 1920,F 18,9:1
Golden Days 1921,N 2,20:1
Robert E Lee 1923,N 21,23:1
Lazybones 1924,S 23,23:1
Cradle Snatchers 1932,N 17,23:2
May, Jim
Greenwillow 1970,D 8,60:1
May, Julie
All in the Family 1935,Jl 24,20:4
May, Leah
Chiffon Girl, The 1924,F 20,23:2
May, Lilly
Hayride 1954,S 14,24:2
May, Marty
Walk With Music 1940,Je 5,33:2
Best Foot Forward 1941,O 2,28:2
Best Foot Forward 1941,O 26,IX,1:3
Artists and Models 1943,N 6,16:6
Annie Get Your Gun 1946,My 17,14:2
Funzapoppin 1949,Jl 1,16:2
Pardon Our French 1950,O 6,22:4
Vaudeville (Palace) 1952,Mr 12,31:2
Hell'z-A-Splashin' 1959,Je 25,22:2
May, Mitchell (Producer)
Happy Town 1959,O 8,49:2
May, Monica
Taming of the Shrew, The 1956,Ag 11,11:2
Taming of the Shrew, The 1956,Ag 26,II,1:1
Once Around the Block 1956,O 29,34:1
Sweet Bird of Youth 1959,Mr 11,39:2
Tempest, The 1959,D 28,19:2
How to Make a Man 1961,F 3,16:1
Natural Affection 1963,F 2,5:2
May, Olive
Daddy Dumplins 1920,N 23,11:1
Scarlet Man, The 1921,Ag 23,10:3
Endless Chain, The 1922,S 5,21:2
Hell's Bells! 1925,Ja 27,14:2
Enemy, The 1925,O 21,20:1
Triumphant Bachelor, The 1927,S 16,21:1
Parisiana 1928,F 10,26:3
May, Pegge
Earthlight Theater 1970,N 4,38:2

May, Val (Director)
War and Peace 1962,Je 16,10:1
Severed Head, A 1964,O 29,40:1
Killing of Sister George, The 1965,Je 18,28:5
Killing of Sister George, The 1966,O 6,57:1
Measure for Measure 1967,F 15,37:1
Hamlet 1967,F 17,44:1
Romeo and Juliet 1967,F 22,18:1
Portrait of a Queen 1968,F 29,29:1
Mrs Mouse Are You Within? 1968,Jl 8,45:1
They Don't Grow on Trees 1968,D 7,63:1
Conduct Unbecoming 1970,O 13,50:1
Conduct Unbecoming 1970,O 25,II,16:2
May, Vicki
Dionysus in 69 1968,Je 7,35:3
May, Vinita
Slightly Delinquent 1954,O 26,32:5
May, Winston
Happy Faculty, The 1967,Ap 19,50:1
King Lear 1968,Je 3,55:4
Trumpets and Drums 1969,O 13,52:1
Maya, Carmen
Golden Streets, The 1970,Ag 14,21:1
Mayall, Herschel
Great Power, The 1928,S 12,25:1
Mayall, Herschel (Director)
Deep Channels 1929,O 19,22:3
Maybaun, Edith
Topsy and Eva 1924,D 24,11:1
Maybaur, Fedor (Colonel) and His Royal Russian /Balalaika Orchestra
Vaudeville (Palace) 1932,S 12,13:5
Maybee, Allen F
Old King's 1924,Mr 12,19:3
Maybee, Roderick
Bottom of the Cup, The 1927,F 1,24:2
Nigger Rich 1929,S 21,16:7
Roadside 1930,S 27,21:1
Sailor, Beware! 1933,S 29,24:4
Forty-Four Below 1935,Jl 23,24:3
Prologue to Glory 1938,Mr 18,22:2
Sea Dogs 1939,N 7,30:3
Two on an Island 1940,Ja 23,17:2
Land Is Bright, The 1941,O 29,26:2
Walking Gentleman, The 1942,My 8,26:2
Sons and Soldiers 1943,My 5,22:2
Love on Leave 1944,Je 21,23:4
Streets Are Guarded, The 1944,N 21,19:7
Mayberry, Arthur
Pick-Up Girl 1944,My 4,25:2
Mayberry, Robert (Director)
Man Who Never Died, The 1958,N 22,27:2
Maye, Anita
Great Scot! 1965,N 12,56:3
Maye, Billie
Vaudeville (Palace) 1926,O 19,27:5
Vaudeville (Palace) 1927,My 24,23:1
Vaudeville (Palace) 1927,My 31,25:1
Vaudeville (Palace) 1927,Je 7,27:3
Vaudeville (Palace) 1927,Ag 23,29:3
Vaudeville (Palace) 1930,O 20,29:1
Maye, Carolyn
Beautiful Dreamer 1960,D 28,22:1
Tattooed Countess, The 1961,My 4,40:2
Maye, Charlotte
Merry Wives of Windsor, The 1938,Ap 15,22:3
Early to Bed 1943,Je 18,16:2
Maye, Edythe
Hello, Yourself 1928,O 31,28:2
Maye, Fred
Ups-A-Daisy 1928,O 9,34:2
Maye, Lola
Garden of Weeds 1924,Ap 29,12:3
Maye, Nick (Producer)
Shadow of My Enemy, A 1957,D 12,35:4
Mayehoff, Eddie
Rhapsody 1944,N 23,37:2
Concert Varieties 1945,Je 2,10:7
Season in the Sun 1950,S 29,31:2
Season in the Sun 1950,O 8,II,1:1
Visit to a Small Planet 1957,F 8,18:1
Visit to a Small Planet 1957,F 24,II,1:1
Rainy Day in Newark, A 1963,O 23,35:1
Mayer, Charles
Bell for Adano, A 1944,D 7,21:2
Now I Lay Me Down to Sleep 1950,Mr 3,21:2
Springtime Folly 1951,F 27,23:4
Jackknife 1958,S 23,36:2
Mayer, Clementine
Wiener Blut 1964,S 12,14:1
Mayer, Edwin Justus (Director)
Children of Darkness 1930,Ja 8,25:1
Mayer, Edwin Justus (Original Author)
Firebird of Florence 1945,Mr 23,13:4
Mayer, Edwin Justus (Playwright)
Firebrand, The 1924,O 16,33:1
Children of Darkness 1930,Ja 8,25:1
Children of Darkness 1930,Ja 19,VIII,1:1
Firebird of Florence 1945,Mr 23,13:4
Last Love of Don Juan, The 1955,N 24,40:1
Children of Darkness 1958,Mr 1,11:4
Mayer, Ella
Hollywood Pinafore 1945,Je 1,20:1

Mayer, Eugene
Lady of the Lamp, The 1920
Mayer, Hans Bruno (Compose
Big Blow 1938,O 3,11:2
Mayer, Harry (Miscellaneous)
Jimmy 1969,O 24,38:1
Mayer, Jerome (Director)
People on the Hill 1931,S
Noah 1935,F 14,25:2
Good Hunting 1938,N 22,
Lucky Sam McCarver 195
Lullaby 1954,F 4,21:2
Mayer, Jerome (Miscellane
Lucky Sam McCarver 19
Mayer, Jerome (Playwrigh
Goodbye in the Night 1
Mayer, Jerome (Producer
Noah 1935,F 14,25:2
Russet Mantle 1936,Ja
Good Hunting 1938,N
Young Couple Wanted
Lullaby 1954,F 4,21:2
Mayer, John C (Miscelle
Ship Comes in, A 193
Mayer, John C (Produc
Co-Respondent Unkn
Mayer, Lottie (Miscelle
Arabian Nights 1954
Arabian Nights 195!
Mayer, Louise Maria (
Kyrill Reist ins Abe
Mayer, Margery
Medium, The 194£
Mayer, Paul Avila (
Six Characters in !
1961,My 11,43:1
Eternal Triangle 1'
Frying Pan, The 1
Bridal Night, The
Mayer, Paul Avila (
Six Characters in
1963,Mr 11,7:2
Mayer, Ray
Vaudeville (Palac
Vaudeville (Palac
Tattle Tales 1933,
Very Warm for M
Weak Link, The
Louisiana Purchas
Mr Big 1941,O 1,2
Banjo Eyes 1941,D
Hear That Trumpet
Mayer, Ted
Born Yesterday 1946,F
Mayer, Tess
Jimmie 1920,N 18,15:3
Mayer, Thomas (Composer)
Dybbuk, The 1954,O 27,33:6
Mayer, Thomas (Miscellaneous)
Cherry Orchard, The 1955,O 19,38:1
Mayer, Thomas (Musical Director)
Three Sisters, The 1955,F 26,13:2
Italian Straw Hat, The 1957,O 1,37:2
Mayer, Timothy
New York Idea, The 1963,Jl 13,12:2
Mayer, Timothy (Lyricist)
William Had the Words! 1964,Mr 30,36:1
No Hard Feelings 1965,Ap 5,33:8
Mayer, Timothy S (Director)
Measure for Measure 1967,Ag 27,II,4:8
Mayerl, Billy (Composer)
Twenty to One 1935,N 13,24:3
Mayers, Ernestine
Silks and Satins 1920,Jl 16,19:1
Mayers, Wilnette
Porgy and Bess 1935,O 11,30:2
Mayes, Doris
Four Saints in Three Acts 1952,Ap 17,35:1
Mayfair, Mitzi
Ziegfeld Follies 1931,Jl 2,30:5
Vaudeville (Hollywood) 1932,Mr 22,17:5
Take a Chance 1932,N 28,11:2
Calling All Stars 1934,N 22,26:1
Calling All Stars 1934,D 14,28:2
Show Is On, The 1936,N 9,22:2
Show Is On, The 1936,N 15,XI,2:1
Show Is On, The 1936,D 26,14:2
Mayfield, Cleo
Look Who's Here 1920,Mr 3,12:2
Blushing Bride, The 1922,F 7,12:1
Innocent Eyes 1924,My 21,22:2
Right Next to Broadway 1944,F 22,26:2
Mayfield, Julian
Lost in the Stars 1949,O 31,21:2
Lost in the Stars 1949,N 6,II,1:1
Mayfield, Julian (Director)
Big Deal, The 1953,Mr 7,13:6
Mayfield, Julian (Playwright)
417 1961,Mr 6,30:1
Mayfield, Kathryn
Sea Legs 1937,My 19,26:5
Mayfield, Menlo (Lyricist)
Greenwich Villagers, The 1927,Ag 19,20:2

,Ag 19,20:2

1

14,52:1
er)
2,18:1
11,25:1
16,37:1
S 15,38:1
,S 13,41:2
7,S 5,33:2
58,S 4,33:2
959,S 4,12:1
1960,S 1,30:1
y (Miscellaneous)
:s 1957,S 5,33:2
arry (Musical Director)
des 1960,S 1,30:1
, Kate
erboard, The 1920,Ag 20,7:2
kerboard, The 1920,Ag 22,VI,1:2
:ca 1920,O 5,12:2
.ly 38 1921,S 14,22:2
.lleted 1922,My 10,22:4
Madre 1923,D 31,9:6
Wonderful Visit, The 1924,F 13,17:3
Small Timers, The 1925,Ja 28,15:3
Wisdom Tooth, The 1926,F 16,22:2
Father, The 1928,My 12,9:4
Beaux' Stratagem, The 1928,Je 5,20:1
Caravan 1928,Ag 30,13:3
Light of Asia, The 1928,O 10,32:2
Vermont 1929,Ja 9,28:1
Jonesy 1929,Ap 10,32:2
Uncle Vanya 1930,Ap 16,26:5
Uncle Vanya 1930,My 4,XI,1:1
Uncle Vanya 1930,S 23,30:3
Peacock 1932,O 12,27:1
Uncle Tom's Cabin 1933,My 30,13:4
Ticket-of-Leave Man, The 1933,Jl 4,16:4
Joyous Season, The 1934,Ja 30,16:3
Farmer Takes a Wife, The 1934,O 31,17:1
Journey by Night 1935,Ap 7,IX,2:1
Journey by Night, A 1935,Ap 17,26:3
Light Behind the Shadow, The 1936,Ja 21,26:6
Alice Takat 1936,F 11,19:2
Amphitryon 38 1937,Je 24,30:2
Mayhew, Stella
Vaudeville (Palace) 1926,Jl 6,19:3
Lace Petticoat 1927,Ja 5,18:2
Hit the Deck! 1927,Ap 26,32:1
Mrs Bumpstead-Leigh 1929,Ap 2,28:3
So This Is Paris 1930,Ap 27,IX,2:3
Hello Paris 1930,N 17,29:3
Mayhood, Orville (Musical Director)
Blossom Time 1922,O 24,18:2
Maykakofski (Playwright)
Bug 1929,Mr 3,III,3:6
Mayla
Artists and Models 1943,N 6,16:6
Mayleas, Ruth
Lulu 1958,S 30,24:1
Maynar, Frederick
Come Angel Band 1936,F 19,17:1
Maynard, Claire
Bright Honor 1936,S 28,14:1
Maynard, Dorothy
Kissing Time 1920,O 12,18:2
Pigeon, The 1930,O 15,26:2
Maynard, Edwin
Thy Name Is Woman 1920,N 16,19:1
They Never Grow Up 1930,Ap 8,27:1
Maynard, Frederick
Nice People 1921,Mr 3,11:1
Maynard, Gertrude
1931 1931,D 11,34:3
Night Over Taos 1932,Mr 10,25:3
Maynard, Mab
Firebird 1932,N 22,25:2
Lone Valley 1933,Mr 11,18:6
Men in White 1933,S 27,24:2
Maynard, Marjorie (Director)
Goodbye Again 1943,N 10,28:4
Maynard, Paul (Director)
Cradle Song 1955,D 2,32:2
Maynard, Ruth
You Can't Take It With You 1951,Ap 7,8:6
Pygmalion 1952,F 9,11:2
Shadow Years, The 1957,Ja 9,26:2
Smokeweaver's Daughter, The 1959,Ap 15,30:1
Best Man, The 1960,Ap 1,39:1
Oliver 1963,Ja 8,5:5
Mayne, Earl
Glory Hallelujah 1926,Ap 7,26:2
Henry's Harem 1926,S 14,25:2
Ballyhoo 1927,Ja 5,18:1
Crime 1927,F 23,27:3
White Eagle, The 1927,D 27,24:4
Killers 1928,Mr 14,28:3

Mayne, Ferdy
Oh Dad, Poor Dad, Mamma's Hung You in the
Closet and I'm Feelin' So Sad 1961,Jl 6,19:2
Mayne, Frank
As You Were 1920,Ja 28,22:3
Our Nell 1922,D 5,24:1
Mayne, Rutherford
Emperor Jones, The 1927,F 13,VII,4:6
Emperor Jones, The 1927,Ag 28,VII,1:1
Mayne, Rutherford (Playwright)
Troth, The 1920,Je 29,9:2
Peter 1930,Mr 2,IX,4:4
Bridgehead 1934,Je 20,24:1
Bridgehead 1935,Ag 7,22:3
Bridge, The 1939,My 28,X,1:3
Mayo, Ann
Little Miss Charity 1920,S 3,6:3
Mayo, Don
Day Before Spring, The 1945,N 23,27:2
Kiss Me, Kate 1948,D 31,10:3
In the Summer House 1953,D 30,17:1
Mayo, Earl
Jefferson Davis 1936,F 19,17:2
Lost Colony, The 1937,Jl 11,X,2:1
Mayo, Flo
Frank Fay's Vaudeville 1939,Mr 3,20:4
Mayo, George
Tick-Tack-Toe 1920,F 24,11:2
Mayo, Harry
Love Birds 1921,Mr 16,12:1
Daffy Dill 1922,Ag 23,14:5
Vaudeville (Palace) 1926,Ag 3,19:2
Mayo, June
Vaudeville (Palace) 1926,My 11,25:3
Vaudeville (Palace) 1926,N 30,27:2
Mayo, Katherine (Original Author)
India 1928,Ja 17,23:3
Mayo, Lisa
Three Plays of the Sea 1970,Ag 20,39:1
Mayo, Lisa (Miscellaneous)
Parasite, The 1965,D 17,43:2
Mayo, Margaret (Playwright)
Seeing Things 1920,Je 18,19:2
Baby Mine 1927,Ap 3,VIII,2:1
Baby Mine 1927,Je 10,21:2
Mayo, Martha
Cave Girl, The 1920,Ag 19,12:2
June Love 1921,Ap 26,20:1
Lawful Larceny 1922,Ja 3,20:2
Endless Chain, The 1922,S 5,21:2
Robert E Lee 1923,N 21,23:1
Paris Bound 1927,D 28,26:3
Whistling in the Dark 1932,Ja 20,16:6
Truly Valiant 1936,Ja 10,17:3
Mayo, Nick (Director)
Best House in Naples, The 1956,O 27,16:2
Mayo, Nick (Producer)
Best House in Naples, The 1956,O 27,16:2
Mayo, Paul (Scenic Designer)
Baptiste 1952,N 13,34:2
South 1955,My 2,17:4
Mayo, Peg
Home Life of a Buffalo; Hope's the Thing
1948,My 12,34:6
Hope Is the Thing With Feathers; Hope's the
Thing 1948,My 12,34:6
Gone Tomorrow; Hope's the Thing
1948,My 12,34:6
Mary Rose 1951,Mr 5,25:2
Mayo, Phyllis
Make Mine Manhattan 1948,Ja 16,26:2
Mayo, Virginia
Banjo Eyes 1941,D 26,20:2
Mayo, Whitman
Amen Corner, The 1965,Ap 16,35:1
Mayo, Winnifred
Groove Tube 1969,O 12,88:3
Mayo and Morton
Banjo Eyes 1941,D 26,20:2
Mayon, Charles
Rain 1935,Ag 27,23:4
Mayon, Helen
Dope 1926,Ja 4,16:3
Adventure 1928,S 26,25:2
Mrs Gibsons' Boys 1949,My 5,35:2
Mayon, Ruth
Great Temptations, The 1926,My 19,29:1
Good News 1927,Ag 14,VII,2:1
Good News 1927,S 7,35:4
Mayor, Edith
Much Ado About Nothing 1929,N 17,30:4
Mayor, Jerry
Alice in Wonderland 1970,O 9,43:1
Mayors, Robert
Little Black Book, The 1932,D 27,11:2
Wednesday's Child 1934,Ja 17,23:2
Come What May 1934,My 16,23:4
Remember the Day 1935,S 26,19:3
Lend Me Your Ears! 1936,O 6,28:5
But for the Grace of God 1937,Ja 13,21:4
Dance Night 1938,O 15,20:5
Mayr, Annemarie
Untitled-Passion Play 1950,My 19,29:6

Mayr, Guido
Untitled-Passion Play 1922,My 10,21:3
Untitled-Passion Play 1930,My 9,9:1
Untitled-Passion Play 1930,My 12,1:5
Mayr, Klara
Untitled-Passion Play 1934,My 18,12:1
Mayring, Lothar
Passion Play, The 1929,Ap 30,32:1
Passion Play, The 1929,My 5,IX,1:1
Mayro, Jacqueline
Gypsy 1959,My 22,31:6
Cindy 1964,Mr 20,24:1
Who's Who, Baby? 1968,Ja 30,36:1
Just for Love 1968,O 18,40:1
Mays, Gayle
Orange Blossoms 1922,S 20,18:1
Lucky Break 1925,Ag 12,16:2
Mays, Kenneth (Miscellaneous)
Wayward Stork, The 1966,Ja 20,27:1
Mazaud, Emile (Playwright)
Dardamelle 1935,Je 30,X,1:4
Mazelle, Belle
Rose of Stamboul, The 1922,Mr 8,11:2
Mazen, Glenn
Danton's Death 1965,O 22,46:1
Caucasian Chalk Circle, The 1966,Mr 25,35:1
Alchemist, The 1966,O 14,48:1
Yerma 1966,D 9,60:1
Galileo 1967,Ap 14,31:1
Mazes, Des
Peu de Musique, Un 1923,N 6,22:1
Mazette and Lewis
Greenwich Village Follies 1920,Ag 31,7:3
Mazin, Stan
Where's Charley? 1966,My 26,57:1
Mazini, Khalil Oglou
Little Racketeer, The 1932,Ja 19,24:4
Mazo, Ricardo
Road to Happiness, The 1927,My 3,24:1
Romantic Young Lady, The 1927,My 5,30:2
Girl and the Cat, The 1927,My 6,21:2
Blind Heart, The 1927,My 8,30:2
Mazo, Sara
Mascaiada 1929,D 28,10:6
Mazurki, Mike
Oh, Kay! 1960,Ap 18,37:2
Mazursky, Paul
Shoestring '57 1956,N 6,31:1
Mazursky, Paul (Director)
Kaleidoscope 1957,Je 14,20:2
Mazza, Alfred
You're a Good Man, Charlie Brown 1969,N 14,39:1
Mazza, Richard
Tiger Rag, The 1961,F 17,20:2
Mazzei, Vi
Climate of Eden, The 1953,N 21,11:2
Mazzini, Herbert
Show Boat 1956,Je 22,16:1
Show Boat 1957,Je 28,30:2
Ben Franklin in Paris 1964,O 28,52:1
Mazzone, Carlo
Cock-A-Doodle Dandy 1958,N 13,39:2
Mazzone and the Abbott Dancers
Hilarities 1948,S 10,20:2
Meacham, Anne
Long Watch, The 1952,Mr 21,19:5
Ondine 1954,F 19,23:1
Immortal Husband, The 1955,F 15,32:2
Eugenia 1957,Ja 31,20:1
Garden District; Suddenly Last Summer
1958,Ja 8,23:4
Garden District; Suddenly Last Summer
1958,Ja 9,II,1:1
Legend of Lizzie, The 1959,F 10,39:1
Moonbirds 1959,O 10,13:1
Hedda Gabler 1960,N 10,61:1
Lady Akane, The 1960,N 16,51:4
Hedda Gabler 1960,N 25,24:3
Passage to India, A 1962,F 1,23:1
Passage to India, A 1962,F 11,II,1:1
Seagull, The 1964,Ap 6,36:1
Crucible, The 1964,Ap 7,30:2
Wives, The 1965,My 18,35:4
Elizabeth the Queen 1966,N 4,30:1
Rosencrantz and Guildenstern Are Dead
1967,O 17,53:1
In the Bar of a Tokyo Hotel 1969,My 12,54:1
In the Bar of a Tokyo Hotel 1969,My 25,II,5:4
Meacham, Mary Lora
Pied Piper of Hamelin, The 1950,Ap 3,19:2
Meacham, Meribeth (Miscellaneous)
Coriolanus 1965,Je 21,36:1
Meacham, Michael
Macbeth 1962,F 7,32:2
Romeo and Juliet 1962,F 14,39:1
Saint Joan 1962,F 21,57:4
Meacham, Michael (Miscellaneous)
Galileo 1968,D 1,88:4
Meacham, Monte (Director)
Indian Captive, The 1949,Ja 31,15:2
Pied Piper of Hamelin, The 1950,Ap 3,19:2
Dick Whittington and His Remarkable Cat
1950,N 25,10:5

Ali Baba 1951,Mr 27,34:2
Meacham, Paul
Dead End 1935,O 29,17:2
Adding Machine, The 1970,D 5,40:1
Mead, George (Lyricist)
Once Over Lightly 1942,N 20,26:2
Mead, Jack
Conflict 1929,Mr 7,22:4
Jonesy 1929,Ap 10,32:2
Mead, Mary
Charm School, The 1920,Ag 3,12:1
Lawyers' Dilemma, The 1928,Jl 10,17:2
Mead, Shepherd (Original Author)
How to Succeed in Business Without Really Trying
1961,O 16,34:1
How to Succeed in Business Without Really Trying
1966,Ap 21,45:1
Mead, Taylor
Conquest of the Universe 1967,N 27,60:1
Meade, Ada
Elsie 1923,Ap 3,26:1
Meade, Anna
Jeanne d'Arc 1922,Ap 22,9:3
Meade, Caroline
Hamlet 1928,Ja 5,33:2
Caponsacchi 1928,Ja 25,20:3
Henry V 1928,Mr 16,26:2
Light of Asia, The 1928,O 10,32:2
Bonds of Interest, The 1929,O 15,34:2
Meade, Claire
Try and Get It 1943,Ag 3,13:2
What's Up 1943,N 12,24:6
Meade, Dwight A
Easy Street 1924,Ag 15,16:4
Meade, Frances
Rendezvous 1932,O 13,22:3
Meade, Harold B
Many Waters 1929,S 26,27:1
Meade, James
Free Soul, A 1928,Ja 13,26:5
Meade, Joseph
Wings Over Europe 1936,Mr 4,24:7
Meade, Julia
Family Reunion, The 1947,N 29,9:2
Tender Trap, The 1954,O 14,37:2
Double in Hearts 1956,O 17,41:7
Roman Candle 1960,F 4,34:2
Front Page, The 1969,My 12,54:2
Meade, Marie Louise
Jackpot 1944,Ja 14,15:2
Meade, Marion (Miscellaneous)
Alcestis Comes Back 1962,Ap 24,33:1
At Sea 1962,Ap 24,33:1
Meade, Sarah
Plough and the Stars, The 1956,Ap 6,14:1
Meade, Tommy
Breakfast in Bed 1920,F 4,12:1
Crooked Gamblers 1920,Ag 2,12:1
Weather Clear, Track Fast 1927,O 19,24:5
Meader, George
Cat and the Fiddle, The 1931,S 27,VIII,3:1
Cat and the Fiddle, The 1931,O 16,26:4
Champagne, Sec 1933,O 16,20:2
Only Girl, The 1934,My 22,28:2
Chimes of Corneville, The 1934,Je 29,16:2
Taming of the Shrew, The 1935,O 1,27:3
Idiot's Delight 1936,Mr 25,25:2
Amphitryon 38 1937,Je 24,30:2
Amphitryon 38 1937,N 2,32:2
Red Mill, The 1945,O 17,16:2
Meader, William
Shady Lady 1933,Jl 6,26:3
Meadow, Frieda
Life Is a Dream 1962,Ja 15,22:3
Meadow, Leslie
Around the World in 80 Days 1964,Je 29,33:2
Meadows, Jayne
Gazebo, The 1958,D 13,2:7
Meadows, Johnny
Confederacy, The 1958,Jl 3,20:1
Meadows, Margaret
Clubs Are Trumps 1924,O 15,27:1
Meadows, Pauline
Girl From Wyoming, The 1938,O 31,12:1
Meakins, Beth
Criss Cross 1926,O 13,20:2
Black Crook, The 1929,Mr 12,26:5
Mealey, John
Vagabond King, The 1925,S 22,23:3
White Eagle, The 1927,D 27,24:4
O'Flynn, The 1934,D 28,24:1
Vagabond King, The 1935,N 29,22:7
Meaney, Patrick
Louisiana Lady 1947,Je 3,35:2
Mear, Michael (Scenic Designer)
Family Reunion, The 1947,N 29,9:2
Meara, Anne
Silver Tassie, The 1949,Jl 22,16:5
Love in Our Time 1952,O 4,14:3
Montserrat 1954,My 26,34:2
Queen After Death 1956,Mr 13,33:2
Month in the Country, A 1956,Ap 4,23:1
Three Times Three; Box and Cox 1956,My 24,27:2

Meara, Anne—Cont
Three Times Three; How He Lied to Her Husband
1956,My 24,27:2
Three Times Three; Merrye Playe, A
1956,My 24,27:2
Good Woman of Setzuan, The 1956,D 19,41:2
Two Gentlemen of Verona 1957,Jl 23,21:5
Macbeth 1957,Ag 16,11:2
Miss Lonelyhearts 1957,O 4,26:2
As You Like It 1958,Ja 21,33:6
Power of Dreams, A 1958,Mr 11,33:1
Ulysses in Nighttown 1958,Je 6,30:1
Cock-A-Doodle Dandy 1958,N 13,39:2
Puntila 1959,My 15,26:2
Mearian, Mike
Spiro Who? 1969,My 19,55:1
Mears, DeAnn
Decameron, The 1961,Ap 13,32:1
Sound of Silence, A 1965,Mr 9,30:1
Tiny Alice 1969,S 30,42:1
Tiny Alice 1969,O 12,II,9:1
Mears, Edna
Queer People 1934,F 16,16:2
Mears, Elizabeth
Judy 1927,F 8,20:2
Queen at Home 1930,D 30,25:2
Singapore 1932,N 15,24:2
Mears, John Henry (Producer)
Judy 1927,F 8,20:2
Brothers 1928,D 26,14:3
Nut Farm, The 1929,O 15,34:3
Queen at Home 1930,N 2,VIII,3:5
Queen at Home 1930,D 30,25:2
Singapore 1932,N 15,24:2
Mears, Marian
Not so Fast 1923,My 23,18:4
Sweet Seventeen 1924,Mr 18,24:2
Judy Drops In 1924,O 6,24:2
Mears, McDonald
Hasty Heart, The 1959,S 15,45:2
Mears, Stannard (Playwright)
Hello, Lola! 1926,Ja 13,30:1
Mearson, Lyon (Playwright)
People Don't Do Such Things 1927,N 24,28:3
Our Wife 1933,Mr 3,13:2
Measor, Beryl
Separate Tables 1955,My 22,II,1:1
Separate Tables 1956,O 26,33:1
Separate Tables 1957,S 15,II,1:1
Mechler, Evelyn
Sharon's Grave 1961,N 9,39:2
Medalis, Joseph
Galileo 1968,D 1,88:4
Dandelion 1969,D 24,12:1
Medcraft, Russell
Sonny 1921,Ag 17,12:2
Golden Days 1921,N 2,20:1
Medcraft, Russell (Director)
Her Supporting Cast 1931,My 5,33:3
Cradle Snatchers 1932,N 17,23:2
Medcraft, Russell (Playwright)
Cradle Snatchers 1925,S 8,28:2
Buy, Buy Baby 1926,O 8,26:2
Cradle Snatchers 1932,N 17,23:2
Medford, Donald (Producer)
Cry of the Peacock 1950,Ap 12,33:2
Medford, Kay
Paint Your Wagon 1951,N 13,32:2
Maya 1953,Je 10,35:1
Little Clay Cart, The 1953,Jl 1,25:1
Lullaby 1954,F 4,21:2
Black-Eyed Susan 1954,D 24,7:5
Almost Crazy 1955,Je 21,37:1
Wake Up, Darling 1956,My 3,34:2
Hole in the Head, A 1957,Mr 1,15:1
Hole in the Head, A 1957,Mr 10,II,1:1
Carousel 1957,S 12,38:2
Handful of Fire 1958,O 2,45:3
Bye Bye Birdie 1960,Ap 15,13:4
In the Counting House 1962,D 15,5:5
Heroine, The 1963,F 21,5:5
Pal Joey 1963,My 30,21:1
Heroine, The 1963,Je 16,II,1:1
Funny Girl 1964,Mr 27,15:1
Don't Drink the Water 1966,N 18,37:1
Don't Drink the Water 1966,D 25,II,1:1
Medico, Michael Del
I Dreamt I Dwelt in Bloomingdale's 1970,F 13,26:1
Medina, Benigno
Top-Notchers 1942,My 30,8:5
Medina, Christopher
Golden Streets, The 1970,Ag 14,21:1
Medina, Manuel
Cabalgata 1949,Jl 8,14:2
Medina, Patricia
Calculated Risk 1962,N 1,35:1
Medinets, Al
Oklahoma! 1958,Mr 8,15:2
Medlen, Barbara Ann
Shunned 1960,D 21,39:1
Medley and Dupree
Vaudeville (Palace) 1928,F 7,30:5
Vaudeville (Palace) 1928,Ap 17,26:2

Medlin, Janet
  Sweethearts 1947,Ja 22,31:2
Medlinsky, Harvey
  Time to Go 1960,Mr 23,33:1
Medlinsky, Harvey (Miscellaneous)
  Time to Go 1960,Mr 23,33:1
  Coggerers, The 1960,Mr 23,33:1
  Barefoot in the Park 1963,O 24,36:2
  Luv 1964,N 12,43:1
  Odd Couple, The 1965,Mr 11,36:1
  There's a Girl in My Soup 1967,O 19,58:1
  Plaza Suite; Visitor From Hollywood
    1968,F 15,49:1
  Plaza Suite; Visitor From Forest Hills
    1968,F 15,49:1
  Plaza Suite; Visitor From Mamaroneck
    1968,F 15,49:1
Mednick, Murray (Playwright)
  Sand 1967,Mr 26,II,1:2
  Hawk, The 1968,Ap 18,54:1
Medoff, David
  Love for Sale 1936,Ja 24,14:2
  Voice of Israel, The 1948,O 26,40:2
  Hershel, The Jester 1948,D 14,39:2
Medoff, Samuel (Composer)
  Berl and Shmerl Corporation 1934,Ap 2,12:5
Medrande, Doro
  Fulton of Oak Falls 1937,Ja 2,15:3
Medvedev, Mikhail
  Kremlin Chimes 1965,F 25,23:1
Medwall, Henry (Playwright)
  Fulgens and Lucrece 1936,Mr 24,26:5
Medwin, Michael (Miscellaneous)
  Keep It in the Family 1967,S 28,59:1
Medwin, Michael (Producer)
  Joe Egg 1968,F 2,26:1
Mee, Kirk
  King Lear 1964,Jl 23,18:1
  Henry VI, Part I 1964,Jl 23,18:1
  Merchant of Venice, The 1964,Jl 23,18:1
Meech, Gaylord
  Golem, The 1959,F 26,38:2
Meech, Owen
  Sun-Up 1923,My 25,28:1
  Assumption of Hannele, The 1924,F 16,16:2
  Small Timers, The 1925,Ja 28,15:3
  Lally 1927,F 9,16:3
  Jacob Slovak 1927,O 6,28:4
  Merry Wives of Windsor, The 1928,Mr 20,20:1
  Beaux' Stratagem, The 1928,Je 5,20:1
  Becky Sharp 1929,Je 4,29:1
  Inspector General, The 1930,D 24,19:2
  Alchemist, The 1931,Je 5,27:1
  Reunion in Vienna 1931,N 17,31:1
Meegan, Thomas
  Samson and Delilah 1920,N 18,18:1
  Minick 1924,S 25,20:1
  Canary Dutch 1925,S 9,22:1
  Brothers Karamazov, The 1927,Ja 4,20:1
  Salvation 1928,F 1,31:1
Meehan, Aileen
  No Other Girl 1924,Ag 14,10:4
  June Days 1925,Ag 7,12:5
  Kitty's Kisses 1926,My 7,12:2
Meehan, Danny
  Whoop-Up 1958,D 23,2:7
  Ping-Pong 1959,Ap 17,22:1
  O, Oysters! 1961,Ja 31,23:1
  Smiling the Boy Fell Dead 1961,Ap 20,28:1
  Thracian Horses, The 1961,S 28,58:2
  Funny Girl 1964,Mr 27,15:1
  Ben Bagley's New Cole Porter Revue
    1965,D 23,20:1
Meehan, Danny (Miscellaneous)
  O, Oysters! 1961,Ja 31,23:1
Meehan, Elva
  Friday Night; River, The 1965,F 9,42:5
Meehan, Harry
  Naughty-Naught '00 1937,Ja 25,23:2
  Naughty-Naught ('00) 1937,Jl 13,22:3
  Fireman's Flame, The 1937,O 11,26:2
  Knickerbocker Holiday 1938,O 20,26:2
  American Jubilee 1940,My 13,20:5
  Johnny on the Spot 1942,Ja 9,24:2
  Up in Central Park 1945,Ja 29,17:2
  Up in Central Park 1947,My 20,29:2
Meehan, John
  Friars Club Frolic 1921,Je 13,16:2
  Song and Dance Man, The 1924,Ja 1,21:2
  Ringside 1928,Ag 30,13:2
Meehan, John (Director)
  Home Towners, The 1926,Ag 24,19:3
  Yellow 1926,S 22,30:1
  Bless You, Sister 1927,D 27,24:5
  Lady for a Night, A 1928,Ap 17,26:4
Meehan, John (Playwright)
  Barnum Was Right 1923,Mr 13,19:3
  Tantrum, The 1924,My 18,VII,2:4
  Tantrum, The 1924,S 5,20:2
  Bluffing Bluffers 1924,D 23,17:2
  Bless You, Sister 1927,D 27,24:5
  Lady Lies, The 1928,N 11,X,2:4
  Lady Lies, The 1928,N 27,36:2

Meehan, John Jr
  Talk About Girls 1927,Je 15,31:3
Meehan, John Jr (Playwright)
  Rosalinda; Fledermaus, Die 1942,O 29,26:5
  Helen Goes to Troy 1944,Ap 25,17:2
  Helen Goes to Troy 1944,Ap 30,II,1:1
Meehan, Leighton
  Mystery Ship, The 1927,Mr 15,28:2
Meehan, Mary
  Yellow 1926,S 22,30:1
Meehan, Michael
  Slightly Scandalous 1944,Je 14,16:2
Meehan, William
  Headquarters 1929,D 5,32:4
Meehan's Canines
  Vaudeville (Palace) 1926,Mr 16,22:2
Meek, Barbara
  Brother to Dragons 1968,D 8,86:1
  Wilson in the Promise Land 1970,Ja 11,78:1
  Wilson in the Promise Land 1970,My 27,41:1
Meek, Donald
  Hottentot, The 1920,Mr 2,9:1
  Little Old New York 1920,S 9,9:2
  Six-Cylinder Love 1921,Ag 26,8:2
  Tweedles 1923,Ag 14,10:1
  Potters, The 1923,D 10,21:4
  Potters, The 1923,D 16,IX,1:1
  Easy Terms 1925,S 23,22:2
  Fool's Bells 1925,D 24,8:3
  Love 'Em and Leave 'Em 1926,F 4,20:4
  Shelf, The 1926,S 28,31:1
  Spread Eagle 1927,Ap 5,30:2
  Ivory Door, The 1927,O 19,24:5
  Mr Moneypenny 1928,O 17,26:2
  Jonesy 1929,F 24,IX,4:1
  Jonesy 1929,Ap 10,32:2
  Arms and the Man 1929,Ag 13,23:4
  Broken Dishes 1929,N 6,28:3
  After Tomorrow 1930,Ag 10,VIII,2:3
  Oh, Promise Me 1930,N 25,31:1
  After Tomorrow 1931,Ag 27,22:4
  Take My Tip 1932,Ap 12,25:2
Meek, Walter
  Marching By 1932,Mr 4,17:1
Meek, William
  Good Boy 1928,S 6,23:2
Meeker, Douglas
  Ruy Blas 1957,D 14,16:3
Meeker, Elinor
  Black Crook, The 1929,Mr 12,26:5
Meeker, George
  Judy Drops In 1924,O 6,24:2
  Lady's Virtue, A 1925,N 24,28:2
  Buy, Buy Baby 1926,O 8,26:2
  Judy 1927,F 8,20:2
  Back Here 1928,N 27,36:3
  Conflict 1929,Mr 7,22:4
  Dread 1929,O 27,IX,2:1
Meeker, Jess (Miscellaneous)
  Seventeen 1951,Je 22,16:6
  Seventeen 1951,Jl 1,II,9:5
Meeker, Leward
  Anna Ascends 1920,S 23,14:1
  Drifting 1922,Ja 3,20:3
Meeker, Ralph
  Strange Fruit 1945,N 30,18:6
  Cyrano de Bergerac 1946,O 9,33:2
  Cyrano de Bergerac 1947,Ja 17,27:2
  Mister Roberts 1948,F 19,27:2
  Streetcar Named Desire, A 1949,Je 12,II,1:1
  Picnic 1953,F 20,14:7
  Picnic 1953,Mr 1,II,1:1
  Cloud 7 1958,F 15,15:2
  Something About a Soldier 1962,Ja 5,36:2
  After the Fall 1964,Ja 24,18:1
  But for Whom Charlie 1964,Mr 13,42:2
  Mrs Dally 1965,S 25,5:7
Meekins, Mildred
  Natural Man 1941,My 8,20:4
Meenan, John
  Journey by Night, A 1935,Ap 17,26:3
Meer, Cassie (Miscellaneous)
  Sharon's Grave 1961,N 9,39:2
Meer, Cassie (Producer)
  School for Wives 1957,Je 20,23:4
  Bonds of Interest, The 1958,My 7,43:1
Meer, June
  Inside Story 1942,O 30,22:2
Meeres, Paul
  Constant Sinner, The 1931,S 15,30:1
Meers, Thelma
  Blackberries of 1932 1932,Ap 5,27:5
Meersman, Peter
  Cradle Will Rock, The 1964,N 9,40:4
Meffre, Armand
  Three Musketeers, The 1968,Je 26,43:1
Megaw, Harry W
  It's the Valet 1933,D 15,25:4
  Fiesta 1933,D 16,12:2
Megley, Macklin (Director)
  Forbidden Melody 1936,N 3,33:1
Megley, Macklin (Miscellaneous)
  Who's Who 1938,Mr 2,16:2

Meglup, Henry
  Beggar on Horseback 1924,F 13,17:2
Megna, Ave Maria
  Morning Sun 1963,O 7,36:2
Megna, John
  Greenwillow 1960,Mr 9,38:1
  Greenwillow 1960,Mr 20,II,1:1
  All the Way Home 1960,D 1,42:1
  All the Way Home 1960,D 18,II,3:1
  All the Way Home 1960,D 27,26:7
Mego, Joe
  Dear Judas 1947,O 6,26:4
  Devil's Disciple, The 1950,Ja 26,23:2
Megrew, Miss
  Stella Brady 1931,O 11,VIII,4:3
Megrue, Roi Cooper (Playwright)
  Honors Are Even 1921,Ag 11,8:2
Mehaffey, Harry
  Little A 1947,Ja 16,31:2
  Design For A Stained Glass Window
    1950,Ja 24,26:2
  His and Hers 1954,Ja 8,18:2
  Four Winds 1957,S 26,21:2
Mehan, Dodd
  Ladies Don't Lie 1929,O 11,36:3
  Venetian Glass Nephew, The 1931,F 24,26:3
Mehegan, John (Composer)
  Traveling Lady 1954,O 28,45:2
Mehegan, John (Miscellaneous)
  Orpheus Descending 1957,Mr 22,28:1
Mehegan, John (Musical Director)
  Traveling Lady 1954,O 28,45:2
Mehl, Brynar
  Annie Get Your Gun 1966,Je 1,42:2
Mehlman, George (Miscellaneous)
  Cocktails of 1934 1934,My 5,22:1
Mehlman, Lily
  Iron Flowers 1933,Je 13,22:2
Mehlmann, Lily (Choreographer)
  Life and Death of an American 1939,My 20,11:2
Mehr, Rachel (Costume Designer)
  King of the Whole Damn World 1962,Ap 16,32:2
Mehring, Walter (Playwright)
  Merchant of Berlin, The 1929,O 27,IX,4:1
Mehrmann, Helen
  Shannons of Broadway, The 1927,S 27,30:4
  That's Gratitude 1930,S 12,28:1
  That's Gratitude 1930,S 21,IX,1:1
  That's Gratitude 1932,Je 17,24:3
Mehta, Xerxes (Director)
  Julius Caesar 1962,My 12,14:1
Mehta, Xerxes (Producer)
  Julius Caesar 1962,My 12,14:1
Mehta, Xerxes (Scenic Designer)
  Julius Caesar 1962,My 12,14:1
Meier, Charles
  Titus Andronicus 1956,D 3,40:2
  Shadow Years, The 1957,Ja 9,26:2
Meier, Charles (Director)
  Night of the Auk 1963,My 22,35:2
Meier, Charles (Producer)
  Night of the Auk 1963,My 22,35:2
Meier, Joseph
  Passion Play, The 1929,Ap 30,32:1
Meier, June
  Give Us This Day 1933,O 28,20:6
  Let Freedom Ring 1935,N 7,26:2
Meier, Lee
  Hamlet 1954,Ap 24,15:2
Meiers, Hal
  City of Kings 1949,F 18,27:2
  Right You Are (If You Think You Are)
    1950,Je 29,37:2
Meiggs, Amanda
  Young and Beautiful, The 1959,My 29,13:1
Meighan, James
  Montmartre 1922,F 14,20:1
  God of Vengeance, The 1922,D 20,22:5
  Antony and Cleopatra 1924,F 20,22:1
  All God's Chillun Got Wings 1924,My 16,22:3
  All God's Chillun Got Wings 1924,Ag 19,9:1
  Saint, The 1924,O 13,20:3
  S S Glencairn 1924,N 4,31:4
  Paolo and Francesca 1924,D 3,24:2
  Diff'rent 1925,F 11,19:3
  Michel Auclair 1925,Mr 5,23:1
  Love for Love 1925,Ap 1,21:2
  Hamlet 1925,N 10,23:1
  My Maryland 1927,S 13,37:2
  These Few Ashes 1928,O 31,28:1
  Octoroon, The 1929,Mr 13,28:3
  Under the Gaslight 1929,Ap 3,27:1
  Privilege Car 1931,Mr 4,33:1
Meigs, Ben
  Holy Terror, A 1925,S 29,31:2
Meigs, Thomas
  Emperor Jones, The 1945,Ja 17,18:4
Meilhac, Henri
  Carmen Jones 1946,Ap 8,32:2
Meilhac, Henri (Original Author)
  Carmen Jones 1943,D 19,II,9:1
Meilhac, Henri (Playwright)
  Perichole, La 1926,D 29,24:4

Meilhac, Henri (Playwright)—Cont

Blue Beard 1929,Jl 7,VIII,2:1
Fledermaus, Die 1929,Jl 14,IX,2:1
Fair Helen 1931,Ag 30,VIII,2:1
Fair Helen 1932,Jl 17,IX,1:2
Carmen Jones 1943,D 3,26:2
Carmen Jones 1945,My 3,26:5
Carmen Jones 1959,Ag 18,25:1
Vie Parisienne, La 1964,Mr 11,34:2

Meiman, Marian
Trees Die Standing, The 1969,O 13,52:1

Meinert, Arthur C
Night of January 16 1935,D 16,22:5

Meinhard, Carl (Playwright)
Johannes Kreisler 1922,D 25,20:3

Meinrad, Josef
Professor Bernhardi 1968,Mr 20,38:1
Jux Will Er Sich Machen, Einen 1968,Ap 3,41:1

Meinrad, Josef (Director)
Konzert, Das 1968,Mr 25,52:1

Meirhold (Director)
Woe to Wit 1936,S 13,X,1:1

Meisel, Bella
Golden Ring, The 1930,F 1,14:7
Motke From Slobodke 1930,Ap 12,23:3

Meisel, Hyman
One Life for Another 1920,D 18,11:2

Meisel, Kurt
Professor Bernhardi 1968,Mr 20,38:1

Meisel, Kurt (Director)
Professor Bernhardi 1968,Mr 20,38:1

Meisel, Kurt (Producer)
Wall, The 1961,N 9,40:3

Meiser, Edith
Fata Morgana 1924,Mr 4,16:3
Guardsman, The 1924,O 14,23:1
Garrick Gaieties 1925,My 18,12:2
Chief Thing, The 1926,Mr 23,24:2
Garrick Gaieties 1926,My 11,25:2
Peggy-Ann 1926,D 28,16:3
Vaudeville (Palace) 1928,F 7,30:5
Airways, Inc 1929,F 21,30:5
Garrick Gaieties 1930,Je 5,29:2
Greater Love 1931,Mr 3,39:1
He 1931,S 22,33:1
Woman's a Fool-To Be Clever, A 1938,O 19,18:6
Strangler Fig, The 1940,My 7,31:2
Jupiter Laughs 1940,S 10,27:1
Let's Face It 1941,O 30,26:2
Mexican Hayride 1944,Ja 29,9:6
Round Trip 1945,My 30,16:4
Rich Full Life, The 1945,N 10,9:2
I Gotta Get Out 1947,S 26,27:2
Getting Married 1951,My 14,28:5
Magic and the Loss, The 1954,Ap 10,10:3
Carefree Tree, The 1955,O 12,37:2
King John 1956,Je 28,33:5
Measure for Measure 1956,Je 29,16:1
Unsinkable Molly Brown, The 1960,N 4,28:1
Murder in the Cathedral 1966,Je 21,38:1
Comedy of Errors, The 1968,F 28,40:2

Meiser, Edith (Director)
Double Dummy 1936,N 12,30:1

Meiser, Edith (Playwright)
Strangler Fig, The 1940,My 7,31:2

Meisler, Bess
Partition 1948,O 29,31:2

Meisner, Sanford
Prunella; Love in a Garden 1926,Je 16,23:3
Juarez and Maximilian 1926,O 12,31:1
Four Walls 1927,S 20,33:1
Marco Millions 1928,Ja 10,28:2
Volpone 1928,Ap 10,32:1
Marco Millions 1930,Mr 4,24:4
Volpone 1930,Mr 11,24:5
Gods of the Lightning 1931,F 19,21:4
1931 1931,D 11,34:3
Night Over Taos 1932,Mr 10,25:3
American Dream; 1933 1933,F 22,24:5
Men in White 1933,S 27,24:2
Gold Eagle Guy 1934,N 29,33:4
Awake and Sing! 1935,F 20,23:2
Paradise Lost 1935,D 10,31:5
Case of Clyde Griffiths 1936,Mr 14,10:4
Johnny Johnson 1936,N 20,26:3
All the Living 1938,Mr 25,14:4
Rocket to the Moon 1938,N 25,18:2
Awake and Sing! 1939,Mr 8,18:2
Night Music 1940,F 23,18:2
They Should Have Stood in Bed 1942,F 14,18:5
Embezzled Heaven 1944,N 1,20:2
Whole World Over, The 1947,Mr 28,28:2
Crime and Punishment 1947,D 23,29:3
Bird Cage, The 1950,F 23,32:2
Cold Wind and the Warm, The 1958,D 9,55:1

Meisner, Sanford (Director)
Waiting for Lefty 1935,F 11,14:5
Criminals, The 1941,D 22,24:3
Playboy of Newark, The 1943,Mr 20,11:2

I'll Take the High Road 1943,N 10,28:3
Listen Professor! 1943,D 23,22:1
Time of Your Life, The 1955,Ja 20,34:1
Time of Your Life, The 1955,Ja 30,II,1:1

Meisner, Sanford (Playwright)
Group Theatre Sketches 1935,F 11,14:5

Meisner, Vicki
Nathan the Wise 1962,Mr 23,29:1

Meister, Barbara
Mikado, The 1959,O 2,24:1
Pirates of Penzance, The 1960,O 7,29:1
Mikado, The 1961,Ja 18,26:1
Gondoliers, The 1961,Ja 26,33:2
Most Happy Fella, The 1966,My 12,55:1
Guys and Dolls 1966,Je 9,55:2

Meister, Fred (Choreographer)
Wiener Blut 1964,S 12,14:1

Meister, Philip (Director)
Breaking Wall, The 1960,Ja 26,27:5
Hop, Signor! 1962,My 8,45:2
Happy Ending 1965,N 16,56:1
Day of Absence 1965,N 16,56:1

Meister, Philip (Producer)
Homeward Look, The 1954,Je 4,26:2
Breaking Wall, The 1960,Ja 26,27:5
Hop, Signor! 1962,My 8,45:2

Meitz, Millie
Shoemaker and the Peddler, The 1960,O 15,27:4

Meizel, Herman
Andersh; New Worlds 1922,S 26,18:2

Mejia, Carlos
Love Call, The 1927,O 25,33:1

Mekler, Gene
Cyanamide 1954,Mr 26,17:6

Melad, Ajan (Miscellaneous)
Narrow Road to the Deep North 1969,D 2,64:1

Meland, Gregory C (Director)
Two Times One; Last Straw, The 1970,Ap 5,76:4

Melanos, Jack
Capacity for Wings 1957,Ja 10,25:2

Melanos, Jack (Miscellaneous)
Capacity for Wings 1957,Ja 10,25:2

Melato, Maria
Daughter of Iorio 1927,S 12,6:4

Melburn, Arline
Nightingale, The 1927,Ja 4,20:4

Melcarth, Edward (Scenic Designer)
Tartuffe 1957,O 9,39:1

Melcher, Edward De S
Gentlemen, the Queen 1927,Ap 23,14:3

Melcher, Edward De S (Playwright)
Forty-Four Below 1935,Jl 23,24:3

Melcher, Marguerite F (Playwright)
Rose in the Wilderness 1949,Ja 5,21:2

Melcher, Martin (Producer)
Perfect Setup, The 1962,O 25,47:1

Melchior, Lauritz
Vaudeville (Palace) 1952,F 27,22:2
Arabian Nights 1954,Je 25,15:2
Arabian Nights 1955,Je 24,16:1

Meldegg, Stephan (Miscellaneous)
Ecole des Femmes, L' 1961,Ap 28,23:1

Meldon, Austin
Katie Roche 1937,O 4,17:4
Far-Off Hills, The 1937,O 12,30:4
In the Train 1937,N 22,14:5
Juno and the Paycock 1937,D 7,32:5
Drama at Inish 1937,D 14,33:2
Devil Came From Dublin, The! 1955,Je 3,27:2

Meldrum, Margaret
Ice Follies 1961,Ja 11,25:2
Ice Follies 1962,Ja 10,24:6

Meldrum, Marlene
Ice Follies 1961,Ja 11,25:2
Ice Follies 1962,Ja 10,24:6

Meldrum Twins
Ice Follies 1960,Ja 13,20:1

Mele, Fred (Musical Director)
Ca. . . C'Est Paris 1927,F 6,VII,4:1

Mele, Louise
Princess April 1924,D 2,23:2

Melfi, Leonard (Miscellaneous)
Oh! Calcutta! 1969,Je 18,33:1

Melfi, Leonard (Playwright)
Birdbath 1966,Ap 12,43:1
Times Square 1968,Ja 27,16:3
Collision Course; Stars and Stripes 1968,My 9,55:2
Night 1968,D 8,II,5:4
Oh! Calcutta! 1969,Je 29,II,1:7

Melfo, Frank
Apollo of Bellac, The 1957,Ap 10,39:1
Virtuous Island, The 1957,Ap 10,39:1

Melford, Austin (Lyricist)
Optimists, The 1928,Ja 31,28:2

Melford, Austin (Playwright)
Dare Devil, The 1924,F 3,VII,1:4
Optimists, The 1928,Ja 31,28:2
Ladies' Night 1933,N 19,IX,3:7

Melford, Jack
Flirting 1923,My 31,12:5
Antony and Cleopatra 1951,D 21,22:2

Meli, Samuel
Shorty 1948,N 14,I,70:6

Melia, Venti (Costume Designer)
Every Other Evil 1961,Ja 23,20:2

Melinand, Monique
Ecole des Femmes, L'; School for Wives 1951,Mr 19,22:1

Melkonian, Arax
Echmiadzin 1946,O 21,27:3

Mell, Joseph
Tenth Man, The 1967,N 9,54:1

Mellas, Spiro (Playwright)
Goats, The 1923,N 4,VIII,2:7
House Divided, The 1923,N 12,14:1

Mellblom, Marnie
Cradle of Willow, A 1961,D 16,20:2

Mellencamp, Emma (Costume Designer)
Third Person 1955,D 30,13:4

Mellencamp, Robert (Lighting Director)
Third Person 1955,D 30,13:4

Mellencamp, Robert (Scenic Designer)
Third Person 1955,D 30,13:4

Meller, Harro
Candle in the Wind 1941,O 23,26:2
Russian People, The 1942,D 30,17:2
Shuffle Along 1952,My 9,20:5

Meller, Harro (Playwright)
No Tears for Tony 1954,Je 3,32:6

Meller, Miss (Playwright)
Lieutenant Comma 1932,N 13,IX,3:7

Meller, Raquel
Raquel Meller 1926,Ap 15,24:1
Untitled-One Woman Show 1926,Ap 25,VIII,1:1
Raquel Meller 1926,O 26,25:1

Meller, Tina
Wake Up and Dream 1929,Ap 14,X,1:8
Wake Up and Dream 1929,D 31,14:3
Wake Up and Dream 1930,Ja 12,9:1
Wake Up and Dream 1930,Ja 12,VIII,1:1

Mellish, Fuller
Light of the World, The 1920,Ja 7,17:1
Genius and the Crowd 1920,S 7,20:1
Rosa Machree 1922,Ja 10,15:2
Madame Pierre 1922,F 16,11:1
On the Stairs 1922,S 26,18:2
Merchant of Venice, The 1922,D 22,13:1
Dancers, The 1923,O 18,17:2
What Price Glory 1924,S 6,14:3
Student Prince, The 1924,D 3,25:3
Black Boy 1926,O 7,30:2
Peggy-Ann 1926,D 28,16:3
My Maryland 1927,S 13,37:2
Present Arms 1928,Ap 27,16:2
Mrs Bumpstead-Leigh 1929,Ap 2,28:3
Traitor, The 1930,My 3,23:4
I Love an Actress 1931,S 18,29:2
Border-Land 1932,Mr 30,15:5
Other One, The 1932,O 4,26:3
Dark Hours, The 1932,N 15,24:2
Chinese Nightingale, The 1934,O 6,20:4
Living Dangerously 1935,Ja 14,10:3
Journey by Night, A 1935,Ap 17,26:3
Woman of Destiny, A 1936,Mr 3,25:2

Mellish, Harold
Peggy-Ann 1926,D 28,16:3

Mellish, Mary
Natja 1925,F 17,19:2

Mellish, Vera Fuller
Genius and the Crowd 1920,S 7,20:1
Dancers, The 1923,O 18,17:2
Shall We Join the Ladies? 1925,Ja 14,19:1
Ladies Leave 1929,O 2,28:3
Napi 1931,Mr 12,22:5
Cynara 1931,N 3,31:1
Within the Gates 1934,O 23,23:1
Puritan, The 1936,Ja 24,14:3
Grey Farm 1940,My 4,12:7
Our Town 1944,Ja 11,24:5
Sheppey 1944,Ap 19,27:2
Town House 1948,S 24,31:2
Small Hours, The 1951,F 16,22:1
Fancy Meeting You Again 1952,Ja 15,23:2
Men of Distinction 1953,My 1,18:4
Solid Gold Cadillac, The 1953,N 6,24:2

Mello, Al (Choreographer)
Lovely Ladies, Kind Gentlemen 1970,D 29,38:1

Mello, Al (Miscellaneous)
Hit the Deck 1960,Je 24,32:1

Mellon, Hyacinth
Diamond Lil 1948,N 30,33:2

Melloni, Vittorio
Venetian Twins, The 1968,My 29,23:1

Mellor, James
Twelfth Night 1958,D 10,54:2
Hamlet 1958,D 17,2:7
Persecution and Assassination of Marat As
  Performed by the Inmates of the Asylum of
  Charenton Under the Direction of the Marquis de
  Sade, The 1965,D 28,35:1

Mellor, Kenneth (Scenic Designer)
Measure for Measure 1969,Je 13,41:3

Mellow, Stephen (Producer)
Education of H*Y*M*A*N K*A*P*L*A*N, The 1968,Ap 5,57:1
How to Steal an Election 1968,O 14,56:1

Melly, Andree
Mixed Doubles 1969,Ap 12,43:2
Melman, Marian
Mirele Efros 1967,O 20,55:1
Mother Courage 1967,N 17,55:1
Mirele Efros 1969,D 26,41:1
Melmud, Helen
Last Torture, The 1927,Ja 13,28:4
Melnick, Daniel (Miscellaneous)
Royal Hunt of the Sun, The 1965,O 27,36:2
Melnick, Daniel (Producer)
Kelly 1965,F 8,28:2
All in Good Time 1965,F 19,25:1
Brief Lives 1967,D 19,60:4
Melodee Four
Yeah-Man 1932,My 27,27:3
Melody, Charles
Our Town 1944,Ja 11,24:5
Melody, Deanna
Annie Get Your Gun 1966,Je 1,42:2
Meloney, William Brown (Producer)
Outrageous Fortune 1943,N 4,28:5
Doctors Disagree 1943,D 29,15:2
Soldier's Wife 1944,O 5,18:6
Hallams, The 1948,Mr 5,18:2
Melrose, Bert
Patience 1933,My 23,22:6
Mels, Irving
Blossom Time 1921,S 30,10:1
Mels and Hiles
Passing Show of 1921, The 1920,D 30,16:2
Melson, Ben
Subway, The 1929,Ja 26,15:1
Melti, Leonard (Playwright)
Night 1968,N 29,52:1
Melton, Robert
Airways, Inc 1929,F 21,30:5
Melton, Sid
Magic Touch, The 1947,S 4,30:1
Meltzer, Charles Henry (Translator)
Assumption of Hannele, The 1924,F 16,16:2
Meltzer, Newton (Playwright)
In the Groove 1938,Ap 22,14:5
Meltzer, William (Playwright)
Yankee Fable 1938,O 23,IX,3:5
Melville, Alan (Lyricist)
Bet Your Life 1952,F 19,26:6
Melville, Alan (Playwright)
Castle in the Air 1950,Ja 8,II,3:7
Bet Your Life 1952,F 19,26:6
Dear Charles 1952,D 21,44:5
Dear Charles 1953,Ap 20,22:4
Dear Charles 1954,S 16,37:2
Dear Charles 1954,S 26,II,1:1
Simon And Laura 1954,D 12,II,5:1
Melville, Bert
Sonny 1921,Ag 17,12:2
Main Street 1921,O 6,21:1
Merton of the Movies 1922,N 14,16:2
Cafe de Danse 1929,Ja 16,22:2
Melville, G S
Vaudeville (Palace) 1924,Ap 1,18:1
Melville, Herman (Original Author)
Uniform of Flesh 1949,Ja 31,15:2
Billy Budd 1951,F 12,18:3
Billy Budd 1951,F 18,II,1:1
Billy Budd 1951,Ap 15,II,1:1
Billy Budd 1951,My 6,II,1:1
Moby Dick 1955,Ap 26,25:3
Billy Budd 1955,My 4,35:1
Moby Dick 1955,Je 17,18:8
Moby Dick 1955,Jl 24,II,1:6
Billy Budd 1959,F 28,13:3
Moby Dick 1961,Ap 11,41:2
Moby Dick 1962,N 4,82:6
Moby Dick 1962,N 29,45:1
Benito Cereno 1964,N 2,62:2
Old Glory, The 1964,N 15,II,1:1
Billy 1969,Mr 24,56:1
Moby Dick 1970,Je 3,52:1
Melville, Herman (Playwright)
Bartleby 1961,Ja 25,28:1
Melville, Lee (Miscellaneous)
Projection Room, The 1969,Ja 15,38:2
Neighbors 1969,Ja 15,38:2
Melville, Nina
Merry-Go-Round 1932,Ap 23,11:2
Melville, William
Right to Love, The 1925,Je 9,16:4
House of Doom, The 1932,Ja 26,20:4
Angeline Moves In 1932,Ap 20,27:5
Whistling in the Dark 1932,N 4,25:2
Turpentine 1936,Je 27,21:6
Case of Philip Lawrence, The 1937,Je 9,31:1
Melvin, Allan
Stalag 17 1951,My 9,41:2
Melvin, Donnie
Summertree 1968,Mr 4,29:1
Cyrano de Bergerac 1968,Ap 26,30:1
Wrong Way Light Bulb, The 1969,Mr 5,40:1
Melvin, Henry
Peter Pan; Boy Who Would Not Grow Up, The
1928,N 27,36:3

Would-Be Gentleman, The 1930,Ap 30,29:2
Melvin, Joseph
Make Mine Manhattan 1948,Ja 16,26:2
Melvin, Maureen
Iolanthe 1955,S 28,38:1
Yeomen of the Guard, The 1955,O 4,39:2
Princess Ida 1955,O 14,22:3
Melvin, Murray
Oh What a Lovely War 1964,O 1,30:1
Melvin Brothers, The Three
Vaudeville (Palace) 1926,Je 22,21:3
Melvin Sisters
I'll Say She Is 1924,My 20,15:1
Melzard, Alyce
Afgar 1920,N 9,13:2
Melzer, Margaret
Blaue Boll, Der 1931,Ja 25,VIII,4:1
Gestern und Heute 1931,My 24,VIII,2:1
One Woman 1931,D 14,16:4
Membrives, Lola
Anna Christie 1930,Je 11,33:3
Anna Christie 1930,Je 12,30:2
Mena, Sonia
Remolienda, La; Bawdy Party 1968,F 3,20:1
Menace, Len
Wild Rose, The 1926,O 21,23:1
Menagh, Thomas
Paradise 1931,My 12,29:2
Menand, Howard Jr (Miscellaneous)
What a Relief 1935,D 14,10:6
Menander (Miscellaneous)
Girl From Samos, The 1954,N 24,17:1
Menard, Paul
Twelfth Night 1949,O 4,33:2
Armor of Light 1950,F 24,26:4
Menard, Paul (Producer)
Salome 1956,F 14,24:4
Florentine Tragedy, The 1956,F 14,24:4
Mence, Len
Golden Dawn 1927,D 1,32:3
Sweet Adeline 1929,S 4,33:1
Re-Echo 1934,Ja 12,28:4
Eternal Road, The 1937,Ja 8,14:2
Three Waltzes 1937,D 27,10:2
Glorious Morning 1938,N 28,10:3
Woman Brown, The 1939,D 9,18:5
Golden Wings 1941,D 9,46:6
Thank You Svoboda 1944,Mr 2,13:2
King and I, The 1951,Mr 30,26:2
Oh, Kay! 1960,Ap 18,37:2
Mencher, Murray (Composer)
Sketch Book 1935,Je 5,22:2
Mencher, Murray (Lyricist)
Sketch Book 1935,Je 5,22:2
Mencher, Steven
When Did You Last See My Mother?
1967,Ja 5,27:5
Antigone 1967,Ja 14,18:1
Mende, William
Great Lady 1938,D 2,26:6
Devil and Daniel Webster, The 1939,My 19,26:1
Sleepy Hollow 1948,Je 4,26:3
Mendell, Dale
Stronger, The 1949,Je 15,38:2
Mendelsohn, Ann (Miscellaneous)
Queen After Death 1956,Mr 13,33:2
Mendelsohn, Bernice
Merry-Go-Rounders, The 1956,N 22,50:1
Mendelsohn, Bernice (Choreographer)
Merry-Go-Rounders, The 1956,N 22,50:1
Mendelsohn, Joseph
Blossom Time 1923,My 22,14:3
Blossom Time 1923,Je 1,22:2
Mendelssohn, Edward
We Are No Longer Children 1932,Ap 1,17:2
Mendelssohn, Edward (Director)
Good-Bye Please 1934,O 25,26:6
Mendelssohn, Edward (Miscellaneous)
Squaring the Circle 1935,O 4,24:6
Mendelssohn, Edward (Producer)
Good-Bye Please 1934,O 25,26:6
Mendelssohn, Eleonora
Daughters of Atreus 1936,O 15,33:1
Flight to the West 1940,D 15,I,59:5
Flight to the West 1940,D 31,19:1
Flight to the West 1941,Ja 19,IX,1:1
Flight to the West 1941,Mr 7,16:3
Russian People, The 1942,D 30,17:2
Secret Room, The 1945,N 8,16:2
Madwoman of Chaillot, The 1950,Je 14,41:2
Mendelssohn, Felix (Composer)
Midsummer Night's Dream, A 1925,Mr 8,VII,2:1
Midsummer Night's Dream, A 1927,N 18,21:1
Midsummer Night's Dream, A 1930,D 28,VIII,3:5
Midsummer Night's Dream, A 1932,Jl 13,15:1
Midsummer Night's Dream, A 1934,S 19,15:1
Athalie 1939,My 14,XI,6:5
Swingin' the Dream 1939,N 30,24:2
Heimkehr aus der Fremde, Die; Stranger, The
1949,S 2,14:1
Midsummer Night's Dream, A 1954,S 22,33:1
Midsummer Night's Dream, A 1954,D 16,50:2
Midsummer Night's Dream, A 1970,Ag 28,15:1

Mendelssohn, Francesco von (Director)
Threepenny Opera, The 1933,Ap 14,22:4
Mendenhall, Dean (Lighting Director)
Geese 1969,Ja 13,26:6
Parents and Children 1969,Ja 13,26:6
Mendenhall, Jim (Producer)
Geese 1969,Ja 13,26:6
Parents and Children 1969,Ja 13,26:6
Mendes, Catulle (Playwright)
Reine Flammette, La 1928,N 11,X,2:7
Mendes, H Pereira (Rev Dr) (Playwright)
Eternal Problem, The 1937,Ap 12,14:5
Mendes, John
This Is the Army 1942,Jl 5,28:2
Mendes, Lothar (Miscellaneous)
Inspector Calls, An 1947,O 22,38:2
Mendes, Richard H P
Eternal Problem, The 1937,Ap 12,14:5
Mendez, A
Don Juan Tenorio 1953,N 20,18:5
Mendez, Jola
Vaudeville (Palace) 1926,Ap 13,28:3
Mendez, Lucilla
Little Jessie James 1923,Ag 16,10:4
My Girl 1924,N 25,27:2
Merry Merry 1925,S 25,24:3
My Girl Friday! 1929,F 13,20:2
Mendez-Ballester, Manuel (Playwright)
Miracle, The 1960,D 5,42:3
Mendi, Joe
Vaudeville (Palace) 1930,F 10,20:3
Vaudeville (Palace) 1930,Mr 3,18:5
Mendick, Charles
Dance Night 1938,O 15,20:5
Where Do We Go From Here? 1938,N 16,26:2
Stop Press 1939,Mr 20,13:2
Night Music 1940,F 23,18:2
No for an Answer 1941,Ja 6,10:6
Lily of the Valley 1942,Ja 27,25:2
Eve of St Mark, The 1942,O 8,30:2
Volpone 1948,Ja 9,24:6
Affair of Honor 1956,Ap 7,12:3
Sixth Finger in a Five Finger Glove 1956,O 9,31:4
Mendillo, Stephen
Revenger's Tragedy, The 1970,D 2,58:1
Mendoza, Alfredo
Holiday on Ice 1965,S 2,38:4
Holiday on Ice 1966,S 1,30:1
Holiday on Ice 1967,Ag 31,29:2
Holiday on Ice 1969,Ag 28,44:1
Mendoza, David (Musical Director)
Hats Off to Ice 1944,Je 23,15:2
Icetime 1946,Je 21,20:5
Icetime 1947,My 29,28:2
Howdy Mr Ice 1948,Je 25,28:5
Howdy, Mr Ice of 1950 1949,My 27,24:2
Mendrek, William
Pigeon, The 1930,O 15,26:2
Room Service 1937,My 20,16:1
Room Service 1937,D 16,35:4
What a Life 1938,Ap 14,26:2
At War With the Army 1949,Mr 9,32:2
Mendrek, William (Producer)
Room Service 1937,D 16,35:4
Mendum, Georgie Drew
Neighbors 1923,D 27,11:1
Close Harmony 1924,D 2,23:1
Still Waters 1926,Mr 2,23:1
Kingdom of God, The 1928,D 21,30:2
Scarlet Sister Mary 1930,N 26,19:2
Laura Garnett 1934,Jl 17,24:4
Aiglon, L' 1934,N 5,22:2
School for Scandal, The 1940,Je 18,29:5
School for Scandal, The 1940,Je 23,IX,1:1
Menefee, Peg
Long Watch, The 1952,Mr 21,19:5
Menefee, Richard
Children of Darkness 1930,Ja 8,25:1
Meneg, Robert
Vincent 1959,O 1,40:1
Menendez, Emilio
Don Juan Tenorio 1953,N 20,18:5
El Alcalde De Zalamea 1953,N 23,32:5
Menerth, Ed Jr (Producer)
Obbligato 1958,F 19,22:2
Meng, Constance
Foxy 1964,F 17,26:1
Certain Young Man, A 1967,D 27,45:1
Menge, Robert
Drunkard, The; Fallen Saved, The 1959,Je 24,37:2
Mengel, Ralph
What a Relief 1935,D 14,10:6
Mengelberg, Willem (Musical Director)
Retablo de Maese Pedro, El 1925,D 30,10:1
Menger, Walter A
Grey Heir, The 1926,Ap 6,29:2
Menges, Herbert (Composer)
Richard of Bordeaux 1934,F 25,IX,1:1
Richard II 1940,Ap 2,31:2
Henry IV, Part I 1946,My 7,25:2
Henry IV, Part II 1946,My 8,33:4
Henry IV 1946,My 12,II,1:1
Richard II 1951,Ja 25,21:2

nges, Herbert (Composer)—Cont
Caesar and Cleopatra 1951,D 20,43:2
Antony and Cleopatra 1951,D 21,22:2
Venus Observed 1952,F 14,24:2
nges, Herbert (Miscellaneous)
Peer Gynt 1935,S 24,28:2
nges, Herbert (Musical Director)
Henry IV, Part I 1946,My 7,25:2
Henry IV, Part II 1946,My 8,33:4
Oedipus; Critic, The 1946,My 21,19:2
Oedipus 1946,My 21,19:2
enhinick, Enid
Middle Watch, The 1929,O 17,27:1
Stepdaughters of War 1930,O 7,27:1
enken, Grace
Girl With Carmine Lips, The 1920,Ag 11,6:1
2 Girls Wanted 1926,S 10,25:3
Gossipy Sex, The 1927,Ap 20,28:3
Brothers 1928,D 26,14:3
enken, Helen
Triumph of X, The 1921,Ag 25,8:2
Mad Dog, The 1921,N 9,20:1
Drifting 1922,Ja 22,VI,1:1
Seventh Heaven 1922,O 31,11:1
Seventh Heaven 1922,N 5,VIII,1:1
Makropoulos Secret, The 1926,Ja 22,12:4
Little Eyolf 1926,F 3,22:1
Captive, The 1926,S 30,23:1
Captive, The 1926,O 10,VIII,1:1
Vaudeville (Palace) 1927,Ap 19,24:3
Seventh Heaven 1927,S 3,13:1
Seventh Heaven 1927,S 25,VIII,2:1
Beaux' Stratagem, The 1928,Je 5,20:1
Beaux' Stratagem, The 1928,Je 10,VIII,1:1
Vaudeville (Palace) 1928,Jl 31,13:5
Saturday Night 1928,Jl 31,13:5
Congai 1928,O 28,IX,4:6
Congai 1928,N 28,24:3
Infinite Shoeblack, The 1929,D 1,X,4:7
Infinite Shoeblack, The 1930,F 18,28:1
Lily White 1930,My 18,VIII,3:1
Rock Me, Julie 1931,Ja 4,VIII,2:3
Rock Me, Julie 1931,F 4,21:1
Merchant of Venice, The 1931,N 17,31:1
Julius Caesar 1931,N 18,26:3
Hamlet 1931,N 19,26:6
Saint Wench 1933,Ja 3,19:3
Mary of Scotland 1933,N 19,IX,2:5
Mary of Scotland 1933,N 28,28:3
Old Maid, The 1935,Ja 8,26:1
Laughing Woman, The 1936,Jl 8,14:7
Laughing Woman, The 1936,O 14,30:1
Skin of Our Teeth, The 1961,Mr 28,40:2
Skin of Our Teeth, The 1961,My 1,35:3
Menken, Helen (Producer)
Saint Wench 1933,Ja 3,19:3
Sotoba Komachi 1961,F 1,15:1
Damask Drum, The 1961,F 4,15:1
Hans's Crime 1961,F 4,15:1
Menken, Shepard
Criminals, The 1941,D 22,24:3
Menkes, Nina
Shylock and His Daughter 1947,S 30,22:2
Menkin, Abraham
Kith and Kin 1930,My 14,31:1
Menkin, Lawrence
Black Diamond 1933,F 24,12:2
Raw Meat 1933,Mr 23,13:2
Mennen, Alida
Green Table, The 1942,Ja 22,12:2
Prodigal Son, The 1942,F 18,22:2
Menotti, Gian-Carlo (Composer)
Medium, The 1947,My 2,28:2
Telephone, The 1947,My 2,28:2
Telephone, The 1947,My 11,II,1:1
Medium, The 1947,My 11,II,1:1
Telephone, The 1948,Ap 30,26:3
Medium, The 1948,Ap 30,26:3
Medium, The 1948,D 8,41:6
Telephone, The 1948,D 8,41:6
Medium, The 1949,N 7,32:4
Old Maid and the Thief, The 1949,N 7,32:4
Consul, The 1950,Mr 2,32:3
Consul, The 1950,Mr 26,II,1:1
Consul, The 1950,Ap 2,II,7:1
Consul, The 1950,My 14,II,1:1
Medium, The 1950,S 3,II,1:1
Consul, The 1951,Mr 4,82:4
Consul, The 1951,Mr 4,II,3:7
Consul, The 1951,My 4,30:8
Consul, The 1951,S 8,9:3
Consul, The 1951,S 23,II,3:1
Consul, The 1952,O 30,41:2
Saint of Bleecker Street, The 1955,Ja 2,II,1:1
Consul, The 1957,S 4,40:3
Maria Golovin 1958,N 30,II,11:1
Saint of Bleecker Street, The 1965,Mr 19,28:1
Leper, The 1970,Ap 24,40:1
Amahl and the Night Visitors 1970,D 24,10:2
Help! Help! the Globolinks 1970,D 24,10:2
Amahl and the Night Visitors 1970,D 26,11:1
Menotti, Gian-Carlo (Director)
Telephone, The 1947,My 2,28:2
Medium, The 1947,My 2,28:2

Telephone, The 1948,D 8,41:6
Medium, The 1948,D 8,41:6
Consul, The 1950,Mr 16,41:1
Consul, The 1950,Mr 26,II,1:1
Medium, The 1950,Jl 20,22:5
Telephone, The 1950,Jl 20,22:5
Saint of Bleecker Street, The 1954,D 28,21:1
Saint of Bleecker Street, The 1955,Ja 2,II,1:1
Maria Golovin 1958,N 6,43:1
Saint of Bleecker Street, The 1965,Mr 19,28:1
Medea 1966,D 21,42:1
Menotti, Gian-Carlo (Lyricist)
Medium, The 1947,My 2,28:2
Telephone, The 1947,My 2,28:2
Telephone, The 1948,D 8,41:6
Medium, The 1948,D 8,41:6
Menotti, Gian-Carlo (Musical Director)
Saint of Bleecker Street, The 1954,D 28,21:1
Menotti, Gian-Carlo (Original Author)
Telephone, The 1948,D 8,41:6
Medium, The 1948,D 8,41:6
Menotti, Gian-Carlo (Playwright)
Medium, The 1947,My 2,28:2
Telephone, The 1947,My 2,28:2
Consul, The 1950,Mr 16,41:1
Consul, The 1950,Mr 26,II,1:1
Telephone, The 1950,Jl 20,22:5
Medium, The 1950,Jl 20,22:5
Saint of Bleecker Street, The 1954,D 28,21:1
Saint of Bleecker Street, The 1955,Ja 2,II,1:1
Maria Golovin 1958,N 6,43:1
Leper, The 1970,Ap 24,40:1
Menotti, Gian-Carlo (Producer)
Amahl and the Night Visitors 1970,D 24,10:2
Menowitz, Fred (Producer)
Gantry 1970,F 16,44:1
Mensch, William
Brothers Ashkenazi, The 1970,N 17,53:2
Mensching, Herbert
Mitschuldigen, Die 1966,Ap 6,34:1
Wozzeck 1966,Ap 6,34:1
Mensching, William H (Scenic Designer)
Bidding High 1932,S 29,17:2
Menteer, Gary (Choreographer)
Lovely Ladies, Kind Gentlemen 1970,D 29,38:1
Menten, Dale F (Composer)
House of Leather, The 1970,Mr 19,56:1
Menten, Dale F (Lyricist)
House of Leather, The 1970,Mr 19,56:1
Menten, Dale F (Musical Director)
House of Leather, The 1970,Mr 19,56:1
Mention, Michel (Musical Director)
Zizi 1964,N 23,51:1
Mentz, Arthur
Nathan the Wise 1962,Mr 7,29:1
Before Sundown 1962,Mr 14,43:1
Menz, Clifford
May Wine 1935,D 6,30:3
Menzel, Heinz (Director)
Dallas-November 22d 1965,N 12,54:1
Menzel, Jiri (Producer)
Mandragola 1970,Ap 19,74:3
Menzies, Angus
Set to Music 1939,Ja 19,16:2
Menzies, Archie (Playwright)
Astonished Ostrich, The 1936,D 18,30:3
Astonished Ostrich, The 1937,Ja 17,X,2:1
Menzies, Heather
We Have Always Lived in the Castle 1966,O 20,53:1
Menzies, William Cameron (Scenic Designer)
Anna Christie 1941,Ag 10,IX,1:8
Menzing, Ralph
Hamlet 1930,Mr 25,34:4
Macbeth 1930,Mr 26,24:6
Merchant of Venice, The 1930,Mr 27,24:7
Twelfth Night 1930,Mr 27,24:7
Taming of the Shrew, The 1930,Mr 28,22:8
Richard III 1930,Mr 31,24:1
King Lear 1930,Ap 1,34:6
As You Like It 1930,Ap 3,32:5
Julius Caesar 1930,Ap 4,22:3
King Lear 1930,D 26,18:2
Merchant of Venice, The 1931,N 17,31:1
Julius Caesar 1931,N 18,26:3
Hamlet 1931,N 19,26:6
Meottel, Frank (Miscellaneous)
Uncle Vanya 1956,F 1,25:2
Merande, Doro
Loose Moments 1935,F 5,22:3
One Good Year 1935,N 28,38:3
Fulton of Oak Falls 1937,F 11,18:2
Red Harvest 1937,Mr 31,29:2
Angel Island 1937,O 21,26:2
Our Town 1938,F 5,18:3
Love's Old Sweet Song 1940,My 3,16:3
Beverly Hills 1940,N 8,24:2
More the Merrier, The 1941,S 16,19:3
Hope for a Harvest 1941,N 27,28:2
Three's a Family 1943,My 6,24:2
Naked Genius, The 1943,O 22,20:5
Our Town 1944,Ja 11,24:5
Pick-Up Girl 1944,My 4,25:2
Violet 1944,O 25,16:1

Merande, Doro—Cont
Hope for the Best 1945,F 8,14:4
Apple of His Eye 1946,F 6,18:2
Silver Whistle, The 1948,N 25,49:2
Rat Race, The 1949,D 23,16:2
Four Twelves Are 48 1951,Ja 18,30:2
Lo and Behold! 1951,D 13,45:2
Diary of a Scoundrel 1956,N 5,41:1
Her Master's Voice 1964,D 28,33:2
Music Man, The 1965,Je 17,26:4
Front Page, The 1969,My 12,54:2
Front Page, The 1969,My 25,II,1:1
Merano, Cora
Bomboola 1929,Je 27,17:3
Mercedes
Vaudeville (Hippodrome) 1924,O 21,21:2
Harry Delmar's Revels 1927,N 29,30:2
Mercedes (Scenic Designer)
Who's Who 1938,Mr 2,16:2
Mercedes and Albano
Ice Capades 1957,S 5,33:2
Mercer, Beryl
Three Live Ghosts 1920,S 30,12:1
Three Live Ghosts 1920,O 10,VI,1:2
Ever Green Lady, The 1922,O 12,25:2
49ers, The 1922,N 7,14:1
Queen Victoria 1923,N 16,15:1
Queen Victoria 1923,N 25,VIII,1:1
Outward Bound 1924,Ja 8,26:1
Outward Bound 1924,Ja 13,VII,1:1
Quarantine 1924,D 17,19:7
Bit o' Love, A 1925,My 13,24:2
Fool's Bells 1925,D 24,8:3
Pygmalion 1926,N 16,24:1
Right You Are (If You Think You Are) 1927,F 24,27:1
Brass Buttons 1927,D 6,26:3
Mercer, David (Playwright)
Ride a Cock Horse 1965,Je 25,36:1
Flint 1970,Jl 26,49:2
Mercer, Ernestine
Boy on the Straight-Back Chair 1969,Mr 18,36:1
Mercer, Frances
Very Warm for May 1939,N 18,23:2
Mercer, Jack
Second Mate, The 1930,Mr 25,34:5
Mercer, Johnny (Composer)
Three After Three 1939,N 25,13:5
Star and Garter 1942,Je 25,26:2
Top Banana 1951,N 2,19:2
Mercer, Johnny (Lyricist)
Garrick Gaieties 1930,Je 5,29:2
Lew Leslie's Blackbirds of 1939 1939,F 13,12:2
Three After Three 1939,N 25,13:5
Walk With Music 1940,Je 5,33:2
Star and Garter 1942,Je 25,26:2
St Louis Woman 1946,Ap 1,22:2
Texas Li'l Darlin' 1949,N 26,10:5
Top Banana 1951,N 2,19:2
Li'l Abner 1956,N 16,24:2
Li'l Abner 1956,N 25,II,1:1
Saratoga 1959,D 8,59:4
Free and Easy 1959,D 15,51:4
Free and Easy 1959,D 20,II,3:2
Foxy 1962,Jl 4,12:2
Foxy 1964,F 17,26:1
Harold Arlen Songbook, The 1967,Mr 1,48:1
Mercer, Johnny (Miscellaneous)
Two Weeks With Pay 1940,Je 25,28:3
Mercer, Mabel
Consul, The 1950,Mr 16,41:1
Mercer, Marian
New Faces of 1962 1962,F 2,25:1
Hotel Passionato 1965,O 23,16:1
Your Own Thing 1968,Ja 15,33:1
Promises, Promises 1968,D 2,59:3
Promises, Promises 1968,D 15,II,3:1
Place for Polly, A 1970,Ap 20,45:1
Hay Fever 1970,N 10,55:1
Hay Fever 1970,N 22,II,18:6
Mercer, Olive
American Tragedy, An 1926,O 12,31:2
Mercer, Richard
Tell Me Pretty Maiden 1937,D 17,33:5
Mercer, Ruby
Forbidden Melody 1936,N 3,33:1
White Plume, The 1939,D 27,16:1
Vie Parisienne, La 1941,N 6,20:3
New Moon, The 1942,Ag 19,14:2
Mercer, William
Hilda Cassidy 1933,My 5,18:3
Merchant, Abby (Playwright)
Ever Green Lady, The 1922,O 12,25:2
New Englander, The 1924,F 8,22:2
Your Loving Son 1941,Ap 5,13:2
Merchant, Vivien
Lover, The 1963,S 19,21:1
Homecoming, The 1967,Ja 6,29:1
Mixed Doubles 1969,Ap 12,43:2
Flint 1970,Jl 26,49:2
Untitled-Recital 1970,S 3,36:1
Exiles 1970,N 19,42:4
Mercier, Mary
Roots 1961,Mr 7,40:2

Mercier, Mary—Cont
French Way, The; Deceased, The 1962,Mr 21,36:2
Fun Couple, The 1962,O 27,15:2
Mercier, Mary (Playwright)
Johnny No-Trump 1967,O 9,60:2
Mercouri, Melina
Illya Darling 1967,Ap 12,37:1
Illya Darling 1967,Ap 30,II,1:1
Illya Darling 1967,N 2,58:1
Marcur, Wolf
60,000 Heroes 1935,Ja 28,11:5
Mercure, Jean (Director)
Cardinal of Spain, The 1960,D 22,16:6
Mercure, Jean (Original Author)
Strong Are Lonely, The 1953,S 30,38:3
Mere, Charles (Playwright)
Masked Woman, The 1922,D 23,14:2
Nuit au Bouge, Une 1923,O 16,18:1
Trois Masques, Les 1923,N 6,22:1
Danse de Minuit, La 1924,Mr 23,VIII,1:3
Plaisir, Le 1927,Ja 9,VII,2:5
Berlioz 1927,F 20,VII,2:1
Carnaval de l'Amour, Le 1928,Mr 11,VIII,2:7
Chair, La 1930,O 19,IX,2:2
Zizippe 1935,D 29,IX,2:1
Indiana 1935,D 29,IX,2:1
Meredith, Anne
Bluebeard's Eighth Wife 1921,S 20,12:2
Meredith, Binard
Holiday 1930,F 6,21:2
Meredith, Burgess
Romeo and Juliet 1930,Ap 22,33:1
Siegfried 1930,O 21,34:1
People on the Hill 1931,S 26,25:5
Liliom 1932,O 27,23:2
Alice in Wonderland 1932,D 12,18:3
Threepenny Opera, The 1933,Ap 14,22:4
Little Ol' Boy 1933,Ap 25,15:5
She Loves Me Not 1933,N 21,22:4
Hide and Seek 1934,Ag 7,20:2
Hipper's Holiday 1934,O 19,26:2
Battleship Gertie 1935,Ja 19,9:2
Barretts of Wimpole Street, The 1935,F 26,16:2
Flowers of the Forest 1935,Ap 9,25:2
Mad Morning 1935,Je 25,14:1
Winterset 1935,S 26,19:2
Winterset 1936,Je 2,35:2
High Tor 1936,D 31,20:3
High Tor 1937,Ja 11,15:2
High Tor 1937,Ja 17,X,1:1
Star-Wagon, The 1937,S 17,28:5
Star-Wagon, The 1937,S 30,18:5
Star-Wagon, The 1937,O 10,XI,1:1
Five Kings 1939,Mr 5,X,3:1
Liliom 1940,Mr 26,17:2
Liliom 1940,Mr 31,IX,1:1
Candida 1942,Ap 28,24:4
Candida 1942,My 3,VIII,1:1
Playboy of the Western World, The 1946,O 28,18:3
Happy as Larry 1950,Ja 7,11:2
ANTA Album 1950,Ja 30,13:2
Little Blue Light, The 1951,Ap 30,17:2
Remarkable Mr Pennypacker, The 1953,D 31,11:2
Hamlet 1956,My 8,28:5
Major Barbara 1956,O 31,27:1
Death of Cuchulain, The 1959,Ap 13,34:4
Hughie 1963,Je 11,29:4
I Was Dancing 1964,N 9,40:4
Meredith, Burgess (Director)
Happy as Larry 1950,Ja 7,11:2
Season in the Sun 1950,S 29,31:2
Season in the Sun 1950,O 8,II,1:1
Out West of Eighth 1951,S 21,20:3
Lo and Behold! 1951,D 13,45:2
Frogs of Spring, The 1953,O 21,36:2
Ulysses in Nighttown 1958,Je 6,30:1
Ulysses in Nighttown 1958,Je 15,II,1:1
God and Kate Murphy 1959,F 27,21:2
Thurber Carnival, A 1960,F 27,13:2
Thurber Carnival, A 1960,Mr 6,II,1:1
Thurber Carnival, A 1960,S 13,41:1
Midgie Purvis 1961,F 2,25:3
Midgie Purvis 1961,F 12,II,1:1
Blues for Mister Charlie 1964,Ap 24,24:1
Blues for Mister Charlie 1965,My 5,52:1
Of Love Remembered 1967,F 20,46:5
Latent Heterosexual, The 1968,Mr 22,52:1
Latent Heterosexual, The 1968,Mr 31,II,3:1
Meredith, Burgess (Playwright)
Ulysses in Nighttown 1958,Je 6,30:1
Thurber Carnival, A 1960,F 27,13:2
Meredith, Burgess (Producer)
Speaking of Murder 1956,D 20,37:1
Meredith, Charles
Starlight 1925,Mr 4,17:2
Village Wooing 1934,Ap 18,22:5
Meredith, Charles (Director)
Village Wooing 1934,Ap 18,22:5
Song of the Bridge 1942,Ap 7,27:5
Meredith, Eleanor
Squaring the Circle 1936,Ag 12,15:3
Meredith, Hoyt
Broadway Nights 1929,Jl 16,23:2

Meredith, Jane
His Chinese Wife 1920,My 18,9:3
Enter Madame 1920,Ag 17,11:2
Ever Green Lady, The 1922,O 12,25:2
One Man's Woman 1926,My 26,25:1
Meredith, Joan
Creeping Fire 1935,Ja 17,22:3
Meredith, Katherine
Man in Evening Clothes, The 1924,D 6,13:4
Embers 1926,F 2,20:3
Meredith, Lois
Czarina, The 1922,F 1,22:1
Number 7 1926,S 9,21:3
Meredith, Lucille
Happy Valley, Limited 1936,Je 30,15:1
Meredith, Madeline
Vaudeville (Palace) 1925,Ap 21,18:1
Broadway Nights 1929,Jl 16,23:2
Meredith, Morley
Christine 1960,Ap 29,27:1
Meredith, Nicholas
Macbeth 1962,F 7,32:2
Saint Joan 1962,F 21,57:4
Meredith, Norman
Vaudeville (Palace) 1925,Ap 21,18:1
Meredith, Peggy
Criminals, The 1941,D 22,24:3
Playboy of Newark, The 1943,Mr 20,11:2
Embezzled Heaven 1944,N 1,20:2
Truckline Cafe 1946,F 28,19:4
All My Sons 1947,Ja 30,21:2
Peer Gynt 1951,Ja 29,15:2
Golden Boy 1952,Mr 13,24:3
Meredith, Ruth
Soliloquy 1938,N 29,26:4
Meredith, Suzette
Gypsy Lady 1946,S 18,25:6
Meredith, Sylvia
Year of Pilar, The 1952,Ja 7,14:3
Meredith, William
Sonny 1921,Ag 17,12:2
Merediths, The
Vaudeville (Palace) 1926,My 8,29:2
Vaudeville (Palace) 1926,D 7,24:3
Vaudeville (Palace) 1927,Je 14,33:3
Greenwich Village Follies 1928,Ap 10,32:2
Broadway Nights 1929,Je 23,VIII,2:4
Vaudeville (Palace) 1931,F 16,16:3
Merejkovsky (Playwright)
Paul I 1927,O 23,VIII,4:1
Mereman, Bessie
Broken Engagement, The 1921,My 12,20:2
Merensky, John
Disintegration of James Cherry, The
1970,Ja 30,33:3
Mergendahl, Charles (Playwright)
Me and Harry 1942,Ap 3,24:6
Mergentime, Neale
Patience 1935,S 3,24:4
Merian, Leon
Silk Stockings 1955,F 25,17:3
Meric, Maurice
Voyage de Monsieur Perrichon, Le 1937,N 2,32:3
Knock 1937,N 17,26:3
Roi Cerf, Le 1937,N 30,26:3
Jean de la Lune 1937,D 14,33:3
Nationale 6 1938,Ja 11,26:6
Y'Avait un Prisonnier 1938,Ja 25,24:3
Fantasio 1938,F 8,17:2
Bal des Voleurs, Le 1938,N 29,26:4
Precieuses Ridicules, Les 1938,D 13,30:3
Fourberies de Scapin, Les 1938,D 13,30:3
Faiseur, Le; Promoter, The 1938,D 27,12:3
Paquebot Tenacity, Le 1939,Ja 10,16:4
Chacun Sa Verite 1939,Ja 24,17:1
37 Sous de M Montaudoin, Les 1939,F 7,17:2
Enterrement, L' 1939,F 7,17:2
Siegfried 1939,F 21,15:2
Mericle, Leona
Moon Is a Gong, The 1926,Mr 13,21:3
Merighi, Augusta
Rose Tattoo, The 1951,F 5,19:2
Aspern Papers, The 1962,F 8,26:1
Merigold, Jack (Miscellaneous)
H M S Pinafore 1960,S 8,41:1
Pirates of Penzance, The 1961,S 7,41:1
Meril, Ann
Thirsty Soil 1937,F 4,16:2
Merill, Milton
Burlesque 1946,D 26,30:3
Merimee, Prosper (Original Author)
Carmen Jones 1945,My 3,26:5
Carmen Jones 1959,Ag 18,25:1
Merimee, Prosper (Playwright)
Carrosse du Saint-Sacrement, Le 1926,O 3,VIII,2:1
Carrosse du Saint-Sacrement, Le 1930,Mr 9,IX,2:7
Occasion, L' 1939,Ja 10,16:4
Carmen Jones 1943,D 3,26:2
Carmen Jones 1951,S 22,8:6
Carmen Jones 1956,Je 1,28:2
Merin, Eda Reiss
Sophie 1944,D 26,22:7
Macbeth 1959,Ag 1,9:2

Merin, Eda Reiss—Cont
Far Country, A 1961,Ap 5,32:1
Square in the Eye 1965,My 20,54:1
Huui, Huui 1968,N 25,58:1
Inner Journey, The 1969,Mr 21,42:1
Good Woman of Setzuan, The 1970,N 6,51:1
Merin, Jennifer
Marie Vison, La 1970,Jl 15,29:1
Merindol, Mme
Poulette et Son Poulain 1924,Je 15,VII,1:4
Merinow, Victor
Call on Kuprin, A 1961,My 26,29:3
Merivale, Bernard (Playwright)
Marriage By Instalments 1923,Ap 8,VIII,1:7
Unguarded Hour, The 1935,Ag 25,X,1:3
Merivale, H C (Playwright)
Foot-Loose 1920,My 11,12:1
Merivale, Jack
Lorelei 1938,N 30,21:2
Journey's End 1939,S 19,29:2
Journey's End 1939,S 24,IX,1:1
Romeo and Juliet 1940,My 10,27:1
Lady Windermere's Fan 1946,O 15,29:2
Merivale, John
Inspector Calls, An 1947,O 22,38:2
Anne of the Thousand Days 1948,D 9,49:2
Day After Tomorrow 1950,O 27,25:2
Getting Married 1951,My 14,28:5
Venus Observed 1952,F 14,24:2
Deep Blue Sea, The 1952,N 6,38:3
Reluctant Debutante, The 1956,O 11,50:1
Reluctant Debutante, The 1956,O 21,II,1:1
Duel of Angels 1960,Ap 20,42:2
Ivanov 1966,My 4,50:1
Merivale, Philip
Tragedy of Nan, The 1920,F 18,9:1
Tragedy of Nan, The 1920,F 22,III,6:1
Call the Doctor 1920,S 1,14:1
Merchant of Venice, The 1922,D 22,13:1
Swan, The 1923,O 24,15:3
Grounds for Divorce 1924,S 24,20:1
Antonia 1925,O 21,20:1
Monkey Talks, The 1925,D 29,20:1
Henry IV, Part I 1926,Je 1,29:1
Scotch Mist 1926,S 21,32:3
Head or Tail 1926,N 10,24:1
Road to Rome, The 1927,F 1,24:2
Hidden 1927,S 25,VIII,4:8
Hidden 1927,O 5,30:4
Road to Rome, The 1928,Je 10,VIII,1:3
Jealous Moon, The 1928,N 21,32:2
Paolo and Francesca 1929,Ap 2,28:2
Death Takes a Holiday 1929,N 24,X,4:5
Death Takes a Holiday 1929,D 27,26:4
Death Takes a Holiday 1931,F 17,29:1
Dr Harmer 1931,Mr 22,VIII,4:3
Cynara 1931,N 3,31:1
Mary of Scotland 1933,N 19,IX,2:5
Mary of Scotland 1933,N 28,28:3
Mary of Scotland 1933,D 3,IX,5:1
Valley Forge 1934,N 27,26:4
Valley Forge 1934,D 11,28:3
Valley Forge 1934,D 23,IX,1:1
Othello 1935,S 13,19:2
Macbeth 1935,S 17,26:3
Othello 1935,S 22,X,2:5
Othello 1935,S 28,13:2
Macbeth 1935,O 8,26:4
Call It a Day 1936,Ja 21,26:7
Call It a Day 1936,Ja 29,15:2
Call It a Day 1936,F 9,X,1:1
White Christmas 1936,Jl 7,22:2
And Now Goodbye 1937,Ja 19,29:1
And Now Goodbye 1937,F 3,26:4
Close Quarters 1937,Ap 18,II,3:5
Good-Bye to Yesterday 1937,N 21,XI,3:6
Dodsworth 1938,F 23,26:2
Dodsworth 1938,Mr 13,XI,3:1
Lysistrata 1938,Ag 7,IX,1:5
Lorelei 1938,N 30,21:2
Ladies and Gentlemen 1939,S 24,IX,2:5
Ladies and Gentlemen 1939,O 18,30:2
Ladies and Gentlemen 1939,O 22,IX,1:3
Ladies and Gentlemen 1939,O 29,IX,1:3
Talley Method, The 1941,F 25,26:3
Talley Method, The 1941,Mr 2,IX,1:1
Rose Burke 1942,Ja 25,IX,2:5
Duke in Darkness, The 1944,Ja 25,15:2
Public Relations 1944,Ap 7,23:3
Merivale, Philip (Playwright)
White Christmas 1936,Jl 7,22:2
Merivale, Philip (Producer)
Spring Meeting 1938,D 9,30:4
Merivale, Rosamund
Foolscap 1933,Ja 12,21:2
Meriwether, Susan (Playwright)
Flight 1929,F 19,22:3
Flight 1929,Mr 24,X,1:1
Meriwether, William (Translator)
Troubled Waters 1965,Je 4,40:2
Merkel, Una
Gossipy Sex, The 1927,Ap 20,28:3
Coquette 1927,N 9,23:1
Coquette 1927,N 13,IX,1:1

Merkel, Una—Cont
Salt Water 1929,N 27,30:3
Summer and Smoke 1950,O 29,II,3:7
Remarkable Mr Pennypacker, The 1953,D 31,11:2
Ponder Heart, The 1956,F 17,14:2
Ponder Heart, The 1956,F 26,II,1:1
Take Me Along 1959,O 23,22:2
Take Me Along 1959,N 1,II,1:1
Merkey, Ryland
Days Between, The 1965,Je 4,39:1
Merkow, Edward (Miscellaneous)
War Games 1969,Ap 18,37:1
Merkt, Marilyn
Carousel 1945,Ap 20,24:2
Merkulova, Nina
Aladdin and His Wonderful Lamp 1963,O 21,39:1
Merkur, Wolf
Bread 1932,D 14,27:3
Merkyl, John
Six-Fifty, The 1921,O 25,20:1
Our Nell 1922,D 5,24:1
Merla, Patrick
Bead-Tangle 1970,Jl 16,38:1
Merle, Janet
Love Expert, The 1929,S 24,29:1
Merle, Margaret
My Maryland 1927,S 13,37:2
Broadway Nights 1929,Jl 16,23:2
Nine Fifteen Revue, The 1930,F 12,26:2
Merlin, Eleanor
Bad Girl 1930,O 3,30:2
Merlin, Frank
Lesson in Love, A 1923,S 25,10:1
Tantrum, The 1924,S 5,20:2
Kathleen 1948,F 4,26:2
Send Me No Flowers 1960,D 6,54:1
Merlin, Frank (Director)
Castles in the Air 1926,S 7,19:2
Triple Crossed 1927,My 6,21:2
King Can Do No Wrong, The 1927,N 17,28:4
Rope 1928,F 23,18:3
Napoleon 1928,Mr 9,21:1
Zeppelin 1929,Ja 15,22:3
Hobo 1931,F 12,24:4
Take My Tip 1932,Ap 12,25:2
Run, Little Chillun! 1933,Mr 2,21:3
World Waits, The 1933,O 26,22:5
False Dreams, Farewell 1934,Ja 16,18:3
Saluta 1934,Ag 29,13:4
Tomorrow's Harvest 1934,D 6,26:5
Prisoners of War 1935,Ja 29,24:1
Hook-Up, The 1935,My 9,24:6
Smile at Me 1935,Ag 24,18:4
Alice Takat 1936,F 11,19:2
Woman's a Fool-To Be Clever, A 1938,O 19,18:6
Scene of the Crime, The 1940,Mr 29,24:1
Try and Get It 1943,Ag 3,13:2
Foenix in Choir 1958,O 28,40:2
Merlin, Frank (Miscellaneous)
Return Engagement 1940,N 2,19:2
Merlin, Frank (Playwright)
New Gallantry, The 1925,S 25,24:2
Triple Crossed 1927,My 6,21:2
King Can Do No Wrong, The 1927,N 17,28:4
Hobo 1931,F 12,24:4
Good Men and True 1935,O 26,12:4
Foenix in Choir 1958,O 28,40:2
I Got Shoes 1963,Ja 25,12:2
Merlin, Frank (Producer)
World Waits, The 1933,O 26,22:5
False Dreams, Farewell 1934,Ja 16,18:3
Prisoners of War 1935,Ja 29,24:1
Good Men and True 1935,O 26,12:4
Merlin, Frank (Scenic Designer)
I Must Love Someone 1939,F 8,18:7
Merlin, Joanna
Pigeon, The 1957,My 17,19:2
Winter's Tale, The 1958,Jl 21,17:4
No Trifling With Love 1959,N 10,55:3
Merry Death, A 1959,N 10,55:3
Breaking Wall, The 1960,Ja 26,27:5
Rules of the Game, The 1960,D 20,44:1
Becket 1961,My 9,44:1
Emperor, The 1963,Ap 17,30:1
Thistle in My Bed 1963,N 20,48:1
Fiddler on the Roof 1964,S 23,56:2
Merlin, Max (Composer)
Time of Your Life, The 1955,Ja 20,34:1
Merlin, Ving
Hairpin Harmony 1943,O 2,18:5
Merlin, Ving (Musical Director)
Lady Says Yes, A 1945,Ja 11,18:5
Merling, Howard
Romeo and Juliet 1922,D 28,20:1
Play, A 1925,F 11,19:2
Merling, Howard (Director)
Killers 1928,Mr 14,28:3
Merling, Howard (Playwright)
Killers 1928,Mr 14,28:3
Merlis, Iris (Miscellaneous)
Hang Down Your Head and Die 1964,O 19,38:1
Sound of Silence, A 1965,Mr 9,30:1
Summertree 1969,D 10,60:1

Merman, Ethel
Vaudeville (Palace) 1930,S 15,29:2
Girl Crazy 1930,O 15,27:1
Girl Crazy 1930,D 28,VIII,1:1
Vaudeville (Palace) 1931,Jl 20,20:3
George White's Scandals 1931,S 15,30:1
Vaudeville (Palace) 1932,Ap 25,18:3
Vaudeville (Palace) 1932,My 2,13:2
Humpty Dumpty 1932,S 18,IX,2:1
Take a Chance 1932,N 28,11:2
Anything Goes 1934,N 18,IX,1:7
Anything Goes 1934,N 22,26:1
Anything Goes 1935,S 15,IX,1:1
Red, Hot and Blue! 1936,O 8,26:1
Red, Hot and Blue! 1936,O 11,X,3:1
Red, Hot and Blue! 1936,O 30,26:3
Stars in Your Eyes 1939,F 10,18:2
Stars in Your Eyes 1939,Mr 5,X,1:2
Du Barry 1939,N 19,X,3:4
Du Barry Was a Lady 1939,D 7,34:2
Du Barry 1939,D 24,IX,1:1
Panama Hattie 1940,O 4,28:4
Panama Hattie 1940,O 31,28:2
Panama Hattie 1940,N 10,IX,1:1
Something for the Boys 1943,Ja 17,VIII,1:1
Annie Get Your Gun 1946,Mr 29,18:2
Annie Get Your Gun 1946,My 17,14:2
Annie Get Your Gun 1946,My 26,II,1:1
Annie Get Your Gun 1946,S 29,II,1:1
Call Me Madam 1950,O 13,25:1
Call Me Madam 1950,O 22,II,1:1
Call Me Madam 1951,My 20,II,1:1
Happy Hunting 1956,D 7,30:1
Happy Hunting 1956,D 16,II,3:1
Gypsy 1959,My 22,31:6
Gypsy 1959,My 31,II,1:1
Annie Get Your Gun 1966,Je 1,42:2
Hello, Dolly! 1970,Mr 30,52:1
Hello, Dolly! 1970,Ap 12,II,3:7
Merman, Ruth
Heaven on Earth 1948,S 17,29:2
Mero, Ruth
Only 38 1921,S 14,22:2
Devils 1926,Mr 18,26:4
Whirlpool 1929,D 4,37:3
Mero-Irion, Yolanda (Producer)
Merry Widow, The 1943,Ag 5,19:2
Helen Goes to Troy 1944,Ap 25,17:2
Merry Widow, The 1944,O 9,17:1
Topaze 1947,D 29,21:5
Merode, Jean
Just Because 1922,Mr 23,11:1
Meroff, Benny
Vaudeville (Palace) 1931,N 2,26:2
Meroff, Diane
Firebird of Florence 1945,Mr 23,13:4
Meroff, Sonia
Vaudeville (Hippodrome) 1924,O 21,21:2
Merrall, Mary
Dover Road, The 1924,My 4,VIII,2:4
Mr What's-His-Name 1927,My 29,VII,1:3
Canaries Sometimes Sing 1930,O 21,34:2
Ladies in Retirement 1939,D 24,IX,1:7
Foolish Gentlewoman, The 1949,Ap 3,II,3:1
Women of Twilight 1952,Mr 4,22:2
Merredith, Jane
Mister Romeo 1927,S 6,35:3
Merrell, Richard
As You Like It 1955,O 29,12:2
Romeo and Juliet 1955,D 16,36:3
Changeling, The 1956,My 4,20:3
Aria Da Capo 1958,My 21,40:1
Aria Da Capo 1958,Je 27,18:5
Merrell, Richard (Scenic Designer)
Opening of a Window, The 1961,S 26,32:2
Merriam, David E (Composer)
Atmosphere 1925,Ap 4,17:1
Merriam, Leone
Half-Caste, The 1926,Mr 30,20:4
Merriam, Mylor
Taming of the Shrew, The 1927,O 26,26:4
When Crummles Played 1928,O 2,34:3
Merriam, Pauline
Deburau 1920,D 24,14:3
Merrick, Alma
Challenge of Youth 1930,Ja 21,28:5
Merrick, Ann
Serpent's Tooth, A 1922,Ag 25,8:5
Merrick, David (Miscellaneous)
Jeb 1946,F 22,20:2
Clutterbuck 1949,D 5,29:2
Merrick, David (Producer)
Willow and I, The 1942,D 11,32:2
Bright Boy 1944,Mr 3,19:5
Fanny 1954,N 5,16:1
Matchmaker, The 1955,D 6,45:6
Look Back in Anger 1957,O 2,28:2
Romanoff and Juliet 1957,O 11,24:1
Jamaica 1957,N 1,32:2
Entertainer, The 1958,F 13,22:2
World of Suzie Wong, The 1958,O 15,47:1

Merrick, David (Producer)—Cont
Epitaph for George Dillon 1958,N 5,44:1
Maria Golovin 1958,N 6,43:1
Plume de Ma Tante, La 1958,N 12,42:1
Destry Rides Again 1959,Ap 24,24:1
Gypsy 1959,My 22,31:6
Take Me Along 1959,O 23,22:2
Good Soup, The 1960,Mr 3,26:4
Vintage '60 1960,S 13,41:1
Irma la Douce 1960,S 30,31:2
Taste of Honey, A 1960,O 5,46:1
Becket 1960,O 6,50:1
Do Re Mi 1960,D 27,23:2
Do Re Mi 1961,Ja 8,II,1:1
Carnival! 1961,Ap 14,22:2
Becket 1961,My 9,44:1
Taste of Honey, A 1961,My 17,43:1
Sunday in New York 1961,N 10,40:1
Ross 1961,D 27,20:2
Subways Are for Sleeping 1961,D 28,22:1
I Can Get It for You Wholesale 1962,Mr 23,29:1
Stop the World-I Want to Get Off 1962,S 17,39:3
Stop the World-I Want to Get Off 1962,O 4,45:4
Tchin-Tchin 1962,O 26,26:2
Oliver 1963,Ja 8,5:5
Rattle of a Simple Man 1963,Ap 18,39:1
Luther 1963,S 11,46:3
Rehearsal, The 1963,S 24,45:2
Luther 1963,S 26,41:1
110 in the Shade 1963,O 25,37:1
Arturo Ui 1963,N 12,49:1
One Flew Over the Cuckoo's Nest 1963,N 14,40:2
Milk Train Doesn't Stop Here Anymore, The
1964,Ja 2,33:1
Hello, Dolly! 1964,Ja 17,22:1
Foxy 1964,F 17,26:1
Oh What a Lovely War 1964,O 1,30:1
Severed Head, A 1964,O 29,40:1
I Was Dancing 1964,N 9,40:4
Roar of the Greasepaint-the Smell of the Crowd
1965,My 17,46:2
Hello, Dolly! 1965,S 11,17:1
Cactus Flower 1965,D 9,60:2
We Have Always Lived in the Castle
1966,O 20,53:1
Don't Drink the Water 1966,N 18,37:1
I Do! I Do! 1966,D 6,58:1
Breakfast at Tiffany's 1966,D 15,60:1
Astrakhan Coat, The 1967,Ja 13,18:1
Hello, Dolly! 1967,Mr 2,30:4
Hello, Dolly! 1967,Je 14,38:1
Keep It in the Family 1967,S 28,59:1
Rosencrantz and Guildenstern Are Dead
1967,O 29,II,1:1
Hello, Dolly! 1967,N 13,61:1
How Now, Dow Jones 1967,D 8,53:1
Happy Time, The 1968,Ja 19,32:2
Seven Descents of Myrtle, The 1968,Mr 28,54:1
Rockefeller and the Red Indians 1968,O 25,37:1
Promises, Promises 1968,D 2,59:3
Promises, Promises 1968,D 15,II,3:1
Forty Carats 1968,D 27,45:1
Play It Again, Sam 1969,F 13,52:3
Play It Again, Sam 1969,Jl 13,II,1:1
Private Lives 1969,D 5,52:1
Forty Carats 1970,Ja 6,48:1
Play on Love 1970,Ja 16,31:1
Hello, Dolly! 1970,Ja 25,70:6
Child's Play 1970,F 18,39:1
Hello, Dolly! 1970,Mr 30,52:1
Merrick, Gordon
Importance of Being Earnest, The 1936,O 22,31:2
Time of Their Lives 1937,O 26,19:1
Man Who Came to Dinner, The 1939,O 17,31:1
Merrick, Gordon (Playwright)
Second Shot, The 1937,Ap 20,28:4
Merrick, Harold E
That's That 1924,Ap 30,19:2
Joan of Arkansas 1925,Ap 5,16:1
Sale and a Sailor, A, or Glory! What Price!
1926,Ap 25,30:4
Merrick, James
Montserrat 1954,My 26,34:2
Merrick, John
Lady in the Dark 1952,Mr 8,11:3
Merrick, Mahlon (Musical Director)
Jack Benny 1963,Mr 1,10:5
Merrifield, Don
Crooked Gamblers 1920,Ag 2,12:1
Inspector Kennedy 1929,D 21,16:3
Merrigal, Alice (Costume Designer)
My Beginning 1962,Ja 31,21:1
Lady of Mexico 1962,O 20,13:2
Daddy Come Home 1963,Ap 17,33:1
Eternal Sabbath 1963,O 19,17:2
Comforter, The 1964,Ap 22,41:1
Go, Go, Go, God is Dead! 1966,O 12,37:1
Man Who Washed His Hands, The 1967,F 16,33:1
Happy Faculty, The 1967,Ap 19,50:1
Guimpes and Saddles 1967,O 11,36:3
Babes Don't Cry Anymore 1968,F 21,55:1
Ballad of John Ogilvie, The 1968,O 9,42:4
Priest in the Cellar, The 1969,F 19,39:1
Reunion of Sorts 1969,O 15,40:1

Merrill, Art (Lighting Director)
Connelly vs Connelly 1961,F 18,11:3
Anthony on Overtime 1961,O 21,13:2
Merrill, Art (Scenic Designer)
Anthony on Overtime 1961,O 21,13:2
Merrill, Beth
Fashions for Men 1922,D 6,22:1
White Desert 1923,O 19,17:3
Lazybones 1924,S 23,23:1
Ladies of the Evening 1924,D 24,11:2
Lily Sue 1926,N 17,22:2
Lily Sue 1926,N 28,VIII,1:1
Hidden 1927,S 25,VIII,4:8
Hidden 1927,O 5,30:4
Menagerie 1935,Jl 2,24:3
Julie the Great 1936,Ja 15,15:3
Christmas Eve 1939,D 28,17:2
Lady Who Came to Stay, The 1941,Ja 3,13:2
Autumn Hill 1942,Ap 14,17:4
All My Sons 1947,Ja 30,21:2
All My Sons 1947,F 9,II,1:1
Merrill, Blanche (Playwright)
Greenwich Village Follies 1921,S 1,18:3
Earl Carroll's Vanities 1925,Jl 7,24:1
Merrill, Bob (Composer)
New Girl in Town 1957,My 15,40:1
New Girl in Town 1957,My 26,II,1:1
Take Me Along 1959,O 23,22:2
Take Me Along 1959,N 1,II,1:1
Carnival! 1961,Ap 14,22:2
Carnival! 1961,Ap 23,II,1:1
Breakfast at Tiffany's 1966,D 15,60:1
Henry, Sweet Henry 1967,O 24,51:2
Henry, Sweet Henry 1967,N 5,II,3:1
Carnival! 1968,D 13,58:1
Merrill, Bob (Lyricist)
New Girl in Town 1957,My 15,40:1
Take Me Along 1959,O 23,22:2
Take Me Along 1959,N 1,II,1:1
Carnival! 1961,Ap 14,22:2
Carnival! 1961,Ap 23,II,1:1
Funny Girl 1964,Mr 27,15:1
Breakfast at Tiffany's 1966,D 15,60:1
Henry, Sweet Henry 1967,O 24,51:2
Carnival! 1968,D 13,58:1
Merrill, Clinton
Orange Blossoms 1922,S 20,18:1
Merrill, David
Ten Million Ghosts 1936,O 24,23:7
Merrill, Dina
Mermaids Singing, The 1945,N 29,26:6
Major Barbara 1965,My 18,33:1
Merrill, Dorritt
Edith Piaf 1947,O 30,30:2
Merrill, Ellen
No for an Answer 1941,Ja 6,10:6
Trojan Women, The 1941,Ap 9,32:5
Victory Belles 1943,O 27,26:3
Merrill, Gary
See My Lawyer 1939,S 28,29:1
Winged Victory 1943,N 22,24:1
Yellow Jack 1944,Ap 7,23:3
Born Yesterday 1946,F 5,18:2
Born Yesterday 1946,F 10,II,1:1
Born Yesterday 1947,My 18,II,1:1
At War With the Army 1949,Mr 9,32:2
World of Carl Sandburg, The 1959,O 13,44:6
World of Carl Sandburg, The 1959,O 26,53:3
Step on a Crack 1962,O 18,48:1
Merrill, Howard (Producer)
Oh Captain! 1958,F 5,21:2
Merrill, James (Playwright)
Immortal Husband, The 1955,F 15,32:2
Merrill, Joan
Priorities of 1942 1942,Mr 13,23:2
Merrill, Lynn
From Morn Till Midnight 1948,D 7,41:6
Lunatics and Lovers 1954,D 14,44:2
Merrill, Mabbs
Rosmersholm 1946,N 23,11:5
Merrill, Marguerite
Tommy 1933,Ag 8,22:5
Merrill, Marion
Fuente Ovejuna; Sheep Well, The 1936,My 3,II,4:1
Merrill, Mary (Costume Designer)
Double Door 1933,S 22,15:5
Laughing Woman, The 1936,O 14,30:1
Tobias and the Angel 1937,Ap 29,16:5
Prologue to Glory 1938,Mr 18,22:2
Big Blow 1938,O 3,11:2
Sing for Your Supper 1939,Ap 25,18:6
Merrill, Mary (Scenic Designer)
Your Young Men 1935,Ag 8,13:2
Merrill, Mary M
Trojan Women, The 1941,Ap 9,32:5
Merrill, Nathaniel (Director)
Porgy and Bess 1965,O 20,53:3
Merrill, Ray (Pvt)
Winged Victory 1943,N 22,24:1
Merrill, Scott
Threepenny Opera, The 1954,Mr 11,26:5
Threepenny Opera, The 1954,Mr 21,II,1:1
Threepenny Opera, The 1954,Ap 4,II,7:1

Immortal Husband, The 1955,F 15,32:2
Seventh Heaven 1955,My 27,16:2
Threepenny Opera, The 1955,S 21,38:1
Threepenny Opera, The 1956,Mr 11,II,1:1
Eugenia 1957,Ja 31,20:1
Threepenny Opera, The 1960,S 15,44:3
Merriman, Dan
Saint of Bleecker Street, The 1954,D 28,21:1
Merriman, Robert (Director)
Capacity for Wings 1957,Ja 10,25:2
Music Man, The 1961,Mr 18,17:3
Merriman, Robert (Miscellaneous)
Dandy Dick 1956,Ja 11,37:2
Merriman, Robert (Producer)
Thieves' Carnival 1955,F 2,21:1
Morning's at Seven 1955,Je 23,25:1
Merriman, Robert (Scenic Designer)
Dragon's Mouth 1955,N 17,45:1
Merrimore, Joy
Memphis Bound 1945,My 25,23:2
Merrit, Gordon
Good Boy 1928,S 6,23:2
Merritt, Arnold
J B 1958,D 12,2:7
Merritt, Bob
Jacobowsky and the Colonel 1944,Mr 15,17:2
Merritt, Franklin
Round Table, The 1930,F 28,20:5
Merritt, George
Hairy Ape, The 1928,F 19,VIII,4:1
Blaue vom Himmel, Das 1930,Ap 20,VIII,2:1
Magda 1930,Je 1,VIII,2:8
Last Enemy, The 1930,O 31,21:1
Merritt, Larry
Fourth Avenue North 1961,S 28,50:2
Merritt, Ray
Tall Story 1959,Ja 30,33:2
Merritt, Theresa
Carmen Jones 1945,My 3,26:5
Carmen Jones 1946,Ap 8,32:2
Our Lan' 1947,S 29,16:5
Carmen Jones 1951,S 22,8:6
Mamba's Daughters 1953,Mr 21,12:6
Trumpets of the Lord 1963,D 23,22:3
Amen Corner, The 1965,Je 13,82:4
Trumpets of the Lord 1969,Ap 30,37:1
Five on the Black Hand Side 1970,Ja 2,32:2
Merritt, Toni
Straw Hat, The 1937,D 31,8:2
Merry, Eileen
Uncle Willie 1956,D 21,17:1
Merry-Macs
Frank Fay's Vaudeville 1939,Mr 3,20:4
Merryman, Joseph
Simon Called Peter 1924,N 11,20:2
Mersereau, Claire
Sophie 1920,Mr 3,12:2
American Born 1925,O 6,31:3
Mershon, Bernice
Princess Ida 1925,Ap 14,27:2
Patience 1925,My 24,23:2
Mlle Modiste 1929,O 8,34:1
Fifty Million Frenchmen 1929,N 28,34:4
Merson, Billy
Rose Marie 1925,Mr 21,16:2
Lad, The 1929,Ja 13,VIII,4:5
Merson, Isobel
Little Poor Man, The 1925,Ag 6,14:1
Merson, Marc (Producer)
Basement, The 1967,O 3,56:1
Fragments 1967,O 3,56:1
Mertens, Patricia
My Beginning 1962,Ja 31,21:1
Merton, Ivy
Her Unborn Child 1928,Mr 7,28:3
Parade 1929,S 1,VIII,1:1
Merton, Martha
Earl Carroll's Vanities 1928,Ag 7,25:2
Mertz, Franz (Costume Designer)
Don Carlos 1964,N 25,40:1
Mertz, Franz (Scenic Designer)
Don Carlos 1964,N 25,40:1
Mertz, Ralph
Curse You, Jack Dalton 1935,Jl 16,24:1
Mervis, Barry
Love's Call 1925,S 11,20:1
Mervis, Harry
If I Were You 1931,S 24,21:1
Bloody Laughter 1931,D 5,20:6
Wolves 1932,Ja 7,26:3
Mervyn, William
Tumbler, The 1960,F 25,32:2
Merwin, Samuel
Nantucket Follies 1927,Jl 30,13:2
Way of the World, The 1931,Je 2,34:3
Merwin, Samuel (Playwright)
Girl Outside, The 1932,O 25,24:3
Merwin, W S (Translator)
Yerma 1966,D 9,60:1
Mery, Andree
Lac Sale, Le 1926,O 3,VIII,2:1
Meryem, Jane
Au Rat Mort, Cabinet No 6 1923,O 16,18:1

Meryem, Jane—Cont
Nounouche 1923,O 23,16:1
Alcide Pepis 1923,O 30,17:2
Prenez Ma Dame 1923,N 27,23:5
Griffe, La 1923,N 27,23:5
Meschke, Michael (Director)
Threepenny Opera, The 1966,O 28,33:1
Meservey, A R
You and I 1925,O 20,29:1
Meshkoff, Janice
Crucible, The 1958,Mr 12,36:1
Nervous Set, The 1959,My 13,43:1
Meshonek, June
Carnival! 1961,Ap 14,22:2
Meskil, Katherine
Ceiling Zero 1935,Ap 11,26:2
Feather in the Breeze 1936,Jl 14,22:2
Chalked Out 1937,Mr 26,24:2
Reno 1937,Ag 10,22:7
Mrs O'Brien Entertains 1939,F 9,16:3
They Should Have Stood in Bed 1942,F 14,18:5
Sun Field, The 1942,D 10,33:2
Ziegfeld Follies 1943,Ap 2,16:2
Death of Cuchulain, The 1959,Ap 13,34:4
Meskin, Aaron
Dybbuk, The 1926,D 14,24:2
Eternal Jew, The 1926,D 21,21:2
Jacob's Dream 1927,Ja 4,20:2
Golem, The 1927,F 5,13:2
David's Crown 1948,My 10,26:2
Golem, The 1948,My 17,22:3
Oedipus Rex 1948,My 24,23:2
Meskin, Amnon
Seven at Dawn, The 1961,Ap 18,43:1
Children of the Shadows 1964,F 27,26:1
Meslin, Louis
Heart of a City 1942,F 13,24:6
Meslow, Sophie
Iron Flowers 1933,Je 13,22:2
Mesot, Frederic
Gay Blades 1937,N 12,26:6
Gay Blades 1937,N 16,27:1
Messager, Andre (Composer)
Deburau 1926,N 14,VIII,2:1
Passionement 1928,Ja 15,VIII,2:1
Coup de Roulis 1928,O 21,IX,5:6
Passionement; Passionately 1929,Mr 8,31:4
Messel, Oliver (Costume Designer)
Cochran's 1930 Revue 1930,Ap 13,X,1:6
Helen 1932,Ja 31,I,5:2
Country Wife, The 1936,O 7,32:3
Romeo and Juliet 1951,Mr 12,21:2
House of Flowers 1954,D 31,11:2
Dark Is Light Enough, The 1955,F 24,20:1
Dark Is Light Enough, The 1955,Mr 6,II,1:1
Rashomon 1959,Ja 28,36:2
Traveller Without Luggage 1964,S 18,26:2
Messel, Oliver (Miscellaneous)
Miracle, The 1932,Ap 10,I,18:1
Lady's Not for Burning, The 1950,N 9,42:2
Messel, Oliver (Scenic Designer)
Cochran's 1930 Revue 1930,Ap 13,X,1:6
Glamorous Night 1935,My 3,23:6
Country Wife, The 1936,O 7,32:3
Country Wife, The 1936,D 2,34:1
Country Wife, The 1936,D 13,XI,3:1
Play's the Thing, The 1948,Ap 29,19:2
Tough at the Top 1949,Jl 17,58:5
Romeo and Juliet 1951,Ja 23,24:8
Romeo and Juliet 1951,Mr 12,21:2
Romeo and Juliet 1951,Mr 25,II,1:1
Little Hut, The 1953,O 8,37:2
House of Flowers 1954,D 31,11:2
Dark Is Light Enough, The 1955,F 24,20:1
Dark Is Light Enough, The 1955,Mr 6,II,1:1
Rashomon 1959,Ja 28,36:2
Rashomon 1959,F 8,II,1:1
Traveller Without Luggage 1964,S 18,26:2
Messidis, Emeleos
Medea 1964,S 1,31:1
Messinger, Martha
Lancelot and Elaine 1921,S 13,12:1
Great Way, The 1921,N 8,28:2
Messner, Marland
Lucky Sam McCarver 1950,Ap 15,10:6
Billy Budd 1955,My 4,35:1
Messuri, Anthony
Song of Bernadette 1946,Mr 27,22:2
Mestayer, Harry
Poppy God, The 1921,Ag 30,10:1
Right to Strike 1921,O 25,20:1
Madeleine and the Movies 1922,Mr 7,11:1
Gypsy Jim 1924,Ja 15,17:4
Ariadne 1925,F 24,17:1
Monkey Talks, The 1925,D 29,20:1
Vaudeville (Palace) 1928,Ag 14,15:5
R U R 1930,F 18,28:1
Marco Millions 1930,Mr 4,24:4
Trick for Trick 1932,F 19,14:2
Music in the Air 1932,N 9,28:2
Sleeping Clergyman, A 1934,O 9,16:1
Music Hath Charms 1934,D 31,8:2
If a Body 1935,My 1,25:3
Achilles Had a Heel 1935,O 14,20:2

Mestayer, Harry—Cont

Hamlet 1936,O 9,30:2
Three Waltzes 1937,D 27,10:2
Glorious Morning 1938,N 28,10:3

Mestayer, Henry
Volpone 1930,Mr 11,24:5

Mestel, Jacob
Wolves 1924,D 31,9:4
Dybbuk, The 1926,Ja 6,16:2
Gold Diggers, The 1927,D 3,19:2
Jew Suss 1929,O 19,22:3
Angels on Earth 1929,D 11,34:7
Roaming Stars 1930,Ja 25,12:2
Chains 1930,F 23,29:2
Witch of Castile, The 1930,O 25,21:1
Man With the Portfolio, The 1931,F 12,24:6
Armored Train No 1469 1931,N 28,20:3
New Man, The 1932,Ap 22,23:2
He, She and the Ox 1934,F 21,22:7
In-Laws 1934,O 25,28:2
60,000 Heroes 1935,Ja 28,11:5
Parnosseh 1935,F 16,8:8
'Round the Family Table 1938,O 8,10:3
Voice of Israel, The 1948,O 26,40:2
Hershel, The Jester 1948,D 14,39:2
Yosele the Nightingale 1949,O 21,30:4
House on Grand Street, A 1953,O 10,12:6
Hole in the Head, A 1957,Mr 1,15:1

Mestel, Jacob (Director)
Treasure, The 1934,D 18,25:5
Awake and Sing! 1938,D 23,16:6
Father and Son 1956,O 20,17:4

Mestel, Jacob (Miscellaneous)
Armored Train No 1469 1931,N 28,20:3

Mestelle, Helen
Susanna, Don't You Cry 1939,My 23,27:2

Mester, A C (Producer)
Two Strange Women 1933,Ja 11,23:3

Meszel, Max (Lyricist)
To Be or Not to Be-What Kind of a Question Is
That? 1970,O 20,39:1

Meta, Max (Musical Director)
Aquashow 1954,Je 23,20:4

Metalik, Morris
Witch of Castile, The 1930,O 25,21:1

Metaxa, Georges
Cat and the Fiddle, The 1931,S 27,VIII,3:1
Cat and the Fiddle, The 1931,O 16,26:4
$25 an Hour 1933,My 11,14:4
Revenge With Music 1934,N 29,33:5

Metcalf, David
Richard III 1957,N 26,41:1
As You Like It 1958,Ja 21,33:6
Crucible, The 1958,Mr 12,36:1
Curate's Play, The 1961,D 18,41:3
Immoralist, The 1963,N 8,36:2
Prince of Peasantmania 1970,F 22,88:1

Metcalf, David (Director)
Time of Vengeance 1959,D 11,39:1
Time of Vengeance 1959,D 27,II,1:1

Metcalf, Henriette (Playwright)
Camille 1956,S 19,33:1

Metcalf, Henriette (Translator)
Lady of the Camellias, The 1931,Ja 27,21:2
Camille 1932,O 28,23:2

Metcalf, William
Pirates of Penzance, The 1960,O 7,29:1
Gondoliers, The 1961,Ja 26,33:2
Gondoliers, The 1962,Ap 19,34:2
Patience 1968,My 16,52:1

Metcalfe, Arthur
Three Live Ghosts 1920,S 30,12:1
Red Poppy, The 1922,D 21,18:2
Dancing Mothers 1924,Ag 12,12:2
Tyrant, The 1930,N 13,33:1
Lady With a Lamp, The 1931,N 20,27:2
Firebird 1932,N 22,25:2

Metcalfe, Edward
I'll Say She Is 1924,My 20,15:1

Metcalfe, Felicia (Playwright)
Come Easy 1933,Ag 30,22:5

Metcalfe, Gerald
Julius Caesar 1955,Jl 13,20:1
Tempest, The 1955,Ag 2,18:2
Mister Roberts 1956,D 6,46:2

Metcalfe, James
Little Theatre Tournament; Aristocrat, The
1929,My 8,34:4
Silver Tassie, The 1929,O 25,26:1
General John Regan 1930,Ja 30,16:5
Moon Over Mulberry Street 1935,S 5,24:6

Metcalfe, Jolliffe (Playwright)
Finished Abroad 1934,Mr 7,23:7

Metcalfe, Nondas
Caesar and Cleopatra 1935,Ag 22,21:1
Whatever Goes Up 1935,N 26,28:2
Let Us Be Gay 1937,Je 29,18:3
Worse Things Happen at Sea 1937,S 1,15:3
What Every Woman Knows 1938,Ag 30,14:5

Meteskey, George
Chicago 70 1970,My 26,33:1
Chicago 70 1970,Je 7,II,3:1

Meth, Max (Musical Director)
Brights Lights of 1944 1943,S 17,27:4

Dream With Music 1944,My 19,15:2
Up in Central Park 1945,Ja 29,17:2
Finian's Rainbow 1948,Ag 29,II,1:1
As the Girls Go 1948,N 15,21:2
Great to Be Alive! 1950,Mr 24,28:2
Pal Joey 1952,Ja 4,17:6
Aquashow 1953,Je 24,29:2
Seventh Heaven 1955,My 27,16:2
Ziegfeld Follies 1957,Mr 2,19:2
Finian's Rainbow 1960,Ap 28,31:1

Methling, Svend (Producer)
Cant 1931,D 20,VIII,1:6

Methot, Mayo
Mad Honeymoon, The 1923,Ag 8,10:1
Song and Dance Man, The 1924,Ja 1,21:2
Deacon, The 1925,N 25,14:3
What Ann Brought Home 1927,F 22,22:2
Song Writer, The 1928,Ag 14,15:2
All the King's Men 1929,F 5,27:1
Now-A-Days 1929,Ag 6,29:3
Great Day! 1929,O 18,24:3
Half Gods 1929,D 23,18:5
Torch Song 1930,Ag 28,23:1
Torch Song 1930,S 7,IX,1:1
Strip Girl 1935,O 21,22:6

Methven, Jeannetta
Tangerine 1921,Ag 10,8:2

Metrick, Cy (Miscellaneous)
Grass Is Always Greener, The 1955,F 16,25:2
Miser, The 1955,Mr 18,34:2

Metropolitan Players
Saturday It Rained 1932,D 14,27:3
Way Out, The 1932,D 14,27:3
March Heir, The 1932,D 14,27:3
White Dress, The 1932,D 14,27:3
Family Exit, The 1932,D 14,27:3

Mette, Jack
Eccentricities of Davy Crockett, The 1961,Ja 4,26:1
Joyful Noise, A 1966,D 16,57:1

Metternich, Mary Lynne
Music Man, The 1963,Ag 15,24:1

Metz, Ben
Marching Song 1937,F 18,18:2
Biggest Thief in Town 1949,Mr 31,31:2

Metz, Jerome (Producer)
Vida es Sueno, La 1964,Mr 18,49:1
Life Is a Dream 1964,Mr 20,24:1

Metz, John
Golden Dog, The 1929,D 25,21:2

Metz, John A Jr
Caesar and Cleopatra 1927,N 6,IX,2:1
Zuider Zee 1928,D 19,24:4

Metz, Lucius
Florodora 1920,Ap 6,18:1
Blossom Time 1921,S 30,10:1
Student Prince, The 1924,D 3,25:3

Metzger, Otto (Miscellaneous)
In Heaven and Earth 1936,Mr 27,24:8

Metzger, Otto (Producer)
Woman of Destiny, A 1936,Mr 3,25:2

Metzger, Rita
Pirates of Penzance, The 1960,O 7,29:1
Happiest Girl in the World, The 1961,Ap 4,42:1
Anya 1965,N 30,48:1
Most Happy Fella, The 1966,My 12,55:1

Metzl, Lothar (Lyricist)
From Vienna 1939,Je 21,26:2

Metzl, Lothar (Playwright)
From Vienna 1939,Je 21,26:2
Reunion in New York 1940,F 22,28:4

Metzler, Larry (Miscellaneous)
Young and Beautiful, The 1959,My 29,13:1

Metzler, Lawrence (Lighting Director)
Macbeth 1966,Ag 29,23:4
Volpone 1967,Je 30,29:1
Hamlet 1968,Jl 4,15:1
Electra 1969,Ag 8,14:1
Sambo 1970,Jl 23,24:1

Metzner, James
Bacchae, The 1969,Mr 15,24:1

Metzner, Ralph (Playwright)
Reincarnation of Christ Show, The 1966,D 4,II,5:1

Metzo, William
Bald Soprano, The 1963,S 18,35:4
Papers 1968,D 3,54:1

Meurneuf, Philip
Taming of the Shrew, The 1957,F 21,30:2

Mew, Marian
Shakuntala 1959,S 10,41:2

Mews, Peter
Measure for Measure 1954,Je 30,23:1
Taming of the Shrew, The 1954,Jl 1,22:2

Mexican Apollonians
Vaudeville (Palace) 1932,Ap 25,18:3

Mexican Tipica Orchestra
Vaudeville (Palace) 1928,Mr 13,23:2
Vaudeville (Palace) 1928,Mr 20,20:2

Mexwell, Edwin (Director)
Not Herbert 1926,Ja 27,16:2

Meyako, Esther
Perfect Fool, The 1921,N 8,28:2

Meyako, Florence
Perfect Fool, The 1921,N 8,28:2

Meyako, George
Perfect Fool, The 1921,N 8,28:2

Meyendorff, Irene von
Victoria Regina 1938,Ap 17,X,2:1

Meyer, Adolph E (Translator)
Phantom Lover, The 1928,S 5,25:1

Meyer, Anders (Lighting Director)
Lovely Light, A 1964,Ja 21,24:2

Meyer, Anders (Miscellaneous)
Lovely Light, A 1964,Ja 21,24:2

Meyer, Anders (Scenic Designer)
Lovely Light, A 1964,Ja 21,24:2

Meyer, Andy (Miscellaneous)
Rules of the Game, The 1960,D 20,44:1

Meyer, Annie Nathan (Playwright)
Advertising of Kate, The 1922,My 9,22:2
Black Souls 1932,Mr 31,25:1

Meyer, B A (Producer)
Crooked Friday, The 1925,O 9,27:3

Meyer, Barbara
Greenwillow 1970,D 8,60:1

Meyer, Beatrice
Lady From the Sea, The 1935,D 14,11:3

Meyer, Beatrice (Miscellaneous)
Nine Till Six 1936,Mr 14,10:3

Meyer, Charles W
Come Seven 1920,Jl 20,10:1

Meyer, Dede (Composer)
She Shall Have Music 1959,Ja 23,18:4
'Toinette 1961,N 21,46:1

Meyer, Dede (Lyricist)
She Shall Have Music 1959,Ja 23,18:4
'Toinette 1961,N 21,46:1

Meyer, Dede (Producer)
She Shall Have Music 1959,Ja 23,18:4

Meyer, Edgar
Greatest Man Alive!, The 1957,My 9,37:2
Dial 'M' for Murder 1958,F 8,12:2

Meyer, Edwin (Lighting Director)
Three Sisters, The 1968,Mr 18,56:1

Meyer, Ellen (Scenic Designer)
Gods of the Mountain, The 1950,My 25,36:2
Aria Da Capo 1950,My 25,36:2
Once Around the Block 1950,My 25,36:2

Meyer, Enoch
Armored Train No 1469 1931,N 28,20:3

Meyer, Ethel O'Dea
Man Who Married a Dumb Wife, The
1930,My 9,20:5

Meyer, Eva
Legend 1930,My 7,25:1

Meyer, Florence
Eternal Road, The 1937,Ja 8,14:2

Meyer, George W (Composer)
Dixie to Broadway 1924,O 30,22:1

Meyer, Greta
Lenz 1926,Ap 29,20:4
Tonight or Never 1930,N 19,19:3

Meyer, Hans Bruno (Composer)
It Can't Happen Here 1936,O 28,30:1
Prologue to Glory 1938,Mr 18,22:2

Meyer, Hans Bruno (Musical Director)
Treasure Island 1938,My 15,II,2:3

Meyer, Harry (Producer)
Shady Lady 1933,Jl 6,26:3

Meyer, Henry W (Musical Director)
Pirates of Penzance, The 1938,Je 3,16:2

Meyer, Hyman
Johannes Kreisler 1922,D 25,20:3

Meyer, Jean
Bourgeois Gentilhomme, Le 1955,O 26,26:1
Barbier de Seville, Le 1955,N 9,40:1

Meyer, Jean (Director)
Bourgeois Gentilhomme, Le 1955,O 26,26:1
Bourgeois Gentilhomme, Le 1955,O 30,II,1:1
Turlututu 1962,S 29,14:2
Femmes Savaantes, Les 1970,F 14,12:1

Meyer, Joan
Ten Nights in a Barroom 1932,Ja 21,17:1

Meyer, Johannes
Victory 1937,N 14,XI,2:5

Meyer, Joseph
Winged Victory 1943,N 22,24:1
Yellow Jack 1944,Ap 7,23:3

Meyer, Joseph (Composer)
Big Boy 1925,Ja 8,28:2
Sweetheart Time 1926,Ja 20,23:2
Just Fancy! 1927,O 12,30:2
Here's Howe! 1928,My 2,19:3
Lady Fingers 1929,F 1,22:4
Jonica 1930,Mr 30,VIII,2:7
Jonica 1930,Ap 8,27:1

Meyer, Joseph (Lyricist)
Ziegfeld Follies 1934,Ja 5,24:3

Meyer, Joseph (Miscellaneous)
Shuffle Along 1952,My 9,20:5

Meyer, Joseph (Playwright)
Ziegfeld Follies 1934,Ja 5,24:3

Meyer, Leo (Costume Designer)
Opera Opera 1955,D 22,19:1
Hungerers, The 1955,D 22,19:1
Hello Out There 1955,D 22,19:1
Floydada to Matador 1955,D 22,19:1

Meyer, Leo (Costume Designer)—Cont
Me, Candido! 1956,O 16,36:2
Right You Are (If You Think You Are)
1957,Mr 5,37:1
Lady's Not for Burning, The 1959,Ja 31,13:2
Meyer, Leo (Lighting Director)
Pajama Tops 1963,Je 1,15:1
What Did We Do Wrong? 1967,O 23,56:1
De Sade Illustrated 1969,My 13,42:4
Foreplay 1970,D 11,58:2
Meyer, Leo (Scenic Designer)
Follies of 1910, The 1960,Ja 15,37:3
Pajama Tops 1963,Je 1,15:1
International Playgirls '64 1964,My 22,40:2
Wives, The 1965,My 18,35:4
Girl in the Freudian Slip, The 1967,My 19,34:3
Minor Adjustment, A 1967,O 7,33:3
Foreplay 1970,D 11,58:2
Meyer, Lester (Producer)
Calico Wedding 1945,Mr 8,18:6
I Gotta Get Out 1947,S 26,27:2
Never Say Never 1951,N 21,21:2
Meyer, Loraine
Galileo 1968,D 1,88:4
Meyer, Lucien
Eisrevue 1969,O 23,55:1
Meyer, Martin (Producer)
Saintliness of Margery Kempe, The 1959,F 3,35:6
Meyer, Mary
Abraham; Dulcitus; Callimachus 1926,Mr 29,24:2
Hamlet 1936,N 11,54:2
Meyer, Michael (Translator)
Hedda Gabler 1960,N 10,61:1
Peer Gynt 1969,Jl 17,56:1
Meyer, Miller C
Taming of the Shrew, The 1957,F 21,30:2
Meyer, Mr (Producer)
Enchanted Cottage, The 1922,Mr 2,21:4
Meyer, Oscar
For Valor 1935,N 19,27:5
Meyer, Perry
Bright Honor 1936,S 28,14:1
Meyer, Ray
Bare Facts 1927,Ag 17,27:5
Malinda 1929,D 4,37:2
Meyer, Steven
Major Barbara 1951,F 24,10:2
Meyer, Virginia
It's About Time 1942,Mr 31,28:3
Meyer, Walter W (Miscellaneous)
Henry V 1969,Je 9,57:1
All's Well That Ends Well 1970,Je 16,53:1
Othello 1970,Je 22,43:1
Meyer Davis's Orchestra
Wonder World 1964,My 18,32:1
Meyer-Foerster (Playwright)
Alt Heidelberg; Student Prince, The
1932,N 20,IX,3:3
Meyerberg, Michael (Producer)
Waiting for Godot 1957,Ja 22,25:1
Meyerhold (Director)
Mandate 1926,F 15,19:1
Last Defensive, The 1931,S 27,VIII,3:2
Meyerhold (Original Author)
Dame aux Camelias, La 1934,Je 10,IX,2:5
Meyerhold (Producer)
Destruction of Europe, The 1925,Ja 11,VII,2:7
Revisor 1927,My 1,II,6:8
Last Defensive, The 1931,S 27,VIII,3:2
Meyerink, Hubert von
Unentbehrliche, Der 1937,O 24,XI,3:1
Meyerowitz, Jan (Composer)
Barrier, The 1950,N 3,32:2
Meyers, David G (Miscellaneous)
Gingham Dog, The 1969,Ap 24,41:1
Meyers, David G (Producer)
Honest-to-God Schnozzola, The 1969,Ap 22,40:2
Leader, The 1969,Ap 22,40:2
Place for Polly, A 1970,Ap 20,45:1
Meyers, Don
Shoemaker and the Peddler, The 1960,O 15,27:4
Meyers, Edward M (Producer)
Man in the Glass Booth, The 1968,S 27,41:1
Meyers, Ernest
At Home Abroad 1935,S 20,17:4
Meyers, Jerry
Kismet 1965,Je 23,45:1
Meyers, John Bernard (Producer)
Gertrude Stein's First Reader 1969,D 16,56:1
Meyers, Lanny (Composer)
Jack in the Box 1960,My 19,43:3
Meyers, Lanny (Lyricist)
Jack in the Box 1960,My 19,43:3
Meyers, Lanny (Miscellaneous)
O Say Can You See! 1962,O 9,45:1
Hooray!! It's a Glorious Day. . .And All That
1966,Mr 10,28:1
Leonard Sillman's New Faces of 1968
1968,My 3,43:1
Meyers, Lorna Lynn
Doll's House, A 1937,D 28,28:6
Meyers, Louise
Honey Girl 1920,My 4,9:1

Meyers, Martin
Guide, The 1968,Mr 7,50:1
Zorba 1968,N 18,58:1
Gandhi 1970,O 21,37:1
Meyers, Norton
As You Like It 1923,Ap 24,24:1
Meyers, Richard (Composer)
Street Singer, The 1929,S 18,35:2
Americana 1932,O 6,19:3
Meyers, Richard (Lyricist)
Ziegfeld Follies 1934,Ja 5,24:3
Meyers, Richard (Playwright)
Ziegfeld Follies 1934,Ja 5,24:3
Meyers, Ruth
Oresteia 1961,N 8,43:5
Judith 1962,Je 21,25:4
Meyers, Vera
Pirates of Penzance, The 1938,Je 3,16:2
Meyers, Warren
Compulsion 1957,O 25,21:1
Meyers, Warren (Composer)
Cast of Characters 1959,Je 11,37:2
Meyers, William
Rehearsal, The 1952,My 27,30:5
Meyers, William (Playwright)
Spiro Who? 1969,My 19,55:1
Spiro Who? 1969,Je 15,II,3:6
Meyers and Hanford
Greenwich Village Follies 1920,Ag 31,7:3
Meyerson, Eileen
New Freedom, The 1930,My 15,32:4
New Freedom, The 1930,My 17,21:4
Meyn, Karen
Proposition, The 1968,Ap 20,25:3
Meyrand, Pierre
Three Musketeers, The 1968,Je 26,43:1
George Dandin 1968,Je 28,36:1
Miacahua
Vaudeville (Hippodrome) 1924,Mr 18,25:1
Mianna, Moses
Set My People Free 1948,N 4,38:2
Micawber, Dora
What Every Woman Knows 1926,Ap 14,20:2
Miceli, Peter
Arms and the Girl 1950,F 3,28:2
Michael
Peg o' My Heart 1921,F 15,7:1
Michael, Angela
Night Watch In Syria 1943,Ja 5,15:5
Michael, G
Josephus 1933,D 1,22:5
Michael, Gerry
Golden Screw, The 1967,Ja 31,52:1
Michael, Gertrude
Caught Wet 1931,N 5,29:1
Round-Up, The 1932,Mr 8,19:4
Damn Deborah 1937,Ag 17,23:1
Michael, Jerome (Miscellaneous)
Viet Rock 1966,N 11,38:1
Fortune and Men's Eyes 1967,F 24,29:1
Michael, Joseph
Five Posts in the Market Place 1961,Mr 6,30:1
Michael, Keith (Lighting Director)
Gloria and Esperanza 1970,F 5,32:1
Gloria and Esperanza 1970,F 15,II,7:5
Michael, Kevin
Golden Screw, The 1967,Ja 31,52:1
Michael, Lewis
Trial of Mary Dugan, The 1927,S 20,33:1
Michael, Mary
Final Balance, The 1928,O 31,28:3
Distant Drums 1932,Ja 19,24:3
Distant Drums 1932,Ja 31,VIII,1:1
Mary of Scotland 1933,N 28,28:3
Accent on Youth 1935,Jl 2,24:3
Wingless Victory, The 1936,D 24,20:2
Madame Capet 1938,O 26,26:2
Two on an Island 1940,Ja 23,17:2
Yours, A Lincoln 1942,Jl 10,12:3
Damask Cheek, The 1942,O 23,24:2
Portrait in Black 1947,My 15,30:2
Mrs McThing 1952,F 21,22:1
Color of Darkness: An Evening in the World of
James Purdy; You Reach for Your Hat
1963,O 1,34:1
Color of Darkness: An Evening in the World of
James Purdy; Cracks 1963,O 1,24:1
Michael, Patricia
Divorce Me, Darling 1965,F 2,29:6
Michael, Paul
Whoop-Up 1958,D 23,2:7
13 Daughters 1961,Mr 3,17:2
Sing Muse 1961,D 7,52:1
Sweet Miani 1962,S 26,33:2
Tovarich 1963,Mr 20,5:1
Hang Down Your Head and Die 1964,O 19,38:1
Zorba 1968,N 18,58:1
Michael, Paul (Producer)
Time of the Cuckoo, The 1958,O 28,40:2
Clearing in the Woods, A 1959,F 13,32:1
Michael, Peter
Green Table, The 1942,Ja 22,12:2
Prodigal Son, The 1942,F 18,22:2

Michael, Ralph
Love Goes to Press 1947,Ja 2,22:2
Day After Tomorrow 1950,O 27,25:2
Michael, Robin
Pride's Crossing 1950,N 21,37:5
Barefoot in Athens 1951,N 1,35:2
White Devil, The 1955,Mr 15,32:5
Michael, Timmy
Seven Days of Mourning 1969,D 17,64:1
Michaelesko, Michal
Of One Mother 1937,Ja 18,21:3
Michaelis, Karen (Original Author)
White Villa, The 1921,F 20,VI,1:1
Michaelis, Karen (Playwright)
White Villa, The 1921,F 15,7:1
Michaels, Barry (Miscellaneous)
Sold to the Movies; Life Size 1970,Je 18,54:2
Sold to the Movies; Crossing the Gap
1970,Je 18,54:2
Sold to the Movies; Type 424 Meet Type Oh-Oh,
No! 1970,Je 18,54:2
Michaels, Bert
Baker Street 1965,F 17,36:1
Grosse Valise, La 1965,D 15,52:1
Cabaret 1966,N 21,62:1
Canterbury Tales, The 1969,F 4,34:1
Michaels, Bert (Miscellaneous)
Canterbury Tales; Wife of Bath's Tale, The
1969,F 4,34:1
Canterbury Tales; Pilgrims, The 1969,F 4,34:1
Canterbury Tales; Merchant's Tale, The
1969,F 4,34:1
Canterbury Tales; Miller's Tale, The 1969,F 4,34:1
Canterbury Tales; Steward's Tale, The
1969,F 4,34:1
Michaels, Dan
Kilpatrick's Old-Time Minstrels 1930,Ap 21,20:2
Ol' Man Satan 1932,O 4,26:3
How Come Lawd? 1937,O 1,18:5
Michaels, Edwin
Queen High 1926,S 9,21:2
Tobias and the Angel 1937,Ap 29,16:5
Pinocchio 1939,Ja 3,19:2
Michaels, Florence
High Button Shoes 1955,Mr 12,10:6
Michaels, Frankie
Mame 1966,My 25,41:1
Michaels, Gil
Pantagleize 1967,D 1,54:1
Michaels, Henry
Pillar to Post 1943,D 11,11:2
Our Town 1944,Ja 11,24:5
Michaels, Iris (Producer)
All the King's Men 1959,O 17,27:2
Michaels, Jacqueline
You'll See Stars 1943,Ja 1,26:6
Cradle Song 1955,D 2,32:2
Michaels, Jill
Tragical Historie of Doctor Faustus, The
1964,O 6,34:2
Michaels, Joyce
Mother Courage and Her Children 1964,My 12,32:
Michaels, Kay
Mike Downstairs 1968,Ap 19,35:1
Michaels, Kim
Cyrano de Bergerac 1968,Ap 26,30:1
Michaels, Laura
Richard III 1966,Ag 11,26:1
Midsummer Night's Dream, A 1967,Je 19,42:1
Me Nobody Knows, The 1970,My 19,42:1
Michaels, Lynn
Private Life of the Master Race, The
1956,Ja 31,33:3
Deirdre of the Sorrows 1959,O 15,46:1
Michaels, Lynn (Miscellaneous)
Private Life of the Master Race, The
1956,Ja 31,33:3
Michaels, Lynn (Producer)
Deep Are the Roots 1960,O 4,47:1
Hop, Signor! 1962,My 8,45:2
Michaels, Paul (Miscellaneous)
Sweeney Todd 1957,Ag 28,21:4
Michaels, Peter
Two Executioners, The 1964,Mr 25,46:2
Michaels, Raf
Kiss Me, Kate 1954,Mr 27,13:2
And the Wind Blows 1959,Ap 29,28:1
Taming of the Shrew, The 1963,Mr 8,9:1
Michaels, Robert
Orange Blossoms 1922,S 20,18:1
Michaels, Saul
Treasure, The 1920,O 5,13:1
Michaels, Sidney
Marco Polo and the Drum of Ahmad
1950,D 18,34:2
Michaels, Sidney (Lyricist)
Ben Franklin in Paris 1964,O 28,52:1
Michaels, Sidney (Playwright)
Tchin-Tchin 1962,O 9,37:3
Tchin-Tchin 1962,O 26,26:2
Tchin-Tchin 1962,N 25,II,1:1
Dylan 1964,Ja 20,18:1
Ben Franklin in Paris 1964,O 28,52:1

Michaels, Stephen (Composer)
Metamorphoses 1969,D 12,69:1
Michaels, Sully
Last Analysis, The 1964,O 2,30:1
Michalek, Stanislaw (Composer)
Jacob and the Angel 1965,Ja 6,32:1
Post Office, The 1965,Ja 6,32:1
Jaselka 1965,Ja 6,32:1
Book, The 1965,Ja 6,32:1
Labyrinth, The 1965,Ja 6,32:1
Kernel and the Shell, The 1965,Ja 6,32:1
Woman, The 1965,Ja 6,32:1
Nightmare, The 1965,Ja 6,32:1
Michales, Anthony (Director)
Burn Me to Ashes 1963,N 20,48:1
Michalesko, Michal
Song of Love, The 1928,S 25,31:2
Golden Ring, The 1930,F 1,14:7
Three in Love 1931,S 26,25:5
Untitled-Benefit 1933,Ja 25,13:3
Holiday in Town, A 1935,S 30,12:3
Secret of Love, The 1936,F 24,15:2
Souls for Sale 1936,S 21,27:6
Stepsisters 1936,O 13,32:3
Farblondjete Honeymoon 1955,S 27,42:1
Michalesko, Michal (Producer)
Golden Ring, The 1930,F 1,14:7
Farblondjete Honeymoon 1955,S 27,42:1
Michalopoulou, R
Electra 1952,N 20,38:2
Michalovitch, Michal
Prince Reuvaini 1967,N 19,83:1
Oh What a Wedding! 1969,O 20,60:1
Michalow, Michael
As You Like It 1936,Ap 24,18:4
Michaux, Anna Dortch
When the Roll Is Called Up Yonder
1930,My 9,20:5
Michedelov (Choreographer)
Dybbuk, The 1964,F 4,30:2
Michel, Frank
It's Up to You 1921,Mr 29,20:1
Michel, Jean-Claude
Proces, Le; Trial, The 1952,N 18,36:2
Amphitryon 1952,N 21,21:2
Occupe-Toi d'Amelie; Keep Your Eyes on Amelie
1952,N 25,35:2
Hamlet 1952,D 2,39:1
Michel, Leon (Director)
Springtime Folly 1951,F 27,23:4
Michel, Leonard
Conversation Piece 1934,O 24,24:1
Michel, Lillian
Talk About Girls 1927,Je 15,31:3
Michel, Lois
Challenge of Youth 1930,Ja 21,28:5
Michel, Lucia
Zunguru 1938,Ag 7,IX,8:2
Michel, Marc (Original Author)
That Hat! 1964,S 24,45:1
Michel, Scott (Playwright)
Angels Kiss Me 1951,Ap 18,37:6
Sixth Finger in a Five Finger Glove 1956,O 9,31:4
Michel, Trudi (Producer)
Angels Kiss Me 1951,Ap 18,37:6
Michel, Werner (Composer)
From Vienna 1939,Je 21,26:2
Reunion in New York 1940,F 22,28:4
Michel, Werner (Playwright)
From Vienna 1939,Je 21,26:2
Reunion in New York 1940,F 22,28:4
Michel, Werner (Translator)
From Vienna 1939,Je 21,26:2
Michel (Original Author)
Horse Eats Hat 1936,S 28,14:2
Micheladze, Gayane
Bridge of Sighs 1939,Jl 2,IX,1:4
Michelena, Vera
Ziegfeld Follies 1921,Je 22,10:1
Love Dreams 1921,O 11,22:2
Michell, Keith
Irma la Douce 1960,S 30,31:2
Irma la Douce 1960,O 16,II,1:1
Chances, The 1962,Jl 4,11:2
Broken Heart, The 1962,Jl 10,28:2
Rehearsal, The 1963,S 24,45:2
King's Mare, The 1966,Jl 21,23:1
Man of La Mancha 1970,Ja 25,70:6
Michell, Leonard
Winslow Boy, The 1947,O 30,32:2
Michell, Lillian
Tip-Toes 1925,D 29,20:2
Michelotti, Angelo
Rugantino 1964,F 7,34:1
Michels, Rand (Miscellaneous)
Susie Is a Good Girl 1968,N 5,53:2
Grab Bag, The 1968,N 5,53:2
Subscriber, The 1968,N 5,53:2
Michelson, Lottie (Playwright)
Faith and Prudence 1952,O 15,40:2
Michener, Dean
Golden Apple, The 1954,Mr 12,15:2
Guys and Dolls 1959,Jl 22,22:2

Michener, James A (Original Author)
South Pacific 1949,Ap 8,30:2
South Pacific 1949,Ap 17,II,1:1
South Pacific 1949,Je 5,II,1:1
South Pacific 1955,My 5,39:5
South Pacific 1957,Ag 25,35:1
South Pacific 1961,Ap 27,26:3
South Pacific 1965,Je 3,25:1
South Pacific 1967,Je 13,56:1
South Pacific 1969,Jl 7,27:1
Michnikowski, Wieslaw
Visit With the Family, A 1957,O 17,42:5
Michoels
Journey of Benjamin III, The 1928,Je 24,VIII,1:4
Michon, Joe
Vaudeville (Palace) 1928,Ag 28,27:3
Nine Fifteen Revue, The 1930,F 12,26:2
Vaudeville (Palace) 1930,Mr 10,24:4
Michon, M
Revisor; Inspector General, The 1935,F 18,19:6
Poverty Is No Crime 1935,F 21,22:5
Enemies 1935,Mr 19,24:7
Michon, Michel
Chauve-Souris of 1943 1943,Ag 13,13:2
Michon, Michel (Director)
Chauve-Souris of 1943 1943,Ag 13,13:2
Michon, Pete
Vaudeville (Palace) 1928,Ag 28,27:3
Nine Fifteen Revue, The 1930,F 12,26:2
Vaudeville (Palace) 1930,Mr 10,24:4
Michon Brothers, The
Vaudeville (Palace) 1930,Jl 7,22:2
Mick, Hetty Louise (Playwright)
Christmas Carol, A 1921,D 23,18:3
Rose and the Ring, The 1931,D 24,20:7
Mickens, Ernest
Swing It 1937,Jl 23,17:2
Micolucci, Felicia
Blood Wedding 1958,Ap 1,35:1
Micone, Alexander
Subway Express 1929,S 25,34:3
O Evening Star 1936,Ja 9,24:6
Othello 1937,Ja 7,16:4
Micunis, Gordon (Costume Designer)
Iolanthe 1962,Ap 12,42:4
Good Soldier Schweik, The 1963,Ap 9,57:1
Antigone 1967,Je 19,43:1
Up Eden 1968,N 27,42:1
Micunis, Gordon (Scenic Designer)
Rules of the Game, The 1960,D 20,44:1
Iolanthe 1962,Ap 12,42:4
Iolanthe 1962,Ag 8,34:2
Good Soldier Schweik, The 1963,Ap 9,57:1
Jo 1964,F 13,25:1
Up Eden 1968,N 27,42:1
Middlemass, Frank
Measure for Measure 1967,F 15,37:1
Hamlet 1967,F 17,44:1
Romeo and Juliet 1967,F 22,18:1
Middlemass, Robert
Lambs Gambol 1922,Ja 30,16:1
Up the Ladder 1922,Mr 7,11:2
For All of Us 1923,O 16,19:4
Izzy 1924,S 17,16:2
Handy Man, The 1925,Mr 10,19:2
Butter and Egg Man, The 1925,S 24,28:1
Butter and Egg Man, The 1927,Ag 31,19:3
Clutching Claw, The 1928,F 15,20:1
Gang War 1928,Ag 21,27:2
Gambling 1929,Ag 27,31:2
Tavern, The 1930,My 20,32:1
Song and Dance Man, The 1930,Je 17,25:5
Miracle at Verdun 1931,Mr 17,34:6
Unexpected Husband 1931,Je 3,29:4
Criminal at Large 1932,O 11,26:3
Small Miracle 1934,S 27,24:3
Little Shot 1935,Ja 18,28:4
Middlemass, Robert (Playwright)
Lambs Gambol 1922,Ja 30,16:1
Little Theatre Tournament; Valiant, The
1926,My 5,24:5
Valiant, The 1927,F 22,22:5
Valiant, The 1929,S 22,24:6
Budget, The 1932,S 21,26:4
Middleton, Ann
Blue Butterfly, The 1929,F 17,29:3
Blue Butterfly, The 1929,My 4,17:2
Would-Be Gentleman, The 1930,Ap 30,29:2
Midsummer Night's Dream, A 1932,N 18,22:2
Saint Wench 1933,Ja 3,19:3
Middleton, Berry
Antigone 1923,My 4,18:4
Middleton, Charles
January Thaw 1946,F 5,18:2
Middleton, Edgar (Playwright)
Potiphar's Wife 1927,S 4,VII,2:1
Tin Gods 1928,F 19,VIII,4:1
Potiphar's Wife 1928,D 24,10:7
England Expects 1936,Ap 14,18:5
Middleton, Emanuel
Conjur' Man Dies 1936,Mr 12,18:5

Middleton, George (Playwright)
Light of the World, The 1920,Ja 7,17:1
Cave Girl, The 1920,Ag 19,12:2
Unknown Lady, The 1923,N 6,22:1
Other Rose, The 1923,D 16,IX,2:4
Other Rose, The 1923,D 21,15:2
Other Rose, The 1923,D 30,VII,1:1
Road Together, The 1924,Ja 18,21:2
Accused 1925,S 30,20:1
Blood Money 1927,Ag 23,29:2
Big Pond, The 1928,Ag 22,25:1
Polly 1929,Ja 9,28:3
Hiss-Boom-Blah 1936,Ap 18,18:3
Madame Capet 1938,O 26,26:2
Middleton, Guy
French Without Tears 1937,S 26,II,4:3
French Without Tears 1937,S 29,19:1
Middleton, Horace (Composer)
Antigone 1923,My 4,18:4
Seventh Trumpet, The 1941,N 22,10:6
Middleton, Jane
Made in Heaven 1946,O 25,28:2
Love Goes to Press 1947,Ja 2,22:2
Bathsheba 1947,Mr 27,40:2
Light Up the Sky 1948,N 19,34:2
Collector's Item 1952,F 9,11:2
Middleton, Jill
Dolly Jordan 1922,O 4,26:1
World We Live In, The 1922,N 1,16:1
Alloy 1924,O 28,27:1
Middleton, Kathleen
Beranger 1923,Ap 20,20:3
Bit o' Love, A 1925,My 13,24:2
Charley's Aunt 1925,Je 2,16:2
Middleton, Patricia
Unto Such Glory 1937,My 7,28:2
Middleton, Ray
Roberta 1933,N 20,18:4
Knickerbocker Holiday 1938,O 20,26:2
Scandals 1939,Ag 29,17:2
Scandals 1939,S 3,IX,1:1
American Jubilee 1940,My 13,20:5
Winged Victory 1943,N 22,24:1
Annie Get Your Gun 1946,Mr 29,18:2
Annie Get Your Gun 1946,My 17,14:2
Annie Get Your Gun 1946,My 26,II,1:1
Annie Get Your Gun 1946,S 29,II,1:1
Love Life 1948,O 8,31:2
ANTA Album 1951,My 7,22:7
Too True to Be Good 1963,Mr 14,8:2
Too True to Be Good 1963,Mr 23,5:6
South Pacific 1965,Je 3,25:1
Man of La Mancha 1965,N 23,52:1
Man of La Mancha 1967,N 24,61:1
Middleton, Robert
Wild Duck, The 1951,D 27,17:1
Red Rainbow, A 1953,S 15,37:4
Ondine 1954,F 19,23:1
Ondine 1954,F 28,II,1:1
Middleton, Roger
Getting Married 1970,Ja 20,46:1
Middleton, Thomas (Playwright)
Changeling, The 1956,My 4,20:3
Changeling, The 1964,O 30,32:2
Middleton, Tony
Cabin in the Sky 1964,Ja 22,32:1
Porgy and Bess 1964,My 7,32:1
Mider, Mary
Keating 1927,D 26,26:6
Midgley, Raymond (Choreographer)
Merry-Go-Round 1927,Je 1,25:4
Red Robe, The 1928,D 26,15:1
Midgley, Richard
Sun Field, The 1942,D 10,33:2
Three's a Family 1943,My 6,24:2
Tea and Sympathy 1953,O 1,35:1
Midgley, Robin (Director)
Those That Play the Clowns 1966,N 25,48:1
Midolla, Stephen
Best Foot Forward 1956,Mr 3,16:1
Miele, Donald
Scapegoat, The 1950,Ap 20,36:5
Miele, Elizabeth (Lyricist)
Hit the Trail 1954,D 3,31:2
Miele, Elizabeth (Miscellaneous)
Magic 1942,S 30,28:2
Hello Out There 1942,S 30,28:2
Miele, Elizabeth (Playwright)
City Haul 1929,D 31,14:4
Did I Say No? 1931,S 23,19:4
Miele, Elizabeth (Producer)
Best Years 1932,S 8,16:2
Jamboree 1932,N 25,18:4
Anybody's Game 1932,D 22,21:4
Come Easy 1933,Ag 30,22:5
Halfway to Hell 1934,Ja 3,22:3
Triumph 1935,O 15,18:5
Holmeses of Baker Street, The 1936,D 10,34:3
Hit the Trail 1954,D 3,31:2
Mielziner, Jo
Failures, The 1923,N 23,20:1
Saint Joan 1923,D 29,8:4
No Time for Comedy 1939,Ap 18,26:4

Mielziner, Jo—Cont

Mr and Mrs North 1941,Ja 13,11:2
Mielziner, Jo (Costume Designer)
Pygmalion 1926,N 16,24:1
Right You Are (If You Think You Are)
  1927,F 24,27:1
Barretts of Wimpole Street, The 1931,F 10,25:1
House Beautiful, The 1931,Mr 13,20:4
Romeo and Juliet 1934,D 4,23:2
Barretts of Wimpole Street, The 1935,F 26,16:2
Pride and Prejudice 1935,N 3,X,1:5
Pride and Prejudice 1935,N 6,32:4
Pride and Prejudice 1935,N 17,IX,1:1
Romeo and Juliet 1935,D 24,10:2
Ethan Frome 1936,Ja 7,24:7
Ethan Frome 1936,Ja 22,15:2
Saint Joan 1936,Mr 10,27:4
St Helena 1936,O 7,32:1
Hamlet 1936,O 9,30:2
St Helena 1936,O 11,X,1:1
Antony and Cleopatra 1937,N 11,30:2
Yr Obedient Husband 1937,N 27,21:2
Mrs O'Brien Entertains 1939,F 9,16:3
Foolish Notion 1945,Mr 14,23:2
Barretts of Wimpole Street, The 1945,Mr 27,23:6
Mielziner, Jo (Director)
I Married an Angel 1938,My 22,XI,1:1
Mielziner, Jo (Lighting Director)
Panic 1935,Mr 16,18:4
Boys From Syracuse, The 1938,N 24,36:1
Too Many Girls 1939,O 19,26:2
Two on an Island 1940,Ja 23,17:2
Journey to Jerusalem 1940,O 7,21:2
Pal Joey 1940,D 26,22:2
Candle in the Wind 1941,O 23,26:2
Land Is Bright, The 1941,O 29,26:2
Seventh Trumpet, The 1941,N 22,10:6
Firebird of Florence 1945,Mr 23,13:4
Hollywood Pinafore 1945,Je 1,20:1
Carib Song 1945,S 28,17:2
Beggars Are Comming to Town 1945,O 29,16:2
Rugged Path, The 1945,N 12,17:2
Dream Girl 1945,D 15,13:2
Jeb 1946,F 22,20:2
Annie Get Your Gun 1946,My 17,14:2
Happy Birthday 1946,N 1,31:2
Another Part of the Forest 1946,N 21,42:2
Big Two, The 1947,Ja 9,21:2
Street Scene 1947,Ja 10,17:2
Chocolate Soldier, The 1947,Mr 13,34:2
Barefoot Boy With Cheek 1947,Ap 4,20:2
Command Decision 1947,O 2,30:2
Allegro 1947,O 11,10:2
Streetcar Named Desire, A 1947,D 4,42:2
Mister Roberts 1948,F 19,27:2
Sleepy Hollow 1948,Je 4,26:3
Summer and Smoke 1948,O 7,33:2
Anne of the Thousand Days 1948,D 9,49:2
Death of a Salesman 1949,F 11,27:2
South Pacific 1949,Ap 8,30:2
Man, The 1950,Ja 20,28:2
Dance Me a Song 1950,Ja 21,10:5
Innocents, The 1950,F 2,30:2
Innocents, The 1950,F 12,II,1:1
Wisteria Trees, The 1950,Mr 30,39:1
Streetcar Named Desire, A 1950,My 24,36:1
King and I, The 1951,Mr 30,26:2
Tree Grows in Brooklyn, A 1951,Ap 20,24:3
Top Banana 1951,N 2,19:2
Point of No Return 1951,D 14,35:2
Flight Into Egypt 1952,Mr 19,33:2
Wish You Were Here 1952,Je 26,26:6
Gambler, The 1952,O 14,40:1
Picnic 1953,F 20,14:7
Can-Can 1953,My 8,28:1
Me and Juliet 1953,My 29,17:1
Tea and Sympathy 1953,O 1,35:1
Kind Sir 1953,N 5,41:2
By the Beautiful Sea 1954,Ap 9,20:1
All Summer Long 1954,S 24,26:2
Fanny 1954,N 5,16:1
Silk Stockings 1955,F 25,17:3
Cat on a Hot Tin Roof 1955,Mr 25,18:2
Island of Goats 1955,O 5,40:1
Lark, The 1955,N 18,20:1
Pipe Dream 1955,D 1,44:1
Middle of the Night 1956,F 9,39:1
Most Happy Fella, The 1956,My 4,20:1
Mister Roberts 1956,D 6,46:2
Happy Hunting 1956,D 7,30:1
Miss Lonelyhearts 1957,O 4,26:2
Square Root of Wonderful, The 1957,O 31,40:1
Look Homeward, Angel 1957,N 29,33:1
Oh Captain! 1958,F 5,21:2
Day the Money Stopped, The 1958,F 21,19:4
Handful of Fire 1958,O 2,45:3
World of Suzie Wong, The 1958,O 15,47:1
Gazebo, The 1958,D 13,2:7
Whoop-Up 1958,D 23,2:7
Rashomon 1959,Ja 28,36:2
Rashomon 1959,F 8,II,1:1
Most Happy Fella, The 1959,F 11,50:2
Sweet Bird of Youth 1959,Mr 11,39:2
Sweet Bird of Youth 1959,Mr 22,II,1:1

Gypsy 1959,My 22,31:6
Gang's All Here, The 1959,O 2,23:1
Silent Night, Lonely Night 1959,D 4,36:1
There Was a Little Girl 1960,Mr 1,28:1
Best Man, The 1960,Ap 1,39:1
Christine 1960,Ap 29,27:1
Period of Adjustment 1960,N 11,34:1
Little Moon of Alban 1960,D 2,34:1
Everybody Loves Opal 1961,O 12,40:2
All American 1962,Mr 20,44:1
Mr President 1962,O 22,34:2
Milk Train Doesn't Stop Here Anymore, The
  1963,Ja 18,7:1
After the Fall 1964,Ja 24,18:1
But for Whom Charlie 1964,Mr 13,42:2
Owl and the Pussycat, The 1964,N 19,48:1
Danton's Death 1965,O 22,46:1
Playroom, The 1965,D 6,49:1
Don't Drink the Water 1966,N 18,37:1
My Sweet Charlie 1966,D 7,56:1
Paisley Convertible, The 1967,F 13,42:1
That Summer-That Fall 1967,Mr 17,33:1
Daphne in Cottage D 1967,O 16,56:1
Prime of Miss Jean Brodie, The 1968,Ja 17,39:1
I Never Sang for My Father 1968,Ja 26,30:1
Seven Descents of Myrtle, The 1968,Mr 28,54:1
Possibilities 1968,D 5,60:1
1776 1969,Mr 17,46:2
Child's Play 1970,F 18,39:1
Georgy 1970,F 27,26:1
Look to the Lilies 1970,Mr 30,59:1
Mielziner, Jo (Miscellaneous)
Two on an Island 1940,Ja 23,17:2
Guys and Dolls 1965,Ap 29,39:1
Mielziner, Jo (Producer)
Co-Respondent Unknown 1936,F 12,24:4
Summer and Smoke 1948,O 17,II,1:1
Happy Hunting 1956,D 7,30:1
Mielziner, Jo (Scenic Designer)
Guardsman, The 1924,O 14,23:1
Guardsman, The 1924,O 19,VIII,1:1
Wild Duck, The 1925,F 25,16:4
First Flight 1925,S 18,26:2
Caught 1925,O 6,31:2
Call of Life, The 1925,O 10,10:1
Lucky Sam McCarver 1925,O 22,22:1
Little Eyolf 1926,F 3,22:1
Masque of Venice, The 1926,Mr 3,27:3
Seed of the Brute 1926,N 2,34:3
Pygmalion 1926,N 16,24:1
Saturday's Children 1927,Ja 27,13:1
Right You Are (If You Think You Are)
  1927,F 24,27:1
Mariners 1927,Mr 29,22:2
Second Man, The 1927,Ap 12,24:3
Marquise, The 1927,N 15,26:4
Doctor's Dilemma, The 1927,N 22,33:1
Fallen Angels 1927,D 2,20:4
Cock Robin 1928,Ja 13,26:6
Strange Interlude 1928,Ja 31,28:1
Grey Fox, The 1928,O 23,32:3
Jealous Moon, The 1928,N 21,32:2
Lady Lies, The 1928,N 27,36:2
Most Immoral Lady, A 1928,N 27,36:1
Street Scene 1929,Ja 11,20:4
Skyrocket, The 1929,Ja 12,14:7
Street Scene 1929,Ja 20,VIII,1:1
Judas 1929,Ja 25,20:4
Meet the Prince 1929,F 26,30:5
Young Alexander 1929,Mr 13,28:2
Little Show, The 1929,My 1,28:5
Street Scene 1929,My 19,IX,1:1
First Mortgage 1929,O 11,36:1
Amorous Antic, The 1929,D 3,29:2
Uncle Vanya 1930,Ap 16,26:5
Second Little Show, The 1930,S 3,36:1
Solid South 1930,O 15,27:1
Mr Gilhooley 1930,O 1,26:1
Sweet and Low 1930,N 18,28:5
Anatol 1931,Ja 17,23:3
Barretts of Wimpole Street, The 1931,F 10,25:1
House Beautiful, The 1931,Mr 13,20:4
Third Little Show, The 1931,Je 2,34:3
I Love an Actress 1931,S 18,29:2
Brief Moment 1931,N 10,28:2
Of Thee I Sing 1931,D 28,20:1
Never No More 1932,Ja 8,27:1
Distant Drums 1932,Ja 19,24:3
Distant Drums 1932,Ja 31,VIII,1:1
Bloodstream 1932,Mr 31,25:1
Bridal Wise 1932,My 31,15:5
Hey, Nonny, Nonny! 1932,Je 7,22:3
Gay Divorce 1932,N 30,23:4
Biography 1932,D 13,25:3
Champagne, Sec 1933,O 16,20:2
Divine Drudge 1933,O 27,22:3
I Was Waiting for You 1933,N 14,23:3
Dark Tower, The 1933,N 27,20:3
Lake, The 1933,D 27,24:2
By Your Leave 1934,Ja 25,15:3
Dodsworth 1934,F 26,20:4
Yellow Jack 1934,Mr 7,22:6
Yellow Jack 1934,Mr 18,IX,1:1
Pure in Heart, The 1934,Mr 21,24:3
Romeo and Juliet 1934,D 4,23:2

Mielziner, Jo (Scenic Designer)—Cont

Romeo and Juliet 1934,D 21,30:3
Accent on Youth 1934,D 26,19:1
De Luxe 1935,F 24,VIII,3:4
Barretts of Wimpole Street, The 1935,F 26,16:2
De Luxe 1935,Mr 6,22:2
Panic 1935,Mr 16,18:4
Flowers of the Forest 1935,Ap 9,25:2
Kind Lady 1935,Ap 24,24:5
Kind Lady 1935,Ap 28,X,1:1
Jubilee 1935,S 23,20:3
Winterset 1935,S 26,19:2
Winterset 1935,O 6,XI,1:1
Jubilee 1935,O 14,20:1
Pride and Prejudice 1935,N 3,X,1:5
Pride and Prejudice 1935,N 6,32:4
Romeo and Juliet 1935,D 24,10:2
Ethan Frome 1936,Ja 7,24:7
Room in Red and White, A 1936,Ja 20,23:3
Ethan Frome 1936,Ja 22,15:2
Ethan Frome 1936,F 2,IX,1:1
Postman Always Rings Twice, The 1936,F 7,14:4
Co-Respondent Unknown 1936,F 12,24:4
Postman Always Rings Twice, The 1936,F 26,17:2
Saint Joan 1936,Mr 10,27:4
On Your Toes 1936,Ap 13,14:4
Hamlet 1936,O 1,28:3
St Helena 1936,O 7,32:1
Hamlet 1936,O 9,30:2
St Helena 1936,O 11,X,1:1
Daughters of Atreus 1936,O 15,33:1
Wingless Victory, The 1936,D 24,20:2
Women, The 1936,D 28,13:1
High Tor 1937,Ja 11,15:2
Susan and God 1937,Ap 11,II,12:3
Star-Wagon, The 1937,S 30,18:5
Susan and God 1937,O 8,26:4
Antony and Cleopatra 1937,N 11,30:2
Too Many Heroes 1937,N 16,26:2
Father Malachy's Miracle 1937,N 18,26:4
Yr Obedient Husband 1937,N 27,21:2
Barchester Towers 1937,D 1,27:1
Yr Obedient Husband 1938,Ja 11,26:5
Father Malachy's Miracle 1938,Ja 23,XI,1:6
On Borrowed Time 1938,F 4,16:4
Save Me the Waltz 1938,Mr 1,19:2
I Married an Angel 1938,My 12,26:2
Sing Out the News 1938,S 26,12:5
Abe Lincoln in Illinois 1938,O 17,12:2
Knickerbocker Holiday 1938,O 20,26:2
Boys From Syracuse, The 1938,N 24,36:1
Mrs O'Brien Entertains 1939,F 9,16:3
Stars in Your Eyes 1939,F 10,18:2
Too Many Girls 1939,O 19,26:2
Morning's at Seven 1939,N 7,30:2
Key Largo 1939,N 19,X,3:4
Key Largo 1939,N 28,30:2
Morning's at Seven 1939,D 1,26:2
Christmas Eve 1939,D 28,17:2
Two on an Island 1940,Ja 16,18:4
Two on an Island 1940,F 4,IX,1:1
Higher and Higher 1940,Ap 5,24:3
Journey to Jerusalem 1940,O 7,21:2
Flight to the West 1940,D 15,I,59:5
Pal Joey 1940,D 26,22:2
Flight to the West 1940,D 31,19:1
Cream in the Well, The 1941,Ja 21,19:2
Talley Method, The 1941,F 25,26:3
Watch on the Rhine 1941,Ap 2,26:2
Wookey, The 1941,S 11,20:5
Candle in the Wind 1941,S 16,19:6
Candle in the Wind 1941,O 23,26:2
Best Foot Forward 1941,O 26,IX,1:3
Best Foot Forward 1941,O 2,28:2
Land Is Bright, The 1941,O 29,26:2
Seventh Trumpet, The 1941,N 22,10:6
Solitaire 1942,Ja 28,22:2
By Jupiter 1942,Je 4,22:1
Susan and God 1943,D 14,30:2
Glass Menagerie, The 1945,Ja 14,II,2:4
Foolish Notion 1945,Mr 14,23:2
Foolish Notion 1945,Mr 18,II,1:1
Firebird of Florence 1945,Mr 23,13:4
Barretts of Wimpole Street, The 1945,Mr 27,23:6
Glass Menagerie, The 1945,Ap 2,15:5
Carousel 1945,Ap 20,24:2
Hollywood Pinafore 1945,Je 1,20:1
Carib Song 1945,S 28,17:2
Beggars Are Comming to Town 1945,O 29,16:2
Rugged Path, The 1945,N 12,17:2
Dream Girl 1945,D 15,13:2
Jeb 1946,F 22,20:2
Annie Get Your Gun 1946,My 17,14:2
Annie Get Your Gun 1946,My 26,II,1:1
Happy Birthday 1946,N 1,31:2
Happy Birthday 1946,N 10,II,1:1
Another Part of the Forest 1946,N 21,42:2
Big Two, The 1947,Ja 9,21:2
Street Scene 1947,Ja 10,17:2
Finian's Rainbow 1947,Ja 11,23:2
Street Scene 1947,Ja 19,II,1:1
Finian's Rainbow 1947,Ja 26,II,1:1
Chocolate Soldier, The 1947,Mr 13,34:2
Barefoot Boy With Cheek 1947,Ap 4,20:2
Command Decision 1947,O 2,30:2
Allegro 1947,O 11,10:2

Mielziner, Jo (Scenic Designer)—Cont
Allegro 1947,N 2,II,1:1
Streetcar Named Desire, A 1947,D 4,42:2
Allegro 1948,Ja 18,II,3:5
Mister Roberts 1948,F 19,27:2
Mister Roberts 1948,F 29,II,1:1
Sleepy Hollow 1948,Je 4,26:3
Finian's Rainbow 1948,Ag 29,II,1:1
Summer and Smoke 1948,O 7,33:2
Anne of the Thousand Days 1948,D 9,49:2
Carousel 1949,Ja 26,28:2
Carousel 1949,F 6,II,1:1
Death of a Salesman 1949,F 11,27:2
Death of a Salesman 1949,F 20,II,1:1
South Pacific 1949,Ap 8,30:2
Man, The 1950,Ja 20,28:2
Dance Me a Song 1950,Ja 21,10:5
Innocents, The 1950,F 2,30:2
Innocents, The 1950,F 12,II,1:1
Wisteria Trees, The 1950,Mr 30,39:1
Streetcar Named Desire, A 1950,My 24,36:1
Mister Roberts 1950,Jl 20,22:4
Burning Bright 1950,O 19,40:2
Guys and Dolls 1950,N 25,11:2
King and I, The 1951,Mr 30,26:2
King and I, The 1951,Ap 8,II,1:1
Tree Grows in Brooklyn, A 1951,Ap 20,24:3
Tree Grows in Brooklyn, A 1951,Ap 29,II,1:1
Top Banana 1951,N 2,19:2
Point of No Return 1951,D 14,35:2
Point of No Return 1951,D 23,II,3:1
Flight Into Egypt 1952,Mr 19,33:2
Wish You Were Here 1952,Je 26,26:6
Gambler, The 1952,O 14,40:1
Picnic 1953,F 20,14:7
Picnic 1953,Mr 1,II,1:1
Can-Can 1953,My 8,28:1
Can-Can 1953,My 17,II,1:1
Me and Juliet 1953,My 29,17:1
Me and Juliet 1953,Je 7,II,1:1
Kind Sir 1953,S 28,21:2
Tea and Sympathy 1953,O 1,35:1
King and I, The 1953,O 9,33:3
Tea and Sympathy 1953,O 11,II,1:1
Kind Sir 1953,N 5,41:2
Kind Sir 1953,N 15,II,1:1
By the Beautiful Sea 1954,Ap 9,20:1
By the Beautiful Sea 1954,Ap 18,II,1:1
All Summer Long 1954,S 24,26:2
All Summer Long 1954,O 3,II,1:1
Fanny 1954,N 5,16:1
Fanny 1954,N 21,II,1:1
Silk Stockings 1955,F 25,17:3
Cat on a Hot Tin Roof 1955,Mr 25,18:2
Cat on a Hot Tin Roof 1955,Ap 3,II,1:1
Guys and Dolls 1955,Ap 21,32:2
South Pacific 1955,My 5,39:5
Island of Goats 1955,O 5,40:1
Lark, The 1955,N 18,20:1
Lark, The 1955,N 27,II,1:1
Pipe Dream 1955,D 1,44:1
Middle of the Night 1956,F 9,39:1
Streetcar Named Desire, A 1956,F 16,24:1
King and I, The 1956,Ap 19,35:4
Most Happy Fella, The 1956,My 4,20:1
Most Happy Fella, The 1956,My 13,II,1:1
Mister Roberts 1956,D 6,46:2
Happy Hunting 1956,D 7,30:1
South Pacific 1957,Ap 25,35:1
Miss Lonelyhearts 1957,O 4,26:2
Square Root of Wonderful, The 1957,O 31,40:1
Look Homeward, Angel 1957,N 29,33:1
Oh Captain! 1958,F 5,21:2
Day the Money Stopped, The 1958,F 21,19:4
Handful of Fire 1958,O 2,45:3
World of Suzie Wong, The 1958,O 15,47:1
World of Suzie Wong, The 1958,O 19,II,1:1
Gazebo, The 1958,D 13,2:7
Whoop-Up 1958,D 23,2:7
Most Happy Fella, The 1959,F 11,50:2
Sweet Bird of Youth 1959,Mr 11,39:2
Sweet Bird of Youth 1959,Mr 22,II,1:1
Gypsy 1959,My 22,31:6
Gypsy 1959,My 31,II,1:1
Gang's All Here, The 1959,O 2,23:1
Gang's All Here, The 1959,O 11,II,1:1
Silent Night, Lonely Night 1959,D 4,36:1
There Was a Little Girl 1960,Mr 1,28:1
Best Man, The 1960,Ap 1,39:1
Christine 1960,Ap 29,27:1
Period of Adjustment 1960,N 11,34:1
Period of Adjustment 1960,N 20,II,1:1
Little Moon of Alban 1960,D 2,34:1
Devil's Advocate, The 1961,Mr 10,20:1
Devil's Advocate, The 1961,Mr 19,II,1:1
Everybody Loves Opal 1961,O 12,40:2
All American 1962,Mr 20,44:1
Mr President 1962,O 22,34:2
After the Fall 1964,Ja 24,18:1
But for Whom Charlie 1964,Mr 13,42:2
Owl and the Pussycat, The 1964,N 19,48:1
South Pacific 1965,Je 3,25:1
Danton's Death 1965,O 22,46:1
Playroom, The 1965,D 6,49:1

Most Happy Fella, The 1966,My 12,55:1
Don't Drink the Water 1966,N 18,37:1
My Sweet Charlie 1966,D 7,56:1
Don't Drink the Water 1966,D 25,II,1:1
Paisley Convertible, The 1967,F 13,42:1
That Summer-That Fall 1967,Mr 17,33:1
Daphne in Cottage D 1967,O 16,56:1
Prime of Miss Jean Brodie, The 1968,Ja 17,39:1
I Never Sang for My Father 1968,Ja 26,30:1
Prime of Miss Jean Brodie, The 1968,Ja 28,II,1:1
Seven Descents of Myrtle, The 1968,Mr 28,54:1
Seven Descents of Myrtle, The 1968,Ap 7,II,1:5
Possibilities 1968,D 5,60:1
1776 1969,Mr 17,46:2
1776 1969,Mr 23,II,1:1
Child's Play 1970,F 18,39:1
Georgy 1970,F 27,26:1
Child's Play 1970,Mr 1,II,1:4
Look to the Lilies 1970,Mr 30,59:1
Look to the Lilies 1970,Ap 12,II,3:7
Mielziner, Jo (Scenic Director)
That Awful Mrs Eaton! 1924,S 30,27:1
Karl and Anna 1929,O 8,34:1
Jenny 1929,O 9,34:4
Barretts of Wimpole Street, The 1931,F 15,VIII,1:8
Gay Divorce 1932,N 13,IX,1:7
Milk Train Doesn't Stop Here Anymore, The 1963,Ja 18,7:1
King and I, The 1963,Je 13,30:2
Mierre
Trumpets and Drums 1969,O 13,52:1
Macbeth 1969,D 23,25:1
Mierse, Frieda
Whoopee 1928,D 5,34:3
Simple Simon 1931,Mr 10,23:2
Laugh Parade, The 1931,N 3,31:2
Mifelow, Al
End as a Man 1953,S 16,39:1
Late Arrival 1953,O 20,35:5
Migan, Paul
Guys and Dolls 1950,N 25,11:2
Guys and Dolls 1955,Ap 21,32:2
Migatz, Marshall (Miscellaneous)
Two for Fun 1961,F 14,45:3
Migenes, Julia
West Side Story 1964,Ap 9,24:2
Fiddler on the Roof 1964,S 23,56:2
Mignon
Frivolities of 1920 1920,Ja 9,22:2
Miguel, Muriel
Viet Rock 1966,N 11,38:1
Mihaly, Stephen (Playwright)
Bela Is 26 1930,Mr 9,IX,8:5
Mihanovich, Sergio (Composer)
David Show, The 1968,N 1,34:2
Mihok, Andrew (Lighting Director)
Hamlet 1956,O 29,34:1
Mihok, Andrew (Miscellaneous)
Ballad of Jazz Street, The 1959,N 12,28:1
Taming of the Shrew, The 1963,Mr 8,9:1
Plot Against the Chase Manhattan Bank, The 1963,N 27,29:1
Memorandum, The 1968,My 6,55:1
Huui, Huui 1968,N 25,58:1
Mijanovi, Bessie
Saint of Bleecker Street, The 1954,D 28,21:1
Mijares
Cinderella on Broadway 1920,Je 25,18:1
Vaudeville (Palace) 1927,D 20,33:4
Vaudeville (Palace) 1929,N 18,22:4
Mikhalkov, Sergei (Playwright)
I Want to Go Home 1949,Je 5,15:3
Miko, Joyce
Utopia, Limited 1960,Ap 8,27:2
Grand Duke, The 1961,My 12,24:1
Princess Ida 1961,My 19,23:1
Student Prince, The 1961,Jl 14,14:1
Merry Widow, The 1961,O 27,28:2
Vagabond King, The 1961,N 24,36:1
Gondoliers, The 1961,D 8,44:1
Miksak, Joseph
Antony and Cleopatra 1963,S 14,12:4
Mikszath, Kalman (Original Author)
Case of the Noszty Boy and Mary Toth, The 1927,Mr 20,VIII,4:3
Siege of Besztercze, The 1929,F 3,VIII,2:1
Mikulewicz, Bil (Miscellaneous)
Endgame 1970,My 6,47:1
Mikulewicz, Bil (Scenic Designer)
Until the Monkey Comes 1966,Je 21,38:1
Jumping Fool, The 1970,F 10,53:1
Milakin, Paul
Moon for the Misbegotten, A 1958,Je 7,10:6
Milan, Dolores
Dream With Music 1944,My 19,15:2
Milan, Frank
Mama Loves Papa 1926,F 23,26:2
Great Necker, The 1928,Mr 7,28:2
Penal Law 2010 1930,Ap 19,14:2
Petrified Forest, The 1935,Ja 8,26:1
Desk Set, The 1955,O 25,36:7
Who Was That Lady I Saw You With? 1958,Mr 4,33:2

Milan, Frank—Cont
Once More With Feeling 1958,O 22,39:1
Highest Tree, The 1959,N 5,41:1
Brigadoon 1963,F 1,6:2
Milan, Joe
Miss Liberty 1949,Jl 16,6:5
Guys and Dolls 1950,N 25,11:2
Wish You Were Here 1952,Je 26,26:6
Boy Friend, The 1954,O 1,20:1
Pal Joey 1961,Je 1,32:1
Milan, Joe (Choreographer)
Another Evening With Harry Stoones 1961,O 23,22:2
Ice Capades 1966,Je 2,50:2
Milan, Kay
Legend of Leonora, The 1926,My 1,10:1
Milan, Michael
Caught Wet 1931,N 5,29:1
Milana, Vincent
Color of Darkness: An Evening in the World of James Purdy; Everything Under the Sun 1963,O 1,34:1
Cannibals, The 1968,N 4,60:1
Milanese, Bob
Hi, Paisano 1961,O 2,36:2
Milano, Rosa
Pigeon, The 1930,O 15,26:2
Milaon, Robert (Producer)
Sandalwood 1926,S 23,23:1
Milbank, Robbins
Fratricide Punished 1925,Ap 21,19:1
Milbert, Seymour
King Lear 1940,D 16,27:2
Circle of Chalk, The 1941,Mr 27,28:4
Milbert, Seymour (Miscellaneous)
Island of Goats 1955,O 5,40:1
Tamburlaine the Great 1956,Ja 20,19:1
Lovers 1956,My 11,23:1
Too Late the Phalarope 1956,O 12,35:1
Milburn, Ann
Top Hole 1924,S 2,22:3
Sky High 1925,Mr 3,21:4
Cherry Blossoms 1927,Mr 29,22:3
Milburn, Ellsworth
Committee, The 1964,S 17,53:1
Milburn, Mary
Girl in the Spotlight, The 1920,Jl 13,9:3
Ziegfeld Follies 1921,Je 22,10:1
Molly Darling 1922,S 2,10:2
Sweetheart Time 1926,Ja 20,23:2
Gay Paree 1926,N 10,24:2
Mile, Saul
Merton of the Movies 1922,N 14,16:2
Miles, Arthur
Holy Terror, A 1925,S 29,31:2
Miles, Beatrice
Ever Green Lady, The 1922,O 12,25:2
You and I 1923,F 20,12:1
You and I 1923,F 25,VII,1:1
Mask and the Face, The 1924,S 11,27:3
Beware of Widows 1925,N 8,VIII,2:1
Beware of Widows 1925,D 2,22:3
Miles, Bernard (Director)
Witch of Edmonton, The 1962,N 23,32:2
Miles, Bernard (Producer)
Henry V 1960,F 26,22:1
Miles, Bernard (Miscellaneous)
Tempest, The 1970,Ag 29,14:1
Miles, Carlton (Playwright)
Nine Pine Street 1933,Ap 28,15:5
Portrait of Gilbert 1934,D 29,11:5
Miles, Cherrilyn (Playwright)
X Has No Value 1970,F 17,35:1
Miles, Christopher
Romeo and Juliet 1967,F 22,18:1
Miles, Dorothy
Gianni Schicci 1969,F 25,36:1
Sganarelle 1970,Ja 13,41:1
Songs From Milk Wood 1970,Ja 13,41:1
Miles, Dorothy (Miscellaneous)
Songs From Milk Wood 1970,Ja 13,41:1
Miles, Emily
Passing Show of 1921, The 1920,D 30,16:2
Passing Show of 1922, The 1922,S 21,18:2
Sky High 1925,Mr 3,21:4
Miles, Eugene
Edward II 1958,F 12,32:5
Heloise 1958,S 25,28:4
Heloise 1958,O 5,II,1:1
Miles, George
Clara's Ole Man 1968,Mr 9,23:2
Miles, Henry (Playwright)
Hook'n Ladder 1952,Ap 30,31:2
Miles, Homer
Solid Ivory 1925,N 17,29:3
Yours, A Lincoln 1942,Jl 10,12:3
Arsenic and Old Lace 1944,Jl 3,7:3
Miles, Jackie
Vaudeville (Palace) 1952,Mr 12,31:2
Vaudeville (Palace) 1952,Mr 16,II,1:1
Miles, Joanna
Walk-Up 1961,F 24,24:1
Cave Dwellers, The 1961,O 16,34:2
Once in a Lifetime 1964,Ja 29,20:1

Miles, Joanna—Cont
Home Free! 1965,F 11,45:1
Drums in the Night 1967,My 18,54:1
Miles, Joyce
Building Blocks 1954,My 8,14:4
Miles, Julia
Red Eye of Love 1961,Je 13,28:1
Miles, Julia (Miscellaneous)
Red Eye of Love 1961,Je 13,28:1
Fortuna 1962,Ja 4,26:1
Three Times Three; Not Enough Rope
1962,Mr 2,24:1
Three Times Three; George Washington Crossing
the Delaware 1962,Mr 2,24:1
Three Times Three; Twenty-Five Cent White Cap,
The 1962,Mr 2,24:1
Miles, Julian
Sweet River 1936,O 29,30:2
Brown Sugar 1937,D 3,29:2
Miles, Lotta
I'll Say She Is 1924,My 20,15:1
Miles, Maralyn
Carnival! 1968,D 13,58:1
Miles, Nadine (Director)
Heloise 1958,S 25,28:4
Heloise 1958,O 5,II,1:1
Miles, Peter
I Was Waiting for You 1933,N 14,23:3
Miles, Roland
Show Boat 1954,My 6,44:1
Miles, Ruth
Strange Bedfellows 1948,Ja 15,27:3
Miles, Sarah
Vivat! Vivat Regina! 1970,My 24,80:1
Vivat! Vivat Regina! 1970,Jl 20,21:2
Miles, Sylvia
Stone for Danny Fisher, A 1954,O 22,24:2
Balcony, The 1960,Mr 4,21:1
Witch, The 1962,F 16,35:2
Riot Act, The 1963,Mr 9,5:2
Matty and the Moron and Madonna
1965,Mr 30,53:1
Play That on Your Old Piano 1965,O 15,49:1
Kitchen, The 1966,Je 14,50:1
Miles, Terrin
Golden Boy 1964,O 21,56:1
Miles, Victoria
Tangerine 1921,Ag 10,8:2
Miles, William
Jason 1942,Ja 22,12:2
Miles, William (Director)
In Old Kentucky 1935,Ag 27,23:4
Take It Away 1936,D 15,30:5
Mariette 1937,Je 29,18:3
Bicentennial 1939,Ag 29,18:2
Miles, William (Original Author)
Nine Pine Street 1933,Ap 28,15:5
Miles, William (Playwright)
Going Gay 1933,Ag 4,18:5
Miles, William (Producer)
As Husbands Go 1935,Jl 2,24:3
Trelawney of the 'Wells' 1935,Jl 16,24:1
All This While 1935,Jl 30,17:2
Berkeley Square 1935,Ag 20,25:1
They Knew What They Wanted 1936,Jl 7,17:2
Octoroon, The 1936,S 1,24:2
Many Mansions 1937,Ag 3,20:5
Mileston, Kenn
Devil's Disciple, The 1950,Ja 26,23:2
Miley, June
Abie's Irish Rose 1937,My 13,30:2
Miley, Kathryn
Jim Jam Jems 1920,O 5,13:2
China Rose 1925,Ja 20,18:1
Miley, William
School for Husbands, The 1933,O 17,26:5
Milgram, Frieda
Cyanamide 1954,Mr 26,17:6
Milgrim, Lynn
New York Idea, The 1963,Jl 13,12:2
Paradise Gardens East 1969,Mr 11,39:1
Conerico Was Here to Stay 1969,Mr 11,39:1
Crimes of Passion; Erpingham Camp, The
1969,O 27,54:1
Charley's Aunt 1970,Jl 6,38:1
Milhan, Guy
Nice People 1921,Mr 3,11:1
Pyramids 1926,Jl 20,17:2
Milhaud, Darius (Composer)
Boeuf sur le Toit, Le 1930,Ap 25,28:4
Faiseur, Le 1936,Ja 12,IX,3:7
Macbeth 1937,N 27,21:3
Bal des Voleurs, Le 1938,N 29,26:4
Christophe Colomb 1957,Ja 31,20:5
Milholland, Bruce (Original Author)
Twentieth Century 1950,D 25,23:6
Milhott, Tom (Producer)
Shout From the Rooftops 1964,O 29,40:1
Milian, Tom
Maidens and Mistresses at Home at the Zoo
1958,O 29,31:1
Milic, Nikola
Ubu Roi 1968,Je 29,20:1

Milicevic, Jovan
Hamlet 1959,Ag 19,34:1
Miliev, Sarah
Little Inn, The 1935,Ag 20,25:1
Milikin, Paul
Trial, The 1955,Je 15,35:2
Spring's Awakening 1955,O 10,30:2
Quare Fellow, The 1958,N 28,34:1
John Brown's Body 1968,F 13,49:2
Comedy of Errors, The 1968,F 28,40:2
She Stoops to Conquer 1968,Ap 1,58:3
Milivoievic, Radomir
Progress of Bora, The Tailor, The 1968,Je 27,49:2
Mill, Callum (Director)
Doctor and the Devils, The 1962,Ag 22,28:1
Mill, Marion
Burning Deck, The 1940,Mr 2,9:2
Milland, Ray
Hostile Witness 1966,F 18,26:1
Millang, Charles (Choreographer)
Streets of Paris, The 1939,Je 20,25:2
Millar, Beatrice
Fan, The 1921,O 4,10:1
Millar, Bertram
Shannons of Broadway, The 1927,S 27,30:4
Silver Tassie, The 1929,O 25,26:1
Tree, The 1932,Ap 13,23:5
Crucible 1933,S 5,22:4
Millar, David B S Jr
Betty Behave 1927,Mr 9,28:4
Millar, Dorothy
Spoon River Anthology 1964,Je 27,15:2
Millar, Geoffrey
Bulldog Drummond 1921,D 27,10:2
Aren't We All? 1923,My 22,14:2
These Charming People 1925,O 7,31:2
Millar, Jonathan (Director)
Twelfth Night 1970,Ja 1,18:1
Millar, Lee
Toto 1921,Mr 22,15:2
Face Value 1921,D 27,10:2
Egotist, The 1922,D 27,12:1
Millar, Lee C (Director)
Three Men and a Woman 1932,Ja 12,29:2
Millar, Robins (Playwright)
Thunder in the Air 1928,My 6,IX,2:4
Thunder in the Air 1929,N 12,34:3
Millar, Ronald (Playwright)
Waiting For Gillian 1954,Ap 22,36:2
New Men, The 1962,S 7,35:2
Affair, The 1962,S 21,34:2
Affair, The 1962,O 7,II,1:1
Masters, The 1963,Je 1,16:8
They Don't Grow on Trees 1968,D 7,63:1
Millard, Buddy
This Rock 1943,F 19,23:2
Millard, Dickie
This Rock 1943,F 19,23:2
Millard, Elinor
How's Your Health? 1929,N 27,30:3
Millard, Helene
Roman Servant, A 1934,D 3,14:5
Millard, Jack
Jubilee 1935,O 14,20:1
Millard, Marjorie
Goodbye Again 1943,N 10,28:4
Pardon Our French 1950,O 6,22:4
Millars, Ariel
Good Boy 1928,S 6,23:2
Millay, Diana
Fair Game 1957,N 4,39:1
Drink to Me Only 1958,O 9,47:4
Boeing-Boeing 1965,F 3,30:1
Millay, Edna St Vincent (Original Author)
Lovely Light, A 1964,Ja 21,24:2
Millay, Edna St Vincent (Playwright)
Aria Da Capo 1923,My 13,16:2
Launzi 1923,O 11,16:3
Aria Da Capo 1950,My 25,36:2
Aria Da Capo 1958,My 21,40:1
Aria Da Capo 1958,Je 27,18:5
Lovely Light, A 1960,F 9,27:4
Conversation at Midnight 1964,N 13,27:1
Millay, Norma
Saint, The 1924,O 13,20:3
Desire Under the Elms 1924,N 12,20:7
Patience 1924,D 30,15:1
Love for Love 1925,S 15,29:3
Me 1925,N 24,28:1
Not Herbert 1926,Ja 27,16:2
Finta Giardiniera, La 1927,Ja 19,20:5
Key Largo 1939,N 28,30:2
Millay, Rachel
Walk Into My Parlor 1941,N 20,38:2
Millay, Snooksie
Days of Our Youth, The 1941,N 29,15:2
Millbanks, Edith (Playwright)
Tancred 1923,Jl 17,14:4
Mille, Louis E
Countess Maritza 1926,S 20,21:1
Mille, Pierre (Original Author)
Pauvre Napoleon 1929,My 5,IX,2:4

Millen, James Knox (Playwright)
Never No More 1932,Ja 8,27:1
Never No More 1932,Ja 17,VIII,1:1
Bough Breaks, The 1937,N 20,21:4
Miller, A K
Inspector General, The 1923,My 1,24:1
Miller, Agnes Heron
Too Hot for Maneuvers 1945,My 3,26:5
Miller, Al (Playwright)
God Is Back, Black and Singing Gospel at the
Fortune Theater 1969,N 19,48:1
Miller, Albert
In the Night Watch 1921,Ja 31,10:1
Miller, Albert (Playwright)
Joan of Arkansas 1925,Ap 5,16:1
Hoot Mon, or Clans Across the Sea 1927,My 8,29:4
Sellout, The 1933,S 7,17:2
Miller, Albert G Jr
Joan of Arkansas 1925,Ap 5,16:1
Sale and a Sailor, A, or Glory! What Price!
1926,Ap 25,30:4
Miller, Albert G Jr (Playwright)
Sale and a Sailor, A, or Glory! What Price!
1926,Ap 25,30:4
Miller, Alfred (Musical Director)
God Is Back, Black and Singing Gospel at the
Fortune Theater 1969,N 19,48:1
Miller, Alice Duer (Original Author)
Charm School, The 1920,Ag 3,12:1
Roberta 1933,N 20,18:4
Miller, Alice Duer (Playwright)
Charm School, The 1920,Ag 3,12:1
Magnolia Lady, The 1924,N 26,17:2
June Days 1925,Ag 7,12:5
June Days 1925,Ag 23,VII,1:1
Springboard, The 1927,O 2,VIII,4:6
Springboard, The 1927,O 13,23:1
Miller, Allan
Devil's Disciple, The 1950,Ja 26,23:2
Entertain a Ghost 1962,Ap 10,48:1
Miller, Allen (Playwright)
Doctor X 1930,Jl 31,12:4
Doctor X 1931,F 10,25:1
Miller, Ann
Dead End 1935,O 29,17:2
Scandals 1939,Ag 20,IX,2:1
Scandals 1939,Ag 29,17:2
Scandals 1939,S 3,IX,1:1
Mame 1969,Je 20,36:1
Miller, Anna
Afgar 1920,N 9,13:2
Passion Play, The 1929,Ap 30,32:1
Miller, Arthur (Miscellaneous)
Enemy of the People, An 1951,Ja 7,II,1:1
Miller, Arthur (Playwright)
Man Who Had All the Luck, The 1944,N 24,18:5
All My Sons 1947,Ja 30,21:2
All My Sons 1947,F 9,II,1:1
All My Sons 1947,S 7,II,1:1
All My Sons 1948,My 12,33:3
Death of a Salesman 1949,F 11,27:2
Death of a Salesman 1949,F 20,II,1:1
Death of a Salesman 1949,Mr 27,II,1:2
Death of a Salesman 1949,My 15,II,1:1
Death of a Salesman 1949,Jl 29,12:5
Death of a Salesman 1949,Ag 7,II,1:4
Death of a Salesman 1949,Ag 28,VI,11:1
All My Sons 1949,O 18,34:4
Death of a Salesman 1950,Mr 4,10:7
Death of a Salesman 1950,Mr 12,II,1:1
Death of a Salesman 1950,Mr 16,41:4
Death of a Salesman 1950,Ap 28,25:4
Death of a Salesman 1950,S 21,20:5
Enemy of the People, An 1950,D 29,14:1
Crucible, The 1953,Ja 23,15:2
Crucible, The 1953,F 1,II,1:1
Crucible, The 1953,Mr 15,II,1:1
Crucible, The 1953,Jl 2,20:2
Sorcieres de Salem, Les 1955,F 27,II,3:1
View From the Bridge, A 1955,Ag 31,16:8
Memory of Two Mondays, A 1955,S 30,21:1
View From the Bridge, A 1955,S 30,21:1
Memory of Two Mondays, A 1955,O 9,II,1:1
View From the Bridge, A 1955,O 9,II,1:1
Crucible, The 1956,Ap 11,28:3
View From the Bridge, A 1956,O 12,35:3
View From the Bridge, A 1956,N 9,34:4
Crucible, The 1958,Mr 12,36:1
Crucible, The 1958,Mr 17,21:1
Crucible, The 1958,Je 1,II,1:1
Enemy of the People, An 1959,F 5,24:4
Death of a Salesman 1963,Jl 20,11:2
After the Fall 1964,Ja 24,18:1
After the Fall 1964,D 20,II,3:1
Crucible, The 1964,Ap 7,30:2
Incident at Vichy 1964,D 4,44:1
Incident at Vichy 1964,D 20,II,3:1
Crucible, The 1965,Ja 20,35:1
After the Fall 1965,Ja 25,21:6
View From the Bridge, A 1965,Ja 29,24:1
Incident at Vichy 1966,Ja 27,28:5
After the Fall 1966,F 1,26:1
Price, The 1968,F 8,37:1

Miller, Arthur (Playwright)—Cont
Price, The 1968,F 18,II,1:1
Price, The 1968,O 19,29:1
Price, The 1968,O 30,39:1
Price, The 1969,Mr 6,36:2
Miller, Ashley (Director)
Sellout, The 1933,S 7,17:2
Miller, Ashley (Playwright)
Challenge of Youth 1930,Ja 21,28:5
Sellout, The 1933,S 7,17:2
Miller, Babe
Look Who's Here 1932,O 31,18:5
Miller, Barbara (Scenic Designer)
Love and Let Love 1968,Ja 4,30:1
Miller, Beatrice
Three Live Ghosts 1920,S 30,12:1
Creaking Chair, The 1926,F 23,26:1
Midsummer Night's Dream, A 1927,Je 27,25:1
Booster, The 1929,O 25,26:2
Red Planet 1932,D 19,19:2
Miller, Belle
Yankee Princess, The 1922,O 3,22:1
Miller, Benjamin
Barefoot Boy With Cheek 1947,Ap 4,20:2
Miller, Bernard (Playwright)
Tomorrow With Pictures 1960,Je 3,26:3
Miller, Bertram
Walk Together Chillun 1936,F 5,15:2
Conjur' Man Dies 1936,Mr 12,18:5
Turpentine 1936,Je 27,21:6
Case of Philip Lawrence, The 1937,Je 9,31:1
Miller, Beth
Parisiana 1928,F 10,26:3
Miller, Betty
Girl on the Via Flaminia, The 1954,F 10,37:1
Girl on the Via Flaminia, The 1954,Ap 6,35:5
Ronde, La 1955,Je 28,24:2
Cradle Song 1955,D 2,32:2
Exiles 1957,Mr 13,27:1
Power and the Glory, The 1958,D 12,2:7
Beaux' Stratagem, The 1959,F 25,35:4
Macbeth 1959,Ag 1,9:2
Balcony, The 1960,Mr 4,21:1
Someone From Assisi 1962,Ja 12,28:1
Childhood 1962,Ja 12,28:1
King Lear 1962,Ag 14,35:1
Macbeth 1962,N 17,16:2
Matty and the Moron and Madonna
  1965,Mr 30,53:1
You Can't Take It With You 1965,N 24,32:1
Right You Are (If You Think You Are)
  1966,N 23,34:2
Wild Duck, The 1967,Ja 12,49:1
Cherry Orchard, The 1968,Mr 20,41:1
Cherry Orchard, The 1968,Ap 7,II,3:7
Misanthrope, The 1968,O 10,59:1
Misanthrope, The 1968,O 20,II,1:1
Cock-A-Doodle Dandy 1969,Ja 21,40:1
Hamlet 1969,Mr 4,34:1
Gandhi 1970,O 21,37:1
Miller, Bob
All Around the Town 1952,Mr 26,33:2
I Feel Wonderful 1954,O 19,22:5
Riot 1968,D 20,64:1
Miller, Bob (Lyricist)
O Say Can You See! 1962,O 9,45:1
Miller, Bob (Playwright)
O Say Can You See! 1962,O 9,45:1
Miller, Brenda
Merry Duchess, The 1943,Je 24,25:1
Miller, Burton J (Costume Designer)
I've Got Sixpence 1952,D 3,44:2
Miller, Buzz
Two's Company 1952,D 16,43:5
Me and Juliet 1953,My 29,17:1
Me and Juliet 1953,Je 7,II,1:1
Pajama Game, The 1954,My 14,20:2
Pajama Game, The 1954,My 30,II,1:1
Arabian Nights 1955,Je 24,16:1
Redhead 1959,F 6,21:1
Bravo Giovanni 1962,My 21,41:2
Hot Spot 1963,Ap 20,17:2
Funny Girl 1964,Mr 27,15:1
Miller, Buzz (Miscellaneous)
Bravo Giovanni 1962,My 21,41:2
Miller, Charles (Miscellaneous)
Penny Friend, The 1966,D 27,46:1
In the Nick of Time 1967,Je 2,36:1
Miller, Chester
Reflected Glory 1936,S 18,19:5
Reflected Glory 1936,S 22,30:2
Miller, Chris
Trumpets and Drums 1969,O 13,52:1
Miller, D D
It's Only Natural 1922,Ap 21,13:2
Miller, David
Tableaux 1961,D 18,41:3
Nathan Weinstein, Mystic, Connecticut
  1966,F 26,15:2
Miller, Denning (Playwright)
Wetward Ho 1921,Ap 22,13:2
Miller, Dick
It's a Bird . . . It's a Plane . . . It's Superman
  1966,Mr 30,34:1

Miller, Doreen
Sound of Music, The 1970,Jl 3,13:1
Miller, Dorothy
Papavert 1931,D 30,25:1
Mr Papavert 1932,Ja 23,18:6
Off Your Marx 1936,Ap 2,28:2
Borstal Boy 1970,Ap 1,38:1
Miller, Duquesne
Say When 1928,Je 27,29:3
Miller, Edward
Student Gypsy, The; Prince of Liederkranz, The
  1963,O 1,34:1
Babes in the Wood 1964,D 29,21:2
Miller, Edward (Producer)
Move On 1926,Ja 19,30:1
Miller, Elaine
Brights Lights of 1944 1943,S 17,27:4
Miller, Elinor
Shoemaker and the Peddler, The 1960,O 15,27:4
Miller, Ernest
Bombo 1921,O 7,20:2
Miller, Estelle
Nativity Play, The 1937,D 21,29:1
Miller, Eva
Town Lunatics 1933,F 6,11:4
Miller, Everett (Composer)
Garrick Gaieties 1930,Je 5,29:2
Miller, F Ben
Diamond Lil 1949,F 7,16:2
Miller, F E
Shuffle Along 1921,My 23,16:2
Runnin' Wild 1923,O 30,17:3
Miller, F E (Playwright)
Shuffle Along 1921,My 23,16:2
Runnin' Wild 1923,O 30,17:3
Miller, Fanchon
Doctored Wife, The 1950,Jl 12,33:2
Son, The 1950,Ag 16,24:6
Miller, Florence
Cradle Song 1921,Mr 1,18:2
Way of the World, The 1924,N 18,23:4
Wild Birds 1925,Ap 10,16:1
Miller, Flournoy
Keep Shufflin' 1928,F 28,18:3
Lew Leslie's Blackbirds of 1930 1930,O 23,34:5
Sugar Hill 1931,D 26,15:2
Shuffle Along of 1933 1932,D 27,11:3
Harlem Cavalcade 1942,My 2,11:2
Shuffle Along 1952,My 9,20:5
Miller, Flournoy (Playwright)
Keep Shufflin' 1928,F 28,18:3
Lew Leslie's Blackbirds of 1930 1930,O 23,34:5
Shuffle Along of 1933 1932,D 27,11:3
Shuffle Along 1952,My 9,20:5
Miller, Foster
Zaporogetz Za Dunayem 1937,My 9,II,5:3
Miller, Frank
Wheel, The 1921,Ag 30,10:1
Elsie Janis and Her Gang 1922,Ja 17,13:2
Tantrum, The 1924,S 5,20:2
Two by Two 1925,F 24,17:1
Two Seconds 1931,O 10,20:6
Coriolanus 1938,F 2,14:5
Miller, Frank (Composer)
Thespis 1953,Ja 17,13:5
Miller, Frank B
Veils 1928,Mr 14,28:5
Fast Life 1928,S 27,35:2
Subway Express 1929,S 25,34:3
Miller, Frank H
In the Night Watch 1921,Ja 31,10:1
Miller, Franklin Gail (Costume Designer)
Ruy Blas 1957,D 14,16:3
Miller, Franklin Gail (Scenic Designer)
Ruy Blas 1957,D 14,16:3
Miller, Fred
Robert E Lee 1923,N 21,23:1
Fedora 1924,Ja 24,14:2
Crime in the Whistler Room, The 1924,O 10,22:2
Lulu Belle 1926,F 10,20:1
Betty Behave 1927,Mr 9,28:4
Buckaroo 1929,Mr 18,31:1
Savage Rhythm 1932,Ja 1,30:4
Angels Don't Kiss 1932,Ap 6,22:5
Ol' Man Satan 1932,O 4,26:3
Strange Gods 1933,Ap 17,16:6
They Shall Not Die 1934,F 22,24:4
Roll Sweet Chariot 1934,O 3,24:3
Inherit the Wind 1955,Ap 22,20:2
Take Me Along 1959,O 23,22:2
Apple, The 1961,D 8,44:1
King and I, The 1964,Jl 7,26:1
Miller, Freda (Composer)
Rehearsal, The 1952,My 27,30:5
Miller, Freda (Miscellaneous)
Rehearsal, The 1952,My 27,30:5
Miller, Gail Franklin (Costume Designer)
What Shall We Tell Caroline? 1961,N 22,24:2
Dock Brief, The 1961,N 22,24:2
Miller, Gene
City Haul 1929,D 31,14:4
Man With the Golden Arm, The 1956,My 22,28:1

Miller, George
Tide Rising 1937,Ja 26,17:2
Young Madame Conti 1937,Ap 1,18:4
Many Loves 1959,Ja 14,28:1
Cave at Machpelah, The 1959,Jl 1,25:1
Mountain Giants, The 1961,Ap 5,32:3
House of Leather, The 1970,Mr 19,56:1
Miller, George L (Producer)
Spring 3100 1928,F 16,14:2
Dinner Is Served 1929,Ag 16,18:4
Boy Friend, The 1932,Je 8,22:3
Louisiana 1933,F 28,15:5
Are You Decent? 1934,Ap 20,16:2
Kick Back, The 1934,Je 23,27:3
Miller, Gilbert (Director)
Captive, The 1926,S 30,23:1
Captive, The 1926,O 10,VIII,1:1
Dantons Tod 1927,D 21,28:3
Er Ist an Allem Schuld; He Is to Blame for
  Everything 1928,Ja 10,28:3
Diener Zweier Herren; Servant of Two Masters,
  The 1928,Ja 10,28:3
Kabale und Liebe 1928,Ja 17,22:3
Patriot, The 1928,Ja 20,15:1
Lebende Leichnam, Der, Der; Living Corpse, The
  1928,Ja 24,26:2
Olympia 1928,O 17,26:1
Sacred Flame, The 1928,N 20,28:2
Candle-Light 1929,O 1,28:2
Marseilles 1930,N 18,28:2
Petticoat Influence 1930,D 16,34:6
Tomorrow and Tomorrow 1931,Ja 14,26:3
Sex Fable, The 1931,O 21,26:1
Good Fairy, The 1931,N 25,17:1
Animal Kingdom, The 1932,Ja 13,26:4
Late Christopher Bean, The 1932,N 1,24:3
Firebird 1932,N 22,25:2
Victoria Regina 1935,D 27,15:2
Pride and Prejudice 1936,Ag 30,IX,1:1
Tovarich 1936,O 16,31:4
Country Wife, The 1936,D 2,34:1
Promise 1936,D 31,20:4
Once Is Enough 1938,F 16,16:2
Victoria Regina 1938,O 4,20:2
Delicate Story 1940,D 5,32:2
Anne of England 1941,O 8,26:2
Heart of a City 1942,F 13,24:6
For Keeps 1944,Je 15,17:5
Rich Full Life, The 1945,N 10,9:2
Play's the Thing, The 1948,Ap 29,19:2
Play's the Thing, The 1948,My 9,II,1:1
Ring Around the Moon 1950,N 24,30:1
Miller, Gilbert (Miscellaneous)
Our Betters 1928,F 21,18:2
Love Duel, The 1929,Ap 16,32:3
Twelfth Night 1940,N 20,26:3
Antigone 1946,F 19,21:3
Candida 1946,Ap 4,33:2
Play's the Thing, The 1948,Ap 29,19:2
Miller, Gilbert (Playwright)
Journey's End 1930,Ag 5,26:4
Miller, Gilbert (Producer)
Polly With a Past 1921,Mr 3,13:6
Nervous Wreck, The 1924,O 19,VIII,2:1
Her Cardboard Lover 1927,Mr 22,30:5
Interference 1927,O 19,24:3
Midsummer Night's Dream, A 1927,N 18,21:1
Jedermann 1927,D 8,33:2
Peripherie 1928,Ja 3,29:1
Patriot, The 1928,Ja 20,15:1
Patriot, The 1928,Ja 29,VIII,1:1
Happy Husband, The 1928,My 8,25:2
Paris 1928,O 9,34:3
Olympia 1928,O 17,26:1
Sacred Flame, The 1928,N 20,28:2
Age of Innocence, The 1928,N 28,24:2
Skyrocket, The 1929,Ja 12,14:7
Journey's End 1929,Mr 23,23:1
Candle Light 1929,S 22,IX,2:6
Candle-Light 1929,O 1,28:2
Hundred Years Old, A 1929,O 2,28:2
Berkeley Square 1929,N 5,32:4
Journey's End 1930,Ja 27,24:7
Michael and Mary 1930,F 2,5:1
Dishonored Lady 1930,F 5,27:1
Journey's End 1930,Ag 5,26:4
Journey's End 1930,Ag 24,VIII,1:1
Violet, The 1930,S 30,24:2
Marseilles; Marius 1930,N 9,IX,3:2
Marseilles 1930,N 18,28:2
Petticoat Influence 1930,D 16,34:6
Tomorrow and Tomorrow 1931,Ja 14,26:3
Payment Deferred 1931,O 1,24:2
Sex Fable, The 1931,O 21,26:1
Good Fairy, The 1931,N 15,VIII,4:1
Good Fairy, The 1931,N 25,17:1
Animal Kingdom, The 1932,Ja 3,VIII,3:1
Animal Kingdom, The 1932,Ja 13,26:4
There's Always Juliet 1932,F 16,24:2
Behold We Live 1932,Ag 17,13:2
Firebird 1932,S 25,IX,1:3
Late Christopher Bean, The 1932,N 1,24:3
Firebird 1932,N 22,25:2

Miller, Gilbert (Producer)—Cont
This Side Idolatry 1933,O 20,15:4
Reunion in Vienna 1934,Ja 4,17:1
Bride of Torozko, The 1934,Jl 10,24:7
Bride of Torozko, The 1934,S 14,24:2
Ode to Liberty 1934,D 11,28:2
Petrified Forest, The 1934,D 21,31:6
Ode to Liberty 1934,D 22,20:2
Petrified Forest, The 1935,Ja 8,26:1
Laburnum Grove 1935,Ja 15,23:5
Ringmaster, The 1935,Mr 12,24:5
Tovarich 1935,Ap 25,19:8
Libel! 1935,D 3,32:8
Libel! 1935,D 8,X,5:8
Victoria Regina 1935,D 13,30:5
Libel! 1935,D 21,10:5
Victoria Regina 1935,D 27,15:2
Country Wife, The 1936,O 7,32:3
Tovarich 1936,O 16,31:4
Tovarich 1936,O 25,X,1:1
Country Wife, The 1936,D 2,34:1
Promise 1936,D 31,20:4
Amazing Dr. Clitterhouse, The 1937,Mr 3,26:4
Yes, My Darling Daughter 1937,Je 4,26:2
Old Music 1937,S 5,X,2:1
French Without Tears 1937,S 26,II,4:3
Victoria Regina 1937,S 26,XI,3:6
French Without Tears 1937,S 29,19:1
Silent Knight, The 1937,N 17,26:4
Once Is Enough 1938,F 16,16:2
Murder in the Cathedral 1938,F 17,16:2
Victoria Regina 1938,O 4,20:2
I Have Been Here Before 1938,O 14,26:2
Ladies and Gentlemen 1939,O 18,30:2
Geneva 1940,Ja 31,15:2
Ladies in Retirement 1940,Mr 27,24:3
Twelfth Night 1940,O 18,26:7
Twelfth Night 1940,O 27,IX,1:5
Delicate Story 1940,D 5,32:2
Anne of England 1941,O 8,26:2
Lily of the Valley 1942,Ja 27,25:2
Heart of a City 1942,F 13,24:6
Lifeline 1942,D 1,20:3
Flare Path 1942,D 24,20:2
Harriet 1943,Mr 4,24:2
Harriet 1943,Mr 14,V,1:1
For Keeps 1944,Je 15,17:5
Harriet 1944,S 28,26:1
Rich Full Life, The 1945,N 10,9:2
Antigone 1946,F 24,II,1:1
Dear Ruth 1946,Mr 1,17:3
Candida 1946,Ap 14,II,1:1
Play's the Thing, The 1948,My 9,II,1:1
Edward, My Son 1948,O 1,30:2
Montserrat 1949,O 31,21:4
Cocktail Party, The 1950,Ja 23,17:2
Caesar and Cleopatra 1951,D 20,43:2
Antony and Cleopatra 1951,D 21,22:2
Horses in Midstream 1953,Ap 3,18:7
Living Room, The 1954,N 18,41:1
Witness for the Prosecution 1954,D 17,35:2
Reluctant Debutante, The 1956,O 11,50:1
Sleeping Prince, The 1956,N 2,31:1
Under Milk Wood 1957,O 16,42:5
Rope Dancers, The 1957,N 21,39:1
Look After Lulu 1959,Mr 4,35:1
Golden Fleecing 1959,O 16,24:5
Caretaker, The 1961,O 5,42:3
White House, The 1964,My 20,39:1
Diamond Orchid 1965,F 11,44:4
Miller, Gilbert (Translator)
Delicate Story 1940,D 5,32:2
Miller, Gladys
Chiffon Girl, The 1924,F 20,23:2
Oh! Oh! Nurse 1925,D 8,28:4
Miller, Grady
Princess Virtue 1921,My 5,20:2
Miller, Griffith (Playwright)
News Item 1935,Ag 6,20:3
Miller, Harold
All-Star Jamboree 1921,Jl 14,18:1
Silver Swan, The 1929,N 28,34:5
Little Cantor, The 1930,S 24,26:2
Cocktails of 1934 1934,My 5,22:1
60,000 Heroes 1935,Ja 28,11:5
Journey of the Fifth Horse, The 1966,Ap 22,36:1
Richard II 1968,Je 24,42:3
Androcles and the Lion 1968,Je 27,47:1
Perfect Party, The 1969,Mr 21,42:1
Miller, Helene
George White's Scandals 1935,D 26,20:2
Miller, Henry
Famous Mrs Fair, The 1920,Ap 24,20:4
Tendresse, La 1922,S 26,18:1
Tendresse, La 1922,O 1,VII,1:1
Pasteur 1923,Mr 13,19:1
Pasteur 1923,Mr 18,VII,1:1
Changelings, The 1923,Ag 26,VI,2:1
Changelings, The 1923,S 18,16:3
Changelings, The 1923,S 30,II,1:1
Untitled-Recital 1923,D 29,8:2
Man in Evening Clothes, The 1924,D 6,13:4
Embers 1926,F 2,20:3

Miller, Henry (Director)
Grounds for Divorce 1924,S 24,20:1
Man in Evening Clothes, The 1924,D 6,13:4
Miller, Henry (Playwright)
Just Wild About Harry 1963,Jl 5,14:1
Miller, Henry (Producer)
Pasteur 1923,Mr 18,VII,1:1
Pasteur 1923,Mr 25,VIII,1:1
Fanshastics 1924,Ja 17,13:2
Man in Evening Clothes, The 1924,D 6,13:4
Miller, Henry L
Tableaux 1961,D 18,41:3
Miller, Hope
It's A Gift 1945,Mr 13,18:7
Now I Lay Me Down to Sleep 1950,Mr 3,21:2
Miller, Howard
Shooting Shadows 1924,Je 27,16:5
Long Road, The 1930,S 10,30:2
Triumph 1935,O 15,18:5
Tide Rising 1937,Ja 26,17:2
Cat and the Canary, The 1937,Je 15,26:3
American Landscape 1938,D 5,19:2
Miller, Hugh
Pickwick 1927,Mr 13,VII,1:1
Pickwick 1927,S 6,35:2
Merchant of Venice, The 1928,Ja 17,22:2
When Crummles Played 1928,O 2,34:3
Whispering Gallery, The 1929,F 12,22:2
Lolly 1929,O 17,26:2
Novice and the Duke, The 1929,D 11,37:2
Mayfair 1930,Mr 18,30:5
One Chaste Man 1930,Je 11,33:5
His Majesty's Car 1930,O 24,30:1
Give Me Yesterday 1931,Mr 5,32:1
Marching By 1932,Mr 4,17:1
Dark Hours, The 1932,N 15,24:2
Cabbages and Kings 1933,N 22,22:3
Counsellor-at-Law 1934,My 1,24:3
Counsellor-at-Law 1934,My 6,IX,2:5
Rocket to the Moon 1948,Mr 23,30:4
Don't Listen, Ladies 1948,D 29,16:2
Miller, Hugh (Director)
One Chaste Man 1930,Je 11,33:5
Cabbages and Kings 1933,N 22,22:3
Miller, Huntington
Coriolanus 1927,Je 18,8:3
Miller, Ira
From the Second City 1969,O 15,34:1
Miller, Irvin C
Put and Take 1921,Ag 24,12:3
Liza 1922,N 28,24:1
Miller, Irvin C (Playwright)
Put and Take 1921,Ag 24,12:3
Liza 1922,N 28,24:1
Miller, Ivan
Getting Gertie's Garter 1921,Ag 2,16:2
Alloy 1924,O 28,27:1
She Means Business 1931,Ja 27,21:2
Peter Flies High 1931,N 10,28:3
Bidding High 1932,S 29,17:2
It's a Wise Child 1933,My 17,15:2
Dodsworth 1934,F 26,20:4
Highland Fling, A 1944,Ap 29,13:2
Miller, Jack
Alive and Kicking 1950,Ja 18,25:5
Miller, James
Scandals 1920,Je 8,9:1
George White's Scandals 1921,Jl 12,14:1
George White's Scandals 1923,Je 19,22:5
Scandals 1924,Jl 1,16:1
George White's Scandals 1926,Je 15,23:2
Miller, James E
Big Mogul, The 1925,My 12,26:3
Miller, James H (Scenic Designer)
Importance of Being Earnest, The 1936,O 22,31:2
Miller, Jane
Side-Show 1931,My 16,13:1
Miller, Jason
Pequod 1969,Je 30,33:1
Happiness Cage, The 1970,O 5,56:4
Miller, Jason (Playwright)
Nobody Hears A Broken Drum 1970,Mr 20,55:1
Miller, Jerry
Arms and the Girl 1950,F 3,28:2
Miller, Jessie
Victory Belles 1943,O 27,26:3
Miller, Jill
Pursuit of Happiness, The 1935,Jl 16,24:2
Sojourner Truth 1948,Ap 22,35:2
Miller, Joan
Lady Precious Stream 1936,Ja 28,15:2
Tiger, The 1936,S 15,36:5
Awake and Sing! 1938,F 21,15:1
Importance of Wearing Clothes, The 1951,D 11,44:7
Man, The 1953,Ja 25,II,3:1
Pin to See the Peepshow, A 1953,S 18,17:2
Pin to See the Peepshow, A 1953,N 8,II,1:1
Wooden Dish, The 1954,Jl 30,9:4
Rope Dancers, The 1959,Jl 15,26:2
Hidden Stranger 1963,Ja 10,5:5
Miller, Joe
Henry V 1965,Je 29,27:2

Miller, Joe E
Jim Jam Jems 1920,O 5,13:2
Miller, John
Doctor Cupid 1952,Ag 14,19:6
Aunt Caroline's Will 1954,Ag 11,21:1
Death of Cuchulain, The 1959,Ap 13,34:4
Miller, John (Skins)
Sleep No More 1944,S 1,11:5
Miller, Jonathan
Beyond the Fringe 1961,Je 25,II,3:5
Beyond the Fringe 1962,O 29,36:1
Miller, Jonathan (Director)
My Kinsman, Major Molineux 1964,N 2,62:2
Benito Cereno 1964,N 2,62:2
Old Glory, The 1964,N 15,II,1:1
Prometheus Bound 1967,My 11,52:1
Merchant of Venice, The 1970,My 10,II,3:1
Merchant of Venice, The 1970,Jl 30,39:1
Tempest, The 1970,Ag 29,14:1
Hamlet 1970,D 28,40:1
Miller, Jonathan (Miscellaneous)
Come Live With Me 1967,Ja 27,29:1
Miller, Jonathan (Playwright)
Beyond the Fringe 1962,O 29,36:1
Miller, Joshua (Producer)
Mime and Me, The 1960,Ap 8,27:3
Miller, Joyce
Mamba's Daughters 1939,Ja 4,24:2
Porgy and Bess 1942,Ja 23,16:2
Miller, Julian
Midsummer Night's Dream, A 1957,Je 27,21:3
Androcles and the Lion 1958,F 22,8:3
Philoctetes 1959,Ja 14,28:1
Merry Wives of Windsor, The 1959,Jl 9,23:2
Nekros 1960,O 26,44:1
Tragical Historie of Doctor Faustus, The 1964,O 6,34:2
Falstaff 1966,Je 20,27:1
Twelfth Night 1966,Je 23,28:1
Miller, June
Where People Gather 1967,O 26,56:1
Miller, June (Miscellaneous)
Miss Julie 1965,N 11,59:1
Stronger, The 1965,N 11,59:1
Miller, June (Producer)
Miss Julie 1965,N 11,59:1
Stronger, The 1965,N 11,59:1
Miller, Kathleen
House of Leather, The 1970,Mr 19,56:1
Butterflies Are Free 1970,D 3,60:2
Miller, Kathryn (Costume Designer)
For Keeps 1944,Je 15,17:5
Living Room, The 1954,N 18,41:1
Reluctant Debutante, The 1956,O 11,50:1
Miller, Kathryn (Miscellaneous)
Witness for the Prosecution 1954,D 17,35:2
Under Milk Wood 1957,O 16,42:5
Miller, Kay
Man Who Reclaimed His Head 1932,S 9,17:3
One Flight Down 1937,D 14,32:4
Miller, Kellis
Porgy and Bess 1965,Mr 6,17:1
Miller, Kermit
Her Man of Wax 1933,O 12,32:3
Miller, Laurence (Playwright)
Head-On Crash 1933,F 26,IX,3:1
Miller, Lavita
Grey Fox, The 1928,O 23,32:3
Miller, Lawrence McK
Little Father of the Wilderness, The 1930,Je 3,27:1
Miller, Leatta
Not So Long Ago 1920,My 5,14:1
Appearances 1925,O 15,27:3
He Who Gets Slapped 1946,Mr 21,31:4
Miller, Lee (Director)
Great Big Doorstep, The 1950,Mr 18,8:6
Miller, Lew
Royal Family, The 1940,Ag 13,15:3
Miller, Lilyan
Madame Bovary 1937,N 17,26:2
Miller, Lois
Murder in the Cathedral 1938,F 17,16:2
Miller, Lorna
Girl From Wyoming, The 1938,O 31,12:1
Miller, Lorraine
Happy Birthday 1946,N 1,31:2
Magdalena 1948,S 21,31:2
Miller, Louis
Bitter Sweet 1929,N 6,30:2
First Night 1930,N 27,32:3
Blue Monday 1932,Je 3,23:2
Miller, Louis (Playwright)
Clinton Street 1939,O 13,27:2
Miller, M S (Lighting Director)
Jo 1964,F 13,25:1
Miller, Madeline
Slow Dance on the Killing Ground 1970,My 14,43:1
Miller, Marian
Father Malachy's Miracle 1937,N 18,26:4
Wine, Women and Song 1942,S 29,18:3
Miller, Marilyn
Sally 1920,D 22,16:1

Miller, Marilyn—Cont

Peter Pan 1924,N 7,16:2
Sunny 1925,S 23,22:1
Rosalie 1927,D 18,IX,2:3
Rosalie 1928,Ja 11,26:3
Smiles 1930,N 2,VIII,1:3
Smiles 1930,N 19,19:2
As Thousands Cheer 1933,S 10,II,5:3
As Thousands Cheer 1933,O 2,22:1
As Thousands Cheer 1933,O 15,IX,1:1
Miller, Marilyn S (Lighting Director)
Beautiful Dreamer 1960,D 28,22:1
Purple Canary, The 1963,Ap 23,31:1
Miller, Marilyn S (Miscellaneous)
Purple Canary, The 1963,Ap 23,31:1
Miller, Marion
Strike Up the Band 1930,Ja 15,29:1
Miller, Martha
Julius Caesar 1957,O 24,39:1
Miller, Marty
Too Hot for Maneuvers 1945,My 3,26:5
Wind Is Ninety, The 1945,Je 22,12:2
Sky Drift 1945,N 14,25:2
On Whitman Avenue 1946,My 9,28:2
Daphne Laureola 1950,S 19,38:6
Miller, Mary
Faith of Our Fathers 1950,Ag 6,72:2
Flies, The 1954,S 10,18:2
Trial, The 1955,Je 15,35:2
Spring's Awakening 1955,O 10,30:2
Miller, Mary Beth
Gianni Schicci 1969,F 25,36:1
Sganarelle 1970,Ja 13,41:1
Songs From Milk Wood 1970,Ja 13,41:1
Miller, Meri
Show Boat 1954,My 6,44:1
Miller, Michael
Thistle in My Bed 1963,N 20,48:1
Ivanov 1966,My 4,50:1
Black Comedy 1967,F 13,42:1
Tom Paine 1968,Mr 26,38:1
Camino Real 1970,Ja 9,42:1
Operation Sidewinder 1970,Mr 13,33:1
Miller, Midgie
Jim Jam Jems 1920,O 5,13:2
Spice of 1922 1922,Jl 7,12:4
Polly of Hollywood 1927,F 22,22:3
Keep It Clean 1929,Je 25,35:5
Hoboken Hoboes 1929,D 28,10:8
Will Morrissey's Folies Bergere Revue
  1930,Ap 16,26:6
Miller, Midgie (Director)
Hot Rhythm 1930,Ag 22,18:5
Miller, Mildred
Mister Pitt 1924,Ja 23,15:3
Miller, Miriam
Good Times 1920,Ag 10,10:1
Mimic World of 1921, The 1921,Ag 18,9:2
Good Morning, Dearie 1921,N 2,20:2
Miller, Mitch (Producer)
Here's Where I Belong 1968,Mr 4,32:1
Miller, Mitzi
Child of Manhattan 1932,Mr 2,15:1
What a Life 1938,Ap 14,26:2
Miller, Moi Yo
Sim Sala Bim 1940,S 10,27:1
Miller, Morris
Royal Family, The 1951,Ja 11,28:2
Picnic 1953,F 20,14:7
Best House in Naples, The 1956,O 27,16:2
Miller, Myrtle
Treat 'Em Rough 1926,O 5,26:2
K Guy, The 1928,O 16,28:4
Wild Duck, The 1938,Ap 16,16:5
Miller, Neal
Slice It Thin 1945,My 11,22:5
Miller, Niels
Cherry Orchard, The 1960,Je 4,17:2
Mr Simian 1963,O 22,44:1
Too Much Johnson 1964,Ja 16,29:1
Miller, Norma
Cotton Club Revue of 1957 1957,Jl 10,23:4
Miller, Norman
Criminal Code, The 1929,O 3,28:2
Miller, Norman (Director)
Gasoline Gypsies 1931,Je 8,21:3
Miller, Norman (Producer)
Gasoline Gypsies 1931,Je 8,21:3
Miller, Norman H
This Mad Whirl 1937,Ja 10,II,4:8
Right Next to Broadway 1944,F 22,26:2
Miller, Olive
It's the Valet 1933,D 15,25:4
Hook-Up, The 1935,My 9,24:6
Miller, Oscar
Victory Belles 1943,O 27,26:3
Miller, Patsy Ruth
White Man 1936,O 19,22:4
Miller, Patsy Ruth (Playwright)
Music in My Heart 1947,O 3,30:2
Miller, Paula
Katerina 1929,F 26,30:3
Mademoiselle Bourrat 1929,O 8,34:3
Women Have Their Way, The 1930,Ja 28,28:1

Night Over Taos 1932,Mr 10,25:3
Men in White 1933,S 27,24:2
Waiting for Lefty 1935,F 11,14:5
Till the Day I Die 1935,Mr 27,24:5
Waiting for Lefty 1935,Mr 27,24:5
Weep for the Virgins 1935,D 2,18:1
Case of Clyde Griffiths 1936,Mr 14,10:4
Johnny Johnson 1936,N 20,26:3
Many Mansions 1937,O 28,28:6
Cafe Crown 1942,Ja 24,12:5
Me and Molly 1948,F 27,27:2
Miller, Phil
Big Two, The 1947,Ja 9,21:2
Miller, Philip
Trojan Women, The 1923,My 27,10:2
Miller, Quintard
Liza 1922,N 28,24:1
Miller, Ray
Caviar 1934,Je 8,19:2
Jumbo 1935,N 18,20:2
Eternal Road, The 1937,Ja 8,14:2
Miller, Ray and His Arcadia Orchestra
Vaudeville (Palace) 1924,S 30,27:5
Miller, Richard A
Wonderful Town 1967,My 18,50:1
Mahagonny 1970,Ap 29,51:1
Miller, Richard A (Lighting Director)
Greenwillow 1970,D 8,60:1
Moon on a Rainbow Shawl 1970,D 18,52:1
Miller, Richard A (Scenic Designer)
Don't Bother Me, I Can't Cope 1970,O 8,60:3
Moon on a Rainbow Shawl 1970,D 18,52:1
Miller, Robert Ellis
Mother, The 1935,N 20,26:3
Revolt of the Beavers, The 1937,My 21,19:2
Prologue to Glory 1938,Mr 18,22:2
Twelfth Night 1954,N 10,42:2
Merchant of Venice, The 1955,F 23,23:2
Miller, Robert Ellis (Director)
Umbrella, The 1965,My 27,31:1
Miller, Robert Ellis (Producer)
Tonight in Samarkand 1955,F 17,22:2
Miller, Robin (Lyricist)
Dames at Sea 1968,D 21,46:1
Dames at Sea 1970,S 24,60:1
Miller, Robin (Playwright)
Dames at Sea 1968,D 21,46:1
Dames at Sea 1970,S 24,60:1
Miller, Roger
John Brown's Body 1953,F 16,17:2
Miller, Ruby (Playwright)
Big Ben 1939,S 10,IX,2:2
Miller, Ruth
From Morn Till Midnight 1948,D 7,41:6
Miller, Sam
Vaudeville (Palace) 1921,Jl 5,15:1
Miller, Sheila
Nights of Wrath; Nuits de la Colere, Les
  1947,D 1,26:4
Miller, Sigmund (Playwright)
One Bright Day 1952,Mr 20,37:2
One Bright Day 1956,Ap 8,II,3:1
Masquerade 1959,Mr 17,42:1
Miller, Skedge
Relapse, The 1950,N 23,54:2
Salvation on a String; No Count Boy, The
  1954,Jl 7,23:1
Last Love of Don Juan, The 1955,N 24,40:1
Dandy Dick 1956,Ja 11,37:2
Affair of Honor 1956,Ap 7,12:3
Doctor in Spite of Himself, The 1957,F 28,18:4
Enchanted, The 1958,Ap 23,41:1
Twelfth Night 1958,Ag 7,21:4
She Shall Have Music 1959,Ja 23,18:4
Gay Divorce 1960,Ap 4,37:1
Tobacco Road 1960,My 11,44:2
Midsummer Night's Dream, A 1964,Je 30,23:2
Miller, Stanley
So Proudly We Hail 1938,Ap 9,11:1
Miller, Stanley (Composer)
So Proudly We Hail 1938,Ap 9,11:1
Miller, Stella
Little Poor Man, The 1925,Ag 6,14:1
Miller, Susan
Earl Carroll's Vanities 1940,Ja 15,11:2
Beat the Band 1942,O 15,26:1
For Your Pleasure 1943,F 6,9:2
Miller, Sylvia
Nautical but Nice 1931,Ap 19,31:6
Miller, Taps
Shuffle Along of 1933 1932,D 27,11:3
Miller, Thad
Bonds of Interest, The 1958,My 7,43:1
Miller, Tim (Miscellaneous)
Tarot 1970,D 12,19:1
Miller, Timothy
Good Soldier Schweik, The 1963,Ap 9,57:1
Miller, Tod
Here's Where I Belong 1968,Mr 4,32:1
Canterbury Tales; Merchant's Tale, The
  1969,F 4,34:1
Miller, Tommy
You Said It 1931,Ja 20,21:3

Miller, Tony
Career Angel 1944,My 24,23:7
Miller, Tootsie
Awake and Sing! 1939,Mr 8,18:2
Miller, Vic
Dream Play 1960,N 23,22:1
Miller, Victoria
Jumbo 1935,N 18,20:2
Miller, Wade (Miscellaneous)
Glass Menagerie, The 1965,My 5,53:2
I Do! I Do! 1966,D 6,58:1
Three Men on a Horse 1969,O 17,35:1
Look to the Lilies 1970,Mr 30,59:1
Miller, Walter
Simpleton of the Unexpected Isles, The
  1954,Ja 12,19:1
Adding Machine, The 1956,F 10,17:1
Poppa Is Home 1961,D 20,37:1
Gogo Loves You 1964,O 10,19:2
Colombe 1965,F 24,33:1
Miller, Warren (Original Author)
Cool World, The 1960,F 23,38:2
Miller, Warren (Playwright)
Cool World, The 1960,F 23,38:2
Miller, William
LeMaire's Affairs 1927,Mr 29,22:4
Miller, William Frederick 3d
This Mad Whirl 1937,Ja 10,II,4:8
Miller, William R
Carousel 1966,D 16,56:2
Miller, William Stanley
Off the Record; Mayor Answers the Newspapers!
  Wow! 1935,Je 19,23:3
Miller, Woods
Vanities 1931,Ag 16,VIII,1:1
Earl Carroll's Vanities 1931,Ag 28,18:7
Murder at the Vanities 1933,S 13,22:4
Chimes of Corneville, The 1934,Je 29,16:2
Keep Moving 1934,Ag 24,10:2
At Home Abroad 1935,S 20,17:4
Miller, Wynne
By Hex 1956,Je 19,25:1
Thurber Carnival, A 1960,F 27,13:2
Thurber Carnival, A 1960,Mr 6,II,1:1
Tenderloin 1960,O 18,47:2
Miller, Yola (Miscellaneous)
Flahooley 1951,My 15,39:1
Miller and Lyles
George White's Scandals 1925,Je 23,24:2
Great Temptations, The 1926,My 19,29:1
Great Temptations, The 1926,My 23,VIII,1:1
Rang Tang 1927,Jl 13,20:1
Vaudeville (Palace) 1928,Jl 3,19:2
Great Day! 1929,O 18,24:3
Miller and Mack
Earl Carroll's Vanities 1924,S 11,23:6
Miller and Ryan
O K 1925,My 4,16:1
Miller Brothers and Lois
Harlem Cavalcade 1942,My 2,11:2
Milleron, Horace
Salome 1922,My 23,12:4
Millership, Florrie
Mary 1920,O 19,12:1
Millet, Paco
Cabalgata 1949,Jl 8,14:2
Millet, Tully
Caviar 1934,Je 8,19:2
Milletaire, Carl
Magdalena 1948,S 21,31:2
Millette, Buddy
Diamond Lil 1948,N 30,33:2
Diamond Lil 1949,F 7,16:2
Millhauser, Bertram (Playwright)
Ragged Army 1934,F 27,16:5
Millholland, Charles Bruce
Faun 1935,N 25,23:5
Millholland, Charles Bruce (Playwright)
20th Century 1932,D 30,15:1
Faun 1935,N 25,23:5
Faun 1935,D 1,XI,6:3
Millhollin, James
Praise Of Folly 1954,F 24,23:2
Slightly Delinquent 1954,O 26,32:5
No Time for Sergeants 1955,O 21,32:2
Girls in 509, The 1958,O 16,47:1
Saratoga 1959,D 8,59:4
Milli, Camillo
Venetian Twins, The 1968,My 29,23:1
Milli, Mary Jane
Ticket-of-Leave Man, The 1961,D 23,15:1
Milli, Robert
Oedipus Rex 1959,Ap 30,36:1
Write Me a Murder 1961,O 27,28:2
Ross 1961,D 27,20:2
Hamlet 1964,Ap 10,30:1
Severed Head, A 1964,O 29,40:1
Way of the World, The 1965,Je 2,40:1
Richard III 1965,Je 3,26:1
Front Page, The 1968,O 20,85:5
Front Page, The 1969,My 12,54:2
Front Page, The 1969,N 2,86:1

Milliard, Marjorie
Hickory Stick 1944,My 9,15:6
Man and Superman 1953,F 21,11:2
Beautiful Changes, The 1956,Mr 24,15:2
Millican, Jane
To Account Rendered 1931,F 15,VIII,2:5
Milligan, Alva
My Sister Eileen 1940,D 27,23:2
Milligan, Andy
Girl on the Via Flaminia, The 1954,F 10,37:1
Where People Gather 1967,O 26,56:1
Milligan, Andy (Costume Designer)
Picture of Dorian Gray, The 1956,Ag 18,15:5
Milligan, Andy (Director)
Picture of Dorian Gray, The 1956,Ag 18,15:5
Fall 1957,N 22,19:1
Mrs Warren's Profession 1963,Ap 25,39:1
Picture of Dorian Gray, The 1963,Ag 29,37:4
Milligan, Andy (Playwright)
Picture of Dorian Gray, The 1963,Ag 29,37:4
Milligan, Andy (Producer)
Picture of Dorian Gray, The 1956,Ag 18,15:5
Fall 1957,N 22,19:1
Milligan, Andy (Scenic Designer)
Picture of Dorian Gray, The 1956,Ag 18,15:5
Milligan, Byron
Sunny River 1941,D 5,28:2
Of V We Sing 1942,F 16,20:3
Milligan, John
Matchmaker, The 1955,D 6,45:6
First Gentleman, The 1957,Ap 26,22:2
Winter's Tale, The 1958,Jl 23,34:3
Love and Libel 1960,D 8,44:1
One Way Pendulum 1961,S 19,38:2
Henry V 1963,Je 14,37:1
John Brown's Body 1964,Je 29,33:1
Devils, The 1965,N 17,51:2
Milligan, Robert J
Merry-Go-Round 1932,Ap 23,11:2
Milligan, Sam
Power of Dreams, A 1958,Mr 11,33:1
Millikan, Max
Hippolytus 1935,Je 15,20:4
Milliken, A
Galloper, The 1924,D 19,26:2
Milliken, Al
Star of Bengal 1929,S 26,27:2
Milliken, Conrad (Producer)
Black Crook, The 1929,Mr 12,26:5
Milliken, Max
In the Days of the Turbins 1934,Mr 7,22:5
Milliman, Grace
New Faces of 1936 1936,My 20,24:5
Millin, Henry
Medea 1960,Jl 26,25:2
Millington, Norris
Straw, The 1921,N 11,16:2
Milliott, Tom (Director)
Shout From the Rooftops 1964,O 29,40:1
Millman, Bird
Greenwich Village Follies 1921,S 1,18:3
Vaudeville (Hippodrome) 1924,Ja 22,15:6
Millman, L'Estrange
Purple Mask, The 1920,Ja 6,18:1
Americans in France, The 1920,Ag 4,14:1
Man in Evening Clothes, The 1924,D 6,13:4
Nirvana 1926,Mr 4,19:1
Joan of Arc 1927,Ap 15,26:2
Behavior of Mrs Crane, The 1928,Mr 21,30:1
Cape Cod Follies 1929,S 19,37:2
Six Characters in Search of an Author
    1931,Ap 16,29:2
Tom Sawyer 1931,D 26,15:3
Millocker, Carl (Composer)
Beggar Student, The 1921,Ja 8,9:3
Du Barry 1931,S 20,VIII,2:7
Du Barry 1932,My 8,VIII,1:6
Du Barry 1932,N 13,IX,1:8
Du Barry 1932,N 23,15:2
Beggar Student, The 1942,S 26,11:4
Millott, Tom E
Billy Budd 1959,F 28,13:3
Mills, Alison
Our Town 1968,D 14,62:1
Mills, Anna
Queen Mother 1938,D 26,29:4
Schwartse Mamme 1939,Ja 16,11:3
Mills, Billy
Liza 1922,N 28,24:1
Africana 1927,Jl 12,29:2
Yeah-Man 1932,My 27,27:3
Mills, Billy (Miscellaneous)
Yeah-Man 1932,My 27,27:3
Mills, Carley (Playwright)
World's My Oyster, The 1956,Ag 10,10:4
Mills, Charles (Composer)
Lion in Love, The 1963,Ap 26,28:3
Mills, David H
New York Idea, The 1963,Jl 13,12:2
Mills, Donna
Don't Drink the Water 1966,N 18,37:1
Mills, Edwin
Zander the Great 1923,Ap 10,24:2

Starlight 1925,Mr 4,17:2
Mismates 1925,Ap 14,27:2
Human Nature 1925,S 25,24:3
Once in a Lifetime 1930,S 25,22:3
Lean Harvest 1931,O 14,26:3
Air-Minded 1932,F 11,17:3
Achilles Had a Heel 1935,O 14,20:2
Bright Honor 1936,S 28,14:1
Dame Nature 1938,S 27,24:3
Mills, Evelyn
Lean Harvest 1931,O 14,26:3
I'd Rather Be Right 1937,N 3,28:2
Case History 1938,O 22,15:2
Mills, Florence
Plantation Revue, The 1922,Jl 18,18:4
Dixie to Broadway 1924,O 30,22:1
Blackbirds 1926,S 25,21:5
Mills, Frank
Hair 1969,F 5,36:1
Mills, Fred
Macbeth 1968,N 30,49:3
Mills, George
Once Over Lightly 1955,Mr 16,39:1
Mills, Gordon
Present Laughter 1946,O 30,31:2
Sabrina Fair 1953,N 12,37:1
Mills, Grace
Makropoulos Secret, The 1926,Ja 22,12:4
Spellbound 1927,N 15,26:2
Midsummer Night's Dream, A 1932,N 18,22:2
Comedy of Errors, The 1932,N 22,25:3
We the People 1933,Ja 23,9:5
Crime Marches on 1935,O 24,19:1
Hedda Gabler 1936,N 17,34:4
Doll's House, A 1937,D 28,28:6
White Steed, The 1939,Ja 11,16:2
Boyd's Daughter 1940,O 12,20:2
Good Neighbor 1941,O 22,26:2
Decision 1944,F 3,23:2
Men to the Sea 1944,O 4,25:2
Little Women 1944,D 13,29:2
Live Life Again 1945,O 1,14:7
Present Laughter 1946,O 30,31:2
Medea 1947,O 21,27:2
Minnie and Mr Williams 1948,O 28,37:2
Mills, Grant
Nightcap, The 1921,Ag 16,18:3
Old Soak, The 1922,Ag 23,14:5
Silence 1924,N 13,18:2
Poor Nut, The 1925,Ap 28,18:1
Lady Screams, The 1927,My 3,24:2
By Request 1928,S 28,30:2
Merry Andrew 1929,Ja 22,22:2
Week-end 1929,O 23,26:4
So Was Napoleon 1930,Ja 9,22:2
Once in a Lifetime 1930,S 7,IX,2:4
Once in a Lifetime 1930,S 25,22:3
American, Very Early 1934,Ja 31,21:2
Merrily We Roll Along 1934,O 1,14:1
Remember the Day 1935,Jl 9,24:3
Stag at Bay, The 1935,Jl 30,17:1
Little Inn, The 1935,Ag 20,25:1
Rain 1935,Ag 27,23:4
Remember the Day 1935,S 26,19:3
Feather in the Breeze 1936,Jl 14,22:2
Reno 1937,Ag 10,22:7
Sea Dogs 1939,N 7,30:3
Little Dark Horse 1941,N 17,14:4
Mills, Hugh (Playwright)
Laughter in Court 1936,S 10,29:4
Laughter in Court 1936,S 27,X,3:5
Little Glass Clock, The 1954,D 12,II,5:1
Little Glass Clock, The 1956,Mr 27,40:2
Mills, Jack
I'd Rather Be Right 1937,N 3,28:2
Mills, Jerry
Keep Shufflin' 1928,F 28,18:3
Mills, John
Jill Darling 1934,D 20,29:8
Aren't Men Beasts? 1936,My 15,29:1
Floodlight 1937,Je 24,30:3
Of Mice and Men 1939,Ap 30,XI,3:5
Men in Shadow 1942,S 27,VIII,2:1
Ross 1961,D 27,20:2
Ross 1962,Ja 7,II,1:1
Mills, John (Director)
Men in Shadow 1942,S 27,VIII,2:1
Mills, Joy
Once in a Lifetime 1962,O 30,30:1
Mills, Juliet
Five Finger Exercise 1959,D 3,45:4
Five Finger Exercise 1959,D 13,II,3:1
Alfie 1964,D 18,27:1
She Stoops to Conquer 1969,Ag 18,28:1
Mills, Kirk and Martin
Vaudeville (Palace) 1932,Ap 25,18:3
Mills, Master Edwin
Napoleon's Barber 1927,F 2,22:4
Mills, Parker
Cyrano de Bergerac 1926,F 19,18:1
When Crummles Played 1928,O 2,34:3
Mills, Richard
King and I, The 1960,My 12,40:1

Mills, Robert
Lady in the Dark 1941,Ja 24,14:2
Mills, Ruth
Last Waltz, The 1921,My 11,20:3
Mills, Shirley
Marie Antoinette in Pennsylvania 1949,My 12,26:2
Mills, Stephen
Three Little Girls 1930,Ap 15,29:1
Prometheus Bound 1967,My 11,52:1
We Bombed in New Haven 1967,D 7,58:1
Mills, Steve
Lady Says Yes, A 1945,Ja 11,18:5
This Was Burlesque 1962,Mr 7,29:1
This Was Burlesque 1965,Mr 17,55:3
This Was Burlesque 1970,F 12,31:1
Mills, Warren
Lean Harvest 1931,O 14,26:3
To My Husband 1936,Je 2,35:2
Stork Mad 1936,O 1,28:4
I'd Rather Be Right 1937,N 3,28:2
Madame Capet 1938,O 26,26:2
Dear Octopus 1939,Ja 12,22:2
Lady in the Dark 1941,Ja 24,14:2
War and Peace 1942,My 22,26:3
Mills, William
Escape Me Never! 1935,Ja 22,22:2
Mills and Shea
Vaudeville (Palace) 1930,Mr 31,24:2
Millstein, Jack
Seven Against One 1930,My 7,25:1
Millstein, Jack (Producer)
Dames at Sea 1968,D 21,46:1
Dames at Sea 1970,S 24,60:1
Millward, Charles
Launzi 1923,O 11,16:3
Beware of Widows 1925,N 8,VIII,2:1
Beware of Widows 1925,D 2,22:3
Arabian Nightmare, The 1927,Ja 11,36:3
Security 1929,Mr 29,20:1
Stripped 1929,O 22,26:1
Millward, James
Poppy God, The 1921,Ag 30,10:1
Milne, A A (Original Author)
Winnie the Pooh 1967,D 23,28:1
Milne, A A (Playwright)
Mr Pim Passes By 1921,Mr 1,18:1
Mr Pim Passes By 1921,Mr 6,VI,1:2
Great Broxopp, The 1921,N 16,22:1
Dover Road, The 1921,D 24,7:2
Truth About Blayds, The 1922,Ja 15,VI,1:7
Truth About Blayds, The 1922,Mr 15,22:1
Truth About Blayds, The 1922,Mr 26,VI,1:2
Belinda 1922,Jl 30,VI,1:7
Romantic Age, The 1922,N 15,22:1
Romantic Age, The 1922,N 19,VII,1:1
Lucky One, The 1922,N 21,15:2
Lucky One, The 1922,D 3,VIII,1:1
Wurzel-Flummery 1923,Ja 17,22:2
Great Broxopp, The 1923,Mr 11,VIII,2:4
Success 1923,Jl 8,VI,1:1
Dover Road, The 1924,My 4,VIII,2:4
To Have the Honor 1924,My 11,VIII,2:7
Dover Road, The 1924,D 20,18:2
Ariadne 1925,F 24,17:1
Ariadne 1925,My 3,VIII,2:1
Dover Road, The 1926,Ap 29,20:3
Mr Pim Passes By 1927,Ap 19,24:1
Mr Pim Passes By 1927,My 22,VIII,1:1
Ivory Door, The 1927,O 19,24:5
Fourth Wall, The 1928,Mr 25,IX,1:3
Perfect Alibi, The 1928,N 28,24:2
Meet the Prince 1929,F 26,30:5
Meet the Prince 1929,Mr 10,X,1:1
Ivory Door, The 1929,My 5,IX,1:3
Michael and Mary 1929,D 14,23:3
Toad of Toad Hall 1929,D 23,5:2
Michael and Mary 1929,D 29,VIII,2:4
Michael and Mary 1930,F 2,5:1
Michael and Mary 1930,F 23,VIII,2:1
Make-Believe 1930,N 8,21:1
Toad of Toad Hall 1931,Ja 4,VIII,2:5
Give Me Yesterday 1931,Mr 5,32:1
Give Me Yesterday 1931,Mr 15,IX,1:1
They Don't Mean Any Harm 1932,F 24,25:2
Truth About Blayds, The 1932,Ap 12,25:2
Other People's Lives; They Don't Mean Any
    Harm 1932,D 4,IX,3:6
Meet the Prince 1935,Jl 9,24:5
Meet the Prince 1935,Ag 6,20:4
Mr Pim Passes By 1935,Ag 7,22:2
Sarah Simple 1937,My 5,28:4
Sarah Simple 1937,My 23,X,2:1
Gentleman Unknown 1938,N 17,29:2
Gentleman Unknown 1938,D 4,X,7:5
Sarah Simple 1940,N 18,22:5
Winnie the Pooh 1967,N 25,33:1
Milne, Elizabeth
Merchant of Venice, The 1970,Je 10,39:1
Milne, Gwendolyn
Sons o' Guns 1929,N 27,30:4
Milne, Lennox
Prime of Miss Jean Brodie, The 1968,Ja 17,39:1
Prime of Miss Jean Brodie, The 1968,Ja 28,II,1:1

Milne, Lewis
Grey Fox, The 1928,O 23,32:3
Troika 1930,Ap 2,32:6
Milne, Minnie
Enter Madame 1920,Ag 17,11:2
Square Peg, A 1923,Ja 29,10:2
Mister Pitt 1924,Ja 23,15:3
Milne, Virginia
Tight Britches 1934,S 12,26:2
Milner, Elsa
All Around the Town 1952,Mr 26,33:2
Milner, Johnny
Midsummer Night's Dream, A 1959,Jl 29,34:1
Milner, M (Composer)
Jacob's Dream 1927,Ja 4,20:2
Golem, The 1948,My 17,22:3
Milner, Martin
Ninety Day Mistress, The 1967,N 7,49:1
Milner, Roger (Playwright)
How's the World Treating You? 1966,O 25,50:1
Milner, Ronald (Playwright)
Who's Got His Own 1966,O 13,52:1
Who's Got His Own 1967,O 14,13:3
Warning, The-A Theme for Linda 1969,Ap 27,92:1
Black Quartet, A; Warning, The-A Theme for Linda 1969,Jl 31,28:1
Warning, The-A Theme for Linda 1969,Ag 3,II,1:4
Black Quartet, A 1969,S 22,36:1
Warning, The: A Theme for Linda 1969,S 22,36:1
Milnor, Frank Richmond 2d
This Mad Whirl 1937,Ja 10,II,4:8
Milo, Christopher
Our Town 1968,D 14,62:1
Milroy, Nancy
Out of My House 1942,Ja 8,28:6
Milstead, Alma
Hansel and Gretel 1929,D 25,21:1
Milstein, Sylvia
Cocktails of 1934 1934,My 5,22:1
Miltern, Frances
Vaudeville (Palace) 1926,Ap 13,28:3
Miltern, John
Ruined Lady, The 1920,Ja 21,10:2
Persons Unknown 1922,O 26,12:1
Changelings, The 1923,Ag 26,VI,2:1
Fanshastics 1924,Ja 17,13:2
Canary Dutch 1925,S 9,22:1
Trapped 1928,S 12,25:3
Be Your Age 1929,F 5,27:1
Sherlock Holmes 1929,N 26,28:3
Yellow Jack 1934,Mr 7,22:6
Allure 1934,O 30,22:6
Romeo and Juliet 1934,D 21,30:3
Coquette 1935,My 22,23:4
Miltiades, Milton (Choreographer)
Electra 1958,My 10,17:7
Miltiades, Milton (Director)
Electra 1958,My 10,17:7
Milton, Barbara
Call the Doctor 1920,S 1,14:1
Milton, Beth
Honor Code, The 1931,My 19,25:3
Milton, Billy
Fools Rush In 1934,D 26,19:2
Milton, David
Pirates of Penzance, The 1936,Ap 21,27:5
Money Mad 1937,My 25,32:5
Taming of the Shrew, The 1957,F 21,30:2
Song of Songs 1958,O 29,31:1
Milton, David Scott
Cave Dwellers, The 1961,O 16,34:2
Milton, David Scott (Playwright)
Two Times One; Duet for Solo Voice 1970,Ap 5,76:4
Milton, Ernest
Loyalties 1922,Jl 9,VI,1:1
Untitled-Play 1925,D 27,VII,2:1
Dybbuk, The 1927,My 1,VIII,2:7
Moving Finger, The 1928,S 16,IX,1:4
Mock Emperor, The 1929,F 17,IX,2:1
Mafro, Darling! 1929,Mr 17,X,1:4
Rope's End 1929,S 20,34:5
Little Eyolf 1930,N 2,VIII,2:6
John Brown's Body 1931,F 1,VIII,2:4
Grand Hotel 1931,S 27,VIII,1:4
Merchant of Venice, The 1932,Ap 29,13:4
Othello 1932,My 1,VIII,2:2
Dizzy 1932,O 30,IX,2:2
Untitled-Play 1933,Ap 2,IX,2:4
Night's Candles 1933,Je 25,IX,1:3
Night's Candles 1933,S 21,22:1
Dark Tower, The 1933,N 27,20:3
Paganini 1935,F 10,VIII,3:1
Delusion 1935,Mr 29,26:4
Timon of Athens 1935,D 15,XI,5:6
Victoria Regina 1937,Jl 11,X,1:7
Scandal in Assyria 1939,My 28,X,2:5
Milton, Ernest (Playwright)
Mary of Magdala 1946,Mr 26,24:5
Milton, Ernest (Producer)
Mock Emperor, The 1929,F 17,IX,2:1
Mafro, Darling! 1929,Mr 17,X,1:4
Merchant of Venice, The 1932,Ap 29,13:4

Milton, Frank
On the Town 1944,D 29,11:4
If the Shoe Fits 1946,D 6,29:4
Happy as Larry 1950,Ja 7,11:2
Out of This World 1950,D 22,17:3
Bells Are Ringing 1956,N 29,43:4
Bells Are Ringing 1956,N 30,18:2
Milton, George
Green Pastures, The 1935,F 27,16:2
Milton, Gerald
On Borrowed Time 1953,F 11,34:1
Stockade 1954,F 5,14:2
Milton, Gilbert
Heel, The 1954,My 27,33:2
Milton, James
Three Sisters, The 1969,O 10,38:1
Milton, John
Lawbreaker, The 1922,F 7,12:1
Doctor Faustus 1961,Ap 26,36:1
Milton, Joseph
Light of Asia, The 1928,O 10,32:2
Milton, Maud
Sacred and Profane Love 1920,F 24,11:1
Peg o' My Heart 1921,F 15,7:1
Milton, Paul R (Playwright)
Cabbages and Kings 1933,Je 28,24:5
Milton, Robert
Catskill Dutch 1924,My 4,VIII,2:1
Connelly vs Connelly 1961,F 18,11:3
Feast of Panthers 1961,Mr 21,32:1
My Beginning 1962,Ja 31,21:1
Milton, Robert (Director)
Outward Bound 1924,Ja 8,26:1
Outsider, The 1924,Mr 4,16:4
Catskill Dutch 1924,My 11,VIII,1:1
Far Cry, The 1924,S 28,VII,2:1
Far Cry, The 1924,O 1,24:1
Youngest, The 1924,D 23,17:1
Bit o' Love, A 1925,My 13,24:2
Enemy, The 1925,O 21,20:1
Last Night of Don Juan, The 1925,N 10,23:2
Bride of the Lamb 1926,Mr 31,20:3
Peggy-Ann 1926,D 28,16:3
Patience 1927,My 24,23:2
Revelry 1927,S 13,37:1
Paradise 1927,D 26,26:4
Napoleon 1928,Mr 9,21:1
Marriage Bed, The 1929,Ja 8,35:1
Dark Victory 1934,N 10,18:2
O'Flynn, The 1934,D 28,24:1
Season Changes, The 1935,D 24,10:2
Among Those Sailing 1936,F 12,24:4
Black Limelight 1936,N 10,31:1
Sea Gull, The 1938,Mr 29,19:2
Here Come the Clowns 1938,D 8,36:2
Burning Deck, The 1940,Mr 2,9:2
Viva O'Brien 1941,O 10,27:2
Golden Wings 1941,D 9,46:6
Milton, Robert (Miscellaneous)
Bride of the Lamb 1926,Mr 31,20:3
Milton, Robert (Playwright)
Charm School, The 1920,Ag 3,12:1
Dark Angel, The 1925,Ja 18,VII,2:8
June Days 1925,Ag 7,12:5
June Days 1925,Ag 23,VII,1:1
Milton, Robert (Producer)
God Bless Our Home 1924,N 23,VIII,2:4
Youngest, The 1924,D 23,17:1
Revelry 1927,S 13,37:1
Paradise 1927,D 26,26:4
Season Changes, The 1935,D 24,10:2
Golden Wings 1941,N 25,33:3
Golden Wings 1941,D 9,46:6
Miltos, M
Slight Case of Murder, A 1935,S 12,28:5
Milward, Jo
Cock Robin 1928,Ja 13,26:6
Milward, Jo (Playwright)
Life Is Like That 1930,D 23,24:3
Theodora, the Queen 1934,F 1,15:3
Milwit, Georgette
Cocktails of 1934 1934,My 5,22:1
Mimmo, Harry
John Murray Anderson's Almanac 1953,D 11,42:2
Mims, Mavis
Dream With Music 1944,My 19,15:2
Mims, Stuart
Midsummer Night's Dream, A 1931,Ag 19,19:3
Mims, Stuart (Playwright)
Russian Bank 1940,My 25,20:2
Minard, Leah-Marie
Medea 1920,Mr 23,12:2
Minciotti, Ernestine (Director)
Passion Play 1937,Mr 22,26:6
Minciotti, Esther
That Lady 1949,O 20,38:8
That Lady 1949,N 23,18:4
Best House in Naples, The 1956,O 27,16:2
Minciotti, Rachel
Vita Nuova; Life Begins Again 1935,F 26,16:2
Minciotti, Silvio
Tristi Amori; Unhappy Loves 1930,O 27,17:6
Vita Nuova; Life Begins Again 1935,F 26,16:2
Signo Della Croce, Il 1935,O 7,11:1

Minciotti, Silvio—Cont
Walk Into My Parlor 1941,N 20,38:2
Bell for Adano, A 1944,D 7,21:2
Best House in Naples, The 1956,O 27,16:2
Mindell, Fania (Costume Designer)
Hedda Gabler 1926,Ja 27,16:5
Easter 1926,Mr 19,24:3
One Day More 1926,Mr 19,24:3
Inspector General, The 1930,D 24,19:2
Mother, The 1935,N 20,26:3
Mindell, Norma
Fourth Pig, The 1965,Ja 27,24:6
Mindis, Arleen
Lysistrata 1968,N 15,42:1
Mindlin, Michael (Producer)
Sweet Chariot 1930,O 24,30:2
Mindlin, Michael Jr (Miscellaneous)
World of Suzie Wong, The 1958,O 15,47:1
Maria Golovin 1958,N 6,43:1
Plume de Ma Tante, La 1958,N 12,42:1
Destry Rides Again 1959,Ap 24,24:1
Gypsy 1959,My 22,31:6
Mine, Naboru
Coney Island Play 1970,O 31,34:2
Minehart, Glory
Topsy and Eva 1924,D 24,11:1
Minehart, Murray
Lady in Ermine, The 1922,O 3,22:2
Mineo, John
Henry, Sweet Henry 1967,O 24,51:2
George M! 1968,Ap 11,48:1
Mineo, Sal
Rose Tattoo, The 1951,F 5,19:2
Dinosaur Wharf 1951,N 9,23:2
Something About a Soldier 1962,Ja 5,36:2
Mineo, Sal (Director)
Fortune and Men's Eyes 1969,O 23,55:1
Fortune and Men's Eyes 1970,Ja 18,II,1:1
Miner, C Worthington (Director)
Top O' the Hill 1929,N 27,30:4
Miner, Henry C Jr (Playwright)
Man From Earth, The 1923,Ja 3,6:2
Miner, Jan
Vaudeville (Palace) 1952,F 27,22:2
Obbligato 1958,F 19,22:2
Viva Madison Avenue 1960,Ap 7,42:1
Decameron, The 1961,Ap 13,32:1
Dumbbell People in a Barbell World 1962,F 15,25:1
Intimate Relations 1962,N 2,27:1
Lady of the Camellias, The 1963,Mr 22,7:1
Wives, The 1965,My 18,35:4
Falstaff 1966,Je 20,27:1
Murder in the Cathedral 1966,Je 21,38:1
Androcles and the Lion 1968,Je 27,47:1
Lemonade 1968,D 14,60:1
Autograph Hound, The 1968,D 14,60:1
All's Well That Ends Well 1970,Je 16,53:1
Othello 1970,Je 22,43:1
Othello 1970,Je 28,II,1:1
Othello 1970,S 15,51:1
Miner, Kenneth
White Gold 1925,N 3,34:5
Miner, Mary
Mountain Fury 1929,S 26,27:2
As You Desire Me 1931,Ja 29,21:2
Miner, Nina Melville
Father, The 1937,Ap 21,18:5
Miner, Peter
Dame Nature 1938,S 27,24:3
Miner, Ranlet
Who's Who 1924,Ap 18,19:2
Miner, Worthington
Fallen Angels 1927,D 2,20:4
On to Fortune 1935,F 5,22:2
Miner, Worthington (Director)
Week-end 1929,O 23,26:4
Up Pops the Devil 1930,S 2,19:1
Sweet Stranger 1930,O 22,23:3
Five Star Final 1930,D 31,11:1
House Beautiful, The 1931,Mr 13,20:4
House Beautiful, The 1931,Mr 22,VIII,1:1
Reunion in Vienna 1931,N 17,31:1
Wild Waves 1932,Ja 24,VIII,3:3
Wild Waves 1932,F 20,11:4
I Loved You Wednesday 1932,O 12,27:1
Both Your Houses 1933,Mr 7,20:3
Her Master's Voice 1933,O 24,24:3
Revenge With Music 1934,N 29,33:5
On to Fortune 1935,Ja 15,23:2
On to Fortune 1935,F 5,22:2
Coward, The 1935,Jl 16,24:1
Blind Alley 1935,S 25,19:6
Let Freedom Ring 1935,N 7,26:2
Bury the Dead 1936,Mr 16,21:2
On Your Toes 1936,Ap 13,14:4
Bury the Dead 1936,Ap 20,17:4
Prelude 1936,Ap 20,17:4
200 Were Chosen 1936,N 21,21:1
Jane Eyre 1937,Ja 3,X,2:1
Excursion 1937,Ap 10,11:4
Excursion 1937,Ap 18,XI,1:1
Father Malachy's Miracle 1937,N 18,26:4
Father Malachy's Miracle 1937,D 5,XII,5:1
Stop-Over 1938,Ja 12,16:5
Father Malachy's Miracle 1938,Ja 23,XI,1:6

Miner, Worthington (Director)—Cont
Washington Jitters 1938,My 3,19:1
Dame Nature 1938,S 27,24:3
Jeremiah 1939,F 4,11:2
Susannah and the Elders 1940,O 30,28:2
Somewhere in France 1941,Ap 29,16:8
Home Is the Hero 1954,S 23,42:2
Miner, Worthington (Playwright)
Jeremiah 1939,F 4,11:2
Miner, Worthington (Producer)
Dame Nature 1938,S 27,24:3
Home Is the Hero 1954,S 23,42:2
Four Winds 1957,S 26,21:2
Mines, Mabou (Producer)
Red Horse Animation, The 1970,N 20,32:1
Minetti, Bernhard
Goetz von Berlichingen 1930,D 14,IX,4:1
Heilige Crispin, Der 1933,Je 25,IX,1:2
Revisor 1935,O 6,XI,3:7
Richard III 1937,My 30,X,2:2
Michael Kramer 1938,F 20,XI,2:1
Mineur, Henry J
Life Begins in '40 1940,Ap 5,24:2
Hit the Road 1941,Ap 4,18:3
Minevitch, Borrah
Puzzles of 1925 1925,F 3,25:3
Vaudeville (Palace) 1926,S 7,24:6
Betsy 1926,D 29,24:3
Good Boy 1928,S 6,23:2
Sweet and Low 1930,N 18,28:5
Vaudeville (Palace) 1930,D 1,19:1
Vaudeville (Palace) 1931,Jl 6,24:6
Vaudeville (Palace) 1931,O 26,22:3
Vaudeville (Hollywood) 1932,Ap 19,25:5
Man Who Came to Dinner, The 1940,F 10,19:5
Man Who Came to Dinner, The 1940,F 18,IX,3:6
Minevitch, Borrah and His Harmonica Rascals
Vaudeville (Palace) 1952,Ap 14,23:2
Vaudeville (Palace) 1952,Ap 27,II,1:1
Aquashow 1952,Je 25,25:1
Miney, H C (Lyricist)
Espanola 1921,D 30,13:1
Minford, Robert
Johnny Johnson 1956,O 22,24:1
Minger, Harold
Miles of Heaven, The 1937,Ag 31,27:4
Minizer, William (Lighting Director)
Prince of Peasantmania 1970,F 22,88:1
Minjer, Harold
Little Clay Cart, The 1924,D 6,13:3
Critic, The 1925,My 9,12:4
Dybbuk, The 1925,D 16,22:2
Apothecary, The 1926,Mr 17,28:1
Romantic Young Lady, The 1926,My 5,24:3
Grand Street Follies, The 1926,Je 16,23:2
New York Exchange 1926,D 31,11:2
Grand Street Follies, The 1928,My 29,16:2
Mink, David
Mother Courage and Her Children 1964,My 12,32:2
Mink, Edna
What's the Use? 1926,S 7,19:1
Mink, Janice
Cabaret 1966,N 21,62:1
Minkin, Vladimir
Moscow Circus on Ice 1970,D 9,63:1
Minkoff, Fran (Composer)
Leonard Sillman's New Faces of 1968 1968,My 3,43:1
Minkoff, Fran (Lyricist)
Leonard Sillman's New Faces of 1968 1968,My 3,43:1
Minkus, Barbara
Education of H*Y*M*A*N K*A*P*L*A*N, The 1968,Ap 5,57:1
Rondelay 1969,N 6,55:1
Minnelli, Liza
Diary of Anne Frank, The 1962,Jl 31,19:2
Best Foot Forward 1963,Ap 3,43:1
Untitled-Revue 1964,N 10,56:2
Flora, the Red Menace 1965,My 12,41:2
Minnelli, Vincente (Costume Designer)
Vanities 1932,S 28,22:4
Du Barry 1932,N 23,15:2
At Home Abroad 1935,S 20,17:4
Ziegfeld Follies 1935,D 31,10:1
Ziegfeld Follies 1936,Ja 31,17:2
Ziegfeld Follies 1936,S 15,37:1
Minnelli, Vincente (Director)
At Home Abroad 1935,S 20,17:4
Show Is On, The 1936,N 9,22:2
Show Is On, The 1936,N 15,XI,2:1
Show Is On, The 1936,D 26,14:2
Show Is On, The 1937,S 20,18:4
Hooray for What! 1937,D 2,32:5
Very Warm for May 1939,N 18,23:2
Minnelli, Vincente (Miscellaneous)
Earl Carroll's Vanities 1931,Ag 28,18:7
Show Is On, The 1936,D 26,14:2
Show Is On, The 1937,S 20,18:4
Hooray for What! 1937,D 2,32:5
Minnelli, Vincente (Playwright)
Dance Me a Song 1950,Ja 21,10:5
Minnelli, Vincente (Producer)
At Home Abroad 1935,O 27,IX,1:1

Minnelli, Vincente (Scenic Designer)
Vanities 1932,S 28,22:4
Du Barry 1932,N 23,15:2
At Home Abroad 1935,S 20,17:4
At Home Abroad 1935,O 27,IX,8:1
Ziegfeld Follies 1935,D 31,10:1
Ziegfeld Follies 1936,Ja 5,IX,3:1
Ziegfeld Follies 1936,Ja 31,17:2
Ziegfeld Follies 1936,S 15,37:1
Show Is On, The 1936,N 9,22:2
Show Is On, The 1937,S 20,18:4
Hooray for What! 1937,N 7,XI,2:4
Hooray for What! 1937,D 2,32:5
Very Warm for May 1939,N 18,23:2
Minney, R J (Playwright)
Clive of India 1934,F 18,IX,3:7
Minnick, Maurice
Comes the Revelation 1942,My 27,26:2
Barber Had Two Sons, The 1943,F 2,22:2
Minoff, Lee (Playwright)
Come Live With Me 1967,Ja 27,29:1
Minor, A J (Playwright)
Masks and Faces 1933,Mr 20,18:5
Minor, Kiki
My Fair Lady 1964,My 21,43:2
My Fair Lady 1968,Je 14,42:1
Minor, Nina Melville (Mrs)
Volpone 1937,N 16,26:4
Life and Death of Sir John Falstaff, The 1938,Mr 15,19:5
Minor, Philip
King and the Duke, The 1955,Je 2,25:2
Ronde, La 1955,Je 28,24:2
He Who Gets Slapped 1956,F 2,18:1
Queen After Death 1956,Mr 13,33:2
Alchemist, The 1964,S 15,33:1
Hamlet 1969,Mr 4,34:1
Minor, Philip (Director)
Bonds of Interest, The 1958,My 7,43:1
Under the Sycamore Tree 1960,Mr 8,37:2
Misalliance 1961,S 26,32:2
Duchess of Malfi, The 1962,Mr 5,27:1
Yes is for a Very Young Man 1963,Mr 6,7:5
Arms and the Man 1967,Je 23,44:2
Cocktail Party, The 1968,O 8,42:1
Millionairess, The 1969,Mr 3,28:1
Minor, Philip (Producer)
Bonds of Interest, The 1958,My 7,43:1
Misalliance 1961,S 26,32:2
Minor, Philip (Translator)
Bonds of Interest, The 1958,My 7,43:1
Minosuke
Chushingura; Treasury of Loyal Retainers, The 1969,S 11,53:1
Momiji-Gari 1969,S 18,64:1
Minot, Anna
Nine Till Six 1936,Mr 14,10:3
Strings, My Lord, Are False, The 1942,My 20,24:2
Russian People, The 1942,D 30,17:2
Visitor, The 1944,O 18,24:5
Enemy of the People, An 1950,D 29,14:1
Sands of the Negev 1954,O 20,32:1
Ivanov 1966,My 4,50:1
Minot, Dominique
P S I Love You 1964,N 20,40:1
Minotis, Alexis
Electra 1930,D 27,16:1
Iphigenia 1931,Ja 6,24:1
Oedipus Tyrannus 1952,N 25,35:2
Minotis, Alexis (Director)
Oedipus Tyrannus 1952,N 25,35:2
Minotis, M
Hamlet 1939,Jl 9,IX,1:6
Minotti, Tatjana
Tales of Hoffmann 1932,Ja 10,VIII,1:6
Mins, Leonard (Playwright)
Temper the Wind 1946,D 28,10:2
Temper the Wind 1947,Ja 12,II,1:1
Minshall, Mickey
Tall Kentuckian, The 1953,Je 17,30:1
Minsky (Producer)
Republic Frolics 1932,O 13,22:2
Minsky Brothers (Producer)
Untitled-Revue 1922,S 16,18:2
Minster, Jack
Not for Children 1935,N 25,23:8
Minster, Jack (Director)
Lady Windermere's Fan 1946,O 15,29:2
Rainmaker, The 1956,Je 1,26:7
Boeing-Boeing 1965,F 3,30:1
Minter, Hilda
Revolt of the Beavers, The 1937,My 21,19:2
Minton, Augustus
Bunch and Judy, The 1922,N 29,20:1
Minton, Gus
Tip-Top 1920,O 6,13:2
Mintun, John
Get Thee to Canterbury 1969,Ja 26,74:1

Minturn, Garrett
Porgy 1927,O 11,26:2
Minturn, Harry
Blue Flame, The 1920,Mr 16,18:1
Endless Chain 1922,S 5,21:2
Forbidden 1923,O 2,10:2
Lonely Lee 1923,N 11,VIII,2:6
Road Together, The 1924,Ja 18,21:2
Myrtie 1924,F 5,21:2
Easy Street 1924,Ag 15,16:4
Minturn, Harry (Director)
Swing Mikado, The 1939,Mr 2,18:2
Minturn, Harry (Playwright)
Swing Mikado, The 1939,Mr 2,18:2
Minty, Dazma
Bitter Oleander 1935,F 12,24:3
Mintz, Billy
Sunup to Sundown 1938,F 2,14:3
Mintz, Claudine
Field God, The 1927,Ap 22,18:2
Mintz, Claudius
Hamlet 1930,Mr 25,34:4
Macbeth 1930,Mr 26,24:6
Twelfth Night 1930,Mr 27,24:7
Merchant of Venice, The 1930,Mr 27,24:7
Taming of the Shrew, The 1930,Mr 28,22:8
Richard III 1930,Mr 31,24:1
As You Like It 1930,Ap 3,32:5
Merchant of Venice, The 1931,N 17,31:1
Julius Caesar 1931,N 18,26:3
Hamlet 1931,N 19,26:6
Mintz, Eli
Chair, The 1930,O 4,15:4
God's Thieves 1930,O 27,17:4
Me and Molly 1948,F 27,27:2
49th Cousin, The 1960,O 28,22:1
Worm in Horseradish, A 1961,Mr 14,32:3
I Was Dancing 1964,N 9,40:4
Catch Me if You Can 1965,Mr 10,50:1
Jimmy Shine 1968,D 6,52:1
Mintz, J Mylong
Her Great Mistake 1940,F 5,12:6
Mintz, Nat
Eternal Road, The 1937,Ja 8,14:2
Sunup to Sundown 1938,F 2,14:3
Mintz, Rose
Innocent Idea, An 1920,My 26,9:4
Mintz, Thelma
Family Mishmash, A 1958,O 20,36:1
Bei Mir Bistu Schoen 1961,O 23,22:2
Cowboy in Israel, A 1962,O 29,36:2
My Wife With Conditions 1963,O 21,39:1
Good Luck 1964,O 19,38:3
Hello Charlie 1965,O 25,47:2
Bride Got Farblondjet, The 1967,N 6,61:6
It's Never Too Late for Happiness 1968,O 21,59:3
Oh What a Wedding! 1969,O 20,60:1
President's Daughter, The 1970,N 4,41:2
Mintzer, Freya
Legend of Lovers 1959,O 28,40:3
Mintzer, William (Lighting Director)
Take Me to Bed 1969,Je 14,24:1
Time for Bed 1969,Je 14,24:1
Passing Through From Exotic Places; Son Who Hunted Tigers in Jakarta, The 1969,D 8,60:4
Passing Through From Exotic Places; Burial of Esposito, The 1969,D 8,60:4
Passing Through From Exotic Places; Sunstroke 1969,D 8,60:4
Exchange 1970,F 9,47:2
Moths, The 1970,My 12,46:1
Candaules, Commissioner 1970,My 29,15:1
Carpenters, The 1970,D 22,40:1
Mio, Eva
Eastward in Eden 1956,Ap 18,25:4
Mio, Tesore
Caviar 1934,Je 8,19:2
Miquel, Pablo
Top-Notchers 1942,My 30,8:5
Miracle, Chester (Playwright)
Noye's Fludde 1959,Mr 17,41:2
Miramova, Elena
Anatol 1931,Ja 17,23:3
Grand Hotel 1931,S 27,VIII,1:4
Theodora, the Queen 1934,F 1,15:3
Times Have Changed 1935,F 26,16:1
Two Mrs Carrolls, The 1935,Je 13,26:1
Two Mrs Carrolls, The 1935,Ag 4,IX,1:3
Close Quarters 1939,Mr 7,19:2
Dark Eyes 1943,Ja 15,20:2
Dark Eyes 1943,Ja 31,II,1:3
Miramova, Elena (Playwright)
Dark Eyes 1943,Ja 15,20:2
Dark Eyes 1943,Ja 31,II,1:1
Dark Eyes 1948,Mr 25,34:4
Miranda, Carmen
Streets of Paris, The 1939,Je 20,25:2
Streets of Paris, The 1939,Je 25,IX,1:1
Sons o' Fun 1941,D 2,28:2
Family, The 1943,Mr 31,22:4
Tidbits of 1946 1946,Jl 9,17:2
Miranda, Edgard da Rocha (Playwright)
And the Wind Blows 1959,Ap 29,28:1

Miranda, Edgard da Rocha (Playwright)—Cont
And the Wind Blows 1959,My 17,II,1:1
Miranda, John
Mandragola 1958,My 29,23:2
Geranium Hat, The 1959,Mr 18,45:1
Drunkard, The; Fallen Saved, The 1959,Je 24,37:2
Guitar 1959,N 11,42:5
Emmanuel 1960,D 5,42:2
Montserrat 1961,Ja 9,30:5
Five Posts in the Market Place 1961,Mr 6,30:1
Miranda, John (Miscellaneous)
I Got Shoes 1963,Ja 25,12:2
Miranda, John M
People vs Ranchman, The 1968,O 28,56:1
Mirande, T (Original Author)
Matrimonial Bed, The 1927,O 13,23:2
Mirande, Yves (Lyricist)
Trois Jeunes Filles Nues; Three Young Maids From
the Folies Bergere 1929,Mr 5,28:2
Ta Bouche 1929,Mr 15,28:5
Mirande, Yves (Original Author)
Man in Dress Clothes, The 1937,Ag 24,24:4
Mirande, Yves (Playwright)
Blue Kitten, The 1922,Ja 14,9:3
One Kiss 1923,N 28,14:2
Man in Evening Clothes, The 1924,D 6,13:4
Baigneuse du Lido, La 1928,Jl 1,VIII,1:8
Trou Dans le Mur, Le 1929,F 24,IX,1:8
Trois Jeunes Filles Nues; Three Young Maids From
the Folies Bergere 1929,Mr 5,28:2
Ta Bouche 1929,Mr 15,28:5
Attachee, L' 1929,My 19,IX,2:1
Homme nu, L' 1932,Ap 3,VIII,2:1
Mirante, Arnold
Fiesta 1929,S 18,35:1
Mirbeau, d'Octave (Playwright)
Affaires Son les Affaires, Les 1924,Mr 11,17:1
Mirbeau, Octave (Original Author)
Jardin des Supplices, Le 1929,Ap 21,X,2:7
Mireaieva, Mme
Revue Russe, The 1922,O 6,28:1
Mirecka, Rena
Constant Prince, The 1969,O 18,36:1
Acropolis 1969,N 5,40:1
Mireille (Mlle)
Odeon-Revue 1927,My 22,VIII,2:7
Bitter Sweet 1929,O 27,IX,2:1
Bitter Sweet 1929,N 6,30:2
Mireno, Gigi
Retabililo de Don Cristobal, El; Puppet Theater of
Don Cristobal, The; Zapatera Prodigiosa, La;
Shoemaker's Prodigious Wife, The 1964,S 3,23:2
Mirick, G S (Miscellaneous)
Second Man, The 1930,My 2,23:2
Mirisch, Lawrence (Producer)
March March, The 1966,N 15,51:4
Neighbors 1966,N 15,51:4
Miro, Bartholomew Jr
Fortune and Men's Eyes 1969,O 23,55:1
Miroff, Seymour
Time Remembered 1957,N 13,41:2
Miromaya, Elene
Grand Hotel 1931,S 4,22:7
Mirr, Dorothy
Show Boat 1954,My 6,44:1
Mirren, Helen
Troilus and Cressida 1969,Jl 31,26:1
Silver Tassle, The 1969,S 12,35:2
Hamlet 1970,Ag 3,37:3
Mirris, Du B S Jr
It's the Valet 1933,D 15,25:4
Mirsak, Joseph
Waiting for Godot 1958,Ag 6,22:1
Mirsky, Alexander
Valley Forge 1934,D 11,28:3
Mirt, S K
Dole Brothers 1932,Mr 26,17:7
Mirval, Yvonne (Mme)
Homme Qui Assassina, L' 1924,N 11,20:1
Homme et Ses Fantomes, L' 1924,N 14,16:1
Merchant of Venice, The 1924,N 18,23:2
Mirvish, E (Producer)
Minor Adjustment, A 1967,O 7,33:3
Mirvish, R (Producer)
Minor Adjustment, A 1967,O 7,33:3
Mirzayantz, Simeon
War and Peace 1942,My 22,26:3
Mischa (Composer)
Happy as Larry 1950,Ja 7,11:2
Misener, Helen
Power Without Glory 1948,Ja 14,30:2
Misenoff, Joseph
Alt Heidelberg 1926,My 31,10:5
Misevic, Radenko (Scenic Designer)
Progress of Bora, The Tailor, The 1968,Je 27,49:2
Misgen, Florence
Greenwich Village Follies 1928,Ap 10,32:2
Mish, Eleanor
Craig's Wife 1925,O 13,21:2
Light of Asia, The 1928,O 10,32:2
Mishima, Yukio (Playwright)
Lady Akane, The 1960,N 16,51:4
Hanjo 1960,N 16,51:4
Sotoba Komachi 1961,F 1,15:1

Damask Drum, The 1961,F 4,15:1
Mishler, James
Great Day in the Morning 1962,Mr 29,29:1
Mishler, James (Producer)
Friday Night; Mary Agnes Is Thirty-Five
1965,F 9,42:5
Friday Night; Passport 1965,F 9,42:5
Friday Night; River, The 1965,F 9,42:5
Mishon Brothers
Night in Venice, A 1929,My 22,30:2
Misita, Mike
Applause 1970,Mr 31,35:1
Misko, Jah
Mima 1928,D 13,24:2
Misrock, Henry R (Playwright)
Bright Honor 1936,S 28,14:1
Family Affair, A 1946,N 28,41:2
Mistinguett
Innocent Eyes 1924,My 21,22:2
Ca. . . C'Est Paris 1927,F 6,VII,4:1
Mistral, Nati
Man of La Mancha 1966,O 5,42:5
Mitchel, Ann
Playboy of the Western World, The 1930,Ja 3,20:4
Mitchel, Helene
Small Timers, The 1925,Ja 28,15:3
Not Herbert 1926,Ja 27,16:2
Challenge of Youth 1930,Ja 21,28:5
Mitchell, Abbie
In Abraham's Bosom 1926,D 31,10:2
In Abraham's Bosom 1927,F 20,VII,1:1
House of Shadows, The 1927,Ap 22,18:4
Coquette 1927,N 9,23:1
Stevedore 1934,O 2,18:2
Porgy and Bess 1935,O 11,30:2
Little Foxes, The 1939,F 16,16:2
On Whitman Avenue 1946,My 9,28:2
Mitchell, Adrian (Lyricist)
US 1966,N 6,II,1:5
Mitchell, Adrian (Miscellaneous)
Persecution and Assassination of Marat As
Performed by the Inmates of the Asylum of
Charenton Under the Direction of the Marquis de
Sade, The 1966,Ja 9,II,1:1
Mitchell, Adrian (Playwright)
Persecution and Assassination of Marat As
Performed by the Inmates of the Asylum of
Charenton Under the Direction of the Marquis de
Sade, The 1965,D 28,35:1
Persecution and Assassination of Marat As
Performed by the Inmates of the Asylum of
Charenton Under the Direction of the Marquis de
Sade, The 1967,Ja 4,34:1
Criminals, The 1970,F 26,33:2
Mitchell, Ann
Amorous Flea, The 1964,F 18,26:1
Mitchell, Anne
Love's Call 1925,S 11,20:1
General John Regan 1930,Ja 30,16:5
Mitchell, Arnuard
Shake Hands With the Devil 1949,O 21,30:4
Mitchell, Arthur
Kiss Me, Kate 1956,My 10,27:2
Noel Coward's Sweet Potato 1968,S 30,59:1
Noel Coward's Sweet Potato 1968,O 13,II,5:1
Mitchell, Barry
Winged Victory 1943,N 22,24:1
Diamond Lil 1948,N 30,33:2
Mitchell, Basil (Playwright)
Holmeses of Baker Street, The 1936,D 10,34:3
Mitchell, Bill
Valmouth 1960,O 7,29:1
Mitchell, Bobby
Horse Fever 1940,N 25,21:2
Mitchell, Byron
Qudrille 1954,N 4,39:2
Copper and Brass 1957,O 18,19:2
Crystal Heart, The 1960,F 16,31:2
Irma la Douce 1960,S 30,31:2
Tovarich 1963,Mr 20,5:1
Mitchell, Cameron
Jeremiah 1939,F 4,11:2
Taming of the Shrew, The 1940,F 6,17:2
Trojan Women, The 1941,Ap 9,32:5
Death of a Salesman 1949,F 11,27:2
Death of a Salesman 1950,Mr 12,II,1:1
Southern Exposure 1950,S 27,36:3
Blancs, Les 1970,N 16,48:4
Blancs, Les 1970,N 29,II,3:5
Blancs, Les 1970,N 29,II,3:1
Mitchell, Carl (Costume Designer)
Merry Wives of Windsor, The 1954,F 17,27:1
Cock-A-Doodle Dandy 1955,N 4,26:5
Mitchell, Charles
Lucky 1927,Mr 23,28:3
Mitchell, David (Director)
Hamlet 1968,Jl 4,15:1
Mitchell, David (Miscellaneous)
No Place to Be Somebody 1969,D 31,17:1
Mitchell, David (Scenic Designer)
Medea 1965,N 29,46:1
Macbeth 1966,Je 29,38:1
Macbeth 1966,Ag 29,23:4

Mitchell, David (Scenic Designer)—Cont
Macbeth 1966,Ag 30,34:1
Volpone 1967,Je 30,29:1
Hamlet 1967,D 27,45:1
Increased Difficulty of Concentration, The
1969,D 5,48:1
Grin and Bare It 1970,Mr 17,36:1
Postcards 1970,Mr 17,36:1
Steambath 1970,Jl 1,49:1
Steambath 1970,Jl 12,II,1:3
Trelawny of the 'Wells' 1970,O 12,48:1
Colette 1970,O 15,58:1
Mitchell, David I (Costume Designer)
Increased Difficulty of Concentration, The
1969,D 5,48:1
Mitchell, Dodson
Tavern, The 1920,S 28,14:1
Personality 1921,Ag 29,14:3
Like a King 1921,O 4,10:1
National Anthem, The 1922,Ja 24,16:3
Night Call, The 1922,Ap 27,12:2
Listening In 1922,D 5,24:1
Home Fires 1923,Ag 21,12:1
Izzy 1924,S 17,16:2
Red Falcon, The 1924,O 8,22:1
Wild Birds 1925,Ap 10,16:1
Beau Gallant 1926,Ap 6,26:3
Behold This Dreamer 1927,N 1,20:4
First Mortgage 1929,O 11,36:1
Her Supporting Cast 1931,My 5,33:3
In Times Square 1931,N 24,29:3
Black Sheep 1932,O 14,22:6
Jamboree 1932,N 25,18:4
Little Black Book, The 1932,D 27,11:2
Stevedore 1934,Ap 19,33:2
Errant Lady 1934,S 18,18:2
Within the Gates 1934,O 23,23:1
Woman of the Soil, A 1935,Mr 26,23:6
Jane Brady-Editor 1935,Jl 2,24:3
Noble Prize, The 1935,Jl 9,24:3
If This Be Treason 1935,Jl 30,17:1
Good Men and True 1935,O 26,12:4
Mid-West 1936,Ja 8,22:4
Ten Million Ghosts 1936,O 24,23:7
Around the Corner 1936,D 29,17:2
Enemy of the People, An 1937,F 16,19:1
Mitchell, Dodson (Playwright)
Cornered 1920,D 9,18:2
In Times Square 1931,N 24,29:3
Mitchell, Donald
Have I Got a Girl for You! 1963,D 3,53:2
Mitchell, Donald J (Miscellaneous)
Best Laid Plans, The 1966,Mr 26,15:2
Mitchell, Earle
Night Call, The 1922,Ap 27,12:2
Egotist, The 1922,D 27,12:1
Thumbs Down 1923,Ag 7,20:1
Bully, The 1924,D 26,18:1
Dove, The 1925,F 12,17:3
Chivalry 1925,D 16,22:3
Desert Song, The 1926,D 1,24:2
New Moon, The 1928,S 20,33:1
Under the Gaslight 1929,Ap 3,27:1
House Afire 1930,Ap 1,34:7
Uncle Tom's Cabin 1933,My 30,13:4
How Beautiful With Shoes 1935,N 29,24:1
Madame Capet 1938,O 26,26:2
Mitchell, Edward R (Director)
Winners and Losers 1947,F 27,27:2
Our Lan' 1947,Ap 19,11:2
Alice Adams 1947,Ag 5,26:1
G-II 1948,My 28,27:3
Mitchell, Edward R (Miscellaneous)
Our Lan' 1947,Ap 19,11:2
Our Lan' 1947,S 29,16:5
Mitchell, Edward R (Scenic Designer)
Winners and Losers 1947,F 27,27:2
Deputy of Paris, The 1947,Mr 22,9:5
G-II 1948,My 28,27:3
Mitchell, Eileen
Poker Session, The 1967,S 20,42:2
Glorious Ruler, The 1969,Jl 1,31:1
Mitchell, Esther
Madras House, The 1921,O 31,18:2
Green Ring, The 1922,Ap 5,22:1
Makers of Light 1922,My 24,22:3
This Fine-Pretty World 1923,D 27,11:1
Time Is a Dream 1924,Ap 23,24:2
Grand Street Follies, The 1925,Je 19,24:1
Chief Thing, The 1926,Mr 23,24:2
Lovers and Enemies 1927,S 21,27:1
Cherry Orchard, The 1928,Mr 6,20:1
Meet the Prince 1929,F 26,30:5
Cyrano de Bergerac 1932,D 27,11:2
Lake, The 1933,D 27,24:2
Within the Gates 1934,O 23,23:1
Call It a Day 1936,Ja 29,15:2
Spring Thaw 1938,Mr 22,18:1
Lorelei 1938,N 30,21:2
Mr Banks of Birmingham 1939,Ja 21,18:4
Red Velvet Goat, The 1939,Ja 21,18:4
Miss Swan Expects 1939,F 21,15:2
Leave Her to Heaven 1940,F 28,16:2
Wind in the Sails 1940,Ag 1,24:6

Mitchell, Esther—Cont

Jupiter Laughs 1940,S 10,27:1
Boyd's Daughter 1940,O 12,20:2
Corn Is Green, The 1943,My 4,18:3
O Mistress Mine 1946,Ja 24,25:2
I Know My Love 1949,N 3,36:1
Mitchell, Ewing
Song of Norway 1944,Ag 22,20:2
Mitchell, Fanny Todd (Playwright)
Angela 1928,D 4,28:2
Boom Boom 1929,Ja 29,26:4
Music in May 1929,Ap 2,29:1
Wonderful Night, A; Fledermaus, Die
1929,N 1,23:3
Mitchell, Frank
Vaudeville (Palace) 1928,D 31,9:3
Earl Carroll's Vanities 1931,Ag 28,18:7
Mitchell, Fred (Miscellaneous)
John Henry 1940,Ja 11,18:2
Mitchell, Fred M
Kibitzer, The 1929,F 19,22:5
Mitchell, Garry
Falstaff 1966,Je 20,27:1
Julius Caesar 1966,Je 24,29:2
Antigone 1967,Je 19,43:1
Whistle in the Dark, A 1968,F 17,32:2
Moon for the Misbegotten, A 1968,Je 13,55:2
We Bombed in New Haven 1968,O 17,51:1
Nobody Hears A Broken Drum 1970,Mr 20,55:1
Blancs, Les 1970,N 16,48:4
Mitchell, Gay
Drifting Apart: or, The Fisherman's Child
1941,Ag 20,16:6
Mitchell, Geneva
Yours Truly 1927,Ja 26,16:5
Take the Air 1927,N 23,28:2
Mitchell, George
Man About Town, A 1921,Mr 22,15:1
Beggar on Horseback 1924,F 13,17:2
Merry Widow, The 1942,Jl 16,22:1
New Moon, The 1942,Ag 19,14:2
Patriots, The 1943,Ja 30,11:2
Blossom Time 1943,S 6,21:2
New Moon, The 1944,My 18,16:2
Throng o' Scarlet 1947,D 2,37:2
Goodbye My Fancy 1948,N 18,35:2
Day After Tomorrow 1950,O 27,25:2
Desire Under the Elms 1952,Ja 17,23:4
Crucible, The 1953,Ja 23,15:2
Roots 1961,Mr 7,40:2
This Here Nice Place 1966,N 2,35:2
Harpers Ferry 1967,Je 6,52:2
House of Atreus, The; Bringers of Offerings, The
1967,Jl 24,23:1
Visit, The 1967,S 13,41:1
Indians 1969,O 14,51:1
Indians 1969,O 19,II,1:1
Mitchell, Grant
Champion, The 1921,Ja 4,11:1
Champion, The 1921,Ja 9,VI,1:1
Hero, The 1921,Mr 15,14:1
Hero, The 1921,Mr 20,VI,1:1
Kempy 1922,My 16,14:2
School for Scandal, The 1923,Je 5,24:3
Whole Town's Talking, The 1923,Ag 30,8:2
Whole Town's Talking, The 1923,S 9,VII,1:1
Habitual Husband, The 1924,D 25,27:3
Spooks 1925,Je 2,16:4
One of the Family 1925,D 23,22:3
Vaudeville (Palace) 1926,Ag 31,15:3
Baby Cyclone, The 1927,S 13,37:4
All the King's Men 1929,F 5,27:1
Tailor-Made Man, A 1929,O 22,26:3
Tide Rising 1937,Ja 26,17:2
Ringside Seat 1938,N 23,24:5
Mitchell, Gwenn
X Has No Value 1970,F 17,35:1
Immaculate Misconception, The 1970,O 28,63:3
Mitchell, Harry (Lighting Director)
Mandragola 1958,My 29,23:2
Mitchell, Harvey
Peg o' My Heart 1948,Ag 25,29:2
Mitchell, Helene
Jimmie's Women 1927,S 27,30:3
Penal Law 2010 1930,Ap 19,14:2
Mitchell, Helene (Playwright)
Cafe de Danse 1929,Ja 16,22:2
Mitchell, Hollis
Boy Meets Girl 1937,Jl 6,23:1
Mitchell, Irving
Tweedles 1923,Ag 14,10:1
This Thing Called Love 1935,Jl 2,24:4
Sister Oakes 1949,Ap 25,19:4
Gentlemen Prefer Blondes 1949,D 9,35:3
Mitchell, Jacqueline
Iolanthe 1962,N 28,42:1
Mitchell, James
Million Dollar Baby 1945,D 22,17:2
Brigadoon 1947,Mr 14,28:2
Brigadoon 1947,Mr 23,II,1:1
Paint Your Wagon 1951,N 13,32:2
Paint Your Wagon 1951,N 18,II,1:1
Livin' the Life 1957,Ap 29,20:1
Carousel 1957,S 12,38:2

Winkelberg 1958,Ja 15,26:2
First Impressions 1959,Mr 20,28:1
First Impressions 1959,Mr 29,II,1:1
Carnival! 1961,Ap 14,22:2
Deputy, The 1964,F 27,26:1
Mitchell, James (Miscellaneous)
Come Summer 1969,Mr 19,43:1
Mitchell, Jennifer
Dirtiest Show in Town, The 1970,Je 29,43:2
Mitchell, Joseph
Poor Nut, The 1925,Ap 28,18:1
Carolinian, The 1925,N 3,34:2
Othello 1955,S 8,27:2
Boo Hoo! East Lynne 1959,S 9,50:4
Macbeth 1969,D 23,25:1
Mitchell, Joseph (Playwright)
Satellite 1935,N 21,27:5
Bajour 1964,N 24,42:1
Mitchell, Julian (Costume Designer)
Castles in the Air 1926,S 7,19:2
Mitchell, Julian (Director)
Ziegfeld Follies 1924,Je 25,26:1
Mitchell, Julian (Playwright)
Heritage and Its History, A 1965,My 19,42:1
Mitchell, Katherine
Caesar and Cleopatra 1927,N 6,IX,2:1
Mitchell, Kay
Journey to the Day 1963,N 12,49:1
Mitchell, Ken
Boy Friend, The 1970,Ap 15,54:1
Mitchell, Kenneth
Policy Kings 1938,D 31,6:2
Mitchell, Kevin
Opening of a Window, The 1961,S 26,32:2
Ticket-of-Leave Man, The 1961,D 23,15:1
Color of Darkness: An Evening in the World of
James Purdy; Everything Under the Sun
1963,O 1,34:1
Color of Darkness: An Evening in the World of
James Purdy; Encore 1963,O 1,34:1
Tragical Historie of Doctor Faustus, The
1964,O 6,34:2
Mitchell, Kolly
Ol' Man Satan 1932,O 4,26:3
Mitchell, L Pearl
Long Moment, The 1950,My 22,16:6
Mitchell, Langdon (Playwright)
Kreutzer Sonata, The 1924,My 15,22:3
Becky Sharp 1929,Je 4,29:1
New York Idea, The 1948,Ag 18,29:2
New York Idea, The 1963,Jl 13,12:2
Mitchell, Lathrop
Regular Guy, A; Man's Man, A 1931,Je 5,27:1
Aries Is Rising 1939,N 22,16:5
Plan M 1942,F 21,15:2
Major Barbara 1951,F 24,10:2
Mitchell, Lloyd
Blackbirds 1928,My 10,31:3
Mitchell, Loften (Playwright)
Land Beyond the River, A 1957,Mr 29,15:7
Land Beyond the River, A 1957,Je 2,II,1:1
Ballad for Bimshire 1963,O 16,54:1
Mitchell, Mabel
Unto Such Glory 1937,My 7,28:2
Mitchell, Margaret
Mikado, The 1947,D 30,18:2
Iolanthe 1948,Ja 13,29:3
Gondoliers, The 1948,Ja 27,31:2
Patience 1948,F 10,27:2
Mikado, The 1951,Ja 30,21:2
Gondoliers, The 1951,F 13,27:2
Iolanthe 1951,F 16,22:1
Mitchell, Margaret (Original Author)
Gone With the Wind 1941,O 21,28:3
Scarlett 1970,Ja 3,19:1
Mitchell, Mary
Caution: A Love Story 1969,Ap 4,45:1
Dirtiest Show in Town, The 1970,My 2,21:1
Mitchell, Mary (Miscellaneous)
Confederates, The 1959,S 29,45:1
Mitchell, Mavis
Madam Will You Walk 1953,D 2,2:4
Mitchell, Mildred
Third Day, The 1929,Ag 13,23:4
Headquarters 1929,D 5,32:4
Topaze 1930,F 13,25:3
Mitchell, Millard
Holy Terror, A 1925,S 29,31:2
Broadway 1926,S 17,19:3
Gentlemen of the Press 1928,Ag 28,27:2
Town Boy 1929,O 5,22:4
Seven 1929,D 28,10:5
Great Scott! 1929,S 3,25:1
Penny Arcade 1930,Mr 11,24:5
Singin' the Blues 1931,S 17,21:3
Louder, Please! 1931,N 13,26:4
Nona 1932,O 5,26:4
Great Magoo, The 1932,D 3,20:7
Man Bites Dog 1933,Ap 26,11:2
World Waits, The 1933,O 26,22:5
False Dreams, Farewell 1934,Ja 16,18:3
Yellow Jack 1934,Mr 7,22:6
Picnic 1934,My 3,15:2

Mitchell, Millard—Cont

Love on an Island 1934,Jl 24,20:5
Three Men on a Horse 1935,Ja 22,22:7
Three Men on a Horse 1935,Ja 31,22:3
Star Spangled 1936,Mr 11,23:1
Something for Nothing 1937,D 10,33:5
How to Get Tough About It 1938,F 9,16:2
Kiss the Boys Goodbye 1938,S 29,30:2
See My Lawyer 1939,S 28,29:1
Goodbye in the Night 1940,Mr 19,31:2
Horse Fever 1940,N 25,21:2
Mr and Mrs North 1941,Ja 13,11:2
More the Merrier, The 1941,S 16,19:3
Sons and Soldiers 1943,My 5,22:2
Naked Genius, The 1943,O 22,20:5
Naked Genius, The 1943,N 7,II,1:6
Storm Operation 1944,Ja 12,28:2
Love on Leave 1944,Je 21,23:4
Lovely Me 1946,D 26,30:4
Great Campaign, The 1947,Ap 1,33:2
Cup of Trembling, The 1948,Ap 21,33:5
Mitchell, Myron
Crime and Crime 1963,D 17,51:2
Mitchell, Norma
March Hares 1921,Ag 12,8:3
To the Ladies! 1922,F 21,20:1
Goldfish, The 1922,Ap 18,15:3
Why Not? 1922,D 25,20:1
All Gummed Up 1923,Ja 29,11:2
March Hares 1923,Mr 13,19:5
New Poor, The 1924,Ja 8,26:1
Dancing Mothers 1924,Ag 12,12:2
Men Must Fight 1931,Ap 12,IX,2:1
Post Road 1935,Jl 23,24:3
Mitchell, Norma (Playwright)
Cradle Snatchers 1925,S 8,28:2
Buy, Buy Baby 1926,O 8,26:2
When Hell Froze 1930,O 5,IX,4:6
Cradle Snatchers 1932,N 17,23:2
Post Road 1934,D 5,28:3
Post Road 1935,Jl 23,24:3
Post Road 1936,Ag 5,15:4
Autumn Hill 1942,Ap 14,17:4
Post Road 1949,Ap 28,27:3
Mitchell, Peter
Point of Honor, A 1937,F 12,26:2
Mitchell, Peter J
Touch 1970,N 9,52:1
Mitchell, Pinkie
This Is the Army 1942,Jl 5,28:2
Mitchell, Priscilla
Bad Habits of 1925 1925,F 9,17:1
Mitchell, Rena
Jezebel 1933,D 20,26:3
There's Always a Breeze 1938,Mr 3,16:2
Mamba's Daughters 1939,Ja 4,24:2
Mamba's Daughters 1939,Mr 25,10:4
Native Son 1941,Mr 25,26:5
Native Son 1942,O 24,10:6
S S Glencairn; Moon of the Caribbees
1948,My 21,21:2
Mitchell, Robert D (Scenic Designer)
Saintliness of Margery Kempe, The 1959,F 3,35:6
Tango 1968,Ja 1,11:1
She Stoops to Conquer 1968,Ja 1,11:1
Sudden and Accidental Re-education of Horse
Johnson, The 1968,D 19,63:1
Someone's Comin' Hungry 1969,Ap 1,51:1
Mitchell, Ronald
Gondoliers, The 1969,My 10,35:1
Pirates of Penzance, The 1970,Jl 26,49:5
Pirates of Penzance, The 1970,D 6,84:6
Mitchell, Ruth
Hitchy-Koo, 1920 1920,O 20,11:3
Werewolf, The 1924,Ag 26,6:1
Mitchell, Ruth (Miscellaneous)
West Side Story 1957,S 27,14:4
Gypsy 1959,My 22,31:6
Fiorello! 1959,N 24,45:3
Tenderloin 1960,O 18,47:2
Call on Kuprin, A 1961,My 26,29:3
Funny Thing Happened on the Way to the Forum,
A 1962,My 9,49:1
She Loves Me 1963,Ap 24,39:1
Fiddler on the Roof 1964,S 23,56:2
Poor Bitos 1964,N 16,40:2
Baker Street 1965,F 17,36:1
It's a Bird . . . It's a Plane . . . It's Superman
1966,Mr 30,34:1
Cabaret 1966,N 21,62:1
Zorba 1968,N 18,58:1
Fiddler on the Roof 1969,Je 26,47:1
Company 1970,Ap 27,40:1
Mitchell, Stephen (Miscellaneous)
Browning Version, The 1949,O 13,32:2
Harlequinade 1949,O 13,32:2
Separate Tables 1956,O 26,33:1
Mitchell, Stephen (Producer)
Day by the Sea, A 1955,S 27,42:1
Mitchell, Thomas
Not So Long Ago 1920,My 5,14:1
Kiki 1921,N 30,13:1
Wisdom Tooth, The 1926,F 16,22:2

Mitchell, Thomas—Cont

Wisdom Tooth, The 1926,F 28,VIII,1:1
Blood Money 1927,Ag 23,29:2
Nightstick 1927,N 11,20:4
Little Accident 1928,O 10,32:3
Cloudy With Showers 1931,Ag 23,VIII,2:5
Cloudy With Showers 1931,S 2,17:5
Riddle Me This! 1932,F 26,22:5
Clear All Wires! 1932,S 15,19:1
Clear All Wires! 1932,S 25,IX,1:1
Honeymoon 1932,D 24,11:2
Fly Away Home 1935,Ja 16,20:4
Stick-in-the-Mud 1935,D 2,18:2
Inspector Calls, An 1947,O 22,38:2
Biggest Thief in Town 1949,Mr 31,31:2
Death of a Salesman 1950,S 21,20:5
Hazel Flagg 1953,F 12,22:2
Cut of the Axe 1960,F 2,38:2

Mitchell, Thomas (Director)

Little Accident 1928,O 10,32:3
Cloudy With Showers 1931,S 2,17:5
Honeymoon 1932,D 24,11:2
Forsaking All Others 1933,Mr 2,21:2
$25 an Hour 1933,My 11,14:4
Calling All Stars 1934,D 14,28:2
Fly Away Home 1935,Ja 16,20:4
Something Gay 1935,Ap 30,12:2
At Home Abroad 1935,S 20,17:4
Stick-in-the-Mud 1935,D 2,18:2

Mitchell, Thomas (Playwright)

Glory Hallelujah 1926,Ap 7,26:2
Glory Hallelujah 1926,Ap 11,VIII,1:1
Little Accident 1928,O 10,32:3
Little Accident 1929,S 22,IX,4:1
Cloudy With Showers 1931,Ag 23,VIII,2:5
Cloudy With Showers 1931,S 2,17:5

Mitchell, Thomas (Producer)

$25 an Hour 1933,My 11,14:4

Mitchell, Tressa

Sugar Hill 1931,D 26,15:2

Mitchell, Warren

Dutch Uncle 1969,Mr 28,41:1
Council of Love 1970,Ag 21,21:2
Council of Love 1970,S 12,32:2

Mitchell, William (Composer)

Oh, Hector! 1929,Mr 6,33:2

Mitchell, Yvonne

Immoralist, The 1954,N 4,39:5
Wall, The 1960,O 12,44:4
Wall, The 1960,O 23,II,1:1
Oresteia 1961,N 8,43:5

Mitchell and Durant

George White's Scandals 1929,S 24,29:1
Vaudeville (Palace) 1930,S 22,23:2
Vaudeville (Palace) 1931,Mr 9,25:7
Vanities 1931,Ag 11,28:4
Vanities 1931,Ag 16,VIII,1:1
Vaudeville (Palace) 1932,My 2,13:2
Vaudeville (Palace) 1932,My 9,19:3

Mitchen, George

Playboy of the Western World, The 1930,Ja 3,20:4
General John Regan 1930,Ja 30,16:5

Mitford, Nancy (Playwright)

Little Hut, The 1953,O 8,37:2

Mitropoulos, Dimitri (Composer)

Electra 1952,N 20,38:2
Hippolytus 1968,N 20,38:3

Mitros, Billy (Costume Designer)

Wizard of Oz, The 1968,N 28,69:2

Mittelhoelzer, Edgar (Director)

Climate of Eden, The 1952,N 16,II,1:1

Mittelholzer, Edgar (Original Author)

Climate of Eden, The 1952,N 7,20:2
Climate of Eden, The 1953,N 21,11:2

Mittler, Leo (Director)

Chicago 1927,D 18,IX,1:8
Crime 1928,Je 24,VIII,1:4
Topaze 1947,D 29,21:5
Teahouse of the August Moon, The 1954,S 18,13:4
Diary of Anne Frank, The 1956,O 3,30:1

Mitty, Germaine

Ziegfeld Follies 1921,Je 22,10:1

Mitty, Nomi

Tree Grows in Brooklyn, A 1951,Ap 20,24:3

Mitty and Tillio

Follies 1924,O 31,19:3
LeMaire's Affairs 1927,Mr 29,22:4

Mitzel, Max

Beyond the Horizon 1920,F 4,12:1

Mitzi

Lady Billy 1920,D 15,18:2
Magic Ring, The 1923,O 2,10:1
Naughty Riquette 1926,S 14,25:2
Naughty Riquette 1926,S 19,IX,1:1
Madcap, The 1928,F 1,31:2
Sari 1930,Ja 29,27:1

Miville, Rene

Hit the Trail 1954,D 3,31:2

Mix, Ruth Rodeo Revue

Vaudeville (Palace) 1929,Jl 1,31:4

Mixon, Alan

Sweet Bird of Youth 1956,Ap 17,27:2
Garden District; Suddenly Last Summer 1958,Ja 8,23:4

Garden District; Suddenly Last Summer 1958,Ja 19,II,1:1
Something About a Soldier 1962,Ja 5,36:2
Duchess of Malfi, The 1962,Mr 5,27:1
Trojan Women, The 1963,D 24,7:6
Alchemist, The 1964,S 15,33:1
Child Buyer, The 1964,D 22,35:1
Devils, The 1965,N 17,51:2
Whitman Portrait, A 1966,O 12,37:1
Unknown Soldier and His Wife, The 1967,Jl 7,22:1
Iphigenia in Aulis 1967,N 22,40:2
Iphigenia in Aulis 1967,D 3,II,1:1
Mr and Mrs Lyman 1968,Mr 6,35:1
Iphigenia in Aulis 1968,Ap 6,43:1

Mixon, Tom

I Feel Wonderful 1954,O 19,22:5
By Hex 1956,Je 19,25:1
Kaleidoscope 1957,Je 14,20:2
Tobias and the Angel 1957,O 21,29:5
On the Town 1959,Ja 16,36:1

Mixteco Trio

Mexicana 1939,Ap 22,14:4
Mexicana 1939,My 7,X,3:1
Flower Drum Song 1958,D 7,II,5:1

Miya, Yuriko

Flower Drum Song 1958,D 7,II,5:1

Mizbin, Benny

Gold Diggers, The 1927,D 3,19:2

Mizutani, Yaeko

Teahouse of the August Moon, The 1955,Ag 7,60:3

Mizzaro, Romeo

PS 193 1962,O 31,33:1

Mizzy, Vic (Composer)

Lew Leslie's Blackbirds of 1939 1939,F 13,12:2

Mizzy, Vic (Lyricist)

Cocktails of 1934 1934,My 5,22:1
Lew Leslie's Blackbirds of 1939 1939,F 13,12:2

Mjannes, Otto

Softly, and Consider the Nearness 1964,My 12,32:1
Home Movies 1964,My 12,32:1

Mjoen, Fridtjof

Lauter Luegen 1937,O 24,XI,3:1

Mladova, Milada

Merry Widow, The 1943,Ag 5,19:2
Merry Widow, The 1943,Ag 22,II,5:1
Allah Be Praised! 1944,Ap 21,14:2
Sadie Thompson 1944,N 17,25:2
All for Love 1949,Ja 24,16:5

Mlakar, Veronika

Riding Hood Revisited 1961,Ja 4,26:1

Mlle Helene and the Lockfords

Passing Show of 1922, The 1922,S 21,18:2

Moana, Ralph

White Eagle, The 1927,D 27,24:4

Mobbs, Kenneth (Composer)

Engaged! or Cheviot's Choice 1965,Ap 24,19:2

Mobbs, Kenneth (Miscellaneous)

Engaged! or Cheviot's Choice 1965,Ap 24,19:2

Moberg, Vilhelm (Playwright)

Kyskhet 1939,Jl 9,IX,2:1

Moberly, Robert

Come Slowly, Eden 1966,D 7,56:1
Millionairess, The 1969,Mr 3,28:1
Place for Polly, A 1970,Ap 20,45:1

Mobley, Constance

Doctor Faustus Lights the Lights 1951,D 3,23:4

Mobley, J W

Kilpatrick's Old-Time Minstrels 1930,Ap 21,20:2
Savage Rhythm 1932,Ja 1,30:4

Mobley, Lushanya

Rose Marie 1936,Jl 22,22:6
Blossom Time 1936,Jl 29,23:1

Mobley, Mary Ann

Nowhere to Go But Up 1962,N 12,36:2

Mochizuki, Tatsuhachiro (Composer)

Fishing for Wives 1966,Mr 16,50:1
General's Daughter, The 1966,Mr 16,50:1
Greengrocer's Daughter, The 1966,Mr 16,50:1

Mock, Ed (Choreographer)

Three Sisters, The 1969,O 10,38:1

Mocollum, Barry

John Ferguson 1921,My 24,20:1

Modal, Holy Rounders (Composer)

Operation Sidewinder 1970,Mr 13,33:1

Modal, Holy Rounders (Musical Director)

Operation Sidewinder 1970,Mr 13,33:1

Modelski, Peff

Antigone 1967,Je 19,43:1
Macbeth 1967,Jl 31,21:1

Modena's Fantastic Revue

Vaudeville (Palace) 1926,Ap 13,28:3

Modernaires, The

Walk With Music 1940,Je 5,33:2

Modes, Theo (Director)

Everyman 1931,Jl 19,III,8:6

Modick, Murray

Pins and Needles 1939,Ap 21,26:2
New Pins and Needles 1939,N 21,19:2

Modo, Michel

Grosse Valise, La 1965,D 15,52:1

Modugno, Domenic (Composer)

Rinaldo in Campo 1962,My 12,14:5

Moe

One Eye Closed 1954,N 25,45:2
Happy Hunting 1956,D 7,30:1

Moe, Alice

Scarlet Fox, The 1928,Mr 28,31:1

Moe, John

Wall Street Scene 1937,O 19,29:2

Moebes, Hans Joachim

Journey's End 1929,S 22,IX,4:1

Moeller, Alfred (Playwright)

Raetzel um Beate 1936,N 8,X,2:1

Moeller, Alma

Triumph of X, The 1921,Ag 25,8:2

Moeller, Eberhard Wolfgang (Playwright)

Douaumont 1929,D 22,VIII,4:3

Moeller, Philip (Director)

Race With the Shadow, The 1924,Ja 21,20:5
Fata Morgana 1924,Mr 4,16:3
Fata Morgana 1924,Mr 9,VIII,1:1
Guardsman, The 1924,O 14,23:1
They Knew What They Wanted 1924,N 25,27:1
Processional 1925,Ja 13,17:1
Ariadne 1925,F 24,17:1
Caesar and Cleopatra 1925,Ap 14,27:1
Arms and the Man 1925,S 15,28:1
Glass Slipper, The 1925,O 20,29:1
Androcles and the Lion 1925,N 24,28:1
Man of Destiny, The 1925,N 24,28:1
Merchants of Glory 1925,D 15,28:3
Chief Thing, The 1926,Mr 23,24:2
At Mrs Beam's 1926,Ap 26,24:3
Juarez and Maximilian 1926,O 12,31:1
Pygmalion 1926,N 16,24:1
Ned McCobb's Daughter 1926,N 30,26:2
Right You Are (If You Think You Are) 1927,F 24,27:1
Second Man, The 1927,Ap 12,24:3
Mr Pim Passes By 1927,Ap 19,24:1
Strange Interlude 1928,Ja 31,28:1
Strange Interlude 1928,F 5,VIII,1:1
Volpone 1928,Ap 10,32:1
Strange Interlude 1928,Jl 1,VIII,3:5
Major Barbara 1928,N 20,28:4
Caprice 1929,Ja 1,61:1
Caprice 1929,Ja 13,VIII,1:1
Dynamo 1929,F 12,22:1
Camel Through the Needle's Eye, The 1929,Ap 16,32:2
Camel Through the Needle's Eye, The 1929,Ap 28,IX,1:1
Karl and Anna 1929,O 8,34:1
Meteor 1929,D 24,15:1
Apple Cart, The 1930,F 25,30:1
Volpone 1930,Mr 11,24:5
Hotel Universe 1930,Ap 15,29:1
Elizabeth the Queen 1930,N 4,37:1
Midnight 1930,D 30,25:1
Getting Married 1931,Mr 31,25:5
Mourning Becomes Electra; Haunted, The 1931,O 27,22:1
Mourning Becomes Electra; Homecoming 1931,O 27,22:1
Mourning Becomes Electra; Hunted, The 1931,O 27,22:1
Mourning Becomes Electra 1931,N 1,VIII,1:1
Moon in the Yellow River, The 1932,Mr 1,19:3
Moon in the Yellow River, The 1932,Mr 13,VIII,1:1
Mourning Becomes Electra 1932,Ap 10,VIII,1:1
Mourning Becomes Electra; Hunted, The 1932,My 10,25:2
Mourning Becomes Electra; Homecoming 1932,My 10,25:2
Mourning Becomes Electra; Haunted, The 1932,My 10,25:2
Good Earth, The 1932,O 18,23:4
Biography 1932,D 13,25:3
American Dream; 1849 1933,F 22,24:5
American Dream; 1650 1933,F 22,24:5
American Dream; 1933 1933,F 22,24:5
Mask and the Face, The 1933,My 9,20:2
Ah, Wilderness! 1933,O 3,28:2
Days Without End 1934,Ja 9,19:1
They Shall Not Die 1934,F 22,24:4
They Shall Not Die 1934,Mr 11,X,1:1
Jig Saw 1934,My 1,26:3
Sleeping Clergyman, A 1934,O 9,16:1
Rain From Heaven 1934,D 16,XI,2:1
Rain From Heaven 1934,D 25,28:4
Love Is Not So Simple 1935,N 5,33:1
End of Summer 1936,Ja 31,17:1
End of Summer 1936,F 18,26:4
And Stars Remain 1936,O 13,32:2
Prelude to Exile 1936,N 17,34:6
Prelude to Exile 1936,N 22,XI,3:2
Prelude to Exile 1936,D 1,31:1
Masque of the Kings, The 1937,F 9,19:4
Storm Over Patsy 1937,Mr 2,16:4
Storm Over Patsy 1937,Mr 9,26:4
To Quito and Back 1937,O 7,30:4

Moeller, Philip (Miscellaneous)

Too True to Be Good 1932,Ap 5,27:5
Mary of Scotland 1933,N 28,28:3

Moeller, Philip (Miscellaneous)—Cont
And Stars Remain 1936,O 13,32:2
Moeller, Philip (Playwright)
Sophie 1920,Mr 3,12:2
Caprice 1929,Ja 1,61:1
Camel Through the Needle's Eye, The
1929,Ap 16,32:2
Love Is Not So Simple 1935,N 5,33:1
Love Is Not So Simple 1935,N 10,IX,1:6
Moeller, Philip (Producer)
Prelude to Exile 1936,D 1,31:1
Masque of the Kings, The 1937,F 9,19:4
Storm Over Patsy 1937,Mr 9,26:4
To Quito and Back 1937,S 21,29:1
To Quito and Back 1937,O 7,30:4
Moeller, Philip (Translator)
Caprice 1929,Ja 1,61:1
Caprice 1929,Ja 13,VIII,1:1
Moen, Yvonne
Sonya's Search for the Christmas Star
1929,D 14,24:6
Moerel, Jan (Miscellaneous)
Midsummer Night's Dream, A 1967,Je 30,23:1
Boesman and Lena 1970,Je 23,35:1
Moerk, Donald
Twelfth Night 1954,D 12,II,3:1
Moerk, Donald (Composer)
Much Ado About Nothing 1955,Ag 20,20:4
Moes-Hake, Dorothea (Miscellaneous)
Wicked Cooks, The 1967,Ja 24,42:1
Moffat, Alice
Dream Girl, The 1924,Ag 21,12:2
If 1927,O 26,26:2
Happy Husband, The 1928,My 8,25:2
Moffat, Donald
Under Milk Wood 1957,O 16,42:5
Bald Soprano, The 1958,Je 4,39:2
Jack 1958,Je 4,39:2
Come Play With Me 1959,My 1,33:5
Much Ado About Nothing 1959,S 18,25:2
Tumbler, The 1960,F 25,32:2
Duel of Angels 1960,Ap 20,42:2
Full Moon in March, A 1960,S 20,48:1
Misalliance 1961,S 26,32:2
Passage to India, A 1962,F 1,23:1
Affair, The 1962,S 21,34:2
Taming of the Shrew, The 1963,Mr 8,9:1
Caretaker, The 1964,Ja 31,16:1
Man and Superman 1964,D 7,45:2
War and Peace 1965,Ja 12,32:1
You Can't Take It With You 1965,N 24,32:1
Right You Are (If You Think You Are)
1966,N 23,34:2
Right You Are (If You Think You Are)
1966,D 11,II,3:1
Wild Duck, The 1967,Ja 12,49:1
Wild Duck, The 1967,Ja 22,II,1:1
War and Peace 1967,Mr 22,42:1
War and Peace 1967,Ap 2,II,1:1
Cherry Orchard, The 1968,Mr 20,41:1
Cherry Orchard, The 1968,Ap 7,II,3:7
Cock-A-Doodle Dandy 1969,Ja 21,40:1
Hamlet 1969,Mr 4,34:1
Moffat, Donald (Director)
Cock-A-Doodle Dandy 1969,Ja 21,40:1
Moffat, Erica
Country Wife, The 1931,Ap 19,31:5
Moffat, Graham
Don't Tell 1920,S 29,12:1
Moffat, Graham (Mrs)
Don't Tell 1920,S 29,12:1
Moffat, Graham (Playwright)
Don't Tell 1920,S 29,12:1
Granny 1927,Ja 2,VII,2:5
Moffat, Joyce Anne
Purple Canary, The 1963,Ap 23,31:1
Moffat, Margaret
Camel's Back, The 1923,N 4,19:2
Leave Her to Heaven 1940,F 28,16:2
At the Stroke of Eight 1940,My 21,29:2
Moffat, Winifred
Don't Tell 1920,S 29,12:1
Moffatt, J A (Lighting Director)
Jo 1964,F 13,25:1
Moffatt, James
Founders, The 1957,My 14,39:1
Moffatt, John
Country Wife, The 1957,N 28,56:1
Luther 1963,S 26,41:1
Way of the World, The 1969,Ag 7,29:1
Hedda Gabler 1970,Jl 18,12:1
Moffatt, June
Founders, The 1957,My 14,39:1
Moffet, Harold
Road to Rome, The 1927,F 1,24:2
Judas 1929,Ja 25,20:4
Buckaroo 1929,Mr 18,31:1
Little Show, The 1929,My 1,28:5
Three's a Crowd 1930,O 16,28:3
Of Thee I Sing 1931,D 28,20:1
Let 'Em Eat Cake 1933,O 23,18:1
Yellow Jack 1934,Mr 7,22:6
Merrily We Roll Along 1934,O 1,14:1
Hook-Up, The 1935,My 9,24:6

Is This a Zither? 1935,Je 11,24:3
Wild Justice 1935,Jl 9,24:3
Drums Professor, The 1935,Jl 30,17:2
Paths of Glory 1935,S 19,29:1
Paths of Glory 1935,S 27,24:2
I Want a Policeman! 1936,Ja 15,15:5
Crab Apple 1936,Jl 8,14:2
Iron Men 1936,O 20,30:6
High Tor 1937,Ja 11,15:2
Siege 1937,D 9,31:4
Tortilla Flat 1938,Ja 13,16:2
Sea Gull, The 1938,Mr 29,19:2
Moffet, Sally
Young and Fair, The 1948,N 23,35:2
Moffett, Miles R
Betty Behave 1927,Mr 9,28:4
Moffitt, John (Lighting Director)
By Hex 1956,Je 19,25:1
Moffitt, John C (Playwright)
It Can't Happen Here 1936,O 28,30:1
It Can't Happen Here 1936,O 28,30:3
It Can't Happen Here 1936,O 28,30:1
It Can't Happen Here 1936,N 8,X,1:1
It Can't Happen Here 1936,N 29,XII,3:3
It Can't Happen Here 1938,Jl 26,22:2
Mogck, David
Zulu and the Zayda, The 1965,N 11,59:1
Mogee, Anita
Little Dark Horse 1941,N 17,14:4
Mogilesco (Composer)
Jewish Heart, The 1939,Ja 25,16:6
Mogilesco (Lyricist)
Jewish Heart, The 1939,Ja 25,16:6
Mogulesko, Bessie
Andersh; New Worlds 1922,S 26,18:2
Brownsville Grandfather, The 1935,Ap 19,24:6
Mohan, Frances (Musical Director)
Seven Mirrors 1945,O 26,17:2
Mohan, Philip V
What a Relief 1935,D 14,10:6
Mohapeloa, J P (Miscellaneous)
Sponono 1964,Ap 3,28:1
Mohica, Victor
West Side Story 1968,Je 25,32:1
Gandhi 1970,O 21,37:1
Mohler, Gladys Hamilton
Little Theatre Tournament; Trifles 1928,My 11,28:1
Mohr, Gary
Point of Honor, A 1937,F 12,26:2
Mohr, Howard K (Playwright)
Here's Howe 1923,Ap 26,19:3
This Way Out 1929,Ap 28,24:4
Mohr, Isabel
Earl Carroll's Vanities 1926,Ag 25,19:4
Mohr, Marcia
Harold Arlen Songbook, The 1967,Mr 1,48:1
Mohr, Max (Playwright)
Improvisations in June 1928,F 27,16:5
Mohyeddin, Zia
Passage to India, A 1962,F 1,23:1
Passage to India, A 1962,F 11,II,1:1
Guide, The 1968,Mr 7,50:1
Moir, Bruce
Barbara's Wedding 1931,O 9,21:1
Moir, Edward
Little Theatre Tournament; Shall We Join the
Ladies? 1929,My 9,34:3
Shall We Join the Ladies? 1929,My 12,28:3
Moir, Ted
Rogues and Vagabonds 1930,My 8,32:5
Moise, Ginna
Carousel 1945,Ap 20,24:2
Moiseiwitsch, Pamela
Lunatic the Secret Sportsman and the Woman
Next 1968,D 5,58:4
Moiseiwitsch, Tanya (Costume Designer)
Uncle Vanya 1946,My 14,18:2
Oedipus; Critic, The 1946,My 21,19:2
Taming of the Shrew, The 1954,Jl 4,II,1:1
Measure for Measure 1954,Jl 4,II,1:1
Matchmaker, The 1955,D 6,45:6
Henry V 1956,Je 24,II,1:1
Two Gentlemen of Verona 1958,Mr 19,35:1
Broken Jug, The 1958,Ap 2,36:1
Hamlet 1963,My 19,II,1:1
Cymbeline 1970,Ag 23,II,1:6
Moiseiwitsch, Tanya (Miscellaneous)
Measure for Measure 1954,Jl 4,II,1:1
Taming of the Shrew, The 1954,Jl 4,II,1:1
Julius Caesar 1955,Je 29,23:3
Moiseiwitsch, Tanya (Scenic Designer)
Village Wooing 1935,O 27,IX,2:5
Noah 1935,D 1,XI,6:4
Uncle Vanya 1946,My 14,18:2
Oedipus; Critic, The 1946,My 21,19:2
Bless the Bride 1947,My 11,II,3:7
Richard III 1953,Jl 15,22:2
All's Well That Ends Well 1953,Jl 16,18:2
Measure for Measure 1954,Je 30,23:1
Taming of the Shrew, The 1954,Jl 1,22:2
Oedipus Rex 1954,Jl 17,6:6
Matchmaker, The 1955,My 8,II,1:1
Matchmaker, The 1955,D 6,45:6

Moiseiwitsch, Tanya (Scenic Designer)—Cont
Matchmaker, The 1955,D 18,II,3:1
Henry V 1956,Je 20,27:2
Merry Wives of Windsor, The 1956,Je 21,34:4
Twelfth Night 1957,Jl 4,16:4
Two Gentlemen of Verona 1958,Mr 19,35:1
Broken Jug, The 1958,Ap 2,36:1
Henry IV, Part I 1958,Je 25,23:3
Winter's Tale, The 1958,Jl 23,34:3
Much Ado About Nothing 1958,Ag 27,34:6
King John 1960,Je 29,26:2
Romeo and Juliet 1960,Jl 1,14:1
Coriolanus 1961,Je 21,31:2
Love's Labour's Lost 1961,Je 23,19:1
Love's Labour's Lost 1961,Jl 2,II,1:1
Taming of the Shrew, The 1962,Je 21,25:1
Cyrano de Bergerac 1962,Ag 1,21:1
Hamlet 1963,My 9,41:1
Miser, The 1963,My 10,39:1
Cyrano de Bergerac 1963,Je 20,30:1
Three Sisters, The 1963,Jl 22,19:2
Saint Joan 1964,My 14,41:1
Volpone 1964,Jl 20,18:3
Way of the World, The 1965,Je 2,40:1
Cherry Orchard, The 1965,Ag 2,17:2
Skin of Our Teeth, The 1966,Je 2,51:1
As You Like It 1966,Je 4,19:1
House of Atreus, The; Agamemnon 1967,Jl 24,23:1
House of Atreus, The; Bringers of Offerings, The
1967,Jl 24,23:1
House of Atreus, The; Furies, The 1967,Jl 24,23:1
Antony and Cleopatra 1967,Ag 2,25:1
Antony and Cleopatra 1967,O 29,83:4
House of Atreus, The 1968,D 18,55:1
Moissi, Alexander
Everyman 1926,Ag 9,1:1
Hamlet 1927,O 30,IX,4:7
Midsummer Night's Dream, A 1927,N 18,21:1
Jedermann 1927,D 8,33:2
Er Ist an Allem Schuld; He Is to Blame for
Everything 1928,Ja 10,28:3
Kabale und Liebe 1928,Ja 17,22:3
Lebende Leichnam, Der, Der; Living Corpse, The
1928,Ja 24,26:2
Gespenster, Die; Ghosts 1928,F 8,28:6
Redemption: Lebende Leichnam, Der; Living
Corpse, The 1928,N 20,28:2
Redemption 1929,F 5,27:2
Ghosts; Gespenster 1929,F 6,30:3
Ghosts 1929,F 17,IX,1:1
Everyman 1929,Ag 5,25:1
Antony and Cleopatra 1932,F 7,VIII,1:5
Dinner at Eight 1933,O 17,26:2
Moissi, Johanna Terwin
Jedermann 1927,D 8,33:2
Moissi, Sandro
Hamlet 1924,Mr 18,25:2
Living Corpse, The 1924,Mr 18,25:2
Moitoza, Rob
Earthlight Theater 1970,N 4,38:2
Mok, Kai Fook
Mu Lan 1921,F 25,16:2
Moka
Geraniums in My Window 1934,O 27,20:6
Mokae, Zakes
Boesman and Lena 1970,Je 23,35:1
Moke and Poke
Harlem Cavalcade 1942,My 2,11:2
Mokranjac, Danica
Victor, or The Children Take Over 1968,Jl 10,22:4
Molander, Olav (Director)
Green Pastures, The 1932,O 30,IX,2:4
Dream Play 1935,D 8,X,4:5
Molchanov, Kirill (Composer)
Orpheus Descending 1961,Ag 28,21:2
Moldoff, Gladys
Seven Mirrors 1945,O 26,17:2
Moldow, Deborah
Enchanted, The 1958,Ap 23,41:1
Moldow, Edwin Bruce
Sunny River 1941,D 5,28:2
Mole, Jean-Michel
Grosse Valise, La 1965,D 15,52:1
Molenadyk, E
Slight Case of Murder, A 1935,S 12,28:5
Moliere (Miscellaneous)
Love Doctor, The 1959,O 14,52:4
Moliere (Original Author)
Imaginary Invalid, The 1922,Jl 26,26:2
School for Husbands, The 1933,O 17,26:5
Would-Be Gentleman, The 1946,Ja 20,II,1:1
Dr Willy Nilly 1959,Je 5,18:2
'Toinette 1961,N 21,46:1
Bungler, The 1968,Ag 2,24:1
Sganarelle 1970,Ja 13,41:1
Moliere (Playwright)
Misanthrope, Le 1922,N 22,18:2
Tartuffe 1922,N 23,21:3
Avare, L'; Miser, The 1924,Mr 12,17:3
George Dandin 1924,Ap 7,15:5
Bourgeois Gentilhomme, Le 1924,N 20,21:2
Amphitryon 1926,O 24,VIII,2:1
Malade Imaginaire, Le 1926,N 14,VIII,2:1
Misanthrope, Le 1926,D 10,31:2

Moliere (Playwright)—Cont

Would-Be Gentleman, The 1928,O 2,34:1
Bourgeois Gentilhomme, Le 1929,Mr 17,30:4
Bourgeois Gentilhomme, Le 1929,Mr 24,X,2:3
Malade Imaginaire 1929,Ap 14,X,2:1
Avare, L' 1930,F 2,VIII,4:1
Would-Be Gentleman, The 1930,Ap 30,29:2
Ecole des Femmes, L' 1930,N 2,VIII,3:1
School for Husbands, The 1933,D 3,IX,6:5
School for Wives 1934,N 14,22:2
Ecole des Femmes, L' 1936,Je 21,IX,2:4
Would-Be Gentleman, The 1936,Ag 4,15:1
Misanthrope, The 1937,F 24,18:6
Medecin Malgre Lui, Le 1937,D 28,28:7
Jalousie du Barbouille, La 1937,D 28,28:7
Precieuses Ridicules, Les 1938,D 13,30:3
Fourberies de Scapin, Les 1938,D 13,30:3
Ecole des Maris, L' 1939,Mr 19,XI,3:1
Doctor in Spite of Himself, The 1949,Ap 23,10:2
Bourgeois Gentleman, The 1949,Ag 31,27:2
Doctored Wife, The 1950,Jl 12,33:2
Gay Invalid, The 1951,F 11,II,3:1
Ecole des Femmes, L'; School for Wives
  1951,Mr 19,22:1
Fourberies de Scapin, Les 1952,N 21,21:2
Amphitryon 1952,N 21,21:2
Bourgeois Gentilhomme, Le 1954,Ap 14,26:7
Miser, The 1955,Mr 18,34:2
Bourgeois Gentilhomme, Le 1955,O 26,26:1
Bourgeois Gentilhomme, Le 1955,O 30,II,1:1
Don Juan; Feast With the Statue, The
  1956,Ja 4,21:4
Misanthrope, Le 1957,Ja 8,26:1
Misanthrope, Le 1957,F 8,19:1
Doctor in Spite of Himself, The 1957,F 28,18:4
School for Wives 1957,Je 20,23:4
Tartuffe 1957,O 9,39:1
Malade Imaginaire, Le; Imaginary Invalid, The
  1958,Ap 30,28:2
Sganarelle; Imaginary Cuckold, The 1958,My 7,43:1
Mariage Force, Le; Forced Wedding, The
  1958,My 7,43:1
Jalousie du Barbouille, La; Jealousy of the
  Barbouille, The 1958,My 7,43:1
Don Juan 1958,O 29,29:1
Fourberies de Scapin, Les 1961,F 22,30:1
Impromptu de Versailles, L' 1961,F 22,30:1
Tartuffe 1961,Mr 1,28:1
Ecole des Femmes, L' 1961,Ap 28,23:1
Miser, The 1963,My 10,39:1
Miser, The 1963,My 19,II,1:1
Tartuffe 1964,Mr 10,42:2
Impromptu at Versailles 1964,Mr 10,43:1
Scapin 1964,Mr 10,43:1
Tartuffe 1965,Ja 15,23:1
Avare, L', L'; Miser, The 1966,F 9,32:1
Femmes Savantes, Les 1967,F 7,34:2
Imaginary Invalid, The 1967,My 2,53:1
Tartuffe 1967,S 18,60:1
Imaginary Invalid, The 1968,My 28,41:1
Tartuffe 1968,Je 12,39:1
Tartuffe 1968,Je 23,II,1:1
George Dandin 1968,Je 28,36:1
Tartuffe 1968,Jl 3,28:2
George Dandin 1968,Jl 7,II,1:1
Misanthrope, The 1968,O 10,59:1
Misanthrope, The 1968,O 20,II,1:1
Miser, The 1969,My 9,35:1
Miser, The 1969,My 25,II,1:1
Troupe Du Roi, La 1970,F 4,38:1
Amphitryon 1970,F 4,38:1
Don Juan 1970,F 7,24:2
Femmes Savaantes, Les 1970,F 14,12:1
Malade Imaginaire, Le 1970,F 18,40:2
Show Me Where the Good Times Are
  1970,Mr 6,32:1
Don Juan 1970,My 26,32:1
Don Juan 1970,My 31,II,1:6
Georges Dandin 1970,O 19,50:1

Molik, Zygmunt
Constant Prince, The 1969,O 18,36:1
Acropolis 1969,N 5,40:1
Apocalypsis cum Figuris 1969,N 20,60:2

Molina, Carmen
Mexicana 1939,My 7,X,3:1

Molina, Jose
Mexicana 1939,Ap 22,14:4

Molina, Tirso de (Original Author)
Esta Noche... Teatro 1968,O 15,40:1

Molinaro, Tom
Boy Friend, The 1958,Ja 27,24:4
Diversions 1958,N 8,14:4

Molinaro, Ursule (Translator)
Egoists, The 1959,O 14,52:2

Molineaux, Constance
All Wet 1925,Jl 7,24:1

Molins, Carmen
Mexicana 1939,Ap 22,14:4

Moll, Elick (Original Author)
Seidman and Son 1962,O 16,32:2

Moll, Elick (Playwright)
Seidman and Son 1962,O 16,32:2

Moll, Howard
Way of the World, The 1950,Ap 9,73:5

Moll, Mariquita
Sunny River 1941,D 5,28:2
Show Boat 1952,Je 6,19:5

Moll, William (Lyricist)
Jonica 1930,Mr 30,VIII,2:7
Jonica 1930,Ap 8,27:1

Moller, Eberhard Wolfgang (Playwright)
Rothschild Siegt bei Waterloo 1937,Ja 3,X,2:5

Moller, Lindsay
Milk Train Doesn't Stop Here Anymore, The
  1965,Jl 27,25:1

Moller, Theodore H
Little Theatre Tournament; White Peacock, The
  1928,My 11,28:1

Moller, Wilson
Shipwrecked 1924,N 13,18:1

Mollette Sisters
Passing Show of 1921, The 1920,D 30,16:2

Mollien, Roger
Lorenzaccio 1958,O 15,44:2
Triomphe de l'Amour, Le 1958,O 17,32:1
Marie Tudor 1958,O 22,39:1
Don Juan 1958,O 29,29:1
Cid, Le 1958,O 31,35:2

Mollison, Clifford
Business With America 1933,Ja 1,IX,1:3
Lights Up 1940,F 18,IX,2:5

Mollison, Henry
London Wall 1931,My 24,VIII,1:6
Richard of Bordeaux 1934,F 15,16:2

Mollison, William (Director)
Murder on the Second Floor 1929,S 12,35:1
Meet My Sister 1930,D 31,11:1
Wonder Bar, The 1931,Mr 18,23:4
Everybody's Welcome 1931,O 14,26:3
Richard of Bordeaux 1934,F 15,16:2

Mollison, William (Producer)
Richard of Bordeaux 1934,F 15,16:2
Satyr 1937,Je 17,18:5

Molloy, Edward A (Rev) (Playwright)
Finis for Oscar Wilde 1964,F 15,15:1
Comforter, The 1964,O 22,42:1
Guimpes and Saddles 1967,O 11,36:3
Five Star Saint 1970,F 11,41:2

Molloy, Francetta
Mayflowers 1925,N 25,14:2

Molloy, John
Double Dublin 1963,D 27,16:2

Molloy, Michael (Playwright)
King of Friday's Men, The 1951,F 22,26:2
Will and the Way, The 1957,D 3,46:5

Molnar, Ferenc (Director)
Miracle in the Mountains 1947,Ap 26,10:2

Molnar, Ferenc (Original Author)
Play's the Thing, The 1927,Mr 20,VIII,4:3
Mima 1928,D 23,VIII,1:1
Carousel 1945,Ap 29,II,1:1
Carousel 1949,Ja 26,28:2
Carousel 1949,F 6,II,1:1
Carousel 1950,Je 8,37:2
Carousel 1954,Je 13,II,1:1
Carousel 1957,S 12,38:2

Molnar, Ferenc (Playwright)
Liliom 1921,Ap 21,18:1
Liliom 1921,Ap 24,VI,1:1
Liliom 1921,My 1,VII,1:1
Devil, The 1921,My 15,VI,1:6
Liliom 1921,S 10,12:3
Love Letter, The 1921,O 5,20:1
Fashions for Men 1922,D 6,22:1
Fashions for Men 1922,D 24,VII,1:1
Launzi 1923,O 11,16:3
Swan, The 1923,O 14,VIII,2:4
Swan, The 1923,O 24,15:3
Swan, The 1923,O 28,VIII,1:1
Guardsman, The 1924,O 14,23:1
Guardsman, The 1924,O 19,VIII,1:1
Carnival 1924,N 30,VIII,2:1
Carnaval 1924,D 30,15:1
Carnival 1925,Ja 4,VII,1:1
Tale of the Wolf, The 1925,S 27,VII,2:1
Tale of the Wolf, The 1925,O 8,31:2
Tale of the Wolf, The 1925,O 18,IX,1:2
Glass Slipper, The 1925,O 20,29:1
Glass Slipper, The 1925,O 25,VIII,1:1
Riviera 1925,D 25,22:2
Play's the Thing, The 1926,N 4,25:1
Play's the Thing, The 1926,N 14,VIII,1:1
Liliom 1927,Ja 2,30:1
Liliom 1927,Ja 9,VII,2:1
Olympia 1928,Mr 3,6:3
Olympia 1928,Mr 25,IX,4:1
Olympia 1928,O 17,26:1
A Farkas 1928,O 28,IX,2:1
Mima 1928,D 13,24:2
Play's the Thing, The 1928,D 23,VIII,4:7
One, Two, Three 1929,O 5,22:4
One, Two, Three 1929,N 17,IX,4:7
Marshal, The 1929,N 17,IX,4:7
Marshall 1930,My 10,25:1
Swan, The 1930,Jl 27,VIII,1:8
One, Two, Three! 1930,S 30,24:2
Violet, The 1930,S 30,24:2

Molnar, Ferenc (Playwright)—Cont

Good Fairy, The 1930,O 13,31:2
Good Fairy, The 1930,D 23,24:2
Fee, Die; Fairy, The 1931,F 8,VIII,2:1
Good Fairy, The 1931,N 15,VIII,4:1
Good Fairy, The 1931,N 25,17:1
Jemand; Somebody 1931,D 13,VIII,3:6
Jemand 1932,Ja 17,VIII,2:2
Liliom 1932,O 27,23:2
Story of the Wolf 1932,N 6,IX,3:4
Harmony 1932,N 13,IX,3:7
Good Fairy, The 1932,N 18,22:3
Great Love, The 1935,O 22,17:3
Great Love, The 1935,D 24,11:5
Miracle in the Mountain 1936,My 9,11:4
Swan, The 1936,Je 30,15:1
Girl Unknown 1936,S 17,18:2
Girl Unknown 1936,O 4,IX,3:7
Good Fairy, The 1937,My 15,23:3
Delila 1937,S 18,15:1
Still Life 1937,D 13,22:8
Good Fairy, The 1939,Ag 30,15:5
Liliom 1940,Mr 26,17:2
Liliom 1940,Mr 31,IX,1:1
Delicate Story 1940,D 5,32:2
King's Maid, The 1941,Ag 27,15:3
Carousel 1945,Ap 20,24:2
Miracle in the Mountains 1947,Ap 26,10:2
Play's the Thing, The 1948,Ap 29,19:2
Play's the Thing, The 1948,My 9,II,1:1
Make a Wish 1951,Ap 19,38:1
Carousel 1954,Je 3,32:2
Swan, The 1954,Ag 17,16:6
Liliom 1956,F 18,12:5
There Is a Play Tonight 1961,F 16,24:2
Guardsman, The 1969,Ag 17,II,5:1

Molnar, Lee
Doctor Faustus 1937,Ja 9,21:2

Molnar, Robert
Every Other Evil 1961,Ja 23,20:2
Here Be Dragons 1970,D 21,52:1

Molnar-Darvas, Lili
Great Love, The 1935,O 22,17:3

Molock, Robert
In the Matter of J Robert Oppenheimer
  1969,Mr 7,28:1
Miser, The 1969,My 9,35:1

Molodowsky, Kadia (Playwright)
House on Grand Street, A 1953,O 10,12:6

Moloney, Andrew
Red Falcon, The 1924,O 8,22:1

Molony, Kathleen
Fair Circassian, The 1921,D 7,22:3

Molson, Martin
Brother to Dragons 1968,D 8,86:1
Wilson in the Promise Land 1970,Ja 11,78:1
Wilson in the Promise Land 1970,My 27,41:1

Molthen, Ida
Married Woman, The 1921,D 26,21:1
Romantic Age, The 1922,N 15,22:1

Molthen, John (Miscellaneous)
Ben Bagley's New Cole Porter Revue
  1965,D 23,20:1

Molyneaux, Tosheen
Picnic on the Battlefield 1960,My 17,42:2

Molyneux, William (Costume Designer)
O Mistress Mine 1946,Ja 24,25:2
Black-Eyed Susan 1954,D 24,7:5

Molyneux, William (Miscellaneous)
Black Chiffon 1950,S 28,39:2

Molyneux, William (Scenic Designer)
Daphne Laureola 1950,S 19,38:6
Black-Eyed Susan 1954,D 24,7:5

Mommsen (Original Author)
Caesar and Cleopatra 1950,Ja 8,II,1:1

Momoulian, Rouben (Director)
Marco Millions 1930,Mr 4,24:4

Momoulian, Rouben (Playwright)
Month in the Country, A 1930,Mr 18,30:5

Mompere, Robert
Vagabond King, The 1935,N 29,22:7

Mona
Life of Reilly, The 1942,Ap 30,13:2

Monachino, Francis
Heimkehr aus der Fremde, Die; Stranger, The
  1949,S 2,14:1
Consul, The 1950,Mr 16,41:1

Monaco, Jimmy (Composer)
Harry Delmar's Revels 1927,N 29,30:2

Monagas, Lionel
Salome 1923,My 8,22:2
Comedy of Errors, The 1923,My 16,22:5
Runnin' Wild 1923,O 30,17:3
Appearances 1925,O 15,27:3
My Magnolia 1926,Jl 13,19:2
Ol' Man Satan 1932,O 4,26:3
Louisiana 1933,F 28,15:5
Hummin' Sam 1933,Ap 10,8:8
Blackbirds 1933,D 4,22:3
Walk Together Chillun 1936,F 5,15:2
Conjur' Man Dies 1936,Mr 12,18:5
One-Act Plays of the Sea; Bound East for Cardiff
  1937,O 30,23:2

Monagas, Lionel—Cont
One-Act Plays of the Sea; In the Zone 1937,O 30,23:2
One-Act Plays of the Sea; Long Voyage Home, The 1937,O 30,23:2
Big White Fog 1940,O 23,26:2
Peepshow 1944,F 4,12:2
Anna Lucasta 1944,Je 17,10:1
Monahan, Dick
High Kickers 1941,N 1,21:2
Great Big Doorstep, The 1942,N 27,26:2
Monahan, Thomas G
Come Marching Home 1946,My 20,18:6
Monaster, Nate (Playwright)
Something More! 1964,N 11,36:1
Moncion, Francisco
Chocolate Soldier, The 1947,Mr 13,34:2
Moncrieff, Mary Jane
Around the World in 80 Days 1963,Je 24,22:1
Around the World in 80 Days 1964,Je 29,33:2
Mondaaye, Jay
Creoles 1927,S 23,33:3
Green Pastures, The 1930,F 27,26:1
Conjur' Man Dies 1936,Mr 12,18:5
Mondo, Peggy
Music Man, The 1957,D 20,31:1
Monelli, Silvia
Venetian Twins, The 1968,My 29,23:1
Monet, Gaby
By the Beautiful Sea 1954,Ap 9,20:1
Mask and Gown 1957,S 11,29:1
Russell Patterson's Sketch-Book 1960,F 8,35:1
Monette, Richard
Falstaff; Henry IV, Part II 1965,Jl 1,35:1
Julius Caesar 1965,Jl 2,18:1
Henry V 1966,Je 8,38:1
Twelfth Night 1966,Je 10,51:2
Antony and Cleopatra 1967,Ag 2,25:1
Merry Wives of Windsor, The 1967,Ag 4,18:1
Soldiers 1968,My 2,58:1
Moneypenny, Guy
Victoria Regina 1935,D 27,15:2
Victoria Regina 1938,O 4,20:2
Ladies and Gentlemen 1939,O 18,30:2
Candle in the Wind 1941,O 23,26:2
Pirate, The 1942,N 26,39:2
Monica, Corbett
Agatha Sue, I Love You 1966,D 15,61:1
Monici, Andre (Musical Director)
Variations of 1940 1940,Ja 29,12:1
Monif, Layelah
Man Who Died Twice, The 1925,D 14,19:1
Monk, John
Trial of Dr Beck, The 1937,Ag 10,22:2
Innocent Voyage, The 1943,N 16,27:2
Hamlet 1954,Ap 24,15:2
Merchant of Venice, The 1955,F 23,23:2
Monk, Marylyn
Time of Your Life, The 1940,S 24,27:2
Take It As It Comes 1944,F 11,17:2
Monk, Meredith (Playwright)
Juice 1969,D 9,67:2
Monk, Terence
Rondelay 1969,N 6,55:1
Monk, William
Henry IV, Part I 1946,My 7,25:2
Henry IV, Part II 1946,My 8,33:4
Uncle Vanya 1946,My 14,18:2
Oedipus; Critic, The 1946,My 21,19:2
Monkhouse, Mr (Playwright)
Conquering Hero, The 1924,Ap 13,VIII,1:3
Monkman, Phyllis
Sunshine Sisters 1933,N 26,IX,3:6
Monks, James
Brother Rat 1936,D 17,34:5
Yesterday's Magic 1942,Ap 15,27:2
Eve of St Mark, The 1942,O 8,30:2
Othello 1943,O 20,18:1
Story of Mary Surratt, The 1947,F 10,25:2
Town House 1948,S 24,31:2
Auntie Mame 1956,N 1,47:2
Monks, John Jr
Rendezvous 1932,O 13,22:3
Monks, John Jr (Playwright)
Brother Rat 1936,D 8,30:6
Brother Rat 1936,D 17,34:5
Lew Leslie's Blackbirds of 1939 1939,F 13,12:2
Monks, Marjorie
Fencing Master, The 1936,Ap 1,29:1
Mlle Modiste 1937,My 5,28:5
Monne, Marilyn
Sea Shells 1935,Jl 16,24:2
Monnier, Henry (Playwright)
Enterrement, L' 1939,F 7,17:2
Monnot, Marguerite (Composer)
Irma la Douce 1960,S 30,31:2
Monod, Roland
Phedre 1969,Mr 1,20:1
Monod, Roland (Director)
Phedre 1969,Mr 1,20:1
Monro, Harold (Playwright)
Elsa Lanchester-Herself 1961,F 6,28:1
Monro, Ronnie (Miscellaneous)
Plume de Ma Tante, La 1958,N 12,42:1

Monroe, Allen
Yerma 1952,F 8,18:4
Miss Julie 1954,Mr 29,24:3
All the King's Men 1959,O 17,27:2
Monroe, Anita
Lady Billy 1920,D 15,18:2
Monroe, Bob
Show Boat 1966,Jl 20,48:1
South Pacific 1967,Je 13,56:1
Monroe, Dale
Chic 1959,My 19,28:2
Monroe, Donna
Girl Who Came to Supper, The 1963,D 9,49:1
Oklahoma! 1969,Je 24,37:1
Monroe, Frank
When We Are Young 1920,N 23,11:1
All-Star Jamboree 1921,Jl 14,18:1
Thank You 1921,O 4,10:2
Haunted House, The 1924,S 3,12:1
Holy Terror, A 1925,S 29,31:2
Deacon, The 1925,N 25,14:3
2 Girls Wanted 1926,S 10,25:3
Wild Duck, The 1928,N 19,17:1
Town's Woman, The 1929,Mr 12,26:2
Apron Strings 1930,F 18,28:2
Ladies of Creation 1931,Ag 30,VIII,1:7
Ladies of Creation 1931,S 9,25:1
Divine Drudge 1933,Jl 4,16:4
Divine Drudge 1933,O 27,22:3
Uncle Tom's Cabin 1934,Jl 6,15:1
Woman of the Soil, A 1935,Mr 26,23:6
Ragged Edge, The 1935,N 26,28:3
Monroe, Franklyn
Witness for the Prosecution 1954,D 17,35:2
Monroe, Gladys
Goat Alley 1921,Je 21,20:2
Monroe, Lois
Out of This World 1950,D 22,17:3
Monroe, Lucy
Criss Cross 1926,O 13,20:2
Hello, Yourself 1928,O 31,28:2
Polly 1929,Ja 9,28:3
Chimes of Corneville, The 1934,Je 29,16:2
O'Flynn, The 1934,D 28,24:1
Three Waltzes 1938,Je 26,II,7:5
American Jubilee 1940,My 13,20:5
Monroe, Tommy
Well of Romance, The 1930,N 8,21:2
Monroe, Vic
Hot-Cha! 1932,Mr 9,17:3
Monroe, Walter
Jackpot 1944,Ja 14,15:2
Monroe and Grant
Vaudeville (Loew's State) 1932,Je 13,19:7
Mons
Streets of Paris, The 1939,Je 20,25:2
Monsanto, Liston
Medea 1960,Jl 26,25:2
Monsees, William
Earth Journey 1944,Ap 28,24:2
Monsell, J R (Composer)
Rivals, The 1935,S 25,19:6
Monsell, J R (Lyricist)
Rivals, The 1935,S 25,19:6
Monsell, Roy
His and Hers 1954,Ja 8,18:2
Age and Grace 1956,F 21,38:2
Across the Board on Tomorrow Morning 1961,O 23,22:5
Monson, Lex
Blacks, The 1961,My 5,23:1
Moby Dick 1962,N 29,45:1
Trumpets of the Lord 1963,D 23,22:3
Trumpets of the Lord 1967,Je 1,51:3
Trumpets of the Lord 1969,Ap 30,37:1
Montagna, Carlo
Game of Heroes, The 1966,F 22,14:2
Montague, Harry
School for Scandal, The 1923,Mr 13,19:2
Montague, Joey
Fast Service 1931,N 18,26:3
Montague, John (Playwright)
Boy Friend, The 1932,Je 8,22:3
Montague, Lee
Climate of Eden, The 1952,N 7,20:2
Climate of Eden, The 1952,N 16,II,1:1
Entertaining Mr Sloane 1965,O 13,41:1
Montaigne, Larry
Shinbone Alley 1957,Ap 15,23:2
Montalban, Carlos
Me, Candido! 1956,O 16,36:2
Montalban, Helena
Our Town 1961,Ap 4,34:3
Montalban, Ricardo
Seventh Heaven 1955,My 27,16:2
Jamaica 1957,N 1,32:2
Jamaica 1957,N 10,II,1:1
Montalvo, Frank
Harlequinade 1959,F 14,15:1
Montana
Vaudeville (Palace) 1923,Ap 3,26:4
Vaudeville (Palace) 1923,N 20,23:4

Montana, Dajalna
Silver Tassie, The 1929,O 25,26:1
Montand, Yves
Evening With Yves Montand, An 1959,S 23,45:1
Evening With Yves Montand, An 1961,O 25,30:1
Montand, Yves (Director)
Evening With Yves Montand, An 1959,S 23,45:1
Evening With Yves Montand, An 1961,O 25,30:1
Montand, Yves (Lighting Director)
Evening With Yves Montand, An 1959,S 23,45:1
Evening With Yves Montand, An 1961,O 25,30:1
Montaner, Joaquin
Student of Vich 1929,Ja 3,25:2
Montanye, C S (Playwright)
Sue, Dear 1922,Jl 11,16:2
Montaya, Carlos
Top-Notchers 1942,My 30,8:5
Monte, Barbara
Kelly 1965,F 8,28:2
On a Clear Day You Can See Forever 1965,O 18,44:1
Billy 1969,Mr 24,56:1
Monte, Elisa
Carousel 1957,S 12,38:2
Monte, Evelyn
Ethan Frome 1936,Ja 22,15:2
Monte, Joseph
Mikado, The 1942,F 4,22:2
Pirates of Penzance, The 1942,F 18,22:2
Iolanthe 1942,F 24,26:4
Gondoliers, The 1942,Mr 4,22:3
Mr Strauss Goes to Boston 1945,S 7,20:2
Montealegre, Felicia
Merchant of Venice, The 1953,Mr 5,20:2
International Set, The 1953,Je 12,19:3
Henry V 1956,Jl 7,11:2
Pelleas and Melisande 1957,F 20,38:1
Little Foxes, The 1968,Ja 6,24:4
Montedoro, Marco (Costume Designer)
Vie Parisienne, La 1941,N 6,20:3
Montedoro, Marco (Scenic Designer)
Vie Parisienne, La 1941,N 6,20:3
Montefiore, Gene
Beautiful Jailer, The 1957,My 17,19:2
Montefiore, Gene (Director)
What a Killing 1961,Mr 28,41:1
Montefiori, Polly
Fuente Ovejuna; Sheep Well, The 1936,My 3,II,4:1
Monteil, Robert
South Pacific 1968,Je 30,54:2
South Pacific 1969,Jl 7,27:1
Monteiro, Linda
Pericas, Las 1969,N 2,86:5
Montel, Blanche
Attachee, L' 1929,My 19,IX,2:1
Montelion, Pat
Cocktails of 1934 1934,My 5,22:1
Montell, Eleanor
Come Seven 1920,Jl 20,10:1
Mary the 3d 1923,F 6,14:2
Montepin, Severio (Original Author)
Medico Delle Pazze, Il; Physician of Mad Woman, The 1937,S 27,24:2
Monterey, Carlotta
Ruined Lady, The 1920,Ja 21,10:2
Bavu 1922,F 27,16:1
Voltaire 1922,Mr 21,17:1
Fashions of 1924 1923,Jl 19,18:2
Other Rose, The 1923,D 21,15:2
Red Falcon, The 1924,O 8,22:1
Man in Evening Clothes, The 1924,D 6,13:4
Monteria, Mata
Duchess Misbehaves, The 1946,F 14,32:2
Montero, Mario
Pinwheel Revel 1922,Je 16,20:6
Montes, Conchita
To My Love 1956,Je 7,35:3
Montes, Robert
Play of Daniel, The 1966,Ja 2,64:4
Montesanto, Leroy
Princess Virtue 1921,My 5,20:2
Montesole, Max
Mongrel, The 1924,D 16,28:2
Tangletoes 1925,F 18,17:1
New Gallantry, The 1925,S 25,24:2
School for Scandal, The 1925,O 24,19:1
Othello 1930,My 20,33:1
Montessi, Robert
Play of Daniel, The 1960,D 27,23:6
Play of Daniel, The 1961,D 28,22:6
Montevecchi, Liliane
Come Play With Me 1959,My 1,33:5
Folies Bergere 1964,Je 3,36:1
Monteverde, Giorgio
Idiot's Delight 1936,Mr 25,25:2
Montez, Mario
Bluebeard 1970,My 5,58:1
Montez, Mayita
Stars on Ice 1942,Jl 3,12:2
Montgomery, Barbara
Ubu Roi 1970,F 17,33:1
Street Sounds 1970,O 23,32:1

Montgomery, Billy
Hoboken Hoboes 1929,D 28,10:8
Montgomery, Bruce (Composer)
Amorous Flea, The 1964,F 18,26:1
Montgomery, Bruce (Lyricist)
Amorous Flea, The 1964,F 18,26:1
Montgomery, Candace
Three to Make Ready 1946,Mr 8,16:2
Toplitzky of Notre Dame 1946,D 27,13:4
Montgomery, Catherine
Kind Lady 1937,Jl 21,19:3
Fly Away Home 1937,Jl 28,15:1
Whiteheaded Boy, The 1937,Ag 11,27:3
Montgomery, Dick
Carmen Jones 1943,D 3,26:2
Montgomery, Douglass
God Loves Us 1926,O 20,22:2
Crime 1927,F 23,27:3
Women Go on Forever 1927,S 8,25:1
Garden of Eden, The 1927,S 28,28:1
Faust 1928,O 9,34:1
Caprice 1929,Ja 1,61:1
Caprice 1929,Ja 13,VIII,1:1
Caprice 1929,Je 23,VIII,1:3
Meteor 1929,D 24,15:1
Many a Slip 1930,F 4,29:2
Nikki 1931,S 30,23:4
Fata Morgana 1931,D 26,15:3
Men Must Fight 1932,O 15,13:4
American Dream; 1933 1933,F 22,24:5
American Dream; 1650 1933,F 22,24:5
Merely Murder 1937,N 16,26:1
They Knew What They Wanted 1939,O 3,19:1
Vigil, The 1948,My 11,28:1
Detective Story 1950,Mr 27,18:2
Legend of Lizzie, The 1959,F 10,39:1
Montgomery, Earl
Summer and Smoke 1948,O 7,33:2
Relapse, The 1950,N 23,54:2
Mr Pickwick 1952,S 18,36:3
Love's Labour's Lost 1953,F 5,20:3
Love's Labour's Lost 1953,F 8,II,1:1
Merchant of Venice, The 1953,Mr 5,20:2
Strong Are Lonely, The 1953,S 30,38:3
White Devil, The 1955,Mr 15,32:5
Moby Dick 1955,Ap 26,25:3
Heavenly Twins, The 1955,N 5,23:2
Lovers 1956,My 11,23:1
Henry V 1956,Jl 7,11:2
Saint Joan 1956,S 12,42:1
Visit to a Small Planet 1957,F 8,18:1
Look After Lulu 1959,Mr 4,35:1
Becket 1960,O 6,50:1
Becket 1961,My 9,44:1
Romulus 1962,Ja 11,27:1
Seagull, The 1962,Mr 22,42:1
Tavern, The 1962,Ap 5,29:1
Lady of the Camellias, The 1963,Mr 22,7:1
Rehearsal, The 1963,S 24,45:2
Caucasian Chalk Circle, The 1966,Mr 25,35:1
Alchemist, The 1966,O 14,48:1
East Wind, The 1967,F 10,30:1
Galileo 1967,Ap 14,31:1
Saint Joan 1968,Ja 5,42:1
Tiger at the Gates 1968,Mr 1,30:1
Cyrano de Bergerac 1968,Ap 26,30:1
Her First Roman 1968,O 21,53:3
Montgomery, Edward Poor (Playwright)
Years Between, The 1931,Ap 23,28:5
Years Between, The 1931,My 10,VIII,2:1
Double Harness 1933,Ja 13,18:5
Montgomery, Elizabeth
Late Love 1953,O 14,35:2
Montgomery, Elizabeth (Costume Designer)
Doctor's Dilemma, The 1941,Mr 12,18:2
Montgomery, Gladys
Sally 1920,D 22,16:1
Montgomery, Goodee
Hassard Short's Ritz Revue 1924,S 18,19:1
Piggy 1927,Ja 12,22:2
Montgomery, James (Composer)
Ziegfeld Follies 1920,Je 23,14:1
Montgomery, James (Lyricist)
Ziegfeld Follies 1920,Je 23,14:1
Montgomery, James (Playwright)
Ziegfeld Follies 1920,Je 23,14:1
Glory 1922,D 26,10:1
City Chap, The 1925,O 27,21:1
Yes, Yes, Yvette 1927,O 4,32:3
Stella Brady 1931,O 11,VIII,4:3
Tell Her the Truth 1932,O 29,18:2
Montgomery, James (Producer)
Brain Sweat 1934,Ap 5,24:4
Montgomery, Janice Lynne
Sambo 1969,D 22,42:1
Montgomery, John A Jr
This Mad Whirl 1937,Ja 10,II,4:8
Montgomery, John E
Earth Journey 1944,Ap 28,24:2
Montgomery, Laried
Finian's Rainbow 1967,Ap 6,44:1
My Fair Lady 1968,Je 14,42:1
Billy 1969,Mr 24,56:1

Montgomery, Lois
All the Living 1938,Mr 25,14:4
Montgomery, Lucy Maud (Original Author)
Anne 1965,Ag 22,82:2
Anne of Green Gables 1969,Ap 18,39:1
Montgomery, Mabel
Easy Terms 1925,S 23,22:2
Chivalry 1925,D 16,22:3
Bride of the Lamb 1926,Mr 31,20:3
Sandalwood 1926,S 23,23:1
New York Exchange 1926,D 31,11:2
Madame X 1927,Jl 7,29:3
Celebrity 1927,D 27,24:3
Lady for a Night, A 1928,Ap 17,26:4
Elmer Gantry 1928,Ag 10,9:4
Love Expert, The 1929,S 24,29:1
Charm 1929,N 29,24:5
Up Pops the Devil 1930,S 2,19:1
Blind Alley 1935,S 25,19:6
Chalked Out 1937,Mr 26,24:2
Montgomery, Monty
Beclch 1968,D 17,59:1
Montgomery, Patricia
Kai Khosru 1925,Ap 27,14:2
Montgomery, Patricia (Costume Designer)
Strange Fruit 1945,N 30,18:6
Jeb 1946,F 22,20:2
This Time Tomorrow 1947,N 4,31:2
Story for a Sunday Evening, A 1950,N 18,10:5
Montgomery, Robert
Mask and the Face, The 1924,S 11,27:3
Dawn 1924,N 25,27:1
Complex, The 1925,Mr 4,17:2
Carolinian, The 1925,N 3,34:2
Bad Habits of 1926 1926,My 1,11:1
High Hatters, The 1928,My 11,28:2
Possession 1928,O 3,35:1
Montgomery, Robert (Director)
Big Two, The 1947,Ja 9,21:2
Desperate Hours, The 1955,F 11,20:2
Desperate Hours, The 1955,F 20,II,1:1
Calculated Risk 1962,O 17,33:3
Calculated Risk 1962,N 1,35:1
Montgomery, Robert (Miscellaneous)
Place of Our Own, A 1945,Ap 3,23:7
Montgomery, Robert (Producer)
All in Favor 1942,Ja 21,20:6
Big Two, The 1947,Ja 9,21:2
Montgomery, Thomas
County Chairman, The 1936,My 26,26:5
Montgomery, Victoria (Playwright)
Blind Alleys 1924,N 18,23:3
Month, Christopher
All the Way Home 1960,D 1,42:1
Montherlant, Henri de (Playwright)
Port-Royal 1955,F 27,II,3:1
Queen After Death 1956,Mr 13,33:2
Port-Royal 1960,Ap 26,41:1
Cardinal of Spain, The 1960,D 22,16:6
Reine Morte, La; Dead Queen, The 1966,F 9,32:1
Reine Morte, La 1966,F 16,52:1
Monti, Fred
Pigeon, The 1922,F 3,13:1
Mask and the Face, The 1924,S 11,27:3
Pickwick 1927,S 6,35:2
Squealer, The 1928,N 26,30:3
Journey's End 1930,Ag 5,26:4
Monticue, Ethel
Young Visitors, The 1920,D 5,VII,1:1
Young Visitors, The 1920,D 26,VI,3:2
Montignac, Georges (Playwright)
Sur la Dalle 1923,O 30,17:2
Montillier, Georges
Boys in the Band, The 1969,S 20,21:2
Montojo, Fausto
Pluma en el Viento; Feather in the Wind
1932,Ap 2,13:4
Montor, Max
Dance of Death, The; Totentanz 1923,D 17,23:3
Rosmersholm 1924,F 8,22:3
Hamlet 1925,O 12,19:2
Montresor, Beni (Costume Designer)
Marco Millions 1964,F 21,33:1
Do I Hear a Waltz? 1965,Mr 19,28:1
Montresor, Beni (Scenic Designer)
Do I Hear a Waltz? 1965,Mr 19,28:1
Do I Hear a Waltz? 1965,Mr 28,II,1:1
Montrose, Edmund
Wings Over Europe 1936,Mr 4,24:7
Montrose, Helen
Right Girl, The 1921,Mr 16,12:1
Montrose, Muriel
By the Way 1925,D 29,20:3
This Year of Grace 1928,N 8,27:1
Montroy, Kent
Visit, The 1958,My 6,40:1
Monty, Gloria (Director)
Rose in the Wilderness 1949,Ja 5,21:2
Don't Go Away Mad 1949,My 10,28:2
Building 222 1950,F 3,28:2
Tread the Green Grass 1950,Ap 21,19:4
On Baile's Strand 1959,Ap 13,34:4
Death of Cuchulain, The 1959,Ap 13,34:4

Monty, Gloria (Producer)
Don't Go Away Mad 1949,My 10,28:2
Monya
Mercenary Mary 1925,Ap 14,27:3
Moody, A
Let Freedom Ring 1935,N 7,26:2
Moody, David
Big Time Buck White 1968,D 9,58:1
Buck White 1969,D 3,63:1
Moody, Eileen
Gondoliers, The 1934,S 4,23:1
Mikado, The; Town of Titipu, The 1934,S 18,18:1
Ruddigore 1934,S 25,25:2
Moody, Jacquelynne
Pirates of Penzance, The 1961,Ja 20,24:5
Moody, James
Old Judge Mose Is Dead 1969,Ag 29,25:1
Moody, Phil (Miscellaneous)
Holiday on Ice 1969,Ag 28,44:1
Moody, Richard
Streets of New York, The 1934,Jl 21,14:5
Coquette 1935,Jl 10,24:1
Hay Fever 1935,Jl 24,20:4
Camille 1935,Jl 31,21:1
Mr Pim Passes By 1935,Ag 7,22:2
Vinegar Tree, The 1935,Ag 14,16:1
Double Door 1935,Ag 21,22:2
Late Christopher Bean, The 1935,Ag 28,13:1
Moody, Robert King
Doctor Faustus Lights the Lights 1951,D 3,23:4
Moog, Heinz
Professor Bernhardi 1968,Mr 20,38:1
Maria Stuart 1968,Mr 27,38:1
Moon, David (Lighting Director)
Yes is for a Very Young Man 1963,Mr 6,7:5
Wet Paint 1965,Ap 13,33:1
Moon, David (Scenic Designer)
I Want You 1961,S 15,29:1
Yes is for a Very Young Man 1963,Mr 6,7:5
Route 1 1964,N 18,52:3
Wet Paint 1965,Ap 13,33:1
Moon, Eugene
Magistrate, The 1959,My 14,30:6
Moon, Frank
My House Is Your House 1970,O 16,53:2
Moon, Joseph (Composer)
In April Once 1955,Mr 14,29:3
Moon, Joseph (Miscellaneous)
If the Shoe Fits 1946,D 6,29:4
Portofino 1958,F 22,8:3
Dr Willy Nilly 1959,Je 5,18:2
Beautiful Dreamer 1960,D 28,22:1
Moon, Keith
Tommy 1969,O 26,82:1
Moon, Sylvia
Ballad for Bimshire 1963,O 16,54:1
Moon, William
John Ferguson 1921,My 24,20:1
Mooney
Dew Drop Inn 1923,My 18,26:4
Mooney, Martin (Playwright)
Town's Woman, The 1929,Mr 12,26:2
Sisters of the Chorus 1930,My 18,VIII,3:1
Sisters of the Chorus 1930,O 21,34:3
Ghost Writer, The 1933,Je 20,22:4
Mooney, Martin (Producer)
Town's Woman, The 1929,Mr 12,26:2
Mooney, Maureen
Mod Donna 1970,My 4,48:1
Mooney, Ria
Juno and the Paycock 1927,D 20,32:2
Would-Be Gentleman, The 1928,O 2,34:1
Invitation au Voyage, L' 1928,O 5,17:1
Lady From Alfaqueque, The; Consulesa, La
1929,Ja 15,22:3
Katerina 1929,F 26,30:3
Living Corpse, The 1929,D 7,19:1
Women Have Their Way, The 1930,Ja 28,28:1
Things That Are Caesar's, The 1932,O 18,23:4
Far-Off Hills, The 1932,O 19,22:4
Playboy of the Western World, The 1932,O 21,25:1
Words Upon the Window Pane, The
1932,O 29,18:2
Crabbed Youth and Age 1932,N 4,25:1
Big House, The 1933,Ja 5,19:3
Parnell of Avondale 1934,O 3,24:4
Village Wooing 1935,O 27,IX,2:5
Armlet of Jade 1936,Ap 15,25:3
Katie Roche 1937,O 4,17:4
Playboy of the Western World, The 1937,N 22,14:5
In the Train 1937,N 22,14:5
Drama at Inish 1937,D 14,33:2
Long Day's Journey Into Night 1959,Ap 29,30:2
Long Day's Journey Into Night 1962,S 30,85:8
Mooney, Ria (Director)
Bugle in the Blood, The 1949,Mr 15,34:5
Mooney, Samuel
Yeomen of the Guard, The 1934,S 21,28:3
Mooney, William
Sotoba Komachi 1961,F 1,15:1
Damask Drum, The 1961,F 4,15:1
Spoon River Anthology 1964,Je 27,15:2
Half Horse, Half Alligator 1964,S 20,120:3

Mooney, William—Cont
Half Horse, Half Alligator 1966,Mr 14,37:2
Place for Polly, A 1970,Ap 20,45:1
Mooney, William (Miscellaneous)
Half Horse, Half Alligator 1966,Mr 14,37:2
Mooney, William (Playwright)
Half Horse, Half Alligator 1966,Mr 14,37:2
Moonshine
Gypsy Fires 1925,D 8,28:3
Moor, Bill
Christmas in the Market Place 1960,D 10,26:1
Love Nest, The 1963,Ja 28,7:6
Sweet Enemy, The 1965,F 16,39:1
Measure for Measure 1966,Jl 14,27:1
Fortune and Men's Eyes 1967,F 24,29:1
King Lear 1968,N 8,43:1
Cry of Players, A 1968,N 15,40:1
Moor, Edward
Great Sebastians, The 1956,Ja 5,27:1
Visit, The 1958,My 6,40:1
Happy as Larry 1961,Ap 26,36:1
Moor, George
Processional 1937,O 14,23:1
Moor, Regina
Night Watch In Syria 1943,Ja 5,15:5
Moor, William
Dandy Dick 1956,Ja 11,37:2
Moorat, Joseph (Composer)
Prunella; Love in a Garden 1926,Je 16,23:3
Moore, Ada
House of Flowers 1954,D 31,11:2
Moore, Adrienne
Lady in the Dark 1943,Mr 1,14:2
Dream Girl 1951,My 10,39:1
Moore, Al
Rhapsody in Black 1931,My 5,33:2
Accent on Youth 1934,D 26,19:1
Cabin in the Sky 1940,O 26,19:2
Moore, Albert
Gang War 1928,Ag 21,27:2
Moore, Alfred
Abraham Lincoln 1929,O 22,26:3
Moore, Allen
Four in Hand 1923,S 7,10:2
Lazybones 1924,S 23,23:1
Weak Sisters 1925,O 14,31:3
Tightwad, The 1927,Ap 18,18:2
Moore, Alphonse
Androcles and the Lion 1938,D 17,10:5
Moore, Arnold
Mandingo 1961,My 23,43:6
Moore, Arthur
Policy Kings 1938,D 31,6:2
Moore, Augustus L Jr
Great Guns 1939,N 18,23:4
Moore, Baker
Dear Me 1921,Ja 18,14:1
Moore, Bernie
Persecution and Assassination of Marat As
Performed by the Inmates of the Asylum of
Charenton Under the Direction of the Marquis de
Sade, The 1967,Ja 4,34:1
Moore, Bolton
Desert Flower, The 1924,N 19,18:2
Moore, Brennan
Jenny Kissed Me 1948,D 24,12:2
Alley of the Sunset 1959,D 31,11:1
Tiger Rag, The 1961,F 17,20:2
Moore, C Barnard
Paddy the Next Best Thing 1920,Ag 28,5:5
Moore, Candy
J B 1958,D 12,2:7
Moore, Carlyle
Ink 1927,N 2,24:2
Moore, Carlyle (Playwright)
Listening In 1922,D 5,24:1
Moore, Carroll (Playwright)
Make a Million 1958,O 24,39:2
Send Me No Flowers 1960,D 6,54:1
Moore, Catherine
Pirates of Penzance, The 1938,Je 3,16:2
Moore, Charles
New York Exchange 1926,D 31,11:2
Meek Mose 1928,F 7,30:1
Green Pastures, The 1930,F 27,26:1
Green Pastures, The 1931,Mr 1,VIII,1:1
Green Pastures, The 1935,F 27,16:2
Point of Honor, A 1937,F 12,26:2
Aria Da Capo 1950,My 25,36:2
Ballad for Bimshire 1963,O 16,54:1
House of Flowers 1968,Ja 29,26:2
Bill Noname 1970,Mr 3,37:1
Blancs, Les 1970,N 16,48:4
Moore, Charles Werner (Director)
Does a Tiger Wear a Necktie? 1967,F 4,17:1
Fire! 1968,My 12,II,7:1
Fire! 1969,Ja 29,26:1
Moore, Chester (Director)
No Exit 1967,O 31,38:2
Moore, Constance
By Jupiter 1942,Je 4,22:1
By Jupiter 1942,Ag 30,VIII,1:1
Moore, Daphne
Twelfth Night 1941,D 3,32:2

Moore, Darby
School for Brides 1944,Ag 2,19:4
Moore, Deidre
Tartuffe 1965,Ja 15,23:1
Moore, Dennie
Lady in Love, A 1927,F 22,22:1
Trial of Mary Dugan, The 1927,S 20,33:1
Jarnegan 1928,S 25,29:2
Conflict 1929,Mr 7,22:4
Cross Roads 1929,N 12,34:2
Phantoms 1930,Ja 14,24:3
Torch Song 1930,Ag 3,VIII,3:4
Torch Song 1930,Ag 28,23:1
Gone Hollywood 1930,D 28,VIII,2:1
Anatol 1931,Ja 17,23:3
East Wind 1931,O 28,19:1
East Wind 1931,D 11,VIII,4:3
Man Who Reclaimed His Head 1932,S 9,17:3
Great Magoo, The 1932,D 3,20:7
20th Century 1932,D 30,15:1
Man Bites Dog 1933,Ap 26,11:2
Pursuit of Happiness, The 1933,O 10,24:4
Pursuit of Happiness, The 1934,Je 24,IX,1:4
Say When 1934,N 9,24:2
Swing Your Lady 1936,O 19,22:4
Hitch Your Wagon! 1937,Ap 9,18:2
In Clover 1937,O 14,23:1
Off the Record 1940,D 1,63:5
Ah, Wilderness! 1941,O 3,26:2
Johnny on the Spot 1942,Ja 9,24:2
Over Twenty-One 1944,Ja 4,20:2
Seven Lively Arts 1944,D 8,26:6
Star Spangled Family 1945,Ap 11,18:6
Fundamental George, The 1949,Ag 17,19:4
Rat Race, The 1949,D 23,16:2
Diary of Anne Frank, The 1955,O 6,24:2
No Exit 1967,O 31,38:2
Moore, Diane
Woman Is My Idea 1968,S 26,61:1
Moore, Dick
Too Many Heroes 1937,N 16,26:2
Saint Joan 1956,S 12,42:1
Moore, Don
Darker Flower, A 1963,Mr 11,7:2
As You Like It 1963,Jl 17,19:2
Moore, Doris
Hole in the Wall, The 1920,Mr 27,11:1
Great Lady 1938,D 2,26:6
Moore, Douglas (Composer)
Headless Horseman, The 1937,Mr 6,10:4
Devil and Daniel Webster, The 1939,My 21,X,1:1
Moore, Douglas (Playwright)
Devil and Daniel Webster, The 1939,My 19,26:1
Moore, Dudley
Beyond the Fringe 1962,O 29,36:1
Beyond the Fringe 1964 1964,Ja 10,18:1
Moore, Dudley (Composer)
Emperor Jones, The 1964,Ag 6,20:4
Emperor Jones, The 1964,Ag 16,II,5:1
Serjeant Musgrave's Dance 1966,Mr 9,44:1
Moore, Dudley (Playwright)
Beyond the Fringe 1962,O 29,36:1
Moore, Ed
Revolt of the Beavers, The 1937,My 21,19:2
Shadow Years, The 1957,Ja 9,26:2
Moore, Edward J
After the Rain 1967,O 10,54:1
White House Murder Case, The 1970,F 19,59:1
Moore, Elena
Hamlet 1954,Ap 24,15:2
Moore, Elizabeth
First Crocus, The 1942,Ja 3,14:6
Galileo 1947,D 8,34:2
Long Gallery, The 1958,Mr 7,17:2
Trip to Bountiful, The 1959,F 27,20:4
Anvil, The 1962,O 31,33:3
Rimers of Eldritch, The 1967,F 21,53:1
Moore, Erin O'Brien
Him 1928,Ap 19,23:3
Yoshe Kalb 1933,D 29,27:2
Moore, Ernest
Pinocchio 1939,Ja 3,19:2
Moore, Eulabelle
Sweet River 1936,O 29,30:2
Jason 1942,Ja 22,12:2
Skin of Our Teeth, The 1942,N 19,29:5
You Can't Take It With You 1945,Mr 27,23:7
Streetcar Named Desire, A 1950,My 24,36:1
Four Twelves Are 48 1951,Ja 18,30:2
Male Animal, The 1952,My 1,35:1
Girl Can Tell, A 1953,O 30,28:2
Debut 1956,F 23,32:1
Jolly's Progress 1959,D 7,42:2
Cool World, The 1960,F 23,38:2
Goose, The 1960,Mr 16,44:1
Great Day in the Morning 1962,Mr 29,29:1
Moore, Eva
Cabbages and Kings 1933,N 22,22:3
Moore, Evelyn
Man in Possession, The 1930,N 3,19:1
Moore, Feroll
Cocktail Impromptu 1927,Ja 13,28:4

Moore, Florence
Breakfast in Bed 1920,F 4,12:1
Untitled-Benefit 1921,My 2,12:3
Irving Berlin's Music Box Revue 1921,S 23,18:2
Music Box Revue 1923,S 24,5:3
Greenwich Village Follies 1925,D 25,23:3
Greenwich Village Follies 1926,Mr 16,22:2
She Couldn't Say No! 1926,S 1,27:3
She Couldn't Say No! 1926,S 12,VIII,1:1
Vaudeville (Palace) 1927,Mr 1,31:2
Artists and Models 1927,N 16,28:2
Vaudeville (Palace) 1928,Jl 24,13:4
Vaudeville (Palace) 1928,D 24,10:8
International Revue 1930,F 9,VIII,4:2
International Revue 1930,F 26,22:2
Cradle Snatchers 1932,N 17,23:2
Moore, Frances
Sweethearts 1929,S 23,25:1
Babes in Toyland 1929,D 24,15:3
Babes in Toyland 1930,D 22,17:1
Gondoliers, The 1931,Je 2,34:4
Patience 1931,Je 16,30:4
Pirates of Penzance, The; Slave of Duty, The
1931,Je 30,23:6
Ruddigore 1931,Ag 11,28:3
Merry Widow, The 1931,S 8,39:1
Yeomen of the Guard, The 1933,My 2,20:4
Patience 1933,My 23,22:6
Pirates of Penzance, The 1933,Ag 8,22:4
Yeomen of the Guard, The 1933,Ag 15,20:5
Moore, Francis D
Hades, the Ladies 1934,Mr 29,25:3
Moore, Francis D (Composer)
Foemen of the Yard 1935,Ap 6,10:4
Moore, Francis D (Lyricist)
Foemen of the Yard 1935,Ap 6,10:4
Moore, Frank
These Are the Times 1950,My 11,37:2
All Around the Town 1952,Mr 26,33:2
Hair 1970,Ja 13,39:1
Moore, Frank (Composer)
After the Angels 1961,F 11,27:5
Moore, Franka
Marathon 1933,Ja 28,8:8
Moore, Gar
Dark of the Moon 1945,Mr 15,27:2
Not for Children 1951,F 14,35:2
Moore, Gene (Costume Designer)
If Five Years Pass 1962,My 11,37:1
Moore, Geoff (Playwright)
Accumulator; Duo 1970,F 4,36:1
Moore, George
Porgy 1927,O 11,26:2
Vaudeville (Palace) 1927,N 15,27:2
One Thing After Another 1937,D 29,17:2
Moore, George (Playwright)
Making of an Immortal, The 1928,Ap 3,32:4
Making of an Immortal, The 1928,Ap 29,IX,1:3
Passing of the Essenes, The 1930,O 19,IX,4:1
Moore, Georgia
Ups-A-Daisy 1928,O 9,34:2
Moore, Gerald
Lace Petticoat 1927,Ja 5,18:2
Moore, Grace
Hitchy-Koo, 1920 1920,O 20,11:3
Up in the Clouds 1922,Ja 3,20:3
Music Box Revue 1923,S 24,5:3
Music Box Revue 1924,D 2,23:3
Du Barry 1932,N 13,IX,1:8
Du Barry 1932,N 23,15:2
Gay Divorce 1932,N 30,23:4
Moore, H Thomas (Miscellaneous)
Dynamite Tonight 1967,Mr 16,52:2
Moore, Harry
Untitled-Revue 1926,O 26,18:3
Moore, Helen
Cloudy With Showers 1931,S 2,17:5
Moore, Henrietta
Sable Brush, The 1956,N 28,41:1
Moore, Herbert
Iolanthe 1954,Ap 28,36:8
Sorcerer, The 1954,My 26,34:3
Moore, Herbert (Scenic Designer)
Wonderful Night, A; Fledermaus, Die
1929,N 1,23:3
Nina Rosa 1930,My 31,19:3
Merchant of Venice, The 1931,N 9,22:2
Growing Pains 1933,N 24,24:2
Night of January 16 1935,S 17,26:4
Moore, Hilda
At Mrs Beam's 1923,Mr 11,VIII,2:4
Interference 1927,F 27,VII,1:3
Moore, Honor (Producer)
Nest, The 1970,Ap 10,46:1
Moore, Ida
Strings, My Lord, Are False, The 1942,My 20,24:2
Moore, Irene
New Faces of 1936 1936,My 20,24:5
Now I Lay Me Down to Sleep 1950,Mr 3,21:2
Seven Year Itch, The 1952,N 21,21:2
Painted Days, The 1961,Ap 7,24:1
Moore, Jack
Red Roses for Me 1955,D 29,15:2

Moore, James
My Princess 1927,O 7,24:2
Plutocrat, The 1930,F 21,23:3
Purity 1930,D 26,18:2
Judgment Day 1934,S 13,26:4
Schoolhouse on the Lot 1938,Mr 23,18:4
Naked Genius, The 1943,O 22,20:5
Plain and Fancy 1955,Ja 28,14:2
New Faces of 1962 1962,F 2,25:1
Hot Spot 1963,Ap 20,17:2
West Side Story 1964,Ap 9,24:2
Moore, James (Choreographer)
New Faces of 1962 1962,F 2,25:1
Moore, James (Miscellaneous)
Drat! the Cat! 1965,O 11,54:2
Moore, Jan
Girl Friend, The 1926,Mr 18,26:5
Moore, Jane
Merry World, The 1926,Je 9,18:3
Naughty Riquette 1926,S 14,25:2
Bitter Sweet 1929,N 6,30:2
Sketch Book 1935,Je 5,22:2
Women, The 1936,D 28,13:1
Family Reunion, The 1960,D 10,26:1
Moore, Jann
Night of Love 1941,Ja 8,14:2
Vagabond King, The 1943,Je 30,24:2
Moore, Jill Esmond
Bird in Hand 1928,My 13,IX,2:7
Bird in Hand 1929,Ap 5,28:2
Moore, Jim
Seventeen 1951,Je 22,16:6
On the Town 1959,Ja 16,36:1
Moore, Joanne
Mikado, The 1962,N 14,43:1
Gondoliers, The 1962,N 16,25:2
H M S Pinafore 1962,N 23,32:4
Iolanthe 1962,N 28,42:1
Moore, John J
Love Song, The 1925,Ja 14,19:4
Yoshe Kalb 1933,D 29,27:2
Jubilee 1935,O 14,20:1
Pirates of Penzance, The 1936,Ap 21,27:5
Knights of Song 1938,O 18,29:2
They Walk Alone 1941,Mr 13,24:2
Wookey, The 1941,S 11,20:5
Theatre 1941,N 13,34:2
Escapade 1953,N 19,40:1
Time Remembered 1955,My 4,35:1
Herne's Egg, The 1960,S 20,48:1
After the Angels 1961,F 11,27:5
Moore, John J (Choreographer)
Idiot's Delight 1957,F 23,14:2
Moore, John J (Lighting Director)
Fisherman, The 1965,Ja 27,24:6
Fourth Pig, The 1965,Ja 27,24:6
How to Be a Jewish Mother 1967,D 29,18:1
Moore, John J (Scenic Designer)
Fourth Pig, The 1965,Ja 27,24:6
Fisherman, The 1965,Ja 27,24:6
Clara's Ole Man 1968,Mr 9,23:2
Electronic Nigger, The 1968,Mr 9,23:2
Son, Come Home, A 1968,Mr 9,23:2
Moore, John W
Last Warning, The 1922,O 25,23:1
Moore, Jonathan
Dylan 1964,Ja 20,18:1
1776 1969,Mr 17,46:2
Moore, Joyce
Yellow Sands 1927,S 12,29:3
Moore, Juanita
Raisin in the Sun, A 1959,Ag 5,32:3
Amen Corner, The 1965,Ap 16,35:1
Moore, Karen
Gypsy 1959,My 22,31:6
Moore, Kent
Tempest, The 1970,F 15,67:1
Moore, Laurens
Only in America 1959,N 20,35:1
Jonah! 1967,S 22,52:2
Moore, Lee (Costume Designer)
Eagle Has Two Heads, The 1956,D 14,37:2
Moore, Lela
Earl Carroll's Vanities 1940,Ja 15,11:2
Moore, Leon
Climate of Eden, The 1952,N 7,20:2
Moore, Leslie
Carry Nation 1932,O 31,18:2
Moore, Lucia
Tavern, The 1920,S 28,14:1
Mountain Man, The 1921,D 13,24:2
Anything Might Happen 1923,F 21,22:3
Whole Town's Talking, The 1923,Ag 30,8:2
Patsy, The 1925,D 24,8:5
Saturday's Children 1927,Ja 27,13:1
Take My Advice 1927,N 2,24:3
Girl Trouble 1928,O 26,22:3
Patsy, The 1929,Ja 6,VIII,1:4
Coastwise 1931,D 1,23:1
Moore, Mabel
Servant in the House, The 1921,My 3,20:1
Taming of the Shrew, The 1921,My 12,20:2
Merchant of Venice, The 1921,My 14,10:4

Cyrano de Bergerac 1923,N 2,14:1
Merchant of Venice, The 1925,D 28,12:1
Cyrano de Bergerac 1926,F 19,18:1
Servant in the House, The 1926,My 4,30:1
Immortal Thief, The 1926,O 4,21:1
Enemy of the People, An 1927,O 4,32:5
Hamlet 1928,Ja 5,33:2
Caponsacchi 1928,Ja 25,20:3
Henry V 1928,Mr 16,26:2
Light of Asia, The 1928,O 10,32:2
Bonds of Interest, The 1929,O 15,34:2
If Love Were All 1931,N 14,14:5
Cyrano de Bergerac 1932,D 27,11:2
Richelieu 1934,My 22,28:1
Hamlet 1934,D 26,19:3
Richard III 1934,D 28,24:3
Achilles Had a Heel 1935,O 14,20:2
Cyrano de Bergerac 1936,Ap 28,17:1
Enemy of the People, An 1937,F 16,19:1
Passing of the Third Floor Back, The
1937,Ag 3,20:6
Moore, Margaret
Sunup to Sundown 1938,F 2,14:3
Moore, Margery
Keep Off the Grass 1940,My 24,22:6
Moore, Marilyn
Doctored Wife, The 1950,Jl 12,33:2
Son, The 1950,Ag 16,24:6
Moore, Marion
Billy the Kid 1951,Ag 21,23:2
Moore, Marjorie
Lady Comes Across, The 1942,Ja 10,10:2
By Jupiter 1942,Ag 16,VIII,2:1
Moore, Martha
Doctor Cupid 1952,Ag 14,19:6
Aunt Caroline's Will 1954,Ag 11,21:1
Moore, Mary
Don Juan 1921,S 8,14:2
Seventh Heart, The 1927,My 3,24:4
Veils 1928,Mr 14,28:5
Henry VIII 1946,N 7,42:2
What Every Woman Knows 1946,N 9,13:2
John Gabriel Borkman 1946,N 13,33:2
Allegro 1952,S 18,36:3
Red Rainbow, A 1953,S 15,37:4
Moore, Mary Laura
Martinique 1920,Ap 27,18:2
Moore, Mary Tyler
Breakfast at Tiffany's 1966,D 15,60:1
Moore, Mavor
Measure for Measure 1954,Je 30,23:1
Moore, McElbert (Lyricist)
Night in Paris, A 1926,Ja 6,16:3
Matinee Girl, The 1926,F 2,20:3
Happy 1927,D 6,26:3
Moore, McElbert (Playwright)
Matinee Girl, The 1926,F 2,20:3
Happy 1927,D 6,26:3
Zeppelin 1929,Ja 15,22:3
Moore, Melba
Hair 1968,Ap 30,40:2
Purlie 1970,F 15,II,1:1
Purlie 1970,Mr 16,53:1
Purlie Victorious 1970,Mr 22,II,3:1
Moore, Melton
My Romance 1948,O 20,38:5
Moore, Mercedes (Costume Designer)
Murder in the Cathedral 1935,D 21,11:3
Moore, Meriel
Not for Children 1935,D 29,IX,2:1
Skin of Our Teeth, The 1945,N 18,II,2:5
John Bull's Other Island 1948,F 11,33:4
Old Lady Says No, The 1948,F 18,35:1
Where Stars Walk 1948,F 25,27:2
Moore, Michael
Pal Joey 1940,D 26,22:2
Moore, Michael D (Miscellaneous)
Jumping Fool, The 1970,F 10,53:1
Moore, Mickey
Jubilee 1935,O 14,20:1
Moore, Monetta
Messin' Around 1929,Ap 23,26:3
Flying Colors 1932,S 16,24:2
Moore, Monica
By Jupiter 1942,Je 4,22:1
Louisiana Lady 1947,Je 3,35:2
Moore, Muriel
Red, White and Maddox 1969,Ja 27,27:1
Moore, Napier (Playwright)
Illustrators' Show, The 1936,Ja 23,25:3
Moore, Neil
Ballyhoo 1930,D 23,24:1
Melody 1933,F 15,17:4
Broadway Interlude 1934,Ap 20,16:3
Horse Fever 1940,N 25,21:2
Moore, Patricia
Capacity for Wings 1957,Ja 10,25:2
Moore, Patti
Vaudeville (Palace) 1926,Je 22,21:3
Moore, Pauline
Easiest Way, The 1921,S 7,14:1
Kiki 1921,N 30,13:1
Man and the Masses 1924,Ap 15,25:1

Moore, Pauline—Cont
Fountain, The 1925,D 11,26:1
Prisoner, The 1927,D 30,22:2
Murder at the Vanities 1933,S 13,22:4
Dance With Your Gods 1934,O 8,14:3
Moore, Peggy
Chiaroscuro; Maggie French Understands
1963,Je 6,40:8
Moore, Percy
Daddy Dumplins 1920,N 23,11:1
Pot-Luck 1921,S 30,10:1
Cat and the Canary, The 1922,F 8,13:1
Green Beetle, The 1924,S 3,12:3
Out of Step 1925,Ja 30,12:1
Lucky Break 1925,Ag 12,16:2
Henry IV, Part I 1926,Je 1,29:1
Scotch Mist 1926,S 21,32:3
Arabian Nightmare, The 1927,Ja 11,36:3
Shannons of Broadway, The 1927,S 27,30:4
Play Without a Name, A 1928,N 26,30:5
Jonesy 1929,Ap 10,32:2
Young Sinners 1929,N 29,24:4
Brass Ankle 1931,Ap 24,26:4
Men Must Fight 1932,O 15,13:4
Red Planet 1932,D 19,19:2
Young Sinners 1933,Mr 7,20:4
Order Please 1934,O 10,21:2
Seven Keys to Baldpate 1935,My 28,30:2
Meet the Prince 1935,Ag 6,20:4
Slight Case of Murder, A 1935,S 12,28:5
Moore, Ralph
Everyman Today 1958,Ja 16,32:4
Moore, Randy
Latent Heterosexual, The 1968,Mr 22,52:1
Macbeth 1968,N 30,49:3
Moore, Randy (Lighting Director)
Macbeth 1968,N 30,49:3
Moore, Raymond
Good Morning, Dearie 1921,N 2,20:2
Moore, Raymond (Miscellaneous)
Divine Drudge 1933,Jl 4,16:4
Spring Dance 1936,Jl 7,22:2
Moore, Raymond (Producer)
Ladies of Creation 1931,S 9,25:1
Berlin 1931,D 31,16:1
Strange Orchestra 1933,N 29,23:2
Whatever Possessed Her 1934,Ja 26,21:2
Fresh Fields 1935,Jl 24,20:4
All Bow Down 1935,Ag 6,20:4
Romance 1935,Ag 27,23:4
Marriage Royal 1937,Jl 15,16:2
Western Union 1937,Ag 10,22:7
Hamlet 1937,Ag 24,24:4
Moore, Richard
Higher and Higher 1940,Ap 5,24:3
Moore, Robert
This Is the Army 1942,Jl 5,28:2
Cactus Flower 1965,D 9,60:2
Everything in the Garden 1967,N 30,60:1
Everything in the Garden 1967,D 10,II,5:1
Moore, Robert (Costume Designer)
Naughty-Naught '00 1946,O 21,27:5
Tenting Tonight 1947,Ap 3,32:2
Moore, Robert (Director)
Ticket-of-Leave Man, The 1961,D 23,15:1
Boys in the Band, The 1968,Ap 15,48:1
Boys in the Band, The 1968,Ap 28,II,1:6
Promises, Promises 1968,D 2,59:3
Boys in the Band, The 1969,F 18,36:1
Last of the Red Hot Lovers 1969,D 29,37:1
Gingerbread Lady, The 1970,D 14,58:3
Gingerbread Lady, The 1970,D 20,II,3:7
Moore, Robert (Original Author)
Promises, Promises 1968,D 15,II,3:1
Moore, Roger
Pin to See the Peepshow, A 1953,S 18,17:2
Concept, The 1968,My 7,51:1
Moore, Roger G
They All Come to Moscow 1933,My 12,20:6
Moore, Ronald
Mandingo 1961,My 23,43:6
Moore, Rosalind
Dominant Sex, The 1935,Ap 2,24:5
Moore, Rudy
Annie Get Your Gun 1957,Mr 9,15:5
Moore, Sam (Original Author)
Texas Li'l Darlin' 1949,N 26,10:5
Moore, Samuel R
If Booth Had Missed 1931,My 14,27:1
Moore, Scott
Musk 1920,Mr 15,13:1
Criminal at Large 1932,O 11,26:3
Shooting Star 1933,Je 13,22:2
Pure in Heart, The 1934,Mr 21,24:3
Three Wise Fools 1936,Mr 2,12:2
Tide Rising 1937,Ja 26,17:2
Bet Your Life 1937,Ap 6,20:2
Money Mad 1937,My 25,32:5
Thanks for Tomorrow 1938,S 28,28:2
Cue for Passion 1940,D 20,33:4
More the Merrier, The 1941,S 16,19:3
Dark Hammock 1944,D 12,27:8
Wind Is Ninety, The 1945,Je 22,12:2
Show Boat 1946,Ja 7,17:2

Moore, Scott—Cont

Show Boat 1956,Je 22,16:1
Show Boat 1957,Je 28,30:2
Show Boat 1961,Ap 13,32:1
Talking to You 1961,O 23,22:5
Little Eyolf 1964,Mr 17,31:1

Moore, Simeon

Ed Wynn's Carnival 1920,Ap 6,18:2

Moore, Sonia (Director)

Painted Days, The 1961,Ap 7,24:1
Sharon's Grave 1961,N 9,39:2

Moore, Sonia (Miscellaneous)

Painted Days, The 1961,Ap 7,24:1

Moore, Stan

Anvil, The 1962,O 31,33:3
Night of the Auk 1963,My 22,35:2
Live Like Pigs 1965,Je 8,48:2

Moore, Stanley (Scenic Designer)

Joyce Grenfell Requests the Pleasure
1955,O 11,48:1

Moore, Stephen (Director)

One-Act Variety Theatre; Devil Is a Good Man,
The 1940,Mr 20,36:2

Moore, Sue

Scarlet Pages 1929,S 10,26:3
Violet, The 1930,S 30,24:2
America's Sweetheart 1931,F 11,23:1
Berlin 1931,D 31,16:1
Between Two Worlds 1934,O 26,24:2

Moore, Sybil

Horse Play 1937,Ag 28,8:3

Moore, Tedde

Midsummer Night's Dream, A 1968,Je 13,54:1
Alchemist, The 1969,Je 12,51:1
Measure for Measure 1969,Je 13,41:3

Moore, Tim

Lucky Sambo 1925,Je 8,19:4
Blackbirds 1928,My 10,31:3
Blackberries of 1932 1932,Ap 5,27:5
Lew Leslie's Blackbirds of 1939 1939,F 13,12:2
Harlem Cavalcade 1942,My 2,11:2

Moore, Tom

Cup, The 1923,N 13,25:1
Beggar's Holiday 1946,D 27,13:3
She Stoops to Conquer 1949,D 29,21:3

Moore, Vera

Teaspoon Every Four Hours, A 1969,Je 16,57:1

Moore, Victor

Easy Come, Easy Go 1925,O 27,20:2
Oh, Kay! 1926,N 9,31:3
Allez-Opp! 1927,Ag 3,29:3
Funny Face 1927,N 23,28:2
Hold Everything 1928,O 11,24:2
Me for You 1929,S 22,IX,2:6
Heads Up! 1929,N 12,34:1
Prince Charming 1930,O 14,31:1
She Lived Next to the Firehouse 1931,F 11,23:1
Vaudeville (Palace) 1931,My 18,21:1
Of Thee I Sing 1931,D 28,20:1
Of Thee I Sing 1932,Mr 20,VIII,1:1
Lambs Gambol 1932,Ap 25,18:2
Of Thee I Sing 1932,My 8,VIII,1:1
Lambs Gambol 1933,Ap 24,10:1
Let 'Em Eat Cake 1933,O 23,18:1
Let 'Em Eat Cake 1933,N 12,IX,1:1
Anything Goes 1934,N 18,IX,1:7
Anything Goes 1934,N 22,26:1
Anything Goes 1935,S 15,IX,1:1
Leave It to Me! 1938,O 23,IX,3:5
Leave It to Me! 1938,N 10,32:2
Leave It to Me! 1938,N 20,IX,1:1
Leave It to Me! 1939,S 10,IX,1:1
Leave It to Me! 1940,Ja 18,27:2
Louisiana Purchase 1940,My 29,19:2
Louisiana Purchase 1940,Je 16,IX,1:1
Keep 'Em Laughing 1942,Ap 25,9:2
Hollywood Pinafore 1945,Je 1,20:1
Hollywood Pinafore 1945,Je 10,II,1:1
Nellie Bly 1946,Ja 22,32:2
Nellie Bly 1946,Ja 27,II,1:1
ANTA Album 1951,My 7,22:7
On Borrowed Time 1953,Ja 1,19:1
On Borrowed Time 1953,F 11,34:1
Carousel 1957,S 12,38:2

Moore, Virginia Lee

Polly Preferred 1923,Ja 12,13:3
Silence 1924,N 13,18:2

Moore, Walker

Sancho Panza 1923,N 27,23:1
Carolinian, The 1925,N 3,34:2

Moore, William

Bombo 1921,O 7,20:2

Moore, William Angus 2d

Merry Wives of Windsor, The 1954,F 17,27:1

Moore and Powell

Vaudeville (Palace) 1927,O 11,27:2

Moorefield, Olive

My Darlin' Aida 1952,O 28,36:4
Porgy and Bess 1965,O 20,53:3

Moorehead, Agnes

Untitled-Recital 1932,F 8,21:1
Don Juan in Hell 1951,O 23,34:4
Don Juan in Hell 1951,N 4,II,1:1
Lord Pengo 1962,N 20,41:2

Moorehead, Jean

Du Barry Was a Lady 1939,D 7,34:2
Laffing Room Only 1944,D 25,15:4

Moorehead, Natalie

Baby Cyclone, The 1927,S 13,37:4

Moorehead, S P

It's Only Natural 1922,Ap 21,13:2

Moorehouse, Marian

This Fine-Pretty World 1923,D 27,11:1
Saint, The 1924,O 13,20:3
Paolo and Francesca 1924,D 3,24:2
Mr Moneypenny 1928,O 17,26:2

Moores, Clara

Shavings 1920,F 17,18:1
Pot-Luck 1921,S 30,10:1
Cobra 1924,Ag 23,24:1
Cobra 1924,Ap 27,VIII,1:1

Moorfield, Olive

Kiss Me, Kate 1959,Ag 10,24:1

Moorhead, Natalie

Lady in Love, A 1927,F 22,22:1

Mooring, Mark (Costume Designer)

Greenwich Village Follies 1925,D 25,23:3
Song of the Flame 1925,D 31,10:2
Peggy-Ann 1926,D 28,16:3
Hit the Deck! 1927,Ap 26,32:1
Polly 1929,Ja 9,28:3

Moorman, Charlotte

Originale 1964,S 9,46:1

Moors, Dudley

Beyond the Fringe 1961,Je 25,II,3:5

Mooser, George

No Foolin' 1926,Je 25,25:1

Moosholzer, A

Wozzeck 1966,Ap 6,34:1

Mopsy (Costume Designer)

Match-Play 1966,O 12,37:1
Party for Divorce, A 1966,O 12,37:1

Mopsy (Miscellaneous)

Me Nobody Knows, The 1970,My 19,42:1

Mor, Tikva

Dybbuk, The 1964,F 4,30:2
Children of the Shadows 1964,F 27,26:1

Mora, Gene

Take a Giant Step 1956,S 26,30:1

Morales, Carmen

Bajour 1964,N 24,42:1
Sweet Charity 1966,Ja 31,22:1

Morales, Daniel

In the Summer House 1953,D 30,17:1

Morales, Maria

Flowers of Virtue, The 1942,F 6,22:2

Morales, Santiago

Tragedia del Faro, La; Tragedy of the Lighthouse,
The 1932,Je 3,23:2

Moran, Alan

Bye Bye Bonnie 1927,Ja 14,15:3

Moran, Alan (Composer)

Howdy Mr Ice 1948,Je 25,28:5
Howdy, Mr Ice of 1950 1949,My 27,24:2
Arabian Nights 1954,Je 25,15:2

Moran, Alan (Lyricist)

Howdy, Mr Ice of 1950 1949,My 27,24:2

Moran, Betty

One Flight Down 1937,D 14,32:4
Let's Face It 1941,O 30,26:2

Moran, Charles

Big Boy 1925,Ja 8,28:2
Canary Dutch 1925,S 9,22:1
Wild Man of Borneo, The 1927,S 14,29:2

Moran, Don

Love and Let Love 1968,Ja 4,30:1

Moran, Eddie

Gang's All Here, The 1931,F 19,21:3

Moran, Eileen

Iolanthe 1952,N 11,26:3

Moran, Francis

Lady Dedlock 1929,Ja 1,61:2
Young Alexander 1929,Mr 13,28:2
Lucrece 1932,D 21,22:2
Alien Corn 1933,F 21,17:2

Moran, Frank

American Tragedy, An 1926,O 12,31:2
Long Frontier, The 1935,Jl 23,24:4

Moran, George

Earl Carroll's Vanities 1927,Ja 5,18:1

Moran, Gertrude

Four Flusher, The 1925,Ap 14,27:4
Half-Caste, The 1926,Mr 30,20:4
Garrick Gaieties 1926,My 11,25:2
These Days 1928,N 13,36:2
Stepping Sisters 1930,Ap 23,24:2

Moran, James

He Who Gets Slapped 1956,F 2,18:1

Moran, Janet

Peter and the Wolf 1969,N 30,85:5

Moran, Joe

Sisters of the Chorus 1930,My 18,VIII,3:1

Moran, John

Dream Play 1926,Ja 21,18:2
East Lynne 1926,Mr 11,18:4

Moran, Kathleen

Pride and Prejudice 1935,N 6,32:4

Moran, Kathleen—Cont

Tomorrow's a Holiday! 1935,D 31,10:2
Duchess of Malfi, The 1946,O 16,35:2

Moran, Lois

This Is New York 1930,N 29,21:1
Of Thee I Sing 1931,D 28,20:1
Let 'Em Eat Cake 1933,O 23,18:1

Moran, Mary

Rope Dancers, The 1959,Mr 14,26:1

Moran, Mike

Instructions for the Running of Trains, etc on the
Erie Railway to Go Into Effect January 1,1862
1970,Ja 7,36:2

Moran, Monica

Fireworks; Fireworks for a Hot Fourth
1969,Je 12,51:1
Fireworks; Report, The 1969,Je 12,51:1

Moran, Patricia

Madre, La 1959,F 12,24:1

Moran, Rosie

Rain or Shine 1928,F 10,26:3
Sea Legs 1937,My 19,26:5
Three Waltzes 1937,D 27,10:2

Moran, Tom

Six Characters in Search of an Author
1934,D 5,29:1

Moran and Mack

Ziegfeld Follies 1920,Je 23,14:1
Greenwich Village Follies 1924,S 17,16:1
Vaudeville (Hippodrome) 1925,S 1,18:3
Greenwich Village Follies 1926,My 23,VIII,1:1
No Foolin' 1926,Je 25,25:1
Earl Carroll's Vanities 1926,Ag 25,19:4
Vanities 1927,F 22,19:1
Vaudeville (Palace) 1927,My 31,25:1
Vaudeville (Palace) 1932,My 2,13:2

Moran and Wiser

Mimic World of 1921, The 1921,Ag 18,9:2
Sons o' Fun 1941,D 2,28:2

Morand, Eugene (Translator)

Hamlet 1932,Je 12,X,1:1

Morand, Paul (Playwright)

Voyageur et l'Amour, Le 1932,Ap 3,VIII,2:2

Morando, Estelle (Playwright)

Shady Lady 1933,Jl 6,26:3

Morange, Edward (Scenic Designer)

For Valor 1935,N 19,27:5

Morard, Rene

George Dandin 1968,Je 28,36:1
Tartuffe 1968,Jl 3,28:2

Morarity, Rita

Jeweled Tree, The 1926,O 8,26:2

Morath, Max

Evening With Max Morath at the Turn of the
Century, An 1969,F 18,35:1
Evening With Max Morath at the Turn of the
Century, An 1969,Ap 3,47:1
Evening With Max Morath at the Turn of the
Century, An 1969,My 4,II,3:1

Moray, Mona

Babes in Toyland 1929,D 24,15:3
Prince of Pilsen, The 1930,Ja 14,24:3
Man Who Reclaimed His Head 1932,S 9,17:3
If I Were You 1938,Ja 25,24:2
Fabulous Invalid, The 1938,O 10,15:1
Beverly Hills 1940,N 8,24:2
Comes the Revelation 1942,My 27,26:2

Moray, Paul

Golden Dog, The 1929,D 25,21:2

Morazinski, Robert

Trial of Dmitri Karamazov, The 1958,Ja 28,30:1

Morcom, James (Costume Designer)

Thumbs Up! 1934,D 28,24:1

Morcom, James (Scenic Designer)

Case History 1938,O 22,15:2
Native Son 1941,Mr 25,26:5
Native Son 1942,O 24,10:6
Native Son 1942,N 1,VIII,1:1

Mordant, Edwin

Partners Again 1922,My 2,22:2
Carolinian, The 1925,N 3,34:2
King Can Do No Wrong, The 1927,N 17,28:4

Mordecai, David (Composer)

Show Boat 1948,S 9,33:2

Mordecai, David (Miscellaneous)

Let Freedom Sing 1942,O 6,18:2

Mordecai, David (Musical Director)

Carmen Jones 1945,My 3,26:5
Carmen Jones 1946,Ap 8,32:2
Sally 1948,My 7,31:2

Mordecai, James

Swing It 1937,Jl 23,17:2

Mordecai, Joyce

Mamba's Daughters 1953,Mr 21,12:6

Morden, Roger

Three by Ferlinghetti; Three Thousand Red Ants
1970,S 23,43:1
Three by Ferlinghetti; Victims of Amnesia, The
1970,S 23,43:1
Three by Ferlinghetti; Alligation, The
1970,S 23,43:1

Mordente, Tony

West Side Story 1957,S 27,14:4

Mordente, Tony (Choreographer)
Here's Where I Belong 1968,Mr 4,32:1
Mordente, Tony (Director)
Here's Where I Belong 1968,Mr 4,32:1
Mordkin, Michael (Choreographer)
Revenge With Music 1934,N 29,33:5
Mordkin, Mikhail
Greenwich Village Follies 1924,N 25,26:2
More, Herbert
Blood Wedding 1949,F 7,16:2
More, J Neil
Man in Possession, The 1930,N 3,19:1
More, Jay (Lighting Director)
Teaspoon Every Four Hours, A 1969,Je 16,57:1
More, Julian (Lyricist)
Irma la Douce 1960,S 30,31:2
More, Julian (Playwright)
Irma la Douce 1960,S 30,31:2
More, Kenneth
Deep Blue Sea, The 1953,Ap 4,8:6
Our Man Crichton 1964,D 23,21:1
Secretary Bird, The 1968,O 18,40:5
Secretary Bird, The 1969,S 14,94:4
More, Kent
King Midas and the Golden Touch 1948,O 25,28:3
More, Lawrence (Producer)
Manhatters, The 1927,Jl 19,27:3
More, Louise
King Midas and the Golden Touch 1948,O 25,28:3
More, Richard
Silver Tassle, The 1969,S 12,35:2
Morea, Gabor
Steambath 1970,Jl 1,49:1
Morea, Robert
Italian Straw Hat, The 1957,O 1,37:2
Romeo and Juliet 1962,Ap 3,42:1
Moreau, Adrien (Playwright)
Madame Sans-Gene 1924,N 4,30:1
Moreau, Andre (Miscellaneous)
Sixieme Etage 1938,Je 12,X,2:3
Moreau, Andree
Girofle-Girofla 1926,N 23,26:3
Moreau, Emile (Playwright)
Trial of Joan of Arc, The 1921,Mr 28,8:2
Trial of Joan of Arc, The 1921,Ap 17,VI,1:1
Moreau, Jean-Luc
Malade Imaginaire, Le 1970,F 18,40:2
Moreau, Peter (Producer)
Before You Go 1968,Ja 12,20:1
Moondreamers, The 1969,D 9,68:1
Moree, John
Transplanting Jean 1921,Ja 4,11:2
Morehouse, Edward
Good Woman of Setzuan, The 1956,D 19,41:2
Morehouse, Edward (Director)
Undercover Man 1966,Je 3,30:2
Conditioned Reflex 1967,Ja 11,51:1
Morehouse, Ralph
Deacon, The 1925,N 25,14:3
Philadelphia 1929,S 17,34:5
Ode to Liberty 1935,Jl 2,24:3
Room Service 1937,My 20,16:1
Mrs O'Brien Entertains 1939,F 9,16:3
Goodbye in the Night 1940,Mr 19,31:2
Russian Bank 1940,My 25,20:2
Morehouse, Ward (Playwright)
Gentlemen of the Press 1928,Ag 28,27:2
Gentlemen of the Press 1928,S 2,VII,1:1
Miss Quis 1937,Ap 2,18:5
Miss Quis 1937,Ap 8,20:5
Morel, Devah
Blood and Sand 1921,S 21,16:2
49ers, The 1922,N 7,14:1
Deep Tangled Wildwood, The 1923,N 6,22:1
Morel, Eugene (Playwright)
Untitled-Play 1924,F 3,VII,1:4
Morel, Isabel
In the Summer House 1953,D 30,17:1
Moreland, Barry (Choreographer)
Beaux' Stratagem, The 1970,F 10,50:2
Moreland, Beatrice
Bonehead, The 1920,Ap 13,12:1
Eyvind of the Hills 1921,F 2,14:1
Minick 1924,S 25,20:1
Something to Brag About 1925,Ag 14,14:3
Jacob Slovak 1927,O 6,28:4
Friendship 1931,S 1,30:2
Mourning Becomes Electra; Homecoming 1932,My 10,25:2
Mourning Becomes Electra; Hunted, The 1932,My 10,25:2
But for the Grace of God 1937,Ja 13,21:4
Victoria Regina 1938,O 4,20:2
Moreland, Don (Composer)
Bohikee Creek 1966,Ap 29,39:1
Moreland, Donald
John Brown's Body 1960,Je 22,31:1
Moreland, Donald (Director)
Bohikee Creek 1966,Ap 29,39:1
Moreland, Mantan
Blackbirds 1928,My 10,31:3
Lew Leslie's Blackbirds of 1930 1930,O 23,34:5
Singin' the Blues 1931,Ap 12,IX,2:1

Singin' the Blues 1931,S 17,21:3
Blackberries of 1932 1932,Ap 5,27:5
Yeah-Man 1932,My 27,27:3
Shuffle Along of 1933 1932,D 27,11:3
Waiting for Godot 1957,Ja 22,25:1
Moreland, Margaret
Cradle Snatchers 1925,S 8,28:2
Morell, Andre
Timon of Athens 1952,Je 8,II,3:1
South 1955,My 2,17:4
Uncle Vanya 1962,Jl 17,18:4
Morell, Carol
Slow Dance on the Killing Ground 1968,N 3,87:1
Morell, Dene
Lady Windermere's Fan 1927,F 27,VII,2:3
Morelli, Carlos
Leyenda del Beso, La 1942,N 20,26:4
Morelli, Marcel
Lady, The 1923,D 5,23:2
Morelli, Wanda
Paese dei Campanelli, Il; Land of Bells, The 1935,My 10,25:4
Morely, Carol
Dames at Sea 1970,S 24,60:1
Morely, Ruth (Costume Designer)
Billy Budd 1951,F 18,II,1:1
Morely, Victor
Love for Love 1936,Je 30,15:4
Morencey, Germaine
Farmer's Wife, The 1924,O 10,22:3
Moreno
Mot de Cambronne, Le 1936,O 25,X,3:8
Moreno, Hilda
Smiles 1930,N 19,19:2
Cuando Los Hijos De Eva No Son Los Hijos De Adan 1937,My 1,17:4
Moreno, J L (Dr)
Untitled-Play 1931,Ap 6,24:4
Moreno, James
I Was Waiting for You 1933,N 14,23:3
Moreno, Jim
They Knew What They Wanted 1949,F 17,28:2
Out West of Eighth 1951,S 21,20:3
Moreno, Marguerite
Folle de Chaillot, La 1945,D 20,17:4
Moreno, Paco
Pleasure Bound 1929,F 19,22:4
Moreno, Rita
Sign in Sidney Brustein's Window, The 1964,O 16,32:1
Gantry 1970,F 16,44:1
Moreno, Rosita
Pleasure Bound 1929,F 19,22:4
All in Fun 1940,N 22,26:2
Moreno, Yolanda
Wonderful World of Burlesque, The 1965,Ap 29,38:1
Morenschildt, Mme
Revue Russe, The 1922,O 6,28:1
Morenus, David (Miscellaneous)
Cocktails of 1934 1934,My 5,22:1
Moret, Solange
Avril 1932,O 16,IX,2:2
Moreto (Playwright)
Donna Diana 1936,Je 28,IX,2:1
Moretti, Marcello
Arlecchino, the Servant of Two Masters 1956,Ag 28,31:1
Servant of Two Masters, The 1960,F 24,42:2
Servant of Two Masters, The 1960,F 29,31:5
Moretti, Raoul (Composer)
Trois Jeunes Filles Nues; Three Young Maids From the Folies Bergere 1929,Mr 5,28:2
Comte Obligado 1929,Mr 12,26:2
Soeurs Hortensias, Les 1934,My 13,IX,2:2
Joies du Capitole, Les 1935,Ap 21,IX,2:1
Moreux, Christiane
Ice Capades 1956,S 13,41:2
Morey, Art
Dirtiest Show in Town, The 1970,My 2,21:1
Dirtiest Show in Town, The 1970,Je 29,43:2
Morey, Cynthia
Iolanthe 1955,S 28,38:1
Mikado, The 1955,S 30,20:2
Princess Ida 1955,O 14,22:3
Ruddigore 1955,O 21,32:2
Morey, James T
Not Herbert 1926,Ja 27,16:2
Trapped 1928,S 12,25:3
Noble Experiment, The 1930,O 28,21:4
Morey, Larry (Composer)
Ice Follies 1957,Ja 16,36:1
Ice Follies 1958,Ja 15,26:2
Ice Follies 1959,Ja 14,30:1
Ice Follies 1960,Ja 13,20:1
Ice Follies 1961,Ja 11,25:2
Ice Follies 1962,Ja 10,24:6
Ice Follies 1963,Ja 10,5:2
Ice Follies 1964,Ja 8,41:2
Ice Follies 1965,Ja 13,35:1
Ice Follies 1966,Ja 12,27:6
Morey, Larry (Lyricist)
Ice Follies 1962,Ja 10,24:6

Morey, Larry (Lyricist)—Cont
Ice Follies 1964,Ja 8,41:2
Morey, Luella
Trimmed in Scarlet 1920,F 3,18:1
Octoroon, The 1929,Mr 13,28:3
Morey, Molly
Merry Merry 1925,S 25,24:3
Morfogen, George
Trial of Dmitri Karamazov, The 1958,Ja 28,30:1
Othello 1958,Jl 4,16:1
Cave Dwellers, The 1961,O 16,34:2
Good Soldier Schweik, The 1963,Ap 9,57:1
Once in a Lifetime 1964,Ja 29,20:1
Morfogen, George (Director)
Golem, The 1959,F 26,38:2
Morfogen, George (Producer)
Golem, The 1959,F 26,38:2
Morfogen, James
Bluebeard 1970,My 5,58:1
Morford, B F Vail
Caesar and Cleopatra 1927,N 6,IX,2:1
Morford, S D
Caesar and Cleopatra 1927,N 6,IX,2:1
Morgan, Adrian
Erminie 1921,Ja 4,11:1
Morgan, Agnes
Madras House, The 1921,O 31,18:2
Morgan, Agnes (Director)
Little Clay Cart, The 1924,D 6,13:3
Romantic Young Lady, The 1926,My 5,24:3
Grand Street Follies, The 1926,Je 16,23:2
Lovers and Enemies 1927,S 21,27:1
If 1927,O 26,26:2
If 1927,O 30,IX,1:1
Love Nest, The 1927,D 23,17:1
Maya 1928,F 22,19:1
Grand Street Follies, The 1928,My 29,16:2
Grand Street Follies, The 1929,My 2,20:4
If Love Were All 1931,N 14,14:5
American Holiday 1936,F 22,13:3
Inconstant Moon, The 1937,Ag 18,15:2
Jeannie 1940,N 13,29:2
Papa Is All 1942,Ja 7,22:2
I Killed the Count 1942,S 4,18:1
Morgan, Agnes (Lyricist)
Grand Street Follies, The 1925,Je 19,24:1
Grand Street Follies, The 1926,Je 16,23:2
Grand Street Follies, The 1927,My 20,22:3
Grand Street Follies, The 1928,My 29,16:2
Grand Street Follies, The 1929,My 2,20:4
Hero Is Born, A 1937,O 2,18:6
Morgan, Agnes (Musical Director)
Hero Is Born, A 1937,O 2,18:6
Morgan, Agnes (Playwright)
Grand Street Follies, The 1925,Je 19,24:1
Grand Street Follies, The 1926,Je 16,23:2
Grand Street Follies, The 1927,My 20,22:3
Grand Street Follies, The 1928,My 29,16:2
Grand Street Follies, The 1929,My 2,20:4
Morgan, Agnes (Producer)
I Killed the Count 1942,S 4,18:1
Morgan, Al (Playwright)
Oh Captain! 1958,F 5,21:2
Minor Miracle 1965,O 8,4:3
Morgan, Alfred D
Rosalinda; Fledermaus, Die 1942,O 29,26:5
Morgan, Angela
Clouds of the Sun 1922,My 6,11:2
Morgan, Aniko
Here's Where I Belong 1968,Mr 4,32:1
Morgan, Ann
Truckline Cafe 1946,F 28,19:4
Morgan, Brewster (Producer)
Macbeth 1930,F 13,9:6
Macbeth 1930,Mr 2,IX,2:4
Morgan, Bruce
Dora Mobridge 1930,Ap 21,20:2
Morgan, Buddy
Inside Story 1942,O 30,22:2
Morgan, C S Jr (Playwright)
Don Quixote, Esquire 1920,My 7,12:6
Morgan, C William
Trial by Jury 1934,S 14,24:3
Yeomen of the Guard, The 1934,S 21,28:3
Trial by Jury 1936,S 1,24:4
Yeomen of the Guard, The 1936,S 15,37:2
Trial by Jury 1939,Ja 6,25:1
Yeomen of the Guard, The 1939,Ja 24,17:1
Trial by Jury 1948,Ja 6,27:2
Yeomen of the Guard, The 1948,F 3,30:2
Patience 1948,F 10,27:2
Morgan, Carey (Composer)
Greenwich Village Follies 1921,S 1,18:3
Morgan, Charles
Desert Song, The 1926,D 1,24:2
Morgan, Charles (Director)
That's That 1924,Ap 30,19:2
Joan of Arkansas 1925,Ap 5,16:1
Sale and a Sailor, A, or Glory! What Price! 1926,Ap 25,30:4
Hoot Mon, or Clans Across the Sea 1927,My 8,29:4
Morgan, Charles (Playwright)
Flashing Stream, The 1938,S 2,21:4
Flashing Stream, The 1938,S 18,X,1:4

Morgan, Charles (Playwright)—Cont

Flashing Stream, The 1939,Ap 11,19:2
Flashing Stream, The 1939,Ap 16,X,1:1
River Line, The 1952,S 7,II,3:1
River Line, The 1952,N 9,II,3:2
Burning Glass, The 1954,Mr 5,15:2
Burning Glass, The 1954,Mr 14,II,1:1
Burning Glass, The 1954,Ap 11,II,2:1
River Line, The 1957,Ja 3,29:2

Morgan, Charles S Jr (Director)

Don Quixote, Esquire 1920,My 7,12:6
Here's Howe 1923,Ap 26,19:3

Morgan, Charles S Jr (Miscellaneous)

Somebody's Lion 1921,Ap 13,20:1

Morgan, Chuck

Teahouse of the August Moon, The 1953,O 16,32:1

Morgan, Clark

Major Barbara 1954,Je 30,23:2
Merchant of Venice, The 1955,Ja 8,9:7
Juno and the Paycock 1955,F 24,20:4
Egg and I, The 1958,S 11,43:4
Mandingo 1961,My 23,43:6
Flora, the Red Menace 1965,My 12,41:2

Morgan, Claudia

Top O' the Hill 1929,N 27,30:4
Dancing Partner 1930,Ag 6,24:2
Modern Virgin, A 1931,My 21,33:4
People on the Hill 1931,S 26,25:5
Marriage for Three 1931,N 12,30:5
Thoroughbred 1933,N 7,29:2
False Dreams, Farewell 1934,Ja 16,18:3
Gentlewoman 1934,Mr 23,28:4
Are You Decent? 1934,Ap 20,16:2
Bridal Quilt 1934,O 11,28:5
Lord Blesses the Bishop, The 1934,N 28,24:5
Lady Detained, A 1935,Ja 10,23:3
De Luxe 1935,Mr 6,22:2
On Stage 1935,O 30,16:6
Call It a Day 1936,Ja 29,15:2
Call It a Day 1936,F 9,X,1:1
Dr Knock 1936,Jl 14,22:1
And Stars Remain 1936,O 13,32:2
Masque of Kings, The 1937,Ja 31,XI,2:1
Masque of the Kings, The 1937,F 9,19:4
Storm Over Patsy 1937,Mr 2,16:4
Storm Over Patsy 1937,Mr 9,26:4
In Clover 1937,S 21,29:1
In Clover 1937,O 14,23:1
Merely Murder 1937,N 16,26:1
Merely Murder 1937,D 4,21:4
Wine of Choice 1938,F 22,18:4
Wine of Choice 1938,F 27,X,1:1
Gas Light 1939,Ag 30,20:8
Man Who Came to Dinner, The 1940,F 10,19:5
Man Who Came to Dinner, The 1940,F 18,IX,3:6
Sun Field, The 1942,D 10,33:2
Ten Little Indians 1944,Je 28,21:2
Venus Observed 1952,F 14,24:2
Apple Cart, The 1956,O 19,23:1
Fig Leaf in Her Bonnet, A 1961,Je 15,50:1

Morgan, Dan

Afternoon Storm 1948,Ap 12,24:2
Miss Lonelyhearts 1957,O 4,26:2
Guests of the Nation 1958,Je 27,18:5
Foenix in Choir 1958,O 28,40:2
Confederates, The 1959,S 29,45:1
Endecott and the Red Cross 1968,My 7,50:1
Nobody Hears A Broken Drum 1970,Mr 20,55:1

Morgan, Dannie

Earth 1927,Mr 10,23:1

Morgan, David

If This Be Treason 1935,S 24,28:2

Morgan, David (Miscellaneous)

Bench, The 1968,Mr 5,35:2

Morgan, Diana (Lyricist)

Your Number's Up 1936,D 24,22:2

Morgan, Diana (Playwright)

Your Number's Up 1936,D 24,22:2
Bats in the Belfry 1937,Mr 12,19:4
Bats in the Belfry 1937,Ap 4,X,2:4
House in the Square 1940,Ap 14,IX,1:6
Starcross Story, The 1954,Ja 14,25:2

Morgan, Dixon

Fol-De-Rol 1937,D 11,22:4

Morgan, Dixon (Composer)

Fol-De-Rol 1937,D 11,22:4

Morgan, Dixon (Director)

Made in France 1930,N 12,21:1
Mimie Scheller 1936,O 1,28:4
Curtain Call 1937,Ap 23,24:7

Morgan, Dixon (Lyricist)

Fol-De-Rol 1937,D 11,22:4

Morgan, Dixon (Scenic Designer)

Downstream 1926,Ja 12,28:1

Morgan, Eddie

How's Your Health? 1929,N 27,30:3

Morgan, Elizabeth

Mimic World of 1921, The 1921,Ag 18,9:2
Elsie Janis and Her Gang 1922,Ja 17,13:2
American Holiday 1936,F 22,13:3

Morgan, Ellen

Without Love 1942,N 11,28:1

Morgan, Eugene

Cabaret 1966,N 21,62:1

Morgan, Fisher

Iolanthe 1955,S 28,38:1
Mikado, The 1955,S 30,20:2
Yeomen of the Guard, The 1955,O 4,39:2
Pirates of Penzance, The 1955,O 7,21:1
Princess Ida 1955,O 14,22:3
Ruddigore 1955,O 21,32:2

Morgan, Frank

Her Family Tree 1920,D 28,9:2
White Villa, The 1921,F 15,7:1
Triumph of X, The 1921,Ag 25,8:2
Dream Maker, The 1921,N 22,17:1
Seventh Heaven 1922,O 31,11:1
Lullaby, The 1923,S 19,5:3
Firebrand, The 1924,O 16,33:1
Weak Woman, A 1926,Ja 27,16:3
Gentlemen Prefer Blondes 1926,S 29,23:1
Puppets of Passion 1927,F 25,24:4
Hearts Are Trumps! 1927,Ap 8,21:1
Tenth Avenue 1927,Ag 16,31:1
Rosalie 1928,Ja 11,26:3
Among the Married 1929,O 4,24:3
Amorous Antic, The 1929,D 3,29:2
Topaze 1930,F 13,25:3
Topaze 1930,Mr 2,IX,1:1
Band Wagon, The 1931,My 17,VIII,3:2
Band Wagon, The 1931,Je 4,31:3
Band Wagon, The 1931,Je 14,VIII,1:1
Band Wagon, The 1931,S 27,VIII,3:7
Hey, Nonny, Nonny! 1932,Je 7,22:3

Morgan, Gabrielle

Caesar and Cleopatra 1935,Ag 22,21:1
Romeo and Juliet 1935,D 24,10:2
County Chairman, The 1936,My 26,26:5

Morgan, Gary

Comic Strip 1958,My 15,26:2
Gift of Time, A 1962,F 23,34:1

Morgan, George

Great Way, The 1921,N 8,28:2
Jazz a La Carte 1922,Je 3,8:3
What a Relief 1935,D 14,10:6
Ronde, La 1960,My 10,44:2
Borak 1960,D 14,51:1
Noontide 1961,Je 2,37:1
Don Carlos 1962,F 28,27:5
Storm, The 1962,Mr 31,17:2

Morgan, Gilbert

Family Upstairs, The 1933,O 28,20:6
Distant City, The 1941,S 23,27:5

Morgan, Helen

George White's Scandals 1925,Je 23,24:2
Vaudeville (Palace) 1927,Ja 25,18:3
Show Boat 1927,D 28,26:1
Show Boat 1928,Ja 8,VIII,1:1
Ziegfeld's Midnight Frolic 1929,F 19,22:4
Sweet Adeline 1929,Ag 25,VIII,3:1
Sweet Adeline 1929,S 4,33:1
Vaudeville (Palace) 1930,Mr 31,24:2
Vaudeville (Palace) 1931,F 2,23:3
Ziegfeld Follies 1931,Jl 2,30:5
Show Boat 1932,My 20,22:2
Memory 1934,My 13,IX,2:6

Morgan, Henry (Miscellaneous)

Alive and Kicking 1950,Ja 18,25:5

Morgan, Howard

Guest of Honor, The 1920,S 21,12:1
Twelve Miles Out 1925,N 17,29:2
Excess Baggage 1927,D 27,24:2
Show Girl 1929,Jl 3,19:3
Jamboree 1932,N 25,18:4
All the King's Horses 1934,Ja 31,21:3

Morgan, Jack

Oh, Promise Me 1930,N 25,31:1

Morgan, Jane

Ziegfeld Follies 1957,Mr 2,19:2
Jack Benny 1963,Mr 1,10:5
Mame 1969,Ja 5,79:4

Morgan, Jim Band

Vaudeville (Hippodrome) 1925,D 29,21:2

Morgan, Joan

Mrs Patterson 1954,D 2,37:1
Who Was That Lady I Saw You With?
1958,Mr 4,33:2
Loss of Roses, A 1959,N 30,27:1

Morgan, Joan (Playwright)

This Was a Woman 1944,Ap 30,II,1:3

Morgan, John

Opportunity 1920,Jl 31,5:1

Morgan, Johnny

What's Up 1943,N 12,24:6
New Moon, The 1944,My 18,16:2

Morgan, Judson

Yanqui and the Senorita, The 1952,Ag 8,8:7

Morgan, Juliana (Producer)

All Editions 1936,D 23,17:2
Penny Wise 1937,Ap 20,28:6

Morgan, Kate

Cradle Song 1921,Mr 1,18:2
Two Blocks Away 1921,Ag 31,8:3
Shadow, The 1922,Ap 25,14:2
Roger Bloomer 1923,Mr 2,18:3
Easy Mark, The 1924,Ag 27,14:2
Sam Abramovitch 1927,Ja 20,20:5

Morgan, Kate—Cont

Elmer the Great 1928,S 25,29:1
Distant Drums 1932,Ja 19,24:3
Good Earth, The 1932,O 18,23:4

Morgan, L G (Mrs)

One Woman's Husband 1920,Mr 23,9:3

Morgan, Lee (Original Author)

Shakuntala 1959,S 10,41:2

Morgan, Leone

Anything Might Happen 1923,F 25,VII,1:1

Morgan, Mabel

Half-Caste, The 1926,Mr 30,20:4

Morgan, Marion Dancers

Vaudeville (Palace) 1923,My 15,22:2
Vaudeville (Hippodrome) 1924,Ja 22,15:6

Morgan, Mary

Respectfully Yours 1947,My 14,29:4

Morgan, Michele

Post Road 1949,Ap 28,27:3

Morgan, Miles (Miscellaneous)

Relapse, The 1950,N 23,54:2
Henry V 1956,Jl 7,11:2
Saint Joan 1956,S 12,42:1

Morgan, Miles (Musical Director)

Beggar's Opera, The 1957,Mr 14,35:1

Morgan, Miss (Playwright)

Grand Street Follies, The 1928,Je 3,VIII,1:1

Morgan, Mona

So That's That 1925,D 15,28:3

Morgan, Norman

Burlesque 1946,D 26,30:3

Morgan, Paris

Born Yesterday 1946,F 5,18:2

Morgan, Patricia

Laughing Woman, The 1936,O 14,30:1

Morgan, Paul

An und Aus 1926,D 5,VIII,8:7
Casanova 1928,N 4,IX,2:1

Morgan, Philip

Founders, The 1957,My 14,39:1

Morgan, Ralph

Poppy God, The 1921,Ag 30,10:1
Poppy God, The 1921,S 4,VI,1:1
National Anthem, The 1922,Ja 24,16:3
In Love With Love 1923,Ag 7,20:1
Cobra 1924,Ap 23,24:1
Cobra 1924,Ap 27,VIII,1:1
Dagger, The 1925,S 10,28:1
Joker, The 1925,N 17,29:1
Weak Woman, A 1926,Ja 27,16:3
Damn the Tears 1927,Ja 22,11:1
Woman of Bronze, The 1927,Je 16,25:4
Romancing 'Round 1927,O 4,32:4
Take My Advice 1927,N 2,24:3
Clutching Claw, The 1928,F 15,20:1
Strange Interlude 1928,D 18,37:3
Sweet Stranger 1930,O 22,23:3
Strange Interlude 1931,F 22,VIII,1:3
Fledgling 1940,N 28,29:2
Moon Is Down, The 1942,Ap 8,22:2
This, Too, Shall Pass 1946,My 1,32:4
Three Wishes for Jamie 1952,Mr 22,9:2

Morgan, Robbi

Curley McDimple 1969,N 25,53:1

Morgan, Robert

Story of Mary Surratt, The 1947,F 10,25:2
Sister Oakes 1949,Ap 25,19:4
Post Road 1949,Ap 28,27:3

Morgan, Roger (Lighting Director)

Witches' Sabbath 1962,Ap 20,22:2
At Sea 1962,Ap 24,33:1
Alcestis Comes Back 1962,Ap 24,33:1
We're Civilized? 1962,N 9,30:1
Knack, The 1964,My 28,42:2
Kiss Mama 1964,O 2,30:1
Othello 1964,O 13,48:1
Room, The 1964,D 10,62:1
Slight Ache, A 1964,D 10,62:1
Friday Night; Mary Agnes Is Thirty-Five
1965,F 9,42:5
Friday Night; River, The 1965,F 9,42:5
Friday Night; Passport 1965,F 9,42:5
Great Western Union, The 1965,F 10,45:1
Baal 1965,My 7,33:2
Troubled Waters 1965,Je 4,40:2
Medea 1965,N 29,46:1
Jonah! 1966,F 16,52:1
Half Horse, Half Alligator 1966,Mr 14,37:2
Journey of the Fifth Horse, The 1966,Ap 22,36:1
World of Gunter Grass, The 1966,Ap 27,38:1
Long Christmas Dinner, The 1966,S 7,53:1
Queens of France 1966,S 7,53:1
Happy Journey to Trenton and Camden, The
1966,S 7,53:1
Who's Got His Own 1966,O 13,52:1
Under the Weather 1966,O 28,35:1
Fragments 1967,O 3,56:1
Basement, The 1967,O 3,56:1
Ceremony of Innocence, The 1968,Ja 2,33:1
I Only Want an Answer 1968,F 6,36:1
Saturday Night 1968,F 26,43:1
Electronic Nigger, The 1968,Mr 9,23:2
Clara's Ole Man 1968,Mr 9,23:2
Son, Come Home, A 1968,Mr 9,23:2

Morgan, Roger (Lighting Director)—Cont

Endecott and the Red Cross 1968,My 7,50:1
Sweet Eros 1968,N 22,38:1
Witness 1968,N 22,38:1
Brother to Dragons 1968,D 8,86:1
Sudden and Accidental Re-education of Horse
Johnson, The 1968,D 19,63:1
Peace 1969,Ja 28,49:1
World War 2 1/2 1969,Mr 25,40:1
Honest-to-God Schnozzola, The 1969,Ap 22,40:2
Leader, The 1969,Ap 22,40:2
Papp 1969,My 6,39:1
Mercy Street 1969,O 28,43:1
Wilson in the Promise Land 1970,Ja 11,78:1
Dr Galley 1970,Ja 23,25:1
Transfers 1970,Ja 23,25:1
Rooming House, The 1970,Ja 23,25:1
Forensic and the Navigators 1970,Ap 2,43:1
Unseen Hand, The 1970,Ap 2,43:1
Two Times One; Last Straw, The 1970,Ap 5,76:4
Two Times One; Duet for Solo Voice
1970,Ap 5,76:4
Nest, The 1970,Ap 10,46:1
Wilson in the Promise Land 1970,My 27,41:1
Colette 1970,O 15,58:1
Gandhi 1970,O 21,37:1
Saved 1970,O 29,57:1
Sunday Dinner 1970,N 3,28:1
Castro Complex, The 1970,N 19,40:1
One Night Stands of a Noisy Passenger; Last
Stand 1970,D 31,8:3
One Night Stands of a Noisy Passenger; Passage,
Un 1970,D 31,8:3
One Night Stands of a Noisy Passenger; Noisy
Passenger, The 1970,D 31,8:3
Morgan, Ruth
Whoopee 1929,Ag 6,29:4
Smiles 1930,N 19,19:2
Morgan, Sonny
Kongi's Harvest 1968,Ap 15,49:1
Malcochon 1969,Ap 2,37:1
Morgan, Stuart Dancers
High Kickers 1941,N 1,21:2
Keep 'Em Laughing 1942,Ap 25,9:2
Morgan, Sydney
White-Headed Boy, The 1921,S 16,20:1
Plough and the Stars, The 1927,N 29,30:2
Juno and the Paycock 1927,D 20,32:2
Hairy Ape, The 1931,My 12,29:4
Morgan, Ted (Sport)
Top Banana 1951,N 2,19:2
Morgan, Terry
Corn Is Green, The 1940,N 27,27:2
Skin of Our Teeth, The 1945,Mr 20,22:8
Morgan, Tom
He Loved the Ladies 1927,My 11,29:2
John Brown 1934,Ja 23,22:3
Sweet River 1936,O 29,30:2
Mr Peebles and Mr Hooker 1946,O 11,29:2
Morgan, Victor
Two Seconds 1931,O 10,20:6
Devil's Little Game, The 1932,Ag 2,20:4
Morgan, Virginia
First Flight 1925,S 18,26:2
Playing the Game 1927,D 20,32:5
Blue and the Gray, The; War Is Hell Gray, The
1929,D 27,26:4
Young and Beautiful, The 1955,O 3,23:2
Morgan, William
Dawn 1924,N 25,27:1
Off the Record; Mayor Answers the Newspapers!
Wow! 1935,Je 19,23:3
Window Shopping 1938,D 24,13:2
Morgan and Mack
Greenwich Village Follies 1924,S 28,VII,1:1
Morgan and Stone
Vaudeville (Palace) 1931,Ag 3,15:7
Morganstern, C W (Producer)
Sex 1926,Ap 27,22:4
57 Bowery 1928,Ja 27,14:3
Morganstern, Constance
Homme et Ses Fantomes, L' 1924,N 14,16:1
Sex 1926,Ap 27,22:4
Morganthaler, Leonard
Magdalena 1948,S 21,31:2
Morganti, James
Veronica's Veil 1950,F 12,II,1:5
Morgensen, Angel
Trojan Women, The 1941,Ap 9,32:5
Morgenstein, Joseph (Playwright)
Lovey 1965,Mr 26,27:1
Morgenstern, Albert
Sound of Hunting, A 1954,Ap 7,41:1
Night Circus, The 1958,D 3,44:1
Morgenstern, Sam (Composer)
Tom Sawyer - Ballad of the Mississippi
1947,D 27,11:3
Merchant of Venice, The 1962,F 3,13:2
Morgenstern, Sam (Miscellaneous)
O Marry Me 1961,O 28,13:1
Mori, Masayuki
Othello 1960,S 11,II,7:1
Mori, Torao (Miscellaneous)
Rashomon 1959,Ja 28,36:2

Moriang, Lillian
One Woman's Husband 1920,Mr 23,9:3
Moriarty, Michael
Antony and Cleopatra 1963,Je 21,33:1
As You Like It 1963,Jl 17,19:2
Winter's Tale, The 1963,Ag 16,14:1
Love's Labour's Lost 1965,Je 16,46:1
Troilus and Cressida 1965,Ag 13,17:1
Skin of Our Teeth, The 1966,Je 2,51:1
As You Like It 1966,Je 4,19:1
Shoemaker's Holiday, The 1967,Je 3,19:1
Harpers Ferry 1967,Je 6,52:2
Visit, The 1967,S 13,41:1
Master Builder, The 1968,Je 22,26:1
Resistible Rise of Arturo Ui, The 1968,Ag 8,25:1
Merton of the Movies 1968,S 26,62:1
Resistible Rise of Arturo Ui, The 1968,D 23,44:1
Mourning Becomes Electra 1969,S 7,II,1:2
Jungle of Cities 1970,Mr 1,75:2
Moriarty, Paul
Contractor, The 1970,Ag 17,32:1
Moricz, Sigmund (Playwright)
Uri Muri 1928,Ap 15,IX,4:1
Nem Elhetek Muzsikaszo Nelkul
1928,D 30,VIII,4:4
Be Good Till You Die 1929,D 29,VIII,4:1
Lottery, The 1930,N 23,IX,3:5
Mories, Fred G
Power of Darkness, The 1920,Ja 22,22:1
Morill, Theodore
Gondoliers, The 1964,Mr 28,14:1
Morin, Albert
What Price Glory 1949,Mr 3,33:2
Morin, Pierre
Procureur Hallers, Le 1924,N 13,18:1
Homme et Ses Fantomes, L' 1924,N 14,16:1
Merchant of Venice, The 1924,N 18,23:2
Bourgeois Gentilhomme, Le 1924,N 20,21:2
Taming of the Shrew, The 1924,N 25,27:3
Morino, Ione
Donna Del Mare, La; Lady From the Sea, The
1923,O 30,17:1
Cosi Sia; Thy Will be Done 1923,N 14,29:2
Porta Chiusa, La; Closed Door, The 1923,N 21,23:1
Citta Morta, La; Dead City, The 1923,N 28,14:1
Morino, Maria
Spretti; Ghosts 1923,N 7,14:1
Cosi Sia; Thy Will be Done 1923,N 14,29:2
Moris, Boris
Motel Peissi, The Contor's Kid 1934,N 29,33:3
Morishige, Hisaya
Fiddler on the Roof 1967,S 7,50:1
Morison, Elizabeth
Watched Pot, The 1933,My 5,13:7
Panic 1935,Mr 16,18:4
Morison, Patricia
Two Bouquets, The 1938,Je 1,19:2
Allah Be Praised! 1944,Ap 21,14:2
Kiss Me, Kate 1948,D 31,10:3
Kiss Me, Kate 1951,Mr 9,30:5
Kiss Me, Kate 1965,My 13,31:1
Morison, Rose
Laugh, Clown, Laugh! 1923,N 29,30:1
Diff'rent 1938,Ja 26,26:4
Pygmalion 1938,Ja 27,16:3
Captain Jinks of the Horse Marines 1938,Ja 28,16:2
Coriolanus 1938,F 2,14:5
Moriss
Diloy le Chemineau 1926,N 14,VIII,2:1
Morissey, Will (Producer)
All-Star Idlers of 1921, The 1921,Jl 16,5:2
Morisson, Joseph
In the Night Watch 1921,Ja 31,10:1
Moritz, Al
Follies of 1910, The 1960,Ja 15,37:3
Moritz, Al (Composer)
Slice It Thin 1945,My 11,22:5
Blue Holiday 1945,My 22,13:3
Moritz, Al (Director)
Hook'n Ladder 1952,Ap 30,31:2
Sable Brush, The 1956,N 28,41:1
Moritz, Al (Playwright)
Follies of 1910, The 1960,Ja 15,37:3
Moritz, Al (Producer)
Hook'n Ladder 1952,Ap 30,31:2
Moriya, Shizu
Teahouse of the August Moon, The 1953,O 16,32:1
Teahouse of the August Moon, The 1956,N 9,33:2
Mork, Ania Romaine
Romeo and Juliet 1956,F 24,20:4
Mork, Donald
Hamlet 1954,Ap 24,15:2
Twelfth Night 1954,N 10,42:2
Merchant of Venice, The 1955,F 23,23:2
Moby Dick 1955,Ap 26,25:3
Julius Caesar 1955,Jl 13,20:1
Midsummer Night's Dream, A 1956,Ja 14,12:2
Romeo and Juliet 1956,F 24,20:4
Morka, Madeleine
Remains to be Seen 1951,O 4,37:1
Arms and the Man 1956,O 2,39:4
Morka, Madelon
They Knew What They Wanted 1949,F 17,28:2

Morlacchi, Lucilla
Venetian Twins, The 1968,My 29,23:1
Morlay, Gaby
Felix 1926,O 10,VIII,2:1
Melo 1929,Ap 7,X,1:3
Morley, Carol
Adaptation 1969,F 11,27:1
Adaptation 1970,Mr 12,46:1
Morley, Charles
Joyful Noise, A 1966,D 16,57:1
Morley, Christopher
Our Town 1940,Je 30,35:5
Morley, Christopher (Composer)
Shoestring Revue 1929,N 23,19:2
Morley, Christopher (Lyricist)
Shoestring Revue 1929,N 23,19:2
Morley, Christopher (Original Author)
Thunder on the Left 1928,Ag 19,VII,1:1
Thunder on the Left 1933,N 1,25:2
Morley, Christopher (Playwright)
Thursday Evening 1923,My 9,14:4
Thunder on the Left 1928,O 21,IX,1:3
Pleased to Meet You 1928,O 30,27:2
Second Mate, The 1930,Mr 25,34:5
Bare Facts of Today 1930,Ap 17,24:4
Rag Picker of Paris, The: or, Modest Modiste
1935,N 12,23:7
Soft Shoulders 1940,Jl 18,22:5
Trojan Horse, The 1940,O 31,28:3
Morley, Christopher (Producer)
After Dark 1928,D 11,35:2
Black Crook, The 1929,Mr 12,26:5
Star of Bengal 1929,S 26,27:2
Shoestring Revue 1929,N 23,19:2
Blue and the Gray, The; War Is Hell Gray, The
1929,D 27,26:4
Morley, Heinz (Playwright)
Music in May 1929,Ap 2,29:1
Morley, James
Me and Harry 1942,Ap 3,24:6
Pin to See the Peepshow, A 1953,S 18,17:2
Morley, John
Emperor Jones, The 1936,Ag 11,24:6
Othello 1937,Ja 7,16:4
Afternoon Storm 1948,Ap 12,24:2
Lost in the Stars 1949,O 31,21:2
Investigation, The 1966,O 5,40:1
Morley, Karen
Somewhere in France 1941,Ap 29,16:8
Walrus and the Carpenter, The 1941,N 10,20:2
Hedda Gabler 1942,Ja 30,22:2
Little Darling 1942,O 28,26:2
Major Barbara 1954,Je 30,23:2
Banker's Daughter, The 1962,Ja 23,37:1
Morley, Malcolm (Director)
Barbara's Wedding 1930,O 9,21:1
Father, The 1931,O 9,21:1
Morley, Malcolm (Playwright)
Emperor of Make-Believe, The 1936,Mr 17,25:5
Emperor of Make-Believe, The 1936,Jl 5,IX,1:8
Morley, Natalja
Musk 1920,Mr 15,13:1
Morley, Robert
All-Star Idlers of 1921, The 1921,Jl 16,5:2
Oscar Wilde 1936,S 30,29:4
Oscar Wilde 1936,O 18,X,3:8
Great Romancer, The 1937,Je 16,26:3
Great Romancer, The 1937,Jl 4,X,1:4
Oscar Wilde 1938,O 11,20:2
Oscar Wilde 1938,O 16,IX,1:1
First Gentleman, The 1945,Jl 19,18:8
First Gentleman, The 1945,Ag 5,II,1:2
Edward, My Son 1948,O 1,30:2
Edward My Son 1948,O 10,II,1:1
Likely Tale, A 1956,Ap 8,II,3:1
Majority of One, A 1960,Mr 10,37:5
Time to Laugh, A 1962,Ap 25,31:4
Halfway up the Tree 1967,N 24,60:4
How the Other Half Loves 1970,Ag 7,23:1
How the Other Half Loves 1970,S 11,33:2
Morley, Robert (Director)
Once More With Feeling 1959,Jl 10,30:1
Morley, Robert (Playwright)
Short Story 1935,N 5,33:2
Short Story 1935,D 1,XI,5:3
Goodness, How Sad 1938,O 19,18:6
Goodness, How Sad 1938,O 6,IX,3:5
Edward, My Son 1948,O 1,30:2
Edward My Son 1948,O 10,II,1:1
Morley, Robert (Producer)
Tunnel of Love, The 1957,D 5,47:2
Morley, Ruth (Costume Designer)
Mrs Warren's Profession 1950,O 26,39:2
Cellar and the Well, The 1950,D 11,30:2
Billy Budd 1951,F 12,18:3
Night Music 1951,Ap 9,29:6
Long Days, The 1951,Ap 21,10:5
Scarecrow, The 1953,Je 17,31:1
Little Clay Cart, The 1953,Jl 1,25:1
Pin to See the Peepshow, A 1953,S 18,17:2
Knight of the Burning Pestle, The 1953,O 24,13:2
Doll's House, A 1954,N 15,32:2
Troublemakers, The 1954,D 31,11:3

Morley, Ruth (Costume Designer)—Cont

Merchant of Venice, The 1955,Ja 8,9:7
Miser, The 1955,Mr 18,34:2
Inherit the Wind 1955,Ap 22,20:2
Moon for the Misbegotten, A 1957,My 3,21:2
Cave Dwellers, The 1957,O 21,29:2
Clerambard 1957,N 8,22:3
Clerambard 1957,N 17,II,1:1
Who Was That Lady I Saw You With?
  1958,Mr 4,33:2
Shadow of a Gunman, The 1958,N 21,26:1
Most Happy Fella, The 1959,F 11,50:2
Miracle Worker, The 1959,O 20,44:1
Only in America 1959,N 20,35:1
Roman Candle 1960,F 4,34:2
Long Dream, The 1960,F 18,36:2
Toys in the Attic 1960,F 26,23:2
Brouhaha 1960,Ap 27,31:2
Thousand Clowns, A 1962,Ap 6,31:2
In the Counting House 1962,D 15,5:5
Wonderful Town 1963,F 15,10:2
Dylan 1964,Ja 20,18:1
Cafe Crown 1964,Ap 18,32:1
Victims of Duty 1964,My 28,40:2
New Tenant, The 1964,My 28,40:2
Dreigroschenoper, Die 1965,Mr 12,24:1
Square in the Eye 1965,My 20,54:1
Xmas in Las Vegas 1965,N 5,31:1
Wait Until Dark 1966,F 3,21:1
Here's Where I Belong 1968,Mr 4,32:1
Cannibals, The 1968,N 4,60:1
Mahagonny 1970,Ap 29,51:1

Morley, Ruth (Miscellaneous)
River Line, The 1957,Ja 3,29:2
Pajama Game, The 1957,My 16,27:1
Wonderful Town 1958,Mr 6,32:4
Lute Song 1959,Mr 13,24:1

Morley, Victor
My Golden Girl 1920,F 3,18:2
All-Star Idlers of 1921, The 1921,Jl 16,5:2
Suzette 1921,N 25,18:3
Blue Kitten, The 1922,Ja 14,9:3
Four in Hand 1923,S 7,10:2
Lady, The 1923,D 5,23:2
Is Zat So? 1925,Ja 6,23:4
Wooden Soldier, The 1931,Je 23,28:4
Ziegfeld Follies 1934,Ja 5,24:3
Country Wife, The 1935,Jl 2,24:2
Matrimony, PFD 1936,N 6,28:4
Matrimony, PFD 1936,N 13,26:3
Roberta 1937,Je 27,II,6:1
Three Waltzes 1937,D 27,10:2
Kiss for Cinderella, A 1942,Mr 11,22:2

Morley, Victor (Director)
Sunshine 1926,Ag 18,15:2
Brass Buttons 1927,D 6,26:3
Skull, The 1928,Ap 24,28:3
Back Here 1928,N 27,36:3
Booster, The 1929,O 25,26:2
Room 349 1930,Ap 23,24:5
Mystery Moon 1930,Je 24,23:4
School for Virtue 1931,Ap 22,29:2
Wooden Soldier, The 1931,Je 23,28:4

Morlin, William
Two Blocks Away 1921,Ag 31,8:3

Morlock, Martin (Playwright)
Why Do I Deserve This? 1966,Ja 19,31:2

Morlowe, Ann
Sunny River 1941,D 5,28:2

Morn, Edna
Three Showers 1920,Ap 6,18:1
Sally, Irene and Mary 1922,S 5,21:2

Mornay, Joy
Pirates of Penzance, The 1955,O 7,21:1
Trial by Jury 1964,N 20,40:1

Morne, Maryland
In Love With Love 1923,Ag 7,20:1

Morningside Players
Sun and I, The 1933,Ap 4,15:2

Morningstar, Carter (Costume Designer)
Beg, Borrow or Steal 1960,F 11,39:4

Morningstar, Carter (Lighting Director)
Beg, Borrow or Steal 1960,F 11,39:4

Morningstar, Carter (Scenic Designer)
Shoestring Revue 1955,Mr 1,22:2
Beg, Borrow or Steal 1960,F 11,39:4

Morny, John
Speak of the Devil! 1939,O 7,21:7
She Gave Him All She Had 1939,D 2,20:7
Man Who Killed Lincoln, The 1939,D 30,9:1
Man Who Killed Lincoln, The 1940,Ja 18,26:4
Return of the Vagabond, The 1940,My 14,27:2
Hope for a Harvest 1941,N 27,28:2
Great Big Doorstep, The 1942,N 27,26:2

Moro, George (Choreographer)
Folies Bergere 1939,D 25,28:2

Moro, Russ
J B 1958,Ap 24,37:1

Moroccans, The
Arabian Nights 1954,Je 25,15:2

Morocco
International Playgirls '64 1964,My 22,40:2
I Had a Ball 1964,D 16,50:1

Moroney, C J Jr
Tiger Smiles, The 1930,D 18,29:1

Moroney, Ed
When Differences Disappear 1941,Je 3,17:4
Trial Honeymoon 1947,N 4,31:2

Moros
Maitresse de Roi 1926,D 1,24:1

Morosco, Bee
Beyond Evil 1926,Je 8,23:2
Black Cockatoo, The 1926,D 31,11:1
Park Avenue, Ltd 1932,Mr 4,17:1

Morosco, Oliver (Lyricist)
Love Dreams 1921,O 11,22:2

Morosco, Oliver (Playwright)
Letty Pepper 1922,Ap 11,22:2

Morosco, Oliver (Producer)
Head First 1926,Ja 7,22:4

Moroso, John A (Playwright)
Canary Dutch 1925,S 9,22:1

Moross, Jerome
Mother, The 1935,N 20,26:3

Moross, Jerome (Composer)
Parade 1935,My 21,22:2
Would-Be Gentleman, The 1946,Ja 10,29:2
Blood Wedding 1949,F 7,16:2
Golden Apple, The 1954,Mr 12,15:2
Golden Apple, The 1954,Mr 21,II,1:1
Riding Hood Revisited 1961,Ja 4,26:1
Eccentricities of Davy Crockett, The 1961,Ja 4,26:1
Willie the Weeper 1961,Ja 4,26:1
Ballet Ballads 1961,Ja 4,26:1
Golden Apple, The 1962,F 13,38:2

Morot, Edouard (Sir) (Miscellaneous)
Cantatrice Chauve, La 1962,Ja 16,30:1
Huis Clos 1962,Ja 16,30:1
Annonce Faite a Marie, L' 1965,Ap 6,33:2

Morra, Gino
View From the Bridge, A 1965,Ja 29,24:1

Morrell
Vierge Folle, La; Foolish Virgin, The
  1924,Mr 22,12:2

Morrell, Don
Taming of the Shrew, The 1940,F 6,17:2

Morrell, Henry
Blue Lagoon, The 1921,S 15,16:1
Loyalties 1922,S 28,18:1
If Winter Comes 1923,Ap 3,26:1
Hassan 1924,S 23,23:1
Old English 1924,D 24,11:2
Merchant of Venice, The 1928,Ja 17,22:2
Her Friend the King 1929,O 8,34:5
Othello 1935,S 28,13:2
Macbeth 1935,O 8,26:4
Lady Precious Stream 1936,Ja 28,15:2

Morrell, Louis
Mary Jane McKane 1923,D 26,13:2
Man in Evening Clothes, The 1924,D 6,13:4
Whoopee 1928,D 5,34:3
Ghost Writer, The 1933,Je 20,22:4
All the King's Horses 1934,Ja 31,21:3
Potash and Perlmutter 1935,Ap 6,11:3

Morrell, Peter (Playwright)
Turpentine 1936,Je 27,21:6

Morrell, Stanleigh
Green Pastures, The 1930,F 27,26:1

Morrelli, Antonio (Musical Director)
Touch and Go 1949,O 14,34:2

Morrice, Ella
Ethan Frome 1936,Ja 22,15:2

Morrigal, Alice (Costume Designer)
Patrick--The First 1965,F 19,25:1

Morrill, Alan
Tapestry in Gray 1935,D 28,10:2

Morrill, Alan (Producer)
Page Pygmalion 1932,Ag 4,17:5

Morrill, Herbert
Mother Sings 1935,N 13,24:1

Morrill, Katherine (Playwright)
Distant Bell, A 1960,Ja 14,29:1

Morrill, Priscilla
When the Bough Breaks 1950,Mr 9,25:5
Relapse, The 1950,N 23,54:2
Love's Labour's Lost 1953,F 5,20:3
Way of the World, The 1954,S 30,38:2
Duchess of Malfi, The 1957,Mr 20,33:1
Alley of the Sunset 1959,D 31,11:1
Sudden End of Anne Cinquefoil, The
  1961,Ja 11,25:2
Firebugs, The 1963,F 13,7:2
Macbeth 1964,Jl 27,22:3
Touch of the Poet, A 1967,My 3,38:2
Still Life 1967,My 4,34:1

Morrill, Theodore
Gondoliers, The 1963,Je 5,33:2
Pirates of Penzance, The 1966,My 24,54:1
H M S Pinafore 1966,Je 8,41:2

Morring, Mark (Costume Designer)
Wild Rose, The 1926,O 21,23:1

Morris, Adrian
Fast Life 1928,S 27,35:2

Morris, Aldyth (Playwright)
Carefree Tree, The 1955,O 12,37:2
Secret Concubine, The 1960,Mr 22,29:2

Morris, Amarilla
Pal Joey 1940,D 26,22:2

Morris, Arthur C
Spellbound 1927,F 16,17:2
Mystery Ship, The 1927,Mr 15,28:2
Madame X 1927,Jl 7,29:3
Atlas and Eva 1928,F 7,30:2
Pleased to Meet You 1928,O 30,27:2
After Dark 1928,D 11,35:2
Adams' Wife 1931,D 29,27:1
Carry Nation 1932,O 31,18:2

Morris, Aubrey
Richard II 1956,O 24,44:1
Romeo and Juliet 1956,O 25,41:1
Macbeth 1956,O 30,42:2
Troilus and Cressida 1956,D 27,21:1
Hostage, The 1960,S 21,42:1

Morris, Bobby
Lady Says Yes, A 1945,Ja 11,18:5

Morris, Chester
Mountain Man, The 1921,D 13,24:2
Exciters, The 1922,S 23,10:4
Extra 1923,Ja 24,22:3
Home Towners, The 1926,Ag 24,19:3
Yellow 1926,S 22,30:1
Crime 1927,F 23,27:3
Whispering Friends 1928,F 21,18:3
Fast Life 1928,S 27,35:2
Girl of the Golden West, The 1957,N 6,44:1
Blue Denim 1958,F 28,17:1
Blue Denim 1958,Ap 20,II,1:1
Advise and Consent 1960,N 18,25:1

Morris, Corbet
Rita Coventry 1923,F 20,12:2
Spring 3100 1928,F 16,14:2
Cape Cod Follies 1929,S 19,37:2
Housewarming 1932,Ap 8,25:1

Morris, David
Yo Ho Hum 1927,My 7,15:1
Silver Swan, The 1929,N 28,34:5
Sari 1930,Ja 29,27:1
Old Rascal, The 1930,Mr 25,34:4
Fine and Dandy 1930,S 24,26:1
In The Best of Families 1931,F 3,29:1
Berlin 1931,D 31,16:1
Scrap Book 1932,Ag 2,20:3
Cradle Snatchers 1932,N 17,23:2
Young Sinners 1933,Mr 7,20:4
Hilda Cassidy 1933,My 5,18:3
Fly by Night 1933,Je 3,16:2
Come Easy 1933,Ag 30,22:5
Big Hearted Herbert 1934,Ja 2,17:3
Dream Child 1934,S 28,26:2
Squaring the Circle 1935,S 22,X,3:2
Squaring the Circle 1935,O 4,24:6
On Your Toes 1936,Ap 13,14:4
On Your Toes 1937,Ag 3,21:2
One Flight Down 1937,D 14,32:4
Stars in Your Eyes 1939,F 10,18:2
Morning Star 1940,Ap 17,26:4
All in Fun 1940,D 28,11:2
Vie Parisienne, La 1945,Ja 13,14:5

Morris, Denise
Romance 1921,Mr 1,18:2
Scarlet Sister Mary 1930,N 26,19:2

Morris, Diane
Ice Follies 1965,Ja 13,35:1

Morris, Dorothy (Lighting Director)
Holiday on Ice 1965,S 2,38:4
Holiday on Ice 1966,S 1,30:1
Holiday on Ice 1967,Ag 31,29:2
Holiday on Ice 1968,Ag 29,44:1
Holiday on Ice 1969,Ag 28,44:1

Morris, Douglas (Miscellaneous)
Measure for Measure 1967,F 15,37:1
Hamlet 1967,F 17,44:1
Romeo and Juliet 1967,F 22,18:1

Morris, Duane
Finis for Oscar Wilde 1964,F 15,15:1

Morris, E B (Playwright)
Take It As It Comes 1944,F 11,17:2

Morris, Edmund (Playwright)
Wooden Dish, The 1954,Jl 30,9:4
Wooden Dish, The 1954,Ag 15,II,1:4
Wooden Dish, The 1955,O 7,20:1
Fifth Commandment, The 1965,N 15,48:4

Morris, Edwin H (Miscellaneous)
Shoestring '57 1956,N 6,31:1

Morris, Garrett
Bible Salesman, The 1960,F 22,12:2
Bible Salesman, The 1961,F 21,40:1
Porgy and Bess 1964,My 7,32:1
Show Boat 1966,Jl 20,48:1
I'm Solomon 1968,Ap 24,51:1
Slave Ship 1969,N 22,46:1
Transfers 1970,Ja 23,25:1
Operation Sidewinder 1970,Mr 13,33:1
Street Sounds 1970,O 23,32:1
Ododo 1970,N 25,26:1

Morris, George (Director)
Ginger Snaps 1930,Ja 1,30:5

Morris, George (Lyricist)
Ginger Snaps 1930,Ja 1,30:5

Morris, George (Playwright)
Ginger Snaps 1930,Ja 1,30:5
Morris, Gordon (Playwright)
Jack in the Pulpit 1925,Ja 7,33:1
Morris, Hayward (Miscellaneous)
Your Own Thing 1968,Ja 15,33:1
In the Bar of a Tokyo Hotel 1969,My 12,54:1
Morris, Howard
Hamlet 1945,D 14,25:2
Gentlemen Prefer Blondes 1949,D 9,35:3
Finian's Rainbow 1960,Ap 28,31:1
Morris, Ivan (Translator)
Hans's Crime 1961,F 4,15:1
Morris, James
In April Once 1955,Mr 14,29:3
Beautiful Dreamer 1960,D 28,22:1
Morris, Janie
Holiday on Ice 1965,S 2,38:4
Holiday on Ice 1966,S 1,30:1
Morris, Jeremiah
Failures, The 1959,Ja 6,30:2
Daughter of Silence 1961,D 1,28:1
Andorra 1963,F 11,5:5
Jennie 1963,O 18,35:2
Sourball 1969,Ag 6,29:2
Sheep on the Runway 1970,F 2,28:3
Sheep on the Runway 1970,F 8,II,5:5
Morris, Jerry
Time Limit! 1956,Ja 25,27:2
Diary of a Scoundrel 1956,N 5,41:1
Morris, Joanna
Alfie 1964,D 18,27:1
Boeing-Boeing 1965,F 3,30:1
Morris, Joe
Sharlee 1923,N 23,20:1
Vaudeville (Palace) 1926,Ap 13,28:3
Vaudeville (Hippodrome) 1926,Ap 27,22:3
Vaudeville (Palace) 1926,N 9,30:3
Vaudeville (Palace) 1930,My 26,25:2
Vaudeville (Palace) 1932,Jl 18,9:7
Morris, John
You Never Can Tell 1958,Je 17,25:1
Morris, John (Choreographer)
Bells Are Ringing 1956,N 30,18:2
First Impressions 1959,Mr 20,28:1
All American 1962,Mr 20,44:1
Baker Street 1965,F 17,36:1
Sherry! 1967,Mr 29,39:1
Look to the Lilies 1970,Mr 30,59:1
Morris, John (Composer)
Phoenix '55 1955,Ap 25,20:2
My Mother, My Father and Me 1963,Mr 25,5:5
As You Like It 1963,Jl 17,19:2
Electra 1964,Ag 12,42:1
Sing to Me Through Open Windows
1965,Mr 16,45:1
Day the Whores Came Out to Play Tennis, The
1965,Mr 16,45:1
Love's Labour's Lost 1965,Je 16,46:1
Time for Singing, A 1966,My 23,48:2
Richard III 1966,Ag 11,26:1
Comedy of Errors, The 1967,Je 15,58:4
Titus Andronicus 1967,Ag 10,43:2
Memorandum, The 1968,My 6,55:1
Henry IV, Part I 1968,Je 30,54:7
Henry IV, Part II 1968,Jl 2,33:1
Take One Step 1968,Jl 5,17:1
Romeo and Juliet 1968,Ag 16,19:1
King Lear 1968,N 8,43:1
Invitation to a Beheading 1969,Mr 18,36:1
Peer Gynt 1969,Jl 17,56:1
Electra 1969,Ag 8,14:1
Morris, John (Lyricist)
As You Like It 1963,Jl 17,19:2
Love's Labour's Lost 1965,Je 16,46:1
Time for Singing, A 1966,My 23,48:2
Henry IV, Part I 1968,Je 30,54:7
Henry IV, Part II 1968,Jl 2,33:1
Peer Gynt 1969,Jl 17,56:1
Morris, John (Miscellaneous)
Shangri-La 1956,Je 14,40:1
Bells Are Ringing 1956,N 29,43:4
Shinbone Alley 1957,Ap 15,23:2
Copper and Brass 1957,O 18,19:2
Girls Against the Boys, The 1959,N 3,26:1
Bye Bye Birdie 1960,Ap 15,13:4
Kwamina 1961,O 24,42:1
Cities in Bezique; Beast's Story, A 1969,Ja 13,26:1
Cities in Bezique; Owl Answers, The
1969,Ja 13,26:1
Sambo 1969,D 22,42:1
Morris, John (Musical Director)
Wildcat 1960,D 17,20:2
All American 1962,Mr 20,44:1
Hair 1967,O 30,55:1
Hamlet 1967,D 27,45:1
Hamlet 1968,Jl 4,15:1
Morris, John (Playwright)
Time for Singing, A 1966,My 23,48:2
Morris, Jonathan
Conversation Piece 1957,N 19,38:2
As You Like It 1958,Ja 21,33:6
Christine 1960,Ap 29,27:1

Saving Grace, The 1963,Ap 19,28:1
Morris, Kirk (Miscellaneous)
Exhibition 1969,My 16,41:1
Morris, Lily
Vaudeville (Palace) 1928,Ja 24,26:4
Vaudeville (Palace) 1928,Ja 31,29:2
Babes in Toyland 1930,D 22,17:1
Morris, Lloyd (Playwright)
Damask Cheek, The 1942,O 23,24:2
Damask Cheek, The 1942,N 8,VIII,1:1
Morris, M
Stepping Stones 1923,N 7,14:3
Morris, Marcia
Portrait of a Lady 1954,D 22,27:6
Twelfth Night 1957,Jl 4,16:4
Richard III 1957,N 26,41:1
Edward II 1958,F 12,32:5
Morris, Margaret
Yankee Princess, The 1922,O 3,22:1
Dew Drop Inn 1923,My 18,26:4
Morris, Marilyn
Ice Capades 1958,S 4,33:2
Morris, Marion
Misalliance 1955,F 12,10:6
Clandestine on the Morning Line 1959,D 5,18:2
Come Share My House 1960,F 19,20:2
Ticket-of-Leave Man, The 1961,D 23,15:1
Morris, Mary
Fashion 1924,F 5,21:2
Fashion 1924,F 10,VII,1:1
Crime in the Whistler Room, The 1924,O 10,22:2
Desire Under the Elms 1924,N 12,20:7
Hidden 1927,O 5,30:4
Would-Be Gentleman, The 1928,O 2,34:1
Cross Roads 1929,N 12,34:2
At the Bottom 1930,Ja 10,24:3
Sea Gull, The 1930,F 26,22:2
Life Is Like That 1930,D 23,24:3
House of Connelly, The 1931,S 29,22:4
1931 1931,D 11,34:3
Night Over Taos 1932,Mr 10,25:3
Camille 1932,N 2,23:3
Peace Palace 1933,Je 6,30:2
Double Door 1933,S 22,15:5
Within the Gates 1934,O 23,23:1
Jane Brady-Editor 1935,Jl 2,24:3
Mother Sings 1935,N 13,24:1
Granite 1936,Ja 14,24:6
Queen's Husband, The 1936,Je 2,33:2
Mrs Moonlight 1936,Je 16,21:3
Granite Fires 1936,Jl 22,22:4
Plumes in the Dust 1936,N 7,14:2
Plumes in the Dust 1936,N 15,XI,1:1
Behind the Red Lights 1937,Ja 14,17:4
Suspect 1937,F 17,16:2
Suspect 1937,Mr 7,XI,2:1
Roosty 1938,F 15,21:2
Empress of Destiny 1938,Mr 10,16:2
Cream in the Well, The 1941,Ja 21,19:2
Father, The 1949,N 17,36:2
Fire-Weed 1950,Mr 30,38:2
Young Elizabeth, The 1952,Ap 3,45:1
Coriolanus 1953,Ag 21,9:2
Month in the Country, A 1956,Ap 4,23:1
Morris, Maurice
Dracula 1931,Ap 14,33:3
Great Lover, The 1932,O 12,27:3
Night of January 16 1935,S 17,26:4
Morris, Michael
Good Times 1920,Ag 10,10:1
Monkey Talks, The 1925,D 29,20:1
Morris, Nelson (Miscellaneous)
Bicycle Ride to Nevada 1963,S 25,38:1
Morris, Nick
Deburau 1920,D 24,14:3
Morris, Nobuko (Miscellaneous)
Conduct Unbecoming 1970,O 13,50:1
Morris, Patricia
Scarlet Man, The 1921,Ag 23,10:3
Morris, Phil (Producer)
Just a Minute 1928,O 9,34:3
Morris, R F Jr (Playwright)
Storm Child 1935,Jl 16,24:1
Morris, Ralph
Pagan Lady 1930,O 21,34:2
Creeping Fire 1935,Ja 17,22:3
Morris, Richard
Talent '49 1949,Ap 13,39:4
Morris, Richard (Playwright)
Unsinkable Molly Brown, The 1960,N 4,28:1
Morris, Robert
Blue Blood 1924,Ap 3,21:2
Lady in the Dark 1952,Mr 8,11:3
Taming of the Shrew, The 1957,F 21,30:2
House of Breath, The 1957,Ap 15,23:2
Midnight Caller, The 1958,Jl 2,25:1
Morris, Robert A (Rev) (Miscellaneous)
Angelic Doctor 1953,Ap 14,30:2
Morris, Ruth
Garrick Gaieties 1926,My 11,25:2
Morris, S (Composer)
It's the Valet 1933,D 15,25:4

Morris, S (Lyricist)
It's the Valet 1933,D 15,25:4
Morris, Sandi
Sambo 1970,Jl 23,24:1
Morris, Virginia
They All Want Something 1926,O 13,20:2
Morris, Wayne
Cave Dwellers, The 1957,O 21,29:2
Cave Dwellers, The 1957,O 27,II,1:1
Morris, Wilhelmina
One Way Street 1928,D 25,31:2
Morris, William
Call the Doctor 1920,S 1,14:1
Scarlet Man, The 1921,Ag 23,10:3
Dream Maker, The 1921,N 22,17:1
Chains 1923,S 20,5:2
Baby Cyclone, The 1927,S 13,37:4
Fast Life 1928,S 27,35:2
Vaudeville (Palace) 1928,N 6,35:2
Dodsworth 1934,F 26,20:4
Play, Genius, Play! 1935,O 31,17:2
Ethan Frome 1936,Ja 22,15:2
I Want You 1961,S 15,29:1
Morris, William E
Lights Out 1922,Ag 18,8:4
Barnum Was Right 1923,Mr 13,19:3
We Americans 1926,O 13,20:4
Spider, The 1927,Mr 23,29:1
Poppa 1928,D 25,31:1
This Man's Town 1930,Mr 11,24:4
Old Man Murphy 1931,My 19,25:2
Mr Papavert 1932,Ja 23,18:6
Lambs Gambol 1932,Ap 25,18:2
Keeping Expenses Down 1932,O 21,25:2
Drums Professor, The 1935,Jl 30,17:2
Iron Men 1936,O 20,30:6
Othello 1937,Ja 7,16:4
Morris, William E (Director)
Singing Rabbi, The 1931,S 11,24:4
Morris, Wolfe
Teahouse of the August Moon, The
1955,My 10,24:1
Morris and Campbell
Artists and Models 1924,O 16,33:3
Morrise, Richard
Spanish Love 1920,Ag 18,6:1
Morrisey, Agnes
Little Jessie James 1923,Ag 16,10:4
Morrisey, Mary
Sex 1926,Ap 27,22:4
Morrish, Ann
Twelfth Night 1957,Jl 4,16:4
Two Gentlemen of Verona 1958,Mr 19,35:1
Broken Jug, The 1958,Ap 2,36:1
Much Ado About Nothing 1958,Je 26,22:1
Winter's Tale, The 1958,Jl 23,34:3
As You Like It 1959,Jl 1,27:1
Othello 1959,Jl 2,17:2
Morrison, Adrienne
Merchant of Venice, The 1921,Ap 2,14:2
March Hares 1921,Ag 12,8:3
Makers of Light 1922,My 24,22:3
Fool, The 1922,O 24,18:1
March Hares 1923,Mr 13,19:5
Launzi 1923,O 11,16:3
Business Widow, The 1923,D 11,27:1
Piker, The 1925,Ja 16,14:1
Love for Love 1925,Ap 1,21:2
Love for Love 1925,S 15,29:3
Hamlet 1925,N 10,23:1
Grey Farm 1940,My 4,12:7
Morrison, Adrienne (Director)
Forest Ring, The 1930,Ap 26,11:2
Make-Believe 1930,N 8,21:1
Little Princess, The 1931,F 7,11:3
Racketty Packetty House 1931,N 7,16:1
Morrison, Albert
Egotist, The 1922,D 27,12:1
Business Widow, The 1923,D 11,27:1
Embers 1926,F 2,20:3
Morrison, Anne
Bat, The 1920,Ag 24,6:1
Within Four Walls 1923,Ap 18,24:1
Aloma of the South Seas 1925,Ap 21,18:1
Morning After, The 1925,Jl 28,24:2
Proud Woman, A 1926,N 16,24:1
Lally 1927,F 9,16:3
Triumphant Bachelor, The 1927,S 16,21:1
Morrison, Anne (Playwright)
Wild Westcotts, The 1923,D 25,26:2
Pigs 1924,Je 8,VII,1:8
Pigs 1924,S 2,22:5
Jonesy 1929,F 24,IX,4:1
Jonesy 1929,Ap 10,32:2
Morrison, B
It's the Valet 1933,D 15,25:4
Morrison, Carl (Lighting Director)
Too True to Be Good 1963,Mr 14,8:2
Morrison, Carl (Scenic Designer)
Too True to Be Good 1963,Mr 14,8:2
Morrison, Caroline
Autumn Fire 1926,O 27,25:3
Exceeding Small 1928,O 23,32:2

Morrison, Caroline—Cont
She Loves Me Not 1933,N 21,22:4
Morrison, Charles (Director)
Doctor in Spite of Himself, The 1957,F 28,18:4
Morrison, Charles (Miscellaneous)
Vaudeville (Palace) 1928,Ap 24,29:2
Palm Tree in a Rose Garden, A 1957,N 27,26:2
Ulysses in Nighttown 1958,Je 6,30:1
Morrison, Charles (Scenic Designer)
Conversation at Midnight 1964,N 13,27:1
Morrison, Donald
Then Came the Dawn 1935,Ag 29,25:4
County Chairman, The 1936,My 26,26:5
Morrison, Dorothy
Her Family Tree 1920,D 28,9:2
Smile at Me 1935,Ag 24,18:4
Slice It Thin 1945,My 11,22:5
Morrison, Eleanor
Girl From Wyoming, The 1938,O 31,12:1
Morrison, Ethel
Farmer's Wife, The 1924,O 10,22:3
Mayflowers 1925,N 25,14:2
Madcap, The 1928,F 1,31:2
Yellow Jacket, The 1928,N 8,27:3
Falstaff 1928,D 26,14:2
Everything's Jake 1930,Ja 17,20:4
Bitter Sweet 1934,My 8,28:4
Yr Obedient Husband 1938,Ja 11,26:5
Lady in Waiting 1940,Mr 28,19:1
My Fair Ladies 1941,Mr 24,12:7
All Men Are Alike 1941,O 7,27:2
What Big Ears! 1942,Ap 21,18:5
I Killed the Count 1942,S 4,18:1
This Rock 1943,F 19,23:2
Morrison, Florence
Her Family Tree 1920,D 28,9:2
Last Waltz, The 1921,My 11,20:3
Queen O' Hearts 1922,O 11,22:1
Fashions of 1924 1923,Jl 19,18:2
Student Prince, The 1924,D 3,25:3
Circus Princess, The 1927,Ap 26,32:2
Morrison, George (Director)
Epitaph for George Dillon 1960,D 29,17:1
Sudden and Accidental Re-education of Horse
Johnson, The 1968,D 19,63:1
Morrison, Harry
Yoshe Kalb 1933,D 29,27:2
Morrison, Jack
Pins and Needles 1922,F 2,20:1
Morrison, James
Two Orphans, The 1926,Ap 6,26:2
Queen's Husband, The 1928,Ja 26,17:2
Green Pastures, The 1935,F 27,16:2
Morrison, Janet
Josef Suss 1930,Ja 21,28:5
Morrison, Jennings
Van Dyck, The 1921,O 12,18:2
Morrison, Kay (Costume Designer)
Gold Eagle Guy 1934,N 29,33:4
Mother Lode 1934,D 24,16:5
May Wine 1935,D 6,30:3
Morrison, Kent (Pvt)
Winged Victory 1943,N 22,24:1
Morrison, Lee (Director)
Provincetown Follies, The 1935,N 4,24:3
Morrison, Lucille
Woman of Bronze, The 1927,Je 16,25:4
Morrison, Mary Horne
Adorable Liar, The 1926,Ag 31,15:2
Growing Pains 1933,N 24,24:2
Errant Lady 1934,S 18,18:2
There's Wisdom in Women 1935,O 31,17:1
Battle Hymn 1936,My 23,12:1
Howdy Stranger 1937,Ja 15,17:5
Morrison, Morris
Sex Fable, The 1931,O 21,26:1
Morrison, Patricia
Growing Pains 1933,N 24,24:2
Kiss Me, Kate 1949,Ja 16,II,1:1
Morrison, Paul
Till the Day I Die 1935,Mr 27,24:5
Paradise Lost 1935,D 10,31:5
Case of Clyde Griffiths 1936,Mr 14,10:4
Skin of Our Teeth, The 1955,Ag 18,16:1
Morrison, Paul (Costume Designer)
Thunder Rock 1939,N 15,18:1
Apology 1943,Mr 23,14:2
John Gabriel Borkman 1946,N 13,33:2
All My Sons 1947,Ja 30,21:2
Uniform of Flesh 1949,Ja 31,15:2
Getting Married 1951,My 14,28:5
Golden Boy 1952,Mr 13,24:3
Four Saints in Three Acts 1952,Ap 17,35:1
On Borrowed Time 1953,F 11,34:1
Confidential Clerk, The 1954,F 12,22:1
Abie's Irish Rose 1954,N 19,19:1
Bus Stop 1955,Mr 3,23:2
Once Upon a Tailor 1955,My 24,36:2
Man With the Golden Arm, The 1956,My 22,28:1
Loud Red Patrick, The 1956,O 4,28:1
Cantilevered Terrace, The 1962,Ja 18,24:1
Worlds of Shakespeare, The 1963,D 5,58:1
Morrison, Paul (Director)
Cyrano de Bergerac 1953,N 13,24:3

Morrison, Paul (Lighting Director)
Closing Door, The 1949,D 2,36:2
Cellar and the Well, The 1950,D 11,30:2
Golden Boy 1952,Mr 13,24:3
On Borrowed Time 1953,F 11,34:1
Confidential Clerk, The 1954,F 12,22:1
Arabian Nights 1954,Je 25,15:2
Tender Trap, The 1954,O 14,37:2
Abie's Irish Rose 1954,N 19,19:1
Bus Stop 1955,Mr 3,23:2
Once Upon a Tailor 1955,My 24,36:2
Joyce Grenfell Requests the Pleasure
1955,O 11,48:1
Tamburlaine the Great 1956,Ja 20,19:1
Man With the Golden Arm, The 1956,My 22,28:1
Loud Red Patrick, The 1956,O 4,28:1
Sixth Finger in a Five Finger Glove 1956,O 9,31:4
Separate Tables 1956,O 26,33:1
Cranks 1956,N 27,32:1
Candide 1956,D 3,40:2
Ziegfeld Follies 1957,Mr 2,19:2
Sin of Pat Muldoon, The 1957,Mr 14,35:1
Maybe Tuesday 1958,Ja 30,18:3
Visit, The 1958,My 6,40:1
Make a Million 1958,O 24,39:2
Masquerade 1959,Mr 17,42:1
Nervous Set, The 1959,My 13,43:1
Much Ado About Nothing 1959,S 18,25:2
Happy Town 1959,O 8,49:2
Flowering Cherry 1959,O 22,46:1
Shadow and Substance 1959,N 4,42:1
Lysistrata 1959,N 25,19:4
Thurber Carnival, A 1960,F 27,13:2
Visit, The 1960,Mr 9,38:3
Jeannette 1960,Mr 25,20:2
Duel of Angels 1960,Ap 20,42:2
Invitation to a March 1960,O 31,27:2
Rape of the Belt, The 1960,N 7,46:1
Porgy and Bess 1961,My 18,40:1
Caretaker, The 1961,O 5,42:3
Complaisant Lover, The 1961,N 2,43:2
Man for All Seasons, A 1961,N 23,51:1
Cantilevered Terrace, The 1962,Ja 18,24:1
Student Gypsy, The; Prince of Liederkranz, The
1963,O 1,34:1
Man for All Seasons, A 1964,Ja 28,24:2
Sponono 1964,Ap 3,28:1
Babes in the Wood 1964,D 29,21:2
Price, The 1968,F 8,37:1
Morrison, Paul (Miscellaneous)
Tiger at the Gates 1955,O 4,40:1
Man With the Golden Arm, The 1956,My 22,28:1
Separate Tables 1956,O 26,33:1
Cranks 1956,N 27,32:1
Much Ado About Nothing 1959,S 18,25:2
South Pacific 1961,Ap 27,26:3
Caretaker, The 1961,O 5,42:3
Sponono 1964,Ap 3,28:1
Conduct Unbecoming 1970,O 13,50:1
Morrison, Paul (Scenic Designer)
Royal Family, The 1940,Ag 13,15:3
Walk Into My Parlor 1941,N 20,38:2
Hedda Gabler 1942,Ja 30,22:2
I'll Take the High Road 1943,N 10,28:3
Mrs January & Mr Ex 1944,Ap 1,10:2
That Old Devil 1944,Je 6,14:2
Love on Leave 1944,Je 21,23:4
What Every Woman Knows 1946,N 9,13:2
John Gabriel Borkman 1946,N 13,33:2
Young and Fair, The 1948,N 23,35:2
Uniform of Flesh 1949,Ja 31,15:2
Closing Door, The 1949,D 2,36:2
Deirdre of the Sorrows 1949,D 15,51:2
Building 222 1950,F 3,28:2
Affairs of State 1950,S 26,37:2
Arms and the Man 1950,O 20,34:2
Cellar and the Well, The 1950,D 11,30:2
Billy Budd 1951,F 12,18:3
Billy Budd 1951,F 18,II,1:1
Getting Married 1951,My 14,28:5
Twilight Walk 1951,S 25,25:4
Faithfully Yours 1951,O 19,22:5
Golden Boy 1952,Mr 13,24:3
Four Saints in Three Acts 1952,Ap 17,35:1
On Borrowed Time 1953,F 11,34:1
Confidential Clerk, The 1954,F 12,22:1
Confidential Clerk, The 1954,F 21,II,1:1
Tender Trap, The 1954,O 14,37:2
Abie's Irish Rose 1954,N 19,19:1
Man With the Golden Arm, The 1956,My 22,28:1
Loud Red Patrick, The 1956,O 4,28:1
Sixth Finger in a Five Finger Glove 1956,O 9,31:4
Maybe Tuesday 1958,Ja 30,18:3
Make a Million 1958,O 24,39:2
Masquerade 1959,Mr 17,42:1
Nervous Set, The 1959,My 13,43:1
Jeannette 1960,Mr 25,20:2
Mousetrap, The 1960,N 7,46:1
Rape of the Belt, The 1960,N 7,46:1
Cantilevered Terrace, The 1962,Ja 18,24:1
Worlds of Shakespeare, The 1963,D 5,58:1
Babes in the Wood 1964,D 29,21:2
Cat and the Canary, The 1965,Ja 5,26:1

Morrison, Paul (Scenic Designer)—Cont
After the Rain 1967,O 10,54:1
Morrison, Peggy (Costume Designer)
Harvest of Years 1948,Ja 13,29:2
Mikado, The 1949,O 5,35:2
Pirates of Penzance, The 1949,O 11,41:2
H M S Pinafore 1949,O 18,34:2
Trial by Jury 1949,O 18,34:2
Tickets, Please! 1950,Ap 28,25:2
Four Twelves Are 48 1951,Ja 18,30:2
Mikado, The 1952,O 21,35:2
Pirates of Penzance, The 1952,O 28,36:4
Trial by Jury 1952,N 4,32:2
H M S Pinafore 1952,N 4,32:2
Iolanthe 1952,N 11,26:3
Morrison, Priestly
Master of the Revels 1935,Ag 14,16:2
Life's Too Short 1935,S 21,18:5
Stage Door 1936,O 23,26:3
Morrison, Priestly (Director)
Easy Come, Easy Go 1925,O 27,20:2
Deacon, The 1925,N 25,14:3
One Man's Woman 1926,My 26,25:1
Pyramids 1926,Jl 20,17:2
Barker, The 1927,Ja 19,20:6
Barker, The 1927,Ja 23,VII,1:1
Married-And How! 1928,Je 15,30:2
Courage 1928,O 9,34:2
Jealous Moon, The 1928,N 21,32:2
All the King's Men 1929,F 5,27:1
Marry the Man! 1929,Ap 23,26:3
Claire Adams 1929,N 20,26:3
Earl Carroll's Vanities 1930,Jl 2,28:3
Paging Danger 1931,F 27,19:2
Did I Say No? 1931,S 23,19:4
Sentinels 1931,D 26,15:1
Best Years 1932,S 8,16:2
Girl Outside, The 1932,O 25,24:3
Strange Gods 1933,Ap 17,16:6
Errant Lady 1934,S 18,18:2
So Many Paths 1934,D 7,26:5
Triumph 1935,O 15,18:5
Suddenly a Stranger 1936,Ag 4,15:2
Morrison, Priestly (Mrs)
Lightnin' 1938,S 16,17:2
Man Who Came to Dinner, The 1939,O 17,31:1
More the Merrier, The 1941,S 16,19:3
Late George Apley, The 1944,O 20,16:4
Late George Apley, The 1944,N 22,26:2
Four Twelves Are 48 1951,Ja 18,30:2
Morrison, Ralph
Circle of Chalk, The 1941,Mr 27,28:4
Swing Sister Wac Swing 1944,Ja 4,20:4
Morrison, Russell
Plot Thickens, The 1922,S 6,16:1
Six Characters in Search of an Author
1922,O 31,11:2
Love Set, The 1923,Mr 20,24:2
Hamlet 1923,N 27,23:6
Macbeth 1924,Mr 17,18:1
New Gallantry, The 1925,S 25,24:2
Blonde Sinner, The 1926,Jl 15,21:2
Mixed Doubles 1927,Ap 27,22:3
World Waits, The 1933,O 26,22:5
Hook-Up, The 1935,My 9,24:6
Good Men and True 1935,O 26,12:4
Whatever Goes Up 1935,N 26,28:2
Marching Song 1937,F 18,18:2
Without Warning 1937,My 3,23:2
Ringside Seat 1938,N 23,24:5
Cue for Passion 1940,D 20,33:4
They Should Have Stood in Bed 1942,F 14,18:5
Strings, My Lord, Are False, The 1942,My 20,24:2
Brights Lights of 1944 1943,S 17,27:4
Suds in Your Eye 1944,Ja 13,15:5
Woman Bites Dog 1946,Ap 18,21:2
Six Characters in Search of an Author
1955,D 12,38:1
Morrison, Russell (Director)
Furnished Rooms 1934,My 30,14:6
Morrison, Ruth
Louisiana 1933,F 28,15:5
Rumpelstiltskin 1948,Mr 15,27:3
Indian Captive, The 1949,Ja 31,15:2
Morrison, Sam (Miscellaneous)
Summer Wives 1936,Ap 14,18:1
Morrison, Thomas V
Chivalry 1925,D 16,22:3
He Loved the Ladies 1927,My 11,29:2
Coriolanus 1927,Je 18,8:3
Skidding 1928,My 22,18:5
With Privileges 1930,S 16,30:2
Did I Say No? 1931,S 23,19:4
Lady Refuses, The 1933,Mr 8,18:6
Amourette 1933,S 28,25:2
Night Remembers, The 1934,N 28,24:3
Knock on Wood 1935,My 29,16:2
Menagerie 1935,Jl 2,24:3
Woman of Destiny, A 1936,Mr 3,25:2
Professor Mamlock 1937,Ap 14,30:3
Prologue to Glory 1938,Mr 18,22:2
Johnny on the Spot 1942,Ja 9,24:2
Flamingo Road 1946,Mr 20,18:2
Christopher Blake 1946,D 2,33:2

Morrison, Viola
Deacon, The 1925,N 25,14:3
Morrison, Walter
Keep Kool 1924,My 23,16:4
Morriss, Ann
Ah, Wilderness! 1954,Ag 21,20:4
Morrissey, Betty
Young and Fair, The 1948,N 23,35:2
Pygmalion 1952,F 9,11:2
Scrapbooks 1953,N 6,24:2
Curious Savage, The 1956,Mr 17,12:3
Morrissey, Eamon
Philadelphia, Here I Come! 1966,F 17,28:1
Lovers; Finders 1967,S 24,II,1:4
Lovers; Winners 1968,Jl 26,21:4
Morrissey, Jack
Hold Your Horses 1933,S 26,26:4
Morrissey, John
Elton Case, The 1921,S 12,16:2
Partners Again 1922,My 2,22:2
Breaking Point, The 1923,Ag 17,8:4
Jack in the Pulpit 1925,Ja 7,33:1
Holy Terror, A 1925,S 29,31:2
Deacon, The 1925,N 25,14:3
First Night 1930,N 27,32:3
Blessed Event 1932,F 13,23:2
Boy Friend, The 1932,Je 8,22:3
Carry Nation 1932,O 31,18:2
Both Your Houses 1933,Mr 7,20:3
Furnished Rooms 1934,My 30,14:6
Roll Sweet Chariot 1934,O 3,24:3
Woman of Destiny, A 1936,Mr 3,25:2
Big Blow 1938,O 3,11:2
Morrissey, John (Musical Director)
Off Your Marx 1936,Ap 2,28:2
Morrissey, John H
Nine Pine Street 1933,Ap 28,15:5
Morrissey, John P
Tarzan of the Apes 1921,S 8,14:3
Morrissey, John S
So This Is Politics 1924,Je 17,22:2
Morrissey, Madelyn
Kid Boots 1924,Ja 1,21:3
Morrissey, Marguerite
Highland Fling, A 1944,Ap 29,13:2
Life With Mother 1948,O 21,32:2
Morrissey, Will
Buzzin' Around 1920,Jl 7,14:1
Will Morrissey's Newcomers 1923,Ag 9,16:2
Keep It Clean 1929,Je 25,35:5
Hoboken Hoboes 1929,D 28,10:8
Will Morrissey's Folies Bergere Revue 1930,Ap 16,26:6
Morrissey, Will (Composer)
Buzzin' Around 1920,Jl 7,14:1
Keep It Clean 1929,Je 25,35:5
Hot Rhythm 1930,Ag 22,18:5
Morrissey, Will (Director)
Hot Rhythm 1930,Ag 22,18:5
Morrissey, Will (Lyricist)
Buzzin' Around 1920,Jl 7,14:1
Keep It Clean 1929,Je 25,35:5
Will Morrissey's Folies Bergere Revue 1930,Ap 16,26:6
Hot Rhythm 1930,Ag 22,18:5
Saluta 1934,Ag 29,13:4
Morrissey, Will (Original Author)
Saluta 1934,Ag 29,13:4
Morrissey, Will (Playwright)
Buzzin' Around 1920,Jl 7,14:1
Newcomers 1923,Jl 15,VI,1:2
Will Morrissey's Newcomers 1923,Ag 9,16:2
Polly of Hollywood 1927,F 22,22:3
Keep It Clean 1929,Je 25,35:5
Hoboken Hoboes 1929,D 28,10:8
Hot Rhythm 1930,Ag 22,18:5
Time, Place and the Girl, The 1942,O 22,24:3
Morrissey, Will (Producer)
Dawn of Ireland, The 1920,O 1,14:2
All-Star Idlers of 1921, The 1921,Ag 9,16:3
Hoboken Hoboes 1929,D 28,10:8
Will Morrissey's Folies Bergere Revue 1930,Ap 16,26:6
Morrissy, Harry
George White's Scandals 1926,Je 15,23:2
Morro
Diamond Lil 1949,F 7,16:2
Morros, Boris (Producer)
Waltz King, The 1943,N 28,II,1:1
Morrow, Betty
House of Bernarda Alba, The 1951,Ja 8,14:6
Morrow, Constance
Noah 1935,N 6,32:2
Tomorrow's Monday 1936,Jl 16,15:6
Morrow, Doretta
Where's Charley? 1948,O 12,33:2
King and I, The 1951,Mr 30,26:2
King and I, The 1951,Ap 8,II,1:1
Kismet 1953,D 4,2:4
Kismet 1955,My 1,II,3:1
Kismet 1955,My 17,33:4
Morrow, Helen
Murder in the Cathedral 1936,Mr 21,13:5

Class of '29 1936,My 16,10:3
It Can't Happen Here 1936,O 28,30:1
Hero Is Born, A 1937,O 2,18:6
Morrow, Irving
Penal Law 2010 1930,Ap 19,14:2
Once in a Lifetime 1930,S 25,22:3
Midsummer Night's Dream, A 1932,Jl 13,15:1
Midsummer Night's Dream, A 1932,N 18,22:2
Twelfth Night 1932,N 19,20:5
Comedy of Errors, The 1932,N 22,25:3
Merchant of Venice, The 1932,N 24,34:5
Romeo and Juliet 1933,F 3,21:5
Romeo and Juliet 1934,D 21,30:3
Barretts of Wimpole Street, The 1935,F 26,16:2
Romeo and Juliet 1935,D 24,10:2
Saint Joan 1936,Mr 10,27:4
If I Were You 1938,Ja 9,II,3:2
If I Were You 1938,Ja 25,24:2
All the Living 1938,Mr 25,14:4
Twelfth Night 1940,N 20,26:3
Macbeth 1941,N 12,30:2
Talking to You 1942,Ag 18,17:1
Across the Board on Tomorrow Morning 1942,Ag 18,17:1
January Thaw 1946,F 5,18:2
Morrow, Jeff
Mr Peebles and Mr Hooker 1946,O 11,29:2
Diamond Lil 1949,F 7,16:2
Lady From the Sea, The 1950,Ag 8,23:2
Billy Budd 1951,F 12,18:3
Lace on Her Petticoat 1951,S 5,40:3
Three Wishes for Jamie 1952,Mr 22,9:2
Morrow, Joan
Hamlet 1967,F 17,44:1
Morrow, Karen
Sing Muse 1961,D 7,52:1
Boys From Syracuse, The 1963,Ap 16,31:1
Boys From Syracuse, The 1963,Je 2,II,1:1
I Had a Ball 1964,D 16,50:1
Oklahoma! 1965,D 16,62:1
Most Happy Fella, The 1966,My 12,55:1
Joyful Noise, A 1966,D 16,57:1
Brigadoon 1967,D 14,59:2
I'm Solomon 1968,Ap 24,51:1
Carnival! 1968,D 13,58:1
Morrow, Macklin (Composer)
Last Night of Don Juan, The 1925,N 10,23:2
Morrow, Mary Jane
Trojan Horse, The 1940,O 31,28:3
Morrow, Milo (Costume Designer)
Sambo 1969,D 22,42:1
X Has No Value 1970,F 17,35:1
Mod Donna 1970,My 4,48:1
Sambo 1970,Jl 23,24:1
Morrow, Portia
Plumes in the Dust 1936,N 7,14:2
Life With Father 1939,N 9,26:2
Morrow, Priscilla
On the Town 1959,F 14,15:1
Morrow, Robert
Scene of the Crime, The 1940,Mr 29,24:1
Morrow, Russ
Sweet Confession 1959,Ap 15,30:1
Morrow, Stephen
Johnny 2X4 1942,Mr 17,24:6
Meet a Body 1944,O 17,19:5
Star Spangled Family 1945,Ap 11,18:6
Morrow, Vic
Deathwatch 1958,O 10,34:2
Morse, Barry
Hide and Seek 1957,Ap 3,26:1
Three Sisters, The 1968,Mr 18,56:1
Coriolanus 1968,My 26,II,7:1
Hadrian VII 1969,S 20,20:1
Morse, Barry (Director)
Salad Days 1958,N 11,24:1
Staircase 1968,Ja 11,41:2
Morse, Barry (Miscellaneous)
Salad Days 1958,N 11,24:1
Morse, Ben
Duchess of Malfi, The 1946,O 16,35:2
Medea 1947,O 21,27:2
Morse, Ben (Costume Designer)
Well of the Saints, The 1959,Ap 11,15:4
Workhouse Ward, The 1959,Ap 11,15:4
Morse, Ben (Playwright)
Daughters of the Late Colonel, The 1951,O 15,21:2
Morse, Charles R (Scenic Designer)
Dover Road, The 1926,Ap 29,20:3
Morse, Donald
Cup of Trembling, The 1959,My 1,33:5
Morse, Edwin
Dover Road, The 1921,D 24,7:2
Anathema 1923,Ap 11,16:2
Mrs Partridge Presents 1925,Ja 6,23:3
Dishonored Lady 1930,F 5,27:1
Brief Moment 1931,N 10,28:2
Morse, Edwin (Director)
Whirlpool 1929,D 4,37:3
Morse, Florence
Unsophisticates, The 1929,D 31,14:5
Morse, George
Night Is Black Bottles, The 1962,D 5,56:1

Morse, George—Cont
Purple Canary, The 1963,Ap 23,31:1
Morse, Grace
Bad Girl 1930,O 3,30:2
Morse, Harold (Miscellaneous)
Cocktails of 1934 1934,My 5,22:1
Morse, Hayward
Merry Wives of Windsor, The 1956,Je 21,34:4
King John 1960,Je 29,26:2
Morse, Joan (Costume Designer)
Rattle of a Simple Man 1963,Ap 18,39:1
Morse, Josephine
What Do We Know 1927,D 24,8:1
First Mortgage 1929,O 11,36:1
Life and Death of an American 1939,My 20,11:2
Morse, Lee
Artists and Models 1923,Ag 21,12:2
Morse, Melanie
Merchant of Venice, The 1970,Je 10,39:1
Morse, Muriel (Producer)
That 5 A.M. Jazz 1964,O 20,42:2
Morse, N Brewster (Playwright)
Half-Naked Truth, The 1926,Je 8,23:1
Morse, Peggy
Dooley Cashes In 1935,Ag 17,18:6
Morse, Richard
Girl From Samos, The 1954,N 24,17:1
Country Wife, The 1955,Ap 6,35:1
Thor, With Angels 1956,O 15,29:4
Makropoulos Secret, The 1957,D 4,52:4
Sign of Winter 1958,My 8,35:1
All Kinds of Giants 1961,D 19,40:1
Stone Tower, The 1962,Je 24,14:2
Mother Courage and Her Children 1963,Mr 30,5:5
Romeo and Juliet 1965,Je 21,36:3
Coriolanus 1965,Je 21,36:1
Taming of the Shrew, The 1965,Je 24,32:2
King Lear 1965,Je 25,39:1
World of Gunter Grass, The 1966,Ap 27,38:1
Fiddler on the Roof 1970,F 28,20:1
Morse, Robert
Matchmaker, The 1955,D 6,45:6
Matchmaker, The 1955,D 18,II,3:1
Say Darling 1958,Ap 4,17:1
Say Darling 1958,Ap 13,II,1:1
Say Darling 1959,F 26,38:2
Take Me Along 1959,O 23,22:2
Take Me Along 1959,N 1,II,1:1
How to Succeed in Business Without Really Trying 1961,O 16,34:1
Morse, Robin
Duchess of Malfi, The 1946,O 16,35:2
Morse, Tilda (Choreographer)
Fourth Avenue North 1961,S 28,50:2
Morselli, Olga
Untitled-Revue 1924,F 19,12:1
Morske, James (Miscellaneous)
Frankie and Johnny 1952,O 29,37:2
Morson, Beatrice
Prince Charlie and Flora 1931,Ag 29,16:5
Morson, Leslie
Pigeon, The 1930,O 15,26:2
Devil's Little Game, The 1932,Ag 2,20:4
Morstatt, Ben (Lighting Director)
Movie Man 1959,O 28,40:4
Abortion 1959,O 28,40:4
Sniper, The 1959,O 28,40:4
Morstatt, Ben (Scenic Designer)
Sniper, The 1959,O 28,40:4
Abortion 1959,O 28,40:4
Movie Man 1959,O 28,40:4
Mortensen, John
Wrong Number 1934,Mr 14,23:6
Mortiea, Ann
Love and Maple Syrup 1970,Ja 8,47:1
Mortimer, Alfred (Playwright)
Divin Aretin, Le 1930,O 5,IX,4:3
Machiavel 1931,O 18,VIII,4:4
Mortimer, Charles
Bitter Sweet 1929,O 27,IX,2:1
Bitter Sweet 1929,N 6,30:2
Mortimer, Dorothy
Just Married 1921,Ap 27,21:1
Primer for Lovers, A 1929,N 19,26:5
Mortimer, Ellen
Maggie, the Magnificent 1929,O 22,26:1
Mortimer, Henry
Musk 1920,Mr 15,13:1
Don Juan 1921,S 8,14:2
Your Woman and Mine 1922,F 28,17:2
Her Temporary Husband 1922,S 1,16:2
World We Live In, The 1922,N 1,16:1
Steadfast 1923,O 31,12:1
Macbeth 1924,Mr 17,18:1
Her Way Out 1924,Je 24,18:3
No Other Girl 1924,Ag 14,10:4
Fall Guy, The 1925,Mr 11,19:1
Paid 1925,N 26,32:1
Dope 1926,Ja 4,16:3
Dream Play 1926,Ja 21,18:2
Unchastened Woman, The 1926,F 17,12:1
Ladder, The 1927,O 7,24:2
Becky Sharp 1929,Je 4,29:1
Little Father of the Wilderness, The 1930,Je 3,27:1

Mortimer, Henry—Cont

Mr Samuel 1930,N 11,28:4
Paging Danger 1931,F 27,19:2
Enemy Within 1931,O 6,35:3
Mortimer, John (Playwright)
Dock Brief, The 1961,N 22,24:2
What Shall We Tell Caroline? 1961,N 22,24:2
Come as You Are 1970,Ag 12,32:1
Voyage Round My Father, A 1970,N 28,20:2
Mortimer, John (Translator)
Flea in Her Ear, A 1967,O 29,II,5:1
Flea in Her Ear, A 1967,O 30,59:1
Mortimer, Lillian (Original Author)
No Mother to Guide Her 1933,D 26,18:5
Mortimer, Trisha
Picture of Dorian Gray, The 1963,Ag 29,37:4
Mortin, Winn (Costume Designer)
Lyle 1970,Mr 21,16:2
Mortman, Mike (Playwright)
Teaspoon Every Four Hours, A 1969,Je 16,57:1
Morton
Locus Solus 1922,D 9,11:4
Morton, Benny
Regina 1949,N 1,32:2
Morton, Betty Lee
Rope 1928,F 23,18:3
Morton, Blaise
My Kinsman, Major Molineux 1964,N 2,62:2
Morton, Brooks
Say Darling 1959,F 26,38:2
Come Out, Carlo! 1962,My 4,27:2
Riverwind 1962,D 14,5:5
Marathon '33 1963,D 23,20:1
West Side Story 1964,Ap 9,24:2
Three Sisters, The 1964,Je 23,24:1
Prime of Miss Jean Brodie, The 1968,Ja 17,39:1
Her First Roman 1968,O 21,53:3
Penny Wars, The 1969,O 16,52:1
Sunday Dinner 1970,N 3,28:1
Morton, David
Student Prince, The 1931,Ja 30,18:1
Melody 1933,F 15,17:4
Morton, Edna
Comedy of Errors, The 1923,My 16,22:5
Morton, Frederic (Original Author)
Rothschilds, The 1970,O 20,40:1
Rothschilds, The 1970,N 1,II,1:1
Morton, Gregory
King Lear 1940,D 16,27:2
Nathan the Wise 1942,Mr 12,25:4
Nathan the Wise 1942,Ap 4,18:4
Nathan the Wise 1944,F 22,26:3
War President 1944,Ap 25,17:3
Mayor of Zalamea, The 1946,Ja 28,15:5
Flag Is Born, A 1946,S 7,10:6
Montserrat 1949,O 31,21:4
Now I Lay Me Down to Sleep 1950,Mr 3,21:2
Romeo and Juliet 1951,Mr 12,21:2
Sherlock Holmes 1953,O 31,11:2
Sands of the Negev 1954,O 20,32:1
Who Was That Lady I Saw You With?
1958,Mr 4,33:2
Morton, Harold (Director)
School for Brides 1944,Ag 2,19:4
Morton, Harry K
Sweetheart Shop, The 1920,S 1,13:4
Love Dreams 1921,O 11,22:2
Springtime of Youth 1922,O 27,15:1
Love Song, The 1925,Ja 14,19:4
Countess Maritza 1926,Mr 30,20:3
Countess Maritza 1926,S 20,21:1
Polly 1929,Ja 9,28:3
Street Singer, The 1929,S 18,35:2
Rose Marie 1936,Jl 22,22:6
Countess Maritza 1936,Ag 19,18:2
Bitter Sweet 1936,Ag 26,17:3
Naughty Marietta 1936,S 2,19:5
Nina Rosa 1937,Ag 26,24:3
Circus Princess, The 1937,Ag 31,26:6
Blossom Time 1938,D 27,12:2
Blossom Time 1943,S 6,21:2
Morton, Howard
Hasty Heart, The 1954,Mr 13,10:1
Ever Since Paradise 1957,Jl 12,18:4
Ignorants Abroad, The 1960,My 24,43:2
Morton, Howard E (Playwright)
Dream Maker, The 1921,N 22,17:1
Morton, Hugh (Composer)
Belle of New York, The 1948,D 2,36:6
Morton, Hugh (Playwright)
Whirl of New York, The 1921,Je 14,18:1
Morton, J Maddison (Playwright)
Cox and Box 1934,S 7,24:3
Morton, James C
Spice of 1922 1922,Jl 7,12:4
Holka Polka 1925,O 15,27:2
Lace Petticoat 1927,Ja 5,18:2
Circus Princess, The 1927,Ap 26,32:2
Hobo 1931,F 12,24:4
Morton, James G
Dear Me 1921,Ja 18,14:1
Roger Bloomer 1923,Mr 2,18:3
School for Scandal, The 1925,O 24,19:1
Spellbound 1927,F 16,17:2

Field God, The 1927,Ap 22,18:2
Playing the Game 1927,D 20,32:5
Up Pops the Devil 1930,S 2,19:1
Morton, Joan
Buttrio Square 1952,O 15,40:2
Almost Crazy 1955,Je 21,37:1
Morton, Joe
Bolls of Cotton 1925,D 22,18:3
Month of Sundays 1968,S 17,50:1
Salvation 1969,S 25,55:1
Morton, John
Connecticut Yankee, A 1927,N 4,24:2
Morton, John Maddison (Playwright)
Three Times Three; Box and Cox 1956,My 24,27:2
Most Unwarrantable Intrusion, A 1968,Jl 9,30:2
Most Unwarrantable Intrusion, A 1968,Jl 14,II,4:5
Morton, Jonnie
Young Provincials, The 1958,S 19,22:4
Morton, Joseph (Scenic Designer)
Hamp 1967,Mr 10,32:1
Morton, Leon
Evergreen 1930,D 21,VIII,1:6
Morton, Lewis (Director)
Century Revue and the Midnight Rounders, The
1920,Jl 13,9:1
Katja 1926,O 19,27:3
Nightingale, The 1927,Ja 4,20:4
Cherry Blossoms 1927,Mr 29,22:3
Luckee Girl 1928,S 17,28:6
Pleasure Bound 1929,F 19,22:4
Music in May 1929,Ap 2,29:1
Night in Venice, A 1929,My 22,30:2
Morton, Linda
War 1929,S 19,37:3
Morton, Maddison (Playwright)
Cox and Box 1936,S 29,34:2
Cox and Box 1948,Ja 20,26:2
Cox and Box 1951,F 20,21:2
Morton, Madison (Lyricist)
Cox and Box 1939,Ja 17,27:5
Morton, Martha
Honeymoon Lane 1926,S 21,32:3
Vaudeville (Palace) 1929,Mr 11,22:5
Morning's at Seven 1955,Je 23,25:1
Morton, Michael (Playwright)
In the Night Watch 1921,Ja 31,10:1
Woman to Woman 1921,S 10,12:3
Guilty One, The 1922,Ag 13,VI,1:3
Guilty One, The 1923,Mr 21,19:1
Guilty One, The 1923,Mr 25,VIII,1:1
Riceyman Steps 1926,D 12,VIII,4:7
Fatal Alibi, The 1932,F 10,26:6
Signor Bracoli 1932,O 2,IX,2:3
Morton, Paul
Hoboken Blues 1928,F 18,10:1
Strip Girl 1935,O 21,22:6
Morton, Richard
Hamlet 1923,N 27,23:6
Morton, Roy
Legitimate Steal, The 1958,Ap 1,35:1
Morton, Sam
Sidewalks of New York 1927,O 4,33:1
Morton, Tommy
Make Mine Manhattan 1948,Ja 16,26:2
Lend an Ear 1948,D 17,38:2
Littlest Revue, The 1956,My 23,37:2
Morton, Vance M (Director)
Tread the Green Grass 1932,Jl 24,IX,1:3
Morton, Winn (Costume Designer)
Paradise Island 1961,Je 24,11:1
Paradise Island 1962,Je 28,22:1
Around the World in 80 Days 1963,Je 24,22:1
Around the World in 80 Days 1964,Je 29,33:2
Mardi Gras! 1965,Je 28,33:2
Mardi Gras! 1966,Jl 11,32:2
By Jupiter 1967,Ja 20,28:2
Arabian Nights 1967,Jl 3,12:1
Spofford 1967,D 15,54:3
Avanti 1968,F 1,29:1
Education of H*Y*M*A*N K*A*P*L*A*N, The
1968,Ap 5,57:1
Leonard Sillman's New Faces of 1968
1968,My 3,43:1
West Side Story 1968,Je 25,32:1
South Pacific 1968,Je 30,54:2
Spiro Who? 1969,My 19,55:1
South Pacific 1969,Jl 7,27:1
Sound of Music, The 1970,Jl 3,13:1
Morton, Winn (Scenic Designer)
Leonard Sillman's New Faces of 1968
1968,My 3,43:1
Morton and Glass
Vaudeville (Palace) 1923,Mr 6,26:1
Morum, William (Playwright)
Edwina Black 1950,N 22,20:5
Morvil, Harry
Bat, The 1920,Ag 24,6:1
Garden of Weeds 1924,Ap 29,12:3
Mory, Janos von (Composer)
Valliere, La 1933,Ap 16,IX,2:5
Mory y Ragon, Don Jaime de
Decent People Frighten Me 1964,Ja 26,82:3

Mosby, Walter
Pirate, The 1942,N 26,39:2
Run, Little Chillun 1943,Ag 14,6:1
Show Boat 1948,S 9,33:2
Mosca, Roy
Compulsion 1957,O 25,21:1
Mosco, Natalie (Miscellaneous)
Hair 1970,Ja 13,39:1
Mosconi, Louis
Hitchy-Koo, 1920 1920,O 20,11:3
Mosconi, Vera
Hitchy-Koo, 1920 1920,O 20,11:3
Mosconi Brothers
Vaudeville (Palace) 1923,Ja 30,12:2
Vaudeville (Palace) 1924,Ja 1,21:1
Friars Club Frolic 1933,My 15,16:4
Mosconi Family
All-Star Jamboree 1921,Jl 14,18:1
Moscovitch, Maurice
Torch, The 1922,O 8,VI,1:7
Angelo 1923,Mr 30,14:4
Josef Suss 1930,Ja 21,28:5
Merchant of Venice, The 1930,N 16,VIII,3:1
Merchant of Venice, The 1930,D 3,29:2
Moscovitz, Jennie
Partners Again 1922,My 2,22:2
Moscow Art Trio
Vaudeville (Palace) 1926,Mr 23,24:3
Moscow Theatrical Society
Porgy and Bess 1945,Je 17,II,4:3
Moscowitz, Jennie
Kosher Kitty Kelly 1925,Je 16,24:2
Song Writer, The 1928,Ag 14,15:2
Wooden Soldier, The 1931,Je 23,28:4
Counsellor-at-Law 1931,N 7,17:2
Counsellor-at-Law 1932,S 13,17:2
Excursion 1937,Ap 10,11:4
Excursion 1937,Ap 18,XI,1:1
Counsellor-at-Law 1942,N 25,17:2
Mosel, George
At War With the Army 1949,Mr 9,32:2
Mosel, Tad (Playwright)
All the Way Home 1960,D 1,42:1
All the Way Home 1960,D 18,II,3:1
Madame Aphrodite 1961,D 30,13:1
Moseley, C S
Front Page, The 1937,N 12,27:2
Moseley, Peggy
George White's Scandals 1926,Je 15,23:2
George White's Scandals 1931,S 15,30:1
Music Hall Varieties 1932,N 23,15:3
Melody 1933,F 15,17:4
George White's Scandals 1935,D 26,20:2
Moseley, Thomas
House of Shadows, The 1927,Ap 22,18:4
Meek Mose 1928,F 7,30:1
Goin' Home 1928,Ag 24,23:2
Brown Buddies 1930,O 8,29:1
Tree, The 1932,Ap 13,23:5
Sailor, Beware! 1935,My 7,28:4
Turpentine 1936,Je 27,21:6
Mosely
In Abraham's Bosom 1927,F 20,VII,1:1
Mosely, Thomas
Case of Philip Lawrence, The 1937,Je 9,31:1
Androcles and the Lion 1938,D 17,10:5
Mosenson, Yigal (Playwright)
Struggle for the Negev 1953,D 14,45:5
Moser
Abie's Irish Rose 1927,O 23,VIII,2:4
Moser, Barbara
Liar, The 1950,My 19,30:2
Moser, Hans
Midsummer Night's Dream, A 1927,N 18,21:1
Jedermann 1927,D 8,33:2
Dantons Tod 1927,D 21,28:3
Peripherie 1928,Ja 3,29:1
Er Ist an Allem Schuld; He Is to Blame for
Everything 1928,Ja 10,28:3
Diener Zweier Herren; Servant of Two Masters,
The 1928,Ja 10,28:3
Artisten; Burlesque 1928,S 23,IX,2:2
Dreimal Hochzeit 1929,Ap 28,IX,1:4
Fledermaus, Die 1931,N 14,IX,2:1
Journey to Pressburg, The 1931,Mr 8,VIII,2:7
Fair Helen 1931,Ag 30,VIII,2:1
Moser, James (Lighting Director)
Ice Capades 1969,Ja 8,42:1
Moser, Margot
Carousel 1949,Ja 26,28:2
Carousel 1949,F 6,II,1:1
Guys and Dolls 1959,Jl 22,22:2
Brigadoon 1967,D 14,59:2
Yeomen of the Guard, The 1968,My 9,53:1
Moser, Simone
Everyman 1941,My 9,19:2
Moses, Elliot S
So's Your Old Antique 1930,My 8,32:5
Moses, Elsa (Producer)
Western Waters 1937,D 29,17:1
Moses, Gilbert
Good Soldier Schweik, The 1963,Ap 9,57:1

Moses, Gilbert (Composer)
Slave Ship 1969,N 22,46:1
Moses, Gilbert (Director)
Slave Ship 1969,N 22,46:1
Slave Ship 1969,N 23,II,3:1
Moses, Harry (Miscellaneous)
Grand Hotel 1930,N 14,30:4
Drama at Inish 1934,N 15,24:2
Moses, Harry (Mrs) (Elsa Lazareff) (Director)
Dangerous Corner 1932,O 28,23:1
Moses, Harry (Producer)
Warrior's Husband, The 1932,Mr 12,19:4
Dangerous Corner 1932,O 28,23:1
Is Life Worth Living? 1933,N 10,24:6
Old Maid, The 1935,Ja 8,26:1
O Evening Star 1936,Ja 9,24:6
Moses, J
Passion Play, The 1929,Ap 30,32:1
Moses, John (Miscellaneous)
Mr Winkle's Holliday 1946,Je 24,27:6
Moses, John (Producer)
Pretty Little Parlor 1944,Ap 18,24:8
Kiss Them for Me 1945,MR 21,27:2
Moses, Julia
Make Me Know It 1929,N 5,32:5
Moses, Montero
Malinda 1929,D 4,37:2
Moses, Sam
Doctor's Dilemma, The 1969,Je 24,37:1
Moses, Tim
Trumpets and Drums 1969,O 13,52:1
Mosheim, Grete
Baby Mine 1927,Ap 3,VIII,2:1
This Was a Man 1928,My 20,VIII,2:1
Burlesque; Artisten 1928,Je 10,17:2
Street Scene 1930,Mr 16,IX,4:1
Phaea 1930,Ag 31,VIII,2:1
Fee, Die; Fairy, The 1931,F 8,VIII,2:1
Kommt ein Vogel Geflogen 1931,My 10,VIII,1:4
Waterloo Bridge 1931,N 29,VIII,4:1
Faust 1932,Je 19,IX,1:3
Two Share a Dwelling 1935,O 9,26:3
Two Share a Dwelling 1935,N 3,X,1:7
Letters to Lucerne 1941,D 24,14:2
Calico Wedding 1945,Mr 8,18:6
Mosher, Hugh
Story of Mary Surratt, The 1947,F 10,25:2
Flies, The 1954,S 10,18:2
Mosia, Meshack (Miscellaneous)
Sponono 1964,Ap 3,28:1
Mosier, Marguerite
Liliom 1921,Ap 21,18:1
Swifty 1922,O 17,14:1
Lady of the Rose 1925,My 20,26:4
Right Age to Marry, The 1926,F 16,22:3
Half-Naked Truth, The 1926,Je 8,23:1
My Country 1926,Ag 10,19:1
Slaves All 1926,D 7,24:4
Junk 1927,Ja 6,25:1
Moskovina, Mlle
As You Were 1920,Ja 28,22:3
Moskvin, Ivan
Czar Feodor 1922,O 22,VIII,1:6
Tsar Fyodor Ivanovitch 1923,Ja 9,26:1
Tsar Fyodor Ivanovitch 1923,Ja 11,25:1
Tsar Fyodor Ivanovitch 1923,Ja 14,VII,1:1
Lower Depths, The 1923,Ja 16,16:1
Cherry Orchard, The 1923,Ja 23,18:1
Cherry Orchard, The 1923,Ja 28,VII,1:1
Brothers Karamazov, The 1923,F 27,14:2
Brothers Karamazov, The 1923,Mr 4,VII,1:1
Tsar Fyodor Ivanovitch 1923,My 22,14:3
Death of Pazukhin, The 1924,F 12,20:1
Brothers Karamazov, The 1924,My 6,25:2
Moscow Art Theatre 1924,My 13,25:2
Mosle, H B
Galloper, The 1924,D 19,26:2
Mosler, Arthur J Jr
Upon My Soul 1927,Ap 22,19:1
Mosler, Arthur K Jr
Betty Behave 1927,Mr 9,28:4
Mosler, Enid
House of Flowers 1954,D 31,11:2
Mosler, Margaret
Not So Long Ago 1920,My 5,14:1
Mosley, Alice
Tarzan of the Apes 1921,S 8,14:3
Mosley, Fred
Peter Weston 1923,S 20,5:2
Mosley, Louise
Macbeth 1968,N 30,49:3
Mosley, Thomas
In Abraham's Bosom 1926,D 31,10:2
Mosnar, Paul
Patriots, The 1943,D 21,22:5
Moss, A George
Oedipus Rex 1965,Jl 9,17:1
Moss, Al
It's About Time 1942,Mr 31,28:3
Moss, Al (Composer)
'Tis of Thee 1940,O 28,21:3
It's About Time 1942,Mr 31,28:3

Moss, Alexandra
Silk Stockings 1955,F 25,17:3
Moss, Arnold
Living Corpse, The 1929,D 7,19:1
Romeo and Juliet 1930,Ap 22,33:1
Siegfried 1930,O 21,34:1
Fifth Column, The 1940,Mr 7,18:2
Fifth Column, The 1940,Mr 17,X,1:1
Hold On to Your Hats 1940,S 12,30:3
Journey to Jerusalem 1940,O 7,21:2
Flight to the West 1940,D 31,19:1
Land Is Bright, The 1941,O 29,26:2
Land Is Bright, The 1941,N 9,IX,1:1
Tempest, The 1945,Ja 26,17:2
Tempest, The 1945,F 4,II,1:1
Tempest, The 1945,N 13,24:6
Front Page, The 1946,S 5,22:4
Front Page, The 1946,S 15,II,21:1
Twelfth Night 1949,O 4,33:2
Twelfth Night 1949,O 9,II,1:1
King Lear 1950,D 26,18:1
King Lear 1950,D 31,II,1:1
Evening With Will Shakespeare, An 1952,D 7,86:5
Dark Is Light Enough, The 1955,F 24,20:1
Medea 1955,Je 16,35:4
King John 1956,Je 28,33:5
Measure for Measure 1956,Je 29,16:1
Measure for Measure 1957,Ja 23,24:1
Measure for Measure 1957,F 3,II,1:1
Back to Methuselah 1958,Mr 27,41:5
Back to Methuselah 1958,Ap 6,II,1:1
Moss, Arnold (Miscellaneous)
Back to Methuselah 1958,Mr 27,41:5
Back to Methuselah 1958,Ap 6,II,1:1
Moss, Arnold (Playwright)
Back to Methuselah 1958,Mr 27,41:5
Moss, David
Enemy of the People, An 1958,F 26,24:2
Moss, David (Producer)
Tobacco Road 1960,My 11,44:2
Moss, Frank L (Playwright)
Lambent Flame, The 1935,Jl 16,24:2
Moss, George
Tell My Story 1939,Mr 16,26:6
Moss, Harry
Lebende Leichnam, Der, Der; Living Corpse, The 1928,Ja 24,26:2
Broken Chain, The 1929,F 21,30:4
Moss, Jeffrey (Scenic Designer)
Me and Juliet 1970,My 15,42:1
Moss, Joe
Vaudeville (Palace) 1932,Jl 4,14:5
Moss, Marjorie
City Chap, The 1925,O 27,21:1
Diable 1926,O 31,VIII,2:4
Vaudeville (Palace) 1928,Ja 31,29:2
This Year of Grace 1928,N 8,27:1
Moss, Mary
Merry Widow, The 1931,S 8,39:1
Geisha, The 1931,O 6,35:4
Moss, Milt
Highway Robbery 1955,N 8,36:1
Moss, Paul (Miscellaneous)
Grand Street Follies, The 1929,My 2,20:4
Moss, Paul F (Producer)
Whole World Over, The 1947,Mr 28,28:2
Moss, Peter
Medea 1947,O 21,27:2
Moss, Richard (Miscellaneous)
Man With a Load of Mischief, The 1966,N 7,65:1
Moss, Richard (Producer)
Three Plays of the Sea 1970,Ag 20,39:1
Moss, Robert
Too Much Johnson 1964,Ja 16,29:1
You Can't Take It With You 1965,N 24,32:1
Moss, Robert (Director)
Club Bedroom, The 1967,D 6,41:1
Mrs Snow 1970,Ja 6,48:3
Moss, Robert (Miscellaneous)
All in Love 1961,N 11,15:2
Half-Past Wednesday 1962,Ap 7,16:2
Barroom Monks, The 1962,My 29,21:1
Portrait of the Artist as a Young Man, A 1962,My 29,21:1
Dumbwaiter, The 1962,N 27,44:1
Collection, The 1962,N 27,44:1
Maids, The 1963,N 15,29:1
Man and Superman 1964,D 7,45:2
War and Peace 1965,Ja 12,32:1
Judith 1965,Mr 25,42:2
You Can't Take It With You 1965,N 24,32:1
Moss, Stewart
Seidman and Son 1962,O 16,32:2
Moss, Stillman (Miscellaneous)
King Lear 1963,N 23,22:1
Moss, Wolf William (Miscellaneous)
My House Is Your House 1970,O 16,53:2
Moss and Fontana
Vaudeville (Palace) 1928,F 7,30:5
International Revue 1930,F 9,VIII,4:2
International Revue 1930,F 26,22:2
Sweet and Low 1930,N 18,28:5

Moss and Frye
Vaudeville (Hippodrome) 1925,D 29,21:2
Vaudeville (Palace) 1927,Ja 4,21:2
Vaudeville (Palace) 1927,O 11,27:2
Vaudeville (Palace) 1929,O 7,22:4
Mosse, Spencer (Lighting Director)
Coriolanus 1968,My 26,II,7:1
Brass Butterfly, The 1970,Ja 31,34:1
Mosse, Walter M (Dr) (Miscellaneous)
Sign of Jonah, The 1957,My 2,27:1
Mossee, Michael (Scenic Designer)
Early Morning 1970,N 26,57:1
Mossensohn, Yigal (Playwright)
Sands of the Negev 1954,O 20,32:1
Mosser, Jack (Costume Designer)
Pardon Our French 1950,O 6,22:4
Mossfield, Harry
H M S Pinafore 1960,S 8,41:1
Pirates of Penzance, The 1961,S 7,41:1
Mossi, Alexander
Robbers, The 1928,Ag 10,9:2
Mossinson, Yigal (Playwright)
Casablan 1954,N 13,13:1
Mossman, Earl
Her Family Tree 1920,D 28,9:2
Mosso, Vincent
Dracula Sabbat 1970,O 2,28:2
Mostel, Barbara
My Mother, My Father and Me 1963,Mr 25,5:5
Bicycle Ride to Nevada 1963,S 25,38:1
Mostel, Zero
Keep 'Em Laughing 1942,Ap 25,9:2
Top-Notchers 1942,My 30,8:5
Concert Varieties 1945,Je 2,10:7
Beggar's Holiday 1946,D 27,13:3
Flight Into Egypt 1952,Mr 19,33:2
Flight Into Egypt 1952,Mr 30,II,1:1
Stone for Danny Fisher, A 1954,O 22,24:2
Once Over Lightly 1955,Mr 16,39:1
Good Woman of Setzuan, The 1956,D 19,41:2
Good Woman of Setzuan, The 1956,D 30,II,1:1
Good as Gold 1957,Mr 8,22:2
Ulysses in Nighttown 1958,Je 6,30:1
Ulysses in Nighttown 1958,Je 15,II,1:1
Rhinoceros 1961,Ja 10,27:1
Rhinoceros 1961,Ja 22,II,1:1
Funny Thing Happened on the Way to the Forum, A 1962,My 9,49:1
Funny Thing Happened on the Way to the Forum, A 1962,My 20,II,1:1
Funny Thing Happened on the Way to the Forum, A 1962,Jl 6,22:5
Funny Thing Happened on the Way to the Forum, A 1963,Je 2,II,1:1
Fiddler on the Roof 1964,S 23,56:2
Fiddler on the Roof 1964,O 4,II,1:1
Fiddler on the Roof 1964,O 6,36:5
Latent Heterosexual, The 1968,Mr 22,52:1
Latent Heterosexual, The 1968,Mr 31,II,3:1
Fiddler on the Roof 1969,Ag 8,10:2
Mosten, Maurice
Homo 1969,Ap 12,40:2
Mostol, Tommy
Pins and Needles 1922,F 2,20:1
Mostoller (Costume Designer)
Affair, The 1962,S 21,34:2
Wet Paint 1965,Ap 13,33:1
Mostovoy
Chauve-Souris 1929,Ja 23,20:2
Moten, Edna
Sugar Hill 1931,D 26,15:2
Moten, Etta
Zombie 1932,F 11,17:2
Porgy and Bess 1943,S 14,26:2
Porgy and Bess 1944,F 8,13:2
Lysistrata 1946,O 18,27:5
Motha, Sidney
Sponono 1964,Ap 3,28:1
Mothers of Invention
Absolutely Freeee 1967,My 25,58:1
Motherwell, Marie
Wind Remains, The 1943,Mr 31,16:6
Motileva, V
Poverty Is No Crime 1935,F 21,22:5
Strange Child 1935,F 26,16:1
Marriage 1935,Mr 12,24:8
Enemies 1935,Mr 19,24:7
Motley, Robert (Scenic Designer)
Doll's House, A 1956,My 8,29:2
Firebugs, The 1963,N 22,41:1
King Lear 1963,N 23,22:1
Bedlam Galore, for Two or More 1965,Mr 8,34:1
Impromptu, L' 1965,Mr 8,34:1
Foursome 1965,Mr 8,34:1
Leader, The 1965,Mr 8,34:1
Motley, Warren
Jungle of Cities 1970,Mr 1,75:2
Motley (Costume Designer)
Charles the King 1936,O 10,20:6
Romeo and Juliet 1940,My 10,27:1
Doctor's Dilemma, The 1941,Mr 30,IX,1:1
Cherry Orchard, The 1944,Ja 26,22:1
Tempest, The 1945,Ja 26,17:2

Motley (Costume Designer)—Cont

Carib Song 1945,S 28,17:2
Sky Drift 1945,N 14,25:2
Pygmalion 1945,D 27,16:1
He Who Gets Slapped 1946,Mr 21,31:4
Second Best Bed 1946,Je 4,20:2
Anne of the Thousand Days 1948,D 9,49:2
Happy as Larry 1950,Ja 7,11:2
Innocents, The 1950,F 2,30:2
Peter Pan 1950,Ap 25,27:2
Peter Pan 1950,Ap 30,II,1:1
Liar, The 1950,My 19,30:2
Grand Tour, The 1951,D 11,45:2
Mademoiselle Colombe 1954,Ja 17,II,1:1
Immoralist, The 1954,F 14,II,1:1
Peter Pan 1954,O 31,II,1:1
Honeys, The 1955,Ap 29,26:1
Middle of the Night 1956,F 9,39:1
Rivalry, The 1959,F 9,24:2
Rivalry, The 1959,F 15,II,1:1
Kwamina 1961,O 24,42:1
Complaisant Lover, The 1961,N 2,43:2
Man for All Seasons, A 1961,N 23,51:1
Lorenzo 1963,F 16,5:2
Tovarich 1963,Mr 20,5:1
Patience 1964,Mr 26,42:1
Ben Franklin in Paris 1964,O 28,52:1
Baker Street 1965,F 17,36:1
Devils, The 1965,N 17,51:2
Unknown Soldier and His Wife, The 1967,Jl 7,22:1
Dance of Death, The 1967,O 20,50:1
Motley (Director)
Happy as Larry 1950,Ja 7,11:2
Motley (Miscellaneous)
Importance of Being Earnest, The 1947,Mr 4,30:2
Motley (Scenic Designer)
Spring, 1600 1934,F 1,14:1
Happy Hypocrite, The 1936,Ap 9,21:6
Happy Hypocrite, The 1936,My 10,X,1:1
Anteroom, The 1936,S 6,IX,1:1
Charles the King 1936,O 10,20:6
Romeo and Juliet 1940,My 10,27:1
Cherry Orchard, The 1944,Ja 26,22:1
Tempest, The 1945,Ja 26,17:2
Tempest, The 1945,F 4,II,1:1
Hope for the Best 1945,F 8,14:4
You Touched Me! 1945,S 26,27:2
You Touched Me! 1945,S 30,II,1:1
Sky Drift 1945,N 14,25:2
He Who Gets Slapped 1946,Mr 21,31:4
Second Best Bed 1946,Je 4,20:2
Dancer, The 1946,Je 6,16:5
Requiem for a Nun 1959,F 8,II,1:1
Complaisant Lover, The 1961,N 2,43:2
Man for All Seasons, A 1961,N 23,51:1
Patience 1964,Mr 26,42:1
Unknown Soldier and His Wife, The 1967,Jl 7,22:1
Dance of Death, The 1967,O 20,50:1
Moto, George
Enter Madame 1920,Ag 17,11:2
Mott, Clara
Untitled-Passion Play 1926,Mr 30,20:2
Mott, Hamilton
Mr Moneypenny 1928,O 17,26:2
Mott, Jane
Tragicomedy of Don Cristobita and Dona Rosita,
The 1958,My 30,12:2
Mott, John
Ridgeway's Late Joys 1939,O 22,IX,3:5
Mott, Michael (Costume Designer)
Merry Widow, The 1961,O 27,28:2
Mott, Peter
Betty, Be Good 1920,My 5,14:2
Jimmie 1920,N 18,15:3
Mott, Will (Lighting Director)
Terminal 1970,Ap 15,51:2
Endgame 1970,My 6,47:1
Serpent, The 1970,Je 2,35:1
Mott, Will (Miscellaneous)
Love Your Crooked Neighbor 1969,D 30,40:1
Motte, Jack
Out of the Night 1927,O 18,32:3
Philadelphia 1929,S 17,34:5
Mottel, Syens (Director)
For the Time Being 1957,D 18,42:7
Mottinpreger, Sonja
Kiss Me, Kate 1959,Ag 10,24:1
Motto, Thomas
Come of Age 1952,Ja 24,22:2
Mottus, Maie
Electronic Nigger, The 1968,Mr 9,23:2
Mottyleff, Ilia (Director)
Empress of Destiny 1938,Mr 10,16:2
Ghost for Sale 1941,S 30,27:4
Mottyleff, Ilia (Producer)
Empress of Destiny 1938,Mr 10,16:2
Motz, Lucius
Phoebe of Quality Street 1921,My 10,20:1
Mouezy-Eon (Original Author)
Matrimonial Bed, The 1927,O 13,23:2
Mouezy-Eon (Playwright)
Plein aux As 1926,O 31,VIII,2:4
Monsieur Qui Se Regrette, Un 1928,D 9,X,2:7
Amour a l'Americaine, L' 1930,Ap 13,X,2:7

Moulan, Frank
H M S Pinafore 1920,Ja 13,10:2
Secret of Suzanne, The 1920,Ja 13,10:2
Ruddigore 1920,Ja 20,11:2
Little Miss Charity 1920,S 3,6:3
Princess Virtue 1921,My 5,20:2
Just Because 1922,Mr 23,11:1
Mikado, The; Town of Titipu, The 1931,My 5,33:2
H M S Pinafore 1931,My 19,25:2
Gondoliers, The 1931,Je 2,34:4
Patience 1931,Je 16,30:4
Pirates of Penzance, The; Slave of Duty, The
1931,Je 30,23:6
Iolanthe 1931,Jl 14,21:5
Trial by Jury 1931,Jl 28,17:6
H M S Pinafore 1931,Jl 28,17:6
Ruddigore 1931,Ag 11,28:3
Mikado, The 1931,Ag 25,17:7
Iolanthe 1932,Ja 5,20:2
Gondoliers, The 1932,Ja 12,29:1
Mikado, The 1933,Ap 18,13:4
Yeomen of the Guard, The 1933,My 2,20:4
H M S Pinafore 1933,My 9,20:3
Trial by Jury 1933,My 9,20:3
Patience 1933,My 23,22:6
Pirates of Penzance, The 1933,Ag 8,22:4
Yeomen of the Guard, The 1933,Ag 15,20:5
Mikado, The 1934,My 22,28:2
Mikado, The 1935,Jl 16,24:4
Pirates of Penzance, The 1935,Jl 23,24:2
Yeomen of the Guard, The 1935,Jl 30,16:4
Gondoliers, The 1935,Ag 6,20:5
Trial by Jury 1935,Ag 13,20:6
H M S Pinafore 1935,Ag 13,20:6
Mikado, The 1936,Ap 11,18:4
Pirates of Penzance, The 1936,Ap 21,27:5
H M S Pinafore 1936,Ap 28,17:2
Trial by Jury 1936,Ap 28,17:2
Iolanthe 1936,My 5,26:2
Moulan, Frank (Director)
Mikado, The 1936,Ap 11,18:4
Pirates of Penzance, The 1936,Ap 21,27:5
H M S Pinafore 1936,Ap 28,17:2
Trial by Jury 1936,Ap 28,17:2
Iolanthe 1936,My 5,26:2
Moulder, Walter
Romeo and Juliet 1961,F 24,24:1
Take Her, She's Mine 1961,D 22,19:1
Moulinot, Jean-Paul
Marie Tudor 1958,O 22,39:1
Don Juan 1958,O 29,29:1
Cid, Le 1958,O 31,35:2
Moulton, Eda
Spring 3100 1928,F 16,14:2
Moulton, Harold
Devil Within, The 1925,Mr 17,19:4
Saturday Night 1926,O 26,25:1
Three Sisters, The 1926,O 27,24:1
Twelfth Night 1926,D 21,21:4
Inheritors 1927,Mr 8,23:1
Good Hope, The 1927,O 19,24:2
2 + 2 = 5 1927,N 29,30:3
Improvisations in June 1928,F 27,16:5
Would-Be Gentleman, The 1928,O 2,34:1
Cherry Orchard, The 1928,O 16,28:5
Peter Pan; Boy Who Would Not Grow Up, The
1928,N 27,36:3
On the High Road 1929,Ja 15,22:3
Katerina 1929,F 26,30:3
Sea Gull, The 1929,S 17,34:1
Mademoiselle Bourrat 1929,O 8,34:3
Living Corpse, The 1929,D 7,19:1
Romeo and Juliet 1930,Ap 22,33:1
Siegfried 1930,O 21,34:1
Lady of the Camellias, The 1931,Ja 27,21:2
Liliom 1932,O 27,23:2
Camille 1932,O 28,23:2
Dear Jane 1932,N 15,24:3
Alice in Wonderland 1932,D 12,18:3
Alice in Wonderland 1932,D 25,IX,1:1
Cherry Orchard, The 1933,Mr 7,20:3
First Legion, The 1934,O 2,18:2
Take It As It Comes 1944,F 11,17:2
Moulton, Lee
Boo Hoo! East Lynne 1959,S 9,50:4
Moulton, Lee (Scenic Designer)
Boo Hoo! East Lynne 1959,S 9,50:4
Moulton, Robert (Choreographer)
As You Like It 1966,Je 4,19:1
Twelfth Night 1968,Je 15,40:1
Serjeant Musgrave's Dance 1968,Je 16,52:4
Merton of the Movies 1968,S 26,62:1
Moulton, Zita
Smooth as Silk 1921,F 23,18:3
Moultrie, Jane
Tom Sawyer - Ballad of the Mississippi
1947,D 27,11:3
Outside the Door 1949,Mr 2,33:2
Burning Bush, The 1949,D 17,15:5
Circle of Chalk, The 1950,D 2,8:3
Curious Savage, The 1956,Mr 17,12:3
Cast of Characters 1959,Je 11,37:2
Cheri 1959,O 13,44:1

Moultrie, Jane (Playwright)
Cast of Characters 1959,Je 11,37:2
Mound City Blue Blowers
City Chap, The 1925,O 27,21:1
Mounet-Sully, Mr
Hamlet 1932,Jl 3,IX,1:1
Mounsey, Duncan (Miscellaneous)
Louisiana Lady 1947,Je 3,35:2
Mount, Peggy
Sailor, Beware! 1955,Mr 6,II,3:1
Mount-Burke, William (Director)
Pirates of Penzance, The 1970,Jl 26,49:5
Mountain, Lone
To Quito and Back 1937,O 7,30:4
Mounties, The
Vaudeville (Palace) 1928,Jl 24,13:4
Mountjoy, Louis
Fall and Rise of Susan Lenox, The 1920,Je 11,11:2
Mouray, Henry
Honors Are Even 1921,Ag 11,8:2
Mourguet, Michel (Playwright)
Amitie 1932,F 14,VIII,2:5
Moussorgsky, Modest (Composer)
Great Catherine, The 1927,Ap 3,VIII,4:7
Mum's the Word 1940,D 6,28:5
Moutrie, Jane
Yes is for a Very Young Man 1949,Je 7,27:2
Moutsios, G
Oedipus Tyrannus 1952,N 25,35:2
Mowat, Mary Jane
Twelfth Night 1970,Ja 1,18:1
Mowatt, Anna Cora (Playwright)
Fashion 1924,F 5,21:2
Fashion 1924,F 10,VII,1:1
Fashion 1959,Ja 21,27:1
Mowbray, Alan
Sport of Kings, The 1926,My 5,24:2
These Modern Women 1928,F 14,26:2
Dinner Is Served 1929,Ag 16,18:4
Amorous Antic, The 1929,D 3,29:2
Apple Cart, The 1930,N 3,IX,1:3
Enter Laughing 1963,Mr 15,8:1
Enter Laughing 1963,Je 16,II,1:1
Mowbray, Alan (Director)
Dinner Is Served 1929,Ag 16,18:4
Mowbray, Alan (Playwright)
Dinner Is Served 1929,Ag 16,18:4
Dinner Is Served 1930,F 8,13:4
Mowbray, Henry
Shall We Join the Ladies? 1925,Ja 14,19:1
Starlight 1925,Mr 4,17:2
Last of Mrs Cheyney, The 1925,N 10,23:5
Ghost Train, The 1926,Ag 26,17:2
Great Adventure, The 1926,D 23,23:1
Courage 1927,Ja 20,20:1
Lucky 1927,Mr 23,28:3
Merry Wives of Windsor, The 1928,Mr 20,20:1
Merry Wives of Windsor, The 1938,Ap 15,22:3
Knights of Song 1938,O 18,29:2
When We Are Married 1939,D 26,22:3
Johnny Belinda 1940,S 19,26:2
Wookey, The 1941,S 11,20:5
Patriots, The 1943,Ja 30,11:2
Another Love Story 1943,O 13,29:2
Mowell, Shelley (Composer)
Razzle Dazzle 1951,F 20,21:1
Shoestring '57 1956,N 6,31:1
Mower, Margaret
Welcome Stranger 1920,S 14,12:1
Fair Circassian, The 1921,D 7,22:3
Crowns 1922,N 10,20:3
Why Not? 1922,D 25,20:1
Time 1923,N 27,23:3
Wonderful Visit, The 1924,F 13,17:3
Wonderful Visit, The 1924,My 18,VII,1:1
Don't Bother Mother 1925,F 4,18:2
Lady of the Rose 1925,My 20,26:4
Napoleon 1928,Mr 9,21:1
Jarnegan 1928,S 25,29:2
Week-end 1929,O 23,26:4
Vikings, The 1930,My 13,27:3
Siegfried 1930,O 21,34:1
Within the Gates 1934,O 23,23:1
Sail Away 1961,O 4,48:5
Mowery, Irl
Man and Superman 1953,F 21,11:2
Mowery, Irl (Director)
Villa of Madame Vidac, The 1959,O 1,40:1
Mowery, Irl (Miscellaneous)
God and Kate Murphy 1959,F 27,21:2
From A to Z 1960,Ap 21,23:2
Mowery, Irl (Producer)
Lullaby 1954,F 4,21:2
Mowls, Shirley
John Gabriel Borkman 1959,N 26,57:4
Mowry, William
Meet the Prince 1935,Jl 9,24:5
Julius Caesar 1937,N 12,26:6
Shoemaker's Holiday, The 1938,Ja 3,17:2
Danton's Death 1938,N 3,26:2
Sea Dogs 1939,N 7,30:3
Moxzer, Jieno
Cabin in the Sky 1940,O 26,19:2

Moyan, Joe
Bridge, The 1930,My 6,33:1
Moyer, Charles
Hilda Cassidy 1933,My 5,18:3
Moyer, Christine
New York Idea, The 1948,Ag 18,29:2
Moyer, David (Miscellaneous)
Drunkard, The 1970,Ap 14,54:1
Moyer, Margaret
First Man, The 1922,Mr 6,9:2
Moyes, Patricia (Playwright)
Time Remembered 1955,My 4,35:1
Time Remembered 1957,N 13,41:2
Time Remembered 1957,N 24,II,1:1
Moylan, Ben
Bridge, The 1930,My 6,33:1
Moylan, Mary Ellen
Day Before Spring, The 1945,N 23,27:2
Chocolate Soldier, The 1947,Mr 13,34:2
Merry Widow, The 1957,Ap 11,36:6
Moylan, Richard
Cockeyed Kite 1961,S 14,27:1
Moyles, Dan
Zander the Great 1923,Ap 10,24:2
Holy Terror, A 1925,S 29,31:2
Solitaire 1929,Mr 13,28:3
Devil's Host, The 1931,N 20,27:2
Moyles, Earnest W
Shake Hands With the Devil 1949,O 21,30:4
Moynahan, G B
Laugh It Off 1925,Ap 25,18:4
Moynahan, J
It's Only Natural 1922,Ap 21,13:2
Who's Who 1924,Ap 18,19:2
Moynihan, Daniel
Romeo and Juliet 1956,O 25,41:1
Moyseenko, M
1860: or, Aris; 1860, or an Interrupted Festival 1931,O 22,27:1
Chauve-Souris; Romantic Adventure of an Italian Ballerina and a Marquis, A 1931,O 22,27:1
Moyseenko, Nicholas
Chauve-Souris; Queen of Spades, The 1931,O 22,27:1
Mozart, Wolfgang Amadeus (Composer)
Finta Giardiniera, La 1927,Ja 19,20:5
Finta Giardiniera, La 1927,F 6,VII,1:1
Philosophy in the Boudoir 1969,My 22,55:2
Man and Superman 1970,F 24,48:1
Mozer, Harvey
Building Blocks 1954,My 8,14:4
Mqomo, Phyllis
Sponono 1964,Ap 3,28:1
Mrozek, Slawomir (Playwright)
Policemen, The 1961,N 22,24:2
At Sea 1962,Ap 24,33:1
Tango 1968,Ja 1,11:1
Tango 1969,Ja 20,33:1
Tango 1969,F 9,II,12:1
Vatzlav 1970,Ag 23,II,1:6
Mtschedelow, W L (Director)
Eternal Jew, The 1926,D 21,21:2
Mucci, Gino
Rugantino 1964,F 7,34:1
Muchnick, Ronald (Producer)
Half Horse, Half Alligator 1966,Mr 14,37:2
Mucklow, Robert
Caesar and Cleopatra 1935,Ag 22,21:1
Mudell, Tommy
Curtain Call 1937,Ap 23,24:7
Mudge, Burton
Drake's Drum 1923,D 26,17:7
Mudge, Gertrude
Phoebe of Quality Street 1921,My 10,20:1
Blushing Bride, The 1922,F 7,12:1
Singing Rabbi, The 1931,S 11,24:4
Marilyn's Affairs 1933,Mr 16,21:5
Ladies' Money 1934,N 2,26:6
Play, Genius, Play! 1935,O 31,17:2
Summer Wives 1936,Ap 14,18:1
Mudge, Haidee
It Happened Tomorrow 1933,My 6,11:5
Mudie, Leonard
Mr Pim Passes By 1921,Mr 1,18:1
Merchant of Venice, The 1921,Ap 2,14:2
East of Suez 1922,S 22,16:3
Lullaby, The 1923,S 19,5:3
Man in Evening Clothes, The 1924,D 6,13:4
Embers 1926,F 2,20:3
Red Dust 1928,Ja 3,29:2
Twelve Thousand 1928,Mr 13,23:1
Macbeth 1928,N 20,28:3
Soldiers and Women 1929,Ag 25,VIII,3:1
Soldiers and Women 1929,S 3,25:1
Ledge, A 1929,N 19,26:3
Novice and the Duke, The 1929,D 11,37:2
Lean Harvest 1931,O 14,26:3
Time for Elizabeth 1948,S 28,32:3
Muehlhofer, George
Everyman 1931,Jl 19,III,8:6
Muehsam, Erich (Lyricist)
Pepper Mill 1937,Ja 6,19:4

Muehsam, Erich (Playwright)
Sacco and Vanzetti 1929,Ap 23,26:5
Pepper Mill 1937,Ja 6,19:4
Muelhel, Lothar
Saint Joan 1924,N 9,VII,2:3
Mueller, Darvin
Little Theatre Tournament; Edna 1929,My 11,22:2
Mueller, Frederic
Calvary 1960,Jl 22,13:1
Delightful Season, A 1960,S 29,30:1
Mueller, Gerda
Lulu 1927,Ja 30,VII,4:3
Mueller, Hans (Original Author)
Depths, The 1925,F 8,VII,1:1
Cafe de Danse 1929,Ja 16,22:2
Mueller, Hans (Playwright)
Depths, The 1925,Ja 28,15:3
Mueller, Karl
For Valor 1935,N 19,27:5
Mueller, Marion
Tell Me More 1925,Ap 14,27:3
Mueller, Traugott (Scenic Designer)
Mensch aus Erde Gemacht 1933,N 5,IX,3:1
Bride of Messina, The 1933,D 10,X,5:1
Richard III 1937,My 30,X,2:2
Michael Kramer 1938,F 20,XI,2:1
Mueller, Zizi
Carmilla 1970,D 1,61:2
Mueller and Pepe
Ice Capades 1970,Ja 7,35:1
Muench, Shirley
York Nativity Play, The 1956,D 5,49:2
Muenz, Hans
Americans on the Rhine 1934,O 11,28:4
Versunkene Glocke, Die 1936,N 20,26:3
Muenz, Hans (Director)
Americans on the Rhine 1934,O 11,28:4
Versunkene Glocke, Die 1936,N 20,26:3
Muenz, Hans (Playwright)
Americans on the Rhine 1934,O 11,28:4
Mueser, Barbara
Play of Daniel, The 1961,D 28,22:6
Muethel, Lothar
Liebestrank 1927,Ja 30,VII,4:3
Muethel, Lothar (Director)
Faust 1933,Ja 22,IX,1:1
Bride of Messina, The 1933,D 10,X,5:1
Michael Kramer 1938,F 20,XI,2:1
Muggsie
To Quito and Back 1937,O 7,30:4
Muhl, Fred
Untitled-Passion Play 1926,Mr 30,20:2
Muhlfelder, Charles H
Seven Against One 1930,My 7,25:1
Muhs, Jack (Costume Designer)
Disney on Parade 1970,S 24,63:1
Muhs, Jack (Miscellaneous)
Disney on Parade 1970,S 24,63:1
Muir, Esther
Lady Fingers 1929,F 1,22:4
My Girl Friday! 1929,F 13,20:2
International Revue 1930,F 26,22:2
Good-Bye to Love 1940,Je 8,18:1
Muir, Gavin
Enter Madame 1920,Ag 17,11:2
Lady Cristilinda, The 1922,D 26,11:2
Love Set, The 1923,Mr 20,24:2
Camel's Back, The 1923,N 4,19:2
Best People, The 1924,Ag 20,8:1
Hay Fever 1925,O 5,25:1
Beaten Track, The 1926,F 9,23:2
Man From Toronto, The 1926,Je 18,27:2
Mr Pim Passes By 1927,Ap 19,24:1
Mystery Square 1929,Ap 5,28:3
Primer for Lovers, A 1929,N 19,26:5
Nancy's Private Affair 1930,Ja 14,24:3
That's the Woman 1930,S 4,27:2
They Don't Mean Any Harm 1932,F 24,25:2
Silent House, The 1932,N 9,28:3
Springtime for Henry 1933,My 2,20:5
Dangerous Corner 1933,Jl 18,20:4
Play, Genius, Play! 1935,O 31,17:2
Puritan, The 1936,Ja 24,14:3
Bachelor Born 1938,Ja 26,26:3
Muir, Jean
Pride and Prejudice 1937,Ag 3,20:5
People at Sea 1937,N 25,38:2
Tenting Tonight 1947,Ap 3,32:2
Semi-Detached 1960,Mr 11,20:2
Muir, Jean (Producer)
Listen Professor! 1943,D 23,22:1
Muir, William (Director)
Moon Over Mulberry Street 1935,S 5,24:6
Mukherji, Pannalal
Ramayana 1931,Ja 13,35:4
Mulady, James
Salvation 1928,F 1,31:1
Mulcahy, Lance (Composer)
Park 1970,Ap 23,47:1
Mulcaster, G H
Anne-One Hundred 1927,Je 26,VIII,1:3
Mulcay, Jimmy
Star Time 1944,S 13,16:2

Mulcay, Mildred
Star Time 1944,S 13,16:2
Muldaur, Diana
Seidman and Son 1962,O 16,32:2
Poor Bitos 1964,N 16,40:2
Muldener, Louis
Wasp, The 1923,Mr 28,14:3
Muldener, Louise
Magda 1926,Ja 27,16:2
Mulders, Betty
Three Love Affairs; Still Life 1958,Mr 11,33:1
Muldoon, Johnny
Rise of Rosie O'Reilly, The 1923,D 26,13:4
Muldowney, John Humphrey
Pleasure Bound 1929,F 10,IX,2:1
Artists and Models 1930,Je 11,33:2
Vaudeville (Palace) 1931,Ja 26,21:5
Crazy Quilt 1931,My 20,28:4
Mulford, Courtland Cramp
This Mad Whirl 1937,Ja 10,II,4:8
Mulgrew, Felix A
Coriolanus 1927,Je 18,8:3
Mulhall, Jack
Blackouts of 1949 1949,S 7,39:2
Mulhare, Edward
My Fair Lady 1957,F 5,27:2
My Fair Lady 1958,Mr 9,II,1:1
My Fair Lady 1959,Ja 19,24:6
Devil's Advocate, The 1961,Mr 10,20:1
Devil's Advocate, The 1961,Mr 19,II,1:1
Tristram 1962,O 29,36:1
Mulhern, Frolie
Ever the Twain 1929,O 20,III,3:5
Plough and the Stars, The 1934,N 13,22:2
Drama at Inish 1934,N 15,24:2
Look at the Heffernans 1934,N 17,13:2
Well of the Saints, The 1934,N 22,26:2
Far-Off Hills, The 1937,O 12,30:4
In the Train 1937,N 22,14:5
Playboy of the Western World, The 1937,N 22,14:5
Juno and the Paycock 1937,D 7,32:5
Drama at Inish 1937,D 14,33:2
Mulhern, Leonard
Twelfth Night 1957,Ja 5,12:2
Mulhern, Leonard (Producer)
Crimes of Passion; Erpingham Camp, The 1969,O 27,54:1
Crimes of Passion; Ruffian on the Stair, The 1969,O 27,54:1
Mulheron, Frank W (Miscellaneous)
Everyman Today 1958,Ja 16,32:4
Mulholland, Ethel
Happy-Go-Lucky 1926,O 1,27:2
Mulholland, Kathryn
Polly 1925,O 12,19:1
Mulie, Ida
Chinese Lily, A 1925,Mr 24,26:5
Mulinos, Angela
Three Sisters, The 1930,Ja 9,22:2
Glass of Water, A 1930,Mr 6,16:3
Mulisch, Harry (Director)
Reconstruction 1969,Jl 8,36:1
Mulisch, Harry (Playwright)
Reconstruction 1969,Jl 8,36:1
Mullally, Don (Director)
Wanted 1928,Jl 3,19:2
Recapture 1930,Ja 30,16:4
Noble Experiment, The 1930,O 28,21:4
Camels Are Coming, The 1931,O 3,20:4
Coastwise 1931,D 1,23:1
Mullally, Don (Playwright)
Conscience 1924,S 12,19:3
Maggie 1924,N 2,VII,2:3
Desert Flower, The 1924,N 19,18:2
Laff That Off 1925,N 3,34:2
Wanted 1928,Jl 3,19:2
Conscience 1929,O 25,26:1
Camels Are Coming, The 1931,O 3,20:4
Coastwise 1931,D 1,23:1
Mullally, Don (Producer)
Camels Are Coming, The 1931,O 3,20:4
Mullaney, William
Donogoo 1961,Ja 19,25:3
Mulle, Henry (Costume Designer)
Sally 1948,My 7,31:2
Mulle, Ida
Mecca 1920,O 5,12:2
Gift, The 1924,Ja 23,15:4
Squall, The 1926,N 12,20:1
Becky Sharp 1929,Je 4,29:1
Mullen, Barbara
Jeannie 1940,F 18,IX,2:5
Jeannie 1940,Ap 14,IX,1:7
Mullen, Bob
Season of the Beast 1958,Mr 14,29:2
Mullen, Bob (Miscellaneous)
Secret Life of Walter Mitty, The 1964,O 27,44:5
Mullen, Clare
Devil Came From Dublin, The! 1955,Je 3,27:2
Mullen, Gordon
Paid 1925,N 26,32:1
Great Gatsby, The 1926,F 3,22:1
Immoral Isabella 1927,O 28,20:3

Mullen, Joseph
Tyrants 1924,Mr 5,14:1
Mullen, Joseph (Scenic Designer)
Wild Birds 1925,Ap 10,16:1
Drift 1925,N 25,15:3
Garden of Eden, The 1927,S 28,28:1
Gala Night 1930,F 26,22:4
Paging Danger 1931,F 27,19:2
Mullen, Kenneth
Ice Capades 1953,S 11,25:1
Ice Capades 1954,S 16,37:1
Mullen, Margaret
Straight Thru the Door 1928,O 5,17:2
Inspector Kennedy 1929,D 21,16:3
Old Rascal, The 1930,Mr 25,34:4
Affair of State, An 1930,N 20,30:3
Betty, Be Careful 1931,My 5,33:3
Fata Morgana 1931,D 26,15:3
Broomsticks Amen! 1934,F 10,20:4
Ladies' Money 1934,N 2,26:6
Three Men on a Horse 1935,Ja 31,22:3
Dead End 1935,O 29,17:2
Sweet River 1936,O 29,30:2
Red Harvest 1937,Mr 31,29:2
Room Service 1937,My 20,16:1
Mrs O'Brien Entertains 1939,F 9,16:3
Yankee Point 1942,N 24,28:2
Anya 1965,N 30,48:1
Mullen, Ronn
Man and Superman 1970,F 24,48:1
Mullen, Walter
Watched Pot, The 1947,O 29,31:4
Mister Roberts 1948,F 19,27:2
Grass Harp, The 1953,My 24,II,1:1
Mullen, Walter (Director)
Watched Pot, The 1947,O 29,31:4
Mullen Twins
Sons o' Fun 1941,D 2,28:2
Muller, Adolf (Composer)
Jux Will Er Sich Machen, Einen 1968,Ap 3,41:1
Muller, Gerda
Antony and Cleopatra 1932,F 7,VIII,1:5
Muller, Hans (Playwright)
Im Weissen Roessel 1931,Ja 4,VIII,3:5
Casanova 1932,Je 19,IX,2:1
White Horse Inn 1936,O 2,28:5
Muller, Harrison
Early to Bed 1943,Je 18,16:2
Allegro 1947,O 11,10:2
Seventeen 1951,Je 22,16:6
Muller, Joseph (Scenic Designer)
Right to Kill, The 1926,F 16,22:2
Muller, N F
Betty Behave 1927,Mr 9,28:4
Muller, Robert (Playwright)
Night Conspirators 1963,My 23,31:4
Muller, Romeo
Saint Joan 1950,Mr 4,10:6
Muller, Romeo (Original Author)
Month of Sundays 1968,S 17,50:1
Muller, Romeo (Playwright)
Month of Sundays 1968,S 17,50:1
Muller, Vera
Mikado, The 1942,F 4,22:2
Pirates of Penzance, The 1942,F 18,22:2
Iolanthe 1942,F 24,26:4
Gondoliers, The 1942,Mr 4,22:3
Muller's Chimpanzees
Holiday on Ice 1969,Ag 28,44:1
Mullery, C W
Tiger Smiles, The 1930,D 18,29:1
Mullett, Gilda
Carousel 1966,D 16,56:2
Mulligan, Archie
Stephen D 1966,Ag 5,17:1
Mulligan, Charles J (Director)
Banshee, The 1927,D 6,26:2
Mulligan, Charles J (Miscellaneous)
On Call 1928,N 10,20:7
Mulligan, Charles J (Producer)
Lady Screams, The 1927,My 3,24:2
John Ferguson 1928,Ja 18,23:1
Mulligan, Mary (Miscellaneous)
Stephen D 1966,Ag 5,17:1
Mulligan, Michael
Stephen D 1966,Ag 5,17:1
Mulligan, R J
Hold Your Horses 1933,S 26,26:4
Mulligan, Richard
Nobody Loves an Albatross 1963,D 20,20:1
Nobody Loves an Albatross 1964,Ja 5,II,1:1
Mating Dance 1965,N 4,58:1
Mulligan, Robert
Round-Up, The 1932,Mr 8,19:4
Many Mansions 1937,O 28,28:6
Mulligan, Robert (Director)
Comes a Day 1958,N 7,22:1
Mulligan, Robert J
Merry-Go-Round 1932,Ap 23,11:2
I Myself 1934,My 10,24:6
Night Remembers, The 1934,N 28,24:3
Dead End 1935,O 29,17:2
Double Dummy 1936,N 12,30:1

But for the Grace of God 1937,Ja 13,21:4
Chalked Out 1937,Mr 26,24:2
Sea Dogs 1939,N 7,30:3
Pal Joey 1940,D 26,22:2
Mulligan, Tom
Shadow and Substance 1956,Mr 14,38:1
Mulligan, Tom (Miscellaneous)
Riders to the Sea 1957,Mr 7,24:1
Tinker's Wedding, The 1957,Mr 7,24:1
In the Shadow of the Glen 1957,Mr 7,24:1
Playboy of the Western World, The 1958,My 9,19:2
Mulligan, William
Jefferson Davis 1936,F 19,17:2
Mullikin, Allen
Rope Dancers, The 1959,Mr 14,26:1
Mullikin, Bill
New Faces of 1952 1952,My 17,23:2
South Pacific 1957,Ap 25,35:1
Boy Friend, The 1958,Ja 27,24:4
Mullin, Bobby
All the King's Men 1929,F 5,27:1
Mullin, James
Miss Gulliver Travels 1931,N 26,36:4
Mullin, June
Ladies of the Jury 1929,O 22,26:2
Did I Say No? 1931,S 23,19:4
Great Lover, The 1932,O 12,27:3
Mullin, Stephen (Scenic Designer)
Cambridge Circus 1964,O 7,53:1
Mullins, Bartlett
Don't Listen, Ladies 1948,D 29,16:2
Mully, George (Miscellaneous)
Deadly Game, The 1960,F 3,27:2
Mulqueen, Catherine
Molly Darling 1922,S 2,10:2
Mulqueen, Kathleen
Tomorrow 1928,D 29,20:2
Mulroy, McNeece and Ridge
Vaudeville (Palace) 1926,Jl 27,15:4
Mulvaney, Ninette (Scenic Designer)
Don Juan; Feast With the Statue, The 1956,Ja 4,21:4
Mulvey, Ben
Tickle Me 1920,Ag 18,9:1
Daffy Dill 1922,Ag 23,14:5
Mumaw, Barton
Promised Valley 1947,Jl 23,18:3
Out of This World 1950,D 22,17:3
Mumaw, Barton (Choreographer)
Dark of the Moon 1958,F 27,22:2
Mumford, Peter B (Director)
March March, The 1966,N 15,51:4
Neighbors 1966,N 15,51:4
Mumford, Peter B (Miscellaneous)
Carpenters, The 1970,D 22,40:1
Mumford, Robert
Does a Tiger Wear a Necktie? 1967,F 4,17:1
Mumma, Kar de (Playwright)
Tattar-Adel 1939,S 17,X,2:4
Munch, Eduard (Costume Designer)
Ghosts; Gespenster 1929,F 6,30:3
Munch, Eduard (Scenic Designer)
Ghosts; Gespenster 1929,F 6,30:3
Munck, Dieter (Director)
Amphitryon 1970,N 18,40:1
Munday, Arthur (Costume Designer)
Gondoliers, The 1969,My 10,35:1
H M S Pinafore 1969,D 8,61:2
Pirates of Penzance, The 1970,D 6,84:6
Munday, Penelope
Lady's Not for Burning, The 1950,N 9,42:2
Climate of Eden, The 1952,N 7,20:2
Climate of Eden, The 1952,N 16,II,1:1
Mundi, Billy
Absolutely Freeee 1967,My 25,58:1
Mundin, Herbert
Charlot's Revue 1924,Ja 10,18:1
Charlot's Revue 1924,Ap 6,VIII,1:1
Charlot's Revue 1924,Ap 15,25:2
Charlot's Revue 1925,N 11,27:1
Charlot's Revue 1925,N 15,VIII,1:1
Earl Carroll's Vanities 1927,Ja 5,18:1
Mundson, Edna (Scenic Designer)
When Differences Disappear 1941,Je 3,17:4
Mundy, Charles
Pullman Car Hiawatha 1962,D 4,46:2
Desire Under the Elms 1963,Ja 11,5:6
Mundy, James (Composer)
Vamp, The 1955,N 11,30:1
Mundy, James (Musical Director)
Vamp, The 1955,N 11,30:1
Mundy, John (Composer)
Liar, The 1950,My 19,30:2
Mundy, Meg
Ten Million Ghosts 1936,O 24,23:7
Three to Make Ready 1946,Mr 8,16:2
How I Wonder 1947,O 1,34:2
Respectful Prostitute, The 1948,F 10,27:2
Respectful Prostitute, The 1948,F 15,II,1:1
Respectful Prostitute, The 1948,Mr 21,II,1:1
Detective Story 1949,Mr 24,34:2
Detective Story 1949,Ap 3,II,1:1
Love's Labour's Lost 1953,F 5,20:3

Mundy, Meg—Cont
Love Me Little 1958,Ap 15,42:2
Lysistrata 1959,My 20,40:2
Munford, Gordon (Musical Director)
Autumn's Here 1966,O 26,40:1
Muni, Paul
This One Man 1930,O 22,32:3
Rock Me, Julie 1931,Ja 4,VIII,2:3
Rock Me, Julie 1931,F 4,21:1
Counsellor-at-Law 1931,N 7,17:2
Counsellor-at-Law 1932,S 13,17:2
Key Largo 1939,O 31,26:6
Key Largo 1939,N 19,X,3:4
Key Largo 1939,N 28,30:2
Key Largo 1939,D 3,IX,5:3
Key Largo 1939,D 10,X,3:1
Yesterday's Magic 1942,Ap 15,27:2
Counsellor-at-Law 1942,N 25,17:2
Flag Is Born, A 1946,S 7,10:6
Flag Is Born, A 1946,S 15,II,21:1
They Knew What They Wanted 1949,F 17,28:2
Death of a Salesman 1949,Jl 29,12:5
Death of a Salesman 1949,Ag 7,II,1:4
Death of a Salesman 1949,Ag 28,VI,11:1
Inherit the Wind 1955,Ap 22,20:2
At the Grand 1958,Ag 13,24:3
Munier, Ferdinand
Miles of Heaven, The 1937,Ag 31,27:4
Munier, Leon (Lighting Director)
Merry Wives of Windsor, The 1954,F 17,27:1
Munier, Leon (Scenic Designer)
Ninety Day Mistress, The 1967,N 7,49:1
Munier, Mason (Costume Designer)
Servant of Two Masters, The 1958,F 11,35:2
Munk, Kaj (Playwright)
Cant 1931,D 20,VIII,1:6
Victory 1937,N 14,XI,2:5
He Sits in a Crucible 1939,Ap 2,X,2:4
Munker, Ariane
Happy Birthday, Wanda June 1970,O 8,58:2
Munn, Bradford and Van Alst
Vaudeville (Palace) 1930,O 13,31:3
Munn, Elizabeth
Victoria Regina 1935,D 27,15:2
Munn, Frank
Hitch Your Wagon! 1937,Ap 9,18:2
Munn, Gary (Playwright)
Judas Applause, The 1969,My 4,II,1:5
Munn, Margaret Crosby (Original Author)
Passionate Pilgrim, The 1932,O 20,24:3
Munn, Margaret Crosby (Playwright)
Passionate Pilgrim, The 1932,O 20,24:3
Munn, Tom (Scenic Designer)
Evening for Merlin Finch, An 1968,D 30,25:1
Great Career, A 1968,D 30,25:1
Brightower 1970,Ja 29,32:1
Munnell, Franklin
Right Girl, The 1921,Mr 16,12:1
Adam Had Two Sons 1932,Ja 21,17:1
Collision 1932,F 17,19:2
Strangers at Home 1934,S 15,20:5
Munnis, Hal
What's Your Wife Doing? 1923,O 2,10:3
Lawyers' Dilemma, The 1928,Jl 10,17:2
Munore, Walter
Long Road, The 1930,S 10,30:2
Munro, C K (Playwright)
At Mrs Beam's 1923,Mr 11,VIII,2:4
Progress 1924,Ja 27,VII,2:4
Storm 1924,Ag 24,VII,1:3
At Mrs Beam's 1926,Ap 26,24:3
Beau-Strings 1926,Ap 27,22:2
At Mrs Beam's 1926,My 2,VIII,1:1
Beau-Strings 1926,My 2,VIII,1:1
Cocks and Hens 1927,Ap 3,VIII,1:4
Mr Eno: His Birth, Death and Life 1930,N 9,IX,2:1
Bluestone Quarry 1931,N 29,VIII,2:2
Ding and Company 1934,N 20,24:2
Ding and Company 1934,D 9,X,3:1
At Mrs Beam's 1937,Jl 27,24:2
Coronation at Mrs. Beam's 1938,Ag 4,14:4
Munro, Chaddock
Legend of Lovers 1951,D 27,17:1
Munro, Charles B
It's Only Natural 1922,Ap 21,13:2
Munro, George (Playwright)
Murder Gang 1935,N 16,19:2
Murder Gang 1935,D 15,XI,5:6
Munro, H H (Saki) (Playwright)
Watched Pot, The 1947,O 29,31:4
Munro, Iseth
White Gold 1925,N 3,34:5
Ashes of Love 1926,Mr 23,24:3
Plutocrat, The 1930,F 21,23:3
Munro, Jock
Streets of New York, The 1931,O 7,29:1
Munro, Mae
Beautiful Jailer, The 1957,My 17,19:2
Munro, Neil
Romeo and Juliet 1968,Je 11,55:2
Munro, Norma (Playwright)
Eternal Spring, The 1924,F 3,VII,1:4
Munro, Victor
Kid Boots 1924,Ja 1,21:3

Munro, Victor—Cont
Manhattan Mary 1927,S 27,30:3
You Said It 1931,Ja 20,21:3
Munro, Viola
Babbling Brookes 1927,F 26,13:2
Munroe, David
Revelry 1927,S 13,37:1
Munroe, Mildred
Trial Honeymoon 1947,N 4,31:2
Munroe, Norma (Playwright)
Basalik 1935,Ap 8,22:5
Munroe, Walter
Funny Face 1927,N 23,28:2
Silver Swan, The 1929,N 28,34:5
O'Flynn, The 1934,D 28,24:1
New Moon, The 1942,Ag 19,14:2
Munroe, William
O'Daniel 1947,F 25,32:2
Munsell, Warren P (Producer)
Love Goes to Press 1947,Ja 2,22:2
Munshin, Jules
Call Me Mister 1946,Ap 19,26:2
Call Me Mister 1946,Ap 28,II,1:1
Bless You All 1950,D 15,42:2
Mrs McThing 1952,F 21,22:1
Mrs McThing 1952,Mr 2,II,1:1
Good Soup, The 1960,Mr 3,26:4
Hit the Deck 1960,Je 24,32:1
Show Girl 1961,Ja 13,37:1
Show Girl 1961,Ja 23,II,1:1
Gay Life, The 1961,N 20,38:1
Oklahoma! 1965,D 16,62:1
Latent Heterosexual, The 1968,Mr 22,52:1
Latent Heterosexual, The 1968,Mr 31,II,3:1
Munso, Felix
Tiger at the Gates 1955,O 4,40:1
Cook for Mr General, A 1961,O 20,39:1
Pilgrim's Progress 1962,Mr 21,36:2
Munson, David
Half-Caste, The 1926,Mr 30,20:4
Munson, Estella
Yeomen of the Guard, The 1965,Jl 8,34:1
Ruddigore 1965,Ag 27,16:1
Munson, Jerry
'Tis of Thee 1940,O 28,21:3
Munson, John
Wedding in Japan 1949,N 11,29:1
There Is No End 1950,F 17,27:4
Munson, Lei Lehua
One Man's Woman 1926,My 26,25:1
Munson, Ona
Manhattan Mary 1927,S 27,30:3
Hold Everything 1928,O 11,24:2
Hold Your Horses 1933,Ag 31,20:4
Hold Your Horses 1933,S 26,26:4
Petticoat Fever 1935,Mr 5,22:2
Ghosts 1935,D 13,30:6
First Lady 1952,My 29,18:5
Munson, Patrice
Merry Widow, The 1964,Ag 18,24:2
Munter, Leo
Enemies Don't Send Flowers 1957,F 20,38:1
Mur, Neville
White Cargo 1960,D 30,12:1
Mura, Corinna
Mexican Hayride 1944,Ja 29,9:6
Mexican Hayride 1944,F 6,II,1:1
Mura, Ester
Earl Carroll's Vanities 1925,D 29,20:3
Vanities 1926,Ja 10,VII,1:1
Murai, Ilona
Touch and Go 1949,O 14,34:2
Goldilocks 1958,O 13,33:1
Girl Who Came to Supper, The 1963,D 9,49:1
Murai, Kikobi
Take the Air 1927,N 23,28:2
Mural, Arnold
Inspector General, The 1923,My 1,24:1
Murand and Girton
Vaudeville (Palace) 1928,Jl 31,13:5
Murashima, Sumiko
Sacco-Vanzetti 1969,F 9,78:1
Murati, (Mme)
Miracle in the Mountain 1936,My 9,11:4
Murati, Goth
Miracle in the Mountain 1936,My 9,11:4
Murawski, C (Lighting Director)
Better Luck Next Time 1966,Ja 28,21:1
Walk in Dark Places, A 1966,Ja 28,21:1
Duet for Three 1966,My 20,41:1
Big Man 1966,My 20,41:1
Beard, The 1967,O 25,40:1
Goa 1968,F 23,46:1
Four Seasons, The 1968,Mr 15,32:1
Ordinary Man, An 1968,S 10,39:1
Front Page, The 1968,O 20,85:5
Papers 1968,D 3,54:1
Shoot Anything With Hair That Moves
  1969,F 3,29:1
Lime Green 1969,Mr 27,54:2
Khaki Blue 1969,Mr 27,54:2
License, The 1969,Ap 23,42:1
Man With the Flower in His Mouth, The
  1969,Ap 23,42:1

Jar, The 1969,Ap 23,42:1
Unfair to Goliath 1970,Ja 26,27:1
Murawski, C (Scenic Designer)
Better Luck Next Time 1966,Ja 28,21:1
Walk in Dark Places, A 1966,Ja 28,21:1
Big Man 1966,My 20,41:1
Duet for Three 1966,My 20,41:1
Golden Screw, The 1967,Ja 31,52:1
Fortune and Men's Eyes 1967,F 24,29:1
Poker Session, The 1967,S 20,42:2
Goa 1968,F 23,46:1
Four Seasons, The 1968,Mr 15,32:1
Ordinary Man, An 1968,S 10,39:1
Front Page, The 1968,O 20,85:5
Papers 1968,D 3,54:1
Shoot Anything With Hair That Moves
  1969,F 3,29:1
Lime Green 1969,Mr 27,54:2
Khaki Blue 1969,Mr 27,54:2
Jar, The 1969,Ap 23,42:1
Man With the Flower in His Mouth, The
  1969,Ap 23,42:1
License, The 1969,Ap 23,42:1
Passing Through From Exotic Places; Burial of
  Esposito, The 1969,D 8,60:4
Passing Through From Exotic Places; Sunstroke
  1969,D 8,60:4
Passing Through From Exotic Places; Son Who
  Hunted Tigers in Jakarta, The 1969,D 8,60:4
Unfair to Goliath 1970,Ja 26,27:1
Murcell, George
Patriot for Me, A 1965,Jl 11,II,1:4
Murch, Robert
Harangues, The 1970,Ja 14,42:1
Conduct Unbecoming 1970,O 13,50:1
Murchie, D
Gentlemen, the Queen 1927,Ap 23,14:3
Murcott, Derek
Connelly vs Connelly 1961,F 18,11:3
Feast of Panthers 1961,Mr 21,32:1
Murden, Dolores
Show Boat 1957,Je 28,30:2
Murdoch, Helen
County Chairman, The 1936,My 26,26:5
Blow Ye Winds 1937,S 24,17:4
Loco 1946,O 17,29:2
Murdoch, Iris (Original Author)
Severed Head, A 1963,Je 28,22:1
Severed Head, A 1964,O 29,40:1
Italian Girl, The 1968,Jl 4,14:1
Murdoch, Iris (Playwright)
Severed Head, A 1963,Je 28,22:1
Severed Head, A 1964,O 29,40:1
Italian Girl, The 1968,Jl 4,14:1
Murdock, Edgar
Tapestry in Gray 1935,D 28,10:2
Murdock, George
Conversation at Midnight 1964,N 13,27:1
Murdock, Janet
Rotters, The 1922,My 23,12:4
Plot Thickens, The 1922,S 6,16:1
Magic Ring, The 1923,O 2,10:1
Murdock, Kermit
Saint's Parade 1930,N 1,23:4
No More Frontier 1931,O 22,27:1
Merry-Go-Round 1932,Ap 23,11:2
Just Suppose 1935,Jl 2,24:3
Lamp at Midnight 1947,D 22,29:2
Sun and I, The 1949,Mr 21,18:4
Bruno and Sidney 1949,My 4,38:2
Strong Are Lonely, The 1953,S 30,38:3
Man Who Never Died, The 1958,N 22,27:2
Idiot, The 1960,S 26,38:1
Emmanuel 1960,D 5,42:2
More Stately Mansions 1967,N 1,40:1
Murdock, Red
Elsie Janis and Her Gang 1922,Ja 17,13:2
Murdock, Sue
Tragical Historie of Doctor Faustus, The
  1964,O 6,34:2
Murdock, Teck
Broadway Brevities, 1920 1920,S 30,12:2
Murdock, Teck and Company
Vaudeville (Palace) 1928,F 21,19:2
Murdock, William J (Playwright)
Dossers 1962,S 27,31:5
Murelle, Felicia
Chocolate Soldier, The 1921,D 13,24:2
Murfi, Lidie
Ladies Night in a Turkish Bath 1961,Mr 22,38:1
Murfin, Jane (Playwright)
Stripped 1929,Je 9,VIII,1:2
Stripped 1929,O 13,IX,5:1
Stripped 1929,O 22,26:1
Murkett, Peter (Scenic Designer)
Gertrude 1970,N 13,29:1
Murkin, Cyril
Education of H*Y*M*A*N K*A*P*L*A*N, The
  1968,Ap 5,57:1
Murphree, Benjamin (Miscellaneous)
Wet Paint 1965,Ap 13,33:1
Murphy, A W
Front Page, The 1937,N 12,27:2

Murphy, Alec
Wives, The 1965,My 18,35:4
Elizabeth the Queen 1966,N 4,30:1
Murphy, Althea
First Lady 1952,My 29,18:5
Murphy, Ann
Young and Fair, The 1948,N 23,35:2
Murphy, Bart
Good Woman of Setzuan, The 1956,D 19,41:2
Murphy, Ben
Barefoot Boy With Cheek 1947,Ap 4,20:2
Murphy, Brian
Oh What a Lovely War 1964,O 1,30:1
Murphy, Charles
Jonah! 1967,S 22,52:2
Lend an Ear 1969,O 29,32:1
What the Butler Saw 1970,My 5,56:1
Murphy, Dean
Ziegfeld Follies 1943,Ap 2,16:2
Murphy, Donald
Try and Get It 1943,Ag 3,13:2
For Keeps 1944,Je 15,17:5
Signature 1945,F 15,25:2
Common Ground 1945,Ap 26,27:2
Wonderful Journey 1946,D 26,30:2
Dear Barbarians 1952,F 22,15:2
Time of the Cuckoo, The 1952,O 16,37:4
Murphy, Donaldson
Hamlet 1936,O 9,30:2
Murphy, Drew
Drunkard, The 1970,Ap 14,54:1
Murphy, Edward Jr
Hair 1967,O 30,55:1
Murphy, Elliott (Playwright)
Elliott Murphy's Aquashow 1955,Je 23,25:1
Murphy, Elliott (Producer)
Mr Winkle's Holliday 1946,Je 24,27:6
Aquashow 1952,Je 25,25:1
Aquashow 1953,Je 24,29:2
Aquashow 1954,Je 23,20:4
Elliott Murphy's Aquashow 1956,Je 20,26:2
Murphy, Ernest
Play of Herod, The 1963,D 10,55:2
Murphy, Francis
Dear Sir 1924,S 24,21:3
Murphy, Frank
Comedian, The 1956,O 18,36:4
Child of the Morning 1958,Ap 22,40:2
Murphy, George
Shoot the Works! 1931,Jl 22,19:5
Of Thee I Sing 1931,D 28,20:1
Roberta 1933,N 20,18:4
Murphy, Gertrude
White-Headed Boy, The 1921,S 16,20:1
Murphy, Harold
Doughgirls, The 1942,D 31,19:2
Murphy, Honoria
Occasion, L' 1939,Ja 10,16:4
Murphy, Hugh Francis
Lucky 1927,Mr 23,28:3
Murphy, Jack (Miscellaneous)
Mandragola 1958,My 29,23:2
Murphy, John Daly
Bonehead, The 1920,Ap 13,12:1
Nightcap, The 1921,Ag 16,18:3
It's a Boy! 1922,S 20,18:3
Dragon, The 1922,D 27,12:1
Forbidden 1923,O 2,10:2
Dumb-Bell 1923,N 27,23:2
She Stoops to Conquer 1924,Je 10,24:3
Top Hole 1924,S 2,22:3
Four Flusher, The 1925,Ap 14,27:4
Virgin, The 1926,F 23,26:1
Julie 1927,My 10,24:4
Storm Center 1927,D 1,33:2
Free Soul, A 1928,Ja 13,26:5
Beaux' Stratagem, The 1928,Je 5,20:1
Wild Duck, The 1928,N 19,17:1
Lady From the Sea 1929,Mr 19,36:1
Ziegfeld Follies 1931,Jl 2,30:5
Hamlet 1931,N 6,28:4
Moon in the Yellow River, The 1932,Mr 1,19:3
Moon in the Yellow River, The
  1932,Mr 13,VIII,1:1
Bulls, Bears and Asses 1932,My 7,11:3
Firebird 1932,N 22,25:2
Two Strange Women 1933,Ja 11,23:3
Uncle Tom's Cabin 1933,My 30,13:4
Thoroughbred 1933,N 7,29:2
False Dreams, Farewell 1934,Ja 16,18:3
Within the Gates 1934,O 23,23:1
Murphy, Judson
Romio and Julietta 1925,Ap 21,19:1
Murphy, Katherine
Jeremiah 1939,F 4,11:2
World We Make, The 1939,N 21,19:1
Murphy, Kathleen
American Mime Theatre 1958,S 25,28:4
Murphy, Lars
Our Lan' 1947,Ap 19,11:2
Murphy, Lillian
Music in the Air 1951,O 9,32:2
Music in the Air 1951,O 21,II,1:1

Murphy, Lillian—Cont
Mikado, The 1952,O 21,35:2
Pirates of Penzance, The 1952,O 28,36:4
H M S Pinafore 1952,N 4,32:2
Iolanthe 1952,N 11,26:3
Murphy, Madeline
Daddy Dumplins 1920,N 23,11:1
Murphy, Marilyn
Something More! 1964,N 11,36:1
Murphy, Melissa C
Unknown Soldier and His Wife, The 1967,Jl 7,22:1
Murphy, Owen (Composer)
Mimic World of 1921, The 1921,Ag 18,9:2
Red Pepper 1922,My 30,8:3
Top Hole 1924,S 2,22:3
Greenwich Village Follies 1925,D 25,23:3
Rainbow Rose 1926,Mr 17,28:2
Rain or Shine 1928,F 10,26:3
Murphy, Owen (Lyricist)
Mimic World of 1921, The 1921,Ag 18,9:2
Red Pepper 1922,My 30,8:3
Spice of 1922 1922,Jl 7,12:4
Top Hole 1924,S 2,22:3
Greenwich Village Follies 1925,D 25,23:3
Rainbow Rose 1926,Mr 17,28:2
Gang's All Here, The 1931,F 19,21:3
Murphy, Owen (Playwright)
Mimic World of 1921, The 1921,Ag 18,9:2
Earl Carroll's Vanities 1925,Jl 7,24:1
Murphy, Patricia
Ballyhoo 1930,D 23,24:1
Murphy, Peter
When We Dead Awaken 1966,Ap 19,37:2
Murphy, Ralph
K Guy, The 1928,O 16,28:4
Murphy, Ralph (Director)
High Hatters, The 1928,My 11,28:2
Get Me in the Movies 1928,My 22,18:3
Town's Woman, The 1929,Mr 12,26:2
Unsophisticates, The 1929,D 31,14:5
I Want My Wife 1930,Mr 21,30:7
What Price Glory 1949,Mr 3,33:2
Murphy, Ralph (Lyricist)
Flossie 1924,Je 4,25:2
Murphy, Ralph (Playwright)
Handy Man, The 1925,Mr 10,19:2
Sure Fire! 1926,O 21,23:1
Pardon Me 1927,O 2,VIII,4:6
Sh! The Octopus 1928,F 22,19:2
Cortez 1929,N 5,32:2
Black Tower 1932,Ja 12,29:2
Murphy, Reri
Ziegfeld Follies 1931,Jl 2,30:5
Murphy, Rosemary
Detective Story 1954,F 13,11:2
Macbeth 1955,O 8,12:6
Look Homeward, Angel 1957,N 29,33:1
Look Homeward, Angel 1958,Ag 31,II,1:1
Period of Adjustment 1960,N 11,34:1
Period of Adjustment 1960,N 20,II,1:1
King Lear 1963,Je 10,37:1
Comedy of Errors, The 1963,Je 13,28:1
Caesar and Cleopatra 1963,Ag 1,18:2
Any Wednesday 1964,F 19,34:1
Delicate Balance, A 1966,S 23,44:1
Delicate Balance, A 1966,O 2,II,1:1
Weekend 1968,Mr 14,50:2
Death of Bessie Smith, The 1968,O 3,55:1
Butterflies Are Free 1970,D 3,60:2
Murphy, Ruth
Thesmophoriazusae, The; Goddesses of Athens,
The 1955,D 14,52:4
Murphy, Susan
Salad of the Mad Cafe, The 1964,Ap 1,43:1
Murphy, Thomas
If Booth Had Missed 1932,F 5,24:2
Murphy, Thomas (Playwright)
Whistle in the Dark, A 1968,F 17,32:2
Whistle in the Dark, A 1969,O 9,55:1
Whistle in the Dark, A 1969,N 9,II,3:1
Murphy, Tim
First Year, The 1920,O 21,11:2
First Year, The 1920,O 31,VI,1:1
Handy Man, The 1925,Mr 10,19:2
Murphy, Walter
General John Regan 1930,Ja 30,16:5
Murphy, William
Elizabethans, The 1962,Ja 22,19:1
Murray, Alan
Biff, Bing, Bang 1921,My 10,20:1
Murray, Anita
Collision 1932,F 17,19:2
Murray, Ann
Abortion 1959,O 28,40:4
Murray, Annabella
Wrecker, The 1928,F 28,18:2
First Mrs Fraser, The 1929,D 30,16:2
Gray Shadow 1931,Mr 11,23:4
Murray, Barbara
In the Counting House 1962,D 15,5:5
Murray, Betty
Playboy of the Western World, The 1930,Ja 3,20:4
Well of the Saints, The 1932,Ja 22,15:2

Murray, Billy
Bad Habits of 1926 1926,My 1,11:1
Murray, Bob
Carnival 1961,Ap 14,22:2
Murray, Bonnie
Ramblers, The 1926,S 21,32:2
Murray, Braham (Choreographer)
Hang Down Your Head and Die 1964,O 19,38:1
Murray, Braham (Director)
Hang Down Your Head and Die 1964,O 19,38:1
She Stoops to Conquer 1969,Ag 18,28:1
Murray, Brian
Hamlet 1961,Ap 12,46:1
Romeo and Juliet 1961,Ag 16,36:3
Macbeth 1962,Je 6,35:2
King Lear 1964,My 19,43:2
All in Good Time 1965,F 19,25:1
Rosencrantz and Guildenstern Are Dead
1967,O 17,53:1
Rosencrantz and Guildenstern Are Dead
1967,O 29,II,1:1
Murray, Brian (Director)
Scent of Flowers, A 1969,O 21,42:1
Place Without Doors, A 1970,D 1,60:1
Murray, Charlie
Vaudeville (Palace) 1929,S 16,30:4
Murray, Charlotte
Deep River 1926,O 5,26:2
Murray, Dennis
Bombo 1921,O 7,20:2
Murray, Don
Rose Tattoo, The 1951,F 5,19:2
Rose Tattoo, The 1951,F 11,II,1:1
Skin of Our Teeth, The 1955,Je 29,25:3
Skin of Our Teeth, The 1955,Ag 18,16:1
Skin of Our Teeth, The 1955,Ag 28,II,1:1
Hot Corner, The 1956,Ja 26,25:2
Murray, Dorothy
Jonica 1930,Ap 8,27:1
Murray, Douglas (Playwright)
Man From Toronto, The 1926,Je 18,27:2
Murray, Dudley (Director)
Red Peppers; Tonight at Eight 1940,Ag 6,15:3
Murray, Edgar Roland
Every Man for Himself 1940,D 10,32:3
Murray, Edward
East of Broadway 1932,Ja 27,19:3
Murray, Elizabeth
Love Birds 1921,Mr 16,12:1
Sidewalks of New York 1927,O 4,33:1
Murray, Floy
Virtue (?) 1922,N 17,14:1
Murray, Frances
Daddy Dumplins 1920,N 23,11:1
Murray, Frank
H M S Pinafore 1944,F 15,14:4
Gondoliers, The 1944,F 22,26:3
Patience 1944,F 26,11:4
Yeomen of the Guard, The 1944,Mr 5,34:3
Murray, Frederick
Captain Jinks 1925,S 9,22:1
Murray, George (Playwright)
Chiffon Girl, The 1924,F 20,23:2
Murray, Gerard M (Playwright)
Career Angel 1943,N 19,24:2
Career Angel 1944,My 24,23:7
Murray, Gilbert (Playwright)
Electra 1958,My 10,17:7
Murray, Gilbert (Translator)
Medea 1920,Mr 23,12:2
Trojan Women, The 1923,My 27,10:2
Oedipus Rex 1923,O 26,14:1
Trojan Women, The 1923,N 8,17:6
Hippolytus 1935,F 12,25:4
Hippolytus 1935,Je 15,20:4
Trojan Women, The 1941,Ap 9,32:5
Electra 1962,Mr 22,42:1
Murray, Grace M
Getting Even 1929,Ag 20,31:1
Murray, Harold
As Thousands Cheer 1933,O 2,22:1
Thumbs Up! 1934,D 28,24:1
Jubilee 1935,O 14,20:1
Between the Devil 1937,D 23,24:5
Nellie Bly 1946,Ja 22,32:2
Murray, Harry
Topaze 1930,F 13,25:3
Murray, Harvey
Ballyhoo 1930,D 23,24:1
Murray, Henry
Midsummer Night's Dream, A 1968,D 9,59:1
Murray, Honey
You'll See Stars 1943,Ja 1,26:6
Early to Bed 1943,Je 18,16:2
What's Up 1943,N 12,24:6
Murray, Irving
Room Service 1953,Ap 7,34:1
Murray, J Harold
Passing Show of 1921, The 1920,D 30,16:2
Whirl of New York, The 1921,Je 14,18:1
Make It Snappy 1922,Ap 14,20:2
Springtime of Youth 1922,O 27,15:1
Caroline 1923,F 1,13:2

Murray, J Harold—Cont
Vogues of 1924 1924,Mr 28,14:3
China Rose 1925,Ja 20,18:1
Captain Jinks 1925,S 9,22:1
Castles in the Air 1926,S 7,19:2
Rio Rita 1927,F 3,18:3
East Wind 1931,O 28,19:1
East Wind 1931,D 11,VIII,4:3
Face the Music 1932,F 18,24:5
Murray, J K
Merton of the Movies 1922,N 14,16:2
Murray, J P (Composer)
Ziegfeld Follies 1931,Jl 2,30:5
Murray, J P (Playwright)
Ziegfeld Follies 1931,Jl 2,30:5
Murray, J S
Tyrant, The 1930,N 13,33:1
Murray, Jack
West Side Story 1957,S 27,14:4
Juno 1959,Mr 10,41:1
Murray, James
Three Cheers 1928,O 16,28:1
Naughty Marietta 1929,O 22,26:2
Naughty Marietta 1931,N 17,31:2
Fiddler's House, The 1941,Mr 28,27:5
Murray, Jan
Music in My Heart 1947,O 3,30:2
Guys and Dolls 1966,Je 9,55:2
Murray, Jan (Producer)
Power of Darkness, The 1959,S 30,33:1
Murray, Jane
Shake Hands With the Devil 1949,O 21,30:4
Murray, Janet (Scenic Designer)
Summertree 1969,D 10,60:1
Murray, Jay
Something to Brag About 1925,Ag 14,14:3
Murray, Jefferson
In the Night Watch 1921,Ja 31,10:1
Murray, John
Baby Pompadour 1934,D 28,24:2
Shylock and His Daughter 1947,S 30,22:2
Murray, John (Miscellaneous)
Room Service 1953,Ap 7,34:1
Room Service 1970,My 13,49:1
Charley's Aunt 1970,Jl 6,38:1
Murray, John (Playwright)
Room Service 1935,N 17,II,7:7
Room Service 1937,My 20,16:1
Room Service 1937,My 30,X,1:1
Room Service 1937,D 16,35:4
Sing for Your Supper 1939,Ap 25,18:6
Room Service 1953,Ap 7,34:1
Room Service 1970,My 13,49:1
Room Service 1970,Jl 5,II,1:2
Murray, John T
Florodora 1920,Ap 6,18:1
Cinderella on Broadway 1920,Je 25,18:1
Whirl of New York, The 1921,Je 14,18:1
Yankee Princess, The 1922,O 3,22:1
Matrimonial Bed, The 1927,O 13,23:2
Vaudeville (Palace) 1927,O 25,33:2
Vaudeville (Palace) 1929,Je 3,27:4
Murray, Kathi
Go-Go 1923,Mr 13,19:4
Murray, Kathleen
Bonds of Interest, The 1951,D 1,7:2
Yerma 1952,F 8,18:4
Summer and Smoke 1952,Ap 25,19:5
Ronde, La 1955,Je 28,24:2
Purple Dust 1956,D 28,15:1
Leave It to Jane 1959,My 26,30:2
Kittiwake Island 1960,O 13,43:1
Ordinary Man, An 1968,S 10,39:1
Murray, Kel (Musical Director)
Mr Winkle's Holliday 1946,Je 24,27:6
Murray, Ken
Vaudeville (Palace) 1928,Ap 24,29:2
Vaudeville (Palace) 1928,O 23,32:5
Vaudeville (Palace) 1928,D 24,10:8
Vaudeville (Palace) 1929,S 2,16:3
Vaudeville (Palace) 1929,D 9,33:2
Vaudeville (Palace) 1930,N 3,19:2
Vaudeville (Palace) 1930,N 10,17:1
Vaudeville (Palace) 1930,D 8,27:2
Vaudeville (Palace) 1932,Ap 4,13:4
Sketch Book 1935,Je 5,22:2
Blackouts of 1949 1949,S 7,39:2
Murray, Ken (Director)
Blackouts of 1949 1949,S 7,39:2
Murray, Ken (Playwright)
Blackouts of 1949 1949,S 7,39:2
Murray, Ken (Producer)
Blackouts of 1949 1949,S 7,39:2
Murray, Kitty
Sons o' Fun 1941,D 2,28:2
Murray, Lawrence
Richard II 1937,F 6,14:2
Murray, Lewis (Miscellaneous)
Winterset 1966,F 10,32:2
Murray, Lyn (Composer)
Ice Capades 1966,Je 2,50:2
Murray, Lyn (Lyricist)
Ice Capades 1966,Je 2,50:2

urray, Lyn (Miscellaneous)
ce Capades 1962,Ag 30,34:1
ce Capades 1963,Ag 29,37:2
ice Capades 1967,Je 2,33:1
urray, Lyn Singers
Hollywood Pinafore 1945,Je 1,20:1
urray, Mae
Untitled-Benefit 1922,My 8,14:5
Vaudeville (Palace) 1930,My 5,27:5
urray, Marcia
Shake Hands With the Devil 1949,O 21,30:4
urray, Marguerite
Ramblers, The 1926,S 21,32:2
urray, Marion
Vaudeville (Palace) 1921,Jl 5,15:1
urray, Mary
Cradle Snatchers 1925,S 8,28:2
Paris Bound 1927,D 28,26:3
Paris Bound 1928,Ja 15,VIII,1:1
Paris Bound 1929,Jl 20,8:3
So Was Napoleon 1930,Ja 9,22:2
Nine Fifteen Revue, The 1930,F 12,26:2
Little Orchard Annie 1930,Ap 22,33:1
Betty, Be Careful 1931,My 5,33:3
Dinner at Eight 1932,O 24,18:2
Journey by Night, A 1935,Ap 17,26:3
Women, The 1936,D 28,13:1
American Way, The 1939,Ja 23,9:2
Murray, Michael
King Lear 1964,My 19,43:2
Comedy of Errors, The 1964,My 21,43:1
Murray, Michael (Director)
House of Breath, The 1957,Ap 15,23:2
Murray, Michael (Miscellaneous)
Iceman Cometh, The 1956,My 8,38:1
Murray, Myra
Don Juan 1921,S 8,14:2
Murray, Paul (Miscellaneous)
By the Way 1925,D 29,20:3
Murray, Paul (Producer)
And On We Go 1937,Ap 22,19:5
Murray, Peg
Great Sebastians, The 1956,Ja 5,27:1
Gypsy 1959,My 22,31:6
Blood, Sweat & Stanley Poole 1961,O 6,31:1
Anyone Can Whistle 1964,Ap 6,36:1
Something More! 1964,N 11,36:1
Cabaret 1966,N 21,62:1
Fiddler on the Roof 1970,F 28,20:1
Murray, Peter
Power Without Glory 1948,Ja 14,30:2
Murray, Robert T
Promis' Lan', De 1930,My 28,31:2
Murray, Rosemary (Producer)
There Is a Play Tonight 1961,F 16,24:2
Murray, Sidney
Joseph 1930,F 13,25:3
Murray, Stephen
Abraham Lincoln 1940,Ap 28,IX,1:7
School for Scandal, The 1970,Je 11,51:1
Murray, T C (Playwright)
Birthright, The 1920,My 25,14:2
Autumn Fire 1926,Ap 15,25:1
Autumn Fire 1926,O 27,25:3
Pipe in the Fields, The 1927,O 23,VIII,4:4
Blind Wolf, The 1928,My 27,VIII,2:7
Flutter of Wings, A 1931,Ja 4,VIII,3:4
Pipe in the Fields, The 1931,Mr 14,23:4
Birthright 1932,N 4,25:1
Autumn Fire 1932,D 29,16:3
Murray, Vangi
Go-Go 1923,Mr 13,19:4
Murray, Vera (Director)
Laura Garnett 1934,Jl 17,24:4
Murray, Vera (Producer)
Laura Garnett 1934,Jl 17,24:4
Bridal Quilt 1934,O 11,28:5
Murray, Virginia
Ladies of the Jury 1929,O 22,26:2
Murray, Warren
People on the Hill 1931,S 26,25:5
Murray, Warren (Lyricist)
Atmosphere 1925,Ap 4,17:1
Murray, Warren (Playwright)
Atmosphere 1925,Ap 4,17:1
Murray, William
Creoles 1927,S 23,33:3
Murray, William (Director)
An Evening With G B S; Press Cuttings 1957,F 19,35:7
Evening With G B S, An; O'Flaherty, V C 1957,F 19,35:7
Murray, William (Playwright)
Rules of the Game, The 1960,D 20,44:1
Murray, William (Producer)
Evening With G B S, An; O'Flaherty, V C 1957,F 19,35:7
An Evening With G B S; Press Cuttings 1957,F 19,35:7
Murray, William (Translator)
To Clothe the Naked 1967,Ap 28,30:1
Jar, The 1969,Ap 23,42:1

Man With the Flower in His Mouth, The 1969,Ap 23,42:1
License, The 1969,Ap 23,42:1
Murray, William B (Translator)
We Are No Longer Children 1932,Ap 1,17:2
Murray, Wynn
Babes in Arms 1937,Ap 15,18:4
Boys From Syracuse, The 1938,N 24,36:1
American Jubilee 1940,My 13,20:5
All in Fun 1940,D 28,11:2
Lady Comes Across, The 1942,Ja 10,10:2
Heaven on Earth 1948,S 17,29:2
Murray and Garrish
Vaudeville (Palace) 1923,Ja 16,16:3
Murrey, Bertha (Playwright)
Lady-in-Law, The 1927,O 23,VIII,4:1
Murrill, Herbert (Composer)
Dog Beneath the Skin, The 1936,F 23,X,1:3
Murrin, Tom (Playwright)
Son of Cock-Strong 1970,Mr 9,43:1
Murry, Belle
Toto 1921,Mr 22,15:2
For All of Us 1923,O 16,19:4
Murry, Ted (Composer)
Take a Bow 1944,Je 16,15:3
Murtagh, Jack
Ever Green Lady, The 1922,O 12,25:2
Sport of Kings, The 1926,My 5,24:2
Murtah, Kate
Texas Li'l Darlin' 1949,N 26,10:5
Murtah Sisters
Take a Bow 1944,Je 16,15:3
Murtaugh, J Harry
Suppressed Desires 1920,F 10,10:2
Magnanimous Lover, The 1920,F 10,10:2
Girl in the Coffin, The 1920,F 10,10:2
Murtaugh, James F
Firebugs, The 1968,Jl 2,36:1
Murtoe, Lionel
Teahouse of the August Moon, The 1954,My 2,II,3:1
Teahouse of the August Moon, The 1955,My 10,24:1
Musante, Tony
Bertha 1962,F 12,27:1
Match-Play 1966,O 12,37:1
Night of the Dunce 1966,D 29,21:1
Musarra, Anthony
Once Over Lightly 1942,N 20,26:2
Muscari, Alfred
Hamlet 1954,Ap 24,15:2
Androcles and the Lion 1958,F 22,8:3
Mandragola 1958,My 29,23:2
Muscat, Robert
It's A Gift 1945,Mr 13,18:7
Musco, Angelo
Aria del Continente, L' 1927,O 5,30:2
Muse, Clarence (Director)
Run, Little Chillun 1943,Ag 14,6:1
Muselli, Fred
Moondreamers, The 1969,D 9,68:1
Musgrove, Gertrude
Heart of a City 1942,F 13,24:6
Three Sisters, The 1942,D 22,31:2
Three Sisters, The 1942,D 27,VIII,1:1
Storm Operation 1944,Ja 12,28:2
Constant Wife, The 1951,D 10,34:3
Mushtakova, Iraida
My Fair Lady 1964,D 29,22:1
Musk, Cecil
Much Ado About Nothing 1929,N 17,30:4
Musketeers, The
Americana 1932,O 6,19:3
Musolino, Angelo (Miscellaneous)
Meet Peter Grant 1961,My 11,41:4
Musselman, Lillian
Mikado, The 1935,Ag 24,17:5
Musser, Tharon (Lighting Director)
Lucky Sam McCarver 1950,Ap 15,10:6
Naked 1950,S 7,39:2
Long Day's Journey Into Night 1956,N 8,47:2
Shinbone Alley 1957,Ap 15,23:2
Much Ado About Nothing 1957,Ag 8,15:2
Monique 1957,O 23,38:1
Makropoulos Secret, The 1957,D 4,52:4
Lesson, The 1958,Ja 10,20:3
Chairs, The 1958,Ja 10,20:3
Infernal Machine, The 1958,F 4,33:1
Entertainer, The 1958,F 13,22:2
Firstborn, The 1958,My 1,35:1
Firstborn, The 1958,My 11,II,1:1
Midsummer Night's Dream, A 1958,Je 23,19:1
Shadow of a Gunman, The 1958,N 21,26:1
J B 1958,D 12,2:7
Rivalry, The 1959,F 9,24:2
Rivalry, The 1959,F 15,II,1:1
Beaux' Stratagem, The 1959,F 25,35:4
Once Upon a Mattress 1959,My 12,40:1
Romeo and Juliet 1959,Je 15,31:1
Merry Wives of Windsor, The 1959,Jl 9,23:2
Great God Brown, The 1959,O 7,48:1
Only in America 1959,N 20,35:1
Five Finger Exercise 1959,D 3,45:4

Musser, Tharon (Lighting Director)—Cont
Five Finger Exercise 1959,D 13,II,3:1
Peer Gynt 1960,Ja 13,21:1
Long Dream, The 1960,F 18,36:2
Tumbler, The 1960,F 25,32:2
Twelfth Night 1960,Je 9,29:4
Tempest, The 1960,Je 20,35:1
Antony and Cleopatra 1960,Ag 1,19:1
As You Like It 1961,Je 17,13:2
Macbeth 1961,Je 19,31:1
Garden of Sweets, The 1961,N 1,35:1
Giants, Sons of Giants 1962,Ja 8,26:2
Calculated Risk 1962,N 1,35:1
Nowhere to Go But Up 1962,N 12,36:2
Andorra 1963,F 11,5:5
Mother Courage and Her Children 1963,Mr 30,5:5
King Lear 1963,Je 10,37:1
Comedy of Errors, The 1963,Je 13,28:1
Henry V 1963,Je 14,37:1
Here's Love 1963,O 4,28:1
Marathon '33 1963,D 23,20:1
Any Wednesday 1964,F 19,34:1
Seagull, The 1964,Ap 6,36:1
Crucible, The 1964,Ap 7,30:2
Much Ado About Nothing 1964,Je 11,26:2
Richard III 1964,Je 12,44:2
Hamlet 1964,Jl 4,9:1
Golden Boy 1964,O 21,56:1
Alfie 1964,D 18,27:1
Kelly 1965,F 8,28:2
All in Good Time 1965,F 19,25:1
Flora, the Red Menace 1965,My 12,41:2
Coriolanus 1965,Je 21,36:1
Romeo and Juliet 1965,Je 21,36:3
Taming of the Shrew, The 1965,Je 24,32:2
King Lear 1965,Je 25,39:1
Malcolm 1966,Ja 12,29:1
Great Indoors, The 1966,F 2,23:1
Lion in Winter, The 1966,Mr 4,23:1
Mame 1966,My 25,41:1
Falstaff 1966,Je 20,27:1
Murder in the Cathedral 1966,Je 21,38:1
Twelfth Night 1966,Je 23,28:1
Julius Caesar 1966,Je 24,29:2
Delicate Balance, A 1966,S 23,44:1
Hallelujah, Baby! 1967,Ap 27,51:1
Imaginary Invalid, The 1967,My 2,53:1
Touch of the Poet, A 1967,My 3,38:2
Ways and Means 1967,My 4,34:1
Still Life 1967,My 4,34:1
Fumed Oak 1967,My 4,34:1
Antigone 1967,Je 19,43:1
Midsummer Night's Dream, A 1967,Je 19,42:1
Merchant of Venice, The 1967,Je 22,46:2
Birthday Party, The 1967,O 4,40:2
After the Rain 1967,O 10,54:1
Promise, The 1967,N 15,38:1
Everything in the Garden 1967,N 30,60:1
House of Flowers 1968,Ja 29,26:2
John Brown's Body 1968,F 13,49:2
Comedy of Errors, The 1968,F 28,40:2
As You Like It 1968,Je 24,42:3
Androcles and the Lion 1968,Je 27,47:1
Lovers; Winners 1968,Jl 26,21:4
Lovers; Losers 1968,Jl 26,21:4
Maggie Flynn 1968,O 24,52:1
Fig Leaves Are Falling, The 1969,Ja 3,19:1
Gingham Dog, The 1969,Ap 24,41:1
Blood Red Roses 1970,Mr 23,48:1
Applause 1970,Mr 31,35:1
Boy Friend, The 1970,Ap 15,54:1
Musser, Tharon (Miscellaneous)
Measure for Measure 1957,Ja 23,24:1
Taming of the Shrew, The 1957,F 21,30:2
All in Good Time 1965,F 19,25:1
Musser, Tharon (Scenic Designer)
Entertainer, The 1958,F 13,22:2

Musser, Walt
Macbeth 1955,O 8,12:6

Musset, Alfred (Director)
Night's Candles 1933,Je 25,IX,1:3
Lorenzaccio 1958,O 15,44:2
Musset, Alfred de (Playwright)
Pas Avec l'Amour 1926,Ap 14,20:2
Nuit Venitienne, La 1930,F 2,VIII,4:1
Caprices de Marianne 1936,Ja 12,IX,3:7
Chandelier, Le 1939,Mr 19,XI,3:1
On Ne Badine Pas Avec l'Amour; No Trifling With Love 1968,Mr 5,35:1
Mussett, Charles
Peter Ibbetson 1931,Ap 9,30:3
Mussolini, Benito (Playwright)
Campo di Maggio 1931,Je 5,4:3
Hundred Days 1931,N 17,31:3
Campo di Maggio; Hundred Days 1932,F 7,III,3:7
Villa Franca 1932,Mr 17,16:5
Napoleon: The Hundred Days 1932,Ap 19,25:2
Napoleon: The Hundred Days 1932,My 8,VIII,1:3
Hundred Days 1934,Ap 29,IX,2:3
Musson, Bennett
Holy Terror, A 1925,S 29,31:2
Musson, Bennett (Playwright)
Scalawag, The 1927,Mr 30,22:3

Mustard, Tom
Hatfields & McCoys 1970,Je 23,34:1
Muston, Jeff (Miscellaneous)
World of Paul Slickey, The 1959,My 6,48:7
Musumeci, Eileen
Miracle Worker, The 1959,O 20,44:1
Muth, May
Sunny River 1941,D 5,28:2
Liar, The 1950,My 19,30:2
Courtin' Time 1951,Je 14,30:2
Muth, May (Miscellaneous)
I Was Dancing 1964,N 9,40:4
Celebration 1969,Ja 23,55:2
Muth, Muriel
Forbidden Melody 1936,N 3,33:1
Muthel, Lothar (Director)
Twelfth Night 1932,O 23,IX,3:1
Muti, Lorenzo
Maria Golovin 1958,N 6,43:1
Mydell, Joseph
Volpone 1967,Je 30,29:1
Myer, Jean (Director)
Amphitryon 1970,F 4,38:1
Myer, Richmond
Fuente Ovejuna; Sheep Well, The 1936,My 3,II,4:1
Myerberg, Michael (Director)
Balloon 1946,Ag 13,30:3
Dear Judas 1947,O 6,26:4
Myerberg, Michael (Playwright)
Dear Judas 1947,Ag 5,26:1
Dear Judas 1947,O 6,26:4
Myerberg, Michael (Producer)
Candide 1933,My 16,15:6
Symphony 1935,Ap 27,20:3
Skin of Our Teeth, The 1942,N 19,29:5
Skin of Our Teeth, The 1943,Ja 3,VIII,1:1
Lute Song 1946,F 7,29:2
Lute Song 1946,F 17,II,1:1
Dear Judas 1947,O 6,26:4
Cradle Will Rock, The 1947,D 27,11:2
Barrier, The 1950,N 3,32:2
Waiting for Godot 1956,Ap 20,21:2
Compulsion 1957,O 25,21:1
What Did We Do Wrong? 1967,O 23,56:1
Myers, Addison
Sidewalks and the Sound of Crying 1956,O 29,34:1
Myers, Ann
Princess Ida 1925,Ap 14,27:2
Myers, Barbara
Clearing in the Woods, A 1957,Ja 11,20:2
Rope Dancers, The 1957,N 21,39:1
Ice Follies 1958,Ja 15,26:2
Ice Follies 1959,Ja 14,30:1
Ice Follies 1960,Ja 13,20:1
Ice Follies 1961,Ja 11,25:2
Ice Follies 1962,Ja 10,24:6
Ice Follies 1963,Ja 10,5:2
Myers, Bill
Temporary Island, A 1948,Mr 15,27:3
Myers, Carmel
Vaudeville (Palace) 1929,N 4,29:1
Myers, Chandler
Cape Smoke 1925,F 17,19:1
Myers, Edward (Costume Designer)
Pilgrim's Progress 1962,Mr 21,36:2
Myers, Eileen
Papavert 1931,D 30,25:1
Lady Luck 1936,Ap 16,21:2
Myers, Florence
Vaudeville (Palace) 1928,Ja 17,23:3
Myers, Fran
Carving a Statue 1968,My 1,43:1
Myers, Frank
Anne of the Thousand Days 1948,D 9,49:2
Myers, Gayther
Simple Life, A 1964,My 18,36:1
Myers, Gordon
Shadow of My Enemy, A 1957,D 12,35:4
Play of Daniel, The 1958,Ja 3,15:3
Play of Daniel, The 1959,Ja 6,30:2
Play of Daniel, The 1960,D 27,23:6
Play of Daniel, The 1961,D 28,22:6
Golden Age, The 1963,N 19,49:2
Myers, Harry (Playwright)
Me 1925,N 24,28:1
Myers, Henry
Checkerboard, The 1920,Ag 20,7:2
Myers, Henry (Composer)
Meet the People 1940,D 26,22:2
Meet the People 1941,Ja 12,IX,1:1
Myers, Henry (Lyricist)
Bare Facts 1926,Jl 19,13:3
New Yorkers, The 1927,Mr 11,24:3
Garrick Gaieties 1930,Je 5,29:2
Meet the People 1940,D 26,22:2
Meet the People 1941,Ja 12,IX,1:1
These Are the Times 1950,My 11,37:2
Myers, Henry (Miscellaneous)
Kilpatrick's Old-Time Minstrels 1930,Ap 21,20:2
Myers, Henry (Original Author)
Gypsy Lady 1946,S 18,25:6
Myers, Henry (Playwright)
First Fifty Years, The 1922,Mr 14,11:2

Blonde Beast, The 1923,Mr 3,9:3
Good Boy 1928,S 6,23:2
Kilpatrick's Old-Time Minstrels 1930,Ap 21,20:2
Other One, The 1932,O 4,26:3
Hallowe'en 1936,F 21,20:3
Work Is for Horses 1937,N 22,14:6
Meet the People 1940,D 26,22:2
They Can't Get You Down 1941,N 2,IX,3:5
These Are the Times 1950,My 11,37:2
Happiest Girl in the World, The 1961,Ap 4,42:1
Myers, Henry (Producer)
New Meet the People, The 1943,Ag 22,II,1:6
Myers, Joanne
Yoshe Kalb 1933,D 29,27:2
Myers, John Bernard (Miscellaneous)
Immortal Husband, The 1955,F 15,32:2
Myers, John Bernard (Producer)
Absalom 1956,My 17,37:2
Myers, Joseph
Taming of the Shrew, The 1957,F 21,30:2
Myers, Lee
Priorities of 1942 1942,Mr 13,23:2
Myers, Margot
49ers, The 1922,N 7,14:1
Myers, Marguerite
Sweet Nell of Old Drury 1923,My 19,16:4
Myers, Martin
Every Man for Himself 1940,D 10,32:3
Myers, Maryn
Path of Flowers, The 1936,S 18,19:3
Myers, Michaele
Getting Married 1951,My 14,28:5
One by One 1964,D 2,60:1
Great Western Union, The 1965,F 10,45:1
Hogan's Goat 1965,N 12,56:1
This Here Nice Place 1966,N 2,35:2
Angela 1969,O 31,33:1
Myers, Mr (Lyricist)
Pajama Lady, The 1930,O 12,VIII,4:1
Myers, Pamela
Company 1970,Ap 27,40:1
Company 1970,My 3,II,1:4
Company 1970,Jl 29,31:1
Myers, Paulene (Playwright)
World of My America, The 1966,O 4,53:1
Myers, Pauline
Growing Pains 1933,N 24,24:2
Plumes in the Dust 1936,N 7,14:2
Willow and I, The 1942,D 11,32:2
Naked Genius, The 1943,O 22,20:5
Dear Ruth 1944,D 14,29:2
Sister Oakes 1949,Ap 25,19:4
Son, The 1950,Ag 16,24:6
You Can't Take It With You 1951,Ap 7,8:6
Take a Giant Step 1953,O 4,II,1:1
Anniversary Waltz 1954,Ap 8,34:1
Myers, Richard (Composer)
Allez-Opp! 1927,Ag 3,29:3
Hello, Yourself 1928,O 31,28:2
Nine Fifteen Revue, The 1930,F 12,26:2
Here Goes the Bride 1931,N 4,31:2
Murder at the Vanities 1933,S 13,22:4
Pure in Heart, The 1934,Mr 21,24:3
Without Love 1942,N 11,28:1
Ziegfeld Follies 1957,Mr 2,19:2
Myers, Richard (Lyricist)
Nine Fifteen Revue, The 1930,F 12,26:2
Murder at the Vanities 1933,S 13,22:4
Ziegfeld Follies 1957,Mr 2,19:2
Myers, Richard (Miscellaneous)
John Bull's Other Island 1948,F 11,33:4
Old Lady Says No, The 1948,F 18,35:1
Where Stars Walk 1948,F 25,27:2
Goodbye My Fancy 1948,N 18,35:2
Caesar and Cleopatra 1949,D 22,28:2
Myers, Richard (Producer)
Give Us This Day 1933,O 28,20:6
I Want a Policeman! 1936,Ja 15,15:5
Tide Rising 1937,Ja 26,17:2
Lorelei 1938,N 30,21:2
Importance of Being Earnest, The 1939,Ja 13,16:2
Margin for Error 1939,N 4,11:3
My Dear Children 1940,F 1,16:2
Cue for Passion 1940,D 20,33:4
Plan M 1942,F 21,15:2
Sons and Soldiers 1943,My 5,22:2
Mrs January & Mr Ex 1944,Ap 1,10:2
Calico Wedding 1945,Mr 8,18:6
Four Twelves Are 48 1951,Ja 18,30:2
Girl Can Tell, A 1953,O 30,28:2
Dear Charles 1954,S 16,37:2
Little Glass Clock, The 1956,Mr 27,40:2
Hotel Paradiso 1957,Ap 12,22:2
Interlock 1958,F 7,18:1
Requiem for a Nun 1959,Ja 31,13:2
Myers, Richardson (Miscellaneous)
Be So Kindly 1937,F 9,19:4
Myers, Robert
Lower North 1944,Ag 26,15:4
Myers, Sellwyn
Fireman's Flame, The 1937,O 11,26:2
Two on an Island 1940,Ja 23,17:2
Out of the Frying Pan 1941,F 12,24:2

Myers, Sylvia
Show Boat 1948,S 9,33:2
Myers, Vera
Chimes of Normandy, The 1931,N 3,31:3
Myers, Vernon
Cotton Stockings 1923,D 19,16:2
Myers, William
Shoemaker's Prodigious Wife, The 1949,Je 15,38:2
Liar, The 1950,My 19,30:2
School for Scandal, The 1953,Je 24,29:2
Cretan Woman, The 1954,Jl 8,18:2
Joan of Lorraine 1955,Mr 26,12:2
Antigone 1956,Ap 3,32:2
Tevya and His Daughters 1957,S 17,38:2
Monique 1957,O 23,38:1
Quare Fellow, The 1958,N 28,34:1
Measure for Measure 1960,Jl 27,33:1
Idiot, The 1960,S 26,38:1
Bring Me a Warm Body 1962,Ap 17,29:3
King Lear 1963,N 23,22:1
Ox Cart, The 1966,D 20,58:1
Macbeth 1967,Jl 31,21:1
King Lear 1968,N 8,43:1
Inner Journey, The 1969,Mr 21,42:1
Miser, The 1969,My 9,35:1
Year Boston Won the Pennant, The 1969,My 23,38:1
Wars of the Roses, The (Part II) 1970,Jl 3,15:1
Myers, William (Director)
Stronger, The 1949,Je 15,38:2
Myers, William (Producer)
Good as Gold 1957,Mr 8,22:2
Myers, Z (Lyricist)
Blue Eyes 1921,F 22,11:2
Myerson, Alan (Director)
This Music Crept by Me Upon the Waters 1959,N 25,19:4
Committee, The 1964,S 17,53:1
Myerson, Jessica
Critic, The 1965,Jl 26,15:2
Myerson, Leonard
Boutique Fantasque, La 1929,D 28,10:6
Myerson, Robert
Gioconda Smile, The 1950,O 9,21:2
Mygatt, Royal E (Producer)
Caesar and Cleopatra 1927,N 6,IX,2:1
Myhers, John
Mandragola 1958,My 29,23:2
Chic 1959,My 19,28:2
Golden Fleecing 1959,O 16,24:5
Good Soup, The 1960,Mr 3,26:4
Antony and Cleopatra 1960,Ag 1,19:1
Myland, Leona (Miscellaneous)
Dance of Death, The 1960,S 14,51:1
Myles, Marian
Great White Hope, The 1967,D 14,58:1
Myles, Meg
Enter Laughing 1963,Mr 15,8:1
Collision Course; Jew! 1968,My 9,55:2
Collision Course; Thoughts on the Instant of Greeting a Friend on the Street 1968,My 9,55:2
Collision Course; Unexpurgated Memoirs of Bernard Mergendeiler, The 1968,My 9,55:2
Collision Course; Stars and Stripes 1968,My 9,55:2
Young Master Dante, The 1968,D 31,19:1
Myles, Raymond
Sweeney Todd 1957,Ag 28,21:4
Ignorants Abroad, The 1960,My 24,43:2
Mylroie, Jayme
It's a Bird . . . It's a Plane . . . It's Superman 1966,Mr 30,34:1
Cabaret 1966,N 21,62:1
Mylroie, Kathryne
All for Love 1949,Ja 24,16:5
Two on the Aisle 1951,Jl 20,13:6
Myra, Olga
Vaudeville (Palace) 1926,Je 15,23:3
Myrat, C
Electra 1952,N 20,38:2
Myrat, Rita
Electra 1952,N 20,38:2
Myrck, Malvin
All God's Chillun Got Wings 1924,My 16,22:3
All God's Chillun Got Wings 1924,Ag 19,9:1
Myrick, George
Kilpatrick's Old-Time Minstrels 1930,Ap 21,20:2
Myrick, William
So Proudly We Hail 1938,Ap 9,11:1
Myrie, Monica (Costume Designer)
Ododo 1970,N 25,26:1
Myron, William
Champion, The 1925,Ap 24,16:4
Pressing Business 1930,N 18,28:5
Myrtil, Odette
Vogues of 1924 1924,Mr 28,14:3
Vogues and Frolics 1924,Je 26,21:7
Love Song, The 1925,Ja 14,19:4
Vaudeville (Hippodrome) 1925,D 29,21:2
Countess Maritza 1926,Mr 30,20:3
Countess Maritza 1926,S 20,21:1
White Lilacs 1928,S 11,31:2
Broadway Nights 1929,Je 23,VIII,2:4
Broadway Nights 1929,Jl 16,23:2

Myrtil, Odette—Cont
Tattle Tales 1930,Jl 20,VIII,2:1
Cat and the Fiddle, The 1931,S 27,VIII,3:1
Cat and the Fiddle, The 1931,O 16,26:4
Red Mill, The 1945,O 17,16:2
Maggie 1953,F 19,20:2
Saratoga 1959,D 8,59:4

Myrtill, Horam
Untitled-Revue 1930,N 30,IX,3:3

Myrtill & Pacaud
Michael Todd's Peep Show 1950,Je 29,37:2

Mysell, Bella
Papirossen 1936,S 18,19:3
Give Me Back My Heart 1937,O 4,17:6
Semele's Bar Mitzvah 1938,Ja 17,11:2

Mysell, Bella (Lyricist)
It's a Funny World 1956,O 22,24:1
My Son and I 1960,O 24,24:2
Go Fight City Hall 1961,N 3,28:5

Mysell, Bella (Miscellaneous)
Uncle Sam in Israel 1952,D 8,38:5

Myselsi, George (Lyricist)
Difficult Woman, The 1962,Ap 26,22:7

Myser, Marion
Abie's Irish Rose 1954,N 19,19:1

N

Nabokov, Dmitri (Translator)
Waltz Invention, The 1969,Ja 12,II,20:4

Nabokov, Vladimir (Original Author)
Invitation to a Beheading 1969,Mr 30,II,1:1

Nabokov, Vladimir (Playwright)
Waltz Invention, The 1969,Ja 12,II,20:4
Invitation to a Beheading 1969,Mr 18,36:1

Nabors, Frances
Glorious Morning 1938,N 28,10:3

Naboudet, Gigi
Ice Capades 1956,S 13,41:2

Nacamee, Fredi
Building Blocks 1954,My 8,14:4
Eastward in Eden 1956,Ap 18,25:4

Nachbush, Noah
Dybbuk, The 1924,Ja 29,17:7
Yoshe Kalb 1932,N 6,IX,2:1
Bread 1932,D 14,27:3
Untitled-Revue 1935,N 11,21:2
Kapores 1936,S 28,14:3
Philosopher, A - A Drunkard 1936,S 28,14:3
Jealousy 1936,S 28,14:3

Nachemin, Meyer
Pirates of Penzance, The 1942,F 20,20:2

Nachman, William
Jazz a La Carte 1922,Je 3,8:3

Nachmann, Fred
Lebende Leichnam, Der, Der; Living Corpse, The 1928,Ja 24,26:2

Nachmann, Heins
Dantons Tod 1927,D 21,28:3

Nacic, Tasko
Ubu Roi 1968,Je 29,20:1
Victor, or The Children Take Over 1968,Jl 10,22:4

Nacional, Trio
Mexicana 1939,Ap 22,14:4

Nack, Allie
Plain Jane 1924,My 13,24:2

Nada, Sankha
Mahabharata 1970,N 28,22:1

Nadal, Michele
Good Woman of Setzuan, The 1960,D 25,II,5:1

Nadal, Sr (Director)
Tragedia del Faro, La; Tragedy of the Lighthouse, The 1932,Je 3,23:2

Nadder, Robert
Midsummer Night's Dream, A 1964,Je 30,23:2

Nadeau, Nicky (Scenic Designer)
Poupees de Paris, Les 1962,D 13,8:2
Poupees de Paris, Les 1964,My 16,11:1

Nadel, Arlene
Red, White and Maddox 1969,Ja 27,27:1
Romeo and Jeanette 1969,D 16,53:1
Brass Butterfly, The 1970,Ja 31,34:1
Trelawny of the 'Wells' 1970,O 12,48:1

Nadell, Melvin
Jack and the Beanstalk 1947,N 3,28:2

Nadell, Rosalind
Helen Goes to Troy 1944,Ap 25,17:2
Let's Make an Opera 1950,D 14,50:2

Nadir, Moishe (Miscellaneous)
Untitled-Poetry Reading 1967,Jl 18,29:1

Nadler, Freeman
Boutique Fantasque, La 1929,D 28,10:6

Nadler, Jacob (Original Author)
Jacques Bergson 1936,O 31,24:6

Nadler, Seymour I (Lyricist)
Off Your Marx 1936,Ap 2,28:2

Nadler, Seymour I (Playwright)
Off Your Marx 1936,Ap 2,28:2
Some of the People 1937,Mr 11,20:1

Nadolsky, Sonia
One Woman 1931,D 14,16:4

Nador, Michael (Playwright)
Love Song, The 1925,Ja 14,19:4

Nadzo, Guido
Lady's Virtue, A 1925,N 24,28:2
What Never Dies 1926,D 29,24:2
Skin Deep 1927,O 18,32:1
Merchant of Venice, The 1928,Ja 17,22:2
Most Immoral Lady, A 1928,N 27,36:1
Divided Honors 1929,O 1,28:2
Seven Year Love 1929,O 27,IX,2:1
Tristi Amori; Unhappy Loves 1930,O 27,17:6
Cena Delle Beffe, La; Jest, The 1930,N 24,26:4
Romeo and Juliet 1933,F 3,21:5
Allure 1934,O 30,22:6
Naked Man, The 1935,Jl 2,24:3
Curtain Call 1937,Ap 23,24:7
Spring Thaw 1938,Mr 22,18:1

Naegele, Genevieve
Sweethearts 1929,S 23,25:1

Nagai, Toru
Long and the Short and the Tall, The 1962,Mr 30,28:2

Nagel, Allen
Magnanimous Lover, The 1933,F 1,13:5
One Day More 1933,F 1,13:5

Nagel, Conrad
First Apple, The 1933,D 17,IX,4:2
First Apple, The 1933,D 28,25:1
Faust 1938,Ag 28,IX,2:5
Susan and God 1943,D 14,30:2
Goose for the Gander, A 1945,Ja 24,16:4
Goodbye My Fancy 1948,N 18,35:2
Goodbye My Fancy 1948,N 28,II,1:1
Music in the Air 1951,O 9,32:2
Music in the Air 1951,O 21,II,1:1
Be Your Age 1953,Ja 15,24:2
Four Winds 1957,S 26,21:2
Captains and the Kings, The 1962,Ja 3,25:2

Nagel, Leonard
Last Pad, The 1970,D 8,61:1

Nagel, Paul
Sweet Bird of Youth 1956,Ap 17,27:2

Nagel, Richard
John Turner Davis 1958,Jl 2,25:1

Nager, A (Playwright)
Little Cantor, The 1930,S 24,26:2

Nagle, Alice
Gertie 1926,N 16,24:2

Nagle, Allen
Shame Woman, The 1923,O 17,14:1
Fashion 1924,F 5,21:2
Crime in the Whistler Room, The 1924,O 10,22:2
Desire Under the Elms 1924,N 12,20:7
East Lynne 1926,Mr 11,18:4
Mystery Man, The 1928,Ja 27,14:2
Gentlemen of the Press 1928,Ag 28,27:2
Fiesta 1929,S 18,35:1
Louder, Please! 1931,N 13,26:4

Nagle, Jack
Banjo Eyes 1941,D 26,20:2

Nagle, Jessie
Two Blocks Away 1921,Ag 31,8:3
Advertising of Kate, The 1922,My 9,22:2

Nagle, Urban (Rev) (Playwright)
Savonarola 1942,Ap 24,20:2
Lady of Fatima 1948,F 13,27:4
City of Kings 1949,F 18,27:2
Armor of Light 1950,F 24,26:4

Nagle, Walter
Marching By 1932,Mr 4,17:1

Nagler, A N (Original Author)
Rhapsody 1944,N 23,37:2

Nagley, Hazel
Jewel Robbery 1932,Ja 14,17:2

Nagoh, Leahcim (Playwright)
Idiot, The 1926,S 26,VIII,2:1

Nagoshiner, S
Aristocrats 1935,My 2,16:2
Haunch, Paunch and Jowl 1935,D 27,22:4
Hirsh Lekert 1936,Mr 11,23:2

Nagrin, Daniel
Of V We Sing 1942,F 16,20:3
It's About Time 1942,Mr 31,28:3
Up in Central Park 1945,Ja 29,17:2
Annie Get Your Gun 1946,My 17,14:2
Touch and Go 1949,O 14,34:2
Touch and Go 1949,O 30,II,1:1
Doll's House, A 1954,N 15,32:2
Plain and Fancy 1955,Ja 28,14:2
Plain and Fancy 1955,F 6,II,6:6

Nagrin, Daniel (Choreographer)
Volpone 1957,Ja 8,27:1
Emperor Jones, The 1964,Ag 6,20:4
Emperor Jones, The 1964,Ag 16,II,5:1

Nagrin, Daniel (Miscellaneous)
Volpone 1957,Ja 13,II,10:1
Firebugs, The 1963,F 13,7:2

Nagrom, Neleh
Minuet, A 1927,Mr 5,12:2

Nagy
Untitled-Passion Play 1922,Je 15,4:5

Nagy, Elmer (Scenic Designer)
Frogs, The 1941,N 14,25:3
Fledermaus, Die 1954,My 20,38:5

Nagy, John F
Laugh It Off 1934,Ap 5,24:2

Nahabedian, Charles
Richard III 1949,F 9,33:2

Naify, Marshall (Miscellaneous)
House of Leather, The 1970,Mr 19,56:1

Nail, Robert (Playwright)
Time of Their Lives 1937,O 26,19:1

Nail, Victor
Caesar and Cleopatra 1935,Ag 22,21:1

Naill, Mahlon
Bystander 1937,S 15,27:1
Emperor Jones, The 1945,Ja 17,18:4
Flamingo Road 1946,Mr 20,18:2
Peer Gynt 1951,Ja 29,15:2

Naill, Mahlon (Lighting Director)
Emperor Jones, The 1945,Ja 17,18:4

Naill, Mahlon (Scenic Designer)
Emperor Jones, The 1945,Ja 17,18:4

Nair, Evelyn
Hello, Yourself 1928,O 31,28:2

Nair, Kunchu
Mahabharata 1970,N 28,22:1

Nair, Madavoor Vasudevan
Mahabharata 1970,N 28,22:1

Nair, Padmanabhan
Mahabharata 1970,N 28,22:1

Nair, Ramankutty
Mahabharata 1970,N 28,22:1

Nairn, Ralph
Lassie 1920,Ap 7,9:2
Play's the Thing, The 1926,N 4,25:1
Collision 1932,F 17,19:2

Nairnes, Carey
One Way Pendulum 1961,S 19,38:2
Importance of Being Earnest, The 1963,F 27,5:2
Girl Who Came to Supper, The 1963,D 9,49:1

Nairobi City Players
King and I, The 1961,Mr 19,22:5

Naish, J Carrol
Broken Chain, The 1929,F 21,30:4
Crooks' Convention, The 1929,S 19,37:4
View From the Bridge, A 1955,Ag 31,16:8
Memory of Two Mondays, A 1955,S 30,21:1
View From the Bridge, A 1955,S 30,21:1
View From the Bridge, A 1955,O 9,II,1:1

Naismith, Laurence
Lark, The 1955,My 13,21:2
School for Scandal, The 1963,Ja 26,5:2
Here's Love 1963,O 4,28:1
Time for Singing, A 1966,My 23,48:2
Billy 1969,Mr 24,56:1

Naiven, Albert
As You Like It 1936,Ap 24,18:4

Najan, Nala (Choreographer)
Shakuntala 1959,S 10,41:2

Naka, Yoshi
Auntie Mame 1958,Ag 12,33:2

Nakagawa, Setsuko
Golden Bat 1970,Ag 16,II,1:1
Coney Island Play 1970,O 31,34:2

Nakamura, Eileen
Merry Wives of Windsor, The 1954,F 17,27:1
Flower Drum Song 1958,D 2,44:1

Nakamura, Eileen (Choreographer)
Merry Wives of Windsor, The 1954,F 17,27:1

Nakamura, Eileen (Lighting Director)
Servant of Two Masters, The 1958,F 11,35:2

Nakanosuke, Nakamura
Musume Dojoji; Maiden at the Dojo Temple, The 1960,Je 10,37:1
Musume Dojoji; Maiden at the Dojo Temple, The 1960,Je 17,35:4

Nakasuke, Nakamura
Kagotsurube; Courtesan, The 1960,Je 3,26:1
Musume Dojoji; Maiden at the Dojo Temple, The 1960,Je 10,37:1
Musume Dojoji; Maiden at the Dojo Temple, The 1960,Je 17,35:4

Nakimura, Tura
Teahouse of the August Moon, The 1956,N 9,33:2

Naldi
Crazy With the Heat 1941,Ja 31,15:2
Take a Bow 1944,Je 16,15:3

Naldi, Nita
Bonehead, The 1920,Ap 13,12:1
Opportunity 1920,Jl 31,5:1
Firebird 1932,N 22,25:2
Queer People 1934,F 16,16:2
In Any Language 1952,O 9,40:2

Naletov, A
Revisor; Inspector General, The 1935,F 18,19:6
White Guard, The; Days of the Turbins 1935,Mr 7,27:5

Nalkowska, Sophy (Playwright)
Women's House, The 1930,Ap 27,IX,3:1

Nally, William
Tin Pan Alley 1928,N 2,29:1

Nam, Bonnie
Tonight We Improvise 1959,N 7,27:4

Namara, Marguerite
Mikado, The 1925,Ap 13,25:1
Vaudeville (Hippodrome) 1925,D 8,28:6

Namara, Marguerite—Cont
H M S Pinafore 1926,Ap 7,26:3
Night of Love 1941,Ja 8,14:2
Nambissan, Neelakantan
Mahabharata 1970,N 28,22:1
Namboodiri, Sankaran
Mahabharata 1970,N 28,22:1
Namboodiripad, Vasudevan (Miscellaneous)
Mahabharata 1970,N 28,22:1
Namboodirl, Nelliyode Vasudevan
Mahabharata 1970,N 28,22:1
Nambu, K
Commodore Marries, The 1929,S 5,26:3
Nammack, Charles H
Sonya's Search for the Christmas Star
1929,D 14,24:6
Nan, Lao
Love in the Tropics 1927,O 19,24:3
Nancarrow, David (Lighting Director)
Deuces Wild; It's All Yours 1962,Ap 25,31:1
Deuces Wild; Thus 1962,Ap 25,31:1
Charlatans; Summer Ghost, A 1962,Ap 27,26:1
Charlatans; On Circe's Island 1962,Ap 27,26:1
Nance, Clarence
Black Scandals 1928,O 27,23:2
Naneris, Nicky
Milk Train Doesn't Stop Here Anymore, The
1962,Jl 12,19:8
Nani
One Man's Woman 1926,My 26,25:1
Nanine, Frances
Rat, The 1925,F 11,19:3
Nannary, Edward F
Madeleine and the Movies 1922,Mr 7,11:1
Paid 1925,N 26,32:1
Lulu Belle 1926,F 10,20:1
Ivory Door, The 1927,O 19,24:5
Gambling 1929,Ag 27,31:2
Tavern, The 1930,My 20,32:1
Song and Dance Man, The 1930,Je 17,25:5
Great Man, The 1931,Ap 8,20:6
Moon in the Yellow River, The 1932,Mr 1,19:3
Moon in the Yellow River, The
1932,Mr 13,VIII,1:1
Pigeons and People 1933,Ja 17,22:3
Stork Mad 1936,O 1,28:4
Merchant of Yonkers, The 1938,D 29,14:2
Beautiful People, The 1941,Ap 22,27:2
Across the Board on Tomorrow Morning
1942,Ag 18,17:1
Sons and Soldiers 1943,My 5,22:2
Mrs January & Mr Ex 1944,Ap 1,10:2
Woman Bites Dog 1946,Ap 18,21:2
Story for Strangers, A 1948,S 22,39:2
Nanon-Kiam
Garden District; Suddenly Last Summer
1958,Ja 8,23:4
Garden District; Suddenly Last Summer
1958,Ja 19,II,1:1
Ping-Pong 1959,Ap 17,22:1
Nansen, Kaji
Student Prince, The 1931,Ja 30,18:1
Nantary, Edward F
Wild Man of Borneo, The 1927,S 14,29:2
Naomi, Leah
Dybbuk, The 1924,Ja 29,17:7
Motke Ganef 1932,D 30,15:2
Revolt 1933,Ja 12,21:3
Verdict, The 1934,S 22,12:5
In-Laws 1934,O 25,28:2
60,000 Heroes 1935,Ja 28,11:5
Parnosseh 1935,F 16,8:8
Motke Ganef 1935,Mr 18,15:2
Sappho 1935,Mr 22,26:4
Brothers Ashkenazi, The 1937,S 21,28:6
Hershel, The Jester 1948,D 14,39:2
Naos, C
Oedipus Tyrannus 1952,N 25,35:2
Naoya, Shiga (Playwright)
Hans's Crime 1961,F 4,15:1
Napier, Alan
Borrowed Life, The 1931,Ja 4,VIII,2:6
Dark Hester 1931,My 17,VIII,1:3
Firebird 1932,S 25,IX,1:3
Sweet Aloes 1934,N 1,24:1
Gentle Rain 1936,S 20,IX,1:4
Time and the Hour 1936,O 5,24:1
Lady in Waiting 1940,Mr 28,19:1
Gertie 1952,Ja 31,23:1
Coriolanus 1954,Ja 20,34:2
Coriolanus 1954,Ja 24,II,1:1
Too Late the Phalarope 1956,O 12,35:1
Napier, John
Sweet Bird of Youth 1959,Mr 11,39:2
Happiest Girl in the World, The 1961,Ap 4,42:1
Everybody Loves Opal 1961,O 12,40:2
Napier, John (Scenic Designer)
Isabel's a Jezebel 1970,D 27,II,3:1
Napier, Russell
Murder in the Cathedral 1938,F 17,16:2
Napoleon, Lou
Golem, The 1959,F 26,38:2
Here Come the Clowns 1960,S 20,48:1

Napoleon, Lou (Miscellaneous)
All the King's Men 1959,O 17,27:2
Here Come the Clowns 1960,S 20,48:1
Napoles, Felipe (Miscellaneous)
Toothbrush, The 1970,S 27,84:5
Napoli, Enzio (Miscellaneous)
In the Shadow of the Glen 1957,Mr 7,24:1
Riders to the Sea 1957,Mr 7,24:1
Tinker's Wedding, The 1957,Mr 7,24:1
Napoli, Nola
Good Earth, The 1932,O 18,23:4
Narai, Kuniko
Annie Get Your Gun 1966,Je 1,42:2
Narayan, R K (Original Author)
Guide, The 1968,Mr 7,50:1
Narcejac, Thomas (Original Author)
Monique 1957,O 23,38:1
Narcisin
Rapacino 1927,D 23,16:4
Pibe de Corralon, El 1927,D 23,16:4
Narciso, Grazia
Take It As It Comes 1944,F 11,17:2
Sadie Thompson 1944,N 17,25:2
Narcisse, Henrietta
Girofle-Girofla 1926,N 23,26:3
Cloches de Cornville, Les; Chimes of Normandy,
The 1926,D 14,24:4
Perichole, La 1926,D 29,24:4
Narcy, John
Aquarama 1960 1960,Jl 1,14:6
Nard, Maude
Nativity Play, The 1937,D 21,29:1
Nardi, Corrado (Miscellaneous)
Servant of Two Masters, The 1960,F 24,42:2
Nardi, Dino
Casa di Tutti, La; Everybody's Home 1932,D 5,21:4
Nardin, Terry
Coriolanus 1954,Ja 20,34:2
Nares, Geoffrey (Scenic Designer)
George and Margaret 1937,S 23,32:2
Nares, Owen
Charm School, The 1921,F 27,VI,1:6
Love Among the Paint Pots 1921,My 29,VI,1:7
Enchanted Cottage, The 1922,Mr 2,21:4
If Winter Comes 1923,F 11,VII,1:4
Romance 1926,N 4,VIII,4:7
These Few Ashes 1929,My 5,IX,1:3
Desire 1930,Jl 27,VIII,1:8
Counsel's Opinion 1931,S 13,IX,2:5
Once a Husband 1932,N 20,IX,3:6
When Ladies Meet 1933,Ap 27,15:4
Man Proposes 1933,D 24,IX,2:2
Nineties; Double Door 1934,Mr 22,24:6
Double Door 1934,Ap 15,X,2:2
All's Over, Then? 1934,Je 10,IX,1:1
Lover's Leap 1934,O 26,24:3
Youth at the Helm 1935,F 21,22:1
Call It a Day 1935,O 31,17:2
Call It a Day 1935,N 24,IX,1:2
They Came by Night 1937,Jl 8,21:1
They Came by Night 1937,Jl 25,X,1:3
Robert's Wife 1937,N 24,20:2
Robert's Wife 1937,D 19,XI,3:7
Rebecca 1940,Ap 14,IX,1:6
Petrified Forest, The 1943,Ja 10,VIII,1:6
Nares, Owen (Producer)
Enchanted Cottage, The 1922,Mr 2,21:4
Lover's Leap 1934,O 26,24:3
Narizzano, Dino
Misanthrope, The 1956,N 13,44:1
Othello 1957,Je 24,19:2
Bivouac at Lucca 1957,O 30,26:1
Hamlet of Stepney Green 1958,N 14,21:1
Romeo and Juliet 1959,Je 15,31:1
Merry Wives of Windsor, The 1959,Jl 9,23:2
All's Well That Ends Well 1959,Ag 3,20:4
Moonbirds 1959,O 10,13:1
Prodigal, The 1960,F 12,23:1
Prodigal, The 1960,F 21,II,1:1
Full Moon in March, A 1960,S 20,48:1
One Way Pendulum 1961,S 19,38:2
If Five Years Pass 1962,My 11,37:1
Month in the Country, A 1963,My 29,39:2
Francesca da Rimini 1967,S 12,54:1
Narke, Robin
Walk-Up 1961,F 24,24:1
Seven at Dawn, The 1961,Ap 18,43:1
Narris, Donald
Pirates of Penzance, The 1951,F 20,21:2
Nasca, Lorenzo (Scenic Designer)
Glorious Ruler, The 1969,Jl 1,31:1
Naselius, G E (Lighting Director)
Mother Courage and Her Children 1964,My 12,32:2
Nash, B D
It's Only Natural 1922,Ap 21,13:2
Nash, Chris (Miscellaneous)
Twelfth Night 1970,Ja 1,18:1
Nash, Dick
Vaudeville (Palace) 1929,N 11,20:5
Nash, Edward R Jr
Laugh It Off 1925,Ap 25,18:4
Nash, Florence
Mirage, The 1920,O 1,14:1

Nash, Florence—Cont
Merton of the Movies 1922,N 14,16:2
Merton of the Movies 1922,N 19,VII,1:1
Lady's Virtue, A 1925,N 24,28:2
Lady's Virtue, A 1925,D 16,VIII,5:1
Two Orphans, The 1926,Ap 6,26:2
Two Orphans, The 1926,Ap 11,VIII,1:1
Fate's Messenger 1927,Ja 4,21:2
Meet Lady Clara 1930,Mr 30,VIII,2:7
Lady Clara 1930,Ap 18,28:7
Nash, Frank (Miscellaneous)
Spring's Awakening 1955,O 10,30:2
Nash, George
Trilby 1921,D 24,7:2
Merchants of Glory 1925,D 15,28:3
Noose, The 1926,O 21,23:3
Creoles 1927,S 23,33:3
Gringa, La 1928,F 2,17:1
Luana 1930,S 18,28:1
If I Were You 1931,S 24,21:1
Other One, The 1932,O 4,26:3
Yellow Jack 1934,Mr 7,22:6
Old Maid, The 1935,Ja 8,26:1
Hamlet 1936,O 9,30:2
Ghost of Yankee Doodle, The 1937,O 28,28:5
Ghost of Yankee Doodle, The 1937,N 23,26:3
How to Get Tough About It 1938,F 9,16:2
Nash, H Randolph
Petrified Forest, The 1943,N 2,30:6
Nash, Henry
Pirates of Penzance, The 1942,F 20,20:2
Nash, J
Carmen Jones 1956,Je 1,28:2
Nash, James F
Elsie Janis and Her Gang 1922,Ja 17,13:2
Nash, Joseph
Mary of Magdala 1946,Mr 26,24:5
Nash, Kenneth (Pvt)
Winged Victory 1943,N 22,24:1
Nash, Leo
Immortal Thief, The 1926,O 4,21:1
Rainbow 1928,N 22,25:1
Nash, Mabel
Career 1943,O 29,22:6
Nash, Margaret
Measure for Measure 1964,Jl 27,22:3
Nash, Marie
Higher and Higher 1940,Ap 5,24:3
Two Weeks With Pay 1940,Je 25,28:3
Higher and Higher 1940,Ag 6,15:4
Higher and Higher 1940,Ag 11,IX,1:1
All in Fun 1940,D 28,11:2
Crazy With the Heat 1941,Ja 15,18:2
Viva O'Brien 1941,O 10,27:2
Nash, Mary
Thy Name Is Woman 1920,N 16,19:1
Captain Applejack 1921,D 31,14:2
Mysterious Way, The 1923,O 28,VIII,2:1
Lady, The 1923,D 5,23:2
Lady, The 1923,D 16,IX,1:1
Hassan 1924,S 23,23:1
Lady's Virtue, A 1925,N 24,28:2
Lady's Virtue, A 1925,D 16,VIII,5:1
Two Orphans, The 1926,Ap 6,26:2
Two Orphans, The 1926,Ap 11,VIII,1:1
Fate's Messenger 1927,Ja 4,21:2
Command to Love, The 1927,S 11,VIII,1:3
Command to Love, The 1927,S 21,27:1
Strong Man's House, A 1929,Je 30,VIII,1:2
Strong Man's House, A 1929,S 17,34:3
Diana 1929,D 10,37:1
Woman Denied, A 1931,F 26,21:1
Devil Passes, The 1932,Ja 5,20:3
Devil Passes, The 1932,Ja 10,VIII,1:1
Uncle Tom's Cabin 1933,My 30,13:4
Nash, N Richard (Director)
Second Best Bed 1946,Je 4,20:2
Nash, N Richard (Original Author)
110 in the Shade 1963,O 25,37:1
Nash, N Richard (Playwright)
Second Best Bed 1946,Je 4,20:2
Young and Fair, The 1948,N 23,35:2
Young and Fair, The 1949,Jl 1,14:3
See the Jaguar 1952,D 4,46:2
Rainmaker, The 1954,O 29,28:1
Rainmaker, The 1954,N 7,II,1:1
Rainmaker, The 1956,Je 1,26:7
Girls of Summer 1956,N 20,45:1
Handful of Fire 1958,O 2,45:3
Wildcat 1960,D 17,20:2
110 in the Shade 1963,O 25,37:1
Happy Time, The 1968,Ja 19,32:2
Nash, N Richard (Producer)
Wildcat 1960,D 17,20:2
Nash, Ogden (Composer)
Littlest Revue, The 1956,My 23,37:2
Nash, Ogden (Lyricist)
One Touch of Venus 1943,O 8,14:1
Two's Company 1952,D 16,43:5
Two's Company 1952,D 21,II,3:1
Littlest Revue, The 1956,My 23,37:2
Whores, Wars & Tin Pan Alley 1969,Je 17,37:1
Nash, Ogden (Miscellaneous)
Hey, Nonny, Nonny! 1932,Je 7,22:3

Nash, Ogden (Playwright)
Hey, Nonny, Nonny! 1932,Je 7,22:3
One Touch of Venus 1943,O 8,14:1
One Touch of Venus 1943,O 17,II,1:1
Nash, Robert
Meet the People 1940,D 26,22:2
Nash, Wally (Producer)
Fractured Follies of 1966 1965,D 18,35:1
Nashelsky, Pavel (Miscellaneous)
Obratsov Russian Pupper Theater in an Unusual
Concert 1963,O 3,28:1
Aladdin and His Wonderful Lamp 1963,O 21,39:1
Nason, Gardner A
What a Relief 1935,D 14,10:6
Nassau, Paul (Composer)
New Faces of 1956 1956,Je 15,32:1
Fallout 1959,My 21,36:2
Happy Town 1959,O 8,49:2
Joyful Noise, A 1966,D 16,57:1
Education of H*Y*M*A*N K*A*P*L*A*N, The
1968,Ap 5,57:1
Leonard Sillman's New Faces of 1968
1968,My 3,43:1
Nassau, Paul (Lyricist)
New Faces of 1956 1956,Je 15,32:1
Fallout 1959,My 21,36:2
Happy Town 1959,O 8,49:2
Joyful Noise, A 1966,D 16,57:1
Education of H*Y*M*A*N K*A*P*L*A*N, The
1968,Ap 5,57:1
Leonard Sillman's New Faces of 1968
1968,My 3,43:1
Nasser, Sam (Producer)
Little A 1947,Ja 16,31:2
Nastasi, Frank
Bonds of Interest, The 1958,My 7,43:1
Nathan the Wise 1962,Mr 23,29:1
Chief Thing, The 1963,Ap 30,27:2
Cindy 1964,Mr 20,24:1
Avanti 1968,F 1,29:1
Natalie
Folly Town 1920,My 18,9:2
Natalie, Lois
Vaudeville (Palace) 1923,Ja 23,18:2
Natanson, Jacques (Original Author)
I Was Waiting for You 1933,N 14,23:3
Natanson, Jacques (Playwright)
Knock Out 1927,Mr 27,VII,4:8
40 CV du Roi, La 1927,O 23,VIII,2:2
Lady of the Orchids, The 1928,D 14,37:3
Je T'Attendais 1929,Ja 20,VIII,1:8
Michel 1932,Ap 3,VIII,2:1
Ete, L' 1934,D 2,X,2:1
Natapoff, Cecil
Wall Street Scene 1937,O 19,29:2
Natelli, Mr (Composer)
Menaechmi 1925,Je 9,16:2
Nathal, Marc
Vaudeville (Palace) 1929,S 30,22:3
Nathan, A Jr (Composer)
They Never Come Back 1920,D 19,I,22:3
Nathan, Adele (Director)
Subway, The 1929,Ja 26,15:1
Attack 1942,S 8,13:4
Nathan, Adele (Original Author)
Knights of Song 1938,O 18,29:2
Nathan, Adele (Playwright)
Attack 1942,S 8,13:4
Nathan, Alfred Jr (Composer)
So's Your Old Manhattan 1927,My 5,30:5
Manhatters, The 1927,Jl 19,27:3
Manhatters, The 1927,Ag 4,25:4
Nathan, Joe
Spring Production 1944,My 20,12:4
Walk Hard 1944,D 1,28:2
Nathan, Paul (Playwright)
Double in Hearts 1956,O 17,41:7
Nathan, Vivian
Montserrat 1949,O 31,21:4
Rose Tattoo, The 1951,F 5,19:2
Camino Real 1953,Mr 20,26:1
Bullfight 1954,Ja 13,25:2
Anastasia 1954,D 30,13:1
Anastasia 1955,Ja 16,II,1:1
Lovers 1956,My 11,23:1
Semi-Detached 1960,Mr 11,20:2
Investigation, The 1966,O 5,40:1
Watering Place, The 1969,Mr 13,51:1
Nathanson, Anna
Some Girl 1927,D 24,8:2
Nathanson, Charles
Parisian Love 1927,Ja 28,15:5
Nathanson, Gerry
Riot 1968,D 20,64:1
Nathanson, Julius
Organ Grinder, The 1934,Ja 1,28:3
Happy Days 1934,Ap 2,12:5
Little Bandit 1935,Ap 19,24:2
David and Esther 1938,O 12,34:3
Street Singers 1938,D 12,25:6
Queen Mother 1938,D 26,29:4
Schwartse Mamme 1939,Ja 16,11:3

National Theatre of Peiping
Untitled-Pantomime 1955,Je 5,48:1
Nations, Arthur (Translator)
Purification, The 1954,My 29,12:1
Apollo of Bellac, The 1954,My 29,12:1
Apollo of Bellac, The 1954,Je 6,II,1:1
Nations, Curt (Scenic Designer)
Happy Town 1959,O 8,49:2
Natter, Dorothy (Producer)
Sing Till Tomorrow 1953,D 29,17:2
Nattova, Natacha
Greenwich Village Follies 1926,Mr 16,22:2
Vaudeville (Palace) 1928,N 26,31:2
Natwick, Mildred
Carry Nation 1932,O 31,18:2
Amourette 1933,S 28,25:2
Spring in Autumn 1933,O 25,22:5
Wind and the Rain, The 1934,F 2,20:6
Distaff Side, The 1934,S 26,17:2
Royal Family, The 1935,Je 25,14:5
Post Road 1935,Jl 23,24:3
Caste 1935,Ag 13,20:3
Elizabeth Sleeps Out 1935,Ag 27,23:4
Night in the House 1935,N 8,19:5
End of Summer 1936,Ja 31,17:1
End of Summer 1936,F 9,X,2:3
End of Summer 1936,F 18,26:4
Book of Charm, The 1936,Je 30,15:1
Elizabeth the Queen 1936,Jl 28,23:4
Middle Man 1936,S 8,23:1
Love From a Stranger 1936,S 22,31:5
Love From a Stranger 1936,S 30,28:1
Candida 1937,Mr 11,20:2
Busman's Honeymoon, A 1937,Jl 13,22:3
At Mrs Beam's 1937,Jl 27,24:2
Star-Wagon, The 1937,S 30,18:5
Star-Wagon, The 1937,O 10,XI,1:1
Missouri Legend 1938,S 20,27:2
Missouri Legend 1938,S 25,IX,1:1
Stars in Your Eyes 1939,F 10,18:2
Christmas Eve 1939,D 28,17:2
Lady Who Came to Stay, The 1941,Ja 3,13:2
Blithe Spirit 1941,N 6,26:2
Blithe Spirit 1941,N 16,IX,1:1
Candida 1942,Ap 28,24:4
Candida 1942,My 3,VIII,1:1
Blithe Spirit 1943,S 12,II,1:1
Candida 1946,Ap 4,33:2
Candida 1946,Ap 14,II,1:1
Playboy of the Western World, The 1946,O 28,18:3
Grass Harp, The 1952,Mr 28,26:2
Grass Harp, The 1952,Ap 6,II,1:1
International Set, The 1953,Je 12,19:3
Coriolanus 1954,Ja 20,34:2
Coriolanus 1954,Ja 24,II,1:1
Medea 1955,Je 16,35:4
Waltz of the Toreadors, The 1957,Ja 18,17:2
Waltz of the Toreadors, The 1957,Ja 27,II,1:1
Day the Money Stopped, The 1958,F 21,19:4
Firstborn, The 1958,My 1,35:1
Firstborn, The 1958,My 11,II,1:1
Good Soup, The 1960,Mr 3,26:4
Critic's Choice 1960,D 15,61:3
Barefoot in the Park 1963,O 24,36:2
Our Town 1969,N 28,50:1
Our Town 1969,D 7,II,7:1
Landscape 1970,Ap 3,43:1
Landscape 1970,Ap 12,II,3:1
Natzler, Grete
Casanova 1932,Je 19,IX,2:1
Naughton, Bill
Contractor, The 1970,Ag 17,32:1
Naughton, Bill (Original Author)
Keep It in the Family 1968,Ja 25,32:4
Naughton, Bill (Playwright)
Alfie 1964,D 18,27:1
All in Good Time 1965,F 19,25:1
Keep It in the Family 1967,S 28,59:1
Keep It in the Family 1967,O 8,II,1:6
Naughton, Charles
Just to Remind You 1931,S 8,39:1
Naughton, Harry
Drat! the Cat! 1965,O 11,54:2
Naughton, Harry (Miscellaneous)
Valmouth 1960,O 7,29:1
Naughton, James
Bacchae, The 1969,Mr 15,24:1
Don Juan 1970,My 26,32:1
Three Philip Roth Stories; Conversion of the Jews
1970,Jl 31,14:1
Three Philip Roth Stories; Defender of the Faith
1970,Jl 31,14:1
Three Philip Roth Stories; Epstein 1970,Jl 31,14:1
Cops and Horrors; Dracula 1970,Ag 11,27:1
Cops and Horrors; Fly Paper 1970,Ag 11,27:1
Story Theater Repertory; Gimpel the Food
1970,O 21,40:1
Story Theater Repertory; Saint Julian the
Hospitaler 1970,O 21,40:1
Revenger's Tragedy, The 1970,D 2,58:1
Naughton, Robert
Brothers 1928,D 26,14:3

Naughton and Gold
Vaudeville (Hippodrome) 1926,Ap 13,28:2
Vaudeville (Palace) 1927,N 8,33:3
Vaudeville (Palace) 1930,Mr 31,24:2
Naumann, Ernst
Fedora 1924,Ja 24,14:2
Tanzgraefin, Die 1925,S 18,26:3
Navarre, Paul
Passenger to Bali, A 1940,Mr 15,26:2
Navarro, Brave Bird
Virtuous Island, The 1957,Ap 10,39:1
Navarro, Mercedes
Tragedia del Faro, La; Tragedy of the Lighthouse,
The 1932,Je 3,23:2
Navarro, Sra (Director)
Tragedia del Faro, La; Tragedy of the Lighthouse,
The 1932,Je 3,23:2
Navas, Anthony
Don Juan in the Russian Manner 1954,Ap 23,23:2
Nay, Fred
Jubilee 1935,O 14,20:1
Higher and Higher 1940,Ap 5,24:3
Let's Face It 1941,O 30,26:2
Naya, Ramon (Playwright)
Mexican Mural; Patio With Flamingo
1942,Ap 27,19:2
Mexican Mural; Moonlight e 1942,Ap 27,19:2
Mexican Mural; Vera C _.ior 1942,Ap 27,19:2
Mexican Mural; Miracle Painting 1942,Ap 27,19:2
Naylor, Charles (Composer)
Hear! Hear! 1955,S 28,38:1
Skits-Oh-Frantics 1967,Ap 3,39:2
Naylor, Charles (Lyricist)
Skits-Oh-Frantics 1967,Ap 3,39:2
Naylor, Charles (Playwright)
Hear! Hear! 1955,S 28,38:1
Naylor, Kathleen
Trial by Jury 1936,S 1,24:4
Pirates of Penzance, The 1936,S 1,24
Iolanthe 1936,S 22,30:3
Princess Ida 1936,O 13,32:2
Ruddigore 1936,O 23,26:4
Nayor, Edward
They Knew What They Wanted 1939,O 3,19:1
Nayor, Edward (Miscellaneous)
High Named Today 1954,D 11,11:2
Nazarro, Nat Jr
Passing Show of 1922, The 1922,S 21,18:2
Passing Show of 1923, The 1923,Je 15,24:6
Nic-Nax of 1926 1926,Ag 5,19:1
Nazfys, The
Jumbo 1935,N 18,20:2
Nazimova
Dagmar 1923,Ja 23,18:2
Vaudeville (Palace) 1923,O 30,16:1
Unknown Lady, The 1923,N 6,22:1
That Sort 1926,Ap 20,24:6
Vaudeville (Palace) 1926,Ap 20,24:6
Woman of the Earth, A 1927,F 1,24:6
Woman of the Earth, A 1927,My 31,25:1
Woman of the Earth, A 1927,S 27,31:3
Vaudeville (Palace) 1927,S 27,31:3
India 1928,Ja 17,23:3
Vaudeville (Palace) 1928,Ja 17,23:3
Cherry Orchard, The 1928,O 16,28:5
Cherry Orchard, The 1928,N 18,IX,1:2
On the High Road 1929,Ja 15,22:3
Katerina 1929,F 26,30:3
Cherry Orchard, The 1929,Je 2,VIII,1:1
Month in the Country, A 1930,Mr 18,30:5
Mourning Becomes Electra; Hunted, The
1931,O 27,22:1
Mourning Becomes Electra; Homecoming
1931,O 27,22:1
Mourning Becomes Electra 1931,N 1,VIII,1:1
Mourning Becomes Electra 1932,Ap 10,VIII,1:1
Good Earth, The 1932,S 25,IX,1:6
Good Earth, The 1932,O 18,23:4
Good Earth, The 1932,O 23,IX,1:1
Cherry Orchard, The 1933,Mr 7,20:3
Doctor Monica 1933,N 7,29:3
Simpleton of the Unexpected Isles, The
1935,F 19,27:5
Simpleton of the Unexpected Isles, The
1935,F 24,VIII,1:1
Ghosts 1935,D 13,30:6
Ghosts 1936,My 12,26:8
Hedda Gabler 1936,O 25,X,1:5
Hedda Gabler 1936,N 17,34:4
Mother, The 1939,Ap 26,26:2
Nazimova (Director)
Ghosts 1935,D 13,30:6
Hedda Gabler 1936,O 25,X,1:5
Hedda Gabler 1936,N 17,34:4
Nazimova (Producer)
Dagmar 1923,F 11,VII,1:1
Ghosts 1936,My 12,26:8
Nazimova (Translator)
Hedda Gabler 1936,O 25,X,1:5
Nazzaro, Nat Jr
Topics of 1923 1923,N 21,23:2
Nazzo, Angelo
People vs Ranchman, The 1968,O 28,56:1

Neal, Cathleen
Truce of the Bear 1957,O 24,39:1
Neal, Coby
Signature 1945,F 15,25:2
Neal, Gerald
Tall Kentuckian, The 1953,Je 17,30:1
Neal, Jeffrey
Traveller Without Luggage 1964,S 18,26:2
Neal, Lloyd
Eyvind of the Hills 1921,F 2,14:1
Autumn Fire 1926,O 27,25:3
Tommy 1927,Ja 11,36:4
Neal, Patricia
Seven Mirrors 1945,O 26,17:2
Another Part of the Forest 1946,N 21,42:2
Children's Hour, The 1952,D 19,35:2
Children's Hour, The 1952,D 28,II,1:1
Scarecrow, The 1953,Je 17,31:1
School for Scandal, The 1953,Je 24,29:2
Roomful of Roses, A 1955,O 18,48:1
Miracle Worker, The 1959,O 20,44:1
Miracle Worker, The 1959,N 1,II,1:1
Neal, Ralph (Playwright)
Power and Glory 1938,My 1,X,2:5
Neal, Ruth
Henry VIII 1946,N 7,42:2
Neal, Sally
Kismet 1965,Je 23,45:1
I'm Solomon 1968,Ap 24,51:1
Neal, Tom
If This Be Treason 1935,S 24,28:2
Spring Dance 1936,Ag 26,17:4
Daughters of Atreus 1936,O 15,33:1
Neal, Walter (Miscellaneous)
Small War on Murray Hill 1957,Ja 4,19:1
Once There Was a Russian 1961,F 20,32:2
Neal Sisters
Vaudeville (Palace) 1930,Ag 18,24:3
Neale, Joe
Hot Money 1931,N 9,22:2
Neale, Ralph (Translator)
This for Remembrance 1937,Mr 17,31:1
Nealy, Richard
Anything Goes 1934,N 22,26:1
Neary, Bernie
Little Black Book, The 1932,D 27,11:2
Far Away Horses 1933,Mr 22,21:6
Nebauer, Charles
First Lady 1937,O 9,17:2
Nedd, Stuart
Assassin, The 1945,O 18,20:2
Dream Girl 1945,D 15,13:2
Nedell, Bernard
Broadway 1927,Ja 9,VII,2:1
Royal Family, The 1951,Ja 11,28:2
Nederlander, James (Producer)
Not Now Darling 1970,O 30,33:1
Nedick, Art
U S A 1956,D 19,41:4
Nedzvetsky, Yuri
Cherry Orchard, The 1965,F 10,46:1
Kremlin Chimes 1965,F 25,23:1
Neebe, Joseph (Producer)
Apple Cart, The 1956,O 19,23:1
Needham, Ann
Buttrio Square 1952,O 15,40:2
Plain and Fancy 1955,F 6,II,6:6
Needham, Leo
Would-Be Gentleman, The 1930,Ap 30,29:2
Experience Unnecessary 1931,D 31,16:2
Experience Unnecessary 1932,Mr 28,10:2
Man Bites Dog 1933,Ap 26,11:2
Growing Pains 1933,N 24,24:2
Not in Our Stars 1941,Ap 26,20:5
Needham, Peter
Macbeth 1956,O 30,42:2
Romeo and Juliet 1960,Jl 1,14:1
Henry VIII 1961,Je 22,22:1
Needles, William
All's Well That Ends Well 1953,Jl 16,18:2
Measure for Measure 1954,Je 30,23:1
Taming of the Shrew, The 1954,Jl 1,22:2
Oedipus Rex 1954,Jl 17,6:6
Soldier's Tale, A 1955,Jl 13,21:2
Henry V 1956,Je 20,27:2
Glass Cage, The 1957,Mr 11,21:2
As You Like It 1959,Jl 1,27:1
Othello 1959,Jl 2,17:2
Romeo and Juliet 1960,Jl 1,14:1
Henry VIII 1961,Je 22,22:1
Love's Labour's Lost 1961,Je 23,19:1
Love's Labour's Lost 1961,Jl 2,II,1:1
Taming of the Shrew, The 1962,Je 21,25:1
Tempest, The 1962,Je 22,14:1
Cyrano de Bergerac 1962,Ag 1,21:1
Moby Dick 1962,N 29,45:1
Troilus and Cressida 1963,Je 19,40:2
Cyrano de Bergerac 1963,Je 20,30:1
Comedy of Errors, The 1963,Je 21,35:3
Next Time I'll Sing to You 1963,N 28,69:2
Richard II 1964,Je 17,47:1
Bourgeois Gentilhomme, Le 1964,Je 18,28:2
King Lear 1964,Je 19,36:1

Henry IV, Part I 1965,Je 30,42:1
Falstaff; Henry IV, Part II 1965,Jl 1,35:1
Cherry Orchard, The 1965,Ag 2,17:2
Henry V 1966,Je 8,38:1
Henry VI 1966,Je 9,55:2
Box-Mao-Box; Quotations From Chairman Mao
Tse-Tung 1968,Mr 8,48:1
Hadrian VII 1969,Ja 9,22:1
Cherry Orchard, The 1970,My 7,63:2
Neely, Billy
Ups-A-Daisy 1928,O 9,34:2
Neely, Dick
Good Boy 1928,S 6,23:2
Neely, George
Last Enemy, The 1934,Jl 13,14:4
Neely, Neill
First Flight 1925,S 18,26:2
Neergaard, Beatrice de
Letters to Lucerne 1941,D 24,14:2
Neff, Adele
Earl Carroll's Vanities 1925,Jl 7,24:1
Neff, Helen
Jimmie 1920,N 18,15:3
Neff, Hildegarde
Silk Stockings 1955,F 25,17:3
Silk Stockings 1955,Mr 27,II,1:1
Neff, John (Playwright)
Time, Place and the Girl, The 1942,O 22,24:3
Neff, Morty (Lyricist)
Difficult Woman, The 1962,Ap 26,22:7
Neff, Robert
Story of Mary Surratt, The 1947,F 10,25:2
Negin, Louis
Tamburlaine the Great 1956,Ja 20,19:1
Good Woman of Setzuan, The 1956,D 19,41:2
Camino Real 1960,My 17,42:2
Henry VIII 1961,Je 22,22:1
Merchant of Venice, The 1962,F 3,13:2
Love and Maple Syrup 1970,Ja 8,47:1
Negin, Louis (Miscellaneous)
Love and Maple Syrup 1970,Ja 8,47:1
Negin, Louis (Playwright)
Love and Maple Syrup 1970,Ja 8,47:1
Negin, Mark (Scenic Designer)
Gondoliers, The 1962,Jl 7,9:4
Comedy of Errors, The 1963,Je 21,35:3
Negley, Howard
Them's the Reporters 1935,My 30,21:4
Mulatto 1935,O 25,25:2
Biography 1937,Ap 11,II,12:8
Boy Meets Girl 1937,Jl 6,23:1
Negley, John
Pleased to Meet You 1928,O 30,27:2
Kansas City Kitty 1929,S 26,27:4
Negri, Addi
Milk and Honey 1961,O 11,52:1
Negri, Pola
Vaudeville (Palace) 1932,S 12,13:5
Negri, Richard (Scenic Designer)
As You Like It 1961,Jl 5,30:1
Peer Gynt 1962,S 27,33:7
Public Eye, The 1963,O 10,51:1
Private Ear, The 1963,O 10,51:1
Negri, Rino
Best House in Naples, The 1956,O 27,16:2
Negrin, Rae D
Kith and Kin 1930,My 14,31:1
Negrita
Cave Dwellers, The 1957,O 21,29:2
Negro, Dante
Cardinale, Il 1933,Ja 9,24:2
Romanticismo 1933,My 1,10:5
Conte di Monte Cristo, Il 1934,Ja 22,13:2
Negro Ensemble Company
Ceremonies in Dark Old Men 1969,F 23,II,5:1
Nehaus, Lavina
Everyman 1941,My 9,19:2
Neher, Carola
Ich Tanze um die Welt mit Dir 1930,Ag 31,VIII,2:1
Marguerite Divided by Three 1930,S 28,VIII,4:4
Neher, Carole
Chicago 1927,D 18,IX,1:8
Neher, Caspar (Miscellaneous)
Threepenny Opera, The 1933,Ap 14,22:4
Neher, Caspar (Scenic Designer)
Hamlet 1927,F 13,VII,2:3
Threepenny Opera, The 1928,D 2,X,4:4
Oliver Cromwells Sendung 1933,Mr 19,IX,2:2
Neidhardt (Playwright)
Prosit Gypsy 1929,Je 2,VIII,2:6
Neiditch, Max
Thousand and One Nights 1959,D 16,53:2
Enchanting Melody 1964,N 25,40:1
Fifth Commandment, The 1965,N 15,48:4
Melody Lingers On, The 1969,N 17,55:1
Neiditch, Michael
Mother's Sabbath Days 1960,N 21,33:2
Neidlinger, Gertrude
Musical Mishaps 1949,Mr 21,18:2
Neighbors, George
Summer of Daisy Miller, The 1963,My 28,33:1
Neihouse, S
Father and Son 1956,O 20,17:4

Neil, Bert
Flies, The; Mouches, Les 1947,Ap 18,26:3
Neil, Dan
Lady Behave 1943,N 17,30:1
Neil, Franklin
Ali Baba 1951,Mr 27,34:2
Neil, James Jr
Richard III 1930,Mr 31,24:1
Neil, Milton
Delicate Story 1940,D 5,32:2
Neil, Nelly
Adorable Liar, The 1926,Ag 31,15:2
General John Regan 1930,Ja 30,16:5
Neil, Sally
Show Boat 1966,Jl 20,48:1
Neil, Terence
Her Cardboard Lover 1927,Mr 22,30:5
Neil, William (1st Lieut)
Winged Victory 1943,N 22,24:1
Neilan, Jack
Censored 1938,F 28,18:2
Neilan, John
Cue for Passion 1940,D 20,33:4
Neill, Grace
Parson's Bride, The 1929,Ja 22,22:3
Neill, James
Days of Our Youth, The 1941,N 29,15:2
Neill, James Jr
Hamlet 1930,Mr 25,34:4
Macbeth 1930,Mr 26,24:6
Twelfth Night 1930,Mr 27,24:7
Merchant of Venice, The 1930,Mr 27,24:7
Taming of the Shrew, The 1930,Mr 28,22:8
King Lear 1930,Ap 1,34:6
As You Like It 1930,Ap 3,32:5
Julius Caesar 1930,Ap 4,22:3
Neill, John
Them's the Reporters 1935,My 30,21:4
Neill, Louise
Days of Our Youth, The 1941,N 29,15:2
Neill, Merritt
Utopia, Limited 1960,Ap 8,27:2
Neill, Terence
Sport of Kings, The 1926,My 5,24:2
This Was a Man 1926,N 24,27:1
Adventurous Age, The 1927,F 8,20:1
Dracula 1927,O 6,29:1
Lady Clara 1930,Ap 18,28:7
Marriage for Three 1931,N 12,30:5
Hay Fever 1931,D 30,25:1
Green Waters 1936,N 5,34:4
Neilsen, Karl (Director)
White Flame 1929,N 5,32:7
Neilson, Frances
His Chinese Wife 1920,My 18,9:3
We Girls 1921,N 10,26:3
Green Ring, The 1922,Ap 5,22:1
That Day 1922,Jl 9,VI,1:4
That Day 1922,O 4,27:3
Ice-Bound 1923,F 12,16:2
Chivalry 1925,D 16,22:3
Company's Coming! 1931,Ap 21,35:5
Neilson, Fred
Mob, The 1920,O 11,18:1
Neilson, George
Alchemist, The 1969,Je 12,51:1
Measure for Measure 1969,Je 13,41:3
Neilson, James (Director)
Happiest Years, The 1949,Ap 26,29:8
Neilson, James (Producer)
All Paris Knows 1934,Jl 24,20:1
Clap Hands 1934,Ag 21,12:7
Neilson, Lester
Sport of Kings, The 1926,My 5,24:2
Good Fellow, The 1926,O 6,22:1
Neilson, Nigel
Love Goes to Press 1947,Ja 2,22:2
Neilson, Perlita
Lace on Her Petticoat 1951,S 5,40:3
Diary of Anne Frank, The 1957,Ja 20,II,3:7
Neilson, Richard
Song Out of Sorrow 1955,N 1,27:3
Heloise 1958,S 25,28:4
Heloise 1958,O 5,II,1:1
O Say Can You See! 1962,O 9,45:1
Neilson, Vera
Caste 1927,D 24,8:1
Freddy 1929,Jl 17,23:4
Amorous Antic, The 1929,D 3,29:2
Neilson-Terry, Dennis
Offence, The 1925,N 16,25:1
Devil, The 1930,F 2,VIII,2:4
Neilson-Terry, Phyllis
Roof and Four Walls, A 1923,Ja 21,VII,1:3
Elizabeth of England 1931,O 18,VIII,1:3
Twelfth Night 1932,Ag 7,IX,1:6
Philomel 1932,D 4,IX,3:8
Six of Calais, The 1934,Ag 12,IX,1:3
Cinderella 1935,Ja 13,IX,3:1
Separate Tables 1955,My 22,II,1:1
Separate Tables 1956,O 26,33:1
Neiman, Austra
Jubilee 1935,O 14,20:1

Neiman, Hal
Keep Off the Grass 1940,My 24,22:6
I Gotta Get Out 1947,S 26,27:2
Neiman, Irving Gaynor (Playwright)
Button Your Lip 1943,Je 15,16:1
Neimark, Bert
Hamlet 1948,D 4,9:2
We're Civilized? 1962,N 9,30:1
Neimark, Henry
Moby Dick 1970,Je 3,52:1
Neimeyer, Joe
Cinderella on Broadway 1920,Je 25,18:1
Neise, George
Grandma's Diary 1948,S 23,36:2
Neistat, Louis (T/5)
Yellow Jack 1944,Ap 7,23:3
Neitendam, Nicolai
Victory 1937,N 14,XI,2:5
Neitendam, Nicolai (Director)
Victory 1937,N 14,XI,2:5
NeJame, George
Henry, Sweet Henry 1967,O 24,51:2
Nelda, Merial
Bare Facts 1927,Ag 17,27:5
Nelidoff, Wladimir (Director)
Abraham; Dulcitus; Callimachus 1926,Mr 29,24:2
Nelidova, Helen
Mimic World of 1921, The 1921,Ag 18,9:2
Rose of Stamboul, The 1922,Mr 8,11:2
Nell, Edward Jr
New Moon, The 1928,S 20,33:1
Silver Swan, The 1929,N 28,34:5
Student Prince, The 1931,Ja 30,18:1
Chimes of Normandy, The 1931,N 3,31:3
Nelle, Anthony (Choreographer)
Patience 1927,My 24,23:2
Lady From Paris, The 1950,S 27,36:1
Nelle, Gay
Merry Merry 1925,S 25,24:3
Nelles, A Douglas (Dr)
It Happens on Ice 1940,O 11,24:3
It Happens on Ice 1941,Ap 5,13:2
Stars on Ice 1942,Jl 3,12:2
Nelle's Belles
Best of Burlesque 1957,S 30,27:2
Nellhaus, Gerhard (Playwright)
Puntila 1959,My 15,26:2
Nellhaus, Gerhard (Translator)
In the Jungle of Cities 1960,D 21,39:1
Man Is Man 1962,S 19,31:1
Nels, Gorris
Foolscap 1933,Ja 12,21:2
Nelson, Alberta
Once There Was a Russian 1961,F 20,32:2
Nelson, Arvid (Lighting Director)
Heartbreak House 1963,Je 28,24:1
Nelson, Barry
Winged Victory 1943,N 22,24:1
Light Up the Sky 1948,N 19,34:2
Rat Race, The 1949,D 23,16:2
Moon Is Blue, The 1951,Mr 9,29:2
Wake Up, Darling 1956,My 3,34:2
No Time for Sergeants 1956,Ag 24,15:8
Mary, Mary 1961,Mr 9,24:2
Cactus Flower 1965,D 9,60:2
Everything in the Garden 1967,N 30,60:1
Everything in the Garden 1967,D 10,II,5:1
Only Game in Town, The 1968,My 21,42:1
Fig Leaves Are Falling, The 1969,Ja 3,19:1
Engagement Baby, The 1970,My 22,40:1
Nelson, Barry (Director)
Only Game in Town, The 1968,My 21,42:1
Nelson, Beau
Russell Patterson's Sketch-Book 1960,F 8,35:1
Nelson, Bert
Complaisant Lover, The 1961,N 2,43:2
Nelson, Bob
Red Pepper 1922,My 30,8:3
Passing Show of 1923, The 1923,Je 15,24:6
Artists and Models 1923,Ag 21,12:2
Happy 1927,D 6,26:3
Nelson, C M (Costume Designer)
Little Eyolf 1964,Mr 17,31:1
Nelson, Carl
Merry Widow, The 1942,Jl 16,22:1
New Moon, The 1942,Ag 19,14:2
New Moon, The 1944,My 18,16:2
Nelson, Carol
New Faces of 1952 1952,My 17,23:2
Nelson, Charles
Blackouts of 1949 1949,S 7,39:2
Master Builder, The 1955,Mr 2,23:2
Othello 1955,S 8,27:2
Nelson, Del
Oklahoma! 1958,Mr 8,15:2
Nelson, DeWitt
Winter's Tale, The 1963,Ag 16,14:1
Nelson, Dorothyann
Ice Follies 1963,Ja 10,5:2
Ice Follies 1964,Ja 8,41:2
Ice Follies 1965,Ja 13,35:1
Ice Follies 1966,Ja 12,27:6
Ice Follies 1967,Ja 11,51:1

Nelson, Duane
Elsie Janis and Her Gang 1922,Ja 17,13:2
Good Morning 1937,D 4,20:7
Nelson, Duane (Director)
Madcap, The 1928,F 1,31:2
Nelson, Ed G (Composer)
Brown Buddies 1930,O 8,29:1
Nelson, Eddie
Sun-Kist 1921,My 24,20:2
Sharlee 1923,N 23,20:1
Vaudeville (Palace) 1926,N 16,24:3
Vaudeville (Palace) 1927,N 29,30:4
Boom Boom 1929,Ja 29,26:4
Woof, Woof 1929,D 26,20:4
Nelson, Edgar
Blue Bonnet 1920,Ag 30,12:1
Just Because 1922,Mr 23,11:1
Humming Bird, The 1923,Ja 16,16:2
Lucky Break 1925,Ag 12,16:2
Yours Truly 1927,Ja 26,16:5
Katy Did 1927,My 10,24:3
Nightstick 1927,N 11,20:4
Tin Pan Alley 1928,N 2,29:1
Black Crook, The 1929,Mr 12,26:5
Long Road, The 1930,S 10,30:2
Betty, Be Careful 1931,My 5,33:3
Shoot the Works! 1931,Jl 22,19:5
Masks and Faces 1933,Mr 20,18:5
Fly by Night 1933,Je 3,16:2
Sailor, Beware! 1933,S 29,24:4
Mid-West 1936,Ja 8,22:4
Come Angel Band 1936,F 19,17:1
Cross-Town 1937,Mr 18,21:5
Nelson, Eldon
Peter Pan 1924,N 7,16:2
Nelson, Eva Mudge
Skin of Our Teeth, The 1942,N 19,29:5
Nelson, Frances
New Toys 1924,F 19,12:1
Nelson, Fred
Mima 1928,D 13,24:2
Nelson, Gene
Lend an Ear 1948,D 17,38:2
Oklahoma! 1958,Mr 20,32:3
Hit the Deck 1960,Je 24,32:1
Nelson, Gil
Don't Go Away Mad 1949,My 10,28:2
Building 222 1950,F 3,28:2
Gods of the Mountain, The 1950,My 25,36:2
Nelson, Gordon
Park Avenue, Ltd 1932,Mr 4,17:1
Take My Tip 1932,Ap 12,25:2
Ticket-of-Leave Man, The 1933,Jl 4,16:4
Mahogany Hall 1934,Ja 18,18:5
Panic 1935,Mr 16,18:4
Puritan, The 1936,Ja 24,14:3
Prelude 1936,Ap 20,17:4
Bury the Dead 1936,Ap 20,17:4
So Proudly We Hail 1936,S 23,28:4
200 Were Chosen 1937,N 21,21:1
There's Always a Breeze 1938,Mr 3,16:2
Jeremiah 1939,F 4,11:2
Tell My Story 1939,Mr 16,26:6
Delicate Story 1940,D 5,32:2
Strings, My Lord, Are False, The 1942,My 20,24:2
Broken Journey 1942,Je 24,22:2
Strip for Action 1942,O 1,26:2
Boy Meets Girl 1943,Je 23,15:5
Goodbye Again 1943,N 10,28:4
Streets Are Guarded, The 1944,N 21,19:7
Rugged Path, The 1945,N 12,17:2
Beggar's Holiday 1946,D 27,13:3
Cyrano de Bergerac 1953,N 13,24:3
Witness for the Prosecution 1954,D 17,35:2
Nelson, Harriet
Diamond Lil 1949,F 7,16:2
Nelson, Harry
Crooked Friday, The 1925,O 9,27:3
Offence, The 1925,N 16,25:1
Mongolia 1927,D 27,24:5
Skull, The 1928,Ap 24,28:3
Congai 1928,N 28,24:3
Nelson, Helen
Ol' Man Satan 1932,O 4,26:3
Nelson, Herbert
Night Before Christmas, The 1941,Ap 11,25:2
First Crocus, The 1942,Ja 3,14:6
Blithe Spirit 1946,Je 5,17:3
His and Hers 1954,Ja 8,18:2
Abe Lincoln in Illinois 1963,Ja 23,5:2
Othello 1964,Jl 15,29:1
Othello 1964,O 13,48:1
Baal 1965,My 7,33:2
Coriolanus 1965,Jl 15,23:1
Miracle in Brooklyn 1966,Je 24,30:2
Pin Up 1966,Je 24,30:2
Venus-Shot 1966,Je 24,30:2
Nelson, J L
Kid Himself, The 1925,D 25,23:2
Nelson, Jack T (Playwright)
Remote Control 1929,S 11,24:5
Nelson, James
Big Mogul, The 1925,My 12,26:3

Nelson, Jen
Russell Patterson's Sketch-Book 1960,F 8,35:1
Hit the Deck 1960,Je 24,32:1
Aspern Papers, The 1962,F 8,26:1
Sunday Man, The 1964,My 14,41:3
Nelson, Jerry
Davy Jones's Locker 1966,D 25,48:5
People Is the Thing That the World Is Fullest Of
1967,F 21,53:1
Wizard of Oz, The 1968,N 28,69:2
Nelson, John
Pirates of Penzance, The 1970,Jl 26,49:5
Nelson, John O
Hamlet 1927,Ap 7,23:3
Nelson, Joseph
Here's Where I Belong 1968,Mr 4,32:1
Nelson, Juana
Don Q Jr 1926,Ja 28,16:3
Nelson, Kenneth
Seventeen 1951,Je 22,16:6
Seventeen 1951,Jl 1,II,1:1
Kaleidoscope 1957,Je 14,20:2
Fantasticks, The 1960,My 4,55:2
Sap of Life, The 1961,O 3,44:1
Boys in the Band, The 1968,Ap 15,48:1
Boys in the Band, The 1968,Ap 28,II,1:6
Lovely Ladies, Kind Gentlemen 1970,D 29,38:1
Nelson, Loy
R U R 1942,D 4,30:2
Nelson, Maggi
Oklahoma! 1953,S 1,19:1
Nelson, Marjorie
World of Sholom Aleichem, The 1953,S 12,13:2
Our Town 1959,Mr 24,46:2
Camino Real 1960,My 17,42:2
Firebugs, The 1963,N 22,41:1
King Lear 1963,N 23,22:1
Nelson, Mervyn
'Tis of Thee 1940,O 28,21:3
Snark Was a Boojum, The 1943,S 2,14:4
Nelson, Mervyn (Director)
Tickets, Please! 1950,Ap 28,25:2
Babes in Arms 1951,Mr 10,7:3
Year Round, The 1953,My 6,38:7
Secret Life of Walter Mitty, The 1964,O 27,44:5
Nelson, Mervyn (Miscellaneous)
Hilarities 1948,S 10,20:2
Cotton Club Revue of 1957 1957,Jl 10,23:4
Secret Life of Walter Mitty, The 1964,O 27,44:5
Nelson, Mervyn (Playwright)
Ivy Green, The 1949,Ap 6,37:2
Nelson, Mervyn (Producer)
Jazz Train 1955,Ap 28,26:4
Nelson, Miriam (Choreographer)
Disney on Parade 1970,S 24,63:1
Nelson, Norma
Shoestring Revue 1929,N 23,19:2
Secret Garden, The 1931,N 8,31:4
Trial of Dr Beck, The 1937,Ag 10,22:2
Nelson, Novella
House of Flowers 1968,Ja 29,26:2
Unto Thee a Garden 1968,O 28,55:3
Horseman, Pass By 1969,Ja 16,46:4
Purlie 1970,F 15,II,1:1
Purlie 1970,Mr 16,53:1
Purlie Victorious 1970,Mr 22,II,3:1
Nelson, Paul
Macbeth 1955,O 20,42:2
Nelson, Peggy
Number, The 1951,O 31,33:2
Long Watch, The 1952,Mr 21,19:5
Much Ado About Nothing 1952,My 2,20:1
Whistler's Grandmother 1952,D 12,40:2
Nelson, Phyllis
Many Loves 1959,Ja 14,28:1
Nelson, Portia
Golden Apple, The 1954,Mr 12,15:2
Nelson, Portia (Composer)
Almost Crazy 1955,Je 21,37:1
Nelson, Portia (Lyricist)
Almost Crazy 1955,Je 21,37:1
Nelson, R E (Miscellaneous)
Firebugs, The 1963,N 22,41:1
King Lear 1963,N 23,22:1
Nelson, Ralph
Romeo and Juliet 1934,D 21,30:3
Othello 1935,S 28,13:2
Macbeth 1935,O 8,26:4
Taming of the Shrew, The 1940,F 6,17:2
There Shall Be No Night 1940,Ap 30,25:2
Nelson, Ralph (Director)
Man in the Dog Suit, The 1958,O 31,34:2
Nelson, Ralph (Playwright)
Mail Call 1943,Je 15,16:1
Wind Is Ninety, The 1945,Je 22,12:2
Nelson, Ralph (Producer)
Look to the Lilies 1970,Mr 30,59:1
Nelson, Raymond
Reunion 1938,Ap 12,26:4
Nelson, Richard (Lighting Director)
Hamlet of Stepney Green 1958,N 14,21:1
Redemptor, The 1959,My 5,40:1
What Did You Say "What" For? 1959,My 5,40:1

Nelson, Richard (Lighting Director)—Cont
Drunkard, The; Fallen Saved, The 1959,Je 24,37:2
Vincent 1959,O 1,40:1
Curtains Up! 1959,N 3,26:3
Guitar 1959,N 11,42:5
Time of Vengeance 1959,D 11,39:1
Marching Song 1959,D 29,20:1
Oh, Kay! 1960,Ap 18,37:2
Idiot, The 1960,S 26,38:1
Nat Turner 1960,N 7,46:3
Man and Superman 1960,N 7,46:2
Emmanuel 1960,D 5,42:2
Montserrat 1961,Ja 9,30:5
Five Posts in the Market Place 1961,Mr 6,30:1
Hobo 1961,Ap 11,41:2
Not While I'm Eating 1961,D 20,37:1
Mummers and Men 1962,Mr 27,41:6
Storm, The 1962,Mr 31,17:2
Firebugs, The 1963,N 22,41:1
King Lear 1963,N 23,22:1
Caucasian Chalk Circle, The 1966,Mr 25,35:1
Crimes of Passion; Ruffian on the Stair, The 1969,O 27,54:1
Crimes of Passion; Erpingham Camp, The 1969,O 27,54:1
Criss-Crossing 1970,Ja 22,30:1
Watercolor 1970,Ja 22,30:1
Nelson, Richard D
Grey Heir, The 1926,Ap 6,29:2
Nelson, Richard E (Producer)
Thorntons, The 1956,F 15,26:1
Nelson, Rowland
How Revolting! 1932,Mr 11,14:6
Laugh It Off 1934,Ap 5,24:2
Nelson, Ruth
Martine 1928,Ap 5,19:3
Sea Gull, The 1929,Ap 10,32:2
Red Rust 1929,D 18,31:1
House of Connelly, The 1931,S 29,22:4
Night Over Taos 1932,Mr 10,25:3
Success Story 1932,S 27,24:4
Big Night 1933,Ja 18,16:2
Men in White 1933,S 27,24:2
Waiting for Lefty 1935,F 11,14:5
Waiting for Lefty 1935,Mr 27,24:5
Till the Day I Die 1935,Mr 27,24:5
Weep for the Virgins 1935,D 2,18:1
Case of Clyde Griffiths 1936,Mr 14,10:4
Johnny Johnson 1936,N 20,26:3
Rocket to the Moon 1938,N 25,18:2
Thunder Rock 1939,N 15,18:1
Night Music 1940,F 23,18:2
Retreat to Pleasure 1940,D 18,32:2
Grass Harp, The 1952,Mr 28,26:2
Hamlet 1963,My 9,41:1
Three Sisters, The 1963,Jl 22,19:2
Henry V 1964,My 13,52:1
Glass Menagerie, The 1964,Jl 20,18:3
Richard III 1965,Je 3,26:1
Cherry Orchard, The 1965,Ag 2,17:2
Skin of Our Teeth, The 1966,Je 2,51:1
Country People 1970,Ja 19,35:1
Colette 1970,O 15,58:1
Nelson, Stanley
Dark of the Moon 1945,Mr 15,27:2
Nelson, Terese (Playwright)
From Here to There; Real Strange One, A 1958,Ap 24,37:3
Nelson, Vesper
East of Broadway 1932,Ja 27,19:3
Nelson, Walter
Vaudeville (Palace) 1928,Ja 31,29:2
Nelson, William
Power of Darkness, The 1920,Ja 22,22:1
Fair Circassian, The 1921,D 7,22:3
Oh, Promise Me 1930,N 25,31:1
Paid Companions 1931,Je 23,28:4
Nelson, William (Lighting Director)
Bacchae, The 1963,Ap 25,39:5
Nelson, William J
One Sunday Afternoon 1933,F 16,23:5
Nelson Sisters, The
Ice Follies 1937,D 22,29:1
Nelsons, The Seven
Vaudeville (Palace) 1929,S 16,30:4
Nemeroff (Costume Designer)
Josephus 1933,D 1,22:5
Nemerov, Howard (Original Author)
Tall Story 1959,Ja 30,33:2
Nemeth, Laurel
Blossom Time 1922,O 24,18:2
Blossom Time 1923,My 22,14:3
Blossom Time 1923,Je 1,22:2
Nemetz, Lee
John Brown 1950,My 4,32:7
Nemetz, Lee (Director)
Wedding in Japan 1957,Mr 12,37:7
Shoemaker and the Peddler, The 1960,O 15,27:4
Nemetz, Lee (Producer)
Once Over Lightly 1955,Mr 16,39:1
Wedding in Japan 1957,Mr 12,37:7
Nemiroff, Robert (Miscellaneous)
To Be Young Gifted and Black; World of Lorraine Hansberry, The 1969,Ja 3,15:1

Blancs, Les 1970,N 29,II,3:5
Nemiroff, Robert (Playwright)
To Be Young Gifted and Black; World of Lorraine Hansberry, The 1969,Ja 3,15:1
To Be Young, Gifted and Black: The World of Lorraine Hansberry 1969,My 25,II,1:5
To Be Young, Gifted and Black: The World of Lorraine Hansberry 1969,S 22,36:1
Blancs, Les 1970,N 16,48:4
Nemiroff, Robert (Producer)
Sign in Sidney Brustein's Window, The 1964,O 16,32:1
Postmark Zero 1965,N 2,28:1
Nemirovich-Danchenko, Vladimir (Director)
Lysistrata 1925,Ja 11,VII,2:7
Anna Karenina 1937,Ap 25,IV,4:5
Three Sisters, The 1965,F 12,15:1
Kremlin Chimes 1965,F 25,23:1
Nemitoff, Betty (Costume Designer)
Son, The 1950,Ag 16,24:6
Nemo, Edward
Rainbow 1928,N 22,25:1
Nemuth, Harold (Composer)
How Revolting! 1932,Mr 11,14:6
Nepoty, Lucien (Playwright)
In the Night Watch 1921,Ja 31,10:1
Merchant of Venice, The 1924,N 18,23:2
Neradoff, Jacques
Clear All Wires! 1932,S 15,19:1
Neri, Phillip
Idiot's Delight 1957,F 23,14:2
Nerivale, Bernard (Playwright)
Wrecker, The 1928,F 28,18:2
Nerney, Edwin Mackin
Criminal Code, The 1929,O 3,28:2
Nertz, Louis (Playwright)
Booster, The 1929,O 25,26:2
Nerudo, Pablo (Translator)
Romeo y Julieta 1965,Ag 28,13:3
Nerval, Natalie
Volpone 1957,F 5,27:2
Misanthrope, Le 1957,F 8,19:1
Nuits de La Colere, Les; Nights of Fury 1957,F 12,31:1
Intermezzo 1957,F 15,20:4
Chien du Jardinier, Le; Gardener's Dog, The 1957,F 19,36:1
Adieux, Les 1957,F 19,36:1
Nervo, Jimmy
Pins and Needles 1922,F 2,20:1
Nervo and Knox
Ziegfeld Follies 1922,Je 6,18:2
Vaudeville (Palace) 1926,S 7,24:6
Nerz, Louis (Playwright)
Dr David's Dad 1924,Ag 14,10:3
Nesbit, Estelle
Her Family Tree 1920,D 28,9:2
Nesbit, Tom
Secrets 1922,D 26,11:1
Nesbitt, Cathleen
Sweet William 1921,My 29,VI,1:7
Constant Nymph, The 1926,O 3,VIII,2:1
Diversion 1928,Ja 6,26:3
Diversion 1928,Ja 12,25:1
Fame 1929,Mr 10,X,4:6
Shanghai Gesture, The 1929,Je 2,VIII,2:7
Maedchen in Uniform 1932,N 6,IX,1:3
Ringmaster, The 1935,Mr 12,24:5
Thou Shalt Not- 1938,S 25,IX,3:5
King Lear 1940,Ap 28,IX,1:7
Cocktail Party, The 1949,Ag 23,28:6
Cocktail Party, The 1950,Ja 23,17:2
Gigi 1951,N 26,20:4
Sabrina Fair 1953,N 12,37:1
Sabrina Fair 1953,N 22,II,1:1
Portrait of a Lady 1954,D 22,27:6
My Fair Lady 1956,Mr 16,20:2
My Fair Lady 1956,Mr 25,II,1:1
Sleeping Prince, The 1956,N 2,31:1
Second String, A 1960,Ap 14,36:2
Romulus 1962,Ja 11,27:1
Amazing Grace 1967,D 10,82:1
Nesbitt, Kayton
Regina 1952,Je 2,25:4
Nesbitt, Murray
Pirates of Penzance, The 1970,D 6,84:6
Nesbitt, Richard (Director)
Hamlet 1968,Je 10,59:1
Nesbitt, Richard (Miscellaneous)
Harry, Noon and Night 1965,My 6,44:1
Nesbitt, Robert
Tom Paine 1969,Mr 30,71:2
Nesbitt, Robert (Miscellaneous)
Catch a Star! 1955,S 7,35:2
Nesbitt, Robert (Producer)
And On We Go 1937,Ap 22,19:5
Nesbitt, Tom
Mary Rose 1920,Ag 8,VI,1:1
Mary Rose 1920,D 23,9:2
Mary Rose 1920,D 26,VI,3:1
Faithful Heart, The 1922,O 11,22:1
Faithful Heart, The 1922,O 15,VIII,1:1
Way Things Happen, The 1924,Ja 29,17:5

Nesbitt, Tom—Cont
Way Things Happen, The 1924,F 3,VII,1:1
Nancy Ann 1924,Ap 1,18:1
Nancy Ann 1924,Ap 6,VIII,1:1
Carnaval 1924,D 30,15:1
Habit 1926,N 4,VIII,4:7
Nesi, James (Director)
Love, Honor and Oh Baby 1940,Mr 29,25:2
Neslo, Henry Craig
Dark Hours, The 1932,N 15,24:2
Late One Evening 1933,Ja 10,27:3
Harriet 1944,S 28,26:1
Witness for the Prosecution 1954,D 17,35:2
Nesor, Al
Guys and Dolls 1955,Ap 21,32:2
Kiss Me, Kate 1956,My 10,27:2
Li'l Abner 1956,N 16,24:2
Do Re Mi 1960,D 27,23:2
One Flew Over the Cuckoo's Nest 1963,N 14,40:2
I Had a Ball 1964,D 16,50:1
Pousse-Cafe 1966,Mr 19,19:2
Three Men on a Horse 1969,O 17,35:1
How Much, How Much? 1970,Ap 21,49:1
Nessler (Composer)
Trumpeter of Sakkingen 1921,Ja 15,11:3
Nestoada, Josefina
Pluma en el Viento; Feather in the Wind 1932,Ap 2,13:4
Nestor, John J (Producer)
My House Is Your House 1970,O 16,53:2
Nestor, Michael
Sophie 1963,Ap 16,32:1
Nestor, Mitchell (Director)
Fortune and Men's Eyes 1967,F 24,29:1
Winter Journey 1968,Mr 13,39:1
Nestor, Mitchell (Producer)
Fortune and Men's Eyes 1967,F 24,29:1
Winter Journey 1968,Mr 13,39:1
Nestosa, Josefina
Pluma en el Viento; Feather in the Wind 1932,Ap 2,13:4
Tambor y Cascabel; Drum and Bell 1932,Ap 21,25:4
De Muy Buena Familia; Of Very Good Family 1932,Ap 29,13:3
Nestroy, Johann (Original Author)
Merchant of Yonkers, The 1938,D 29,14:2
Nestroy, Johann (Playwright)
Jux Will Er Sich Machen, Einen 1968,Ap 3,41:1
Nesville, Carmen
Back Pay 1921,Ag 31,8:2
Nethersole, Olga
Writing on the Wall, The 1923,Jl 3,25:2
Writing on the Wall, The 1923,Jl 8,VI,1:1
Nett, George
Deirdre of the Sorrows 1949,D 15,51:2
Nettleton, Lois
Biggest Thief in Town 1949,Mr 31,31:2
Darkness at Noon 1951,Ja 15,13:4
Merchant of Venice, The 1957,Jl 11,19:5
Much Ado About Nothing 1957,Ag 8,15:2
God and Kate Murphy 1959,F 27,21:2
Silent Night, Lonely Night 1959,D 4,36:1
Wayward Stork, The 1966,Ja 20,27:1
Nettum, Richard
Henry V 1965,Je 29,27:2
Now You See It 1967,N 20,59:1
Nettum, William
Student Prince, The 1924,D 3,25:3
Netzel, Sally
Macbeth 1968,N 30,49:3
Neu, Harry
Stags at Bay 1934,D 15,9:2
Neu, Thea (Costume Designer)
Midsummer Night's Dream, A 1958,Je 23,19:1
Neu, Thea (Miscellaneous)
Luther 1963,S 26,41:1
Neu, Thea (Scenic Designer)
Julius Caesar 1962,F 22,19:6
Neubach, Ernest (Playwright)
Marching By 1932,Mr 4,17:1
Neuberg, Vivian
Ivanov 1958,O 8,42:1
Neuberger, Harold S
Zuleika 1928,Mr 7,28:7
Neuberry, Barbara
Betsy 1926,D 29,24:3
Neuburger, Harold S (Playwright)
Upon My Soul 1927,Ap 22,19:1
Neudahl, Clifford
Sunday Nights at 9 1935,N 11,21:1
Neudell, Mort
Lamp at Midnight 1947,D 22,29:2
Blood Wedding 1949,F 7,16:2
Sun and I, The 1949,Mr 21,18:4
Neufeld, Jane (Miscellaneous)
Mod Donna 1970,My 4,48:1
Happiness Cage, The 1970,O 5,56:4
Neuhaus, Max
Originale 1964,S 9,46:1
Neukum, Bob
Gentlemen Prefer Blondes 1949,D 9,35:3
Neuman, Alfred E (Director)
Mad Show, The 1966,Ja 10,16:1

Neuman, Audrey
Resistible Rise of Arturo Ui, The 1968,Ag 8,25:1
Neuman, David
Vamp, The 1955,N 11,30:1
Neuman, Elisabeth
From Vienna 1939,Je 21,26:2
Neuman, Lucille
Boutique Fantasque, La 1929,D 28,10:6
Neumann, Alfred (Miscellaneous)
War and Peace 1962,Je 16,10:1
Neumann, Alfred (Playwright)
Patriot, The 1928,Ja 20,15:1
Patriot, The 1928,Ja 29,VIII,1:1
Such Men Are Dangerous 1928,O 7,IX,2:7
War and Peace 1942,My 22,26:3
War and Peace 1965,Ja 12,32:1
War and Peace 1965,Ja 31,II,1:1
War and Peace 1967,Mr 22,42:1
Neumann, Charles P
Once Over Lightly 1938,D 10,13:4
Neumann, Curt
Vaudeville (Hippodrome) 1925,D 29,21:2
Neumann, Dorothy
Post Road 1936,Ag 5,15:4
Royal Family, The 1936,Ag 12,15:1
Neumann, Dorothy (Costume Designer)
Pursuit of Happiness, The 1936,Jl 15,14:1
Neumann, Elizabeth
If You Get It, Do You Want It? 1938,D 1,28:2
Shakespeare's Merchant 1939 1939,Ja 10,16:3
Reunion in New York 1940,F 22,28:4
Private Life of the Master Race, The
1945,Je 13,28:3
Whole World Over, The 1947,Mr 28,28:2
Crime and Punishment 1947,D 23,29:3
Neumann, Frederick
In White America 1965,F 9,42:5
Neumann, Leone
Through the Years 1932,Ja 29,13:3
Nevada, Lloyd
Vaudeville (Palace) 1926,Ag 24,19:3
Nevans, Roy N (Producer)
Gandhi 1970,O 21,37:1
Nevard, Billy
Patriots, The 1943,Ja 30,11:2
Violet 1944,O 25,16:1
Too Hot for Maneuvers 1945,My 3,26:5
Strange Bedfellows 1948,Ja 15,27:3
Nevard, Buddy
Too Hot for Maneuvers 1945,My 3,26:5
Nevard, Ruth (Mrs)
Too Hot for Maneuvers 1945,My 3,26:5
Nevel, Dave (Miscellaneous)
John Brown 1950,My 4,32:7
Nevens, Paul
Hamlet 1938,O 13,28:1
Purple Canary, The 1963,Ap 23,31:1
Neveux, Georges (Playwright)
Juliette, ou La Cle des Songes 1930,Mr 30,VIII,2:4
Chien du Jardinier, Le; Gardener's Dog, The
1957,F 19,36:1
Nevil, Charles
Career Angel 1944,My 24,23:7
January Thaw 1946,F 5,18:2
Nevill, Hugh
Pride and Prejudice 1935,N 6,32:4
Neville, Ada C
Nancy Ann 1924,Ap 1,18:1
Neville, Anthony
Bitter Sweet 1929,N 6,30:2
Neville, Carlton
White Eagle, The 1927,D 27,24:4
Neville, Charles
Marching Song 1937,F 18,18:2
Neville, Dorothy
Earl Carroll's Vanities 1923,Jl 6,8:2
Greenwich Village Follies 1924,S 17,16:1
House of Bernarda Alba, The 1963,N 25,23:2
Neville, Edgar (Playwright)
To My Love 1956,Je 7,35:3
Neville, George
Across the Street 1924,Mr 25,24:1
Move On 1926,Ja 19,30:1
Babbling Brookes 1927,F 26,13:2
Squealer, The 1928,N 13,36:3
Decision 1929,My 28,37:3
Fine and Dandy 1930,S 24,26:1
Neville, Harry
Candida 1922,Mr 23,11:1
Enchanted Cottage, The 1923,Ap 2,22:3
Fake, The 1924,O 7,26:3
Butter and Egg Man, The 1925,S 24,28:1
Service for Two 1926,Ag 31,15:1
Playing the Game 1927,D 20,32:5
Embezzled Heaven 1944,N 1,20:2
Neville, John
Henry IV 1955,My 15,II,1:1
Othello 1956,Mr 11,II,3:1
Romeo and Juliet 1956,Je 13,45:8
Richard II 1956,Jl 4,15:1
Romeo and Juliet 1956,S 19,34:6
Richard II 1956,O 24,44:1
Romeo and Juliet 1956,O 25,41:1

Macbeth 1956,O 30,42:2
Troilus and Cressida 1956,D 27,21:1
Twelfth Night 1958,Ag 27,32:1
Twelfth Night 1958,D 10,54:2
Hamlet 1958,D 17,2:7
Once More With Feeling 1959,Jl 10,30:1
School for Scandal, The 1962,Ap 6,31:3
Chances, The 1962,Jl 4,11:2
Broken Heart, The 1962,Jl 10,28:2
Coriolanus 1963,D 17,52:1
Boswell's Life of Johnson 1970,S 4,19:1
Much Ado About Nothing 1970,S 4,19:1
Neville, John (Director)
Coriolanus 1963,D 17,52:1
Honor and Offer 1969,My 14,36:1
Neville, Margot (Original Author)
Love at Second Sight 1927,S 11,VIII,2:4
Neville, Margot (Playwright)
Once a Husband 1932,N 20,IX,3:6
Neville, Marie
They All Come to Moscow 1933,My 12,20:6
Neville, Oliver
Twelfth Night 1958,D 10,54:2
Hamlet 1958,D 17,2:7
Henry V 1958,D 26,2:7
Nevills, George
Shavings 1920,F 17,18:1
Nevin, Hardwick
They Knew What They Wanted 1924,N 25,27:1
Taming of the Shrew, The 1925,D 19,14:1
Garrick Gaieties 1926,My 11,25:2
Nevin, Hardwick (Playwright)
Young Alexander 1929,Mr 13,28:2
Whatever Possessed Her 1934,Ja 26,21:2
Nevin, Hazel
Red, Hot and Blue! 1936,O 30,26:3
Nevins, April
It's a Bird . . . It's a Plane . . . It's Superman
1966,Mr 30,34:1
Nevins, Claudette
Wall, The 1960,O 12,44:4
Emperor, The 1963,Ap 17,30:1
In White America 1963,N 1,26:1
Danton's Death 1965,O 22,46:1
Plaza Suite; Visitor From Mamaroneck
1968,F 15,49:1
Plaza Suite; Visitor From Forest Hills
1968,F 15,49:1
Nevins, Don
Flight to the West 1940,D 31,19:1
Nevins, Frances
Just Fancy! 1927,O 12,30:2
Nevins, Zebra
Boys From Syracuse, The 1963,Ap 16,31:1
Funny Thing Happened on the Way to the Forum,
A 1963,Je 2,II,1:1
Where's Charley? 1966,My 26,57:1
New, Arnold
Diamond Lil 1949,F 7,16:2
Diamond Lil 1951,S 15,8:2
New, Babette
Italian Straw Hat, The 1957,O 1,37:2
New, Derek
Troilus and Cressida 1956,D 27,21:1
New, Thea (Scenic Designer)
Importance of Being Earnest, The 1963,F 27,5:2
New Stagers
Happy Journey to Trenton and Camden, The
1948,Mr 21,II,1:1
Respectful Prostitute, The 1948,Mr 21,II,1:1
New York Pro Musica
Play of Daniel, The 1958,Ja 3,15:3
Play of Herod, The 1963,D 10,55:2
Play of Herod, The 1965,D 29,24:2
Newall, Guy
When Blue Hills Laughed 1927,O 9,VIII,2:1
Newall, Guy (Playwright)
When Blue Hills Laughed 1927,O 9,VIII,2:1
Neway, Patricia
Consul, The 1950,Mr 2,32:3
Consul, The 1950,Mr 16,41:1
Consul, The 1950,Mr 26,II,1:1
Consul, The 1951,My 4,30:8
Lord Byron's Love Letter 1955,Ja 19,23:2
Consul, The 1957,S 4,40:3
Maria Golovin 1958,N 6,43:1
Sound of Music, The 1959,N 17,40:2
Sound of Music, The 1959,N 22,II,1:1
Morning Sun 1963,O 7,36:2
King and I, The 1964,Jl 7,26:1
Carousel 1966,D 16,56:2
Leper, The 1970,Ap 24,40:1
Newbaker, Frances
Warrior's Husband, The 1932,Mr 12,19:4
Newbegin, H W
Rose, The 1922,D 30,13:4
Newberry, Barbara
Oh, Ernest! 1927,My 10,24:3
Golden Dawn 1927,D 1,32:3
Good Boy 1928,S 6,23:2
Show Girl 1929,Jl 3,19:3
Heads Up! 1929,N 12,34:1
Pajama Lady, The 1930,O 12,VIII,4:1

Newberry, Barbara—Cont
Vaudeville (Palace) 1931,Je 15,23:5
Little Racketeer, The 1932,Ja 19,24:4
Vaudeville (Loew's State) 1932,O 3,15:5
Pardon My English 1933,Ja 21,11:4
Newberry, Barbara (Choreographer)
Gay Divorce 1932,N 30,23:4
Newberry, Cammann (Composer)
Foemen of the Yard 1935,Ap 6,10:4
Newberry, Cammann (Playwright)
Come Across 1937,Ap 10,10:7
Newberry, Doyle
Hole, The 1961,Ap 4,42:2
Plot Against the Chase Manhattan Bank, The
1963,N 27,29:1
Newberry, Steve (Miscellaneous)
Queen After Death 1956,Mr 13,33:2
Newbigin, Margaret
This Way to the Tomb 1961,D 9,21:1
Newbold, Robinson
Lady of the Lamp, The 1920,Ag 18,6:4
O'Brien Girl, The 1921,O 4,10:2
Irving Berlin's New Music Box Revue
1922,O 24,18:1
Moonlight 1924,Ja 31,13:7
China Rose 1925,Ja 20,18:1
Princess Ida 1925,Ap 14,27:2
Merry Malones, The 1927,S 27,30:2
Billie 1928,O 2,34:2
Du Barry 1932,N 13,IX,1:8
Du Barry 1932,N 23,15:2
Newborn, Barbary
Delightful Season, A 1960,S 29,30:1
Newby, Herbert (Director)
Mikado, The 1962,N 14,43:1
Pirates of Penzance, The 1962,N 21,28:1
Trial by Jury 1962,N 23,32:4
H M S Pinafore 1962,N 23,32:4
Iolanthe 1962,N 28,42:1
Iolanthe 1964,N 18,52:1
Trial by Jury 1964,N 20,40:1
H M S Pinafore 1964,N 20,40:1
Pirates of Penzance, The 1964,N 27,43:1
Ruddigore 1964,D 4,44:1
Pirates of Penzance, The 1966,N 16,54:1
Mikado, The 1966,N 18,36:1
Ruddigore 1966,N 23,28:1
H M S Pinafore 1966,N 24,64:1
Patience 1966,N 30,58:1
Mikado, The 1968,N 2,29:4
Pirates of Penzance, The 1968,N 7,54:1
Iolanthe 1968,N 9,37:3
Newby, Herbert (Miscellaneous)
H M S Pinafore 1968,O 30,35:1
Newby, Jerry
Boy Friend, The 1954,O 1,20:1
Newcomb, Caroline
Roger Bloomer 1923,Mr 2,18:3
First Flight 1925,S 18,26:2
Jay Walker, The 1926,F 9,23:1
Playing the Game 1927,D 20,32:5
Rope 1928,F 23,18:3
Caprice 1929,Ja 1,61:1
Puritan, The 1936,Ja 24,14:3
Newcomb, Frank
Casanova 1923,S 27,10:2
Newcomb, Jean
Riddle Me This! 1933,Mr 15,21:3
Newcomb, Jessamine
Phoebe of Quality Street 1921,My 10,20:1
K Guy, The 1928,O 16,28:4
Little Inn, The 1935,Ag 20,25:1
Remember the Day 1935,O 13,IX,1:1
Life With Father 1939,Ag 15,14:4
Newcomb, Mary
Woman on the Jury, The 1923,Ag 16,10:4
Night Hawk 1925,F 25,16:4
Bridge of Distances, The 1925,S 29,30:1
Bridge of Distances, The 1925,O 4,IX,1:1
Distant Drum, A 1928,Ja 21,13:1
Jealousy 1928,D 6,31:2
Emma Hamilton 1929,O 13,IX,4:1
Healthy, Wealthy and Wise 1930,Mr 2,26:3
Healthy, Wealthy and Wise 1930,Mr 23,IX,2:3
Marriage Has Been Disarranged, A 1930,D 10,28:2
Merchant of Venice, The 1932,Ap 29,13:4
When Ladies Meet 1933,My 14,IX,2:2
Angel 1933,D 8,31:1
Angel 1933,D 24,IX,2:2
There's Always Tomorrow 1934,My 13,IX,2:6
Antony and Cleopatra 1934,S 18,18:2
Much Ado About Nothing 1934,N 9,24:3
Saint Joan 1934,N 27,27:2
Hippolytus 1935,F 12,25:4
Major Barbara 1935,Mr 5,23:2
Newcombe, Caroline
Aglavaine and Selysette 1922,Ja 4,11:1
Play, A 1925,F 11,19:2
Ruint 1925,Ap 8,24:2
American Tragedy, An 1926,O 12,31:2
This Man's Town 1930,Mr 11,24:4
Brass Ankle 1931,Ap 24,26:4
Little Women 1931,D 8,36:2
Peace on Earth 1933,N 30,39:2

Newcombe, Caroline—Cont
Days Without End 1934,Ja 9,19:1
Post Road 1934,D 5,28:3
Newcombe, James
Henry-Behave 1926,Ag 24,19:4
Newcombe, Jean
Sophie 1920,Mr 3,12:2
Lady Billy 1920,D 15,18:2
Blue Kitten, The 1922,Ja 14,9:3
Adrienne 1923,My 29,10:4
Booster, The 1929,O 25,26:2
Diana 1929,D 10,37:1
Wonder Bar, The 1931,Mr 18,23:4
Everybody's Welcome 1931,O 14,26:3
Girls in Uniform 1932,D 31,10:3
O'Flynn, The 1934,D 28,24:1
Jefferson Davis 1936,F 19,17:2
Newcombe, Jessamine
Courage 1927,Ja 20,20:1
Outsider, The 1928,Ap 10,32:2
Cold in Sables 1931,D 24,20:7
Cradle Snatchers 1932,N 17,23:2
Girls in Uniform 1932,D 31,10:3
Sophisticrats, The 1933,F 14,19:5
Nine Pine Street 1933,Ap 28,15:5
Within the Gates 1934,O 23,23:1
Remember the Day 1935,Jl 9,24:3
Remember the Day 1935,S 26,19:3
Feather in the Breeze 1936,Jl 14,22:2
White Man 1936,O 19,22:4
Fulton of Oak Falls 1937,Ja 2,15:3
Fulton of Oak Falls 1937,F 11,18:2
Two Time Mary 1937,Ag 3,20:5
Reno 1937,Ag 10,22:7
Prodigal Father, The 1937,Ag 17,23:1
Merely Murder 1937,D 4,21:4
Woman Brown, The 1939,D 9,18:5
Ladies in Retirement 1940,Mr 27,24:3
Newcombe, Mary
Easy Street 1924,Ag 15,16:4
When Ladies Meet 1933,Ap 27,15:4
Newcomer, Ray
Springtime Folly 1951,F 27,23:4
Newdahl, Clifford
Prince Chu Chang 1930,O 12,VIII,4:1
Blossom Time 1931,Mr 5,32:1
Vie Parisienne, La 1941,N 6,20:3
Newell, Billy
Vaudeville (Palace) 1927,Jl 19,27:6
Vaudeville (Palace) 1929,Je 10,22:6
Vaudeville (Palace) 1929,D 9,33:2
Artists and Models 1943,N 6,16:6
Newell, David
Phantom Lover, The 1928,S 5,25:1
Newell, Dorothy
Little Nellie Kelly 1922,N 14,16:1
Newell, Elsa
Vaudeville (Palace) 1927,Jl 19,27:6
Vaudeville (Palace) 1929,Je 10,22:6
Vaudeville (Palace) 1929,D 9,33:2
Newell, Frank
Celebration 1969,Ja 23,55:2
Newell, Gertrude (Costume Designer)
Age of Innocence, The 1928,N 28,24:2
Newell, Gertrude (Miscellaneous)
Maya 1928,F 22,19:1
Newell, Gertrude (Scenic Designer)
Age of Innocence, The 1928,N 28,24:2
Newell, Helen Broderick
Vaudeville (Palace) 1926,Ap 20,24:6
Newell, Hope
Pursuit of Happiness, The 1952,Mr 22,9:2
Newell, Joan
Power Without Glory 1948,Ja 14,30:2
Under Milk Wood 1957,O 16,42:5
Newell, Kevin
Aquarama 1960 1960,Jl 1,14:6
Newell, Michael
Winslow Boy, The 1947,O 30,32:2
Newfield, Lincoln
Poisoned Kiss, The 1937,Ap 22,19:1
Newgord, William
Summer Wives 1936,Ap 14,18:1
Frederika 1937,F 5,16:5
Three Waltzes 1937,D 27,10:2
Newhall, Patricia (Director)
No Exit 1956,Ag 15,23:1
Tinker's Wedding, The 1957,Mr 7,24:1
Riders to the Sea 1957,Mr 7,24:1
In the Shadow of the Glen 1957,Mr 7,24:1
Riders to the Sea 1957,Mr 17,II,1:1
Blood Wedding 1958,Ap 1,35:1
Ronde, La 1960,My 10,44:2
Don Carlos 1962,F 28,27:5
Goa 1968,F 23,46:1
Newhall, Patricia (Miscellaneous)
No Exit 1956,Ag 15,23:1
King of the Dark Chamber 1961,F 10,21:1
Newhall, Patricia (Producer)
Blood Wedding 1958,Ap 1,35:1
Shakuntala 1959,S 10,41:2
Newhall, Patricia (Translator)
Ronde, La 1960,My 10,44:2

Newham-Davis, Mary
All Men Are Alike 1941,O 7,27:2
Newill, James
Sadie Thompson 1944,N 17,25:2
Newing, De Witt (Playwright)
Big Mogul, The 1925,My 12,26:3
Newkirk, Phyllis
My Princess 1927,O 7,24:2
Newland, John
Once an Actor 1950,Ag 1,19:8
Grand Prize, The 1955,Ja 27,17:1
Newley, Anthony
Cranks 1956,My 14,23:1
Cranks 1956,N 27,32:1
Stop the World-I Want to Get Off 1962,S 17,39:3
Stop the World-I Want to Get Off 1962,O 4,45:4
Stop the World-I Want to Get Off 1962,O 14,II,1:1
Roar of the Greasepaint-the Smell of the Crowd
1965,My 17,46:2
Newley, Anthony (Composer)
Stop the World-I Want to Get Off 1962,S 17,39:3
Stop the World-I Want to Get Off 1962,O 4,45:4
Stop the World-I Want to Get Off 1962,O 14,II,1:1
Newley, Anthony (Director)
Stop the World-I Want to Get Off 1962,S 17,39:3
Stop the World-I Want to Get Off 1962,O 4,45:4
Roar of the Greasepaint-the Smell of the Crowd
1965,My 17,46:2
Newley, Anthony (Lyricist)
Stop the World-I Want to Get Off 1962,S 17,39:3
Stop the World-I Want to Get Off 1962,O 4,45:4
Stop the World-I Want to Get Off 1962,O 14,II,1:1
Newley, Anthony (Playwright)
Stop the World-I Want to Get Off 1962,S 17,39:3
Stop the World-I Want to Get Off 1962,O 4,45:4
Stop the World-I Want to Get Off 1962,O 14,II,1:1
Roar of the Greasepaint-the Smell of the Crowd
1965,My 17,46:2
Newman, Arthur
Vie Parisienne, La 1945,Ja 13,14:5
Insect Comedy, The 1948,Je 4,26:3
Night in Venice, A 1952,Je 27,18:6
Night in Venice, A 1953,Je 26,15:2
Show Boat 1954,My 6,44:1
Show Boat 1954,O 29,28:4
Newman, Barry
Nature's Way 1957,O 17,42:2
Maybe Tuesday 1958,Ja 30,18:3
Mousetrap, The 1960,N 7,46:1
Oklahoma! 1963,My 16,40:1
What Makes Sammy Run? 1964,F 28,19:1
Newman, Bob
Gordon Reilly 1952,N 26,20:5
Newman, Bronia
Jacques Bergson 1936,O 31,24:6
Jacques Bergson 1936,N 29,XII,3:3
Newman, Charles
Audition of the Apprentice Theatre 1939,Je 2,26:2
Newman, Charles (Composer)
Sketch Book 1935,Je 5,22:2
Newman, Charles (Lyricist)
Sketch Book 1935,Je 5,22:2
Newman, David (Miscellaneous)
Oh! Calcutta! 1969,Je 18,33:1
Newman, David (Playwright)
It's a Bird . . . It's a Plane . . . It's Superman
1966,Mr 30,34:1
Newman, Dean
Garden of Time 1945,Mr 10,13:7
Newman, Dorothy
Audition of the Apprentice Theatre 1939,Je 2,26:2
Newman, Dov
Hedda Gabler 1970,Ja 18,78:1
Newman, Frank D
Hamlet 1931,Ap 24,26:4
Newman, Franne (Costume Designer)
Universal Nigger, The 1970,Mr 21,18:1
Newman, Franne (Scenic Designer)
Alice in Wonderland 1970,O 9,43:1
Saved 1970,O 29,57:1
Newman, Greatrex (Lyricist)
Optimists, The 1928,Ja 31,28:2
Newman, Greatrex (Playwright)
Optimists, The 1928,Ja 31,28:2
Stop Press 1935,Mr 17,VIII,1:4
Newman, Harold K
Sleuth 1970,N 13,25:1
Newman, Howard
Stick-in-the-Mud 1935,D 2,18:2
Newman, Howard (Playwright)
Brooklyn Biarritz 1941,F 28,16:2
Newman, J K
Woman Disputed, A 1926,S 29,23:2
Newman, Joel
Twelfth Night 1954,N 10,42:2
Midsummer Night's Dream, A 1956,Ja 14,12:2
Newman, Judy
It's a Bird . . . It's a Plane . . . It's Superman
1966,Mr 30,34:1
Newman, Julie
Li'l Abner 1956,N 16,24:2
Newman, Kathryn
Yeomen of the Guard, The 1964,Ag 3,16:1

Newman, Lewis
Half a Widow 1927,S 13,37:3
Newman, Mark (Producer)
Late Wisdom 1934,Ap 24,27:4
Newman, Martin
Julius Caesar 1950,Je 21,30:1
Borned in Texas 1950,Ag 22,30:6
Shrike, The 1952,Ja 16,20:2
Shrike, The 1953,N 26,51:2
Newman, Mildred
Well of Romance, The 1930,N 8,21:2
Newman, Naomi
Annie Get Your Gun 1957,Mr 9,15:5
Newman, Patricia (Choreographer)
Seven Mirrors 1945,O 26,17:2
Newman, Paul
Picnic 1953,F 20,14:7
Picnic 1953,Mr 1,II,1:1
Picnic 1953,Ag 30,II,1:1
Desperate Hours, The 1955,F 11,20:2
Desperate Hours, The 1955,F 20,II,1:1
Sweet Bird of Youth 1959,Mr 11,39:2
Sweet Bird of Youth 1959,Mr 22,II,1:1
Baby Want a Kiss 1964,Ap 20,32:1
Newman, Phyllis
I Feel Wonderful 1954,O 19,22:5
First Impressions 1959,Mr 20,28:1
Moonbirds 1959,O 10,13:1
Subways Are for Sleeping 1961,D 28,22:1
Newman, Red
Biff, Bing, Bang 1921,My 10,20:1
Newman, Robert
Private Lives 1931,My 12,29:3
Newman, Robert V (Producer)
Off Key 1927,F 9,16:2
So Was Napoleon 1930,Ja 9,22:2
Bad Girl 1930,O 3,30:2
Old Man Murphy 1931,My 19,25:2
Trick for Trick 1932,F 19,14:2
Newman, Ronnie
Ballad of John Ogilvie, The 1968,O 9,42:4
Universal Nigger, The 1970,Mr 21,18:1
Newman, William
Legend of Leonora, The 1927,Mr 30,22:4
Firebugs, The 1963,N 22,41:1
Newmann, Dorothy
Kind Lady 1937,Jl 21,19:3
Newmann, Dorothy (Scenic Designer)
Fly Away Home 1937,Jl 28,15:1
Newmar, Julie
Silk Stockings 1955,F 25,17:3
Marriage-Go-Round, The 1958,O 30,37:1
Marriage-Go-Round, The 1958,N 9,II,1:1
Once There Was a Russian 1961,F 20,32:2
Newmark, V P
Humble, The 1926,O 14,22:2
Witch, The 1926,N 19,22:5
Newmayer, Sarah (Playwright)
Susanna, Don't You Cry 1939,My 23,27:2
Newnham-Davis, Mary
Perfect Alibi, The 1928,N 28,24:2
Peter Ibbetson 1931,Ap 9,30:3
Cynara 1931,N 3,31:1
Thousand Summers, A 1932,My 25,23:4
Strange Orchestra 1933,N 29,23:2
Victoria Regina 1935,D 27,15:2
Newport, Beatrice
Love's Old Sweet Song 1940,My 3,16:3
Good Night Ladies 1945,Ja 18,16:2
Newport, Rosalyn
Power of Darkness, The 1959,S 30,33:1
Semi-Detached 1960,Mr 11,20:2
Bring Me a Warm Body 1962,Ap 17,29:3
Newsom, Charles
Lovely Lady 1925,O 15,27:1
Subway Express 1929,S 25,34:3
Precedent 1931,Ap 15,24:5
Newsom, Robert M (Miscellaneous)
Too True to Be Good 1963,Mr 14,8:2
Newton, Adele
Show Boat 1954,My 6,44:1
Show Boat 1954,O 29,28:4
Newton, Christopher
Henry V 1966,Je 8,38:1
Henry VI 1966,Je 9,55:2
Twelfth Night 1966,Je 10,51:2
Richard III 1967,Je 14,43:1
Government Inspector, The 1967,Je 15,55:1
Antony and Cleopatra 1967,Ag 2,25:1
Government Inspector, The 1967,O 28,34:1
Romeo and Juliet 1968,Je 11,55:2
Midsummer Night's Dream, A 1968,Je 13,54:1
Three Musketeers, The 1968,Jl 24,49:2
Newton, Craig
Vagabond King, The 1943,Je 30,24:2
Newton, Daphne
Visit, The 1958,My 6,40:1
Newton, Flo
Perfect Fool, The 1921,N 8,28:2
Newton, Florence
Vaudeville (Palace) 1928,O 23,32:5
Newton, George
King Oedipus 1933,Ja 16,12:4

Newton, George A Jr
Napoleon Passes 1927,D 21,29:2
Newton, Iris
Du Barry 1932,N 23,15:2
Newton, Joan
Junior Miss 1941,N 19,28:2
Junior Miss 1941,N 30,IX,1:1
Newton, John
Point of No Return 1957,Mr 23,17:2
Weekend 1968,Mr 14,50:2
Transgressor Rides Again, The 1969,My 21,42:1
Newton, Johnny
Hayride 1954,S 14,24:2
Newton, Mildred
Forbidden Melody 1936,N 3,33:1
Newton, P W
Dover Road, The 1924,D 20,18:2
Newton, Priscilla
Farm of Three Echoes 1939,N 29,18:3
Mexican Mural; Vera Cruz Interior 1942,Ap 27,19:2
Mexican Mural; Moonlight Scene 1942,Ap 27,19:2
Newton, Richard
Faithful, The 1935,Ja 20,X,3:8
Duchess of Malfi, The 1946,O 16,35:2
Edward, My Son 1948,O 1,30:2
Confidential Clerk, The 1954,F 12,22:1
Newton, Rita
Inherit the Wind 1955,Ap 22,20:2
Newton, Robert
Pirates of Penzance, The 1942,F 20,20:2
Newton, Ruth
Inherit the Wind 1955,Ap 22,20:2
Mating Dance 1965,N 4,58:1
Newton, Ruth (Miscellaneous)
Exiles 1957,Mr 13,27:1
Girl of the Golden West, The 1957,N 6,44:1
Newton, Sylvia
Trimmed in Scarlet 1920,F 3,18:1
Newton, Theodore
Elmer the Great 1928,S 25,29:1
Vermont 1929,Ja 9,28:1
Solitaire 1929,Mr 13,28:3
Gambling 1929,Ag 27,31:2
Tavern, The 1930,My 20,32:1
Sleeping Clergyman, A 1934,O 9,16:1
Accent on Youth 1934,D 26,19:1
Dead End 1935,O 29,17:2
Wise Tomorrow 1937,O 16,22:5
Wine of Choice 1938,F 22,18:4
American Landscape 1938,D 5,19:2
Man Who Came to Dinner, The 1939,O 17,31:1
Susannah and the Elders 1940,O 13,47:7
Susannah and the Elders 1940,O 30,28:2
Apology 1943,Mr 23,14:2
Land's End 1946,D 12,37:5
Joy to the World 1948,Mr 19,28:2
Big Knife, The 1949,F 25,27:5
Lady From the Sea, The 1950,Ag 8,23:2
Royal Family, The 1951,Ja 11,28:2
Ney, Marie
She Stoops to Conquer 1928,S 2,VII,2:1
Savonarola Brown 1930,F 26,22:3
Machines 1930,N 23,IX,2:4
London Wall 1931,My 24,VIII,1:6
Dangerous Corner 1932,My 11,15:3
Lake, The 1933,Mr 26,IX,1:1
Touch Wood 1934,Jl 1,X,1:3
Mrs Nobby Clark 1935,F 28,16:2
Love From a Stranger 1936,F 3,20:7
Love From a Stranger 1936,Ap 1,28:7
Love From a Stranger 1936,Ap 26,IX,2:2
To Have and to Hold 1937,Je 27,X,1:3
She, Too, Was Young 1938,S 4,X,2:1
Gioconda Smile, The 1948,Je 20,II,2:3
Young and Fair, The 1949,Jl 1,14:3
Ney, Richard (Lyricist)
Portofino 1958,F 22,8:3
Ney, Richard (Playwright)
Portofino 1958,F 22,8:3
Ney, Richard (Producer)
Portofino 1958,F 22,8:3
Neye, Betty
His Queen 1925,My 12,26:1
Neylin, James
Spring's Awakening 1955,O 10,30:2
Righteous Are Bold, The 1955,D 23,12:1
First Gentleman, The 1957,Ap 26,22:2
Mary Stuart 1957,O 9,39:1
Ngakane, Lionel
Sponono 1964,Ap 3,28:1
Ngoetjana, Joe
Sponono 1964,Ap 3,28:1
Niblo, Fred
Quiet, Please! 1940,O 20,IX,2:3
Quiet, Please! 1940,N 9,20:3
Nicander, Edwin
Bonehead, The 1920,Ap 13,12:1
True to Form 1921,S 13,12:1
Plot Thickens, The 1922,S 6,16:1
Fashions for Men 1922,D 6,22:1
Fashions for Men 1922,D 24,VII,1:1
Moon-Flower, The 1924,Ja 27,VII,2:7
Moon-Flower, The 1924,F 26,15:1

Werewolf, The 1924,Ag 26,6:1
Oh! Mama 1925,Ag 20,22:2
Oh! Mama 1925,Ag 30,VII,1:1
Morals 1925,D 1,22:2
Embers 1926,F 2,20:3
No Trespassing! 1926,S 8,19:1
Buy, Buy Baby 1926,O 8,26:2
Mulberry Bush, The 1927,O 27,33:1
Paris Bound 1927,D 28,26:3
Paris Bound 1928,Ja 15,VIII,1:1
Final Fling, The 1928,O 7,IX,2:3
Kiss the Boys Goodbye 1938,S 29,30:2
Niccodemi, Dario (Playwright)
Stolen Fruit 1925,O 8,31:4
Stolen Fruit 1925,N 8,VIII,1:1
Stronger Than Love 1925,D 29,20:2
Nemica, La 1926,S 7,24:6
Alba, Il Gioro, La Notte, L'; Dawn, the Day, the
Night, The 1931,My 18,21:4
Religione e Patria 1936,Mr 23,22:4
Nicholai, Boris
This Is New York 1930,N 29,21:1
Modern Virgin, A 1931,My 21,33:4
Happy Landing 1932,Mr 28,10:5
Nicholas, Carl
Poisoned Kiss, The 1937,Ap 22,19:1
Detective Story 1954,F 13,11:2
Fledermaus, Die 1954,My 20,38:5
Music Man, The 1957,D 20,31:1
110 in the Shade 1963,O 25,37:1
Most Happy Fella, The 1966,My 12,55:1
Guys and Dolls 1966,Je 9,55:2
Walking Happy 1966,N 28,47:1
Darling of the Day 1968,Ja 29,26:2
Jimmy 1969,O 24,38:1
Rothschilds, The 1970,O 20,40:1
Nicholas, Denise
Song of the Lusitanian Bogey, The 1968,Ja 3,52:1
Kongi's Harvest 1968,Ap 15,49:1
Daddy Goodness 1968,Je 5,37:1
Nicholas, Fayard
Babes in Arms 1937,Ap 15,18:4
St Louis Woman 1946,Ap 1,22:2
Nicholas, Harold
Babes in Arms 1937,Ap 15,18:4
St Louis Woman 1946,Ap 1,22:2
Free and Easy 1959,D 15,51:4
Free and Easy 1959,D 20,II,3:2
Nicholas, M J (Producer)
Black Velvet 1927,S 28,28:1
Skin Deep 1927,O 18,32:1
Up and Up, The 1930,S 9,25:2
Nicholas, Paul
Hair 1969,S 13,30:1
Nicholas, Peter
So Proudly We Hail 1938,Ap 9,11:1
Nicholas, Ronald
Enemy of the People, An 1959,F 5,24:4
Sunday in New York 1961,N 10,40:1
Nicholas Brothers
Ziegfeld Follies 1936,Ja 31,17:2
Nicholls, Anthony
Midsummer Night's Dream, A 1954,S 22,33:1
Ross 1961,D 27,20:2
Love for Love 1967,O 21,17:1
Love for Love 1967,O 30,59:1
Merchant of Venice, The 1970,Jl 30,39:1
Nicholls, Beatrice
He Walked in Her Sleep 1929,Ap 5,28:2
Nicholls, Elmer
Swifty 1922,O 17,14:1
Nicholls, Fred J
Deep Tangled Wildwood, The 1923,N 6,22:1
Nicholls, Jack (Playwright)
Doyen, The 1962,Mr 11,41:4
Nicholls, Richard
Wise-Crackers, The 1925,D 17,26:1
Half-Naked Truth, The 1926,Je 8,23:1
Jeweled Tree, The 1926,O 8,26:2
Aiglon, L' 1927,D 27,24:3
Forbidden Roads 1928,Ap 17,26:4
Jealous Moon, The 1928,N 21,32:2
Jade God, The 1929,My 14,28:3
Gray Shadow 1931,Mr 11,23:4
Lark, The 1955,N 18,20:1
Jane Eyre 1958,My 2,31:1
Distant Bell, A 1960,Ja 14,29:1
Burning, The 1963,D 4,57:1
Abraham Cochrane 1964,F 18,26:1
Hadrian VII 1969,Ja 9,22:1
Nicholls, Sandy
Chemmy Circle, The 1968,Ag 10,17:2
Nichols, Alberta (Composer)
Gay Paree 1926,N 10,24:2
Angela 1928,D 4,28:2
Rhapsody in Black 1931,My 5,33:2
Blackbirds 1933,D 4,22:3
Nichols, Alberta (Lyricist)
Gay Paree 1926,N 10,24:2
Rhapsody in Black 1931,My 5,33:2
Blackbirds 1933,D 4,22:3
Nichols, Alberta (Miscellaneous)
Hey, Nonny, Nonny! 1932,Je 7,22:3

Nichols, Ann (Playwright)
Just Married 1921,Ap 27,21:1
Love Dreams 1921,O 11,22:2
Nearly Married 1929,S 22,IX,4:1
Nichols, Anne (Director)
Her Week-End 1936,Mr 20,28:5
Pre-Honeymoon 1936,My 1,19:4
Hey Diddle Diddle 1937,Ja 22,24:2
Abie's Irish Rose 1937,My 13,30:2
Abie's Irish Rose 1954,N 19,19:1
Nichols, Anne (Playwright)
Abie's Irish Rose 1922,My 24,22:4
Abie's Irish Rose 1926,Ag 29,VII,1:1
Abie's Irish Rose 1927,Mr 29,23:3
Abie's Irish Rose 1927,Ap 12,24:5
Abie's Irish Rose 1927,O 23,VIII,2:4
Abie's Irish Rose 1928,Je 10,VIII,2:8
Her Week-End 1936,Mr 20,28:5
Pre-Honeymoon 1936,My 1,19:4
Abie's Irish Rose 1937,My 13,30:2
Abie's Irish Rose 1954,N 19,19:1
Nichols, Anne (Producer)
Puppy Love 1925,O 4,IX,2:1
Puppy Love 1926,Ja 28,16:3
Howdy King 1926,O 17,VIII,2:4
Howdy King 1926,D 14,24:4
Sam Abramovitch 1926,D 19,VII,6:1
Sam Abramovitch 1927,Ja 20,20:5
Abie's Irish Rose 1927,Ap 12,24:5
Her Week-End 1936,Mr 20,28:5
Pre-Honeymoon 1936,My 1,19:4
Hey Diddle Diddle 1937,Ja 22,24:2
Nichols, Barbara
Pal Joey 1952,Ja 4,17:6
Let It Ride 1961,O 13,27:4
Nichols, Beatrice
I Will IF You Will 1922,Ag 30,10:4
Polly Preferred 1923,Ja 12,13:3
Tangletoes 1925,F 18,17:1
Mismates 1925,Ap 14,27:2
Weak Sisters 1925,O 14,31:3
Blood Money 1927,Ag 23,29:2
Killers 1928,Mr 14,28:3
Gang War 1928,Ag 21,27:2
One Way Street 1928,D 25,31:2
Short Cut, The 1930,Ja 28,28:2
Live and Learn 1930,Ap 10,24:6
Nichols, Beth
Lady in the Dark 1941,Ja 24,14:2
Lady in the Dark 1941,S 3,26:6
Nichols, Beverley (Composer)
Cochran's 1930 Revue 1930,Ap 13,X,1:6
Floodlight 1937,Je 24,30:3
Nichols, Beverley (Lyricist)
Floodlight 1937,Je 24,30:3
Nichols, Beverley (Original Author)
Evensong 1932,Jl 1,19:6
Evensong 1932,Jl 24,IX,2:1
Evensong 1933,F 1,13:4
Nichols, Beverley (Playwright)
Stag, The 1929,Ap 21,IX,2:1
Cochran's 1930 Revue 1930,Ap 13,X,1:6
Avalanche 1932,F 14,VIII,1:8
Evensong 1932,Jl 1,19:6
Evensong 1932,Jl 24,IX,2:1
Evensong 1933,F 1,13:4
Floodlight 1937,Je 24,30:3
Nichols, Bobb (Costume Designer)
Tempest, The 1959,D 28,19:2
Tiger Rag, The 1961,F 17,20:2
Nichols, Dandy
Home 1970,Ag 17,32:1
Home 1970,N 18,41:1
Home 1970,N 29,II,1:1
Nichols, Dianne
Eccentricities of Davy Crockett, The 1961,Ja 4,26:1
Nichols, Dominie (Playwright)
Doyen, The 1962,Mr 11,41:4
Nichols, Dudley (Playwright)
Come Angel Band 1936,F 19,17:1
Nichols, Frank B (Director)
Next President, The 1958,Ap 10,34:3
Nichols, Frank B (Producer)
Next President, The 1958,Ap 10,34:3
Nichols, Frederick H
Take a Brace 1923,Ap 20,20:3
Nichols, George 3d (Playwright)
Now I Lay Me Down to Sleep 1950,Mr 3,21:2
Nichols, George 3d (Producer)
Small Wonder 1948,S 16,33:5
Nichols, Guy
Blood and Sand 1921,S 21,16:2
Our Nell 1922,D 5,24:1
Laugh, Clown, Laugh! 1923,N 29,30:1
Lucky Sam McCarver 1925,O 22,22:1
Henry IV, Part I 1926,Je 1,29:1
Gentle Grafters 1926,O 28,23:1
Midsummer Night's Dream, A 1927,Je 27,25:1
Shannons of Broadway, The 1927,S 27,30:4
Nichols, Harriet
Cock-A-Doodle Dandy 1955,N 4,26:5
Nichols, James
Annie Get Your Gun 1957,Mr 9,15:5

Nichols, Josephine
Adding Machine, The 1956,F 10,17:1
Prodigal, The 1960,F 12,23:1
Prodigal, The 1960,F 21,II,1:1
Rendezvous at Senlis 1961,F 28,39:2
Storm, The 1962,Mr 31,17:2
On an Open Roof 1963,Ja 30,7:3
Nichols, Joy
Redhead 1959,F 6,21:1
Girls Against the Boys, The 1959,N 3,26:1
Girls Against the Boys, The 1959,N 8,II,1:1
Darling of the Day 1968,Ja 29,26:2
Nichols, Lawrence
Hades, the Ladies 1934,Mr 29,25:3
Foemen of the Yard 1935,Ap 6,10:4
Nichols, Marjorie
Moonbirds 1959,O 10,13:1
Nichols, Mike
Evening With Mike Nichols and Elaine May, An
1960,O 10,37:1
Nichols, Mike (Director)
Barefoot in the Park 1963,O 24,36:2
Knack, The 1964,My 28,42:2
Knack, The 1964,Je 7,II,1:1
Luv 1964,N 12,43:1
Luv 1964,N 22,II,1:1
Odd Couple, The 1965,Mr 11,36:1
Odd Couple, The 1965,Mr 21,II,1:1
Passionella 1966,O 19,53:1
Lady or the Tiger?, The 1966,O 19,53:1
Diary of Adam and Eve, The 1966,O 19,53:1
Apple Tree, The 1966,O 30,II,1:1
Apple Tree, The 1967,O 12,56:1
Little Foxes, The 1967,O 27,53:1
Little Foxes, The 1967,N 5,II,1:1
Plaza Suite; Visitor From Hollywood
1968,F 15,49:1
Plaza Suite; Visitor From Mamaroneck
1968,F 15,49:1
Plaza Suite; Visitor From Forest Hills
1968,F 15,49:1
Plaza Suite 1968,F 25,II,1:1
Nichols, Mike (Playwright)
Evening With Mike Nichols and Elaine May, An
1960,O 10,37:1
Nichols, Noreen
Lyle 1970,Mr 21,16:2
Nichols, Peter (Miscellaneous)
Georgy 1970,F 27,26:1
Nichols, Peter (Playwright)
Joe Egg 1968,F 2,26:1
Joe Egg 1968,F 11,II,1:1
Joe Egg 1968,Ap 27,43:2
National Health 1969,O 19,75:1
Nichols, Red and His Orchestra
Strike Up the Band 1930,Ja 15,29:1
Girl Crazy 1930,O 15,27:1
Nichols, Richard
John 1927,N 5,16:4
Nichols, Robert (Playwright)
Wings Over Europe 1928,D 11,35:1
Wings Over Europe 1928,D 23,VIII,1:1
Wings Over Europe 1932,My 15,VIII,1:8
Nichols, Ruddy
Regina 1949,N 1,32:2
Nichols, William
Sailors of Cattaro 1934,D 11,28:4
Weep for the Virgins 1935,D 2,18:1
Black Eye, The 1938,Mr 8,22:4
Pastoral 1939,N 2,26:2
Elizabeth the Queen 1941,O 17,27:2
Macbeth 1941,N 12,30:2
Alchemist, The 1948,My 7,31:4
Richard III 1949,F 9,33:2
Nichols, William (Producer)
Cockeyed Kite 1961,S 14,27:1
Nichols, William Jr
If You Get It, Do You Want It? 1938,D 1,28:2
Shakespeare's Merchant 1939 1939,Ja 10,16:3
Nicholson, Arthur
Biff, Bing, Bang 1921,My 10,20:1
Nicholson, Dianne
Riding Hood Revisited 1961,Ja 4,26:1
Nicholson, John
Mecca 1920,O 5,12:2
Pearl of Great Price, The 1926,N 2,34:3
Padre, The 1926,D 28,16:3
If Booth Had Missed 1932,F 5,24:2
Mountain, The 1933,S 12,28:6
Nicholson, John (Director)
One More Honeymoon 1934,Ap 2,13:5
Nicholson, John (Producer)
One More Honeymoon 1934,Ap 2,13:5
Nicholson, Kenyon (Director)
Sailor, Beware! 1933,S 29,24:4
Flying Gerardos, The 1940,D 30,21:4
Nicholson, Kenyon (Playwright)
Barker, The 1927,Ja 19,20:6
Barker, The 1927,Ja 23,VII,1:1
Love Is Like That 1927,Ap 19,24:1
Confession 1927,My 3,24:3
Town Hall Tonight 1927,N 27,IX,2:1
Eva the Fifth 1928,Jl 22,VII,1:7

Eva the Fifth 1928,Ag 29,19:3
Before You're 25 1929,Ap 17,30:2
Torch Song 1930,Ag 3,VIII,3:4
Torch Song 1930,Ag 28,23:1
Torch Song 1930,S 7,IX,1:1
Stepdaughters of War 1930,O 7,27:1
Vanderbilt Revue, The 1930,N 6,22:6
Sailor, Beware! 1933,S 29,24:4
Sailor, Beware! 1935,My 7,28:4
Swing Your Lady 1935,N 16,19:4
Swing Your Lady 1936,O 19,22:4
Dance Night 1938,O 15,20:5
Flying Gerardos, The 1940,D 30,21:4
Apple of His Eye 1946,F 6,18:2
Out West of Eighth 1951,S 21,20:3
Nicholson, Nora
Rope's End 1929,S 20,34:5
Lady's Not for Burning, The 1950,N 9,42:2
Millionairess, The 1952,O 18,17:2
Living Room, The 1954,N 18,41:1
Living Room, The 1954,N 28,II,1:1
Nicholson, Paul
Red Light Annie 1923,Ag 22,10:3
Nicholson, Ragnar
Good Morning 1937,D 4,20:7
Nicholson, Stanley
Fuente Ovejuna; Sheep Well, The 1936,My 3,II,4:1
Nicholson, William (Costume Designer)
Marquise, The 1927,Mr 20,VIII,2:7
Nicholson, William (Scenic Designer)
Cox and Box 1934,S 7,24:3
Nichtern, Claire (Producer)
Banker's Daughter, The 1962,Ja 23,37:1
Tiger, The 1963,F 6,5:2
Typists, The 1963,F 6,5:2
Luv 1964,N 12,43:1
Jimmy Shine 1968,D 6,52:1
Nicita, Jean
Pins and Needles 1939,Ap 21,26:2
Nick, Bobby
Seeds in the Wind 1948,Ap 26,27:2
Seeds in the Wind 1948,My 26,29:2
Me, The Sleeper 1949,My 16,18:6
Nickell-Lean, Elizabeth
Gondoliers, The 1934,S 4,23:1
Pirates of Penzance, The; Slave of Duty, The
1934,S 7,24:3
Iolanthe 1934,S 11,24:3
Mikado, The; Town of Titipu, The 1934,S 18,18:1
Ruddigore 1934,S 25,25:2
Princess Ida; Castle Adamant 1934,S 28,26:3
Mikado, The 1936,Ag 21,13:2
Pirates of Penzance, The 1936,S 1,24:4
Gondoliers, The 1936,S 8,23:1
Iolanthe 1936,S 22,30:3
Patience 1936,O 6,28:6
Nickerson, Connie
Squaring the Circle 1936,Ag 12,15:3
As You Like It 1937,N 1,25:2
Nickerson, Dawn
Riverwind 1962,D 14,5:5
Nickerson, Denise
Our Town 1969,N 28,50:1
Nickerson, Gregg
Riding Hood Revisited 1961,Ja 4,26:1
Grand Duke, The 1961,My 12,24:1
South Pacific 1965,Je 3,25:1
Nickerson, Wendy
Wildcat 1960,D 17,20:2
Nicklisch, Franz
Don Carlos 1964,N 25,40:1
Nicks, Walter
Carmen Jones 1956,Je 1,28:2
Nicks, Walter (Choreographer)
World's My Oyster, The 1956,Ag 10,10:4
Niclas, Emmie
Blue Eyes 1921,F 22,11:2
Blossom Time 1921,S 30,10:1
Nicodemi, Dario (Playwright)
Shadow, The 1923,D 15,16:2
Aube, le Jour Et la Nuit, L' 1929,Je 9,VIII,2:4
Dawn, Noon, Eve 1930,Mr 9,IX,8:5
Shadow, The 1930,N 17,21:2
Nicodemus
Swingin' the Dream 1939,N 30,24:2
Louisiana Purchase 1940,My 29,19:2
Nicol, Alex
Sundown Beach 1948,S 8,37:1
Nicol, Alexander
Hamlet 1939,D 5,35:2
Return Engagement 1940,N 2,19:2
Nicol, Eric (Playwright)
Minor Adjustment, A 1967,O 7,33:3
Nicol, Lesslie
Man With a Load of Mischief, The 1966,N 7,65:1
Nicola
Vaudeville (Hippodrome) 1926,My 8,29:2
Vaudeville (Palace) 1927,Mr 1,31:2
Nicolaeff, Ariadne (Miscellaneous)
Ivanov 1966,My 4,50:1
Nicolaeff, Ariadne (Translator)
Promise, The 1967,N 15,38:1

Nicolai, Marquita
Red, Hot and Blue! 1936,O 30,26:3
Nicolaidis, Freddie
Hair 1970,Ja 13,39:1
Nicolaj, Aldo (Playwright)
Apricot Season, The 1962,O 4,43:8
Nicoletti, L A
Naughty-Naught '00 1946,O 21,27:5
Nicoletti, Susi
Konzert, Das 1968,Mr 25,52:1
Nicoli, Tamara
Right of Happiness 1931,Ap 3,34:2
Nicolina, Mme
Vaudeville (Palace) 1929,My 13,26:3
Nicoll, Tamara
Left Bank, The 1931,O 6,35:3
Nicoloudi, Zouzou (Choreographer)
Bacchae, The 1963,Ap 25,39:5
Nicols, William
Trojan Women, The 1941,Ap 9,32:5
Nicolson, Olive
Pal Joey 1940,D 26,22:2
Niday, Kathleen
Loves of Lulu, The 1925,My 12,26:1
Gambling 1929,Ag 27,31:2
Tavern, The 1930,My 20,32:1
Niedermoser, Otto (Costume Designer)
Silent Knight, The 1937,D 5,XII,5:8
Niedermoser, Otto (Scenic Designer)
Silent Knight, The 1937,D 5,XII,5:8
Niedzialkowski, Stefan
Woman, The 1965,Ja 6,32:1
Book, The 1965,Ja 6,32:1
Kernel and the Shell, The 1965,Ja 6,32:1
Jaselka 1965,Ja 6,32:1
Jacob and the Angel 1965,Ja 6,32:1
Post Office, The 1965,Ja 6,32:1
Nightmare, The 1965,Ja 6,32:1
Labyrinth, The 1965,Ja 6,32:1
Niehoff, H Richard
Volpone 1937,N 16,26:4
Nielsen, Claire
Cue for Passion 1940,D 20,33:4
Nielsen, Francis
Life of Reilly, The 1942,Ap 30,13:2
Hasty Heart, The 1945,Ja 4,14:2
Nielsen, Gertrude
Ziegfeld Follies 1935,D 31,10:1
Ziegfeld Follies 1936,Ja 31,17:2
Nielsen, Glen
Admirable Bashville, The 1956,F 21,38:1
Nielsen, Glenn
Admirable Bashville, The 1956,F 21,38:1
Nielsen, Herbert (Director)
Every Other Evil 1961,Ja 23,20:2
Nielsen, Herbert (Scenic Designer)
Every Other Evil 1961,Ja 23,20:2
Nielsen, John
Carmen Jones 1956,Je 1,28:2
Nielsen, Karl (Director)
Paris Bound 1929,Jl 20,8:3
Little Black Book, The 1932,D 27,11:2
Cross Ruff 1935,F 20,23:3
Nielsen, Karl (Miscellaneous)
Time Limit! 1956,Ja 25,27:2
Tunnel of Love, The 1957,F 14,31:4
Third Best Sport 1958,D 31,15:3
Desert Incident, A 1959,Mr 25,40:1
Jolly's Progress 1959,D 7,42:2
One More River 1960,Mr 19,12:2
49th Cousin, The 1960,O 28,22:1
Seidman and Son 1962,O 16,32:2
Nielsen, Lavina
Green Table, The 1942,Ja 22,12:2
Beggar's Holiday 1946,D 27,13:3
Nielsen, Leslie
Seagulls Over Sorrento 1952,S 12,18:4
Nielson, Glenn (Miscellaneous)
Gloria and Esperanza 1970,F 5,32:1
Nielson, James (Producer)
Musical Chairs 1934,Jl 31,20:7
Nude in Washington Square, The 1934,Ag 7,20:1
Nielson, Julia
Borderer, The 1923,Mr 18,VII,1:1
Nielson, Karl (Director)
Master of the Revels 1935,Ag 14,16:2
Nielson, Lavina
Prodigal Son, The 1942,F 18,22:2
It's About Time 1942,Mr 31,28:3
Nielson, Lester
Spread Eagle 1927,Ap 5,30:2
Royal Family, The 1927,D 29,26:4
Nielson, Richard (Lighting Director)
Gloria and Esperanza 1970,F 5,32:1
Nielson, Thor
Hamlet 1954,Ap 24,15:2
Nielson, Vera
Loose Ends 1926,N 2,34:2
Nielson-Terry, Dennis
Crooked Friday, The 1925,O 9,27:3
Nielson-Terry, Dennis (Director)
Crooked Friday, The 1925,O 9,27:3

iemar, Gert
Alt Heidelberg; Student Prince, The 1932,N 20,IX,3:3

iemela, Aina
Our Town 1959,Mr 24,46:2
Visit, The 1960,Mr 9,38:3
Duel of Angels 1960,Ap 20,42:2
Arms and the Man 1965,Je 24,32:5

iemeyer, Charles
Mother, The 1935,N 20,26:3
Searching for the Sun 1936,F 20,22:6
Swing Your Lady 1936,O 19,22:4
Golden Boy 1937,N 5,18:5
Cradle Will Rock, The 1938,Ja 4,19:3

iemeyer, Joseph
Little Nellie Kelly 1922,N 14,16:1

iiemeyer, W H
Find the Fox 1930,Je 21,20:4

iieminski, Joseph (Scenic Designer)
Tom Paine 1969,Mr 30,71:2

iier, Rosa
Johannes Kreisler 1922,D 25,20:3

iierendorf, Phyllis
Poupees de Paris, Les 1964,My 16,11:1
Davy Jones's Locker 1966,D 25,48:5
People Is the Thing That the World Is Fullest Of 1967,F 21,53:1
Wizard of Oz, The 1968,N 28,69:2

iiesen, Claire
Empress of Destiny 1938,Mr 10,16:2
Talley Method, The 1941,F 25,26:3

iiesen, Gertrude
Casino Varieties 1934,Ap 3,26:4
Calling All Stars 1934,D 14,28:2
Ziegfeld Follies 1936,Ja 5,IX,3:1
Follow the Girls 1944,Ap 10,15:2
Follow the Girls 1944,Ap 16,II,1:2

iiessner, Tony (Director)
Wiener Blut 1964,S 12,14:1

iiessner, Tony (Playwright)
Wiener Blut 1964,S 12,14:1

iieves, Maria
New Faces of 1962 1962,F 2,25:1

iieves, Richard
Boys From Syracuse, The 1963,Ap 16,31:1
Zorba 1968,N 18,58:1
Lovely Ladies, Kind Gentlemen 1970,D 29,38:1

iieves, Robert
Handful of Fire 1958,O 2,45:3

iievinsky, J (Scenic Designer)
Golem, The 1948,My 17,22:3

iiggli, Josephinna (Playwright)
Red Velvet Goat, The 1939,Ja 21,18:4

iightingale, John
Beaux' Stratagem, The 1970,F 10,50:2
Three Sisters, The 1970,F 12,30:1

iijinskaya, Mrs (Choreographer)
Tales of Hoffmann 1932,Ja 10,VIII,1:6

iikalajewna, Genia
Alt Heidelberg; Student Prince, The 1932,N 20,IX,3:3

iiki, Mariko
Teahouse of the August Moon, The 1953,O 16,32:1
Teahouse of the August Moon, The 1953,O 25,II,1:1
Teahouse of the August Moon, The 1954,S 12,II,1:1

iiki, Yuriko
Teahouse of the August Moon, The 1955,Ag 7,60:3

iikiforaki, Titika
Electra 1964,S 8,33:1

iikitina, (Mlle)
Chauve-Souris; Romantic Adventure of an Italian Ballerina and a Marquis, A 1931,O 22,27:1

iikolai of Wilkowieck (Original Author)
Story of the Glorious Resurrection of Our Lord, The 1962,Je 10,II,1:1

iikolaieva, Maria
Lower Depths, The 1923,Ja 16,16:1
Death of Pazukhin, The 1924,F 12,20:1

iikolas, Lucile
Time 1923,N 27,23:3
Across the Street 1924,Mr 25,24:1
Beaten Track, The 1926,F 9,23:2
Tightwad, The 1927,Ap 18,18:2
Big Pond, The 1928,Ag 22,25:1

iikowitz, Erich
Rendezvous in Wien 1956,S 5,23:1

Niles, DeWaymond
Horse Play 1937,Ag 28,8:3

Niles, Marian
Show Boat 1954,O 29,28:4

Niles, Marion
Girl From Nantucket, The 1945,N 9,17:2

Niles, Mary Ann
Carnival! 1968,D 13,58:1

Niles, Melva
Magdalena 1948,S 21,31:2

Niles, Richard
Sourball 1969,Ag 6,29:2

Nilioff, G (Playwright)
Doctor Herzl 1945,D 21,25:4

Nillo, David
Call Me Mister 1946,Ap 19,26:2

Great to Be Alive! 1950,Mr 24,28:2
Out of This World 1950,D 22,17:3
Beggar's Opera, The 1957,Mr 14,35:1
Goldilocks 1958,O 13,33:1
Bench, The 1968,Mr 5,35:2

Nillo, David (Director)
One-Woman Show, A 1962,My 22,31:1

Nillo, David (Miscellaneous)
If Five Years Pass 1962,My 11,37:1
Double Dublin 1963,D 27,16:2

Nillson, Carlotta
Delicate Story 1940,D 5,32:2

Nils, Georg J
Father, The 1962,My 15,49:1

Nilson, Einar (Composer)
Jedermann 1927,D 8,33:2
Passion Play, The 1929,Ap 30,32:1

Nilson, Einar (Musical Director)
Miracle, The 1927,F 1,24:5
Miracle, The 1927,Ap 15,27:1
Midsummer Night's Dream, A 1927,Ag 8,6:1

Nilson, Loy
Suds in Your Eye 1944,Ja 13,15:5
Arsenic and Old Lace 1944,Jl 3,7:3
Make Yourself at Home 1945,S 14,21:2

Nilson, Ralph
Way of the World, The 1950,Ap 9,73:5

Nilsson, Walter
Hellzapoppin 1938,S 23,34:2
New Hellzapoppin, The 1939,D 12,36:4

Nimer, Damian
Hidden Horizon 1946,S 20,42:2

Nimitz, Leo
Voice of Israel, The 1948,O 26,40:2

Nimura, Y
Lilies of the Field 1921,O 5,20:1

Nimura, Yeichi (Choreographer)
Lute Song 1959,Mr 13,24:1

Nimura, Yeichi (Costume Designer)
Lute Song 1946,F 7,29:2

Nin, Joaquin (Composer)
Autobiography 1956,O 3,29:2

Ninchi, Annibale
Daughter of Iorio 1927,S 12,6:4

Nine, Annette
Red, Hot and Blue! 1936,O 30,26:3

Nineteen-Thirty Players
Love From a Stranger 1936,F 3,20:7

Ninio, Avraham
Dybbuk, The 1964,F 4,30:2
Each Had Six Wings 1964,Mr 12,39:1

Ninio, Avraham (Director)
Struggle for the Negev 1953,D 14,45:5
Each Had Six Wings 1964,Mr 12,39:1

Nino (Miscellaneous)
Aunt Caroline's Will 1954,Ag 11,21:1

Ninubirg, Vera
Enough Stupidity in Every Wise Man 1923,D 6,23:1

Nip, Tom
Frivolities of 1920 1920,Ja 9,22:2
Passing Show of 1923, The 1923,Je 15,24:6

Nip, Tom (Choreographer)
Fine and Dandy 1930,S 24,26:1

Nirdlinger, Samuel F E (Miscellaneous)
Party, A 1933,Ag 24,18:4

Nirska
Tales of Rigo 1927,My 31,25:3
Rose Marie 1928,Mr 31,23:2
Sketch Book 1935,Je 5,22:2
Earl Carroll's Vanities 1940,Ja 15,11:2
Funzapoppin 1949,Jl 1,16:2
Arabian Nights 1955,Je 24,16:1

Nirvana, Nirva (Costume Designer)
Britannicus 1958,N 29,17:2

Nisbet, Bob
Macbeth 1962,Je 20,41:1

Nishri
Grand Music Hall of Israel, The 1968,F 7,42:1

Nissen, Greta
No Foolin' 1926,Je 25,25:1
This Queen of Sheba 1928,D 2,X,4:2

Nissen, Hanns Heinz
Consul, The 1951,S 8,9:3

Nistikakis, Alan
Displaced Person, The 1966,D 30,15:1

Nit, Johnny
Dixie to Broadway 1924,O 30,22:1

Nita, Ann
Bye Bye, Barbara 1924,Ag 26,6:3

Nita, Marta
Is It Murder? 1951,Je 3,54:5

Nita, Marta (Choreographer)
Is It Murder? 1951,Je 3,54:5

Nitke, Herbert (Producer)
Dark of the Moon 1970,Ap 4,21:2

Nitke, Maurice (Composer)
Firebrand, The 1924,O 16,33:1
Strange Prince, The 1926,D 8,24:2

Nitos, The Three
Vaudeville (Palace) 1926,Mr 23,24:3

Nittajo, Mlle
Night in Paris, A 1926,Ja 6,16:3

Niven, David
Nina 1951,D 6,44:3

Niven, Sally
Now Is the Time for all Good Men 1967,S 27,42:1

Nivoix, Paul (Playwright)
Merchants of Glory 1925,D 15,28:3
Merchants of Glory 1925,D 27,VII,1:1
Eve Toute Nue 1927,O 30,IX,4:7
Echec a la Reine 1928,D 23,VIII,2:1
Amours 1929,Ja 13,VIII,2:7
Deux Sous de Fleurs 1933,O 1,IX,1:3
Mariee Eperdue, La 1935,My 26,XI,2:2

Nivoy, Jacqueline
We're All in the Gutter 1927,Mr 5,12:2

Nixon, Gaynelle
Dream Girl 1945,D 15,13:2

Nixon, George W
Bottom of the Cup, The 1927,F 1,24:2
Kilpatrick's Old-Time Minstrels 1930,Ap 21,20:2
Macbeth 1936,Ap 15,24:4
Case of Philip Lawrence, The 1937,Je 9,31:1
Nativity Play, The 1937,D 21,29:1

Nixon, J W
It's the Valet 1933,D 15,25:4

Nixon, Marni
New Moon, The; Desert Song, The 1955,Jl 1,13:1
My Fair Lady 1964,My 21,43:2

Nizer, Louis (Playwright)
Case of Libel, A 1963,O 11,43:2

Nkomo, William (Dr)
Next Phase, The 1957,Ag 4,38:3

Nkonyeni, Ruth
Sponono 1964,Ap 3,28:1

Noa, Julian
Mud Turtle, The 1925,Ag 21,8:2
Lady in Love, A 1927,F 22,22:1
Eva the Fifth 1928,Ag 29,19:3
Zeppelin 1929,Ja 15,22:3
Joseph 1930,F 13,25:3
This Man's Town 1930,Mr 11,24:4

Noack, Robert
Romeo and Juliet 1933,F 3,21:5

Noah, Mordecai Manuel (Playwright)
Marion, or the Hero of Lake George 1932,Ap 23,11:3

Noah, Robert (Playwright)
Advocate, The 1963,O 15,46:7
Advocate, The 1963,O 27,II,1:1

Noah, Vernon
Last Enemy, The 1934,Jl 13,14:4

Noakes, John
Chips With Everything 1963,O 2,49:1

Noall, Hugh F
Midsummer Night's Dream, A 1932,N 18,22:2
Twelfth Night 1932,N 19,20:5
Comedy of Errors, The 1932,N 22,25:3
Merchant of Venice, The 1932,N 24,34:5
Romeo and Juliet 1933,F 3,21:5

Noam Singers, The
Holiday in Israel 1968,O 14,55:2

Nobel, Marion
Trojan Women, The 1941,Ap 9,32:5

Nobel, Michael
Man and Superman 1970,F 24,48:1
Moby Dick 1970,Je 3,52:1

Nobel, Michael (Miscellaneous)
Man and Superman 1970,F 24,48:1

Nobili, Lila de (Costume Designer)
Midsummer Night's Dream, A 1962,Ap 18,30:3

Nobili, Lila de (Scenic Designer)
Streetcar Named Desire, A 1949,O 19,36:6
Midsummer Night's Dream, A 1962,Ap 18,30:3

Noble, Ann
One Is a Lonely Number 1964,Je 19,37:3

Noble, Dennis
Great Waltz, The 1934,S 24,14:4

Noble, Duncan (Choreographer)
Tom Sawyer 1958,Jl 15,21:8

Noble, Emily
Harvest of Years 1948,Ja 13,29:2

Noble, Eulalie
Girl From Samos, The 1954,N 24,17:1
Romeo and Juliet 1957,Je 28,30:2
Richard III 1957,N 26,41:1
Mrs Warren's Profession 1958,Je 26,22:1
Romeo and Juliet 1959,Je 15,31:1
Marcus in the High Grass 1960,N 22,38:6

Noble, Jack Friend (Director)
Who Is Leslie? 1941,My 20,15:5

Noble, Jack Friend (Playwright)
Who Is Leslie? 1941,My 20,15:5

Noble, James
Hi Ho Figaro 1947,Jl 23,18:8
Velvet Glove, The 1949,D 27,26:2
Come of Age 1952,Ja 24,22:2
American Mime Theatre 1958,S 25,28:4
Far Country, A 1961,Ap 5,32:1
Dynamite Tonight 1964,Mr 16,36:2
Happy Journey to Trenton and Camden, The 1966,S 7,53:1
Long Christmas Dinner, The 1966,S 7,53:1
Night of the Dunce 1966,D 29,21:1

Noble, James—Cont

Rimers of Eldritch, The 1967,F 21,53:1
Death of the Well-Loved Boy, The 1967,My 16,48:1
Acquisition, The 1968,D 31,19:1
Scent of Flowers, A 1969,O 21,42:1

Noble, Joel (Choreographer)

Cotton Club Revue of 1957 1957,Jl 10,23:4

Noble, Louise

Heel, The 1954,My 27,33:2
Purification, The 1954,My 29,12:1
Apollo of Bellac, The 1954,My 29,12:1

Noble, Mae

Humble, The 1926,O 14,22:2
Grand Street Follies, The 1927,My 20,22:3
Grand Street Follies, The 1928,Je 3,VIII,1:1
Grand Street Follies, The 1929,My 2,20:4
Grand Street Follies, The 1929,My 12,IX,1:2
Merry Wives of Windsor, The 1938,Ap 15,22:3

Noble, Margaret

Don't Tell 1920,S 29,12:1

Noble, Martin

Broken Chain, The 1929,F 21,30:4
Channel Road, The 1929,O 18,24:2
Unsophisticates, The 1929,D 31,14:5
Out of a Blue Sky 1930,F 10,20:6
Troika 1930,Ap 2,32:6
This Is New York 1930,N 29,21:1
Hotel Alimony 1934,Ja 30,16:2
American Holiday 1936,F 22,13:3

Noble, Mary

Company's Coming! 1931,Ap 21,35:5

Noble, Mary MacArthur (Producer)

Wall Street Scene 1937,O 19,29:2

Noble, May

On Your Toes 1936,Ap 13,14:4

Noble, Robert

Wandering Jew, The 1921,O 27,22:1
Spring Cleaning 1923,N 10,16:3
Shall We Join the Ladies? 1925,Ja 14,19:1
White Gold 1925,N 3,34:5
One, Two, Three! 1930,S 30,24:2
Miss Gulliver Travels 1931,N 26,36:4

Noble, Robert Peel (Director)

Nirvana 1926,Mr 4,19:1

Noble, Sally

Doctor Faustus 1961,Ap 26,36:1
Candida 1961,Ap 27,26:1

Noble, Sheldon (Playwright)

One Thing After Another 1937,D 29,17:2

Noble, William

Carnival in Flanders 1953,S 9,38:2

Noble, William (Playwright)

Blue Denim 1958,F 28,17:1
Blue Denim 1958,Ap 20,II,1:1

Nobles, Milton

Lightnin' 1920,Jl 27,11:2
She Stoops to Conquer 1924,Je 10,24:3

Noboru, Mine

Golden Bat 1970,Je 27,18:2

Nodin, Gerald

Bitter Sweet 1929,O 27,IX,2:1
Bitter Sweet 1929,N 6,30:2

Noe, Robert

Make Yourself at Home 1945,S 14,21:2

Noe, Yvan (Playwright)

Marge des Tombes, En 1927,Ja 16,VII,2:1
Monsieur le Comte 1933,F 12,IX,3:4
Teddy and Partner 1933,F 12,IX,3:4
Christian 1936,D 13,XI,5:1
Christian 1937,F 25,18:6

Noel, Alan

Firebird of Florence 1945,Mr 23,13:4

Noel, Bernard

Luv 1965,N 16,56:4

Noel, Christopher (Producer)

This Our House 1935,D 12,33:3

Noel, Edwin

Deburau 1920,D 24,14:3
Czarina, The 1922,F 1,22:1

Noel, Emil

Adieux, Les 1957,F 19,36:1
Chien du Jardinier, Le; Gardener's Dog, The 1957,F 19,36:1

Noel, Harvey

Early Morning 1970,N 26,57:1

Noel, Hattie

Good-Bye to Love 1940,Je 8,18:1
Try and Get It 1943,Ag 3,13:2

Noel, Hubert

Britannicus 1958,N 29,17:2

Noel, Jacques (Costume Designer)

Good Soup, The 1960,Mr 3,26:4
Overcoat, The 1960,S 7,45:1
Salut a Moliere 1964,Mr 4,33:2
Pieton de L'Air, Le 1964,Mr 4,33:2
Avare, L', L'; Miser, The 1966,F 9,32:1
Chaises, Les 1970,My 6,49:1
Jeune Fille a Marier, La 1970,My 6,49:1
Lacune, La 1970,My 6,49:1

Noel, Jacques (Scenic Designer)

Good Soup, The 1960,Mr 3,26:4
Overcoat, The 1960,S 7,45:1
Huis Clos 1962,Ja 16,30:1

Avare, L', L'; Miser, The 1966,F 9,32:1
Jeune Fille a Marier, La 1970,My 6,49:1
Chaises, Les 1970,My 6,49:1
Lacune, La 1970,My 6,49:1

Noel, Joseph (Playwright)

Morgue, The 1927,F 2,22:4

Noel, M (Costume Designer)

Cantatrice Chauve, La 1962,Ja 16,30:1

Noel, M (Scenic Designer)

Cantatrice Chauve, La 1962,Ja 16,30:1

Noel, Maurice (Playwright)

Daniel Boone 1967,D 23,28:1

Noel, Renee

Melody Man, The 1924,My 14,14:2

Noel, Tom

Children of Darkness 1958,Mr 1,11:4
Of Mice and Men 1958,D 5,38:1
Hit the Deck 1960,Je 24,32:1
Young Abe Lincoln 1961,Ap 26,36:1
Paradise Island 1961,Je 24,11:1
Banker's Daughter, The 1962,Ja 23,37:1
Man With a Load of Mischief, The 1966,N 7,65:1

Noelnetter, Bob (Miscellaneous)

Ziegfeld Follies 1957,Mr 2,19:2

Noemi, Leah

Chaver, Nachman 1939,O 2,15:2

Nofer, Ferd

Behold Your God 1936,Ap 22,28:3
Kit Marlowe 1936,My 24,35:1
Arms and the Man 1937,Jl 20,19:3
Too True to Be Good 1937,Jl 27,24:2

Noffke, William (Scenic Designer)

Simpleton of the Unexpected Isles, The 1954,Ja 12,19:1

Noh (Playwright)

Fishing for Wives 1966,Mr 16,50:1

Noiret, Philippe

Lorenzaccio 1958,O 15,44:2
Marie Tudor 1958,O 22,39:1
Don Juan 1958,O 29,29:1
Cid, Le 1958,O 31,35:2

Noizeux, Paulette

Maitresse de Roi 1926,D 1,24:1
Dame aux Camelias, La 1926,D 7,24:2
Misanthrope, Le 1926,D 10,31:2
Aventuriere, L' 1926,D 17,27:3

Nola, John

On Your Toes 1954,O 12,24:4

Nola, John (Choreographer)

Carnival! 1968,D 13,58:1

Nola, V

Cena Delle Beffe, La; Jest, The 1930,N 24,26:4

Nolan, Arthur (Playwright)

Pigeon, The 1957,My 17,19:2

Nolan, Bonnie

Make Yourself at Home 1945,S 14,21:2

Nolan, Charlotte

Rehearsal, The 1952,My 27,30:5

Nolan, Doris

Night of January 16 1935,S 10,26:1
Night of January 16 1935,S 17,26:4
Night of January 16 1935,D 16,22:5
Arrest That Woman 1936,S 19,20:4
Tell Me Pretty Maiden 1937,D 17,33:5
Lorelei 1938,N 30,21:2
Man Who Came to Dinner, The 1940,F 10,19:5
Man Who Came to Dinner, The 1940,F 18,IX,3:6
Cue for Passion 1940,D 20,33:4
Cat Screams, The 1942,Je 17,26:5
Doughgirls, The 1942,D 31,19:2
Doughgirls, The 1943,Ja 10,VIII,1:1
Closing Door, The 1949,D 2,36:2

Nolan, Dorothee

God of Vengeance, The 1922,D 20,22:5
Crime in the Whistler Room, The 1924,O 10,22:2
S S Glencairn 1924,N 4,31:4
East Lynne 1926,Mr 11,18:4
Exceeding Small 1928,O 23,32:2
S S Glencairn 1929,Ja 10,24:5
Prisoners of War 1935,Ja 29,24:1

Nolan, George

Dover Road, The 1921,D 24,7:2
K Guy, The 1928,O 16,28:4

Nolan, James

Sunday Breakfast 1952,My 30,12:2
Lunatics and Lovers 1954,D 14,44:2

Nolan, James V

Remote Control 1929,S 11,24:5

Nolan, Jeannette

Macbeth 1947,My 30,25:1

Nolan, Kathleen

Love in E Flat 1967,F 14,38:1
South Pacific 1968,Je 30,54:2

Nolan, Kathy

Peter Pan 1954,Jl 20,15:3
Peter Pan 1954,O 21,30:2
Peter Pan 1954,O 31,II,1:1

Nolan, Lloyd

Cape Cod Follies 1929,S 19,37:2
Blue and the Gray, The; War Is Hell Gray, The 1929,D 27,26:4
Sweet Stranger 1930,O 22,23:3
Reunion in Vienna 1931,N 17,31:1

Nolan, Lloyd—Cont

Americana 1932,O 6,19:3
One Sunday Afternoon 1933,F 16,23:5
One Sunday Afternoon 1933,Mr 19,IX,1:1
One Sunday Afternoon 1933,S 17,X,2:4
Ragged Army 1934,F 27,16:5
Gentlewoman 1934,Mr 23,28:4
Caine Mutiny Court-Martial, The 1953,O 14,35:1
Caine Mutiny Court-Martial, The 1953,D 15,52:8
Caine Mutiny Court-Martial, The 1954,Ja 21,27:2
Caine Mutiny Court-Martial, The 1954,Ja 31,II,1:1
Caine Mutiny Court-Martial, The 1956,Je 14,40:1
One More River 1960,Mr 19,12:2

Nolan, Mabel

Blue Butterfly, The 1929,F 17,29:3

Nolan, Maire (Playwright)

Mourners' Bench, The 1950,S 22,35:7

Nolan, Maude

Main Street 1921,O 6,21:1
Subway Express 1929,S 25,34:3
I Love an Actress 1931,S 18,29:2

Nolan, Patrick

John Bull's Other Island 1948,F 11,33:4

Nolan, Peter (Composer)

Garrick Gaieties 1930,Je 5,29:2

Noland, Nancy

New Faces of 1936 1936,My 20,24:5
Common Ground 1945,Ap 26,27:2

Nolden, Ruth

Please Do Not Disturb 1936,Je 23,27:1

Noles, Conrad

First American Dictator 1939,Mr 15,18:2
King Lear 1940,D 16,27:2

Nolfi, Edward

Cabaret 1966,N 21,62:1
Zorba 1968,N 18,58:1

Noll, Edward (Choreographer)

Angel in the Wings 1947,D 12,36:4

Noll, Nancy

All in Fun 1940,N 22,26:2

Noll, Ronald (Musical Director)

Engaged! or Cheviot's Choice 1965,Ap 24,19:2
Princess Ida 1967,Ap 17,46:2
Mikado, The 1967,D 4,65:3
Gondoliers, The 1969,My 10,35:1
H M S Pinafore 1969,D 8,61:2
Patience 1970,My 10,72:4
Pirates of Penzance, The 1970,D 6,84:6

Noll, Sara-Ann

Mikado, The 1967,D 4,65:3
Gondoliers, The 1969,My 10,35:1
H M S Pinafore 1969,D 8,61:2
Pirates of Penzance, The 1970,D 6,84:6

Nolley, Edmonia

Comedian, The 1923,Mr 14,14:1
Dr David's Dad 1924,Ag 14,10:3
Guest Room, The 1931,O 7,29:2
First Apple, The 1933,D 28,25:1
Children's Hour, The 1934,N 21,23:2
Infernal Machine, The 1937,D 13,22:7
War and Peace 1942,My 22,26:3
Naked Genius, The 1943,O 22,20:5
Pick-Up Girl 1944,My 4,25:2
And Be My Love 1945,F 22,30:4

Nollman, Barbara (Lighting Director)

Importance of Being Earnest, The 1963,F 27,5:2
Pocket Watch, The 1966,Ja 6,18:1
Winterset 1966,F 10,32:2
Coop, The 1966,Mr 2,48:1
Hawk, The 1968,Ap 18,54:1
God Bless You, Harold Fineberg 1969,Mr 31,30:2
Silhouettes 1969,S 9,41:1

Nolte, Carolyn

Sidewalks of New York 1927,O 4,33:1
Harry Delmar's Revels 1927,N 29,30:2
George White's Scandals 1929,S 24,29:1
Strike Me Pink 1933,Mr 6,16:3

Nolte, Charles

Tin Top Valley 1947,Mr 1,11:2
Antony and Cleopatra 1947,N 27,49:2
Uniform of Flesh 1949,Ja 31,15:2
Design For A Stained Glass Window 1950,Ja 24,26:2
Billy Budd 1951,F 12,18:3
Billy Budd 1951,F 18,II,1:1
Caine Mutiny Court-Martial, The 1954,Ja 21,27:2
Do Not Pass Go 1965,Ap 20,44:1

Nolte, Charles (Playwright)

Do Not Pass Go 1965,Ap 20,44:1

Nolte, Claire

Remote Control 1929,S 11,24:5
Marathon 1933,Ja 28,8:8
All Editions 1936,D 23,17:2
Woman Brown, The 1939,D 9,18:5

Nomicos, Vanda

Rose Marie 1925,D 4,26:1

Nonchalants, The

Earl Carroll's Vanities 1940,Ja 15,11:2
Priorities of 1942 1942,Mr 13,23:2
Red White and Blue 1950,O 8,64:5

Noon, Paisley

Will Morrissey's Newcomers 1923,Ag 9,16:2
Topics of 1923 1923,N 21,23:2
Betty Lee 1924,D 26,18:2

oon, Paisley—Cont
Rainbow Rose 1926,Mr 17,28:2

Noonan, Felix
Ruddigore 1931,Ag 11,28:3

Noonan, John Ford (Playwright)
Year Boston Won the Pennant, The 1969,My 23,38:1
Year Boston Won the Pennant, The 1969,Je 8,II,1:7

Noonan, Padear
Hall of Healing 1952,My 8,35:6

Noonan, Tom
Men to the Sea 1944,O 4,25:2

Noonan, Tommy
How to Make a Man 1961,F 3,16:1

Norager, Thomas
Play of Herod, The 1963,D 10,55:2

Norbo, Zahra
Italian Straw Hat, The 1957,O 1,37:2

Norcross, Hale
First Year, The 1920,O 21,11:2
Like a King 1921,O 4,10:1
Celebrity 1927,D 27,24:3
Jealous Moon, The 1928,N 21,32:2
Paolo and Francesca 1929,Ap 2,28:2
Last Mile, The 1930,F 14,21:2
Bloodstream 1932,Mr 31,25:1
They Shall Not Die 1934,F 22,24:4
Distant Shore, The 1935,F 22,26:2
Caesar and Cleopatra 1935,Ag 22,21:1
Stick-in-the-Mud 1935,D 2,18:2
Stork Mad 1936,O 1,28:4
Kindred 1939,D 27,17:2
Juno and the Paycock 1940,Ja 17,24:2
At the Stroke of Eight 1940,My 21,29:2
Susannah and the Elders 1940,O 30,28:2
Tanyard Street 1941,F 5,16:2
Ah, Wilderness! 1941,O 3,26:2
Strings, My Lord, Are False, The 1942,My 20,24:2
Dunnigan's Daughter 1945,D 27,16:1

Norcross, Richard (Playwright)
Brother Cain 1941,S 13,21:5

Nord, Al
Hello, Yourself 1928,O 31,28:2

Nord, Aliki
Bacchants, The 1967,F 25,14:1

Nord, Eric
Eternal Sabbath 1963,O 19,17:2

Nord, Hedda
Orpheus Descending 1959,O 6,45:2

Nord, Paul (Playwright)
God Strikes Back 1943,F 27,11:2

Nord, Paul (Producer)
God Strikes Back 1943,F 27,11:2

Nord, Paul (Translator)
Oedipus Rex 1965,Jl 9,17:1
Bacchants, The 1967,F 25,14:1

Nordegg, Sepp (Director)
Maria Stuart 1968,Mr 27,38:1

Nordegg, Sepp (Lighting Director)
Maria Stuart 1968,Mr 27,38:1

Norden, Christine
Tenderloin 1960,O 18,47:2
Butter and Egg Man, The 1966,O 18,49:1
Persecution and Assassination of Marat As Performed by the Inmates of the Asylum of Charenton Under the Direction of the Marquis de Sade, The 1967,Ja 4,34:1
Scuba Duba 1967,O 11,36:1

Norden, Peter
Antigone 1967,Je 19,43:1

Norden, Thomas
Greenwillow 1960,Mr 9,38:1

Nordenson, Lars (Producer)
Bird Cage, The 1950,F 23,32:2
Enemy of the People, An 1950,D 29,14:1

Nordio, Mario (Translator)
Kiss Me, Kate 1959,Ag 10,24:1

Nordlund, Aili (Mrs)
Betrothal, The 1959,F 16,52:2

Nordoff, Paul (Composer)
Romeo and Juliet 1934,D 21,30:3
Romeo and Juliet 1935,D 24,10:2
Saint Joan 1936,Mr 10,27:4
Antony and Cleopatra 1947,N 27,49:2

Nordon, Denise
My Wife and I 1966,O 11,53:2

Nordstrom, Clarence
June Love 1921,Ap 26,20:1
Blushing Bride, The 1922,F 7,12:1
Molly Darling 1922,S 2,10:2
Vaudeville (Palace) 1924,F 19,12:1
Follies 1925,Mr 11,19:2
Follies 1925,Jl 7,24:3
Queen High 1926,S 9,21:2
Cross My Heart 1928,S 18,32:7
Knickerbocker Holiday 1938,O 20,26:2
First Crocus, The 1942,Ja 3,14:6
Visit, The 1958,My 6,40:1
Donnybrook! 1961,My 19,23:1
Brigadoon 1964,D 24,9:1
Guys and Dolls 1965,Ap 29,39:1
Guys and Dolls 1966,Je 9,55:2

Nordstrom, Frances (Playwright)
Ruined Lady, The 1920,Ja 21,10:2

Irving Berlin's Music Box Revue 1921,S 23,18:2
Lady Bug 1922,Ap 18,15:3
Irving Berlin's New Music Box Revue 1922,O 24,18:1

Nordstrom, Marie
Bought and Paid For 1921,D 8,17:5
Vaudeville (Winter Garden) 1922,F 14,21:1
Lady Bug 1922,Ap 18,15:3
Fashions of 1924 1923,Jl 19,18:2
Sweetheart Time 1926,Ja 20,23:2
Mirrors 1928,Ja 19,17:1
Once in a Lifetime 1931,F 1,VIII,1:3
Forty-Four Below 1935,Jl 23,24:3
Sap Runs High, The 1936,F 1,9:4
Sap Runs High, The 1936,F 5,15:3

Nordt, Richard (Choreographer)
Ice Capades 1954,S 16,37:1
Ice Capades 1956,S 13,41:2

Norell, Henry
Order Please 1934,O 10,21:2
Post Road 1934,D 5,28:3
Swing Your Lady 1936,O 19,22:4
Solid Gold Cadillac, The 1953,N 6,24:2

Norell, Michael
Cactus Flower 1967,D 16,48:1

Norell, S Henry
School for Virtue 1931,Ap 22,29:2
Whistling in the Dark 1932,Ja 20,16:6

Norfolk, Edgar
No More Ladies 1934,S 19,14:4
Dark Victory 1934,N 10,18:2
Eden End 1935,O 22,17:1

Noric, Leona
Drink to Me Only 1958,O 9,47:4

Norin, Vonda
Anybody's Game 1932,D 22,21:4
Music Hath Charms 1934,D 31,8:2

Norman, Al
Earl Carroll's Vanities 1931,Ag 28,18:7

Norman, Alan
Closing Door, The 1949,D 2,36:2

Norman, Ann
Vaudeville (Palace) 1924,Ap 29,12:2
Vaudeville (Palace) 1928,S 4,21:3

Norman, Annette
Merry Widow, The 1944,O 9,17:1

Norman, Bruce
There You Are! 1932,My 17,25:4

Norman, Carl (Miscellaneous)
Penny Friend, The 1966,D 27,46:1

Norman, Christine
Nest, The 1922,F 2,20:1
Great Music 1924,O 6,24:1

Norman, Duke
Time, Place and the Girl, The 1942,O 22,24:3

Norman, Frank (Playwright)
Inside Out 1969,D 2,64:1

Norman, Fredericka
Songs From Milk Wood 1970,Ja 13,41:1
Sganarelle 1970,Ja 13,41:1

Norman, George (Mrs) (Playwright)
Young Visitors, The 1920,N 30,14:1

Norman, Hal
Pousse-Cafe 1966,Mr 19,19:2
Carricknabauna 1967,Mr 31,30:1

Norman, Harold
Music in My Heart 1947,O 3,30:2

Norman, Jay
West Side Story 1957,S 27,14:4
My Fair Lady 1963,S 2,19:4
West Side Story 1964,Ap 9,24:2
Baker Street 1965,F 17,36:1
Passionella 1966,O 19,53:1
Lady or the Tiger?, The 1966,O 19,53:1

Norman, John G (Producer)
Before Morning 1933,F 10,13:4

Norman, Karyl
Vaudeville (Palace) 1923,My 15,22:2
Vaudeville (Palace) 1924,S 16,26:5
Lady Do 1927,Ap 19,24:2
Vaudeville (Palace) 1931,Mr 9,25:7

Norman, Kay
Madre, La 1959,F 12,24:1

Norman, Kirk
Lovely Ladies, Kind Gentlemen 1970,D 29,38:1

Norman, Lon (Composer)
Ice Capades 1970,Ja 7,35:1

Norman, Lon (Lyricist)
Ice Capades 1970,Ja 7,35:1

Norman, Lucille
Show Time 1942,S 17,20:2

Norman, Marsha
New Faces of 1936 1936,My 20,24:5

Norman, Monty (Lyricist)
Irma la Douce 1960,S 30,31:2

Norman, Monty (Playwright)
Irma la Douce 1960,S 30,31:2

Norman, Natalie
My Romance 1948,O 20,38:5

Norman, Percy
Bachelor's Brides 1925,My 29,20:2

Norman, Perry
Aiglon, L' 1927,D 27,24:3

Norman, Perry—Cont
Sign of the Leopard 1928,D 12,34:4
Suspense 1930,Ag 13,22:3
First Night 1930,N 27,32:3
In The Best of Families 1931,F 3,29:1
Tree, The 1932,Ap 13,23:5
Criminal at Large 1932,O 11,26:3

Norman, Peter
Maggie Flynn 1968,O 24,52:1

Norman, Richard
Mlle Modiste 1937,My 5,28:5

Norman, Rolla
Maitresse de Roi 1926,D 1,24:1
Dame aux Camelias, La 1926,D 7,24:2
Misanthrope, Le 1926,D 10,31:2
Aventuriere, L' 1926,D 17,27:3

Norman, Rosalie
Holiday 1928,N 27,36:1
Bright Star 1935,O 16,26:2
Places, Please 1937,N 13,10:6

Norman and Blake
Lew Leslie's Blackbirds of 1939 1939,F 13,12:2

Normandeau, Alice
Little Mouse, The 1925,S 8,21:5

Normandeau, Alice
Little Theatre Tournament; Father Returns, The 1929,My 7,28:1

Normandy, Jean
Walk Hard 1946,Mr 28,34:2

Normann, Harda
Empress of Destiny 1938,Mr 10,16:2
Heart of a City 1942,F 13,24:6

Normington, John
Homecoming, The 1967,Ja 6,29:1

Normund, Rolla
Bitter Stream 1936,Mr 31,16:6

Norree
Vaudeville (Palace) 1926,Jl 20,17:4

Norris, Arthur (Composer)
Foolish Notion 1945,Mr 14,23:2

Norris, Arthur (Miscellaneous)
Hit the Trail 1954,D 3,31:2
On the Town 1959,F 14,15:1

Norris, Arthur (Musical Director)
Hairpin Harmony 1943,O 2,18:5
Hit the Trail 1954,D 3,31:2
On the Town 1959,F 14,15:1

Norris, Bob
Lady Comes Across, The 1942,Ja 10,10:2

Norris, Christopher
Roar Like a Dove 1964,My 22,40:2
Secret Life of Walter Mitty, The 1964,O 27,44:5
Playroom, The 1965,D 6,49:1

Norris, Craig
Shake Hands With the Devil 1949,O 21,30:4

Norris, Dallett
Peace 1969,Ja 28,49:1

Norris, Edmund
Married Woman, The 1921,D 26,21:1
Uptown West 1923,Ap 4,22:2
Wonderful Visit, The 1924,F 13,17:3
Episode 1925,F 5,23:2
Penny Arcade 1930,Mr 11,24:5

Norris, Edward
Blood and Sand 1921,S 21,16:2
Nativity Play, The 1937,D 21,29:1

Norris, Edwin
Madre 1923,D 31,9:6

Norris, Ethel
Rain or Shine 1928,F 10,26:3
Great Day! 1929,O 18,24:3
Crazy Quilt 1931,My 20,28:4
Marching By 1932,Mr 4,17:1
Scrap Book 1932,Ag 2,20:3
Stork Is Dead, The 1932,S 24,18:2

Norris, Herbert (Costume Designer)
Josef Suss 1930,Ja 21,28:5

Norris, James
Saint Joan 1923,D 29,8:4
Manhatters, The 1927,Jl 19,27:3
Manhatters, The 1927,Ag 4,25:4
Music in May 1929,Ap 2,29:1
Shoestring Revue 1929,N 23,19:2
Short Cut, The 1930,Ja 28,28:2
Little Orchard Annie 1930,Ap 22,33:1
Garrick Gaieties 1930,Je 5,29:2
Lady Luck 1936,Ap 16,21:2

Norris, Jay
Strange Fruit 1945,N 30,18:6

Norris, Jerry
Jonica 1930,Ap 8,27:1
Sweet and Low 1930,N 18,28:5
Third Little Show, The 1931,My 10,VIII,2:4
Third Little Show, The 1931,Je 2,34:3
Hey, Nonny, Nonny! 1932,Je 7,22:3
Walk a Little Faster 1932,D 8,24:4
Thoroughbred 1933,N 7,29:2

Norris, Leonard
Engagement Baby, The 1970,My 22,40:1

Norris, Margherite
This Our House 1935,D 12,33:3
Steps Leading Up 1941,Ap 19,20:6

Norris, Monte
Policy Kings 1938,D 31,6:2

Norris, Natalie
Paging Danger 1931,F 27,19:2
Norris, Richard
Caine Mutiny Court-Martial, The 1953,O 14,35:1
Norris, Ruth
Black Eye, The 1938,Mr 8,22:4
Norris, Ruth Ann
Happy Faculty, The 1967,Ap 19,50:1
Where People Gather 1967,O 26,56:1
Norris, Shirley
John Brown 1950,My 4,32:7
Comrades 1956,Je 6,38:1
Wedding in Japan 1957,Mr 12,37:7
Shoemaker and the Peddler, The 1960,O 15,27:4
Norris, William
Kissing Time 1920,O 12,18:2
Van Dyck, The 1921,O 12,18:2
Dove, The 1925,F 12,17:3
White Wings 1926,O 16,15:1
Connecticut Yankee, A 1927,N 4,24:2
Norstrand, Suzannah
Hair 1968,Ap 30,40:2
North, Alan
Never Live Over a Pretzel Factory 1964,Mr 30,37:1
South Pacific 1965,Je 3,25:1
Spofford 1967,D 15,54:3
North, Alex
Mother, The 1935,N 20,26:3
North, Alex (Composer)
Life and Death of an American 1939,My 20,11:2
'Tis of Thee 1940,O 28,21:3
Of V We Sing 1942,F 16,20:3
O'Daniel 1947,F 25,32:2
Great Campaign, The 1947,Ap 1,33:2
Death of a Salesman 1949,F 11,27:2
Death of a Salesman 1949,F 20,II,1:1
Death of a Salesman 1949,Mr 27,II,1:2
Richard III 1953,D 10,65:2
Coriolanus 1954,Ja 20,34:2
Coriolanus 1954,Ja 24,II,1:1
Innocents, The 1959,Ap 21,41:2
North, Alex (Miscellaneous)
Innocents, The 1959,Ap 21,41:2
North, Alex (Playwright)
Of V We Sing 1941,O 26,I,39:1
North, Caroline (Playwright)
Aries Is Rising 1939,N 22,16:5
North, Carrington
Garden of Weeds 1924,Ap 29,12:3
North, Carrington (Playwright)
Dr David's Dad 1924,Ag 14,10:3
North, Clyde
Night Lodging 1920,Ap 14,18:2
Varying Shore, The 1921,D 6,24:1
Peter Weston 1923,S 20,5:2
What Price Glory 1924,S 6,14:3
North, Clyde (Director)
Remote Control 1929,S 11,24:5
In Times Square 1931,N 24,29:3
Marathon 1933,Ja 28,8:8
All Editions 1936,D 23,17:2
North, Clyde (Original Author)
If I Was Rich 1926,S 3,15:2
North, Clyde (Playwright)
Lambs Gambol 1922,Ja 30,16:1
Yours Truly 1927,Ja 26,16:5
Remote Control 1929,S 11,24:5
In Times Square 1931,N 24,29:3
All Editions 1936,D 23,17:2
North, Edmund (Playwright)
Vanderbilt Revue, The 1930,N 6,22:6
Drums Professor, The 1935,Jl 30,17:2
North, Elizabeth
Rubicon, The 1922,F 22,13:1
Garden of Weeds 1924,Ap 29,12:3
North, Harry
Hobo 1931,F 12,24:4
North, Heather
Girl in the Freudian Slip, The 1967,My 19,34:3
North, Katherine (Playwright)
Melody That Got Lost, The 1938,F 6,X,1:2
North, Madge
Magic Ring, The 1923,O 2,10:1
Decoy, The 1932,Ap 2,13:4
North, Robert
Harriet 1944,S 28,26:1
North, Sheree
Hazel Flagg 1953,F 12,22:2
I Can Get It for You Wholesale 1962,Mr 23,29:1
North, Sherle
My Dear Public 1943,S 10,28:1
If the Shoe Fits 1946,D 6,29:4
North, Zeme
Parade at the Devil's Bridge 1957,F 19,35:7
Doctor Faustus 1957,F 19,35:7
Take Me Along 1959,O 23,22:2
Northern, Bessie
Come Angel Band 1936,F 19,17:1
Northern, Chauncey
Come Angel Band 1936,F 19,17:1
Northern, Felix
Come Angel Band 1936,F 19,17:1

Northern, Ida May
Come Angel Band 1936,F 19,17:1
Northern, Sarah
Come Angel Band 1936,F 19,17:1
Northrop, D D
Kid Himself, The 1925,D 25,23:2
Northrop, D D (Composer)
Kid Himself, The 1925,D 25,23:2
Northrop, Jill
Silver Swan, The 1929,N 28,34:5
Northrop, Patricia
Oklahoma! 1951,My 30,15:2
Pal Joey 1952,Ja 4,17:6
Northrup, Charles C
What a Relief 1935,D 14,10:6
Take It Away 1936,D 15,30:5
Take It Away 1936,D 22,32:3
Norton, Audree
Gianni Schicci 1969,F 25,36:1
Tale of Kasane, The 1969,F 25,36:1
Norton, B Lorain
Front Page Stuff 1926,D 29,24:4
Norton, Bert J
Mirage, The 1920,O 1,14:1
Farmer Takes a Wife, The 1934,O 31,17:1
Processional 1937,O 14,23:1
Norton, Bert J (Director)
One Shot Fired 1927,N 8,32:5
Norton, Betty
Young Madame Conti 1937,Ap 1,18:4
Norton, Carolyne
Censored 1938,F 28,18:2
Norton, Charles (Lighting Director)
Bitch of Waverly Place, The 1965,Ap 2,26:1
Blind Angel, The 1965,Ap 2,26:1
Norton, Cliff
Comic Strip 1958,My 15,26:2
Norton, Coe
Tattooed Countess, The 1961,My 4,40:2
Francesca da Rimini 1967,S 12,54:1
Norton, Coleman
Little Ol' Boy 1933,Ap 25,15:5
Norton, Dean
Night Before Christmas, The 1941,Ap 11,25:2
Outrageous Fortune 1943,N 4,28:5
Hallams, The 1948,Mr 5,18:2
Norton, Edgar
World We Live In, The 1922,N 1,16:1
As You Like It 1923,Ap 24,24:1
Norton, Fletcher
Roger Bloomer 1923,Mr 2,18:3
Norton, Harold
Blackberries of 1932 1932,Ap 5,27:5
Norton, Helen
Mill Shadows 1932,F 29,20:7
Norton, Hugh
Hamlet 1936,N 11,54:2
Lightnin' 1938,S 16,17:2
Norton, Inez
Room 349 1930,Ap 23,24:5
Norton, Jack
Earl Carroll's Vanities 1925,Jl 7,24:1
Florida Girl 1925,N 3,34:1
Norton, Jim
Contractor, The 1970,Ag 17,32:1
Norton, Joe
Salvation 1969,Mr 13,53:1
Norton, Laura
Fields Beyond, The 1936,Mr 7,11:2
Norton, Lillian
First Lady 1935,N 27,17:4
Women, The 1936,D 28,13:1
Norton, Marjorie
On Location 1937,S 28,19:1
Norton, Marybelle
Liar, The 1950,My 19,30:2
Norton, Mimi
Song of Bernadette 1946,Mr 27,22:2
Norton, Robert
Jazz a La Carte 1922,Je 3,8:3
Karl and Anna 1929,O 8,34:1
Game of Love and Death, The 1929,N 26,28:4
Norton, Ruby
Vaudeville (Palace) 1927,My 24,23:1
Vaudeville (Palace) 1927,D 27,25:2
Norton, Virginia
Paolo and Francesca 1929,Ap 2,28:2
Norton, William A
Extra 1923,Ja 24,22:3
Inspector General, The 1923,My 1,24:1
Out of the Seven Seas 1923,N 20,23:3
Lady Killer, The 1924,Mr 13,14:2
Desert Flower, The 1924,N 19,18:2
Piker, The 1925,Ja 16,14:1
Solid Ivory 1925,N 17,29:3
Still Waters 1926,Mr 2,23:1
Wooden Kimono 1926,D 28,16:2
Tin Pan Alley 1928,N 2,29:1
Great Man, The 1931,Ap 8,20:6
They Shall Not Die 1934,F 22,24:4
Play, Genius, Play! 1935,O 31,17:2
Norval, Carl
Mother, The 1939,Ap 26,26:2

Norvals, R
Slight Case of Murder, A 1935,S 12,28:5
Norvas, Bill
Tickets, Please! 1950,Ap 28,25:2
Norvell, Jane
Salome 1956,F 14,24:4
Norvelle, Lenore
Malvaloca 1922,O 3,22:1
Norvello, Mitzi
Hilarities 1948,S 10,20:2
Norvig, Irvin
American Tragedy, An 1931,F 21,15:5
Norville, Hubert
Two Misers, The 1943,D 9,30:5
Pirates of Penzance, The 1946,My 17,14:6
Pirates of Penzance, The 1946,S 21,19:2
Norwick, Douglas
Rosencrantz and Guildenstern Are Dead 1967,O 17,53:1
Norwood, Bashti
Sentinels 1931,D 26,15:1
Norwood, Jean
Night Before Christmas, The 1941,Ap 11,25:2
Norworth, Jack
Vaudeville (Palace) 1926,My 4,31:2
Vaudeville (Palace) 1926,Jl 13,19:4
Vaudeville (Palace) 1927,Mr 22,31:1
On Location 1937,S 28,19:1
Fabulous Invalid, The 1938,O 10,15:1
Norworth, Ned
Artists and Models 1924,O 16,33:3
Nossen, Bram
Dark Hours, The 1932,N 15,24:2
Love Kills 1934,My 2,25:3
Twelfth Night 1934,Jl 17,24:5
Henrietta the Eighth 1935,Je 25,15:4
Othello 1935,S 28,13:2
Macbeth 1935,O 8,26:4
Bright Honor 1936,S 28,14:1
Richard II 1937,F 6,14:2
Kind Lady 1937,Jl 6,23:1
Censored 1938,F 28,18:2
Madame Capet 1938,O 26,26:2
Family Portrait 1939,Mr 9,18:4
Medicine Show 1940,Ap 13,20:6
Johnny Belinda 1940,S 19,26:2
Days of Our Youth, The 1941,N 29,15:2
Pie in the Sky 1941,D 23,26:5
Nathan the Wise 1942,Mr 12,25:4
Nathan the Wise 1942,Ap 4,18:4
Magic 1942,S 30,28:2
Star Spangled Family 1945,Ap 11,18:6
Tempest, The 1945,N 13,24:6
Oedipus Rex 1945,D 17,16:7
Buoyant Billions 1959,My 27,32:2
Getting Married 1959,Je 5,18:2
Gang's All Here, The 1959,O 2,23:1
Notara, Darrell
Seventeen 1951,Je 22,16:6
Carousel 1966,D 16,56:2
Hallelujah, Baby! 1967,Ap 27,51:1
Notkins, Ruth Wilk (Miscellaneous)
Entertain a Ghost 1962,Ap 10,48:1
Noto, Lore
Shake Hands With the Devil 1949,O 21,30:4
Italian Straw Hat, The 1957,O 1,37:2
Lulu 1958,S 30,24:1
Failures, The 1959,Ja 6,30:2
Noto, Lore (Miscellaneous)
Failures, The 1959,Ja 6,30:2
Noto, Lore (Playwright)
Yearling, The 1965,D 11,25:1
Noto, Lore (Producer)
Fantasticks, The 1960,My 4,55:2
Yearling, The 1965,D 11,25:1
Nouri, Michael
Forty Carats 1968,D 27,45:1
Nourse, Allen
Dora Mobridge 1930,Ap 21,20:2
Man Who Reclaimed His Head 1932,S 9,17:3
Foolscap 1933,Ja 12,21:2
Masks and Faces 1933,Mr 20,18:5
Scorpion, The 1933,N 28,28:4
Night Remembers, The 1934,N 28,24:3
Class of '29 1936,My 16,10:3
Enemy of the People, An 1937,F 16,19:1
Craig's Wife 1947,F 13,35:2
Advocate, The 1963,O 15,46:7
Nourse, Joan (Playwright)
Happy Faculty, The 1967,Ap 19,50:1
Nourse, Philip (Playwright)
Happy Faculty, The 1967,Ap 19,50:1
Nova, Lou
Guys and Dolls 1955,Ap 21,32:2
Happiest Millionaire, The 1956,N 21,21:3
Rosalie 1957,Je 26,28:2
Nova, Olga
Four Walls 1927,S 20,33:1
Nova, Sandra
Trojan Women, The 1941,Ap 9,32:5
Novak, David
Darker Flower, A 1963,Mr 11,7:2

Novak, Norma
Hedda Gabler 1970,Ja 18,78:1
Novella, Alba
Colonello Bridall, L' 1934,Ap 16,20:3
Miserabili I, 1934,O 1,14:2
Romanzo di un Giovane Povero, Il 1935,F 25,12:3
Paese dei Campanelli, Il; Land of Bells, The
1935,My 10,25:4
Novelle Brothers
Vaudeville (Loew's State) 1932,Je 13,19:7
Novello, Ivor
Rat, The 1924,Je 15,VII,1:4
Liliom 1927,Ja 2,30:1
Liliom 1927,Ja 9,VII,2:1
Sirocco 1927,D 18,IX,4:1
Truth Game, The 1928,O 21,IX,1:3
Symphony in Two Flats 1930,S 17,30:4
Truth Game, The 1930,D 29,19:1
I Lived With You 1932,Ap 24,VIII,1:1
Proscenium 1933,Je 15,21:2
Murder at Mayfair 1934,S 6,23:5
Murder in Mayfair 1934,S 23,X,3:6
Glamorous Night 1935,My 3,23:6
Royal Exchange 1935,D 7,22:3
Happy Hypocrite, The 1936,Ap 9,21:6
Happy Hypocrite, The 1936,My 10,X,1:1
Crest of the Wave 1937,S 19,XI,3:1
Novello, Ivor (Composer)
Glamorous Night 1935,My 3,23:6
Careless Rapture 1936,S 12,20:6
Novello, Ivor (Miscellaneous)
Wake Up and Dream 1929,D 31,14:3
Novello, Ivor (Playwright)
Rat, The 1924,Je 15,VII,1:4
Rat, The 1924,Je 29,VII,1:8
Symphony in Two Flats 1930,S 17,30:4
Truth Game, The 1930,D 29,19:1
I Lived With You 1932,Ap 24,VIII,1:1
Party, A 1932,Jl 10,IX,1:2
Fresh Fields 1933,F 5,IX,3:5
Proscenium 1933,Je 15,21:2
Party, A 1933,Ag 24,18:4
Party, A 1933,S 3,IX,1:1
Sunshine Sisters 1933,N 26,IX,3:6
Fresh Fields 1934,Jl 15,X,1:1
Murder at Mayfair 1934,S 6,23:5
Murder in Mayfair 1934,S 23,X,3:6
Glamorous Night 1935,My 3,23:6
Fresh Fields 1935,Jl 24,20:4
Full House 1935,Ag 22,20:3
Full House 1935,S 22,X,3:3
Fresh Fields 1936,F 11,19:2
Fresh Fields 1936,Je 23,27:3
Careless Rapture 1936,S 12,20:6
Crest of the Wave 1937,S 19,XI,3:1
Comedienne 1938,Jl 3,IX,2:1
Dancing Years, The 1939,Ap 16,X,2:3
Ladies Into Action 1940,Ap 21,IX,1:6
Novello, Jay
License, The 1969,Ap 23,42:1
Jar, The 1969,Ap 23,42:1
Man With the Flower in His Mouth, The
1969,Ap 23,42:1
Novello, Richard
Romeo and Juliet 1962,Ap 3,42:1
Macbeth 1967,Jl 31,21:1
Novello (Costume Designer)
Romeo and Juliet 1962,Ap 3,42:1
Novick, Janet
Trumpets and Drums 1969,O 13,52:1
Novick, Judith
Tom Sawyer - Ballad of the Mississippi
1947,D 27,11:3
Novik, Nora
Midsummer Night's Dream, A 1932,N 18,22:2
Novikoff, Rashel
World of Mrs Solomon, The; Another Chance
1969,Je 4,37:1
Novins, Dolores
Make Mine Manhattan 1948,Ja 16,26:2
Novis, Donald
Luana 1930,S 18,28:1
Jumbo 1935,N 18,20:2
Novoa, Sofia
Logia a la Natividad de Nuestro Senor Jesucristo,
El 1937,D 14,33:4
Novosel, Olga
Familiar Pattern 1943,S 3,15:6
Novotna, Jarmila
Fair Helen 1931,Ag 30,VIII,2:1
Tales of Hoffmann 1932,Ja 10,VIII,1:6
Giuditta 1934,Ja 21,30:1
Variations of 1940 1940,Ja 29,12:1
Helen Goes to Troy 1944,Ap 25,17:2
Helen Goes to Troy 1944,Ap 30,II,1:1
Sherlock Holmes 1953,O 31,11:2
Novotney, Irene
Love Dreams 1921,O 11,22:2
Nowell, Christine (Choreographer)
Jotham Valley 1951,F 7,37:2
Nowell, Helen
Green Goddess, The 1921,Ja 19,14:1

Noy, Wilfred
Dancers, The 1923,O 18,17:2
Noyes, Ann (Miscellaneous)
Fancy Meeting You Again 1952,Ja 15,23:2
Of Thee I Sing 1952,My 6,34:2
Noyes, Beatrice
Tragedy of Nan, The 1920,F 18,9:1
Fall and Rise of Susan Lenox, The 1920,Je 11,11:2
Marry the Poor Girl 1920,S 27,18:3
Lights Out 1922,Ag 18,8:4
Spite Corner 1922,S 26,18:1
Seventh Heaven 1922,O 31,11:1
Fall Guy, The 1925,Mr 11,19:1
After Tomorrow 1930,Ag 10,VIII,2:3
Noyes, Crosby E
Frogs, The 1941,N 14,25:3
Noyes, Helen
Show Boat 1966,Jl 20,48:1
Sound of Music, The 1967,Ap 27,52:1
Sound of Music, The 1970,Jl 3,13:1
Noyes, Linda
Wicked Cooks, The 1967,Ja 24,42:1
Harold 1967,My 10,39:1
Noyes, Richard
Parlor Story 1947,Mr 5,29:2
Noyes, Thomas
Now I Lay Me Down to Sleep 1950,Mr 3,21:2
Small Hours, The 1951,F 16,22:1
Noyes, Thomas (Producer)
Frogs of Spring, The 1953,O 21,36:2
Portrait of a Lady 1954,D 22,27:6
Joyce Grenfell Requests the Pleasure
1955,O 11,48:1
Copper and Brass 1957,O 18,19:2
Nozawa, Katsuhei (Miscellaneous)
General's Daughter, The 1966,Mr 16,50:1
Fishing for Wives 1966,Mr 16,50:1
Greengrocer's Daughter, The 1966,Mr 16,50:1
Nozawa, Katsutaro (Miscellaneous)
Greengrocer's Daughter, The 1966,Mr 16,50:1
General's Daughter, The 1966,Mr 16,50:1
Fishing for Wives 1966,Mr 16,50:1
Nozawa, Matsunosuke (Miscellaneous)
Fishing for Wives 1966,Mr 16,50:1
Greengrocer's Daughter, The 1966,Mr 16,50:1
General's Daughter, The 1966,Mr 16,50:1
Noziere, Fernand (Original Author)
Cafe de Danse 1929,Ja 16,22:2
Noziere, Fernand (Playwright)
Notre Amour 1926,O 31,VIII,2:4
Vieille Maman, La 1927,N 6,IX,4:1
Robe de Perles, La 1928,Ja 15,VIII,2:3
Bapteme, Le 1928,Mr 11,VIII,2:7
Lelia 1928,D 2,X,2:1
Lady Hamilton 1929,N 17,IX,2:6
Cette Vieille Canaille 1930,D 7,IX,4:2
Untitled-Play 1932,Ja 31,VIII,3:1
Nuchtern, Jean
Greenwillow 1970,D 8,60:1
Nuckles, Rolla
Chinese Nightingale, The 1934,O 6,20:4
Nudell, Sam
Tenth Man, The 1967,N 9,54:1
Nudelman, M (Playwright)
Let's Sing Yiddish 1966,N 10,63:1
Nudsen, Evita
Personality 1921,Ag 29,14:3
Nuetzman, Delmar
Slice It Thin 1945,My 11,22:5
City of Kings 1949,F 18,27:2
Nugent, Eddie
One Thing After Another 1937,D 29,17:2
Flying Ginzburgs, The 1938,N 13,IX,2:2
See My Lawyer 1939,S 28,29:1
Strangler Fig, The 1940,My 7,31:2
Your Loving Son 1941,Ap 5,13:2
Snookie 1941,Je 4,26:2
Brooklyn, U S A 1941,D 22,24:2
Brooklyn, U S A 1941,D 28,IX,1:1
Star Spangled Family 1945,Ap 11,18:6
Round Trip 1945,My 30,16:4
Nugent, Elliott
Dulcy 1921,Ag 15,14:1
Kempy 1922,My 16,14:2
Wild Westcotts, The 1923,D 25,26:2
Rising Son, The 1924,O 28,27:2
Poor Nut, The 1925,Ap 19,IX,2:1
Poor Nut, The 1925,Ap 28,18:1
Kempy 1927,My 12,25:2
Breaks, The 1928,Ap 17,26:3
By Request 1928,Ag 26,VII,2:1
By Request 1928,S 28,30:2
Wife's Away, The 1930,N 23,IX,3:5
Fast Service 1931,N 18,26:3
Male Animal, The 1940,Ja 10,17:2
Male Animal, The 1940,Ja 21,IX,1:1
Without Love 1942,Mr 5,20:7
Without Love 1942,Ap 28,17:4
Without Love 1942,N 11,28:1
Without Love 1942,N 29,VIII,1:1
Voice of the Turtle 1943,D 9,30:3
Voice of the Turtle, The 1943,D 19,II,3:1
Voice of the Turtle, The 1944,D 19,27:2

Nugent, Elliott—Cont
Fundamental George, The 1949,Ag 17,19:4
Not for Children 1951,F 14,35:2
Male Animal, The 1952,My 1,35:1
Male Animal, The 1952,My 18,II,1:1
Nugent, Elliott (Director)
All in Favor 1942,Ja 21,20:6
Tomorrow the World 1943,Ap 15,22:2
Tomorrow the World 1943,Ap 25,II,1:1
Mrs January & Mr Ex 1944,Ap 1,10:2
Place of Our Own, A 1945,Ap 3,23:7
Message for Margaret 1947,Ap 17,34:2
Fundamental George, The 1949,Ag 17,19:4
Greatest Man Alive!, The 1957,My 9,37:2
Nugent, Elliott (Miscellaneous)
Place of Our Own, A 1945,Ap 3,23:7
Seven Year Itch, The 1952,N 21,21:2
Wayward Saint, The 1955,F 18,17:1
Greatest Man Alive!, The 1957,My 9,37:2
Nugent, Elliott (Playwright)
Kempy 1922,My 16,14:2
Dumb-Bell 1923,N 27,23:2
Apartment to Let 1924,Ap 1,18:1
Rising Son, The 1924,O 28,27:2
Poor Nut, The 1925,Ap 19,IX,2:1
Poor Nut, The 1925,Ap 28,18:1
Human Nature 1925,S 25,24:3
Trouper, The 1926,Mr 9,21:1
Nightstick 1927,N 11,20:4
Breaks, The 1928,Ap 17,26:3
By Request 1928,Ag 26,VII,2:1
By Request 1928,S 28,30:2
Fast Service 1931,N 18,26:3
World's My Onion, The 1935,Je 16,X,1:8
Fight's On, The; Uneasy Virtue; Pardon My Back
1937,Ag 4,14:1
Male Animal, The 1940,Ja 10,17:2
Male Animal, The 1940,Ja 21,IX,1:1
Male Animal, The 1941,Jl 9,24:6
Place of Our Own, A 1945,Ap 3,23:7
Male Animal, The 1952,My 1,35:1
Male Animal, The 1952,My 18,II,1:1
Nugent, Elliott (Producer)
All in Favor 1942,Ja 21,20:6
Big Two, The 1947,Ja 9,21:2
Seven Year Itch, The 1952,N 21,21:2
Wayward Saint, The 1955,F 18,17:1
Nugent, Howard
Nemesis 1921,Ap 5,24:3
Pot-Luck 1921,S 30,10:1
Wild Oats Lane 1922,S 7,12:1
Nugent, J C
Kempy 1922,My 16,14:2
Dumb-Bell 1923,N 27,23:2
Rising Son, The 1924,O 28,27:2
Trouper, The 1926,Mr 9,21:1
Vaudeville (Palace) 1926,My 11,25:3
God Loves Us 1926,O 20,22:2
God Loves Us 1926,O 31,VIII,1:4
Comic, The 1927,Ap 20,28:2
Kempy 1927,My 12,25:2
Kempy 1927,My 22,VIII,1:1
Mister Romeo 1927,S 6,35:3
Breaks, The 1928,Ap 17,26:3
By Request 1928,Ag 26,VII,2:1
By Request 1928,S 28,30:2
Skyrocket, The 1929,Ja 12,14:7
Fast Service 1931,N 18,26:3
That's Gratitude 1932,Je 17,24:3
Humpty Dumpty 1932,S 18,IX,2:1
Big Hearted Herbert 1934,Ja 2,17:3
Dream Child 1934,Jl 31,20:2
Dream Child 1934,S 28,26:2
World's My Onion, The 1935,Je 16,X,1:8
Mr Shaddy 1936,Jl 15,14:4
When We Are Married 1939,N 21,19:5
When We Are Married 1939,D 10,X,5:6
When We Are Married 1939,D 26,22:3
Snookie 1941,Je 4,26:2
More the Merrier, The 1941,S 16,19:3
All in Favor 1942,Ja 21,20:6
That Old Devil 1944,Je 6,14:2
Place of Our Own, A 1945,Ap 3,23:7
Playboy of the Western World, The 1946,O 28,18:3
Nugent, J C (Director)
Comic, The 1927,Ap 20,28:2
That Old Devil 1944,Je 6,14:2
Nugent, J C (Playwright)
Kempy 1922,My 16,14:2
Dumb-Bell 1923,N 27,23:2
Rising Son, The 1924,O 28,27:2
Poor Nut, The 1925,Ap 19,IX,2:1
Poor Nut, The 1925,Ap 28,18:1
Human Nature 1925,S 25,24:3
Trouper, The 1926,Mr 9,21:1
Nightstick 1927,N 11,20:4
Breaks, The 1928,Ap 17,26:3
By Request 1928,Ag 26,VII,2:1
By Request 1928,S 28,30:2
Fast Service 1931,N 18,26:3
Dream Child 1934,Jl 31,20:2
Dream Child 1934,S 28,26:2
World's My Onion, The 1935,Je 16,X,1:8
Mr Shaddy 1936,Jl 15,14:4

Nugent, J C (Playwright)—Cont
That Old Devil 1944,Je 6,14:2
Nugent, Judy
Penny Wars, The 1969,O 16,52:1
Nugent, Lee
Precedent 1931,Ap 15,24:5
Fundamental George, The 1949,Ag 17,19:4
Nugent, Margaret
Little Old New York 1920,S 9,9:2
Wild Oats Lane 1922,S 7,12:1
Nugent, Moya
Conversation Piece 1934,O 24,24:1
Hands Across the Sea 1936,N 25,17:2
Shadow Play 1936,N 28,13:1
We Were Dancing 1936,N 28,13:1
Fumed Oak 1936,N 28,13:1
Family Album 1936,D 1,31:1
Still Life 1936,D 1,31:1
Ways and Means 1936,D 1,31:1
George and Margaret 1937,S 23,32:2
Set to Music 1939,Ja 19,16:2
Nugent, Nancy
Tomorrow the World 1943,Ap 15,22:2
Tomorrow the World 1943,Ap 25,II,1:1
Male Animal, The 1952,My 1,35:1
Male Animal, The 1952,My 18,II,1:1
Billygoat Eddie 1964,Ap 21,43:2
Nugent, Nelle (Miscellaneous)
Feast of Panthers 1961,Mr 21,32:1
Clandestine on the Morning Line 1961,O 31,28:1
Angels of Anadarko 1962,O 11,47:1
Home Fires 1969,Ap 8,42:1
Cop-Out 1969,Ap 8,42:1
Nugent, Paul
At Mrs Beam's 1926,Ap 26,24:3
Buckaroo 1929,Mr 18,31:1
Young Sinners 1929,N 29,24:4
Nugent, Ruth
Kempy 1922,My 16,14:2
Dumb-Bell 1923,N 27,23:2
Neighbors 1923,D 27,11:1
Rising Son, The 1924,O 28,27:2
Family Upstairs, The 1925,Ag 18,14:2
Trouper, The 1926,Mr 9,21:1
Vaudeville (Palace) 1926,My 11,25:3
Kempy 1927,My 12,25:2
Mr Moneypenny 1928,O 17,26:2
American Tragedy, An 1931,F 21,15:5
Fly by Night 1933,Je 3,16:2
Dream Child 1934,Jl 31,20:2
Dream Child 1934,S 28,26:2
Mr Shaddy 1936,Jl 15,14:4
Nugent, William
Strip Girl 1935,O 21,22:6
Double Dummy 1936,N 12,30:1
Nugent (Mr)
Hoosiers Abroad; Man From Home, The 1927,O 2,VIII,4:6
Nugents, The (Playwright)
By Request 1928,O 7,IX,1:1
Nulens, Arthur
Long Road, The 1930,S 10,30:2
Numark, Harry E
Alt Heidelberg 1926,My 31,10:5
Numes, Mr
Roi, Le 1931,Ap 5,VIII,3:1
Nun, William
Grand Hotel 1930,N 14,30:4
Nunan, Peadar
Playboy of the Western World, The 1958,My 9,19:2
Nunes, George P
Cardinale, Il; Cardinal, The 1931,Ja 12,24:2
Nunes, Morris (Miscellaneous)
Best Foot Forward 1941,S 12,24:4
Nunn, Alan
Hamlet 1957,Jl 3,15:2
Henry IV, Part I 1958,Je 25,23:3
Much Ado About Nothing 1958,Je 26,22:1
Winter's Tale, The 1958,Jl 23,34:3
Hostage, The 1961,D 13,55:4
Nunn, Alice
Fourth Avenue North 1961,S 28,50:2
Nunn, Barbara
Heaven on Earth 1948,S 17,29:2
Nunn, Juanita
Airways, Inc 1929,F 21,30:5
Nunn, Trevor (Director)
King Lear 1968,Ap 12,42:5
Much Ado About Nothing 1968,O 16,33:1
Winter's Tale, The 1969,Je 1,II,4:5
Much Ado About Nothing 1969,S 1,13:1
Henry VIII 1969,O 11,42:1
Hamlet 1970,Je 5,23:1
Hamlet 1970,Ag 3,37:3
Nunn, Trevor (Playwright)
Winter's Tale, The 1969,S 1,13:1
Nunn, Trevor (Producer)
Winter's Tale, The 1969,My 17,18:1
Nunn, Wayne
Tangerine 1921,Ag 10,8:2
Crucible 1933,S 5,22:4
Eight Bells 1933,O 30,14:2
Mahogany Hall 1934,Ja 18,18:5

Nunn, William
Octoroon, The 1929,Mr 13,28:3
Night Remembers, The 1934,N 28,24:3
Mother Sings 1935,N 13,24:1
One Thing After Another 1937,D 29,17:2
Clash by Night 1941,D 29,20:2
My Dear Public 1943,S 10,28:1
Joy Forever, A 1946,Ja 8,20:2
Nunn, William Company
Vaudeville (Palace) 1930,My 5,27:5
Nurnberg, Maxwell (Playwright)
Chalk Dust 1936,Mr 5,24:5
Nuroc, Kirk (Musical Director)
Salvation 1969,Mr 13,53:1
Nurock, Kirk (Composer)
Sunday Dinner 1970,N 3,28:1
Dream Out of Time, A 1970,N 9,52:1
Nurock, Kirk (Miscellaneous)
Salvation 1969,S 25,55:1
Nusbaum, Jane C (Producer)
Half a Sixpence 1965,Ap 26,38:2
Hallelujah, Baby! 1967,Ap 27,51:1
Riot 1968,D 20,64:1
Nusbaum, Sally (Scenic Designer)
Familiar Pattern 1943,S 3,15:6
Career 1943,O 29,22:6
Partition 1948,O 29,31:2
Nussbaum, Louis
Diamond Lil 1928,Ap 10,32:1
Diamond Lil 1948,N 30,33:2
Diamond Lil 1949,F 7,16:2
Diamond Lil 1951,S 15,8:2
Nussbaum, M
Roaming Stars 1930,Ja 25,12:2
Nussbaum, Norma
Nautical but Nice 1931,Ap 19,31:6
Nutter, Eileen (Playwright)
Hummin' Sam 1933,Ap 10,8:8
Nuyen, France
World of Suzie Wong, The 1958,O 15,47:1
World of Suzie Wong, The 1958,O 19,II,1:1
Nxumalo, Gideon (Miscellaneous)
Sponono 1964,Ap 3,28:1
Nyberg, Peter
Alchemist, The 1966,O 14,48:1
Yerma 1966,D 9,60:1
Nybloc, Margaret
Great Broxopp, The 1921,N 16,22:1
Nye, Carrie
Second String, A 1960,Ap 14,36:2
As You Like It 1961,Je 17,13:2
Macbeth 1961,Je 19,31:1
As You Like It 1961,Je 25,II,1:1
Troilus and Cressida 1961,Jl 24,15:1
Ghosts 1961,S 22,29:1
Importance of Being Earnest, The 1963,F 27,5:2
King Lear 1963,Je 10,37:1
Comedy of Errors, The 1963,Je 13,28:1
Caesar and Cleopatra 1963,Ag 1,18:2
Trojan Women, The 1963,D 24,7:6
Half a Sixpence 1965,Ap 26,38:2
Very Rich Woman, A 1965,O 5,5:8
White Devil, The 1965,D 7,56:1
Macbeth 1967,Jl 31,21:1
Home Fires 1969,Ap 8,42:1
Nye, Gene
Too Much Johnson 1964,Ja 16,29:1
Birds, The 1966,Jl 1,40:1
Elizabeth the Queen 1966,N 4,30:1
Trelawny of the 'Wells' 1970,O 12,48:1
Nye, Louis
Inside U S A 1948,My 1,19:2
Touch and Go 1949,O 14,34:2
Flahooley 1951,My 15,39:1
Charley's Aunt 1970,Jl 6,38:1
Nye, Pat
Caesar and Cleopatra 1951,D 20,43:2
Antony and Cleopatra 1951,D 21,22:2
Apple Cart, The 1956,O 19,23:1
Rape of the Belt, The 1960,N 7,46:1
Nye, Richard
Androcles and the Lion 1925,N 24,28:1
Prunella; Love in a Garden 1926,Je 16,23:3
Nye, Sally
If You Get It, Do You Want It? 1938,D 1,28:2
Shakespeare's Merchant 1939 1939,Ja 10,16:3
Nygren, James (Choreographer)
Night in Venice, A 1952,Je 27,18:6
Night in Venice, A 1953,Je 26,15:2
Nygren, James (Director)
Best Foot Forward 1956,Mr 3,16:1
Nyitray, Emil (Playwright)
Broken Branches 1922,Mr 7,11:1
What's Your Wife Doing? 1923,O 2,10:3
Mercenary Mary 1925,Ap 14,27:3
Nylander, Betty
You Said It 1931,Ja 20,21:3
Nyman, Betty Anne
Best Foot Forward 1941,S 12,24:4
Best Foot Forward 1941,O 2,28:2
Annie Get Your Gun 1946,My 17,14:2
Annie Get Your Gun 1946,My 26,II,1:1

Nype, Russell
Regina 1949,N 1,32:2
Great to Be Alive! 1950,Mr 24,28:2
Call Me Madam 1950,O 13,25:1
Call Me Madam 1950,O 22,II,1:1
Regina 1952,Je 2,25:4
Wake Up, Darling 1956,My 3,34:2
Carousel 1957,S 12,38:2
Goldilocks 1958,O 13,33:1
Goldilocks 1958,O 19,II,1:1
Brouhaha 1960,Ap 27,31:2
Brigadoon 1963,F 1,6:2
Once for the Asking 1963,N 21,42:2
My Fair Lady 1964,My 21,43:2
Girl in the Freudian Slip, The 1967,My 19,34:3
Brigadoon 1967,D 14,59:2
Private Lives 1968,My 20,59:1
Hello, Dolly! 1970,Mr 30,52:1
Hello, Dolly! 1970,Ap 12,II,3:7

O

O-Gidayu, Takemoto
Chushingura; Treasury of Loyal Retainers, The 1969,S 11,53:1
Kumagai Jinya 1969,S 18,64:1
Oaker, Jane
Lightnin' 1921,S 11,VI,1:6
Butter and Egg Man, The 1927,Ag 31,19:3
Los Angeles 1927,D 20,32:3
Oakes, Arthur
On the Level 1937,Mr 26,24:4
Oakes, Betty
Of Thee I Sing 1952,My 6,34:2
Of Thee I Sing 1952,My 11,II,1:1
Sandhog 1954,N 24,17:1
Epitaph for George Dillon 1960,D 29,17:1
All American 1962,Mr 20,44:1
Oakes, Gary
On the Town 1959,F 14,15:1
Boys From Syracuse, The 1963,Ap 16,31:1
Shoemaker's Holiday, The 1967,Mr 3,25:1
Oakes, George W Jr
Caesar and Cleopatra 1927,N 6,IX,2:1
Oakland, Ben (Composer)
Ziegfeld Follies 1931,Jl 2,30:5
Hold Your Horses 1933,S 26,26:4
Oakland, Ben (Lyricist)
Hold Your Horses 1933,S 26,26:4
Oakland, Ben (Playwright)
Ziegfeld Follies 1931,Jl 2,30:5
Oakland, Dagmar
Orange Blossoms 1922,S 20,18:1
One Kiss 1923,N 28,14:2
Student Prince, The 1924,D 3,25:3
Pearl of Great Price, The 1926,N 2,34:3
Show Boat 1927,D 28,26:1
Wonder Bar, The 1931,Mr 18,23:4
Oakland, Simon
Skipper Next to God 1948,Ja 5,14:5
Light Up the Sky 1948,N 19,34:2
Caesar and Cleopatra 1949,D 22,28:2
Sands of the Negev 1954,O 20,32:1
Men in White 1955,F 26,13:2
Great Sebastians, The 1956,Ja 5,27:1
Trial of Dmitri Karamazov, The 1958,Ja 28,30:1
Five Evenings 1963,My 10,37:3
Have I Got a Girl for You! 1963,D 3,53:2
Angela 1969,O 31,33:1
Oakland, Vivian
Betty, Be Good 1920,My 5,14:2
Century Revue and the Midnight Rounders, The 1920,Jl 13,9:1
Bombo 1921,O 7,20:2
Vaudeville (Palace) 1927,O 25,33:2
Vaudeville (Palace) 1929,Je 3,27:4
Oakland, Will
All-Star Jamboree 1921,Jl 14,18:1
Spice of 1922 1922,Jl 7,12:4
Vaudeville (Palace) 1932,My 16,19:2
Oakleaf, Gilda
Noble Experiment, The 1930,O 28,21:4
Christopher Comes Across 1932,Je 1,19:2
Daughters of Atreus 1936,O 15,33:1
But for the Grace of God 1937,Ja 13,21:4
Oakley, Barbara
Republic, The 1970,Ap 28,49:1
Oakley, Catherine
What Next 1920,Ja 27,7:2
Oakley, Hal
Poupees de Paris, Les 1964,My 16,11:1
Oakley, Jane
Chinese Nightingale, The 1934,O 6,20:4
Oakley, Roger
Madwoman of Chaillot, The 1970,Mr 23,48:3
Oaks, J Vernon
Flora, the Red Menace 1965,My 12,41:2
Oakwood, Elliott
Paradise 1931,My 12,29:2
Oas-Heim, Gordon
Beaux' Stratagem, The 1957,Jl 9,25:4
Romeo and Juliet 1961,F 24,24:1

Oates, Cicely
Red Blinds 1926,O 1,27:1
Payment Deferred 1931,O 1,24:2
Oates, Joan
Strip Girl 1935,O 21,22:6
Oates, Joyce Carol (Playwright)
Sweet Enemy, The 1965,F 16,39:1
Sunday Dinner 1970,N 3,28:1
Sunday Dinner 1970,N 8,II,1:1
Oates, Simon
Rockefeller and the Red Indians 1968,O 25,37:1
Oates, Warren
Wisteria Trees, The 1955,F 3,20:2
Oates, Whitney (Playwright)
Thesmophoriazusae, The; Goddesses of Athens,
The 1955,D 14,52:4
Obayashi, Kazu (Translator)
Fishing for Wives 1966,Mr 16,50:1
General's Daughter, The 1966,Mr 16,50:1
Greengrocer's Daughter, The 1966,Mr 16,50:1
Obayashi, Toby
Good Woman of Setzuan, The 1970,N 6,51:1
Ober, Dillon
Here's Howe! 1928,My 2,19:3
Ober, Philip
Technique 1931,My 15,21:1
She Loves Me Not 1933,N 21,22:4
Personal Appearance 1934,O 18,26:7
Spring Dance 1936,Jl 7,22:2
Spring Dance 1936,Ag 26,17:4
Without Warning 1937,My 3,23:2
Hill Between, The 1938,Mr 12,12:5
Eye on the Sparrow 1938,My 4,26:3
Kiss the Boys Goodbye 1938,S 29,30:2
Out From Under 1940,My 6,13:2
Mr and Mrs North 1941,Ja 13,11:2
Junior Miss 1941,N 19,28:2
Another Love Story 1943,O 13,29:2
Naked Genius, The 1943,N 7,II,1:6
Doctors Disagree 1943,D 29,15:2
Craig's Wife 1947,F 13,35:2
Craig's Wife 1947,Mr 30,II,1:1
Light Up the Sky 1948,N 19,34:2
Ober, Robert
Humming Bird, The 1923,Ja 16,16:2
Unexpected Husband 1931,Je 3,29:4
Lambs Gambol 1932,Ap 25,18:2
Back Fire 1932,Je 14,26:3
Ann Adams, Spinster 1933,Mr 27,12:4
Katy Did So What? 1935,N 6,32:3
Bat, The 1937,Je 1,27:5
Cat and the Canary, The 1937,Je 15,26:3
Savonarola 1942,Ap 24,20:2
Victory Belles 1943,O 27,26:3
Assassin, The 1945,O 18,20:2
Fundamental George, The 1949,Ag 17,19:4
Ober, Robert (Director)
Brain Sweat 1934,Ap 5,24:4
Yesterday's Orchids 1934,O 6,20:4
Ober, Robert (Playwright)
Ann Adams, Spinster 1933,Mr 27,12:4
Ober, William
If Booth Had Missed 1932,F 5,24:2
Ober-Reich, Robert
Marching Song 1937,F 18,18:2
Oberle, William
Fatal Lady, The 1936,Mr 19,23:7
Oberley, Charlet
Shoemaker's Prodigious Wife, The 1949,Je 15,38:2
Oberlin, James
Henry IV, Part I 1955,S 22,34:2
Oberlin, Richard
Doctor Faustus 1961,Ap 26,36:1
Candida 1961,Ap 27,26:1
Oberlin, Russell
Duchess of Malfi, The 1957,Mr 20,33:1
Merchant of Venice, The 1957,Jl 11,19:5
Much Ado About Nothing 1957,Ag 8,15:2
Play of Daniel, The 1958,Ja 3,15:3
Midsummer Night's Dream, A 1958,Je 23,19:1
Winter's Tale, The 1958,Jl 21,17:4
Play of Daniel, The 1959,Ja 6,30:2
Twelfth Night 1959,Jl 11,10:2
Play of Daniel, The 1959,D 28,17:6
Obermeier, Emma
Doctor Knock 1928,F 24,15:2
Obermeyer, Erna
Trumpet Shall Sound, The 1926,D 11,15:2
Obey, Andre (Playwright)
Wife With a Smile, The 1921,N 29,20:1
Noe 1931,Jl 5,VIII,1:3
Viol de Lucrece, Le 1931,Jl 5,VIII,1:6
Bataille de la Marne 1931,D 20,VIII,2:7
Bataille de la Marne 1932,F 21,VIII,1:8
Lucrece 1932,N 30,22:8
Lucrece 1932,D 4,IX,3:3
Lucrece 1932,D 21,22:2
Lucrece 1933,Ja 1,IX,1:1
Venus et Adonis 1933,Jl 23,IX,1:3
Don Juan 1934,F 27,16:5
Noah 1935,F 14,25:2
Noah 1935,Ag 4,IX,1:3

Noah 1935,D 1,XI,6:4
Trompeur de Seville, Le 1937,My 16,X,2:5
Hoboes in Heaven 1947,O 29,31:4
Noah 1954,O 11,32:2
Obey, Andre (Translator)
Richard III 1933,D 3,IX,7:7
Obileye, Yomi
Madmen and Specialists 1970,Ag 3,38:1
Obolensky, Alexis
Music in the Air 1932,N 9,28:2
Y'Avait un Prisonnier 1938,Ja 25,24:3
Obolensky, Serge (Prince)
Variations of 1940 1940,Ja 29,12:1
Oboler, Arch (Playwright)
Night of the Auk 1956,D 4,50:2
Night of the Auk 1963,My 22,35:2
O'Brady, Hope
Red Mill, The 1945,O 17,16:2
O'Brady, Katey
Something More! 1964,N 11,36:1
O'Brady, Mary
Righteous Are Bold, The 1955,D 23,12:1
Obratsov, Sergei (Director)
Obratsov Russian Pupper Theater in an Unusual
Concert 1963,O 3,28:1
Aladdin and His Wonderful Lamp 1963,O 21,39:1
Obratsov, Sergei (Playwright)
Obratsov Russian Pupper Theater in an Unusual
Concert 1963,O 3,28:1
O'Brennan, J A (Playwright)
Scrap 1931,S 27,VIII,2:8
O'Brian, Hugh
First Love 1961,D 26,20:2
Guys and Dolls 1966,Je 9,55:2
O'Brien, Adale
Doctor Faustus 1961,Ap 26,36:1
Candida 1961,Ap 27,26:1
Cat and the Canary, The 1965,Ja 5,26:1
O'Brien, Bernard
Yeomen of the Guard, The 1941,D 19,34:3
Cox and Box 1942,F 20,20:2
Pirates of Penzance, The 1942,F 20,20:2
O'Brien, Bill
Trouble in July 1949,D 2,36:2
Captain Brassbound's Conversion 1950,D 28,21:1
Glory in the Flower 1959,D 9,57:5
O'Brien, Bill (Miscellaneous)
Family Way, The 1965,Ja 14,44:5
O'Brien, Blanche
Little Jessie James 1923,Ag 16,10:4
My Girl 1924,N 25,27:2
O'Brien, Charles
Frivolities of 1920 1920,Ja 9,22:2
O'Brien, Chester (Choreographer)
Fools Rush In 1934,D 26,19:2
O'Brien, Chester (Miscellaneous)
Fools Rush In 1934,D 26,19:2
Guys and Dolls 1959,Jl 22,22:2
Music Man, The 1965,Je 17,26:4
Carousel 1966,D 16,56:2
O'Brien, Chet
Who's Who 1938,Mr 2,16:2
Rosalie 1957,Je 26,28:2
O'Brien, Chet (Miscellaneous)
Duchess Misbehaves, The 1946,F 14,32:2
Most Happy Fella, The 1959,F 11,50:2
Lute Song 1959,Mr 13,24:1
Show Boat 1961,Ap 13,32:1
Brigadoon 1962,My 31,21:4
Brigadoon 1963,F 1,6:2
Oklahoma! 1965,D 16,62:1
Most Happy Fella, The 1966,My 12,55:1
Wonderful Town 1967,My 18,50:1
O'Brien, Conor Cruise (Playwright)
Murderous Angels 1970,F 8,70:1
Murderous Angels 1970,Mr 15,II,1:4
O'Brien, Dan
Hurricane 1923,D 26,13:4
O'Brien, Daniel
Arms and the Girl 1950,F 3,28:2
O'Brien, David
Tomorrow the World 1944,S 10,II,2:6
Passage to India, A 1962,F 1,23:1
Time for Singing, A 1966,My 23,48:2
King John 1967,Jl 14,19:1
Henry IV, Part I 1968,Je 30,54:7
Henry IV, Part II 1968,Jl 2,33:1
Henry IV, Part II 1968,Jl 14,II,1:1
Boys in the Band, The 1969,F 18,36:1
O'Brien, Edmond
Daughters of Atreus 1936,O 15,33:1
Star-Wagon, The 1937,S 30,18:5
Henry IV, Part I 1939,Ja 31,17:2
Henry IV 1939,F 5,IX,1:1
Leave Her to Heaven 1940,F 28,16:2
Romeo and Juliet 1940,My 10,27:1
Winged Victory 1943,N 22,24:1
I've Got Sixpence 1952,D 3,44:2
I've Got Sixpence 1952,D 7,II,5:1
O'Brien, Edward
Birthday Party, The 1961,My 15,34:6
O'Brien, Eugene
Vaudeville (Palace) 1928,Ap 10,32:4

O'Brien, Eugene V
Sun-Up 1930,My 10,25:1
O'Brien, George
What Price Glory 1949,Mr 3,33:2
O'Brien, Gerald (Miscellaneous)
Glass Cage, The 1957,Mr 11,21:2
Far Country, A 1961,Ap 5,32:1
Everybody Loves Opal 1961,O 12,40:2
Bertha 1962,F 12;27:1
Endgame 1962,F 12,27:1
Month in the Country, A 1963,My 29,39:2
Keep It in the Family 1967,S 28,59:1
Everything in the Garden 1967,N 30,60:1
O'Brien, Geraldine
Gold 1921,Je 2,14:2
Varying Shore, The 1921,D 6,24:1
Faithful Heart, The 1922,O 11,22:1
Tale of the Wolf, The 1925,O 8,31:2
O'Brien, Greg
Seventeen 1951,Je 22,16:6
O'Brien, Gypsy
Happy-Go-Lucky 1920,Ag 25,6:1
Happy-Go-Lucky 1920,Ag 29,VI,1:1
Right to Strike, The 1921,O 25,20:1
East of Suez 1922,S 22,16:3
My Aunt From Ypsilanti 1923,My 2,22:6
Casanova 1923,S 27,10:2
Parasites 1924,N 20,21:1
Morning After, The 1925,Jl 28,24:2
Easy Virtue 1925,D 8,28:2
Beau Gallant 1926,Ap 6,26:3
Ghost Train, The 1926,Ag 26,17:2
O'Brien, Jack (Director)
Cock-A-Doodle Dandy 1969,Ja 21,40:1
O'Brien, Jack (Lyricist)
Pantagleize 1967,D 1,54:1
O'Brien, Jack (Miscellaneous)
War and Peace 1967,Mr 22,42:1
Pantagleize 1967,D 1,54:1
Cherry Orchard, The 1968,Mr 20,41:1
Cocktail Party, The 1968,O 8,42:1
Hamlet 1969,Mr 4,34:1
O'Brien, James
Edgar Allan Poe 1925,O 6,31:1
Great Power, The 1928,S 12,25:1
Othello 1953,O 30,28:2
Hamlet 1954,Ap 24,15:2
O'Brien, Jay (Miscellaneous)
Candida 1957,F 9,14:1
O'Brien, Jean
Son, The 1950,Ag 16,24:6
O'Brien, Jimmy
Vaudeville (Palace) 1928,Ag 28,27:3
O'Brien, Joan
House of Bernarda Alba, The 1963,N 25,23:2
O'Brien, Joan (Composer)
Three Times Three; George Washington Crossing
the Delaware 1962,Mr 2,24:1
O'Brien, Joe
Lamp at Midnight 1947,D 22,29:2
O'Brien, Joe (Director)
Ardele 1958,Ap 9,39:4
Hamlet of Stepney Green 1958,N 14,21:1
O'Brien, Joe (Producer)
Eastward in Eden 1956,Ap 18,25:4
Palm Tree in a Rose Garden, A 1957,N 27,26:2
Ardele 1958,Ap 9,39:4
Hamlet of Stepney Green 1958,N 14,21:1
O'Brien, John
Mr Jiggins of Jigginstown 1936,D 18,30:2
Make Me Disappear 1969,My 14,34:1
O'Brien, John S
Voltaire 1922,Mr 21,17:1
Hamlet 1922,N 17,14:1
O'Brien, Julie
Storm Operation 1944,Ja 12,28:2
O'Brien, Justin (Playwright)
Caligula 1960,F 17,31:1
Caligula 1960,F 28,II,1:1
Condemned of Altona, The 1966,F 4,21:1
O'Brien, Kate (Original Author)
Anteroom, The 1936,Ag 15,6:7
Anteroom, The 1936,S 6,IX,1:1
That Lady 1949,N 23,18:4
That Lady 1949,D 4,II,5:1
O'Brien, Kate (Playwright)
Distinguished Villa, A 1926,Jl 14,19:4
Anteroom, The 1936,Ag 15,6:7
Anteroom, The 1936,S 6,IX,1:1
That Lady 1949,N 23,18:4
That Lady 1949,D 4,II,5:1
O'Brien, Lawrence C
Tired Business Man, The 1929,Je 5,32:5
Love Expert, The 1929,S 24,29:1
Headquarters 1929,S 5,32:4
Merry-Go-Round 1932,Ap 23,11:2
Man Bites Dog 1933,Ap 26,11:2
Is Life Worth Living? 1933,N 10,24:6
Jayhawker 1934,N 6,34:2
Jefferson Davis 1936,F 19,17:2
To What Red Hell 1940,My 5,I,54:8
At the Stroke of Eight 1940,My 21,29:2
Old Foolishness, The 1940,D 21,20:2

O'Brien, Liam (Playwright)
Remarkable Mr Pennypacker, The 1953,D 31,11:2
O'Brien, Lois
Rumple 1957,N 7,42:2
Oklahoma! 1958,Mr 20,32:3
O'Brien, Louise
Oklahoma! 1963,F 28,8:2
Oklahoma! 1963,My 16,40:1
Brigadoon 1964,D 24,9:1
O'Brien, Margaret
Gondoliers, The 1934,S 4,23:1
Iolanthe 1934,S 11,24:3
Child of the Morning 1951,N 17,9:7
O'Brien, Marianne
Johnny 2X4 1942,Mr 17,24:6
O'Brien, Marietta
Topics of 1923 1923,N 21,23:2
Artists and Models 1927,N 16,28:2
O'Brien, Mary
Sweetheart Shop, The 1920,S 1,13:4
Boy Friend, The 1932,Je 8,22:3
O'Brien, Maureen
Merchant of Venice, The 1970,Je 10,39:1
Merchant of Venice, The 1970,Je 21,II,1:1
Cymbeline 1970,Jl 24,17:2
Cymbeline 1970,Ag 23,II,1:6
O'Brien, Michael Miguel
Send Me No Flowers 1960,D 6,54:1
O'Brien, Mort
Who's Who 1938,Mr 2,16:2
O'Brien, Nora
Straw, The 1921,N 11,16:2
O'Brien, Pat
Henry-Behave 1926,Ag 24,19:4
Gertie 1926,N 16,24:2
This Man's Town 1930,Mr 11,24:4
Up and Up, The 1930,S 9,25:2
Up and Up, The 1930,S 14,VIII,1:1
Overture 1930,N 25,31:2
Overture 1930,D 8,26:4
What Price Glory 1949,Mr 3,33:2
Miss Lonelyhearts 1957,O 4,26:2
O'Brien, Paul
War Song, The 1928,S 25,29:3
O'Brien, Raymond
We All Do 1927,Mr 1,30:3
Three Musketeers, The 1928,Mr 14,28:1
Poppa 1928,D 25,31:1
Three Little Girls 1930,Ap 15,29:1
Luana 1930,S 18,28:1
Silent House, The 1932,N 9,28:3
Mad Hopes, The 1932,D 2,26:3
Our Wife 1933,Mr 3,13:2
O'Flynn, The 1934,D 28,24:1
Patience 1935,S 3,24:4
Ghosts 1935,D 13,30:6
O'Brien, Richard
Midsummer Night's Dream, A 1956,Ja 14,12:2
O'Brien, Robert
Hold Everything 1928,O 11,24:2
Two on an Island 1940,Ja 23,17:2
O'Brien, Sean (Lighting Director)
Butter and Egg Man, The 1966,O 18,49:1
O'Brien, Shaun
Polonaise 1945,O 8,20:2
Sleepy Hollow 1948,Je 4,26:3
O'Brien, Sylvia
Every Other Evil 1961,Ja 23,20:2
Moon Shines on Kylenamoe, The 1962,O 31,33:1
Loves of Cass McGuire, The 1966,O 7,36:1
Conduct Unbecoming 1970,O 13,50:1
O'Brien, Timothy (Scenic Designer)
Poor Bitos 1964,N 16,40:2
O'Brien, Vera
O'Brien Girl, The 1921,O 4,10:2
O'Brien, Vince
Leave It to Jane 1959,My 26,30:2
Promises, Promises 1968,D 2,59:3
O'Brien, Virginia
Chocolate Soldier, The 1921,D 13,24:2
Jack and Jill 1923,Mr 23,17:2
Rise of Rosie O'Reilly, The 1923,D 26,13:4
Vaudeville (Palace) 1924,S 16,26:5
Princess Ida 1925,Ap 14,27:2
How's Your Health? 1929,N 27,30:3
Merry Widow, The 1931,S 8,39:1
Merry Widow, The 1932,N 27,IX,1:2
Keep Off the Grass 1940,My 5,X,1:6
Keep Off the Grass 1940,My 24,22:6
O'Brien, W J P
You Can't Win 1926,F 17,12:1
O'Brien, William
J B 1958,Ap 24,37:1
O'Brien-Moore, Erin
Makropoulos Secret, The 1926,Ja 22,12:4
My Country 1926,Ag 10,19:1
Street Scene 1929,Ja 11,20:4
Street Scene 1930,S 10,14:2
Street Scene 1930,S 28,VIII,2:4
Riddle Me This! 1932,F 26,22:5
Men Must Fight 1932,O 15,13:4
Tortilla Flat 1938,Ja 13,16:2
Apology 1943,Mr 23,14:2

O'Brionn, Leon (Translator)
Children of the Moon 1930,My 4,XI,3:1
O'Bryan, James
Medea 1960,Jl 26,25:2
O'Bryne, Patricia
Canteen Show, The 1942,S 4,18:1
O'Byrne, Bryan
Mis-Guided Tour 1959,O 13,44:7
O'Byrne, Robert (Director)
Tread the Green Grass 1950,Ap 21,19:4
O'Byrne, Robert (Producer)
Don't Go Away Mad 1949,My 10,28:2
O'Callaghan, Deirdre
Double Dublin 1963,D 27,16:2
O'Casey, Sean (Original Author)
I Know at the Door 1957,S 30,27:2
Juno 1959,Mr 10,41:1
Juno 1959,Mr 15,II,1:1
Pictures in the Hallway 1959,D 28,19:1
I Knock at the Door 1964,N 26,53:2
Pictures in the Hallway 1964,D 17,51:1
O'Casey, Sean (Playwright)
Juno and the Paycock 1925,N 22,VIII,1:8
Juno and the Paycock 1926,Mr 16,22:1
Juno and the Paycock 1926,Mr 21,VIII,1:1
Plough and the Stars, The 1926,Mr 21,VIII,2:6
Shadow of a Gunman, The 1927,Je 26,VIII,1:3
Plough and the Stars, The 1927,N 29,30:2
Plough and the Stars, The 1927,D 4,X,1:1
Juno and the Paycock 1927,D 20,32:2
Silver Tassie, The 1929,O 25,26:1
Silver Tassie, The 1929,N 3,IX,4:1
Silver Tassie, The 1929,N 10,X,1:1
Juno and the Paycock 1932,O 20,24:3
Shadow of a Gunman, The 1932,O 31,18:1
Within the Gates 1933,D 24,IX,2:2
Within the Gates 1934,F 8,14:4
Within the Gates 1934,F 25,IX,3:7
Within the Gates 1934,O 23,23:1
Within the Gates 1934,O 28,IX,1:1
Plough and the Stars, The 1934,N 13,22:2
Within the Gates; Plough and the Stars, The 1934,N 25,IX,1:1
Silver Tassie, The 1935,Ag 14,16:1
Juno and the Paycock 1937,Ag 29,X,2:1
Plough and the Stars, The 1937,O 8,26:5
Juno and the Paycock 1937,D 7,32:5
Juno and the Paycock 1940,Ja 17,24:2
Juno and the Paycock 1940,Ja 21,IX,1:2
Juno and the Paycock 1940,Ja 28,IX,1:1
Star Turns Red, The 1940,Mr 24,IX,2:5
Life, Laughter And Tears 1942,F 26,15:2
Red Roses for Me 1946,Mr 10,II,2:1
Pound on Demand 1946,D 20,29:3
Silver Tassie, The 1949,Jl 22,16:5
Silver Tassie, The 1949,S 4,II,1:1
Cock-A-Doodle Dandy 1949,D 12,29:4
Cock-A-Doodle Dandy 1950,F 1,26:2
Plough and the Stars, The 1950,Ap 2,II,1:1
Juno and the Paycock 1950,D 31,II,3:7
Red Roses for Me 1951,Ap 26,35:8
Hall of Healing 1952,My 8,35:6
Bedtime Story 1952,My 8,35:6
Time to Go 1952,My 8,35:6
Juno and the Paycock 1955,F 24,20:4
Bishop's Bonfire, The 1955,Mr 1,22:8
Bishop's Bonfire, The 1955,Mr 6,II,3:1
Cock-A-Doodle Dandy 1955,N 4,26:5
Red Roses for Me 1955,D 29,15:2
Red Roses for Me 1956,Ja 8,II,1:1
I Knock at the Door 1956,Mr 19,27:5
Plough and the Stars, The 1956,Ap 6,14:1
Pictures in the Hallway 1956,My 28,23:1
Pictures in the Hallway 1956,S 17,23:2
Pictures in the Hallway 1956,S 23,II,1:1
Purple Dust 1956,D 28,15:1
Purple Dust 1957,Ja 6,II,1:1
Bedtime Story 1957,Ap 1,21:2
Three Love Affairs; Bedtime Story 1958,Mr 11,33:1
Bedtime Story 1958,Mr 16,II,1:1
Cock-A-Doodle Dandy 1958,N 13,39:2
Shadow of a Gunman, The 1958,N 21,26:1
Cock-A-Doodle Dandy 1958,N 23,II,1:1
Shadow of a Gunman, The 1958,N 30,II,1:1
Bedtime Story 1959,Ap 16,28:1
Pound on Demand, A 1959,Ap 16,28:1
Pound on Demand, A 1959,Ap 26,II,1:1
Bedtime Story 1959,Ap 26,II,1:1
Cock-A-Doodle Dandy 1959,S 8,43:5
Time to Go 1960,Mr 23,33:1
Drums Under the Windows 1960,O 14,26:1
Plough and the Stars, The 1960,D 7,56:2
Red Roses for Me 1961,F 11,26:5
Friends and Lovers; End of the Beginning, The 1961,My 11,43:1
Bishop's Bonfire, The 1961,Jl 27,22:2
Red Roses for Me 1961,N 28,41:1
Stars Turn Red, The 1962,O 25,47:1
Figuro in the Night 1962,O 31,33:1
Moon Shines on Kylenamoe, The 1962,O 31,33:1
Juno and the Paycock 1964,My 6,41:1
Juno and the Paycock 1966,Ag 3,40:1
Cock-A-Doodle Dandy 1969,Ja 21,40:1

O'Casey, Sean (Playwright)—Cont
Cock-A-Doodle Dandy 1969,F 2,II,1:1
Silver Tassle, The 1969,S 12,35:2
Ocasio, Jose
Ox Cart, The 1966,D 20,58:1
Plaza Suite; Visitor From Mamaroneck 1968,F 15,49:1
Plaza Suite; Visitor From Hollywood 1968,F 15,49:1
Occent, Yvonne
No Foolin' 1926,Je 25,25:1
O'Cedar
Very Warm for May 1939,N 18,23:2
Ochart, Ray
Shakuntala 1959,S 10,41:2
Ochs, Al
If I Was Rich 1926,S 3,15:2
Lucky 1927,Mr 23,28:3
Take the Air 1927,N 23,28:2
Remote Control 1929,S 11,24:5
Miss Gulliver Travels 1931,N 26,36:4
Warrior's Husband, The 1932,Mr 12,19:4
Swing Your Lady 1936,O 19,22:4
Ochs, Phil (Composer)
Spiro Who? 1969,My 19,55:1
Ocko, Bernard
Jazz a La Carte 1922,Je 3,8:3
Ocko, Daniel
Baby Pompadour 1934,D 28,24:2
First Lady 1935,N 27,17:4
What a Life 1938,Ap 14,26:2
Mrs O'Brien Entertains 1939,F 9,16:3
Horse Fever 1940,N 25,21:2
Cafe Crown 1942,Ja 24,12:5
Trial of Dmitri Karamazov, The 1958,Ja 28,30:1
O'Connell, Arthur
How Long Till Summer 1949,D 28,30:3
Child of the Morning 1951,N 17,9:7
Anna Christie 1952,Ja 10,33:1
Golden Boy 1952,Mr 13,24:3
Picnic 1953,F 20,14:7
Picnic 1953,Mr 1,II,1:1
Lunatics and Lovers 1954,D 14,44:2
Comes a Day 1958,N 7,22:1
Remote Asylum 1970,D 13,II,3:1
O'Connell, Bland
Magnolia Lady, The 1924,N 26,17:2
O'Connell, Burke
Not in Our Stars 1941,Ap 26,20:5
O'Connell, Eileen
Shadow and Substance 1956,Mr 14,38:1
O'Connell, Hazel
Chameleon, The 1932,Jl 19,20:4
Her Tin Soldier 1933,Ap 7,22:6
Locked Room, The 1933,D 26,18:5
Mr Jiggins of Jigginstown 1936,D 18,30:2
O'Connell, Hugh
Face Value 1921,D 27,10:2
Zeno 1923,Ag 27,14:2
Cousin Sonia 1925,D 8,28:3
Wisdom Tooth, The 1926,F 16,22:2
Sure Fire! 1926,O 21,23:1
Ballyhoo 1927,Ja 5,18:1
Fog 1927,F 8,20:1
Racket, The 1927,N 23,28:3
Racket, The 1927,D 18,IX,1:1
Gentlemen of the Press 1928,Ag 28,27:2
Gentlemen of the Press 1928,S 2,VII,1:1
Week-end 1929,O 23,26:4
So Was Napoleon 1930,Ja 9,22:2
Once in a Lifetime 1930,S 7,IX,2:4
Once in a Lifetime 1930,S 25,22:3
Once in a Lifetime 1930,D 7,IX,1:1
Face the Music 1932,F 4,25:4
Face the Music 1932,F 18,24:5
Saturday Night 1933,Mr 1,13:2
Saturday Night 1933,Mr 19,IX,1:1
Lambs Gambol 1933,Ap 24,10:1
Milky Way, The 1934,My 9,23:2
Milky Way, The 1934,My 20,IX,1:1
Ziegfeld Follies 1935,D 31,10:1
Ziegfeld Follies 1936,Ja 5,IX,3:1
Ziegfeld Follies 1936,Ja 31,17:2
Spring Tonic 1936,My 11,16:1
Run Sheep Run 1938,N 4,26:2
Off the Record 1940,D 1,63:5
O'Connell, James
Matty and the Moron and Madonna 1965,Mr 30,53:1
O'Connell, James (Miscellaneous)
Whistle in the Dark, A 1969,O 9,55:1
O'Connell, Jeremiah
Twisting Road, The; Jewel of the South, The 1957,N 18,36:5
Brothers Karamazov, The 1957,D 9,39:4
O'Connell, Jeremiah (Miscellaneous)
Zoo Story, The 1960,Ja 15,37:2
Krapp's Last Tape 1960,Ja 15,37:2
O'Connell, Kathleen
Low Bridge 1933,F 10,13:4
O'Connell, Margaret
Jayhawker 1934,N 6,34:2
O'Connell, Milton V
You'll Never Know 1921,Ap 21,9:2

'onnell, Patricia
rpheus in Hades 1930,D 16,30:1
ledermaus, Die 1933,My 14,II,3:8
aintliness of Margery Kempe, The 1959,F 3,35:6
tephen D 1966,Ag 5,17:1
Irs Snow 1970,Ja 6,48:3
riss-Crossing 1970,Ja 22,30:1
'onnell, Quinn
rom Morn Till Midnight 1948,D 7,41:6
'onnell, Richard (Miscellaneous)
eronica's Veil 1950,F 12,II,1:5
'onnell, Richard L (Translator)
lood Wedding 1949,F 7,16:2
Iouse of Bernarda Alba, The 1951,Ja 8,14:6
erma 1952,F 8,18:4
llood Wedding 1958,Ap 1,35:1
f Five Years Pass 1962,My 11,37:1
Iouse of Bernarda Alba, The 1963,N 25,23:2
Conner, Gertrude
Jp in the Clouds 1922,Ja 3,20:3
Connor, Adeline
Cradle Song 1921,Mr 1,18:2
Connor, Agnes
Marry the Poor Girl 1920,S 27,18:3
Connor, Aideen
*lough and the Stars, The 1934,N 13,22:2
Drama at Inish 1934,N 15,24:2
Look at the Heffernans 1934,N 17,13:2
Church Street 1934,N 20,24:5
Well of the Saints, The 1934,N 22,26:2
*ar-Off Hills, The 1937,O 12,30:4
Playboy of the Western World, The 1937,N 22,14:5
New Gossoon, The 1937,N 30,26:2
Juno and the Paycock 1937,D 7,32:5
Drama at Inish 1937,D 14,33:2
Spring Meeting 1938,D 9,30:4
Kindred 1939,D 27,17:2
Juno and the Paycock 1940,Ja 17,24:2
Tanyard Street 1941,F 5,16:2
Connor, Anna (Mrs)
Marry the Poor Girl 1920,S 27,18:3
'Connor, Arthur (Director)
Brighten the Corner 1945,D 13,33:2
'Connor, Ayn (Ayn Rand)
Night of January 16 1935,S 17,26:4
'Connor, Bob
Artists and Models 1923,Ag 21,12:2
'Connor, Carroll
Ulysses in Nighttown 1958,Je 6,30:1
Big Knife, The 1959,N 13,25:1
Heartbreak House 1963,Je 8,14:2
Heartbreak House 1963,Je 28,24:1
'Connor, Charles F
Kosher Kitty Kelly 1925,Je 16,24:2
Racket, The 1927,N 23,28:3
Man on Stilts, The 1931,S 10,23:2
Queer People 1934,F 16,16:2
Farmer Takes a Wife, The 1934,O 31,17:1
St Helena 1936,O 7,32:1
Father Malachy's Miracle 1937,N 18,26:4
I Gotta Get Out 1947,S 26,27:2
'Connor, Colleen (Miscellaneous)
Sophie 1963,Ap 16,32:1
'Connor, Consuelo
Miracle in the Mountains 1947,Ap 26,10:2
'Connor, Eavan
Scarecrow, The 1953,Je 17,31:1
'Connor, Edward
Rising of the Moon, The 1920,Je 22,9:1
Minute's Wait, A 1920,Je 22,9:1
Guest of Honor, The 1920,S 21,12:1
Sally, Irene and Mary 1922,S 5,21:2
My Country 1926,Ag 10,19:1
Ten Per Cent 1927,S 14,29:3
Street Wolf, The 1929,Ja 1,61:1
Silver Tassie, The 1929,O 25,26:1
'Connor, Edwin (Playwright)
I Was Dancing 1964,N 9,40:4
'Connor, Eugene B
Fiesta 1933,D 16,12:2
'Connor, Flannery (Playwright)
Displaced Person, The 1966,D 30,15:1
'Connor, Frank
Unconquered, The 1940,F 14,25:2
'Connor, Frank (Original Author)
In the Train 1937,N 22,14:5
Guests of the Nation 1958,My 21,40:1
Guests of the Nation 1958,Je 27,18:5
Guests of the Nation 1958,Ag 31,II,1:1
Bridal Night, The 1966,N 8,45:1
Frying Pan, The 1966,N 8,45:1
Eternal Triangle 1966,N 8,45:1
O'Connor, Frank (Playwright)
When I Was a Child 1960,D 9,38:1
O'Connor, Gloria
Miracle in the Mountains 1947,Ap 26,10:2
O'Connor, Helen
Cyrano de Bergerac 1932,D 27,11:2
O'Connor, Iris (Miscellaneous)
Whispers in the Wind 1970,Je 4,50:1
Gandhi 1970,O 21,37:1
O'Connor, Jack
Comforter, The 1964,O 22,42:1

O'Connor, John
Moon in the Yellow River, The 1932,Mr 1,19:3
Caesar and Cleopatra 1935,Ag 22,21:1
Kind Lady 1937,Jl 6,23:1
Pride and Prejudice 1937,Ag 3,20:5
Idiot's Delight 1937,Ag 10,22:7
Worse Things Happen at Sea 1937,S 1,15:3
Madame Bovary 1937,N 17,26:2
If I Were You 1938,Ja 25,24:2
Mamba's Daughters 1940,Mr 25,10:4
Harriet 1944,S 28,26:1
He Who Gets Slapped 1946,Mr 21,31:4
Cyrano de Bergerac 1946,O 9,33:2
Cyrano de Bergerac 1947,Ja 17,27:2
Eastward in Eden 1947,N 19,33:2
Young Provincials, The 1958,S 19,22:4
O'Connor, Jonathan
Seven Mirrors 1945,O 26,17:2
O'Connor, Kathleen
Hostage, The 1960,S 21,42:1
O'Connor, Kevin
Up to Thursday 1965,F 11,45:1
Thank You, Miss Victoria 1966,Ap 12,43:1
This Is the Rill Speaking 1966,Ap 12,43:1
Birdbath 1966,Ap 12,43:1
War 1966,Ap 13,36:1
Chicago 1966,Ap 13,36:1
Rimers of Eldritch, The 1967,F 21,53:1
Times Square 1968,Ja 27,16:3
Tom Paine 1968,Mr 26,38:1
Boy on the Straight-Back Chair 1969,Mr 18,36:1
Gloria and Esperanza 1970,F 5,32:1
Dear Janet Rosenberg, Dear Mr Kooning
   1970,Ap 6,46:1
Dear Janet Rosenberg, Dear Mr Kooning
   1970,Ap 26,II,5:7
O'Connor, Kitty
Paddy the Next Best Thing 1920,Ag 28,5:5
Take the Air 1927,N 23,28:2
O'Connor, Larry (Playwright)
Roman Servant, A 1934,D 3,14:5
O'Connor, Norman
Caution: A Love Story 1969,Ap 4,45:1
O'Connor, Patricia
Kiss in a Taxi, The 1925,Ag 26,14:1
Potash and Perlmutter, Detectives; Poisoned by
   Pictures 1926,S 1,27:3
She Lived Next to the Firehouse 1931,F 11,23:1
O'Connor, Patrick
Corn Is Green, The 1943,My 4,18:3
Ten Little Indians 1944,Je 28,21:2
O'Connor, Peggy
Street Wolf, The 1929,Ja 1,61:1
Girl Crazy 1930,O 15,27:1
There You Are! 1932,My 17,25:4
Young and Fair, The 1948,N 23,35:2
O'Connor, Raymond
Marry the Poor Girl 1920,S 27,18:3
O'Connor, Richard
Barber Had Two Sons, The 1943,F 2,22:2
O'Connor, Rita
Most Happy Fella, The 1966,My 12,55:1
Guys and Dolls 1966,Je 9,55:2
Show Boat 1966,Jl 20,48:1
Cabaret 1966,N 21,62:1
Promises, Promises 1968,D 2,59:3
Coco 1969,D 19,66:1
O'Connor, Robert
My Golden Girl 1920,F 3,18:2
Deluge, The 1922,Ja 28,14:2
Blushing Bride, The 1922,F 7,12:1
Old Soak, The 1922,Ag 23,14:5
Glory 1922,D 26,10:1
New Toys 1924,F 19,12:1
Ladies of the Evening 1924,D 24,11:2
City Chap, The 1925,O 27,21:1
Circus Princess, The 1927,Ap 26,32:2
Prince of Pilsen, The 1930,Ja 14,24:3
Blossom Time 1931,Mr 5,32:1
All the King's Horses 1934,Ja 31,21:3
O'Connor, Sean
Tom Paine 1969,Mr 30,71:2
O'Connor, Tim
Macbeth 1955,O 20,42:2
Romeo and Juliet 1956,F 24,20:4
Hamlet 1956,O 29,34:1
Obbligato 1958,F 19,22:2
Guests of the Nation 1958,Je 27,18:5
First Love 1961,D 26,20:2
General Seeger 1962,Mr 1,26:2
Emperor, The 1963,Ap 17,30:1
Tonight in Living Color; Golden Fleece, The
   1969,Je 11,43:1
O'Connor, Timothy
Good Times 1920,Ag 10,10:1
O'Connor, Tom
Minstrel Boy, The 1948,O 15,28:2
O'Connor, Una
Fake, The 1924,O 7,26:3
Autumn Fire 1926,O 27,25:3
Chance Acquaintance 1927,N 27,IX,4:1
Ryan Girl, The 1945,S 25,28:2
Linden Tree, The 1948,Mr 3,28:2

O'Connor, Una—Cont
Shop at Sly Corner, The 1949,Ja 19,35:2
Enchanted, The 1950,Ja 19,34:2
Child of the Morning 1951,N 17,9:7
Starcross Story, The 1954,Ja 14,25:2
Witness for the Prosecution 1954,D 17,35:2
Witness for the Prosecution 1954,D 26,II,1:1
O'Connor, Vince
Hostage, The 1961,D 13,55:4
O'Conor, Joseph
Hamlet 1958,D 17,2:7
Henry V 1958,D 26,2:7
O'Daniels, Barrie
Three Men and a Woman 1932,Ja 12,29:2
Walk With Music 1940,Je 5,33:2
O'Daniels, Barrie (Director)
Night of Love 1941,Ja 8,14:2
O'Daniels, Mark
For Love or Money 1947,N 5,36:2
Auntie Mame 1958,Ag 12,33:2
O'Dare, Eileen
Hell'z-A-Splashin' 1959,Je 25,22:2
O'Dare, Tewks
Philadelphia 1929,S 17,34:5
O'Day, Eileen
Family Upstairs, The 1933,O 28,20:6
O'Day, Nell
Fine and Dandy 1930,S 7,IX,2:4
Fine and Dandy 1930,S 24,26:1
Many Mansions 1937,O 28,28:6
One for the Money 1939,F 6,9:2
Many Happy Returns 1945,Ja 6,15:5
Oddie, Bill
Cambridge Circus 1964,O 7,53:1
New Cambridge Circus, The 1965,Ja 15,22:2
Oddie, Bill (Composer)
Cambridge Circus 1964,O 7,53:1
Oddie, Bill (Playwright)
New Cambridge Circus, The 1965,Ja 15,22:2
O'Dea, Anthony
Ballyhoo 1930,D 23,24:1
O'Dea, Denis
Things That Are Caesar's, The 1932,O 18,23:4
Juno and the Paycock 1932,O 20,24:3
Rising of the Moon, The 1932,O 21,25:1
New Gossoon, The 1932,O 22,18:2
Cathleen ni Houlihan 1932,O 31,18:1
Shadow of a Gunman, The 1932,O 31,18:1
Crabbed Youth and Age 1932,N 4,25:1
Birthright 1932,N 4,25:1
Autumn Fire 1932,D 29,16:3
Big House, The 1933,Ja 5,19:3
King Oedipus 1933,Ja 16,12:4
Bridgehead 1934,Je 20,24:1
Plough and the Stars, The 1934,N 13,22:2
Drama at Inish 1934,N 15,24:2
Look at the Heffernans 1934,N 17,13:2
Resurrection 1934,N 20,24:5
Church Street 1934,N 20,24:5
Well of the Saints, The 1934,N 22,26:2
Coiner, The 1934,N 22,26:2
Bridgehead 1935,Ag 7,22:3
Puritan, The 1936,Ja 24,14:3
Green Waters 1936,N 5,34:4
Katie Roche 1937,O 4,17:4
In the Train 1937,N 22,14:5
Playboy of the Western World, The 1937,N 22,14:5
New Gossoon, The 1937,N 30,26:2
Juno and the Paycock 1937,D 7,32:5
Drama at Inish 1937,D 14,33:2
Marks and Mabel 1945,S 9,II,1:4
Righteous Are Bold, The 1955,D 23,12:1
O'Dea, John (Playwright)
Where E'er We Go 1943,Je 15,16:1
Where E'er We Go 1943,Je 20,II,1:1
O'Dea, June
Queen High 1926,S 9,21:2
Here's Howe! 1928,My 2,19:3
Billie 1928,O 2,34:2
Jonica 1930,Mr 30,VIII,2:7
Jonica 1930,Ap 8,27:1
Of Thee I Sing 1931,D 28,20:1
O'Dea, Sunnie
Ballyhoo of 1932 1932,S 7,14:2
Sketch Book 1935,Je 5,22:2
Keep Off the Grass 1940,My 5,X,1:6
Keep Off the Grass 1940,My 24,22:6
Let's Face It 1941,O 30,26:2
Lunchtime Follies, The 1942,Je 23,22:3
Wallflower 1944,Ja 27,14:2
Good Night Ladies 1945,Ja 18,16:2
Odegaard, Myron (Lighting Director)
Cage, The 1961,Mr 6,30:1
417 1961,Mr 6,30:1
Odegaard, Myron (Miscellaneous)
417 1961,Mr 6,30:1
Cage, The 1961,Mr 6,30:1
God, Man & You, Baby! 1963,O 30,47:1
Odegaard, Myron (Scenic Designer)
God, Man & You, Baby! 1963,O 30,47:1
Odell, Donald Edwards
Pigeon, The 1930,O 15,26:2

Odell, George
Little Theatre Tournament; Monkey's Paw, The 1929,My 10,32:2
Odell, Helen
Skylark 1921,Jl 26,10:6
O'Dell, Janice
Valmouth 1960,O 7,29:1
O'Dell, Larry
Mikado, The 1944,F 12,11:3
Polonaise 1945,O 8,20:2
Odell, Maude
Sally, Irene and Mary 1922,S 5,21:2
Dream Girl, The 1924,Ag 21,12:2
Princess Flavia 1925,N 3,34:3
Lady Do 1927,Ap 19,24:2
Little Orchard Annie 1930,Ap 22,33:1
Purity 1930,D 26,18:2
Child of Manhattan 1932,Mr 2,15:1
Her Tin Soldier 1933,Ap 7,22:6
Tobacco Road 1933,D 5,31:2
O'Dempsey, Phillip
Purple Dust 1956,D 28,15:1
O'Denishawn, Florence
Hitchy-Koo, 1920 1920,O 20,11:3
Ziegfeld Follies 1921,Je 22,10:1
Rose Briar 1922,D 26,11:3
Music Box Revue 1923,S 24,5:3
Love Spell, The 1925,N 25,14:2
Honeymoon Lane 1926,S 21,32:3
Odets, Clifford
Midnight 1930,D 30,25:1
House of Connelly, The 1931,S 29,22:4
1931 1931,D 11,34:3
Night Over Taos 1932,Mr 10,25:3
Big Night 1933,Ja 18,16:2
They All Come to Moscow 1933,My 12,20:6
Men in White 1933,S 27,24:2
Gold Eagle Guy 1934,N 29,33:4
Waiting for Lefty 1935,F 11,14:5
Waiting for Lefty 1935,Mr 27,24:5
Odets, Clifford (Director)
Waiting for Lefty 1935,F 11,14:5
Country Girl, The 1950,N 11,10:6
Golden Boy 1952,Mr 13,24:3
Flowering Peach, The 1954,D 29,19:2
Odets, Clifford (Original Author)
Golden Boy 1964,O 21,56:1
Two by Two 1970,N 11,37:1
Two by Two 1970,N 22,II,1:1
Odets, Clifford (Playwright)
Waiting for Lefty 1935,F 11,14:5
Group Theatre Sketches 1935,F 11,14:5
Awake and Sing! 1935,F 20,23:2
Awake and Sing! 1935,Mr 10,VIII,1:1
Till the Day I Die 1935,Mr 27,24:5
Waiting for Lefty 1935,Mr 27,24:5
Paradise Lost 1935,D 10,31:5
Paradise Lost 1935,D 29,IX,1:1
Golden Boy 1937,N 5,18:5
Golden Boy 1937,N 21,XI,1:1
Golden Boy 1938,Ja 23,XI,1:6
Awake and Sing! 1938,F 21,15:1
Golden Boy 1938,Je 22,27:5
Golden Boy 1938,Jl 10,IX,1:5
Rocket to the Moon 1938,N 25,18:2
Rocket to the Moon 1938,D 4,X,5:1
Awake and Sing! 1938,D 23,16:6
Paradise Lost 1939,Ja 8,IX,1:4
Awake and Sing! 1939,Mr 8,18:2
Awake and Sing! 1939,Mr 26,X,1:2
Night Music 1940,F 23,18:2
Night Music 1940,Mr 3,X,1:1
Clash by Night 1941,D 29,20:2
Clash by Night 1942,Ja 11,IX,1:1
Russian People, The 1942,D 16,21:3
Russian People, The 1942,D 30,17:2
Rocket to the Moon 1948,Mr 23,30:4
Rocket to the Moon 1948,Ap 11,II,3:1
Big Knife, The 1949,F 25,27:5
Big Knife, The 1949,Mr 6,II,1:1
Country Girl, The 1950,N 11,10:6
Country Girl, The 1950,N 19,II,1:1
Night Music 1951,Ap 9,29:6
Golden Boy 1952,Mr 13,24:3
Golden Boy 1952,Mr 23,II,1:1
Winter Journey; Country Girl, The 1952,Ap 4,21:1
Winter Journey; Country Girl, The 1952,Ap 13,II,3:7
Big Knife, The 1954,Ja 3,I,64:4
Big Knife, The 1954,Ja 17,II,4:4
Flowering Peach, The 1954,D 29,19:2
Flowering Peach, The 1955,Ja 9,II,1:1
Big Knife, The 1959,N 13,25:1
Golden Boy 1964,O 21,56:1
Golden Boy 1964,N 1,II,1:1
Country Girl, The 1966,S 30,55:1
Waiting for Lefty 1967,D 19,58:2
Winter Journey 1968,Mr 13,39:1
Awake and Sing! 1970,My 28,35:1
Awake and Sing! 1970,Je 7,II,1:1
Awake and Sing! 1970,Jl 5,II,1:2
Odets, Clifford (Producer)
Awake and Sing! 1942,My 31,VIII,2:3

Odets, Florence
Night Music 1940,F 23,18:2
Odinor, Shirley
Champion, The 1925,Ap 24,16:4
Odiva
Vaudeville (Hippodrome) 1926,Ap 20,24:6
Odlin, Richard
Circle of Chalk, The 1941,Mr 27,28:4
Everyman 1941,My 9,19:2
Any Day Now 1941,Je 10,28:2
O'Doherty, Mignon
Secrets 1922,D 26,11:1
Fanshastics 1924,Ja 21,17:3
Carnaval 1924,D 30,15:1
O'Doherty, Molly
Great Temptations, The 1926,My 19,29:1
White Lights 1927,O 12,30:4
Odone, Ardelle
Son, The 1950,Ag 16,24:6
O'Donnell, Alice
Count of Luxembourg, The 1930,F 18,28:2
O'Donnell, Anne
Greenwillow 1970,D 8,60:1
O'Donnell, C H
When in Rome 1929,Je 16,VIII,2:1
O'Donnell, Charles
Town's Woman, The 1929,Mr 12,26:2
O'Donnell, E P (Original Author)
Great Big Doorstep, The 1942,N 27,26:2
O'Donnell, Gene
Another Part of the Forest 1946,N 21,42:2
Our Lan' 1947,S 29,16:5
Point of No Return 1951,D 14,35:2
O'Donnell, George
Sitting Pretty 1924,Ap 9,24:2
O'Donnell, Gerald
Clouds of the Sun 1922,My 6,11:2
O'Donnell, Helen
Veils 1928,Mr 14,28:5
Bedfellows 1929,Jl 3,19:2
O'Donnell, Jack
Becky Sharp 1929,Je 4,29:1
Little Father of the Wilderness, The 1930,Je 3,27:1
O'Donnell, Jack (Original Author)
So Was Napoleon 1930,Ja 9,22:2
O'Donnell, Jack (Playwright)
So Was Napoleon 1930,Ja 9,22:2
O'Donnell, James
Joan of Arc-The Warrior Maid 1931,N 9,21:6
Veronica's Veil 1933,F 20,11:7
O'Donnell, Judson (Playwright)
What Big Ears! 1942,Ap 21,18:5
O'Donnell, Judson (Producer)
Untitled-One Woman Show 1938,O 31,12:2
O'Donnell, Lillian
Priorities of 1942 1942,Mr 13,23:2
O'Donnell, Maire
Righteous Are Bold, The 1946,O 27,II,1:3
Juno and the Paycock 1964,My 6,41:1
O'Donnell, Margaret
Low Bridge 1933,F 10,13:4
Hook-Up, The 1935,My 9,24:6
Wild Justice 1935,Jl 9,24:3
O'Donnell, May (Choreographer)
Pelleas and Melisande 1957,F 20,38:1
O'Donnell, Peggy
Whatever Goes Up 1935,N 26,28:2
Spring Dance 1936,Jl 7,22:2
Spring Dance 1936,Ag 26,17:4
Tide Rising 1937,Ja 26,17:2
On Borrowed Time 1938,F 4,16:4
O'Donnell, Richard
Little Theatre Tournament; White Peacock, The 1928,My 11,28:1
O'Donnell, Shirley
Commedia Dell' Arte 1957,Jl 5,13:2
O'Donnell and Blair
Ziegfeld Follies 1921,Je 22,10:1
Puzzles of 1925 1925,F 3,25:3
O'Donovan, Desmond
Moon in the Yellow River, The 1932,Mr 1,19:3
O'Donovan, Desmond (Director)
Royal Hunt of the Sun, The 1964,Jl 8,40:6
O'Donovan, Robert
Brother Rat 1936,D 17,34:5
O'Dowd, Michael
Deadly Game, The 1966,F 14,34:1
Odry
Siberia 1928,Ap 15,IX,4:1
O'Duel, Merritt
Corn Is Green, The 1940,N 27,27:2
O'Dwyer, Fred
Mr Big 1941,O 1,24:2
Oehler, Gretchen
Mira 1970,Je 3,51:1
Oehlschlaeger, Anne
Dracula Sabbat 1970,O 2,28:2
Oelbaum, Jack
Thomas Paine 1930,Mr 21,30:7
Oelkers, Edmund
Ten Nights in a Barroom 1928,Mr 28,31:2
Oenslager, Donald (Costume Designer)
Pinwheel 1927,F 4,16:4

Oenslager, Donald (Costume Designer)—Cont
Pinwheel 1927,F 13,VII,1:1
Uncle Tom's Cabin 1933,My 30,13:4
Eastward in Eden 1947,N 19,33:2
Life With Mother 1948,O 21,32:2
Life With Mother 1949,Mr 27,II,1:1
Paris '90 1952,Mr 5,33:2
Oenslager, Donald (Lighting Director)
On Whitman Avenue 1946,My 9,28:2
Park Avenue 1946,N 5,31:2
Fatal Witness, The 1946,N 20,43:2
Lovely Me 1946,D 26,30:4
Portrait in Black 1947,My 15,30:2
How I Wonder 1947,O 1,34:2
Angel in the Wings 1947,D 12,36:4
Men We Marry, The 1948,Ja 17,11:2
Town House 1948,S 24,31:2
Leading Lady 1948,O 19,33:1
Goodbye My Fancy 1948,N 18,35:2
Smile of the World, The 1949,Ja 13,26:5
Father, The 1949,N 17,36:2
Rat Race, The 1949,D 23,16:2
Liar, The 1950,My 19,30:2
Live Wire, The 1950,Ag 18,16:2
Second Threshold 1951,Ja 3,23:2
Peer Gynt 1951,Ja 29,15:2
Candida 1952,Ap 23,23:6
Horses in Midstream 1953,Ap 3,18:7
Sabrina Fair 1953,N 12,37:1
Dear Charles 1954,S 16,37:2
Wooden Dish, The 1955,O 7,20:1
Roomful of Roses, A 1955,O 18,48:1
Janus 1955,N 25,37:2
Major Barbara 1956,O 31,27:1
Mary Stuart 1957,O 9,39:1
Nature's Way 1957,O 17,42:2
Shadow of My Enemy, A 1957,D 12,35:4
Girls in 509, The 1958,O 16,47:1
Pleasure of His Company, The 1958,O 23,36:1
Marriage-Go-Round, The 1958,O 30,37:1
Man in the Dog Suit, The 1958,O 31,34:2
Majority of One, A 1959,F 17,28:2
Highest Tree, The 1959,N 5,41:1
Far Country, A 1961,Ap 5,32:1
Call on Kuprin, A 1961,My 26,29:3
Blood, Sweat & Stanley Poole 1961,O 6,31:1
First Love 1961,D 26,20:2
Venus at Large 1962,Ap 13,30:1
Irregular Verb to Love, The 1963,S 19,22:2
Case of Libel, A 1963,O 11,43:2
One by One 1964,D 2,60:1
Love in E Flat 1967,F 14,38:1
Spofford 1967,D 15,54:3
Avanti 1968,F 1,29:1
Wrong Way Light Bulb, The 1969,Mr 5,40:1
Oenslager, Donald (Producer)
Horses in Midstream 1953,Ap 3,18:7
Oenslager, Donald (Scenic Designer)
Bit o' Love, A 1925,My 13,24:2
Morals 1925,D 1,22:2
Pinwheel 1927,F 4,16:4
Pinwheel 1927,F 13,VII,1:1
Good News 1927,S 7,35:4
Anna 1928,My 17,25:2
New Moon, The 1928,S 20,33:1
Follow Thru 1929,Ja 10,24:3
Stepping Out 1929,My 21,29:1
Heads Up! 1929,N 12,34:1
Girl Crazy 1930,O 15,27:1
Overture 1930,D 8,26:4
You Said It 1931,Ja 20,21:3
America's Sweetheart 1931,Ja 25,VIII,2:4
Rock Me, Julie 1931,F 4,21:1
America's Sweetheart 1931,F 11,23:1
Free for All 1931,S 9,25:1
Singin' the Blues 1931,S 17,21:3
East Wind 1931,O 28,19:1
East Wind 1931,D 11,VIII,4:3
Whistling in the Dark 1932,Ja 20,16:6
Adam Had Two Sons 1932,Ja 21,17:1
Thousand Summers, A 1932,My 25,23:4
King's Coat, The 1933,Ja 12,21:4
Forsaking All Others 1933,Mr 2,21:2
Uncle Tom's Cabin 1933,My 30,13:4
Keeper of the Keys 1933,O 19,23:2
Jezebel 1933,D 20,26:3
Lady From the Sea, The 1934,My 2,25:2
Divided by Three 1934,O 3,24:2
Dance With Your Gods 1934,O 8,14:3
Farmer Takes a Wife, The 1934,O 31,17:1
Farmer Takes a Wife, The 1934,N 11,IX,1:1
Gold Eagle Guy 1934,N 18,IX,1:7
Anything Goes 1934,N 18,IX,1:1
Anything Goes 1934,N 22,26:1
Gold Eagle Guy 1934,N 29,33:4
Gold Eagle Guy 1934,D 9,X,1:1
Something Gay 1935,Ap 30,12:2
Sweet Mystery of Life 1935,O 12,13:3
First Lady 1935,N 27,17:4
Tapestry in Gray 1935,D 28,10:2
Russet Mantle 1936,Ja 17,15:5
Timber House 1936,S 21,27:5
Stage Door 1936,S 29,35:1
Stage Door 1936,O 23,26:3

Oenslager, Donald (Scenic Designer)—Cont

Ten Million Ghosts 1936,O 24,23:7
Sweet River 1936,O 29,30:2
Red, Hot and Blue! 1936,O 30,26:3
Matrimony, PFD 1936,N 13,26:3
Johnny Johnson 1936,N 20,26:3
200 Were Chosen 1936,N 21,21:1
You Can't Take It With You 1936,D 1,30:8
You Can't Take It With You 1936,D 6,XII,6:2
You Can't Take It With You 1936,D 15,31:1
Miss Quis 1937,Ap 8,20:5
Of Mice and Men 1937,D 12,XI,3:1
Good, The 1938,O 6,27:2
Fabulous Invalid, The 1938,O 10,15:1
Woman's a Fool-To Be Clever, A 1938,O 19,18:6
American Way, The 1939,Ja 23,9:2
Off to Buffalo! 1939,F 22,18:2
From Vienna 1939,Je 21,26:2
Skylark 1939,O 12,32:2
Margin for Error 1939,O 15,48:7
Man Who Came to Dinner, The 1939,O 17,31:1
Margin for Error 1939,N 4,11:3
I Know What I Like 1939,N 25,13:5
Young Couple Wanted 1940,Ja 25,16:2
Man Who Came to Dinner, The 1940,F 10,19:5
Beverly Hills 1940,N 8,24:2
Retreat to Pleasure 1940,D 18,32:2
Old Foolishness, The 1940,D 21,20:2
My Sister Eileen 1940,D 27,23:2
Lady Who Came to Stay, The 1941,Ja 3,13:2
Claudia 1941,F 13,24:2
Doctor's Dilemma, The 1941,Mr 12,18:2
Mr Big 1941,O 1,24:2
Spring Again 1941,N 11,28:2
Theatre 1941,N 13,34:2
Pie in the Sky 1941,D 23,26:5
Rose Burke 1942,Ja 25,IX,2:5
Flowers of Virtue, The 1942,F 6,22:2
Hairpin Harmony 1943,O 2,18:5
Pygmalion 1945,D 27,16:1
Born Yesterday 1946,F 5,18:2
Three to Make Ready 1946,Mr 8,16:2
On Whitman Avenue 1946,My 9,28:2
Loco 1946,O 17,29:2
Present Laughter 1946,O 30,31:2
Park Avenue 1946,N 5,31:2
Fatal Witness, The 1946,N 20,43:2
Years Ago 1946,D 4,44:2
Land's End 1946,D 12,37:5
Lovely Me 1946,D 26,30:4
Eagle Has Two Heads, The 1947,Mr 20,39:2
Message for Margaret 1947,Mr 17,34:2
Portrait in Black 1947,My 15,30:2
How I Wonder 1947,O 1,34:2
Eastward in Eden 1947,N 19,33:2
Angel in the Wings 1947,D 12,36:4
Men We Marry, The 1948,Ja 17,11:2
Life With Mother 1948,Je 9,36:3
Leading Lady 1948,S 15,38:1
Town House 1948,S 24,31:2
Leading Lady 1948,O 19,33:1
Life With Mother 1948,O 21,32:2
Life With Mother 1948,O 31,II,1:1
Goodbye My Fancy 1948,N 18,35:2
Smile of the World, The 1949,Ja 13,26:5
At War With the Army 1949,Mr 9,32:2
Life With Mother 1949,Mr 27,II,1:1
Father, The 1949,N 17,36:2
Rat Race, The 1949,D 23,16:2
Velvet Glove, The 1949,D 27,26:2
Liar, The 1950,My 19,30:2
Live Wire, The 1950,Ag 18,16:2
Second Threshold 1951,Ja 3,23:2
Second Threshold 1951,Ja 14,II,1:1
Peer Gynt 1951,Ja 29,15:2
Small Hours, The 1951,F 16,22:1
Constant Wife, The 1951,D 10,34:3
Constant Wife, The 1951,D 16,II,6:1
Paris '90 1952,Mr 5,33:2
Paris '90 1952,Mr 16,II,1:1
Candida 1952,Ap 23,23:6
To Be Continued 1952,Ap 24,37:2
Horses in Midstream 1953,Ap 3,18:7
Sabrina Fair 1953,N 12,37:1
Escapade 1953,N 19,40:1
Sabrina Fair 1953,N 22,II,1:1
Madam Will You Walk 1953,D 2,2:4
Prescott Proposals, The 1953,D 17,53:1
Prescott Proposals, The 1953,D 27,II,3:1
Coriolanus 1954,Ja 20,34:2
Coriolanus 1954,Ja 24,II,1:1
Dear Charles 1954,S 16,37:2
Dear Charles 1954,S 26,II,1:1
Wooden Dish, The 1955,O 7,20:1
Roomful of Roses, A 1955,O 18,48:1
Janus 1955,N 25,37:2
Major Barbara 1956,O 31,27:1
Four Winds 1957,S 26,21:2
Mary Stuart 1957,O 9,39:1
Nature's Way 1957,O 17,42:2
Shadow of My Enemy, A 1957,D 12,35:4
J B 1958,Ap 24,37:1
J B 1958,My 4,II,1:1
Girls in 509, The 1958,O 16,47:1

Pleasure of His Company, The 1958,O 23,36:1
Marriage-Go-Round, The 1958,O 30,37:1
Man in the Dog Suit, The 1958,O 31,34:2
Pleasure of His Company, The 1958,N 2,II,1:1
Marriage-Go-Round, The 1958,N 9,II,1:1
Majority of One, A 1959,F 17,28:2
Mikado, The 1959,O 2,24:1
Highest Tree, The 1959,N 5,41:1
Dear Liar 1960,Mr 18,19:2
Mikado, The 1961,Ja 18,26:1
Far Country, A 1961,Ap 5,32:1
Call on Kuprin, A 1961,My 26,29:3
Blood, Sweat & Stanley Poole 1961,O 6,31:1
First Love 1961,D 26,20:2
Venus at Large 1962,Ap 13,30:1
Irregular Verb to Love, The 1963,S 19,22:2
Case of Libel, A 1963,O 11,43:2
One by One 1964,D 2,60:1
Love in E Flat 1967,F 14,38:1
Antigone 1967,Je 19,43:1
Spofford 1967,D 15,54:3
Avanti 1968,F 1,29:1
Mikado, The 1968,My 2,59:1
Wrong Way Light Bulb, The 1969,Mr 5,40:1
Oenslager, Otto (Scenic Designer)
My Dear Children 1940,F 1,16:2
Oertel, Millie
Her Family Tree 1920,D 28,9:2
Oeser, Helmut
Minna von Barnhelm 1968,N 13,37:1
Schloss, Das 1968,N 20,35:3
Oestbye, Niels Johan
Untitled-One Woman Show 1956,Ap 9,23:5
Oesterman, Philip (Director)
To Bury a Cousin 1967,My 17,38:3
Parents and Children 1969,Ja 13,26:6
Geese 1969,Ja 13,26:6
Oesterreicher, Rudolph (Playwright)
Garden of Eden, The 1927,S 28,28:1
Mikado, The 1927,O 30,IX,4:6
Konto X 1930,N 2,VIII,3:1
Auslandreise 1932,N 20,IX,3:5
Oestreicher, Gerard (Miscellaneous)
But, Seriously... 1969,F 28,29:1
Oestreicher, Gerard (Producer)
Milk and Honey 1961,O 11,52:1
Girl Could Get Lucky, A 1964,S 21,36:1
Royal Hunt of the Sun, The 1965,O 27,36:2
But, Seriously... 1969,F 28,29:1
Oestvig, Aagard
Rose Marie 1928,Mr 31,23:2
Rose Marie 1928,Ap 29,IX,2:8
Oettinger, Elmer
How Beautiful With Shoes 1935,N 29,24:1
O'Faillon, Taugh
Quare Fellow, The 1958,N 28,34:1
Our Town 1959,Mr 24,46:2
O'Fallon, Mary
King of Friday's Men, The 1951,F 22,26:2
Courtin' Time 1951,Je 14,30:2
O'Farrell, Mairin (Composer)
Heart's a Wonder, The 1958,S 19,23:2
O'Farrell, Mairin (Playwright)
Heart's a Wonder, The 1958,S 19,23:2
O'Farrell, Margaret
Plough and the Stars, The 1927,N 29,30:2
O'Farrell, Nuala (Composer)
Heart's a Wonder, The 1958,S 19,23:2
O'Farrell, Nuala (Playwright)
Heart's a Wonder, The 1958,S 19,23:2
O'Farrell, Shaun
Chiffon Girl, The 1924,F 20,23:2
Offenbach, Jacques (Composer)
Hubby in Distress 1921,Ap 17,VI,1:1
Orpheus in der Unterwelt 1922,F 5,VI,1:7
Perichole, La 1926,D 28,12:2
Perichole, La 1926,D 29,24:4
Fair Helen 1928,Ap 1,IX,2:4
Blue Beard 1929,Jl 7,VIII,2:1
Grand Duchess 1929,D 17,29:2
Orpheus in Hades 1930,D 16,30:1
Blaue Hemd von Ithaka, Das 1931,Mr 15,IX,2:4
Fair Helen 1931,Ag 30,VIII,2:1
1860: or, Aris; 1860, or an Interrupted Festival 1931,O 22,27:1
Tales of Hoffmann 1932,Ja 10,VIII,1:6
Helen 1932,Ja 31,I,5:2
Fair Helen 1932,Jl 17,IX,1:2
Princess of Trapezunt 1933,F 19,IX,3:1
Belle Helene, La 1941,Jl 8,14:1
Vie Parisienne, La 1941,N 6,20:3
Helen Goes to Troy 1944,Ap 30,II,1:1
Vie Parisienne, La 1945,Ja 13,14:5
Happiest Girl in the World, The 1961,Ap 4,42:1
Vie Parisienne, La 1964,Mr 11,34:2
Perichole, La 1970,Mr 9,42:1
Offer, Harold
Smiling Faces 1932,Ag 31,12:3
Offer, Herman
Kith and Kin 1930,My 14,31:1
Offer, Richard
Topaze 1930,F 13,25:3

Offerman, George
Little Poor Man, The 1925,Ag 6,14:1
Enemy of the People, An 1927,O 4,32:5
Music in May 1929,Ap 2,29:1
Subway Express 1929,S 25,34:3
Simple Simon 1930,F 19,22:1
Would-Be Gentleman, The 1930,Ap 30,29:2
Simple Simon 1931,Mr 10,23:2
Incubator 1932,N 2,23:3
Sleep No More 1944,S 1,11:5
Offerman, Marie
Sam Abramovitch 1927,Ja 20,20:5
Subway Express 1929,S 25,34:3
Offley, Hilda
Ol' Man Satan 1932,O 4,26:3
Walk Together Chillun 1936,F 5,15:2
One-Act Plays of the Sea; Long Voyage Home, The 1937,O 30,23:2
Androcles and the Lion 1938,D 17,10:5
Big White Fog 1940,O 23,26:2
Offner, Mortimer (Composer)
Meet the People 1940,D 26,22:2
Offner, Mortimer (Director)
Room Service 1953,Ap 7,34:1
Offner, Mortimer (Lyricist)
Meet the People 1940,D 26,22:2
Offner, Mortimer (Miscellaneous)
Meet the People 1940,D 26,22:2
Offner, Mortimer (Playwright)
Meet the People 1940,D 26,22:2
O'Flaherty, Liam (Original Author)
Mr Gilhooley 1930,O 1,26:1
Puritan, The 1936,Ja 24,14:3
O'Flaherty, Robert
Captain Brassbound's Conversion 1950,D 28,21:1
O'Flynn, Damian
Hide and Seek 1934,Ag 7,20:2
Eldest, The 1935,F 12,24:3
Bright Star 1935,O 16,26:2
Tulips Are Blooming, The 1935,D 4,27:6
Mrs Moonlight 1936,Je 16,21:3
At the Theatre 1937,Ag 4,14:1
Barchester Towers 1937,D 1,27:1
Empress of Destiny 1938,Mr 10,16:2
Brown Danube, The 1939,My 18,30:4
Foreigners 1939,D 6,30:2
Anna Christie 1941,Ag 10,IX,1:8
Winged Victory 1943,N 22,24:1
O'Gatty, Packey
Ringside 1928,Ag 30,13:2
Ogden, Angela
Will Shakespeare 1923,Ja 2,14:1
Ogden, Leslie (Producer)
Man in the Glass Booth, The 1968,S 27,41:1
Ogden, Pat
Jackpot 1944,Ja 14,15:2
Ogden, Richard
O Evening Star 1936,Ja 9,24:6
Hamlet 1936,N 11,54:2
Ogelthorpe, Selma
Walk-Up 1961,F 24,24:1
Ogg, Roberta
Canteen Show, The 1942,S 4,18:1
Ogle, Carla
Daughters of Atreus 1936,O 15,33:1
Ogle, Haakon
Arms for Venus 1937,Mr 12,18:7
Reunion 1938,Ap 12,26:4
Oglesby, Carl (Playwright)
Season of the Beast 1958,Mr 14,29:2
Oglesby, Marshall
Macbeth 1968,N 30,49:3
O'Gorman, W
Plough and the Stars, The 1934,N 13,22:2
Drama at Inish 1934,N 15,24:2
Resurrection 1934,N 20,24:5
Coiner, The 1934,N 22,26:2
O'Grady, Mary (Director)
Mikado, The 1939,Mr 11,15:6
O'Grady, Patricia
Macbeth 1957,Ag 16,11:2
Richard III 1957,N 26,41:1
Playboy of the Western World, The 1958,My 9,19:2
Macbeth 1959,Ag 1,9:2
Ogunyemi, Wale
Madmen and Specialists 1970,Ag 3,38:1
O'Hagan, John
Deirdre of the Sorrows 1949,D 15,51:2
O'Hagen, Casey
Birds, The 1967,My 7,67:1
O'Hagen, Ita
Sharon's Grave 1961,N 9,39:2
O'Halloran, George
Nobody's Child 1956,Ag 23,25:2
O'Hanlon, Dorothy
Case of Youth, A 1940,Mr 25,10:3
O'Hanlon, Kathleen
Century Revue and the Midnight Rounders, The 1920,Jl 13,9:1
Century Review, The 1920,Jl 22,9:5
O'Hanlon and Sambuni
Vaudeville (Palace) 1924,Ap 1,18:1

O'Hara, Barry
Ondine 1954,F 19,23:1
O'Hara, Don
Nobody Hears A Broken Drum 1970,Mr 20,55:1
O'Hara, Edith (Producer)
Touch 1970,N 9,52:1
O'Hara, Eileen
Daphne Laureola 1950,S 19,38:6
O'Hara, Fiske
Big Mogul, The 1925,My 12,26:3
Sidewalks of New York 1927,O 4,33:1
Jerry for Short 1929,Ag 13,23:4
O'Hara, Geoffrey
Half a Widow 1927,S 13,37:3
O'Hara, Geoffrey (Composer)
Rogues and Vagabonds 1930,My 8,32:5
O'Hara, Gerry
Promises, Promises 1968,D 2,59:3
O'Hara, Hamilton (Miscellaneous)
Three by Ferlinghetti; Victims of Amnesia, The
  1970,S 23,43:1
Three by Ferlinghetti; Three Thousand Red Ants
  1970,S 23,43:1
Three by Ferlinghetti; Alligation, The
  1970,S 23,43:1
O'Hara, Helen
New Faces 1934,Mr 16,24:5
O'Hara, Jenny
Dylan 1964,Ja 20,18:1
Hang Down Your Head and Die 1964,O 19,38:1
Play With a Tiger 1964,D 31,14:2
Fig Leaves Are Falling, The 1969,Ja 3,19:1
Sambo 1969,D 22,42:1
My House Is Your House 1970,O 16,53:2
O'Hara, Jill
Hang Down Your Head and Die 1964,O 19,38:1
Hair 1967,O 30,55:1
Hair 1967,N 14,50:1
George M! 1968,Ap 11,48:1
Promises, Promises 1968,D 2,59:3
Promises, Promises 1968,D 15,II,3:1
Promises, Promises 1970,Ja 18,II,7:1
O'Hara, John (Miscellaneous)
Pal Joey 1940,D 26,22:2
O'Hara, John (Original Author)
Pal Joey 1940,D 26,22:2
Pal Joey 1952,Ja 13,II,1:1
O'Hara, John (Playwright)
Pal Joey 1952,Ja 4,17:6
Searching Sun, The 1952,My 8,37:3
Pal Joey 1961,Je 1,32:1
Pal Joey 1963,My 30,21:1
O'Hara, Kenny (Lighting Director)
Murder in the Cathedral 1958,Mr 22,12:4
O'Hara, Lyle
Tour De Four 1963,Je 19,41:1
O'Hara, Maureen
What Price Glory 1949,Mr 3,33:2
Christine 1960,Ap 29,27:1
O'Hara, Michael (Playwright)
Derryowen 1946,O 29,34:2
O'Hara, Patricia Quinn
Kiss Them for Me 1945,Mr 21,27:2
Qudrille 1954,N 4,39:2
O'Hara, Riggs
Hamlet 1969,Je 30,33:1
Henry V 1969,N 11,43:1
O'Hara, Shirley
Button, Button 1929,O 24,26:1
Meteor 1929,D 24,15:1
O'Hara, Tom
Blue Flame, The 1920,Mr 16,18:1
Jimmie 1920,N 18,15:3
O'Hare, Jack
Good Boy 1928,S 6,23:2
O'Hare, John
Sister Oakes 1949,Ap 25,19:4
Enchanted, The 1950,Ja 19,34:2
Long Days, The 1951,Ap 21,10:5
Pink Elephant, The 1953,Ap 23,37:2
Bad Seed, The 1954,D 9,42:1
Auntie Mame 1956,N 1,47:2
O'Hare, Michael
City of Kings 1949,F 18,27:2
O'Hare, Tom
Sun Showers 1923,F 6,14:2
O'Hare, Ursula
Tip-Top 1920,O 6,13:2
O'Hay, Irving
Passing Show of 1921, The 1920,D 30,16:2
O'Hearn, Patricia
Behold This Dreamer 1927,N 1,20:4
Salt Water 1929,N 27,30:3
O'Hearn, Robert (Costume Designer)
Relapse, The 1950,N 23,54:2
O'Hearn, Robert (Lighting Director)
Festival 1955,Ja 19,22:1
Apple Cart, The 1956,O 19,23:1
Child of Fortune 1956,N 14,41:1
Abraham Cochrane 1964,F 18,26:1
O'Hearn, Robert (Scenic Designer)
Relapse, The 1950,N 23,54:2
Love's Labour's Lost 1953,F 5,20:3

Date With April, A 1953,Ap 16,36:2
Festival 1955,Ja 19,22:1
Othello 1955,S 8,27:2
Henry IV, Part I 1955,S 22,34:2
Henry V 1956,Jl 7,11:2
Apple Cart, The 1956,O 19,23:1
Child of Fortune 1956,N 14,41:1
As You Like It 1961,Je 17,13:2
Macbeth 1961,Je 19,31:1
As You Like It 1961,Je 25,II,1:1
Troilus and Cressida 1961,Jl 24,15:1
Abraham Cochrane 1964,F 18,26:1
Kiss Me, Kate 1965,My 13,31:1
Porgy and Bess 1965,O 20,53:3
O'Herlihy, Daniel
Ivy Green, The 1949,Ap 6,37:2
O'Higgins, Brian
Bugle in the Blood, The 1949,Mr 15,34:5
O'Higgins, Harvey (Playwright)
Wrong Number, The 1921,Jl 17,VI,1:8
Main Street 1921,Jl 24,VI,1:1
Main Street 1921,O 6,21:1
Sweet Seventeen 1924,Mr 18,24:2
Ohle, Bob
Billy Budd 1955,My 4,35:1
Ohlson, Barbara
Utopia, Limited 1960,Ap 8,27:2
Cradle of Willow, A 1961,D 16,20:2
Ohm, Alba (Director)
He Who Gets Slapped 1956,F 2,18:1
Ohm, Alba (Translator)
He Who Gets Slapped 1956,F 2,18:1
Ohman, Phil
Lady Be Good 1924,D 2,23:4
Tip-Toes 1925,D 29,20:2
Treasure Girl 1928,N 9,22:1
Vaudeville (Palace) 1929,Ja 21,18:3
Spring Is Here 1929,Mr 12,26:1
Heads Up! 1929,N 12,34:1
Ohmead, Isobel
Bitter Sweet 1929,N 6,30:2
Good Companions, The 1931,O 2,31:1
Ohnet, Georges (Original Author)
Padrone Delle Ferriere, Il 1934,Mr 19,13:5
O'Hollewitt, Brett
City of Kings 1949,F 18,27:2
Shake Hands With the Devil 1949,O 21,30:4
O'Horgan, Tom (Composer)
Tempest, The 1959,D 28,19:2
Open Season at Second City 1964,Ja 23,25:1
Thank You, Miss Victoria 1966,Ap 12,43:1
This Is the Rill Speaking 1966,Ap 12,43:1
Birdbath 1966,Ap 12,43:1
Recluse, The 1966,Ap 13,36:1
Chicago 1966,Ap 13,36:1
War 1966,Ap 13,36:1
Futz 1968,Je 14,39:1
Tom Paine 1969,Mr 30,71:2
O'Horgan, Tom (Director)
This Is the Rill Speaking 1966,Ap 12,43:1
Thank You, Miss Victoria 1966,Ap 12,43:1
Birdbath 1966,Ap 12,43:1
War 1966,Ap 13,36:1
Chicago 1966,Ap 13,36:1
Recluse, The 1966,Ap 13,36:1
Tom Paine 1967,N 12,II,17:6
Times Square 1968,Ja 27,16:3
Tom Paine 1968,Mr 26,38:1
Hair 1968,Ap 30,40:2
Hair 1968,My 19,II,3:3
Futz 1968,Je 14,39:1
Tom Paine 1968,Je 30,II,1:1
Futz 1968,Je 30,II,1:1
Futz 1968,O 22,37:1
Hair 1969,F 5,36:1
Hair 1970,Ja 13,39:1
Hair 1970,S 27,II,1:2
O'Horgan, Tom (Original Author)
Massachusetts Trust 1968,S 1,II,1:1
Ohrbach's (Costume Designer)
Democratic Body, A 1942,F 13,24:7
Ohse, Bernard (Translator)
Sign of Jonah, The 1957,My 2,27:1
Ohta, Takashi
If This Be Treason 1935,S 24,28:2
Family, The 1943,Mr 31,22:4
Oisher, Moishe
Vacation Follies 1939,Ag 30,15:6
O'Judy, Judy
Strings, My Lord, Are False, The 1942,My 20,24:2
Oke, Richard (Original Author)
Frolic Wind 1935,Mr 14,19:7
O'Keefe, Arthur J
His Majesty the Queen 1926,Mr 9,8:1
O'Keefe, Dennis
Never Live Over a Pretzel Factory 1964,Mr 30,37:1
O'Keefe, Lester
Scandals 1920,Je 8,9:1
Plain Jane 1924,My 13,24:2
O'Keefe, Paul
Sail Away 1961,O 4,48:5
O'Keefe, Walter
Third Little Show, The 1931,My 10,VIII,2:4

O'Keefe, Walter—Cont
Third Little Show, The 1931,Je 2,34:3
Casino Varieties 1934,Ap 3,26:4
Spring Tonic 1936,My 11,16:1
Hymn to the Rising Sun 1937,My 7,28:2
Top-Notchers 1942,My 30,8:5
O'Keefe, Walter (Lyricist)
Just a Minute 1928,O 9,34:3
O'Keefe, Winston
Parnell 1935,N 12,24:2
Parnell 1936,My 5,26:2
Hamlet 1936,N 11,54:2
Private Lives 1937,Jl 14,17:4
Kind Lady 1937,Jl 21,19:3
Fly Away Home 1937,Jl 28,15:1
Candida 1937,Ag 4,14:5
Ode to Liberty 1937,Ag 18,15:2
Elizabeth the Queen 1937,Ag 25,24:3
Richard II 1937,S 16,28:2
Two Bouquets, The 1938,Je 1,19:2
Knights of Song 1938,O 18,29:2
Glorious Morning 1938,N 28,10:3
As You Like It 1939,My 9,28:4
As You Like It; Midsummer Night's Dream, A;
  Comedy of Errors, The; Taming of the Shrew,
  The 1939,My 9,28:4
When We Are Married 1939,D 26,22:3
O'Keefe, Winston (Director)
Parnell 1936,My 5,26:2
O'Keeffe, Judith
Merry Wives of Windsor, The 1954,F 17,27:1
Doctor and the Devils, The 1959,Ja 21,27:8
O'Kelly, Aideen
Playboy of the Western World, The 1968,S 4,40:1
O'Kelly, Alex
Devil Came From Dublin, The! 1955,Je 3,27:2
Okemah, Caddo
Arrow-Maker, The 1956,O 5,20:1
Okerson, Doris
Saint of Bleecker Street, The 1954,D 28,21:1
Okhlopkov, Nikolai (Producer)
Hamlet 1955,Ja 4,24:5
Okninski, Janusz
Kernel and the Shell, The 1965,Ja 6,32:1
Woman, The 1965,Ja 6,32:1
Nightmare, The 1965,Ja 6,32:1
Labyrinth, The 1965,Ja 6,32:1
Book, The 1965,Ja 6,32:1
Jacob and the Angel 1965,Ja 6,32:1
Jaselka 1965,Ja 6,32:1
Post Office, The 1965,Ja 6,32:1
Okomoto, Michi
Wedding in Japan 1949,N 11,29:1
Okorotchenkoff, (Messr)
Chauve-Souris 1925,Ja 15,25:1
Okotie-Barrett, Betty
Madmen and Specialists 1970,Ag 3,38:1
Okum, Arthur
Babes in Arms 1951,Mr 10,7:3
O'Kun, Lan (Miscellaneous)
Best Foot Forward 1956,Mr 3,16:1
Okun, Lillian
Pelican, The 1929,N 14,25:1
Carry Nation 1932,O 31,18:2
Threepenny Opera, The 1933,Ap 14,22:4
Okun, Yale
Iron Men 1936,O 20,30:6
Olaf, Pierre
Plume de Ma Tante, La 1958,N 12,42:1
Plume de Ma Tante, La 1959,S 13,II,1:1
Carnival! 1961,Ap 14,22:2
Murderer Among Us, A 1964,Mr 26,43:1
That Hat! 1964,S 24,45:1
Carnival! 1968,D 13,58:1
Olakh, Latsy
Porgy and Bess 1945,Je 17,II,4:3
Olarra, Jose
Fuerza Ciega, La 1927,D 6,26:1
Olcott, Charles
Johnny on the Spot 1942,Ja 9,24:2
Olcott, Chauncey
Macushla 1920,My 18,9:3
Olcott, Helen
Eyvind of the Hills 1921,F 2,14:1
Old Gotham Town Players
Petticoat Fever 1937,Jl 20,19:3
Old Smoothies, The
Ice Capades 1952,S 12,18:1
Ice Capades 1953,S 11,25:1
Ice Capades 1954,S 15,38:1
Ice Capades 1955,S 15,38:1
Ice Capades 1956,S 13,41:2
Ice Capades 1957,S 5,33:2
Ice Capades 1958,S 4,33:2
Ice Capades 1960,S 1,30:1
Old Vic Company
Cherry Orchard, The 1941,S 7,IX,2:5
Oldbridge, Harry
Edgar Allan Poe 1925,O 6,31:1
Pomeroy's Past 1926,Ap 20,24:4
Olden, Charles
Salome 1923,My 8,22:2
Comedy of Errors, The 1923,My 16,22:5
Comedy of Errors, The 1923,My 20,VII,1:1

Olden, Charles—Cont
Runnin' Wild 1923,O 30,17:3

Olden, Courtenaye
On Strivers' Row 1946,Mr 1,17:2
Green Pastures, The 1951,Mr 16,35:2

Olden, Peggy
Red, Hot and Blue! 1936,O 30,26:3

Oldfield, Edward
Elizabeth the Queen 1930,N 4,37:1
Macbeth 1935,O 8,26:4
Libel! 1935,D 21,10:5

Oldfield, Emmett
Life Begins at 8:40 1934,Ag 28,24:2
Life Begins at 8:40 1934,S 2,IX,1:1

Oldfield, Julian (Miscellaneous)
Chips With Everything 1963,O 2,49:1

Oldham, Christopher
Hamlet 1937,Ag 8,X,1:7

Oldham, Derek
Gondoliers, The 1934,S 4,23:1
Pirates of Penzance, The; Slave of Duty, The 1934,S 7,24:3
Gondoliers, The 1934,S 9,IX,1:1
Iolanthe 1934,S 11,24:3
H M S Pinafore 1934,S 14,24:3
Mikado, The; Town of Titipu, The 1934,S 18,18:1
Yeomen of the Guard, The 1934,S 21,28:3
Princess Ida; Castle Adamant 1934,S 28,26:3
Mikado, The 1936,Ag 21,13:2
Gondoliers, The 1936,S 8,23:1
Yeomen of the Guard, The 1936,S 15,37:2
Iolanthe 1936,S 22,30:3
H M S Pinafore 1936,S 29,34:2
Princess Ida 1936,O 13,32:2

Oldham, Lynn Mary
Lend Me Your Ears! 1936,O 6,28:5

Oldmixon, Blanche
Offence, The 1925,N 16,25:1

Oldridge, Alfred
Patience 1966,N 30,58:1

Oldridge, Harry
Manhattan Mary 1927,S 27,30:3

Oldridge, Henry
Edgar Allan Poe 1925,O 6,31:1

Oldroyd, Margery
Sleepy Hollow 1948,Je 4,26:3
Alive and Kicking 1950,Ja 18,25:5
Liar, The 1950,My 19,30:2
Guys and Dolls 1950,N 25,11:2

O'Leary, Barbara
Hamlet 1948,D 4,9:2

O'Leary, Hannah
King of Friday's Men, The 1951,F 22,26:2

O'Leary, John
Detective Story 1954,F 13,11:2
Venice Preserv'd 1955,D 13,54:4
Picture of Dorian Gray, The 1956,Ag 18,15:5
Rimers of Eldritch, The 1967,F 21,53:1
Front Page, The 1968,O 20,85:5

O'Leary, Kevin
Happy Hypocrite, The 1968,S 6,38:1

O'Leary, Margaret (Playwright)
Woman, The 1929,O 6,IX,4:2

O'Leary, Ray
Saint Joan 1950,Mr 4,10:6

O'Leary, William
H M S Pinafore 1949,Jl 29,13:2

Olfson, Ken
Scuba Duba 1967,O 11,36:1

Olga and Mishka
Tickle Me 1920,Ag 18,9:1

Olgin, M (Playwright)
Third Parade, The 1933,O 23,18:2

Oliansky, Joel
Merry Wives of Windsor, The 1959,Mr 14,23:1

Oliansky, Joel (Playwright)
Here Comes Santa Claus 1962,My 18,34:1

Olicker, I
Love, Honor and Oh Baby 1940,Mr 29,25:2

Oligny, Huguette
Ti-Coq 1951,F 10,10:2
Malade Imaginaire, Le; Imaginary Invalid, The 1958,Ap 13,30:28:2
Sganarelle; Imaginary Cuckold, The 1958,My 7,43:1
Mariage Force, Le; Forced Wedding, The 1958,My 7,43:1

Olim, Dorothy (Miscellaneous)
Fantasticks, The 1960,My 4,55:2

Olim, Dorothy (Producer)
Worm in Horseradish, A 1961,Mr 14,32:3
Golden Apple, The 1962,F 13,38:2
Lion in Love, The 1963,Ap 26,28:3
Pimpernel! 1964,Ja 7,26:6

Oliphant, Moliclare
Macbeth 1928,N 20,28:3

Olive, Harry
Second Hurricane 1937,Ap 22,18:4

Olivenbaum, S H
My Little Girl 1931,F 2,22:4

Olivencia, Jaime
And the Wind Blows 1959,Ap 29,28:1

Oliver
Are You With It? 1945,N 12,17:3

Oliver, Annette
Antigone 1967,Ja 14,18:1

Oliver, Anthony
Gently Does It 1953,O 29,43:4
Gently Does It 1953,N 8,II,1:1
After the Rain 1967,O 10,54:1

Oliver, Barrie
New Yorkers, The 1930,N 16,VIII,3:1
New Yorkers, The 1930,D 9,31:1
Provincetown Follies, The 1935,N 4,24:3
Nine O'Clock Revue 1936,Jl 8,14:3

Oliver, Barrie (Playwright)
Provincetown Follies, The 1935,N 4,24:3

Oliver, Beatrice
If 1927,O 26,26:2

Oliver, Burns
Great Sebastians, The 1956,Ja 5,27:1

Oliver, Charles
Aunt Caroline's Will 1954,Ag 11,21:1

Oliver, Clarence
Rosalie 1928,Ja 11,26:3

Oliver, De Wayne
People vs Ranchman, The 1968,O 28,56:1
Billy 1969,Mr 24,56:1

Oliver, Don
Night of January 16 1935,S 17,26:4
Boy Meets Girl 1937,Jl 6,23:1
Empress of Destiny 1938,Mr 10,16:2

Oliver, Edna May
My Golden Girl 1920,F 3,18:2
Half-Moon, The 1920,N 2,15:2
Wait Till We're Married 1921,S 27,14:1
Her Salary Man 1921,N 29,20:1
Rubicon, The 1922,F 22,13:1
Wild Oats Lane 1922,S 7,12:1
Ice-Bound 1923,F 12,16:2
In His Arms 1924,O 14,23:1
Isabel 1925,Ja 14,19:1
Cradle Snatchers 1925,S 8,28:2
Show Boat 1927,D 28,26:1
Show Boat 1928,Ja 8,VIII,1:1
Show Boat 1932,My 20,22:2

Oliver, George
Strange Fruit 1945,N 30,18:6
Cyrano de Bergerac 1946,O 9,33:2
Cyrano de Bergerac 1947,Ja 17,27:2
Our Lan' 1947,S 29,16:5

Oliver, George W (Playwright)
Port O' London 1926,F 10,20:2

Oliver, Gordon
Walrus and the Carpenter, The 1941,N 10,20:2
Golden Wings 1941,D 9,46:6
Cat Screams, The 1942,Je 17,26:5
R U R 1942,D 4,30:2

Oliver, Henry
Portrait of a Madonna 1957,Ap 1,21:2
Bedtime Story 1957,Ap 1,21:2
Good Soldier Schweik, The 1963,Ap 9,57:1
Seven Scenes for Yeni 1963,My 13,36:2
Time of the Key, A 1963,S 12,33:3
Mutilated, The 1966,F 23,42:1
Investigation, The 1966,O 5,40:1
Midsummer Night's Dream, A 1967,Je 30,23:1

Oliver, James
Meet the Prince 1935,Jl 9,24:5

Oliver, John
Mr Strauss Goes to Boston 1945,S 7,20:2

Oliver, Larry
Room 349 1930,Ap 23,24:5
Torch Song 1930,Ag 28,23:1
Farmer Takes a Wife, The 1934,O 31,17:1
Next Half Hour, The 1945,O 30,14:6
Born Yesterday 1946,F 5,18:2
Born Yesterday 1946,F 10,II,1:1

Oliver, Laurence (Director)
Beaux' Stratagem, The 1970,F 10,50:2

Oliver, Lili-Ann
Idiot's Delight 1957,F 23,14:2

Oliver, Margaret
Girls in Uniform 1932,D 31,10:3

Oliver, Margaret Scott
Paolo and Francesca 1924,D 3,24:2

Oliver, Nina
Blue Bird, The 1923,D 26,13:3

Oliver, Norman
Well of the Saints, The 1959,Ap 11,15:4

Oliver, Olive
Sacred and Profane Love 1920,F 24,11:1
Piper, The 1920,Mr 20,14:2
White Villa, The 1921,F 15,7:1
Good Woman, The 1921,Je 14,15:2
Macbeth 1921,D 27,10:3
Bully, The 1924,D 26,18:1
Macbeth 1928,N 20,28:3

Oliver, Paula
Our Lan' 1947,S 29,16:5

Oliver, Pilar
Don Juan Tenorio 1953,N 20,18:5

Oliver, Regina
Boo Hoo! East Lynne 1959,S 9,50:4

Oliver, Richard
Carousel 1965,Ag 11,39:1

Oliver, Robin
House on Grand Street, A 1953,O 10,12:6
King and the Duke, The 1955,Je 2,25:2

Oliver, Rochelle
Brothers Karamazov, The 1957,D 9,39:4
Jackknife 1958,S 23,36:2
Vincent 1959,O 1,40:1
Vincent 1959,O 11,II,1:1
Toys in the Attic 1960,F 26,23:2
Toys in the Attic 1960,Mr 6,II,1:1
Harold 1962,N 30,27:1
Happily Never After 1966,Mr 11,37:1
Stop, You're Killing Me; Terrible Jim Fitch 1969,Mr 20,53:1

Oliver, Roland (Playwright)
Night Hawk 1925,F 25,16:4
Night Hawk 1926,D 27,21:3
Footlights 1927,Ag 20,8:2
Forbidden Roads 1928,Ap 17,26:4
On Call 1928,N 10,20:7
Kansas City Kitty 1929,S 26,27:4

Oliver, Sherling
God Loves Us 1926,O 20,22:2
Mystery Ship, The 1927,Mr 15,28:2
One Way Street 1928,D 25,31:2
Silver Tassie, The 1929,O 25,26:1
Silver Tassie, The 1929,N 10,X,1:1
Launcelot and Elaine 1930,Mr 10,24:3
Lady Windermere's Fan 1932,Ja 27,19:3
Web, The 1932,Je 28,24:4
Invitation to a Murder 1934,My 18,26:3
Nowhere Bound 1935,Ja 23,20:2
Symphony 1935,Ap 27,20:3
This Our House 1935,D 12,33:3
Home Sweet Home 1936,Jl 1,29:2
Richard II 1937,F 6,14:2
Love in My Fashion 1937,D 4,21:4
Wuthering Heights 1939,Ap 28,30:4
Without Love 1942,N 11,28:1
Magnificent Yankee, The 1946,Ja 2,23:6
Magnificent Yankee, The 1946,Ja 23,21:2

Oliver, Smith
Escurial 1956,O 3,29:2

Oliver, Susan
Ronde, La 1955,Je 28,24:2
Small War on Murray Hill 1957,Ja 4,19:1

Oliver, Sy (Miscellaneous)
New Faces of 1962 1962,F 2,25:1

Oliver, Thelma
Fly Blackbird 1962,F 6,26:2
Cindy 1964,Mr 20,24:1
Sweet Charity 1966,Ja 31,22:1
Sweet Charity 1967,Jl 1,13:1
House of Flowers 1968,Ja 29,26:2

Oliver, Thelma (Choreographer)
Man Dies, A 1968,Jl 16,35:1

Oliver, Vic
Follow the Sun 1935,D 24,10:3
Get a Load of This 1941,N 30,IX,3:1

Oliver, Viola
Playing With Love 1929,F 27,16:4

Oliver, William I (Translator)
Tragicomedy of Don Cristobita and Dona Rosita, The 1958,My 30,12:2

Oliver-Smith, Gerald
Strange Orchestra 1933,N 29,23:2
Red Cat, The 1934,S 20,21:1

Olivet, Carmen
Fuerza Ciega, La 1927,D 6,26:1

Olivette, Nina
Irving Berlin's New Music Box Revue 1922,O 24,18:1
George White's Scandals 1923,Je 19,22:5
Sweet Little Devil 1924,Ja 22,15:4
Captain Jinks 1925,S 9,22:1
Hold Everything 1928,O 11,24:2
Vaudeville (Palace) 1930,Ap 21,20:7
Roberta 1937,Je 27,II,6:1
On Your Toes 1937,Ag 3,21:2
Roberta 1937,S 7,16:4

Olivia
Watched Pot, The 1947,O 29,31:4
Family Reunion, The 1947,N 29,9:2

Olivier, Ellen
Narrow Road to the Deep North 1969,D 2,64:1

Olivier, Laurence
Beau Geste 1929,F 17,IX,2:1
Journey's End 1929,Jl 14,IX,5:1
Murder on the Second Floor 1929,S 12,35:1
Private Lives 1930,O 12,VIII,1:8
Private Lives 1931,Ja 28,24:1
Green Bay Tree, The 1933,O 21,11:5
Green Bay Tree, The 1933,O 29,IX,1:1
Biography 1934,My 20,IX,2:4
Theatre Royal 1934,N 11,IX,1:1
Ringmaster, The 1935,Mr 12,24:5
Ringmaster, The 1935,Ap 7,IX,1:6
Romeo and Juliet 1935,O 18,27:5
Romeo and Juliet 1935,O 17,IX,2:4
Romeo and Juliet 1935,D 29,IX,1:3
Bees on the Boat Deck 1936,My 6,27:2
Bees on the Boat Deck 1936,Je 7,IX,2:1
Hamlet 1937,Ja 6,19:4

Olivier, Laurence—Cont

Hamlet 1937,Je 4,26:6
Macbeth 1937,N 27,21:3
Macbeth 1937,D 19,XI,3:7
Othello 1938,F 27,X,1:4
King of Nowhere, The 1938,Ap 3,XI,1:8
No Time for Comedy 1939,Ap 18,26:4
No Time for Comedy 1939,Ap 30,XI,1:1
Romeo and Juliet 1940,My 10,27:1
Arms and the Man 1944,O 1,II,1:3
Richard III 1944,O 1,II,1:3
Uncle Vanya 1945,Mr 25,II,2:4
Henry IV, Part I 1945,S 27,24:5
Henry IV 1945,O 14,II,2:3
Critic, The 1945,N 11,II,2:5
Oedipus Rex 1945,N 11,II,2:5
Henry IV, Part I 1946,My 7,25:2
Henry IV, Part II 1946,My 8,33:4
Henry IV 1946,My 12,II,1:1
Uncle Vanya 1946,My 14,18:2
Uncle Vanya 1946,My 19,II,1:1
Oedipus; Critic, The 1946,My 21,19:2
Oedipus 1946,My 21,19:2
King Lear 1946,S 25,39:4
King Lear 1946,O 13,II,2:3
School for Scandal, The 1949,Ja 21,24:5
Venus Observed 1950,Ja 19,35:2
Venus Observed 1950,N 26,II,1:1
Caesar and Cleopatra 1951,My 11,32:8
Caesar and Cleopatra 1951,D 20,43:2
Antony and Cleopatra 1951,D 21,22:2
Antony and Cleopatra 1951,D 30,II,1:1
Caesar and Cleopatra 1951,D 30,II,1:1
Sleeping Prince, The 1953,S 29,25:1
Sleeping Prince, The 1953,N 6,24:4
Sleeping Prince, The 1953,D 20,II,4:2
Sleeping Prince, The 1954,F 9,22:8
Twelfth Night 1955,My 1,II,3:1
Twelfth Night 1955,Je 7,37:4
Macbeth 1955,Je 19,II,1:1
Titus Andronicus 1957,Jl 2,33:8
Entertainer, The 1958,F 13,22:2
Entertainer, The 1958,F 23,II,1:1
Coriolanus 1959,Jl 8,24:5
Rhinoceros 1960,Ap 30,15:3
Becket 1960,O 6,50:1
Becket 1960,O 16,II,1:1
Becket 1960,O 18,36:3
Becket 1961,My 9,44:1
Broken Heart, The 1962,Jl 10,28:2
Uncle Vanya 1962,Jl 17,18:4
Semi-Detached 1962,D 6,54:3
Uncle Vanya 1963,Jl 2,16:2
Othello 1964,Ap 22,56:1
Othello 1964,Jl 23,18:4
Othello 1965,S 8,51:4
Dance of Death, The 1967,O 20,50:1
Love for Love 1967,O 21,17:1
Dance of Death 1967,O 29,II,5:1
Love for Love 1967,O 29,II,5:1
Flea in Her Ear, A 1967,O 29,II,5:1
Love for Love 1967,O 30,59:1
Flea in Her Ear, A 1967,O 30,59:1
Merchant of Venice, The 1970,My 10,II,3:1
Merchant of Venice, The 1970,Jl 30,39:1

Olivier, Laurence (Director)

Romeo and Juliet 1940,My 10,27:1
Born Yesterday 1947,F 9,II,3:7
Streetcar Named Desire, A 1949,S 29,38:1
Venus Observed 1952,F 14,24:2
Venus Observed 1952,F 24,II,1:1
Tumbler, The 1960,F 25,32:2
Chances, The 1962,Jl 4,11:2
Broken Heart, The 1962,Jl 10,28:2
Uncle Vanya 1962,Jl 17,18:4
Hamlet 1963,O 23,37:2
Crucible, The 1965,Ja 20,35:1
Love's Labour's Lost 1968,D 22,54:3
Three Sisters, The 1970,F 12,30:1
Three Sisters, The 1970,F 22,II,1:1

Olivier, Laurence (Miscellaneous)

Romeo and Juliet 1940,My 10,27:1
Daphne Laureola 1950,S 19,38:6
Tumbler, The 1960,F 25,32:2
One More River 1960,Mr 19,12:2
As You Like It 1967,O 6,33:4
Love's Labour's Lost 1969,Ja 5,II,3:1

Olivier, Laurence (Producer)

Bees on the Boat Deck 1936,My 6,27:2
Romeo and Juliet 1940,My 10,27:1
Skin of Our Teeth, The 1945,Mr 20,22:8
King Lear 1946,S 25,39:4
Born Yesterday 1947,F 9,II,3:7
Fading Mansion 1949,S 1,25:4
Streetcar Named Desire, A 1949,S 29,38:1
Streetcar Named Desire, A 1949,O 13,33:6
Uncle Vanya 1963,Jl 2,16:2
Crucible, The 1965,Ja 20,35:1
Othello 1965,S 8,51:4

Olivier, Stuart (Playwright)

Bride, The 1924,My 6,25:1
Beau Gallant 1926,Ap 6,26:3

Olivier, Vic

Vaudeville (Palace) 1931,Jl 13,13:4

Ollington, Charles

As You Like It 1947,F 21,16:2

Ollivierre, Lawrence

Does a Tiger Wear a Necktie? 1967,F 4,17:1

Olman, Wynn (Miscellaneous)

Worm in Horseradish, A 1961,Mr 14,32:3

Olmer, Vit

Matter of Days, A 1969,My 20,40:1

Olmi, Arthur

Spooks 1925,Je 2,16:4

Olmstead, Frederick

Tide Rising 1937,Ja 26,17:2
Stop Press 1939,Mr 20,13:2

Olmstead, John

Prunella 1929,Ap 10,23:3

Olmsted, Remington

Fireman's Flame, The 1937,O 11,26:2
Sadie Thompson 1944,N 17,25:2
Polonaise 1945,O 8,20:2

Olney, Dorothy (Miscellaneous)

Village Green 1941,Je 17,24:7

Olney, Dorothy (Producer)

Village Green 1941,S 4,24:4

Olney, Joseph

Hilda Cassidy 1933,My 5,18:3
Caviar 1934,Je 8,19:2
Tapestry in Gray 1935,D 28,10:2
Pirates of Penzance, The 1936,Ap 21,27:5
Excursion 1937,Ap 10,11:4
Tell My Story 1939,Mr 16,26:6
Doughgirls, The 1942,D 31,19:2

Olney, Joseph (Miscellaneous)

Someone Waiting 1956,F 15,26:1
Moonbirds 1959,O 10,13:1
Julia, Jake, and Uncle Joe 1961,Ja 30,19:1
Look: We've Come Through 1961,O 26,40:1
Hidden Stranger 1963,Ja 10,5:5
Sunday Man, The 1964,My 14,41:3

Olney, Julian (Miscellaneous)

Village Green 1941,Je 17,24:7

Olney, Julian (Mrs) (Producer)

Robin Hood 1935,Jl 15,20:6

Olney, Julian (Producer)

Village Green 1941,S 4,24:4

Olney, Julian Jr

Village Green 1941,S 4,24:4

O'Loghlen, Clement

Kathleen ni Houlihan 1920,Je 29,9:2
Lady, The 1923,D 5,23:2
Emperor Jones, The 1924,My 7,18:1
S S Glencairn 1924,N 4,31:4
Man in Evening Clothes, The 1924,D 6,13:4
Love for Love 1925,Ap 1,21:2
Man Who Died Twice, The 1925,D 14,19:1
Weak Woman, A 1926,Ja 27,16:3
Two Orphans, The 1926,Ap 6,26:2
Autumn Fire 1926,O 27,25:3
Hangman's House 1926,D 17,27:2
Road to Rome, The 1927,F 1,24:2
Infinite Shoeblack, The 1930,F 18,28:1
Mr Gilhooley 1930,O 1,26:1
Cynara 1931,N 3,31:1
Parnell 1935,N 12,24:2
Parnell 1936,My 5,26:2
Storm Over Patsy 1937,Mr 9,26:4
Father Malachy's Miracle 1937,N 18,26:4
Mr Banks of Birmingham 1939,Ja 21,18:4
Coggerers, The 1939,Ja 21,18:4
Not in Our Stars 1941,Ap 26,20:5

Olon-Scrymgeour, John (Director)

Shoemaker's Holiday, The 1967,Je 3,19:1

Olonova, Olga

Samson and Delilah 1920,N 18,18:1
Daddy's Gone A-Hunting 1921,S 1,18:3
Quarantine 1924,D 17,19:7

O'Loughlin, Gerald

Golden Boy 1952,Mr 13,24:3
Streetcar Named Desire, A 1956,F 16,24:1
Shadow of a Gunman, The 1958,N 21,26:1
Shadow of a Gunman, The 1958,N 30,II,1:1
Machinal 1960,Ap 8,27:1
Machinal 1960,Ap 17,II,1:1
Cook for Mr General, A 1961,O 20,39:1
Who'll Save the Plowboy? 1962,Ja 10,24:2
Calculated Risk 1962,N 1,35:1
One Flew Over the Cuckoo's Nest 1963,N 14,40:2
Harry, Noon and Night 1965,My 6,44:1
Happily Never After 1966,Mr 11,37:1
Lovers and Other Strangers 1968,S 19,63:1

Olrich, April

Wait a Minim! 1966,Mr 8,43:1

Olsen, Carolyn

Send Me No Flowers 1960,D 6,54:1
Bring Me a Warm Body 1962,Ap 17,29:3

Olsen, Charles (Director)

Admirable Bashville, The 1956,F 21,38:1
Dark Lady of the Sonnets, The 1956,F 21,38:1
This Property Is Condemned 1956,O 29,34:1
Career 1957,My 1,42:6
Career 1957,My 19,II,1:1
Androcles and the Lion 1958,F 22,8:3
Augustus Does His Bit 1958,F 22,8:3
Sign of Winter 1958,My 8,35:1

Olsen, Charles (Director)—Cont

Smokeweaver's Daughter, The 1959,Ap 15,30:1
Place for Chance, The 1964,My 15,44:2
Rose 1969,O 29,30:1

Olsen, Charles (Miscellaneous)

Typewriter, The 1955,Jl 29,8:3

Olsen, Charles (Producer)

Career 1957,My 1,42:6
Smokeweaver's Daughter, The 1959,Ap 15,30:1

Olsen, Dickie

Salvation on a String; Chair Endowed 1954,Jl 7,23:1

Olsen, E Oliver (Costume Designer)

Beaver Coat, The 1956,Mr 29,22:5
Sappho 1960,Ja 12,22:1

Olsen, E Oliver (Miscellaneous)

Tobias and the Angel 1957,O 21,29:5
Nathan the Wise 1962,Mr 23,29:1

Olsen, Fin

Higher and Higher 1940,Ap 5,24:3
If the Shoe Fits 1946,D 6,29:4
Happy as Larry 1950,Ja 7,11:2

Olsen, Garda

Mademoiselle 1932,O 19,22:4

Olsen, George

Good News 1927,S 7,35:4

Olsen, George and His Orchestra

Kid Boots 1924,Ja 1,21:3
Ziegfeld Follies 1924,Je 25,26:1
Sunny 1925,S 23,22:1
City Chap, The 1925,O 27,21:1
Good News 1927,S 7,35:4

Olsen, George Band

Lambs Gambol 1925,Ap 27,15:1

Olsen, Irene

Daffy Dill 1922,Ag 23,14:5
9 O'Clock Revue 1923,O 5,22:1
Nic-Nax of 1926 1926,Ag 5,19:1

Olsen, Leona

Banjo Eyes 1941,D 26,20:2

Olsen, Maureen

Back Pay 1921,Ag 31,8:2

Olsen, Moroni

Medea 1920,Mr 23,12:2
Trial of Joan of Arc, The 1921,Mr 28,8:2
Iphigenia in Aulis 1921,Ap 8,18:2
Great Way, The 1921,N 8,28:2
Mr Faust 1922,Ja 31,11:2
Candida 1922,Mr 23,11:1
Her Man of Wax 1933,O 12,32:3
Mary of Scotland 1933,N 28,28:3
Romeo and Juliet 1934,D 21,30:3
Barretts of Wimpole Street, The 1935,F 26,16:2

Olsen, Ole

Vaudeville (Palace) 1923,My 15,22:2
Vaudeville (Palace) 1928,N 12,18:7
Sons o' Fun 1941,D 2,28:2
Laffing Room Only 1944,D 25,15:4
Funzapoppin 1949,Jl 1,16:2
Pardon Our French 1950,O 6,22:4
Hell'z-A-Splashin' 1959,Je 25,22:2

Olsen, Ole (Composer)

Funzapoppin 1949,Jl 1,16:2

Olsen, Ole (Lyricist)

Funzapoppin 1949,Jl 1,16:2
Pardon Our French 1950,O 6,22:4

Olsen, Ole (Miscellaneous)

Count Me In 1942,O 9,24:2

Olsen, Ole (Playwright)

Hellzapoppin 1938,O 2,IX,1:1
New Hellzapoppin, The 1939,D 12,36:4
Sons o' Fun 1941,D 2,28:2
Laffing Room Only 1944,D 25,15:4
Pardon Our French 1950,O 6,22:4

Olsen, Ole (Producer)

Hellzapoppin 1938,S 23,34:2
Streets of Paris, The 1939,Je 20,25:2
New Hellzapoppin, The 1939,D 12,36:4
Snookie 1941,Je 4,26:2
Sons o' Fun 1941,N 1,20:1
Laffing Room Only 1944,D 25,15:4

Olsen, Olive

Who Cares 1930,Jl 9,27:1
Meet My Sister 1930,D 31,11:1
Vanities 1931,Ag 11,28:4
Vanities 1931,Ag 16,VIII,1:1
Earl Carroll's Vanities 1931,Ag 28,18:7
Salute to Spring 1937,Jl 14,16:2

Olsen, Oliver (Costume Designer)

Enemy of the People, An 1959,F 5,24:4
Ping-Pong 1959,Ap 17,22:1

Olsen, Stephen

New Hellzapoppin, The 1939,D 12,36:4

Olsen & Shirley

Show Time 1942,S 17,20:2

Olsen and Johnson

Vaudeville (Palace) 1929,O 14,20:4
Atrocities of 1932 1932,Ag 22,20:3
New Hellzapoppin, The 1939,D 12,36:4
Actors Fund Fete 1942,F 23,24:5
Laffing Room Only 1945,S 20,31:1
Hellzapoppin 1948,F 25,27:2
Vaudeville (Palace) 1952,Mr 12,31:2
Vaudeville (Palace) 1952,Mr 16,II,1:1

Olsen's Orchestra
Black Cockatoo, The 1926,D 31,11:1
Olshanetsky, Alexander
Untitled-Benefit 1933,Ja 25,13:3
What Girls Do 1935,Ja 14,10:4
Olshanetsky, Alexander (Composer)
Soul of a Woman, The 1930,F 22,13:1
Motke From Slobodke 1930,Ap 12,23:3
Song of the Ghetto, The 1932,O 3,15:5
Organ Grinder, The 1934,Ja 1,28:3
Happy Days 1934,Ap 2,12:5
Lucky Boy 1935,D 2,19:5
Secret of Love, The 1936,F 24,15:2
Water Carrier, The 1936,D 25,20:2
Long Live America 1939,Ja 2,28:3
Polish Rabbi, The 1939,Mr 20,13:3
Olshanetsky, Alexander (Musical Director)
Long Live America 1939,Ja 2,28:3
Olshanetsky, Alexander (Playwright)
Three in Love 1933,N 8,32:5
My Baby's Wedding 1938,O 10,15:3
Olshever, Rochelle
Shadow Years, The 1957,Ja 9,26:2
Olshin, Milton (Miscellaneous)
Coco 1969,D 19,66:1
Olson, Bob (Scenic Designer)
Of Thee I Sing 1969,Mr 8,19:1
Olson, Brad
Joan of Lorraine 1955,Mr 26,12:2
My 3 Angels 1956,F 4,24:2
Olson, Glenn
Brigadoon 1957,Mr 28,37:1
Olson, James
Moby Dick 1955,Ap 26,25:3
Julius Caesar 1955,Jl 13,20:1
Young and Beautiful, The 1955,O 3,23:2
Sin of Pat Muldoon, The 1957,Mr 14,35:1
Hamlet 1958,Je 21,11:1
Midsummer Night's Dream, A 1958,Je 23,19:1
Winter's Tale, The 1958,Jl 21,17:4
J B 1958,D 12,2:7
Romulus 1962,Ja 11,27:1
Chinese Prime Minister, The 1964,Ja 3,14:1
Three Sisters, The 1964,Je 23,24:1
Three Sisters, The 1964,Jl 5,II,1:1
Gnadiges Fraulein, The 1966,F 23,42:1
Mutilated, The 1966,F 23,42:1
Of Love Remembered 1967,F 20,46:5
Olson, Joyce
Most Happy Fella, The 1966,My 12,55:1
My Fair Lady 1968,Je 14,42:1
Olson, Kurt
Oklahoma! 1969,Je 24,37:1
Olson, Mabel
Caroline 1923,F 1,13:2
Olson, Murray
Now Is the Time for all Good Men 1967,S 27,42:1
Olson, Nancy
Tunnel of Love, The 1957,F 14,31:4
Send Me No Flowers 1960,D 6,54:1
Olson, Paul
Kiss Me, Kate 1949,Ja 30,II,6:5
Alive and Kicking 1950,Ja 18,25:5
Brigadoon 1964,D 24,9:1
Olson, Uta (Costume Designer)
Mother Courage and Her Children 1964,My 12,32:2
Oltarsh, Martin
Recruiting Officer, The 1958,F 8,12:2
Olvin, Laurence (Miscellaneous)
Land Beyond the River, A 1957,Mr 29,15:7
Simply Heavenly 1957,My 22,28:2
Courageous One, The 1958,Ja 21,33:6
Olvis, William
My Darlin' Aida 1952,O 28,36:4
Candide 1956,D 3,40:2
Candide 1956,D 9,II,5:1
Song of Norway 1959,Je 26,16:2
O'Madigan, Isabel
Just Married 1921,Ap 27,21:1
That Awful Mrs Eaton! 1924,S 30,27:1
Half-Caste, The 1926,Mr 30,20:4
Potash and Perlmutter, Detectives; Poisoned by
  Pictures 1926,S 1,27:3
White Eagle, The 1927,D 27,24:4
Money Lender, The 1928,Ag 28,27:3
Polly 1929,Ja 9,28:3
Smiling Faces 1932,Ag 31,12:3
Slightly Married 1943,O 26,19:2
O'Mahony, Nora
School for Wives 1934,N 14,22:2
Six Characters in Search of an Author
  1934,D 5,29:1
John Bull's Other Island 1948,F 11,33:4
Where Stars Walk 1948,F 25,27:2
Righteous Are Bold, The 1955,D 23,12:1
Little Moon of Alban 1960,D 2,34:1
O'Maley, Natalie
Patience 1929,D 16,34:5
O'Malley, Ellen
Unknown, The 1920,Ag 29,VI,1:4
O'Malley, Etain
New York Idea, The 1963,Jl 13,12:2
Cocktail Party, The 1968,O 8,42:1

O'Malley, Gloria
Pal Joey 1952,Ja 4,17:6
O'Malley, Grania
Playboy of the Western World, The 1930,Ja 3,20:4
Well of the Saints, The 1932,Ja 22,15:2
Juno and the Paycock 1940,Ja 17,24:2
At the Stroke of Eight 1940,My 21,29:2
Lily of the Valley 1942,Ja 27,25:2
Snark Was a Boojum, The 1943,S 2,14:4
Laura 1947,Je 27,16:1
King of Friday's Men, The 1951,F 22,26:2
Three Wishes for Jamie 1952,Mr 22,9:2
Shadow and Substance 1956,Mr 14,38:1
Guests of the Nation 1958,My 21,40:1
Guests of the Nation 1958,Je 27,18:5
Sharon's Grave 1961,N 9,39:2
Hogan's Goat 1965,N 12,56:1
Lovers; Losers 1968,Jl 26,21:4
O'Malley, J Edward
What's Your Wife Doing? 1923,O 2,10:3
O'Malley, J Pat
But Not Goodbye 1944,Ap 12,19:2
Ten Little Indians 1944,Je 28,21:2
Of Thee I Sing 1952,My 6,34:2
Seagulls Over Sorrento 1952,S 12,18:4
Home Is the Hero 1954,S 23,42:2
O'Malley, John
Golden Boy 1937,N 5,18:5
My Heart's in the Highlands 1939,Ap 14,29:2
Heavenly Express 1940,Ap 19,24:2
Johnny on the Spot 1942,Ja 9,24:2
O'Malley, Mary
Lady of Mexico 1962,O 20,13:2
O'Malley, Muriel
Chocolate Soldier, The 1947,Mr 13,34:2
Allegro 1947,O 11,10:2
Touch and Go 1949,O 14,34:2
Music in the Air 1951,O 9,32:2
Allegro 1951,S 18,36:3
Carousel 1953,My 6,38:1
Song of Norway 1958,Je 23,19:2
Song of Norway 1959,Je 26,16:2
Sound of Music, The 1959,N 17,40:2
O'Malley, Neill
Easy Come, Easy Go 1925,O 27,20:2
Rendezvous 1932,O 13,22:3
Is Life Worth Living? 1933,N 10,24:6
Gentlewoman 1934,Mr 23,28:4
Stevedore 1934,Ap 19,33:2
Bury the Dead 1936,Ap 20,17:4
Prelude 1936,Ap 20,17:4
200 Were Chosen 1936,N 21,21:1
O'Malley, Neill (Director)
Strange Prince, The 1926,D 8,24:2
O'Malley, Neill (Producer)
Strange Prince, The 1926,D 8,24:2
O'Malley, Pat
Dial 'M' for Murder 1953,N 8,II,1:1
O'Malley, Power (Scenic Designer)
Well of the Saints, The 1932,Ja 22,15:2
O'Malley, Rex
Strange Prince, The 1926,D 8,24:2
Comic, The 1927,Ap 20,28:2
Marquise, The 1927,N 15,26:4
Bachelor Father, The 1928,F 29,28:2
Apple Cart, The 1930,F 25,30:1
Lost Sheep 1930,My 6,33:2
Wonder Bar, The 1931,Mr 18,23:4
Experience Unnecessary 1931,D 31,16:2
Mad Hopes, The 1932,My 29,VIII,2:2
Mad Hopes, The 1932,D 2,26:3
No More Ladies 1934,Ja 24,20:3
Red Cat, The 1934,S 20,21:1
Revenge With Music 1934,N 29,33:5
Simpleton of the Unexpected Isles, The
  1935,F 19,27:5
Petticoat Fever 1935,Jl 2,24:4
Love for Love 1936,Je 30,15:4
Difficulty of Getting Married, The 1936,Jl 7,22:1
Matrimony, PFD 1936,N 6,28:4
Matrimony, PFD 1936,N 13,26:3
Merely Murder 1937,D 4,21:4
You Never Know 1938,Mr 4,16:3
You Never Know 1938,S 22,26:3
Shadow Play 1939,Ag 15,14:5
Man Who Came to Dinner, The 1940,F 10,19:5
Man Who Came to Dinner, The 1940,F 18,IX,3:6
Naked Genius, The 1943,O 22,20:5
Cherry Orchard, The 1944,Ja 26,22:1
Many Happy Returns 1945,Ja 6,15:5
Devils Galore 1945,S 13,27:2
Lute Song 1946,F 7,29:2
Charley's Aunt 1953,D 23,22:2
Sleeping Prince, The 1956,N 2,31:1
Lady of the Camellias, The 1963,Mr 22,7:1
Say Nothing 1965,Ja 28,21:2
O'Malley, Sheila
Too Hot for Maneuvers 1945,My 3,26:5
O'Malley, Tom (Lyricist)
Bella 1961,N 17,40:1
O'Malley, Tom (Playwright)
Bella 1961,N 17,40:1

Oman, Julia Trevelyan (Scenic Designer)
Brief Lives 1967,D 19,60:4
Merchant of Venice, The 1970,Jl 30,39:1
Omar, Jemela
Zorba 1968,N 18,58:1
O'Mara, Brian
Broken Hearts of Broadway 1944,Je 13,16:2
Down to Miami 1944,S 12,23:5
Mr Strauss Goes to Boston 1945,S 7,20:2
O'Meara, John
Half-Caste, The 1926,Mr 30,20:4
Crime 1927,F 23,27:3
Judas 1929,Ja 25,20:4
As You Desire Me 1931,Ja 29,21:2
Omens, Estelle
Summer and Smoke 1952,Ap 25,19:5
Grass Harp, The 1953,Ap 28,32:2
Grass Harp, The 1953,My 24,II,1:1
Pullman Car Hiawatha 1962,D 4,46:2
Pocket Watch, The 1966,Ja 6,18:1
Brownstone Urge, The 1969,D 18,63:1
Gandhi 1970,O 21,37:1
Omeron, Guen
Night in Venice, A 1952,Je 27,18:6
Night in Venice, A 1953,Je 26,15:2
Fledermaus, Die 1954,My 20,38:5
O'Moor, Maureen
Furies, The 1928,Mr 8,23:1
When Crummles Played 1928,O 2,34:3
Sign of the Leopard 1928,D 12,34:4
O'Moore, Colin
Lassie 1920,Ap 7,9:2
O'Moore, Patrick
Ladies in Retirement 1940,Mr 27,24:3
Yesterday's Magic 1942,Ap 15,27:2
O'Morrison, Kevin
Deirdre of the Sorrows 1959,O 15,46:1
Rose Tattoo, The 1966,O 21,36:2
Oms, Alba
Comrades 1956,Je 6,38:1
O'Murphy, W
Winter's Tale, The 1958,Jl 23,34:3
Ondine
Conquest of the Universe 1967,N 27,60:1
O'Neal, Charles (Original Author)
Three Wishes for Jamie 1952,Mr 22,9:2
O'Neal, Charles (Playwright)
Three Wishes for Jamie 1952,Mr 22,9:2
O'Neal, Charon (Composer)
Great Magician, The 1951,N 22,45:1
O'Neal, Cynthia
Sign in Sidney Brustein's Window, The
  1964,O 16,32:1
O'Neal, Frederick
Natural Man 1941,My 8,20:4
Three's a Family 1943,N 19,24:3
Anna Lucasta 1944,Je 17,10:1
Anna Lucasta 1944,Ag 31,15:1
Anna Lucasta 1944,S 24,II,1:5
Henri Christophe 1945,Je 7,24:5
Henri Christophe 1945,Je 17,II,1:1
Anna Lucasta 1947,O 30,31:3
Take a Giant Step 1953,O 4,II,1:1
Winner, The 1954,F 18,34:1
Salvation on a String; Supper for the Dead
  1954,Jl 7,23:1
House of Flowers 1954,D 31,11:2
Man With the Golden Arm, The 1956,My 22,28:1
Twelfth Night 1959,Jl 11,10:2
God's Trombones 1960,F 10,43:4
God's Trombones 1960,F 21,II,1:1
Ballad for Bimshire 1963,O 16,54:1
Iceman Cometh, The 1968,Ap 1,58:1
Madwoman of Chaillot, The 1970,Mr 23,48:3
O'Neal, Harry
O K 1925,My 4,16:1
Night in Paris, A 1926,Ja 6,16:3
Night in Paris, A 1926,Jl 27,15:4
Artists and Models 1927,N 16,28:2
O'Neal, Patrick
Lulu 1958,S 30,24:1
Coming Forth by Day of Osiris Jones, The; Kid,
  The 1961,Mr 15,45:2
Far Country, A 1961,Ap 5,32:1
Night of the Iguana, The 1961,D 29,10:1
Night of the Iguana, The 1962,Ja 7,II,1:1
Ginger Man, The 1963,N 22,42:1
O'Neal, Ron
Americana Pastoral 1968,D 11,51:1
No Place to Be Somebody 1969,My 5,53:3
No Place to Be Somebody 1969,My 18,II,22:1
No Place to Be Somebody 1969,My 18,II,1:1
No Place to Be Somebody 1969,D 31,17:1
O'Neal, William
Dream Girl, The 1924,Ag 21,12:2
Mayflowers 1925,N 25,14:2
Desert Song, The 1926,D 1,24:2
George White's Scandals 1928,Jl 3,19:1
New Moon, The 1928,S 20,33:1
Shoot the Works! 1931,Jl 22,19:5
Sunny River 1941,D 5,28:2
Annie Get Your Gun 1946,My 17,14:2
Annie Get Your Gun 1946,My 17,14:2

O'Neal, William—Cont
Annie Get Your Gun 1957,Ag 31,18:2
O'Neal, Zelma
Good News 1927,Ag 14,VII,2:1
Good News 1927,S 7,35:4
Follow Thru 1929,Ja 10,24:3
Vaudeville (Palace) 1930,N 10,17:1
Gang's All Here, The 1931,F 19,21:3
Jack o' Diamonds 1935,F 26,17:3
Swing Along 1936,S 20,IX,1:4
O'Neal Sisters, The
Vaudeville (Palace) 1923,O 23,18:2
O'Neall Sisters, The
Vaudeville (Hippodrome) 1924,Mr 18,25:1
O'Neil, Barbara
Saint's Parade 1930,N 1,23:4
Carry Nation 1932,O 31,18:2
Forsaking All Others 1933,Mr 2,21:2
Is Life Worth Living? 1933,N 10,24:6
Mother Lode 1934,D 24,16:5
Reprise 1935,My 2,16:2
Ten Million Ghosts 1936,O 24,23:7
Miles of Heaven, The 1937,Ag 31,27:4
Willow and I, The 1942,D 11,32:2·
Counterattack 1943,F 4,27:2
Counterattack 1943,F 14,II,1:1
Doctors Disagree 1943,D 29,15:2
Searching Wind, The 1944,Ap 13,25:2
Searching Wind, The 1944,Ap 23,II,1:1
Affairs of State 1950,S 26,37:2
Portrait of a Lady 1954,D 22,27:6
Sea Gull, The 1956,O 23,38:1
Little Moon of Alban 1960,D 2,34:1
O'Neil, Betty
Kiss Me, Kate 1954,Mr 27,13:2
O'Neil, Bill
Carmen Jones 1945,My 3,26:5
Carmen Jones 1946,Ap 8,32:2
O'Neil, Bobby
Sue, Dear 1922,Jl 11,16:2
O'Neil, Brian
School for Scandal, The 1925,D 7,18:2
O'Neil, Charles
Lady Dedlock 1929,Ja 1,61:2
O'Neil, Dennie
Silks and Satins 1920,Jl 16,19:1
O'Neil, Dick
Man of Destiny, The 1957,Ap 1,21:2
O'Neil, F J
Bella 1961,N 17,40:1
O'Neil, George (Playwright)
American Dream; 1849 1933,F 22,24:5
American Dream; 1933 1933,F 22,24:5
American Dream; 1650 1933,F 22,24:5
American Dream 1933,Mr 5,IX,1:1
Mother Lode 1934,D 24,16:5
Something to Live For 1935,Ja 20,X,2:4
O'Neil, Harry
Three 1928,D 4,28:2
O'Neil, Henry
Mob, The 1920,O 11,18:1
Fountain, The 1925,D 11,26:1
You Can't Win 1926,F 17,12:1
O'Neil, Horton (Scenic Designer)
Flying Gerardos, The 1940,D 30,21:4
O'Neil, J R (Choreographer)
Noble Rogue, A 1929,Ag 20,31:2
O'Neil, Jack
Don't, George! 1944,N 4,18:6
O'Neil, James
Alice in Arms 1945,F 1,18:4
Sweeney Todd 1957,Ag 28,21:4
O'Neil, Joyce
Funny Girl 1964,Mr 27,15:1
O'Neil, Nance
Passion Flower, The 1920,Ja 14,12:1
Untitled-Benefit 1921,My 2,12:3
Madre 1923,D 31,9:6
Stronger Than Love 1925,D 29,20:2
Fog-Bound 1927,Ap 2,21:2
Lily, The 1927,Ag 2,19:1
House of Women, The 1927,S 11,VIII,1:3
House of Women, The 1927,O 4,32:2
House of Women, The 1927,O 9,VIII,1:1
Vaudeville (Palace) 1928,Ap 3,32:5
Bitter Oleander 1935,F 12,24:3
Long Frontier, The 1935,Jl 23,24:4
Night in the House 1935,N 8,19:5
Ruy Blas 1938,Jl 24,IX,2:1
O'Neil, Nance (Playwright)
Stronger Than Love 1925,D 20,VII,4:1
O'Neil, Patrick
Shipwrecked 1924,N 13,18:1
O'Neil, R F Jr
1776 1926,Ap 24,11:2
O'Neil, Randall
Monkey 1932,F 12,25:2
She Loves Me Not 1933,N 21,22:4
O'Neil, Raymond (Director)
Comedy of Errors, The 1923,My 16,22:5
Salome 1923,My 20,VII,1:1
Comedy of Errors, The 1923,My 20,VII,1:1
Chip Woman's Fortune, The 1923,My 20,VII,1:1

O'Neil, Raymond (Playwright)
Triumph of the Egg, The 1925,F 11,19:3
O'Neil, Sally
Manhattan Medley 1932,S 25,IX,1:6
When We Are Married 1939,D 26,22:3
O'Neil, Sherry
Desert Song, The 1946,Ja 9,20:2
O'Neil, Tricia
Two by Two 1970,N 11,37:1
Two by Two 1970,N 22,II,1:1
O'Neil, William
Countess Maritza 1926,Mr 30,20:3
Porgy and Bess 1935,O 11,30:2
O'Neill, Barry
Dark Angel, The 1925,F 11,19:2
Sex 1926,Ap 27,22:4
Man With Red Hair, A 1928,N 9,22:2
Potiphar's Wife 1928,D 24,10:7
Borrowed Love 1929,Je 18,29:2
Merchant of Venice, The 1931,N 9,22:2
Shooting Star 1933,Je 13,22:2
O'Neill, Bobby
Rise of Rosie O'Reilly, The 1923,D 26,13:4
O'Neill, Dick
Bedtime Story 1957,Ap 1,21:2
Can-Can 1959,Ag 26,25:4
Skyscraper 1965,N 15,48:1
Have I Got One for You 1968,Ja 8,32:1
Promises, Promises 1968,D 2,59:3
O'Neill, Eugene (Miscellaneous)
Ancient Mariner, The 1924,Ap 7,15:5
Ancient Mariner, The 1924,Ap 13,VIII,1:1
Love for Love 1925,S 15,29:3
O'Neill, Eugene (Original Author)
New Girl in Town 1957,My 26,II,1:1
Take Me Along 1959,O 23,22:2
Take Me Along 1959,N 1,II,1:1
Marco Millions 1964,F 21,33:1
O'Neill, Eugene (Playwright)
Beyond the Horizon 1920,F 4,12:1
Beyond the Horizon 1920,F 8,VIII,2:1
Beyond the Horizon 1920,Mr 10,9:2
Exorcism 1920,Ap 4,VI,6:1
Emperor Jones, The 1920,N 7,VII,1:3
Emperor Jones, The 1920,D 28,9:1
Diff'rent 1920,D 29,8:1
Emperor Jones, The 1921,Ja 2,VI,3:1
Gold 1921,Je 2,14:2
Anna Christie 1921,N 3,22:1
Anna Christie 1921,N 6,VI,1:1
Straw, The 1921,N 11,16:2
Anna Christie 1921,N 13,VI,1:1
Anna Christie 1922,Ja 15,III,3:1
First Man, The 1922,Mr 6,9:2
Hairy Ape, The 1922,Mr 10,18:2
Hairy Ape, The 1922,Ap 16,VI,1:1
Anna Christie 1923,Ap 11,16:2
Anna Christie 1923,Ap 15,VII,2:4
Emperor Jones, The 1923,N 1,24:1
Anna Christie 1923,N 18,VIII,2:8
Emperor Jones, The 1923,N 18,VIII,2:8
Emperor Jones, The 1924,Ja 10,18:2
Welded 1924,Mr 9,VIII,2:3
Welded 1924,Mr 18,24:1
Welded 1924,Mr 23,VIII,1:1
Emperor Jones, The 1924,My 7,18:1
All God's Chillun Got Wings 1924,My 16,22:3
All God's Chillun Got Wings 1924,My 18,VII,1:1
Anna Christie 1924,Je 24,18:4
All God's Chillun Got Wings 1924,Ag 19,9:1
All God's Chillun Got Wings 1924,Ag 24,VII,1:1
S S Glencairn 1924,N 4,31:4
Desire Under the Elms 1924,N 12,20:7
Desire Under the Elms 1924,D 7,VIII,5:1
S S Glencairn 1924,D 28,VII,1:1
Diff'rent 1925,F 11,19:3
Emperor Jones, The 1925,S 11,20:1
Desire Under the Elms 1925,N 1,VIII,1:3
Fountain, The 1925,D 11,26:1
Fountain, The 1925,D 20,VII,3:1
Great God Brown, The 1926,Ja 25,26:1
Great God Brown, The 1926,Ja 31,VII,1:1
Great God Brown, The 1926,Ap 11,VIII,1:1
Emperor Jones, The 1926,My 18,28:3
Beyond the Horizon 1926,D 1,24:2
Beyond the Horizon 1926,D 26,VII,1:1
Emperor Jones, The 1927,F 13,VII,4:6
Great God Brown, The 1927,Jl 24,VII,1:7
Emperor Jones, The 1927,Ag 28,VII,1:1
Marco Millions 1928,Ja 10,28:2
Marco Millions 1928,Ja 22,VIII,1:1
Strange Interlude 1928,Ja 31,28:1
Strange Interlude 1928,F 5,VIII,1:1
Hairy Ape, The 1928,F 19,VIII,4:1
Lazarus Laughed 1928,Ap 10,33:1
Lazarus Laughed 1928,Ap 22,IX,2:3
Marco Millions 1928,Ap 22,IX,1:1
Little Theatre Tournement; Where The Cross Is Made 1928,My 10,31:1
Hairy Ape, The 1928,Je 10,VIII,2:8
Strange Interlude 1928,Jl 1,VIII,3:5
Hairy Ape, The 1928,D 2,X,2:1
Strange Interlude 1928,D 18,37:3

O'Neill, Eugene (Playwright)—Cont
S S Glencairn 1929,Ja 10,24:5
S S Glencairn; Moon of the Caribbees, The; Bound East for Cardiff; Long Voyage Home, The; In the Zone 1929,Ja 27,IX,1:1
Dynamo 1929,F 12,22:1
Dynamo 1929,F 17,IX,1:1
Before Breakfast 1929,Mr 6,33:1
Little Theatre Tournament; Thirst 1929,My 10,32:2
Hairy Ape, The 1929,S 23,27:2
Hairy Ape, The 1929,S 29,IX,4:7
Strange Interlude 1929,O 1,34:8
In the Zone 1930,F 9,VIII,2:1
Marco Millions 1930,Mr 4,24:4
Emperor Jones, The 1930,Ap 1,10:1
Anna Christie 1930,My 4,XI,3:1
Emperor Jones, The 1930,My 25,IX,1:8
Anna Christie 1930,Je 11,33:3
Anna Christie 1930,Je 12,30:2
Desire Under the Elms 1930,Ag 3,23:4
Strange Interlude 1931,F 4,22:1
Strange Interlude 1931,F 22,VIII,1:3
Hairy Ape, The 1931,Ap 15,24:4
Hairy Ape, The 1931,My 12,29:4
Mourning Becomes Electra; Haunted, The 1931,O 27,22:1
Mourning Becomes Electra; Homecoming 1931,O 27,22:1
Mourning Becomes Electra; Hunted, The 1931,O 27,22:1
Mourning Becomes Electra 1931,N 1,VIII,1:1
Mourning Becomes Electra 1932,F 21,VIII,2:6
All God's Chillun Got Wings 1932,Mr 27,VIII,3:3
Mourning Becomes Electra 1932,Ap 10,VIII,1:1
Mourning Becomes Electra; Hunted, The 1932,My 10,25:2
Mourning Becomes Electra; Homecoming 1932,My 10,25:2
Mourning Becomes Electra; Haunted, The 1932,My 10,25:2
Mourning Becomes Electra 1932,My 22,VIII,1:1
All God's Chillun Got Wings 1933,Mr 14,19:4
Mourning Becomes Electra 1933,My 7,IX,2:3
Ah, Wilderness! 1933,S 26,26:3
Ah, Wilderness! 1933,O 3,28:2
Desire Under the Elms 1933,N 12,IX,1:1
Emperor Jones, The 1933,D 26,18:6
Days Without End 1933,D 31,IX,2:2
Days Without End 1934,Ja 9,19:1
Days Without End 1934,Ja 14,IX,1:1
Days Without End 1934,F 4,IX,1:1
Days Without End 1934,Ap 24,26:7
Ah, Wilderness! 1934,My 1,26:3
Ah, Wilderness! 1934,O 30,23:1
Days Without End 1935,F 5,23:2
Days Without End 1935,Mr 3,VIII,1:3
Ah, Wilderness! 1935,Ag 20,25:1
Ah, Wilderness! 1936,My 5,26:1
Ah, Wilderness! 1936,Je 7,IX,2:1
Great God Brown, The 1936,Je 28,IX,1:6
Ah, Wilderness! 1936,Je 28,IX,1:6
Emperor Jones, The 1936,Ag 11,24:6
Strange Interlude 1937,Ja 5,19:1
One-Act Plays of the Sea; Moon of the Caribbees 1937,O 30,23:2
One-Act Plays of the Sea; In the Zone 1937,O 30,23:2
One-Act Plays of the Sea; Bound East for Cardiff 1937,O 30,23:2
One-Act Plays of the Sea; Long Voyage Home, The 1937,O 30,23:2
Diff'rent 1937,N 21,II,10:7
Mourning Becomes Electra 1937,D 12,XI,3:8
Diff'rent 1938,Ja 26,26:4
Mourning Becomes Electra 1938,Ja 30,X,1:3
Beyond the Horizon 1938,Mr 20,XI,3:1
Marco Millions 1938,N 24,36:2
Marco Millions 1939,Ja 15,IX,3:1
Emperor Jones, The 1939,Je 20,25:2
Ah, Wilderness! 1940,Ag 20,23:2
Anna Christie 1941,Ag 10,IX,1:8
Ah, Wilderness! 1941,O 3,26:2
Ah, Wilderness! 1941,O 12,IX,1:1
Emperor Jones, The 1945,Ja 17,18:4
Iceman Cometh, The 1946,O 10,31:3
Iceman Cometh, The 1946,O 20,II,1:1
Iceman Cometh, The 1946,O 27,II,1:1
Moon for the Misbegotten, A 1947,F 21,16:2
Lazarus Laughed 1948,Ap 9,27:4
S S Glencairn; Bound East for Cardiff 1948,My 21,21:2
S S Glencairn; Moon of the Caribbees 1948,My 21,21:2
S S Glencairn; Long Voyage Home, The 1948,My 21,21:2
S S Glencairn; In the Zone 1948,My 21,21:2
S S Glencairn; Long Voyage Home, The; Moon of the Caribbees; In the Zone; Bound East for Cardiff 1948,My 30,II,1:1
Iceman Cometh, The 1948,Je 9,35:1
Desire Under the Elms 1951,N 22,45:1
Anna Christie 1952,Ja 10,33:1
Desire Under the Elms 1952,Ja 17,23:4
Desire Under the Elms 1952,Ja 20,II,1:1

O'Neill, Eugene (Playwright)—Cont

Anna Christie 1952,Ja 20,II,1:1
Ah, Wilderness! 1953,F 7,10:6
Ah, Wilderness! 1953,F 15,II,1:1
Desire Under the Elms 1953,N 29,II,3:1
Ah, Wilderness! 1954,Ag 21,20:4
Anna Christie 1955,N 22,41:1
Long Day's Journey Into Night 1956,F 11,12:6
Long Day's Journey Into Night 1956,F 19,II,1:6
Iceman Cometh, The 1956,My 8,38:1
Iceman Cometh, The 1956,My 20,II,1:1
Long Day's Journey Into Night 1956,O 17,40:1
Long Day's Journey Into Night 1956,N 8,47:2
Long Day's Journey Into Night 1956,N 18,II,1:1
Touch of the Poet, A 1957,Mr 30,12:5
Touch of the Poet, A 1957,Ap 7,II,3:1
Moon for the Misbegotten, A 1957,My 3,21:2
Moon for the Misbegotten, A 1957,My 12,II,1:1
New Girl in Town 1957,My 15,40:1
Long Day's Journey Into Night 1957,Jl 3,14:1
Long Day's Journey Into Night 1957,Jl 6,9:5
Iceman Cometh, The 1958,Ja 30,18:3
Before Breakfast 1958,Mr 12,36:1
Moon for the Misbegotten, A 1958,Je 7,10:6
Hughie 1958,S 9,24:5
Long Day's Journey Into Night 1958,S 9,40:4
Long Day's Journey Into Night 1958,S 26,21:2
Touch of the Poet, A 1958,O 3,23:2
Touch of the Poet, A 1958,O 12,II,1:1
Long Day's Journey Into Night 1959,Ap 29,30:2
Great God Brown, The 1959,O 7,48:1
Hughie 1959,O 15,48:1
Great God Brown, The 1959,O 18,II,1:1
Movie Man 1959,O 28,40:4
Abortion 1959,O 28,40:4
Sniper, The 1959,O 28,40:4
Moon for the Misbegotten, A 1960,Ja 22,14:8
Friends and Lovers; In the Zone; Bound East for
  Cardiff 1961,My 11,43:1
Touch of the Poet, A 1961,My 15,34:6
Diff'rent 1961,O 18,52:1
Mourning Becomes Electra 1961,N 22,24:3
Long Voyage Home, The 1961,D 5,49:1
Long Day's Journey Into Night 1962,My 16,35:4
Touch of the Poet, A 1962,S 30,85:8
Long Day's Journey Into Night 1962,S 30,85:8
Beyond the Horizon 1962,O 26,27:2
More Stately Mansions 1962,N 10,16:4
Desire Under the Elms 1963,Ja 11,5:6
Strange Interlude 1963,Mr 13,5:2
In the Zone; Before Breakfast 1963,Je 11,29:4
Hughie 1963,Je 11,29:4
Strange Interlude 1963,Je 18,34:6
Long Day's Journey Into Night 1963,Je 27,25:1
Marco Millions 1964,Mr 1,II,1:1
Emperor Jones, The 1964,Ag 6,20:4
Emperor Jones, The 1964,Ag 16,II,5:1
Hughie 1964,D 23,21:2
Enchaines; Welded 1965,Mr 13,17:1
Touch of the Poet, A 1967,My 3,38:2
More Stately Mansions 1967,S 14,54:1
More Stately Mansions 1967,N 1,40:1
More Stately Mansions 1967,N 12,II,1:1
Iceman Cometh, The 1968,Ap 1,58:1
Moon for the Misbegotten, A 1968,Je 13,55:2
Moon for the Misbegotten, A 1968,Je 30,II,1:1
Mourning Becomes Electra 1969,S 7,II,1:2
Ah, Wilderness! 1969,N 9,86:1
Three Plays of the Sea 1970,Ag 20,39:1

O'Neill, Eugene Jr
Oedipus Rex 1945,D 17,16:7
Mayor of Zalamea, The 1946,Ja 28,15:5

O'Neill, Eugene Jr (Playwright)
Thesmophoriazusae, The; Goddesses of Athens,
  The 1955,D 14,52:4

O'Neill, Frank (Playwright)
Hit the Trail 1954,D 3,31:2

O'Neill, Gerald
Cyrano de Bergerac 1932,D 27,11:2
Cyrano de Bergerac 1936,Ap 28,17:1

O'Neill, Henry
Kathleen ni Houlihan 1920,Je 29,9:2
Verge, The 1921,N 15,23:2
Mr Faust 1922,Ja 31,11:2
Hairy Ape, The 1922,Mr 10,18:2
Taboo 1922,Ap 5,22:1
Chains of Dew 1922,Ap 28,20:2
Staircase, The 1923,Ja 29,11:2
Love for Love 1925,S 15,29:3
Last Night of Don Juan, The 1925,N 10,23:2
Dream Play 1926,Ja 21,18:2
Squall, The 1926,N 12,20:1
Jarnegan 1928,S 25,29:2
Solitaire 1929,Mr 13,28:3
Hawk Island 1929,S 17,34:7
Last Mile, The 1930,F 14,21:2
Old Man Murphy 1931,My 19,25:2
Wonder Boy 1931,O 24,20:1
Trick for Trick 1932,F 19,14:2
I Loved You Wednesday 1932,O 12,27:1
Foolscap 1933,Ja 12,21:2
Conquest 1933,F 20,11:3
Shooting Star 1933,Je 13,22:2
What Price Glory 1949,Mr 3,33:2

O'Neill, Jack
Career Angel 1943,N 19,24:2

O'Neill, James
As You Like It 1941,O 21,29:2
Pirate, The 1942,N 26,39:2
Enchanted, The 1950,Ja 19,34:2

O'Neill, Joan
Rosalinda; Fledermaus, Die 1942,O 29,26:5

O'Neill, John
Blossom Time 1943,S 6,21:2
Wonder World 1964,My 18,32:1

O'Neill, Kathleen
Home Is Tomorrow 1950,Je 2,27:2

O'Neill, Kathryn
Cynara 1931,N 3,31:1

O'Neill, Macgowan (Producer)
Fountain, The 1925,D 11,26:1

O'Neill, Maire
White-Headed Boy, The 1921,S 16,20:1
Send for Dr O'Grady 1923,Jl 29,VI,1:6
Plough and the Stars, The 1927,N 29,30:2
Plough and the Stars, The 1927,D 4,X,1:1
Juno and the Paycock 1927,D 20,32:2
Real McCoy, The 1928,Jl 15,VIII,2:1
Mr Gilhooley 1930,O 1,26:1
Old Man Murphy 1931,My 19,25:2
Juno and the Paycock 1937,Ag 29,X,2:1

O'Neill, Margaret
Affair of Honor 1956,Ap 7,12:3
Coming Forth by Day of Osiris Jones, The; Kid,
  The 1961,Mr 15,45:2
Julius Caesar 1962,F 22,19:6
Marathon '33 1963,D 23,20:1
Deer Park, The 1967,F 1,27:2

O'Neill, Mary
Men in White 1955,F 26,13:2

O'Neill, Michael (Playwright)
Life Price 1969,Ja 14,36:2

O'Neill, Norman (Composer)
Mary Rose 1920,My 16,VI,1:7
Mary Rose 1920,Ag 8,VI,1:1
Last Enemy, The 1930,O 31,21:1

O'Neill, Pat
Sweet Bird of Youth 1956,Ap 17,27:2

O'Neill, Peggy
Just Fancy! 1927,O 12,30:2
Treasure Girl 1928,N 9,22:1
Who Cares 1930,Jl 9,27:1

O'Neill, Randall (Director)
Alexander Hamilton 1949,Mr 30,29:2

O'Neill, Randall (Scenic Designer)
Alexander Hamilton 1949,Mr 30,29:2

O'Neill, Robert
If a Body 1935,My 1,25:3
There Is No End 1950,F 17,27:4

O'Neill, Sally
Old Foolishness, The 1940,D 21,20:2

O'Neill, Sheila (Choreographer)
Kiss Me, Kate 1970,D 26,10:4

O'Neill, Standish (Producer)
Moon Over Mulberry Street 1935,S 5,24:6

O'Neill, William
Last Man In, The 1930,My 8,32:5

O'Neill, William J (Director)
Low Bridge 1933,F 10,13:4
They All Come to Moscow 1933,My 12,20:6

Oneto, Richard
Kismet 1953,D 4,2:4

Ongley, Amy
Innocent Idea, An 1920,My 26,9:4
Bachelor's Night, A 1921,O 18,20:1
Broken Branches 1922,Mr 7,11:1
Night Duel, The 1926,F 16,22:3

Onibon-Okuta, Ademola
Madmen and Specialists 1970,Ag 3,38:1

O'Nil, Suzette
Palace aux Femmes 1926,O 10,VIII,2:1

Onoe, Kikunojo
Azuma Kabuki Dancers and Musicians
  1954,F 19,22:3
Azuma Kabuki Dancers and Musicians
  1954,F 28,II,4:1
Azuma Kabuki Dancers and Musicians
  1954,Mr 10,29:4

Onri, Archie
Black Crook, The 1929,Mr 12,26:5
Pinocchio 1939,Ja 3,19:2

Onslow, Alexander
Sacred and Profane Love 1920,F 24,11:1
French Leave 1920,N 9,13:1
March Hares 1921,Ag 12,8:3
March Hares 1921,Ag 21,VI,1:1
It Is the Law 1922,N 30,28:2
Five Star Final 1930,D 31,11:1

Onstott, Kyle (Original Author)
Mandingo 1961,My 23,43:6

Ontanon, Santiago (Miscellaneous)
Bitter Oleander 1935,F 12,24:3

Opalach, Dorothy
Modern Statuary 1968,My 28,41:1

Opalinsky, Dorothy
Cocktails of 1934 1934,My 5,22:1

Opatoshu, David
Night Music 1940,F 23,18:2
Mexican Mural; Moonlight Scene 1942,Ap 27,19:2
Me and Molly 1948,F 27,27:2
Flight Into Egypt 1952,Mr 19,33:2
Reclining Figure 1954,O 8,26:5
Silk Stockings 1955,F 25,17:3
Wall, The 1960,O 12,44:4
Bravo Giovanni 1962,My 21,41:2
Bravo Giovanni 1962,My 27,II,1:1
Lorenzo 1963,F 16,5:2
Does a Tiger Wear a Necktie? 1969,F 26,38:1
Does a Tiger Wear a Necktie? 1969,Mr 9,II,1:1

Open Window
Oh! Calcutta! 1969,Je 18,33:1

Open Window (Composer)
Oh! Calcutta! 1969,Je 18,33:1

Open Window (Lyricist)
Oh! Calcutta! 1969,Je 18,33:1

Openshaw, C E (Playwright)
All the King's Horses 1928,Je 17,VIII,1:6
Convict, The 1935,F 5,23:2

Operti, Le Roi
George Washington 1920,Mr 2,9:1
Hamlet 1920,Mr 17,14:2
Servant in the House, The 1921,My 3,20:1
Taming of the Shrew, The 1921,My 12,20:2
Merchant of Venice, The 1921,My 14,10:4
Jolly Roger, The 1923,Ag 31,10:4
Cyrano de Bergerac 1923,N 2,14:1
Little Poor Man, The 1925,Ag 6,14:1
Hamlet 1925,O 12,19:2
Merchant of Venice, The 1925,D 28,12:1
Cyrano de Bergerac 1926,F 19,18:1
Joan of Arc 1926,Ap 24,21:2
Servant in the House, The 1926,My 4,30:1
Honeymooning 1927,Mr 18,25:3
Footlights 1927,Ag 20,8:2
Light of Asia, The 1928,O 10,32:2
Gray Shadow 1931,Mr 11,23:4
Alchemist, The 1931,Je 5,27:1
Great Lover, The 1932,O 12,27:3
Firebird 1932,N 22,25:2
All Good Americans 1933,D 6,29:2
Richelieu 1934,My 22,28:1
Twelfth Night 1934,Jl 17,24:5
Hamlet 1934,D 26,19:3
Richard III 1934,D 28,24:3
Rip Van Winkle 1935,Ag 7,22:2
Master of the Revels 1935,Ag 14,16:2
Taming of the Shrew, The 1935,O 1,27:3
Idiot's Delight 1936,Mr 25,25:2
Moroni 1936,Ag 19,19:1
Cradle Will Rock, The 1938,Ja 4,19:3
Merry Wives of Windsor, The 1938,Ap 15,22:3
Madame Capet 1938,O 26,26:2
Good Hunting 1938,N 22,26:5
American Way, The 1939,Ja 23,9:2
Mr Big 1941,O 1,24:2
They Should Have Stood in Bed 1942,F 14,18:5
Kiss for Cinderella, A 1942,Mr 11,22:2
I Killed the Count 1942,S 4,18:1
Meet a Body 1944,O 17,19:5
Would-Be Gentleman, The 1946,Ja 10,29:2
Magic Touch, The 1947,S 4,30:1
Volpone 1948,Ja 9,24:6
Make a Wish 1951,Ap 19,38:1
First Gentleman, The 1957,Ap 26,22:2
Time Remembered 1957,N 13,41:2
Henry IV, Part I 1962,Je 18,20:4
Richard II 1962,Je 18,20:2
Hamlet 1964,Je 17,49:1

Operti, Le Roi (Director)
Joan of Arc 1926,Ap 24,21:2

Ophir, Shai K
Lute Song 1959,Mr 13,24:1
41 in a Sack 1960,Mr 26,15:2
My Fair Lady 1964,F 20,24:4

Ophir, Shai K (Director)
41 in a Sack 1960,Mr 26,15:2

Ophir, Shai K (Playwright)
41 in a Sack 1960,Mr 26,15:2

Ophir, Shai K (Producer)
41 in a Sack 1960,Mr 26,15:2

Ophuls, Max (Director)
Royal Family, The 1931,Ap 12,IX,1:3

Opitz, Larry (Director)
Republic, The 1970,Ap 28,49:1

Opler, Alfred
Sweetheart Shop, The 1920,S 1,13:4

Opoku, Albert (Miscellaneous)
Kwamina 1961,O 24,42:1

Opp, Joe
Century Revue and the Midnight Rounders, The
  1920,Jl 13,9:1
Make It Snappy 1922,Ap 14,20:2

Oppenheim, David (Producer)
Last Analysis, The 1964,O 2,30:1

Oppenheim, E Phillips (Original Author)
Evelyne 1928,F 19,VIII,2:1

Oppenheim, Menashe
Untitled-Revue 1939,Ap 5,31:2
Melody Lingers On, The 1969,N 17,55:1
Brothers Ashkenazi, The 1970,N 17,53:2

Oppenheimer, Alan
Clandestine on the Morning Line 1959,D 5,18:2
Caucasian Chalk Circle, The 1961,N 1,35:1
Burning of the Lepers, The 1962,Ap 5,29:1
Once in a Lifetime 1962,O 30,30:1
Burning, The 1963,D 4,57:1
Lonesome Train, The 1965,Je 17,25:1
Hard Travelin' 1965,Je 17,25:1

Oppenheimer, George (Lyricist)
So's Your Old Manhattan 1927,My 5,30:5
Manhatters, The 1927,Jl 19,27:3
Manhatters, The 1927,Ag 4,25:4

Oppenheimer, George (Playwright)
Manhatters, The 1927,Jl 19,27:3
Manhatters, The 1927,Ag 4,25:4
Here Today 1932,S 7,14:2
Here Today 1932,S 18,IX,1:1
Another Love 1934,Mr 20,26:3
Dance Me a Song 1950,Ja 21,10:5
Mighty Man Is He, A 1960,Ja 7,25:2

Oppenheimer, George (Translator)
Another Love 1934,Mr 20,26:3

Oppenheimer, J (Producer)
Tales of Rigo 1927,My 31,25:3

Oppenheimer, Jacob (Producer)
Just Life 1926,S 15,33:3

Opperman, Joseph
Emperor's New Clothes, The 1941,D 27,15:5

Opperman, Joseph (Playwright)
Emperor's New Clothes, The 1941,D 27,15:5

Opunui, Charles
Half-Caste, The 1926,Mr 30,20:4

O'Quinn, Beauton
Chocolate Soldier, The 1921,D 13,24:2
All Wet 1925,Jl 7,24:1

Oram, Harold L (Producer)
Believers, The 1968,My 10,57:4

O'Ramey, Georgia
Daffy Dill 1922,Ag 23,14:5
Jack and Jill 1923,Mr 23,17:2
No, No, Nanette 1925,S 17,20:2
Ramblers, The 1926,S 21,32:2

Oran, Bob
Of Thee I Sing 1952,My 6,34:2

Orange, Ruby
Henri Christophe 1945,Je 7,24:5

Orb, Forrest
Philadelphia Story, The 1939,Mr 29,21:1

Orbach, Jerry
Fantasticks, The 1960,My 4,55:2
Carnival! 1961,Ap 14,22:2
Carnival! 1961,Ap 23,II,1:1
Cradle Will Rock, The 1964,N 9,40:4
Guys and Dolls 1965,Ap 29,39:1
Carousel 1965,Ag 11,39:1
Annie Get Your Gun 1966,Je 1,42:2
Natural Look, The 1967,Mr 13,45:2
Scuba Duba 1967,O 11,36:1
Scuba Duba 1967,O 22,II,3:7
Scuba Duba 1968,Ja 7,II,1:5
Promises, Promises 1968,D 2,59:3
Promises, Promises 1968,D 15,II,3:1
Scuba Duba 1969,Ap 7,51:1
Promises, Promises 1970,Ja 18,II,7:1

Orbera, Rafael Marti (Playwright)
Madre 1923,D 31,9:6

Orbok, Attileo (Playwright)
40 CV du Roi, La 1927,O 23,VIII,2:2

Orchard, Edward
Red Robe, The 1928,D 26,15:1
Merry Widow, The 1931,S 8,39:1
Geisha, The 1931,O 6,35:4

Orchard, Geoffrey
Republic, The 1970,Ap 28,49:1

Orczy, Baroness (Original Author)
Pimpernel! 1964,Ja 7,26:6

Ord, Robert (Playwright)
Paddy the Next Best Thing 1920,Ag 28,5:5

Ord, Simon (Producer)
Rising Sun, The 1929,O 27,IX,2:2

Ord, Winifred
Marigold 1930,O 9,23:1

Orde, Knox
In the Night Watch 1921,Ja 31,10:1
Danger 1921,D 23,18:3

Ordinatsky, Janet
Fifth Commandment, The 1965,N 15,48:4

Ordon, Edmund (Translator)
Policemen, The 1961,N 22,24:2

Ordway, Eugene
John Hawthorne 1921,Ja 24,16:1
Pearl of Great Price, The 1926,N 2,34:3
Broken Chain, The 1929,F 21,30:4

O'Rear, Betty
Billygoat Eddie 1964,Ap 21,43:2

O'Rear, James
Shoemaker's Holiday, The 1938,Ja 3,17:2
My Heart's in the Highlands 1939,Ap 14,29:2
World We Make, The 1939,N 21,19:1

Heavenly Express 1940,Ap 19,24:2
Glamour Preferred 1940,N 16,13:2
Eight O'Clock Tuesday 1941,Ja 7,18:2
Happy Time, The 1950,Ja 25,24:1
Maya 1953,Je 10,35:1
Loss of Roses, A 1959,N 30,27:1
Caligula 1960,F 17,31:1
Promises to Keep 1965,Jl 22,25:1

Oreck, Marvin
Crime 1927,F 23,27:3

O'Regan, George
Juno and the Paycock 1940,Ja 17,24:2

O'Regan, Kathleen
Professor Tim 1927,Ap 17,VII,1:4
Young Woodley 1928,Mr 11,VIII,1:3
Black Magic 1931,S 6,VIII,2:1

O'Regan, Michael
Henry V 1966,Je 8,38:1
Twelfth Night 1966,Je 10,51:2

O'Reiley, Francis
Night Hostess 1928,S 13,31:2

O'Reilly, Emmet
Magnanimous Lover, The 1920,F 10,10:2
Girl in the Coffin, The 1920,F 10,10:2
Suppressed Desires 1920,F 10,10:2
Minute's Wait, A 1920,Je 22,9:1
Rising of the Moon, The 1920,Je 22,9:1
O'Flaherty, V C 1920,Je 22,9:1
Drums of Jeopardy, The 1922,My 30,8:4
Dream Play 1926,Ja 21,18:2
Juno and the Paycock 1926,Mr 16,22:1
Hangman's House 1926,D 17,27:2

O'Reilly, J Francis
Wheel, The 1921,My 8,VI,1:1
Wheel, The 1921,Ag 30,10:1
Walk Together Chillun 1936,F 5,15:2

O'Reilly, Kathleen
Shewing-Up of Blanco Posnet, The 1959,S 19,26:7

O'Reilly, Larry
Dawn of Ireland, The 1920,O 1,14:2

O'Reilly, Nan (Playwright)
Four O'Clock 1933,F 14,19:6

O'Reilly, Rosalie
Los Angeles 1927,D 20,32:3

O'Reilly, Rosemary
New Faces of 1952 1952,My 17,23:2
New Faces of 1952 1952,My 25,II,1:1
Johnny Johnson 1956,O 22,24:1

Orfaly, Alexander
How Now, Dow Jones 1967,D 8,53:1
End of All Things Natural, The 1969,S 12,38:1

Orff, Carl (Composer)
Midsummer Night's Dream, A 1956,Jl 20,9:5

Orin, Renee
Great Magician, The 1951,N 22,45:1
Cafe Crown 1964,Ap 18,32:1
Mutilated, The 1966,F 23,42:1
Show Me Where the Good Times Are 1970,Mr 6,32:1

Oringer, Harold
Three Plays of the Sea 1970,Ag 20,39:1

O'Riordan, Blanche
Crime at Blossoms, The 1937,Jl 17,12:8

O'Riordan, Patricia
South Pacific 1965,Je 3,25:1

Orkow, B Harrison (Playwright)
Milgrim's Progress 1924,D 23,17:1
Napoleon 1928,Mr 9,21:1
Star Spangled Family 1945,Ap 11,18:6

Orlandi, Felice
Grass Harp, The 1953,Ap 28,32:2
Girl on the Via Flaminia, The 1954,F 10,37:1
Girl on the Via Flaminia, The 1954,Ap 6,35:5
27 Wagons Full of Cotton 1955,Ja 19,23:2
All in One; 27 Wagons Full of Cotton 1955,Ap 20,40:3
Ronde, La 1955,Je 28,24:2
Brigadoon 1963,F 1,6:2
Matty and the Moron and Madonna 1965,Mr 30,53:1

Orlandini, Leo
Donna Del Mare, La; Lady From the Sea, The 1923,O 30,17:1
Spretti; Ghosts 1923,N 7,14:1
Cosi Sia; Thy Will be Done 1923,N 14,29:2
Porta Chiusa, La; Closed Door, The 1923,N 21,23:1
Rain 1925,S 27,28:6

Orlando, Guido
Flame of Love 1924,Ap 22,19:2

Orlando, Joyce
Of Thee I Sing 1969,Mr 8,19:1

Orlando, Phil (Miscellaneous)
Hobo 1961,Ap 11,41:2

Orlando and his horses
Better Times 1922,S 4,14:2

Orleans, Leslie
Kingdom of God, The 1928,D 21,30:2

Orley, Malcolm (Playwright)
Emperor of Make-Believe, The 1936,Je 4,27:2

Orlob, Harold (Composer)
Talk About Girls 1927,Je 15,31:3
Hairpin Harmony 1943,O 2,18:5

Orlob, Harold (Lyricist)
Hairpin Harmony 1943,O 2,18:5

Orlob, Harold (Playwright)
Hairpin Harmony 1943,O 2,18:5

Orlob, Harold (Producer)
Hairpin Harmony 1943,O 2,18:5

Orloff, Nicholas
On Your Toes 1954,O 12,24:4
Pipe Dream 1955,D 1,44:1

Orlova, Margarita
Shanghai Gesture, The 1926,F 2,20:2

Orlova, Sonia
Rosalinda; Fledermaus, Die 1942,O 29,26:5
Song of Norway 1944,Ag 22,20:2

Orlovetsky, Emil
West Side Story 1965,Je 25,37:2

Orman, Roscoe
Party on Greenwich Avenue, The 1967,My 11,52:1
Who's Got His Own 1967,O 14,13:3
Clara's Ole Man 1968,Mr 9,23:2
Electronic Nigger, The 1968,Mr 9,23:2

Ormay, Lucille
Anatomist, The 1957,F 27,21:5

Orme, Gordon
New Faces 1934,Mr 16,24:5

Orme, Michel (Playwright)
Tiger Cats 1924,O 22,18:1
Blaue vom Himmel, Das 1930,Ap 20,VIII,2:1

Ormiston, George
Leonard Sillman's New Faces of 1968 1968,My 3,43:1

Ormiston, Robert
Sunny River 1941,D 5,28:2

Ormonde, Viola Cecil
Straw, The 1921,N 11,16:2

Ormsby, Ken
Ice Follies 1966,Ja 12,27:6
Ice Follies 1970,My 23,27:1

Ormsby, Margaret
Escape This Night 1938,Ap 23,18:1

Ormsby, Paulette
Ice Follies 1966,Ja 12,27:6
Ice Follies 1970,My 23,27:1

Ormsbys, The
Ice Follies 1969,My 23,38:1

Orna, Adolphe (Playwright)
Mademoiselle le Feu 1924,My 18,VII,2:8
Peche, Le 1930,F 2,VIII,4:1

Ornadel, Cyril (Composer)
Pickwick 1963,Jl 5,13:2
Pickwick 1965,O 6,5:3

Ornadel, Cyril (Lyricist)
Pickwick 1965,O 6,5:3

Ornbo, Robert (Lighting Director)
Company 1970,Ap 27,40:1

Ornest, Otto (Director)
Thirty Pieces of Silver 1951,Mr 18,42:1

Ornest, Otto (Translator)
Thirty Pieces of Silver 1951,Mr 18,42:1

Ornitz, Samuel (Original Author)
Haunch, Paunch and Jowl 1935,D 27,22:4

Ornitz, Samuel (Playwright)
Geraniums in My Window 1934,O 27,20:6
Haunch, Paunch and Jowl 1935,D 27,22:4

Ornstein, J Alan (Producer)
Friday Night; River, The 1965,F 9,42:5
Friday Night; Passport 1965,F 9,42:5
Friday Night; Mary Agnes Is Thirty-Five 1965,F 9,42:5

Ornstein, Leo (Composer)
Lysistrata 1930,Ap 29,30:5
Lysistrata 1930,Je 6,20:1

Oro, Charles
Lady of the Lamp, The 1920,Ag 18,6:4

O'Rourke, Betty
Viva O'Brien 1941,O 10,27:2

O'Rourke, Charles
Infernal Machine, The 1937,D 13,22:7

O'Rourke, Cliff
Betty Lee 1924,D 26,18:2
Vaudeville (Palace) 1927,Jl 5,19:3
Allez-Opp! 1927,Ag 3,29:3

O'Rourke, J A
Plough and the Stars, The 1927,N 29,30:2
Juno and the Paycock 1927,D 20,32:2
New Gossoon, The 1931,Ap 27,24:5
Anatomist, The 1931,O 25,VIII,2:6

O'Rourke, Jerry
Forbidden Melody 1936,N 3,33:1

O'Rourke, John
White-Headed Boy, The 1921,S 16,20:1

O'Rourke, Mary
Flossie 1924,Je 4,25:2
Squaring the Circle 1936,Ag 12,15:3

O'Rourke, Nancy
Ladies Night in a Turkish Bath 1961,Mr 22,38:1

O'Rourke, Pat
Song of Norway 1944,Ag 22,20:2
Too Hot for Maneuvers 1945,My 3,26:5

O'Rourke, Paul A
Born Yesterday 1958,Mr 22,12:6

Orr, Ann
Death Takes a Holiday 1929,N 24,X,4:5

Orr, Ann—Cont

Death Takes a Holiday 1929,D 27,26:4
Orr, Charlotte
As You Desire Me 1931,Ja 29,21:2
Cloudy With Showers 1931,S 2,17:5
Electra 1932,Ja 9,21:4
Orr, David
Aria Da Capo 1950,My 25,36:2
Liliom 1956,F 18,12:5
Orr, Forrest
Peter Flies High 1931,N 10,28:3
Sophisticrats, The 1933,F 14,19:5
Big Hearted Herbert 1934,Ja 2,17:3
Pursuit of Happiness, The 1934,Je 24,IX,1:4
Lost Horizons 1934,O 16,31:2
Dear Old Darling 1936,Mr 3,25:1
County Chairman, The 1936,My 26,26:5
Red, Hot and Blue! 1936,O 30,26:3
Washington Jitters 1938,My 3,19:1
Dame Nature 1938,S 27,24:3
Night Before Christmas, The 1941,Mr 30,I,48:2
Night Before Christmas, The 1941,Ap 11,25:2
Meet a Body 1944,O 17,19:5
Man Who Had All the Luck, The 1944,N 24,18:5
Calico Wedding 1945,Mr 8,18:6
Oh, Herbert! 1945,Je 20,26:3
C·r, M M (Costume Designer)
·s the Valet 1933,D 15,25:4
·r, M M (Scenic Designer)
It's the Valet 1933,D 15,25:4
Orr, Mary
Berlin 1931,D 31,16:1
Child of Manhattan 1932,Mr 2,15:1
Julie the Great 1936,Ja 15,15:3
Jupiter Laughs 1940,S 10,27:1
Jeannie 1940,N 13,29:2
Malice Domestic 1942,Jl 21,22:1
Wallflower 1944,Ja 27,14:2
Dark Hammock 1944,D 12,27:8
Sherlock Holmes 1953,O 31,11:2
Desperate Hours, The 1955,F 11,20:2
Orr, Mary (Original Author)
Applause 1970,Mr 31,35:1
Applause 1970,Ap 5,II,1:1
Orr, Mary (Playwright)
Wallflower 1944,Ja 27,14:2
Dark Hammock 1944,D 12,27:8
Round Trip 1945,My 30,16:4
Be Your Age 1953,Ja 15,24:2
Orr, Metta Louise
Jack and Jill 1923,Mr 23,17:2
Orrick, David
Romeo and Juliet 1935,D 24,10:2
Saint Joan 1936,Mr 10,27:4
All That Glitters 1938,Ja 20,18:2
Come Across 1938,S 15,28:3
George Washington Slept Here 1940,O 19,20:3
Doctor's Dilemma, The 1941,Mr 12,18:2
Antony and Cleopatra 1947,N 27,49:2
Deirdre of the Sorrows 1949,D 15,51:2
Orrick, Martha
Camille 1956,S 19,33:1
Waltz of the Toreadors, The 1958,Mr 5,37:1
Well of the Saints, The 1959,Ap 11,15:4
Workhouse Ward, The 1959,Ap 11,15:4
Farewell, Farewell Eugene 1960,S 28,35:1
Orrison, Jack
Doll's House, A 1956,My 8,29:2
Orsatti, June-Ellen
Crucible, The 1958,Mr 17,21:1
Orsell, Renee
I Know My Love 1949,N 3,36:1
Orselli, Raimonda
Much Ado About Nothing 1952,My 2,20:1
Virtuous Island, The 1957,Ap 10,39:1
Orson, Barbara
Brother to Dragons 1968,D 8,86:1
Ortega, Eva
Set to Music 1939,Ja 19,16:2
Ortega, L Garcia
Road to Happiness, The 1927,My 3,24:1
Romantic Young Lady, The 1927,My 5,30:2
Girl and the Cat, The 1927,My 6,21:2
Blind Heart, The 1927,My 8,30:2
Fragila Rosina 1927,My 10,24:4
Cradle Song 1927,My 10,24:4
Pygmalion 1927,My 12,25:2
Ortega, Margarita Garcia
Pluma en el Viento; Feather in the Wind
1932,Ap 2,13:4
De Muy Buena Familia; Of Very Good Family
1932,Ap 29,13:3
Ortega, Rosario Garcia
Pluma en el Viento; Feather in the Wind
1932,Ap 2,13:4
Tambor y Cascabel; Drum and Bell
1932,Ap 21,25:4
Cuando Los Hijos De Eva No Son Los Hijos De
Adan; When Eve's Children Are Not Adam's
1932,Ap 23,11:2
De Muy Buena Familia; Of Very Good Family
1932,Ap 29,13:3
Ortega, Santos
What's the Use? 1926,S 7,19:1

What Never Dies 1926,D 29,24:2
Puppets of Passion 1927,F 25,24:4
Marilyn's Affairs 1933,Mr 16,21:5
Jeb 1946,F 22,20:2
Ortell, George
Saluta 1934,Ag 29,13:4
Orth, Betina
Desert Song, The 1946,Ja 9,20:2
Orth, Elisabeth
Wozzeck 1966,Ap 6,34:1
Mitschuldigen, Die 1966,Ap 6,34:1
Ratten, Die 1966,Ap 13,36:1
Orth, Frank L Jr
Wings Over Europe 1936,Mr 4,24:7
Orth, Louise
Madeleine and the Movies 1922,Mr 7,11:1
Ortiz, Elsa
Toothbrush, The 1970,S 27,84:5
Ortman, George (Miscellaneous)
Lesson, The 1956,O 3,29:2
Escurial 1956,O 3,29:2
Ortman, George (Producer)
By Hex 1956,Je 19,25:1
Ortman, George (Scenic Designer)
Escurial 1956,O 3,29:2
Ortmann, Will (Composer)
Holka Polka 1925,O 15,27:2
Ortmayr, Heinrich
Before Sundown 1962,Mr 14,43:1
Ortn, Louise
Mandarin, The 1920,N 10,18:2
Ortner, Heinz (Playwright)
Wer Will Unter die Soldaten? 1931,My 10,VIII,3:2
Orton, Evelyn
Dice of the Gods, The 1923,Ap 6,20:2
Orton, Jack
He Who Gets Slapped 1946,Mr 21,31:4
Orton, Joe (Playwright)
Entertaining Mr Sloane 1964,Je 30,21:1
Entertaining Mr Sloane 1965,O 13,41:1
Entertaining Mr Sloane 1965,O 24,II,1:1
Loot 1968,Mr 19,40:2
Loot 1968,Mr 31,II,1:1
What the Butler Saw 1969,Mr 7,27:7
Crimes of Passion; Ruffian on the Stair, The
1969,O 27,54:1
Crimes of Passion; Erpingham Camp, The
1969,O 27,54:1
Crimes of Passion; Erpingham Camp, The; Ruffian
on the Stair, The 1969,N 9,II,1:1
What the Butler Saw 1970,My 5,56:1
What the Butler Saw 1970,My 17,II,1:1
What the Butler Saw 1970,O 14,38:1
Ortway, Frank
One Heluva Night 1924,Je 5,18:1
Orval, Whitlege
Vaudeville (Palace) 1932,O 3,15:5
Orville, William
Foolscap 1933,Ja 12,21:2
Orvis, Franklin
Fortuno 1925,D 23,22:1
Orwig, Joyce
Hamlet 1954,Ap 24,15:2
O'Ryan, Anna Wynne (Playwright)
Just Because 1922,Mr 23,11:1
Orzazewski, Kasia
World We Make, The 1939,N 21,19:1
Brother Cain 1941,S 13,21:5
Suds in Your Eye 1944,Ja 13,15:5
One-Man Show 1945,F 9,21:2
Swan Song 1946,My 16,29:2
Orzel, Richard
Rimers of Eldritch, The 1967,F 21,53:1
Orzello, Harry
Triumph of Robert Emmet, The 1969,My 8,54:1
Osato, Sono
One Touch of Venus 1943,O 8,14:1
One Touch of Venus 1943,O 17,II,1:1
On the Town 1944,D 29,11:4
On the Town 1945,Ja 7,II,1:1
Peer Gynt 1951,Ja 29,15:2
Maya 1953,Je 10,35:1
Little Clay Cart, The 1953,Jl 1,25:1
Once Over Lightly 1955,Mr 16,39:1
Osborn, Conrad
Corn Is Green, The 1954,F 27,10:2
Osborn, John (Playwright)
Luther 1963,S 11,46:3
Osborn, Leonard
Trial by Jury 1939,Ja 6,25:1
Gondoliers, The 1939,Ja 20,14:2
Yeomen of the Guard, The 1939,Ja 24,17:1
Iolanthe 1948,Ja 13,29:3
Cox and Box 1948,Ja 20,26:2
Gondoliers, The 1948,Ja 27,31:2
Yeomen of the Guard, The 1948,F 3,30:2
Patience 1948,F 10,27:2
Trial by Jury 1951,F 6,24:2
Gondoliers, The 1951,F 13,27:2
Iolanthe 1951,F 16,22:1
Cox and Box 1951,F 20,21:2
Iolanthe 1955,S 28,38:1
Yeomen of the Guard, The 1955,O 4,39:2

Osborn, Leonard—Cont

Princess Ida 1955,O 14,22:3
Ruddigore 1955,O 21,32:2
Osborn, Lincoln (Playwright)
Uptown West 1923,Ap 4,22:2
Secret Service Smith 1927,S 4,VII,2:4
Osborn, Paul (Director)
Innocent Voyage, The 1943,N 16,27:2
Osborn, Paul (Original Author)
On Borrowed Time 1938,O 6,27:5
Osborn, Paul (Playwright)
Hotbed 1928,N 10,20:7
Ledge, A 1929,N 19,26:3
Vinegar Tree, The 1930,N 20,30:3
Vinegar Tree, The 1930,D 7,IX,1:1
Vinegar Tree, The 1931,N 15,VIII,4:1
Vinegar Tree, The 1932,Je 9,27:7
Vinegar Tree, The 1932,Jl 10,IX,1:3
Oliver Oliver 1934,Ja 6,18:5
Vinegar Tree, The 1935,Ag 14,16:1
Tomorrow's Monday 1936,Jl 16,15:6
On Borrowed Time 1938,F 4,16:4
On Borrowed Time 1938,N 6,IX,1:1
Morning's at Seven 1939,N 7,30:2
Morning's at Seven 1939,N 12,IX,2:3
Morning's at Seven 1939,D 1,26:2
Morning's at Seven 1939,D 10,X,5:6
Morning's at Seven 1939,D 17,IX,3:1
Innocent Voyage, The 1943,N 16,27:2
Bell for Adano, A 1944,N 10,24:6
Bell for Adano, A 1944,D 7,21:2
Bell for Adano, A 1944,D 17,II,3:2
Bell for Adano, A 1945,S 20,31:1
Point of No Return 1951,O 31,32:2
Point of No Return 1951,D 14,35:2
Point of No Return 1951,D 23,II,3:1
On Borrowed Time 1953,F 11,34:1
Morning's at Seven 1955,Je 23,25:1
Morning's at Seven 1956,Ja 8,II,3:1
Point of No Return 1957,Mr 23,17:2
World of Suzie Wong, The 1958,O 15,47:1
World of Suzie Wong, The 1958,O 19,II,1:1
Osborn, Peter
Gentle Rain 1936,S 20,IX,1:4
Osborne, Brian
Comedy of Errors, The 1964,My 21,43:1
Osborne, Eunice
Dice of the Gods, The 1923,Ap 6,20:2
Helena's Boys 1924,Ap 8,22:2
Polly 1925,O 12,19:1
When We Dead Awaken 1926,My 18,29:3
Ladies of the Jury 1929,O 22,26:2
Little Princess, The 1931,F 7,11:3
Anatomist, The 1932,O 25,24:3
Osborne, Hubert (Director)
Witch, The 1926,N 19,22:5
Closed Room, The 1934,Jl 24,20:2
Osborne, Hubert (Original Author)
Hit the Deck! 1927,Ap 26,32:1
Osborne, Hubert (Playwright)
Shore Leave 1922,Ag 9,20:2
Rita Coventry 1923,F 20,12:2
Blue Bandanna, The 1924,Je 24,18:4
Two Worlds 1926,Je 27,VII,3:1
Eve's Complaint 1928,My 20,VIII,1:3
Osborne, Innis G (Playwright)
Biarritz 1929,Ag 11,VIII,2:1
Osborne, J A
Fan, The 1921,O 4,10:1
Osborne, John
This Our House 1935,D 12,33:3
Osborne, John (Director)
World of Paul Slickey, The 1959,My 6,48:7
Osborne, John (Lyricist)
World of Paul Slickey, The 1959,My 6,48:7
Osborne, John (Playwright)
Look Back in Anger 1957,O 2,28:2
Look Back in Anger 1957,O 13,II,1:1
Epitaph for George Dillon 1958,F 12,33:8
Entertainer, The 1958,F 13,22:2
Entertainer, The 1958,F 23,II,1:1
Epitaph for George Dillon 1958,N 5,44:1
Epitaph for George Dillon 1958,N 16,II,1:1
World of Paul Slickey, The 1959,My 6,48:7
Epitaph for George Dillon 1960,D 29,17:1
Luther 1961,Jl 8,9:2
Luther 1961,Jl 28,10:2
Blood of the Bambergs, The; Under Plain Cover
1962,Jl 20,15:3
Luther 1963,S 26,41:1
Luther 1963,O 6,II,1:1
Inadmissible Evidence 1964,S 10,31:1
Luther 1965,F 15,30:4
Patriot for Me, A 1965,Jl 11,II,1:4
Inadmissible Evidence 1965,D 1,52:1
Time Present 1968,My 25,38:1
Time Present 1968,Je 2,II,3:6
Time Present 1968,Jl 5,20:1
Hotel in Amsterdam, The 1968,Jl 21,II,12:1
Hotel in Amsterdam, The 1968,Ag 17,17:1
Look Back in Anger 1968,N 1,38:1
Patriot for Me, A 1969,O 6,58:1
Patriot for Me, A 1969,O 12,II,1:1

Osborne, Kipp
Butterflies Are Free 1970,D 3,60:2
Osborne, Loyall Allan Jr (Playwright)
Bicentennial 1939,Ag 29,18:2
Osborne, Lucille
Everybody's Welcome 1931,O 14,26:3
Osborne, Nancy
Mystery of the Finding of the Cross, The
1959,Ja 16,35:2
Osborne, Paul (Playwright)
On Borrowed Time 1953,Ja 1,19:1
World of Suzie Wong, The 1959,N 18,49:6
Osborne, Peggy
Daddy Come Home 1963,Ap 17,33:1
Colombe 1965,F 24,33:1
Osborne, Rafaele
Femme d'Amour, La 1927,Je 5,VII,2:1
Osborne, Seymour
Russian People, The 1942,D 30,17:2
Osborne, Sidney (Playwright)
Gestaendris 1921,Jl 24,VI,1:7
Osborne, Suzanne
Romulus 1962,Ja 11,27:1
Tragical Historie of Doctor Faustus, The
1964,O 6,34:2
Osborne, Thomas Mott (Composer)
Little Town of Bethlehem, The 1920,D 27,11:1
Osborne, Vivienne
Bonehead, The 1920,Ap 13,12:1
Silver Fox, The 1921,S 6,13:1
Love Child, The 1922,N 15,22:1
Scaramouche 1923,O 25,14:2
New Toys 1924,F 19,12:1
New Toys 1924,F 24,VII,1:1
Blue Bandanna, The 1924,Je 24,18:4
Houses of Sand 1925,F 18,17:1
Aloma of the South Seas 1925,Ap 21,18:1
Fog 1927,F 8,20:1
One Glorious Hour 1927,Ap 15,27:2
Three Musketeers, The 1928,Mr 4,IX,2:3
Three Musketeers, The 1928,Mr 14,28:1
Three Musketeers, The 1928,Mr 25,IX,1:1
Week-end 1929,O 23,26:4
Elizabeth and Essex 1930,Mr 2,IX,4:7
Royal Virgin, The 1930,Mr 18,30:5
As Good As New 1930,N 4,37:3
Order Please 1934,O 10,21:2
Osborne, Will
Vaudeville (Palace) 1930,N 10,17:1
Radio Carnival 1932,Mr 14,13:3
Osbourne, Lloyd (Playwright)
Little Father of the Wilderness, The 1930,Je 3,27:1
Osburn, Oran
Maggie 1953,F 19,20:2
Li'l Abner 1956,N 16,24:2
Destry Rides Again 1959,Ap 24,24:1
Oscapella, Edward
Twelfth Night 1957,Jl 4,16:4
Oscar, Henry
Othello 1932,My 1,VIII,2:2
Future That Was, The 1936,Ap 23,21:3
Waltz in Goose Step 1938,N 2,26:2
Oscar, Henry (Director)
Future That Was, The 1936,Ap 23,21:3
Oscare, Jules
Mountain, The 1933,S 12,28:6
Oseka, Janusz
Visit With the Family, A 1957,O 17,42:5
Osena, Alex
Wedding in Japan 1949,N 11,29:1
Burning Bush, The 1949,D 17,15:5
Scapegoat, The 1950,Ap 20,36:5
Oser, Julie
West Side Story 1957,S 27,14:4
Osgood, Alfred A
What a Relief 1935,D 14,10:6
Osgood, Henry
That's the Woman 1930,S 4,27:2
Osgood, Herbert
Fratricide Punished 1925,Ap 21,19:1
Romio and Julietta 1925,Ap 21,19:1
Osgood, Lawrence (Playwright)
Pigeons 1965,Mr 4,37:1
Osgood, Pearl
Flying High 1930,F 9,VIII,4:2
Flying High 1930,Mr 4,24:4
Ziegfeld Follies 1931,Jl 2,30:5
Canteen Show, The 1942,S 4,18:1
O'Shaughnessy, John
Six Miracle Plays; Miraculous Birth and the
Midwives, The; Lamentation of the Virgin Mary,
The; Magdalen, The; Trois Rois, Les; Trois
Maries, Les; Nativite, La 1933,F 12,IX,2:1
Panic 1935,Mr 16,18:4
Let Freedom Ring 1935,N 7,26:2
Bury the Dead 1936,Ap 20,17:4
200 Were Chosen 1936,N 21,21:1
Excursion 1937,Ap 10,11:4
Journeyman 1938,Ja 31,14:2
Washington Jitters 1938,My 3,19:1
Boys From Syracuse, The 1938,N 24,36:1
Johnny Doodle 1942,Mr 19,28:2
Great Campaign, The 1947,Ap 1,33:2

Street Sounds 1970,O 23,32:1
O'Shaughnessy, John (Director)
Command Decision 1947,O 2,30:2
Command Decision 1947,O 12,II,1:1
Last Dance, The 1948,Ja 28,27:2
Church Street 1948,F 10,27:2
Afternoon Storm 1948,Ap 12,24:2
Sleepy Hollow 1948,Je 4,26:3
Riders to the Sea 1949,F 4,30:2
Freight 1949,F 4,30:2
Phoenix Too Frequent, A 1950,Ap 27,36:2
Freight 1950,Ap 27,36:2
Red Roses for Me 1951,Ap 26,35:8
Red Roses for Me 1955,D 29,15:2
Red Roses for Me 1956,Ja 8,II,1:1
Portrait of a Madonna 1957,Ap 1,21:2
Bedtime Story 1957,Ap 1,21:2
Man of Destiny, The 1957,Ap 1,21:2
Asmodee 1958,Mr 26,42:2
Cut of the Axe 1960,F 2,38:2
Figuro in the Night 1962,O 31,33:1
Moon Shines on Kylenamoe, The 1962,O 31,33:1
O'Shaughnessy, John (Playwright)
Prelude 1936,Ap 20,17:4
O'Shaughnessy, Patrick
Who'll Save the Plowboy? 1962,Ja 10,24:2
O'Shay, William
Nellie Bly 1946,Ja 22,32:2
O'Shea, Dan
Twelfth Night 1959,Jl 11,10:2
O'Shea, Eddie
Eve of St Mark, The 1942,O 8,30:2
O'Shea, Helen
Spice of 1922 1922,Jl 7,12:4
Moonlight 1924,Ja 31,13:7
Vaudeville (Hippodrome) 1926,Ap 27,22:3
No Foolin' 1926,Je 25,25:1
O'Shea, John
Growing Pains 1933,N 24,24:2
O'Shea, Kevin
As You Like It 1939,My 9,28:4
Dream Girl 1945,D 15,13:2
O'Shea, Madalyn
Three Sisters, The 1930,Ja 9,22:2
Coquette 1935,Jl 10,24:1
Beaux' Stratagem, The 1935,Jl 17,22:5
Hay Fever 1935,Jl 24,20:4
Camille 1935,Jl 31,21:1
Mr Pim Passes By 1935,Ag 7,22:2
Double Door 1935,Ag 21,22:2
Late Christopher Bean, The 1935,Ag 28,13:1
Candida 1937,Ag 4,14:5
Whiteheaded Boy, The 1937,Ag 11,27:3
Elizabeth the Queen 1937,Ag 25,24:3
O'Shea, Michael
Red Mill, The 1945,O 17,16:2
Red Mill, The 1945,O 28,II,1:1
O'Shea, Milo
Staircase 1968,Ja 11,41:2
Staircase 1968,Ja 21,II,3:7
Dear World 1969,F 7,33:1
O'Shea, Patsy
Love's Old Sweet Song 1940,My 3,16:3
Delicate Story 1940,D 5,32:2
Kiss for Cinderella, A 1942,Mr 11,22:2
Inside Story 1942,O 30,22:2
Tinker's Dam 1943,Ja 29,22:2
Arsenic and Old Lace 1943,D 13,18:6
O'Shea, Tessie
Girl Who Came to Supper, The 1963,D 9,49:1
Time for Singing, A 1966,My 23,48:2
O'Shiel, Fiona
Walk Hard 1946,Mr 28,34:2
Heiress, The 1947,S 30,22:2
Oshier, Irene
Crime and Punishment 1935,Ja 23,20:3
Coggerers, The 1939,Ja 21,18:4
Oshima, K (Translator)
Coney Island Play 1970,O 31,34:2
Oshima, W U
Airways, Inc 1929,F 21,30:5
Oshins, Julie
This Is the Army 1942,Jl 5,28:2
This Is the Army 1942,Ag 16,VIII,1:1
Oshlag, Arthur
Angel in the Pawnshop 1951,Ja 19,20:3
Long Watch, The 1952,Mr 21,19:5
Sing Till Tomorrow 1953,D 29,17:2
Witness for the Prosecution 1954,D 17,35:2
Oshrin, Harry H (Producer)
Talk About Girls 1927,Je 15,31:3
Oshrin, Sidney S (Producer)
I Feel Wonderful 1954,O 19,22:5
Osin, Fred
Have I Got One for You 1968,Ja 8,32:1
Osipow, Benjamin
Moon Is a Gong, The 1926,Mr 13,21:3
Window Panes 1927,F 22,22:2
Loud Speaker 1927,Mr 3,27:2
Belt, The 1927,O 20,33:1
Oslin, Kay
West Side Story 1968,Je 25,32:1

Osmond, Herman
Dead End 1935,O 29,17:2
Osmond, Marion (Playwright)
Chinese Bungalow, The 1929,F 3,VIII,2:1
Osmun, Leighton (Playwright)
Manhattan 1922,Ag 16,7:5
Sylvia 1923,Ap 26,22:1
Peter Weston 1923,S 20,5:2
Peter Weston 1923,S 30,II,1:1
Peter Weston 1924,Je 15,VII,1:4
Paging Danger 1931,F 27,19:2
Osnath-Halevy, Sarah
Eternal Road, The 1937,Ja 8,14:2
Ospina, Mercedes
Seidman and Son 1962,O 16,32:2
Ostendorf, John
Help! Help! the Globolinks 1970,D 24,10:2
Oster, Jimmy
Once Upon a Tailor 1955,My 24,36:2
Ostergren, Christopher
Crimes and Crimes 1970,Ja 19,35:1
Osterhout, Anne
Mary of Magdala 1946,Mr 26,24:5
Osterloh, Robert
Nights of Wrath; Nuits de la Colere, Les
1947,D 1,26:4
All the King's Men 1948,Ja 19,19:2
Osterman, Jack
All-Star Jamboree 1921,Jl 14,18:1
Vaudeville (Palace) 1924,Mr 18,25:1
Night in Paris, A 1926,Ja 6,16:3
Night in Paris, A 1926,Jl 27,15:4
Artists and Models 1927,N 16,28:2
Vaudeville (Palace) 1932,Ap 18,19:5
Smile at Me 1935,Ag 24,18:4
Osterman, Jack (Lyricist)
Artists and Models 1927,N 16,28:2
Osterman, Lester (Miscellaneous)
Loss of Roses, A 1959,N 30,27:1
Osterman, Lester (Producer)
Miss Lonelyhearts 1957,O 4,26:2
Say Darling 1958,Ap 4,17:1
Loss of Roses, A 1959,N 30,27:1
Cool World, The 1960,F 23,38:2
Face of a Hero 1960,O 21,29:5
Isle of Children 1962,Mr 17,16:2
High Spirits 1964,Ap 8,34:1
Fade Out--Fade In 1964,My 27,45:1
Something More! 1964,N 11,36:1
Fade Out--Fade In 1965,F 16,40:2
Dinner at Eight 1966,S 28,38:1
Weekend 1968,Mr 14,50:2
Rothschilds, The 1970,O 20,40:1
Osterman, Lester Jr (Miscellaneous)
Mr Wonderful 1956,Mr 23,23:2
Candide 1956,D 3,40:2
Ostermayer, Christine
Ratten, Die 1966,Ap 13,36:1
Ostermeler, Doheos (Dr)
Jumbo 1935,N 18,20:2
Ostertag, Bernard
Lancashire Lass, The 1931,D 31,16:3
Anatomist, The 1932,O 25,24:3
Nine Pine Street 1933,Ap 28,15:5
Divine Drudge 1933,Jl 4,16:4
No Questions Asked 1934,F 6,24:3
Crime and Punishment 1935,Ja 23,20:3
Trelawney of the 'Wells' 1935,Jl 16,24:1
Murder in the Cathedral 1936,Mr 21,13:5
Help Yourself! 1936,Jl 15,15:1
Fabulous Invalid, The 1938,O 10,15:1
Trojan Women, The 1941,Ap 9,32:5
Osterwald, Bibi
Broken Hearts of Broadway 1944,Je 13,16:2
Sing Out, Sweet Land! 1944,D 28,24:2
Three to Make Ready 1946,Mr 8,16:2
Sally 1948,My 7,31:2
Magnolia Alley 1949,Ap 19,29:2
Golden Apple, The 1954,Mr 12,15:2
Golden Apple, The 1954,Mr 21,II,1:1
Vamp, The 1955,N 11,30:1
Look Homeward, Angel 1957,N 29,33:1
Look Homeward, Angel 1957,D 8,II,5:1
Look Homeward, Angel 1958,Ag 31,II,1:1
Family Affair, A 1962,Ja 29,17:1
Osterweil, Leon (Mrs)
Bad Habits of 1925 1925,F 9,17:1
Ostrander, A A (Playwright)
Littlest Circus, The 1959,D 26,5:6
Ostrander, A A (Scenic Designer)
Where There's a Will 1939,Ja 18,16:6
Case of Youth, A 1940,Mr 25,10:3
All for All 1943,S 30,25:2
Sleep No More 1944,S 1,11:5
Duchess Misbehaves, The 1946,F 14,32:2
Ostrander, Don
Our Betters 1937,Jl 22,16:2
Ostrander, Leslie
Othello 1937,Ja 7,16:4
Ostraska, George
Don Carlos 1962,F 28,27:5
Storm, The 1962,Mr 31,17:2

trin, Art
Time of Your Life, The 1955,Ja 20,34:1
Othello 1955,S 8,27:2
South Pacific 1961,Ap 27,26:3
Around the World in 80 Days 1964,Je 29,33:2
Gnadiges Fraulein, The 1966,F 23,42:1
Promenade 1969,Je 5,56:1
trin, Arthur (Costume Designer)
Babes in Arms 1951,Mr 10,7:3
tro, Pauline (Musical Director)
Mikado, The 1939,Mr 11,15:6
troff, Oscar (Playwright)
Game of Love, A 1934,O 25,26:6
troff, Peter
Hippolytus 1948,N 22,25:5
trofsky, Samuel (Scenic Designer)
Anathema 1923,F 9,10:2
strom, Esther
Side-Show 1931,My 16,13:1
strov, Dmitri (Director)
Doctor Monica 1933,N 7,29:3
Are You Decent? 1934,Ap 20,16:2
Gypsy Blonde 1934,Je 26,22:5
Lady of Letters 1935,Mr 29,26:6
Squaring the Circle 1935,O 4,24:6
strov, Dmitri (Producer)
Gypsy Blonde 1934,Je 26,22:5
Lady of Letters 1935,Mr 29,26:6
strovksy, Sam (Scenic Designer)
Witch of Castile, The 1930,O 25,21:1
strovsky, Alexander (Playwright)
Enough Stupidity in Every Wise Man
1923,D 6,23:1
Poverty Is No Crime 1928,My 13,IX,2:7
Poverty Is No Crime 1928,Je 3,VIII,2:1
Storm, The 1929,D 29,VIII,2:1
Poverty Is No Crime 1935,F 21,22:5
Diary of a Scoundrel 1956,N 5,41:1
Storm, The 1962,Mr 31,17:2
strovsky, Boris
Doctor in Spite of Himself, The 1957,F 28,18:4
strow, Rayla
Take It Easy 1950,D 25,23:6
strow, Stuart (Director)
Here's Love 1963,O 4,28:1
strow, Stuart (Producer)
Here's Love 1963,O 4,28:1
Diary of Adam and Eve, The 1966,O 19,53:1
Passionella 1966,O 19,53:1
Lady or the Tiger?, The 1966,O 19,53:1
1776 1969,Mr 17,46:2
Ostrowsky, Chaim
Rich Man, Poor Man 1950,F 13,15:4
O'Sullivan, Arthur
Loves of Cass McGuire, The 1966,O 7,36:1
O'Sullivan, David
Five Star Saint 1970,F 11,41:2
O'Sullivan, Eugene (Director)
Whistler's Grandmother 1952,D 12,40:2
O'Sullivan, James
South Pacific 1968,Je 30,54:2
O'Sullivan, Lawrence
Excess Baggage 1927,D 27,24:2
Buzzard, The 1928,Mr 15,29:1
Inspector Kennedy 1929,D 21,16:3
Spook House 1930,Je 4,33:3
She Lived Next to the Firehouse 1931,F 11,23:1
Old Man Murphy 1931,My 19,25:2
When in Rome 1934,F 28,22:6
O'Sullivan, Mairin D
Philadelphia, Here I Come! 1966,F 17,28:1
Borstal Boy 1970,Ap 1,38:1
O'Sullivan, Maureen
Never Too Late 1962,N 28,42:1
Keep It in the Family 1967,S 28,59:1
Charley's Aunt 1970,Jl 6,38:1
O'Sullivan, Michael
King Lear 1961,My 15,34:6
Six Characters in Search of an Author
1963,Mr 11,7:2
In White America 1963,N 1,26:1
White House, The 1964,My 20,39:1
Tartuffe 1965,Ja 15,23:1
It's a Bird . . . It's a Plane . . . It's Superman
1966,Mr 30,34:1
Alchemist, The 1966,O 14,48:1
Love and Let Love 1968,Ja 4,30:1
Bench, The 1968,Mr 5,35:2
Flea in Her Ear, A 1969,O 4,25:1
Three Sisters, The 1969,O 10,38:1
Flea in Her Ear, A 1969,O 12,II,9:1
O'Sullivan, Terry
Intimate Relations 1962,N 2,27:1
Osuna, Jess
Hanjo 1960,N 16,51:4
This Side of Paradise 1962,F 22,19:6
Veronica 1965,N 19,31:1
Bugs 1965,N 19,31:1
Make Like a Dog 1966,Mr 7,22:1
Young Marrieds Play Monopoly 1966,Mr 7,22:1
Infantry, The 1966,N 15,51:1
Hamp 1967,Mr 10,32:1
Goodbye People, The 1968,D 4,52:1

Osuna, Jess (Miscellaneous)
This Side of Paradise 1962,F 22,19:6
Osuna, Jess (Producer)
This Side of Paradise 1962,F 22,19:6
Oswald, Raymond E
Betty, Be Good 1920,My 5,14:2
Jimmie 1920,N 18,15:3
Oswald, Virginia
Small Wonder 1948,S 16,33:5
Brigadoon 1950,My 3,36:2
Brigadoon 1957,Mr 28,37:1
Oswalda, Ossie
Rose of Florida, The 1929,F 23,17:1
Oswalk, Raymond
Betty, Be Good 1920,My 5,14:2
Otero, Anibal (Scenic Designer)
Crossroads 1969,Ag 7,28:1
Othon, Yvonne
West Side Story 1961,Mr 31,22:3
Otis
Theatre 1941,O 26,IX,2:3
Otis, Benjamin
Masque of the Kings, The 1937,F 9,19:4
Otis, Betty
39 Steps 1938,Mr 12,13:1
Otis, Helen Chichester (Director)
Pot Boiler, The 1923,My 11,20:3
Otis, Patricia
Mystery Square 1929,Ap 5,28:3
Otiz, Olive
Bottomland 1927,Je 28,29:3
Otoo, Paul
This Was a Man 1928,My 20,VIII,2:1
O'Toole, Peter
Merchant of Venice, The 1960,Ap 13,46:5
Hamlet 1963,O 23,37:2
Ride a Cock Horse 1965,Je 25,36:1
Juno and the Paycock 1966,Ag 3,40:1
Ott, Dorothy
Guimpes and Saddles 1967,O 11,36:3
Ott, Edgar
Don Carlos 1964,N 25,40:1
Ott, John
Don Juan in the Russian Manner 1954,Ap 23,23:2
Ottaviano, Robert
In Any Language 1952,O 9,40:2
Ottenfeld, Eddison von (Composer)
Pinocchio 1939,Ja 3,19:2
Ottenheimer, Albert
In Splendid Error 1954,O 27,33:6
Juno and the Paycock 1955,F 24,20:4
Affair of Honor 1956,Ap 7,12:3
Virtuous Island, The 1957,Ap 10,39:1
Apollo of Bellac, The 1957,Ap 10,39:1
Italian Straw Hat, The 1957,O 1,37:2
West Side Story 1960,Ap 28,31:1
Call It Virtue 1963,Mr 28,8:2
Immoralist, The 1963,N 8,36:2
Deputy, The 1964,F 27,26:1
Good Day 1965,O 19,51:1
Deadly Game, The 1966,F 14,34:1
Ottiano, Raffaela
Sweeney Todd 1924,Jl 19,10:4
Diamond Lil 1928,Ap 10,32:1
Grand Hotel 1930,N 14,30:4
Ottinger, Leonora
Genius and the Crowd 1920,S 7,20:1
Ottinger, Maurice
Dial 'M' for Murder 1958,F 8,12:2
Come Share My House 1960,F 19,20:2
Otto
Trial of Mary Dugan, The 1928,Je 24,VIII,1:4
Miss Gulliver Travels 1931,N 26,36:4
Otto, Annaliese
Wilhelm Tell 1925,Mr 2,15:1
Otto, Arthur F
All the King's Horses 1934,Ja 31,21:3
Otto, Ernest
Gypsy Baron, The 1930,Ap 22,22:8
Otto, Frank
Genius and the Crowd 1920,S 7,20:1
Little Nellie Kelly 1922,N 14,16:1
Howdy King 1926,D 14,24:4
Merry Malones, The 1927,S 27,30:2
June Moon 1929,O 10,34:5
Air-Minded 1932,F 11,17:3
Queer People 1934,F 16,16:2
Sun Field, The 1942,D 10,33:2
Marriage Is for Single People 1945,N 22,38:2
Born Yesterday 1946,F 5,18:2
Born Yesterday 1947,My 18,II,1:1
Otto, Jeanne (Producer)
Nathan Weinstein, Mystic, Connecticut
1966,F 26,15:2
Otto, K L (Scenic Designer)
Alcestiade 1957,Je 29,11:5
Otto, Linda (Producer)
People vs Ranchman, The 1968,O 28,56:1
Calling in Crazy 1969,O 7,42:2
Otto, Liz
Plot Against the Chase Manhattan Bank, The
1963,N 27,29:1
I Dreamt I Dwelt in Bloomingdale's 1970,F 13,26:1

Otto, Teo (Scenic Designer)
Good Woman of Setzuan, The 1956,D 19,41:2
Visit, The 1958,My 6,40:1
Visit, The 1960,Mr 9,38:3
Faust, Part I; Prologue in Heaven 1961,F 5,27:2
Faust, Part I; Play, The 1961,F 5,27:2
Faust, Part I; Prelude in the Theater 1961,F 5,27:2
Irish Faustus, An 1963,D 19,40:1
Otvos, A (Composer)
Paradise Alley 1924,Ap 2,17:3
Otvos, Dorian (Playwright)
Nine Fifteen Revue 1930,F 12,26:2
Garrick Gaieties 1930,Je 5,29:2
Calling All Stars 1934,D 14,28:2
It's A Gift 1945,Mr 13,18:7
Otway, Howard
Barretts of Wimpole Street, The 1945,Mr 27,23:6
Otway, Howard (Director)
This Nice Place 1966,N 2,35:2
Otway, Howard (Playwright)
This Here Nice Place 1966,N 2,35:2
Otway, Howard (Producer)
One Night Stands of a Noisy Passenger; Passage,
Un 1970,D 31,8:3
One Night Stands of a Noisy Passenger; Last
Stand 1970,D 31,8:3
One Night Stands of a Noisy Passenger; Noisy
Passenger, The 1970,D 31,8:3
Otway, Thomas (Playwright)
Venice Preserv'd 1955,D 13,54:4
Otway, Travers (Playwright)
Hidden Years, The 1948,F 15,II,3:1
Ouellet
Bourgeois Gentilhomme, Le 1955,O 26,26:1
Ould, Hermon (Playwright)
Dance of Life, The 1927,N 27,IX,4:7
Oulukanoff, Nicolai
Diana 1929,D 10,37:1
Oura, Saki (Miscellaneous)
Family, The 1943,Mr 31,22:4
Rhinoceros 1961,Ja 10,27:1
Oursler, Fulton (Original Author)
Sandalwood 1926,S 23,23:1
Behold This Dreamer 1927,N 1,20:4
Oursler, Fulton (Playwright)
Spider, The 1927,F 13,VII,1:4
Spider, The 1927,Mr 23,29:1
Spider, The 1927,Mr 27,VII,1:1
Behold This Dreamer 1927,O 16,IX,2:4
Behold This Dreamer 1927,N 1,20:4
All the King's Men 1929,F 5,27:1
Walking Gentleman, The 1942,My 8,26:2
Oursler, Helen
Launcelot and Elaine 1930,Mr 10,24:3
Ouspenskaya, Maria
Saint, The 1924,O 13,20:3
Jest, The 1926,F 5,22:2
Jest, The 1926,F 14,VIII,1:1
Witch, The 1926,N 19,22:5
Taming of the Shrew, The 1927,O 26,26:4
Taming of the Shrew, The 1927,N 13,IX,1:1
Three Sisters, The 1930,Ja 9,22:2
Passing Present, The 1931,D 8,36:2
Dodsworth 1934,F 26,20:4
Dodsworth 1934,Ag 21,12:3
Abide With Me 1935,N 22,19:2
Daughters of Atreus 1936,O 15,33:1
Outrageous Fortune 1943,N 4,28:5
Ouspensky, A (Playwright)
Red Rust 1929,D 18,31:1
Outin, Regis
Fausses Confidences, Les 1952,N 13,34:2
Proces, Le; Trial, The 1952,N 18,36:2
Amphitryon 1952,N 21,21:2
Fourberies de Scapin, Les 1952,N 21,21:2
Occupe-Toi d'Amelie; Keep Your Eyes on Amelie
1952,N 25,35:2
Hamlet 1952,D 2,39:1
Christophe Colomb 1957,Ja 31,20:5
Nuits de La Colere, Les; Nights of Fury
1957,F 12,31:1
Intermezzo 1957,F 15,20:4
Chien du Jardinier, Le; Gardener's Dog, The
1957,F 19,36:1
Adieux, Les 1957,F 19,36:1
Mariage de Figaro, Le 1964,F 26,41:2
Pieton de L'Air, Le 1964,Mr 4,33:2
Salut a Moliere 1964,Mr 4,33:2
Vie Parisienne, La 1964,Mr 11,34:2
Ouzoroff, Anna
Clear All Wires! 1932,S 15,19:1
Ouzounoff, Paul (Scenic Designer)
Sing High, Sing Low 1931,N 13,26:4
Over, Robert D
From Morn Till Midnight 1948,D 7,41:6
Overend, Dorothy
Offence, The 1925,N 16,25:1
Overman, Charles
Lost Colony, The 1937,Jl 11,X,2:1
Overman, Lynne
Honey Girl 1920,My 4,9:1
Just Married 1921,Ap 27,21:1
Vaudeville (Palace) 1923,O 23,18:2

Overman, Lynne—Cont

Just Married 1924,D 16,29:6
Just Married 1924,D 21,VII,1:8
Gossipy Sex, The 1927,Ap 20,28:3
Mr What's-His-Name 1927,S 4,VII,2:4
People Don't Do Such Things 1927,N 24,28:3
Sunny Days 1928,F 9,29:1
Little Accident 1929,Ap 28,IX,1:4
Button, Button 1929,O 24,26:1
Dancing Partner 1930,Jl 27,VIII,2:3
Dancing Partner 1930,Ag 6,24:2
Company's Coming! 1931,Ap 21,35:5
Stella Brady 1931,O 11,VIII,4:3
Hot-Cha! 1932,Mr 9,17:3
Budget, The 1932,S 21,26:4

Overton, Frank

Johnny Doodle 1942,Mr 19,28:2
Jacobowsky and the Colonel 1944,Mr 15,17:2
Truckline Cafe 1946,F 28,19:4
Trip to Bountiful, The 1953,N 4,30:3
Dark at the Top of the Stairs, The 1957,D 6,38:1

Overton, Frank E (Scenic Designer)

Democratic Body, A 1942,F 13,24:7

Overton, Hall (Composer)

Julius Caesar 1950,Je 21,30:1

Overton, Jane

Hassard Short's Ritz Revue 1924,S 18,19:1
Dearest Enemy 1925,S 19,9:2

Ovid (Original Author)

Metamorphoses 1969,D 12,69:1
Metamorphosis 1970,F 15,II,1:1

Owen, Alice

Thesmophoriazusae, The; Goddesses of Athens,
The 1955,D 14,52:4

Owen, Alun (Playwright)

There'll Be Some Changes Made 1969,O 2,56:2

Owen, Bill

As You Like It 1950,Ja 27,27:2

Owen, Catherine Dale

Mountain Man, The 1921,D 13,24:2
Bootleggers, The 1922,N 28,24:1
Love Set, The 1923,Mr 20,24:2
Whole Town's Talking, The 1923,Ag 30,8:2
Whole Town's Talking, The 1923,S 9,VII,1:1
Trelawney of the 'Wells' 1925,Je 2,16:2
Canary Dutch 1925,S 9,22:1
Love City, The 1926,Ja 26,18:2
Play's the Thing, The 1926,N 4,25:1
Mr Moneypenny 1928,O 17,26:2
Happy Landing 1932,Mr 28,10:5

Owen, Cecil

Musk 1920,Mr 15,13:1
Mask of Hamlet, The 1921,Ag 23,10:3
Johannes Kreisler 1922,D 25,20:3
For Value Received 1923,My 8,22:3
Spooks 1925,Je 2,16:4
Cradle Snatchers 1925,S 8,28:2
Bye Bye Bonnie 1927,Ja 14,15:3
Sidewalks of New York 1927,O 4,33:1
Anna 1928,My 17,25:2

Owen, Cecil (Director)

Lombardi, Ltd 1927,Je 7,27:3
Madame X 1927,Jl 7,29:3

Owen, Cliff

Comedian, The 1956,O 18,36:4
Tartuffe 1957,O 9,39:1

Owen, Clinton

Madre 1923,D 31,9:6

Owen, David

Carolinian, The 1925,N 3,34:2

Owen, Deirdre

Monique 1957,O 23,38:1
Back to Methuselah 1958,Mr 27,41:5
Back to Methuselah 1958,Ap 6,II,1:1

Owen, Esther

Mr Jiggins of Jigginstown 1936,D 18,30:2
All the Living 1938,Mr 25,14:4
Next Half Hour, The 1945,O 30,14:6

Owen, Ethel

Three's a Family 1943,My 6,24:2
Laffing Room Only 1944,D 25,15:4
Show Boat 1946,Ja 7,17:2
Show Boat 1946,Ja 13,II,1:1
Once an Actor 1950,Ag 1,19:8

Owen, Francine

Tartuffe 1957,O 9,39:1

Owen, Glyn

Luther 1963,S 26,41:1

Owen, Gregory

Babes in Arms 1951,Mr 10,7:3
Macbeth 1957,Ag 16,11:2
Richard III 1957,N 26,41:1

Owen, Guy

Gay Blades 1937,N 12,26:6
Gay Blades 1937,N 16,27:1
International Ice Frolics, The 1938,My 7,18:3

Owen, Hanna

My Fair Lady 1968,Je 14,42:1

Owen, Harrison (Playwright)

Happy Husband, The 1927,Jl 10,VII,2:3
Happy Husband, The 1928,My 8,25:2
Happy Husband, The 1928,My 27,VIII,1:1
Dr Pygmalion 1932,Ap 24,VIII,1:1

Owen, J

Boo Hoo! East Lynne 1959,S 9,50:4

Owen, Jan

Pygmalion 1952,F 9,11:2
Blood Wedding 1958,Ap 1,35:1
Spots of the Leopard, The 1963,S 25,38:1

Owen, Janet

Legend of Leonora, The 1926,My 1,10:1

Owen, Jay Jr

Everywhere I Roam 1938,D 30,10:4

Owen, Jeanne

Way of the World, The 1924,N 18,23:4
Polly 1925,O 12,19:1

Owen, John

Boo Hoo! East Lynne 1959,S 9,50:4

Owen, Larry (Miscellaneous)

Hit the Deck 1960,Je 24,32:1

Owen, Lichfield

Best People, The 1924,Ag 20,8:1

Owen, Lillian Marionettes

Christmas Carol, A 1921,D 23,18:3

Owen, Margaret Dale

Rotters, The 1922,My 23,12:4

Owen, Michael

Where Do We Go From Here? 1938,N 16,26:2

Owen, Muriel

Sisters of the Chorus 1930,My 18,VIII,3:1

Owen, Paul

Friends and Lovers; In the Zone; Bound East for
Cardiff 1961,My 11,43:1

Owen, Paul (Costume Designer)

Galileo 1968,D 1,88:4

Owen, Paul (Lighting Director)

Long Day's Journey Into Night 1963,Je 27,25:1

Owen, Paul (Scenic Designer)

Six Characters in Search of an Author
1961,My 11,43:1
Long Day's Journey Into Night 1963,Je 27,25:1
Effect of Gamma Rays on Man-in-the-Moon
Marigolds, The 1965,Je 7,48:1

Owen, Reginald

Carolinian, The 1925,N 3,34:2
Little Eyolf 1926,F 3,22:1
Importance of Being Earnest, The 1926,My 4,30:1
Play's the Thing, The 1926,N 4,25:1
Skin Deep 1927,O 18,32:1
Marquise, The 1927,N 15,26:4
Three Musketeers, The 1928,Mr 4,IX,2:3
Three Musketeers, The 1928,Mr 14,28:1
Three Musketeers, The 1928,Mr 25,IX,1:1
Candle-Light 1929,O 1,28:2
Out of a Blue Sky 1930,F 10,20:6
Jack's Up 1930,N 23,IX,3:5
Petticoat Influence 1930,D 16,34:6
Through the Years 1932,Ja 29,13:3
Child of Manhattan 1932,Mr 2,15:1
We Were Dancing; Tonight at Eight 1940,Ag 6,15:3
Tonight at 8:30 1940,Ag 11,IX,11:2
Affairs of State 1950,S 26,37:2

Owen, Reginald (Playwright)

Jack's Up 1930,N 23,IX,3:5

Owen, Rita

Ziegfeld Follies 1922,Je 6,18:2

Owen, Terence

Daphne Laureola 1950,S 19,38:6
Caesar and Cleopatra 1951,D 20,43:2

Owen, Teri

Adding Machine, The 1970,D 5,40:1

Owen, Tudor

King of Friday's Men, The 1951,F 22,26:2

Owen, Vernon Band

Vaudeville (Hippodrome) 1924,S 30,27:5

Owen, Walter

Girofle-Girofla 1926,N 24,26:2

Owens, Adelynn

Thanks for Tomorrow 1938,S 28,28:2

Owens, Deirdre

Tread the Green Grass 1950,Ap 21,19:4
Much Ado About Nothing 1952,My 2,20:1
Country Wife, The 1955,Ap 6,35:1

Owens, Edwin

Romeo and Juliet 1965,Je 21,36:3
Coriolanus 1965,Je 21,36:1
King Lear 1965,Je 25,39:1
Hamlet 1969,Je 30,33:1
Conduct Unbecoming 1970,O 13,50:1

Owens, Elizabeth

Candida 1969,F 3,29:1
Trumpets and Drums 1969,O 13,52:1
Macbeth 1969,D 23,25:1
Oedipus 1970,F 23,30:1

Owens, Janet (Scenic Designer)

Adding Machine, The 1948,N 18,35:2

Owens, Jean

Indian Captive, The 1949,Ja 31,15:2

Owens, Jeanette

Red, Hot and Blue! 1936,O 30,26:3

Owens, Juanita

Long Moment, The 1950,My 22,16:6

Owens, Maggie

Eastward in Eden 1956,Ap 18,25:4
Right You Are (If You Think You Are)
1957,Mr 5,37:1

Owens, Maggie—Cont

Ardele 1958,Ap 9,39:4

Owens, Margaret

Blood Wedding 1949,F 7,16:2

Owens, Peter

Moon on a Rainbow Shawl 1962,Ja 16,30:1

Owens, Regina

Lazarus Laughed 1948,Ap 9,27:4

Owens, Rochelle (Playwright)

Futz 1968,Je 14,39:1
Futz 1968,Je 30,II,1:1
Futz 1968,O 22,37:1
Beclch 1968,D 17,59:1
Queen of Greece, The 1969,Ap 12,40:2
Homo 1969,Ap 12,40:2

Owens, Walter J

Long Road, The 1930,S 10,30:2
Merchant of Venice, The 1930,D 3,29:2

Owsley, Monroe

Young Blood 1925,N 25,15:1
Holiday 1928,N 27,36:1

Oxford, Earl

Nine Fifteen Revue, The 1930,F 12,26:2
Three's a Crowd 1930,O 16,28:3
Life Begins at 8:40 1934,Ag 7,20:7
Life Begins at 8:40 1934,Ag 28,24:2
Parade 1935,My 21,22:2
Scandals 1935,O 30,17:1
Illustrators' Show, The 1936,Ja 23,25:3
Sally, Irene and Mary 1938,Jl 5,13:4
Firefly, The 1938,Jl 12,15:4
Two Weeks With Pay 1940,Je 25,28:3
This Is the Army 1942,Jl 5,28:2
Great to Be Alive! 1950,Mr 24,28:2

Oxford Playhouse Company

Oresteia 1961,N 8,43:5

Oxford Trio, The

Vaudeville (Hippodrome) 1926,My 4,31:2

Oxley, Frederic

Symphony in Two Flats 1930,S 17,30:4

Oxley, John (Miscellaneous)

Measure for Measure 1967,F 15,37:1

Oxtoby, Emily J (Director)

Ah! Wah! 1932,My 11,15:2

Oxton, Charles (Playwright)

Late Arrival 1953,O 20,35:5

Oyebola, Ifatumbo

Akokawe 1970,Je 5,21:1

Oyelana, Tunli

Madmen and Specialists 1970,Ag 3,38:1

Oyra, Jan

Night in Paris, A 1926,Jl 27,15:4
Artists and Models 1927,N 16,28:2

Oysher, Fraydele

It's Never Too Late for Happiness 1968,O 21,59:3

Oyster, Jim

Cretan Woman, The 1954,Jl 8,18:2
White Devil, The 1955,Mr 15,32:5
Titus Andronicus 1956,D 3,40:2
Lady's Not for Burning, The 1959,Ja 31,13:2
Man and Superman 1960,N 7,46:2
Sound of Music, The 1967,Ap 27,52:1
Sound of Music, The 1970,Jl 3,13:1

Oyster, Jim (Costume Designer)

Dark Lady of the Sonnets, The 1956,F 21,38:1
Admirable Bashville, The 1956,F 21,38:1

Ozab, Freddie J

Night Duel, The 1926,F 16,22:3

Ozark Mountain Boy (Zag)

Hayride 1954,S 14,24:2

Ozeray, Madeleine

Tessa 1935,Ja 6,IX,2:1

P

Paaz, Nira

41 in a Sack 1960,Mr 26,15:2

Pabon, Ramon

Retabilillo de Don Cristobal, El; Puppet Theater of
Don Cristobal, The; Zapatera Prodigiosa, La;
Shoemaker's Prodigious Wife, The 1964,S 3,23:2
Romeo y Julieta 1965,Ag 28,13:3

Pabst, E (Composer)

Untitled-Passion Play 1933,Jl 16,II,4:7

Pace, Don

Cradle of Willow, A 1961,D 16,20:2

Pace, Gian (Miscellaneous)

Matter of Like Life and Death, A 1963,O 3,28:2
Opening Night 1963,O 3,28:2

Pace, Jean (Costume Designer)

Buck White 1969,D 3,63:1

Pace, Jean (Director)

Buck White 1969,D 3,63:1

Pace, Jean and Sivuca

Joy 1970,Ja 28,50:1

Pace, Merna

Personal Appearance 1934,O 18,26:7

Pace (Scenic Designer)

Jardin des Delices, Le 1969,N 4,54:1

Pacetti, Elizabeth

Seventeen 1951,Je 22,16:6

Pacetti, Joseph (Miscellaneous)

If Five Years Pass 1962,My 11,37:1

Pacheco, Don Carlos Maria (Playwright)
  Rapacino 1927,D 23,16:4
Pacheco, Gil
  Last Pad, The 1970,D 8,61:1
Pacile, Aldo
  Signora Dalle Camelie, La; Dame aux Camelias, La
    1937,O 9,16:3
Pacino, Al
  Indian Wants the Bronx, The 1968,Ja 18,47:2
  Does a Tiger Wear a Necktie? 1969,F 26,38:1
  Does a Tiger Wear a Necktie? 1969,Mr 9,II,1:1
  Does a Tiger Wear a Necktie? 1969,Mr 16,II,4:5
  Local Stigmatic, The 1969,N 4,55:2
  Camino Real 1970,Ja 9,42:1
  Camino Real 1970,Ja 18,II,1:1
Pacitti, Joe (Lighting Director)
  Once in a Lifetime 1964,Ja 29,20:1
  When Did You Last See My Mother?
    1967,Ja 5,27:5
Pack, Charles Lloyd
  School for Scandal, The 1963,Ja 26,5:2
  Arms and the Man 1970,Ag 26,36:1
Pack, Muriel
  Stars on Ice (2d Edition) 1943,Je 25,13:2
Packard, Frank L (Original Author)
  Miracle Man, The 1935,My 14,17:5
  Miracle Man, The 1935,Je 9,IX,1:1
Packard, Fred
  Hello Paris 1930,N 17,29:3
Packard, Theodore (Playwright)
  Crab Apple 1936,Jl 8,14:2
Packard, William (Playwright)
  Phedre 1966,F 11,36:1
Packer, Doris
  Back Fire 1932,Je 14,26:3
  Strip Girl 1935,O 21,22:6
Packer, Jerry
  Are You With It? 1945,N 12,17:3
Packer, Jerry (Miscellaneous)
  Let It Ride 1961,O 13,27:4
Packer, Netta
  Guys and Dolls 1950,N 25,11:2
Packer, Robert
  Twelfth Night 1959,Jl 11,10:2
  Unto Thee a Garden 1968,O 28,55:3
Packer, Sidney
  Chinese Nightingale, The 1934,O 6,20:4
  Sailors of Cattaro 1934,D 11,28:4
  Black Pit 1935,Mr 21,26:6
  Bitter Stream 1936,Mr 31,16:6
  But for the Grace of God 1937,Ja 13,21:4
Packer, William
  Ship Comes in, A 1934,S 20,21:1
  Rip Van Winkle 1935,Ag 7,22:2
  Master of the Revels 1935,Ag 14,16:2
  Victoria Regina 1935,D 27,15:2
  Call It a Day 1936,Ja 29,15:2
  Bachelor Born 1938,Ja 26,26:3
  Leave Her to Heaven 1940,F 28,16:2
  Golden Wings 1941,D 9,46:6
Packwood, Harry
  Cuban Thing, The 1968,S 25,36:2
  But, Seriously... 1969,F 28,29:1
Paco
  White Lilacs 1928,S 11,31:2
Padden, Sarah
  Night of January 16 1935,S 17,26:4
Paddick, Hugh
  Country Wife, The 1969,Ag 30,10:3
  Antony and Cleopatra 1969,Ag 30,10:3
Paddock, Robert Rowe (Scenic Designer)
  Yellow Jack 1944,Ap 7,23:3
  Burlesque 1946,D 26,30:3
  Alice in Wonderland 1947,Ap 7,19:2
Padeloup, Donna
  Playing the Game 1927,D 20,32:5
Padgett, Donald (Scenic Designer)
  But Never Jam Today 1969,Ap 24,40:1
Padgitt, G Newton
  Fiesta 1933,D 16,12:2
Padgurski, Joe
  Aquashow 1954,Je 23,20:4
Padian, Thomas H F (Composer)
  Tinker's Dam 1943,Ja 29,22:2
Padilla, Jose
  Montmarte aux Nues 1926,O 3,VIII,2:1
Padilla, Jose (Composer)
  Ca. . . C'Est Paris 1927,F 6,VII,4:1
  Pibe de Corralon, El 1927,D 23,16:4
Padilla, Nicholas J (Costume Designer)
  Rope Dancers, The 1959,Mr 14,26:1
Padovani, Gianfranco (Costume Designer)
  Venetian Twins, The 1968,My 29,23:1
Padovani, Gianfranco (Scenic Designer)
  Venetian Twins, The 1968,My 29,23:1
Paduit, Anna
  Dybbuk, The 1926,D 14,24:2
  Golem, The 1927,F 5,13:2
Padula, Edward (Director)
  Day Before Spring, The 1945,N 23,27:2
  Joyful Noise, A 1966,D 16,57:1
Padula, Edward (Miscellaneous)
  No Time for Sergeants 1955,O 21,32:2

Rumple 1957,N 7,42:2
God and Kate Murphy 1959,F 27,21:2
Saratoga 1959,D 8,59:4
Padula, Edward (Playwright)
  Joyful Noise, A 1966,D 16,57:1
Padula, Edward (Producer)
  Bye Bye Birdie 1960,Ap 15,13:4
  All American 1962,Mr 20,44:1
  Bajour 1964,N 24,42:1
  Joyful Noise, A 1966,D 16,57:1
  Red, White and Maddox 1969,Ja 27,27:1
  Park 1970,Ap 23,47:1
Padula, Marguerite
  Vaudeville (Palace) 1927,Jl 12,29:3
Padula, Nick
  Winterset 1966,F 10,32:2
Paffrath, John (Producer)
  Marilyn's Affairs 1933,Mr 16,21:5
Pagan, Anna
  Fig Leaves Are Falling, The 1969,Ja 3,19:1
Pagan, Norma Iris
  Romeo y Julieta 1965,Ag 28,13:3
Pagan, Peter
  Escapade 1953,N 19,40:1
  Portrait of a Lady 1954,D 22,27:6
  Child of Fortune 1956,N 14,41:1
  Villa of Madame Vidac, The 1959,O 1,40:1
  13 Daughters 1961,Mr 3,17:2
  Girl Who Came to Supper, The 1963,D 9,49:1
  Hostile Witness 1966,F 18,26:1
Pagano, Ernest (Playwright)
  Homeward Look, The 1954,Je 4,26:2
Pagano, Jerry
  Blood Bugle, The 1961,Je 29,26:1
  Cockeyed Kite 1961,S 14,27:1
Paganuzzi, Victor (Scenic Designer)
  Fundamental George, The 1949,Ag 17,19:4
Page, Anderson
  Foemen of the Yard 1935,Ap 6,10:4
Page, Anne
  Princess Virtue 1921,My 5,20:2
Page, Anthony (Director)
  Inadmissible Evidence 1965,D 1,52:1
  Time Present 1968,Jl 5,20:1
  Hotel in Amsterdam, The 1968,Ag 17,17:1
  Look Back in Anger 1968,N 1,38:1
  Uncle Vanya 1970,Mr 15,II,7:3
Page, Arthur
  George White's Scandals 1928,Jl 3,19:1
  Hot-Cha! 1932,Mr 9,17:3
  Gypsy Blonde 1934,Je 26,22:5
Page, Bradley
  What Do We Know 1927,D 24,8:1
Page, Don
  Shoemaker and the Peddler, The 1960,O 15,27:4
Page, Donald
  Veils 1928,Mr 14,28:5
Page, Dorothy
  Dear Judas 1947,O 6,26:4
Page, Edna
  George White's Scandals 1935,D 26,20:2
Page, Eileen
  Harlequinade 1949,O 13,32:2
Page, Evelyn
  Tattle Tales 1933,Je 2,22:6
  Boy Friend, The 1958,Ja 27,24:4
  Canterbury Tales; Merchant's Tale, The
    1969,F 4,34:1
  Canterbury Tales; Pilgrims, The 1969,F 4,34:1
  Canterbury Tales; Steward's Tale, The
    1969,F 4,34:1
Page, Frank (Costume Designer)
  Fun City 1968,Mr 7,53:2
Page, Genevieve
  Lorenzaccio 1958,O 15,44:2
  Andromaque 1964,F 29,13:2
Page, George
  O'Brien Girl, The 1921,O 4,10:2
Page, Geraldine
  Seven Mirrors 1945,O 26,17:2
  Yerma 1952,F 8,18:4
  Summer and Smoke 1952,Ap 25,19:5
  Summer and Smoke 1952,My 4,II,1:1
  Mid-Summer 1953,Ja 22,19:1
  Mid-Summer 1953,Mr 15,II,1:1
  Immoralist, The 1954,F 2,18:7
  Immoralist, The 1954,F 9,22:1
  Immoralist, The 1954,F 14,II,1:1
  Rainmaker, The 1954,O 29,28:1
  Rainmaker, The 1954,N 7,II,1:1
  Anna Christie 1955,N 22,41:1
  Innkeepers, The 1956,F 3,19:1
  Rainmaker, The 1956,Je 1,26:7
  Separate Tables 1957,S 15,II,1:1
  Sweet Bird of Youth 1959,Mr 11,39:2
  Sweet Bird of Youth 1959,Mr 22,II,1:1
  Strange Interlude 1963,Mr 13,5:2
  Strange Interlude 1963,Je 18,34:6
  Strange Interlude 1964,Mr 1,II,1:1
  Three Sisters, The 1964,Je 23,24:1
  Three Sisters, The 1964,Jl 5,II,1:1
  P S I Love You 1964,N 20,40:1
  Great Indoors, The 1966,F 2,23:1

Page, Geraldine—Cont
  Black Comedy; White Lies 1967,F 13,42:1
  Black Comedy 1967,F 13,42:1
  White Lies 1967,F 26,II,1:5
  White Lies 1967,O 19,58:1
  Angela 1969,O 31,33:1
  Angela 1969,N 9,II,1:1
Page, Gertrude (Original Author)
  Paddy the Next Best Thing 1920,Ag 28,5:5
Page, Jane
  Marie Antoinette 1921,N 23,16:1
Page, Jocelyne
  King Lear 1950,Ag 30,26:2
Page, Joy Ann
  Hidden Horizon 1946,S 20,42:2
Page, Lucille
  Vaudeville (Hollywood) 1932,Ap 19,25:5
  Casino Varieties 1934,Ap 3,26:4
  Hats Off to Ice 1944,Je 23,15:2
Page, Mann (Playwright)
  Lights Out 1922,Ag 8,8:4
  Backslapper, The 1925,Ap 13,25:2
  Mama Loves Papa 1926,F 23,26:2
  Hush Money 1926,Mr 16,22:3
  House Afire 1930,Ap 1,34:7
  Greatness Comes to the Maronies 1937,Ag 18,15:2
Page, Norman (Director)
  Marigold 1930,O 9,23:1
Page, Peggy
  Vaudeville (Palace) 1928,N 12,18:7
Page, Peter
  Poisoned Kiss, The 1937,Ap 22,19:1
Page, Phyllis (Miscellaneous)
  Rose Marie 1928,Ap 29,IX,2:8
Page, Prunella
  Nine Till Six 1930,S 29,17:2
Page, Richmond
  Carousel 1949,Ja 26,28:2
Page, Robert (Miscellaneous)
  Jo 1964,F 13,25:1
Page, Rosamond
  Greatness Comes to the Maronies 1937,Ag 18,15:2
Page, Ruth
  Untitled-Benefit 1922,My 8,14:5
  Irving Berlin's New Music Box Revue
    1922,O 24,18:1
Page, Ruth (Choreographer)
  Music in My Heart 1947,O 3,30:2
Page, Sherrold
  Mister Romeo 1927,S 6,35:3
Page, Stan
  Golden Apple, The 1962,F 13,38:2
  South Pacific 1965,Je 3,25:1
  Mame 1966,My 25,41:1
Page, Tamara
  Desert Song, The 1946,Ja 9,20:2
Page, Tom
  School for Scandal, The 1925,O 24,19:1
Page, Tommy
  Thomas Paine 1930,Mr 21,30:7
Page, Virginia
  Way of the Cross, The 1959,Ja 16,35:2
  Mystery of the Finding of the Cross, The
    1959,Ja 16,35:2
Page, Virginia (Playwright)
  Quem Quaeritis 1954,My 2,II,1:1
Page, William A (Playwright)
  Bootleggers, The 1922,N 28,24:1
Pagent, Robert
  Carousel 1945,Ap 20,24:2
  Rape of Lucretia, The 1948,D 30,24:2
  Miss Liberty 1949,Jl 16,6:5
  Carousel 1953,My 6,38:1
  Fledermaus, Die 1954,My 20,38:5
  Carousel 1954,Je 3,32:2
  Carousel 1957,S 12,38:2
Pagent, Robert (Choreographer)
  Fledermaus, Die 1954,My 20,38:5
Pagent, Robert (Director)
  Carousel 1954,Je 3,32:2
  Carousel 1957,S 12,38:2
Pagent, Robert (Miscellaneous)
  Carousel 1957,S 12,38:2
Paget, Daniel (Musical Director)
  Love and Let Love 1968,Ja 4,30:1
Paget, Lily
  Allegro 1947,O 11,10:2
  Call Me Madam 1950,O 13,25:1
  Ondine 1954,F 19,23:1
Pagett, Nicola
  Boston Story, A 1968,S 21,26:2
Pagni, Eros
  Venetian Twins, The 1968,My 29,23:1
Pagnol, Marcel (Original Author)
  Fanny 1954,N 5,16:1
  Fanny 1954,N 21,II,1:1
  Fanny 1956,D 2,II,3:1
Pagnol, Marcel (Playwright)
  Merchants of Glory 1925,D 15,28:3
  Merchants of Glory 1925,D 27,VII,1:1
  Jazz 1927,Ja 23,VII,2:1
  Topaze 1928,N 4,IX,4:4
  Marius 1929,Mr 31,VIII,2:7
  Topaze 1930,F 13,25:3

Pagnol, Marcel (Playwright)—Cont
Topaze 1930,Mr 2,IX,1:1
Marseilles; Marius 1930,N 9,IX,3:2
Marseilles 1930,N 18,28:2
Topaze 1931,F 17,29:1
Roi, Le 1931,Ap 5,VIII,3:1
Fanny 1931,D 27,VIII,3:4
Marius 1956,F 6,27:4
Pagnol, Marcel (Translator)
Topaze 1947,D 29,21:5
Pagowski, Walter
Swing Sister Wac Swing 1944,Ja 4,20:4
Pahitu, Kuruks
Strong Are Lonely, The 1953,S 30,38:3
Pahl, Ellen (Director)
Blitzstein! 1966,D 1,58:2
Pahl, Naida
Everybody's Welcome 1931,O 14,26:3
Paige, Barbara
Escape This Night 1938,Ap 23,18:1
Paige, Betty
Prince of Peasantmania 1970,F 22,88:1
Paige, Jacqueline
Idiot's Delight 1936,Mr 10,26:7
Idiot's Delight 1936,Mr 25,25:2
Amphitryon 38 1937,Je 24,30:2
Night of January 16 1937,Jl 20,19:3
Idiot's Delight 1937,Ag 10,22:7
Amphitryon 38 1937,N 2,32:2
Sea Gull, The 1938,Mr 29,19:2
Ladies and Gentlemen 1939,O 18,30:2
Happy Birthday 1946,N 1,31:2
Detective Story 1949,Mr 24,34:2
Paige, Janis
Remains to Be Seen 1951,O 4,37:1
Pajama Game, The 1954,My 14,20:2
Pajama Game, The 1954,My 15,12:1
Here's Love 1963,O 4,28:1
Mame 1968,Ap 20,25:1
Paige, Judith
Noah 1954,O 11,32:2
Abie's Irish Rose 1954,N 19,19:1
Three by Thurber; Imperturbable Spirit, The 1955,Mr 8,23:2
Three by Thurber; Middle Years, The 1955,Mr 8,23:2
Paige, Louis Stanley
Hamlet 1951,Jl 20,13:6
Paige, Mabel
Lost Horizons 1934,O 16,31:2
Murder in the Cathedral 1936,Mr 21,13:5
Western Union 1937,Ag 10,22:7
Western Waters 1937,D 29,17:1
Out of the Frying Pan 1941,F 12,24:2
Two Blind Mice 1949,Mr 3,32:2
Gramercy Ghost 1951,Ap 27,20:2
Paige, Margaret
He Walked in Her Sleep 1929,Ap 5,28:2
Paige, Norman
Mikado, The 1954,Mr 24,31:1
Pirates of Penzance, The 1954,Mr 31,32:5
Gondoliers, The 1954,Ap 14,24:3
Ruddigore 1954,Ap 21,36:4
Iolanthe 1954,Ap 28,36:8
Yeomen of the Guard, The 1954,My 5,36:2
H M S Pinafore 1954,My 19,36:8
Sorcerer, The 1954,My 26,34:3
Paige, Peggy
County Chairman, The 1936,My 26,26:5
Paige, Rita
That Ferguson Family 1928,D 24,10:7
Paige, Sammy
Blackberries of 1932 1932,Ap 5,27:5
Paige, Shirley
Pal Joey 1940,D 26,22:2
Keep 'Em Laughing 1942,Ap 25,9:2
Paige, Thelma
Shame Woman, The 1923,O 17,14:1
That Ferguson Family 1928,D 24,10:7
Best People, The 1933,Mr 16,21:5
Paige, William
Paradise 1931,My 12,29:2
Painchaud, Janice
Happiest Girl in the World, The 1961,Ap 4,42:1
Paine, Ann
Streetcar Named Desire, A 1955,Mr 4,18:2
Paine, G L
It's Only Natural 1922,Ap 21,13:2
Paine, Helen
Lady Billy 1920,D 15,18:2
Paine, Kenneth
Billy Budd 1951,F 12,18:3
Bonds of Interest, The 1951,D 1,7:2
Infernal Machine, The 1954,Mr 22,22:2
Paine, Kenneth (Lighting Director)
Detective Story 1954,F 13,11:2
Paine, Kenneth (Miscellaneous)
Ernest in Love 1960,My 5,39:4
Elsa Lanchester-Herself 1961,F 6,28:1
Paine, Ray
Riot 1968,D 20,64:1
Painter, Clarke (Producer)
Arabian Nightmare, The 1927,Ja 11,36:3

Painter, Eleanor
Florodora 1920,Ap 6,18:1
Last Waltz, The 1921,My 11,20:3
Exile, The 1923,Ap 10,24:2
Chiffon Girl, The 1924,F 20,23:2
Nightingale, The 1927,Ja 4,20:4
Painting, Norman
King Lear 1950,Ag 30,26:2
Paipert, Beatrice
Doctor and the Devils, The 1959,Ja 21,27:8
Paisley, Frederick
Heaven and Charing Cross 1939,Ap 16,X,2:4
Paisner, Dina
Cave at Machpelah, The 1959,Jl 1,25:1
Montserrat 1961,Ja 9,30:5
Sap of Life, The 1961,O 3,44:1
If Five Years Pass 1962,My 11,37:1
Troubled Waters 1965,Je 4,40:2
Oresteia 1966,Je 30,29:1
Paiva, Jeanne
Herne's Egg, The 1960,S 20,48:1
Pakewitz, Irving
John Brown 1950,My 4,32:7
Pakington, Mary (Playwright)
Pirate Mallory 1935,O 8,26:3
Pakkanen, John
Grass Harp, The 1953,Ap 28,32:2
Pakula, Alan J (Playwright)
Jennie 1963,O 18,35:2
Pakula, Alan J (Producer)
Comes a Day 1958,N 7,22:1
Pakulski, Jerzy (Composer)
Post Office, The 1965,Ja 6,32:1
Woman, The 1965,Ja 6,32:1
Nightmare, The 1965,Ja 6,32:1
Labyrinth, The 1965,Ja 6,32:1
Jaselka 1965,Ja 6,32:1
Kernel and the Shell, The 1965,Ja 6,32:1
Jacob and the Angel 1965,Ja 6,32:1
Book, The 1965,Ja 6,32:1
Pal, Niranjan (Playwright)
Magic Crystal, The 1924,Jl 13,VII,1:6
Pal, Sital
Ramayana 1931,Ja 13,35:4
Palace, Johnny
Vaudeville (Palace) 1926,O 19,27:5
Vaudeville (Palace) 1927,Je 7,27:3
Palacine, Anita
Private Lives 1968,My 20,59:1
Palagy, Lajos
Campo di Maggio 1931,Je 5,4:3
Palance, Jack
Silver Tassie, The 1949,Jl 22,16:5
Silver Tassle, The 1949,S 4,II,1:1
Julius Caesar 1955,Jl 13,20:1
Tempest, The 1955,Ag 2,18:2
Tempest, The 1955,Ag 7,II,1:1
Palance, Walter
Big Two, The 1947,Ja 9,21:2
Temporary Island, A 1948,Mr 15,27:3
Vigil, The 1948,My 22,8:6
Darkness at Noon 1951,Ja 15,13:4
Palau
Nuit, Une 1935,Je 16,X,1:1
Palazzi, M Charles
Americana 1926,Jl 27,15:3
Treat 'Em Rough 1926,O 5,26:2
Woman of Bronze, The 1927,Je 16,25:4
Liane, Le (Ties That Bind); Ties That Bind (Le Liane) 1929,Ap 22,22:1
Piacere Del'Onesta, Il; Happiness of Probity, The 1930,N 10,16:4
Cena Delle Beffe, La; Jest, The 1930,N 24,26:4
In Fondo Al Cuore; Depths of the Heart, The 1930,D 8,27:1
Delitto e Castigo; Crime and Punishment 1931,Ja 26,20:5
Society Girl 1931,D 31,16:1
Collision 1932,F 17,19:2
Last Enemy, The 1934,Jl 13,14:4
Paleologue, Content
Voice From the Minaret, The 1922,Ja 31,11:2
Palermo, Alex
On the Town 1959,F 14,15:1
Miss Emily Adam 1960,Mr 30,43:1
Palermo, Alex (Choreographer)
Miss Emily Adam 1960,Mr 30,43:1
Tattooed Countess, The 1961,My 4,40:2
Palermo, Mario
Paese dei Campanelli, Il; Land of Bells, The 1935,My 10,25:4
Palester, Franz
Bajadere, Die 1925,O 2,26:2
Palestrant, Judith (Playwright)
Shunned 1960,D 21,39:1
Palestrant, Stephen (Lighting Director)
Taming of the Shrew, The 1956,Ag 11,11:2
Titus Andronicus 1956,D 3,40:2
Shunned 1960,D 21,39:1
King of the Dark Chamber 1961,F 10,21:1
Palestrant, Stephen (Scenic Designer)
Shunned 1960,D 21,39:1

Paley, Paul K (Playwright)
Right Next to Broadway 1944,F 22,26:2
Paley, Paul K (Producer)
Right Next to Broadway 1944,F 22,26:2
Paley, Selma
Head First 1926,Ja 7,22:4
Paley, Stanley (Playwright)
Sweet Confession 1959,Ap 15,30:1
Paley, Stephen
Take Her, She's Mine 1961,D 22,19:1
Palfi, Lotta
Place of Our Own, A 1945,Ap 3,23:7
Palin, Pat
Shoemaker and the Peddler, The 1960,O 15,27:4
Palitzsch, Hansheinrich (Costume Designer)
Schloss, Das 1968,N 20,35:3
Palitzsch, Hansheinrich (Scenic Designer)
Schloss, Das 1968,N 20,35:3
Kleinburgerhochzeit, Die 1970,N 25,25:1
Kurve, Die 1970,N 25,25:1
Palitzsch, Peter (Director)
Guerrillas 1970,My 17,91:3
Palkowich, Joseph
Pinocchio 1939,Ja 3,19:2
Pall, James
Chicago 1926,D 31,11:1
Congai 1928,N 28,24:3
Pallas, Elvira
Nervous Set, The 1959,My 13,43:1
Pallenberg, Max
Weisse Laemmchen, Das 1921,Mr 6,VI,1:7
Jonny's Busenfreund 1921,D 11,VI,1:4
Everyman 1926,Ag 9,1:1
Mikado, The 1927,O 30,IX,4:6
Adventures of the Worthy Soldier Schwejk, The 1928,Mr 4,IX,2:1
Fair Helen 1928,Ap 1,IX,2:4
Bourgeois Gentilhomme, Le 1929,Mr 24,X,2:3
Absconders, The; Defraudanten, Die 1931,Ja 25,VIII,4:1
Pallenberg's Bears
Vaudeville (Palace) 1927,O 25,33:2
Vaudeville (Palace) 1929,D 23,19:1
Pallet, Dolores (Choreographer)
Aquashow 1954,Je 23,20:4
Elliott Murphy's Aquashow 1956,Je 20,26:2
Pallet, Dolores (Composer)
Holiday on Ice 1965,S 2,38:4
Pallet, Dolores (Director)
Aquashow 1954,Je 23,20:4
Elliott Murphy's Aquashow 1956,Je 20,26:2
Pallet, Dolores (Miscellaneous)
Holiday on Ice 1965,S 2,38:4
Holiday on Ice 1966,S 1,30:1
Pallet, Dolores (Producer)
Holiday on Ice 1967,Ag 31,29:2
Pallis, V
Screwball, The 1957,My 25,24:7
Palloy, Charles
May Wine 1935,D 6,30:3
Palm, Walter
Marching By 1932,Mr 4,17:1
Palma, Anthony (Playwright)
There Is No End 1950,F 17,27:4
Palma, Joseph
Face of a Hero 1960,O 21,29:5
Palme, Leslie
Thank You 1921,O 4,10:2
Palme, Ulf
Long Day's Journey Into Night 1956,F 19,II,1:6
Long Day's Journey Into Night 1962,My 16,35:4
Miss Julie 1962,My 17,31:1
Palmer, Anthony
Macbeth 1962,N 17,16:2
Passion of Josef D, The 1964,F 12,29:1
Traveller Without Luggage 1964,S 18,26:2
Galileo 1968,D 1,88:4
Whistle in the Dark, A 1969,O 9,55:1
Whistle in the Dark, A 1969,N 9,II,3:1
Nobody Hears A Broken Drum 1970,Mr 20,55:1
Palmer, Artie
Russell Patterson's Sketch-Book 1960,F 8,35:1
Palmer, Audrey
Leave It to Me! 1938,N 10,32:2
Du Barry Was a Lady 1939,D 7,34:2
Palmer, Betsy
Grand Prize, The 1955,Ja 27,17:1
Affair of Honor 1956,Ap 7,12:3
Roar Like a Dove 1964,My 22,40:2
South Pacific 1965,Je 3,25:1
Cactus Flower 1967,D 16,48:1
Palmer, Betty
Nine Till Six 1936,Mr 14,10:3
Palmer, Byron
Where's Charley? 1948,O 12,33:2
Bless You All 1950,D 15,42:2
Palmer, Carter
Frogs, The 1941,N 14,25:3
Palmer, Christene
Pirates of Penzance, The 1966,N 16,54:1
Mikado, The 1966,N 18,36:1
Ruddigore 1966,N 23,28:1
H M S Pinafore 1966,N 24,64:1

almer, Christene—Cont
Patience 1966,N 30,58:1
H M S Pinafore 1968,O 30,35:1
Mikado, The 1968,N 2,29:4
Pirates of Penzance, The 1968,N 7,54:1
Iolanthe 1968,N 9,37:3

almer, Christy
South Pacific 1957,Ap 25,35:1

'almer, Clara
Sally, Irene and Mary 1922,S 5,21:2
Dream Girl, The 1924,Ag 21,12:2
Not Herbert 1926,Ja 27,16:2
Nightingale, The 1927,Ja 4,20:4
Brothers 1928,D 26,14:3
Queen at Home 1930,D 30,25:2
Budget, The 1932,S 21,26:4
Little Black Book, The 1932,D 27,11:2
Under Glass 1933,O 31,24:3
Come of Age 1934,Ja 13,16:6
Queer People 1934,F 16,16:2
Ragged Edge, The 1935,N 26,28:3

Palmer, Cort (Playwright)
Rain Before Seven 1935,Ag 13,20:3

Palmer, Craig
Ruddigore 1965,Ag 27,16:1

Palmer, David
Iolanthe 1964,N 18,52:1
H M S Pinafore 1964,N 20,40:1
Ruddigore 1964,D 4,44:1
Mikado, The 1966,N 18,36:1
Ruddigore 1966,N 23,28:1
H M S Pinafore 1966,N 24,64:1

Palmer, David (Composer)
Cambridge Circus 1964,O 7,53:1

Palmer, David (Miscellaneous)
Salad Days 1958,N 11,24:1
Cambridge Circus 1964,O 7,53:1

Palmer, Effie
Untitled-Recital 1932,F 8,21:1

Palmer, Elaine
Half-Moon, The 1920,N 2,15:2
Bunch and Judy, The 1922,N 29,20:1
One Kiss 1923,N 28,14:2

Palmer, Frank
Carmen Jones 1946,Ap 8,32:2

Palmer, Gaston
Vaudeville (Hippodrome) 1926,My 4,31:2
Diable 1926,O 31,VIII,2:4
Vaudeville (Palace) 1932,Jl 18,9:7

Palmer, Irving
God Strikes Back 1943,F 27,11:2

Palmer, Jeanne
Russian Bank 1940,My 25,20:2

Palmer, John A
Hoot Mon, or Clans Across the Sea 1927,My 8,29:4

Palmer, Kiki
Famiglia Barrett, La 1933,N 19,IX,1:3

Palmer, Leland
Joyful Noise, A 1966,D 16,57:1
Your Own Thing 1968,Ja 15,33:1
Dames at Sea 1970,S 24,60:1

Palmer, Leslie
Light of the World, The 1920,Ja 7,17:1
Richard III 1920,Mr 8,7:1
Young Visitors, The 1920,N 30,14:1
Mary Stuart 1921,Mr 22,15:1
Comedienne 1924,O 22,18:1
Buccaneer, The 1925,O 3,10:2
Last of Mrs Cheyney, The 1925,N 10,23:5
Novice and the Duke, The 1929,D 11,37:2

Palmer, Lester
Horse Play 1937,Ag 28,8:3

Palmer, Lilli
Tree of Eden 1938,O 30,IX,1:2
Little Ladyship 1939,F 26,IX,3:5
My Name is Aquilon 1949,F 10,38:2
Caesar and Cleopatra 1949,D 22,28:2
Caesar and Cleopatra 1950,Ja 8,II,1:1
ANTA Album 1950,Ja 30,13:2
Bell, Book and Candle 1950,N 15,37:4
Bell, Book and Candle 1950,D 17,II,3:1
Venus Observed 1952,F 14,24:2
Venus Observed 1952,F 24,II,1:1
Love of Four Colonels, The 1953,Ja 16,17:2
Bell, Book and Candle 1954,O 6,30:8
Song at Twilight, A 1966,Ap 17,86:5
Shadows of the Evening; Come Into the Garden, Maud 1966,Ap 27,38:1

Palmer, Maria
Moon Is Down, The 1942,Ap 8,22:2
Vigil, The 1948,My 22,8:6

Palmer, Marian
Street Singer, The 1929,S 18,35:2

Palmer, Mary E
Way of the World, The 1950,Ap 9,73:5

Palmer, Maurice (Playwright)
Place for Chance, The 1964,My 15,44:2

Palmer, Melba
Big Blow 1938,O 3,11:2

Palmer, Osna
Flowering Peach, The 1954,D 29,19:2
Flowering Peach, The 1955,Ja 9,II,1:1

Palmer, Pat
Gay Divorce 1932,N 30,23:4

Palmer, Patricia
Merrily We Roll Along 1934,O 1,14:1
American Landscape 1938,D 5,19:2

Palmer, Peter
Li'l Abner 1956,N 16,24:2
Li'l Abner 1956,N 25,II,1:1
Brigadoon 1962,My 31,21:4
Brigadoon 1963,F 1,6:2
Oklahoma! 1963,F 28,8:2
Oklahoma! 1963,My 16,40:1
Brigadoon 1964,D 24,9:1

Palmer, Renzo
Rugantino 1964,F 7,34:1

Palmer, Rita Dallas (Director)
Ice Capades 1966,Je 2,50:2
Ice Capades 1970,Ja 7,35:1

Palmer, Rose A (Playwright)
Caponsacchi 1926,O 27,24:2
Caponsacchi 1928,Ja 25,20:3

Palmer, Sidney
Othello 1937,Ja 7,16:4
Sun Kissed 1937,Mr 11,20:2

Palmer, Skip (Lighting Director)
Now 1968,Je 6,53:1

Palmer, Steve
Threepenny Opera, The 1955,S 21,38:1

Palmer, Thomas
Here Come the Clowns 1938,D 8,36:2
Mother, The 1939,Ap 26,26:2
Alice Adams 1947,Ag 5,26:1
I Know My Love 1949,N 3,36:1
Blithe Spirit 1952,F 23,7:5

Palmer, Virginia
Trojan Women, The 1938,Ja 25,24:2

Palmer, William
Heartbreak House 1950,Mr 22,33:2

Palmer, Winthrop (Miscellaneous)
Miss Emily Adam 1960,Mr 30,43:1

Palmer, Winthrop (Playwright)
Miss Emily Adam 1960,Mr 30,43:1
Place for Chance, The 1964,My 15,44:2

Palmeri, Amleto (Playwright)
'Il Tesoro D'Isacco; Treasure of Isaac, The 1928,Ja 26,17:1

Palmerston, Hugh
Faith of Our Fathers 1950,Ag 6,72:2
Taming of the Shrew, The 1956,Ag 11,11:2
Taming of the Shrew, The 1956,Ag 26,II,1:1
Enemy of the People, An 1958,F 26,24:2
Heloise 1958,S 25,28:4

Palmieri, Joseph
Henry V 1965,Je 29,27:2
Measure for Measure 1966,Jl 14,27:1
Butter and Egg Man, The 1966,O 18,49:1
Cyrano de Bergerac 1968,Ap 26,30:1

Palmieri, Peter
Christmas Eve 1939,D 28,17:2

Palmstierna-Weiss, Gunilla (Costume Designer)
Persecution and Assassination of Marat As Performed by the Inmates of the Asylum of Charenton Under the Direction of the Marquis de Sade, The 1965,D 28,35:1

Paltrow, Bruce W (Producer)
Someone's Comin' Hungry 1969,Ap 1,51:1
Whispers on the Wind 1970,Je 4,50:1

Paluchiewicz, Andrzei
Acropolis 1969,N 5,40:1

Palumbo, Gene (Musical Director)
Untitled-Judy Garland 1967,D 26,45:1

Pam, Mlle
Chiffon Girl, The 1924,F 20,23:2

Pambrun, Marcella (Miscellaneous)
Song Out of Sorrow 1955,N 1,27:3
Comedian, The 1956,O 18,36:4
Child of the Morning 1958,Ap 22,40:2
Madre, La 1959,F 12,24:1
Egoists, The 1959,O 14,52:2
Madame Lafayette 1960,Mr 4,21:1
Connelly vs Connelly 1961,F 18,11:3
Lady of Mexico 1962,O 20,13:2
Daddy Come Home 1963,Ap 17,33:1
Eternal Sabbath 1963,O 19,17:2

Pan, Hermes (Choreographer)
As the Girls Go 1948,N 15,21:2

Pan, Vesso
Blue and the Gray, The; War Is Hell Gray, The 1929,D 27,26:4

Panama, Norman (Playwright)
Li'l Abner 1956,N 16,24:2
Li'l Abner 1956,N 25,II,1:1

Panama, Norman (Producer)
Li'l Abner 1956,N 16,24:2

Panama & Frank (Playwright)
Keep Off the Grass 1940,My 24,22:6

Panama Francis Quartet
Never Live Over a Pretzel Factory 1964,Mr 30,37:1

Panara, Robert (Playwright)
Sganarelle 1970,Ja 13,41:1

Panas, Alexander
Electra 1964,Ag 12,42:1
Volpone 1967,Je 30,29:1

Panayiotou, Popy
Electra 1930,D 27,16:1

Pandel, Ted (Composer)
Kumquat in the Persimmon Tree, The 1962,Je 19,27:2

Panell, Raymond (Composer)
Three Musketeers, The 1968,Jl 24,49:2

Panenko, Anthoni (Scenic Designer)
Ship, The 1929,N 21,24:7

Panetta, George (Original Author)
Comic Strip 1958,My 15,26:2
King of the Whole Damn World 1962,Ap 16,32:2

Panetta, George (Playwright)
Comic Strip 1958,My 15,26:2
Viva Madison Avenue 1960,Ap 7,42:1
King of the Whole Damn World 1962,Ap 16,32:2
Kiss Mama 1964,O 2,30:1
Mike Downstairs 1968,Ap 19,35:1

Pangborn, Franklin
Parasites 1924,N 20,21:1

Panich, David (Composer)
Put It in Writing 1963,My 14,31:1

Panich, David (Miscellaneous)
Fallout 1959,My 21,36:2

Panich, David (Playwright)
Fallout 1959,My 21,36:2
Put It in Writing 1963,My 14,31:1

Panish, Paul
Shunned 1960,D 21,39:1
Good Soldier Schweik, The 1963,Ap 9,57:1

Panizza, Oscar (Original Author)
Council of Love 1970,Ag 21,21:2
Council of Love 1970,S 12,32:2

Pankiewicz, Krysztof (Costume Designer)
Book, The 1965,Ja 6,32:1
Labyrinth, The 1965,Ja 6,32:1
Post Office, The 1965,Ja 6,32:1
Nightmare, The 1965,Ja 6,32:1
Jacob and the Angel 1965,Ja 6,32:1
Woman, The 1965,Ja 6,32:1
Kernel and the Shell, The 1965,Ja 6,32:1
Jaselka 1965,Ja 6,32:1

Panko, Tom (Choreographer)
Not While I'm Eating 1961,D 20,37:1
Golden Rainbow 1968,F 5,27:1

Panko, Tom (Miscellaneous)
Grosse Valise, La 1965,D 15,52:1
Mame 1966,My 25,41:1
Illya Darling 1967,Ap 12,37:1

Pann, Peter
Dark Hours, The 1932,N 15,24:2
Signature 1945,F 15,25:2

Pannell, Raymond (Composer)
Government Inspector, The 1967,Je 15,55:1
Government Inspector, The 1967,O 28,34:1
Measure for Measure 1969,Je 13,41:3

Panoch, Kenneth (Miscellaneous)
Time for Bed 1969,Je 14,24:1
Take Me to Bed 1969,Je 14,24:1

Pantaleoni, Michael (Producer)
Memory Bank, The 1970,Ja 12,24:3

Panteleieff, Maxim
Doughgirls, The 1942,D 31,19:2

Panter, John
Louisiana Purchase 1940,My 29,19:2
Girl From Nantucket, The 1945,N 9,17:2

Pantopias, Doris
Mikado, The 1942,F 4,22:2
Pirates of Penzance, The 1942,F 18,22:2
Iolanthe 1942,F 24,26:4
Gondoliers, The 1942,Mr 4,22:3

Panvini, Grace
Great Lady 1938,D 2,26:6
Once Over Lightly 1942,N 20,26:2

Panzer, Marty (Playwright)
Now 1968,Je 6,53:1

Paoli, Diana
Christopher's Wonders 1960,S 27,41:1

Paolucci, Henry (Composer)
Liola 1964,S 9,30:3

Paone, Jove
In Any Language 1952,O 9,40:2

Paone, Marian
Changeling, The 1956,My 4,20:3
Good Woman of Setzuan, The 1956,D 19,41:2

Papaconstantinou, N
Oedipus Tyrannus 1952,N 25,35:2

Papadachis, St
Oedipus Tyrannus 1952,N 25,35:2

Papadakis, M
Screwball, The 1957,My 25,24:7

Papas, Irene
That Summer-That Fall 1967,Mr 17,33:1
Phedre 1967,Ap 2,II,1:1
Iphigenia in Aulis 1967,N 22,40:2
Iphigenia in Aulis 1967,D 3,II,1:1

Papathanassiou, A
Electra 1961,S 20,23:4
Eumenides 1961,S 27,32:4
Choephori 1961,S 27,32:4
Electra 1964,S 8,33:1

Papay, Raymond
Gondoliers, The 1963,Je 5,33:2

Pape, Alice
Becky Sharp 1929,Je 4,29:1

Pape, Eric
Becky Sharp 1929,Je 4,29:1
Pape, Eric (Costume Designer)
Little Father of the Wilderness, The 1930,Je 3,27:1
Pape, Eric (Scenic Designer)
Little Father of the Wilderness, The 1930,Je 3,27:1
Pape, Joan
Prometheus Bound 1967,My 11,52:1
Three Sisters, The 1968,Mr 18,56:1
Don Juan 1970,My 26,32:1
Pape, Katie (Miscellaneous)
Mighty Man Is He, A 1960,Ja 7,25:2
Pape, Lionel
Young Visitors, The 1920,N 30,14:1
June Love 1921,Ap 26,20:1
Faithful Heart, The 1922,O 11,22:1
Lady Butterfly 1923,Ja 23,18:1
Second Mrs Tanqueray, The 1924,O 28,27:1
Last of Mrs Cheyney, The 1925,N 10,23:5
High Road, The 1928,S 11,31:1
Suspense 1930,Ag 13,22:3
As Good As New 1930,N 4,37:3
Heat Wave 1931,F 18,14:6
Payment Deferred 1931,O 1,24:2
Fatal Alibi, The 1932,F 10,26:6
Lake, The 1933,D 27,24:2
Lake, The 1934,Ja 7,X,1:1
While Parents Sleep 1934,Je 5,28:2
Birthday 1934,D 27,24:2
Simpleton of the Unexpected Isles, The
  1935,F 19,27:5
Simpleton of the Unexpected Isles, The
  1935,F 24,VIII,1:1
Pape, Richard
Tall Kentuckian, The 1953,Je 17,30:1
Pape, Suzanne
Tall Kentuckian, The 1953,Je 17,30:1
Papell, Lee
In Any Language 1952,O 9,40:2
Wonderful Town 1953,F 26,22:3
Paperin, Faye
Cocktails of 1934 1934,My 5,22:1
Papez, Idi
Ice Follies 1937,D 22,29:1
Papezik, Rudolf
Button, Button 1970,O 20,41:1
Papirofsky, Joseph (Miscellaneous)
Hall of Healing 1952,My 8,35:6
Time to Go 1952,My 8,35:6
Bedtime Story 1952,My 8,35:6
Papoigny, Mr
Aiglon, L' 1924,O 21,21:1
Papp, Joseph (Director)
Twelfth Night 1958,Ag 7,21:4
Antony and Cleopatra 1959,Ja 14,28:1
Henry V 1960,Je 30,23:1
Romeo and Juliet 1961,F 24,24:1
Much Ado About Nothing 1961,Jl 7,17:1
Julius Caesar 1962,F 22,19:6
Merchant of Venice, The 1962,Je 22,1:4
King Lear 1962,Ag 14,35:1
Antony and Cleopatra 1963,Je 21,33:1
Twelfth Night 1963,O 9,47:1
Hamlet 1964,Je 17,49:1
Henry V 1965,Je 29,27:2
Taming of the Shrew, The 1965,Jl 3,10:5
Troilus and Cressida 1965,Ag 13,17:1
All's Well That Ends Well 1966,Je 17,39:1
King John 1967,Jl 14,19:1
Hamlet 1967,D 27,45:1
Memorandum, The 1968,My 6,55:1
Romeo and Juliet 1968,Ag 16,19:1
Huui, Huui 1968,N 25,58:1
Huui, Huui 1968,D 8,II,5:4
Twelfth Night 1969,Ag 14,29:2
Mod Donna 1970,My 4,48:1
Papp, Joseph (Miscellaneous)
Comes a Day 1958,N 7,22:1
Papp, Joseph (Producer)
As You Like It 1955,O 29,12:2
Romeo and Juliet 1955,D 16,36:3
Taming of the Shrew, The 1956,Ag 11,11:2
Taming of the Shrew, The 1956,Ag 26,II,1:1
Titus Andronicus 1956,D 3,40:2
Romeo and Juliet 1957,Je 28,30:2
Two Gentlemen of Verona 1957,Jl 23,21:5
Macbeth 1957,Ag 16,11:2
Richard III 1957,N 26,41:1
As You Like It 1958,Ja 21,33:6
Othello 1958,Jl 4,16:1
Twelfth Night 1958,Ag 7,21:4
Julius Caesar 1959,Ag 4,30:1
Julius Caesar 1959,Ag 16,II,1:1
Measure for Measure 1960,Jl 27,33:1
Taming of the Shrew, The 1960,Ag 20,17:1
Romeo and Juliet 1961,F 24,24:1
Much Ado About Nothing 1961,Jl 7,17:1
Midsummer Night's Dream, A 1961,Ag 3,13:1
Richard II 1961,Ag 30,25:1
Julius Caesar 1962,F 22,19:6
Merchant of Venice, The 1962,Je 22,1:4
Tempest, The 1962,Jl 17,18:2
King Lear 1962,Ag 14,35:1

Macbeth 1962,N 17,16:2
Antony and Cleopatra 1963,Je 21,33:1
Winter's Tale, The 1963,Ag 16,14:1
Twelfth Night 1963,O 9,47:1
Midsummer Night's Dream, A 1964,Je 30,23:2
Midsummer Night's Dream, A 1964,Jl 12,II,1:1
Othello 1964,Jl 15,29:1
Electra 1964,Ag 12,42:1
Retabilillo de Don Cristobal, El; Puppet Theater of
  Don Cristobal, The; Zapatera Prodigiosa, La;
  Shoemaker's Prodigious Wife, The 1964,S 3,23:2
Love's Labour's Lost 1965,Je 16,46:1
Coriolanus 1965,Jl 15,23:1
Romeo y Julieta 1965,Ag 28,13:3
All's Well That Ends Well 1966,Je 17,39:1
Macbeth 1966,Je 29,38:1
Measure for Measure 1966,Jl 14,27:1
Richard III 1966,Ag 11,26:1
Macbeth 1966,Ag 29,23:4
Comedy of Errors, The 1967,Je 15,58:4
Volpone 1967,Je 30,29:1
King John 1967,Jl 14,19:1
Titus Andronicus 1967,Ag 10,43:2
Hair 1967,O 30,55:1
Hair 1967,N 19,II,1:1
Hamlet 1968,Ja 7,II,1:5
Memorandum, The 1968,My 6,55:1
Hamlet 1968,My 12,II,1:1
Skywriting 1968,My 19,II,1:1
Thoughts on the Instant of Greeting a Friend on
  the Street 1968,My 19,II,1:1
Chuck 1968,My 19,II,1:1
Collision Course 1968,My 19,II,1:1
Henry IV, Part I 1968,Je 30,54:7
Henry IV, Part II 1968,Jl 2,33:1
Hamlet 1968,Jl 4,15:1
Romeo and Juliet 1968,Ag 16,19:1
Huui, Huui 1968,N 25,58:1
Huui, Huui 1968,D 8,II,5:4
Cities in Bezique; Owl Answers, The
  1969,Ja 13,26:1
Cities in Bezique; Beast's Story, A 1969,Ja 13,26:1
Invitation to a Beheading 1969,Mr 18,36:1
Invitation to a Beheading 1969,Mr 30,II,1:1
No Place to Be Somebody 1969,My 5,53:3
No Place to Be Somebody 1969,My 18,II,22:1
Peer Gynt 1969,Jl 17,56:1
Electra 1969,Ag 8,14:1
Twelfth Night 1969,Ag 14,29:2
Stomp 1969,N 17,60:1
Stomp 1969,N 23,II,1:1
Sambo 1969,D 22,42:1
No Place to Be Somebody 1969,D 31,17:1
X Has No Value 1970,F 17,35:1
Mod Donna 1970,My 4,48:1
Mod Donna 1970,My 10,II,1:1
Mod Donna 1970,My 10,II,1:1
Wars of the Roses, The (Part I) 1970,Jl 2,30:1
Wars of the Roses, The (Part II) 1970,Jl 3,15:1
Richard III 1970,Jl 4,11:1
Henry VI, Parts I, II, III 1970,Jl 5,II,3:1
Sambo 1970,Jl 23,24:1
Happiness Cage, The 1970,O 5,56:4
Trelawny of the 'Wells' 1970,O 12,48:1
Jack MacGowran in the Works of Samuel Beckett
  1970,N 20,32:1
Jack MacGowran in the Works of Samuel Beckett
  1970,N 27,46:1
Pappa, K
Electra 1961,S 20,23:4
Choephori 1961,S 27,32:4
Pappas, Cleopatra A (Costume Designer)
Sextet 1958,N 27,53:1
Pappas, George
Joan of Lorraine 1947,N 14,29:1
Pappas, Mrs
Poisoned Kiss, The 1937,Ap 22,19:1
Pappas, William
Mother Courage and Her Children 1964,My 12,32:2
Papps, Frank (Playwright)
Purple Canary, The 1963,Ap 23,31:1
Papps, Krinio
Hippolytus 1968,N 20,38:3
Paquin, Lawrence (Director)
Blue Blood 1924,Ap 3,21:2
Paquis, Gerard
Femmes Savantes, Les 1967,F 7,34:2
Parades, Jean
Vie Parisienne, La 1964,Mr 11,34:2
Paradine, Thomas
Low Bridge 1933,F 10,13:4
They All Come to Moscow 1933,My 12,20:6
Paradis, Marjorie Bartholomew (Playwright)
New Freedom, The 1930,My 15,32:4
New Freedom, The 1930,My 17,21:4
Parady, Paul (Costume Designer)
Stephen D 1966,Ag 5,17:1
Paramore, Edward E Jr (Playwright)
Set a Thief 1927,F 22,22:1
Ringside 1928,Ag 30,13:2
Mr Peebles and Mr Hooker 1946,O 11,29:2
Paraskevas, Nicos
Oedipus Tyrannus 1952,N 25,35:2

Parber, Victor
Story for Strangers, A 1948,S 22,39:2
Pardee, Richard
Happy Ending 1936,Jl 15,14:3
Pardell, David M (Miscellaneous)
Leading Lady 1948,O 19,33:1
Pardello, Leo
Big Fight, The 1928,S 19,33:1
Pardoll, David (Miscellaneous)
Sunday in New York 1961,N 10,40:1
Gift of Time, A 1962,F 23,34:1
Come on Strong 1962,O 5,29:1
I Was Dancing 1964,N 9,40:4
We Have Always Lived in the Castle
  1966,O 20,53:1
Pardoll, David (Producer)
Talent '49 1949,Ap 13,39:4
Pardos, John (Miscellaneous)
Tobias and the Angel 1957,O 21,29:5
Pardue, William
Dracula Sabbat 1970,O 2,28:2
Pardy, Edmond J
Eyvind of the Hills 1921,F 2,14:1
Pardy, Richard
Stephen D 1966,Ag 5,17:1
Paredes, Jean
Pieton de L'Air, Le 1964,Mr 4,33:2
Salut a Moliere 1964,Mr 4,33:2
Parella, Anthony (Director)
Mourners' Bench, The 1950,S 22,35:7
Parella, Anthony (Miscellaneous)
Hostile Witness 1966,F 18,26:1
Parella, Anthony (Producer)
Sacred Flame, The 1952,O 8,35:2
Whistler's Grandmother 1952,D 12,40:2
Harbor Lights 1956,O 5,20:1
Parella, John
Noye's Fludde 1959,Mr 17,41:2
Parent, Gail (Composer)
Leonard Sillman's New Faces of 1968
  1968,My 3,43:1
Parent, Gail (Lyricist)
Leonard Sillman's New Faces of 1968
  1968,My 3,43:1
Parent, Gail (Playwright)
Leonard Sillman's New Faces of 1968
  1968,My 3,43:1
Parent, Lair
Tempest, The 1959,D 28,19:2
Parent, Nicole
Plume de Ma Tante, La 1958,N 12,42:1
Parente, Jerry
Chiaroscuro; Judges, The 1963,Je 6,40:8
Parente, Noel
View From the Bridge, A 1965,Ja 29,24:1
Pares (Composer)
Lulu 1927,O 2,VIII,2:4
Parfitt, Judy
Time Remembered 1955,My 4,35:1
Hotel in Amsterdam, The 1968,Jl 21,II,12:1
Parfrey, Woodrow
All the King's Men 1948,Ja 19,19:2
Millionairess, The 1949,Ap 7,38:5
Rehearsal, The 1952,My 27,30:5
Room Service 1953,Ap 7,34:1
Moby Dick 1955,Ap 26,25:3
Cradle Song 1955,D 2,32:2
All That Fall 1957,O 8,41:2
Winesburg, Ohio 1958,F 6,22:2
Rivalry, The 1959,F 9,24:2
Advise and Consent 1960,N 18,25:1
Giants, Sons of Giants 1962,Ja 8,26:2
Parichy, Dennis (Lighting Director)
Little Eyolf 1964,Mr 17,31:1
Arms and the Man 1964,Ap 28,41:1
Acquisition, The 1968,D 31,19:1
This Bird of Dawning Singeth All Night Long
  1968,D 31,19:1
Young Master Dante, The 1968,D 31,19:1
Boy on the Straight-Back Chair 1969,Mr 18,36:1
War Games 1969,Ap 18,37:1
Transgressor Rides Again, The 1969,My 21,42:1
Jumping Fool, The 1970,F 10,53:1
Shepherd of Avenue B, The 1970,My 16,30:1
Steal the Old Man's Bundle 1970,My 16,30:1
Parigot, Guy (Director)
Femmes Savantes, Les 1967,F 7,34:2
Paris, Eugen de
Mediterranee 1926,N 7,VIII,2:7
Paris, Irene
Recruiting Officer, The 1958,F 8,12:2
Paris, J D
Betty Behave 1927,Mr 9,28:4
Paris, Jackie
Cry of Players, A 1968,N 15,40:1
Paris, Jean-Louis
Malade Imaginaire, Le; Imaginary Invalid, The
  1958,Ap 30,28:2
Jalousie du Barbouille, La; Jealousy of the
  Barbouille, The 1958,My 7,43:1
Sganarelle; Imaginary Cuckold, The 1958,My 7,43:1
Mariage Force, Le; Forced Wedding, The
  1958,My 7,43:1

Paris, Jerry
Anna Christie 1952,Ja 10,33:1
Paris, Lila
Stronger, The 1949,Je 15,38:2
Paris, Lila (Director)
Right You Are (If You Think You Are)
1950,Je 29,37:2
Paris, Norman (Miscellaneous)
Owl and the Pussycat, The 1964,N 19,48:1
Paris, Ronnie (Director)
Nat Turner 1960,N 7,46:3
Paris, Ronnie (Playwright)
Yes, Yes, No No 1969,Ja 1,16:1
Paris Rive Gauche
Untitled-Revue 1968,O 21,55:4
Parisette, Mildred
Melody 1933,F 15,17:4
Parish, Dorothy
Chief Thing, The 1963,Ap 30,27:2
Parish, Frank
Merry Wives of Windsor, The 1938,Ap 15,22:3
Parish, James (Playwright)
Distinguished Gathering 1935,O 8,26:3
Distinguished Gathering 1935,N 3,X,1:7
Good-Bye to Yesterday 1937,N 21,XI,3:6
Cheapside 1938,F 28,18:2
Message for Margaret 1946,S 2,13:2
Message for Margaret 1947,Ap 17,34:2
Parish, Michael
Falstaff 1966,Je 20,27:1
Twelfth Night 1966,Je 23,28:1
Julius Caesar 1966,Je 24,29:2
Yerma 1966,D 9,60:1
Richard II 1968,Je 24,42:3
Androcles and the Lion 1968,Je 27,47:1
Hamlet 1969,Je 30,33:1
Three Sisters, The 1969,Ag 4,29:1
Henry V 1969,N 11,43:1
Parish, Mitchell (Composer)
Lew Leslie's Blackbirds of 1939 1939,F 13,12:2
Parish, Mitchell (Lyricist)
Lew Leslie's Blackbirds of 1939 1939,F 13,12:2
Parisi, Anita
Ice Capades 1958,S 4,33:2
Parisian Redheads, The
Vaudeville (Palace) 1928,Ap 3,32:5
Parisys, Miss
Youki 1932,O 16,IX,2:3
Parizet, Lucienne (Mme)
Homme et Ses Fantomes, L' 1924,N 14,16:1
Merchant of Venice, The 1924,N 18,23:2
Bourgeois Gentilhomme, Le 1924,N 20,21:2
Taming of the Shrew, The 1924,N 25,27:3
Petit Peche 1926,O 24,VIII,2:1
Mauvais Ange, Le 1927,Je 5,VII,2:1
Park, Andy (Composer)
Joe Egg 1968,F 2,26:1
Park, Dave
Ice Capades 1961,Ag 31,24:4
Park, George
Petrified Forest, The 1942,Ag 19,14:3
Park, John
Crooked Square, The 1923,S 11,10:2
Chiffon Girl, The 1924,F 20,23:2
Top Hole 1924,S 2,22:3
Matinee Girl, The 1926,F 2,20:3
Tyrant, The 1930,N 13,33:1
Park, Mae
Find the Fox 1930,Je 21,20:4
Park, Richard
My Fair Lady 1964,My 21,43:2
Park, S John (Director)
Philadelphia 1929,S 17,34:5
Park, S John (Playwright)
Philadelphia 1929,S 17,34:5
Lily White 1930,My 18,VIII,3:1
Park, Sam J
Enemy Within 1931,O 6,35:3
Locked Room, The 1933,D 26,18:5
Park, Sam J (Playwright)
Black Widow 1936,F 13,24:3
Park, Thomas
Yeomen of the Guard, The 1964,Ag 3,16:1
Park, Vincent
Tempest, The 1970,F 15,67:1
Parke, Gladys
American Holiday 1936,F 22,13:3
Parke, Larry
Great Big Doorstep, The 1950,Mr 18,8:6
Parke, Peter
Young Alexander 1929,Mr 13,28:2
Parke, William
Creoles 1927,S 23,33:3
Troika 1930,Ap 2,32:6
Jefferson Davis 1936,F 19,17:2
Arsenic and Old Lace 1941,Ja 11,13:2
Parker, Alison
Iolanthe 1968,N 9,37:3
Parker, Ann
Vaudeville (Palace) 1928,D 17,23:3
Parker, Audrey
Vaudeville (Palace) 1932,Ap 18,19:5

Parker, Austin (Playwright)
Week-end 1929,O 23,26:4
With All My Heart 1935,Jl 30,17:1
Parker, Barnett
Hotel Mouse, The 1922,Mr 14,11:3
Caroline 1923,F 1,13:2
Passing Show of 1923, The 1923,Je 15,24:6
Topics of 1923 1923,N 21,23:2
Artists and Models 1924,O 16,33:3
Night in Paris, A 1926,Ja 6,16:3
Night in Paris, A 1926,Jl 27,15:4
Red Robe, The 1928,D 26,15:1
Going Gay 1933,Ag 4,18:5
Red Cat, The 1934,S 20,21:1
Thumbs Up! 1934,D 28,24:1
Parker, Betzie
March March, The 1966,N 15,51:4
Parker, Beverly
Knock on Wood 1935,My 29,16:2
Parker, Blaine
Richard III 1967,Je 14,43:1
Parker, Brian
Henry IV, Part II 1946,My 8,33:4
Parker, Caroline
Right to Kill, The 1926,F 16,22:2
Parker, Carolyn (Costume Designer)
Death of a Salesman 1963,Jl 20,11:2
She Stoops to Conquer 1968,Ja 1,11:1
Tango 1968,Ja 1,11:1
Parker, Carolyn (Miscellaneous)
House of Atreus, The; Bringers of Offerings, The
1967,Jl 24,23:1
House of Atreus, The; Agamemnon 1967,Jl 24,23:1
House of Atreus, The; Furies, The 1967,Jl 24,23:1
Parker, Carolyn (Scenic Designer)
Skin of Our Teeth, The 1966,Je 2,51:1
Thieves' Carnival 1967,Je 5,52:1
Romeo and Juliet 1968,Je 11,55:2
Parker, Catherine
My Magnolia 1926,Jl 13,19:2
Parker, Cecil
Shadow, The 1936,Ap 26,II,12:6
Innocent Party, The 1938,F 13,X,3:3
Little Ladyship 1939,F 26,IX,3:5
French for Love 1939,N 12,IX,1:8
Skin of Our Teeth, The 1945,Mr 20,22:8
Daphne Laureola 1950,S 19,38:6
Daphne Laureola 1950,S 24,II,1:1
Parker, Charles
Blithe Spirit 1941,Jl 13,IX,1:4
Parker, Charlotte
Fashion 1937,Mr 21,II,7:8
Parker, Curtis
Battle Hymn 1936,My 23,12:1
Unto Such Glory 1937,My 7,28:2
Parker, Cynthia
Rivals, The 1969,O 18,37:1
Parker, Del
Follow the Girls 1944,Ap 10,15:2
Knight of the Burning Pestle, The 1953,O 24,13:2
Moon in Capricorn 1953,O 28,37:2
Midsummer Night's Dream, A 1957,Je 27,21:3
Parker, Don (Playwright)
Nuns, The 1970,Je 2,35:1
Parker, Don (Producer)
Nuns, The 1970,Je 2,35:1
Parker, Dorothy (Lyricist)
Candide 1956,D 3,40:2
Candide 1956,D 9,II,5:1
Parker, Dorothy (Original Author)
After Such Pleasures 1934,Ja 6,18:6
After Such Pleasures 1934,F 8,15:2
Parker, Dorothy (Playwright)
49ers, The 1922,N 7,14:1
49ers, The 1922,N 12,VIII,1:1
Close Harmony 1924,D 2,23:1
Coast of Illyria, The 1949,Ap 5,37:4
Coast of Illyria, The 1949,Ap 13,39:2
Ladies of the Corridor, The 1953,O 22,33:5
Ladies of the Corridor, The 1953,N 1,II,1:1
Parker, Edward
Elizabeth Sleeps Out 1936,Ap 21,27:6
Parker, Edwin S
Little Theatre Tournament; Another Room for
Rent 1929,My 7,28:1
Parker, Eleanor
Is Zat So? 1925,Ja 6,23:4
Parker, Elizabeth
Liliom 1921,Ap 21,18:1
Parker, Florence
Bye Bye Bonnie 1927,Ja 14,15:3
White Lights 1927,O 12,30:4
Parker, Frank
Just Life 1926,S 15,33:3
My Princess 1927,O 7,24:2
Untitled-Dance 1930,F 13,25:2
Howdy Stranger 1937,Ja 15,17:5
Follow the Girls 1944,Ap 10,15:2
Parker, George
Mr Moneypenny 1928,O 17,26:2
Parker, Gerald (Scenic Designer)
General Seeger 1962,Mr 1,26:2

Parker, Hal
Keep Kool 1924,My 23,16:4
Vaudeville (Palace) 1928,Ja 10,28:5
Parker, Henry
Oklahoma! 1951,S 13,38:2
Parker, Irene
Earth Journey 1944,Ap 28,24:2
Parker, James
Midnight 1930,D 30,25:1
Conjur 1938,N 1,27:2
Mandragola 1956,Mr 1,36:4
Ivory Branch, The 1956,My 25,27:1
Parker, Janet
Tree Grows in Brooklyn, A 1951,Ap 20,24:3
Children's Hour, The 1952,D 19,35:2
Parker, Janet Lee
Gogo Loves You 1964,O 10,19:2
Live Like Pigs 1965,Je 8,48:2
Parker, Jean
Loco 1946,O 17,29:2
Burlesque 1946,D 26,30:3
Parker, Jim
Happy Faculty, The 1967,Ap 19,50:1
Parker, John S Jr
Assorted Nuts 1940,Ap 7,I,44:6
Parker, Joy
Love's Labour's Lost 1961,Je 23,19:1
Parker, Kay
Way of the World, The 1954,S 30,38:2
Parker, Ken
As You Like It 1968,Je 24,42:3
Androcles and the Lion 1968,Je 27,47:1
Love's Labour's Lost 1968,Je 28,36:1
All's Well That Ends Well 1970,Je 16,53:1
Othello 1970,Je 22,43:1
Devil's Disciple, The 1970,Je 30,48:1
Othello 1970,S 15,51:1
Parker, Ken (Director)
Four Flights Up 1948,Ja 8,29:1
Parker, Ken (Playwright)
Four Flights Up 1948,Ja 8,29:1
Parker, Ken (Producer)
Four Flights Up 1948,Ja 8,29:1
Parker, Lara
Woman Is My Idea 1968,S 26,61:1
Lulu; Earth Spirit 1970,Mr 28,32:1
Parker, Larry (Lighting Director)
Streetcar Named Desire, A 1955,Mr 4,18:2
Journey With Strangers, A 1958,N 27,53:1
Parker, Larry (Miscellaneous)
Simply Heavenly 1957,My 22,28:2
Journey With Strangers, A 1958,N 27,53:1
Dear Liar 1962,Mr 19,36:1
Parker, Lenore
Pirates of Penzance, The 1946,My 17,14:6
Parker, Leonard
Fly Blackbird 1962,Ap 29,II,1:1
One Flew Over the Cuckoo's Nest 1963,N 14,40:2
Physicists, The 1964,O 14,52:1
Parker, Leroy
Criminal Code, The 1929,O 3,28:2
Parker, Lew
Spring Is Here 1929,Mr 12,26:1
Heads Up! 1929,N 12,34:1
Girl Crazy 1930,O 15,27:1
Red, Hot and Blue! 1936,O 30,26:3
Are You With It? 1945,N 12,17:3
Front Page, The 1946,S 5,22:4
Front Page, The 1946,S 15,II,21:1
Ankles Aweigh 1955,Ap 19,27:1
Amorous Flea, The 1964,F 18,26:1
Parker, Lida-Virginia
Mystery of the Finding of the Cross, The
1959,Ja 16,35:2
Parker, Lloyd
When the Roll Is Called Up Yonder
1930,My 9,20:5
Parker, Lois
Little Orchard Annie 1930,Ap 22,33:1
Parker, Lou
Tell Her the Truth 1932,O 29,18:2
Parker, Louis N (Original Author)
Cardinale, Il 1933,Ja 9,24:2
Parker, Louis N (Playwright)
Marjolaine 1922,Ja 25,16:1
Johannes Kreisler 1922,D 25,20:3
Angelo 1923,Mr 30,14:4
Monkey's Paw, The 1923,My 12,15:4
Minuet, A 1927,Mr 5,12:2
Disraeli 1927,My 4,29:1
Cardinale Giovanni de Medici, Il 1935,D 9,24:8
Parker, Louis N (Translator)
Aiglon, L' 1927,D 27,24:3
Cardinale, Il; Cardinal, The 1931,Ja 12,24:2
Parker, Lucette
Try It With Alice 1924,Je 24,18:4
Parker, Lucille
Like a King 1921,O 4,10:1
Parker, Mary
Audition of the Apprentice Theatre 1939,Je 2,26:2
Let's Face It 1941,O 30,26:2
Parker, Midge
Tickets, Please! 1950,Ap 28,25:2

Parker, Nancy Lee
Song of Norway 1958,Je 23,19:2
Parker, Patricia
Alternate Current 1939,D 23,8:3
Parker, Peter
King Lear 1950,Ag 30,26:2
Parker, Priscilla
Buzzin' Around 1920,Jl 7,14:1
Parker, Rena
Peacock 1932,O 12,27:1
Parker, Ross
Plume de Ma Tante, La 1958,N 12,42:1
Plume de Ma Tante, La 1959,S 13,II,1:1
Parker, Ross (Lyricist)
Plume de Ma Tante, La 1958,N 12,42:1
Parker, Rusty
Journey With Strangers, A 1958,N 27,53:1
Parker, Stephen
Macbeth 1928,N 20,28:3
Parker, Tommy
Fifth Horseman, The 1949,Je 14,26:6
Parker, Warren
Queen Bee 1929,N 13,25:1
Sellout, The 1933,S 7,17:2
Keeper of the Keys 1933,O 19,23:2
Rip Van Winkle 1935,Ag 7,22:2
Master of the Revels 1935,Ag 14,16:2
Swing Your Lady 1936,O 19,22:4
Love Goes to Press 1947,Ja 2,22:2
Parker, Willard
Johnny Belinda 1940,S 19,26:2
Lady in the Dark 1941,S 3,26:6
Lady in the Dark 1943,Mr 1,14:2
Parker, Woody
Abie's Irish Rose 1954,N 19,19:1
Mary Stuart 1956,Ap 28,10:2
Capacity for Wings 1957,Ja 10,25:2
Parker and Porthole
Sons o' Fun 1941,D 2,28:2
Parkes, Clifford
H M S Pinafore 1968,O 30,35:1
Parkes, Elizabeth
Jamboree 1932,N 25,18:4
Parkes, George
Ethan Frome 1936,Ja 22,15:2
Parkes, Gerard
Hadrian VII 1969,Ja 9,22:1
Parkes, Timothy
Richard II 1956,O 24,44:1
Romeo and Juliet 1956,O 25,41:1
Parkham, Florence
Put and Take 1921,Ag 24,12:3
Parkhirst, Douglass
Let Freedom Ring 1935,N 7,26:2
Prelude 1936,Ap 20,17:4
Bury the Dead 1936,Ap 20,17:4
200 Were Chosen 1936,N 21,21:1
Washington Jitters 1938,My 3,19:1
Good, The 1938,O 6,27:2
Male Animal, The 1941,Jl 9,24:6
Holiday 1941,Jl 23,15:2
Drifting Apart: or, The Fisherman's Child
1941,Ag 20,16:6
Tread the Green Grass 1950,Ap 21,19:4
Thunder Rock 1956,F 27,18:1
Potting Shed, The 1958,N 3,49:2
Parkhurst, Penelope H (Miscellaneous)
When Did You Last See Your Mother?
1967,Ja 5,27:5
Parkington, Mary (Playwright)
Little Theatre Tournament; House With the Twisty
Windows, The 1929,My 8,34:4
House With the Twisty Windows, The
1930,My 8,32:5
Parkins, Will
Foxy 1964,F 17,26:1
Parkinson, John
Demon Mirror, The 1968,Mr 13,42:1
Parkinson, John (Composer)
Now You See It 1967,N 20,59:1
Parkinson, John (Director)
Venturi, The: A Squeeze Play 1970,Mr 21,17:1
Parkinson, John (Lighting Director)
Demon Mirror, The 1968,Mr 13,42:1
Parkinson, John (Playwright)
Venturi, The: A Squeeze Play 1970,Mr 21,17:1
Parkinson, John (Producer)
Venturi, The: A Squeeze Play 1970,Mr 21,17:1
Parks, Alice
Gift, The 1924,Ja 23,15:4
Parks, Bernice
Beggar's Holiday 1946,D 27,13:3
Beggar's Holiday 1947,Ja 26,II,1:1
Parks, Bert
Music Man, The 1965,Je 17,26:4
Parks, Clifford
Mikado, The 1968,N 2,29:4
Parks, Cora
Malinda 1929,D 4,37:2
Swing It 1937,Jl 23,17:2
Parks, Don (Lyricist)
From A to Z 1960,Ap 21,23:2
Jo 1964,F 13,25:1

Parks, Don (Playwright)
Jo 1964,F 13,25:1
Parks, Freeman (Miscellaneous)
Autumn's Here 1966,O 26,40:1
Skits-Oh-Frantics 1967,Ap 3,39:2
Parks, Gower (Scenic Designer)
Henry IV, Part I 1946,My 7,25:2
Henry IV, Part II 1946,My 8,33:4
Henry IV 1946,My 12,II,1:1
Parks, Hildy
Bathsheba 1947,Mr 27,40:2
Summer and Smoke 1948,O 7,33:2
Magnolia Alley 1949,Ap 19,29:2
To Dorothy, A Son 1951,N 20,37:2
Be Your Age 1953,Ja 15,24:2
Parks, Hildy (Miscellaneous)
Baker Street 1965,F 17,36:1
Devils, The 1965,N 17,51:2
Time for Singing, A 1966,My 23,48:2
Black Comedy 1967,F 13,42:1
Black Comedy; White Lies 1967,F 13,42:1
Little Murders 1967,Ap 26,38:1
Unknown Soldier and His Wife, The 1967,Jl 7,22:1
Halfway up the Tree 1967,N 8,52:1
Dear World 1969,F 7,33:1
Home 1970,N 18,41:1
Parks, Jarvin (Scenic Designer)
Lovers in the Metro, The 1962,Ja 31,21:1
Keyhole, The 1962,Ja 31,21:1
Information Bureau, The 1962,Ja 31,21:1
Parks, Larry
Beg, Borrow or Steal 1960,F 11,39:4
Love and Kisses 1963,D 19,39:1
Parks, Mama Lu
Take One Step 1968,Jl 5,17:1
Parks, Melvin
Daughters of Atreus 1936,O 15,33:1
Hamlet 1939,D 5,35:2
Macbeth 1941,N 12,30:2
Parks, Melvin (Producer)
Pygmalion 1947,F 6,29:4
Parks, Paul
Falstaff 1928,D 26,14:2
Way of the World, The 1931,Je 2,34:3
County Chairman, The 1936,My 26,26:5
I'd Rather Be Right 1937,N 3,28:2
Love for Love 1940,Je 4,19:5
Pretty Little Parlor 1944,Ap 18,24:8
Allegro 1947,O 11,10:2
Parks, Sam
Jimmie's Women 1927,S 27,30:3
Parks, Trina
House of Flowers 1968,Ja 29,26:2
Parlan, Stanley
Barretts of Wimpole Street, The 1945,Mr 27,23:6
Parlow, Julia
Trip to Scarborough, A 1929,Mr 18,31:2
Parmalee, Walter W
Fiesta 1933,D 16,12:2
Parmeggiani, E
Assalto, L' 1929,My 20,23:2
Parmegiani, A
Tutto Per Bene; All's Well That Ends Well
1929,Je 3,27:1
Cena Delle Beffe, La; Jest, The 1930,N 24,26:4
Parmegiani, Alberto
In Fondo Al Cuore; Depths of the Heart, The
1930,D 8,27:1
Cardinale, Il; Cardinal, The 1931,Ja 12,24:2
Parmegiani, Angelo
Marchese di Priola, Il 1931,Mr 2,19:3
Parmegiani, Antonio
Arzigogolo, L'; Whim, The 1931,Ap 27,24:4
Giuochi di Prestigio 1931,N 2,26:1
Zia Morta, La; Dead Aunt, The 1931,N 30,16:3
Parnahay, Alicia
Strange Play, A 1944,Je 2,20:3
Parnall, William E
Cotton Stockings 1923,D 19,16:2
Parnell, Emory
Mr Adam 1949,My 26,34:6
Parnell, Keith
Case of Libel, A 1963,O 11,43:2
Paroll, David (Miscellaneous)
Sweet Bird of Youth 1959,Mr 11,39:2
Parone, Edward (Director)
Dutchman 1964,Mr 25,46:2
Two Executioners, The 1964,Mr 25,46:2
Pigeons 1965,Mr 4,37:1
Lovey 1965,Mr 26,27:1
Displaced Person, The 1966,D 30,15:1
Collision Course; Skywriting 1968,My 9,55:2
Collision Course; Tour 1968,My 9,55:2
Collision Course; Wandering 1968,My 9,55:2
Collision Course; Unexpurgated Memoirs of
Bernard Mergendeiler, The 1968,My 9,55:2
Collision Course; Metaphors 1968,My 9,55:2
Collision Course; Chuck 1968,My 9,55:2
Collision Course; Rats 1968,My 9,55:2
Collision Course; Stars and Stripes 1968,My 9,55:2
Collision Course; Thoughts on the Instant of
Greeting a Friend on the Street 1968,My 9,55:2
Collision Course; Jew! 1968,My 9,55:2

Parone, Edward (Director)—Cont
Collision Course; Camera Obscura 1968,My 9,55:2
Rats 1968,Je 30,II,1:1
Dozens, The 1969,Mr 14,51:1
L A Under Siege 1970,Ag 16,II,1:7
Remote Asylum 1970,D 13,II,3:1
Parone, Edward (Miscellaneous)
Terrible Swift Sword, The 1955,N 16,42:1
Anna Christie 1955,N 22,41:1
Adding Machine, The 1956,F 10,17:1
Queen After Death 1956,Mr 13,33:2
Parone, Edward (Producer)
Venice Preserv'd 1955,D 13,54:4
Parotte, M
Aventuriere, L' 1922,N 14,16:1
Parr, Allan
Cafe 1930,Ag 29,11:1
Parr, Antoinette
Green Hat, The 1925,S 16,23:2
Parr, Antony
King John 1960,Je 29,26:2
Parr, Gladene
Madame Bovary 1937,N 17,26:2
Parr, Hazel
Aquashow 1953,Je 24,29:2
Parraga, Graziella
Mexicana 1939,Ap 22,14:4
Parriot, John
Tarot 1970,D 12,19:1
Parriott, John
House of Leather, The 1970,Mr 19,56:1
Parris, Steve
Comforter, The 1964,O 22,42:1
License, The 1969,Ap 23,42:1
Jar, The 1969,Ap 23,42:1
Parrish, Anne (Original Author)
Journey With Strangers, A 1958,N 27,53:1
Parrish, Claire (Playwright)
Maid in the Ozarks 1946,Jl 16,20:3
Parrish, Elizabeth
Cock-A-Doodle-Doo 1949,F 28,16:5
Lady in the Dark 1952,Mr 8,11:3
Scrapbooks 1953,N 6,24:2
Johnny Johnson 1956,O 22,24:1
Redemptor, The 1959,My 5,40:1
Little Mary Sunshine 1959,N 19,49:3
Little Mary Sunshine 1959,N 29,II,1:1
Riverwind 1962,D 14,5:5
Twelfth Night 1966,Je 23,28:1
Julius Caesar 1966,Je 24,29:2
Rivals, The 1969,O 18,37:1
Don Juan 1970,My 26,32:1
Three Philip Roth Stories; Epstein 1970,Jl 31,14:1
Cops and Horrors; Fly Paper 1970,Ag 11,27:1
Cops and Horrors; Dracula 1970,Ag 11,27:1
Story Theater Repertory; Gimpel the Food
1970,O 21,40:1
Story Theater Repertory; Saint Julian the
Hospitaler 1970,O 21,40:1
Revenger's Tragedy, The 1970,D 2,58:1
Parrish, Gladys (Playwright)
Borrowed Life, The 1931,Ja 4,VIII,2:6
Parrish, Grady
Movie Man 1959,O 28,40:4
Parrish, John
Malvaloca 1922,O 3,22:1
Romeo and Juliet 1923,Ja 25,16:1
Lord Byron's Cain 1925,Ap 9,20:3
Patriot, The 1928,Ja 20,15:1
Maya 1928,F 22,19:1
Furies, The 1928,Mr 8,23:1
Journey's End 1930,Ag 5,26:4
Happy Landing 1932,Mr 28,10:5
Carry Nation 1932,O 31,18:2
Mountain, The 1933,S 12,28:6
Love Kills 1934,My 2,25:3
Prisoners of War 1935,Ja 29,24:1
Hamlet 1936,N 11,54:2
Holmeses of Baker Street, The 1936,D 10,34:3
Antony and Cleopatra 1937,N 11,30:2
Unconquered, The 1940,F 14,25:2
Steps Leading Up 1941,Ap 19,20:6
Mr Big 1941,O 1,24:2
Macbeth 1941,N 12,30:2
Richard III 1943,Mr 27,8:3
Parrish, Judy
Dance Night 1938,O 15,20:5
Pastoral 1939,N 2,26:2
Horse Fever 1940,N 25,21:2
Hope for a Harvest 1941,N 27,28:2
Kiss and Tell 1943,Mr 18,22:1
Flamingo Road 1946,Mr 20,18:2
Happiest Years, The 1949,Ap 26,29:8
As You Like It 1950,Ja 27,27:2
Legend of Sarah 1950,O 12,42:4
Parrish, Lex
Abe Lincoln in Illinois 1938,O 17,12:2
Parrish, Mitchell (Lyricist)
Italian Straw Hat, The 1957,O 1,37:2
Parrish, Robert
Hot Mikado, The 1939,Mr 24,26:2
Parry, John C
Great Guns 1939,N 18,23:4

Parry, Joseph
Tomorrow 1928,D 29,20:2
Parry, Lee
When We Are Married 1939,D 26,22:3
Pillar to Post 1943,D 11,11:2
Metropole 1949,D 7,43:2
Parry, Natasha
Fighting Cock, The 1959,D 9,57:3
Fighting Cock, The 1959,D 20,II,3:1
Parry, Ray (Playwright)
Sea Shells 1935,Jl 16,24:2
Parshall, Jean (Costume Designer)
Waiting for Godot 1958,Ag 6,22:1
Parson, Carola
Suzette 1921,N 25,18:3
Blue Kitten, The 1922,Ja 14,9:3
Is Zat So? 1925,Ja 6,23:4
Skull, The 1928,Ap 24,28:3
Parson, Jean (Producer)
Evening of European Theatre, An 1960,Ap 26,41:1
Sap of Life, The 1961,O 3,44:1
Parson, Milton
At Your Service 1937,Ag 17,23:1
Parson, William (Musical Director)
Hot Mikado, The 1939,Mr 24,26:2
Parsonett, Mario
Candida 1925,D 19,14:2
Dear Brutus 1926,Jl 15,21:3
Parsons, Betty (Costume Designer)
Wizard of Oz, The 1968,N 28,69:2
Parsons, Billy
Best Foot Forward 1941,O 2,28:2
Heaven on Earth 1948,S 17,29:2
Tree Grows in Brooklyn, A 1951,Ap 20,24:3
Parsons, C J
Virginia Reel 1947,Ap 15,28:2
Parsons, Cathy
Caukey 1944,F 18,15:4
Walk Hard 1944,D 1,28:2
John Brown 1950,My 4,32:7
Parsons, Chauncey
Artists and Models 1927,N 16,28:2
Parsons, Donovan (Miscellaneous)
Earl Carroll's Vanities 1927,Ja 5,18:1
Wake Up and Dream 1929,D 31,14:3
Parsons, Estelle
Happy Hunting 1956,D 7,30:1
Beg, Borrow or Steal 1960,F 11,39:4
Threepenny Opera, The 1960,S 15,44:3
Automobile Graveyard, The 1961,N 14,46:2
Mrs Dally Has a Lover 1962,O 2,47:1
Next Time I'll Sing to You 1963,N 28,69:2
In the Summer House 1964,Mr 26,43:1
Ready When You Are, C. B.! 1964,D 8,55:1
Malcolm 1966,Ja 12,29:1
Suburban Tragedy 1966,Mr 7,22:1
Princess Rebecca Birnbaum 1966,Mr 7,22:1
East Wind, The 1967,F 10,30:1
Galileo 1967,Ap 14,31:1
We Bombed in New Haven 1967,D 7,58:1
Seven Descents of Myrtle, The 1968,Mr 28,54:1
Seven Descents of Myrtle, The 1968,Ap 7,II,1:5
Our Town 1968,S 29,77:4
Front Page, The 1968,O 20,85:5
Honor and Offer 1968,D 1,II,3:1
Peer Gynt 1969,Jl 17,56:1
Mahagonny 1970,Ap 29,51:1
Mahagonny 1970,My 10,II,15:1
Mahagonny 1970,My 10,II,1:1
Parsons, Eugene W (Producer)
Behavior of Mrs Crane, The 1928,Mr 21,30:1
Parsons, Frank
Virgin, The 1926,F 23,26:1
Parsons, Frederick
Vaudeville (Hippodrome) 1926,Ap 13,28:2
Parsons, George
Her Temporary Husband 1922,S 1,16:2
Merrily We Roll Along 1934,O 1,14:1
First Lady 1935,N 27,17:4
Parsons, Harriet (Producer)
Rape of the Belt, The 1960,N 7,46:1
Parsons, Hubert (Playwright)
Dancers, The 1923,F 25,VII,1:7
Parsons, J Palmer (Playwright)
White Gold 1925,N 3,34:5
Parsons, Jack
First Crocus, The 1942,Ja 3,14:6
Johnny 2X4 1942,Mr 17,24:6
Parsons, Jane
Pirates of Penzance, The 1942,F 20,20:2
Parsons, Jeanne
Oklahoma! 1951,My 30,15:2
Parsons, Joel
Venice Preserv'd 1955,D 13,54:4
Two Gentlemen of Verona 1957,Jl 23,21:5
As You Like It 1958,Ja 21,33:6
Twelfth Night 1958,Ag 7,21:4
Parsons, John
Three Musketeers, The 1921,My 20,18:5
Parsons, Joseph
Good Times 1920,Ag 10,10:1
Parsons, Kate (Playwright)
Blow the Man Down 1929,Ag 25,VIII,3:1

Commodore Marries, The 1929,S 5,26:3
Commodore Marries, The 1929,S 15,IX,1:1
Parsons, Milton
Royal Virgin, The 1930,Mr 18,30:5
Unto the Third 1933,Ap 21,24:8
Right This Way 1938,Ja 6,22:3
Vigil, The 1948,My 22,8:6
Now I Lay Me Down to Sleep 1949,Jl 23,7:3
Now I Lay Me Down to Sleep 1950,Mr 3,21:2
Parsons, Patti
Oklahoma! 1953,S 1,19:1
Parsons, Robert
Much Ado About Nothing 1927,N 19,14:6
Trip to Scarborough, A 1929,Mr 18,31:2
Dragon, The 1929,Mr 26,34:2
Life Line, The 1930,D 29,19:3
Parsons, Sally Ann
Now I Lay Me Down to Sleep 1950,Mr 3,21:2
Parsons, Sally Ann (Miscellaneous)
House of Bernarda Alba, The 1963,N 25,23:2
Parsons, Wellman
Golden Days 1921,N 2,20:1
Pigeon, The 1922,F 3,13:1
Parsons, William (Musical Director)
Up in Central Park 1947,My 20,29:2
Partello, Billy
Macbeth 1961,Je 19,31:1
Richard III 1964,Je 12,44:2
Antigone 1967,Je 19,43:1
Partikian, Edwin
Magistrate, The 1959,My 14,30:6
Partington, Arthur
High Button Shoes 1947,O 10,32:2
Talent '49 1949,Ap 13,39:4
Call Me Madam 1950,O 13,25:1
Shoestring Revue 1955,Mr 1,22:2
Partington, Arthur (Choreographer)
Most Happy Fella, The 1959,F 11,50:2
Show Boat 1961,Ap 13,32:1
Partington, Dorothy
Lady Comes Across, The 1942,Ja 10,10:2
Partington, Jeanne (Costume Designer)
Hear! Hear! 1955,S 28,38:1
Harbor Lights 1956,O 5,20:1
Shoestring '57 1956,N 6,31:1
Partington, Rex
Lunatics and Lovers 1954,D 14,44:2
Partington, Rex (Miscellaneous)
Hamlet 1963,My 9,41:1
Miser, The 1963,My 10,39:1
Henry V 1964,My 13,52:1
Saint Joan 1964,My 14,41:1
Cherry Orchard, The 1965,Ag 2,17:2
Partner, Mycroft
Evening With the Times Square Two, An 1967,My 21,83:6
Partnow, Elaine
Awakening of Spring, The 1964,My 13,50:1
Partridge, Bellamy (Original Author)
January Thaw 1946,F 5,18:2
Partridge, Roland
Gondoliers, The 1944,F 22,26:3
Patience 1944,F 26,11:4
Parver, Michael (Miscellaneous)
Lord Pengo 1962,N 20,41:2
Parver, Michael (Producer)
Anything Goes 1962,My 16,35:1
Parwell, Gertrude
Streetcar Named Desire, A 1955,Mr 4,18:2
Pary, Mlle
Untitled-Revue 1924,Je 15,VII,1:4
Paryla, Herr
Love Is Not So Simple 1935,N 20,26:7
Parys, George de (Playwright)
Lulu 1928,O 28,IX,2:1
Pasalbessy, Helen
Lysistrata 1968,N 15,42:1
Pasatieri, Thomas (Composer)
Bacchants, The 1967,F 25,14:1
Pascal, Andre (Playwright)
Lorsqu'on Aime 1921,D 25,VI,1:8
Risk, The; Caducee, Le 1922,Jl 30,VI,1:7
Moulin de la Galette, Le 1923,Ja 28,VII,2:7
Vocation, La 1926,D 19,VII,3:3
Circe 1929,Mr 31,VIII,2:7
Pascal, Ernest (Director)
Amorous Antic, The 1929,D 3,29:2
Pascal, Ernest (Original Author)
Marriage Bed, The 1928,D 30,VIII,1:6
Marriage Bed, The 1929,Ja 8,35:1
Pascal, Ernest (Playwright)
Charlatan, The 1922,Ap 25,14:2
Marriage Bed, The 1928,D 30,VIII,1:6
Marriage Bed, The 1929,Ja 8,35:1
Amorous Antic, The 1929,D 3,29:2
American Primitive 1937,Ag 13,12:5
I Am My Youth 1938,Mr 8,22:4
Peepshow 1944,F 4,12:2
Pascal, Ernest (Producer)
Peepshow 1944,F 4,12:2
Pascal, Fran (Playwright)
George M! 1968,Ap 11,48:1

Pascal, Gabriel (Miscellaneous)
Red Gloves 1948,D 6,28:2
Pascal, Gordon
Three Sisters, The 1926,O 27,24:1
Twelfth Night 1926,D 21,21:4
Inheritors 1927,Mr 8,23:1
Pascal, John (Playwright)
George M! 1968,Ap 11,48:1
Pascal, Milton (Composer)
Illustrators' Show, The 1936,Ja 23,25:3
Artists and Models 1943,N 6,16:6
Follow the Girls 1944,Ap 10,15:2
Follow the Girls 1944,Ap 16,II,1:2
Along Fifth Avenue 1949,Ja 14,28:2
Pascal, Milton (Lyricist)
Oh, Hector! 1929,Mr 6,33:2
Artists and Models 1943,N 6,16:6
Follow the Girls 1944,Ap 10,15:2
Along Fifth Avenue 1949,Ja 14,28:2
Pascal, Roy
Partition 1948,O 29,31:2
Pascale, Elizabeth
Headless Horseman, The 1937,Mr 6,10:4
Pasch, Claire
Oklahoma! 1951,My 30,15:2
Pasch, Reginald
Merry Widow, The 1921,S 6,13:1
Clinging Vine, The 1922,D 25,20:2
Golden Dawn 1927,D 1,32:3
Paschall, Alfred
Hamlet 1938,O 13,28:1
Henry IV, Part I 1939,Ja 31,17:2
Hamlet 1939,D 5,35:2
Richard II 1940,Ap 2,31:2
Macbeth 1941,N 12,30:2
Paschall, John
Gentlemen of the Press 1928,Ag 28,27:2
Paschall, Robert
This Happy Breed 1952,Ap 4,23:2
Howie 1958,S 18,35:2
Paschall, Robert (Director)
Cry of the Raindrop 1961,Mr 8,38:1
Paschall, Robert (Miscellaneous)
Pictures in the Hallway 1956,S 17,23:2
I Know at the Door 1957,S 30,27:2
Genius and the Goddess, The 1957,D 11,41:1
Jane Eyre 1958,My 2,31:1
Beg, Borrow or Steal 1960,F 11,39:4
Send Me No Flowers 1960,D 6,54:1
Pasco, Richard
Entertainer, The 1958,F 13,22:2
Measure for Measure 1967,F 15,37:1
Hamlet 1967,F 17,44:1
Italian Girl, The 1968,Jl 4,14:1
Pascoe, Paul
Young Madame Conti 1937,Ap 1,18:4
Pasdeloup, Donna
Philip Goes Forth 1931,Ja 13,35:4
Pasha Four
Folly Town 1920,My 18,9:2
Pashalinski, Lola
Bluebeard 1970,My 5,58:1
Pashennaya, Vera
Tsar Fyodor Ivanovitch 1923,Ja 11,25:1
Cherry Orchard, The 1923,Ja 23,18:1
Three Sisters, The 1923,Ja 30,12:2
Long Live Spain! 1937,Ja 10,X,3:3
Pashennaya, Vera (Director)
Long Live Spain! 1937,Ja 10,X,3:3
Pashkova, Galina
Sea Gull, The 1954,Jl 7,22:1
Pashley, Anne
Yeomen of the Guard, The 1962,Jl 11,28:1
Pasic, Petar (Scenic Designer)
Who's Afraid of Virginia Woolf? 1968,Jl 4,13:1
Paskin, Murray
Many Loves 1959,Ja 14,28:1
Cave at Machpelah, The 1959,Jl 1,25:1
In the Jungle of Cities 1960,D 21,39:1
Blind Angel, The 1965,Ap 2,26:1
Pasle-Green, Jeanne
Grin and Bare It 1970,Mr 17,36:1
Pasmore, Edward H
Flying Blind 1930,My 16,20:2
Pasmore, Evelyn
Flying Blind 1930,My 16,20:2
Pasner, Eleanor
Good, The 1938,O 6,27:2
Paso, Alfonso (Playwright)
Las Que Tienen Gue Servir 1962,D 18,5:1
Song of the Grasshopper 1967,S 29,52:2
Paso, Antonio Jr (Playwright)
Leyenda del Beso, La 1942,N 20,26:4
Pasquali
Procureur Hallers, Le 1924,N 13,18:1
Homme et Ses Fantomes, L' 1924,N 14,16:1
Merchant of Venice, The 1924,N 18,23:2
Bourgeois Gentilhomme, Le 1924,N 20,21:2
Teddy and Partner 1933,F 12,IX,3:4
Pasquali, Alfred
Taming of the Shrew, The 1924,N 25,27:3
Pasquali Brothers
Vogues of 1924 1924,Mr 28,14:3

Pasquali Brothers, The and Wallace
Vaudeville (Hippodrome) 1926,Mr 30,20:4
Passa, Katy
Hippolytus 1968,N 20,38:3
Passantino, Anthony
Hamlet 1964,Je 17,49:1
Othello 1964,Jl 15,29:1
Hamlet 1969,Je 30,33:1
Henry V 1969,N 11,43:1
Passeltiner, Bernie
Sourball 1969,Ag 6,29:2
Passeur, Steve (Playwright)
A Quoi Penses-Tu? 1928,O 28,IX,2:7
Suzanne 1929,F 17,IX,4:2
Acheteuse, L' 1930,My 4,XI,2:6
Chaine, La 1931,My 10,VIII,2:4
Marriage by Purchase 1931,Je 21,VIII,1:3
Defense d'Afficher 1931,S 27,VIII,2:7
Tricheurs, Les 1932,Ap 3,VIII,2:2
Vilaine Femme, Une 1933,Ja 1,IX,3:4
Amour Gai, L' 1933,N 12,IX,3:4
Bete Noire, La 1934,My 13,IX,2:2
Je Vivrai un Grand Amour 1935,Jl 21,IX,1:6
Temoin, Le 1936,F 23,X,2:3
Chateau de Cartes, Le 1937,F 14,X,2:3
Passloff, Aileen
Dybbuk, The 1954,O 27,33:6
Full Moon in March, A 1960,S 20,48:1
Last Triangle, The (An Embroidered Camp)
1968,Mr 19,41:1
Passloff, Aileen (Choreographer)
Full Moon in March, A 1960,S 20,48:1
Last Triangle, The (An Embroidered Camp)
1968,Mr 19,41:1
Only a Countess May Dance When She's Crazy
(An Almost Historical Camp) 1968,Mr 19,41:1
Passy, Antonio
If I Were You 1931,S 24,21:1
Bloody Laughter 1931,D 5,20:6
Wolves 1932,Ja 7,26:3
Pastell, George
King and I, The 1955,My 17,33:4
Pastene, Robert
First Crocus, The 1942,Ja 3,14:6
Hamlet 1945,D 14,25:2
King Midas and the Golden Touch 1948,O 25,28:3
Me, The Sleeper 1949,My 16,18:6
Saint Joan 1950,Mr 4,10:6
Taming of the Shrew, The 1951,Ap 26,35:2
Saint Joan 1951,O 5,23:2
Children's Hour, The 1952,D 19,35:2
Time of the Cuckoo, The 1958,O 28,40:2
Policemen, The 1961,N 22,24:2
In the Counting House 1962,D 15,5:5
Hamlet 1963,My 9,41:1
Miser, The 1963,My 10,39:1
Three Sisters, The 1963,Jl 22,19:2
Journey to the Day 1963,N 12,49:1
Henry V 1964,My 13,52:1
Saint Joan 1964,My 14,41:1
Volpone 1964,Jl 20,18:3
Way of the World, The 1965,Je 2,40:1
Richard III 1965,Je 3,26:1
Cherry Orchard, The 1965,Ag 2,17:2
Dance of Death, The 1966,Je 3,31:1
As You Like It 1966,Je 4,19:1
Harpers Ferry 1967,Je 6,52:2
House of Atreus, The; Agamemnon 1967,Jl 24,23:1
House of Atreus, The; Bringers of Offerings, The
1967,Jl 24,23:1
Visit, The 1967,S 13,41:1
She Stoops to Conquer 1968,Ja 1,11:1
Master Builder, The 1968,Je 22,26:1
Resistible Rise of Arturo Ui, The 1968,Ag 8,25:1
Merton of the Movies 1968,S 26,62:1
House of Atreus, The 1968,D 18,55:1
Resistible Rise of Arturo Ui, The 1968,D 23,44:1
Murderous Angels 1970,F 8,70:1
Pasteras, Peter (Miscellaneous)
Sextet 1958,N 27,53:1
Pasternack, Louis
All the King's Men 1948,Ja 19,19:2
Pasternak, Boris (Translator)
Henry IV 1969,My 11,4:1
Romeo and Juliet 1970,My 28,28:1
Pasternak, Marfa
Crime and Punishment 1935,Ja 23,20:3
Paston, George (Playwright)
Gold Fields 1920,Jl 11,VI,1:6
Pastor, Enrique
Mexicana 1939,Ap 22,14:4
Pastore, Donna
Miracle Worker, The 1959,O 20,44:1
Pastorfield, Camille
John Hawthorne 1921,Ja 24,16:1
Golden Days 1921,N 2,20:1
Patachou
International Soiree 1958,Mr 13,25:1
Folies Bergere 1964,Je 3,36:1
Pataki, Michael
Jumping Fool, The 1970,F 10,53:1
Patchen, Anna
Night of January 16 1935,D 16,22:5

Patchen, Kenneth (Playwright)
Now You See It 1967,N 20,59:1
Patchova, Mme
Man Platonof, The 1929,Mr 3,VIII,3:1
Pate, Bernard
Air-Minded 1932,F 11,17:3
Haiti 1938,Mr 3,16:1
Day Will Come, The 1944,S 8,17:2
Pate, Mayon
In Heaven and Earth 1936,Mr 27,24:8
Patelis, George
Shoemaker and the Peddler, The 1960,O 15,27:4
Patent, Will
Macbeth 1969,D 23,25:1
Paterno, Yolanda
Henri Christophe 1945,Je 7,24:5
Paterson, Ian
Oh What a Lovely War 1964,O 1,30:1
Paterson, Kenneth
Time for Elizabeth 1948,S 28,32:3
Paterson, Patrick (Playwright)
Roses Are Real, The 1964,Ja 23,27:1
Paterson, William
Hamlet 1968,Je 10,59:1
Three Sisters, The 1969,O 10,38:1
Pates, Gwendolyn
Mating Season, The 1927,Jl 19,27:6
Pathe, Bernard
Milky Way, The 1934,My 9,23:2
Patinkin, Sheldon (Director)
Return of Second City in "20,000 Frozen
Grenadiers," The 1966,Ap 22,36:1
Paton, Alan (Original Author)
Lost in the Stars 1949,O 31,21:2
Lost in the Stars 1949,N 6,II,1:1
Too Late the Phalarope 1956,O 12,35:1
Paton, Alan (Playwright)
Mkhumbhane 1960,Mr 31,29:2
Sponono 1964,Ap 3,28:1
Sponono 1964,Ap 12,II,1:1
Paton, Angela
Hamlet 1968,Je 10,59:1
Three Sisters, The 1969,O 10,38:1
Three Sisters, The 1969,O 19,II,3:1
Paton, Lee
Man of Destiny, The 1956,Ap 26,38:1
Fall 1957,N 22,19:1
Paton, Lee (Director)
Blood Bugle, The 1961,Je 29,26:1
West of the Moon 1961,Je 29,26:1
Paton, Lee (Miscellaneous)
On the Harmfulness of Tobacco 1956,Ap 26,38:1
Man of Destiny, The 1956,Ap 26,38:1
From Here to There; Slow Dusk 1958,Ap 24,37:3
From Here to There; Real Strange One, A
1958,Ap 24,37:3
From Here to There; Otherwise Engaged
1958,Ap 24,37:3
Geranium Hat, The 1959,Mr 18,45:1
Paton, Lee (Producer)
Sweeney Todd 1957,Ag 28,21:4
Power of Dreams, A 1958,Mr 11,33:1
Jack 1958,Je 4,39:2
Bald Soprano, The 1958,Je 4,39:2
Patou Sisters
Revels of 1936 1935,S 30,12:4
Patrice, Gloria
Life With Mother 1948,Je 9,36:3
Peter Pan 1950,Ap 25,27:2
Courtin' Time 1951,Je 14,30:2
Patrick, Albert
Hymn to the Rising Sun 1937,My 7,28:2
Patrick, Dennis
Wayward Saint, The 1955,F 18,17:1
Saint Joan 1956,S 12,42:1
Persecution and Assassination of Marat As
Performed by the Inmates of the Asylum of
Charenton Under the Direction of the Marquis de
Sade, The 1967,Ja 4,34:1
Patrick, Fred
Aunt Caroline's Will 1954,Ag 11,21:1
Patrick, Harold
Robin Hood 1944,N 8,28:2
Cradle Will Rock, The 1947,D 27,11:2
Patrick, Jerome
Nightcap, The 1921,Ag 16,18:3
Zander the Great 1923,Ap 10,24:2
Patrick, John (Director)
Story of Mary Surratt, The 1947,F 10,25:2
Patrick, John (Lighting Director)
Red Horse Animation, The 1970,N 20,32:1
Patrick, John (Playwright)
Hell Freezes Over 1935,D 30,14:2
Cat Screams, The 1942,Je 17,26:5
Willow and I, The 1942,D 11,32:2
Hasty Heart, The 1945,Ja 4,14:2
Hasty Heart, The 1945,Ja 14,II,1:1
Story of Mary Surratt, The 1947,F 10,25:2
Curious Savage, The 1950,O 25,44:3
Lo and Behold! 1951,D 13,45:2
Teahouse of the August Moon, The 1953,O 16,32:1
Teahouse of the August Moon, The
1953,O 25,II,1:1

Patrick, John (Playwright)—Cont
Teahouse of the August Moon, The
1954,Mr 10,30:2
Hasty Heart, The 1954,Mr 13,10:1
Teahouse of the August Moon, The
1954,Ap 23,23:5
Teahouse of the August Moon, The
1954,My 2,II,3:1
Teahouse of the August Moon, The
1954,My 20,37:1
Teahouse of the August Moon, The 1954,S 12,II,1:1
Teahouse of the August Moon, The 1954,S 18,13:4
Teahouse of the August Moon, The
1955,My 10,24:1
Teahouse of the August Moon, The
1955,Ag 14,II,1:5
Curious Savage, The 1956,Mr 17,12:3
Teahouse of the August Moon, The 1956,Je 4,25:4
Teahouse of the August Moon, The 1956,N 9,33:2
Good as Gold 1957,Mr 8,22:2
Hasty Heart, The 1959,S 15,45:2
Everybody Loves Opal 1961,O 12,40:2
Love Is a Time of Day 1969,D 23,21:3
Love Is a Time of Day 1970,Ja 4,II,5:1
Lovely Ladies, Kind Gentlemen 1970,D 29,38:1
Patrick, Julian
Golden Apple, The 1954,Mr 12,15:2
Juno 1959,Mr 10,41:1
Fiorello! 1959,N 24,45:3
Patrick, Lee
Green Beetle, The 1924,S 3,12:3
Undercurrent, The 1925,F 4,18:2
Backslapper, The 1925,Ap 13,25:2
Bachelor's Brides 1925,My 29,20:2
It All Depends 1925,Ag 11,16:4
Shelf, The 1926,S 28,31:1
Baby Mine 1927,Je 10,21:2
Matrimonial Bed, The 1927,O 13,23:2
Nightstick 1927,N 11,20:4
Common Sin, The 1928,O 16,28:2
June Moon 1929,O 10,34:5
Room of Dreams 1930,N 6,22:4
Rock Me, Julie 1931,Ja 4,VIII,2:3
Privilege Car 1931,Mr 4,33:1
Friendship 1931,S 1,30:2
Little Women 1931,D 8,36:2
Blessed Event 1932,F 13,23:2
Girl Outside, The 1932,O 25,24:3
June Moon 1933,My 16,15:5
Shooting Star 1933,Je 13,22:2
Slightly Delirious 1935,Ja 1,25:3
Knock on Wood 1935,My 29,16:2
Curse You, Jack Dalton 1935,Jl 16,24:1
Abide With Me 1935,N 22,19:2
Stage Door 1936,S 29,35:1
Stage Door 1936,O 23,26:3
Stage Door 1936,N 1,X,1:1
Michael Drops In 1938,D 28,24:3
Patrick, Leonard
Strip for Action 1942,O 1,26:2
Miracle in the Mountains 1947,Ap 26,10:2
Command Decision 1947,O 2,30:2
Shrike, The 1953,N 26,51:2
Patrick, Leonard (Miscellaneous)
Epitaph for George Dillon 1958,N 5,44:1
Romulus 1962,Ja 11,27:1
Advocate, The 1963,O 15,46:7
Patrick, Nigel
Escapade 1953,Ap 8,37:2
Pleasure of His Company, The 1959,Ap 24,22:3
Best of Friends 1970,F 21,22:1
Patrick, Nigel (Director)
Pleasure of His Company, The 1959,Ap 24,22:3
Avanti 1968,F 1,29:1
Patrick, Pat (Composer)
Trials of Brother Jero, The 1967,N 10,60:1
Strong Breed, The 1967,N 10,60:1
Kongi's Harvest 1968,Ap 15,49:1
Patrick, Robert (Playwright)
Warhol Machine, The 1967,O 4,43:1
Collision Course; Camera Obscura 1968,My 9,55:2
Haunted Host, The 1969,O 28,43:1
Bad Place to Get Your Head, A 1970,Jl 16,38:1
Bead-Tangle 1970,Jl 16,38:1
Patrick, Roy
Hamlet 1958,D 17,2:7
Patrick (Dog)
Baby Want a Kiss 1964,Ap 20,32:1
Patrick and Francisco
Better Times 1922,S 4,14:2
Patricola, Miss
Vaudeville (Palace) 1926,Jl 13,19:4
Vaudeville (Proctor's) 1927,My 17,27:4
Vaudeville (Palace) 1928,Jl 17,15:5
Patricola, Tom
Vaudeville (Palace) 1923,My 15,22:2
George White's Scandals 1923,Je 19,22:5
Scandals 1924,Jl 1,16:1
George White's Scandals 1925,Je 23,24:2
George White's Scandals 1926,Je 15,23:2
George White's Scandals 1928,Jl 3,19:1
Vaudeville (Palace) 1930,D 22,16:5
Music Hall Varieties 1933,Ja 3,19:4
Hold Your Horses 1933,Ag 31,20:4

Patricola, Tom—Cont
Hold Your Horses 1933,S 26,26:4
Let's Play Fair 1938,Ja 19,26:4
Patrikiou, Lela
Electra 1930,D 27,16:1
Patrimmo, G P
Skylark 1921,Jl 26,10:6
Patron, Eli
Melody Lingers On, The 1969,N 17,55:1
Brothers Ashkenazi, The 1970,N 17,53:2
Patston, Doris
Louie the 14th 1925,Mr 4,17:1
Katja 1926,O 19,27:3
Lovely Lady 1927,D 30,22:1
Smiling Faces 1932,Ag 31,12:3
All the King's Horses 1934,Ja 31,21:3
Florodora 1936,Ag 23,II,8:2
Frederika 1937,F 5,16:5
Roberta 1937,Je 27,II,6:1
Gay Divorce 1937,Jl 20,19:4
Gay Divorce 1937,Ag 11,27:2
Nina Rosa 1937,Ag 26,24:3
Roberta 1937,S 7,16:4
Firefly, The 1938,Jl 12,15:4
Kiss for Cinderella, A 1942,Mr 11,22:2
Chocolate Soldier, The 1942,Je 24,22:2
New Moon, The 1942,Ag 19,14:2
Flare Path 1942,D 24,20:2
Sheppey 1944,Ap 19,27:2
Sadie Thompson 1944,N 17,25:2
Therese 1945,O 10,24:2
Toplitzky of Notre Dame 1946,D 27,13:4
My Romance 1948,O 20,38:5
Gigi 1951,N 26,20:4
Starcross Story, The 1954,Ja 14,25:2
Patsy and Mickey
Vaudeville (Palace) 1930,Mr 31,24:2
Patten, Dorothy
Subway Express 1929,S 25,34:3
One Chaste Man 1930,Je 11,33:5
Stepdaughters of War 1930,O 7,27:1
House of Connelly, The 1931,S 29,22:4
Night Over Taos 1932,Mr 10,25:3
Success Story 1932,S 27,24:4
Big Night 1933,Ja 18,16:2
Mask and the Face, The 1933,My 9,20:2
Men in White 1933,S 27,24:2
Till the Day I Die 1935,Mr 27,24:5
Waiting for Lefty 1935,Mr 27,24:5
Weep for the Virgins 1935,D 2,18:1
Case of Clyde Griffiths 1936,Mr 14,10:4
Greatest Show on Earth, The 1938,Ja 6,22:2
Hill Between, The 1938,Mr 12,12:5
Retreat to Pleasure 1940,D 18,32:2
Lamp at Midnight 1947,D 22,29:2
Church Street 1948,F 10,27:2
Rose in the Wilderness 1949,Ja 5,21:2
Blood Wedding 1949,F 7,16:2
Deirdre of the Sorrows 1949,O 15,51:2
Romeo and Juliet 1951,Mr 12,21:2
Pony Cart, The 1954,S 15,39:2
Anastasia 1954,D 30,13:1
Anastasia 1955,Ja 16,II,1:1
Duchess of Malfi, The 1957,Mr 20,33:1
Brothers Karamazov, The 1957,D 9,39:4
On Baile's Strand 1959,Ap 13,34:4
Death of Cuchulain, The 1959,Ap 13,34:4
Drums Under the Windows 1960,O 14,26:1
Diff'rent 1961,O 18,52:1
Long Voyage Home, The 1961,D 5,49:1
Saving Grace, The 1963,Ap 19,28:1
Patten, Goldwin
Letter of the Law, The; Robe Rouge, La 1920,F 24,11:1
Americans in France, The 1920,Ag 4,14:1
Apache, The 1923,My 9,14:3
Rapid Transit 1927,Ap 8,21:2
Stairs, The 1927,N 8,32:7
Hot Pan 1928,F 16,14:1
Patten, Mary
Afternoon Storm 1948,Ap 12,24:2
Patten, Moultrie
One Eye Closed 1954,N 25,45:2
Girl of the Golden West, The 1957,N 6,44:1
Andersonville Trial, The 1959,D 30,15:1
Brigadoon 1962,My 31,21:4
Long Day's Journey Into Night 1963,Je 27,25:1
Patterson, Agnes
Girl in the Spotlight, The 1920,Jl 13,9:3
Patterson, Albert
Temper the Wind 1946,D 28,10:2
Patterson, Dick
Vintage '60 1960,S 13,41:1
Billy Barnes People, The 1961,Je 14,10:3
Fade Out--Fade In 1964,My 27,45:1
Fade Out--Fade In 1965,F 16,40:2
Patterson, Dorothy
Wanhope Building, The 1947,F 11,36:5
Patterson, Elinor
Miracle, The 1926,D 28,16:2
Patterson, Elizabeth
Piper, The 1920,Mr 20,14:2
Intimate Strangers, The 1921,N 8,28:1
Lady Cristilinda, The 1922,D 26,11:2

Magnolia 1923,Ag 28,12:3
Gypsy Jim 1924,Ja 15,17:4
Lazybones 1924,S 23,23:1
Book of Charm, The 1925,S 4,26:3
Spellbound 1927,N 15,26:2
Paradise 1927,D 26,26:4
Carry On 1928,Ja 24,26:1
Rope 1928,F 23,18:3
Rope 1928,Mr 4,IX,1:1
Box Seats 1928,Ap 20,27:2
Marriage Bed, The 1929,Ja 8,35:1
Man's Estate 1929,Ap 2,28:2
Man's Estate 1929,Ap 28,IX,1:1
Solid South 1930,My 11,IX,2:6
Solid South 1930,O 15,27:1
Her Master's Voice 1933,O 24,24:3
Spring Freshet 1934,O 5,28:3
Yankee Point 1942,N 24,28:2
But Not Goodbye 1944,Ap 12,19:2
His and Hers 1954,Ja 8,18:2
Patterson, Frederick
Twelfth Night 1934,Jl 17,24:5
This Is Today 1935,Jl 30,17:2
Patterson, George
Tonight in Living Color; David Show, The 1969,Je 11,43:1
Patterson, Helen
Just a Minute 1928,O 9,34:3
Blue Butterfly, The 1929,F 17,29:3
Patterson, Henry
Fratricide Punished 1925,Ap 21,19:1
Romio and Julietta 1925,Ap 21,19:1
Watched Pot, The 1933,My 5,13:7
Patterson, Herbert
Bird in Hand 1942,O 20,24:2
Patterson, Howard
Shipwrecked 1924,N 13,18:1
Patterson, James
Brothers Karamazov, The 1957,D 9,39:4
Brothers Karamazov, The 1957,D 22,II,3:1
Tomorrow With Pictures 1960,Je 3,26:3
Epitaph for George Dillon 1960,D 29,17:1
Collection, The 1962,N 27,44:1
Conversation at Midnight 1964,N 13,27:1
Birthday Party, The 1967,O 4,40:2
Wrong Way Light Bulb, The 1969,Mr 5,40:1
Silence 1970,Ap 3,43:1
Amphitryon 1970,My 29,13:1
Patterson, Joe
Spring Again 1941,N 11,28:2
Patterson, John A
Elizabeth the Queen 1941,O 17,27:2
Patterson, Joseph Medill (Playwright)
Dope 1926,Ja 4,16:3
Patterson, Kenneth
Her Man of Wax 1933,O 12,32:3
Meet the People 1940,D 26,22:2
Patterson, Lee
P S I Love You 1964,N 20,40:1
Patterson, Marjorie
New Freedom, The 1930,My 15,32:4
New Freedom, The 1930,My 17,21:4
Patterson, Mary
Merry Widow, The 1929,D 3,29:1
Patterson, Massie
Porgy and Bess 1935,O 11,30:2
Patterson, McKay
Blue Blood 1924,Ap 3,21:2
Patterson, Mildred
Pal Joey 1940,D 26,22:2
Patterson, Neva
Druid Circle, The 1947,O 23,29:5
Ivy Green, The 1949,Ap 6,37:2
Ring Around the Moon 1950,N 24,30:1
Long Days, The 1951,Ap 21,10:5
Lace on Her Petticoat 1951,S 5,40:3
Seven Year Itch, The 1952,N 21,21:2
Double in Hearts 1956,O 17,41:7
Speaking of Murder 1956,D 20,37:1
Make a Million 1958,O 24,39:2
Patterson, Pat
Gazebo, The 1958,D 13,2:7
Patterson, Russell (Costume Designer)
Gang's All Here, The 1931,F 19,21:3
Ballyhoo of 1932 1932,S 7,14:2
Hold Your Horses 1933,S 26,26:4
Ziegfeld Follies 1934,Ja 5,24:3
Fools Rush In 1934,D 26,19:2
Patterson, Russell (Director)
Ballyhoo of 1932 1932,S 7,14:2
Patterson, Russell (Producer)
Ballyhoo of 1932 1932,S 7,14:2
Russell Patterson's Sketch-Book 1960,F 8,35:1
Patterson, Russell (Scenic Designer)
Ballyhoo of 1932 1932,S 7,14:2
Hold Your Horses 1933,S 26,26:4
Fools Rush In 1934,D 26,19:2
Scandals 1935,O 30,17:1
George White's Scandals 1935,D 26,20:2
Patterson, Ruth
Smiles 1930,N 19,19:2
Patterson, Ruth Cleary (Composer)
Russell Patterson's Sketch-Book 1960,F 8,35:1

Patterson, Ruth Cleary (Musical Director)
Russell Patterson's Sketch-Book 1960,F 8,35:1
Patterson, Starke
Sweetheart Time 1926,Ja 20,23:2
Merry World, The 1926,Je 9,18:3
Chee-Chee 1928,S 26,25:1
Patterson, Ted
Play's the Thing, The 1948,Ap 29,19:2
Patterson, Todd
Good as Gold 1957,Mr 8,22:2
Patterson, Yvonne
Rosalinda; Fledermaus, Die 1942,O 29,26:5
Lady From Maxim's, The 1970,Je 1,41:1
Patterson Twins
Earl Carroll's Vanities 1926,Ag 25,19:4
Patteson, John
Hats Off to Ice 1944,Je 23,15:2
Pattison, B Patrick
Crucible 1933,S 5,22:4
Pattison, Diantha
Secrets 1922,D 26,11:1
Paolo and Francesca 1924,D 3,24:2
Habitual Husband, The 1924,D 25,27:3
Fall of Eve, The 1925,S 1,18:1
Beware of Widows 1925,N 8,VIII,2:1
Beware of Widows 1925,D 2,22:3
Weak Woman, A 1926,Ja 27,16:3
No Trespassing! 1926,S 8,19:1
Out of the Night 1927,O 18,32:3
Divorce a la Carte 1928,Mr 27,30:3
Golden Age, The 1928,Ap 25,31:3
Indiscretion 1929,Mr 5,28:1
Nancy's Private Affair 1930,Ja 14,24:3
Between Two Worlds 1934,O 26,24:2
First Lady 1935,N 27,17:4
Ring Around Elizabeth 1941,N 18,32:2
Patton, Barbara
My Romance 1948,O 20,38:5
Patton, Frank
Cornered 1920,D 9,18:2
Patton, Fred
Robin Hood 1932,Ja 28,25:4
Patton, Jack
Earl Carroll's Vanities 1923,Jl 6,8:2
Patton, Joey (Miscellaneous)
Three Men on a Horse 1969,O 17,35:1
Patton, Lucille
Winter's Tale, The 1946,Ja 16,18:6
Topaze 1947,D 29,21:5
Joy to the World 1948,Mr 19,28:2
Cry of the Peacock 1950,Ap 12,33:2
Peer Gynt 1951,Ja 29,15:2
Camino Real 1953,Mr 20,26:1
Heavenly Twins, The 1955,N 5,23:2
Ulysses in Nighttown 1958,Je 6,30:1
Failures, The 1959,Ja 6,30:2
Three Sisters, The 1959,S 22,46:1
Rhinoceros 1961,Ja 10,27:1
Marathon '33 1963,D 23,20:1
Last Analysis, The 1964,O 2,30:1
Dinner at Eight 1966,S 28,38:1
Box-Mao-Box; Quotations From Chairman Mao Tse-Tung 1968,Mr 8,48:1
Yes, Yes, No No 1969,Ja 1,16:1
Strada, La 1969,D 15,63:1
Patton, Mary
Big Knife, The 1949,F 25,27:5
Hour Glass, The 1955,O 17,33:1
Pattrick, Shela
Conversation Piece 1934,O 24,24:1
Paudler, Maria
Five From the Jazz Band; Fuenf von der Jazzband 1927,N 20,IX,4:7
Pauker, John (Playwright)
Moonbirds 1959,O 10,13:1
Paul, Betty
Maggie 1953,F 19,20:2
Paul, Cedar (Translator)
Jeremiah 1939,F 4,11:2
Paul, Charles
Passing of the Third Floor Back, The 1937,Ag 3,20:6
Paul, Charles (Composer)
On Baile's Strand 1959,Ap 13,34:4
Death of Cuchulain, The 1959,Ap 13,34:4
Notes From the Underground 1960,Ja 20,26:1
Paul, Charles (Miscellaneous)
First Love 1961,D 26,20:2
Paul, Curt
Climate of Eden, The 1953,N 21,11:2
Paul, David
Dance Night 1938,O 15,20:5
Paul, Dorothy
Goat Alley 1927,Ap 21,24:3
Porgy 1927,O 11,26:2
Never No More 1932,Ja 8,27:1
Conjur' Man Dies 1936,Mr 12,18:5
Case of Philip Lawrence, The 1937,Je 9,31:1
Mamba's Daughters 1939,Ja 4,24:2
Paul, Eden (Translator)
Jeremiah 1939,F 4,11:2
Paul, Edgerton
Horse Eats Hat 1936,S 28,14:2

Paul, Edgerton—Cont
Doctor Faustus 1937,Ja 9,21:2
But for the Grace of God 1937,Ja 13,21:4
Danton's Death 1938,N 3,26:2
Paul, Elliot
Antigone 1967,Je 19,43:1
Goa 1968,F 23,46:1
Paul, Elsa
Well of Romance, The 1930,N 8,21:2
Paul, Estelle
Don Juan 1921,S 8,14:2
Paul, Eugene
Church Street 1948,F 10,27:2
Paul, Eugene (Producer)
Pink Elephant, The 1953,Ap 23,37:2
Paul, Eva
Knights of Song 1938,O 18,29:2
Paul, G Lester
Crashing Through 1928,O 30,26:5
Let and Sub-Let 1930,My 20,32:2
Cinderelative 1930,S 19,18:4
Heigh-Ho, Everybody 1932,My 26,31:2
Paul, Gene
Rockbound 1929,Ap 20,23:2
Paul, Gene (Miscellaneous)
Shadow of a Gunman, The 1958,N 21,26:1
Paul, Genevieve
Privilege Car 1931,Mr 4,33:1
Crucible 1933,S 5,22:4
Paul, Guy
Song Out of Sorrow 1941,D 12,34:5
Paul, Ike
Frankie and Johnny 1930,S 26,16:5
Nativity Play, The 1937,D 21,29:1
Paul, Inge
Eisrevue 1969,O 23,55:1
Paul, Isaac (Playwright)
Broadway Boy 1932,My 4,23:5
Paul, James
Macbeth 1955,O 20,42:2
Lower Depths, The 1956,O 3,29:2
King Lear 1959,Ja 3,11:2
Paul, Jo Anne
Life With Mother 1948,O 21,32:2
Paul, John
Our Town 1944,Ja 11,24:5
Day Will Come, The 1944,S 8,17:2
Brigadoon 1947,Mr 14,28:2
Paul, John (Director)
Lute Song 1959,Mr 13,24:1
Paul, John (Miscellaneous)
Waiting for Godot 1956,Ap 20,21:2
Waiting for Godot 1957,Ja 22,25:1
Compulsion 1957,O 25,21:1
Paul, Kent (Director)
Fireworks; Football 1969,Je 12,51:1
Fireworks; Report, The 1969,Je 12,51:1
Fireworks; Fireworks for a Hot Fourth 1969,Je 12,51:1
Paul, Leslie
Major Barbara 1951,F 24,10:2
Paul, Lester
Lady in Love, A 1927,F 22,22:1
Paul, Lewis
Battle Hymn 1936,My 23,12:1
Paul, Logan
Mima 1928,D 13,24:2
Paul, Louis
Meet the People 1940,D 26,22:2
Paul, Louis (Playwright)
Cup of Trembling, The 1948,Ap 21,33:5
Paul, Max
In-Laws 1960,O 17,32:4
Life Is a Dream 1962,Ja 15,22:3
Paul, Max (Lighting Director)
Life Is a Dream 1962,Ja 15,22:3
Paul, Max (Miscellaneous)
Life Is a Dream 1962,Ja 15,22:3
Paul, Michael (Costume Designer)
Snark Was a Boojum, The 1943,S 2,14:4
Paul, N S
Front Page, The 1937,N 12,27:2
Paul, Priscilla
Just Because 1922,Mr 23,11:1
Paul, Rene
Now I Lay Me Down to Sleep 1950,Mr 3,21:2
Collector's Item 1952,F 9,11:2
Holiday for Lovers 1957,F 15,20:1
Conversation Piece 1957,N 19,38:2
Paul, Richard
Truckline Cafe 1946,F 28,19:4
Decameron, The 1961,Ap 13,32:1
Mother Courage and Her Children 1964,My 12,32:2
Paul, Robert
H M S Pinafore 1949,Jl 29,13:2
Ice Capades 1960,S 1,30:1
Ice Capades 1962,Ag 30,34:1
Paul, Steven
Lyle 1970,Mr 21,16:2
Lemon Sky 1970,My 18,40:1
Happy Birthday, Wanda June 1970,O 8,58:2
Paul, Thomas
Saint of Bleecker Street, The 1965,Mr 19,28:1

Paul, W J
Baby Mine 1927,Je 10,21:2
Paul, Wauna
Father Malachy's Miracle 1937,N 18,26:4
Kindred 1939,D 27,17:2
Little Dark Horse 1941,N 17,14:4
Uncle Harry 1942,My 21,24:1
Embezzled Heaven 1944,N 1,20:2
Big Two, The 1947,Ja 9,21:2
Crime and Punishment 1947,D 23,29:3
Paul, Wauna (Miscellaneous)
Gently Does It 1953,O 29,43:4
Paul, William
Red Poppy, The 1922,D 21,18:2
Victory Belles 1943,O 27,26:3
Paula, Chona
He Loved the Ladies 1927,My 11,29:2
Paulding, James Kirke (Playwright)
Half Horse, Half Alligator 1966,Mr 14,37:2
Paule, Dorothy
Farewell to Arms, A 1930,S 23,30:3
Paulee, Mona
Most Happy Fella, The 1956,My 4,20:1
Most Happy Fella, The 1956,My 13,II,1:1
Madame Aphrodite 1961,D 30,13:1
Pauley
Miracle, Un 1927,D 25,VIII,4:3
Untitled-Play 1928,Je 17,VIII,1:4
Three Men on a Horse 1936,Je 7,IX,1:1
Pauley, Ann
Love Dreams 1921,O 11,22:2
Pauli, Agneta (Miscellaneous)
Threepenny Opera, The 1966,O 28,33:1
Pauli, Ken
Cyrano de Bergerac 1963,Je 20,30:1
Timon of Athens 1963,Jl 31,19:2
Paulina, Anna
Hamlet 1959,S 11,21:4
Paulina, Anna (Choreographer)
Hamlet 1959,S 11,21:4
Paulina, Anna (Costume Designer)
Shakuntala 1959,S 10,41:2
Paulina, Anna (Miscellaneous)
King of the Dark Chamber 1961,F 10,21:1
Paulinger, Minnie
Tenth Commandment, The 1926,N 18,27:1
Pauliny, Paul
Mary Stuart 1956,Ap 28,10:2
Pauliny, Paul (Lighting Director)
Mary Stuart 1956,Ap 28,10:2
Paull, Morgan
That Thing at the Cherry Lane 1965,My 19,42:1
Paulo, Liano
Rain 1922,N 8,18:2
Paulsen, Albert
Three Sisters, The 1964,Je 23,24:1
Papp 1969,My 6,39:1
Papp 1969,Je 8,II,1:7
Paulsen, David
Widowers' Houses 1959,Mr 3,39:2
Three Sisters, The 1964,Je 23,24:1
Paulsen, David (Miscellaneous)
Widowers' Houses 1959,Mr 3,39:2
Paulsen, Harald
Broadway 1928,Ap 15,IX,4:7
Threepenny Opera, The 1928,D 2,X,4:4
Phaea 1930,Ag 31,VIII,2:1
Journalisten, Die 1932,Jl 17,IX,1:1
Paulson, Albert
Don Juan; Feast With the Statue, The 1956,Ja 4,21:4
Infernal Machine, The 1958,F 4,33:1
Night Circus, The 1958,D 3,44:1
Paulson, Arvid
Goin' Home 1928,Ag 24,23:2
This Man's Town 1930,Mr 11,24:4
Pigeons and People 1933,Ja 17,22:3
Mother Lode 1934,D 24,16:5
Bat, The 1937,Je 1,27:5
Innocent Voyage, The 1943,N 16,27:2
Paulson, Myron
Where's Your Husband? 1927,Ja 15,10:3
Women Go on Forever 1927,S 8,25:1
Doctor Faustus 1937,Ja 9,21:2
Processional 1937,O 14,23:1
Big Blow 1938,O 3,11:2
Paulson Sisters
Vaudeville (Palace) 1929,Ap 22,22:6
Paulton, Edward (Lyricist)
It's Up to You 1921,Mr 29,20:1
Paulton, Edward (Playwright)
Look Who's Here 1920,Mr 3,12:2
Her Temporary Husband 1922,S 1,16:2
Her Temporary Husband 1923,My 13,VIII,3:5
Street Wolf, The 1929,Ja 1,61:1
Paulton, Harry (Lyricist)
Erminie 1921,Ja 4,11:1
Paulton, Harry (Playwright)
Erminie 1921,Ja 4,11:1
Paulus, Paul
Ripples 1930,F 12,26:1
Paulus, Richard
Family Reunion, The 1960,D 10,26:1

Paulus, Robert
Child of the Morning 1958,Ap 22,40:2
Pauly, Hedwig
Jedermann 1927,D 8,33:2
Dantons Tod 1927,D 21,28:3
Er Ist an Allem Schuld; He Is to Blame for Everything 1928,Ja 10,28:3
Lebende Leichnam, Der, Der; Living Corpse, The 1928,Ja 24,26:2
Gespenster, Die; Ghosts 1928,F 8,28:6
Pauncefort, George
Just Suppose 1920,N 2,15:1
Mad Honeymoon, The 1923,Ag 8,10:1
What's Your Wife Doing? 1923,O 2,10:3
Bride, The 1924,My 6,25:1
Joker, The 1925,N 17,29:1
Honeymoon Lane 1926,S 21,32:3
Ups-A-Daisy 1928,O 9,34:2
Take a Chance 1932,N 28,11:2
Paust, Einar B
Upon My Soul 1927,Ap 22,19:1
Pavek, Janet
Christine 1960,Ap 29,27:1
Mikado, The 1961,Ja 18,26:1
Gondoliers, The 1961,Ja 26,33:2
Pavelko, John
Twilight Walk 1951,S 25,25:4
Maya 1953,Je 10,35:1
Pavell, Barbara
She Shall Have Music 1959,Ja 23,18:4
Pavenelli, Livio
Strictly Dishonorable 1931,Ap 12,IX,1:3
Paver, Charles (Original Author)
Land of Fame 1943,S 22,31:5
Paver, Chaver (Original Author)
Clinton Street 1939,O 13,27:2
Paver, Chaver (Playwright)
Haunch, Paunch and Jowl 1935,D 27,22:4
Outlaw, The 1937,O 6,28:1
Awake and Sing! 1938,D 23,16:6
Pavey, Marie
East Lynne 1926,Mr 11,18:4
Pavia, Judith
Harlequinade 1959,F 14,15:1
Pavia, Marcia
Harlequinade 1959,F 14,15:1
Pavicevic, Bozidar
Progress of Bora, The Tailor, The 1968,Je 27,49:2
Ubu Roi 1968,Je 29,20:1
Pavley-Oukrainsky Ballet Troupe
Vaudeville (Palace) 1929,Ap 8,32:7
Pavlik, Nicholas (Miscellaneous)
Delightful Season, A 1960,S 29,30:1
Pavlo, Hattie May (Playwright)
Alexander Hamilton 1949,Mr 30,29:2
Pavlov, P
Revisor; Inspector General, The 1935,F 18,19:6
Poverty Is No Crime 1935,F 21,22:5
Strange Child 1935,F 26,16:1
White Guard, The; Days of the Turbins 1935,Mr 7,27:5
Marriage 1935,Mr 12,24:8
Pavlovska, Vera
Chauve-Souris of 1943 1943,Ag 13,13:2
Pavlow, Muriel
Odd Man In 1957,Jl 17,21:3
Pawle, Lennox
Marjolaine 1922,Ja 25,16:1
Jack and Jill 1923,Mr 23,17:2
Mountebank, The 1923,My 8,22:2
Mary, Mary, Quite Contrary 1923,S 12,14:1
Werewolf, The 1924,Ag 26,6:1
Harem, The 1924,N 16,VIII,2:8
Harem, The 1924,D 3,24:1
Matrimonial Bed, The 1927,O 13,23:2
Mima 1928,D 13,24:2
Simple Simon 1930,F 19,22:1
Collision 1932,F 17,19:2
Pawley, Anthony
Street Scene 1929,Ja 11,20:4
Doctor X 1930,Jl 31,12:4
American Tragedy, An 1931,F 21,15:5
Camels Are Coming, The 1931,O 3,20:4
If Booth Had Missed 1932,F 5,24:2
Pawley, Edward
Shame Woman, The 1923,O 17,14:1
Elmer Gantry 1928,Ag 10,9:4
Man's Estate 1929,Ap 2,28:2
Now-A-Days 1929,Ag 6,29:3
Subway Express 1929,S 25,34:3
Life Is Like That 1930,D 23,24:3
Regular Guy, A; Man's Man, A 1931,Je 5,27:1
Two Seconds 1931,O 10,20:6
Distant Drums 1932,Ja 19,24:3
Life Begins; Birth 1932,Mr 20,VIII,2:4
Willow and I, The 1942,D 11,32:2
Pawley, William
Holy Terror, A 1925,S 29,31:2
Four Walls 1927,S 20,33:1
Gentlemen of the Press 1928,Ag 28,27:2
Subway Express 1929,S 25,34:3
Bad Girl 1930,O 3,30:2

ax, Paulette
 Great Catherine, The 1927,Ap 3,VIII,4:7
axinou, Katina
 Electra 1930,D 27,16:1
 Electra 1939,Jl 9,IX,1:6
 Hedda Gabler 1942,Ja 30,22:2
 Sophie 1944,D 26,22:7
 House of Bernarda Alba, The 1951,Ja 8,14:6
 Electra 1952,N 20,38:2
 Oedipus Tyrannus 1952,N 25,35:2
 Garden of Sweets, The 1961,N 1,35:1
 Bacchae, The 1962,Je 19,30:1
Paxinou, Katina (Composer)
 Oedipus Tyrannus 1952,N 25,35:2
Paxton, Glenn (Composer)
 First Impressions 1959,Mr 20,28:1
Paxton, Glenn (Lyricist)
 First Impressions 1959,Mr 20,28:1
Paxton, Guy (Playwright)
 Quitter, The 1934,F 6,24:4
Paxton, Marie
 Pickwick 1927,S 6,35:2
 Napoleon 1928,Mr 9,21:1
 Kind Lady 1935,Ap 24,24:5
 Passing of the Third Floor Back, The
  1937,Ag 3,20:6
 Kind Lady 1940,S 4,28:3
 Three Sisters, The 1942,D 22,31:2
 O Mistress Mine 1946,Ja 24,25:2
 Pin to See the Peepshow, A 1953,S 18,17:2
 Escapade 1953,N 19,40:1
 Chalk Garden, The 1955,O 27,29:1
 Hadrian VII 1969,Ja 9,22:1
 Boy Friend, The 1970,Ap 15,54:1
Paxton, Sidney
 Werewolf, The 1924,Ag 26,6:1
 Loves of Lulu, The 1925,My 12,26:1
 School for Scandal, The 1925,O 24,19:1
 Constant Nymph, The 1926,D 10,31:1
 Great Necker, The 1928,Mr 7,28:2
Paxton, Steve
 Eccentricities of Davy Crockett, The 1961,Ja 4,26:1
Paya (Composer)
 Rapacino 1927,D 23,16:4
Payant, Lee
 In White America 1965,F 9,42:5
Paydyl, Franz (Musical Director)
 Untitled-Passion Play 1927,Jl 31,VII,1:6
Payen
 Girofle-Girofla 1926,N 23,26:3
 Cloches de Cornville, Les; Chimes of Normandy,
  The 1926,D 14,24:4
 Perichole, La 1926,D 29,24:4
Payer, Harry
 Goldne Meistern 1927,O 25,33:4
Payn, Graham
 Pacific 1860 1946,D 20,30:4
 Tonight at 8:30; Ways and Means 1948,F 21,8:2
 Tonight at 8:30; Red Peppers 1948,F 21,8:2
 Tonight at 8:30; Family Album 1948,F 21,8:2
 Tonight at 8:30; Hands Across the Sea
  1948,F 24,20:4
 Tonight at 8:30; Shadow Play 1948,F 24,20:4
 Ace of Clubs 1950,Jl 8,7:2
Payne, B Iden
 Great Broxopp, The 1921,N 16,22:1
Payne, B Iden (Director)
 Weak Woman, A 1926,Ja 27,16:3
 Service for Two 1926,Ag 31,15:1
 Way of the World, The 1931,Je 2,34:3
 Antony and Cleopatra 1935,Ap 16,26:7
 Taming of the Shrew, The 1936,Ap 14,18:4
 Embezzled Heaven 1944,N 1,20:2
 Winter's Tale, The 1946,Ja 16,18:6
 Much Ado About Nothing 1964,Jl 24,15:2
Payne, B Iden (Playwright)
 Dolly Jordan 1922,O 4,26:1
 Mary Goes to See 1938,Mr 6,XI,3:6
 Winter's Tale, The 1946,Ja 16,18:6
Payne, B Iden (Producer)
 Antony and Cleopatra 1935,Ap 16,26:7
Payne, Barbara (Producer)
 Deep Mrs Sykes, The 1945,Mr 20,22:6
 Three to Make Ready 1946,Mr 8,16:2
 Message for Margaret 1947,Ap 17,34:2
Payne, Benny
 Golden Boy 1964,O 21,56:1
Payne, Burt
 Henry's Harem 1926,S 14,25:2
Payne, Carol
 Pelleas and Melisande 1957,F 20,38:1
Payne, Charles
 Blancs, Les 1970,N 16,48:4
Payne, Dorothy
 Dream Play 1926,Ja 21,18:2
 Fast Life 1928,S 27,35:2
Payne, Frederick B (Mrs)
 Variations of 1940 1940,Ja 29,12:1
Payne, Gavin
 Hostage, The 1961,D 13,55:4
Payne, Jessie
 Boom Boom 1929,Ja 29,26:4

Payne, Jimmy (Choreographer)
 Policy Kings 1938,D 31,6:2
Payne, John
 Abe Lincoln in Illinois 1938,O 17,12:2
Payne, John Howard (Playwright)
 Love in Humble Life 1937,Mr 10,27:2
Payne, Nina
 Vaudeville (Hippodrome) 1924,S 30,27:5
 Vaudeville (Hippodrome) 1924,O 21,21:2
Payne, Robert
 Stars on Ice (2d Edition) 1943,Je 25,13:2
Payne, Sunny
 Swingin' the Dream 1939,N 30,24:2
Payne, Sylvester
 Black Souls 1932,Mr 31,25:1
Payne, Virginia
 Lucky Sam McCarver 1950,Ap 15,10:6
 Right You Are (If You Think You Are)
  1950,Je 29,37:2
 Liliom 1956,F 18,12:5
 Thunder Rock 1956,F 27,18:1
 House of Breath, The 1957,Ap 15,23:2
 Tattooed Countess, The 1961,My 4,40:2
 Long Day's Journey Into Night 1963,Je 27,25:1
 Fade Out--Fade In 1964,My 27,45:1
 Galileo 1968,D 1,88:4
Payne and Hilliard
 Vaudeville (Palace) 1928,Ja 24,26:4
Payne-Jennings, Victor (Producer)
 Whiteoaks 1938,Mr 24,20:2
 Flashing Stream, The 1939,Ap 11,19:2
 Mother, The 1939,Ap 26,26:2
 Farm of Three Echoes 1939,N 29,18:3
 Wind in the Sails 1940,Ag 1,24:6
 Rebecca 1944,Ap 30,II,1:1
 Rebecca 1945,Ja 19,17:2
 Happily Ever After 1945,Mr 16,21:2
 Therese 1945,O 10,24:2
 Song of Bernadette 1946,Mr 27,22:2
Paynter, Corone
 Tantrum, The 1924,S 5,20:2
Paynter, Henry (Playwright)
 Tabloid 1929,S 29,IX,5:1
Payson, Herta (Choreographer)
 Romeo and Juliet 1957,Je 28,30:2
 Two Gentlemen of Verona 1957,Jl 23,21:5
 Richard III 1957,N 26,41:1
 As You Like It 1958,Ja 21,33:6
Payson, Robert
 Empress of Destiny 1938,Mr 10,16:2
 Red Velvet Goat, The 1939,Ja 21,18:4
 Mr Banks of Birmingham 1939,Ja 21,18:4
Payson, W F (Playwright)
 Joker, The 1925,N 17,29:1
Payter, Peggy
 Trimmed in Scarlet 1920,F 3,18:1
Payton, James
 Ulysses in Nighttown 1958,Je 6,30:1
Payton, Lew
 Harlem 1929,F 21,30:3
 Boundry Line, The 1930,F 6,21:1
 Solid South 1930,O 15,27:1
 Never No More 1932,Ja 8,27:1
 Bridal Wise 1932,My 31,15:5
 Jezebel 1933,D 20,26:3
Payton, Lew (Playwright)
 Chocolate Dandies, The 1924,S 2,22:2
Payton, Raymond (Producer)
 Dead End 1937,Ag 17,23:1
Payton-Wright, Pamela
 Show-Off, The 1967,D 6,40:2
 Exit the King 1968,Ja 10,48:1
 Exit the King 1968,Ja 21,II,1:2
 Cherry Orchard, The 1968,Mr 20,41:1
 Cherry Orchard, The 1968,Ap 7,II,3:7
 Jimmy Shine 1968,D 6,52:1
 Effect of Gamma Rays on Man-in-the-Moon
  Marigolds, The 1970,Ap 8,32:1
 Effect of Gamma Rays on Man-in-the-Moon
  Marigolds, The 1970,Ap 19,II,1:1
Paz, Claudia
 Remolienda, La; Bawdy Party 1968,F 3,20:1
Pazdera, Vashek
 Pirates of Penzance, The 1970,Jl 26,49:5
Pazumba, S
 Hindu, The 1922,Mr 22,13:3
Pazzi-Preval, Mr
 Trois Jeunes Filles Nues; Three Young Maids From
  the Folies Bergere 1929,Mr 5,28:2
Peabody, Helen
 Meet the Prince 1935,Jl 9,24:5
 Bright Honor 1936,S 28,14:1
Peabody, Josephine Preston (Playwright)
 Piper, The 1920,Mr 20,14:2
Peabody, Judith (Miscellaneous)
 Sudden End of Anne Cinquefoil, The
  1961,Ja 11,25:2
Peabody, Katrina Trask (Playwright)
 Without the Walls 1921,Mr 28,8:1
 Without the Walls 1922,Ap 17,17:1
 Little Town of Bethlehem, The 1922,D 26,15:4
Peabody, Sandra
 Tarot 1970,D 12,19:1

Peacey, Howard (Miscellaneous)
 Venetian, The 1931,N 2,26:1
Peacey, Howard (Playwright)
 Magic Hours 1925,My 3,VIII,2:1
Peach, Du Garde (Playwright)
 Night Sky 1937,Ja 7,28:7
 Night Sky 1937,Ja 31,XI,3:1
Peacock, Bertram
 H M S Pinafore 1920,Ja 13,10:2
 Blossom Time 1921,S 30,10:1
 Blossom Time 1921,O 9,VI,1:1
 Princess Ida 1925,Ap 14,27:2
 Lambs Gambol 1925,Ap 27,15:1
 Girofle-Girofla 1926,N 24,26:2
 Houseboat on the Styx, The 1928,D 26,14:3
 Mikado, The 1935,Jl 16,24:4
 Pirates of Penzance, The 1935,Jl 23,24:2
 Yeomen of the Guard, The 1935,Jl 30,16:4
 Gondoliers, The 1935,Ag 6,20:5
 Trial by Jury 1935,Ag 13,20:6
 H M S Pinafore 1935,Ag 13,20:6
 Iolanthe 1936,My 5,26:2
 H M S Pinafore 1942,Ja 22,12:2
 Mikado, The 1942,F 4,22:2
 Pirates of Penzance, The 1942,F 18,22:2
 Gondoliers, The 1942,Mr 4,22:3
 Mikado, The 1944,F 12,11:3
 Trial by Jury 1944,F 15,14:4
 H M S Pinafore 1944,F 15,14:4
 Pirates of Penzance, The 1944,F 18,15:5
 Patience 1944,F 26,11:4
 Ruddigore 1944,Mr 3,19:5
 Yeomen of the Guard, The 1944,Mr 5,34:3
Peacock, Kim
 Stepping Out 1929,My 21,29:1
Peacock, Kim (Playwright)
 Battle Royal 1934,Ap 19,33:4
 Under One Roof 1941,My 4,IX,1:6
Peacock, Thomas Love (Original Author)
 Nightmare Abbey 1952,Mr 16,II,3:8
Peacock, Trevor
 She Stoops to Conquer 1969,Ag 18,28:1
 Erb 1970,Ap 9,49:1
Peacock, Trevor (Composer)
 Erb 1970,Ap 9,49:1
Peacock, Trevor (Playwright)
 Erb 1970,Ap 9,49:1
Peacocke, Leslie T
 Comedy of Women, A 1929,S 14,17:4
Peacocks, The
 Holiday on Ice 1967,Ag 31,29:2
Peadon, Pamela
 Celebration 1969,Ja 23,55:2
Peake, Bladon (Producer)
 School for Wives 1934,N 14,22:2
 Six Characters in Search of an Author
  1934,D 5,29:1
Peale, Patricia
 Sonya's Search for the Christmas Star
  1929,D 14,24:6
Pearce, Alice
 New Faces of 1943 1942,D 23,22:2
 On the Town 1944,D 29,11:4
 Look, Ma, I'm Dancin' 1948,Ja 30,20:2
 Small Wonder 1948,S 16,33:5
 Gentlemen Prefer Blondes 1949,D 9,35:3
 Grass Harp, The 1952,Mr 28,26:2
 Dear Charles 1954,S 16,37:2
 Dear Charles 1954,S 26,II,1:1
 Fallen Angels 1956,Ja 18,27:1
 Copper and Brass 1957,O 18,19:2
 Ignorants Abroad, The 1960,My 24,43:2
 Midgie Purvis 1961,F 2,25:3
 Sail Away 1961,O 4,48:5
Pearce, Ann
 Vigil, The 1948,My 22,8:6
Pearce, Billy
 Steadfast 1923,O 31,12:1
Pearce, J Robert
 Harpers Ferry 1967,Je 6,52:2
 Visit, The 1967,S 13,41:1
Pearce, Jan
 As You Like It 1966,Je 4,19:1
Pearce, Nayan
 Artists and Models 1927,N 16,28:2
 Vaudeville (Palace) 1932,O 3,15:5
 Roberta 1933,N 20,18:4
 Keep Moving 1934,Ag 24,10:2
Pearce, Nelson
 Candida 1925,D 19,14:2
Pearce, Norman
 Big Fight, The 1928,S 19,33:1
 Town's Woman, The 1929,Mr 12,26:2
Pearce, Phyllis
 Bye Bye, Barbara 1924,Ag 26,6:3
 Music Box Revue 1924,D 2,23:3
 Criss Cross 1926,O 13,20:2
Pearce, Sam
 Aiglon, L' 1934,N 5,22:2
Pearce, Sam (Producer)
 Pygmalion 1947,F 6,29:4
Pearce, Stella Mary (Costume Designer)
 Murder in the Cathedral 1938,F 17,16:2

Pearce, Vera
Dear Love 1930,My 18,VIII,3:1
Artists and Models 1930,Je 11,33:2
Night of January 16 1936,S 30,29:3
Big Business 1937,F 19,15:3
Shephard's Pie 1941,My 18,IX,1:5
Fun and Games 1941,Ag 31,IX,1:4
Hotel Paradiso 1957,Ap 12,22:2
Hotel Paradiso 1957,Ap 21,II,1:1
Pearce, Walter
Oedipus Rex 1923,O 26,14:1
Via Crucis 1923,N 13,25:2
Burgomaster of Stilemonde, The 1923,N 16,15:3
Hamlet 1923,N 20,23:3
Pearce, William
Tendresse, La 1922,S 26,18:1
Pasteur 1923,Mr 13,19:1
Pelleas and Melisande 1923,D 5,23:2
Starlight 1925,Mr 4,17:2
Little Eyolf 1926,F 3,22:1
Hangman's House 1926,D 17,27:2
Road to Rome, The 1927,F 1,24:2
Pearce, Wynn
No Time for Sergeants 1955,O 21,32:2
Maybe Tuesday 1958,Ja 30,18:3
Peardon, Patricia
Hook-Up, The 1935,My 9,24:6
Junior Miss 1941,N 19,28:2
Junior Miss 1941,N 30,IX,1:1
Desperate Hours, The 1955,F 11,20:2
Desperate Hours, The 1955,F 20,II,1:1
Candida 1957,F 9,14:1
Jackass, The 1960,Mr 24,39:2
Cherry Orchard, The 1960,Je 4,17:2
Comedy of Errors, The 1963,Je 13,28:1
Henry V 1963,Je 14,37:1
Caesar and Cleopatra 1963,Ag 1,18:2
Much Ado About Nothing 1964,Je 11,26:2
Richard III 1964,Je 12,44:2
Twelfth Night 1966,Je 23,28:1
Pearl, Barry
Teaspoon Every Four Hours, A 1969,Je 16,57:1
Pearl, Irwin
Invitation to a Beheading 1969,Mr 18,36:1
Minnie's Boys 1970,Mr 27,27:1
Minnie's Boys 1970,Ap 5,II,3:1
Pearl, Jack
Dancing Girl, The 1923,Ja 25,16:2
Night in Paris, A 1926,Ja 6,16:3
Night in Paris, A 1926,Jl 27,15:4
Artists and Models 1927,N 16,28:2
Vaudeville (Palace) 1928,Je 26,29:4
Vaudeville (Palace) 1928,S 25,29:4
Vaudeville (Palace) 1928,O 2,35:1
Vaudeville (Palace) 1928,O 23,32:5
Pleasure Bound 1929,F 10,IX,2:1
Pleasure Bound 1929,F 19,22:4
International Revue 1930,F 9,VIII,4:2
International Revue 1930,F 26,22:2
Vaudeville (Palace) 1930,N 17,21:2
Ziegfeld Follies 1931,Jl 2,30:5
Pardon My English 1932,D 11,IX,5:2
Pardon My English 1933,Ja 21,11:4
One Flight Down 1937,D 14,32:4
All for All 1943,S 30,25:2
Pearl, Leatrice
East Wind 1931,O 28,19:1
Pearl, Lorraine
East Wind 1931,O 28,19:1
Pearlman, Nan (Miscellaneous)
Engagement Baby, The 1970,My 22,40:1
Pearlman, Rhea
Dracula Sabbat 1970,O 2,28:2
Pearlman, Stephen
Spoon River Anthology 1963,My 2,40:5
Time of the Key, A 1963,S 12,33:3
Pimpernel! 1964,Ja 7,26:6
Falstaff 1966,Je 20,27:1
Twelfth Night 1966,Je 23,28:1
Julius Caesar 1966,Je 24,29:2
Strada, La 1969,D 15,63:1
Pearly, Fred (Composer)
Ca. . . C'Est Paris 1927,F 6,VII,4:1
Pearman, Michael
Richard of Bordeaux 1934,F 15,16:2
Pearre, Elizabeth
Saint Joan 1923,D 29,8:4
Pearsall, Janet
Few Are Chosen 1935,S 18,19:3
Pearse, Jack Faulkner
This Mad Whirl 1937,Ja 10,II,4:8
Pearse, Padraic H (Playwright)
Singer, The 1920,My 25,14:2
Pearson, Anne
Clearing in the Woods, A 1957,Ja 11,20:2
Much Ado About Nothing 1961,Jl 7,17:1
Pearson, Barbara
Pursuit of Happiness, The 1936,Jl 15,14:1
Post Road 1936,Ag 5,15:4
Art and Mrs Bottle 1936,S 2,18:1
Pearson, Beatrice
Get Away Old Man 1943,N 25,40:2
Over Twenty-One 1944,Ja 4,20:2

Mermaids Singing, The 1945,N 29,26:6
Mermaids Singing, The 1945,D 9,II,5:1
Day After Tomorrow 1950,O 27,25:2
Pearson, Bud
Music Box Revue 1924,D 2,23:3
Vaudeville (Palace) 1926,Je 8,23:1
London, Paris and New York 1926,Je 8,23:1
Take the Air 1927,N 23,28:2
Pearson, Bud (Director)
Too Hot for Maneuvers 1945,My 3,26:5
Pearson, Bud (Miscellaneous)
Ziegfeld Follies 1943,Ap 2,16:2
Pearson, Bud (Playwright)
Too Hot for Maneuvers 1945,My 3,26:5
Pearson, Celia
Oy, Is Dus a Leben!; Oh, What a Life!
1942,O 13,19:2
Song of Dnieper 1946,O 26,10:5
Pearson, Donna
Lunatics and Lovers 1954,D 14,44:2
Pearson, Eppy
Panama Hattie 1940,O 31,28:2
Star and Garter 1942,Je 25,26:2
Pearson, Ginger
It Pays to Sin 1933,N 4,18:6
Pearson, Hesketh
Matriarch, The 1930,Mr 19,24:5
Pearson, Humphrey (Playwright)
They Never Grow Up 1930,Ap 8,27:1
Pearson, Jack
Music Box Revue 1924,D 2,23:3
London, Paris and New York 1926,Je 8,23:1
Vaudeville (Palace) 1926,Je 8,23:1
Take the Air 1927,N 23,28:2
Pearson, Malcolm (Miscellaneous)
Season in the Sun 1950,S 29,31:2
Genius and the Goddess, The 1957,D 11,41:1
Pearson, Malcolm (Producer)
Out West of Eighth 1951,S 21,20:3
Pearson, Malcolm L (Producer)
I Myself 1934,My 10,24:6
Little Shot 1935,Ja 18,28:4
Abide With Me 1935,N 22,19:2
Hitch Your Wagon! 1937,Ap 9,18:2
Pearson, Mark
Play of Risen Christ, The 1970,Mr 9,44:1
Pearson, Mollie
Jane's Legacy 1935,Ag 13,20:3
Pearson, Molly
Lassie 1920,Ap 7,9:2
Dover Road, The 1921,D 24,7:2
Dark Angel, The 1925,F 11,19:2
Little Minister, The 1925,Mr 24,21:1
Trelawney of the 'Wells' 1925,Je 2,16:2
White Flame 1929,N 5,32:7
Unsophisticates, The 1929,D 31,14:5
Lean Harvest 1931,O 14,26:3
They Don't Mean Any Harm 1932,F 24,25:2
Housewarming 1932,Ap 8,25:1
Anatomist, The 1932,O 25,24:3
Closed Room, The 1934,Jl 24,20:2
Good-Bye Please 1934,O 25,26:6
Laburnum Grove 1935,Ja 15,23:5
Lady Precious Stream 1936,Ja 28,15:2
Lady Precious Stream 1936,F 23,X,1:1
Young Mr Disraeli 1937,N 10,30:5
Love of Women 1937,D 14,33:2
Save Me the Waltz 1938,Mr 1,19:2
Knights of Song 1938,O 18,29:2
Pearson, Nancy
Idiot's Delight 1951,My 24,46:3
Pearson, Newport and Pearson
Vaudeville (Hippodrome) 1924,Mr 18,25:1
Vaudeville (Palace) 1926,Mr 30,20:4
Pearson, Pearl
Hey You, Light Man! 1963,Mr 2,5:2
Pearson, Pearl (Director)
Mrs Warren's Profession 1956,Je 7,35:2
Pearson, R Vereda (Composer)
Natural Man 1941,My 8,20:4
Pearson, Richard
Vivat! Vivat Regina! 1970,Jl 20,21:2
Pearson, Scott
Joyful Noise, A 1966,D 16,57:1
Promises, Promises 1968,D 2,59:3
Pearson, Shelly
Pericas, Las 1969,N 2,86:5
Pearson, Susan
No Place to Be Somebody 1969,My 5,53:3
No Place to Be Somebody 1969,My 18,II,22:1
No Place to Be Somebody 1969,My 18,II,1:1
No Place to Be Somebody 1969,D 31,17:1
Pearson, Theodore (Composer)
Who's Who 1924,Ap 18,19:2
Pearson, Walter
Folly Town 1920,My 18,9:2
High Hatters, The 1928,My 11,28:2
Challenge of Youth 1930,Ja 21,28:5
Pease, George
His Majesty the Queen 1926,Mr 9,8:1
Pease, James
Gondoliers, The 1940,O 1,29:2
Pirates of Penzance, The 1946,S 21,19:2

Peaslee, Richard (Composer)
Persecution and Assassination of Marat As
Performed by the Inmates of the Asylum of
Charenton Under the Direction of the Marquis de
Sade, The 1965,D 28,35:1
Persecution and Assassination of Marat As
Performed by the Inmates of the Asylum of
Charenton Under the Direction of the Marquis de
Sade, The 1966,Ja 9,II,1:1
US 1966,N 6,II,1:5
Persecution and Assassination of Marat As
Performed by the Inmates of the Asylum of
Charenton Under the Direction of the Marquis de
Sade, The 1967,Ja 4,34:1
Persecution and Assassination of Marat As
Performed by the Inmates of the Asylum of
Charenton Under the Direction of the Marquis de
Sade, The 1967,Ja 15,II,1:1
Merchant of Venice, The 1967,Je 22,46:2
Niggerlovers, The; Demonstration, The
1967,O 2,54:2
Niggerlovers, The; Man and Dog 1967,O 2,54:2
Endecott and the Red Cross 1968,My 7,50:1
Cry of Players, A 1968,N 15,40:1
Bacchae, The 1969,Mr 15,24:1
Flight of Lindbergh, The 1969,My 26,55:2
Lesson in Consent, A 1969,My 26,55:2
Indians 1969,My 27,43:1
Indians 1969,O 14,51:1
Don Juan 1970,My 26,32:1
Midsummer Night's Dream, A 1970,Ag 28,15:1
Midsummer Night's Dream, A 1970,S 13,II,7:1
Revenger's Tragedy, The 1970,D 2,58:1
Peaslee, Richard (Miscellaneous)
Bacchae, The 1969,Mr 15,24:1
Serpent, The 1970,Je 2,35:1
Revenger's Tragedy, The 1970,D 2,58:1
Pecheur, Bruce
Moke Eaters, The 1968,O 28,55:3
Pecheur, Marie
Genius and the Crowd 1920,S 7,20:1
Pechner, Gerhard
Magdalena 1948,S 21,31:2
Pechy, Miss
Bitter Sweet 1929,D 29,VIII,4:1
Peck, Allen
Kismet 1965,Je 23,45:1
Peck, Charles K Jr (Lyricist)
Christine 1960,Ap 29,27:1
Peck, Charles K Jr (Playwright)
Christine 1960,Ap 29,27:1
Strada, La 1969,D 15,63:1
Peck, Charles K Jr (Producer)
Strada, La 1969,D 15,63:1
Peck, Ed
Homeward Look, The 1954,Je 4,26:2
No Time for Sergeants 1955,O 21,32:2
Peck, Edgar
What Women Do? 1925,Jl 21,26:4
Peck, Elcie
Lace Petticoat 1927,Ja 5,18:2
Peck, Esther (Costume Designer)
Burmese Pwe, A 1926,Mr 17,28:1
Ritornell 1927,Ap 6,24:3
Peck, Esther (Scenic Designer)
Burmese Pwe, A 1926,Mr 17,28:1
Ritornell 1927,Ap 6,24:3
Peck, Frank
Personality 1921,Ag 29,14:3
Peck, Gregory
Morning Star, The 1942,S 15,18:4
Morning Star, The 1942,S 20,VIII,1:1
Willow and I, The 1942,D 11,32:2
Sons and Soldiers 1943,My 5,22:2
What Price Glory 1949,Mr 3,33:2
Peck, Helene (Costume Designer)
Trumpet Shall Sound, The 1926,D 11,15:2
Peck, Norman
Tempest, The 1945,Ja 26,17:2
Peck, Norman (Director)
Twelfth Night 1954,N 10,42:2
Twelfth Night 1954,D 12,II,3:1
Midsummer Night's Dream, A 1956,Ja 14,12:2
Peck, Raymond W (Lyricist)
Right Girl, The 1921,Mr 16,12:1
Castles in the Air 1926,S 7,19:2
Peck, Raymond W (Playwright)
Right Girl, The 1921,Mr 16,12:1
Castles in the Air 1926,S 7,19:2
Peck, Roy
Hello Paris 1930,N 17,29:3
Peck, Shirley
Trumpets and Drums 1969,O 13,52:1
Peck, Theodorea
Naked Man, The 1935,Jl 2,24:3
Pecker, Victor
Armored Train No 1469 1931,N 28,20:3
Laugh Night 1936,S 14,25:1
Peckett, Neil
Drums in the Night 1967,My 18,54:1
Peckham, Edna
Second Mrs Tanqueray, The 1924,O 28,27:1

Peckham, Harry
Billy Budd 1955,My 4,35:1
Peckham, Ted
Reunion 1938,Ap 12,26:4
Peddie, Frank
Glass Cage, The 1957,Mr 11,21:2
Peddie, James
Henry IV, Part I 1958,Je 25,23:3
As You Like It 1959,Jl 1,27:1
Romeo and Juliet 1960,Jl 1,14:1
Henry VIII 1961,Je 22,22:1
Peddy, Elaine
Glamour Preferred 1940,N 16,13:2
Peden, Emily
Life With Father 1967,O 20,53:2
Pedersen, Deborah
Merton of the Movies 1968,S 26,62:1
Pedersen, Harry
Lady Comes Across, The 1942,Ja 10,10:2
Take It As It Comes 1944,F 11,17:2
Pedersen, Michael
Beyond Desire 1967,O 11,36:1
Pederson, Arthur
Gods of the Lightning 1928,O 25,27:2
Pederson, Dorothy
Fall 1957,N 22,19:1
Pederson, Michael Frank
Here Be Dragons 1970,D 21,52:1
Pedi, Tom
Brooklyn, U S A 1941,D 22,24:2
Johnny Doodle 1942,Mr 19,28:2
Beggars Are Comming to Town 1945,O 29,16:2
Iceman Cometh, The 1946,O 10,31:3
Death of a Salesman 1949,F 11,27:2
Guys and Dolls 1950,N 25,11:2
Guys and Dolls 1950,D 3,II,1:1
Guys and Dolls 1951,O 7,II,1:1
Guys and Dolls 1955,Ap 21,32:2
Memory of Two Mondays, A 1955,S 30,21:1
View From the Bridge, A 1955,S 30,21:1
Beaver Coat, The 1956,Mr 29,22:5
Kiss Me, Kate 1956,My 10,27:2
Hole in the Head, A 1957,Mr 1,15:1
Courageous One, The 1958,Ja 21,33:6
Comic Strip 1958,My 15,26:2
Antigone 1959,S 16,46:2
Stage Affair, A 1962,Ja 17,30:2
King of the Whole Damn World 1962,Ap 16,32:2
My Mother, My Father and Me 1963,Mr 25,5:5
Kiss Mama 1964,O 2,30:1
Guys and Dolls 1965,Ap 29,39:1
South Pacific 1965,Je 3,25:1
Guys and Dolls 1966,Je 9,55:2
Investigation, The 1966,O 5,40:1
Mike Downstairs 1968,Ap 19,35:1
Pedrick, Lloyd
Ramblers, The 1926,S 21,32:2
Top Speed 1929,D 26,20:1
Pedro, Antonio
Arena Conta Zumbi 1969,Ag 19,31:1
Pedroza, Alfonsa
Mexican Hayride 1944,Ja 29,9:6
Peebles, Arlene
Master of the Revels 1935,Ag 14,16:2
Peebles, May
Sweet River 1936,O 29,30:2
Peel, Eileen
Tread Softly 1935,D 8,X,5:1
Shadow, The 1936,Ap 26,II,12:6
Cocktail Party, The 1950,Ja 23,17:2
Venus Observed 1952,F 14,24:2
Sherlock Holmes 1953,O 31,11:2
Elder Statesman, The 1958,Ag 31,II,3:1
Peel, Robert
Poppy God, The 1921,Ag 30,10:1
Peele, Fanny
Zunguru 1938,Ag 7,IX,8:2
Peele, George (Playwright)
David and Bethsabe 1932,D 25,IX,1:6
Peeler, Yorke
Cup of Trembling, The 1959,My 1,33:5
Cranmer of Canterbury 1959,D 4,36:1
Peely, Farrell
Wind in the Sails 1940,Ag 1,24:6
Peeples, Joseph
Hamlet 1954,Ap 24,15:2
Peer, Ronald
Moby Dick 1970,Je 3,52:1
Hamlet 1970,O 27,54:2
Rosencrantz and Guildenstern Are Dead 1970,N 19,39:3
Peerce, Alice (Producer)
Megilla of Itzik Manger, The 1968,O 10,60:1
Megilla of Itzik Manger, The 1969,Ap 21,55:1
Peers, Joan
Marry the Man! 1929,Ap 23,26:3
Peever, Henry
Reunion in New York 1940,F 22,28:4
Peggs, Marjorie
Tinker's Dam 1943,Ja 29,22:2
Peggy
Boom Boom 1929,Ja 29,26:4
Nina Rosa 1930,My 31,19:3

Nina Rosa 1930,S 22,22:5
King of Hearts 1954,Ap 2,23:1
Peggy, Helen
Bombo 1921,O 7,20:2
Pegler, Arthur James (Playwright)
She Gave Him All She Had 1939,D 2,20:7
Pegram, Florence
New Freedom, The 1930,My 15,32:4
New Freedom, The 1930,My 17,21:4
Pegram, Nigel
Wait a Minim! 1966,Mr 8,43:1
Pegues, Charles
Operation Sidewinder 1970,Mr 13,33:1
Street Sounds 1970,O 23,32:1
Peine, Virginia
Lady in the Dark 1941,Ja 24,14:2
Lady in the Dark 1941,S 3,26:6
Heart of a City 1942,F 13,24:6
Peior Brothers
Danny Kaye's International Show 1953,Ja 19,20:2
Peirce, Evelyn
Royal Family, The 1936,Ag 12,15:1
Peirce, Morrie
Family Portrait 1939,My 6,48:2
Fortuna 1962,Ja 4,26:1
Pilgrim's Progress 1962,Mr 21,36:2
Peiro Brothers
Peep Show 1950,Jl 9,II,1:1
Peisley, Frederick
To What Red Hell 1928,N 18,IX,2:3
Heaven and Charing Cross 1939,Ap 16,X,2:3
Peladan, Josephin (Playwright)
Prometheide 1926,N 21,VIII,2:1
Oedipus and the Sphinx 1928,Mr 11,VIII,2:7
Pelham, David
Schoolhouse on the Lot 1938,Mr 23,18:4
Pelham, Jimmy
Great White Hope, The 1967,D 14,58:1
Great White Hope, The 1968,O 4,40:1
Pelham, Robert
Schoolhouse on the Lot 1938,Mr 23,18:4
Pelican, Frankie
Aquashow 1954,Je 23,20:4
Pelish, Thelma
All Around the Town 1952,Mr 26,33:2
Pajama Game, The 1954,My 14,20:2
Pajama Game, The 1957,My 16,27:1
Handful of Fire 1958,O 2,45:3
Ladies Night in a Turkish Bath 1961,Mr 22,38:1
Milk and Honey 1961,O 11,52:1
Pelissier, Anthony
Red Peppers 1936,N 25,17:2
Hands Across the Sea 1936,N 25,17:2
Astonished Heart, The 1936,N 25,17:2
We Were Dancing 1936,N 28,13:1
Shadow Play 1936,N 28,13:1
Family Album 1936,D 1,31:1
Still Life 1936,D 1,31:1
Ways and Means 1936,D 1,31:1
Set to Music 1939,Ja 19,16:2
Pelissier, Constance
Dulcy 1921,Ag 15,14:1
Lake, The 1933,D 27,24:2
Richard III 1934,D 28,24:3
Othello 1935,S 28,13:2
Macbeth 1935,O 8,26:4
Cyrano de Bergerac 1936,Ap 28,17:1
Enemy of the People, An 1937,F 16,19:1
Pell, Isabel
Fools Errant 1922,Ag 22,12:3
Pell, Peter
Dear Charles 1954,S 16,37:2
Pell, Peter (Miscellaneous)
Eugenia 1957,Ja 31,20:1
Mask and Gown 1957,S 11,29:1
Second String, A 1960,Ap 14,36:2
Pell, Peter (Producer)
Chic 1959,My 19,28:2
Pell, W II
Man From Earth, The 1923,Ja 3,6:2
Pellar, Rudolf
Laterna Magika 1964,Ag 4,21:1
Pellatt, Thomas (Playwright)
Dizzy 1932,O 30,IX,2:2
Pellegrini, Gene
Best Foot Forward 1956,Mr 3,16:1
Julius Caesar 1957,O 24,39:1
Jackass, The 1960,Mr 24,39:2
Penny Change 1963,O 25,37:1
Pellerin, Jean Victor (Playwright)
Cris des Coeurs 1928,Je 3,VIII,2:5
Terrain Vague 1931,Mr 1,VIII,2:6
Cris des Coeurs 1936,Ja 12,IX,3:7
Pelletier, Denise
Ti-Coq 1951,F 10,10:2
Malade Imaginaire, Le; Imaginary Invalid, The 1958,Ap 30,28:2
Sganarelle; Imaginary Cuckold, The 1958,My 7,43:1
Mariage Force, Le; Forced Wedding, The 1958,My 7,43:1
Jalousie du Barbouille, La; Jealousy of the Barbouille, The 1958,My 7,43:1
Henry V 1966,Je 8,38:1

Pelletier, Denise—Cont
Henry VI 1966,Je 9,55:2
Seagull, The 1968,Jl 25,27:2
Pelletier, Gilles
P S I Love You 1964,N 20,40:1
Pelletier, Louis Jr (Playwright)
Howdy Stranger 1937,Ja 15,17:5
Pelletier, Wilfrid (Musical Director)
Toy Box 1955,D 18,95:3
Pelletti, John
Hazel Flagg 1953,F 12,22:2
Time of Your Life, The 1955,Ja 20,34:1
Mr Wonderful 1956,Mr 23,23:2
Pelletz, Pietro
Great Way, The 1921,N 8,28:2
Pellissier, Raoul (Translator)
No Trifling With Love 1959,N 10,55:3
Pellman, Arthur
Simple Life, A 1964,My 18,36:1
Pellow, Clifford
Pullman Car Hiawatha 1962,D 4,46:2
Desire Under the Elms 1963,Ja 11,5:6
Matty and the Moron and Madonna 1965,Mr 30,53:1
Fortune and Men's Eyes 1967,F 24,29:1
Plebeians Rehearse the Uprising, The 1968,S 8,II,11:1
Tango 1969,Ja 20,33:1
Pelly, Anthony
Caesar and Cleopatra 1951,D 20,43:2
Antony and Cleopatra 1951,D 21,22:2
Pelly, F S
Dragon, The 1922,D 27,12:1
Pelly, Farrell
Storm Over Patsy 1937,Mr 9,26:4
What Every Woman Knows 1938,Ag 30,14:5
White Steed, The 1939,Ja 11,16:2
Beautiful People, The 1941,Ap 22,27:2
Magic 1942,S 30,28:2
Hello Out There 1942,S 30,28:2
Hickory Stick 1944,My 9,15:6
What Every Woman Knows 1954,D 23,16:2
Miser, The 1955,Mr 18,34:2
Red Roses for Me 1955,D 29,15:2
Iceman Cometh, The 1956,My 8,38:1
Moon for the Misbegotten, A 1958,Je 7,10:6
Touch of the Poet, A 1958,O 3,23:2
Peloquin, Noella
Night in Venice, A 1953,Je 26,15:2
Pelt, Tim
Slave Ship 1969,N 22,46:1
Pelto, Matt
As You Like It 1955,O 29,12:2
Romeo and Juliet 1955,D 16,36:3
Thorntons, The 1956,F 15,26:1
Peltz, David (Original Author)
Johnny on the Spot 1942,Ja 9,24:2
Peluso, Emanuel (Playwright)
Good Day 1965,O 19,51:1
Peluso, Tom (Composer)
Blackberries of 1932 1932,Ap 5,27:5
Peluso, Tom (Lyricist)
Blackberries of 1932 1932,Ap 5,27:5
Peman, Jose Maria (Playwright)
Saint in a Hurry, A 1935,D 29,IX,2:1
Pember, Clifford (Playwright)
Caravan 1928,Ag 30,13:3
Pember, Clifford (Scenic Designer)
Dodsworth 1938,F 23,26:2
Under the Counter 1947,O 4,10:2
Pemberton, Antonia
Semi-Detached 1963,O 8,49:1
Straight Up 1970,S 2,30:2
Pemberton, Brock
Ceiling Zero 1935,Ap 2,24:3
Harvey 1947,S 14,II,1:6
Pemberton, Brock (Director)
Puppets 1925,Mr 10,19:1
Masque of Venice, The 1926,Mr 3,27:3
Loose Ankles 1926,Ag 17,15:1
Ladder, The 1926,O 23,15:1
Goin' Home 1928,Ag 24,23:2
Hotbed 1928,N 10,20:7
Strictly Dishonorable 1929,S 19,37:1
Strictly Dishonorable 1929,S 29,IX,1:1
Three Times the Hour 1931,Ag 26,15:5
Christopher Comes Across 1932,Je 1,19:2
Personal Appearance 1934,O 18,26:7
Love Me Long 1949,N 8,34:5
Mr Barry's Etchings 1950,F 1,26:2
Pemberton, Brock (Playwright)
Lady in Waiting 1940,Mr 28,19:1
Pemberton, Brock (Producer)
Love Habit, The 1923,Mr 25,VIII,1:1
Mister Pitt 1924,Ja 6,VII,1:4
Living Mask, The 1924,Ja 22,15:1
Mister Pitt 1924,Ja 23,15:3
Marionette Man, The 1924,Ja 27,VII,2:7
Little Angel, The 1924,S 29,10:3
Puppets 1925,Mr 10,19:1
Masque of Venice, The 1926,Mr 3,27:3
Ladder, The 1926,Je 27,VII,3:1
Loose Ankles 1926,Ag 17,15:1
Ladder, The 1926,S 26,VIII,2:7

Pemberton, Brock (Producer)—Cont

Ladder, The 1926,O 23,15:1
Say It With Flowers 1926,D 6,29:1
Goin' Home 1928,Ag 24,23:2
Hotbed 1928,N 10,20:7
Strictly Dishonorable 1929,S 19,37:1
Seven Year Love 1929,O 27,IX,2:1
Strictly Dishonorable 1929,D 17,29:2
Gone Hollywood 1930,D 28,VIII,2:1
Three Times the Hour 1931,Ag 26,15:5
Christopher Comes Across 1932,Je 1,19:2
Nude in Washington Square, The 1934,Ag 7,20:1
Personal Appearance 1934,O 18,26:7
Ceiling Zero 1935,Ap 11,26:2
Ceiling Zero 1935,Ap 21,IX,1:1
Personal Appearance 1935,D 8,X,5:8
Now You've Done It 1937,Mr 6,10:4
Chalked Out 1937,Mr 26,24:2
Red Harvest 1937,Mr 31,29:2
Kiss the Boys Goodbye 1938,S 29,30:2
Lady in Waiting 1940,Mr 28,19:1
Out From Under 1940,My 6,13:2
Glamour Preferred 1940,N 16,13:2
Cuckoos on the Hearth 1941,S 17,26:2
Janie 1942,S 11,24:2
Pillar to Post 1943,D 11,11:2
Harvey 1944,N 2,23:2
Harvey 1944,N 12,II,1:1
Harvey 1947,S 14,II,1:6
Love Me Long 1949,N 8,34:5
Mr Barry's Etchings 1950,F 1,26:2

Pemberton, Goldie

Squealer, The 1928,N 13,36:3

Pemberton, Henry W

Immodest Violet 1920,Ag 25,6:2
Bride, The 1924,My 6,25:1
Devil Within, The 1925,Ja 25,VII,1:4
Devil Within, The 1925,Mr 17,19:4
Edgar Allan Poe 1925,O 6,31:1
Golden Dawn 1927,D 1,32:3
It Is to Laugh 1927,D 27,24:2
Rainbow 1928,N 22,25:1
Scarlet Pages 1929,S 10,26:3
Through the Night 1930,Ag 19,19:1
Perfectly Scandalous 1931,My 14,27:2
Pygmalion 1938,Ja 27,16:3
Coriolanus 1938,F 2,14:5

Pemberton, Idalie

Belle Helene, La 1941,Jl 8,14:1

Pemberton, Madge (Playwright)

Son of the Man, The 1934,D 4,22:1
King of Rome, The 1935,My 15,26:1
Emperor of Make-Believe, The 1936,Mr 17,25:5
Emperor of Make-Believe, The 1936,Je 4,27:2
Emperor of Make-Believe, The 1936,Jl 5,IX,1:8

Pemberton, Margaret (Costume Designer)

Love Me Long 1949,N 8,34:5
Mr Barry's Etchings 1950,F 1,26:2

Pemberton, Murdock (Playwright)

Ladder, The 1927,O 7,24:2
Sing High, Sing Low 1931,N 13,26:4

Pemberton, Virginia

Master of the Inn, The 1925,D 23,22:2
Caravan 1928,Ag 30,13:3

Pemberton-Billing, Noel (Playwright)

High Treason 1928,N 25,X,2:3

Pembroke, George

Poppy God, The 1921,Ag 30,10:1
Man on Stilts, The 1931,S 10,23:2
Inside Story, The 1932,F 23,23:2
Wednesday's Child 1934,Ja 17,23:2
One More Honeymoon 1934,Ap 2,13:5
Paradise Lost 1935,D 10,31:5
Chalk Dust 1936,Mr 5,24:5

Pen, John (Original Author)

Thank You Svoboda 1944,Mr 2,13:2

Penagos, Isabel

Fiesta in Madrid 1969,My 29,49:1

Penalosa, Albert E

There Was a Young Man 1940,F 27,17:4
Jim Dandy 1941,N 8,10:5

Penalosa, Albert E (Director)

Jim Dandy 1941,N 8,10:5

Penberthy, Beverly

But, Seriously... 1969,F 28,29:1

Pendelton, Elizabeth

Glass Slipper, The 1925,O 20,29:1

Pender, O A

Laugh It Off 1925,Ap 25,18:4

Pendergast, Shirley (Lighting Director)

Ceremonies in Dark Old Men 1969,F 6,33:1
Five on the Black Hand Side 1970,Ja 2,32:2

Pendergast, W H

Paid 1925,N 26,32:1

Pender's Comedians

Good Times 1920,Ag 10,10:1

Pendleton, Ann

Merry Wives of Windsor, The 1938,Ap 15,22:3

Pendleton, Austin

Oh Dad, Poor Dad, Mamma's Hung You in the
  Closet and I'm Feelin' So Sad 1962,F 27,28:1
Fiddler on the Roof 1964,S 23,56:2
Hail Scrawdyke! 1966,N 29,50:1
Little Foxes, The 1967,O 27,53:1

Last Sweet Days of Isaac, The 1970,Ja 27,49:1
Last Sweet Days of Isaac, The 1970,F 8,II,1:6

Pendleton, David

Knack With Horses, A 1970,D 21,52:1

Pendleton, Eleanor

Fall and Rise of Susan Lenox, The 1920,Je 11,11:2

Pendleton, Eloise

Desire Under the Elms 1924,N 12,20:7

Pendleton, Florence

Tweedles 1923,Ag 14,10:1
Goose Hangs High, The 1924,Ja 30,16:1
Magda 1926,Ja 27,16:2
Pearl of Great Price, The 1926,N 2,34:3
Veils 1928,Mr 14,28:5
Eva the Fifth 1928,Ag 29,19:3
Penal Law 2010 1930,My 19,14:2
Grand Hotel 1930,N 14,30:4
Come Marching Home 1946,My 20,18:6

Pendleton, Gaylord

Cold Feet 1923,My 22,14:2
Helena's Boys 1924,Ap 8,22:2
Coquette 1927,N 9,23:1
Coquette 1935,My 22,23:4

Pendleton, George

Little Theatre Tournament; Little Italy
  1928,My 10,31:1

Pendleton, Nat

Naughty Cinderella 1925,N 10,23:6
Grey Fox, The 1928,O 23,32:3
My Girl Friday! 1929,F 13,20:2

Pendleton, Wyman

Cradle of Willow, A 1961,D 16,20:2
Corruption in the Palace of Justice 1963,O 9,49:2
Giants' Dance, The 1964,N 17,48:2
Child Buyer, The 1964,D 22,35:1
Malcolm 1966,Ja 12,29:1
Butter and Egg Man, The 1966,O 18,49:1
Comedy of Errors, The 1968,F 28,40:2
She Stoops to Conquer 1968,Ap 1,58:3
Quotations From Chairman Mao Tse-Tung
  1968,O 1,39:1
Happy Days 1968,O 14,54:1
Henry V 1969,Je 9,57:1
Much Ado About Nothing 1969,Je 16,57:1
Hamlet 1969,Je 30,33:1
Henry V 1969,N 11,43:1
Othello 1970,Je 22,43:1
Devil's Disciple, The 1970,Je 30,48:1
Othello 1970,S 15,51:1

Penella, Manuel (Composer)

Wildcat, The 1921,N 28,16:2

Penella, Manuel (Playwright)

Wildcat, The 1921,N 28,16:2

Penfold, Maurice

Merry-Go-Round 1927,Je 1,25:4

Penhallow, David

Golden Six, The 1958,O 27,31:2

Penman, Charles

Sweeney Todd 1924,Jl 19,10:4
Bombasters Furioso 1924,Jl 19,10:4
Charley's Aunt 1925,Je 2,16:2
Spring Fever 1925,Ag 4,14:2
Royal Box, The 1928,N 21,32:3
Sakura 1928,D 26,14:4
Traitor, The 1930,My 3,23:4
My Fair Lady 1964,My 21,43:2

Penman, Lea

Just Life 1926,S 15,33:3
Mirrors 1928,Ja 19,17:1
Her Unborn Child 1928,Mr 7,28:3
House of Fear, The 1929,O 8,34:2
Headquarters 1929,D 5,32:4
Venetian, The 1931,N 2,26:1
Absent Father 1932,O 18,23:5
Comic Artist, The 1933,Ap 20,20:3
After Such Pleasures 1934,Ja 6,18:6
After Such Pleasures 1934,F 8,15:2
So Many Paths 1934,D 7,26:5
Life's Too Short 1935,S 21,18:5
Boy Meets Girl 1935,N 28,38:2
Angel Island 1937,O 21,26:2
What a Life 1938,Ap 14,26:2
Unconquered, The 1940,F 14,25:2
International Incident, An 1940,Ap 3,18:2
Beverly Hills 1940,N 8,24:2
Ring Around Elizabeth 1941,N 18,32:2
Cat Screams, The 1942,Je 17,26:5
Pirate, The 1942,N 26,39:2
Annie Get Your Gun 1946,My 17,14:2

Penn, Albert (Miscellaneous)

Magnificent Hugo, The 1961,Ap 8,12:2

Penn, Albert (Producer)

Cantilevered Terrace, The 1962,Ja 18,24:1

Penn, Arthur (Director)

Lovers 1956,My 11,23:1
Two for the Seesaw 1958,Ja 17,15:1
Two for the Seesaw 1958,Ja 26,II,1:1
Miracle Worker, The 1959,O 20,44:1
Miracle Worker, The 1959,N 1,II,1:1
Miracle Worker, The 1959,D 20,II,5:1
Toys in the Attic 1960,F 26,23:2
Toys in the Attic 1960,Mr 6,II,1:1

Penn, Arthur (Director)—Cont

Evening With Mike Nichols and Elaine May, An
  1960,O 10,37:1
All the Way Home 1960,D 1,42:1
All the Way Home 1960,D 18,II,3:1
In the Counting House 1962,D 15,5:5
Lorenzo 1963,F 16,5:2
Golden Boy 1964,O 21,56:1
Golden Boy 1964,N 1,II,1:1
Wait Until Dark 1966,F 3,21:1

Penn, Bill

Boy With a Cart, The 1954,Ap 5,19:2
Noah 1954,O 11,32:2
In April Once 1955,Mr 14,29:3
Hour Glass, The 1955,O 17,33:1
Infernal Machine, The 1958,F 4,33:1

Penn, Bill (Director)

By Hex 1956,Je 19,25:1
Lesson, The 1956,O 3,29:2
Thor, With Angels 1956,O 15,29:4
Box of Watercolors, A 1957,F 18,22:2
Oscar Wilde 1957,Ap 20,21:3
Tobias and the Angel 1957,O 21,29:5
Marvellous History of Saint Bernard, The
  1958,F 24,16:3
Potting Shed, The 1958,N 3,49:2
Susannah and the Elders 1959,O 19,37:3
Bible Salesman, The 1960,F 22,12:2
Tobacco Road 1960,My 11,44:2
Miracle, The 1960,D 5,42:3
Bartleby 1961,Ja 25,28:1
Bible Salesman, The 1961,F 21,40:1
Oldest Trick in the World, The 1961,F 21,40:1
Sing Muse 1961,D 7,52:1
Put It in Writing 1963,My 14,31:1
That Thing at the Cherry Lane 1965,My 19,42:1

Penn, Bill (Producer)

Country Wife, The 1955,Ap 6,35:1

Penn, Bill (Scenic Designer)

Lesson, The 1956,O 3,29:2

Penn, Cynthia (Costume Designer)

Victims, The; Victims of Duty 1968,Mr 6,34:1
Victims, The; On the Hazards of Smoking Tobacco
  1968,Mr 6,34:1
Victims, The; Escurial 1968,Mr 6,34:1

Penn, Ed

Queen and the Rebels, The 1965,F 26,16:1
My Wife and I 1966,O 11,53:2
Of Thee I Sing 1969,Mr 8,19:1
Greenwillow 1970,D 8,60:1

Penn, Elizabeth (Costume Designer)

And People All Around 1968,F 12,46:1

Penn, Leo

Dinosaur Wharf 1951,N 9,23:2
Maya 1953,Je 10,35:1
School for Scandal, The 1953,Je 24,29:2
Girl on the Via Flaminia, The 1954,F 10,37:1
Girl on the Via Flaminia, The 1954,Ap 6,35:5
Girl on the Via Flaminia, The 1954,O 13,26:5
View From the Bridge, A 1955,S 30,21:1
Memory of Two Mondays, A 1955,S 30,21:1
Henry V 1956,Jl 7,11:2
Of Mice and Men 1958,D 5,38:1

Penn, Leo (Director)

Midnight Caller, The 1958,Jl 2,25:1
John Turner Davis 1958,Jl 2,25:1

Penn, Leonard

Between Two Worlds 1934,O 26,24:2
Field of Ermine 1935,F 9,10:4
Paths of Glory 1935,S 19,29:1
Paths of Glory 1935,S 27,24:2
Lady in Waiting 1940,Mr 28,19:1
Distant City, The 1941,S 23,27:5

Penn, Nina

Molly Darling 1922,S 2,10:2
Top Hole 1924,S 2,22:3
Florida Girl 1925,N 3,34:1

Penn, Robert

Sing Out, Sweet Land! 1944,D 28,24:2
Private Life of the Master Race, The
  1945,Je 13,28:3
If the Shoe Fits 1946,D 6,29:4
Liar, The 1950,My 19,30:2
Paint Your Wagon 1951,N 13,32:2
Can-Can 1953,My 8,28:1
Guitar 1959,N 11,42:5
Crystal Heart, The 1960,F 16,31:2
Paradise Island 1961,Je 24,11:1
Kean 1961,N 3,28:2
Cafe Crown 1964,Ap 18,32:1

Penna, Tarver

Berkeley Square 1929,N 5,32:4

Pennell, Daniel

Your Woman and Mine 1922,F 28,17:2
Yellow 1923,S 22,30:1

Penner, David

Hour Glass, The 1955,O 17,33:1

Penner, Joe

Tattle Tales 1930,Jl 20,VIII,2:1
Vanderbilt Revue, The 1930,O 26,VIII,3:5
Vanderbilt Revue, The 1930,N 6,22:6
East Wind 1931,O 28,19:1
East Wind 1931,D 11,VIII,4:3
Vaudeville (Palace) 1932,Jl 4,14:5

⸱ner, Richard
Tour Glass, The 1955,O 17,33:1
⸱nese, Giuseppe
Rugantino 1964,F 7,34:1
⸱nning, Estelle
Perfect Fool, The 1921,N 8,28:2
⸱nnington, Ann
Scandals 1920,Je 8,9:1
George White's Scandals 1921,Jl 12,14:1
Jack and Jill 1923,Mr 23,17:2
Follies 1923,Je 26,14:5
Ziegfeld Follies 1924,Mr 18,25:2
Ziegfeld Follies 1924,Je 25,26:1
Follies 1925,Mr 11,19:2
George White's Scandals 1926,Je 15,23:2
George White's Scandals 1928,Jl 3,19:1
Vaudeville (Palace) 1930,F 17,18:4
New Yorkers, The 1930,N 16,VIII,3:1
New Yorkers, The 1930,D 9,31:1
Everybody's Welcome 1931,S 20,VIII,3:2
Everybody's Welcome 1931,O 14,26:3
Flying Ginzburgs, The 1938,N 13,IX,2:2
Student Prince, The 1943,Je 9,16:2
⸱nnington, Buck
Howdy Mr Ice 1948,Je 25,28:5
Howdy, Mr Ice of 1950 1949,My 27,24:2
⸱nnington, Michael
Hamlet 1969,My 2,38:1
⸱nnington, Theo
Trial by Jury 1931,Jl 28,17:6
H M S Pinafore 1931,Jl 28,17:6
⸱nnington, Theodore A (Miscellaneous)
Autumn's Here 1966,O 26,40:1
Beclch 1968,D 17,59:1
⸱nnock, Christopher
Patriot for Me, A 1969,O 6,58:1
⸱nnsylvanians, The
Hear! Hear! 1955,S 28,38:1
⸱nnwarden, Duncan
Chinese Lily, A 1925,Mr 24,26:5
⸱nny, Don
Drink to Me Only 1958,O 9,47:4
There Is a Play Tonight 1961,F 16,24:2
⸱enon, Agustin (Playwright)
Song of the Grasshopper 1967,S 29,52:2
⸱enrose, Gibbs
Say When 1928,Je 27,29:3
Out of a Blue Sky 1930,F 10,20:6
Farmer Takes a Wife, The 1934,O 31,17:1
Liliom 1940,Mr 26,17:2
Porgy and Bess 1942,Ja 23,16:2
⸱enrose, Tudor
Polly 1929,Ja 9,28:3
⸱enry-Jones, Peter
Dance of Death, The 1967,O 20,50:1
Love for Love 1967,O 21,17:1
⸱enta, Michael C (Choreographer)
Of Thee I Sing 1969,Mr 8,19:1
⸱entecost, George
Tavern, The 1964,Mr 6,39:2
Impromptu at Versailles 1964,Mr 10,43:1
Scapin 1964,Mr 10,43:1
Lower Depths, The 1964,Mr 31,30:1
You Can't Take It With You 1965,N 24,32:1
School for Scandal, The 1966,N 22,33:2
Wild Duck, The 1967,Ja 12,49:1
War and Peace 1967,Mr 22,42:1
Pantagleize 1967,D 1,54:1
Show-Off, The 1967,D 6,40:2
Cherry Orchard, The 1968,Mr 20,41:1
Boys in the Band, The 1970,Ap 18,34:1
Pentzoldt, Ernst (Playwright)
Portugalische Schlacht, Die 1931,Je 7,VIII,2:5
Penue, Violet
Many Waters 1929,S 26,27:1
Penven, Alice
Trois Jeunes Filles Nues; Three Young Maids From
the Folies Bergere 1929,Mr 5,28:2
Comte Obligado 1929,Mr 12,26:2
Ta Bouche 1929,Mr 15,28:5
Penwarden, Duncan
Is Zat So? 1925,Ja 6,23:4
Scarlet Lily, The 1927,Ja 31,12:3
Scalawag, The 1927,Mr 30,22:3
Clutching Claw, The 1928,F 15,20:1
Gentlemen of the Press 1928,Ag 28,27:2
Now-A-Days 1929,Ag 6,29:3
Broken Dishes 1929,N 6,28:3
Penwarden, Hazel
Lark, The 1955,My 13,21:2
Penwarn, Joan
Ice Capades 1955,S 15,38:1
Ice Capades 1956,S 13,41:2
Ice Capades 1957,S 5,33:2
Penwell, Jack
Cyrano de Bergerac 1936,Ap 28,17:1
Penyen, Alice
Bon Garcon, Un 1929,Mr 19,36:2
Penzner, Seymour
Pirates of Penzance, The 1942,F 20,20:2
Coriolanus 1965,Jl 15,23:1
Troilus and Cressida 1965,Ag 13,17:1

Pepin, Clermont (Composer)
Malade Imaginaire, Le; Imaginary Invalid, The
1958,Ap 30,28:2
Pepin, Clermont (Miscellaneous)
Jalousie du Barbouille, La; Jealousy of the
Barbouille, The 1958,My 7,43:1
Sganarelle; Imaginary Cuckold, The 1958,My 7,43:1
Mariage Force, Le; Forced Wedding, The
1958,My 7,43:1
Pepine, Arthur (Miscellaneous)
Epitaph for George Dillon 1960,D 29,17:1
Three Times Three; George Washington Crossing
the Delaware 1962,Mr 2,24:1
Three Times Three; Twenty-Five Cent White Cap,
The 1962,Mr 2,24:1
Three Times Three; Not Enough Rope
1962,Mr 2,24:1
Giants' Dance, The 1964,N 17,48:2
Pepito
Vaudeville (Palace) 1932,Jl 11,11:6
Peppard, George
Beautiful Changes, The 1956,Mr 24,15:2
Girls of Summer 1956,N 20,45:1
Pleasure of His Company, The 1958,O 23,36:1
Pleasure of His Company, The 1958,N 2,II,1:1
Peppe, Audrey
Stars on Ice (2d Edition) 1943,Je 25,13:2
Pepper, Bessie
Lightnin' 1938,S 16,17:2
Pepper, Jack
Vaudeville (Palace) 1929,Je 17,29:3
Pepper, Jessica
Red, Hot and Blue! 1936,O 30,26:3
Between the Devil 1937,D 23,24:5
Pepper, Lawrence
Garden of Time 1945,Mr 10,13:7
Pepper, Llewelyn
Nobody's Child 1956,Ag 23,25:2
Pepusch, Johann Christoph (Composer)
Beggar's Opera, The 1963,Jl 17,20:1
Beggar's Opera, The 1965,Mr 21,II,13:1
Peques, Charles
Instructions for the Running of Trains, etc on the
Erie Railway to Go Into Effect January 1,1862
1970,Ja 7,36:2
Perah, Pnina
Children of the Shadows 1964,F 27,26:1
Peralta, Delfor
Esta Noche... Teatro 1968,O 15,40:1
Peralta, Delfor (Director)
Esta Noche... Teatro 1968,O 15,40:1
Percel (Miss)
Great Love, The 1935,O 22,17:3
Percelly, Juanita
Holiday on Ice 1965,S 2,38:4
Holiday on Ice 1966,S 1,30:1
Holiday on Ice 1967,Ag 31,29:2
Holiday on Ice 1968,Ag 29,44:1
Holiday on Ice 1969,Ag 28,44:1
Perceval, Robert
Teahouse of the August Moon, The
1955,My 10,24:1
Percival
Midsummer Night's Dream, A 1932,Jl 13,15:1
Percival, David (Playwright)
Girlfriend 1970,F 19,59:1
Percival, Elsie
Good Boy 1928,S 6,23:2
Percival, James
Audition of the Apprentice Theatre 1939,Je 2,26:2
Percival, Julie Helene (Playwright)
Bully, The 1924,D 26,18:1
Percival, Lionel
Buccaneer, The 1925,O 3,10:2
Percival, W I
Merchant of Venice, The 1922,D 22,13:1
Percival, W I (Producer)
Find Daddy 1926,Mr 9,21:3
Percival, Walter C
Henky 1924,Ap 27,VIII,2:3
Percival, Walter C (Playwright)
Swifty 1922,O 17,14:1
Percy, Edward (Playwright)
If Four Walls Told 1922,My 21,VI,1:6
Slaves All 1926,D 7,24:4
Misdoings of Charley Peace, The 1929,S 29,IX,2:1
Object of Virtue, An 1930,N 5,28:3
Object of Virtue, An 1930,N 23,IX,2:4
Suspect 1937,F 17,16:2
Ladies in Retirement 1939,D 24,IX,1:7
Ladies in Retirement 1940,Mr 27,24:3
Suspect 1940,Ap 10,30:4
Malice Domestic 1942,Jl 21,22:1
Shop at Sly Corner, The 1949,Ja 19,35:2
Percy, Esme
Byron 1929,F 10,IX,4:7
Douaumont 1929,D 22,VIII,4:3
Colonel Satan 1931,Ja 18,I,28:6
Success Story 1934,Ja 2,17:4
Peter Petrolus 1937,Ap 5,16:5
Peter Petrolus 1937,Ap 25,X,1:1
She, Too, Was Young 1938,S 4,X,2:1

Percy, Esme—Cont
Lady's Not for Burning, The 1950,N 9,42:2
Lady's Not for Burning, The 1950,N 26,II,1:1
Colombe 1951,D 15,13:2
Percy, Esme (Director)
Success Story 1934,Ja 2,17:4
Far Fetched Fables 1950,S 7,39:7
Percy, Neville
Criminal at Large 1932,O 11,26:3
Living Dangerously 1935,Ja 14,10:3
Laughing Woman, The 1936,O 14,30:1
Percy, William Alexander (Playwright)
In April Once 1955,Mr 14,29:3
Percyval, T Wigney
Bunch and Judy, The 1922,N 29,20:1
Mountebank, The 1923,My 8,22:2
Way Things Happen, The 1924,Ja 29,17:5
Outsider, The 1924,Mr 4,16:4
All Dressed Up 1925,S 10,28:1
Slaves All 1926,D 7,24:4
Mariners 1927,Mr 29,22:2
Garden of Eden, The 1927,S 28,28:1
Caste 1927,D 24,8:1
Lady Clara 1930,Ap 18,28:7
Silent Witness, The 1931,Mr 24,31:5
Percyval, T Wigney (Playwright)
One Wife or Another 1933,F 7,23:6
Perdriere, Miss
Ligne du Coeur, La 1931,O 25,VIII,1:7
Pere, Alexander (Musical Director)
Quo Vadis 1932,O 17,18:2
Perea, Carol
Old Bucks and New Wings 1962,N 6,39:4
Perelman, Laura (Playwright)
All Good Americans 1933,D 6,29:2
Perelman, S J (Playwright)
Walk a Little Faster 1932,D 8,24:4
All Good Americans 1933,D 6,29:2
Night Before Christmas, The 1941,Mr 30,I,48:2
Night Before Christmas, The 1941,Ap 11,25:2
One Touch of Venus 1943,O 8,14:1
One Touch of Venus 1943,O 17,II,1:1
Beauty Part, The 1962,D 28,5:2
Beauty Part, The 1963,Ja 5,5:1
Beauty Part, The 1969,S 7,II,1:2
Perelmutter, Marcel (Miscellaneous)
Who's Who, Baby? 1968,Ja 30,36:1
Perera, Lydia
For Charity 1937,Ag 25,24:3
Night Music 1940,F 23,18:2
Peress, Maurice
Rivalry, The 1959,F 9,24:2
Peress, Maurice (Musical Director)
West Side Story 1968,Je 25,32:1
Peretti, Hugo (Composer)
Maggie Flynn 1968,O 24,52:1
Maggie Flynn 1968,N 3,II,1:1
Peretti, Hugo (Lyricist)
Maggie Flynn 1968,O 24,52:1
Peretti, Hugo (Playwright)
Maggie Flynn 1968,O 24,52:1
Peretz, I L (Original Author)
Rich Man, Poor Man 1950,F 13,15:4
World of Sholom Aleichem, The 1953,S 20,II,1:1
Peretz, I L (Playwright)
Theater of Peretz, The 1963,N 6,35:2
Melody Lingers On, The 1969,N 17,55:1
Peretz, J L
We Live and Laugh 1936,My 9,10:3
Perez, Bobby
Mrs January & Mr Ex 1944,Ap 1,10:2
Perez, Everett A
200 Were Chosen 1936,N 21,21:1
Perez, Francois
Femmes Savantes, Les 1967,F 7,34:2
Perez, Giuseppe
Promessi Sposi I,; Betrothed, The 1934,O 22,13:2
Perez, Inez Yvette
Difunta, La 1969,N 2,86:5
Emerald Slippers, The 1970,S 2,31:2
Perez, Jose
Time of the Cuckoo, The 1952,O 16,37:4
Me, Candido! 1956,O 16,36:2
Square in the Eye 1965,My 20,54:1
Ox Cart, The 1966,D 20,58:1
Goa 1968,F 23,46:1
Does a Tiger Wear a Necktie? 1969,F 26,38:1
Camino Real 1970,Ja 9,42:1
Perez, Lazaro
Does a Tiger Wear a Necktie? 1967,F 4,17:1
Does a Tiger Wear a Necktie? 1969,F 26,38:1
Perez, Luis
Fuerza Ciega, La 1927,D 6,26:1
Perez, Pia
Promessi Sposi I,; Betrothed, The 1934,O 22,13:2
Perez, Ray (Choreographer)
Rainbow Rose 1926,Mr 17,28:2
White Lights 1927,O 12,30:4
Houseboat on the Styx, The 1928,D 26,14:3
Perez, Raymond
County Chairman, The 1936,My 26,26:5
Perez, Raymond B (Choreographer)
1776 1926,Ap 24,11:2

Perez, Royce
County Chairman, The 1936,My 26,26:5
Perfect, Rose
George White's Scandals 1926,Je 15,23:2
George White's Scandals 1928,Jl 3,19:1
Vaudeville (Palace) 1929,S 2,16:3
Vaudeville (Palace) 1930,O 13,31:3
Mr Strauss Goes to Boston 1945,S 7,20:2
Night in Venice, A 1952,Je 27,18:6
Night in Venice, A 1953,Je 26,15:2
Pergament, Lola (Lyricist)
O Marry Me 1961,O 28,13:1
Pergament, Lola (Playwright)
2 for Fun; Switch in Time, A 1955,My 26,34:1
O Marry Me 1961,O 28,13:1
Pergola, Joseph
Jubilee 1935,O 14,20:1
Peri, Arnold (Miscellaneous)
Sandhog 1954,N 24,17:1
Pericet, Angelo
Rugantino 1964,F 7,34:1
Perier, Jean
Divin Mensonge 1926,N 14,VIII,2:1
Berlioz 1927,F 20,VII,2:1
Perin, Ceci
People vs Ranchman, The 1968,O 28,56:1
Perine, Louise
Crooks' Convention, The 1929,S 19,37:4
Perkins, Albert
Blue Blood 1924,Ap 3,21:2
Perkins, Alberta
My Magnolia 1926,Jl 13,19:2
Change Your Luck 1930,Je 7,10:2
Louisiana 1933,F 28,15:5
Point Valaine 1935,Ja 17,22:2
Walk Together Chillun 1936,F 5,15:2
Case of Philip Lawrence, The 1937,Je 9,31:1
Swingin' the Dream 1939,N 30,24:2
Harriet 1943,Mr 4,24:2
Anna Lucasta 1944,Je 17,10:1
Harriet 1944,S 28,26:1
Perkins, Anthony
Tea and Sympathy 1954,Ag 15,II,1:1
Look Homeward, Angel 1957,N 29,33:1
Look Homeward, Angel 1957,D 8,II,5:1
Greenwillow 1960,Mr 9,38:1
Greenwillow 1960,Mr 20,II,1:1
Harold 1962,N 8,50:7
Harold 1962,N 30,27:1
Star-Spangled Girl, The 1966,D 22,38:1
Steambath 1970,Jl 1,49:1
Steambath 1970,Jl 12,II,1:3
Steambath 1970,O 11,II,1:1
Perkins, Anthony (Director)
Steambath 1970,Jl 1,49:1
Steambath 1970,Jl 12,II,1:3
Perkins, Bobbie
Tantrum, The 1924,S 5,20:2
June Days 1925,Ag 7,12:5
Garrick Gaieties 1926,My 11,25:2
Betsy 1926,D 29,24:3
Hit the Deck! 1927,Ap 26,32:1
Animal Crackers 1928,O 24,26:2
Perkins, Catherine
Enemy of the People, An 1958,F 26,24:2
Perkins, Cy (Pvt)
Winged Victory 1943,N 22,24:1
Perkins, David
Watched Pot, The 1947,O 29,31:4
Family Reunion, The 1947,N 29,9:2
Hamlet 1948,D 4,9:2
She Stoops to Conquer 1949,D 29,21:3
Love and Let Love 1951,O 20,11:2
Corn Is Green, The 1954,F 27,10:2
Perkins, Don
King Lear 1963,N 23,22:1
Borstal Boy 1970,Ap 1,38:1
Wars of the Roses, The (Part I) 1970,Jl 2,30:1
Perkins, Dorothy (Choreographer)
Merchant of Venice, The 1950,My 3,37:2
Perkins, Garwood
Porgy and Bess 1964,My 7,32:1
Porgy and Bess 1965,Mr 6,17:1
Perkins, Grace
Lullaby, The 1923,S 19,5:3
Her Way Out 1924,Je 24,18:3
Perkins, Grace (Playwright)
Walking Gentleman, The 1942,My 8,26:2
Perkins, H
Under the Gaslight 1929,Ap 3,27:1
Perkins, Jackson
God Innis 1937,Ag 25,24:3
As You Like It 1939,My 9,28:4
Hamlet 1939,D 5,35:2
Richard II 1940,Ap 2,31:2
Perkins, John
Little Racketeer, The 1932,Ja 19,24:4
Romeo and Juliet 1951,Mr 12,21:2
Wish You Were Here 1952,Je 26,26:6
Balcony, The 1960,Mr 4,21:1
Physicists, The 1964,O 14,52:1
Perkins, Joseph
Two Orphans, The 1926,Ap 6,26:2

Perkins, Julius
Porgy and Bess 1942,Ja 23,16:2
Perkins, Kenneth (Playwright)
Creoles 1927,S 23,33:3
Dance With Your Gods 1934,O 8,14:3
Louisiana Lady 1947,Je 3,35:2
Perkins, Martin
Criminal Code, The 1929,O 3,28:2
Perkins, Max (Producer)
Vintage '60 1960,S 13,41:1
Perkins, Osgood
Beggar on Horseback 1924,F 13,17:2
Weak Sisters 1925,O 14,31:3
Masque of Venice, The 1926,Mr 3,27:3
Pomeroy's Past 1926,Ap 20,24:4
Loose Ankles 1926,Ag 17,15:1
Loose Ankles 1926,Ag 29,VII,1:1
Say It With Flowers 1926,D 6,29:1
Spread Eagle 1927,Ap 5,30:2
Women Go on Forever 1927,S 8,25:1
Salvation 1928,F 1,31:1
Front Page, The 1928,Ag 15,19:2
Front Page, The 1928,Ag 26,VII,1:1
Uncle Vanya 1930,Ap 16,26:5
Uncle Vanya 1930,My 4,XI,1:1
Uncle Vanya 1930,S 23,30:3
Tomorrow and Tomorrow 1931,Ja 14,26:3
Tomorrow and Tomorrow 1931,Ja 25,VIII,1:1
Tomorrow and Tomorrow 1931,F 1,VIII,2:1
Wiser They Are, The 1931,Jl 7,31:1
Wild Waves 1932,Ja 24,VIII,3:3
Wild Waves 1932,F 20,11:4
Foreign Affairs 1932,Ap 14,25:5
Thousand Summers, A 1932,My 25,23:4
Chrysalis 1932,N 16,15:2
Goodbye Again 1932,D 29,16:4
Dream of Sganarelle, The 1933,O 17,26:5
School for Husbands, The 1933,O 17,26:5
Point Valaine 1934,O 30,IX,1:6
Point Valaine 1935,Ja 17,22:2
Point Valaine 1935,F 3,VIII,1:1
Ceiling Zero 1935,Ap 2,24:3
Ceiling Zero 1935,Ap 11,26:2
On Stage 1935,Jl 23,24:4
On Stage 1935,O 30,16:6
End of Summer 1936,Ja 31,17:1
End of Summer 1936,F 9,X,2:3
End of Summer 1936,F 18,26:4
Tovarich 1937,Ap 25,X,2:4
Perkins, Ray
Sunday Nights at Nine 1934,Mr 5,18:5
Perkins, Ray (Composer)
It's Up to You 1921,Mr 29,20:1
Spider, The 1927,Mr 23,29:1
Greenwich Village Follies 1928,Ap 10,32:2
Say When 1928,Je 27,29:3
Perkins, Ray (Lyricist)
Say When 1928,Je 27,29:3
Perkins, Shirley
Gondoliers, The 1963,Je 5,33:2
Perkins, Susan
Tiger Rag, The 1961,F 17,20:2
Perkins, Tom
Sweethearts 1947,Ja 22,31:2
Allegro 1947,O 11,10:2
Perkins, Walter
No Mother to Guide Her 1933,D 26,18:5
Perkinson, Coleridge-Taylor (Choreographer)
Billy 1969,Mr 24,56:1
Perkinson, Coleridge-Taylor (Composer)
Othello 1953,O 30,28:2
To Damascus 1961,F 15,40:2
Song of the Lusitanian Bogey, The 1968,Ja 3,52:1
God Is a (Guess What?) 1968,D 18,56:1
God Is a (Guess What?) 1968,D 29,II,1:1
Malcochon 1969,Ap 2,37:1
Contribution 1969,Ap 2,37:1
String 1969,Ap 2,37:1
Man Better Man 1969,Jl 3,22:1
Man Better Man 1969,Jl 13,II,3:6
Perkinson, Coleridge-Taylor (Lyricist)
God Is a (Guess What?) 1968,D 29,II,1:1
Perl, Adam (Miscellaneous)
No Place to Be Somebody 1969,My 5,53:3
Sambo 1969,D 22,42:1
Perl, Arnold (Miscellaneous)
Tevya and His Daughters 1957,S 17,38:2
Perl, Arnold (Playwright)
World of Sholom Aleichem, The 1953,S 12,13:2
World of Sholom Aleichem, The 1953,S 20,II,1:1
World of Sholom Aleichem, The 1955,Ja 12,22:4
Tevya and His Daughters 1957,S 17,38:2
Tevya and His Daughters 1957,S 29,II,1:1
Perl, Arnold (Producer)
World of Sholom Aleichem, The 1953,S 12,13:2
Best of Burlesque 1957,S 30,27:2
All That Fall 1957,O 8,41:2
Quare Fellow, The 1958,N 28,34:1
Perl, Gitta
No Strings 1942,Je 14,VIII,2:1
Perl, Lothar (Composer)
All for Love 1938,Ap 5,19:4
Two for Fun 1961,F 14,45:3

Perleno, Hilda
Messin' Around 1929,Ap 23,26:3
Bomboola 1929,Je 27,17:3
Hot Rhythm 1930,Ag 22,18:5
Yeah-Man 1932,My 27,27:3
Perlman, Max
Honeymoon in Israel, A 1962,O 15,33:5
Don't Worry Brother! 1963,O 14,35:2
Good Luck 1964,O 19,38:3
Hello Charlie 1965,O 25,47:2
It's Never Too Late for Happiness 1968,O 21,59:3
Oh What a Wedding! 1969,O 20,60:1
Perlman, Max (Director)
Honeymoon in Israel, A 1962,O 15,33:5
Don't Worry Brother! 1963,O 14,35:2
Good Luck 1964,O 19,38:3
Perlman, Max (Playwright)
Oh What a Wedding! 1969,O 20,60:1
Perlman, Murray
Ali Baba 1951,Mr 27,34:2
Perlman, William J (Playwright)
My Country 1926,Ag 1,VII,4:1
My Country 1926,Ag 10,19:1
My Country 1926,Ag 29,VII,1:1
Bottom of the Cup, The 1927,F 1,24:2
Broken Chain, The 1929,F 21,30:4
House of Remsen 1934,Ap 3,26:4
Perlman, William J (Producer)
Comic, The 1927,Ap 20,28:2
Perlmutter, Erwin
Laugh It Off 1934,Ap 5,24:2
Flair-Flair the Idol of Paree 1935,Mr 13,16:1
Perlmutter, Sholom (Playwright)
Abi Gezunt 1949,O 10,19:4
Perloff, J
Three Musketeers, The 1921,My 20,18:5
Perloff, Michael (Miscellaneous)
Hop, Signor! 1962,My 8,45:2
Blood Knot, The 1964,Mr 3,30:2
Perlowen, Ginny
Rumple 1957,N 7,42:2
Perlowin, Elizabeth
Dead End 1935,O 29,17:2
Perlowin, Gene
Twilight Walk 1951,S 25,25:4
Perlowin, Gene (Miscellaneous)
Moon for the Misbegotten, A 1957,My 3,21:2
Moby Dick 1962,N 29,45:1
To Broadway With Love 1964,Ap 30,28:6
Severed Head, A 1964,O 29,40:1
Roar of the Greasepaint-the Smell of the Crowd 1965,My 17,46:2
Girl in the Freudian Slip, The 1967,My 19,34:3
Permane, Constantin
Silks and Satins 1920,Jl 16,19:1
Permane, Henry
Music Box Revue 1924,D 2,23:3
Ramblers, The 1926,S 21,32:2
Permett, Dolores
Crucible, The 1958,Mr 17,21:1
Pernice, Sal
Baker Street 1965,F 17,36:1
Peroff, Ella
Dancing Mothers 1924,Ag 12,12:2
Perone, Guy
Make a Million 1958,O 24,39:2
Peronne, Fred
Sunny River 1941,D 5,28:2
Perot, Cynthea
Hotel Mouse, The 1922,Mr 14,11:3
Perott, Ruth
At Mrs Beam's 1937,Jl 27,24:2
Perovic, Slobodan
Who's Afraid of Virginia Woolf? 1968,Jl 4,13:1
Perr, Harvey (Playwright)
Collision Course; Jew! 1968,My 9,55:2
Perras, John (Miscellaneous)
Pictures in the Hallway 1959,D 28,19:1
Perrault, Georges
Ecole des Femmes, L' 1961,Ap 28,23:1
Perrault, Robert
Minstrel Boy, The 1948,O 15,28:2
Perrault, Serge
Baptiste 1952,N 13,34:2
Amphitryon 1952,N 21,21:2
Fourberies de Scapin, Les 1952,N 21,21:2
Hamlet 1952,D 2,39:1
Perret, Edith
Overcoat, The 1960,S 7,45:1
Perrey-Chappuis, Charles du (Playwright)
Frenesie 1938,Mr 27,X,2:1
Perri, Irene
She Shall Have Music 1959,Ja 23,18:4
Not While I'm Eating 1961,D 20,37:1
Perri, Rick
Wonderful World of Burlesque, The 1965,Ap 29,38:1
Perrie, Ernestine (Director)
Scrapbooks 1953,N 6,24:2
In April Once 1955,Mr 14,29:3
Thunder Rock 1956,F 27,18:1
Enchanted, The 1958,Ap 23,41:1
Beautiful Dreamer 1960,D 28,22:1

'errie, Ernestine (Director)—Cont
Worlds of Shakespeare, The 1963,D 5,58:1
'errie, Ernestine (Playwright)
Worlds of Shakespeare, The 1963,D 5,58:1
'errier, Francois
Shock Troops 1969,F 22,36:1
'errier, Jean
Napoleon Unique 1936,N 13,27:3
'errin, Adrian S (Choreographer)
Bunk of 1926 1926,F 17,12:3
Noble Rogue, A 1929,Ag 20,31:2
'errin, Adrian S (Director)
Noble Rogue, A 1929,Ag 20,31:2
'errin, Ceci
People vs Ranchman, The 1968,N 10,II,5:1
Perfect Party, The 1969,Mr 21,42:1
Electra 1969,Ag 8,14:1
'errin, Jacques
Shock Troops 1969,F 22,36:1
'errin, Marguerite
Cantatrice Chauve, La 1962,Ja 16,30:1
Huis Clos 1962,Ja 16,30:1
'errin, Marie
Elizabeth Sleeps Out 1936,Ap 21,27:6
'errin, Nat (Playwright)
Glory for All 1937,F 9,18:2
'errin, Sam (Playwright)
Are You With It? 1945,N 12,17:3
'errine, Mary
Pied Piper of Hamelin, The 1950,Ap 3,19:2
Macbeth 1959,Ag 1,9:2
'errins, Ford
Sonya's Search for the Christmas Star
  1929,D 14,24:6
'errins, Leslie
Insult; Dolle Hans 1930,My 4,XI,1:3
Insult 1930,S 16,30:2
Elizabeth of England 1931,O 18,VIII,1:3
'erron, Lawrence
Antony and Cleopatra 1947,N 27,49:2
'errone, James
Doctored Wife, The 1950,Jl 12,33:2
Son, The 1950,Ag 16,24:6
'erroni, Patsy
Diamond Lil 1948,N 30,33:2
Diamond Lil 1951,S 15,8:2
'errot, Francois (Director)
Diary of a Madman 1967,Mr 24,25:1
'errot, Irma
Amour Magicien, L' 1926,D 26,VII,2:1
Perry, Albert
Heartbreak House 1920,N 11,11:1
Heartbreak House 1920,N 21,VI,1:2
Liliom 1921,Ap 21,18:1
Cloister, The 1921,Je 6,16:3
Children of the Moon 1923,Ag 18,10:3
Saint Joan 1923,D 29,8:4
Ned McCobb's Daughter 1926,N 30,26:2
Seven Keys to Baldpate 1930,Ja 8,25:2
Perry, Albert (Miscellaneous)
Time for Bed 1969,Je 14,24:1
Take Me to Bed 1969,Je 14,24:1
Perry, Antoinette
Mister Pitt 1924,Ja 23,15:3
Minick 1924,S 25,20:1
Dunce Boy, The 1925,Ap 4,20:2
Engaged! or Cheviot's Choice 1925,Je 19,24:2
Caught 1925,O 6,31:2
Masque of Venice, The 1926,Mr 3,27:3
Ladder, The 1926,O 23,15:1
Electra 1927,D 2,20:6
Perry, Antoinette (Director)
Hotbed 1928,N 10,20:7
Strictly Dishonorable 1929,S 19,37:1
Strictly Dishonorable 1929,S 29,IX,1:1
Strictly Dishonorable 1929,D 17,29:2
Three Times the Hour 1931,Ag 26,15:5
Divorce Me, Dear 1931,O 7,29:2
Christopher Comes Across 1932,Je 1,19:2
Noble Prize, The 1933,Jl 4,16:4
Personal Appearance 1934,O 18,26:7
Ceiling Zero 1935,Ap 11,26:2
Now You've Done It 1937,Mr 6,10:4
Chalked Out 1937,Mr 26,24:2
Red Harvest 1937,Mr 31,29:2
Kiss the Boys Goodbye 1938,S 29,30:2
Lady in Waiting 1940,Mr 28,19:1
Out From Under 1940,My 6,13:2
Glamour Preferred 1940,N 16,13:2
Cuckoos on the Hearth 1941,S 17,26:2
Janie 1942,S 11,24:2
Pillar to Post 1943,D 11,11:2
Harvey 1944,N 2,23:2
Perry, Antoinette (Miscellaneous)
Ceiling Zero 1935,Ap 21,IX,1:1
Audition of the Apprentice Theatre 1939,Je 2,26:2
Perry, Antoinette (Playwright)
Lady in Waiting 1940,Mr 28,19:1
Perry, Barbara
Blue Butterfly, The 1929,F 17,29:3
Swan Song 1946,My 16,29:2
If the Shoe Fits 1946,D 6,29:4
Happy as Larry 1950,Ja 7,11:2
Rumple 1957,N 7,42:2

Perry, Douglas
Babes in Arms 1937,Ap 15,18:4
Help! Help! the Globolinks 1970,D 24,10:2
Amahl and the Night Visitors 1970,D 24,10:2
Perry, Elaine
Trojan Women, The 1941,Ap 9,32:5
Pillar to Post 1943,D 11,11:2
Perry, Elaine (Director)
Race of Hairy Men!, A 1965,Ap 30,42:1
Perry, Elaine (Producer)
Touchstone 1953,F 4,33:2
King of Hearts 1954,Ap 2,23:1
Anastasia 1954,D 30,13:1
Race of Hairy Men!, A 1965,Ap 30,42:1
How's the World Treating You? 1966,O 25,50:1
Perry, Elizabeth
Royal Gambit 1959,Mr 5,34:2
Here Be Dragons 1970,D 21,52:1
Perry, Flo
Luckee Girl 1928,S 17,28:6
Perry, Frank (Miscellaneous)
Party With Betty Comden and Adolph Green, A
  1958,D 24,2:7
Perry, Frank (Producer)
Pretender, The 1960,My 25,42:1
Perry, Fred
Zunguru 1938,Ag 3,14:5
Zunguru 1938,Ag 7,IX,8:2
Perry, Frederick
Nice People 1921,Mr 3,11:1
Gringo 1922,D 15,26:3
Dagmar 1923,Ja 23,18:2
Song and Dance Man, The 1924,Ja 1,21:2
Silence 1924,N 13,18:2
Stronger Than Love 1925,D 29,20:2
Half-Caste, The 1926,Mr 30,20:4
Saturday's Children 1927,Ja 27,13:1
In the Meantime 1930,D 7,IX,1:6
Midnight 1930,D 30,25:1
Marriage for Three 1931,N 12,30:5
Her Master's Voice 1933,O 24,24:3
Perry, Gertrude
Mrs Jimmie Thompson 1920,Mr 30,9:1
Penal Law 2010 1930,Ap 19,14:2
Perry, Harold R (Director)
Romeo and Juliet 1940,Ap 16,28:4
Perry, Herald (Scenic Designer)
Little Red Riding Hood 1948,Ja 12,15:3
Perry, Jack
Is Zat So? 1925,Ja 6,23:4
Perry, Jean
Prodigal Son, The 1965,My 21,19:1
Perry, John (Playwright)
Spring Meeting 1938,Je 19,IX,2:1
Spring Meeting 1938,D 9,30:4
Perry, John Bennett
Now Is the Time for all Good Men 1967,S 27,42:1
Month of Sundays 1968,S 17,50:1
Show Me Where the Good Times Are
  1970,Mr 6,32:1
Perry, Joseph
But Never Jam Today 1969,Ap 24,40:1
Perry, Kathryn
Blackbirds 1933,D 4,22:3
Perry, M J (Miscellaneous)
Dossier, The 1961,Ja 14,15:2
Perry, Margaret
Strictly Dishonorable 1929,D 17,29:2
Strictly Dishonorable 1931,Mr 11,23:5
After All 1931,D 4,28:4
Ceiling Zero 1935,Ap 11,26:2
Now You've Done It 1937,Mr 6,10:4
Worse Things Happen at Sea 1937,S 1,15:3
Greatest Show on Earth, The 1938,Ja 6,22:2
Perry, Margaret (Director)
Shop at Sly Corner, The 1949,Ja 19,35:2
Love Me Long 1949,N 8,34:5
Mr Barry's Etchings 1950,F 1,26:2
Perry, Mary
In His Arms 1924,O 14,23:1
Let Freedom Ring 1935,N 7,26:2
Prelude 1936,Ap 20,17:4
Bury the Dead 1936,Ap 20,17:4
Iron Men 1936,O 20,30:6
Susanna, Don't You Cry 1939,My 23,27:2
Comes the Revelation 1942,My 27,26:2
Last Stop 1944,S 6,17:2
Out West of Eighth 1951,S 21,20:3
Traveling Lady 1954,O 28,45:2
Uncle Vanya 1956,F 1,25:2
Uncle Vanya 1956,F 12,II,1:1
Midnight Caller, The 1958,Jl 2,25:1
Three Sisters, The 1959,S 22,46:1
Perry, Mitzi
My Dear Public 1943,S 10,28:1
What's Up 1943,N 12,24:6
Perry, Nettie
Policy Kings 1938,D 31,6:2
Perry, Nick
Winter Soldiers 1942,N 30,19:2
Perry, Peter (Producer)
Drunkard, The 1970,Ap 14,54:1

Perry, Peter J (Miscellaneous)
Red, White and Maddox 1969,Ja 27,27:1
Perry, Robert E
Devil's Host, The 1931,N 20,27:2
Crime Marches on 1935,O 24,19:1
Woman of Destiny, A 1936,Mr 3,25:2
It Can't Happen Here 1936,O 28,30:1
Years Between, The 1942,F 7,13:2
Othello 1943,O 20,18:1
Perry, Robert E (Director)
Dark of the Moon 1945,Mr 15,27:2
Devils Galore 1945,S 13,27:2
Young Man's Fancy, A 1947,Ap 30,33:2
Hold It! 1948,My 6,31:5
They Knew What They Wanted 1949,F 17,28:2
Perry, Rod
To Broadway With Love 1964,Ap 30,28:6
Leonard Sillman's New Faces of 1968
  1968,My 3,43:1
New Faces of 1968 1968,My 12,II,7:1
Perry, Sara
Launcelot and Elaine 1930,Mr 10,24:3
Bridal Wise 1932,My 31,15:5
Come What May 1934,My 16,23:4
So Many Paths 1934,D 7,26:5
Constant Wife, The 1935,Jl 3,20:2
Tobacco Road 1942,S 7,34:2
Tobacco Road 1943,S 6,21:3
Trio 1944,D 30,13:4
Perry, Shauneille
Goose, The 1960,Mr 16,44:1
Clandestine on the Morning Line 1961,O 31,28:1
Perry, Steve
Just for Love 1968,O 18,40:1
Perry, Tileston
Hamlet 1936,N 11,54:2
Shoemaker's Holiday, The 1938,Ja 3,17:2
Danton's Death 1938,N 3,26:2
Perry, Ty
At War With the Army 1949,Mr 9,32:2
Make a Million 1958,O 24,39:2
Perry, Wanda
We Never Learn 1928,Ja 24,26:1
Pershing, D'Vaughn
Blackouts of 1949 1949,S 7,39:2
Pershing, Francis Warren (Mrs)
Variations of 1940 1940,Ja 29,12:1
Pershon, Frederic
Nina Rosa 1930,My 31,19:3
Persip, Charles
Evening With Yves Montand, An 1959,S 23,45:1
Persky, Lester (Producer)
Mutilated, The 1966,F 23,42:1
Gnadiges Fraulein, The 1966,F 23,42:1
De Sade Illustrated 1969,My 13,42:4
Persoff, Nehemiah
Flies, The; Mouches, Les 1947,Ap 18,26:3
Galileo 1947,D 8,34:2
Sundown Beach 1948,S 8,37:1
Richard III 1949,F 9,33:2
Montserrat 1949,O 31,21:4
Peter Pan 1950,Ap 25,27:2
King Lear 1950,D 26,18:1
Peer Gynt 1951,Ja 29,15:2
Flahooley 1951,My 15,39:1
Mademoiselle Colombe 1954,Ja 7,26:1
Reclining Figure 1954,O 8,26:5
Tiger at the Gates 1955,O 4,40:1
Only in America 1959,N 20,35:1
Person, William (Musical Director)
Small Wonder 1948,S 16,33:5
Personette, Joan (Costume Designer)
New Hellzapoppin, The 1939,D 12,36:4
Two on the Aisle 1951,Jl 20,13:6
Persson, Frederic
Iolanthe 1931,Jl 14,21:5
H M S Pinafore 1931,Jl 28,17:6
Trial by Jury 1931,Jl 28,17:6
Iolanthe 1932,Ja 5,20:2
Yeoman of the Guard, The 1933,My 2,20:4
Trial by Jury 1933,My 9,20:3
H M S Pinafore 1933,My 9,20:3
Patience 1933,My 23,22:6
Yeomen of the Guard, The 1933,Ag 15,20:5
Her Man of Wax 1933,O 12,32:3
They Shall Not Die 1934,F 22,24:4
Iolanthe 1934,My 1,26:4
Sunny River 1941,D 5,28:2
H M S Pinafore 1942,Ja 22,12:2
Mikado, The 1942,F 4,22:2
Pirates of Penzance, The 1942,F 18,22:2
Iolanthe 1942,F 24,26:4
Gondoliers, The 1942,Mr 4,22:3
Would-Be Gentleman, The 1946,Ja 10,29:2
Years Ago 1946,D 4,44:2
Persson, Gene (Miscellaneous)
Slave, The 1964,D 17,51:1
Toilet, The 1964,D 17,51:1
Persson, Gene (Producer)
Journey to the Day 1963,N 12,49:1
Walk in Dark Places, A 1966,Ja 28,21:1
Better Luck Next Time 1966,Ja 28,21:1
Big Man 1966,My 20,41:1

Persson, Gene (Producer)—Cont

Duet for Three 1966,My 20,41:1
You're a Good Man, Charlie Brown 1967,Mr 8,51:1
Trial of Lee Harvey Oswald, The 1967,N 6,64:1
Sudden and Accidental Re-education of Horse
  Johnson, The 1968,D 19,63:1
Watering Place, The 1969,Mr 13,51:1

Pertwee, Jon
There's a Girl in My Soup 1967,O 19,58:1
There's a Girl in My Soup 1967,N 12,II,5:6

Pertwee, Michael (Playwright)
Come Across 1938,S 15,28:3

Pertwee, Roland (Playwright)
I Serve 1922,O 8,VI,1:7
Creaking Chair, The 1924,Jl 27,VII,1:8
Creaking Chair, The 1926,F 23,26:1
Interference 1927,F 20,VII,1:4
Interference 1927,F 27,VII,1:3
Interference 1927,O 19,24:3
Interference 1927,D 18,IX,1:1
Heat Wave 1931,F 18,14:6
Counsel's Opinion 1932,D 14,27:3
This Inconstancy 1933,Mr 25,13:6
This Inconstancy 1933,Ap 16,IX,1:3
Evening Dress Indispensable 1934,Mr 22,24:6
To Kill a Cat 1939,Jl 2,IX,1:6
Pink String and Sealing Wax 1943,S 19,II,1:5
Pink String and Sealing Wax 1957,S 6,13:1

Perutz, Leo (Playwright)
Journey to Pressburg, The 1931,Mr 8,VIII,2:7
Trip to Pressburg, A 1933,Mr 12,IX,2:7
Journey by Night 1935,Ap 7,IX,2:1
Journey by Night, A 1935,Ap 17,26:3
Tomorrow's a Holiday! 1935,D 31,10:2

Peruzzi, Michele
Republic, The 1970,Ap 28,49:1

Perven, Alice
Pas Sur La Bouche; Not on the Lips
  1929,Mr 26,34:3

Peryalis, Notis (Playwright)
Masks of Angels 1965,Ja 20,33:1

Perz, June (Miscellaneous)
Rat's Mass, A 1969,N 1,39:1

Pesacov, Bill
Nautical but Nice 1931,Ap 19,31:6

Pesek, Ladislav
Fiddler on the Roof 1968,F 22,36:2

Peshkin, Blanche
Boutique Fantasque, La 1929,D 28,10:6

Pesso, Paul
Mourners' Bench, The 1950,S 22,35:7

Petchey, Briain
Henry IV, Part I 1965,Je 30,42:1
Falstaff; Henry IV, Part II 1965,Jl 1,35:1
Julius Caesar 1965,Jl 2,18:1
Cherry Orchard, The 1965,Ag 2,17:2
Henry V 1966,Je 8,38:1
Henry VI 1966,Je 9,55:2
Twelfth Night 1966,Je 10,51:2
Richard III 1967,Je 14,43:1
Antony and Cleopatra 1967,Ag 2,25:1
Play by Aleksandr Solzhenitsyn, A 1970,O 18,94:1
Play by Aleksandr Solzhenitsyn, A 1970,O 25,II,1:3

Petek, Marie
Pirates of Penzance, The 1949,O 11,41:2
H M S Pinafore 1949,O 18,34:2
Trial by Jury 1949,O 18,34:2

Petell, Frank
Three Musketeers, The 1921,My 20,18:5

Peter, Eleanor Parke Custis
Faith of Our Fathers 1950,Ag 6,72:2

Peter, Frances
Delightful Season, A 1960,S 29,30:1
Sold to the Movies; Life Size 1970,Je 18,54:2
Sold to the Movies; Crossing the Gap
  1970,Je 18,54:2

Peter, Jon
Adding Machine, The 1970,D 5,40:1

Peter, Paul (Playwright)
Stevedore 1934,O 2,18:2

Peter, Rene (Playwright)
Naughty Cinderella 1925,N 10,23:6

Petera, Gordon
Sister Oakes 1949,Ap 25,19:4

Peterkin, Julia (Original Author)
Scarlet Sister Mary 1930,O 5,IX,4:6
Scarlet Sister Mary 1930,N 26,19:2

Peters, Anne
Idiot, The 1960,S 26,38:1
Emmanuel 1960,D 5,42:2

Peters, Bernadette
Penny Friend, The 1966,D 27,46:1
Johnny No-Trump 1967,O 9,60:2
Curley McDimple 1967,N 23,59:2
George M! 1968,Ap 11,48:1
Dames at Sea 1968,D 21,46:1
Dames at Sea 1969,Ja 5,II,1:3
Strada, La 1969,D 15,63:1

Peters, Brandon
Cave Girl, The 1920,Ag 19,12:2
John Ferguson 1921,My 24,20:1
Cloister, The 1921,Je 6,16:3
John Ferguson 1921,Je 21,20:2
March Hares 1921,Ag 12,8:3

Lady, The 1923,D 5,23:2
Strong, The 1924,F 27,15:3
Flame of Love 1924,Ap 22,19:2
Top Hole 1924,S 2,22:3
Buccaneer, The 1925,O 3,10:2
Creaking Chair, The 1926,F 23,26:1
Potash and Perlmutter, Detectives; Poisoned by
  Pictures 1926,S 1,27:3
Devil in the Cheese, The 1926,D 30,22:4
Window Panes 1927,F 22,22:2
As You Desire Me 1931,Ja 29,21:2
Cold in Sables 1931,D 24,20:7
Singapore 1932,N 15,24:2
They Shall Not Die 1934,F 22,24:4
Too Many Boats 1934,S 12,26:3
Woman of the Soil 1935,Mr 26,23:6
Jane Brady-Editor 1935,Jl 2,24:3
Noble Prize, The 1935,Jl 9,24:3
Curse You, Jack Dalton 1935,Jl 16,24:1
She Cried for the Moon 1935,Jl 23,24:3
Love on the Dole 1936,F 25,23:3
Fulton of Oak Falls 1937,Ja 2,15:3
Fulton of Oak Falls 1937,F 11,18:2
One Thing After Another 1937,D 29,17:2
Savonarola 1942,Ap 24,20:2
Malice Domestic 1942,Jl 21,22:1
Day Will Come, The 1944,S 8,17:2
Curious Savage, The 1950,O 25,44:3
Grey-Eyed People, The 1952,D 18,41:2

Peters, Brock
Mister Johnson 1956,Mr 30,11:1
King of the Dark Chamber 1961,F 10,21:1
King of the Dark Chamber 1961,Ap 9,II,1:1
Kwamina 1961,O 24,42:1
Caucasian Chalk Circle, The 1966,Mr 25,35:1

Peters, Charles
War Song, The 1928,S 25,29:3
Still Life 1936,D 1,31:1

Peters, Don
Wanhope Building, The 1947,F 11,36:5
Eastward in Eden 1947,N 19,33:2

Peters, Florence (Costume Designer)
Merry-Go-Rounders, The 1956,N 22,50:1

Peters, Frank
Spanish Love 1920,Ag 18,6:1
Twelfth Night 1921,N 1,17:1
Merchant of Venice, The 1921,N 22,17:1
Fashions for Men 1922,D 6,22:1
Cymbeline 1923,O 3,12:1
House of Shadows, The 1927,Ap 22,18:4
Banshee, The 1927,D 6,26:2
Yellow Jacket, The 1928,N 8,27:3
Falstaff 1928,D 26,14:2
King Lear 1930,D 26,18:2
Merchant of Venice, The 1931,N 17,31:1
Julius Caesar 1931,N 18,26:3
Hamlet 1931,N 19,26:6

Peters, Fred
Nellie Bly 1946,Ja 22,32:2

Peters, George
Whatever Goes Up 1935,N 26,28:2

Peters, George (Miscellaneous)
All in Love 1961,N 11,15:2

Peters, Gerald
Hostile Witness 1966,F 18,26:1

Peters, Glen
Emerald Slippers, The 1970,S 2,31:2

Peters, Gordon
Daughters of Atreus 1936,O 15,33:1
Straw Hat, The 1937,D 31,8:2
Comedy of Good and Evil, A 1938,Ap 8,16:3
Dance Night 1938,O 15,20:5
Criminals, The 1941,D 22,24:3
Pal Joey 1952,Ja 4,17:6
My 3 Angels 1956,F 4,24:2
Oscar Wilde 1957,Ap 20,21:3
Clerambard 1957,N 8,22:3
'Tis Pity She's a Whore 1958,D 6,21:1

Peters, Grace
Rollo's Wild Oat 1920,N 24,14:1

Peters, Holly
Engagement Baby, The 1970,My 22,40:1

Peters, Jeff
Wars of the Roses, The (Part II) 1970,Jl 3,15:1

Peters, Johanna
Yeomen of the Guard, The 1962,Jl 11,28:1

Peters, John
Henry IV, Part I 1955,S 22,34:2
Girl of the Golden West, The 1957,N 6,44:1
Crucible, The 1958,Mr 12,36:1
All the King's Men 1963,Jl 12,12:1

Peters, Kelly Jean
Crucible, The 1964,Ap 7,30:2
Midsummer Night's Dream, A 1964,Je 30,23:2
Giants' Dance, The 1964,N 17,48:2

Peters, Lauri
First Impressions 1959,Mr 20,28:1
Sound of Music, The 1959,N 17,40:2
Murderer Among Us, A 1964,Mr 26,43:1
Cradle Will Rock, The 1964,N 9,40:4
Twelfth Night 1968,Je 15,40:1
Master Builder, The 1968,Je 22,26:1
Merton of the Movies 1968,S 26,62:1

Peters, Lena
To Quito and Back 1937,O 7,30:4

Peters, Leonard
Man and Superman 1964,D 7,45:2

Peters, Michael
Billy 1969,Mr 24,56:1

Peters, Paul (Lyricist)
Parade 1935,My 21,22:2

Peters, Paul (Playwright)
Third Parade, The 1933,O 23,18:2
Stevedore 1934,Ap 19,33:2
Stevedore 1934,Ap 29,IX,1:1
Parade 1935,My 7,26:1
Parade 1935,My 12,X,2:5
Parade 1935,My 21,22:2
Parade 1935,My 26,XI,1:1
Stevedore 1949,F 23,30:2
Nat Turner 1960,N 7,46:3

Peters, Paul (Translator)
Mother, The 1935,N 20,26:3

Peters, Robert
Yeomen of the Guard, The 1964,Ag 3,16:1

Peters, Rollo
Mixed Marriage 1920,D 15,18:2
Varying Shore, The 1921,D 6,24:1
Malvaloca 1922,O 3,22:1
Romeo and Juliet 1923,Ja 25,16:1
Romeo and Juliet 1923,F 4,VII,1:1
Romeo and Juliet 1923,Ap 22,VII,1:1
Pelleas and Melisande 1923,D 5,23:2
Pelleas and Melisande 1923,D 16,IX,1:1
Antony and Cleopatra 1924,F 20,22:1
Antony and Cleopatra 1924,F 24,VII,1:1
Antony and Cleopatra 1924,Mr 2,VIII,1:1
Antony and Cleopatra 1924,Mr 9,VIII,1:1
Depths, The 1925,Ja 28,15:3
Stolen Fruit 1925,O 8,31:4
Stolen Fruit 1925,N 8,VIII,1:1
Taming of the Shrew, The 1925,D 19,14:1
Taming of the Shrew, The 1925,D 27,VII,1:1
Eskimo, The 1926,Je 20,VII,3:1
Trelawney of the 'Wells' 1927,F 1,24:4
Trelawney of the 'Wells' 1927,F 6,VII,1:1
Out of the Sea 1927,D 6,26:2
Diplomacy 1928,My 29,16:3
Diplomacy 1928,Je 3,VIII,1:1
Age of Innocence, The 1928,N 28,24:2
Arms and the Man 1929,Ag 13,23:4
Rivals, The 1930,Mr 14,24:4
Cafe 1930,Ag 29,11:1
Streets of New York, The 1931,O 7,29:1
Pillars of Society, The 1931,O 15,19:1

Peters, Rollo (Costume Designer)
Taming of the Shrew, The 1925,D 19,14:1

Peters, Rollo (Scenic Designer)
Prince and the Pauper, The 1920,N 7,VII,1:1
Prince and the Pauper, The 1920,N 21,VI,1:4
Romeo and Juliet 1923,F 4,VII,1:1
Romeo and Juliet 1923,Ap 22,VII,1:1
Antony and Cleopatra 1924,F 24,VII,1:1
Taming of the Shrew, The 1925,D 19,14:1
Diversion 1928,Ja 12,25:1
Streets of New York, The 1931,O 7,29:1
Pillars of Society, The 1931,O 15,19:1

Peters, Stephen
Incident at Vichy 1964,D 4,44:1
School for Scandal, The 1966,N 22,33:2
Picnic on the Battlefield 1967,S 9,25:2

Peters, Susan
Volpone 1967,Je 30,29:1

Peters, Val (Miscellaneous)
Cuban Thing, The 1968,S 25,36:2

Peters, Warde
Knickerbocker Holiday 1938,O 20,26:2

Peters, William
Revenger's Tragedy, The 1970,D 2,58:1

Peters Sisters
Harlem Cavalcade 1942,My 2,11:2
Artists and Models 1943,N 6,16:6

Petersen, David O
Route 1 1964,N 18,52:3

Petersen, Don (Playwright)
Does a Tiger Wear a Necktie? 1967,F 4,17:1
Does a Tiger Wear a Necktie? 1969,F 26,38:1
Does a Tiger Wear a Necktie? 1969,Mr 9,II,1:1
Does a Tiger Wear a Necktie? 1969,Mr 16,II,4:5

Petersen, Elsa
Mikado, The 1925,Ap 13,25:1

Petersen, Elza
Queen O' Hearts 1922,O 11,22:1

Petersen, Erika
I Dreamt I Dwelt in Bloomingdale's 1970,F 13,26:1

Peterson, Alan
Lend an Ear 1959,S 25,20:5
Joyful Noise, A 1966,D 16,57:1
Hallelujah, Baby! 1967,Ap 27,51:1
Mike Downstairs 1968,Ap 19,35:1

Peterson, Arleigh (Choreographer)
Shuffle Along 1952,My 9,20:5

Peterson, Arthur
Heartbreak House 1963,Je 8,14:2
Heartbreak House 1963,Je 28,24:1

Peterson, Caleb
Run, Little Chillun 1943,Ag 14,6:1
Peterson, Carol
Hamlet 1948,D 4,9:2
Shoemaker's Prodigious Wife, The 1949,Je 15,38:2
Peterson, Charles
Girl Trouble 1928,O 26,22:3
Peterson, Colleen
Hair 1970,Ja 13,39:1
Peterson, Curt
Madame Pompadour 1924,N 12,20:6
Peterson, Dorothy
Cobra 1924,Ap 23,24:1
Fall Guy, The 1925,Mr 11,19:1
Find Daddy 1926,Mr 9,21:3
Pomeroy's Past 1926,Ap 20,24:4
God Loves Us 1926,O 20,22:2
Dracula 1927,O 6,29:1
Subway Express 1929,S 25,34:3
Who'll Save the Plowboy? 1962,Ja 10,24:2
Love of Two Hours, The 1962,O 27,16:2
Little Eyolf 1964,Mr 17,31:1
Peterson, Ed (Lighting Director)
Ivory Branch, The 1956,My 25,27:1
Peterson, Elwood
In White America 1965,F 9,42:5
Peterson, Fern
Blind Mice 1930,O 16,28:2
Peterson, Florence
Mister Pitt 1924,Ja 23,15:3
Dawn 1924,N 25,27:1
Peterson, G F
It's the Valet 1933,D 15,25:4
Peterson, Gary (Miscellaneous)
Bernard Shaw Story, The 1965,N 19,31:1
Peterson, Harry
On Your Toes 1936,Ap 13,14:4
Peterson, James (Miscellaneous)
Ice Capades 1963,Ag 29,37:2
Ice Capades 1966,Je 2,50:2
Peterson, James (Musical Director)
Ice Capades 1962,Ag 30,34:1
Ice Capades 1966,Je 2,50:2
Peterson, Jon (Producer)
Local Stigmatic, The; Request Stop 1969,N 4,55:2
Local Stigmatic, The; Interview 1969,N 4,55:2
Local Stigmatic, The; That's All 1969,N 4,55:2
Local Stigmatic, The; That's Your Trouble 1969,N 4,55:2
Local Stigmatic, The; Trouble in the Works 1969,N 4,55:2
Local Stigmatic, The; Applicant 1969,N 4,55:2
Local Stigmatic, The; Last to Go 1969,N 4,55:2
Local Stigmatic, The 1969,N 4,55:2
Peterson, Karen
Not Herbert 1926,Ja 27,16:2
Women, The 1939,Ap 21,21:2
Peterson, Kurt
West Side Story 1968,Je 25,32:1
Dear World 1969,F 7,33:1
Dames at Sea 1970,S 24,60:1
Peterson, Lenka
Bathsheba 1947,Mr 27,40:2
Harvest of Years 1948,Ja 13,29:2
Sundown Beach 1948,S 8,37:1
Young and Fair, The 1948,N 23,35:2
Grass Harp, The 1952,Mr 28,26:2
Time of Your Life, The 1955,Ja 20,34:1
Time of Your Life, The 1955,Ja 30,II,1:1
Girls of Summer 1956,N 20,45:1
Look Homeward, Angel 1958,Ag 31,II,1:1
All the Way Home 1960,D 1,42:1
Peterson, Louis
Young American, A 1946,Ja 18,14:5
Our Lan' 1947,Ap 19,11:2
Our Lan' 1947,S 29,16:5
Peterson, Louis (Playwright)
Take a Giant Step 1953,O 4,II,1:1
Take a Giant Step 1956,S 26,30:1
Entertain a Ghost 1962,Ap 10,48:1
Peterson, Marjorie
Greenwich Village Follies 1922,S 13,18:2
Annie 1924,O 12,VIII,2:1
Annie Dear 1924,N 5,25:3
Earl Carroll's Vanities 1925,Jl 7,24:1
Countess Maritza 1926,Mr 30,20:3
Countess Maritza 1926,S 20,21:1
Kiss Me! 1927,Jl 22,17:1
Red Robe, The 1928,D 26,15:1
Perfumed Lady, The 1934,Mr 13,27:2
Creeping Fire 1935,Ja 17,22:3
Pre-Honeymoon 1936,My 1,19:4
Censored 1938,F 28,18:2
Pie in the Sky 1941,D 23,26:5
It's A Gift 1945,Mr 13,18:7
Great to Be Alive! 1950,Mr 24,28:2
Date With April, A 1953,Ap 16,36:2
Peterson, Milton A (Composer)
Tambourine 1925,D 30,10:2
Front Page Stuff 1926,D 29,24:4
Peterson, Milton A (Lyricist)
Front Page Stuff 1926,D 29,24:4

Peterson, Milton A (Playwright)
Front Page Stuff 1926,D 29,24:4
Peterson, Nat
LeMaire's Affairs 1927,Mr 29,22:4
Peterson, Nels (Lighting Director)
Desert Song, The 1946,Ja 9,20:2
Peterson, Otto (Playwright)
Lenz 1926,Ap 29,20:4
Peterson, Ruth
Second Comin', The 1931,D 9,32:4
Peterson, Sylvia
Cherry Blossoms 1927,Mr 29,22:3
Peterson, Thom (Costume Designer)
Dynamite Tonight 1967,Mr 16,52:2
Henry IV 1968,F 7,40:1
Peterson, Wally
Passage to India, A 1962,F 1,23:1
Dinner at Eight 1966,S 28,38:1
Peterson, Wally (Miscellaneous)
Painted Days, The 1961,Ap 7,24:1
Never Too Late 1962,N 28,42:1
Mating Dance 1965,N 4,58:1
Peterson, Walter
Duchess of Malfi, The 1946,O 16,35:2
Peterson, William (Scenic Designer)
Girl From Samos, The 1954,N 24,17:1
Petgen, Dorothea
Blessed Event 1932,F 13,23:2
School for Husbands, The 1933,O 17,26:5
Plumes in the Dust 1936,N 7,14:2
Petherbridge, Edward
Love for Love 1967,O 21,17:1
Dance of Death 1967,O 29,II,5:1
Love for Love 1967,O 30,59:1
Flea in Her Ear, A 1967,O 30,59:1
Petho
Nem Elhetek Muzsikaszo Nelkul 1928,D 30,VIII,4:4
Petina, Irra
Song of Norway 1944,Ag 22,20:2
Song of Norway 1944,Ag 27,II,1:1
Magdalena 1948,Jl 28,27:2
Magdalena 1948,S 21,31:2
Hit the Trail 1954,D 3,31:2
Candide 1956,D 3,40:2
Candide 1956,D 9,II,5:1
Anya 1965,N 30,48:1
Petit, Charles (Original Author)
Chee-Chee 1928,S 26,25:1
Petit, Michel
Lorenzaccio 1958,O 15,44:2
Petit, Roland (Director)
Zizi 1964,N 23,51:1
Petit, Roland (Playwright)
Zizi 1964,N 23,51:1
Petitjean, Simone
French Without Tears 1937,S 29,19:1
Petker, Boris
Dead Souls 1965,F 5,34:1
Kremlin Chimes 1965,F 25,23:1
Petley, Arthur
Vaudeville (Palace) 1931,Ag 3,15:7
Petley, Frank
Bird in Hand 1929,Ap 5,28:2
Good Companions, The 1931,O 2,31:1
Petraitis, Peter
Music in May 1929,Ap 2,29:1
Petrarca, George
Grass Harp, The 1953,Ap 28,32:2
Matty and the Moron and Madonna 1965,Mr 30,53:1
Petri, Carol
Applause 1970,Mr 31,35:1
Petri, Helene
Lady Detained, A 1935,Ja 10,23:3
Petri, Morgens (Scenic Designer)
Black Souls 1932,Mr 31,25:1
Petri, Roland (Director)
Ne Reveillez pas Madame 1970,O 24,29:5
Petri, Walter
Devil Within, The 1925,Mr 17,19:4
Jeweled Tree, The 1926,O 8,26:2
Petrides, Alex
Zorba 1968,N 18,58:1
Petrides, Avra
Love Me Little 1958,Ap 15,42:2
Golden Six, The 1958,O 27,31:2
Who's Afraid of Virginia Woolf? 1962,N 1,34:1
Young Marrieds Play Monopoly 1966,Mr 7,22:1
Petrie, Daniel
Kiss Them for Me 1945,Mr 21,27:2
Petrie, Daniel (Director)
Shadow of My Enemy, A 1957,D 12,35:4
Who'll Save the Plowboy? 1962,Ja 10,24:2
Morning Sun 1963,O 7,36:2
Princess Rebecca Birnbaum 1966,Mr 7,22:1
Suburban Tragedy 1966,Mr 7,22:1
Young Marrieds Play Monopoly 1966,Mr 7,22:1
Make Like a Dog 1966,Mr 7,22:1
Petrie, Frank
Game of Love and Death, The 1929,N 26,28:4
Petrie, George
Girl From Wyoming, The 1938,O 31,12:1

Petrie, George—Cont
Night Before Christmas, The 1941,Ap 11,25:2
Mr Big 1941,O 1,24:2
Cafe Crown 1942,Ja 24,12:5
Winged Victory 1943,N 22,24:1
Brighten the Corner 1945,D 13,33:2
Petrie, Gordon
Marigold 1930,O 9,23:1
Petrie, Hay
Road to Ruin 1937,F 12,26:2
Petrie, Valerie
Carolinian, The 1925,N 3,34:2
Petrie, Walter
Constant Sinner, The 1931,Ag 30,VIII,1:6
Constant Sinner, The 1931,S 15,30:1
Diamond Lil 1949,F 7,16:2
Diamond Lil 1951,S 15,8:2
Petrone, Susan
Age and Grace 1956,F 21,38:2
Petrov, Helen
Topaze 1931,F 17,29:1
Petrov, Mikhail
Aladdin and His Wonderful Lamp 1963,O 21,39:1
Petrov, S
Revisor; Inspector General, The 1935,F 18,19:6
Petrov, Viktor
Kremlin Chimes 1965,F 25,23:1
Petrova, Olga
White Peacock, The 1921,D 27,10:2
Hurricane 1923,D 26,13:4
Vaudeville (Hippodrome) 1925,O 20,29:2
What Do We Know 1927,D 24,8:1
Petrova, Olga (Playwright)
White Peacock, The 1921,D 27,10:2
Hurricane 1923,D 26,13:4
What Do We Know 1927,D 24,8:1
Petrow, Mischa (Costume Designer)
Corner of the Bed, A 1969,F 27,35:2
Rose 1969,O 29,30:1
Petrow, Mischa (Scenic Designer)
Corner of the Bed, A 1969,F 27,35:2
World of Mrs Solomon, The; Another Chance 1969,Je 4,37:1
World of Mrs Solomon, The; Second Mrs Aarons, The 1969,Je 4,37:1
Rose 1969,O 29,30:1
And I Met a Man 1970,Ap 11,20:3
Petrucelli, Rick
Last Pad, The 1970,D 8,61:1
Petrushka, Gina
Between Two Thieves 1960,F 12,23:1
Opening of a Window, The 1961,S 26,32:2
Petry, Else
Wiener Blut 1964,S 12,14:1
Petry, Gedda
Lady in the Dark 1941,Ja 24,14:2
Lady in the Dark 1941,S 3,26:6
Lady in the Dark 1943,Mr 1,14:2
Firebird of Florence 1945,Mr 23,13:4
Call on Kuprin, A 1961,My 26,29:3
Pett, Aaron
Clear All Wires! 1932,S 15,19:1
Petter, Edith (Choreographer)
Eisrevue 1969,O 23,55:1
Petter, Will (Director)
Eisrevue 1969,O 23,55:1
Petterson, John
Broken Hearts of Broadway 1944,Je 13,16:2
Pettersson, John
Nautical but Nice 1931,Ap 19,31:6
Pettes, Marie
Phoebe of Quality Street 1921,My 10,20:1
Main Street 1921,O 6,21:1
Springtime of Youth 1922,O 27,15:1
Artists and Models 1923,Ag 21,12:2
Pearl of Great Price, The 1926,N 2,34:3
Speakeasy 1927,S 27,30:1
Subway Express 1929,S 25,34:3
Amourette 1933,S 28,25:2
Pettet, Joanna
Chinese Prime Minister, The 1964,Ja 3,14:1
Poor Richard 1964,D 3,59:1
Pettett, Madeleine
Desire Under the Elms 1963,Ja 11,5:6
Pettie, Charles (Original Author)
Son of the Grand Eunuch 1937,Ja 15,17:8
Pettingell, Frank
Present From Margate, The 1933,D 15,28:1
Magnolia Street 1934,Mr 9,22:6
Touch Wood 1934,Jl 1,X,1:3
Black Eye, The 1935,N 10,IX,3:1
Susannah and the Elders 1937,N 21,XI,3:6
When We Are Married 1938,O 30,IX,1:2
Lifeline 1942,Jl 12,VIII,1:4
Arsenic and Old Lace 1943,Ja 1,26:5
Pettinger, Charles
Second Hurricane 1937,Ap 22,18:4
Pettis, Jack
Vaudeville (Palace) 1930,F 17,18:4
Pettis, Mary
Here Goes the Bride 1931,N 4,31:2
Pettit, Anne
Awhile to Work 1937,Mr 20,23:1

Pettit, Paul
Career Angel 1943,N 19,24:2
Pettit, Roberta
Dream Play 1926,Ja 21,18:2
Pettit, Wilfrid H (Playwright)
Nine Girls 1943,Ja 14,26:2
Pettus, Thomas
Malice in Wonderland 1953,D 17,51:3
Petty, Jane Reid (Producer)
Home Away From, A 1969,Ap 29,40:3
Petty, Margaret
Lulu Belle 1926,F 10,20:1
Goat Alley 1927,Ap 21,24:3
Pevney, Joseph
Battle Hymn 1936,My 23,12:1
Johnny Johnson 1936,N 20,26:3
World We Make, The 1939,N 21,19:1
World We Make, The 1939,D 3,IX,5:1
Horse Fever 1940,N 25,21:2
Native Son 1941,Mr 25,26:5
Lily of the Valley 1942,Ja 27,25:2
Counsellor-at-Law 1942,N 25,17:2
Home of the Brave 1945,D 28,13:2
Home of the Brave 1946,Ja 6,II,1:1
Pevney, Joseph (Director)
Press Time 1938,N 28,10:4
Let Freedom Sing 1942,O 6,18:2
Swan Song 1946,My 16,29:2
Peyrou, Pierre
Pique-Nique en Campagne 1969,My 1,50:1
Guernica 1969,My 1,50:1
Peyrou, Pierre (Director)
Pique-Nique en Campagne 1969,My 1,50:1
Guernica 1969,My 1,50:1
Peyton, Charles
Springtime of Youth 1922,O 27,15:1
Miracle, The 1924,Ja 16,17:1
Miracle, The 1924,Ag 19,9:1
Racket, The 1927,N 23,28:3
Aiglon, L' 1927,D 27,24:3
Red Rust 1929,D 18,31:1
Jefferson Davis 1936,F 19,17:2
Doctor Faustus 1937,Ja 9,21:2
Peyton, John
Theatre of the Soul 1942,Mr 21,13:5
Across the Board on Tomorrow Morning
1942,Mr 21,13:5
Peyton, Sara
Between Two Worlds 1934,O 26,24:2
Two on an Island 1940,Ja 23,17:2
New Life, A 1943,S 16,26:6
Pezet, A W
Shoot 1922,Je 8,14:2
Pezet, A W (Director)
Schoolgirl 1930,N 21,31:1
Hotel Alimony 1934,Ja 30,16:2
Pezet, A W (Playwright)
Schoolgirl 1930,N 2,VIII,3:5
Schoolgirl 1930,N 21,31:1
Hotel Alimony 1934,Ja 30,16:2
In Heaven and Earth 1936,Mr 27,24:8
Pfeiffer, Edward
On Your Toes 1954,O 12,24:4
Pfeiffer, Jack (Composer)
Vamp, The 1955,N 11,30:1
Pfeiffer, Jules (Producer)
Maid in the Ozarks 1946,Jl 16,20:3
Pfeiffer, P L
Magistrate, The 1959,My 14,30:6
Pfeil, Eugenia
Legend of Leonora, The 1926,My 1,10:1
Pfeiler, Max
Professor Bernhardi 1968,Mr 20,38:1
Konzert, Das 1968,Mr 25,52:1
Pfluger, Helmuth P
Upon My Soul 1927,Ap 22,19:1
Pfoutz, S F (Original Author)
Call Me by My Rightful Name 1961,F 1,31:1
Phalen, Robert
Birthday Party, The 1961,My 15,34:6
Caretaker, The 1963,N 25,23:2
Alchemist, The 1966,O 14,48:1
Yerma 1966,D 9,60:1
Galileo 1967,Ap 14,31:1
Tiger at the Gates 1968,Mr 1,30:1
Cyrano de Bergerac 1968,Ap 26,30:1
King Lear 1968,N 8,43:1
In the Matter of J Robert Oppenheimer
1969,Mr 7,28:1
Operation Sidewinder 1970,Mr 13,33:1
Beggar on Horseback 1970,My 15,47:2
Good Woman of Setzuan, The 1970,N 6,51:1
Phalon, Beverly
Growing Pains 1933,N 24,24:2
Body Beautiful, The 1935,N 1,24:3
Don't Look Now! 1936,N 4,41:3
All That Glitters 1938,Ja 20,18:2
Pharr, Kelsey
Big White Fog 1940,O 23,26:2
Belle Helene, La 1941,Jl 8,14:1
Me and Harry 1942,Ap 3,24:6
Memphis Bound 1945,My 25,23:2

Pharr, Walter
Rain or Shine 1928,F 10,26:3
Phauls, Laura
Nativity Play, The 1937,D 21,29:1
Phebe, Mlle
Greenwich Village Follies 1920,Ag 31,7:3
Pheffer, Phil
Iceman Cometh, The 1956,My 8,38:1
Phelan, Betty Anne
Gypsy Baron, The 1944,Je 15,17:3
Phelan, Frank
Leper, The 1970,Ap 24,40:1
Phelan, Katharine
Crime and Punishment 1935,Ja 23,20:3
Phelan, Kathy
Praise Of Folly 1954,F 24,23:2
Phelan, Martin (Scenic Designer)
Short Cut, The 1930,Ja 28,28:2
Phelan, Mary Lou
Young and Fair, The 1948,N 23,35:2
Phelan, Phil (Miscellaneous)
Macbeth 1969,N 21,51:1
Renard 1970,Mr 25,36:4
Only Jealousy of Emer, The 1970,Mr 25,36:4
Phelan, Tom
Midsummer Night's Dream, A 1963,Jl 1,19:2
Phelps, Don
Walk-Up 1961,F 24,24:1
Streets of New York, The 1963,O 30,47:1
Phelps, Eleanor
Queen Bee 1929,N 13,25:1
Six Characters in Search of an Author
1931,Ap 16,29:2
Steel 1931,N 19,26:5
Trick for Trick 1932,F 19,14:2
We the People 1933,Ja 23,9:5
Give Us This Day 1933,O 28,20:6
Bridal Quilt 1934,O 11,28:5
Seen But Not Heard 1936,S 18,19:2
Naughty-Naught '00 1937,Ja 25,23:2
Richard II 1937,S 16,28:2
Mr Big 1941,S 7,I,51:3
Mr Big 1941,O 1,24:2
Garden District; Something Unspoken
1958,Ja 8,23:4
Garden District; Suddenly Last Summer
1958,Ja 8,23:4
Garden District; Suddenly Last Summer
1958,Ja 19,II,1:1
Disenchanted, The 1958,D 4,53:4
Color of Darkness: An Evening in the World of
James Purdy; Cracks 1963,O 1,24:1
Phelps, Florine
Three Cheers 1928,O 16,28:1
Phelps, George
Laughing Woman, The 1936,Jl 8,14:7
Ghost of Elsinore, The 1949,Ap 16,10:2
Phelps, Harman
Man in Possession, The 1930,N 3,19:1
Phelps, Irene
Three Cheers 1928,O 16,28:1
Phelps, Jacks (Composer)
How Revolting! 1932,Mr 11,14:6
Phelps, John
Uncle Willie 1956,D 21,17:1
Phelps, Lyon (Lyricist)
Do You Know the Milky Way? 1961,O 17,45:1
Phelps, Mable
Star of Bengal 1929,S 26,27:2
Phelps, Pauline (Playwright)
Shavings 1920,F 17,18:1
Phelps, Robert (Miscellaneous)
Colette 1970,My 7,60:1
Phelps, Robert (Playwright)
Colette 1970,O 15,58:1
Phelps, Stowe
Call Me Madam 1950,O 13,25:1
Phelps, Tracey
One Is a Lonely Number 1964,Je 19,37:3
Phelps, William
Hearts Are Trumps! 1927,Ap 8,21:1
Sun and I, The 1937,F 27,9:5
Phelps Twins, The
Sketch Book 1929,Jl 2,33:5
Phenice, Izella
Professor Mamlock 1937,Ap 14,30:3
Phifer, Edward
Long Dream, The 1960,F 18,36:2
Philbrick, Will H
Whoopee 1928,D 5,34:3
Merry Widow, The 1931,S 8,39:1
One More Honeymoon 1934,Ap 2,13:5
O'Flynn, The 1934,D 28,24:1
Vagabond King, The 1943,Je 30,24:2
Philcox, Lester (Director)
One Is a Lonely Number 1964,Je 19,37:3
Philiber, John
Wooden Slipper, The 1934,Ja 4,16:3
Philip, John
Evening With Beatrice Lillie, An 1952,O 3,17:2
Evening With Beatrice Lillie, An 1952,O 12,II,1:1
Ziegfeld Follies 1957,Mr 2,19:2

Philipe, Gerard
Lorenzaccio 1958,O 15,44:2
Cid, Le 1958,O 31,35:2
Philipe, Gerard (Director)
Lorenzaccio 1958,O 15,44:2
Philipp, Adolf (Original Author)
Hotel Alimony 1934,Ja 30,16:2
Philipp, Adolf (Playwright)
Kultur 1933,S 27,24:3
Philippe, Pierre (Composer)
Jalousie du Barbouille, La; Jealousy of the
Barbouille, The 1958,My 7,43:1
Mariage Force, Le; Forced Wedding, The
1958,My 7,43:1
Sganarelle; Imaginary Cuckold, The 1958,My 7,43:1
Philippe, St John
Sherlock Holmes 1953,O 31,11:2
Philips, Andy (Lighting Director)
Beaux' Stratagem, The 1970,F 10,50:2
Philips, Anita (Playwright)
Touch of Brimstone, A 1935,S 23,20:1
Philips, Edwin
Wisdom Tooth, The 1926,F 16,22:2
Damn the Tears 1927,Ja 22,11:1
These Days 1928,N 13,36:2
Vikings, The 1930,My 13,27:3
Little Ol' Boy 1930,Ap 25,15:5
So Proudly We Hail 1936,S 23,28:4
Woman's a Fool-To Be Clever, A 1938,O 19,18:6
Unconquered, The 1940,F 14,25:2
First Crocus, The 1942,Ja 3,14:6
They Should Have Stood in Bed 1942,F 14,18:5
What Big Ears! 1942,Ap 21,18:5
Three's a Family 1943,My 6,24:2
Me and Juliet 1953,My 29,17:1
Philips, Elliot
Threepenny Opera, The 1955,S 21,38:1
Philips, Georgia
High Button Shoes 1955,Mr 12,10:6
Philips, Lee
Middle of the Night 1956,F 9,39:1
Middle of the Night 1956,F 19,II,1:1
U S A 1956,D 19,41:4
Philips, Leonora
Wisdom Tooth, The 1926,F 16,22:2
Philips, Mary
Old Soak, The 1922,Ag 23,14:5
Wisdom Tooth, The 1926,F 16,22:2
2 Girls Wanted 1926,S 10,25:3
Gambling 1929,Ag 27,31:2
Tavern, The 1930,My 20,32:1
Song and Dance Man, The 1930,Je 17,25:5
Oh, Promise Me 1930,N 25,31:1
House Beautiful, The 1931,Mr 13,20:4
Both Your Houses 1933,Mr 7,20:3
Both Your Houses 1933,My 23,22:2
All Good Americans 1933,D 6,29:2
Come What May 1934,My 16,23:4
Merrily We Roll Along 1934,O 1,14:1
Merrily We Roll Along 1934,O 7,IX,1:1
Touch of Brimstone, A 1935,S 23,20:1
Postman Always Rings Twice, The 1936,F 7,14:4
Postman Always Rings Twice, The 1936,F 26,17:2
Spring Thaw 1938,Mr 22,18:1
Chicken Every Sunday 1944,Ap 16,II,1:1
Philips, Minna
Go West, Young Man 1923,N 13,25:2
Philips, Nelson
King John 1960,Je 29,26:2
Philliber, John
Winterset 1935,S 26,19:2
High Tor 1937,Ja 11,15:2
Star-Wagon, The 1937,S 30,18:5
Missouri Legend 1938,S 20,27:2
Pastoral 1939,N 2,26:2
Two on an Island 1940,Ja 23,17:2
Lily of the Valley 1942,Ja 27,25:2
Mr Sycamore 1942,N 14,13:2
Phillipi, Henry
Spider, The 1927,Mr 23,29:1
Big Fight, The 1928,S 19,33:1
Phillips, Agatha
Pleasure Bound 1929,F 19,22:4
Phillips, Albert
Play, A 1925,F 11,19:2
Gypsy Fires 1925,D 8,28:3
American Tragedy, An 1926,O 12,31:2
Wasp's Nest, The 1927,O 26,26:3
Abraham Lincoln 1929,O 22,26:3
Launcelot and Elaine 1930,Mr 10,24:3
Abe Lincoln in Illinois 1938,O 4,20:1
Abe Lincoln in Illinois 1938,O 17,12:2
Phillips, Allen D
Bachelor Born 1938,Ag 17,23:1
Phillips, Anita (Playwright)
All Bow Down 1935,Ag 6,20:4
Phillips, Barbara-Mae (Miscellaneous)
Great Career, A 1968,D 30,25:1
Evening for Merlin Finch, An 1968,D 30,25:1
Operation Sidewinder 1970,Mr 13,33:1
Good Woman of Setzuan, The 1970,N 6,51:1
Phillips, Barney
Meet the People 1940,D 26,22:2

hillips, Carole M (Miscellaneous)
Ivory Branch, The 1956,My 25,27:1
hillips, Clyde
Frugal Noon 1964,My 23,15:2
Acid Wine 1964,My 23,15:2
hillips, Darius V (Producer)
Silhouettes 1969,S 9,41:1
hillips, David
Letter to the Times, A 1966,D 5,63:1
hillips, David Graham (Original Author)
Fall and Rise of Susan Lenox, The 1920,Je 11,11:2
hillips, Diane
Coco 1969,D 19,66:1
hillips, Donald K
Betty Behave 1927,Mr 9,28:4
Zuleika 1928,Mr 7,28:7
hillips, Donald K (Composer)
Zuleika 1928,Mr 7,28:7
hillips, Eddie
Miss Liberty 1949,Jl 16,6:5
Guys and Dolls 1950,N 25,11:2
Damn Yankees 1955,My 6,17:1
New Girl in Town 1957,My 15,40:1
Oh, Kay! 1960,Ap 18,37:2
Tenderloin 1960,O 18,47:2
Guys and Dolls 1966,Je 9,55:2
Show Boat 1966,Jl 20,48:1
hillips, Edis
Well of Romance, The 1930,N 8,21:2
hillips, Edwin
Farmer's Wife, The 1924,O 10,22:3
Four Walls 1927,S 20,33:1
Henry V 1928,Mr 16,26:2
Courage 1928,O 9,34:2
Those We Love 1930,F 20,22:2
Fly Away Home 1935,Ja 16,20:4
Searching for the Sun 1936,F 20,22:6
Sunrise at Campobello 1958,Ja 31,25:1
Phillips, Ferman
Our Lan' 1947,S 29,16:5
Sojourner Truth 1948,Ap 22,35:2
Phillips, Frank
Journeyman 1938,Ja 31,14:2
Phillips, Garry
Eastward in Eden 1956,Ap 18,25:4
Romeo and Juliet 1957,Je 28,30:2
Time of the Cuckoo, The 1958,O 28,40:2
Phillips, George (Scenic Designer)
Professor Mamlock 1937,Ap 14,30:3
Phillips, Gerald
Cradle Snatchers 1925,S 8,28:2
Phillips, Gerard
Mirrors 1928,Ja 19,17:1
Phillips, Guy
King Can Do No Wrong, The 1927,N 17,28:4
Sign of the Leopard 1928,D 12,34:4
Phillips, H I (Lyricist)
Ziegfeld Follies 1934,Ja 5,24:3
Phillips, H I (Playwright)
Greenwich Village Follies 1921,S 1,18:3
Ziegfeld Follies 1934,Ja 5,24:3
Life Begins at 8:40 1934,Ag 28,24:2
Calling All Stars 1934,N 22,26:1
Calling All Stars 1934,D 14,28:2
Thumbs Up! 1934,D 28,24:1
Michael Todd's Peep Show 1950,Je 29,37:2
Phillips, Hamilton
Half Moon Inn 1925,Mr 10,14:1
Howdy King 1926,D 14,24:4
Phillips, Harry (Costume Designer)
Five Queens 1963,S 11,46:2
Phillips, Helen
Show Boat 1954,My 6,44:1
Phillips, Howard
Orestes 1926,Je 20,II,3:6
Electra 1927,D 2,20:6
Patriarch, The 1929,N 26,28:5
Last Mile, The 1930,F 14,21:2
Hilda Cassidy 1933,My 5,18:3
Phillips, Irving (Playwright)
Rumple 1957,N 7,42:2
Phillips, James
Du Barry 1932,N 23,15:2
Knickerbocker Holiday 1938,O 20,26:2
Louisiana Purchase 1940,My 29,19:2
Viva O'Brien 1941,O 10,27:2
Time, Place and the Girl, The 1942,O 22,24:3
Phillips, Jason (Scenic Designer)
Tango 1969,Ja 20,33:1
Gondoliers, The 1969,My 10,35:1
Slow Dance on the Killing Ground
1970,My 14,43:1
Phillips, Joe
Vaudeville (Palace) 1926,O 26,24:2
Broadway Nights 1929,Je 23,VIII,2:4
Broadway Nights 1929,Jl 16,23:2
Phillips, Juliette
Dragon, The 1929,Mr 26,34:2
Phillips, June
Confederacy, The 1958,Jl 3,20:1
Phillips, L C
Broadway Shadows 1930,Ap 1,34:6
Saluta 1934,Ag 29,13:4

Phillips, Lee
Mademoiselle Colombe 1954,Ja 7,26:1
Phillips, Lee (Miscellaneous)
Trial of Dmitri Karamazov, The 1958,Ja 28,30:1
Phillips, Leslie
Accounting for Love 1954,D 2,37:6
Phillips, Lorraine
Utopia, Limited; Flowers of Progress, The
1957,F 27,21:1
Mikado, The 1957,Ap 24,28:2
Pirates of Penzance, The 1957,My 8,43:1
Yeomen of the Guard, The 1957,My 22,28:3
Gondoliers, The 1957,My 29,34:2
From Here to There; Real Strange One, A
1958,Ap 24,37:3
Phillips, Mable
Nine Till Six 1936,Mr 14,10:3
Phillips, Madelyn
Hamlet 1936,N 11,54:2
Phillips, Marcy
Most Happy Fella, The 1966,My 12,55:1
Phillips, Margaret
Proof Thro' the Night 1942,D 26,14:2
Late George Apley, The 1944,O 20,16:4
Late George Apley, The 1944,N 22,26:2
Late George Apley, The 1944,D 3,II,1:1
Another Part of the Forest 1946,N 21,42:2
Another Part of the Forest 1946,D 1,II,1:1
Summer and Smoke 1948,O 7,33:2
Summer and Smoke 1948,O 17,II,1:1
Heiress, The 1950,F 9,34:2
Second Threshold 1951,Ja 3,23:2
Second Threshold 1951,Ja 14,II,1:1
Merchant of Venice, The 1953,Mr 5,20:2
Fallen Angels 1956,Ja 18,27:1
Lady's Not for Burning, The 1957,F 22,26:2
Prometheus Bound 1957,Ag 9,11:6
Under the Sycamore Tree 1960,Mr 8,37:2
Twelfth Night 1960,Je 9,29:4
Ginger Man, The 1963,N 22,42:1
Richard III 1964,Je 12,44:2
Hamlet 1964,Jl 4,9:1
Mourning Becomes Electra 1969,S 7,II,1:2
Phillips, Mario
Hotel Mouse, The 1922,Mr 14,11:3
Phillips, Marjorie
Five O'Clock Girl, The 1927,O 11,26:3
Rivals, The 1969,O 18,37:1
Phillips, Mary
Nerves 1924,S 2,22:2
One of the Family 1925,D 23,22:3
Five O'Clock Girl, The 1927,O 11,26:3
Skyrocket, The 1929,Ja 12,14:7
House Beautiful, The 1931,Mr 22,VIII,1:1
Black Sheep 1932,O 14,22:6
Remember the Day 1935,Jl 9,24:3
All Bow Down 1935,Ag 6,20:4
Chicken Every Sunday 1944,Ap 6,27:2
Phillips, Michael (Scenic Designer)
H M S Pinafore 1969,D 8,61:2
Phillips, Minna
Mrs Jimmie Thompson 1920,Mr 30,9:1
We Girls 1921,N 10,26:3
Captive, The 1926,S 30,23:1
Love Is Like That 1927,Ap 19,24:1
Month in the Country, A 1930,Mr 18,30:5
After All 1931,D 4,28:4
Too True to Be Good 1932,Mr 1,19:2
Too True to Be Good 1932,Ap 5,27:5
Autumn Crocus 1932,N 21,20:2
Personal Appearance 1934,O 18,26:7
Love From a Stranger 1936,S 30,28:1
Merchant of Yonkers, The 1938,D 29,14:2
Male Animal, The 1940,Ja 10,17:2
Phillips, Miriam
Heartbreak House 1935,Jl 23,24:3
Arms and the Man 1937,Jl 20,19:3
House Remembered, A 1957,F 7,20:2
Waltz of the Toreadors, The 1958,Mr 5,37:1
Hamlet of Stepney Green 1958,N 14,21:1
Legend of Lizzie, The 1959,F 10,39:1
Anniversary, The 1961,Ap 21,26:2
Wedding, The 1961,Ap 21,26:2
Caucasian Chalk Circle, The 1961,N 1,35:1
Wretched the Lionhearted 1962,S 13,31:2
Anvil, The 1962,O 31,33:3
Lion in Love, The 1963,Ap 26,28:3
Phaedra 1967,My 22,50:2
Phillips, Miriam (Director)
Emperor Jones, The 1945,Ja 17,18:4
Phillips, Murray (Director)
Tragic 18 1926,O 11,18:2
Blue Jeans 1933,Ap 9,31:5
Fly by Night 1933,Je 3,16:2
Phillips, Murray (Miscellaneous)
Bare Facts 1926,Jl 19,13:3
Tragic 18 1926,O 11,18:2
Phillips, Murray (Producer)
One Glorious Hour 1927,Ap 15,27:2
Kempy 1927,My 12,25:2
Kempy 1927,My 22,VIII,1:1
Lombardi, Ltd 1927,Je 7,27:3
Woman of Bronze, The 1927,Je 16,25:4

Phillips, Murray (Producer)—Cont
Madame X 1927,Jl 7,29:3
Mister Romeo 1927,S 6,35:3
Happy 1927,D 6,26:3
Lady Dedlock 1929,Ja 1,61:2
Mystery Square 1929,Ap 5,28:3
Freddy 1929,Jl 17,23:4
What a Question 1930,F 23,VIII,2:5
I Want My Wife 1930,Mr 21,30:7
Back Fire 1932,Je 14,26:3
Phillips, Nancie
Leonard Sillman's New Faces of 1968
1968,My 3,43:1
Phillips, Nelson
Tempest, The 1962,Je 22,14:1
Troilus and Cressida 1963,Je 19,40:2
Comedy of Errors, The 1963,Je 21,35:3
Royal Hunt of the Sun, The 1965,O 27,36:2
Birds, The 1966,Jl 1,40:1
Death of the Well-Loved Boy, The
1967,My 16,48:1
Phillips, Norma
Love's Call 1925,S 11,20:1
Phillips, Norman
George White's Scandals 1925,Je 23,24:2
Vaudeville (Palace) 1926,O 19,27:5
Phillips, Norman (Mrs)
George White's Scandals 1925,Je 23,24:2
Phillips, Owen (Director)
Blithe Spirit 1946,Je 5,17:3
Phillips, P
Journey by Night, A 1935,Ap 17,26:3
Phillips, Paul (Miscellaneous)
Thorntons, The 1956,F 15,26:1
Shadow and Substance 1956,Mr 14,38:1
Take Her, She's Mine 1961,D 22,19:1
Phillips, Paul J (Lighting Director)
Hasty Heart, The 1959,S 15,45:2
Phillips, Peggy
Yeah-Man 1932,My 27,27:3
Phillips, Peggy (Playwright)
Listen Professor! 1943,D 23,22:1
Phillips, R Hart (Playwright)
Is It Murder? 1951,Je 3,54:5
Phillips, Randolph
Oh, Hector! 1929,Mr 6,33:2
Phillips, Redmond
Potting Shed, The 1958,Mr 16,II,3:1
Hamlet 1961,Ap 12,46:1
Phillips, Rufus (Director)
Lady Has a Heart, The 1937,S 27,24:1
Ringside Seat 1938,N 23,24:5
Phillips, Rufus (Miscellaneous)
Lady Has a Heart, The 1937,S 27,24:1
Phillips, Rufus (Producer)
Lady Has a Heart, The 1937,S 27,24:1
Lady Has a Heart, The 1937,O 3,XI,1:1
Ringside Seat 1938,N 23,24:5
Phillips, Ruth
Crucible, The 1958,Mr 17,21:1
Phillips, Sidney (Producer)
Blessed Event 1932,F 13,23:2
Girls in Uniform 1932,D 31,10:3
Phillips, Stanley
Lifeline 1942,D 1,20:3
Milky Way, The 1943,Je 10,17:2
Boy Meets Girl 1943,Je 23,15:5
Victory Belles 1943,O 27,26:3
Cherry Orchard, The 1944,Ja 26,22:1
Armor of Light 1950,F 24,26:4
Phillips, Stanley (Director)
What's Up 1953,O 28,37:2
Darwin's Theories 1960,O 19,53:2
Phillips, Stephen (Playwright)
Paolo and Francesca 1924,D 3,24:2
Paolo and Francesca 1924,D 7,VIII,5:1
Paolo and Francesca 1929,Ap 2,28:2
Phillips, Steven
Wedding in Japan 1957,Mr 12,37:7
Phillips, Stevenson
Spots of the Leopard, The 1963,S 25,38:1
Phillips, Terence
Hamlet 1959,S 11,21:4
Phillips, Teri
Hang Down Your Head and Die 1964,O 19,38:1
Phillips, Theodore J Jr
That's That 1924,Ap 30,19:2
Hoot Mon, or Clans Across the Sea 1927,My 8,29:4
Phillips, Thomas
Music Hall Varieties 1932,N 23,15:3
Phillips, Vinnie
Tobacco Road 1942,S 7,34:2
Tobacco Road 1943,S 6,21:3
Phillips, Wendell Jr
Saturday Night 1968,F 26,43:1
Phillips, Wendell K
Sailors of Cattaro 1934,D 11,28:4
Till the Day I Die 1935,Mr 27,24:5
Mother Sings 1935,N 13,24:1
Case of Clyde Griffiths 1936,Mr 14,10:4
Many Mansions 1937,O 28,28:6
Abe Lincoln in Illinois 1938,O 17,12:2
Fifth Column, The 1940,Mr 7,18:2
Fifth Column, The 1940,Mr 17,X,1:1

Phillips, Wendell K—Cont
Comes the Revelation 1942,My 27,26:2
Yours, A Lincoln 1942,Jl 10,12:3
R U R 1942,D 4,30:2
Petrified Forest, The 1943,N 2,30:6
South Pacific 1943,D 30,11:2
Rosmersholm 1946,N 23,11:5
Anne of the Thousand Days 1948,D 9,49:2
Small Hours, The 1951,F 16,22:1
Solid Gold Cadillac, The 1953,N 6,24:2
Love Nest, The 1963,Ja 28,7:6
Investigation, The 1966,O 5,40:1
Winterset 1968,Jl 23,28:2
Phillips, Wendell K (Director)
War President 1944,Ap 25,17:3
Rosmersholm 1946,N 23,11:5
Phillips, Wendell K (Scenic Designer)
Ghost Bereft 1933,F 1,13:5
Black Diamond 1933,F 24,12:2
Phillips, William
Wrong Number 1934,Mr 14,23:6
Jackson White 1935,Ap 22,14:6
Lightnin' 1938,S 16,17:2
Phillipson, Charlotte (Director)
39 Steps 1938,Mr 12,13:1
Phillis, Pat
Lonesome West, The 1936,Je 30,15:1
Phillpotts, Adelaide (Playwright)
Yellow Sands 1926,N 21,VIII,4:1
Yellow Sands 1927,S 12,29:3
Yellow Sands 1927,S 18,VII,1:1
My Lady's Mill 1928,Jl 22,VII,1:3
Good Old Days, The 1935,F 19,27:3
Phillpotts, Eden (Playwright)
Shadow, The 1922,Ap 25,14:2
Farmer's Wife, The 1924,Mr 16,VIII,1:7
Farmer's Wife, The 1924,O 10,22:3
Devonshire Cream 1924,D 28,VII,2:2
Yellow Sands 1926,N 21,VIII,4:1
Yellow Sands 1927,S 12,29:3
Yellow Sands 1927,S 18,VII,1:1
My Lady's Mill 1928,Jl 22,VII,1:3
Runaways, The 1928,D 2,X,4:1
Jane's Legacy 1930,D 17,30:4
Good Old Days, The 1935,F 19,27:3
Jane's Legacy 1935,Ag 13,20:3
Courtin' Time 1951,Je 14,30:2
Phillpotts, Eden (Producer)
Jane's Legacy 1930,D 17,30:4
Phills, Samuel
Mister Johnson 1956,Mr 30,11:1
Philson, Betty
Sweet River 1936,O 29,30:2
Phinney, William
Song and Dance Man, The 1924,Ja 1,21:2
Clean Beds 1939,My 26,21:2
Phipps, Jennifer
Measure for Measure 1969,Je 13,41:3
Phipps, Leslie
Sweet River 1936,O 29,30:2
Phipps, Roger
Flame of Love 1924,Ap 22,19:2
Phipps, Sally
Once in a Lifetime 1930,S 7,IX,2:4
Once in a Lifetime 1930,S 25,22:3
Knock on Wood 1935,My 29,16:2
Phipps, Thomas W (Playwright)
Four Winds 1957,S 26,21:2
Phite, William
Merry Widow, The 1929,D 3,29:1
Phocas, Antonios (Costume Designer)
Electra 1952,N 20,38:2
Oedipus Tyrannus 1952,N 25,35:2
Physioc, Joseph (Scenic Designer)
Dracula 1927,O 6,29:1
Philadelphia 1929,S 17,34:5
Kansas City Kitty 1929,S 26,27:4
Piacentini, Anne
Greenwillow 1970,D 8,60:1
Piacentini, Vincent Jr (Scenic Designer)
Devils, The 1963,N 5,25:1
Vida es Sueno, La 1964,Mr 18,49:1
Life Is a Dream 1964,Mr 20,24:1
Piaf, Edith
Untitled-Revue 1947,N 23,II,1:1
Petite Lili, La 1951,Mr 11,7:1
Piane, Carlo Delle
Rugantino 1964,F 7,34:1
Piani, George
Lucky Sam McCarver 1925,O 22,22:1
Piat, Jean
Bourgeois Gentilhomme, Le 1955,O 26,26:1
Bourgeois Gentilhomme, Le 1955,O 30,II,1:1
Arlequin Poli par l'Amour 1955,N 9,40:1
Barbier de Seville, Le 1955,N 9,40:1
Troupe Du Roi, La 1970,F 4,38:1
Amphitryon 1970,F 4,38:1
Troupe Du Roi, La 1970,F 4,38:1
Piatov, Sascha
As You Were 1920,Ja 28,22:3
Vaudeville (Palace) 1923,Ja 23,18:2
Piatov and Mlle Natalie
Good Times 1920,Ag 10,10:1

Piazza, Ben
Winesburg, Ohio 1958,F 6,22:2
Kataki 1959,Ap 10,24:1
Second String, A 1960,Ap 14,36:2
American Dream, The 1961,Ja 25,28:1
I Am a Camera 1961,Jl 10,26:1
Zoo Story, The 1961,Jl 10,26:1
Endgame 1962,F 12,27:1
Fun Couple, The 1962,O 27,15:2
Zoo Story, The 1965,Je 9,42:3
Krapp's Last Tape 1965,Je 9,42:3
Song of the Grasshopper 1967,S 29,52:2
Death of Bessie Smith, The 1968,O 3,55:1
Zoo Story, The 1968,O 11,41:1
Piazza, Ben (Playwright)
Khaki Blue 1969,Mr 27,54:2
Lime Green 1969,Mr 27,54:2
Piazza, Frank (Lighting Director)
Bad Place to Get Your Head, A 1970,Jl 16,38:1
Bead-Tangle 1970,Jl 16,38:1
Piazza, Marguerite
Gypsy Baron, The 1944,N 15,20:3
Rape of Lucretia, The 1948,D 30,24:2
Happy as Larry 1950,Ja 7,11:2
Piazza, Rita
Walk Into My Parlor 1941,N 20,38:2
Picard, Andre (Original Author)
Man in Dress Clothes, The 1937,Ag 24,24:4
Picard, Andre (Playwright)
Kiki 1921,N 30,13:1
Red Poppy, The 1922,D 21,18:2
Marriage of Fredaine, The 1924,Mr 2,VIII,1:3
Man in Evening Clothes, The 1924,D 6,13:4
Kiss of Importance, A 1930,D 2,31:3
Picard, Daphne
Girl From Wyoming, The 1938,O 31,12:1
Picard, Frank
From Morn Till Midnight 1948,D 7,41:6
Butter and Egg Man, The 1949,Ap 29,27:1
Picasso, Pablo (Playwright)
Desire Caught by the Tail 1950,F 18,9:8
Picasso, Sara
Coney Island Play 1970,O 31,34:2
Picciano, Eugene
Macbeth 1955,O 8,12:6
Piccoli
Theatre of the Piccoli 1940,Mr 22,22:2
Piccoli, Michel
Shock Troops 1969,F 22,36:1
Piccolo Teatro di Milano
Servant of Two Masters, The 1960,F 29,31:5
Picconi, G
Piacere Dell 'Onesta, Il 1929,Mr 25,33:1
Pichel, Irving
Lazarus Laughed 1928,Ap 10,33:1
Pichette, Joseph
West Side Story 1968,Je 25,32:1
Triumph of Robert Emmet, The 1969,My 8,54:1
Haunted Host, The 1969,O 28,43:1
Pichette, Louise
Malade Imaginaire, Le; Imaginary Invalid, The
1958,Ap 30,28:2
Pichler, Maria
From Vienna 1939,Je 21,26:2
Reunion in New York 1940,F 22,28:4
Pichon, Gerard
Three Musketeers, The 1968,Je 26,43:1
Piciano, Eugene
Girl of the Golden West, The 1957,N 6,44:1
Pickard, Alison
Much Ado About Nothing 1929,N 17,30:4
Pickard, Helena
Country Wife, The 1936,D 2,34:1
Time and the Conways 1938,Ja 4,19:2
Flare Path 1942,D 24,20:2
Pickard, John
Yr Obedient Husband 1938,Ja 11,26:5
Pickard, Margery
Laburnum Grove 1935,Ja 15,23:5
Pickens, Jane
Ziegfeld Follies 1936,S 15,37:1
Boys and Girls Together 1940,S 5,28:6
Boys and Girls Together 1940,O 2,19:2
Beggar's Opera, The 1941,Ag 12,14:6
Regina 1949,N 1,32:2
Music in the Air 1951,O 9,32:2
Music in the Air 1951,O 21,II,1:1
Regina 1952,Je 2,25:4
Pickens Sisters
Thumbs Up! 1934,D 28,24:1
Pickering, Donald
School for Scandal, The 1963,Ja 26,5:2
Conduct Unbecoming 1969,Jl 26,14:1
Conduct Unbecoming 1970,O 13,50:1
Pickering, Silas 2d
Measure for Measure 1966,Jl 14,27:1
Pickert, Rollo
Babes in Arms 1937,Ap 15,18:4
Pickert, Rolly
Mr Winkle's Holliday 1946,Je 24,27:6
Pickett, Albert
Philoctetes 1964,Ag 19,29:1

Pickett, George (Playwright)
Silent House, The 1927,Jl 3,VII,1:4
Silent House, The 1928,F 8,28:5
Silent House, The 1932,N 9,28:3
Pickett, Jack
Dinner at Eight 1966,S 28,38:1
Pickett, William
Tall Kentuckian, The 1953,Je 17,30:1
Pickford, Mary
Coquette 1935,My 22,23:4
Pickles, Ann
Gondoliers, The 1957,My 29,34:2
Pickles, Christine
Measure for Measure 1960,Jl 27,33:1
Taming of the Shrew, The 1960,Ag 20,17:1
Duchess of Malfi, The 1962,Mr 5,27:1
Right You Are (If You Think You Are)
1964,Mr 5,37:1
Tavern, The 1964,Mr 6,39:2
Scapin 1964,Mr 10,43:1
Impromptu at Versailles 1964,Mr 10,43:1
Severed Head, A 1964,O 29,40:1
War and Peace 1965,Ja 12,32:1
White Devil, The 1965,D 7,56:1
War and Peace 1967,Mr 22,42:1
Misanthrope, The 1968,O 10,59:1
Misanthrope, The 1968,O 20,II,1:1
Cock-A-Doodle Dandy 1969,Ja 21,40:1
Hamlet 1969,Mr 4,34:1
Pickman, Daisy
Bachelor Born 1938,Ag 17,23:1
Pickman, Jane
Bachelor Born 1938,Ag 17,23:1
Pickney, Lloyd
Great Magoo, The 1932,D 3,20:7
Pickup, Ronald
As You Like It 1967,O 6,33:4
As You Like It 1967,O 15,II,9:3
Oedipus 1968,Mr 31,II,5:1
As You Like It 1968,Jl 6,9:1
In His Own Write 1968,Jl 9,30:2
Oedipus 1968,Jl 31,29:1
Love's Labour's Lost 1968,D 22,54:3
Beaux' Stratagem, The 1970,F 10,50:2
Three Sisters, The 1970,F 12,30:1
Three Sisters, The 1970,F 22,II,1:1
Picon, Isidore (Lyricist)
Radio Girl, The 1929,O 19,22:4
Picon, Lillian (Lyricist)
Radio Girl, The 1929,O 19,22:4
Picon, Molly
Kid Mother 1927,F 27,VII,1:1
Kid Mother 1927,Mr 6,VII,1:6
Some Girl 1927,O 24,8:2
Circus Girl, The 1928,O 21,IX,1:1
Vaudeville (Palace) 1929,Je 24,27:4
Vaudeville (Palace) 1929,Jl 1,31:4
Vaudeville (Palace) 1929,Jl 8,17:6
Vaudeville (Palace) 1929,S 9,30:5
Radio Girl, The 1929,O 19,22:4
Jolly Orphan, The 1929,D 23,18:6
Little Clown, The 1930,Mr 15,23:3
Girl of Yesterday, The 1930,S 27,21:2
Love Thief, The 1931,Ja 19,24:5
Here Runs the Bride 1934,S 20,21:3
Here Runs the Bride 1934,N 4,IX,2:1
One in a Million 1934,N 17,13:2
Motel Peissi, The Contor's Kid 1934,N 29,33:3
What Girls Do 1935,Ja 14,10:4
My Malkele 1937,S 20,18:6
Bublitchki 1938,Ja 17,11:2
Vaudeville Marches On 1938,D 30,11:1
Morning Star 1940,Ap 17,26:4
Oy, Is Dus a Leben!; Oh, What a Life!
1942,O 13,19:2
For Heaven's Sake Mother 1948,N 17,33:4
Abi Gezunt 1949,O 10,19:4
Sadie Is a Lady 1950,Ja 28,9:2
Mazel Tov, Molly 1950,O 2,18:1
Take It Easy 1950,D 25,23:6
Farblondjete Honeymoon 1955,S 27,42:1
Kosher Widow, The 1959,N 2,40:2
Majority of One, A 1960,Mr 10,37:5
Milk and Honey 1961,O 11,52:1
How to Be a Jewish Mother 1967,D 29,18:1
Paris Is Out! 1970,F 3,35:1
Paris Is Out! 1970,F 22,II,5:5
Picon, Molly (Lyricist)
Radio Girl, The 1929,O 19,22:4
Jolly Orphan, The 1929,D 23,18:6
Oy, Is Dus a Leben!; Oh, What a Life!
1942,O 13,19:2
Abi Gezunt 1949,O 10,19:4
Sadie Is a Lady 1950,Ja 28,9:2
Mazel Tov, Molly 1950,O 2,18:1
Kosher Widow, The 1959,N 2,40:2
Picow, George (Miscellaneous)
How to Steal an Election 1968,O 14,56:1
Picquet, A L
Star of Bengal 1929,S 26,27:2
Picture, Kay
Look Who's Here 1932,O 31,18:5
Keep Moving 1934,Ag 24,10:2

cture, Kay—Cont

Red, Hot and Blue! 1936,O 8,26:1
Red, Hot and Blue! 1936,O 30,26:3
Leave It to Me! 1938,N 10,32:2
Very Warm for May 1939,N 18,23:2

dcock, Robin (Scenic Designer)
Joe Egg 1968,F 2,26:1

dgeon, Walter
Puzzles of 1925 1925,F 3,25:3
No More Ladies 1934,S 4,23:2
Something Gay 1935,Ap 30,12:2
There's Wisdom in Women 1935,Jl 16,24:1
Night of January 16 1935,S 17,26:4
There's Wisdom in Women 1935,O 31,17:1
Happiest Millionaire, The 1956,N 21,21:3
Happiest Millionaire, The 1956,D 2,II,1:1
Take Me Along 1959,O 23,22:2
Take Me Along 1959,N 1,II,1:1
Dinner at Eight 1966,S 28,38:1
Dinner at Eight 1966,O 9,II,1:1

echaud, Martial (Playwright)
Quatrieme, Le 1928,Ap 29,IX,2:3

eczuro, Jan
Labyrinth, The 1965,Ja 6,32:1
Jacob and the Angel 1965,Ja 6,32:1
Jaselka 1965,Ja 6,32:1
Book, The 1965,Ja 6,32:1
Kernel and the Shell, The 1965,Ja 6,32:1
Nightmare, The 1965,Ja 6,32:1
Post Office, The 1965,Ja 6,32:1
Woman, The 1965,Ja 6,32:1

iel, David
Francesca da Rimini 1967,S 12,54:1
We Bombed in New Haven 1968,O 17,51:1

ielot, Francis
Storm Over Patsy 1937,Mr 9,26:4

ieng, Charles (Original Author)
Americans on the Rhine 1934,O 11,28:4

ienne, Yvette
Marigold 1930,O 9,23:1

ier, Garrett Chatfield (Playwright)
Jeweled Tree, The 1926,O 8,26:2

ierantoni, Joseph
See Naples and Die 1929,S 27,30:4

ierantozzi, Victor
Sweet Miani 1962,S 26,33:2

ierce, Arthur
Polly Preferred 1923,Ja 12,13:3

Pierce, Barbara
Love Set, The 1923,Mr 20,24:2
Circle of Chalk, The 1950,D 2,8:3

Pierce, Betty
Julie 1927,My 10,24:4

Pierce, Burton
Sing Out the News 1938,S 26,12:5

Pierce, Charles I
What a Relief 1935,D 14,10:6
Take It Away 1936,D 15,30:5

Pierce, Evelyn (Director)
Truth About Blayds, The 1936,Ag 19,18:5
Art and Mrs Bottle 1936,S 2,18:1
Elizabeth the Queen 1937,Ag 25,24:3
Arms and the Man 1938,Ag 10,14:1
Circle, The 1939,Jl 12,17:2
What a Life 1939,Ag 2,17:5
White Steed, The 1939,Ag 16,21:3

Pierce, Glenn (Director)
Teahouse of the August Moon, The
  1954,Ap 23,23:6

Pierce, Harry
Tickle Me 1920,Ag 18,9:1

Pierce, Henry
County Chairman, The 1936,My 26,26:5
Tomorrow's Monday 1936,Jl 16,15:6

Pierce, Jack
Mister Roberts 1948,F 19,27:2

Pierce, Jean
Best of Burlesque 1957,S 30,27:2

Pierce, John
Motel Peissi, The Contor's Kid 1934,N 29,33:3

Pierce, John (Choreographer)
Meet My Sister 1930,D 31,11:1

Pierce, John (Director)
Chocolate Soldier, The 1942,Je 24,22:2
Merry Widow, The 1942,Jl 16,22:1
New Moon, The 1942,Ag 19,14:2

Pierce, John (Musical Director)
Girl From Wyoming, The 1938,O 31,12:1

Pierce, Lewis
Paul Bunyan 1941,My 6,25:1
Mikado, The 1944,F 12,11:3
Gondoliers, The 1944,F 22,26:3
Iolanthe 1944,F 23,17:1
Ruddigore 1944,Mr 3,19:5
Yeomen of the Guard, The 1944,Mr 5,34:3
Would-Be Gentleman, The 1946,Ja 10,29:2
Mary and the Fairy 1956,Mr 24,15:2
Fortunato 1956,Mr 24,15:2
Anvil, The 1962,O 31,33:3
Utopia! 1963,My 7,47:4

Pierce, Lewis (Miscellaneous)
Pirates of Penzance, The 1949,O 11,41:2

Pierce, Lewis (Producer)
H M S Pinafore 1949,O 18,34:2

Trial by Jury 1949,O 18,34:2

Pierce, Lola
O K 1925,My 4,16:1

Pierce, Marion
New Faces of 1936 1936,My 20,24:5
Three Waltzes 1937,D 27,10:2
I Must Love Someone 1939,F 8,18:7

Pierce, Michael
As You Like It 1966,Je 4,19:1
Harpers Ferry 1967,Je 6,52:2
Visit, The 1967,S 13,41:1

Pierce, Nat (Composer)
Ballad of Jazz Street, The 1959,N 12,28:1

Pierce, Nathalie F
Little Theatre Tournament; Fancy Free
  1929,My 9,34:3

Pierce, Noel (Playwright)
Shooting Star 1933,Je 13,22:2

Pierce, Randy
Infantry, The 1966,N 15,51:1

Pierce, Rik
Call It Virtue 1963,Mr 28,8:2
Experiment, The 1967,My 9,54:2
Avanti 1968,F 1,29:1

Pierce, Roy
Sign of the Leopard 1928,D 12,34:4

Pierce, Samuel
Did I Say No? 1931,S 23,19:4

Pierce, Susanna
Fuente Ovejuna; Sheep Well, The 1936,My 3,II,4:1

Pierce, Virginia
Richard of Bordeaux 1934,F 15,16:2

Pierce, Wesley
Lovely Lady 1927,D 30,22:1
Dear Love 1930,My 18,VIII,3:1
Artists and Models 1930,Je 11,33:2

Pierce, Willard
Aunt Caroline's Will 1954,Ag 11,21:1

Pierce and Harris
Revels of 1935 1934,O 3,24:2

Pierlot, Francis
Show-Off, The 1924,F 6,16:2
Fanny 1926,S 22,30:1
Women Go on Forever 1927,S 8,25:1
Gentlemen of the Press 1928,Ag 28,27:2
Whirlpool 1929,D 4,37:3
Midnight 1930,D 30,25:1
Band Wagon, The 1931,Je 4,31:3
Band Wagon, The 1931,S 27,VIII,3:7
Her Master's Voice 1933,O 24,24:3
Bride of Torozko, The 1934,Jl 10,24:7
Bride of Torozko, The 1934,S 14,24:2
Farmer Takes a Wife, The 1934,O 31,17:1
Journey by Night, A 1935,Ap 17,26:3
Ethan Frome 1936,Ja 22,15:2
St Helena 1936,O 7,32:1
Be So Kindly 1937,F 9,19:4
Too Many Heroes 1937,N 16,26:2
Save Me the Waltz 1938,Mr 1,19:2
Washington Jitters 1938,My 3,19:1
Knickerbocker Holiday 1938,O 20,26:2

Piero Brothers
Michael Todd's Peep Show 1950,Je 29,37:2

Pierpont, Laura
Wonder Bar, The 1931,Mr 18,23:4
Village Green 1941,S 4,24:4
Village Green 1941,S 14,IX,1:1
Winged Victory 1943,N 22,24:1
Sleepy Hollow 1948,Je 4,26:3
Leading Lady 1948,O 19,33:1
Smile of the World, The 1949,Ja 13,26:5
Two Blind Mice 1949,Mr 3,32:2
Time Out for Ginger 1952,N 27,50:4
J B 1958,D 12,2:7

Pierrard, Gisele
Dancers, The 1923,O 18,17:2

Pierre, Alford
Carmen Jones 1943,D 3,26:2

Pierre, Edna
Tangerine 1921,Ag 10,8:2

Pierre, Gloria
Cross-Town 1937,Mr 18,21:5
Censored 1938,F 28,18:2

Pierre, Roberta
Rat, The 1925,F 11,19:3
Du Barry 1932,N 23,15:2

Pierrin, Sara
John Hawthorne 1921,Ja 24,16:1

Pierry, Marguerite
Divin Mensonge 1926,N 14,VIII,2:1
Comme le Temps Passe 1927,O 30,IX,4:7
Vingt ans, Madame 1928,Ap 8,VIII,4:1
Trou Dans le Mur, Le 1929,F 24,IX,1:8
Petite Catherine, La 1930,N 2,VIII,2:1

Piers, Gwendolyn
Eyvind of the Hills 1921,F 2,14:1

Piers, Walter
Once Is Enough 1938,F 16,16:2

Pierson, Arthur
Remote Control 1929,S 11,24:5
Queer People 1934,F 16,16:2
Broadway Interlude 1934,Ap 20,16:3
Lost Horizons 1934,O 16,31:2

Pierson, Arthur—Cont

Woman of the Soil, A 1935,Mr 26,23:6
If a Body 1935,My 1,25:3
Jane Brady-Editor 1935,Jl 2,24:3
Night of January 16 1935,S 17,26:4
Remember the Day 1936,Je 30,15:1
Othello 1936,N 27,26:5
Othello 1937,Ja 7,16:4
One Thing After Another 1937,D 29,17:2
What a Life 1938,Ap 14,26:2
Unconquered, The 1940,F 14,25:2

Pierson, Arthur (Director)
Name Your Poison 1936,Ja 21,27:4
Assorted Nuts 1940,Ap 7,I,44:6
What Big Ears! 1942,Ap 21,18:5
Cat Screams, The 1942,Je 17,26:5

Pierson, Arthur (Miscellaneous)
Ziegfeld Follies 1943,Ap 2,16:2

Pierson, Arthur (Playwright)
What's Up 1943,N 12,24:6

Pierson, Barbara
Truth About Blayds, The 1936,Ag 19,18:5

Pierson, Edward
Porgy and Bess 1965,Mr 6,17:1
Play of Risen Christ, The 1970,Mr 9,44:1
Amahl and the Night Visitors 1970,D 24,10:2

Pierson, Gardiner H
Assorted Nuts 1940,Ap 7,I,44:6
One on the House 1941,Mr 30,I,47:3

Pierson, Harold
Cabin in the Sky 1964,Ja 22,32:1
Sweet Charity 1966,Ja 31,22:1

Pierson, Harry
Singing Rabbi, The 1931,S 11,24:4

Pierson, John
Mecca 1920,O 5,12:2
Elmer the Great 1928,S 25,29:1

Pierson, Lin
Love Me Little 1958,Ap 15,42:2
Foenix in Choir 1958,O 28,40:2
Family Portrait 1959,My 6,48:2

Pierson, Malcolm (Producer)
Noble Prize, The 1935,Jl 9,24:3
She Cried for the Moon 1935,Jl 23,24:3

Pierson, Paul
Wolf! Wolf! 1925,O 30,21:1

Pierson, Paul R B
Technique 1931,My 15,21:1

Pierson, Robert
Cradle Will Rock, The 1947,D 27,11:2

Pierson, Susanne
What Next 1920,Ja 27,7:2

Pierson, William
Stalag 17 1951,My 9,41:2
High Button Shoes 1955,Mr 12,10:6
Guitar 1959,N 11,42:5
Sing Muse 1961,D 7,52:1

Piesowocki, Kazimierz
Jaselka 1965,Ja 6,32:1
Labyrinth, The 1965,Ja 6,32:1
Kernel and the Shell, The 1965,Ja 6,32:1
Nightmare, The 1965,Ja 6,32:1
Post Office, The 1965,Ja 6,32:1
Book, The 1965,Ja 6,32:1
Woman, The 1965,Ja 6,32:1
Jacob and the Angel 1965,Ja 6,32:1

Pieters, Barbara
Earthlight Theater 1970,N 4,38:2

Pieters, Rick
Earthlight Theater 1970,N 4,38:2

Pietropinto, Angela
Alice in Wonderland 1970,O 9,43:1

Piette, W Fredric
Paul Bunyan 1941,My 6,25:1

Pigott, Dolores
Mr Pickwick 1952,S 18,36:3

Pihale, Franz
Untitled-Passion Play 1927,Jl 31,VII,1:6

Pike, Robert
Duchess of Malfi, The 1946,O 16,35:2
Command. Decision 1947,O 2,30:2
Two Blind Mice 1949,Mr 3,32:2
Golden State, The 1950,N 27,29:3

Pike, William
Strawberry Blonde, The 1927,F 8,20:3
She Got What She Wanted 1929,Mr 5,28:1
Another Language 1932,Ap 26,25:3
Another Language 1933,My 9,20:2
Tomorrow's a Holiday! 1935,D 31,10:2

Pike Davis's Continental Orchestra
Rhapsody in Black 1931,My 5,33:2
Blackbirds 1933,D 4,22:3

Pilar, Mario
Phedre 1969,Mr 1,20:1

Pilares, Jay
Murder in the Cathedral 1958,Mr 22,12:4

Pilbeam, Nova
Peter Pan 1935,D 27,14:4

Pilbrow, Richard (Lighting Director)
Rosencrantz and Guildenstern Are Dead
  1967,O 17,53:1
Love for Love 1967,O 21,17:1
Rosencrantz and Guildenstern Are Dead
  1967,O 29,II,1:1

Pilbrow, Richard (Lighting Director)—Cont
Love for Love 1967,O 30,59:1
Zorba 1968,N 18,58:1
Three Sisters, The 1970,F 12,30:1
Rothschilds, The 1970,O 20,40:1
Pilbrow, Richard (Miscellaneous)
Golden Boy 1964,O 21,56:1
Dear Janet Rosenberg, Dear Mr Kooning 1970,Ap 6,46:1
Jakey Fat Boy 1970,Ap 6,46:1
Pilbrow, Richard (Scenic Designer)
Golden Boy 1964,N 1,II,1:1
Pilcer, Elsie
Vaudeville (Palace) 1926,Je 15,23:3
Pilcer, Harry
Pins and Needles 1922,F 2,20:1
Vaudeville (Palace) 1926,Je 15,23:3
Palace aux Femmes 1926,O 10,VIII,2:1
Vive la Femme 1927,My 29,VII,2:1
Pilcer and Douglass
Vaudeville (Palace) 1928,S 18,34:6
Pilchard, Frances
Awhile to Work 1937,Mr 20,23:1
If You Get It, Do You Want It? 1938,D 1,28:2
Pilcher, Lee (Costume Designer)
Aria Da Capo 1958,My 21,40:1
Pilditch, Charles R (Translator)
Ox Cart, The 1966,D 20,58:1
Pile, Seifert
Lulu Belle 1926,F 10,20:1
Pilgrim Players
Sleep of Prisoners, A 1951,My 16,46:6
Pilgrims, Robert O'Brien
Embezzled Heaven 1944,N 1,20:2
Pilhofer, Herbert (Composer)
Hamlet 1963,My 9,41:1
Henry V 1964,My 13,52:1
Richard III 1965,Je 3,26:1
Thieves' Carnival 1967,Je 5,52:1
Visit, The 1967,S 13,41:1
Resistible Rise of Arturo Ui, The 1968,Ag 8,25:1
Resistible Rise of Arturo Ui, The 1968,D 23,44:1
Good Woman of Setzuan, The 1970,N 6,51:1
Pilhofer, Herbert (Lyricist)
Good Woman of Setzuan, The 1970,N 6,51:1
Pilhofer, Herbert (Miscellaneous)
Way of the World, The 1965,Je 2,40:1
Skin of Our Teeth, The 1966,Je 2,51:1
Dance of Death, The 1966,Je 3,31:1
Merton of the Movies 1968,S 26,62:1
Pilhofer, Herbert (Musical Director)
Three Sisters, The 1963,Jl 22,19:2
Pillai, Gopala (Costume Designer)
Mahabharata 1970,N 28,22:1
Pillai, Gopala (Miscellaneous)
Mahabharata 1970,N 28,22:1
Pillar, Gary
Wayward Stork, The 1966,Ja 20,27:1
Pillard, Earl
Legal Murder 1934,F 16,16:2
Pillard, Etta
Artists and Models 1923,Ag 21,12:2
Piller & Curtin
Ice Capades 1952,S 12,18:1
Pillsbury, Walter (Miscellaneous)
Pale Horse, Pale Rider 1957,O 30,26:1
Pilmmer, Harry
Vaudeville (Palace) 1926,S 14,25:3
Pilotto, Camillo
Famiglia Barrett, La 1933,N 19,IX,1:3
Pils and Tabet
Continental Varieties 1935,D 27,15:3
Pilzer, Dorothy
Ruddigore 1927,My 21,25:2
Pimley, John
Story of Mary Surratt, The 1947,F 10,25:2
Pimmer, Harry
Victoria Regina 1938,O 4,20:2
Pinard, Jean (Playwright)
Moonflowers 1936,Ap 6,19:4
Pinault, Jean Burt
Marshall 1930,My 10,25:1
Pinch, Esther
Merton of the Movies 1922,N 14,16:2
Pinchot, Rosamond
Miracle, The 1924,Ja 16,17:1
Miracle, The 1924,Ja 26,10:1
Miracle, The 1924,Ag 19,9:1
Miracle, The 1925,Ag 17,10:4
Pardon My Glove 1926,My 23,VIII,1:1
Henry IV, Part I 1926,Je 1,29:1
Miracle, The 1927,Ap 15,27:1
Miracle, The 1927,Je 8,23:2
Midsummer Night's Dream, A 1927,Ag 8,6:1
Midsummer Night's Dream, A 1927,N 18,21:1
Midsummer Night's Dream, A 1927,D 4,X,6:1
Dantons Tod 1927,D 21,28:3
Swan, The 1936,Je 30,15:1
St Helena 1936,S 29,35:1
St Helena 1936,O 7,32:1
Eternal Road, The 1937,Ja 8,14:2
Pinckard, Marie
Madras House, The 1921,O 31,18:2

Pinckert, Addison
Order Please 1934,O 10,21:2
Pincus, Irvin
Anything Goes 1934,N 22,26:1
Pincus, Irvin (Miscellaneous)
Higher and Higher 1940,Ap 5,24:3
Pincus, Irvin (Playwright)
More the Merrier, The 1941,S 16,19:3
Pincus, Irvin (Producer)
Good, The 1938,O 6,27:2
Pincus, Norman (Producer)
Good, The 1938,O 6,27:2
More the Merrier, The 1941,S 16,19:3
Pincus, Warren
Electronic Nigger, The 1968,Mr 9,23:2
Last Pad, The 1970,D 8,61:1
Pincus-Gani, Lidia (Costume Designer)
Sage of Rottenburg, The 1963,N 20,48:1
Pincus-Gani, Lidia (Scenic Designer)
Sage of Rottenburg, The 1963,N 20,48:1
Pine, Ellie
All You Need Is One Good Break 1950,F 10,20:3
Pine, La Verne
Panic 1935,Mr 16,18:4
Pine, Larry
Cyrano de Bergerac 1968,Ap 26,30:1
Alice in Wonderland 1970,O 9,43:1
Alice in Wonderland 1970,O 18,II,3:1
Pine, Les
Talent '54 1954,Ap 13,40:1
Pine, Margaret
No Place to Be Somebody 1969,D 31,17:1
Pine, Phillip
Counterattack 1943,F 4,27:2
Lower North 1944,Ag 26,15:4
All You Need Is One Good Break 1950,F 10,20:3
One Bright Day 1952,Mr 20,37:2
See the Jaguar 1952,D 4,46:2
Little Clay Cart, The 1953,Jl 1,25:1
Stone for Danny Fisher, A 1954,O 22,24:2
Pine, Sandra
Red Roses for Me 1955,D 29,15:2
Pinelli, Tullio (Playwright)
Sweet Charity 1966,Ja 31,22:1
Pinero, Arthur Wing (Sir)
Caste 1929,F 24,IX,4:3
Pinero, Arthur Wing (Sir) (Playwright)
Enchanted Cottage, The 1922,Mr 2,21:4
Second Mrs Tanqueray, The 1922,Jl 9,VI,1:1
Enchanted Cottage, The 1923,Ap 2,22:3
Gay Lord Quex 1923,Ap 8,VIII,1:7
Enchanted Cottage, The 1923,Ap 8,VIII,1:1
Second Mrs Tanqueray, The 1924,S 28,VII,2:1
Second Mrs Tanqueray, The 1924,O 19,VIII,1:1
Second Mrs Tanqueray, The 1924,O 28,27:1
Second Mrs Tanqueray, The 1924,N 2,VII,1:1
Trelawney of the 'Wells' 1925,Je 2,16:2
Trelawney of the 'Wells' 1927,F 1,24:4
Trelawney of the 'Wells' 1927,F 6,VII,1:1
Untitled-Play 1928,Je 10,VIII,1:3
Dr Harmer 1931,Mr 22,VIII,4:3
Trelawney of the 'Wells' 1935,Jl 16,24:1
Benefit of the Doubt, The 1935,Ag 4,IX,1:3
Second Mrs Tanqueray, The 1950,O 8,II,3:7
His House in Order 1951,Ag 12,II,1:4
Dandy Dick 1956,Ja 11,37:2
Magistrate, The 1959,My 14,30:6
Trelawny of the 'Wells' 1970,O 12,48:1
Trelawny of the 'Wells' 1970,O 25,II,16:1
Pinget, Robert (Playwright)
Lettre Morte 1960,Mr 29,47:6
Old Tune, The 1961,Mr 24,37:1
Lettre Morte 1970,Ap 16,55:1
Architruc 1970,Ap 16,55:1
Pinheiro, Victor
Miser, The 1950,Mr 27,19:5
Pinillos, Jose Lopez (Playwright)
Forbidden Roads 1928,Ap 17,26:4
Pink, S B
Eight Bells 1933,O 30,14:2
Pink, Shirley B
Secrets 1922,D 26,11:1
Pink, Wal (Playwright)
Pins and Needles 1922,F 2,20:1
Pinkard, Fred
In White America 1963,N 1,26:1
Shoemaker's Holiday, The 1967,Je 3,19:1
Harpers Ferry 1967,Je 6,52:2
Visit, The 1967,S 13,41:1
I'm Solomon 1968,Ap 24,51:1
Pinkard, Macco (Composer)
Pansy 1929,My 15,36:3
Pinkard, Macco (Lyricist)
Liza 1922,N 28,24:1
Pinkard, Macco (Producer)
Pansy 1929,My 15,36:3
Pinkerton, Harry (Lighting Director)
Treatment, The 1968,My 10,54:7
Soap Opera 1968,My 10,54:7
Pinkham, Charles H
To Quito and Back 1937,O 7,30:4
Pinkham, Daniel (Composer)
Beggar's Opera, The 1957,Mr 14,35:1

Pinkston, Frank S
Tall Kentuckian, The 1953,Je 17,30:1
Pinkston, Robert
Prodigal Son, The 1965,My 21,19:1
Pinner, Alfred
What Every Woman Knows 1926,Ap 14,20:2
Pinney, Colin
And People All Around 1968,F 12,46:1
Pinnock, Tommy
But Never Jam Today 1969,Ap 24,40:1
Pinon, Lee (Miscellaneous)
Volpone 1957,Ja 8,27:1
Pins, Murnai
Priorities of 1942 1942,Mr 13,23:2
Pinski, David (Playwright)
Treasure, The 1920,O 5,13:1
Treasure, The 1920,O 24,VI,1:1
Eternal Jew, The 1926,D 21,21:2
Final Balance, The 1928,O 31,28:3
Three 1928,D 4,28:2
Zwie Family, The 1934,Mr 2,22:8
Treasure, The 1934,D 18,25:5
Power That Builds, The 1935,Mr 9,18:4
Tailor Becomes a Storekeeper, The 1938,Ap 14,26:3
Pinter, Harold (Director)
Man in the Glass Booth, The 1967,Jl 29,12:1
Man in the Glass Booth, The 1967,Ag 27,II,1:1
Man in the Glass Booth, The 1968,S 27,41:1
Man in the Glass Booth, The 1968,O 6,II,5:1
Man in the Glass Booth, The 1969,Ap 17,58:1
Exiles 1970,N 19,42:4
Pinter, Harold (Playwright)
Birthday Party, The 1961,My 15,34:6
Caretaker, The 1961,O 5,42:3
Caretaker, The 1961,O 15,II,1:1
Dumbwaiter, The 1962,N 27,44:1
Collection, The 1962,N 27,44:1
Dumbwaiter, The; Collection, The 1962,D 9,II,5:1
Lover, The 1963,S 19,21:1
Dwarf, The 1963,S 19,21:1
Caretaker, The 1963,N 25,23:2
Lover, The 1964,Ja 6,35:1
Caretaker, The 1964,Ja 31,16:1
Slight Ache, A 1964,D 10,62:1
Room, The 1964,D 10,62:1
Homecoming, The 1965,Je 4,38:8
Homecoming, The 1967,Ja 6,29:1
Homecoming, The 1967,Ja 15,II,1:1
Homecoming, The 1967,Ja 22,II,1:4
Birthday Party, The 1967,O 4,40:2
Homecoming, The 1967,O 5,47:3
Birthday Party, The 1967,O 15,II,1:1
Tea Party 1968,O 16,40:1
Basement, The 1968,O 16,40:1
Basement, The 1968,N 3,II,7:4
Tea Party 1968,N 3,II,7:4
Mixed Doubles 1969,Ap 12,43:2
Silence 1969,Jl 13,II,8:1
Landscape 1969,Jl 13,II,8:1
Landscape; Silence 1969,Jl 25,34:1
Local Stigmatic, The; That's Your Trouble 1969,N 4,55:2
Local Stigmatic, The; Last to Go 1969,N 4,55:2
Local Stigmatic, The; That's All 1969,N 4,55:2
Local Stigmatic, The; Applicant 1969,N 4,55:2
Local Stigmatic, The; Request Stop 1969,N 4,55:2
Local Stigmatic, The 1969,N 4,55:2
Local Stigmatic, The; Trouble in the Works 1969,N 4,55:2
Local Stigmatic, The; Interview 1969,N 4,55:2
Landscape 1970,Ap 3,43:1
Silence 1970,Ap 3,43:1
Landscape 1970,Ap 12,II,3:1
Silence 1970,Ap 12,II,3:1
Pinter, Richard
Brother to Dragons 1968,D 8,86:1
Knack With Horses, A 1970,D 21,52:1
Pinto, Dorothea
As the Girls Go 1948,N 15,21:2
Pinto, Effingham
Anna Ascends 1920,S 23,14:1
On the Stairs 1922,S 26,18:2
Blonde Beast, The 1923,Mr 3,9:3
Gift, The 1924,Ja 23,15:4
Virgin of Bethulia, The 1925,F 24,17:2
Climax, The 1926,My 18,29:3
One Glorious Hour 1927,Ap 15,27:2
Love in the Tropics 1927,O 19,24:3
Pinto, Marion
Sextet 1958,N 27,53:1
Pinto, Thea
Hold On to Your Hats 1940,S 12,30:3
Pinza, Carla
Ox Cart, The 1966,D 20,58:1
House of Flowers 1968,Ja 29,26:2
Cuban Thing, The 1968,S 25,36:2
Pinza, Ezio
South Pacific 1949,Ap 8,30:2
South Pacific 1949,Ap 17,II,1:1
Fanny 1954,N 5,16:1
Fanny 1954,N 21,II,1:1
Pio-Ulsky, Konstantin
Anya 1965,N 30,48:1

Pious, Minerva
Dear Me, the Sky Is Falling 1963,Mr 4,9:1
Last Analysis, The 1964,O 2,30:1
Piozet, Nina
Girofle-Girofla 1926,N 24,26:2
Pip, Buddy
South 1955,My 2,17:4
Piper, Frank
Decameron, The 1961,Ap 13,32:1
Piper, John (Costume Designer)
Rape of Lucretia, The 1948,D 30,24:2
Piper, John (Scenic Designer)
Oedipus 1946,My 21,19:2
Rape of Lucretia, The 1948,D 30,24:2
Cranks 1956,My 14,23:1
Cranks 1956,N 27,32:1
Piper, Will (Playwright)
Enemy Within 1931,O 6,35:3
Pipers, Dagenham
Ice Capades 1958,S 4,33:2
Pipitone, Nino Jr
Slightly Scandalous 1944,Je 14,16:2
Pippin, Donald (Musical Director)
Oliver 1963,Ja 8,5:5
110 in the Shade 1963,O 25,37:1
Foxy 1964,F 17,26:1
Ben Franklin in Paris 1964,O 28,52:1
Mame 1966,My 25,41:1
Dear World 1969,F 7,33:1
Applause 1970,Mr 31,35:1
Pippin, Horace (Scenic Designer)
Porgy and Bess 1952,S 8,18:2
Piquer, Conchita
Wildcat, The 1921,N 28,16:2
Make It Snappy 1922,Ap 14,20:2
Pirandello, Luigi (Original Author)
Chacun Sa Verite 1939,Ja 24,17:1
Pirandello, Luigi (Playwright)
Six Characters in Search of an Author
1922,O 31,11:2
Six Characters in Search of an Author
1922,N 5,VIII,1:1
Floriani's Wife 1923,O 1,10:1
Floriani's Wife 1923,O 7,IX,1:1
Living Mask, The 1924,Ja 22,15:1
Naked 1924,O 28,27:2
Naked 1924,N 2,VII,1:1
Sagra del Signore Della Nave 1925,Ap 4,20:2
Festival of the Saviour of the Seamen, The
1925,Ap 26,VIII,1:3
Six Characters in Search of an Author
1925,Je 16,26:4
Naked 1926,N 9,31:2
Say It With Flowers 1926,D 6,29:1
Right You Are (If You Think You Are)
1927,F 24,27:1
Right You Are (If You Think You Are)
1927,Mr 6,VIII,1:1
Diana e la Tuda 1927,Mr 13,II,9:3
Naked 1927,Ap 17,VII,1:4
Six Characters in Search of an Author
1928,Je 24,VIII,4:2
Signora Morli-One and Two 1928,D 16,IX,2:1
Mock Emperor, The 1929,F 17,IX,2:1
Piacere Dell 'Onesta, Il 1929,Mr 25,33:1
Tutto Per Bene; All's Well That Ends Well
1929,Je 3,27:1
Lazzaro 1929,Jl 10,31:1
Lazzaro 1929,Ag 4,VIII,1:7
Vie Que Je T'Ai Donnee, La 1930,Ap 6,IX,2:3
Piacere Del'Onesta, Il; Happiness of Probity, The
1930,N 10,16:4
As You Desire Me 1930,N 30,IX,3:6
As You Desire Me 1931,Ja 29,21:2
Lazzaro 1931,F 22,VIII,4:1
Six Characters in Search of an Author
1931,Ap 16,29:2
Life I Gave You, The 1931,My 12,29:3
Berretto a Songali, Il; Cap With Bells, The
1931,N 30,16:3
Homme, la Bete et la Vertu, L'; Say It With
Flowers 1931,D 13,VIII,2:2
He, She and the Ox 1934,F 21,22:7
As You Desire Me 1934,O 2,18:3
As You Desire Me 1934,O 28,IX,3:4
Life That I Gave Him, The 1934,O 28,IX,3:4
Six Characters in Search of an Author
1934,D 5,29:1
Non si Sa Come 1934,D 20,29:4
Ce Soir on Improvise 1935,F 17,VIII,3:7
Tonight We Improvise 1936,D 20,XI,3:8
Right You Are (If You Think You Are)
1950,Je 29,37:2
Naked 1950,S 7,39:2
Six Characters in Search of an Author
1955,D 12,38:1
Six Characters in Search of an Author
1955,D 25,II,3:1
Right You Are (If You Think You Are)
1957,Mr 5,37:1
Tonight We Improvise 1959,N 7,27:4
Rules of the Game, The 1960,D 20,44:1
Mountain Giants, The 1961,Ap 5,32:3

Six Characters in Search of an Author
1961,My 11,43:1
Six Characters in Search of an Author
1963,Mr 11,7:2
Call It Virtue 1963,Mr 28,8:2
Right You Are (If You Think You Are)
1964,Mr 5,37:1
Liola 1964,S 9,30:3
Right You Are (If You Think You Are)
1966,D 11,II,3:1
To Clothe the Naked 1967,Ap 28,30:1
Henry IV 1968,F 7,40:1
License, The 1969,Ap 23,42:1
Man With the Flower in His Mouth, The
1969,Ap 23,42:1
Jar, The 1969,Ap 23,42:1
License, The; Jar, The; Man With the Flower in His
Mouth, The 1969,My 4,II,3:1
Pirk, Robert
Fools Are Passing Through 1958,Ap 3,24:2
Pirnikoff, Serge
Ziegfeld Follies 1922,Je 6,18:2
Piro, Phillip
Birds, The 1966,Jl 1,40:1
Stop, You're Killing Me; Bad Bad Jo-Jo
1969,Mr 20,53:1
Piro, Pia
Dracula Sabbat 1970,O 2,28:2
Pisacane, Joseph
Hello Out There 1955,D 22,19:1
Hungerers, The 1955,D 22,19:1
Floydada to Matador 1955,D 22,19:1
Pisacane, Joseph (Producer)
Hungerers, The 1955,D 22,19:1
Opera Opera 1955,D 22,19:1
Hello Out There 1955,D 22,19:1
Floydada to Matador 1955,D 22,19:1
Pisani, Remo
Cherry Orchard, The 1962,N 15,46:2
Piscator, Erwin (Director)
Robbers, The 1926,N 21,VIII,1:3
What Price Glory 1929,Ap 28,IX,1:4
Kaisers Kulis, Des 1930,O 19,IX,2:4
King Lear 1940,D 16,27:2
War and Peace 1942,My 22,26:3
Last Stop 1944,S 6,17:2
All the King's Men 1948,Ja 19,19:2
Outside the Door 1949,Mr 2,33:2
Burning Bush, The 1949,D 17,15:5
Scapegoat, The 1950,Ap 20,36:5
All the King's Men 1950,Jl 19,25:6
In der Sache J Robert Oppenheimer 1964,N 3,27:2
200,000 1966,F 15,33:5
Piscator, Erwin (Miscellaneous)
245 1930,D 28,VIII,3:5
Flies, The; Mouches, Les 1947,Ap 18,26:3
Nights of Wrath; Nuits de la Colere, Les
1947,D 1,26:4
Piscator, Erwin (Original Author)
Case of Clyde Griffiths 1936,Mr 14,10:4
Piscator, Erwin (Playwright)
King Lear 1940,D 16,27:2
War and Peace 1942,My 22,26:3
Circle of Chalk, The 1950,D 2,8:3
War and Peace 1962,Je 16,10:1
War and Peace 1965,Ja 12,32:1
War and Peace 1965,Ja 31,II,1:1
War and Peace 1967,Mr 22,42:1
Piscator, Erwin (Producer)
Hoppla, Wir Leben! 1927,D 11,IX,4:1
Adventures of the Worthy Soldier Schwejk, The
1928,Mr 4,IX,2:1
Merchant of Berlin, The 1929,O 27,IX,4:1
Saint Joan 1940,Mr 11,10:6
Nathan the Wise 1942,Ap 4,18:4
Winter Soldiers 1942,N 30,19:2
Nathan the Wise 1944,F 22,26:3
Burning Bush, The 1949,D 17,15:5
Scapegoat, The 1950,Ap 20,36:5
Iphigenia in Aulis; Agamemnon's Death; Electra;
Iphigenia in Delphi 1962,N 11,82:4
Stellvertreter, Der 1963,F 23,7:8
Investigation, The 1965,O 21,55:3
Piscator, Erwin (Scenic Designer)
All the King's Men 1948,Ja 19,19:2
Piscator, Erwin (Translator)
Outside the Door 1949,Mr 2,33:2
Piscator, Maria Ley (Director)
Bobino 1944,Ap 7,23:4
Nights of Wrath; Nuits de la Colere, Les
1947,D 1,26:4
Home Is Tomorrow 1950,Je 2,27:2
Pisharoty, Vasudeva
Mahabharata 1970,N 28,22:1
Pitcher, Barbara
Young Provincials, The 1958,S 19,22:4
Pitcher, Oliver
On Strivers' Row 1946,Mr 1,17:2
Pitchmen, The
Sons o' Fun 1941,D 2,28:2
Pitchon, Jack
Around the World 1946,Je 1,9:5

Piteoff (Producer)
Plus Jamais ca 1932,My 29,VIII,1:7
Pitkin, Robert
Princess Virtue 1921,My 5,20:2
All-Star Idlers of 1921, The 1921,Jl 16,5:2
Little Nellie Kelly 1922,N 14,16:1
Lambs Gambol 1925,Ap 27,15:1
Merry Merry 1925,S 25,24:3
Polly of Hollywood 1927,F 22,22:3
Lawyers' Dilemma, The 1928,Jl 10,17:2
Silver Swan, The 1929,N 28,34:5
Who Cares 1930,Jl 9,27:1
Ghost Writer, The 1933,Je 20,22:4
Come Angel Band 1936,F 19,17:1
Man Who Killed Lincoln, The 1940,Ja 18,26:4
Louisiana Purchase 1940,My 29,19:2
H M S Pinafore 1942,Ja 22,12:2
Mikado, The 1942,F 4,22:2
Pirates of Penzance, The 1942,F 18,22:2
Iolanthe 1942,F 24,26:4
Gondoliers, The 1942,Mr 4,22:3
Mikado, The 1944,F 12,11:3
H M S Pinafore 1944,F 15,14:4
Trial by Jury 1944,F 15,14:4
Pirates of Penzance, The 1944,F 18,15:5
Gondoliers, The 1944,F 22,26:3
Iolanthe 1944,F 23,17:1
Patience 1944,F 26,11:4
Ruddigore 1944,Mr 3,19:5
Yeomen of the Guard, The 1944,Mr 5,34:3
Finian's Rainbow 1947,Ja 11,23:2
Pitkin, William (Costume Designer)
Threepenny Opera, The 1955,S 21,38:1
Child of Fortune 1956,N 14,41:1
Something About a Soldier 1962,Ja 5,36:2
Henry V 1963,Je 14,37:1
Pitkin, William (Lighting Director)
Beauty Part, The 1962,D 28,5:2
Pitkin, William (Miscellaneous)
Good Soup, The 1960,Mr 3,26:4
Pitkin, William (Scenic Designer)
Threepenny Opera, The 1954,Mr 11,26:5
Threepenny Opera, The 1954,Ap 4,II,7:1
Threepenny Opera, The 1955,S 21,38:1
Threepenny Opera, The 1956,Mr 11,II,1:1
Potting Shed, The 1957,Ja 30,32:1
Moon for the Misbegotten, A 1957,My 3,21:2
Cave Dwellers, The 1957,O 21,29:2
Invitation to a March 1960,O 31,27:2
Conquering Hero, The 1961,Ja 17,40:2
Something About a Soldier 1962,Ja 5,36:2
Seidman and Son 1962,O 16,32:2
Beauty Part, The 1962,D 28,5:2
Henry V 1963,Je 14,37:1
Taming of the Shrew, The 1965,Je 24,32:2
Impossible Years, The 1965,O 14,55:1
John Brown's Body 1968,F 13,49:2
Comedy of Errors, The 1968,F 28,40:2
Guide, The 1968,Mr 7,50:1
She Stoops to Conquer 1968,Ap 1,58:3
Next 1969,F 11,27:1
Adaptation 1969,F 11,27:1
Dr Fish 1970,Mr 11,42:2
Chinese, The 1970,Mr 11,42:2
Pitlik, Noam
Roots 1961,Mr 7,40:2
Pitman, Keith
Would-Be Gentleman, The 1930,Ap 30,29:2
Pitman, Richard
It's a Boy! 1922,S 20,18:3
Pitoeff, Georges
Jean le Mauranc 1927,Ja 2,VII,2:1
Hamlet 1927,Ja 23,VII,2:1
Saint Joan 1930,Je 29,VIII,1:4
Pitoeff, Georges (Producer)
Saint Joan 1930,Je 29,VIII,1:4
Pitoeff, Georges Jr
Annonce Faite a Marie, L'; Tidings Brought to
Mary, The 1942,My 21,24:1
Pitoeff, Ludmilla
Mademoiselle Bourrat 1923,F 4,VII,1:4
Sainte Jeanne 1925,D 27,VII,2:1
Mademoiselle Bourrat 1926,N 21,VIII,2:1
Jean le Mauranc 1927,Ja 2,VII,2:1
Hamlet 1927,Ja 23,VII,2:1
Mixture 1927,N 20,IX,4:4
Heartbreak House 1928,F 12,VIII,1:3
Living Corpse, The 1928,N 25,X,4:7
Caesar and Cleopatra 1929,Ja 6,VIII,4:7
Caesar and Cleopatra 1929,Ja 6,VIII,4:7
Three Sisters 1929,F 17,IX,4:2
Three Sisters 1929,F 17,IX,4:2
Vray Proces de Jehane d'Arc, Le
1929,Je 16,VIII,2:3
Saint Joan 1930,Je 29,VIII,1:4
Belle au Bois, La 1932,Ap 3,VIII,2:1
Ce Soir on Improvise 1935,F 17,VIII,3:7
Folle du Ciel, La 1936,My 31,X,2:1
Escape Me Never! 1936,Je 21,IX,2:4
Sauvage, La 1938,Mr 27,X,2:1
Annonce Faite a Marie, L'; Tidings Brought to
Mary, The 1942,My 21,24:1
House in Paris, The 1944,Mr 21,17:1

Pitoeff, Ludmilla (Director)
Mademoiselle Bourrat 1923,F 4,VII,1:4
Mixture 1927,N 20,IX,4:4
Annonce Faite a Marie, L'; Tidings Brought to Mary, The 1942,My 21,24:1

Pitoeff, Ludmilla (Producer)
Sainte Jeanne 1925,D 27,VII,2:1
Heartbreak House 1928,F 12,VIII,1:3
Celebre Histoire, La 1928,My 13,IX,2:2
Adam et Eve et Cie 1928,Je 17,VIII,1:4
Living Corpse, The 1928,N 25,X,4:7
Caesar and Cleopatra 1929,Ja 6,VIII,4:7
Three Sisters 1929,F 17,IX,4:2
Vray Proces de Jehane d'Arc, Le 1929,Je 16,VIII,2:3
Mixture 1929,N 10,X,4:1
Criminals 1929,D 29,VIII,2:6
Joe et Cie; Patrasket 1932,Je 12,X,1:2
Folle du Ciel, La 1936,My 31,X,2:1
Annonce Faite a Marie, L'; Tidings Brought to Mary, The 1942,My 21,24:1

Pitoeff, Ludmilla (Translator)
Living Corpse, The 1928,N 25,X,4:7
Three Sisters 1929,F 17,IX,4:2
Three Sisters 1929,F 17,IX,4:2

Pitoeff, Miss
Fourberies de Scapin, Les 1938,D 13,30:3

Pitoeff, Svetlana
Knock 1937,N 17,26:3
Roi Cerf, Le 1937,N 30,26:3
Jean de la Lune 1937,D 14,33:3
Nationale 6 1938,Ja 11,26:6
Y'Avait un Prisonnier 1938,Ja 25,24:3
Fantasio 1938,F 8,17:2
Bal des Voleurs, Le 1938,N 29,26:4
Precieuses Ridicules, Les 1938,D 13,30:3
Faiseur, Le; Promoter, The 1938,D 27,12:3
Occasion, L' 1939,Ja 10,16:4
Chacun Sa Verite 1939,Ja 24,17:1
Enterrement, L' 1939,F 7,17:2
37 Sous de M Montaudoin, Les 1939,F 7,17:2
Enterrement, L' 1939,F 7,17:2
37 Sous de M Montaudoin, Les 1939,F 7,17:2
Barbier de Seville, Le 1939,Mr 7,19:2

Pitoeff, Varvara
Annonce Faite a Marie, L'; Tidings Brought to Mary, The 1942,My 21,24:1

Pitoeffs, The
Plus Jamais ca 1932,My 29,VIII,1:7

Pitoniak, Anne
Gay Apprentice, The 1960,F 3,27:2

Pitot, Genevieve (Choreographer)
Miss Liberty 1949,Jl 16,6:5
Milk and Honey 1961,O 11,52:1

Pitot, Genevieve (Composer)
It's About Time 1942,Mr 31,28:3
Inside U S A 1948,My 1,19:2
Kiss Me, Kate 1948,D 31,10:3
Touch and Go 1949,O 14,34:2
Two's Company 1952,D 16,43:5

Pitot, Genevieve (Miscellaneous)
Two on the Aisle 1951,Jl 20,13:6
Kiss Me, Kate 1952,Ja 9,24:6
Can-Can 1953,My 8,28:1
Can-Can 1953,My 17,II,1:1
Shangri-La 1956,Je 14,40:1
Li'l Abner 1956,N 16,24:2
Livin' the Life 1957,Ap 29,20:1
Body Beautiful, The 1958,Ja 24,15:2
Destry Rides Again 1959,Ap 24,24:1
Saratoga 1959,D 8,59:4
Sophie 1963,Ap 16,32:1
Girl Who Came to Supper, The 1963,D 9,49:1
Drat! the Cat! 1965,O 11,54:2

Pitot, Genevieve (Musical Director)
Out of This World 1950,D 22,17:3

Pitou, Diana
Song of Norway 1958,Je 23,19:2

Pitou, Peggy
Unsophisticates, The 1929,D 31,14:5

Pitray, Paul (Playwright)
Diloy le Chemineau 1926,N 14,VIII,2:1

Pitre, Anthony
Mikado, The 1942,F 4,22:2
Pirates of Penzance, The 1942,F 18,22:2
Iolanthe 1942,F 24,26:4
Gondoliers, The 1942,Mr 4,22:3

Pitt, Addison
Saturday Night 1933,Mr 1,13:2
Room Service 1935,N 17,II,7:7

Pitt, Addison (Director)
Them's the Reporters 1935,My 30,21:4

Pitt, Annette
Made for Each Other 1924,S 30,27:2

Pitt, Charles
Divorce a la Carte 1928,Mr 27,30:3

Pitt, Charles (Director)
Adam's Apple 1929,Je 11,27:5

Pitt, Dave
Ice Capades 1963,Ag 29,37:2

Pitt, Frances
Move On 1926,Ja 19,30:1
Right to Kill, The 1926,F 16,22:2

Pitt, George Didbin (Playwright)
Sweeney Todd 1924,Jl 19,10:4
Sweeney Todd 1957,Ag 28,21:4

Pitt, Hedy
From Vienna 1939,Je 21,26:2

Pitt, Margaret
Wanted 1928,Jl 3,19:2
Through the Night 1930,Ag 19,19:1

Pittenger, Martha (Playwright)
No Laughter in Heaven 1938,My 17,26:5

Pittman, Arthur (Playwright)
Possibilities 1968,D 5,60:1

Pittman, Tillmon
Androcles and the Lion 1938,D 17,10:5

Pitts, Dave
Ice Capades 1964,Ag 27,27:2
Ice Capades 1966,Je 2,50:2
Ice Capades 1969,Ja 8,42:1
Ice Capades 1970,Ja 7,35:1

Pitts, Spanky
Ice Capades 1966,Je 2,50:2

Pitts, Stanley
All Summer Long 1953,Ja 29,23:1
Cretan Woman, The 1954,My 21,17:2
Typewriter, The 1955,Jl 29,8:3

Pitts, ZaSu
Ramshackle Inn 1944,Ja 6,17:5
Bat, The 1953,Ja 21,28:2

Piven, Byrne
Rich Man, Poor Man 1950,F 13,15:4
Year of Pilar, The 1952,Ja 7,14:3
Thunder Rock 1956,F 27,18:1
Good Woman of Setzuan, The 1956,D 19,41:2
House Remembered, A 1957,F 7,20:2
Johnny Summit 1957,S 25,23:4
Infernal Machine, The 1958,F 4,33:1
Of Mice and Men 1958,D 5,38:1
Too Close for Comfort 1960,F 3,27:2
Jackass, The 1960,Mr 24,39:2
Electra 1962,Mr 22,42:1
Alcestis Comes Back 1962,Ap 24,33:1
At Sea 1962,Ap 24,33:1
Macbeth 1962,N 17,16:2
Galileo 1968,D 1,88:4

Piven, Byrne (Director)
Jackknife 1958,S 23,36:2

Pixley, Frank (Playwright)
Prince of Pilsen, The 1930,Ja 14,24:3

Pizella
Lulu 1927,O 2,VIII,2:4

Pizhova, Olga
Mistress of the Inn, The; Locandiera, La 1923,N 22,16:1
In the Claws of Life 1923,N 30,23:4
Enough Stupidity in Every Wise Man 1923,D 6,23:1

Pizon, Mr
Farandula, La 1930,Mr 25,34:6

Pizzi, Donna
Sunset 1966,My 13,34:1
Gandhi 1970,O 21,37:1

Plamondon, Andre
Beyond Desire 1967,O 11,36:1

Plamondon, Carol
Utopia, Limited; Flowers of Progress, The 1957,F 27,21:1
Mikado, The 1957,Ap 24,28:2
H M S Pinafore 1957,My 1,42:6
Pirates of Penzance, The 1957,My 8,43:1
Yeomen of the Guard, The 1957,My 22,28:3
Gondoliers, The 1957,My 29,34:2

Planchon, Roger (Director)
Tartuffe 1964,Mr 10,42:2
Three Musketeers, The 1968,Je 26,43:1
George Dandin 1968,Je 28,36:1
Tartuffe 1968,Jl 3,28:2

Planchon, Roger (Playwright)
Three Musketeers, The 1968,Je 26,43:1

Planchon, Roger (Producer)
Three Musketeers, The 1968,Jl 7,II,1:1

Plane, Liane
West Side Story 1957,S 27,14:4

Plank, Tom
Utopia, Limited; Flowers of Progress, The 1957,F 27,21:1
Mikado, The 1957,Ap 24,28:2
H M S Pinafore 1957,My 1,42:6
Pirates of Penzance, The 1957,My 8,43:1
Yeomen of the Guard, The 1957,My 22,28:3
Gondoliers, The 1957,My 29,34:2

Plankenton, Elsie
Mulatto 1935,Ag 8,13:2

Planquette, Robert (Composer)
Surcouf 1926,N 14,VIII,2:1
Cloches de Cornville, Les; Chimes of Normandy, The 1926,D 14,24:4
Chimes of Normandy, The 1931,N 3,31:3
Chimes of Corneville, The 1934,Je 29,16:2

Plant, Mark
Jubilee 1935,S 23,20:3

Plant, Mark—Cont
Jubilee 1935,O 14,20:1
Broadway Sho-Window 1936,Ap 13,14:5

Plant, Mary
Yokel Boy 1939,Jl 7,12:2

Plant, Michael (Playwright)
Miss Isobel 1957,D 27,22:1

Plantation Orchestra, The
Blackbirds 1928,My 10,31:3

Plantation Quartet, The
Plantation Revue, The 1922,Jl 18,18:4

Plante, Louis
Three Sisters, The 1968,Mr 18,56:1
Rivals, The 1969,O 18,37:1
Metamorphoses 1969,D 12,69:1
Crimes and Crimes 1970,Ja 19,35:1
Metamorphosis 1970,F 15,II,1:1
Don Juan 1970,My 26,32:1
Three Philip Roth Stories; Epstein 1970,Jl 31,14:1
Three Philip Roth Stories; Defender of the Faith 1970,Jl 31,14:1
Three Philip Roth Stories; Conversion of the Jews 1970,Jl 31,14:1
Cops and Horrors; Dracula 1970,Ag 11,27:1
Cops and Horrors; Fly Paper 1970,Ag 11,27:1
Story Theater Repertory; Saint Julian the Hospitaler 1970,O 21,40:1
Story Theater Repertory; Gimpel the Food 1970,O 21,40:1
Revenger's Tragedy, The 1970,D 2,58:1

Plante, Oscar
Memphis Bound 1945,My 25,23:2

Plants, Harvey Jack (Director)
Time of Their Lives 1937,O 26,19:1

Plasencia, V
Road to Happiness, The 1927,My 3,24:1
Girl and the Cat, The 1927,My 6,21:2
Cradle Song 1927,My 10,24:4
Fragila Rosina 1927,My 10,24:4

Plater, Louise
Sonya's Search for the Christmas Star 1929,D 14,24:6

Platfoot, Priscilla
Tidings Brought to Mary, The 1922,D 25,20:1

Platnova, Mme
Revue Russe, The 1922,O 6,28:1

Platt, David (Lighting Director)
Mandragola 1956,Mr 1,36:4

Platt, David (Scenic Designer)
Mandragola 1956,Mr 1,36:4

Platt, Edward
H M S Pinafore 1942,Ja 22,12:2
Mikado, The 1942,F 4,22:2
Pirates of Penzance, The 1942,F 18,22:2
Iolanthe 1942,F 24,26:4
Gondoliers, The 1942,Mr 4,22:3
Allegro 1947,O 11,10:2
Silver Whistle, The 1948,N 25,49:2
Texas Li'l Darlin' 1949,N 26,10:5
Twentieth Century 1950,D 25,23:6
Shrike, The 1952,Ja 16,20:2
Oh Captain! 1958,F 5,21:2

Platt, Evelyn
Four Walls 1927,S 20,33:1
Kansas City Kitty 1929,S 26,27:4

Platt, Fred
Betty Behave 1927,Mr 9,28:4

Platt, George (Miscellaneous)
Golden Boy 1964,O 21,56:1
Best Laid Plans, The 1966,Mr 26,15:2
Oh! Calcutta! 1969,Je 18,33:1

Platt, Harvey
Wooden Idol, The 1930,My 13,27:2

Platt, Jack (Director)
Legitimate Steal, The 1958,Ap 1,35:1

Platt, Jack (Playwright)
Legitimate Steal, The 1958,Ap 1,35:1

Platt, Joseph B (Scenic Designer)
Suds in Your Eye 1944,Ja 13,15:5
In Bed We Cry 1944,N 15,20:2

Platt, Livingston (Costume Designer)
Play of the Shepherds, The; Play of the Offering of the Shepherds, The; Play of the Adoration of the Magi, The 1923,D 26,15:4
Electra 1927,My 4,28:3
Launcelot and Elaine 1930,Mr 10,24:3

Platt, Livingston (Lighting Director)
When Ladies Meet 1932,O 7,19:1

Platt, Livingston (Miscellaneous)
When Ladies Meet 1932,O 7,19:1

Platt, Livingston (Producer)
Dinner at Eight 1932,O 24,18:2

Platt, Livingston (Scenic Designer)
Play of the Shepherds, The; Play of the Offering of the Shepherds, The; Play of the Adoration of the Magi, The 1923,D 26,15:4
Outsider, The 1924,Mr 4,16:4
Far Cry, The 1924,O 5,VIII,1:1
Two Married Men 1925,Ja 14,19:1
Pierrot the Prodigal; Enfant Prodigue, L' 1925,Mr 7,8:1
Stronger Than Love 1925,D 29,20:2
Puppy Love 1926,Ja 28,16:3
Creaking Chair, The 1926,F 23,26:1

Platt, Livingston (Scenic Designer)—Cont

Devils 1926,Mr 18,26:4
Sport of Kings, The 1926,My 5,24:2
Humble, The 1926,O 14,22:2
Daisy Mayme 1926,O 26,24:2
Witch, The 1926,N 19,22:5
Dark, The 1927,F 2,22:5
Strawberry Blonde, The 1927,F 8,20:3
Lally 1927,F 9,16:3
Puppets of Passion 1927,F 25,24:4
Thou Desperate Pilot 1927,Mr 8,23:1
Honeymooning 1927,Mr 18,25:3
Savages Under the Skin 1927,Mr 25,25:2
Legend of Leonora, The 1927,Mr 30,22:4
House of Shadows, The 1927,Ap 22,18:4
Electra 1927,My 4,28:3
Electra 1927,My 15,VIII,1:1
Baby Mine 1927,Je 10,21:2
A la Carte 1927,Ag 18,25:3
Racket, The 1927,N 23,28:3
Storm Center 1927,D 1,33:2
Venus 1927,D 26,26:5
Behold the Bridegroom 1927,D 27,24:1
Distant Drum, A 1928,Ja 21,13:1
Carry On 1928,Ja 24,26:1
Queen's Husband, The 1928,Ja 26,17:2
Outsider, The 1928,Ap 10,32:2
Say When 1928,Je 27,29:3
Great Power, The 1928,S 12,25:1
Pleasure Man 1928,O 2,34:7
Tomorrow 1928,D 29,20:2
Lady Dedlock 1929,Ja 1,61:2
Precious 1929,Ja 15,22:5
Flight 1929,F 19,22:3
Strong Man's House, A 1929,S 17,34:3
Maggie, the Magnificent 1929,O 22,26:1
Thunder in the Air 1929,N 12,34:3
First Mrs Fraser, The 1929,D 30,16:2
Greeks Had a Word for It, The 1930,S 26,16:5
Guest Room, The 1931,O 7,29:2
Church Mouse, A 1931,O 13,26:4
Berlin 1931,D 31,16:1
Alice Sit-By-The-Fire 1932,Mr 8,19:3
Round-Up, The 1932,Mr 8,19:4
Old Lady Shows Her Medals, The 1932,Mr 8,19:3
We Are No Longer Children 1932,Ap 1,17:2
Domino 1932,Ag 17,13:2
Man Who Reclaimed His Head 1932,S 9,17:3
Lilly Turner 1932,S 20,26:1
Stork Is Dead, The 1932,S 24,18:2
Mademoiselle 1932,O 19,22:4
Dinner at Eight 1933,Ja 7,11:5
Hangman's Whip 1933,F 25,20:2
Saturday Night 1933,Mr 1,13:2
Her Tin Soldier 1933,Ap 7,22:6
For Services Rendered 1933,Ap 13,15:5
$25 an Hour 1933,My 11,14:4
Party, A 1933,Ag 24,18:4
Pursuit of Happiness, The 1933,O 10,24:4
Three and One 1933,O 26,22:6

Platt, Louise

Caesar and Cleopatra 1935,Ag 22,21:1
Room in Red and White, A 1936,Ja 20,23:3
Mrs Moonlight 1936,Je 16,21:3
Spring Dance 1936,Jl 7,22:2
Spring Dance 1936,Ag 26,17:4
You Can't Take It With You 1936,D 1,30:8
You Can't Take It With You 1936,D 6,XII,6:2
Promise 1936,D 31,20:4
In Clover 1937,S 21,29:1
In Clover 1937,O 14,23:1
Five Alarm Waltz 1941,Mr 14,16:2
Anne of the Thousand Days 1948,D 9,49:2
Traitor, The 1949,Ap 1,30:2

Platt, Marc

Lady Comes Across, The 1942,Ja 10,10:2
Oklahoma! 1943,Ap 1,27:1
Oklahoma! 1943,My 9,II,6:4
Maggie 1953,F 19,20:2

Platt, Polly (Costume Designer)

Women at the Tomb, The 1961,Ap 25,41:1
Red Roses for Me 1961,N 28,41:1
Once in a Lifetime 1964,Ja 29,20:1

Platt, Richard (Miscellaneous)

Sixth Finger in a Five Finger Glove 1956,O 9,31:4

Platt, Waddill

It's the Valet 1933,D 15,25:4

Platte, Rudolf

Don Juan's Raincoat 1933,O 22,IX,2:3

Platts, Ronald

Merry-Go-Rounders, The 1956,N 22,50:1
Prodigal Son, The 1965,My 21,19:1

Plaut, Fred (Miscellaneous)

Hamlet 1957,Ja 29,27:1

Plaut, J S (Composer)

Pudding on the Ritz 1932,Ap 9,18:3

Plaut, J S (Lyricist)

Pudding on the Ritz 1932,Ap 9,18:3

Plautus (Miscellaneous)

Funny Thing Happened on the Way to the Forum,
A 1963,Je 2,II,1:1

Plautus (Original Author)

Funny Thing Happened on the Way to the Forum,
A 1962,My 9,49:1

Plautus (Playwright)

Menaechmi 1925,Je 9,16:2

Plaxen, Barnett Wolfe (Producer)

Grin and Bare It 1970,Mr 17,36:1
Postcards 1970,Mr 17,36:1

Player's Company

Escape Into Glory 1941,Mr 20,24:2

Players From Japan

Kage-No-Chikara; Shadow Man, The
1930,Mr 5,26:7
Matsuri; Festival 1930,Mr 5,26:7
Koi No Yozakura; Romance in Cherry Blossom
Lane 1930,Mr 5,26:7

Players Theatre

Clandestine Marriage, The 1954,O 17,II,1:1

Playfair, Nigel (Sir)

Beaux' Stratagem, The 1927,F 13,VII,2:1
She Stoops to Conquer 1928,S 2,VII,2:1
When Crummles Played 1928,S 23,IX,2:2
Savonarola Brown 1930,F 26,22:3
Blaue vom Himmel, Das 1930,Ap 20,VIII,2:1
Twelve Pound Look, The 1934,F 6,24:4

Playfair, Nigel (Sir) (Director)

Savonarola Brown 1930,F 26,22:3

Playfair, Nigel (Sir) (Playwright)

R U R 1930,F 18,28:1

Playfair, Nigel (Sir) (Producer)

She Stoops to Conquer 1928,S 2,VII,2:1
Critic, The 1928,N 11,X,4:1
Importance of Being Earnest, The
1930,Jl 27,VIII,1:8
Devil and the Lady, The 1930,Ag 10,VIII,1:3
Marriage a la Mode 1930,O 26,VIII,2:1
Those Naughty Nineties 1931,S 13,IX,2:7

Playten, Alice

Oliver 1963,Ja 8,5:5
Hello, Dolly! 1964,Ja 17,22:1
Henry, Sweet Henry 1967,O 24,51:2
Promenade 1969,Je 5,56:1
Promenade 1969,Je 15,II,1:1

Playwin, Ella

Home Is the Hero 1945,Ja 20,16:4
Innocents, The 1950,F 2,30:2

Plaza, Isabel

Cuando Los Hijos De Eva No Son Los Hijos De
Adan; When Eve's Children Are Not Adam's
1932,Ap 23,11:2

Pleadwell, Theodora

Wingless Victory, The 1936,D 24,20:2

Pleasence, Angela

Ha-Ha, The 1968,Je 15,38:2
Tempest, The 1970,Ag 29,14:1

Pleasence, Donald

Caesar and Cleopatra 1951,D 20,43:2
Antony and Cleopatra 1951,D 21,22:2
Lark, The 1955,My 13,21:2
Caretaker, The 1961,O 5,42:3
Caretaker, The 1961,O 15,II,1:1
Poor Bitos 1964,N 16,40:2
Man in the Glass Booth, The 1967,Jl 29,12:1
Man in the Glass Booth, The 1967,Ag 27,II,1:1
Man in the Glass Booth, The 1968,S 27,41:1
Man in the Glass Booth, The 1968,O 6,II,5:1
Man in the Glass Booth, The 1969,Ap 17,58:1

Plehn, Nancy

Children's Hour, The 1952,D 19,35:2

Plesa, Branko

Progress of Bora, The Tailor, The 1968,Je 27,49:2

Plesa, Branko (Director)

Progress of Bora, The Tailor, The 1968,Je 27,49:2

Pleshette, Eugene (Miscellaneous)

Holiday on Ice 1967,Ag 31,29:2

Pleshette, Eugene (Producer)

Holiday on Ice 1966,S 1,30:1

Pleshette, John

Sound of Silence, A 1965,Mr 9,30:1
Love's Labour's Lost 1965,Je 16,46:1
Zulu and the Zayda, The 1965,N 11,59:1
Measure for Measure 1966,Jl 14,27:1
Richard III 1966,Ag 11,26:1
MacBird! 1967,F 23,38:1
It's Called the Sugar Plum 1968,Ja 18,47:2
Jimmy Shine 1968,D 6,52:1

Pleshette, Suzanne

Cold Wind and the Warm, The 1958,D 9,55:1
Golden Fleecing 1959,O 16,24:5
Miracle Worker, The 1961,F 7,40:2

Pletzke, Marvin (Miscellaneous)

Awake and Sing! 1970,My 28,35:1

Plimmer, Denis

Off Your Marx 1936,Ap 2,28:2

Plimmer, Harry

Blue Lagoon, The 1921,S 15,16:1
Laughing Lady, The 1923,F 13,25:1
Shall We Join the Ladies? 1925,Ja 14,19:1
Antonia 1925,O 21,20:1
Pickwick 1927,S 6,35:2
Kingdom of God, The 1928,D 21,30:2
School for Scandal, The 1931,N 11,26:4
Firebird 1932,N 22,25:2
Victoria Regina 1935,D 27,15:2
Billy Draws a Horse 1939,D 22,14:5

Plimmer, Peggy

Top Secret 1960,S 6,40:1

Plimmer, Walter Jr

Home Towners, The 1926,Ag 24,19:3
Ten Per Cent 1927,S 14,29:3

Plimpton, Shelley

Hair 1967,O 30,55:1
Hair 1967,N 14,50:1
Hair 1968,Ap 30,40:2
Hair 1969,F 5,36:1

Plinge, George

If Love Were All 1931,N 14,14:5

Plinge, Walter

Crooked Friday, The 1925,O 9,27:3
Just Beyond 1925,D 2,22:4
John 1927,N 5,16:4
Jarnegan 1928,S 25,29:2
Infinite Shoeblack, The 1930,F 18,28:1
Lost Sheep 1930,My 6,33:2
Tyrant, The 1930,N 13,33:1
King Lear 1930,D 26,18:2
Julius Caesar 1931,N 18,26:3
Cyrano de Bergerac 1932,D 27,11:2
Richelieu 1934,My 22,28:1
Richard III 1934,D 28,24:3
American Holiday 1936,F 22,13:3
Cyrano de Bergerac 1936,Ap 28,17:1

Plinton, Ursula

Our Lan' 1947,S 29,16:5

Plivier, Theodor (Original Author)

Kaisers Kulis, Des 1930,O 19,IX,2:4

Plivier, Theodor (Playwright)

Kaisers Kulis, Des 1930,O 19,IX,2:4

Plotz, Charles

Life Begins in '40 1940,Ap 5,24:2
Hit the Road 1941,Ap 4,18:3

Plowden, R S

Playboy of the Western World, The 1930,Ja 3,20:4

Plowden, Roger

Russian Bank 1940,My 25,20:2
Song of Songs 1958,O 29,31:1
Three Sisters, The 1959,S 22,46:1
Marching Song 1959,D 29,20:1

Plowright, Hilda

Tale of the Wolf, The 1925,O 8,31:2
Cradle Song 1927,Ja 25,18:2
When Crummles Played 1928,O 2,34:3
Michael and Mary 1929,D 14,23:3
Heat Wave 1931,F 18,14:6
Lady With a Lamp, The 1931,N 20,27:2
Good Fairy, The 1932,N 18,22:3
Party's Over, The 1933,Mr 28,23:3
Distaff Side, The 1934,S 26,17:2
For Valor 1935,N 19,27:5
Eastwood Ho 1936,Jl 8,14:2
And Now Goodbye 1937,F 3,26:4
Leave Her to Heaven 1940,F 28,16:2

Plowright, Joan

Lesson, The 1958,Ja 10,20:3
Chairs, The 1958,Ja 10,20:3
Entertainer, The 1958,F 13,22:2
Chairs, The; Lesson, The 1958,F 16,II,1:1
Entertainer, The 1958,F 23,II,1:1
Taste of Honey, A 1960,O 5,46:1
Taste of Honey, A 1960,N 6,II,1:1
Chances, The 1962,Jl 4,11:2
Uncle Vanya 1962,Jl 17,18:4
Saint Joan 1963,Je 25,23:1
Uncle Vanya 1963,Jl 2,16:2
Love's Labour's Lost 1968,D 22,54:3
Merchant of Venice, The 1970,My 10,II,3:1
Merchant of Venice, The 1970,Jl 30,39:1

Plowright, Joan (Producer)

Travails of Sancho Panza, The 1969,D 20,35:1

Ployharova, Vlasta

Laterna Magika 1964,Ag 4,21:1

Plucinski, Dan

Wilson in the Promise Land 1970,Ja 11,78:1
Wilson in the Promise Land 1970,My 27,41:1

Plugge, D E

If Booth Had Missed 1931,My 14,27:1

Plugge, Domis

R U R 1922,O 10,16:1

Plugge, Mary Lou

If Booth Had Missed 1931,My 14,27:1

Plumador, Evelyn

Yankee Princess, The 1922,O 3,22:1

Plumby, Don (Miscellaneous)

Zizi 1964,N 23,51:1

Plumley, Don

Cage, The 1961,Mr 6,30:1
Saving Grace, The 1963,Ap 19,28:1
Whistle in the Dark, A 1968,F 17,32:2
Whistle in the Dark, A 1969,O 9,55:1
Whistle in the Dark, A 1969,N 9,II,3:1
Operation Sidewinder 1970,Mr 13,33:1

Plummer, Avalon

Warrior's Husband, The 1932,Mr 12,19:4

Plummer, Christopher

Starcross Story, The 1954,Ja 14,25:2
Home Is the Hero 1954,S 23,42:2
Dark Is Light Enough, The 1955,F 24,20:1
Medea 1955,Je 16,35:4

Plummer, Christopher—Cont
Julius Caesar 1955,Jl 13,20:1
Tempest, The 1955,Ag 2,18:2
Tempest, The 1955,Ag 7,II,1:1
Lark, The 1955,N 18,20:1
Lark, The 1955,N 27,II,1:1
Henry V 1956,Je 20,27:2
Henry V 1956,Je 24,II,1:1
Henry V 1956,Ag 29,25:3
Night of the Auk 1956,D 4,50:2
Hamlet 1957,Jl 3,15:2
Twelfth Night 1957,Jl 4,16:4
Twelfth Night 1957,Jl 7,II,1:1
Hamlet 1957,Jl 7,II,1:1
Henry IV, Part I 1958,Je 25,23:3
Much Ado About Nothing 1958,Je 26,22:1
Winter's Tale, The 1958,Jl 23,34:3
J B 1958,D 12,2:7
King John 1960,Je 29,26:2
Romeo and Juliet 1960,Jl 1,14:1
Much Ado About Nothing 1961,Ap 5,31:1
Richard III 1961,My 25,32:3
Richard III 1961,Je 25,II,3:5
Becket 1961,Jl 12,35:6
Macbeth 1962,Je 20,41:1
Cyrano de Bergerac 1962,Ag 1,21:1
Arturo Ui 1963,N 12,49:1
Arturo Ui 1963,N 24,II,1:1
Royal Hunt of the Sun, The 1965,O 27,36:2
Royal Hunt of the Sun, The 1965,N 14,II,1:1
Antony and Cleopatra 1967,Ag 2,25:1
Antony and Cleopatra 1967,S 17,II,1:1
Antony and Cleopatra 1967,O 29,83:4
Plummer, Earl
Music in May 1929,Ap 2,29:1
Plummer, Inez
Broken Wing, The 1920,N 30,14:1
Broken Wing, The 1920,D 5,VII,1:1
Dust Heap, The 1924,Ap 25,20:2
Octoroon, The 1929,Mr 13,28:3
Plummer, Joseph
Ticket-of-Leave Man, The 1961,D 23,15:1
Plummer, Tel
For Heaven's Sake Mother 1948,N 17,33:4
Plumptre, Edward Hayes (Translator)
Electra 1927,My 4,28:3
Electra 1927,My 15,VIII,1:1
Electra 1927,D 2,20:6
Plunkett, Albert
Biff, Bing, Bang 1921,My 10,20:1
Plunkett, Cy
Lights Out 1922,Ag 18,8:4
Spooks 1925,Je 2,16:4
Plunkett, E M (Scenic Designer)
John Gabriel Borkman 1959,N 26,57:4
Plunkett, M W (Captain)
Biff, Bing, Bang 1921,My 10,20:1
Plunkett, Morley
Biff, Bing, Bang 1921,My 10,20:1
Plunkett, Randolph (Hon Mrs)
Variations of 1940 1940,Ja 29,12:1
Plunkett, Walter
Out of the Seven Seas 1923,N 20,23:3
Man Who Ate the Popomack, The 1924,Mr 25,24:1
Plunkett, William
Lady of the Lamp, The 1920,Ag 18,6:4
Woof, Woof 1929,D 26,20:4
Children of Darkness 1930,Ja 8,25:1
Pluta, Steve
Stockade 1954,F 5,14:2
Mister Roberts 1956,D 6,46:2
Big Knife, The 1959,N 13,25:1
Pober, Leon (Composer)
Beg, Borrow or Steal 1960,F 11,39:4
Pobers, Tatiana
Chauve-Souris of 1943 1943,Ag 13,13:2
Pocaro, Marie
Paradise 1931,My 12,29:2
Poch, Leon (Costume Designer)
Hershel, The Jester 1948,D 14,39:2
Poch, Leon (Scenic Designer)
Hershel, The Jester 1948,D 14,39:2
Pockriss, Hal (Playwright)
Egg and I, The 1958,S 11,43:4
Pockriss, Lee (Composer)
Ernest in Love 1960,My 5,39:4
Tovarich 1963,Ja 23,5:6
Tovarich 1963,Mr 20,5:1
Pocock, Roger (Playwright)
Crime and Punishment 1927,Mr 6,VIII,2:1
Dr Jeckyll and Mr Hyde 1927,Ap 24,VII,2:3
Pocorobba, Tom
By Hex 1956,Je 19,25:1
Pocta, Frank
You and I 1925,O 20,29:1
Podgorny, Nikolai
Tsar Fyodor Ivanovitch 1923,Ja 9,26:1
Cherry Orchard, The 1923,Ja 23,18:1
Cherry Orchard, The 1923,Ja 28,VII,1:1
Three Sisters, The 1923,Ja 30,12:2
Brothers Karamazov, The 1923,N 20,23:4
In the Claws of Life 1923,N 30,23:4
Podmore, William
Charlatan, The 1922,Ap 25,14:2

School for Scandal, The 1923,Mr 13,19:2
Uptown West 1923,Ap 4,22:2
Lady of the Rose 1925,My 20,26:4
White Gold 1925,N 3,34:5
Easy Virtue 1925,D 8,28:2
Age of Innocence, The 1928,N 28,24:2
Mr Pickwick 1952,S 18,36:3
Whistler's Grandmother 1952,D 12,40:2
Ondine 1954,F 19,23:1
Dark Is Light Enough, The 1955,F 24,20:1
Separate Tables 1956,O 26,33:1
Separate Tables 1957,S 15,II,1:1
Podrecca, Vittorio
Untitled-Marionettes 1932,D 23,22:2
Untitled-Puppet Show 1934,Ja 9,19:2
Podrecca, Vittorio (Director)
Theatre of the Piccoli 1940,Mr 22,22:2
Podrecca, Vittorio (Producer)
Piccoli, The 1933,Ja 20,20:5
Poduval, Appukutty
Mahabharata 1970,N 28,22:1
Poe, Aileen
Poor Little Ritz Girl 1920,Jl 29,7:1
Broken Branches 1922,Mr 7,11:1
Royal Fandango, A 1923,N 13,25:1
Seventh Heart, The 1927,My 3,24:4
Berlin 1931,D 31,16:1
They All Come to Moscow 1933,My 12,20:6
Bright Honor 1936,S 28,14:1
Babes in Arms 1937,Ap 15,18:4
Aries Is Rising 1939,N 22,16:5
Feathers in a Gale 1943,D 22,26:2
Six Characters in Search of an Author
1955,D 12,38:1
Failures, The 1959,Ja 6,30:2
Fade Out--Fade In 1964,My 27,45:1
Poe, Gary
Henry IV, Part II 1968,Jl 2,33:1
Romeo and Juliet 1968,Ag 16,19:1
People vs Ranchman, The 1968,O 28,56:1
All's Well That Ends Well 1970,Je 16,53:1
Othello 1970,Je 22,43:1
Othello 1970,S 15,51:1
Poe, Virginia
Million Dollar Baby 1945,D 22,17:2
Poel, William (Director)
Conspiracy and Tragedy of the Duke of Byron,
The 1929,Ag 18,VIII,1:3
Poel, William (Producer)
David and Bethsabe 1932,D 25,IX,1:6
Pogany, Bella
Milgrim's Progress 1924,D 23,17:1
Captain Jinks 1925,S 9,22:1
Pogany, Willy (Costume Designer)
Little Angel, The 1924,S 29,10:3
Sari 1930,Ja 29,27:1
Pogany, Willy (Scenic Designer)
Liliom 1921,S 10,12:3
Little Angel, The 1924,S 29,10:3
Queen High 1926,S 9,21:2
Jeweled Tree, The 1926,O 8,26:2
Houseboat on the Styx, The 1928,D 26,14:3
Hawk Island 1929,S 17,34:7
Divided Honors 1929,O 1,28:2
Sari 1930,Ja 29,27:1
Pogodin, N (Playwright)
Aristocrats 1936,O 11,X,1:4
Pogodin, Nikolai (Playwright)
Missouri Waltz 1950,F 15,23:2
Kremlin Chimes 1964,Je 23,26:3
Kremlin Chimes 1965,F 25,23:1
Kremlin Chimes 1965,Mr 7,II,1:1
Pogostin, S Lee (Playwright)
Sidewalks and the Sound of Crying 1956,O 29,34:1
Pogue, Kenneth
Bourgeois Gentilhomme, Le 1964,Je 18,28:2
Henry IV, Part I 1965,Je 30,42:1
Falstaff; Henry IV, Part II 1965,Jl 1,35:1
Julius Caesar 1965,Jl 2,18:1
Henry V 1966,Je 8,38:1
Henry VI 1966,Je 9,55:2
Richard III 1967,Je 14,43:1
Antony and Cleopatra 1967,Ag 2,25:1
Merry Wives of Windsor, The 1967,Ag 4,18:1
Romeo and Juliet 1968,Je 11,55:2
Tartuffe 1968,Je 12,39:1
Midsummer Night's Dream, A 1968,Je 13,54:1
Three Musketeers, The 1968,Jl 24,49:2
Hamlet 1969,Je 11,37:1
Alchemist, The 1969,Je 12,51:1
Measure for Measure 1969,Je 13,41:1
Pogue, William
Miser, The 1963,My 10,39:1
Henry V 1964,My 13,52:1
Saint Joan 1964,My 14,41:1
Pohl, Elsa
Boy With a Cart, The 1954,Ap 5,19:2
Pohl, Frederick J (Playwright)
Brittle Heaven 1934,N 14,22:5
Pohle, Lawrence (Playwright)
Wise Girl 1932,Mr 20,VIII,2:5
Alley Cat 1934,S 18,18:1

Poidlous, Charles (Playwright)
Crucified, Les 1923,Ap 8,VIII,1:7
Crucifies, Les 1923,O 30,17:2
Poindexter, H R (Lighting Director)
Mrs Warren's Profession 1958,Je 26,22:1
Story Theater 1970,O 27,54:1
Poindexter, H R (Miscellaneous)
My Sweet Charlie 1966,D 7,56:1
Poindexter, Marlin
Chalked Out 1937,Mr 26,24:2
Poindexter, Rose
One-Act Plays of the Sea; Moon of the Caribbees
1937,O 30,23:2
Pointer, Priscilla
Gift of Fury, A 1958,Mr 24,21:4
Country Wife, The 1965,D 10,58:2
Condemned of Altona, The 1966,F 4,21:1
Caucasian Chalk Circle, The 1966,Mr 25,35:1
Alchemist, The 1966,O 14,48:1
Yerma 1966,D 9,60:1
Summertree 1968,Mr 4,29:1
Evening for Merlin Finch, An 1968,D 30,25:1
Inner Journey, The 1969,Mr 21,42:1
Time of Your Life, The 1969,N 7,37:1
Time of Your Life, The 1969,N 16,II,1:4
Camino Real 1970,Ja 9,42:1
Disintegration of James Cherry, The
1970,Ja 30,33:3
Amphitryon 1970,My 29,13:1
Good Woman of Setzuan, The 1970,N 6,51:1
Pointing, Audrey
Bitter Sweet 1929,N 6,30:2
Private Lives 1931,My 12,29:3
Poirer, Kathryn
Gypsy Baron, The 1944,Je 15,17:3
Poiret, Paul (Costume Designer)
Afgar 1920,N 14,VI,1:1
Beux Billes de Cadix, Les 1923,Ja 21,VII,1:3
Naughty Cinderella 1925,N 10,23:6
Poiret, Paul (Playwright)
Vogue 1921,O 23,22:2
Poiret, Paul (Scenic Designer)
Naughty Cinderella 1925,N 10,23:6
Poirier, Shirley
Achilles Had a Heel 1935,O 14,20:2
Let Freedom Ring 1935,N 7,26:2
Victoria Regina 1935,D 27,15:2
Greatest Show on Earth, The 1938,Ja 6,22:2
Dear Octopus 1939,Ja 12,22:2
Poirier, Sidney
Journeyman 1938,Ja 31,14:2
Poisner, Dina
Gandhi 1970,O 21,37:1
Poitier, Juanita (Miscellaneous)
Day of Absence 1965,N 16,56:1
Happy Ending 1965,N 16,56:1
Poitier, Sidney
Lysistrata 1946,O 18,27:5
Freight 1949,F 4,30:2
Raisin in the Sun, A 1959,Mr 12,27:1
Raisin in the Sun, A 1959,Mr 29,II,1:1
Poitier, Sidney (Director)
Carry Me Back to Morningside Heights
1968,F 28,41:1
Pokrass, Samuel
Satellite 1935,N 21,27:5
Pokrass, Samuel (Composer)
White Plume, The 1939,D 27,16:1
Pokrass, Samuel (Lyricist)
Ziegfeld Follies 1934,Ja 5,24:3
Pokrass, Samuel (Playwright)
Ziegfeld Follies 1934,Ja 5,24:3
Pokrovsky, Aleksei
Cherry Orchard, The 1965,F 10,46:1
Three Sisters, The 1965,F 12,15:1
Kremlin Chimes 1965,F 25,23:1
Pola, Edward (Composer)
Woof, Woof 1929,D 26,20:4
Pola, Edward (Lyricist)
Woof, Woof 1929,D 26,20:4
Polacek, Louis
Silk Stockings 1955,F 25,17:3
Most Happy Fella, The 1956,My 4,20:1
Christine 1960,Ap 29,27:1
Polacheck, Charles
Two on an Island 1940,Ja 23,17:2
No for an Answer 1941,Ja 6,10:6
Polah, Andre
Susanna, Don't You Cry 1939,My 23,27:2
Polakov, Lester (Costume Designer)
Reunion in New York 1940,F 22,28:4
Crazy With the Heat 1941,Ja 31,15:2
Crime and Punishment 1947,D 23,29:3
Member of the Wedding, The 1950,Ja 6,26:6
Winner, The 1954,F 18,34:1
Purple Dust 1956,D 28,15:1
Empire Builders, The 1968,O 2,34:1
Polakov, Lester (Lighting Director)
Member of the Wedding, The 1950,Ja 6,26:6
Little Blue Light, The 1951,Ap 30,17:2
Mrs McThing 1952,F 21,22:1
Emperor's Clothes, The 1953,F 10,24:2
Master Builder, The 1955,Mr 2,23:2

olakov, Lester (Lighting Director)—Cont

Purple Dust 1956,D 28,15:1
Winkelberg 1958,Ja 15,26:2
Cock-A-Doodle Dandy 1958,N 13,39:2
Great Day in the Morning 1962,Mr 29,29:1
Empire Builders, The 1968,O 2,34:1

olakov, Lester (Miscellaneous)

I Know at the Door 1957,S 30,27:2

olakov, Lester (Scenic Designer)

Mother, The 1939,Ap 26,26:2
Call Me Mister 1946,Ap 19,26:2
Nineteenth Hole of Europe, The 1949,Mr 28,16:2
Golden State, The 1950,N 27,29:3
Little Blue Light, The 1951,Ap 30,17:2
Mrs McThing 1952,F 21,22:1
Mrs McThing 1952,Mr 2,II,1:1
Emperor's Clothes, The 1953,F 10,24:2
Winner, The 1954,F 18,34:1
Skin of Our Teeth, The 1955,Ag 18,16:1
Purple Dust 1956,D 28,15:1
Winkelberg 1958,Ja 15,26:2
Cock-A-Doodle Dandy 1958,N 13,39:2
Cock-A-Doodle Dandy 1958,N 23,II,1:1
Twelfth Night 1959,Jl 11,10:2
Great Day in the Morning 1962,Mr 29,29:1
Empire Builders, The 1968,O 2,34:1
Candaules, Commissioner 1970,My 29,15:1

Polan, Barron (Producer)

Can-Can 1959,Ag 26,25:4

Polan, Lou

Bootleggers, The 1922,N 28,24:1
Cyrano de Bergerac 1923,N 2,14:1
Three Doors 1925,Ap 24,16:4
Cyrano de Bergerac 1926,F 19,18:1
Immortal Thief, The 1926,O 4,21:1
Caponsacchi 1926,O 27,24:2
Electra 1927,My 4,28:3
Hamlet 1928,Ja 5,33:2
Henry V 1928,Mr 16,26:2
Light of Asia, The 1928,O 10,32:2
Cyrano de Bergerac 1928,D 26,14:4
Bonds of Interest, The 1929,O 15,34:2
Richelieu 1929,D 26,20:3
Merchant of Venice, The 1930,D 3,29:2
Merchant of Venice, The 1931,N 9,22:2
Firebird 1932,N 22,25:2
Yoshe Kalb 1933,D 29,27:2
Sweet Mystery of Life 1935,O 12,13:3
Julie the Great 1936,Ja 15,15:3
Hymn to the Rising Sun 1937,My 7,28:2
Haiti 1938,Mr 3,16:1
All the Living 1938,Mr 25,14:4
Night Music 1940,F 23,18:2
Walk Into My Parlor 1941,N 20,38:2
Cafe Crown 1942,Ja 24,12:5
Oklahoma! 1943,N 14,II,1:1
Whole World Over, The 1947,Mr 28,28:2
Gentleman From Athens, The 1947,D 10,42:4
Golden State, The 1950,N 27,29:3
Desire Under the Elms 1952,Ja 17,23:4
Coriolanus 1954,Ja 20,34:2
Sea Gull, The 1954,My 12,38:1
Bus Stop 1955,Mr 3,23:2
Bus Stop 1955,Mr 13,II,1:1
Sea Gull, The 1956,O 23,38:1
Drink to Me Only 1958,O 9,47:4
Legend of Lizzie, The 1959,F 10,39:1
Hamlet 1964,Je 17,49:1
Tenth Man, The 1967,N 9,54:1

Polanco, Iraida

Song for a Certain Midnight 1959,S 17,49:1

Poland, Albert (Miscellaneous)

Futz 1968,Je 14,39:1

Poland, Albert (Producer)

Now Is the Time for all Good Men 1967,S 27,42:1
Peace 1969,Ja 28,49:1
Forensic and the Navigators 1970,Ap 2,43:1
Unseen Hand, The 1970,Ap 2,43:1

Poland, Edward

Like a King 1921,O 4,10:1
Ghosts 1922,F 7,12:1
Lady Bug 1922,Ap 18,15:3
Faithful Heart, The 1922,O 11,22:1
Extra 1923,Ja 24,22:3
Bachelor's Brides 1925,My 29,20:2
What Ann Brought Home 1927,F 22,22:2
Midsummer Night's Dream, A 1927,Je 27,25:1
Paradise 1927,D 26,26:4
Did I Say No? 1931,S 23,19:4

Pole, Frances

'Tis Pity She's a Whore 1958,D 6,21:1

Pole, Reginald

Great Way, The 1921,N 8,28:2
Hamlet 1922,N 17,14:1
King Lear 1923,Mr 10,9:4
Hamlet 1923,N 27,23:6
Great Adventure, The 1926,D 23,23:1
Courage 1927,Ja 20,20:1
Possessed, The 1939,O 25,26:2

Pole, Reginald (Director)

Great Adventure, The 1926,D 23,23:1

Pole, Reginald (Producer)

Great Adventure, The 1926,D 23,23:1

Pole, Rupert

No for an Answer 1941,Ja 6,10:6
Mr Sycamore 1942,N 14,13:2
Common Ground 1945,Ap 26,27:2
Duchess of Malfi, The 1946,O 16,35:2

Polen, Nat

Blood, Sweat & Stanley Poole 1961,O 6,31:1

Poleo, Dominic (Costume Designer)

Grin and Bare It 1970,Mr 17,36:1
Postcards 1970,Mr 17,36:1

Poleo, Dominic (Lighting Director)

Hi, Paisano 1961,O 2,36:2

Poleri, David

Belle of New York, The 1948,D 2,36:6
Saint of Bleecker Street, The 1954,D 28,21:1
Saint of Bleecker Street, The 1955,Ja 2,II,1:1

Polesie, Herbert

We Americans 1926,O 13,20:4

Polesie, Herbert (Playwright)

Heigh-Ho, Everybody 1932,My 26,31:2

Polgar, Alfred (Playwright)

Absconders, The; Defraudanten, Die
    1931,Ja 25,VIII,4:1

Polgar, Alfred (Translator)

Harvey 1949,Mr 24,34:1

Poliakoff, Vera

Love's Labour's Lost 1932,Ag 7,IX,1:7

Poliakova, (Mlle)

Chauve-Souris; Romantic Adventure of an Italian
    Ballerina and a Marquis, A 1931,O 22,27:1

Polianov, Alexis

Samson and Delilah 1920,N 18,18:1
Face Value 1921,D 27,10:2
Egotist, The 1922,D 27,12:1
Puppets 1925,Mr 10,19:1
Kibitzer, The 1929,F 19,22:5
Mr Samuel 1930,N 11,28:4
Hot Money 1931,N 9,22:2
Great Lover, The 1932,O 12,27:3

Police Band, The

Off the Record; Mayor Answers the Newspapers!
    Wow! 1935,Je 19,23:3

Polinoff, Tatiana

Faust 1927,Ja 4,20:1

Polinoff, Tessie

Faust 1927,Ja 4,20:1

Polinoff, Xenia

Launzi 1923,O 11,16:3

Polis, Daniel

Darkness at Noon 1951,Ja 15,13:4
Fortress of Glass 1952,S 5,19:2

Polis, Daniel (Director)

Fortress of Glass 1952,S 5,19:2

Polis, Daniel (Playwright)

Fortress of Glass 1952,S 5,19:2

Politis, Photos (Translator)

Oedipus Tyrannus 1952,N 25,35:2

Polito, Philip

1776 1969,Mr 17,46:2

Polizzotto, Marie (Baby)

Broadway Shadows 1930,Ap 1,34:6

Polk, Gordon

Happy Hunting 1956,D 7,30:1

Polk, Olvester

Johnny on the Spot 1942,Ja 9,24:2
Flamingo Road 1946,Mr 20,18:2

Polk, Oscar

Trial of Mary Dugan, The 1927,S 20,33:1
Cross Roads 1929,N 12,34:2
Once in a Lifetime 1930,S 25,22:3
Face the Music 1932,F 18,24:5
Nona 1932,O 5,26:4
Face the Music 1933,F 1,13:4
Both Your Houses 1933,Mr 7,20:3
Pursuit of Happiness, The 1933,O 10,24:4
Green Pastures, The 1935,F 27,16:2
You Can't Take It With You 1936,D 15,31:1
Swingin' the Dream 1939,N 30,24:2
Mr Big 1941,O 1,24:2
Sunny River 1941,D 5,28:2
Walking Gentleman, The 1942,My 8,26:2
Dark Eyes 1943,Ja 15,20:2
Dark Eyes 1943,Ja 31,II,1:1

Polk, Pauline

Tyranny of Love, The 1921,Mr 2,7:3

Polky, S S

Arabian Nights 1955,Je 24,16:1

Polky, S S Jr

Arabian Nights 1955,Je 24,16:1

Poll, Martin H (Producer)

Brights Lights of 1944 1943,S 17,27:4
Viva Madison Avenue 1960,Ap 7,42:1

Pollack, Bernard

Major Barbara 1951,F 24,10:2

Pollack, Herbert (Scenic Designer)

Mikado, The 1967,D 4,65:3

Pollack, Lew

Vaudeville (Palace) 1929,Jl 8,17:6
Vaudeville (Palace) 1931,Jl 20,20:3
Vaudeville (Palace) 1931,Ag 3,15:7
Vaudeville (Palace) 1932,My 30,16:7

Pollack, Lew (Composer)

Mimic World of 1921, The 1921,Ag 18,9:2

Pollack, Max

Bronx Express, 1968 1968,N 16,43:3
Brothers Ashkenazi, The 1970,N 17,53:2

Pollack, Sydney

Dark Is Light Enough, The 1955,F 24,20:1

Pollack, Ted (Playwright)

Wedding in Japan 1957,Mr 12,37:7

Pollak, Joseph (Producer)

All Rights Reserved 1934,N 7,33:5

Pollak, Martha

Let's Sing Yiddish 1966,N 10,63:1

Pollard, Alice

Pins and Needles 1922,F 2,20:1

Pollard, Avril

Here's Josephine Premice 1966,Ap 26,54:4

Pollard, Daphne

Greenwich Village Follies 1923,S 21,4:6
Vaudeville (Palace) 1926,N 2,35:2
Vaudeville (Palace) 1927,Ja 25,18:3
Vaudeville (Palace) 1932,Mr 7,13:4

Pollard, Michael J

Comes a Day 1958,N 7,22:1
Our Town 1959,Mr 24,46:2
Loss of Roses, A 1959,N 30,27:1
Bye Bye Birdie 1960,Ap 15,13:4
Enter Laughing 1963,Mr 15,8:1
Enter Laughing 1963,Je 16,II,1:1

Pollard, Sherrand

Girl From Wyoming, The 1938,O 31,12:1

Poller, Fred

New Moon, The 1944,My 18,16:2
Broken Hearts of Broadway 1944,Je 13,16:2

Pollick, Teno

Steambath 1970,Jl 1,49:1

Pollitt, Josephine (Original Author)

Brittle Heaven 1934,N 14,22:5

Pollock, Al

County Chairman, The 1936,My 26,26:5

Pollock, Allan

Bill of Divorcement, A 1921,O 11,22:2
Bill of Divorcement, A 1921,O 16,VI,1:1
Pinch Hitter, A 1922,Je 2,20:4

Pollock, Arthur (Playwright)

Melo 1931,Ap 17,26:6
Melo 1931,O 20,29:3

Pollock, Bernard

Private Life of the Master Race, The
    1956,Ja 31,33:3
Lady From the Sea, The 1956,D 13,49:5

Pollock, Bernard (Miscellaneous)

Beggar's Opera, The 1957,Mr 14,35:1
Heroine, The 1963,F 21,5:5
Norman, Is That You? 1970,F 20,30:1

Pollock, Bert (Miscellaneous)

Leave It to Jane 1959,My 26,30:2

Pollock, Channing (Playwright)

Ziegfeld Follies 1921,Je 22,10:1
Fool, The 1922,Jl 30,VI,1:3
Fool, The 1922,O 24,18:1
Fool, The 1922,O 29,VII,1:1
Fool, The 1923,Ja 15,18:4
Enemy, The 1925,O 21,20:1
Enemy, The 1928,Ag 19,VII,1:1
Mr Moneypenny 1928,S 30,IX,2:7
Mr Moneypenny 1928,O 17,26:2
Mr Moneypenny 1928,O 28,IX,1:1
House Beautiful, The 1931,Mr 13,20:4
House Beautiful, The 1931,Mr 22,VIII,1:1

Pollock, Channing (Producer)

Mr Moneypenny 1928,O 17,26:2

Pollock, Ellen

On the Rocks 1933,N 26,II,2:8
No Ordinary Lady 1936,O 1,28:3
Far Fetched Fables 1950,S 7,39:7

Pollock, Ernest

Hell's Bells! 1925,Ja 27,14:2
Elmer Gantry 1928,Ag 10,9:4
Back Here 1928,N 27,36:3
Philadelphia 1929,S 17,34:5
Adams' Wife 1931,D 29,27:1
If Booth Had Missed 1932,F 5,24:2
Carry Nation 1932,O 31,18:2

Pollock, Frank

What Next 1920,Ja 27,7:2

Pollock, Gordon W (Producer)

Time Out for Ginger 1952,N 27,50:4
Black-Eyed Susan 1954,D 24,7:5
Red Roses for Me 1955,D 29,15:2
Innkeepers, The 1956,F 3,19:1
Wake Up, Darling 1956,My 3,34:2

Pollock, Horace

Skin Game, The 1920,O 21,11:1
Honors Are Even 1921,Ag 11,8:2
Peter Pan 1924,N 7,16:2
Cape Smoke 1925,F 17,19:1
This Was a Man 1926,N 24,27:1
White Eagle, The 1927,D 27,24:4
Money Lender, The 1928,Ag 28,27:3
Josef Suss 1930,Ja 21,28:5
Three Times the Hour 1931,Ag 26,15:5
Money in the Air 1932,Mr 8,19:3

Pollock, John (Playwright)

Damaged Goods 1937,My 18,27:2

Pollock, John (Producer)
Three's a Family 1943,My 6,24:2
Pollock, Kate M (Miscellaneous)
Cannibals, The 1968,N 4,60:1
Boy on the Straight-Back Chair 1969,Mr 18,36:1
Pollock, Lew (Composer)
Whirl of New York, The 1921,Je 14,18:1
Pollock, Michael
Show Boat 1954,O 29,28:4
Pollock, Michael (Miscellaneous)
Sophie 1963,Ap 16,32:1
Pollock, Muriel (Composer)
Pleasure Bound 1929,F 19,22:4
Pollock, Nancy R
Church Street 1948,F 10,27:2
Blood Wedding 1949,F 7,16:2
Sun and I, The 1949,Mr 21,18:4
Grass Is Always Greener, The 1955,F 16,25:2
Middle of the Night 1956,F 9,39:1
Middle of the Night 1956,F 19,II,1:1
Power of Darkness, The 1959,S 30,33:1
Gay Apprentice, The 1960,F 3,27:2
Too Close for Comfort 1960,F 3,27:2
Period of Adjustment 1960,N 11,34:1
In the Counting House 1962,D 15,5:5
Have I Got a Girl for You! 1963,D 3,53:2
Dream of Swallows, A 1964,Ap 15,46:1
Ceremony of Innocence, The 1968,Ja 2,33:1
Front Page, The 1968,O 20,85:5
Wrong Way Light Bulb, The 1969,Mr 5,40:1
Pollock, Percy
Only 38 1921,S 14,22:2
Spite Corner 1922,S 26,18:1
Pollock, Robert
Sonny 1921,Ag 17,12:2
Pollock, Sidney
Stone for Danny Fisher, A 1954,O 22,24:2
Pollock, Ted (Playwright)
Wedding in Japan 1949,N 11,29:1
Polonska, Tamara (Miscellaneous)
Victor, or The Children Take Over 1968,Jl 10,22:4
Poltorak, Henryka
Aunt Caroline's Will 1954,Ag 11,21:1
Polyakov, Vladimir (Miscellaneous)
Happy Landing 1942,D 6,VIII,1:6
Polynack, Mary
Pirates of Penzance, The 1946,My 17,14:6
Pomada, Maxime
Pickwick 1927,S 6,35:2
Pomeranz, Sally
Jack and the Beanstalk 1947,N 3,28:2
Many Moons 1947,D 15,35:2
Rumpelstiltskin 1948,Mr 15,27:3
Pomeroy, David
Family Reunion, The 1960,D 10,26:1
Pomes, Don
Christmas in the Market Place 1960,D 10,26:1
God, Man & You, Baby! 1963,O 30,47:1
Pomfret, J E (Mrs)
Dr Faustus 1926,O 27,25:5
Pommier, Jean
Annonce Faite a Marie, L' 1965,Ap 6,33:2
Pompa, Anne
Paradise 1931,My 12,29:2
Pompeii, Jim
Greenwich Village U S A 1960,S 29,30:5
Boys From Syracuse, The 1963,Ap 16,31:1
Pompianov, Mischa
New Faces of 1936 1936,My 20,24:5
Pompoff, The
Judy Garland's New Variety Show 1956,S 27,43:2
Poms, The Three
Blue Holiday 1945,My 22,13:3
Ponazecki, Joe
Port-Royal 1960,Ap 26,41:1
Send Me No Flowers 1960,D 6,54:1
West of the Moon 1961,Je 29,26:1
Take Her, She's Mine 1961,D 22,19:1
Dragon, The 1963,Ap 10,32:1
Dragon, The 1963,Ap 10,32:1
Fiddler on the Roof 1964,S 23,56:2
Xmas in Las Vegas 1965,N 5,31:1
3 Bags Full 1966,Mr 7,22:1
Love in E Flat 1967,F 14,38:1
Witness 1968,N 22,38:1
Harvey 1970,F 25,41:1
Ponazecki, Joe (Miscellaneous)
Port-Royal 1960,Ap 26,41:1
Ponce, Miguel (Director)
Subscriber, The 1968,N 5,53:2
Grab Bag, The 1968,N 5,53:2
Susie Is a Good Girl 1968,N 5,53:2
Pond, Barbara
War President 1944,Ap 25,17:3
Pygmalion 1945,D 27,16:1
Rosmersholm 1946,N 23,11:5
Madwoman of Chaillot, The 1950,Je 14,41:2
Pond, Donald (Composer)
Yanqui and the Senorita, The 1952,Ag 8,8:7
Pond, Helen (Lighting Director)
Palm Tree in a Rose Garden, A 1957,N 27,26:2
O Marry Me 1961,O 28,13:1
Can-Can 1962,My 17,32:2

Double Dublin 1963,D 27,16:2
What Makes Sammy Run? 1964,F 28,19:1
Roar Like a Dove 1964,My 22,40:2
Pond, Helen (Scenic Designer)
Floydada to Matador 1955,D 22,19:1
Opera Opera 1955,D 22,19:1
Hello Out There 1955,D 22,19:1
Hungerers, The 1955,D 22,19:1
Liliom 1956,F 18,12:5
Beaver Coat, The 1956,Mr 29,22:5
Idiot's Delight 1957,F 23,14:2
Right You Are (If You Think You Are) 1957,Mr 5,37:1
Palm Tree in a Rose Garden, A 1957,N 27,26:2
Oklahoma! 1958,Mr 8,15:2
Ardele 1958,Ap 9,39:4
Hamlet of Stepney Green 1958,N 14,21:1
She Shall Have Music 1959,Ja 23,18:4
Time of Vengeance 1959,D 11,39:1
Time of Vengeance 1959,D 27,II,1:1
Gay Divorce 1960,Ap 4,37:1
Ronde, La 1960,My 10,44:2
Idiot, The 1960,S 26,38:1
Man and Superman 1960,N 7,46:2
Emmanuel 1960,D 5,42:2
Montserrat 1961,Ja 9,30:5
Five Posts in the Market Place 1961,Mr 6,30:1
Smiling the Boy Fell Dead 1961,Ap 20,28:1
O Marry Me 1961,O 28,13:1
Merchant of Venice, The 1962,F 3,13:2
Can-Can 1962,My 17,32:2
I Got Shoes 1963,Ja 25,12:2
Boys From Syracuse, The 1963,Ap 16,31:1
Double Dublin 1963,D 27,16:2
What Makes Sammy Run? 1964,F 28,19:1
Roar Like a Dove 1964,My 22,40:2
Great Scot! 1965,N 12,56:3
By Jupiter 1967,Ja 20,28:2
Peddler, The 1967,D 9,62:1
Dodo Bird, The 1967,D 9,62:1
Private Lives 1968,My 20,59:1
Little Boxes; Trevor 1969,D 4,71:2
Little Boxes; Coffee Lace, The 1969,D 4,71:2
Pond, James B (Playwright)
Unknown Warrior, The 1931,O 23,28:4
Pond, James B (Producer)
Untitled-Revue 1928,N 19,16:2
Untitled-One Woman Show 1929,N 18,22:6
Ponder, Nancy
Typewriter, The 1955,Jl 29,8:3
Pongetti, Henrique (Translator)
My Fair Lady 1962,Ag 23,24:6
Ponkard, Macco (Composer)
Liza 1922,N 28,24:1
Ponnelle, Jean-Pierre (Scenic Designer)
Nathan the Wise 1962,Mr 7,29:1
Ponomareva, Irene
Moscow Circus on Ice 1970,D 9,63:1
Pons, Beatrice
Mahogany Hall 1934,Ja 18,18:5
Panic 1935,Mr 16,18:4
Bride in the Morning, A 1960,My 26,38:2
Valmouth 1960,O 7,29:1
Sunset 1966,My 13,34:1
Pons, Helene (Costume Designer)
Golden Journey, The 1936,S 16,28:6
Babes in Arms 1937,Ap 15,18:4
Madame Capet 1938,O 26,26:2
Primrose Path, The 1939,Ja 5,16:3
Two on an Island 1940,Ja 23,17:2
Ladies in Retirement 1940,Mr 27,24:3
Five Alarm Waltz 1941,Mr 14,16:2
Watch on the Rhine 1941,Ap 2,26:2
Distant City, The 1941,S 23,27:5
Portrait in Black 1947,My 15,30:2
Duet for Two Hands 1947,O 8,28:3
Men We Marry, The 1948,Ja 17,11:2
Paris '90 1952,Mr 5,33:2
Paris '90 1952,Mr 16,II,1:1
Time of the Cuckoo, The 1952,O 16,37:4
Skin of Our Teeth, The 1955,Ag 18,16:1
View From the Bridge, A 1955,S 30,21:1
Memory of Two Mondays, A 1955,S 30,21:1
Diary of Anne Frank, The 1955,O 6,24:2
Heavenly Twins, The 1955,N 5,23:2
Holiday for Lovers 1957,F 15,20:1
Romanoff and Juliet 1957,O 11,24:1
Monique 1957,O 23,38:1
Lovely Light, A 1960,F 9,27:4
Semi-Detached 1960,Mr 11,20:2
Sail Away 1961,O 4,48:5
Daughter of Silence 1961,D 1,28:1
Love and Kisses 1963,D 19,39:1
Lovely Light, A 1964,Ja 21,24:2
Pons, Helene (Miscellaneous)
Epitaph for George Dillon 1958,N 5,44:1
Ponsov, A D (Miscellaneous)
Three Sisters, The 1965,F 12,15:1
Ponterio, Robin
Song of the Grasshopper 1967,S 29,52:2
Pontilena, Carmine
Failures, The 1959,Ja 6,30:2

Pontilena, Carmine (Miscellaneous)
Winter Journey 1968,Mr 13,39:1
Ponto, Erich
Threepenny Opera, The 1928,D 2,X,4:4
Ponzini, Anthony
Anthony on Overtime 1961,O 21,13:2
Ponzini, Nicholas
Breaking Wall, The 1960,Ja 26,27:5
Poo, (Mme)
Satellite 1935,N 21,27:5
Poodles Hanneford and Family
Circus Princess, The 1927,Ap 26,32:2
Pool, John (Producer)
Billy Barnes People, The 1961,Je 14,10:3
Poole, Daniel
Criminal Code, The 1929,O 3,28:2
If Booth Had Missed 1932,F 5,24:2
If Booth Had Missed 1932,F 14,VIII,1:1
Best Years 1932,S 8,16:2
Poole, Newtt
Poupees de Paris, Les 1962,D 13,8:2
Poole, Patricia
Courtin' Time 1951,Je 14,30:2
Poole, Robert
Cage, The 1970,Je 19,25:1
Poole, Roy
Under Milk Wood 1953,My 29,17:1
Cretan Woman, The 1954,Jl 8,18:2
Cretan Woman, The 1954,S 5,II,1:1
Clandestine Marriage, The 1954,O 4,23:2
Firstborn, The 1957,Ja 7,29:2
Macbeth 1957,Ag 16,11:2
I Know at the Door 1957,S 30,27:2
Quare Fellow, The 1958,N 28,34:1
Macbeth 1959,Ag 1,9:2
Flowering Cherry 1959,O 22,46:1
Balcony, The 1960,Mr 4,21:1
Face of a Hero 1960,O 21,29:5
Moon in the Yellow River, The 1961,F 7,40:2
Witches' Sabbath 1962,Ap 20,22:2
King Lear 1962,Ag 14,35:1
Moby Dick 1962,N 29,45:1
Poor Bitos 1964,N 16,40:2
King Lear 1965,Je 25,39:1
1776 1969,Mr 17,46:2
Poole, Wakefield (Miscellaneous)
Do I Hear a Waltz? 1965,Mr 19,28:1
Pooler, Alfred
Stag at Bay, The 1935,Jl 30,17:1
Little Inn, The 1935,Ag 20,25:1
Pooley, Edward
Bombo 1921,O 7,20:2
Poor, Daniel S
Assorted Nuts 1940,Ap 7,I,44:6
Poor, Priscilla
Male Animal, The 1941,Jl 9,24:6
Holiday 1941,Jl 23,15:2
Drifting Apart: or, The Fisherman's Child 1941,Ag 20,16:6
Poore, Sadie
Black Eye, The 1938,Mr 8,22:4
Poore, William
Jumping Fool, The 1970,F 10,53:1
Popa, Alda
Intermezzo 1957,F 15,20:4
Pope, Carmelita
Streetcar Named Desire, A 1949,Je 12,II,1:1
Pope, Cathleen
Vaudeville (Palace) 1928,Jl 24,13:4
Pope, Glen
Frank Fay's Vaudeville 1939,Mr 3,20:4
Pope, Lenox
Trial of Joan of Arc, The 1921,Mr 28,8:2
Pope, Milton
Power of Darkness, The 1920,Ja 22,22:1
Romeo and Juliet 1923,Ja 25,16:1
Antony and Cleopatra 1924,F 20,22:1
Pope, Patty
Slightly Married 1943,O 26,19:2
Goodbye My Fancy 1948,N 18,35:2
Pope, Peggy
Doctor's Dilemma, The 1955,Ja 12,22:1
Master Builder, The 1955,Mr 2,23:2
Volpone 1957,Ja 8,27:1
Moonbirds 1959,O 10,13:1
Shadow and Substance 1959,N 4,42:1
Viva Madison Avenue 1960,Ap 7,42:1
Sudden End of Anne Cinquefoil, The 1961,Ja 11,25:2
Cockeyed Kite 1961,S 14,27:1
Across the Board on Tomorrow Morning 1961,O 23,22:5
We're Civilized? 1962,N 9,30:1
Uncommon Denominator, The 1963,My 8,35:2
Twelfth Night 1963,O 9,47:1
Kiss Mama 1964,O 2,30:1
Rose Tattoo, The 1966,O 21,36:2
Muzeeka 1968,Ap 29,47:2
Ah, Wilderness! 1969,N 9,86:1
Harvey 1970,F 25,41:1
Pope, Peggy (Playwright)
Uncommon Denominator, The 1963,My 8,35:2

Pope, Reginald
Hamlet 1923,N 27,23:6
Pope, Robert
St Louis Woman 1946,Ap 1,22:2
Popesco, Elvire
Tu m'ePouseras 1927,Mr 13,VII,2:7
Amant de Madame Vidal, L' 1928,Mr 25,IX,4:6
Course a l'Etoile, La 1928,D 9,X,2:7
Rendez-Vous, Le 1930,O 26,VIII,2:1
Tovarich 1933,D 3,IX,7:7
Vive le Roi 1935,N 24,IX,3:7
Tovarich 1953,N 29,II,3:1
Popiel, Ruth (Miscellaneous)
Loss of Roses, A 1959,N 30,27:1
Popikoff, Don
Hooray for What! 1937,D 2,32:5
Popkiewicz, Maria
Isabel's a Jezebel 1970,D 27,II,3:1
Poplar, Dorothy
Pal Joey 1940,D 26,22:2
Popoff, Michael
Nowhere Bound 1935,Ja 23,20:2
Popov, K (Scenic Designer)
Poverty Is No Crime 1935,F 21,22:5
Strange Child 1935,F 26,16:1
Popov, Konstantin (Director)
Porgy and Bess 1945,Je 17,II,4:3
Popov, Vladimir
Three Sisters, The 1965,F 12,15:1
Kremlin Chimes 1965,F 25,23:1
Popov, Vladimir (Miscellaneous)
Three Sisters, The 1965,F 12,15:1
Popova, Nina
Merry Widow, The 1944,O 9,17:1
Moscow Circus on Ice 1970,D 9,63:1
Popovic, Alexander (Playwright)
Progress of Bora, The Tailor, The 1968,Je 27,49:2
Popovic, Mica (Director)
Victor, or The Children Take Over 1968,Jl 10,22:4
Popovic, Mica (Scenic Designer)
Victor, or The Children Take Over 1968,Jl 10,22:4
Popovic, Vladimir
Who's Afraid of Virginia Woolf? 1968,Jl 4,13:1
Victor, or The Children Take Over 1968,Jl 10,22:4
Popowa, Mrs
Russian Isba 1920,F 17,19:2
Popp, Andre (Miscellaneous)
Irma la Douce 1960,S 30,31:2
Popp, Kaye
Best Foot Forward 1941,O 2,28:2
Popp, Wilhelm
Wiener Blut 1964,S 12,14:1
Poppe, Herman
Flea in Her Ear, A 1969,O 4,25:1
Poppen, Detmar
Chocolate Soldier, The 1921,D 13,24:2
Lady in Ermine, The 1922,O 3,22:2
Princess Ida 1925,Ap 14,27:2
Dearest Enemy 1925,S 19,9:2
Three Musketeers, The 1928,Mr 4,IX,2:3
Three Musketeers, The 1928,Mr 14,28:1
Three Musketeers, The 1928,Mr 25,IX,1:1
Sweethearts 1929,S 23,25:1
Mlle Modiste 1929,O 8,34:1
Fortune Teller, The 1929,N 5,32:3
Chocolate Soldier, The 1931,S 22,33:3
Geisha, The 1931,O 6,35:4
Chimes of Normandy, The 1931,N 3,31:3
Naughty Marietta 1931,N 17,31:2
Firefly, The 1931,D 1,23:2
Merry Widow, The 1932,N 27,IX,1:2
Bohemian Girl, The 1933,Jl 28,18:5
Chocolate Soldier, The 1934,My 3,15:3
Revenge With Music 1934,N 29,33:5
Lady Precious Stream 1936,Ja 28,15:2
Hooray for What! 1937,D 2,32:5
Chocolate Soldier, The 1942,Je 24,22:2
Student Prince, The 1943,Je 9,16:2
Popper, David
Golden Ring, The 1930,F 1,14:7
Soul of a Woman, The 1930,F 22,13:1
Little Bandit 1935,Ap 19,24:2
Souls for Sale 1936,S 21,27:6
Of One Mother 1937,Ja 18,21:3
Who Is Who? 1938,D 24,13:3
Yoshe Kalb 1939,F 6,9:2
Popper, Felix (Director)
H M S Pinafore 1968,Ap 29,47:2
Mikado, The 1968,My 2,59:1
Popper, Felix (Miscellaneous)
Pirates of Penzance, The 1968,Ap 26,32:1
Yeomen of the Guard, The 1968,My 9,53:1
Patience 1968,My 16,52:1
Popper, Felix (Musical Director)
H M S Pinafore 1964,Mr 21,13:4
Gondoliers, The 1964,Mr 28,14:1
H M S Pinafore 1965,Ap 15,39:1
Popper, Lila
Girl in Pink Tights, The 1954,Mr 6,13:2
Dybbuk, The 1954,O 27,33:6
Pops and Louie
Casino Varieties 1934,Ap 3,26:4
Harlem Cavalcade 1942,My 2,11:2

Popular Theatre
Johnny Johnson 1941,My 3,20:2
Popwell, Albert
Pirate, The 1942,N 26,39:2
Innocent Voyage, The 1943,N 16,27:2
Hickory Stick 1944,My 9,15:6
Inside U S A 1948,My 1,19:2
Show Boat 1957,Je 28,30:2
Body Beautiful, The 1958,Ja 24,15:2
Cabin in the Sky 1964,Ja 22,32:1
Popwell, Albert (Choreographer)
South Pacific 1965,Je 3,25:1
Porcasi, Paul
Jimmie 1920,N 18,15:3
National Anthem, The 1922,Ja 24,16:3
Texas Nightingale, The 1922,N 21,15:2
Oh! Mama 1925,Ag 20,22:2
Broadway 1926,S 17,19:3
Broadway 1926,S 26,VIII,1:1
Porcelain, Syd
Alternate Current 1939,D 23,8:3
Porcelain, Syd (Playwright)
Alternate Current 1939,D 23,8:3
Porcelli, Fred
Silver Tassie, The 1949,Jl 22,16:5
There Is No End 1950,F 17,27:4
In Any Language 1952,O 9,40:2
Porche, Francois (Playwright)
Knight of Columbus, The 1922,O 27,17:1
Virgin With a Big Heart, The 1925,F 1,VII,2:1
Sam Abramovitch 1927,Ja 20,20:5
Untitled-Play 1931,N 15,VIII,2:1
Race Errante, La 1932,Ap 10,VIII,2:5
Paix, La 1933,Ja 15,IX,2:1
Roi, Deux Dames et un Valet, Un 1935,Mr 3,VIII,2:3
Tsar Lenin 1937,Jl 18,X,1:4
Porcher, Nananne (Lighting Director)
Child Buyer, The 1962,My 14,35:1
Porgy and Bess 1964,My 7,32:1
Pordum, Herbert
Yeomen of the Guard, The 1964,Mr 19,29:2
Porel, Jacqueline
French Without Tears 1937,S 29,19:1
Poret, Janine
Can-Can 1959,Ag 26,25:4
Poret, Luc
Can-Can 1959,Ag 26,25:4
Porfiriewa, E
Blue Bird, The 1932,Ap 22,23:2
Porise, Daniele
Snookie 1941,Je 4,26:2
More the Merrier, The 1941,S 16,19:3
Porretta, Frank
Mikado, The 1959,O 2,24:1
Pirates of Penzance, The 1960,O 7,29:1
Mikado, The 1961,Ja 18,26:1
Pirates of Penzance, The 1961,Ja 20,24:5
H M S Pinafore 1961,F 2,26:6
King and I, The 1964,Jl 7,26:1
Merry Widow, The 1964,Ag 18,24:2
Pirates of Penzance, The 1968,Ap 26,32:1
Mikado, The 1968,My 2,59:1
Yeomen of the Guard, The 1968,My 9,53:1
Mahagonny 1970,Ap 29,51:1
Mahagonny 1970,My 10,II,1:1
Porta, Juan
Fuerza Ciega, La 1927,D 6,26:1
Todo un Hombre 1937,Ap 28,19:2
Cuando Los Hijos De Eva No Son Los Hijos De Adan 1937,My 1,17:4
Tierra Baja 1937,My 8,22:4
Portal, M (Composer)
Jardin des Delices, Le 1969,N 4,54:1
Porter, Alfred
Pillar to Post 1943,D 11,11:2
Our Town 1944,Ja 11,24:5
Helen Goes to Troy 1944,Ap 25,17:2
Merry Widow, The 1944,O 9,17:1
Porter, Annabelle
Crime 1927,N 6,IX,2:5
Porter, Arthur
Green Pastures, The 1930,F 27,26:1
Long Road, The 1930,S 10,30:2
Green Pastures, The 1935,F 27,16:2
Porter, Arthur D
Runnin' Wild 1923,O 30,17:3
Porter, Arthur Gould
Within the Gates 1934,O 23,23:1
Porter, Barbara
Up Eden 1968,N 27,42:1
Porter, Beth
Sunset 1966,My 13,34:1
Tom Paine 1968,Mr 26,38:1
Futz 1968,Je 14,39:1
Porter, Cole (Composer)
Greenwich Village Follies 1924,S 17,16:1
Out o' Luck 1925,D 19,15:1
Paris 1928,O 9,34:3
Wake Up and Dream 1929,Ap 14,X,1:8
Fifty Million Frenchmen 1929,N 28,34:4
Wake Up and Dream 1929,D 31,14:3
Fifty Million Frenchmen 1930,Ja 5,VIII,1:8

Porter, Cole (Composer)—Cont
Wake Up and Dream 1930,Ja 5,VIII,1:8
New Yorkers, The 1930,N 16,VIII,3:1
New Yorkers, The 1930,D 9,31:1
Gay Divorce 1932,N 13,IX,1:7
Gay Divorce 1932,N 30,23:4
Nymph Errant 1933,O 7,18:2
Nymph Errant 1933,O 29,IX,1:6
Gay Divorce 1933,N 19,IX,3:7
Anything Goes 1934,N 18,IX,1:7
Anything Goes 1934,N 22,26:1
Anything Goes 1935,S 15,IX,1:1
Jubilee 1935,S 23,20:3
Jubilee 1935,S 29,X,1:1
Jubilee 1935,O 14,20:1
Jubilee 1935,O 27,IX,1:1
Red, Hot and Blue! 1936,O 11,X,3:1
Red, Hot and Blue! 1936,O 30,26:3
Gay Divorce 1937,Jl 20,19:4
Gay Divorce 1937,Ag 11,27:2
Anything Goes 1937,Ag 17,23:4
Anything Goes 1937,Ag 26,24:3
You Never Know 1938,Mr 4,16:3
You Never Know 1938,S 22,26:3
Leave It to Me! 1938,O 23,IX,3:5
Leave It to Me! 1938,N 10,32:2
Leave It to Me! 1938,N 20,IX,1:1
Leave It to Me! 1939,S 10,IX,1:1
Du Barry 1939,N 19,X,3:4
Du Barry Was a Lady 1939,D 7,34:2
Du Barry 1939,D 24,IX,1:1
Two Weeks With Pay 1940,Je 25,28:3
Panama Hattie 1940,O 4,28:4
Panama Hattie 1940,O 31,28:2
Panama Hattie 1940,N 10,IX,1:1
Let's Face It 1941,O 10,27:1
Let's Face It 1941,O 30,26:2
Du Barry 1942,N 1,VIII,2:2
Let's Face It 1942,N 29,VIII,2:1
Something for the Boys 1943,Ja 17,VIII,1:1
Mexican Hayride 1944,Ja 29,9:6
Mexican Hayride 1944,F 6,II,1:1
Seven Lively Arts 1944,D 8,26:6
Seven Lively Arts 1944,D 17,II,3:1
Around the World 1946,Je 1,9:5
Around the World 1946,Je 9,II,1:1
Kiss Me, Kate 1948,D 31,10:3
Kiss Me, Kate 1949,Ja 16,II,1:1
Kiss Me, Kate 1952,Ja 9,24:6
Can-Can 1953,My 8,28:1
Can-Can 1953,My 17,II,1:1
Kiss Me, Kate 1954,Mr 27,13:2
Can-Can 1954,O 24,II,3:1
Silk Stockings 1955,F 25,17:3
Silk Stockings 1955,Mr 27,II,1:1
Out of This World 1955,O 13,35:2
Out of This World 1955,N 10,44:2
Kiss Me, Kate 1956,My 10,27:2
Kiss Me, Kate 1959,Ag 10,24:1
Gay Divorce 1960,Ap 4,37:1
Anything Goes 1962,My 16,35:1
Can-Can 1962,My 17,32:2
Kiss Me, Kate 1963,D 1,184:3
Kiss Me, Kate 1964,F 16,29:1
Kiss Me, Kate 1965,My 13,31:1
Kiss Me, Kate 1970,D 26,10:4
Porter, Cole (Lyricist)
Greenwich Village Follies 1924,S 17,16:1
Out o' Luck 1925,D 19,15:1
Fifty Million Frenchmen 1929,N 28,34:4
Wake Up and Dream 1929,D 31,14:3
Fifty Million Frenchmen 1930,Ja 5,VIII,1:8
New Yorkers, The 1930,D 9,31:1
Gay Divorce 1932,N 13,IX,1:7
Gay Divorce 1932,N 30,23:4
Nymph Errant 1933,O 7,18:2
Nymph Errant 1933,O 29,IX,1:6
Anything Goes 1934,N 18,IX,1:7
Anything Goes 1934,N 22,26:1
Anything Goes 1935,S 15,IX,1:1
Jubilee 1935,S 23,20:3
Jubilee 1935,S 29,X,1:1
Jubilee 1935,O 14,20:1
Jubilee 1935,O 27,IX,1:1
Red, Hot and Blue! 1936,O 11,X,3:1
You Never Know 1938,Mr 4,16:3
You Never Know 1938,S 22,26:3
Leave It to Me! 1938,N 10,32:2
Du Barry Was a Lady 1939,D 7,34:2
Panama Hattie 1940,O 31,28:2
Panama Hattie 1940,N 10,IX,1:1
Let's Face It 1941,O 10,27:1
Let's Face It 1941,O 30,26:2
Something for the Boys 1943,Ja 17,VIII,1:1
Seven Lively Arts 1944,D 8,26:6
Around the World 1946,Je 1,9:5
Around the World 1946,Je 9,II,1:1
Kiss Me, Kate 1948,D 31,10:3
Out of This World 1950,D 22,17:3
Kiss Me, Kate 1952,Ja 9,24:6
Can-Can 1953,My 17,II,1:1
Kiss Me, Kate 1954,Mr 27,13:2
Can-Can 1954,O 24,II,3:1

Porter, Cole (Lyricist)—Cont
Silk Stockings 1955,F 25,17:3
Silk Stockings 1955,Mr 27,II,1:1
Out of This World 1955,N 10,44:2
Kiss Me, Kate 1956,My 10,27:2
Gay Divorce 1960,Ap 4,37:1
Anything Goes 1962,My 16,35:1
Can-Can 1962,My 17,32:2
Kiss Me, Kate 1964,F 16,29:1
Kiss Me, Kate 1965,My 13,31:1
Kiss Me, Kate 1966,F 5,32:1
Porter, Cole (Miscellaneous)
Rosalie 1957,Je 26,28:2
Porter, Cole (Playwright)
Gay Divorce 1937,Ag 11,27:2
Anything Goes 1937,Ag 17,23:4
You Never Know 1938,Mr 4,16:3
Leave It to Me! 1938,O 23,IX,3:5
Out of This World 1955,N 10,44:2
Kiss Me, Kate 1958,My 31,7:4
Can-Can 1959,Ag 26,25:4
Porter, Dee
Anything Goes 1934,N 22,26:1
Porter, Del
Ripples 1930,F 12,26:1
Girl Crazy 1930,O 15,27:1
Porter, Don
Any Wednesday 1964,F 19,34:1
Front Page, The 1969,My 12,54:2
Plaza Suite 1970,Mr 22,90:3
Porter, Edna
Magnanimous Lover, The 1920,F 10,10:2
Suppressed Desires 1920,F 10,10:2
Girl in the Coffin, The 1920,F 10,10:2
Porter, Eric
Visit, The 1958,My 6,40:1
Visit, The 1958,S 7,II,1:1
Twelfth Night 1960,My 18,48:6
Richard III 1961,My 25,32:3
Becket 1961,Jl 12,35:6
Macbeth 1962,Je 6,35:2
Cymbeline 1962,Jl 18,21:2
Jew of Malta, The 1965,Ap 17,9:1
Merchant of Venice, The 1965,Ap 17,9:1
King Lear 1968,Ap 12,42:5
Dr Faustus 1968,Je 29,20:1
Porter, Ethel
Gala Night 1930,F 26,22:4
Porter, Harry
Latent Heterosexual, The 1968,Mr 22,52:1
Macbeth 1968,N 30,49:3
Porter, Henry (Playwright)
Sap Runs High, The 1936,F 1,9:4
Sap Runs High, The 1936,F 5,15:3
Two Angry Women of Abingdon 1936,S 14,25:1
Porter, Henry Jr
Rogues and Vagabonds 1930,My 8,32:5
Porter, Hugh (Prof) (Musical Director)
Jericho-Jim Crow 1964,Ja 13,25:3
Porter, Hugh Gospel Singers
Jericho-Jim Crow 1968,Mr 23,22:2
Porter, Isabel (Playwright)
Singing Girl, The 1952,Je 4,31:8
Porter, Joan
Fun City 1968,Mr 7,53:2
Lend an Ear 1969,O 29,32:1
Porter, Katherine
What Next 1920,Ja 27,7:2
Porter, Katherine Anne (Original Author)
Pale Horse, Pale Rider 1957,O 30,26:1
Porter, Katherine Anne (Playwright)
When I Was a Child 1960,D 9,38:1
Porter, Ken
Commedia Dell' Arte 1957,Jl 5,13:2
Porter, L Ross
On the Level 1937,Mr 26,24:4
Porter, Mary (Miscellaneous)
Troubled Waters 1965,Je 4,40:2
Porter, Michael
Kibitzer, The 1929,F 19,22:5
Porter, Norman
Stop Press 1939,Mr 20,13:2
Brown Danube, The 1939,My 18,30:4
She Gave Him All She Had 1939,D 2,20:7
Years Between, The 1942,F 7,13:2
Porter, Nyree Dawn
Duel, The 1968,Ap 18,56:1
Porter, Paul
Little Old New York 1920,S 9,9:2
Close Harmony 1924,D 2,23:1
Kosher Kitty Kelly 1925,Je 16,24:2
Port O' London 1926,F 10,20:2
She Couldn't Say No! 1926,S 1,27:3
Pickwick 1927,Mr 13,VII,1:1
Burlesque 1927,S 2,15:3
Half Gods 1929,D 23,18:5
Torch Song 1930,Ag 28,23:1
Man on Stilts, The 1931,S 10,23:2
Wild Waves 1932,F 20,11:4
Heigh-Ho, Everybody 1932,My 26,31:2
St Helena 1936,O 7,32:1
Miss Quis 1937,Ap 8,20:5
Father Malachy's Miracle 1937,N 18,26:4
Run Sheep Run 1938,N 4,26:2

Porter, Paul (Director)
Page Pygmalion 1932,Ag 4,17:5
Porter, Paul (Lyricist)
Florida Girl 1925,N 3,34:1
Porter, Paul (Playwright)
Florida Girl 1925,N 3,34:1
Porter, Paul E (Miscellaneous)
Othello 1934,Jl 22,23:4
Porter, Paul Jr
Tomorrow the World 1943,Ap 15,22:2
Arsenic and Old Lace 1943,D 13,18:6
Porter, Paul W (Director)
Nic-Nax of 1926 1926,Ag 5,19:1
Porter, Paul W (Playwright)
Nic-Nax of 1926 1926,Ag 5,19:1
Porter, Pauline
Pickwick 1927,S 6,35:2
Porter, Paull (Miscellaneous)
Ladies Night in a Turkish Bath 1961,Mr 22,38:1
Porter, Quincy (Composer)
Merry Wives of Windsor, The 1954,F 17,27:1
Porter, Rose Albert (Playwright)
Chrysalis 1932,N 16,15:2
Porter, Stan
Hello Solly! 1967,Ap 6,44:3
Porter, Stephen (Director)
Misanthrope, The 1956,N 13,44:1
Country Wife, The 1957,Je 27,22:1
Philoctetes 1959,Ja 14,28:1
Right You Are (If You Think You Are) 1964,Mr 5,37:1
Impromptu at Versailles 1964,Mr 10,43:1
Scapin 1964,Mr 10,43:1
Alchemist, The 1964,S 15,33:1
Man and Superman 1964,D 7,45:2
Right You Are (If You Think You Are) 1966,N 23,34:2
Right You Are (If You Think You Are) 1966,D 11,II,3:1
Wild Duck, The 1967,Ja 12,49:1
Phaedra 1967,My 22,50:2
Thieves' Carnival 1967,Je 5,52:1
Show-Off, The 1967,D 6,40:2
Master Builder, The 1968,Je 22,26:1
As You Like It 1968,Je 24,42:3
Misanthrope, The 1968,O 10,59:1
Misanthrope, The 1968,O 20,II,1:1
Wrong Way Light Bulb, The 1969,Mr 5,40:1
Guardsman, The 1969,Ag 17,II,5:1
Private Lives 1969,D 5,52:1
Private Lives 1969,D 14,II,3:3
Harvey 1970,F 25,41:1
Porter, Stephen (Playwright)
Philoctetes 1959,Ja 14,28:1
Porter, Stephen (Producer)
Country Wife, The 1957,Je 27,22:1
Porter, Stephen (Scenic Designer)
Country Wife, The 1957,Je 27,22:1
Porter, Stephen (Translator)
Scapin 1964,Mr 10,43:1
Impromptu at Versailles 1964,Mr 10,43:1
Porter, Tom (Miscellaneous)
Little Foxes, The 1967,O 27,53:1
Porter, Vivian
Music Hall Varieties 1932,N 23,15:3
Porter, Willie
Bottomland 1927,Je 28,29:3
Portercliffe, H
Merchant of Venice, The 1920,D 30,16:2
Porterfield, Gordon (Playwright)
Universal Nigger, The 1970,Mr 21,18:1
Porterfield, Robert
Town Boy 1929,O 5,22:4
Petrified Forest, The 1935,Ja 8,26:1
Let Freedom Ring 1935,N 7,26:2
Prelude 1936,Ap 20,17:4
Bury the Dead 1936,Ap 20,17:4
200 Were Chosen 1936,N 21,21:1
Washington Jitters 1938,My 3,19:1
Everywhere I Roam 1938,D 30,10:4
Porterfield, Robert (Director)
Petrified Forest, The 1935,N 24,II,9:3
Macbeth 1937,O 11,26:3
Hill Between, The 1938,Mr 12,12:5
Porterfield, Robert (Miscellaneous)
Two Angry Women of Abingdon 1936,S 14,25:1
Everywhere I Roam 1938,D 30,10:4
Porterfield, Robert (Producer)
For Charity 1937,Ag 25,24:3
Hill Between, The 1938,Mr 12,12:5
9 by Six: A Cry of Players 1956,D 5,49:2
Porterfield, Robert H (Miscellaneous)
Blithe Spirit 1946,Je 5,17:3
Porterport, John (Director)
Shewing-Up of Blanco Posnet, The 1959,S 19,26:7
Portman, Eric
Madame Bovary 1937,O 6,28:4
Madame Bovary 1937,N 17,26:2
Masque of Kings, The 1938,My 8,X,1:7
I Have Been Here Before 1938,O 14,26:2
Harlequinade 1948,O 10,II,3:7
Moment of Truth 1951,D 9,II,7:7
Living Room, The 1953,Ap 17,29:5

Portman, Eric—Cont
Separate Tables 1954,S 23,42:1
Separate Tables 1955,My 22,II,1:1
Separate Tables 1956,O 26,33:1
Separate Tables 1956,N 4,II,1:1
Separate Tables 1957,S 15,II,1:1
Jane Eyre 1958,My 2,31:1
Touch of the Poet, A 1958,O 3,23:2
Touch of the Poet, A 1958,O 12,II,1:1
Flowering Cherry 1959,O 22,46:1
Passage to India, A 1962,F 1,23:1
Passage to India, A 1962,F 11,II,1:1
Creeper, The 1965,Jl 15,21:1
Portman, Julie (Director)
Riot 1968,D 20,64:1
Portman, Julie (Miscellaneous)
Riot 1968,D 20,64:1
Portnoff, Wesley (Composer)
Happy as Larry 1950,Ja 7,11:2
Portnow, Richard
Give My Regards to Off Off Broadway 1966,D 9,57:1
Portnoy, Lenore
Pirates of Penzance, The 1946,S 21,19:2
Porto, Eddo
Taming of the Shrew, The 1940,F 6,17:2
Porto-Riche, Georges de (Playwright)
Tyranny of Love, The 1921,Mr 6,VI,1:2
Tyranny of Love, The 1921,My 3,20:2
Tyranny of Love, The 1921,My 8,VI,1:1
Portser, John Sarver
This Mad Whirl 1937,Ja 10,II,4:8
Pos, William
Thank You 1921,O 4,10:2
Pose, Walter
Rape of the Sabine Women, The 1949,F 5,10:5
Posemkowski, M
Revue Russe, The 1922,O 6,28:1
Posford, George (Composer)
Balalaika 1936,D 23,17:4
Posin, Kathryn (Choreographer)
Salvation 1969,S 25,55:1
Dream Out of Time, A 1970,N 9,52:1
Posner, Arie (Miscellaneous)
41 in a Sack 1960,Mr 26,15:2
Posner, Shulamith
Uncle Moses 1930,N 29,21:3
Posnick, Michael
Three Sisters, The 1968,Mr 18,56:1
Posnick, Michael (Composer)
'Tis Pity She's a Whore 1967,O 21,15:2
Metamorphoses 1969,D 12,69:1
Poss, Stanley
Danton's Death 1938,N 3,26:2
Posselt, Maria
Versunkene Glocke, Die 1936,N 20,26:3
Post, Ani
Ardele 1958,Ap 9,39:4
Post, Charles Gordon
Lady From the Sea, The 1935,D 14,11:3
No More Peace 1937,F 27,9:1
Post, David
Waterloo Bridge 1930,Ja 7,29:2
Post, Guy Bates
Climax, The 1927,S 25,VIII,2:1
Climax, The 1933,Je 14,22:2
Shatter'd Lamp, The 1934,Mr 22,26:3
Post, Guy Bates (Director)
Wrecker, The 1928,F 28,18:2
Climax, The 1933,Je 14,22:2
Post, Guy Bates (Producer)
Wrecker, The 1928,F 28,18:2
Post, Kenneth M (Miscellaneous)
Ah, Wilderness! 1969,N 9,86:1
Post, Langdon W
Off the Record; Mayor Answers the Newspapers! Wow! 1935,Je 19,23:3
Post, Leo
Good Times 1920,Ag 10,10:1
Post, Melville Davisson (Original Author)
Signature 1945,F 15,25:2
Post, Mildred
Peg o' My Heart 1921,F 15,7:1
Post, Sara
Mikado, The 1939,Mr 11,15:6
Post, Shelley
Hamlet 1959,S 11,21:4
Post, Ted (Director)
Rain 1948,F 2,15:2
Post, Tom
Joseph 1930,F 13,25:3
Post, W H
Ballyhoo 1927,Ja 5,18:1
Post, W H (Lyricist)
Vagabond King, The 1925,S 22,23:3
White Eagle, The 1927,D 27,24:4
Vagabond King, The 1935,N 29,22:7
Post, W H (Playwright)
June Love 1921,Ap 26,20:1
Vagabond King, The 1925,S 22,23:3
White Eagle, The 1927,D 27,24:4
Vagabond King, The 1935,N 29,22:7
Vagabond King, The 1961,N 24,36:1

Post, William
Seventh Heaven 1922,O 31,11:1
Aiglon, L' 1925,O 31,20:3
Glass of Water, A 1930,Mr 6,16:3
Clap Hands 1934,Ag 21,12:7
Many Mansions 1937,O 28,28:6
Calico Wedding 1945,Mr 8,18:6
Post, William D
Judas 1929,Ja 25,20:4
Three Sisters, The 1930,Ja 9,22:2
Boeuf sur le Toit, Le 1930,Ap 25,28:4
Post, William Jr
Faun, The 1924,Mr 28,17:2
Galloper, The 1924,D 19,26:2
Doctor Knock 1928,F 24,15:2
When the Bough Breaks 1932,F 17,19:2
Ah, Wilderness! 1933,O 3,28:2
Strangers at Home 1934,S 15,20:5
Eldest, The 1935,F 12,24:3
Prodigal Father, The 1935,Jl 2,24:2
Beginner's Luck 1935,Jl 23,24:4
Touch of Brimstone, A 1935,S 23,20:1
Three Wise Fools 1936,Mr 2,12:2
Richard II 1937,F 6,14:2
Apron Strings 1937,Jl 13,22:3
Merry Wives of Windsor, The 1938,Ap 15,22:3
Madame Capet 1938,O 26,26:2
Boyd's Daughter 1940,O 12,20:2
My Sister Eileen 1940,D 27,23:2
Love Goes to Press 1947,Ja 2,22:2
Richard III 1953,D 10,65:2
Postal, Martin
Topaze 1930,F 13,25:3
Postance, William
Quarantine 1924,D 17,19:7
Easy Terms 1925,S 23,22:2
Possession 1928,O 3,35:1
Lady of the Orchids, The 1928,D 14,37:3
Sherlock Holmes 1929,N 26,28:3
Touch of Brimstone, A 1935,S 23,20:1
Postance, William (Director)
Sherlock Holmes 1929,N 26,28:3
Admirable Crichton, The 1931,Mr 10,23:2
Poston, Richard
Stalag 17 1951,My 9,41:2
Chase, The 1952,Ap 16,30:2
School for Scandal, The 1953,Je 24,29:2
Gazebo, The 1958,D 13,2:7
Viva Madison Avenue 1960,Ap 7,42:1
Once for the Asking 1963,N 21,42:2
Poston, Thomas
Jack and the Beanstalk 1947,N 3,28:2
Many Moons 1947,D 15,35:2
Little Red Riding Hood 1948,Ja 12,15:3
Insect Comedy, The 1948,Je 4,26:3
Poston, Tom
Stockade 1954,F 5,14:2
Grand Prize, The 1955,Ja 27,17:1
Goodbye Again 1956,Ap 25,38:1
Best of Burlesque 1957,S 30,27:2
Drink to Me Only 1958,O 9,47:4
Come Play With Me 1959,My 1,33:5
Golden Fleecing 1959,O 16,24:5
Conquering Hero, The 1961,Ja 17,40:2
But, Seriously... 1969,F 28,29:1
Poswolsky, Jay (Lighting Director)
In Circles 1967,O 14,12:1
Pote, John
Ivory Door, The 1927,O 19,24:5
Broken Chain, The 1929,F 21,30:4
Life and Death of an American 1939,My 20,11:2
Poth, Clark
Then Came the Dawn 1935,Ag 29,25:4
Mulatto 1935,O 25,25:2
Petrified Forest, The 1943,N 2,30:6
Last Stop 1944,S 6,17:2
Bell for Adano, A 1944,D 7,21:2
Pothen, Yvonne
Tom Sawyer - Ballad of the Mississippi
1947,D 27,11:3
Potkin, Irving
Pirates of Penzance, The 1942,F 20,20:2
Potocka, Przybycko
Apple Cart, The 1929,Je 15,6:2
Potter, Ada
These Days 1928,N 13,36:2
Rebound 1930,F 4,29:1
Lean Harvest 1931,O 14,26:3
Plumes in the Dust 1936,N 7,14:2
Potter, Alan
Petrified Forest, The 1942,Ag 19,14:3
Potter, Arthur J (Dr) (Composer)
Scatterin', The 1960,S 15,44:2
Potter, Betsey (Costume Designer)
Getting Married 1970,Ja 20,46:1
Greenwillow 1970,D 8,60:1
Potter, Don
What a Killing 1961,Mr 28,41:1
Sunset 1966,My 13,34:1
You're a Good Man, Charlie Brown 1969,N 14,39:1
Potter, Edward
Distant Drums 1932,Ja 19,24:3
New Faces 1934,Mr 16,24:5

Fools Rush In 1934,D 26,19:2
Hamlet 1936,N 11,54:2
Potter, H C
Out o' Luck 1925,D 19,15:1
Orestes 1926,Je 20,II,3:6
Man Who Married a Dumb Wife, The
1930,My 9,20:5
Potter, H C (Director)
Button, Button 1929,O 24,26:1
Doctor X 1930,Jl 31,12:4
Experience Unnecessary 1931,D 31,16:2
Double Door 1933,S 22,15:5
Wednesday's Child 1934,Ja 17,23:2
Post Road 1934,D 5,28:3
Kind Lady 1935,Ap 24,24:5
Bell for Adano, A 1944,N 10,24:6
Bell for Adano, A 1944,D 7,21:2
Bell for Adano, A 1945,S 20,31:1
Anne of the Thousand Days 1948,D 9,49:2
Point of No Return 1951,D 14,35:2
Point of No Return 1951,D 23,II,3:1
Sabrina Fair 1953,N 12,37:1
Sabrina Fair 1953,N 22,II,1:1
Potter, H C (Miscellaneous)
Button, Button 1929,O 24,26:1
Potter, H C (Producer)
Coriolanus 1927,Je 18,8:3
Double Door 1933,S 22,15:5
Wednesday's Child 1934,Ja 17,23:2
Post Road 1934,D 5,28:3
Kind Lady 1935,Ap 24,24:5
Potter, Joan
King Lear 1962,Ag 14,35:1
Potter, John H (Producer)
Good Woman, Poor Thing, A 1933,Ja 10,27:3
Potter, Judy
Thesmophoriazusae, The; Goddesses of Athens,
The 1955,D 14,52:4
Potter, Lois
Red Mill, The 1945,O 17,16:2
Potter, Natalie
Let Us Be Gay 1929,F 22,19:1
Those We Love 1930,F 20,22:2
Potter, Paul
Meet a Body 1944,O 17,19:5
Hope for the Best 1945,F 8,14:4
It's an Ill Wind 1957,Ap 24,28:1
Potter, Paul M (Playwright)
Honor of the Family, The 1926,D 27,21:1
Potter, Penelope (Miscellaneous)
Chip, The 1960,My 17,42:2
Sandbox, The 1960,My 17,42:2
Picnic on the Battlefield 1960,My 17,42:2
Two Executioners, The 1960,My 17,42:2
Potter, Philip
Gondoliers, The 1962,N 16,25:2
Pirates of Penzance, The 1962,N 21,28:1
Trial by Jury 1962,N 23,32:4
Iolanthe 1962,N 28,42:1
Trial by Jury 1964,N 20,40:1
Mikado, The 1964,N 27,43:1
Pirates of Penzance, The 1964,N 27,43:1
Pirates of Penzance, The 1966,N 16,54:1
Patience 1966,N 30,58:1
Mikado, The 1968,N 2,29:4
Pirates of Penzance, The 1968,N 7,54:1
Potter, Shirley
Coco 1969,D 19,66:1
Pottle, Emery (Playwright)
Hero, The 1921,Mr 15,14:1
Hero, The 1921,Mr 20,VI,1:1
Pottle, Sam
Curious Evening With Gypsy Rose Lee, A
1961,My 10,53:1
Pottle, Sam (Composer)
J B 1958,Ap 24,37:1
All Kinds of Giants 1961,D 19,40:1
Leonard Sillman's New Faces of 1968
1968,My 3,43:1
Pottle, Sam (Lyricist)
Leonard Sillman's New Faces of 1968
1968,My 3,43:1
Pottle, Sam (Musical Director)
Mad Show, The 1966,Ja 10,16:1
Cry for Us All 1970,Ap 9,48:2
Pottlitzer, Joanne (Director)
Remolienda, La; Bawdy Party 1968,F 3,20:1
Potts, Nancy (Costume Designer)
Right You Are (If You Think You Are)
1964,Mr 5,37:1
Tavern, The 1964,Mr 6,39:2
Scapin 1964,Mr 10,43:1
Impromptu at Versailles 1964,Mr 10,43:1
Lower Depths, The 1964,Mr 31,30:1
Man and Superman 1964,D 7,45:2
War and Peace 1965,Ja 12,32:1
Judith 1965,Mr 25,42:2
You Can't Take It With You 1965,N 24,32:1
School for Scandal, The 1966,N 22,33:2
Right You Are (If You Think You Are)
1966,N 23,34:2
We Comrades Three 1966,D 21,46:1
Wild Duck, The 1967,Ja 12,49:1

Potts, Nancy (Costume Designer)—Cont
War and Peace 1967,Mr 22,42:1
Pantagleize 1967,D 1,54:1
Show-Off, The 1967,D 6,40:2
Exit the King 1968,Ja 10,48:1
Cherry Orchard, The 1968,Mr 20,41:1
Hair 1968,Ap 30,40:2
Cocktail Party, The 1968,O 8,42:1
Misanthrope, The 1968,O 10,59:1
Horseman, Pass By 1969,Ja 16,46:4
Cock-A-Doodle Dandy 1969,Ja 21,40:1
Hamlet 1969,Mr 4,34:1
Strada, La 1969,D 15,63:1
Hair 1970,Ja 13,39:1
Harvey 1970,F 25,41:1
Criminals, The 1970,F 26,33:2
Persians, The 1970,Ap 16,53:1
Early Morning 1970,N 26,57:1
Potts, Nancy (Miscellaneous)
Persians, The 1970,Ap 16,53:1
Pouch, Martin
As You Like It 1936,Ap 24,18:4
Poucil, Rene
Saint Wench 1933,Ja 3,19:3
Poulain, Bernard
Scuba Duba 1967,O 11,36:1
Poulenc, Francis (Composer)
Intermezzo 1933,Mr 26,IX,2:1
Enchanted, The 1950,Ja 19,34:2
Ring Around the Moon 1950,N 24,30:1
Amphitryon 1952,N 21,21:2
Intermezzo 1957,F 15,20:4
Enchanted, The 1958,Ap 23,41:1
Poulos, Angi O
Love's Old Sweet Song 1940,My 3,16:3
Brooklyn Biarritz 1941,F 28,16:2
Snookie 1941,Je 4,26:2
Poulsen, Johannes
Cant 1931,D 20,VIII,1:6
Poulter, Walter
Mating Season, The 1927,Jl 19,27:6
Pouncy, Gert
Road to Rome, The 1927,F 1,24:2
Pound, Ezra (Playwright)
Women of Trachis 1960,Je 23,18:3
Poupart, Homer (Miscellaneous)
Beyond Desire 1967,O 11,36:1
Pous, James
Breaking Wall, The 1960,Ja 26,27:5
Poutous, Constantine
Moondreamers, The 1969,D 9,68:1
Povah, Phyllis
Mr Pim Passes By 1921,Mr 1,18:1
Hospitality 1922,N 14,16:1
Ice-Bound 1923,F 12,16:2
Windows 1923,O 9,17:2
Minick 1924,S 25,20:1
Paolo and Francesca 1924,D 3,24:2
Tale of the Wolf, The 1925,S 27,VII,2:1
Tale of the Wolf, The 1925,O 8,31:2
Virgin, The 1926,F 23,26:1
Blood Money 1927,Ag 23,29:2
Marriage on Approval 1928,Mr 2,28:2
Vermont 1929,Ja 9,28:1
Hotel Universe 1930,Ap 15,29:1
Re-Echo 1934,Ja 12,28:4
Co-Respondent Unknown 1936,F 12,24:4
Women, The 1936,D 28,13:1
Dear Octopus 1939,Ja 12,22:2
Land Is Bright, The 1941,O 21,28:5
Land Is Bright, The 1941,O 29,26:2
Land Is Bright, The 1941,N 9,IX,1:1
Broken Journey 1942,Je 24,22:2
Naked Genius, The 1943,O 22,20:5
Dear Ruth 1944,D 14,29:2
Light Up the Sky 1948,N 19,34:2
Light Up the Sky 1948,D 5,II,5:1
Gently Does It 1953,O 29,43:4
Anniversary Waltz 1954,Ap 8,34:1
Poveda, Jose
Don Juan Tenorio 1953,N 20,18:5
El Alcalde De Zalamea 1953,N 23,32:5
Povia, Charlotte
Iolanthe 1962,Ag 8,34:2
Povitch, Stanley
But for the Grace of God 1937,Ja 13,21:4
Sunup to Sundown 1938,F 2,14:3
Powe, Dorothy
Pied Piper of Hamelin, The 1950,Ap 3,19:2
Powel, Robert Hare (Playwright)
Beware of the Bull 1933,My 30,13:7
Divine Moment, A 1934,Ja 8,21:8
Powell, Ackland
Revolt 1928,N 1,25:3
Red Rust 1929,D 18,31:1
Penny Arcade 1930,Mr 11,24:5
After Such Pleasures 1934,Ja 6,18:6
After Such Pleasures 1934,F 15,15:2
Sunday Nights at Nine 1934,Mr 5,18:5
Powell, Addison
First in Heart, The 1947,N 14,29:2
Pygmalion 1952,F 9,11:2
Shrike, The 1953,N 26,51:2
Fragile Fox 1954,O 13,27:1

Powell, Addison—Cont

Iceman Cometh, The 1956,My 8,38:1
Camino Real 1960,My 17,42:2
Powell, Anthony (Costume Designer)
School for Scandal, The 1963,Ja 26,5:2
Comedy of Errors, The 1964,My 21,43:1
Powell, Anthony (Scenic Designer)
School for Scandal, The 1962,Ap 6,31:3
School for Scandal, The 1963,Ja 26,5:2
Powell, Bertha
Promis' Lan', De 1930,My 28,31:2
Run, Little Chillun! 1933,Mr 2,21:3
Run, Little Chillun 1943,Ag 14,6:1
Louisiana Lady 1947,Je 3,35:2
Set My People Free 1948,N 4,38:2
Powell, Buddug-Mair
Under Milk Wood 1957,O 16,42:5
Powell, David
Winter's Tale, The 1946,Ja 16,18:6
Powell, Dawn (Original Author)
Lady Comes Across, The 1942,Ja 10,10:2
Powell, Dawn (Playwright)
Big Night 1933,Ja 18,16:2
Jig Saw 1934,My 1,26:3
Powell, Dick (Director)
Caine Mutiny Court-Martial, The 1953,O 14,35:1
Powell, E J
Galloper, The 1924,D 19,26:2
Powell, Ed
Fortuna 1962,Ja 4,26:1
Powell, Edward
Zeppelin 1929,Ja 15,22:3
Ladies of the Jury 1929,O 22,26:2
It's a Grand Life 1930,F 11,30:3
Powell, Eleanor
Optimists, The 1928,Ja 31,28:2
Follow Thru 1929,Ja 10,24:3
Fine and Dandy 1930,S 24,26:1
Music Hall Varieties 1932,N 23,15:3
At Home Abroad 1935,S 4,22:3
At Home Abroad 1935,S 8,IX,1:1
At Home Abroad 1935,S 20,17:4
At Home Abroad 1935,O 27,IX,1:1
Powell, Elmer (Producer)
Dinner Is Served 1929,Ag 16,18:4
Powell, Florence
Night in Venice, A 1929,My 22,30:2
Powell, Hagen
Tragical Historie of Doctor Faustus, The 1964,O 6,34:2
Powell, Jack
Laugh Parade, The 1931,N 3,31:2
Laugh Parade, The 1931,D 6,VIII,1:1
Powell, Jack Jr (Pvt)
Winged Victory 1943,N 22,24:1
Powell, Jerry (Composer)
Leonard Sillman's New Faces of 1968 1968,My 3,43:1
Powell, Jerry (Lyricist)
Leonard Sillman's New Faces of 1968 1968,My 3,43:1
Powell, Jerry (Playwright)
That Thing at the Cherry Lane 1965,My 19,42:1
Powell, Lee
Sap of Life, The 1961,O 3,44:1
Powell, Lewis M
Smyth With a Y 1937,Je 30,19:5
Powell, Lovelady
Riverwind 1962,D 14,5:5
Powell, Michael Warren
Home Free! 1965,F 11,45:1
Thank You, Miss Victoria 1966,Ap 12,43:1
This Is the Rill Speaking 1966,Ap 12,43:1
Chicago 1966,Ap 13,36:1
War 1966,Ap 13,36:1
Powell, Michael Warren (Costume Designer)
Tom Paine 1968,Mr 26,38:1
Powell, Pepper
This Was Burlesque 1970,F 12,31:1
Powell, Rae
Free for All 1931,S 9,25:1
Powell, Richard
Lace Petticoat 1927,Ja 5,18:2
Sweethearts 1929,S 23,25:1
Mlle Modiste 1929,O 8,34:1
Naughty Marietta 1929,O 22,26:2
Merry Widow, The 1929,D 3,29:1
Powell, Rosa
Roseanne 1923,D 31,9:5
Powell, Templer
Dancers, The 1923,O 18,17:2
Powell, Thomas R
Show Boat 1954,My 6,44:1
Fledermaus, Die 1954,My 20,38:5
Powell, William
Mary Stuart 1956,Ap 28,10:2
Powell, William (Producer)
Revolt 1928,N 1,25:3
Powell, William H
Spanish Love 1920,Ag 18,6:1
Bavu 1922,F 27,16:1
Woman Who Laughed, The 1922,Ag 17,14:3
Power, Arthur (Playwright)
Drapier Letters, The 1927,S 18,VII,2:1

Power, Edward
Back Pay 1921,Ag 31,8:2
Crooked Square, The 1923,S 11,10:2
Conscience 1924,S 12,19:3
Mismates 1925,Ap 14,27:2
Young Madame Conti 1937,Ap 1,18:4
Power, Harry C
Unwritten Chapter, The 1920,O 12,18:1
Power, Hartley
Dolly Jordan 1922,O 4,26:1
Pasteur 1923,Mr 13,19:1
Dawn 1924,N 25,27:1
Fall Guy, The 1925,Mr 11,19:1
Potash and Perlmutter, Detectives; Poisoned by Pictures 1926,S 1,27:3
Broadway 1927,Ja 9,VII,2:1
Dishonored Lady 1930,My 25,IX,2:4
Sweet Aloes 1934,N 1,24:1
To Have and to Hold 1937,Je 27,X,1:3
Room Service 1937,D 16,35:4
Alien Corn 1939,Jl 23,IX,2:3
Born Yesterday 1947,F 9,II,3:7
Power, Margaret
Pillar to Post 1943,D 11,11:2
Power, Mary
Tomorrow's a Holiday! 1935,D 31,10:2
Power, Stella
Murray Anderson's Almanac 1929,Ag 15,20:3
Power, Tyrone
Wandering Jew, The 1921,O 27,22:1
Wandering Jew, The 1921,O 30,VI,1:1
Rivals, The 1922,Je 6,18:2
Hamlet 1922,N 17,14:1
Julius Caesar 1927,Je 7,27:2
Venus 1927,D 26,26:5
Diplomacy 1928,My 29,16:3
Unknown Warrior, The 1928,O 30,26:6
Julius Caesar 1929,N 19,26:5
Merchant of Venice, The 1931,N 17,31:1
Julius Caesar 1931,N 18,26:3
Hamlet 1931,N 19,26:6
Power, Tyrone Jr
Romeo and Juliet 1935,D 24,10:2
Saint Joan 1936,Mr 10,27:4
Mister Roberts 1950,Jl 20,22:4
Mister Roberts 1950,Jl 23,II,1:6
John Brown's Body 1952,N 3,25:8
John Brown's Body 1952,D 16,43:5
John Brown's Body 1953,F 16,17:2
John Brown's Body 1953,F 22,II,1:1
Dark Is Light Enough, The 1955,F 24,20:1
Dark Is Light Enough, The 1955,Mr 6,II,1:1
Back to Methuselah 1958,Mr 27,41:5
Back to Methuselah 1958,Ap 6,II,1:1
Power, Walter
Crime 1927,F 23,27:3
Power-Waters, Pierce (Miscellaneous)
Parnell 1936,My 5,26:2
Lorelei 1938,N 30,21:2
Powers, Adrian
Little Theatre Tournament; House With the Twisty Windows, The 1929,My 8,34:4
Powers, Albert
Lights Out 1922,Ag 18,8:4
Ever Green Lady, The 1922,O 12,25:2
As You Like It 1923,Ap 24,24:1
Powers, Alonzo J 2d (Miscellaneous)
Caesar and Cleopatra 1927,N 6,IX,2:1
Powers, Bessie
Sojourner Truth 1948,Ap 22,35:2
Riders to the Sea 1949,F 4,30:2
Powers, Bill (Choreographer)
Broadway Sho-Window 1936,Ap 13,14:5
Powers, Charles
Kingdom of God, The 1928,D 21,30:2
Midnight 1930,D 30,25:1
Breadwinner, The 1931,S 23,19:4
Little Ol' Boy 1933,Ap 25,15:5
Dodsworth 1934,F 26,20:4
Bright Honor 1936,S 28,14:1
Tell Me Pretty Maiden 1937,D 17,33:5
Once Upon a Time 1939,D 21,28:2
Powers, Ed
Birds, The 1967,My 7,67:1
Nighthawks 1967,D 30,14:2
Powers, Edward
Charlatan, The 1922,Ap 25,14:2
Powers, Eleanor
Kingdom of God, The 1928,D 21,30:2
Spring Freshet 1934,O 5,28:3
Daughters of Atreus 1936,O 15,33:1
Powers, Eugene
Woman of Bronze, The 1920,S 8,9:2
Trial of Joan of Arc, The 1921,Mr 28,8:2
Iphigenia in Aulis 1921,Ap 8,18:2
Madras House, The 1921,O 31,18:2
First Man, The 1922,Mr 6,9:2
Bronx Express 1922,Ap 27,12:2
Ever Green Lady, The 1922,O 12,25:2
Lady Cristilinda, The 1922,D 26,11:2
Rita Coventry 1923,F 20,12:2
Home Fires 1923,Ag 21,12:1
Robert E Lee 1923,N 21,23:1

Powers, Eugene—Cont

Outward Bound 1924,Ja 8,26:1
Episode 1925,F 5,23:2
Episode 1925,F 8,VII,1:1
Green Hat, The 1925,S 16,23:2
Immoral Isabella 1927,O 28,20:3
Buzzard, The 1928,Mr 15,29:1
Light of Asia, The 1928,O 10,32:2
Kibitzer, The 1929,F 19,22:5
Children of Darkness 1930,Ja 8,25:1
Uncle Vanya 1930,Ap 16,26:5
Uncle Vanya 1930,My 4,XI,1:1
Uncle Vanya 1930,S 23,30:3
Inspector General, The 1930,D 24,19:2
Six Characters in Search of an Author 1931,Ap 16,29:2
He 1931,S 22,33:1
Jewel Robbery 1932,Ja 14,17:2
Troilus and Cressida 1932,Je 7,22:3
Red Planet 1932,D 19,19:2
Powers, Florence Colebrook (Miscellaneous)
These Are My Loves 1960,Ap 19,41:2
Powers, Geoffrey
Cradle Will Rock, The 1937,D 6,19:4
Cradle Will Rock, The 1938,Ja 4,19:3
Powers, Grace
Major Barbara 1951,F 24,10:2
Powers, Gudrun (Playwright)
Thistle in My Bed 1963,N 20,48:1
Powers, Hartley
Petrified Forest, The 1943,Ja 10,VIII,1:6
Powers, James T
Untitled-Benefit 1921,My 2,12:3
Rivals, The 1922,Je 6,18:2
Rivals, The 1923,My 9,14:2
Casanova 1923,S 27,10:2
Henry IV, Part I 1926,Je 1,29:1
Henry IV, Part I 1926,Je 6,VIII,1:1
Julius Caesar 1927,Je 7,27:2
Beaux' Stratagem, The 1928,Je 5,20:1
Beaux' Stratagem, The 1928,Je 10,VIII,1:1
Becky Sharp 1929,Je 4,29:1
Rivals, The 1930,Mr 14,24:4
Geisha, The 1931,O 6,35:4
Seven Keys to Baldpate 1935,My 28,30:2
Powers, James T (Playwright)
Lady Butterfly 1923,Ja 23,18:1
Powers, Jeanne
Cradle Song 1921,Mr 1,18:2
Adam Solitaire 1925,N 7,19:2
House of Ussher, The 1926,Ja 14,18:4
Powers, Jimmy
Untitled-Benefit 1922,My 8,14:5
Powers, Leona
Best Years 1932,S 8,16:2
Errant Lady 1934,S 18,18:2
Return to Folly 1935,Jl 23,24:3
Whatever Goes Up 1935,N 26,28:2
Golden Journey, The 1936,S 16,28:6
Aged 26 1936,D 22,32:1
Red Harvest 1937,Mr 31,29:2
Right This Way 1938,Ja 6,22:3
There's Always a Breeze 1938,Mr 3,16:2
Good, The 1938,O 6,27:2
When We Are Married 1939,D 26,22:3
Return Engagement 1940,N 2,19:2
Little Dark Horse 1941,N 17,14:4
Pie in the Sky 1941,D 23,26:5
Moon Is Down, The 1942,Ap 8,22:2
Malice Domestic 1942,Jl 21,22:1
Mr Sycamore 1942,N 14,13:2
Wallflower 1944,Ja 27,14:2
Home Life of a Buffalo; Hope's the Thing 1948,My 12,34:6
Hope Is the Thing With Feathers; Hope's the Thing 1948,My 12,34:6
Gone Tomorrow; Hope's the Thing 1948,My 12,34:6
Big Knife, The 1949,F 25,27:5
Drink to Me Only 1958,O 9,47:4
My Mother, My Father and Me 1963,Mr 25,5:5
Bicycle Ride to Nevada 1963,S 25,38:1
Once for the Asking 1963,N 21,42:2
Powers, Lou
Luckee Girl 1928,S 17,28:6
Powers, Louise
Prunella; Love in a Garden 1926,Je 16,23:3
Powers, Mala
Absence of a Cello 1964,S 22,45:1
Powers, Manila
Artists and Models 1927,N 16,28:2
Red Robe, The 1928,D 26,15:1
Count of Luxembourg, The 1930,F 18,28:2
Roberta 1937,Je 27,II,6:1
Powers, Marcella
My Dear Children 1941,Jl 22,22:6
Good Neighbor 1941,O 22,26:2
Powers, Marie
Medium, The 1947,My 2,28:2
Medium, The 1947,My 11,II,1:1
Medium, The 1948,Ap 30,26:3
Medium, The 1948,D 8,41:6
Medium, The 1949,N 7,32:4
Old Maid and the Thief, The 1949,N 7,32:4

Powers, Marie—Cont
Consul, The 1950,Mr 2,32:3
Consul, The 1950,Mr 16,41:1
Consul, The 1950,Mr 26,II,1:1
Consul, The 1950,Ap 2,II,7:1
Consul, The 1951,My 4,30:8
Carousel 1957,S 12,38:2
Becket 1960,O 6,50:1
Becket 1961,My 9,44:1
Powers, Maude
Vaudeville (Palace) 1927,Mr 1,31:2
A la Carte 1927,Ag 18,25:3
Powers, Nancy
Cabaret 1966,N 21,62:1
Powers, Neville (Lighting Director)
Live Like Pigs 1965,Je 8,48:2
Powers, Neville (Miscellaneous)
Softly, and Consider the Nearness 1964,My 12,32:1
Home Movies 1964,My 12,32:1
Powers, Nicky
Song of Norway 1958,Je 23,19:2
Powers, Peter
Lady of Letters 1935,Mr 29,26:6
Hook-Up, The 1935,My 9,24:6
Whatever Goes Up 1935,N 26,28:2
Powers, Puck
House in the Country, A 1937,Ja 12,18:3
Powers, Rea (Dr)
Veronica's Veil 1950,F 12,II,1:5
Powers, Richard
Barber Had Two Sons, The 1943,F 2,22:2
Powers, S B
Night at an Inn, A 1930,My 10,25:1
Powers, Susan
First Lady 1935,N 27,17:4
Powers, Suzanne
Evil Doers of Good, The 1923,Ja 17,22:2
Blue Bird, The 1923,D 26,13:3
Powers, Tom
Bab 1920,O 19,12:1
Love Dreams 1921,O 11,22:2
Steamship Tenacity 1922,Ja 3,20:2
First Fifty Years, The 1922,Mr 14,11:2
Hospitality 1922,N 14,16:1
Why Not? 1922,D 25,20:1
Cat Comes Back, The 1923,Ja 29,11:2
Tarnish 1923,O 2,10:1
Great Music 1924,O 6,24:1
Great Music 1924,O 12,VIII,1:1
Wild Duck, The 1925,F 25,16:4
Androcles and the Lion 1925,N 24,28:1
Man of Destiny, The 1925,N 24,28:1
Arms and the Man 1926,Ja 21,18:3
Love in a Mist 1926,Ap 13,28:3
White Wings 1926,O 16,15:1
For Better or Worse 1927,F 1,24:3
House of Shadows, The 1927,Ap 22,18:4
Strange Interlude 1928,Ja 31,28:1
Strange Interlude 1928,F 5,VIII,1:1
Apple Cart, The 1930,F 25,30:1
Milestones 1930,Je 3,27:1
Untitled-Play 1930,Jl 13,VIII,2:1
He 1931,S 22,33:1
Smiling Through 1932,Ja 3,VIII,3:1
Mackerel Skies 1934,Ja 24,20:4
Pure in Heart, The 1934,Mr 21,24:3
Sailors of Cattaro 1934,D 11,28:4
Ugly Runts, The 1935,Je 11,24:4
Country Wife, The 1935,Jl 2,24:2
Coward, The 1935,Jl 16,24:1
If This Be Treason 1935,Jl 30;17:1
Bishop Misbehaves, The 1935,Ag 27,23:4
If This Be Treason 1935,S 24,28:2
End of Summer 1936,F 18,26:4
House in the Country, A 1937,Ja 12,18:3
Never Trouble Trouble 1937,Ag 18,15:2
Julius Caesar 1938,Ja 30,X,3:1
Gloriana 1938,N 26,18:4
Ring Two 1939,N 23,38:2
When We Are Married 1939,D 26,22:3
Fledgling 1940,N 28,29:2
Broken Journey 1942,Je 24,22:2
Three Sisters, The 1942,D 22,31:2
Three Sisters, The 1942,D 27,VIII,1:1
Allah Be Praised! 1944,Ap 21,14:2
Powers, Tom (Director)
For Better or Worse 1927,F 1,24:3
Bridal Quilt 1934,O 11,28:5
Gloriana 1938,N 26,18:4
Powers, Tom (Playwright)
Untitled-Play 1930,Jl 13,VIII,2:1
Bridal Quilt 1934,O 11,28:5
Powers, Walter
Tin Pan Alley 1928,N 2,29:1
First Night 1930,N 27,32:3
Powers, William H
Ziegfeld Follies 1927,Ag 17,27:3
Powers, William V
Rain or Shine 1928,F 10,26:3
Powers's Performing Elephants
Good Times 1920,Ag 10,10:1
Get Together 1921,S 5,12:2
Better Times 1922,S 4,14:2

Pownall, Leon
Richard II 1964,Je 17,47:1
Bourgeois Gentilhomme, Le 1964,Je 18,28:2
Henry IV, Part I 1965,Je 30,42:1
Falstaff; Henry IV, Part II 1965,Jl 1,35:1
Julius Caesar 1965,Jl 2,18:1
Henry V 1966,Je 8,38:1
Henry VI 1966,Je 9,55:2
Richard III 1967,Je 14,43:1
Government Inspector, The 1967,Je 15,55:1
Antony and Cleopatra 1967,Ag 2,25:1
Merry Wives of Windsor, The 1967,Ag 4,18:1
Government Inspector, The 1967,O 28,34:1
Romeo and Juliet 1968,Je 11,55:2
Tartuffe 1968,Je 12,39:1
Midsummer Night's Dream, A 1968,Je 13,54:1
Merchant of Venice, The 1970,Je 10,39:1
School for Scandal, The 1970,Je 11,51:1
Powys, Stephen (Guy Bolton) (Original Author)
Walk With Music 1940,Je 5,33:2
Powys, Stephen (Playwright)
Wise Tomorrow 1937,F 18,19:1
Wise Tomorrow 1937,O 5,29:2
Wise Tomorrow 1937,O 16,22:5
Powys, Stephen (Translator)
Don't Listen, Ladies 1948,D 29,16:2
Poynter, Beulah (Playwright)
One Way Street 1928,D 25,31:2
Poynter, Edward
Elton Case, The 1921,S 12,16:2
Four Flusher, The 1925,Ap 14,27:4
Poynter, J Thompson (Lighting Director)
Milk Train Doesn't Stop Here Anymore, The 1965,Jl 27,25:1
Pozer, Edna
Glass Cage, The 1957,Mr 11,21:2
Pozzi, Gina
Piacere Del'Onesta, Il; Happiness of Probity, The 1930,N 10,16:4
Cena Delle Beffe, La; Jest, The 1930,N 24,26:4
In Fondo Al Cuore; Depths of the Heart, The 1930,D 8,27:1
Pradillo, Carmen
Don Juan Tenorio 1953,N 20,18:5
El Alcalde De Zalamea 1953,N 23,32:5
Prado, Francisco
Macbeth 1966,Ag 29,23:4
Praga, Marco (Playwright)
Porta Chiusa, La; Closed Door, The 1923,N 21,23:1
Prager, Elaine
Legend of Leonora, The 1926,My 1,10:1
Prager, Jack
Upon My Soul 1927,Ap 22,19:1
Prager, Jacob (Playwright)
Water Carrier, The 1936,D 25,20:2
Prager, Regina
Little Clown, The 1930,Mr 15,23:3
Mother's Son 1931,N 26,36:4
Longing for Home 1933,S 22,15:1
Prager, Richard (Lighting Director)
Mourners' Bench, The 1950,S 22,35:7
Prager, Sammy
Danny Kaye's International Show 1953,Ja 19,20:2
Prager, Sigfried (Dr) (Musical Director)
Anneliese von Dessau 1926,F 26,24:3
Prager, Stanley
Big White Fog 1940,O 23,26:2
Skin of Our Teeth, The 1942,N 19,29:5
Two on the Aisle 1951,Jl 20,13:6
Two on the Aisle 1951,Jl 29,II,1:1
Two's Company 1952,D 16,43:5
Room Service 1953,Ap 7,34:1
Pajama Game, The 1954,My 14,20:2
Pajama Game, The 1957,My 16,27:1
Prager, Stanley (Director)
Once Over Lightly 1955,Mr 16,39:1
Come Blow Your Horn 1961,F 23,31:3
Let It Ride 1961,O 13,27:4
Bravo Giovanni 1962,My 21,41:2
Bravo Giovanni 1962,My 27,II,1:1
Don't Drink the Water 1966,N 18,37:1
Who's Happy Now? 1969,N 18,39:1
Minnie's Boys 1970,Mr 27,27:1
Prague Pantomime Theatre
Twenty-four Inventions 1964,Ag 11,37:5
Prahar, Irene
Ah! Wah! 1932,My 11,15:2
Prahl, Richard
Midgie Purvis 1961,F 2,25:3
Prainee, Marcelle
Vacances de Paques, Les 1927,Ja 2,VII,2:1
Praino, Frank
Man Who Washed His Hands, The 1967,F 16,33:1
Pramsky, John (Producer)
Bagels and Yox 1951,S 13,38:2
Pransky, John (Miscellaneous)
Agatha Sue, I Love You 1966,D 15,61:1
Praskins, Leonard (Playwright)
Charlatan, The 1922,Ap 25,14:2
Prather, Tom Ross (Director)
My Wife and I 1966,O 11,53:2
Prato, Neil
Honest Liars 1926,Jl 20,17:2

Praton, Alain
Avare, L', L'; Miser, The 1966,F 9,32:1
Reine Morte, La 1966,F 16,52:1
Fil a la Paite, Un 1966,F 18,25:1
Pratsch, Kurt
My Fair Lady 1962,S 7,34:1
Pratt, A
Pudding on the Ritz 1932,Ap 9,18:3
Pratt, Betty
You and I 1925,O 20,29:1
Pratt, Charles
Pink Elephant, The 1953,Ap 23,37:2
Pratt, Charles Jr
Nineteenth Hole of Europe, The 1949,Mr 28,16:2
Pratt, Charles Jr (Producer)
Enchanted, The 1958,Ap 23,41:1
Pratt, Dallas B
Wings Over Europe 1936,Mr 4,24:7
Pratt, Henry N
It's Only Natural 1922,Ap 21,13:2
Take a Brace 1923,Ap 20,20:3
Who's Who 1924,Ap 18,19:2
Pratt, John (Costume Designer)
Swing Mikado, The 1939,Mr 2,18:2
American Legend 1941,My 12,13:2
Look, Ma, I'm Dancin' 1948,Ja 30,20:2
Fourth Avenue North 1961,S 28,50:2
Pratt, Judson
Popsy 1941,F 11,26:2
Billy Budd 1951,F 12,18:3
Hook'n Ladder 1952,Ap 30,31:2
Desperate Hours, The 1955,F 11,20:2
Pratt, Lynn
Romance 1921,Mr 1,18:2
Merton of the Movies 1922,N 14,16:2
Flame of Love 1924,Ap 22,19:2
Pratt, Mlle
Bourgeois Gentilhomme, Le 1955,O 26,26:1
Pratt, Neil
Solid Ivory 1925,N 17,29:3
Not Herbert 1926,Ja 27,16:2
One Shot Fired 1927,N 8,32:5
Los Angeles 1927,D 20,32:3
Kidding Kidders 1928,Ag 24,28:3
Song Writer, The 1928,Ag 14,15:2
Pratt, Peter
Mikado, The 1947,D 30,18:2
Yeomen of the Guard, The 1948,F 3,30:2
Gondoliers, The 1951,F 13,27:2
Iolanthe 1955,S 28,38:1
Mikado, The 1955,S 30,20:2
Yeomen of the Guard, The 1955,O 4,39:2
Pirates of Penzance, The 1955,O 7,21:1
Princess Ida 1955,O 14,22:3
H M S Pinafore 1955,O 18,48:1
Ruddigore 1955,O 21,32:2
Pratt, Purnell
Crooked Gamblers 1920,Ag 2,12:1
Just Married 1921,Ap 27,21:1
Charlatan, The 1922,Ap 25,14:2
Thumbs Down 1923,Ag 7,20:1
Vagabond, The 1923,D 28,13:4
Goose Hangs High, The 1924,Ja 30,16:1
Her Way Out 1924,Je 24,18:3
Cock o' the Roost 1924,O 14,23:1
Tenth Avenue 1927,Ag 16,31:1
Pratt, Richard
Summer of the Seventeenth Doll 1958,Ja 23,23:2
Pratt, Stanley (Director)
Roll Sweet Chariot 1934,O 3,24:3
Pratt, Theodore (Original Author)
Big Blow 1938,O 3,11:2
Pratt, Theodore (Playwright)
Revolt of the Mummies, The 1923,My 8,22:3
Big Blow 1938,O 3,11:2
Pratt, W P
Gentlemen, the Queen 1927,Ap 23,14:3
Pratt, Wilda
Big Blow 1938,O 3,11:2
Pratt, William W (Playwright)
Ten Nights in a Barroom 1928,Mr 28,31:2
Ten Nights in a Barroom 1932,Ja 21,17:1
Praver, Harriet
Bonds of Interest, The 1951,D 1,7:2
Prawy, Marcel (Producer)
Kiss Me, Kate 1956,F 19,94:1
Porgy and Bess 1965,O 20,53:3
Prawy, Marcel (Translator)
Kiss Me, Kate 1959,Ag 10,24:1
Praxy, Raoul (Playwright)
Poulette et Son Poulain 1924,Je 15,VII,1:4
Pray, James
Is Zat So? 1925,Ap 25,18:2
Preble, Ed
An Evening With G B S; Press Cuttings 1957,F 19,35:7
Beautiful Jailer, The 1957,My 17,19:2
Failures, The 1959,Ja 6,30:2
Fig Leaf in Her Bonnet, A 1961,Je 15,50:1
Hamlet 1963,My 9,41:1
Miser, The 1963,My 10,39:1
Hamlet 1963,My 19,II,1:1
Three Sisters, The 1963,Jl 22,19:2

Preble, Ed—Cont
Family Way, The 1965,Ja 14,44:5
Calling in Crazy 1969,O 7,42:2
Preble, Ed (Playwright)
Laugh Parade, The 1931,N 3,31:2
Preble, Edwin
Treasure Girl 1928,N 9,22:1
Precht, Donna
Gondoliers, The 1964,Mr 28,14:1
Pred, Suzanne
Americana Pastoral 1968,D 11,51:1
Preece, Marion
Clouds of the Sun 1922,My 6,11:2
Preece, Tim
Hail Scrawdyke! 1966,N 29,50:1
Preedy, George (Marjorie Bowen) (Playwright)
Court Cards 1934,N 9,24:3
Preer, Evelyn
Chip Woman's Fortune, The 1923,My 8,22:2
Salome 1923,My 8,22:2
Comedy of Errors, The 1923,My 16,22:5
Salome 1923,My 20,VII,1:1
Lulu Belle 1926,F 10,20:1
Rang Tang 1927,Jl 13,20:1
Preillerman, Geraldine
Three's a Family 1943,N 19,24:3
Preillerman, Geraldine (Scenic Designer)
Three's a Family 1943,N 19,24:3
Preische, Henry
Betty Behave 1927,Mr 9,28:4
Preisinger, Anton
Untitled-Passion Play 1950,My 19,29:6
Passion of Christ, The 1960,My 18,46:1
Preisinger, Johanna
Untitled-Passion Play 1930,My 9,9:1
Preisser, Cherry
Vaudeville (Palace) 1932,Ag 1,11:5
Ziegfeld Follies 1934,Ja 5,24:3
Ziegfeld Follies 1936,S 15,37:1
Preisser, June
Ziegfeld Follies 1936,Ja 31,17:2
Preito, Nick
Evening With Yves Montand, An 1959,S 23,45:1
Premice, Josephine
Blue Holiday 1945,My 22,13:3
Caribbean Carnival 1947,D 6,12:2
Mister Johnson 1956,Mr 30,11:1
Mister Johnson 1956,Ap 8,II,1:1
Jamaica 1957,N 1,32:2
Here's Josephine Premice 1966,Ap 26,54:4
Hand Is on the Gate, A 1966,S 22,54:1
Mister Mayor! 1967,Ap 4,36:3
House of Flowers 1968,Ja 29,26:2
Electra 1969,Ag 8,14:1
Premice, Josephine (Choreographer)
Garden of Time 1945,Mr 10,13:7
Preminger, Jetti
Virginia Reel 1947,Ap 15,28:2
Preminger, Otto
Margin for Error 1939,O 15,48:7
Margin for Error 1939,N 4,11:3
Margin for Error 1939,N 12,IX,1:1
Preminger, Otto (Director)
Libel! 1935,D 21,10:5
Outward Bound 1938,D 23,16:5
Margin for Error 1939,O 15,48:7
Margin for Error 1939,N 4,11:3
Margin for Error 1939,N 12,IX,1:1
My Dear Children 1940,F 1,16:2
Beverly Hills 1940,N 8,24:2
Cue for Passion 1940,D 20,33:4
More the Merrier, The 1941,S 16,19:3
Four Twelves Are 48 1951,Ja 18,30:2
Moon Is Blue, The 1951,Mr 9,29:2
Critic's Choice 1960,D 15,61:3
Preminger, Otto (Producer)
Beverly Hills 1940,N 8,24:2
More the Merrier, The 1941,S 16,19:3
In Time to Come 1941,D 29,20:2
Four Twelves Are 48 1951,Ja 18,30:2
Moon Is Blue, The 1951,Mr 9,29:2
Critic's Choice 1960,D 15,61:3
Prendergast, Frank
Muzeeka 1968,Ap 29,47:2
Prendergast, Shirley (Lighting Director)
Summer of the Seventeenth Doll 1968,F 21,59:1
Who's Happy Now? 1969,N 18,39:1
Prendergast, W H
Red Light Annie 1923,Ag 22,10:3
Prentice, Don
Divina Pastora, La 1931,Mr 4,33:2
Sparkin' 1931,Mr 4,33:2
Psychological Moment, The 1931,Mr 4,33:2
Prentice, George
Laugh Parade, The 1931,N 3,31:2
Virginia 1937,S 3,13:2
Virginia 1937,O 5,29:1
Prentice, Georgia
Wisdom Tooth, The 1926,F 16,22:2
Prentice, Henrietta (Director)
Jeanne d'Arc 1922,Ap 22,9:3
Prentice, Herbert (Producer)
Counsellor-at-Law 1934,Ap 11,24:3

Prentice, Keith
Boys in the Band, The 1968,Ap 15,48:1
Prentiss, Brett
Prometheus Bound 1967,My 11,52:1
'Tis Pity She's a Whore 1967,O 21,15:2
Prentiss, Eleanor
Naked Genius, The 1943,O 22,20:5
Hollywood Pinafore 1945,Je 1,20:1
Dream Play 1960,N 23,22:1
Prentiss, Henrietta (Prof) (Director)
Yellow Jacket, The 1923,Ap 20,20:3
Prentiss, Paula
As You Like It 1963,Jl 17,19:2
Arf 1969,My 28,36:1
Great Airplane Snatch, The 1969,My 28,36:1
Prescod, Pearl
Crucible, The 1965,Ja 20,35:1
Prescott, Bettina
Texas Town 1941,Ap 30,22:3
Prescott, Jack
Love for Love 1940,Je 4,19:5
Prescott, John A (Producer)
Cradle Will Rock, The 1964,N 9,40:4
Prescott, Norman
Earl Carroll's Vanities 1926,Ag 25,19:4
Prescott, Tina
Louisiana Lady 1947,Je 3,35:2
Dance Me a Song 1950,Ja 21,10:5
Present, Jack (Miscellaneous)
On Borrowed Time 1953,F 11,34:1
Present, Marion
Fourth Pig, The 1965,Ja 27,24:6
Preses, Peter
Circle of Chalk, The 1941,Mr 27,28:4
Presnell, Harve
Unsinkable Molly Brown, The 1960,N 4,28:1
Presnell, Robert (Playwright)
Rust 1924,F 1,12:1
Saturday Night 1924,F 11,18:1
Press, Barbara
Play It Again, Sam 1969,F 13,52:3
Press, Steve
Doctor in Spite of Himself, The 1957,F 28,18:4
Pressler, Lorraine
Pillar to Post 1943,D 11,11:2
Hickory Stick 1944,My 9,15:6
Pressler and Klaiss
Vaudeville (Hippodrome) 1924,Ja 22,15:6
Pressman, David
Romeo and Juliet 1933,F 3,21:5
Brooklyn, U S A 1941,D 22,24:2
Eve of St Mark, The 1942,O 8,30:2
Dream Girl 1945,D 15,13:2
Pressman, David (Director)
Emperor's Clothes, The 1953,O 23,19:7
Pony Cart, The 1954,S 15,39:2
Disenchanted, The 1958,D 4,53:4
Disenchanted, The 1959,Ja 11,II,1:1
Roman Candle 1960,F 4,34:2
Pressman, David (Original Author)
Summertree 1968,Mr 4,29:1
Pressman, Kenneth (Playwright)
Hunting the Jingo Birds 1965,Mr 26,27:1
Mrs Snow 1970,Ja 6,48:3
Steal the Old Man's Bundle 1970,My 16,30:1
Pressman, Lawrence
Go Show Me a Dragon 1961,O 28,18:1
Never Live Over a Pretzel Factory 1964,Mr 30,37:1
Hunting the Jingo Birds 1965,Mr 26,27:1
Man in the Glass Booth, The 1967,Jl 29,12:1
As You Like It 1968,Je 24,42:3
Richard II 1968,Je 24,42:3
Love's Labour's Lost 1968,Je 28,36:1
Man in the Glass Booth, The 1968,S 27,41:1
Great Airplane Snatch, The 1969,My 28,36:1
Arf 1969,My 28,36:1
Play It Again, Sam 1970,F 7,25:2
Pressman, Peter (Composer)
Moby Dick 1955,Ap 26,25:3
Presson, Jay
Pal Joey 1949,Mr 7,17:2
Preston, Ann
Broadway 1926,S 17,19:3
Preston, Arnold
Foolscap 1933,Ja 12,21:2
Preston, Barry
Joyful Noise, A 1966,D 16,57:1
Preston, David
Jubilee 1935,O 14,20:1
Preston, Don
Absolutely Freeee 1967,My 25,58:1
Preston, Edna
Out West of Eighth 1951,S 21,20:3
Tovarich 1952,My 15,39:2
Mademoiselle Colombe 1954,Ja 7,26:1
Fanny 1954,N 5,16:1
Preston, Edward (Miscellaneous)
Education of H*Y*M*A*N K*A*P*L*A*N, The 1968,Ap 5,57:1
Preston, Erme
Judy Garland's New Variety Show 1956,S 27,43:2
Preston, Frances
Kai Khosru 1925,Ap 27,14:2

Preston, Harold
Scarecrow, The 1953,Je 17,31:1
Preston, J A
King John 1967,Jl 14,19:1
Henry IV, Part I 1968,Je 30,54:7
Henry IV, Part II 1968,Jl 2,33:1
Death of Bessie Smith, The 1968,O 3,55:1
Persians, The 1970,F 15,II,1:1
Persians, The 1970,Ap 16,53:1
Persians, The 1970,Ap 26,II,1:3
Preston, James (Miscellaneous)
This Property Is Condemned 1956,O 29,34:1
Once Around the Block 1956,O 29,34:1
Sidewalks and the Sound of Crying 1956,O 29,34:1
Annie Get Your Gun 1957,Mr 9,15:5
Preston, James (Producer)
Career 1957,My 1,42:6
Preston, Mark
Mahogany Hall 1934,Ja 18,18:5
Creeping Fire 1935,Ja 17,22:3
Preston, Nancy
Quiet, Please! 1940,N 9,20:3
Preston, Philip
Tableaux 1961,D 18,41:3
Preston, Randolph
Behind the Red Lights 1937,Ja 14,17:4
World We Make, The 1939,N 21,19:1
My Fair Ladies 1941,Mr 24,12:7
In Time to Come 1941,D 29,20:2
They Should Have Stood in Bed 1942,F 14,18:5
Preston, Robert
Male Animal, The 1952,My 1,35:1
Male Animal, The 1952,My 18,II,1:1
Men of Distinction 1953,My 1,18:4
His and Hers 1954,Ja 8,18:2
Magic and the Loss, The 1954,Ap 10,10:3
Tender Trap, The 1954,O 14,37:2
Janus 1955,N 25,37:2
Hidden River, The 1957,Ja 24,32:1
Music Man, The 1957,D 20,31:1
Music Man, The 1958,S 28,II,1:1
Too True to Be Good 1963,Mr 14,8:2
Too True to Be Good 1963,Mr 23,5:6
Nobody Loves an Albatross 1963,D 20,20:1
Nobody Loves an Albatross 1964,Ja 5,II,1:1
Ben Franklin in Paris 1964,O 28,52:1
Lion in Winter, The 1966,Mr 4,23:1
Lion in Winter, The 1966,Mr 13,II,1:1
I Do! I Do! 1966,D 6,58:1
I Do! I Do! 1966,D 18,II,3:1
Preston, Sandee
Children's Hour, The 1952,D 19,35:2
Preston, Walter J
Springtime of Youth 1922,O 27,15:1
Prestons, The
Howdy, Mr Ice of 1950 1949,My 27,24:2
Preval, Pazzi
Bon Garcon, Un 1929,Mr 19,36:2
Prevert, Jacques (Playwright)
Baptiste 1952,N 13,34:2
Prevete, Pete
Aquashow 1954,Je 23,20:4
Prevete, Tony
Aquashow 1953,Je 24,29:2
Previn, Andre (Composer)
Party With Betty Comden and Adolph Green, A 1958,D 24,2:7
Coco 1969,D 19,66:1
Coco 1969,D 28,II,1:1
Prevon, Katya
Bought and Paid For 1921,D 8,17:5
Prevost, Jacqueline
House in Berlin, A (Als der Kreig zu Ende War); Als der Krieg zu Ende War (A House in Berlin) 1950,D 27,32:3
Prevost, Robert
Malade Imaginaire, Le; Imaginary Invalid, The 1958,Ap 30,28:2
Prevost, Robert (Scenic Designer)
Malade Imaginaire, Le; Imaginary Invalid, The 1958,Ap 30,28:2
Mariage Force, Le; Forced Wedding, The 1958,My 7,43:1
Sganarelle; Imaginary Cuckold, The 1958,My 7,43:1
Jalousie du Barbouille, La; Jealousy of the Barbouille, The 1958,My 7,43:1
Othello 1959,Jl 2,17:2
Comedy of Errors, The 1963,Je 21,35:3
Bourgeois Gentilhomme, Le 1964,Je 18,28:2
Tartuffe 1968,Je 12,39:1
Pribor, Richard (Miscellaneous)
Make a Wish 1951,Ap 19,38:1
3 for Tonight 1955,Ap 7,23:2
Priborsky, Richard (Composer)
Small Wonder 1948,S 16,33:5
Pribulsky, Roslyn
Eleventh Inheritor, The 1962,N 22,43:5
Price, Alan (Composer)
Home 1970,N 18,41:1
Price, Alonzo
Polly 1929,Ja 9,28:3
Price, Alonzo (Director)
They All Want Something 1926,O 13,20:2

Price, Alonzo (Director)—Cont
Silver Swan, The 1929,N 28,34:5
Chocolate Soldier, The 1934,My 3,15:3
Mrs Kimball Presents 1944,Mr 1,17:3
Price, Alonzo (Playwright)
Bye Bye, Barbara 1924,Ag 26,6:3
Silver Swan, The 1929,N 28,34:5
Mrs Kimball Presents 1944,Mr 1,17:3
Price, Audrey (Costume Designer)
Hamlet 1967,F 17,44:1
Price, Dennis
Heartbreak House 1959,O 19,37:1
Price, Don
Follies of 1910, The 1960,Ja 15,37:3
Price, Drew
Tomorrow and Tomorrow 1931,Ja 14,26:3
Washington Heights 1931,S 30,23:4
Carry Nation 1932,O 31,18:2
Price, Elizabeth
Vaudeville (Palace) 1923,Ap 3,26:4
Price, Evadne (Playwright)
Big Ben 1939,S 10,IX,2:2
Price, Frank
Star and Garter 1942,Je 25,26:2
Once Over Lightly 1942,N 20,26:2
Price, George
Century Revue and the Midnight Rounders, The
 1920,Jl 13,9:1
Vaudeville (Palace) 1926,Ag 10,19:4
Precedent 1931,Ap 15,24:5
Lost Boy 1932,Ja 6,24:4
Price, George N
Dear Me 1921,Ja 18,14:1
Moon Is a Gong, The 1926,Mr 13,21:3
Belt, The 1927,O 20,33:1
International, The 1928,Ja 16,24:4
Hoboken Blues 1928,F 18,10:1
Box Seats 1928,Ap 20,27:2
That Ferguson Family 1928,D 24,10:7
Dead End 1935,O 29,17:2
Price, Georgie
Cinderella on Broadway 1920,Je 25,18:1
Vaudeville (Forty-Fourth Street Theatre)
 1921,S 20,12:2
Spice of 1922 1922,Jl 7,12:4
Night in Spain, A 1927,My 4,28:2
Song Writer, The 1928,Ag 14,15:2
Vaudeville (Palace) 1929,Ja 21,18:3
Vaudeville (Palace) 1930,O 13,31:3
Price, Georgie (Composer)
Song Writer, The 1928,Ag 14,15:2
Price, Georgie (Lyricist)
Song Writer, The 1928,Ag 14,15:2
Price, Gerald
Naked 1950,S 7,39:2
Threepenny Opera, The 1954,Mr 11,26:5
Threepenny Opera, The 1954,Mr 21,II,1:1
Fanny 1954,N 5,16:1
Italian Straw Hat, The 1957,O 1,37:2
Girl of the Golden West, The 1957,N 6,44:1
Power of Dreams, A 1958,Mr 11,33:1
Price, Gilbert
Fly Blackbird 1962,F 6,26:2
Jericho-Jim Crow 1964,Ja 13,25:3
Midsummer Night's Dream, A 1964,Je 30,23:2
Roar of the Greasepaint-the Smell of the Crowd
 1965,My 17,46:2
Promenade 1969,Je 5,56:1
Promenade 1969,Je 15,II,1:1
Price, Hal
Red Mill, The 1945,O 17,16:2
Price, Hildred
Brooklyn Biarritz 1941,F 28,16:2
Steps Leading Up 1941,Ap 19,20:6
Guest in the House 1942,F 25,25:2
Price, James (Director)
Saintliness of Margery Kempe, The 1959,F 3,35:6
Price, Leontyne
Four Saints in Three Acts 1952,Ap 17,35:1
Porgy and Bess 1952,S 8,18:2
Porgy and Bess 1952,S 18,36:5
Porgy and Bess 1952,O 10,21:4
Porgy and Bess 1953,F 17,21:1
Porgy and Bess 1953,Mr 10,25:5
Porgy and Bess 1953,Mr 15,II,1:1
Price, Loren E (Miscellaneous)
Mime and Me, The 1960,Ap 8,27:3
Price, Loretta
Hook'n Ladder 1952,Ap 30,31:2
Price, Lorin E (Producer)
Tiger Rag, The 1961,F 17,20:2
Moon Besieged, The 1962,D 6,54:1
Natural Look, The 1967,Mr 13,45:2
To Clothe the Naked 1967,Ap 28,30:1
George M! 1968,Ap 11,48:1
Price, Maitland
Solid Ivory 1925,N 17,29:3
Price, Michael (Lighting Director)
Josephine Baker and Her Company 1964,F 5,30:1
Price, Nancy
Trifles 1932,Ja 30,13:6
Nurse Cavell 1934,Ap 1,X,1:7
Life That I Gave Him, The 1934,O 28,IX,3:4
Whiteoaks 1936,Ap 15,25:2

Thou Shalt Not- 1938,S 25,IX,3:5
Price, Nancy (Director)
Trifles 1932,Ja 30,13:6
Hangman, The 1935,O 23,18:6
Price, Paton
Schoolhouse on the Lot 1938,Mr 23,18:4
Price, Paul B
Banquet for the Moon, A 1961,Ja 20,24:2
O Say Can You See! 1962,O 9,45:1
Medea 1965,N 29,46:1
Room Service 1970,My 13,49:1
Price, Philip
Corn Is Green, The 1954,F 27,10:2
Price, Roger
Tickets, Please! 1950,Ap 28,25:2
Price, Stanley
Adam's Apple 1929,Je 11,27:5
Price, Stanley (Playwright)
Come Live With Me 1967,Ja 27,29:1
Price, Vincent
Victoria Regina 1935,D 27,15:2
Victoria Regina 1936,Ja 5,IX,1:1
Elizabeth the Queen 1936,Jl 28,23:4
Princess Turandot 1937,Ag 3,20:5
Romance 1937,Ag 17,23:1
Lady Has a Heart, The 1937,S 27,24:1
Shoemaker's Holiday, The 1938,Ja 3,17:2
Shoemaker's Holiday, The 1938,Ja 9,X,1:1
Heartbreak House 1938,Ap 30,18:2
Outward Bound 1938,D 23,16:5
Angel Street 1941,D 6,15:2
Yours, A Lincoln 1942,Jl 10,12:3
Richard III 1953,D 10,65:2
Black-Eyed Susan 1954,D 24,7:5
Darling of the Day 1968,Ja 29,26:2
Darling of the Day 1968,F 11,II,3:1
Price, Vola
If I Was Rich 1926,S 3,15:2
Price, Walter
Run, Little Chillun! 1933,Mr 2,21:3
John Brown 1934,Ja 23,22:3
Sweet River 1936,O 29,30:2
Price, William
Many Mansions 1937,O 28,28:6
Prichard, Charles
Ruy Blas 1957,D 14,16:3
Prickett, Oliver B
All the Comforts of Home 1942,My 26,24:5
Priddy, Nancy
Hamlet 1968,Jl 4,15:1
Pride, Malcolm (Costume Designer)
Chances, The 1962,Jl 4,11:2
Pride, Malcolm (Lighting Director)
Twelfth Night 1955,Je 7,37:4
All's Well That Ends Well 1955,Je 7,37:4
Prideaux, James (Playwright)
Postcards 1967,D 6,41:1
Autograph Hound, The 1968,D 14,60:1
Lemonade 1968,D 14,60:1
Postcards 1970,Mr 17,36:1
Prideaux, Tom (Playwright)
Prodigal Father, The 1935,Jl 2,24:2
Priesser, Cherry
Ziegfeld Follies 1936,Ja 31,17:2
Priesser, Cherry and June
Vaudeville (Palace) 1932,My 16,19:2
Priesser, June
Vaudeville (Palace) 1932,Ag 1,11:5
Ziegfeld Follies 1934,Ja 5,24:3
Ziegfeld Follies 1936,S 15,37:1
You Never Know 1938,S 22,26:3
Count Me In 1942,O 9,24:2
Priest, Dan
Deep Are the Roots 1960,O 4,47:1
Night Is Black Bottles, The 1962,D 5,56:1
View From the Bridge, A 1965,Ja 29,24:1
Investigation, The 1966,O 5,40:1
Trial of Lee Harvey Oswald, The 1967,N 6,64:1
Priest, John (Miscellaneous)
Under the Sycamore Tree 1960,Mr 8,37:2
Priest, Martin
Mister Roberts 1962,O 12,27:2
Time of the Key, A 1963,S 12,33:3
Duet for Three 1966,My 20,41:1
Priest, Natalie
God Bless You, Harold Fineberg 1969,Mr 31,30:2
Priestley, J B (Director)
Duet in Floodlight 1935,Je 5,22:1
Priestley, J B (Miscellaneous)
Time and the Conways 1938,Ja 4,19:2
Priestley, J B (Original Author)
Good Companions, The 1931,My 15,20:8
Good Companions, The 1931,My 31,VIII,2:6
Good Companions, The 1931,O 2,31:1
Good Companions, The 1931,O 11,VIII,1:1
Priestley, J B (Playwright)
Good Companions, The 1931,My 15,20:8
Good Companions, The 1931,My 31,VIII,2:6
Good Companions, The 1931,O 2,31:1
Good Companions, The 1931,O 11,VIII,1:1
Dangerous Corner 1932,My 11,15:3
Dangerous Corner 1932,Je 5,X,2:2
Dangerous Corner 1932,O 28,23:1

Priestley, J B (Playwright)—Cont
Dangerous Corner 1933,Jl 18,20:4
Laburnum Grove 1933,N 29,23:4
Laburnum Grove 1933,D 17,IX,4:2
Eden End 1934,S 15,20:7
Eden End 1934,S 30,IX,3:1
Laburnum Grove 1935,Ja 15,23:5
Laburnum Grove 1935,Ja 20,X,1:1
Duet in Floodlight 1935,F 14,24:3
Cornelius 1935,Mr 21,27:4
Cornelius 1935,Ap 14,IX,1:1
Duet in Floodlight 1935,Je 5,22:1
Eden End 1935,O 22,17:1
Bees on the Boat Deck 1936,My 6,27:2
Bees on the Boat Deck 1936,Je 7,IX,2:1
Time and the Conways 1937,Ag 27,23:3
Time and the Conways 1937,S 12,XI,2:1
I Have Been Here Before 1937,S 23,32:3
I Have Been Here Before 1937,O 10,XI,1:4
People at Sea 1937,N 25,38:2
People at Sea 1937,D 19,XI,3:7
Time and the Conways 1938,Ja 4,19:2
Music at Night 1938,Ag 3,14:8
Music at Night 1938,Ag 21,IX,2:1
When We Are Married 1938,O 12,34:1
I Have Been Here Before 1938,O 14,26:2
When We Are Married 1938,O 30,IX,1:2
Johnson Over Jordan 1939,Mr 12,XI,3:5
Johnson Over Jordan 1939,Ap 2,X,1:6
When We Are Married 1939,N 21,19:5
When We Are Married 1939,D 10,X,5:6
When We Are Married 1939,D 26,22:3
Good Night, Children 1942,F 15,VIII,3:6
They Came to a City 1943,Je 6,II,1:6
Desert Highway 1944,Ja 2,II,1:5
How Are They at Home? 1944,My 28,II,1:3
Inspector Calls, An 1946,O 13,II,2:3
Linden Tree, The 1947,S 14,II,3:7
Inspector Calls, An 1947,O 22,38:2
Linden Tree, The 1948,Mr 3,28:2
Home Is Tomorrow 1948,N 22,25:4
Home Is Tomorrow 1948,D 12,II,4:7
Summer Day's Dream 1949,S 9,28:5
Summer Day's Dream 1949,O 9,II,3:7
Home Is Tomorrow 1950,Je 2,27:2
Dragon's Mouth 1952,Je 8,II,3:1
Dragon's Mouth 1955,N 17,45:1
Glass Cage, The 1957,Mr 11,21:2
Ever Since Paradise 1957,Jl 12,18:4
Severed Head, A 1963,Je 28,22:1
Severed Head, A 1964,O 29,40:1
Priestly, Harriet
Audition of the Apprentice Theatre 1939,Je 2,26:2
Priestly, Joseph
It's an Ill Wind 1957,Ap 24,28:1
Priestman, Brian (Musical Director)
Hollow Crown, The 1963,Ja 31,5:1
Prieur, Don
Look to the Lilies 1970,Mr 30,59:1
Prillerman, Geraldine
Caukey 1944,F 18,15:4
Prim, Suzy
Livree de M le Comte, La 1927,N 20,IX,4:4
Aube, le Jour Et la Nuit, L' 1929,Je 9,VIII,2:4
Guignol 1930,Mr 30,VIII,2:4
Deodat 1931,Ap 19,VIII,2:8
Quand Jouons-Nous La Comedie? 1935,O 27,IX,2:1
Trois, Six, Neuf 1936,Je 21,IX,2:4
Prima, Miss
Will Morrissey's Folies Bergere Revue
 1930,Ap 16,26:6
Primm, John
Devil's Disciple, The 1950,Ja 26,23:2
Primont, Marian
As You Like It 1936,Ap 24,18:4
Primont, Marion
Anatomist, The 1957,F 27,21:5
Richard III 1957,N 26,41:1
Primrose, Alek
Golem, The 1959,F 26,38:2
Rules of the Game, The 1960,D 20,44:1
Troilus and Cressida 1961,Jl 24,15:1
Incident at Vichy 1964,D 4,44:1
Tartuffe 1965,Ja 15,23:1
Kitchen, The 1966,Je 14,50:1
Master Builder, The 1968,Je 22,26:1
Resistible Rise of Arturo Ui, The 1968,Ag 8,25:1
Merton of the Movies 1968,S 26,62:1
Resistible Rise of Arturo Ui, The 1968,D 23,44:1
Room Service 1970,My 13,49:1
Room Service 1970,My 24,II,1:1
Primus, Barry
King and the Duke, The 1955,Je 2,25:2
Nervous Set, The 1959,My 13,43:1
Camino Real 1960,My 17,42:2
Red Eye of Love 1961,Je 13,28:1
Cayenne Pepper 1961,D 13,55:5
After the Fall 1964,Ja 24,18:1
Marco Millions 1964,F 21,33:1
Changeling, The 1964,O 30,32:2
Henry IV, Part I 1968,Je 30,54:7
Henry IV, Part II 1968,Jl 2,33:1
Huui, Huui 1968,N 25,58:1
Indians 1969,My 27,43:1

Primus, Barry—Cont
Criminals, The 1970,F 26,33:2
Primus, Marc
High John De Conquer 1969,Ap 23,39:1
Primus, Marc (Director)
High John De Conquer 1969,Ap 23,39:1
Primus, Pearl
Show Boat 1946,Ja 7,17:2
Show Boat 1946,Ja 13,II,1:1
Caribbean Carnival 1947,D 6,12:2
Primus, Pearl (Choreographer)
Caribbean Carnival 1947,D 6,12:2
Mister Johnson 1956,Ap 8,II,1:1
Primus, Pearl (Miscellaneous)
Mister Johnson 1956,Mr 30,11:1
Prince, Adelaide
Her Salary Man 1921,N 29,20:1
What Every Woman Knows 1926,Ap 14,20:2
Springboard, The 1927,O 13,23:1
Free Soul, A 1928,Ja 13,26:5
Mr Samuel 1930,N 11,28:4
Prince, Aladar
Bruder Straubinger 1921,N 16,22:3
Prince, Arthur
Vaudeville (Palace) 1926,N 2,35:2
Vaudeville (Palace) 1926,N 9,30:3
Prince, Eileen
Grandma's Diary 1948,S 23,36:2
Prince, Esther (Producer)
Bench, The 1968,Mr 5,35:2
Prince, Frank (Miscellaneous)
Dr Cook's Garden 1967,S 26,52:1
Conerico Was Here to Stay 1969,Mr 11,39:1
Paradise Gardens East 1969,Mr 11,39:1
Prince, Frank (Producer)
Look: We've Come Through 1961,O 26,40:1
Prince, Harold (Director)
Family Affair, A 1962,Ja 29,17:1
She Loves Me 1963,Ap 24,39:1
She Loves Me 1963,My 5,II,1:1
Baker Street 1965,F 17,36:1
It's a Bird . . . It's a Plane . . . It's Superman
1966,Mr 30,34:1
Cabaret 1966,N 21,62:1
Mister Mayor! 1967,Ap 4,36:3
Zorba 1968,N 18,58:1
Zorba 1968,N 24,II,1:1
Company 1970,Ap 27,40:1
Company 1970,My 3,II,1:4
Company 1970,Jl 29,31:1
Prince, Harold (Producer)
Pajama Game, The 1954,My 14,20:2
Damn Yankees 1955,My 6,17:1
New Girl in Town 1957,My 15,40:1
West Side Story 1957,S 27,14:4
Fiorello! 1959,N 24,45:3
West Side Story 1960,Ap 28,31:1
Tenderloin 1960,O 18,47:2
Call on Kuprin, A 1961,My 26,29:3
Take Her, She's Mine 1961,D 22,19:1
Funny Thing Happened on the Way to the Forum,
A 1962,My 9,49:1
She Loves Me 1963,Ap 24,39:1
Fiddler on the Roof 1964,S 23,56:2
Poor Bitos 1964,N 16,40:2
Flora, the Red Menace 1965,My 12,41:2
It's a Bird . . . It's a Plane . . . It's Superman
1966,Mr 30,34:1
Cabaret 1966,N 21,62:1
Zorba 1968,N 18,58:1
Zorba 1968,N 24,II,1:1
Fiddler on the Roof 1969,Je 26,47:1
Fiddler on the Roof 1969,Ag 8,10:2
Company 1970,Ap 27,40:1
Prince, Hudson
Walk Together Chillun 1936,F 5,15:2
Prince, Hughie (Composer)
Girl From Nantucket, The 1945,N 9,17:2
Prince, Jack
Destry Rides Again 1959,Ap 24,24:1
Prince, Michael
Under Milk Wood 1962,O 6,13:4
Othello 1964,Jl 15,29:1
Coach With the Six Insides, The 1967,My 12,50:1
Prince, Neal (Director)
Man and Superman 1953,F 21,11:2
Prince, Peter
Time of Storm 1954,F 26,14:2
Prince, Robert (Choreographer)
Something More! 1964,N 11,36:1
Prince, Robert (Composer)
Oh Dad, Poor Dad, Mamma's Hung You in the
Closet and I'm Feelin' So Sad 1962,F 27,28:1
Oh Dad, Poor Dad, Mamma's Hung You in the
Closet and I'm Feelin' So Sad 1963,Ag 28,28:2
Tragical Historie of Doctor Faustus, The
1964,O 6,34:2
Prince, Robert (Miscellaneous)
Half a Sixpence 1965,Ap 26,38:2
Prince, Van
Mr Peebles and Mr Hooker 1946,O 11,29:2
Lost in the Stars 1949,O 31,21:2
Twentieth Century 1950,D 25,23:6
Green Pastures, The 1951,Mr 16,35:2

Shrike, The 1953,N 26,51:2
Prince, William
Richard II 1937,S 16,28:2
Hamlet 1938,O 13,28:1
Henry IV, Part I 1939,Ja 31,17:2
Steps Leading Up 1941,Ap 19,20:6
Ah, Wilderness! 1941,O 3,26:2
Guest in the House 1942,F 25,25:2
Across the Board on Tomorrow Morning
1942,Ag 18,17:1
Eve of St Mark, The 1942,O 8,30:2
John Loves Mary 1947,F 5,29:2
Forward the Heart 1949,Ja 29,9:2
As You Like It 1950,Ja 27,27:2
I Am a Camera 1951,N 29,39:6
I Am a Camera 1951,D 9,II,5:1
Affair of Honor 1956,Ap 7,12:3
Third Best Sport 1958,D 31,15:3
Highest Tree, The 1959,N 5,41:1
Venus at Large 1962,Ap 13,30:1
Strange Interlude 1963,Mr 13,5:2
Strange Interlude 1963,Je 18,34:6
Ballad of the Sad Cafe, The 1963,O 31,27:1
Ballad of the Sad Cafe, The 1963,N 10,II,1:1
Stephen D 1967,S 25,58:1
Stephen D 1967,O 8,II,1:6
Little Foxes, The 1967,O 27,53:1
Mercy Street 1969,O 28,43:1
Mercy Street 1969,N 2,II,3:1
Princeton Theatre Intime (Producer)
Volpone 1937,N 16,26:4
Prindle, Roderic
Patrick--The First 1965,F 19,25:1
Prine, Andrew
Mrs Patterson 1957,F 6,20:2
Look Homeward, Angel 1958,Ag 31,II,1:1
Distant Bell, A 1960,Ja 14,29:1
Borak 1960,D 14,51:1
Prine, Gilbert
Marie Vison, La 1970,Jl 15,29:1
Pringle, Bryan
Richard II 1956,O 24,44:1
Romeo and Juliet 1956,O 25,41:1
Pringle, Casha
Sacred Flame, The 1928,N 20,28:2
Pringle, Gerald (Scenic Designer)
Catiline 1936,Ja 28,14:6
Pringle, James
Purification, The 1954,My 29,12:1
Apollo of Bellac, The 1954,My 29,12:1
Pringle, James (Lighting Director)
Season of the Beast 1958,Mr 14,29:2
Pringle, James (Scenic Designer)
Season of the Beast 1958,Mr 14,29:2
Pringle, Joan
Camino Real 1970,Ja 9,42:1
Operation Sidewinder 1970,Mr 13,33:1
Pringle, Shirley
Pirates of Penzance, The 1952,O 28,36:4
Pringle, Val
Moon Besieged, The 1962,D 6,54:1
Mahagonny 1970,Ap 29,51:1
Pringle, William
Passing Show of 1921, The 1920,D 30,16:2
Passing Show of 1923, The 1923,Je 15,24:6
Princess Flavia 1925,N 3,34:3
Cherry Blossoms 1927,Mr 29,22:3
Luana 1930,S 18,28:1
Student Prince, The 1931,Ja 30,18:1
Student Prince, The 1943,Je 9,16:2
Day Will Come, The 1944,S 8,17:2
I Remember Mama 1944,O 20,16:2
Printemps, Yvonne
Jacqueline 1921,N 20,VI,1:3
Grand Duc, Le 1922,Jl 30,VI,1:7
Springtime 1924,My 11,VIII,1:4
Mozart 1925,D 27,VII,6:7
Mozart 1925,D 27,VII,2:1
Mozart 1926,Jl 4,VII,1:3
Deburau 1926,N 14,VIII,2:1
Mozart 1926,D 28,16:1
Deburau 1926,D 28,16:1
Mozart 1927,Ja 2,VII,1:1
Illusioniste, L' 1927,Ja 11,36:5
Desire 1927,My 29,VII,2:7
Mariette 1928,O 21,IX,5:6
Histoires de France 1929,O 27,IX,2:4
Et Vive le Theatre! 1930,Ap 20,VIII,2:8
Frans Hals 1931,Ap 26,VIII,2:5
Rapide de Minuit, Le; Last Mile, The
1932,Ap 3,VIII,2:1
Bonheur 1933,My 14,IX,1:4
Conversation Piece 1934,F 17,20:5
Conversation Piece 1934,Mr 11,X,3:6
Conversation Piece 1934,O 24,24:1
Conversation Piece 1934,N 18,IX,1:1
O Mistress Mine 1936,D 4,30:3
O Mistress Mine 1936,D 20,XI,3:3
Printz, Edward
Johnny Johnson 1956,O 22,24:1
Legend of Lizzie, The 1959,F 10,39:1
Printzlau, Olga (Playwright)
Jay Walker, The 1926,F 9,23:1

Printzlau, Olga (Playwright)—Cont
Window Panes 1927,F 22,22:2
Back Here 1928,N 27,36:3
Prinz, Aladar
Fruehlingsluft 1921,N 29,17:4
Prinz, Eddie (Choreographer)
Earl Carroll's Vanities 1940,Ja 15,11:2
Prinz, LeRoy (Choreographer)
Fioretta 1929,F 6,30:3
Sketch Book 1929,Jl 2,33:5
Great Day! 1929,O 18,24:3
Silver Swan, The 1929,N 28,34:5
Top Speed 1929,D 26,20:1
Earl Carroll's Vanities 1930,Jl 1,28:3
Prinz, LeRoy (Miscellaneous)
Tattle Tales 1933,Je 2,22:6
Prinz, LeRoy (Producer)
Red White and Blue 1950,O 8,64:5
Prinz, Rosemary
Indian Captive, The 1949,Ja 31,15:2
Grey-Eyed People, The 1952,D 18,41:2
Homeward Look, The 1954,Je 4,26:2
Tonight in Samarkand 1955,F 17,22:2
Three Men on a Horse 1969,O 17,35:1
Prioio, Susan
Utbu 1966,Ja 5,24:1
Prior, Allan
Topics of 1923 1923,N 21,23:2
Passing Show of 1924, The 1924,S 4,13:4
Love Song, The 1925,Ja 14,19:4
Katja 1926,O 19,27:3
White Eagle, The 1927,D 27,24:4
Rainbow 1928,N 22,25:1
Prior, Hays
Goat Alley 1927,Ap 21,24:3
Too Many Boats 1934,S 12,26:3
Prior, Shirley Ann
Out of This World 1950,D 22,17:3
Wish You Were Here 1952,Je 26,26:6
Prisant, Hymie
Bublitchki 1938,Ja 17,11:2
Pritchard, Ann
Artists and Models 1923,Ag 21,12:2
Greenwich Village Follies 1928,Ap 10,32:2
Ned Wayburn's Gambols 1929,Ja 16,22:3
Slightly Delinquent 1954,O 26,32:5
Pritchard, David
Crow's Nest, The 1923,My 10,22:3
Town Boy 1929,O 5,22:4
Pritchard, Ellis
Holy Night 1941,D 22,23:3
Pritchard, Margaret
Cherry Pie 1926,Ap 15,24:4
Pritchard, Ogmore
Songs From Milk Wood 1970,Ja 13,41:1
Pritchard, Thelma
Los Angeles 1927,D 20,32:3
Pritchett, James
Wayside 1957,Ap 18,34:1
Auntie Mame 1958,Ag 12,33:2
Killer, The 1960,Mr 23,33:1
Embers 1960,O 26,44:1
Fam and Yam 1960,O 26,44:1
Sail Away 1961,O 4,48:5
Love of Two Hours, The 1962,O 27,16:2
Emperor, The 1963,Ap 17,30:1
Phedre 1966,F 11,36:1
Round With Ring, A 1969,O 30,56:1
Pritchett, Lizabeth
Happy Town 1959,O 8,49:2
Cindy 1964,Mr 20,24:1
Pritchett, Willie
Simply Heavenly 1957,My 22,28:2
Prival, Bert
Iolanthe 1926,Ap 20,24:2
Pirates of Penzance, The; Slave of Duty, The
1926,D 7,25:1
Belmont Varieties 1932,S 29,17:2
Privette, Pamela
Autumn's Here 1966,O 26,40:1
Prizant, Hyman
My Malkele 1937,S 20,18:6
Proach, Henry
Many Loves 1959,Ja 14,28:1
Cave at Machpelah, The 1959,Jl 1,25:1
Connection, The 1959,Jl 16,30:2
Marrying Maiden, The 1960,Je 23,18:3
In the Jungle of Cities 1960,D 21,39:1
Apple, The 1961,D 8,44:1
Man Is Man 1962,S 19,31:1
Brig, The 1963,My 16,40:1
Wicked Cooks, The 1967,Ja 24,42:1
Cuban Thing, The 1968,S 25,36:2
Sheep on the Runway 1970,F 2,28:3
Probert, George
Mad Honeymoon, The 1923,Ag 8,10:1
Houses of Sand 1925,F 18,17:1
New York 1927,N 15,26:2
Murder on the Second Floor 1929,S 12,35:1
Great Barrington, The 1931,F 20,18:1
Boy Friend, The 1932,Je 8,22:3
American Holiday 1936,F 22,13:3
Help Yourself! 1936,Jl 15,15:1
Sun and I, The 1937,F 27,9:5

⋯ert, George—Cont
⋯g Blow 1938,O 3,11:2
⋯an Who Came to Dinner, The 1939,O 17,31:1
⋯ost, Ben
⋯enry V 1928,Mr 16,26:2
⋯ima 1928,D 13,24:2
⋯enny Arcade 1930,Mr 11,24:5
⋯ost, Gerry
⋯ew Faces of 1936 1936,My 20,24:5
⋯ost, Nicholas
⋯amlet 1956,O 29,34:1
⋯mall War on Murray Hill 1957,Ja 4,19:1
⋯chnicka, Lidia
⋯Iisalliance 1961,S 26,32:2
⋯Icestis Comes Back 1962,Ap 24,33:1
⋯chnik, Bruce
⋯Dliver 1962,S 27,32:3
⋯Dliver 1963,Ja 8,5:5
⋯copio, Rennie (Costume Designer)
⋯hunder Rock 1956,F 27,18:1
⋯ly Hex 1956,Je 19,25:1
⋯esson, The 1956,O 3,29:2
⋯escurial 1956,O 3,29:2
⋯hor, With Angels 1956,O 15,29:4
⋯ox of Watercolors, A 1957,F 18,22:2
⋯Dscar Wilde 1957,Ap 20,21:3
⋯octer, Robert
⋯Drunkard, The; Fallen Saved, The 1959,Je 24,37:2
⋯octer, Robert (Composer)
⋯Hamlet of Stepney Green 1958,N 14,21:1
⋯Drunkard, The; Fallen Saved, The 1959,Je 24,37:2
⋯octer, Wynn (Playwright)
⋯Savages Under the Skin 1927,Mr 25,25:2
⋯octor, Buddy
⋯Three Little Girls 1930,Ap 15,29:1
⋯Six Characters in Search of an Author 1931,Ap 16,29:2
⋯Counsellor-at-Law 1931,N 7,17:2
⋯Between Two Worlds 1934,O 26,24:2
⋯roctor, Catherine
⋯Mirage, The 1920,O 1,14:1
⋯Ambush 1921,O 11,22:1
⋯Wife With a Smile, The 1921,N 29,20:1
⋯East of Suez 1922,S 22,16:3
⋯Macbeth 1924,Mr 17,18:1
⋯Steam Roller, The 1924,N 11,20:2
⋯Ariadne 1925,F 24,17:1
⋯Importance of Being Earnest, The 1926,My 4,30:1
⋯Aiglon, L' 1927,D 27,24:3
⋯Royal Box, The 1928,N 21,32:3
⋯Sakura 1928,D 26,14:4
⋯Ghost Parade, The 1929,O 31,28:4
⋯Greater Love 1931,Mr 3,39:1
⋯If Booth Had Missed 1932,F 5,24:2
⋯Nine Pine Street 1933,Ap 28,15:5
⋯Puritan, The 1936,Ja 24,14:3
⋯Howdy Stranger 1937,Ja 15,17:5
⋯Late George Apley, The 1944,N 22,26:2
⋯Proctor, Charles
⋯Sunup to Sundown 1938,F 2,14:3
⋯Twilight Walk 1951,S 25,25:4
⋯Bat, The 1953,Ja 21,28:2
⋯Proctor, Doris
⋯Shakespeare in Harlem 1959,O 28,40:7
⋯Proctor, Florence
⋯Ambush 1921,O 16,VI,1:1
⋯Proctor, Gerald E (Scenic Designer)
⋯Digging for Apples 1962,S 28,29:4
⋯Proctor, Hubert
⋯Mill Shadows 1932,F 29,20:7
⋯Proctor, John
⋯Ten Million Ghosts 1936,O 24,23:7
⋯Anna Lucasta 1944,Je 17,10:1
⋯Anna Lucasta 1944,Ag 31,15:1
⋯Proctor, John (Scenic Designer)
⋯Walk Hard 1944,D 1,28:2
⋯Proctor, Philip
⋯Cherry Orchard, The 1962,N 15,46:2
⋯Thistle in My Bed 1963,N 20,48:1
⋯Amorous Flea, The 1964,F 18,26:1
⋯Time for Singing, A 1966,My 23,48:2
⋯Proctor, Vouletti
⋯What Next 1920,Ja 27,7:2
⋯Proctor, Warren
⋯Erminie 1921,Ja 4,11:1
⋯Phoebe of Quality Street 1921,My 10,20:1
⋯Natja 1925,F 17,19:2
Prodromides, Jean (Composer)
⋯Trojan Women, The 1963,D 24,7:6
Profanato, Gene
⋯Lovely Ladies, Kind Gentlemen 1970,D 29,38:1
Profit, Herman
⋯Lulu Belle 1926,F 10,20:1
Prokofiev, Serge (Composer)
⋯Peter and the Wolf 1969,N 30,85:5
Prokop, Albert
⋯Don Carlos 1962,F 28,27:5
Prol, Julio
⋯Brothers Karamazov, The 1957,D 9,39:4
Pronko, Leonard G (Translator)
⋯Anna Kleiber 1965,Ja 20,33:1
Propper, Judith
⋯Alchemist, The 1966,O 14,48:1
⋯Yerma 1966,D 9,60:1

Proser, Monte (Producer)
⋯High Button Shoes 1947,O 10,32:2
⋯Heaven on Earth 1948,S 17,29:2
⋯All You Need Is One Good Break 1950,F 10,20:3
⋯Eddie Fisher at the Winter Garden 1962,O 3,47:1
Prosk, Gerald
⋯Show Boat 1948,S 9,33:2
Prosky, Robert
⋯Pale Horse, Pale Rider 1957,O 30,26:1
⋯Month in the Country, A 1959,Mr 2,32:2
⋯Caucasian Chalk Circle, The 1961,N 1,35:1
⋯Devils, The 1963,N 5,25:1
⋯Lonesome Train, The 1965,Je 17,25:1
⋯Hard Travelin' 1965,Je 17,25:1
⋯Iceman Cometh, The 1968,Ap 1,58:1
⋯Indians 1969,My 27,43:1
Prosper, Charles
⋯Bellamy Trial, The 1928,Ag 20,21:1
Prosper and Maret
⋯Gay Paree 1925,Ag 19,14:3
Prospery, George
⋯Star Time 1944,S 13,16:2
Prosser, Joseph
⋯For Better or Worse 1927,F 1,24:3
⋯Killers 1928,Mr 14,28:3
Prothen, Yvonne
⋯Nights of Wrath; Nuits de la Colere, Les 1947,D 1,26:4
Prothero, James H Jr
⋯Here's Howe 1923,Ap 26,19:3
⋯That's That 1924,Ap 30,19:2
Protopapas, Vangel
⋯Screwball, The 1957,My 25,24:7
Prouse, Derek (Playwright)
⋯Amedee: or, How to Disentangle Yourself 1955,N 1,27:3
Prouse, Derek (Translator)
⋯Rhinoceros 1961,Ja 10,27:1
Prouty, Jed
⋯Girl From Home, The 1920,My 4,9:2
⋯Some Party 1922,Ap 17,22:1
⋯And Be My Love 1945,F 22,30:4
⋯Too Hot for Maneuvers 1945,My 3,26:5
⋯Heads or Tails 1947,My 3,10:6
Prouty, Olive Higgins (Original Author)
⋯Stella Dallas 1924,Ja 20,VII,2:8
Prova, Sreemati
⋯Ramayana 1931,Ja 13,35:4
Providence, Roy
⋯What Did We Do Wrong? 1967,O 23,56:1
Provost, Jack
⋯Narrow Road to the Deep North 1969,D 2,64:1
Provost, Jeanne
⋯Cyrano de Bergerac 1926,Ja 24,II,8:5
⋯Amants 1928,Mr 4,IX,4:5
⋯Monsieur le Comte 1933,F 12,IX,3:4
Provost, Robert (Costume Designer)
⋯Othello 1959,Jl 5,II,1:1
Provost, Robert (Scenic Designer)
⋯Othello 1959,Jl 5,II,1:1
Prowse, Juliet
⋯Eddie Fisher at the Winter Garden 1962,O 3,47:1
⋯Sweet Charity 1967,O 13,34:3
Prud'Homme, Cameron
⋯Tide Rising 1937,Ja 26,17:2
⋯See the Jaguar 1952,D 4,46:2
⋯By the Beautiful Sea 1954,Ap 9,20:1
⋯Rainmaker, The 1954,O 29,28:1
⋯Rainmaker, The 1954,N 7,II,1:1
⋯New Girl in Town 1957,My 15,40:1
⋯New Girl in Town 1957,My 26,II,1:1
⋯Drink to Me Only 1958,O 9,47:4
⋯Desert Incident, A 1959,Mr 25,40:1
⋯Unsinkable Molly Brown, The 1960,N 4,28:1
Prud'Homme, June
⋯Blood Wedding 1949,F 7,16:2
⋯Bruno and Sidney 1949,My 4,38:2
⋯Henry V 1969,Je 9,57:1
⋯Much Ado About Nothing 1969,Je 16,57:1
⋯Henry V 1969,N 11,43:1
Prudkin, A
⋯Dybbuk, The 1926,D 14,24:2
⋯Deluge, The 1927,Ja 11,36:2
Prudkin, Mark
⋯Kremlin Chimes 1965,F 25,23:1
Prudkin, S
⋯Eternal Jew, The 1926,D 21,21:2
Prue, Edwina
⋯Gentlemen Prefer Blondes 1926,S 29,23:1
Prufer, Guntram (Miscellaneous)
⋯War and Peace 1962,Je 16,10:1
Prufer, Guntram (Playwright)
⋯War and Peace 1965,Ja 12,32:1
⋯War and Peace 1965,Ja 31,II,1:1
⋯War and Peace 1967,Mr 22,42:1
Prumbs, Lucille (Playwright)
⋯Five Alarm Waltz 1941,Mr 14,16:2
⋯I'll Take the High Road 1943,N 10,28:3
Pruneau, Phillip
⋯Winner, The 1954,F 18,34:1
⋯There Was a Little Girl 1960,Mr 1,28:1
⋯Last Analysis, The 1964,O 2,30:1

Pruneau, Phillip (Director)
⋯I Am a Camera 1956,O 10,47:2
Pruneau, Phillip (Miscellaneous)
⋯I Am a Camera 1956,O 10,47:2
Pruneau, Phillip (Playwright)
⋯Cellar and the Well, The 1950,D 11,30:2
⋯Sophie 1963,Ap 16,32:1
Prussing, Louise
⋯Mayor of Casterbridge, The 1926,S 9,20:1
⋯Berkeley Square 1929,N 5,32:4
⋯Counsellor-at-Law 1931,N 7,17:2
⋯Singapore 1932,N 15,24:2
⋯Before Morning 1933,F 10,13:4
⋯Beginner's Luck 1935,Jl 23,24:4
⋯King's Messenger, The 1935,Ag 14,16:3
Pruvot, Lydie
⋯Labyrinth, The 1968,S 22,II,1:6
Pruyn, R L
⋯Laugh It Off 1925,Ap 25,18:4
⋯1776 1926,Ap 24,11:2
Pryce, Richard (Playwright)
⋯Old House, The 1920,Jl 11,VI,1:6
⋯Thunder on the Left 1928,Ag 19,VII,1:1
⋯Thunder on the Left 1928,O 21,IX,1:3
⋯Frolic Wind 1935,Mr 14,19:7
Pryde, James (Scenic Designer)
⋯Othello 1930,My 20,33:1
Pryme, Alberta
⋯Born Yesterday 1954,Ja 1,16:6
Pryne, Eleanor
⋯Johnny 2X4 1942,Mr 17,24:6
Pryor, Ainslie
⋯Caine Mutiny Court-Martial, The 1954,Ja 21,27:2
Pryor, Allan
⋯Great Day! 1929,O 18,24:3
Pryor, C H (Playwright)
⋯Autocrat, The 1929,Je 9,VIII,2:4
Pryor, Elinor (Original Author)
⋯First in Heart, The 1947,N 14,29:2
Pryor, F R (Playwright)
⋯Marigold 1927,My 29,VII,1:3
⋯Autocrat, The 1929,Je 9,VIII,2:4
⋯Marigold 1930,O 9,23:1
Pryor, Hayes
⋯Earth 1927,Mr 10,23:1
⋯Porgy 1927,O 11,26:2
⋯Second Comin', The 1931,D 9,32:4
⋯Marriage of Cana, The 1932,F 3,22:4
⋯Black Souls 1932,Mr 31,25:1
⋯Ol' Man Satan 1932,O 4,26:3
⋯Jayhawker 1934,N 6,34:2
⋯Sailor, Beware! 1935,My 7,28:4
⋯Zunguru 1938,Ag 7,IX,8:2
⋯Mamba's Daughters 1939,Ja 4,24:2
Pryor, Joan
⋯Mulatto 1967,N 16,61:4
⋯Black Quartet, A; Warning, The-A Theme for Linda 1969,Jl 31,28:1
⋯Warning, The-A Theme for Linda 1969,Ag 3,II,1:4
Pryor, Martha
⋯I'll Say She Is 1924,My 20,15:1
⋯Murder at the Vanities 1933,S 13,22:4
Pryor, Maureen
⋯Boeing-Boeing 1965,F 3,30:1
⋯After the Rain 1967,O 10,54:1
⋯Little Boxes; Coffee Lace, The; Trevor 1968,Jl 5,20:1
Pryor, Nicholas
⋯Egghead, The 1957,O 10,39:1
⋯Love Me Little 1958,Ap 15,42:2
⋯Howie 1958,S 18,35:2
⋯Borak 1960,D 14,51:1
⋯Party for Divorce, A 1966,O 12,37:1
Pryor, Robert
⋯Dark of the Moon 1945,Mr 15,27:2
Pryor, Roger
⋯Backslapper, The 1925,Ap 13,25:2
⋯Sea Woman, The 1925,Ag 25,12:2
⋯Paid 1925,N 26,32:1
⋯Vaudeville (Palace) 1926,Je 8,23:1
⋯Thieves 1926,Je 8,23:1
⋯Saturday's Children 1927,Ja 27,13:1
⋯Sisters 1927,D 26,26:5
⋯Royal Family, The 1927,D 29,26:4
⋯See Naples and Die 1929,S 27,30:4
⋯Apron Strings 1930,F 18,28:2
⋯Up Pops the Devil 1930,S 2,19:1
⋯Modern Virgin, A 1931,My 21,33:4
⋯Blessed Event 1932,Ja 31,VIII,1:6
⋯Blessed Event 1932,F 13,23:2
⋯Blessed Event 1932,F 21,VIII,1:1
⋯There's Always Juliet 1932,O 28,23:2
⋯Message for Margaret 1947,Ap 17,34:2
Pryor, Roger (Playwright)
⋯Here Goes the Bride 1931,N 4,31:2
Pryor, Sara Sherman (Playwright)
⋯Rut, The 1923,My 8,22:3
Pryor, William
⋯Edgar Allan Poe 1925,O 6,31:1
Pryse, Hugh
⋯Sleep of Prisoners, A 1951,O 17,36:2
⋯Time Remembered 1955,My 4,35:1

Przgrodska, Olga
Button, Button 1970,O 20,41:1
Przybylko, Mary
Women's House, The 1930,Ap 27,IX,3:1
Psacharopoulos, Nikos (Director)
Play of Daniel, The 1958,Ja 3,15:3
Play of Daniel, The 1958,Ja 26,II,1:1
Tambourines to Glory 1963,N 4,47:1
Play of Herod, The 1963,D 10,55:2
Play of Herod, The 1965,D 29,24:2
Androcles and the Lion 1968,Je 27,47:1
Psachos, Constantine (Composer)
Prometheus Unbound 1927,My 29,VII,6:7
Psathas, Demetrios (Playwright)
Screwball, The 1957,My 25,24:7
Pshepurka, Leo
Thousand and One Nights 1959,D 16,53:2
Ptagek, Joseph
Low Bridge 1933,F 10,13:4
Puck, Eva
Greenwich Village Follies 1923,S 21,4:6
Melody Man, The 1924,My 14,14:2
Girl Friend, The 1926,Mr 18,26:5
Show Boat 1927,D 28,26:1
Show Boat 1928,Ja 8,VIII,1:1
Vaudeville (Palace) 1929,Ag 19,23:1
Vaudeville (Palace) 1931,O 19,28:5
Show Boat 1932,My 20,22:2
Puck, Harry
Tangerine 1921,Ag 10,8:2
Lollipop 1924,Ja 22,15:3
My Girl 1924,N 25,27:2
Merry Merry 1925,S 25,24:3
Madcap, The 1928,F 1,31:2
Luckee Girl 1928,S 17,28:6
Three Little Girls 1930,Mr 30,VIII,2:7
Three Little Girls 1930,Ap 15,29:1
Vaudeville (Palace) 1932,My 23,18:7
Puck, Harry (Choreographer)
Madcap, The 1928,F 1,31:2
Puck, Harry (Director)
Twinkle Twinkle 1926,N 17,22:2
Puck, Harry (Miscellaneous)
Luckee Girl 1928,S 17,28:6
Pudaloff, L
Golem, The 1927,F 5,13:2
Pudalowa, L
Eternal Jew, The 1926,D 21,21:2
Puel, Rene
Ada Beats the Drum 1930,My 9,20:4
Puget, Claude-Andre (Original Author)
Happy Days 1941,My 14,24:2
Puget, Claude Andre (Playwright)
Ligne du Coeur, La 1931,O 25,VIII,1:7
Pugh, Ed
Africana 1927,Jl 12,29:2
Pugh, Ted
In the Nick of Time 1967,Je 2,36:1
Have I Got One for You 1968,Ja 8,32:1
Now 1968,Je 6,53:1
Lend an Ear 1969,O 29,32:1
Pugh, Ted (Playwright)
In the Nick of Time 1967,Je 2,36:1
Pughe, George
Vaudeville (Palace) 1927,My 17,27:4
Whistling in the Dark 1933,D 6,29:3
Puglia, Francesco
Mother Martyr 1935,Ja 28,10:3
Signori, Il Figlio E' Nato 1935,Je 8,13:7
Pugsley, Jean
Dear Judas 1947,O 6,26:4
For Heaven's Sake Mother 1948,N 17,33:4
Pujol, Rene (Playwright)
Nuit, Une 1935,Je 16,X,1:1
Puknat, Joan (Choreographer)
Christmas in the Market Place 1960,D 10,26:1
Puleo, Johnny
Vaudeville (Palace) 1952,Ap 14,23:2
Vaudeville (Palace) 1952,Ap 27,II,1:1
Aquashow 1952,Je 25,25:1
Puleo, Robert
Galileo 1967,Ap 14,31:1
Amahl and the Night Visitors 1970,D 24,10:2
Pulitzer, Ralph (Mrs) (Playwright)
Divided by Three 1934,O 3,24:2
Pullen, Miriam
Walk Hard 1946,Mr 28,34:2
Pulleyn, Robert
Half Moon Inn 1923,Mr 21,19:2
Pullman, Victor
Jubilee 1935,O 14,20:1
Pully, B S
Guys and Dolls 1950,N 25,11:2
Guys and Dolls 1950,D 3,II,1:1
Guys and Dolls 1951,O 7,II,1:1
Guys and Dolls 1966,Je 9,55:2
Pulman, Jack (Playwright)
Happy Apple, The 1970,Jl 26,49:2
Pulsifer, Fay (Playwright)
Go West, Young Man 1923,N 13,25:2
Pulsifer, Ken
Great Day! 1929,O 18,24:3

Pulver, Enid
Hamlet 1948,D 4,9:2
Pulver, Mary Brecht (Original Author)
Helena's Boys 1924,Ap 8,22:2
Puma, Marie
Romeo and Jeanette 1969,D 16,53:1
Engagement Baby, The 1970,My 22,40:1
Pumock, Mildred
Only the Heart 1944,Ap 5,17:2
Punk (Cat)
Years Ago 1946,D 4,44:2
Punsley, Bea
Dead End 1935,O 29,17:2
Punsly, Bernard
Dead End 1935,O 29,17:2
Pupp, Anally
Florida Girl 1925,N 3,34:1
Purcell, Charles
Poor Little Ritz Girl 1920,Jl 29,7:1
Rose Girl, The 1921,F 12,11:1
Vaudeville (Winter Garden) 1922,F 14,21:1
Swanee River 1923,Jl 15,VI,1:2
Lambs Gambol 1925,Ap 27,15:1
Dearest Enemy 1925,S 19,9:2
Oh, Please! 1926,D 22,24:3
Judy 1927,F 8,20:2
Chocolate Soldier, The 1930,Ja 28,28:1
Chocolate Soldier, The 1931,S 22,33:3
Shady Lady 1933,Jl 6,26:3
Chocolate Soldier, The 1934,My 3,15:3
Park Avenue 1946,N 5,31:2
Purcell, Charles (Producer)
Chocolate Soldier, The 1934,My 3,15:3
Purcell, Dick
Paths of Glory 1935,S 27,24:2
Purcell, Gertrude
March Hares 1923,Mr 13,19:5
Great Temptations, The 1926,My 19,29:1
Purcell, Gertrude (Playwright)
Voltaire 1922,Mr 21,17:1
Tangletoes 1925,F 18,17:1
Wolf! Wolf! 1925,O 30,21:1
Just Fancy! 1927,O 12,30:2
Madcap, The 1928,F 1,31:2
Luckee Girl 1928,S 17,28:6
Three Little Girls 1930,Mr 30,VIII,2:7
Three Little Girls 1930,Ap 15,29:1
Purcell, Harold (Lyricist)
Under the Counter 1947,O 4,10:2
Purcell, Helen
Simon's Wife 1945,Mr 9,16:4
Purcell, Henry (Composer)
In Good King Charles's Golden Days
1957,Ja 25,16:1
Tempest, The: or, The Enchanted Forest
1959,Je 10,42:2
Way of the World, The 1965,Je 2,40:1
King Arthur 1968,N 3,87:1
Purcell, Irene
New Poor, The 1924,Ja 8,26:1
Helena's Boys 1924,Ap 8,22:2
What Women Do? 1925,Jl 21,26:4
Ladder, The 1926,O 23,15:1
Sisters 1927,D 26,26:5
Great Necker, The 1928,Mr 7,28:2
Cross Roads 1929,N 12,34:2
Dancing Partner 1930,Jl 27,VIII,2:3
Dancing Partner 1930,Ag 6,24:2
Good Woman, Poor Thing, A 1933,Ja 10,27:3
First Apple, The 1933,D 28,25:1
Accent on Youth 1934,D 26,19:1
Penny Wise 1937,Ap 20,28:6
Contrast, The 1940,Mr 26,17:2
Royal Family, The 1940,Ag 13,15:3
Purcell, Irene (Playwright)
Royal Family, The 1940,Ag 13,15:3
Purcell, Jack
Three to Make Ready 1946,Mr 8,16:2
Hit the Trail 1954,D 3,31:2
Ankles Aweigh 1955,Ap 19,27:1
Purcell, Matthew
Dead End 1935,O 29,17:2
Purcell, Noel
Devil Came From Dublin, The! 1955,Je 3,27:2
Purcell, Ray
Fall 1957,N 22,19:1
Purcell, Raymond
Troubled Waters 1965,Je 4,40:2
Purcell, Vivian
Gentlemen Prefer Blondes 1926,S 29,23:1
Purcella, Frank
Whirl of New York, The 1921,Je 14,18:1
Purcella, Raymond
Whirl of New York, The 1921,Je 14,18:1
Purcella Brothers
Century Revue and the Midnight Rounders, The
1920,Jl 13,9:1
Purdell, Reginald
Years Between, The 1931,My 10,VIII,2:1
Jack o' Diamonds 1935,F 26,17:3
Purdom, C B (Director)
Mr Sampson 1927,My 8,30:1

Purdom, Edmund
Caesar and Cleopatra 1951,D 20,43:2
Antony and Cleopatra 1951,D 21,22:2
Child of Fortune 1956,N 14,41:1
Purdom, J Robert (Miscellaneous)
Folies Bergere 1964,Je 3,36:1
Purdue, Lillian
Mikado, The 1942,F 4,22:2
Pirates of Penzance, The 1942,F 18,22:2
Iolanthe 1942,F 24,26:4
Gondoliers, The 1942,Mr 4,22:3
Purdum, Ralph
Paradise Island 1961,Je 24,11:1
All Kinds of Giants 1961,D 19,40:1
Paradise Island 1962,Je 28,22:1
Children From Their Games 1963,Ap 12,33:1
Mardi Gras! 1965,Je 28,33:2
Mardi Gras! 1966,Jl 11,32:2
Blancs, Les 1970,N 16,48:4
Blancs, Les 1970,N 29,II,3:1
Purdy, Claude
Dutchman; Slave, The 1965,N 17,53:7
Purdy, Elsa
Jotham Valley 1951,F 7,37:2
Purdy, James (Original Author)
Malcolm 1966,Ja 12,29:1
Purdy, John
Macbeth 1968,N 30,49:3
Purdy, Merlyn
Beautiful Changes, The 1956,Mr 24,15:2
Richard III 1957,N 26,41:1
Purdy, Richard
Crime and Punishment 1947,D 23,29:3
Peer Gynt 1951,Ja 29,15:2
Fancy Meeting You Again 1952,Ja 15,23:2
Misalliance 1953,F 19,20:1
Can-Can 1953,My 8,28:1
Saint Joan 1956,S 12,42:1
Hamlet 1957,Ja 29,27:1
Purdy, Richard A (Playwright)
Across the Street 1924,Mr 16,VIII,2:1
Across the Street 1924,Mr 25,24:1
Purdy, Robert E
On the Level 1937,Mr 26,24:4
Purefoy, Tom
School for Wives 1934,N 14,22:2
Purlans, Brothers and June
Vaudeville (Palace) 1932,Jl 4,14:5
Purnell, Louise
Love's Labour's Lost 1968,D 22,54:3
Beaux' Stratagem, The 1970,F 10,50:2
Three Sisters, The 1970,F 12,30:1
Idiot, The 1970,Jl 17,18:1
Purnell, Roger
Sleuth 1970,N 13,25:1
Purnello, Ethel
Run, Little Chillun! 1933,Mr 2,21:3
Sweet River 1936,O 29,30:2
Hitch Your Wagon! 1937,Ap 9,18:2
Cat and the Canary, The 1937,Je 15,26:3
Mamba's Daughters 1939,Ja 4,24:2
Mamba's Daughters 1940,Mr 25,10:4
Green Pastures, The 1951,Mr 16,35:2
Pursell, Charles S
Corn Is Green, The 1940,N 27,27:2
Miser, The 1950,Mr 27,19:5
How to Make a Man 1961,F 3,16:1
Pursley, David
Peace 1969,Ja 28,49:1
Pursley, David (Costume Designer)
Days Between, The 1965,Je 4,39:1
Pursley, David (Scenic Designer)
Days Between, The 1965,Je 4,39:1
Pursley, Mona
Macbeth 1968,N 30,49:3
Pursley, Patricia
George White's Scandals 1926,Je 15,23:2
Purviance, Roy
Made in America 1925,O 15,27:2
Purvin, Beverly
Tree Grows in Brooklyn, A 1951,Ap 20,24:3
Can-Can 1953,My 8,28:1
Purvis, Mary (Scenic Designer)
Women of Twilight 1952,Mr 4,22:2
Pushkin, Alexander (Playwright)
Chauve-Souris 1922,O 11,22:2
Boris Godunoff 1925,F 27,14:1
Chauve-Souris; Queen of Spades, The
1931,O 22,27:1
Pusilo, Robert J (Costume Designer)
Goa 1968,F 23,46:1
Believers, The 1968,My 10,57:4
License, The 1969,Ap 23,42:1
Man With the Flower in His Mouth, The
1969,Ap 23,42:1
Jar, The 1969,Ap 23,42:1
Putch, William (Miscellaneous)
Come Share My House 1960,F 19,20:2
Putnam, A M
Baby Pompadour 1934,D 28,24:2
Putnam, Alice
Scarlet Man, The 1921,Ag 23,10:3

Putnam, Christine
Faust 1928,O 9,34:1
Putnam, Marilyn
Summer and Smoke 1947,Jl 9,18:5
Putnam, Oliver
Bootleggers, The 1922,N 28,24:1
Baby Cyclone, The 1927,S 13,37:4
Mourning Becomes Electra; Hunted, The 1931,O 27,22:1
Mourning Becomes Electra; Haunted, The 1931,O 27,22:1
Putnam, Polly
Prunella 1929,Ap 10,23:3
Putnam, William B D (Playwright)
Assorted Nuts 1940,Ap 7,I,44:6
Putney, Harold B
If Booth Had Missed 1931,My 14,27:1
Putney, Jay
Steel 1939,D 20,30:2
Putnoe, Marton
Nautical but Nice 1931,Ap 19,31:6
Putz, Egon (Musical Director)
Bruder Straubinger 1921,N 16,22:3
Puzinger, Emmi
Eisrevue 1969,O 23,55:1
Puzo, Billy (Scenic Designer)
Greenwillow 1970,D 8,60:1
Pvopesco, Elvire
Elvire 1940,F 11,IX,2:5
Pyatt, Richard
Reckoning, The 1969,S 5,28:1
Pyle, Richard
Girl in the Spotlight, The 1920,Jl 13,9:3
Pyle, Seifert C
Commodore Marries, The 1929,S 5,26:3
Pyne, Alison
Variations of 1940 1940,Ja 29,12:1
Pyne, Frederick
Dance of Death, The 1967,O 20,50:1
Love for Love 1967,O 21,17:1
Pyzel, Robert (Playwright)
Anybody Home 1949,F 26,10:5

Q

Quadflieg, Will
Faust, Part I; Prelude in the Theater 1961,F 5,27:2
Faust, Part I; Play, The 1961,F 5,27:2
Irish Faustus, An 1963,D 19,40:1
Quadri, Therese
Cornered 1920,D 9,18:2
Private Lives 1931,Ja 28,24:1
Mrs January & Mr Ex 1944,Ap 1,10:2
Private Lives 1948,O 5,30:2
Eugenia 1957,Ja 31,20:1
Nude With Violin 1957,N 15,36:1
Quadruplets, Gale
George White's Scandals 1931,S 15,30:1
Qualen, John M
Street Scene 1929,Ja 11,20:4
Counsellor-at-Law 1931,N 7,17:2
Qualters, Tot
Century Revue and the Midnight Rounders, The 1920,Jl 13,9:1
Passing Show of 1921, The 1920,D 30,16:2
Make It Snappy 1922,Ap 14,20:2
Vogues and Frolics 1924,Je 26,21:7
Qualtinger, Helmut
Satiric Evening 1963,O 24,36:2
Qualtinger, Helmut (Playwright)
Satiric Evening 1963,O 24,36:2
Quam, Mylo
Curate's Play, The 1961,D 18,41:3
Bertha 1962,F 12,27:1
Royal Hunt of the Sun, The 1965,O 27,36:2
Midsummer Night's Dream, A 1967,Je 19,42:1
Merchant of Venice, The 1967,Je 22,46:2
Macbeth 1967,Jl 31,21:1
Collision Course; Tour 1968,My 9,55:2
Quaney, Barbara
I Want You 1961,S 15,29:1
Quaranta, Giuseppe
Conte di Monte Cristo, Il 1934,Ja 22,13:2
Padrone Delle Ferriere, Il 1934,Mr 19,13:5
Colonello Bridall, L' 1934,Ap 16,20:3
Romanticismo 1934,My 14,20:2
Miserabili I, 1934,S 24,15:1
Miserabili I, 1934,O 1,14:2
Signora Dalle Camelie, La; Camille 1934,O 22,13:2
Processo dei Veleni, Il; Case of Poisons, The 1935,Ja 21,18:2
Romanzo di un Giovane Povero, Il 1935,F 25,12:3
Signo Della Croce, Il 1935,O 7,11:1
Due Orfanelle, Le; Two Orphans, The 1936,O 5,24:4
Morte Civile, La; Civic Death 1936,N 9,23:4
Tombola, La; Lottery, The 1936,N 9,23:4
Feudalismo Oppure La Terra Bassa; Feudalism or the Lowland 1937,Mr 8,22:2
Quarante, Joseph
In Time to Come 1941,D 29,20:2

Quarrier, Helen
Ponder Heart, The 1956,F 17,14:2
Lady From the Sea, The 1956,D 13,49:5
Hotel Paradiso 1957,Ap 12,22:2
Quarry, Richard
Georgy 1970,F 27,26:1
Quarry, Robert
As You Like It 1950,Ja 27,27:2
Taming of the Shrew, The 1951,Ap 26,35:2
Friends and Lovers; Proposal, The 1961,My 11,43:1
Friends and Lovers; In the Zone; Bound East for Cardiff 1961,My 11,43:1
Six Characters in Search of an Author 1961,My 11,43:1
Caucasian Chalk Circle, The 1961,N 1,35:1
Burning of the Lepers, The 1962,Ap 5,29:1
Quartell, John
Iron Men 1936,O 20,30:6
Quartermaine, Charles
Loyalties 1922,S 28,18:1
Loose Ends 1926,N 2,34:2
Quartermaine, Leon
Crooked Billet, The 1927,N 6,IX,2:5
Return of the Soldier, The 1928,Jl 8,VIII,1:7
Mrs Moonlight 1928,D 23,VIII,4:7
Journey's End 1929,Mr 23,23:1
Journey's End 1929,Mr 31,VIII,1:1
Journey's End 1929,Jl 14,IX,5:1
Journey's End 1930,Ja 27,24:7
Twelfth Night 1930,S 14,VIII,2:8
Twelfth Night 1930,O 16,28:2
Twelfth Night 1930,N 2,VIII,1:1
Art and Mrs Bottle 1930,N 19,19:3
Hamlet 1931,N 6,28:4
Hamlet 1931,N 15,VIII,1:1
King, Queen, Knave 1932,Mr 6,VIII,2:4
Tomorrow Will Be Friday 1932,S 18,IX,1:1
Mocking Bird, The 1933,Je 23,18:2
Escape Me Never! 1935,Ja 22,22:2
Seagull, The 1936,Je 21,IX,1:5
Seagull, The 1936,Ag 30,IX,1:1
Antony and Cleopatra 1936,N 1,X,3:7
Boy David, The 1936,N 22,VI,7:1
Merchant of Venice, The 1938,My 15,X,1:5
Call Home the Heart 1947,Ap 13,I,54:2
Quarterman, Edward
Fuente Ovejuna; Sheep Well, The 1936,My 3,II,4:1
Quave, Tony
Marvellous History of Saint Bernard, The 1958,F 24,16:3
Quayle, Anna
Stop the World-I Want to Get Off 1962,S 17,39:3
Stop the World-I Want to Get Off 1962,O 4,45:4
Stop the World-I Want to Get Off 1962,O 14,II,1:1
Quayle, Anthony
Magnolia Street 1934,Mr 9,22:6
Country Wife, The 1936,D 2,34:1
Silent Knight, The 1937,N 17,26:4
Coriolanus 1952,Mr 14,26:2
Coriolanus 1952,Ap 13,II,3:8
Tamburlaine the Great 1956,Ja 20,19:1
Tamburlaine the Great 1956,Ja 29,II,1:1
View From the Bridge, A 1956,O 12,35:3
Firstborn, The 1958,My 1,35:1
Firstborn, The 1958,My 11,II,1:1
Firstborn, The 1958,Jl 4,16:3
Long Day's Journey Into Night 1958,S 9,40:4
Long Day's Journey Into Night 1958,S 26,21:2
Incident at Vichy 1966,Ja 27,28:5
Galileo 1967,Ap 14,31:1
Galileo 1967,Ap 23,II,1:1
Halfway up the Tree 1967,N 8,52:1
Halfway up the Tree 1967,N 19,II,1:1
Sleuth 1970,N 13,25:1
Sleuth 1970,N 22,II,18:1
Quayle, Anthony (Director)
Richard II 1951,Mr 25,75:3
Henry V 1951,Ag 12,II,1:4
Coriolanus 1952,Mr 14,26:2
Coriolanus 1952,Ap 13,II,3:8
Firstborn, The 1958,My 1,35:1
Firstborn, The 1958,My 11,II,1:1
Firstborn, The 1958,Jl 4,16:3
Tiger at the Gates 1968,Mr 1,30:1
Idiot, The 1970,Jl 30,39:1
Quayle, Anthony (Miscellaneous)
Relapse, The 1950,N 23,54:2
Quayle, Anthony (Producer)
Tiger at the Gates 1968,Mr 10,II,1:1
Idiot, The 1970,Jl 17,18:1
Quealy, Harry
Rain 1922,N 8,18:2
Queen, Elinor
Bright Honor 1936,S 28,14:1
Queen, Ellery (Playwright)
Danger-Men Working 1936,F 7,14:4
Queen, Murray Jay (Producer)
Russet Mantle 1936,Ja 17,15:5
House in the Country, A 1937,Ja 12,18:3
Queenan, Charles
Caribbean Carnival 1947,D 6,12:2
Quentin, John
Romeo and Juliet 1962,F 14,39:1

Quentin, John—Cont
1776 1970,Je 18,54:4
Quentin, Pol (Playwright)
Luther 1965,F 15,30:4
Quentin, Pol (Translator)
Man for All Seasons, A 1963,My 11,15:1
Quessy, Alice
Holiday on Ice 1965,S 2,38:4
Holiday on Ice 1966,S 1,30:1
Holiday on Ice 1967,Ag 31,29:2
Holiday on Ice 1968,Ag 29,44:1
Holiday on Ice 1969,Ag 28,44:1
Quest, Christopher
Time and the Conways 1938,Ja 4,19:2
Quest, Josephine
By the Way 1925,D 29,20:3
Questel, Mae
Vaudeville (Palace) 1930,Mr 31,24:2
Doctor Social 1948,F 12,29:5
Majority of One, A 1959,F 17,28:2
Bajour 1964,N 24,42:1
Quevli, Marie Louise
May Wine 1935,D 6,30:3
Forbidden Melody 1936,N 3,33:1
I Married an Angel 1938,My 12,26:2
Quevli, Truman
Steel 1931,N 19,26:5
Tree, The 1932,Ap 13,23:5
Achilles Had a Heel 1935,O 14,20:2
Cyrano de Bergerac 1936,Ap 28,17:1
Quick, Diana
Midsummer Night's Dream, A 1968,D 9,59:1
Quick, George
Merry Widow, The 1964,Ag 18,24:2
Quick, George (Miscellaneous)
Pygmalion 1952,F 9,11:2
Protective Custody 1956,D 29,8:7
Oh Captain! 1958,F 5,21:2
Once Upon a Mattress 1959,My 12,40:1
Banker's Daughter, The 1962,Ja 23,37:1
West Side Story 1968,Je 25,32:1
Quick, Louise
Half a Sixpence 1965,Ap 26,38:2
Fig Leaves Are Falling, The 1969,Ja 3,19:1
Quigg, John
Arsenic and Old Lace 1941,Ja 11,13:2
Up in Central Park 1945,Ja 29,17:2
Up in Central Park 1947,My 20,29:2
Quigley, Charles
Arabian Nightmare, The 1927,Ja 11,36:3
Light of Asia, The 1928,O 10,32:2
Cyrano de Bergerac 1928,D 26,14:4
Bonds of Interest, The 1929,O 15,34:2
Diana 1929,D 10,37:1
Scarlet Sister Mary 1930,N 26,19:2
Her Tin Soldier 1933,Ap 7,22:6
World Waits, The 1933,O 26,22:5
False Dreams, Farewell 1934,Ja 16,18:3
Quigley, Dorothea
Genius and the Crowd 1920,S 7,20:1
Quigley, Godfrey
Mundy Scheme, The 1969,D 12,75:1
Quigley, Jack
Right to Kill, The 1926,F 16,22:2
American Tragedy, An 1926,O 12,31:2
Wall Street 1927,Ap 21,24:4
Quigley, Jack (Producer)
Curtain Call 1937,Ap 23,24:7
Quigley, Robert
Fools Rush In 1934,D 26,19:2
Quilan, Joseph (Original Author)
Nellie Bly 1946,Ja 22,32:2
Quillan, Joe (Playwright)
Banjo Eyes 1941,N 8,10:6
Banjo Eyes 1941,D 26,20:2
Quilter, Roger (Composer)
Julia 1936,D 27,X,7:8
Quimby, Cassius C
Eternal Road, The 1937,Ja 8,14:2
Quimby, George H
Beggarman, Thief 1935,Jl 16,24:1
Quin, Mike (Composer)
Meet the People 1940,D 26,22:2
Quin, Mike (Lyricist)
Meet the People 1940,D 26,22:2
Quin, Mike (Playwright)
Meet the People 1940,D 26,22:2
Quin, Philip
Hamlet 1930,Mr 25,34:4
Macbeth 1930,Mr 26,24:6
Merchant of Venice, The 1930,Mr 27,24:7
Taming of the Shrew, The 1930,Mr 28,22:8
Richard III 1930,Mr 31,24:1
King Lear 1930,Ap 1,34:6
As You Like It 1930,Ap 3,32:5
Julius Caesar 1930,Ap 4,22:3
King Lear 1930,D 26,18:2
Decoy, The 1932,Ap 2,13:4
Quinby, George H
Double Door 1933,S 22,15:5
Quinby, George H (Miscellaneous)
Doctor X 1930,Jl 31,12:4
Quince, Louis V
Taming of the Shrew, The 1925,D 19,14:1

Quince, Louis V—Cont
Straw Hat, The 1926,O 15,20:2
Trumpet Shall Sound, The 1926,D 11,15:2
Big Lake 1927,Ap 9,17:2
Madame Capet 1938,O 26,26:2
Cock-A-Doodle Dandy 1950,F 1,26:2
Country Girl, The 1950,N 11,10:6
Quine, Donald
All the King's Men 1959,O 17,27:2
Quine, Richard
Very Warm for May 1939,N 18,23:2
My Sister Eileen 1940,D 27,23:2
Quinlan, Dan
Red Pepper 1922,My 30,8:3
Quinlan, Frank (Lighting Director)
Phaedra 1967,My 22,50:2
Quinlan, Gertrude
Intimate Relations 1932,Mr 29,23:2
Quinlan, Gus
Good Boy 1928,S 6,23:2
Quinlan, John
Madame Pompadour 1924,N 12,20:6
Quinlan, Neil
Plot Thickens, The 1922,S 6,16:1
Romeo and Juliet 1923,Ja 25,16:1
Quinlan, Roger
Paths of Glory 1935,S 27,24:2
Woman of Destiny, A 1936,Mr 3,25:2
Woman Bites Dog 1946,Ap 18,21:2
Quinlivan, Charles
Cradle Song 1955,D 2,32:2
Quinlivan, Maurice
Irving Berlin's Music Box Revue 1921,S 23,18:2
Quinlivan, Michael
Master Builder, The 1955,Mr 2,23:2
Quinn, Anthony
Gentleman From Athens, The 1947,N 30,I,78:2
Gentleman From Athens, The 1947,D 10,42:4
Streetcar Named Desire, A 1950,My 24,36:1
Borned in Texas 1950,Ag 22,30:6
Becket 1960,O 6,50:1
Becket 1960,O 16,II,1:1
Becket 1960,O 18,36:3
Tchin-Tchin 1962,O 9,37:3
Tchin-Tchin 1962,O 26,26:2
Tchin-Tchin 1962,N 25,II,1:1
Quinn, Barbara
Instructions for the Running of Trains, etc on the
Erie Railway to Go Into Effect January 1,1862
1970,Ja 7,36:2
Quinn, Billy
Blue Bird, The 1923,D 26,13:3
Don Q Jr 1926,Ja 28,16:3
That Smith Boy 1926,F 20,13:1
They All Want Something 1926,O 13,20:2
Buzzard, The 1928,Mr 15,29:1
Gentlemen of the Press 1928,Ag 28,27:2
Houseparty 1929,S 10,26:5
As Good As New 1930,N 4,37:3
Angels Don't Kiss 1932,Ap 6,22:5
Winterset 1935,S 26,19:2
Frogs of Spring, The 1953,O 21,36:2
Remarkable Mr Pennypacker, The 1953,D 31,11:2
Speaking of Murder 1956,D 20,37:1
Genius and the Goddess, The 1957,D 11,41:1
Quinn, Ed
Coming of Christ, The 1957,D 23,29:8
Quinn, Edith
Paradise 1931,My 12,29:2
Quinn, Edward
Firebrand, The 1924,O 16,33:1
Wisdom Tooth, The 1926,F 16,22:2
Quinn, James
Diamond Lil 1948,N 30,33:2
Diamond Lil 1949,F 7,16:2
Quinn, Jessica
Sound of Music, The 1967,Ap 27,52:1
Quinn, Louise
Woman Disputed, A 1926,S 29,23:2
Whirlpool 1929,D 4,37:3
Quinn, Marie
Exiles 1925,F 20,20:2
Quinn, Michael
New Girl in Town 1957,My 15,40:1
Fiorello! 1959,N 24,45:3
South Pacific 1965,Je 3,25:1
Anya 1965,N 30,48:1
Walking Happy 1966,N 28,47:1
Quinn, Patricia
Jerry for Short 1929,Ag 13,23:4
Keeping Expenses Down 1932,O 21,25:2
Tobacco Road 1933,D 5,31:2
Portrait of Gilbert 1934,D 29,11:5
Golden Six, The 1958,O 27,31:2
Marathon '33 1963,D 23,20:1
Blues for Mister Charlie 1964,Ap 24,24:1
Quinn, Robert
Take a Giant Step 1956,S 26,30:1
Quinn, Rosie
Century Revue and the Midnight Rounders, The
1920,Jl 13,9:1
Quinn, Stanley J (Playwright)
What a Relief 1935,D 14,10:6

Quinn, Tony
Plough and the Stars, The 1927,N 29,30:2
Juno and the Paycock 1927,D 20,32:2
Quinn, William
Fanshastics 1924,Ja 17,13:2
Little Minister, The 1925,Mr 24,21:1
Is Zat So? 1925,Ap 25,18:2
Crooked Friday, The 1925,O 9,27:3
Offence, The 1925,N 16,25:1
Spring Dance 1936,Jl 7,22:2
Quinney, Maureen
Country Wife, The 1957,N 28,56:1
Quinson, Gustave (Playwright)
Blue Kitten, The 1922,Ja 14,9:3
Quinson (Producer)
Touche-A-Tout 1929,O 20,IX,4:4
Quint, Nancy
Good Woman of Setzuan, The 1956,D 19,41:2
Quint, Robert
All in Love 1961,N 11,15:2
Quintana, Rosita
Carnival 1962,Je 6,37:1
Quintavalla, Tony (Lighting Director)
Harold Arlen Songbook, The 1967,Mr 1,48:1
Brownstone Urge, The 1969,D 18,63:1
Quintero, Joaquin Alvarez (Playwright)
Malvaloca 1922,O 3,22:1
Fortunato; Lady From Alfaqueque, The
1928,N 11,X,4:1
Hundred Years Old, A 1928,D 9,X,2:1
Lady From Alfaqueque, The; Consulesa, La
1929,Ja 15,22:3
Hundred Years Old, A 1929,Ap 19,27:5
Hundred Years Old, A 1929,O 2,28:2
Women Have Their Way, The 1930,Ja 28,28:1
Tambor y Cascabel; Drum and Bell
1932,Ap 21,25:4
Fortunato 1956,Mr 24,15:2
Quintero, Jose (Director)
Yerma 1952,F 8,18:4
Summer and Smoke 1952,Ap 25,19:5
Summer and Smoke 1952,My 4,II,1:1
Grass Harp, The 1953,Ap 28,32:2
Grass Harp, The 1953,My 24,II,1:1
American Gothic 1953,N 11,35:6
In the Summer House 1953,D 30,17:1
In the Summer House 1954,Ja 10,II,1:1
Girl on the Via Flaminia, The 1954,F 10,37:1
Girl on the Via Flaminia, The 1954,Ap 6,35:5
Portrait of a Lady 1954,D 22,27:6
King and the Duke, The 1955,Je 2,25:2
Ronde, La 1955,Je 28,24:2
Cradle Song 1955,D 2,32:2
Innkeepers, The 1956,F 3,19:1
Iceman Cometh, The 1956,My 8,38:1
Iceman Cometh, The 1956,My 20,II,1:1
Long Day's Journey Into Night 1956,N 8,47:2
Long Day's Journey Into Night 1956,N 18,II,1:1
Children of Darkness 1958,Mr 1,11:4
Long Day's Journey Into Night 1958,S 9,40:4
Quare Fellow, The 1958,N 28,34:1
Our Town 1959,Mr 24,46:2
Our Town 1959,Ap 5,II,1:1
Macbeth 1959,Ag 1,9:2
Balcony, The 1960,Mr 4,21:1
Balcony, The 1960,Mr 20,II,1:1
Camino Real 1960,My 17,42:2
Camino Real 1960,My 29,II,1:1
Look: We've Come Through 1961,O 26,40:1
Childhood 1962,Ja 12,28:1
Infancy 1962,Ja 12,28:1
Someone From Assisi 1962,Ja 12,28:1
Plays for Bleecker Street 1962,Ja 12,28:1
Plays for Bleecker Street; Infancy; Childhood;
Someone From Assisi 1962,Ja 21,II,1:1
Great Day in the Morning 1962,Mr 29,29:1
Pullman Car Hiawatha 1962,D 4,46:2
Desire Under the Elms 1963,Ja 11,5:6
Strange Interlude 1963,Mr 13,5:2
Marco Millions 1964,F 21,33:1
Hughie 1964,D 23,21:2
Diamond Orchid 1965,F 11,44:4
Matty and the Moron and Madonna
1965,Mr 30,53:1
Pousse-Cafe 1966,Mr 19,19:2
More Stately Mansions 1967,S 14,54:1
More Stately Mansions 1967,N 1,40:1
More Stately Mansions 1967,N 12,II,1:1
Seven Descents of Myrtle, The 1968,Mr 28,54:1
Seven Descents of Myrtle, The 1968,Ap 7,II,1:5
Gandhi 1970,O 21,37:1
Remote Asylum 1970,D 13,II,3:1
Quintero, Jose (Miscellaneous)
Iceman Cometh, The 1956,My 8,38:1
Camino Real 1960,My 17,42:2
Quintero, Jose (Producer)
Cradle Song 1955,D 2,32:2
Long Day's Journey Into Night 1956,N 8,47:2
House of Breath, The 1957,Ap 15,23:2
Children of Darkness 1958,Mr 1,11:4
Moon for the Misbegotten, A 1958,Je 7,10:6
Quare Fellow, The 1958,N 28,34:1
Our Town 1959,Mr 24,46:2

Quintero, Jose (Producer)—Cont
Childhood 1962,Ja 12,28:1
Infancy 1962,Ja 12,28:1
Someone From Assisi 1962,Ja 12,28:1
Plays for Bleecker Street 1962,Ja 12,28:1
Pullman Car Hiawatha 1962,D 4,46:2
Desire Under the Elms 1963,Ja 11,5:6
Quintero, Serafin (Playwright)
Malvaloca 1922,O 3,22:1
Fortunato; Lady From Alfaqueque, The
1928,N 11,X,4:1
Hundred Years Old, A 1928,D 9,X,2:1
Lady From Alfaqueque, The; Consulesa, La
1929,Ja 15,22:3
Hundred Years Old, A 1929,Ap 19,27:5
Hundred Years Old, A 1929,O 2,28:2
Women Have Their Way, The 1930,Ja 28,28:1
Tambor y Cascabel; Drum and Bell
1932,Ap 21,25:4
Fortunato 1956,Mr 24,15:2
Quintina, Ada
Mother Martyr 1935,Ja 28,10:3
Quinto, Stephen (Director)
Calvary 1960,Jl 22,13:1
Escurial 1960,Jl 22,13:1
Santa Claus 1960,Jl 22,13:1
Quinton, Albert
Romeo and Juliet 1957,Je 28,30:2
Two Gentlemen of Verona 1957,Jl 23,21:5
Macbeth 1957,Ag 16,11:2
Othello 1958,Jl 4,16:1
Twelfth Night 1958,Ag 7,21:4
Ivanov 1958,O 8,42:1
Ivanov 1958,O 19,II,1:1
Power and the Glory, The 1958,D 12,2:7
Beaux' Stratagem, The 1959,F 25,35:4
Ping-Pong 1959,Ap 17,22:1
Great God Brown, The 1959,O 7,48:1
Peer Gynt 1960,Ja 13,21:1
Henry IV 1960,Mr 2,42:1
Henry IV 1960,Ap 19,41:1
Henry IV, Part II 1960,Ap 24,II,1:1
Henry V 1960,Je 30,23:1
Measure for Measure 1960,Jl 27,33:1
Taming of the Shrew, The 1960,Ag 20,17:1
She Stoops to Conquer 1960,N 2,42:5
She Stoops to Conquer 1960,N 15,36:3
Plough and the Stars, The 1960,D 7,56:2
Much Ado About Nothing 1961,Jl 7,17:1
Midsummer Night's Dream, A 1961,Ag 3,13:1
Richard II 1961,Ag 30,25:1
Passage to India, A 1962,F 1,23:1
Merchant of Venice, The 1962,Je 22,1:4
Antony and Cleopatra 1963,Je 21,33:1
Twelfth Night 1963,O 9,47:1
Henry V 1965,Je 29,27:2
Taming of the Shrew, The 1965,Jl 3,10:5
Macbeth 1966,Jl 14,27:2
Comedy of Errors, The 1967,Je 15,58:4
King John 1967,Jl 14,19:1
Hamlet 1967,D 27,45:1
Hamlet 1968,Jl 4,15:1
Romeo and Juliet 1968,Ag 16,19:1
Twelfth Night 1969,Ag 14,29:2
Quinton, Albert (Miscellaneous)
Twelfth Night 1969,Ag 14,29:2
Quinton, Dolores
Right You Are (If You Think You Are)
1957,Mr 5,37:1
Quinton, Pat
Robin Hood 1932,Ja 28,25:4
Quinton, Patrick
Ruddigore 1931,Ag 11,28:3
Quiroga, Camila
Fuerza Ciega, La 1927,D 6,26:1
Quist, Harlin
Ivanov 1958,O 8,42:1
Quist, Harlin (Miscellaneous)
Ivanov 1958,O 8,42:1
Quitak, Oscar
Mixed Doubles 1969,Ap 12,43:2
Quitman, Cleo
Black Nativity 1961,D 12,54:2
Quitzow, Diane
Everyman Today 1958,Ja 16,32:4
Quong, Rose
Circle of Chalk, The 1941,Mr 27,28:4
Flower Drum Song 1958,D 2,44:1

R

Raab, Max L (Miscellaneous)
Hail Scrawdyke! 1966,N 29,50:1
Raab, Nancy Jean
Annie Get Your Gun 1946,My 17,14:2
Raae, Marin
All for Love 1938,Ap 5,19:4
Raaf, Vici
I Gotta Get Out 1947,S 26,27:2
Raasche
Borscht Capades 1951,S 18,38:3
Rabaud, Henri (Miscellaneous)
Neighborhood Playhouse Program 1930,F 21,23:1

abb, Ellis
Moby Dick 1955,Ap 26,25:3
Thesmophoriazusae, The; Goddesses of Athens,
The 1955,D 14,52:4
Midsummer Night's Dream, A 1956,Ja 14,12:2
Misanthrope, The 1956,N 13,44:1
Measure for Measure 1957,Ja 23,24:1
Hamlet 1957,Ja 29,27:1
Taming of the Shrew, The 1957,F 21,30:2
Duchess of Malfi, The 1957,Mr 20,33:1
Mary Stuart 1957,O 9,39:1
Mary Stuart 1957,O 20,II,1:1
Hamlet 1958,Je 21,11:1
Midsummer Night's Dream, A 1958,Je 23,19:1
Winter's Tale, The 1958,Jl 21,17:4
Philoctetes 1959,Ja 14,28:1
Look After Lulu 1959,Mr 4,35:1
Jolly's Progress 1959,D 7,42:2
Right You Are (If You Think You Are)
1964,Mr 5,37:1
Tavern, The 1964,Mr 6,39:2
Impromptu at Versailles 1964,Mr 10,43:1
Scapin 1964,Mr 10,43:1
Lower Depths, The 1964,Mr 31,30:1
Man and Superman 1964,D 7,45:2
School for Scandal, The 1966,N 22,33:2
School for Scandal, The 1966,D 11,II,3:1
Pantagleize 1967,D 1,54:1
Pantagleize 1967,D 17,II,3:7
Cock-A-Doodle Dandy 1969,Ja 21,40:1
Cock-A-Doodle Dandy 1969,F 2,II,1:1
Hamlet 1969,Mr 4,34:1
Hamlet 1969,Mr 23,II,3:1
Rabb, Ellis (Director)
Midsummer Night's Dream, A 1957,Je 27,21:3
Seagull, The 1960,Je 2,26:4
School for Scandal, The 1962,Mr 19,36:1
Seagull, The 1962,Mr 22,42:1
Tavern, The 1962,Ap 5,29:1
We Comrades Three 1962,O 12,26:1
Midsummer Night's Dream, A 1963,Jl 1,19:2
Caesar and Cleopatra 1963,Ag 1,18:2
Tavern, The 1964,Mr 6,39:2
Lower Depths, The 1964,Mr 31,30:1
War and Peace 1965,Ja 12,32:1
War and Peace 1965,Ja 31,II,1:1
Judith 1965,Mr 25,42:2
Judith 1965,Ap 4,II,1:1
You Can't Take It With You 1965,N 24,32:1
You Can't Take It With You 1965,D 5,II,5:1
School for Scandal, The 1966,N 22,33:2
School for Scandal, The 1966,D 11,II,3:1
We Comrades Three 1966,D 21,46:1
War and Peace 1967,Mr 22,42:1
Pantagleize 1967,D 1,54:1
Show-Off, The 1967,D 6,40:2
Pantagleize 1967,D 17,II,3:7
Exit the King 1968,Ja 10,48:1
Hamlet 1968,Jl 21,II,21:2
Cocktail Party, The 1968,O 8,42:1
Cock-A-Doodle Dandy 1969,Ja 21,40:1
Hamlet 1969,Mr 4,34:1
Hamlet 1969,Mr 23,II,3:1
Rabb, Ellis (Miscellaneous)
Cherry Orchard, The 1968,Mr 20,41:1
Misanthrope, The 1968,O 10,59:1
Rabb, Ellis (Playwright)
Philoctetes 1959,Ja 14,28:1
Rabb, Ellis (Translator)
Scapin 1964,Mr 10,43:1
Impromptu at Versailles 1964,Mr 10,43:1
Rabb, Jo
Way of the World, The 1954,S 30,38:2
Men in White 1955,F 26,13:2
Rabbino, D Bruce
I Want You 1961,S 15,29:1
Rabe, Martin (Playwright)
Unentbehrliche, Der 1937,O 24,XI,3:1
Rabier, Benjamin (Playwright)
Court Circuit, Le 1923,O 16,18:1
Rabinowitch, Dave
Brothers Ashkenazi, The 1955,N 12,24:4
Rabinowitz, Julian
Life Begins in '40 1940,Ap 5,24:2
Rabinowitz, Tillie
Love Thief, The 1931,Ja 19,24:5
Twice 100,000 1931,N 22,VIII,3:1
Little Bandit 1935,Ap 19,24:2
Schlemihl 1936,S 19,20:4
Straw Hero, The 1936,N 24,35:1
My Malkele 1937,S 20,18:6
Bublitchki 1938,Ja 17,11:2
Wise Fool, The 1938,O 10,15:3
Mazel Tov, Rabbi 1938,N 28,10:4
Jewish Heart, The 1939,Ja 25,16:6
Three Men and a Girl 1939,F 6,9:3
Oy, Is Dus a Leben!; Oh, What a Life!
1942,O 13,19:2
House on Grand Street, A 1953,O 10,12:6
Life Is a Dream 1962,Ja 15,22:3
Rabke, Harry
Blossom Time 1931,Mr 5,32:1

Rabke, Henry
Bitter Sweet 1934,My 8,28:4
Rabkin, Gerald
Right You Are (If You Think You Are)
1950,Je 29,37:2
Raboid, Rajah
Vaudeville (Belmont) 1931,Ja 6,24:1
Raby, John
Triumph 1935,O 15,18:5
O Evening Star 1936,Ja 9,24:6
London Assurance 1937,F 19,14:5
Chalked Out 1937,Mr 26,24:2
Good, The 1938,O 6,27:2
Don't Throw Glass Houses 1938,D 28,24:4
Raby, Peter (Playwright)
Government Inspector, The 1967,Je 15,55:1
Government Inspector, The 1967,O 28,34:1
Three Musketeers, The 1968,Jl 24,49:2
Raccine, Jules
Wind in the Sails 1940,Ag 1,24:6
Race, Kempton
Once in a Lifetime 1930,S 25,22:3
Merry-Go-Round 1932,Ap 23,11:2
Racey, Edward
Common Sin, The 1928,O 16,28:2
Jonesy 1929,Ap 10,32:2
Young Sinners 1929,N 29,24:4
Rachel, Annie
Half a Sixpence 1965,Ap 26,38:2
Hallelujah, Baby! 1967,Ap 27,51:1
Salvation 1969,Mr 13,53:1
Salvation 1969,S 25,55:1
Steambath 1970,Jl 1,49:1
Steambath 1970,Jl 12,II,1:3
Rachelle, Bernie
Nighthawks 1967,D 30,14:2
Rachins, Alan
After the Rain 1967,O 10,54:1
Oh! Calcutta! 1969,Je 18,33:1
Rachleff, Owen (Playwright)
Javelin 1966,N 10,63:1
Rachmaninoff, Sergei (Composer)
Climax, The 1933,Je 14,22:2
Racine, Eugene
Well of Romance, The 1930,N 8,21:2
Racine, Jean (Original Author)
Andromaque 1964,F 29,13:2
Racine, Jean (Playwright)
Phedre 1930,Mr 23,IX,2:3
Athalie 1939,My 14,XI,6:5
Athalie 1942,Mr 18,29:2
Britannicus 1958,N 29,17:2
Britannicus 1961,Mr 3,17:1
Phedre 1963,O 21,39:1
Berenice 1963,O 30,46:1
Phedre 1966,F 11,36:1
Phaedra 1967,My 22,50:2
Phaedra 1967,Je 11,II,1:1
Phedre 1969,Mr 1,20:1
Racine, Jules
Let Freedom Sing 1942,O 6,18:2
Sing Out, Sweet Land! 1944,D 28,24:2
Winter's Tale, The 1946,Ja 16,18:6
Grass Harp, The 1952,Mr 28,26:2
No Time for Sergeants 1955,O 21,32:2
Racioppi, James
Silhouettes 1969,S 9,41:1
Rackerby, Don
Noah 1954,O 11,32:2
Thor, With Angels 1956,O 15,29:4
Rackow, Sanford (Miscellaneous)
Postmark Zero 1965,N 2,28:1
Racolin, Alexander E (Producer)
Woman, The 1965,O 21,56:1
Undercover Man 1966,Je 3,30:2
Arms and the Man 1967,Je 23,44:2
Hawk, The 1968,Ap 18,54:1
Carving a Statue 1968,My 1,43:1
In Circles 1968,Je 28,36:1
Millionairess, The 1969,Mr 3,28:1
Racolin, Dina (Producer)
Woman, The 1965,O 21,56:1
Undercover Man 1966,Je 3,30:2
Arms and the Man 1967,Je 23,44:2
Hawk, The 1968,Ap 18,54:1
Carving a Statue 1968,My 1,43:1
In Circles 1968,Je 28,36:1
Millionairess, The 1969,Mr 3,28:1
Racomar, Ramon
Tin Pan Alley 1928,N 2,29:1
Lady Beyond the Moon 1931,Ap 1,36:5
Rad, Richard H
Laugh It Off 1934,Ap 5,24:2
Radabaugh, Ed
Three Love Affairs; Bedtime Story 1958,Mr 11,33:1
Radaelli
International Revue 1930,F 26,22:2
Radaelli, Paolo (Producer)
Orlando Furioso 1970,N 5,59:1
Radai
Great Love, The 1935,O 22,17:3
Radakovic, Theodore
Mother Courage and Her Children 1964,My 12,32:2

Radano, Gene (Playwright)
Opening of a Window, The 1961,S 26,32:2
Radcliff and Williams
Vaudeville (Palace) 1930,N 24,26:3
Radcliffe, Vernon
Little Clay Cart, The 1924,D 6,13:3
Radclyffe, Cecilia
Lady, The 1923,D 5,23:2
Farmer's Wife, The 1924,O 10,22:3
Freddy 1929,Jl 17,23:4
Radd, Ronald
Hotel Paradiso 1957,Ap 12,22:2
Hotel Paradiso 1957,Ap 21,II,1:1
My Fair Lady 1958,Mr 9,II,1:1
Ivanov 1966,My 4,50:1
1776 1970,Je 18,54:4
Raddatz, Carl
Captain of Koepenick, The 1964,D 2,60:1
Raddock, Charles (Playwright)
Magic Touch, The 1947,S 4,30:1
Radecki, Anthony
Medea 1949,My 3,31:2
That Lady 1949,N 23,18:4
Raden, Ernst (Director)
Last Warning, The 1927,Ap 3,VIII,2:1
Rader, Frank
Twelfth Night 1941,D 3,32:2
Radford, Basil
Spring Tide 1936,Ag 9,IX,1:5
Warn That Man 1942,Ja 4,IX,1:4
Radford, Frank
Macbeth 1955,O 8,12:6
Radin, Lucille
Mascaiada 1929,D 28,10:6
Radin, Robin
Path of Flowers, The 1936,S 18,19:3
Radina, Sonia
Tenth Commandment, The 1926,N 18,27:1
It Is to Laugh 1927,D 27,24:2
Radio Aces
New Priorities of 1943 1942,S 16,28:2
Artists and Models 1943,N 6,16:6
Radio Rogues, The
Hellzapoppin 1938,S 23,34:2
Radiscev Dancers
Fun With Music 1946,N 25,38:5
Radmilovic, Zoran
Ubu Roi 1968,Je 29,20:1
Radnitz, Robert (Miscellaneous)
Frogs of Spring, The 1953,O 21,36:2
Radnitz, Robert (Producer)
Young and Beautiful, The 1955,O 3,23:2
Rado, James
Hang Down Your Head and Die 1964,O 19,38:1
Lion in Winter, The 1966,Mr 4,23:1
Infantry, The 1966,N 15,51:1
Hair 1968,Ap 30,40:2
Hair 1968,My 19,II,3:3
Rado, James (Director)
Hair 1970,Ja 13,39:1
Rado, James (Lyricist)
Hair 1967,O 30,55:1
Hair 1968,Ap 30,40:2
Hair 1969,F 5,36:1
Hair 1969,S 13,30:1
Hair 1970,Ja 13,39:1
Rado, James (Miscellaneous)
School for Wives 1957,Je 20,23:4
Rado, James (Playwright)
Hair 1967,O 30,55:1
Hair 1967,N 14,50:1
Hair 1968,Ap 30,40:2
Hair 1968,My 19,II,3:3
Hair 1969,F 5,36:1
Hair 1970,Ja 13,39:1
Hair 1970,S 27,II,1:2
Rado, Ted
Guimpes and Saddles 1967,O 11,36:3
Radon, Dolores
Don't Go Away Mad 1949,My 10,28:2
Radosch, Louis
Alt Heidelberg 1926,My 31,10:5
Radosta, John S (Miscellaneous)
Cocktails of 1934 1934,My 5,22:1
Radowsky, Phillip (Composer)
Singing Girl, The 1952,Je 4,31:8
Radus, Herbert
Sweeney Todd 1924,Jl 19,10:4
Rae, Audree
One Way Pendulum 1961,S 19,38:2
Saving Grace, The 1963,Ap 19,28:1
Mr Grossman 1964,My 6,43:1
Rae, Charlotte
Three Wishes for Jamie 1952,Mr 22,9:2
Threepenny Opera, The 1954,Mr 11,26:5
Threepenny Opera, The 1954,Mr 21,II,1:1
Threepenny Opera, The 1954,Ap 4,II,7:1
Littlest Revue, The 1956,My 23,37:2
Li'l Abner 1956,N 16,24:2
Li'l Abner 1956,N 25,II,1:1
Beauty Part, The 1962,D 28,5:2
New Tenant, The 1964,My 28,40:2
Victims of Duty 1964,My 28,40:2

Rae, Charlotte—Cont

Pickwick 1965,O 6,5:3
Henry IV, Part I 1968,Je 30,54:7
Henry IV, Part II 1968,Jl 2,33:1
Henry IV, Part II 1968,Jl 14,II,1:1
Romeo and Juliet 1968,Ag 16,19:1
Morning 1968,N 29,52:1
Noon 1968,N 29,52:1
Night 1968,N 29,52:1
Dr Fish 1970,Mr 11,42:2
Dr Fish 1970,Mr 22,II,3:1
Rae, Claude
Long and the Short and the Tall, The 1962,Mr 30,28:2
Rae, D Bagnell
Show-Off, The 1932,D 13,25:4
Rae, Dorothy
Gay Paree 1925,Ag 19,14:3
Rae, Florence
Ice Follies 1957,Ja 16,36:1
Ice Follies 1958,Ja 15,26:2
Ice Follies 1959,Ja 14,30:1
Rae, Helen
Babes in Toyland 1929,D 24,15:3
Rae, Kathryn
Night in Paris, A 1926,Ja 6,16:3
Rae, Leonore
Bathsheba 1947,Mr 27,40:2
Rae, Melba
Trojan Horse, The 1940,O 31,28:3
Happily Ever After 1945,Mr 16,21:2
Rae, Nan
Keep Off the Grass 1940,My 5,X,1:6
Keep Off the Grass 1940,My 24,22:6
Rae, Nelson
Pal Joey 1940,D 26,22:2
Rae, Oliver (Miscellaneous)
Naughty-Naught '00 1946,O 21,27:5
Rae, Phyllis
She's My Baby 1928,Ja 4,22:2
Three Cheers 1928,O 16,28:1
How's Your Health? 1929,N 27,30:3
Rae, Sara
Divina Pastora, La 1931,Mr 4,33:2
Sparkin' 1931,Mr 4,33:2
Psychological Moment, The 1931,Mr 4,33:2
Rae, Sarah
Old Maid, The 1949,Ja 27,20:6
Post Road 1949,Ap 28,27:3
Raeburn, Burt
Blossom Time 1938,D 27,12:2
Raeburn, Henzie
Murder in the Cathedral 1938,F 17,16:2
Family Reunion, The 1960,D 10,26:1
Raeburn, Henzie (Director)
Way of the Cross, The 1959,Ja 16,35:2
Mystery of the Finding of the Cross, The 1959,Ja 16,35:2
Raeburn, Henzie (Miscellaneous)
Cranmer of Canterbury 1959,D 4,36:1
Raeder, Lois
Trial, The 1955,Je 15,35:2
Spring's Awakening 1955,O 10,30:2
Beautiful Jailer, The 1957,My 17,19:2
Raedler, Dorothy (Choreographer)
Utopia, Limited; Flowers of Progress, The 1957,F 27,21:1
Mikado, The 1957,Ap 24,28:2
H M S Pinafore 1957,My 1,42:6
Pirates of Penzance, The 1957,My 8,43:1
Raedler, Dorothy (Director)
H M S Pinafore 1949,Jl 29,13:2
Mikado, The 1954,Mr 24,31:1
Pirates of Penzance, The 1954,Mr 31,32:5
Gondoliers, The 1954,Ap 14,24:3
Ruddigore 1954,Ap 21,36:4
Yeomen of the Guard, The 1954,My 5,36:2
Sorcerer, The 1954,My 26,34:3
Utopia, Limited; Flowers of Progress, The 1957,F 27,21:1
Mikado, The 1957,Ap 24,28:2
H M S Pinafore 1957,My 1,42:6
Pirates of Penzance, The 1957,My 8,43:1
Yeomen of the Guard, The 1957,My 22,28:3
Gondoliers, The 1957,My 29,34:2
From Here to There; Slow Dusk 1958,Ap 24,37:3
From Here to There; Otherwise Engaged 1958,Ap 24,37:3
From Here to There; Real Strange One, A 1958,Ap 24,37:3
H M S Pinafore 1960,Ja 29,14:1
Gondoliers, The 1960,F 7,II,1:1
Utopia, Limited 1960,Ap 8,27:2
Pirates of Penzance, The 1960,O 7,29:1
Mikado, The 1961,Ja 18,26:1
Pirates of Penzance, The 1961,Ja 20,24:5
Gondoliers, The 1961,Ja 26,33:2
Yeomen of the Guard, The 1961,Ap 28,23:1
Mikado, The 1961,My 5,23:1
Grand Duke, The 1961,My 12,24:1
Princess Ida 1961,My 19,23:1
Iolanthe 1961,My 26,29:6
H M S Pinafore 1961,Je 9,29:5
Student Prince, The 1961,Jl 14,14:1

Merry Widow, The 1961,O 27,28:2
Vagabond King, The 1961,N 24,36:1
Gondoliers, The 1961,D 8,44:1
Iolanthe 1962,Ap 12,42:4
Gondoliers, The 1962,Ap 19,34:2
Iolanthe 1962,Ag 8,34:2
Gondoliers, The 1963,Je 5,33:2
Gondoliers, The 1964,Mr 28,14:1
Iolanthe 1965,My 19,42:1
Yeomen of the Guard, The 1965,Jl 8,34:1
Ruddigore 1965,Ag 27,16:1
Pirates of Penzance, The 1966,My 24,54:1
H M S Pinafore 1966,Je 8,41:2
Trial by Jury 1966,Je 8,41:2
Patience 1967,O 13,32:1
Iolanthe 1967,O 18,40:1
Mikado, The 1967,O 25,42:2
Gondoliers, The 1967,O 29,83:1
H M S Pinafore 1967,N 1,40:1
Raedler, Dorothy (Miscellaneous)
Mikado, The 1959,O 2,24:1
Patience 1964,Mr 26,42:1
Raedler, Dorothy (Producer)
Mikado, The 1954,Mr 24,31:1
Utopia, Limited; Flowers of Progress, The 1957,F 27,21:1
Utopia, Limited 1957,Mr 17,II,1:1
Yeomen of the Guard, The 1957,My 22,28:3
Gondoliers, The 1957,My 29,34:2
From Here to There; Otherwise Engaged 1958,Ap 24,37:3
From Here to There; Real Strange One, A 1958,Ap 24,37:3
From Here to There; Slow Dusk 1958,Ap 24,37:3
Yeomen of the Guard, The 1961,Ap 28,23:1
Mikado, The 1961,My 5,23:1
Grand Duke, The 1961,My 12,24:1
Princess Ida 1961,My 19,23:1
Iolanthe 1961,My 26,29:6
H M S Pinafore 1961,Je 9,29:5
Student Prince, The 1961,Jl 14,14:1
Merry Widow, The 1961,O 27,28:2
Raemier, Valerie
Furnished Rooms 1934,My 30,14:6
Raevsky, Iosif (Miscellaneous)
Three Sisters, The 1965,F 12,15:1
Rafael, Elena
Camille 1956,S 19,33:1
Beaux' Stratagem, The 1957,Jl 9,25:4
Rafale, Sarah
Mediterranee 1926,N 7,VIII,2:7
Rafart, Carlos
Vida es Sueno, La 1964,Mr 18,49:1
Raff, Alice
Peter Ibbetson 1926,Mr 26,24:7
Raffaei, Jack
So Was Napoleon 1930,Ja 9,22:2
Raffael, Alain
Ecole des Femmes, L' 1961,Ap 28,23:1
Raffael, Alain (Miscellaneous)
Cantatrice Chauve, La 1962,Ja 16,30:1
Huis Clos 1962,Ja 16,30:1
Raffael, Jack
Checkerboard, The 1920,Ag 20,7:2
Nightcap, The 1921,Ag 16,18:3
Sporting Thing to Do, The 1923,F 20,12:2
Raffalt, Reinhard (Playwright)
Successor, The 1964,F 26,43:2
Raffayette's Dogs
Vaudeville (Palace) 1923,F 13,25:1
Raffell, Anthony
Gondoliers, The 1962,N 16,25:2
H M S Pinafore 1962,N 23,32:4
H M S Pinafore 1964,N 20,40:1
Trial by Jury 1964,N 20,40:1
Pirates of Penzance, The 1964,N 27,43:1
Pirates of Penzance, The 1966,N 16,54:1
H M S Pinafore 1966,N 24,64:1
Rafferty, Ewing (Playwright)
Happy Valley, Limited 1936,Je 30,15:1
Rafferty, James
Come Marching Home 1946,My 20,18:6
Rafferty, Patrick
My Girl 1924,N 25,27:2
Peggy-Ann 1926,D 28,16:3
Raffles, Gerry (Producer)
Oh What a Lovely War 1964,O 1,30:1
Raffloer, Jack
Aquashow 1953,Je 24,29:2
Hollywood Ice Revue 1954,Ja 15,16:2
Raft, Georgie
Vaudeville (Palace) 1927,Ja 18,23:2
Raftopoulou, A
Electra 1952,N 20,38:2
Ragan, James
Mother Courage and Her Children 1964,My 12,32:2
Ragazzino, Edward
Flies, The 1954,S 10,18:2
Raghan, Michael
Henry IV, Part I 1946,My 7,25:2
Henry IV, Part II 1946,My 8,33:4
Oedipus; Critic, The 1946,My 21,19:2

Ragin, John
Hamlet 1957,Ja 29,27:1
Duchess of Malfi, The 1957,Mr 20,33:1
Trial of Dmitri Karamazov, The 1958,Ja 28,30:1
Hamlet 1958,Je 21,11:1
Winter's Tale, The 1958,Jl 21,17:4
Romeo and Juliet 1959,Je 15,31:1
All's Well That Ends Well 1959,Ag 3,20:4
All the King's Men 1959,O 17,27:2
Tempest, The 1960,Je 20,35:1
Antony and Cleopatra 1960,Ag 1,19:1
Tavern, The 1964,Mr 6,39:2
Lower Depths, The 1964,Mr 31,30:1
Raglan, James
Insult 1930,S 16,30:2
Ragland, Oscar
Tip-Top 1920,O 6,13:2
Stepping Stones 1923,N 7,14:3
Criss Cross 1926,O 13,20:2
Three Cheers 1928,O 16,28:1
Nine Fifteen Revue, The 1930,F 12,26:2
New Yorkers, The 1930,D 9,31:1
Take a Chance 1932,N 28,11:2
White Horse Inn 1936,O 2,28:5
Ragland, Rags
Who's Who 1938,Mr 2,16:2
Panama Hattie 1940,O 31,28:2
Panama Hattie 1940,N 10,IX,1:1
Raglyn, Cynthia
Power of Darkness, The 1948,O 11,28:2
Ragni, Gerome
Legend of Lovers 1959,O 28,40:3
Hang Down Your Head and Die 1964,O 19,38:1
Viet Rock 1966,N 11,38:1
Hair 1967,O 30,55:1
Hair 1967,N 14,50:1
Hair 1968,Ap 30,40:2
Ragni, Gerome (Director)
Hair 1970,Ja 13,39:1
Ragni, Gerome (Lyricist)
Hair 1967,O 30,55:1
Hair 1967,N 14,50:1
Hair 1968,Ap 30,40:2
Hair 1969,F 5,36:1
Hair 1969,S 13,30:1
Hair 1970,Ja 13,39:1
Ragni, Gerome (Playwright)
Hair 1967,O 30,55:1
Hair 1968,Ap 30,40:2
Hair 1969,F 5,36:1
Hair 1970,Ja 13,39:1
Hair 1970,S 27,II,1:2
Ragno, Joseph
Worm in Horseradish, A 1961,Mr 14,32:3
Rago, Joe (Choreographer)
Ballad for a Firing Squad 1968,D 12,64:2
Ragotzy, Jack (Director)
Mamba's Daughters 1953,Mr 21,12:6
Point of No Return 1957,Mr 23,17:2
Time of the Cuckoo, The 1958,O 28,40:2
Clearing in the Woods, A 1959,F 13,32:1
Come Share My House 1960,F 19,20:2
King of the Whole Damn World 1962,Ap 16,32:2
Angela 1969,O 31,33:1
Ragozzino, Edward
Building Blocks 1954,My 8,14:4
Ragsdale, Howard
Charlatan, The 1922,Ap 25,14:2
Raher, David
Wind Remains, The 1943,Mr 31,16:6
Rahila
King of the Dark Chamber 1961,F 10,21:1
Rahill, Marion
Bridal Crown, The 1938,F 7,11:2
Rahmid, Dolores
Witness for the Prosecution 1954,D 17,35:2
Rahn, Muriel
Come of Age 1934,Ja 13,16:6
Pirate, The 1942,N 26,39:2
Carmen Jones 1943,D 3,26:2
Barrier, The 1950,N 3,32:2
ANTA Album 1951,My 7,22:7
Carmen Jones 1951,S 22,8:6
Come of Age 1952,Ja 24,22:2
Ivory Branch, The 1956,My 25,27:1
Raht, Katharine
For Charity 1937,Ag 25,24:3
Heiress, The 1947,S 30,22:2
Good Housekeeping 1949,Ag 17,19:3
Heiress, The 1950,F 9,34:2
Sabrina Fair 1953,N 12,37:1
Happiest Millionaire, The 1956,N 21,21:3
Love and Kisses 1963,D 19,39:1
Rai, Jhoreck
Summer Wives 1936,Ap 14,18:1
Raibuel, Phil (Scenic Designer)
Slightly Married 1943,O 26,19:2
Raiche, Edmund
Ice Capades 1953,S 11,25:1
Ice Capades 1954,S 16,37:1
Raichle, Donald
Black Eye, The 1938,Mr 8,22:4

Raider-Wexler, Victor
Universal Nigger, The 1970,Mr 21,18:1
Raiff, Stan (Producer)
Damn You, Scarlett O'Hara 1964,F 5,30:1
All My Pretty Little Ones 1964,F 5,30:1
Raiford, Richard
Jumping Fool, The 1970,F 10,53:1
Raiford, Roger
Jumping Fool, The 1970,F 10,53:1
Raigh, Angela
Jarnegan 1928,S 25,29:2
Raiguel, Phil (Scenic Designer)
Barber Had Two Sons, The 1943,F 2,22:2
Mr Adam 1949,My 26,34:6
Railing, Curtis Burnley (Mrs)
Brother Rat 1936,D 17,34:5
Railton, Margo
Walking Gentleman, The 1942,My 8,26:2
Raimon
Aquacircus 1958,Je 30,24:6
Raimond, Anthony
Clean Beds 1939,My 26,21:2
Raimu
Diable a Paris, Le 1927,N 13,IX,4:2
1928 1928,Ap 8,VIII,4:1
Coup de Roulis 1928,O 21,IX,5:6
Marius 1929,Mr 31,VIII,2:7
Raimund, Ferdinand (Playwright)
Gefesselte Phantasie, Die 1936,N 8,X,2:1
Rain, Douglas
Richard III 1953,Jl 15,22:2
Measure for Measure 1954,Je 30,23:1
Taming of the Shrew, The 1954,Jl 1,22:2
Oedipus Rex 1954,Jl 17,6:6
Julius Caesar 1955,Je 29,23:3
Soldier's Tale, A 1955,Jl 13,21:2
Tamburlaine the Great 1956,Ja 20,19:1
Henry V 1956,Je 20,27:2
Merry Wives of Windsor, The 1956,Je 21,34:4
Hamlet 1957,Jl 3,15:2
Twelfth Night 1957,Jl 4,16:4
Twelfth Night 1957,Jl 7,II,1:1
Two Gentlemen of Verona 1958,Mr 19,35:1
Broken Jug, The 1958,Ap 2,36:1
Henry IV, Part I 1958,Je 25,23:3
Winter's Tale, The 1958,Jl 23,34:3
Winter's Tale, The 1958,Jl 27,II,1:1
As You Like It 1959,Jl 1,27:1
Othello 1959,Jl 2,17:2
Othello 1959,Jl 5,II,1:1
King John 1960,Je 29,26:2
Romeo and Juliet 1960,Jl 1,14:1
Henry VIII 1961,Je 22,22:1
Love's Labour's Lost 1961,Je 23,19:1
Henry VIII 1961,Jl 2,II,1:1
Cyrano de Bergerac 1962,Ag 1,21:1
Troilus and Cressida 1963,Je 19,40:2
Comedy of Errors, The 1963,Je 21,35:3
Timon of Athens 1963,Jl 31,19:2
Golden Age, The 1963,N 19,49:2
Bourgeois Gentilhomme, Le 1964,Je 18,28:2
King Lear 1964,Je 19,36:1
Country Wife, The 1964,Ag 3,16:1
Henry IV, Part I 1965,Je 30,42:1
Falstaff; Henry IV, Part II 1965,Jl 1,35:1
Henry V 1966,Je 8,38:1
Henry VI 1966,Je 9,55:2
Twelfth Night 1966,Je 10,51:2
Tartuffe 1968,Je 12,39:1
Midsummer Night's Dream, A 1968,Je 13,54:1
Tartuffe 1968,Je 23,II,1:1
Three Musketeers, The 1968,Jl 24,49:2
Raine, Deane
Good Hunting 1938,N 22,26:5
Raine, Gillian
Semi-Detached 1963,O 8,49:1
Raine, Harry
Forbidden Melody 1936,N 3,33:1
Raine, Jack
Fast Service 1931,N 18,26:3
Anthony and Anna 1935,D 8,X,5:1
Sherlock Holmes 1953,O 31,11:2
Raine, Jennifer
Legend of Lovers 1951,D 27,17:1
Raine, Lola
Merry World, The 1926,Je 9,18:3
Passions of 1926 1926,Ag 3,19:4
Greenwich Village Follies 1928,Ap 10,32:2
Modern Virgin, A 1931,My 21,33:4
Raine, Norman Reilly (Playwright)
Hangman's Whip 1933,F 25,20:2
Raine, Patricia
Separate Tables 1955,My 22,II,1:1
Rainer
Everyman 1926,Ag 9,1:1
Rainer, Beatrice (Composer)
Merry-Go-Rounders, The 1956,N 22,50:1
Rainer, Frances
Allegro 1947,O 11,10:2
Rainer, Louis
Miracle, The 1924,Ja 16,17:1
Rosmersholm 1924,F 8,22:3
Miracle, The 1927,F 1,24:5

Miracle, The 1927,Ap 15,27:1
Rainer, Luise
Behold the Bride 1939,My 24,28:3
Behold the Bride 1939,Je 11,IX,2:5
Saint Joan 1940,Mr 11,10:6
Kiss for Cinderella, A 1942,Mr 11,22:2
Kiss for Cinderella, A 1942,Mr 15,VIII,1:1
Lady From the Sea, The 1950,Ag 8,23:2
Raineri, Orestes (Scenic Designer)
Singing Rabbi, The 1931,S 11,24:4
Bough Breaks, The 1937,N 20,21:4
Raines, Arlyne
Tonight We Improvise 1959,N 7,27:4
Raines, Ella
Wisteria Trees, The 1955,F 3,20:2
Raines, Quinton (Miscellaneous)
Failures, The 1959,Ja 6,30:2
Hedda Gabler 1960,N 10,61:1
Pocket Watch, The 1966,Ja 6,18:1
Raines, Quinton (Scenic Designer)
Pocket Watch, The 1966,Ja 6,18:1
Coop, The 1966,Mr 2,48:1
Nighthawks 1967,D 30,14:2
Raines, R C
Kilpatrick's Old-Time Minstrels 1930,Ap 21,20:2
Raines, Robert
Porgy and Bess 1935,O 11,30:2
Raines, Walter
House of Flowers 1968,Ja 29,26:2
Rainey, Ford
Infernal Machine, The 1937,D 13,22:7
Possessed, The 1939,O 25,26:2
Twelfth Night 1941,D 3,32:2
Wanhope Building, The 1947,F 11,36:5
Crucible, The 1958,Mr 12,36:1
Crucible, The 1958,Je 1,II,1:1
On Baile's Strand 1959,Ap 13,34:4
Legend of Lovers 1959,O 28,40:3
Between Two Thieves 1960,F 12,23:1
Rainey, William S
Spring, The 1921,F 6,VI,1:2
Red Geranium, The 1922,My 9,22:3
Man Who Ate the Popomack, The 1924,Mr 25,24:1
Way of the World, The 1924,N 18,23:4
Polly 1925,O 12,19:1
Shelter 1926,Ja 26,18:2
Cherry Pie 1926,Ap 15,24:4
Damn the Tears 1927,Ja 22,11:1
Way of the World, The 1931,Je 2,34:3
Rainey, William S (Director)
Drift 1925,N 25,15:3
Rainger, Ralph (Composer)
Nine Fifteen Revue, The 1930,F 12,26:2
Tattle Tales 1933,Je 2,22:6
Rainger, Ralph (Lyricist)
Nine Fifteen Revue, The 1930,F 12,26:2
Tattle Tales 1933,Je 2,22:6
Rainger and Carroll
Little Show, The 1929,My 1,28:5
Rainnie, Hedley
Alexander Hamilton 1949,Mr 30,29:2
Rains, Charles
Glamour Preferred 1940,N 16,13:2
Rains, Claude
Iphigenie in Tauris 1915,Je 1,15:5
Constant Nymph, The 1926,D 10,31:1
Lally 1927,F 9,16:3
Out of the Sea 1927,D 6,26:2
Camel Through the Needle's Eye, The
1929,Ap 16,32:2
Karl and Anna 1929,O 8,34:1
Game of Love and Death, The 1929,N 26,28:4
Apple Cart, The 1930,F 25,30:1
Miracle at Verdun 1931,Mr 17,34:6
He 1931,S 22,33:1
Moon in the Yellow River, The 1932,F 21,VIII,2:1
Moon in the Yellow River, The 1932,Mr 1,19:3
Moon in the Yellow River, The
1932,Mr 13,VIII,1:1
Too True to Be Good 1932,Ap 5,27:5
Man Who Reclaimed His Head 1932,S 9,17:3
Good Earth, The 1932,O 18,23:4
Good Earth, The 1932,O 23,IX,1:1
American Dream; 1849 1933,F 22,24:5
Peace Palace 1933,Je 6,30:2
They Shall Not Die 1934,F 22,24:4
They Shall Not Die 1934,Mr 4,IX,1:3
They Shall Not Die 1934,Mr 11,X,1:1
Darkness at Noon 1951,Ja 15,13:4
Darkness at Noon 1951,Ja 21,II,1:1
Evening With Will Shakespeare, An 1952,D 7,86:5
Confidential Clerk, The 1954,F 12,22:1
Confidential Clerk, The 1954,F 21,II,1:1
Night of the Auk 1956,D 4,50:2
Rains, Jack
Wonderful Town 1958,Mr 6,32:4
Rains, Lee
When the Bough Breaks 1950,Mr 9,25:5
Rains, Robert
Constant Sinner, The 1931,S 15,30:1
Rainsford, Nan
Last Waltz, The 1921,My 11,20:3

Raisbeck, Kenneth (Playwright)
Torches, The 1923,My 11,20:3
Rock Me, Julie 1931,F 4,21:1
Raison, Milton (Miscellaneous)
Shoot the Works! 1931,Jl 22,19:5
Raiter, Frank
Cock-A-Doodle Dandy 1955,N 4,26:5
Raitt, John
Carousel 1945,Ap 20,24:2
Carousel 1945,Ap 29,II,1:1
Magdalena 1948,Jl 28,27:2
Magdalena 1948,S 21,31:2
Three Wishes for Jamie 1952,Mr 22,9:2
Carnival in Flanders 1953,S 9,38:2
Pajama Game, The 1954,My 14,20:2
Pajama Game, The 1954,My 15,12:1
Pajama Game, The 1954,My 30,II,1:1
Annie Get Your Gun 1957,Ag 31,18:2
Carousel 1965,Ag 11,39:1
Joyful Noise, A 1966,D 16,57:1
Rake, Georginia
Alexander Hamilton 1949,Mr 30,29:2
Raker, Lorin
Getting Gertie's Garter 1921,Ag 2,16:2
Lights Out 1922,Ag 18,8:4
Queen O' Hearts 1922,O 11,22:1
Mama Loves Papa 1926,F 23,26:2
Arabian Nightmare, The 1927,Ja 11,36:3
Honeymooning 1927,Mr 18,25:3
Raksin, David (Composer)
If the Shoe Fits 1946,D 6,29:4
Rale, M W
Good Earth, The 1932,O 18,23:4
Rale, Michael
Arabian, The 1927,N 1,20:5
Sakura 1928,D 26,14:4
Raleigh, Evangeline
Sunny Days 1928,F 9,29:1
Three Cheers 1928,O 16,28:1
Three Little Girls 1930,S 28,VIII,2:5
Raleigh, James
Alternate Current 1939,D 23,8:3
Rall, Tommy
Look, Ma, I'm Dancin' 1948,Ja 30,20:2
Look, Ma, I'm Dancin' 1948,F 8,II,2:1
Small Wonder 1948,S 16,33:5
Miss Liberty 1949,Jl 16,6:5
Miss Liberty 1949,Jl 24,II,1:1
Miss Liberty 1949,Ag 7,II,6:4
Call Me Madam 1950,O 13,25:1
Juno 1959,Mr 10,41:1
Juno 1959,Mr 15,II,1:1
Milk and Honey 1961,O 11,52:1
Cafe Crown 1964,Ap 18,32:1
Cry for Us All 1970,Ap 9,48:2
Ralley, Barbara
Viet Rock 1966,N 11,38:1
Ralli, Margarita
Cute Gata.....Oute Zhmia; Neither Cat . . . Nor
Damage 1957,D 20,31:1
Ralph, Charles
Rainbow 1928,N 22,25:1
Ralph, George
King Lear 1946,S 25,39:4
Everyman Today 1958,Ja 16,32:4
Cup of Trembling, The 1959,My 1,33:5
Cranmer of Canterbury 1959,D 4,36:1
Ralph, Jessie
Malvaloca 1922,O 3,22:1
Romeo and Juliet 1923,Ja 25,16:1
Pelleas and Melisande 1923,D 5,23:2
Depths, The 1925,Ja 28,15:3
Depths, The 1925,F 8,VII,1:1
Man With a Load of Mischief, The 1925,O 27,20:1
Taming of the Shrew, The 1925,D 19,14:1
Virgin, The 1926,F 23,26:1
Shelf, The 1926,S 28,31:1
Road to Rome, The 1927,F 1,24:2
Paolo and Francesca 1929,Ap 2,28:2
Road to Rome, The 1929,N 23,19:1
Twelfth Night 1930,O 16,28:2
Twelfth Night 1930,N 2,VIII,1:1
Child of Manhattan 1932,Mr 2,15:1
Good Earth, The 1932,O 18,23:4
Ralph, Julia
Ladies' Night 1920,Ag 10,10:1
Roger Bloomer 1923,Mr 2,18:3
Arabesque 1925,O 21,20:2
Bride of the Lamb 1926,Mr 31,20:3
Veils 1928,Mr 14,28:5
Ralston, Alfred (Miscellaneous)
Oh What a Lovely War 1964,O 1,30:1
Ralston, Bob
Slave Ship 1969,N 22,46:1
Ralston, Esther
Vaudeville (Palace) 1929,D 9,33:2
Ralston, Gilbert
Lady Precious Stream 1936,Ja 28,15:2
Ralston, Louis (Mrs)
One Woman's Husband 1920,Mr 23,9:3
Ralston, Marjorie (Playwright)
Suddenly a Stranger 1936,Ag 4,15:2

Ralston, Teri
Company 1970,Ap 27,40:1
Company 1970,My 3,II,1:4
Ram, Jerry
Guide, The 1968,Mr 7,50:1
Rama IX, King of Thailand (Composer)
Peep Show 1950,Je 7,34:5
Ramage, Cecile
Last Enemy, The 1930,O 31,21:1
When Ladies Meet 1933,Ap 27,15:4
Ramage, Jack
When We Dead Awaken 1966,Ap 19,37:2
Rambeau, Marjorie
Daddy's Gone A-Hunting 1921,S 1,18:3
Daddy's Gone A-Hunting 1921,S 25,VI,1:1
Goldfish, The 1922,Ap 18,15:3
Untitled-Benefit 1922,My 8,14:5
As You Like It 1923,Ap 24,24:1
As You Like It 1923,Ap 29,VII,1:1
Road Together, The 1924,Ja 18,21:2
Valley of Content, The 1925,Ja 14,19:2
Antonia 1925,O 11,VIII,2:6
Antonia 1925,O 21,20:1
Night Duel, The 1926,F 16,22:3
Just Life 1926,S 15,33:3
Just Life 1926,S 19,IX,1:1
Madame Alias 1927,S 4,VII,2:4
Story to Be Whispered 1937,Ag 20,21:4
Rambeau, Zella
Princess Virtue 1921,My 5,20:2
Rambova, Natacha
Set a Thief 1927,F 22,22:1
Creoles 1927,S 23,33:3
Rambova, Natacha (Costume Designer)
These Few Ashes 1928,O 31,28:1
Ramer, Jack (Lyricist)
I Dreamt I Dwelt in Bloomingdale's 1970,F 13,26:1
Ramer, Jack (Playwright)
I Dreamt I Dwelt in Bloomingdale's 1970,F 13,26:1
Ramet, Karl (Scenic Designer)
Housewarming 1932,Ap 8,25:1
Ramey, Bette
Liliom 1956,F 18,12:5
Ramey, Cortell
Battle Hymn 1936,My 23,12:1
Ramey, Pierre de
Atout... Coeur 1936,Mr 27,25:4
Son Mari 1936,Ap 17,17:3
Ramin, Sid (Composer)
Agatha Sue, I Love You 1966,D 15,61:1
Ramin, Sid (Miscellaneous)
West Side Story 1957,S 27,14:4
West Side Story 1957,O 13,II,9:1
Gypsy 1959,My 22,31:6
Girls Against the Boys, The 1959,N 3,26:1
West Side Story 1960,Ap 28,31:1
Wildcat 1960,D 17,20:2
Conquering Hero, The 1961,Ja 17,40:2
Kwamina 1961,O 24,42:1
I Can Get It for You Wholesale 1962,Mr 23,29:1
Funny Thing Happened on the Way to the Forum,
A 1962,My 9,49:1
Sophie 1963,Ap 16,32:1
West Side Story 1968,Je 25,32:1
Ramirez, Carlos
Crazy With the Heat 1941,Ja 31,15:2
Ramirez, Coco
South Pacific 1961,Ap 27,26:3
In the Summer House 1964,Mr 26,43:1
Ramirez, Frank
Romeo y Julieta 1965,Ag 28,13:3
Ramirez, Jose
To Quito and Back 1937,O 7,30:4
Ramirez, Ray
Harold Arlen Songbook, The 1967,Mr 1,48:1
Ramirez, Ray (Producer)
Harold Arlen Songbook, The 1967,Mr 1,48:1
Ramirez, Tim
Wonderful Town 1967,My 18,50:1
Billy 1969,Mr 24,56:1
Rammelkamp, Rhoda
Saint's Parade 1930,N 1,23:4
Young Go First, The 1935,My 29,16:2
Rammelkamp, Rhoda (Original Author)
Treasure Island 1938,My 15,II,2:3
Ramon, Maurice
As You Desire Me 1931,Ja 29,21:2
Ramond, Cyril
Dover Road, The 1924,My 4,VIII,2:4
Ramondetta, John
Brothers Karamazov, The 1957,D 9,39:4
Brothers Karamazov, The 1957,D 22,II,3:1
Golden Six, The 1958,O 27,31:2
Orpheus Descending 1959,O 6,45:2
Caligula 1960,F 17,31:1
Ramonov, Nadya
Sojourner Truth 1948,Ap 22,35:2
Ramos, George
West Side Story 1968,Je 25,32:1
Ramos, Louis
Moondreamers, The 1969,D 9,68:1
Ramos, N
Screwball, The 1957,My 25,24:7

Ramos, Richard
Harpers Ferry 1967,Je 6,52:2
House of Atreus, The; Bringers of Offerings, The
1967,Jl 24,23:1
Visit, The 1967,S 13,41:1
She Stoops to Conquer 1968,Ja 1,11:1
Twelfth Night 1968,Je 15,40:1
Resistible Rise of Arturo Ui, The 1968,Ag 8,25:1
Merton of the Movies 1968,S 26,62:1
House of Atreus, The 1968,D 18,55:1
Resistible Rise of Arturo Ui, The 1968,D 23,44:1
Adaptation 1970,Mr 12,46:1
Ramoska, Biruta
Music in the Air 1951,O 9,32:2
Ramoy, Pearl
Cafe de Danse 1929,Ja 16,22:2
Purity 1930,D 26,18:2
Rampino, Lewis (Miscellaneous)
Macbeth 1969,N 21,51:1
Ramsay, Allan
Menace 1927,Mr 15,28:2
Three Times the Hour 1931,Ag 26,15:5
Ramsay, Franklin
Ghosts 1925,D 2,23:2
Ramsay, J Nelson
Courting 1925,S 14,17:1
Ramsay, Percy
Twelfth Disciple, The 1930,My 17,21:4
Ramsay, Remak
Hang Down Your Head and Die 1964,O 19,38:1
Sheep on the Runway 1970,F 2,28:3
Sheep on the Runway 1970,F 8,II,5:5
Lovely Ladies, Kind Gentlemen 1970,D 29,38:1
Ramsdell, Roger
Anatol 1931,Ja 17,23:3
Ramsdell, Roger (Miscellaneous)
Daphne Laureola 1950,S 19,38:6
Ramsen, Alan
Lullaby 1954,F 4,21:2
Ramsen, Robert
Career Angel 1944,My 24,23:7
Ramsey, Alan
Master Builder, The 1955,Mr 2,23:2
Ramsey, Alice
Second Comin', The 1931,D 9,32:4
Marriage of Cana, The 1932,F 3,22:4
Ol' Man Satan 1932,O 4,26:3
Ramsey, Alicia (Playwright)
Byron 1929,F 10,IX,4:7
Ramsey, Allan
American Born 1925,O 6,31:3
Ramsey, Barbara
Lost 1927,Mr 29,22:2
Ramsey, Bob (Scenic Designer)
Watched Pot, The 1947,O 29,31:4
Ramsey, Dorothy
Rosalinda; Fledermaus, Die 1942,O 29,26:5
New Moon, The 1944,My 18,16:2
Ramsey, Edna
Blind Alley 1935,S 25,19:6
Laughing Woman, The 1936,O 14,30:1
Ramsey, George
Mr Adam 1949,My 26,34:6
Ramsey, Gordon
Autumn's Here 1966,O 26,40:1
Ramsey, Harriet
Achilles Had a Heel 1935,O 14,20:2
Ramsey, Helen
Garrick Gaieties 1926,My 11,25:2
Ramsey, James
Madwoman of Chaillot, The 1950,Je 14,41:2
Ramsey, John
Sunset 1966,My 13,34:1
Tango 1968,Ja 1,11:1
Ramsey, Logan
Devil's Disciple, The 1950,Ja 26,23:2
High Ground, The 1951,F 21,31:2
Pursuit of Happiness, The 1952,Mr 22,9:2
In the Summer House 1953,D 30,17:1
Johnny Johnson 1956,O 22,24:1
Good Woman of Setzuan, The 1956,D 19,41:2
Fall 1957,N 22,19:1
Making of Moo, The 1958,Je 12,34:1
Sweet Bird of Youth 1959,Mr 11,39:2
Sweet Bird of Youth 1959,Mr 22,II,1:1
Tiger Rag, The 1961,F 17,20:2
'Toinette 1961,N 21,46:1
Marathon '33 1963,D 23,20:1
My Kinsman, Major Molineux 1964,N 2,62:2
Great Indoors, The 1966,F 2,23:1
Ramsey, Logan (Producer)
Fall 1957,N 22,19:1
Ramsey, Margretta
As You Like It 1945,Jl 4,10:4
Ramsey, Packer
Liza 1922,N 28,24:1
Ramsey, Percy
Right of Possession 1930,My 9,20:5
Ramsey, Robert (Costume Designer)
God's Trombones 1960,F 10,43:4
Shakespeare in Harlem 1960,F 10,43:4
Ramsey, Robert (Lighting Director)
God's Trombones 1960,F 10,43:4

Ramsey, Robert (Lighting Director)—Cont
Shakespeare in Harlem 1960,F 10,43:4
Ramsey, Robert (Scenic Designer)
Creditors 1949,N 22,36:5
Heartbreak House 1950,Mr 22,33:2
Shakespeare in Harlem 1960,F 10,43:4
God's Trombones 1960,F 10,43:4
Ramsey, Robert L (Costume Designer)
U S A 1959,O 29,38:1
Ramsey, Robert L (Lighting Director)
Desire Under the Elms 1951,N 22,45:1
Ramsey, Robert L (Scenic Designer)
Peg o' My Heart 1948,Ag 25,29:2
Desire Under the Elms 1951,N 22,45:1
U S A 1959,O 29,38:1
U S A 1959,N 8,II,1:1
Bring Me a Warm Body 1962,Ap 17,29:3
Figuro in the Night 1962,O 31,33:1
Moon Shines on Kylenamoe, The 1962,O 31,33:1
Ramsey, Robert R (Costume Designer)
Death of Satan, The 1960,Ap 6,49:1
Ramsey, Robert R (Lighting Director)
Death of Satan, The 1960,Ap 6,49:1
Ramsey, Robert R (Scenic Designer)
Death of Satan, The 1960,Ap 6,49:1
Ramsey, Ruth
Ruddigore 1927,My 21,25:2
Mame 1966,My 25,41:1
Ramson, Ralph
Ol' Man Satan 1932,O 4,26:3
Cradle Will Rock, The 1937,D 6,19:4
Ramus, Tucky (Miscellaneous)
Entertain a Ghost 1962,Ap 10,48:1
Ramuz, C F (Playwright)
Soldier's Tale, A 1955,Jl 13,21:2
Ramuz, G F (Playwright)
Tale of the Soldier, The 1927,Ag 14,VII,1:7
Ranck, Carty (Playwright)
Mountain, The 1933,S 12,28:6
Ranck, John (Miscellaneous)
Madrigal of Shakespeare, A 1968,F 14,56:2
Rand, Ayn (Original Author)
Unconquered, The 1940,F 14,25:2
Rand, Ayn (Playwright)
Night of January 16 1935,S 10,26:1
Night of January 16 1935,S 17,26:4
Night of January 16 1936,S 30,29:3
Night of January 16 1937,Jl 20,19:3
Unconquered, The 1940,F 14,25:2
Rand, Edith
Survivors, The 1948,Ja 20,27:2
Rand, Edwin
Red Harvest 1937,Mr 31,29:2
Tell My Story 1939,Mr 16,26:6
Rand, Florence
Venetian Glass Nephew, The 1931,F 24,26:3
Rand, Florence (Miscellaneous)
Here Come the Clowns 1960,S 20,48:1
Rand, Florence (Producer)
Women at the Tomb, The 1961,Ap 25,41:1
Philoktetes 1961,Ap 25,41:1
Rand, Jay
Thomas Paine 1930,Mr 21,30:7
Rand, Jerry
Lower North 1944,Ag 26,15:4
Rand, Leigh (Costume Designer)
Ah, Wilderness! 1969,N 9,86:1
Room Service 1970,My 13,49:1
Rand, Leslie
Gondoliers, The 1934,S 9,IX,1:1
Rand, Marguerite
Musk 1920,Mr 15,13:1
Rand, Raymond
Try and Get It 1943,Ag 3,13:2
Rand, Sally
Vaudeville (Palace) 1928,S 25,29:4
Rain 1935,Ag 27,23:4
Let's Play Fair 1938,Ja 19,26:4
Randal, Carl
Countess Maritza 1926,S 20,21:1
Randall, Addison
Victory Belles 1943,O 27,26:3
Randall, Andre
Vanities 1932,S 18,IX,2:1
Vanities 1932,S 28,22:4
Randall, Anthony
Circle of Chalk, The 1941,Mr 27,28:4
Antony and Cleopatra 1947,N 27,49:2
To Tell You the Truth 1948,Ap 19,28:6
Caesar and Cleopatra 1949,D 22,28:2
Randall, Bernard
Ziegfeld Follies 1922,Je 6,18:2
Honeymoon Lane 1926,S 21,32:3
My Girl Friday! 1929,F 13,20:2
In Time to Come 1941,D 29,20:2
Flamingo Road 1946,Mr 20,18:2
Miracle in the Mountains 1947,Ap 26,10:2
Randall, Bill
Let Freedom Sing 1942,O 6,18:2
Randall, Bob
Utopia, Limited 1960,Ap 8,27:2
Grand Duke, The 1961,My 12,24:1
Student Prince, The 1961,Jl 14,14:1
'Toinette 1961,N 21,46:1

ndall, Carl
Ziegfeld Midnight Frolic 1920,Mr 17,14:2
Ziegfeld Follies 1920,Je 23,14:1
Sonny 1921,Ag 17,12:2
Midnight Frolic 1921,N 19,11:3
Greenwich Village Follies 1922,S 13,18:2
Music Box Revue 1924,D 2,23:3
Lambs Gambol 1925,Ap 27,15:1
Vaudeville (Palace) 1925,O 6,31:3
Countess Maritza 1926,Mr 30,20:3
Sunny Days 1928,F 9,29:1
New Americana 1928,N 30,32:4
Vaudeville (Palace) 1930,Mr 7,21:2
Third Little Show, The 1931,My 10,VIII,2:4
Third Little Show, The 1931,Je 2,34:3
Little Racketeer, The 1932,Ja 19,24:4
Vaudeville (Loew's State) 1932,O 3,15:5
Pardon My English 1933,Ja 21,11:4
Crazy With the Heat 1941,Ja 15,18:2
andall, Carl (Choreographer)
Countess Maritza 1926,S 20,21:1
Gay Divorce 1932,N 30,23:4
Illustrators' Show, The 1936,Ja 23,25:3
Knickerbocker Holiday 1938,O 20,26:2
Stars in Your Eyes 1939,F 10,18:2
Louisiana Purchase 1940,My 29,19:2
High Kickers 1941,N 1,21:2
Sunny River 1941,D 5,28:2
Time, Place and the Girl, The 1942,O 22,24:3
andall, Carl (Miscellaneous)
Crazy With the Heat 1941,Ja 31,15:2
Randall, Charles
2 for Fun; Switch in Time, A 1955,My 26,34:1
2 for Fun; Anniversary, The 1955,My 26,34:1
Adding Machine, The 1956,F 10,17:1
Brothers Karamazov, The 1957,D 9,39:4
Susan Slept Here 1961,Jl 12,35:2
Cherry Orchard, The 1962,N 15,46:2
Enter Laughing 1963,Mr 15,8:1
Trial of Lee Harvey Oswald, The 1967,N 6,64:1
Randall, Clifford
Blue Blood 1924,Ap 3,21:2
Randall, Dick (Producer)
Aquarama 1960 1960,Jl 1,14:6
How to Make a Man 1961,F 3,16:1
Once There Was a Russian 1961,F 20,32:2
Tattooed Countess, The 1961,My 4,40:2
Mermaid's Holiday 1961,Jl 1,8:1
Randall, Dorothy
Gasoline Gypsies 1931,Je 8,21:3
Randall, George
Chocolates 1967,Ap 11,51:1
Randall, John
Little Old New York 1920,S 9,9:2
Randall, Joyce
Six Characters in Search of an Author
1961,My 11,43:1
Randall, Juliet
Lysistrata 1959,N 25,19:4
Henry IV 1960,Mr 2,42:1
Henry IV 1960,Mr 13,II,1:1
Henry IV 1960,Ap 19,41:1
Idiot, The 1960,S 26,38:1
She Stoops to Conquer 1960,N 2,42:5
Plough and the Stars, The 1960,D 7,56:2
Octoroon, The 1961,Ja 28,13:1
Hamlet 1961,Mr 17,17:1
Tristram 1962,O 29,36:1
Taming of the Shrew, The 1963,Mr 8,9:1
Randall, Keith
Hamlet 1936,N 11,54:2
Randall, Kenn
Moroni 1936,Ag 19,19:1
Randall, L
Pansy 1929,My 15,36:3
Randall, Lee
O'Flynn, The 1934,D 28,24:1
Randall, Margaret
Glorious Morning 1938,N 28,10:3
Don't Throw Glass Houses 1938,D 28,24:4
Randall, Martha
Be Your Age 1953,Ja 15,24:2
Randall, Pat
Marathon '33 1963,D 23,20:1
Blues for Mister Charlie 1964,Ap 24,24:1
Randall, Paul
Iron Men 1936,O 20,30:6
Randall, Robert
Free for All 1931,S 9,25:1
Summer and Smoke 1952,Ap 25,19:5
Randall, Robert (Lighting Director)
Summer and Smoke 1952,My 4,II,1:1
Randall, Rosalie
Hear! Hear! 1955,S 28,38:1
Randall, Sharon
Song of Norway 1944,Ag 22,20:2
Randall, Skip
Make Mine Manhattan 1948,Ja 16,26:2
Randall, Susann
Yes, Yes, No No 1969,Ja 1,16:1
Randall, Tony
Inherit the Wind 1955,Ap 22,20:2
Inherit the Wind 1955,S 25,II,1:1

Oh Captain! 1958,F 5,21:2
Utbu 1966,Ja 5,24:1
Randall, William R
Robert E Lee 1923,N 21,23:1
Catskill Dutch 1924,My 7,18:1
That Awful Mrs Eaton! 1924,S 30,27:1
Black Cockatoo, The 1926,D 31,11:1
Road to Rome, The 1927,F 1,24:2
Jealous Moon, The 1928,N 21,32:2
Paolo and Francesca 1929,Ap 2,28:2
Ledge, A 1929,N 19,26:3
Plutocrat, The 1930,F 21,23:3
Reunion in Vienna 1931,N 17,31:1
Her Tin Soldier 1933,Ap 7,22:6
Randall Sisters
Her Family Tree 1920,D 28,9:2
Randalu, Juliet
Henry IV, Part II 1960,Ap 24,II,1:1
Randau, Carl (Original Author)
Visitor, The 1944,O 18,24:5
Randel, Elinor
Sands of the Negev 1954,O 20,32:1
Randell, Pamela
Bloomer Girl 1944,O 6,18:5
Hollywood Pinafore 1945,Je 1,20:1
Randell, Ron
Browning Version, The 1949,O 13,32:2
Harlequinade 1949,O 13,32:2
Browning Version, The 1949,O 23,II,1:1
Candida 1952,Ap 23,23:6
World of Suzie Wong, The 1958,O 15,47:1
Randels, Marilyn
Let's Face It 1941,O 30,26:2
Randol, George
My Magnolia 1926,Jl 13,19:2
Bomboola 1929,Je 27,17:3
Green Pastures, The 1930,F 27,26:1
Green Pastures, The 1935,F 27,16:2
Porgy and Bess 1943,S 14,26:2
Anna Lucasta 1944,Ag 31,15:1
Randole, Leo (Mme) (Playwright)
Caviar 1934,Je 8,19:2
Randole, Leo (Translator)
Chief Thing, The 1963,Ap 30,27:2
Randolf, Michael
Surgeon, The 1932,O 28,23:1
Randolph, Amanda
Chocolate Dandies, The 1924,S 2,22:2
Male Animal, The 1940,Ja 10,17:2
Harlem Cavalcade 1942,My 2,11:2
Willow and I, The 1942,D 11,32:2
Randolph, Cathryn
Window Panes 1927,F 22,22:2
Randolph, Clemence (Playwright)
Rain 1922,O 15,VIII,1:8
Rain 1922,N 8,18:2
Rain 1926,O 12,27:1
Rain 1935,F 13,24:1
Rain 1935,F 17,VIII,1:1
Sadie Thompson 1944,N 17,25:2
Rain 1948,F 2,15:2
Randolph, Donald
Fatal Alibi, The 1932,F 10,26:6
Strange Gods 1933,Ap 17,16:6
Errant Lady 1934,S 18,18:2
It's You I Want 1935,F 6,23:3
Reprise 1935,My 2,16:2
Crime Marches on 1935,O 24,19:1
Richard II 1937,F 6,14:2
Richard II 1937,S 16,28:2
Man From Cairo, The 1938,My 5,26:5
Hamlet 1938,O 13,28:1
Henry IV, Part I 1939,Ja 31,17:2
Hamlet 1939,D 5,35:2
Richard II 1940,Ap 2,31:2
Lady in the Dark 1941,Ja 24,14:2
Lady in the Dark 1941,S 3,26:6
Yours, A Lincoln 1942,Jl 10,12:3
Sun Field, The 1942,D 10,33:2
Naked Genius, The 1943,O 22,20:5
I Like It Here 1946,Mr 23,8:6
Randolph, Dorothy
Green Pastures, The 1930,F 27,26:1
Randolph, George
Porgy and Bess 1944,F 8,13:2
Randolph, Isabel
If I Was Rich 1926,S 3,15:2
Ink 1927,N 2,24:2
Randolph, James
Carmen Jones 1959,Ag 18,25:1
Porgy and Bess 1961,My 18,40:1
Porgy and Bess 1965,O 20,53:3
Randolph, Jimmy
John Brown 1950,My 4,32:7
Carmen Jones 1956,Je 1,28:2
Ballad for Bimshire 1963,O 16,54:1
Porgy and Bess 1965,Mr 6,17:1
Randolph, John
Captain Jinks of the Horse Marines 1938,Ja 28,16:2
No More Peace 1938,Ja 29,13:2
Coriolanus 1938,F 2,14:5
Medicine Show 1940,Ap 13,20:6
Hold On to Your Hats 1940,S 12,30:3

Randolph, John—Cont
Any Day Now 1941,Je 10,28:2
Command Decision 1947,O 2,30:2
Sun and I, The 1949,Mr 21,18:4
Come Back, Little Sheba 1950,F 16,28:5
Golden State, The 1950,N 27,29:3
Peer Gynt 1951,Ja 29,15:2
Paint Your Wagon 1951,N 13,32:2
Seagulls Over Sorrento 1952,S 12,18:4
Grey-Eyed People, The 1952,D 18,41:2
Room Service 1953,Ap 7,34:1
Maya 1953,Je 10,35:1
Madam Will You Walk 1953,D 2,2:4
Coriolanus 1954,Ja 20,34:2
All Summer Long 1954,S 24,26:2
All Summer Long 1954,O 3,II,1:1
Time of Your Life, The 1955,Ja 20,34:1
Time of Your Life, The 1955,Ja 30,II,1:1
Wooden Dish, The 1955,O 7,20:1
Miss Isobel 1957,D 27,22:1
Visit, The 1958,My 6,40:1
Portrait of a Madonna 1959,Ap 16,28:1
Portrait of a Madonna 1959,Ap 26,II,1:1
Sound of Music, The 1959,N 17,40:2
Mother Courage and Her Children 1963,Mr 30,5:5
Case of Libel, A 1963,O 11,43:2
Hamlet 1964,Je 17,49:1
Conversation at Midnight 1964,N 13,27:1
Evening's Frost, An 1965,O 12,56:1
My Sweet Charlie 1966,D 7,56:1
Dodo Bird, The 1967,D 9,62:1
Peddler, The 1967,D 9,62:1
In the Matter of J Robert Oppenheimer
1968,Je 7,31:1
In the Matter of J Robert Oppenheimer
1968,Je 9,II,1:1
Our Town 1969,N 28,50:1
Our Town 1969,D 7,II,7:1
Randolph, John (Playwright)
Portrait of the Artist as a Young Man, A
1962,My 29,21:1
Randolph, Joyce
Lucky Sam McCarver 1950,Ap 15,10:6
Brandy Is My True Love's Name 1953,Je 18,38:5
Hopalong--Freud 1953,Je 18,38:5
California 1953,Je 18,38:5
Where There's a Will 1953,Je 18,38:5
Voice of the Turtle, The 1961,Je 28,41:1
Randolph, Louise
Cradle Song 1921,Mr 1,18:2
Shadow, The 1922,Ap 25,14:2
Nancy Ann 1924,Ap 1,18:1
Juno and the Paycock 1926,Mr 16,22:1
My Country 1926,Ag 10,19:1
Randolph, Marion
Sojourner Truth 1948,Ap 22,35:2
Randolph, Mimi
Partition 1948,O 29,31:2
All in Love 1961,N 11,15:2
Dear Me, the Sky Is Falling 1963,Mr 4,9:1
Jo 1964,F 13,25:1
Pocket Watch, The 1966,Ja 6,18:1
Randolph, Patricia
Symphony 1935,Ap 27,20:3
Randolph, Ralph
Carmen Jones 1951,S 22,8:6
Randolph, Renita
Out of Step 1925,Ja 30,12:1
Moon Is a Gong, The 1926,Mr 13,21:3
Donovan Affair, The 1926,Ag 31,15:2
Rockbound 1929,Ap 20,23:2
Randolph, Robert (Costume Designer)
Saint of Bleecker Street, The 1954,D 28,21:1
Desperate Hours, The 1955,F 11,20:2
Saint of Bleecker Street, The 1965,Mr 19,28:1
Randolph, Robert (Lighting Director)
How to Succeed in Business Without Really Trying
1961,O 16,34:1
Bravo Giovanni 1962,My 21,41:2
Little Me 1962,N 19,41:3
Sophie 1963,Ap 16,32:1
Foxy 1964,F 17,26:1
Funny Girl 1964,Mr 27,15:1
Something More! 1964,N 11,36:1
Xmas in Las Vegas 1965,N 5,31:1
Skyscraper 1965,N 15,48:1
Sweet Charity 1966,Ja 31,22:1
It's a Bird . . . It's a Plane . . . It's Superman
1966,Mr 30,34:1
Walking Happy 1966,N 28,47:1
Sherry! 1967,Mr 29,39:1
Henry, Sweet Henry 1967,O 24,51:2
Golden Rainbow 1968,F 5,27:1
Angela 1969,O 31,33:1
Randolph, Robert (Scenic Designer)
Saint of Bleecker Street, The 1954,D 28,21:1
Bye Bye Birdie 1960,Ap 15,13:4
How to Succeed in Business Without Really Trying
1961,O 16,34:1
Bravo Giovanni 1962,My 21,41:2
Calculated Risk 1962,N 1,35:1
Little Me 1962,N 19,41:3
Sophie 1963,Ap 16,32:1
Foxy 1964,F 17,26:1

Randolph, Robert (Scenic Designer)—Cont

Any Wednesday 1964,F 19,34:1
Funny Girl 1964,Mr 27,15:1
Something More! 1964,N 11,36:1
Saint of Bleecker Street, The 1965,Mr 19,28:1
Xmas in Las Vegas 1965,N 5,31:1
Skyscraper 1965,N 15,48:1
Anya 1965,N 30,48:1
Sweet Charity 1966,Ja 31,22:1
It's a Bird . . . It's a Plane . . . It's Superman 1966,Mr 30,34:1
Walking Happy 1966,N 28,47:1
Sherry! 1967,Mr 29,39:1
Henry, Sweet Henry 1967,O 24,51:2
How to Be a Jewish Mother 1967,D 29,18:1
Golden Rainbow 1968,F 5,27:1
Teaspoon Every Four Hours, A 1969,Je 16,57:1
Angela 1969,O 31,33:1
Applause 1970,Mr 31,35:1

Randolph, Shannon

Song of Norway 1944,Ag 22,20:2

Rands, Leslie

Gondoliers, The 1934,S 4,23:1
Iolanthe 1934,S 11,24:3
Trial by Jury 1934,S 14,24:3
H M S Pinafore 1934,S 14,24:3
Mikado, The; Town of Titipu, The 1934,S 18,18:1
Yeomen of the Guard, The 1934,S 21,28:3
Princess Ida; Castle Adamant 1934,S 28,26:3
Patience 1934,O 12,32:2
Mikado, The 1936,Ag 21,13:2
Trial by Jury 1936,S 1,24:4
Gondoliers, The 1936,S 8,23:1
Yeomen of the Guard, The 1936,S 15,37:2
Iolanthe 1936,S 22,30:3
H M S Pinafore 1936,S 29,34:2
Patience 1936,O 6,28:6
Princess Ida 1936,O 13,32:2
Trial by Jury 1939,Ja 6,25:1
Mikado, The 1939,Ja 10,16:3
Iolanthe 1939,Ja 13,16:3
H. M. S. Pinafore 1939,Ja 17,27:5
Gondoliers, The 1939,Ja 20,14:2
Yeomen of the Guard, The 1939,Ja 24,17:1
Patience 1939,Ja 27,16:3

Ranelli, J (Director)

Songs From Milk Wood 1970,Ja 13,41:1

Ranevsky, Boris

Pelican, The 1925,S 22,23:2

Raney, Jim

Thurber Carnival, A 1960,F 27,13:2

Ranger, Nell

Patience 1935,S 3,24:4

Rangers, The

Vaudeville (Palace) 1929,D 23,19:1

Ranier, Richard

Don Juan 1921,S 8,14:2
Arabian, The 1927,N 1,20:5
Royal Box, The 1928,N 21,32:3
Sakura 1928,D 26,14:4

Rank, Paul H

Grey Heir, The 1926,Ap 6,29:2

Rankin, Arthur Jr (Producer)

Month of Sundays 1968,S 17,50:1

Rankin, Doris

Letter of the Law, The; Robe Rouge, La 1920,F 24,11:1
Letter of the Law, The 1920,F 29,V,5:1
Claw, The 1921,O 18,20:1
Rose Bernd 1922,S 27,17:1
Chivalry 1925,D 16,22:3
Vaudeville (Palace) 1926,S 14,25:3
Seed of the Brute 1926,N 2,34:3
Garden of Eden, The 1927,S 28,28:1
Big Pond, The 1928,Ag 22,25:1
Six Characters in Search of an Author 1931,Ap 16,29:2

Rankin, Earle

Cock-A-Doodle Dandy 1955,N 4,26:5
Country Scandal, A 1960,My 6,21:8

Rankin, Linda

Carnival! 1968,D 13,58:1

Ranney, Frank

These Charming People 1925,O 7,31:2

Ransan, Andre (Playwright)

Parade Amoureuse 1928,Mr 4,IX,4:5
Je Veux d'Etre Heureux 1928,My 13,IX,2:2
Grande Enfant, La 1931,D 13,VIII,2:2

Ranseer, Mignon

Kiki 1921,N 30,13:1
Dove, The 1925,F 12,17:3

Ransom, Herbert

Nirvana 1926,Mr 4,19:1
Beaux' Stratagem, The 1928,Je 5,20:1
Romeo and Juliet 1951,Mr 12,21:2

Ransom, Nellie

Dead End 1935,O 29,17:2

Ransom, Paul

Patriots, The 1943,D 21,22:5
All the King's Men 1948,Ja 19,19:2
Outside the Door 1949,Mr 2,33:2
Burning Bush, The 1949,D 17,15:5

Ransom, Paul (Director)

Flies, The; Mouches, Les 1947,Ap 18,26:3

Ransome, Ernie

Trial of Dr Beck, The 1937,Ag 10,22:2

Ranson, Herbert

Green Goddess, The 1921,Ja 19,14:1
Merchant of Venice, The 1922,D 22,13:1
School for Scandal, The 1923,Mr 13,19:2
If Winter Comes 1923,Ap 3,26:1
Bit o' Love, A 1925,My 13,24:2
Hamlet 1925,N 10,23:1
Schweiger 1926,Mr 24,20:4
Henry IV, Part I 1926,Je 1,29:1
Old Bill, M P 1926,N 11,22:2
Junk 1927,Ja 6,25:1
Julius Caesar 1927,Je 7,27:2
Candida 1927,Ag 31,19:4
Banshee, The 1927,D 6,26:2
Becky Sharp 1929,Je 4,29:1
General John Regan 1930,Ja 30,16:5
Milestones 1930,Je 3,27:1
Suspense 1930,Ag 13,22:3
Tyrant, The 1930,N 13,33:1
Hamlet 1931,N 6,28:4
Lancashire Lass, The 1931,D 31,16:3
Troilus and Cressida 1932,Je 7,22:3
Dark Hours, The 1932,N 15,24:2
One Wife or Another 1933,F 7,23:6
Hamlet 1934,D 26,19:3
Richard III 1934,D 28,24:3
Rain 1935,F 13,24:1
Hamlet 1935,N 11,54:2
Julius Caesar 1938,Ja 30,X,3:1
Love for Love 1940,Je 4,19:5
King Lear 1940,D 16,27:2
Much Ado About Nothing 1959,S 18,25:2

Ranson, Herbert (Director)

One Wife or Another 1933,F 7,23:6

Ranson, Marcelle

Britannicus 1958,N 29,17:2

Ranson, Nellie

Young Madame Conti 1937,Ap 1,18:4
Annie Get Your Gun 1946,My 17,14:2

Ranson, Ralph

Cradle Will Rock, The 1938,Ja 4,19:3

Ransone, John W

Praying Curve 1927,Ja 25,18:2

Ranzato, V (Composer)

Paese dei Campanelli, Il; Land of Bells, The 1935,My 10,25:4

Raoul-Henry

Parisienne 1924,N 25,26:2
Amoureuse 1924,N 28,13:1

Raph, Gerry

New Freedom, The 1930,My 15,32:4
New Freedom, The 1930,My 17,21:4
Mlle Modiste 1937,My 5,28:5

Raphael

Continental Varieties 1934,O 4,18:3
Continental Varieties 1934,N 15,24:3

Raphael, Alice (Translator)

Faust, Part I; Prologue in Heaven 1961,F 5,27:2
Faust, Part I; Play, The 1961,F 5,27:2
Faust, Part I; Prelude in the Theater 1961,F 5,27:2

Raphael, Bette-Jane

Fourth Wall, The 1968,S 5,53:1

Raphael, Enid

Make Me Know It 1929,N 5,32:5
Marseilles 1930,N 18,28:2
Heat Wave 1931,F 18,14:6
Second Comin', The 1931,D 9,32:4
Never No More 1932,Ja 8,27:1
Tree, The 1932,Ap 13,23:5
Policy Kings 1938,D 31,6:2

Raphael, Gerrianne

Goodbye My Fancy 1948,N 18,35:2
Threepenny Opera, The 1954,Mr 11,26:5
Seventh Heaven 1955,My 27,16:2
Boy Friend, The 1958,Ja 27,24:4
Saratoga 1959,D 8,59:4
Ernest in Love 1960,My 5,39:4
Fourth Avenue North 1961,S 28,50:2
Man of La Mancha 1965,N 23,52:1

Raphael, Henry

Mr Papavert 1932,Ja 23,18:6

Raphael, Jerome

Connection, The 1960,F 7,II,1:1

Raphael, John N (Playwright)

Potash and Perlmutter 1926,N 14,VIII,2:1
Madame X 1927,Jl 7,29:3
Peter Ibbetson 1931,Ap 9,30:3

Raphael, Lennox (Playwright)

Che! 1969,Mr 24,56:1
Che! 1969,My 4,II,3:5
Che! 1970,Ja 18,II,1:1

Raphael, Marilyn

Penny Change 1963,O 25,37:1

Raphael, William

If Booth Had Missed 1931,My 14,27:1

Raphaelson, Samson (Director)

Wooden Slipper, The 1934,Ja 4,16:3
Skylark 1939,O 12,32:2
Jason 1942,Ja 22,12:2

Raphaelson, Samson (Director)—Cont

Perfect Marriage, The 1944,O 27,17:6

Raphaelson, Samson (Playwright)

Jazz Singer, The 1925,S 15,29:2
Young Love 1928,Ag 12,VII,1:2
Young Love 1928,S 30,IX,2:7
Young Love 1928,O 31,28:1
Young Love 1929,Jl 4,8:4
Wooden Slipper, The 1934,Ja 4,16:3
Accent on Youth 1934,D 26,19:1
Accent on Youth 1935,Jl 11,24:3
Accent on Youth 1935,Ag 13,20:3
Accent on Youth 1935,S 29,X,1:6
White Man 1936,O 19,22:4
Skylark 1939,Mr 19,XI,2:5
Skylark 1939,O 12,32:2
Skylark 1939,O 22,IX,1:3
Jason 1942,Ja 22,12:2
Skylark 1942,Ap 12,VIII,1:6
Perfect Marriage, The 1944,O 27,17:6
Perfect Marriage, The 1944,N 5,II,1:2
Hilda Crane 1950,N 2,38:2
Heel, The 1954,My 27,33:2

Raphel, Jerome

Cave at Machpelah, The 1959,Jl 1,25:1
Connection, The 1959,Jl 16,30:2
Marrying Maiden, The 1960,Je 23,18:3
Full Moon in March, A 1960,S 20,48:1
Cayenne Pepper 1961,D 13,55:5
Grand Vizier, The 1961,D 13,55:5
Julius Caesar 1962,F 22,19:6
Man Is Man 1962,S 19,31:1
Lorenzo 1963,F 16,5:2
Seagull, The 1964,Ap 6,36:1
Crucible, The 1964,Ap 7,30:2
Slave, The 1964,D 17,51:1
Tonight in Living Color; David Show, The 1969,Je 11,43:1
Mercy Street 1969,O 28,43:1

Rapkin, Stephanie

Beyond the Horizon 1962,O 26,27:2

Rapone, Luigi

My Wife Is Different 1931,Ap 27,24:4

Rapoport, Herbert

Dybbuk, The 1954,O 27,33:6

Raposo, Joseph (Composer)

Sing Muse 1961,D 7,52:1
Man's a Man, A 1962,S 20,30:2

Raposo, Joseph (Miscellaneous)

Sing Muse 1961,D 7,52:1
Great Scot! 1965,N 12,56:3
You're a Good Man, Charlie Brown 1967,Mr 8,51:1
Trial of Lee Harvey Oswald, The 1967,N 6,64:1

Raposo, Joseph (Musical Director)

Great Scot! 1965,N 12,56:3
House of Flowers 1968,Ja 29,26:2

Rapovsky, Istvan

Judy Garland's New Variety Show 1956,S 27,43:2

Rapp, Barney

Look Who's Here 1932,O 31,18:5

Rapp, Carl

R U R 1942,D 4,30:2

Rapp, Marvin

Young Visitors, The 1920,N 30,14:1

Rapp, William Jourdan (Playwright)

Harlem 1929,F 21,30:3
Harlem 1929,Mr 3,VIII,1:1
Whirlpool 1929,D 4,37:3
Substitute for Murder 1935,O 23,18:6
Holmeses of Baker Street, The 1936,D 10,34:3

Rappel, Malvina

Untitled-Revue 1939,Ap 5,31:2

Rapper, Irving H

Crime 1927,F 23,27:3

Rapport, Betsy (Lighting Director)

Tartuffe 1957,O 9,39:1

Rapport, Helena

Passion Flower, The 1920,Ja 14,12:1
Booster, The 1929,O 25,26:2
Berlin 1931,D 31,16:1
$25 an Hour 1933,My 11,14:4
All Good Americans 1933,D 6,29:2
Nowhere Bound 1935,Ja 23,20:2
Doctor Faustus 1937,Ja 9,21:2

Rapport, Paul

Sweet Genevieve 1945,Mr 21,27:3

Rapps and Tapps

Girl From Nantucket, The 1945,N 9,17:2

Raquello, Edward

Smiles 1930,N 19,19:2
New York to Cherbourg 1932,F 20,11:4
Our Wife 1933,Mr 3,13:2
Come Easy 1933,Ag 30,22:5
Wind and the Rain, The 1934,F 2,20:6
Nowhere Bound 1935,Ja 23,20:2
Idiot's Delight 1936,Mr 10,26:7
Idiot's Delight 1936,Mr 25,25:2
Amphitryon 38 1937,Je 24,30:2
There Shall Be No Night 1940,Ap 30,25:2
Rugged Path, The 1945,N 12,17:2

Rasbury, Andy (Miscellaneous)

Cicero 1961,F 9,37:2
Go Show Me a Dragon 1961,O 28,18:1
Living Room, The 1962,N 22,43:5

Rasbury, Andy (Miscellaneous)—Cont
Hamp 1967,Mr 10,32:1

Rasch, Albertina
Vaudeville (Hippodrome) 1924,F 12,20:2
Vaudeville (Hippodrome) 1924,F 19,12:1
Vaudeville (Palace) 1925,D 8,28:6
Vaudeville (Palace) 1932,Ap 4,13:4

Rasch, Albertina (Choreographer)
Three Musketeers, The 1928,Mr 14,28:1
Vaudeville (Palace) 1928,O 9,35:2
Show Girl 1929,Jl 3,19:3
Sons o' Guns 1929,N 27,30:4
Sons o' Guns 1930,Ja 12,VIII,1:1
Three's a Crowd 1930,O 5,IX,4:6
Pajama Lady, The 1930,O 12,VIII,4:1
Prince Charming 1930,O 14,31:1
Three's a Crowd 1930,O 16,28:3
Three's a Crowd 1930,O 26,VIII,1:1
Vaudeville (Palace) 1930,D 8,27:2
Band Wagon, The 1931,Je 4,31:3
Band Wagon, The 1931,Je 14,VIII,1:1
Ziegfeld Follies 1931,Jl 2,30:5
Cat and the Fiddle, The 1931,O 16,26:4
Laugh Parade, The 1931,N 3,31:2
Little Racketeer, The 1932,Ja 19,24:4
Face the Music 1932,F 4,25:4
Face the Music 1932,F 18,24:5
Flying Colors 1932,O 9,IX,1:1
Great Waltz, The 1934,S 24,14:4
Jubilee 1935,O 14,20:1
Jubilee 1935,N 24,IX,8:1
Very Warm for May 1939,N 18,23:2
Boys and Girls Together 1940,O 2,19:2
Lady in the Dark 1941,Ja 24,14:2
Lady in the Dark 1941,F 2,IX,1:1
Lady in the Dark 1941,S 3,26:6
Star and Garter 1942,Je 25,26:2
Lady in the Dark 1943,Mr 1,14:2
Marinka 1945,Jl 19,19:2

Rasch, Albertina (Director)
Sari 1930,Ja 29,27:1
Flying Colors 1932,S 16,24:2
Walk a Little Faster 1932,D 8,24:4

Rasch, Albertina Ballet
Vaudeville (Hippodrome) 1924,Ap 1,18:1
Vaudeville (Hippodrome) 1926,My 11,25:3
Vaudeville (Palace) 1926,Jl 20,17:4

Rasch, Albertina Dancers
Vaudeville (Hippodrome) 1926,My 4,31:2

Rasch, Albertina Girls
Vaudeville (Palace) 1926,Jl 6,19:3
Vaudeville (Palace) 1929,D 2,28:6

Rasch, Albertina Specialty Dancers
Ballyhoo of 1932 1932,S 7,14:2

Rasch, Albertina Troupe
Vaudeville (Hippodrome) 1926,Ap 27,22:3
Vaudeville (Hippodrome) 1926,My 8,29:2
Vaudeville (Palace) 1928,D 17,23:3

Raseac (Miscellaneous)
Happy Ending 1965,N 16,56:1
Day of Absence 1965,N 16,56:1

Rasehouba, Valentina
Savages Under the Skin 1927,Mr 25,25:2

Raselli, Daisy T
Serata D'Inverno; Winter Evening, A
1929,Ap 8,32:5

Rasely, George
Greenwich Village Follies 1922,S 13,18:2
Greenwich Village Follies 1924,S 17,16:1
Devil and Daniel Webster, The 1939,My 19,26:1
Vie Parisienne, La 1941,N 6,20:3
Helen Goes to Troy 1944,Ap 25,17:2

Raset, Val (Choreographer)
Girl From Nantucket, The 1945,N 9,17:2

Rasey, Adelle
Mutilated, The 1966,F 23,42:1
Ballad for a Firing Squad 1968,D 12,64:2

Rash, Philip
South Pacific 1965,Je 3,25:1

Rashid, Dolores
Blood Wedding 1958,Ap 1,35:1
Mandragola 1958,My 29,23:2
Royal Gambit 1959,Mr 5,34:2

Raskin, Saul (Costume Designer)
Shepherd King, The 1955,O 13,36:2

Raskin, Saul (Scenic Designer)
Shepherd King, The 1955,O 13,36:2

Raskin, Thomas
Body Beautiful, The 1958,Ja 24,15:2
Illya Darling 1967,Ap 12,37:1

Raskin (Costume Designer)
Josephus 1933,D 1,22:5

Raskyn, Sam
Johnny 2X4 1942,Mr 17,24:6

Rasley, George
Hollywood Pinafore 1945,Je 1,20:1

Rasoumov, M
Revisor; Inspector General, The 1935,F 18,19:6
Strange Child 1935,F 26,16:1
White Guard, The; Days of the Turbins
1935,Mr 7,27:5
Marriage 1935,Mr 12,24:8
Enemies 1935,Mr 19,24:7

Rasponi, Lanfranco (Count)
Variations of 1940 1940,Ja 29,12:1

Rassaerts, Inge
Nathan der Weise 1966,D 10,45:2
Minna von Barnhelm 1968,N 13,37:1
Schloss, Das 1968,N 20,35:3
Amphitryon 1970,N 18,40:1
Kleinburgerhochzeit, Die 1970,N 25,25:1

Rastede, Hans (Playwright)
Tomorrow's Harvest 1934,D 6,26:5

Rastegar-Nejad, Nasser (Composer)
Persians, The 1970,Ap 16,53:1

Rastelli
Vaudeville (Palace) 1928,N 12,18:7

Rastellis, The
Wonder World 1964,My 18,32:1

Rasumny, Mikhail
Russian Bank 1940,My 25,20:2
Mademoiselle Colombe 1954,Ja 7,26:1

Rasumny, Mikhail (Director)
Simple Woman, The 1937,Mr 29,14:1
'Round the Family Table 1938,O 8,10:3

Ratcliffe, Harry
Rio Rita 1927,F 3,18:3
Miss Gulliver Travels 1931,N 26,36:4

Ratcliffe, Sandy
Dracula Sabbat 1970,O 2,28:2
Coney Island Play 1970,O 31,34:2

Ratcliffe-Graff, Wilton (Mrs)
Shall We Join the Ladies? 1929,Mr 17,30:4

Rateci, Hella
Soul of a Woman, The 1930,F 22,13:1

Ratel, Janine
Logia a la Natividad de Nuestro Senor Jesucristo,
El 1937,D 14,33:4

Rath, E J (Original Author)
Will You Kiss Me? 1920,D 5,VII,1:4
They All Want Something 1926,O 13,20:2

Rath, E J (Playwright)
Nervous Wreck, The 1923,O 10,16:1

Rath, Frederick (Miscellaneous)
Her Tin Soldier 1933,Ap 7,22:6

Rath, Frederick (Original Author)
Her Tin Soldier 1933,Ap 7,22:6

Rath, Frederick (Playwright)
Solitaire 1929,Mr 13,28:3
First Night 1930,N 27,32:3

Rath, Frederick Jr
Ah, Wilderness! 1935,Ag 20,25:1

Rath Brothers
Spice of 1922 1922,Jl 7,12:4
Irving Berlin's New Music Box Revue
1922,O 24,18:1
Gay Paree 1926,N 10,24:2
Vaudeville (Palace) 1928,Ja 3,29:3
Artists and Models 1930,Je 11,33:2
Vaudeville (Palace) 1931,O 26,22:3

Rathay, Maria
Penny Change 1963,O 25,37:1

Rathbone, Basil
Unknown, The 1920,Ag 29,VI,1:4
Czarina, The 1922,F 1,22:1
Swan, The 1923,O 14,VIII,2:4
Swan, The 1923,O 24,15:3
Assumption of Hannele, The 1924,F 16,16:2
Grand Duchess and the Waiter, The
1925,O 14,31:1
Port O' London 1926,F 10,20:2
Captive, The 1926,S 30,23:1
Captive, The 1926,O 10,VIII,1:1
Love Is Like That 1927,Ap 19,24:1
Julius Caesar 1927,Je 7,27:2
Command to Love, The 1927,S 11,VIII,1:3
Command to Love, The 1927,S 21,27:1
Judas 1929,Ja 25,20:4
Kiss of Importance, A 1930,D 2,31:3
Heat Wave 1931,F 18,14:6
Melo 1931,Ap 17,26:6
Devil Passes, The 1932,Ja 5,20:3
Devil Passes, The 1932,Ja 10,VIII,1:1
Romeo and Juliet 1933,N 30,38:5
Romeo and Juliet 1934,D 4,23:2
Romeo and Juliet 1934,D 21,30:3
Romeo and Juliet 1934,D 30,IX,1:1
Astonished Heart, The; Tonight at Eight
1940,Ag 6,15:3
Tonight at 8:30 1940,Ag 11,IX,11:2
Obsession 1946,O 2,39:2
Heiress, The 1947,S 30,22:2
Heiress, The 1947,O 5,II,1:1
Heiress, The 1950,F 9,34:2
Julius Caesar 1950,Je 21,30:1
Gioconda Smile, The 1950,O 9,21:2
Gioconda Smile, The 1950,O 15,II,1:1
Jane 1952,F 2,10:2
Jane 1952,F 10,II,1:1
Sherlock Holmes 1953,O 31,11:2
Sherlock Holmes 1953,N 8,II,1:1
Untitled-Dramatic Reading 1955,O 7,21:1
Midsummer Night's Dream, A 1956,Jl 20,9:5
Hide and Seek 1957,Ap 3,26:1

Rathbone, Basil (Director)
Heiress, The 1950,F 9,34:2

Rathbone, Basil (Playwright)
Judas 1929,Ja 25,20:4

Rathbone, Dounia
Riding Hood Revisited 1961,Ja 4,26:1

Rathbone, George
Passing of the Third Floor Back, The
1937,Ag 3,20:6

Rathbone, Ouida (Playwright)
Sherlock Holmes 1953,O 31,11:2
Sherlock Holmes 1953,N 8,II,1:1

Rathbun, Janet
Decoy, The 1932,Ap 2,13:4
Man Who Reclaimed His Head 1932,S 9,17:3
Pigeons and People 1933,Ja 17,22:3
American Holiday 1936,F 22,13:3
Hero Is Born, A 1937,O 2,18:6

Rathbun, Ruth
Yokel Boy 1939,Jl 7,12:2

Rathbun, William (Director)
Treasure Island 1938,My 15,II,2:3

Rathburn, Elizabeth
Charm 1929,N 29,24:5

Rathke, H W
Marie Antoinette 1921,N 23,16:1

Rathke, Herbert
Lawbreaker, The 1922,F 7,12:1

Ratib, Gamil
Othello 1964,Ag 3,16:6

Ratkay, Martin
Liliom 1921,S 10,12:3

Ratkovic, Zoran
Progress of Bora, The Tailor, The 1968,Je 27,49:2
Ubu Roi 1968,Je 29,20:1

Ratner, Herbert
House of Connelly, The 1931,S 29,22:4
Night Over Taos 1932,Mr 10,25:3
Big Night 1933,Ja 18,16:2
Men in White 1933,S 27,24:2
Waiting for Lefty 1935,F 11,14:5
Till the Day I Die 1935,Mr 27,24:5
Waiting for Lefty 1935,Mr 27,24:5
Paradise Lost 1935,D 10,31:5
Having Wonderful Time 1937,F 22,12:5
Brooklyn Biarritz 1941,F 28,16:2
Native Son 1942,O 24,10:6
Richard III 1943,Mr 27,8:3
Joy to the World 1948,Mr 19,28:2
Julius Caesar 1950,Je 21,30:1
Darkness at Noon 1951,Ja 15,13:4

Ratner, Herbert (Director)
Mummers and Men 1962,Mr 27,41:6

Ratner, Judy
Rose Tattoo, The 1951,F 5,19:2
Crucible, The 1953,Jl 2,20:2

Ratoff, Gregory
Castles in the Air 1926,S 7,19:2
Tenth Avenue 1927,Ag 16,31:1
Cafe de Danse 1929,Ja 16,22:2
Out of a Blue Sky 1930,F 10,20:6
Wonder Boy 1931,O 24,20:1

Ratoff, Gregory (Director)
Cafe de Danse 1929,Ja 16,22:2
Nina 1951,D 6,44:3
Fifth Season, The 1953,Ja 24,13:2
Black-Eyed Susan 1954,D 24,7:5

Ratoff, M
Revue Russe, The 1922,O 6,28:1

Ratousheff, Andrew
Talking to You 1942,Ag 18,17:1
Skin of Our Teeth, The 1942,N 19,29:5

Ratschof, Frank J
Fifty-Fifty 1937,D 5,II,3:4

Rattigan, Terence (Playwright)
First Episode 1934,S 18,18:1
French Without Tears 1937,S 26,II,4:3
French Without Tears 1937,S 29,19:1
After the Dance 1939,Jl 16,IX,2:3
Grey Farm 1940,My 4,12:7
Flare Path 1942,Ag 23,VII,1:6
Flare Path 1942,D 24,20:2
While the Sun Shines 1944,S 20,21:3
While the Sun Shines 1944,S 24,II,1:1
Love in Idleness 1944,D 22,13:2
Love in Idleness 1945,Ja 7,II,2:3
O Mistress Mine 1946,Ja 24,25:2
O Mistress Mine 1946,F 3,II,1:1
O Mistress Mine 1946,S 1,II,1:1
Winslow Boy, The 1947,O 30,32:2
Winslow Boy, The 1947,N 9,II,1:1
Harlequinade 1948,O 10,II,3:7
Browning Version, The 1948,O 10,II,3:7
Adventure Story 1949,Mr 19,11:2
Browning Version, The 1949,O 13,32:2
Harlequinade 1949,O 13,32:2
Harlequinade 1949,O 23,II,1:1
Browning Version, The 1949,O 23,II,1:1
Who Is Sylvia? 1950,O 25,45:7
Deep Blue Sea, The 1952,Mr 16,II,3:7
Deep Blue Sea, The 1952,N 6,38:3
Deep Blue Sea, The 1952,D 7,II,7:2
Deep Blue Sea, The 1952,D 14,II,3:1
Deep Blue Sea, The 1953,Ap 4,8:6
Sleeping Prince, The 1953,S 29,25:1

Rattigan, Terence (Playwright)—Cont
Sleeping Prince, The 1953,N 6,24:4
Sleeping Prince, The 1953,D 20,II,4:2
Separate Tables 1954,S 23,42:1
Separate Tables 1954,O 24,II,3:3
Separate Tables 1955,My 22,II,1:1
Separate Tables 1956,O 26,33:1
Sleeping Prince, The 1956,N 2,31:1
Separate Tables 1956,N 4,II,1:1
Separate Tables 1957,S 15,II,1:1
Browning Version, The 1958,Mr 7,17:2
Variations on a Theme 1958,My 9,16:5
Harlequinade 1959,F 14,15:1
Ross; Lawrence d'Arabie 1961,O 8,II,3:4
Ross 1961,D 27,20:2
Ross 1962,Ja 7,II,1:1
Man and Boy 1963,S 5,28:1
Man and Boy 1963,N 13,34:1
Man and Boy 1963,D 1,II,1:1
Girl Who Came to Supper, The 1963,D 9,49:1
Bequest to the Nation, A 1970,S 25,36:1
Rau, James
Tom Paine 1969,Mr 30,71:2
Rau, Santha Rama (Playwright)
Passage to India, A 1960,Ap 21,23:1
Passage to India, A 1962,F 1,23:1
Passage to India, A 1962,F 11,II,1:1
Rauber, Richard
Sea Shells 1935,Jl 16,24:2
Murder in the Old Red Barn, The 1936,F 3,20:4
Richard II 1937,S 16,28:2
Man From Cairo, The 1938,My 5,26:5
Raucci, Aida
Anthony on Overtime 1961,O 21,13:2
Rauch, Maurice (Composer)
Jacques Bergson 1936,O 31,24:6
Outlaw, The 1937,O 6,28:1
In A Jewish Grocery 1939,O 2,15:2
Hello Charlie 1965,O 25,47:2
Rauch, Maurice (Musical Director)
We Live and Laugh 1936,My 9,10:3
Rauch, Morris (Composer)
God's Thieves 1930,O 27,17:4
Rauch, Victoria
Route 1 1964,N 18,52:3
Raucher, Gary
Trumpets and Drums 1969,O 13,52:1
Macbeth 1969,D 23,25:1
Minnie's Boys 1970,Mr 27,27:1
Raucher, Herman (Playwright)
Harold 1962,N 30,27:1
Rauh, Al
Hobo 1931,F 12,24:4
Brass Ankle 1931,Ap 24,26:4
Hot Money 1931,N 9,22:2
Rauh, Ida
Power of Darkness, The 1920,Ja 22,22:1
Rauh, Stanley (Playwright)
Earl Carroll's Vanities 1926,Ag 25,19:4
Raushenbush, Stephen (Playwright)
Bugles at Noon 1936,Jl 18,18:4
Rautenberg, Alice
Bruder Straubinger 1921,N 16,22:3
Rautenberg, Eugene (Musical Director)
Beggar Student, The 1921,Ja 8,9:3
Rautnen, Victor
Betrothal, The 1959,F 16,52:2
Ravaioli, Adele
Piacere Del'Onesta, Il; Happiness of Probity, The 1930,N 10,16:4
Cena Delle Beffe, La; Jest, The 1930,N 24,26:4
Cardinale, Il; Cardinal, The 1931,Ja 12,24:2
Delitto e Castigo; Crime and Punishment 1931,Ja 26,20:5
Sansone; Samson 1931,F 9,25:1
Civil Death, The 1932,Ja 25,20:3
Ravaioli, Luigi
Barbara 1929,N 18,24:5
Ravel, Anne
Saint Wench 1933,Ja 3,19:3
Ravel, Billy
Sketch Book 1935,Je 5,22:2
Ravel, Charles
Good Times 1920,Ag 10,10:1
Ravel (Composer)
Du Barry 1932,My 8,VIII,1:6
Ravell, Paul
Green Grow the Lilacs 1931,Ja 27,21:2
Raven, Elsa
Quick Years, The 1953,N 26,51:2
Legend of Lizzie, The 1959,F 10,39:1
Paradise Island 1961,Je 24,11:1
In the Bar of a Tokyo Hotel 1969,My 12,54:1
Raven, Marc
Edge of the Sword, The 1949,N 10,40:3
Building 222 1950,F 3,28:2
Tread the Green Grass 1950,Ap 21,19:4
Gods of the Mountain, The 1950,My 25,36:2
Raven, Wendy
Girl From Samos, The 1954,N 24,17:1
Ravenell, Henrietta
This Is New York 1930,N 29,21:1
Ravenscroft, Edward (Playwright)
Anatomist, The 1957,F 27,21:5

Ravenski, Boris (Director)
Power of Darkness, The 1962,Je 21,26:1
Raveson, Sherman (Scenic Designer)
If Booth Had Missed 1931,My 14,27:1
Ravet, Louis
Aventuriere, L' 1922,N 14,16:1
Duel, The 1922,N 16,22:2
Megere Apprivoisee, La 1922,N 20,21:2
Misanthrope, Le 1922,N 22,18:2
Tartuffe 1922,N 23,21:3
Maitresse de Roi 1926,D 1,24:1
Dame aux Camelias, La 1926,D 7,24:2
Misanthrope, Le 1926,D 10,31:2
Aventuriere, L' 1926,D 17,27:3
Ravette, Gene
Frankie and Johnny 1930,S 26,16:5
Ravine, Gabrielle
Mountebank, The 1923,My 8,22:2
Ravinett, Theodore
Story Theater Repertory; Gimpel the Food 1970,O 21,40:1
Story Theater Repertory; Saint Julian the Hospitaler 1970,O 21,40:1
Revenger's Tragedy, The 1970,D 2,58:1
Ravold, John
Deluge, The 1922,Ja 28,14:2
New Brooms 1924,N 18,23:5
Enchanted April, The 1925,Ag 25,12:3
Downstream 1926,Ja 12,28:1
Mama Loves Papa 1926,F 23,26:2
Money From Home 1927,Mr 1,30:2
Trial of Mary Dugan, The 1927,S 20,33:1
Distant Drums 1932,Ja 19,24:3
Ghosts 1933,My 24,24:5
American, Very Early 1934,Ja 31,21:2
All Editions 1936,D 23,17:2
Sun Kissed 1937,Mr 11,20:2
Virginia 1937,S 3,13:2
Night Before Christmas, The 1941,Ap 11,25:2
Village Green 1941,S 4,24:4
Our Town 1944,Ja 11,24:5
Thank You Svoboda 1944,Mr 2,13:2
Rawitser, Rae
Bursting the Barriers 1930,My 7,25:1
Rawley, Joseph
Creoles 1927,S 23,33:3
Rawlings, Judy
Oklahoma! 1951,My 30,15:2
Oklahoma! 1953,S 1,19:1
Rawlings, Lester
Cretan Woman, The 1954,My 21,17:2
Macbeth 1955,O 20,42:2
Reckoning, The 1969,S 14,II,1:1
Rawlings, Margaret
Venetian, The 1931,Mr 15,IX,4:3
Salome 1931,Je 21,VIII,1:4
Venetian, The 1931,O 11,VIII,4:5
Venetian, The 1931,N 2,26:1
This Side Idolatry 1933,N 5,IX,1:3
Napoleon 1934,S 4,23:2
Greeks Had a Word for It, The 1934,N 23,22:2
Roulette 1935,Je 16,X,1:1
Parnell 1935,N 12,24:2
Parnell 1936,Ap 24,19:5
Parnell 1936,My 24,IX,1:7
Parnell 1936,My 31,X,1:5
Antony and Cleopatra 1936,N 1,X,3:7
Parnell 1936,N 8,X,3:4
Parnell 1936,N 22,XI,1:3
Macbeth 1937,Mr 7,XI,2:1
Black Limelight 1937,My 2,XI,2:1
Flashing Stream, The 1938,S 2,21:4
Flashing Stream, The 1938,S 18,X,1:4
Flashing Stream, The 1939,Ap 11,19:2
House in the Square 1940,Ap 14,IX,1:6
Sappho 1961,Ag 23,28:5
Rawlings, Marjorie Kinnan (Original Author)
Yearling, The 1965,D 11,25:1
Rawlings, Martha
Sons o' Fun 1941,D 2,28:2
Rawlings, Ray
Park Avenue, Ltd 1932,Mr 4,17:1
Jefferson Davis 1936,F 19,17:2
Rawlings, Robert
Henry VIII 1946,N 7,42:2
Androcles and the Lion 1946,D 20,29:2
Yellow Jack 1947,F 28,26:2
Alice in Wonderland 1947,Ap 7,19:2
Rawlins, Lester
Othello 1955,S 8,27:2
Henry IV, Part I 1955,S 22,34:2
King Lear 1956,Ja 13,17:1
Romeo and Juliet 1956,F 24,20:4
Lovers 1956,My 11,23:1
Hamlet 1956,O 29,34:1
Richard III 1957,N 26,41:1
Endgame 1958,Ja 29,32:4
Endgame 1958,F 16,II,1:1
Quare Fellow, The 1958,N 28,34:1
Camino Real 1960,My 17,42:2
Camino Real 1960,My 29,II,1:1
Hedda Gabler 1960,N 10,61:1
Man for All Seasons, A 1961,N 23,51:1

Rawlins, Lester—Cont
King Lear 1963,Je 10,37:1
Golden Age, The 1963,N 19,49:2
Benito Cereno 1964,N 2,62:2
Child Buyer, The 1964,D 22,35:1
Winterset 1966,F 10,32:2
In the Bar of a Tokyo Hotel 1969,My 12,54:1
Reckoning, The 1969,S 5,28:1
Rawlins, W H
Afgar 1920,N 9,13:2
Rawlinson, A R (Playwright)
Magnolia Street 1934,Mr 9,22:6
Magnolia Street 1934,Ap 1,X,1:7
Rawlinson, Herbert
City Haul 1929,D 31,14:4
She Means Business 1931,Ja 27,21:2
Right of Happiness 1931,Ap 3,34:2
Modern Virgin, A 1931,My 21,33:4
When Ladies Meet 1932,O 7,19:1
Baby Pompadour 1934,D 28,24:2
Rawls, Berrell (Miscellaneous)
Prima Donna 1929,D 12,36:4
Rawls, Eugenia
Children's Hour, The 1934,N 21,23:2
To Quito and Back 1937,O 7,30:4
Journeyman 1938,Ja 31,14:2
As You Like It; Midsummer Night's Dream, A; Comedy of Errors, The; Taming of the Shrew, The 1939,My 9,28:4
As You Like It 1939,My 9,28:4
Man Who Had All the Luck, The 1944,N 24,18:5
Strange Fruit 1945,N 30,18:6
Great Sebastians, The 1956,Ja 5,27:1
Poker Session, The 1967,S 20,42:2
Rawls, James
Take It As It Comes 1944,F 11,17:2
Rawls, R Birrell
Between Two Worlds 1934,O 26,24:2
Crime Marches on 1935,O 24,19:1
Black Limelight 1936,N 10,31:1
Rawson, Graham (Playwright)
Faust 1928,O 9,34:1
Rudolph of Austria 1932,Ap 10,VIII,3:7
Rawson, Graham (Translator)
Race With the Shadow, The 1924,Ja 21,20:5
Weibsteufel, Der 1927,My 8,VII,1:5
Road to Damascus, The; Nach Damaskus 1937,My 30,X,2:5
Queen Christina 1937,N 29,18:1
Rawson, Richard
Great Gatsby, The 1926,F 3,22:1
Legend of Leonora, The 1927,Mr 30,22:4
Rawson, Ronald (Producer)
Farewell, Farewell Eugene 1960,S 28,35:1
Rawson, Ruth (Director)
Hour Glass, The 1955,O 17,33:1
Comic Strip 1958,My 15,26:2
Kiss Mama 1964,O 2,30:1
Rawson, Tristan
Mrs Fischer's War 1931,Ag 9,VIII,1:3
Rawson, Tristan (Playwright)
Faust 1928,O 9,34:1
Rawson, Tristan (Translator)
Race With the Shadow, The 1924,Ja 21,20:5
Weibsteufel, Der 1927,My 8,VII,1:5
Rawsthorne, Alan (Composer)
Practical Cats 1954,Ag 27,11:5
Ray, Alan
You'll See Stars 1943,Ja 1,26:6
Ray, Andrew
Flowering Cherry 1959,O 22,46:1
Taste of Honey, A 1960,O 5,46:1
Taste of Honey, A 1960,N 6,II,1:1
Oh Dad, Poor Dad, Mamma's Hung You in the Closet and I'm Feelin' So Sad 1961,Jl 6,19:2
Ray, Anje (Composer)
Believers, The 1968,My 10,57:4
Ray, Anje (Lyricist)
Believers, The 1968,My 10,57:4
Ray, Anna
Lingering Past, The 1932,Je 30,26:5
Ray, Anthony
Dark at the Top of the Stairs, The 1957,D 6,38:1
Before Breakfast 1958,Mr 12,36:1
Moonbirds 1959,O 10,13:1
Philoktetes 1961,Ap 25,41:1
Ray, Arthur
Salome 1923,My 8,22:2
Chip Woman's Fortune, The 1923,My 8,22:2
Comedy of Errors, The 1923,My 16,22:5
Meek Mose 1928,F 7,30:1
Ray, Charles
Within the Law 1928,Mr 6,20:1
Ray, Charlotte
Beggar's Opera, The 1957,Mr 14,35:1
Ray, Ellen
Bells Are Ringing 1956,N 29,43:4
Bells Are Ringing 1956,N 30,18:2
Ray, Ellen (Choreographer)
Can-Can 1962,My 17,32:2
By Jupiter 1967,Ja 20,28:2
Ray, Ellis and La Rue
Vaudeville (Palace) 1929,D 9,33:2

ay, Frank
Steel 1931,N 19,26:5
Broadway Boy 1932,My 4,23:5
Field of Ermine 1935,F 9,10:4
ay, Helen
Strangers at Home 1934,S 15,20:5
Brittle Heaven 1934,N 14,22:5
Beggarman, Thief 1935,Jl 16,24:1
Fields Beyond, The 1936,Mr 7,11:2
Stage Door 1936,O 23,26:3
My Sister Eileen 1940,D 27,23:2
Signature 1945,F 15,25:2
State of the Union 1945,N 15,25:2
Prescott Proposals, The 1953,D 17,53:1
In the Jungle of Cities 1960,D 21,39:1
ay, Ina
Melody 1933,F 15,17:4
Ziegfeld Follies 1934,Ja 5,24:3
ay, James
Angela 1928,D 4,28:2
King and the Duke, The 1955,Je 2,25:2
Venice Preserv'd 1955,D 13,54:4
Comedian, The 1956,O 18,36:4
Henry V 1960,Je 30,23:1
Wall, The 1960,O 12,44:4
As You Like It 1961,Je 17,13:2
Macbeth 1961,Je 19,31:1
Creditors 1962,Ja 26,19:1
Henry IV, Part I 1962,Je 18,20:4
Richard II 1962,Je 18,20:2
Henry IV, Part I 1962,Je 24,II,1:1
Collection, The 1962,N 27,44:1
King Lear 1963,Je 10,37:1
Henry V 1963,Je 14,37:1
Caesar and Cleopatra 1963,Ag 1,18:2
Dylan 1964,Ja 20,18:1
Tragical Historie of Doctor Faustus, The
   1964,O 6,34:2
Love's Labour's Lost 1965,Je 16,46:1
Untitled-Poetry Reading 1967,Jl 18,29:1
Henry IV, Part I 1968,Je 30,54:7
Henry IV, Part II 1968,Jl 2,33:1
Henry IV, Part II 1968,Jl 14,II,1:1
Basement, The 1968,O 16,40:1
Disintegration of James Cherry, The
   1970,Ja 30,33:3
Amphitryon 1970,My 29,13:1
Sensations 1970,O 26,48:2
ay, Jimmy
Hello, Yourself 1928,O 31,28:2
Vanderbilt Revue, The 1930,O 26,VIII,3:5
Vanderbilt Revue, The 1930,N 6,22:6
Ray, Joey
Earl Carroll's Vanities 1928,Ag 7,25:2
Second Little Show, The 1930,S 3,36:1
Right This Way 1938,Ja 6,22:3
Ray, John
Blue Bandanna, The 1924,Je 24,18:4
Journey by Night, A 1935,Ap 17,26:3
Ray, Kathryn
Earl Carroll's Vanities 1925,Jl 7,24:1
Night in Paris, A 1926,Jl 27,15:4
Ray, Leslie
Trumpets and Drums 1969,O 13,52:1
Ray, Madeline
Pelican, The 1929,N 14,25:1
Drunkard, The; Fallen Saved, The 1929,D 31,14:6
Ray, Martha
Calling All Stars 1934,D 14,28:2
Ray, Mary Ellen
All's Well That Ends Well 1970,Je 16,53:1
Devil's Disciple, The 1970,Je 30,48:1
Ray, Mavis
Carousel 1949,Ja 26,28:2
Carousel 1954,Je 3,32:2
Ray, Mavis (Choreographer)
Riding Hood Revisited 1961,Ja 4,26:1
Ray, Mavis (Miscellaneous)
Oklahoma! 1963,My 16,40:1
Ray, Michel
Journey With Strangers, A 1958,N 27,53:1
Ray, Naomi
Earl Carroll's Vanities 1930,Jl 2,28:3
Murder at the Vanities 1933,S 13,22:4
Ray, Nicholas (Director)
Beggar's Holiday 1946,D 27,13:3
Ray, Nik
Young Go First, The 1935,My 29,16:2
Ray, Rene
Inspector Calls, An 1947,O 22,38:2
Ray, Robert
Cranmer of Canterbury 1959,D 4,36:1
Ray, Ruth
From Here to There; Slow Dusk 1958,Ap 24,37:3
Patience 1967,O 13,32:1
Iolanthe 1967,O 18,40:1
Mikado, The 1967,O 25,42:2
Gondoliers, The 1967,O 29,83:1
H M S Pinafore 1967,N 1,40:1
Ray, Sonnie
This Year of Grace 1928,N 8,27:1
Ray (Producer)
Wild Waves 1932,Ja 24,VIII,3:3

Ray Bloch's Orchestra
Mermaid's Holiday 1961,Jl 1,8:1
Ray-James, Jim
Marco Millions 1964,F 21,33:1
Rayburn, Gene
Aqua Carnival 1962,Je 29,15:1
Raycelle, Ilya
Parisiana 1928,F 10,26:3
Raycelle, Maria
Parisiana 1928,F 10,26:3
Rayder, Sidney
Electra 1958,My 10,17:7
Raydi, Maria
Fledermaus, Die 1929,Jl 14,IX,2:1
Raye, Carol
Fun and Games 1941,Ag 31,IX,1:4
Raye, Martha
Vaudeville (Hollywood) 1932,Ap 19,25:5
Vaudeville (Loew's State) 1932,Jl 18,9:7
Hold On to Your Hats 1940,Jl 17,25:3
Hold On to Your Hats 1940,S 12,30:3
Hold On to Your Hats 1940,S 29,IX,1:1
Hello, Dolly! 1967,Mr 2,30:4
Raye, Mary
Crazy With the Heat 1941,Ja 31,15:2
Take a Bow 1944,Je 16,15:3
Raye, Sally
Revolt of the Beavers, The 1937,My 21,19:2
Rayes, Billy
Sketch Book 1935,Je 5,22:2
Scandals 1939,Ag 29,17:2
Rayevskaya, Yevgenia
Ivanoff 1923,N 27,23:2
Enemy of the People, An 1923,D 4,25:1
Enough Stupidity in Every Wise Man
   1923,D 6,23:1
Uncle Vanya 1924,Ja 29,16:2
Rayevsky, Iosit (Director)
Kremlin Chimes 1965,F 25,23:1
Rayfiel, David (Playwright)
PS 193 1962,O 31,33:1
Nathan Weinstein, Mystic, Connecticut
   1966,F 26,15:2
Rayfield, Florence
Red Pepper 1922,My 30,8:3
Rayman, Sylvia (Playwright)
Women of Twilight 1952,Mr 4,22:2
Raymo, Albert
Bell for Adano, A 1944,D 7,21:2
Raymon, Allen (Miscellaneous)
Fall 1957,N 22,19:1
Raymond, Al
East of Broadway 1932,Ja 27,19:3
Strip Girl 1935,O 21,22:6
Raymond, Alan
Romantic Mr Dickens 1940,D 3,33:2
Raymond, Allen
Blossom Time 1938,D 27,12:2
Raymond, Babette
Silks and Satins 1920,Jl 16,19:1
Raymond, Billy
Vaudeville (Palace) 1930,Mr 24,24:5
Raymond, Cyril
Mandarin, The 1920,N 10,18:2
Red Blinds 1926,O 1,27:1
Josef Suss 1930,Ja 21,28:5
There's Always Juliet 1932,F 16,24:2
Shining Hour, The 1934,F 14,22:6
French Without Tears 1937,S 26,II,4:3
French Without Tears 1937,S 29,19:1
Raymond, Cyril (Director)
Love in the Tropics 1927,O 19,24:3
Raymond, Dean
Potters, The 1923,D 10,21:4
Square Crooks 1926,Mr 2,23:2
Trial of Mary Dugan, The 1927,S 20,33:1
Great Scott! 1929,S 3,25:1
Babes in Toyland 1929,D 24,15:3
This One Man 1930,O 22,32:3
Raymond, Dorothy
Eve's Leaves 1925,Mr 27,22:2
Jazz Singer, The 1925,S 15,29:2
Wild Duck, The 1928,F 19,VIII,2:1
Broken Chain, The 1929,F 21,30:4
Woman of Destiny, A 1936,Mr 3,25:2
Big Blow 1938,O 3,11:2
Uncle Willie 1956,D 21,17:1
Walk in Dark Places, A 1966,Ja 28,21:1
Rose Tattoo, The 1966,O 21,36:2
Raymond, Ellen (Director)
Peter Ibbetson 1926,Mr 26,24:7
Raymond, Estelle
Having Wonderful Time 1937,F 22,12:5
It's About Time 1942,Mr 31,28:3
Raymond, F
Murder at the Vanities 1933,S 13,22:4
Raymond, Frank
Macbeth 1928,N 20,28:3
Raymond, Frederick
Little Miss Charity 1920,S 3,6:3
Nobody's Money 1921,Ag 18,9:3
Across the Street 1924,Mr 25,24:1
Quicksand 1928,F 14,26:3

Raymond, Frederick—Cont
Mima 1928,D 13,24:2
Strip Girl 1935,O 21,22:6
Raymond, Gene (Raymond Guion)
Shadow of My Enemy, A 1957,D 12,35:4
Raymond, George
Sweet Adeline 1929,S 4,33:1
Raymond, Guy
Hook'n Ladder 1952,Ap 30,31:2
Pipe Dream 1955,D 1,44:1
Raymond, Helen
Stepping Sisters 1930,Ap 23,24:2
Peacock 1932,O 12,27:1
Du Barry 1932,N 23,15:2
It Happened Tomorrow 1933,My 6,11:5
Shady Lady 1933,Jl 6,26:3
False Dreams, Farewell 1934,Ja 16,18:3
Anything Goes 1934,N 22,26:1
Private Affair, A 1936,My 15,28:7
Salute to Spring 1937,Jl 14,16:2
Empress of Destiny 1938,Mr 10,16:2
One Touch of Venus 1943,O 8,14:1
Girl From Nantucket, The 1945,N 9,17:2
Show Boat 1956,Je 22,16:1
Show Boat 1957,Je 28,30:2
Music Man, The 1957,D 20,31:1
Music Man, The 1958,S 28,II,1:1
Raymond, Howard
Good Boy 1928,S 6,23:2
Raymond, Jack
Dr David's Dad 1924,Ag 14,10:3
Raymond, Janet
Streets of New York, The 1963,O 30,47:1
Raymond, Janet (Miscellaneous)
Saving Grace, The 1963,Ap 19,28:1
Raymond, Janice (Miscellaneous)
Darker Flower, A 1963,Mr 11,7:2
Raymond, Joseph
Shannons of Broadway, The 1927,S 27,30:4
Raymond, Ken
E-MC2 1948,Je 16,36:2
Raymond, Louis
Homme Qui Assassina, L' 1924,N 11,20:1
Procureur Hallers, Le 1924,N 13,18:1
Homme et Ses Fantomes, L' 1924,N 14,16:1
Bourgeois Gentilhomme, Le 1924,N 20,21:2
Taming of the Shrew, The 1924,N 25,27:3
Raymond, Marjorie
Bitter Sweet 1929,N 6,30:2
Raymond, Nicky
Janie 1942,S 11,24:2
Raymond, Peter
Meanest Man in the World, The 1920,O 13,18:2
Myrtie 1924,F 5,21:2
Across the Street 1924,Mr 25,24:1
Raymond, Ray
Blue Eyes 1921,F 22,11:2
Letty Pepper 1922,Ap 11,22:2
When You Smile 1925,O 6,31:2
Raymond, Robin
See My Lawyer 1939,S 28,29:1
Raymond, Roy
Magdalena 1948,S 21,31:2
Raymond, Royal
Brother Cain 1941,S 13,21:5
O'Daniel 1947,F 25,32:2
Raymond, Ruth
Tell Me More 1925,Ap 14,27:3
Dagger, The 1925,S 10,28:1
Raymond, Sid
Something About a Soldier 1962,Ja 5,36:2
Golden Rainbow 1968,F 5,27:1
Raymond, William
Cat-Bird, The 1920,F 17,18:1
Merchant of Venice, The 1921,Ap 2,14:2
Aglavaine and Selysette 1922,Ja 4,11:1
Master Builder, The 1925,N 11,27:1
Raymond-Girard
Homme Qui Assassina, L' 1924,N 11,20:1
Procureur Hallers, Le 1924,N 13,18:1
Homme et Ses Fantomes, L' 1924,N 14,16:1
Merchant of Venice, The 1924,N 18,23:2
Bourgeois Gentilhomme, Le 1924,N 20,21:2
Taming of the Shrew, The 1924,N 25,27:3
Raymonde, Ruth
Havoc 1924,S 2,22:2
Gentlemen Prefer Blondes 1926,S 29,23:1
Raynal, Paul (Original Author)
Unknown Warrior, The 1928,Mr 4,IX,4:7
Raynal, Paul (Playwright)
Unknown Warrior, The 1928,O 30,26:6
Tombeau Sous l'Arc de Triomphe
   1929,Je 16,VIII,2:3
Francerie 1933,Ap 30,IX,2:3
Napoleon Unique 1936,N 13,27:3
Napoleon Unique 1936,N 29,XII,2:4
Raynaud, Herb (Costume Designer)
Hamlet 1954,Ap 24,15:2
Raynaud, Herb (Lighting Director)
Hamlet 1954,Ap 24,15:2
Raynaud, Herb (Scenic Designer)
Hamlet 1954,Ap 24,15:2
Rayner, John
Othello 1964,Jl 15,29:1

Rayner, John—Cont
Othello 1964,O 13,48:1
Rayner, Minnie
Symphony in Two Flats 1930,S 17,30:4
Rayner, Suki
Pink Elephant, The 1953,Ap 23,37:2
Rayner, Sydney
Street Scene 1947,Ja 10,17:2
Reynolds, Robert (Playwright)
Ugly Runts, The 1935,Je 11,24:4
Raynor, Grace
Dear Charles 1954,S 16,37:2
Debut 1956,F 23,32:1
Wake Up, Darling 1956,My 3,34:2
Raynor, Tom
Little Clay Cart, The 1953,Jl 1,25:1
Dear Charles 1954,S 16,37:2
Raynore, Katherine
Street Wolf, The 1929,Ja 1,61:1
War 1929,S 19,37:3
Rayon, Pierre
Simply Heavenly 1957,My 22,28:2
Rayson-Cousens, E
Voice From the Minaret, The 1922,Ja 31,11:2
Fedora 1922,F 11,18:1
Raysor, Roberta
Kongi's Harvest 1968,Ap 15,49:1
Raysor, Roberta (Scenic Designer)
In the Wine Time 1968,D 22,II,7:1
Raywin, Hal (Director)
Half-Past Wednesday 1962,Ap 7,16:2
Transgressor Rides Again, The 1969,My 21,42:1
Raywin, Hal (Producer)
Half-Past Wednesday 1962,Ap 7,16:2
Raz, Rivka
My Fair Lady 1964,F 20,24:4
Razaf, Andy (Composer)
Lew Leslie's Blackbirds of 1930 1930,O 23,34:5
Razaf, Andy (Lyricist)
Keep Shufflin' 1928,F 28,18:3
Hot Chocolates 1929,Je 21,17:4
Lew Leslie's Blackbirds of 1930 1930,O 23,34:5
Rea, Alec (Producer)
Dark Horizon 1934,Ap 21,13:3
Rea, Oliver (Miscellaneous)
Medea 1949,My 3,31:2
Rea, Oliver (Producer)
Medea 1947,O 21,27:2
Crime and Punishment 1947,D 23,29:3
Member of the Wedding, The 1950,Ja 6,26:6
Juno 1959,Mr 10,41:1
Rea, Peggy
Streetcar Named Desire, A 1950,My 24,36:1
Out of This World 1950,D 22,17:3
Rea, William J
Oliver Cromwell 1923,F 25,VII,1:7
Read, Charlotte
You and I 1925,O 20,29:1
Read, David
Planctus Mariae 1968,Ap 29,49:1
Read, Edward C K (Lyricist)
Assorted Nuts 1940,Ap 7,I,44:6
Read, John B (Lighting Director)
Dance of Death, The 1967,O 20,50:1
Flea in Her Ear, A 1967,O 30,59:1
Read, Mary (Choreographer)
Provincetown Follies, The 1935,N 4,24:3
Read, Sue
Sunday Nights at Nine 1933,N 13,20:7
Reade, Gail
Old Maid, The 1935,Ja 8,26:1
Reade, Gilbert
Antony and Cleopatra 1947,N 27,49:2
Reade, Janet
Ballyhoo 1930,D 23,24:1
Vaudeville (Palace) 1931,N 2,26:2
Reade, Leslie (Playwright)
Shatter'd Lamp, The 1934,Mr 22,26:3
Stranger, The 1945,F 13,21:2
Stranger, The 1945,F 18,II,1:2
Reade, Maida
Dr David's Dad 1924,Ag 14,10:3
Made for Each Other 1924,S 30,27:2
Strawberry Blonde, The 1927,F 8,20:3
Oh, Professor 1930,My 2,19:6
That's Gratitude 1930,S 12,28:1
That's Gratitude 1930,S 21,IX,1:1
That's Gratitude 1932,Je 17,24:3
Best People, The 1933,Mr 16,21:5
Tommy 1933,Ag 8,22:5
Dream Child 1934,Jl 31,20:2
Dream Child 1934,S 28,26:2
Forty-Four Below 1935,Jl 23,24:3
Stick-in-the-Mud 1935,D 2,18:2
Behind the Red Lights 1937,Ja 14,17:4
Dance Night 1938,O 15,20:5
Merchant of Yonkers, The 1938,D 29,14:2
Day in the Sun 1939,My 17,29:2
Royal Family, The 1940,Ag 13,15:3
Village Green 1941,S 4,24:4
Me and Harry 1942,Ap 3,24:6
Arsenic and Old Lace 1944,Jl 3,7:3
For Love or Money 1947,N 5,36:2

Reade, Walter (Producer)
Boy Meets Girl 1937,Jl 6,23:1
Excursion 1937,Jl 27,24:3
Passing of the Third Floor Back, The
1937,Ag 3,20:6
Reader, Ann
Vagabond, The 1923,D 28,13:4
Shooting Shadows 1924,Je 27,16:5
Sex 1926,Ap 27,22:4
57 Bowery 1928,Ja 27,14:3
Reader, Nina
Qudrille 1954,N 4,39:2
Pink String and Sealing Wax 1957,S 6,13:1
Genius and the Goddess, The 1957,D 11,41:1
Reader, Ralph
June Days 1925,Ag 7,12:5
Reader, Ralph (Choreographer)
Yours Truly 1927,Ja 26,16:5
Cherry Blossoms 1927,Mr 29,22:3
Artists and Models 1927,N 16,28:2
Take the Air 1927,N 23,28:2
Sunny Days 1928,F 9,29:1
Greenwich Village Follies 1928,Ap 10,32:2
Reader, Ralph (Miscellaneous)
Night in Spain, A 1927,My 4,28:2
Readick, Bob
George Washington Slept Here 1940,O 19,20:3
All in Favor 1942,Ja 21,20:6
Readick, Dorothy
Chalk Dust 1936,Mr 5,24:5
Readick, Frank
Nemesis 1921,Ap 5,24:3
Solid Ivory 1925,N 17,29:3
Readick, Robert
Biggest Thief in Town 1949,Mr 31,31:2
In the Penal Colony 1962,My 4,27:2
Reading, Bertice
Jazz Train 1955,Ap 28,26:4
Requiem for a Nun 1959,Ja 31,13:2
Requiem for a Nun 1959,F 8,II,1:1
Valmouth 1960,O 7,29:1
Reading, Edwin
Mouthpiece, The 1929,Je 16,VIII,2:1
Readinger, Jeanne
Streets of Paris, The 1939,Je 20,25:2
Readinger, Jo
Streets of Paris, The 1939,Je 20,25:2
Readis, Hattie King (Composer)
Tin Top Valley 1947,Mr 1,11:2
Reagan, Marie
Night Boat, The 1920,F 3,18:1
Reais, Grace
Handy Man, The 1925,Mr 10,19:2
Real, Marthe
Maitresse de Roi 1926,D 1,24:1
Reale, Joseph
In the Matter of J Robert Oppenheimer
1968,Je 7,31:1
Reals, Grace
When We Are Young 1920,N 23,11:1
Mountain Man, The 1921,D 13,24:2
Reals, Nancy (Miscellaneous)
Best of Burlesque 1957,S 30,27:2
Reamer, Robert
Man Who Killed Lincoln, The 1940,Ja 18,26:4
Reams, Lee Roy
Sweet Charity 1966,Ja 31,22:1
Oklahoma! 1969,Je 24,37:1
Applause 1970,Mr 31,35:1
Reano, Robert
Good Times 1920,Ag 10,10:1
Reardon, Dennis J (Playwright)
Happiness Cage, The 1970,O 5,56:4
Happiness Cage, The 1970,O 11,II,1:1
Reardon, Edward (Sgt)
Winged Victory 1943,N 22,24:1
Reardon, Frank (Lyricist)
Rumple 1957,N 7,42:2
Dream of Swallows, A 1964,Ap 15,46:1
Reardon, Greg
Beaux' Stratagem, The 1957,Jl 9,25:4
Listen to the Quiet 1958,O 28,40:2
Reardon, Greg (Producer)
Anniversary, The 1961,Ap 21,26:2
Wedding, The 1961,Ap 21,26:2
On the High Road 1961,Ap 21,26:2
When We Dead Awaken 1966,Ap 19,37:2
Reardon, John
Saint of Bleecker Street, The 1954,D 28,21:1
Saint of Bleecker Street, The 1954,D 28,21:1
New Faces of 1956 1956,Je 15,32:1
Song of Norway 1959,Je 26,16:2
Do Re Mi 1960,D 27,23:2
Do Re Mi 1961,Ja 8,II,1:1
Reardon, Leo F (Playwright)
One More Honeymoon 1934,Ap 2,13:5
Reardon, Marian
All Summer Long 1953,Ja 29,23:1
Cretan Woman, The 1954,My 21,17:2
Tonight in Samarkand 1955,F 17,22:2
Miss Lonelyhearts 1957,O 4,26:2
Ivanov 1958,O 8,42:1
All the King's Men 1959,O 17,27:2

Reardon, Marian—Cont
Play 1964,Ja 6,35:1
Play 1964,Mr 25,46:2
Two Executioners, The 1964,Mr 25,46:2
Child Buyer, The 1964,D 22,35:1
Pigeons 1965,Mr 4,37:1
Reardon, Nancy
Moon Shines on Kylenamoe, The 1962,O 31,33:1
Figuro in the Night 1962,O 31,33:1
Summer of Daisy Miller, The 1963,My 28,33:1
Poor Bitos 1964,N 16,40:2
Love's Labour's Lost 1965,Je 16,46:1
Twelfth Night 1968,Je 15,40:1
Resistible Rise of Arturo Ui, The 1968,Ag 8,25:1
Resistible Rise of Arturo Ui, The 1968,D 23,44:1
Reaske, Herbert E
Coriolanus 1927,Je 18,8:3
Reason, James
South Pacific 1943,D 30,11:2
Reavey, Jean (Playwright)
Place for Chance, The 1964,My 15,44:2
Reavin, Sara (Playwright)
Ivory Branch, The 1956,My 25,27:1
Reavis, Hattie King
Natural Man 1941,My 8,20:4
Rebenalt, A M (Director)
Raetzel um Beate 1936,N 8,X,2:1
Rebiroff, Jacques
Sally 1920,D 22,16:1
Rebla
Bing Boys Are Here, The 1934,D 19,26:6
Reboux, Paul (Original Author)
Trio 1929,Mr 17,X,2:7
Rebroff, Ivan
Fiddler on the Roof 1969,N 16,82:6
Recco, Ernest
Hold Your Horses 1933,S 26,26:4
Rechelle, Lizzie
Commodore Marries, The 1929,S 5,26:3
Recht, Charles (Translator)
Morals 1925,D 1,22:2
Rechtzeit, Jack
Mazel Tov, Rabbi 1938,N 28,10:4
Three Men and a Girl 1939,F 6,9:3
Nice People 1958,O 20,36:1
Honeymoon in Israel, A 1962,O 15,33:5
Country Boy, The 1963,O 28,20:1
Prince Reuvaini 1967,N 19,83:1
Bronx Express, 1968 1968,N 16,43:3
Trees Die Standing, The 1969,O 13,52:1
President's Daughter, The 1970,N 4,41:2
Rechtzeit, Jack (Composer)
Country Boy, The 1963,O 28,20:1
Rechtzeit, Jack (Director)
Country Boy, The 1963,O 28,20:1
Rechtzeit, Jack (Lyricist)
Country Boy, The 1963,O 28,20:1
Rechtzeit, Jack (Playwright)
Country Boy, The 1963,O 28,20:1
Rechtzeit, Jacob
Parisian Love 1927,Ja 28,15:5
Jewish Heart, The 1939,Ja 25,16:6
Chaver, Nachman 1939,O 2,15:2
Song of Dnieper 1946,O 26,10:5
Wandering Stars 1946,D 14,18:2
Rechtzeit, Seymour
Stranger, The 1935,N 7,26:2
Freidel Becomes a Bride 1936,F 10,14:3
Sins of Mothers 1937,Mr 30,20:2
With Open Eyes 1938,O 27,27:2
It Could Happen to You 1957,O 28,30:5
Good Luck 1964,O 19,38:3
Reckel, Lore
Pirates of Penzance, The 1954,Mr 31,32:5
Sorcerer, The 1954,My 26,34:3
Rect, Charles (Playwright)
Rapid Transit 1927,Ap 8,21:2
Rector, Eddie
Hot Rhythm 1930,Ag 22,18:5
Yeah-Man 1932,My 27,27:3
Rector, Eddie (Choreographer)
Messin' Around 1929,Ap 23,26:3
Rector, Eddie (Director)
Hot Rhythm 1930,Ag 22,18:5
Rector and Cooper
Vaudeville (Palace) 1928,N 26,31:2
Red, Clarence
Out of My House 1942,Ja 8,28:6
Red, Rhythm
Hoofers, The 1969,Jl 30,23:4
Red and Curley
Harlem Cavalcade 1942,My 2,11:2
Red and Struggy
Brown Buddies 1930,O 8,29:1
Redalieu, Joseph
Judas 1929,Ja 25,20:4
Redd, Clarence
Kongo 1926,Mr 31,20:5
Goin' Home 1928,Ag 24,23:2
Christopher Comes Across 1932,Je 1,19:2
Hangman's Whip 1933,F 25,20:2
Processional 1937,O 14,23:1
Redd, Florence
World We Make, The 1939,N 21,19:1

d, Freddie
onnection, The 1959,Jl 16,30:2
d, Freddie (Composer)
onnection, The 1959,Jl 16,30:2
ld, Veronica
ambo 1970,Jl 23,24:1
lden, Melvin
rince of Pilsen, The 1930,Ja 14,24:3
ddick, Betty
ello, Yourself 1928,O 31,28:2
ddick, Cecil (Director)
topia! 1963,My 7,47:4
ddick, Grant
Merchant of Venice, The 1955,Jl 1,13:1
Henry V 1956,Je 20,27:2
Harlequinade 1959,F 14,15:1
welfth Night 1959,Jl 11,10:2
ort-Royal 1960,Ap 26,41:1
ddick, Walter
Hello, Yourself 1928,O 31,28:2
ddick, William J (Musical Director)
Grand Duchess 1929,D 17,29:2
Gypsy Baron, The 1930,Ap 22,22:8
Orpheus in Hades 1930,D 16,30:1
ddicks, The
Hello, Yourself 1928,O 31,28:2
ddie, Milton (Playwright)
Swing It 1937,Jl 23,17:2
dding, Earl
Top Hole 1924,S 2,22:3
Gang War 1928,Ag 21,27:2
Out of a Blue Sky 1930,F 10,20:6
Life Begins 1932,Mr 29,23:2
Riddle Me This! 1933,Mr 15,21:3
Crucible 1933,S 5,22:4
Brigadoon 1947,Mr 14,28:2
edding, Eddie
Brass Ankle 1931,Ap 24,26:4
edding, Edward
Black Boy 1926,O 7,30:2
adding, Edwin
Scarlet Lily, The 1927,Ja 31,12:3
Scalawag, The 1927,Mr 30,22:3
Good News 1927,Ag 14,VII,2:1
Good News 1927,S 7,35:4
Phantoms 1930,Ja 14,24:3
Hot Money 1931,N 9,22:2
Happy Landing 1932,Mr 28,10:5
Whistling in the Dark 1932,N 4,25:2
Riddle Me This! 1933,Mr 15,21:3
Crucible 1933,S 5,22:4
Little Inn, The 1935,Ag 20,25:1
Strip Girl 1935,O 21,22:6
Fulton of Oak Falls 1937,Ja 2,15:3
Fulton of Oak Falls 1937,F 11,18:2
Redding, Eugene
Whirl of New York, The 1921,Je 14,18:1
Pride 1923,My 3,22:3
Tell Me More 1925,Ap 14,27:3
Redding, Harry
Right Girl, The 1921,Mr 16,12:1
Casanova 1923,S 27,10:2
John 1927,N 5,16:4
Mr Samuel 1930,N 11,28:4
Parnell 1935,N 12,24:2
Parnell 1936,My 5,26:2
Hero Is Born, A 1937,O 2,18:6
Young Mr Disraeli 1937,N 10,30:5
Redding, Ida F (Miscellaneous)
Dandy Dick 1956,Ja 11,37:2
Redfern, Anthony
Blue Boy in Black, The 1963,My 1,32:1
Redfield, Billie
Swing Your Lady 1936,O 19,22:4
Redfield, Clare
David Garrick 1929,Ag 2,17:5
Redfield, Liza (Composer)
John Brown's Body 1968,F 13,49:2
Comedy of Errors, The 1968,F 28,40:2
Redfield, Liza (Musical Director)
Miss Emily Adam 1960,Mr 30,43:1
Ernest in Love 1960,My 5,39:4
Sophie 1963,Ap 16,32:1
Music Man, The 1965,Je 17,26:4
Mod Donna 1970,My 4,48:1
Redfield, Orrin
Antony and Cleopatra 1947,N 27,49:2
Richard III 1949,F 9,33:2
Redfield, William
Excursion 1937,Ap 10,11:4
Virginia 1937,S 3,13:2
Stop-Over 1938,Ja 12,16:5
Our Town 1938,F 5,18:3
Junior Miss 1941,N 19,28:2
Snafu 1944,O 26,19:5
Barefoot Boy With Cheek 1947,Ap 4,20:2
Bruno and Sidney 1949,My 4,38:2
Montserrat 1949,O 31,21:4
Out of This World 1950,D 22,17:3
Misalliance 1953,F 19,20:1
Misalliance 1953,Mr 22,II,1:1
Double in Hearts 1956,O 17,41:7
Making of Moo, The 1958,Je 12,34:1

U S A 1959,O 29,38:1
U S A 1959,N 8,II,1:1
Midgie Purvis 1961,F 2,25:3
Man for All Seasons, A 1961,N 23,51:1
Man for All Seasons, A 1961,D 3,II,1:1
Man for All Seasons, A 1962,S 23,II,1:1
Hamlet 1964,Ap 10,30:1
Minor Adjustment, A 1967,O 7,33:3
You Know I Can't Hear You When the Water's
Running 1968,Mr 29,33:1
Redford, Leslie
Bicycle Ride to Nevada 1963,S 25,38:1
Sponge Room, The 1964,F 25,24:1
Squat Betty 1964,F 25,24:1
Play With a Tiger 1964,D 31,14:2
Hamp 1967,Mr 10,32:1
Redford, Robert
Highest Tree, The 1959,N 5,41:1
Little Moon of Alban 1960,D 2,34:1
Sunday in New York 1961,N 10,40:1
Barefoot in the Park 1963,O 24,36:2
Redford, William
Keep Kool 1924,My 23,16:4
Keep Moving 1934,Ag 24,10:2
Redgrave, Corin
Chips With Everything 1963,O 2,49:1
Redgrave, Lynn
Black Comedy 1967,F 13,42:1
Black Comedy 1967,F 26,II,1:5
Zoo, Zoo, Widdershins, Zoo 1969,S 5,30:1
Two of Us, The 1970,Ag 1,13:2
Two of Us, The 1970,S 11,33:2
Redgrave, Michael
Three Set Out 1937,Je 23,29:3
Twelfth Night 1938,D 18,IX,5:6
Thunder Rock 1940,Ag 11,IX,2:4
Duke in Darkness, The 1942,O 18,VIII,1:4
Uncle Harry 1944,Ap 30,II,1:4
Jacobowsky and the Colonel 1945,Je 24,II,1:3
Macbeth 1947,D 19,34:3
Macbeth 1948,Ap 11,II,1:1
Love's Labour's Lost 1949,O 24,18:3
She Stoops to Conquer 1950,Je 18,34:4
Richard II 1951,Mr 25,75:3
Winter Journey; Country Girl, The 1952,Ap 4,21:1
Winter Journey; Country Girl, The
1952,Ap 13,II,3:7
Antony and Cleopatra 1953,My 10,II,1:1
King Lear 1953,Ag 9,II,1:2
Tiger at the Gates 1955,Je 3,27:1
Tiger at the Gates 1955,Je 12,II,1:1
Tiger at the Gates 1955,O 4,40:1
Tiger at the Gates 1955,O 23,II,1:1
Sleeping Prince, The 1956,N 2,31:1
Much Ado About Nothing 1958,Ag 27,34:6
Aspern Papers, The 1959,Ag 13,21:5
Tiger and the Horse, The 1960,Ag 25,26:5
Complaisant Lover, The 1961,N 2,43:2
Uncle Vanya 1962,Jl 17,18:4
Uncle Vanya 1963,Jl 2,16:2
Hamlet 1963,O 23,37:2
Master Builder, The 1964,Je 10,50:2
Redgrave, Michael (Director)
Month in the Country, A 1956,Ap 4,23:1
Month in the Country, A 1956,Ap 15,II,1:1
Sleeping Prince, The 1956,N 2,31:1
Redgrave, Michael (Miscellaneous)
Importance of Being Oscar, The 1961,Mr 15,45:2
Redgrave, Michael (Playwright)
Aspern Papers, The 1959,Ag 13,21:5
Aspern Papers, The 1962,F 8,26:1
Aspern Papers, The 1962,F 18,II,1:1
Redgrave, Michael (Producer)
Aspern Papers, The 1959,Ag 13,21:5
Redgrave, Vanessa
Midsummer Night's Dream, A 1959,Je 3,30:1
As You Like It 1961,Jl 5,30:1
Taming of the Shrew, The 1962,Ap 24,33:3
Cymbeline 1962,Jl 18,21:2
Daniel Deronda 1969,Ja 11,22:2
Redin, Vladimir
Moscow Circus on Ice 1970,D 9,63:1
Redington, Michael
Midsummer Night's Dream, A 1954,S 22,33:1
Redish, Sidney (Scenic Designer)
Dutchman's Farm, A 1941,My 11,I,43:3
Redlich, Don
Golden Apple, The 1954,Mr 12,15:2
Thieves' Carnival 1955,F 2,21:1
Redlich, Don (Choreographer)
Thieves' Carnival 1955,F 2,21:1
Redman, Don
House of Flowers 1954,D 31,11:2
Redman, George (Playwright)
It Pays to Sin 1933,N 4,18:6
Redman, Joyce
Arms and the Man 1944,O 1,II,1:3
Henry IV, Part II 1946,My 8,33:4
Henry IV 1946,My 12,II,1:1
Uncle Vanya 1946,My 14,18:2
Uncle Vanya 1946,My 19,II,1:1
Oedipus; Critic, The 1946,My 21,19:2
Oedipus 1946,My 21,19:2

Redman, Joyce—Cont
King Lear 1946,O 13,II,2:3
Duet for Two Hands 1947,O 8,28:3
Anne of the Thousand Days 1948,D 9,49:2
Anne of the Thousand Days 1948,D 19,II,3:1
Anne of the Thousand Days 1949,S 18,II,1:1
Colombe 1951,D 15,13:2
Affairs of State 1952,Ag 22,12:2
All's Well That Ends Well 1955,Je 7,37:4
Rape of the Belt, The 1960,N 7,46:1
Crucible, The 1965,Ja 20,35:1
Love for Love 1967,O 21,17:1
Love for Love 1967,O 30,59:1
Lionel Touch, The 1969,N 6,57:2
Redmond, Henry S (Composer)
Samarkand 1926,D 22,24:4
Redmond, Jack
Earl Carroll's Vanities 1925,D 29,20:3
Redmond, John
Green Hat, The 1925,S 16,23:2
Redmond, Johnston L (Mrs)
Variations of 1940 1940,Ja 29,12:1
Redmond, Laurence
Honors Are Even 1921,Ag 11,8:2
Redmond, Liam
White Steed, The 1939,Ja 11,16:2
Wayward Saint, The 1955,F 18,17:1
Wayward Saint, The 1955,F 27,II,1:1
Devil Came From Dublin, The! 1955,Je 3,27:2
Loves of Cass McGuire, The 1966,O 7,36:1
Loot 1968,Mr 19,40:2
Redmond, Marge
Phoenix '55 1955,Ap 25,20:2
Redmond, Marjorie
Royal Family, The 1951,Ja 11,28:2
Redmond, Mary
Inside Story, The 1932,F 23,23:2
Redmond, Maurice
Well of the Saints, The 1932,Ja 22,15:2
Redmond, Moira
Early Morning 1968,Ap 9,58:1
Flint 1970,Jl 26,49:2
Redouin, Edmee
Folies Bergere 1964,Je 3,36:1
Redpath, Ralph
All's Well That Ends Well 1970,Je 16,53:1
Redstone, Michael (Producer)
Artists and Models 1943,N 6,16:6
Redway, Norman
Stephen D 1962,S 25,31:3
Redwine, Skip (Miscellaneous)
Vintage '60 1960,S 13,41:1
Redwine, Skip (Musical Director)
Decline and Fall of the Entire World As Seen
Through the Eyes of Cole Porter Revisited, The
1965,Mr 31,24:2
Ree, Sushelagh
Enchanted, The 1958,Ap 23,41:1
Reebie, Earl S
Life and Death of Sir John Falstaff, The
1938,Mr 15,19:5
Reece, Brian
Seven Year Itch, The 1953,My 18,26:8
Reece, Kathryn
Iolanthe 1926,Ap 20,24:2
Pirates of Penzance, The; Slave of Duty, The
1926,D 7,25:1
Enchanted Isle 1927,S 20,33:2
Falstaff 1928,D 26,14:2
Shoestring Revue 1929,N 23,19:2
Pirates of Penzance, The 1944,F 18,15:5
Iolanthe 1944,F 23,17:1
Patience 1944,F 26,11:4
Ruddigore 1944,Mr 3,19:5
Yeomen of the Guard, The 1944,Mr 5,34:3
Reece, Lucille
Enchanted Isle 1927,S 20,33:2
Happy 1927,D 6,26:3
Reece, Ted
Floydada to Matador 1955,D 22,19:1
Hello Out There 1955,D 22,19:1
Opera Opera 1955,D 22,19:1
Reed, Ada May
Post Road 1934,D 5,28:3
Reed, Alan
Love's Old Sweet Song 1940,Ap 14,IX,3:3
Love's Old Sweet Song 1940,My 3,16:3
Hope for a Harvest 1941,N 27,28:2
Hope for a Harvest 1941,D 7,X,5:1
Lunchtime Follies, The 1942,Je 23,22:3
Pirate, The 1942,N 26,39:2
Reed, Albert
Cat-Bird, The 1920,F 17,18:1
Not So Long Ago 1920,My 5,14:1
Romeo and Juliet 1922,D 28,20:1
Wonderful Visit, The 1924,F 13,17:3
Father, The 1928,My 12,9:4
Reed, Alex
Liliom 1956,F 18,12:5
Lady From the Sea, The 1956,D 13,49:5
Point of No Return 1957,Mr 23,17:2
Edward II 1958,F 12,32:5
Lady's Not for Burning, The 1959,Ja 31,13:2
All the King's Men 1959,O 17,27:2

Reed, Alex—Cont

Death of Satan, The 1960,Ap 6,49:1
Physicists, The 1964,O 14,52:1
Reed, Alexander
Arsenic and Old Lace 1970,N 5,59:1
Reed, Anthony
Million Dollar Baby 1945,D 22,17:2
Reed, Bernard
Apollo of Bellac, The 1957,Ap 10,39:1
Career 1957,My 1,42:6
Trial of Dmitri Karamazov, The 1958,Ja 28,30:1
Dinny and the Witches 1959,D 10,53:3
Seven at Dawn, The 1961,Ap 18,43:1
I Want You 1961,S 15,29:1
Chief Thing, The 1963,Ap 30,27:2
Reed, Bert
Johnny 2X4 1942,Mr 17,24:6
Reed, Betty Lou
Rosalinda; Fledermaus, Die 1942,O 29,26:5
Reed, Billy
Fifty Million Frenchmen 1929,N 28,34:4
Big Deal, The 1953,Mr 7,13:6
Reed, Bonnie
New Hellzapoppin, The 1939,D 12,36:4
Reed, Carl
Weak Woman, A 1926,Ja 27,16:3
Head or Tail 1926,N 10,24:1
Black Cockatoo, The 1926,D 31,11:1
One Glorious Hour 1927,Ap 15,27:2
Tales of Rigo 1927,My 31,25:3
Reed, Carl (Miscellaneous)
Electra 1930,D 27,16:1
Reed, Carl (Producer)
Stronger Than Love 1925,D 29,20:2
Creaking Chair, The 1926,F 23,26:1
Sport of Kings, The 1926,My 5,24:2
Humble, The 1926,O 14,22:2
Witch, The 1926,N 19,22:5
Lally 1927,F 9,16:3
Savages Under the Skin 1927,Mr 25,25:2
Venus 1927,D 26,26:5
Carry On 1928,Ja 24,26:1
Say When 1928,Je 27,29:3
Pleasure Man 1928,O 2,34:7
Berlin 1931,D 31,16:1
Round-Up, The 1932,Mr 8,19:4
Reed, Carol (Director)
On the Spot 1930,O 30,33:3
Reed, Daniel
Unknown Warrior, The 1931,O 23,28:4
Hope Is the Thing With Feathers 1948,Ap 12,24:2
Home Life of a Buffalo; Hope's the Thing
  1948,My 12,34:6
Hope Is the Thing With Feathers; Hope's the
  Thing 1948,My 12,34:6
Gone Tomorrow; Hope's the Thing
  1948,My 12,34:6
Vigil, The 1948,My 22,8:6
Love Me Long 1949,N 8,34:5
My Heart's in the Highlands 1949,N 22,36:7
Spoon River Anthology 1950,Ja 16,18:5
Come Back, Little Sheba 1950,F 16,28:5
Borned in Texas 1950,Ag 22,30:6
Mary Rose 1951,Mr 5,25:2
Mary Rose 1951,Mr 11,II,1:1
Barefoot in Athens 1951,N 1,35:2
Time of the Cuckoo, The 1952,O 16,37:4
Carousel 1954,Je 3,32:2
Shadow of a Gunman, The 1958,N 21,26:1
Shadow of a Gunman, The 1958,N 30,II,1:1
Man and Superman 1960,Ag 17,35:3
Reed, Daniel (Playwright)
Scarlet Sister Mary 1930,O 5,IX,4:6
Scarlet Sister Mary 1930,N 26,19:2
Reed, Dean and Reed
Hellzapoppin 1938,S 23,34:2
Reed, Donald
It Happened Tomorrow 1933,My 6,11:5
Reed, Dorothy
Major Barbara 1954,Je 30,23:2
Reed, Edna May
George White's Scandals 1923,Je 19,22:5
Reed, Elizabeth
Sonya's Search for the Christmas Star
  1929,D 14,24:6
Reed, Eugenie
Threepenny Opera, The 1933,Ap 14,22:4
Reed, Florence
Mirage, The 1920,O 1,14:1
Untitled-Benefit 1922,My 8,14:5
East of Suez 1922,S 22,16:3
Hail and Farewell 1923,F 20,12:1
Lullaby, The 1923,S 9,VII,2:4
Lullaby, The 1923,S 19,5:3
Lullaby, The 1923,O 7,IX,1:1
Lullaby, The 1923,D 16,IX,1:1
Ashes 1924,Je 1,VII,4:3
Ashes 1924,O 21,21:2
Shanghai Gesture, The 1926,F 2,20:2
Vaudeville (Palace) 1928,Mr 13,23:2
Macbeth 1928,N 20,28:3
Purity 1930,D 7,IX,1:6
Purity 1930,D 26,18:2
Mourning Becomes Electra 1932,F 21,VIII,2:6

Mourning Becomes Electra; Homecoming
  1932,My 10,25:2
Mourning Becomes Electra; Hunted, The
  1932,My 10,25:2
Mourning Becomes Electra 1932,My 22,VIII,1:1
Thoroughbred 1933,N 7,29:2
Murder With Pen and Ink 1935,Jl 30,17:2
Murder With Pen and Ink 1935,Ag 20,25:1
Romeo and Juliet 1935,D 24,10:2
Point of Honor, A 1937,Ja 31,II,10:4
Point of Honor, A 1937,F 12,26:2
Herod and Mariamne 1938,O 27,27:2
Outward Bound 1938,D 23,16:5
Outward Bound 1939,Ja 1,IX,1:1
Flying Gerardos, The 1940,D 30,21:4
Athalie 1942,Mr 18,29:2
Attack 1942,S 8,13:4
Skin of Our Teeth, The 1942,N 19,29:5
Skin of Our Teeth, The 1942,N 22,VIII,1:1
Rebecca 1944,Ap 30,II,1:1
Rebecca 1945,Ja 19,17:2
Rebecca 1945,Ja 28,II,1:2
Winter's Tale, The 1946,Ja 16,18:6
Winter's Tale, The 1946,Ja 20,II,1:1
Medea 1947,O 21,27:2
Medea 1947,O 26,II,1:1
Richard III 1953,D 10,65:2
Skin of Our Teeth, The 1955,Je 29,25:3
Skin of Our Teeth, The 1955,Ag 18,16:1
Skin of Our Teeth, The 1955,Ag 28,II,1:1
Family Reunion, The 1958,O 21,39:1
Family Reunion, The 1958,O 26,II,1:1
Reed, Gene
Judy Garland's New Variety Show 1956,S 27,43:2
Reed, H Ellis
Great Way, The 1921,N 8,28:2
Reed, Henry (Playwright)
Island of Goats 1955,O 5,40:1
Reed, Henry (Translator)
Corruption in the Palace of Justice 1963,O 9,49:2
Reed, Herman
Shuffle Along of 1933 1932,D 27,11:3
Reed, Ione
New Faces of 1936 1936,My 20,24:5
Reed, Jack
Camels Are Coming, The 1931,O 3,20:4
Reed, Jacqueline
Italian Straw Hat, The 1957,O 1,37:2
Reed, Janet
Look, Ma, I'm Dancin' 1948,Ja 30,20:2
Look, Ma, I'm Dancin' 1948,F 8,II,2:1
'Tis Pity She's a Whore 1958,D 6,21:1
Reed, Jared
Leaf and Bough 1949,Ja 22,10:2
Texas Li'l Darlin' 1949,N 26,10:5
Missouri Legend 1951,F 10,10:4
Paint Your Wagon 1951,N 13,32:2
Well of the Saints, The 1959,Ap 11,15:4
Workhouse Ward, The 1959,Ap 11,15:4
She Stoops to Conquer 1960,N 2,42:5
Plough and the Stars, The 1960,D 7,56:2
Hamlet 1961,Mr 17,17:1
Jackhammer, The 1962,F 6,26:2
Reed, Jared (Composer)
Octoroon, The 1961,Ja 28,13:1
Reed, Jared (Miscellaneous)
Octoroon, The 1961,Ja 28,13:1
Reed, Jessie
Ziegfeld Follies 1920,Je 23,14:1
Ziegfeld Follies 1921,Je 22,10:1
Reed, Joe
Four in Hand 1923,S 7,10:2
Reed, Joel M (Producer)
End of All Things Natural, The 1969,S 12,38:1
Reed, John
Yeomen of the Guard, The 1955,O 4,39:2
Trial by Jury 1955,O 18,48:1
Mikado, The 1962,N 14,43:1
Gondoliers, The 1962,N 16,25:2
Pirates of Penzance, The 1962,N 21,28:1
H M S Pinafore 1962,N 23,32:4
Iolanthe 1962,N 28,42:1
Iolanthe 1964,N 18,52:1
H M S Pinafore 1964,N 20,40:1
Mikado, The 1964,N 27,43:1
Pirates of Penzance, The 1964,N 27,43:1
Pirates of Penzance, The 1966,N 16,54:1
Mikado, The 1966,N 18,36:1
Ruddigore 1966,N 23,28:1
H M S Pinafore 1966,N 24,64:1
Patience 1966,N 30,58:1
H M S Pinafore 1968,O 30,35:1
Patience 1968,N 1,34:1
Mikado, The 1968,N 2,29:4
Pirates of Penzance, The 1968,N 7,54:1
Reed, John (Choreographer)
Gondoliers, The 1962,N 16,25:2
Reed, John H
Erminie 1921,Ja 4,11:1
Reed, Joseph Verner (Producer)
Children of Darkness 1930,Ja 8,25:1
Twelfth Night 1930,S 14,VIII,2:8

Reed, Joseph Verner (Producer)—Cont

When Hell Froze 1930,O 5,IX,4:6
Twelfth Night 1930,O 16,28:2
Art and Mrs Bottle 1930,N 19,19:3
Lean Harvest 1931,O 4,VIII,2:2
Lean Harvest 1931,O 14,26:3
Lady With a Lamp, The 1931,N 20,27:2
Springtime for Henry 1931,D 10,29:2
Henry V 1969,N 11,43:1
Devil's Disciple, The 1970,Je 30,48:1
Othello 1970,S 15,51:1
Reed, Karen Lynn
Stop the World-I Want to Get Off 1962,O 4,45:4
Reed, Leslie
Virtuous Island, The 1957,Ap 10,39:1
Reed, Lew
Vaudeville (Palace) 1926,O 26,24:2
Reed, Luther (Playwright)
Dear Me 1921,Ja 18,14:1
Dear Me 1921,Ja 30,VI,1:1
Reed, Lydia
Number, The 1951,O 31,33:2
Mrs McThing 1952,F 21,22:1
Mrs McThing 1952,Mr 2,II,1:1
Reed, Mark (Playwright)
Skyrocket, The 1929,Ja 12,14:7
Petticoat Fever 1935,Mr 5,22:2
Petticoat Fever 1936,F 21,21:1
Yes, My Darling Daughter 1937,F 10,19:2
Yes, My Darling Daughter 1937,F 28,XI,1:1
Petticoat Fever 1937,Mr 21,II,7:3
Petticoat Fever 1937,Jl 6,23:1
Petticoat Fever 1937,Jl 20,19:3
Yes, My Darling Daughter 1938,Jl 13,19:2
Reed, Mary
George White's Scandals 1922,Ag 29,10:1
Reed, Mary Ann (Costume Designer)
Three Sisters, The 1959,S 22,46:1
Burning Bright 1959,O 17,27:2
Country Scandal, A 1960,My 6,21:8
Moon in the Yellow River, The 1961,F 7,40:2
Meet Peter Grant 1961,My 11,41:4
Intimate Relations 1962,N 2,27:1
Reed, Mary Ann (Scenic Designer)
Tobacco Road 1960,My 11,44:2
Moon in the Yellow River, The 1961,F 7,40:2
Feast of Panthers 1961,Mr 21,32:1
Intimate Relations 1962,N 2,27:1
Reed, Mel
New Hellzapoppin, The 1939,D 12,36:4
Reed, Napoleon
Carmen Jones 1943,D 3,26:2
Carmen Jones 1945,My 3,26:5
Carmen Jones 1946,Ap 8,32:2
Carmen Jones 1946,Ap 14,II,1:2
Shuffle Along 1952,My 9,20:5
Reed, Ned (Composer)
Brown Buddies 1930,O 8,29:1
Reed, Paul
Gondoliers, The 1940,O 1,29:2
Trojan Women, The 1941,Ap 9,32:5
New Moon, The 1942,Ag 19,14:2
Up in Central Park 1945,Ja 29,17:2
Up in Central Park 1947,My 20,29:2
Hold It! 1948,My 6,31:5
All for Love 1949,Ja 24,16:5
Great to Be Alive! 1950,Mr 24,28:2
Guys and Dolls 1950,N 25,11:2
Carnival in Flanders 1953,S 9,38:2
By the Beautiful Sea 1954,Ap 9,20:1
Music Man, The 1957,D 20,31:1
How to Succeed in Business Without Really Trying
  1961,O 16,34:1
Here's Love 1963,O 4,28:1
I'm Solomon 1968,Ap 24,51:1
Promises, Promises 1968,D 2,59:3
Reed, Penelope
Prince of Peasantmania 1970,F 22,88:1
Reed, Philip
Reflected Glory 1936,S 22,30:2
My Dear Children 1939,Mr 25,19:6
My Dear Children 1940,F 1,16:2
Reed, Phyllis
Pinocchio 1939,Ja 3,19:2
Reed, Richard
Touch and Go 1949,O 14,34:2
Making of Moo, The 1958,Je 12,34:1
Reed, Robbie
Shadow of Heroes 1961,D 6,59:1
Child's Play 1970,F 18,39:1
Reed, Robert
Sailors of Cattaro 1934,D 11,28:4
Let Freedom Ring 1935,N 7,26:2
Marching Song 1937,F 18,18:2
Too Many Heroes 1937,N 16,26:2
Avanti 1968,F 1,29:1
Reed, Ruth
These Days 1928,N 13,36:2
Reed, Sam
Wren, The 1921,O 11,22:1
Chicken Feed 1923,S 25,10:2
Reed, Stori
John Gabriel Borkman 1959,N 26,57:4

Reed, Susan
Coming Forth by Day of Osiris Jones, The; Kid, The 1961,Mr 15,45:2
Reed, Taylor
Something More! 1964,N 11,36:1
Here's Where I Belong 1968,Mr 4,32:1
Cry for Us All 1970,Ap 9,48:2
Reed, Vern
Music Man, The 1957,D 20,31:1
Music Man, The 1965,Je 17,26:4
Reed, Virginia
Odds on Mrs Oakley, The 1944,O 3,18:8
Reed, Walter (Pvt)
Winged Victory 1943,N 22,24:1
Reed, Will (Composer)
Jotham Valley 1951,F 7,37:2
Reed and Duthers
Vaudeville (Palace) 1929,Ag 19,23:1
Reeder, George
Buttrio Square 1952,O 15,40:2
Li'l Abner 1956,N 16,24:2
Destry Rides Again 1959,Ap 24,24:1
Funny Girl 1964,Mr 27,15:1
And Puppy Dog Tails 1969,O 20,60:1
Reeder, Nancy (Costume Designer)
Gertrude 1970,N 13,29:1
Reeder, Pierre de (Musical Director)
Student Prince, The 1937,Jl 28,15:1
Gay Divorce 1937,Ag 11,27:2
Of Thee I Sing 1937,Ag 18,14:4
Anything Goes 1937,Ag 26,24:3
Reeder, Pierre de (Playwright)
Firefly, The 1937,Ag 4,14:1
Reeds, John
He Who Gets Slapped 1956,F 2,18:1
Reedy, Eleanor
Broadway Whirl, The 1921,Je 9,10:4
Reedy, William
As the Girls Go 1948,N 15,21:2
Reehling, Larry (Miscellaneous)
Those That Play the Clowns 1966,N 25,48:1
Reehling, Larry (Scenic Designer)
Happiness Is Just a Little Thing Called a Rolls Royce 1968,My 13,54:5
Reel, Adelle
Madre, La 1959,F 12,24:1
Reel, Arthur (Director)
Lower Depths, The 1956,O 3,29:2
Enemy of the People, An 1958,F 26,24:2
Hamlet 1959,S 11,21:4
Cage, The 1961,Mr 6,30:1
417 1961,Mr 6,30:1
Stronger, The 1965,N 11,59:1
Miss Julie 1965,N 11,59:1
Reel, Arthur (Playwright)
Enemy of the People, An 1958,F 26,24:2
Miss Julie 1965,N 11,59:1
Stronger, The 1965,N 11,59:1
Reel, Arthur (Producer)
Hamlet 1959,S 11,21:4
Reel, Arthur (Scenic Designer)
Lower Depths, The 1956,O 3,29:2
Enemy of the People, An 1958,F 26,24:2
Hamlet 1959,S 11,21:4
417 1961,Mr 6,30:1
Cage, The 1961,Mr 6,30:1
Stronger, The 1965,N 11,59:1
Miss Julie 1965,N 11,59:1
Reener, Katherine
Angeline Moves In 1932,Ap 20,27:5
Reep, Phil
Street Singer, The 1929,S 18,35:2
Rees, Alys
Love for Love 1925,Ap 1,21:2
Beaten Track, The 1926,F 9,23:2
Rees, Betsy
Vaudeville (Palace) 1926,Je 15,23:3
Night in Venice, A 1929,My 22,30:2
Fine and Dandy 1930,S 24,26:1
Rees, Carlyle
Post Road 1949,Ap 28,27:3
Rees, Crosby
Cotton Stockings 1923,D 19,16:2
Rees, Judson
Winter's Tale, The 1946,Ja 16,18:6
Lost in the Stars 1949,O 31,21:2
Barefoot in Athens 1951,N 1,35:2
Rees, Milton
Patience 1948,F 10,27:2
Rees, Roland (Producer)
How Do You Do? 1969,Ap 13,II,3:3
Rees, William
Case of Youth, A 1940,Mr 25,10:3
Reese, Bob (Miscellaneous)
Billy Barnes Revue, The 1959,Je 10,42:2
Reese, Edward
Youth 1920,O 27,14:3
White Villa, The 1921,F 15,7:1
Verge, The 1921,N 15,23:2
Chains of Dew 1922,Ap 28,20:2
Torch Bearers, The 1922,Ag 30,10:2
Grounds for Divorce 1924,S 24,20:1
Androcles and the Lion 1925,N 24,28:1

Man of Destiny, The 1925,N 24,28:1
Moon Is a Gong, The 1926,Mr 13,21:3
Beyond Evil 1926,Je 8,23:2
Gertie 1926,N 16,24:2
Half Gods 1929,D 23,18:5
Short Cut, The 1930,Ja 28,28:2
Gold Braid 1930,My 14,31:2
Reese, Gregory
When Did You Last See My Mother? 1967,Ja 5,27:5
Antigone 1967,Ja 14,18:1
Reese, Henry
Magdalena 1948,S 21,31:2
Reese, Jack
Icetime 1946,Je 21,20:5
Reese, James
Festival 1955,Ja 19,22:1
Sweet Bird of Youth 1956,Ap 17,27:2
Sunrise at Campobello 1958,Ja 31,25:1
Potting Shed, The 1958,N 3,49:2
Reese, John
Remarkable Mr Pennypacker, The 1953,D 31,11:2
Lark, The 1955,N 18,20:1
Diary of a Scoundrel 1956,N 5,41:1
Pale Horse, Pale Rider 1957,O 30,26:1
Reese, Joy
Ivy Green, The 1949,Ap 6,37:2
Reese, Lloyd
Fanny 1954,N 5,16:1
Reese, Ned
Live and Learn 1930,Ap 10,24:6
Reese, Stephen
Come of Age 1952,Ja 24,22:2
Reese, Trevor (Playwright)
Before I Wake 1968,O 14,56:1
Reeve, Ada
Vaudeville (Palace) 1928,Ja 24,26:4
They Came to a City 1943,Je 6,II,1:6
Reeve, Constance
Noah 1935,N 6,32:2
Tomorrow's Monday 1936,Jl 16,15:6
Reeve, Frederick E Jr
Importance of Being Earnest, The 1936,O 22,31:2
Reeve, Mary Ann
Lute Song 1946,F 7,29:2
Reeve-Smith, Olive
Bachelor's Brides 1925,My 29,20:2
Reeves, Allen
Nativity Play, The 1937,D 21,29:1
Possessed, The 1939,O 25,26:2
Reeves, Edwin
He Who Gets Slapped 1956,F 2,18:1
Reeves, Geoffrey (Director)
God Bless 1968,N 3,II,1:1
Reeves, George (Sgt)
Winged Victory 1943,N 22,24:1
Yellow Jack 1944,Ap 7,23:3
Reeves, Jean
Kiss for Cinderella, A 1942,Mr 11,22:2
Show Boat 1946,Ja 7,17:2
Reeves, Kynaston
Much Ado About Nothing 1929,N 17,30:4
King's Leisure, The 1936,My 31,II,6:8
Affair, The 1962,S 21,34:2
Reeves, Mary
Save Me the Waltz 1938,Mr 1,19:2
Reeves, McKinley
Earth 1927,Mr 10,23:1
Green Pastures, The 1930,F 27,26:1
Green Pastures, The 1935,F 27,16:2
Abe Lincoln in Illinois 1938,O 17,12:2
Reeves, Nancy
Song of Norway 1958,Je 23,19:2
Song of Norway 1959,Je 26,16:2
Reeves, Richard
Yesterday's Orchids 1934,O 6,20:4
This Is the Army 1942,Jl 5,28:2
Reeves, Robert
200 Were Chosen 1936,N 21,21:1
But for the Grace of God 1937,Ja 13,21:4
Sweethearts 1947,Ja 22,31:2
Reeves, Rosalie
County Chairman, The 1936,My 26,26:5
Reeves, Steve
Vamp, The 1955,N 11,30:1
Reeves, Theodore (Playwright)
Beggars Are Comming to Town 1945,O 29,16:2
Wedding Breakfast 1954,N 22,29:2
Wedding Breakfast 1954,D 5,II,5:1
Reeves-Smith, H
Road Together, The 1924,Ja 18,21:2
Grounds for Divorce 1924,S 24,20:1
We All Do 1927,Mr 1,30:3
Just Fancy! 1927,O 12,30:2
High Road, The 1928,S 11,31:1
Vinegar Tree, The 1930,N 20,30:3
Great Waltz, The 1934,S 24,14:4
Great Waltz, The 1935,Ag 6,20:5
Reeves-Smith, Olive
Henry's Harem 1926,S 14,25:2
Constant Nymph, The 1926,D 10,31:1
Stepdaughters of War 1930,O 7,27:1
Cold in Sables 1931,D 24,20:7

Reeves-Smith, Olive—Cont
Bulls, Bears and Asses 1932,My 7,11:3
Budget, The 1932,S 21,26:4
Pigeons and People 1933,Ja 17,22:3
Dangerous Corner 1933,Jl 18,20:4
Party, A 1933,Ag 24,18:4
Richard of Bordeaux 1934,F 15,16:2
Laura Garnett 1934,Jl 17,24:4
Jubilee 1935,O 14,20:1
Love From a Stranger 1936,S 30,28:1
Black Limelight 1936,N 10,31:1
Susan and God 1937,Ap 11,II,12:3
Susan and God 1937,Ap 25,X,2:6
Meet the Wife 1937,Jl 6,23:1
Wise Tomorrow 1937,O 16,22:5
Whiteoaks 1938,Mr 24,20:2
Wookey, The 1941,S 11,20:5
Bloomer Girl 1947,Ja 7,33:2
My Fair Lady 1956,Mr 16,20:2
My Fair Lady 1964,My 21,43:2
Reflow, Mabel
O K 1925,My 4,16:1
Refregier, Anton (Scenic Designer)
Pepper Mill 1937,Ja 6,19:4
Regal, Danis
Victims, The; Victims of Duty 1968,Mr 6,34:1
Regal, Henry
Ed Wynn's Carnival 1920,Ap 6,18:2
Vaudeville (Hippodrome) 1924,Ja 22,15:6
Regal, Henry & Co
Vaudeville (Hippodrome) 1925,D 29,21:2
Regal and Moore
Vaudeville (Forty-Fourth Street Theatre) 1921,S 20,12:2
Regali, Alfred L
57 Bowery 1928,Ja 27,14:3
Regamey, Giana
Little Theatre Tournament; Rain 1929,My 11,22:2
Regan, Charles
Make Me Disappear 1969,My 14,34:1
Regan, J D (Lighting Director)
Believers, The 1968,My 10,57:4
Regan, J Pat (Miscellaneous)
Believers, The 1968,My 10,57:4
Regan, Jack
Ledge, A 1929,N 19,26:3
Regan, Joe (Costume Designer)
'Toinette 1961,N 21,46:1
Regan, Joe (Miscellaneous)
That 5 A.M. Jazz 1964,O 20,42:2
Regan, John
She Couldn't Say No! 1926,S 1,27:3
Pickwick 1927,S 6,35:2
Storm Center 1927,D 1,33:2
Pleased to Meet You 1928,O 30,27:2
Halfway to Hell 1934,Ja 3,22:3
Love's Old Sweet Song 1940,My 3,16:3
All the Comforts of Home 1942,My 26,24:5
Goodbye Again 1943,N 10,28:4
French Touch, The 1945,D 10,18:2
Billy the Kid 1951,Ag 21,23:2
Time to Go 1952,My 8,35:6
Regan, Larry
False Dreams, Farewell 1934,Ja 16,18:3
Regan, Patti
Ah, Wilderness! 1954,Ag 21,20:4
Billy Barnes Revue, The 1959,Je 10,42:2
Billy Barnes People, The 1961,Je 14,10:3
Regan, Robert
In the Jungle of Cities 1960,D 21,39:1
Regan, Robert (Miscellaneous)
Mountain Giants, The 1961,Ap 5,32:3
Regan, Sylvia (Playwright)
Morning Star 1940,Ap 17,26:4
Great to Be Alive! 1950,Mr 24,28:2
Fifth Season, The 1953,Ja 24,13:2
Fifth Season, The 1954,F 25,24:5
Zelda 1969,Mr 6,38:1
Regan, Walter
Glory 1922,D 26,10:1
Cinders 1923,Ap 4,22:1
Sunshine 1926,Ag 18,15:2
Philadelphia 1929,S 17,34:5
Half Gods 1929,D 23,18:5
Regas, George
Zombie 1932,F 11,17:2
Regay, Pearl
Vaudeville (Palace) 1921,My 17,20:3
George White's Scandals 1922,Ag 29,10:1
Vaudeville (Palace) 1924,Ja 15,17:3
Rose Marie 1924,S 3,12:2
Rose Marie 1925,D 4,26:1
Desert Song, The 1926,D 1,24:2
Regensburg, Irwin
Bad Habits of 1925 1925,F 9,17:1
Regent, Glenn
Signature 1945,F 15,25:2
Regina, Vera
Arena Conta Zumbi 1969,Ag 19,31:1
Regina-Camier, Mme
Famille Lavolette, La 1926,O 10,VIII,2:1
Regis, Basha
Top Banana 1951,N 2,19:2

Regis, Leon (Playwright)
Chagrins d'Amour 1926,N 14,VIII,2:1
Grandee Penitence, La 1926,N 14,VIII,2:1
Brout 1928,N 11,X,2:7
Register, Vincent
Neighbors 1966,N 15,51:4
Regnier, Marthe
Moulin de la Galette, Le 1923,Ja 28,VII,2:7
Debauche 1929,Mr 24,X,2:1
Machine Infernale, La 1934,My 13,IX,2:2
Chateau de Cartes, Le 1937,F 14,X,2:3
Reguera, Rogelio
International Soiree 1958,Mr 13,25:1
Regy, Claude (Producer)
Jardin des Delices, Le 1969,N 4,54:1
Rehak, Frank
Copper and Brass 1957,O 18,19:2
Rehan, Mary
Prince and the Pauper, The 1920,N 2,15:1
Rehan, Reneice
Tobacco Road 1933,D 5,31:2
Rehfisch, Hans (Original Author)
I Accuse 1937,O 26,19:1
Rehfisch, Hans (Playwright)
Dreyfus Affair, The 1930,Mr 30,VIII,4:1
Brest-Litovsk 1930,N 30,IX,2:1
Rehnolds, Lette
Secret Life of Walter Mitty, The 1964,O 27,44:5
Rehrig, Geraldine
Legend of Lizzie, The 1959,F 10,39:1
Reich, George
Touch and Go 1949,O 14,34:2
Reich, George (Choreographer)
Folies Bergere 1964,Je 3,36:1
Reich, John
Nautical but Nice 1931,Ap 19,31:6
Reich, John (Director)
Hippolytus 1948,N 22,25:5
Sacred Flame, The 1952,O 8,35:2
Tom Paine 1969,Mr 30,71:2
Reich, John (Playwright)
Mary Stuart 1957,O 9,39:1
Mary Stuart 1957,O 20,II,1:1
Reich, John (Producer)
Hippolytus 1948,N 22,25:5
Mother Courage and Her Children 1964,My 12,32:2
Reich, Richard (Playwright)
Pets 1969,My 15,41:2
Silver Grey Toy Poodle 1969,My 15,41:2
Baby With a Knife 1969,My 15,41:2
Reich, Rita
Mother's Sabbath Days 1960,N 21,33:2
Reich-Baxter, John (Director)
Mrs Warren's Profession 1950,O 26,39:2
Reichard, Loise
Having Wonderful Time 1937,F 22,12:5
Reichardt, Marie
Return of Peter Grimm, The 1921,S 22,12:2
Steadfast 1923,O 31,12:1
Dr David's Dad 1924,Ag 14,10:3
Milgrim's Progress 1924,D 23,17:1
Joker, The 1925,N 17,29:1
That French Lady 1927,Mr 16,29:3
Reichberg, Walter
Mighty Nimrod, The 1931,My 13,23:1
Reichel, John Jr
What a Relief 1935,D 14,10:6
Reichenbach, Olivier (Miscellaneous)
Diary of a Madman 1967,Mr 24,25:1
Reicher, Emanuel (Director)
Treasure, The 1920,O 24,VI,1:1
Reicher, Frank
Mary Stuart 1921,Mr 22,15:1
Cloister, The 1921,Je 6,16:3
Ambush 1921,O 11,22:1
Ambush 1921,O 16,VI,1:1
He Who Gets Slapped 1922,Ja 10,15:1
From Morn to Midnight 1922,My 22,17:2
Morn to Midnight 1922,Je 27,16:4
Goat Song 1926,Ja 26,18:1
Reicher, Frank (Director)
From Morn to Midnight 1922,My 22,17:2
Romeo and Juliet 1923,F 4,VII,1:1
Fake, The 1924,O 7,26:3
Carnaval 1924,D 30,15:1
Isabel 1925,Ja 14,19:1
Shall We Join the Ladies? 1925,Ja 14,19:1
Tale of the Wolf, The 1925,O 8,31:2
Grand Duchess and the Waiter, The
1925,O 14,31:1
Monkey Talks, The 1925,D 29,20:1
Song of the Flame 1925,D 31,10:2
Reicher, James (Miscellaneous)
Five on the Black Hand Side 1970,Ja 2,32:2
Reicher, S Bickley (Composer)
Great Guns 1939,N 18,23:4
Reicher, S Bickley (Lyricist)
Great Guns 1939,N 18,23:4
Reichert, Heinz (Original Author)
Blossom Time 1923,My 22,14:3
Blossom Time 1931,Mr 5,32:1
Great Waltz, The 1934,S 24,14:4
Blossom Time 1938,D 27,12:2

Reichert, Heinz (Playwright)
Blossom Time 1921,S 30,10:1
Blossom Time 1943,S 6,21:2
Reichert, James (Composer)
Father Uxbridge Wants to Marry 1967,O 30,57:1
Young Master Dante, The 1968,D 31,19:1
Prince of Peasantmania 1970,F 22,88:1
Effect of Gamma Rays on Man-in-the-Moon
Marigolds, The 1970,Ap 8,32:1
Candaules, Commissioner 1970,My 29,15:1
Early Morning 1970,N 26,57:1
Reichert, James (Miscellaneous)
Mr Grossman 1964,My 6,43:1
Dark Corners 1964,My 6,43:1
Father Uxbridge Wants to Marry 1967,O 30,57:1
Muzeeka 1968,Ap 29,47:2
Red Cross 1968,Ap 29,47:2
Firebugs, The 1968,Jl 2,36:1
Ordinary Man, An 1968,S 10,39:1
Does a Tiger Wear a Necktie? 1969,F 26,38:1
Cop-Out 1969,Ap 8,42:1
Home Fires 1969,Ap 8,42:1
Papp 1969,My 6,39:1
Reckoning, The 1969,S 5,28:1
Calling in Crazy 1969,O 7,42:2
Mercy Street 1969,O 28,43:1
Day of Absence 1970,Mr 18,39:1
Brotherhood 1970,Mr 18,39:1
Two Times One; Duet for Solo Voice
1970,Ap 5,76:4
Two Times One; Last Straw, The 1970,Ap 5,76:4
Carpenters, The 1970,D 22,40:1
Reichert, Kurt
From Vienna 1939,Je 21,26:2
Reichner, Morgan
Samarkand 1926,D 22,24:4
Reichner, Morgan (Lyricist)
Samarkand 1926,D 22,24:4
Reichstetter, Jannette
Salvation 1928,F 1,31:1
Reid, Arthur (Playwright)
People in Love 1937,My 28,17:5
Reid, Barbara
Here Comes Santa Claus 1962,My 18,34:1
Reid, Beryl
Killing of Sister George, The 1965,Je 18,28:5
Killing of Sister George, The 1966,O 6,57:1
Killing of Sister George, The 1966,O 16,II,1:1
Blithe Spirit 1970,S 17,57:1
Reid, Carl Benton
Fiesta 1929,S 18,35:1
Lancashire Lass, The 1931,D 31,16:3
Foreign Affairs 1932,Ap 14,25:5
Sophisticrats, The 1933,F 14,19:5
Her Man of Wax 1933,O 12,32:3
Red Harvest 1937,Mr 31,29:2
At the Theatre 1937,Ag 4,14:1
Sunup to Sundown 1938,F 2,14:3
Little Foxes, The 1939,F 16,16:2
Little Foxes, The 1939,F 26,IX,1:1
Papa Is All 1942,Ja 7,22:2
Papa Is All 1942,Ja 18,IX,1:1
You Touched Me! 1943,O 17,II,2:4
Cherry Orchard, The 1944,Ja 26,22:1
Iceman Cometh, The 1946,O 10,31:3
Strange Bedfellows 1948,Ja 15,27:3
Twelfth Night 1949,O 4,33:2
Twelfth Night 1949,O 9,II,1:1
Reid, Charles
Jack in the Box 1960,My 19,43:3
Reid, David W (Playwright)
Let's Laugh Again 1937,Ag 24,24:5
Reid, Dixie
Sweet Chariot 1930,O 24,30:2
Reid, Edith Atuka
Our Lan' 1947,S 29,16:5
Reid, Elliott
Shoemaker's Holiday, The 1938,Ja 3,17:2
Two Blind Mice 1949,Mr 3,32:2
Live Wire, The 1950,Ag 18,16:2
Two on the Aisle 1951,Jl 20,13:6
Two on the Aisle 1951,Jl 29,II,1:1
From A to Z 1960,Ap 21,23:2
Reid, Eugenie
Cortez 1929,N 5,32:2
Reid, Frances
Where There's a Will 1939,Ja 18,16:6
Not in Our Stars 1941,Ap 26,20:5
Rivals, The 1941,N 18,32:2
Rivals, The 1942,Ja 15,24:2
Bird in Hand 1942,O 20,24:2
Patriots, The 1943,Ja 30,11:2
Listen Professor! 1943,D 23,22:1
Highland Fling, A 1944,Ap 29,13:2
Little Women 1944,D 13,29:2
Star Spangled Family 1945,Ap 11,18:6
Wind Is Ninety, The 1945,Je 22,12:2
Hamlet 1945,D 14,25:2
Hamlet 1945,D 23,II,3:1
Hamlet 1946,Je 4,18:4
Cyrano de Bergerac 1946,O 9,33:2
Cyrano de Bergerac 1947,Ja 17,27:2
Rip Van Winkle 1947,Jl 16,28:2

Reid, Frances—Cont
On the Harmfulness of Tobacco 1948,F 6,29:2
Bear, The 1948,F 6,29:2
Tragedian in Spite of Himself, A 1948,F 6,29:2
Wedding, The 1948,F 6,29:2
Richard III 1949,F 9,33:2
Richard III 1949,F 13,II,1:1
Twelfth Night 1949,O 4,33:2
Twelfth Night 1949,O 9,II,1:1
Touch of the Poet, A 1961,My 15,34:6
Reid, Gregory
Julius Caesar 1965,Jl 2,18:1
Reid, Helen
Return Engagement 1940,N 2,19:2
Reid, Helen Wicks (Choreographer)
Captain Jinks of the Horse Marines 1938,Ja 28,16:2
Reid, J Speed
Hamlet 1928,Je 2,11:3
Reid, Janet
Glass Cage, The 1957,Mr 11,21:2
Reid, Johnny
Singin' the Blues 1931,S 17,21:3
Reid, Justin
John Turner Davis 1958,Jl 2,25:1
Midnight Caller, The 1958,Jl 2,25:1
Reid, Kate
As You Like It 1959,Jl 1,27:1
Othello 1959,Jl 2,17:2
Othello 1959,Jl 5,II,1:1
Midsummer Night's Dream, A 1960,Je 30,23:5
Romeo and Juliet 1960,Jl 1,14:1
Henry VIII 1961,Je 22,22:1
Love's Labour's Lost 1961,Je 23,19:1
Henry VIII 1961,Jl 2,II,1:1
Macbeth 1962,Je 20,41:1
Taming of the Shrew, The 1962,Je 21,25:1
Who's Afraid of Virginia Woolf? 1962,N 1,34:1
Troilus and Cressida 1963,Je 19,40:2
Cyrano de Bergerac 1963,Je 20,30:1
Comedy of Errors, The 1963,Je 21,35:3
Dylan 1964,Ja 20,18:1
Julius Caesar 1965,Jl 2,18:1
Cherry Orchard, The 1965,Ag 2,17:2
Gnadiges Fraulein, The 1966,F 23,42:1
Mutilated, The 1966,F 23,42:1
Price, The 1968,F 8,37:1
Price, The 1968,F 18,II,1:1
Price, The 1968,O 30,39:1
Hamlet 1969,Je 30,33:1
Hamlet 1969,Jl 6,II,1:1
Three Sisters, The 1969,Ag 4,29:1
Three Sisters, The 1969,Ag 10,II,3:1
Friends, The 1970,Jl 24,17:2
Friends, The 1970,Ag 30,II,1:1
Reid, Kenneth
Love of Two Hours, The 1962,O 27,16:2
Reid, Lewis
Elsie Janis and Her Gang 1922,Ja 17,13:2
Reid, Maria
Come Share My House 1960,F 19,20:2
Reid, Marita
In the Summer House 1953,D 30,17:1
Reid, Marshall
Everyman 1941,My 9,19:2
Milky Way, The 1943,Je 10,17:2
Boy Meets Girl 1943,Je 23,15:5
Reid, Muriel
It Is to Laugh 1927,D 27,24:2
Reid, Nat (Playwright)
Booster, The 1929,O 25,26:2
Reid, Paul-Rodger
Black Quartet, A; Great Goodness of Life (A Coon
Show) 1969,Jl 31,28:1
Reid, Philip
Reflected Glory 1936,S 18,19:5
Reid, Scott
Cops and Horrors; Dracula 1970,Ag 11,27:1
Reid, Sheila
Beaux' Stratagem, The 1970,F 10,50:2
Three Sisters, The 1970,F 12,30:1
Reid, Ted
Julius Caesar 1937,N 12,26:6
Reid, Warren
Country Wife, The 1936,D 2,34:1
Reid, William
Ruy Blas 1957,D 14,16:3
Reide, Evelyn
Blossom Time 1931,Mr 5,32:1
Little Racketeer, The 1932,Ja 19,24:4
Reif, Paul (Composer)
Murderer Among Us, A 1964,Mr 26,43:1
Reiff, Almer
Hamlet 1928,Je 2,11:3
Bourgeois Gentilhomme, Le 1929,Mr 17,30:4
Reigbert, Erna
Last Warning, The 1927,Ap 3,VIII,2:1
Constant Wife, The 1928,My 20,VIII,2:1
Reigel, Charles
Fools Errant 1922,Ag 22,12:3
Reigeluth, John B
Wings Over Europe 1936,Mr 4,24:7
Reighard, Catherine (Playwright)
Pan Pipes and Donkeys' Ears 1929,D 27,26:5

iker, Don
Wretched the Lionhearted 1962,S 13,31:2
Toy for the Clowns, A 1962,S 13,31:2
iko, Nagai
Golden Bat 1970,Je 27,18:2
iley, Orrin
Applause 1970,Mr 31,35:1
illey, Estelle
Boyd's Daughter 1940,O 12,20:2
illey, Victor
Once Over Lightly 1955,Mr 16,39:1
illy
Anna Christie 1921,N 3,22:1
illy, Alfred
Respectfully Yours 1947,My 14,29:4
illy, Anastasia
No Foolin' 1926,Je 25,25:1
Yours Truly 1927,Ja 26,16:5
illy, Betty
Paradise 1931,My 12,29:2
illy, Bill
Seventeen 1951,Je 22,16:6
Enemy of the People, An 1959,F 5,24:4
illy, Charles
Black Crook, The 1929,Mr 12,26:5
Shoestring Revue 1929,N 23,19:2
illy, Charles Nelson
Best Foot Forward 1956,Mr 3,16:1
Three Times Three; Merrye Playe, A
  1956,My 24,27:2
Three Times Three; How He Lied to Her Husband
  1956,My 24,27:2
Three Times Three; Box and Cox 1956,My 24,27:2
Saintliness of Margery Kempe, The 1959,F 3,35:6
Fallout 1959,My 21,36:2
Lend an Ear 1959,S 25,20:5
Parade 1960,Ja 21,27:4
Bye Bye Birdie 1960,Ap 15,13:4
How to Succeed in Business Without Really Trying
  1961,O 16,34:1
Hello, Dolly! 1964,Ja 17,22:1
Skyscraper 1965,N 15,48:1
illy, Frank C (Playwright)
Mr Pickwick 1927,F 20,VII,2:6
Pickwick 1927,Mr 13,VII,1:1
Pickwick 1927,S 6,35:2
Pickwick 1927,O 2,VIII,1:1
illy, Frank C (Producer)
Pickwick 1927,F 16,17:4
Pickwick 1927,Mr 13,VII,1:1
Pickwick 1927,S 6,35:2
Pickwick 1927,S 11,VIII,1:1
Play Without a Name, A 1928,N 26,30:5
illy, Greg
Golden Bat 1970,Je 27,18:2
illy, Howard
Don Carlos 1962,F 28,27:5
illy, Hugh
Young Man's Fancy, A 1947,Ap 30,33:2
Curious Savage, The 1950,O 25,44:3
Second Threshold 1951,Ja 3,23:2
Second Threshold 1951,Ja 14,II,1:1
Never Say Never 1951,N 21,21:2
Dear Charles 1954,S 16,37:2
Dear Charles 1954,S 26,II,1:1
Fair Game 1957,N 4,39:1
illy, James
Emperor Jones, The 1936,Ag 11,24:6
illy, Jameson
King Lear 1923,Mr 10,9:4
illy, John
Henry IV, Part I 1946,My 7,25:2
illy, Joseph
This Mad Whirl 1937,Ja 10,II,4:8
Nativity Play, The 1937,D 21,29:1
illy, Kenneth D
Life Begins in '40 1940,Ap 5,24:2
illy, Lawrence
Oedipus Tyrannus 1941,My 10,13:8
Martyr Without Tears 1942,N 23,19:2
illy, Maurice
Half Moon Inn 1923,Mr 21,19:2
Old King's 1924,Mr 12,19:3
illy, Michael
Our Town 1959,Mr 24,46:2
illy, Phemy
Song for a Certain Midnight 1959,S 17,49:1
illy, Robert
Sharon's Grave 1961,N 9,39:2
Mister Roberts 1962,O 12,27:2
illy, Walter (Miscellaneous)
Highest Tree, The 1959,N 5,41:1
Unsinkable Molly Brown, The 1960,N 4,28:1
Devil's Advocate, The 1961,Mr 10,20:1
Something About a Soldier 1962,Ja 5,36:2
illy, Will Charles
Macbeth 1969,D 23,25:1
illy, William
On a Clear Day You Can See Forever
  1965,O 18,44:1
Three Philip Roth Stories; Conversion of the Jews
  1970,Jl 31,14:1
Cops and Horrors; Fly Paper 1970,Ag 11,27:1

Reillys, Five
Hooray for What! 1937,D 2,32:5
Reim, Robert
Kiss Me, Kate 1956,My 10,27:2
Reiman, Elise
Lady Comes Across, The 1942,Ja 10,10:2
Rosalinda; Fledermaus, Die 1942,O 29,26:5
Reimann, Hans (Playwright)
Adventures of the Worthy Soldier Schwejk, The
  1928,Mr 4,IX,2:1
Reimer, Helen
Ruined Lady, The 1920,Ja 21,10:2
Mob, The 1920,O 11,18:1
Deburau 1920,D 24,14:3
Deburau 1921,Ja 2,VI,3:1
Pot-Luck 1921,S 30,10:1
Partners Again 1922,My 2,22:2
Catskill Dutch 1924,My 7,18:1
Reimherr, George
Natja 1925,F 17,19:2
Rein, Fred (Miscellaneous)
Alchemist, The 1964,S 15,33:1
Reindel, Carl
Dark at the Top of the Stairs, The 1957,D 6,38:1
Moonbirds 1959,O 10,13:1
Something About a Soldier 1962,Ja 5,36:2
Reineke, Gary
Hamlet 1969,Je 11,37:1
Alchemist, The 1969,Je 12,51:1
Reiner, Carl
Inside U S A 1948,My 1,19:2
Alive and Kicking 1950,Ja 18,25:5
Reiner, Carl (Director)
Something Different 1967,N 29,52:1
Reiner, Carl (Original Author)
Enter Laughing 1963,Mr 15,8:1
Enter Laughing 1963,Je 16,II,1:1
Reiner, Carl (Playwright)
Something Different 1967,N 29,52:1
Something Different 1967,D 10,II,15:6
Reiner, E Susan (Scenic Designer)
Kill the One-Eyed Man 1965,O 21,56:1
Reiner, Earl
Bourgeois Gentilhomme, Le 1964,Je 18,28:2
Reiner, Ethel Linder (Miscellaneous)
Four Saints in Three Acts 1952,Ap 17,35:1
Reiner, Ethel Linder (Producer)
Camino Real 1953,Mr 20,26:1
Rainmaker, The 1954,O 29,28:1
Candide 1956,D 3,40:2
Maybe Tuesday 1958,Ja 30,18:3
Roman Candle 1960,F 4,34:2
Reiner, Fritz (Musical Director)
Devil and Daniel Webster, The 1939,My 19,26:1
Devil and Daniel Webster, The 1939,My 21,X,1:1
Reiner, Hanne Marie
On a Clear Day You Can See Forever
  1965,O 18,44:1
Reiner, Michelle
Guys and Dolls 1955,Ap 21,32:2
Goodbye Charlie 1959,D 17,50:1
Reines, Bernard
Prescott Proposals, The 1953,D 17,53:1
Reines, Bernard (Playwright)
Forward the Heart 1949,Ja 29,9:2
Reinglas, Fred (Miscellaneous)
New Tenant, The 1964,My 28,40:2
Victims of Duty 1964,My 28,40:2
That 5 A.M. Jazz 1964,O 20,42:2
Great Scot! 1965,N 12,56:3
Hooray!! It's a Glorious Day....And All That
  1966,Mr 10,28:1
Butterfly Dream, The 1966,My 20,41:1
Hair 1968,Ap 30,40:2
Reinhardt, Beatrice
George Washington 1920,Mr 2,9:1
Reinhardt, Edith
Belmont Varieties 1932,S 29,17:2
Reinhardt, Gottfried
Europa A G 1932,O 2,IX,1:2
Reinhardt, Gottfried (Director)
Europa A G 1932,O 2,IX,1:2
Reinhardt, Gottfried (Playwright)
Rosalinda; Fledermaus, Die 1942,O 29,26:5
Helen Goes to Troy 1944,Ap 25,17:2
Helen Goes to Troy 1944,Ap 30,II,1:1
Polonaise 1945,O 8,20:2
Reinhardt, Max
Miracle, The 1927,My 29,II,2:5
Reinhardt, Max (Director)
Orpheus in der Unterwelt 1922,F 5,VI,1:7
Miracle, The 1924,Ja 16,17:1
Miracle, The 1924,Ja 20,VII,1:1
Miracle, The 1924,Ja 27,VII,1:1
Miracle, The 1924,F 3,VII,1:1
Miracle, The 1924,F 17,4:3
Miracle, The 1924,Ag 19,9:1
Midsummer Night's Dream, A 1925,Mr 8,VII,2:1
Miracle, The 1925,Ag 17,10:4
Miracle, The 1925,S 29,31:6
King Lear 1925,O 12,18:1
Miracle, The 1925,O 29,29:1
Rain 1925,N 25,23:5

Reinhardt, Max (Director)—Cont
Riviera 1925,D 25,22:2
Captive, The 1926,O 24,VIII,2:1
Peripherie 1926,D 19,VII,4:4
Miracle, The 1926,D 28,16:2
Miracle, The 1927,My 29,II,2:5
Miracle, The 1927,Je 8,23:2
Midsummer Night's Dream, A 1927,Ag 8,6:1
Midsummer Night's Dream, A 1927,N 27,IX,1:1
Midsummer Night's Dream, A 1927,D 4,X,6:1
Dantons Tod 1928,Ja 1,VIII,3:1
Redemption: Lebende Leichnam, Der; Living
  Corpse, The 1928,N 20,28:2
Fledermaus, Die 1929,Jl 14,IX,2:1
Everyman 1929,Ag 5,25:1
Kreatur, Die 1930,My 25,IX,1:8
Weaker Sex, The 1931,Mr 1,VIII,1:3
Fair Helen 1931,Ag 30,VIII,2:1
Tales of Hoffmann 1932,Ja 10,VIII,1:6
Helen 1932,Ja 31,I,5:2
Vor Sonnenuntergang; Before Sunset
  1932,Mr 13,VIII,2:7
Grosses Welttheater 1933,Ap 16,IX,2:5
Welttheater 1933,Je 25,IX,1:2
Merchant of Venice, The 1934,Ag 12,IX,5:5
Eternal Road, The 1937,Ja 8,14:2
Eternal Road, The 1937,Ap 25,X,1:6
Merchant of Yonkers, The 1938,D 13,30:1
Merchant of Yonkers, The 1938,D 18,IX,3:2
Merchant of Yonkers, The 1938,D 29,14:2
Sons and Soldiers 1943,My 5,22:2
Family Portrait; Familie, Eine 1946,N 11,44:1
Reinhardt, Max (Miscellaneous)
Miracle, The 1932,Ap 10,I,18:1
Eternal Road, The 1937,Ja 8,14:2
Rosalinda; Fledermaus, Die 1942,O 29,26:5
Reinhardt, Max (Original Author)
Eternal Road, The 1937,Ja 24,X,1:1
Reinhardt, Max (Playwright)
Miracle, The 1924,Ja 16,17:1
Miracle, The 1924,Ag 19,9:1
Reinhardt, Max (Producer)
Midsummer Night's Dream, A 1921,My 15,VI,1:6
Saint Joan 1924,N 9,VII,2:3
Midsummer Night's Dream, A 1925,Mr 8,VII,2:1
Emperor Jones, The 1926,My 18,28:3
Everyman 1926,Ag 9,1:1
Periphery 1926,O 2,40:6
Dorothea Angermann 1926,N 22,28:2
Peripherie 1926,D 19,VII,4:4
Miracle, The 1927,Ap 15,27:1
Everyman 1927,Ag 1,4:3
Midsummer Night's Dream, A 1927,Ag 8,6:1
Abie's Irish Rose 1927,S 30,29:3
Midsummer Night's Dream, A 1927,N 18,21:1
Midsummer Night's Dream, A 1927,D 4,X,6:1
Jedermann 1927,D 8,33:2
Jedermann 1927,D 18,IX,6:1
Dantons Tod 1927,D 21,28:3
Danton's Death 1928,Ja 1,VIII,1:1
Peripherie 1928,Ja 3,29:1
Er Ist an Allem Schuld; He Is to Blame for
  Everything 1928,Ja 10,28:3
Diener Zweier Herren; Servant of Two Masters,
  The 1928,Ja 10,28:3
Kabale und Liebe 1928,Ja 17,22:3
Servant of Two Masters, The 1928,Ja 22,VIII,6:1
Lebende Leichnam, Der, Der; Living Corpse, The
  1928,Ja 24,26:2
Gespenster, Die; Ghosts 1928,F 8,28:6
Dorothea Angermann 1928,F 19,VIII,2:1
Trial of Mary Dugan, The 1928,My 4,31:3
Burlesque; Artisten 1928,Je 10,17:2
Robbers, The 1928,Ag 10,9:2
Artisten; Burlesque 1928,S 23,IX,2:2
Romeo and Juliette 1928,D 2,X,4:4
Fledermaus, Die 1929,Jl 14,IX,2:1
Apple Cart, The 1930,Mr 9,IX,4:3
Phaea 1930,Ag 31,VIII,2:1
Schwierige, Der 1930,N 30,IX,2:1
Good Fairy, The 1930,D 23,24:2
Kabale und Liebe 1931,N 1,VIII,4:2
Rebound 1931,N 1,VIII,4:1
Before Sunset 1932,F 17,19:3
Vor Sonnenuntergang; Before Sunset
  1932,Mr 13,VIII,2:7
Miracle, The 1932,My 8,VIII,2:2
Journalisten, Die 1932,Jl 17,IX,1:1
Fair Helen 1932,Jl 17,IX,1:2
Grosses Welttheater 1933,Ap 16,IX,2:5
Midsummer Night's Dream, A 1934,S 19,15:1
Oedipus Rex 1936,O 18,X,3:8
Faust 1938,Ag 28,IX,2:5
Sons and Soldiers 1943,My 5,22:2
Russian Question, The 1947,My 4,I,54:3
Reinhardt, Ray
Brothers Karamazov, The 1957,D 9,39:4
Brothers Karamazov, The 1957,D 22,II,3:1
Song of Songs 1958,O 29,31:1
Puntila 1959,My 15,26:2
Julius Caesar 1959,Ag 4,30:1
Great God Brown, The 1959,O 7,48:1
Lysistrata 1959,N 25,19:4
Henry IV 1960,Mr 2,42:1

Reinhardt, Ray—Cont
Henry IV 1960,Ap 19,41:1
Henry IV, Part II 1960,Ap 24,II,1:1
She Stoops to Conquer 1960,N 2,42:5
She Stoops to Conquer 1960,N 13,II,1:1
She Stoops to Conquer 1960,N 15,36:3
Plough and the Stars, The 1960,D 7,56:2
Octoroon, The 1961,Ja 28,13:1
Hamlet 1961,Mr 17,17:1
Caucasian Chalk Circle, The 1961,N 1,35:1
Burning of the Lepers, The 1962,Ap 5,29:1
Once in a Lifetime 1962,O 30,30:1
Devils, The 1963,N 5,25:1
Helen 1964,D 11,55:4
Hamlet 1968,Je 10,59:1
Tiny Alice 1969,S 30,42:1
Flea in Her Ear, A 1969,O 4,25:1

Reinhardt, Stephen
West Side Story 1968,Je 25,32:1
Minnie's Boys 1970,Mr 27,27:1

Reinhart, Frances
Curtain Call 1937,Ap 23,24:7

Reinhart, Robert
School for Husbands, The 1933,O 17,26:5

Reinheart, Alice
Papavert 1931,D 30,25:1
Mr Papavert 1932,Ja 23,18:6
Foolscap 1933,Ja 12,21:2
Mask and the Face, The 1933,My 9,20:2
Drums Begin, The 1933,N 25,10:5
Wooden Slipper, The 1934,Ja 4,16:3
Journey to Jerusalem 1940,O 7,21:2
Leaf and Bough 1949,Ja 22,10:2

Reinholdt, Robert (Lighting Director)
Antony and Cleopatra 1967,O 29,83:4
Seagull, The 1968,Jl 25,27:2

Reinholt, George
Misalliance 1961,S 26,32:2
Chiaroscuro; Judges, The 1963,Je 6,40:8
Bald Soprano, The 1963,S 18,35:4
Colombe 1965,F 24,33:1

Reinle, Ernest
When the Bough Breaks 1950,Mr 9,25:5
Gods of the Mountain, The 1950,My 25,36:2

Reino, Richard
B J One 1931,My 7,21:3

Reinold, Bernard A
Unwritten Chapter, The 1920,O 12,18:1
Deburau 1920,D 24,14:3
Drums of Jeopardy, The 1922,My 30,8:4
Flame of Love 1924,Ap 22,19:2
Quarantine 1924,D 17,19:7
Beware of Widows 1925,D 2,22:3

Reis, Hilda
Stevedore 1934,O 2,18:2
Weep for the Virgins 1935,D 2,18:1
Revolt of the Beavers, The 1937,My 21,19:2
Many Mansions 1937,O 28,28:6

Reis, Kurt (Director)
Friends, The 1970,Jl 24,17:2

Reis, Maxene (Miscellaneous)
Digging for Apples 1962,S 28,29:4

Reisbeck, Kenneth (Playwright)
Rock Me, Julie 1931,Ja 4,VIII,2:3

Reisdorff, Kenn
Man of Destiny, The 1956,Ap 26,38:1
Beaux' Stratagem, The 1957,Jl 9,25:4
Magistrate, The 1959,My 14,30:6

Reisel, Robert
Homo 1969,Ap 12,40:2

Reisel, Zvi (Playwright)
To Be or Not to Be-What Kind of a Question Is
That? 1970,O 20,39:1

Reiselt, Susan
Tobacco Road 1960,My 11,44:2

Reiser, Al
After Such Pleasures 1934,F 8,15:2
For Your Pleasure 1943,F 6,9:2

Reiser, Anna
King Lear 1968,Je 3,55:4
Dance of Death, The 1969,My 26,53:1

Reiser, Catherine
Kit Marlowe 1936,My 24,35:1

Reiser, Lee
After Such Pleasures 1934,F 8,15:2
For Your Pleasure 1943,F 6,9:2

Reiser, Robert
Criss-Crossing 1970,Ja 22,30:1

Reisman, Barbara
Oklahoma! 1953,S 1,19:1

Reisman, Jane (Lighting Director)
Shadow of Heroes 1961,D 6,59:1
Man's a Man, A 1962,S 20,30:2
Amorous Flea, The 1964,F 18,26:1

Reisman, Joe (Musical Director)
Poupees de Paris, Les 1964,My 16,11:1

Reisman, Sylvia
Women at the Tomb, The 1961,Ap 25,41:1

Reiss, Amanda
Blithe Spirit 1970,S 17,57:1

Reiss, Eda
My Heart's in the Highlands 1939,Ap 14,29:2
No for an Answer 1941,Ja 6,10:6
Everyman 1941,My 9,19:2

Mexican Mural; Vera Cruz Interior 1942,Ap 27,19:2

Reiss, Jeffrey C (Miscellaneous)
Ofay Watcher, The 1969,S 16,40:1

Reiss, Jeffrey C (Producer)
Tonight in Living Color; David Show, The
1969,Je 11,43:1
Tonight in Living Color; Golden Fleece, The
1969,Je 11,43:1

Reiss, Marvin (Costume Designer)
Highest Tree, The 1959,N 5,41:1

Reiss, Marvin (Lighting Director)
Back to Methuselah 1958,Mr 27,41:5
Party With Betty Comden and Adolph Green, A
1958,D 24,2:7
Love and Kisses 1963,D 19,39:1
Portrait of a Queen 1968,F 29,29:1

Reiss, Marvin (Miscellaneous)
Summer of the Seventeenth Doll 1958,Ja 23,23:2
Requiem for a Nun 1959,Ja 31,13:2

Reiss, Marvin (Scenic Designer)
Home Is the Hero 1954,S 23,42:2
Back to Methuselah 1958,Mr 27,41:5
Party With Betty Comden and Adolph Green, A
1958,D 24,2:7
Third Best Sport 1958,D 31,15:3
Thurber Carnival, A 1960,F 27,13:2
Thurber Carnival, A 1960,Mr 6,II,1:1
Evening With Mike Nichols and Elaine May, An
1960,O 10,37:1
Love and Kisses 1963,D 19,39:1
Portrait of a Queen 1968,F 29,29:1

Reiss, Ronald
Family Portrait 1939,Mr 9,18:4
Woman Brown, The 1939,D 9,18:5
Medicine Show 1940,Ap 13,20:6
Harriet 1943,Mr 4,24:2

Reiss-Merlin, Eda
Private Life of the Master Race, The
1945,Je 13,28:3

Reissman, Carl
Seven Against One 1930,My 7,25:1

Reiter, Ann
Song of Norway 1959,Je 26,16:2

Reiter, Ronny (Costume Designer)
Maria Stuart 1968,Mr 27,38:1

Reiter, Ruth
Music Hath Charms 1934,D 31,8:2
Countess Maritza 1936,Ag 19,18:2

Reith, Kapi (Costume Designer)
Ludlow Fair 1966,Mr 23,42:1
Madness of Lady Bright, The 1966,Mr 23,42:1

Reitnel, Georges
Heure du Berger, L'; Propitious Moment, The
1936,N 12,30:1
Martine 1936,N 26,38:2
Dejeuner d'Amoureax, Un; Lovers Breakfast, A
1936,N 26,38:2
Homme Que J'Ai Tue, L'; Man Whom I Have
Killed, The 1936,D 10,34:3
Bichon; Little Dear 1936,D 31,20:5
Sexe Fort, Le; Strong Sex, The 1937,Ja 14,17:4
Si Je Voulais; If I Wished to 1937,Ja 28,22:5
Dans Le Noir; In the Dark 1937,F 11,18:3
Christian 1937,F 25,18:6

Reitzell, William
Fiesta 1933,D 16,12:2

Rek, Paul
Killers 1928,Mr 14,28:3

Rekoma
Earl Carroll's Vanities 1923,Jl 6,8:2

Relis, Rachela
Brothers Ashkenazi, The 1955,N 12,24:4
Enchanting Melody 1964,N 25,40:1
Trees Die Standing, The 1969,O 13,52:1
Mirele Efros 1969,D 26,41:1
President's Daughter, The 1970,N 4,41:2

Relkin, Edwin A (Producer)
Wild Man, The 1930,My 17,21:5
Money Mad 1937,My 25,32:5
Oy, Is Dus a Leben!; Oh, What a Life!
1942,O 13,19:2

Rella, Ettore (Playwright)
Sign of Winter 1958,My 8,35:1

Reller, Elizabeth
Abe Lincoln in Illinois 1938,O 17,12:2
Day in the Sun 1939,My 17,29:2

Relph, George
Home Chat 1927,N 13,IX,2:1
Henry IV, Part I 1946,My 7,25:2
Henry IV, Part II 1946,My 8,33:4
Henry IV 1946,My 12,II,1:1
Uncle Vanya 1946,My 14,18:2
Oedipus; Critic, The 1946,My 21,19:2
Oedipus 1946,My 21,19:2
King Lear 1946,O 13,II,2:3
Gioconda Smile, The 1950,O 9,21:2
Gioconda Smile, The 1950,O 15,II,1:1
Entertainer, The 1958,F 13,22:2
Entertainer, The 1958,F 23,II,1:1

Remar, Philip
Ceiling Zero 1935,Ap 11,26:2

Remarque, Erich Maria (Playwright)
Berlin 1945 1956,S 22,20:6

Rembach, Frank (Lighting Director)
Wait a Minim! 1966,Mr 8,43:1

Rembach, Frank (Scenic Designer)
Wait a Minim! 1966,Mr 8,43:1

Rembova, Lisa
Chalk Dust 1936,Mr 5,24:5
Path of Flowers, The 1936,S 18,19:3
Big Blow 1938,O 3,11:2

Remer, Philip
Crime and Punishment 1935,Ja 23,20:3
Virginia Reel 1947,Ap 15,28:2
Wild Duck, The 1951,D 27,17:1

Remey, Ethel
Rose Briar 1922,D 26,11:3
Connie Goes Home 1923,S 7,10:1
Such Is Life 1927,S 1,27:3
Virtue's Bed 1930,Ap 16,26:5
Take My Tip 1932,Ap 12,25:2
Forsaking All Others 1933,Mr 2,21:2
I'll Take the High Road 1943,N 10,28:3
Our Town 1944,Ja 11,24:5
Chicken Every Sunday 1944,Ap 6,27:2
Tenting Tonight 1947,Ap 3,32:2
Family Portrait 1959,My 6,48:2

Remi, Jean-Francois
Lorenzaccio 1958,O 15,44:2
Marie Tudor 1958,O 22,39:1

Remick, Lee
Be Your Age 1953,Ja 15,24:2
Anyone Can Whistle 1964,Ap 6,36:1
Wait Until Dark 1966,F 3,21:1

Remick, William
Red Rainbow, A 1953,S 15,37:4

Remington, Barbara
On a Clear Day You Can See Forever
1965,O 18,44:1

Remington, Barbara (Costume Designer)
Escurial 1960,Jl 22,13:1
Calvary 1960,Jl 22,13:1
Santa Claus 1960,Jl 22,13:1

Remington, Barbara (Scenic Designer)
Santa Claus 1960,Jl 22,13:1
Escurial 1960,Jl 22,13:1
Calvary 1960,Jl 22,13:1

Remington, Emily
Romeo and Juliet 1940,Ap 16,28:4

Remington, William
Out Goes She 1928,D 30,VIII,4:1

Remisoff (Scenic Designer)
Chauve-Souris 1922,O 11,22:2

Remley, Ralph M
Ah, Wilderness! 1934,My 1,26:3

Remo, Kenneth
Sleepy Hollow 1948,Je 4,26:3

Remo, Ray
Dancing Girl, The 1923,Ja 25,16:2

Remos, Susanne
Of V We Sing 1942,F 16,20:3

Rempel, Oskar (Benjamin M Kaye) (Playwright)
Curtain Rises, The 1933,O 20,15:2

Rempell, Harriet
Babies a La Carte 1927,Ag 16,31:1

Remsen, Bert
Doctored Wife, The 1950,Jl 12,33:2
Son, The 1950,Ag 16,24:6
Diamond Lil 1951,S 15,8:2
Diary of a Scoundrel 1956,N 5,41:1

Remsen, Deborah
Me and Juliet 1953,My 29,17:1

Remsten, H L
S S Glencairn 1924,N 4,31:4
S S Glencairn 1929,Ja 10,24:5

Remus, Jorie
Potting Shed, The 1958,N 3,49:2
Hi, Paisano 1961,O 2,36:2

Remy, Constant
Bourgeoise, La 1927,O 2,VIII,2:4
Yes 1928,F 19,VIII,4:4

Remy, Dick
Boys and Girls Together 1940,S 5,28:6
Boys and Girls Together 1940,O 2,19:2

Remy, Dot
Boys and Girls Together 1940,S 5,28:6
Boys and Girls Together 1940,O 2,19:2
Blackouts of 1949 1949,S 7,39:2

Remy, Maurice
Topaze 1931,F 17,29:1

Rena, Gita
Wiener Blut 1964,S 12,14:1

Renan, Emile
Gypsy Baron, The 1944,N 15,20:3
Pirates of Penzance, The 1946,My 17,14:6
Pirates of Penzance, The 1946,S 21,19:2
Rape of Lucretia, The 1948,D 30,24:2
Miss Liberty 1949,Jl 16,6:5
Consul, The 1957,S 4,40:3
Patience 1964,Mr 26,42:1
Patience 1965,Ap 16,34:1
Pirates of Penzance, The 1965,Ap 21,50:6
Patience 1968,My 16,52:1

Renard, David
Teahouse of the August Moon, The 1956,N 9,33:2

enard, Eileen
Big White Fog 1940,O 23,26:2
enard, Ken
Sailor, Beware! 1935,My 7,28:4
Patriots, The 1943,D 21,22:5
Strange Fruit 1945,N 30,18:6
Mr Peebles and Mr Hooker 1946,O 11,29:2
Long Way From Home, A 1948,F 9,25:2
Answered the Flute 1960,Mr 10,37:4
Renatsky (Composer)
Deux Sous de Fleurs 1933,O 1,IX,1:3
Renaud, Alfred
What Price Glory 1924,S 6,14:3
Renaud, Andre
Vanities 1932,S 18,IX,2:1
Vanities 1932,S 28,22:4
Renaud, Madeleine
Roi Dagobert, Le 1926,N 14,VIII,2:1
Jalousie, La 1932,D 4,IX,3:6
Chandelier, Le 1939,Mr 19,XI,3:1
Baptiste 1952,N 13,34:2
Fausses Confidences, Les 1952,N 13,34:2
Baptiste 1952,N 13,34:2
Proces, Le; Trial, The 1952,N 18,36:2
Amphitryon 1952,N 21,21:2
Occupe-Toi d'Amelie; Keep Your Eyes on Amelie
1952,N 25,35:2
Repetition, La; Rehearsal, The 1952,N 28,22:2
Pour Lucrece 1953,N 29,II,3:1
Sleep of Prisoners, A 1955,Ja 15,10:5
Misanthrope, Le 1957,Ja 8,26:1
Christophe Colomb 1957,Ja 31,20:5
Misanthrope, Le 1957,F 8,19:1
Nuits de La Colere, Les; Nights of Fury
1957,F 12,31:1
Feu la Mere de Madame; Dear Departed
Mother-in-Law 1957,F 12,31:1
Chien du Jardinier, Le; Gardener's Dog, The
1957,F 19,36:1
Adieux, Les 1957,F 19,36:1
Repetition, La 1957,S 3,23:2
Mariage de Figaro, Le 1964,F 26,41:2
Pieton de L'Air, Le 1964,Mr 4,33:2
Salut a Moliere 1964,Mr 4,33:2
Happy Days 1965,S 14,45:2
Journees Entieres dans les Arbres, Des
1965,D 4,20:1
Paravents, Les 1966,Ap 22,36:3
Oh, Les Beaux Jours 1970,Ap 25,32:3
Beaux Jours, Les 1970,My 20,32:1
Rabelais 1970,My 20,32:1
Renaud, Madeleine (Director)
Mariage de Figaro, Le 1964,F 26,41:2
Andromaque 1964,F 29,13:2
Salut a Moliere 1964,Mr 4,33:2
Pieton de L'Air, Le 1964,Mr 4,33:2
Renaud, Madeleine (Producer)
Misanthrope, Le 1957,F 8,19:1
Renaud, William
Paradise Alley 1924,Ap 2,17:3
Renault, Charles
Colonel Satan 1931,Ja 12,24:1
Renault, Francis
Passing Show of 1922, The 1922,S 21,18:2
Renault, Louis
Pasteur 1923,Mr 13,19:1
Renault, Norma
Salad Days 1958,N 11,24:1
Renault, Paul
Get Thee to Canterbury 1969,Ja 26,74:1
Renavent, Georges
Genius and the Crowd 1920,S 7,20:1
Cloister, The 1921,Je 6,16:3
Pigeon, The 1922,F 3,13:1
Texas Nightingale, The 1922,N 21,15:2
Crooked Square, The 1923,S 11,10:2
Grounds for Divorce 1924,S 24,20:1
Antonia 1925,O 21,20:1
Last Torture, The 1927,Ja 13,28:4
Claw, The 1927,Ja 13,28:4
Florentine Tragedy, A 1927,F 2,22:4
Napoleon's Barber 1927,F 2,22:4
Minuet, A 1927,Mr 5,12:2
Diplomacy 1928,My 29,16:3
Goin' Home 1928,Ag 24,23:2
Renavent, Georges (Playwright)
Last Torture, The 1927,Ja 13,28:4
Renavent, Gladys
Cocktail Impromptu 1927,Ja 13,28:4
Renda, Joey
Infernal Machine, The 1958,F 4,33:1
Rendel, Robert
Circle, The 1921,S 13,12:1
Four in Hand 1923,S 7,10:2
Right to Kill, The 1926,F 16,22:2
Ghost Train, The 1926,Ag 26,17:2
Wings Over Europe 1928,D 11,35:1
Josef Suss 1930,Ja 21,28:5
One Chaste Man 1930,Je 11,33:5
Rendel, Robert (Director)
Enchantment 1927,Ap 28,27:3
Rendina, Victor
They Knew What They Wanted 1949,F 17,28:2

Rendl, Paula
Untitled-Passion Play 1922,My 10,21:3
Rene
Mexicana 1939,Ap 22,14:4
Mexicana 1939,My 7,X,3:1
Rene, A W
Samson and Delilah 1920,N 18,18:1
Rene, Fernand
Ecole des Femmes, L'; School for Wives
1951,Mr 19,22:1
Rene, Henri (Miscellaneous)
Pirates of Penzance, The 1961,S 7,41:1
Renee, Carol
Sunny River 1941,D 5,28:2
Renee, Helen
Madame Capet 1938,O 26,26:2
Dear Octopus 1939,Ja 12,22:2
Susanna, Don't You Cry 1939,My 23,27:2
Two on an Island 1940,Ja 23,17:2
Flight to the West 1940,D 31,19:1
Renee-Devillers, Mme
Homme et Ses Fantomes, L' 1924,N 14,16:1
Merchant of Venice, The 1924,N 18,23:2
Bourgeois Gentilhomme, Le 1924,N 20,21:2
Taming of the Shrew, The 1924,N 25,27:3
Renfroe, Steve
Red, White and Maddox 1969,Ja 27,27:1
Rengier, John (Miscellaneous)
By Hex 1956,Je 19,25:1
Rengier, John (Playwright)
By Hex 1956,Je 19,25:1
Renie (Costume Designer)
Ice Follies 1959,Ja 14,30:1
Ice Follies 1962,Ja 10,24:6
Renn, Charles G
Madame Lafayette 1960,Mr 4,21:1
Rennick, Jack
Trip to Scarborough, A 1929,Mr 18,31:2
Dragon, The 1929,Mr 26,34:2
Rennick, Jack (Miscellaneous)
Revolt of the Beavers, The 1937,My 21,19:2
Rennick, Nancy
Career 1957,My 1,42:6
Career 1957,My 19,II,1:1
Rennie, Hugh
Porgy 1927,O 11,26:2
Intimate Relations 1932,Mr 29,23:2
Goodbye Again 1932,D 29,16:4
Spring in Autumn 1933,O 25,22:5
Oliver Oliver 1934,Ja 6,18:5
They Shall Not Die 1934,F 22,24:4
Picnic 1934,My 3,15:2
Lord Blesses the Bishop, The 1934,N 28,24:5
On to Fortune 1935,F 5,22:2
Golden Journey, The 1936,S 16,28:6
You Can't Take It With You 1936,D 15,31:1
Family Portrait 1939,Mr 9,18:4
Journey's End 1939,S 19,29:2
Weak Link, The 1940,Mr 5,19:2
Craig's Wife 1947,F 13,35:2
Joy to the World 1948,Mr 19,28:2
Remains to Be Seen 1951,O 4,37:1
Rennie, Hugh (Director)
Meet the Wife 1937,Jl 6,23:1
Apron Strings 1937,Jl 13,22:3
Ten Minute Alibi 1937,Jl 20,19:3
Rennie, James
Spanish Love 1920,Ag 18,6:1
Pot-Luck 1921,S 30,10:1
Madeleine and the Movies 1922,Mr 7,11:1
Shore Leave 1922,Ag 9,20:2
Love Habit, The 1923,Mr 15,17:1
Best People, The 1924,Ag 20,8:1
Cape Smoke 1925,F 17,19:1
Spring Fever 1925,Ag 4,14:2
Great Gatsby, The 1926,F 3,22:1
Crime Wave, The 1927,F 13,VII,1:4
Crime 1927,F 23,27:3
Julius Caesar 1927,Je 7,27:2
Vaudeville (Palace) 1927,Jl 5,19:3
Mulberry Bush, The 1927,O 27,33:1
Young Love 1928,Ag 12,VII,1:2
Young Love 1928,S 30,IX,2:7
Young Love 1928,O 31,28:1
Biarritz 1929,Ag 11,VIII,2:1
Jehovah Joe 1929,Ag 25,VIII,3:1
Gala Night 1930,F 26,22:4
Trick for Trick 1932,F 19,14:2
Bridal Wise 1932,My 31,15:5
Alien Corn 1933,F 14,19:5
Alien Corn 1933,F 21,17:2
Alien Corn 1933,F 26,IX,1:1
Murder at the Vanities 1933,Ag 31,20:1
Murder at the Vanities 1933,S 13,22:4
Love on an Island 1934,Jl 24,20:5
Divided by Three 1934,O 3,24:2
Knock on Wood 1935,My 29,16:2
Drums Professor, The 1935,Jl 30,17:2
Abide With Me 1935,N 22,19:2
Co-Respondent Unknown 1936,F 12,24:4
Miss Quis 1937,Ap 2,18:5
Miss Quis 1937,Ap 8,20:5
I Must Love Someone 1939,F 8,18:7

Rennie, James—Cont
Christmas Eve 1939,D 28,17:2
Russian Bank 1940,My 25,20:2
One-Man Show 1945,F 9,21:2
One-Man Show 1945,F 18,II,1:1
Four Winds 1957,S 26,21:2
Annie Get Your Gun 1958,F 20,29:2
Rennie, James (Playwright)
Jehovah Joe 1929,Ag 25,VIII,3:1
Rennie, Michael
Mary, Mary 1961,Mr 9,24:2
Renno, Vincent
Legal Grounds 1940,D 2,18:4
Reno, Muriel
Canteen Show, The 1942,S 4,18:1
Renoff, Renova, and Bekefi
Vaudeville (Palace) 1932,Je 6,18:2
Renoff and Renova
Earl Carroll's Vanities 1923,Jl 6,8:2
Renoir, Pierre
Siegfried 1928,My 20,VIII,1:3
Suzanne 1929,F 17,IX,4:2
Jean de la Lune 1929,My 12,IX,5:3
Amphitryon 38 1929,D 1,X,4:1
Eau Fraiche, L' 1931,Je 7,VIII,3:5
Taciturne, Un 1931,N 22,VIII,1:6
Margrave, La 1932,D 18,X,3:6
Intermezzo 1933,Mr 26,IX,2:1
Chateau de Cartes, Le 1937,F 14,X,2:3
Ecole des Femmes, L'; School for Wives
1951,Mr 19,22:1
Renouardt, Jane
Facon de Se Donner, La 1925,D 27,VII,2:1
Homme Qui Jouait du Banjo, L' 1926,O 24,VIII,2:1
Vacances de Paques, Les 1927,Ja 2,VII,2:1
Par le Temps Qui Court 1930,O 5,IX,4:3
Pierre ou Jack? 1931,Ap 19,VIII,2:7
Renouardt, Jane (Producer)
Lulu 1927,O 2,VIII,2:4
Renschler, George
Anthony on Overtime 1961,O 21,13:2
Rate of Exchange 1968,Ap 2,50:1
Renton, Edward (Musical Director)
Porgy and Bess 1952,O 10,21:4
Renwick, Katherine
So's Your Old Manhattan 1927,My 5,30:5
Manhatters, The 1927,Jl 19,27:3
Manhatters, The 1927,Ag 4,25:4
Ritzy 1930,F 11,30:4
Renwick, Kenneth
Macbeth 1936,Ap 15,25:4
Trial of Dr Beck, The 1937,Ag 10,22:2
One-Act Plays of the Sea; Long Voyage Home,
The 1937,O 30,23:2
Renwick, Peter
Who's Who 1938,Mr 2,16:2
Renys, Roberta
Straw Hat, The 1926,O 15,20:2
Renzi, Ada
Romanticismo 1933,My 1,10:5
Renzi, Silvio
Processo dei Veleni, Il; Case of Poisons, The
1935,Ja 21,18:2
Reoyo, Enrique (Playwright)
Leyenda del Beso, La 1942,N 20,26:4
Repp, Ellen
Street Scene 1947,Ja 10,17:2
Sleepy Hollow 1948,Je 4,26:3
Repp, Guy
Paths of Glory 1935,S 27,24:2
Bicycle Ride to Nevada 1963,S 25,38:1
Deputy, The 1964,F 27,26:1
Repp, Stafford
Ah, Wilderness! 1954,Ag 21,20:4
Reppa, David (Lighting Director)
Minstrel Boy, The 1948,O 15,28:2
Idiot's Delight 1957,F 23,14:2
Rope Dancers, The 1959,Mr 14,26:1
Reppa, David (Scenic Designer)
Respectfully Yours 1947,My 14,29:4
Minstrel Boy, The 1948,O 15,28:2
Rope Dancers, The 1959,Mr 14,26:1
Painted Days, The 1961,Ap 7,24:1
Don Carlos 1962,F 28,27:5
Storm, The 1962,Mr 31,17:2
Man's a Man, A 1962,S 20,30:2
Reppil, R A (Arthur Lipper Jr) (Producer)
Saluta 1934,Ag 29,13:4
Rescigno, Nicola (Musical Director)
Lord Byron's Love Letter 1955,Ja 19,23:2
Resin, Dan
Young Abe Lincoln 1961,Ap 26,36:1
Fade Out--Fade In 1964,My 27,45:1
On a Clear Day You Can See Forever
1965,O 18,44:1
Month of Sundays 1968,S 17,50:1
Resley, Robert
Flame of Love 1924,Ap 22,19:2
Resnick, L (Playwright)
Recruits 1934,O 13,10:4
Recruits 1935,Ja 20,X,3:1
Resnick, Matt
Anna Christie 1952,Ja 10,33:1

Resnick, Murray
Mighty Nimrod, The 1931,My 13,23:1
Resnick, Victor (Miscellaneous)
Leader, The 1969,Ap 22,40:2
Honest-to-God Schnozzola, The 1969,Ap 22,40:2
Resnickoff, Leo
Russian People, The 1942,D 30,17:2
Chauve-Souris of 1943 1943,Ag 13,13:2
Resnik, Muriel (Playwright)
Any Wednesday 1964,F 19,34:1
Respighi, Carlo
Storm Operation 1944,Ja 12,28:2
Respighi (Miscellaneous)
Boutique Fantasque, La 1929,D 28,10:6
Ress, Charles
Family Reunion, The 1947,N 29,9:2
Ressler, Benjamin
Chair, The 1930,O 4,15:4
God's Thieves 1930,O 27,17:4
Ressler, Benjamin (Playwright)
Love Thief, The 1931,Ja 19,24:5
Girl From Warsaw, The 1931,S 14,15:5
60,000 Heroes 1935,Ja 28,11:5
Worlds Apart 1941,Ja 23,19:3
Uncle Sam in Israel 1952,D 8,38:5
Ressler, Benjamin (Translator)
It Can't Happen Here 1936,O 28,30:1
Restand, Edmond (Playwright)
Cyrano de Bergerac 1936,Ap 28,17:1
Reta, Patti Ann
Song of Norway 1958,Je 23,19:2
Retford, Ella
Vaudeville (Palace) 1926,O 19,27:5
Rethy, J B (Original Author)
If I Was Rich 1926,S 3,15:2
Retik, Jozef
Mother Courage 1967,N 17,55:1
Retinue, Papalin
Embezzled Heaven 1944,N 1,20:2
Retsof, Elinor
Trigger 1927,D 7,32:1
Retter, Dezso
Merry World, The 1926,Je 9,18:3
Merry World, The 1926,Je 13,VII,1:1
Passions of 1926 1926,Ag 3,19:4
Vaudeville (Palace) 1930,Mr 7,21:2
Retter, Oscar (Playwright)
Phantom Ship, The 1926,Je 27,VII,3:1
Rettig, George P
Grey Heir, The 1926,Ap 6,29:2
Rettig, Samuel
Mother Courage 1967,N 17,55:1
Reud, Robert (Producer)
Two Mrs Carrolls, The 1943,Ag 4,14:1
Ramshackle Inn 1944,Ja 6,17:5
Odds on Mrs Oakley, The 1944,O 3,18:8
Duet for Two Hands 1947,O 8,28:3
Reumert, Anna
Victory 1937,N 14,XI,2:5
Reumert, Paul
Journey's End 1930,Mr 30,VIII,3:4
Swedenhielms 1931,Mr 1,VIII,3:1
Reuss, Leo
Brest-Litovsk 1930,N 30,IX,2:1
Revallos, Elaine
Don Juan 1921,S 8,14:2
Reve, Germaine
Untitled-Revue 1926,N 21,VIII,2:1
Reveaux, Edward (Director)
Are You With It? 1945,N 12,17:3
All for Love 1949,Ja 24,16:5
Razzle Dazzle 1951,F 20,21:1
Reveaux, Edward (Playwright)
Tom Sawyer 1958,Jl 15,21:8
Revecz, Lazlo (Miscellaneous)
Fools Are Passing Through 1958,Ap 3,24:2
Reveges, Domingo A (Miscellaneous)
Smiling the Boy Fell Dead 1961,Ap 20,28:1
Revel, Billie
Ziegfeld Follies 1923,O 22,17:2
Revel, Harry (Composer)
Ziegfeld Follies 1931,Jl 2,30:5
Marching By 1932,Mr 4,17:1
Smiling Faces 1932,Ag 31,12:3
Are You With It? 1945,N 12,17:3
Revel, Harry (Lyricist)
Marching By 1932,Mr 4,17:1
Revel, Harry (Playwright)
Ziegfeld Follies 1931,Jl 2,30:5
Revelers, The
Vaudeville (Palace) 1929,My 20,22:8
Revelle, Hamilton
Captain Applejack 1921,D 31,14:2
Lonely Lee 1923,N 11,VIII,2:6
Reverby, Milton (Miscellaneous)
Red Roses for Me 1961,N 28,41:1
Revere, Amy
Tip-Toes 1925,D 29,20:2
Good News 1927,Ag 14,VII,2:1
Manhattan Mary 1927,S 27,30:3
Revere, Anne
Great Barrington, The 1931,F 20,18:1
Lady With a Lamp, The 1931,N 20,27:2

Wild Waves 1932,F 20,11:4
Double Door 1933,S 22,15:5
Children's Hour, The 1934,N 21,23:2
As You Like It 1937,N 1,25:2
As You Like It 1937,N 8,18:2
Three Sisters, The 1939,O 16,23:1
Four Twelves Are 48 1951,Ja 18,30:2
Cue for Passion 1958,N 26,25:2
Jolly's Progress 1959,D 7,42:2
Toys in the Attic 1960,F 26,23:2
Toys in the Attic 1960,Mr 6,II,1:1
Night of the Dunce 1966,D 29,21:1
Revere, Eugene
Bunch and Judy, The 1922,N 29,20:1
Sitting Pretty 1924,Ap 9,24:2
City Chap, The 1925,O 27,21:1
Reverelly
White Horse Inn 1936,O 2,28:5
Revil, Rudi (Composer)
Crazy With the Heat 1941,Ja 15,18:2
Crazy With the Heat 1941,Ja 31,15:2
Gabrielle 1941,Mr 26,26:2
Revill, Clive
Mr Pickwick 1952,S 18,36:3
Irma la Douce 1960,S 30,31:2
Irma la Douce 1960,O 16,II,1:1
Oliver 1962,S 27,32:3
Oliver 1963,Ja 8,5:5
Persecution and Assassination of Marat As
Performed by the Inmates of the Asylum of
Charenton Under the Direction of the Marquis de
Sade, The 1964,Ag 21,14:2
Sherry! 1967,Mr 29,39:1
Sherry! 1967,Ap 9,II,1:1
Skin of Our Teeth, The 1968,S 12,55:1
Revner, Katherine
Valley of Content, The 1925,Ja 14,19:2
Rat, The 1925,F 11,19:3
Bells, The 1926,Ap 14,20:3
They All Want Something 1926,O 13,20:2
Off Key 1927,F 9,16:2
Rewalt, Lothar
From Vienna 1939,Je 21,26:2
Reunion in New York 1940,F 22,28:4
Winter Soldiers 1942,N 30,19:2
Private Life of the Master Race, The
1945,Je 13,28:3
Iphigenie in Tauris 1949,Ap 9,8:1
Stalag 17 1951,My 9,41:2
Winner, The 1954,F 18,34:1
Rexford, Orlo
Knights of Song 1938,O 18,29:2
Rexsite, Seymour
It's a Funny World 1956,O 22,24:1
Bei Mir Bistu Schoen 1961,O 23,22:2
Cowboy in Israel, A 1962,O 29,36:2
My Wife With Conditions 1963,O 21,39:1
Hello Charlie 1965,O 25,47:2
Bride Got Farblondjet, The 1967,N 6,61:6
It's Never Too Late for Happiness 1968,O 21,59:3
From Israel With Laughter 1969,O 17,34:1
Light, Lively and Yiddish 1970,O 28,58:1
Rey, Antonia
Bajour 1964,N 24,42:1
Fiesta in Madrid 1969,My 29,49:1
Camino Real 1970,Ja 9,42:1
Engagement Baby, The 1970,My 22,40:1
Rey, Billy
Music Hath Charms 1934,D 31,8:2
Rey, Frank (Choreographer)
Cross and the Sword, The 1965,Je 28,32:6
Rey, Frederico
Top-Notchers 1942,My 30,8:5
Rey, Veronica
Hundred Years Old, A 1929,O 2,28:2
Reyburn, A T
Caesar and Cleopatra 1927,N 6,IX,2:1
Reyde, Gwendolyn
Hot Mikado, The 1939,Mr 24,26:2
Reydova, Elizabeth
Pinocchio 1939,Ja 3,19:2
Reyes, Angel
Fuerza Ciega, La 1927,D 6,26:1
Reyes, Aurea
Cabalgata 1949,Jl 8,14:2
Reyes, Eva
Mexican Hayride 1944,Ja 29,9:6
Hilarities 1948,S 10,20:2
Reyes, Paul
Mexican Hayride 1944,Ja 29,9:6
Hilarities 1948,S 10,20:2
Reyes, Roberto
Camino Real 1970,Ja 9,42:1
Reyes, Trini
Vaudeville (Palace) 1953,O 15,42:1
Reyher, Ferdinand (Original Author)
Quiet, Please! 1940,O 20,IX,2:3
Quiet, Please! 1940,N 9,20:3
Reyman, Frank
Howdy King 1926,D 14,24:4
Romancing 'Round 1927,O 4,32:4
Fast Life 1928,S 27,35:2
Oh, Professor 1930,My 2,19:6

Furnished Rooms 1934,My 30,14:6
Reymert, Martin L H (Scenic Designer)
Haunted Host, The 1969,O 28,43:1
Reyna, Marc
Tempest, The 1959,D 28,19:2
Reyna, Marc (Miscellaneous)
Tempest, The 1959,D 28,19:2
Reynal, E St R (Lyricist)
Who's Who 1924,Ap 18,19:2
Reynal, Eugene
Take a Brace 1923,Ap 20,20:3
Reynal, Paul (Playwright)
Au Soleil de l'Instinct 1932,Mr 20,VIII,2:2
Reynal, Pierre
Lorenzaccio 1958,O 15,44:2
Reynolds, Abe
Vaudeville (Palace) 1927,D 13,33:5
Let 'Em Eat Cake 1933,O 23,18:1
Reynolds, Alan
Cranmer of Canterbury 1959,D 4,36:1
Reynolds, Alfred (Composer)
1066 and All That 1935,My 26,XI,2:5
Reynolds, Anne
Three Times the Hour 1931,Ag 26,15:5
Reynolds, Betty
Merrily We Roll Along 1934,O 1,14:1
Reynolds, Bill
Story of Mary Surratt, The 1947,F 10,25:2
Reynolds, Bruce (Playwright)
Playing the Game 1927,D 20,32:5
Reynolds, Buddy
Mister Roberts 1956,D 6,46:2
Reynolds, Burt
Look: We've Come Through 1961,O 26,40:1
Reynolds, Carolyn
Afgar 1920,N 9,13:2
Last Waltz, The 1921,My 11,20:3
Reynolds, Cecil
Tyrant, The 1930,N 13,33:1
Reynolds, Champ
Kiss Me, Kate 1954,Mr 27,13:2
Reynolds, Charles
Passion of Gross, The 1955,Ja 24,20:2
Pal Joey 1961,Je 1,32:1
Reynolds, Charlotte
Kultur 1933,S 27,24:3
Birthright 1933,N 22,22:3
When in Rome 1934,F 28,22:6
Satellite 1935,N 21,27:5
Reynolds, Chauncey
Our Lan' 1947,Ap 19,11:2
Our Lan' 1947,S 29,16:5
Stevedore 1949,F 23,30:2
Reynolds, Dale
De Sade Illustrated 1969,My 13,42:4
Reynolds, Dexter
Guns 1928,Ag 7,25:2
Reynolds, Dorothy
Heritage and Its History, A 1965,My 19,42:1
Reynolds, Dorothy (Lyricist)
Salad Days 1958,N 11,24:1
Reynolds, Dorothy (Playwright)
Salad Days 1958,N 11,24:1
Reynolds, E Vivian
Fedora 1922,F 11,18:1
Reynolds, Edith (Translator)
Lady of the Camellias, The 1930,Mr 23,IX,2:3
Reynolds, Elizabeth
Bombo 1921,O 7,20:2
Rose of Stamboul, The 1922,Mr 8,11:2
Reynolds, Eugene
Five on the Black Hand Side 1970,Ja 2,32:2
Reynolds, Florence
Ten Nights in a Barroom 1932,Ja 21,17:1
Angelic Doctor 1953,Ap 14,30:2
Reynolds, Frank
Razzle Dazzle 1951,F 20,21:1
Reynolds, Frank (Producer)
Importance of Being Earnest, The 1926,O 3,VIII,2:1
Reynolds, George
Soliloquy 1938,N 29,26:4
My Dear Children 1939,Mr 25,19:6
My Dear Children 1940,F 1,16:2
Reynolds, Gertrude
Girl in the Spotlight, The 1920,Jl 13,9:3
Reynolds, Helen, Skaters
Priorities of 1942 1942,Mr 13,23:2
Reynolds, Helene
Too Hot for Maneuvers 1945,My 3,26:5
Reynolds, Howard (Director)
Jotham Valley 1951,F 7,37:2
Reynolds, Howard (Producer)
Jotham Valley 1951,F 7,37:2
Reynolds, Iona
Sweet River 1936,O 29,30:2
Reynolds, Jack
Swing Your Lady 1936,O 19,22:4
I'd Rather Be Right 1937,N 3,28:2
Reynolds, James (Costume Designer)
Music Box Revue 1924,D 2,23:3
Bird Cage, The 1925,Je 3,26:2
Oh, Please! 1926,D 22,24:3
Ballyhoo 1927,Ja 5,18:1

Reynolds, James (Costume Designer)—Cont
Bridal Veil, The 1928,Ja 27,15:2
Trip to Scarborough, A 1929,Mr 18,31:2
Fifty Million Frenchmen 1929,N 28,34:4
Sweet and Low 1930,N 18,28:5
Within the Gates 1934,O 23,23:1
Within the Gates 1934,O 28,IX,1:1
O'Flynn, The 1934,D 28,24:1
Thumbs Up! 1934,D 28,24:1
Jumbo 1935,N 18,20:2
Daughters of Atreus 1936,O 15,33:1
Reynolds, James (Miscellaneous)
Come of Age 1952,Ja 24,22:2
Reynolds, James (Scenic Designer)
Bird Cage, The 1925,Je 3,26:2
Last Night of Don Juan, The 1925,N 10,23:2
Criss Cross 1926,O 13,20:2
On Approval 1926,O 19,27:1
Oh, Please! 1926,D 22,24:3
Ballyhoo 1927,Ja 5,18:1
White Eagle, The 1927,D 27,24:4
Royal Family, The 1927,D 29,26:4
Furies, The 1928,Mr 8,23:1
Sorcerer, The 1928,Je 24,VIII,1:1
Trip to Scarborough, A 1929,Mr 18,31:2
Going Gay 1933,Ag 4,18:5
Come of Age 1934,Ja 13,16:6
Within the Gates 1934,O 23,23:1
Within the Gates 1934,O 28,IX,1:1
O'Flynn, The 1934,D 28,24:1
Thumbs Up! 1934,D 28,24:1
Vagabond King, The 1943,Je 30,24:2
Reynolds, Jonathan
Comedy of Errors, The 1967,Je 15,58:4
Titus Andronicus 1967,Ag 10,43:2
Reynolds, Lee (Producer)
Wet Paint 1965,Ap 13,33:1
Reynolds, Lillian
Tattle Tales 1933,Je 2,22:6
Reynolds, Louise
White Man 1936,O 19,22:4
Reynolds, Malcolm
Dance of Death, The 1967,O 20,50:1
Reynolds, Marsha
Wayward Saint, The 1955,F 18,17:1
Reynolds, Martha
Republic, The 1970,Ap 28,49:1
Reynolds, Mell
Marie Vison, La 1970,Jl 15,29:1
Reynolds, Nellie R
Lulu Belle 1926,F 10,20:1
Reynolds, Paddy
Young Sinners 1933,Mr 7,20:4
Party, A 1933,Ag 24,18:4
Reynolds, Pearl
House of Flowers 1954,D 31,11:2
Reynolds, Quentin
Flag Is Born, A 1946,S 7,10:6
Reynolds, Richard
Family Portrait 1959,My 6,48:2
Reynolds, Roger
Sojourner Truth 1948,Ap 22,35:2
Reynolds, Sarah-Elizabeth
Clubs Are Trumps 1924,O 15,27:1
Reynolds, Stella
Aiglon, L' 1934,N 5,22:2
Reynolds, Stephanie
Pirates of Penzance, The 1961,Ja 20,24:5
Reynolds, Sydney
Princess April 1924,D 2,23:2
Reynolds, Thomas
Laugh, Clown, Laugh! 1923,N 29,30:1
Ladies of the Evening 1924,D 24,11:2
Menace 1927,Mr 15,28:2
Bachelor Father, The 1928,F 29,28:2
Dora Mobridge 1930,Ap 21,20:2
Dancing Partner 1930,Ag 6,24:2
Did I Say No? 1931,S 23,19:4
Marriage for Three 1931,N 12,30:5
Happy Landing 1932,Mr 28,10:5
Best Years 1932,S 8,16:2
Face the Music 1933,F 1,13:4
Me, The Sleeper 1949,My 16,18:6
Mr Barry's Etchings 1950,F 1,26:2
Shrike, The 1952,Ja 16,20:2
Ah, Wilderness! 1953,F 7,10:6
Shrike, The 1953,N 26,51:2
Rainmaker, The 1954,O 29,28:1
Rainmaker, The 1954,N 7,II,1:1
Look Homeward, Angel 1957,N 29,33:1
Reynolds, Tim (Playwright)
Peace 1969,Ja 28,49:1
Reynolds, Timothy (Translator)
Peace 1968,N 10,87:1
Reynolds, Tobi
Meet Peter Grant 1961,My 11,41:4
Reynolds, William W
Carousel 1954,Je 3,32:2
Reynolds, Wilson
Bad Man, The 1920,Ag 31,7:1
Pasteur 1923,Mr 13,19:1
Woman on the Jury, The 1923,Ag 16,10:4
Dove, The 1925,F 12,17:3
Honor of the Family, The 1926,D 27,21:1

Mother Sings 1935,N 13,24:1
Reynolds and Donegan
Vaudeville (Hippodrome) 1924,Ap 1,18:1
Reynosa, Angelita
Seven Mirrors 1945,O 26,17:2
Reznikoff, Peter
Richard III 1966,Ag 11,26:1
Rhea, James
Life Begins in '40 1940,Ap 5,24:2
Rhea and Santora
Vaudeville (Hippodrome) 1926,My 4,31:2
Rheinfeld, Leslie
Lute Song 1946,F 7,29:2
Rheinfrank, Rita
Warrior's Husband, The 1932,Mr 12,19:4
Rheingold, Betty
Dead End 1935,O 29,17:2
Rheis-Gromes, Hill (Costume Designer)
Wiener Blut 1964,S 12,14:1
Rhene-Baton (M) (Musical Director)
Berlioz 1927,F 20,VII,2:1
Rhett, Alicia
Contrast, The 1940,Mr 26,17:2
Rheubottom, Doris
Hot Rhythm 1930,Ag 22,18:5
Rhinelander, Annie
Lulu Belle 1926,F 10,20:1
Rhoades, Richard
Sleepy Hollow 1948,Je 4,26:3
Rhodes, Arthur
Fool's Bells 1925,D 24,8:3
Rhodes, Barbara
This Was Burlesque 1965,Mr 17,55:3
Rhodes, Barbara (Miscellaneous)
Of Love Remembered 1967,F 20,46:5
Rhodes, Betty
Beg, Borrow or Steal 1960,F 11,39:4
Rhodes, Billy
Tangerine 1921,Ag 10,8:2
Rhodes, Burt (Miscellaneous)
Stop the World-I Want to Get Off 1962,O 4,45:4
Rhodes, Dale
Merrily We Roll Along 1936,Je 30,15:1
Rhodes, Donnelly
Troilus and Cressida 1963,Je 19,40:2
Cyrano de Bergerac 1963,Je 20,30:1
Rhodes, Elise
Phoenix '55 1955,Ap 25,20:2
Rhodes, Erik
Gay Divorce 1932,N 30,23:4
Gay Divorce 1933,N 19,IX,3:7
Great Campaign, The 1947,Ap 1,33:2
Dance Me a Song 1950,Ja 21,10:5
Collector's Item 1952,F 9,11:2
Can-Can 1953,My 8,28:1
Right You Are (If You Think You Are)
  1957,Mr 5,37:1
Shinbone Alley 1957,Ap 15,23:2
Shinbone Alley 1957,Ap 28,II,1:1
Jamaica 1957,N 1,32:2
Song of Norway 1958,Je 23,19:2
Can-Can 1959,Ag 26,25:4
How to Make a Man 1961,F 3,16:1
My Fair Lady 1968,Je 14,42:1
Madwoman of Chaillot, The 1970,Mr 23,48:3
Colette 1970,O 15,58:1
Rhodes, Grandon
Antony and Cleopatra 1924,F 20,22:1
Lost Horizons 1934,O 16,31:2
Ceiling Zero 1935,Ap 11,26:2
Flight to the West 1940,D 31,19:1
Deep Mrs Sykes, The 1945,Mr 20,22:6
Boy Who Lived Twice, A 1945,S 12,31:2
Rhodes, Harrison (Original Author)
Cherry Blossoms 1927,Mr 29,22:3
Rhodes, Harrison (Playwright)
Her Friend the King 1929,O 8,34:5
Rhodes, Jordan
Night Is Black Bottles, The 1962,D 5,56:1
Rhodes, Jordan (Composer)
Night Is Black Bottles, The 1962,D 5,56:1
Rhodes, Lilt
It's Up to You 1921,Mr 29,20:1
Rhodes, Loretta
Night in Paris, A 1926,Jl 27,15:4
Rhodes, Marjorie
Love in a Mist 1941,N 30,IX,3:1
Power Without Glory 1948,Ja 14,30:2
Edwina Black 1950,N 22,20:5
All in Good Time 1965,F 19,25:1
Rhodes, Robert
Mecca 1920,O 5,12:2
Earl Carroll's Vanities 1926,Ag 25,19:4
Noble Rogue, A 1929,Ag 20,31:2
Mlle Modiste 1929,O 8,34:1
Singing Rabbi, The 1931,S 11,24:4
Music in the Air 1932,N 9,28:2
Summer Night 1939,N 3,17:1
Mr Big 1941,O 1,24:2
Suds in Your Eye 1944,Ja 13,15:5
Rhodes, Russell
Bride the Sun Shines On, The 1931,D 28,20:2
Midsummer Night's Dream, A 1932,N 18,22:2

Rhodes, Russell—Cont
Twelfth Night 1932,N 19,20:5
Comedy of Errors, The 1932,N 22,25:3
Merchant of Venice, The 1932,N 24,34:5
Closed Room, The 1934,Jl 24,20:2
Loose Moments 1935,F 5,22:3
Savonarola 1942,Ap 24,20:2
Rhodes, W Barnes (Playwright)
Bombasters Furioso 1924,Jl 19,10:4
Rhodes, Walter
Brooklyn Biarritz 1941,F 28,16:2
Color of Darkness: An Evening in the World of
  James Purdy; Cracks 1963,O 1,24:1
Color of Darkness: An Evening in the World of
  James Purdy; Sermon 1963,O 1,34:1
Route 1 1964,N 18,52:3
Rhodes, Willard (Prof) (Musical Director)
Belle of New York, The 1948,D 2,36:6
Rhodes, William
Back Pay 1921,Ag 31,8:2
Rhodes and Watson
Night in Paris, A 1926,Ja 6,16:3
Rhomm, Sophie
Will Morrissey's Newcomers 1923,Ag 9,16:2
Rhoni, Rita
Summer Night 1939,N 3,17:1
Rhyness, Murry
Growing Pains 1933,N 24,24:2
Rhys, William
Does a Tiger Wear a Necktie? 1967,F 4,17:1
Tale of Kasane, The 1969,F 25,36:1
Songs From Milk Wood 1970,Ja 13,41:1
Sganarelle 1970,Ja 13,41:1
Rhythm Dancers
Vaudeville (Palace) 1931,N 2,26:2
Rhythmaires, The
Count Me In 1942,O 9,24:2
Ziegfeld Follies 1943,Ap 2,16:2
Riabouchinska, Tania
Waltz King, The 1943,N 28,II,1:1
Polonaise 1945,O 8,20:2
Rial, Vira
Three Times the Hour 1931,Ag 26,15:5
Riane, L
Homme Que J'Ai Tue, L'; Man Whom I Have
  Killed, The 1936,D 10,34:3
Riane, Louza
Recapture 1930,Ja 19,VIII,2:6
Recapture 1930,Ja 30,16:4
Ada Beats the Drum 1930,My 9,20:4
All Good Americans 1933,D 6,29:2
Rianna
Bombo 1921,O 7,20:2
Riano, Jack
Vaudeville (Loew's State) 1932,O 3,15:5
More the Merrier, The 1941,S 16,19:3
Sunny River 1941,D 5,28:2
Mr Winkle's Holliday 1946,Je 24,27:6
Riano, Rene
Irving Berlin's Music Box Revue 1921,S 23,18:2
Music Box Revue 1923,My 20,VII,1:3
Greenwich Village Follies 1925,D 25,23:3
Greenwich Village Follies 1926,Mr 16,22:2
Vaudeville (Palace) 1927,N 15,27:2
Man Who Came to Dinner, The 1940,F 10,19:5
Ribaudo, Guy
Cocktails of 1934 1934,My 5,22:1
Ribb, Leon
Annie Get Your Gun 1946,My 17,14:2
Ribbink, Tom (Choreographer)
Forever This Land 1951,Jl 29,II,1:1
Beautiful Dreamer 1960,D 28,22:1
Ribla, Gertrude
Lord Byron's Love Letter 1955,Ja 19,23:2
Ribman, Ronald (Playwright)
Harry, Noon and Night 1965,My 6,44:1
Journey of the Fifth Horse, The 1966,Ap 22,36:1
Journey of the Fifth Horse, The 1966,My 8,II,1:1
Ceremony of Innocence, The 1968,Ja 2,33:1
Ceremony of Innocence, The 1968,Ja 14,II,1:1
Passing Through From Exotic Places; Burial of
  Esposito, The 1969,D 8,60:4
Passing Through From Exotic Places; Son Who
  Hunted Tigers in Jakarta, The 1969,D 8,60:4
Passing Through From Exotic Places; Sunstroke
  1969,D 8,60:4
Passing Through From Exotic Places
  1969,D 21,II,3:1
Ribuca, Linda
Flower Drum Song 1958,D 7,II,5:1
Ribuca, Yvonne
Flower Drum Song 1958,D 7,II,5:1
Ricard, Leila
Irving Berlin's New Music Box Revue
  1922,O 24,18:1
Ricard, Lelia
Hassard Short's Ritz Revue 1924,S 18,19:1
Ricard, Mary
Red Geranium, The 1922,My 9,22:3
Main Line, The 1924,Mr 26,19:4
Devil to Pay, The 1925,D 4,26:2
Poppa 1928,D 25,31:1
Is Life Worth Living? 1933,N 10,24:6
Old Maid, The 1935,Ja 8,26:1

Ricardel, Molly
Broadway 1926,S 17,19:3
Gods of the Lightning 1928,O 25,27:2
Ricardel, Molly (Playwright)
I Loved You Wednesday 1932,O 12,27:1
Clap Hands 1934,Ag 21,12:7
Ricardo, Billie
Whistling in the Dark 1933,D 6,29:3
Ricardo, Irene
Vaudeville (Palace) 1924,S 16,26:5
Vaudeville (Palace) 1928,F 21,19:2
Vaudeville (Palace) 1929,F 18,29:1
Ricards, Mary
Great Broxopp, The 1921,N 16,22:1
Riccardo, Dorothea
Patience 1929,D 16,34:5
Riccardo, Irene
Earl Carroll's Vanities 1923,Jl 6,8:2
Ricci, Jose
Mountain Giants, The 1961,Ap 5,32:3
Caucasian Chalk Circle, The 1961,N 1,35:1
Ricci, Mark
When the Bough Breaks 1950,Mr 9,25:5
Ricci, Paul
Three...With Women in Mind; I Hear It Kissing Me
Ladies 1970,N 28,22:1
Three...With Women in Mind; Jeff Chandler
1970,N 28,22:1
Three...With Women in Mind; How a Nice Girl
Named Janet Contracted Syphilis 1970,N 28,22:1
Ricci, Renzo
Long Day's Journey Into Night 1956,O 17,40:1
Ricci, Renzo (Producer)
Long Day's Journey Into Night 1956,O 17,40:1
Ricciardi, William
Mister Malatesta 1923,F 27,14:2
Money Business 1926,Ja 21,18:1
Treat 'Em Rough 1926,O 5,26:2
Big Fight, The 1928,S 19,33:1
Strictly Dishonorable 1929,S 19,37:1
Great Lover, The 1932,O 12,27:3
Ricciardi, William (Playwright)
Mister Malatesta 1923,F 27,14:2
Rice, Adnia
Beggar's Opera, The 1957,Mr 14,35:1
Music Man, The 1957,D 20,31:1
Little Me 1962,N 19,41:3
Music Man, The 1965,Je 17,26:4
Rice, Allyn
As You Like It 1941,O 21,29:2
Rice, Allyn (Producer)
Set My People Free 1948,N 4,38:2
Set My People Free 1948,N 14,II,1:1
Rice, Andy (Miscellaneous)
LeMaire's Affairs 1927,Mr 29,22:4
Rice, Andy (Playwright)
Scandals 1920,Je 8,9:1
George White's Scandals 1922,Ag 29,10:1
Rice, Andy Jr
Ballyhoo 1930,D 23,24:1
Rice, Bob
Good News 1927,S 7,35:4
Whoopee 1928,D 5,34:3
Orchids Preferred 1937,My 12,26:5
Rice, Dorothy
Under Milk Wood 1957,O 16,42:5
Rice, Edison
Boy Meets Girl 1935,N 28,38:2
Boy Meets Girl 1937,Jl 6,23:1
Too Many Girls 1939,O 19,26:2
Pal Joey 1940,D 26,22:2
Rice, Edison (Director)
Paese dei Campanelli, Il; Land of Bells, The
1935,My 10,25:4
Rice, Edmund (Playwright)
Tickets, Please! 1950,Ap 28,25:2
Rice, Elmer (Director)
Street Scene 1929,Ja 11,20:4
See Naples and Die 1929,S 27,30:4
Left Bank, The 1931,O 6,35:3
Counsellor-at-Law 1931,N 7,17:2
Black Sheep 1932,O 14,22:6
We the People 1933,Ja 23,9:5
Judgment Day 1934,S 13,26:4
Judgment Day 1934,S 23,X,1:1
Between Two Worlds 1934,O 26,24:2
Abe Lincoln in Illinois 1938,O 17,12:2
Abe Lincoln in Illinois 1938,O 23,IX,1:1
American Landscape 1938,D 5,19:2
Abe Lincoln in Illinois 1939,Ap 23,X,1:1
Two on an Island 1940,Ja 23,17:2
Two on an Island 1940,F 4,IX,1:1
Journey to Jerusalem 1940,O 7,21:2
Flight to the West 1940,D 31,19:1
New Life, A 1943,S 12,VI,14:4
New Life, A 1943,S 16,26:6
Dream Girl 1945,D 15,13:2
Not for Children 1951,F 14,35:2
Grand Tour, The 1951,D 11,45:2
Winner, The 1954,F 18,34:1
Cue for Passion 1958,N 26,25:2
Cue for Passion 1958,D 7,II,5:1

Rice, Elmer (Miscellaneous)
Counsellor-at-Law 1942,N 25,17:2
Rice, Elmer (Original Author)
Street Scene 1947,Ja 10,17:2
Skyscraper 1965,N 15,48:1
Rice, Elmer (Playwright)
Wake Up, Jonathan 1921,Ja 18,14:1
Wake Up, Jonathan 1921,Ja 23,VI,1:6
Wake Up, Jonathan 1921,Ja 23,VI,1:1
It Is the Law 1922,N 30,28:2
Adding Machine, The 1923,Mr 20,24:1
Adding Machine, The 1923,Mr 25,VIII,1:1
Adding Machine, The 1923,Ap 1,VII,1:1
Adding Machine, The 1924,Mr 23,VIII,1:3
Close Harmony 1924,D 2,23:1
Mongrel, The 1924,D 16,28:2
Cock Robin 1928,Ja 13,26:6
Adding Machine, The 1928,Ja 29,VIII,2:6
Street Scene 1929,Ja 11,20:4
Street Scene 1929,Ja 20,VIII,1:1
Subway, The 1929,Ja 26,15:1
Street Scene 1929,My 19,IX,1:1
Subway, The 1929,Jl 15,25:4
See Naples and Die 1929,S 27,30:4
Passing of Chow-Chow, The 1929,O 4,24:4
Street Scene 1929,N 17,IX,2:6
Street Scene 1929,N 29,24:5
Street Scene 1930,Mr 16,IX,4:1
Street Scene 1930,S 10,14:2
Street Scene 1930,S 28,VIII,2:4
Left Bank, The 1931,O 6,35:3
Left Bank, The 1931,O 18,VIII,1:1
Counsellor-at-Law 1931,N 7,17:2
Counsellor-at-Law 1932,Mr 27,VIII,3:2
Counsellor-at-Law 1932,S 13,17:2
Black Sheep 1932,O 14,22:6
We the People 1933,Ja 23,9:5
We the People 1933,F 5,IX,1:1
Counsellor-at-Law 1934,Ap 11,24:3
Counsellor-at-Law 1934,My 6,IX,2:5
Judgment Day 1934,S 13,26:4
Judgment Day 1934,S 23,X,1:1
Between Two Worlds 1934,O 26,24:2
Not for Children 1935,N 25,23:8
Not for Children 1935,D 22,IX,3:3
Not for Children 1935,D 29,IX,2:1
Not for Children 1936,Mr 1,IX,2:2
Judgment Day 1937,My 20,16:1
Judgment Day 1937,Je 20,X,1:7
American Landscape 1938,D 5,19:2
American Landscape 1938,D 11,X,3:1
Judgment Day 1939,D 3,IX,7:6
Two on an Island 1940,Ja 16,18:4
Two on an Island 1940,Ja 23,17:2
Two on an Island 1940,Ja 28,IX,1:2
Two on an Island 1940,F 4,IX,1:1
Flight to the West 1940,D 15,I,59:5
Flight to the West 1940,D 31,19:1
Flight to the West 1941,Ja 19,IX,1:1
Flight to the West 1941,Mr 7,16:3
Counsellor-at-Law 1942,N 25,17:2
New Life, A 1943,S 12,VI,14:4
New Life, A 1943,S 16,26:6
Dream Girl 1945,D 15,13:2
Dream Girl 1945,D 23,II,3:1
Street Scene 1947,Ja 10,17:2
Street Scene 1947,Ja 19,II,1:1
Adding Machine, The 1948,N 18,35:2
Not for Children 1951,F 14,35:2
Dream Girl 1951,My 10,39:1
Grand Tour, The 1951,D 11,45:2
Winner, The 1954,F 18,34:1
Adding Machine, The 1956,F 10,17:1
Cue for Passion 1958,N 26,25:2
Cue for Passion 1958,D 7,II,5:1
Love Among the Ruins 1963,My 5,85:6
Adding Machine, The 1970,D 5,40:1
Rice, Elmer (Producer)
Left Bank, The 1931,O 6,35:3
Counsellor-at-Law 1931,N 7,17:2
Black Sheep 1932,O 14,22:6
We the People 1933,Ja 23,9:5
We the People 1933,F 5,IX,1:1
Judgment Day 1934,S 13,26:4
Judgment Day 1934,S 23,X,1:1
Between Two Worlds 1934,O 26,24:2
Abe Lincoln in Illinois 1938,O 17,12:2
New Life, A 1943,S 12,VI,14:4
Time Remembered 1957,N 13,41:2
Rope Dancers, The 1957,N 21,39:1
Rice, Felix
Celebration 1969,Ja 23,55:2
Rice, Florence
June Moon 1929,Ag 4,VIII,1:6
June Moon 1929,O 10,34:5
She Loves Me Not 1933,N 21,22:4
Proof Thro' the Night 1942,D 26,14:2
Rice, Gitz
All-Star Idlers of 1921, The 1921,Jl 16,5:2
Nic-Nax of 1926 1926,Ag 5,19:1
Rice, Gitz (Composer)
Nic-Nax of 1926 1926,Ag 5,19:1
19th Hole, The 1927,O 12,30:3

Rice, Gitz (Playwright)
Princess Virtue 1921,My 5,20:2
Rice, Gordon O
Cotton Stockings 1923,D 19,16:2
Rice, Hazel L (Mrs) (Miscellaneous)
Judgment Day 1934,S 13,26:4
Rice, Helen
Dear Judas 1947,O 6,26:4
Rice, J Clifford
Hello Paris 1930,N 17,29:3
Rice, Jack
Passing Show of 1921, The 1920,D 30,16:2
Passing Show of 1923, The 1923,Je 15,24:6
Rice, Jarvis
Good, The 1938,O 6,27:2
Audition of the Apprentice Theatre 1939,Je 2,26:2
Rice, John
Streetcar Named Desire, A 1955,Mr 4,18:2
Rice, Linda
Alchemist, The 1969,Je 12,51:1
Measure for Measure 1969,Je 13,41:3
Rice, Lorin E (Producer)
Show Me Where the Good Times Are
1970,Mr 6,32:1
Rice, Michael
Banshee, The 1927,D 6,26:2
John Ferguson 1928,Ja 18,23:1
Caravan 1928,Ag 30,13:3
Rice, Patricia
Window Shopping 1938,D 24,13:2
Rice, Peter (Costume Designer)
Time Remembered 1955,My 4,35:1
Pickwick 1965,O 6,5:3
Rice, Peter (Scenic Designer)
Time Remembered 1955,My 4,35:1
Joyce Grenfell Requests the Pleasure
1955,O 11,48:1
Young Visitors, The 1968,D 26,48:1
Arms and the Man 1970,Jl 10,18:1
Rice, Rosemary
Naked Genius, The 1943,O 22,20:5
Pick-Up Girl 1944,My 4,25:2
Love on Leave 1944,Je 21,23:4
Bees and the Flowers, The 1946,S 27,19:3
Rice, Sunny
Dream With Music 1944,My 19,15:2
Rice, Sydney
Don Juan in the Russian Manner 1954,Ap 23,23:2
Rice, Terry (Harris)
Journey to Jerusalem 1940,O 7,21:2
Rice, Timothy (Miscellaneous)
Whisper in God's Ear, A 1962,O 12,27:2
Rice, True
Perfect Fool, The 1921,N 8,28:2
Rice, William
Please, Mrs. Garibaldi 1939,Mr 17,24:3
Rich, Adele
Three Waltzes 1937,D 27,10:2
Rich, Allan
I'll Take the High Road 1943,N 10,28:3
Career Angel 1944,My 24,23:7
Darkness at Noon 1951,Ja 15,13:4
Emperor's Clothes, The 1953,F 10,24:2
Grass Is Always Greener, The 1955,F 16,25:2
Miser, The 1955,Mr 18,34:2
Journey of the Fifth Horse, The 1966,Ap 22,36:1
Rich, Arthur
Emperor Jones, The 1945,Ja 17,18:4
Rich, Bernie (Miscellaneous)
Eddie Fisher at the Winter Garden 1962,O 3,47:1
Rich, Carla
Love of Two Hours, The 1962,O 27,16:2
Summer of Daisy Miller, The 1963,My 28,33:1
Rich, Doris
Get Me in the Movies 1928,My 22,18:3
Electra 1932,Ja 9,21:4
Mad Hopes, The 1932,D 2,26:3
O'Flynn, The 1934,D 28,24:1
Taming of the Shrew, The 1935,O 1,27:3
Sophie 1944,D 26,22:7
Flamingo Road 1946,Mr 20,18:2
Strange Bedfellows 1948,Ja 15,27:3
Madwoman of Chaillot, The 1949,S 11,II,1:1
Affair of Honor 1956,Ap 7,12:3
Redhead 1959,F 6,21:1
Physicists, The 1964,O 14,52:1
Utbu 1966,Ja 5,24:1
We Have Always Lived in the Castle
1966,O 20,53:1
Warm Body, A 1967,Ap 17,44:2
Antigone 1967,Je 19,43:1
Rich, Eddie (Miscellaneous)
Girl of the Golden West, The 1957,N 6,44:1
Rich, Eddie (Producer)
Someone Waiting 1956,F 15,26:1
Rich, Eleanor (Costume Designer)
Legend of Leonora, The 1926,My 1,10:1
Rich, Frances
Brief Moment 1931,N 10,28:2
Rich, Franklin
Two Orphans, The 1926,Ap 6,26:2
Rich, Helen
Tip-Top 1920,O 6,13:2

Rich, Helen—Cont

Irving Berlin's New Music Box Revue
1922,O 24,18:1

Rich, Irene
Ask Your Wife 1929,O 14,20:4
Vaudeville (Palace) 1929,O 14,20:4
Any Woman 1934,Ag 28,24:4
Seven Keys to Baldpate 1935,My 28,30:2
As Husbands Go 1935,Jl 2,24:3
As Husbands Go 1935,Jl 10,24:1
As the Girls Go 1948,N 15,21:2

Rich, Jane
Father, The 1937,Ap 21,18:5

Rich, Joan
Recruiting Officer, The 1958,F 8,12:2

Rich, Lucille
Naughty-Naught '00 1937,Ja 25,23:2

Rich, Max
Idiot's Delight 1936,Mr 25,25:2
Pirate, The 1942,N 26,39:2

Rich, Max (Composer)
Keep Moving 1934,Ag 24,10:2

Rich, Ron
Big Time Buck White 1968,D 9,58:1
Buck White 1969,D 3,63:1

Rich, Ron (Miscellaneous)
Big Time Buck White 1968,D 9,58:1

Rich, Roy (Director)
Affairs of State 1952,Ag 22,12:2

Rich, Vernon
Man Who Died Twice, The 1925,D 14,19:1
Dream Play 1926,Ja 21,18:2
Pleased to Meet You 1928,O 30,27:2
Unsophisticates, The 1929,D 31,14:5
Miss Gulliver Travels 1931,N 26,36:4

Richar, Georges
Architruc 1970,Ap 16,55:1

Richar, Georges (Costume Designer)
Architruc 1970,Ap 16,55:1
Lettre Morte 1970,Ap 16,55:1

Richar, Georges (Scenic Designer)
Architruc 1970,Ap 16,55:1
Lettre Morte 1970,Ap 16,55:1

Richard
Are You With It? 1945,N 12,17:3

Richard, Chris
Latent Heterosexual, The 1968,Mr 22,52:1

Richard, Claire
Let's Make an Opera 1950,D 14,50:2

Richard, Darryl
King of Hearts 1954,Ap 2,23:1
High Named Today 1954,D 11,11:2
Cat on a Hot Tin Roof 1955,Mr 25,18:2
Roomful of Hearts, A 1955,O 18,48:1
Harbor Lights 1956,O 5,20:1
Portofino 1958,F 22,8:3

Richard, Doreen
Prodigal, The 1960,F 12,23:1
Prodigal, The 1960,F 21,II,1:1

Richard, Frieda
Lady Windermere's Fan 1927,F 27,VII,2:3

Richard, Henry
Age of Innocence, The 1928,N 28,24:2

Richard, Jean
Ecole des Femmes, L'; School for Wives
1951,Mr 19,22:1
Four Pieces sur Jardin 1969,F 18,35:1

Richard, Josee
King Lear 1950,Ag 30,26:2

Richard, Lee
Summer and Smoke 1952,Ap 25,19:5

Richard, Paul
Hatful of Rain, A 1955,D 4,II,1:1

Richard, Viola
Geraniums in My Window 1934,O 27,26:5

Richard, Ward
Merry Widow, The 1944,O 9,17:1

Richards, Addison
One Bright Day 1952,Mr 20,37:2
First Lady 1952,My 29,18:5

Richards, Al
Blackbirds 1933,D 4,22:3

Richards, Al (Choreographer)
Lew Leslie's Blackbirds of 1930 1930,O 23,34:5

Richards, Albert
Witness for the Prosecution 1954,D 17,35:2

Richards, Allen
Jamaica 1957,N 1,32:2

Richards, Beah
Take a Giant Step 1956,S 26,30:1
Miracle Worker, The 1959,O 20,44:1
Purlie Victorious 1961,S 29,29:1
Purlie Victorious 1961,O 8,II,1:1
Amen Corner, The 1965,Ap 16,35:1
Amen Corner, The 1965,Ap 25,II,1:2
Little Foxes, The 1967,O 27,53:1
Little Foxes, The 1967,N 5,II,1:1

Richards, Bill
Body Beautiful, The 1958,Ja 24,15:2
Wildcat 1960,D 17,20:2

Richards, Cain
Life and Times of J Walter Smintheus, The
1970,D 10,59:1

Richards, Charles
This Is New York 1930,N 29,21:1
Just to Remind You 1931,S 8,39:1
Happy Landing 1932,Mr 28,10:5

Richards, Dal
It's a Bird . . . It's a Plane . . . It's Superman
1966,Mr 30,34:1
1776 1969,Mr 17,46:2

Richards, Dennis
Make a Million 1958,O 24,39:2

Richards, Don
Johnny 2X4 1942,Mr 17,24:6
Count Me In 1942,O 9,24:2

Richards, Donald
Winged Victory 1943,N 22,24:1
Finian's Rainbow 1947,Ja 11,23:2
Along Fifth Avenue 1949,Ja 14,28:2

Richards, Elayne
Lost in the Stars 1949,O 31,21:2

Richards, Frank
Brown Danube, The 1939,My 18,30:4
World We Make, The 1939,N 21,19:1
Embezzled Heaven 1944,N 1,20:2
Wanhope Building, The 1947,F 11,36:5

Richards, Fred
Busybody, The 1924,S 30,27:5

Richards, Gerald
Our Town 1959,Mr 24,46:2
Cave Dwellers, The 1961,O 16,34:2
General Seeger 1962,Mr 1,26:2

Richards, Gordon
Adventurous Age, The 1927,F 8,20:1
Caste 1927,D 24,8:1
Wings Over Europe 1928,D 11,35:1
Noble Rogue, A 1929,Ag 20,31:2
Let and Sub-Let 1930,My 20,32:2
Noble Experiment, The 1930,O 28,21:4
Society Girl 1931,D 31,16:1
Money in the Air 1932,Mr 8,19:3
Masks and Faces 1933,Mr 20,18:5
Whatever Possessed Her 1934,Ja 26,21:2
Virginia 1937,S 3,13:2
I Am My Youth 1938,Mr 8,22:4
Oscar Wilde 1938,O 11,20:2
Springtime for Henry 1940,F 27,16:3
Second Threshold 1951,Ja 3,23:2
Second Threshold 1951,Ja 14,II,1:1

Richards, Grant
Halfway to Hell 1934,Ja 3,22:3
Every Man for Himself 1940,D 10,32:3
They Should Have Stood in Bed 1942,F 14,18:5
Winged Victory 1943,N 22,24:1
Yellow Jack 1944,Ap 7,23:3

Richards, Greta (Costume Designer)
As You Like It 1958,Ja 21,33:6
Power of Dreams, A 1958,Mr 11,33:1
Bonds of Interest, The 1958,My 7,43:1
Misalliance 1961,S 26,32:2

Richards, Guy
Orestes 1926,Je 20,II,3:6

Richards, Henry
Twelfth Night 1930,O 16,28:2
Jezebel 1933,D 20,26:3
Lightnin' 1938,S 16,17:2
Calico Wedding 1945,Mr 8,18:6

Richards, Hope
Creeping Fire 1935,Ja 17,22:3

Richards, Houston
Boundry Line, The 1930,F 6,21:1
Lysistrata 1930,Ap 29,30:5
Lysistrata 1930,Je 6,20:1
She Means Business 1931,Ja 27,21:2
Monkey 1932,F 12,25:2
Two Strange Women 1933,Ja 11,23:3
House of Remsen 1934,Ap 3,26:4
Anything Goes 1934,N 22,26:1
County Chairman, The 1936,My 26,26:5
Red, Hot and Blue! 1936,O 30,26:3
Let's Face It 1941,O 30,26:2
Jackpot 1944,Ja 14,15:2
Lovely Me 1946,D 26,30:4

Richards, Jack
Bitter Sweet 1934,My 8,28:4
Say When 1934,N 9,24:2
Between the Devil 1937,D 23,24:5
Yokel Boy 1939,Jl 7,12:2

Richards, Jean
Madwoman of Chaillot, The 1970,Mr 23,48:3

Richards, Jeff
Boy Friend, The 1970,Ap 15,54:1

Richards, Jerome
Slightly Delinquent 1954,O 26,32:5

Richards, Jess
Blood Red Roses 1970,Mr 23,48:1

Richards, Jon
Pink Elephant, The 1953,Ap 23,37:2
Leave It to Jane 1959,My 26,30:2
Sail Away 1961,O 4,48:5
3 Bags Full 1966,Mr 7,22:1
Elizabeth the Queen 1966,N 4,30:1
Woman Is My Idea 1968,S 26,61:1
Does a Tiger Wear a Necktie? 1969,F 26,38:1
Indians 1969,O 14,51:1

Richards, Ken
On a Clear Day You Can See Forever
1965,O 18,44:1

Richards, Kenneth
They All Want Something 1926,O 13,20:2

Richards, Kurt
Miss Swan Expects 1939,F 21,15:2
Hamlet 1939,D 5,35:2
Richard II 1940,Ap 2,31:2
Counsellor-at-Law 1942,N 25,17:2
Wallflower 1944,Ja 27,14:2
Sophie 1944,D 26,22:7
Winter's Tale, The 1946,Ja 16,18:6
Edge of the Sword, The 1949,N 10,40:3
Julius Caesar 1950,Je 21,30:1
King Lear 1950,D 26,18:1
Mr Pickwick 1952,S 18,36:3
Tall Kentuckian, The 1953,Je 17,30:1

Richards, Lamonte
Let Them Down, Gently; On Vacation
1968,Ja 31,28:2

Richards, Laura
Expressing Willie 1924,Ap 17,22:1

Richards, Lee
Summer and Smoke 1952,My 4,II,1:1

Richards, Lex
Wanhope Building, The 1947,F 11,36:5
First Mrs Fraser, The 1947,N 6,36:2

Richards, Lex (Director)
Gayden 1949,My 11,34:4
Where There's a Will 1953,Je 18,38:5

Richards, Lex (Playwright)
Dear Barbarians 1952,F 22,15:2
Where There's a Will 1953,Je 18,38:5

Richards, Lisa
Tragical Historie of Doctor Faustus, The
1964,O 6,34:2
Nobody Hears A Broken Drum 1970,Mr 20,55:1

Richards, Lloyd
Stevedore 1949,F 23,30:2
Trouble in July 1949,D 2,36:2
Freight 1950,Ap 27,36:2
Egghead, The 1957,O 10,39:1

Richards, Lloyd (Director)
Raisin in the Sun, A 1959,Mr 12,27:1
Raisin in the Sun, A 1959,Mr 29,II,1:1
Long Dream, The 1960,F 18,36:2
Moon Besieged, The 1962,D 6,54:1
I Had a Ball 1964,D 16,50:1
Amen Corner, The 1965,Je 13,82:4
Yearling, The 1965,D 11,25:1
Who's Got His Own 1966,O 13,52:1
Ox Cart, The 1966,D 20,58:1

Richards, Lois
These Are the Times 1950,My 11,37:2

Richards, Luciel
Tobacco Road 1943,S 6,21:3

Richards, Nick
Jane Eyre 1958,My 2,31:1

Richards, Paul E
Voice of Israel, The 1948,O 26,40:2
Hershel, The Jester 1948,D 14,39:2
Finian's Rainbow 1953,Mr 7,13:2
End as a Man 1953,S 16,39:1
End As a Man 1953,S 27,II,1:1
Saint Joan 1954,S 18,12:1
Hatful of Rain, A 1955,N 10,44:1
Tevya and His Daughters 1957,S 17,38:2
Tevya and His Daughters 1957,S 29,II,1:1
Once More With Feeling 1958,O 22,39:1
Viva Madison Avenue 1960,Ap 7,42:1
Alligators, The 1960,N 15,47:1
Rosemary 1960,N 15,47:1
In the Counting House 1962,D 15,5:5
All Women Are One 1965,Ja 8,21:1
Exception and the Rule, The 1965,My 21,19:1

Richards, Paul E (Director)
Spanish Armada, The 1962,Ap 4,38:1
Man Out Loud, Girl Quiet 1962,Ap 4,38:1

Richards, Percy
Daddy Dumplins 1920,N 23,11:1
Three Musketeers, The 1921,My 20,18:5

Richards, Rudy
Stars on Ice (2d Edition) 1943,Je 25,13:2
Hats Off to Ice 1944,Je 23,15:2
Howdy Mr Ice 1948,Je 25,28:5

Richards, Shelah
Plough and the Stars, The 1927,N 29,30:2
Days Without End 1934,Ap 24,26:7
Gallant Cassian 1934,N 14,22:2
Six Characters in Search of an Author
1934,D 5,29:1
Spring Meeting 1938,D 9,30:4

Richards, Shirley
Ned Wayburn's Gambols 1929,Ja 16,22:3
Top Speed 1929,D 26,20:1
Sweet and Low 1930,N 18,28:5

Richards, Stanley (Playwright)
Marriage Is for Single People 1945,N 22,38:2

Richards, Stephen (Composer)
Hello Out There 1955,D 22,19:1
Hungerers, The 1955,D 22,19:1
Opera Opera 1955,D 22,19:1

Richards, Stephen (Composer)—Cont

Floydada to Matador 1955,D 22,19:1

Richards, Stephen Jr (Composer)

When I Was a Child 1960,D 9,38:1

Richards, Wayne

Beautiful Jailer, The 1957,My 17,19:2

Richardsen, Roseanna (Costume Designer)

Pastry Shop, The 1970,Je 12,28:1

Young Among Themselves, The 1970,Je 12,28:1

Richardson, Abby Sage (Playwright)

Prince and the Pauper, The 1920,N 2,15:1

Prince and the Pauper, The 1920,N 21,VI,1:4

Richardson, Anna Mae

Green Pastures, The 1951,Mr 16,35:2

Richardson, Anna Steese (Original Author)

Big Hearted Herbert 1934,Ja 2,17:3

Richardson, Anna Steese (Playwright)

Big Hearted Herbert 1934,Ja 2,17:3

Richardson, Anthony (Director)

Semi-Detached 1963,O 8,49:1

Richardson, Anthony (Original Author)

Semi-Detached 1963,O 20,II,1:1

Richardson, Betty

Enchanted, The 1950,Ja 19,34:2

Hair 1970,Ja 13,39:1

Richardson, Charles O

On the Level 1937,Mr 26,24:4

Richardson, Claibe (Composer)

Shoestring '57 1956,N 6,31:1

Richardson, Don (Director)

Sound of Hunting, A 1945,N 21,16:6

Good Housekeeping 1949,Ag 17,19:3

Have I Got a Girl for You! 1963,D 3,53:2

Richardson, Don (Miscellaneous)

Rugged Path, The 1945,N 12,17:2

Richardson, Doreen

Finian's Rainbow 1953,Mr 7,13:2

Richardson, Dorothy

Milk and Honey 1961,O 11,52:1

Richardson, Douglas

Stephen D 1967,S 25,58:1

Hot Feet 1970,D 22,38:1

Richardson, Ellis

Hamlet 1969,Je 30,33:1

Richardson, Emory

Harlem 1929,F 21,30:3

Green Pastures, The 1930,F 27,26:1

Green Pastures, The 1935,F 27,16:2

Abe Lincoln in Illinois 1938,O 17,12:2

American Landscape 1938,D 5,19:2

Anna Lucasta 1944,Ag 31,15:1

Rugged Path, The 1945,N 12,17:2

Lysistrata 1946,O 18,27:5

Our Lan' 1947,S 29,16:5

Leading Lady 1948,O 19,33:1

Anybody Home 1949,F 26,10:5

Wisteria Trees, The 1950,Mr 30,39:1

Mrs Patterson 1954,D 2,37:1

Richardson, Florence Jazz Band

Vaudeville (Palace) 1930,Mr 24,24:5

Richardson, Foster

Polly 1923,Ap 8,VIII,1:7

Richardson, Frank

Vaudeville (Palace) 1931,My 18,21:1

Richardson, Frederick F

Hamlet 1938,N 8,26:1

Richardson, Henry

Black Scandals 1928,O 27,23:2

Richardson, Howard (Miscellaneous)

Dark of the Moon 1970,Ap 4,21:2

Richardson, Howard (Playwright)

Dark of the Moon 1945,Mr 15,27:2

Dark of the Moon 1945,Mr 25,II,1:1

Design For A Stained Glass Window 1950,Ja 24,26:2

Protective Custody 1956,D 29,8:7

Dark of the Moon 1958,F 27,22:2

Laundry, The 1963,F 19,5:2

Dark of the Moon 1970,Ap 4,21:2

Richardson, Ian

Twelfth Night 1960,My 18,48:6

As You Like It 1961,Jl 5,30:1

Measure for Measure 1962,Ap 11,47:4

Midsummer Night's Dream, A 1962,Ap 18,30:3

King Lear 1964,My 19,43:2

Comedy of Errors, The 1964,My 21,43:1

Persecution and Assassination of Marat As Performed by the Inmates of the Asylum of Charenton Under the Direction of the Marquis de Sade, The 1965,D 28,35:1

Persecution and Assassination of Marat As Performed by the Inmates of the Asylum of Charenton Under the Direction of the Marquis de Sade, The 1966,Ja 9,II,1:1

Merry Wives of Windsor, The 1968,My 4,45:5

Merry Wives of Windsor, The 1968,Jl 31,29:1

Pericles 1969,Ap 11,36:1

Pericles 1969,Je 1,II,4:5

Richard III 1970,Ag 3,37:3

Richardson, Ian (Miscellaneous)

Persecution and Assassination of Marat As Performed by the Inmates of the Asylum of Charenton Under the Direction of the Marquis de Sade, The 1965,D 28,35:1

Richardson, Jack

Will Morrissey's Newcomers 1923,Ag 9,16:2

Richardson, Jack (Playwright)

Prodigal, The 1960,F 12,23:1

Prodigal, The 1960,F 21,II,1:1

Gallows Humor 1961,Ap 19,35:1

Lorenzo 1963,Ja 25,12:5

Lorenzo 1963,F 16,5:2

Xmas in Las Vegas 1965,N 5,31:1

Richardson, Jane

Pitter Patter 1920,S 29,12:2

Just Because 1922,Mr 23,11:1

Spice of 1922 1922,Jl 7,12:4

My Aunt From Ypsilanti 1923,My 2,22:6

Higher and Higher 1940,Ap 5,24:3

Earthlight Theater 1970,N 4,38:2

Richardson, Jazzlips

Hot Chocolates 1929,Je 21,17:4

Lew Leslie's Blackbirds of 1930 1930,O 23,34:5

Richardson, Jazzlips Jr

Green Pastures, The 1935,F 27,16:2

Richardson, Lee

Saint Joan 1956,S 12,42:1

Legend of Lizzie, The 1959,F 10,39:1

Twelfth Night 1959,Jl 11,10:2

Macbeth 1959,Ag 1,9:2

Death of Bessie Smith, The 1961,Mr 2,19:1

Someone From Assisi 1962,Ja 12,28:1

Merchant of Venice, The 1962,Je 22,1:4

King Lear 1962,Ag 14,35:1

Lord Pengo 1962,N 20,41:2

Hamlet 1963,My 9,41:1

Hamlet 1963,My 19,II,1:1

Death of a Salesman 1963,Jl 20,11:2

Three Sisters, The 1963,Jl 22,19:2

Saint Joan 1964,My 14,41:1

Glass Menagerie, The 1964,Jl 20,18:3

Richard III 1965,Je 3,26:1

Cherry Orchard, The 1965,Ag 2,17:2

Skin of Our Teeth, The 1966,Je 2,51:1

Shoemaker's Holiday, The 1967,S 3,19:1

Thieves' Carnival 1967,Je 5,52:1

Harpers Ferry 1967,Je 6,52:2

House of Atreus, The; Agamemnon 1967,Jl 24,23:1

House of Atreus, The; Furies, The 1967,Jl 24,23:1

House of Atreus, The; Agamemnon 1967,Jl 24,23:1

Tango 1968,Ja 1,11:1

Twelfth Night 1968,Je 15,40:1

Serjeant Musgrave's Dance 1968,Je 16,52:4

Resistible Rise of Arturo Ui, The 1968,Ag 8,25:1

House of Atreus, The 1968,D 18,55:1

Resistible Rise of Arturo Ui, The 1968,D 23,44:1

Mourning Becomes Electra 1969,S 7,II,1:2

Henry V 1969,N 11,43:1

Othello 1970,Je 22,43:1

Othello 1970,Je 28,II,1:1

Devil's Disciple, The 1970,Je 30,48:1

Devil's Disciple, The 1970,Jl 12,II,1:3

Othello 1970,S 15,51:1

Revenger's Tragedy, The 1970,D 2,58:1

Richardson, Lee (Miscellaneous)

Othello 1970,Je 22,43:1

Richardson, Louise

Merry-Go-Round 1927,Je 1,25:4

Richardson, Michael

Moby Dick 1970,Je 3,52:1

Richardson, Norma

Bye Bye Birdie 1960,Ap 15,13:4

Richardson, Ralph

Taming of the Shrew, The 1928,My 27,VIII,1:8

Othello 1930,My 20,33:1

Marriage Is No Joke 1934,F 7,16:2

Romeo and Juliet 1935,D 24,10:2

Promise 1936,Mr 22,XI,1:7

Bees on the Boat Deck 1936,My 6,27:2

Bees on the Boat Deck 1936,Je 7,IX,2:1

Silent Knight, The 1937,N 17,26:4

Silent Knight, The 1937,D 5,XII,5:8

Othello 1938,F 27,X,1:4

Johnson Over Jordan 1939,Mr 12,XI,3:5

Arms and the Man 1944,O 1,II,1:3

Peer Gynt 1944,O 1,II,1:3

Uncle Vanya 1945,Mr 25,II,2:4

Henry IV, Part I 1945,S 27,24:5

Henry IV 1945,O 14,II,2:3

Henry IV, Part I 1946,My 7,25:2

Henry IV, Part II 1946,My 8,33:4

Henry IV 1946,My 12,II,1:1

Uncle Vanya 1946,My 14,18:2

Uncle Vanya 1946,My 19,II,1:1

Oedipus 1946,My 21,19:2

Oedipus; Critic, The 1946,My 21,19:2

Inspector Calls, An 1946,O 13,II,2:3

Cyrano de Bergerac 1946,N 3,I,54:6

Cyrano de Bergerac 1946,N 10,II,3:2

Heiress, The 1949,F 3,26:2

Heiress, The 1949,F 13,II,3:7

Home at Seven 1950,Mr 8,34:5

Richardson, Ralph—Cont

Tempest, The 1952,Ap 13,II,3:8

Macbeth 1952,Jl 6,II,1:7

Day by the Sea, A 1953,N 27,22:3

Day by the Sea, A 1953,D 20,II,4:2

Waltz of the Toreadors, The 1956,D 22,14:8

Waltz of the Toreadors, The 1957,Ja 18,17:2

Waltz of the Toreadors, The 1957,Ja 27,II,1:1

Complaisant Lover, The 1959,Je 19,28:3

School for Scandal, The 1962,Ap 6,31:3

School for Scandal, The 1962,N 30,27:1

School for Scandal, The 1963,Ja 26,5:2

Carving a Statue 1964,S 18,25:1

What the Butler Saw 1969,Mr 7,27:7

Home 1970,Je 20,23:1

Home 1970,Ag 17,32:1

Home 1970,N 18,41:1

Home 1970,N 29,II,1:1

Richardson, Ralph (Director)

Richard II 1947,My 11,II,3:7

What the Butler Saw 1969,Mr 7,27:7

Richardson, Ralph (Producer)

Bees on the Boat Deck 1936,My 6,27:2

Richardson, Robert E (Miscellaneous)

Who's Who, Baby? 1968,Ja 30,36:1

Richardson, Robert E (Producer)

Bill Noname 1970,Mr 3,37:1

Richardson, Roy S (Playwright)

Pequod 1969,Je 30,33:1

Richardson, Susan (Producer)

Death of the Well-Loved Boy, The 1967,My 16,48:1

Scent of Flowers, A 1969,O 21,42:1

One Night Stands of a Noisy Passenger; Last Stand 1970,D 31,8:3

One Night Stands of a Noisy Passenger; Noisy Passenger, The 1970,D 31,8:3

One Night Stands of a Noisy Passenger; Passage, Un 1970,D 31,8:3

Richardson, Susan M (Miscellaneous)

Bring Me a Warm Body 1962,Ap 17,29:3

Richardson, Suzanne

Yeomen of the Guard, The 1961,Ap 28,23:1

Richardson, Tony (Director)

Crucible, The 1956,Ap 11,28:3

Look Back in Anger 1957,O 2,28:2

Look Back in Anger 1957,O 13,II,1:1

Lesson, The 1958,Ja 10,20:3

Chairs, The 1958,Ja 10,20:3

Entertainer, The 1958,F 13,22:2

Chairs, The; Lesson, The 1958,F 16,II,1:1

Requiem for a Nun 1959,Ja 31,13:2

Requiem for a Nun 1959,F 8,II,1:1

Othello 1959,Ap 8,41:3

Othello 1959,Ap 12,II,3:1

Taste of Honey, A 1960,O 5,46:1

Taste of Honey, A 1960,N 6,II,1:1

Luther 1961,Jl 8,9:2

Luther 1961,Jl 28,10:2

Semi-Detached 1962,D 6,54:3

Natural Affection 1963,F 2,5:2

Luther 1963,S 26,41:1

Luther 1963,O 6,II,1:1

Arturo Ui 1963,N 12,49:1

Arturo Ui 1963,N 24,II,1:1

Milk Train Doesn't Stop Here Anymore, The 1964,Ja 2,33:1

St Joan of the Stockyards 1964,Je 12,45:1

Hamlet 1969,Mr 2,II,3:1

Hamlet 1969,My 2,38:1

Hamlet 1969,My 11,II,1:1

Richardson, Tony (Producer)

Hamlet 1969,F 19,38:1

Richardson, Virginia

Brigadoon 1950,My 3,36:2

Richardson, W

Under the Gaslight 1929,Ap 3,27:1

Richardson, Walter

Ol' Man Satan 1932,O 4,26:3

Black Rhythm 1936,D 21,19:2

Richardson, Wayne (Director)

Camille 1956,S 19,33:1

Trojan Women, The 1957,Mr 19,42:7

Richardson, Wayne (Miscellaneous)

Taming of the Shrew, The 1956,Ag 11,11:2

Richardson, Wayne (Producer)

Camille 1956,S 19,33:1

Richardson, Webb

Malinda 1929,D 4,37:2

Richardson, Wells

Fast Life 1928,S 27,35:2

His Majesty's Car 1930,O 24,30:1

Park Avenue, Ltd 1932,Mr 4,17:1

Between Two Worlds 1934,O 26,24:2

Hook-Up, The 1935,My 9,24:6

Duke in Darkness, The 1944,Ja 25,15:2

Buy Me Blue Ribbons 1951,O 18,33:2

Bad Seed, The 1954,D 9,42:1

Donogoo 1961,Ja 19,25:3

Cherry Orchard, The 1962,N 15,46:2

Richardson, William

Jezebel 1933,D 20,26:3

Porgy and Bess 1942,Ja 23,16:2

Richardson, Willis (Playwright)
Chip Woman's Fortune, The 1923,My 8,22:2
Chip Woman's Fortune, The 1923,My 16,22:5
Chip Woman's Fortune, The 1923,My 20,VII,1:1
Richart, Sheila
To Quito and Back 1937,O 7,30:4
Richaud, Andre de (Playwright)
Chateau des Papes, Le 1932,N 13,IX,2:5
Richemont, Robert
Zizi 1964,N 23,51:1
Richepin, Jacques (Miscellaneous)
Notre Dame du Cinema 1936,Ja 19,IX,3:4
Richetelle, Charles
Dracula Sabbat 1970,O 2,28:2
Richfield, Don
Hindu, The 1922,Mr 22,13:3
Richling, Louis
Trumpeter of Sakkingen 1921,Ja 15,11:3
Richman, Arthur (Playwright)
Not So Long Ago 1920,My 5,14:1
Not So Long Ago 1920,Ag 29,VI,1:3
Ambush 1921,O 11,22:1
Ambush 1921,O 16,VI,1:1
Serpent's Tooth, A 1922,Ag 25,8:5
Awful Truth, The 1922,S 19,14:3
Awful Truth, The 1922,S 24,VI,1:1
Far Cry, The 1924,S 28,VII,2:1
Far Cry, The 1924,O 1,24:1
Far Cry, The 1924,O 5,VIII,1:1
Isabel 1925,Ja 14,19:1
All Dressed Up 1925,S 10,28:1
Antonia 1925,O 21,20:1
Mayflowers 1925,N 25,14:2
Proud Woman, A 1926,N 16,24:1
Heavy Traffic 1928,S 6,23:3
Violet, The 1930,S 30,24:2
Season Changes, The 1935,D 24,10:2
Richman, Charles
Bought and Paid For 1921,D 8,17:5
School for Scandal, The 1923,Je 5,24:3
Home Fires 1923,Ag 21,12:1
Best People, The 1924,Ag 20,8:1
Dagger, The 1925,S 10,28:1
We All Do 1927,Mr 1,30:3
Love Is Like That 1927,Ap 19,24:1
Ink 1927,N 2,24:2
Ladies Don't Lie 1929,O 11,36:3
In The Best of Families 1931,F 3,29:1
Berlin 1931,D 31,16:1
Riddle Me This! 1932,F 26,22:5
Girl Outside, The 1932,O 25,24:3
Biography 1932,D 13,25:3
Biography 1934,F 6,24:4
Jig Saw 1934,My 1,26:3
And Stars Remain 1936,S 29,35:2
And Stars Remain 1936,O 13,32:2
Richman, Harry
Queen O' Hearts 1922,O 11,22:1
George White's Scandals 1926,Je 15,23:2
George White's Scandals 1928,Jl 3,19:1
International Revue 1930,F 26,22:2
Vaudeville (Palace) 1930,Ag 4,13:2
Vaudeville (Palace) 1930,S 22,23:2
Simple Simon 1930,N 23,IX,1:3
Vaudeville (Palace) 1931,Ja 19,25:3
Ziegfeld Follies 1931,Jl 2,30:5
Vaudeville (Hollywood) 1932,Mr 22,17:5
Music Hall Varieties 1932,N 23,15:3
Music Hall Varieties 1933,Ja 3,19:4
Say When 1934,O 28,IX,3:1
Say When 1934,N 9,24:2
New Priorities of 1943 1942,S 16,28:2
Richman, Ken
Courtyard 1960,Mr 1,28:1
Richman, Lorraine
Matty and the Moron and Madonna
1965,Mr 30,53:1
Richman, Mark
End as a Man 1953,S 16,39:1
End As a Man 1953,S 27,II,1:1
Masquerade 1959,Mr 17,42:1
Richman, Rebecca
Bei Mir Bistu Schoen 1961,O 23,22:2
Cowboy in Israel, A 1962,O 29,36:2
My Wife With Conditions 1963,O 21,39:1
Richman, Robert
Kith and Kin 1930,My 14,31:1
Richman, Susan Jo
Abortion 1959,O 28,40:4
Richmond, Bernice
Salvation 1928,F 1,31:1
Richmond, David
Cherry Orchard, The 1970,My 7,63:2
Richmond, Edna
Get Me in the Movies 1928,My 22,18:3
Richmond, Eric
Land Beyond the River, A 1957,Mr 29,15:7
Richmond, George
Banjo Eyes 1941,D 26,20:2
Richmond, June
Are You With It? 1945,N 12,17:3
Richmond, Katherine
Pirates of Penzance, The 1938,Je 3,16:2

Richmond, Marion
Bare Facts 1927,Ag 17,27:5
Richmond, Maude
Hail and Farewell 1923,F 20,12:1
Dora Mobridge 1930,Ap 21,20:2
Too Much Party 1934,Mr 6,28:4
Lady Luck 1936,Ap 16,21:2
Richmond, Virginia
Brother Elks 1925,S 15,29:2
Richmond, Warren
John Ferguson 1921,My 24,20:1
Richmond, Wynne
Dream Girl, The 1924,Ag 21,12:2
Hello, Lola! 1926,Ja 13,30:1
Richter, Barbara (Lighting Director)
Shadow and Substance 1956,Mr 14,38:1
Richter, Berna
Aria Da Capo 1958,Je 27,18:5
Richter, Gosta E
Polly Preferred 1923,Ja 12,13:3
Richter, I S (Playwright)
Chalk Circle, The 1933,Ag 22,20:5
Richter, Irmgard
Redemption: Lebende Leichnam, Der; Living
Corpse, The 1928,N 20,28:2
Ghosts; Gespenster 1929,F 6,30:3
Richter, Joe
Say Darling 1959,F 26,38:2
Richter, Will
Athenian Touch, The 1964,Ja 15,25:4
Richter, Will (Miscellaneous)
Certain Young Man, A 1967,D 27,45:1
Happy Hypocrite, The 1968,S 6,38:1
Rickabaugh, Clive (Scenic Designer)
Swing Mikado, The 1939,Mr 2,18:2
Rickaby, Ruth
Soldiers and Women 1929,S 3,25:1
Rickard, Gwen (Miscellaneous)
Where's Charley? 1948,O 12,33:2
Rickard, Gwen (Producer)
Where's Charley? 1951,Ja 30,21:7
Rickards, Shirley
Shadow and Substance 1956,Mr 14,38:1
Playboy of the Western World, The 1958,My 9,19:2
Ricketson, J H
Who's Who 1924,Ap 18,19:2
Rickett, Charles (Costume Designer)
Elizabeth of England 1931,O 18,VIII,1:3
Rickett, Edmond
Little Clay Cart, The 1924,D 6,13:3
Stigma 1927,F 11,19:1
Rickett, Edmond (Producer)
Stigma 1927,F 11,19:1
Rickett, Edmond W (Composer)
Dream of Sganarelle, The 1933,O 17,26:5
School for Husbands, The 1933,O 17,26:5
School for Husbands, The 1933,D 3,IX,6:5
Ricketts, Charles (Costume Designer)
Mikado, The 1926,O 10,VIII,2:1
Macbeth 1927,Ja 16,VII,4:3
Coming of Christ, The 1928,My 29,6:2
Gondoliers, The 1934,S 4,23:1
Gondoliers, The 1934,S 9,IX,1:1
Mikado, The; Town of Titipu, The 1934,S 18,18:1
Mikado, The 1936,Ag 21,13:2
Gondoliers, The 1936,S 8,23:1
Mikado, The 1947,D 30,18:2
Gondoliers, The 1948,Ja 27,31:2
Mikado, The 1951,Ja 30,21:2
Mikado, The 1955,S 30,20:2
Mikado, The 1962,N 14,43:1
Gondoliers, The 1962,N 16,25:2
Mikado, The 1964,N 27,43:1
Mikado, The 1966,N 18,36:1
Mikado, The 1968,N 2,29:4
Ricketts, Charles (Miscellaneous)
Gondoliers, The 1936,S 8,23:1
Ricketts, Charles (Scenic Designer)
Macbeth 1927,Ja 16,VII,4:3
Gondoliers, The 1934,S 4,23:1
Mikado, The; Town of Titipu, The 1934,S 18,18:1
Mikado, The 1936,Ag 21,13:2
Gondoliers, The 1936,S 8,23:1
Mikado, The 1947,D 30,18:2
Gondoliers, The 1948,Ja 27,31:2
Mikado, The 1951,Ja 30,21:2
Rickey, Al (Musical Director)
Almost Crazy 1955,Je 21,37:1
Rickie Layne and Velvel
Bagels and Yox 1951,S 13,38:2
Rickman, Carl (Playwright)
Brown Buddies 1930,O 8,29:1
Ricks, John T
I Must Love Someone 1939,F 8,18:7
Rico, Roger
South Pacific 1951,Jl 10,30:5
South Pacific 1951,S 2,II,1:1
Riddell, George
Beyond the Horizon 1920,F 4,12:1
Peg o' My Heart 1921,F 15,7:1
Right to Strike, The 1921,O 25,20:1
Dover Road, The 1921,D 24,7:2
In the Next Room 1923,N 28,14:1

Riddell, George—Cont
Blue Peter, The 1925,Mr 25,25:3
Engaged! or Cheviot's Choice 1925,Je 19,24:2
All Dressed Up 1925,S 10,28:1
Henry IV, Part I 1926,Je 1,29:1
Devil in the Cheese, The 1926,D 30,22:4
Bachelor Father, The 1928,F 29,28:2
General John Regan 1930,Ja 30,16:5
Little Father of the Wilderness, The 1930,Je 3,27:1
Tyrant, The 1930,N 13,33:1
Barretts of Wimpole Street, The 1931,F 10,25:1
Huui, Huui 1968,N 25,58:1
Riddle, Gladys
Henry V 1965,Je 29,27:2
Riddle, Hal
Have I Got a Girl for You! 1963,D 3,53:2
Riddleberger, H H (Director)
Underground 1952,F 13,33:2
Riddleberger, H H (Scenic Designer)
Life Begins in '40 1940,Ap 5,24:2
Hit the Road 1941,Ap 4,18:3
Rideamus, Edward (Composer)
Caroline 1923,F 1,13:2
Rideamus, Edward (Playwright)
Caroline 1923,F 1,13:2
Rose Marie 1928,Ap 29,IX,2:8
Rideamus, Edward (Translator)
Rose Marie 1928,Mr 31,23:2
Ridenour, Nina (Playwright)
My Name Is Legion 1952,Ap 21,23:7
Rideout, Douglas
Brigadoon 1950,My 3,36:2
Girl in Pink Tights, The 1954,Mr 6,13:2
Rideout, Ransom (Playwright)
Goin' Home 1928,Ag 24,23:2
Goin' Home 1928,S 2,VII,1:1
Rider, Frederick (Miscellaneous)
I Am a Camera 1956,O 10,47:2
Rider, Ivan
Arms and the Man 1964,Ap 28,41:1
Rider, Ivan (Director)
Home Away From, A 1969,Ap 29,40:3
Rider, Ivan (Miscellaneous)
Arms and the Man 1964,Ap 28,41:1
Rider, James F
In the Night Watch 1921,Ja 31,10:1
Rider, Tom
Sweet Adeline 1929,S 4,33:1
Rider, William
Ice Capades 1963,Ag 29,37:2
Ice Capades 1964,Ag 27,27:2
Ridge, Albert
Scarlet Sister Mary 1930,N 26,19:2
Ridge, Frank
Ed Wynn's Carnival 1920,Ap 6,18:2
Passing Show of 1921, The 1920,D 30,16:2
Ridge, John
Triumph of Robert Emmet, The 1969,My 8,54:1
Ridge, John David (Costume Designer)
Paradise Gardens East 1969,Mr 11,39:1
Conerico Was Here to Stay 1969,Mr 11,39:1
Jumping Fool, The 1970,F 10,53:1
Ridges, Stanley
Sally 1920,D 22,16:1
Elsie 1923,Ap 3,26:1
Mary Jane McKane 1923,D 26,13:2
Her Way Out 1924,Je 24,18:3
Bye Bye, Barbara 1924,Ag 26,6:3
Lambs Gambol 1925,Ap 27,15:1
Bride Retires, The 1925,My 18,12:3
Boom Boom 1929,Ja 29,26:4
Nancy's Private Affair 1930,Ja 14,24:3
Made in France 1930,N 12,21:1
Air-Minded 1932,F 11,17:3
Inside Story, The 1932,F 23,23:2
Dangerous Corner 1932,O 28,23:1
American Dream; 1849 1933,F 22,24:5
American Dream; 1933 1933,F 22,24:5
Mask and the Face, The 1933,My 9,20:2
Mary of Scotland 1933,N 28,28:3
Days Without End 1934,Ja 9,19:1
Days Without End 1934,Ja 14,IX,1:1
Valley Forge 1934,N 27,26:4
Valley Forge 1934,D 11,28:3
First Lady 1935,N 27,17:4
Ridgeway, Guy
This Island Is Mine 1959,Jl 1,26:4
Ridgewell, Andrew
Eastwood Ho 1936,Jl 8,14:2
Ridgwell, Audrey
Peter Pan 1924,N 7,16:2
Scotch Mist 1926,S 21,32:3
Old Bill, M P 1926,N 11,22:2
Lombardi, Ltd 1927,Je 7,27:3
Potiphar's Wife 1928,D 24,10:7
Chinese O'Neill 1929,My 23,27:1
Family Affairs 1929,D 11,34:6
Apple Cart, The 1930,F 25,30:1
Milestones 1930,Je 3,27:1
One Chaste Man 1930,Je 11,33:5
Merchant of Venice, The 1931,N 9,22:2
Anatomist, The 1932,O 25,24:3
Late One Evening 1933,Ja 10,27:3

Ridgwell, Audrey—Cont
Lake, The 1933,D 27,24:2
Fresh Fields 1934,Jl 15,X,1:1
Fresh Fields 1936,F 11,19:2
Father Malachy's Miracle 1937,N 18,26:4
Circle, The 1938,Ap 19,24:2
Claudia 1941,F 13,24:2
Sleep, My Pretty One 1944,N 3,26:8
Under Milk Wood 1957,O 16,42:5
Ridley, Arnold (Playwright)
Ghost Train, The 1926,Ag 26,17:2
Wrecker, The 1928,F 28,18:2
Keepers of Youth 1929,Je 9,VIII,2:4
Third Time Lucky 1929,D 8,X,2:5
Glory Be 1935,Mr 8,25:6
Ridley, Mabel
Deep Harlem 1929,Ja 8,35:2
Ridley, Michael
Slave Ship 1969,N 22,46:1
Ridoni, Relda
Servant of Two Masters, The 1960,F 24,42:2
Ridout, Godfrey
Country Wife, The 1964,Ag 3,16:1
Ridwell, Raye (Capt)
Winged Victory 1943,N 22,24:1
Rieck, Milton
Bunk of 1926 1926,F 17,12:3
Rieck, Waldemar
Bolls of Cotton 1925,D 22,18:3
Riede, Dimples
Oh, Ernest! 1927,My 10,24:3
Rain or Shine 1928,F 10,26:3
Riedinger, Mary
Pirates of Penzance, The 1942,F 20,20:2
Riegen, Deric (Director)
Bed Time 1958,Ap 11,20:2
Riegen, Deric (Playwright)
Bed Time 1958,Ap 11,20:2
Rieger, Grete
Armseligen Besenbinder, Die 1928,N 19,16:2
Rieger, Josephine
Trojan Women, The 1923,My 27,10:2
Riegger, Wallingford (Composer)
Trojan Incident 1938,Ap 22,15:2
Trojan Incident 1938,My 1,X,8:3
Riehl, Bob
Autumn's Here 1966,O 26,40:1
Riekman, Ruth
Polonaise 1945,O 8,20:2
Rielly, Bobo
How Beautiful With Shoes 1935,N 29,24:1
Riely and Wilkins
Africana 1927,Jl 12,29:2
Rieman, Margot
Varying Shore, The 1921,D 6,24:1
Riemann, Johannes
This Was a Man 1928,My 20,VIII,2:1
Riemer, Walter
Laura 1947,Je 27,16:1
Porgy and Bess 1953,Mr 10,25:5
Porgy and Bess 1964,My 7,32:1
Riemer, Walter (Miscellaneous)
Man's a Man, A 1962,S 20,30:2
Riendeau, Leonard J (Producer)
Beautiful Jailer, The 1957,My 17,19:2
Rienhard, John
Girl in the Spotlight, The 1920,Jl 13,9:3
Ries, Hilda
Uncle Tom's Cabin 1934,Jl 6,15:1
Ries, Nina
Beggar Student, The 1921,Ja 8,9:3
Riese, Laura (Translator)
Soldier's Tale, A 1955,Jl 13,21:2
Riesenberg, Felix (Playwright)
Second Mate, The 1930,Mr 25,34:5
Riesenfeld, Hugo (Dr)
Vaudeville (Hippodrome) 1925,D 8,28:6
Riesenfeld, Hugo (Dr) (Musical Director)
Lambs Gambol 1925,Ap 27,15:1
Riesenfeld, Hugo Dr (Composer)
Betty, Be Good 1920,My 5,14:2
Ziegfeld Follies 1931,Jl 2,30:5
Riesenfeld, Hugo Dr (Playwright)
Ziegfeld Follies 1931,Jl 2,30:5
Rieser, Allan (Playwright)
Brownstone Urge, The 1969,D 18,63:1
Riess, Bernard
Alt Heidelberg 1926,My 31,10:5
Rieth, Zita
Circle of Chalk, The 1941,Mr 27,28:4
Big Two, The 1947,Ja 9,21:2
Scarecrow, The 1953,Je 17,31:1
Rieti, Vittorio (Composer)
House of Bernarda Alba, The 1951,Ja 8,14:6
Ecole des Femmes, L'; School for Wives
1951,Mr 19,22:1
Rietz, Robert
Midsummer Night's Dream, A 1956,Ja 14,12:2
Romeo and Juliet 1956,F 24,20:4
Riewerts, J P (Playwright)
Blue Ghost, The 1930,Mr 11,24:5
Rifenburgh, Guinevere
Without the Walls 1921,Mr 28,8:1

Rifkin, Leo (Playwright)
They Should Have Stood in Bed 1942,F 14,18:5
Rigali, Alfred
Cup, The 1923,N 13,25:1
Izzy 1924,S 17,16:2
Badges 1924,D 4,25:1
Love's Call 1925,S 11,20:1
Rigali, Alfred L
Chivalry 1925,D 16,22:3
Rigat, Tina
Banjo Eyes 1941,D 26,20:2
Rigau, Angel
Handful of Fire 1958,O 2,45:3
Rigaud, George
Mr Strauss Goes to Boston 1945,S 7,20:2
Rigault, Jean de (Director)
Guernica 1969,My 1,50:1
Pique-Nique en Campagne 1969,My 1,50:1
Rigbie, Isabel
Menonite 1936,Mr 20,29:6
Rigby, Edward
Peter Pan 1924,N 7,16:2
Bit o' Love, A 1925,My 13,24:2
Kiss in a Taxi, The 1925,Ag 26,14:1
This Woman Business 1926,D 8,25:1
Enchantment 1927,Ap 28,27:3
Ivory Door, The 1927,O 19,24:5
Queen's Husband, The 1928,Ja 26,17:2
Cherry Orchard, The 1928,Mr 6,20:1
Young Alexander 1929,Mr 13,28:2
Chinese O'Neill 1929,My 23,27:1
Scotland Yard 1929,S 28,16:6
Game of Love and Death, The 1929,N 26,28:4
Dear Old England 1930,Mr 26,24:6
Inspector General, The 1930,D 24,19:2
Give Me Yesterday 1931,Mr 5,32:1
He 1931,S 22,33:1
Rigby, Edward (Director)
This Woman Business 1926,D 8,25:1
Rigby, Harry (Producer)
Make a Wish 1951,Ap 19,38:1
John Murray Anderson's Almanac 1953,D 11,42:2
Harlequinade 1959,F 14,15:1
Electra 1959,F 14,15:1
Hallelujah, Baby! 1967,Ap 27,51:1
Riot 1968,D 20,64:1
Rigby, Terence
Homecoming, The 1967,Ja 6,29:1
Rigdon, Edna May (Playwright)
Alice in Wonderland 1935,N 10,43:5
Rigdon, Walt (Lighting Director)
Lower Depths, The 1956,O 3,29:2
Rigg, Diana
Taming of the Shrew, The 1962,Ap 24,33:3
Macbeth 1962,Je 6,35:2
King Lear 1964,My 19,43:2
Comedy of Errors, The 1964,My 21,43:1
Riggin, Aileen
Vaudeville (Hippodrome) 1926,My 4,31:2
Vaudeville (Hippodrome) 1926,My 8,29:2
Vaudeville (Hippodrome) 1926,My 11,25:3
Riggins, Norman
Arabian Nights 1967,Jl 3,12:1
Riggio, James
House in Berlin, A (Als der Kreig zu Ende War);
Als der Krieg zu Ende War (A House in Berlin)
1950,D 27,32:3
Riggs, Helen
Sarah Simple 1940,N 18,22:5
Riggs, Joel
Borak 1960,D 14,51:1
If Five Years Pass 1962,My 11,37:1
Riggs, Lynn (Original Author)
Oklahoma! 1943,Ap 11,II,1:1
Oklahoma! 1953,S 1,19:1
Oklahoma! 1953,S 6,II,1:1
Oklahoma! 1955,Je 21,37:7
Oklahoma! 1958,Mr 8,15:2
Oklahoma! 1958,Mr 20,32:3
Oklahoma! 1965,D 16,62:1
Oklahoma! 1969,Je 24,37:1
Riggs, Lynn (Playwright)
Big Lake 1927,Ap 9,17:2
Roadside 1930,S 27,21:1
Green Grow the Lilacs 1930,D 14,IX,3:1
Green Grow the Lilacs 1931,Ja 27,21:2
Green Grow the Lilacs 1931,F 8,VIII,1:1
Cherokee Night, The 1932,Je 21,19:4
Cherokee Night, The 1932,Je 26,IX,1:1
Russet Mantle 1936,Ja 17,15:5
Russet Mantle 1936,Ja 26,IX,1:1
Lonesome West, The 1936,Je 30,15:1
Russet Mantle 1936,Ag 18,15:2
Cream in the Well, The 1941,Ja 21,19:2
Oklahoma! 1943,Ap 1,27:1
Borned in Texas 1950,Ag 22,30:6
Oklahoma! 1951,My 30,15:2
Year of Pilar, The 1952,Ja 7,14:3
Oklahoma! 1963,F 28,8:2
Oklahoma! 1963,My 16,40:1
Riggs, Otis (Scenic Designer)
Trip to Bountiful, The 1953,N 4,30:3

Riggs, Ralph
Grab Bag, The 1924,O 7,26:2
Oh, Ernest! 1927,My 10,24:3
Of Thee I Sing 1931,D 28,20:1
Lambs Gambol 1932,Ap 25,18:2
Let 'Em Eat Cake 1933,O 23,18:1
Farmer Takes a Wife, The 1934,O 31,17:1
Parade 1935,My 21,22:2
How Beautiful With Shoes 1935,N 29,24:1
Dr Knock 1936,Jl 14,22:1
Would-Be Gentleman, The 1936,Ag 4,15:1
Show Is On, The 1936,D 26,14:2
How to Get Tough About It 1938,F 9,16:2
Yokel Boy 1939,Jl 7,12:2
Louisiana Purchase 1940,My 29,19:2
Oklahoma! 1943,Ap 1,27:1
Mikado, The 1949,O 5,35:2
Pirates of Penzance, The 1949,O 11,41:2
Trial by Jury 1949,O 18,34:2
H M S Pinafore 1949,O 18,34:2
Riggs, Ralph (Choreographer)
Oh, Ernest! 1927,My 10,24:3
Riggs, Ralph (Miscellaneous)
Blonde Sinner, The 1926,Jl 15,21:2
Riggs, Rita (Costume Designer)
Nuns, The 1970,Je 2,35:1
Riggs, Robert
Operation Sidewinder 1970,Mr 13,33:1
Riggs, Sally
Celebration 1969,Ja 23,55:2
Riggs, Seth
Guys and Dolls 1955,Ap 21,32:2
Finian's Rainbow 1955,My 19,25:1
King and I, The 1960,My 12,40:1
110 in the Shade 1963,O 25,37:1
Riggs, Sydney
Tendresse, La 1922,S 26,18:1
Exile, The 1923,Ap 10,24:2
Is Zat So? 1925,Ja 6,23:4
Skull, The 1928,Ap 24,28:3
So Was Napoleon 1930,Ja 9,22:2
Ritzy 1930,F 11,30:4
Company's Coming! 1931,Ap 21,35:5
Girl Outside, The 1932,O 25,24:3
Play, Genius, Play! 1935,O 31,17:2
Riggs and Witchie
Grab Bag, The 1924,O 7,26:2
Nic-Nax of 1926 1926,Ag 5,19:1
Rightor, Hack
Man Who Never Died, The 1958,N 22,27:2
Rignold, Hugo (Musical Director)
Midsummer Night's Dream, A 1954,S 22,33:1
Rignold, Stanley
Free Soul, A 1928,Ja 13,26:5
Rigo, Jack
Treat 'Em Rough 1926,O 5,26:2
Sign of the Leopard 1928,D 12,34:4
Wild Waves 1932,F 20,11:4
Sellout, The 1933,S 7,17:2
Ladies' Money 1934,N 2,26:6
How to Get Tough About It 1938,F 9,16:2
Rigsby, Gordon
Doctored Wife, The 1950,Jl 12,33:2
Rigsby, Howard (Playwright)
South Pacific 1943,D 30,11:2
Riki
Shoemaker's Prodigious Wife, The 1962,S 2,44:4
Riley, Bradford
Dirtiest Show in Town, The 1970,My 2,21:1
Dirtiest Show in Town, The 1970,Je 29,43:2
Riley, Charles
Carmen Jones 1951,S 22,8:6
Riley, Ed
Front Page, The 1969,My 12,54:2
Riley, Edward (Playwright)
Before Morning 1933,F 10,13:4
Riley, Eulabel
Conjur 1938,N 1,27:2
Carib Song 1945,S 28,17:2
Riley, Francis
Three Little Girls 1930,Ap 15,29:1
Riley, J Flashe
Native Son 1941,Mr 25,26:5
Riley, Jack
Girl From Wyoming, The 1938,O 31,12:1
Riley, James
Greenwillow 1970,D 8,60:1
Riley, James (Miscellaneous)
Spofford 1967,D 15,54:3
Soldiers 1968,My 2,58:1
Riley, James (Scenic Designer)
Wilderness Road 1955,Je 30,20:4
Wedding in Japan 1957,Mr 12,37:7
Confederacy, The 1958,Jl 3,20:1
Riley, Janet
Tender Trap, The 1954,O 14,37:2
Riley, Jay
Peter Pan 1950,Ap 25,27:2
Mamba's Daughters 1953,Mr 21,12:6
Finian's Rainbow 1955,My 19,25:1
Mister Johnson 1956,Mr 30,11:1
Making of Moo, The 1958,Je 12,34:1
Shakespeare in Harlem 1959,O 28,40:7

Riley, Jay—Cont

Shakespeare in Harlem 1960,F 10,43:4
God's Trombones 1960,F 10,43:4
Blacks, The 1961,My 5,23:1
Trumpets of the Lord 1967,Je 1,51:3

Riley, Jay (Choreographer)
Making of Moo, The 1958,Je 12,34:1

Riley, Jay (Miscellaneous)
Making of Moo, The 1958,Je 12,34:1

Riley, John
Lingering Past, The 1932,Je 30,26:5
Sweeney Todd 1957,Ag 28,21:4

Riley, Kevin
Merchant of Venice, The 1953,Mr 5,20:2

Riley, Lawrence (Playwright)
Personal Appearance 1934,O 18,26:7
Personal Appearance 1936,Je 16,23:4
Return Engagement 1940,N 2,19:2

Riley, Louise
Magistrate, The 1959,My 14,30:6

Riley, Maggie
Dance of Death, The 1967,O 20,50:1
Love for Love 1967,O 30,59:1

Riley, Margot
Shoot the Works! 1931,Jl 22,19:5

Riley, Marin
Courageous One, The 1958,Ja 21,33:6

Riley, Peter (Miscellaneous)
Pirates of Penzance, The 1966,N 16,54:1
Mikado, The 1966,N 18,36:1
Ruddigore 1966,N 23,28:1
H M S Pinafore 1966,N 24,64:1
Patience 1966,N 30,58:1

Riley, Sherman
Immoral Support 1935,S 3,24:3

Riley, Theodore
Moon Is a Gong, The 1926,Mr 13,21:3

Riley, Tim
Othello 1970,Je 22,43:1
Devil's Disciple, The 1970,Je 30,48:1
Othello 1970,S 15,51:1

Riley, William T
It's the Valet 1933,D 15,25:4
Fiesta 1933,D 16,12:2

Rill, Eli
Pursuit of Happiness, The 1952,Mr 22,9:2
End as a Man 1953,S 16,39:1
2 for Fun; Anniversary, The 1955,My 26,34:1
2 for Fun; Switch in Time, A 1955,My 26,34:1

Rill, Eli (Director)
Evening With Shaw, An; Excerpts From Shaw
1955,Ag 13,6:6
Evening With Shaw, An; Village Wooing
1955,Ag 13,6:6
Glimpse of the Domesticity of Franklyn Barnabas,
A 1960,Mr 7,24:2

Rimac, Ciro
Follow the Sun 1936,F 5,15:8

Rimaldo, Bruce
Blue and the Gray, The; War Is Hell Gray, The
1929,D 27,26:4

Rimp, Jack
Anna Kleiber 1965,Ja 20,33:1
Masks of Angels 1965,Ja 20,33:1

Rimsky-Korsakoff (Composer)
Great Catherine, The 1927,Ap 3,VIII,4:7

Rimson, Jonas
Mikado, The 1939,Mr 11,15:6

Rinaldi, Don
Madame Lafayette 1960,Mr 4,21:1

Rinaldi, Frank (Lighting Director)
Don Juan in the Russian Manner 1954,Ap 23,23:2
Pigeon, The 1957,My 17,19:2

Rinaldi, Frank (Scenic Designer)
Don Juan in the Russian Manner 1954,Ap 23,23:2

Rinaldi, Joy
Satisfaction Guaranteed 1969,F 12,31:1

Rinaldi, Nick (Miscellaneous)
Sing Muse 1961,D 7,52:1

Rind, Maurice (Producer)
Just for Love 1968,O 18,40:1

Rinehart, Dora
Cry for Us All 1970,Ap 9,48:2

Rinehart, Mary Roberts (Original Author)
Bab 1920,O 19,12:1
Bat, The 1920,N 14,VI,1:1

Rinehart, Mary Roberts (Playwright)
Spanish Love 1920,Ag 18,6:1
Bat, The 1920,Ag 24,6:1
Bat, The 1920,N 14,VI,1:1
Bat, The 1922,Ap 30,VII,1:1
Breaking Point, The 1923,Jl 1,VI,1:4
Breaking Point, The 1923,Ag 17,8:4
Breaking Point, The 1923,Ag 26,VI,1:1
Bat, The 1953,Ja 21,28:2

Rinehart, Patricia (Playwright)
Guide, The 1968,Mr 7,50:1

Rines, Robert (Composer)
Drums Under the Windows 1960,O 14,26:1
Diff'rent 1961,O 18,52:1
Long Voyage Home, The 1961,D 5,49:1
Creditors 1962,Ja 26,19:1
Whitman Portrait, A 1966,O 12,37:1

Ring, Blanche
Broadway Whirl, The 1921,Je 9,10:4
Untitled-Benefit 1922,My 8,14:5
Alarm Clock, The 1923,D 25,26:2
Vaudeville (Palace) 1924,F 19,12:1
Vaudeville (Hippodrome) 1924,Ap 29,12:2
Henry IV, Part I 1926,Je 1,29:1
Great Necker, The 1928,Mr 7,28:2
Houseboat on the Styx, The 1928,D 26,14:3
Strike Up the Band 1930,Ja 15,29:1
Once in a Lifetime 1930,S 7,IX,2:4
Intimate Relations 1932,Mr 29,23:2
De Luxe 1935,Mr 6,22:2
Right This Way 1938,Ja 6,22:3
Madame Capet 1938,O 26,26:2

Ring, Cyril
Back Seat Drivers 1928,D 26,14:4

Ring, Gerda (Director)
Abraham's Offering 1938,D 18,IX,4:2

Ring, Joyce
By Jupiter 1942,Je 4,22:1

Ring, Julie
Strawberry Blonde, The 1927,F 8,20:3
Intimate Relations 1932,Mr 29,23:2

Ring, Lillian
Americana 1926,Jl 27,15:3

Ringer, Titus
Restless Flame, The 1952,Ap 15,30:6

Ringham, Walter
Richard III 1920,Mr 8,7:1
Marie Antoinette 1921,N 23,16:1
Dolly Jordan 1922,O 4,26:1
Red Falcon, The 1924,O 8,22:1
Right Age to Marry, The 1926,F 16,22:3
Ghosts 1927,Ja 11,36:3

Ringland, Byron (Miscellaneous)
Moby Dick 1961,Ap 11,41:2
Plays for Bleecker Street 1962,Ja 12,28:1
Infancy 1962,Ja 12,28:1
Someone From Assisi 1962,Ja 12,28:1
Childhood 1962,Ja 12,28:1
Six Characters in Search of an Author
1963,Mr 11,7:2

Ringling, Edith C (Miscellaneous)
All the Comforts of Home 1942,My 26,24:5

Ringo, James (Composer)
Thesmophoriazusae, The; Goddesses of Athens,
The 1955,D 14,52:4

Ringwald, Roy (Composer)
Hear! Hear! 1955,S 28,38:1

Ringwald, Roy (Playwright)
Hear! Hear! 1955,S 28,38:1

Ringwood, Susan
Cherry Orchard, The 1965,Ag 2,17:2

Rinn, Joseph F (Playwright)
Zeno 1923,Ag 27,14:2

Rinner, Walter
Firebird of Florence 1945,Mr 23,13:4
Dear Judas 1947,O 6,26:4

Rio, Amelia del (Director)
Logia a la Natividad de Nuestro Senor Jesucristo,
El 1937,D 14,33:4

Riofrancos, Osvaldo
Shoemaker's Prodigious Wife, The 1962,S 2,44:4
Retabilillo de Don Cristobal, El; Puppet Theater of
Don Cristobal, The; Zapatera Prodigiosa, La;
Shoemaker's Prodigious Wife, The 1964,S 3,23:2
Romeo y Julieta 1965,Ag 28,13:3
Macbeth 1966,Ag 29,23:4

Riofrancos, Osvaldo (Director)
Retabilillo de Don Cristobal, El; Puppet Theater of
Don Cristobal, The; Zapatera Prodigiosa, La;
Shoemaker's Prodigious Wife, The 1964,S 3,23:2
Romeo y Julieta 1965,Ag 28,13:3

Riofrancos, Osvaldo (Original Author)
Macbeth 1966,Ag 29,23:4

Riordan, Irene
Brothers Karamazov, The 1957,D 9,39:4
Smokeweaver's Daughter, The 1959,Ap 15,30:1
Committee, The 1964,S 17,53:1

Riordan, John
Taming of the Shrew, The 1956,Ag 11,11:2

Riordan, Joseph
Gondoliers, The 1962,N 16,25:2

Riordan, Naomi
Velvet Glove, The 1949,D 27,26:2

Riordan, Patricia
Skin of Our Teeth, The 1942,N 19,29:5

Rios, Augie
Jamaica 1957,N 1,32:2
Saratoga 1959,D 8,59:4
Christine 1960,Ap 29,27:1

Rios, Jorge
Lady of Mexico 1962,O 20,13:2

Rios, Juanita
Star and Garter 1942,Je 25,26:2

Rios, Laura de los
Logia a la Natividad de Nuestro Senor Jesucristo,
El 1937,D 14,33:4

Rios, Louis (Lighting Director)
Emerald Slippers, The 1970,S 2,31:2

Rios, Rosita
Mexicana 1939,Ap 22,14:4

Rip (Playwright)
Untitled-Revue 1924,My 25,VIII,1:8
Surcouf 1926,N 14,VIII,2:1
Untitled-Revue 1927,O 9,VIII,2:4
Comme le Temps Passe 1927,O 30,IX,4:7
Untitled-Revue 1928,N 18,IX,2:1
A la Mode de Chez Nous 1929,My 26,IX,4:1
Untitled-Revue 1929,O 20,IX,4:4
Par le Temps Qui Court 1930,O 5,IX,4:3
Untitled-Revue 1931,My 3,VIII,1:7

Ripa, Bob
Vaudeville (Palace) 1930,Mr 31,24:2
Vaudeville (Palace) 1932,Je 6,18:2

Ripley, Arthur (Director)
Every Man for Himself 1940,D 10,32:3
Happy Days 1941,My 14,24:2

Ripley, Arthur (Producer)
Every Man for Himself 1940,D 10,32:3

Ripley, Constance (Costume Designer)
Band Wagon, The 1931,Je 4,31:3
Flying Colors 1932,S 16,24:2
Flying Colors 1932,O 9,IX,1:1
Great Magoo, The 1932,D 3,20:7
Revenge With Music 1934,N 29,33:5
Red, Hot and Blue! 1936,O 30,26:3

Ripley, Cornelia
Medea 1920,Mr 23,12:2

Ripley, Dillion
Wings Over Europe 1936,Mr 4,24:7

Ripley, Edward
Arms and the Man 1938,Ag 10,14:1

Ripley, Everett
Peter Ibbetson 1931,Ap 9,30:3
One Sunday Afternoon 1933,F 16,23:5
Richard of Bordeaux 1934,F 15,16:2
Animal Kingdom, The 1938,Jl 27,14:5
Biography 1938,Ag 3,14:7
Bachelor Born 1938,Ag 17,23:1
Hamlet 1938,O 13,28:1
Henry IV, Part I 1939,Ja 31,17:2
Journey's End 1939,S 19,29:2
They Knew What They Wanted 1939,O 3,19:1
Richard II 1940,Ap 2,31:2
Wookey, The 1941,S 11,20:5
Lifeline 1942,D 1,20:3
This Rock 1943,F 19,23:2
Richard II 1951,Ja 25,21:2

Ripley, Lou
Up She Goes 1922,N 7,14:2
Unchastened Woman, The 1926,F 17,12:1
Trial Marriage 1927,F 1,24:3
Marriage on Approval 1928,Mr 2,28:2

Ripley, Patricia
Be Your Age 1953,Ja 15,24:2
Henry V 1956,Jl 7,11:2
Major Barbara 1956,O 31,27:1
Sweet Bird of Youth 1959,Mr 11,39:2
Great God Brown, The 1959,O 7,48:1
Lysistrata 1959,N 25,19:4
Hostage, The 1961,D 13,55:4

Ripley, Ramon R
School for Virtue 1931,Mr 11,23:4

Ripley, Trescott
Half a Sixpence 1965,Ap 26,38:2
Measure for Measure 1966,Jl 14,27:1

Ripple, Pacie
Great Adventure, The 1921,F 26,9:2
Farmer's Wife, The 1924,O 10,22:3
Complex, The 1925,Mr 4,17:2
Three Doors 1925,Ap 24,16:4
Sex 1926,Ap 27,22:4
Wrecker, The 1928,F 28,18:2
New Moon, The 1928,S 20,33:1
Little Father of the Wilderness, The 1930,Je 3,27:1
Overture 1930,D 8,26:4
Barrister, The 1932,N 22,25:2
Under Glass 1933,O 31,24:3
Anything Goes 1934,N 22,26:1

Rippner, William W (Producer)
Pequod 1969,Je 30,33:1

Rippy, Robert
Arms and the Girl 1950,F 3,28:2
Vamp, The 1955,N 11,30:1

Riquier, Georges
Ecole des Femmes, L'; School for Wives
1951,Mr 19,22:1
Marie Tudor 1958,O 22,39:1
Don Juan 1958,O 29,29:1
Cid, Le 1958,O 31,35:2

Riquier, Georges (Director)
Red Roses for Me 1961,F 11,26:5

Risch, Pierre
Otage, L' 1959,O 27,42:1

Riscoe, Arthur
Jill Darling 1934,D 20,29:8
Going Places 1936,O 25,X,2:4
Shephard's Pie 1941,My 18,IX,1:5
Fun and Games 1941,Ag 31,IX,1:4

Risdon, Elizabeth
Foot-Loose 1920,My 11,12:1
Heartbreak House 1920,N 11,11:1
Heartbreak House 1920,N 21,VI,1:2
Nightcap, The 1921,Ag 16,18:3

Risdon, Elizabeth—Cont

Lady, The 1923,D 5,23:2
Rabbit's Foot, The 1924,Ap 27,VIII,2:3
Cock o' the Roost 1924,O 14,23:1
Artistic Temperament 1924,D 10,20:2
Thrills 1925,Ap 17,24:3
Enchanted April, The 1925,Ag 25,12:3
Lovely Lady 1925,O 15,27:1
Proud Woman, A 1926,N 16,24:1
Silver Cord, The 1926,D 21,21:1
Right You Are (If You Think You Are) 1927,F 24,27:1
Midsummer Night's Dream, A 1927,Je 27,25:1
Springboard, The 1927,O 13,23:1
We Never Learn 1928,Ja 24,26:1
Silver Cord, The 1928,F 19,VIII,2:1
For Services Rendered 1933,Ap 13,15:5
Uncle Tom's Cabin 1933,My 30,13:4
Big Hearted Herbert 1934,Ja 2,17:3
Laburnum Grove 1935,Ja 15,23:5

Risdon, Marianne

Round-Up, The 1932,Mr 8,19:4

Riselle, Miriam

Who Is Who? 1938,D 24,13:3
Salvation 1939,S 29,19:2

Riseman, Naomi

Lady's Not for Burning, The 1959,Ja 31,13:2
Boo Hoo! East Lynne 1959,S 9,50:4
Romeo and Juliet 1962,Ap 3,42:1
Will the Mail Train Run Tonight? 1964,Ja 10,18:1

Risien, Clarence

Trapped 1928,S 12,25:3

Riskin, A E (Producer)

She Couldn't Say No! 1926,S 1,27:3
Lady in Love, A 1927,F 22,22:1
Bless You, Sister 1927,D 27,24:5

Riskin, R R (Producer)

She Couldn't Say No! 1926,S 1,27:3
Lady in Love, A 1927,F 22,22:1
Bless You, Sister 1927,D 27,24:5

Riskin, Robert (Director)

Many a Slip 1930,F 4,29:2

Riskin, Robert (Playwright)

Bless You, Sister 1927,D 27,24:5
Many a Slip 1930,F 4,29:2
Nine Fifteen Revue, The 1930,F 12,26:2
It Happened One Night; On the Road to New York 1944,Je 21,23:4

Riskin, Susan

Winter's Tale, The 1958,Jl 21,17:4

Risler, Jeannie

Magnificent Hugo, The 1961,Ap 8,12:2

Risley, Carl

Betty Behave 1927,Mr 9,28:4

Risser, Carol

This Side of Paradise 1962,F 22,19:6

Risser, Marguerite

Monster, The 1922,Ag 10,20:3
Naked 1926,N 9,31:2
Scarlet Lily, The 1927,Ja 31,12:3

Rissler, Suzanne (Mme)

Topaze 1931,F 17,29:1

Rissman, Herbert

Oklahoma! 1943,Ap 1,27:1

Rissman, Hope

Best House in Naples, The 1956,O 27,16:2

Risto, Manuel

To Quito and Back 1937,O 7,30:4

Rita, Palma

Creoles 1927,S 23,33:3

Ritch, Rozanne

Kill the One-Eyed Man 1965,O 21,56:1

Ritchard, Cyril

Puzzles of 1925 1925,F 3,25:3
People in Love 1937,My 28,17:5
Sigh No More 1945,S 2,II,1:2
Love for Love 1947,My 27,30:2
Make Way for Lucia 1948,D 23,23:5
Relapse, The 1950,N 23,54:2
Millionairess, The 1952,Je 28,12:2
Millionairess, The 1952,O 18,17:2
Peter Pan 1954,Jl 20,15:3
Peter Pan 1954,O 21,30:2
Peter Pan 1954,O 31,II,1:1
Visit to a Small Planet 1957,F 8,18:1
Visit to a Small Planet 1957,F 24,II,1:1
Pleasure of His Company, The 1958,O 23,36:1
Pleasure of His Company, The 1958,N 2,II,1:1
Happiest Girl in the World, The 1961,Ap 4,42:1
Romulus 1962,Ja 11,27:1
Too True to Be Good 1963,Mr 14,8:2
Too True to Be Good 1963,Mr 23,5:6
Too True to Be Good 1963,Ap 9,28:1
Irregular Verb to Love, The 1963,S 19,22:2
Irregular Verb to Love, The 1963,S 29,II,1:1
Roar of the Greasepaint-the Smell of the Crowd 1965,My 17,46:2
Midsummer Night's Dream, A 1967,Je 19,42:1
Devil's Disciple, The 1970,Je 30,48:1
Devil's Disciple, The 1970,Jl 12,II,1:3

Ritchard, Cyril (Director)

Relapse, The 1950,N 23,54:2
Buy Me Blue Ribbons 1951,O 18,33:2
Jane 1952,F 2,10:2

Jane 1952,F 10,II,1:1
Misalliance 1953,F 19,20:1
Misalliance 1953,Mr 22,II,1:1
John Murray Anderson's Almanac 1953,D 11,42:2
Almanac 1954,Ja 3,II,1:1
Heavenly Twins, The 1955,N 5,23:2
Reluctant Debutante, The 1956,O 11,50:1
Reluctant Debutante, The 1956,O 23,II,1:1
Visit to a Small Planet 1957,F 8,18:1
Pleasure of His Company, The 1958,O 23,36:1
Look After Lulu 1959,Mr 4,35:1
Happiest Girl in the World, The 1961,Ap 4,42:1
Everybody Loves Opal 1961,O 12,40:2
Irregular Verb to Love, The 1963,S 19,22:2
Roar Like a Dove 1964,My 22,40:2
Midsummer Night's Dream, A 1967,Je 19,42:1
Devil's Disciple, The 1970,Je 30,48:1
Devil's Disciple, The 1970,Jl 12,II,1:3

Ritchey, Camilia

Ah, Wilderness! 1969,N 9,86:1
Seven Days of Mourning 1969,D 17,64:1

Ritchie, Adam (Lighting Director)

Sometime Jam Today 1967,F 13,41:1

Ritchie, Adam (Scenic Designer)

Sometime Jam Today 1967,F 13,41:1

Ritchie, Adele

Little Theatre Tournament; Little Italy 1928,My 10,31:1

Ritchie, Charles

No More Women 1926,Ag 4,17:2
No Trespassing! 1926,S 8,19:1
Gentle Grafters 1926,O 28,23:1
Romancing 'Round 1927,O 4,32:4
Undertow 1929,N 10,X,4:8
Claire Adams 1929,N 20,26:3
House Afire 1930,Ap 1,34:7
Mr Samuel 1930,N 11,28:4

Ritchie, Estelle

Detective Story 1954,F 13,11:2
Buffalo Skinner, The 1959,F 20,18:1
Delightful Season, A 1960,S 29,30:1
Man and Superman 1960,N 7,46:2
Poppa Is Home 1961,D 20,37:1

Ritchie, Gertrude

Blue and the Gray, The; War Is Hell Gray, The 1929,D 27,26:4
American Tragedy, An 1931,F 21,15:5
Regular Guy, A; Man's Man, A 1931,Je 5,27:1
Whistling in the Dark 1932,N 4,25:2
Riddle Me This! 1933,Mr 15,21:3
It's a Wise Child 1933,My 17,15:2

Ritchie, Harry (Director)

Angel Comes to Babylon, An 1962,S 29,15:2

Ritchie, Ralph K

Fiesta 1933,D 16,12:2

Ritchie, Robert (Producer)

Hi-Ya Gentlemen 1940,D 4,34:2

Ritchie, Sharon

Brigadoon 1964,D 24,9:1
Sweet Charity 1966,Ja 31,22:1

Ritchy, A

Deburau 1926,D 28,16:1
Mozart 1926,D 28,16:1

Ritchy, Mlle

Illusioniste, L' 1927,Ja 11,36:5

Ritman, William (Costume Designer)

Russell Patterson's Sketch-Book 1960,F 8,35:1
Bartleby 1961,Ja 25,28:1
American Dream, The 1961,Ja 25,28:1
Death of Bessie Smith, The 1961,Mr 2,19:1
Birthday Party, The 1967,O 4,40:2
Johnny No-Trump 1967,O 9,60:2
Box-Mao-Box; Quotations From Chairman Mao Tse-Tung 1968,Mr 8,48:1
Box-Mao-Box; Box 1968,Mr 8,48:1

Ritman, William (Lighting Director)

On the Town 1959,F 14,15:1
Zoo Story, The 1960,Ja 15,37:2
Krapp's Last Tape 1960,Ja 15,37:2
Russell Patterson's Sketch-Book 1960,F 8,35:1
Killer, The 1960,Mr 23,33:1
Sudden End of Anne Cinquefoil, The 1961,Ja 11,25:2
Bartleby 1961,Ja 25,28:1
American Dream, The 1961,Ja 25,28:1
Death of Bessie Smith, The 1961,Mr 2,19:1
Fortuna 1962,Ja 4,26:1
King of the Whole Damn World 1962,Ap 16,32:2
Place for Chance, The 1964,My 15,44:2
Absence of a Cello 1964,S 22,45:1
Come Live With Me 1967,Ja 27,29:1
Johnny No-Trump 1967,O 9,60:2
Loot 1968,Mr 19,40:2
Box 1968,O 1,39:1
Quotations From Chairman Mao Tse-Tung 1968,O 1,39:1
American Dream, The 1968,O 3,55:1
Death of Bessie Smith, The 1968,O 3,55:1
Krapp's Last Tape 1968,O 11,41:1
Zoo Story, The 1968,O 11,41:1
Happy Days 1968,O 14,54:1
Mundy Scheme, The 1969,D 12,75:1
How Much, How Much? 1970,Ap 21,49:1

Ritman, William (Lighting Director)—Cont

Sleuth 1970,N 13,25:1

Ritman, William (Producer)

Killing of Sister George, The 1966,O 6,57:1

Ritman, William (Scenic Designer)

On the Town 1959,F 14,15:1
Zoo Story, The 1960,Ja 15,37:2
Krapp's Last Tape 1960,Ja 15,37:2
Russell Patterson's Sketch-Book 1960,F 8,35:1
Killer, The 1960,Mr 23,33:1
Kukla, Burr and Ollie 1960,N 1,47:2
Sudden End of Anne Cinquefoil, The 1961,Ja 11,25:2
Bartleby 1961,Ja 25,28:1
American Dream, The 1961,Ja 25,28:1
Death of Bessie Smith, The 1961,Mr 2,19:1
Gallows Humor 1961,Ap 19,35:1
Happy Days 1961,S 18,36:1
Fortuna 1962,Ja 4,26:1
Endgame 1962,F 12,27:1
Mrs Dally Has a Lover 1962,O 2,47:1
Whisper Into My Good Ear 1962,O 2,47:1
Who's Afraid of Virginia Woolf? 1962,O 15,33:1
Dumbwaiter, The 1962,N 27,44:1
Collection, The 1962,N 27,44:1
Riot Act, The 1963,Mr 9,5:2
Corruption in the Palace of Justice 1963,O 9,49:2
Lover, The 1964,Ja 6,35:1
Play 1964,Ja 6,35:1
Funnyhouse of a Negro 1964,Ja 15,25:3
Play 1964,Mr 25,46:2
Dutchman 1964,Mr 25,46:2
Two Executioners, The 1964,Mr 25,46:2
Place for Chance, The 1964,My 15,44:2
Midsummer Night's Dream, A 1964,Je 30,23:2
Absence of a Cello 1964,S 22,45:1
Giants' Dance, The 1964,N 17,48:2
Tiny Alice 1964,D 30,14:2
Tiny Alice 1965,Ja 10,II,1:1
Do Not Pass Go 1965,Ap 20,44:1
Entertaining Mr Sloane 1965,O 13,41:1
Play That on Your Old Piano 1965,O 15,49:1
Malcolm 1966,Ja 12,29:1
Delicate Balance, A 1966,S 23,44:1
Delicate Balance, A 1966,O 2,II,1:1
Night of the Dunce 1966,D 29,21:1
Come Live With Me 1967,Ja 27,29:1
Rimers of Eldritch, The 1967,F 21,53:1
Birthday Party, The 1967,O 4,40:2
Johnny No-Trump 1967,O 9,60:2
Promise, The 1967,N 15,38:1
Everything in the Garden 1967,N 30,60:1
Box-Mao-Box; Quotations From Chairman Mao Tse-Tung 1968,Mr 8,48:1
Box-Mao-Box; Box 1968,Mr 8,48:1
Loot 1968,Mr 19,40:2
Lovers; Winners 1968,Jl 26,21:4
Lovers; Losers 1968,Jl 26,21:4
Quotations From Chairman Mao Tse-Tung 1968,O 1,39:1
Box 1968,O 1,39:1
American Dream, The 1968,O 3,55:1
Death of Bessie Smith, The 1968,O 3,55:1
Krapp's Last Tape 1968,O 11,41:1
Zoo Story, The 1968,O 11,41:1
Happy Days 1968,O 14,54:1
Play It Again, Sam 1969,F 13,52:3
Gingham Dog, The 1969,Ap 24,41:1
Three Sisters, The 1969,Ag 4,29:1
Hello and Goodbye 1969,S 19,54:1
Penny Wars, The 1969,O 16,52:1
Crimes of Passion; Ruffian on the Stair, The 1969,O 27,54:1
Crimes of Passion; Erpingham Camp, The 1969,O 27,54:1
Mundy Scheme, The 1969,D 12,75:1
Nature of the Crime 1970,Mr 24,41:1
How Much, How Much? 1970,Ap 21,49:1
What the Butler Saw 1970,My 5,56:1
Devil's Disciple, The 1970,Je 30,48:1
Bob and Ray-The Two and Only 1970,S 25,36:1
Bob and Ray-The Two and Only 1970,O 4,II,3:1

Ritner, George

Juno 1959,Mr 10,41:1

Ritt, Martin

Golden Boy 1937,N 5,18:5
Gentle People, The 1939,Ja 6,25:1
Two on an Island 1940,Ja 23,17:2
No for an Answer 1941,Ja 6,10:6
Criminals, The 1941,D 22,24:3
They Should Have Stood in Bed 1942,F 14,18:5
Eve of St Mark, The 1942,O 8,30:2
Winged Victory 1943,N 22,24:1
Men of Distinction 1953,My 1,18:4
Maya 1953,Je 10,35:1
Flowering Peach, The 1954,D 29,19:2
Flowering Peach, The 1955,Ja 9,II,1:1

Ritt, Martin (Director)

Yellow Jack 1944,Ap 7,23:3
Mr Peebles and Mr Hooker 1946,O 11,29:2
Yellow Jack 1947,F 28,26:2
Set My People Free 1948,N 4,38:2
Man, The 1950,Ja 20,28:2
Cry of the Peacock 1950,Ap 12,33:2

Ritt, Martin (Director)—Cont
View From the Bridge, A 1955,S 30,21:1
Memory of Two Mondays, A 1955,S 30,21:1
View From the Bridge, A 1955,O 9,II,1:1
Very Special Baby, A 1956,N 15,43:2

Rittenhouse, Florence
Red Geranium, The 1922,My 9,22:3
Swanee River 1923,Jl 15,VI,1:2
Shame Woman, The 1923,O 17,14:1
Praying Curve 1927,Ja 25,18:2
Tonight at 12 1928,N 16,28:1

Rittenhouse, Martin H Jr
What a Relief 1935,D 14,10:6

Ritter, Blake
Doodle Dandy of the U S A 1942,O 19,15:2
Doodle Dandy of the U S A 1942,O 19,15:2
Carousel 1945,Ap 20,24:2
Allegro 1947,O 11,10:2

Ritter, Evan
Moondreamers, The 1969,D 9,68:1

Ritter, Ilse
Wozzeck 1966,Ap 6,34:1

Ritter, J C
Adam Solitaire 1925,N 7,19:2

Ritter, Margaret
Sleepy Hollow 1948,Je 4,26:3
Heimkehr aus der Fremde, Die; Stranger, The 1949,S 2,14:1

Ritter, Ted (Miscellaneous)
Redhead 1959,F 6,21:1

Ritter, Tex
Round-Up, The 1932,Mr 8,19:4
Mother Lode 1934,D 24,16:5

Ritter, Thelma
Shelf, The 1926,S 28,31:1
In Times Square 1931,N 24,29:3
New Girl in Town 1957,My 15,40:1
New Girl in Town 1957,My 26,II,1:1
Ubu 1966,Ja 5,24:1

Ritter, Thomas Frederick
This Mad Whirl 1937,Ja 10,II,4:8

Ritter, Woodward
Green Grow the Lilacs 1931,Ja 27,21:2

Ritterbusch, Robert
Highest Tree, The 1959,N 5,41:1

Ritterman, H (Playwright)
To Be or Not to Be-What Kind of a Question Is That? 1970,O 20,39:1

Rittman, Trude (Choreographer)
Look, Ma, I'm Dancin' 1948,Ja 30,20:2
Two by Two 1970,N 11,37:1

Rittman, Trude (Composer)
Climate of Eden, The 1952,N 7,20:2
Peter Pan 1954,Jl 20,15:3
Peter Pan 1954,O 21,30:2
Darling of the Day 1968,Ja 29,26:2

Rittman, Trude (Miscellaneous)
Allegro 1948,Ja 18,II,3:5
Miss Liberty 1949,Ag 7,II,6:4
Peter Pan 1950,Ap 25,27:2
Paint Your Wagon 1951,N 13,32:2
Wish You Were Here 1952,Je 26,26:6
Girl in Pink Tights, The 1954,Mr 6,13:2
Fanny 1954,N 5,16:1
My Fair Lady 1956,Mr 16,20:2
Sound of Music, The 1959,N 17,40:2
Christine 1960,Ap 29,27:1
Camelot 1960,D 5,42:1
All American 1962,Mr 20,44:1
Hot Spot 1963,Ap 20,17:2
Jennie 1963,O 18,35:2
My Fair Lady 1964,My 21,43:2
On a Clear Day You Can See Forever 1965,O 18,44:1
My Fair Lady 1968,Je 14,42:1
Maggie Flynn 1968,O 24,52:1
Come Summer 1969,Mr 19,43:1

Rittman, Trude (Musical Director)
Out of This World 1950,D 22,17:3
Sound of Music, The 1970,Jl 3,13:1

Rittman, William (Scenic Designer)
We Bombed in New Haven 1968,O 17,51:1

Rittner, Thaddeus (Playwright)
Tyrants 1924,Mr 5,14:1

Ritz, Harry
Everybody's Welcome 1931,S 20,VIII,3:2

Ritz, Robert (Playwright)
Alloy 1924,O 12,VIII,2:1
Alloy 1924,O 28,27:1

Ritz Brothers
Vaudeville (Palace) 1929,Mr 25,33:2
Vaudeville (Palace) 1932,Mr 7,13:4
Casino Varieties 1934,Ap 3,26:4

Riva, Maria
Burning Glass, The 1954,Mr 5,15:2
Burning Glass, The 1954,Mr 14,II,1:1

Riva, William (Lighting Director)
Telephone, The 1950,Jl 20,22:5
Medium, The 1950,Jl 20,22:5
Stone for Danny Fisher, A 1954,O 22,24:2

Riva, William (Scenic Designer)
Trial by Fire 1947,D 5,31:5
Lazarus Laughed 1948,Ap 9,27:4

Medium, The 1950,Jl 20,22:5
Telephone, The 1950,Jl 20,22:5
Razzle Dazzle 1951,F 20,21:1
Stone for Danny Fisher, A 1954,O 22,24:2
Shoestring '57 1956,N 6,31:1

Rivain, Mme
Vie Que Je T'Ai Donnee, La 1930,Ap 6,IX,2:3

Rivas, Cherif, Cipriano (Playwright)
Custom, The 1946,Je 29,22:6

Rivas, Cherif, Cipriano (Producer)
Custom, The 1946,Je 29,22:6

Rivas, Cherif, Cipriano (Scenic Designer)
Custom, The 1946,Je 29,22:6

Rivas, Jose
Love's Call 1925,S 11,20:1
Yellow 1926,S 22,30:1
Spread Eagle 1927,Ap 5,30:2

Rivas, Linares (Playwright)
Hoy 1929,Ja 3,25:2

Rivera, Al
Carmen Jones 1951,S 22,8:6

Rivera, Chita
Shoestring Revue 1955,Mr 1,22:2
Seventh Heaven 1955,My 27,16:2
Mr Wonderful 1956,Mr 23,23:2
West Side Story 1957,S 27,14:4
Bye Bye Birdie 1960,Ap 15,13:4
Bye Bye Birdie 1961,Je 25,II,3:5
Wonder World 1964,My 18,32:1
Bajour 1964,N 24,42:1
Mister Mayor! 1967,Ap 4,36:3

Rivera, Chita (Choreographer)
Man Dies, A 1968,Jl 16,35:1

Rivera, Fred
Much Ado About Nothing 1969,Je 16,57:1
Hamlet 1969,Je 30,33:1
Tarot 1970,D 12,19:1

Rivera, Lelane
Hansel and Gretel 1929,D 25,21:1
Through the Years 1932,Ja 29,13:3

Rivero, Amalia
Cradle Song 1927,My 10,24:4

Rivers, Anthony
American Primitive 1937,Ag 13,12:5

Rivers, Carlton
Helena's Boys 1924,Ap 8,22:2
Set a Thief 1927,F 22,22:1
Wrecker, The 1928,F 28,18:2

Rivers, Cecil
Hummin' Sam 1933,Ap 10,8:8

Rivers, Chief
Girl Crazy 1930,O 15,27:1

Rivers, Clarice
Tinguely Machine Mystery, or the Love Suicide at Kaluka, The 1965,D 24,15:5

Rivers, Diana
Chicken Every Sunday 1944,Ap 6,27:2

Rivers, Edna
Polly Preferred 1923,Ja 12,13:3

Rivers, Frank
Nativity Play, The 1937,D 21,29:1

Rivers, Grace
Her Family Tree 1920,D 28,9:2

Rivers, Jimmy
Penny Friend, The 1966,D 27,46:1

Rivers, Joseph
Heat Lightning 1933,S 16,9:6

Rivers, Larry
Tinguely Machine Mystery, or the Love Suicide at Kaluka, The 1965,D 24,15:5

Rivers, Larry (Miscellaneous)
Mahagonny 1970,Ap 29,51:1

Rivers, Larry (Scenic Designer)
Toilet, The 1964,D 17,51:1
Slave, The 1964,D 17,51:1

Rivers, Laurence (Producer)
Green Pastures, The 1930,F 27,26:1
Philip Goes Forth 1931,Ja 13,35:4
Antony and Cleopatra 1937,O 14,23:2

Rivers, Leslie
417 1961,Mr 6,30:1
Funnyhouse of a Negro 1964,Ja 15,25:3
Warning, The-A Theme for Linda 1969,Ap 27,92:1
Electra 1969,Ag 8,14:1

Rivers, Max (Choreographer)
This Year of Grace 1928,N 8,27:1
Wake Up and Dream 1929,D 31,14:3
White Horse Inn 1936,O 2,28:5

Rivers, Pamela
Pick-Up Girl 1944,My 4,25:2
Next Half Hour, The 1945,O 30,14:6
Song of Bernadette 1946,Mr 27,22:2
Jenny Kissed Me 1948,D 24,12:2

Rivers, Walter
Schoolgirl 1930,N 21,31:1

Rives, Amelie (Playwright)
Prince and the Pauper, The 1920,N 2,15:1
Sea-Woman's Cloak, The 1925,N 5,28:1
Love in a Mist 1926,Ap 13,28:3
Say When 1928,Je 27,29:3

Riviere, Maya
Tobias and the Angel 1937,Ap 29,16:5

Rivinus, David
So Proudly We Hail 1938,Ap 9,11:1

Rivituso, Danny
King and the Duke, The 1955,Je 2,25:2

Rivkin, Allen (Playwright)
Knock on Wood 1935,My 29,16:2

Rivoire, Andre (Playwright)
Roi Dagobert, Le 1926,N 14,VIII,2:1
Pardon, Madame 1930,F 9,VIII,2:6

Rivoire, Mary
Mascaiada 1929,D 28,10:6
Iron Flowers 1933,Je 13,22:2

Rivollet, Georges (Translator)
Oedipe a Colone 1924,S 7,III,12:4

Rix, Mary
Blossom Time 1936,Jl 29,23:1
Countess Maritza 1936,Ag 19,18:2
Bitter Sweet 1936,Ag 26,17:3

Rizer, Elsie
Tavern, The 1920,S 28,14:1
Night Call, The 1922,Ap 27,12:2

Rizzo, Gino (Translator)
Troubled Waters 1965,Je 4,40:2

Rizzo, Judy
Birds, The 1967,My 7,67:1

Rizzo, Patty Anne
Birds, The 1967,My 7,67:1

Rizzo, Ray
Strong Are Lonely, The 1953,S 30,38:3
Admirable Bashville, The 1956,F 21,38:1

Rizzo, Raymond (Producer)
Liola 1964,S 9,30:3

Roach, Jeanette
Gondoliers, The 1962,N 16,25:2

Roach, John
Mob, The 1920,O 11,18:1

Roach, Walter
Forest Ring, The 1930,Ap 26,11:2
Little Princess, The 1931,F 7,11:3
Anybody's Game 1932,D 22,21:4

Roache, Viola
Woman Disputed, A 1926,S 29,23:2
Bachelor Father, The 1928,F 29,28:2
Sweet Stranger 1930,O 22,23:3
Bellamy Trial, The 1931,Ap 23,28:6
Alchemist, The 1931,Je 5,27:1
Merchant of Venice, The 1931,N 17,31:1
Julius Caesar 1931,N 18,26:3
Hamlet 1931,N 19,26:6
Midsummer Night's Dream, A 1932,Jl 13,15:1
Distaff Side, The 1934,S 26,17:2
Simpleton of the Unexpected Isles, The 1935,F 19,27:5
Simpleton of the Unexpected Isles, The 1935,F 24,VIII,1:1
Royal Family, The 1935,Je 25,14:5
Patsy, The 1935,Jl 16,24:1
Post Road 1935,Jl 23,24:3
Hay Fever 1935,Ag 6,20:3
Caste 1935,Ag 13,20:3
Caesar and Cleopatra 1935,Ag 22,21:1
Pride and Prejudice 1935,N 6,32:4
Call It a Day 1936,Ja 21,26:7
Call It a Day 1936,Ja 29,15:2
Pomeroy's Past 1936,Ag 4,15:2
Russet Mantle 1936,Ag 18,15:2
Jane Eyre 1937,F 7,X,1:1
Kind Lady 1937,Jl 6,23:1
Night of January 16 1937,Jl 20,19:3
Pride and Prejudice 1937,Ag 3,20:5
Worse Things Happen at Sea 1937,S 1,15:3
Madame Bovary 1937,N 17,26:2
I Am My Youth 1938,Mr 8,22:4
Man From Cairo, The 1938,My 5,26:5
What Every Woman Knows 1938,Ag 30,14:5
Lorelei 1938,N 30,21:2
Wuthering Heights 1939,Ap 28,30:4
Man in Possession, The 1939,S 26,21:4
Theatre 1941,O 26,IX,2:3
Bird in Hand 1942,O 20,24:2
Sweet Charity 1942,D 29,26:4
No Way Out 1944,O 31,23:1
Hand in Glove 1944,D 5,19:1
Haven, The 1946,N 14,39:4
Craig's Wife 1947,F 13,35:2
Craig's Wife 1947,Mr 30,II,1:1
Angel in the Wings 1947,D 12,36:4
Make Way for Lucia 1948,D 23,23:5
Cyrano de Bergerac 1953,N 13,24:3
What Every Woman Knows 1954,D 23,16:2
My Fair Lady 1956,Mr 16,20:2
My Fair Lady 1958,Mr 9,II,1:1

Road, Michael
Moon Vine, The 1943,F 12,22:2
Tenting Tonight 1947,Ap 3,32:2

Roader, James
Valley Forge 1934,D 11,28:3

Roane, Frank
Lost in the Stars 1949,O 31,21:2
Lost in the Stars 1949,N 6,II,1:1

Roark, Jonathan
Movie Man 1959,O 28,40:4

Roark, Peter
Have I Got One for You 1968,Ja 8,32:1
Roat, Richard
Miracle, The 1960,D 5,42:3
Julius Caesar 1962,F 22,19:6
Roatina, Adeline
Viva O'Brien 1941,O 10,27:2
Roattino, Adelina
Enchanted April, The 1925,Ag 25,12:3
Creeping Fire 1935,Ja 17,22:3
Moon Over Mulberry Street 1935,S 5,24:6
Robando, Rose
Rose Girl, The 1921,F 12,11:1
Robards, Jason Jr
Spite Corner 1922,S 26,18:1
Many Moons 1947,D 15,35:2
Little Red Riding Hood 1948,Ja 12,15:3
American Gothic 1953,N 11,35:6
Iceman Cometh, The 1956,My 8,38:1
Long Day's Journey Into Night 1956,N 8,47:2
Long Day's Journey Into Night 1956,N 18,II,1:1
Long Day's Journey Into Night 1957,Jl 3,14:1
Henry IV, Part I 1958,Je 25,23:3
Winter's Tale, The 1958,Jl 23,34:3
Disenchanted, The 1958,D 4,53:4
Disenchanted, The 1959,Ja 11,II,1:1
Macbeth 1959,Ag 1,9:2
Toys in the Attic 1960,F 26,23:2
Toys in the Attic 1960,Mr 6,II,1:1
Big Fish, Little Fish 1961,Mr 16,42:2
Big Fish, Little Fish 1961,Mr 26,II,1:1
Thousand Clowns, A 1962,Ap 6,31:2
Thousand Clowns, A 1962,Ap 15,II,1:1
After the Fall 1964,Ja 24,18:1
After the Fall 1964,F 2,II,1:1
But for Whom Charlie 1964,Mr 13,42:2
Hughie 1964,D 23,21:2
Devils, The 1965,N 17,51:2
Devils, The 1965,N 28,II,1:1
We Bombed in New Haven 1968,O 17,51:1
We Bombed in New Haven 1968,O 27,II,1:1
Robb, Frank
Will Morrissey's Newcomers 1923,Ag 9,16:2
Robb, John
Daddy's Gone A-Hunting 1921,S 1,18:3
Goldfish, The 1922,Ap 18,15:3
We've Got to Have Money 1923,Ag 21,12:1
High Hatters, The 1928,My 11,28:2
Blessed Event 1932,F 13,23:2
Father Malachy's Miracle 1937,N 18,26:4
Sea Dogs 1939,N 7,30:3
Kind Lady 1940,S 4,28:3
Feathers in a Gale 1943,D 22,26:2
Highland Fling, A 1944,Ap 29,13:2
Girl From Nantucket, The 1945,N 9,17:2
On Your Toes 1954,O 12,24:4
Robb, Lotus
Rollo's Wild Oat 1920,N 24,14:1
Rollo's Wild Oat 1921,Ja 23,VI,1:1
Kempy 1922,My 16,14:2
Johannes Kreisler 1922,D 25,20:3
Johannes Kreisler 1923,Ja 21,VII,1:1
Devil's Disciple, The 1923,Ap 24,24:3
Out of the Seven Seas 1923,N 20,23:3
Badges 1924,D 4,25:1
Constant Nymph, The 1926,D 10,31:1
Constant Nymph, The 1926,D 19,VII,3:1
And Be My Love 1945,F 22,30:4
Robb, Romola
Don't, George! 1944,N 4,18:6
Coast of Illyria, The 1949,Ap 5,37:4
Robb, Willard (Miscellaneous)
Confederacy, The 1958,Jl 3,20:1
Robb, Willard (Musical Director)
Confederacy, The 1958,Jl 3,20:1
Robbe, Michel
Lettre Morte 1970,Ap 16,55:1
Robbeloth, Cletus
Little Theatre Tournament; Yellow Triangle, The 1929,My 10,32:2
Robbenolt, Roger
York Nativity Play, The 1956,D 5,49:2
Robbian, Alden
What a Life 1939,Ag 2,17:5
Robbiano, Giacomo
Ora di Diana, L' 1937,My 17,22:3
Robbins, Alexandra
Everyman Today 1958,Ja 16,32:4
Robbins, Archie (Pvt)
Winged Victory 1943,N 22,24:1
Robbins, B N (Scenic Designer)
Buckaroo 1929,Mr 18,31:1
Robbins, Barbara
Overture 1930,N 25,31:2
Overture 1930,D 8,26:4
Men Must Fight 1931,Ap 12,IX,2:1
After Tomorrow 1931,Ag 27,22:4
Dangerous Corner 1932,O 28,23:1
No Questions Asked 1934,F 6,24:3
Abide With Me 1935,N 22,19:2
All Desirable Young Men 1936,Jl 22,22:5
Now You've Done It 1937,Mr 6,10:4
Ghost of Yankee Doodle, The 1937,N 23,26:3

Mr Banks of Birmingham 1939,Ja 21,18:4
Red Velvet Goat, The 1939,Ja 21,18:4
Junior Miss 1941,N 19,28:2
Bees and the Flowers, The 1946,S 27,19:3
Robbins, Barbara (Producer)
London Assurance 1937,F 19,14:5
Robbins, Carrie Fishbein (Costume Designer)
Millionairess, The 1969,Mr 3,28:1
Inner Journey, The 1969,Mr 21,42:1
Year Boston Won the Pennant, The 1969,My 23,38:1
Time of Your Life, The 1969,N 7,37:1
Look to the Lilies 1970,Mr 30,59:1
Good Woman of Setzuan, The 1970,N 6,51:1
Robbins, China
Snapshots of 1921 1921,Je 3,19:2
Robbins, Cindy
By the Beautiful Sea 1954,Ap 9,20:1
Happy Town 1959,O 8,49:2
Robbins, Edmund
When You Smile 1925,O 6,31:2
Robbins, Elinor (Costume Designer)
Saint Joan 1951,O 5,23:2
Robbins, Gil
Month of Sundays 1968,S 17,50:1
Robbins, Greg
Trial of Joan of Arc, The 1921,Mr 28,8:2
Robbins, Gregory
Big Blow 1938,O 3,11:2
Heads or Tails 1947,My 3,10:6
Dinosaur Wharf 1951,N 9,23:2
Robbins, Harold (Original Author)
Stone for Danny Fisher, A 1954,O 22,24:2
Robbins, Helen
Richard III 1920,Mr 8,7:1
Macbeth 1921,F 18,16:1
Daddy's Gone A-Hunting 1921,S 1,18:3
Way Things Happen, The 1924,Ja 29,17:5
Second Mrs Tanqueray, The 1924,O 28,27:1
Robbins, J J (Translator)
Listen Professor! 1943,D 23,22:1
Robbins, James
Seperate Rooms 1940,Mr 25,10:3
Robbins, Jane Marla
Beyond Desire 1967,O 11,36:1
Dear Nobody 1968,Jl 31,33:1
Morning 1968,N 29,52:1
Noon 1968,N 29,52:1
Night 1968,N 29,52:1
Robbins, Jane Marla (Playwright)
Dear Nobody 1968,Jl 31,33:1
Robbins, Jean
Bride in the Morning, A 1960,My 26,38:2
Triumph of Robert Emmet, The 1969,My 8,54:1
Robbins, Jerome (Choreographer)
On the Town 1944,D 29,11:4
On the Town 1945,Ja 7,II,1:1
Million Dollar Baby 1945,D 22,17:2
Billion Dollar Baby 1945,D 30,II,1:1
High Button Shoes 1947,O 10,32:2
High Button Shoes 1947,N 23,II,1:1
Look, Ma, I'm Dancin' 1948,Ja 30,20:2
Look, Ma, I'm Dancin' 1948,F 8,II,2:1
Miss Liberty 1949,Je 14,26:6
Miss Liberty 1949,Jl 16,6:5
Miss Liberty 1949,Jl 24,II,1:1
Miss Liberty 1949,Ag 7,II,6:4
Call Me Madam 1950,O 13,25:1
Call Me Madam 1950,O 22,II,1:1
King and I, The 1951,Mr 30,26:2
King and I, The 1951,Ap 8,II,1:1
Wish You Were Here 1952,Ag 31,II,1:1
Two's Company 1952,D 16,43:5
Two's Company 1952,D 21,II,3:1
Peter Pan 1954,O 21,30:2
Peter Pan 1954,O 31,II,1:1
King and I, The 1956,Ap 19,35:4
Bells Are Ringing 1956,N 29,43:4
Bells Are Ringing 1956,N 30,18:2
West Side Story 1957,S 27,14:4
West Side Story 1957,O 6,II,1:1
West Side Story 1957,O 27,II,15:3
Gypsy 1959,My 22,31:6
West Side Story 1960,Ap 28,31:1
West Side Story 1960,My 8,II,1:1
King and I, The 1963,Je 13,30:2
West Side Story 1964,Ap 9,24:2
King and I, The 1964,Jl 7,26:1
Fiddler on the Roof 1964,S 23,56:2
Fiddler on the Roof 1964,O 4,II,1:1
Fiddler on the Roof 1965,Je 9,40:1
Fiddler on the Roof 1967,F 17,50:1
King and I, The 1968,My 24,39:1
West Side Story 1968,S 1,II,20:4
Robbins, Jerome (Director)
High Button Shoes 1947,O 10,32:2
Miss Liberty 1949,Jl 16,6:5
Pajama Game, The 1954,My 14,20:2
Pajama Game, The 1954,My 30,II,1:1
Peter Pan 1954,Jl 20,15:3
Peter Pan 1954,O 31,II,1:1
Bells Are Ringing 1956,N 29,43:4
Bells Are Ringing 1956,N 30,18:2

Robbins, Jerome (Director)—Cont
West Side Story 1957,S 27,14:4
West Side Story 1957,O 6,II,1:1
West Side Story 1957,O 27,II,15:3
Gypsy 1959,My 22,31:6
Gypsy 1959,My 31,II,1:1
West Side Story 1960,Ap 28,31:1
Oh Dad, Poor Dad, Mamma's Hung You in the Closet and I'm Feelin' So Sad 1962,F 27,28:1
Oh Dad, Poor Dad, Mamma's Hung You in the Closet and I'm Feelin' So Sad 1962,Mr 11,II,1:1
Oh Dad, Poor Dad, Mamma's Hung You in the Closet and I'm Feelin' So Sad 1962,Ap 29,II,3:1
Mother Courage and Her Children 1963,Mr 30,5:5
Oh Dad, Poor Dad, Mamma's Hung You in the Closet and I'm Feelin' So Sad 1963,Ag 28,28:2
West Side Story 1964,Ap 9,24:2
Fiddler on the Roof 1964,S 23,56:2
Fiddler on the Roof 1964,O 4,II,1:1
Fiddler on the Roof 1967,F 17,50:1
Fiddler on the Roof 1967,S 28,59:2
West Side Story 1968,S 1,II,20:4
Fiddler on the Roof 1969,Je 26,47:1
Fiddler on the Roof 1969,Ag 8,10:2
Robbins, Jerome (Miscellaneous)
Ankles Aweigh 1955,Ap 19,27:1
Pajama Game, The 1957,My 26,II,1:1
King and I, The 1960,My 12,40:1
Robbins, Jerome (Original Author)
On the Town 1959,Ja 25,II,1:1
Robbins, Jerome (Playwright)
On the Town 1944,D 29,11:4
Look, Ma, I'm Dancin' 1948,Ja 30,20:2
West Side Story 1957,S 27,14:4
On the Town 1959,Ja 16,36:1
On the Town 1959,F 14,15:1
West Side Story 1960,Ap 28,31:1
West Side Story 1964,Ap 9,24:2
West Side Story 1968,Je 25,32:1
Robbins, Jerome (Producer)
Mother Courage and Her Children 1963,Mr 30,5:5
Funny Girl 1964,Mr 27,15:1
Robbins, Jerome & Co
Concert Varieties 1945,Je 2,10:7
Robbins, Jerry
Robin Hood 1944,N 8,28:2
Robbins, John Franklyn
War and Peace 1962,Je 16,10:1
Measure for Measure 1967,F 15,37:1
Hamlet 1967,F 17,44:1
Robbins, Lanthrop (Miscellaneous)
Romeo and Juliet 1961,F 24,24:1
Robbins, Larry
Sleepy Hollow 1948,Je 4,26:3
Robbins, Lawrence S Jr
Coriolanus 1927,Je 18,8:3
Robbins, Leo (Original Author)
Her Great Mistake 1940,F 5,12:6
Robbins, Leo (Playwright)
Province 1936,Ap 4,10:4
Robbins, Mac
Teaspoon Every Four Hours, A 1969,Je 16,57:1
Robbins, Mary
Bedrock 1934,N 18,II,6:3
Robbins, Mary Ann
Strada, La 1969,D 15,63:1
Robbins, Nance
Our Town 1944,Ja 11,24:5
Night Music 1951,Ap 9,29:6
Finian's Rainbow 1953,Mr 7,13:2
Robbins, Patricia
Bathsheba 1947,Mr 27,40:2
Robbins, R N (Scenic Designer)
Box Seats 1928,Ap 20,27:2
Gentlemen of the Press 1928,Ag 28,27:2
Ringside 1928,Ag 30,13:2
Courage 1928,O 9,34:2
Poppa 1928,D 25,31:1
Heigh-Ho, Everybody 1932,My 26,31:2
Robbins, Ralph
Blue Eyes 1921,F 22,11:2
Robbins, Rex
Servant of Two Masters, The 1958,F 11,35:2
Glory in the Flower 1959,D 9,57:5
Henry IV 1960,Ap 19,41:1
One Flew Over the Cuckoo's Nest 1963,N 14,40:2
Richard II 1968,Je 24,42:3
As You Like It 1968,Je 24,42:3
Androcles and the Lion 1968,Je 27,47:1
Robbins, Rex (Miscellaneous)
Purification, The 1959,D 9,57:5
Glory in the Flower 1959,D 9,57:5
Robbins, Richard
Savonarola 1942,Ap 24,20:2
Egghead, The 1957,O 10,39:1
Sunrise at Campobello 1958,Ja 31,25:1
Robbins, Richard (Director)
Richard III 1957,N 26,41:1
As You Like It 1958,Ja 21,33:6
Robbins, Richard L (Miscellaneous)
Midsummer Night's Dream, A 1964,Je 30,23:2
Robbins, Stewart
Robert E Lee 1923,N 21,23:1

Robbins, Tamar
Golem, The 1927,F 5,13:2
Robbins, Wilma
H M S Pinafore 1949,Jl 29,13:2
Robbins (Scenic Designer)
Woman Denied, A 1931,F 26,21:1
Great Man, The 1931,Ap 8,20:6
Lightnin' 1938,S 16,17:2
Robeling, Paul
Milk Train Doesn't Stop Here Anymore, The
1963,Ja 18,7:1
Robenette, Camille
Love Song, The 1925,Ja 14,19:4
Robenne, Anna
Night in Paris, A 1926,Jl 27,15:4
Rober, Katherine
Right to Strike, The 1921,O 25,20:1
Rober, Richard
Banjo Eyes 1941,D 26,20:2
Ramshackle Inn 1944,Ja 6,17:5
Roberson, John
Show Boat 1966,Jl 20,48:1
Robert, Alfredo
Donna Del Mare, La; Lady From the Sea, The
1923,O 30,17:1
Cosi Sia; Thy Will be Done 1923,N 14,29:2
Porta Chiusa, La; Closed Door, The 1923,N 21,23:1
Robert, Chapman
Salvation 1969,S 25,55:1
Salvation 1969,O 5,II,1:1
Robert, Enif
Donna Del Mare, La; Lady From the Sea, The
1923,O 30,17:1
Cosi Sia; Thy Will be Done 1923,N 14,29:2
Porta Chiusa, La; Closed Door, The 1923,N 21,23:1
Citta Morta, La; Dead City, The 1923,N 28,14:1
Robert, Ernst
Bruder Straubinger 1921,N 16,22:3
Fruehlingsluft 1921,N 29,17:4
Late One Evening 1933,Ja 10,27:3
One Sunday Afternoon 1933,F 16,23:5
Night Remembers, The 1934,N 28,24:3
Robert, Eugen (Director)
Liebestrank 1927,Ja 30,VII,4:3
Broadway 1928,Ap 15,IX,4:7
Robert, Eugen (Dr) (Miscellaneous)
Gestaendris 1921,Jl 24,VI,1:7
Robert, Eugen (Producer)
X Y Z 1929,Ap 7,X,4:4
Robert, Hans
It Is the Law 1922,N 30,28:2
Noose, The 1926,O 21,23:3
Dinner at Eight 1932,O 24,18:2
Judgment Day 1934,S 13,26:4
One Good Year 1935,N 28,38:3
Howdy Stranger 1937,Ja 15,17:5
Room Service 1937,My 20,16:1
Too Many Girls 1939,O 19,26:2
What Big Ears! 1942,Ap 21,18:5
Sweet Charity 1942,D 29,26:4
Happily Ever After 1945,Mr 16,21:2
Robert, Jerrold (Playwright)
Back Fire 1932,Je 14,26:3
Robert, Lynn
Boy Friend, The 1954,O 1,20:1
Robert, Muriel
Dance With Your Gods 1934,O 8,14:3
Page Miss Glory 1934,N 28,24:2
Robert, Renee
Vaudeville (Palace) 1926,O 26,24:2
Robert-Lloyd, John (Lighting Director)
Hell'z-A-Splashin' 1959,Je 25,22:2
Robert-Lloyd, John (Scenic Designer)
Hell'z-A-Splashin' 1959,Je 25,22:2
Robert Orton's Teen Aces
Two's Company 1952,D 16,43:5
Robert Williams's trick dog, Red Dust
Sketch Book 1935,Je 5,22:2
Roberti, Lyda
You Said It 1931,Ja 20,21:3
Vaudeville (Palace) 1931,Jl 13,13:4
Vaudeville (Palace) 1931,Jl 20,20:3
Vaudeville (Palace) 1931,Ag 3,15:7
Vaudeville (Hollywood) 1932,F 16,24:3
Vaudeville (Hollywood) 1932,Mr 22,17:5
Pardon My English 1932,D 11,IX,5:2
Pardon My English 1933,Ja 21,11:4
Roberta 1933,N 20,18:4
Scandals 1935,O 30,17:1
New Hellzapoppin, The 1939,D 12,36:4
Roberti, Renato
Assalto, L' 1929,My 20,23:2
Tutto Per Bene; All's Well That Ends Well
1929,Je 3,27:1
Colonello Bridall, L' 1934,Ap 16,20:3
Roberti, Rene
Merry Wives of Windsor, The 1928,Mr 20,20:1
Farewell to Arms, A 1930,S 23,30:3
Strana Avventura, Una; Queer Adventure, A
1930,O 27,17:6
Piacere Del'Onesta, Il; Happiness of Probity, The
1930,N 10,16:4
Cena Delle Beffe, La; Jest, The 1930,N 24,26:4

Fast Service 1931,N 18,26:3
Happy Landing 1932,Mr 28,10:5
Istruttoria, L'; Judicial Inquiry, The 1933,F 13,11:3
Tragedy of the Ages, The 1933,Ap 7,22:7
Romanticismo 1933,My 1,10:5
Romanticismo 1934,My 14,20:2
Miserabili I, 1934,O 1,14:2
Signora Dalle Camelie, La; Camille 1934,O 22,13:2
Conte di Monte Cristo, Il 1935,Ap 1,17:6
Signo Della Croce, Il 1935,O 7,11:1
Religione e Patria 1936,Mr 23,22:4
In Time to Come 1941,D 29,20:2
Roberti and Ray
Hellzapoppin 1938,S 23,34:2
Roberto, Francesca
Saint of Bleecker Street, The 1954,D 28,21:1
Roberton, Guy
Nina Rosa 1929,O 27,IX,2:1
Roberts, Al
Her Family Tree 1920,D 28,9:2
Aloma of the South Seas 1925,Ap 21,18:1
Deacon, The 1925,N 25,14:3
Henry's Harem 1926,S 14,25:2
Barker, The 1927,Ja 19,20:6
Bottled 1928,Ap 11,25:1
Cyclone Lover, The 1928,Je 6,23:3
Eva the Fifth 1928,Ag 29,19:3
Kibitzer, The 1929,F 19,22:5
Tired Business Man, The 1929,Je 5,32:5
Ladies of the Jury 1929,O 22,26:2
Roberts, Al (Director)
Cyclone Lover, The 1928,Je 6,23:3
Roberts, Alan (Composer)
Star and Garter 1942,Je 25,26:2
All for Love 1949,Ja 24,16:5
Roberts, Alan (Lyricist)
Star and Garter 1942,Je 25,26:2
All for Love 1949,Ja 24,16:5
Roberts, Anne Starr
Emperor's Clothes, The 1953,O 23,19:7
Roberts, Anthony
Something About a Soldier 1962,Ja 5,36:2
Last Analysis, The 1964,O 2,30:1
Don't Drink the Water 1966,N 18,37:1
How Now, Dow Jones 1967,D 8,53:1
How Now, Dow Jones 1967,D 24,II,3:2
Play It Again, Sam 1969,F 13,52:3
Play It Again, Sam 1969,F 23,II,1:1
Play It Again, Sam 1969,Jl 13,II,1:1
Roberts, Archie
Artists and Models 1930,Je 11,33:2
Roberts, Arthur
Borstal Boy 1970,Ap 1,38:1
Roberts, Barbara (Costume Designer)
Jeannette 1960,Mr 25,20:2
Roberts, Ben
Inspector General, The 1923,My 1,24:1
One Heluva Night 1924,Je 5,18:1
City Haul 1929,D 31,14:4
Find the Fox 1930,Je 21,20:4
Frankie and Johnny 1930,S 26,16:5
Precedent 1931,Ap 15,24:5
Mr Papavert 1932,Ja 23,18:6
Broadway Boy 1932,My 4,23:5
Tomorrow's a Holiday! 1935,D 31,10:2
On Location 1937,S 28,19:1
Missouri Legend 1938,S 20,27:2
Yokel Boy 1939,Jl 7,12:2
Johnny on the Spot 1942,Ja 9,24:2
Vagabond King, The 1943,Je 30,24:2
Roberts, Ben (Playwright)
Merry Widow, The 1943,Ag 5,19:2
Merry Widow, The 1943,Ag 22,II,5:1
Jackpot 1944,Ja 14,15:2
Dream With Music 1944,My 19,15:2
Merry Widow, The 1944,O 9,17:1
Portrait in Black 1947,My 15,30:2
Merry Widow, The 1957,Ap 11,36:6
Roberts, Beverly
Passionate Pilgrim, The 1932,O 20,24:3
Heart of a City 1942,F 13,24:6
Uncle Harry 1942,My 21,24:1
Roberts, Bob
Mill Shadows 1932,F 29,20:7
Roberts, Bonnie
World We Make, The 1939,N 21,19:1
Roberts, Bradley Louis
Mother, The 1935,N 20,26:3
Roberts, Buddy
Laugh Parade, The 1931,S 20,VIII,3:1
Vaudeville (Loew's State) 1932,Jl 18,9:7
Streets of Paris, The 1939,Je 20,25:2
Roberts, C E Bechhofer (Playwright)
Nurse Cavell 1934,Ap 1,X,1:7
Roberts, C Luckyeth (Composer)
Go-Go 1923,Mr 13,19:4
Sharlee 1923,N 23,20:1
My Magnolia 1926,Jl 13,19:2
Roberts, Catherine
Swords 1921,S 2,9:3
Aglavaine and Selysette 1922,Ja 4,11:1
Roberts, Chapman
Salvation 1969,Mr 13,53:1

Roberts, Cledge
Left Bank, The 1931,O 6,35:3
Between Two Worlds 1934,O 26,24:2
Them's the Reporters 1935,My 30,21:4
Devil Takes a Bride, The 1938,O 8,10:3
Aries Is Rising 1939,N 22,16:5
Walking Gentleman, The 1942,My 8,26:2
Sheppey 1944,Ap 19,27:2
Roberts, Cledge (Director)
Sleep No More 1944,S 1,11:5
Roberts, D L
Go-Go 1923,Mr 13,19:4
Roberts, David
Walk in Darkness 1963,O 29,30:2
Roberts, Davis
Point of No Return 1951,D 14,35:2
Roberts, Desmond
Flashing Stream, The 1938,S 18,X,1:4
Roberts, Dixie
Ziegfeld Follies 1943,Ap 2,16:2
Dream With Music 1944,My 19,15:2
Roberts, Donald
Buzzin' Around 1920,Jl 7,14:1
Fables 1922,F 7,12:2
Native Son 1941,Mr 25,26:5
Roberts, Doris
Time of Your Life, The 1955,Ja 20,34:1
Desk Set, The 1955,O 25,36:7
Color of Darkness: An Evening in the World of
James Purdy; You Reach for Your Hat
1963,O 1,34:1
Color of Darkness: An Evening in the World of
James Purdy; Don't Call Me By My Right Name
1963,O 1,34:1
Marathon '33 1963,D 23,20:1
Natural Look, The 1967,Mr 13,45:2
Last of the Red Hot Lovers 1969,D 29,37:1
Last of the Red Hot Lovers 1970,Ja 4,II,1:1
Roberts, Dorothy
Meet the People 1940,D 26,22:2
Roberts, Douglas
Desire Under the Elms 1963,Ja 11,5:6
Roberts, Edmund
Jay Walker, The 1926,F 9,23:1
Roberts, Edward Barry (Playwright)
Forsaking All Others 1933,Mr 2,21:2
Lady Has a Heart, The 1937,S 27,24:1
Roberts, Elizabeth
Pinocchio 1939,Ja 3,19:2
Roberts, Elizabeth (Miscellaneous)
Foenix in Choir 1958,O 28,40:2
Roberts, Elizabeth (Producer)
Cave Dwellers, The 1961,O 16,34:2
Roberts, Ellis (Playwright)
Peer Gynt 1935,S 24,28:2
Roberts, Eric
World We Make, The 1939,N 21,19:1
Love's Old Sweet Song 1940,My 3,16:3
My Sister Eileen 1940,D 27,23:2
Watch on the Rhine 1941,Ap 2,26:2
Mexican Hayride 1944,Ja 29,9:6
Roberts, Erling (Scenic Designer)
Jotham Valley 1951,F 7,37:2
Roberts, Ernest
God Strikes Back 1943,F 27,11:2
Roberts, Ernest (Miscellaneous)
Private Life of the Master Race, The
1945,Je 13,28:3
Roberts, Eugen (Producer)
Story of the Wolf 1932,N 6,IX,3:4
Roberts, Eve
Big Knife, The 1959,N 13,25:1
All the King's Men 1963,Jl 12,12:1
Once in a Lifetime 1964,Ja 29,20:1
Right You Are (If You Think You Are)
1964,Mr 5,37:1
Scapin 1964,Mr 10,43:1
Impromptu at Versailles 1964,Mr 10,43:1
Lower Depths, The 1964,Mr 31,30:1
Roberts, Evelyn
Journey's End 1929,Mr 23,23:1
Journey's End 1930,Ja 27,24:7
Mulberry Bush, The 1930,My 18,VIII,2:6
O H M S 1931,Mr 29,VIII,2:1
Good Fairy, The 1931,N 25,17:1
No More Ladies 1934,S 19,14:4
Tovarich 1935,Ap 25,19:8
Dear Ruth 1946,Mr 1,17:3
Roberts, Francine
Song of Norway 1958,Je 23,19:2
Roberts, Francis
Arrest That Woman 1936,S 19,20:4
Under the Counter 1947,O 4,10:2
Roberts, Frank
Grand Duchess and the Waiter, The
1925,O 14,31:1
Tragic 18 1926,O 11,18:2
I Myself 1934,My 10,24:6
Closed Room, The 1934,Jl 24,20:2
Jane's Legacy 1935,Ag 13,20:3
Service for Two 1935,Ag 20,25:1
Desk Set, The 1955,O 25,36:7
Goodbye Charlie 1959,D 17,50:1

Roberts, George
Triumphant Bachelor, The 1927,S 16,21:1
Malinda 1929,D 4,37:2
Louisiana Lady 1947,Je 3,35:2
Roberts, Helen
Pirates of Penzance, The 1939,Ja 6,25:1
Iolanthe 1939,Ja 13,16:3
H. M. S. Pinafore 1939,Ja 17,27:5
Gondoliers, The 1939,Ja 20,14:2
Yeomen of the Guard, The 1939,Ja 24,17:1
Pirates of Penzance, The 1948,Ja 6,27:2
Pirates of Penzance, The 1948,Ja 11,II,1:1
H M S Pinafore 1948,Ja 20,26:2
Yeomen of the Guard, The 1948,F 3,30:2
Roberts, Henry
Hymn to the Rising Sun 1937,My 7,28:2
Roberts, Howard
Ghost of Yankee Doodle, The 1937,N 23,26:3
Porgy and Bess 1953,Mr 10,25:5
Shinbone Alley 1957,Ap 15,23:2
Roberts, Howard (Composer)
Trumpets of the Lord 1969,Ap 30,37:1
Roberts, Howard (Musical Director)
Trumpets of the Lord 1963,D 23,22:3
Trumpets of the Lord 1969,Ap 30,37:1
Roberts, J H
Exiled 1929,Jl 7,VIII,1:3
Espionage 1935,N 10,IX,3:1
Roberts, James
Empress of Destiny 1938,Mr 10,16:2
Roberts, Jeff
Body Beautiful, The 1958,Ja 24,15:2
Roberts, Joan
Sunny River 1941,D 5,28:2
Oklahoma! 1943,Ap 1,27:1
Oklahoma! 1943,Ap 11,II,1:1
Marinka 1945,Jl 19,19:2
Are You With It? 1945,N 12,17:3
Roberts, John
Mask and the Face, The 1924,S 11,27:3
Roberts, John (Miscellaneous)
After the Rain 1967,O 10,54:1
Roberts, John (Producer)
New Faces of 1956 1956,Je 15,32:1
Miss Isobel 1957,D 27,22:1
Roberts, Julian
Hit the Road 1941,Ap 4,18:3
Roberts, June
Up in the Clouds 1922,Ja 3,20:3
Roberts, Katharine
Survival of the Fittest 1921,Mr 15,14:1
Trial of Joan of Arc, The 1921,Mr 28,8:2
Hurricane 1923,D 26,13:4
Roberts, Katharine (Playwright)
Divorce Me, Dear 1930,Ag 3,VIII,3:4
Divorce Me, Dear 1931,O 7,29:2
Bonfire to Glory 1936,Jl 28,23:4
Roberts, Kenneth
Hitch Your Wagon! 1937,Ap 9,18:2
Roberts, Lee
Best Foot Forward 1941,O 2,28:2
Roberts, Lee (Composer)
Round With Ring, A 1969,O 30,56:1
Roberts, Lena Sanford
My Magnolia 1926,Jl 13,19:2
Roberts, Leona
Saturday Night 1926,O 26,25:1
Three Sisters, The 1926,O 27,24:1
Cradle Song 1927,Ja 25,18:2
Inheritors 1927,Mr 8,23:1
Good Hope, The 1927,O 19,24:2
2 + 2 = 5 1927,N 29,30:3
First Stone, The 1928,Ja 14,12:2
Hedda Gabler 1928,Mr 27,30:2
Cherry Orchard, The 1928,O 16,28:5
Lady From Alfaqueque, The; Consulesa, La
1929,Ja 15,22:3
Katerina 1929,F 26,30:3
Sea Gull, The 1929,S 17,34:1
Mademoiselle Bourrat 1929,O 8,34:3
Living Corpse, The 1929,D 7,19:1
Women Have Their Way, The 1930,Ja 28,28:1
Romeo and Juliet 1930,Ap 22,33:1
Alison's House 1930,D 2,31:2
Lady of the Camellias, The 1931,Ja 27,21:2
Liliom 1932,O 27,23:2
Camille 1932,O 28,23:2
Dear Jane 1932,N 15,24:3
Alice in Wonderland 1932,D 12,18:3
Alice in Wonderland 1932,D 25,IX,1:1
Cherry Orchard, The 1933,Mr 7,20:3
Noble Prize, The 1933,Jl 4,16:4
Aiglon, L' 1934,N 5,22:2
Hedda Gabler 1934,D 4,22:5
Rosmersholm 1935,D 3,32:5
Searching for the Sun 1936,F 20,22:6
Stage Door 1936,O 23,26:3
Spring in Autumn 1937,Ag 17,23:1
Candle in the Wind 1941,O 23,26:2
Uncle Harry 1942,My 21,24:1
Cherry Orchard, The 1944,Ja 26,22:1
Cherry Orchard, The 1944,F 6,II,1:1

Roberts, Lorraine
Eccentricities of Davy Crockett, The 1961,Ja 4,26:1
Roberts, MacFarlane
Having Wonderful Time 1937,F 22,12:5
Roberts, Margaret
Mary of Magdala 1946,Mr 26,24:5
Roberts, Marilyn
Tom Paine 1968,Mr 26,38:1
Futz 1968,Je 14,39:1
Rat's Mass, A 1969,N 1,39:1
Candaules, Commissioner 1970,My 29,15:1
Roberts, Mark
Stalag 17 1951,My 9,41:2
Sacred Flame, The 1952,O 8,35:2
Roberts, Martha
Sandro Botticelli 1923,Mr 27,24:2
Knights of Song 1938,O 18,29:2
Brother Cain 1941,S 13,21:5
Roberts, Mary Jane
Little Theatre Tournament; Joint Owners in Spain
1929,My 7,28:1
Roberts, Meade (Playwright)
Palm Tree in a Rose Garden, A 1957,N 27,26:2
Maidens and Mistresses at Home at the Zoo
1958,O 29,31:1
Roberts, Mel
My Sister Eileen 1940,D 27,23:2
Pretty Little Parlor 1944,Ap 18,24:8
Roberts, Michael
Night in Venice, A 1952,Je 27,18:6
Roberts, Milton
Mystery Square 1929,Ap 5,28:3
Papavert 1931,D 30,25:1
Roberts, Milton (Director)
Come Easy 1933,Ag 30,22:5
Roberts, Nellie
Flossie 1924,Je 4,25:2
Roberts, Olga
Call Me Madam 1952,Mr 16,84:3
Roberts, Oswald Dale
Misdoings of Charley Peace, The 1929,S 29,IX,2:1
Roberts, Pamela
Collector's Item 1952,F 9,11:2
Roberts, Pat
Spots of the Leopard, The 1963,S 25,38:1
Roberts, Paul
Devil and Daniel Webster, The 1939,My 19,26:1
Susanna, Don't You Cry 1939,My 23,27:2
Roberts, Paul (Director)
Fair Game 1957,N 4,39:1
Roberts, Pernell
Twelfth Night 1954,N 10,42:2
Twelfth Night 1954,D 12,II,3:1
Tonight in Samarkand 1955,F 17,22:2
Othello 1955,S 8,27:2
Henry IV, Part I 1955,S 22,34:2
Macbeth 1955,O 20,42:2
Romeo and Juliet 1956,F 24,20:4
Lovers 1956,My 11,23:1
King John 1956,Je 28,33:5
Measure for Measure 1956,Je 29,16:1
Taming of the Shrew, The 1956,Ag 6,20:1
Clearing in the Woods, A 1957,Ja 11,20:2
Taming of the Shrew, The 1957,F 21,30:2
Duchess of Malfi, The 1957,Mr 20,33:1
Roberts, R D
Half Moon Inn 1923,Mr 21,19:2
Roberts, R Ellis (Translator)
Peer Gynt 1935,O 20,XI,3:7
Roberts, Ralp Arthur (Playwright)
Hau-Ruck 1934,My 6,IX,2:2
Roberts, Ralph
Kingdom of God, The 1928,D 21,30:2
He Walked in Her Sleep 1929,Ap 5,28:2
Candle-Light 1929,O 1,28:2
Bellamy Trial, The 1931,Ap 23,28:6
School for Scandal, The 1931,N 11,26:4
Late One Evening 1933,Ja 10,27:3
Black Eye, The 1935,N 10,IX,3:1
Angel Street 1948,Ja 23,26:6
On the Harmfulness of Tobacco 1948,F 6,29:2
Wedding, The 1948,F 6,29:2
Bear, The 1948,F 6,29:2
Tragedian in Spite of Himself, A 1948,F 6,29:2
S S Glencairn; Long Voyage Home, The
1948,My 21,21:2
S S Glencairn; In the Zone 1948,My 21,21:2
S S Glencairn; Moon of the Caribbees
1948,My 21,21:2
S S Glencairn; Bound East for Cardiff
1948,My 21,21:2
Witness for the Prosecution 1954,D 17,35:2
Lark, The 1955,N 18,20:1
Miracle, The 1960,D 5,42:3
Milk Train Doesn't Stop Here Anymore, The
1964,Ja 2,33:1
Roberts, Ralph Arthur
Chicago 1927,D 18,IX,1:8
Mann mit den Grauen Schlafen, Der; Man Who Is
Getting Gray, The 1932,F 21,VIII,2:3
Tiefstapler, Der 1932,S 4,IX,2:1
Hau-Ruck 1934,My 6,IX,2:2

Roberts, Ralph Arthur (Director)
Fabian, Der Elephant 1933,Ap 30,IX,2:2
Terzett zu Viert 1933,O 22,IX,2:3
Roberts, Ralph Arthur (Producer)
Bargold Lacht 1932,N 6,IX,3:2
Roberts, Rhoda (Lyricist)
Show Me Where the Good Times Are
1970,Mr 6,32:1
Roberts, Richard
Sold to the Movies; Crossing the Gap
1970,Je 18,54:2
Sold to the Movies; Type 424 Meet Type Oh-Oh,
No! 1970,Je 18,54:2
Sold to the Movies; Life Size 1970,Je 18,54:2
Roberts, Ron
Jotham Valley 1951,F 7,37:2
Roberts, Roy
Old Man Murphy 1931,My 19,25:2
Everybody's Welcome 1931,O 14,26:3
Inside Story, The 1932,F 23,23:2
Broadway Boy 1932,My 4,23:5
20th Century 1932,D 30,15:1
Keeper of the Keys 1933,O 19,23:2
Ragged Army 1934,F 27,16:5
Body Beautiful, The 1935,N 1,24:3
Pre-Honeymoon 1936,My 1,19:4
Hooray for What! 1937,D 2,32:5
Ringside Seat 1938,N 23,24:5
Ladies and Gentlemen 1939,O 18,30:2
Old Foolishness, The 1940,D 21,20:2
Actors Fund Fete 1942,F 23,24:5
Carnival in Flanders 1953,S 9,38:2
Roberts, S H
Roof, The 1929,N 24,X,1:6
Roberts, Shepherd D
Seven Mirrors 1945,O 26,17:2
Roberts, Sis
Laugh Parade, The 1931,S 20,VIII,3:1
Vaudeville (Loew's State) 1932,Jl 18,9:7
Roberts, Stephen
Danton's Death 1938,N 3,26:2
Summer Night 1939,N 3,17:1
Native Son 1941,Mr 25,26:5
Day Will Come, The 1944,S 8,17:2
On Whitman Avenue 1946,My 9,28:2
Joan of Lorraine 1946,N 19,40:2
Roberts, Sterling
Ballad of John Ogilvie, The 1968,O 9,42:4
But Never Jam Today 1969,Ap 24,40:1
Five Star Saint 1970,F 11,41:2
Roberts, Ted
Ed Wynn's Carnival 1920,Ap 6,18:2
Roberts, Thayer
Hamlet 1930,Mr 25,34:4
Macbeth 1930,Mr 26,24:6
Twelfth Night 1930,Mr 27,24:7
Merchant of Venice, The 1930,Mr 27,24:7
Taming of the Shrew, The 1930,Mr 28,22:8
Richard III 1930,Mr 31,24:1
King Lear 1930,Ap 1,34:6
As You Like It 1930,Ap 3,32:5
Julius Caesar 1930,Ap 4,22:3
King Lear 1930,D 26,18:2
Merchant of Venice, The 1931,N 17,31:1
Julius Caesar 1931,N 18,26:3
Hamlet 1931,N 19,26:6
Desert Song, The 1946,Ja 9,20:2
On Borrowed Time 1953,F 11,34:1
Roberts, Theodore
Vaudeville (Palace) 1926,N 23,27:3
Man Higher Up, The 1926,N 23,27:3
Roberts, Tom (Choreographer)
Wuziz! 1970,O 2,25:2
Roberts, Velma
Girls in Uniform 1932,D 31,10:3
Roberts, Vincent
Steps Leading Up 1941,Ap 19,20:6
Roberts, Waldo
Kid Boots 1924,Ja 1,21:3
Roberts, Wallis
Merchant of Venice, The 1920,D 30,16:2
Sonya 1921,Ag 16,18:3
Cymbeline 1923,O 3,12:1
Ashes 1924,O 21,21:2
Little Poor Man, The 1925,Ag 6,14:1
Importance of Being Earnest, The 1926,My 4,30:1
Story of Mary Surratt, The 1947,F 10,25:2
Roberts, Walter Charles (Playwright)
Red Harvest 1937,Mr 21,29:2
Damn Deborah 1937,Ag 17,23:1
Roberts, William
Taming of the Shrew, The 1956,Ag 11,11:2
Camille 1956,S 19,33:1
Henry VI, Part I 1964,Jl 23,18:1
Roberts, William (Costume Designer)
Hamlet 1957,Ja 29,27:1
Girl of the Golden West, The 1957,N 6,44:1
Roberts, William (Miscellaneous)
Eternal Road, The 1937,Ap 25,X,1:6
Roberts, William D (Costume Designer)
Saint Joan 1950,Mr 4,10:6
Duchess of Malfi, The 1962,Mr 5,27:1
Roberts, William D (Scenic Designer)
Duchess of Malfi, The 1962,Mr 5,27:1

Robertson, Adele
Talent '49 1949,Ap 13,39:4
Robertson, Alex
Conversation Piece 1934,O 24,24:1
Robertson, Arnold
Lamp at Midnight 1947,D 22,29:2

Victors, The 1948,D 27,17:2
Bruno and Sidney 1949,My 4,38:2
Robertson, Byers (Playwright)
Coincidence 1935,N 6,32:3
Coincidence 1935,D 1,XI,5:3
Robertson, Cliff
Late Love 1953,O 14,35:2
Wisteria Trees, The 1955,F 3,20:2
Orpheus Descending 1957,Mr 22,28:1
Orpheus Descending 1957,Mr 31,II,1:1
Robertson, David A Jr (Playwright)
Bitter Tulips 1936,Mr 5,24:6
Robertson, Eliot
Sea Shells 1935,Jl 16,24:2
Robertson, Guy
Perfect Fool, The 1921,N 8,28:2
Daffy Dill 1922,Ag 23,14:5
Wildflower 1923,F 8,17:2
Song of the Flame 1925,D 31,10:2
Circus Princess, The 1927,Ap 26,32:2
Lovely Lady 1927,D 30,22:1
White Lilacs 1928,S 11,31:2
Street Singer, The 1929,Jl 28,VIII,1:6
Street Singer, The 1929,S 18,35:2
Nina Rosa 1930,My 31,19:3
Nina Rosa 1930,S 22,22:5
Marching By 1931,N 15,VIII,4:2
Marching By 1932,Mr 4,17:1
All the King's Horses 1934,Ja 31,21:3
Great Waltz, The 1934,S 24,14:4
Great Waltz, The 1935,Ag 6,20:5
Salute to Spring 1937,Jl 14,16:2
Right This Way 1938,Ja 6,22:3
Show Boat 1938,Je 30,21:1
Robertson, J Francis
Bride of the Lamb 1926,Mr 31,20:3
Legend of Leonora, The 1927,Mr 30,22:4
Quicksand 1928,F 14,26:3
You Said It 1931,Ja 20,21:3
Saint Wench 1933,Ja 3,19:3
Let 'Em Eat Cake 1933,O 23,18:1
Sap Runs High, The 1936,F 5,15:3
Mr Peebles and Mr Hooker 1946,O 11,29:2
Robertson, Jane
Ben Bagley's Shoestring Revues 1970,O 24,22:1
Robertson, Jean
Nobody's Money 1921,Ag 18,9:3
Madeleine and the Movies 1922,Mr 7,11:1
Robertson, Jim B
Hill Between, The 1938,Mr 12,12:5
Robertson, John
Knight of the Burning Pestle, The 1953,O 24,13:2
Girl From Samos, The 1954,N 24,17:1
Robertson, John (Lighting Director)
Macbeth 1957,Ag 16,11:2
Richard III 1957,N 26,41:1
As You Like It 1958,Ja 21,33:6
Othello 1958,Jl 4,16:1
Twelfth Night 1958,Ag 7,21:4
Julius Caesar 1959,Ag 4,30:1
Henry V 1960,Je 30,23:1
Measure for Measure 1960,Jl 27,33:1
Much Ado About Nothing 1961,Jl 7,17:1
Midsummer Night's Dream, A 1961,Ag 3,13:1
Who'll Save the Plowboy? 1962,Ja 10,24:2
Robertson, John (Miscellaneous)
Cherry Orchard, The 1955,O 19,38:1
Richard III 1957,N 26,41:1
As You Like It 1958,Ja 21,33:6
She Stoops to Conquer 1960,N 2,42:5
Plough and the Stars, The 1960,D 7,56:2
Octoroon, The 1961,Ja 28,13:1
Hamlet 1961,Mr 17,17:1
Androcles and the Lion 1961,N 22,24:2
Robertson, Katherine (Miscellaneous)
Critic, The 1965,Jl 26,15:2
Robertson, Lolita
Six-Fifty, The 1921,O 25,20:1
Love Child, The 1922,N 15,22:1
So This Is Politics 1924,Je 17,22:2
Du Barry 1932,N 23,15:2
Robertson, Margaret
Love and Maple Syrup 1970,Ja 8,47:1
Robertson, Ralph
Wisteria Trees, The 1950,Mr 30,39:1
Enemy of the People, An 1950,D 29,14:1
Robertson, Ronnie
Ice Capades 1956,S 13,41:2
Ice Capades 1957,S 5,33:2
Ice Capades 1958,S 4,33:2
Ice Capades 1959,S 4,12:1
Ice Capades 1960,S 1,30:1
Ice Capades 1961,Ag 31,24:4

Ice Capades 1962,Ag 30,34:1
Holiday on Ice 1966,S 1,30:1
Holiday on Ice 1967,Ag 31,29:2
Holiday on Ice 1968,Ag 29,44:1
Holiday on Ice 1969,Ag 28,44:1
Robertson, Sanchia
Roar China! 1930,O 28,23:1
Robertson, Strowan (Director)
Typewriter, The 1955,Jl 29,8:3
Venice Preserv'd 1955,D 13,54:4
Robertson, Strowen
Little Clay Cart, The 1953,Jl 1,25:1
Robertson, Texas Jim
Out West of Eighth 1951,S 21,20:3
Robertson, Toby (Director)
Edward II 1969,S 4,50:1
Much Ado About Nothing 1970,S 4,19:1
Boswell's Life of Johnson 1970,S 4,19:1
Robertson, Tom (Playwright)
Caste 1929,F 24,IX,4:3
David Garrick 1929,Ag 2,17:5
Caste 1935,Ag 13,20:3
Robertson, Warren
World of Suzie Wong, The 1958,O 15,47:1
Difficult Woman, The 1962,Ap 26,22:7
Robertson, Wes L
New Yorkers, The 1927,Mr 11,24:3
Robertson, Willard
Big Game 1920,Ja 22,23:1
Miss Lulu Bett 1920,D 28,9:1
Detour, The 1921,Ag 24,12:2
Squaw Man, The 1921,D 27,10:3
Whispering Wires 1922,Ag 8,26:2
Ice-Bound 1923,F 12,16:2
Lazybones 1924,S 23,23:1
Tia Juana 1927,N 16,28:4
Racket, The 1927,N 23,28:3
Rope 1928,F 23,18:3
Front Page, The 1928,Ag 15,19:2
Front Page, The 1928,Ag 26,VII,1:1
These Days 1928,N 13,36:2
Winter Bound 1929,N 13,24:6
This Man's Town 1930,Mr 2,IX,4:7
This Man's Town 1930,Mr 11,24:4
Robertson, Willard (Composer)
Garrick Gaieties 1930,Je 5,29:2
Robertson, Willard (Director)
Black Velvet 1927,S 28,28:1
Robertson, Willard (Playwright)
Big Game 1920,Ja 22,23:1
Sea Woman, The 1923,Ja 21,VII,1:6
Sea Woman, The 1925,Ag 25,12:2
Sea Woman, The 1925,Ag 30,VII,1:1
Black Velvet 1927,S 28,28:1
This Man's Town 1930,Mr 2,IX,4:7
This Man's Town 1930,Mr 11,24:4
Robertson, William
Hello, Yourself 1928,O 31,28:2
If You Get It, Do You Want It? 1938,D 1,28:2
Cup of Trembling, The 1948,Ap 21,33:5
Madame Is Served 1949,F 15,28:1
Our Town 1969,N 28,50:1
Last Pad, The 1970,D 8,61:1
Robeson, Erba
Blossom Time 1921,S 30,10:1
Robeson, Paul
Taboo 1922,Ap 5,22:1
Emperor Jones, The 1924,My 7,18:1
All God's Chillun Got Wings 1924,My 16,22:3
All God's Chillun Got Wings 1924,Ag 19,9:1
All God's Chillun Got Wings 1924,Ag 24,VII,1:1
Emperor Jones, The 1925,S 11,20:1
Black Boy 1926,S 26,VIII,2:7
Black Boy 1926,O 7,30:2
Show Boat 1928,My 4,31:3
Show Boat 1928,My 27,VIII,1:8
Show Boat 1928,Je 10,VIII,1:3
Emperor Jones, The 1930,Ap 1,10:1
Othello 1930,My 20,33:1
Emperor Jones, The 1930,My 25,IX,1:8
Emperor Jones, The 1930,S 14,VIII,2:1
Hairy Ape, The 1931,My 12,29:4
Show Boat 1932,My 20,22:2
Show Boat 1932,My 29,VIII,5:6
All God's Chillun Got Wings 1933,Mr 14,19:4
Basalik 1935,Ap 8,22:5
Stevedore 1935,My 7,26:2
Toussaint L'Ouverture 1936,Mr 16,21:6
Emperor Jones, The 1939,Je 20,25:2
John Henry 1939,D 12,36:4
John Henry 1940,Ja 11,18:2
Othello 1942,Ag 16,VIII,1:7
Othello 1943,O 3,VI,15:1
Othello 1943,O 20,18:1
Othello 1943,O 24,II,1:1
Othello 1943,O 31,II,1:1
Othello 1945,My 23,25:4
Othello 1959,Ap 8,41:3
Othello 1959,Ap 12,II,3:1
Robet, Gaston
Topaze 1931,F 17,29:1
Robey, George
Helen 1932,Ja 31,I,5:2

Robey, George—Cont
Jolly Roger 1933,Mr 26,IX,1:1
Here's How 1934,F 23,22:4
Bing Boys Are Here, The 1934,D 19,26:6
Henry IV, Part I 1935,Mr 1,16:1
Henry IV, Part I 1935,Mr 24,VIII,2:3
Untitled-Benefit 1935,Je 23,IX,1:3
Certainly, Sir 1936,S 18,19:5
Laughter Over London 1936,D 8,31:3
Robey, Ken (Playwright)
Hilarities 1948,S 10,20:2
Robey, Ken (Producer)
Hilarities 1948,S 10,20:2
Robey and Gould
Vaudeville (Hippodrome) 1926,Mr 23,24:3
Robi, Armand (Composer)
Flossie 1924,Je 4,25:2
Robi, Armand (Playwright)
Flossie 1924,Je 4,25:2
Robin, Judith (Miscellaneous)
Postcards 1970,Mr 17,36:1
Grin and Bare It 1970,Mr 17,36:1
Robin, Leo (Lyricist)
Judy 1927,F 8,20:2
Hit the Deck! 1927,Ap 26,32:1
Allez-Opp! 1927,Ag 3,29:3
Just Fancy! 1927,O 12,30:2
Hello, Yourself 1928,O 31,28:2
Gentlemen Prefer Blondes 1949,D 9,35:3
Gentlemen Prefer Blondes 1949,D 18,II,3:1
Girl in Pink Tights, The 1954,Mr 6,13:2
Hit the Deck 1960,Je 24,32:1
Harold Arlen Songbook, The 1967,Mr 1,48:1
Robin, Michel
Three Musketeers, The 1968,Je 26,43:1
George Dandin 1968,Je 28,36:1
Robin, Naomi
Awakening of Spring, The 1964,My 13,50:1
Pirates of Penzance, The 1966,My 24,54:1
Robin, Red (Scenic Designer)
Arrow-Maker, The 1956,O 5,20:1
Robin, Sue
Meet the People 1940,D 26,22:2
Robins, A
Vaudeville (Palace) 1926,N 9,30:3
Vaudeville (Palace) 1930,My 5,27:5
Vaudeville (Palace) 1930,N 17,21:2
Jumbo 1935,N 18,20:2
Jumbo 1935,N 24,IX,1:1
Top-Notchers 1942,My 30,8:5
Robins, Barry
King and I, The 1964,Jl 7,26:1
Robins, Edward H
Acquittal, The 1920,Ja 6,18:2
So This Is London 1923,Ap 12,22:1
Bluffing Bluffers 1924,D 23,17:2
Something to Brag About 1925,Ag 14,14:3
Puppy Love 1926,Ja 28,16:3
Paradise 1927,D 26,26:4
Oh, Promise Me 1930,N 25,31:1
Just to Remind You 1931,S 8,39:1
Of Thee I Sing 1931,D 28,20:1
Let 'Em Eat Cake 1933,O 23,18:1
Whatever Goes Up 1935,N 26,28:2
Leave It to Me! 1938,N 10,32:2
Louisiana Purchase 1940,My 29,19:2
Doughgirls, The 1942,D 31,19:2
Nellie Bly 1946,Ja 22,32:2
Front Page, The 1946,S 5,22:4
Robins, Gregory
Rose Bernd 1922,S 27,17:1
Venetian, The 1931,N 2,26:1
According to Law 1944,Je 2,20:3
Last Stop 1944,S 6,17:2
Signature 1945,F 15,25:2
Temporary Island, A 1948,Mr 15,27:3
Mademoiselle Colombe 1954,Ja 7,26:1
Wayside 1957,Ap 18,34:1
Robins, Isobel
Wet Paint 1965,Ap 13,33:1
Robins, Isobel (Producer)
Wet Paint 1965,Ap 13,33:1
Robins, Leo (Composer)
Tattle Tales 1933,Je 2,22:6
Robins, Leo (Lyricist)
Tattle Tales 1933,Je 2,22:6
Robins, Sam (Playwright)
Answered the Flute 1960,Mr 10,37:4
Robins, Tamar
Dybbuk, The 1926,D 14,24:2
Eternal Jew, The 1926,D 21,21:2
Jacob's Dream 1927,Ja 4,20:2
Dybbuk, The 1948,My 3,26:3
Golem, The 1948,My 17,22:3
Robins, Toby
Measure for Measure 1954,Je 30,23:1
Taming of the Shrew, The 1962,Je 21,25:1
Cyrano de Bergerac 1962,Ag 1,21:1
Before You Go 1969,Ap 9,51:1
Robinson, Alma
Hair 1967,O 30,55:1
Robinson, Andy
Phaedra 1967,My 22,50:2
Cannibals, The 1968,N 4,60:1

Robinson, Andy—Cont

Young Master Dante, The 1968,D 31,19:1
Operation Sidewinder 1970,Mr 13,33:1
Robinson, Ann
New Faces of 1943 1942,D 23,22:2
Memphis Bound 1945,My 25,23:2
Robinson, Annette
O Evening Star 1936,Ja 9,24:6
Devil of Pei-Ling 1936,F 21,20:4
Robinson, Armin (Original Author)
Three Waltzes 1937,D 27,10:2
Robinson, Armin L (Producer)
Take It As It Comes 1944,F 11,17:2
Robinson, Bartlett
Sweet River 1936,O 29,30:2
Naughty-Naught 'OO 1937,Ja 25,23:2
Naughty-Naught ('00) 1937,Jl 13,22:3
Merchant of Yonkers, The 1938,D 29,14:2
Dear Ruth 1944,D 14,29:2
Another Part of the Forest 1946,N 21,42:2
Light Up the Sky 1948,N 19,34:2
Point of No Return 1951,Mr 14,35:2
Room Service 1953,Ap 7,34:1
Prescott Proposals, The 1953,D 17,53:1
Robinson, Bertrand
Solid Ivory 1925,N 17,29:3
Robinson, Bertrand (Director)
Tommy 1927,Ja 11,36:4
Your Uncle Dudley 1929,N 19,26:4
Oh, Promise Me 1930,N 25,31:1
Right This Way 1938,Ja 6,22:3
Robinson, Bertrand (Playwright)
Tommy 1927,Ja 11,36:4
Tommy 1927,Mr 27,VII,1:1
Your Uncle Dudley 1929,N 19,26:4
Who Cares 1930,Jl 9,27:1
Oh, Promise Me 1930,N 25,31:1
Tommy 1933,Ag 8,22:5
Crime Marches on 1935,O 24,19:1
Robinson, Bill
Vaudeville (Palace) 1926,Je 22,21:3
Vaudeville (Palace) 1926,Je 29,21:3
Vaudeville (Palace) 1927,Ap 26,33:1
Vaudeville (Palace) 1927,S 20,33:3
Blackbirds 1928,My 10,31:3
Vaudeville (Palace) 1929,Je 3,27:4
Vaudeville (Palace) 1930,F 10,20:3
Vaudeville (Palace) 1930,Ag 11,13:3
Brown Buddies 1930,O 8,29:1
Vaudeville (Palace) 1931,Ja 26,21:5
Vaudeville (Palace) 1932,F 15,13:3
Blackbirds 1933,D 4,22:3
Hot Mikado, The 1939,Mr 24,26:2
Hot Mikado, The 1939,Ap 2,X,1:3
Hot Mikado, The 1939,Je 23,23:4
All in Fun 1940,N 22,26:2
All in Fun 1940,D 28,11:2
Actors Fund Fete 1942,F 23,24:5
Memphis Bound 1945,My 25,23:2
Memphis Bound 1945,Je 10,II,1:1
Swan Song 1951,O 16,35:2
Big Deal, The 1953,Mr 7,13:6
Born Yesterday 1954,Ja 1,16:6
Barroom Monks, The 1962,My 29,21:1
Robinson, Carlo
Violet 1944,O 25,16:1
Robinson, Carol
From the Second City 1969,O 15,34:1
Robinson, Carroll
Patience 1928,Je 26,29:3
Robinson, Charles
Patriarch, The 1929,N 26,28:5
Sailor, Beware! 1933,S 29,24:4
Mahogany Hall 1934,Ja 18,18:5
Sailor, Beware! 1935,My 7,28:4
Swing Your Lady 1936,O 19,22:4
Tall Story 1959,Ja 30,33:2
Good Soup, The 1960,Mr 3,26:4
Robinson, Charles (Playwright)
Swing Your Lady 1935,N 16,19:4
Eastwood Ho 1936,Jl 8,14:2
Flying Gerardos, The 1940,D 30,21:4
Apple of His Eye 1946,F 6,18:2
Robinson, Charley
This Was Burlesque 1962,Mr 7,29:1
Robinson, Chris
Wonderful Town 1953,F 26,22:3
Carousel 1954,Je 3,32:2
Plain and Fancy 1955,Ja 28,14:2
Robinson, Clarence
Keep Shufflin' 1928,F 28,18:3
Robinson, Clarence (Miscellaneous)
Cotton Club Revue of 1957 1957,Jl 10,23:4
Robinson, Clark
Marching Song 1937,F 18,18:2
Robinson, Clark (Costume Designer)
Patience 1927,My 24,23:2
Robinson, Clark (Producer)
Viva O'Brien 1941,O 10,27:2
Robinson, Clark (Scenic Designer)
Music Box Revue 1924,D 2,23:3
Cradle Snatchers 1925,S 8,28:2
Young Blood 1925,N 25,15:1
Just Beyond 1925,D 2,22:4

Greenwich Village Follies 1925,D 25,23:3
No Trespassing! 1926,S 8,19:1
Peggy-Ann 1926,D 28,16:3
LeMaire's Affairs 1927,Mr 29,22:4
Enchantment 1927,Ap 28,27:3
Patience 1927,My 24,23:2
Peggy-Ann 1927,Jl 3,VII,1:1
Jarnegan 1928,S 25,29:2
Fioretta 1929,F 6,30:3
Ghost Parade, The 1929,O 31,28:4
Woof, Woof 1929,D 26,20:4
Nine Fifteen Revue, The 1930,F 12,26:2
Roberta 1933,N 20,18:4
Keep Moving 1934,Ag 24,10:2
Say When 1934,O 28,IX,3:1
Say When 1934,N 9,24:2
Sketch Book 1935,Je 5,22:2
Granite 1936,Ja 14,24:6
Mainly for Lovers 1936,F 22,13:2
Broadway Sho-Window 1936,Ap 13,14:5
Call Me Ziggy 1937,F 13,9:6
Viva O'Brien 1941,O 10,27:2
Robinson, Clarnece
Shuffle Along of 1933 1932,D 27,11:3
Robinson, Cynthia
Tonight We Improvise 1959,N 7,27:4
Robinson, Dee
Fun City 1968,Mr 7,53:2
Robinson, Dewey
Last Warning, The 1922,O 25,23:1
Solid Ivory 1925,N 17,29:3
Robinson, Donald
Journey With Strangers, A 1958,N 27,53:1
Robinson, Donald B (Playwright)
Nautical but Nice 1931,Ap 19,31:6
Robinson, Dorothy
Nine Till Six 1936,Mr 14,10:3
Robinson, Dorothy Marie (Miscellaneous)
Pirates of Penzance, The 1966,My 24,54:1
Trial by Jury 1966,Je 8,41:2
H M S Pinafore 1966,Je 8,41:2
Robinson, Douglas
Not While I'm Eating 1961,D 20,37:1
Robinson, Dwight E Jr
Hippolytus 1935,Je 15,20:4
Robinson, Earl
Young Go First, The 1935,My 29,16:2
Robinson, Earl (Composer)
Pink Slips on Parade 1937,F 1,14:4
Processional 1937,O 14,23:1
Life and Death of an American 1939,My 20,11:2
It's Up to You 1943,Ap 1,19:1
Blue Holiday 1945,My 22,13:3
Robinson, Earl (Lyricist)
Hellzapoppin 1938,S 23,34:2
Robinson, Earl (Miscellaneous)
Let Freedom Sing 1942,O 6,18:2
Robinson, Earl (Playwright)
Sandhog 1954,N 24,17:1
Lonesome Train, The 1965,Je 17,25:1
Lonesome Train, The 1965,Je 27,II,1:1
Robinson, Edna Mae
Born Yesterday 1954,Ja 1,16:6
Robinson, Edward
Night Lodging 1920,Ap 18,VI,2:1
Launzi 1923,O 11,16:3
Fashion 1937,Mr 21,II,7:8
Robinson, Edward G
Samson and Delilah 1920,N 18,18:1
Samson and Delilah 1920,N 28,VI,1:1
Eyvind of the Hills 1921,F 2,14:1
Idle Inn, The 1921,D 21,26:2
Deluge, The 1922,Ja 28,14:2
Banco 1922,S 21,18:1
Peer Gynt 1923,F 6,14:1
Adding Machine, The 1923,Mr 20,24:1
Royal Fandango, A 1923,N 13,25:1
Firebrand, The 1924,O 16,33:1
Man of Destiny, The 1925,N 24,28:1
Androcles and the Lion 1925,N 24,28:1
Androcles and the Lion 1925,N 29,VIII,1:1
Goat Song 1926,Ja 26,18:1
Goat Song 1926,F 7,VII,1:1
Chief Thing, The 1926,Mr 23,24:2
Henry-Behave 1926,Ag 24,19:4
Juarez and Maximilian 1926,O 12,31:1
Ned McCobb's Daughter 1926,N 30,26:2
Brothers Karamazov, The 1927,Ja 4,20:1
Right You Are (If You Think You Are) 1927,F 24,27:1
Racket, The 1927,N 23,28:3
Racket, The 1927,D 18,IX,1:1
Man With Red Hair, A 1928,N 9,22:2
Kibitzer 1929,F 10,IX,2:1
Kibitzer, The 1929,F 19,22:5
Mr Samuel 1930,O 26,VIII,3:5
Mr Samuel 1930,N 11,28:4
Vaudeville (Palace) 1931,S 28,17:5
Lambs Gambol 1933,Ap 24,10:1
Middle of the Night 1956,F 9,39:1
Middle of the Night 1956,F 19,II,1:1
Robinson, Edward G (Playwright)
Kibitzer, The 1929,F 19,22:5

Robinson, Edwin Arlington (Playwright)
Tristram 1962,O 29,36:1
Robinson, Eileen
Trimmed in Scarlet 1920,F 3,18:1
Robinson, Emmett
Master of the Revels 1935,Ag 14,16:2
Robinson, Erik
Mira 1970,Je 3,51:1
Robinson, F G
Poldekin 1920,S 10,12:1
Robinson, Florence
George White's Scandals 1929,S 24,29:1
Midsummer Night's Dream, A 1932,N 18,22:2
Iron Flowers 1933,Je 13,22:2
Personal Appearance 1934,O 18,26:7
Steps Leading Up 1941,Ap 19,20:6
Assassin, The 1945,O 18,20:2
Robinson, Forrest
Transplanting Jean 1921,Ja 4,11:2
Tarzan of the Apes 1921,S 8,14:3
Mad Dog, The 1921,N 9,20:1
Robinson, Frances
Jackpot 1944,Ja 14,15:2
Robinson, Francis
Hamlet 1927,Ap 7,23:3
Robinson, Freddie
Hot Mikado, The 1939,Mr 24,26:2
Robinson, Garrett (Playwright)
Whiteshop, The 1968,Ag 24,24:2
Hamhocks 1968,Ag 24,24:2
Robinson, Gloria
South Pacific 1943,D 30,11:2
Robinson, Gordon (Composer)
Liberace's Variety Bill 1957,Ap 22,29:5
Robinson, Happy
Searching for the Sun 1936,F 20,22:6
Robinson, Horace W (Director)
Dawn's Early Light 1959,Ag 9,76:4
Robinson, Jack
Hoboken Blues 1928,F 18,10:1
Robinson, Jack (Scenic Designer)
Now 1968,Je 6,53:1
Robinson, Jay
Shop at Sly Corner, The 1949,Ja 19,35:2
Gayden 1949,My 11,34:4
As You Like It 1950,Ja 27,27:2
Buy Me Blue Ribbons 1951,O 18,33:2
Much Ado About Nothing 1952,My 2,20:1
Picture of Dorian Gray, The 1963,Ag 29,37:4
Robinson, Jay (Producer)
Buy Me Blue Ribbons 1951,O 18,33:2
Robinson, Jo-Ann
Warning, The-A Theme for Linda 1969,Ap 27,92:1
Black Quartet, A; Warning, The-A Theme for
Linda 1969,Jl 31,28:1
Robinson, John
Savage Rhythm 1932,Ja 1,30:4
Living Room, The 1953,Ap 17,29:5
Miracle Worker, The 1961,Mr 10,19:4
Robinson, Joseph
Overture 1930,D 8,26:4
Robinson, Judith
Dark at the Top of the Stairs, The 1957,D 6,38:1
Dark at the Top of the Stairs, The 1957,D 15,II,3:1
Robinson, Kathleen
Such Is Life 1927,S 1,27:3
Robinson, Kathleen (Miscellaneous)
Mother, The 1939,Ap 26,26:2
Robinson, Kenneth W (Producer)
Reunion 1938,Ap 12,26:4
Robinson, Kitty
Philadelphia 1929,S 17,34:5
Robinson, Larry
Life With Father 1939,N 9,26:2
Richard III 1943,Mr 27,8:3
Victors, The 1948,D 27,17:2
Grass Harp, The 1952,Mr 28,26:2
Time Out for Ginger 1952,N 27,50:4
Dear Charles 1954,S 16,37:2
Iceman Cometh, The 1956,My 8,38:1
Bananas 1968,D 5,60:1
Robinson, Lennox (Composer)
King Oedipus 1933,Ja 16,12:4
Robinson, Lennox (Costume Designer)
Parnell of Avondale 1934,O 3,24:4
Robinson, Lennox (Director)
Cat and the Moon, The 1931,N 8,VIII,4:3
Vigil 1932,D 11,IX,4:5
Is Life Worth Living? 1933,N 10,24:6
Robinson, Lennox (Playwright)
White-Headed Boy, The 1920,O 31,VI,1:4
White-Headed Boy, The 1921,S 16,20:1
Round Table, The 1927,Ag 28,VII,1:1
Far-Off Hills, The 1928,N 11,X,4:8
Give a Dog. . . 1929,Je 9,VIII,3:5
Ever the Twain 1929,O 9,31:3
Ever the Twain 1929,O 20,III,3:5
Ever the Twain 1929,O 27,IX,1:1
Round Table, The 1930,F 28,20:5
Critic, The 1931,F 22,VIII,3:5
Far-Off Hills, The 1932,O 19,22:4
Crabbed Youth and Age 1932,N 4,25:1

Robinson, Lennox (Playwright)—Cont

Big House, The 1933,Ja 5,19:3
Drama at Inish 1933,F 12,II,2:8
Is Life Worth Living? 1933,S 17,X,1:6
Is Life Worth Living? 1933,N 10,24:6
Ever the Twain 1933,D 17,IX,4:2
Big House, The 1934,F 22,24:4
Big House, The 1934,Mr 18,IX,2:3
Church Street 1934,My 23,15:5
All's Over, Then? 1934,Je 10,IX,1:1
Drama at Inish 1934,N 15,24:2
Church Street 1934,N 20,24:5
Whiteheaded Boy, The 1937,Ag 11,27:3
Far-Off Hills, The 1937,O 12,30:4
Drama at Inish 1937,D 14,33:2
Lucky Finger, The 1948,Ja 21,30:5
Church Street 1948,F 10,27:2
Church Street 1948,F 15,II,1:3

Robinson, Lennox (Producer)
Things That Are Caesar's, The 1933,Ja 29,IX,1:3
Saint in a Hurry, A 1935,D 29,IX,2:1

Robinson, Lennox (Scenic Designer)
Parnell of Avondale 1934,O 3,24:4

Robinson, Lenor
Orthee 1962,D 29,5:5
Antigone 1962,D 29,5:5

Robinson, Leslie (Miscellaneous)
Madwoman of Chaillot, The 1970,Mr 23,48:3

Robinson, Linda
J B 1958,Ap 24,37:1
Every Other Evil 1961,Ja 23,20:2

Robinson, Lois
Italian Straw Hat, The 1957,O 1,37:2
Lulu 1958,S 30,24:1

Robinson, Lytton
Story of Mary Surratt, The 1947,F 10,25:2

Robinson, Mabel
Golden Boy 1964,O 21,56:1

Robinson, Madeleine
Soif, La 1949,F 9,33:2
Adorable Julia 1954,N 28,II,3:1

Robinson, Mary
Demi-Virgin, The 1921,O 19,22:1
Los Angeles 1927,D 20,32:3
Trapped 1928,S 12,25:3
Cafe de Danse 1929,Ja 16,22:2
Wild Waves 1932,F 20,11:4

Robinson, McNeil (Composer)
Mercy Street 1969,O 28,43:1

Robinson, Michael (Playwright)
Eastwood Ho 1936,Jl 8,14:2

Robinson, Muriel
Purity 1930,D 26,18:2

Robinson, Paul
Ten Nights in a Barroom 1932,Ja 21,17:1
Man Who Never Died, The 1958,N 22,27:2

Robinson, Pauline
House in Paris, The 1944,Mr 21,17:1

Robinson, Peggy
Sweet Bird of Youth 1956,Ap 17,27:2

Robinson, Percy (Playwright)
To What Red Hell 1928,N 18,IX,2:3
Whispering Gallery, The 1929,Ja 6,VIII,4:4
Whispering Gallery, The 1929,F 12,22:2
Archdupe 1931,D 27,VIII,4:1
Wanted for Murder 1937,Je 29,18:1
Wanted for Murder 1937,Ag 26,25:3
At the Stroke of Eight 1940,My 21,29:2

Robinson, Pernett
West Side Story 1968,Je 25,32:1

Robinson, Peter
Lost Boy 1932,Ja 6,24:4
Dear Octopus 1939,Ja 12,22:2
No Time for Comedy 1939,Ap 18,26:4

Robinson, Philip
Merchant of Venice, The 1930,D 3,29:2
House of Connelly, The 1931,S 29,22:4
1931 1931,D 11,34:3
Night Over Taos 1932,Mr 10,25:3
Valley Forge 1934,D 11,28:3
Young Go First, The 1935,My 29,16:2
Paths of Glory 1935,S 27,24:2
Mayor of Zalamea, The 1946,Ja 28,15:5
Great Campaign, The 1947,Ap 1,33:2
Topaze 1947,D 29,21:5
Hope Is the Thing With Feathers 1948,Ap 12,24:2
Home Life of a Buffalo; Hope's the Thing
  1948,My 12,34:6
Gone Tomorrow; Hope's the Thing
  1948,My 12,34:6
Hope Is the Thing With Feathers; Hope's the
  Thing 1948,My 12,34:6
Saint Joan 1950,Mr 4,10:6
Firstborn, The 1958,My 1,35:1

Robinson, Philip (Director)
Saint Joan 1950,Mr 4,10:6

Robinson, Phyllis (Lyricist)
Cry for Us All 1970,Ap 9,48:2

Robinson, Ralph
Pleased to Meet You 1928,O 30,27:2

Robinson, Raymond
Life Begins in '40 1940,Ap 5,24:2
Hit the Road 1941,Ap 4,18:3

Robinson, Robert
When the Roll Is Called Up Yonder
  1930,My 9,20:5
King Lear 1950,Ag 30,26:2

Robinson, Roberta
Band Wagon, The 1931,My 17,VIII,3:2
Band Wagon, The 1931,Je 4,31:3
Here Goes the Bride 1931,N 4,31:2

Robinson, Roger
Walk in Darkness 1963,O 29,30:2
Who's Got His Own 1966,O 13,52:1
Trials of Brother Jero, The 1967,N 10,60:1
Does a Tiger Wear a Necktie? 1969,F 26,38:1
Does a Tiger Wear a Necktie? 1969,Mr 9,II,1:1
Does a Tiger Wear a Necktie? 1969,Mr 16,II,4:5
Miser, The 1969,My 9,35:1
Rat's Mass, A 1969,N 1,39:1

Robinson, Russel
Vaudeville (Palace) 1926,Jl 27,15:4
Vaudeville (Palace) 1926,Ag 3,19:2

Robinson, Russell J (Composer)
Plantation Revue, The 1922,Jl 18,18:4

Robinson, Russell J (Lyricist)
Plantation Revue, The 1922,Jl 18,18:4

Robinson, Ruth
Theatre of the Soul 1942,Mr 21,13:5
Across the Board on Tomorrow Morning
  1942,Mr 21,13:5

Robinson, Sally Shoemaker
Everyman Today 1958,Ja 16,32:4

Robinson, Scott
Sourball 1969,Ag 6,29:2

Robinson, Sumner
Blue Blood 1924,Ap 3,21:2

Robinson, Susan
Listen Professor! 1943,D 23,22:1

Robinson, Thomas P (Playwright)
Skylark 1921,Jl 26,10:6
Brook 1923,Ag 20,14:3
Artistic Temperament 1924,D 10,20:2
Be Your Age 1929,F 5,27:1

Robinson, Virginia
Harvest of Years 1948,Ja 13,29:2
Blithe Spirit 1952,F 23,7:5
Fig Leaf in Her Bonnet, A 1961,Je 15,50:1

Robinson, Walter
Bottled 1928,Ap 11,25:1
Ol' Man Satan 1932,O 4,26:3

Robinson, William
Nativity Play, The 1937,D 21,29:1
Hamlet 1948,D 4,9:2
Indian Captive, The 1949,Ja 31,15:2
Chameleon, The 1949,F 7,16:2
Dick Whittington and His Remarkable Cat
  1950,N 25,10:5

Robinson, Zeb
Hayride 1954,S 14,24:2

Robinson (Playwright)
White Blackbird, The 1925,N 15,VIII,2:1

Robinson and Wade
Bubble Along 1930,Je 3,27:3

Robison, Joseph
Downstream 1926,Ja 12,28:1
Donovan Affair, The 1926,Ag 31,15:2

Robison, Susan K (Miscellaneous)
Greenwillow 1970,D 8,60:1

Robison, Willard (Composer)
Tattle Tales 1933,Je 2,22:6

Robison, Willard (Lyricist)
Tattle Tales 1933,Je 2,22:6

Robitschek, Kurt (Playwright)
Let's Raise the Curtain 1936,S 29,34:3

Robitschek, Kurt (Producer)
Laughter Over London 1936,D 8,31:3
Vaudeville Marches On 1938,D 30,11:1
Laughter Over Broadway 1939,Ja 16,10:3

Robles, Emmanuel (Original Author)
Montserrat 1961,Ja 9,30:5

Robles, Emmanuel (Translator)
Montserrat 1949,O 31,21:4
Montserrat 1954,My 26,34:2

Robles, Frank
Toothbrush, The 1970,S 27,84:5
Invasores, Los 1970,D 12,20:1

Robles, Maria
Leyenda del Beso, La 1942,N 20,26:4

Robon, Robert
Pastoral 1939,N 2,26:2

Robson, Bryan
Measure for Measure 1967,F 15,37:1
Hamlet 1967,F 17,44:1
Romeo and Juliet 1967,F 22,18:1

Robson, Cecil (Playwright)
Cry of the Peacock 1950,Ap 12,33:2

Robson, Eleanor (Playwright)
In the Next Room 1923,N 28,14:1
In the Next Room 1924,Je 7,16:5

Robson, Flora
Anatomist, The 1931,O 25,VIII,2:6
Dangerous Corner 1932,My 11,15:3
For Services Rendered 1932,N 2,23:5
For Services Rendered 1932,N 27,IX,1:3

Robson, Flora—Cont

All God's Chillun Got Wings 1933,Mr 14,19:4
Touch Wood 1934,Jl 1,X,1:3
Mary Read 1934,N 22,26:7
Mary Read 1934,D 16,XI,3:4
Mary Tudor 1935,D 13,30:6
Mary Tudor 1936,Ja 12,IX,1:5
Satyr 1937,Je 17,18:5
Satyr 1937,Jl 4,X,1:4
Last Train South 1938,S 4,X,2:2
Ladies in Retirement 1940,Mr 27,24:3
Anne of England 1941,O 8,26:2
Damask Cheek, The 1942,O 23,24:2
Damask Cheek, The 1942,N 8,VIII,1:1
Message for Margaret 1946,S 2,13:2
Macbeth 1948,Ap 11,II,1:1
Black Chiffon 1949,Je 11,II,3:1
Black Chiffon 1950,S 28,39:2
Black Chiffon 1950,O 15,II,1:1
Innocents, The 1952,Jl 4,9:7
Time and the Yellow Roses 1961,Je 25,II,3:5
Importance of Being Earnest, The 1968,Jl 6,9:1
Ring Around the Moon 1968,N 2,28:1
Untitled-Recital 1970,S 3,36:1

Robson, Ivor
Holiday on Ice 1965,S 2,38:4
Holiday on Ice 1966,S 1,30:1

Robson, Mary
Bulldog Drummond 1921,D 27,10:2
Dew Drop Inn 1923,My 18,26:4
And So to Bed 1927,N 10,23:1
Maya 1928,F 22,19:1

Robson, May
Two Orphans, The 1926,Ap 6,26:2
Two Orphans, The 1926,Ap 11,VIII,1:1

Robson, Robert
Sancho Panza 1923,N 27,23:1
Conscience 1924,S 12,19:3
Wall Street 1927,Ap 21,24:4
Guinea Pig, The 1929,Ja 8,35:1
Unsophisticates, The 1929,D 31,14:5

Robson, Roy
Arsenic and Old Lace 1943,D 13,18:6
Our Town 1944,Ja 11,24:5
Too Hot for Maneuvers 1945,My 3,26:5

Robson, Stuart (Mrs)
Ladies' Night 1920,Ag 10,10:1

Roby, Stephen
Fratricide Punished 1925,Ap 21,19:1
Romio and Julietta 1925,Ap 21,19:1

Roc, John (Playwright)
Fire! 1968,My 12,II,7:1
Fire! 1969,Ja 29,26:1

Roc, Patricia
Love's Old Sweet Song 1940,My 3,16:3

Roca, Carlos
Melody 1933,F 15,17:4

Rocca, Gino (Playwright)
Liane, Le (Ties That Bind); Ties That Bind (Le
  Liane) 1929,Ap 22,22:1
Liane, Le (Ties That Bind) 1933,Je 12,20:3

Rocca, Robert (Playwright)
Vive la Libe 1964,Ja 9,36:3

Roccardi, Albert
Wheel, The 1921,Ag 30,10:1
Molly Darling 1922,S 2,10:2

Rocco, Joe
Can-Can 1959,Ag 26,25:4
Littlest Circus, The 1959,D 26,5:6
Irma la Douce 1960,S 30,31:2

Rocco, Sonny
Rose Tattoo, The 1966,O 21,36:2

Rocco, Vincenzo
In Time to Come 1941,D 29,20:2

Rocha, Kathleen
Singing Girl, The 1952,Je 4,31:8

Rochberg, George (Composer)
Alchemist, The 1966,O 14,48:1

Roche, Arthur Somers (Playwright)
Crooks' Convention, The 1928,O 21,IX,2:1
Crooks' Convention, The 1929,S 19,37:4

Roche, Con
Trelawny of the 'Wells' 1970,O 12,48:1

Roche, Edward
Run, Little Chillun 1943,Ag 14,6:1
Carmen Jones 1943,D 3,26:2
Carmen Jones 1945,My 3,26:5
Carmen Jones 1946,Ap 8,32:2

Roche, Emeline (Costume Designer)
Papa Is All 1942,Ja 7,22:2
Mr Sycamore 1942,N 14,13:2
Pick-Up Girl 1944,My 4,25:2
Deep Are the Roots 1945,S 27,24:4
Flamingo Road 1946,Mr 20,18:2
Loco 1946,O 17,29:2
Love Goes to Press 1947,Ja 2,22:2
Volpone 1948,Ja 9,24:6
Tragedian in Spite of Himself, A 1948,F 6,29:2
Bear, The 1948,F 6,29:2
Wedding, The 1948,F 6,29:2
On the Harmfulness of Tobacco 1948,F 6,29:2
Alchemist, The 1948,My 7,31:4
S S Glencairn; Bound East for Cardiff
  1948,My 21,21:2

Roche, Emeline (Costume Designer)—Cont
S S Glencairn; Long Voyage Home, The
1948,My 21,21:2
S S Glencairn; Moon of the Caribbees
1948,My 21,21:2
S S Glencairn; In the Zone 1948,My 21,21:2
Insect Comedy, The 1948,Je 4,26:3
Goodbye My Fancy 1948,N 18,35:2
Red Gloves 1948,D 6,28:2
Gayden 1949,My 11,34:4
Corn Is Green, The 1950,Ja 12,33:2
Heiress, The 1950,F 9,34:2
Captain Brassbound's Conversion 1950,D 28,21:1
Royal Family, The 1951,Ja 11,28:2
Richard II 1951,Ja 25,21:2
Taming of the Shrew, The 1951,Ap 26,35:2
Dream Girl 1951,My 10,39:1
Idiot's Delight 1951,My 24,46:3
Anna Christie 1952,Ja 10,33:1
Cyrano de Bergerac 1953,N 13,24:3
Shrike, The 1953,N 26,51:2
Richard III 1953,D 10,65:2
Charley's Aunt 1953,D 23,22:2
Roche, Emeline (Miscellaneous)
Jacobowsky and the Colonel 1944,Mr 15,17:2
Devil's Disciple, The 1950,Ja 26,23:2
As You Like It 1950,Ja 27,27:2
Roche, Emeline (Scenic Designer)
Jeannie 1940,N 13,29:2
Papa Is All 1942,Ja 7,22:2
Anna Christie 1952,Ja 10,33:1
Anna Christie 1952,Ja 20,II,1:1
Roche, Gene
Waiting for Godot 1958,Ag 6,22:1
Valmouth 1960,O 7,29:1
Under Milk Wood 1961,Mr 30,25:1
Blood, Sweat & Stanley Poole 1961,O 6,31:1
Great Day in the Morning 1962,Mr 29,29:1
Mother Courage and Her Children 1963,Mr 30,5:5
White House, The 1964,My 20,39:1
Secret Life of Walter Mitty, The 1964,O 27,44:5
All in Good Time 1965,F 19,25:1
Laughwind 1966,Mr 3,27:1
Father Uxbridge Wants to Marry 1967,O 30,57:1
Roche, Jack (Playwright)
Tickets, Please! 1950,Ap 28,25:2
Roche, James
What Every Woman Knows 1954,D 23,16:2
Roche, John
Whispering Well, The 1920,D 6,19:1
Deburau 1920,D 24,14:3
Great Adventure, The 1921,F 26,9:2
Harlequinade 1921,My 11,20:3
Madras House, The 1921,O 31,18:2
Nature's Nobleman 1921,N 15,23:2
R U R 1922,O 10,16:1
Innocent Voyage, The 1943,N 16,27:2
Roche, John (Director)
Mackerel Skies 1934,Ja 24,20:4
Roche, John F
Makers of Light 1922,My 24,22:3
It Is the Law 1922,N 30,28:2
This Fine-Pretty World 1923,D 27,11:1
Time Is a Dream 1924,Ap 23,24:2
Little Clay Cart, The 1924,D 6,13:3
Lovers and Enemies 1927,S 21,27:1
Love Nest, The 1927,D 23,17:1
Roche, Kathleen
H M S Pinafore 1942,Ja 22,12:2
Mikado, The 1942,F 4,22:2
Pirates of Penzance, The 1942,F 18,22:2
Iolanthe 1942,F 24,26:4
Gondoliers, The 1942,Mr 4,22:3
Mikado, The 1944,F 12,11:3
H M S Pinafore 1944,F 15,14:4
Trial by Jury 1944,F 15,14:4
Pirates of Penzance, The 1944,F 18,15:5
Gondoliers, The 1944,F 22,26:3
Iolanthe 1944,F 23,17:1
Patience 1944,F 26,11:4
Ruddigore 1944,Mr 3,19:5
Yeomen of the Guard, The 1944,Mr 5,34:3
Mikado, The 1949,O 5,35:2
Pirates of Penzance, The 1949,O 11,41:2
H M S Pinafore 1949,O 18,34:2
Roche, Mary
Mikado, The 1942,F 4,22:2
Pirates of Penzance, The 1942,F 18,22:2
Iolanthe 1942,F 24,26:4
Gondoliers, The 1942,Mr 4,22:3
What's Up 1943,N 12,24:6
What's Up 1943,N 21,II,1:1
Seven Lively Arts 1944,D 8,26:6
Mikado, The 1952,O 21,35:2
Pirates of Penzance, The 1952,O 28,36:4
H M S Pinafore 1952,N 4,32:2
Iolanthe 1952,N 11,26:3
Roche, Mazo de la (Original Author)
Whiteoaks 1936,My 17,IX,2:2
Roche, Mazo de la (Playwright)
Whiteoaks 1936,My 17,IX,2:2
Whiteoaks 1938,F 23,26:2
Roche, Tami
This Was Burlesque 1970,F 12,31:1

Roche, Viola
Theatre 1941,N 13,34:2
Rochelle, Drieu La (Playwright)
Eau Fraiche, L' 1931,Je 7,VIII,3:5
Chef, Le 1935,Ja 6,IX,2:1
Rochelle, Rene
You'll See Stars 1943,Ja 1,26:6
Rochelle, Sandy
Tiger at the Gates 1968,Mr 1,30:1
Rocher, Pierre (Playwright)
Chambre d'Hotel 1932,Mr 20,VIII,2:2
Rocher, Rene (Original Author)
Petit Peche 1926,O 24,VIII,2:1
Rocher, Rene (Producer)
J'ai tue 1928,O 28,IX,2:7
Avare, L' 1930,F 2,VIII,4:1
Tartuffe 1930,F 2,VIII,4:1
Dardamelle 1935,Je 30,X,1:4
Elizabeth, la Femme Sans Hommes
1935,N 24,IX,3:7
Rochester, Noble
Ice Capades 1960,S 1,30:1
Ice Capades 1963,Ag 29,37:2
Rochford, Alma
If 1927,O 26,26:2
Rochte, Antoinette
Easy Terms 1925,S 23,22:2
Fata Morgana 1931,D 26,15:3
Life Begins 1932,Mr 29,23:2
Angeline Moves In 1932,Ap 20,27:5
Late One Evening 1933,Ja 10,27:3
Rock, Clarence
Far Away Horses 1933,Mr 22,21:6
Crucible 1933,S 5,22:4
Her Man of Wax 1933,O 12,32:3
Furnished Rooms 1934,My 30,14:6
Lost Horizons 1934,O 16,31:2
Summer Wives 1936,Ap 14,18:1
Rock, Helen Eby
Bunch and Judy, The 1922,N 29,20:1
Dancing Mothers 1924,Ag 12,12:2
City Chap, The 1925,O 27,21:1
Harry Delmar's Revels 1927,N 29,30:2
Rock, Jeff
Jonah! 1966,F 16,52:1
Rock, Kenneth
Banquet for the Moon, A 1961,Ja 20,24:2
Rock, Nicholas (Director)
Foreplay 1970,D 11,58:2
Rock, Norman (Scenic Designer)
Reflected Glory 1936,S 22,30:2
Soliloquy 1938,N 29,26:4
Rock, Stan
Good Boy 1928,S 6,23:2
Rock, William
Silks and Satins 1920,Jl 16,19:1
Rockefeller, Clarence
Immodest Violet 1920,Ag 25,6:2
Rockefeller (Producer)
Virginia 1937,S 12,XI,1:1
Rocklin, Diane
Hamlet 1954,Ap 24,15:2
Rockmore, Robert (Producer)
Triple Crossed 1927,My 6,21:2
These Modern Women 1928,F 14,26:2
Run, Little Chillun! 1933,Mr 2,21:3
Dance Night 1938,O 15,20:5
Rockwell, Doc
Vaudeville (Palace) 1925,Ap 21,18:1
Vaudeville (Palace) 1926,My 8,29:2
Vaudeville (Palace) 1926,D 7,24:3
Vaudeville (Palace) 1927,Je 14,33:3
Greenwich Village Follies 1928,Ap 10,32:2
Broadway Nights 1929,Je 23,VIII,2:4
Broadway Nights 1929,Jl 16,23:2
Vaudeville (Palace) 1931,F 16,16:3
Vaudeville (Palace) 1931,My 25,17:4
Let's Play Fair 1938,Ja 19,26:4
Seven Lively Arts 1944,D 8,26:6
Seven Lively Arts 1944,D 17,II,3:1
Rockwell, George
Scandals 1920,Je 8,9:1
Rockwell, Keith (Producer)
Under the Yum-Yum Tree 1964,My 29,18:1
Rockwell, Mary
Blow Ye Winds 1937,S 24,17:4
Rockwell, Russell
Brothers 1928,D 26,14:3
Let and Sub-Let 1930,My 20,32:2
Rockwood, Jerry
Great Magician, The 1951,N 22,45:1
Man and Superman 1953,F 21,11:2
Mrs Patterson 1957,F 6,20:2
Man of Destiny, The 1957,Ap 1,21:2
Cave Dwellers, The 1961,O 16,34:2
Rockwood, Jerry (Director)
Will and the Way, The 1957,D 3,46:5
Rocky, Leonard
Knights of Song 1938,O 18,29:2
Rodale, J I (Playwright)
Goose, The 1960,Mr 16,44:1
'Toinette 1961,N 21,46:1

Rodale, J I (Producer)
Engagement Baby, The 1970,My 22,40:1
Rodalito, Don
Hobo 1931,F 12,24:4
Rodd, Marcia
Love in E Flat 1967,F 14,38:1
Love and Let Love 1968,Ja 4,30:1
Last of the Red Hot Lovers 1969,D 29,37:1
Last of the Red Hot Lovers 1970,Ja 4,II,1:1
Rodd, Philip
Arms and the Girl 1950,F 3,28:2
Emperor's Clothes, The 1953,F 10,24:2
Rodda, Richard (Miscellaneous)
Peter Pan 1954,O 21,30:2
Roddy, Cornelius
Street Wolf, The 1929,Ja 1,61:1
Rode, Alfredo and his Royal Tzigane Orchestra
Americana 1932,O 6,19:3
Rode, Christian
Minna von Barnhelm 1968,N 13,37:1
Schloss, Das 1968,N 20,35:3
Amphitryon 1970,N 18,40:1
Kleinburgerhochzeit, Die 1970,N 25,25:1
Rode, Richard
Concept, The 1968,My 7,51:1
Roden, Charles (Miscellaneous)
Dark of the Moon 1970,Ap 4,21:2
Roden, Chuck (Miscellaneous)
Reckoning, The 1969,S 5,28:1
Roden, Edelaine
Pride 1923,My 3,22:3
Roden, Illa
From Vienna 1939,Je 21,26:2
From Vienna 1939,Jl 2,IX,1:1
Roden, Maire
O'Flaherty, V C 1920,Je 22,9:1
Dragon, The 1922,D 27,12:1
Rodensky, Shmuel
Each Had Six Wings 1964,Mr 12,39:1
Fiddler on the Roof; Anatevka 1968,F 2,28:1
Roderick, Beatrice (Composer)
Thanks for Tomorrow 1938,S 28,28:2
Roderick, William
Man for All Seasons, A 1964,Ja 28,24:2
Rodes, Mary
Patience 1933,My 23,22:6
Rodewald, Lillian
Alt Heidelberg 1924,D 8,23:2
Wilhelm Tell 1925,Mr 2,15:1
Rodger, Robin (Composer)
While Parents Sleep 1934,Je 5,28:2
Rodger-Reid, Paul
Great Goodness of Life (A Coon Show)
1969,Ap 27,92:1
Black Quartet, A; Warning, The-A Theme for
Linda 1969,Jl 31,28:1
Rodgers, Anton
Pickwick 1965,O 6,5:3
Rodgers, Bob
Billy Barnes Revue, The 1959,Je 10,42:2
Rodgers, Bob (Director)
Billy Barnes Revue, The 1959,Je 10,42:2
Billy Barnes People, The 1961,Je 14,10:3
Rodgers, Bob (Playwright)
Billy Barnes Revue, The 1959,Je 10,42:2
Billy Barnes People, The 1961,Je 14,10:3
Rodgers, Carl
Daughters of Atreus 1936,O 15,33:1
Lysistrata 1937,Jl 20,19:3
Rodgers, Cynthia
Springtime for Henry 1936,Je 30,15:1
Rodgers, Douglas Fletcher
Plain and Fancy 1955,Ja 28,14:2
Ruy Blas 1957,D 14,16:3
Oklahoma! 1958,Mr 20,32:3
Rodgers, Eileen
Chic 1959,My 19,28:2
Fiorello! 1959,N 24,45:3
Fiorello! 1959,N 29,II,1:1
Tenderloin 1960,O 18,47:2
Anything Goes 1962,My 16,35:1
Kelly 1965,F 8,28:2
Rodgers, Enid
Sourball 1969,Ag 6,29:2
Getting Married 1970,Ja 20,46:1
Rodgers, Gaby
Heavenly Twins, The 1955,N 5,23:2
Mister Johnson 1956,Mr 30,11:1
Mister Johnson 1956,Ap 8,II,1:1
Hidden River, The 1957,Ja 24,32:1
Cock-A-Doodle Dandy 1958,N 13,39:2
Under the Sycamore Tree 1960,Mr 8,37:2
Deuces Wild; Thus 1962,Ap 25,31:1
Rodgers, Gaby (Director)
Treatment, The 1968,My 10,54:7
Soap Opera 1968,My 10,54:7
Rodgers, Lou
Illya Darling 1967,Ap 12,37:1
Rodgers, Lou (Composer)
Triumph of Robert Emmet, The 1969,My 8,54:1
Rodgers, Lou (Lyricist)
Triumph of Robert Emmet, The 1969,My 8,54:1

Rodgers, Mark (Miscellaneous)
Flea in Her Ear, A 1969,O 4,25:1
Three Sisters, The 1969,O 10,38:1
Rodgers, Marshall
Shuffle Along of 1933 1932,D 27,11:3
Rodgers, Mary (Composer)
Davy Jones's Locker 1959,Mr 30,25:1
Once Upon a Mattress 1959,My 12,40:1
Once Upon a Mattress 1959,My 17,II,1:1
Davy Jones's Locker 1959,D 28,18:1
From A to Z 1960,Ap 21,23:2
Once Upon a Mattress 1960,S 21,43:4
Hot Spot 1963,Ap 20,17:2
Mad Show, The 1966,Ja 10,16:1
Davy Jones's Locker 1966,D 25,48:5
Rodgers, Mary (Lyricist)
Davy Jones's Locker 1966,D 25,48:5
Rodgers, Pete
Winners and Losers 1947,F 27,27:2
Rodgers, Richard (Composer)
Bad Habits of 1925 1925,F 9,17:1
Garrick Gaieties 1925,My 18,12:2
Dearest Enemy 1925,S 19,9:2
Girl Friend, The 1926,Mr 18,26:5
Garrick Gaieties 1926,My 11,25:2
Peggy-Ann 1926,D 28,16:3
Betsy 1926,D 29,24:3
Connecticut Yankee, A 1927,O 9,VIII,1:3
Connecticut Yankee, A 1927,N 4,24:2
She's My Baby 1928,Ja 4,22:2
Present Arms 1928,Ap 27,16:2
Chee-Chee 1928,S 26,25:1
Spring Is Here 1929,Mr 12,26:1
Me for You 1929,S 22,IX,2:6
Heads Up! 1929,N 12,34:1
Simple Simon 1930,F 19,22:1
Garrick Gaieties 1930,O 17,21:2
America's Sweetheart 1931,Ja 25,VIII,2:4
America's Sweetheart 1931,F 11,23:1
Simple Simon 1931,Mr 10,23:2
Jumbo 1935,N 18,20:2
Jumbo 1935,N 24,IX,1:1
On Your Toes 1936,Mr 23,22:4
On Your Toes 1936,Ap 13,14:4
Babes in Arms 1937,Ap 15,18:4
On Your Toes 1937,Ag 3,21:2
I'd Rather Be Right 1937,O 12,27:6
I'd Rather Be Right 1937,O 17,XI,2:1
I'd Rather Be Right 1937,N 3,28:2
I'd Rather Be Right 1937,N 14,XI,1:1
I Married an Angel 1938,My 12,26:2
I Married an Angel 1938,My 22,XI,1:1
Boys From Syracuse, The 1938,N 13,IX,2:2
Boys From Syracuse, The 1938,N 24,36:1
Too Many Girls 1939,O 19,26:2
Too Many Girls 1939,O 29,IX,1:6
Higher and Higher 1940,Mr 17,X,2:5
Higher and Higher 1940,Ap 5,24:3
Higher and Higher 1940,Ag 6,15:4
Higher and Higher 1940,Ag 11,IX,1:1
Pal Joey 1940,D 26,22:2
It's All Yours 1942,Mr 26,26:2
By Jupiter 1942,Je 4,22:1
By Jupiter 1942,Ag 30,VIII,1:1
Oklahoma! 1943,Ap 1,27:1
Oklahoma! 1943,Ap 11,II,1:1
Oklahoma! 1943,My 9,II,6:4
Connecticut Yankee, A 1943,N 18,30:2
Connecticut Yankee, A 1943,N 21,II,1:1
Carousel 1945,Ap 20,24:2
Carousel 1945,Ap 29,II,1:1
Allegro 1947,O 11,10:2
Allegro 1947,N 2,II,1:1
Carousel 1949,Ja 26,28:2
Carousel 1949,F 6,II,1:1
South Pacific 1949,Ap 8,30:2
South Pacific 1949,Ap 17,II,1:1
South Pacific 1949,Je 5,II,1:1
South Pacific 1950,Ap 26,36:5
Babes in Arms 1951,Mr 10,7:3
King and I, The 1951,Ap 8,II,1:1
Oklahoma! 1951,My 30,15:2
South Pacific 1951,Jl 10,30:5
South Pacific 1951,S 2,II,1:1
Oklahoma! 1951,S 13,38:2
South Pacific 1951,N 2,19:1
South Pacific 1951,N 11,II,3:1
Pal Joey 1952,Ja 4,17:6
Pal Joey 1952,Ja 13,II,1:1
King and I, The 1952,Ap 14,23:1
Allegro 1952,S 18,36:3
King and I, The 1952,O 5,II,1:1
Carousel 1953,My 6,38:1
Me and Juliet 1953,My 29,17:1
Me and Juliet 1953,Je 7,II,1:1
Oklahoma! 1953,S 1,19:1
Oklahoma! 1953,S 6,II,1:1
King and I, The 1953,O 9,33:3
King and I, The 1953,O 18,II,3:1
Pal Joey 1954,Ap 1,40:5
Carousel 1954,Je 3,32:2
Carousel 1954,Je 13,II,1:1
On Your Toes 1954,O 12,24:4

South Pacific 1955,My 5,39:5
King and I, The 1955,My 17,33:4
Oklahoma! 1955,Je 21,37:7
Pipe Dream 1955,D 1,44:1
Pipe Dream 1955,D 11,II,5:1
King and I, The 1956,Ap 19,35:4
South Pacific 1957,Ap 25,35:1
Oklahoma! 1958,Mr 8,15:2
Oklahoma! 1958,Mr 20,32:3
Flower Drum Song 1958,D 2,44:1
Flower Drum Song 1958,D 7,II,5:1
Sound of Music, The 1959,N 17,40:2
Sound of Music, The 1959,N 22,II,1:1
Flower Drum Song 1960,Mr 25,20:4
King and I, The 1960,My 12,40:1
King and I, The 1960,My 22,II,1:1
King and I, The 1961,Mr 19,22:5
Sound of Music, The 1961,My 19,22:6
No Strings 1962,Mr 16,24:1
No Strings 1962,Mr 25,II,1:1
Boys From Syracuse, The 1963,Ap 16,31:1
Oklahoma! 1963,My 16,40:1
Pal Joey 1963,My 30,21:1
Boys From Syracuse, The 1963,Je 2,II,1:1
Boys From Syracuse, The 1963,N 9,14:3
King and I, The 1964,Jl 7,26:1
Do I Hear a Waltz? 1965,Mr 19,28:1
Do I Hear a Waltz? 1965,Mr 28,II,1:1
South Pacific 1965,Je 3,25:1
Carousel 1965,Ag 11,39:1
Oklahoma! 1965,D 16,62:1
Carousel 1966,D 16,56:2
By Jupiter 1967,Ja 20,28:2
Sound of Music, The 1967,Ap 27,52:1
South Pacific 1967,Je 13,56:1
King and I, The 1968,My 24,39:1
South Pacific 1968,Je 30,54:2
Oklahoma! 1969,Je 24,37:1
Oklahoma! 1969,Jl 6,II,1:1
South Pacific 1969,Jl 7,27:1
Sound of Music, The 1970,Jl 3,13:1
Two by Two 1970,N 11,37:1
Two by Two 1970,N 22,II,1:1
Rodgers, Richard (Director)
Kismet 1965,Je 23,45:1
Annie Get Your Gun 1966,Je 1,42:2
Show Boat 1966,Jl 20,48:1
West Side Story 1968,Je 25,32:1
Oklahoma! 1969,Je 24,37:1
Rodgers, Richard (Lyricist)
Simple Simon 1930,F 19,22:1
Jumbo 1935,N 18,20:2
Show Is On, The 1937,S 20,18:4
Two Weeks With Pay 1940,Je 25,28:3
It's All Yours 1942,Mr 26,26:2
By Jupiter 1942,Je 4,22:1
Happy Birthday 1946,N 1,31:2
No Strings 1962,Mr 16,24:1
No Strings 1962,Mr 25,II,1:1
No Strings 1964,Ja 1,17:1
Rodgers, Richard (Miscellaneous)
Kismet 1965,Je 23,45:1
Avanti 1968,F 1,29:1
Rodgers, Richard (Original Author)
Babes in Arms 1937,Ap 15,18:4
I Married an Angel 1938,My 12,26:2
On Your Toes 1954,O 12,24:4
Rodgers, Richard (Playwright)
Evergreen 1930,O 14,31:2
On Your Toes 1936,Ap 13,14:4
By Jupiter 1942,Je 4,22:1
Allegro 1947,N 2,II,1:1
Babes in Arms 1951,Mr 10,7:3
King and I, The 1951,Mr 30,26:2
Carousel 1957,S 12,38:2
South Pacific 1961,Ap 27,26:3
Pal Joey 1961,Je 1,32:1
Oklahoma! 1963,F 28,8:2
King and I, The 1963,Je 13,30:2
By Jupiter 1967,Ja 20,28:2
Me and Juliet 1970,My 15,42:1
Rodgers, Richard (Producer)
By Jupiter 1942,Je 4,22:1
By Jupiter 1942,Ag 30,VIII,1:1
Connecticut Yankee, A 1943,N 18,30:2
Connecticut Yankee, A 1943,N 21,II,1:1
I Remember Mama 1944,O 20,16:2
I Remember Mama 1944,O 21,II,1:1
Annie Get Your Gun 1946,Mr 29,18:2
Annie Get Your Gun 1946,My 17,14:2
Happy Birthday 1946,N 1,31:2
John Loves Mary 1947,F 5,29:2
Show Boat 1948,S 9,33:2
Show Boat 1948,S 19,II,1:1
South Pacific 1949,Ap 8,30:2
Happy Time, The 1950,Ja 25,24:1
Burning Bright 1950,O 19,40:2
King and I, The 1951,Mr 30,26:2
Me and Juliet 1953,My 29,17:1
Oklahoma! 1953,S 1,19:1
Flower Drum Song 1958,D 2,44:1
Sound of Music, The 1959,N 17,40:2
No Strings 1962,Mr 16,24:1

Rodgers, Richard (Producer)—Cont
Do I Hear a Waltz? 1965,Mr 19,28:1
Two by Two 1970,N 11,37:1
Rodgers, Richard C (Composer)
Fly With Me 1920,Mr 25,11:4
Poor Little Ritz Girl 1920,Jl 29,7:1
You'll Never Know 1921,Ap 21,9:2
Jazz a La Carte 1922,Je 3,8:3
Rodgers, Richard C (Musical Director)
Fly With Me 1920,Mr 25,11:4
Rodgers, Richard D (Composer)
Half Moon Inn 1925,Mr 10,14:1
Rodgers, Shev
Man of La Mancha 1965,N 23,52:1
Get Thee to Canterbury 1969,Ja 26,74:1
War Games 1969,Ap 18,37:1
Rodgers, Stephen
Decision 1944,F 3,23:2
Rodgers, Thomas B 3d
What a Relief 1935,D 14,10:6
Rodien, Jean
Waiting for Godot 1968,Ap 23,38:1
Rodin, Gustav
Blaue Hemd von Ithaka, Das 1931,Mr 15,IX,2:4
Rodin, Roberta
Moon Walk 1970,N 27,52:1
Rodis, James
Processional 1937,O 14,23:1
Rodman, David J (Musical Director)
Touch 1970,N 9,52:1
Rodman, Howard (Playwright)
Moby Dick 1955,Ap 26,25:3
Rodman, Lewis
At Your Service 1937,Ag 17,23:1
Rodman, Maia (Translator)
At Sea 1962,Ap 24,33:1
Rodner, Brian
Ticket-of-Leave Man, The 1961,D 23,15:1
Rodney, Jean
Women, The 1936,D 28,13:1
Stop-Over 1938,Ja 12,16:5
All the Living 1938,Mr 25,14:4
Rodney, Jean (Miscellaneous)
Swingin' the Dream 1939,N 30,24:2
Rodney, John
Grand Tour, The 1951,D 11,45:2
Flight Into Egypt 1952,Mr 19,33:2
Rodney, Pauline
Patience 1935,S 3,24:4
Rodrigues, Alfred (Choreographer)
Joyce Grenfell Requests the Pleasure
  1955,O 11,48:1
Love for Love 1967,O 21,17:1
Love for Love 1967,O 30,59:1
Rodriguez, Burt
But Never Jam Today 1969,Ap 24,40:1
Rodriguez, Charlie J
Lovely Ladies, Kind Gentlemen 1970,D 29,38:1
Rodriguez, Domingo A (Costume Designer)
Delightful Season, A 1960,S 29,30:1
Donogoo 1961,Ja 19,25:3
Worm in Horseradish, A 1961,Mr 14,32:3
Gideon 1961,N 10,38:1
Passion of Josef D, The 1964,F 12,29:1
Abraham Cochrane 1964,F 18,26:1
Falstaff 1966,Je 20,27:1
After the Rain 1967,O 10,54:1
Moon for the Misbegotten, A 1968,Je 13,55:2
Lovers and Other Strangers 1968,S 19,63:1
Sudden and Accidental Re-education of Horse
  Johnson, The 1968,D 19,63:1
Trumpets of the Lord 1969,Ap 30,37:1
Rodriguez, Domingo A (Lighting Director)
Pilgrim's Progress 1962,Mr 21,36:2
Rodriguez, Domingo A (Scenic Designer)
Pilgrim's Progress 1962,Mr 21,36:2
Rodriguez, Emilio
Difunta, La 1969,N 2,86:5
Rodriguez, George Luis
White Cargo 1960,D 30,12:1
Rodriguez, Isabel
Last Waltz, The 1921,My 11,20:3
Rodriguez, Josef
Our Town 1968,D 14,62:1
Rodriguez, Nivia
And the Wind Blows 1959,Ap 29,28:1
Rodriguez, Ozzie
Marie Vison, La 1970,Jl 15,29:1
Rodriguez, Percy
Toys in the Attic 1960,F 26,23:2
Blues for Mister Charlie 1964,Ap 24,24:1
Blues for Mister Charlie 1964,My 3,II,1:1
Rodriguez, Roberto
Song for a Certain Midnight 1959,S 17,49:1
Rodriguez, William V
Hit the Deck 1960,Je 24,32:1
Rodriquez, Lucy
Horse Eats Hat 1936,S 28,14:2
Rodway, Norman
Poker Session, The 1964,F 12,30:4
Troilus and Cressida 1968,Ag 9,30:5
Silence 1969,Jl 13,II,8:1
Troilus and Cressida 1969,Jl 31,26:1
Richard III 1970,Ag 3,37:3

Roe, Bart
Young Man's Fancy, A 1947,Ap 30,33:2
Roe, Bertha
Change Your Luck 1930,Je 7,10:2
Roe, Patricia
Bohemian Girl, The 1933,Jl 28,18:5
Jubilee 1935,O 14,20:1
200 Were Chosen 1936,N 21,21:1
Night Circus, The 1958,D 3,44:1
Distant Bell, A 1960,Ja 14,29:1
Tiger Rag, The 1961,F 17,20:2
Night of the Iguana, The 1961,D 29,10:1
Collection, The 1962,N 27,44:1
After the Fall 1964,Ja 24,18:1
But for Whom Charlie 1964,Mr 13,42:2
Tartuffe 1965,Ja 15,23:1
Bananas 1968,D 5,60:1
Rooming House, The 1970,Ja 23,25:1
Transfers 1970,F 1,II,7:2
Roe, Patsy
County Chairman, The 1936,My 26,26:5
Stork Mad 1936,O 1,28:4
Roe, Raymond
House of Remsen 1934,Ap 3,26:4
Jubilee 1935,O 14,20:1
Seen But Not Heard 1936,Jl 22,23:4
Seen But Not Heard 1936,S 18,19:2
Our Town 1938,F 5,18:3
Life With Father 1939,N 9,26:2
Little Dark Horse 1941,N 17,14:4
All in Favor 1942,Ja 21,20:6
Roe, Sandy
Henry IV, Part I 1946,My 7,25:2
Roe, Walter C
Moroni 1936,Ag 19,19:1
Roebling, F W
It's the Valet 1933,D 15,25:4
Roebling, Paul
Homeward Look, The 1954,Je 4,26:2
Dark Is Light Enough, The 1955,F 24,20:1
Lark, The 1955,N 18,20:1
Lark, The 1955,N 27,II,1:1
Desert Incident, A 1959,Mr 25,40:1
Romeo and Juliet 1961,F 24,24:1
This Side of Paradise 1962,F 22,19:6
Milk Train Doesn't Stop Here Anymore, The 1962,Jl 12,19:8
Four Seasons, The 1968,Mr 15,32:1
Roeburt, John (Playwright)
International Playgirls '64 1964,My 22,40:2
Roecker, Edward
Allah Be Praised! 1944,Ap 21,14:2
Vie Parisienne, La 1945,Ja 13,14:5
Roeder, Joseph
Recapture 1930,Ja 19,VIII,2:6
Recapture 1930,Ja 30,16:4
Well of Romance, The 1930,N 8,21:2
Child of Manhattan 1932,Mr 2,15:1
Romeo and Juliet 1935,D 24,10:2
Fields Beyond, The 1936,Mr 7,11:2
Othello 1937,Ja 7,16:4
Whiteoaks 1938,Mr 24,20:2
Roeder, Ralph
Medea 1920,Mr 23,12:2
Heartbreak House 1920,N 11,11:1
Trial of Joan of Arc, The 1921,Mr 28,8:2
Iphigenia in Aulis 1921,Ap 8,18:2
Electra 1927,My 4,28:3
Electra 1927,My 15,VIII,1:1
John 1927,N 5,16:4
Electra 1927,D 2,20:6
Wild Duck, The 1928,N 19,17:1
Hedda Gabler 1929,F 4,20:3
Lonely Way, The 1931,F 22,VIII,4:1
Getting Married 1931,Mr 31,25:5
Roeder, Ralph (Playwright)
Purity 1930,D 7,IX,1:6
Roeder, Ralph (Translator)
Purity 1930,D 26,18:2
Roediger, Rolf
Poupees de Paris, Les 1962,D 13,8:2
Poupees de Paris, Les 1964,My 16,11:1
Roediger, V M (Scenic Designer)
Master of the Revels 1935,Ag 14,16:2
Roediger, Virginia
Saint's Parade 1930,N 1,23:4
Roehrick, William
Romeo and Juliet 1935,D 24,10:2
Saint Joan 1936,Mr 10,27:4
Hamlet 1936,O 9,30:2
At the Theatre 1937,Ag 4,14:1
Our Town 1938,F 5,18:3
Roeland, Augusta
Victoria Regina 1938,O 4,20:2
Heart of a City 1942,F 13,24:6
Embezzled Heaven 1944,N 1,20:2
Open House 1947,Je 4,33:4
Heiress, The 1947,S 30,22:2
Fifth Season, The 1953,Ja 24,13:2
Roelker, Frederick E C
Coriolanus 1927,Je 18,8:3
Roeloff, Wilma
Prince Charming 1930,O 14,31:1

Pardon My English 1933,Ja 21,11:4
Jubilee 1935,O 14,20:1
Roemele, John
Jubilee 1935,O 14,20:1
County Chairman, The 1936,My 26,26:5
Roemer, Kate P
Where's Your Husband? 1927,Ja 15,10:3
Speakeasy 1927,S 27,30:1
Cold in Sables 1931,D 24,20:7
Yoshe Kalb 1933,D 29,27:2
Roen
Chushingura; Treasury of Loyal Retainers, The 1969,S 11,53:1
Momiji-Gari 1969,S 18,64:1
Roen, George
Betty Behave 1927,Mr 9,28:4
Roene, Emeline (Costume Designer)
Angel Street 1948,Ja 23,26:6
Roerick, N
Tonight at 8:30; Hands Across the Sea 1948,F 24,20:4
Roerick, William
Royal Family, The 1940,Ag 13,15:3
Land Is Bright, The 1941,O 29,26:2
Flowers of Virtue, The 1942,F 6,22:2
Autumn Hill 1942,Ap 14,17:4
Magnificent Yankee, The 1946,Ja 23,21:2
Great Campaign, The 1947,Ap 1,33:2
Tonight at 8:30; Ways and Means 1948,F 21,8:2
Tonight at 8:30; Family Album 1948,F 21,8:2
Tonight at 8:30; Shadow Play 1948,F 24,20:4
Madam Will You Walk 1953,D 2,2:4
Burning Glass, The 1954,Mr 5,15:2
Right Honourable Gentleman, The 1965,O 20,50:2
Elizabeth the Queen 1966,N 4,30:1
Come Slowly, Eden 1966,D 7,56:1
Persecution and Assassination of Marat As Performed by the Inmates of the Asylum of Charenton Under the Direction of the Marquis de Sade, The 1967,Ja 4,34:1
We Bombed in New Haven 1968,O 17,51:1
We Bombed in New Haven 1968,O 27,II,1:1
Passage to E M Forster, A 1970,O 28,62:1
Roerick, William (Director)
Passage to E M Forster, A 1970,O 28,62:1
Roerick, William (Playwright)
Happiest Years, The 1949,Ap 26,29:8
Passage to E M Forster, A 1970,O 28,62:1
Roerm, Ned (Composer)
Cock-A-Doodle-Doo 1949,F 28,16:5
Roessler, Karl (Playwright)
Fledermaus, Die 1929,Jl 14,IX,2:1
Millions 1930,O 3,30:4
Verfl--- Geld, Das 1931,N 15,VIII,4:1
Roeusseau, L
Gala Night 1930,F 26,22:4
Roff, Joseph (Rev) (Composer)
Lady of Mexico 1962,O 20,13:2
Roffey, Jack (Playwright)
Hostile Witness 1966,F 18,26:1
Roffman, Frederick
Ruddigore 1965,Ag 27,16:1
Roffman, Richard (Producer)
Five Queens 1963,S 11,46:2
Roffman, Richard H (Miscellaneous)
Dance of Death, The 1960,S 14,51:1
Dream Play 1960,N 23,22:1
Feast of Panthers 1961,Mr 21,32:1
Roffman, Rose
Happy Hypocrite, The 1968,S 6,38:1
Tea Party 1968,O 16,40:1
Rogan, H McKenzie
Josef Suss 1930,Ja 21,28:5
Rogan, Peter
Kitchen, The 1966,Je 14,50:1
Rogan, Peter (Miscellaneous)
Picture of Dorian Gray, The 1963,Ag 29,37:4
Rogati, Marius
Mister Malatesta 1923,F 27,14:2
Vagabond King, The 1925,S 22,23:3
White Eagle, The 1927,D 27,24:4
Big Pond, The 1928,Ag 22,25:1
Strictly Dishonorable 1929,S 19,37:1
Roger, Arthur
Countess Maritza 1926,S 20,21:1
Roger-Reid, Paul
Warning, The-A Theme for Linda 1969,Ap 27,92:1
Rogers, Alex
Taboo 1922,Ap 5,22:1
Rogers, Alex ((Playwright)
My Magnolia 1926,Jl 13,19:2
Rogers, Alex (Director)
My Magnolia 1926,Jl 13,19:2
Rogers, Alex (Lyricist)
Go-Go 1923,Mr 13,19:4
Sharlee 1923,N 23,20:1
My Magnolia 1926,Jl 13,19:2
Rogers, Allan
Vaudeville (Palace) 1924,Ja 15,17:3
Song of the Flame 1925,D 11,26:4
Song of the Flame 1925,D 20,VII,4:1
Vaudeville (Palace) 1928,Ja 17,23:3
White Lilacs 1928,S 11,31:2

Rogers, Allan—Cont
Wonderful Night, A; Fledermaus, Die 1929,N 1,23:3
Rogers, Ann
Seven Mirrors 1945,O 26,17:2
Rogers, Anne
My Fair Lady 1957,Mr 26,33:4
Rogers, Arthur Jensen
Macbeth 1968,N 30,49:3
Rogers, Bob (Costume Designer)
Walk Down Mah Street! 1968,Je 13,54:1
Rogers, Bob (Scenic Designer)
Walk Down Mah Street! 1968,Je 13,54:1
Rogers, Brooks
Mister Roberts 1962,O 12,27:2
Rogers, Bruce
Damaged Goods 1937,My 18,27:2
Rogers, Buddy
Hot-Cha! 1932,F 21,VIII,2:1
Hot-Cha! 1932,Mr 9,17:3
Rogers, C Mitch (Lighting Director)
Slow Dance on the Killing Ground 1970,My 14,43:1
Rogers, Charles
Fedora 1924,Ja 24,14:2
Rogers, Charles R (Miscellaneous)
Lady Comes Across, The 1942,Ja 10,10:2
Rogers, Charlotte
Petrified Forest, The 1943,N 2,30:6
Rogers, Cynthia
Houseparty 1929,S 10,26:5
Garrick Gaieties 1930,Je 5,29:2
Modern Virgin, A 1931,My 21,33:4
Money in the Air 1932,Mr 8,19:3
Tiara, The 1932,D 12,18:3
Mary of Scotland 1933,N 28,28:3
By Your Leave 1934,Ja 25,15:3
Lost Horizons 1934,O 16,31:2
Little Shot 1935,Ja 18,28:4
Double Dummy 1936,N 12,30:1
Fireman's Flame 1937,O 11,26:2
Dance Me a Song 1950,Ja 21,10:5
Ah, Wilderness! 1953,F 7,10:6
Rogers, David
As You Like It 1945,Jl 4,10:4
Rogers, David (Composer)
Ziegfeld Follies 1957,Mr 2,19:2
New Faces of 1962 1962,F 2,25:1
Fun City 1968,Mr 7,53:2
Rogers, David (Director)
Fun City 1968,Mr 7,53:2
Rogers, David (Lyricist)
Ziegfeld Follies 1957,Mr 2,19:2
New Faces of 1962 1962,F 2,25:1
Rogers, David (Playwright)
Ziegfeld Follies 1957,Mr 2,19:2
Fun City 1968,Mr 7,53:2
Rogers, Davie
Faith of Our Fathers 1950,Ag 6,72:2
Rogers, Don Loring
Hats Off to Ice 1944,Je 23,15:2
Rogers, Doug
Copper and Brass 1957,O 18,19:2
Follies of 1910, The 1960,Ja 15,37:3
Rogers, Doug (Miscellaneous)
How to Be a Jewish Mother 1967,D 29,18:1
Rogers, Earl (Miscellaneous)
Ziegfeld Follies 1957,Mr 2,19:2
Rogers, Edmund H (Playwright)
This Way Out 1929,Ap 28,24:4
Rogers, Elaine
Utopia, Limited; Flowers of Progress, The 1957,F 27,21:1
Gondoliers, The 1957,My 29,34:2
Rogers, Emmett
Growing Pains 1933,N 24,24:2
Master of the Revels 1935,Ag 14,16:2
Strip Girl 1935,O 21,22:6
Alice Takat 1936,F 11,19:2
Richard II 1937,S 16,28:2
Hamlet 1938,O 13,28:1
Henry IV, Part I 1939,Ja 31,17:2
Hamlet 1939,D 5,35:2
Richard II 1940,Ap 2,31:2
Jeannie 1940,N 13,29:2
Papa Is All 1942,Ja 7,22:2
Papa Is All 1942,Ja 18,IX,1:1
Hamlet 1945,D 14,25:2
Hamlet 1946,Je 4,18:4
Linden Tree, The 1948,Mr 3,28:2
Shop at Sly Corner, The 1949,Ja 19,35:2
Idiot's Delight 1951,My 24,46:3
Rogers, Emmett (Miscellaneous)
Richard II 1951,Ja 25,21:2
Dial 'M' for Murder 1952,O 30,41:2
No Time for Sergeants 1955,O 21,32:2
Rogers, Emmett (Producer)
Tall Story 1959,Ja 30,33:2
Riot Act, The 1963,Mr 9,5:2
Rogers, Eric (Miscellaneous)
Oliver 1963,Ja 8,5:5
Rogers, Ferne
Red Pepper 1922,My 30,8:3

ogers, Florence
Priest in the Cellar, The 1969,F 19,39:1
ogers, Fred
Wildcat, The 1921,N 28,16:2
ogers, George
Virgin of Bethulia, The 1925,F 24,17:2
Sex 1926,Ap 27,22:4
Half a Widow 1927,S 13,37:3
Veils 1928,Mr 14,28:5
Tin Pan Alley 1928,N 2,29:1
Hot Money 1931,N 9,22:2
Yeomen of the Guard, The 1935,Jl 30,16:4
Gondoliers, The 1935,Ag 6,20:5
Trial by Jury 1935,Ag 13,20:6
ogers, George S Jr (Miscellaneous)
Life Begins in '40 1940,Ap 5,24:2
ogers, Gerald
Light of the World, The 1920,Ja 7,17:1
Unwritten Chapter, The 1920,O 12,18:1
Lancelot and Elaine 1921,S 13,12:1
Squaw Man, The 1921,D 27,10:3
Trelawney of the 'Wells' 1927,F 1,24:4
Silver Box, The 1928,Ja 18,23:1
Bellamy Trial, The 1928,Ag 20,21:1
Rogers, Gil
Ivory Branch, The 1956,My 25,27:1
Great White Hope, The 1967,D 14,58:1
Rose 1969,O 29,30:1
Memory Bank, The 1970,Ja 12,24:3
Rogers, Ginger
Top Speed 1929,D 26,20:1
Girl Crazy 1930,O 15,27:1
Girl Crazy 1930,D 28,VIII,1:1
ANTA Album 1951,My 7,22:7
Love and Let Love 1951,O 20,11:2
Hello, Dolly! 1965,Ag 10,17:2
Mame 1969,F 22,35:5
Rogers, Gladys
Garrick Gaieties 1926,My 11,25:2
Rogers, Grace
Peg o' My Heart 1948,Ag 25,29:2
Rogers, Harriet
Live Like Pigs 1965,Je 8,48:2
Rogers, Harry
Hold Your Horses 1933,S 26,26:4
Rogers, Hilda
My Magnolia 1926,Jl 13,19:2
How Come Lawd? 1937,O 1,18:5
Rogers, Howard (Director)
Luana 1930,S 18,28:1
Rogers, Howard (Lyricist)
Red Pepper 1922,My 30,8:3
Rogers, Howard (Playwright)
Century Revue and the Midnight Rounders, The
1920,Jl 13,9:1
Luana 1930,S 18,28:1
Rogers, Irma
Gondoliers, The 1967,O 29,83:1
Ballad for a Firing Squad 1968,D 12,64:2
Rogers, J
Under the Gaslight 1929,Ap 3,27:1
Rogers, Jaime
My Fair Lady 1963,S 2,19:4
Golden Boy 1964,O 21,56:1
Golden Boy 1964,N 1,II,1:1
Annie Get Your Gun 1966,Je 1,42:2
Rogers, Jaime (Choreographer)
Education of H*Y*M*A*N K*A*P*L*A*N, The
1968,Ap 5,57:1
Rogers, James K
Life Is Like That 1930,D 23,24:3
Rogers, Jane
Rose in the Wilderness 1949,Ja 5,21:2
Rogers, Jean
Carousel 1949,Ja 26,28:2
Rogers, Jeanne
Gay Divorce 1960,Ap 4,37:1
Rogers, Jerry
Laugh Parade, The 1931,N 3,31:2
Rogers, Jessica
Doll's House, A 1937,D 28,28:6
Rogers, Jo Jean
Louisiana Purchase 1940,My 29,19:2
Rogers, John
Blood and Sand 1921,S 21,16:2
Dolly Jordan 1922,O 4,26:1
Fashions for Men 1922,D 6,22:1
Patience 1924,D 30,15:1
Finta Giardiniera, La 1927,Ja 19,20:5
Spider, The 1927,Mr 23,29:1
Pickwick 1927,S 6,35:2
Prunella 1929,Ap 10,23:3
Rogers, Justin
Shadow Years, The 1957,Ja 9,26:2
Rogers, Kieran
Child of the Morning 1958,Ap 22,40:2
Rogers, Lora
Indiscretion 1929,Mr 5,28:1
Ladies' Money 1934,N 2,26:6
Battleship Gertie 1935,Ja 19,9:2
Sweet River 1936,O 29,30:2
Rogers, Lynn
Shoemaker's Prodigious Wife, The 1949,Je 15,38:2

Rogers, Maggie (Miscellaneous)
Mrs Warren's Profession 1963,Ap 25,39:1
Rogers, Marilyn
Sound of Music, The 1959,N 17,40:2
Fiddler on the Roof 1964,S 23,56:2
Rogers, Mary
On to Fortune 1935,F 5,22:2
Ten Minute Alibi 1935,Je 11,24:4
Remember the Day 1935,Jl 9,24:3
Stag at Bay, The 1935,Jl 30,17:1
Crime Marches on 1935,O 24,19:1
Three Wise Fools 1936,Ja 14,25:2
Feather in the Breeze 1936,Jl 14,22:2
Rogers, Mason T
On the Level 1937,Mr 26,24:4
Rogers, Merrill (Playwright)
Her First Affaire 1927,Ag 23,29:2
Thousand Summers, A 1932,My 25,23:4
Rogers, Mickie
Old Bucks and New Wings 1962,N 6,39:4
Rogers, Mildred
Chocolate Soldier, The 1921,D 13,24:2
Rogers, Muriel C
Pressing Business 1930,N 18,28:5
Rogers, Natalie
Bead-Tangle 1970,Jl 16,38:1
Rogers, Pat (Miscellaneous)
Major Barbara 1951,F 24,10:2
Rogers, Paul
Macbeth 1954,S 5,II,3:7
Henry IV 1955,My 15,II,1:1
Macbeth 1956,My 24,27:1
Romeo and Juliet 1956,Je 13,45:8
Richard II 1956,Jl 4,15:1
Romeo and Juliet 1956,S 19,34:6
Richard II 1956,O 24,44:1
Romeo and Juliet 1956,O 25,41:1
Macbeth 1956,O 30,42:2
Troilus and Cressida 1956,D 27,21:1
Elder Statesman, The 1958,Ag 26,35:1
Elder Statesman, The 1958,Ag 31,II,3:1
Macbeth 1961,Ja 10,28:1
Macbeth 1961,F 1,5:7
Photo Finish 1963,F 14,5:2
Homecoming, The 1967,Ja 6,29:1
Here's Where I Belong 1968,Mr 4,32:1
Happy Apple, The 1970,Jl 26,49:2
Rogers, Phyllis
Louisiana Purchase 1940,My 29,19:2
Rogers, R C (Playwright)
It's Only Natural 1922,Ap 21,13:2
Rogers, Radio
New Hellzapoppin, The 1939,D 12,36:4
Rogers, Renee
Best House in Naples, The 1956,O 27,16:2
Rogers, Rick (Composer)
Girl From Nantucket, The 1945,N 9,17:2
Rogers, Robert (Musical Director)
Pimpernel! 1964,Ja 7,26:6
Rogers, Rock
Idiot's Delight 1951,My 24,46:3
Rogers, Rod
Girl of the Golden West, The 1957,N 6,44:1
Shakuntala 1959,S 10,41:2
Rogers, Ronald
Livin' the Life 1957,Ap 29,20:1
Rules of the Game, The 1960,D 20,44:1
Rogers, Ross R
March March, The 1966,N 15,51:4
Rogers, Roy
Vaudeville (Palace) 1929,Ap 8,32:7
Topaze 1947,D 29,21:5
Rogers, Shoshanna
Get Thee to Canterbury 1969,Ja 26,74:1
Rogers, Stanley
Vaudeville (Palace) 1924,Ap 1,18:1
Hassard Short's Ritz Revue 1924,S 18,19:1
Vaudeville (Palace) 1927,O 25,33:2
Night in Venice, A 1929,My 22,30:2
Cherry Lane Follies, The 1930,Je 30,22:4
Rogers, Suzanne
Coco 1969,D 19,66:1
Rogers, Timmie
Blue Holiday 1945,My 22,13:3
Rogers, Will
Midnight Frolic 1921,N 19,11:3
Ziegfeld Follies 1922,Je 6,18:2
Ziegfeld Follies 1923,Ja 30,12:2
Follies 1924,Je 19,25:7
Ziegfeld Follies 1924,Je 25,26:1
Follies 1925,Mr 11,19:2
Lambs Gambol 1925,Ap 27,15:1
Follies 1925,Jl 7,24:3
Untitled-One Man Show 1926,Ap 12,18:1
Vaudeville (Palace) 1927,Mr 29,22:6
Three Cheers 1928,O 7,IX,2:3
Three Cheers 1928,O 16,28:1
Three Cheers 1928,O 21,IX,1:1
Ah, Wilderness! 1934,My 1,26:3
Rogers, Will (Playwright)
Follies 1924,Je 19,25:7
Ziegfeld Follies 1924,Je 25,26:1

Rogers, Will Jr
Ah, Wilderness! 1954,Ag 21,20:4
Rogers, William
Clinging Vine, The 1922,D 25,20:2
Patience 1935,S 3,24:4
Rogers and Allen
Vaudeville (Palace) 1924,Ja 22,15:6
Rogers and Wynne
Vaudeville (Palace) 1929,S 16,30:4
Rogerson, Budd
All for Love 1949,Ja 24,16:5
Roget, Raphael
King's Standards, The 1958,F 14,19:1
Rogge, Florence (Choreographer)
Virginia 1937,S 3,13:2
Roggenkamp, Eddie
Tall Kentuckian, The 1953,Je 17,30:1
Roggers, Henriette
Sujet de Roman, Un 1923,Ja 14,VII,1:1
Rogier, Frank
Medium, The 1947,My 2,28:2
Telephone, The 1947,My 2,28:2
Telephone, The 1947,My 11,II,1:1
As You Like It 1950,Ja 27,27:2
Mikado, The 1952,O 21,35:2
Pirates of Penzance, The 1952,O 28,36:4
Trial by Jury 1952,N 4,32:2
H M S Pinafore 1952,N 4,32:2
Iolanthe 1952,N 11,26:3
Rognan, Lorraine
Vaudeville (Palace) 1949,My 20,32:4
Rognan, Roy
Taming of the Shrew, The 1935,O 1,27:3
Laughter Over Broadway 1939,Ja 16,10:3
Rognoni, Raymond (Director)
Malade Imaginaire, Le 1926,N 14,VIII,2:1
Rogoff, Lena
Mikado, The 1939,Mr 11,15:6
Rogoff, Martin
Tempest, The 1959,D 28,19:2
Rogow, David
Devil's Game, A 1959,N 9,35:6
Fifth Commandment, The 1965,N 15,48:4
Prince Reuvaini 1967,N 19,83:1
Hut a Yid a Landele 1968,O 19,28:1
Melody Lingers On, The 1969,N 17,55:1
Rogow, Lee (Playwright)
Two's Company 1952,D 16,43:5
Rohan, Robert
Comedy of Errors, The 1967,Je 15,58:4
Rohe, Alice (Translator)
Say It With Flowers 1926,D 6,29:1
Roher, David
Dybbuk, The 1954,O 27,33:6
Rohman, Richard (Playwright)
Power of the Press 1936,Ap 6,19:2
Tell My Story 1939,Mr 16,26:6
Rohmann, Paul
Cure for Matrimony 1939,O 26,26:3
Steel 1939,D 20,30:2
Rohmer, Sax (Lyricist)
Nightingale, The 1947,Jl 17,16:4
Rohmier, Blanche
Spring Production 1944,My 20,12:4
Rohr, Morris
Mikado, The 1942,F 4,22:2
Pirates of Penzance, The 1942,F 18,22:2
Iolanthe 1942,F 24,26:4
Gondoliers, The 1942,Mr 4,22:3
Roio, Jerry (Costume Designer)
Macbeth 1969,N 21,51:1
Roiten, Vilma
If You Get It, Do You Want It? 1938,D 1,28:2
Roiton, Elma
Woman of Bronze, The 1927,Je 16,25:4
Rojo, Jerry (Miscellaneous)
Macbeth 1969,N 21,51:1
Rojo, Jerry (Scenic Designer)
Dionysus in 69 1968,Je 7,35:3
Dionysus in 69 1968,N 19,52:1
Sourball 1969,Ag 6,29:2
Commune 1970,D 21,50:1
Roker, Roxie
Ododo 1970,N 25,26:1
Rokusaburo, Onoe
Kanjincho; Subscription List, The 1960,Je 3,26:1
Rokuya
Kagami-Jishi; Mirror Lion Dance, The
1969,S 11,53:1
Rola, Joven E
Eve of St Mark, The 1942,O 8,30:2
Roland, Dawn
Stars in Your Eyes 1939,F 10,18:2
Roland, Frederick
White Cargo 1923,N 6,22:2
R U R 1930,F 18,28:1
Marco Millions 1930,Mr 4,24:4
Volpone 1930,Mr 11,24:5
One, Two, Three! 1930,S 30,24:2
Overture 1930,N 25,31:2
Overture 1930,D 8,26:4
Jewel Robbery 1932,Ja 14,17:2
We Are No Longer Children 1932,Ap 1,17:2

Roland, Frederick—Cont
I Was Waiting for You 1933,N 14,23:3
Twelfth Night 1934,Jl 17,24:5
Sailors of Cattaro 1934,D 11,28:4
Roland, Howard
Student Prince, The 1943,Je 9,16:2
Roland, Janet
Up in Central Park 1947,My 20,29:2
Roland, Kathleen
Amphitryon 38 1937,Je 24,30:2
Amphitryon 38 1937,N 2,32:2
God Strikes Back 1943,F 27,11:2
Design For A Stained Glass Window
  1950,Ja 24,26:2
Saint Joan 1950,Mr 4,10:6
Dark of the Moon 1958,F 27,22:2
Overruled 1959,My 27,32:2
Buoyant Billions 1959,My 27,32:2
Getting Married 1959,Je 5,18:2
Overruled 1959,Ag 21,13:1
Shewing-Up of Blanco Posnet, The 1959,S 19,26:7
Hostage, The 1961,D 13,55:4
Andorra 1963,F 11,5:5
Month in the Country, A 1963,My 29,39:2
Roland, Norman
Vie Parisienne, La 1941,N 6,20:3
Mr Strauss Goes to Boston 1945,S 7,20:2
Caesar and Cleopatra 1949,D 22,28:2
Darkness at Noon 1951,Ja 15,13:4
Saint Joan 1951,O 5,23:2
Richard III 1953,Jl 15,22:2
All's Well That Ends Well 1953,Jl 16,18:2
Richard III 1953,D 10,65:2
Dark of the Moon 1958,F 27,22:2
Harlequinade 1959,F 14,15:1
Electra 1959,F 14,15:1
Buoyant Billions 1959,My 27,32:2
Getting Married 1959,Je 5,18:2
Overruled 1959,Ag 21,13:1
Passion, Poison and Petrifaction 1959,Ag 21,13:1
Dark Lady of the Sonnets, The 1959,Ag 21,13:1
Shewing-Up of Blanco Posnet, The 1959,S 19,26:7
Coggerers, The 1960,Mr 23,33:1
Time to Go 1960,Mr 23,33:1
Fig Leaf in Her Bonnet, A 1961,Je 15,50:1
Hostage, The 1961,D 13,55:4
Roland, Norman (Director)
Dark of the Moon 1958,F 27,22:2
Roland, Norman (Producer)
Buoyant Billions 1959,My 27,32:2
Overruled 1959,My 27,32:2
Getting Married 1959,Je 5,18:2
Dark Lady of the Sonnets, The 1959,Ag 21,13:1
Overruled 1959,Ag 21,13:1
Passion, Poison and Petrifaction 1959,Ag 21,13:1
Shewing-Up of Blanco Posnet, The 1959,S 19,26:7
Roland, Robert
Deburau 1920,D 24,14:3
Roland, Ruth
Vaudeville (Palace) 1931,Ap 13,17:2
Roland, Samuel
Kith and Kin 1930,My 14,31:1
Till the Day I Die 1935,Mr 27,24:5
Waiting for Lefty 1935,Mr 27,24:5
Body Beautiful, The 1935,N 1,24:3
Tapestry in Gray 1935,D 28,10:2
Roland, Steve
Come on Strong 1962,O 5,29:1
110 in the Shade 1963,O 25,37:1
I Had a Ball 1964,D 16,50:1
Roland Petit Corps de Ballet, The
Zizi 1964,N 23,51:1
Rolanda, Rose
Irving Berlin's Music Box Revue 1921,S 23,18:2
Round the Town 1924,My 22,14:3
Garrick Gaieties 1925,My 18,12:2
Garrick Gaieties 1925,Je 28,VIII,1:1
See Naples and Die 1929,S 27,30:4
Rolando
Mexicana 1939,Ap 22,14:4
Mexicana 1939,My 7,X,3:1
Tidbits of 1946 1946,Jl 9,17:2
Rolbein, Theodore (Producer)
Times Have Changed 1935,F 26,16:1
Rolf, Ernst
Rolf's Revue 1930,Jl 13,VIII,2:1
Rolf, Frederick
Saint Joan 1951,O 5,23:2
Strong Are Lonely, The 1953,S 30,38:3
Immortal Husband, The 1955,F 15,32:2
Dark Lady of the Sonnets, The 1956,F 21,38:1
Dark Lady of the Sonnets, The 1956,Mr 4,II,1:1
Taming of the Shrew, The 1956,Ag 6,20:1
Time Remembered 1957,N 13,41:2
Smokeweaver's Daughter, The 1959,Ap 15,30:1
Between Two Thieves 1960,F 12,23:1
Cherry Orchard, The 1960,Je 4,17:2
Hedda Gabler 1960,N 10,61:1
Egg, The 1962,Ja 9,23:2
Call It Virtue 1963,Mr 28,8:2
Play With a Tiger 1964,D 31,14:2
Rolf, Frederick (Director)
Titus Andronicus 1956,D 3,40:2
Hogan's Goat 1965,N 12,56:1

Rolf, Tutta
Barber Had Two Sons, The 1943,F 2,22:2
Rolfe, B A and His Orchestra
Vaudeville (Palace) 1927,Ag 2,19:1
Vaudeville (Palace) 1927,N 8,33:3
Vaudeville (Palace) 1929,N 18,22:4
Rolfe, Frederick (Original Author)
Hadrian VII 1968,Jl 4,14:1
Hadrian VII 1969,Ja 19,II,1:2
Hadrian VII 1969,S 20,20:1
Rolfe, Frederick (Playwright)
Hadrian VII 1969,Ja 9,22:1
Rolfe, Mary
Dance Night 1938,O 15,20:5
Ringside Seat 1938,N 23,24:5
Life and Death of an American 1939,My 20,11:2
See My Lawyer 1939,S 28,29:1
Eve of St Mark, The 1942,O 8,30:2
Wallflower 1944,Ja 27,14:2
Live Life Again 1945,O 1,14:7
Rolfe, Thomas A
Mrs Jimmie Thompson 1920,Mr 30,9:1
We Girls 1921,N 10,26:3
Rolfsen, Katie
Autumn Manoeuvers 1938,N 27,IX,3:6
Rolin, Katherine
Tom Sawyer 1931,D 26,15:3
Jayhawker 1934,N 6,34:2
Roll, Eddie
By the Beautiful Sea 1954,Ap 9,20:1
West Side Story 1957,S 27,14:4
Sophie 1963,Ap 16,32:1
Man of La Mancha 1965,N 23,52:1
Roll, Philip
Boutique Fantasque, La 1929,D 28,10:6
Rolla, Tom (Director)
Applause 1970,Mr 31,35:1
Rollan, Henri
Napoleon Unique 1936,N 13,27:3
Cardinal of Spain, The 1960,D 22,16:6
Rollan, Maria
El Alcalde De Zalamea 1953,N 23,32:5
Rolland, Adele
Ladies' Night 1920,Ag 10,10:1
Getting Gertie's Garter 1921,Ag 2,16:2
Partners Again 1922,My 2,22:2
Rolland, Augustus
In the Night Watch 1921,Ja 31,10:1
Rolland, Elsa
Outside the Door 1949,Mr 2,33:2
Rolland, Grace (Musical Director)
Girl From Wyoming, The 1938,O 31,12:1
Rolland, Gustave
Anna Ascends 1920,S 23,14:1
Romance 1921,Mr 1,18:2
Beware of Dogs 1921,O 4,10:1
Hail and Farewell 1923,F 20,12:1
Moon-Flower, The 1924,F 26,15:1
Blue Bandanna, The 1924,Je 24,18:4
Green Hat, The 1925,S 16,23:2
Chinese O'Neill 1929,My 23,27:1
Recapture 1930,Ja 19,VIII,2:6
Recapture 1930,Ja 30,16:4
Hotel Universe 1930,Ap 15,29:1
Dancing Partner 1930,Jl 27,VIII,2:3
Dancing Partner 1930,Ag 6,24:2
Wonder Bar, The 1931,Mr 18,23:4
Rolland, Kathleen
Harlequinade 1959,F 14,15:1
Rolland, Liza
Shunned 1960,D 21,39:1
Rolland, Romain (Playwright)
Jean Christophe 1924,D 28,VII,1:1
Wolves 1924,D 28,VII,1:1
Wolves 1924,D 31,9:4
Jeu de l'Amour et de la Mort, Le
  1928,F 19,VIII,4:4
Fourteenth of July, The 1928,Mr 11,VIII,1:3
Game of Love and Death, The 1929,N 26,28:4
Wolves 1932,Ja 7,26:3
Rolland, William (Producer)
Dybbuk, The 1924,Ja 29,17:7
Rolle, Esther
Happy Ending 1965,N 16,56:1
Day of Absence 1965,N 16,56:1
Summer of the Seventeenth Doll 1968,F 21,59:1
Summer of the Seventeenth Doll 1968,Mr 3,II,3:1
God Is a (Guess What?) 1968,D 18,56:1
God Is a (Guess What?) 1968,D 29,II,1:1
String 1969,Ap 2,37:1
Contribution 1969,Ap 2,37:1
Contribution 1969,Ap 13,II,1:1
Song of the Lusitanian Bogey, The 1969,My 13,41:1
Man Better Man 1969,F 3,22:1
Day of Absence 1970,Mr 18,39:1
Akokawe 1970,Je 5,21:1
Roller (Professor) (Scenic Designer)
Blue Beard 1929,Jl 7,VIII,2:1
Rolley, Joseph
Frivolities of 1920 1920,Ja 9,22:2
Rollin, Betty
Country Wife, The 1957,Je 27,22:1

Rolling, Hubert (Director)
Romeo and Juliet 1962,Ap 3,42:1
Rollins, Ann
Night Is Black Bottles, The 1962,D 5,56:1
Scarlet Lullaby 1968,Mr 11,48:1
Rollins, Greg
Mother Sings 1935,N 13,24:1
Rollins, Jack (Miscellaneous)
Don't Drink the Water 1966,N 18,37:1
Play It Again, Sam 1969,F 13,52:3
Rollins, Leighton (Director)
Birds, The 1935,Jl 21,II,3:2
Castle Irish 1938,Mr 21,20:1
Rollins, Leighton (Playwright)
Hippolytus 1948,N 22,25:5
Rollins, Pierce (Composer)
Political Party, A 1963,S 27,17:5
Rollins, Pierce (Lyricist)
Political Party, A 1963,S 27,17:5
Rollins, Pierce (Playwright)
Political Party, A 1963,S 27,17:5
Rollins, Rowena
Priorities of 1942 1942,Mr 13,23:2
Rollins, Ruth
Tangerine 1921,Ag 10,8:2
Rollins, Sherwood (Composer)
Assorted Nuts 1940,Ap 7,I,44:6
One on the House 1941,Mr 30,I,47:3
Rollins, Sherwood (Lyricist)
Assorted Nuts 1940,Ap 7,I,44:6
Rollison, Richard
Unto Such Glory 1937,My 7,28:2
Rollo, Billy
Wanhope Building, The 1947,F 11,36:5
Rollo, Esta
Lady Dedlock 1929,Ja 1,61:2
Rollo, Walter (Composer)
Springtime of Youth 1922,O 27,15:1
Rolls, Billy
Earl Carroll's Vanities 1930,Jl 2,28:3
Rolly, Jeanne
Mediterranee 1926,N 7,VIII,2:7
Rolontz, Lela (Miscellaneous)
Elliott Murphy's Aquashow 1956,Je 20,26:2
Rolph, Alice
Miss Julie 1956,F 22,23:2
Rolston, William
Young Madame Conti 1937,Ap 1,18:4
Roltner, Robert
Silver Swan, The 1929,N 28,34:5
Devil's Host, The 1931,N 20,27:2
Roma, Catherine
Playing With Love 1929,F 27,16:4
Romain, Georges
Cape Smoke 1925,F 17,19:1
Just Beyond 1925,D 2,22:4
Gentlemen Prefer Blondes 1926,S 29,23:1
These Few Ashes 1928,O 31,28:1
Romain, Georges (Director)
Chinese O'Neill 1929,My 23,27:1
Romain, Ray
Smiling Faces 1932,Ag 31,12:3
Romain, Tom
Smiling Faces 1932,Ag 31,12:3
Romaine, Anthony
Honor Code, The 1931,My 19,25:3
Romaine, Homer
Vaudeville (Palace) 1926,Mr 30,20:4
Romaine, Rilla
S S Glencairn 1924,N 4,31:4
Romaine, Worthington
Betty, Be Good 1920,My 5,14:2
Last Warning, The 1922,O 25,23:1
Easy Mark, The 1924,Ag 27,14:2
Easy Terms 1925,S 23,23:2
Wooden Kimono 1926,D 28,16:2
Penal Law 2010 1930,Ap 19,14:2
On the Make 1932,My 24,23:2
Strip Girl 1935,O 21,22:6
Romains, Jules (Playwright)
Dictator, The 1926,O 5,26:4
Dictateur, Le 1926,N 7,VIII,2:7
Jean le Mauranc 1927,Ja 2,VII,2:1
Doctor Knock 1928,F 24,15:2
Dictator, The 1928,Ap 29,IX,1:3
Volpone 1928,D 9,X,2:7
Untitled-Play 1929,Mr 3,VIII,4:8
Donogoo 1930,N 16,VIII,2:6
Musse 1930,D 14,IX,2:7
Roi Masque, Le 1932,Ja 17,VIII,1:6
Dr Knock 1936,Jl 14,22:1
Knock 1937,N 17,26:3
Volpone 1957,F 5,27:2
Donogoo 1961,Ja 19,25:3
Romak, Serge
King Oedipus 1933,Ja 16,12:4
Roman, Andrew
In Circles 1968,Je 28,36:1
Roman, Barry
Circle of Chalk, The 1950,D 2,8:3
Roman, Bernard
Burning Bush, The 1949,D 17,15:5

Roman, Bob
Decameron, The 1961,Ap 13,32:1
Roman, Greg
Caine Mutiny Court-Martial, The 1954,Ja 21,27:2
Brouhaha 1960,Ap 27,31:2
Roman, Jane
Out of This World 1955,O 13,35:2
Roman, Joseph
Twilight Walk 1951,S 25,25:4
Child of the Morning 1951,N 17,9:7
Roman, Lawrence (Playwright)
Under the Yum-Yum Tree 1960,N 17,45:1
Under the Yum-Yum Tree 1964,My 29,18:1
P S I Love You 1964,N 20,40:1
Roman, Mark
Child of the Morning 1958,Ap 22,40:2
Roman, Martin (Composer)
41 in a Sack 1960,Mr 26,15:2
Roman, Murray
Night Life 1962,O 24,44:1
Roman, Myron (Miscellaneous)
Judy Garland's New Variety Show 1956,S 27,43:2
Roman, Myron (Musical Director)
Safari! 1955,My 12,32:6
Roman, Paul Reid
Fly Blackbird 1962,F 6,26:2
On a Clear Day You Can See Forever
1965,O 18,44:1
Roman, Pete
Poppa Is Home 1961,D 20,37:1
Roman, Robert
Love's Labour's Lost 1965,Je 16,46:1
Romann, Fidel
All in Love 1961,N 11,15:2
Romann, Susan (Miscellaneous)
Promenade 1969,Je 5,56:1
Romano, Amelia
Plumes in the Dust 1936,N 7,14:2
Plumes in the Dust 1936,N 15,XI,1:1
Marching Song 1937,F 18,18:2
Red Harvest 1937,Mr 31,29:2
Big Blow 1938,O 3,11:2
Mayor of Zalamea, The 1946,Ja 28,15:5
Land's End 1946,D 12,37:5
Romano, Armando (Playwright)
Abisso 1920,O 10,VI,1:8
Romano, Charles
Romance 1921,Mr 1,18:2
Will Shakespeare 1923,Ja 2,14:1
Mountebank, The 1923,My 8,22:2
School for Scandal, The 1925,O 24,19:1
Doctor's Dilemma, The 1927,N 22,33:1
Marco Millions 1928,Ja 10,28:2
Bellamy Trial, The 1928,Ag 20,21:1
Berkeley Square 1929,N 5,32:4
School for Scandal, The 1931,N 11,26:4
Clear All Wires! 1932,S 15,19:1
Clear All Wires! 1932,S 25,IX,1:1
Dark Tower, The 1933,N 27,20:3
Richard of Bordeaux 1934,F 15,16:2
While Parents Sleep 1934,Je 5,28:2
Great Waltz, The 1934,S 24,14:4
Country Wife, The 1935,Jl 2,24:2
Romano, Jane
Out of This World 1955,N 10,44:2
Body Beautiful, The 1958,Ja 24,15:2
Red Eye of Love 1961,Je 13,28:1
Three Times Three; Not Enough Rope
1962,Mr 2,24:1
Romano, Peggy
Virginia 1937,S 3,13:2
Trojan Incident 1938,Ap 22,15:2
Bees and the Flowers, The 1946,S 27,19:3
For Heaven's Sake Mother 1948,N 17,33:4
Villa of Madame Vidac, The 1959,O 1,40:1
Romano, Tom (Lyricist)
Russell Patterson's Sketch-Book 1960,F 8,35:1
Romanoff, Boris
Chauve-Souris; Romantic Adventure of an Italian
Ballerina and a Marquis, A 1931,O 22,27:1
Romanoff, Boris (Choreographer)
Chauve-Souris of 1943 1943,Ag 13,13:2
Romanoff, Boris (Playwright)
Chauve-Souris; Romantic Adventure of an Italian
Ballerina and a Marquis, A 1931,O 22,27:1
Romanoff, Michael
Say When 1934,N 9,24:2
Romanos, The
Ice Capades 1969,Ja 8,42:1
Romanou, Mika
Hippolytus 1968,N 20,38:3
Romanov, Boris (Choreographer)
Chauve-Souris 1925,Ja 25,VII,1:1
Romanov, Michael (Lighting Director)
Ever Since Paradise 1957,Jl 12,18:4
Sweeney Todd 1957,Ag 28,21:4
Romanowsky, Richard
Fee, Die; Fairy, The 1931,F 8,VIII,2:1
Romanski, Frank C Jr (Producer)
Bring Me a Warm Body 1962,Ap 17,29:3
Romantini, Joseph
Infinite Shoeblack, The 1930,F 18,28:1
Peter Ibbetson 1931,Ap 9,30:3

Cynara 1931,N 3,31:1
Romany, Enid
Kiss Me! 1927,Jl 22,17:1
This Thing Called Love 1928,S 18,32:7
Cafe de Danse 1929,Ja 16,22:2
In The Best of Families 1931,F 3,29:1
Late One Evening 1933,Ja 10,27:3
Masks and Faces 1933,Mr 20,18:5
Romanyi, Czara
Maitresse de Roi 1926,D 1,24:1
So Was Napoleon 1930,Ja 9,22:2
Virtue's Bed 1930,Ap 16,26:5
Cafe 1930,Ag 29,11:1
Room of Dreams 1930,N 6,22:4
Marathon 1933,Ja 28,8:8
Romay, Lina
Michael Todd's Peep Show 1950,Je 29,37:2
Peep Show 1950,Jl 9,II,1:1
Romayne, Phil
Ice Capades 1955,S 15,38:1
Ice Capades 1957,S 5,33:2
Ice Capades 1960,S 1,30:1
Ice Capades 1961,Ag 31,24:4
Ice Capades 1962,Ag 30,34:1
Ice Capades 1963,Ag 29,37:2
Ice Capades 1964,Ag 27,27:2
Ice Capades 1966,Je 2,50:2
Ice Capades 1967,Je 2,33:1
Ice Capades 1969,Ja 8,42:1
Romayne and Steele
Ice Capades 1958,S 4,33:2
Ice Capades 1959,S 4,12:1
Romberg, Hugo W (Producer)
Juno and the Paycock 1926,Mr 16,22:1
Red Dust 1928,Ja 3,29:2
Romberg, Sigmund (Choreographer)
Annie Dear 1924,N 5,25:3
Romberg, Sigmund (Composer)
Poor Little Ritz Girl 1920,Jl 29,7:1
Love Birds 1921,Mr 16,12:1
Blossom Time 1921,S 30,10:1
Bombo 1921,O 7,20:2
Blossom Time 1921,O 9,VI,1:1
Blushing Bride, The 1922,F 7,12:1
Rose of Stamboul, The 1922,Mr 8,11:2
Springtime of Youth 1922,O 27,15:1
Innocent Eyes 1924,My 21,22:2
Marjorie 1924,Ag 12,12:2
Passing Show of 1924, The 1924,S 4,13:4
Annie 1924,O 12,VIII,2:1
Artists and Models 1924,O 16,33:3
Student Prince, The 1924,D 3,25:3
Louie the 14th 1925,Mr 4,17:1
Princess Flavia 1925,N 3,34:3
Desert Song, The 1926,D 1,24:2
Cherry Blossoms 1927,Mr 29,22:3
My Golden Girl 1927,S 11,VIII,1:3
My Maryland 1927,S 13,37:2
My Princess 1927,O 7,24:2
Love Call, The 1927,O 25,33:1
Rosalie 1927,D 18,IX,2:3
Rosalie 1928,Ja 11,26:3
New Moon, The 1928,S 20,33:1
Nina Rosa 1929,O 27,IX,2:1
Nina Rosa 1930,My 31,19:3
Nina Rosa 1930,S 22,22:5
East Wind 1931,O 28,19:1
East Wind 1931,D 11,VIII,4:3
Alt Heidelberg; Student Prince, The
1932,N 20,IX,3:3
Melody 1933,F 15,17:4
Rose of France 1933,O 29,II,3:3
May Wine 1935,N 23,23:1
May Wine 1935,D 6,30:3
Student Prince, The 1936,Jl 12,II,5:2
Blossom Time 1936,Jl 29,23:1
My Maryland 1936,Ag 12,14:2
Blossom Time 1936,Ag 30,II,5:8
Forbidden Melody 1936,O 13,30:3
Forbidden Melody 1936,N 3,33:1
Maytime 1937,Jl 6,23:4
Student Prince, The 1937,Jl 28,15:1
Nina Rosa 1937,Ag 26,24:3
Blossom Time 1938,D 27,12:2
Sunny River 1941,D 5,28:2
Student Prince, The 1943,Je 9,16:2
Blossom Time 1943,S 6,21:2
Up in Central Park 1945,Ja 29,17:2
Desert Song, The 1946,Ja 9,20:2
Up in Central Park 1947,My 20,29:2
My Romance 1948,O 20,38:5
Girl in Pink Tights, The 1954,Mr 6,13:2
New Moon, The; Desert Song, The 1955,Jl 1,13:1
Rosalie 1957,Je 26,28:2
Romberg, Sigmund (Musical Director)
Student Prince, The 1931,Ja 30,18:1
Blossom Time 1931,Mr 5,32:1
Romberg, Sigmund (Playwright)
New Moon, The 1942,Ag 19,14:2
New Moon, The 1944,My 18,16:2
Student Prince, The 1961,Jl 14,14:1
Rombola, Ed
White Devil, The 1965,D 7,56:1

Sunset 1966,My 13,34:1
Front Page, The 1968,O 20,85:5
Indians 1969,O 14,51:1
Rome, Harold (Composer)
Pins and Needles 1936,Je 15,24:6
Pins and Needles 1937,N 29,18:6
Pins and Needles 1938,Ja 23,XI,1:1
Sing Out the News 1938,S 26,12:5
Sing Out the News 1938,O 2,IX,1:1
Pins and Needles 1939,Ap 21,26:2
Streets of Paris, The 1939,Je 20,25:2
New Pins and Needles 1939,N 21,19:2
Lunchtime Follies, The 1942,Je 23,22:3
Star and Garter 1942,Je 25,26:2
Let Freedom Sing 1942,O 6,18:2
Call Me Mister 1946,Ap 19,26:2
Call Me Mister 1946,Ap 28,II,1:1
Alive and Kicking 1950,Ja 18,25:5
Michael Todd's Peep Show 1950,Je 29,37:2
Bless You All 1950,D 15,42:2
Wish You Were Here 1952,Je 26,26:6
Wish You Were Here 1952,Ag 31,II,1:1
Fanny 1954,N 5,16:1
Fanny 1954,N 21,II,1:1
Romanoff and Juliet 1957,O 11,24:1
Destry Rides Again 1959,Ap 24,24:1
Destry Rides Again 1959,My 3,II,1:1
I Can Get It for You Wholesale 1962,Mr 23,29:1
Zulu and the Zayda, The 1965,N 11,59:1
Scarlett 1970,Ja 3,19:1
Rome, Harold (Lyricist)
Pins and Needles 1936,Je 15,24:6
Pins and Needles 1937,N 29,18:6
Pins and Needles 1938,Ja 23,XI,1:1
Sing Out the News 1938,S 26,12:5
New Pins and Needles 1939,N 21,19:2
Lunchtime Follies, The 1942,Je 23,22:3
Star and Garter 1942,Je 25,26:2
Let Freedom Sing 1942,O 6,18:2
Call Me Mister 1946,Ap 19,26:2
Call Me Mister 1946,Ap 28,II,1:1
Alive and Kicking 1950,Ja 18,25:5
Michael Todd's Peep Show 1950,Je 29,37:2
Wish You Were Here 1952,Je 26,26:6
Fanny 1954,N 5,16:1
Destry Rides Again 1959,Ap 24,24:1
I Can Get It for You Wholesale 1962,Mr 23,29:1
Zulu and the Zayda, The 1965,N 11,59:1
Grosse Valise, La 1965,D 15,52:1
Scarlett 1970,Ja 3,19:1
Rome, Harold (Miscellaneous)
Ziegfeld Follies 1943,Ap 2,16:2
Rome, Harold (Playwright)
Pins and Needles 1937,N 29,18:6
Sing Out the News 1938,O 2,IX,1:1
Pins and Needles 1939,Ap 21,26:2
Rome, Joe
Vaudeville (Palace) 1923,Ja 30,12:2
Rome, Tina
Red White and Blue 1950,O 8,64:5
Rome and Dunn
Earl Carroll's Vanities 1924,S 11,23:6
Romeo, Angelo
Will Morrissey's Newcomers 1923,Ag 9,16:2
Romeo, Carmelina
'Il Tesoro D'Isacco; Treasure of Isaac, The
1928,Ja 26,17:1
Romeo, Gene
Beclch 1968,D 17,59:1
Romeo, Vincent
Sudden End of Anne Cinquefoil, The
1961,Ja 11,25:2
Bertha 1962,F 12,27:1
Emperor, The 1963,Ap 17,30:1
Romer, Ernst (Musical Director)
Blaue Hemd von Ithaka, Das 1931,Mr 15,IX,2:4
Romer, Jess
Gang War 1928,Ag 21,27:2
Romer, Leila
Clean Beds 1939,My 26,21:2
Romer, Rurik (Miscellaneous)
Uncle Vanya 1960,F 13,13:4
Romer, Tomi
King John 1956,Je 28,33:5
Measure for Measure 1956,Je 29,16:1
Taming of the Shrew, The 1956,Ag 6,20:1
Once in a Lifetime 1964,Ja 29,20:1
Romero, Alex (Choreographer)
Happy Hunting 1956,D 7,30:1
Romero, Cesar
Street Singer, The 1929,S 18,35:2
Dinner at Eight 1932,O 24,18:2
Romero, Elias (Lighting Director)
House of Bernarda Alba, The 1963,N 25,23:2
Romero, Emilo (Playwright)
Decent People Frighten Me 1964,Ja 26,82:3
Romero, Lili
Cabin in the Sky 1940,N 10,IX,2:1
Romero, Ramon (Original Author)
Swan Song 1946,My 16,29:2
Romerowsky, Blanche
Shylock and His Daughter 1947,S 30,22:2

Romiche, Henry
Mamba's Daughters 1953,Mr 21,12:6
Romig, Valerie
Stephen D 1967,S 25,58:1
Romilli, G (Composer)
Fioretta 1929,F 6,30:3
Romilli, G (Lyricist)
Fioretta 1929,F 6,30:3
Romilly, Rita
Genius and the Crowd 1920,S 7,20:1
Crooked Square, The 1923,S 11,10:2
Man's Man, A 1925,O 14,31:2
Unchastened Woman, The 1926,F 17,12:1
Easter 1926,Mr 19,24:3
Living Corpse, The 1929,D 7,19:1
Romley, Virginia
Minstrel Boy, The 1948,O 15,28:2
Romoff
Chauve-Souris 1929,Ja 23,20:2
Romoff, Colin (Composer)
Ziegfeld Follies 1957,Mr 2,19:2
Romoff, Colin (Lyricist)
Ziegfeld Follies 1957,Mr 2,19:2
Romoff, Colin (Miscellaneous)
Say Darling 1958,Ap 4,17:1
Kwamina 1961,O 24,42:1
Romoff, Colin (Musical Director)
Say Darling 1959,F 26,38:2
Kwamina 1961,O 24,42:1
Fade Out--Fade In 1964,My 27,45:1
Romoff, Wood
Moby Dick 1955,Ap 26,25:3
Henry IV, Part I 1955,S 22,34:2
She Loves Me 1963,Ap 24,39:1
Cafe Crown 1964,Ap 18,32:1
Merry Widow, The 1964,Ag 18,24:2
Romor, Ruggero
Time of the Cuckoo, The 1952,O 16,37:4
Rompel, Royal
What Big Ears! 1942,Ap 21,18:5
Lower North 1944,Ag 26,15:4
Ronan, Robert
Tragical Historie of Doctor Faustus, The 1964,O 6,34:2
Colombe 1965,F 24,33:1
Troilus and Cressida 1965,Ag 13,17:1
All's Well That Ends Well 1966,Je 17,39:1
Richard III 1966,Ag 11,26:1
Shoemaker's Holiday, The 1967,Mr 3,25:1
Memorandum, The 1968,My 6,55:1
Henry IV, Part II 1968,Jl 2,33:1
Henry IV, Part II 1968,Jl 14,II,1:1
Invitation to a Beheading 1969,Mr 18,36:1
Twelfth Night 1969,Ag 14,29:2
Trelawny of the 'Wells' 1970,O 12,48:1
Trelawny of the 'Wells' 1970,O 25,II,16:1
Ronan, Robert (Director)
Trelawny of the 'Wells' 1970,O 12,48:1
Trelawny of the 'Wells' 1970,O 25,II,16:1
Ronconi, Luca (Director)
Orlando Furioso 1970,N 5,59:1
Ronconi, Luca (Playwright)
Orlando Furioso 1970,N 27,46:1
Rondeau, Charles
I Gotta Get Out 1947,S 26,27:2
Rondell, Al
Her Week-End 1936,Mr 20,28:5
Rondell, Gloria
New Faces of 1936 1936,My 20,24:5
Rondelle, Adelaide
Honest Liars 1926,Jl 20,17:2
Bottom of the Cup, The 1927,F 1,24:2
Katy Did 1927,My 10,24:3
Speakeasy 1927,S 27,30:1
Rondinone, Vincent
Honor Code, The 1931,My 19,25:3
Rondiri, Constantina
Hippolytus 1968,N 20,38:3
Rondiris, Dimitrios (Director)
Electra 1952,N 20,38:2
Electra 1961,S 20,23:4
Eumenides 1961,S 27,32:4
Choephori 1961,S 27,32:4
Medea 1964,S 1,31:1
Electra 1964,S 8,33:1
Iphigenia in Aulis 1968,N 13,40:1
Hippolytus 1968,N 20,38:3
Rondo, George (Miscellaneous)
In the Bar of a Tokyo Hotel 1969,My 12,54:1
Last of the Red Hot Lovers 1969,D 29,37:1
Gingerbread Lady, The 1970,D 14,58:3
Ronell, Ann (Composer)
Count Me In 1942,O 9,24:2
Crucible, The 1953,Ja 23,15:2
Ronell, Ann (Lyricist)
Count Me In 1942,O 9,24:2
Ronet
Affaires Son les Affaires, Les 1924,Mr 11,17:1
Avare, L'; Miser, The 1924,Mr 12,17:3
Monsieur Brotonneau 1924,Mr 13,14:1
Blanchette 1924,Mr 19,19:4
Roney, Edmund
Lower Depths, The 1956,O 3,29:2

Aria Da Capo 1958,My 21,40:1
Roney, Edmund (Miscellaneous)
Aria Da Capo 1958,My 21,40:1
Guests of the Nation 1958,My 21,40:1
Ronson, Adele
Sam Abramovitch 1927,Ja 20,20:5
Legend of Leonora, The 1927,Mr 30,22:4
Dorian Gray 1928,My 22,18:4
Great Scott! 1929,S 3,25:1
Gold Braid 1930,My 14,31:2
Happy Ending 1936,Jl 15,14:3
Ronson, Herb
Anatomist, The 1957,F 27,21:5
Ronstadt, Louisa
Deep River 1926,O 5,26:2
Rood, Marcia
Oh, Johnny: or, Jonny Spielt Auf 1970,Mr 15,88:4
Roodney, Cyrel
New Hellzapoppin, The 1939,D 12,36:4
Rook, Edith
Her Family Tree 1920,D 28,9:2
Rook, Willie
Lemon Sky 1970,My 18,40:1
Rooke, Arnold
Wandering Jew, The 1927,F 2,22:4
Rooke, Irene
Old English 1924,N 9,VIII,2:3
Rooks, Lois
Athenian Touch, The 1964,Ja 15,25:4
Rooney, Ed
Vaudeville (Palace) 1928,N 26,31:2
Rooney, Frank
Hamlet 1945,D 14,25:2
Rooney, Gilbert
Fair Circassian, The 1921,D 7,22:3
Rooney, Jenny
Vaudeville (Palace) 1928,N 26,31:2
Rooney, Marion
Abe Lincoln in Illinois 1938,O 17,12:2
Male Animal, The 1941,Jl 9,24:6
Holiday 1941,Jl 23,15:2
Drifting Apart: or, The Fisherman's Child 1941,Ag 20,16:6
Rooney, Mickey
Midsummer Night's Dream, A 1934,S 19,15:1
Rooney, Pat
Love Birds 1921,Mr 16,12:1
Friars Club Frolic 1921,Je 13,16:2
Vaudeville (Palace) 1923,F 13,25:1
Lambs Gambol 1925,Ag 27,15:1
Vaudeville (Palace) 1926,Mr 30,20:4
Vaudeville (Palace) 1926,Je 29,21:3
Vaudeville (Palace) 1928,My 15,17:1
Vaudeville (Palace) 1929,O 7,22:4
Vaudeville (Palace) 1932,Ap 18,19:5
Friars Club Frolic 1933,My 15,16:4
Friars Club Frolic 1933,My 15,16:4
Take a Bow 1944,Je 16,15:3
Guys and Dolls 1950,N 25,11:2
Guys and Dolls 1950,D 3,II,1:1
ANTA Album 1951,My 7,22:7
Guys and Dolls 1951,O 7,II,1:1
Rooney, Susanne
Little Red Riding Hood 1948,Ja 12,15:3
Rooney, W Edgar
Who Was That Lady I Saw You With? 1958,Mr 4,33:2
Rooney, Wallace
Pepper Mill 1937,Ja 6,19:4
Audition of the Apprentice Theatre 1939,Je 2,26:2
White Steed, The 1939,Ag 16,21:3
Blind Alley 1939,Ag 23,18:8
Girl of the Golden West, The 1957,N 6,44:1
Who Was That Lady I Saw You With? 1958,Mr 4,33:2
Whoop-Up 1958,D 23,2:7
Investigation, The 1966,O 5,40:1
Spofford 1967,D 15,54:3
Rooney, Wallace (Director)
Sarah Simple 1940,N 18,22:5
Rooney, William
Mundy Scheme, The 1969,D 12,75:1
Roony, Jeannette
Stone for Danny Fisher, A 1954,O 22,24:2
Hamlet of Stepney Green 1958,N 14,21:1
Roop, Reno
Medea 1965,N 29,46:1
Roope, Fay
One Heluva Night 1924,Je 5,18:1
What Price Glory 1924,S 6,14:3
Biggest Thief in Town 1949,Mr 31,31:2
Madwoman of Chaillot, The 1950,Je 14,41:2
Roos, Audrey (Playwright)
Speaking of Murder 1956,D 20,37:1
Roos, Casper
Show Boat 1956,Je 22,16:1
Merry Widow, The 1957,Ap 11,36:6
Show Boat 1957,Je 28,30:2
Walking Happy 1966,N 28,47:1
Here's Where I Belong 1968,Mr 4,32:1
Minnie's Boys 1970,Mr 27,27:1
Roos, Delmar
Pilgrim's Progress 1962,Mr 21,36:2

Roos, Delmar (Costume Designer)
Magistrate, The 1959,My 14,30:6
Roos, Gene
Minnie's Boys 1970,Mr 27,27:1
Roos, Joanna
Harlequinade 1921,My 11,20:3
Idle Inn, The 1921,D 21,26:2
Green Ring, The 1922,Ap 5,22:1
This Fine-Pretty World 1923,D 27,11:1
Loggerheads 1925,F 10,21:1
Makropoulos Secret, The 1926,Ja 22,12:4
Strange Prince, The 1926,D 8,24:2
Stigma 1927,F 11,19:1
Lovers and Enemies 1927,S 21,27:1
Grand Street Follies, The 1928,Je 3,VIII,1:1
Veneer 1929,N 13,24:5
Veneer 1929,N 24,X,1:1
Uncle Vanya 1930,Ap 16,26:5
Uncle Vanya 1930,My 4,XI,1:1
Torch Song 1930,Ag 3,VIII,3:4
Schoolgirl 1930,N 2,VIII,3:5
Schoolgirl 1930,N 21,31:1
Lonely Way, The 1931,F 22,VIII,4:1
Washington Heights 1931,S 30,23:4
Little Women 1931,D 8,36:2
Life Begins; Birth 1932,Mr 20,VIII,2:4
Life Begins 1932,Mr 29,23:2
Picnic 1934,My 3,15:2
Tight Britches 1934,S 12,26:2
Panic 1935,Mr 16,18:4
Remember the Day 1935,Jl 9,24:3
Stag at Bay, The 1935,Jl 30,17:1
Little Inn, The 1935,Ag 20,25:1
Rain 1935,Ag 27,23:4
Black Widow 1936,F 13,24:3
Daughters of Atreus 1936,O 15,33:1
Inconstant Moon, The 1937,Ag 18,15:2
Trojan Women, The 1941,Ap 9,32:5
Lottie Dundass 1941,Ag 22,19:5
War President 1944,Ap 25,17:3
Joan of Lorraine 1946,N 19,40:2
Maya 1953,Je 10,35:1
School for Scandal, The 1953,Je 24,29:2
Orpheus Descending 1957,Mr 22,28:1
Orpheus Descending 1957,Mr 31,II,1:1
Peer Gynt 1960,Ja 13,21:1
School for Scandal, The 1962,Mr 19,36:1
Seagull, The 1962,Mr 22,42:1
Tavern, The 1962,Ap 5,29:1
Right You Are (If You Think You Are) 1964,Mr 5,37:1
Tavern, The 1964,Mr 6,39:2
Impromptu at Versailles 1964,Mr 10,43:1
Lower Depths, The 1964,Mr 31,30:1
Man and Superman 1964,D 7,45:2
War and Peace 1965,Ja 12,32:1
All's Well That Ends Well 1966,Je 17,39:1
Roos, William (Original Author)
As the Girls Go 1948,N 15,21:2
Roos, William (Playwright)
Triple Play 1937,Ag 24,24:4
Life of Reilly, The 1942,Ap 30,13:2
January Thaw 1946,F 5,18:2
Michael Todd's Peep Show 1950,Je 29,37:2
Courtin' Time 1951,Je 14,30:2
Speaking of Murder 1956,D 20,37:1
Roose, Olwen
Civilian Clothes 1923,Jl 26,13:2
Roose-Evans, James (Director)
Two Character Play, The 1967,D 13,54:5
Dreams; Deaths and Entrances 1970,Je 3,51:2
Roosevelt, John
Lid's Off, The 1936,Ap 4,11:6
Roosevelt, Theodore 3d
Hades, the Ladies 1934,Mr 29,25:3
Roosin, Adele
Yellow Jacket, The 1923,Ap 20,20:3
Root, George F
Nantucket Follies 1927,Jl 30,13:2
Root, Jack
What Do We Know 1927,D 24,8:1
Root, John (Lighting Director)
Mrs Gibsons' Boys 1949,My 5,35:2
Not for Children 1951,F 14,35:2
Root, John (Scenic Designer)
Nude in Washington Square, The 1934,Ag 7,20:1
Piper Paid 1934,D 26,19:1
Cross Ruff 1935,F 20,23:3
Ceiling Zero 1935,Ap 11,26:2
Return to Folly 1935,Jl 23,24:3
With All My Heart 1935,Jl 30,17:1
Thy People 1935,Ag 13,20:3
If This Be Treason 1935,S 24,28:2
Substitute for Murder 1935,O 23,18:6
Crime Marches on 1935,O 24,19:1
There's Wisdom in Women 1935,O 31,17:1
Hell Freezes Over 1935,D 30,14:2
White Christmas 1936,Jl 7,22:2
Seen But Not Heard 1936,S 18,19:2
So Proudly We Hail 1936,S 23,28:4
Now You've Done It 1937,Mr 6,10:4
Sun Kissed 1937,Mr 11,20:2
Chalked Out 1937,Mr 26,24:2

Root, John (Scenic Designer)—Cont

Red Harvest 1937,Mr 31,29:2
Angel Island 1937,O 21,26:2
One Thing After Another 1937,D 29,17:2
Greatest Show on Earth, The 1938,Ja 6,22:2
All That Glitters 1938,Ja 20,18:2
Kiss the Boys Goodbye 1938,S 29,30:2
Run Sheep Run 1938,N 4,26:2
Brown Danube, The 1939,My 18,30:4
Pastoral 1939,N 2,26:2
Sea Dogs 1939,N 7,30:3
Ring Two 1939,N 23,38:2
Lady in Waiting 1940,Mr 28,19:1
Out From Under 1940,My 6,13:2
George Washington Slept Here 1940,O 19,20:3
Glamour Preferred 1940,N 16,13:2
Cuckoos on the Hearth 1941,S 17,26:2
Jason 1942,Ja 22,12:2
Cat Screams, The 1942,Je 17,26:5
Janie 1942,S 11,24:2
Nine Girls 1943,Ja 14,26:2
Counterattack 1943,F 4,27:2
Kiss and Tell 1943,Mr 18,22:1
Get Away Old Man 1943,N 25,40:2
Pillar to Post 1943,D 11,11:2
Doctors Disagree 1943,D 29,15:2
Highland Fling, A 1944,Ap 29,13:2
Snafu 1944,O 26,19:5
Harvey 1944,N 2,23:2
Boy Who Lived Twice, A 1945,S 12,31:2
It Takes Two 1947,F 4,33:4
Tenting Tonight 1947,Ap 3,32:2
Mrs Gibsons' Boys 1949,My 5,35:2
Love Me Long 1949,N 8,34:5
Mr Barry's Etchings 1950,F 1,26:2
Not for Children 1951,F 14,35:2
Root, Juan
Stop Press 1939,Mr 20,13:2
Root, Lin S (Mrs) (Playwright)
One Good Year 1935,N 28,38:3
Root, Lula
Mikado, The 1924,Jl 29,9:1
Root, Lynn
Chippies 1929,My 30,23:3
City Haul 1929,D 31,14:4
Sing High, Sing Low 1931,N 13,26:4
Blessed Event 1932,F 13,23:2
Stork Mad 1936,O 1,28:4
Root, Lynn (Original Author)
Cabin in the Sky 1940,O 26,19:2
Root, Lynn (Playwright)
Milky Way, The 1934,My 9,23:2
Milky Way, The 1934,My 20,IX,1:1
Stork Mad 1936,O 1,28:4
Cabin in the Sky 1940,N 3,IX,1:1
Milky Way, The 1943,Je 10,17:2
Cabin in the Sky 1964,Ja 22,32:1
Root, Phebe
Moon Over Mulberry Street 1935,S 5,24:6
Root, T E
Richelieu 1934,My 22,28:1
Rootstein, Mark
Brass Butterfly, The 1970,Ja 31,34:1
Roper, James
Firebird 1932,N 22,25:2
Roper, John
Wann und Wo 1927,D 18,IX,1:8
Roper, June
Wann und Wo 1927,D 18,IX,1:8
Ropp, Margaret
Shrike, The 1953,N 26,51:2
Roquemore, Larry
Anyone Can Whistle 1964,Ap 6,36:1
Rordam, Annie (Choreographer)
Weathercock, The 1948,Ag 6,22:3
Rordam, Annie (Costume Designer)
Weathercock, The 1948,Ag 6,22:3
Rorem, Ned (Composer)
Hippolytus 1948,N 22,25:5
Garden District; Something Unspoken
  1958,Ja 8,23:4
Garden District; Suddenly Last Summer
  1958,Ja 8,23:4
Cave at Machpelah, The 1959,Jl 1,25:1
Lady of the Camellias, The 1963,Mr 22,7:1
Color of Darkness: An Evening in the World of
  James Purdy; Encore 1963,O 1,34:1
Color of Darkness: An Evening in the World of
  James Purdy; You Reach for Your Hat
  1963,O 1,34:1
Color of Darkness: An Evening in the World of
  James Purdy; Cracks 1963,O 1,24:1
Color of Darkness: An Evening in the World of
  James Purdy; Sermon 1963,O 1,34:1
Color of Darkness: An Evening in the World of
  James Purdy; Everything Under the Sun
  1963,O 1,34:1
Color of Darkness: An Evening in the World of
  James Purdy; Don't Call Me By My Right Name
  1963,O 1,34:1
Milk Train Doesn't Stop Here Anymore, The
  1964,Ja 2,33:1
Pastry Shop, The 1970,Je 12,28:1
Young Among Themselves, The 1970,Je 12,28:1

Rorem, Ned (Musical Director)
Hippolytus 1948,N 22,25:5
Rorem, Ned (Playwright)
Young Among Themselves, The 1970,Je 12,28:1
Pastry Shop, The 1970,Je 12,28:1
Rork, Ann (Miscellaneous)
Family Way, The 1965,Ja 14,44:5
Rorke, Hayden
If Booth Had Missed 1932,F 5,24:2
Birthright 1933,N 22,22:3
Richelieu 1934,My 22,28:1
As You Like It 1937,N 1,25:2
Save Me the Waltz 1938,Mr 1,19:2
Philadelphia Story, The 1939,Mr 29,21:1
Rorke, Ina
Clair de Lune 1921,Ap 19,15:1
Six Characters in Search of an Author
  1931,Ap 16,29:2
Mad Hopes, The 1932,D 2,26:3
Henrietta the Eighth 1935,Je 25,15:4
Rorl, Carl (Producer)
Pleasure Man 1928,O 2,34:7
Rosa, Caracolillo
International Soiree 1958,Mr 13,25:1
Rosa, Carl
Peter Pan 1924,N 7,16:2
Rosa, Dennis (Director)
World of Gunter Grass, The 1966,Ap 27,38:1
Rosa, Dennis (Playwright)
World of Gunter Grass, The 1966,Ap 27,38:1
Rosa, Ledia
South Pacific 1943,D 30,11:2
Rosa, Maria
International Soiree 1958,Mr 13,25:1
Rosaire, Robert
Good Times 1920,Ag 10,10:1
Sancho Panza 1923,N 27,23:1
Rosaly, Kenneth
Does a Tiger Wear a Necktie? 1969,F 26,38:1
Rosanka, Vera
In-Laws 1960,O 17,32:4
World Is a Stage, The 1962,N 5,37:4
Rosario and Antonio
Sons o' Fun 1941,D 2,28:2
Concert Varieties 1945,Je 2,10:7
Rosato, Catherine
Enchanted, The 1958,Ap 23,41:1
Rosay, Francoise
Once Upon a Russian 1961,F 20,32:2
Aspern Papers, The 1962,F 8,26:1
Aspern Papers, The 1962,F 18,II,1:1
Rosche, Viola
Two Bouquets, The 1938,Je 1,19:2
Roscoe, Lee
Kitchen, The 1966,Je 14,50:1
Roscoe, Maxine
Straw Hat, The 1937,D 31,8:2
Rose, Anita
High Flyers 1927,Je 26,VIII,1:1
Rose, Arthur (Playwright)
Return of Sherlock Holmes 1923,O 11,23:7
Rose, Austin I
Pre-Honeymoon 1936,My 1,19:4
Rose, Belle
Steps Leading Up 1941,Ap 19,20:6
Rose, Bill (Miscellaneous)
Playroom, The 1965,D 6,49:1
Rose, Billy (Choreographer)
Harry Delmar's Revels 1927,N 29,30:2
Rose, Billy (Composer)
Crazy Quilt 1931,My 20,28:4
Rose, Billy (Director)
Crazy Quilt 1931,My 20,28:4
Rose, Billy (Lyricist)
Padlocks of 1927 1927,Jl 6,23:4
Harry Delmar's Revels 1927,N 29,30:2
Fioretta 1929,F 6,30:3
Ziegfeld Follies 1934,Ja 5,24:3
Let's Play Fair 1938,Ja 19,26:4
New Aquacade Revue, The 1940,My 13,20:5
Harold Arlen Songbook, The 1967,Mr 1,48:1
Rose, Billy (Original Author)
Let's Play Fair 1938,Ja 19,26:4
Rose, Billy (Playwright)
Ziegfeld Follies 1934,Ja 5,24:3
Rose, Billy (Producer)
Sweet and Low 1930,N 18,28:5
Crazy Quilt 1931,My 20,28:4
Great Magoo, The 1932,D 3,20:7
Jumbo 1935,N 18,20:2
Jumbo 1935,N 24,IX,1:1
Let's Play Fair 1938,Ja 19,26:4
Aquacade 1939,My 5,26:2
Aquacade 1939,My 14,XI,1:1
New Aquacade Revue, The 1940,My 13,20:5
Clash by Night 1941,D 29,20:2
Carmen Jones 1943,O 20,17:2
Carmen Jones 1943,D 3,26:2
Carmen Jones 1943,D 12,II,3:1
Carmen Jones 1943,D 19,II,9:1
Seven Lively Arts 1944,D 8,26:6
Seven Lively Arts 1944,D 17,II,3:1
Carmen Jones 1945,My 3,26:5

Rose, Billy (Producer)—Cont

Concert Varieties 1945,Je 2,10:7
Carmen Jones 1946,Ap 8,32:2
Carmen Jones 1946,Ap 14,II,1:2
Immoralist, The 1954,F 2,18:7
Immoralist, The 1954,F 9,22:1
Wall, The 1960,O 12,44:4
Rose, Carl
Melody 1933,F 15,17:4
Rose, Clifford
King Lear 1964,My 19,43:2
Comedy of Errors, The 1964,My 21,43:1
Persecution and Assassination of Marat As
  Performed by the Inmates of the Asylum of
  Charenton Under the Direction of the Marquis de
  Sade, The 1965,D 28,35:1
Silver Tassie, The 1969,S 12,35:2
Boswell's Life of Johnson 1970,S 4,19:1
Rose, David
Lulu 1958,S 30,24:1
Rose, David (Composer)
Winged Victory 1943,N 22,24:1
Winged Victory 1943,N 28,II,1:1
Red White and Blue 1950,O 8,64:5
Rose, David (Musical Director)
Winged Victory 1943,N 22,24:1
Winged Victory 1943,N 28,II,1:1
Red White and Blue 1950,O 8,64:5
Rose, Donald
War President 1944,Ap 25,17:3
Lute Song 1946,F 7,29:2
Seeds in the Wind 1948,Ap 26,27:2
Seeds in the Wind 1948,My 26,29:2
Design For A Stained Glass Window
  1950,Ja 24,26:2
Rose, Edmund
Apollo of Bellac, The 1957,Ap 10,39:1
Virtuous Island, The 1957,Ap 10,39:1
Dark of the Moon 1958,F 27,22:2
Rose, Edward
Immoral Isabella 1927,O 28,20:3
Sherlock Holmes 1928,F 21,18:4
Within the Law 1928,Mr 6,20:1
Lady for a Night, A 1928,Ap 17,26:4
Rose, Edward E (Playwright)
Rosa Machree 1922,Ja 10,15:2
Three Doors 1925,Ap 24,16:4
Rose, Emmett
Best of Burlesque 1957,S 30,27:2
Littlest Circus, The 1959,D 26,5:6
Russell Patterson's Sketch-Book 1960,F 8,35:1
Rose, F H (Playwright)
Whispering Well, The 1920,D 6,19:1
Rose, George
Henry IV, Part I 1946,My 7,25:2
Henry IV, Part II 1946,My 8,33:4
Oedipus; Critic, The 1946,My 21,19:2
Much Ado About Nothing 1959,S 18,25:2
Much Ado About Nothing 1959,S 27,II,1:1
Man for All Seasons, A 1961,N 23,51:1
Man for All Seasons, A 1961,D 3,II,1:1
Man for All Seasons, A 1962,S 23,II,1:1
Hamlet 1964,Ap 10,30:1
Slow Dance on the Killing Ground 1964,D 1,50:1
Royal Hunt of the Sun, The 1965,O 27,36:2
Royal Hunt of the Sun, The 1965,N 14,II,1:1
Walking Happy 1966,N 28,47:1
Loot 1968,Mr 19,40:2
Loot 1968,Mr 31,II,1:1
My Fair Lady 1968,Je 14,42:1
Canterbury Tales; Miller's Tale, The 1969,F 4,34:1
Canterbury Tales; Merchant's Tale, The
  1969,F 4,34:1
Canterbury Tales; Pilgrims, The 1969,F 4,34:1
Canterbury Tales 1969,F 16,II,1:1
Coco 1969,D 19,66:1
Coco 1969,D 28,II,1:1
Coco 1970,Ag 7,28:1
Rose, Harry
George White's Scandals 1921,Jl 12,14:1
O'Brien Girl, The 1921,O 4,10:2
Merry Malones, The 1927,S 27,30:2
Rose, Irving
Last Waltz, The 1921,My 11,20:3
Music Box Revue 1924,D 2,23:3
Rose, Irwin (Producer)
Fortress of Glass 1952,S 5,19:2
Rose, Isobel
Sea Shells 1935,Jl 16,24:2
News Item 1935,Ag 6,20:3
Goodbye Again 1943,N 10,28:4
Rose, Jack
Scandals 1920,Je 8,9:1
Passing Show of 1924, The 1924,S 4,13:4
Vagabond King, The 1925,S 22,23:3
Rose, Jack (Playwright)
Jimmy 1969,O 24,38:1
Rose, Jan
Heartbreak House 1959,O 19,37:1
Rose, Jane
Trojan Women, The 1938,Ja 25,24:2
Out of My House 1942,Ja 8,28:6
Playboy of Newark, The 1943,Mr 20,11:2
Time of the Cuckoo, The 1952,O 16,37:4

Rose, Jane—Cont
Wooden Dish, The 1955,O 7,20:1
Antigone 1956,Ap 3,32:2
Orpheus Descending 1957,Mr 22,28:1
Gazebo, The 1958,D 13,2:7
All's Well That Ends Well 1966,Je 17,39:1
Measure for Measure 1966,Jl 14,27:1
Richard III 1966,Ag 11,26:1
Arms and the Man 1967,Je 23,44:2
Rose, Jane (Director)
Out of My House 1942,Ja 8,28:6
Rose, Jane Phin
Texas Town 1941,Ap 30,22:3
Rose, Jennifer
Carnival! 1968,D 13,58:1
Rose, Jerry (Choreographer)
Hatfields & McCoys 1970,Je 23,34:1
Rose, Jurgen (Costume Designer)
Wozzeck 1966,Ap 6,34:1
Mitschuldigen, Die 1966,Ap 6,34:1
Ratten, Die 1966,Ap 13,36:1
Rose, Jurgen (Scenic Designer)
Mitschuldigen, Die 1966,Ap 6,34:1
Wozzeck 1966,Ap 6,34:1
Ratten, Die 1966,Ap 13,36:1
Rose, L Arthur (Playwright)
Twenty to One 1935,N 13,24:3
Rose, Leo (Miscellaneous)
New Moon, The 1942,Ag 19,14:2
Rose, Martin
Wasp, The 1923,Mr 28,14:3
Rose, Maximilian
Vaudeville (Hippodrome) 1926,My 4,31:2
Rose, Michael (Producer)
Abie's Irish Rose 1954,N 19,19:1
Rose, Mimi
Moral Fabric 1932,N 22,25:3
Rose, Mr and His Friends (Composer)
Sweet and Low 1930,N 18,28:5
Rose, Mr and His Friends (Lyricist)
Sweet and Low 1930,N 18,28:5
Rose, Norman
Emperor's New Clothes, The 1941,D 27,15:5
Richard III 1943,Mr 27,8:3
Land of Fame 1943,S 22,31:5
Fifth Season, The 1953,Ja 24,13:2
Deadfall 1955,O 28,20:1
Lovers 1956,My 11,23:1
U S A 1956,D 19,41:4
Career 1957,My 1,42:6
Career 1957,My 19,II,1:1
Wicked Cooks, The 1967,Ja 24,42:1
Empire Builders, The 1968,O 2,34:1
Rose, Norman (Director)
In the Penal Colony 1962,My 4,27:2
Rose, Norman (Miscellaneous)
Respectful Prostitute, The 1948,F 10,27:2
Church Street 1948,F 10,27:2
Trial of Dmitri Karamazov, The 1958,Ja 28,30:1
Rose, Norman (Playwright)
Mrs Warren's Profession 1950,O 26,39:2
Trial of Dmitri Karamazov, The 1958,Ja 28,30:1
Rose, Norman (Producer)
To Tell You the Truth 1948,Ap 19,28:6
Rose, Norman S (Playwright)
Mrs Jimmie Thompson 1920,Mr 30,9:1
Rose, Paul (Director)
Rothschild Siegt bei Waterloo 1937,Ja 3,X,2:5
Rose, Pegeen
King's Standards, The 1958,F 14,19:1
Listen to the Quiet 1958,O 28,40:2
Rose, Philip (Director)
Ninety Day Mistress, The 1967,N 7,49:1
Purlie 1970,Mr 16,53:1
Rose, Philip (Producer)
Raisin in the Sun, A 1959,Mr 12,27:1
Semi-Detached 1960,Mr 11,20:2
Purlie Victorious 1961,S 29,29:1
Bravo Giovanni 1962,My 21,41:2
Heroine, The 1963,F 21,5:5
Nobody Loves an Albatross 1963,D 20,20:1
Cafe Crown 1964,Ap 18,32:1
Owl and the Pussycat, The 1964,N 19,48:1
Nathan Weinstein, Mystic, Connecticut 1966,F 26,15:2
Ninety Day Mistress, The 1967,N 7,49:1
Does a Tiger Wear a Necktie? 1969,F 26,38:1
Purlie 1970,Mr 16,53:1
Rose, Phyllis
Royal Family, The 1927,D 29,26:4
Rose, R A
Noble Rogue, A 1929,Ag 20,31:2
Rose, R P
Who's Who 1924,Ap 18,19:2
Rose, Ralph (Director)
Brown Buddies 1930,O 8,29:1
Rose, Ralph Jr (Playwright)
Free for All 1947,S 18,28:2
Rose, Reginald (Playwright)
Black Monday 1962,Mr 7,29:1
Rose, Reva
Time of the Cuckoo, The 1958,O 28,40:2
Look After Lulu 1959,Mr 4,35:1
You're a Good Man, Charlie Brown 1967,Mr 8,51:1

You're a Good Man, Charlie Brown 1967,Ap 9,II,1:1
Rose, Rhonda
Cherry Orchard, The 1970,My 7,63:2
Rose, Richard M (Lighting Director)
Raisin' Hell in the Son 1962,Jl 3,13:2
Rose, Robert (Pvt)
Yellow Jack 1944,Ap 7,23:3
Rose, Ruth
Pietro 1920,Ja 20,10:2
Rose, Sam (Choreographer)
Matinee Girl, The 1926,F 2,20:3
A la Carte 1927,Ag 18,25:3
Hold Everything 1928,O 11,24:2
Bomboola 1929,Je 27,17:3
Rose, Sam (Director)
Make Me Know It 1929,N 5,32:5
Rose, Stewart
Wonderful Town 1963,F 15,10:2
Rose, Teddy
Arsenic and Old Lace 1943,D 13,18:6
Our Town 1944,Ja 11,24:5
War President 1944,Ap 25,17:3
Wind Is Ninety, The 1945,Je 22,12:2
Lute Song 1946,F 7,29:2
Seeds in the Wind 1948,Ap 26,27:2
Seeds in the Wind 1948,My 26,29:2
Rose, Upson
Made for Each Other 1924,S 30,27:2
Rose, Virginia
Fiesta 1929,S 18,35:1
Rose, William (Lyricist)
Great Day! 1929,O 18,24:3
Rose and Moon
Vaudeville (Palace) 1923,Ja 30,12:2
Rose Mary
Processional 1937,O 14,23:1
Rosebrook, Leon (Composer)
Silks and Satins 1920,Jl 16,19:1
Ice Capades 1952,S 12,18:1
Rosecrans, J O D
1776 1926,Ap 24,11:2
Rosecrans, J Q
Laugh It Off 1925,Ap 25,18:4
Rosedale, Harry
Dew Drop Inn 1923,My 18,26:4
Rosedale, Lillian
Red Pepper 1922,My 30,8:3
Roseen, Irene
Visit, The 1967,S 13,41:1
She Stoops to Conquer 1968,Ja 1,11:1
Roseleigh, Jack
You Can't Win 1926,F 17,12:1
Menace 1927,Mr 15,28:2
Big Fight, The 1928,S 19,33:1
Mountain Fury 1929,S 26,27:2
Troika 1930,Ap 2,32:6
Paths of Glory 1935,S 19,29:1
Paths of Glory 1935,S 27,24:2
Without Warning 1937,My 3,23:2
Roseleigh, Jack (Director)
He Loved the Ladies 1927,My 11,29:2
Roseleigh, John
Scarlet Sister Mary 1930,N 26,19:2
Rosellat, Robert
Pardon Our French 1950,O 6,22:4
Roselle, Max
Dew Drop Inn 1923,My 18,26:4
Roselle, Richard
Hamlet 1920,Mr 17,14:2
Roselle, William
Marry the Poor Girl 1920,S 27,18:3
Bachelor's Night, A 1921,O 18,20:1
I Will IF You Will 1922,Ag 30,10:4
Ziegfeld Follies 1923,O 22,17:2
Mama Loves Papa 1926,F 23,26:2
Connecticut Yankee, A 1927,N 4,24:2
Tonight at 12 1928,N 16,28:1
Veneer 1929,N 13,24:5
Papavert 1931,D 30,25:1
Mr Papavert 1932,Ja 23,18:6
Bulls, Bears and Asses 1932,My 7,11:3
Masks and Faces 1933,Mr 20,18:5
Queer People 1934,F 16,16:2
Woman of Destiny, A 1936,Mr 3,25:2
Strangler Fig, The 1940,My 7,31:2
Roselli, Jimmy
Jimmy Roselli Show, The 1969,My 3,39:1
Rosello
Circus-Madison Square Garden 1939,Ap 6,23:5
Roseman, Edward
Caravan 1928,Ag 30,13:3
Street Wolf, The 1929,Ja 1,61:1
Roseman, Ralph (Producer)
Major Barbara 1965,My 18,33:1
Roseman, William
Free Soul, A 1928,Ja 13,26:5
Rosemary
Irving Berlin's New Music Box Revue 1922,O 24,18:1
Rosemont, Norman (Producer)
Drat! the Cat! 1965,O 11,54:2

Rosemont, Walter L (Composer)
Battling Buttler 1923,O 9,17:2
Rosemont Troubadours, The
Vaudeville (Hippodrome) 1926,Ap 13,28:2
Rosen, Abigail
Beclch 1968,D 17,59:1
Rosen, Al (Producer)
One Good Year 1935,N 28,38:3
Good Night Ladies 1945,Ja 18,16:2
Rosen, Albert H (Miscellaneous)
Diamond Lil 1948,N 30,33:2
Rosen, Albert H (Producer)
Diamond Lil 1949,F 7,16:2
High Ground, The 1951,F 21,31:2
Never Say Never 1951,N 21,21:2
Rosen, Andrea (Miscellaneous)
Noontide 1961,Je 2,37:1
Rosen, Arnie (Playwright)
Ziegfeld Follies 1957,Mr 2,19:2
Rosen, Arthur
Ethan Frome 1936,Ja 22,15:2
Othello 1937,Ja 7,16:4
Rosen, Bernice
Bad Habits of 1925 1925,F 9,17:1
Rosen, Charles (Scenic Designer)
Clandestine Marriage, The 1954,O 4,23:2
Clandestine Marriage, The 1954,O 17,II,1:1
Virtuous Island, The 1957,Ap 10,39:1
Apollo of Bellac, The 1957,Ap 10,39:1
Buffalo Skinner, The 1959,F 20,18:1
Rosen, David
Design For A Stained Glass Window 1950,Ja 24,26:2
Rosen, Edward
Alt Heidelberg 1926,My 31,10:5
Rosen, Estelle
Bad Habits of 1925 1925,F 9,17:1
Rosen, George
Half Moon Inn 1925,Mr 10,14:1
Rosen, Gerta
Brothers Ashkenazi, The 1937,S 21,28:6
Rosen, Harry
Country Boy, The 1963,O 28,20:1
Rosen, Harry (Producer)
Trial Honeymoon 1947,N 4,31:2
Rosen, Hershel
Both Kooney Lemels 1964,O 12,37:2
Rosen, Irwin
Winterset 1966,F 10,32:2
Awake and Sing! 1970,My 28,35:1
Rosen, James
No Mother to Guide Her 1933,D 26,18:5
Rosen, Jimmie
Black Velvet 1927,S 28,28:1
Rosen, Lewis (Miscellaneous)
Dear Janet Rosenberg, Dear Mr Kooning 1970,Ap 6,46:1
Jakey Fat Boy 1970,Ap 6,46:1
Rosen, Lewis (Mixcellaneous)
To Clothe the Naked 1967,Ap 28,30:1
Goa 1968,F 23,46:1
Rosen, Lia
Dybbuk, The 1926,Ja 6,16:2
Rosen, Louis
It's About Time 1942,Mr 31,28:3
Rosen, Max
Dybbuk, The 1954,O 27,33:6
Rosen, Mordecai
House on Grand Street, A 1953,O 10,12:6
Rosen, Nanette
West Side Story 1957,S 27,14:4
Rosen, Richard (Miscellaneous)
U S A 1959,O 29,38:1
Rosen, Sam (Director)
White Cargo 1960,D 30,12:1
Rosen, Samuel
Man and the Masses 1924,Ap 15,25:1
Androcles and the Lion 1925,N 24,28:1
Schweiger 1926,Mr 24,20:4
Midnight 1930,D 30,25:1
Rosen, Samuel (Director)
As You Like It 1937,N 1,25:2
Androcles and the Lion 1938,D 17,10:5
Three Sisters, The 1939,O 16,23:1
Rosen, Samuel (Playwright)
Three Sisters, The 1939,O 16,23:1
Rosen, Willi (Composer)
Liebling Adieu 1931,N 29,VIII,4:2
Rosen, Zvi (Composer)
Children of the Shadows 1964,F 27,26:1
Rosenbaum, Abraham
Mother Courage 1967,N 17,55:1
Rosenbaum, David
Cave Dwellers, The 1961,O 16,34:2
Rosenbaum, Ed Jr (Producer)
Matinee Girl, The 1926,F 2,20:3
Rosenbaum, Norman M
Babes Don't Cry Anymore 1968,F 21,55:1
Rosenberg
Signor Bracoli 1932,O 2,IX,2:3
Rosenberg, Bella (Miscellaneous)
Entertain a Ghost 1962,Ap 10,48:1

Rosenberg, Bella (Producer)
Play With a Tiger 1964,D 31,14:2
Rosenberg, Israel
In-Laws 1960,O 17,32:4
Going to America 1961,O 30,33:7
Rosenberg, Israel (Composer)
Going to America 1961,O 30,33:7
Rosenberg, Israel (Director)
Going to America 1961,O 30,33:7
Rosenberg, Israel (Lyricist)
Sonitchka 1930,Mr 8,21:3
Rosenberg, Israel (Miscellaneous)
Family Mishmash, A 1958,O 20,36:1
Honeymoon in Israel, A 1962,O 15,33:5
Rosenberg, Israel (Playwright)
Sonitchka 1930,Mr 8,21:3
Berdichever Bridegroom, The 1930,S 24,26:2
Berl and Shmerl Corporation 1934,Ap 2,12:5
Saint and Sinners 1935,D 30,15:2
Jolly Village, The 1937,N 15,15:5
Family Mishmash, A 1958,O 20,36:1
Going to America 1961,O 30,33:7
Rosenberg, Israel (Producer)
In-Laws 1960,O 17,32:4
Rosenberg, J B (Miscellaneous)
New Faces of 1943 1942,D 23,22:2
Rosenberg, James N (Playwright)
Wall Street 1927,Ap 21,24:4
Rosenberg, Jerome (Director)
Love, Honor and Oh Baby 1940,Mr 29,25:2
Rosenberg, Michael
Tenth Commandment, The 1926,N 18,27:1
Othello 1929,F 4,21:2
Major Noah 1929,F 23,17:2
Man With the Portfolio, The 1931,F 12,24:6
Armored Train No 1469 1931,N 28,20:3
Yoshe Kalb 1932,O 3,15:5
Yoshe Kalb 1932,N 6,IX,2:1
Chayim Lederer 1932,N 15,24:4
Motke Ganef 1932,D 30,15:2
Revolt 1933,Ja 12,21:3
Wise Men of Chelm, The 1933,O 18,24:4
Organ Grinder, The 1934,Ja 1,28:3
Happy Days 1934,Ap 2,12:5
Here Runs the Bride 1934,S 20,21:3
Here Runs the Bride 1934,N 4,IX,2:1
One in a Million 1934,N 17,13:2
Motel Peissi, The Contor's Kid 1934,N 29,33:3
Secret of Love, The 1936,F 24,15:2
Jacques Bergson 1936,N 29,XII,3:3
Water Carrier, The 1936,D 25,20:2
Brothers Ashkenazi, The 1937,S 21,28:6
'Round the Family Table 1938,O 8,10:3
One Sabbath Afternoon 1939,Ja 17,27:5
In a Jewish Grocery 1939,O 2,15:2
Her Great Mistake 1940,F 5,12:6
Uncle Sam in Israel 1952,D 8,38:5
Hello Solly! 1967,Ap 6,44:3
Rosenberg, Michel
Jacques Bergson 1936,O 31,24:6
Highway Robbery 1955,N 8,36:1
Rosenberg, Mr
Dame de Chambre, La 1924,Je 1,VII,1:7
Rosenberg, Mr (Producer)
Dame de Chambre, La 1924,Je 1,VII,1:7
Rosenberg, Philip (Lighting Director)
Courtyard 1960,Mr 1,28:1
Rosenberg, Philip (Scenic Designer)
Courtyard 1960,Mr 1,28:1
Mr Simian 1963,O 22,44:1
Rosenberg, Phillip (Scenic Designer)
Brouhaha 1960,Ap 27,31:2
Rosenberg, Ralph P
Alt Heidelberg 1926,My 31,10:5
Rosenberg, Rebecca
Revolt of the Beavers, The 1937,My 21,19:2
Rosenberg, Stanley (Miscellaneous)
Bacchae, The 1969,Mr 15,24:1
Bacchae, The 1969,Mr 23,II,11:1
Rosenberg, Susie Wolter
Bacchae, The 1969,Mr 15,24:1
Rosenberg, Victor
For Valor 1935,N 19,27:5
Rosenblatt, Josef
Vaudeville (Palace) 1925,D 8,28:6
Rosenblatt, Max
Jolly Orphan, The 1929,D 23,18:6
My Little Girl 1931,F 2,22:4
Honeymoon for Three, A 1933,Ja 30,9:6
Jewish Melody, The 1933,Mr 27,12:4
Rosenblatt (Cantor)
Vaudeville (Hippodrome) 1926,Ap 20,24:6
Rosenblum, Al
Revolt of the Beavers, The 1937,My 21,19:2
Rosenblum, Ava
Touch 1970,N 9,52:1
Rosenblum, M Edger (Producer)
When I Was a Child 1960,D 9,38:1
Rosenblum, Pauly
Enchanting Melody 1964,N 25,40:1
Rosenblum, Ralph (Producer)
Jakey Fat Boy 1970,Ap 6,46:1

Dear Janet Rosenberg, Dear Mr Kooning
1970,Ap 6,46:1
Rosenblum, Robert (Composer)
Blue Boy in Black, The 1963,My 1,32:1
Up Eden 1968,N 27,42:1
Rosenblum, Robert (Lyricist)
Up Eden 1968,N 27,42:1
Rosenblum, Robert (Playwright)
Up Eden 1968,N 27,42:1
Rosenblum, Susan
Touch 1970,N 9,52:1
Rosendahl, Henry (Playwright)
Yesterday's Orchids 1934,O 6,20:4
Strip Girl 1935,O 21,22:6
Rosene, John
Tinker's Dam 1943,Ja 29,22:2
Earth Journey 1944,Ap 28,24:2
Slice It Thin 1945,My 11,22:5
Rosener, George
Artists and Models 1923,Ag 21,12:2
Artists and Models 1925,Je 25,16:2
My Maryland 1927,S 13,37:2
Keep Moving 1934,Ag 24,10:2
Rosener, George (Director)
Keep Moving 1934,Ag 24,10:2
Music Hath Charms 1934,D 31,8:2
If a Body 1935,My 1,25:3
One Good Year 1935,N 28,38:3
Rosener, George (Lyricist)
Music Hath Charms 1934,D 31,8:2
Rosener, George (Playwright)
Speakeasy 1927,S 27,30:1
She Got What She Wanted 1929,Mr 5,28:1
Music Hath Charms 1934,D 31,8:2
If a Body 1935,Ap 21,II,8:3
If a Body 1935,My 1,25:3
Rosenfeld, Jerome E (Producer)
At War With the Army 1949,Mr 9,32:2
Rosenfeld, Moisha
Mirele Efros 1969,D 26,41:1
Rosenfeld, Morris (Miscellaneous)
Untitled-Poetry Reading 1967,Jl 18,29:1
Rosenfeld, Morris (Playwright)
Let's Sing Yiddish 1966,N 10,63:1
Rosenfeld, Mort
Dream Play 1960,N 23,22:1
Rosenfeld, Richard
Flies, The; Mouches, Les 1947,Ap 18,26:3
Rosenfeld, Sydney (Playwright)
Forbidden 1923,O 2,10:2
Rosenfeld-Boushover
We Live and Laugh 1936,My 9,10:3
Rosenfels, Daniel (Miscellaneous)
Hot Feet 1970,D 22,38:1
Rosenfield, Grace (Miscellaneous)
Shuffle Along 1952,My 9,20:5
Rosenfield, Jerome (Miscellaneous)
Semi-Detached 1963,O 8,49:1
Rosengardt, Thelma
What of It? 1929,Mr 9,24:2
Rosenmerkel, Jack
Jubilee 1935,O 14,20:1
Rosenova, Olga
It Pays to Sin 1933,N 4,18:6
Rosenquist, Holger (Choreographer)
Threepenny Opera, The 1966,O 28,33:1
Rosenschein, Matthew
Life Begins in '40 1940,Ap 5,24:2
Rosenstein, Samuel
Love and Politics 1929,O 21,30:7
Rosenstock, Joseph (Musical Director)
Medium, The 1949,N 7,32:4
Rosenstock, Milton (Miscellaneous)
Two's Company 1952,D 16,43:5
Rosenstock, Milton (Musical Director)
Barefoot Boy With Cheek 1947,Ap 4,20:2
High Button Shoes 1947,O 10,32:2
Gentlemen Prefer Blondes 1949,D 9,35:3
Make a Wish 1951,Ap 19,38:1
Can-Can 1953,My 8,28:1
Vamp, The 1955,N 11,30:1
Bells Are Ringing 1956,N 29,43:4
Bells Are Ringing 1956,N 30,18:2
Gypsy 1959,My 22,31:6
Subways Are for Sleeping 1961,D 28,22:1
Stop the World-I Want to Get Off 1962,O 4,45:4
Hot Spot 1963,Ap 20,17:2
Funny Girl 1964,Mr 27,15:1
Come Summer 1969,Mr 19,43:1
Jimmy 1969,O 24,38:1
Look to the Lilies 1970,Mr 30,59:1
Rosental, Chayele
Hello Charlie 1965,O 25,47:2
Rosenthal, Andrew (Composer)
Horses in Midstream 1953,Ap 3,18:7
Innocent as Hell 1960,Je 30,2:6
Rosenthal, Andrew (Lyricist)
Innocent as Hell 1960,Je 30,2:6
Rosenthal, Andrew (Playwright)
Burning Deck, The 1940,Mr 2,9:2
Broken Journey 1942,Je 24,22:2
Third Person 1951,N 1,35:3
Red Letter Day, The 1952,F 22,14:4

Rosenthal, Andrew (Playwright)—Cont
Red Letter Day 1952,Mr 1,9:3
Red Letter Day 1952,Mr 16,II,3:7
Horses in Midstream 1953,Ap 3,18:7
Third Person 1955,D 30,13:4
Innocent as Hell 1960,Je 30,2:6
Rosenthal, Boris
Love and Politics 1929,O 21,30:7
Slaves of Luxury 1930,F 8,13:3
Sonitchka 1930,Mr 8,21:3
Russian Love 1930,N 27,32:3
Great Miracle, The 1931,D 12,23:5
Big Surprise, The 1932,O 17,18:3
Traveling Salesman, The 1932,N 1,24:4
Honeymoon for Three, A 1933,Ja 30,9:6
Germany Aflame 1933,O 28,20:5
Little Giants 1933,D 2,9:5
Organ Grinder, The 1934,Ja 1,28:3
Holiday in Town, A 1935,S 30,12:3
Rosenthal, Boris (Lyricist)
His Wife's Lover 1929,O 21,30:6
Village Wedding, A 1930,S 24,26:2
Night in the Woods, A 1931,Mr 2,19:3
Big Surprise, The 1932,O 17,18:3
Rosenthal, Chayele
President's Daughter, The 1970,N 4,41:2
Rosenthal, Harry
June Moon 1929,Ag 4,VIII,1:6
June Moon 1929,O 10,34:5
Heigh-Ho, Everybody 1932,My 26,31:2
June Moon 1933,My 16,15:5
Rosenthal, Helen
Whispering Well, The 1920,D 6,19:1
Rosenthal, Hermann (Miscellaneous)
Don Carlos 1964,N 25,40:1
Captain of Koepenick, The 1964,D 2,60:1
Rosenthal, Jean (Lighting Director)
Richard III 1943,Mr 27,8:3
Telephone, The 1947,My 2,28:2
Medium, The 1947,My 2,28:2
Medium, The 1947,My 11,II,1:1
Joy to the World 1948,Mr 19,28:2
Sundown Beach 1948,S 8,37:1
Medium, The 1948,D 8,41:6
Telephone, The 1948,D 8,41:6
Caesar and Cleopatra 1949,D 22,28:2
Consul, The 1950,Mr 16,41:1
Consul, The 1950,Mr 26,II,1:1
Medium, The 1950,S 3,II,1:1
Climate of Eden, The 1952,N 7,20:2
Climate of Eden, The 1952,N 16,II,1:1
Ondine 1954,F 19,23:1
Show Boat 1954,My 6,44:1
Fledermaus, Die 1954,My 20,38:5
Carousel 1954,Je 3,32:2
Qudrille 1954,N 4,39:2
Saint of Bleecker Street, The 1954,D 28,21:1
House of Flowers 1954,D 31,11:2
Time of Your Life, The 1955,Ja 20,34:1
Julius Caesar 1955,Jl 13,20:1
Tempest, The 1955,Ag 2,18:2
Tempest, The 1955,Ag 7,II,1:1
Great Sebastians, The 1956,Ja 5,27:1
King and I, The 1956,Ap 19,35:4
Kiss Me, Kate 1956,My 10,27:2
King John 1956,Je 28,33:5
Measure for Measure 1956,Je 29,16:1
Taming of the Shrew, The 1956,Ag 6,20:1
Measure for Measure 1957,Ja 23,24:1
Taming of the Shrew, The 1957,F 21,30:2
Hole in the Head, A 1957,Mr 1,15:1
Hole in the Head, A 1957,Mr 10,II,1:1
Beggar's Opera, The 1957,Mr 14,35:1
Duchess of Malfi, The 1957,Mr 20,33:1
Othello 1957,Je 24,19:2
Othello 1957,Je 30,II,1:1
Merchant of Venice, The 1957,Jl 11,19:5
West Side Story 1957,S 27,14:4
West Side Story 1957,O 27,II,15:3
Jamaica 1957,N 1,32:2
Dark at the Top of the Stairs, The 1957,D 6,38:1
Winesburg, Ohio 1958,F 6,22:2
Hamlet 1958,Je 21,11:1
Winter's Tale, The 1958,Jl 21,17:4
Disenchanted, The 1958,D 4,53:4
Redhead 1959,F 6,21:1
Destry Rides Again 1959,Ap 24,24:1
Judy Garland 1959,My 12,40:1
All's Well That Ends Well 1959,Ag 3,20:4
Take Me Along 1959,O 23,22:2
Sound of Music, The 1959,N 17,40:2
Saratoga 1959,D 8,59:4
Caligula 1960,F 17,31:1
Caligula 1960,F 28,II,1:1
Henry IV 1960,Mr 2,42:1
Dear Liar 1960,Mr 18,19:2
Henry IV 1960,Ap 19,41:1
West Side Story 1960,Ap 28,31:1
Taste of Honey, A 1960,O 5,46:1
Becket 1960,O 6,50:1
Conquering Hero, The 1961,Ja 17,40:2
Becket 1961,My 9,44:1
Gay Life, The 1961,N 20,38:1
Daughter of Silence 1961,D 1,28:1

Rosenthal, Jean (Lighting Director)—Cont
Night of the Iguana, The 1961,D 29,10:1
Gift of Time, A 1962,F 23,34:1
Funny Thing Happened on the Way to the Forum,
A 1962,My 9,49:1
Lord Pengo 1962,N 20,41:2
On an Open Roof 1963,Ja 30,7:3
Beast in Me, The 1963,My 17,29:1
Jennie 1963,O 18,35:2
Barefoot in the Park 1963,O 24,36:2
Ballad of the Sad Cafe, The 1963,O 31,27:1
Chinese Prime Minister, The 1964,Ja 3,14:1
Hello, Dolly! 1964,Ja 17,22:1
West Side Story 1964,Ap 9,24:2
Hamlet 1964,Ap 10,30:1
To Broadway With Love 1964,Ap 30,28:6
Fiddler on the Roof 1964,S 23,56:2
Luv 1964,N 12,43:1
Poor Bitos 1964,N 16,40:2
Incident at Vichy 1964,D 4,44:1
Baker Street 1965,F 17,36:1
Odd Couple, The 1965,Mr 11,36:1
Country Wife, The 1965,D 10,58:2
Happily Never After 1966,Mr 11,37:1
Ivanov 1966,My 4,50:1
Time for Singing, A 1966,My 23,48:2
Show Boat 1966,Jl 20,48:1
Diary of Adam and Eve, The 1966,O 19,53:1
Lady or the Tiger?, The 1966,O 19,53:1
Passionella 1966,O 19,53:1
Cabaret 1966,N 21,62:1
I Do! I Do! 1966,D 6,58:1
Star-Spangled Girl, The 1966,D 22,38:1
Illya Darling 1967,Ap 12,37:1
Hello, Dolly! 1967,N 13,61:1
Happy Time, The 1968,Ja 19,32:2
Plaza Suite; Visitor From Hollywood
1968,F 15,49:1
Plaza Suite; Visitor From Mamaroneck
1968,F 15,49:1
Plaza Suite; Visitor From Forest Hills
1968,F 15,49:1
Weekend 1968,Mr 14,50:2
Exercise, The 1968,Ap 25,54:1
Twelfth Night 1968,Je 15,40:1
Dear World 1969,F 7,33:1
Rosenthal, Jean (Miscellaneous)
Seventh Trumpet, The 1941,N 22,10:6
Measure for Measure 1957,Ja 23,24:1
Duchess of Malfi, The 1957,Mr 20,33:1
Othello 1957,Je 24,19:2
Merchant of Venice, The 1957,Jl 11,19:5
Much Ado About Nothing 1957,Ag 8,15:2
Poor Bitos 1964,N 16,40:2
Rosenthal, Jean (Producer)
Native Son 1941,Mr 25,26:5
King John 1956,Je 28,33:5
Measure for Measure 1956,Je 29,16:1
Rosenthal, Jean (Scenic Designer)
Conquering Hero, The 1961,Ja 17,40:2
On an Open Roof 1963,Ja 30,7:3
Beast in Me, The 1963,My 17,29:1
Rosenthal, Larry
Mikado, The 1939,Mr 11,15:6
Rosenthal, Laurence (Composer)
Clearing in the Woods, A 1957,Ja 11,20:2
Clearing in the Woods, A 1957,Ja 20,II,1:1
Rashomon 1959,Ja 28,36:2
Clearing in the Woods, A 1959,F 13,32:1
Becket 1960,O 6,50:1
Becket 1961,My 9,44:1
Dylan 1964,Ja 20,18:1
Sherry! 1967,Mr 29,39:1
Patriot for Me, A 1969,O 6,58:1
Rosenthal, Laurence (Miscellaneous)
Music Man, The 1957,D 20,31:1
Goldilocks 1958,O 13,33:1
Take Me Along 1959,O 23,22:2
Donnybrook! 1961,My 19,23:1
Music Man, The 1965,Je 17,26:4
George M! 1968,Ap 11,48:1
Rosenthal, Max
Othello 1929,F 4,21:2
Major Noah 1929,F 23,17:2
Rosenthal, Raymond (Translator)
Sunset 1966,My 13,34:1
Rosenthal, Ruth L
Blue Jeans 1933,Ap 9,31:5
Rosenthal, Yasha
He, She and the Ox 1934,F 21,22:7
Flag Is Born, A 1946,S 7,10:6
Rosenwald, Patricia
Pigeon, The 1957,My 17,19:2
Rosenzweig, Ben (Lighting Director)
In-Laws 1960,O 17,32:4
Rosenzweig, Ben (Scenic Designer)
Father and Son 1956,O 20,17:4
In-Laws 1960,O 17,32:4
Going to America 1961,O 30,33:7
Life Is a Dream 1962,Ja 15,22:3
Rosenzweig, Rose
Go Fight City Hall 1961,N 3,28:5
Rosenzweig, Rose Lee
Wedding March, The 1955,O 17,33:1

Devil's Game, A 1959,N 9,35:6
Roseray and Capella
Great Temptations, The 1926,My 19,29:1
Rosevich, Joseph D
Demon Mirror, The 1968,Mr 13,42:1
Roshanara
Greenwich Village Follies 1924,S 17,16:1
Rosi, Alfredo (Playwright)
My Wife Is Different 1931,Ap 27,24:4
Rosica, Tom
Hamlet 1968,Jl 4,15:1
Moondreamers, The 1969,D 9,68:1
Gloria and Esperanza 1970,F 23,32:1
Forensic and the Navigators 1970,Ap 2,43:1
Unseen Hand, The 1970,Ap 2,43:1
Rosie and Black-Eyed Susan
Hayride 1954,S 14,24:2
Rosing, Bodil
Fools Errant 1922,Ag 22,12:3
Rosita and Ramon
Vaudeville (Palace) 1927,D 27,25:2
New Moon, The 1928,S 20,33:1
Vaudeville (Palace) 1929,O 14,20:4
Vaudeville (Palace) 1930,D 22,16:5
Rosito, Anthony
They Knew What They Wanted 1939,O 3,19:1
Roskam, Cathryn
Gandhi 1970,O 21,37:1
Roskin, Miriam (Miscellaneous)
Coach With the Six Insides, The 1962,N 27,44:1
Rosley, Adrian
Mike Angelo 1923,Ja 9,26:2
Gentlemen Prefer Blondes 1926,S 29,23:1
Lovely Lady 1927,D 30,22:1
Little Accident 1928,O 10,32:3
Rhapsody, The 1930,S 16,30:3
Smiles 1930,N 19,19:2
Wonder Bar, The 1931,Mr 18,23:4
Cloudy With Showers 1931,S 2,17:5
There You Are! 1932,My 17,25:4
Roslyn, Agnes
Cock o' the Roost 1924,O 14,23:1
Rosmer, Milton
12 Miles Out 1927,F 20,VII,1:4
Gas Light 1939,F 19,IX,3:1
Rosne, Michael
Story of Mary Surratt, The 1947,F 10,25:2
Rosner, Jacques (Miscellaneous)
Three Musketeers, The 1968,Je 26,43:1
Rosner, Louis
Trapped 1928,S 12,25:3
Rosner, Paul (Lyricist)
Shoestring '57 1956,N 6,31:1
Rosoff, Charles (Composer)
Judy 1927,F 8,20:2
Earl Carroll's Vanities 1940,Ja 15,11:2
Roson, Samuel
Crown Prince, The 1927,Mr 24,23:2
Rosovskaya, Mira
Mexican Mural; Miracle Painting 1942,Ap 27,19:2
Rosovsky, Shlomo (Composer)
David's Crown 1948,My 10,26:2
Rosow, Judith
Yellow Jacket, The 1923,Ap 20,20:3
Rosqui, Tom
Merchant of Venice, The 1955,Ja 8,9:7
Gift of Fury, A 1958,Mr 24,21:4
Caretaker, The 1963,N 25,23:2
Danton's Death 1965,O 22,46:1
Condemned of Altona, The 1966,F 4,21:1
Condemned of Altona, The 1966,F 13,II,1:1
Alchemist, The 1966,O 14,48:1
Yerma 1966,D 9,60:1
East Wind, The 1967,F 10,30:1
'Tis Pity She's a Whore 1967,O 21,15:2
Collision Course; Rats 1968,My 9,55:2
Collision Course; Tour 1968,My 9,55:2
Collision Course; Stars and Stripes 1968,My 9,55:2
Collision Course; Camera Obscura 1968,My 9,55:2
Collision Course; Skywriting 1968,My 9,55:2
Collision Course; Wandering 1968,My 9,55:2
Brotherhood 1970,Mr 18,39:1
Day of Absence 1970,Mr 18,39:1
What the Butler Saw 1970,My 5,56:1
What the Butler Saw 1970,O 14,38:1
Ross, Adrian (Lyricist)
Merry Widow, The 1921,S 6,13:1
Merry Widow, The 1929,D 3,29:1
Count of Luxembourg, The 1930,F 18,28:2
Merry Widow, The 1942,Jl 16,22:1
Merry Widow, The 1943,Ag 5,19:2
Merry Widow, The 1944,O 9,17:1
Merry Widow, The 1957,Ap 11,36:6
Merry Widow, The 1961,O 27,28:2
Ross, Alan
Small Wonder 1948,S 16,33:5
Dance Me a Song 1950,Ja 21,10:5
Tragicomedy of Don Cristobita and Dona Rosita,
The 1958,My 30,12:2
Ross, Allan
Hatfields & McCoys 1970,Je 23,34:1
Ross, Allie
Blackbirds 1928,My 10,31:3

Ross, Alma
Present Arms 1928,Ap 27,16:2
Hot Money 1931,N 9,22:2
Hot-Cha! 1932,Mr 9,17:3
Spring Song 1934,O 2,18:2
Summer Wives 1936,Ap 14,18:1
Bell for Adano, A 1944,D 7,21:2
Annie Get Your Gun 1946,My 17,14:2
Ross, Annabelle
Porgy and Bess 1935,O 11,30:2
Porgy and Bess 1942,Ja 23,16:2
Ross, Annie
Cranks 1956,My 14,23:1
Cranks 1956,N 27,32:1
Stiffkey Scandals of 1932, The 1969,Je 14,24:3
Ross, Anthony
Whistling in the Dark 1932,N 4,25:2
Riddle Me This! 1933,Mr 15,21:3
Fly by Night 1933,Je 3,16:2
This Is Today 1935,Jl 30,17:2
Case of Clyde Griffiths 1936,Mr 14,10:4
Prelude 1936,Ap 20,17:4
200 Were Chosen 1936,N 21,21:1
But for the Grace of God 1937,Ja 13,21:4
Excursion 1937,Ap 10,11:4
Too Many Heroes 1937,N 16,26:2
Greatest Show on Earth, The 1938,Ja 6,22:2
Washington Jitters 1938,My 3,19:1
Devil Takes a Bride, The 1938,O 8,10:3
Richard II 1940,Ap 2,31:2
Twelfth Night 1940,N 20,26:3
Arsenic and Old Lace 1941,Ja 11,13:2
Elizabeth the Queen 1941,O 17,27:2
Winged Victory 1943,N 22,24:1
Glass Menagerie, The 1945,Ap 2,15:5
Glass Menagerie, The 1945,Ap 8,II,1:1
It Takes Two 1947,F 4,33:4
Survivors, The 1948,Ja 20,27:2
Cup of Trembling, The 1948,Ap 21,33:5
Leaf and Bough 1949,Ja 22,10:2
Season in the Sun 1950,S 29,31:2
Season in the Sun 1950,O 8,II,1:1
Sunday Breakfast 1952,My 30,12:2
Emperor's Clothes, The 1953,F 10,24:2
Frogs of Spring, The 1953,O 21,36:2
Starcross Story, The 1954,Ja 14,25:2
Bus Stop 1955,Mr 3,23:2
Bus Stop 1955,Mr 13,II,1:1
Ross, Arthur
Gentlemen Prefer Blondes 1926,S 29,23:1
Lombardi, Ltd 1927,Je 7,27:3
Elmer Gantry 1928,Ag 10,9:4
Kibitzer, The 1929,F 19,22:5
Enemy Within 1931,O 6,35:3
Whistling in the Dark 1932,N 4,25:2
Potash and Perlmutter 1935,Ap 6,11:3
Ross, Arthur H (Miscellaneous)
Culbin Sands 1935,Mr 23,10:3
Ross, Auriel
Tattle Tales 1930,Jl 20,VIII,2:1
Ross, Ben
Young Go First, The 1935,My 29,16:2
Revolt of the Beavers, The 1937,My 21,19:2
Medicine Show 1940,Ap 13,20:6
No for an Answer 1941,Ja 6,10:6
Brooklyn, U S A 1941,D 22,24:2
Ross, Betsy
Dead End 1935,O 29,17:2
Ross, Bill (Director)
Nineteenth Hole of Europe, The 1949,Mr 28,16:2
Ross, Bill (Miscellaneous)
Clearing in the Woods, A 1957,Ja 11,20:2
Winesburg, Ohio 1958,F 6,22:2
Marriage-Go-Round, The 1958,O 30,37:1
Best Man, The 1960,Ap 1,39:1
Under the Yum-Yum Tree 1960,N 17,45:1
Rhinoceros 1961,Ja 10,27:1
Mary, Mary 1961,Mr 9,24:2
Captains and the Kings, The 1962,Ja 3,25:2
110 in the Shade 1963,O 25,37:1
Chinese Prime Minister, The 1964,Ja 3,14:1
Last Analysis, The 1964,O 2,30:1
Kismet 1965,Je 23,45:1
Ross, Bob
They Shall Not Die 1934,F 22,24:4
They Shall Not Die 1934,Mr 4,IX,1:3
Ross, Carmel (Miscellaneous)
Cherry Orchard, The 1962,N 15,46:2
Ross, Carmel (Playwright)
Ghosts 1961,S 22,29:1
Doll's House, A 1963,F 4,5:6
Month in the Country, A 1963,My 29,39:2
Ross, Carmel (Translator)
Rosmersholm 1962,Ap 12,42:1
Ross, Clark (Producer)
Oh! Oh! Nurse 1925,D 8,28:4
Love in the Tropics 1927,O 19,24:3
Ross, Constance (Costume Designer)
In the Matter of J Robert Oppenheimer
1969,Mr 7,28:1
Ross, Corinne
Humbug, The 1929,N 28,34:5
Rebound 1930,F 4,29:1

Ross, Dan
Ah, Wilderness! 1954,Ag 21,20:4
Ross, David
Dybbuk, The 1954,O 27,33:6
Easter 1957,Ja 17,35:2
Failures, The 1959,Ja 6,30:2
Ross, David (Director)
Dybbuk, The 1954,O 27,33:6
Three Sisters, The 1955,F 26,13:2
Three Sisters, The 1955,Mr 20,II,1:1
Cherry Orchard, The 1955,O 19,38:1
Uncle Vanya 1956,F 1,25:2
Sea Gull, The 1956,O 23,38:1
Easter 1957,Ja 17,35:2
Easter 1957,F 3,II,1:1
Italian Straw Hat, The 1957,O 1,37:2
Lulu 1958,S 30,24:1
Failures, The 1959,Ja 6,30:2
Three Sisters, The 1959,S 22,46:1
Three Sisters, The 1959,O 4,II,1:1
Hedda Gabler 1960,N 10,61:1
Ghosts 1961,S 22,29:1
Rosmersholm 1962,Ap 12,42:1
Rosmersholm 1962,Ap 22,II,1:1
Cherry Orchard, The 1962,N 15,46:2
Doll's House, A 1963,F 4,5:6
Month in the Country, A 1963,My 29,39:2
Ross, David (Mrs) (Miscellaneous)
Doll's House, A 1963,F 4,5:6
Ross, David (Mrs) (Translator)
Rosmersholm 1962,Ap 22,II,1:1
Ross, David (Producer)
Rehearsal, The 1952,My 27,30:5
Dybbuk, The 1954,O 27,33:6
Three Sisters, The 1955,F 26,13:2
Cherry Orchard, The 1955,O 19,38:1
Uncle Vanya 1956,F 1,25:2
Uncle Vanya 1956,F 12,II,1:1
Sea Gull, The 1956,O 23,38:1
Easter 1957,Ja 17,35:2
Italian Straw Hat, The 1957,O 1,37:2
Lulu 1958,S 30,24:1
Failures, The 1959,Ja 6,30:2
Three Sisters, The 1959,S 22,46:1
Hedda Gabler 1960,N 25,24:3
Ghosts 1961,S 22,29:1
Rosmersholm 1962,Ap 12,42:1
Rosmersholm 1962,Ap 22,II,1:1
Cherry Orchard, The 1962,N 15,46:2
Doll's House, A 1963,F 4,5:6
Month in the Country, A 1963,My 29,39:2
Ross, Don
Ziegfeld Follies 1934,Ja 5,24:3
Ross, Don (Miscellaneous)
Artists and Models 1943,N 6,16:6
Ross, Don (Producer)
Artists and Models 1943,N 6,16:6
Ross, Donald (Playwright)
Shoot Anything With Hair That Moves
1969,F 3,29:1
Ross, Douglas
Macbeth 1928,N 20,28:3
Ross, Douglas (Director)
Macbeth 1928,N 4,IX,1:3
Macbeth 1928,N 20,28:3
Ross, Duncan (Director)
Winter's Tale, The 1963,Je 29,13:1
Macbeth 1964,Jl 27,22:3
Ross, Duncan (Lighting Director)
Narrow Road to the Deep North 1969,D 2,64:1
Ross, Eddie
Vaudeville (Palace) 1921,Jl 5,15:1
Career Angel 1943,N 19,24:2
Ross, Edwin
Light of Asia, The 1928,O 10,32:2
Richelieu 1934,My 22,28:1
Hamlet 1934,D 26,19:3
Richard III 1934,D 28,24:3
Cyrano de Bergerac 1936,Ap 28,17:1
If in the Green Wood 1947,Ja 17,27:6
Skipper Next to God 1948,Ja 5,14:5
Fifth Horseman, The 1949,Je 14,26:6
Bourgeois Gentleman, The 1949,Ag 31,27:2
Ross, Eleanor
Hello Out There 1955,D 22,19:1
Floydada to Matador 1955,D 22,19:1
Ross, Elizabeth
Song of Bernadette 1944,Jl 27,15:3
Song of Bernadette 1946,Mr 27,22:2
Story of Mary Surratt, The 1947,F 10,25:2
Minnie and Mr Williams 1948,O 28,37:2
Burning Bush, The 1949,D 17,15:5
In the Summer House 1953,D 30,17:1
Ross, Emily
On Call 1928,N 10,20:7
Passionate Pilgrim, The 1932,O 20,24:3
Barrister, The 1932,N 22,25:2
Naked Genius, The 1943,O 22,20:5
Million Dollar Baby 1945,D 22,17:2
Family Affair, A 1946,N 28,41:2
Ross, Etna
Piper, The 1920,Mr 20,14:2
Idiot's Delight 1936,Mr 25,25:2

Ross, Evelyn
Macbeth 1928,N 20,28:3
Ross, Evelyne
Carousel 1949,Ja 26,28:2
Ross, Florence
Family Upstairs, The 1933,O 28,20:6
Ross, Frank
Genius and the Crowd 1920,S 7,20:1
Sailor, Beware! 1935,My 7,28:4
Ross, Frank (Producer)
Man With Blonde Hair, The 1941,N 5,30:2
Ross, Frederick
Shoemaker's Holiday, The 1938,Ja 3,17:2
Ross, Gene
Corn Is Green, The 1943,My 4,18:3
Ross, George (Playwright)
Sophie 1944,D 26,22:7
Calculated Risk 1962,N 1,35:1
Ross, George (Producer)
Sophie 1944,D 26,22:7
Gently Does It 1953,O 29,43:4
Drink to Me Only 1958,O 9,47:4
Ross, George H R
Once Over Lightly 1938,D 10,13:4
Ross, George Maxim (Playwright)
Philoktetes 1961,Ap 25,41:1
Ross, Grace
Seven Mirrors 1945,O 26,17:2
Ross, Gregory
Courtyard 1960,Mr 1,28:1
Ross, Harold
Tragicomedy of Don Cristobita and Dona Rosita,
The 1958,My 30,12:2
Ross, Harriet
My Girl 1924,N 25,27:2
Wooden Idol, The 1930,My 13,27:2
Ross, Helen
Persecution and Assassination of Marat As
Performed by the Inmates of the Asylum of
Charenton Under the Direction of the Marquis de
Sade, The 1967,Ja 4,34:1
Our Town 1969,N 28,50:1
Ross, Herbert (Choreographer)
Tree Grows in Brooklyn, A 1951,Ap 20,24:3
Body Beautiful, The 1958,Ja 24,15:2
Finian's Rainbow 1960,Ap 28,31:1
Gay Life, The 1961,N 20,38:1
Tovarich 1963,Mr 20,5:1
Anyone Can Whistle 1964,Ap 6,36:1
Kelly 1965,F 8,28:2
Do I Hear a Waltz? 1965,Mr 19,28:1
On a Clear Day You Can See Forever
1965,O 18,44:1
Ross, Herbert (Director)
House of Flowers 1954,D 31,11:2
Finian's Rainbow 1960,Ap 28,31:1
I Can Get It for You Wholesale 1962,Mr 23,29:1
Hot Spot 1963,Ap 20,17:2
Kelly 1965,F 8,28:2
Ross, Herbert (Miscellaneous)
Wonderful Town 1958,Mr 6,32:4
Passionella 1966,O 19,53:1
Lady or the Tiger?, The 1966,O 19,53:1
Diary of Adam and Eve, The 1966,O 19,53:1
Ross, Hugh (Musical Director)
Paul Bunyan 1941,My 6,25:1
Golden Apple, The 1954,Mr 12,15:2
Golden Apple, The 1954,Mr 21,II,1:1
Tempest, The 1955,S 3,8:6
Midsummer Night's Dream, A 1956,Jl 20,9:5
Ross, J A (Playwright)
Happily Never After 1966,Mr 11,37:1
Ross, Jack
Everybody's Welcome 1931,O 14,26:3
Ross, James
Last Man In, The 1930,My 8,32:5
O'Flynn, The 1934,D 28,24:1
Ross, Jamie
Moon Besieged, The 1962,D 6,54:1
Penny Friend, The 1966,D 27,46:1
Ross, Jerry
Dream With Music 1944,My 19,15:2
Rhapsody 1944,N 23,37:2
Ross, Jerry (Composer)
John Murray Anderson's Almanac 1953,D 11,42:2
Pajama Game, The 1954,My 14,20:2
Pajama Game, The 1954,My 15,12:1
Pajama Game, The 1954,My 30,II,1:1
Damn Yankees 1955,My 6,17:1
Pajama Game, The 1957,My 16,27:1
Pajama Game, The 1957,My 26,II,1:1
Ross, Jerry (Lyricist)
John Murray Anderson's Almanac 1953,D 11,42:2
Pajama Game, The 1954,My 14,20:2
Pajama Game, The 1954,My 15,12:1
Pajama Game, The 1954,My 30,II,1:1
Damn Yankees 1955,My 6,17:1
Pajama Game, The 1957,My 16,27:1
Ross, Jerry (Miscellaneous)
Razzle Dazzle 1951,F 20,21:1
Ross, Joe
Billie 1928,O 2,34:2
Body Beautiful, The 1958,Ja 24,15:2

Ross, Joe—Cont
Fallout 1959,My 21,36:2
Crystal Heart, The 1960,F 16,31:2
She Loves Me 1963,Ap 24,39:1
Cafe Crown 1964,Ap 18,32:1
That Hat! 1964,S 24,45:1
Guys and Dolls 1966,Je 9,55:2
Ross, John
Riff-Raff 1926,F 9,18:6
Prunella 1929,Ap 10,23:3
Mrs Moonlight 1930,S 30,24:3
Few Wild Oats, A 1932,Mr 25,22:6
Beware of the Bull 1933,My 30,13:7
Ross, John (Composer)
Masque of Reason, The 1959,N 25,19:4
Ross, John (Scenic Designer)
Cave Dwellers, The 1961,O 16,34:2
Ross, Joseph
Antigone 1967,Ja 14,18:1
Ross, Joyce
As We Forgive Our Debtors 1947,Mr 11,37:2
Ross, Julia
Golden Apple, The 1962,F 13,38:2
Ross, Katherine
Talent '54 1954,Ap 13,40:1
Ronde, La 1955,Je 28,24:2
Cradle Song 1955,D 2,32:2
Long Day's Journey Into Night 1956,N 8,47:2
Long Day's Journey Into Night 1956,N 18,II,1:1
Long Day's Journey Into Night 1957,Jl 3,14:1
Matty and the Moron and Madonna
1965,Mr 30,53:1
Ross, Kay
Street Singer, The 1929,S 18,35:2
Ross, Kenelm (Director)
Flora 1935,O 30,17:4
Ross, Lancelot P
Orestes 1926,Je 20,II,3:6
Ross, Lanny
Petticoat Fever 1935,Je 25,14:5
Pursuit of Happiness, The 1935,Jl 16,24:2
Ross, Len (Miscellaneous)
Billy Liar 1965,Mr 18,26:1
Golden Screw, The 1967,Ja 31,52:1
Ross, Lillian
Bab 1920,O 19,12:1
Nevertheless 1920,D 28,9:1
Six-Fifty, The 1921,O 25,20:1
Six-Fifty, The 1921,O 30,VI,1:1
Vaudeville (Palace) 1923,Ja 23,18:2
Home Fires 1923,Ag 21,12:1
Solid Ivory 1925,N 17,29:3
What's the Big Idea? 1926,Mr 24,20:3
He Loved the Ladies 1927,My 11,29:2
Ross, Linda
Fiddler on the Roof 1964,S 23,56:2
Ross, Liz
These Are the Times 1950,My 11,37:2
Ross, Lois
Little Poor Man, The 1925,Ag 6,14:1
Stronger Than Love 1925,D 29,20:2
Fog-Bound 1927,Ap 2,21:2
Ten Nights in a Barroom 1928,Mr 28,31:2
Under the Gaslight 1929,Ap 3,27:1
Ross, Lynn
West Side Story 1957,S 27,14:4
First Impressions 1959,Mr 20,28:1
Fiorello! 1959,N 24,45:3
Ross, Marguerite
Broadway Whirl, The 1921,Je 9,10:4
Ross, Marilyn
Flahooley 1951,My 15,39:1
Ross, Marion
Pirates of Penzance, The 1926,D 12,VIII,3:1
Roberta 1933,N 20,18:4
Pirates of Penzance, The 1936,Ap 21,27:5
Variations of 1940 1940,Ja 29,12:1
This Is Edwin Booth 1958,Ag 27,32:7
Edwin Booth 1958,N 25,37:1
Ross, Martin
We're Civilized? 1962,N 9,30:1
Once for the Asking 1963,N 21,42:2
Cabaret 1968,Ja 12,19:1
Cabaret 1969,F 2,74:2
Ross, Michael (Director)
Vintage '60 1960,S 13,41:1
Wet Paint 1965,Ap 13,33:1
Hotel Passionato 1965,O 23,16:1
Ross, Myrtle
O Evening Star 1936,Ja 9,24:6
Ross, Natalie
Lady's Not for Burning, The 1959,Ja 31,13:2
Butterfly Dream, The 1966,My 20,41:1
Ross, Neill
Midsummer Night's Dream, A 1968,D 9,59:1
Ross, Norris
Recruiting Officer, The 1958,F 8,12:2
Ross, Oriel
Admirable Crichton, The 1931,Mr 10,23:2
Ross, Paul
Enemy of the People, An 1959,F 5,24:4
Ross, Richard
Straw, The 1921,N 11,16:2
Lost Boy 1932,Ja 6,24:4

Ross, Richard—Cont

Paths of Glory 1935,S 27,24:2
Cyrano de Bergerac 1936,Ap 28,17:1
Tide Rising 1937,Ja 26,17:2
Enemy of the People, An 1937,F 16,19:1
Antony and Cleopatra 1937,N 11,30:2

Ross, Robert

Twelfth Night 1926,D 21,21:4
Inheritors 1927,Mr 8,23:1
Good Hope, The 1927,O 19,24:2
2 + 2 = 5 1927,N 29,30:3
Would-Be Gentleman, The 1928,O 2,34:1
Invitation au Voyage, L' 1928,O 5,17:1
Cherry Orchard, The 1928,O 16,28:5
Peter Pan; Boy Who Would Not Grow Up, The
  1928,N 27,36:3
Lady From Alfaqueque, The; Consulesa, La
  1929,Ja 15,22:3
On the High Road 1929,Ja 15,22:3
Katerina 1929,F 26,30:3
Sea Gull, The 1929,S 17,34:1
Mademoiselle Bourrat 1929,O 8,34:3
Living Corpse, The 1929,D 7,19:1
Women Have Their Way, The 1930,Ja 28,28:1
Romeo and Juliet 1930,Ap 22,33:1
Siegfried 1930,O 21,34:1
Alison's House 1930,D 2,31:2
Lady of the Camellias, The 1931,Ja 27,21:2
Liliom 1932,O 27,23:2
Camille 1932,O 28,23:2
Dear Jane 1932,N 15,24:3
Cherry Orchard, The 1933,Mr 7,20:3
Farmer Takes a Wife, The 1934,O 31,17:1
Stars in Your Eyes 1939,F 10,18:2
Christmas Eve 1939,D 28,17:2
Point of No Return 1951,O 31,32:2
Point of No Return 1951,D 14,35:2
Point of No Return 1951,D 23,II,3:1
Kind Sir 1953,S 28,21:2
Kind Sir 1953,N 5,41:2

Ross, Robert (Director)

Distant Shore, The 1935,F 22,26:2
On Stage 1935,Jl 23,24:4
On Stage 1935,O 30,16:6
Black Eye, The 1938,Mr 8,22:4
On the Rocks 1938,Je 16,20:2
Girl From Wyoming, The 1938,O 31,12:1
They Knew What They Wanted 1939,O 3,19:1
Aries Is Rising 1939,N 22,16:5
Romeo and Juliet 1940,My 10,27:1
Royal Family, The 1940,Ag 13,15:3
Porgy and Bess 1942,Ja 23,16:2
Yours, A Lincoln 1942,Jl 10,12:3
Count Me In 1942,O 9,24:2
Porgy and Bess 1943,S 14,26:2
Porgy and Bess 1944,F 8,13:2
Memphis Bound 1945,My 25,23:2
Tower Beyond Tragedy, The 1950,N 27,29:1
Tower Beyond Tragedy, The 1950,D 10,II,5:1

Ross, Robert (Miscellaneous)

Dance Me a Song 1950,Ja 21,10:5

Ross, Ron

Hamlet 1959,S 11,21:4

Ross, Rosalind

All in Good Time 1965,F 19,25:1

Ross, Roslyn

Mikado, The 1942,F 4,22:2
Pirates of Penzance, The 1942,F 18,22:2
Iolanthe 1942,F 24,26:4
Gondoliers, The 1942,Mr 4,22:3

Ross, Roy

Du Barry Was a Lady 1939,D 7,34:2

Ross, Sam (Playwright)

My House Is Your House 1970,O 16,53:2

Ross, Shirley

Higher and Higher 1940,Mr 17,X,2:5
Higher and Higher 1940,Ap 5,24:3

Ross, Sidney (Miscellaneous)

If 1927,O 26,26:2
Love Nest, The 1927,D 23,17:1

Ross, Sidney (Producer)

Marquise, The 1927,N 15,26:4
Young Love 1928,O 31,28:1

Ross, Stanley

Sons o' Fun 1941,D 2,28:2

Ross, Steven

End as a Man 1953,S 16,39:1

Ross, Ted

Buck White 1969,D 3,63:1

Ross, Terry (Composer)

Fortune and Men's Eyes 1967,F 24,29:1

Ross, Terry (Miscellaneous)

Goa 1968,F 23,46:1
Little Murders 1969,Ja 6,38:1
Nobody Hears A Broken Drum 1970,Mr 20,55:1

Ross, Thomas W

Wheel, The 1921,My 8,VI,1:1
Wheel, The 1921,Ag 30,10:1
Bombo 1921,O 7,20:2
Polly Preferred 1923,Ja 12,13:3
Scandals 1924,Jl 1,16:1
Laff That Off 1925,N 3,34:2
Gossipy Sex, The 1927,Ap 20,28:3
Family Upstairs, The 1933,O 28,20:6

Service for Two 1935,Ag 20,25:1
Saturday's Children 1936,Jl 7,22:5
High Tor 1937,Ja 11,15:2
Our Town 1938,Ja 23,II,10:6
Our Town 1938,F 5,18:3
Our Town 1938,F 13,X,1:1
World's Full of Girls, The 1943,D 7,31:2

Ross, Tony

Black Pit 1935,Mr 21,26:6
Mother, The 1935,N 20,26:3

Ross, Trudy

Plough and the Stars, The 1956,Ap 6,14:1

Ross, Vera

Three Showers 1920,Ap 6,18:1
Wildcat, The 1921,N 28,16:2
Passing Show of 1923, The 1923,Je 15,24:6
Iolanthe 1926,Ap 20,24:2
Pirates of Penzance, The; Slave of Duty, The
  1926,D 7,25:1
Mikado, The; Town of Titipu, The 1927,S 19,30:1
Chocolate Soldier, The 1930,Ja 28,28:1
Mikado, The; Town of Titipu, The 1931,My 5,33:2
Gondoliers, The 1931,Je 2,34:4
Iolanthe 1931,Jl 14,21:5
Iolanthe 1932,Ja 5,20:2
Gondoliers, The 1932,Ja 12,29:1
Mikado, The 1933,Ap 18,13:4
Yeomen of the Guard, The 1933,My 2,20:4
H M S Pinafore 1933,My 9,20:3
Patience 1933,My 23,22:6
Pirates of Penzance, The 1933,Ag 8,22:4
Yeomen of the Guard, The 1933,Ag 15,20:5
Mikado, The 1934,Ap 3,26:3
Pirates of Penzance, The 1934,Ap 10,26:5
H M S Pinafore 1934,Ap 17,27:2
Iolanthe 1934,My 1,26:4
Mikado, The 1935,Jl 16,24:4
Pirates of Penzance, The 1935,Jl 23,24:2
Yeomen of the Guard, The 1935,Jl 30,16:4
Gondoliers, The 1935,Ag 6,20:5
H M S Pinafore 1935,Ag 13,20:6
Mikado, The 1936,Ap 11,18:4
Pirates of Penzance, The 1936,Ap 21,27:5
H M S Pinafore 1936,Ap 28,17:2
Iolanthe 1936,My 5,26:2

Ross, William (Miscellaneous)

Hostage, The 1960,S 21,42:1
Slow Dance on the Killing Ground 1964,D 1,50:1
Annie Get Your Gun 1966,Je 1,42:2
Borstal Boy 1970,Ap 1,38:1

Ross, Winston

Taming of the Shrew, The 1935,O 1,27:3
Idiot's Delight 1936,Mr 25,25:2
Hidden Horizon 1946,S 20,42:2
S S Glencairn; In the Zone 1948,My 21,21:2
S S Glencairn; Bound East for Cardiff
  1948,My 21,21:2
Uniform of Flesh 1949,Ja 31,15:2
Twelfth Night 1949,O 4,33:2
Design For A Stained Glass Window
  1950,Ja 24,26:2
Julius Caesar 1950,Je 21,30:1
Billy Budd 1951,F 12,18:3
Idiot's Delight 1951,My 24,46:3
Red Rainbow, A 1953,S 15,37:4

Ross (Miscellaneous)

Ordinary Man, An 1968,S 10,39:1

Ross Sisters

Count Me In 1942,O 9,24:2

Rossato (Playwright)

Delitto e Castigo; Crime and Punishment
  1931,Ja 26,20:5

Rossbach, Richard M

Whispering Gallery, The 1935,D 1,II,12:6

Rossback, A

Lady of the Lamp, The 1920,Ag 18,6:4

Rosse, Herman (Costume Designer)

Americana 1928,O 31,28:2

Rosse, Herman (Scenic Designer)

Americana 1928,O 31,28:2
Hello, Daddy! 1928,D 27,26:5
Hamlet 1930,Mr 25,34:4
Macbeth 1930,Mr 26,24:6
Twelfth Night 1930,Mr 27,24:7
Merchant of Venice, The 1930,Mr 27,24:7
Richard III 1930,Mr 31,24:1
Great Magoo, The 1932,D 3,20:7
Ulysses in Nighttown 1958,Je 6,30:1

Rousseau, Marcel

Caravan 1928,Ag 30,13:3

Rossellini, Roberto (Director)

Joan At The Stake 1954,Je 25,15:3

Rossen, Carol

Entertain a Ghost 1962,Ap 10,48:1
Nobody Loves an Albatross 1963,D 20,20:1
Nobody Loves an Albatross 1964,Ja 5,II,1:1
Square in the Eye 1965,My 20,54:1

Rossen, Frances H (Miscellaneous)

Sniper, The 1959,O 28,40:4
Movie Man 1959,O 28,40:4
Abortion 1959,O 28,40:4

Rossen, Robert (Director)

Thomas Paine 1930,Mr 21,30:7

Rossen, Robert (Director)—Cont

Tree, The 1932,Ap 13,23:5
Birthright 1933,N 22,22:3
Body Beautiful, The 1935,N 1,24:3
Cool World, The 1960,F 23,38:2

Rossen, Robert (Playwright)

Body Beautiful, The 1935,N 1,24:3
Cool World, The 1960,F 23,38:2

Rossen, Robert (Producer)

Birthright 1933,N 22,22:3

Rosset, Allan

Many Loves 1959,Ja 14,28:1

Rossi, Adele

Tristi Amori; Unhappy Loves 1930,O 27,17:6

Rossi, Alfred

Hamlet 1963,My 9,41:1
Miser, The 1963,My 10,39:1
Death of a Salesman 1963,Jl 20,11:2

Rossi, David B (Director)

Squaring the Circle 1931,Ap 27,24:4
Dole Brothers 1932,Mr 26,17:7

Rossi, Helen (Playwright)

Squaring the Circle 1931,Ap 27,24:4

Rossi, Mario

Shewing-Up of Blanco Posnet, The 1959,S 19,26:7

Rossi, Max

Great Way, The 1921,N 8,28:2

Rossi, Susanna

Laugh, Clown, Laugh! 1923,N 29,30:1
Dove, The 1925,F 12,17:3

Rossilli, Gastone

Pantagleize 1967,D 1,54:1
Iphigenia in Aulis 1968,Ap 6,43:1
Brass Butterfly, The 1970,Ja 31,34:1

Rossington, Norman

Midsummer Night's Dream, A 1954,S 22,33:1

Rossini (Composer)

Boutique Fantasque, La 1929,D 28,10:6
Once Over Lightly 1942,N 20,26:2

Rossiter, Leonard

Semi-Detached 1963,O 8,49:1
Semi-Detached 1963,O 20,II,1:1
Resistible Rise of Arturo Ui, The 1968,Ag 30,22:2
Resistible Rise of Arturo Ui, The 1969,Ag 18,28:1

Rossiter, P T (Producer)

Oh, Ernest! 1927,My 10,24:3

Rossler, Karl (Playwright)

Blaue Hemd von Ithaka, Das 1931,Mr 15,IX,2:4

Rossman, Arthur

Chinese O'Neill 1929,My 23,27:1

Rossman, Herman (Original Author)

Ace, The 1933,S 17,X,1:6

Rosso, Joseph

Beggars Are Comming to Town 1945,O 29,16:2

Rossum, George

Strip Girl 1935,O 21,22:6

Rostaing, Jeanne

Exhibition 1969,My 16,41:1

Rostand, Edmond (Original Author)

White Plume, The 1939,D 27,16:1
Cyrano de Bergerac 1953,N 13,24:3

Rostand, Edmond (Playwright)

Cyrano de Bergerac 1920,Mr 20,14:3
Faraway Princess, The 1922,D 6,3:2
Cyrano de Bergerac 1923,N 2,14:1
Cyrano de Bergerac 1923,N 11,VIII,1:1
Aiglon, L' 1924,O 21,21:1
Aiglon, L' 1925,O 31,20:3
Last Night of Don Juan, The 1925,N 10,23:2
Cyrano de Bergerac 1926,Ja 24,II,8:5
Cyrano de Bergerac 1926,F 19,18:1
Aiglon, L' 1926,O 3,29:5
Chantecler 1927,N 6,IX,4:1
Cyrano de Bergerac 1927,N 27,IX,4:1
Aiglon, L' 1927,D 27,24:3
Princesse Lointaine, La 1929,N 17,IX,2:6
Romanesques, Les 1930,Mr 2,IX,4:2
Cyrano de Bergerac 1932,D 27,11:2
Aiglon, L' 1934,N 5,22:2
Chantecler 1937,D 10,33:6
Cyrano de Bergerac 1946,N 3,II,1:1
Cyrano de Bergerac 1946,N 3,I,54:6
Cyrano de Bergerac 1946,N 10,II,3:2
Cyrano de Bergerac 1947,Ja 17,27:2
Fantasticks, The 1960,My 4,55:2
Cyrano de Bergerac 1962,Ag 1,21:1
Cyrano de Bergerac 1963,Je 20,30:1
Cyrano de Bergerac 1968,Ap 26,30:1

Rostand, Maurice

Deserteuse, La 1926,N 21,VIII,2:1

Rostand, Maurice (Playwright)

Gloire, La 1921,O 23,22:2
Phoenix, The 1923,Ja 11,21:4
Phoenix, The 1923,Ja 21,VII,1:3
Secret of the Sphinx 1924,Mr 2,VIII,1:3
Archangel, The 1925,Mr 26,21:5
Deserteuse, La 1926,N 21,VIII,2:1
Trouble, Le 1928,Ap 29,IX,2:3
Deserteuse, La 1928,S 23,IX,2:1
Napoleon IV 1928,O 7,IX,5:3
Homme Que J'ai Tue, L' 1930,F 9,VIII,2:6
Marchands de Canons, Les 1933,Je 4,IX,1:6
Trial of Oscar Wilde, The 1935,Ap 21,IX,2:1
Homme Que J'Ai Tue, L'; Man Whom I Have
  Killed, The 1936,D 10,34:3

and, Maurice (Playwright)—Cont
therine Empereur 1938,Je 12,X,2:3

en, Herman (Director)
agic Touch, The 1947,S 4,30:1

en, Leo (Original Author)
lucation of H*Y*M*A*N K*A*P*L*A*N, The
1968,Ap 14,II,1:1

en, Leo (Playwright)
lucation of H*Y*M*A*N K*A*P*L*A*N, The
1968,Ap 5,57:1

en, Norman (Playwright)
rst Stop to Heaven 1941,Ja 6,10:7
ister Johnson 1956,Mr 30,11:1
ister Johnson 1956,Ap 8,II,1:1
me Slowly, Eden 1966,D 7,56:1

tetter, Alice
ream Play 1926,Ja 21,18:2

toff, P
evisor; Inspector General, The 1935,F 18,19:6

ton, Ronald
ne Is a Lonely Number 1964,Je 19,37:3
arrow Road to the Deep North 1969,D 2,64:1

ton, Ronald (Miscellaneous)
ne Is a Lonely Number 1964,Je 19,37:3

tova, Luba
razy With the Heat 1941,Ja 15,18:2
ady Comes Across, The 1942,Ja 10,10:2

tova, Mira
ea Gull, The 1954,My 12,38:1
ea Gull, The 1954,My 23,II,1:1

tova, Mira (Playwright)
ea Gull, The 1954,My 12,38:1

tovtseva, Klementina
herry Orchard, The 1965,F 10,46:1
hree Sisters, The 1965,F 12,15:1
remlin Chimes 1965,F 25,23:1

tovzev, Ivan
ncle Vanya 1960,F 13,13:4

switha (Playwright)
braham; Dulcitus; Callimachus 1926,Mr 29,24:2

ra, Kiki
ippolytus 1968,N 20,38:3

ra, Nino (Composer)
omeo and Juliet 1962,F 14,39:1

tante, Rick
unset 1966,My 13,34:1

tante, Rick (Miscellaneous)
Walk Down Mah Street! 1968,Je 13,54:1
acco-Vanzetti 1969,F 9,78:1
hepherd of Avenue B, The 1970,My 16,30:1
teal the Old Man's Bundle 1970,My 16,30:1

tet
Bourgeois Gentilhomme, Le 1924,N 20,21:2

th, Ann
straight Thru the Door 1928,O 5,17:2
Here Goes the Bride 1931,N 4,31:2

th, Ann (Costume Designer)
Maybe Tuesday 1958,Ja 30,18:3
Edward II 1958,F 12,32:5
Make a Million 1958,O 24,39:2
Disenchanted, The 1958,D 4,53:4
Desert Incident, A 1959,Mr 25,40:1
Cool World, The 1960,F 23,38:2
Gay Divorce 1960,Ap 4,37:1
Ernest in Love 1960,My 5,39:4
Face of a Hero 1960,O 21,29:5
Far Country, A 1961,Ap 5,32:1
Purlie Victorious 1961,S 29,29:1
Look: We've Come Through 1961,O 26,40:1
This Side of Paradise 1962,F 22,19:6
Isle of Children 1962,Mr 17,16:2
Venus at Large 1962,Ap 13,30:1
Portrait of the Artist as a Young Man, A
1962,My 29,21:1
Barroom Monks, The 1962,My 29,21:1
Natural Affection 1963,F 2,5:2
Hey You, Light Man! 1963,Mr 2,5:2
Children From Their Games 1963,Ap 12,33:1
Case of Libel, A 1963,O 11,43:2
In the Summer House 1964,Mr 26,43:1
Last Analysis, The 1964,O 2,30:1
Slow Dance on the Killing Ground 1964,D 1,50:1
I Had a Ball 1964,D 16,50:1
Odd Couple, The 1965,Mr 11,36:1
Romeo and Juliet 1965,Je 21,36:3
Impossible Years, The 1965,O 14,55:1
Wayward Stork, The 1966,Ja 20,27:1
Star-Spangled Girl, The 1966,D 22,38:1
Deer Park, The 1967,F 1,27:2
Beard, The 1967,O 25,40:1
Something Different 1967,N 29,52:1
Happiness Is Just a Little Thing Called a Rolls
Royce 1968,My 13,54:5
Play It Again, Sam 1969,F 13,52:3
My Daughter, Your Son 1969,My 14,36:2
Tiny Alice 1969,S 30,42:1
Three Sisters, The 1969,O 10,38:1
Gantry 1970,F 16,44:1
Purlie 1970,Mr 16,53:1
What the Butler Saw 1970,My 5,56:1
Engagement Baby, The 1970,My 22,40:1

Roth, Ann (Scenic Designer)
We Comrades Three 1962,O 12,26:1
Roth, Beatrice
Man Who Never Died, The 1958,N 22,27:2
Roth, Dennis
Lovely Ladies, Kind Gentlemen 1970,D 29,38:1
Roth, Elliot
Love Letter, The 1921,O 5,20:1
Revolt 1928,N 1,25:3
Mendel, Inc 1929,N 26,28:5
Roth, George
Heimkehr aus der Fremde, Die; Stranger, The
1949,S 2,14:1
Roth, Lillian
Shavings 1920,F 17,18:1
Padlocks of 1927 1927,Jl 6,23:4
Earl Carroll's Vanities 1928,Ag 7,25:2
Vaudeville (Palace) 1930,N 3,19:2
Vanities 1931,Ag 11,28:4
Vanities 1931,Ag 16,VIII,1:1
Earl Carroll's Vanities 1931,Ag 28,18:7
Revels of 1935 1934,O 3,24:2
I Can Get It for You Wholesale 1962,Mr 23,29:1
Roth, Ludwig
Everyman 1941,My 9,19:2
God Strikes Back 1943,F 27,11:2
Private Life of the Master Race, The
1945,Je 13,28:3
Faust 1947,N 29,9:2
Rape of the Sabine Women, The 1949,F 5,10:5
Stalag 17 1951,My 9,41:2
Sherlock Holmes 1953,O 31,11:2
Flowering Peach, The 1954,D 29,19:2
Roth, Manuel L (Miscellaneous)
Homeward Look, The 1954,Je 4,26:2
Roth, Marc (Costume Designer)
High Button Shoes 1955,Mr 12,10:6
Roth, Mary
Great Scott! 1929,S 3,25:1
Infinite Shoeblack, The 1930,F 18,28:1
Murder in the Cathedral 1936,Mr 21,13:5
Help Yourself! 1936,Jl 15,15:1
Roth, Nancy
Kismet 1965,Je 23,45:1
Roth, Philip
Three Times Three; George Washington Crossing
the Delaware 1962,Mr 2,24:1
Three Times Three; Twenty-Five Cent White Cap,
The 1962,Mr 2,24:1
Roth, Philip (Original Author)
Three Philip Roth Stories; Defender of the Faith
1970,Jl 31,14:1
Three Philip Roth Stories; Epstein 1970,Jl 31,14:1
Three Philip Roth Stories; Conversion of the Jews
1970,Jl 31,14:1
Roth, Wolfgang (Costume Designer)
Good Woman of Setzuan, The 1956,D 19,41:2
Roth, Wolfgang (Lighting Director)
Wanhope Building, The 1947,F 11,36:5
Twentieth Century 1950,D 25,23:6
Medea 1955,Je 16,35:4
Johnny Johnson 1956,O 22,24:1
Deadly Game, The 1960,F 3,27:2
Secret Concubine, The 1960,Mr 22,29:2
Cannibals, The 1968,N 4,60:1
Roth, Wolfgang (Playwright)
Littlest Circus, The 1959,D 26,5:6
Roth, Wolfgang (Scenic Designer)
First Million, The 1943,Ap 29,27:4
Too Hot for Maneuvers 1945,My 3,26:5
Wanhope Building, The 1947,F 11,36:5
Yellow Jack 1947,F 28,26:2
Oh, Mr Meadowbrook! 1948,D 27,17:2
Cock-A-Doodle-Doo 1949,F 28,16:5
Now I Lay Me Down to Sleep 1950,Mr 3,21:2
Tower Beyond Tragedy, The 1950,N 27,29:1
Tower Beyond Tragedy, The 1950,D 10,II,5:1
Twentieth Century 1950,D 25,23:6
Porgy and Bess 1952,S 8,18:2
Porgy and Bess 1953,Mr 10,25:5
Medea 1955,Je 16,35:4
Johnny Johnson 1956,O 22,24:1
Good Woman of Setzuan, The 1956,D 19,41:2
Good Woman of Setzuan, The 1956,D 30,II,1:1
River Line, The 1957,Ja 3,29:2
Portofino 1958,F 22,8:3
Littlest Circus, The 1959,D 26,5:6
Deadly Game, The 1960,F 3,27:2
Secret Concubine, The 1960,Mr 22,29:2
Brecht on Brecht 1962,Ja 4,26:1
Typists, The 1963,F 6,5:2
Tiger, The 1963,F 6,5:2
Lion in Love, The 1963,Ap 26,28:3
Dreigroschenoper, Die 1965,Mr 12,24:1
Cannibals, The 1968,N 4,60:1
Cannibals, The 1968,N 10,II,5:1
Rotha, Wanda
Queen Christina 1937,N 29,18:1
Elisabeth of Austria 1938,N 20,IX,1:8
Rothblatt, Philip
Sound of Hunting, A 1954,Ap 7,41:1
Rothblum, I
Tenth Commandment, The 1926,N 18,27:1

Rothblum, I—Cont
It Can't Happen Here 1936,O 28,30:1
Rothe, Anita
Mrs Jimmie Thompson 1920,Mr 30,9:1
White Villa, The 1921,F 15,7:1
Rose Bernd 1922,S 27,17:1
Queen Victoria 1923,N 16,15:1
Kingdom of God, The 1928,D 21,30:2
Love Duel, The 1929,Ap 16,32:3
Scarlet Sister Mary 1930,N 26,19:2
School for Scandal, The 1931,N 11,26:4
Achilles Had a Heel 1935,O 14,20:2
Rothe, Frank
One, Two, Three! 1930,S 30,24:2
Hamlet 1931,N 6,28:4
When in Rome 1934,F 28,22:6
Ringside Seat 1938,N 23,24:5
Rothe, Hans (Miscellaneous)
Merry Wives of Windsor 1929,Mr 24,X,2:3
Rothe, Hans (Playwright)
Night Arrival 1938,D 25,IX,5:4
Rothe, Hans (Translator)
Troilus and Cressida 1927,N 20,IX,4:7
Little Accident 1929,S 22,IX,4:1
Antony and Cleopatra 1932,F 7,VIII,1:5
Twelfth Night 1932,O 23,IX,3:1
Two Gentlemen of Verona 1936,Je 28,IX,2:1
Rothenberg, David (Producer)
Viet Rock 1966,N 11,38:1
Fortune and Men's Eyes 1967,F 24,29:1
Rothenberg, Jerome (Playwright)
Deputy, The 1964,F 27,26:1
Rothenberg, John (Miscellaneous)
Beaux' Stratagem, The 1970,F 10,50:2
Three Sisters, The 1970,F 12,30:1
Rother, Artur (Musical Director)
Consul, The 1951,S 8,9:3
Rothgeb, John (Lighting Director)
Candida 1957,F 9,14:1
Rothgeb, John (Scenic Designer)
Candida 1957,F 9,14:1
Rothier, Leon
Bell for Adano, A 1944,N 10,24:6
Bell for Adano, A 1944,D 7,21:2
Rothlein, Arlene
In Circles 1967,O 14,12:1
In Circles 1968,Je 28,36:1
Peace 1968,N 10,87:1
Peace 1969,Ja 28,49:1
Rothman, Barbara (Costume Designer)
Angels of Anadarko 1962,O 11,47:1
Rothman, Benjamin (Producer)
House on Grand Street, A 1953,O 10,12:6
Sands of the Negev 1954,O 20,32:1
Family Mishmash, A 1958,O 20,36:1
Rothman, Bernard
Outside the Door 1949,Mr 2,33:2
Rothman, Harry
Alt Heidelberg 1926,My 31,10:5
Rothman, Lawrence (Producer)
Sands of the Negev 1954,O 20,32:1
Rothmel, Bill
Last Pad, The 1970,D 8,61:1
Rothrock, Richard
House of Breath, The 1957,Ap 15,23:2
Rothrock, Rusti
Master Builder, The 1957,D 18,42:7
Roths, Frank
Mademoiselle 1932,O 19,22:4
Rothschild, Henride (Playwright)
Moulin de la Galette, Le 1923,Ja 28,VII,2:7
Vocation, La 1926,D 19,VII,3:3
Circe 1929,Mr 31,VIII,2:7
Rothschild, Keith
Macbeth 1968,N 30,49:3
Rothschild, William
Treasure, The 1920,O 5,13:1
Great Adventure, The 1921,F 26,9:2
Rothstein, Norman (Miscellaneous)
Postmark Zero 1965,N 2,28:1
Rothstein, Raphael (Miscellaneous)
Children of the Shadows 1964,F 27,26:1
Rothstein, Raphael (Translator)
Mother Courage 1967,N 17,55:1
Mirele Efros 1969,D 26,41:1
Rotoli, Francesca
Mask of Hamlet, The 1921,Ag 23,10:3
Rotolo, Carla (Lighting Director)
World of Kurt Weill in Song, The 1964,My 13,53:1
Rotolo, Carla (Miscellaneous)
World of Kurt Weill in Song, The 1964,My 13,53:1
Rotondo, Guy
To Broadway With Love 1964,Ap 30,28:6
Rotov, Alex
Dream With Music 1944,My 19,15:2
Rott
Abie's Irish Rose 1928,Je 10,VIII,2:8
Rott, Adolf (Director)
Consul, The 1951,S 8,9:3
Rott, Adolf (Miscellaneous)
Dreigroschenoper, Die 1965,Mr 12,24:1
Rotter, Alfred (Producer)
Marietta 1929,D 8,X,4:4
Land des Laechelns, Das 1929,D 8,X,4:4

Rotter, Fritz (Playwright)
Letters to Lucerne 1941,D 9,47:6
Letters to Lucerne 1941,D 24,14:2
Rotter, Fritz (Producer)
Marietta 1929,D 8,X,4:4
Land des Laechelns, Das 1929,D 8,X,4:4
Lied der Liebe, Das 1932,F 7,VIII,1:3
Rotter (Composer)
Liselott 1932,My 22,VIII,2:3
Rotter (Lyricist)
Liselott 1932,My 22,VIII,2:3
Rotter Brothers
Veilchen von Montmartre 1931,Mr 29,VIII,3:1
Rotter Brothers (Producer)
Blue Beard 1929,Jl 7,VIII,2:1
Veilchen von Montmartre 1931,Mr 29,VIII,3:1
Maria Stuart 1932,Je 19,IX,1:3
Katharina 1932,O 2,IX,3:1
Frau Die Weiss Was Sie Will, Eine 1932,O 9,IX,3:7
Rouba, Pawel
Woman, The 1965,Ja 6,32:1
Jaselka 1965,Ja 6,32:1
Kernel and the Shell, The 1965,Ja 6,32:1
Nightmare, The 1965,Ja 6,32:1
Post Office, The 1965,Ja 6,32:1
Jacob and the Angel 1965,Ja 6,32:1
Book, The 1965,Ja 6,32:1
Labyrinth, The 1965,Ja 6,32:1
Roubanis, Nicholas (Composer)
Song of Daphnis, The 1938,Je 23,26:5
Roubanis, Nicholas (Musical Director)
Song of Daphnis, The 1938,Je 23,26:5
Roud, Richard (Translator)
Chairs, The 1958,Ja 10,20:3
Lesson, The 1958,Ja 10,20:3
Rouda, Mitchell
Mirele Efros 1969,D 26,41:1
Rouda, Neil
Mirele Efros 1969,D 26,41:1
Roudenko, Lubov
Merry Widow, The 1943,Ag 5,19:2
Merry Widow, The 1943,Ag 22,II,5:1
Nellie Bly 1946,Ja 22,32:2
Annie Get Your Gun 1946,My 17,14:2
Pardon Our French 1950,O 6,22:4
Rouer, Germaine
Homme Qui Assassina, L' 1924,N 11,20:1
Homme et Ses Fantomes, L' 1924,N 14,16:1
Bourgeois Gentilhomme, Le 1955,O 26,26:1
Rouffe, Alida
Marius 1929,Mr 31,VIII,2:7
Rougeri, Carmen
Hippolytus 1968,N 20,38:3
Roughton, A I (Translator)
Judge, The 1958,My 14,36:2
Rouleau, Philipp
Boys in the Band, The 1969,S 20,21:2
Rouleau, Raymond (Director)
Gigi 1951,N 26,20:4
Orpheus Descending 1959,Mr 18,44:6
Hedda Gabler 1962,D 13,8:5
Rouleau, Raymond (Producer)
Sorcieres de Salem, Les 1955,F 27,II,3:1
Rouledge, Patricia
How's the World Treating You? 1966,O 25,50:1
Rouler, Bill
Macbeth 1969,D 23,25:1
Roulet, Bill
Macbeth 1969,D 23,25:1
Round, Thomas
Mikado, The 1947,D 30,18:2
Pirates of Penzance, The 1948,Ja 6,27:2
Pirates of Penzance, The 1948,Ja 11,II,1:1
H M S Pinafore 1948,Ja 20,26:2
Gondoliers, The 1948,Ja 27,31:2
Yeomen of the Guard, The 1962,Jl 11,28:1
Mikado, The 1962,N 14,43:1
Gondoliers, The 1962,N 16,25:2
H M S Pinafore 1962,N 23,32:4
Rounds, David
You Never Can Tell 1958,Je 17,25:1
Foxy 1964,F 17,26:1
Child's Play 1970,F 18,39:1
Child's Play 1970,Mr 1,II,1:4
Rounds, David (Lighting Director)
Philanderer, The 1958,My 13,26:2
Rounds, David (Scenic Designer)
School for Wives 1957,Je 20,23:4
Philanderer, The 1958,My 13,26:2
You Never Can Tell 1958,Je 17,25:1
Rounds, Frank W Jr
What a Relief 1935,D 14,10:6
Take It Away 1936,D 22,32:3
Rounds, Frank W Jr (Playwright)
Take It Away 1936,D 15,30:5
Rounds, Gene
Walk Down Mah Street! 1968,Je 13,54:1
Rounds, Irene
Paradise 1931,My 12,29:2
Roundtree, Jean
Roll Sweet Chariot 1934,O 3,24:3
Roundtree, Richard
Man Better Man 1969,Jl 3,22:1

Rounseville, Robert
Babes in Arms 1937,Ap 15,18:4
Knickerbocker Holiday 1938,O 20,26:2
Higher and Higher 1940,Ap 5,24:3
Mikado, The 1952,O 21,35:2
Pirates of Penzance, The 1952,O 28,36:4
H M S Pinafore 1952,N 4,32:2
Show Boat 1954,My 6,44:1
Show Boat 1954,O 29,28:4
Candide 1956,D 3,40:2
Candide 1956,D 9,II,5:1
Brigadoon 1957,Mr 28,37:1
Song of Norway 1958,Je 23,19:2
Show Boat 1961,Ap 13,32:1
Yeomen of the Guard, The 1964,Mr 19,29:2
H M S Pinafore 1964,Mr 19,29:2
Man of La Mancha 1965,N 23,52:1
Man of La Mancha 1967,N 24,61:1
Rourke, Betty
Happy 1927,D 6,26:3
Rourke, Vincent
Sojourner Truth 1948,Ap 22,35:2
Pursuit of Happiness, The 1952,Mr 22,9:2
Philanderer, The 1958,My 13,26:2
Rousby, Harry
I Have Been Here Before 1938,O 14,26:2
Rouskaya, Norka
Century Revue and the Midnight Rounders, The 1920,Jl 13,9:1
Roussakis, Nicolas
Full Moon in March, A 1960,S 20,48:1
Herne's Egg, The 1960,S 20,48:1
Purgatory 1960,S 20,48:1
Rousseau, Marcel
Tickle Me 1920,Ag 18,9:1
Voltaire 1922,Mr 21,17:1
Agent 666, L' 1923,My 30,10:5
Homme et Ses Fantomes, L' 1924,N 14,16:1
Taming of the Shrew, The 1924,N 25,27:3
Sapphire Ring, The 1925,Ap 16,25:2
Naughty Cinderella 1925,N 10,23:6
Sweetheart Time 1926,Ja 20,23:2
Manhattan Mary 1927,S 27,30:3
So Was Napoleon 1930,Ja 9,22:2
Ada Beats the Drum 1930,My 9,20:4
Weather Permitting 1935,My 24,24:5
Hooray for What! 1937,D 2,32:5
Trojan Incident 1938,Ap 22,15:2
Naked Genius, The 1943,O 22,20:5
Rousseau, Virginia
Stage Door 1936,O 23,26:3
Roussel, Albert (Playwright)
Aunt Caroline's Will 1954,Ag 11,21:1
Roussel, Raymond (Playwright)
Locus Solus 1922,D 9,11:4
Etoile au Front, L' 1924,My 11,VIII,1:4
Roussey, Fernande
Aiglon, L' 1924,O 21,21:1
Madame Sans-Gene 1924,N 4,30:1
Amoureuse 1924,N 28,13:1
Roussillon, Jean-Paul
Troupe Du Roi, La 1970,F 4,38:1
Don Juan 1970,F 7,24:2
Roussillon, Jean-Paul (Director)
Georges Dandin 1970,O 19,50:1
Roussilon, Jean-Paul
Troupe Du Roi, La 1970,F 4,38:1
Roussin, Andre
Bal des Voleurs, Le 1938,N 29,26:4
Faiseur, Le; Promoter, The 1938,D 27,12:3
Paquebot Tenacity, Le 1939,Ja 10,16:4
Chacun Sa Verite 1939,Ja 24,17:1
37 Sous de M Montaudoin, Les 1939,F 7,17:2
Enterrement, L' 1939,F 7,17:2
Siegfried 1939,F 21,15:2
Roussin, Andre (Playwright)
Nina 1951,D 6,44:3
Helen 1952,D 15,22:6
Little Hut, The 1953,O 8,37:2
Little Hut, The 1961,Jl 26,34:2
Roussin, Mr
Precieuses Ridicules, Les 1938,D 13,30:3
Fourberies de Scapin, Les 1938,D 13,30:3
Roussou, Matel (Playwright)
Beau Reve, Un 1928,Je 3,VIII,2:5
Fin du Monde, La 1930,F 2,VIII,4:1
Rousten, Herman (Director)
Comes the Revelation 1942,My 27,26:2
Routledge, Patricia
Darling of the Day 1968,Ja 29,26:2
Darling of the Day 1968,F 11,II,3:1
Country Wife, The 1969,Ag 30,10:3
Rouvel, Otto
Nathan the Wise 1962,Mr 7,29:1
Before Sundown 1962,Mr 14,43:1
Rouverol, Aurania (Playwright)
Skidding 1928,My 22,18:5
It Never Rains 1929,N 20,26:4
It Never Rains 1931,D 25,29:3
Growing Pains 1933,N 24,24:2
All in Marriage 1936,O 29,31:3
Places, Please 1937,N 13,10:6

Rouverol, Jean
Growing Pains 1933,N 24,24:2
So Proudly We Hail 1936,S 23,28:4
Roux, Jean-Louis
Henry V 1956,Je 20,27:2
Malade Imaginaire, Le; Imaginary Invalid, The 1958,Ap 30,28:2
Mariage Force, Le; Forced Wedding, The 1958,My 7,43:1
Henry V 1966,Je 8,38:1
Henry VI 1966,Je 9,55:2
Roux, Marie-Ange
Femmes Savantes, Les 1967,F 7,34:2
Rovano, Antonio
Desert Song, The 1946,Ja 9,20:2
Rove, Korena
Congai 1928,N 28,24:3
Rover, Dominic (Rev) (Playwright)
Age and Grace 1956,F 21,38:2
Rovetta, Gerolamo (Playwright)
Romanticismo 1933,My 1,10:5
Romanticismo 1934,My 14,20:2
Rovida, Maya
Green Table, The 1942,Ja 22,12:2
Rovin, Robert
Pousse-Cafe 1966,Mr 19,19:2
House of Leather, The 1970,Mr 19,56:1
Rovina, Anna
Dybbuk, The 1926,D 14,24:2
Eternal Jew, The 1926,D 21,21:2
Golem, The 1927,F 5,13:2
Rovina, Hanna
Dybbuk, The 1948,My 3,26:3
David's Crown 1948,My 10,26:2
Golem, The 1948,My 17,22:3
Oedipus Rex 1948,My 24,23:2
Row, Arthur William
Richard III 1920,Mr 8,7:1
Merchant of Venice, The 1920,D 30,16:2
School for Scandal, The 1923,Mr 13,19:2
Man Who Ate the Popomack, The 1924,Mr 25,24:1
Airways, Inc 1929,F 21,30:5
Joy of Serpents 1930,Ap 4,22:4
Colonel Satan 1931,Ja 12,24:1
Country Wife, The 1931,Ap 19,31:5
Ship Comes in, A 1934,S 20,21:1
Streetcar Named Desire, A 1950,My 24,36:1
Wild Duck, The 1951,D 27,17:1
Row, Arthur William (Director)
Lady Windermere's Fan 1932,Ja 27,19:3
Row, Charles
Scotland Yard 1929,S 28,16:6
Rowan, Ernest
George Washington 1920,Mr 2,9:1
Hamlet 1920,Mr 17,14:2
Servant in the House, The 1921,My 3,20:1
Taming of the Shrew, The 1921,My 12,20:2
Merchant of Venice, The 1921,My 14,10:4
Jolly Roger, The 1923,Ag 31,10:4
Cyrano de Bergerac 1923,N 2,14:1
Othello 1925,Ja 12,11:1
Bit o' Love, A 1925,My 13,24:2
Hamlet 1925,O 12,19:2
Merchant of Venice, The 1925,D 28,12:1
Cyrano de Bergerac 1926,F 19,18:1
Servant in the House, The 1926,My 4,30:1
Immortal Thief, The 1926,O 4,21:1
Caponsacchi 1926,O 27,24:2
Enemy of the People, An 1927,O 4,32:5
Hamlet 1928,Ja 5,33:2
Caponsacchi 1928,Ja 25,20:3
Henry V 1928,Mr 16,26:2
Light of Asia, The 1928,O 10,32:2
Cyrano de Bergerac 1928,D 26,14:4
Becky Sharp 1929,Je 4,29:1
Bonds of Interest, The 1929,O 15,34:2
Richelieu 1929,D 26,20:3
Frankie and Johnny 1930,S 26,16:5
Way of the World, The 1931,Je 2,34:3
School for Scandal, The 1931,N 11,26:4
Cyrano de Bergerac 1932,D 27,11:2
Sailor, Beware! 1933,S 29,24:4
Richelieu 1934,My 22,28:1
Hamlet 1934,D 26,19:3
Richard III 1934,D 28,24:3
Cyrano de Bergerac 1936,Ap 28,17:1
Dead End 1936,S 20,IX,3:7
Brown Sugar 1937,D 3,29:2
All the Living 1938,Mr 25,14:4
Jeremiah 1939,F 4,11:2
Goodbye in the Night 1940,Mr 19,31:2
Snafu 1944,O 26,19:5
Antony and Cleopatra 1947,N 27,49:2
Corn Is Green, The 1950,Ja 12,33:2
Rowan, Frank
Daisy Mayme 1926,O 26,24:2
A la Carte 1927,Ag 18,25:3
Vermont 1929,Ja 9,28:1
Maggie, the Magnificent 1929,O 22,26:1
Penny Arcade 1930,Mr 11,24:5
Blessed Event 1932,F 13,23:2
Marathon 1933,Ja 28,8:8
All Good Americans 1933,D 6,29:2

Rowan, Frank—Cont
Portrait of Gilbert 1934,D 29,11:5
Holy Night 1941,D 22,23:3
Cellar and the Well, The 1950,D 11,30:2
Anna Christie 1952,Ja 10,33:1
First Lady 1952,My 29,18:5
Rowan, John
Three Doors 1925,Ap 24,16:4
Nowhere Bound 1935,Ja 23,20:2
Rowan, Marc
Annie Get Your Gun 1966,Je 1,42:2
Rowan, Ted
Hall of Healing 1952,My 8,35:6
Rowe, Alfred
Kind Lady 1935,Ap 24,24:5
Heartbreak House 1935,Jl 23,24:3
Arms and the Man 1937,Jl 20,19:3
Rowe, Arthur
Living Dangerously 1935,Ja 14,10:3
Kit Marlowe 1936,My 24,35:1
Rowe, Charles (Producer)
East of Broadway 1932,Ja 27,19:3
Rowe, Crayton
Orpheus Descending 1959,O 6,45:2
Rowe, Earl
Man Who Never Died, The 1958,N 22,27:2
Viva Madison Avenue 1960,Ap 7,42:1
Rowe, Eleanor
Melody Man, The 1924,My 14,14:2
Rowe, Frances
They Came to a City 1943,Je 6,II,1:6
Man and Superman 1947,O 9,31:2
Man and Superman 1947,O 19,II,1:1
Man and Superman 1949,My 17,28:6
Rowe, Hansford
We Bombed in New Haven 1968,O 17,51:1
Ah, Wilderness! 1969,N 9,86:1
Arsenic and Old Lace 1970,N 5,59:1
Rowe, James
Aquashow 1954,Je 23,20:4
Rowe, Jeremy
Cherry Orchard, The 1970,My 7,63:2
Rowe, Joan
Faith of Our Fathers 1950,Ag 6,72:2
Rowe, John
State of the Union 1945,N 15,25:2
Rowe, John Boyne
Middle Watch, The 1929,O 17,27:1
Rowe, Kim (Miscellaneous)
Wuziz! 1970,O 2,25:2
Rowe, Leonard
Don Juan 1921,S 8,14:2
Mountain Man, The 1921,D 13,24:2
Rowe, Norman L
Grey Heir, The 1926,Ap 6,29:2
Rowe, Peter
Founders, The 1957,My 14,39:1
Rowe, Raymond
Life With Father 1939,Ag 15,14:4
Rowel, Kenneth (Scenic Designer)
Hamlet 1953,Ag 25,18:6
Edward II 1969,S 4,50:1
Rowell, George (Miscellaneous)
Engaged! or Cheviot's Choice 1965,Ap 24,19:2
Rowell, George (Playwright)
Engaged! or Cheviot's Choice 1965,Ap 24,19:2
Rowen, Don
Sunny 1925,S 23,22:1
Rowen, Rebecca
Summer Night 1939,N 3,17:1
Rowen, Ruth
Great Campaign, The 1947,Ap 1,33:2
Rowland, Adele
Vaudeville (Palace) 1921,My 17,20:3
Spice of 1922 1922,Jl 7,12:4
Vaudeville (Palace) 1928,Jl 10,17:3
Rowland, Douglas
Wild Duck, The 1928,N 19,17:1
Naughty-Naught '00 1937,Ja 25,23:2
London Assurance 1937,F 19,14:5
First Stop to Heaven 1941,Ja 6,10:7
Rowland, Frank (Producer)
Money in the Air 1932,Mr 8,19:3
Rowland, Helen
Roof, The 1931,O 31,22:4
Audition of the Apprentice Theatre 1939,Je 2,26:2
Rowland, Henry
Right to Love, The 1925,Je 9,16:4
Winged Victory 1943,N 22,24:1
Rowland, Jada
That Lady 1949,O 20,38:8
That Lady 1949,N 23,18:4
House of Bernarda Alba, The 1951,Ja 8,14:6
Sunday Breakfast 1952,My 30,12:2
Cold Wind and the Warm, The 1958,D 9,55:1
Rowland, Jeffrey
Sunrise at Campobello 1958,Ja 31,25:1
J B 1958,D 12,2:7
Invitation to a March 1960,O 31,27:2
Rowland, Mabel
Untitled-One Woman Show 1923,N 19,19:1
Nine O'Clock Revue 1936,Jl 8,14:3
Rowland, Mabel (Director)
Nine O'Clock Revue 1936,Jl 8,14:3

Rowland, Mabel (Playwright)
Nine O'Clock Revue 1936,Jl 8,14:3
Rowland, Penelope
Big Pond, The 1928,Ag 22,25:1
Rowland, Toby
Comedy of Good and Evil, A 1938,Ap 8,16:3
Rowlands, Gena
Middle of the Night 1956,F 9,39:1
Middle of the Night 1956,F 19,II,1:1
Rowles, Polly
Dark Eyes 1948,Mr 25,34:4
Richard III 1949,F 9,33:2
Golden State, The 1950,N 27,29:3
Small Hours, The 1951,F 16,22:1
Gertie 1952,Ja 31,23:1
Time Out for Ginger 1952,N 27,50:4
Julius Caesar 1955,Jl 13,20:1
Wooden Dish, The 1955,O 7,20:1
Goodbye Again 1956,Ap 25,38:1
Auntie Mame 1956,N 1,47:2
Auntie Mame 1956,N 11,II,1:1
Look After Lulu 1959,Mr 4,35:1
Mighty Man Is He, A 1960,Ja 7,25:2
No Strings 1962,Mr 16,24:1
No Strings 1962,Mr 25,II,1:1
Best Laid Plans, The 1966,Mr 26,15:2
Killing of Sister George, The 1966,O 6,57:1
Forty Carats 1968,D 27,45:1
Forty Carats 1969,Ja 5,II,1:3
Rowley, Belinha
Night Thoreau Spent in Jail, The 1970,N 2,66:1
Rowley, Edward
Round Trip 1945,My 30,16:4
Rowley, Frank (Miscellaneous)
Tableaux 1961,D 18,41:3
Curate's Play, The 1961,D 18,41:3
Her Master's Voice 1964,D 28,33:2
Rowley, Samuel (Playwright)
When You See Me You Know Me
1927,Ag 14,VII,1:7
Rowley, William (Playwright)
Changeling, The 1956,My 4,20:3
Witch of Edmonton, The 1962,N 23,32:2
Changeling, The 1964,O 30,32:2
Rowthorn, Jeffrey
Cup of Trembling, The 1959,My 1,33:5
Rox, John (Composer)
All in Fun 1940,D 28,11:2
John Murray Anderson's Almanac 1953,D 11,42:2
New Faces of 1956 1956,Je 15,32:1
Rox, John (Lyricist)
All in Fun 1940,D 28,11:2
John Murray Anderson's Almanac 1953,D 11,42:2
New Faces of 1956 1956,Je 15,32:1
Roxan, William (Producer)
Red Roses for Me 1951,Ap 26,35:8
Roxanne
Black Crook, The 1929,Mr 12,26:5
Roxlo, Conrado Nale (Original Author)
Difficult Woman, The 1962,Ap 26,22:7
Roy, Dorothy
Peggy-Ann 1926,D 28,16:3
Connecticut Yankee, A 1927,N 4,24:2
Hello, Daddy! 1928,D 27,26:5
Roy, Etienne (Playwright)
Ce Que Femme Veut 1924,F 3,VII,1:4
Roy, Harold W
Sale and a Sailor, A, or Glory! What Price!
1926,Ap 25,30:4
Roy, Hazel (Costume Designer)
Lace on Her Petticoat 1951,S 5,40:3
To Dorothy, A Son 1951,N 20,37:2
Gertie 1952,Ja 31,23:1
Evening With Mike Nichols and Elaine May, An
1960,O 10,37:1
Zelda 1969,Mr 6,38:1
Roy, Jesse L
Guns 1928,Ag 7,25:2
Roy, Jules (Playwright)
Cyclones, Les 1955,F 27,II,3:1
Red River, The 1961,Ja 10,27:2
Roy, Margaret
H M S Pinafore 1942,Ja 22,12:2
Mikado, The 1942,F 4,22:2
Pirates of Penzance, The 1942,F 18,22:2
Iolanthe 1942,F 24,26:4
Gondoliers, The 1942,Mr 4,22:3
Roy, Nell
Jonica 1930,Mr 30,VIII,2:7
Jonica 1930,Ap 8,27:1
Roy, Renee
Nature's Way 1957,O 17,42:2
Zelda 1969,Mr 6,38:1
Roy, Rob
Mrs Moonlight 1952,N 21,21:1
Roy, Sheila
Coach With the Six Insides, The 1962,N 27,44:1
Roy, Susan
Cock-A-Doodle-Doo 1949,F 28,16:5
Infernal Machine, The 1954,Mr 22,22:2
Doll's House, A 1954,N 15,32:2

Roy, Susan (Director)
French Way, The; Grand Vizier, The
1962,Mr 21,36:2
French Way, The; Deceased, The 1962,Mr 21,36:2
French Way, The; Edward and Agrippina
1962,Mr 21,36:2
Roy, Walter
Hunky Dory 1922,S 5,21:2
Little Minister, The 1925,Mr 24,21:1
Marigold 1930,O 9,23:1
Roy, Will
Most Happy Fella, The 1966,My 12,55:1
H M S Pinafore 1968,Ap 29,47:2
Roy, William (Composer)
Maggie 1953,F 19,20:2
Roy, William (Lyricist)
Maggie 1953,F 19,20:2
Roy, William (Musical Director)
Ben Bagley's New Cole Porter Revue
1965,D 23,20:1
Roy, William (Playwright)
Penny Friend, The 1966,D 27,46:1
Roy Campbell's Continentals
At Home Abroad 1935,S 20,17:4
Show Is On, The 1936,D 26,14:2
Royal, Daniel
Steel 1931,N 19,26:5
Royal, Ted (Composer)
Hold It! 1948,My 6,31:5
Where's Charley? 1948,O 12,33:2
As the Girls Go 1948,N 15,21:2
Tickets, Please! 1950,Ap 28,25:2
Royal, Ted (Miscellaneous)
Brigadoon 1950,My 3,36:2
Guys and Dolls 1950,N 25,11:2
Flahooley 1951,My 15,39:1
Seventeen 1951,Je 22,16:6
Paint Your Wagon 1951,N 13,32:2
New Faces of 1952 1952,My 17,23:2
John Murray Anderson's Almanac 1953,D 11,42:2
Mr Wonderful 1956,Mr 23,23:2
New Faces of 1956 1956,Je 15,32:1
Happy Hunting 1956,D 7,30:1
Rumple 1957,N 7,42:2
Body Beautiful, The 1958,Ja 24,15:2
New Faces of 1962 1962,F 2,25:1
Royal, Ted (Musical Director)
Make Mine Manhattan 1948,Ja 16,26:2
Sleepy Hollow 1948,Je 4,26:3
Small Wonder 1948,S 16,33:5
Boy Friend, The 1954,O 1,20:1
House of Flowers 1954,D 31,11:2
Guys and Dolls 1955,Ap 21,32:2
Almost Crazy 1955,Je 21,37:1
Boy Friend, The 1970,Ap 15,54:1
Royal Pekin Troupe of Chinese Wonder Workers
Vaudeville (Hippodrome) 1924,Ap 1,18:1
Royall, W Allen
When the Roll Is Called Up Yonder
1930,My 9,20:5
Royall, W Allen (Playwright)
When the Roll Is Called Up Yonder
1930,My 9,20:5
Royce, Allen
Walk in Darkness 1963,O 29,30:2
Royce, Brigham
Miss Lulu Bett 1920,D 28,9:1
Royce, Burt B Jr
Patience 1928,Je 26,29:3
Royce, Ed (Miscellaneous)
You're a Good Man, Charlie Brown 1967,Mr 8,51:1
Royce, Edward (Director)
Midnight Frolic 1920,Ag 4,7:1
Annie 1924,O 12,VIII,2:1
Annie Dear 1924,N 5,25:3
Louie the 14th 1925,Mr 4,17:1
No Foolin' 1926,Je 25,25:1
Merry Malones, The 1927,S 27,30:2
She's My Baby 1928,Ja 4,22:2
Billie 1928,O 2,34:2
Royce, Edward (Miscellaneous)
Student Gypsy, The; Prince of Liederkranz, The
1963,O 1,34:1
Babes in the Wood 1964,D 29,21:2
This Here Nice Place 1966,N 2,35:2
Royce, Edward (Playwright)
Fritzi 1935,D 21,10:3
Royce, Elizabeth
Father Malachy's Miracle 1937,N 18,26:4
Jeremiah 1939,F 4,11:2
Royce, Julian
Anne-One Hundred 1927,Je 26,VIII,1:3
Death Takes a Holiday 1931,F 17,29:1
Gentle Rain 1936,S 20,IX,1:4
Royce, Lynn and Vanya
Star and Garter 1942,Je 25,26:2
Royce, Margie
Bye Bye Bonnie 1927,Ja 14,15:3
Royce, Marguerite
Showboat Revue 1935,Ag 18,13:2
Royce, Ray L
Dorian Gray 1928,My 22,18:4

Royce, Rosita
Night in Venice, A 1952,Je 27,18:6
Night in Venice, A 1953,Je 26,15:2
Royce, Virginia
Merchant of Venice, The 1955,Ja 8,9:7
Royce-Garrett (Baroness)
Vaudeville (Hippodrome) 1924,S 30,27:5
Royde-Smith, Naomi (Playwright)
Mafro, Darling! 1929,Mr 17,X,1:4
Roye, Harry
Vaudeville (Palace) 1926,O 19,27:5
Vaudeville (Palace) 1927,My 24,23:1
Vaudeville (Palace) 1927,My 31,25:1
Vaudeville (Palace) 1927,Je 7,27:3
Vaudeville (Palace) 1927,Ag 23,29:3
Chee-Chee 1928,S 26,25:1
Vaudeville (Palace) 1929,Ja 14,20:3
Vaudeville (Palace) 1930,O 20,29:1
Roye, Maye
Vaudeville (Palace) 1927,Je 14,33:3
Roye, Ruth
Vaudeville (Palace) 1921,Je 14,18:2
Vaudeville (Palace) 1923,Ja 23,18:2
Royle, Edwin Milton
Milestones 1930,Je 3,27:1
Royle, Edwin Milton (Original Author)
White Eagle, The 1927,D 27,24:4
Royle, Edwin Milton (Playwright)
Lancelot and Elaine 1921,S 13,12:1
Squaw Man, The 1921,D 27,10:3
Her Way Out 1924,Je 24,18:3
Launcelot and Elaine 1930,Mr 10,24:3
Royle, Josephine
Lancelot and Elaine 1921,S 13,12:1
Squaw Man, The 1921,D 27,10:3
Tyrants 1924,Mr 5,14:1
Her Way Out 1924,Je 24,18:3
Magda 1926,Ja 27,16:2
Launcelot and Elaine 1930,Mr 10,24:3
Royle, Selena
Lancelot and Elaine 1921,S 13,12:1
Golden Days 1921,N 2,20:1
Her Temporary Husband 1922,S 1,16:2
Peer Gynt 1923,F 6,14:1
Rust 1924,F 1,12:1
She Stoops to Conquer 1924,Je 10,24:3
Jane-Our Stranger 1925,O 9,27:2
Masque of Venice, The 1926,Mr 3,27:3
Yellow 1926,S 22,30:1
Paradise 1927,D 26,26:4
Napoleon 1928,Mr 9,21:1
Thunder in the Air 1929,N 12,34:3
Launcelot and Elaine 1930,Mr 10,24:3
Milestones 1930,Je 3,27:1
Merchant of Venice, The 1930,D 3,29:2
Heat Wave 1931,F 18,14:6
Way of the World, The 1931,Je 2,34:3
Roof, The 1931,O 31,22:4
Roof, The 1931,N 8,VIII,1:1
When Ladies Meet 1932,O 7,19:1
When Ladies Meet 1932,O 16,IX,1:1
Days Without End 1934,Ja 9,19:1
Good-Bye Please 1934,O 25,26:6
Portrait of Gilbert 1934,D 29,11:5
Hippolytus 1935,Je 15,20:4
Mad Morning 1935,Je 25,14:1
Meet the Prince 1935,Jl 9,24:5
Meet the Prince 1935,Ag 6,20:4
On Stage 1935,O 30,16:6
Among Those Sailing 1936,F 12,24:4
Curtain Call 1937,Ap 23,24:7
Reno 1937,Ag 10,22:7
Prodigal Father, The 1937,Ag 17,23:1
Young Mr Disraeli 1937,N 10,30:5
Royse, Roberta
Twisting Road, The; Housekeeper, The
1957,N 18,36:5
Lady's Not for Burning, The 1959,Ja 31,13:2
Country Scandal, A 1960,My 6,21:8
Country Scandal, A 1960,My 15,II,1:1
Here Come the Clowns 1960,S 20,48:1
Anniversary, The 1961,Ap 21,26:2
On the High Road 1961,Ap 21,26:2
Wedding, The 1961,Ap 21,26:2
Call It Virtue 1963,Mr 28,8:2
Royster, H P
Tiger Smiles, The 1930,D 18,29:1
Royster, Hubert (Composer)
Samarkand 1926,D 22,24:4
Royston, George
Green Pastures, The 1951,Mr 16,35:2
Royston, Roy
Peg o' My Dreams 1924,My 6,25:3
Marjorie 1924,Ag 12,12:2
June Days 1925,Ag 7,12:5
Ups-A-Daisy 1928,O 9,34:2
Smiling Faces 1931,D 13,VIII,2:5
Smiling Faces 1932,Ag 31,12:3
Royton, Helen
American, Very Early 1934,Ja 31,21:2
Dooley Cashes In 1935,Ag 17,18:6
Royton, Velma
All Men Are Alike 1941,O 7,27:2

Little Women 1944,D 13,29:2
Little Women 1945,D 24,18:2
Pursuit of Happiness, The 1952,Mr 22,9:2
Rozahegyi
Nem Elhetek Muzsikaszo Nelkul
1928,D 30,VIII,4:4
Rozakis, Gregory
Natural Affection 1963,F 2,5:2
Dirty Old Man, The 1964,My 5,53:1
Royal Hunt of the Sun, The 1965,O 27,36:2
What Did We Do Wrong? 1967,O 23,56:1
Cannibals, The 1968,N 4,60:1
Rozan, Dominique
Volpone 1957,F 5,27:2
Rozan, Gerta
Window Shopping 1938,D 24,13:2
Rozan, Gertrude
Grandma's Diary 1948,S 23,36:2
Rozanka, Vera
Going to America 1961,O 30,33:7
Country Boy, The 1963,O 28,20:1
Both Kooney Lemels 1964,O 12,37:2
Rozano, Jennie (Pfc)
Swing Sister Wac Swing 1944,Ja 4,20:4
Roze, Edmond (Director)
Mediterranee 1926,N 7,VIII,2:7
Rozenberg, Lucien
Maitre Bolbec et son Mari 1926,N 14,VIII,2:1
Ma Soeur et Moi 1926,Ap 29,IX,2:3
Untitled-Play 1928,N 11,X,2:7
Manquait un Homme, Il 1929,Ap 14,X,2:1
Bloch de Chicago 1933,O 15,IX,1:8
Rozet
Homme Qui Assassina, L' 1924,N 11,20:1
Procureur Hallers, Le 1924,N 13,18:1
Merchant of Venice, The 1924,N 18,23:2
Taming of the Shrew, The 1924,N 25,27:3
Rozewicz, Tadeusz (Playwright)
Dossier, The 1961,Ja 14,15:2
Rozier, Sheva
International Playgirls '64 1964,My 22,40:2
Rub, Christian
Bruder Straubinger 1921,N 16,22:3
Fruehlingsluft 1921,N 29,17:4
Rubain, Lenny
Hajj Malik, El 1970,O 4,II,5:1
Rubans, Maurice (Composer)
Broadway Nights 1929,Jl 16,23:2
Rubber, Violla (Miscellaneous)
Night of the Iguana, The 1961,D 29,10:1
Rubber, Violla (Producer)
Haven, The 1946,N 14,39:4
Rubber Band
Tarot 1970,D 12,19:1
Rubber Duck, The
Tarot 1970,D 12,19:1
Rubber Duck, The (Playwright)
Tarot 1970,D 12,19:1
Rubber Duck, The and Robert Kalfin (Director)
Tarot 1970,D 12,19:1
Ruben, Florence (Musical Director)
Jeanne d'Arc 1922,Ap 22,9:3
Ruben, Jose
Sacred and Profane Love 1920,F 24,11:1
Sacred and Profane Love 1920,F 29,V,5:2
Maker of Dreams, The 1920,Ap 28,9:3
Untitled-Benefit 1920,My 2,VI,2:2
Checkerboard, The 1920,Ag 20,7:2
Checkerboard, The 1920,Ag 22,VI,1:2
Thy Name Is Woman 1920,N 16,19:1
Swords 1921,S 2,9:3
Gringo 1922,D 15,26:3
Gringo 1922,D 24,VII,1:1
Exile, The 1923,Ap 10,24:2
Vierge Folle, La; Foolish Virgin, The
1924,Mr 22,12:2
Leah Kleschna 1924,Ap 22,19:2
Leah Kleschna 1924,Ap 27,VIII,1:1
Bewitched 1924,O 2,26:3
Merchants of Glory 1925,D 15,28:3
Merchants of Glory 1925,D 27,VII,1:1
Ghosts 1926,Mr 17,28:2
Two Orphans, The 1926,Ap 6,26:2
Two Orphans, The 1926,Ap 11,VIII,1:1
Jacob Slovak 1927,O 6,28:4
Red Robe, The 1928,D 26,15:1
Red Robe, The 1929,Ja 13,VIII,1:1
As You Desire Me 1931,Ja 29,21:2
Cat and the Fiddle, The 1931,O 16,26:4
Drums Begin, The 1933,N 25,10:5
Rain From Heaven 1934,D 25,28:4
Matrimony, PFD 1936,N 6,28:4
Matrimony, PFD 1936,N 13,26:3
Madame Capet 1938,O 26,26:2
Vagabond King, The 1943,Je 30,24:2
Great Sebastians, The 1956,Ja 5,27:1
Ruben, Jose (Director)
First Mortgage 1929,O 11,36:1
Wonderful Night, A; Fledermaus, Die
1929,N 1,23:3
Cafe 1930,Ag 29,11:1
Sweet Chariot 1930,O 24,30:2
Cat and the Fiddle, The 1931,O 16,26:4

Ruben, Jose (Director)—Cont
All the King's Horses 1934,Ja 31,21:3
Strip Girl 1935,O 21,22:6
May Wine 1935,D 6,30:3
Forbidden Melody 1936,N 3,33:1
Matrimony, PFD 1936,N 13,26:3
Orchids Preferred 1937,My 12,26:5
Madame Capet 1938,O 26,26:2
Susanna, Don't You Cry 1939,My 23,27:2
Chocolate Soldier, The 1942,Je 24,22:2
New Moon, The 1944,My 18,16:2
Flamingo Road 1946,Mr 20,18:2
Toplitzky of Notre Dame 1946,D 27,13:4
Lady From Paris, The 1950,S 27,36:1
Ruben, Jose (Miscellaneous)
Red Robe, The 1928,D 26,15:1
Ruben, Jose (Playwright)
Light Behind the Shadow, The 1936,Ja 21,26:6
Alice Takat 1936,F 11,19:2
Rubens, Maurie (Composer)
Sky High 1925,Mr 3,21:4
Artists and Models 1925,Je 25,16:2
Gay Paree 1925,Ag 19,14:3
Night in Paris, A 1926,Ja 6,16:3
Great Temptations, The 1926,My 19,29:1
Merry World, The 1926,Je 9,18:3
Night in Paris, A 1926,Jl 27,15:4
Artists and Models 1927,N 16,28:2
Madcap, The 1928,F 1,31:2
Greenwich Village Follies 1928,Ap 10,32:2
Luckee Girl 1928,S 17,28:6
Music in May 1929,Ap 2,29:1
Night in Venice, A 1929,My 22,30:2
Hello Paris 1930,N 17,29:3
Rubens, Paul (Lyricist)
Florodora 1920,Ap 6,18:1
Florodora 1936,Ag 23,II,8:2
Rubenstein, Albert
Road to Rio, The 1930,My 7,25:1
Rubenstein, Bath-Zion
Golem, The 1948,My 17,22:3
Rubenstein, Rosa
Gondoliers, The 1932,Ja 12,29:1
Rubien, William
Shake Hands With the Devil 1949,O 21,30:4
Rubin, Aaron (Director)
Girls Against the Boys, The 1959,N 3,26:1
Rubin, Arthur
Silk Stockings 1955,F 25,17:3
Most Happy Fella, The 1956,My 4,20:1
Juno 1959,Mr 10,41:1
Kean 1961,N 3,28:2
Here's Love 1963,O 4,28:1
Rubin, Benny
Half a Widow 1927,S 13,37:3
Vaudeville (Palace) 1927,S 27,31:3
Vaudeville (Palace) 1927,O 4,34:3
Vaudeville (Palace) 1930,D 1,19:1
Vaudeville (Palace) 1930,D 8,27:2
Radio Carnival 1932,Mr 14,13:3
Vaudeville (Palace) 1932,Ap 25,18:3
Rubin, Daniel (Playwright)
Night Duel, The 1926,F 16,22:3
Devils 1926,Mr 18,26:4
Women Go on Forever 1927,S 8,25:1
Undertow 1929,N 10,X,4:8
Claire Adams 1929,N 20,26:3
Riddle Me This! 1932,F 26,22:5
Riddle Me This! 1933,Mr 15,21:3
Move on, Sister 1933,O 25,22:4
Rubin, David
Without Warning 1937,My 3,23:2
Rubin, Evelyn
Playing With Love 1929,F 27,16:4
Rubin, Flora (Musical Director)
Faraway Princess, The 1922,D 6,3:2
Rubin, Gershon
Green Fields 1920,Mr 26,11:2
Naomi 1920,My 7,12:2
Andersh; New Worlds 1922,S 26,18:2
Three Little Business Men, The 1923,S 4,12:1
Some Girl 1927,D 24,8:2
Major Noah 1929,F 23,17:2
Stempenu, the Fiddler 1929,Mr 9,24:7
Jew Suss 1929,O 19,22:3
Angels on Earth 1929,D 11,34:7
Roaming Stars 1930,Ja 25,12:2
Chains 1930,F 23,29:2
Chair, The 1930,O 4,15:4
God's Thieves 1930,O 27,17:4
Rubin, Harry
Backlane Center 1961,N 23,51:1
Sage of Rottenburg, The 1963,N 20,48:1
Fifth Commandment, The 1965,N 15,48:4
Prince Reuvaini 1967,N 19,83:1
Melody Lingers On, The 1969,N 17,55:1
Rubin, Ira
Don Carlos 1962,F 28,27:5
Storm, The 1962,Mr 31,17:2
Hop, Signor! 1962,My 8,45:2
Rubin, Jeff
Adding Machine, The 1970,D 5,40:1
Rubin, Jose
Couturiere de Luneville, La 1924,Mr 26,16:2

Rubin, Joseph
Mighty Nimrod, The 1931,My 13,23:1
Rubin, Leon
Tell Me Pretty Maiden 1937,D 17,33:5
Rubin, Martin (Miscellaneous)
Susan Slept Here 1961,Jl 12,35:2
Little Hut, The 1961,Jl 26,34:2
Rubin, Martin (Producer)
World of Gunter Grass, The 1966,Ap 27,38:1
Diary of a Madman 1967,Mr 24,25:1
Tango 1969,Ja 20,33:1
Rubin, Menachem
Twice 100,000 1931,N 22,VIII,3:1
Happy Family, A 1934,S 24,15:2
Twice 100,000 1934,N 23,22:6
East Side Wedding, An 1935,Ja 21,18:2
Lovka Maladetz 1935,Mr 27,25:5
Heaven on Earth 1935,O 8,26:2
Tevye the Dairyman 1935,O 25,25:1
Wise Fool, The 1938,O 10,15:3
Mazel Tov, Rabbi 1938,N 28,10:4
Jewish Heart, The 1939,Ja 25,16:6
Three Men and a Girl 1939,F 6,9:3
Doctor Herzl 1945,D 21,25:4
Song of Dnieper 1946,O 26,10:5
Wandering Stars 1946,D 14,18:2
Shepherd King, The 1955,O 13,36:2
Hamlet of Stepney Green 1958,N 14,21:1
Go Fight City Hall 1961,N 3,28:5
Rubin, Menachem (Director)
Twice 100,000 1934,N 23,22:6
Mazel Tov, Rabbi 1938,N 28,10:4
Nice People 1958,O 20,36:1
Go Fight City Hall 1961,N 3,28:5
Rubin, Menachem (Playwright)
Tevye the Dairyman 1935,O 25,25:1
Rubin, Menachem (Producer)
Twice 100,000 1931,N 22,VIII,3:1
Rubin, Milton
Kith and Kin 1930,My 14,31:1
Rubin, Myra
Man and Superman 1970,F 24,48:1
Rubin, Myron
Outside the Door 1949,Mr 2,33:2
Rubin, Pedro
Rio Rita 1927,F 3,18:3
Rubina, Fania
Schlemihl 1936,S 19,20:4
Warson at Night 1938,Ja 31,14:3
Rubina, Fanya
Mazel Tov, Molly 1950,O 2,18:1
Take It Easy 1950,D 25,23:6
Wedding March, The 1955,O 17,33:1
Rubinate, Dan
Power of Dreams, A 1958,Mr 11,33:1
Rubincyzk, Israel
Each Had Six Wings 1964,Mr 12,39:1
Rubine, Sarah
To Be or Not to Be-What Kind of a Question Is
 That? 1970,O 20,39:1
Rubinek, Saul
Hamlet 1969,Je 11,37:1
Alchemist, The 1969,Je 12,51:1
Measure for Measure 1969,Je 13,41:3
Rubini, Miriam
Day of Judgement, The 1941,O 9,27:3
Rubinsky, Robert I
Hair 1968,Ap 30,40:2
Rubinson, David (Producer)
Cradle Will Rock, The 1964,N 9,40:4
Rubinstein, Arthur (Composer)
Androcles and the Lion 1968,Je 27,47:1
Spitting Image 1969,Mr 3,28:1
Rubinstein, Arthur (Miscellaneous)
Love and Let Love 1968,Ja 4,30:1
Rubinstein, Arthur (Musical Director)
Gantry 1970,F 16,44:1
Whispers on the Wind 1970,Je 4,50:1
Rubinstein, Carol (Lighting Director)
Now Is the Time for all Good Men 1967,S 27,42:1
Rubinstein, Edwin V (Original Author)
Love, Honor and Oh Baby 1940,Mr 29,25:2
Rubinstein, Eli (Composer)
To Be or Not to Be-What Kind of a Question Is
 That? 1970,O 20,39:1
Light, Lively and Yiddish 1970,O 28,58:1
Rubinstein, Eli (Musical Director)
To Be or Not to Be-What Kind of a Question Is
 That? 1970,O 20,39:1
Rubinstein, Eva
Girl in Pink Tights, The 1954,Mr 6,13:2
Dybbuk, The 1954,O 27,33:6
Diary of Anne Frank, The 1955,O 6,24:2
Rubinstein, Ida
Secret of the Sphinx 1924,Mr 2,VIII,1:3
Dame aux Camelias, La 1926,N 21,VIII,2:1
Rubinstein, Ida (Mme) (Producer)
Imperatrice aux Rochers, L' 1927,Mr 20,VIII,2:4
Rubinstein, Jehuda
Dybbuk, The 1948,My 3,26:3
David's Crown 1948,My 10,26:2
Oedipus Rex 1948,My 24,23:2

Rubinstein, Jehudah (Miscellaneous)
David's Crown 1948,My 10,26:2
Rubinstein, Ruth
Pins and Needles 1939,Ap 21,26:2
Rubio, Emery (Playwright)
Sunday Breakfast 1952,My 30,12:2
Rubio, Jose Lopez (Playwright)
Max and Mr Max 1932,Ja 24,VIII,3:5
Rublee, Juliet Barrett (Producer)
Moon Is a Gong, The 1926,Mr 13,21:3
Ruby, Adeline
Subway, The 1929,Ja 26,15:1
Ruby, Elialee
First Flight 1925,S 18,26:2
Footlights 1927,Ag 20,8:2
Ruby, Harry
All-Star Jamboree 1921,Jl 14,18:1
Ruby, Harry (Composer)
Helen of Troy, New York 1923,Je 20,22:6
No Other Girl 1924,Ag 14,10:4
By the Way 1925,D 29,20:3
Ramblers, The 1926,S 21,32:2
Twinkle Twinkle 1926,N 17,22:2
Five O'Clock Girl, The 1927,O 11,26:3
Good Boy 1928,S 6,23:2
Animal Crackers 1928,O 24,26:2
High Kickers 1941,N 1,21:2
Ruby, Harry (Lyricist)
Helen of Troy, New York 1923,Je 20,22:6
No Other Girl 1924,Ag 14,10:4
Ramblers, The 1926,S 21,32:2
Twinkle Twinkle 1926,N 17,22:2
Lucky 1927,Mr 23,28:3
Five O'Clock Girl, The 1927,O 11,26:3
Good Boy 1928,S 6,23:2
Animal Crackers 1928,O 24,26:2
High Kickers 1941,N 1,21:2
Ruby, Harry (Playwright)
Broadway Brevities, 1920 1920,S 30,12:2
Holka Polka 1925,O 15,27:2
Ramblers, The 1926,S 21,32:2
Twinkle Twinkle 1926,N 17,22:2
Lucky 1927,Mr 23,28:3
She's My Baby 1928,Ja 4,22:2
Top Speed 1929,N 17,IX,4:1
Top Speed 1929,D 26,20:1
High Kickers 1941,N 1,21:2
Ruby, Toby (Miscellaneous)
Lullaby 1954,F 4,21:2
Ruby, Vera
Afgar 1920,N 9,13:2
Rudashefsky, Herman
Alt Heidelberg 1926,My 31,10:5
Rudaw, Geoffrey (Lighting Director)
Recruiting Officer, The 1958,F 8,12:2
Rudd, Dorothy
Wall Street 1927,Ap 21,24:4
Rudd, Enid (Playwright)
Peterpat 1965,Ja 7,27:1
Peterpat; Dual Marriage Way 1965,Ag 19,34:3
Rudd, Eric (Playwright)
Song of Songs 1958,O 29,31:1
Diary of a Madman 1964,Ap 17,29:2
Rudd, Paul
King Lear 1968,N 8,43:1
Evening for Merlin Finch, An 1968,D 30,25:1
In the Matter of J Robert Oppenheimer
 1969,Mr 7,28:1
Rudd, Wayland
Sentinels 1931,D 26,15:1
Marriage of Cana, The 1932,F 3,22:4
Bloodstream 1932,Mr 31,25:1
Ruddy, Muriel
Yellow Jacket, The 1923,Ap 20,20:3
Rude, Roberta
Latent Heterosexual, The 1968,Mr 22,52:1
Macbeth 1968,N 30,49:3
Rudel, Julius (Director)
Mikado, The 1961,Ja 18,26:1
Rudel, Julius (Miscellaneous)
Gondoliers, The 1961,Ja 26,33:2
Show Boat 1961,Ap 13,32:1
Oklahoma! 1963,F 28,8:2
Oklahoma! 1963,My 16,40:1
Yeomen of the Guard, The 1964,Mr 19,29:2
Rudel, Julius (Musical Director)
Pirates of Penzance, The 1946,My 17,14:6
Pirates of Penzance, The 1946,S 21,19:2
Show Boat 1954,My 6,44:1
Carousel 1954,Je 3,32:2
Show Boat 1954,O 29,28:4
Finian's Rainbow 1955,My 19,25:1
Kiss Me, Kate 1956,F 15,27:6
Carmen Jones 1956,Je 1,28:2
Brigadoon 1957,Mr 28,37:1
Carousel 1957,S 12,38:2
Pirates of Penzance, The 1961,Ja 20,24:5
Show Boat 1961,Ap 13,32:1
South Pacific 1961,Ap 27,26:3
Porgy and Bess 1961,My 18,40:1
Iolanthe 1962,Ap 12,42:4
Gondoliers, The 1962,Ap 19,34:2
Brigadoon 1962,My 31,21:4

Rudel, Julius (Musical Director)—Cont
Brigadoon 1963,F 1,6:2
Wonderful Town 1963,F 15,10:2
Oklahoma! 1963,F 28,8:2
Oklahoma! 1963,My 16,40:1
Patience 1964,Mr 26,42:1
Porgy and Bess 1964,My 7,32:1
Brigadoon 1964,D 24,9:1
Dreigroschenoper, Die 1965,Mr 12,24:1
Patience 1965,Ap 16,34:1
Yeomen of the Guard, The 1965,Ap 22,26:1
Rudell, Billie
Dove, The 1925,F 12,17:3
Rudell and Dunigan
Vaudeville (Palace) 1929,Ap 22,22:6
Rudenski, Marian
Mirele Efros 1967,O 20,55:1
Mother Courage 1967,N 17,55:1
Rudenski, Shmuel
Dybbuk, The 1964,F 4,30:2
Ruder, Lucius S (Musical Director)
Blue Blood 1924,Ap 3,21:2
Ruderman, Mikhail (Playwright)
Counterattack 1943,F 4,27:2
Rudge, Jerry
Make Me Disappear 1969,My 14,34:1
Rudi, Richard
Yankee Point 1942,N 24,28:2
Counterattack 1943,F 4,27:2
Rudie, Robert
Heure du Berger, L'; Propitious Moment, The
 1936,N 12,30:1
Si Je Voulais; If I Wished to 1937,Ja 28,22:5
Rudie, Yvonne
Si Je Voulais; If I Wished to 1937,Ja 28,22:5
Rudin, Frederick
Zeppelin 1929,Ja 15,22:3
Airways, Inc 1929,F 21,30:5
Tyrant, The 1930,N 13,33:1
Flag Is Born, A 1946,S 7,10:6
Rudin, Herman
Whisper in God's Ear, A 1962,O 12,27:2
Rudish, David (Costume Designer)
Say Nothing 1965,Ja 28,21:2
Rudkin, David (Playwright)
Afore Night Come 1964,Je 26,34:1
Rudley, Herbert
Did I Say No? 1931,S 23,19:4
Black Tower 1932,Ja 12,29:2
We the People 1933,Ja 23,9:5
Threepenny Opera, The 1933,Ap 14,22:4
Mother, The 1935,N 20,26:3
Eternal Road, The 1937,Ja 8,14:2
Abe Lincoln in Illinois 1938,O 17,12:2
World We Make, The 1939,N 21,19:1
World We Make, The 1939,D 3,IX,5:1
Another Sun 1940,F 24,8:6
Eight O'Clock Tuesday 1941,Ja 7,18:2
Macbeth 1941,N 12,30:2
Sons and Soldiers 1943,My 5,22:2
Rudley, Herbert (Director)
How Long Till Summer 1949,D 28,30:3
Rudley, Herbert (Playwright)
How Long Till Summer 1949,D 28,30:3
Rudley, Marian
Processional 1937,O 14,23:1
Cradle Will Rock, The 1937,D 6,19:4
Cradle Will Rock, The 1938,Ja 4,19:3
Rudley, Sarett (Playwright)
How Long Till Summer 1949,D 28,30:3
Rudman, Michael (Director)
Straight Up 1970,S 2,30:2
Rudney, Edward
Hamlet 1964,Jl 4,9:1
Falstaff; Henry IV, Part II 1965,Jl 1,35:1
Julius Caesar 1965,Jl 2,18:1
Falstaff 1966,Je 20,27:1
Twelfth Night 1966,Je 23,28:1
Julius Caesar 1966,Je 24,29:2
Those That Play the Clowns 1966,N 25,48:1
Antigone 1967,Je 19,43:1
Henry IV, Part I 1968,Je 30,54:7
Henry IV, Part II 1968,Jl 2,33:1
Rudnick, Max (Producer)
Hot Rhythm 1930,Ag 22,18:5
Blackberries of 1932 1932,Ap 5,27:5
Cradle Snatchers 1932,N 17,23:2
Rudnicki, Stefan
'Tis Pity She's a Whore 1967,O 21,15:2
Rudofsky, Bernard (Costume Designer)
Barefoot in Athens 1951,N 1,35:2
Rudolf, Eugene (Lighting Director)
Merry Widow, The 1961,O 27,28:2
Rudolf, Eugene (Scenic Designer)
Merry Widow, The 1961,O 27,28:2
Rudolf, Gene (Lighting Director)
Vagabond King, The 1961,N 24,36:1
Gondoliers, The 1961,D 8,44:1
Rudolf, Gene (Scenic Designer)
Vagabond King, The 1961,N 24,36:1
Gondoliers, The 1961,D 8,44:1
Rudolf, Heinz
Armseligen Besenbinder, Die 1928,N 19,16:2

Rudolph, Jerome (Miscellaneous)
How to Make a Man 1961,F 3,16:1
Rudolph, Jerome (Producer)
Half-Past Wednesday 1962,Ap 7,16:2
Transgressor Rides Again, The 1969,My 21,42:1
Rudolph, Phyllis
Canteen Show, The 1942,S 4,18:1
Rudolph, Vernon
White Lilacs 1928,S 11,31:2
Rudsten, Dan
Storm Over Patsy 1937,Mr 9,26:4
Rudsten, Daniel (Playwright)
Golden Falcon, The 1948,Mr 26,25:4
Rudy, Martin
Joan of Lorraine 1946,N 19,40:2
To Dorothy, A Son 1951,N 20,37:2
Strong Are Lonely, The 1953,S 30,38:3
Uncle Willie 1956,D 21,17:1
Infernal Machine, The 1958,F 4,33:1
Luther 1963,S 26,41:1
Play That on Your Old Piano 1965,O 15,49:1
Sunset 1966,My 13,34:1
Man in the Glass Booth, The 1968,S 27,41:1
Rudy, Martin B
Noontide 1961,Je 2,37:1
Rudzki, Kazimeirz
Visit With the Family, A 1957,O 17,42:5
Rue, Robert
Juno 1959,Mr 10,41:1
Rueckert, Jean
Tall Kentuckian, The 1953,Je 17,30:1
Rueckert, Ted
Tall Kentuckian, The 1953,Je 17,30:1
Ruediger, Virginia (Costume Designer)
Culbin Sands 1935,Mr 23,10:3
Ruesch, Hans (Playwright)
Papers 1968,D 3,54:1
Ruff, Alton
Chaparral 1958,S 10,38:2
Happiest Girl in the World, The 1961,Ap 4,42:1
Ruffin, J A
Night at an Inn, A 1930,My 10,25:1
Ruffin, Leonard (Choreographer)
Malinda 1929,D 4,37:2
Ruffino, Val
There Was a Little Girl 1960,Mr 1,28:1
Ruffner, Edmund
Princess Flavia 1925,N 3,34:3
Circus Princess, The 1927,Ap 26,32:2
Rufo, Paul
Hunting the Jingo Birds 1965,Mr 26,27:1
Rufsnyder, Gregory
Fratricide Punished 1925,Ap 21,19:1
Rugel, Yvette
Earl Carroll's Vanities 1926,Ag 25,19:4
Vaudeville (Palace) 1927,N 22,33:2
Vaudeville (Palace) 1928,Jl 24,13:4
Vaudeville (Palace) 1929,Ap 8,32:7
Ruggere, Michael
Marie Vison, La 1970,Jl 15,29:1
Ruggeri, Ada
Promessi Sposi I,; Betrothed, The 1934,O 22,13:2
Ruggeri, Nino
Marchese di Priola, Il 1931,Mr 2,19:3
Arzigogolo, L'; Whim, The 1931,Ap 27,24:4
Ladro, Il; Thief, The 1932,F 22,23:4
Conte di Monte Cristo, Il 1934,Ja 22,13:2
Padrone Delle Ferriere, Il 1934,Mr 19,13:5
Colonello Bridall, L' 1934,Ap 16,20:3
Romanticismo 1934,My 14,20:2
Miserabili I, 1934,S 24,15:1
Miserabili I, 1934,O 1,14:2
Signora Dalle Camelie, La; Camille 1934,O 22,13:2
Processo dei Veleni, Il; Case of Poisons, The 1935,Ja 21,18:2
Romanzo di un Giovane Povero, Il 1935,F 25,12:3
Signo Della Croce, Il 1935,O 7,11:1
Adventurer, The 1935,N 11,21:1
Cardinale Giovanni de Medici, Il 1935,D 9,24:8
Religione e Patria 1936,Mr 23,22:4
Testamento della Zia d'America, Il; American Aunt's Will, The 1936,Mr 23,22:4
Due Orfanelle, Le; Two Orphans, The 1936,O 5,24:4
Tombola, La; Lottery, The 1936,N 9,23:4
Morte Civile, La; Civic Death 1936,N 9,23:4
Sansone; Samson 1936,N 30,25:2
Asino di Buridano, L' 1936,N 30,25:2
Feudalismo Oppure La Terra Bassa; Feudalism or the Lowland 1937,Mr 8,22:2
Lucrezia Borgia 1937,Mr 8,22:2
Fantasmi 1937,Mr 22,26:5
Sposa e la Cavalla, La 1937,Mr 22,26:5
Medico Delle Pazze, Il; Physician of Mad Woman, The 1937,S 27,24:2
Signora Dalle Camelie, La; Dame aux Camelias, La 1937,O 9,16:3
Ruggiero, Gabrielle
Saint of Bleecker Street, The 1954,D 28,21:1
Ruggiero, Joseph
H M S Pinafore 1931,Jl 28,17:6
Ruggiero, Osvaldo
Medea 1966,D 21,42:1

Ruggles, Charles
Ladies' Night 1920,Ag 10,10:1
Demi-Virgin, The 1921,O 19,22:1
Battling Buttler 1923,O 9,17:2
Queen High 1926,S 9,21:2
Rainbow 1928,N 22,25:1
Rainbow 1928,D 16,IX,1:1
Spring Is Here 1929,Mr 12,26:1
Vaudeville (Palace) 1929,D 30,16:3
Ruggles, Charlie
Pleasure of His Company, The 1958,O 23,36:1
Pleasure of His Company, The 1958,N 2,II,1:1
Captains and the Kings, The 1962,Ja 3,25:2
Roar Like a Dove 1964,My 22,40:2
Rugoff, David
Honeymoon in Israel, A 1962,O 15,33:5
Don't Worry Brother! 1963,O 14,35:2
Rugoff, David (Miscellaneous)
Don't Worry Brother! 1963,O 14,35:2
Ruhberg, Emily
Yes is for a Very Young Man 1963,Mr 6,7:5
Yerma 1966,D 9,60:1
Ruick, Barbara
Kiss Me, Kate 1956,My 10,27:2
Ruick, Melville
My Romance 1948,O 20,38:5
Come of Age 1952,Ja 24,22:2
Ruisinger, Thomas
Season of the Beast 1958,Mr 14,29:2
Warm Peninsula, The 1959,O 21,46:2
Thracian Horses, The 1961,S 28,58:2
Captains and the Kings, The 1962,Ja 3,25:2
Coriolanus 1965,Je 21,36:1
Taming of the Shrew, The 1965,Je 24,32:2
King Lear 1965,Je 25,39:1
Richard II 1968,Je 24,42:3
Love's Labour's Lost 1968,Je 28,36:1
Papers 1968,D 3,54:1
Ruiz, Albert
Pal Joey 1940,D 26,22:2
Ruiz, Jose
Hamlet 1923,N 27,23:6
Ruiz, Jose Martinez (Playwright)
Old Spain 1927,My 8,VII,2:3
Ruiz, Ruben
Tragedia del Faro, La; Tragedy of the Lighthouse, The 1932,Je 3,23:2
Ruiz and Bonita
Vaudeville (Palace) 1927,N 22,33:2
Rukoff, Carl
Body Beautiful, The 1935,N 1,24:3
Rule, Charles
Oklahoma! 1953,S 1,19:1
Henry, Sweet Henry 1967,O 24,51:2
Maggie Flynn 1968,O 24,52:1
1776 1969,Mr 17,46:2
Cry for Us All 1970,Ap 9,48:2
Rule, Janice
Picnic 1953,F 20,14:7
Picnic 1953,Mr 1,II,1:1
Flowering Peach, The 1954,D 29,19:2
Flowering Peach, The 1955,Ja 9,II,1:1
Carefree Tree 1955,O 12,37:2
Night Circus, The 1958,D 3,44:1
Happiest Girl in the World, The 1961,Ap 4,42:1
Rule, Jim (Lighting Director)
Salad of the Mad Cafe, The 1964,Ap 1,43:1
Rule, Jim (Scenic Designer)
Salad of the Mad Cafe, The 1964,Ap 1,43:1
Rulh, Michel
Tartuffe 1968,Jl 3,28:2
Rulon-Miller, B T (Playwright)
Stags at Bay 1934,D 15,9:2
Rulsinger, Thomas
As You Like It 1968,Je 24,42:3
Ruman, Sig
Once There Was a Russian 1961,F 20,32:2
Rumann, S Albon (Major)
War Song, The 1928,S 25,29:3
Rumann, Siegfried
Fedora 1924,Ja 24,14:2
Channel Road, The 1929,O 18,24:2
Channel Road, The 1929,O 27,IX,1:1
Half Gods 1929,D 23,18:5
Grand Hotel 1930,N 14,30:4
Grand Hotel 1930,N 23,IX,1:1
Alien Corn 1933,F 14,19:5
Alien Corn 1933,F 21,17:2
Alien Corn 1933,F 26,IX,1:1
Eight Bells 1933,O 30,14:2
Eight Bells 1933,N 5,IX,1:1
Lily of the Valley 1942,Ja 27,25:2
Rumann, Siegfried (Musical Director)
Tanzgraefin, Die 1925,S 18,26:3
Rumbold, Hugo (Costume Designer)
Patience 1948,F 10,27:2
Rumiantseff, Nikolai
Brothers Karamazov, The 1923,N 20,23:4
Ivanoff 1923,N 27,23:2
In the Claws of Life 1923,N 30,23:4
Uncle Vanya 1924,Ja 29,16:2
Rummery, David
South Pacific 1969,Jl 7,27:1

Rummler, Tom
Once There Was a Russian 1961,F 20,32:2
All Kinds of Giants 1961,D 19,40:1
Rumshinsky, Joseph (Composer)
Kid Mother 1927,F 27,VII,1:1
Some Girl 1927,D 24,8:2
Circus Girl, The 1928,O 21,IX,1:1
Radio Girl, The 1929,O 19,22:4
Jolly Orphan, The 1929,D 23,18:6
Joseph 1930,F 13,25:3
Little Clown, The 1930,Mr 15,23:3
Girl of Yesterday, The 1930,S 27,21:2
Love Thief, The 1931,Ja 19,24:5
Singing Rabbi, The 1931,S 11,24:4
Girl From Warsaw, The 1931,S 14,15:5
Mother's Son 1931,N 26,36:4
Pleasure 1931,D 28,20:2
Under One Roof 1932,F 8,21:2
Longing for Home 1933,S 22,15:1
Singing Thief, The 1933,D 4,22:4
Here Runs the Bride 1934,S 20,21:3
Here Runs the Bride 1934,N 4,IX,2:1
Perfect Fishel, The 1935,S 30,12:4
Schlemihl 1936,S 19,20:4
Straw Hero, The 1936,N 24,35:1
Galician Rabbi, The 1937,F 13,9:7
Yossel and His Wives 1937,S 19,II,8:3
Jolly Village, The 1937,N 15,15:5
Little Tailor, The 1938,Mr 21,18:2
Wise Fool, The 1938,O 10,15:3
Three Men and a Girl 1939,F 6,9:3
Oy, Is Dus a Leben!; Oh, What a Life! 1942,O 13,19:2
Doctor Herzl 1945,D 21,25:4
Song of Dnieper 1946,O 26,10:5
Wandering Stars 1946,N 14,18:2
Shylock and His Daughter 1947,S 30,22:2
Hershel, The Jester 1948,D 14,39:2
Abi Gezunt 1949,O 10,19:4
Sadie Is a Lady 1950,Ja 28,9:2
Mazel Tov, Molly 1950,O 2,18:1
Take It Easy 1950,D 25,23:6
Wish Me Luck! 1954,N 1,37:2
Wedding March, The 1955,O 17,33:1
Rumshinsky, Joseph (Director)
Untitled-Benefit 1933,Ja 25,13:3
Rumshinsky, Joseph (Miscellaneous)
Borscht Capades 1951,S 18,38:3
Rumshinsky, Joseph (Musical Director)
Little Tailor, The 1938,Mr 21,18:2
Mazel Tov, Rabbi 1938,N 28,10:4
Voice of Israel, The 1948,O 26,40:2
Rumshinsky, Joseph (Playwright)
Sacrifice of Isaac, The 1933,N 22,22:4
Jewish Heart, The 1939,Ja 25,16:6
Rumshinsky, Joseph (Producer)
Radio Girl, The 1929,O 19,22:4
Little Clown, The 1930,Mr 15,23:3
Rumshinsky, Murray (Composer)
Go Fight City Hall 1961,N 3,28:5
Oh What a Wedding! 1969,O 20,60:1
President's Daughter, The 1970,N 4,41:2
Runanin, Boris (Choreographer)
Allegro 1952,S 18,36:3
Phoenix '55 1955,Ap 25,20:2
Pipe Dream 1955,D 1,44:1
Girls Against the Boys, The 1959,N 3,26:1
Runaway Four
Vaudeville (Hippodrome) 1924,F 19,12:1
Music Box Revue 1924,D 2,23:3
Vaudeville (Palace) 1926,N 9,30:3
Vaudeville (Palace) 1927,O 4,34:3
Vaudeville (Palace) 1930,D 22,16:5
Runciman, Jean
Don't Tell 1920,S 29,12:1
Rundt, Arthur (Playwright)
Kyrill Reist ins Abendland 1933,Ja 8,IX,2:1
Runey, Edmund
Mary Stuart 1956,Ap 28,10:2
Runge, Karl
Armseligen Besenbinder, Die 1928,N 19,16:2
Runitch, Emma
Blue Bird, The 1932,Ap 22,23:2
Continental Varieties 1934,O 4,18:3
Runner, Joe
Clandestine on the Morning Line 1959,D 5,18:2
Runyon, Damon (Director)
Slight Case of Murder, A 1935,S 12,28:5
Runyon, Damon (Original Author)
Guys and Dolls 1950,D 3,II,1:1
Guys and Dolls 1951,O 7,II,1:1
Guys and Dolls 1952,My 29,17:5
Guys and Dolls 1953,Je 7,II,1:3
Guys and Dolls 1966,Je 9,55:2
Runyon, Damon (Playwright)
Slight Case of Murder, A 1935,S 12,28:5
Slight Case of Murder, A 1935,S 22,X,1:1
Guys and Dolls 1950,N 25,11:2
Guys and Dolls 1955,Ap 21,32:2
Guys and Dolls 1959,Jl 22,22:2
Guys and Dolls 1965,Ap 29,39:1
Runyon, Eddie
Ice Capades 1954,S 16,37:1

nyon, Virginia
All in the Family 1935,Jl 24,20:4
Mother Sings 1935,N 13,24:1
All the Comforts of Home 1942,My 26,24:5
pert, Gene
Midsummer Night's Dream, A 1956,Ja 14,12:2
Romeo and Juliet 1956,F 24,20:4
Arms and the Man 1956,O 2,39:4
Twelfth Night 1957,Ja 5,12:2
Coggerers, The 1960,Mr 23,33:1
Time to Go 1960,Mr 23,33:1
Valmouth 1960,O 7,29:1
Square in the Eye 1965,My 20,54:1
Time for Singing, A 1966,My 23,48:2
pert, Mike
Happy Time, The 1968,Ja 19,32:2
pp, Louis
Well of Romance, The 1930,N 8,21:2
scio, Al
Captain Brassbound's Conversion 1950,D 28,21:1
Idiot's Delight 1957,F 23,14:2
Pigeon, The 1957,My 17,19:2
sco, James (Producer)
Two's Company 1952,D 16,43:5
ush, James (Playwright)
Not a Way of Life 1967,Mr 23,28:1
ush, John F
Comforter, The 1964,O 22,42:1
Go, Go, Go, God is Dead! 1966,O 12,37:1
Happy Faculty, The 1967,Ap 19,50:1
ush, Madge
Look Who's Here 1920,Mr 3,12:2
ush, Myra
Coquette 1935,Jl 10,24:1
ush, Peggy
If Winter Comes 1923,Ap 3,26:1
ush, Renee
57 Bowery 1928,Ja 27,14:3
ush, Ronald
Pirates of Penzance, The 1954,Mr 31,32:5
Sorcerer, The 1954,My 26,34:3
ush, Susan
Drunkard, The 1970,Ap 14,54:1
ushing, Shirley
High John De Conquer 1969,Ap 23,39:1
ushkin, Shimen
God Man and Devil 1935,Mr 6,22:3
ushmore, Vivian
Merchants of Venus 1920,S 28,14:2
ushton, Roland
It All Depends 1925,Ag 11,16:4
uskay, Everett (Playwright)
Meanest Man in the World, The 1920,O 13,18:2
uskin, Abbott Lee
Festival 1955,Ja 19,22:1
uskin, Coby
Sing for Your Supper 1939,Ap 25,18:6
No for an Answer 1941,Ja 6,10:6
Man With Blonde Hair, The 1941,N 5,30:2
Jacobowsky and the Colonel 1944,Mr 15,17:2
uskin, Coby (Director)
One-Act Variety Theatre; What D' You Call It? 1940,Mr 20,36:2
Woman Bites Dog 1946,Ap 18,21:2
Bathsheba 1947,Mr 27,40:2
Open House 1947,Je 4,33:4
Kathleen 1948,F 4,26:2
uskin, Coby (Miscellaneous)
Another Part of the Forest 1946,N 21,42:2
uskin, Harry (Director)
Hot Chocolates 1929,Je 21,17:4
uskin, Harry (Lyricist)
Ballyhoo 1930,D 14,IX,3:1
Ballyhoo 1930,D 23,24:1
uskin, Harry (Playwright)
Murray Anderson's Almanac 1929,Ag 15,20:3
Ballyhoo 1930,D 14,IX,3:1
Ballyhoo 1930,D 23,24:1
Hey, Nonny, Nonny! 1932,Je 7,22:3
uskin, John (Playwright)
King of the Golden River, The 1929,D 27,26:5
uskin, Joseph
King's Darling, The 1951,Jl 25,17:2
Montserrat 1954,My 26,34:2
Midsummer Night's Dream, A 1956,Ja 14,12:2
Romeo and Juliet 1956,F 24,20:4
Hamlet 1956,O 29,34:1
Twelfth Night 1957,Ja 5,12:2
Julius Caesar 1957,O 24,39:1
King Lear 1959,Ja 3,11:2
In the Matter of J Robert Oppenheimer 1968,Je 7,31:1
Murderous Angels 1970,F 8,70:1
Ruskin, Jospeh
King Lear 1964,Jl 28,18:2
Ruskin, Leonard (Miscellaneous)
Song of Norway 1958,Je 23,19:2
Ruskin, Leonard (Producer)
Song of Norway 1959,Je 26,16:2
Cook for Mr General, A 1961,O 20,39:1
Ruskin, Shimen
Town Lunatics 1933,F 6,11:4
Salt and Pepper 1933,Ap 24,10:2

Organ Grinder, The 1934,Ja 1,28:3
Chalk Dust 1936,Mr 5,24:5
Path of Flowers, The 1936,S 18,19:3
Having Wonderful Time 1937,F 22,12:5
All You Need Is One Good Break 1950,F 10,20:3
Whisper in God's Ear, A 1962,O 12,27:2
Enter Laughing 1963,Mr 15,8:1
Saturday Night 1968,F 26,43:1
Happiness Is Just a Little Thing Called a Rolls Royce 1968,My 13,54:5
Little Murders 1969,Ja 6,38:1
Seven Days of Mourning 1969,D 17,64:1
Seven Days of Mourning 1970,Ja 4,II,5:1
Ruslander, Daniel
Political Party, A 1963,S 27,17:5
Ruslander, Daniel (Musical Director)
Political Party, A 1963,S 27,17:5
Rusleton, Roland (Director)
Clubs Are Trumps 1924,O 15,27:1
Rusling, Jacqueline
Growing Pains 1933,N 24,24:2
Children's Hour, The 1934,N 21,23:2
Russ, Alfred
Nina Rosa 1930,My 31,19:3
Music in the Air 1932,N 9,28:2
Russ, Gloria
Little Theatre Tournament; House With the Twisty Windows, The 1929,My 8,34:4
Russ, Toby
Amen Corner, The 1965,Ap 16,35:1
Russ Morgan and his orchestra
Aquacircus 1958,Je 30,24:6
Russak, Gerard
Difficult Woman, The 1962,Ap 26,22:7
Persecution and Assassination of Marat As Performed by the Inmates of the Asylum of Charenton Under the Direction of the Marquis de Sade, The 1967,Ja 4,34:1
Zorba 1968,N 18,58:1
Russel, Elizabeth
Trojan Women, The 1923,My 27,10:2
Russel, John
Sleepy Hollow 1948,Je 4,26:3
Russel, Mark
Caution: A Love Story 1969,Ap 4,45:1
Dirtiest Show in Town, The 1970,My 2,21:1
Russel, S K (Composer)
All in Fun 1940,D 28,11:2
Russel, S K (Lyricist)
All in Fun 1940,D 28,11:2
Russell, A J (Playwright)
Bravo Giovanni 1962,My 21,41:2
Bravo Giovanni 1962,My 27,II,1:1
Winnie the Pooh 1967,N 25,33:1
Winnie the Pooh 1967,D 23,28:1
Russell, Alfred
On the Harmfulness of Tobacco 1956,Ap 26,38:1
Man of Destiny, The 1956,Ap 26,38:1
Sweeney Todd 1957,Ag 28,21:4
Russell, Alfred (Scenic Designer)
Jack 1958,Je 4,39:2
Bald Soprano, The 1958,Je 4,39:2
Russell, Anna
Untitled-One Woman Show 1952,D 13,18:6
Anna Russell and Her Little Show 1953,S 8,27:2
One Way Pendulum 1961,S 19,38:2
Flora, the Red Menace 1965,My 12,41:2
Ice Follies 1969,My 23,38:1
Russell, Anna (Composer)
Anna Russell and Her Little Show 1953,S 8,27:2
All by Myself 1964,Je 16,47:1
Russell, Anna (Lyricist)
Anna Russell and Her Little Show 1953,S 8,27:2
All by Myself 1964,Je 16,47:1
Russell, Anna (Playwright)
All by Myself 1964,Je 16,47:1
Russell, Arthur
Woman Bites Dog 1946,Ap 18,21:2
Snow Maiden, The 1960,Ap 5,43:3
Russell, Byron
Right to Strike, The 1921,O 25,20:1
Red Poppy, The 1922,D 21,18:2
Devil's Disciple, The 1923,Ap 24,24:1
When Crummles Played 1928,O 2,34:3
S S Glencairn 1929,Ja 10,24:5
Scotland Yard 1929,S 28,16:6
Sherlock Holmes 1929,N 26,28:3
Tyrant, The 1930,N 13,33:1
Pipe in the Fields, The 1931,Mr 14,23:4
Three Times the Hour 1931,Ag 26,15:5
Merchant of Venice, The 1931,N 9,22:2
King Oedipus 1933,Ja 16,12:4
Is Life Worth Living? 1933,N 10,24:6
Twelfth Night 1934,Jl 17,24:5
Passing of the Third Floor Back, The 1937,Ag 3,20:6
Come Across 1938,S 15,28:3
Jeremiah 1939,F 4,11:2
Kindred 1939,D 27,17:2
Juno and the Paycock 1940,Ja 17,24:2
At the Stroke of Eight 1940,My 21,29:2
Wookey, The 1941,S 11,20:5
Patriots, The 1943,Ja 30,11:2

Russell, Byron—Cont
Naked Genius, The 1943,O 22,20:5
Strange Play, A 1944,Je 2,20:3
Late George Apley, The 1944,O 20,16:4
Late George Apley, The 1944,N 22,26:2
Park Avenue 1946,N 5,31:2
Legend of Lovers 1951,D 27,17:1
Too Late the Phalarope 1956,O 12,35:1
Taming of the Shrew, The 1957,F 21,30:2
Cheri 1959,O 13,44:1
Sharon's Grave 1961,N 9,39:2
Russell, C E (Playwright)
Biarritz 1929,Ag 11,VIII,2:1
Russell, Charles L (Miscellaneous)
Sail Away 1961,O 4,48:5
Russell, Charles L (Playwright)
Five on the Black Hand Side 1970,Ja 2,32:2
Five on the Black Hand Side 1970,Ja 11,II,1:1
Russell, Charles L (Producer)
Nude With Violin 1957,N 15,36:1
Look After Lulu 1959,Mr 4,35:1
Russell, Donn (Scenic Designer)
Junebug Graduates Tonight! 1967,F 27,35:1
Russell, Dorothy N S
Daddy Come Home 1963,Ap 17,33:1
Russell, Dorothy Peabody
Sherlock Holmes 1929,N 26,28:3
Russell, Eddie
Good Times 1920,Ag 10,10:1
Rise of Rosie O'Reilly, The 1923,D 26,13:4
Madame X 1927,Jl 7,29:3
Kiss Me! 1927,Jl 22,17:1
Russell, Edith
Land Is Bright, The 1941,O 29,26:2
Russell, Edna
New Faces of 1936 1936,My 20,24:5
Who's Who 1938,Mr 2,16:2
Russell, Edward
Ballad of Jazz Street, The 1959,N 12,28:1
Russell, Eileen (Playwright)
Retreat From Folly 1937,F 25,18:2
Retreat From Folly 1937,Je 29,18:3
Russell, Elizabeth T
Sonya's Search for the Christmas Star 1929,D 14,24:6
Russell, Emerson
Wild Duck, The 1938,Ap 16,16:5
Russell, Evelyn
Copper and Brass 1957,O 18,19:2
On the Town 1959,Ja 16,36:1
On the Town 1959,Ja 25,II,1:1
Chic 1959,My 19,28:2
Sail Away 1961,O 4,48:5
That Thing at the Cherry Lane 1965,My 19,42:1
Warm Body, A 1967,Ap 17,44:2
Place for Polly, A 1970,Ap 20,45:1
Russell, Frank
Robert E Lee 1923,N 21,23:1
Russell, Franklin L (Playwright)
Great Barrington, The 1931,F 20,18:1
Russell, Gilbert
Wookey, The 1941,S 11,20:5
Hollywood Pinafore 1945,Je 1,20:1
Gypsy Lady 1946,S 18,25:6
Russell, Gordon
Major Barbara 1951,F 24,10:2
Children's Hour, The 1952,D 19,35:2
Russell, Grace
Her Family Tree 1920,D 28,9:2
Russell, Guy
Auntie Mame 1958,Ag 12,33:2
Russell, Harriet
Joy of Serpents 1930,Ap 4,22:4
Child of Manhattan 1932,Mr 2,15:1
Black Sheep 1932,O 14,22:6
Russell, Hazel
Legend of Leonora, The 1926,My 1,10:1
Russell, Helene
Eyvind of the Hills 1921,F 2,14:1
Russell, Henry
Orchids Preferred 1937,My 12,26:5
Russell, Herbert
Ed Wynn's Carnival 1920,Ap 6,18:2
Russell, Hooper
Bitter Sweet 1929,N 6,30:2
Russell, Jack
Heaven on Earth 1948,S 17,29:2
As the Girls Go 1948,N 15,21:2
Alive and Kicking 1950,Ja 18,25:5
Night in Venice, A 1952,Je 27,18:6
Night in Venice, A 1952,Jl 13,II,1:1
Night in Venice, A 1953,Je 26,15:2
Fledermaus, Die 1954,My 20,38:5
Difficult Woman, The 1962,Ap 26,22:7
Russell, James (Scenic Designer)
Happiest Years, The 1949,Ap 26,29:8
Russell, Janet
Kai Khosru 1925,Ap 27,14:2
Russell, Jeanne
Room Service 1953,Ap 7,34:1
Russell, Jessica
Carmen Jones 1943,D 3,26:2
Russell, Jim
Student Prince, The 1943,Je 9,16:2

Russell, Jim—Cont
New Faces of 1952 1952,My 17,23:2
Teahouse of the August Moon, The 1956,N 9,33:2
Russell, Jim (Choreographer)
Mask and Gown 1957,S 11,29:1
Chic 1959,My 19,28:2
Follies of 1910, The 1960,Ja 15,37:3
Greenwich Village U S A 1960,S 29,30:5
Russell, Jim (Director)
Mask and Gown 1957,S 11,29:1
Russell, John Patton (Playwright)
Tattle Tales 1930,Jl 20,VIII,2:1
Russell, Judith
Stage Door 1936,O 23,26:3
Russell, Keith
Point of No Return 1951,D 14,35:2
Russell, Kennedy (Composer)
Nightingale, The 1947,Jl 17,16:4
Russell, Kennedy (Playwright)
By Appointment 1934,O 13,10:4
Russell, Lewis L
Dead End 1935,O 29,17:2
London Assurance 1937,F 19,14:5
Our Betters 1937,Jl 22,16:2
Bright Rebel 1938,D 28,24:2
Return Engagement 1940,N 2,19:2
Corn Is Green, The 1943,My 4,18:3
Russell, Lillian
Untitled-Benefit 1921,My 2,12:3
Untitled-Benefit 1922,My 8,14:5
Russell, Lloyd
Kibitzer, The 1929,F 19,22:5
So Was Napoleon 1930,Ja 9,22:2
Second Comin', The 1931,D 9,32:4
Russell, Mae
Lovely Lady 1927,D 30,22:1
Russell, Mairhi
Caesar and Cleopatra 1951,D 20,43:2
Antony and Cleopatra 1951,D 21,22:2
Russell, Mande
Dark Eyes 1943,Ja 15,20:2
Russell, Marian
For Heaven's Sake Mother 1948,N 17,33:4
Gioconda Smile, The 1950,O 9,21:2
One Bright Day 1952,Mr 20,37:2
Russell, Maude
Liza 1922,N 28,24:1
Keep Shufflin' 1928,F 28,18:3
Just a Minute 1928,O 9,34:3
Singin' the Blues 1931,S 17,21:3
Black Rhythm 1936,D 21,19:2
Mamba's Daughters 1940,Mr 25,10:4
Big White Fog 1940,O 23,26:2
St Louis Woman 1946,Ap 1,22:2
Russell, Olivia
School for Brides 1944,Ag 2,19:4
Russell, Paul
Lady Windermere's Fan 1946,O 15,29:2
Russell, Peter (Lighting Director)
Jonah! 1967,S 22,52:2
Russell, Renee
Let's Face It 1941,O 30,26:2
My Dear Public 1943,S 10,28:1
Russell, Robert
Jazz Singer, The 1925,S 15,29:2
Whatever Goes Up 1935,N 26,28:2
Arms for Venus 1937,Mr 12,18:7
Russell, Robert (Playwright)
Take Me Along 1959,O 23,22:2
Flora, the Red Menace 1965,My 12,41:2
Russell, Roberta
Persecution and Assassination of Marat As
    Performed by the Inmates of the Asylum of
    Charenton Under the Direction of the Marquis de
    Sade, The 1967,Ja 4,34:1
Russell, Rosalind
Company's Coming! 1931,Ap 21,35:5
Wonderful Town 1953,F 26,22:3
Wonderful Town 1953,Mr 8,II,1:1
Auntie Mame 1956,N 1,47:2
Auntie Mame 1956,N 11,II,1:1
Russell, Roy
Let's Face It 1941,O 30,26:2
Russell, Ruth
Dear Jane 1932,N 15,24:3
Russell, Smith Jr
John Brown's Body 1953,F 16,17:2
Russell, Stuart (Miscellaneous)
King Lear 1956,Ja 13,17:1
Russell, Thomas
Green Pastures, The 1935,F 27,16:2
Russell, Trustam
Romio and Julietta 1925,Ap 21,19:1
Russell, Val
Vaudeville (Palace) 1930,Mr 24,24:5
Russell, Virginia
Wandering Jew, The 1921,O 27,22:1
Behold the Bridegroom 1927,D 27,24:1
Big Pond, The 1928,Ag 22,25:1
Russell, W Stuart (Miscellaneous)
Evening of Rare Pleasures, An 1959,Je 4,26:2
Russell, Walter S (Lighting Director)
Noontide 1961,Je 2,37:1
ne Way Pendulum 1961,S 19,38:2

Thracian Horses, The 1961,S 28,58:2
Eternal Triangle 1966,N 8,45:1
Frying Pan, The 1966,N 8,45:1
Bridal Night, The 1966,N 8,45:1
Russell, Walter S (Miscellaneous)
Fun City 1968,Mr 7,53:2
Russell, Walter S (Scenic Designer)
Frying Pan, The 1966,N 8,45:1
Bridal Night, The 1966,N 8,45:1
Eternal Triangle 1966,N 8,45:1
Russell, Walters
Show Boat 1948,S 9,33:2
Russell, William
Career Angel 1943,N 19,24:2
Macbeth 1961,Ja 10,28:1
Russell, Zella
Sweetheart Shop, The 1920,S 1,13:4
Springtime of Youth 1922,O 27,15:1
Love Song, The 1925,Ja 14,19:4
Countess Maritza 1936,Ag 19,18:2
Circus Princess, The 1937,Ag 31,26:6
Blossom Time 1938,D 27,12:2
Blossom Time 1943,S 6,21:2
Russell Market Dancers
George White's Scandals 1928,Jl 3,19:1
Russi, June
Gianni Schicci 1969,F 25,36:1
Russian Choir
Passion Play, The 1929,Ap 30,32:1
Russino, Tom
Dinosaur Wharf 1951,N 9,23:2
Maya 1953,Je 10,35:1
Russiyan, Nicholas (Miscellaneous)
Phaedra 1967,My 22,50:2
Futz 1968,Je 14,39:1
Our Town 1969,N 28,50:1
Mahagonny 1970,Ap 29,51:1
Russiyan, Nicholas (Scenic Designer)
Futz 1968,Je 14,39:1
Russler, G
Aristocrats 1935,My 2,16:2
Russo, Frank
Wall Street 1927,Ap 21,24:4
Russo, James
Girl From Wyoming, The 1938,O 31,12:1
Royal Family, The 1940,Ag 13,15:3
Right Next to Broadway 1944,F 22,26:2
Public Relations 1944,Ap 7,23:3
Russo, James (Director)
Jenny Kissed Me 1948,D 24,12:2
Russo, James (Miscellaneous)
Last Dance, The 1948,Ja 28,27:2
Play's the Thing, The 1948,Ap 29,19:2
Play's the Thing, The 1948,My 9,II,1:1
Saint of Bleecker Street, The 1954,D 28,21:1
First Gentleman, The 1957,Ap 26,22:2
Russo, James (Producer)
Jenny Kissed Me 1948,D 24,12:2
Courtin' Time 1951,Je 14,30:2
Russo, John
Antony and Cleopatra 1947,N 27,49:2
Russo, Michael
Jackknife 1958,S 23,36:2
Russo, Nasseka
Cute Gata.....Oute Zhmia; Neither Cat . . . Nor
    Damage 1957,D 20,31:1
Russo, Salvatrice
Judith 1965,Mr 25,42:2
Russom, Leon
Cyrano de Bergerac 1968,Ap 26,30:1
Oh! Calcutta! 1969,Je 18,33:1
Wars of the Roses, The (Part II) 1970,Jl 3,15:1
Russotto, Leo (Composer)
Winter's Tale, The 1946,Ja 16,18:6
Rust, A D (Composer)
It's the Valet 1933,D 15,25:4
Rust, A D (Lyricist)
It's the Valet 1933,D 15,25:4
Rust, Diane Elizabeth (Costume Designer)
Mamba's Daughters 1953,Mr 21,12:6
Rustad, John
Othello 1937,Ja 7,16:4
Too Many Heroes 1937,N 16,26:2
Waltz in Goose Step 1938,N 2,26:2
Mamba's Daughters 1939,Ja 4,24:2
Night Music 1940,F 23,18:2
Ruta, Francesca (Miscellaneous)
Great Indoors, The 1966,F 2,23:1
Ruta, John
Twelfth Night 1957,Jl 4,16:4
Ruta, Ken
Under Milk Wood 1961,Mr 30,25:1
Androcles and the Lion 1961,N 22,24:2
Ross 1961,D 27,20:2
Hamlet 1963,My 9,41:1
Miser, The 1963,My 10,39:1
Death of a Salesman 1963,Jl 20,11:2
Devils, The 1963,N 5,25:1
Henry V 1964,My 13,52:1
Saint Joan 1964,My 14,41:1
Volpone 1964,Jl 20,18:3
Way of the World, The 1965,Je 2,40:1
Richard III 1965,Je 3,26:1

Ruta, Ken—Cont
Cherry Orchard, The 1965,Ag 2,17:2
As You Like It 1966,Je 4,19:1
Three Sisters, The 1969,O 10,38:1
Three Sisters, The 1969,O 19,II,3:1
Rutan, A Raymond
Merry Wives of Windsor, The 1954,F 17,27:1
Rutan, Frank
Espanola 1921,D 30,13:1
Rutebeuf of Paris (Playwright)
Theophilus 1942,Ja 7,23:2
Ruteford, E
Trojan Women, The 1941,Ap 9,32:5
Rutenborn, Guenter (Playwright)
Sign of Jonah, The 1957,My 2,27:1
Sign of Jonah, The 1960,S 9,35:1
Ruth, Jack
Next Half Hour, The 1945,O 30,14:6
Solid Gold Cadillac, The 1953,N 6,24:2
Ruth, Joan
My Maryland 1927,S 13,37:2
Ruth, John
Little Women 1944,D 13,29:2
Ruth, Leon (Playwright)
C'est Jeune 1927,O 2,VIII,2:4
Ruth, Paul
Desert Song, The 1946,Ja 9,20:2
Ruth, Robert L
Victims, The; Escurial 1968,Mr 6,34:1
Victims, The; Victims of Duty 1968,Mr 6,34:1
Ruth, Thea
Good Soldier Schweik, The 1963,Ap 9,57:1
Lesson, The 1963,S 18,35:4
Bald Soprano, The 1963,S 18,35:4
Rutherford, Cecil
Great Magician, The 1951,N 22,45:1
No Time for Sergeants 1955,O 21,32:2
Rutherford, Douglas
Deep Are the Roots 1945,S 27,24:4
Hold It! 1948,My 6,31:5
Magnolia Alley 1949,Ap 19,29:2
Abie's Irish Rose 1954,N 19,19:1
Rutherford, Forrest (Playwright)
Her Salary Man 1921,N 29,20:1
Rutherford, Frank
American Tragedy, An 1926,O 12,31:2
Rutherford, Jack
Whoopee 1928,D 5,34:3
Rutherford, John
Two Blocks Away 1921,Ag 31,8:3
He Who Gets Slapped 1922,Ja 10,15:1
R U R 1922,O 10,16:1
Magnolia 1923,Ag 28,12:3
Kid Boots 1924,Ja 1,21:3
City Chap, The 1925,O 27,21:1
Queen High 1926,S 9,21:2
Love Call, The 1927,O 25,33:1
Soliloquy 1938,N 29,26:4
Rutherford, Judith (Producer)
Call Me by My Rightful Name 1961,F 1,31:1
Rutherford, June
Lady in the Dark 1941,Ja 24,14:2
Rutherford, Lisa
Let's Face It 1941,O 30,26:2
Rutherford, Margaret
Short Story 1935,D 1,XI,5:3
Blithe Spirit 1941,Jl 13,IX,1:4
Importance of Being Earnest, The 1947,Ja 24,18:6
Importance of Being Earnest, The 1947,Mr 4,30:2
Importance of Being Earnest, The 1947,Mr 9,II,1:1
Ring Around the Moon 1950,Ja 27,29:2
Way of the World, The 1953,Ap 10,17:1
Time Remembered 1955,My 4,35:1
Farewell, Farewell Eugene 1960,S 28,35:1
Dazzling Prospect 1961,Je 25,II,3:5
Rutherford, Montague
Trimmed in Scarlet 1920,F 3,18:1
Richard III 1920,Mr 8,7:1
Prince and the Pauper, The 1920,N 2,15:1
Swords 1921,S 2,9:3
Madras House, The 1921,O 31,18:2
Anything Might Happen 1923,F 21,22:3
Lucky Sam McCarver 1925,O 22,22:1
Pomeroy's Past 1926,Ap 20,24:4
Rutherford, Tom
Macbeth 1928,N 20,28:3
American Tragedy, An 1931,F 21,15:5
Society Girl 1931,D 31,16:1
New Faces of 1936 1936,My 20,24:5
Canteen Show, The 1942,S 4,18:1
Richard III 1943,Mr 27,8:3
He Who Gets Slapped 1946,Mr 21,31:4
Laura 1947,Je 27,16:1
Billy the Kid 1951,Ag 21,23:2
Shewing-Up of Blanco Posnet, The 1959,S 19,26:7
Rutland, Betty
Daddy Dumplins 1920,N 23,11:1
Deacon, The 1925,N 25,14:3
Rutledge, Ann
Prologue to Glory 1938,Mr 18,22:2
Rutledge, Larney
Failures, The 1959,Ja 6,30:2
Rutledge, Tracy D
Good Hunting 1938,N 22,26:5

Ruto, Paul
Medea 1965,N 29,46:1
Rutten, Joseph
Troilus and Cressida 1963,Je 19,40:2
Timon of Athens 1963,Jl 31,19:2
Richard II 1964,Je 17,47:1
King Lear 1964,Je 19,36:1
Rutter, Barrie
Apprentices, The 1968,Ag 21,40:5
Rutter, Barrie (Producer)
Spring-Heeled Jack 1970,Ag 27,41:2
Ruttledge, Frances
Man in Possession, The 1930,N 3,19:1
Ruttman, Lucien Arnold
Russian People, The 1942,D 30,17:2
Rutyna, Edward (Scenic Designer)
Seven Mirrors 1945,O 26,17:2
Rutz, Anni
Untitled-Passion Play 1930,My 9,9:1
Rutz, Hugo
Untitled-Passion Play 1930,My 9,9:1
Untitled-Passion Play 1930,My 12,1:5
Rutzisky, Edward
Bullfight 1954,Ja 13,25:2
Song Out of Sorrow 1955,N 1,27:3
Ruusunen, Kalle
Betrothal, The 1959,F .16,52:2
Ruymen, Ayn
Gingerbread Lady, The 1970,D 14,58:3
Gingerbread Lady, The 1970,D 20,II,3:7
Ruys, Cor
Born Yesterday 1946,N 5,32:1
Ruys, Cor (Producer)
Born Yesterday 1946,N 5,32:1
Ruysdael, Basil
Topsy and Eva 1924,D 24,11:1
Cocoanuts, The 1925,D 9,30:1
Enchanted Isle 1927,S 20,33:2
Ruyte, Mlle
Avare. L': Miser. The 1924.Mr 12.17:3
Ruzf Nissen Grethe
Beggar on Horseback 1924,F 13,17:2
Beggar on Horseback 1924,F 17,VII,1:1
Rwttigan, Terence (Playwright)
Ross 1960,My 13,26:4
Ryaboushinskaya, (Mlle)
Chauve-Souris; Romantic Adventure of an Italian
Ballerina and a Marquis, A 1931,O 22,27:1
Ryall, David
Dance of Death, The 1967,O 20,50:1
Beaux' Stratagem, The 1970,F 10,50:2
Three Sisters, The 1970,F 12,30:1
Idiot, The 1970,Jl 17,18:1
Ryan, Alfred
Winged Victory 1943,N 22,24:1
Yellow Jack 1944,Ap 7,23:3
Ryan, Allan A Jr (Mrs)
Variations of 1940 1940,Ja 29,12:1
Ryan, Anne
Right of Happiness 1931,Ap 3,34:2
Ryan, Barry
Pal Joey 1952,Ja 4,17:6
Ryan, Benny (Composer)
Keep It Clean 1929,Je 25,35:5
Ryan, Benny (Lyricist)
Keep It Clean 1929,Je 25,35:5
Ryan, Byron Dean (Miscellaneous)
Mikado, The 1968,My 2,59:1
Ryan, Catherine
Volpone 1967,Je 30,29:1
Ryan, Charlene
Never Live Over a Pretzel Factory 1964,Mr 30,37:1
Sweet Charity 1967,Jl 1,13:1
Coco 1969,D 19,66:1
Ryan, Chilton
Criminals, The 1941,D 22,24:3
Ryan, Chris (Miscellaneous)
Egg, The 1962,Ja 9,23:2
Ryan, Clendenin J Jr
Off the Record; Mayor Answers the Newspapers!
Wow! 1935,Je 19,23:3
Ryan, Clint
Hair 1970,Ja 13,39:1
Ryan, Colletta
George White's Scandals 1922,Ag 29,10:1
Here Goes the Bride 1931,N 4,31:2
Ryan, Conny
This Was Burlesque 1962,Mr 7,29:1
Ryan, D D (Costume Designer)
Company 1970,Ap 27,40:1
Ryan, David
Red Roses for Me 1955,D 29,15:2
Plough and the Stars, The 1956,Ap 6,14:1
Diff'rent 1961,O 18,52:1
Long Voyage Home, The 1961,D 5,49:1
Beyond the Horizon 1962,O 26,27:2
Ryan, Dean (Miscellaneous)
Porgy and Bess 1965,Mr 6,17:1
Ryan, Dean (Musical Director)
Pirates of Penzance, The 1965,Ap 21,50:6
Ryan, Dolph
Roger Bloomer 1923,Mr 2,18:3

Ryan, Donald J (Playwright)
Little Theatre Tournament; Rhythm of the City,
The 1929,My 7,28:1
Ryan, Eddie Jr
Let Freedom Ring 1935,N 7,26:2
Ryan, Edmon
Post Road 1934,D 5,28:3
Whatever Goes Up 1935,N 26,28:2
Dream Girl 1945,D 15,13:2
Command Decision 1947,O 2,30:2
Legend of Sarah 1950,O 12,42:4
Dream Girl 1951,My 10,39:1
Date With April, A 1953,Ap 16,36:2
Nature's Way 1957,O 17,42:2
Marriage-Go-Round, The 1958,O 30,37:1
Marriage-Go-Round, The 1958,N 9,II,1:1
Lord Pengo 1962,N 20,41:2
In the Matter of J Robert Oppenheimer
1968,Je 7,31:1
Ryan, Edward Jr
Late One Evening 1933,Ja 10,27:3
Give Us This Day 1933,O 28,20:6
Brittle Heaven 1934,N 14,22:5
Saint Joan 1936,Mr 10,27:4
St Helena 1936,O 7,32:1
French Without Tears 1937,S 29,19:1
Schoolhouse on the Lot 1938,Mr 23,18:4
Knights of Song 1938,O 18,29:2
Ryan, Eileen
Ah, Wilderness! 1953,F 7,10:6
Sing Till Tomorrow 1953,D 29,17:2
Three Sisters, The 1955,F 26,13:2
Brothers Karamazov, The 1957,D 9,39:4
Comes a Day 1958,N 7,22:1
Ryan, Elaine (Playwright)
Now I Lay Me Down to Sleep 1949,Jl 23,7:3
Now I Lay Me Down to Sleep 1950,Mr 3,21:2
Now I Lay Me Down to Sleep 1950,Mr 19,II,1:1
Ryan, Elizabeth
Seven Mirrors 1945,O 26,17:2
Ryan, Elsa
Sweet Land of Liberty 1929,S 24,29:2
Melo 1931,Ap 17,26:6
Family Upstairs, The 1933,O 28,20:6
Wrong Number 1934,Mr 14,23:6
Merrily We Roll Along 1934,O 1,14:1
Ryan, Emmet
Spring Fever 1925,Ag 4,14:2
Ryan, Eugene
Bright Boy 1944,Mr 3,19:5
Ryan, Gail
Caucasian Chalk Circle, The 1961,N 1,35:1
Coach With the Six Insides, The 1967,My 12,50:1
Ryan, Genevieve
Sun-Up 1930,My 10,25:1
Ryan, George
Deburau 1920,D 24,14:3
Dolly Jordan 1922,O 4,26:1
Mima 1928,D 13,24:2
Paths of Glory 1935,S 27,24:2
Ryan, Gertrude
Skylark 1939,O 12,32:2
Ryan, Harry
. This Was Burlesque 1970,F 12,31:1
Ryan, Hayne
Pale Horse, Pale Rider 1957,O 30,26:1
Ping-Pong 1959,Ap 17,22:1
Ryan, James Orr
Hot Water 1929,Ja 22,22:3
Ryan, Jerry
Killers 1928,Mr 14,28:3
Ryan, John
Nobody's Money 1921,Ag 18,9:3
Ryan, John Barry (Miscellaneous)
Mr Wonderful 1956,Mr 23,23:2
Hidden River, The 1957,Ja 24,32:1
Ryan, John P
Serjeant Musgrave's Dance 1966,Mr 9,44:1
Duet for Three 1966,My 20,41:1
Yerma 1966,D 9,60:1
Nobody Hears A Broken Drum 1970,Mr 20,55:1
Ryan, Lawrence
What a Relief 1935,D 14,10:6
Ryan, Mabel (Producer)
Half-Naked Truth, The 1926,Je 8,23:1
Ryan, Madge
Summer of the Seventeenth Doll 1958,Ja 23,23:2
Measure for Measure 1967,F 15,37:1
Hamlet 1967,F 17,44:1
Romeo and Juliet 1967,F 22,18:1
Ryan, Margaret
Dionysus in 69 1968,Je 7,35:3
Ryan, Mary
Turn in the Road, A 1921,Je 12,VI,1:6
Only 38 1921,S 14,22:2
Apache, The 1923,My 9,14:3
Red Light Annie 1923,Ag 22,10:3
That Awful Mrs Eaton! 1924,S 30,27:1
Her Man of Wax 1933,O 12,32:3
County Chairman, The 1936,My 26,26:5
Ryan, Michael
Richard III 1957,N 26,41:1
King Lear 1959,Ja 3,11:2

Ryan, Michael—Cont
Herne's Egg, The 1960,S 20,48:1
Hamlet 1964,Je 17,49:1
Ryan, Mitchell
9 by Six: A Cry of Players 1956,D 5,49:2
Whisper to Me 1960,N 22,38:6
Tempest, The 1962,Jl 17,18:2
As You Like It 1963,Jl 17,19:2
Winter's Tale, The 1963,Ag 16,14:1
Twelfth Night 1963,O 9,47:1
Othello 1964,Jl 15,29:1
Othello 1964,O 13,48:1
Baal 1965,My 7,33:2
Coriolanus 1965,Jl 15,23:1
Wait Until Dark 1966,F 3,21:1
Iphigenia in Aulis 1967,N 22,40:2
Iphigenia in Aulis 1967,D 3,II,1:1
Iphigenia in Aulis 1968,Ap 6,43:1
Moon for the Misbegotten, A 1968,Je 13,55:2
Moon for the Misbegotten, A 1968,Je 30,II,1:1
Sudden and Accidental Re-education of Horse
Johnson, The 1968,D 19,63:1
Ryan, Nancy
Last of Mrs Cheyney, The 1925,N 10,23:5
Happy Husband, The 1928,My 8,25:2
High Road, The 1928,S 11,31:1
Forsaking All Others 1933,Mr 2,21:2
No More Ladies 1934,Ja 24,20:3
Something Gay 1935,Ap 30,12:2
Once Is Enough 1938,F 16,16:2
Ryan, Norah
Secrets 1922,D 26,11:1
Family Upstairs, The 1925,Ag 18,14:2
Ryan, Oscar (Lighting Director)
Swing Mikado, The 1939,Mr 2,18:2
Ryan, Owen (Lighting Director)
Bernard Shaw Story, The 1965,N 19,31:1
Ryan, Owen (Miscellaneous)
White House Murder Case, The 1970,F 19,59:1
Ryan, Owen (Scenic Designer)
Old Bucks and New Wings 1962,N 6,39:4
Ryan, Patricia
Sleep No More 1944,S 1,11:5
Ryan, Patrick (Miscellaneous)
Tree Witch, The 1961,Je 5,39:4
Ryan, Paul
Hair 1970,Ja 13,39:1
Ryan, Peggy
Meet the People 1940,D 26,22:2
Ryan, Phyllis
Devil Came From Dublin, The! 1955,Je 3,27:2
Ryan, Richard
International Revue 1930,F 26,22:2
Vanderbilt Revue, The 1930,N 6,22:6
Ryan, Robert
Clash by Night 1941,D 29,20:2
Coriolanus 1954,Ja 20,34:2
Coriolanus 1954,Ja 24,II,1:1
Antony and Cleopatra 1960,Ag 1,19:1
Mr President 1962,Ag 29,18:4
Mr President 1962,S 26,36:1
Mr President 1962,O 14,II,1:7
Mr President 1962,O 22,34:2
Our Town 1968,S 29,77:4
Front Page, The 1968,O 20,85:5
Front Page, The 1969,My 12,54:2
Front Page, The 1969,My 25,II,1:1
Front Page, The 1969,N 2,86:1
Ryan, Sue
Ziegfeld Follies 1943,Ap 2,16:2
Lady Says Yes, A 1945,Ja 11,18:5
Ryan, T S
Faun, The 1924,Mr 28,17:2
Galloper, The 1924,D 19,26:2
Ryan, Thomas
Headless Horseman, The 1937,Mr 6,10:4
Ryan, Thomas J
Vaudeville (Palace) 1927,N 29,30:4
Ryans, The
Vaudeville (Loew's State) 1932,Jl 18,9:7
Rybrant, Goesta (Translator)
My Fair Lady 1959,F 16,24:1
Ryburn, Marie
New York Idea, The 1948,Ag 18,29:2
Rychtarik, Richard (Costume Designer)
Arabian Nights 1954,Je 25,15:2
Arabian Nights 1955,Je 24,16:1
Rychtarik, Richard (Scenic Designer)
Once Over Lightly 1942,N 20,26:2
Arabian Nights 1954,Je 25,15:2
Arabian Nights 1955,Je 24,16:1
Wonder World 1964,My 18,32:1
Rydeberg, Georg
Long Day's Journey Into Night 1962,My 16,35:4
Rydell, Charles
Secret Life of Walter Mitty, The 1964,O 27,44:5
By Jupiter 1967,Ja 20,28:2
Rydell, Mark
Seagulls Over Sorrento 1952,S 12,18:4
Maya 1953,Je 10,35:1
Handful of Fire 1958,O 2,45:3
Moonbirds 1959,O 10,13:1
Rydell, Mark (Director)
Roots 1961,Mr 7,40:2

Ryder, Alfred
Our Town 1938,F 5,18:3
All the Living 1938,Mr 25,14:4
Jeremiah 1939,F 4,11:2
Awake and Sing! 1939,Mr 8,18:2
Medicine Show 1940,Ap 13,20:6
No for an Answer 1941,Ja 6,10:6
Man With Blonde Hair, The 1941,N 5,30:2
Nathan the Wise 1942,Mr 12,25:4
Nathan the Wise 1942,Ap 4,18:4
Sky Drift 1945,N 14,25:2
Yellow Jack 1947,F 28,26:2
Ghosts 1948,F 17,31:2
Julius Caesar 1950,Je 21,30:1
Tower Beyond Tragedy, The 1950,N 27,29:1
Tower Beyond Tragedy, The 1950,D 10,II,5:1
Volpone 1957,Ja 8,27:1
Volpone 1957,Ja 13,II,10:1
I Rise in Flame, Cried the Phoenix 1959,Ap 15,30:1
One More River 1960,Mr 19,12:2
Hey You, Light Man! 1963,Mr 2,5:2
Hamlet 1964,Je 17,49:1
Ryder, Alfred (Director)
Sweet Confession 1959,Ap 15,30:1
Far Country, A 1961,Ap 5,32:1
Far Country, A 1961,Ap 16,II,1:1
Hey You, Light Man! 1963,Mr 2,5:2
In the Summer House 1964,Mr 26,43:1
Exercise, The 1968,Ap 25,54:1
Ryder, Arthur William (Translator)
Little Clay Cart, The 1924,D 6,13:3
Little Clay Cart, The 1953,Jl 1,25:1
Ryder, Charles
Cross-Town 1937,Mr 18,21:5
Ryder, Donald (Scenic Designer)
Ballad for Bimshire 1963,O 16,54:1
Ryder, John
Cortez 1929,N 5,32:2
Valley Forge 1934,D 11,28:3
Ryder, Klock
Town House 1948,S 24,31:2
Ryder, Maxwell
Hamlet 1920,Mr 17,14:2
Ryder, Philip
Singing Rabbi, The 1931,S 11,24:4
Postman Always Rings Twice, The 1936,F 26,17:2
Ryder, Robert
Once in a Lifetime 1930,S 25,22:3
Rye, Derek (Miscellaneous)
Measure for Measure 1967,F 15,37:1
Hamlet 1967,F 17,44:1
Romeo and Juliet 1967,F 22,18:1
Rye, Frank (Director)
Pansy 1929,My 15,36:3
Rye, Isabella
Hit the Deck 1960,Je 24,32:1
Ryerson, Elena
First Stop to Heaven 1941,Ja 6,10:7
Ryerson, Florence (Playwright)
Glamour Preferred 1940,N 16,13:2
Harriet 1943,Ja 29,22:1
Harriet 1943,Mr 4,24:2
Harriet 1943,Mr 14,V,1:1
Harriet 1944,S 28,26:1
Strange Bedfellows 1948,Ja 15,27:3
Rykey, William
Golden Wings 1941,N 25,33:3
Golden Wings 1941,D 9,46:6
Ryland, George
Fortune and Men's Eyes 1969,O 23,55:1
Ryland, George (Director)
Hamlet 1944,N 19,II,2:4
Duchess of Malfi, The 1946,O 16,35:2
Ryland, George (Miscellaneous)
Ages of Man 1958,S 22,26:1
Ages of Man 1959,Jl 10,28:2
Ryland, George (Playwright)
Ages of Man 1958,D 29,21:1
Ages of Man 1963,Ap 15,36:1
Ryland, Jack
Palm Tree in a Rose Garden, A 1957,N 27,26:2
Song for a Certain Midnight 1959,S 17,49:1
White Rose and the Red, The 1964,Mr 17,31:1
My Kinsman, Major Molineux 1964,N 2,62:2
Benito Cereno 1964,N 2,62:2
Troilus and Cressida 1965,Ag 13,17:1
Merchant of Venice, The 1967,Je 22,46:2
Macbeth 1967,Jl 31,21:1
Henry V 1969,N 11,43:1
Wars of the Roses, The (Part I) 1970,Jl 2,30:1
Wars of the Roses, The (Part II) 1970,Jl 3,15:1
Richard III 1970,Jl 4,11:1
Henry VI, Parts I, II, III 1970,Jl 5,II,3:1
Ryle, Lawrence
Duchess of Malfi, The 1946,O 16,35:2
Winners and Losers 1947,F 27,27:2
Deputy of Paris, The 1947,Mr 22,9:5
Galileo 1947,D 8,34:2·
Faith of Our Fathers 1950,Ag 6,72:2
Ryles, Robert
Two by Two 1925,F 24,17:1
Tell Me More 1925,Ap 14,27:3

Ryley, Phil
Sally 1920,D 22,16:1
Ziegfeld Follies 1924,Je 25,26:1
Betsy 1926,D 29,24:3
Ziegfeld Follies 1927,Ag 17,27:3
Ryman, Lucille (Director)
Blood on the Moon 1934,S 30,IX,3:1
Ryman, Lucille (Producer)
Blood on the Moon 1934,S 30,IX,3:1
Rymer, L
Aristocrats 1935,My 2,16:2
Clinton Street 1939,O 13,27:2
Rynne, John
Prunella; Love in a Garden 1926,Je 16,23:3
Juarez and Maximilian 1926,O 12,31:1
If 1927,O 26,26:2
Love Nest, The 1927,D 23,17:1
Maya 1928,F 22,19:1
Ryskind, Morrie
Ned Wayburn's Gambols 1929,Ja 16,22:3
Ryskind, Morrie (Composer)
Americana 1926,Jl 27,15:3
Ryskind, Morrie (Lyricist)
Buds of 1927 1927,F 22,22:5
Merry-Go-Round 1927,Je 1,25:4
Ryskind, Morrie (Miscellaneous)
Lady Comes Across, The 1942,Ja 10,10:2
Ryskind, Morrie (Musical Director)
Gang's All Here, The 1931,F 19,21:3
Ryskind, Morrie (Original Author)
Louisiana Purchase 1940,My 29,19:2
Ryskind, Morrie (Playwright)
Garrick Gaieties 1925,My 18,12:2
Merry-Go-Round 1927,Je 1,25:4
Animal Crackers 1928,O 24,26:2
Ned Wayburn's Gambols 1929,Ja 16,22:3
Strike Up the Band 1930,Ja 15,29:1
Of Thee I Sing 1931,D 13,VIII,2:4
Of Thee I Sing 1931,D 28,20:1
Of Thee I Sing 1932,Mr 20,VIII,1:1
Of Thee I Sing 1932,My 8,VIII,1:1
Pardon My English 1932,D 11,IX,5:2
Let 'Em Eat Cake 1933,O 3,26:5
Let 'Em Eat Cake 1933,O 23,18:1
Let 'Em Eat Cake 1933,N 12,IX,1:1
Bring on the Girls 1934,O 23,23:2
Of Thee I Sing 1937,Ag 10,22:3
Of Thee I Sing 1952,My 6,34:2
Of Thee I Sing 1952,My 11,II,1:1
Of Thee I Sing 1969,Mr 8,19:1
Rysz, Mary
Geisha, The 1931,O 6,35:4
Ryza, Paul D
Born Yesterday 1958,Mr 22,12:6

S

Saadi, Grenadier
Visit to a Small Planet 1957,F 8,18:1
Saah, Joe
Proposition, The 1968,Ap 20,25:3
Saal, Frederick H Vom
Upon My Soul 1927,Ap 22,19:1
Saari, Charles
Dark at the Top of the Stairs, The 1957,D 6,38:1
Dark at the Top of the Stairs, The 1957,D 15,II,3:1
Behind the Wall 1960,N 1,47:1
Sabadin, Marie
Revolt of the Beavers, The 1937,My 21,19:2
Sabata, Victor de (Composer)
Merchant of Venice, The 1934,Ag 12,IX,5:5
Sabath, Joseph (Judge) (Playwright)
Trial Divorce 1927,Ja 9,30:2
Sabatier, Pierre (Original Author)
Business 1930,Ap 13,X,2:7
Sabatier, Pierre (Playwright)
Demon de la Chair, Le 1927,N 20,IX,4:4
Amour a la Blague, L' 1929,Mr 10,X,1:8
Business 1930,Ap 13,X,2:7
Sabatini, Rafael (Director)
Tyrant, The 1930,N 13,33:1
Sabatini, Rafael (Original Author)
Scaramouche 1923,O 25,14:2
Sabatini, Rafael (Playwright)
Scaramouche 1923,O 25,14:2
Carolinian, The 1925,N 3,34:2
Tyrant, The 1930,N 13,33:1
Sabatini, Rafael (Producer)
In the Snare 1924,Jl 13,VII,1:6
Sabben, James (Playwright)
Lure, The 1924,My 18,VII,2:8
Sabel, Barbara (Costume Designer)
Gondoliers, The 1969,My 10,35:1
H M S Pinafore 1969,D 8,61:2
Pirates of Penzance, The 1970,D 6,84:6
Sabel, David
Wheel, The 1921,Ag 30,10:1
Sabel, Josephine
Earl Carroll's Vanities 1925,Jl 7,24:1
Oh, Please! 1926,D 22,24:3
Sidewalks of New York 1927,O 4,33:1
Vaudeville (Palace) 1931,Mr 2,19:2

Sabella, M
Cena Delle Beffe, La; Jest, The 1930,N 24,26:4
Sabeth, Joseph (Playwright)
Trial Divorce 1927,Ja 16,VII,2:4
Sabetti, Audrey
Carousel 1949,Ja 26,28:2
Sabian, Lloyd
Synthetic Sin 1927,O 11,26:2
Sabin, Charles
Vaudeville (Palace) 1928,Jl 17,15:5
Billie 1928,O 2,34:2
Sabin, David
Much Ado About Nothing 1964,Je 11,26:2
Richard III 1964,Je 12,44:2
Hamlet 1964,Jl 4,9:1
Yearling, The 1965,D 11,25:1
Mutilated, The 1966,F 23,42:1
Now Is the Time for all Good Men 1967,S 27,42:1
Jimmy Shine 1968,D 6,52:1
Gantry 1970,F 16,44:1
Sabin, Evelyn
Puppets of Passion 1927,F 25,24:4
Sabin, Gustav
Tender Trap, The 1961,Ag 26,15:1
Don Carlos 1962,F 28,27:5
Storm, The 1962,Mr 31,17:2
We're Civilized? 1962,N 9,30:1
Sabin, Gustav (Miscellaneous)
Political Party, A 1963,S 27,17:5
International Playgirls '64 1964,My 22,40:2
Sabin, H S
Tiger Smiles, The 1930,D 18,29:1
Sabine, Lloyd
Wanted 1928,Jl 3,19:2
Gods of the Lightning 1928,O 25,27:2
Sabini, Frank
Peek-A-Boo 1921,My 17,20:3
Sabinson, Lee (Producer)
Counterattack 1943,F 4,27:2
Trio 1944,D 30,13:4
Home of the Brave 1945,D 28,13:2
Finian's Rainbow 1947,Ja 11,23:2
Biggest Thief in Town 1949,Mr 31,31:2
Sable, Josephine
Marion Show, The 1923,My 8,22:3
Sablic, Jelisaveta
Progress of Bora, The Tailor, The 1968,Je 27,49:2
Ubu Roi 1968,Je 29,20:1
Victor, or The Children Take Over 1968,Jl 10,22:4
Sabline, Patsy
Dream Out of Time, A 1970,N 9,52:1
Sablon, Jean
Streets of Paris, The 1939,Je 20,25:2
Sablons, Albert (Playwright)
Trio 1929,Mr 17,X,2:7
Sablukova, Anna
Lysistrata 1925,D 15,28:2
Sabo, Oskar
Chicago 1927,D 18,IX,1:8
Sturm im Wasserglas 1930,D 28,VIII,2:4
Sabol, Ed
Where Do We Go From Here? 1938,N 16,26:2
Sabol, Richard
Hostage, The 1961,D 13,55:4
3 Bags Full 1966,Mr 7,22:1
Sabouret, Marie
Bourgeois Gentilhomme, Le 1955,O 26,26:1
Arlequin Poli par l'Amour 1955,N 9,40:1
Caprice, Un 1955,N 16,42:4
Sabourin, Marcel
Henry V 1966,Je 8,38:1
Henry VI 1966,Je 9,55:2
Sacco, Nola
John Brown 1950,My 4,32:7
Sacharow, Lawrence (Director)
Concept, The 1968,My 7,51:1
Sacher, Toby (Composer)
Of V We Sing 1942,F 16,20:3
Sachs, Ann
Wilson in the Promise Land 1970,Ja 11,78:1
Wilson in the Promise Land 1970,My 27,41:1
Sachs, Arieh (Dr) (Director)
Alice in Wonderland 1967,Mr 20,27:1
Sachs, Arthur L
Daughters of Atreus 1936,O 15,33:1
Howdy Stranger 1937,Ja 15,17:5
Richard II 1937,S 16,28:2
As You Like It 1939,My 9,28:4
Two on an Island 1940,Ja 23,17:2
Journey to Jerusalem 1940,O 7,21:2
As You Like It 1941,O 21,29:2
Johnny 2X4 1942,Mr 17,24:6
Swan Song 1946,My 16,29:2
Joan of Lorraine 1946,N 19,40:2
Sachs, Bernard Leon (Lighting Director)
Angels of Anadarko 1962,O 11,47:1
Sachs, Bernard Leon (Scenic Designer)
Angels of Anadarko 1962,O 11,47:1
Sachs, Dorothy (Composer)
Lew Leslie's Blackbirds of 1939 1939,F 13,12:2
Sachs, Dorothy (Lyricist)
Lew Leslie's Blackbirds of 1939 1939,F 13,12:2

Sachs, Ernest (Mrs) (Costume Designer)
Twelfth Disciple, The 1930,My 17,21:4
Sachs, Evelyn
Gondoliers, The 1961,Ja 26,33:2
Yeomen of the Guard, The 1964,Mr 19,29:2
Sachs, Louis
Airways, Inc 1929,F 21,30:5
Sachs, Mary Parmly Koues (Playwright)
Twelfth Disciple, The 1930,My 17,21:4
Sachs, Mr (Playwright)
Liebling Adieu 1931,N 29,VIII,4:2
Sachse, Leopold (Director)
Beggar Student, The 1942,S 26,11:4
Sachtleben, Horst
Wozzeck 1966,Ap 6,34:1
Mitschuldigen, Die 1966,Ap 6,34:1
Sack, August (Scenic Designer)
Boom-Boom Clopper 1940,Ja 6,8:7
Sack, Julanne
Schoolhouse on the Lot 1938,Mr 23,18:4
Sack, Nathaniel
East of Suez 1922,S 22,16:3
Cape Smoke 1925,F 17,19:1
Trapped 1928,S 12,25:3
Schoolhouse on the Lot 1938,Mr 23,18:4
Student Prince, The 1943,Je 9,16:2
Twilight Walk 1951,S 25,25:4
Sack, Penelope
After the Theatre 1942,S 28,13:1
House in Paris, The 1944,Mr 21,17:1
Wanhope Building, The 1947,F 11,36:5
Eastward in Eden 1947,N 19,33:2
Sackeroff, David (Scenic Designer)
Does a Tiger Wear a Necktie? 1967,F 4,17:1
Sackett, Albert
Fall and Rise of Susan Lenox, The 1920,Je 11,11:2
It's Up to You 1921,Mr 29,20:1
Personality 1921,Ag 29,14:3
Zeno 1923,Ag 27,14:2
Sackett, Beatrice
Madras House, The 1921,O 31,18:2
Sackheim, Jerome (Playwright)
When the Bough Breaks 1932,F 17,19:2
Sackler, Harold O (Director)
Hamlet 1957,O 29,34:2
Sackler, Harry (Playwright)
Major Noah 1929,F 23,17:2
Sackler, Howard (Playwright)
Great White Hope, The 1967,D 14,58:1
Great White Hope, The 1967,D 24,II,3:1
Great White Hope, The 1968,O 4,40:1
Great White Hope, The 1968,O 13,II,1:1
Great White Hope, The 1969,S 27,26:1
Sacklett, Albert
Bye Bye, Barbara 1924,Ag 26,6:3
Sacks, Gloria
Show Boat 1954,My 6,44:1
Sacks, Harry
Little Theatre Tournament; Father Returns, The 1929,My 7,28:1
Sacks, Merrylen
Pequod 1969,Je 30,33:1
Sacks, Miv
Thespis 1953,Ja 17,13:5
Sackville-West, Victoria (Original Author)
Edwardians, The 1937,Ap 20,28:4
Edwardians, The 1937,My 9,XI,1:4
Sacre Mont Gypsies
Continental Varieties 1934,O 4,18:3
Continental Varieties 1934,N 15,24:3
Sad Sacks, The
Ice Follies 1957,Ja 16,36:1
Sadang, Rob
Emerald Slippers, The 1970,S 2,31:2
Saddler, Donald
Dance Me a Song 1950,Ja 21,10:5
Bless You All 1950,D 15,42:2
Saddler, Donald (Choreographer)
Wonderful Town 1953,F 26,22:3
Wonderful Town 1953,Mr 8,II,1:1
John Murray Anderson's Almanac 1953,D 11,42:2
Wonderful Town 1954,My 7,II,1:1
Shangri-La 1956,Je 14,40:1
Milk and Honey 1961,O 11,52:1
Sophie 1963,Ap 16,32:1
Morning Sun 1963,O 7,36:2
Saddler, Donald (Miscellaneous)
Wonderful Town 1953,F 26,22:3
To Broadway With Love 1964,Ap 30,28:6
Sader, Ray
Cock-A-Doodle Dandy 1955,N 4,26:5
J B 1958,Ap 24,37:1
J B 1958,My 4,II,1:1
Sadler, Dudley
Man Who Had All the Luck, The 1944,N 24,18:5
Kiss Them for Me 1945,Mr 21,27:2
Kiss Them for Me 1945,Mr 25,II,1:1
Woman Bites Dog 1946,Ap 18,21:2
All My Sons 1947,Ja 30,21:2
Show-Off, The 1950,Je 1,24:5
Borned in Texas 1950,Ag 22,30:6
Sadler, Francis
Madre 1923,D 31,9:6

Sadoff, Fred
South Pacific 1949,Ap 8,30:2
South Pacific 1949,Ap 17,II,1:1
Wish You Were Here 1952,Je 26,26:6
Sadoff, Fred (Director)
Terrible Swift Sword, The 1955,N 16,42:1
Jackhammer, The 1962,F 6,26:2
In the Zone; Before Breakfast 1963,Je 11,29:4
Hughie 1963,Je 11,29:4
Sadoff, Fred (Miscellaneous)
Sleeping Prince, The 1956,N 2,31:1
Importance of Being Oscar, The 1961,Mr 15,45:2
Sadoff, Simon
Rosalinda; Fledermaus, Die 1942,O 29,26:5
Sadoff, Simon (Musical Director)
Good Woman of Setzuan, The 1956,D 19,41:2
Sadoyan, Isabelle
Three Musketeers, The 1968,Je 26,43:1
George Dandin 1968,Je 28,36:1
Tartuffe 1968,Jl 3,28:2
Sadoyan, Isabelle (Costume Designer)
Three Musketeers, The 1968,Je 26,43:1
Sadtler, Francis
He Who Gets Slapped 1922,Ja 10,15:1
Dice of the Gods, The 1923,Ap 6,20:2
Kreutzer Sonata, The 1924,My 15,22:3
Wild Duck, The 1925,F 25,16:4
Nirvana 1926,Mr 4,19:1
Sadun, Icilio
Bombasters Furioso 1924,Jl 19,10:4
Saegers, Mark
Hamlet 1948,D 4,9:2
Buskers, The 1961,O 31,28:1
Saerchinger, Eugene
Life Begins in '40 1940,Ap 5,24:2
Saffon, Dorothy
Warm Body, A 1967,Ap 17,44:2
Safford, Charles L
Master of the Revels 1935,Ag 14,16:2
Safford, Charles L (Composer)
Julius Caesar 1927,Je 7,27:2
Safian, Louis A (Producer)
Phantoms 1930,Ja 14,24:3
Gold Braid 1930,My 14,31:2
Safina, Anthony
Gondoliers, The 1963,Je 5,33:2
Safonova
Chauve-Souris 1929,Ja 23,20:2
Safranac, Gregory
King Lear 1923,Mr 10,9:4
Safranski, Eddie (Composer)
Frankie and Johnny 1952,O 29,37:2
Safranski, Eddie (Musical Director)
Frankie and Johnny 1952,O 29,37:2
Safrian, Louis A (Producer)
Great Scott! 1929,S 3,25:1
Sagal, Boris
Shoemaker's Prodigious Wife, The 1949,Je 15,38:2
Right You Are (If You Think You Are) 1950,Je 29,37:2
Sagall, Solomon (Producer)
I'm Solomon 1968,Ap 24,51:1
Megilla of Itzik Manger, The 1968,O 10,60:1
Megilla of Itzik Manger, The 1969,Ap 21,55:1
Sagalyn, Robert
Twilight Walk 1951,S 25,25:4
Mrs McThing 1952,F 21,22:1
Sagalyn, Robert (Miscellaneous)
Frogs of Spring, The 1953,O 21,36:2
Trial of Dmitri Karamazov, The 1958,Ja 28,30:1
Sagalyn, Robert (Producer)
Trial of Dmitri Karamazov, The 1958,Ja 28,30:1
Sagan, Francoise (Director)
Bonheur, Impair et Passe 1964,Ja 17,23:3
Sagan, Francoise (Playwright)
Bonheur, Impair et Passe 1964,Ja 17,23:3
Piano Dans l'Herbe, Un 1970,S 17,56:1
Sagan, Leontine
Lady Windermere's Fan 1927,F 27,VII,2:3
Sagan, Leontine (Director)
Little Accident 1929,S 22,IX,4:1
Gestern und Heute 1931,My 24,VIII,2:1
Maedchen in Uniform 1932,N 6,IX,1:3
Glamorous Night 1935,My 3,23:6
Two Share a Dwelling 1935,O 9,26:3
O Evening Star 1935,D 26,20:1
O Evening Star 1936,Ja 9,24:6
Sagan, Leontine (Producer)
Balalaika 1936,D 23,17:4
Sage, C Russell
Inspector Kennedy 1929,D 21,16:3
Mother Lode 1934,D 24,16:5
If This Be Treason 1935,S 24,28:2
Tapestry in Gray 1935,D 28,10:2
Ten Million Ghosts 1936,O 24,23:7
Sage, David (Miscellaneous)
Hedda Gabler 1970,Ja 18,78:1
Sage, David Rohan
Mother Courage and Her Children 1964,My 12,32:2
Firebugs, The 1968,Jl 2,36:1
Sage, Frances
It Happened Tomorrow 1933,My 6,11:5
Mahogany Hall 1934,Ja 18,18:5

Sage, Frances—Cont
Valley Forge 1934,D 11,28:3
Sage, Jacque
Afgar 1920,N 9,13:2
Sage, Michael
Daughters of Atreus 1936,O 15,33:1
Fifth Column, The 1940,Mr 7,18:2
Sage, Stuart
Bat, The 1920,Ag 24,6:1
Elton Case, The 1921,S 12,16:2
Hospitality 1922,N 14,16:1
Sager, Bernie
Naughty Marietta 1929,O 22,26:2
Fortune Teller, The 1929,N 5,32:3
Merry Widow, The 1929,D 3,29:1
Babes in Toyland 1929,D 24,15:3
Babes in Toyland 1930,D 22,17:1
Sager, Charles
Smiles 1930,N 19,19:2
Sager, David
Deep River 1926,O 5,26:2
Creoles 1927,S 23,33:3
Aiglon, L' 1927,D 27,24:3
Sager, Ed
Cradle of Willow, A 1961,D 16,20:2
Sager, Jacqueline
Out of This World 1950,D 22,17:3
Sager, Lester W (Producer)
Appearances 1925,O 15,27:3
Sager, Sidney (Composer)
Romeo and Juliet 1967,F 22,18:1
Sagi-Vela, Luis
Man of La Mancha 1966,O 5,42:5
Sahl, Hans (Translator)
Wall, The 1961,N 9,40:3
Sahl, Mike (Miscellaneous)
To Clothe the Naked 1967,Ap 28,30:1
Sahl, Mort
Next President, The 1958,Ap 10,34:3
Sahlins, Bernard (Producer)
From the Second City 1961,S 27,32:1
Return of Second City in "20,000 Frozen Grenadiers," The 1966,Ap 22,36:1
From the Second City 1969,O 15,34:1
Said, Boris (Miscellaneous)
Russian Bank 1940,My 25,20:2
Saidenberg, Eleanore (Producer)
Hot Corner, The 1956,Ja 26,25:2
Disenchanted, The 1958,D 4,53:4
Andersonville Trial, The 1959,D 30,15:1
Cook for Mr General, A 1961,O 20,39:1
Saidenberg, Theodore (Musical Director)
On a Clear Day You Can See Forever 1965,O 18,44:1
Here's Where I Belong 1968,Mr 4,32:1
Mahagonny 1970,Ap 29,51:1
Lovely Ladies, Kind Gentlemen 1970,D 29,38:1
Saidy, Fred (Director)
Flahooley 1951,My 15,39:1
Saidy, Fred (Miscellaneous)
Bloomer Girl 1947,Ja 7,33:2
Flahooley 1951,My 15,39:1
Saidy, Fred (Playwright)
Bloomer Girl 1944,O 6,18:5
Finian's Rainbow 1947,Ja 11,23:2
Finian's Rainbow 1947,Ja 26,II,1:1
Flahooley 1951,My 15,39:1
Flahooley 1951,My 20,II,1:1
Jollyanna; Flahooley 1952,Ag 13,17:7
Finian's Rainbow 1953,Mr 7,13:2
Finian's Rainbow 1955,My 19,25:1
Jamaica 1957,N 1,32:2
Jamaica 1957,N 10,II,1:1
Finian's Rainbow 1960,Ap 28,31:1
Happiest Girl in the World, The 1961,Ap 4,42:1
Finian's Rainbow 1967,Ap 6,44:1
Sailors, The Three
Vaudeville (Palace) 1929,Je 17,29:3
Sainer, Arthur (Playwright)
Bitch of Waverly Place, The 1965,Ap 2,26:1
Blind Angel, The 1965,Ap 2,26:1
Sainer, Lionel
Noble Rogue, A 1929,Ag 20,31:2
Sainpolis, John
Return of Peter Grimm, The 1921,S 22,12:2
Saint, Carroll
Threepenny Opera, The 1955,S 21,38:1
Saint, Eva Marie
Trip to Bountiful, The 1953,N 4,30:3
St Angel, Michael
Cat Screams, The 1942,Je 17,26:5
Janie 1942,S 11,24:2
St Aubyn, Marjorie
Many Waters 1929,S 26,27:1
St Chad, Gordon
Half-Caste, The 1926,Mr 30,20:4
St Clair, Bob
Plain and Fancy 1955,F 6,II,6:6
St Clair, Clare
Dancing Partner 1930,Ag 6,24:2
They Don't Mean Any Harm 1932,F 24,25:2
St Clair, June
Springtime Folly 1951,F 27,23:4

St Clair, Lydia
Flight to the West 1940,D 31,19:1
Flight to the West 1941,Ja 19,IX,1:1
Flight to the West 1941,Mr 7,16:3
Trio 1944,D 30,13:4
Time of the Cuckoo, The 1952,O 16,37:4
St Clair, Stewart (Playwright)
Lace Petticoat 1927,Ja 5,18:2
St Claire, Winifred
When the Bough Breaks 1950,Mr 9,25:5
St Darr, Deborah
Me and Juliet 1970,My 15,42:1
St Denis, Michael
Don Juan 1934,F 27,16:5
St Denis, Michael (Director)
Noah 1935,Ag 4,IX,1:3
Macbeth 1937,D 19,XI,3:7
St Denis, Ruth (Choreographer)
Light of Asia, The 1928,O 10,32:2
Singapore 1932,N 15,24:2
St Dennis, Michael (Director)
Twelfth Night 1938,D 18,IX,5:6
Oedipus 1946,My 21,19:2
St Dennis, Michael (Producer)
Macbeth 1937,N 27,21:3
Three Sisters, The 1938,F 13,X,3:3
White Guard, The 1938,O 23,IX,3:1
Twelfth Night 1938,D 18,IX,5:6
Cherry Orchard, The 1961,D 15,49:1
St Dennis, Michael (Scenic Designer)
Witch of Edmonton, The 1936,D 9,34:1
St Gaudens, Celeste
New York Exchange 1926,D 31,11:2
St George's Choir and Treble Choir
Tableaux 1961,D 18,41:3
St Gilles, De
Folies Bergere 1939,D 25,28:2
St Granier (Playwright)
Vogue 1921,O 23,22:2
J'Aime 1927,Ja 23,VII,2:1
1927 1927,Mr 6,VII,4:4
Untitled-Revue 1930,N 30,IX,3:3
Deux Sous de Fleurs 1933,O 1,IX,1:3
Dame du Promenoir, La 1933,O 1,IX,1:3
St Heller, Ivy
Spread It Abroad 1936,My 3,X,1:2
Don't Listen, Ladies 1948,D 29,16:2
St Ives, Beatrice
Bitter Oleander 1935,F 12,24:3
St Jacques, Raymond
Romeo and Juliet 1959,Je 15,31:1
Cool World, The 1960,F 23,38:2
Henry V 1960,Je 30,23:1
Blacks, The 1961,My 5,23:1
St James, William
Bonehead, The 1920,Ap 13,12:1
Way of the World, The 1924,N 18,23:4
Love Song, The 1925,Ja 14,19:4
Lulu Belle 1926,F 10,20:1
St Jean, Andre
Kismet 1965,Je 23,45:1
St Jean, Mlle
Bourgeois Gentilhomme, Le 1955,O 26,26:1
St John, Adele Rogers (Original Author)
Free Soul, A 1928,Ja 13,26:5
St John, Betta
South Pacific 1949,Ap 8,30:2
South Pacific 1949,Je 5,II,1:1
South Pacific 1951,Jl 10,30:5
South Pacific 1951,N 2,19:1
South Pacific 1951,N 11,II,3:1
Carousel 1953,My 6,38:1
St John, Christopher
No Place to Be Somebody 1969,D 31,17:1
St John, Christopher (Translator)
Rising Sun, The 1929,O 27,IX,2:2
St John, Howard
Blonde Sinner, The 1926,Jl 15,21:2
Trial Marriage 1927,F 1,24:3
Broadway Shadows 1930,Ap 1,34:6
Prince Charming 1930,O 14,31:1
Bulls, Bears and Asses 1932,My 7,11:3
Keeper of the Keys 1933,O 19,23:2
Tomorrow's Harvest 1934,D 6,26:5
Triumph 1935,O 15,18:5
Cuckoos on the Hearth 1941,S 17,26:2
Janie 1942,S 11,24:2
Late George Apley, The 1944,O 20,16:4
Late George Apley, The 1944,N 22,26:2
Fatal Witness, The 1946,N 20,43:2
Two Blind Mice 1949,Mr 3,32:2
Jane 1952,F 2,10:2
Jane 1952,F 10,II,1:1
His and Hers 1954,Ja 8,18:2
Someone Waiting 1956,F 15,26:1
Li'l Abner 1956,N 16,24:2
Li'l Abner 1956,N 25,II,1:1
Highest Tree, The 1959,N 5,41:1
St John, Marco
Angels of Anadarko 1962,O 11,47:1
Poor Bitos 1964,N 16,40:2
Colombe 1965,F 24,33:1

And Things That Go Bump in the Night
1965,Ap 27,27:5
We Comrades Three 1966,D 21,46:1
War and Peace 1967,Mr 22,42:1
Unknown Soldier and His Wife, The 1967,Jl 7,22:1
Weekend 1968,Mr 14,50:2
Hamlet 1968,Jl 21,II,21:2
Forty Carats 1968,D 27,45:1
Forty Carats 1969,Ja 5,II,1:3
St John, Marguerite
Tendresse, La 1922,S 26,18:1
Aren't We All? 1923,My 22,14:2
Beau-Strings 1926,Ap 27,22:2
Becky Sharp 1929,Je 4,29:1
St John, Michael
John Brown 1950,My 4,32:7
Night Circus, The 1958,D 3,44:1
St John, Richard
Ronde, La 1960,My 10,44:2
St John, Theodore
You and I 1925,O 20,29:1
Friend Indeed 1926,Ap 27,22:3
Ghosts 1927,Ja 11,36:3
Marquise, The 1927,N 15,26:4
Paris 1928,O 9,34:3
Paris Bound 1929,Jl 20,8:3
Plutocrat, The 1930,F 21,23:3
His Majesty's Car 1930,O 24,30:1
Blue Monday 1932,Je 3,23:2
Only the Young 1932,S 22,25:2
All This While 1935,Jl 30,17:2
Master of the Revels 1935,Ag 14,16:2
St John, Theodore (Playwright)
Adams' Wife 1931,D 29,27:1
Distant Shore, The 1935,F 22,26:2
All This While 1935,Jl 30,17:2
St John, Wayne
Hair 1970,Ja 13,39:1
St Joseph, Ellis (Playwright)
Passenger to Bali, A 1940,Mr 15,26:2
Saint-Laurent, Yves (Costume Designer)
Mariage de Figaro, Le 1964,F 26,41:2
Zizi 1964,N 23,51:1
St Leger, Frank (Director)
Yeomen of the Guard, The 1939,Jl 16,30:4
Yeomen of the Guard, The 1939,Jl 23,IX,2:1
St Leger, Frank (Producer)
Yeomen of the Guard, The 1939,Jl 23,IX,2:1
St Leo, Leonard
Lollipop 1924,Ja 22,15:3
Song of the Flame 1925,D 31,10:2
St Leon, Ida
Mamma's Affair 1920,Ja 20,10:1
Mama's Affair 1920,Ja 25,VIII,2:1
Wheel, The 1921,My 8,VI,1:1
Wheel, The 1921,Ag 30,10:1
St Louis, Louis
Mahagonny 1970,Ap 29,51:1
Saint-Marc, Boussac de (Playwright)
Sardanapale 1926,N 7,VIII,2:7
Sardanapale 1926,N 21,VIII,2:1
Moloch 1929,Ja 27,IX,2:8
St Maur, Adele
Wise-Crackers, The 1925,D 17,26:1
St Moritz, Ruth (Costume Designer)
Sponono 1964,Ap 3,28:1
St Moritz Orchestra
Vaudeville (Palace) 1930,D 22,16:5
Saint-Pierre, Denyse
Malade Imaginaire, Le; Imaginary Invalid, The
1958,Ap 30,28:2
Sganarelle; Imaginary Cuckold, The 1958,My 7,43:1
Mariage Force, Le; Forced Wedding, The
1958,My 7,43:1
Jalousie du Barbouille, La; Jealousy of the
Barbouille, The 1958,My 7,43:1
St Polis, John
Coquette 1935,My 22,23:4
Saint-Subber, Arnold
More the Merrier, The 1941,S 16,19:3
Saint-Subber, Arnold (Miscellaneous)
Hollywood Pinafore 1945,Je 1,20:1
Park Avenue 1946,N 5,31:2
Loss of Roses, A 1959,N 30,27:1
Little Foxes, The 1967,O 27,53:1
Saint-Subber, Arnold (Playwright)
Out of This World 1950,D 22,17:3
Saint-Subber, Arnold (Producer)
Kiss Me, Kate 1948,D 31,10:3
Kiss Me, Kate 1952,Ja 9,24:6
Grass Harp, The 1952,Mr 28,26:2
My 3 Angels 1953,Mr 12,23:2
House of Flowers 1954,D 31,11:2
Square Root of Wonderful, The 1957,O 31,40:1
Dark at the Top of the Stairs, The 1957,D 6,38:1
Tenth Man, The 1959,N 6,24:2
Loss of Roses, A 1959,N 30,27:1
Look: We've Come Through 1961,O 26,40:1
Harold 1962,N 30,27:1
Barefoot in the Park 1963,O 24,36:2
Odd Couple, The 1965,Mr 11,36:1
Dr Cook's Garden 1967,S 26,52:1
There's a Girl in My Soup 1967,O 19,58:1

Saint-Subber, Arnold (Producer)—Cont
House of Flowers 1968,Ja 29,26:2
Plaza Suite; Visitor From Mamaroneck
1968,F 15,49:1
Plaza Suite; Visitor From Hollywood
1968,F 15,49:1
Plaza Suite; Visitor From Forest Hills
1968,F 15,49:1
Carry Me Back to Morningside Heights
1968,F 28,41:1
Weekend 1968,Mr 14,50:2
Gingerbread Lady, The 1970,D 14,58:3
Saintey, Monique
Lacune, La 1970,My 6,49:1
Sainthill, Loudon (Costume Designer)
Tiger at the Gates 1955,O 4,40:1
Romeo and Juliet 1956,O 25,41:1
Half a Sixpence 1965,Ap 26,38:2
Right Honourable Gentleman, The 1965,O 20,50:2
Canterbury Tales; Pilgrims, The 1969,F 4,34:1
Canterbury Tales; Wife of Bath's Tale, The
1969,F 4,34:1
Canterbury Tales; Miller's Tale, The 1969,F 4,34:1
Canterbury Tales; Steward's Tale, The
1969,F 4,34:1
Canterbury Tales; Merchant's Tale, The
1969,F 4,34:1
Canterbury Tales 1969,F 16,II,1:1
Sainthill, Loudon (Scenic Designer)
Tiger at the Gates 1955,O 4,40:1
Romeo and Juliet 1956,O 25,41:1
Half a Sixpence 1965,Ap 26,38:2
Right Honourable Gentleman, The 1965,O 20,50:2
Saintsbury, H A
Julius Caesar 1932,F 28,VIII,2:4
Sainval, Claude (Producer)
Absence of a Cello; Mal de Test, Le 1965,S 9,36:3
Saito, Shoichi
Golden Bat 1970,Ag 16,II,1:1
Coney Island Play 1970,O 31,34:2
Saito, Shoichi (Translator)
Coney Island Play 1970,O 31,34:2
Saitta, Paul (Lighting Director)
Obbligato 1958,F 19,22:2
Buffalo Skinner, The 1959,F 20,18:1
Confederates, The 1959,S 29,45:1
Miss Emily Adam 1960,Mr 30,43:1
Saix, Guillot de (Playwright)
Gualtier l'Oyseau 1926,D 5,VIII,6:1
Saka, Jean
Watched Pot, The 1947,O 29,31:4
Sakae, Kato
Golden Bat 1970,Je 27,18:2
Sakallarios, A (Playwright)
Cute Gata.....Oute Zhmia; Neither Cat . . . Nor
Damage 1957,D 20,31:1
Sakamoto, Kyu
How to Succeed in Business Without Really Trying
1964,Jl 18,10:1
Sakellariou, Loukia (Choreographer)
Electra 1952,N 20,38:2
Sakhnovsky, V G (Miscellaneous)
Dead Souls 1965,F 5,34:1
Saki
Teahouse of the August Moon, The 1953,O 16,32:1
Saki, Marion
Little Nellie Kelly 1922,N 14,16:1
Plain Jane 1924,My 13,24:2
Sweetheart Time 1926,Ja 20,23:2
Polly 1929,Ja 9,28:3
Saki (Playwright)
Watched Pot, The 1933,My 5,13:7
Watched Pot, The 1947,O 29,31:4
Sakolow, Anna (Director)
Veronica 1965,N 19,31:1
Bugs 1965,N 19,31:1
Saks, Florence
Familiar Pattern 1943,S 3,15:6
Saks, Gene
Outside the Door 1949,Mr 2,33:2
Yes is for a Very Young Man 1949,Je 7,27:2
Bourgeois Gentleman, The 1949,Ag 31,27:2
All You Need Is One Good Break 1950,F 10,20:3
Coriolanus 1954,Ja 20,34:2
Master Builder, The 1955,Mr 2,23:2
South Pacific 1955,My 5,39:5
Good Woman of Setzuan, The 1956,D 19,41:2
Infernal Machine, The 1958,F 4,33:1
Howie 1958,S 18,35:2
Tenth Man, The 1959,N 6,24:2
Love and Libel 1960,D 8,44:1
Shot in the Dark, A 1961,O 19,40:1
Thousand Clowns, A 1962,Ap 6,31:2
Thousand Clowns, A 1962,Ap 15,II,1:1
Saks, Gene (Director)
Enter Laughing 1963,Mr 15,8:1
Enter Laughing 1963,Je 16,II,1:1
Nobody Loves an Albatross 1963,D 20,20:1
Nobody Loves an Albatross 1964,Ja 5,II,1:1
Half a Sixpence 1965,Ap 26,38:2
Generation 1965,O 8,5:6
Mame 1966,My 25,41:1
Mame 1969,Ja 5,79:4
Sheep on the Runway 1970,F 2,28:3

Saks, Jean
Topaze 1947,D 29,21:5
Saks, Michael (Producer)
Village Wedding, A 1930,S 24,26:2
Once Upon a Time 1933,S 22,15:1
Sala, Fernando
Pluma en el Viento; Feather in the Wind 1932,Ap 2,13:4
Tambor y Cascabel; Drum and Bell 1932,Ap 21,25:4
De Muy Buena Familia; Of Very Good Family 1932,Ap 29,13:3
Salacrou, Armand (Playwright)
Patchouli 1930,F 16,IX,4:4
Atlas-Hotel 1931,My 10,VIII,2:6
Vie en Rose, La 1931,D 20,VIII,2:7
Femme Libre, Une 1934,D 2,X,2:1
Frenetiques, Les 1935,Ja 13,IX,2:1
Inconnue d'Arras 1935,D 29,IX,2:1
Homme Comme les Autres, Un 1937,F 28,XI,2:3
Invites de Bon Dieu, Les 1953,N 29,II,3:1
Nuits de La Colere, Les; Nights of Fury 1957,F 12,31:1
Boulevard Durand 1961,O 8,II,3:4
Salacrou, Armand (Translator)
Nights of Wrath; Nuits de la Colere, Les 1947,D 1,26:4
Salama, Andrew
Chauve-Souris 1922,Je 6,17:4
Cricket on the Hearth, The 1925,My 29,20:2
Spring in Autumn 1933,O 25,22:5
Night Remembers, The 1934,N 28,24:3
Salama, Nina
Doctor Faustus 1937,Ja 9,21:2
Salaman, Chattie (Director)
Architect and the Emperor of Assyria, The 1970,Jl 24,17:2
Architect and the Emperor of Assyria, The 1970,Ag 9,II,1:5
Salango, James
Tall Kentuckian, The 1953,Je 17,30:1
Sale, Chic
Common Sense 1923,D 2,VIII,2:1
Gay Paree 1925,Ag 19,14:3
Gay Paree 1926,N 10,24:2
So This Is Paris 1930,Ap 27,IX,2:3
Hello Paris 1930,N 17,29:3
Sale, Virginia
Play, Genius, Play! 1935,O 31,17:2
Salerno, Antonio
Bootleggers, The 1922,N 28,24:1
Mister Malatesta 1923,F 27,14:2
Cyrano de Bergerac 1923,N 2,14:1
Cyrano de Bergerac 1926,F 19,18:1
Deep River 1926,O 5,26:2
Aiglon, L' 1927,D 27,24:3
Salerno, Antonio (Playwright)
Sirena 1931,S 22,33:4
Salerno, Jean (Miscellaneous)
Mariage de Figaro, Le 1964,F 26,41:2
Andromaque 1964,F 29,13:2
Vie Parisienne, La 1964,Mr 11,34:2
Salerno, Ray (Producer)
Salad of the Mad Cafe, The 1964,Ap 1,43:1
Sales, Clifford
Annie Get Your Gun 1946,My 17,14:2
Topaze 1947,D 29,21:5
Happy Journey to Trenton and Camden, The 1948,Mr 21,II,1:1
As the Girls Go 1948,N 15,21:2
Cry of the Peacock 1950,Ap 12,33:2
Sales, Patricia
Mother Said No 1951,Ap 17,34:2
Sales, Soupy
Ice Capades 1966,Je 2,50:2
Come Live With Me 1967,Ja 27,29:1
Come Live With Me 1967,F 5,II,1:1
Sales, Wilferd (Lyricist)
Egg and I, The 1958,S 11,43:4
Salfner, Heinz
Dreimal Hochzeit 1929,Ap 28,IX,1:4
Salgado, Carlos (Producer)
Big Knife, The 1959,N 13,25:1
Salici Puppets
Concert Varieties 1945,Je 2,10:7
Salignac, E Thomas
Perichole, La 1926,D 29,24:4
Salignac, E Thomas (Director)
Perichole, La 1926,D 28,12:2
Salinaro, Dom
Boys From Syracuse, The 1963,Ap 16,31:1
Salinger, Conrad
Beranger 1923,Ap 20,20:3
Salinger, Conrad (Miscellaneous)
George White's Scandals 1935,D 26,20:2
Salinger, Helen
Light Wines and Beer 1930,N 11,28:6
Did I Say No? 1931,S 23,19:4
Biography 1932,D 13,25:3
Curtain Rises, The 1933,O 20,15:2
Tomorrow's Harvest 1934,D 6,26:5
Salisbury, Franklin
Merchant of Venice, The 1925,D 28,12:1

Caponsacchi 1928,Ja 25,20:3
Henry V 1928,Mr 16,26:2
Light of Asia, The 1928,O 10,32:2
Richelieu 1929,D 26,20:3
Richelieu 1934,My 22,28:1
Hamlet 1934,D 26,19:3
Richard III 1934,D 28,24:3
Cyrano de Bergerac 1936,Ap 28,17:1
Salisbury, Jane
Lady in Love, A 1927,F 22,22:1
Salisbury, Jean
Master of the Revels 1935,Ag 14,16:2
Salisbury, Lottie
Spellbound 1927,F 16,17:2
Challenge of Youth 1930,Ja 21,28:5
Salisbury, Mary
Demi-Virgin, The 1921,O 19,22:1
Salisbury, Milton
Glass Slipper, The 1925,O 20,29:1
Salisbury, Winifred
Hamlet 1923,N 27,23:6
Salisian, Richard
Tomorrow's a Holiday! 1935,D 31,10:2
Salkeld, Celia
Hostage, The 1960,S 21,42:1
Hostage, The 1960,O 2,II,1:1
Salkin, Marie Helene
Intermezzo 1957,F 15,20:4
Salko, Lester
Money Lender, The 1928,Ag 28,27:3
Peter Pan; Boy Who Would Not Grow Up, The 1928,N 27,36:3
Salko, Sidney
Family Upstairs, The 1925,Ag 18,14:2
Solid Ivory 1925,N 17,29:3
Salkow, Charlotte
Dead End 1935,O 29,17:2
Salkow, Lester
Up Pops the Devil 1930,S 2,19:1
He 1931,S 22,33:1
Counsellor-at-Law 1931,N 7,17:2
Salkow, Lester (Master)
Mendel, Inc 1929,N 26,28:5
Salkow, Sidney (Director)
Black Tower 1932,Ja 12,29:2
Bloodstream 1932,Mr 31,25:1
Geraniums in My Window 1934,O 27,20:6
Sky's the Limit, The 1934,D 18,25:5
De Luxe 1935,Mr 6,22:2
Salkowitz, Charlotte
Humoresque 1923,F 28,13:2
Salkowitz, Sidney
Bronx Express 1922,Ap 27,12:2
Humoresque 1923,F 28,13:2
Sallade, David
Nervous Set, The 1959,My 13,43:1
Sallee, Hilmar
As You Like It 1955,O 29,12:2
Sallee, Hilmar (Miscellaneous)
As You Like It 1955,O 29,12:2
Portrait of a Madonna 1957,Ap 1,21:2
Man of Destiny, The 1957,Ap 1,21:2
Bedtime Story 1957,Ap 1,21:2
Sallert, Ulla
Kiss Me, Kate 1958,My 31,7:4
My Fair Lady 1959,F 16,24:1
Ben Franklin in Paris 1964,O 28,52:1
Sallis, Peter
Baker Street 1965,F 17,36:1
Inadmissible Evidence 1965,D 1,52:1
Sally, Sommer
Hawk, The 1968,Ap 18,54:1
Dirtiest Show in Town, The 1970,Je 29,43:2
Sally and Ted
George White's Scandals 1929,S 24,29:1
Salmaggi, Carlo (Miscellaneous)
Jackass, The 1960,Mr 24,39:2
Marcus in the High Grass 1960,N 22,38:6
Fig Leaf in Her Bonnet, A 1961,Je 15,50:1
Salmi, Albert
Scarecrow, The 1953,Je 17,31:1
End as a Man 1953,S 16,39:1
End As a Man 1953,S 27,II,1:1
Rainmaker, The 1954,O 29,28:1
Rainmaker, The 1954,N 7,II,1:1
Bus Stop 1955,Mr 3,23:2
Bus Stop 1955,Mr 13,II,1:1
Good Woman of Setzuan, The 1956,D 19,41:2
Good Woman of Setzuan, The 1956,D 30,II,1:1
Howie 1958,S 18,35:2
Failures, The 1959,Ja 6,30:2
Once There Was a Russian 1961,F 20,32:2
Price, The 1968,O 30,39:1
Salmon, Eric (Director)
Happy Haven, The 1963,My 10,40:6
Troubled Waters 1965,Je 4,40:2
Salmon, Patricia
Vaudeville (Hippodrome) 1926,F 23,26:2
Salmon, Scotty
George M! 1968,Ap 11,48:1
Salmonese, Frank
Man Who Washed His Hands, The 1967,F 16,33:1
Priest in the Cellar, The 1969,F 19,39:1

Salner, Arthur (Playwright)
Three...With Women in Mind; I Hear It Kissing Me Ladies 1970,N 28,22:1
Salomon, Ernest
El Cristo 1926,My 9,II,1:4
Salonis, Clark
Finian's Rainbow 1967,Ap 6,44:1
South Pacific 1969,Jl 7,27:1
Salsbury, Colgate
Country Wife, The 1957,Je 27,22:1
Cantilevered Terrace, The 1962,Ja 18,24:1
Poor Richard 1964,D 3,59:1
Kitchen, The 1966,Je 14,50:1
Fireworks; Football 1969,Je 12,51:1
Fireworks; Fireworks for a Hot Fourth 1969,Je 12,51:1
Salsbury, Milton S
Caesar and Cleopatra 1925,Ap 14,27:1
Salt, Jennifer
Watercolor 1970,Ja 22,30:1
Salt, Waldo (Playwright)
Sandhog 1954,N 24,17:1
Davy Jones's Locker 1966,D 25,48:5
Salt and Pepper
Gay Paree 1925,Ag 19,14:3
Merry World, The 1926,Je 9,18:3
Salten, Felix (Playwright)
Abie's Irish Rose 1927,O 23,VIII,2:4
Royal Highness 1949,Ap 14,29:3
Salten, Felix (Translator)
Abie's Irish Rose 1927,S 30,29:3
Saltenburg (Producer)
Zarewitsch, Der 1927,Ap 3,VIII,2:1
Chicago 1927,D 18,IX,1:8
Salter, Harold
Hail and Farewell 1923,F 20,12:1
Whole Town's Talking, The 1923,Ag 30,8:2
Mismates 1925,Ap 14,27:2
Square Crooks 1926,Mr 2,23:2
Salter, John
Everyman 1941,My 9,19:2
Saltuikoff-Shchedrin, Mikhail (Playwright)
Death of Pazukhin, The 1924,F 12,20:1
Saltz, Amy (Director)
Touch 1970,N 9,52:1
Saltz, Amy (Miscellaneous)
Electra 1969,Ag 8,14:1
Saltz, Amy (Playwright)
Touch 1970,N 9,52:1
Saltz, Charles (Miscellaneous)
Crystal Heart, The 1960,F 16,31:2
Saltzman, Esta
Twice 100,000 1934,N 23,22:6
Secret of Love, The 1936,F 24,15:2
Yoina Seeks a Bride 1936,O 20,31:1
Oy, Is Dus a Leben!; Oh, What a Life! 1942,O 13,19:2
Take It Easy 1950,D 25,23:6
Second Marriage 1953,O 12,30:1
Farblondjete Honeymoon 1955,S 27,42:1
Nice People 1958,O 20,36:1
Kosher Widow, The 1959,N 2,40:2
Saltzman, Jack
Lady of the Camellias, The 1931,Ja 27,21:2
Melody 1933,F 15,17:4
Saltzman, Leonard
Nautical but Nice 1931,Ap 19,31:6
Saltzman, Michael (Scenic Designer)
Pinye of Pinchev 1936,S 21,27:5
Let's Get Married 1937,Ja 11,16:2
Abi Gezunt 1949,O 10,19:4
Sadie Is a Lady 1950,Ja 28,9:2
Uncle Sam in Israel 1952,D 8,38:5
Wish Me Luck! 1954,N 1,37:2
Saltzman, Michal (Miscellaneous)
It Could Happen to You 1957,O 28,30:5
Saltzman, Simon L (Miscellaneous)
Weekend 1968,Mr 14,50:2
Saltzman, Simon L (Producer)
Paradise Gardens East 1969,Mr 11,39:1
Conerico Was Here to Stay 1969,Mr 11,39:1
Salvacion, Francisco
They Knew What They Wanted 1949,F 17,28:2
Tenth of an Inch Makes the Difference, A 1962,N 13,44:1
Salvador, Ruby
Circle of Chalk, The 1950,D 2,8:3
Salvatore, Elena
What a Life 1938,Ap 14,26:2
Salve, Juleste
It's a Bird . . . It's a Plane . . . It's Superman 1966,Mr 30,34:1
Salvia, Delia
Grass Is Always Greener, The 1955,F 16,25:2
Salvini, Guido (Director)
Citta Morta, La 1935,S 22,X,7:7
Salvini, Guido (Producer)
Oedipus Rex 1937,My 9,XI,7:5
Salvio, Robert
Awakening of Spring, The 1964,My 13,50:1
Night of the Dunce 1966,D 29,21:1
Hamp 1967,Mr 10,32:1
Billy 1969,Mr 24,56:1

Salvio, Robert—Cont
 Awake and Sing! 1970,My 28,35:1
 Awake and Sing! 1970,Je 7,II,1:1
Salvo, Louis
 There You Are! 1932,My 17,25:4
Salvotti, Vera
 Lauf ins Glueck 1935,My 19,IX,2:5
Salzer, Marcella
 All God's Chillun Got Wings 1932,Mr 27,VIII,3:3
Salzer, Sidney
 Jubilee 1935,O 14,20:1
 Yokel Boy 1939,Jl 7,12:2
Salzman, Ezta
 Mazel Tov, Molly 1950,O 2,18:1
Salzman, Harold Aaron (Producer)
 Once Upon a Time 1939,D 21,28:2
Salzman, M (Scenic Designer)
 Alexander Pushkin 1928,Ja 27,14:2
Sam, Ted and Ray
 George White's Scandals 1935,D 26,20:2
Samach, Samuel (Producer)
 Anna 1928,My 17,25:2
Samalka, Michael
 Sonya's Search for the Christmas Star
  1929,D 14,24:6
Samarie, Janice
 South Pacific 1955,My 5,39:5
Samberg, I A
 Motke Ganef 1932,D 30,15:2
Sambound and O'Hanlon
 Passing Show of 1921, The 1920,D 30,16:2
Sameth, Marten
 On the Town 1944,D 29,11:4
 Barefoot Boy With Cheek 1947,Ap 4,20:2
 Golden Apple, The 1954,Mr 12,15:2
Samford, Mary
 Lower Depths, The 1956,O 3,29:2
 Hamlet 1959,S 11,21:4
Samie, Catherine
 Impromptu de Versailles, L' 1961,F 22,30:1
 Tartuffe 1961,Mr 1,28:1
 Dindon, Le 1961,Mr 8,38:1
 Fil a la Paite, Un 1966,F 18,25:1
 Troupe Du Roi, La 1970,F 4,38:1
 Don Juan 1970,F 7,24:2
 Femmes Savaantes, Les 1970,F 14,12:1
Sammis, Edward R (Playwright)
 Day in the Sun 1939,My 17,29:2
Sammon, Caroline
 Would-Be Gentleman, The 1930,Ap 30,29:2
Sammons, Jeff
 Picture of Dorian Gray, The 1956,Ag 18,15:5
Sammons, Jennie
 Singin' the Blues 1931,S 17,21:3
Sammut, Fred (Costume Designer)
 Chiaroscuro; Maggie French Understands
  1963,Je 6,40:8
 Chiaroscuro; Kitty, I Hardly Knew You
  1963,Je 6,40:8
 Chiaroscuro; Judges, The 1963,Je 6,40:8
Sammut, Fred (Lighting Director)
 On the High Road 1961,Ap 21,26:2
 Anniversary, The 1961,Ap 21,26:2
 Wedding, The 1961,Ap 21,26:2
 Poppa Is Home 1961,D 20,37:1
 Merchant of Venice, The 1962,F 3,13:2
 Chiaroscuro; Maggie French Understands
  1963,Je 6,40:8
 Chiaroscuro; Kitty, I Hardly Knew You
  1963,Je 6,40:8
 Chiaroscuro; Judges, The 1963,Je 6,40:8
Sammut, Fred (Producer)
 Vincent 1959,O 1,40:1
Sammut, Fred (Scenic Designer)
 Mrs Warren's Profession 1958,Je 26,22:1
 Vincent 1959,O 1,40:1
 On the High Road 1961,Ap 21,26:2
 Wedding, The 1961,Ap 21,26:2
 Anniversary, The 1961,Ap 21,26:2
 Poppa Is Home 1961,D 20,37:1
 Chiaroscuro; Judges, The 1963,Je 6,40:8
 Chiaroscuro; Maggie French Understands
  1963,Je 6,40:8
 Chiaroscuro; Kitty, I Hardly Knew You
  1963,Je 6,40:8
 Love Your Crooked Neighbor 1969,D 30,40:1
Sammy
 If a Body 1935,My 1,25:3
Samnis, Edward R (Playwright)
 Day in the Sun 1937,Jl 27,24:3
Samodur, Semyon
 Obratsov Russian Pupper Theater in an Unusual
  Concert 1963,O 3,28:1
 Aladdin and His Wonderful Lamp 1963,O 21,39:1
Samodur, Semyon (Choreographer)
 Obratsov Russian Pupper Theater in an Unusual
  Concert 1963,O 3,28:1
Samoos, William
 Nautical but Nice 1931,Ap 19,31:6
Sampaio, Silveira (Playwright)
 On the Necessity of Being Polygamous
  1964,D 9,61:1
Samples, Howard
 Blossom Time 1931,Mr 5,32:1

Samples, M David
 Forever This Land 1951,Jl 29,II,1:1
 Wedding in Japan 1957,Mr 12,37:7
 Richard III 1957,N 26,41:1
 Cock-A-Doodle Dandy 1958,N 13,39:2
Samples, M David (Director)
 Kataki 1959,D 16,55:1
Samples, M David (Producer)
 Kataki 1959,D 16,55:1
Sampliner, David W (Miscellaneous)
 Education of H*Y*M*A*N K*A*P*L*A*N, The
  1968,Ap 5,57:1
Sampsel, Guy
 Tide Rising 1937,Ja 26,17:2
 Case of Youth, A 1940,Mr 25,10:3
 Cue for Passion 1940,D 20,33:4
 More the Merrier, The 1941,S 16,19:3
 Uncle Harry 1942,My 21,24:1
Sampson, Caroline (Miscellaneous)
 Anatomist, The 1957,F 27,21:5
Sampson, George
 Giants' Dance, The 1964,N 17,48:2
 Queen and the Rebels, The 1965,F 26,16:1
 Royal Hunt of the Sun, The 1965,O 27,36:2
Sampson, Hazel
 Jazz a La Carte 1922,Je 3,8:3
Sampson, Jean
 Susan and God 1943,D 14,30:2
Sampson, June
 Salad Days 1958,N 11,24:1
Sampson, William
 Hole in the Wall, The 1920,Mr 27,11:1
 First Year, The 1920,O 21,11:2
 First Year, The 1920,O 31,VI,1:1
Sampter, Martin (Miscellaneous)
 Noose, The 1926,O 21,23:3
Samrock, Victor (Miscellaneous)
 Inside U S A 1948,My 1,19:2
 Hilda Crane 1950,N 2,38:2
 First Love 1961,D 26,20:2
 Romulus 1962,Ja 11,27:1
 Tiger Tiger Burning Bright 1962,D 24,5:2
 Milk Train Doesn't Stop Here Anymore, The
  1963,Ja 18,7:1
 Children From Their Games 1963,Ap 12,33:1
 Public Eye, The 1963,O 10,51:1
 Private Ear, The 1963,O 10,51:1
 Chinese Prime Minister, The 1964,Ja 3,14:1
 Last Analysis, The 1964,O 2,30:1
 Beekman Place 1964,O 8,50:1
 Poor Richard 1964,D 3,59:1
Samrock, Victor (Producer)
 How I Wonder 1947,O 1,34:2
 Leading Lady 1948,O 19,33:1
Sams, William
 Manhattan 1922,Ag 16,7:5
 Immortal Thief, The 1926,O 4,21:1
 Enemy of the People, An 1927,O 4,32:5
 Hamlet 1928,Ja 5,33:2
 Caponsacchi 1928,Ja 25,20:3
 Henry V 1928,Mr 16,26:2
 Bellamy Trial, The 1928,Ag 20,21:1
 Becky Sharp 1929,Je 4,29:1
 Apple Cart, The 1930,F 25,30:1
 Milestones 1930,Je 3,27:1
 Troilus and Cressida 1932,Je 7,22:3
Samson, John T
 Trapped 1928,S 12,25:3
Samson, Philip
 Prince and the Pauper, The 1920,N 2,15:1
Samuel, Maurice (Original Author)
 World of Sholom Aleichem, The 1953,S 20,II,1:1
Samuels, Al
 Here Goes the Bride 1931,N 4,31:2
Samuels, Alex (Playwright)
 All Kinds of Men 1957,S 20,20:3
Samuels, Arthur (Composer)
 49ers, The 1922,N 7,14:1
 Poppy 1923,S 4,14:2
Samuels, Irene
 High Flyers 1927,Je 26,VIII,1:1
Samuels, Lesser (Playwright)
 Greenwillow 1960,Mr 9,38:1
 Greenwillow 1960,Mr 20,II,1:1
 Greenwillow 1970,D 8,60:1
Samuels, Lucielle (Costume Designer)
 Bright Rebel 1938,D 28,24:2
Samuels, Mark
 Terminal 1970,Ap 15,51:2
 Serpent, The 1970,Je 2,35:1
Samuels, Maurice V (Playwright)
 Flame of Love 1924,Ap 22,19:2
 Drift 1925,N 25,15:3
 Tales of Rigo 1927,My 31,25:3
Samuels, Rae
 Vaudeville (Palace) 1927,D 13,33:5
 Vaudeville (Palace) 1930,O 20,29:1
 Here Goes the Bride 1931,N 4,31:2
Samuels, Walter G (Composer)
 Ned Wayburn's Gambols 1929,Ja 16,22:3
Samuels, Walter G (Miscellaneous)
 Buds of 1927 1927,F 22,22:5

Samuels, Yetta
 Yellow Jacket, The 1923,Ap 20,20:3
Samuelson, Jerome
 Challenge of Youth 1930,Ja 21,28:5
Samuelson, Raphael (Playwright)
 Accent on Youth 1935,Jl 2,24:3
Samuylow, Morris
 Othello 1929,F 4,21:2
 Major Noah 1929,F 23,17:2
 It Can't Happen Here 1936,O 28,30:1
 Flag Is Born, A 1946,S 7,10:6
San Juan, Olga
 Paint Your Wagon 1951,N 13,32:2
 Paint Your Wagon 1951,N 18,II,1:1
San Marco, Rosana
 Rose Tattoo, The 1951,F 5,19:2
 In Any Language 1952,O 9,40:2
 Time of Your Life, The 1955,Ja 20,34:1
San Marzano, Robert de
 Coquette 1935,Jl 10,24:1
 Beaux' Stratagem, The 1935,Jl 17,22:5
 Hay Fever 1935,Jl 24,20:4
 Camille 1935,Jl 31,21:1
 Mr Pim Passes By 1935,Ag 7,22:2
 Vinegar Tree, The 1935,Ag 14,16:1
 Double Door 1935,Ag 21,22:2
 Late Christopher Bean, The 1935,Ag 28,13:1
San Miguel, Nito
 In the Summer House 1964,Mr 26,43:1
San Miguel, Nito (Composer)
 In the Summer House 1964,Mr 26,43:1
San Secondo, Rosso di (Original Author)
 Sirena 1931,S 22,33:4
San Secondo, Rosso di (Playwright)
 Puppets of Passion 1927,F 25,24:4
 Puppets of Passion 1927,Mr 6,VIII,1:1
 Passions de Fantoches 1927,Ap 3,VIII,4:7
Sanasardo, Paul
 Red Roses for Me 1955,D 29,15:2
Sanborn, Fred
 Folies Bergere 1939,D 25,28:2
 Keep 'Em Laughing 1942,Ap 25,9:2
Sanchez, Connie
 Something More! 1964,N 11,36:1
Sanchez, Eduardo
 Beyond Evil 1926,Je 8,23:2
 Spread Eagle 1927,Ap 5,30:2
Sanchez, Florencio (Playwright)
 Barranca Abajo 1963,Je 1,16:2
Sanchez, Jaime
 West Side Story 1957,S 27,14:4
 Song for a Certain Midnight 1959,S 17,49:1
 Othello 1964,Jl 15,29:1
 Toilet, The 1964,D 17,51:1
 Conerico Was Here to Stay 1965,Mr 4,37:1
 Conerico Was Here to Stay 1965,My 9,II,1:2
Sanchez, Lillian
 Does a Tiger Wear a Necktie? 1967,F 4,17:1
Sanchez, Marie
 Emerald Slippers, The 1970,S 2,31:2
Sanchez, Paul
 Marcel Marceau 1956,F 2,18:1
Sanchos, Francisco S (Playwright)
 New Man, The 1932,Ap 22,23:2
Sand, George (Original Author)
 Indiana 1935,D 29,IX,2:1
Sand, George (Playwright)
 Mariage of Victorine, Le 1926,D 19,VII,3:3
Sand, John (Playwright)
 Come Out to Play 1937,F 10,18:5
Sand, L (Playwright)
 Phantoms 1930,Ja 14,24:3
Sand, Paul
 From the Second City 1961,S 27,32:1
 Journey to the Day 1963,N 12,49:1
 Wet Paint 1965,Ap 13,33:1
 Hotel Passionato 1965,O 23,16:1
 Mad Show, The 1966,Ja 10,16:1
 Story Theater 1970,O 27,54:1
 Story Theater 1970,N 8,II,1:1
Sand, Philip
 War President 1944,Ap 25,17:3
Sand, Tom Hughes
 Harlequinade 1949,O 13,32:2
 Royal Family, The 1951,Ja 11,28:2
Sandberg, D F (Composer)
 Don Carlos 1962,F 28,27:5
 Storm, The 1962,Mr 31,17:2
Sandberg, Sara (Playwright)
 In Gold We Trust 1936,S 1,24:1
 Be So Kindly 1937,F 9,19:4
Sandberg, Trish
 Tarot 1970,D 12,19:1
Sandborg, Olof
 His Excellency's Last Will and Testament
  1931,O 11,VIII,4:5
Sandburg, Carl (Miscellaneous)
 World of Carl Sandburg, The 1959,O 13,44:6
 World of Carl Sandburg, The 1959,O 26,53:3
Sandburg, Carl (Original Author)
 World of Carl Sandburg, The 1960,S 25,II,1:1

ndburg, Carl (Playwright)
World of Carl Sandburg, The 1960,S 15,44:1
nde, Margaret
Stop Press 1935,Mr 17,VIII,1:4
nde, Margaret (Choreographer)
Catherine Was Great 1944,Ag 3,16:1
ndeen, Darrell
Young Abe Lincoln 1961,Ap 26,36:1
My Fair Lady 1968,Je 14,42:1
Fig Leaves Are Falling, The 1969,Ja 3,19:1
nder, Alfred
Montserrat 1954,My 26,34:2
In Splendid Error 1954,O 27,33:6
Time Limit! 1956,Ja 25,27:2
nder, Peter
Bacchae, The 1963,Ap 25,39:5
nder, Peter (Director)
Schweik in the Second World War
1967,N 12,II,17:1
nder, Peter (Translator)
Schweik in the Second World War
1967,N 12,II,17:1
anders, A H
If Booth Had Missed 1931,My 14,27:1
anders, Alma (Composer)
Louisiana Lady 1947,Je 3,35:2
anders, Alma (Lyricist)
Louisiana Lady 1947,Je 3,35:2
anders, Andy
Bernardine 1952,O 17,33:4
anders, Ann
York Nativity Play, The 1956,D 5,49:2
anders, Arthur
Scapegoat, The 1950,Ap 20,36:5
anders, Byron
Desk Set, The 1955,O 25,36:7
Friday Night; River, The 1965,F 9,42:5
anders, Donna
Saint of Bleecker Street, The 1954,D 28,21:1
Drunkard, The 1970,Ap 14,54:1
anders, George
Conversation Piece 1934,O 24,24:1
anders, Honey
She Shall Have Music 1959,Ja 23,18:4
Tobacco Road 1960,My 11,44:2
13 Daughters 1961,Mr 3,17:2
Paradise Island 1961,Je 24,11:1
Fortuna 1962,Ja 4,26:1
Paradise Island 1962,Je 28,22:1
South Pacific 1965,Je 3,25:1
Rose Tattoo, The 1966,O 21,36:2
Education of H*Y*M*A*N K*A*P*L*A*N, The
1968,Ap 5,57:1
Sanders, Howard
Black Nativity 1961,D 12,54:2
anders, Ira
Christopher's Wonders 1960,S 27,41:1
Sanders, Ivy
Iolanthe 1936,S 22,30:3
Pirates of Penzance, The 1939,Ja 6,25:1
Iolanthe 1939,Ja 13,16:3
Gondoliers, The 1939,Ja 20,14:2
Patience 1939,Ja 27,16:3
Sanders, Lee
From Morn Till Midnight 1948,D 7,41:6
Dr Cook's Garden 1967,S 26,52:1
Our Town 1969,N 28,50:1
Sanders, Lota
That Awful Mrs Eaton! 1924,S 30,27:1
Simon Called Peter 1924,N 11,20:2
Man From Toronto, The 1926,Je 18,27:2
Sanders, Pauli
Republic, The 1970,Ap 28,49:1
Sanders, Ray
Chameleon, The 1949,F 7,16:2
Sanders, Richard
Counterattack 1943,F 4,27:2
Story of Mary Surratt, The 1947,F 10,25:2
Night Thoreau Spent in Jail, The 1970,N 2,66:1
Sanders, Sandi
Sound of Music, The 1970,Jl 3,13:1
Sanders, Sarah
Andromaque 1964,F 29,13:2
Vie Parisienne, La 1964,Mr 11,34:2
Let Them Down, Gently; Our Man in Madras
1968,Ja 31,28:2
Let Them Down, Gently; On Vacation
1968,Ja 31,28:2
Sanders, Scott
Vaudeville (Palace) 1928,Ja 24,26:4
Vaudeville (Palace) 1928,Ja 31,29:2
Vaudeville (Palace) 1928,Je 26,29:4
Sanders, Steve
Yearling, The 1965,D 11,25:1
Sanders, Tom
Side-Show 1931,My 16,13:1
Sanders, William
Room in Red and White, A 1936,Ja 20,23:3
Madame Capet 1938,O 26,26:2
Tell My Story 1939,Mr 16,26:6
Democratic Body, A 1942,F 13,24:7
Jacobowsky and the Colonel 1944,Mr 15,17:2
Feast of Panthers 1961,Mr 21,32:1

Sanders (Composer)
Oh! Oh! Nurse 1925,D 8,28:4
Sanders (Lyricist)
Oh! Oh! Nurse 1925,D 8,28:4
Sandersen, Alexis
Du Barry 1932,N 23,15:2
Sanderson, Adele
Iolanthe 1926,Ap 20,24:2
Pirates of Penzance, The; Slave of Duty, The
1926,D 7,25:1
Venetian Glass Nephew, The 1931,F 24,26:3
Sanderson, Colfax
Path of Flowers, The 1936,S 18,19:3
Trojan Incident 1938,Ap 22,15:2
Sanderson, George A Jr
Orestes 1926,Je 20,II,3:6
Sanderson, Julia
Hitchy-Koo, 1920 1920,O 20,11:3
Tangerine 1921,Ag 10,8:2
Vaudeville (Palace) 1924,F 12,20:2
Sanderson, May
Ruddigore 1955,O 21,32:2
Sanderson, Oliver
Meek Mose 1928,F 7,30:1
Sanderson, R
Galloper, The 1924,D 19,26:2
Sandes, Stephen
Taming of the Shrew, The 1935,O 1,27:3
Idiot's Delight 1936,Mr 25,25:2
Wind in the Sails 1940,Ag 1,24:6
Sandford, Charles (Musical Director)
Make Mine Manhattan 1948,Ja 16,26:2
Sandford, Kenneth
Mikado, The 1962,N 14,43:1
Gondoliers, The 1962,N 16,25:2
Iolanthe 1962,N 28,42:1
Iolanthe 1964,N 18,52:1
Mikado, The 1964,N 27,43:1
Ruddigore 1964,D 4,44:1
Patience 1966,N 30,58:1
Patience 1968,N 1,34:1
Iolanthe 1968,N 9,37:3
Sandheim, Grete
Shadow, The 1923,D 15,16:2
Sandifur, Virginia
Papers 1968,D 3,54:1
Sandler, Jacob
Airways, Inc 1929,F 21,30:5
Paradise Lost 1935,D 10,31:5
Sandler, Jeanne
Merry Duchess, The 1943,Je 24,25:1
Sandler, Will B (Miscellaneous)
Trumpets of the Lord 1963,D 23,22:3
Sandlin, Dorothy
Desert Song, The 1946,Ja 9,20:2
Sandor, Alfred
Confederates, The 1959,S 29,45:1
Damask Drum, The 1961,F 4,15:1
Hans's Crime 1961,F 4,15:1
On an Open Roof 1963,Ja 30,7:3
Luther 1963,S 26,41:1
Zelda 1969,Mr 6,38:1
Sandor, Gluck
Fiddler on the Roof 1964,S 23,56:2
Fiddler on the Roof 1970,F 28,20:1
Sandor, Gluck (Choreographer)
Mexicana 1939,My 7,X,3:1
Sandor, Gluck (Producer)
Cabbages and Kings 1933,Je 28,24:5
Sandor, Ugo (Translator)
Gli Spettri 1930,D 22,16:4
Sandquist, Hans
Women Go on Forever 1927,S 8,25:1
Scarlet Fox, The 1928,Mr 28,31:1
World Waits, The 1933,O 26,22:5
Sandrich, Mark Jr (Composer)
Ben Franklin in Paris 1964,O 28,52:1
Sandridge, Maynard
Natural Man 1941,My 8,20:4
Sandrock, Adele
Liebestrank 1927,Ja 30,VII,4:3
Royal Family, The 1931,Ap 12,IX,1:3
Story of the Wolf 1932,N 6,IX,3:4
Sands, Ann
Little Jessie James 1923,Ag 16,10:4
Sands, Billy
Press Time 1938,N 28,10:4
I'll Take the High Road 1943,N 10,28:3
Fun With Music 1946,N 25,38:5
Sands, Bob
Hear! Hear! 1955,S 28,38:1
Sands, David
Let Freedom Ring 1935,N 7,26:2
Bury the Dead 1936,Ap 20,17:4
Prelude 1936,Ap 20,17:4
Sands, Diana
Major Barbara 1954,Je 30,23:2
Fortunato 1956,Mr 24,15:2
Mary and the Fairy 1956,Mr 24,15:2
Land Beyond the River, A 1957,Mr 29,15:7
Egg and I, The 1958,S 11,43:4
Raisin in the Sun, A 1959,Mr 12,27:1
Raisin in the Sun, A 1959,Mr 29,II,1:1

Sands, Diana—Cont
Another Evening With Harry Stoones
1961,O 23,22:2
Black Monday 1962,Mr 7,29:1
Tiger Tiger Burning Bright 1962,D 24,5:2
Living Premise, The 1963,Je 14,34:1
Blues for Mister Charlie 1964,Ap 24,24:1
Blues for Mister Charlie 1964,My 3,II,1:1
Owl and the Pussycat, The 1964,N 19,48:1
Owl and the Pussycat, The 1966,Mr 4,25:5
Phaedra 1967,My 22,50:2
Phaedra 1967,Je 11,II,1:1
Saint Joan 1968,Ja 5,42:1
Saint Joan 1968,Ja 14,II,1:1
Tiger at the Gates 1968,Mr 1,30:1
We Bombed in New Haven 1968,O 17,51:1
We Bombed in New Haven 1968,O 27,II,1:1
Gingham Dog, The 1969,Ap 24,41:1
Gingham Dog, The 1969,My 4,II,1:5
Gingham Dog, The 1969,Jl 13,II,1:1
Sands, Dorothy
Catskill Dutch 1924,My 7,18:1
Little Clay Cart, The 1924,D 6,13:3
Exiles 1925,F 20,20:2
Critic, The 1925,My 9,12:4
Grand Street Follies, The 1925,Je 19,24:1
Dybbuk, The 1925,D 16,22:2
Apothecary, The 1926,Mr 17,28:1
Romantic Young Lady, The 1926,My 5,24:3
Grand Street Follies, The 1926,Je 16,23:2
Lion Tamer, The 1926,O 8,26:1
Dybbuk, The 1926,D 17,27:2
Pinwheel 1927,F 4,16:4
Commedia Dell' Arte 1927,Ap 6,24:3
Grand Street Follies, The 1927,My 20,22:3
Grand Street Follies, The 1927,Je 1,24:2
Grand Street Follies, The 1927,Jl 3,VII,1:1
Stairs, The 1927,N 8,32:7
Grand Street Follies, The 1928,My 29,16:2
Grand Street Follies, The 1928,Je 3,VIII,1:1
Sea Gull, The 1929,Ap 10,32:2
Grand Street Follies, The 1929,My 2,20:4
Grand Street Follies, The 1929,My 12,IX,1:2
Grand Street Follies, The 1929,Je 19,34:3
Half Gods 1929,D 23,18:5
Many a Slip 1930,F 4,29:2
Rock Me, Julie 1931,Ja 4,VIII,2:3
Rock Me, Julie 1931,F 4,21:1
Styles in Acting 1932,Ap 3,VIII,13:3
Our Stage and Stars 1933,N 13,20:6
Inconstant Moon, The 1937,Ag 18,15:2
Jeannie 1940,N 13,29:2
Papa Is All 1942,Ja 7,22:2
Papa Is All 1942,Ja 18,IX,1:1
All the Comforts of Home 1942,My 26,24:5
Tomorrow the World 1943,Ap 15,22:2
Joy Forever, A 1946,Ja 8,20:2
American Theatre Highlights 1949,My 11,34:5
Cellar and the Well, The 1950,D 11,30:2
Misalliance 1953,F 19,20:1
Misalliance 1953,Mr 22,II,1:1
Qudrille 1954,N 4,39:2
Quadrille 1954,N 14,II,1:1
Firstborn, The 1957,Ja 7,29:2
First Gentleman, The 1957,Ap 26,22:2
Mary Stuart 1957,O 9,39:1
Mary Stuart 1957,O 20,II,1:1
Family Reunion, The 1958,O 21,39:1
Moonbirds 1959,O 10,13:1
Whisper to Me 1960,N 22,38:6
Once for the Asking 1963,N 21,42:2
My Fair Lady 1964,My 21,43:2
Club Bedroom, The 1967,D 6,41:1
Come Summer 1969,Mr 19,43:1
Paris Is Out! 1970,F 3,35:1
Sands, George
Battling Buttler 1923,O 9,17:2
Sands, Georgia
Vaudeville (Palace) 1928,F 21,19:2
Sands, Hal
Red Pepper 1922,My 30,8:3
Sands, Hal (Director)
Aquacircus 1958,Je 30,24:6
Hell'z-A-Splashin' 1959,Je 25,22:2
Sands, Hal (Lighting Director)
Hell'z-A-Splashin' 1959,Je 25,22:2
Sands, Patricia
Song for a Certain Midnight 1959,S 17,49:1
Sands, Paula
You Said It 1931,Ja 20,21:3
Sands, Peter
Put It in Writing 1963,My 14,31:1
Sands, Regina
When Differences Disappear 1941,Je 3,17:4
Winners and Losers 1947,F 27,27:2
Sands, Walter
From Morn Till Midnight 1948,D 7,41:6
Butter and Egg Man, The 1949,Ap 29,27:1
Sands, William
Heavenly Express 1940,Ap 19,24:2
Rugged Path, The 1945,N 12,17:2
Sandy
Vaudeville (Palace) 1923,Ja 30,12:2
Hummin' Sam 1933,Ap 10,8:8

Sandy, Gary
Pequod 1969,Je 30,33:1
Sandy, William
Othello 1945,My 23,25:4
Sanford, Agnes
Tangletoes 1925,F 18,17:1
Pinocchio 1939,Ja 3,19:2
Sanford, Beth
Effect of Gamma Rays on Man-in-the-Moon Marigolds, The 1965,Je 7,48:1
Sanford, Beth (Miscellaneous)
Galileo 1968,D 1,88:4
Sanford, Bobby (Miscellaneous)
Minskey the Magnificent 1936,D 26,14:3
Sanford, Bobby (Producer)
Showboat Revue 1934,Je 6,24:2
Showboat Revue 1935,Ag 18,13:2
Sanford, Charles (Musical Director)
Duchess Misbehaves, The 1946,F 14,32:2
Park Avenue 1946,N 5,31:2
Little Me 1962,N 19,41:3
Sanford, Charles G (Miscellaneous)
Sadie Thompson 1944,N 17,25:2
Sanford, Erskine
Power of Darkness, The 1920,Ja 22,22:1
Jane Clegg 1920,F 25,14:1
Treasure, The 1920,O 5,13:1
Heartbreak House 1920,N 11,11:1
Mr Pim Passes By 1921,Mr 1,18:1
Liliom 1921,Ap 21,18:1
Cloister, The 1921,Je 6,16:3
Johannes Kreisler 1922,D 25,20:3
Sandro Botticelli 1923,Mr 27,24:2
Failures, The 1923,N 23,20:1
Man and the Masses 1924,Ap 15,25:1
Glass Slipper, The 1925,O 20,29:1
Goat Song 1926,Ja 26,18:1
What's the Big Idea? 1926,Mr 24,20:3
Juarez and Maximilian 1926,O 12,31:1
Witch, The 1926,N 19,22:5
Puppets of Passion 1927,F 25,24:4
Mr Pim Passes By 1927,Ap 19,24:1
Mr Pim Passes By 1927,My 22,VIII,1:1
Roar China! 1930,O 28,23:1
Mourning Becomes Electra; Haunted, The 1931,O 27,22:1
Mourning Becomes Electra; Hunted, The 1931,O 27,22:1
American Dream; 1933 1933,F 22,24:5
Peace Palace 1933,Je 6,30:2
Valley Forge 1934,D 11,28:3
Sweet Mystery of Life 1935,O 12,13:3
Heartbreak House 1938,Ap 30,18:2
Native Son 1941,Mr 25,26:5
Sanford, Gerald (Playwright)
Walk-Up 1961,F 24,24:1
Sanford, Herbert C (Composer)
Fortuno 1925,D 23,22:1
Samarkand 1926,D 22,24:4
Sanford, Herbert C (Lyricist)
Samarkand 1926,D 22,24:4
Sanford, Herbert C (Playwright)
Samarkand 1926,D 22,24:4
Sanford, Isabell
On Strivers' Row 1946,Mr 1,17:2
Egg and I, The 1958,S 11,43:4
Soul Gone Home 1959,O 28,40:7
Shakespeare in Harlem 1959,O 28,40:7
God's Trombones 1960,F 10,43:4
Shakespeare in Harlem 1960,F 10,43:4
Amen Corner, The 1965,Ap 16,35:1
Sanford, Jane
Caution: A Love Story 1969,Ap 4,45:1
Moondreamers, The 1969,D 9,68:1
Gloria and Esperanza 1970,F 5,32:1
Sanford, Judy
Innocents, The 1959,Ap 21,41:2
Fighting Cock, The 1959,D 9,57:3
Sanford, Kenneth
Yeomen of the Guard, The 1962,Jl 11,28:1
Mikado, The 1966,N 18,36:1
Ruddigore 1966,N 23,28:1
Sanford, Lee
Devil's Little Game, The 1932,Ag 2,20:4
Decision 1944,F 3,23:2
Sanford, Peggy
Rape of the Sabine Women, The 1949,F 5,10:5
Sanford, Ralph
Half a Widow 1927,S 13,37:3
Mendel, Inc 1929,N 26,28:5
Great Man, The 1931,Ap 8,20:6
Constant Sinner, The 1931,S 15,30:1
Child of Manhattan 1932,Mr 2,15:1
Hey, Nonny, Nonny! 1932,Je 7,22:3
$25 an Hour 1933,My 11,14:4
They Shall Not Die 1934,F 22,24:4
Saluta 1934,Ag 29,13:4
Between Two Worlds 1934,O 26,24:2
Sanford, Randee
Good Night Ladies 1945,Ja 18,16:2
Mr Peebles and Mr Hooker 1946,O 11,29:2
Sanford, Richard
Million Dollar Baby 1945,D 22,17:2

Sanford, Robert (Choreographer)
Orchids Preferred 1937,My 12,26:5
Sanford, Sallie
In His Arms 1924,O 14,23:1
Right to Kill, The 1926,F 16,22:2
Sanger, Doris
Boundry Line, The 1930,F 6,21:1
Sanger, Malcolm H (Playwright)
You'll Never Know 1921,Ap 21,9:2
Sanger, R H
1776 1926,Ap 24,11:2
Sangiolo, Anita
Live Like Pigs 1965,Je 8,48:2
Sangster, Alfred
Brontes, The 1933,Ap 21,24:8
Brontes, The 1933,My 7,IX,1:4
Sangster, Alfred (Playwright)
Brontes, The 1933,Ap 21,24:8
Brontes, The 1933,My 7,IX,1:4
Napoleon 1934,S 4,23:2
Sangster, Frank
Little Theatre Tournament; Severed Cord, The 1929,My 9,34:3
Sangster, Robert
Little Theatre Tournament; Severed Cord, The 1929,My 9,34:3
Sanguineti, Eduardo (Playwright)
Orlando Furioso 1970,N 5,59:1
Sani, Amru
New Faces of 1956 1956,Je 15,32:1
Sanina, Mlle
Revue Russe, The 1922,O 6,28:1
Sanina, Tanya
Jubilee 1935,O,14,20:1
Sanjuan, Pedro (Musical Director)
Leyenda del Beso, La 1942,N 20,26:4
Sankey, Rosemary
By Jupiter 1942,Je 4,22:1
Sankey, Tom
Golden Screw, The 1967,Ja 31,52:1
Golden Screw, The 1967,Mr 26,II,1:2
Sankey, Tom (Composer)
Golden Screw, The 1967,Ja 31,52:1
Picnic on the Battlefield 1967,S 9,25:2
People vs Ranchman, The 1968,O 28,56:1
Sankey, Tom (Lyricist)
Golden Screw, The 1967,Ja 31,52:1
Sankey, Tom (Playwright)
Golden Screw, The 1967,Ja 31,52:1
Golden Screw, The 1967,Mr 26,II,1:2
Sann, Phillip
Rosmersholm 1946,N 23,11:5
E-MC2 1948,Je 16,36:2
Sanossian, Leon (Miscellaneous)
Charles Aznavour 1970,F 5,32:4
Sansegundo, Carlos (Scenic Designer)
Line of Least Existence, The 1968,Mr 25,53:1
Sansegundo, Ruth (Costume Designer)
Line of Least Existence, The 1968,Mr 25,53:1
Sansho, Shinsui
Golden Bat 1970,Je 27,18:2
Sansom, Mary
Gondoliers, The 1962,N 16,25:2
Pirates of Penzance, The 1962,N 21,28:1
Trial by Jury 1962,N 23,32:4
Iolanthe 1962,N 28,42:1
Sansone, Anthony J
Mima 1928,D 13,24:2
Sansone, Tony (Composer)
Nighthawks 1967,D 30,14:2
Santa Ana, Walter
Projimos, Los 1966,Je 29,38:5
Santa Clara, Abraham A (Original Author)
Beloved Augustine, The 1931,Ap 26,VIII,2:6
Santaliz, Pedro
All's Well That Ends Well 1966,Je 17,39:1
Santamaria, Mario
Let's Make an Opera 1950,D 14,50:2
Santangelo, Michael R (Producer)
Black Nativity 1961,D 12,54:2
Santarelli, Dominique
Salut a Moliere 1964,Mr 4,33:2
Pieton de L'Air, Le 1964,Mr 4,33:2
Vie Parisienne, La 1964,Mr 11,34:2
Santell, Marie
Hi, Paisano 1961,O 2,36:2
Flora, the Red Menace 1965,My 12,41:2
Drunkard, The 1970,Ap 14,54:1
Sensations 1970,O 26,48:2
Santiago, Anthony
Kiss Me, Kate 1965,My 13,31:1
Santiago, Rodrigo
Arena Conta Zumbi 1969,Ag 19,31:1
Santina, Bruno della
Due Orfanelle, Le; Two Orphans, The 1936,O 5,24:4
Morte Civile, La; Civic Death 1936,N 9,23:4
Sansone; Samson 1936,N 30,25:2
Medico Delle Pazze, Il; Physician of Mad Woman, The 1937,S 27,24:2

Santina, Pierina della
Due Orfanelle, Le; Two Orphans, The 1936,O 5,24:4
Santinelli, Ralph
Moon Walk 1970,N 27,52:1
Santini, Ottavia
Canto Della Vita, Il; Song of Life, The 1932,Ap 4,13:3
Santley, Fred
Two Little Girls in Blue 1921,My 4,10:3
Kosher Kitty Kelly 1925,Je 16,24:2
Nic-Nax of 1926 1926,Ag 5,19:1
Kiss Me! 1927,Jl 22,17:1
Happy 1927,D 6,26:3
Vaudeville (Palace) 1928,Mr 6,20:5
Santley, Joseph
Half-Moon, The 1920,N 2,15:2
Irving Berlin's Music Box Revue 1921,S 23,18:2
Music Box Revue 1923,S 24,5:3
Lambs Gambol 1925,Ap 27,15:1
Mayflowers 1925,N 25,14:2
Vaudeville (Palace) 1926,Ap 13,28:3
Wild Rose, The 1926,O 21,23:1
Lucky 1927,Mr 23,28:3
Just Fancy! 1927,O 12,30:2
Vaudeville (Palace) 1927,O 18,32:4
Heigh-Ho, Everybody 1932,My 26,31:2
Santley, Joseph (Director)
Mayflowers 1925,N 25,14:2
Just Fancy! 1927,O 12,30:2
Life Begins 1932,Mr 29,23:2
Lambs Gambol 1933,Ap 24,10:1
Santley, Joseph (Playwright)
Just Fancy! 1927,O 12,30:2
Santley, Joseph (Producer)
London, Paris and New York 1926,Je 8,23:1
Just Fancy! 1927,O 12,30:2
Lady Lies, The 1928,N 27,36:2
Life Begins; Birth 1932,Mr 20,VIII,2:4
Life Begins 1932,Mr 29,23:2
Santley, Zelda
Frivolities of 1920 1920,Ja 9,22:2
Santo, Gaspar
Bruder Straubinger 1921,N 16,22:3
Santon, Charles
Possession 1928,O 3,35:1
Santon, Penny
Rose Tattoo, The 1951,F 5,19:2
Dark Legend 1952,Mr 25,24:2
Santoni, Reni
Witches' Sabbath 1962,Ap 20,22:2
Third Ear, The 1964,My 29,16:1
Umbrella, The 1965,My 27,31:1
Santoni, Reni (Playwright)
Raisin' Hell in the Son 1962,Jl 3,13:2
Santoro, Charles
Don Juan in the Russian Manner 1954,Ap 23,23:2
Santoro, Dean
Play of Herod, The 1968,D 27,40:1
Philosophy in the Boudoir 1969,My 22,55:2
Borstal Boy 1970,Ap 1,38:1
Trelawny of the 'Wells' 1970,O 12,48:1
Trelawney of the 'Wells' 1970,O 25,II,16:1
Santoro, Mr (Playwright)
Princess Liana 1929,Jl 14,IX,6:8
Santrey, Henry
Vaudeville (Palace) 1928,My 1,33:2
Vaudeville (Palace) 1930,Mr 3,18:5
Vaudeville (Palace) 1932,My 9,19:3
Santry, Marion
Du Barry 1932,N 23,15:2
Santvoord, Peg
Marching Song 1959,D 29,20:1
Saparilas, Christopher
Abortion 1959,O 28,40:4
Sapik, Alois
How to Make a Man 1961,F 3,16:1
Sapin, Louis (Playwright)
Daddy Goodness 1968,Je 5,37:1
Sapinsley, Alvin (Playwright)
Clerambard 1957,N 8,22:3
Saposnick, Michael
Grab Bag, The 1968,N 5,53:2
Subscriber, The 1968,N 5,53:2
Susie Is a Good Girl 1968,N 5,53:2
Sapper (Original Author)
Bulldog Drummond 1921,D 27,10:2
Sappington, Fay
Cellar and the Well, The 1950,D 11,30:2
Glad Tidings 1951,O 12,33:2
J B 1958,D 12,2:7
Sudden End of Anne Cinquefoil, The 1961,Ja 11,25:2
Yearling, The 1965,D 11,25:1
Sappington, Margo
Oh! Calcutta! 1969,Je 18,33:1
Oh! Calcutta! 1969,Je 29,II,1:7
Sappington, Margo (Choreographer)
Oh! Calcutta! 1969,Je 18,33:1
Sappir, Jerry
Zorba 1968,N 18,58:1

Sapuppo, Pietro
'Il Tesoro D'Isacco; Treasure of Isaac, The 1928,Ja 26,17:1
Sarah
Vaudeville (Palace) 1924,Ja 22,15:6
Sarandon, Chris
Stephen D 1966,Ag 5,17:1
Rothschilds, The 1970,O 20,40:1
Saranoff, Jules
All-Star Jamboree 1921,Jl 14,18:1
Play, Genius, Play! 1935,O 31,17:2
Sarasohn, Lane (Playwright)
Groove Tube 1969,O 12,88:3
Saratovsky, Pyotr
Lysistrata 1925,D 15,28:2
Sarattos, The
Vaudeville (Palace) 1927,Ja 25,18:3
Sarazen, Gene
Vaudeville (Palace) 1931,Ap 20,16:2
Sarcey, Martine
Britannicus 1958,N 29,17:2
Sardi, Vincent Jr
Master of the Inn, The 1925,D 23,22:2
Sardinas, Donald
Merry Duchess, The 1943,Je 24,25:1
Sardo, Frank
Page Miss Glory 1934,N 28,24:2
Sardou, Victorien (Playwright)
Fedora 1922,F 11,18:1
Fedora 1924,Ja 24,14:2
Diplomacy 1924,Mr 16,VIII,1:7
Madame Sans-Gene 1924,N 4,30:1
Diplomacy 1928,My 29,16:3
Diplomacy 1928,Je 3,VIII,1:1
Processo dei Veleni, Il; Case of Poisons, The 1935,Ja 21,18:2
Sarg, Tony
Don Quixote 1922,D 12,22:2
Nantucket Follies 1927,Jl 30,13:2
Sarg, Tony (Director)
Rip Van Winkle 1920,D 14,22:3
Sarg, Tony (Producer)
Hairy Ape The 1931,Ap 15,24:4
Rose and the Ring, The 1931,D 24,20:7
Sarg, Tony Marionettes
Treasure Island 1925,D 23,22:5
Ali Baba and the Forty Thieves 1926,D 23,23:2
Ali Baba and the Forty Thieves 1927,D 23,16:7
Untitled-Marionettes 1928,D 21,30:3
Rip Van Winkle 1929,D 21,22:7
Alice in Wonderland 1930,D 25,31:3
Sargent, Julie
Henry, Sweet Henry 1967,O 24,51:2
Sargent
Harry Delmar's Revels 1927,N 29,30:2
Sargent, Anne
Boy Who Lived Twice, A 1945,S 12,31:2
Men We Marry, The 1948,Ja 17,11:2
I Know My Love 1949,F 24,29:2
I Know My Love 1949,N 3,36:1
Sargent, Betty
Beyond Evil 1926,Je 8,23:2
Sargent, Brent
Outrageous Fortune 1943,N 4,28:5
Biggest Thief in Town 1949,Mr 31,31:2
Sargent, Dorothy
Night of Love 1941,Ja 8,14:2
Sargent, Jean
Face the Music 1932,F 18,24:5
Flying Colors 1932,S 16,24:2
Sargent, Joe
Nights of Wrath; Nuits de la Colere, Les 1947,D 1,26:4
Chameleon, The 1949,F 7,16:2
Night Music 1951,Ap 9,29:6
Kiss Me, Kate 1954,Mr 27,13:2
Talent '54 1954,Ap 13,40:1
Stone for Danny Fisher, A 1954,O 22,24:2
Once Over Lightly 1955,Mr 16,39:1
Sargent, Joe (Director)
Talent '54 1954,Ap 13,40:1
Sargent, Judy
Show Boat 1957,Je 28,30:2
Sargent, Karen
Beg, Borrow or Steal 1960,F 11,39:4
Sargent, Malcolm (Sir) (Musical Director)
Pilgrim's Progress 1948,Jl 20,27:5
Sargent, Margherita
Macbeth 1921,F 18,16:1
Macbeth 1921,F 27,VI,1:1
Great Gatsby, The 1926,F 3,22:1
Little Father of the Wilderness, The 1930,Je 3,27:1
Distant Drums 1932,Ja 19,24:3
Troilus and Cressida 1932,Je 7,22:3
First Lady 1935,N 27,17:4
Homecoming 1942,N 17,28:5
Inherit the Wind 1955,Ap 22,20:2
Sargent, Mary
No More Ladies 1934,Ja 24,20:3
No More Ladies 1934,S 4,23:2
Post Road 1934,D 5,28:3
Times Have Changed 1935,F 19,28:2
Times Have Changed 1935,F 26,16:1
Fresh Fields 1935,Jl 24,20:4

One Good Year 1935,N 28,38:3
Fresh Fields 1936,F 11,19:2
Fresh Fields 1936,Je 23,27:3
And Stars Remain 1936,O 13,32:2
Sea Legs 1937,My 19,26:5
Case of Youth, A 1940,Mr 25,10:3
My Fair Ladies 1941,Mr 24,12:7
Sweet Charity 1942,D 29,26:4
Ask My Friend Sandy 1943,F 5,16:2
Love on Leave 1944,Je 21,23:4
Calico Wedding 1945,Mr 8,18:6
Sargent, Peter
Face the Music 1932,F 18,24:5
Sargent, William
Golem, The 1959,F 26,38:2
Sargent and Marvin
Vaudeville (Hippodrome) 1924,Ap 1,18:1
Sargia, Jane Ann
Me and Juliet 1970,My 15,42:1
Sargine, Vera
Margrave, La 1932,D 18,X,3:6
Sargon, Simon (Musical Director)
Iolanthe 1965,My 19,42:1
Yeomen of the Guard, The 1965,Jl 8,34:1
Saridis, Angelo
Zorba 1968,N 18,58:1
Sarles, Everett
Patience 1935,S 3,24:4
Sarmatoff, Stanislaw
See Naples and Die 1929,S 27,30:4
Roberta 1933,N 20,18:4
Sarment, Jean
Plus Beaux Yeux du Monde, Les 1925,D 27,VII,2:1
As-tu du Coeur? 1926,O 31,VIII,2:4
Peau d'Espagne 1933,Ap 30,IX,2:3
Sarment, Jean (Original Author)
Peau d'Espagne 1933,Ap 30,IX,2:3
Sarment, Jean (Playwright)
Fisher of Shadows, The 1921,My 1,VII,1:7
Plus Beaux Yeux du Monde, Les 1925,D 27,VII,2:1
As-tu du Coeur? 1926,O 31,VIII,2:4
Leopold le Bien-Aime 1927,O 30,IX,4:7
Bobard 1930,My 4,XI,2:6
Plancher des Vaches, Le 1932,Mr 20,VIII,2:2
Peau d'Espagne 1933,Ap 30,IX,2:3
Madame Quinze 1935,Ap 21,IX,2:1
Untitled-Play 1936,Je 7,IX,1:1
Sarner, Alexander
Josef Suss 1930,Ja 21,28:5
Sarno, Herman B (Miscellaneous)
Bring Me a Warm Body 1962,Ap 17,29:3
Sarno, Janet
Here Comes Santa Claus 1962,My 18,34:1
Dylan 1964,Ja 20,18:1
Sarnoff, Dorothy
Rosalinda; Fledermaus, Die 1942,O 29,26:5
Magdalena 1948,Jl 28,27:2
Magdalena 1948,S 21,31:2
King and I, The 1951,Mr 30,26:2
King and I, The 1951,Ap 8,II,1:1
My Darlin' Aida 1952,O 28,36:4
Saroyan, Lucy
Ah, Wilderness! 1969,N 9,86:1
I Dreamt I Dwelt in Bloomingdale's 1970,F 13,26:1
Room Service 1970,My 13,49:1
Saroyan, William (Director)
Time of Your Life, The 1939,O 26,26:2
Love's Old Sweet Song 1940,My 3,16:3
Time of Your Life, The 1940,S 24,27:2
Beautiful People, The 1941,Ap 22,27:2
Talking to You 1942,Ag 18,17:1
Across the Board on Tomorrow Morning 1942,Ag 18,17:1
Across the Board on Tomorrow Morning 1942,Ag 23,VIII,1:1
Saroyan, William (Lyricist)
Love's Old Sweet Song 1940,My 3,16:3
Saroyan, William (Playwright)
My Heart's in the Highlands 1939,Ap 14,29:2
My Heart's in the Highlands 1939,My 7,X,1:1
Time of Your Life, The 1939,O 26,26:2
Time of Your Life, The 1939,N 5,IX,1:1
Time of Your Life, The 1939,N 26,IX,1:1
Love's Old Sweet Song 1940,Ap 7,I,44:6
Love's Old Sweet Song 1940,Ap 14,IX,3:3
Love's Old Sweet Song 1940,My 3,16:3
Time of Your Life, The 1940,S 24,27:2
Beautiful People, The 1941,Ap 22,27:2
Beautiful People, The 1941,My 4,IX,1:1
Hello Out There 1941,S 11,20:6
Jim Dandy 1941,N 8,10:5
Life, Laughter And Tears 1942,F 26,15:2
Across the Board on Tomorrow Morning 1942,Mr 21,13:5
Talking to You 1942,Ag 18,17:1
Across the Board on Tomorrow Morning 1942,Ag 18,17:1
Across the Board on Tomorrow Morning 1942,Ag 23,VIII,1:1

Saroyan, William (Playwright)—Cont
Hello Out There 1942,S 30,28:2
Get Away Old Man 1943,N 25,40:2
Sam Ego's House 1947,N 1,11:3
Don't Go Away Mad 1949,My 10,28:2
My Heart's in the Highlands 1949,N 22,36:7
My Heart's in the Highlands 1950,F 18,8:4
Son, The 1950,Ap 1,12:4
Once Around the Block 1950,My 25,36:2
Son, The 1950,Ag 16,24:6
Lost Child's Fireflies, A 1954,Jl 16,11:4
Sam Ego's House 1954,N 11,43:1
Time of Your Life, The 1955,Ja 20,34:1
Time of Your Life, The 1955,Ja 30,II,1:1
Floydada to Matador 1955,D 22,19:1
Hello Out There 1955,D 22,19:1
Opera Opera 1955,D 22,19:1
Hungerers, The 1955,D 22,19:1
Once Around the Block 1956,O 29,34:1
Cave Dwellers, The 1957,O 21,29:2
Cave Dwellers, The 1957,O 27,II,1:1
Sam, The Highest Jumper of Them All 1960,Ap 8,24:3
Settled Out of Court 1960,O 20,44:4
Cave Dwellers, The 1961,O 16,34:2
Across the Board on Tomorrow Morning 1961,O 23,22:5
Talking to You 1961,O 23,22:5
Time of Your Life, The 1969,N 7,37:1
Time of Your Life, The 1969,N 16,II,1:4
Saroyan, William (Producer)
Beautiful People, The 1941,Ap 22,27:2
Talking to You 1942,Ag 18,17:1
Across the Board on Tomorrow Morning 1942,Ag 18,17:1
Across the Board on Tomorrow Morning 1942,Ag 23,VIII,1:1
Sarr, Bill
Nowhere to Go But Up 1962,N 12,36:2
Sarracini, Gerald
Sin of Pat Muldoon, The 1957,Mr 14,35:1
Romanoff and Juliet 1957,O 11,24:1
Sarracino, Ernest
He Who Gets Slapped 1946,Mr 21,31:4
At War With the Army 1949,Mr 9,32:2
Buttrio Square 1952,O 15,40:2
Sarros, Dimitrios (Translator)
Medea 1964,S 1,31:1
Iphigenia in Aulis 1968,N 13,40:1
Hippolytus 1968,N 20,38:3
Sarton, May
Living Corpse, The 1929,D 7,19:1
Sartori, Amleto (Miscellaneous)
Servant of Two Masters, The 1960,F 24,42:2
Sartorres, R
Blind Heart, The 1927,My 8,30:2
Sartre, Jean-Paul (Playwright)
Griffe, La 1923,N 27,23:5
Claw, The 1927,Ja 13,28:4
No Exit 1946,N 27,21:1
Unburied Dead, The; Morts Sans Sepulture 1946,D 22,II,4:1
Deferential Prostitute, The; Putain Respectueuse, La 1946,D 22,II,4:2
Flies, The; Mouches, Les 1947,Ap 18,26:3
Respectful Prostitute, The 1948,F 15,II,1:1
Flies, The 1948,F 29,II,2:1
Respectful Prostitute, The 1948,Mr 21,II,1:1
Soiled Hands; Mains Sales, Les 1948,Ap 18,II,1:6
Crime Passionel 1948,Je 18,19:4
Red Gloves; Mains Sales, Les 1948,D 12,II,3:1
Victors, The 1948,D 27,17:2
Victors, The 1949,Ja 2,II,1:1
Diable et le Bon Dieu, Le 1951,Je 8,32:6
Diable et le Bon Dieu, Le 1951,Ag 19,II,1:6
Flies, The 1954,S 10,18:2
No Exit 1956,Ag 15,23:1
Nekrassou 1957,Ag 20,22:1
Altona; Sequestres d'Altona, Les 1961,Je 25,II,3:5
Kean 1961,N 3,28:2
Kean 1961,N 12,II,1:1
Huis Clos 1962,Ja 16,30:1
Trojan Women, The 1965,Mr 18,25:1
Condemned of Altona, The 1966,F 4,21:1
Condemned of Altona, The 1966,F 13,II,1:1
No Exit 1967,O 31,38:2
Sartre, Jean-Paul (Translator)
Red Gloves 1948,D 6,28:2
Sasha, G
Backlane Center 1961,N 23,51:1
Sashka
Squaring the Circle 1935,O 4,24:6
Sassafrass
Sketch Book 1935,Je 5,22:2
Sassano, Ralph
New Moon, The 1944,My 18,16:2
Bloomer Girl 1944,O 6,18:5
Sasse, Heribert
Change 1970,O 13,52:2
Sassmann, Hans (Playwright)
House of Rothschild 1931,Mr 8,VIII,2:7
Tales of Hoffmann 1932,Ja 10,VIII,1:6
Fair Helen 1932,Jl 17,IX,1:2
Sasso, John
As You Like It 1936,Ap 24,18:4

Sasso, Richard (Producer)
Chief Thing, The 1963,Ap 30,27:2
Sasson, Pierre (Playwright)
Light of the World, The 1920,Ja 7,17:1
Sasson, Sam
Love and Politics 1929,O 21,30:7
Sastre, Alfonso (Playwright)
Anna Kleiber 1965,Ja 20,33:1
Sater, Rex
Ah, Wilderness! 1953,F 7,10:6
Satie, Stephanie
Moon Walk 1970,N 27,52:1
Satin, Samuel
Waltz of the Dogs, The 1928,Ap 26,31:3
David Garrick 1929,Ag 2,17:5
Satio (Scenic Designer)
Give My Regards to Off Off Broadway
1966,D 9,57:1
Sato, K (Scenic Designer)
Coney Island Play 1970,O 31,34:2
Sato, Reiko
Kismet 1953,D 4,2:4
Kismet 1965,Je 23,45:1
Satorres, Rafaela
Road to Happiness, The 1927,My 3,24:1
Romantic Young Lady, The 1927,My 5,30:2
Girl and the Cat, The 1927,My 6,21:2
Cradle Song 1927,My 10,24:4
Fragila Rosina 1927,My 10,24:4
Pygmalion 1927,My 12,25:2
Satovsky, Youacca G (George, George S)
/**(Playwright)**
Clean Beds 1939,My 26,21:2
Satow, Mark
King and I, The 1960,My 12,40:1
Satterfield, Maude
Rose of Stamboul, The 1922,Mr 8,11:2
Satterthwait, Ann
J B 1958,Ap 24,37:1
Satterthwaite, T W
1776 1926,Ap 24,11:2
Satterwhite, Alberta
Conjur 1938,N 1,27:2
Sattin, Lonnie
Cotton Club Revue of 1957 1957,Jl 10,23:4
Body Beautiful, The 1958,Ja 24,15:2
Ballad of Jazz Street, The 1959,N 12,28:1
Sattin, Tina
Ballad of Jazz Street, The 1959,N 12,28:1
Skin of Our Teeth, The 1966,Je 2,51:1
Sattler, Dan
Look, Ma, I'm Dancin' 1948,Ja 30,20:2
Satur, Claudio Garcia
Romeo y Julieta 1965,Ag 28,13:3
Saturn, Simeon
Master Builder, The 1955,Mr 2,23:2
Saturnine, Barbara
Cage, The 1961,Mr 6,30:1
Satvro, Sidney
Noble Experiment, The 1930,O 28,21:4
Satz, Ludwig
Three Little Business Men, The 1923,S 4,12:1
Jolly Tailors, The 1923,N 3,13:3
Potash and Perlmutter, Detectives; Poisoned by
Pictures 1926,S 1,27:3
Potash and Perlmutter, Detectives 1926,S 5,VII,1:1
His Wife's Lover 1929,O 21,30:6
Berdichever Bridegroom, The 1930,S 24,26:2
Hello Grandpa! 1931,Ja 2,25:3
Jolly World, A 1931,Ja 24,15:3
Longing for Home 1933,S 22,15:1
Singing Thief, The 1933,D 4,22:4
Slaves of the Public 1934,Mr 10,18:6
Holiday in Town, A 1935,S 30,12:3
Money Mad 1937,My 25,32:5
Chaver, Nachman 1939,O 2,15:2
Life Marches On 1940,Ja 4,18:2
Satz, Ludwig (Director)
His Wife's Lover 1929,O 21,30:6
Jolly World, A 1931,Ja 24,15:3
Longing for Home 1933,S 22,15:1
Satz, Ludwig (Lyricist)
Singing Thief, The 1933,D 4,22:4
Satz, Ludwig (Producer)
His Wife's Lover 1929,O 21,30:6
If the Rabbi Wants 1929,D 23,18:5
Hello Grandpa! 1931,Ja 2,25:3
Jolly World, A 1931,Ja 24,15:3
Slaves of the Public 1934,Mr 10,18:6
Saudio, Carlo
Processo dei Veleni, Il; Case of Poisons, The
1935,Ja 21,18:2
Sauer, Bernard
Let's Sing Yiddish 1966,N 10,63:1
Sing Israel Sing 1967,My 12,50:1
Sauer, Bernard (Lighting Director)
Brothers Ashkenazi, The 1970,N 17,53:2
Sauer, Bernard (Miscellaneous)
Sage of Rottenburg, The 1963,N 20,48:1
Let's Sing Yiddish 1966,N 10,63:1
Sing Israel Sing 1967,My 12,50:1
Megilla of Itzik Manger, The 1968,O 10,60:1
Light, Lively and Yiddish 1970,O 28,58:1

Sauer, Joseph
Gods of the Lightning 1931,F 19,21:4
Sauerman, Carl
Beggar Student, The 1921,Ja 8,9:3
Sauers, Joseph
Inspector General, The 1930,D 24,19:2
Sauguet, Henri (Composer)
Fourberies de Scapin, Les 1952,N 21,21:2
School for Scandal, The 1962,My 18,34:2
Saul, Oscar (Playwright)
Revolt of the Beavers, The 1937,My 21,19:2
Medicine Show 1940,Ap 13,20:6
Saulpaugh, Edwin
Free for All 1931,S 9,25:1
Saulpaugh, Edwin (Director)
Saluta 1934,Ag 29,13:4
Saulter, William Noel (Scenic Designer)
Make Yourself at Home 1945,S 14,21:2
Haven, The 1946,N 14,39:4
Saunder, Herbert
Thank You 1921,O 4,10:2
Saunders, Allan (Lighting Director)
Eagle Has Two Heads, The 1956,D 14,37:2
Saunders, Allan (Miscellaneous)
Eagle Has Two Heads, The 1956,D 14,37:2
'Tis Pity She's a Whore 1958,D 6,21:1
Saunders, Alma
George White's Scandals 1935,D 26,20:2
Saunders, Andrea
Bill Noname 1970,Mr 3,37:1
Saunders, Bernice
Sound of Music, The 1967,Ap 27,52:1
Saunders, Clare
Cue for Passion 1940,D 20,33:4
Saunders, Diana
Golden Rainbow 1968,F 5,27:1
Saunders, Frank
Cherry Pie 1926,Ap 15,24:4
Saunders, Garrett
Nat Turner 1960,N 7,46:3
417 1961,Mr 6,30:1
Trial of Lee Harvey Oswald, The 1967,N 6,64:1
Rate of Exchange 1968,Ap 2,50:1
Take One Step 1968,Jl 5,17:1
Ododo 1970,N 25,26:1
Saunders, George
Edgar Allan Poe 1925,O 6,31:1
Killers 1928,Mr 14,28:3
Saunders, Gertrude
Liza 1922,N 28,24:1
Blackberries of 1932 1932,Ap 5,27:5
Run, Little Chillun 1943,Ag 14,6:1
Saunders, Henry
Antony and Cleopatra 1937,N 11,30:2
Saunders, Herbert
Wheel, The 1921,Ag 30,10:1
Paid 1925,N 26,32:1
2 Girls Wanted 1926,S 10,25:3
Waterloo Bridge 1930,Ja 7,29:2
Saunders, Jack
Desert Song, The 1946,Ja 9,20:2
Saunders, James (Playwright)
Next Time I'll Sing to You 1963,N 28,69:2
Italian Girl, The 1968,Jl 4,14:1
Neighbors 1969,Ja 15,38:2
Scent of Flowers, A 1969,O 21,42:1
Scent of Flowers, A 1969,N 2,II,3:1
Travails of Sancho Panza, The 1969,D 20,35:1
Saunders, John
Romance 1921,Mr 1,18:2
Swords 1921,S 2,9:3
Plot Thickens, The 1922,S 6,16:1
Six Characters in Search of an Author
1922,O 31,11:2
Schemers 1924,S 16,27:1
House of Ussher, The 1926,Ja 14,18:4
Say It With Flowers 1926,D 6,29:1
Lombardi, Ltd 1927,Je 7,27:3
Saunders, John Monk (Playwright)
Nikki 1931,S 30,23:4
Saunders, Joy
Pin to See the Peepshow, A 1953,S 18,17:2
Time of Storm 1954,F 26,14:2
Saunders, Lanna
Marcus in the High Grass 1960,N 22,38:6
Milk and Honey 1961,O 11,52:1
Never Live Over a Pretzel Factory 1964,Mr 30,37:1
Changeling, The 1964,O 30,32:2
Philadelphia, Here I Come! 1966,F 17,28:1
Saunders, Lilian (Translator)
Devil to Pay, The 1925,D 4,26:2
Good Hope, The 1927,O 19,24:2
Saunders, Lois Ann
Great Scot! 1965,N 12,56:3
Saunders, Marilyn
Company 1970,Ap 27,40:1
Saunders, Merl (Miscellaneous)
Buck White 1969,D 3,63:1
Saunders, Merl (Musical Director)
Buck White 1969,D 3,63:1
Saunders, Nellie Peck
George Washington 1920,Mr 2,9:1

Saunders, Nicholas
Lady in the Dark 1943,Mr 1,14:2
New Life, A 1943,S 16,26:6
Highland Fling, A 1944,Ap 29,13:2
Happily Ever After 1945,Mr 16,21:2
Marriage Is for Single People 1945,N 22,38:2
Magnificent Yankee, The 1946,Ja 23,21:2
Call on Kuprin, A 1961,My 26,29:3
Take Her, She's Mine 1961,D 22,19:1
Passion of Josef D, The 1964,F 12,29:1
End of All Things Natural, The 1969,S 12,38:1
Saunders, Pamela
Hamlet 1956,O 29,34:1
Measure for Measure 1957,Ja 23,24:1
Taming of the Shrew, The 1957,F 21,30:2
Born Yesterday 1958,Mr 22,12:6
Kitchen, The 1966,Je 14,50:1
Happy Birthday, Wanda June 1970,O 8,58:2
Happy Birthday, Wanda June 1970,O 18,II,1:1
Saunders, Peter (Miscellaneous)
Hostile Witness 1966,F 18,26:1
Saunders, Peter (Producer)
Witness for the Prosecution 1954,D 17,35:2
Saunders, Rai
Big Deal, The 1953,Mr 7,13:6
Foenix in Choir 1958,O 28,40:2
Hostage, The 1961,D 13,55:4
Saunders, Richard
When You Smile 1925,O 6,31:2
Saunders, Sue
Bye Bye Bonnie 1927,Ja 14,15:3
Saunders, Terry
Music in the Air 1951,O 9,32:2
Music in the Air 1951,O 21,II,1:1
King and I, The 1952,O 5,II,1:1
Saunders, Valentine
Van Dyck, The 1921,O 12,18:2
Saunders, Wandolf
Ol' Man Satan 1932,O 4,26:3
Saunders, Wardell
Conjur' Man Dies 1936,Mr 12,18:5
Macbeth 1936,Ap 15,25:4
One-Act Plays of the Sea; Bound East for Cardiff
1937,O 30,23:2
One-Act Plays of the Sea; In the Zone
1937,O 30,23:2
Androcles and the Lion 1938,D 17,10:5
Native Son 1941,Mr 25,26:5
Native Son 1942,O 24,10:6
According to Law 1944,Je 2,20:3
Jeb 1946,F 22,20:2
Saunier, Rene (Producer)
Pecheresse Innocent, La 1927,Ja 9,VII,2:5
Baccara 1927,Ap 3,VIII,4:7
Sauris, Genevieve
Around the World 1946,Je 1,9:5
Saussen, Edmund
Wozzeck 1966,Ap 6,34:1
Sauter, Eddie (Miscellaneous)
Milk and Honey 1961,O 11,52:1
It's a Bird . . . It's a Plane . . . It's Superman
1966,Mr 30,34:1
Diary of Adam and Eve, The 1966,O 19,53:1
Passionella 1966,O 19,53:1
Lady or the Tiger?, The 1966,O 19,53:1
1776 1969,Mr 17,46:2
Promenade 1969,Je 5,56:1
Strada, La 1969,D 15,63:1
Georgy 1970,F 27,26:1
Sauter, Eddie (Musical Director)
Two by Two 1970,N 11,37:1
Sauter, Edward (Miscellaneous)
Foxy 1964,F 17,26:1
Sauter, Joe (Director)
Along Came a Spider 1963,My 28,33:1
Sauter, Joe (Playwright)
Along Came a Spider 1963,My 28,33:1
Cindy 1964,Mr 20,24:1
Sauter, William
George Washington 1920,Mr 2,9:1
Hamlet 1920,Mr 17,14:2
Servant in the House, The 1921,My 3,20:1
Taming of the Shrew, The 1921,My 12,20:2
Merchant of Venice, The 1921,My 14,10:4
Jolly Roger, The 1923,Ag 31,10:4
Cyrano de Bergerac 1923,N 2,14:1
Othello 1925,Ja 12,11:1
Servant in the House, The 1925,Ap 8,24:2
Hamlet 1925,O 12,19:2
Merchant of Venice, The 1925,D 28,12:1
Cyrano de Bergerac 1926,F 19,18:1
Servant in the House, The 1926,My 4,30:1
Henry V 1928,Mr 16,26:2
Light of Asia, The 1928,O 10,32:2
Cyrano de Bergerac 1928,D 26,14:4
Journey's End 1930,Ag 5,26:4
Roof, The 1931,O 31,22:4
Cyrano de Bergerac 1932,D 27,11:2
Cyrano de Bergerac 1936,Ap 28,17:1
Ruy Blas 1938,Jl 24,IX,2:1
Sauvacool, John K (Playwright)
O'Daniel 1947,F 25,32:2

uvain, Eunice
Vaudeville (Palace) 1926,Ag 3,19:2

uvajon, Marc-Gilbert (Original Author)
Dear Charles 1952,D 21,44:5
Dear Charles 1954,S 26,II,1:1

uvajon, Marc-Gilbert (Playwright)
Dear Charles 1953,Ap 20,22:4
Dear Charles 1954,S 16,37:2
Adorable Julia 1954,N 28,II,3:1

uvaneix, Helene
Otage, L' 1959,O 27,42:1

uvinet, Jeri
Lady Windermere's Fan 1946,O 15,29:2

va, Marusia
Chauve-Souris of 1943 1943,Ag 13,13:2

vacool, John K (Playwright)
Judith 1965,Mr 25,42:2

vacool, John K (Translator)
Judith 1965,Ap 4,II,1:1

vage, Allen (Director)
Jumping Fool, The 1970,F 10,53:1

vage, Archie
Macbeth 1936,Ap 15,25:4
Doctor Faustus 1937,Ja 9,21:2
Case of Philip Lawrence, The 1937,Je 9,31:1
Horse Play 1937,Ag 28,8:3
Cabin in the Sky 1940,O 26,19:2
Cabin in the Sky 1940,N 10,IX,2:1
South Pacific 1949,Ap 8,30:2

vage, Archie (Choreographer)
Porgy and Bess 1965,O 20,53:3

vage, Babs
Case History 1938,O 22,15:2

vage, Bernard
Young Visitors, The 1920,N 30,14:1
Macbeth 1921,F 18,16:1
R U R 1922,O 10,16:1
Cyrano de Bergerac 1923,N 2,14:1
Hamlet 1925,N 10,23:1
Brothers Karamazov, The 1927,Ja 4,20:1
Patriot, The 1928,Ja 20,15:1
Macbeth 1928,N 20,28:3
Suspense 1930,Ag 13,22:3
Hamlet 1931,N 6,28:4
Horse Eats Hat 1936,S 28,14:2
Doctor Faustus 1937,Ja 9,21:2
Come Across 1938,S 15,28:3
Savonarola 1942,Ap 24,20:2
Around the World 1946,Je 1,9:5

vage, Charles McLean
Sam Abramovitch 1927,Ja 20,20:5
Help Yourself! 1936,Jl 15,15:1
On the Rocks 1938,Je 16,20:2

vage, Courtenay (Playwright)
Don't Bother Mother 1925,F 4,18:2
They All Want Something 1926,O 13,20:2
Buzzard, The 1928,Mr 15,29:1
Virtue's Bed 1930,Ap 16,26:5
Loose Moments 1935,F 5,22:3
Home Is the Hero 1945,Ja 20,16:4

vage, Elliot
Rothschilds, The 1970,O 20,40:1

vage, Elliott
Ballad for a Firing Squad 1968,D 12,64:2
Cry for Us All 1970,Ap 9,48:2

vage, Henry W (Producer)
Stolen Fruit 1925,O 8,31:4

vage, Jim
Utopia! 1963,My 7,47:4

vage, John
Sensations 1970,O 26,48:2

vage, Kathie
George M! 1968,Ap 11,48:1

vage, M
Drunkard, The; Fallen Saved, The 1929,D 31,14:6

vage, Mary Lou
Priorities of 1942 1942,Mr 13,23:2

vage, Mr (Producer)
Lass O' Laughter 1924,N 16,VIII,2:8

vage, R Powers (Playwright)
Mike The Angel 1943,Ap 6,25:3

vage, Robert Cosmos (Composer)
Last Triangle, The (An Embroidered Camp) 1968,Mr 19,41:1
Only a Countess May Dance When She's Crazy (An Almost Historical Camp) 1968,Mr 19,41:1

vage, Steele (Costume Designer)
Caviar 1934,Je 8,19:2

vage, Steele (Scenic Designer)
Caviar 1934,Je 8,19:2

vage, Winston
But Never Jam Today 1969,Ap 24,40:1
Old Judge Mose Is Dead 1969,Ag 29,25:1

Savage-Friedman (Miscellaneous)
Four Seasons, The 1968,Mr 15,32:1

Savay, Ruth
Scandals 1920,Je 8,9:1

Savel, Ernest (Miscellaneous)
Wizard of Oz, The 1968,N 28,69:2

Savell, Walter
Rogues and Vagabonds 1930,My 8,32:5

Saveile, M
Half Moon Inn 1923,Mr 21,19:2

Saverino, Anthony
Wildcat 1960,D 17,20:2

Savery, Gerald (Playwright)
George and Margaret 1937,F 26,25:2

Savery, Ronald
Bird Cage, The 1925,Je 3,26:2
Harvest 1925,S 21,16:2
Diamond Lil 1928,Ap 10,32:1
Veneer 1929,N 13,24:5
Penal Law 2010 1930,Ap 19,14:2
Long Road, The 1930,S 10,30:2

Savian, Nick
Edward II 1958,F 12,32:5
Darker Flower, A 1963,Mr 11,7:2
Shoemaker's Holiday, The 1967,Je 3,19:1
Thieves' Carnival 1967,Je 5,52:1
Visit, The 1967,S 13,41:1

Savian, Robert
Unto Thee a Garden 1968,O 28,55:3

Savich, Ray
Great Way, The 1921,N 8,28:2

Savidge, Mary
Salad Days 1958,N 11,24:1
Taming of the Shrew, The 1962,Je 21,25:1
Cyrano de Bergerac 1962,Ag 1,21:1
Richard II 1964,Je 17,47:1
Country Wife, The 1964,Ag 3,16:1
Henry IV, Part I 1965,Je 30,42:1
Falstaff; Henry IV, Part II 1965,Jl 1,35:1
Cherry Orchard, The 1965,Ag 2,17:2

Savidge, Victor
Around the World 1946,Je 1,9:5

Savie
Emerald Slippers, The 1970,S 2,31:2

Savig, Sonja
Merry Widow, The 1957,Ap 11,36:6

Savile, Edith (Playwright)
King's Leisure, The 1936,My 31,II,6:8

Savill, Geoffrey
Second Mrs Tanqueray, The 1924,O 28,27:1

Savilla, Ross
Find Daddy 1926,Mr 9,21:3

Saville, Jane
Shall We Join the Ladies? 1925,Ja 14,19:1
Green Hat, The 1925,S 16,23:2
Constant Nymph, The 1926,D 10,31:1
Lady With a Lamp, The 1931,N 20,27:2
Near to the Stars 1932,F 23,23:2
Few Wild Oats, A 1932,Mr 25,22:6

Saville, Mari (Producer)
Sondra 1967,My 10,39:1
Harold 1967,My 10,39:1
Lulu; Earth Spirit 1970,Mr 28,32:1

Saville, Philip
Shop at Sly Corner, The 1949,Ja 19,35:2
Iphigenie in Tauris 1949,O 22,11:2
Naked 1950,S 7,39:2

Saville, Ruth
Live Life Again 1945,O 1,14:7
I Gotta Get Out 1947,S 26,27:2
Hold It! 1948,My 6,31:5
Jenny Kissed Me 1948,D 24,12:2
House of Bernarda Alba, The 1951,Ja 8,14:6

Saville, T G (Playwright)
Expedition 1936,O 13,32:4

Savin, Lillian
Fata Morgana 1931,D 26,15:3
Mademoiselle 1932,O 19,22:4
Far Away Horses 1933,Mr 22,21:6
John Ferguson 1933,Jl 11,15:7

Savin, M (Composer)
Little Miss Charity 1920,S 3,6:3

Savino, Frank
Medea 1965,N 29,46:1
Firebugs, The 1968,Jl 2,36:1
Room Service 1970,My 13,49:1

Savio, William Lo (Musical Director)
Festa Italiana 1966,S 30,55:1

Savior, Alfred (Playwright)
He 1931,S 22,33:1

Savior, Paul
Picture of Dorian Gray, The 1956,Ag 18,15:5
Escurial 1956,O 3,29:2

Savo, Jimmy
Vogues of 1924 1924,Mr 28,14:3
Vogues and Frolics 1924,Je 26,21:7
Vaudeville (Hippodrome) 1925,D 29,21:2
Vaudeville (Palace) 1926,Jl 6,19:3
Vaudeville (Palace) 1928,N 6,35:2
Murray Anderson's Almanac 1929,Ag 4,VIII,1:6
Murray Anderson's Almanac 1929,Ag 15,20:3
Vaudeville (Palace) 1929,N 11,20:5
Earl Carroll's Vanities 1930,Jl 2,28:3
Lambs Gambol 1932,Ap 25,18:2
Parade 1935,My 12,X,2:5
Parade 1935,My 21,22:2
Parade 1935,My 26,XI,1:1
Would-Be Gentleman, The 1936,Ag 4,15:1
Boys From Syracuse, The 1938,N 13,IX,2:2
Boys From Syracuse, The 1938,N 24,36:1
Mum's the Word 1940,D 6,28:5
Wine, Women and Song 1942,S 29,18:3
What's Up 1943,N 12,24:6

Savo, Jimmy—Cont
What's Up 1943,N 21,II,1:1

Savo, Jimmy (Miscellaneous)
Mum's the Word 1940,D 6,28:5

Savo, Jimmy (Playwright)
Mum's the Word 1940,D 6,28:5

Savo, Jimmy (Producer)
Mum's the Word 1940,D 6,28:5

Savoca, John (Miscellaneous)
Awakening of Spring, The 1964,My 13,50:1

Savoir, Alfred
Huitieme Femme de Barbe-Bleue, La 1936,Ja 27,20:5

Savoir, Alfred (Playwright)
Bluebeard's Eighth Wife 1921,S 20,12:2
Banco 1922,S 21,18:1
Nouvelle Heloise, La 1923,Ap 8,VIII,1:7
Ce Que Femme Veut 1924,F 3,VII,1:4
Couturiere de Luneville, La 1924,Mr 26,16:2
Grande Duchesse et la Garcon d'Etage, La 1924,My 25,VIII,1:8
Grand Duchess and the Waiter, The 1925,O 14,31:1
Dompteur, Le, ou L'Anglais Tel Qu' On La Mange 1926,Ja 10,VII,1:3
Lion Tamer, The 1926,O 8,26:1
Lion Tamer, The 1926,O 17,VIII,1:1
Passy-08-45 1927,F 20,VII,2:1
Deux Amis, Les 1927,Je 12,VII,2:1
Comme le Temps Passe 1927,O 30,IX,4:7
Cocktail 1928,F 5,VIII,2:1
Bapteme, Le 1928,Mr 11,VIII,2:7
Lui 1929,N 17,IX,2:6
Lui 1929,N 24,X,2:1
Petite Catherine, La 1930,O 26,VIII,2:1
Petite Catherine, La 1930,N 2,VIII,2:1
He 1931,My 3,VIII,1:1
Little Catherine 1931,N 19,27:2
Patissiere du Village, La 1932,Ap 3,VIII,2:1
Margrave, La 1932,D 18,X,3:6
Voie Lactee, La 1933,F 26,IX,2:2
Maria 1933,O 29,IX,2:5
All Paris Knows 1934,Jl 24,20:1
Huitieme Femme de Barbe-Bleue, La 1936,Ja 27,20:5

Savoir, Andre (Playwright)
Van Dyck, The 1921,O 12,18:2

Savoir, M (Playwright)
Little Catherine 1931,D 6,VIII,2:7

Savoir, Paul
Teahouse of the August Moon, The 1954,Ap 23,23:6

Savold, Ed
Holy Terror, A 1925,S 29,31:2

Savory, A L C
Riff-Raff 1926,F 9,18:6

Savory, Gerald
Golden Wings 1941,N 25,33:3
Golden Wings 1941,D 9,46:6
Flare Path 1942,D 24,20:2
Sheppey 1944,Ap 19,27:2

Savory, Gerald (Director)
Little Brown Jug 1946,Mr 7,32:2
Virginia Reel 1947,Ap 15,28:2

Savory, Gerald (Original Author)
Hand in Glove 1944,D 5,19:1
Hand in Glove 1944,D 10,II,5:1

Savory, Gerald (Playwright)
George and Margaret 1937,S 23,32:2
Hand in Glove 1944,D 5,19:1
Hand in Glove 1944,D 10,II,5:1
Likely Tale, A 1956,Ap 8,II,3:1

Savoy, Harry
Vaudeville (Palace) 1932,Je 13,19:7

Savoy, Raymond (Scenic Designer)
Temper the Wind 1946,D 28,10:2

Savoy and Brennan
Greenwich Village Follies 1920,Ag 31,7:3
Greenwich Village Follies 1922,S 13,18:2

Savoy Comic Opera
Mikado, The 1932,Jl 29,18:4

Savoye, Adele
Babes in Toyland 1929,D 24,15:3

Sawasho
Christ 1928,D 25,6:1

Sawaya, George
Dream Play 1960,N 23,22:1
After the Angels 1961,F 11,27:5

Sawyer, Bobby
Fly Away Home 1937,Jl 28,15:1

Sawyer, Carl (Miscellaneous)
13 Daughters 1961,Mr 3,17:2

Sawyer, Carol
Fiddler on the Roof 1964,S 23,56:2

Sawyer, Connie
Hilarities 1948,S 10,20:2
Hole in the Head, A 1957,Mr 1,15:1

Sawyer, Conway
Roseanne 1923,D 31,9:5

Sawyer, David (Producer)
Under the Sycamore Tree 1960,Mr 8,37:2

Sawyer, Donald
Her Family Tree 1920,D 28,9:2

Sawyer, Dorie
Hottentot, The 1920,Mr 2,9:1
Sawyer, George
Elmer the Great 1928,S 25,29:1
Poppa 1928,D 25,31:1
Sawyer, Ivy
Half-Moon, The 1920,N 2,15:2
Irving Berlin's Music Box Revue 1921,S 23,18:2
Music Box Revue 1923,S 24,5:3
Mayflowers 1925,N 25,14:2
Vaudeville (Palace) 1926,Ap 13,28:3
Lucky 1927,Mr 23,28:3
Just Fancy! 1927,O 12,30:2
Sawyer, Joseph
Casey Jones 1938,F 21,14:2
Sawyer, Mary Le
Pirates of Penzance, The 1946,S 21,19:2
Sawyer, Mike
Cindy 1964,Mr 20,24:1
Sawyer, Mike (Playwright)
Cindy 1964,Mr 20,24:1
Sawyer, Nesta (Playwright)
Black Magic 1931,S 6,VIII,2:1
Sawyer, Randolph
Zunguru 1938,Ag 3,14:5
Zunguru 1938,Ag 7,IX,8:2
Zunguru 1940,Mr 21,30:5
Carmen Jones 1943,D 3,26:2
Green Pastures, The 1951,Mr 16,35:2
Sawyer, Spencer
You Can't Take It With You 1945,Mr 27,23:7
Sawyer, Tom
Hamlet 1961,Mr 17,17:1
Androcles and the Lion 1961,N 22,24:2
Dark Lady of the Sonnets, The 1961,D 15,48:1
Who'll Save the Plowboy? 1962,Ja 10,24:2
Duchess of Malfi, The 1962,Mr 5,27:1
Richard II 1962,Je 18,20:2
King Lear 1963,Je 10,37:1
Comedy of Errors, The 1963,Je 13,28:1
Henry V 1963,Je 14,37:1
Richard III 1964,Je 12,44:2
Hamlet 1964,Jl 4,9:1
King Lear 1968,N 8,43:1
Cry of Players, A 1968,N 15,40:1
Wars of the Roses, The (Part I) 1970,Jl 2,30:1
Wars of the Roses, The (Part II) 1970,Jl 3,15:1
Richard III 1970,Jl 4,11:1
Sawyer, Tom (Miscellaneous)
H M S Pinafore 1960,S 8,41:1
Warm Body, A 1967,Ap 17,44:2
Song of the Grasshopper 1967,S 29,52:2
Sax, Arline
Uncle Willie 1956,D 21,17:1
Sax, Carol (Director)
Road to Rome, The 1929,N 23,19:1
Road to Rome, The 1929,D 29,VIII,2:6
Holiday 1930,F 6,21:2
Guest Room, The 1931,O 7,29:2
Re-Echo 1934,Ja 12,28:4
Sax, Carol (Producer)
Guest Room, The 1931,O 7,29:2
Re-Echo 1934,Ja 12,28:4
Sax, Carol (Scenic Designer)
Lady Dedlock 1929,Ja 1,61:2
Sax, Joseph
Mother Courage and Her Children 1964,My 12,32:2
Sax, Ray
Hear! Hear! 1955,S 28,38:1
Sax, Ray (Director)
Hear! Hear! 1955,S 28,38:1
Saxby, Barbara
Show Boat 1957,Je 28,30:2
Saxe, Al
Mrs McThing 1952,F 21,22:1
Giants, Sons of Giants 1962,Ja 8,26:2
Saxe, Al (Director)
Young Go First, The 1935,My 29,16:2
Johnny Doodle 1942,Mr 19,28:2
Silver Tassie, The 1949,Jl 22,16:5
Silver Tassie, The 1949,S 4,II,1:1
Saxe, Al (Playwright)
Johnny Doodle 1942,Mr 19,28:2
Saxe, Stephen O (Scenic Designer)
Merry Wives of Windsor, The 1954,F 17,27:1
Porgy and Bess 1961,My 18,40:1
Yeomen of the Guard, The 1964,Mr 19,29:2
Porgy and Bess 1964,My 7,32:1
Porgy and Bess 1965,Mr 6,17:1
Yeomen of the Guard, The 1968,My 9,53:1
Saxelby, Joyce
Captain Jinks of the Horse Marines 1938,Ja 28,16:2
Saxen, Eve
Rutherford and Son 1927,Ap 13,29:2
Vegetable, The, or From President to Postman 1929,Ap 11,32:3
Saxon, David (Composer)
Golden State, The 1950,N 27,29:3
Saxon, Don
Street Scene 1947,Ja 10,17:2
Saxon, Don (Miscellaneous)
Jimmy 1969,O 24,38:1

Saxon, Don (Producer)
Boy Friend, The 1970,Ap 15,54:1
Saxon, Len
Du Barry 1932,N 23,15:2
Saxon, Lou
Bagels and Yox 1951,S 13,38:2
Saxon, Luther
Carmen Jones 1943,D 3,26:2
Saxon, Marie
Battling Buttler 1923,O 9,17:2
My Girl 1924,N 25,27:2
Merry Merry 1925,S 25,24:3
Ramblers, The 1926,S 21,32:2
Ups-A-Daisy 1928,O 9,34:2
Saxon, Mary
Passing Show of 1924, The 1924,S 4,13:4
Saxon Sisters
New Aquacade Revue, The 1940,My 13,20:5
Say, Terry
At Your Service 1937,Ag 17,23:1
Sayblack, Curt
Moon on a Rainbow Shawl 1970,D 18,52:1
Saye, Paul
Apollo of Bellac, The 1954,My 29,12:1
Purification, The 1954,My 29,12:1
Sayer, Archie
Trial of Mary Dugan, The 1927,S 20,33:1
Sayer, Earl
Commedia Dell' Arte 1957,Jl 5,13:2
Sayer, Sorella
This Thing Called Love 1935,Jl 2,24:4
Day in the Sun 1939,My 17,29:2
Sayer, Stanley
Me, Candido! 1956,O 16,36:2
Five Posts in the Market Place 1961,Mr 6,30:1
Pilgrim's Progress 1962,Mr 21,36:2
Walk in Darkness 1963,O 29,30:2
Sayers, Dora
Getting Married 1951,My 14,28:5
Sayers, Dorothy L
Busman's Honeymoon, A 1937,Jl 13,22:3
Sayers, Dorothy L (Original Author)
Busman's Honeymoon, A 1936,D 17,35:2
Sayers, Dorothy L (Playwright)
Busman's Honeymoon, A 1936,D 17,35:2
Busman's Honeymoon, A 1937,Ja 10,X,1:8
Devil to Pay, The 1939,Jl 21,11:1
Devil to Pay, The 1939,Ag 13,IX,2:4
Sayers, Harvey
Lolly 1929,O 17,26:2
Cyrano de Bergerac 1932,D 27,11:2
Creeping Fire 1935,Ja 17,22:3
Cyrano de Bergerac 1936,Ap 28,17:1
Sayers, Jo Ann
My Sister Eileen 1940,D 27,23:2
ANTA Album 1951,My 7,22:7
Sayers, Kchast
Watched Pot, The 1947,O 29,31:4
Sayers, Loretta
Body Beautiful, The 1935,N 1,24:3
Sayers, Michael (Playwright)
Kathleen 1948,F 4,26:2
Sayinka, Wole (Playwright)
Kongi's Harvest 1968,Ap 15,49:1
Sayler, John
View From the Bridge, A 1956,N 9,34:4
Sayler, Oliver M (Miscellaneous)
Ulysses in Nighttown 1958,Je 6,30:1
Saymour, John D
She Stoops to Conquer 1928,My 15,17:1
Sayre, Archie
Scarlet Pages 1929,S 10,26:3
Sayre, Bigelow
Roll Sweet Chariot 1934,O 3,24:3
Hipper's Holiday 1934,O 19,26:2
Menagerie 1935,Jl 2,24:3
Let Freedom Ring 1935,N 7,26:2
Susan and God 1937,O 8,26:4
Pick-Up Girl 1944,My 4,25:2
Sayre, Katherine
Merchant of Venice, The 1920,D 30,16:2
Madras House, The 1921,O 31,18:2
Mister Pitt 1924,Ja 23,15:3
Sayre, Syd and His Orchestra
Summer Wives 1936,Ap 14,18:1
Sayre and Mack
Vaudeville (Hippodrome) 1925,D 8,28:6
Sayres, Evelyn
Boom Boom 1929,Ja 29,26:4
Sayres, Loretta
Boom Boom 1929,Ja 29,26:4
Scaasi, Arnold (Miscellaneous)
P S I Love You 1964,N 20,40:1
Scaife, Chris
Rat, The 1925,F 11,19:3
Scaife, Marvin
So Proudly We Hail 1938,Ap 9,11:1
Scala, Delia
My Fair Lady 1963,N 16,16:1
Scales, Prunella
Matchmaker, The 1955,D 6,45:6
Matchmaker, The 1955,D 18,II,3:1

Scalise, Frank
Nativity Play, The 1937,D 21,29:1
Scals, Nat
Riot 1968,D 20,64:1
Scamman, P R
Humbug, The 1929,N 28,34:5
Scammell, Terence
King Lear 1963,Je 10,37:1
Caesar and Cleopatra 1963,Ag 1,18:2
Richard III 1964,Je 12,44:2
Hamlet 1964,Jl 4,9:1
Giants' Dance, The 1964,N 17,48:2
Coriolanus 1965,Je 21,36:1
Romeo and Juliet 1965,Je 21,36:3
John Brown's Body 1968,F 13,49:2
Comedy of Errors, The 1968,F 28,40:2
She Stoops to Conquer 1968,Ap 1,58:3
Scammon, Howard (Director)
Anatomist, The 1957,F 27,21:5
Founders, The 1957,My 14,39:1
Scammon, Percy
Second Mate, The 1930,Mr 25,34:5
Scandur, Gene
Hunting the Jingo Birds 1965,Mr 26,27:1
We Bombed in New Haven 1968,O 17,51:1
Scandur, Joseph
Pirates of Penzance, The 1936,Ap 21,27:5
Higher and Higher 1940,Ap 5,24:3
Mr Winkle's Holliday 1946,Je 24,27:6
Anna Russell and Her Little Show 1953,S 8,27:2
Scanga, Richard (Miscellaneous)
Cuban Thing, The 1968,S 25,36:2
Steambath 1970,Jl 1,49:1
Scanga, Richard (Producer)
Man in the Glass Booth, The 1968,S 27,41:1
Scanlan, John
Master Builder Solness 1950,My 26,19:3
To Bury a Cousin 1967,My 17,38:3
Beyond Desire 1967,O 11,36:1
Parents and Children 1969,Ja 13,26:6
Geese 1969,Ja 13,26:6
Scanlan, Mark
Lysistrata 1968,N 15,42:1
Scanlon
Coney Island Play 1970,O 31,34:2
Scanlon, Arthur
Young Sinners 1929,N 29,24:4
Young Sinners 1931,Ap 21,35:5
Bright Honor 1936,S 28,14:1
Scanlon, Denno Brothers and Scanlon
Vaudeville (Hippodrome) 1926,Ap 13,28:2
Scanlon, Edward J (Director)
Student Prince, The 1931,Ja 30,18:1
Blossom Time 1931,Mr 5,32:1
Bitter Sweet 1934,My 8,28:4
Rose Marie 1936,Jl 22,22:6
Countess Maritza 1936,Ag 19,18:2
Roberta 1937,Je 27,II,6:1
Maytime 1937,Jl 6,23:4
Anything Goes 1937,Ag 26,24:3
Roberta 1937,S 7,16:4
Show Boat 1938,Je 30,21:1
Blossom Time 1938,D 27,12:2
Scanlon, Edward J (Miscellaneous)
Blossom Time 1936,Jl 29,23:1
Scanlon, Edward J (Original Author)
Circus Princess, The 1937,Ag 31,26:6
Scanlon, Edward J (Producer)
So Many Paths 1934,D 7,26:5
Scanlon, John
Mousetrap, The 1960,N 7,46:1
Scanlon, Marion
Set My People Free 1948,N 4,38:2
Scanlon, Michael
Galileo 1968,D 1,88:4
Scanlon, Morgan (Miscellaneous)
Mrs Warren's Profession 1956,Je 7,35:2
Scannell, John
Night Boat, The 1920,F 3,18:1
Good Morning, Dearie 1921,N 2,20:2
Scarborough, George (Miscellaneous)
Madame Alias 1927,S 4,VII,2:4
Scarborough, George (Playwright)
Blue Bonnet 1920,Ag 30,12:1
Mad Dog, The 1921,N 9,20:1
Heaven-Tappers, The 1927,Mr 9,28:3
Scardino, Don
Seven Scenes for Yeni 1963,My 13,36:2
Shout From the Rooftops 1964,O 29,40:1
Loves of Cass McGuire, The 1966,O 7,36:1
Rimers of Eldritch, The 1967,F 21,53:1
Unknown Soldier and His Wife, The 1967,Jl 7,22:1
Johnny No-Trump 1967,O 9,60:2
My Daughter, Your Son 1969,My 14,36:2
Park 1970,Ap 23,47:1
Scarecrows, The
Ice Follies 1958,Ja 15,26:2
Ice Follies 1960,Ja 13,20:1
Ice Follies 1965,Ja 13,35:1
Ice Follies 1969,My 23,38:1
Ice Follies 1970,My 23,27:1
Scarlett, Frank
Vaudeville (Palace) 1933,Ja 16,13:2

Scarlett, Kathleen
Scarlet Lullaby 1968,Mr 11,48:1
Golden Streets, The 1970,Ag 14,21:1
Scarpato, Bob (Director)
Fourth Pig, The 1965,Ja 27,24:6
Fisherman, The 1965,Ja 27,24:6
Scelzo
Last Mile, The 1930,D 21,VIII,3:1
Schaaf, C Hart (Playwright)
Partition 1948,O 29,31:2
Schaaf, Mrytle
Hassard Short's Ritz Revue 1924,S 18,19:1
Schaal, Dick
Open Season at Second City 1964,Ja 23,25:1
Schaal, Richard
Little Murders 1967,Ap 26,38:1
Story Theater 1970,O 27,54:1
Schacht, Al
Second Guesser 1946,F 20,29:2
Schacht, Gustav
Motke Ganef 1932,D 30,15:2
Revolt 1933,Ja 12,21:3
It Can't Happen Here 1936,O 28,30:1
Awake and Sing! 1938,D 23,16:6
Salvation 1939,S 29,19:2
If I Were Rothschild 1940,Ja 1,28:7
Schacht, Sam
Cannibals, The 1968,N 4,60:1
Increased Difficulty of Concentration, The
1969,D 5,48:1
And I Met a Man 1970,Ap 11,20:3
One Night Stands of a Noisy Passenger; Passage,
Un 1970,D 31,8:3
Schachtel, Irving (Producer)
Curtain Call 1937,Ap 23,24:7
Schachter, Leon
Queen Mother 1938,D 26,29:4
Right Next to Broadway 1944,F 22,26:2
Brothers Ashkenazi, The 1955,N 12,24:4
My Son and I 1960,O 24,24:2
Schachter, Leon (Miscellaneous)
Kosher Widow, The 1959,N 2,40:2
My Son and I 1960,O 24,24:2
Schack, William (Playwright)
Bloody Laughter 1931,D 5,20:6
Schackelford, Margaret
Zeno 1923,Ag 27,14:2
Schaded, Maurice (Miscellaneous)
Donogoo 1961,Ja 19,25:3
Schaded, Maurice (Producer)
Cave Dwellers, The 1961,O 16,34:2
Schaedlich, Edwin (Director)
Marriage of Mr Mississippi, The 1969,N 20,60:5
Schaefer, Frank (Miscellaneous)
Macbeth 1968,N 30,49:3
Schaefer, George
Wonderful Thing, The 1920,F 18,9:1
Squaw Man, The 1921,D 27,10:3
Schaefer, George (Director)
Hamlet 1945,D 14,25:2
Hamlet 1945,D 23,II,3:1
Man and Superman 1947,O 9,31:2
Linden Tree, The 1948,Mr 3,28:2
Man and Superman 1949,My 17,28:6
When the Bough Breaks 1950,Mr 9,25:5
Idiot's Delight 1951,My 24,46:3
Wild Duck, The 1951,D 27,17:1
Anna Christie 1952,Ja 10,33:1
Come of Age 1952,Ja 24,22:2
Male Animal, The 1952,My 1,35:1
Tovarich 1952,My 15,39:2
First Lady 1952,My 29,18:5
Southwest Corner, The 1955,F 4,18:2
Southwest Corner, The 1955,F 13,II,1:1
Apple Cart, The 1956,O 19,23:1
Apple Cart, The 1956,O 28,II,1:1
Body Beautiful, The 1958,Ja 24,15:2
Write Me a Murder 1961,O 27,28:2
Great Indoors, The 1966,F 2,23:1
Schaefer, George (Lighting Director)
Man and Superman 1947,O 9,31:2
Teahouse of the August Moon, The
1955,My 10,24:1
Schaefer, George (Miscellaneous)
Captain Brassbound's Conversion 1950,D 28,21:1
Teahouse of the August Moon, The 1953,O 16,32:1
Schaefer, George (Producer)
Corn Is Green, The 1950,Ja 12,33:2
Devil's Disciple, The 1950,Ja 26,23:2
Heiress, The 1950,F 9,34:2
Royal Family, The 1951,Ja 11,28:2
Richard II 1951,Ja 25,21:2
Taming of the Shrew, The 1951,Ap 26,35:2
Dream Girl 1951,My 10,39:1
To Broadway With Love 1964,Ap 30,28:6
Schaefer, Hal (Miscellaneous)
Funny Thing Happened on the Way to the Forum,
A 1962,My 9,49:1
Foxy 1964,F 17,26:1
Schaefer, Henry
Holy Terror, A 1925,S 29,31:2
Subway Express 1929,S 25,34:3

Schaefer, Jerry
Ben Franklin in Paris 1964,O 28,52:1
Schaefer, Karl
Gay Blades 1937,N 16,27:1
Schaefer, Otis
Once in a Lifetime 1930,S 25,22:3
Merrily We Roll Along 1934,O 1,14:1
Journey by Night, A 1935,Ap 17,26:3
Schaefer, Polly
Merry Merry 1925,S 25,24:3
Schaefer, Rosemary
Best Foot Forward 1941,O 2,28:2
Schaeffer, Mary (Composer)
Provincetown Follies, The 1935,N 4,24:3
Schaeffer, Pierre (Composer)
Phedre 1963,O 21,39:1
Berenice 1963,O 30,46:1
Schaeffer, Ronald
Year Boston Won the Pennant, The
1969,My 23,38:1
Schaeffer, Ronald (Miscellaneous)
Cry of Players, A 1968,N 15,40:1
Schaenen, Lee (Musical Director)
Porgy and Bess 1965,O 20,53:3
Schafer, Karl
Gay Blades 1937,N 12,26:6
Schafer, Milton (Composer)
Bravo Giovanni 1962,My 21,41:2
Bravo Giovanni 1962,My 27,II,1:1
Drat! the Cat! 1965,O 11,54:2
Schafer, Natalie
Trigger 1927,D 7,32:1
March Hares 1928,Ap 3,32:6
Nut Farm, The 1929,O 15,34:3
Ada Beats the Drum 1930,My 9,20:4
Rhapsody, The 1930,S 16,30:3
Great Barrington, The 1931,F 20,18:1
Perfectly Scandalous 1931,My 14,27:2
New York to Cherbourg 1932,F 20,11:4
So Many Paths 1934,D 7,26:5
Why We Misbehave 1935,Jl 25,14:8
Lady Precious Stream 1936,Ja 28,15:2
Goodbye in the Night 1940,Mr 19,31:2
Lady in the Dark 1941,Ja 5,IX,1:7
Lady in the Dark 1941,Ja 24,14:2
Lady in the Dark 1941,S 3,26:6
Doughgirls, The 1942,D 31,19:2
Joy Forever, A 1946,Ja 8,20:2
Forward the Heart 1949,Ja 29,9:2
Six Characters in Search of an Author
1955,D 12,38:1
Six Characters in Search of an Author
1955,D 25,II,3:1
Romanoff and Juliet 1957,O 11,24:1
Highest Tree, The 1959,N 5,41:1
Schafer, Reuben
Happy Faculty, The 1967,Ap 19,50:1
Schafer, Robert
Roberta 1937,Je 27,II,6:1
Schaff, M
Haunch, Paunch and Jowl 1935,D 27,22:4
Schaffer, Laura
Dantons Tod 1927,D 21,28:3
Schaffer, Louis (Director)
Pins and Needles 1938,Ja 23,XI,1:1
Schaffers, Willi
Merry Widow, The 1929,F 17,IX,2:3
Schaffner, Franklin (Director)
Advise and Consent 1960,N 18,25:1
Schallert, William
Son, The 1950,Ap 1,12:4
Trial of the Catonsville Nine, The 1970,Ag 16,II,1:7
Schanche, Ingolf
Bryllupsdager; Noces d'Argent, Les
1930,D 28,VIII,3:5
Schang, Rosalind
Jonah and the Whale 1940,My 5,II,8:4
Schanser (Playwright)
Jugend im Mai 1927,Ja 23,VII,4:5
Schanz, Barbara
Dark Lady of the Sonnets, The 1956,F 21,38:1
Schanzer, R (Playwright)
Naughty Riquette 1926,S 14,25:2
Schanzer, Rudolph (Lyricist)
Spanische Nachtigall, Die 1920,D 12,VI,1:4
Madame Pompadour 1924,N 12,20:6
Schanzer, Rudolph (Playwright)
Spanische Nachtigall, Die 1920,D 12,VI,1:4
Lady in Ermine, The 1922,O 3,22:2
Madame Pompadour 1924,N 12,20:6
Schanzer (Playwright)
Casanova 1928,N 4,IX,2:1
Three Musketeers 1929,O 13,IX,4:7
Casanova 1932,Je 19,IX,2:1
Alt Heidelberg; Student Prince, The
1932,N 20,IX,3:3
Schap-Kevisch, William
Sailors of Cattaro 1934,D 11,28:4
Schaper, Marjorie (Lighting Director)
Don Juan in Hell 1960,O 4,47:3
Schaper, Marjorie (Scenic Designer)
Don Juan in Hell 1960,O 4,47:3

Schapira, Ruth
Cocktails of 1934 1934,My 5,22:1
Schapiro, Estelle
Cocktails of 1934 1934,My 5,22:1
Schapiro, Herbert (Lyricist)
Me Nobody Knows, The 1970,My 19,42:1
Schapiro, Herbert (Playwright)
Me Nobody Knows, The 1970,My 19,42:1
Schaps, Harvey M (Miscellaneous)
From the Second City 1969,O 15,34:1
Scharaff, Irene (Costume Designer)
All in Fun 1940,D 28,11:2
Scharf, Alan
Behind the Wall 1960,N 1,47:1
Scharf, Leon
Betty Behave 1927,Mr 9,28:4
Scharf, Sabrina
Raisin' Hell in the Son 1962,Jl 3,13:2
Scharfe, Theodore
Phantoms 1930,Ja 14,24:3
Scharff, Lester
Home Fires 1923,Ag 21,12:1
Solid Ivory 1925,N 17,29:3
Alice in Wonderland 1932,D 12,18:3
Scharff, Ralph
Othello 1937,Ja 7,16:4
Scharrad, Hilary (Miscellaneous)
Slave Ship 1969,N 22,46:1
Schary, Dore (Director)
Majority of One, A 1959,F 17,28:2
Majority of One, A 1959,F 22,II,1:1
Highest Tree, The 1959,N 5,41:1
Unsinkable Molly Brown, The 1960,N 4,28:1
Devil's Advocate, The 1961,Mr 10,20:1
Something About a Soldier 1962,Ja 5,36:2
Love and Kisses 1963,D 19,39:1
One by One 1964,D 2,60:1
Zulu and the Zayda, The 1965,N 11,59:1
Schary, Dore (Miscellaneous)
Golden Streets, The 1970,Ag 14,21:1
Schary, Dore (Playwright)
Too Many Heroes 1937,N 16,26:2
Sunrise at Campobello 1958,Ja 31,25:1
Sunrise at Campobello 1958,F 9,II,1:1
Highest Tree, The 1959,N 5,41:1
Devil's Advocate, The 1961,Mr 10,20:1
Devil's Advocate, The 1961,Mr 19,II,1:1
One by One 1964,D 2,60:1
Brightower 1970,Ja 29,32:1
Schary, Dore (Producer)
Sunrise at Campobello 1958,Ja 31,25:1
Majority of One, A 1959,F 17,28:2
Portrait of a Madonna 1959,Ap 16,28:1
Pound on Demand, A 1959,Ap 16,28:1
On the Harmful Effects of Tobacco
1959,Ap 16,28:1
Bedtime Story 1959,Ap 16,28:1
Highest Tree, The 1959,N 5,41:1
Unsinkable Molly Brown, The 1960,N 4,28:1
Devil's Advocate, The 1961,Mr 10,20:1
Something About a Soldier 1962,Ja 5,36:2
Love and Kisses 1963,D 19,39:1
One by One 1964,D 2,60:1
Zulu and the Zayda, The 1965,N 11,59:1
Schary, Jeb
Something About a Soldier 1962,Ja 5,36:2
Schary, Jeb (Miscellaneous)
One by One 1964,D 2,60:1
Zulu and the Zayda, The 1965,N 11,59:1
Schat, Peter (Composer)
Reconstruction 1969,Jl 8,36:1
Schatt, Daniel
Winter Soldiers 1942,N 30,19:2
Schatz, Curly
Uniform of Flesh 1949,Ja 31,15:2
Schatz, Holly (Miscellaneous)
Queen of Greece, The 1969,Ap 12,40:2
Homo 1969,Ap 12,40:2
Schatz, Sam
Possessed, The 1939,O 25,26:2
Twelfth Night 1941,D 3,32:2
Schauffler, Elizabeth
Hamlet 1927,Ap 7,23:3
Caesar and Cleopatra 1927,N 6,IX,2:1
Schauffler, Elizabeth (Playwright)
Day I Forgot, The 1933,My 13,16:6
Schauffler, Elsie (Playwright)
Parnell 1935,N 12,24:2
Parnell 1936,Ap 24,19:5
Parnell 1936,My 5,26:2
Parnell 1936,My 24,IX,1:7
Parnell 1936,My 31,X,1:5
Schaughency, Harold
Dolly Jordan 1922,O 4,26:1
Schauler, Eileen
Lady in the Dark 1952,Mr 8,11:3
My Darlin' Aida 1952,O 28,36:4
Gondoliers, The 1962,Ap 19,34:2
Schavlan, Ruth
Mascaiada 1929,D 28,10:6
Schawche, Ingolf
To Damascus 1933,N 12,IX,1:1

Schdanoff, Georg (Playwright)
Crime and Punishment 1935,Ja 23,20:3
Schear, Robert (Miscellaneous)
Ages of Man 1958,D 29,21:1
Schechner, Richard
Dionysus in 69 1968,Je 7,35:3
Schechner, Richard (Director)
Macbeth 1969,N 21,51:1
Makbeth 1969,N 30,II,3:1
Commune 1970,D 21,50:1
Commune 1970,D 27,II,1:1
Schechner, Richard (Playwright)
Dionysus in 69 1968,Je 16,II,1:1
Dionysus in 69 1968,N 19,52:1
Schechter, Bennie
Hello Grandpa! 1931,Ja 2,25:3
Women of New York 1931,Mr 23,24:3
Schechter, Beverley (Producer)
Burlesque As You Expect 1965,D 18,35:1
Schechter, Maxi
He, She and the Ox 1934,F 21,22:7
Schechtman, Frank
What Girls Do 1935,Ja 14,10:4
In a Jewish Grocery 1939,O 2,15:2
Schechtman, Saul (Composer)
Auntie Mame 1956,N 1,47:2
Auntie Mame 1958,Ag 12,33:2
Schechtman, Saul (Miscellaneous)
Fallout 1959,My 21,36:2
Carnival! 1961,Ap 14,22:2
Carnival! 1968,D 13,58:1
Schechtman, Saul (Musical Director)
Kiss Me, Kate 1958,My 31,7:4
Fallout 1959,My 21,36:2
Carnival! 1961,Ap 14,22:2
Hello, Dolly! 1967,N 13,61:1
Scheck, Max (Choreographer)
Say When 1928,Je 27,29:3
Americana 1928,O 31,28:2
Through the Years 1932,Ja 29,13:3
Scheck, Max (Director)
Schoen und Schick 1928,Ag 26,II,1:2
Belmont Varieties 1932,S 29,17:2
Scheer, Estelle
Lady of the Camellias, The 1931,Ja 27,21:2
Dark Hours, The 1932,N 15,24:2
Late One Evening 1933,Ja 10,27:3
Scheerer, Bob
Lend an Ear 1948,D 17,38:2
Dance Me a Song 1950,Ja 21,10:5
Top Banana 1951,N 2,19:2
Boy Friend, The 1954,O 1,20:1
Scheerer, Louise
Clinging Vine, The 1922,D 25,20:2
Scheerer, Maud
Playing With Love 1929,F 27,16:4
Bathsheba 1947,Mr 27,40:2
Fifth Horseman, The 1949,Je 14,26:6
Blithe Spirit 1952,F 23,7:5
Skin of Our Teeth, The 1955,Ag 18,16:1
Six Characters in Search of an Author
1955,D 12,38:1
Six Characters in Search of an Author
1955,D 25,II,3:1
First Gentleman, The 1957,Ap 26,22:2
Dark of the Moon 1958,F 27,22:2
Potting Shed, The 1958,N 3,49:2
Rendezvous at Senlis 1961,F 28,39:2
Scheff, Fritzi
Vaudeville (Palace) 1923,N 13,24:2
Sherlock Holmes 1928,F 21,18:4
Mlle Modiste 1929,O 8,34:1
I Am Different 1938,Ag 28,IX,2:5
Bravo! 1948,N 12,31:2
ANTA Album 1950,Ja 30,13:2
Scheff, Walter
Brigadoon 1947,Mr 14,28:2
Cradle Will Rock, The 1947,N 25,38:3
Cradle Will Rock, The 1947,D 27,11:2
Scheffer, Norman
Innocent Voyage, The 1943,N 16,27:2
Scheglov, Dmitry (Playwright)
First Law, The 1929,My 7,28:4
Schehner, Richard (Playwright)
Macbeth 1969,N 21,51:1
Scheid, Charles W
Betty Behave 1927,Mr 9,28:4
Scheidel, Jack
Sweetheart Shop, The 1920,S 1,13:4
Scheider, Roy R
Romeo and Juliet 1961,F 24,24:1
Duchess of Malfi, The 1962,Mr 5,27:1
Once in a Lifetime 1962,O 30,30:1
Alchemist, The 1964,S 15,33:1
Stephen D 1966,Ag 5,17:1
Stephen D 1967,O 8,II,1:6
Year Boston Won the Pennant, The
1969,My 23,38:1
Year Boston Won the Pennant, The 1969,Je 8,II,1:7
Nuns, The 1970,Je 2,35:1
Schein, Isabel (Translator)
Faraway Princess, The 1922,D 6,3:2

Schein, Joseph (Director)
Wandering Stars 1966,N 14,52:2
Schein, Joseph (Playwright)
Wandering Stars 1966,N 14,52:2
Scheingold, Joseph
One Life for Another 1920,D 18,11:2
Scheinpflugova (Miss)
Hannibal Ante Portas 1929,Jl 7,VIII,2:4
Schell, Howard
Sound of Silence, A 1965,Mr 9,30:1
Schell, Maximilian
Interlock 1958,F 7,18:1
Patriot for Me, A 1965,Jl 11,II,1:4
Patriot for Me, A 1969,O 6,58:1
Patriot for Me, A 1969,O 12,II,1:1
Schellenberg, August
Antony and Cleopatra 1967,Ag 2,25:1
Merry Wives of Windsor, The 1967,Ag 4,18:1
Scheller, James
Giants' Dance, The 1964,N 17,48:2
Schellow, Erich
Don Carlos 1964,N 25,40:1
Amphitryon 1970,N 18,40:1
Schench, H
It's the Valet 1933,D 15,25:4.
Schenck, Elliott (Composer)
Immortal Thief, The 1926,O 4,21:1
Light of Asia, The 1928,O 10,32:2
Schenck, Gracie
Vaudeville (Palace) 1932,S 12,13:5
Schenck, Mary Percy (Costume Designer)
Skin of Our Teeth, The 1942,N 19,29:5
Catherine Was Great 1944,Ag 3,16:1
Hollywood Pinafore 1945,Je 1,20:1
Next Half Hour, The 1945,O 30,14:6
Dear Judas 1947,O 6,26:4
Schenker, David V
Rutherford and Son 1927,Ap 13,29:2
Schenker, Joel (Producer)
Right You Are (If You Think You Are)
1957,Mr 5,37:1
Shadow of a Gunman, The 1958,N 21,26:1
Rivalry, The 1959,F 9,24:2
Long Dream, The 1960,F 18,36:2
Kukla, Burr and Ollie 1960,N 1,47:2
Far Country, A 1961,Ap 5,32:1
Captains and the Kings, The 1962,Ja 3,25:2
Venus at Large 1962,Ap 13,30:1
Seidman and Son 1962,O 16,32:2
Case of Libel, A 1963,O 11,43:2
Darling of the Day 1968,Ja 29,26:2
Indians 1969,O 14,51:1
Schenker, Joel W (Playwright)
This Our House 1935,D 12,33:3
Schenker, Joel W (Producer)
Oedipus Rex 1945,D 17,16:7
Mayor of Zalamea, The 1946,Ja 28,15:5
Schenker, Kurt
Wiener Blut 1964,S 12,14:1
Schenone, Rinaldo
See Naples and Die 1929,S 27,30:4
Scher, Eleanor
Case of Philip Lawrence, The 1937,Je 9,31:1
Schere, Loretta
Rosalinda; Fledermaus, Die 1942,O 29,26:5
Vie Parisienne, La 1945,Ja 13,14:5
Scherkenbach, Bob
It's a Bird . . . It's a Plane . . . It's Superman
1966,Mr 30,34:1
Scherl, Philip (Miscellaneous)
Cocktails of 1934 1934,My 5,22:1
Scherler, Sasha von
Ludlow Fair 1966,Mr 23,42:1
Trelawney of the 'Wells' 1970,O 25,II,16:1
Scherman, Catherine
They Knew What They Wanted 1924,N 25,27:1
Scherman, Pincus
Major Noah 1929,F 23,17:2
Roaming Stars 1930,Ja 25,12:2
Scherman, Thomas
They Knew What They Wanted 1924,N 25,27:1
Scherman, Thomas K (Composer)
Sun and I, The 1937,F 27,9:5
Schermerhorn, Sally
Dream of Swallows, A 1964,Ap 15,46:1
Scherr, Eleanor
Life and Death of an American 1939,My 20,11:2
Scherr, Meyer
Song of Dnieper 1946,O 26,10:5
Schertler, Jean
Month in the Country, A 1959,Mr 2,32:2
Scheuer, Charles (Playwright)
Year Round, The 1953,My 6,38:7
Scheuer, Steven H (Producer)
Phoenix Too Frequent, A 1950,Ap 27,36:2
Freight 1950,Ap 27,36:2
Nowhere to Go But Up 1962,N 12,36:2
Schevers, Susan
Me and Juliet 1970,My 15,42:1
Schevill, James (Playwright)
Lovecraft's Follies 1970,Ap 19,II,12:1
Schewenke, Mildred
Show Boat 1927,D 28,26:1

Schiavelli, Vincent
Instructions for the Running of Trains, etc on the
Erie Railway to Go Into Effect January 1,1862
1970,Ja 7,36:2
Schiavoni, Elisa
Berretto a Songali, Il; Cap With Bells, The
1931,N 30,16:3
Piccolo Santo, Il; Little Saint, The 1931,D 14,16:4
T'Amo E Sarai Mia; I Love You and You'll Be
Mine 1932,Mr 21,19:4
Casa di Tutti, La; Everybody's Home 1932,D 5,21:4
Cardinale, Il 1933,Ja 9,24:2
Schichtl's Marionettes
Vaudeville (Palace) 1926,Je 15,23:3
Schick, A (Costume Designer)
Esterke 1940,O 18,24:2
Schick, George (Musical Director)
Yours Is My Heart 1946,S 6,16:5
Schickele, Peter
Oh! Calcutta! 1969,Je 18,33:1
Schickling, John
Magdalena 1948,S 21,31:2
Out of This World 1950,D 22,17:3
Schiebler, Howard A (Playwright)
George White's Scandals 1935,D 26,20:2
Schieffelin, Elliott
Faun, The 1924,F 6,19:2
Faun, The 1924,Mr 28,17:2
Galloper, The 1924,D 19,26:2
Schiel, Eugene
Stop-Over 1938,Ja 12,16:5
Family Portrait 1939,Mr 9,18:4
First Crocus, The 1942,Ja 3,14:6
Schields, Robert
Little Theatre Tournament; Yellow Triangle, The
1929,My 10,32:2
Schieren, Alma (Miscellaneous)
MacBird! 1967,F 23,38:1
Schierski, Stanislaw
Apocalypsis cum Figuris 1969,N 20,60:2
Schierz, Paul
Oklahoma! 1943,Ap 1,27:1
Schiesske, Alfred
My Fair Lady 1961,O 26,40:1
Schiff, Albert J (Producer)
Gandhi 1970,O 27,37:1
Schiff, Charlotte (Miscellaneous)
Fragments 1967,O 3,56:1
Basement, The 1967,O 3,56:1
Schiff, Charlotte (Producer)
Who's Who, Baby? 1968,Ja 30,36:1
Schiffer, Marcellus (Lyricist)
Ich Tanze um die Welt mit Dir 1930,Ag 31,VIII,2:1
Hundert Meter Glueck 1933,F 19,IX,3:1
Haus Dazwischen, Das 1933,F 19,IX,3:1
Schiffer, Marcellus (Playwright)
Hetaerengespraeche 1927,Ja 9,VII,4:1
Es Liegt in der Luft 1928,S 23,IX,2:2
Fledermaus, Die 1929,Jl 14,IX,2:1
Alles Schwindel 1931,Je 7,VIII,2:5
Schiffrin, Celia
Pirates of Penzance, The 1936,Ap 21,27:5
Schildkraut, Joseph
Pagans 1921,Ja 5,11:1
Liliom 1921,Ap 21,18:1
Liliom 1921,My 1,VII,1:1
Liliom 1921,N 27,VI,1:1
Peer Gynt 1923,F 6,14:1
Peer Gynt 1923,F 11,VII,1:1
Firebrand, The 1924,O 16,33:1
Anatol 1931,Ja 17,23:3
American Tragedy, An 1932,Ap 17,I,19:1
Liliom 1932,O 27,23:2
Camille 1932,O 28,23:2
Dear Jane 1932,N 15,24:3
Alice in Wonderland 1932,D 12,18:3
Alice in Wonderland 1932,D 25,IX,1:1
Between Two Worlds 1934,O 26,24:2
Tomorrow's a Holiday! 1935,D 31,10:2
Clash by Night 1941,D 29,20:2
Clash by Night 1942,Ja 11,IX,1:1
Uncle Harry 1942,My 21,24:1
Cherry Orchard, The 1944,Ja 26,22:1
Cherry Orchard, The 1944,F 6,II,1:1
Green Bay Tree, The 1951,F 2,18:2
Love's Labour's Lost 1953,F 5,20:3
Love's Labour's Lost 1953,F 8,II,1:1
Diary of Anne Frank, The 1955,O 6,24:2
Diary of Anne Frank, The 1955,O 16,II,1:1
Schildkraut, Joseph (Producer)
Tomorrow's a Holiday! 1935,D 31,10:2
Schildkraut, Rudolph
Silent Forces 1920,Ag 30,12:1
Kreutzer Sonata, The 1920,O 3,VI,1:7
Merchant of Venice, The 1920,N 12,15:5
One Life for Another 1920,D 18,11:2
God of Revenge, The 1921,N 4,15:2
God of Vengeance, The 1922,D 20,22:5
Three Little Business Men, The 1923,S 4,12:1
Miracle, The 1924,Ja 16,17:1
Mongrel, The 1924,D 16,28:2
Schildkret, Edward
Nautical but Nice 1931,Ap 19,31:6

Schille, George
Thank You 1921,O 4,10:2
Schiller, Friedrich (Playwright)
Wilhelm Tell 1925,Mr 2,15:1
Robbers, The 1926,N 21,VIII,1:3
Robbers, The 1928,Ag 10,9:2
Fiesco 1930,Jl 13,VIII,2:1
Kabale und Liebe 1931,N 1,VIII,4:2
Maria Stuart 1932,Je 19,IX,1:3
Wilhelm Tell 1932,N 20,IX,3:5
Kabale und Liebe 1933,O 18,24:3
Maria Stuart 1933,D 10,X,5:1
Bride of Messina, The 1933,D 10,X,5:1
Don Karlos 1935,Jl 28,X,1:6
Mary Stuart 1957,O 9,39:1
Mary Stuart 1957,O 20,II,1:1
Mary Stuart 1958,S 3,38:1
Mary Stuart 1959,Jl 30,21:3
Don Carlos 1962,F 28,27:5
Wilhelm Tell 1964,Ja 19,II,5:1
After-Dinner Evening With Oskar Werner, An 1967,Mr 27,39:1
Schiller, George
Blue Eyes 1921,F 22,11:2
Naughty Riquette 1926,S 14,25:2
Padre, The 1926,D 28,16:3
Fine and Dandy 1930,S 24,26:1
Hold Your Horses 1933,S 26,26:4
Music Hath Charms 1934,D 31,8:2
Schiller, Kenneth
Kith and Kin 1930,My 14,31:1
Schiller, Leon (Director)
Julius Caesar 1928,Ap 8,VIII,4:3
Schiller, Mary
Trumpeter of Sakkingen 1921,Ja 15,11:3
Schiller, Mickey
You Can't Take It With You 1951,Ap 7,8:6
Schiller, Miriam
Electra 1932,Ja 9,21:4
Schiller, Rose Marie
Best Foot Forward 1941,O 2,28:2
Schilling, Erich
Midsummer Night's Dream, A 1927,N 18,21:1
Jedermann 1927,D 8,33:2
Dantons Tod 1927,D 21,28:3
Peripherie 1928,Ja 3,29:1
Diener Zweier Herren; Servant of Two Masters, The 1928,Ja 10,28:3
Kabale und Liebe 1928,Ja 17,22:3
Lebende Leichnam, Der, Der; Living Corpse, The 1928,Ja 24,26:2
Schilling, Florence
Mlle Modiste 1937,My 5,28:5
Schilling, Inge
Ice Follies 1963,Ja 10,5:2
Ice Follies 1966,Ja 12,27:6
Ice Follies 1967,Ja 11,51:1
Schilling, Margaret
Merry Widow, The 1921,S 6,13:1
Patience 1927,My 24,23:2
Strike Up the Band 1930,Ja 15,29:1
Schilling, Robert
Don Juan 1921,S 8,14:2
Schilling, Willie
Ice Follies 1963,Ja 10,5:2
Ice Follies 1965,Ja 13,35:1
Ice Follies 1966,Ja 12,27:6
Ice Follies 1967,Ja 11,51:1
Schimelpfenig, Jane
Mystery of the Finding of the Cross, The 1959,Ja 16,35:2
Cup of Trembling, The 1959,My 1,33:5
Schindler, Ellen
Serpent, The 1970,Je 2,35:1
Schindler, Kurt (Playwright)
Mascaiada 1929,D 28,10:6
Schipa, Tito (Composer)
Princess Liana 1929,Jl 14,IX,6:8
Schippers, Leo
Red, Hot and Blue! 1936,O 30,26:3
Schippers, Thomas (Miscellaneous)
Consul, The 1950,Mr 16,41:1
Schippers, Thomas (Musical Director)
Consul, The 1952,O 30,41:2
Saint of Bleecker Street, The 1954,D 28,21:1
Schirmer, Alma
Church Street 1934,N 20,24:5
Schirmer, Elizabeth
Miracle, The 1924,Ag 19,9:1
Versunkene Glocke, Die 1924,N 3,21:2
Schirmer, Frederick (Composer)
Bridge of Distances, The 1925,S 29,30:1
Schirmer, Frederick (Miscellaneous)
Miracle, The 1924,Ja 16,17:1
Miracle, The 1924,Ag 19,9:1
Schirmer, Gus (Director)
Boy Friend, The 1958,Ja 27,24:4
Gay Divorce 1960,Ap 4,37:1
Pal Joey 1961,Je 1,32:1
Can-Can 1962,My 17,32:2
Wonderful Town 1963,F 15,10:2
Pal Joey 1963,My 30,21:1
Guys and Dolls 1965,Ap 29,39:1

Music Man, The 1965,Je 17,26:4
How to Succeed in Business Without Really Trying 1966,Ap 21,45:1
Guys and Dolls 1966,Je 9,55:2
Carousel 1966,D 16,56:2
Finian's Rainbow 1967,Ap 6,44:1
Wonderful Town 1967,My 18,50:1
Life With Father 1967,O 20,53:2
Brigadoon 1967,D 14,59:2
Carnival! 1968,D 13,58:1
Boy Friend, The 1970,Ap 15,54:1
Boy Friend, The 1970,Ap 26,II,5:7
Schirmer, Gus (Miscellaneous)
One Glorious Hour 1927,Ap 15,27:2
Little Women 1944,D 13,29:2
Burlesque 1946,D 26,30:3
Double Dublin 1963,D 27,16:2
Elizabeth the Queen 1966,N 4,30:1
Schisgal, Murray (Playwright)
Ducks and Lovers 1961,O 20,39:1
Tiger, The 1963,F 6,5:2
Typists, The 1963,F 6,5:2
Luv 1964,N 12,43:1
Luv 1964,N 22,II,1:1
Luv 1965,N 16,56:4
Basement, The 1967,O 3,56:1
Fragments 1967,O 3,56:1
Fragments; Basement, The 1967,O 15,II,3:3
Jimmy Shine 1968,D 6,52:1
Jimmy Shine 1968,D 22,II,3:1
Dr Fish 1970,Mr 11,42:2
Chinese, The 1970,Mr 11,42:2
Dr Fish 1970,Mr 22,II,3:1
Chinese, The 1970,Mr 22,II,3:1
Schlader, James
Brigadoon 1950,My 3,36:2
Schlamme, Martha
World of Kurt Weill in Song, The 1964,My 13,53:1
Dreigroschenoper, Die 1965,Mr 12,24:1
Untitled-Poetry Reading 1967,Jl 18,29:1
Month of Sundays 1968,S 17,50:1
Whores, Wars & Tin Pan Alley 1969,Je 17,37:1
Country People 1970,Ja 19,35:1
Schlauch, Helen (Translator)
Thomas Paine 1930,Mr 21,30:7
Schlegel, Jeanne
Ivory Branch, The 1956,My 25,27:1
Beautiful Dreamer 1960,D 28,22:1
Music Man, The 1965,Je 17,26:4
Guys and Dolls 1966,Je 9,55:2
Schlegel, John (Playwright)
Take a Gander 1956,D 14,36:4
Schlegel, Kurt
Anneliese von Dessau 1926,F 26,24:3
Schlegel (Translator)
Taming of the Shrew, The 1933,N 5,IX,3:1
Richard III 1937,My 30,X,2:1
Schlein, Israel
Untitled-Recital 1931,Mr 23,24:3
Schlein, Jack
Mascaiada 1929,D 28,10:6
Schlenk, Josephine
Gala Night 1930,F 26,22:4
Schlesinger, G S (Producer)
Strangers at Home 1934,S 15,20:5
Schlesinger, John
King Lear 1950,Ag 30,26:2
Schlesinger, M S (Producer)
Locked Room, The 1933,D 26,18:5
Strangers at Home 1934,S 15,20:5
Schlesser, Andre
Bal des Voleurs, Le 1938,N 29,26:4
Faiseur, Le; Promoter, The 1938,D 27,12:3
Paquebot Tenacity, Le 1939,Ja 10,16:4
Chacun Sa Verite 1939,Ja 24,17:1
Enterrement, L' 1939,F 7,17:2
37 Sous de M Montaudoin, Les 1939,F 7,17:2
Siegfried 1939,F 21,15:2
Barbier de Seville, Le 1939,Mr 7,19:2
Don Juan 1958,O 29,29:1
Schlessinger, Roslyn
Knight of the Burning Pestle, The 1927,Ap 23,15:1
Schley, Karl Maria
Rhinoceros 1959,N 2,41:1
Hunger und Durst 1965,Ja 19,28:6
Ratten, Die 1966,Ap 13,36:1
Schlichting, Louise
Dear Brutus 1926,Jl 15,21:3
Schlick, Frederick (Playwright)
Joy of Serpents 1930,Ap 4,22:4
Bloodstream 1932,Mr 31,25:1
Schlitt, Edward
Joan of Arc-The Warrior Maid 1931,N 9,21:6
Schlitt, Genia
Three Cities 1938,O 11,20:3
Who Is Who? 1938,D 24,13:3
Water Carrier, The 1939,Jl 2,IX,1:6
Schlitt, Robert (Translator)
Egg, The 1962,Ja 9,23:2
Schloss, Marjorie
H M S Pinafore 1949,Jl 29,13:2
Schloss, Sybele
Pepper Mill 1937,Ja 6,19:4

Schlossberg, Jerry (Producer)
Gantry 1970,F 16,44:1
Room Service 1970,My 13,49:1
Charley's Aunt 1970,Jl 6,38:1
Schlosser, Elise
Legend of Leonora, The 1926,My 1,10:1
Schlosser, Peter (Composer)
Here Be Dragons 1970,D 21,52:1
Schluetter, Giselz
Raetzel um Beate 1936,N 8,X,2:1
Schly, Lucile
Cradle Will Rock, The 1937,D 6,19:4
Cradle Will Rock, The 1938,Ja 4,19:3
Schmid, Aglaja
Maria Stuart 1968,Mr 27,38:1
Schmid, Helen
Diamond Lil 1948,N 30,33:2
Schmid, Helmut
Wozzeck 1966,Ap 6,34:1
Schmid, Josef (Musical Director)
Private Life of the Master Race, The 1945,Je 13,28:3
Galileo 1947,D 8,34:2
Schmid, Lars (Producer)
My Fair Lady 1962,S 7,34:1
Schmidlapp, W Horace (Miscellaneous)
Count Me In 1942,O 9,24:2
South Pacific 1943,D 30,11:2
Schmidlapp, W Horace (Producer)
Walk With Music 1940,Je 5,33:2
Boyd's Daughter 1940,O 12,20:2
Return Engagement 1940,N 2,19:2
Polonaise 1945,O 8,20:2
Schmidt, Adolph
Scarlet Coat, The 1924,D 24,11:1
Schmidt, Ann
Critic, The 1925,My 9,12:4
Wise-Crackers, The 1925,D 17,26:1
Bad Habits of 1926 1926,My 1,11:1
Straw Hat, The 1926,O 15,20:2
Trumpet Shall Sound, The 1926,D 11,15:2
Doctor Knock 1928,F 24,15:2
Schmidt, Barbara
Five Little Peppers, The 1952,My 19,13:1
Schmidt, Carl
Shadow, The 1923,D 15,16:2
Fedora 1924,Ja 24,14:2
Schmidt, Douglas W (Costume Designer)
Landscape 1970,Ap 3,43:1
Silence 1970,Ap 3,43:1
Schmidt, Douglas W (Scenic Designer)
Ox Cart, The 1966,D 20,58:1
To Bury a Cousin 1967,My 17,38:3
King John 1967,Jl 14,19:1
Great White Hope, The 1967,D 14,58:1
Memorandum, The 1968,My 6,55:1
Huui, Huui 1968,N 25,58:1
Acquisition, The 1968,D 31,19:1
This Bird of Dawning Singeth All Night Long 1968,D 31,19:1
Young Master Dante, The 1968,D 31,19:1
Parents and Children 1969,Ja 13,26:6
Geese 1969,Ja 13,26:6
Inner Journey, The 1969,Mr 21,42:1
Twelfth Night 1969,Ag 14,29:2
Time of Your Life, The 1969,N 7,37:1
Disintegration of James Cherry, The 1970,Ja 30,33:3
Paris Is Out! 1970,F 3,35:1
Operation Sidewinder 1970,Mr 13,33:1
Landscape 1970,Ap 3,43:1
Silence 1970,Ap 3,43:1
Good Woman of Setzuan, The 1970,N 6,51:1
Schmidt, Francelia
Lady Says Yes, A 1945,Ja 11,18:5
Schmidt, Frank (Miscellaneous)
Yes is for a Very Young Man 1963,Mr 6,7:5
Schmidt, Harvey (Composer)
Fantasticks, The 1960,My 4,55:2
110 in the Shade 1963,O 25,37:1
I Do! I Do! 1966,D 6,58:1
I Do! I Do! 1966,D 18,II,3:1
I Do! I Do! 1967,N 28,54:1
Celebration 1969,Ja 23,55:2
Colette 1970,My 7,60:1
Colette 1970,My 17,II,1:1
Colette 1970,O 15,58:1
Schmidt, Harvey (Lyricist)
Shoestring '57 1956,N 6,31:1
Schmidt, Harvey (Playwright)
Celebration 1969,F 2,II,3:1
Schmidt, John
Polonaise 1945,O 8,20:2
Out of This World 1950,D 22,17:3
Schmidt, Joseph
Three Musketeers 1929,O 13,IX,4:7
Schmidt, Jules
Elizabeth Sleeps Out 1935,Ag 27,23:4
Romance 1937,Ag 17,23:1
Cradle Will Rock, The 1938,Ja 4,19:3
Schmidt, Lars (Producer)
My Fair Lady 1961,O 26,40:1

Schmidt, M (Scenic Designer)
David's Crown 1948,My 10,26:2
Schmidt, Margarete
Lebende Leichnam, Der, Der; Living Corpse, The 1928,Ja 24,26:2
Schmidt, Marie
Blue Butterfly, The 1929,F 17,29:3
Schmiedel, Hans (Playwright)
Chinese Nightingale, The 1934,O 6,20:4
Schmieder, Willy
Redemption: Lebende Leichnam, Der; Living Corpse, The 1928,N 20,28:2
Schmieit, Wilhelm
Abraham Lincoln 1934,D 1,8:6
Schmitt, Charles
Waiting for Godot 1968,Ap 23,38:1
Schmitt, Frank (Miscellaneous)
Widowers' Houses 1959,Mr 3,39:2
Misalliance 1961,S 26,32:2
Bedlam Galore, for Two or More 1965,Mr 8,34:1
Impromptu, L' 1965,Mr 8,34:1
Foursome 1965,Mr 8,34:1
Leader, The 1965,Mr 8,34:1
Death of the Well-Loved Boy, The 1967,My 16,48:1
Millionairess, The 1969,Mr 3,28:1
Schmitt, Fritz
Passion Play, The 1929,Ap 30,32:1
Schmitt, Gregor (Playwright)
Don Juan's Raincoat 1933,O 22,IX,2:3
Schmoll, Warren
Oklahoma! 1951,My 30,15:2
Schmorr, Robert
Iolanthe 1962,Ag 8,34:2
Schmucki, Norbert (Choreographer)
Malade Imaginaire, Le 1970,F 18,40:2
Schnabel, Stefan
Julius Caesar 1937,N 12,26:6
Shoemaker's Holiday, The 1938,Ja 3,17:2
Glamour Preferred 1940,N 16,13:2
Everyman 1941,My 9,19:2
Land of Fame 1943,S 22,31:5
Cherry Orchard, The 1944,Ja 26,22:1
Around the World 1946,Je 1,9:5
Faust 1947,N 29,9:2
Now I Lay Me Down to Sleep 1950,Mr 3,21:2
Idiot's Delight 1951,My 24,46:3
Love of Four Colonels, The 1953,Ja 16,17:2
Plain and Fancy 1955,Ja 28,14:2
Plain and Fancy 1955,F 6,II,1:1
Small War on Murray Hill 1957,Ja 4,19:1
Small War on Murray Hill 1957,Ja 13,II,1:1
Dreigroschenoper, Die 1965,Mr 12,24:1
Tango 1969,Ja 20,33:1
In the Matter of J Robert Oppenheimer 1969,Mr 7,28:1
Patriot for Me, A 1969,O 6,58:1
Schnapier, Alan Jay
Out West of Eighth 1951,S 21,20:3
Schnee, Charles (Playwright)
Apology 1943,Mr 23,14:2
Schnee, Thelma
Flight Into China 1939,S 12,28:1
World We Make, The 1939,N 21,19:1
World We Make, The 1939,D 3,IX,5:1
Corn Is Green, The 1940,N 27,27:2
Proof Thro' the Night 1942,D 26,14:2
Apology 1943,Mr 23,14:2
Next Half Hour, The 1945,O 30,14:6
Tower Beyond Tragedy, The 1950,N 27,29:1
Schnee, Thelma (Playwright)
Whole World Over, The 1947,Mr 28,28:2
Whole World Over, The 1947,Ap 6,II,1:1
Schneider, Alan
Storm Operation 1944,Ja 12,28:2
Schneider, Alan (Director)
All Summer Long 1953,Ja 29,23:1
Remarkable Mr Pennypacker, The 1953,D 31,11:2
All Summer Long 1954,S 24,26:2
All Summer Long 1954,O 3,II,1:1
Anastasia 1954,D 30,13:1
Anastasia 1955,Ja 16,II,1:1
Skin of Our Teeth, The 1955,Ag 18,16:1
Skin of Our Teeth, The 1955,Ag 28,II,1:1
Little Glass Clock, The 1956,Mr 27,40:2
View From the Bridge, A 1956,N 9,34:4
Glass Menagerie, The 1956,N 22,50:1
Glass Menagerie, The 1956,D 2,II,1:1
Miss Lonelyhearts 1957,O 4,26:2
Endgame 1958,Ja 29,32:4
Endgame 1958,F 16,II,1:1
Kataki 1959,Ap 10,24:1
Summer of the Seventeenth Doll 1959,O 14,52:1
Clandestine on the Morning Line 1959,D 5,18:2
Krapp's Last Tape 1960,Ja 15,37:2
Krapp's Last Tape 1960,Ja 31,II,1:1
Measure for Measure 1960,Jl 27,33:1
American Dream, The 1961,Ja 25,28:1
Happy Days 1961,S 18,36:1
Caucasian Chalk Circle, The 1961,N 1,35:1
Endgame 1962,F 12,27:1
Burning of the Lepers, The 1962,Ap 5,29:1
Who's Afraid of Virginia Woolf? 1962,O 15,33:1

Who's Afraid of Virginia Woolf? 1962,O 28,II,1:1
Who's Afraid of Virginia Woolf? 1962,N 1,34:1
Collection, The 1962,N 27,44:1
Dumbwaiter, The 1962,N 27,44:1
Ballad of the Sad Cafe, The 1963,O 31,27:1
Ballad of the Sad Cafe, The 1963,N 10,II,1:1
Lover, The 1964,Ja 6,35:1
Play 1964,Ja 6,35:1
Play 1964,Mr 25,46:2
Glass Menagerie, The 1964,Jl 20,18:3
Tiny Alice 1964,D 30,14:2
Tiny Alice 1965,Ja 10,II,1:1
Do Not Pass Go 1965,Ap 20,44:1
Krapp's Last Tape 1965,Je 9,42:3
Entertaining Mr Sloane 1965,O 13,41:1
Malcolm 1966,Ja 12,29:1
Gnadiges Fraulein, The 1966,F 23,42:1
Mutilated, The 1966,F 23,42:1
Delicate Balance, A 1966,S 23,44:1
Delicate Balance, A 1966,O 2,II,1:1
You Know I Can't Hear You When the Water's Running; I'll Be Home for Christmas 1967,Mr 14,54:1
You Know I Can't Hear You When the Water's Running; I'm Herbert 1967,Mr 14,54:1
You Know I Can't Hear You When the Water's Running; Shock of Recognition, The 1967,Mr 14,54:1
You Know I Can't Hear You When the Water's Running; Footsteps of Doves, The 1967,Mr 14,54:1
You Know I Can't Hear You When the Water's Running 1967,Mr 26,II,1:1
Birthday Party, The 1967,O 4,40:2
Birthday Party, The 1967,O 15,II,1:1
I Never Sang for My Father 1968,Ja 26,30:1
Box-Mao-Box; Quotations From Chairman Mao Tse-Tung 1968,Mr 8,48:1
Box-Mao-Box; Box 1968,Mr 8,48:1
You Know I Can't Hear You When the Water's Running 1968,Mr 29,33:1
Box 1968,O 1,39:1
Quotations From Chairman Mao Tse-Tung 1968,O 1,39:1
Zoo Story, The 1968,O 11,41:1
Krapp's Last Tape 1968,O 11,41:1
Box 1968,O 13,II,5:1
Quotations From Chairman Mao Tse-Tung 1968,O 13,II,5:1
Happy Days 1968,O 14,54:1
Watering Place, The 1969,Mr 13,51:1
Gingham Dog, The 1969,Ap 24,41:1
Blood Red Roses 1970,Mr 23,48:1
Inquest 1970,Ap 24,38:1
Saved 1970,O 29,57:1
Saved 1970,N 1,II,10:1
Schneider, Alan (Miscellaneous)
From Morn Till Midnight 1948,D 7,41:6
Tonight in Samarkand 1955,F 17,22:2
Strada, La 1969,D 15,63:1
Schneider, Alan (Original Author)
I Never Sang for My Father 1968,F 4,II,1:1
Schneider, Alan (Producer)
Trip to Bountiful, The 1956,Jl 5,25:1
Schneider, Alexander
Soldier's Tale, A 1955,Jl 13,21:2
Schneider, B
Deluge, The 1927,Ja 11,36:2
Schneider, Barbara
Walk in Darkness 1963,O 29,30:2
Schneider, Benno
Dybbuk, The 1926,D 14,24:2
Eternal Jew, The 1926,D 21,21:2
Jacob's Dream 1927,Ja 4,20:2
200,000 1936,N 29,XII,3:3
Schneider, Benno (Director)
Third Parade, The 1933,O 23,18:2
Yegor Bulevitch 1934,Ja 8,21:7
Recruits 1934,O 13,10:4
Dostigayev 1935,Ja 14,10:5
Recruits 1935,Ja 20,X,3:1
Aristocrats 1935,My 2,16:2
Reapers, The 1935,O 7,11:4
Haunch, Paunch and Jowl 1935,D 27,22:4
Hirsh Lekert 1936,Mr 11,23:2
200,000 1936,O 14,30:2
But for the Grace of God 1937,Ja 13,21:4
Outlaw, The 1937,O 6,28:1
Outlaw, The 1937,N 8,18:2
Mazal Tov 1938,My 23,21:3
Liliom 1940,Mr 26,17:2
Strange Bedfellows 1948,Ja 15,27:3
Schneider, Carl
Passion Play, The 1929,Ap 30,32:1
Schneider, Charles (Choreographer)
Your Own Thing 1968,Ja 15,33:1
Schneider, Charles (Miscellaneous)
Ice Capades 1967,Je 2,33:1
Schneider, Charles (Musical Director)
Your Own Thing 1968,Ja 15,33:1
Schneider, Edouard (Playwright)
Exaltation, L' 1929,Mr 10,X,1:8

Schneider, Edward
Devil's Little Game, The 1932,Ag 2,20:4
Tragedy of the Ages, The 1933,Ap 7,22:7
Schneider, Gus (Scenic Designer)
On Borrowed Time 1953,Ja 1,19:1
Schneider, Irving
Merrily We Roll Along 1934,O 1,14:1
Schneider, Irving (Miscellaneous)
Chalk Garden, The 1955,O 27,29:1
Schneider, Phyllis
Measure for Measure 1966,Jl 14,27:1
Schneider, Robert C
Every Other Evil 1961,Ja 23,20:2
Schneider, Roy R
Henry IV, Part I 1962,Je 18,20:4
All the King's Men 1963,Jl 12,12:1
Serjeant Musgrave's Dance 1966,Mr 9,44:1
Stephen D 1967,S 25,58:1
Schneider, Samuel
Centuries, The 1927,N 30,23:1
Singing Jailbirds 1928,D 5,34:4
Airways, Inc 1929,F 21,30:5
First Law, The 1929,My 7,28:4
Man on Stilts, The 1931,S 10,23:2
Keeping Expenses Down 1932,O 21,25:2
Schneider, Schorling
Possibilities 1968,D 5,60:1
Schneider, Selma (Choreographer)
Shylock and His Daughter 1947,S 30,22:2
Hershel, The Jester 1948,D 14,39:2
Schneider, Stan
Threepenny Opera, The 1954,Mr 11,26:5
Schneider, Vern (Original Author)
Teahouse of the August Moon, The 1953,O 25,II,1:1
Teahouse of the August Moon, The 1954,S 12,II,1:1
Schneider, Walter J (Miscellaneous)
Littlest Circus, The 1959,D 26,5:6
Schneiderman, Abraham (Scenic Designer)
Kith and Kin 1930,My 14,31:1
Schneiderman, M
Dostigayev 1935,Ja 14,10:5
Aristocrats 1935,My 2,16:2
Hirsh Lekert 1936,Mr 11,23:2
Schneidler, Ellen
Terminal 1970,Ap 15,51:2
Schneier, Chaim
Neveile, The 1924,F 9,16:2
Schneier, Monroe (Playwright)
Poppa Is Home 1961,D 20,37:1
Schneir, Mirriam (Playwright)
Inquest 1970,Ap 24,38:1
Schneir, Walter (Playwright)
Inquest 1970,Ap 24,38:1
Schnelder, Alan (Director)
Long Way From Home, A 1948,F 9,25:2
Schnell, G H
Redemption: Lebende Leichnam, Der; Living Corpse, The 1928,N 20,28:2
Schneuer, Chaim
He, She and the Ox 1934,F 21,22:7
In-Laws 1934,O 25,28:2
Jealousy 1934,D 20,31:4
60,000 Heroes 1935,Ja 28,11:5
Motke Ganef 1935,Mr 18,15:2
Schnitzer, Henrietta
Naomi 1920,My 7,12:2
One Life for Another 1920,D 18,11:2
Alexander Pushkin 1928,Ja 27,14:2
Mazal Darf Men; You Need Luck 1938,My 18,16:5
Schnitzer, Robert C
Half Moon Inn 1925,Mr 10,14:1
Contrast, The 1926,O 1,26:2
Hamlet 1928,Ja 5,33:2
Caponsacchi 1928,Ja 25,20:3
Richelieu 1929,D 26,20:3
First Night 1930,N 27,32:3
Electra 1932,Ja 9,21:4
Richelieu 1934,My 22,28:1
Hamlet 1934,D 26,19:3
Richard III 1934,D 28,24:3
Cyrano de Bergerac 1936,Ap 28,17:1
Schnitzer, Robert C (Miscellaneous)
Glass Menagerie, The 1961,Je 16,27:3
Schnitzer, Robert C (Producer)
E-MC2 1948,Je 16,36:2
Schnitzler, Arthur (Original Author)
Fraeulein Elsa 1932,D 18,X,5:8
Gay Life, The 1961,N 20,38:1
Schnitzler, Arthur (Playwright)
Last Masks 1920,Ap 4,VI,6:1
Call of Life, The 1925,O 10,10:1
Bridal Veil, The 1928,Ja 27,15:2
Playing With Love 1929,F 27,16:4
Green Cockatoo, The 1930,O 10,20:5
Anatol 1931,Ja 17,23:3
Lonely Way, The 1931,F 22,VIII,4:1
Gang zum Weiher, Der 1931,Ap 5,VIII,1:6
Ronde, La 1932,O 30,IX,3:7
Gallant Cassian 1934,N 14,22:2
Professor Bernhardi 1936,Jl 12,IX,1:8
Ronde, La 1955,Je 28,24:2

Schnitzler, Arthur (Playwright)—Cont
Ronde, La 1960,My 10,44:2
Professor Bernhardi 1968,Mr 20,38:1
Rondelay 1969,N 6,55:1
Schnitzler, Heinrich (Director)
Professor Bernhardi 1936,Jl 12,IX,1:8
Fledgling 1940,N 28,29:2
Schnuzel, Reinhold
Marinka 1945,Jl 19,19:2
Schnyder, Theodore
Bitter Sweet 1934,My 8,28:4
Schoch, Hedwig
Plumes in the Dust 1936,N 7,14:2
Schochen, Seyril (Lyricist)
Tiger Rag, The 1961,F 17,20:2
Schochen, Seyril (Playwright)
Moon Besieged, The 1950,N 4,13:1
Tiger Rag, The 1961,F 17,20:2
Tiger Rag, The 1961,Mr 5,II,1:1
Moon Besieged, The 1962,D 6,54:1
Schockley, Marian
Prodigal Father, The 1937,Ag 17,23:1
Schoctor, Joseph H (Miscellaneous)
Peterpat 1965,Ja 7,27:1
Schoedinger, Ferd P
Little Theatre Tournament; Trifles 1928,My 11,28:1
Schoeller, Fritz
Passion Play, The 1929,Ap 30,32:1
Schoeller, William (Scenic Designer)
Years Between, The 1942,F 7,13:2
Schoeller, William F
Hate Planters 1933,My 26,24:5
Broomsticks Amen! 1934,F 10,20:4
Tomorrow's Harvest 1934,D 6,26:5
Escape Me Never! 1935,Ja 22,22:2
Fifth Column, The 1940,Mr 7,18:2
Searching Wind, The 1944,Ap 13,25:2
Schoemaker, Oscar
Jefferson Davis 1936,F 19,17:2
Schoemann, Albert (Miscellaneous)
Heloise 1958,S 25,28:4
O Marry Me 1961,O 28,13:1
Schoen, Judy
Red, White and Maddox 1969,Ja 27,27:1
Schoenberg, Bessie
Mascaiada 1929,D 28,10:6
Schoenberg, Edgar M (Playwright)
Mystery Ship, The 1927,Mr 15,28:2
People Don't Do Such Things 1927,N 24,28:3
Schoenberg, Mark (Director)
All the King's Men 1959,O 17,27:2
All the King's Men 1959,O 25,II,1:1
Here Come the Clowns 1960,S 20,48:1
Philoktetes 1961,Ap 25,41:1
Schoenemann, Franz
Fedora 1924,Ja 24,14:2
Versunkene Glocke, Die 1924,N 3,21:2
Wilhelm Tell 1925,Mr 2,15:1
Schoenfeld, Adam
Passion Play, The 1929,Ap 30,32:1
Schoenfeld, Barbara
Lysistrata 1968,N 15,42:1
Schoenfeld, Ben Zion
Abi Gezunt 1949,O 10,19:4
Sadie Is a Lady 1950,Ja 28,9:2
Wedding March, The 1955,O 17,33:1
Schoenfeld, Bernard C (Playwright)
Shooting Star 1933,Je 13,22:2
Hitch Your Wagon! 1937,Ap 9,18:2
Schoenfeld, Hannelore
Dallas-November 22d 1965,N 12,54:1
Schoenfeld, Mae
Abi Gezunt 1949,O 10,19:4
Sadie Is a Lady 1950,Ja 28,9:2
Take It Easy 1950,S 25,23:6
Second Marriage 1953,O 12,30:1
Wish Me Luck! 1954,N 1,37:2
Wedding March, The 1955,O 17,33:1
It's a Funny World 1956,O 22,24:1
It Could Happen to You 1957,O 28,30:5
Nice People 1958,O 20,36:1
Kosher Widow, The 1959,N 2,40:2
My Son and I 1960,O 24,24:2
Go Fight City Hall 1961,N 3,28:5
Schoenfelder, Friedrich
My Fair Lady 1962,Je 14,24:1
Schoenfield, Lynn
Miracle Worker, The 1959,O 20,44:1
Schoengold, Joseph
Wild Man, The 1930,My 17,21:5
Schoengold, Joseph (Director)
Wild Man, The 1930,My 17,21:5
Schoengold, Yetta
Spring Song 1934,O 2,18:2
Schoenherr, Carl (Playwright)
Children's Tragedy, The 1921,O 12,18:2
Schoenhut, George
Streets of New York, The 1934,Jl 21,14:5
Vinegar Tree, The 1935,Ag 14,16:1
Schoeni, Helen (Director)
Dutchman's Farm, A 1941,My 11,I,43:3
Schoeni, Helen (Playwright)
Dutchman's Farm, A 1941,My 11,I,43:3

Schoenstein, Waldemar
Passion Play, The 1929,Ap 30,32:1
Schoenthan, Franz (Playwright)
Rape of the Sabine Women, The 1949,F 5,10:5
Schoenthan, Paul V (Playwright)
Rape of the Sabine Women, The 1949,F 5,10:5
Schoesmith, Thomas (Lighting Director)
And I Met a Man 1970,Ap 11,20:3
Schoetz, Joni
Three Philip Roth Stories; Conversion of the Jews 1970,Jl 31,14:1
Cops and Horrors; Fly Paper 1970,Ag 11,27:1
Cops and Horrors; Dracula 1970,Ag 11,27:1
Schofield, Charles (Director)
Scrap Book 1932,Ag 2,20:3
Jefferson Davis 1936,F 19,17:2
Schofield, Charles I
Welcome Stranger 1920,S 14,12:1
New Sin, The 1923,My 28,18:3
Scrap Book 1932,Ag 2,20:3
Schofield, Edgar
Apothecary, The 1926,Mr 17,28:1
Schofield, Frank
Mary of Magdala 1946,Mr 26,24:5
In Good King Charles's Golden Days 1957,Ja 25,16:1
In Good King Charles's Golden Days 1957,F 3,II,1:1
As You Like It 1963,Jl 17,19:2
Twelfth Night 1963,O 9,47:1
Sign in Sidney Brustein's Window, The 1964,O 16,32:1
Troilus and Cressida 1965,Ag 13,17:1
Schofield, Scharles
Clinging Vine, The 1922,D 25,20:2
Scholfield, Eileen
Vaudeville (Palace) 1924,O 21,21:2
Scholl, Danny
Winged Victory 1943,N 22,24:1
Call Me Mister 1946,Ap 19,26:2
Texas Li'l Darlin' 1949,N 26,10:5
Scholl, Jack (Lyricist)
Keep Moving 1934,Ag 24,10:2
Scholl, John Jay (Miscellaneous)
Juno and the Paycock 1926,Mr 16,22:1
Scholl, John Jay (Producer)
Comic, The 1927,Ap 20,28:2
Scholl, Richard (Miscellaneous)
Firstborn, The 1957,Ja 7,29:2
Scholle, Jackie
Remarkable Mr Pennypacker, The 1953,D 31,11:2
Scholle, Lewis
Sleepy Hollow 1948,Je 4,26:3
Ah, Wilderness! 1953,F 7,10:6
Remarkable Mr Pennypacker, The 1953,D 31,11:2
Scholz, August (Playwright)
Lebende Leichnam, Der, Der; Living Corpse, The 1928,Ja 24,26:2
Redemption: Lebende Leichnam, Der; Living Corpse, The 1928,N 20,28:2
Scholz, Edwin
Ruddigore 1965,Ag 27,16:1
Scholz, Walter Rosen (Miscellaneous)
Happy Birthday, Wanda June 1970,O 8,58:2
Scholz, Wilhelm von
Race With the Shadow, The 1927,Ap 7,23:1
Scholz, Wilhelm von (Playwright)
Race With the Shadow, The 1927,Ap 7,23:1
Scholz, Will
Stevedore 1949,F 23,30:2
Peter Pan 1950,Ap 25,27:2
Detective Story 1954,F 13,11:2
Schomberg, Hermann
Faust, Part I; Prelude in the Theater 1961,F 5,27:2
Faust, Part I; Prologue in Heaven 1961,F 5,27:2
Faust, Part I; Play, The 1961,F 5,27:2
Schon, Bonnie
Noel Coward's Sweet Potato 1968,O 13,II,5:1
Schon, John
How to Make a Man 1961,F 3,16:1
Schon, Kenneth
Night in Venice, A 1952,Je 27,18:6
My Darlin' Aida 1952,O 28,36:4
Schonbach, Dieter (Composer)
Schloss, Das 1968,N 20,35:3
Schonbrun, Sheila
Play of Herod, The 1963,D 10,55:2
Play of Daniel, The 1966,Ja 2,64:4
Schoner, Carl (Playwright)
Thy Name Is Woman 1920,N 16,19:1
Schonherr, Karl (Original Author)
Kindertragoedie; Children's Tragedy, The 1931,D 27,VIII,3:1
Schonning, Soffi
Casanova 1932,Je 19,IX,2:1
School, Danny
Call Me Mister 1946,Ap 28,II,1:1
Schooler, Dave (Producer)
Brittle Heaven 1934,N 14,22:5
Schooler, Louis
Cape Smoke 1925,F 17,19:1
Make Me Know It 1929,N 5,32:5

Schooler, Zvi
Back Streets 1933,My 18,17:4
Schools, Victoria
Best Foot Forward 1941,S 12,24:4
Best Foot Forward 1941,O 2,28:2
Schoop, Trudi
All for Love 1938,Ap 5,19:4
Schoop, Trudi (Choreographer)
My L A 1951,D 9,87:1
Schorr, Anschel (Director)
Pinye of Pinchev 1936,S 21,27:5
Schorr, Anschel (Playwright)
One in a Million 1934,N 17,13:2
Mazel Tov, Rabbi 1938,N 28,10:4
Schorr, Bert
Abe Lincoln in Illinois 1938,O 17,12:2
Schorr, Freya
Summer Wives 1936,Ap 14,18:1
Schorr, Salche
Honeymoon for Three, A 1933,Ja 30,9:6
Stepsisters 1936,O 13,32:3
Schorr, Sally
Love and Politics 1929,O 21,30:7
Slaves of Luxury 1930,F 8,13:3
Sonitchka 1930,Mr 8,21:3
Russian Love 1930,N 27,32:3
My Little Girl 1931,F 2,22:4
Night in the Woods, A 1931,Mr 2,19:3
Victims of Life 1931,O 21,26:2
Rich Paupers 1932,Mr 14,13:4
Big Surprise, The 1932,O 17,18:3
Jewish Melody, The 1933,Mr 27,12:4
Longing for Home 1933,S 22,15:1
Slaves of the Public 1934,Mr 10,18:6
Of One Mother 1937,Ja 18,21:3
Me and Molly 1948,F 27,27:2
Schorr, William (Director)
Six Characters in Search of an Author 1931,Ap 16,29:2
Milky Way, The 1934,My 9,23:2
Birthday 1934,D 27,24:2
Stork Mad 1936,O 1,28:4
Ring Around Elizabeth 1941,N 18,32:2
Bloomer Girl 1944,O 6,18:5
Schorr, William (Producer)
Ring Around Elizabeth 1941,N 18,32:2
Schott, Christian (Lighting Director)
Faust, Part I; Prologue in Heaven 1961,F 5,27:2
Faust, Part I; Play, The 1961,F 5,27:2
Faust, Part I; Prelude in the Theater 1961,F 5,27:2
Schoukhaeff, V (Scenic Designer)
Chauve-Souris 1924,D 14,VIII,6:1
Schraeder, Marie B (Playwright)
Wildcat, The 1921,N 28,16:2
Schraffs, Ernest (Costume Designer)
H M S Pinafore 1926,Ap 7,26:3
Schrager, Charlotte
Merchant of Venice, The 1955,Jl 1,13:1
Schrager, Edythe
Mikado, The 1939,Mr 11,15:6
Schramm, Eunice
Patience 1928,Je 26,29:3
Fatal Lady, The 1936,Mr 19,23:7
Schrank, Joseph (Playwright)
Page Miss Glory 1934,N 28,24:2
Good Hunting 1938,N 22,26:5
Pins and Needles 1939,Ap 21,26:2
New Pins and Needles 1939,N 21,19:2
Schrapps, Ernest (Costume Designer)
Two Orphans, The 1926,Ap 6,26:2
Red Robe, The 1928,D 26,15:1
Wonderful Night, A; Fledermaus, Die 1929,N 1,23:3
Three Little Girls 1930,Ap 15,29:1
Artists and Models 1930,Je 11,33:2
Everybody's Welcome 1931,O 14,26:3
School for Scandal, The 1931,N 11,26:4
If Booth Had Missed 1932,F 5,24:2
Perfect Marriage, The 1932,N 17,23:2
Music Hath Charms 1934,D 31,8:2
Corn Is Green, The 1940,N 27,27:2
Romantic Mr Dickens 1940,D 3,33:2
Night of Love 1941,Ja 8,14:2
Corn Is Green, The 1943,My 4,18:3
Catherine Was Great 1944,Ag 3,16:1
Up in Central Park 1945,Ja 29,17:2
Dark of the Moon 1945,Mr 15,27:2
Up in Central Park 1947,My 20,29:2
Set My People Free 1948,N 4,38:2
Silver Whistle, The 1948,N 25,49:2
Schratt, Peter
Professor Bernhardi 1968,Mr 20,38:1
Maria Stuart 1968,Mr 27,38:1
Schreck, Charles (Miscellaneous)
Veronica's Veil 1950,F 12,II,1:5
Schreck, Everett
Saint's Parade 1930,N 1,23:4
Schreck, William F (Miscellaneous)
Veronica's Veil 1950,F 12,II,1:5
Schreiber, Avery
Open Season at Second City 1964,Ja 23,25:1
Schreiber, Avery (Director)
How to Be a Jewish Mother 1967,D 29,18:1

Schreiber, Elizabeth
Bridge, The 1930,My 6,33:1
Schreiber, O
Yegor Bulevitch 1934,Ja 8,21:7
Schreiner, Warner
Apollo of Bellac, The 1958,Mr 7,17:2
Schreuer, Carl (Miscellaneous)
Rats of Norway, The 1948,Ap 16,27:6
Schreuers, Dick (Choreographer)
Mexicana 1939,My 7,X,3:1
Schreyvogel, Friedrich (Translator)
Elizabeth and Essex 1935,N 9,18:8
Schrieber, Maribeth
Yes, My Darling Daughter 1938,Jl 13,19:2
Bachelor Born 1938,Ag 17,23:1
Schrock, Robert
Dirtiest Show in Town, The 1970,My 2,21:1
Dirtiest Show in Town, The 1970,Je 29,43:2
Schrode, Joseph
Passing Show of 1921, The 1920,D 30,16:2
Criss Cross 1926,O 13,20:2
Black Crook, The 1929,Mr 12,26:5
Babes in Toyland 1929,D 24,15:3
Schroder, Friedrich Ludwig (Translator)
Diener Zweier Herren; Servant of Two Masters, The 1928,Ja 10,28:3
Schroeder, Aaron (Producer)
Babes in the Wood 1964,D 29,21:2
Schroeder, Michael
Have I Got One for You 1968,Ja 8,32:1
Schroeder, Mildred
Play, Genius, Play! 1935,O 31,17:2
Frederika 1937,F 5,16:5
Schroeder-Schrom
General Percy Gruendet ein Koenigreich 1932,N 6,IX,3:1
Schroeders, George
High Button Shoes 1955,Mr 12,10:6
Schroer, Joseph
Henry IV, Part I 1968,Je 30,54:7
Henry IV, Part II 1968,Jl 2,33:1
King Lear 1968,N 8,43:1
In the Matter of J Robert Oppenheimer 1969,Mr 7,28:1
Miser, The 1969,My 9,35:1
Year Boston Won the Pennant, The 1969,My 23,38:1
Schrogin, J
Aristocrats 1935,My 2,16:2
Schruers, Edward (Scenic Designer)
Infernal Machine, The 1937,D 13,22:7
On the Rocks 1938,Je 16,20:2
Schubert, Arland
Burning, The 1963,D 4,57:1
Schubert, Bernard S (Playwright)
Don Q Jr 1926,Ja 28,16:3
Schubert, Buddy
Decision 1929,My 28,37:3
City Haul 1929,D 31,14:4
Schubert, Franz (Composer)
Blossom Time 1921,S 30,10:1
Blossom Time 1921,O 9,VI,1:1
Blossom Time 1922,O 24,18:2
Blossom Time 1931,Mr 5,32:1
Blossom Time 1938,D 27,12:2
Blossom Time 1943,S 6,21:2
Schubert, Heinz
Kleinburgerhochzeit, Die 1970,N 25,25:1
Kurve, Die 1970,N 25,25:1
Schuchardt, Emil (Composer)
Why Do I Deserve This? 1966,Ja 19,31:2
Schuchatt, Isidor
Honeymoon for Three, A 1933,Ja 30,9:6
Jewish Melody, The 1933,Mr 27,12:4
Schuck, Karen
My Wife and I 1966,O 11,53:2
Schuette, Ernst (Scenic Designer)
Phaea 1930,Ag 31,VIII,2:1
Alt Heidelberg; Student Prince, The 1932,N 20,IX,3:3
Hamlet in Wittenberg 1936,N 15,XI,2:4
Schuetz, Adolph (Playwright)
Evelyne 1928,F 19,VIII,2:1
Schuh, Fritz (Director)
Irish Faustus, An 1963,D 19,40:1
Schuhplattlers, The
Ice Capades 1957,S 5,33:2
Schulberg, B P (Producer)
Tapestry in Gray 1935,D 28,10:2
Schulberg, Budd (Original Author)
Disenchanted, The 1958,D 4,53:4
What Makes Sammy Run? 1964,F 28,19:1
Schulberg, Budd (Playwright)
Disenchanted, The 1958,D 4,53:4
Disenchanted, The 1959,Ja 11,II,1:1
What Makes Sammy Run? 1964,F 28,19:1
Schulberg, Stuart (Playwright)
What Makes Sammy Run? 1964,F 28,19:1
Schulman, Abraham (Playwright)
Bronx Express, 1968 1968,N 16,43:3
Schulman, Arnold
Come Back, Little Sheba 1950,F 16,28:5

Schulman, Arnold (Original Author)
Hole in the Head, A 1958,N 26,25:2
Schulman, Arnold (Playwright)
Hole in the Head, A 1957,Mr 1,15:1
Hole in the Head, A 1957,Mr 10,II,1:1
Jennie 1963,O 18,35:2
Golden Rainbow 1968,F 5,27:1
Schulman, Elvira
Knight of the Burning Pestle, The 1927,Ap 23,15:1
Schulman, Herman (Sgt)
Swing Sister Wac Swing 1944,Ja 4,20:4
Schulman, Joseph (Playwright)
Springtime Folly 1951,F 27,23:4
Schulman, Rose
Emperor Jones, The 1945,Ja 17,18:4
Schulman, Samuel (Producer)
Uncle Willie 1956,D 21,17:1
Schulmann, Walter Chorus
John Brown's Body 1952,D 16,43:5
Schults, Jeanne
Hamlet 1948,D 4,9:2
Schultz, Barbara
Desire Under the Elms 1952,Ja 17,23:4
Schultz, Bob
Jubilee 1935,O 14,20:1
Schultz, Charles
Never Say Horses 1951,D 7,34:4
Malice in Wonderland 1953,D 17,51:3
Schultz, Charles (Original Author)
You're a Good Man, Charlie Brown 1969,N 14,39:1
Schultz, Charles (Playwright)
You're a Good Man, Charlie Brown 1967,Mr 8,51:1
You're a Good Man, Charlie Brown 1967,Ap 9,II,1:1
Schultz, Charles M (Director)
Kongi's Harvest 1968,Ap 21,II,5:3
Schultz, Charlotte
Redemption: Lebende Leichnam, Der; Living Corpse, The 1928,N 20,28:2
Schultz, Chiz (Miscellaneous)
Witches' Sabbath 1962,Ap 20,22:2
Schultz, Chiz (Producer)
To Be Young Gifted and Black; World of Lorraine Hansberry, The 1969,Ja 3,15:1
Schultz, Elsia
No Mother to Guide Her 1933,D 26,18:5
Schultz, Eva-Katharina
Don Carlos 1964,N 25,40:1
Captain of Koepenick, The 1964,D 2,60:1
Schultz, Fritz
Liebling Adieu 1931,N 29,VIII,4:2
Schultz, Gloria
Kongi's Harvest 1968,Ap 15,49:1
Schultz, Kuni
Elliott Murphy's Aquashow 1956,Je 20,26:2
Schultz, Louis
Straw Hat, The 1937,D 31,8:2
Schultz, Michael
Benito Cereno 1964,N 2,62:2
Operation Sidewinder 1970,Mr 22,II,1:4
Schultz, Michael (Director)
Song of the Lusitanian Bogey, The 1968,Ja 3,52:1
Kongi's Harvest 1968,Ap 15,49:1
God Is a (Guess What?) 1968,D 18,56:1
Does a Tiger Wear a Necktie? 1969,F 26,38:1
Does a Tiger Wear a Necktie? 1969,Mr 16,II,4:5
Reckoning, The 1969,S 5,28:1
Reckoning, The 1969,S 14,II,1:1
Operation Sidewinder 1970,Mr 13,33:1
Sambo 1970,Jl 23,24:1
Schultz, Michael (Lighting Director)
Daddy Goodness 1968,Je 5,37:1
Schultz, Michael (Miscellaneous)
Miracle in Brooklyn 1966,Je 24,30:2
Pin Up 1966,Je 24,30:2
Venus-Shot 1966,Je 24,30:2
Child and the Dragon, The 1966,Je 24,30:2
Schultz, Ray
No Mother to Guide Her 1933,D 26,18:5
Taming of the Shrew, The 1935,O 1,27:3
Taming of the Shrew, The 1940,F 6,17:2
Schultze-Westrum, Edith
Wozzeck 1966,Ap 6,34:1
Schulz, Maximilian (Director)
Iphigenie in Tauris 1949,O 22,11:2
Schulz-Breiden, Eugene (Director)
Soliloquy 1938,N 29,26:4
Schulze-Berge, Rose
Little Theatre Tournament; Shall We Join the Ladies? 1929,My 9,34:3
Shall We Join the Ladies? 1929,My 12,28:3
Schumacher, Jann
Egoists, The 1959,O 14,52:2
Schumacher, Olga
Merry Widow, The 1931,S 8,39:1
Geisha, The 1931,O 6,35:4
Pirates of Penzance, The 1934,Ap 10,26:5
Iolanthe 1934,My 1,26:4
Schumacher, Robert
Awakening of Spring, The 1964,My 13,50:1
Shout From the Rooftops 1964,O 29,40:1
Schuman, Howard (Lyricist)
Up Eden 1968,N 27,42:1

Schuman, Howard (Playwright)
Up Eden 1968,N 27,42:1
Schuman, Wilfred
Brigadoon 1967,D 14,59:2
Schumann, Lieschen
Americans on the Rhine 1934,O 11,28:4
Schumann, Walter
3 for Tonight 1955,Ap 17,II,1:1
Schumann, Walter (Composer)
John Brown's Body 1953,F 16,17:2
3 for Tonight 1955,Ap 7,23:2
Schumann (Composer)
Veritable Histoire de Mignon, La 1927,F 20,VII,2:
Schumer, Henry (Miscellaneous)
Tidbits of 1946 1946,Jl 9,17:2
Schumer, Leo (Composer)
Razzle Dazzle 1951,F 20,21:1
Schumer, Yvette (Miscellaneous)
Plain and Fancy 1955,Ja 28,14:2
New Faces of 1956 1956,Je 15,32:1
Schumer, Yvette (Producer)
Winesburg, Ohio 1958,F 6,22:2
Half Horse, Half Alligator 1966,Mr 14,37:2
Schumm, Hans Josef
Red Rainbow, A 1953,S 15,37:4
Schunzel, Reinhold
He Who Gets Slapped 1946,Mr 21,31:4
He Who Gets Slapped 1946,Mr 31,II,1:1
Temper the Wind 1946,D 10,28:2
Temper the Wind 1947,Ja 12,II,1:1
Big Knife, The 1949,F 25,27:5
Big Knife, The 1949,Mr 6,II,1:1
Montserrat 1949,O 31,21:4
Schustek, Douglas M (Miscellaneous)
Rendezvous at Senlis 1961,F 28,39:2
Schuster, Betty
Candle-Light 1929,O 1,28:2
Schuster, Friedel
Kuss-und Sonst Gar Nichts, Ein 1933,N 19,IX,3:1
Schustik, Bill
Billy 1969,Mr 24,56:1
Love and Maple Syrup 1970,Ja 8,47:1
Schutt, William
Sun Showers 1923,F 6,14:2
Schutte, Ernst (Scenic Designer)
Fair Helen 1931,Ag 30,VIII,2:1
Schutz, George F (Producer)
Pierrot's Journey 1964,Ag 5,23:1
Schutz, Herbert (Miscellaneous)
Razzle Dazzle 1951,F 20,21:1
Schutzman, Harold
It Can't Happen Here 1936,O 28,30:1
Awake and Sing! 1938,D 23,16:6
Schuyler, Adele
Would-Be Gentleman, The 1928,O 2,34:1
Tomorrow and Tomorrow 1931,Ja 14,26:3
Schuyler, Margot Van R (Miscellaneous)
Halfway to Hell 1934,Ja 3,22:3
Schuyler, Phyllis
Magnolia 1923,Ag 28,12:3
Schuyler, Robert (Costume Designer)
Along Came a Spider 1963,My 28,33:1
Schuyler, Robert (Lighting Director)
Along Came a Spider 1963,My 28,33:1
Schuyler, Robert (Miscellaneous)
Along Came a Spider 1963,My 28,33:1
Schuyler, Robert (Scenic Designer)
Along Came a Spider 1963,My 28,33:1
Schwab, Buddy
Boy Friend, The 1954,O 1,20:1
Schwab, Buddy (Choreographer)
Boy Friend, The 1958,Ja 27,24:4
Fallout 1959,My 21,36:2
Step on a Crack 1962,O 18,48:1
Ben Bagley's New Cole Porter Revue 1965,D 23,20:1
Boy Friend, The 1970,Ap 26,II,5:7
Schwab, Buddy (Director)
Ben Bagley's New Cole Porter Revue 1965,D 23,20:1
Boy Friend, The 1970,Ap 15,54:1
Schwab, Buddy (Miscellaneous)
No Strings 1962,Mr 16,24:1
Schwab, Charles M (Composer)
Bare Facts 1926,Jl 19,13:3
New Yorkers, The 1927,Mr 11,24:3
Garrick Gaieties 1930,Je 5,29:2
Schwab, Evah
Subway, The 1929,Ja 26,15:1
Schwab, Laurence (Playwright)
Sweet Little Devil 1924,Ja 22,15:4
Captain Jinks 1925,S 9,22:1
Queen High 1926,S 9,21:2
Good News 1927,S 7,35:4
New Moon, The 1928,S 20,33:1
Follow Thru 1929,Ja 10,24:3
Three's a Crowd 1930,O 26,VIII,1:1
Free for All 1931,S 9,25:1
Humpty Dumpty 1932,S 18,IX,2:1
Take a Chance 1932,N 28,11:2
Hide and Seek 1934,Ag 7,20:2
New Moon, The 1942,Ag 19,14:2
New Moon, The 1944,My 18,16:2

hwab, Laurence (Producer)
Captain Jinks 1925,S 9,22:1
Queen High 1926,S 9,21:2
Desert Song, The 1926,D 1,24:2
Good News 1927,S 7,35:4
Follow Thru 1929,Ja 10,24:3
America's Sweetheart 1931,Ja 25,VIII,2:4
America's Sweetheart 1931,F 11,23:1
Free for All 1931,Ag 16,VIII,1:1
East Wind 1931,O 28,19:1
East Wind 1931,D 11,VIII,4:3
Take a Chance 1932,N 28,11:2
She Loves Me Not 1933,N 21,22:4
Hide and Seek 1934,Ag 7,20:2
Dance With Your Gods 1934,O 8,14:3
Page Miss Glory 1934,N 28,24:2
May Wine 1935,D 6,30:3
Knights of Song 1938,O 18,29:2
Beverly Hills 1940,N 8,24:2
Song of Norway 1951,Ja 11,28:5

hwab, Tony
Ah, Wilderness! 1969,N 9,86:1
Seven Days of Mourning 1969,D 17,64:1

hwab & Mandel (Producer)
Free for All 1931,S 9,25:1

hwaighofer, Hans
Untitled-Passion Play 1950,My 19,29:6
Passion of Christ, The 1960,My 18,46:1

hwalbach, Mary Ellen
Cock-A-Doodle Dandy 1955,N 4,26:5

hwanecke, Ellen
Gestern und Heute 1931,My 24,VIII,2:1
Verfl--- Geld, Das 1931,N 15,VIII,4:1
Frau Die Weiss Was Sie Will, Eine 1932,O 9,IX,3:7
Case of Youth, A 1940,Mr 25,10:3

hwaneke, Victor (Original Author)
Silver Box, The 1928,My 20,VIII,2:1

hwank, Dorothy
Red, Hot and Blue! 1936,O 30,26:3

hwartz, Arthur (Composer)
Grand Street Follies, The 1926,Je 16,23:2
New Yorkers, The 1927,Mr 11,24:3
Ned Wayburn's Gambols 1929,Ja 16,22:3
Little Show, The 1929,My 1,28:5
Grand Street Follies, The 1929,My 2,20:4
Second Little Show, The 1930,Ag 17,VIII,2:2
Second Little Show, The 1930,S 3,36:1
Prince Charming 1930,O 14,31:1
Three's a Crowd 1930,O 16,28:3
Band Wagon, The 1931,Je 7,VIII,8:1
Flying Colors 1932,S 16,24:2
Flying Colors 1932,O 9,IX,1:1
She Loves Me Not 1933,N 21,22:4
Revenge With Music 1934,N 29,33:5
Virginia 1937,S 3,13:2
Virginia 1937,S 12,XI,1:1
Virginia 1937,O 5,29:1
Stars in Your Eyes 1939,F 10,18:2
American Jubilee 1940,My 13,20:5
It's All Yours 1942,Mr 26,26:2
Park Avenue 1946,N 5,31:2
Inside U S A 1948,Mr 30,27:3
Inside U S A 1948,My 1,19:2
Inside U S A 1948,My 23,II,1:1
Tree Grows in Brooklyn, A 1951,Ap 20,24:3
Tree Grows in Brooklyn, A 1951,Ap 29,II,1:1
Tree Grows in Brooklyn, A 1951,My 20,II,1:1
By the Beautiful Sea 1954,Ap 9,20:1
By the Beautiful Sea 1954,Ap 18,II,1:1
Gay Life, The 1961,N 20,38:1
Jennie 1963,O 18,35:2

hwartz, Arthur (Lyricist)
Three's a Crowd 1930,O 16,28:3
Flying Colors 1932,S 16,24:2
Revenge With Music 1934,N 29,33:5
It's All Yours 1942,Mr 26,26:2
Jennie 1963,O 18,35:2

hwartz, Arthur (Miscellaneous)
Wake Up and Dream 1929,D 31,14:3

hwartz, Arthur (Musical Director)
Band Wagon, The 1931,Je 4,31:3

hwartz, Arthur (Playwright)
Revenge With Music 1934,N 29,33:5
At Home Abroad 1935,S 20,17:4
At Home Abroad 1935,O 27,IX,1:1
Between the Devil 1937,O 24,XI,2:1
Between the Devil 1937,D 23,24:5
Hilda Crane 1950,N 2,38:2

hwartz, Arthur (Producer)
Inside U S A 1948,My 1,19:2

hwartz, Ben (Composer)
Tales of Rigo 1927,My 31,25:3

hwartz, Ben (Lyricist)
Tales of Rigo 1927,My 31,25:3

hwartz, Bernie
Flies, The; Mouches, Les 1947,Ap 18,26:3
Tom Sawyer - Ballad of the Mississippi 1947,D 27,11:3

hwartz, Dan
Long Gallery, The 1958,Mr 7,17:2

hwartz, Dora
Straw Hat, The 1926,O 15,20:2

Schwartz, Eugene (Playwright)
Dragon, The 1963,Ap 10,32:1

Schwartz, Frances
Shepherd King, The 1955,O 13,36:2
Brothers Ashkenazi, The 1955,N 12,24:4

Schwartz, Gwen Gibson (Composer)
Political Party, A 1963,S 27,17:5

Schwartz, Gwen Gibson (Lyricist)
Political Party, A 1963,S 27,17:5

Schwartz, Gwen Gibson (Playwright)
Political Party, A 1963,S 27,17:5

Schwartz, Helene
Riot 1968,D 20,64:1

Schwartz, Herbert
Yours Truly 1927,Ja 26,16:5
Subway Express 1929,S 25,34:3

Schwartz, Howard (Director)
Riot 1968,D 20,64:1

Schwartz, Howard (Producer)
God Is Back, Black and Singing Gospel at the
Fortune Theater 1969,N 19,48:1

Schwartz, Jean (Composer)
Century Revue and the Midnight Rounders, The
1920,Jl 13,9:1
Passing Show of 1921, The 1920,D 30,16:2
Mimic World of 1921, The 1921,Ag 18,9:2
Make It Snappy 1922,Ap 14,20:2
Topics of 1923 1923,N 21,23:2
Innocent Eyes 1924,My 21,22:2
Passing Show of 1924, The 1924,S 4,13:4
Night in Spain, A 1927,My 4,28:2
Sunny Days 1928,F 9,29:1
Man in Dress Clothes, The 1937,Ag 24,24:4

Schwartz, Jean (Lyricist)
Man in Dress Clothes, The 1937,Ag 24,24:4

Schwartz, Jerome J (Playwright)
Hotel Passionato 1965,O 23,16:1

Schwartz, Jon W (Producer)
Cast of Characters 1959,Je 11,37:2

Schwartz, Kenneth (Producer)
Once There Was a Russian 1961,F 20,32:2

Schwartz, Leonard (Director)
Nether-World 1938,O 22,15:2
Boom-Boom Clopper 1940,Ja 6,8:7

Schwartz, Maderia
No More Peace 1937,F 27,9:1

Schwartz, Marvin
Grass Is Always Greener, The 1955,F 16,25:2
Brothers Ashkenazi, The 1955,N 12,24:4
Backlane Center 1961,N 23,51:1
Sage of Rottenburg, The 1963,N 20,48:1

Schwartz, Marvin (Director)
Eleventh Inheritor, The 1962,N 22,43:5
Enchanting Melody 1964,N 25,40:1

Schwartz, Marvin (Miscellaneous)
Backlane Center 1961,N 23,51:1
Eleventh Inheritor, The 1962,N 22,43:5
Fifth Commandment, The 1965,N 15,48:4
Melody Lingers On, The 1969,N 17,55:1

Schwartz, Maurice
Andersh; New Worlds 1922,S 26,18:2
Inspector General, The 1922,O 9,15:4
King Saul 1925,S 18,26:3
Dybbuk, The 1926,Ja 6,16:2
Tenth Commandment, The 1926,N 18,27:1
Gardener's Dog, The 1927,O 21,27:1
Gold Diggers, The 1927,D 3,19:2
On Foreign Soil 1927,D 24,8:2
Alexander Pushkin 1928,Ja 27,14:2
American Chasidim 1928,Mr 17,8:8
Cherry Orchard, The 1928,N 8,26:8
God Man and Devil 1928,D 22,14:8
Othello 1929,F 4,21:2
Major Noah 1929,F 23,17:2
Stempenu, the Fiddler 1929,Mr 9,24:7
Jew Suss 1929,O 19,22:3
Angels on Earth 1929,D 11,34:7
Roaming Stars 1930,Ja 25,12:2
Chains 1930,F 23,29:2
Vaudeville (Palace) 1930,Ap 21,20:7
Merchant of Venice, The 1930,Ap 21,20:7
Tobias the Milkman 1930,Je 21,20:4
Witch of Castile, The 1930,O 25,21:1
Uncle Moses 1930,N 29,21:3
Riverside Drive 1931,Ja 6,24:2
Man With the Portfolio, The 1931,F 12,24:6
If I Were You 1931,S 24,21:1
Bloody Laughter 1931,D 5,20:6
Wolves 1932,Ja 7,26:3
New Man, The 1932,Ap 22,23:2
Yoshe Kalb 1932,O 3,15:5
Yoshe Kalb 1932,N 6,IX,2:1
Bread 1932,D 14,27:3
Revolt 1933,Ja 12,21:3
Wise Men of Chelm, The 1933,O 18,24:4
Josephus 1933,D 1,22:5
Yoshe Kalb 1935,Ag 25,X,1:3
Jacques Bergson 1936,O 31,24:6
Jacques Bergson 1936,N 29,XII,3:3
Borderline 1937,F 10,18:6
Brothers Ashkenazi, The 1937,S 21,28:6
Three Cities 1938,O 11,20:3
Who Is Who? 1938,D 24,13:3

Schwartz, Maurice—Cont
Yoshe Kalb 1939,F 6,9:2
Far-Away Corner, A 1939,F 15,15:2
Sarah Adler Testimonial 1939,Mr 15,18:2
Professor Schelling 1939,Jl 2,IX,1:6
Water Carrier, The 1939,Jl 2,IX,1:6
Vacation Follies 1939,Ag 30,15:6
Salvation 1939,S 29,19:2
Worlds Apart 1941,Ja 23,19:3
Day of Judgement, The 1941,O 9,27:3
Family Carnovsky, The 1943,O 19,16:7
Doctor Herzl 1945,D 21,25:4
Song of Dnieper 1946,O 26,10:5
Wandering Stars 1946,D 14,18:2
Shylock and His Daughter 1947,S 30,22:2
Shylock and His Daughter 1947,N 30,II,1:1
Voice of Israel, The 1948,O 26,40:2
Hershel, The Jester 1948,D 14,39:2
Yosele the Nightingale 1949,O 21,30:4
Conscience 1952,My 16,17:6
Grass Is Always Greener, The 1955,F 16,25:2
Miser, The 1955,Mr 18,34:2
Shepherd King, The 1955,O 13,36:2
Brothers Ashkenazi, The 1955,N 12,24:4
Hole in the Head, A 1958,N 26,25:2

Schwartz, Maurice (Director)
Morris, the Fiddler 1920,Ap 9,11:4
Thieves 1920,Ap 9,11:4
King Saul 1925,S 18,26:3
Tenth Commandment, The 1926,N 18,27:1
Gold Diggers, The 1927,D 3,19:2
On Foreign Soil 1927,D 24,8:2
Alexander Pushkin 1928,Ja 27,14:2
Kiddish Hashem 1928,S 30,IX,1:1
Major Noah 1929,F 23,17:2
Stempenu, the Fiddler 1929,Mr 9,24:7
Jew Suss 1929,O 19,22:3
Angels on Earth 1929,D 11,34:7
Roaming Stars 1930,Ja 25,12:2
Chains 1930,F 23,29:2
Witch of Castile, The 1930,O 25,21:1
Riverside Drive 1931,Ja 6,24:2
Man With the Portfolio, The 1931,F 12,24:6
If I Were You 1931,S 24,21:1
Bloody Laughter 1931,D 5,20:6
Wolves 1932,Ja 7,26:3
New Man, The 1932,Ap 22,23:2
Yoshe Kalb 1932,O 3,15:5
Yoshe Kalb 1932,N 6,IX,2:1
Yoshe Kalb 1932,D 18,X,3:1
Motke Ganef 1932,D 30,15:2
Revolt 1933,Ja 12,21:3
Wise Men of Chelm, The 1933,O 18,24:4
Josephus 1933,D 1,22:5
Yoshe Kalb 1933,D 29,27:2
Yoshe Kalb 1935,My 26,XI,2:2
Yoshe Kalb 1935,Jl 31,20:5
Jacques Bergson 1936,O 31,24:6
Jacques Bergson 1936,N 29,XII,3:3
Water Carrier, The 1936,D 25,20:2
Three Cities 1938,O 11,20:3
Who Is Who? 1938,D 24,13:3
Far-Away Corner, A 1939,F 15,15:2
If I Were Rothschild 1940,Ja 1,28:7
Esterke 1940,O 18,24:2
Worlds Apart 1941,Ja 23,19:3
Family Carnovsky, The 1943,O 19,16:7
Wandering Stars 1946,D 14,18:2
Shylock and His Daughter 1947,S 30,22:2
Voice of Israel, The 1948,O 26,40:2
Hershel, The Jester 1948,D 14,39:2
Conscience 1952,My 16,17:6
Grass Is Always Greener, The 1955,F 16,25:2
Miser, The 1955,Mr 18,34:2
Shepherd King, The 1955,O 13,36:2
Brothers Ashkenazi, The 1955,N 12,24:4
Hole in the Head, A 1958,N 26,25:2

Schwartz, Maurice (Miscellaneous)
Shylock and His Daughter 1947,S 30,22:2

Schwartz, Maurice (Playwright)
Tenth Commandment, The 1926,N 18,27:1
Kiddish Hashem 1928,S 30,IX,1:1
Stempenu, the Fiddler 1929,Mr 9,24:7
Jew Suss 1929,O 19,22:3
Roaming Stars 1930,Ja 25,12:2
Yoshe Kalb 1932,N 6,IX,2:1
Yoshe Kalb 1932,D 18,X,3:1
Josephus 1933,D 1,22:5
Brothers Ashkenazi, The 1937,S 21,28:6
Three Cities 1938,O 11,20:3
Yoshe Kalb 1939,F 6,9:2
Salvation 1939,S 29,19:2
If I Were Rothschild 1940,Ja 1,28:7
Day of Judgement, The 1941,O 9,27:3
Shylock and His Daughter 1947,N 30,II,1:1
Brothers Ashkenazi, The 1955,N 12,24:4
Hole in the Head, A 1958,N 26,25:2

Schwartz, Maurice (Producer)
Gardener's Dog, The 1927,O 21,27:1
Stempenu, the Fiddler 1929,Mr 9,24:7
Chains 1930,F 23,29:2
Witch of Castile, The 1930,O 25,21:1
Bloody Laughter 1931,D 5,20:6
Wolves 1932,Ja 7,26:3

Schwartz, Maurice (Producer)—Cont

Yoshe Kalb 1933,Ap 2,IX,6:6
Borderline 1937,F 10,18:6
Esterke 1940,O 18,24:2
Doctor Herzl 1945,D 21,25:4
Song of Dnieper 1946,O 26,10:5
Wandering Stars 1946,D 14,18:2
Yosele the Nightingale 1949,O 21,30:4

Schwartz, Meridee (Miscellaneous)

Dirtiest Show in Town, The 1970,My 2,21:1

Schwartz, Meyer (Playwright)

Kid Mother 1927,F 27,VII,1:1
Kid Mother 1927,Mr 6,VII,1:6
Under One Roof 1932,F 8,21:2
Madame Pagliacci 1935,S 30,12:3

Schwartz, Milton

Criminals, The 1941,D 22,24:3

Schwartz, Morris (Producer)

Untitled-Play 1924,Jl 5,14:4

Schwartz, Mort (Producer)

Wretched the Lionhearted 1962,S 13,31:2
Toy for the Clowns, A 1962,S 13,31:2

Schwartz, Morton C (Mrs)

Variations of 1940 1940,Ja 29,12:1

Schwartz, Noel

Dybbuk, The 1954,O 27,33:6
West Side Story 1957,S 27,14:4
King of the Dark Chamber 1961,F 10,21:1
Firebugs, The 1968,Jl 2,36:1

Schwartz, Noel (Choreographer)

Man With a Load of Mischief, The 1966,N 7,65:1

Schwartz, Risa

Tenth Man, The 1959,N 6,24:2
Tenth Man, The 1959,O 15,II,1:1
Cherry Orchard, The 1962,N 15,46:2

Schwartz, Robert

Flies, The; Mouches, Les 1947,Ap 18,26:3
Nat Turner 1960,N 7,46:3

Schwartz, Sam

Girls in 509, The 1958,O 16,47:1

Schwartz, Sam (Miscellaneous)

Both Kooney Lemels 1964,O 12,37:2

Schwartz, Sammy

Open House 1947,Je 4,33:4

Schwartz, Sid (Playwright)

Something for Nothing 1937,D 10,33:5

Schwartz, Sidney (Composer)

Political Party, A 1963,S 27,17:5

Schwartz, Sidney (Lyricist)

Political Party, A 1963,S 27,17:5

Schwartz, Sidney (Playwright)

Political Party, A 1963,S 27,17:5

Schwartz, Ted

Last Analysis, The 1964,O 2,30:1

Schwartz, William

Soul of a Woman, The 1930,F 22,13:1

Schwartz, Wolfgang

Ice Capades 1970,Ja 7,35:1

Schwartz (Lyricist)

Show Is On, The 1937,S 20,18:4

Schwartz (Miscellaneous)

Band Wagon, The 1931,My 17,VIII,3:2

Schwartzdorf, Jacob (Musical Director)

H M S Pinafore 1935,Ag 17,18:4

Schwartzenreich, Alexander

Alt Heidelberg 1926,My 31,10:5

Schwartzman, Dina

Bronx Express, 1968 1968,N 16,43:3

Schwarz, Eva (Costume Designer)

Captain of Koepenick, The 1964,D 2,60:1

Schwarz, Eva (Scenic Designer)

Captain of Koepenick, The 1964,D 2,60:1

Schwarz, Max

Trumpeter of Sakkingen 1921,Ja 15,11:3

Schwarze, Henry (Choreographer)

Yours Is My Heart 1946,S 6,16:5

Schwarzkopf, Klaus

Wozzeck 1966,Ap 6,34:1

Schwarzwald, Milton (Composer)

Be Yourself! 1924,S 4,13:3

Schweich, Arthur (Miscellaneous)

On the Town 1959,F 14,15:1

Schweid, Mark

Andersh; New Worlds 1922,S 26,18:2
Anathema 1923,F 9,10:2
Wolves 1924,D 31,9:4
King Saul 1925,S 18,26:3
Marco Millions 1928,Ja 10,28:2
Volpone 1928,Ap 10,32:1
Jew Suss 1929,O 19,22:3
Angels on Earth 1929,D 11,34:7
Roaming Stars 1930,Ja 25,12:2
Chains 1930,F 23,29:2
Chair, The 1930,O 4,15:4
God's Thieves 1930,O 27,17:4
One Woman 1931,D 14,16:4
In a Tenement House 1932,Ja 25,20:4
Wedding Chains 1932,Mr 28,10:5
Good Earth, The 1932,O 18,23:4
Yoshe Kalb 1933,D 29,27:2
Love on an Island 1934,Jl 24,20:5
Judgment Day 1934,S 13,26:4
Eternal Road, The 1937,Ja 8,14:2
Tortilla Flat 1938,Ja 13,16:2

Mazal Darf Men; You Need Luck 1938,My 18,16:5
Jeremiah 1939,F 4,11:2
Salvation 1939,S 29,19:2
If I Were Rothschild 1940,Ja 1,28:7
Worlds Apart 1941,Ja 23,19:3
Russian People, The 1942,D 30,17:2
Wandering Stars 1946,D 14,18:2

Schweid, Mark (Director)

Broken Chain, The 1929,F 21,30:4
God's Thieves 1930,O 27,17:4
Good Soldier Schweik, The 1937,D 22,33:2

Schweid, Mark (Playwright)

Othello 1929,F 4,21:2
Good Soldier Schweik, The 1937,D 22,33:2
Mazal Darf Men; You Need Luck 1938,My 18,16:5

Schweiger, Henrich

Wozzeck 1966,Ap 6,34:1

Schweikart, Hans (Director)

Soldiers 1967,O 10,14:3

Schweikart, Hans (Playwright)

Lauter Luegen 1937,O 24,XI,3:1

Schweikert, Ernest G (Composer)

Rumple 1957,N 7,42:2

Schweizer, Theo (Costume Designer)

Marriage of Mr Mississippi, The 1969,N 20,60:5
Philipp Hotz 1969,N 27,52:1
Firebugs, The 1969,N 27,52:1

Schweizer, Theo (Scenic Designer)

Marriage of Mr Mississippi, The 1969,N 20,60:5
Firebugs, The 1969,N 27,52:1
Philipp Hotz 1969,N 27,52:1

Schwelch, Bud (Lighting Director)

Escurial 1956,O 3,29:2
Lesson, The 1956,O 3,29:2

Schweng, Hans

Pinocchio 1939,Ja 3,19:2

Schwenk, Herman

Sudden End of Anne Cinquefoil, The
1961,Ja 11,25:2

Schwenke, Mildred

Show Boat 1932,My 20,22:2

Schwerin, Doris (Composer)

O, Oysters! 1961,Ja 31,23:1
Marco Millions 1964,F 21,33:1

Schwerin, Doris (Miscellaneous)

Marco Millions 1964,F 21,33:1

Schwezoff, Igor (Choreographer)

Vagabond King, The 1943,Je 30,24:2
Pirates of Penzance, The 1946,My 17,14:6

Schwiefert, Fritz (Playwright)

Marguerite Divided by Three 1930,S 28,VIII,4:4

Schwimmer, Walter (Producer)

Right Honourable Gentleman, The 1965,O 20,50:2

Schwindler, Richard

Mecca 1920,O 5,12:2

Schwinn, Ron

How Now, Dow Jones 1967,D 8,53:1

Schwob, Marcel (Translator)

Hamlet 1927,Ja 23,VII,2:1
Hamlet 1932,Je 12,X,1:1

Sciabona, Anthony

All's Well That Ends Well 1966,Je 17,39:1

Sciabona, Tom

Oedipus Rex 1965,Jl 9,17:1

Sciandra, Gian

Hans's Crime 1961,F 4,15:1
Damask Drum, The 1961,F 4,15:1
Poppa Is Home 1961,D 20,37:1

Sciandra, Gian (Miscellaneous)

Wives, The 1965,My 18,35:4

Sciandra, Gian (Producer)

Automobile Graveyard, The 1961,N 14,46:2

Scibilia, Anton F (Producer)

Wicked Age, The 1927,N 5,16:6

Scibona, Angelina

'Il Tesoro D'Isacco; Treasure of Isaac, The
1928,Ja 26,17:1

Scibor, Maria (Composer)

Annonce Faite a Marie, L' 1965,Ap 6,33:2

Scierski, Stanislaw

Constant Prince, The 1969,O 18,36:1
Acropolis 1969,N 5,40:1

Scimonelli, Glen

Matty and the Moron and Madonna
1965,Mr 30,53:1

Scize, Pierre (Playwright)

Lac Sale, Le 1926,O 3,VIII,2:1
Ludo 1932,Je 12,X,1:3

Scmidt, Douglas (Scenic Designer)

Father Uxbridge Wants to Marry 1967,O 30,57:1

Scnlichting, Louise

Ship, The 1929,N 21,24:7

Scoblete, Frank

Don't Go Away Mad 1949,My 10,28:2

Scofield, Pamela (Costume Designer)

Lend an Ear 1969,O 29,32:1
Little Boxes; Trevor 1969,D 4,71:2
Little Boxes; Coffee Lace, The 1969,D 4,71:2
Unfair to Goliath 1970,Ja 26,27:1
Awake and Sing! 1970,My 28,35:1

Scofield, Paul

Hamlet 1948,My 9,II,2:5
Adventure Story 1949,Mr 19,11:2

Scofield, Paul—Cont

Ring Around the Moon 1950,Ja 27,29:2
Richard II 1953,Ja 1,19:1
Richard II 1953,Ja 25,II,3:1
Way of the World, The 1953,Ap 10,17:1
Time Remembered 1955,My 4,35:1
Hamlet 1955,N 24,40:7
Power and the Glory, The 1956,Ap 6,14:3
Power and the Glory, The 1956,My 13,II,3:1
Family Reunion, The 1956,Je 9,13:6
Complaisant Lover, The 1959,Je 19,28:3
Coriolanus 1961,Je 21,31:2
Love's Labour's Lost 1961,Je 23,19:1
Love's Labour's Lost 1961,Jl 2,II,1:1
Coriolanus 1961,Jl 5,30:1
Man for All Seasons, A 1961,N 23,51:1
Man for All Seasons, A 1961,D 3,II,1:1
King Lear 1962,N 7,49:3
King Lear 1964,Ap 3,28:1
King Lear 1964,My 19,43:2
King Lear 1964,My 31,II,1:1
Hotel in Amsterdam, The 1968,Jl 21,II,12:1
Hotel in Amsterdam, The 1968,Ag 17,17:1
Uncle Vanya 1970,Mr 15,II,7:3

Scofield, Thomas

Crow's Nest, The 1923,My 10,22:3

Scofield, Thomas (Miscellaneous)

Room in Red and White, A 1936,Ja 20,23:3

Scofield, Thomas (Playwright)

Rain Before Seven 1935,Ag 13,20:3

Scoggins, Virgil

At Home Abroad 1935,S 20,17:4

Scogin, Robert

Hamlet 1969,Je 30,33:1
Henry V 1969,N 11,43:1

Scognamillo, Gabriel (Scenic Designer)

Ice Capades 1953,S 11,25:1
Ice Capades 1954,S 16,37:1

Scola, John

Blue Blood 1924,Ap 3,21:2

Scolari, Camillo (Playwright)

So Am I 1928,Ja 28,9:1

Scollay, Fred J

High Named Today 1954,D 11,11:2
Truce of the Bear 1957,O 24,39:1
Devil's Advocate, The 1961,Mr 10,20:1

Scollay, Fred J (Director)

King's Standards, The 1958,F 14,19:1
Listen to the Quiet 1958,O 28,40:2

Scollay, Fred J (Playwright)

Listen to the Quiet 1958,O 28,40:2

Scoller, Zvee (Director)

We Live and Laugh 1936,My 9,10:3

Scooler, Esther

Town Lunatics 1933,F 6,11:4

Scooler, Zvee

Command Performance, The 1928,O 4,27:1
God's Thieves 1930,O 27,17:4
One Woman 1931,D 14,16:4
Town Lunatics 1933,F 6,11:4
Once Upon a Time 1933,S 22,15:1
Germany Aflame 1933,O 28,20:5
Little Giants 1933,D 2,9:5
Two Hearts 1935,My 6,22:2
Kibbetzers, Inc 1935,My 13,18:5
Untitled-Revue 1935,S 23,20:2
Jacques Bergson 1936,O 31,24:6
Jacques Bergson 1936,N 29,XII,3:3
Brothers Ashkenazi, The 1937,S 21,28:6
Three Cities 1938,O 11,20:3
Who Is Who? 1938,D 24,13:3
Yoshe Kalb 1939,F 6,9:2
If I Were Rothschild 1940,Ja 1,28:7
Highway Robbery 1955,N 8,36:1
Theater of Peretz, The 1963,N 6,35:2
Fiddler on the Roof 1964,S 23,56:2

Scot, Selwyn

Magda 1926,Ja 27,16:2

Scot Don

Processional 1937,O 14,23:1

Scotford, Sybil

Oh, Kay! 1960,Ap 18,37:2

Scotlin, Michael

Midsummer Night's Dream, A 1967,Je 19,42:1
Antigone 1967,Je 19,43:1

Scott, A C (Playwright)

Butterfly Dream, The 1966,My 20,41:1

Scott, Alice

Eccentricities of Davy Crockett, The 1961,Ja 4,26:1
Riding Hood Revisited 1961,Ja 4,26:1
Decameron, The 1961,Ap 13,32:1

Scott, Allan (Costume Designer)

Stone Tower, The 1962,Ag 24,14:2
Mister Roberts 1962,O 12,27:2

Scott, Allan (Playwright)

Goodbye Again 1932,D 29,16:4
Goodbye Again 1937,S 15,15:1
In Clover 1937,S 21,29:1
In Clover 1937,O 14,23:1
Goodbye Again 1943,N 10,28:4
Joy to the World 1948,Mr 19,28:2
Joy to the World 1948,Mr 28,II,1:1
Goodbye Again 1956,Ap 25,38:1

Scott, Ann
Lord Byron's Love Letter 1955,Ja 19,23:2
Scott, Ashmead
Mask of Hamlet, The 1921,Ag 23,10:3
Scott, Avis
Rape of the Belt, The 1960,N 7,46:1
Scott, Barbara Ann
Hollywood Ice Revue 1953,Ja 16,17:2
Hollywood Ice Revue 1954,Ja 15,16:2
Hollywood Ice Revue 1955 1955,Ja 14,16:1
Scott, Bert
Relations 1928,Ag 21,27:3
Scott, Blake
Grand Street Follies, The 1928,My 29,16:2
Rumanian Rhapsody, No 1 1929,Ap 27,16:4
Living Corpse, The 1929,D 7,19:1
Romeo and Juliet 1930,Ap 22,33:1
Chinese Nightingale, The 1934,O 6,20:4
Master of the Revels 1935,Ag 14,16:2
Scott, Blake (Choreographer)
Would-Be Gentleman, The 1930,Ap 30,29:2
Peter Ibbetson 1931,Ap 9,30:3
Scott, Bobby
Biff, Bing, Bang 1921,My 10,20:1
Taste of Honey, A 1960,O 5,46:1
Scott, Bobby (Composer)
Dinny and the Witches 1959,D 10,53:3
Taste of Honey, A 1960,O 5,46:1
Taste of Honey, A 1960,N 6,II,1:1
Step on a Crack 1962,O 18,48:1
Scott, Bonnie
Vintage '60 1960,S 13,41:1
How to Succeed in Business Without Really Trying
1961,O 16,34:1
Scott, Bruce
Two Married Men 1925,Ja 14,19:1
Richard III 1953,Jl 15,22:2
Lion in Winter, The 1966,Mr 4,23:1
Ballad for a Firing Squad 1968,D 12,64:2
Does a Tiger Wear a Necktie? 1969,F 26,38:1
Does a Tiger Wear a Necktie? 1969,Mr 16,II,4:5
Sensations 1970,O 26,48:2
Scott, C Robert
Slave Ship 1969,N 22,46:1
Scott, C W
John Henry 1940,Ja 11,18:2
Scott, Cecil
Run, Little Chillun! 1933,Mr 2,21:3
Scott, Charles
Conflict 1929,Mr 7,22:4
Hipper's Holiday 1934,O 19,26:2
Co-Respondent Unknown 1936,F 12,24:4
Oklahoma! 1951,My 30,15:2
Oklahoma! 1953,S 1,19:1
Scott, Cheryl
Galileo 1968,D 1,88:4
Scott, Christopher (Scenic Designer)
Bluebeard 1970,My 5,58:1
Scott, Connie
Jennie 1963,O 18,35:2
Scott, Cyril
Paddy the Next Best Thing 1920,Ag 28,5:5
In the Night Watch 1921,Ja 31,10:1
Dancing Girl, The 1923,Ja 25,16:2
New Gallantry, The 1925,S 25,24:2
It's a Grand Life 1930,F 11,30:3
Rock Me, Julie 1931,Ja 4,VIII,2:3
Passing Present, The 1931,D 8,36:2
Paths of Glory 1935,S 19,29:1
Paths of Glory 1935,S 27,24:2
Tomorrow's a Holiday! 1935,D 31,10:2
Holmeses of Baker Street, The 1936,D 10,34:3
Scott, D H Jr
It's the Valet 1933,D 15,25:4
Scott, David (Composer)
Bluebeard 1970,My 5,58:1
Scott, Debbie
Childhood 1962,Ja 12,28:1
Scott, Dennis
Music Man, The 1965,Je 17,26:4
Play That on Your Old Piano 1965,O 15,49:1
Scott, Donna
Once for the Asking 1963,N 21,42:2
Scott, Dorothy
Immortal Thief, The 1926,O 4,21:1
Winter Bound 1929,N 13,24:6
Technique 1931,My 15,21:1
Beauty and the Beast 1932,Ja 10,I,29:2
Pride and Prejudice 1935,N 6,32:4
But for the Grace of God 1937,Ja 13,21:4
You Can't Take It With You 1945,Mr 27,23:7
Jane Eyre 1958,My 2,31:1
Lysistrata 1959,My 20,40:2
Scott, Duncan
Show Boat 1946,Ja 7,17:2
Scott, Ed (Miscellaneous)
Walking Happy 1966,N 28,47:1
Scott, Edgar (Lyricist)
Wetward Ho 1921,Ap 22,13:2
Scott, Edgar (Playwright)
It's Only Natural 1922,Ap 21,13:2
Scott, Edith
Outrageous Mrs Palmer, The 1920,O 13,18:1

Big Boy 1925,Ja 8,28:2
Music in May 1929,Ap 2,29:1
Scott, Elizabeth
Skin of Our Teeth, The 1942,N 19,29:5
Scott, Ethel
Porgy and Bess 1955,Ag 5,14:5
Scott, Evelyn (Playwright)
Love 1921,Mr 6,VI,1:2
Scott, Ewart
Pins and Needles 1922,F 2,20:1
Scott, Francena
Horse Play 1937,Ag 28,8:3
Scott, Frank
Julius Caesar 1930,Ap 4,22:3
Scott, Frederick
Dice of the Gods, The 1923,Ap 6,20:2
Scott, Geoffrey
Lulu; Earth Spirit 1970,Mr 28,32:1
Scott, George C
Richard III 1957,N 26,41:1
As You Like It 1958,Ja 21,33:6
Children of Darkness 1958,Mr 1,11:4
Comes a Day 1958,N 7,22:1
Antony and Cleopatra 1959,Ja 14,28:1
Andersonville Trial, The 1959,D 30,15:1
Andersonville Trial, The 1960,Ja 10,II,1:1
Wall, The 1960,O 12,44:4
Wall, The 1960,O 23,II,1:1
General Seeger 1962,Mr 1,26:2
Merchant of Venice, The 1962,Je 22,1:4
Desire Under the Elms 1963,Ja 11,5:6
Three Sisters, The 1965,My 15,19:4
Little Foxes, The 1967,O 27,53:1
Little Foxes, The 1967,N 5,II,1:1
Plaza Suite; Visitor From Hollywood
1968,F 15,49:1
Plaza Suite; Visitor From Mamaroneck
1968,F 15,49:1
Plaza Suite; Visitor From Forest Hills
1968,F 15,49:1
Plaza Suite 1968,F 25,II,1:1
Scott, George C (Director)
General Seeger 1962,Mr 1,26:2
Scott, George C (Producer)
Great Day in the Morning 1962,Mr 29,29:1
Scott, Glory Van
House of Flowers 1954,D 31,11:2
Fly Blackbird 1962,Ap 29,II,1:1
Scott, Gordon
Twelfth Night 1957,Jl 4,16:4
Scott, Harold
Pride and Prejudice 1935,N 3,X,1:5
Pride and Prejudice 1935,N 6,32:4
Pride and Prejudice 1935,N 17,IX,1:1
Murder in the Cathedral 1938,F 17,16:2
Waters of the Moon 1953,Ap 2,34:3
Egg and I, The 1958,S 11,43:4
Deathwatch 1958,O 10,34:2
Cool World, The 1960,F 23,38:2
Jackass, The 1960,Mr 24,39:2
Calvary 1960,Jl 22,13:1
Santa Claus 1960,Jl 22,13:1
Escurial 1960,Jl 22,13:1
Death of Bessie Smith, The 1961,Mr 2,19:1
After the Fall 1964,Ja 24,18:1
Marco Millions 1964,F 21,33:1
Changeling, The 1964,O 30,32:2
Incident at Vichy 1964,D 4,44:1
Strong Breed, The 1967,N 10,60:1
Trials of Brother Jero, The 1967,N 10,60:1
Cuban Thing, The 1968,S 25,36:2
Boys in the Band, The 1969,F 18,36:1
Blancs, Les 1970,N 16,48:4
Scott, Harold (Producer)
Gingham Dog, The 1969,Ap 24,41:1
Scott, Hazel
Priorities of 1942 1942,Mr 13,23:2
Priorities of 1942 1942,Mr 29,VIII,1:1
Scott, Helen
Swifty 1922,O 17,14:1
Scott, Helena
Me and Juliet 1953,My 29,17:1
Me and Juliet 1953,Je 7,II,1:1
Arabian Nights 1954,Je 25,15:2
Arabian Nights 1955,Je 24,16:1
Merry Widow, The 1957,Ap 11,36:6
Song of Norway 1958,Je 23,19:2
Song of Norway 1959,Je 26,16:2
Most Happy Fella, The 1960,Ap 22,25:3
Banker's Daughter, The 1962,Ja 23,37:1
Scott, Henry B
Long Way From Home, A 1948,F 9,25:2
Riders to the Sea 1949,F 4,30:2
Member of the Wedding, The 1950,Ja 6,26:6
Born Yesterday 1954,Ja 1,16:6
Scott, Henry B (Miscellaneous)
Riders to the Sea 1949,F 4,30:2
Freight 1949,F 4,30:2
Scott, Henry E 3d (Scenic Designer)
Jacques Brel Is Alive and Well and Living in Paris
1968,Ja 23,25:2
Scott, Henry Jr (Scenic Designer)
Merchant of Venice, The 1950,My 3,37:2

Scott, Henry L
Concerto for Fun 1949,My 10,28:3
Scott, Houston
Caesar and Cleopatra 1927,N 6,IX,2:1
Scott, Howard
Go Show Me a Dragon 1961,O 28,18:1
Scott, Hutchinson (Scenic Designer)
Merchant of Venice, The 1953,My 10,II,1:1
Iceman Cometh, The 1958,Ja 30,18:3
Boeing-Boeing 1965,F 3,30:1
Help Stamp Out Marriage 1966,S 30,50:1
There's a Girl in My Soup 1967,O 19,58:1
Flip Side, The 1968,O 11,36:1
Scott, Ivy
Music in the Air 1932,N 9,28:2
Revenge With Music 1934,N 29,33:5
Three Waltzes 1937,D 27,10:2
Too Many Girls 1939,O 19,26:2
Liberty Jones 1941,F 6,24:2
Sunny River 1941,D 5,28:2
Song of Norway 1944,Ag 22,20:2
Song of Norway 1944,Ag 27,II,1:1
Scott, J Blake
Mozart 1926,N 23,26:2
Commedia Dell' Arte 1927,Ap 6,24:3
If 1927,O 26,26:2
Would-Be Gentleman, The 1928,O 2,34:1
Peter Pan; Boy Who Would Not Grow Up, The
1928,N 27,36:3
Katerina 1929,F 26,30:3
Scott, J Blake (Choreographer)
Would-Be Gentleman, The 1928,O 2,34:1
Scott, J Blake (Director)
Peter Pan; Boy Who Would Not Grow Up, The
1928,N 27,36:3
Scott, Jack
Rose of Stamboul, The 1922,Mr 8,11:2
Scott, Jacqueline
Wooden Dish, The 1955,O 7,20:1
Scott, James
Manhattan Mary 1927,S 27,30:3
Mr Gilhooley 1930,O 1,26:1
Scott, Jean
Kiki 1921,N 30,13:1
Red, Hot and Blue! 1936,O 30,26:3
Let's Face It 1941,O 30,26:2
Scott, Jeffrey
Annie Get Your Gun 1966,Je 1,42:2
Scott, Jimmie
Gertie 1926,N 16,24:2
Scott, Joan Clement
Easy Virtue 1925,D 8,28:2
Scott, John
Ziegfeld Follies 1922,Je 6,18:2
New Moon, The 1944,My 18,16:2
Caucasian Chalk Circle, The 1961,N 1,35:1
Scott, John (Miscellaneous)
Wonderful Town 1958,Mr 6,32:4
Scott, Joseph
They Shall Not Die 1934,F 22,24:4
Dance With Your Gods 1934,O 8,14:3
Scott, Kenneth
Relapse, The 1950,N 23,54:2
I'm Solomon 1968,Ap 24,51:1
Scott, Kenyon (Composer)
Noble Rogue, A 1929,Ag 20,31:2
Scott, Kenyon (Lyricist)
Noble Rogue, A 1929,Ag 20,31:2
Scott, Kenyon (Playwright)
Noble Rogue, A 1929,Ag 20,31:2
Scott, Kevin
Carnival in Flanders 1953,S 9,38:2
Almost Crazy 1955,Je 21,37:1
Scott, Lauren
Ruddigore 1965,Ag 27,16:1
Scott, Lea
Electra 1969,Ag 8,14:1
Scott, Lee (Choreographer)
Happy Town 1959,O 8,49:2
Scott, Leonard
White Lights 1927,O 12,30:4
Scott, Leslie
Shuffle Along 1952,My 9,20:5
Porgy and Bess 1953,F 17,21:1
Porgy and Bess 1953,Mr 10,25:5
Porgy and Bess 1953,Mr 15,II,1:1
Porgy and Bess 1955,Ja 21,19:6
Porgy and Bess 1955,Ag 5,14:5
Scott, Lisle
Brown Danube, The 1939,My 18,30:4
Scott, Lorene
Ringside Seat 1938,N 23,24:5
Scott, Lous
Traite d'Auteuil, Le 1921,Jl 17,VI,1:8
Scott, Lucian
R U R 1930,F 18,28:1
Volpone 1930,Mr 11,24:5
What the Butler Saw 1970,My 5,56:1
What the Butler Saw 1970,O 14,38:1
Scott, Lydia
Bunch and Judy, The 1922,N 29,20:1
Stepping Stones 1923,N 7,14:3
Criss Cross 1926,O 13,20:2

Scott, Margaretta
Hamlet 1931,Mr 22,VIII,2:1
Miracle Man, The 1935,Je 9,IX,1:1
Chastity, My Brother 1936,My 9,27:3
Lady's Gentleman, A 1937,D 24,20:5
Flood Tide 1938,Mr 24,20:8
Alien Corn 1939,Jl 6,26:8
Alien Corn 1939,Jl 23,IX,2:3
Much Ado About Nothing 1941,Ap 20,IX,3:3
Young Elizabeth, The 1952,Ap 3,45:1

Scott, Martha
Please Do Not Disturb 1936,Je 23,27:1
Western Union 1937,Ag 10,22:7
Damn Deborah 1937,Ag 17,23:1
Our Town 1938,Ja 23,II,10:6
Our Town 1938,Ja 26,27:4
Our Town 1938,Ja 30,X,3:1
Our Town 1938,F 5,18:3
Foreigners 1939,D 6,30:2
Willow and I, The 1942,D 11,32:2
Our Town 1944,Ja 11,24:5
Soldier's Wife 1944,O 5,18:6
Soldier's Wife 1944,O 15,II,1:1
It Takes Two 1947,F 4,33:4
Design For A Stained Glass Window
   1950,Ja 24,26:2
ANTA Album 1951,My 7,22:7
Number, The 1951,O 31,33:2
Male Animal, The 1952,My 1,35:1
Male Animal, The 1952,My 18,II,1:1
Remarkable Mr Pennypacker, The 1953,D 31,11:2
Cloud 7 1958,F 15,15:2
Distant Bell, A 1960,Ja 14,29:1
Tumbler, The 1960,F 25,32:2
49th Cousin, The 1960,O 28,22:1

Scott, Martha (Miscellaneous)
Front Page, The 1968,O 20,85:5

Scott, Mary
Caesar and Cleopatra 1949,D 22,28:2
Girl on the Via Flaminia, The 1954,O 13,26:5

Scott, Melvin
Goose, The 1960,Mr 16,44:1
Moby Dick 1962,N 29,45:1

Scott, Michael
Plough and the Stars, The 1927,N 29,30:2
Juno and the Paycock 1927,D 20,32:2

Scott, Michael (Producer)
Capacity for Wings 1957,Ja 10,25:2

Scott, Miriam
Kind Lady 1937,Jl 21,19:3
Great Big Doorstep, The 1950,Mr 18,8:6

Scott, Monte
Stars on Ice (2d Edition) 1943,Je 25,13:2

Scott, Murray
Coriolanus 1961,Je 21,31:2
Love's Labour's Lost 1961,Je 23,19:1

Scott, Nathan (Miscellaneous)
3 for Tonight 1955,Ap 7,23:2

Scott, Noel (Playwright)
Half a Loaf 1926,N 28,VIII,1:4

Scott, Patricia
Herne's Egg, The 1960,S 20,48:1

Scott, Paula (Producer)
Here Come the Clowns 1960,S 20,48:1
God Bless You, Harold Fineberg 1969,Mr 31,30:2

Scott, Peter
Christmas Eve 1939,D 28,17:2
International Incident, An 1940,Ap 3,18:2
Happy Days 1941,My 14,24:2
Junior Miss 1941,N 19,28:2

Scott, Phil
Blackbirds 1933,D 4,22:3

Scott, Pippa
Child of Fortune 1956,N 14,41:1
Apollo of Bellac, The 1957,Ap 10,39:1
Miss Lonelyhearts 1957,O 4,26:2

Scott, Raymond (Composer)
Lute Song 1946,F 7,29:2
Lute Song 1946,F 17,II,1:1
Michael Todd's Peep Show 1950,Je 29,37:2
Lute Song 1959,Mr 13,24:1

Scott, Raymond (Lyricist)
Michael Todd's Peep Show 1950,Je 29,37:2

Scott, Robert
Bright Honor 1936,S 28,14:1
Male Animal, The 1940,Ja 10,17:2
Male Animal, The 1940,Ja 21,IX,1:1
Big Two, The 1947,Ja 9,21:2

Scott, Robert C (Scenic Designer)
Trachiniae 1931,Ja 27,21:2

Scott, Robert S (Playwright)
When the Bough Breaks 1950,Mr 9,25:5

Scott, Rod (Costume Designer)
Year Round, The 1953,My 6,38:7

Scott, Roy
Montserrat 1961,Ja 9,30:5

Scott, Russell
Jack and Jill 1923,Mr 23,17:2

Scott, S
Bulls and Belles 1931,Ap 18,17:2

Scott, Sarah
Kilgo Run, The 1953,D 13,105:1

Scott, Seret
Slave Ship 1969,N 22,46:1

Scott, Stanley (Producer)
Before Sunset 1933,S 29,10:7

Scott, Stepen
Caine Mutiny Court-Martial, The 1953,O 14,35:1

Scott, Stephen
Borstal Boy 1970,Ap 1,38:1

Scott, Sydna
Hamlet 1936,O 9,30:2
Days of Our Youth, The 1941,N 29,15:2
He Who Gets Slapped 1946,Mr 21,31:4
Parisienne 1950,Jl 25,24:2

Scott, Ted
Tragicomedy of Don Cristobita and Dona Rosita,
   The 1958,My 30,12:2
Wonder World 1964,My 18,32:1
Cradle Will Rock, The 1964,N 9,40:4

Scott, Thomas Jefferson (Lyricist)
Gloriana 1938,N 26,18:4

Scott, Thurman
All's Well That Ends Well 1966,Je 17,39:1
Open 24 Hours 1969,F 12,31:1
Electra 1969,Ag 8,14:1

Scott, Tom
Collision Course; Rats 1968,My 9,55:2

Scott, Walter F
Pietro 1920,Ja 20,10:2
Broken Wing, The 1920,N 30,14:1
Van Dyck, The 1921,O 12,18:2
Captain Applejack 1921,D 31,14:2
Joan of Arkansas 1925,Ap 5,16:1
Great Power, The 1928,S 12,25:1
Kibitzer, The 1929,F 19,22:5
Hawk Island 1929,S 17,34:7
Little Father of the Wilderness, The 1930,Je 3,27:1
As Good As New 1930,N 4,37:3

Scott, Walter F (Director)
Fool's Bells 1925,D 24,8:3
Kilpatrick's Old-Time Minstrels 1930,Ap 21,20:2

Scott, William R
Hoot Mon, or Clans Across the Sea 1927,My 8,29:4

Scott, Zachary
Circle of Chalk, The 1941,Mr 27,28:4
Ah, Wilderness! 1941,O 3,26:2
Damask Cheek, The 1942,O 23,24:2
This Rock 1943,F 19,23:2
Those Endearing Young Charms 1943,Je 17,16:3
King and I, The 1956,Ap 19,35:4
Subway in the Sky 1957,F 28,19:1
Requiem for a Nun 1959,Ja 31,13:2
Requiem for a Nun 1959,F 8,II,1:1
Twelfth Night 1959,Jl 11,10:2
Rainy Day in Newark, A 1963,O 23,35:1

Scott-Moncrieff, C K (Translator)
Lazzaro 1929,Ag 4,VIII,1:7

Scott Sisters
George White's Scandals 1926,Je 15,23:2
Manhattan Mary 1927,S 27,30:3
George White's Scandals 1929,S 24,29:1

Scott-Smith, Peter
Browning Version, The 1949,O 13,32:2
Harlequinade 1949,O 13,32:2
Browning Version, The 1949,O 23,II,1:1

Scotti, Donald J
Emerald Slippers, The 1970,S 2,31:2

Scotti, Ida
Old Maid, The 1949,Ja 27,20:6
Post Road 1949,Ap 28,27:3
This Happy Breed 1952,Ap 4,23:2
Mrs Moonlight 1952,N 21,21:1

Scotti, Joseph
Farewell to Arms, A 1930,S 23,30:3

Scotti, Louise
This Happy Breed 1952,Ap 4,23:2
Mrs Moonlight 1952,N 21,21:1

Scotti, Vito
Pinocchio 1939,Ja 3,19:2
Steel 1939,D 20,30:2

Scottish Players
Follow Me 1932,D 11,IX,5:3

Scougall, Diana
Romeo and Juliet 1962,F 14,39:1
Saint Joan 1962,F 21,57:4

Scourby, Alexander
Hamlet 1936,N 11,54:2
Infernal Machine, The 1937,D 13,22:7
Black Eye, The 1938,Mr 8,22:4
Hamlet 1938,O 13,28:1
Henry IV, Part I 1939,Ja 31,17:2
Richard II 1940,Ap 2,31:2
Elizabeth the Queen 1941,O 17,27:2
War President 1944,Ap 25,17:3
Deputy of Paris, The 1947,Mr 22,9:5
Crime and Punishment 1947,D 23,29:3
Insect Comedy, The 1948,Je 4,26:3
Victors, The 1948,D 27,17:2
Blood Wedding 1949,F 7,16:2
Detective Story 1949,Mr 24,34:2
Darkness at Noon 1951,Ja 15,13:4
Darkness at Noon 1951,Ja 21,II,1:1
Saint Joan 1951,O 5,23:2
Tonight in Samarkand 1955,F 17,22:2

Month in the Country, A 1956,Ap 4,23:1
Month in the Country, A 1956,Ap 15,II,1:1
Hamlet 1961,Mr 17,17:1
Candida 1962,N 12,35:5
Tovarich 1963,Mr 20,5:1
Whitman Portrait, A 1966,O 12,37:1

Scoville, Ann
Pursuit of Happiness, The 1936,Jl 15,14:1
Post Road 1936,Ag 5,15:4
Royal Family, The 1936,Ag 12,15:1
Truth About Blayds, The 1936,Ag 19,18:5
Art and Mrs Bottle 1936,S 2,18:1
Private Lives 1937,Jl 14,17:4
Kind Lady 1937,Jl 21,19:3
Fly Away Home 1937,Ag 28,15:1
Whiteheaded Boy, The 1937,Ag 11,27:3
Ode to Liberty 1937,Ag 18,15:2
Goodbye Again 1937,S 1,15:1
Yes, My Darling Daughter 1938,Jl 13,19:2
Animal Kingdom, The 1938,Jl 27,14:5

Scribe, Eugene (Playwright)
Betty, Be Good 1920,My 5,14:2
Glass of Water, A 1930,Mr 6,16:3
Glass Wasser, Das 1934,D 30,IX,2:1
Glass Wasser, Das 1935,Jl 28,X,1:6

Scrittorale, Michael
Fiorello! 1959,N 24,45:3

Scroppo, Dennis
Devil's Advocate, The 1961,Mr 10,20:1

Scruggs, Earl
Hayride 1954,S 14,24:2

Scrussi, Emil
Dole Brothers 1932,Mr 26,17:7

Scrymsour, Ella (Playwright)
Bridge of Distances, The 1925,S 29,30:1

Scrymsour, John (Playwright)
Bridge of Distances, The 1925,S 29,30:1

Scudder, Alice
Dance of Death, The 1960,S 14,51:1
Bugs 1965,N 19,31:1

Scudder, Alice (Director)
Texas Steer, A 1968,N 13,39:1

Scudder, Alice (Producer)
This Side of Paradise 1962,F 22,19:6

Scudder, George (Playwright)
Young Go First, The 1935,My 29,16:2

Scudder, George (Producer)
Cage, The 1961,Mr 6,30:1
417 1961,Mr 6,30:1

Scudi, Mike
Solid Ivory 1925,N 17,29:3

Scudi, Santo
Burlesque 1946,D 26,30:3

Scularekes, Venus
Flame of Love 1924,Ap 22,19:2

Sculias, Christina
Song of Bernadette 1946,Mr 27,22:2

Scullin, Robert
Fifty-Fifty 1937,N 20,21:1

Scully, Barbara
Student Prince, The 1943,Je 9,16:2
Blossom Time 1943,S 6,21:2
Robin Hood 1944,N 8,28:2

Scully, Harry
Faith of Our Fathers 1950,Ag 6,72:2

Scully, Joseph
Rumpelstiltskin 1948,Mr 15,27:3
Pied Piper of Hamelin, The 1950,Ap 3,19:2
Dick Whittington and His Remarkable Cat
   1950,N 25,10:5

Scully, Sean
Girl Who Came to Supper, The 1963,D 9,49:1

Scunberg, Robert
Milk Train Doesn't Stop Here Anymore, The
   1965,Jl 27,25:1

Scunda, Sholem (Composer)
Yosele the Nightingale 1949,O 21,30:4

Scupham, Peter
Romeo and Juliet 1968,Je 11,55:2
Hamlet 1969,Je 11,37:1
Alchemist, The 1969,Je 12,51:1
Measure for Measure 1969,Je 13,41:3

Scwartz, Arthur (Composer)
Band Wagon, The 1931,Je 14,VIII,1:1

Seabolt, Frank
Golden Apple, The 1954,Mr 12,15:2
Arabian Nights 1955,Je 24,16:1

Seaborn, Rosanna
Song Out of Sorrow 1941,D 12,34:5

Seabra, Nelson (Miscellaneous)
Lady Comes Across, The 1942,Ja 10,10:2

Seabrook, Gay
Coquette 1935,My 22,23:4
Crime Marches on 1935,O 24,19:1
Three Men on a Horse 1936,Mr 24,26:4
Three Men on a Horse 1942,O 10,10:2

Seabrook, Jeremy (Playwright)
Life Price 1969,Ja 14,36:2

Seabury, William
Vaudeville (Palace) 1924,Ap 29,12:2
Polly 1929,Ja 9,28:3

Seager, John
Paths of Glory 1935,S 27,24:2

Seager, John—Cont
Hallowe'en 1936,F 21,20:3
Seager, Stella
Americana 1928,O 31,28:2
Seagle, Betty Jane
Seventeen 1951,Je 22,16:6
Seagram, Mr
Electra 1931,My 24,VIII,3:5
Seagram, Wilfrid
Loyalties 1922,S 28,18:1
Peter Pan 1924,N 7,16:2
Gay Paree 1925,Ag 19,14:3
School for Scandal, The 1925,O 24,19:1
Great Temptations, The 1926,My 19,29:1
She Stoops to Conquer 1928,My 15,17:1
She Stoops to Conquer 1928,My 20,VIII,1:1
Beaux' Stratagem, The 1928,Je 5,20:1
First Law, The 1929,My 7,28:4
Thunder in the Air 1929,N 12,34:3
Royal Virgin, The 1930,Mr 18,30:5
Journey's End 1930,Ag 5,26:4
Affair of State, An 1930,N 20,30:3
Bellamy Trial, The 1931,Ap 23,28:6
When Ladies Meet 1932,Ag 14,IX,1:7
Red Planet 1932,D 19,19:2
Merrily We Roll Along 1934,O 1,14:1
Caesar and Cleopatra 1935,Ag 22,21:1
Eden End 1935,O 22,17:1
Laughing Woman, The 1936,O 14,30:1
Antony and Cleopatra 1937,N 11,30:2
Once Is Enough 1938,F 16,16:2
Seagram, William
Masque of Venice, The 1926,Mr 3,27:3
Seagrave, Edmund (Lighting Director)
Sourball 1969,Ag 6,29:2
Seagrave, James
Shadow and Substance 1956,Mr 14,38:1
Seagraves, Fred
Tiger at the Gates 1968,Mr 1,30:1
Seal, Elizabeth
Irma la Douce 1960,S 30,31:2
Irma la Douce 1960,O 16,II,1:1
Seal, Lewis A
Fanshastics 1924,Ja 17,13:2
Seal, Slyvia (Miscellaneous)
Present Laughter 1946,O 30,31:2
Sealby, Mabel
Happy Husband, The 1927,Jl 10,VII,2:3
Canaries Sometimes Sing 1929,N 10,X,2:1
Seale, Douglas (Director)
Henry IV 1955,My 15,II,1:1
Henry V 1956,Jl 7,11:2
King John 1960,Je 29,26:2
One Way Pendulum 1961,S 19,38:2
Saint Joan 1962,F 21,57:4
Henry IV, Part I 1962,Je 18,20:4
Henry IV, Part I 1962,Je 24,II,1:1
Importance of Being Earnest, The 1963,F 27,5:2
Comedy of Errors, The 1963,Je 13,28:1
Henry V 1963,Je 14,37:1
Damn You, Scarlett O'Hara 1964,F 5,30:1
All My Pretty Little Ones 1964,F 5,30:1
Tempest, The 1970,F 15,67:1
Seale, Douglas (Producer)
Henry VI (Part III) 1957,O 18,19:5
Much Ado About Nothing 1958,Ag 27,34:6
Tempest, The: or, The Enchanted Forest
1959,Je 10,42:2
Seale, Joan
Hajj Malik, El 1970,O 4,II,5:1
Seals, Charles
Hamlet 1968,Jl 4,15:1
No Place to Be Somebody 1969,My 5,53:3
No Place to Be Somebody 1969,D 31,17:1
Sealy, Charles L
Circle, The 1921,S 13,12:1
Sealy, Lewis
Richard III 1920,Mr 8,7:1
Awful Truth, The 1922,S 19,14:3
Lass O' Laughter 1925,Ja 9,13:2
Merchant of Venice, The 1928,Ja 17,22:2
Dishonored Lady 1930,F 5,27:1
Country Wife, The 1936,D 2,34:1
Seaman, Adelaide
Honeymoon Lane 1926,S 21,32:3
Seaman, Frank
Laugh Parade, The 1931,S 20,VIII,3:1
Laugh Parade, The 1931,N 3,31:2
Laugh Parade, The 1931,D 6,VIII,1:1
Seaman, Gordon (Musical Director)
By Hex 1956,Je 19,25:1
Seaman, Harry
Laugh Parade, The 1931,S 20,VIII,3:1
Laugh Parade, The 1931,N 3,31:2
Laugh Parade, The 1931,D 6,VIII,1:1
Seaman, Margaret
Night Remembers, The 1934,N 28,24:3
Seaman, Mary
On Baile's Strand 1959,Ap 13,34:4
Seaman, Norman (Producer)
'Tis Pity She's a Whore 1958,D 6,21:1
Cicero 1961,F 9,37:2
Seamans, Nina
Twilight Walk 1951,S 25,25:4

Seamark (Playwright)
When Blue Hills Laughed 1927,O 9,VIII,2:1
Seamon, Helen
Vigil, The 1948,My 22,8:6
Now I Lay Me Down to Sleep 1950,Mr 3,21:2
No Exit 1956,Ag 15,23:1
Waltz of the Toreadors, The 1957,Ja 18,17:2
Searchinger, Gene (Director)
Curious Savage, The 1956,Mr 17,12:3
Searis, Margaret
Waterloo Bridge 1930,Ja 7,29:2
Searle, Deborah
Pirates of Penzance, The 1942,F 20,20:2
Searle, Donald
Peter Pan 1924,N 7,16:2
Searle, Jackie
Memory 1934,My 13,IX,2:6
Searle, Judith
New York Idea, The 1963,Jl 13,12:2
Angela 1969,O 31,33:1
Searles, Grace
Polly 1925,O 12,19:1
Sears, David (Playwright)
Juggernaut 1929,My 19,IX,3:2
Dead Ride Fast, The 1931,D 6,VIII,4:5
Sears, Forrest
Cock-A-Doodle Dandy 1955,N 4,26:5
Sears, Fred
Tide Rising 1937,Ja 26,17:2
Censored 1938,F 28,18:2
Lorelei 1938,N 30,21:2
Quiet, Please! 1940,N 9,20:3
Cue for Passion 1940,D 20,33:4
Sears, Harold (Playwright)
Lucky Break 1925,Ag 12,16:2
Sears, Hess T
It's the Valet 1933,D 15,25:4
Fiesta 1933,D 16,12:2
Sears, Lucille
Breaking Point, The 1923,Ag 17,8:4
Lucky Break 1925,Ag 12,16:2
Gentle Grafters 1926,O 28,23:1
See Naples and Die 1929,S 27,30:4
Pigeons and People 1933,Ja 17,22:3
Mulatto 1935,Ag 8,13:2
Call Me Ziggy 1937,F 13,9:6
Two on an Island 1940,Ja 23,17:2
Sears, Miriam
Checkerboard, The 1920,Ag 20,7:2
Dream Maker, The 1921,N 22,17:1
Sap, The 1924,D 16,28:3
Boundry Line, The 1930,F 6,21:1
Sears, Nancy
Master Builder, The 1957,D 18,42:7
John Gabriel Borkman 1959,N 26,57:4
Sears, Winton
Slight Case of Murder, A 1935,S 12,28:5
Stick-in-the-Mud 1935,D 2,18:2
Sears, Zelda
Pygmalion and Galatea 1920,Ap 28,9:3
Untitled-Benefit 1920,My 2,VI,2:2
Lollipop 1924,Ja 22,15:3
Sears, Zelda (Composer)
Lucky Break 1925,Ag 12,16:2
Sears, Zelda (Lyricist)
Lady Billy 1920,D 15,18:2
Clinging Vine, The 1922,D 25,20:2
Magic Ring, The 1923,O 2,10:1
Lollipop 1924,Ja 22,15:3
Sears, Zelda (Original Author)
Rainbow Rose 1926,Mr 17,28:2
Sears, Zelda (Playwright)
Lady Billy 1920,D 15,18:2
Clinging Vine, The 1922,D 25,20:2
Clinging Vine, The 1922,D 31,VII,1:1
Magic Ring, The 1923,O 2,10:1
Lollipop 1924,Ja 22,15:3
Broke 1925,My 3,VIII,2:1
Seastrom, Guje
Utopia! 1963,My 7,47:4
Seastrom, Julie
Burn Me to Ashes 1963,N 20,48:1
Seaton, George (Director)
Love in E Flat 1967,F 14,38:1
Seaton, George (Playwright)
But Not Goodbye 1944,Ap 12,19:2
Here's Love 1963,O 4,28:1
Seaver, Robert E (Director)
Sign of Jonah, The 1957,My 2,27:1
Seaver, Robert E (Producer)
Everyman Today 1958,Ja 16,32:4
Seavey, Erman
High Gear 1927,O 7,24:3
Seavey, Hollis M
On the Level 1937,Mr 26,24:4
Seavy, Erman
What Ann Brought Home 1927,F 22,22:2
Set a Thief 1927,F 22,22:1
Seaward, Sydney
Journey's End 1929,Mr 23,23:1
Journey's End 1930,Ja 27,24:7
Seawell, Brook
Traveling Lady 1954,O 28,45:2

Seawell, Brook—Cont
Wisteria Trees, The 1955,F 3,20:2
Seawell, Donald (Producer)
King Lear 1964,My 19,43:2
Comedy of Errors, The 1964,My 21,43:1
Seay, Bob (Lighting Director)
Riot 1968,D 20,64:1
Sebaldt, Maria
Philipp Hotz 1969,N 27,52:1
Firebugs, The 1969,N 27,52:1
Sebastian, John (Composer)
Jimmy Shine 1968,D 6,52:1
Jimmy Shine 1968,D 22,II,3:1
Sebastian, John (Lyricist)
Jimmy Shine 1968,D 6,52:1
Jimmy Shine 1968,D 22,II,3:1
Sebastian John
Variations of 1940 1940,Ja 29,12:1
Sebastien, Beryl
Medea 1960,Jl 26,25:2
Sebba (Scenic Designer)
Oedipus Rex 1948,My 24,23:2
Sebert, Neva
Forever This Land 1951,Jl 29,II,1:1
Sebesi, Erno (Translator)
Collision 1932,F 17,19:2
Sebree, Charles
Our Lan' 1947,Ap 19,11:2
Sebree, Charles (Costume Designer)
Garden of Time 1945,Mr 10,13:7
Henri Christophe 1945,Je 7,24:5
Sebree, Charles (Lyricist)
Mrs Patterson 1954,D 2,37:1
Sebree, Charles (Playwright)
Mrs Patterson 1954,D 2,37:1
Mrs Patterson 1957,F 6,20:2
Sebree, Charles (Scenic Designer)
Garden of Time 1945,Mr 10,13:7
Henri Christophe 1945,Je 7,24:5
Sechler, Curly
Hayride 1954,S 14,24:2
Secino, Betty
Russell Patterson's Sketch-Book 1960,F 8,35:1
What a Killing 1961,Mr 28,41:1
Seckel, Elizabeth
Children's Hour, The 1934,N 21,23:2
Seckler, Beatrice
Dear Judas 1947,O 6,26:4
Red Roses for Me 1955,D 29,15:2
Secombe, Harry
Pickwick 1963,Jl 5,13:2
Pickwick 1965,O 6,5:3
Secombe, Lesley
Boy Friend, The 1970,Ap 15,54:1
Secon, Norman
Yeomen of the Guard, The 1941,D 19,34:3
Cave Dwellers, The 1957,O 21,29:2
Secoy, Maryalice
Life of Man, The 1923,Ap 17,26:1
Secrest, Cecil W
What Ann Brought Home 1927,F 22,22:2
High Gear 1927,O 7,24:3
Secretan, Ingrid
Kiss Me, Kate 1949,Ja 30,II,6:5
Secretan, Lance
Escapade 1953,Ap 8,37:2
Secter, David (Lyricist)
Get Thee to Canterbury 1969,Ja 26,74:1
Secter, David (Playwright)
Get Thee to Canterbury 1969,Ja 26,74:1
Secter, David (Producer)
Get Thee to Canterbury 1969,Ja 26,74:1
Secunda, Sholom
Untitled-Benefit 1933,Ja 25,13:3
Secunda, Sholom (Composer)
Salt and Pepper 1933,Ap 24,10:2
Happy Family, A 1934,S 24,15:2
Game of Love, A 1934,O 25,26:6
East Side Wedding, An 1935,Ja 21,18:2
Itche Mayer of Warsaw 1935,Ja 31,22:4
Two Hearts 1935,My 6,22:2
Heaven on Earth 1935,O 8,26:2
Oh, You Girls! 1935,D 2,19:5
Pinye of Pinchev 1936,S 21,27:5
Night in Budapest, A 1936,N 3,33:2
His Jewish Girl 1936,D 9,34:1
Let's Get Married 1937,Ja 11,16:2
Street Singers 1938,D 12,25:6
Who Is Who? 1938,D 24,13:3
If I Were Rothschild 1940,Ja 1,28:7
Esterke 1940,O 18,24:2
Bagels and Yox 1951,S 13,38:2
Uncle Sam in Israel 1952,D 8,38:5
Shepherd King, The 1955,O 13,36:2
Brothers Ashkenazi, The 1955,N 12,24:4
It's a Funny World 1956,O 22,24:1
It Could Happen to You 1957,O 28,30:5
Nice People 1958,O 20,36:1
Kosher Widow, The 1959,N 2,40:2
My Son and I 1960,O 24,24:2
Bei Mir Bistu Schoen 1961,O 23,22:2
Cowboy in Israel, A 1962,O 29,36:2
My Wife With Conditions 1963,O 21,39:1
Good Luck 1964,O 19,38:3

Secunda, Sholom (Composer)—Cont
Poor Millionaire, The 1966,O 24,48:2
Bride Got Farblondjet, The 1967,N 6,61:6
Melody Lingers On, The 1969,N 17,55:1
Secunda, Sholom (Musical Director)
It Could Happen to You 1957,O 28,30:5
Secunda, William
Tevye the Dairyman 1935,O 25,25:1
Sedan, Rolfe
All Men Are Alike 1941,O 7,27:2
Little Dark Horse 1941,N 17,14:4
Time, Place and the Girl, The 1942,O 22,24:3
Bell for Adano, A 1944,D 7,21:2
Seder, Audrey
Opera Opera 1955,D 22,19:1
Floydada to Matador 1955,D 22,19:1
Sederholm, Richard
Walking Happy 1966,N 28,47:1
Sedgwick, Anne Douglas (Original Author)
Dark Hester 1931,My 17,VIII,1:3
Sedgwick, Charles
Hades, the Ladies 1934,Mr 29,25:3
Many Mansions 1937,O 28,28:6
Sedgwick, Edna
Boys and Girls Together 1940,O 2,19:2
Sedgwick, Paulita
Demon Mirror, The 1968,Mr 13,42:1
Sedgwick, Paulita (Scenic Designer)
Beclch 1968,D 17,59:1
Sedgwick, Winton
Master Builder Solness 1950,My 26,19:3
Sedley, Roy
Hot-Cha! 1932,Mr 9,17:3
Sedore, Robert
Susannah 1955,F 25,18:4
See, Edmond (Playwright)
Untitled-Play 1921,D 25,VI,1:8
Depositaire, La 1924,My 25,VIII,1:8
Saison d'Amour 1926,O 31,VIII,2:4
Metier d'Amant, Le 1928,Ap 29,IX,2:3
See, Edward
My Golden Girl 1920,F 3,18:2
Toto 1921,Mr 22,15:2
See, John
House of Shadows, The 1927,Ap 22,18:4
Seed and Austin
Vaudeville (Palace) 1923,F 13,25:1
Artists and Models 1924,O 16,33:3
Vaudeville (Hippodrome) 1926,My 11,25:3
Vaudeville (Palace) 1926,Je 8,23:1
Seegan, Sara
At War With the Army 1949,Mr 9,32:2
Seegar, Dorothy
Big Mogul, The 1925,My 12,26:3
Robin Hood 1929,N 20,26:5
Gondoliers, The 1931,Je 2,34:4
Seegar, Miriam
Crime 1927,O 19,24:2
Seegar, Sara
Horse Fever 1940,N 25,21:2
Vickie 1942,S 23,28:1
School for Scandal, The 1953,Je 24,29:2
Ernest in Love 1960,My 5,39:4
Seeger, Sanford
Dybbuk, The 1954,O 27,33:6
Three Sisters, The 1955,F 26,13:2
Cherry Orchard, The 1955,O 19,38:1
Uncle Vanya 1956,F 1,25:2
Uncle Vanya 1956,F 12,II,1:1
Month in the Country, A 1963,My 29,39:2
Seel, Charles
Drift 1925,N 25,15:3
So That's That 1925,D 15,28:3
Killers 1928,Mr 14,28:3
Seel, Jeanne
Every Man for Himself 1940,D 10,32:3
Seel, Peggy
Jubilee 1935,O 14,20:1
Seelen, Arthur
Winners and Losers 1947,F 27,27:2
Deputy of Paris, The 1947,Mr 22,9:5
White Devil, The 1955,Mr 15,32:5
Seelen, Jerry (Composer)
Star and Garter 1942,Je 25,26:2
New Priorities of 1943 1942,S 16,28:2
Seelen, Jerry (Lyricist)
Star and Garter 1942,Je 25,26:2
New Priorities of 1943 1942,S 16,28:2
Seelen, Jerry (Miscellaneous)
Ziegfeld Follies 1943,Ap 2,16:2
Seeley, Blossom
Vaudeville (Palace) 1921,Jl 5,15:1
Vaudeville (Palace) 1923,Mr 13,19:2
Vaudeville (Palace) 1925,Je 18,18:1
Vaudeville (Palace) 1926,My 4,31:2
Vaudeville (Palace) 1926,S 28,30:4
Vaudeville (Palace) 1927,S 20,33:3
Vaudeville (Palace) 1927,O 18,32:4
Vaudeville (Palace) 1927,O 25,33:2
Greenwich Village Follies 1928,Ap 10,32:2
Vaudeville (Palace) 1929,N 18,22:4
Vaudeville (Palace) 1931,Ap 20,16:2
Vaudeville (Hollywood) 1932,Ap 19,25:5

Seeley, Inez
Hot Rhythm 1930,Ag 22,18:5
Seeley, James
Like a King 1921,O 4,10:1
Spite Corner 1922,S 26,18:1
Sandalwood 1926,S 23,23:1
Sure Fire! 1926,O 21,23:1
Judy 1927,F 8,20:2
Behold This Dreamer 1927,N 1,20:4
Adventure 1928,S 26,25:2
Lady Lies, The 1928,N 27,36:2
Brothers 1928,D 26,14:3
Dinner at Eight 1932,O 24,18:2
American, Very Early 1934,Ja 31,21:2
Merrily We Roll Along 1934,O 1,14:1
First Lady 1935,N 27,17:4
Save Me the Waltz 1938,Mr 1,19:2
Ladies and Gentlemen 1939,O 18,30:2
Flight to the West 1940,D 31,19:1
Seeley, John
Hamlet 1970,O 27,54:2
Rosencrantz and Guildenstern Are Dead
1970,N 19,39:3
Sef, Roman (Translator)
My Fair Lady 1964,D 29,22:1
Seff, Linda
Whisper in God's Ear, A 1962,O 12,27:2
Seff, Manuel (Miscellaneous)
Natural Affection 1963,F 2,5:2
Dr Cook's Garden 1967,S 26,52:1
Seff, Manuel (Playwright)
Blessed Event 1932,Ja 31,VIII,1:6
Blessed Event 1932,F 13,23:2
Blessed Event 1932,F 21,VIII,1:1
Sweet Charity 1942,D 29,26:4
Seff, Richard
Hippolytus 1948,N 22,25:5
Darkness at Noon 1951,Ja 15,13:4
Seff, Richard (Playwright)
Paris Is Out! 1970,F 3,35:1
Segal, Alex (Director)
Compulsion 1957,O 25,21:1
Who Was That Lady I Saw You With?
1958,Mr 4,33:2
Jolly's Progress 1959,D 7,42:2
One Flew Over the Cuckoo's Nest 1963,N 14,40:2
Segal, Annette (Miscellaneous)
Evening With Mike Nichols and Elaine May, An
1960,O 10,37:1
Segal, Arthur
Midsummer Night's Dream, A 1931,Ag 19,19:3
Segal, Arthur (Scenic Designer)
Broadway 1926,S 17,19:3
Midsummer Night's Dream, A 1931,Ag 19,19:3
Both Your Houses 1933,Mr 7,20:3
Three-Cornered Moon 1933,Mr 17,20:6
Her Man of Wax 1933,O 12,32:3
First Apple, The 1933,D 28,25:1
But Not for Love 1934,N 27,26:2
Sky's the Limit, The 1934,D 18,25:5
Segal, Ben (Producer)
Fancy Meeting You Again 1952,Ja 15,23:2
Of Thee I Sing 1952,My 6,34:2
Segal, Benet (Miscellaneous)
Billy Budd 1951,F 12,18:3
Segal, Bernardo (Composer)
Maidens and Mistresses at Home at the Zoo
1958,O 29,31:1
Segal, David F (Lighting Director)
Say Nothing 1965,Ja 28,21:2
Madness of Lady Bright, The 1966,Mr 23,42:1
Ludlow Fair 1966,Mr 23,42:1
Private Lives 1968,My 20,59:1
Paradise Gardens East 1969,Mr 11,39:1
Conerico Was Here to Stay 1969,Mr 11,39:1
Home Away From, A 1969,Ap 29,40:3
World's a Stage, The 1969,My 13,42:1
Exhibition 1969,My 16,41:1
Oh! Calcutta! 1969,Je 18,33:1
Pequod 1969,Je 30,33:1
Scent of Flowers, A 1969,O 21,42:1
Summertree 1969,D 10,60:1
Seven Days of Mourning 1969,D 17,64:1
Last Sweet Days of Isaac, The 1970,Ja 27,49:1
White House Murder Case, The 1970,F 19,59:1
Bill Noname 1970,Mr 3,37:1
House of Leather, The 1970,Mr 19,56:1
Whispers on the Wind 1970,Je 4,50:1
Boesman and Lena 1970,Je 23,35:1
Happy Birthday, Wanda June 1970,O 8,58:2
Arsenic and Old Lace 1970,N 5,59:1
Dream Out of Time, A 1970,N 9,52:1
Segal, David F (Scenic Designer)
Say Nothing 1965,Ja 28,21:2
Madness of Lady Bright, The 1966,Mr 23,42:1
Ludlow Fair 1966,Mr 23,42:1
Conerico Was Here to Stay 1969,Mr 11,39:1
Paradise Gardens East 1969,Mr 11,39:1
Exhibition 1969,My 16,41:1
Pequod 1969,Je 30,33:1
House of Leather, The 1970,Mr 19,56:1
Whispers on the Wind 1970,Je 4,50:1
Dream Out of Time, A 1970,N 9,52:1

Segal, Edith
Dybbuk, The 1925,D 16,22:2
Segal, Edward
Fiesta 1929,S 18,35:1
Battle Hymn 1936,My 23,12:1
Unto Such Glory 1937,My 7,28:2
Processional 1937,O 14,23:1
Trojan Incident 1938,Ap 22,15:2
Segal, Erich (Lyricist)
Sing Muse 1961,D 7,52:1
Segal, Erich (Playwright)
Sing Muse 1961,D 7,52:1
Segal, George
Don Juan; Feast With the Statue, The
1956,Ja 4,21:4
Antony and Cleopatra 1959,Ja 14,28:1
Our Town 1959,Mr 24,46:2
Leave It to Jane 1959,My 26,30:2
Gideon 1961,N 10,38:1
Rattle of a Simple Man 1963,Ap 18,39:1
Knack, The 1964,My 28,42:2
Knack, The 1964,Je 7,II,1:1
Segal, Gilles
Untitled-Pantomime 1958,Ja 22,23:1
Segal, Linda
Glory in the Flower 1959,D 9,57:5
Stewed Prunes 1960,N 15,47:1
Untitled-Revue; Second City 1962,Ja 12,30:2
Student Gypsy, The; Prince of Liederkranz, The
1963,O 1,34:1
Conerico Was Here to Stay 1965,Mr 4,37:1
Segal, Linda (Playwright)
Stewed Prunes 1960,N 15,47:1
Segal, Louise
Roger Bloomer 1923,Mr 2,18:3
We've Got to Have Money 1923,Ag 21,12:1
Segal, Morton (Choreographer)
Valmouth 1960,O 7,29:1
Segal, Morton (Miscellaneous)
Deadly Game, The 1960,F 3,27:2
Segal, Morton (Producer)
Once There Was a Russian 1961,F 20,32:2
Segal, Nessa Lynn
Emerald Slippers, The 1970,S 2,31:2
Segal, Richard
Little Ol' Boy 1933,Ap 25,15:5
Segal, Richard Z (Director)
Once Upon a Time 1939,D 21,28:2
Segal, Sara
Revolt of the Beavers, The 1937,My 21,19:2
Segal, Shmuel
Dybbuk, The 1964,F 4,30:2
Children of the Shadows 1964,F 27,26:1
Segal, Susan
Jimmy Shine 1968,D 6,52:1
Segal, Vivienne
Untitled-Benefit 1921,My 2,12:3
Yankee Princess, The 1922,O 3,22:1
Vaudeville (Palace) 1923,Mr 13,19:2
Adrienne 1923,My 29,10:4
Ziegfeld Follies 1924,Je 25,26:1
Follies 1925,Mr 11,19:2
Follies 1925,Jl 7,24:3
Florida Girl 1925,N 3,34:1
Castles in the Air 1926,S 7,19:2
Desert Song, The 1926,D 1,24:2
Three Musketeers, The 1928,Mr 4,IX,2:3
Three Musketeers, The 1928,Mr 14,28:1
Three Musketeers, The 1928,Mr 25,IX,1:1
Chocolate Soldier, The 1931,S 22,33:3
Countess Maritza 1936,Ag 19,18:2
Bitter Sweet 1936,Ag 26,17:3
Maytime 1937,Jl 6,23:4
Wonderful Night, A; Fledermaus, Die
1937,Jl 14,17:1
Of Thee I Sing 1937,Ag 10,22:3
Of Thee I Sing 1937,Ag 18,14:4
Circus Princess, The 1937,Ag 31,26:6
I Married an Angel 1938,My 12,26:2
I Married an Angel 1938,My 22,XI,1:1
Pal Joey 1940,D 26,22:2
Connecticut Yankee, A 1943,N 18,30:2
Music in My Heart 1947,O 3,30:2
Great to Be Alive! 1950,Mr 24,28:2
Pal Joey 1952,Ja 4,17:6
Pal Joey 1952,Ja 13,II,1:1
Segall, Bernardo (Composer)
Camino Real 1953,Mr 20,26:1
Cave Dwellers, The 1957,O 21,29:2
Cave Dwellers, The 1961,O 16,34:2
Camino Real 1970,Ja 9,42:1
Segall, Ely
Anna Christie 1952,Ja 10,33:1
Segall, Harry (Original Author)
Lost Horizons 1934,O 16,31:2
Segall, Harry (Playwright)
Behavior of Mrs Crane, The 1928,Mr 21,30:1
Odds on Mrs Oakley, The 1944,O 3,18:8
Wonderful Journey 1946,D 26,30:2
Segall, Lee (Miscellaneous)
Wake Up, Darling 1956,My 3,34:2
Segar, Richard W (Lighting Director)
Sound of Silence, A 1965,Mr 9,30:1

ıar, Richard W (Scenic Designer)
ound of Silence, A 1965,Mr 9,30:1
ıare, George (Scenic Designer)
ingering Past, The 1932,Je 30,26:5
ıasture, Jack (Producer)
Design For A Stained Glass Window
1950,Ja 24,26:2
ıelcke, Tore
Untitled-One Woman Show 1956,Ap 9,23:5
ıger, Arthur E
Easy Terms 1925,S 23,22:2
ıger, Lucia
Ringside Seat 1938,N 23,24:5
More the Merrier, The 1941,S 16,19:3
ıger, Richard (Costume Designer)
Vida es Sueno, La 1964,Mr 18,49:1
Life Is a Dream 1964,Mr 20,24:1
ıger, Richard (Lighting Director)
Happy Ending 1965,N 16,56:1
Day of Absence 1965,N 16,56:1
ıger, Richard (Scenic Designer)
Day of Absence 1965,N 16,56:1
Happy Ending 1965,N 16,56:1
World of Gunter Grass, The 1966,Ap 27,38:1
Butterflies Are Free 1969,O 22,30:1
ıgree, Rita (Miscellaneous)
Bible Salesman, The 1960,F 22,12:2
ıgrera, Carolina
Vie Parisienne, La 1941,N 6,20:3
ıgur, Countesse de (Original Author)
Diloy le Chemineau 1926,N 14,VIII,2:1
ıgura, Mercedes
De Muy Buena Familia; Of Very Good Family
1932,Ap 29,13:3
ıhnert, Dale
Shoemaker's Prodigious Wife, The 1949,Je 15,38:2
ıibert, Wallace (Choreographer)
Candide 1956,D 3,40:2
ıibert, Wally (Miscellaneous)
Bajour 1964,N 24,42:1
ıibrecht, Florence
Patience 1935,S 3,24:4
ıid, David
Nautical but Nice 1931,Ap 19,31:6
ıid, Gerd
Ides of March, The 1962,N 17,16:4
ıida, Karaji
Teahouse of the August Moon, The 1953,O 16,32:1
Teahouse of the August Moon, The 1956,N 9,33:2
ıeidel, George
Rape of the Sabine Women, The 1949,F 5,10:5
ıeidel, Louise
Take a Chance 1932,N 28,11:2
ıeidel, Tom
Slightly Married 1943,O 26,19:2
Over Twenty-One 1944,Ja 4,20:2
Harvey 1944,N 2,23:2
ıeidelman, Arthur A (Director)
Awakening of Spring, The 1964,My 13,50:1
World of My America, The 1966,O 4,53:1
Hamp 1967,Mr 10,32:1
Ceremony of Innocence, The 1968,Ja 2,33:1
Four Seasons, The 1968,Mr 15,32:1
Billy 1969,Mr 24,56:1
Awake and Sing! 1970,My 28,35:1
Awake and Sing! 1970,Je 7,II,1:1
Seidelman, Arthur A (Playwright)
Awakening of Spring, The 1964,My 13,50:1
Seiden, Natalie (Miscellaneous)
Cocktails of 1934 1934,My 5,22:1
Seiden, Stan (Miscellaneous)
Fair Game for Lovers 1964,F 11,43:2
Seiden, Stan (Producer)
Pajama Tops 1963,Je 1,15:1
Seidenberg, Leon
New Man, The 1932,Ap 22,23:2
Seidenberg, Roderick (Scenic Designer)
Prisoner, The 1927,D 30,22:2
Seidi, Lea
White Horse Inn 1931,Ap 27,24:5
Seidler, Alma
Old Maid, The; Two Mothers, The 1937,F 24,19:3
Seidler, Carol
Flossie 1924,Je 4,25:2
Seidman, Arthur A (Director)
Inherit the Wind 1967,Je 23,50:1
Seidman, Bennie
Golden Ring, The 1930,F 1,14:7
Soul of a Woman, The 1930,F 22,13:1
Seidman, Lloyd
Oh, Hector! 1929,Mr 6,33:2
Great Shakes 1931,Mr 12,22:2
Seidman, M
Matinee Wife 1936,Ap 25,21:3
Seidman, Stanley
Oedipus Rex 1965,Jl 9,17:1
Modern Statuary 1968,My 28,41:1
Seiff, Gerald B (Miscellaneous)
Zelda 1969,Mr 6,38:1
Seig, John (Miscellaneous)
Much Ado About Nothing 1964,Je 11,26:2
Richard III 1964,Je 12,44:2
Hamlet 1964,Jl 4,9:1

Romeo and Juliet 1965,Je 21,36:3
Coriolanus 1965,Je 21,36:1
Taming of the Shrew, The 1965,Je 24,32:2
King Lear 1965,Je 25,39:1
Tiny Alice 1969,S 30,42:1
Seigel, Sylvia
Doctor's Dilemma, The 1969,Je 24,37:1
Seiger, Marvin (Playwright)
Beg, Borrow or Steal 1960,F 11,39:4
Seiger, Marvin L (Director)
Lysistrata 1968,N 15,42:1
Seigh, Eileen
Howdy Mr Ice 1948,Je 25,28:5
Howdy, Mr Ice of 1950 1949,My 27,24:2
Seigner, Francoise
Tartuffe 1968,Jl 3,28:2
Troupe Du Roi, La 1970,F 4,38:1
Femmes Savaantes, Les 1970,F 14,12:1
Malade Imaginaire, Le 1970,F 18,40:2
Seigner, Louis
Bourgeois Gentilhomme, Le 1955,O 26,26:1
Bourgeois Gentilhomme, Le 1955,O 30,II,1:1
Barbier de Seville, Le 1955,N 9,40:1
Impromptu de Versailles, L' 1961,F 22,30:1
Tartuffe 1961,Mr 1,28:1
Britannicus 1961,Mr 3,17:1
Dindon, Le 1961,Mr 8,38:1
Seigner, Louis (Director)
Tartuffe 1961,Mr 1,28:1
Seiler, C Linn (Composer)
Great Music 1924,O 6,24:1
Seiler, Conrad (Playwright)
Censored 1938,F 28,18:2
Seiler, Jacques
Lorenzaccio 1958,O 15,44:2
Seiler, Jay
Vaudeville (Palace) 1932,Jl 11,11:6
Seiller (M)
Demi-Monde, Le 1922,N 15,22:3
Seiltgen, Ernst (Director)
Nathan der Weise 1966,D 10,45:2
Seip, Peter
Coriolanus 1938,F 2,14:5
Seitz, Dran
Ondine 1954,F 19,23:1
Fanny 1954,N 5,16:1
Widowers' Houses 1959,Mr 3,39:2
Moonbirds 1959,O 10,13:1
Becket 1960,O 6,50:1
Happiest Girl in the World, The 1961,Ap 4,42:1
Seitz, Dran (Director)
Mandragola 1958,My 29,23:2
Seitz, John Frank
Cross and the Sword, The 1965,Je 28,32:6
Seitz, Tani
Moon in Capricorn 1953,O 28,37:2
Ondine 1954,F 19,23:1
Fanny 1954,N 5,16:1
Island of Goats 1955,O 5,40:1
Antigone 1956,Ap 3,32:2
No Exit 1956,Ag 15,23:1
Royal Gambit 1959,Mr 5,34:2
Royal Gambit 1959,Mr 15,II,1:1
Nervous Set, The 1959,My 13,43:1
Confederates, The 1959,S 29,45:1
Prodigal, The 1960,F 12,23:1
Prodigal, The 1960,F 21,II,1:1
Noontide 1961,Je 2,37:1
Seitz, W Thomas (Costume Designer)
Streets of New York, The 1963,O 30,47:1
Seizer, Milton
Richard III 1949,F 9,33:2
Seka, Ron
Journey of the Fifth Horse, The 1966,Ap 22,36:1
Sometime Jam Today 1967,F 13,41:1
Sekiya, Yukio (Choreographer)
Fiddler on the Roof 1967,S 7,50:1
Sekiya, Yukio (Director)
Fiddler on the Roof 1967,S 7,50:1
Selbert, Marianne
Cabaret 1966,N 21,62:1
Selbert, Wallace
Along Fifth Avenue 1949,Ja 14,28:2
Selbit
Vaudeville (Hippodrome) 1924,S 30,27:5
Selby, Anne
Theatre of the Soul 1942,Mr 21,13:5
Across the Board on Tomorrow Morning
1942,Mr 21,13:5
Selby, David
Unseen Hand, The 1970,Ap 2,43:1
Devil's Disciple, The 1970,Je 30,48:1
Devil's Disciple, The 1970,Jl 12,II,1:3
Gandhi 1970,O 21,37:1
Selby, Edgar Fordham
This Mad Whirl 1937,Ja 10,II,4:8
Selby, Harriette
Point of No Return 1951,D 14,35:2
Sabrina Fair 1953,N 12,37:1
Selby, Harry
Button, Button 1929,O 24,26:1
Everything's Jake 1930,Ja 17,20:4
Doctor X 1930,Jl 31,12:4

Selby, Harry—Cont
Overture 1930,D 8,26:4
Hamlet 1931,N 6,28:4
I Was Waiting for You 1933,N 14,23:3
Dead End 1935,O 29,17:2
Lady Precious Stream 1936,Ja 28,15:2
Juno and the Paycock 1940,Ja 17,24:2
Strings, My Lord, Are False, The 1942,My 20,24:2
Bell for Adano, A 1944,D 7,21:2
Anne of the Thousand Days 1948,D 9,49:2
Selby, Ott
Reunion of Sorts 1969,O 15,40:1
Five Star Saint 1970,F 11,41:2
Selby, Tony
Enemy 1969,D 19,65:6
Selden, Albert (Composer)
Small Wonder 1948,S 16,33:5
Selden, Albert (Producer)
Grey-Eyed People, The 1952,D 18,41:2
His and Hers 1954,Ja 8,18:2
Body Beautiful, The 1958,Ja 24,15:2
Girls Against the Boys, The 1959,N 3,26:1
Selden, Albert W (Producer)
Man of La Mancha 1965,N 23,52:1
Hallelujah, Baby! 1967,Ap 27,51:1
Portrait of a Queen 1968,F 29,29:1
Come Summer 1969,Mr 19,43:1
Selden, Neil (Playwright)
Someone's Comin' Hungry 1969,Ap 1,51:1
Selden, Samuel
S S Glencairn 1924,N 4,31:4
Selden, Samuel (Director)
Shroud My Body Down 1934,D 9,II,1:6
Lost Colony, The 1937,Jl 11,X,2:1
Forever This Land 1951,Jl 29,II,1:1
Wilderness Road 1955,Je 30,20:4
Confederacy, The 1958,Jl 3,20:1
Selden, Samuel (Miscellaneous)
Forever This Land 1952,Je 30,14:6
Selden, Tom
Faith of Our Fathers 1950,Ag 6,72:2
Seldes, Gilbert (Playwright)
Wise-Crackers, The 1925,D 17,26:1
Lysistrata 1930,Ap 29,30:5
Lysistrata 1930,Je 1,VIII,1:1
Lysistrata 1930,Je 6,20:1
Fall of Berg-Op-Zoom, The 1930,Je 8,IX,2:7
Swingin' the Dream 1939,N 30,24:2
Lysistrata 1946,O 18,27:5
Lysistrata 1959,My 20,40:2
Seldes, Marian
Medea 1947,O 21,27:2
Crime and Punishment 1947,D 23,29:3
Medea 1949,My 3,31:2
That Lady 1949,N 23,18:4
Tower Beyond Tragedy, The 1950,N 27,29:1
Tower Beyond Tragedy, The 1950,D 10,II,5:1
High Ground, The 1951,F 21,31:2
Come of Age 1952,Ja 24,22:2
Ondine 1954,F 19,23:1
Ondine 1954,F 28,II,1:1
Chalk Garden, The 1955,O 27,29:1
Wall, The 1960,O 12,44:4
Diff'rent 1961,O 18,52:1
Long Voyage Home, The 1961,D 5,49:1
Gift of Time, A 1962,F 23,34:1
Ginger Man, The 1963,N 22,42:1
Milk Train Doesn't Stop Here Anymore, The
1964,Ja 2,33:1
All Women Are One 1965,Ja 8,21:1
Delicate Balance, A 1966,S 23,44:1
Before You Go 1968,Ja 12,20:1
Three Sisters, The 1969,Ag 4,29:1
Three Sisters, The 1969,Ag 10,II,3:1
Mercy Street 1969,O 28,43:1
Mercy Street 1969,N 2,II,3:1
Seldin, J (Scenic Designer)
Father and Son 1956,O 20,17:4
Seldin, Timmy
Doll's House, A 1954,N 15,32:2
Selee, Marion
Hansel and Gretel 1929,D 25,21:1
Orpheus in Hades 1930,D 16,30:1
Threepenny Opera, The 1954,Mr 11,26:5
Threepenny Opera, The 1955,S 21,38:1
Seletsky, Harold (Composer)
Wicked Cooks, The 1967,Ja 24,42:1
Self, Clifton
Hell's Bells! 1925,Ja 27,14:2
Appearances 1925,O 15,27:3
Crime 1927,F 23,27:3
Ten Per Cent 1927,S 14,29:3
Rope 1928,F 23,18:3
Crooks' Convention, The 1929,S 19,37:4
Self, Edwin B (Playwright)
Junk 1927,Ja 6,25:1
Two Strange Women 1933,Ja 11,23:3
Distant City, The 1941,S 23,27:5
Self, Lucian
Three and One 1933,O 26,22:6
Times Have Changed 1935,F 26,16:1
Juno and the Paycock 1940,Ja 17,24:2
Pie in the Sky 1941,D 23,26:5
Joy Forever, A 1946,Ja 8,20:2

Selgicke, Tore
Abraham's Offering 1938,D 18,IX,4:2
Selig, Brenda Lorraine
My Heart's in the Highlands 1949,N 22,36:7
My Heart's in the Highlands 1950,F 18,8:4
Selinska, Helen
Chair, The 1930,O 4,15:4
Selinskaya, Fanya
Chauve-Souris 1929,Ja 23,20:2
Trojan Women, The 1938,Ja 25,24:2
Selinsky, Helen
Armored Train No 1469 1931,N 28,20:3
Selkirk, Jerry (Playwright)
Why We Misbehave 1935,Jl 25,14:8
Sell, David (Miscellaneous)
Burn Me to Ashes 1963,N 20,48:1
Junebug Graduates Tonight! 1967,F 27,35:1
Sell, Henry G
Virtue (?) 1922,N 17,14:1
Sell, Janie
George M! 1968,Ap 11,48:1
Dames at Sea 1970,Ja 5,46:3
Dames at Sea 1970,S 24,60:1
Sellar, W C (Original Author)
1066 and All That 1935,My 26,XI,2:5
Sellars, Elizabeth
Tea and Sympathy 1957,Ap 26,22:5
Hamlet 1961,Ap 12,46:1
Italian Girl, The 1968,Jl 4,14:1
Sellars, Lawrence
Street Sounds 1970,O 23,32:1
Seller, Robert
Nuit au Bouge, Une 1923,O 16,18:1
Court Circuit, Le 1923,O 16,18:1
Horrible Experience, L' 1923,O 23,16:1
Alcide Pepis 1923,O 30,17:2
Crucifies, Les 1923,O 30,17:2
Peu de Musique, Un 1923,N 6,22:1
Trois Masques, Les 1923,N 6,22:1
Laboratoire des Hallucinations, Le 1923,N 20,23:3
Petite Bonnie Serieuse 1923,N 27,23:5
Sellers, Arlene (Miscellaneous)
Anyone Can Whistle 1964,Ap 6,36:1
Sellers, Arthur
Camino Real 1970,Ja 9,42:1
Operation Sidewinder 1970,Mr 13,33:1
Sellers, Brother John
Tambourines to Glory 1963,N 4,47:1
Sellers, Clifford
Diff'rent 1925,F 11,19:3
Adam Solitaire 1925,N 7,19:2
Great God Brown, The 1926,Ja 25,26:1
Sellers, Peter
Brouhaha 1958,Ag 28,18:8
Sellery, William
Pride 1923,My 3,22:3
Ballyhoo 1927,Ja 5,18:1
Kiss Me! 1927,Jl 22,17:1
People Don't Do Such Things 1927,N 24,28:3
Eva the Fifth 1928,Ag 29,19:3
Selley, Ernest
Mr Sampson 1927,My 8,30:1
Sellier, Georges
Duel, Le 1922,N 16,22:2
Sellier (M)
Misanthrope, Le 1922,N 22,18:2
Selling, C M (Playwright)
So Am I 1928,Ja 28,9:1
Sellman, Hunton D (Lighting Director)
Tread the Green Grass 1932,Jl 24,IX,1:3
Sellner, Gustav Rudolf (Director)
Don Carlos 1964,N 25,40:1
Sellors, Sue
Vintage '60 1960,S 13,41:1
Sells, Bryant
Rope 1928,F 23,18:3
Sells, Milton
Heartbreak House 1950,Mr 22,33:2
Selman, Joseph
Out of the Seven Seas 1923,N 20,23:3
Shipwrecked 1924,N 13,18:1
Selman, Linda
Criminals, The 1970,F 26,33:2
Selman, Robert
Othello 1937,Ja 7,16:4
Selmar
Maitresse de Roi 1926,D 1,24:1
Dame aux Camelias, La 1926,D 7,24:2
Selmier, Deane
Ballad of the Sad Cafe, The 1963,O 31,27:1
Sels, Jane
George White's Scandals 1926,Je 15,23:2
Selsby, Harvey
Conerico Was Here to Stay 1965,Mr 4,37:1
Selser, E Maxwell
Six-Fifty, The 1921,O 25,20:1
Beggar on Horseback 1924,F 13,17:2
Selser, Maxwell (Playwright)
Eye on the Sparrow 1938,My 4,26:3
Seltzer, Carl (Lighting Director)
Laughwind 1966,Mr 3,27:1
Venus-Shot 1966,Je 24,30:2
Pin Up 1966,Je 24,30:2

Miracle in Brooklyn 1966,Je 24,30:2
Child and the Dragon, The 1966,Je 24,30:2
Seltzer, Dov (Composer)
Megilla of Itzik Manger, The 1968,O 10,60:1
Megilla of Itzik Manger, The 1969,Ap 21,55:1
Seltzer, Edwin (Composer)
Laugh It Off 1934,Ap 5,24:2
Seltzer, Marjorie
Prince of Pilsen, The 1930,Ja 14,24:3
Seltzer, Meyer
Chair, The 1930,O 4,15:4
Armored Train No 1469 1931,N 28,20:3
Seltzer, Thomas (Translator)
Inspector General, The 1923,My 1,24:1
Selver, Paul (Playwright)
R U R 1930,F 18,28:1
Mother, The 1939,Mr 19,XI,3:3
Mother, The 1939,Ap 26,26:2
R U R 1942,D 4,30:2
Selwart, Tonio
Liliom 1932,O 27,23:2
Camille 1932,O 28,23:2
Pursuit of Happiness, The 1933,O 10,24:4
Pursuit of Happiness, The 1934,Je 24,IX,1:4
Laughing Woman, The 1936,O 14,30:1
Flight Into China 1939,S 12,28:1
Russian Bank 1940,My 25,20:2
Candle in the Wind 1941,S 16,19:6
Candle in the Wind 1941,O 23,26:2
Candle in the Wind 1941,N 2,IX,1:1
Temper the Wind 1946,D 28,10:2
Temper the Wind 1947,Ja 12,II,1:1
Seeds in the Wind 1948,Ap 26,27:2
Seeds in the Wind 1948,My 26,29:2
Hidden River, The 1957,Ja 24,32:1
Lute Song 1959,Mr 13,24:1
And the Wind Blows 1959,Ap 29,28:1
Selwyn, Arch (Miscellaneous)
Silver Tassie, The 1929,O 25,26:1
Foreigners 1939,D 6,30:2
Selwyn, Arch (Playwright)
Private Lives 1931,My 12,29:3
Selwyn, Arch (Producer)
Monkey Talks, The 1925,D 29,20:1
Untitled-Magic Show 1926,My 24,24:2
Ghost Train, The 1926,Ag 26,17:2
Garden of Eden, The 1927,S 28,28:1
This Year of Grace 1928,N 8,27:1
Many Waters 1929,S 26,27:1
Middle Watch, The 1929,O 17,27:1
Bitter Sweet 1929,N 6,30:2
Wake Up and Dream 1929,D 31,14:3
Cherries Are Ripe 1930,O 19,IX,3:4
Kiss of Importance, A 1930,D 2,31:3
Devil Passes, The 1932,Ja 5,20:3
Thousand Summers, A 1932,My 25,23:4
Evensong 1933,F 1,13:4
Forsaking All Others 1933,Mr 2,21:2
Lady Jane 1934,S 11,24:2
Continental Varieties 1934,O 4,18:3
Conversation Piece 1934,O 24,24:1
Aiglon, L' 1934,N 5,22:2
Revenge With Music 1934,N 29,33:5
Story to Be Whispered 1937,Ag 20,21:4
Selwyn, Edgar (Director)
Quarantine 1924,D 17,19:7
Adorable Liar, The 1926,Ag 31,15:2
Gentlemen Prefer Blondes 1926,S 29,23:1
Possession 1928,O 3,35:1
Other Men's Wives 1929,N 13,24:4
Fast Service 1931,N 18,26:3
Selwyn, Edgar (Miscellaneous)
Barker, The 1927,Ja 19,20:6
Redemption: Lebende Leichnam, Der; Living
Corpse, The 1928,N 20,28:2
Selwyn, Edgar (Playwright)
Mirage, The 1920,O 1,14:1
Love Chef, The 1921,Je 12,VI,1:6
Anything Might Happen 1923,F 21,22:3
Anything Might Happen 1923,F 25,VII,1:1
Dancing Mothers 1924,My 4,VIII,2:1
Dancing Mothers 1924,Ag 12,12:2
Dear Sir 1924,S 24,21:3
Quarantine 1924,D 17,19:7
Something to Brag About 1925,Jl 12,VII,1:8
Something to Brag About 1925,Ag 14,14:3
Adorable Liar, The 1926,Ag 31,15:2
Possession 1928,Jl 22,VII,1:7
Possession 1928,S 23,IX,2:2
Possession 1928,O 3,35:1
Selwyn, Edgar (Producer)
Quarantine 1924,D 17,19:7
Imaginative Girl, The 1926,Ag 8,VII,3:1
Adorable Liar, The 1926,Ag 31,15:2
Gentlemen Prefer Blondes 1926,S 29,23:1
Proud Woman, A 1926,N 16,24:1
Possession 1928,Jl 22,VII,1:7
Eva the Fifth 1928,Jl 22,VII,1:7
Eva the Fifth 1928,Ag 29,19:3
Possession 1928,O 3,35:1
Ghosts; Gespenster 1929,F 6,30:3
Other Men's Wives 1929,N 13,24:4
Strike Up the Band 1929,D 29,VIII,4:3

Selwyn, Edgar (Producer)—Cont
Strike Up the Band 1930,Ja 15,29:1
Fast Service 1931,N 18,26:3
Wookey, The 1941,S 11,20:5
Selwyn, Florence
Bad Habits of 1926 1926,My 1,11:1
Evensong 1933,F 1,13:4
Lady Jane 1934,S 11,24:2
Selwyn, Ruth (Miscellaneous)
Bachelor Born 1938,Ja 26,26:3
Selwyn, Ruth (Producer)
Nine Fifteen Revue, The 1930,F 12,26:2
Three After Three 1939,N 25,13:5
Walk With Music 1940,Je 5,33:2
Selzer, Milton
Fifth Horseman, The 1949,Je 14,26:6
My Heart's in the Highlands 1949,N 22,36:7
My Heart's in the Highlands 1950,F 18,8:4
Earth Spirit 1950,Je 7,33:4
Julius Caesar 1950,Je 21,30:1
Arms and the Man 1950,O 20,34:2
Scarecrow, The 1953,Je 17,31:1
Bullfight 1954,Ja 13,25:2
Doctor's Dilemma, The 1955,Ja 12,22:1
Once Upon a Tailor 1955,My 24,36:2
Tiger at the Gates 1955,O 4,40:1
Visit, The 1958,My 6,40:1
Selzer, Milton (Miscellaneous)
Tiger Rag, The 1961,F 17,20:2
Selzer, Milton (Musical Director)
All Kinds of Giants 1961,D 19,40:1
By Jupiter 1967,Ja 20,28:2
Blood Red Roses 1970,Mr 23,48:1
Selznick, Daniel (Miscellaneous)
Highest Tree, The 1959,N 5,41:1
Selznick, David O (Producer)
Anna Christie 1941,Ag 10,IX,1:8
Lottie Dundass 1941,Ag 22,19:5
Selznick, Irene (Producer)
Streetcar Named Desire, A 1947,D 4,42:2
Streetcar Named Desire, A 1950,My 24,36:1
Bell, Book and Candle 1950,N 15,37:4
Flight Into Egypt 1952,Mr 19,33:2
Chalk Garden, The 1955,O 27,29:1
Complaisant Lover, The 1961,N 2,43:2
Semal, Jean (Miscellaneous)
Don Carlos 1962,F 28,27:5
Semal, John P (Costume Designer)
Storm, The 1962,Mr 31,17:2
Semal, John P (Miscellaneous)
Storm, The 1962,Mr 31,17:2
Semans, William H (Producer)
House of Leather, The 1970,Mr 19,56:1
Semenoff
Chauve-Souris 1923,S 4,12:1
Seminoff, Betty
Girl From Warsaw, The 1931,S 14,15:5
Semkoff, Sheine Rochel (Playwright)
His Wife's Lover 1929,O 21,30:6
Semmel, Hannah
Legend of Leonora, The 1926,My 1,10:1
Semmes, Margot
You and I 1925,O 20,29:1
Semmler, Alexander (Composer)
Solo 1962,Ap 27,26:1
Semochkin, Serge P (Director)
Moscow Circus on Ice 1970,D 9,63:1
Semon, Marty
Music in the Air 1932,N 9,28:2
Semon, Maxine
Mr Adam 1949,My 26,34:6
Semonin, David (Miscellaneous)
Someone's Comin' Hungry 1969,Ap 1,51:1
Pequod 1969,Je 30,33:1
Semowitch, Sam
Don't Worry Brother! 1963,O 14,35:2
Semple, Lorenzo Jr (Playwright)
Tonight in Samarkand 1955,F 17,22:2
Golden Fleecing 1959,O 16,24:5
Semyonova, Lydia
Greenwich Village Follies 1924,N 25,26:2
Sen, Satu
Antigone 1930,Ap 25,28:4
Sen, Satu (Scenic Designer)
Three Sisters, The 1930,Ja 9,22:2
Sena, Joan
Saint of Bleecker Street, The 1965,Mr 19,28:1
Senac, Rene Marguerite
Mozart 1926,D 28,16:1
Illusioniste, L' 1927,Ja 11,36:5
Senber, Henry
Falstaff 1928,D 26,14:2
Sendrey, Albert (Miscellaneous)
New Faces of 1956 1956,Je 15,32:1
Sendroff, Abraham
Parnosseh 1939,F 20,12:5
Sendry, Albert (Musical Director)
Peter Pan 1954,O 21,30:2
Seneca (Playwright)
Oedipus 1968,Mr 31,II,5:1
Oedipus 1968,Ap 2,54:1
Oedipus 1968,Jl 31,29:1
Senensky, Ralph (Director)
Crucible, The 1958,Mr 17,21:1

enft, Charles
Tick-Tack-Toe 1920,F 24,11:2
enger, John
Penny Friend, The 1966,D 27,46:1
enghor, Lina
Macbeth 1969,D 14,87:1
enie, Richard (Scenic Designer)
Circle, The 1939,Jl 12,17:2
What a Life 1939,Ag 2,17:5
Blind Alley 1939,Ag 23,18:8
enie, Richard Harrison (Scenic Designer)
Saint Joan 1951,O 5,23:2
eniro, W H
Merton of the Movies 1922,N 14,16:2
enius, Martha
Versunkene Glocke, Die 1936,N 20,26:3
enn, Herbert (Lighting Director)
O Marry Me 1961,O 28,13:1
Double Dublin 1963,D 27,16:2
What Makes Sammy Run? 1964,F 28,19:1
Roar Like a Dove 1964,My 22,40:2
enn, Herbert (Scenic Designer)
Opera Opera 1955,D 22,19:1
Hello Out There 1955,D 22,19:1
Hungerers, The 1955,D 22,19:1
Floydada to Matador 1955,D 22,19:1
Liliom 1956,F 18,12:5
Beaver Coat, The 1956,Mr 29,22:5
Idiot's Delight 1957,F 23,14:2
Right You Are (If You Think You Are)
1957,Mr 5,37:1
Brothers Karamazov, The 1957,D 9,39:4
Brothers Karamazov, The 1957,D 22,II,3:1
Oklahoma! 1958,Mr 8,15:2
Ardele 1958,Ap 9,39:4
Hamlet of Stepney Green 1958,N 14,21:1
She Shall Have Music 1959,Ja 23,18:4
Time of Vengeance 1959,D 11,39:1
Time of Vengeance 1959,D 27,II,1:1
Gay Divorce 1960,Ap 4,37:1
Ronde, La 1960,My 10,44:2
Idiot, The 1960,S 26,38:1
Man and Superman 1960,N 7,46:2
Emmanuel 1960,D 5,42:2
Montserrat 1961,Ja 9,30:5
Five Posts in the Market Place 1961,Mr 6,30:1
Smiling the Boy Fell Dead 1961,Ap 20,28:1
O Marry Me 1961,O 28,13:1
Merchant of Venice, The 1962,F 3,13:2
I Got Shoes 1963,Ja 25,12:2
Boys From Syracuse, The 1963,Ap 16,31:1
Double Dublin 1963,D 27,16:2
What Makes Sammy Run? 1964,F 28,19:1
Roar Like a Dove 1964,My 22,40:2
Great Scot! 1965,N 12,56:3
By Jupiter 1967,Ja 20,28:2
Dodo Bird, The 1967,D 9,62:1
Peddler, The 1967,D 9,62:1
Private Lives 1968,My 20,59:1
Little Boxes; Trevor 1969,D 4,71:2
Little Boxes; Coffee Lace, The 1969,D 4,71:2
enna, Charles
Earl Carroll's Vanities 1923,Jl 6,8:2
Hold Your Horses 1933,S 26,26:4
Hooray for What! 1937,D 2,32:5
Ziegfeld Follies 1943,Ap 2,16:2
Laffing Room Only 1944,D 25,15:4
ennett, Earl (Director)
Billy Budd 1955,My 4,35:1
Amedee or, How to Disentangle Yourself
1955,N 1,27:3
Recruiting Officer, The 1958,F 8,12:2
ennett, Earl (Producer)
Recruiting Officer, The 1958,F 8,12:2
ennott, Jean
Caesar and Cleopatra 1935,Ag 22,21:1
ennott, John
Valley Forge 1934,D 11,28:3
ennott, Ruth
Hello, Yourself 1928,O 31,28:2
enroku, Onoe
Kanjincho; Subscription List, The 1960,Je 3,26:1
Kagotsurube; Courtesan, The 1960,Je 3,26:1
Musume Dojoji; Maiden at the Dojo Temple, The
1960,Je 10,37:1
Musume Dojoji; Maiden at the Dojo Temple, The
1960,Je 17,35:4
Kagami-Jishi; Mirror Lion Dance, The
1969,S 11,53:1
Kumagai Jinya 1969,S 18,64:1
enter, Boyd
Vaudeville (Palace) 1931,Je 29,20:1
entes, Pierre
Maitresse de Roi 1926,D 1,24:1
Dame aux Camelias, La 1926,D 7,24:2
enya, Nakamura
Tsubosaka Reigenki; Miracle at Tsubosaka Temple,
The 1960,Je 3,26:1
Kanjincho; Subscription List, The 1960,Je 3,26:1
Kagotsurube; Courtesan, The 1960,Je 3,26:1
Musume Dojoji; Maiden at the Dojo Temple, The
1960,Je 10,37:1

Musume Dojoji; Maiden at the Dojo Temple, The
1960,Je 17,35:4
Seplow, Jerome
Rutherford and Son 1927,Ap 13,29:2
Vegetable, The, or From President to Postman
1929,Ap 11,32:3
Septinelli, A E
Night of January 16 1935,D 16,22:5
Sequeira, Horace
Many Waters 1929,S 26,27:1
South 1955,My 2,17:4
Serabian, Lorraine
Sign of Jonah, The 1960,S 9,35:1
Electra 1962,Mr 22,42:1
Secret Life of Walter Mitty, The 1964,O 27,44:5
Bugs 1965,N 19,31:1
Veronica 1965,N 19,31:1
Zorba 1968,N 18,58:1
Serabian, Lorraine (Scenic Designer)
Bugs 1965,N 19,31:1
Veronica 1965,N 19,31:1
Seranne, Ann (Producer)
Close Quarters 1939,Mr 7,19:2
Serbagi, Roger
Falstaff 1966,Je 20,27:1
Twelfth Night 1966,Je 23,28:1
Julius Caesar 1966,Je 24,29:2
Certain Young Man, A 1967,D 27,45:1
Henry V 1969,Je 9,57:1
Much Ado About Nothing 1969,Je 16,57:1
Henry V 1969,N 11,43:1
Awake and Sing! 1970,My 28,35:1
Awake and Sing! 1970,Je 7,II,1:1
Serbais, Jean
Hedda Gabler 1962,D 13,8:5
Serbaroli, Alexander
John Brown's Body 1953,F 16,17:2
Serber, Barry
Three Plays of the Sea 1970,Ag 20,39:1
Serchio, Tony
Hawk, The 1968,Ap 18,54:1
Serebrier, Jose (Musical Director)
Romeo and Juliet 1965,Je 21,36:3
Coriolanus 1965,Je 21,36:1
Taming of the Shrew, The 1965,Je 24,32:2
King Lear 1965,Je 25,39:1
Serebrov, Muni
Radio Girl, The 1929,O 19,22:4
Jolly Orphan, The 1929,D 23,18:6
Little Clown, The 1930,Mr 15,23:3
Song of the Ghetto, The 1932,O 3,15:5
Here Runs the Bride 1934,S 20,21:3
Here Runs the Bride 1934,N 4,IX,2:1
One in a Million 1934,N 17,13:2
What Girls Do 1935,Ja 14,10:4
Saint and Sinners 1935,D 30,15:2
Freidel Becomes a Bride 1936,F 10,14:3
My Baby's Wedding 1938,O 10,15:3
With Open Eyes 1938,O 27,27:2
Polish Rabbi, The 1939,Mr 20,13:3
In a Jewish Grocery 1939,O 2,15:2
Her Great Mistake 1940,F 5,12:6
Worlds Apart 1941,Ja 23,19:3
Shylock and His Daughter 1947,S 30,22:2
Voice of Israel, The 1948,O 26,40:2
Hershel, The Jester 1948,D 14,39:2
Abi Gezunt 1949,O 10,19:4
Sadie Is a Lady 1950,Ja 28,9:2
Second Marriage 1953,O 12,30:1
Wish Me Luck! 1954,N 1,37:2
Wedding March, The 1955,O 17,33:1
It's a Funny World 1956,O 22,24:1
It Could Happen to You 1957,O 28,30:5
Nice People 1958,O 20,36:1
Hole in the Head, A 1958,N 26,25:2
Kosher Widow, The 1959,N 2,40:2
Between Two Thieves 1960,F 12,23:1
Wall, The 1960,O 12,44:4
Shadow of Heroes 1961,D 6,59:1
Corruption in the Palace of Justice 1963,O 9,49:2
Day the Whores Came Out to Play Tennis, The
1965,Mr 16,45:1
Kitchen, The 1966,Je 14,50:1
Javelin 1966,N 10,63:1
Tenth Man, The 1967,N 9,54:1
Soldiers 1968,My 2,58:1
Winterset 1968,Jl 23,28:2
End of All Things Natural, The 1969,S 12,38:1
Sergava, Katharine
Oklahoma! 1943,Ap 1,27:1
Oklahoma! 1943,My 9,II,6:4
Look, Ma, I'm Dancin' 1948,Ja 30,20:2
Look, Ma, I'm Dancin' 1948,F 8,II,2:1
Edge of the Sword, The 1949,N 10,40:3
Typewriter, The 1955,Jl 29,8:3
Sergel, Christopher (Playwright)
Winesburg, Ohio 1958,F 6,22:2
Sergent, Margherita
First Man, The 1922,Mr 6,9:2
Sergeyeva, Nina
Russian Isba 1920,F 17,19:2
Russian Isba 1920,Mr 12,18:4

Sergine, Vera
Carnaval de l'Amour, Le 1928,Mr 11,VIII,2:7
Phedre 1930,N 30,IX,3:3
Asie 1932,Ja 10,VIII,3:1
Napoleon Unique 1936,N 13,27:3
Serio, Joy
Most Happy Fella, The 1966,My 12,55:1
Serkin, Rudolf
Variations of 1940 1940,Ja 29,12:1
Serle, Christopher
Measure for Measure 1967,F 15,37:1
Hamlet 1967,F 17,44:1
Romeo and Juliet 1967,F 22,18:1
Serlin, Oscar
Jade God, The 1929,My 14,28:3
Serlin, Oscar (Miscellaneous)
Broken Dishes 1929,N 6,28:3
Lost Sheep 1930,My 6,33:2
Serlin, Oscar (Producer)
Life With Father 1939,N 9,26:2
Life With Father 1940,Mr 3,X,2:5
King's Maid, The 1941,Ag 27,15:3
Moon Is Down, The 1942,Ap 8,22:2
Strip for Action 1942,O 1,26:2
Family, The 1943,Mr 31,22:4
Beggars Are Comming to Town 1945,O 29,16:2
Life With Mother 1948,O 21,32:2
Serlin, Sol
Don Juan; Feast With the Statue, The
1956,Ja 4,21:4
Absalom 1956,My 17,37:2
Heloise 1958,S 25,28:4
Go Show Me a Dragon 1961,O 28,18:1
Alcestis Comes Back 1962,Ap 24,33:1
At Sea 1962,Ap 24,33:1
Winterset 1966,F 10,32:2
Sunset 1966,My 13,34:1
Tenth Man, The 1967,N 9,54:1
Serly, Tibor (Composer)
Medea 1947,O 21,27:2
Serly, Tibor (Lyricist)
Medea 1947,O 21,27:2
Serrallonga, Marcello
Rugantino 1964,F 7,34:1
Serrano, Enrique
Amor 1937,Ap 22,18:6
Todo un Hombre 1937,Ap 28,19:2
Tierra Baja 1937,My 8,22:4
Serrano, Vincent
Fools Errant 1922,Ag 22,12:3
Alarm Clock, The 1923,D 25,26:2
Werewolf, The 1924,Ag 26,6:1
Rio Rita 1927,F 3,18:3
Serreau, Jean-Marie
Tableau, Le 1963,S 4,34:3
Serreau, Jean-Marie (Director)
Saison au Congo, Une 1967,D 3,II,10:6
Serries, G E
Front Page, The 1937,N 12,27:2
Serton, Betty
Jack and the Beanstalk 1947,N 3,28:2
Many Moons 1947,D 15,35:2
Little Red Riding Hood 1948,Ja 12,15:3
Indian Captive, The 1949,Ja 31,15:2
Pied Piper of Hamelin, The 1950,Ap 3,19:2
Ali Baba 1951,Mr 27,34:2
Serva, David
Man of La Mancha 1965,N 23,52:1
Servaes, Dagny
Everyman 1926,Ag 9,1:1
Midsummer Night's Dream, A 1927,N 18,21:1
Jedermann 1927,D 8,33:2
Dantons Tod 1927,D 21,28:3
Peripherie 1928,Ja 3,29:1
Diener Zweier Herren; Servant of Two Masters,
The 1928,Ja 10,28:3
Servant of Two Masters, The 1928,Ja 22,VIII,6:1
Robbers, The 1928,Ag 10,9:2
Servais, Ivan
Blossom Time 1921,S 30,10:1
Skin Deep 1927,O 18,32:1
Dancing Partner 1930,Ag 6,24:2
Servatius, Hans
Girofle-Girofla 1926,N 23,26:3
Cloches de Cornville, Les; Chimes of Normandy,
The 1926,D 14,24:4
Perichole, La 1926,D 29,24:4
Trois Jeunes Filles Nues; Three Young Maids From
the Folies Bergere 1929,Mr 5,28:2
Passionement; Passionately 1929,Mr 8,31:4
Comte Obligado 1929,Mr 12,26:2
Ta Bouche 1929,Mr 15,28:5
Bon Garcon, Un 1929,Mr 19,36:2
Servello, Joe
World of Gunter Grass, The 1966,Ap 27,38:1
Servetnik, John
Investigation, The 1966,O 5,40:1
Service, Cel F (Costume Designer)
Anthony on Overtime 1961,O 21,13:2
Servoss, Mary
Merchant of Venice, The 1922,D 22,13:1
Tiger Cats 1924,O 22,18:1
Behold the Bridegroom 1927,D 27,24:1

Servoss, Mary—Cont
Street Scene 1929,Ja 11,20:4
Street Scene 1930,S 28,VIII,2:4
Hamlet 1931,N 6,28:4
Counsellor-at-Law 1932,S 13,17:2
Dangerous Corner 1932,O 28,23:1
Another Love 1934,Mr 20,26:3
Hamlet 1936,O 20,31:3
Hamlet 1936,N 11,54:2
Tortilla Flat 1938,Ja 13,16:2
Dance Night 1938,O 15,20:5
Suspect 1940,Ap 10,30:4
Swan Song 1946,My 16,29:2
Medea 1949,My 3,31:2
Sessions, Almira
Scrap Book 1932,Ag 2,20:3
One More Honeymoon 1934,Ap 2,13:5
Ethan Frome 1936,Ja 22,15:2
White Horse Inn 1936,O 2,28:5
Curtain Call 1937,Ap 23,24:7
Shadow and Substance 1938,Ja 27,16:2
Yokel Boy 1939,Jl 7,12:2
Sessions, Anne
Gondoliers, The 1962,N 16,25:2
Iolanthe 1968,N 9,37:3
Sessions, W E
Hamlet 1928,Je 2,11:3
Seton, Beryl
Finian's Rainbow 1947,O 22,38:4
Seton, Harold
Poppy God, The 1921,Ag 30,10:1
Comedian, The 1923,Mr 14,14:1
Accused 1925,S 30,20:1
Lulu Belle 1926,F 10,20:1
Mima 1928,D 13,24:2
Knock on Wood 1935,My 29,16:2
Seton, Joan
Don't Listen, Ladies 1948,D 29,16:2
Seton, Mary Scott
Secrets 1922,D 26,11:1
Quarantine 1924,D 17,19:7
Letter, The 1927,S 27,30:1
Cynara 1931,N 3,31:1
Setrakian, Ed
Othello 1964,Jl 15,29:1
Othello 1964,O 13,48:1
Baal 1965,My 7,33:2
Coriolanus 1965,Jl 15,23:1
Drums in the Night 1967,My 18,54:1
Setrakian, Ed (Director)
Homo 1969,Ap 12,40:2
Queen of Greece, The 1969,Ap 12,40:2
Setsuko, Nakagawa
Golden Bat 1970,Je 27,18:2
Settimio, Al
Poker Session, The 1967,S 20,42:2
Settles, Alonzo
Legal Murder 1934,F 16,16:2
Seulitrinic, Jack
Mascaiada 1929,D 28,10:6
Sevareid, Michael
Cherry Orchard, The 1962,N 15,46:2
Month in the Country, A 1963,My 29,39:2
Twelfth Night 1968,Je 15,40:1
Resistible Rise of Arturo Ui, The 1968,Ag 8,25:1
Merton of the Movies 1968,S 26,62:1
Resistible Rise of Arturo Ui, The 1968,D 23,44:1
Sevedra, Edward
Child of the Morning 1958,Ap 22,40:2
Seven, John
Story Teller, The 1951,D 15,11:3
Salvage 1957,Ap 10,39:2
Seven, John (Playwright)
Salvage 1957,Ap 10,39:2
Severn, Margaret
Greenwich Village Follies 1920,Ag 31,7:3
Vaudeville (Hippodrome) 1926,Ap 13,28:2
Vaudeville (Palace) 1928,F 14,26:2
Severns, Dorothy
Adam's Apple 1929,Je 11,27:5
Severs, William
Cut of the Axe 1960,F 2,38:2
Blood Bugle, The 1961,Je 29,26:1
Moon Is Blue, The 1961,Ag 9,29:1
Lulu; Earth Spirit 1970,Mr 28,32:1
Sevilla, Jose (Lighting Director)
Birdbath 1966,Ap 12,43:1
Thank You, Miss Victoria 1966,Ap 12,43:1
This Is the Rill Speaking 1966,Ap 12,43:1
War 1966,Ap 13,36:1
Chicago 1966,Ap 13,36:1
Recluse, The 1966,Ap 13,36:1
Sewall, Rachel
Rapid Transit 1927,Ap 8,21:2
Lysistrata 1937,Jl 20,19:3
Princess Turandot 1937,Ag 3,20:5
Romance 1937,Ag 17,23:1
Sewall, Richard Benson (Director)
Shall We Join the Ladies? 1929,Mr 17,30:4
Sewall, Sally
Decameron, The 1961,Ap 13,32:1
Seward, Frederick
Rogues and Vagabonds 1930,My 8,32:5

Seward, Ruth
Cyrano de Bergerac 1926,F 19,18:1
Sewell, Danny
Oliver 1963,Ja 8,5:5
Sewell, George
Oh What a Lovely War 1964,O 1,30:1
Sewell, Marie
Tip-Top 1920,O 6,13:2
Sewell, Miss
Honey Girl 1920,My 4,9:1
Sewell, Rachel
Your Loving Son 1941,Ap 5,13:2
Sexton, Al
Cinderella on Broadway 1920,Je 25,18:1
Hotel Mouse, The 1922,Mr 14,11:3
Greenwich Village Follies 1923,S 21,4:6
Sweetheart Time 1926,Ja 20,23:2
Honeymoon Lane 1926,S 21,32:3
Hello, Yourself 1928,O 31,28:2
Lady Fingers 1929,F 1,22:4
Woof, Woof 1929,D 26,20:4
Thumbs Up! 1934,D 28,24:1
Sexton, Anne (Playwright)
Mercy Street 1969,O 28,43:1
Mercy Street 1969,N 2,II,3:1
Sexton, Eddie
I Loved You Wednesday 1932,O 12,27:1
Sexton, Tony
Traveling Lady 1954,O 28,45:2
Seybolt, Eleanor
Sacred and Profane Love 1920,F 24,11:1
Blood and Sand 1921,S 21,16:2
Main Line, The 1924,Mr 26,19:4
Seyeux, Jean Le (Playwright)
1927 1927,Mr 6,VII,4:4
A la Mode de Chez Nous 1929,My 26,IX,4:1
Seyler, Athene
Gift Horse, The 1926,N 21,VIII,4:1
Country Wife, The 1927,Ja 2,VII,2:5
Transit of Venus, The 1927,My 22,VIII,2:1
These Few Ashes 1929,My 5,IX,1:3
Last Enemy, The 1930,Ja 5,VIII,2:2
Marriage a la Mode 1930,O 26,VIII,2:1
Last of the Ladies, The 1936,Mr 26,26:7
Cherry Orchard, The 1941,S 7,IX,2:5
Watch on the Rhine 1942,My 3,VIII,1:7
Harvey 1949,Ja 6,29:2
Chances, The 1962,Jl 4,11:2
Seymore, Stewart
Spring Fever 1925,Ag 4,14:2
Seymour, Anne
Always You 1920,Ja 6,18:2
Vaudeville (Palace) 1928,My 1,33:2
Night in Venice, A 1929,My 22,30:2
At the Bottom 1930,Ja 10,24:3
Vaudeville (Palace) 1930,Mr 10,24:4
Puppet Show 1930,O 29,26:5
Vaudeville (Palace) 1931,Je 29,20:1
School for Scandal, The 1931,N 11,26:4
Hey, Nonny, Nonny! 1932,Je 7,22:3
Sunrise at Campobello 1958,Ja 31,25:1
Sunrise at Campobello 1958,F 9,II,1:1
Seymour, Blanche
Merry Widow, The 1921,S 6,13:1
Small Timers, The 1925,Ja 28,15:3
Seymour, Harry
Vaudeville (Palace) 1928,My 1,33:2
Vaudeville (Palace) 1930,Mr 10,24:4
Seymour, James
Sing High, Sing Low 1931,N 13,26:4
Hide and Seek 1934,Ag 7,20:2
Pequod 1969,Je 30,33:1
Seymour, Jane
Enemy, The 1925,O 21,20:1
Seed of the Brute 1926,N 2,34:3
Vaudeville (Palace) 1927,Ap 26,33:1
Blind Mice 1930,O 16,28:2
House Beautiful, The 1931,Mr 13,20:4
I Loved You Wednesday 1932,O 12,27:1
Girls in Uniform 1932,D 31,10:3
Both Your Houses 1933,Mr 7,20:3
Sellout, The 1933,S 7,17:2
Broomsticks Amen! 1934,F 10,20:4
Invitation to a Murder 1934,My 18,26:3
Page Miss Glory 1934,N 28,24:2
Remember the Day 1935,S 26,19:3
Remember the Day 1935,O 13,IX,1:1
Lend Me Your Ears! 1936,N 6,28:5
Women, The 1936,D 28,13:1
Susannah and the Elders 1940,O 30,28:2
Moon Is Down, The 1942,Ap 8,22:2
Sweet Charity 1942,D 29,26:4
Harriet 1943,Mr 4,24:2
Harriet 1944,S 28,26:1
Survivors, The 1948,Ja 20,27:2
Survivors, The 1948,Ja 25,II,1:1
Metropole 1949,D 7,43:2
Show-Off, The 1950,Je 1,24:5
Show-Off, The 1950,Je 11,II,1:1
Seymour, John D
She Stoops to Conquer 1924,Je 10,24:3
Cape Smoke 1925,F 17,19:1
Trelawney of the 'Wells' 1925,Je 2,16:2

Seymour, John D—Cont
Right to Love, The 1925,Je 9,16:4
Dearest Enemy 1925,S 19,9:2
Blood Money 1927,Ag 23,29:2
New York 1927,N 15,26:2
57 Bowery 1928,Ja 27,14:3
Mr Moneypenny 1928,O 17,26:2
Falstaff 1928,D 26,14:2
Flight 1929,F 19,22:3
Becky Sharp 1929,Je 4,29:1
Sweet Adeline 1929,S 4,33:1
Barretts of Wimpole Street, The 1931,F 10,25:1
Cyrano de Bergerac 1932,D 27,11:2
Richelieu 1934,My 22,28:1
Hamlet 1934,D 26,19:3
Richard III 1934,D 28,24:3
Pride and Prejudice 1935,N 6,32:4
Tide Rising 1937,Ja 26,17:2
Love for Love 1940,Je 4,19:5
Solitaire 1942,Ja 28,22:2
Moon Is Down, The 1942,Ap 8,22:2
Eastward in Eden 1947,N 19,33:2
Vigil, The 1948,My 22,8:6
Light Up the Sky 1948,N 19,34:2
Father, The 1949,N 17,36:2
Sacred Flame, The 1952,O 8,35:2
Howie 1958,S 18,35:2
Pal Joey 1963,My 30,21:1
King and I, The 1963,Je 13,30:2
Life With Father 1967,O 20,53:2
Seymour, Jonathan
Summer and Smoke 1947,Jl 9,18:5
Throng o' Scarlet 1947,D 2,37:2
Seymour, Jonathan (Director)
Yanqui and the Senorita, The 1952,Ag 8,8:7
Bat, The 1953,Ja 21,28:2
Seymour, Mildred
Jerry Lewis' Variety Show 1957,F 8,18:5
Seymour, Paul
Pins and Needles 1939,Ap 21,26:2
My Sister Eileen 1940,D 27,23:2
Seymour, Robert T (Director)
Poppa Is Home 1961,D 20,37:1
Seymour, Tot (Lyricist)
Innocent Eyes 1924,My 21,22:2
Seymour, William
To the Ladies! 1922,F 21,20:1
To the Ladies! 1922,Mr 12,VI,1:1
Goose Hangs High, The 1924,Ja 30,16:1
School for Scandal, The 1925,D 7,18:2
Two Orphans, The 1926,Ap 6,26:2
Two Orphans, The 1926,Ap 11,VIII,1:1
Strange Prince, The 1926,D 8,24:2
Seymour, William (Director)
She Stoops to Conquer 1924,Je 10,24:3
Trelawney of the 'Wells' 1925,Je 2,16:2
Trelawney of the 'Wells' 1927,F 1,24:4
She Stoops to Conquer 1928,My 15,17:1
Seymour and Jeannette
Vaudeville (Palace) 1925,Ap 21,18:1
Seyrig, Delphine
Jardin des Delices, Le 1969,N 4,54:1
Sforim, Mendele (Original Author)
Journey of Benjamin III, The 1928,Je 24,VIII,1:4
Shaber, David (Miscellaneous)
Gift of Time, A 1962,F 23,34:1
Shaber, David (Producer)
Conversation Piece 1957,N 19,38:2
Shacht, Gustav
Chayim Lederer 1932,N 15,24:4
Shack, Fanny
Vegetable, The, or From President to Postman 1929,Ap 11,32:3
Shack, M (Mrs) (Choreographer)
Some Girl 1927,D 24,8:2
Shackelford, Emmett
Three Live Ghosts 1920,S 30,12:1
Squaw Man, The 1921,D 27,10:3
On the Make 1932,My 24,23:2
Lilly Turner 1932,S 20,26:1
Shackelford, Harry
Circus Princess, The 1927,Ap 26,32:2
Shackelford, Margaret
Only 38 1921,S 14,22:2
My Son 1924,S 18,18:2
Ladder, The 1927,O 7,24:2
Lady Dedlock 1929,Ja 1,61:2
Shackett, Arthur
Hymn to the Rising Sun 1937,My 7,28:2
Shackleton, Robert
Very Warm for May 1939,N 18,23:2
Keep Off the Grass 1940,My 24,22:6
Sweethearts 1947,Ja 22,31:2
Sally 1948,My 7,31:2
Shackman, Harold
Two Seconds 1931,O 10,20:6
Shackner, Alan
Borscht Capades 1951,S 18,38:3
Shackner, Blackie
Time of Your Life, The 1940,S 24,27:2
Shackt, Gustav
Good Neighbor 1941,O 22,26:2
Shadanoff, George (Director)
Twelfth Night 1941,D 3,32:2

hadburne, Sherry
Banjo Eyes 1941,D 26,20:2
Jackpot 1944,Ja 14,15:2
Polonaise 1945,O 8,20:2
hadden, Donna
Let's Sing Yiddish 1966,N 10,63:1
hade, Ellen
Engaged! or Cheviot's Choice 1965,Ap 24,19:2
Iolanthe 1965,My 19,42:1
Yeomen of the Guard, The 1965,Jl 8,34:1
Ruddigore 1965,Ag 27,16:1
Have I Got One for You 1968,Ja 8,32:1
Pirates of Penzance, The 1968,Ap 26,32:1
hade, Lillian
Vanities 1932,S 18,IX,2:1
Vanities 1932,S 28,22:4
hadow, Bert
Sky High 1925,Mr 3,21:4
hadurskawa and Kuderoff
Night in Venice, A 1929,My 22,30:2
haefer, A
Passion Play, The 1929,Ap 30,32:1
haer, Carol Sue
On the Town 1959,Ja 16,36:1
hafer, Clyde
Ten Nights in a Barroom 1932,Ja 21,17:1
hafer, Hal (Scenic Designer)
There Is No End 1950,F 17,27:4
hafer, Natalie
These Few Ashes 1928,O 31,28:1
hafer, Phil
Banjo Eyes 1941,D 26,20:2
hafer, Robert
Student Prince, The 1936,Jl 12,II,5:2
Rose Marie 1936,Jl 22,22:6
Blossom Time 1936,Jl 29,23:1
My Maryland 1936,Ag 12,14:2
Countess Maritza 1936,Ag 19,18:2
Naughty Marietta 1936,S 2,19:5
Show Is On, The 1936,D 26,14:2
Maytime 1937,Jl 6,23:4
Wonderful Night, A; Fledermaus, Die 1937,Jl 14,17:1
Student Prince, The 1937,Jl 28,15:1
Firefly, The 1937,Ag 4,14:1
Nina Rosa 1937,Ag 26,24:3
Roberta 1937,S 7,16:4
Hooray for What! 1937,D 2,32:5
Firefly, The 1938,Jl 12,15:4
Song of Norway 1944,Ag 22,20:2
Allegro 1952,S 18,36:3
Damn Yankees 1955,My 6,17:1
haff, Edmund
Call on Kuprin, A 1961,My 26,29:3
haff, Monty (Miscellaneous)
Tovarich 1963,Mr 20,5:1
Pousse-Cafe 1966,Mr 19,19:2
haffer, Anthony (Playwright)
Sleuth 1970,N 13,25:1
Sleuth 1970,N 22,II,18:1
haffer, Louise
First One Asleep, Whistle 1966,F 28,19:1
haffer, Marjorie
Crucible, The 1958,Mr 12,36:1
haffer, Peter (Playwright)
Five Finger Exercise 1958,Ag 17,II,1:7
Five Finger Exercise 1959,D 3,45:4
Five Finger Exercise 1959,D 13,II,3:1
Public Eye, The 1963,O 10,51:1
Private Ear, The 1963,O 10,51:1
Royal Hunt of the Sun, The 1964,Jl 8,40:6
Black Comedy 1965,Jl 29,19:1
Royal Hunt of the Sun, The 1965,O 27,36:2
Royal Hunt of the Sun, The 1965,N 14,II,1:1
Black Comedy; White Lies 1967,F 13,42:1
Black Comedy 1967,F 13,42:1
Black Comedy 1967,F 26,II,1:5
White Lies 1967,F 26,II,1:5
Black Comedy 1967,O 19,58:1
White Lies 1967,O 19,58:1
Battle of Shrivings, The 1970,F 7,23:1
haftman, Ben (Director)
Exhaustion of Our Son's Love, The 1965,O 19,51:1
Good Day 1965,O 19,51:1
hafton, Jack (Miscellaneous)
Poupees de Paris, Les 1964,My 16,11:1
hah, Krishna (Director)
King of the Dark Chamber 1961,F 10,21:1
Sponono 1964,Ap 3,28:1
hah, Krishna (Playwright)
Sponono 1964,Ap 3,28:1
Sponono 1964,Ap 12,II,1:1
hah, Krishna (Producer)
Shakuntala 1959,S 10,41:2
hahan, Harvey
Gypsy Lady 1946,S 18,25:6
haik, Abdul
Midsummer Night's Dream, A 1956,Ja 14,12:2
haik, Jorge
Shakuntala 1959,S 10,41:2
hain, Carl (Director)
Magnolia Alley 1949,Ap 19,29:2

Shairp, Mordaunt (Playwright)
Offence, The 1925,N 16,25:1
Crime at Blossoms, The 1931,Je 7,VIII,2:1
Green Bay Tree, The 1933,O 21,11:5
Green Bay Tree, The 1933,O 29,IX,1:1
Crime at Blossoms, The 1933,D 17,IX,4:2
Green Bay Tree, The 1951,F 2,18:2
Shakar, Martin
Infantry, The 1966,N 15,51:1
Wicked Cooks, The 1967,Ja 24,42:1
Americana Pastoral 1968,D 11,51:1
No Place to Be Somebody 1969,My 5,53:3
World of Mrs Solomon, The; Second Mrs Aarons, The 1969,Je 4,37:1
Our Town 1969,N 28,50:1
Nobody Hears A Broken Drum 1970,Mr 20,55:1
Sunday Dinner 1970,N 3,28:1
Shakespeare, William (Miscellaneous)
Novice and the Duke, The 1929,D 11,37:2
Boys From Syracuse, The 1938,N 24,36:1
This Island Is Mine 1959,Jl 1,26:4
Ages of Man 1959,Jl 10,28:2
Boys From Syracuse, The 1963,Je 2,II,1:1
Love and Let Love 1968,Ja 4,30:1
Shakespeare, William (Original Author)
Megere Apprivoisee, La 1922,N 20,21:2
Merchant of Venice, The 1924,N 18,23:2
Romio and Julietta 1925,Ap 21,19:1
Fratricide Punished 1925,Ap 21,19:1
Othello 1929,F 4,21:2
Hamlet 1931,Ap 24,26:4
Merchant of Venice, The 1931,N 9,22:2
Merchant of Venice, The 1931,N 17,31:1
Julius Caesar 1931,N 18,26:3
Hamlet 1931,N 19,26:6
Hamlet 1932,N 13,IX,3:8
Lucrece 1932,D 4,IX,3:3
Romeo and Juliet 1933,F 3,21:5
Hamlet 1936,N 11,54:2
Amor Vincit Omnia 1936,N 15,XI,2:4
Othello 1937,Ja 7,16:4
Richard II 1937,F 6,14:2
Richard II 1937,S 16,28:2
As You Like It 1937,N 1,25:2
Antony and Cleopatra 1937,N 11,30:2
Julius Caesar 1937,N 12,26:6
Cymbeline 1937,D 5,XII,5:8
Coriolanus 1938,F 2,14:5
Life and Death of Sir John Falstaff, The 1938,Mr 15,19:5
Shakespeare's Merchant 1939 1939,Ja 10,16:3
Henry IV, Part I 1939,Ja 31,17:2
As You Like It 1939,My 9,28:4
Hamlet 1939,Jl 9,IX,1:6
Swingin' the Dream 1939,N 30,24:2
Taming of the Shrew, The 1940,F 6,17:2
Tempest, The 1945,Ja 26,17:2
Shylock '47 1947,My 28,30:5
King Lear 1950,D 26,18:1
Love's Labour's Lost 1953,F 5,20:3
Merchant of Venice, The 1953,Mr 5,20:2
Lovers, Villains and Fools: A Shakespearean Variety Show 1956,O 24,44:7
Ages of Man 1958,S 22,26:1
Tempest, The: or, The Enchanted Forest 1959,Je 10,42:2
Romeo and Juliet 1959,Je 15,31:1
Romeo and Juliet 1961,F 24,24:1
Hamlet 1961,Mr 17,17:1
White Rose and the Red, The 1964,Mr 17,31:1
Hamlet 1964,Ap 10,30:1
Henry V 1964,My 13,52:1
King Lear 1964,My 19,43:2
Comedy of Errors, The 1964,My 21,43:1
Much Ado About Nothing 1964,Je 11,26:2
Richard III 1964,Je 12,44:2
Bourgeois Gentilhomme, Le 1964,Je 18,28:2
King Lear 1964,Je 19,36:1
Midsummer Night's Dream, A 1964,Je 30,23:2
Hamlet 1964,Jl 4,9:1
Othello 1964,Jl 15,29:1
Othello 1964,O 13,48:1
Kiss Me, Kate 1965,My 13,31:1
Coriolanus 1965,Je 21,36:1
Romeo and Juliet 1965,Je 21,36:3
Taming of the Shrew, The 1965,Je 24,32:2
King Lear 1965,Je 25,39:1
Henry V 1965,Je 29,27:2
Henry IV, Part I 1965,Je 30,42:1
Falstaff; Henry IV, Part II 1965,Jl 1,35:1
Julius Caesar 1965,Jl 2,18:1
Coriolanus 1965,Jl 15,23:1
Troilus and Cressida 1965,Ag 13,17:1
Macbeth 1969,N 21,51:1
Macbeth 1969,N 30,II,3:1
Shakespeare, William (Playwright)
Richard III 1920,Mr 8,7:1
Richard III 1920,Mr 21,VI,6:1
Merchant of Venice, The 1920,My 9,VI,1:7
Henry IV 1920,Je 20,II,9:2
Merchant of Venice, The 1920,N 12,15:5
Hamlet 1920,D 28,9:3
Merchant of Venice, The 1920,D 30,16:2

Shakespeare, William (Playwright)—Cont
Winter's Tale, The 1921,F 13,VI,1:1
Macbeth 1921,F 18,16:1
Macbeth 1921,F 20,VI,1:1
Macbeth 1921,F 27,VI,1:1
Merchant of Venice, The 1921,Ap 2,14:2
Macbeth 1921,Ap 20,11:1
Macbeth 1921,Ap 24,VI,1:1
Taming of the Shrew, The 1921,My 12,20:2
Merchant of Venice, The 1921,My 14,10:4
Twelfth Night 1921,N 1,17:1
Merchant of Venice, The 1921,N 22,17:1
Macbeth 1921,D 27,10:3
Hamlet 1922,N 17,14:1
Hamlet 1922,N 26,VIII,1:1
Hamlet 1922,D 17,VII,1:1
Merchant of Venice, The 1922,D 22,13:1
Romeo and Juliet 1922,D 28,20:1
Merchant of Venice, The 1923,Ja 7,VII,1:1
Romeo and Juliet 1923,Ja 25,16:1
Romeo and Juliet 1923,F 4,VII,1:1
Hamlet 1923,F 6,14:1
Julius Caesar 1923,F 9,10:4
Macbeth 1923,F 11,VII,1:1
King Lear 1923,Mr 10,9:4
Romeo and Juliet 1923,Ap 22,VII,1:1
Hamlet 1923,Ap 22,VII,1:1
As You Like It 1923,Ap 24,24:1
As You Like It 1923,Ap 29,VII,1:1
Comedy of Errors, The 1923,My 16,22:5
Comedy of Errors, The 1923,My 20,VII,1:1
Hamlet 1923,Ag 19,VI,9:2
Cymbeline 1923,O 3,12:1
Cymbeline 1923,O 7,IX,2:2
Cymbeline 1923,O 14,VIII,1:1
Taming of the Shrew, The 1923,O 16,19:3
Twelfth Night 1923,O 23,17:1
Merchant of Venice, The 1923,N 6,22:2
Romeo and Juliet 1923,N 13,25:2
Hamlet 1923,N 20,23:3
Hamlet 1923,N 25,VIII,1:1
Hamlet 1923,N 27,23:6
Antony and Cleopatra 1924,F 20,22:1
Antony and Cleopatra 1924,F 24,VII,1:1
Antony and Cleopatra 1924,Mr 2,VIII,1:1
Antony and Cleopatra 1924,Mr 9,VIII,1:1
Macbeth 1924,Mr 17,18:1
Macbeth 1924,Mr 23,VIII,1:1
Merchant of Venice, The 1924,N 23,VIII,1:1
Taming of the Shrew, The 1924,N 25,27:3
Othello 1925,Ja 18,VII,1:1
Midsummer Night's Dream, A 1925,Mr 8,VII,2:1
Hamlet 1925,Mr 29,VIII,1:1
Twelfth Night 1925,O 25,VIII,1:1
Hamlet 1925,N 22,VIII,1:1
Taming of the Shrew, The 1925,D 19,14:1
Taming of the Shrew, The 1925,D 27,VII,1:1
Merchant of Venice, The 1925,D 28,12:1
Hamlet; Merchant of Venice, The 1926,Ja 3,VII,1:1
Henry IV, Part I 1926,Je 1,29:1
Henry IV, Part I 1926,Je 6,VIII,1:1
Julius Caesar 1926,S 19,28:5
Twelfth Night 1926,D 21,21:4
Romeo and Juliet 1927,Ja 2,VII,2:5
Macbeth 1927,Ja 16,VII,4:3
Hamlet 1927,Mr 12,13:1
King Lear 1927,Mr 13,VII,1:4
Hamlet 1927,Mr 27,VII,2:6
Hamlet 1927,Ap 7,23:3
All's Well That Ends Well 1927,Ap 17,17:6
Taming of the Shrew, The 1927,My 4,29:1
Julius Caesar 1927,Je 7,27:2
Twelfth Night 1927,Je 12,VII,2:1
Coriolanus 1927,Je 18,8:3
Midsummer Night's Dream, A 1927,Je 27,25:1
Midsummer Night's Dream, A 1927,Ag 8,6:1
Measure for Measure 1927,S 18,VII,2:2
Taming of the Shrew, The 1927,O 26,26:4
Taming of the Shrew, The 1927,N 13,IX,1:1
Midsummer Night's Dream, A 1927,N 18,21:1
Much Ado About Nothing 1927,N 19,14:6
Troilus and Cressida 1927,N 20,IX,4:7
Midsummer Night's Dream, A 1927,N 27,IX,1:1
Midsummer Night's Dream, A 1927,D 4,X,6:1
Hamlet 1927,D 9,28:2
Merchant of Venice, The 1928,Ja 10,38:6
Hamlet 1928,Ja 15,VIII,1:8
Merchant of Venice, The 1928,Ja 17,22:2
Henry V 1928,Mr 16,26:2
Merry Wives of Windsor, The 1928,Mr 20,20:1
Henry V; Merry Wives of Windsor, The 1928,Ap 1,IX,1:1
Julius Caesar 1928,Ap 8,VIII,4:3
Two Noble Kinsmen, The 1928,Ap 8,VIII,2:7
Taming of the Shrew, The 1928,My 27,VIII,1:8
Hamlet 1928,Je 2,11:3
Merry Wives of Windsor, The 1928,O 2,24:5
Macbeth 1928,N 20,28:3
Merchant of Venice, The 1929,Ja 27,IX,1:3
Merry Wives of Windsor 1929,Mr 24,X,2:3
King John 1929,Je 23,VIII,2:1
Merry Wives of Windsor, The: 1929 Version 1929,Jl 27,7:2

Shakespeare, William (Playwright)—Cont

Merchant of Venice, The 1929,S 24,28:4
Merry Wives of Windsor, The 1929,O 27,IX,2:4
Much Ado About Nothing 1929,N 17,30:4
Julius Caesar 1929,N 19,26:5
Tempest, The 1929,D 30,16:2
Macbeth 1930,F 13,9:6
Macbeth 1930,Mr 2,IX,2:4
Hamlet 1930,Mr 25,34:4
Macbeth 1930,Mr 26,24:6
Merchant of Venice, The 1930,Mr 27,24:7
Twelfth Night 1930,Mr 27,24:7
Taming of the Shrew, The 1930,Mr 28,22:8
Richard III 1930,Mr 31,24:1
King Lear 1930,Ap 1,34:6
As You Like It 1930,Ap 3,32:5
Julius Caesar 1930,Ap 4,22:3
Romeo and Juliet 1930,Ap 22,33:1
Othello 1930,My 20,33:1
Twelfth Night 1930,S 14,VIII,2:8
As You Like It 1930,S 19,18:5
Richard III 1930,S 21,IX,2:1
Twelfth Night 1930,O 16,28:2
Twelfth Night 1930,O 19,IX,4:5
Twelfth Night 1930,N 2,VIII,1:1
Merchant of Venice, The 1930,N 16,VIII,3:1
Merchant of Venice, The 1930,D 3,29:2
Antony and Cleopatra 1930,D 14,IX,3:1
King Lear 1930,D 26,18:2
Merchant of Venice, The 1931,F 1,VIII,3:3
Hamlet 1931,Mr 22,VIII,2:1
Measure for Measure 1931,Ag 9,VIII,1:3
Midsummer Night's Dream, A 1931,Ag 19,19:3
Merchant of Venice, The 1931,N 4,31:1
Merchant of Venice, The 1932,Ja 10,II,6:4
Antony and Cleopatra 1932,F 7,VIII,1:5
Julius Caesar 1932,F 9,30:7
Julius Caesar 1932,F 28,VIII,2:4
Othello 1932,Mr 6,VIII,2:1
Merchant of Venice, The 1932,Ap 29,13:4
Troilus and Cressida 1932,Je 7,22:3
Hamlet 1932,Je 12,X,1:1
Midsummer Night's Dream, A 1932,Jl 13,15:1
Love's Labour's Lost 1932,Ag 7,IX,1:7
Twelfth Night 1932,O 23,IX,3:1
Midsummer Night's Dream, A 1932,N 18,22:2
Twelfth Night 1932,N 19,20:5
Comedy of Errors, The 1932,N 22,25:3
Merchant of Venice, The 1932,N 24,34:5
Much Ado About Nothing 1933,Ap 30,IX,2:2
Taming of the Shrew, The 1933,N 5,IX,3:1
Romeo and Juliet 1933,N 30,38:5
Richard III 1933,D 3,IX,7:7
Coriolanus 1933,D 17,IV,2:4
Henry V 1934,Ja 28,II,3:4
Tempest, The 1934,F 4,IX,3:4
Hamlet 1934,F 11,IX,3:7
Macbeth 1934,Ap 3,26:4
Tempest, The 1934,Ap 17,26:6
Twelfth Night 1934,Jl 17,24:5
Othello 1934,Jl 22,23:4
Othello 1934,Jl 29,IX,1:3
Merchant of Venice, The 1934,Ag 12,IX,5:5
Twelfth Night 1934,Ag 21,12:4
Antony and Cleopatra 1934,S 18,18:2
Julius Caesar 1934,O 24,25:2
Richard II 1934,N 4,IX,3:1
King Lear 1934,N 4,IX,3:1
Much Ado About Nothing 1934,N 9,24:3
As You Like It 1934,N 11,IX,3:6
Hamlet 1934,D 2,X,3:6
Romeo and Juliet 1934,D 21,30:3
Hamlet 1934,D 26,19:3
Richard III 1934,D 28,24:3
Romeo and Juliet 1934,D 30,IX,1:1
Henry IV, Part I 1935,Mr 1,16:1
Henry IV, Part I 1935,Mr 24,VIII,2:3
Antony and Cleopatra 1935,Ap 16,26:7
Taming of the Shrew, The 1935,Ap 23,24:1
Othello 1935,S 13,19:2
Taming of the Shrew, The 1935,S 22,X,3:2
Othello 1935,S 28,13:2
Taming of the Shrew, The 1935,S 29,X,3:1
Taming of the Shrew, The 1935,O 1,27:3
Macbeth 1935,O 8,26:4
Romeo and Juliet 1935,O 18,27:5
Taming of the Shrew, The 1935,O 20,X,1:1
Romeo and Juliet 1935,N 17,IX,2:4
Timon of Athens 1935,D 15,XI,5:6
Romeo and Juliet 1935,D 24,10:2
Macbeth 1936,Ap 5,IX,1:4
Taming of the Shrew, The 1936,Ap 14,18:4
Macbeth 1936,Ap 15,25:4
Macbeth 1936,Ap 15,25:3
King Lear 1936,Ap 21,27:4
As You Like It 1936,Ap 24,18:4
Two Gentlemen of Verona 1936,Je 28,IX,2:1
Antony and Cleopatra 1936,O 15,32:8
Hamlet 1936,O 18,X,1:1
Hamlet 1936,O 20,31:3
Hamlet 1936,O 25,X,1:5
Henry V 1936,N 30,24:6
As You Like It 1937,Ja 3,X,3:6
Richard II 1937,F 14,X,1:1

Taming of the Shrew, The 1937,Ap 11,XI,2:1
Midsummer Night's Dream, A 1937,Je 2,21:2
Hamlet 1937,Je 4,26:6
Hamlet 1937,Ag 8,X,1:7
Richard II 1937,S 7,16:3
Richard II 1937,S 26,XI,1:1
Coriolanus 1937,O 10,VI,4:7
Antony and Cleopatra 1937,O 14,23:2
As You Like It 1937,N 8,18:2
Merchant of Venice, The 1938,Ja 15,18:8
Merry Wives of Windsor, The 1938,Ap 15,22:3
Hamlet 1938,N 8,26:1
Henry IV 1939,F 5,IX,1:1
As You Like It 1939,Ap 23,X,2:5
Taming of the Shrew, The 1939,Ap 23,X,2:4
As You Like It; Midsummer Night's Dream, A;
  Comedy of Errors, The; Taming of the Shrew,
  The 1939,My 9,28:4
Macbeth 1939,Je 4,IX,2:5
Hamlet 1939,Jl 16,IX,2:1
Midsummer Night's Dream, A 1939,Jl 23,IX,1:3
Hamlet 1939,D 5,35:2
Hamlet 1939,D 10,X,3:1
Tempest, The 1940,My 1,14:2
Richard II 1940,Ap 2,31:2
Romeo and Juliet 1940,Ap 16,28:4
King Lear 1940,Ap 28,IX,1:7
Romeo and Juliet 1940,My 10,27:1
All's Well That Ends Well 1940,O 13,IX,1:5
Twelfth Night 1940,O 18,26:7
Twelfth Night 1940,O 27,IX,1:5
Twelfth Night 1940,N 20,26:3
Much Ado About Nothing 1941,Ap 20,IX,3:3
King John 1941,Ag 3,IX,2:2
As You Like It 1941,O 21,29:2
Macbeth 1941,N 12,30:2
Macbeth 1941,N 23,IX,1:1
Twelfth Night 1941,D 3,32:2
Midsummer Night's Dream, A 1942,Ap 12,VIII,1:7
Othello 1942,Ag 9,VIII,1:7
Richard III 1943,Mr 27,8:3
Othello 1943,O 20,18:1
Othello 1943,O 24,II,1:1
Richard III 1944,O 1,II,1:3
Tempest, The 1945,F 4,II,1:1
Antony and Cleopatra 1945,Ap 25,26:5
As You Like It 1945,Jl 4,10:4
Henry IV 1945,O 14,II,2:3
Tempest, The 1945,N 13,24:6
Hamlet 1945,D 14,25:2
Hamlet 1945,D 23,II,3:1
Winter's Tale, The 1946,Ja 16,18:6
Winter's Tale, The 1946,Ja 20,II,1:1
Henry IV, Part I 1946,My 7,25:2
Henry IV, Part II 1946,My 8,33:4
Henry IV 1946,My 12,II,1:1
Hamlet 1946,Je 4,18:4
Measure for Measure 1946,Ag 24,6:8
King Lear 1946,S 25,39:4
King Lear 1946,O 13,II,2:3
Henry VIII 1946,N 7,42:2
Macbeth 1946,D 1,II,3:7
Othello 1946,D 4,44:2
Hamlet 1947,Ja 8,26:2
King Lear 1947,F 19,32:2
As You Like It 1947,F 21,16:2
Merchant of Venice, The 1947,F 24,16:2
Hamlet 1947,F 27,27:2
Romeo and Juliet 1947,Ap 7,18:5
Richard II 1947,My 11,II,3:7
Macbeth 1947,My 30,25:1
Hamlet 1947,Jl 13,I,47:2
Antony and Cleopatra 1947,N 27,49:2
Antony and Cleopatra 1947,D 7,II,5:1
Macbeth 1947,D 19,34:3
Macbeth 1948,Ap 1,30:2
Macbeth 1948,Ap 11,II,1:1
Hamlet 1948,My 9,II,2:5
Hamlet 1948,S 11,13:3
Hamlet 1948,D 4,9:2
Richard III 1949,F 9,33:2
Richard III 1949,F 13,II,1:1
Othello 1949,My 16,17:4
Twelfth Night 1949,O 4,33:2
Twelfth Night 1949,O 8,9:4
Twelfth Night 1949,O 9,II,1:1
Romeo and Juliet 1949,O 17,19:2
Love's Labour's Lost 1949,O 24,18:3
Measure for Measure 1950,Mr 10,33:5
Tempest, The 1950,S 17,II,3:7
Twelfth Night 1950,D 3,II,3:1
King Lear 1950,D 31,II,1:1
Richard II 1951,Ja 25,21:2
Henry V 1951,F 11,II,3:1
Romeo and Juliet 1951,Mr 12,21:2
Romeo and Juliet 1951,Mr 25,II,1:1
Richard II 1951,Mr 25,75:3
Taming of the Shrew, The 1951,Ap 26,35:2
Henry V 1951,Ag 12,II,1:4
Taming of the Shrew, The 1951,N 18,II,3:1
Antony and Cleopatra 1951,D 21,22:2
Antony and Cleopatra 1951,D 30,II,1:1
Coriolanus 1952,Mr 14,26:2

Shakespeare, William (Playwright)—Cont

Much Ado About Nothing 1952,My 2,20:1
Hamlet 1952,D 2,39:1
Richard II 1953,Ja 25,II,3:1
Love's Labour's Lost 1953,F 8,II,1:1
Antony and Cleopatra 1953,My 10,II,1:1
Merchant of Venice, The 1953,My 10,II,1:1
Richard III 1953,My 10,II,1:1
Romeo and Juliet 1953,My 29,17:5
Richard III 1953,Jl 15,22:2
All's Well That Ends Well 1953,Jl 16,18:2
All's Well That Ends Well 1953,Jl 19,II,1:1
Henry VI 1953,Ag 9,II,1:2
King Lear 1953,Ag 9,II,1:2
Troilus and Cressida 1953,Ag 19,25:2
Pericles 1953,Ag 21,9:2
Coriolanus 1953,Ag 21,9:2
Hamlet 1953,Ag 25,18:6
Hamlet 1953,Ag 30,II,2:1
Othello 1953,O 30,28:2
Richard III 1953,D 10,65:2
Coriolanus 1954,Ja 20,34:2
Coriolanus 1954,Ja 24,II,1:1
Merry Wives of Windsor, The 1954,F 17,27:1
Hamlet 1954,Ap 24,15:2
Hamlet 1954,My 31,9:1
Measure for Measure 1954,Je 30,23:1
Taming of the Shrew, The 1954,Jl 1,22:2
Measure for Measure 1954,Jl 4,II,1:1
Taming of the Shrew, The 1954,Jl 4,II,1:1
Midsummer Night's Dream, A 1954,S 1,31:3
Macbeth 1954,S 5,II,3:7
Midsummer Night's Dream, A 1954,S 19,VI,26:1
Midsummer Night's Dream, A 1954,S 22,33:1
Twelfth Night 1954,N 10,42:2
Twelfth Night 1954,D 12,II,3:1
Midsummer Night's Dream, A 1954,D 16,50:2
Hamlet 1955,Ja 4,24:5
Merchant of Venice, The 1955,Ja 8,9:7
Merchant of Venice, The 1955,F 23,23:2
Twelfth Night 1955,My 1,II,3:1
Henry IV 1955,My 15,II,1:1
Twelfth Night 1955,Je 7,37:4
All's Well That Ends Well 1955,Je 7,37:4
Macbeth 1955,Je 19,II,1:1
Julius Caesar 1955,Je 29,23:3
Merchant of Venice, The 1955,Jl 1,13:1
Julius Caesar 1955,Jl 13,20:1
Julius Caesar 1955,Jl 17,II,1:1
Tempest, The 1955,Ag 2,18:2
Tempest, The 1955,Ag 7,II,1:1
Much Ado About Nothing 1955,Ag 20,20:4
Tempest, The 1955,S 3,8:6
Othello 1955,S 8,27:2
Othello 1955,S 18,II,1:1
Henry IV, Part I 1955,S 22,34:2
Macbeth 1955,O 8,12:6
Macbeth 1955,O 20,42:2
As You Like It 1955,O 29,12:2
Hamlet 1955,N 24,40:7
Romeo and Juliet 1955,D 16,36:3
King Lear 1956,Ja 13,17:1
Midsummer Night's Dream, A 1956,Ja 14,12:2
King Lear 1956,Ja 22,II,1:1
Othello 1956,Mr 11,II,3:1
Troilus and Cressida 1956,Ap 4,22:7
Hamlet 1956,Ap 11,28:1
Romeo and Juliet 1956,Je 13,45:8
Henry V 1956,Je 20,27:2
Merry Wives of Windsor, The 1956,Je 21,34:4
Henry V 1956,Je 24,II,1:1
King John 1956,Je 28,33:5
Measure for Measure 1956,Je 29,16:1
Richard II 1956,Jl 4,15:1
Henry V 1956,Jl 7,11:2
Midsummer Night's Dream, A 1956,Jl 20,9:5
Taming of the Shrew, The 1956,Ag 6,20:1
Taming of the Shrew, The 1956,Ag 11,11:2
Taming of the Shrew, The 1956,Ag 26,II,1:1
Henry V 1956,Ag 29,25:3
Romeo and Juliet 1956,S 19,34:6
Richard II 1956,O 24,44:1
Romeo and Juliet 1956,O 25,41:1
Hamlet 1956,O 29,34:1
Macbeth 1956,O 30,42:2
Richard II; Romeo and Juliet; Macbeth
  1956,N 4,II,1:1
Titus Andronicus 1956,D 3,40:2
Troilus and Cressida 1956,D 27,21:1
Twelfth Night 1957,Ja 5,12:2
Troilus and Cressida 1957,Ja 6,II,1:1
Measure for Measure 1957,Ja 23,24:1
Hamlet 1957,Ja 29,27:1
Measure for Measure 1957,F 3,II,1:1
Taming of the Shrew, The 1957,F 21,30:2
Othello 1957,Je 24,19:2
Midsummer Night's Dream, A 1957,Je 27,21:3
Romeo and Juliet 1957,Je 28,30:2
Othello 1957,Je 30,II,1:1
Hamlet 1957,Jl 3,15:2
Twelfth Night 1957,Jl 4,16:4
Twelfth Night 1957,Jl 7,II,1:1
Hamlet 1957,Jl 7,II,1:1
Merchant of Venice, The 1957,Jl 11,19:5

Shakespeare, William (Playwright)—Cont

Two Gentlemen of Verona 1957,Jl 23,21:5
Much Ado About Nothing 1957,Ag 8,15:2
Tempest, The 1957,Ag 14,21:1
Macbeth 1957,Ag 16,11:2
Much Ado About Nothing 1957,Ag 18,II,1:1
Merchant of Venice, The 1957,Ag 18,II,1:1
Henry VI (Part III) 1957,O 18,19:5
Julius Caesar 1957,O 24,39:1
Measure for Measure 1957,N 20,42:8
Richard III 1957,N 26,41:1
As You Like It 1958,Ja 21,33:6
Two Gentlemen of Verona 1958,Mr 19,35:1
Hamlet 1958,Je 21,11:1
Midsummer Night's Dream, A 1958,Je 23,19:1
Henry IV, Part I 1958,Je 25,23:3
Much Ado About Nothing 1958,Je 26,22:1
Othello 1958,Jl 4,16:1
Winter's Tale, The 1958,Jl 21,17:4
Winter's Tale, The 1958,Jl 23,34:3
Winter's Tale, The 1958,Jl 27,II,1:1
Twelfth Night 1958,Ag 7,21:4
Twelfth Night 1958,Ag 27,32:1
Much Ado About Nothing 1958,Ag 27,34:6
Twelfth Night 1958,D 10,54:2
Hamlet 1958,D 17,2:7
Henry V 1958,D 26,2:7
King Lear 1959,Ja 3,11:2
Antony and Cleopatra 1959,Ja 14,28:1
Merry Wives of Windsor, The 1959,Mr 14,23:1
Othello 1959,Ap 8,41:3
Othello 1959,Ap 12,II,3:1
All's Well That Ends Well 1959,Ap 22,30:3
Midsummer Night's Dream, A 1959,Je 3,30:1
Midsummer Night's Dream, A 1959,Je 5,16:5
Macbeth 1959,Je 7,124:3
Romeo and Juliet 1959,Je 21,II,1:1
As You Like It 1959,Jl 1,27:1
Othello 1959,Jl 2,17:2
As You Like It 1959,Jl 5,II,1:1
Othello 1959,Jl 5,II,1:1
Coriolanus 1959,Jl 8,24:5
Merry Wives of Windsor, The 1959,Jl 9,23:2
Twelfth Night 1959,Jl 11,10:2
Midsummer Night's Dream, A 1959,Jl 29,34:1
Macbeth 1959,Ag 1,9:2
All's Well That Ends Well 1959,Ag 3,20:4
Julius Caesar 1959,Ag 4,30:1
Julius Caesar 1959,Ag 16,II,1:1
King Lear 1959,Ag 19,34:7
Hamlet 1959,S 11,21:4
Much Ado About Nothing 1959,S 18,25:2
Much Ado About Nothing 1959,S 27,II,1:1
Tempest, The 1959,D 28,19:2
Henry V 1960,F 26,22:1
Henry IV 1960,Mr 2,42:1
Henry IV 1960,Mr 13,II,1:1
Two Gentlemen of Verona 1960,Ap 6,47:3
Merchant of Venice, The 1960,Ap 13,46:5
Henry IV 1960,Ap 19,41:1
Henry IV, Part II 1960,Ap 24,II,1:1
Twelfth Night 1960,My 18,48:6
Twelfth Night 1960,Je 9,29:4
Tempest, The 1960,Je 20,35:1
Taming of the Shrew, The 1960,Je 22,29:1
Tempest, The 1960,Je 26,II,1:1
King John 1960,Je 29,26:2
Henry V 1960,Je 30,23:1
Midsummer Night's Dream, A 1960,Je 30,23:5
Romeo and Juliet 1960,Jl 1,14:1
Measure for Measure 1960,Jl 27,33:1
Antony and Cleopatra 1960,Ag 1,19:1
Taming of the Shrew, The 1960,Ag 20,17:1
Othello 1960,S 11,II,7:1
Macbeth 1961,Ja 10,28:1
Much Ado About Nothing 1961,Ap 5,31:1
Hamlet 1961,Ap 12,46:1
Hamlet 1961,Ap 30,II,1:1
King Lear 1961,My 15,34:6
Richard III 1961,My 25,32:3
As You Like It 1961,Je 17,13:2
Macbeth 1961,Je 19,31:1
Coriolanus 1961,Je 21,31:2
Henry VIII 1961,Je 22,22:1
Love's Labour's Lost 1961,Je 23,19:1
Macbeth 1961,Je 25,II,1:1
Richard III 1961,Je 25,II,3:5
As You Like It 1961,Je 25,II,1:1
Henry VIII 1961,Jl 2,II,1:1
Love's Labour's Lost 1961,Jl 2,II,1:1
As You Like It 1961,Jl 5,30:1
Coriolanus 1961,Jl 5,30:1
Much Ado About Nothing 1961,Jl 7,17:1
Troilus and Cressida 1961,Jl 24,15:1
Midsummer Night's Dream, A 1961,Ag 3,13:1
Romeo and Juliet 1961,Ag 16,36:3
Richard II 1961,Ag 30,25:1
Merchant of Venice, The 1962,F 3,13:2
Macbeth 1962,F 7,32:2
Romeo and Juliet 1962,F 14,39:1
Julius Caesar 1962,F 22,19:6
Romeo and Juliet 1962,F 25,II,1:1
Macbeth 1962,F 25,II,1:1
Romeo and Juliet 1962,Ap 3,42:1

Measure for Measure 1962,Ap 11,47:4
Midsummer Night's Dream, A 1962,Ap 18,30:3
Taming of the Shrew, The 1962,Ap 24,33:3
Julius Caesar 1962,My 12,14:1
Macbeth 1962,Je 6,35:2
Henry IV, Part I 1962,Je 18,20:4
Richard II 1962,Je 18,20:2
Macbeth 1962,Je 20,41:1
Taming of the Shrew, The 1962,Je 21,25:1
Merchant of Venice, The 1962,Je 22,1:4
Tempest, The 1962,Je 22,14:1
Henry IV, Part I 1962,Je 24,II,1:1
Richard II 1962,Je 24,II,1:1
Midsummer Night's Dream, A 1962,Jl 2,22:2
Tempest, The 1962,Jl 17,18:2
Cymbeline 1962,Jl 18,21:2
Shakespeare Revisited 1962,Jl 19,19:2
Richard II 1962,Ag 8,36:1
King Lear 1962,Ag 14,35:1
Comedy of Errors, The 1962,S 12,34:2
Othello 1962,S 28,27:1
Macbeth 1962,N 17,16:2
Taming of the Shrew, The 1963,Mr 8,9:1
Tempest, The 1963,Ap 3,43:1
Othello 1963,Ap 13,10:4
Ages of Man 1963,Ap 15,36:1
Boys From Syracuse, The 1963,Ap 16,31:1
Hamlet 1963,My 9,41:1
Hamlet 1963,My 19,II,1:1
King Lear 1963,Je 10,37:1
Comedy of Errors, The 1963,Je 13,28:1
Henry V 1963,Je 14,37:1
Troilus and Cressida 1963,Je 19,40:2
Antony and Cleopatra 1963,Je 21,33:1
Comedy of Errors, The 1963,Je 21,35:3
Winter's Tale, The 1963,Je 29,13:1
Midsummer Night's Dream, A 1963,Jl 1,19:2
Much Ado About Nothing 1963,Jl 15,25:2
As You Like It 1963,Jl 17,19:2
Henry VI 1963,Jl 18,14:1
Timon of Athens 1963,Jl 31,19:2
Winter's Tale, The 1963,Ag 16,14:1
Richard III 1963,Ag 21,37:5
Antony and Cleopatra 1963,S 14,12:4
Twelfth Night 1963,O 9,47:1
King Lear 1963,N 23,22:1
Hamlet 1964,Ap 19,II,1:1
Othello 1964,Ap 22,56:1
Hamlet 1964,Je 17,49:1
Richard II 1964,Je 17,47:1
Midsummer Night's Dream, A 1964,Jl 12,II,1:1
Henry VI, Part I 1964,Jl 21,29:1
King Lear 1964,Jl 23,18:1
Merchant of Venice, The 1964,Jl 23,18:1
Twelfth Night 1964,Jl 23,18:1
Henry VI, Part I 1964,Jl 23,18:1
Othello 1964,Jl 23,18:4
Much Ado About Nothing 1964,Jl 24,15:2
Macbeth 1964,Jl 27,22:3
Much Ado About Nothing 1964,Jl 27,22:3
Measure for Measure 1964,Jl 27,22:3
Othello 1964,Ag 3,16:6
Merchant of Venice, The 1965,Ap 17,9:1
Richard III 1965,Je 3,26:1
Love's Labour's Lost 1965,Je 16,46:1
Taming of the Shrew, The 1965,Jl 3,10:5
Hamlet 1965,Ag 20,18:2
Romeo y Julieta 1965,Ag 28,13:3
Midsummer Night's Dream, A 1965,N 21,123:1
Taming of the Shrew, The 1966,F 5,32:1
As You Like It 1966,Ap 4,19:1
Henry V 1966,Je 8,38:1
Henry VI 1966,Je 9,55:2
Twelfth Night 1966,Je 10,51:2
All's Well That Ends Well 1966,Je 17,39:1
Falstaff 1966,Je 20,27:1
Twelfth Night 1966,Je 23,28:1
Julius Caesar 1966,Je 24,29:2
Measure for Measure 1966,Jl 14,27:1
Richard III 1966,Ag 11,26:1
Measure for Measure 1967,F 15,37:1
Hamlet 1967,F 17,44:1
Romeo and Juliet 1967,F 22,18:1
Richard III 1967,Je 14,43:1
Comedy of Errors, The 1967,Je 15,58:4
Midsummer Night's Dream, A 1967,Je 19,42:1
Merchant of Venice, The 1967,Je 22,46:2
Richard III 1967,Je 25,II,1:2
Midsummer Night's Dream, A 1967,Je 30,23:1
Macbeth 1967,Jl 31,21:1
Antony and Cleopatra 1967,Ag 2,25:1
Merry Wives of Windsor, The 1967,Ag 4,18:1
Measure for Measure 1967,Ag 27,II,4:8
Antony and Cleopatra 1967,S 17,II,1:1
As You Like It 1967,O 6,33:4
As You Like It 1967,O 15,II,9:3
Antony and Cleopatra 1967,O 29,83:4
Hamlet 1967,D 27,45:1
Comedy of Errors, The 1968,F 28,40:2
Merry Wives of Windsor, The 1968,My 4,45:5
Coriolanus 1968,My 26,II,7:1
Hamlet 1968,Je 9,II,1:1
Hamlet 1968,Je 10,59:1

Shakespeare, William (Playwright)—Cont

Romeo and Juliet 1968,Je 11,55:2
Midsummer Night's Dream, A 1968,Je 13,54:1
Twelfth Night 1968,Je 15,40:1
Richard II 1968,Je 24,42:3
As You Like It 1968,Je 24,42:3
Love's Labour's Lost 1968,Je 28,36:1
Henry IV, Part I 1968,Je 30,54:7
Henry IV, Part II 1968,Jl 2,33:1
Hamlet 1968,Jl 4,15:1
As You Like It 1968,Jl 6,9:1
Richard II 1968,Jl 7,II,1:1
Henry IV, Part II 1968,Jl 14,II,1:1
Hamlet 1968,Jl 21,II,21:2
Troilus and Cressida 1968,Ag 9,30:5
Romeo and Juliet 1968,Ag 16,19:1
Much Ado About Nothing 1968,O 16,33:1
King Lear 1968,N 8,43:1
King Lear 1968,N 17,II,1:3
Macbeth 1968,N 30,49:3
Midsummer Night's Dream, A 1968,D 9,59:1
Love's Labour's Lost 1968,D 22,54:3
Love's Labour's Lost 1969,Ja 5,II,3:1
Hamlet 1969,F 19,38:1
Hamlet 1969,Mr 4,34:1
Hamlet 1969,Mr 23,II,3:1
Pericles 1969,Jl 11,36:1
Hamlet 1969,My 2,38:1
Henry IV 1969,My 11,4:1
Hamlet 1969,My 11,II,1:1
Winter's Tale, The 1969,My 17,18:1
Macbeth 1969,Je 1,II,4:5
Winter's Tale, The 1969,Je 1,II,4:5
Pericles 1969,Je 1,II,4:5
Henry V 1969,Je 9,57:1
Hamlet 1969,Je 11,37:1
Measure for Measure 1969,Je 13,41:3
Henry V 1969,Je 15,II,3:1
Much Ado About Nothing 1969,Je 16,57:1
Measure for Measure 1969,Je 22,II,1:7
Hamlet 1969,Je 30,33:1
Troilus and Cressida 1969,Jl 31,26:1
Twelfth Night 1969,Ag 14,29:2
Twelfth Night 1969,S 1,13:1
Winter's Tale, The 1969,S 1,13:1
Much Ado About Nothing 1969,S 1,13:1
Richard II 1969,S 4,50:1
Henry VIII 1969,O 11,42:1
Henry V 1969,N 11,43:1
Macbeth 1969,D 14,87:1
Macbeth 1969,D 23,25:1
Twelfth Night 1970,Ja 1,18:1
Tempest, The 1970,F 15,67:1
Measure for Measure 1970,Ap 5,71:1
Merchant of Venice, The 1970,My 10,II,3:1
Romeo and Juliet 1970,My 28,28:1
Hamlet 1970,Je 5,23:1
Merchant of Venice, The 1970,Je 10,39:1
All's Well That Ends Well 1970,Je 16,53:1
King John 1970,Je 19,27:2
All's Well That Ends Well 1970,Je 21,II,3:2
Merchant of Venice, The 1970,Je 21,II,1:1
Othello 1970,Je 22,43:1
Othello 1970,Je 28,II,1:1
Wars of the Roses, The (Part I) 1970,Jl 2,30:1
Wars of the Roses, The (Part II) 1970,Jl 3,15:1
Richard III 1970,Jl 4,11:1
Henry VI, Parts I, II, III 1970,Jl 5,II,3:1
Cymbeline 1970,Jl 24,17:2
Merchant of Venice, The 1970,Jl 30,39:1
Richard III 1970,Ag 3,37:3
Hamlet 1970,Ag 3,37:3
Cymbeline 1970,Ag 23,II,1:6
Midsummer Night's Dream, A 1970,Ag 28,15:1
Tempest, The 1970,Ag 29,14:1
Much Ado About Nothing 1970,S 4,19:1
Midsummer Night's Dream, A 1970,S 13,II,7:1
Othello 1970,S 15,51:1
Hamlet 1970,O 19,51:1
Sensations 1970,O 26,48:2
Hamlet 1970,O 27,54:2

Shakow, Zara (Director)
Liliom 1956,F 18,12:5
Shaktman, Ben (Director)
Emperor Jones, The 1964,Ag 6,20:4
Square in the Eye 1965,My 20,54:1
Shale, Betty
Conversation Piece 1934,O 24,24:1
Shaler, Anna
Devils, The 1965,N 17,51:2
Iceman Cometh, The 1968,Ap 1,58:1
Philosophy in the Boudoir 1969,My 22,55:2
Shaler, Eleanor
Garrick Gaieties 1926,My 11,25:2
Manhatters, The 1927,Jl 19,27:3
Manhatters, The 1927,Ag 4,25:4
Murray Anderson's Almanac 1929,Ag 15,20:3
How's Your Health? 1929,N 27,30:3
Streets of New York, The 1931,O 7,29:1
Pillars of Society, The 1931,O 15,19:1
Bride the Sun Shines On, The 1931,D 28,20:2
Housewarming 1932,Ap 8,25:1
Pardon My English 1933,Ja 21,11:4

Shalet, Diane
In Good King Charles's Golden Days
  1957,Ja 25,16:1
Beaux' Stratagem, The 1957,Jl 9,25:4
Russell Patterson's Sketch-Book 1960,F 8,35:1
After the Fall 1964,Ja 24,18:1
But for Whom Charlie 1964,Mr 13,42:2
Changeling, The 1964,O 30,32:2
Tartuffe 1965,Ja 15,23:1
Shalfont, Lucille
Whirl of New York, The 1921,Je 14,18:1
Shalleck, Alan J (Miscellaneous)
Curious Savage, The 1956,Mr 17,12:3
Shalleck, Joseph (Playwright)
Good Morning, Corporal 1944,Ag 9,13:7
Shallenberger, Marion (Lighting Director)
Nine Till Six 1936,Mr 14,10:3
Shalom, Bella
Sophie 1963,Ap 16,32:1
Shaloub, Susan
Red, White and Maddox 1969,Ja 27,27:1
Shamir, Moshe (Playwright)
Highway Robbery 1955,N 8,36:1
Shanahan, Alice
Littlest Circus, The 1959,D 26,5:6
Shanahan, William H
Hit the Road 1941,Ap 4,18:3
Shand, Sonia
Pygmalion 1938,Ja 27,16:3
Captain Jinks of the Horse Marines 1938,Ja 28,16:2
Shane, Brooke
Slightly Scandalous 1944,Je 14,16:2
Shane, Margaret (Playwright)
Mr Big 1941,S 7,I,51:3
Mr Big 1941,S 14,IX,2:5
Mr Big 1941,O 1,24:2
Shane, Robert
Miss Emily Adam 1960,Mr 30,43:1
Shane, Theodore
Old King's 1924,Mr 12,19:3
Shaneberger, Hale M
Orestes 1926,Je 20,II,3:6
Coriolanus 1927,Je 18,8:3
Shanet, Howard (Miscellaneous)
Cradle Will Rock, The 1947,D 27,11:2
Shanewise, Lenore
Lazarus Laughed 1928,Ap 10,33:1
Shange, Victor
Sponono 1964,Ap 3,28:1
Shank, Richard C (Director)
Bella 1961,N 17,40:1
Shank, William
Borak 1960,D 14,51:1
Shankar, Ravi (Miscellaneous)
Guide, The 1968,Mr 7,50:1
Shankland, Richard
Virginia Reel 1947,Ap 15,28:2
I Gotta Get Out 1947,S 26,27:2
Shanks, Alec (Director)
Plume de Ma Tante, La 1958,N 12,42:1
Shanks, John
Antonia 1925,O 21,20:1
Treat 'Em Rough 1926,O 5,26:2
Shanley, Robert
Higher and Higher 1940,Ap 5,24:3
Shannon, Arthur
Fortuno 1925,D 23,22:1
Shannon, Barry
Lost Colony, The 1937,Jl 11,X,2:1
Shannon, Danny
Corn Is Green, The 1954,F 27,10:2
Shannon, Effie
Mamma's Affair 1920,Ja 20,10:1
Mama's Affair 1920,Ja 25,VIII,2:1
Heartbreak House 1920,N 11,11:1
Heartbreak House 1920,N 21,VI,1:2
Detour, The 1921,Ag 24,12:2
Sue, Dear 1922,Jl 11,16:2
Other Rose, The 1923,D 21,15:2
She Stoops to Conquer 1924,Je 10,24:3
In His Arms 1924,O 14,23:1
Youngest, The 1924,D 23,17:1
Pearl of Great Price, The 1926,N 2,34:3
Trelawney of the 'Wells' 1927,F 1,24:4
Aiglon, L' 1927,D 27,24:3
Her Unborn Child 1928,Mr 7,28:3
Good Boy 1928,S 6,23:2
Merry Andrew 1929,Ja 13,VIII,2:4
Merry Andrew 1929,Ja 22,22:2
House of Fear, The 1929,O 8,34:2
That's the Woman 1930,S 4,27:2
Admirable Crichton, The 1931,Mr 10,23:2
Admirable Crichton, The 1931,Mr 29,VIII,1:1
Fatal Alibi, The 1932,F 10,26:6
Truth About Blayds, The 1932,Ap 12,25:2
Party's Over, The 1933,Mr 28,23:3
Shatter'd Lamp, The 1934,Mr 22,26:3
But Not for Love 1934,N 27,26:2
Bitter Oleander 1935,F 12,24:3
Kind Lady 1935,Jl 23,24:4
Parnell 1935,N 12,24:2
Parnell 1936,My 5,26:2
Wingless Victory, The 1936,N 25,17:5

Wingless Victory, The 1936,D 24,20:2
Kind Lady 1937,Jl 6,23:1
Barchester Towers 1937,D 1,27:1
Merry Wives of Windsor, The 1938,Ap 15,22:3
Jeremiah 1939,F 4,11:2
Morning's at Seven 1939,N 7,30:2
Morning's at Seven 1939,D 1,26:2
Juno and the Paycock 1940,Ja 17,24:2
Russian Bank 1940,My 25,20:2
Arsenic and Old Lace 1941,Mr 25,26:7
Shannon, Frank
Anna Christie 1921,N 3,22:1
Anna Christie 1922,Ja 15,III,3:1
Anna Christie 1923,Ap 11,16:2
Anna Christie 1923,Ap 15,VII,2:4
White Desert 1923,O 19,17:3
Undercurrent, The 1925,F 4,18:2
Twelve Miles Out 1925,N 17,29:2
Hangman's House 1926,D 17,27:2
Brass Buttons 1927,D 6,26:3
Patriot, The 1928,Ja 20,15:1
Within the Law 1928,Mr 6,20:1
Elmer Gantry 1928,Ag 10,9:4
Common Sin, The 1928,O 16,28:2
Patsy, The 1929,Ja 6,VIII,1:4
Dread 1929,O 27,IX,2:1
Mystery Moon 1930,Je 24,23:4
9th Street Guest, The 1930,Ag 26,24:3
Just to Remind You 1931,S 8,39:1
In Times Square 1931,N 24,29:3
Too True to Be Good 1932,Mr 1,19:2
Too True to Be Good 1932,Mr 6,VIII,1:1
Too True to Be Good 1932,Ap 5,27:5
Web, The 1932,Je 28,24:4
Young Sinners 1933,Mr 7,20:4
Fly by Night 1933,Je 3,16:2
Move on, Sister 1933,O 25,22:4
Too Many Boats 1934,S 12,26:3
Geraniums in My Window 1934,O 27,20:6
Shannon, Harry
Oh, Kay! 1926,N 9,31:3
Hold Everything 1928,O 11,24:2
Jonica 1930,Ap 8,27:1
Simple Simon 1931,Mr 10,23:2
Free for All 1931,S 9,25:1
Pardon My English 1933,Ja 21,11:4
Under Glass 1933,O 31,24:3
Washington Jitters 1938,My 3,19:1
Mrs O'Brien Entertains 1939,F 9,16:3
Shannon, Jack
Dearest Enemy 1925,S 19,9:2
Criss Cross 1926,O 13,20:2
Shannon, James (Scenic Designer)
Marriage of Cana, The 1932,F 3,22:4
Shannon, Jay
Long and the Short and the Tall, The
  1962,Mr 30,28:2
Shannon, Lavinia
Minick 1924,S 25,20:1
Loose Ankles 1926,Ag 17,15:1
Shannon, Mark
Fortune and Men's Eyes 1969,O 23,55:1
Shannon, Mary
Pinocchio 1939,Ja 3,19:2
Shannon, Peggy
What Ann Brought Home 1927,F 22,22:2
High Gear 1927,O 7,24:3
Back Here 1928,N 27,36:3
Now-A-Days 1929,Ag 6,29:3
Cross Roads 1929,N 12,34:2
Damn Your Honor 1929,D 31,14:3
Life Is Like That 1930,D 23,24:3
Napi 1931,Mr 12,22:5
Page Miss Glory 1934,N 28,24:2
Light Behind the Shadow, The 1936,Ja 21,26:6
Larger Than Life 1936,Mr 17,25:3
Shannon, Richard
Roosty 1938,F 15,21:2
Shannon, Zyllah
Youth 1920,O 27,14:3
Shanstrom, David (Miscellaneous)
Now Is the Time for all Good Men 1967,S 27,42:1
Saturday Night 1968,F 26,43:1
Shapero, Lillian
Town Lunatics 1933,F 6,11:4
Salt and Pepper 1933,Ap 24,10:2
Untitled-Revue 1935,S 23,20:2
Shapero, Lillian (Choreographer)
Yoshe Kalb 1932,N 6,IX,2:1
Yoshe Kalb 1933,Ap 2,IX,6:6
Longing for Home 1933,S 22,15:1
Wise Men of Chelm, The 1933,O 18,24:4
Josephus 1933,D 1,22:5
Yoshe Kalb 1933,D 29,27:2
We Live and Laugh 1936,My 9,10:3
Pinye of Pinchev 1936,S 21,27:5
Water Carrier, The 1936,D 25,20:2
Oy, Is Dus a Leben!; Oh, What a Life!
  1942,O 13,19:2
Abi Gezunt 1949,O 10,19:4
Sadie Is a Lady 1950,Ja 28,9:2
Shapiro, Abraham
Clinton Street 1939,O 13,27:2

Shapiro, Al
Pirates of Penzance, The 1942,F 20,20:2
Shapiro, Clarence M (Miscellaneous)
Jenny Kissed Me 1948,D 24,12:2
Shapiro, Dan (Composer)
Artists and Models 1943,N 6,16:6
Follow the Girls 1944,Ap 10,15:2
Follow the Girls 1944,Ap 16,II,1:2
Michael Todd's Peep Show 1950,Je 29,37:2
Shapiro, Dan (Lyricist)
Artists and Models 1943,N 6,16:6
Follow the Girls 1944,Ap 10,15:2
Michael Todd's Peep Show 1950,Je 29,37:2
Ankles Aweigh 1955,Ap 19,27:1
Shapiro, Herb (Playwright)
Kill the One-Eyed Man 1965,O 21,56:1
Shapiro, Herbert
Cherry Orchard, The 1928,O 16,28:5
Sea Gull, The 1929,S 17,34:1
Living Corpse, The 1929,D 7,19:1
Romeo and Juliet 1930,Ap 22,33:1
Siegfried 1930,O 21,34:1
Alison's House 1930,D 2,31:2
Shapiro, Herman (Miscellaneous)
King Lear 1956,Ja 13,17:1
Streetcar Named Desire, A 1956,F 16,24:1
Teahouse of the August Moon, The 1956,N 9,33:2
Glass Menagerie, The 1956,N 22,50:1
Mister Roberts 1956,D 6,46:2
Hide and Seek 1957,Ap 3,26:1
Pajama Game, The 1957,My 16,27:1
Carousel 1957,S 12,38:2
Maybe Tuesday 1958,Ja 30,18:3
Annie Get Your Gun 1958,F 20,29:2
Oklahoma! 1958,Mr 20,32:3
Masquerade 1959,Mr 17,42:1
Judy Garland 1959,My 12,40:1
Finian's Rainbow 1960,Ap 28,31:1
South Pacific 1961,Ap 27,26:3
Pal Joey 1961,Je 1,32:1
Can-Can 1962,My 17,32:2
Fiorello! 1962,Je 14,24:1
Marcel Marceau 1963,Ja 3,5:7
Oklahoma! 1963,F 28,8:2
Oklahoma! 1963,My 16,40:1
King and I, The 1963,Je 13,30:2
Man and Boy 1963,N 13,34:1
West Side Story 1964,Ap 9,24:2
My Fair Lady 1964,My 21,43:2
Guys and Dolls 1965,Ap 29,39:1
South Pacific 1965,Je 3,25:1
Oklahoma! 1965,D 16,62:1
Elizabeth the Queen 1966,N 4,30:1
Carousel 1966,D 16,56:2
Finian's Rainbow 1967,Ap 6,44:1
Life With Father 1967,O 20,53:2
Tenth Man, The 1967,N 9,54:1
Brigadoon 1967,D 14,59:2
My Fair Lady 1968,Je 14,42:1
Carnival! 1968,D 13,58:1
Shapiro, Irvin (Producer)
Blue Holiday 1945,My 22,13:3
Shapiro, Kenneth
Channel One: Underground Television
  1968,Je 3,55:4
Groove Tube 1969,O 12,88:3
Shapiro, Kenneth (Director)
Groove Tube 1969,O 12,88:3
Shapiro, Kenneth (Playwright)
Groove Tube 1969,O 12,88:3
Shapiro, Leonardo (Director)
Yes, Yes, No No 1969,Ja 1,16:1
Shapiro, Marilyn (Producer)
Ever Since Paradise 1957,Jl 12,18:4
Death of Satan, The 1960,Ap 6,49:1
Shapiro, Martin (Miscellaneous)
Sweeney Todd 1957,Ag 28,21:4
Shapiro, Mel (Director)
Visit, The 1967,S 13,41:1
Serjeant Musgrave's Dance 1968,Je 16,52:4
Merton of the Movies 1968,S 26,62:1
Increased Difficulty of Concentration, The
  1969,D 5,48:1
Shapiro, Owen (Scenic Designer)
Frugal Noon 1964,My 23,15:2
Acid Wine 1964,My 23,15:2
Shapiro, Richard (Producer)
House of Leather, The 1970,Mr 19,56:1
Shapiro, Sidney
Dybbuk, The 1926,D 17,27:2
Shapiro, Sonia
Voice of Israel, The 1948,O 26,40:2
Shapiro, Stanley (Playwright)
Engagement Baby, The 1970,My 22,40:1
Shapiro, Ted
High Kickers 1941,N 1,21:2
Shapli, Omar (Director)
Instructions for the Running of Trains, etc on the
  Erie Railway to Go Into Effect January 1,1862
  1970,Ja 7,36:2
Shapli, Omar (Miscellaneous)
Merton of the Movies 1968,S 26,62:1

Shapman, William
Arabian Nights 1954,Je 25,15:2
Shappell, Ruth
Hansel and Gretel 1929,D 25,21:1
Shara, Evelyn (Playwright)
Poisoned Kiss, The 1936,Je 7,IX,5:1
Sharaff, Irene (Costume Designer)
Alice in Wonderland 1932,D 12,18:3
Alice in Wonderland 1932,D 25,IX,1:1
As Thousands Cheer 1933,O 15,IX,1:1
Great Waltz, The 1934,S 24,14:4
Jubilee 1935,S 23,20:3
Jubilee 1935,O 14,20:1
Rosmersholm 1935,D 3,32:5
On Your Toes 1936,Ap 13,14:4
Virginia 1937,S 3,13:2
Virginia 1937,S 12,XI,1:1
Virginia 1937,O 5,29:1
Boys From Syracuse, The 1938,N 24,36:1
American Way, The 1939,Ja 23,9:2
Streets of Paris, The 1939,Je 20,25:2
From Vienna 1939,Je 21,26:2
Boys and Girls Together 1940,O 2,19:2
Lady in the Dark 1941,Ja 24,14:2
Lady in the Dark 1941,F 2,IX,1:1
Lady in the Dark 1941,S 3,26:6
Land Is Bright, The 1941,O 29,26:2
Sunny River 1941,D 5,28:2
By Jupiter 1942,Je 4,22:1
Star and Garter 1942,Je 25,26:2
Count Me In 1942,O 9,24:2
Lady in the Dark 1943,Mr 1,14:2
Hamlet 1945,D 14,25:2
Million Dollar Baby 1945,D 22,17:2
Billion Dollar Baby 1945,D 30,II,1:1
Would-Be Gentleman, The 1946,Ja 10,29:2
Magdalena 1948,Jl 28,27:2
Magdalena 1948,S 21,31:2
Montserrat 1949,O 31,21:4
Dance Me a Song 1950,Ja 21,10:5
Michael Todd's Peep Show 1950,Je 29,37:2
King and I, The 1951,Mr 30,26:2
King and I, The 1951,Ap 8,II,1:1
Tree Grows in Brooklyn, A 1951,Ap 20,24:3
Tree Grows in Brooklyn, A 1951,Ap 29,II,1:1
Of Thee I Sing 1952,My 6,34:2
King and I, The 1952,O 5,II,1:1
Me and Juliet 1953,My 29,17:1
Me and Juliet 1953,Je 7,II,1:1
King and I, The 1953,O 9,33:3
By the Beautiful Sea 1954,Ap 9,20:1
By the Beautiful Sea 1954,Ap 18,II,1:1
On Your Toes 1954,O 12,24:4
King and I, The 1956,Ap 19,35:4
Shangri-La 1956,Je 14,40:1
Candide 1956,D 3,40:2
Happy Hunting 1956,D 7,30:1
Candide 1956,D 9,II,5:1
Small War on Murray Hill 1957,Ja 4,19:1
Small War on Murray Hill 1957,Ja 13,II,1:1
West Side Story 1957,S 27,14:4
Flower Drum Song 1958,D 2,44:1
Flower Drum Song 1958,D 7,II,5:1
Juno 1959,Mr 10,41:1
Judy Garland 1959,My 12,40:1
West Side Story 1960,Ap 28,31:1
Do Re Mi 1960,D 27,23:2
Do Re Mi 1961,Ja 8,II,1:1
King and I, The 1963,Je 13,30:2
Jennie 1963,O 18,35:2
Girl Who Came to Supper, The 1963,D 9,49:1
Funny Girl 1964,Mr 27,15:1
King and I, The 1964,Jl 7,26:1
Sweet Charity 1966,Ja 31,22:1
Hallelujah, Baby! 1967,Ap 27,51:1
Sharaff, Irene (Lighting Director)
Land Is Bright, The 1941,O 21,28:5
Sharaff, Irene (Scenic Designer)
Alice in Wonderland 1932,D 12,18:3
Alice in Wonderland 1932,D 25,IX,1:1
Crime and Punishment 1935,Ja 23,20:3
Rosmersholm 1935,D 3,32:5
Land Is Bright, The 1941,O 21,28:5
Judy Garland 1959,My 12,40:1
Shari, Michael
Antigone 1968,O 11,36:1
Shari, William
Man Is Man 1962,S 19,31:1
Brig, The 1963,My 16,40:1
Shari, William (Miscellaneous)
In the Jungle of Cities 1960,D 21,39:1
Shari, William (Scenic Designer)
Dance of Death, The 1960,S 14,51:1
Sharim, Amiram (Scenic Designer)
Men and Dreams 1966,S 7,51:2
Sharir, David (Scenic Designer)
Children of the Shadows 1964,F 27,26:1
Sharkey
Higher and Higher 1940,Ap 5,24:3
Sharkey, Anna
Divorce Me, Darling 1965,F 2,29:6

Sharkey, Jack (Playwright)
Leonard Sillman's New Faces of 1968
1968,My 3,43:1
Sharkey, John
Lawful Larceny 1922,Ja 3,20:2
Woman on the Jury, The 1923,Ag 16,10:4
Dust Heap, The 1924,Ap 25,20:2
Badges 1924,D 4,25:1
Joker, The 1925,N 17,29:1
Virgin, The 1926,F 23,26:1
Trial of Mary Dugan, The 1927,S 20,33:1
Sweet Land of Liberty 1929,S 24,29:2
Headquarters 1929,D 5,32:4
Sharkey, Susan
Cuba Si 1968,D 10,53:1
Guns of Carrar, The 1968,D 10,53:1
Good Woman of Setzuan, The 1970,N 6,51:1
Sharkey (Seal)
Higher and Higher 1940,Ag 6,15:4
Higher and Higher 1940,Ag 11,IX,1:1
Sharma, Barbara
That Hat! 1964,S 24,45:1
Sweet Charity 1966,Ja 31,22:1
Hallelujah, Baby! 1967,Ap 27,51:1
Her First Roman 1968,O 21,53:3
Come Summer 1969,Mr 19,43:1
Dames at Sea 1970,Ja 5,46:3
Sharmat, Mary (Miscellaneous)
Those That Play the Clowns 1966,N 25,48:1
Sharmat, Stephen W (Miscellaneous)
Monique 1957,O 23,38:1
Sharmat, Stephen W (Producer)
Folies Bergere 1964,Je 3,36:1
Sharoff, Luba
Maya 1951,Ag 9,17:4
Sharoff, Victor
Princess Turandot 1926,N 13,14:2
Sharon, Fran
Song of Songs 1958,O 29,31:1
Never Too Late 1962,N 28,42:1
Sharon, Ula
Broadway Brevities, 1920 1920,S 30,12:2
Greenwich Village Follies 1922,S 13,18:2
Music Box Revue 1924,D 2,23:3
Song of the Flame 1925,D 11,26:4
Song of the Flame 1925,D 31,10:2
She's My Baby 1928,Ja 4,22:2
New Americana 1928,N 30,32:4
Vaudeville (Palace) 1928,D 31,9:3
Sharon, William
Haiti 1938,Mr 3,16:1
Johnny 2X4 1942,Mr 17,24:6
Love Me Long 1949,N 8,34:5
Mr Barry's Etchings 1950,F 1,26:2
King of Hearts 1954,Ap 2,23:1
Sharp, Anthony (Playwright)
Nightmare Abbey 1952,Mr 16,II,3:8
Sharp, Arthur
Hamlet 1927,Ap 7,23:3
Caesar and Cleopatra 1927,N 6,IX,2:1
Sharp, Arthur (Miscellaneous)
Caesar and Cleopatra 1927,N 6,IX,2:1
Sharp, Evelyn (Playwright)
Poisoned Kiss, The 1937,Ap 22,19:1
Sharp, F B J
Many Waters 1929,S 26,27:1
Sharp, George (Producer)
Young Sinners 1931,Ap 21,35:5
Sharp, Henry
Morning Star 1940,Ap 17,26:4
Assassin, The 1945,O 18,20:2
Fifth Horseman, The 1949,Je 14,26:6
Oh, Men! Oh, Women! 1953,D 18,37:2
Island of Goats 1955,O 5,40:1
Idiot's Delight 1957,F 23,14:2
Seven at Dawn, The 1961,Ap 18,43:1
Sharp, Ivan
Green Pastures, The 1930,F 27,26:1
Green Pastures, The 1935,F 27,16:2
Sharp, John
All in Good Time 1965,F 19,25:1
Honor and Offer 1969,My 14,36:1
Sharp, Louis
Conjur' Man Dies 1936,Mr 12,18:5
Turpentine 1936,Je 27,21:6
Case of Philip Lawrence, The 1937,Je 9,31:1
Haiti 1938,Mr 3,16:1
Mamba's Daughters 1939,Ja 4,24:2
Mamba's Daughters 1940,Mr 25,10:4
Cabin in the Sky 1940,O 26,19:2
Run, Little Chillun 1943,Ag 14,6:1
South Pacific 1943,D 30,11:2
St Louis Woman 1946,Ap 1,22:2
Set My People Free 1948,N 4,38:2
Sharp, Margery (Original Author)
Lady in Waiting 1940,Mr 28,19:1
Nutmeg Tree 1941,O 19,IX,2:5
Sharp, Margery (Playwright)
Meeting at Night 1934,Je 15,19:1
Meeting at Night 1934,Jl 15,X,1:3
Lady in Waiting 1940,Mr 28,19:1
Nutmeg Tree 1941,O 19,IX,2:5
Foolish Gentlewoman, The 1949,Ap 3,II,3:1

Sharp, Mordaunt (Playwright)
Crime at Blossoms, The 1937,Jl 17,12:8
Sharp, R Farquharson (Translator)
Doll's House, A 1963,F 4,5:6
Sharp, Robert
Cabaret 1966,N 21,62:1
Sharp, Walter
Top Secret 1960,S 6,40:1
Sharp, William L (Director)
Critic, The 1965,Jl 26,15:2
Sharpe, Albert
Finian's Rainbow 1947,Ja 11,23:2
Finian's Rainbow 1947,Ja 26,II,1:1
Sharpe, Carl M
Holy Night 1941,D 22,23:3
Sharpe, Edith
Good Companions, The 1931,My 15,20:8
Good Companions, The 1931,My 31,VIII,2:6
Night Club Queen 1933,D 3,IX,7:6
Sharpe, Ernest
Most Immoral Lady, A 1928,N 27,36:1
Little Show, The 1929,My 1,28:5
Hey, Nonny, Nonny! 1932,Je 7,22:3
Sharpe, John
Seventeen 1951,Je 22,16:6
Shoestring Revue 1955,Mr 1,22:2
Subways Are for Sleeping 1961,D 28,22:1
Sweet Charity 1966,Ja 31,22:1
Sharpe, John (Choreographer)
Where's Charley? 1966,My 26,57:1
Sharpe, Millicent
Fall and Rise of Susan Lenox, The 1920,Je 11,11:2
Sharpe, Nancy
Brown Buddies 1930,O 8,29:1
Sharpe, R Farquharson (Translator)
Ghosts 1961,S 22,29:1
Sharpe, Robert Redington (Scenic Designer)
Major Barbara 1928,N 20,28:4
Claire Adams 1929,N 20,26:3
Joseph 1930,F 13,25:3
Saint Wench 1933,Ja 3,19:3
Strange Orchestra 1933,N 29,23:2
Tobacco Road 1933,D 5,31:2
Tobacco Road 1942,S 7,34:2
Tobacco Road 1943,S 6,21:3
Sharpe, Ruth
Naughty Marietta 1929,O 22,26:2
Sharpe, Stanley (Producer)
Company's Coming! 1931,Ap 21,35:5
Sharpe, William Jr
Hangman's Whip 1933,F 25,20:2
Shooting Star 1933,Je 13,22:2
Sharples, Wally
Vaudeville (Palace) 1927,Jl 19,27:6
Sharples, Win Jr (Producer)
Cicero 1961,F 9,37:2
Sharr, Yoel
Holiday in Israel 1968,O 14,55:2
To Be or Not to Be-What Kind of a Question Is
That? 1970,O 20,39:1
Sharron, Robert
Of V We Sing 1942,F 16,20:3
Shatner, William
Measure for Measure 1954,Je 30,23:1
Taming of the Shrew, The 1954,Jl 1,22:2
Merchant of Venice, The 1955,Jl 1,13:1
Tamburlaine the Great 1956,Ja 20,19:1
Henry V 1956,Je 20,27:2
Merry Wives of Windsor, The 1956,Je 21,34:4
World of Suzie Wong, The 1958,O 15,47:1
Shot in the Dark, A 1961,O 19,40:1
Remote Asylum 1970,D 13,II,3:1
Shatrov, Mikhail F (Playwright)
30th of August, The; Bolsheviks, The 1969,F 3,3:1
Shattuck, Joseph
Clash by Night 1941,D 29,20:2
Russian People, The 1942,D 30,17:2
Shattuck, Ralph W
Trip to Scarborough, A 1929,Mr 18,31:2
Dragon, The 1929,Mr 26,34:2
Shattuck, Richard
Virginian, The 1937,Ag 10,22:7
Shattuck, Richard (Original Author)
Snark Was a Boojum, The 1943,S 2,14:4
Shattuck, Robert
Ceremony of Innocence, The 1968,Ja 2,33:1
Shatz, Boris
Shylock and His Daughter 1947,S 30,22:2
Shaughnessy, John
Panic 1935,Mr 16,18:4
Shaughnessy, Mickey
Kelly 1965,F 8,28:2
Shaul, Avi (Playwright)
Jew Suss 1936,Ag 16,X,2:5
Shavelson, Melville (Playwright)
Jimmy 1969,O 24,38:1
Shaver, Bob
New Faces of 1956 1956,Je 15,32:1
Shaver, Buster
Vaudeville (Palace) 1929,Mr 11,22:5
Vaudeville (Palace) 1929,N 25,22:4
Vaudeville (Palace) 1931,Je 29,20:1
Variety Anthology 1932,Mr 21,19:4

Shaver, Buster—Cont

Are You With It? 1945,N 12,17:3

Shaver, David (Miscellaneous)
Narrow Road to the Deep North 1969,D 2,64:1

Shaw, Al
Five O'Clock Girl, The 1927,O 11,26:3
Pleasure Bound 1929,F 19,22:4
Vaudeville (Palace) 1930,Ag 18,24:3
Gang's All Here, The 1931,F 19,21:3
Vaudeville (Palace) 1931,S 28,17:5
High Kickers 1941,N 1,21:2

Shaw, Albert
Grab Bag, The 1924,O 7,26:2
White Eagle, The 1927,D 27,24:4

Shaw, Allen
Abe Lincoln in Illinois 1938,O 17,12:2
Steps Leading Up 1941,Ap 19,20:6
Wookey, The 1941,S 11,20:5
Christopher Blake 1946,D 2,33:2

Shaw, Anthony
Bulldog Drummond Hits Out 1937,D 22,33:2

Shaw, Arthur
Yellow Jacket, The 1921,Ja 5,11:1
Ghosts 1922,F 7,12:1
Torch Bearers, The 1922,Ag 30,10:2
New Englander, The 1924,F 8,22:2
Craig's Wife 1925,O 13,21:2
Yellow Jacket, The 1928,N 8,27:3
Falstaff 1928,D 26,14:2
Yellow Jacket, The 1929,Ja 11,21:1
Half Gods 1929,D 23,18:5
Yellow Jacket, The 1934,F 25,IX,2:6

Shaw, Barnett
Latent Heterosexual, The 1968,Mr 22,52:1
Macbeth 1968,N 30,49:3

Shaw, Barnett (Translator)
Flea in Her Ear, A 1969,O 4,25:1

Shaw, Ben
Slightly Scandalous 1944,Je 14,16:2

Shaw, Billie
Gutta Iconoclast 1921,Je 14,15:2

Shaw, Billie (Playwright)
Good Woman, The 1921,Je 14,15:2
Squaring the Triangle 1921,Je 14,15:2
Pearls 1921,Je 14,15:2
Gutta Iconoclast 1921,Je 14,15:2

Shaw, Brian (Director)
Macbeth 1955,O 20,42:2
Romeo and Juliet 1956,F 24,20:4
Romeo and Juliet 1956,Mr 4,II,1:1
Sign of Jonah, The 1960,S 9,35:1
Marcus in the High Grass 1960,N 22,38:6
Cabin in the Sky 1964,Ja 22,32:1

Shaw, Brinsley
Sherlock Holmes 1929,N 26,28:3
Mr Samuel 1930,N 11,28:4

Shaw, Carl
Harry Delmar's Revels 1927,N 29,30:2
Vaudeville (Palace) 1929,O 21,31:2
Vaudeville (Loew's State) 1932,Jl 18,9:7

Shaw, Clay (Producer)
Untitled-One Woman Show 1938,O 31,12:2

Shaw, David (Miscellaneous)
Career Angel 1944,My 24,23:7

Shaw, David (Playwright)
They Should Have Stood in Bed 1942,F 14,18:5
Redhead 1959,F 6,21:1
Tovarich 1963,Mr 20,5:1

Shaw, Dickson
Good Soldier Schweik, The 1963,Ap 9,57:1

Shaw, Edna
Little Miss Charity 1920,S 3,6:3

Shaw, Edward
Lombardi, Ltd 1927,Je 7,27:3
Footlights 1927,Ag 20,8:2
Poppa 1928,D 25,31:1

Shaw, Eleanor
Pomeroy's Past 1926,Ap 20,24:4
What Never Dies 1926,D 29,24:2
Show Boat 1927,D 28,26:1

Shaw, Ernest
Conjur 1938,N 1,27:2

Shaw, Erwin (Playwright)
Bury the Dead 1936,Mr 16,21:2

Shaw, Fernandez (Playwright)
Villana, La 1928,Ja 1,VIII,8:3

Shaw, G Tito
Trials of Brother Jero, The 1967,N 10,60:1

Shaw, George
Hades, the Ladies 1934,Mr 29,25:3

Shaw, George Bernard (Miscellaneous)
Chocolate Soldier, The 1934,My 3,15:3
Jitta's Atonement 1935,Ja 31,22:3
Dear Liar 1960,Mr 18,19:2
Dear Liar 1962,Mr 19,36:1

Shaw, George Bernard (Original Author)
Chocolate Soldier, The 1932,F 9,30:3
Chocolate Soldier, The 1942,Je 24,22:2
Heartbreak House 1950,Mr 22,33:2
My Fair Lady 1956,Mr 25,II,1:1
My Fair Lady 1956,Ap 29,II,17:1
My Fair Lady 1956,Je 3,II,1:1
My Fair Lady 1956,Ag 12,II,1:1
My Fair Lady 1956,O 28,II,1:1

My Fair Lady 1958,Mr 9,II,1:1
Back to Methuselah 1958,Mr 27,41:5
My Fair Lady 1958,My 1,34:5
My Fair Lady 1958,My 4,II,3:1
Arms and the Man 1964,Ap 28,41:1
Saint Joan 1964,My 14,41:1
My Fair Lady 1964,My 21,43:2
My Fair Lady 1964,D 29,22:1
Major Barbara 1965,My 18,33:1
Her First Roman 1968,N 3,II,1:1
Adventures of the Black Girl in Her Search for God, The 1969,Mr 22,24:4

Shaw, George Bernard (Playwright)
O'Flaherty, V C 1920,Je 22,9:1
Heartbreak House 1920,N 11,11:1
Heartbreak House 1920,N 21,VI,1:2
Arms and the Man 1921,Mr 6,VI,1:7
Arms and the Man 1921,Ap 10,VI,1:1
Heartbreak House 1921,N 18,20:3
Chocolate Soldier, The 1921,D 13,24:2
Back to Methuselah (Part II: The Gospel of the Brothers Barnabas); Gospel of the Brothers Barnabas, The (Back to Methuselah, Part II) 1922,F 28,17:2
Back to Methuselah (Part I: In the Beginning); In the Beginning (Back to Methuselah, Part I) 1922,F 28,17:2
Back to Methuselah (Part III: The Thing Happens); Thing Happens, The (Back to Methuselah, Part III) 1922,Mr 7,11:1
Back to Methuselah (Part IV: The Tragedy of an Elderly Gentleman); Tragedy of an Elderly Gentleman, The (Back to Methuselah, Part IV) 1922,Mr 7,11:1
Back to Methuselah (Part V: As Far as Thought Can Reach); As Far as Thought Can Reach (Back to Methuselah, Part V) 1922,Mr 14,11:2
Candida 1922,Mr 23,11:1
Jitta's Atonement 1923,Ja 18,16:3
Devil's Disciple, The 1923,Ap 24,24:1
Devil's Disciple, The 1923,My 6,VII,1:1
You Never Can Tell 1923,Jl 13,18:4
Back to Methuselah 1923,O 14,VIII,1:8
Shewing-Up of Blanco Posnet, The 1923,O 17,14:2
Back to Methuselah 1923,O 21,VIII,2:2
Saint Joan 1923,D 29,8:4
Saint Joan 1924,Ja 6,VII,1:1
Back to Methuselah 1924,F 23,12:2
Saint Joan 1924,Mr 27,16:2
How He Lied to Her Husband 1924,S 30,27:5
Saint Joan 1924,O 26,30:2
Saint Joan 1924,N 9,VII,2:3
Candida 1924,D 13,12:3
Candida 1924,D 21,VII,1:1
Saint Joan 1925,Ja 11,VII,2:7
Candida 1925,Ap 5,IX,1:2
Caesar and Cleopatra 1925,Ap 14,27:1
Caesar and Cleopatra 1925,Ap 19,IX,1:1
Candida 1925,Ap 26,VIII,1:1
Arms and the Man 1925,S 15,28:1
Arms and the Man 1925,O 4,IX,1:1
Candida 1925,N 10,23:4
Man of Destiny, The 1925,N 24,28:1
Androcles and the Lion 1925,N 24,28:1
Androcles and the Lion 1925,N 29,VIII,1:1
Candida 1925,D 19,14:2
Candida 1926,Mr 17,28:3
Man of Destiny, The 1926,My 1,10:1
Fanny's First Play 1926,O 10,VIII,2:1
Candida 1926,O 24,VIII,2:1
Pygmalion 1926,N 16,24:1
Pygmalion 1926,N 21,VIII,1:1
Shewing-Up of Blanco Posnet, The 1926,D 26,VII,4:8
Great Catherine, The 1927,Ap 3,VIII,4:7
Pygmalion 1927,My 12,25:2
Candida 1927,Ag 31,19:4
Caesar and Cleopatra 1927,N 6,IX,2:1
Doctor's Dilemma, The 1927,N 22,33:1
Doctor's Dilemma, The 1927,D 4,X,1:1
Getting Married 1927,D 25,VIII,1:4
Heartbreak House 1928,F 12,VIII,1:3
Major Barbara 1928,N 20,28:4
Major Barbara 1928,D 2,X,1:1
Caesar and Cleopatra 1929,Ja 6,VIII,4:7
Apple Cart, The 1929,Je 15,6:2
Apple Cart, The 1929,Ag 20,30:2
Apple Cart, The 1929,S 8,IX,1:8
Apple Cart, The 1929,S 18,35:1
Apple Cart, The 1930,F 25,30:1
Apple Cart, The 1930,Mr 2,IX,1:1
Apple Cart, The 1930,Mr 9,IX,4:3
Saint Joan 1930,Je 29,VIII,1:4
Devil's Disciple, The 1930,S 21,IX,2:1
Apple Cart, The 1930,N 23,IX,1:3
Getting Married 1931,Mr 31,25:5
O'Flaherty, V C 1931,Ap 11,17:6
Widowers' Houses 1931,Ap 12,IX,2:1
Too True to Be Good 1932,Mr 1,19:2
Too True to Be Good 1932,Mr 6,VIII,1:1
Too True to Be Good 1932,Ap 5,27:5
Too True to Be Good 1932,Ap 10,VIII,1:1
Too True to Be Good 1932,Ag 7,I,23:2

Shaw, George Bernard (Playwright)—Cont

Too True to Be Good 1932,Ag 28,IX,1:1
Too True to Be Good 1932,Ag 28,IX,1:1
Caesar and Cleopatra 1932,O 16,IX,3:7
On the Rocks 1933,N 25,10:1
On the Rocks 1933,N 26,II,2:8
On the Rocks 1933,D 17,IX,4:2
Village Wooing 1934,Ap 18,22:5
Village Wooing 1934,Je 20,24:3
On the Rocks 1934,Jl 11,20:4
Six of Calais, The 1934,Jl 18,20:3
Six of Calais, The 1934,Ag 12,IX,1:3
Saint Joan 1934,N 27,27:2
Simpleton of the Unexpected Isles, The 1935,F 19,27:5
Simpleton of the Unexpected Isles, The 1935,F 24,VIII,1:1
Major Barbara 1935,Mr 5,23:2
Heartbreak House 1935,Jl 23,24:3
Simpleton of the Unexpected Isles, The 1935,Jl 30,17:3
Candida 1935,Ag 20,25:1
Caesar and Cleopatra 1935,Ag 22,21:1
Simpleton of the Unexpected Isles, The 1935,Ag 25,X,1:3
Village Wooing 1935,O 27,IX,2:5
Millionairess, The 1936,Ja 5,39:3
Saint Joan 1936,Mr 10,27:4
Saint Joan 1936,Mr 15,X,1:1
Saint Joan 1936,Jl 26,II,1:3
Millionairess, The 1936,N 18,30:3
Millionairess, The 1936,D 13,XI,5:3
Candida 1937,F 11,19:3
Candida 1937,F 28,XI,1:5
Candida 1937,Mr 11,20:2
Candida 1937,Mr 21,XI,1:1
Pygmalion 1937,Jl 7,26:3
Arms and the Man 1937,Jl 20,19:3
Too True to Be Good 1937,Jl 27,24:2
Candida 1937,Ag 4,14:5
Too True to Be Good 1937,Ag 15,II,5:8
Cymbeline 1937,N 17,26:4
Cymbeline 1937,D 5,XII,5:8
Pygmalion 1938,Ja 27,16:3
Heartbreak House 1938,Ap 30,18:2
Heartbreak House 1938,My 8,X,1:1
On the Rocks 1938,Je 16,20:2
Geneva 1938,Ag 2,15:6
Geneva 1938,Ag 7,IV,5:3
Millionairess, The 1938,Ag 16,22:5
Geneva 1938,Ag 21,IX,2:1
Candida 1938,Ag 31,13:2
Geneva 1938,N 23,25:1
Androcles and the Lion 1938,D 17,10:5
In Good King Charles's Golden Days 1939,Ag 13,28:1
In Good King Charles's Golden Days 1939,Ag 20,IV,2:7
In Good King Charles's Golden Days 1939,S 3,IX,2:1
Geneva 1940,Ja 31,15:2
In Good King Charles's Golden Days 1940,My 19,IX,1:4
Doctor's Dilemma, The 1941,F 18,26:6
Doctor's Dilemma, The 1941,Mr 12,18:2
Doctor's Dilemma, The 1941,Mr 30,IX,1:1
Devil's Disciple, The 1941,S 11,20:6
Candida 1942,Ap 28,24:4
Candida 1942,My 3,VIII,1:1
Arms and the Man 1944,O 1,II,1:3
Candida 1945,Ag 7,25:3
Pygmalion 1945,D 27,16:1
Pygmalion 1946,Ja 6,II,1:1
Candida 1946,Ap 4,33:2
Candida 1946,D 4,44:2
Androcles and the Lion 1946,D 20,29:2
Androcles and the Lion 1946,D 29,II,1:1
Pygmalion 1947,F 6,29:4
Man and Superman 1947,O 9,31:2
Man and Superman 1947,O 19,II,1:1
Saint Joan 1948,Ja 11,II,3:7
John Bull's Other Island 1948,F 11,33:4
You Never Can Tell 1948,Mr 17,31:2
Millionairess, The 1949,Ap 7,38:5
St Joan 1949,Ap 23,10:2
Man and Superman 1949,My 17,28:6
Buoyant Billions 1949,Ag 14,58:3
Buoyant Billions 1949,O 24,18:3
Caesar and Cleopatra 1949,D 22,28:2
Caesar and Cleopatra 1950,Ja 8,II,1:1
Devil's Disciple, The 1950,Ja 26,23:2
Devil's Disciple, The 1950,F 5,II,1:1
Getting Married 1950,Je 14,41:2
Far Fetched Fables 1950,S 7,39:7
Arms and the Man 1950,O 20,34:2
Mrs Warren's Profession 1950,O 26,39:2
Captain Brassbound's Conversion 1950,D 28,21:1
Major Barbara 1951,F 24,10:2
Caesar and Cleopatra 1951,My 11,32:8
Getting Married 1951,My 14,28:5
Saint Joan 1951,O 5,23:2
Saint Joan 1951,O 14,II,1:1
Don Juan in Hell 1951,O 23,34:4
Don Juan in Hell 1951,N 4,II,1:1

Shaw, George Bernard (Playwright)—Cont

Caesar and Cleopatra 1951,D 20,43:2
Caesar and Cleopatra 1951,D 30,II,1:1
Pygmalion 1952,F 9,11:2
Candida 1952,Ap 23,23:6
Millionairess, The 1952,Je 28,12:2
Widowers' Houses 1952,S 21,II,1:1
Millionairess, The 1952,O 18,17:2
Millionairess, The 1952,O 26,II,1:1
In Good King Charles's Golden Days
    1952,D 11,46:2
Misalliance 1953,F 19,20:1
Man and Superman 1953,F 21,11:2
Misalliance 1953,Mr 22,II,1:1
Apple Cart, The 1953,My 8,29:3
Simpleton of the Unexpected Isles, The
    1954,Ja 12,19:1
Major Barbara 1954,Je 30,23:2
Saint Joan 1954,S 18,12:1
Doctor's Dilemma, The 1955,Ja 12,22:1
Doctor's Dilemma, The 1955,Ja 23,II,1:1
Misalliance 1955,F 12,10:6
Saint Joan 1955,F 13,II,3:1
Saint Joan 1955,My 29,II,1:1
Dark Lady of the Sonnets, The 1956,F 21,38:1
Admirable Bashville, The 1956,F 21,38:1
Dark Lady of the Sonnets, The 1956,Mr 4,II,1:1
My Fair Lady 1956,Mr 16,20:2
Man of Destiny, The 1956,Ap 26,38:1
Three Times Three; How He Lied to Her Husband
    1956,My 24,27:2
Mrs Warren's Profession 1956,Je 7,35:2
Village Wooing 1956,S 5,22:6
Fanny's First Play 1956,S 5,22:6
Saint Joan 1956,S 12,42:1
Saint Joan 1956,S 16,II,1:1
Arms and the Man 1956,O 2,39:4
Apple Cart, The 1956,O 19,23:1
Apple Cart, The 1956,O 28,II,1:1
Major Barbara 1956,O 31,27:1
Saint Joan 1956,D 15,20:3
In Good King Charles's Golden Days
    1957,Ja 25,16:1
In Good King Charles's Golden Days
    1957,F 3,II,1:1
Candida 1957,F 9,14:1
Evening With G B S, An; O'Flaherty, V C
    1957,F 19,35:7
An Evening With G B S; Press Cuttings
    1957,F 19,35:7
Man of Destiny, The 1957,Ap 1,21:2
Augustus Does His Bit 1958,F 22,8:3
Androcles and the Lion 1958,F 22,8:3
Back to Methuselah 1958,Ap 6,II,1:1
Philanderer, The 1958,My 13,26:2
You Never Can Tell 1958,Je 17,25:1
Mrs Warren's Profession 1958,Je 26,22:1
Shakes Versus Shaw 1959,Ja 27,27:5
Widowers' Houses 1959,Mr 3,39:2
Buoyant Billions 1959,My 27,32:2
Overruled 1959,My 27,32:2
Getting Married 1959,Je 5,18:2
Passion, Poison and Petrifaction 1959,Ag 21,13:1
Overruled 1959,Ag 21,13:1
Dark Lady of the Sonnets, The 1959,Ag 21,13:1
Shewing-Up of Blanco Posnet, The 1959,S 19,26:7
Shewing-Up of Blanco Posnet, The 1959,O 4,II,1:1
Heartbreak House 1959,O 19,37:1
Heartbreak House 1959,O 25,II,1:1
Glimpse of the Domesticity of Franklyn Barnabas,
    A 1960,Mr 7,24:2
Man and Superman 1960,Ag 17,35:3
Don Juan in Hell 1960,O 4,47:3
Man and Superman 1960,N 7,46:2
Candida 1961,Ap 27,26:1
Misalliance 1961,S 26,32:2
Androcles and the Lion 1961,N 22,24:2
Dark Lady of the Sonnets, The 1961,D 15,48:1
Saint Joan 1962,F 21,57:4
Candida 1962,N 12,35:5
Too True to Be Good 1963,Mr 14,8:2
Too True to Be Good 1963,Mr 23,5:6
Too True to Be Good 1963,Ap 9,28:1
Mrs Warren's Profession 1963,Ap 25,39:1
Heartbreak House 1963,Je 8,14:2
Saint Joan 1963,Je 25,23:1
Heartbreak House 1963,Je 28,24:1
Caesar and Cleopatra 1963,Ag 1,18:2
Man and Superman 1964,D 7,45:2
Man and Superman 1965,Ja 31,II,1:1
Arms and the Man 1965,Je 24,32:5
Arms and the Man 1967,Je 23,44:2
Heartbreak House 1967,Ag 27,II,1:1
Saint Joan 1968,Ja 5,42:1
Saint Joan 1968,Ja 14,II,1:1
My Fair Lady 1968,Je 14,42:1
Androcles and the Lion 1968,Je 27,47:1
Heartbreak House 1968,Jl 6,9:1
Her First Roman 1968,O 21,53:3
Candida 1969,F 3,29:1
Millionairess, The 1969,Mr 3,28:1
Doctor's Dilemma, The 1969,Je 24,37:1
Back to Methuselah 1969,Ag 31,46:3
Getting Married 1970,Ja 20,46:1

Man and Superman 1970,F 24,48:1
Candida 1970,Ap 7,41:1
Devil's Disciple, The 1970,Je 30,48:1
Arms and the Man 1970,Jl 10,18:1
Devil's Disciple, The 1970,Jl 12,II,1:3
Arms and the Man 1970,Ag 26,36:1

Shaw, George Bernard (Translator)
Jitta's Atonement 1925,F 1,VII,2:1
Frau Jitta's Suehne 1930,My 18,VIII,2:6

Shaw, Glen Byam
Cherry Orchard, The 1928,Mr 6,20:1
Lady of the Camellias, The 1930,Mr 23,IX,2:3
Queen of Scots 1934,Jl 15,X,1:3
Merchant of Venice, The 1938,My 15,X,1:5

Shaw, Glen Byam (Director)
Dear Octopus 1939,Ja 12,22:2
Winslow Boy, The 1947,O 30,32:2
Winslow Boy, The 1947,N 9,II,1:1
Henry V 1951,F 11,II,3:1
Antony and Cleopatra 1953,My 10,II,1:1
Merchant of Venice, The 1953,My 10,II,1:1
Richard III 1953,My 10,II,1:1
Macbeth 1955,Je 19,II,1:1
King Lear 1959,Ag 19,34:7
Complaisant Lover, The 1961,N 2,43:2
Ross 1961,D 27,20:2
Dance of Death, The 1967,O 20,50:1

Shaw, Glenn (Translator)
Little Theatre Tournament; Father Returns, The
    1929,My 7,28:1

Shaw, Harold (Director)
Father, The 1962,My 15,49:1
Long Day's Journey Into Night 1962,My 16,35:4
Miss Julie 1962,My 17,31:1

Shaw, Harry
Inherit the Wind 1955,Ap 22,20:2

Shaw, Helen
Genius and the Crowd 1920,S 7,20:1

Shaw, Henry M (Lighting Director)
Billy Budd 1959,F 28,13:3

Shaw, Henry M (Miscellaneous)
Billy Budd 1959,F 28,13:3
Jackass, The 1960,Mr 24,39:2
Fig Leaf in Her Bonnet, A 1961,Je 15,50:1

Shaw, Hollace
Very Warm for May 1939,N 18,23:2
Higher and Higher 1940,Ap 5,24:3

Shaw, Howard (Original Author)
Bravo Giovanni 1962,My 21,41:2
Bravo Giovanni 1962,My 27,II,1:1

Shaw, Irwin (Playwright)
Bury the Dead 1936,Ap 20,17:4
Bury the Dead 1936,Ap 26,IX,1:1
Siege 1937,D 9,31:4
Gentle People, The 1939,Ja 6,25:1
Gentle People, The 1939,Jl 7,12:6
Gentle People, The 1939,Jl 30,IX,1:3
Retreat to Pleasure 1940,D 18,32:2
Sons and Soldiers 1943,My 5,22:2
Assassin, The 1945,Mr 23,13:6
Assassin, The 1945,Ap 1,II,2:3
Assassin, The 1945,O 18,20:2
Survivors, The 1948,Ja 20,27:2
Survivors, The 1948,Ja 25,II,1:1
Gentle People, The 1950,Ap 15,10:5
Children From Their Games 1963,Ap 12,33:1

Shaw, Jack
Whoopee 1928,D 5,34:3

Shaw, Jerome
Candida 1945,Ag 7,25:3
Lost in the Stars 1949,O 31,21:2

Shaw, Joan
Mismates 1925,Ap 14,27:2

Shaw, Joseph
Two Gentlemen of Verona 1957,Jl 23,21:5
Macbeth 1957,Ag 16,11:2
As You Like It 1958,Ja 21,33:6
Macbeth 1962,Je 20,41:1
Taming of the Shrew, The 1962,Je 21,25:1
Troilus and Cressida 1963,Je 19,40:2
Cyrano de Bergerac 1963,Je 20,30:1
Timon of Athens 1963,Jl 31,19:2
Richard II 1964,Je 17,47:1
King Lear 1964,Je 19,36:1
Country Wife, The 1964,Ag 3,16:1
Henry IV, Part I 1965,Je 30,42:1
Falstaff; Henry IV, Part II 1965,Jl 1,35:1
Julius Caesar 1965,Jl 2,18:1
Merry Wives of Windsor, The 1967,Ag 4,18:1
Soldiers 1968,Mr 3,88:2
Soldiers 1968,My 2,58:1

Shaw, Julia
Honor of the Family, The 1926,D 27,21:1

Shaw, K Edwin
As You Like It 1937,N 1,25:2

Shaw, Kendall (Scenic Designer)
Gertrude Stein's First Reader 1969,D 16,56:1

Shaw, Kerry (Playwright)
Satellite 1935,N 21,27:5

Shaw, Krishna (Director)
King of the Dark Chamber 1961,Ap 9,II,1:1

Shaw, Len
Flying High 1930,Mr 4,24:4

Shaw, Leon
Theatre 1941,N 13,34:2
Hamlet 1945,D 14,25:2
Devil's Disciple, The 1950,Ja 26,23:2
King and I, The 1956,Ap 19,35:4
Boy Friend, The 1958,Ja 27,24:4
Living Room, The 1962,N 22,43:5
Around the World in 80 Days 1964,Je 29,33:2
Canterbury Tales; Pilgrims, The 1969,F 4,34:1
Boy Friend, The 1970,Ap 15,54:1

Shaw, Lew
Spots of the Leopard, The 1963,S 25,38:1

Shaw, Lillian
One Flight Down 1937,D 14,32:4

Shaw, Lois
Oedipus Rex 1954,Jl 17,6:6

Shaw, Mac
This Happy Breed 1952,Ap 4,23:2

Shaw, Marguerite
Pajama Game, The 1957,My 16,27:1
Tenderloin 1960,O 18,47:2

Shaw, Marion (Producer)
Absence of a Cello; Mal de Test, Le 1965,S 9,36:3

Shaw, Martha
Detective Story 1954,F 13,11:2

Shaw, Martin
Battle of Shrivings, The 1970,F 7,23:1

Shaw, Martin (Composer)
Trip to Scarborough, A 1929,Mr 18,31:2

Shaw, Mary
Pietro 1920,Ja 20,10:2
Pietro 1920,Ja 25,VIII,2:2
Back Pay 1921,Ag 31,8:2
Idle Inn, The 1921,D 21,26:2
Ghosts 1922,F 7,12:1
Rivals, The 1922,Je 6,18:2
Rivals, The 1923,My 9,14:2
Rivals, The 1923,My 13,VIII,1:1
We Moderns 1924,Mr 12,17:2
We Moderns 1924,Mr 16,VIII,1:1
Rising Son, The 1924,O 28,27:2

Shaw, Maureen
Josef Suss 1930,Ja 21,28:5

Shaw, Maxwell
Hostage, The 1960,S 21,42:1

Shaw, Montague
Soldiers and Women 1929,S 3,25:1
Sherlock Holmes 1929,N 26,28:3
As Good As New 1930,N 4,37:3
Colonel Satan 1931,Ja 12,24:1
Give Me Yesterday 1931,Mr 5,32:1

Shaw, Neeka
Deep Harlem 1929,Ja 8,35:2
Change Your Luck 1930,Je 7,10:2
Lew Leslie's Blackbirds of 1930 1930,O 23,34:5

Shaw, Norton (Dr) (Composer)
Philomel 1932,D 4,IX,3:8

Shaw, Oscar
Half-Moon, The 1920,N 2,15:2
Two Little Girls in Blue 1921,My 4,10:3
Good Morning, Dearie 1921,N 2,20:2
One Kiss 1923,N 28,14:2
Dear Sir 1924,S 24,21:3
Music Box Revue 1924,D 2,23:3
Lambs Gambol 1925,Ap 27,15:1
Oh, Kay! 1926,N 9,31:3
Five O'Clock Girl, The 1927,O 11,26:3
Flying High 1930,Mr 4,24:4
Everybody's Welcome 1931,S 20,VIII,3:2
Everybody's Welcome 1931,O 14,26:3
Lady Detained, A 1935,Ja 10,23:3
Private Affair, A 1936,My 15,28:7
Let's Play Fair 1938,Ja 19,26:4
Pie in the Sky 1941,D 23,26:5

Shaw, Oscar (Producer)
Lady Detained, A 1935,Ja 10,23:3

Shaw, Paula
Digging for Apples 1962,S 28,29:4
Deadly Game, The 1966,F 14,34:1
Experiment, The 1967,My 9,54:2
Geese 1969,Ja 13,26:6

Shaw, Persy (Playwright)
One Wife or Another 1933,F 7,23:6

Shaw, Ray
Guys and Dolls 1955,Ap 21,32:2

Shaw, Reta
It Takes Two 1947,F 4,33:4
Virginia Reel 1947,Ap 15,28:2
Gentlemen Prefer Blondes 1949,D 9,35:3
Picnic 1953,F 20,14:7
Pajama Game, The 1954,My 14,20:2
Pajama Game, The 1954,My 30,II,1:1
Annie Get Your Gun 1957,Ag 31,18:2

Shaw, Robert
Carmen Jones 1943,D 3,26:2
Caretaker, The 1961,O 5,42:3
Caretaker, The 1961,O 15,II,1:1
Physicists, The 1964,O 14,52:1
Physicists, The 1964,O 25,II,1:1
Gantry 1970,F 16,44:1

Shaw, Robert (Miscellaneous)
Carmen Jones 1945,My 3,26:5
Carmen Jones 1946,Ap 8,32:2

My Darlin' Aida 1952,O 28,36:4

Shaw, Robert (Musical Director)
Carmen Jones 1943,D 12,II,3:1
Carmen Jones 1943,D 19,II,9:1

Shaw, Robert (Original Author)
Man in the Glass Booth, The 1967,Jl 29,12:1
Man in the Glass Booth, The 1967,Ag 27,II,1:1
Man in the Glass Booth, The 1968,O 6,II,5:1

Shaw, Robert (Playwright)
Man in the Glass Booth, The 1967,Jl 29,12:1
Man in the Glass Booth, The 1967,Ag 27,II,1:1
Man in the Glass Booth, The 1968,S 27,41:1
Man in the Glass Booth, The 1968,O 6,II,5:1
Man in the Glass Booth, The 1969,Ap 17,58:1

Shaw, Romero (Playwright)
Villana, La 1928,Ja 1,VIII,8:3

Shaw, Rosalind
Gondoliers, The 1931,Je 2,34:4

Shaw, Ruth
Logia a la Natividad de Nuestro Senor Jesucristo,
El 1937,D 14,33:4

Shaw, Sebastian
Rope's End 1929,S 20,34:5
Melo 1931,O 20,29:3
Sunshine Sisters 1933,N 26,IX,3:6
Nineties; Double Door 1934,Mr 22,24:6
Troilus and Cressida 1969,Jl 31,26:1
Measure for Measure 1970,Ap 5,71:1
Hamlet 1970,Ag 3,37:3

Shaw, Steven
Legend of Lovers 1959,O 28,40:3
Comedy of Errors, The 1967,Je 15,58:4
Invitation to a Beheading 1969,Mr 18,36:1

Shaw, Sydney (Composer)
Leonard Sillman's New Faces of 1968
1968,My 3,43:1

Shaw, Sydney (Lyricist)
Leonard Sillman's New Faces of 1968
1968,My 3,43:1

Shaw, Wini
Simple Simon 1931,Mr 10,23:2
Let's Play Fair 1938,Ja 19,26:4

Shaw, Winn
Sharlee 1923,N 23,20:1

Shaw, Woody
Sambo 1970,Jl 23,24:1

Shaw and Lee
Vaudeville (Palace) 1927,Jl 26,16:5
Vaudeville (Palace) 1930,Ag 18,24:3
Vaudeville (Palace) 1931,Ap 20,16:2
Friars Club Frolic 1933,My 15,16:4

Shawhan, April
Hit the Deck 1960,Je 24,32:1
Jo 1964,F 13,25:1
Race of Hairy Men!, A 1965,Ap 30,42:1
3 Bags Full 1966,Mr 7,22:1
Dinner at Eight 1966,S 28,38:1
Hamlet 1967,D 27,45:1
Home Fires 1969,Ap 8,42:1
Oklahoma! 1969,Je 24,37:1
Oklahoma! 1969,Jl 6,II,1:1
Mod Donna 1970,My 4,48:1
Mod Donna 1970,My 10,II,1:1

Shawley, Robert
Stalag 17 1951,My 9,41:2
Rosalie 1957,Je 26,28:2

Shawn, Bill
Moonbirds 1959,O 10,13:1

Shawn, Dick
Vaudeville (Palace) 1953,O 15,42:1
Egg, The 1962,Ja 9,23:2
Peterpat 1965,Ja 7,27:1
Fade Out--Fade In 1965,F 16,40:2
I'm Solomon 1968,Ap 24,51:1

Shawn, Jonathan
Dark at the Top of the Stairs, The 1957,D 6,38:1

Shawn, Peter
Ballad for a Firing Squad 1968,D 12,64:2

Shawn, Richy
For Heaven's Sake Mother 1948,N 17,33:4

Shawn, Silvia
Girl Friend, The 1926,Mr 18,26:5

Shawn, Ted (Choreographer)
Falstaff 1928,D 26,14:2
Doodle Dandy of the U S A 1942,O 19,15:2

Shawn, William (Composer)
Cabbages and Kings 1933,Je 28,24:5

Shawn, William (Lyricist)
Cabbages and Kings 1933,Je 28,24:5

Shay, Alan
Topaze 1947,D 29,21:5
Sleepy Hollow 1948,Je 4,26:3

Shay, Anne
Way, The 1940,O 12,20:3

Shay, David (Producer)
This, Too, Shall Pass 1946,My 1,32:4

Shay, Mildred
Sap Runs High, The 1936,F 5,15:3

Shay, Patricia
It's an Ill Wind 1957,Ap 24,28:1

Shay, Paula
Toto 1921,Mr 22,15:2
Teaser, The 1921,Jl 28,8:3

Shay, Paula (Director)
Dooley Cashes In 1935,Ag 17,18:6

Shay, Rita
By Hex 1956,Je 19,25:1

Shay, Sylvia
Pale Horse, Pale Rider 1957,O 30,26:1
Dinny and the Witches 1959,D 10,53:3
Fourth Avenue North 1961,S 28,50:2

Shayevskaya, Margavita
Moscow Circus on Ice 1970,D 9,63:1

Shayne, Al
Cinderella on Broadway 1920,Je 25,18:1

Shayne, Alan
Nathan the Wise 1944,F 22,26:3
Antony and Cleopatra 1947,N 27,49:2
Madwoman of Chaillot, The 1950,Je 14,41:2
Infernal Machine, The 1954,Mr 22,22:2
Merchant of Venice, The 1955,Ja 8,9:7
Julius Caesar 1955,Jl 13,20:1
Tempest, The 1955,Ag 2,18:2
Jamaica 1957,N 1,32:2
Confederates, The 1959,S 29,45:1
Susannah and the Elders 1959,O 19,37:3

Shayne, Edith
Beware of Dogs 1921,O 4,10:1
Nancy Ann 1924,Ap 1,18:1
Houses of Sand 1925,F 18,17:1
Oh! Mama 1925,Ag 20,22:2
Nirvana 1926,Mr 4,19:1
Happy-Go-Lucky 1926,O 1,27:2
Brass Buttons 1927,D 6,26:3
Veneer 1929,N 13,24:5
Shooting Star 1933,Je 13,22:2
Crime Marches on 1935,O 24,19:1
Good Neighbor 1941,O 22,26:2
He Who Gets Slapped 1946,Mr 21,31:4

Shayne, Robert
Rap, The 1931,Ap 7,31:2
Wild Waves 1932,F 20,11:4
Bulls, Bears and Asses 1932,My 7,11:3
Both Your Houses 1933,Mr 7,20:3
Yellow Jack 1934,Mr 7,22:6
Order Please 1934,O 10,21:2
Mother Lode 1934,D 24,16:5
Cat and the Canary, The 1935,Jl 9,24:4
Night of January 16 1935,S 10,26:1
Night of January 16 1935,S 17,26:4
Devil of Pei-Ling 1936,F 21,20:4
Timber House 1936,S 21,27:5
Don't Look Now! 1936,N 4,41:3
Whiteoaks 1938,F 23,26:2
Whiteoaks 1938,Mr 24,20:2
Beverly Hills 1940,N 8,24:2
Five Alarm Waltz 1941,Mr 14,16:2
Land Is Bright, The 1941,O 29,26:2
Without Love 1942,N 11,28:1

Shayon, Lewis (Playwright)
Life Begins at 8:40 1934,Ag 28,24:2

Shayre, Paul (Playwright)
Pictures in the Hallway 1959,D 28,19:1

Shays, Thurston C
East Lynne Goes West 1931,My 3,I,26:5

Shchegoleff, P E (Playwright)
Rasputin 1929,My 12,IX,2:3

Shdanoff, George
I Forgot 1942,S 28,13:1

Shdanoff, George (Playwright)
Possessed, The 1939,O 25,26:2

Shea, Al
Music Man, The 1957,D 20,31:1
Music Man, The 1965,Je 17,26:4

Shea, Beth
Home Is the Hero 1945,Ja 20,16:4

Shea, George
Don Carlos 1962,F 28,27:5

Shea, Helen
Ziegfeld Follies 1920,Je 23,14:1
Noble Experiment, The 1930,O 28,21:4
Secret Garden, The 1931,N 8,31:4
Mary of Scotland 1933,N 28,28:3

Shea, Hertha
Annie Get Your Gun 1958,F 20,29:2

Shea, Jack B
First Flight 1925,S 18,26:2
Burlesque 1927,S 2,15:3

Shea, Jeanne
Crystal Heart, The 1960,F 16,31:2
My Fair Lady 1968,Je 14,42:1

Shea, John
Lazarus Laughed 1948,Ap 9,27:4

Shea, Joseph
Mr Gilhooley 1930,O 1,26:1

Shea, Joseph E (Producer)
Chivalry 1925,D 16,22:3
Interference 1928,My 8,25:4
Elmer Gantry 1928,Ag 10,9:4
Patriarch, The 1929,N 26,28:5

Shea, Loretto
Mima 1928,D 13,24:2
Gold Braid 1930,My 14,31:2
Purity 1930,D 26,18:2
Marilyn's Affairs 1933,Mr 16,21:5
Unto the Third 1933,Ap 21,24:8

Shea, Marie
My Girl 1924,N 25,27:2

Shea, Norma
You'll See Stars 1943,Ja 1,26:6

Shea, Olive
Blind Mice 1930,O 16,28:2

Shea, Patrick
Twelfth Night 1969,Ag 14,29:2
Child's Play 1970,F 18,39:1

Shea, Robert
Romeo and Jeanette 1969,D 16,53:1

Shea, Stephen (Scenic Designer)
Kill the One-Eyed Man 1965,O 21,56:1

Shea, William
Drums Begin, The 1933,N 25,10:5
John Brown 1934,Ja 23,22:3
Kill That Story 1934,Ag 30,22:2
Creeping Fire 1935,Ja 17,22:3
Lorelei 1938,N 30,21:2
Brown Danube, The 1939,My 18,30:4

Shea, William E
Solid Ivory 1925,N 17,29:3

Shea and Raymond
George White's Scandals 1935,D 26,20:2

Shean, Al
Betsy 1926,D 29,24:3
Vaudeville (Palace) 1927,Ap 19,24:3
Vaudeville (Palace) 1928,Ap 10,32:4
Vaudeville (Palace) 1929,My 13,26:3
Prince of Pilsen, The 1930,Ja 14,24:3
Light Wines and Beer 1930,N 11,28:6
Music in the Air 1932,O 23,IX,3:3
Music in the Air 1932,N 9,28:2
Music in the Air 1932,N 20,IX,1:1
Father Malachy's Miracle 1937,N 18,26:4
Father Malachy's Miracle 1937,D 5,XII,5:1
Father Malachy's Miracle 1938,Ja 23,XI,1:6
Popsy 1941,F 11,26:2
Meet a Body 1944,O 17,19:5
Doctor Social 1948,F 12,29:5

Shear, Josef
King Lear 1947,F 19,32:2
As You Like It 1947,F 21,16:2
Merchant of Venice, The 1947,F 24,16:2
Volpone 1947,F 25,32:2
Hamlet 1947,F 27,27:2

Shear, Orrin
Jane-Our Stranger 1925,O 9,27:2

Shear, Sylvia
Garrick Gaieties 1926,My 11,25:2

Shearer, Ann
Devil's Little Game, The 1932,Ag 2,20:4

Shearer, Carla
Month in the Country, A 1963,My 29,39:2

Shearer, Denny
Up Eden 1968,N 27,42:1

Shearer, Dorothy
Richard II 1968,Je 24,42:3

Shearer, John
Jonah! 1967,S 22,52:2

Shearer, Moira
Midsummer Night's Dream, A 1954,S 1,31:3
Midsummer Night's Dream, A 1954,S 22,33:1
Man of Distinction 1957,Ag 27,33:7

Shearer, Thomas
Poor Nut, The 1925,Ap 28,18:1

Shearing, Jack (Miscellaneous)
Blancs, Les 1970,N 16,48:4

Shearon, James K (Costume Designer)
House of Leather, The 1970,Mr 19,56:1

Shebaya, Peter
Birds, The 1966,Jl 1,40:1

Shechter, Shulamith
Far-Away Corner, A 1939,F 15,15:2

Shechtman, Ephraim'l
Here Runs the Bride 1934,S 20,21:3

Shechtman, Frankie
Little Giants 1933,D 2,9:5
Here Runs the Bride 1934,N 4,IX,2:1

Sheckley, Marian
Dear Old Darling 1936,Mr 3,25:1

Shecter, Ben (Scenic Designer)
Penny Friend, The 1966,D 27,46:1

Shecter, Leon
Shepherd King, The 1955,O 13,36:2

Shecter, Louis E (Playwright)
I Take Care of My Friends 1936,Jl 21,13:2
Window Shopping 1938,D 24,13:2

Shedd, Agnes Jeffrey
Little Theatre Tournament; Trifles 1928,My 11,28:1

Shedlin, Myrna (Choreographer)
Moon Besieged, The 1962,D 6,54:1

Sheean, Vincent (Playwright)
International Incident, An 1940,Mr 21,30:3
International Incident, An 1940,Ap 3,18:2

Sheedy, Bryan (Miscellaneous)
Another City, Another Land 1968,O 9,42:1

Sheehan, Grant
Jumping Fool, The 1970,F 10,53:1

Sheehan, John
Sun-Kist 1921,My 24,20:2
Greenwich Village Follies 1922,S 13,18:2
No Other Girl 1924,Ag 14,10:4

Sheehan, John—Cont

Greenwich Village Follies 1924,S 17,16:1
Katja 1926,O 19,27:3
Twinkle Twinkle 1926,N 17,22:2
Good News 1927,Ag 14,VII,2:1
Good News 1927,S 7,35:4
Lovely Lady 1927,D 30,22:1
Follow Thru 1929,Ja 10,24:3
Nina Rosa 1930,My 31,19:3
Nina Rosa 1930,S 22,22:5
America's Sweetheart 1931,F 11,23:1
Everybody's Welcome 1931,O 14,26:3
Tell Her the Truth 1932,O 29,18:2
Forbidden Melody 1936,N 3,33:1
Roberta 1937,Je 27,II,6:1
Maytime 1937,Jl 6,23:4
Salute to Spring 1937,Jl 14,16:2
Gay Divorce 1937,Jl 20,19:4
Of Thee I Sing 1937,Ag 10,22:3
Of Thee I Sing 1937,Ag 18,14:4
I Must Love Someone 1939,F 8,18:7
Flying Gerardos, The 1940,D 30,21:4
Counsellor-at-Law 1942,N 25,17:2
Lady Behave 1943,N 17,30:1
School for Brides 1944,Ag 2,19:4
Man Who Had All the Luck, The 1944,N 24,18:5
Kathleen 1948,F 4,26:2
As the Girls Go 1948,N 15,21:2
Look Homeward, Angel 1957,N 29,33:1

Sheehan, Lester
Vaudeville (Palace) 1924,Ja 15,17:3

Sheehan, Michael
Sing Till Tomorrow 1953,D 29,17:2

Sheehan, Peter (Playwright)
Inside Story 1942,O 30,22:2

Sheehy, Lester
Strange Interlude 1928,D 18,37:3

Sheehy, W W (Miscellaneous)
Caesar and Cleopatra 1927,N 6,IX,2:1

Sheekman, Arthur (Composer)
It's All Yours 1942,Mr 26,26:2

Sheekman, Arthur (Director)
Crazy With the Heat 1941,Ja 15,18:2
Crazy With the Heat 1941,Ja 31,15:2

Sheekman, Arthur (Lyricist)
It's All Yours 1942,Mr 26,26:2

Sheekman, Arthur (Playwright)
Three's a Crowd 1930,O 26,VIII,1:1
Crazy With the Heat 1941,Ja 15,18:2
Mr Big 1941,S 7,I,51:3
Mr Big 1941,S 14,IX,2:5
Mr Big 1941,O 1,24:2

Sheen, Martin
Calvary 1960,Jl 22,13:1
Purgatory 1960,S 20,48:1
Mountain Giants, The 1961,Ap 5,32:3
Never Live Over a Pretzel Factory 1964,Mr 30,37:1
Subject Was Roses, The 1964,My 26,45:1
Subject Was Roses, The 1964,Je 7,II,1:1
Wicked Cooks, The 1967,Ja 24,42:1
Hamlet 1967,D 27,45:1
Hamlet 1968,Ja 7,II,1:5
Romeo and Juliet 1968,Ag 16,19:1
Hello and Goodbye 1969,S 19,54:1

Sheer, Anita
Look to the Lilies 1970,Mr 30,59:1

Sheer, Rosemarie
Twilight Walk 1951,S 25,25:4
Oh, Kay! 1960,Ap 18,37:2

Sheffer, Isaiah
Highway Robbery 1955,N 8,36:1
Theater of Peretz, The 1963,N 6,35:2

Sheffer, Isaiah (Director)
Theater of Peretz, The 1963,N 6,35:2
Exception and the Rule, The 1965,My 21,19:1

Sheffer, Isaiah (Playwright)
Theater of Peretz, The 1963,N 6,35:2

Sheffey, Gwendolyn
In White America 1965,F 9,42:5

Sheffey, Gwendolyn (Director)
Dutchman; Slave, The 1965,N 17,53:7

Sheffield, Flora
Three Live Ghosts 1920,S 30,12:1
Nightcap, The 1921,Ag 16,18:3
Faithful Heart, The 1922,O 11,22:1
Faithful Heart, The 1922,O 15,VIII,1:1
Haunted House, The 1924,S 3,12:1
Silence 1924,N 13,18:2
Weak Woman, A 1926,Ja 27,16:3
Sour Grapes 1926,S 7,19:1
Constant Nymph, The 1926,D 10,31:1
Savages Under the Skin 1927,Mr 25,25:2
Carry On 1928,Ja 24,26:1
Sign of the Leopard 1928,D 12,34:4
Jehovah Joe 1929,Ag 25,VIII,3:1

Sheffield, Frederick
Successful Calamity, A 1921,Mr 19,11:2
Faun, The 1924,F 6,19:2

Sheffield, Jay
Bonds of Interest, The 1958,My 7,43:1
Galileo 1968,D 1,88:4

Sheffield, Nellie
Yellow Sands 1927,S 12,29:3

Sheffield, Reginald
Youth 1920,O 27,14:3
Romance 1921,Mr 1,18:2
Way Things Happen, The 1924,Ja 29,17:5
Helena's Boys 1924,Ap 8,22:2
Hay Fever 1925,O 5,25:1
Pearl of Great Price, The 1926,N 2,34:3
Slaves All 1926,D 7,24:4
Honeymooning 1927,Mr 18,25:3
Soldiers and Women 1929,S 3,25:1
Dear Old England 1930,Mr 26,24:6
Miles of Heaven, The 1937,Ag 31,27:4

Sheffy, Pearl
Antigone 1959,S 16,46:2

Sheftel, (Messr)
Chauve-Souris 1925,Ja 15,25:1

Shefter, Bert (Musical Director)
Blackouts of 1949 1949,S 7,39:2

Sheidy, Charles Raymond Jr
This Mad Whirl 1937,Ja 10,II,4:8

Sheidy, William
Immortal Husband, The 1955,F 15,32:2

Sheil, Frances
Cinderelative 1930,S 19,18:4

Sheil, Mark Jude
West Side Story 1964,Ap 9,24:2
Baker Street 1965,F 17,36:1

Shein, Niura
Golem, The 1948,My 17,22:3

Sheiner, David
Bourgeois Gentleman, The 1949,Ag 31,27:2
Will Success Spoil Rock Hunter? 1955,O 14,22:2

Sheinin, Lev (Playwright)
Game Without Rules 1961,D 29,4:4

Sheinkman, Mordechai (Composer)
Automobile Graveyard, The 1961,N 14,46:2

Shelaso, Gad
Persians, The 1927,F 27,VII,2:3

Shelburne, James
Three Times the Hour 1931,Ag 26,15:5
Hotel Alimony 1934,Ja 30,16:2
Invitation to a Murder 1934,My 18,26:3
Bury the Dead 1936,Ap 20,17:4
Prelude 1936,Ap 20,17:4
Stop-Over 1938,Ja 12,16:5

Shelby, Ann (Playwright)
Gold Braid 1930,My 14,31:2

Shelby, Jean
Wait Till We're Married 1921,S 27,14:1
Caste 1927,D 24,8:1
Crime Marches on 1935,O 24,19:1

Shelby, Jeanne
Lady in the Dark 1941,Ja 24,14:2
Lady in the Dark 1941,S 3,26:6
Lady in the Dark 1943,Mr 1,14:2
Mexican Hayride 1944,Ja 29,9:6
Music in My Heart 1947,O 3,30:2
Man and Superman 1953,F 21,11:2

Shelby, Laurel
Great Big Doorstep, The 1950,Mr 18,8:6

Shelby, Virginia
Half-Moon, The 1920,N 2,15:2

Sheldon, Bert
Heaven on Earth 1948,S 17,29:2

Sheldon, Charles
Firebird of Florence 1945,Mr 23,13:4

Sheldon, Connie
Girl From Nantucket, The 1945,N 9,17:2

Sheldon, Edith
Honeymoon Lane 1926,S 21,32:3
New Moon, The 1928,S 20,33:1
Garrick Gaieties 1930,Je 5,29:2

Sheldon, Edward (Original Author)
My Golden Girl 1927,S 11,VIII,1:3
My Princess 1927,O 7,24:2

Sheldon, Edward (Playwright)
Jest, The 1920,F 1,VIII,2:2
Romance 1921,Mr 1,18:2
Romance 1921,Mr 6,VI,1:2
Proud Princess, The 1924,F 17,VII,2:8
Bewitched 1924,O 2,26:3
Lulu Belle 1926,F 10,20:1
Lulu Belle 1926,F 14,VIII,1:1
Romance 1926,N 4,VIII,4:7
Jenny 1929,Je 2,VIII,1:2
Jenny 1929,O 9,34:4
Dishonored Lady 1930,Ja 26,VIII,2:1
Dishonored Lady 1930,F 5,27:1
Dishonored Lady 1930,My 25,IX,2:4
Romance 1935,Ag 27,23:4
Romance 1937,Ag 17,23:1
My Romance 1948,O 20,38:5

Sheldon, Elizabeth
Bedrock 1934,N 18,II,6:3

Sheldon, Eloise
Harvey 1944,N 2,23:2

Sheldon, Gene
Priorities of 1942 1942,Mr 13,23:2
Priorities of 1942 1942,Mr 29,VIII,1:1
Take a Bow 1944,Je 16,15:3

Sheldon, H S (Playwright)
Doormat, The 1922,D 8,36:3

Sheldon, Jerome
Zombie 1932,F 11,17:2
News Item 1935,Ag 6,20:3
Chalk Dust 1936,Mr 5,24:5

Sheldon, Jerry
Tragedy of the Ages, The 1933,Ap 7,22:7

Sheldon, Lenore
Nights of Wrath; Nuits de la Colere, Les 1947,D 1,26:4

Sheldon, Louise
Child of Manhattan 1932,Mr 2,15:1

Sheldon, Nan
Money Lender, The 1928,Ag 28,27:3
Old Lady Shows Her Medals, The 1932,Mr 8,19:3
Alice Sit-By-The-Fire 1932,Mr 8,19:3

Sheldon, Neil
Beaver Coat, The 1956,Mr 29,22:5

Sheldon, Orlo
Scaramouche 1923,O 25,14:2

Sheldon, Sidney (Playwright)
Merry Widow, The 1943,Ag 5,19:2
Merry Widow, The 1943,Ag 22,II,5:1
Jackpot 1944,Ja 14,15:2
Dream With Music 1944,My 19,15:2
Merry Widow, The 1944,O 9,17:1
Alice in Arms 1945,F 1,18:4
Merry Widow, The 1957,Ap 11,36:6
Redhead 1959,F 6,21:1
Roman Candle 1960,F 4,34:2

Sheldon, Suzanne
Shannons of Broadway, The 1927,S 27,30:4

Shell, Dale
Walk Hard 1944,D 1,28:2

Shell, David (Producer)
Twisting Road, The; One Tuesday Morning 1957,N 18,36:5
Twisting Road, The; Jewel of the South, The 1957,N 18,36:5
Twisting Road, The; Housekeeper, The 1957,N 18,36:5

Shell, Frances
Let and Sub-Let 1930,My 20,32:2

Shell, Freda Hope
Tall Kentuckian, The 1953,Je 17,30:1

Shell, Suzanne
Under Milk Wood 1957,O 16,42:5

Shelle, Lori
Scarlet Lullaby 1968,Mr 11,48:1
Boy on the Straight-Back Chair 1969,Mr 18,36:1

Sheller, Joan
Idiot's Delight 1957,F 23,14:2

Shelley, Carole
Odd Couple, The 1965,Mr 11,36:1
Astrakhan Coat, The 1967,Ja 13,18:1
Loot 1968,Mr 19,40:2
Noel Coward's Sweet Potato 1968,S 30,59:1
Noel Coward's Sweet Potato 1968,O 13,II,5:1
Little Murders 1969,O 2,54:1
Hay Fever 1970,N 10,55:1
Hay Fever 1970,N 22,II,18:6

Shelley, David
Whatever Goes Up 1935,N 26,28:2
Two Time Mary 1937,Ag 3,20:5
Reno 1937,Ag 10,22:7

Shelley, Elizabeth
Sea Gull, The 1929,S 17,34:1

Shelley, Elsa
Veils 1928,Mr 14,28:5
Caravan 1928,Ag 30,13:3
Sign of the Leopard 1928,D 12,34:4
Courtesan 1930,Ap 30,29:3

Shelley, Elsa (Director)
With a Silk Thread 1950,Ap 13,34:3

Shelley, Elsa (Playwright)
Pick-Up Girl 1944,My 4,25:2
Foxhole in the Parlor 1945,My 24,15:4
With a Silk Thread 1950,Ap 13,34:3

Shelley, Frances
New Americana 1928,N 30,32:4
Wake Up and Dream 1929,D 31,14:3
Mystery Moon 1930,Je 24,23:4

Shelley, Frank
Luther 1963,S 26,41:1

Shelley, George
Silks and Satins 1920,Jl 16,19:1

Shelley, Gladys
Baby Pompadour 1934,D 28,24:2
Moon Over Mulberry Street 1935,S 5,24:6
Money Mad 1937,My 25,32:5

Shelley, Gladys (Lyricist)
Duchess Misbehaves, The 1946,F 14,32:2
Russell Patterson's Sketch-Book 1960,F 8,35:1
Gogo Loves You 1964,O 10,19:2

Shelley, Gladys (Original Author)
Duchess Misbehaves, The 1946,F 14,32:2

Shelley, Hazel
Bunk of 1926 1926,F 17,12:3
Bunk of 1926 1926,Ap 23,25:2

Shelley, Jeanne
Ponder Heart, The 1956,F 17,14:2

Shelley, Joshua
Tidbits of 1946 1946,Jl 9,17:2
Tenting Tonight 1947,Ap 3,32:2

Shelley, Joshua—Cont

Make Mine Manhattan 1948,Ja 16,26:2
Liar, The 1950,My 19,30:2
Four Twelves Are 48 1951,Ja 18,30:2
Girl in Pink Tights, The 1954,Mr 6,13:2
On Your Toes 1954,O 12,24:4
Phoenix '55 1955,Ap 25,20:2
I Want You 1961,S 15,29:1
Shelley, Joshua (Director)
Simply Heavenly 1957,My 22,28:2
Come Live With Me 1967,Ja 27,29:1
Shelley, Mary (Original Author)
Frankenstein 1968,O 3,54:1
Shelley, Mary Anne
Che! 1969,Mr 24,56:1
Shelley, Michael
Escort 1942,S 6,VIII,1:8
Shelley, Percy Bysshe (Original Author)
Cenci, The 1935,Je 16,X,1:1
Cenci, The 1935,Ag 18,IX,1:4
Shelley, William
Lights Out 1922,Ag 18,8:4
Zeno 1923,Ag 27,14:2
What Women Do? 1925,Jl 21,26:4
High Gear 1927,O 7,24:3
Maya 1928,F 22,19:1
Shellie, John
Tom Sawyer 1931,D 26,15:3
Brown Sugar 1937,D 3,29:2
See My Lawyer 1939,S 28,29:1
Lily of the Valley 1942,Ja 27,25:2
Life of Reilly, The 1942,Ap 30,13:2
Woman Bites Dog 1946,Ap 18,21:2
Skipper Next to God 1948,Ja 5,14:5
At War With the Army 1949,Mr 9,32:2
Closing Door, The 1949,D 2,36:2
Bird Cage, The 1950,F 23,32:2
Shely, Elizabeth
Living Corpse, The 1929,D 7,19:1
Women Have Their Way, The 1930,Ja 28,28:1
Shelly, Frances
Nine Fifteen Revue, The 1930,F 12,26:2
Shelly, Mildred
George White's Scandals 1922,Ag 29,10:1
Shelly, Norman
They Came to a City 1943,Je 6,II,1:6
Peter Pan 1950,Ap 25,27:2
Peter Pan 1954,O 21,30:2
Daughter of Silence 1961,D 1,28:1
Cafe Crown 1964,Ap 18,32:1
Promises, Promises 1968,D 2,59:3
Shelly, Norman (Director)
God Slept Here, A 1957,F 20,38:1
Enemies Don't Send Flowers 1957,F 20,38:1
Shelton, Carl
Uniform of Flesh 1949,Ja 31,15:2
Hamlet 1954,Ap 24,15:2
Enemy of the People, An 1958,F 26,24:2
Shelton, Christopher
Our Town 1968,D 14,62:1
Shelton, Don
Birthright 1933,N 22,22:3
After Such Pleasures 1934,Ja 6,18:6
After Such Pleasures 1934,F 8,15:2
Shatter'd Lamp, The 1934,Mr 22,26:3
Ah, Wilderness! 1934,O 30,23:1
Plumes in the Dust 1936,N 7,14:2
Two on an Island 1940,Ja 23,17:2
Eight O'Clock Tuesday 1941,Je 7,18:2
Story of Mary Surratt, The 1947,F 10,25:2
Shelton, Edward (Lighting Director)
Mandragola 1956,Mr 1,36:4
Shelton, Edward (Miscellaneous)
Thistle in My Bed 1963,N 20,48:1
Shelton, Edward (Scenic Designer)
Mandragola 1956,Mr 1,36:4
Shelton, George
Keep Moving 1934,Ag 24,10:2
Shelton, Hall
Slightly Delirious 1935,Ja 1,25:3
Lady Luck 1936,Ap 16,21:2
Mrs Kimball Presents 1944,Mr 1,17:3
Shelton, Hall (Director)
Please, Mrs. Garibaldi 1939,Mr 17,24:3
Shelton, Hall (Miscellaneous)
King Lear 1947,F 19,32:2
Merchant of Venice, The 1947,F 24,16:2
Volpone 1947,F 25,32:2
Hamlet 1947,F 27,27:2
Shelton, Hall (Producer)
Please, Mrs. Garibaldi 1939,Mr 17,24:3
Boy Who Lived Twice, A 1945,S 12,31:2
As You Like It 1947,F 21,16:2
Louisiana Lady 1947,Je 3,35:2
Ivy Green, The 1949,Ap 6,37:2
Shelton, James
New Faces 1934,Mr 16,24:5
Who's Who 1938,Mr 2,16:2
Straw Hat, The 1939,S 30,10:6
Canteen Show, The 1942,S 4,18:1
Almost Crazy 1955,Je 21,37:1
Shelton, James (Composer)
New Faces 1934,Mr 16,24:5
Who's Who 1938,Mr 2,16:2

Straw Hat, The 1939,S 30,10:6
Canteen Show, The 1942,S 4,18:1
Dance Me a Song 1950,Ja 21,10:5
Mrs Patterson 1954,D 2,37:1
Almost Crazy 1955,Je 21,37:1
Shelton, James (Director)
Canteen Show, The 1942,S 4,18:1
Dance Me a Song 1950,Ja 21,10:5
Shelton, James (Lyricist)
Who's Who 1938,Mr 2,16:2
Canteen Show, The 1942,S 4,18:1
Mrs Patterson 1954,D 2,37:1
Almost Crazy 1955,Je 21,37:1
Shelton, James (Playwright)
Dance Me a Song 1950,Ja 21,10:5
Almost Crazy 1955,Je 21,37:1
Shelton, Jerry
For Your Pleasure 1943,F 6,9:2
Shelton, Reid
By the Beautiful Sea 1954,Ap 9,20:1
Saint of Bleecker Street, The 1954,D 28,21:1
Oh What a Lovely War 1964,O 1,30:1
Carousel 1965,Ag 11,39:1
Butterfly Dream, The 1966,My 20,41:1
Man With a Load of Mischief, The 1966,N 7,65:1
Canterbury Tales; Wife of Bath's Tale, The
  1969,F 4,34:1
Canterbury Tales; Pilgrims, The 1969,F 4,34:1
Shelton, Sloane
Imaginary Invalid, The 1967,My 2,53:1
Touch of the Poet, A 1967,My 3,38:2
Fumed Oak 1967,My 4,34:1
I Never Sang for My Father 1968,Ja 26,30:1
Shelvey, Henry
What Price Glory 1924,S 6,14:3
Elmer the Great 1928,S 25,29:1
Just to Remind You 1931,S 8,39:1
Blessed Event 1932,F 13,23:2
Rendezvous 1932,O 13,22:3
Shelvey, Matt (Miscellaneous)
Pinocchio 1939,Ja 3,19:2
Shelving, Paul (Costume Designer)
Yellow Sands 1927,S 12,29:3
Shelving, Paul (Scenic Designer)
Yellow Sands 1927,S 12,29:3
Shemonsky, Herman
Burning Bush, The 1949,D 17,15:5
Shenar, Paul
Tartuffe 1965,Ja 15,23:1
Hamlet 1968,Je 10,59:1
Tiny Alice 1969,S 30,42:1
Three Sisters, The 1969,O 10,38:1
Tiny Alice 1969,O 12,II,9:1
Three Sisters, The 1969,O 19,II,3:1
Tiny Alice 1970,F 15,II,1:1
Shepard, Burt and Company
Vaudeville (Palace) 1927,S 13,36:3
Shepard, Elaine
Panama Hattie 1940,O 31,28:2
Land Is Bright, The 1941,O 29,26:2
Shepard, Ethel
Would-Be Gentleman, The 1930,Ap 30,29:2
Shepard, Joan
Sunny River 1941,D 5,28:2
Strings, My Lord, Are False, The 1942,My 20,24:2
This Rock 1943,F 19,23:2
Foolish Notion 1945,Mr 14,23:2
Foolish Notion 1945,Mr 18,II,1:1
Young Man's Fancy, A 1947,Ap 30,33:2
My Romance 1948,O 20,38:5
Member of the Wedding, The 1950,Ja 6,26:6
Othello 1953,O 30,28:2
Best Foot Forward 1956,Mr 3,16:1
Plot Against the Chase Manhattan Bank, The
  1963,N 27,29:1
Philosophy in the Boudoir 1969,My 22,55:2
Shepard, Karen
Ankles Aweigh 1955,Ap 19,27:1
Sound of Music, The 1959,N 17,40:2
Mardi Gras! 1965,Je 28,33:2
Anya 1965,N 30,48:1
Where's Charley? 1966,My 26,57:1
Mardi Gras! 1966,Jl 11,32:2
Shepard, Lionel
Mime and Me, The 1960,Ap 8,27:3
World of Illusion 1964,Je 25,26:2
Shepard, Lionel (Choreographer)
Mime and Me, The 1960,Ap 8,27:3
Shepard, Lionel (Composer)
Mime and Me, The 1960,Ap 8,27:3
Shepard, Lionel (Director)
Mime and Me, The 1960,Ap 8,27:3
Keyhole, The 1962,Ja 31,21:1
World of Illusion 1964,Je 25,26:2
Shepard, Lionel (Miscellaneous)
Mountain Giants, The 1961,Ap 5,32:3
Shepard, Lionel (Playwright)
Mime and Me, The 1960,Ap 8,27:3
World of Illusion 1964,Je 25,26:2
Shepard, Mabel
Lonesome West, The 1936,Je 30,15:1
Shepard, Martin
Sweet Adeline 1929,S 4,33:1

Shepard, Martin—Cont

Face the Music 1932,F 18,24:5
Shepard, Richard
Heel, The 1954,My 27,33:2
Apollo of Bellac, The 1954,My 29,12:1
Purification, The 1954,My 29,12:1
Terrible Swift Sword, The 1955,N 16,42:1
Jackhammer, The 1962,F 6,26:2
Zoo Story, The 1963,Je 11,29:2
Shepard, Ruth
Girl Who Came to Supper, The 1963,D 9,49:1
Shepard, Sam
Operation Sidewinder 1970,Mr 22,II,1:4
Shepard, Sam (Miscellaneous)
Oh! Calcutta! 1969,Je 18,33:1
Shepard, Sam (Playwright)
Up to Thursday 1965,F 11,45:1
Chicago 1966,Ap 13,36:1
Turista, La 1967,Mr 26,II,1:2
Forensic and the Navigators 1968,Ja 20,22:2
Red Cross 1968,Ap 29,47:2
Turista, La 1969,Ap 13,II,3:3
Oh! Calcutta! 1969,Je 29,II,1:7
Operation Sidewinder 1970,Mr 13,33:1
Unseen Hand, The 1970,Ap 2,43:1
Forensic and the Navigators 1970,Ap 2,43:1
Shepard, Sydney
Wasp, The 1923,Mr 28,14:3
Shepard, Tina
Terminal 1970,Ap 15,51:2
Serpent, The 1970,Je 2,35:1
Shepard, William
Sweet Adeline 1929,S 4,33:1
Makbeth 1969,N 30,II,3:1
Shepeard, Jean
Fruits of Englightenment, The 1928,N 25,X,2:3
Sheperd, Firth (Miscellaneous)
Assassin, The 1945,Mr 23,13:6
Shephard, Bob
Me and Juliet 1970,My 15,42:1
Shephard, Esther (Playwright)
Venetian Hour, A 1934,Mr 22,24:6
Shephard, Michael
Don't Shoot Mable It's Your Husband
  1968,O 23,34:1
Shephard, William
Titus Andronicus 1967,Ag 10,43:2
Dionysus in 69 1968,Je 7,35:3
Macbeth 1969,N 21,51:1
Shepherd, Ann
Sophie 1944,D 26,22:7
Truckline Cafe 1946,F 28,19:4
Shepherd, Elizabeth
Jumping Fool, The 1970,F 10,53:1
Conduct Unbecoming 1970,O 13,50:1
Shepherd, Firth (Miscellaneous)
Living Dangerously 1935,Ja 14,10:3
Shepherd, Firth (Producer)
Fun and Games 1941,Ag 31,IX,1:4
Shepherd, James
J B 1958,Ap 24,37:1
J B 1958,My 4,II,1:1
Shepherd, Jean
Banquet for the Moon, A 1961,Ja 20,24:2
Voice of the Turtle, The 1961,Je 28,41:1
Tender Trap, The 1964,Ag 26,15:1
Untitled-One Man Show 1970,O 31,34:1
Shepherd, Jean (Playwright)
New Faces of 1962 1962,F 2,25:1
Shepherd, John
Macbeth 1968,N 30,49:3
Shepherd, Leonard
Six of Calais, The 1934,Ag 12,IX,1:3
Shepley, Michael
Middle Watch, The 1929,O 17,27:1
Night Must Fall 1936,S 29,34:1
Bulldog Drummond Hits Out 1937,D 22,33:2
Love in a Mist 1941,N 30,IX,3:1
Edwina Black 1950,N 22,20:5
Shepley, Ruth
Her Salary Man 1921,N 29,20:1
Two Fellows and a Girl 1923,Jl 20,8:2
Cape Smoke 1925,F 17,19:1
New York 1927,N 15,26:2
Squealer, The 1928,N 13,36:3
Three and One 1933,O 26,22:6
Dear Old Darling 1936,Mr 3,25:1
Shepp, Archie (Composer)
Junebug Graduates Tonight! 1967,F 27,35:1
Slave Ship 1969,N 22,46:1
Shepp, Archie (Lyricist)
Junebug Graduates Tonight! 1967,F 27,35:1
Sheppard, Billy
Hot Rhythm 1930,Ag 22,18:5
Sheppard, Dick
Marco Polo and the Drum of Ahmad
  1950,D 18,34:2
Sheppard, Dorothy
Noose, The 1926,O 21,23:3
Sheppard, Harry
Behold Your God 1936,Ap 22,28:3
Kit Marlowe 1936,My 24,35:1
Arms and the Man 1937,Jl 20,19:3
Too True to Be Good 1937,Jl 27,24:2

heppard, Harry—Cont

As You Like It 1941,O 21,29:2
Cat Screams, The 1942,Je 17,26:5
Mr Sycamore 1942,N 14,13:2
Hamlet 1946,Je 4,18:4
Leading Lady 1948,O 19,33:1
Saint Joan 1950,Mr 4,10:6
Small War on Murray Hill 1957,Ja 4,19:1

heppard, Hazel
Keep Shufflin' 1928,F 28,18:3

heppard, J T (Translator)
Electra 1932,Ja 9,21:4

heppard, John (Playwright)
Decree Nisi 1936,N 11,54:4

heppard, John R Jr (Miscellaneous)
Strings, My Lord, Are False, The 1942,My 20,24:2

heppard, John R Jr (Producer)
Foolscap 1933,Ja 12,21:2
Mahogany Hall 1934,Ja 18,18:5
Beggar's Holiday 1946,D 27,13:3

heppard, Julie
Royal Hunt of the Sun, The 1965,O 27,36:2

heppard, Ken
Magistrate, The 1959,My 14,30:6

heppard, Madelyn (Composer)
Just Because 1922,Mr 23,11:1

heppard, Martin
Say When 1934,N 9,24:2

heppard, Maxine
Johnny 2X4 1942,Mr 17,24:6

heppard, Morgan
Persecution and Assassination of Marat As
Performed by the Inmates of the Asylum of
Charenton Under the Direction of the Marquis de
Sade, The 1965,D 28,35:1

heppard, Robert
110 in the Shade 1963,O 25,37:1

heppard, Ruth
All Rights Reserved 1934,N 7,33:5

her, Ben (Playwright)
I Gotta Get Out 1947,S 26,27:2

her, Jack (Playwright)
Perfect Setup, The 1962,O 25,47:1

her, Larry
Love in Our Time 1952,O 4,14:3

her, Louis K (Miscellaneous)
Americana Pastoral 1968,D 11,51:1

her, Ruth
Thespis 1953,Ja 17,13:5

Sheraton, Ted
Captain Brassbound's Conversion 1950,D 28,21:1

Sheratsky, Herman
Radio Girl, The 1929,O 19,22:4
Little Clown, The 1930,Mr 15,23:3
Germany Aflame 1933,O 28,20:5

Sherban, Andrei (Director)
Ubu Roi 1970,F 17,33:1
Arden of Faversham 1970,F 17,33:1

Sherbatoff, Alexis
Y'Avait un Prisonnier 1938,Ja 25,24:3

Sherberg, Pincus
Roaming Stars 1930,Ja 25,12:2

Sherbrooke, Michael
Pariah 1927,O 30,IX,2:1
Brass Paperweight, The 1928,N 4,IX,2:4
Bluestone Quarry 1931,N 29,VIII,2:2

Sherek, Henry (Miscellaneous)
Message for Margaret 1947,Ap 17,34:2

Sherek, Henry (Producer)
First Gentleman, The 1945,Jl 19,18:8
Edward, My Son 1948,O 1,30:2
Escapade 1953,N 19,40:1
Confidential Clerk, The 1954,F 12,22:1
Under Milk Wood 1957,O 16,42:5
Affair, The 1962,S 21,34:2

Sherer, Lee
Lamp at Midnight 1947,D 22,29:2

Sheridan, Alex
King Oedipus 1933,Ja 16,12:4

Sheridan, Edith
New Faces 1934,Mr 16,24:5

Sheridan, Farrell S
Hot Pan 1928,F 16,14:1

Sheridan, Frank
Everyday 1921,N 17,15:1
Lawbreaker, The 1922,F 7,12:1
Madeleine and the Movies 1922,Mr 7,11:1
Virtue (?) 1922,N 17,14:1

Sheridan, Helen
Don Juan 1921,S 8,14:2
He Who Gets Slapped 1922,Ja 10,15:1
Mister Pitt 1924,Ja 23,15:3
Fata Morgana 1924,Mr 4,16:3
Finta Giardiniera, La 1927,Ja 19,20:5

Sheridan, Joseph
Blonde Beast, The 1923,Mr 3,9:3

Sheridan, Katherine
Strip Girl 1935,O 21,22:6

Sheridan, Liz
Ballad for a Firing Squad 1968,D 12,64:2
American Hamburger League, The 1969,S 17,51:1

Sheridan, Nancy
Sure Fire! 1926,O 21,23:1
Ten Per Cent 1927,S 14,29:3

Celebrity 1927,D 27,24:3
Vaudeville (Palace) 1928,Ag 28,27:3
Come Easy 1933,Ag 30,22:5
So Many Paths 1934,D 7,26:5
Eldest, The 1935,F 12,24:3
Penny Wise 1937,Ap 20,28:6
Schoolhouse on the Lot 1938,Mr 23,18:4
Farm of Three Echoes 1939,N 29,18:3
Jupiter Laughs 1940,S 10,27:1
Dragon's Mouth 1955,N 17,45:1

Sheridan, Noel
Double Dublin 1963,D 27,16:2

Sheridan, Otis
Out of a Blue Sky 1930,F 10,20:6
Reunion in Vienna 1931,N 17,31:1
Peace Palace 1933,Je 6,30:2
Bright Honor 1936,S 28,14:1
30 Days Hath September 1938,O 1,10:5

Sheridan, Phil
Afgar 1920,N 9,13:2
Bootleggers, The 1922,N 28,24:1
Glory Hallelujah 1926,Ap 7,26:2
White Wings 1926,O 16,15:1
Crime 1927,F 23,27:3
Shannons of Broadway, The 1927,S 27,30:4
Show Boat 1927,D 28,26:1
Hold Everything 1928,O 11,24:2
First Night 1930,N 27,32:3
Two Seconds 1931,O 10,20:6
Show Boat 1932,My 20,22:2
Man Bites Dog 1933,Ap 26,11:2
Murder at the Vanities 1933,S 13,22:4
Personal Appearance 1934,O 18,26:7
Body Beautiful, The 1935,N 1,24:3
But for the Grace of God 1937,Ja 13,21:4
Window Shopping 1938,D 24,13:2
Innocent Voyage, The 1943,N 16,27:2
Mrs January & Mr Ex 1944,Ap 1,10:2
He Who Gets Slapped 1946,Mr 21,31:4

Sheridan, Richard Brinsley (Miscellaneous)
School for Scandal, The 1962,My 18,34:2

Sheridan, Richard Brinsley (Original Author)
Critic, The 1931,F 22,VIII,3:5
New School for Scandal 1937,My 5,28:2
All in Love 1961,N 11,15:2
Critic, The 1969,Mr 9,76:5

Sheridan, Richard Brinsley (Playwright)
Rivals, The 1922,Je 6,18:2
School for Scandal, The 1923,Mr 13,19:2
Rivals, The 1923,My 9,14:2
Rivals, The 1923,My 13,VIII,1:1
School for Scandal, The 1923,Je 5,24:3
Critic, The 1925,My 9,12:4
School for Scandal, The 1925,O 24,19:1
School for Scandal, The 1925,D 7,18:2
School for Scandal, The 1925,D 13,IX,3:1
Critic, The 1928,N 11,X,4:1
Trip to Scarborough, A 1929,Mr 18,31:2
School for Scandal, The 1929,D 15,X,4:2
Rivals, The 1930,Mr 14,24:4
Rivals, The 1930,Mr 23,IX,1:1
School for Scandal, The 1931,N 11,26:4
School for Scandal, The 1931,N 22,VIII,3:1
Rivals, The 1935,S 25,19:6
School for Scandal, The 1940,Je 23,IX,1:1
Rivals, The 1941,N 18,32:2
Rivals, The 1942,Ja 15,24:2
Rivals, The 1942,Ja 25,IX,1:1
Critic, The 1945,N 11,II,2:5
Oedipus; Critic, The 1946,My 21,19:2
School for Scandal, The 1949,Ja 21,24:5
School for Scandal, The 1953,Je 24,29:2
Rivals, The 1956,Mr 11,II,3:1
School for Scandal, The 1962,Mr 19,36:1
School for Scandal, The 1962,Ap 6,31:3
School for Scandal, The 1962,D 30,27:1
School for Scandal, The 1963,Ja 26,5:2
Critic, The 1965,Jl 26,15:2
School for Scandal, The 1966,N 22,33:2
Rivals, The 1969,O 18,37:1
School for Scandal, The 1970,Je 11,51:1
School for Scandal, The 1970,Je 21,II,1:1

Sheridan, Rose
Tragedy of the Ages, The 1933,Ap 7,22:7

Sheridan, Wayne
Brigadoon 1950,My 3,36:2

Sheriff, Noam (Composer)
Men and Dreams 1966,S 7,51:2

Sheriff, Paul (Costume Designer)
Macbeth 1948,Ap 1,30:2

Sheriff, Paul (Scenic Designer)
Macbeth 1948,Ap 1,30:2

Sherin, Edwin
Romeo and Juliet 1957,Je 28,30:2
Macbeth 1957,Ag 16,11:2
As You Like It 1958,Ja 21,33:6
Othello 1958,Jl 4,16:1
Twelfth Night 1958,Ag 7,21:4
Antony and Cleopatra 1959,Ja 14,28:1
Dr Willy Nilly 1959,Je 5,18:2
Henry IV 1960,Mr 2,42:1
Henry IV 1960,Mr 13,II,1:1
Henry IV 1960,Ap 19,41:1

Sherin, Edwin—Cont

Face of a Hero 1960,O 21,29:5
Diff'rent 1961,O 18,52:1
Romulus 1962,Ja 11,27:1

Sherin, Edwin (Director)
Deirdre of the Sorrows 1959,O 15,46:1
Mister Roberts 1962,O 12,27:2
White Rose and the Red, The 1964,Mr 17,31:1
Hard Travelin' 1965,Je 17,25:1
Lonesome Train, The 1965,Je 17,25:1
Great White Hope, The 1967,D 14,58:1
Great White Hope, The 1967,D 24,II,3:1
Iceman Cometh, The 1968,Ap 1,58:1
Great White Hope, The 1968,O 4,40:1
Great White Hope, The 1968,O 13,II,1:1
Great White Hope, The 1969,S 27,26:1

Sherin, Edwin (Miscellaneous)
Great White Hope, The 1967,D 14,58:1

Sheringham, George (Costume Designer)
Venetian, The 1931,N 2,26:1
Iolanthe 1934,S 11,24:3
H M S Pinafore 1934,S 14,24:3
Pirates of Penzance, The 1948,Ja 6,27:2
Trial by Jury 1948,Ja 6,27:2
H M S Pinafore 1948,Ja 20,26:2
Patience 1948,F 10,27:2
H M S Pinafore 1951,F 6,24:2
Trial by Jury 1951,F 6,24:2
Pirates of Penzance, The 1951,F 20,21:2
Pirates of Penzance, The 1955,O 7,21:1
Trial by Jury 1955,O 18,48:1
H M S Pinafore 1955,O 18,48:1
Trial by Jury 1962,N 23,32:4
Trial by Jury 1964,N 20,40:1

Sheringham, George (Scenic Designer)
Patience 1948,F 10,27:2

Sherkot
Streamline 1934,S 29,13:1
Streamline 1934,O 21,IX,1:3

Sherlock, Frank
Bachelor's Brides 1925,My 29,20:2
Kiss in a Taxi, The 1925,Ag 26,14:1

Sherlock, John
Holka Polka 1925,O 15,27:2

Sherman, Adah
Wait Till We're Married 1921,S 27,14:1

Sherman, Allan (Lyricist)
Fig Leaves Are Falling, The 1969,Ja 3,19:1

Sherman, Allan (Playwright)
Fig Leaves Are Falling, The 1969,Ja 3,19:1

Sherman, Ann
Veils 1928,Mr 14,28:5
Secret Garden, The 1931,N 8,31:4

Sherman, Arthur (Director)
World War 2 1/2 1969,Mr 25,40:1
Dream of a Blacklisted Actor 1969,D 18,64:1

Sherman, Arthur (Lyricist)
Not While I'm Eating 1961,D 20,37:1

Sherman, Arthur (Playwright)
Not While I'm Eating 1961,D 20,37:1

Sherman, Ben
Cocktails of 1934 1934,My 5,22:1

Sherman, Cecile
Scrap Book 1932,Ag 2,20:3
Fledermaus, Die 1933,My 14,II,3:8
Mr Strauss Goes to Boston 1945,S 7,20:2
Dear Judas 1947,O 6,26:4

Sherman, Charles
Stars on Ice (2d Edition) 1943,Je 25,13:2

Sherman, Charles (Miscellaneous)
Ziegfeld Follies 1943,Ap 2,16:2

Sherman, Charles (Playwright)
Sketch Book 1935,Je 5,22:2
Streets of Paris, The 1939,Je 20,25:2
All in Fun 1940,D 28,11:2
Brights Lights of 1944 1943,S 17,27:4
Seven Lively Arts 1944,D 8,26:6
Seven Lively Arts 1944,D 17,II,3:1
Magic Touch, The 1947,S 4,30:1
Along Fifth Avenue 1949,Ja 14,28:2
Two's Company 1952,D 16,43:5

Sherman, Edith
Sister Oakes 1949,Ap 25,19:4

Sherman, Eleanor
Sweet Bird of Youth 1956,Ap 17,27:2

Sherman, Ethel
Let Freedom Sing 1942,O 6,18:2

Sherman, Fred
Best Years 1932,S 8,16:2
Them's the Reporters 1935,My 30,21:4
Petticoat Fever 1935,Jl 2,24:4
As Husbands Go 1935,Jl 10,24:1
Whatever Goes Up 1935,N 26,28:2
Frederika 1937,F 5,16:5
Roberta 1937,Je 27,II,6:1
Three Waltzes 1937,D 27,10:2
Sun Field, The 1942,D 10,33:2

Sherman, Garry (Miscellaneous)
Purlie 1970,Mr 16,53:1

Sherman, Garry (Musical Director)
Purlie 1970,Mr 16,53:1

Sherman, George L (Director)
Come Play With Me 1959,My 1,33:5
Gallows Humor 1961,Ap 19,35:1

Sherman, George L (Director)—Cont
Little Murders 1967,Ap 26,38:1
Volpone 1967,Je 30,29:1
Happiness 1967,N 11,25:2
Walking to Waldheim 1967,N 11,25:2
Guide, The 1968,Mr 7,50:1
Great Career, A 1968,D 30,25:1
Evening for Merlin Finch, An 1968,D 30,25:1

Sherman, Grant
Hindu, The 1922,Mr 22,13:3

Sherman, Gretchen
Roberta 1933,N 20,18:4

Sherman, Hal
Irving Berlin's New Music Box Revue
   1922,O 24,18:1
Music Box Revue 1924,D 2,23:3
Lambs Gambol 1925,Ap 27,15:1
Vaudeville (Palace) 1931,My 11,15:5
Vaudeville (Palace) 1932,My 23,18:7
Hellzapoppin 1938,S 23,34:2
New Hellzapoppin, The 1939,D 12,36:4

Sherman, Harold (Playwright)
Her Supporting Cast 1931,My 5,33:3
Little Black Book, The 1932,D 27,11:2
Girl From Nantucket, The 1945,N 9,17:2
Second Guesser 1946,F 20,29:2

Sherman, Henry (Playwright)
Once Upon a Tailor 1955,My 24,36:2

Sherman, Hiram
Midsummer Night's Dream, A 1931,Ag 19,19:3
Horse Eats Hat 1936,S 28,14:2
Julius Caesar 1937,N 12,26:6
Cradle Will Rock, The 1937,D 6,19:4
Shoemaker's Holiday, The 1938,Ja 3,17:2
Shoemaker's Holiday, The 1938,Ja 9,X,1:1
Shoemaker's Holiday, The 1938,Ja 23,XI,1:6
Sing Out the News 1938,S 26,12:5
Sing Out the News 1938,O 2,IX,1:1
As You Like It 1939,My 9,28:4
As You Like It; Midsummer Night's Dream, A;
   Comedy of Errors, The; Taming of the Shrew,
   The 1939,My 9,28:4
Midsummer Night's Dream, A 1939,My 14,XI,1:1
Very Warm for May 1939,N 18,23:2
Contrast, The 1940,Mr 26,17:2
Two Weeks With Pay 1940,Je 25,28:3
Boyd's Daughter 1940,O 12,20:2
Mum's the Word 1940,D 6,28:5
Talley Method, The 1941,F 25,26:3
Cyrano de Bergerac 1946,O 9,33:2
Cyrano de Bergerac 1947,Ja 17,27:2
Alchemist, The 1948,My 7,31:4
Town House 1948,S 24,31:2
Brigadoon 1949,Ap 16,11:1
Four Twelves Are 48 1951,Ja 18,30:2
Two's Company 1952,D 16,43:5
Two's Company 1952,D 21,II,3:1
Frogs of Spring, The 1953,O 21,36:2
3 for Tonight 1955,Ap 7,23:2
3 for Tonight 1955,Ap 17,II,1:1
Goodbye Again 1956,Ap 25,38:1
King John 1956,Je 28,33:5
Measure for Measure 1956,Je 29,16:1
Measure for Measure 1957,Ja 23,24:1
International Soiree 1958,Mr 13,25:1
Hamlet 1958,Je 21,11:1
Midsummer Night's Dream, A 1958,Je 23,19:1
Winter's Tale, The 1958,Jl 21,17:4
Romeo and Juliet 1959,Je 15,31:1
Romeo and Juliet 1959,Je 21,II,1:1
Merry Wives of Windsor, The 1959,Jl 9,23:2
All's Well That Ends Well 1959,Ag 3,20:4
Killer, The 1960,Mr 23,33:1
Killer, The 1960,Ap 3,II,1:1
As You Like It 1961,Je 17,13:2
Macbeth 1961,Je 19,31:1
As You Like It 1961,Je 25,II,1:1
Troilus and Cressida 1961,Jl 24,15:1
Where's Daddy? 1966,Mr 3,27:1
How Now, Dow Jones 1967,D 8,53:1
How Now, Dow Jones 1967,D 24,II,3:2
Anne of Green Gables 1969,Ap 18,39:1
Anne of Green Gables 1969,Ag 25,41:1

Sherman, Hiram (Director)
Midsummer Night's Dream, A 1931,Ag 19,19:3
Boyd's Daughter 1940,O 12,20:2

Sherman, Hiram (Playwright)
Too Much Party 1934,Mr 6,28:4

Sherman, Howard
Daughters of Atreus 1936,O 15,33:1
Doll's House, A 1937,D 28,28:6
Abe Lincoln in Illinois 1938,O 17,12:2
Delicate Story 1940,D 5,32:2

Sherman, Joseph T (Musical Director)
Beggar's Opera, The 1952,S 26,17:4

Sherman, Judy
Pygmalion 1952,F 9,11:2

Sherman, L C
Big Boy 1925,Ja 8,28:2

Sherman, Larry
Maid in the Ozarks 1946,Jl 16,20:3
Traitor, The 1949,Ap 1,30:2

Sherman, Lee (Choreographer)
Nellie Bly 1946,Ja 22,32:2

Sherman, Lee (Director)
Catch a Star! 1955,S 7,35:2
Banker's Daughter, The 1962,Ja 23,37:1

Sherman, Lowell
Man's Name, The 1921,N 16,22:1
Lawful Larceny 1922,Ja 3,20:2
Fool, The 1922,O 24,18:1
Masked Woman, The 1922,D 23,14:2
Morphia 1923,Mr 7,20:2
Casanova 1923,S 16,VII,2:8
Casanova 1923,S 27,10:2
Casanova 1923,O 2,10:3
Leah Kleschna 1924,Ap 22,19:2
Leah Kleschna 1924,Ap 27,VIII,1:1
High Stakes 1924,S 10,21:3
Passionate Prince, The 1925,O 11,VIII,2:6
Woman Disputed, A 1926,S 29,23:2
Vaudeville (Palace) 1927,Ap 5,30:2

Sherman, Manning (Composer)
Nine Fifteen Revue, The 1930,F 12,26:2

Sherman, Manning (Lyricist)
Nine Fifteen Revue, The 1930,F 12,26:2

Sherman, Milt (Choreographer)
Mardi Gras! 1965,Je 28,33:2

Sherman, Milt (Miscellaneous)
Paradise Island 1961,Je 24,11:1
Paradise Island 1962,Je 28,22:1

Sherman, Murray (Scenic Designer)
Climate of Eden, The 1953,N 21,11:2

Sherman, Nathan (Director)
Late Wisdom 1934,Ap 24,27:4

Sherman, Nathan (Playwright)
Late Wisdom 1934,Ap 24,27:4
First American Dictator 1939,Mr 15,18:2
War President 1944,Ap 25,17:3

Sherman, Orville
Buttrio Square 1952,O 15,40:2
Wooden Dish, The 1955,O 7,20:1

Sherman, Orville (Director)
High Button Shoes 1955,Mr 12,10:6

Sherman, Paul (Musical Director)
Soldier's Tale, A 1955,Jl 13,21:2

Sherman, Philip
Wolves 1924,D 31,9:4
Roaming Stars 1930,Ja 25,12:2
Chains 1930,F 23,29:2

Sherman, Pincus
Tenth Commandment, The 1926,N 18,27:1
Jew Suss 1929,O 19,22:3
Angels on Earth 1929,D 11,34:7
Witch of Castile, The 1930,O 25,21:1
Man With the Portfolio, The 1931,F 12,24:6

Sherman, Rita
For All of Us 1923,O 16,19:4

Sherman, Robert J (Playwright)
Spooks 1925,Je 2,16:4

Sherman, Roger
This Island Is Mine 1959,Jl 1,26:4

Sherman, Roger (Lighting Director)
Common Glory, The 1947,Jl 19,11:2
Founders, The 1957,My 14,39:1

Sherman, Roger (Miscellaneous)
Founders, The 1957,My 14,39:1

Sherman, Roger (Scenic Designer)
Common Glory, The 1947,Jl 19,11:2
Founders, The 1957,My 14,39:1

Sherman, Ronald
Texas Town 1941,Ap 30,22:3
Out of My House 1942,Ja 8,28:6

Sherman, Shirley
Blossom Time 1922,O 24,18:2
Rainbow Rose 1926,Mr 17,28:2
Happy 1927,D 6,26:3

Sherman, Susanne (Costume Designer)
Common Glory, The 1947,Jl 19,11:2
Faith of Our Fathers 1950,Ag 6,72:2
Founders, The 1957,My 14,39:1

Sherman, Teddi
Slightly Married 1943,O 26,19:2

Sherman, Vincent
Marco Millions 1930,Mr 4,24:4
Elizabeth the Queen 1930,N 4,37:1
Hairy Ape, The 1931,Ap 15,24:4
Good Earth, The 1932,O 18,23:4
Judgment Day 1934,S 13,26:4
Black Pit 1935,Mr 21,26:6
Paradise Lost 1935,D 10,31:5
Bitter Stream 1936,Mr 31,16:6

Sherman, Vincent (Director)
Battle Hymn 1936,My 23,12:1
It Can't Happen Here 1936,O 28,30:1

Sherman, Willis
Henry V 1964,My 13,52:1

Shermet, Hazel
Cradle Will Rock, The 1947,D 27,11:2

Sherrald, Charles
Zunguru 1938,Ag 7,IX,8:2

Sherrer, Hugh (Miscellaneous)
School for Wives 1957,Je 20,23:4

Sherriff, Paul (Scenic Designer)
Crime and Punishment 1947,D 23,29:3
Crime and Punishment 1948,Ja 4,II,1:1

Sherriff, R C (Playwright)
Journey's End 1928,D 30,VIII,4:1
Journey's End 1929,F 10,IX,4:7
Journey's End 1929,Mr 23,23:1
Journey's End 1929,Mr 31,VIII,1:1
Journey's End 1929,S 15,IX,2:6
Journey's End 1929,S 22,IX,4:1
Journey's End 1930,Mr 23,4:3
Journey's End 1930,Mr 30,VIII,3:4
Journey's End 1930,Ag 5,26:4
Journey's End 1930,Ag 24,VIII,1:1
Windfall 1934,F 27,17:8
St Helena 1936,F 5,15:8
St Helena 1936,Mr 8,IX,1:1
St Helena 1936,S 29,35:1
St Helena 1936,O 7,32:1
St Helena 1936,O 11,X,1:1
Journey's End 1939,S 19,29:2
Journey's End 1939,S 24,IX,1:1
Miss Mabel 1948,D 12,II,4:8
Home at Seven 1950,Mr 8,34:5
Journey's End 1968,O 28,55:3

Sherrill, Joya
Long Dream, The 1960,F 18,36:2

Sherrill, Martha
Geese 1969,Ja 13,26:6

Sherrill, Ruth
Hamlet 1938,N 8,26:1
World We Make, The 1939,N 21,19:1

Sherrock, Irene E
Vie Parisienne, La 1945,Ja 13,14:5

Sherry, Ann
Bright Honor 1936,S 28,14:1

Sherry, Avery
Scarlet Coat, The 1924,D 24,11:1
Fortuno 1925,D 23,22:1
Samarkand 1926,D 22,24:4

Sherry, Avery (Composer)
Samarkand 1926,D 22,24:4

Sherry, Edna (Playwright)
Inspector Kennedy 1929,D 21,16:3

Sherry, Gordon
Earl Carroll's Vanities 1927,Ja 5,18:1

Sherry, Gordon (Playwright)
Black Limelight 1936,N 10,31:1
Black Limelight 1937,My 2,XI,2:1

Sherry, Jack
Earth Journey 1944,Ap 28,24:2
Seven Mirrors 1945,O 26,17:2

Sherry, John (Playwright)
Abraham Cochrane 1964,F 18,26:1

Sherry, Laura
Mister Pitt 1924,Ja 23,15:3

Sherry, Laura (Mrs) (Producer)
Crime and Punishment 1935,Ja 23,20:3

Sherry, Susan (Choreographer)
'Tis Pity She's a Whore 1967,O 21,15:2

Sherry, Virginia
Public Relations 1944,Ap 7,23:3

Shertzer, Sidney
Night Music 1951,Ap 9,29:6

Sherwell, Yvonne
Contributions; Plantation 1970,Mr 10,53:1

Sherwin, Albert
I Love an Actress 1931,S 18,29:2

Sherwin, Albert (Composer)
Life Begins in '40 1940,Ap 5,24:2
Hit the Road 1941,Ap 4,18:3
Step a Little Closer 1948,My 28,26:6

Sherwin, Harry
Petrified Forest, The 1935,Ja 8,26:1

Sherwin, Jeannette
Loyalties 1922,S 28,18:1
Little Miss Bluebeard 1923,Ag 29,12:1
Othello 1925,Ja 12,11:1
Vortex, The 1925,S 17,20:1
Constant Wife, The 1926,N 30,26:3
Kingdom of God, The 1928,D 21,30:2
Love Duel, The 1929,Ap 16,32:3
Thunder in the Air 1929,N 12,34:3

Sherwin, Manning (Composer)
Bad Habits of 1926 1926,My 1,11:1
Everybody's Welcome 1931,S 20,VIII,3:2
Under the Counter 1947,O 4,10:2

Sherwin, Walter
Prince and the Pauper, The 1920,N 2,15:1

Sherwood, Alison
Sound of Music, The 1967,Ap 27,52:1

Sherwood, Arthur
Jumbo 1935,N 18,20:2

Sherwood, Betty
Lolly 1929,O 17,26:2

Sherwood, Bill
Getting Married 1970,Ja 20,46:1

Sherwood, Bob
Vaudeville (Palace) 1926,Je 1,29:5

Sherwood, Bobby
Hear That Trumpet 1946,O 8,19:2

Sherwood, Carlotta
Romeo and Juliet 1956,F 24,20:4

herwood, Carlotta—Cont

Ronde, La 1960,My 10,44:2
herwood, Cynthia
If This Be Treason 1935,S 24,28:2
Laughing Woman, The 1936,O 14,30:1
herwood, Dawn
Sound of Music, The 1967,Ap 27,52:1
herwood, Gale
Vaudeville (Palace) 1926,Je 1,29:5
Red White and Blue 1950,O 8,64:5
herwood, Garrison P
County Chairman, The 1936,My 26,26:5
Egoists, The 1959,O 14,52:2
herwood, George
Fanny 1926,S 22,30:1
Satellite 1935,N 21,27:5
herwood, George (Director)
Zombie 1932,F 11,17:2
herwood, George (Producer)
Zombie 1932,F 11,17:2
herwood, Henry
Broadway 1926,S 17,19:3
Elmer Gantry 1928,Ag 10,9:4
Headquarters 1929,D 5,32:4
City Haul 1929,D 31,14:4
Five Star Final 1930,D 31,11:1
Bellamy Trial, The 1931,Ap 23,28:6
Louder, Please! 1931,N 13,26:4
Mr Papavert 1932,Ja 23,18:6
Rendezvous 1932,O 13,22:3
20th Century 1932,D 30,15:1
Tomorrow's a Holiday! 1935,D 31,10:2
Woman of Destiny, A 1936,Mr 3,25:2
Waltz in Goose Step 1938,N 2,26:2
Return of the Vagabond, The 1940,My 14,27:2
Good Neighbor 1941,O 22,26:2
Twentieth Century 1950,D 25,23:6
Shuffle Along 1952,My 9,20:5
herwood, Holly
Half-Past Wednesday 1962,Ap 7,16:2
Annie Get Your Gun 1966,Je 1,42:2
Sound of Music, The 1967,Ap 27,52:1
herwood, James
Mister Roberts 1948,F 19,27:2
herwood, James P (Producer)
Dial 'M' for Murder 1952,O 30,41:2
herwood, Jan
Day Will Come, The 1944,S 8,17:2
As You Like It 1950,Ja 27,27:2
Paint Your Wagon 1951,N 13,32:2
Ondine 1954,F 19,23:1
herwood, Kyle
Sound of Music, The 1967,Ap 27,52:1
herwood, Lorraine
Nic-Nax of 1926 1926,Ag 5,19:1
Footlights 1927,Ag 20,8:2
Sherwood, Lydia
Brass Paperweight, The 1928,N 4,IX,2:4
Roof, The 1929,N 6,30:4
Insult 1930,S 16,30:2
Brontes, The 1933,My 7,IX,1:4
King of Rome, The 1935,My 15,26:1
I Have Been Here Before 1938,O 14,26:2
Sherwood, Madeleine
Scapegoat, The 1950,Ap 20,36:5
All the King's Men 1950,Jl 19,25:6
Crucible, The 1953,Ja 23,15:2
Crucible, The 1953,Jl 2,20:2
Cat on a Hot Tin Roof 1955,Mr 25,18:2
Cat on a Hot Tin Roof 1955,Ap 3,II,1:1
Sweet Bird of Youth 1959,Mr 11,39:2
Sweet Bird of Youth 1959,Mr 22,II,1:1
Invitation to a March 1960,O 31,27:2
Garden of Sweets, The 1961,N 1,35:1
Hey You, Light Man! 1963,Mr 2,5:2
Arturo Ui 1963,N 12,49:1
Do I Hear a Waltz? 1965,Mr 19,28:1
Inadmissible Evidence 1965,D 1,52:1
Sherwood, Mary Elizabeth (Producer)
Petrified Forest, The 1943,N 2,30:6
Petrified Forest, The 1943,N 7,II,1:1
Goodbye Again 1943,N 10,28:4
Sherwood, Mindy
Sound of Music, The 1967,Ap 27,52:1
Sherwood, Naomi
To Damascus 1961,F 15,40:2
Sherwood, Robert
Processional 1937,O 14,23:1
Sherwood, Robert (Miscellaneous)
Untitled-Revue 1941,My 18,IX,1:1
Second Threshold 1951,Ja 14,II,1:1
Sherwood, Robert E (Original Author)
Miss Liberty 1949,Jl 16,6:5
Sherwood, Robert E (Playwright)
49ers, The 1922,N 7,14:1
Road to Rome, The 1927,F 1,24:2
Road to Rome, The 1927,F 6,VII,1:1
Love Nest, The 1927,D 23,17:1
Queen's Husband, The 1928,Ja 26,17:2
Queen's Husband, The 1928,F 12,VIII,1:1
Love Nest, The 1928,My 27,VIII,1:1
Road to Rome, The 1928,Je 10,VIII,1:3
Hannibal Ante Portas 1929,Ap 15,22:2
Hannibal Ante Portas 1929,Jl 7,VIII,2:4

Road to Rome, The 1929,N 10,X,4:8
Waterloo Bridge 1929,D 1,X,4:7
Road to Rome, The 1929,D 29,VIII,2:6
Waterloo Bridge 1930,Ja 7,29:2
This Is New York 1930,N 29,21:1
This Is New York 1930,D 7,IX,1:1
Reunion in Vienna 1931,O 11,VIII,4:6
Queen's Husband, The 1931,N 15,VIII,2:1
Reunion in Vienna 1931,N 17,31:1
Reunion in Vienna 1931,N 29,VIII,1:1
Waterloo Bridge 1931,N 29,VIII,4:1
Acropolis 1933,N 24,25:8
Acropolis 1933,D 10,X,3:6
Reunion in Vienna 1934,Ja 4,17:1
Reunion in Vienna 1934,Ja 28,IX,3:4
Petrified Forest, The 1934,D 21,31:6
Petrified Forest, The 1934,D 30,IX,1:6
Petrified Forest, The 1935,Ja 8,26:1
Petrified Forest, The 1935,Ja 13,IX,1:1
Petrified Forest, The 1935,Ja 20,X,1:3
Tovarich 1935,Ap 25,19:8
Tovarich 1935,My 19,IX,1:1
Petrified Forest, The 1935,N 24,II,9:3
Petrified Forest, The 1936,Mr 1,II,12:7
Idiot's Delight 1936,Mr 10,26:7
Idiot's Delight 1936,Mr 25,25:2
Idiot's Delight 1936,Ap 12,IX,1:1
Queen's Husband, The 1936,Je 2,33:2
Idiot's Delight 1936,S 1,24:5
Tovarich 1936,S 29,35:2
Tovarich 1936,O 16,31:4
Tovarich 1936,O 25,X,1:1
Idiot's Delight 1938,Mr 23,19:3
Idiot's Delight 1938,Ap 10,X,2:1
Abe Lincoln in Illinois 1938,O 4,20:1
Abe Lincoln in Illinois 1938,O 17,12:2
Abe Lincoln in Illinois 1938,O 23,IX,1:1
Abe Lincoln in Illinois 1939,Ap 23,X,1:1
There Shall Be No Night 1940,Mr 30,11:2
There Shall Be No Night 1940,Ap 30,25:2
There Shall Be No Night 1940,My 5,X,1:1
There Shall Be No Night 1940,S 10,27:3
There Shall Be No Night 1940,S 22,IX,1:1
Petrified Forest, The 1943,Ja 10,VIII,1:6
Petrified Forest, The 1943,N 2,30:6
Petrified Forest, The 1943,N 7,II,1:1
There Shall Be No Night 1943,D 16,34:5
There Shall Be No Night 1944,Ja 2,II,1:5
Rugged Path, The 1945,N 12,17:2
Rugged Path, The 1945,N 18,II,1:1
Miss Liberty 1949,Je 14,26:6
Miss Liberty 1949,Jl 24,II,1:1
Second Threshold 1951,Ja 3,23:2
Idiot's Delight 1951,My 24,46:3
Tovarich 1952,My 15,39:2
Second Threshold 1952,S 25,38:8
Second Threshold 1952,N 9,II,3:2
Petrified Forest, The 1955,Mr 19,6:2
Small War on Murray Hill 1957,Ja 4,19:1
Small War on Murray Hill 1957,Ja 13,II,1:1
Idiot's Delight 1957,F 23,14:2
Abe Lincoln in Illinois 1963,Ja 23,5:2
Tovarich 1963,Mr 20,5:1
Idiot's Delight 1970,Mr 24,39:1
Sherwood, Robert E (Producer)
Abe Lincoln in Illinois 1938,O 17,12:2
Miss Liberty 1949,Jl 16,6:5
Sherwood, Robin
Don Carlos 1964,N 25,40:1
Sound of Music, The 1967,Ap 27,52:1
Sherwood, Wayne
Catch a Star! 1955,S 7,35:2
Wonderful Town 1958,Mr 6,32:4
Shevelove, Burt (Director)
Frogs, The 1941,N 14,25:3
Small Wonder 1948,S 16,33:5
Small Wonder 1948,S 26,II,1:1
Kiss Me, Kate 1956,My 10,27:2
Bil and Cora Baird's Marionette Theater; Ali Baba and the Forty Thieves 1956,S 3,10:1
Davy Jones's Locker 1959,Mr 30,25:1
Too Much Johnson 1964,Ja 16,29:1
Butter and Egg Man, The 1966,O 18,49:1
Davy Jones's Locker 1966,D 25,48:5
People Is the Thing That the World Is Fullest Of 1967,F 21,53:1
Hallelujah, Baby! 1967,Ap 27,51:1
Rockefeller and the Red Indians 1968,O 25,37:1
Shevelove, Burt (Miscellaneous)
Beggar's Opera, The 1957,Mr 14,35:1
Davy Jones's Locker 1959,Mr 30,25:1
Davy Jones's Locker 1966,D 25,48:5
Shevelove, Burt (Musical Director)
Bil and Cora Baird's Marionette Theater 1955,D 27,29:2
Shevelove, Burt (Playwright)
Funny Thing Happened on the Way to the Forum, A 1962,My 9,49:1
Funny Thing Happened on the Way to the Forum, A 1962,My 20,II,1:1
Funny Thing Happened on the Way to the Forum, A 1963,Je 2,II,1:1
Too Much Johnson 1964,Ja 16,29:1

Shevlin, Rosemary
Make Me Disappear 1969,My 14,34:1
Shevtchenko, Faina
Lower Depths, The 1923,Ja 16,16:1
Ivanoff 1923,N 27,23:2
Enough Stupidity in Every Wise Man 1923,D 6,23:1
Death of Pazukhin, The 1924,F 12,20:1
Shibley, Pat
Let Freedom Sing 1942,O 6,18:2
Shiel, Stella
Sky High 1925,Mr 3,21:4
Princess Flavia 1925,N 3,34:3
Shield, Gina
Quick Years, The 1953,N 26,51:2
Shield, Gina (Miscellaneous)
Imaginary Invalid, The 1967,My 2,53:1
Touch of the Poet, A 1967,My 3,38:2
Ways and Means 1967,My 4,34:1
Fumed Oak 1967,My 4,34:1
Still Life 1967,My 4,34:1
John Brown's Body 1968,F 13,49:2
Shields, Arthur
White-Headed Boy, The 1921,S 16,20:1
Far-Off Hills, The 1932,O 19,22:4
Juno and the Paycock 1932,O 20,24:3
Playboy of the Western World, The 1932,O 21,25:5
Rising of the Moon, The 1932,O 21,25:1
New Gossoon, The 1932,O 22,18:2
Words Upon the Window Pane, The 1932,O 29,18:2
Cathleen ni Houlihan 1932,O 31,18:1
Shadow of a Gunman, The 1932,O 31,18:1
Birthright 1932,N 4,25:1
Crabbed Youth and Age 1932,N 4,25:1
Shadow of the Glen, The 1932,N 4,25:1
Autumn Fire 1932,D 29,16:3
Big House, The 1933,Ja 5,19:3
King Oedipus 1933,Ja 16,12:4
Days Without End 1934,Ap 24,26:7
Church Street 1934,My 23,15:5
Plough and the Stars, The 1934,N 13,22:2
Drama at Inish 1934,N 15,24:2
Look at the Heffernans 1934,N 17,13:2
Church Street 1934,N 20,24:5
Bridgehead 1935,Ag 7,22:3
Candida 1935,O 27,IX,2:5
Katie Roche 1937,O 4,17:4
Far-Off Hills, The 1937,O 12,30:4
In the Train 1937,N 22,14:5
Playboy of the Western World, The 1937,N 22,14:5
New Gossoon, The 1937,N 30,26:2
Juno and the Paycock 1937,D 7,32:5
Drama at Inish 1937,D 14,33:2
Spring Meeting 1938,D 9,30:4
Kindred 1939,D 27,17:2
Juno and the Paycock 1940,Ja 17,24:2
Tanyard Street 1941,F 5,16:2
Shields, Arthur (Director)
King Oedipus 1933,Ja 16,12:4
Juno and the Paycock 1940,Ja 17,24:2
Tanyard Street 1941,F 5,16:2
Shields, Arthur (Producer)
Kindred 1939,D 27,17:2
Juno and the Paycock 1940,Ja 17,24:2
Shields, Barbara
Double Door 1933,S 22,15:5
Kind Lady 1935,Ap 24,24:5
Shields, Betty
Masked Woman, The 1922,D 23,14:2
Shields, Bobby
Whoop-Up 1958,D 23,2:7
Shields, Ella
Vaudeville (Palace) 1926,N 2,35:2
Vaudeville (Palace) 1928,Ja 24,26:4
Vaudeville (Palace) 1928,Ja 31,29:2
Shields, Frank
Mikado, The 1932,Jl 29,18:4
Shields, George
White Eagle, The 1927,D 27,24:4
Pardon My English 1933,Ja 21,11:4
O'Flynn, The 1934,D 28,24:1
Pygmalion 1938,Ja 27,16:3
Captain Jinks of the Horse Marines 1938,Ja 28,16:2
Coriolanus 1938,F 2,14:5
Shields, Helen
Petticoat Fever 1935,Jl 2,24:4
As Husbands Go 1935,Jl 10,24:1
Strip Girl 1935,O 21,22:6
Washington Jitters 1938,My 3,19:1
Devil Takes a Bride, The 1938,O 8,10:3
Young Couple Wanted 1940,Ja 25,16:2
Liliom 1940,Mr 26,17:2
Barefoot in Athens 1951,N 1,35:2
Apollo of Bellac, The 1957,Ap 10,39:1
Virtuous Island, The 1957,Ap 10,39:1
Egghead, The 1957,O 10,39:1
Moon Besieged, The 1962,D 6,54:1
Shields, Marie
Marigold 1930,O 9,23:1
Shields, Peggy
Man and Superman 1960,Ag 17,35:3

Shields, Ruth
Street Singer, The 1929,S 18,35:2
Shields, Sidney
Hindu, The 1922,Mr 22,13:3
Shields, Sydney
New York Exchange 1926,D 31,11:2
Such Is Life 1927,S 1,27:3
Red Dust 1928,Ja 3,29:2
White Flame 1929,N 5,32:7
Spring Freshet 1934,O 5,28:3
Shields, Vincent
Hot Mikado, The 1939,Mr 24,26:2
Shields, Virginia
Sweet Mystery of Life 1935,O 12,13:3
Shiels, George (Playwright)
Professor Tim 1927,Ap 17,VII,1:4
Cartney and Kevney 1928,Ja 1,VIII,2:8
Mountain Dew 1929,Mr 31,VIII,4:2
New Gossoon, The 1930,My 11,IX,2:7
New Gossoon, The 1931,Ap 27,24:5
New Gossoon, The 1932,O 22,18:2
New Gossoon, The 1937,N 30,26:2
Shiers, Paul
Girl From Nantucket, The 1945,N 9,17:2
Rat Race, The 1949,D 23,16:2
Shiffrin, A B (Playwright)
Love on Leave 1944,Je 21,23:4
I Like It Here 1946,Mr 23,8:6
Angel in the Pawnshop 1951,Ja 19,20:3
Twilight Walk 1951,S 25,25:4
Black-Eyed Susan 1954,D 24,7:5
Shigekawa, Joan (Producer)
Fireworks; Fireworks for a Hot Fourth
1969,Je 12,51:1
Fireworks; Report, The 1969,Je 12,51:1
Fireworks; Football 1969,Je 12,51:1
Shigorin, James (Director)
Jesters, The 1938,Mr 14,13:3
Shih, Joseph Tso
Ask My Friend Sandy 1943,F 5,16:2
Family, The 1943,Mr 31,22:4
Shilfko, Ola
Yosele the Nightingale 1949,O 21,30:4
Shilkret, Nathaniel (Musical Director)
Paris '90 1952,Mr 5,33:2
Paris '90 1952,Mr 16,II,1:1
Shiller, George S
Jonica 1930,Ap 8,27:1
Shilling, Billie
June Love 1921,Ap 26,20:1
Shilling, William A (Director)
Ol' Man Satan 1932,O 4,26:3
Shillo, Michael
Rashomon 1959,Ja 28,36:2
Rashomon 1959,F 8,II,1:1
Secret Concubine, The 1960,Mr 22,29:2
Magnificent Hugo, The 1961,Ap 8,12:2
Shimoda, Dana
South Pacific 1965,Je 3,25:1
South Pacific 1968,Je 30,54:2
Lovely Ladies, Kind Gentlemen 1970,D 29,38:1
Shimizu, Keenan
South Pacific 1965,Je 3,25:1
South Pacific 1968,Je 30,54:2
Shimizu, Sachi
Lovely Ladies, Kind Gentlemen 1970,D 29,38:1
Shimizu, Sadako
Wedding in Japan 1957,Mr 12,37:7
Shimkin, Arthur (Producer)
Young Abe Lincoln 1961,Ap 26,36:1
Shimoda, I (Composer)
Marie Vison, La 1970,Jl 15,29:1
Coney Island Play 1970,O 31,34:2
Shimoda, Yuki
Teahouse of the August Moon, The 1953,O 16,32:1
Auntie Mame 1956,N 1,47:2
Shimoda, Yuki (Choreographer)
Singing Girl, The 1952,Je 4,31:8
Shimono, Sab
South Pacific 1965,Je 3,25:1
Mame 1966,My 25,41:1
Lovely Ladies, Kind Gentlemen 1970,D 29,38:1
Shindel, Larry
Mikado, The 1942,F 4,22:2
Pirates of Penzance, The 1942,F 18,22:2
Iolanthe 1942,F 24,26:4
Gondoliers, The 1942,Mr 4,22:3
Shindell, Nathan
Monkey Talks, The 1925,D 29,20:1
Shine, John L
Deburau 1920,D 24,14:3
Deburau 1921,Ja 2,VI,3:1
Grand Duke, The 1921,N 2,20:1
Will Shakespeare 1923,Ja 2,14:1
Scaramouche 1923,O 25,14:2
Man in Evening Clothes, The 1924,D 6,13:4
Autumn Fire 1926,O 27,25:3
Shine, John L (Producer)
Autumn Fire 1926,O 27,25:3
Shine, Ted (Playwright)
Contribution 1969,Ap 2,37:1
Contribution 1969,Ap 13,II,1:1
Contributions; Contribution 1970,Mr 10,53:1

Contributions; Plantation 1970,Mr 10,53:1
Contributions; Shoes 1970,Mr 10,53:1
Contributions 1970,Mr 29,II,1:1
Shiner, Evelyn
Voice of Israel, The 1948,O 26,40:2
Shinn, Everett (Costume Designer)
Roadside 1930,S 27,21:1
Shinnal, Vern
Guys and Dolls 1965,Ap 29,39:1
Shinsui, Sansho
Coney Island Play 1970,O 31,34:2
Shinsui, Sansho (Miscellaneous)
Coney Island Play 1970,O 31,34:2
Shipley, Victor
Wasp's Nest, The 1927,O 26,26:3
Killers 1928,Mr 14,28:3
Shipman, Helen
Lady in Ermine, The 1922,O 3,22:2
Caroline 1923,F 1,13:2
Passing Show of 1923, The 1923,Je 15,24:6
Topics of 1923 1923,N 21,23:2
Paradise Alley 1924,Ap 2,17:3
Kosher Kitty Kelly 1925,Je 16,24:2
Padlocks of 1927 1927,Jl 6,23:4
Great Power, The 1928,S 12,25:1
Room 349 1930,Ap 23,24:5
Life Is Like That 1930,D 23,24:3
Society Girl 1931,D 31,16:1
Shipman, Louis Evan (Playwright)
Fools Errant 1922,Ag 22,12:3
Poor Richard 1924,N 16,VIII,2:8
Poor Richard 1930,Ja 18,2:7
Shipman, Samuel (Playwright)
Crooked Gamblers 1920,Ag 2,12:1
Unwritten Chapter, The 1920,O 12,18:1
Nature's Nobleman 1921,N 15,23:2
Lawful Larceny 1922,Ja 3,20:2
Crooked Square, The 1923,S 11,10:2
Crooked Square, The 1923,S 16,VII,1:1
Cheaper to Marry 1924,Ap 16,26:1
Cheaper to Marry 1924,Ap 20,VIII,1:1
No More Women 1926,Ag 4,17:2
Crime Wave, The 1927,F 13,VII,1:4
Crime 1927,F 23,27:3
That French Lady 1927,Mr 16,29:3
Creoles 1927,S 23,33:3
Crime 1927,O 19,24:2
Crime 1928,My 13,IX,2:2
Crime 1928,My 19,7:4
Crime 1928,Je 24,VIII,1:4
Trapped 1928,Ag 26,VII,2:1
Trapped 1928,S 12,25:3
Fast Life 1928,S 27,35:2
Scarlet Pages 1929,S 1,VIII,1:1
Scarlet Pages 1929,S 10,26:3
Scarlet Pages 1929,S 22,IX,1:1
She Means Business 1931,Ja 27,21:2
Alley Cat 1934,S 18,18:1
Lady Detained, A 1935,Ja 10,23:3
Behind the Red Lights 1937,Ja 14,17:4
Louisiana Lady 1947,Je 3,35:2
Shipp, Cameron
Rogues and Vagabonds 1930,My 8,32:5
Shipp, J A
Green Pastures, The 1930,F 27,26:1
Shipp, J A (Director)
Kilpatrick's Old-Time Minstrels 1930,Ap 21,20:2
Shipp, Reuben (Playwright)
It's About Time 1942,Mr 31,28:3
Shippey, Lee (Original Author)
Great American Family, The 1939,D 10,X,5:6
Shipstad, Bob (Director)
Ice Follies 1967,Ja 11,51:1
Ice Follies 1969,My 23,38:1
Ice Follies 1970,My 23,27:1
Shipstad, Eddie
Ice Follies 1937,D 22,29:1
Ice Follies 1941,D 2,32:2
Shipstad, Eddie (Producer)
Ice Follies 1957,Ja 16,36:1
Ice Follies 1958,Ja 15,26:2
Ice Follies 1959,Ja 14,30:1
Ice Follies 1960,Ja 13,20:1
Ice Follies 1961,Ja 11,25:2
Ice Follies 1962,Ja 10,24:6
Ice Follies 1963,Ja 10,5:2
Ice Follies 1964,Ja 8,41:2
Ice Follies 1965,Ja 13,35:1
Ice Follies 1966,Ja 12,27:6
Ice Follies 1967,Ja 11,51:1
Ice Follies 1969,My 23,38:1
Ice Follies 1970,My 23,27:1
Shipstad, Jill
Ice Follies 1962,Ja 10,24:6
Ice Follies 1964,Ja 8,41:2
Ice Follies 1965,Ja 13,35:1
Ice Follies 1966,Ja 12,27:6
Ice Follies 1970,My 23,27:1
Shipstad, Joe
Ice Follies 1963,Ja 10,5:2
Shipstad, Roy
Ice Follies 1937,D 22,29:1
Ice Follies 1939,D 5,38:2
Ice Follies 1941,D 2,32:2

Shipstad, Roy (Producer)
Ice Follies 1941,D 2,32:2
Ice Follies 1957,Ja 16,36:1
Ice Follies 1958,Ja 15,26:2
Ice Follies 1959,Ja 14,30:1
Ice Follies 1960,Ja 13,20:1
Ice Follies 1961,Ja 11,25:2
Ice Follies 1962,Ja 10,24:6
Ice Follies 1963,Ja 10,5:2
Ice Follies 1964,Ja 8,41:2
Ice Follies 1965,Ja 13,35:1
Ice Follies 1966,Ja 12,27:6
Ice Follies 1967,Ja 11,51:1
Ice Follies 1969,My 23,38:1
Ice Follies 1970,My 23,27:1
Shipstad and Johnson
Ice Follies 1939,D 5,38:2
Shipworth, Alison
Lilies of the Field 1921,O 5,20:1
Lily of the Valley 1942,Ja 27,25:2
Shirah, Milton
Jeb 1946,F 22,20:2
Shire, David (Composer)
Sap of Life, The 1961,O 3,44:1
Unknown Soldier and His Wife, The 1967,Jl 7,22:1
Leonard Sillman's New Faces of 1968
1968,My 3,43:1
Shire, David (Lyricist)
Leonard Sillman's New Faces of 1968
1968,My 3,43:1
Shire, David (Miscellaneous)
Sap of Life, The 1961,O 3,44:1
Shire, David (Musical Director)
'Toinette 1961,N 21,46:1
Shirley, Alfred
Purple Mask, The 1920,Ja 6,18:1
Mob, The 1920,O 11,18:1
Macbeth 1921,F 18,16:1
Great Broxopp, The 1921,N 16,22:1
Ashes 1924,O 21,21:2
Serena Blandish 1929,Ja 24,30:3
Shirley, Bill
Pardon Our French 1950,O 6,22:4
Shirley, Don Jr (Costume Designer)
Shakespeare Revisited 1962,Jl 19,19:2
Shirley, Don Jr (Scenic Designer)
Shakespeare Revisited 1962,Jl 19,19:2
Wonder World 1964,My 18,32:1
Shirley, Florence
Why Men Leave Home 1922,Jl 30,VI,1:3
Why Men Leave Home 1922,S 13,18:2
My Aunt From Ypsilanti 1923,My 2,22:6
Locked Door, The 1924,Je 20,17:2
Poor Nut, The 1925,Ap 28,18:1
Embers 1926,F 2,20:3
Doctor X 1931,F 10,25:1
Fast Service 1931,N 18,26:3
Take My Tip 1932,Ap 12,25:2
Alice in Arms 1945,F 1,18:4
Shirley, Irene
Rose Bernd 1922,S 27,17:1
Launzi 1923,O 11,16:3
Madre 1923,D 31,9:6
Devil Within, The 1925,Mr 17,19:4
They All Want Something 1926,O 13,20:2
Wanted 1928,Jl 3,19:2
Brothers 1928,D 26,14:3
Little Father of the Wilderness, The 1930,Je 3,27:1
People on the Hill 1931,S 26,25:5
Heigh-Ho, Everybody 1932,My 26,31:2
Lost Horizons 1934,O 16,31:2
Lady of Letters 1935,Mr 29,26:6
Shirley, Mercedes
Naked 1950,S 7,39:2
Shirley, Ralph
Woman of Bronze, The 1920,S 8,9:2
Helena's Boys 1924,Ap 8,22:2
Right to Dream, The 1924,My 27,14:2
Stork, The 1925,Ja 27,14:2
Shirley, Stanla
Heartbreak House 1950,Mr 22,33:2
Shirley, Tom
Advise and Consent 1960,N 18,25:1
Giants, Sons of Giants 1962,Ja 8,26:2
Shishkin, Sergei
Diana 1929,D 10,37:1
Shishkina, Mme
Revue Russe, The 1922,O 6,28:1
Shkolnick, Sylvia (Costume Designer)
Don Juan in the Russian Manner 1954,Ap 23,23:2
Shkvarkin, V (Playwright)
Strange Child 1935,F 26,16:1
Shlifko, Ola
Mazel Tov, Rabbi 1938,N 28,10:4
Song of Dnieper 1946,O 26,10:5
Shlonsky, Verdina (Composer)
Brothers Ashkenazi, The 1955,N 12,24:4
Shloymeh
Wish Me Luck! 1954,N 1,37:2
Shmunes, Helena
Mirele Efros 1969,D 26,41:1

Shneierman, Zelda
Brothers Ashkenazi, The 1955,N 12,24:4
Shneour, Zalman (Original Author)
Song of Dnieper 1946,O 26,10:5
Shneyur, Chaim
Dybbuk, The 1924,Ja 29,17:7
King Saul 1925,S 18,26:3
Tailor Becomes a Storekeeper, The 1938,Ap 14,26:3
Shnitzer, Henrietta
On Foreign Soil 1927,D 24,8:2
Shnitzer, Robert C
Henry V 1928,Mr 16,26:2
Shoaff, Charlotte
Here Come the Clowns 1954,My 5,36:2
Shobey, Norman
Joy 1970,Ja 28,50:1
Shochat, Leib
Brothers Ashkenazi, The 1955,N 12,24:4
Shockley, Marian
Abie's Irish Rose 1937,My 13,30:2
Two Time Mary 1937,Ag 3,20:5
Reno 1937,Ag 10,22:7
Censored 1938,F 28,18:2
Shoctor, Joseph H (Miscellaneous)
Hamp 1967,Mr 10,32:1
Billy 1969,Mr 24,56:1
Shoctor, Joseph H (Producer)
Hamlet 1969,My 2,38:1
Shoemaker, Ann
Great God Brown, The 1926,Ja 25,26:1
Noose, The 1926,O 21,23:3
We All Do 1927,Mr 1,30:3
Speakeasy 1927,S 27,30:1
Whispering Friends 1928,F 21,18:3
Tonight at 12 1928,N 16,28:1
Button, Button 1929,O 24,26:1
Novice and the Duke, The 1929,D 11,37:2
Silent Witness, The 1931,Mr 24,31:5
Black Sheep 1932,O 14,22:6
Ah, Wilderness! 1934,My 1,26:3
Ah, Wilderness! 1941,O 3,26:2
Proof Thro' the Night 1942,D 26,14:2
Rich Full Life, The 1945,N 10,9:2
Woman Bites Dog 1946,Ap 18,21:2
Dream Girl 1951,My 10,39:1
Twilight Walk 1951,S 25,25:4
Living Room, The 1954,N 18,41:1
Living Room, The 1954,N 28,II,1:1
Separate Tables 1957,S 15,II,1:1
Importance of Being Earnest, The 1963,F 27,5:2
Half a Sixpence 1965,Ap 26,38:2
Shoemaker, Dorothy
Man's Name, The 1921,N 16,22:1
Shoemaker, George
Final Balance, The 1928,O 31,28:3
Red Rust 1929,D 18,31:1
Shoemaker, Leonard W
Billy Budd 1959,F 28,13:3
Shoemaker, Richard (Scenic Designer)
On the Necessity of Being Polygamous
  1964,D 9,61:1
Shoenfeld, Ben Zion
Germany Aflame 1933,O 28,20:5
Shoenfeld, Mae
Topsy-Turvy 1939,F 13,12:3
Parnosseh 1939,F 20,12:5
Mazel Tov, Molly 1950,O 2,18:1
Shoenfeld, May
Golden Ring, The 1930,F 1,14:7
Soul of a Woman, The 1930,F 22,13:1
Shoengold, Albert
Yours Is My Heart 1946,S 6,16:5
Shoengold, Joseph
His Wife's Lover 1929,O 21,30:6
Millions 1930,O 3,30:4
Untitled-Benefit 1933,Ja 25,13:3
Slaves of the Public 1934,Mr 10,18:6
Madame Pagliacci 1935,S 30,12:3
Stranger, The 1935,N 7,26:2
Saint and Sinners 1935,D 30,15:2
Golden Stream, The 1936,F 13,25:1
Topsy-Turvy 1939,F 13,12:3
Parnosseh 1939,F 20,12:5
Sarah Adler Testimonial 1939,Mr 15,18:2
Chaver, Nachman 1939,O 2,15:2
Shoengold, Joseph (Director)
Millions 1930,O 3,30:4
Shoenthal, Sidney D
Blue Jeans 1933,Ap 9,31:5
Shoichi, Saito
Golden Bat 1970,Je 27,18:2
Sholes, Maxwell
Say It With Flowers 1926,D 6,29:1
What Do We Know 1927,D 24,8:1
Hot Pan 1928,F 16,14:1
Sholz, Edwin
Iolanthe 1965,My 19,42:1
Yeomen of the Guard, The 1965,Jl 8,34:1
Sholz, Edwin (Miscellaneous)
Ah, Wilderness! 1969,N 9,86:1
Shomer, Miriam (Playwright)
Singing Thief, The 1933,D 4,22:4

Shomer, Rose (Playwright)
One of the Many 1921,O 4,10:3
Singing Thief, The 1933,D 4,22:4
Shone, Hermione
Back Pay 1921,Ag 31,8:2
Shook, Maggie
On the Necessity of Being Polygamous
  1964,D 9,61:1
Shook, Rodey
Marie Vison, La 1970,Jl 15,29:1
Shore, Elaine
Junebug Graduates Tonight! 1967,F 27,35:1
Next 1969,F 11,27:1
Next 1970,Mr 12,46:1
Shore, Herma
Vincent 1959,O 1,40:1
John Brown's Body 1964,Je 29,33:1
Shore, Lewis
Will Shakespeare 1923,Ja 2,14:1
Shore, Lois
Mob, The 1920,O 11,18:1
Whispering Well, The 1920,D 6,19:1
Miss Lulu Bett 1920,D 28,9:1
Little Clay Cart, The 1924,D 6,13:3
Exiles 1925,F 20,20:2
Treat 'Em Rough 1926,O 5,26:2
We're All in the Gutter 1927,Mr 5,12:2
Eva the Fifth 1928,Ag 29,19:3
Buckaroo 1929,Mr 18,31:1
Shoestring Revue 1929,N 23,19:2
Drunkard, The; Fallen Saved, The 1929,D 31,14:6
This Man's Town 1930,Mr 11,24:4
Forest Ring, The 1930,Ap 26,11:2
Little Princess, The 1931,F 7,11:3
Uncle Tom's Cabin 1933,My 30,13:4
Shore, Viola Brothers (Lyricist)
New Faces 1934,Mr 16,24:5
Shore, Viola Brothers (Playwright)
New Faces 1934,Mr 16,24:5
Piper Paid 1934,D 26,19:1
Fools Rush In 1934,D 26,19:2
Is This a Zither? 1935,Je 11,24:3
Shores, Byron
Bloody Laughter 1931,D 5,20:6
Wolves 1932,Ja 7,26:3
Round-Up, The 1932,Mr 8,19:4
Lilly Turner 1932,S 20,26:1
One Day More 1933,F 1,13:5
One Sunday Afternoon 1933,F 16,23:5
Ragged Army 1934,F 27,16:5
Boys From Syracuse, The 1938,N 24,36:1
Too Many Girls 1939,O 19,26:2
Shoroku
Chushingura; Treasury of Loyal Retainers, The
  1969,S 11,53:1
Kumagai Jinya 1969,S 18,64:1
Shoroku, Onoe II
Kanjincho; Subscription List, The 1960,Je 3,26:1
Migawari Zazen; Substitute, The 1960,Je 10,37:1
Chushingura; Forty-Seven Ronin, The
  1960,Je 10,37:1
Chushingura; Forty-Seven Ronin, The
  1960,Je 17,35:4
Chushingura; Treasury of Loyal Retainers, The
  1969,S 11,53:1
Shorr, William
Dream of a Blacklisted Actor 1969,D 18,64:1
Shorr, William (Miscellaneous)
Dream of a Blacklisted Actor 1969,D 18,64:1
Short, Antrim
Carnival 1929,Ap 25,32:5
Short, Bobby
Kiss Me, Kate 1956,My 10,27:2
Night Life 1962,O 24,44:1
Ben Bagley's New Cole Porter Revue
  1965,D 23,20:1
Short, Florence
Romance 1921,Mr 1,18:2
Romance 1921,Mr 6,VI,1:2
Drifting 1922,Ja 3,20:3
Starlight 1925,Mr 4,17:2
Tonight at 12 1928,N 16,28:1
Short, Frank Lea (Director)
Way, The 1940,O 12,20:3
Short, George
Shall We Join the Ladies? 1925,Ja 14,19:1
Short, Gertrude
Arrest That Woman 1936,S 19,20:4
Short, Gloria
Funzapoppin 1949,Jl 1,16:2
Short, Harry
It's Up to You 1921,Mr 29,20:1
Ziegfeld Follies 1923,O 22,17:2
Kid Boots 1924,Ja 1,21:3
China Rose 1925,Ja 20,18:1
Nic-Nax of 1926 1926,Ag 5,19:1
Sidewalks of New York 1927,O 4,33:1
Mystery Moon 1930,Je 24,23:4
She Lived Next to the Firehouse 1931,F 11,23:1
On the Make 1932,My 24,23:2
Monster, The 1933,F 11,11:5
Night of January 16 1935,S 17,26:4

Short, Hassard (Director)
Untitled-Benefit 1921,My 2,12:3
Peg o' My Dreams 1924,My 6,25:3
Hassard Short's Ritz Revue 1924,S 18,19:1
Sunny 1925,S 23,22:1
Greenwich Village Follies 1925,D 25,23:3
No Trespassing! 1926,S 8,19:1
Oh, Please! 1926,D 22,24:3
Lucky 1927,Mr 23,28:3
Sunny Days 1928,F 9,29:1
Three's a Crowd 1930,O 16,28:3
Three's a Crowd 1930,O 26,VIII,1:1
Band Wagon, The 1931,Je 4,31:3
Band Wagon, The 1931,Je 14,VIII,1:1
Face the Music 1932,F 4,25:4
Face the Music 1932,F 18,24:5
As Thousands Cheer 1933,O 2,22:1
As Thousands Cheer 1933,O 15,IX,1:1
Roberta 1933,N 20,18:4
Great Waltz, The 1934,S 24,14:4
Great Waltz, The 1934,S 30,IX,1:1
Stop Press 1935,F 22,26:4
Jubilee 1935,S 29,X,1:1
Jubilee 1935,O 14,20:1
Frederika 1937,F 5,16:5
Three Waltzes 1937,N 15,15:6
Between the Devil 1937,D 23,24:5
Three Waltzes 1937,D 27,10:2
Hot Mikado, The 1939,Mr 24,26:2
Hot Mikado, The 1939,Ap 2,X,1:3
Banjo Eyes 1941,D 26,20:2
Star and Garter 1942,Je 25,26:2
Something for the Boys 1943,Ja 17,VIII,1:1
Carmen Jones 1943,O 20,17:2
Carmen Jones 1943,D 3,26:2
Carmen Jones 1943,D 12,II,3:1
Mexican Hayride 1944,Ja 29,9:6
Seven Lively Arts 1944,D 8,26:6
Carmen Jones 1945,My 3,26:5
Marinka 1945,Jl 19,19:2
Show Boat 1946,Ja 7,17:2
Carmen Jones 1946,Ap 14,II,1:2
Music in My Heart 1947,O 3,30:2
Show Boat 1948,S 9,33:2
Show Boat 1948,S 19,II,1:1
Michael Todd's Peep Show 1950,Je 29,37:2
Seventeen 1951,Jl 1,II,1:1
Short, Hassard (Lighting Director)
Three's a Crowd 1930,O 26,VIII,1:1
As Thousands Cheer 1933,O 2,22:1
Roberta 1933,N 20,18:4
Great Waltz, The 1934,S 24,14:4
Stop Press 1935,Mr 17,VIII,1:4
Jubilee 1935,O 14,20:1
Three Waltzes 1937,N 15,15:6
American Way, The 1939,Ja 23,9:2
Lady in the Dark 1941,Ja 24,14:2
Lady in the Dark 1941,F 2,IX,1:1
Lady in the Dark 1941,S 3,26:6
Banjo Eyes 1941,D 26,20:2
Lady in the Dark 1943,Mr 1,14:2
Carmen Jones 1943,D 3,26:2
Carmen Jones 1943,D 12,II,3:1
Mexican Hayride 1944,Ja 29,9:6
Seven Lively Arts 1944,D 8,26:6
Carmen Jones 1945,My 3,26:5
Carmen Jones 1946,Ap 8,32:2
Music in My Heart 1947,O 3,30:2
Make Mine Manhattan 1948,Ja 16,26:2
Michael Todd's Peep Show 1950,Je 29,37:2
My Darlin' Aida 1952,O 28,36:4
Short, Hassard (Miscellaneous)
Sandalwood 1926,S 23,23:1
Great Waltz, The 1935,Ag 6,20:5
Frederika 1937,F 5,16:5
American Way, The 1939,Ja 23,9:2
Lady in the Dark 1941,Ja 24,14:2
Lady in the Dark 1941,S 3,26:6
Carmen Jones 1943,D 3,26:2
Carmen Jones 1946,Ap 8,32:2
Short, Hassard (Playwright)
Hassard Short's Ritz Revue 1924,S 18,19:1
Greenwich Village Follies 1925,D 25,23:3
Short, Hassard (Producer)
No Trespassing! 1926,S 8,19:1
Sunny Days 1928,F 9,29:1
Jubilee 1935,O 27,IX,1:1
Lady in the Dark 1943,Mr 1,14:2
Short, Hassard (Scenic Designer)
Carmen Jones 1946,Ap 8,32:2
Make Mine Manhattan 1948,Ja 16,26:2
Short, Jane
Weak Sisters 1925,O 14,31:3
Short, Marcia
Beaux' Stratagem, The 1957,Jl 9,25:4
Short, Marie Ney
Ghosts 1937,N 28,XI,2:1
Short, Marion (Original Author)
Shavings 1920,F 17,18:1
Short, Marion (Playwright)
Golden Days 1921,N 2,20:1
Short, Paul (Scenic Designer)
Dynamite Tonight 1967,Mr 16,52:2

Short, Robin (Playwright)
Last Dance, The 1948,Ja 28,27:2
Short, Roger (Director)
Eh? 1966,O 17,47:1
Short, Seabury T (Mrs)
Nantucket Follies 1927,Jl 30,13:2
Short, Sylvia
Clandestine Marriage, The 1954,O 4,23:2
Clandestine Marriage, The 1954,O 17,II,1:1
Passion of Gross, The 1955,Ja 24,20:2
Carefree Tree, The 1955,O 12,37:2
King Lear 1956,Ja 13,17:1
King Lear 1956,Ja 22,II,1:1
Measure for Measure 1956,Je 29,16:1
Family Reunion, The 1958,O 21,39:1
Beaux' Stratagem, The 1959,F 25,35:4
Golden Apple, The 1962,F 13,38:2
Shorter, Carl
Green Pastures, The 1935,F 27,16:2
Shorter, Del
Make Me Disappear 1969,My 14,34:1
Shortt, Paul (Scenic Designer)
Three Sisters, The 1968,Mr 18,56:1
Shorty and Esalene
Singin' the Blues 1931,S 17,21:3
Shoshana, Rose
House on Grand Street, A 1953,O 10,12:6
Shepherd King, The 1955,O 13,36:2
Brothers Ashkenazi, The 1955,N 12,24:4
In-Laws 1960,O 17,32:4
World Is a Stage, The 1962,N 5,37:4
Country Boy, The 1963,O 28,20:1
Shoshana, Rose (Producer)
World Is a Stage, The 1962,N 5,37:4
Shostac, Percy
Love Is Like That 1927,Ap 19,24:1
Shostakovich, Dmitri (Composer)
Russian People, The 1942,Jl 18,8:2
Hamlet 1954,My 31,9:1
Moskvo Cheremushki 1959,Ja 25,27:7
Shotter, Billie
By the Way 1925,D 29,20:3
Shotwell, Hudson
Romeo and Juliet 1935,D 24,10:2
Saint Joan 1936,Mr 10,27:4
Othello 1937,Ja 7,16:4
Key Largo 1939,N 28,30:2
Shotwell, Judith (Costume Designer)
Black Monday 1962,Mr 7,29:1
Shotwell, Judith (Scenic Designer)
Black Monday 1962,Mr 7,29:1
Shotwell, Marie
School for Scandal, The 1923,Mr 13,19:2
Incubator 1932,N 2,23:3
Shoua, Howard (Costume Designer)
Red White and Blue 1950,O 8,64:5
Shoukhaev (Scenic Designer)
Chauve-Souris 1925,Ja 25,VII,1:1
Shoup, Howard (Sgt) (Costume Designer)
Winged Victory 1943,N 22,24:1
Showalter, David
Knights of Song 1938,O 18,29:2
Showalter, Gordon
Lute Song 1946,F 7,29:2
Showalter, Max
Show Boat 1946,Ja 7,17:2
John Loves Mary 1947,F 5,29:2
Make Mine Manhattan 1948,Ja 16,26:2
Showell, Jill
Just for Love 1968,O 18,40:1
Showell, Jill (Playwright)
Just for Love 1968,O 18,40:1
Shower, Mary
Hamlet 1936,N 11,54:2
Shown, John (Scenic Designer)
Hamlet 1970,O 27,54:2
Rosencrantz and Guildenstern Are Dead
1970,N 19,39:3
Shown, Suzan
Hamlet 1970,O 27,54:2
Rosencrantz and Guildenstern Are Dead
1970,N 19,39:3
Shoztic, Michael
Life Is a Dream 1964,Mr 20,24:1
Shpaisman, Ziporah
Mother's Sabbath Days 1960,N 21,33:2
Backlane Center 1961,N 23,51:1
Eleventh Inheritor, The 1962,N 22,43:5
Shreve, Jerry
Jack Jack 1968,Je 23,74:5
Shreve, Lucy
Hail and Farewell 1923,F 20,12:1
Sylvia 1923,Ap 26,22:1
Crime in the Whistler Room, The 1924,O 10,22:2
Drunkard, The; Fallen Saved, The 1929,D 31,14:6
Shrewsbury, Lillian
What's the Use? 1926,S 7,19:1
Prologue to Glory 1938,Mr 18,22:2
Shrewsbury, Robert
Western Waters 1937,D 29,17:1
Shriner, Herb
Inside U S A 1948,My 1,19:2
Vaudeville (Palace) 1952,Ap 14,23:2

Vaudeville (Palace) 1952,Ap 27,II,1:1
Shrode, Joseph
Three Cheers 1928,O 16,28:1
Shrog, Maurice
Rumpelstiltskin 1948,Mr 15,27:3
Sun and I, The 1949,Mr 21,18:4
She Stoops to Conquer 1949,D 29,21:3
Ah, Wilderness! 1953,F 7,10:6
Montserrat 1961,Ja 9,30:5
Devil's Advocate, The 1961,Mr 10,20:1
Shropshire, Anne
Father, The 1949,Ag 21,II,1:1
Right You Are (If You Think You Are)
1950,Je 29,37:2
Naked 1950,S 7,39:2
Gang's All Here, The 1959,O 2,23:1
Sudden End of Anne Cinquefoil, The
1961,Ja 11,25:2
Trial of Lee Harvey Oswald, The 1967,N 6,64:1
Spiro Who? 1969,My 19,55:1
Shrubb, Albert
Young Visitors, The 1920,N 30,14:1
Macbeth 1921,F 18,16:1
Shryock, Raymond Des
That's That 1924,Ap 30,19:2
Joan of Arkansas 1925,Ap 5,16:1
Sale and a Sailor, A, or Glory! What Price!
1926,Ap 25,30:4
Shryver, Harold
Birds, The 1967,My 7,67:1
Shtok, Zvi (Translator)
Struggle for the Negev 1953,D 14,45:5
Shuartser, Veniamin
Beyond the Ocean 1970,Ag 19,30:1
Shube, Bernard
Roberta 1937,Je 27,II,6:1
Shubert, Eddie
Greenwich Village Follies 1928,Ap 10,32:2
Broadway Nights 1929,Jl 16,23:2
Shubert, Elaine
Casa di Tutti, La; Everybody's Home 1932,D 5,21:4
Shubert, J J (Director)
Century Revue and the Midnight Rounders, The
1920,Jl 13,9:1
Night in Paris, A 1926,Jl 27,15:4
Three Little Girls 1930,Ap 15,29:1
Nina Rosa 1930,S 22,22:5
Student Prince, The 1943,Je 9,16:2
Blossom Time 1943,S 6,21:2
Lady Says Yes, A 1945,Ja 11,18:5
Shubert, J J (Miscellaneous)
Music Hath Charms 1934,D 31,8:2
Anything Goes 1937,Ag 26,24:3
Robin Hood 1944,N 8,28:2
Ti-Coq 1951,F 10,10:2
Shubert, J J (Producer)
Century Review, The 1920,Jl 22,9:5
Vaudeville (Forty-Fourth Street Theatre)
1921,S 20,12:2
Countess Maritza 1926,Mr 30,20:3
Red Robe, The 1928,My 2,18:5
Broadway Nights 1929,Je 23,VIII,2:4
On the Spot 1930,O 30,33:3
Going Gay 1933,Ag 4,18:5
Hold Your Horses 1933,S 26,26:4
Student Prince, The 1936,Jl 12,II,5:2
Rose Marie 1936,Jl 22,22:6
Green Waters 1936,N 5,34:4
Wonderful Night, A; Fledermaus, Die
1937,Jl 14,17:1
Nina Rosa 1937,Ag 26,24:3
Circus Princess, The 1937,Ag 31,26:6
Roberta 1937,S 7,16:4
Show Boat 1938,Je 30,21:1
Sally, Irene and Mary 1938,Jl 5,13:4
Firefly, The 1938,Jl 12,15:4
Off the Record 1940,D 1,63:5
Night of Love 1941,Ja 8,14:2
Johnny on the Spot 1942,Ja 9,24:2
Count Me In 1942,O 9,24:2
Lady Says Yes, A 1945,Ja 11,18:5
Yes, M'Lord 1949,O 5,35:2
Day After Tomorrow 1950,O 27,25:2
Julia, Jake, and Uncle Joe 1961,Ja 30,19:1
Shubert, John (Lyricist)
Music Hath Charms 1934,D 31,8:2
Shubert, John (Miscellaneous)
Hold Your Horses 1933,S 26,26:4
Shubert, John (Playwright)
Music Hath Charms 1934,D 31,8:2
Shubert, Lawrence (Producer)
Congratulations 1929,My 1,28:4
Shubert, Lee (Miscellaneous)
Thief, The 1927,Ap 23,15:2
Peter Ibbetson 1931,Ap 9,30:3
Green Bay Tree, The 1933,O 21,11:5
I Was Waiting for You 1933,N 14,23:3
Ziegfeld Follies 1936,S 15,37:1
Katie Roche 1937,O 4,17:4
Juno and the Paycock 1937,D 7,32:5
Drama at Inish 1937,D 14,33:2
Hellzapoppin 1938,S 23,34:2
Snookie 1941,Je 4,26:2

Shubert, Lee (Miscellaneous)—Cont
Bird in Hand 1942,O 20,24:2
You Touched Me! 1945,S 26,27:2
Ti-Coq 1951,F 10,10:2
Shubert, Lee (Producer)
Vaudeville (Forty-Fourth Street Theatre)
1921,S 20,12:2
Man With a Load of Mischief, The 1925,O 27,20:1
Right Age to Marry, The 1926,F 16,22:3
Countess Maritza 1926,Mr 30,20:3
What Every Woman Knows 1926,Ap 14,20:2
Judge's Husband, The 1926,S 28,31:1
Heaven-Tappers, The 1927,N 9,28:3
And So to Bed 1927,N 10,23:1
Silent House, The 1928,F 8,28:5
Red Robe, The 1928,My 2,18:5
Sign of the Leopard 1928,D 12,34:4
Security 1929,Mr 29,20:1
Bird in Hand 1929,Ap 5,28:2
Love Duel, The 1929,Ap 16,32:3
Broadway Nights 1929,Je 23,VIII,2:4
Rope's End 1929,S 20,34:5
Nigger Rich 1929,S 21,16:7
Thunder in the Air 1929,N 12,34:3
Death Takes a Holiday 1929,D 27,26:4
Topaze 1930,F 13,25:3
Infinite Shoeblack, The 1930,F 18,28:1
Matriarch, The 1930,Mr 19,24:5
Up Pops the Devil 1930,S 2,19:1
Insult 1930,S 16,30:2
Nine Till Six 1930,S 29,17:2
On the Spot 1930,O 30,33:3
Man in Possession, The 1930,N 3,19:1
Scarlet Sister Mary 1930,N 26,19:2
Purity 1930,D 26,18:2
Truth Game, The 1930,D 29,19:1
As You Desire Me 1931,Ja 29,21:2
Wonder Bar, The 1931,Mr 6,26:6
Silent Witness, The 1931,Mr 24,31:5
Melo 1931,Ap 17,26:6
Silent Witness, The 1931,My 10,VIII,3:5
Alison's House 1931,My 12,29:2
Good Companions, The 1931,O 2,31:1
Father, The 1931,O 9,21:1
Barbara's Wedding 1931,O 9,21:1
Cynara 1931,N 3,31:1
Marriage for Three 1931,N 12,30:5
Americana 1932,O 6,19:3
Autumn Crocus 1932,N 21,20:2
Best Sellers 1933,My 4,20:2
Her Man of Wax 1933,O 12,32:3
Ten Minute Alibi 1933,O 18,24:3
Growing Pains 1933,N 24,24:2
First Apple, The 1933,D 28,25:1
No More Ladies 1934,Ja 24,20:3
Spring Freshet 1934,O 5,28:3
Night of January 16 1935,S 17,26:4
Ziegfeld Follies 1936,Ja 31,17:2
Reflected Glory 1936,S 22,30:2
Close Quarters 1937,Ap 18,II,3:5
Show Is On, The 1937,S 20,18:4
Far-Off Hills, The 1937,O 12,30:4
Hooray for What! 1937,D 2,32:5
Between the Devil 1937,D 23,24:5
Show Boat 1938,Je 30,21:1
Sally, Irene and Mary 1938,Jl 5,13:4
I Am Different 1938,Ag 28,IX,2:5
Billy Draws a Horse 1939,D 22,14:5
Boyd's Daughter 1940,O 12,20:2
Return Engagement 1940,N 2,19:2
Wine, Women and Song 1942,S 29,18:3
Count Me In 1942,O 9,24:2
Proof Thro' the Night 1942,D 26,14:2
Yes, M'Lord 1949,O 5,35:2
Shubert, Lynn
Rugged Path, The 1945,N 12,17:2
Shubert, Messrs (Miscellaneous)
Priorities of 1942 1942,Mr 13,23:2
Shubert, Messrs (Producer)
Three Little Girls 1930,Mr 30,VIII,2:7
Ladies All 1930,Jl 20,VIII,2:1
Babes in Toyland 1930,D 22,17:1
Ziegfeld Follies 1943,Ap 2,16:2
Student Prince, The 1943,Je 9,16:2
Blossom Time 1943,S 6,21:2
Dark of the Moon 1945,Mr 15,27:2
Dark of the Moon 1945,Mr 25,II,1:1
Under the Counter 1947,O 4,10:2
Power Without Glory 1948,Ja 14,30:2
My Romance 1948,O 20,38:5
Shubert, Milton (Director)
Green Waters 1936,N 5,34:4
Shubert, Milton (Miscellaneous)
Her Man of Wax 1933,O 12,32:3
First Episode 1934,S 18,18:1
Laburnum Grove 1935,Ja 15,23:5
Shubert, Milton (Producer)
Nina Rosa 1930,My 31,19:3
Eden End 1935,O 22,17:1
Swing Your Lady 1935,N 16,19:4
Case of Clyde Griffiths 1936,Mr 14,10:4
Swing Your Lady 1936,O 19,22:4
Love of Women 1937,D 14,33:2
Bachelor Born 1938,Ja 26,26:3

Shubert, Milton (Producer)—Cont
Dial 'M' for Murder 1952,O 14,41:5
Shubert, Mr (Producer)
Venetian, The 1931,O 11,VIII,4:5
Little Racketeer, The 1931,O 11,VIII,4:7
Marching By 1931,N 15,VIII,4:2
Smiling Faces 1931,D 13,VIII,2:5
Keep Off the Grass 1940,My 5,X,1:6
Night of Love 1940,O 29,32:6
Shubert, Roberta
Endecott and the Red Cross 1968,My 7,50:1
Shubert (Miscellaneous)
New Hellzapoppin, The 1939,D 12,36:4
Shubert (Producer)
Pleasure Bound 1929,F 10,IX,2:1
Nina Rosa 1929,O 27,IX,2:1
Duchess of Chicago, The 1929,N 17,IX,4:1
Only Girl, The 1934,My 22,28:2
My Maryland 1936,Ag 12,14:2
Countess Maritza 1936,Ag 19,18:2
Florodora 1936,Ag 23,II,8:2
Blossom Time 1936,Ag 30,II,5:8
Frederika 1937,F 5,16:5
Maytime 1937,Jl 6,23:4
Gay Divorce 1937,Jl 20,19:4
Student Prince, The 1937,Jl 28,15:1
On Your Toes 1937,Ag 3,21:2
Firefly, The 1937,Ag 4,14:1
Of Thee I Sing 1937,Ag 10,22:3
Gay Divorce 1937,Ag 11,27:2
Anything Goes 1937,Ag 17,23:4
Between the Devil 1937,O 24,XI,2:1
Hooray for What! 1937,N 7,XI,2:4
Three Waltzes 1937,N 15,15:6
Blossom Time 1938,D 27,12:2
Streets of Paris, The 1939,Je 20,25:2
Three After Three 1939,N 25,13:5
Foreigners 1939,D 6,30:2
Laffing Room Only 1944,D 25,15:4
Shuberts, The (Miscellaneous)
Venetian, The 1931,N 2,26:1
Shatter'd Lamp, The 1934,Mr 22,26:3
Come Angel Band 1936,F 19,17:1
Iolanthe 1942,F 24,26:4
Shuberts, The (Producer)
Red Robe, The 1929,Ja 13,VIII,1:1
Street Singer, The 1929,Jl 28,VIII,1:6
Three Little Girls 1930,Ap 15,29:1
Lady Clara 1930,Ap 18,28:7
Dear Love 1930,My 18,VIII,3:1
Artists and Models 1930,Je 11,33:2
Symphony in Two Flats 1930,S 17,30:4
Hello Paris 1930,N 17,29:3
Meet My Sister 1930,D 31,11:1
Modern Virgin, A 1931,My 21,33:4
If I Were You 1931,S 24,21:1
Everybody's Welcome 1931,O 14,26:3
Little Racketeer, The 1932,Ja 19,24:4
Happy Landing 1932,Mr 28,10:5
Smiling Faces 1932,Ag 31,12:3
There's Always Juliet 1932,O 28,23:2
Silent House, The 1932,N 9,28:3
Cyrano de Bergerac 1932,N 13,IX,1:6
Blue Widow, The 1933,Ag 31,20:2
Double Door 1933,S 22,15:5
Ziegfeld Follies 1934,Ja 5,24:3
Bitter Sweet 1934,My 8,28:4
Life Begins at 8:40 1934,Ag 12,IX,1:1
Life Begins at 8:40 1934,Ag 28,24:2
First Episode 1934,S 18,18:1
Music Hath Charms 1934,D 31,8:2
Mid-West 1936,Ja 8,22:4
Show Is On, The 1936,N 9,22:2
Three Waltzes 1937,D 27,10:2
You Never Know 1938,S 22,26:3
Close Quarters 1939,Mr 7,19:2
Keep Off the Grass 1940,My 24,22:6
Walk With Music 1940,Je 5,33:2
Sons o' Fun 1941,D 2,28:2
Green Table, The 1942,Ja 22,12:2
Prodigal Son, The 1942,F 18,22:2
Gondoliers, The 1942,Mr 4,22:3
Keep 'Em Laughing 1942,Ap 25,9:2
Top-Notchers 1942,My 30,8:5
Wind Is Ninety, The 1945,Je 22,12:2
Ryan Girl, The 1945,S 25,28:2
Hidden Horizon 1946,S 20,42:2
Singing Girl, The 1952,Je 4,31:8
Starcross Story, The 1954,Ja 14,25:2
Shuchart, Isidor
Once Upon a Time 1933,S 22,15:1
Shudraka, King (Playwright)
Little Clay Cart, The 1924,D 14,VIII,3:1
Little Clay Cart, The 1953,Jl 1,25:1
Shuffa, Ethel
Jennie 1963,O 18,35:2
Shuffle, Ted (Miscellaneous)
Holiday on Ice 1965,S 2,38:4
Shuffle Along Four, The
Vaudeville (Hippodrome) 1926,My 8,29:2
Shugrue, J Edward (Director)
Timber House 1936,S 21,27:5
Journeyman 1938,Ja 31,14:2

Shugrue, J Edward (Miscellaneous)
200 Were Chosen 1936,N 21,21:1
Shugrue, J Edward (Playwright)
Prelude 1936,Ap 20,17:4
Shull, Leo (Producer)
Virtuous Island, The 1957,Ap 10,39:1
Apollo of Bellac, The 1957,Ap 10,39:1
Shull, Mark
Rosalie 1928,Ja 11,26:3
Shull, Richard B
Wake Up, Darling 1956,My 3,34:2
American Hamburger League, The 1969,S 17,51:1
Minnie's Boys 1970,Mr 27,27:1
Shull, Richard B (Miscellaneous)
Purple Dust 1956,D 28,15:1
Have I Got a Girl for You! 1963,D 3,53:2
Shulman, A (Lyricist)
Light, Lively and Yiddish 1970,O 28,58:1
Shulman, A (Playwright)
Light, Lively and Yiddish 1970,O 28,58:1
Shulman, Alan (Composer)
Chinese Nightingale, The 1934,O 6,20:4
Shulman, Daniel (Playwright)
No Hard Feelings 1965,Ap 5,33:8
Shulman, Itzhak
David's Crown 1948,My 10,26:2
Oedipus Rex 1948,My 24,23:2
Shulman, Joe
Me and Juliet 1953,My 29,17:1
Shulman, Max (Miscellaneous)
All for Love 1949,Ja 24,16:5
Shulman, Max (Playwright)
Barefoot Boy With Cheek 1947,Ap 4,20:2
Tender Trap, The 1954,O 14,37:2
Tender Trap, The 1961,Ag 26,15:1
How Now, Dow Jones 1967,D 8,53:1
Shulskaya, Elizabeth
Three Sisters, The 1923,Ja 30,12:2
Shults, Mae
Technique 1931,My 15,21:1
Mother Sings 1935,N 13,24:1
Shumaker, David (Director)
Three...With Women in Mind; Jeff Chandler 1970,N 28,22:1
Three...With Women in Mind; How a Nice Girl Named Janet Contracted Syphilis 1970,N 28,22:1
Three...With Women in Mind; I Hear It Kissing Me Ladies 1970,N 28,22:1
Shumaker, David (Playwright)
Three...With Women in Mind; Jeff Chandler 1970,N 28,22:1
Three...With Women in Mind; How a Nice Girl Named Janet Contracted Syphilis 1970,N 28,22:1
Shuman, Andrew
Rogues and Vagabonds 1930,My 8,32:5
Shuman, Earl (Lyricist)
Secret Life of Walter Mitty, The 1964,O 27,44:5
Shuman, Lewis
Big Fight, The 1928,S 19,33:1
Shuman, Mort
Jacques Brel Is Alive and Well and Living in Paris 1968,Ja 23,25:2
Jacques Brel Is Alive and Well and Living in Paris 1970,Ja 21,34:1
Jacques Brel Is Alive and Well and Living in Paris 1970,F 15,II,1:1
Shuman, Mort (Lyricist)
Jacques Brel Is Alive and Well and Living in Paris 1968,Ja 23,25:2
Shuman, Mort (Miscellaneous)
Jacques Brel Is Alive and Well and Living in Paris 1970,Ja 21,34:1
Shuman, Mort (Musical Director)
Jacques Brel Is Alive and Well and Living in Paris 1968,Ja 23,25:2
Shuman, Roy
Silver Tassie, The 1949,Jl 22,16:5
Dial 'M' for Murder 1958,F 8,12:2
Henry V 1965,Je 29,27:2
Taming of the Shrew, The 1965,Jl 3,10:5
Shumlin, Diana (Producer)
Rooming House, The 1970,Ja 23,25:1
Transfers 1970,Ja 23,25:1
Dr Galley 1970,Ja 23,25:1
Shumlin, Herman (Director)
Grand Hotel 1930,N 14,30:4
Grand Hotel 1930,N 23,IX,1:1
Clear All Wires! 1932,S 15,19:1
Clear All Wires! 1932,S 25,IX,1:1
Ten Minute Alibi 1933,O 18,24:3
Bride of Torozko, The 1934,Jl 10,24:7
Bride of Torozko, The 1934,S 14,24:2
Children's Hour, The 1934,N 21,23:2
Children's Hour, The 1934,D 2,X,1:1
Sweet Mystery of Life 1935,O 12,13:3
Days to Come 1936,D 16,35:1
Wine of Choice 1938,F 22,18:4
Wine of Choice 1938,F 27,X,1:1
Little Foxes, The 1939,F 16,16:2
Little Foxes, The 1939,F 26,IX,1:1
Male Animal, The 1940,Ja 10,17:2
Male Animal, The 1940,Ja 21,IX,1:1
Passenger to Bali, A 1940,Mr 15,26:2

Shumlin, Herman (Director)—Cont
Corn Is Green, The 1940,N 27,27:2
Corn Is Green, The 1940,D 1,X,1:1
Watch on the Rhine 1941,Ap 2,26:2
Watch on the Rhine 1941,Ap 13,IX,1:1
Watch on the Rhine 1941,Ag 24,IX,1:1
Great Big Doorstep, The 1942,N 27,26:2
Corn Is Green, The 1943,My 4,18:3
Searching Wind, The 1944,Ap 13,25:2
Visitor, The 1944,O 18,24:5
Kiss Them for Me 1945,Mr 21,27:2
Jeb 1946,F 22,20:2
Jeb 1946,Mr 3,II,1:1
Biggest Thief in Town 1949,Mr 31,31:2
Corn Is Green, The 1950,Ja 12,33:2
High Ground, The 1951,F 21,31:2
Lace on Her Petticoat 1951,S 5,40:3
To Dorothy, A Son 1951,N 20,37:2
Gertie 1952,Ja 31,23:1
Candida 1952,Ap 23,23:6
Gambler, The 1952,O 14,40:1
Wedding Breakfast 1954,N 22,29:2
Inherit the Wind 1955,Ap 22,20:2
Inherit the Wind 1955,S 25,II,1:1
Tall Story 1959,Ja 30,33:2
Only in America 1959,N 20,35:1
Little Moon of Alban 1960,D 2,34:1
Dear Me, the Sky Is Falling 1963,Mr 4,9:1
Bicycle Ride to Nevada 1963,S 25,38:1
Deputy, The 1964,F 27,26:1
Spofford 1967,D 15,54:3
Rooming House, The 1970,Ja 23,25:1
Transfers 1970,Ja 23,25:1
Dr Galley 1970,Ja 23,25:1
Shumlin, Herman (Miscellaneous)
Daphne Laureola 1950,S 19,38:6
Shumlin, Herman (Playwright)
Spofford 1967,D 15,54:3
Spofford 1967,D 24,II,3:2
Shumlin, Herman (Producer)
Celebrity 1927,D 27,24:3
Command Performance, The 1928,O 4,27:1
Tonight at 12 1928,N 16,28:1
Button, Button 1929,O 24,26:1
Last Mile, The 1930,F 14,21:2
Grand Hotel 1930,N 14,30:4
Clear All Wires! 1932,S 15,19:1
Bride of Torozko, The 1934,S 14,24:2
Children's Hour, The 1934,N 21,23:2
Sweet Mystery of Life 1935,O 12,13:3
Days to Come 1936,D 16,35:1
Merchant of Yonkers, The 1938,D 29,14:2
Little Foxes, The 1939,F 16,16:2
Male Animal, The 1940,Ja 10,17:2
Corn Is Green, The 1940,N 27,27:2
Corn Is Green, The 1940,D 1,X,1:1
Watch on the Rhine 1941,Mr 25,26:7
Watch on the Rhine 1941,Ap 2,26:2
Great Big Doorstep, The 1942,N 27,26:2
Corn Is Green, The 1943,My 4,18:3
Searching Wind, The 1944,Ap 13,25:2
Visitor, The 1944,O 18,24:5
Jeb 1946,F 22,20:2
Lace on Her Petticoat 1951,S 5,40:3
To Dorothy, A Son 1951,N 20,37:2
Gertie 1952,Ja 31,23:1
Inherit the Wind 1955,Ap 22,20:2
Only in America 1959,N 20,35:1
Bicycle Ride to Nevada 1963,S 25,38:1
Deputy, The 1964,F 27,26:1
Soldiers 1968,My 2,58:1
Transfers 1970,Ja 23,25:1
Dr Galley 1970,Ja 23,25:1
Rooming House, The 1970,Ja 23,25:1
Shumski (Composer)
Lovka Maladetz 1935,Mr 27,25:5
Shumway, Donald
Anna Kleiber 1965,Ja 20,33:1
Masks of Angels 1965,Ja 20,33:1
Shure, Barbara
Years Between, The 1942,F 7,13:2
Shure, Robert (Playwright)
Sourball 1969,Ag 6,29:2
Shurr, Buff
Finian's Rainbow 1953,Mr 7,13:2
Brandy Is My True Love's Name 1953,Je 18,38:5
California 1953,Je 18,38:5
Where There's a Will 1953,Je 18,38:5
Hopalong--Freud 1953,Je 18,38:5
Madam Will You Walk 1953,D 2,2:4
Kiss Me, Kate 1954,Mr 27,13:2
Pimpernel! 1964,Ja 7,26:6
Shurr, Buff (Director)
California 1953,Je 18,38:5
Shurr, Gertrude (Choreographer)
Sojourner Truth 1948,Ap 22,35:2
Shurtleff, Michael (Miscellaneous)
Carousel 1954,Je 3,32:2
King and I, The 1956,Ap 19,35:4
Kiss Me, Kate 1956,My 10,27:2
Carmen Jones 1956,Je 1,28:2
Best House in Naples, The 1956,O 27,16:2
Shadow of My Enemy, A 1957,D 12,35:4

Shurtleff, Michael (Playwright)
Call Me by My Rightful Name 1961,F 1,31:1
Shurtleff, Michael (Producer)
Fledermaus, Die 1954,My 20,38:5
Shust, William
Macbeth 1955,O 8,12:6
Last Love of Don Juan, The 1955,N 24,40:1
Misanthrope, The 1956,N 13,44:1
Trojan Women, The 1957,Mr 19,42:7
Tartuffe 1957,O 9,39:1
Julius Caesar 1959,Ag 4,30:1
Taming of the Shrew, The 1963,Mr 8,9:1
Shuster, Mary
Kai Khosru 1925,Ap 27,14:2
Shute, James
Moon Is a Gong, The 1926,Mr 13,21:3
Shute, James (Scenic Designer)
Trumpet Shall Sound, The 1926,D 11,15:2
Shuter, E Mortimer (Director)
Cotton Stockings 1923,D 19,16:2
Tambourine 1925,D 30,10:2
Front Page Stuff 1926,D 29,24:4
Shuter, E Mortimer (Miscellaneous)
Rainbow's End 1928,D 26,14:6
Shutta, Ethel
Passing Show of 1922, The 1922,S 21,18:2
Marjorie 1924,Ag 12,12:2
Louie the 14th 1925,Mr 4,17:1
Follies 1925,Jl 7,24:3
Whoopee 1928,D 5,34:3
My Dear Public 1943,S 10,28:1
Shutta, George
It Pays to Sin 1933,N 4,18:6
Shutta, Jack
Vaudeville (Loew's State) 1932,O 3,15:5
Shuttleworth, Bertram
Millionairess, The 1952,O 18,17:2
Shuttleworth, W W
Nightcap, The 1921,Ag 16,18:3
Silence 1924,N 13,18:2
Good Fellow, The 1926,O 6,22:1
Praying Curve 1927,Ja 25,18:2
Fog-Bound 1927,Ap 2,21:2
Los Angeles 1927,D 20,32:3
Crashing Through 1928,O 30,26:5
Inside Story, The 1932,F 23,23:2
Marathon 1933,Ja 28,8:8
Undesirable Lady, An 1933,O 10,24:4
Queer People 1934,F 16,16:2
Come What May 1934,My 16,23:4
Nowhere Bound 1935,Ja 23,20:2
Play, Genius, Play! 1935,O 31,17:2
Shvartser, Veniamin (Director)
Beyond the Ocean 1970,Ag 19,30:1
Shvedoff, C (Composer)
Turandot 1929,Ja 12,14:4
Shwarz, Henry
Green Table, The 1942,Ja 22,12:2
Prodigal Son, The 1942,F 18,22:2
Shweid, Mark
Song of Dnieper 1946,O 26,10:5
Shweid, Mark (Translator)
Jealousy 1934,D 20,31:4
Shy, Gus
Lollipop 1924,Ja 22,15:3
Matinee Girl, The 1926,F 2,20:3
Wild Rose, The 1926,O 21,23:1
Good News 1927,S 7,35:4
New Moon, The 1928,S 20,33:1
America's Sweetheart 1931,Ja 25,VIII,2:4
America's Sweetheart 1931,F 11,23:1
Shy, Gus (Choreographer)
Zuider Zee 1928,D 19,24:4
Shy, Gus (Director)
Ballyhoo of 1932 1932,S 7,14:2
Shy, Martha
Book of Job, The 1962,F 10,13:1
Shy, Robert
Book of Job, The 1962,F 10,13:1
Shyre, Paul
Joan of Lorraine 1955,Mr 26,12:2
I Knock at the Door 1956,Mr 19,27:5
Pictures in the Hallway 1956,My 28,23:1
Pictures in the Hallway 1956,S 17,23:2
Pictures in the Hallway 1956,S 23,II,1:1
Purple Dust 1956,D 28,15:1
I Know at the Door 1957,S 30,27:2
Othello 1958,Jl 4,16:1
Cock-A-Doodle Dandy 1958,N 13,39:2
Cock-A-Doodle Dandy 1958,N 23,II,1:1
I Knock at the Door 1964,N 26,53:2
Pictures in the Hallway 1964,D 17,51:1
Shyre, Paul (Director)
This Happy Breed 1952,Ap 4,23:2
U S A 1959,O 29,38:1
Drums Under the Windows 1960,O 14,26:1
Diff'rent 1961,O 18,52:1
Long Voyage Home, The 1961,D 5,49:1
Creditors 1962,Ja 26,19:1
Child Buyer, The 1962,My 14,35:1
Beyond the Horizon 1962,O 26,27:2
Fair Game for Lovers 1964,F 11,43:2
I Knock at the Door 1964,N 26,53:2

Pictures in the Hallway 1964,D 17,51:1
Queen and the Rebels, The 1965,F 26,16:1
Whitman Portrait, A 1966,O 12,37:1
Shyre, Paul (Miscellaneous)
U S A 1956,D 19,41:4
Shyre, Paul (Playwright)
I Knock at the Door 1956,Mr 19,27:5
Pictures in the Hallway 1956,My 28,23:1
Pictures in the Hallway 1956,S 17,23:2
I Know at the Door 1957,S 30,27:2
U S A 1959,O 29,38:1
U S A 1959,N 8,II,1:1
Drums Under the Windows 1960,O 14,26:1
Creditors 1962,Ja 26,19:1
Child Buyer, The 1962,My 14,35:1
I Knock at the Door 1964,N 26,53:2
Pictures in the Hallway 1964,D 17,51:1
Child Buyer, The 1964,D 22,35:1
Whitman Portrait, A 1966,O 12,37:1
Shyre, Paul (Producer)
I Knock at the Door 1956,Mr 19,27:5
Pictures in the Hallway 1956,My 28,23:1
Purple Dust 1956,D 28,15:1
I Know at the Door 1957,S 30,27:2
Cock-A-Doodle Dandy 1958,N 13,39:2
Cock-A-Doodle Dandy 1958,N 23,II,1:1
Sibelius, Jean (Composer)
Lady From the Sea, The 1935,D 14,11:3
Tempest, The 1955,S 3,8:6
Life Is a Dream 1962,Ja 15,22:3
Sibello, Tino
Tia Juana 1927,N 16,28:4
Siblot
Roi Dagobert, Le 1926,N 14,VIII,2:1
Sica, Carol
Here Be Dragons 1970,D 21,52:1
Sica, Joy Lynne
On the Town 1959,F 14,15:1
Fallout 1959,My 21,36:2
Sica, Lina
Ora di Diana, L' 1937,My 17,22:3
Sicari, Joseph R
Parasite, The 1965,D 17,43:2
Comedy of Errors, The 1967,Je 15,58:4
Love and Let Love 1968,Ja 4,30:1
Henry IV, Part II 1968,Jl 2,33:1
Dames at Sea 1968,D 21,46:1
Dames at Sea 1970,Ja 5,46:3
Siccama, Ellen
On an Open Roof 1963,Ja 30,7:3
Sidimus, Joyce Anne
Commedia Dell' Arte 1957,Jl 5,13:2
Sidlauskas, Francis W (Producer)
Seven Scenes for Yeni 1963,My 13,36:2
Sidman, Alice Fleming (Playwright)
Blind Alleys 1924,N 18,23:3
Sidman, Sam
Humoresque 1923,F 28,13:2
Antonia 1925,O 21,20:1
Just a Minute 1928,O 9,34:3
Potash and Perlmutter 1935,Ap 6,11:3
For Valor 1935,N 19,27:5
Lady Luck 1936,Ap 16,21:2
Sidney, Andrey
Waltz of the Dogs, The 1928,Ap 26,31:3
Sidney, Carl (Costume Designer)
Illustrators' Show, The 1936,Ja 23,25:3
Sidney, Charles
Blue Jeans 1933,Ap 9,31:5
Sidney, Clara
One 1920,S 15,12:2
Merton of the Movies 1922,N 14,16:2
Sidney, D Jay
Green Pastures, The 1935,F 27,16:2
Sidney, E
Cradle Will Rock, The 1937,D 6,19:4
Sidney, George
Welcome Stranger 1920,S 14,12:1
Give and Take 1923,Ja 19,13:1
Vaudeville (Palace) 1928,My 15,17:1
Window Shopping 1938,D 24,13:2
Sidney, Howard
19th Hole, The 1927,O 12,30:3
Sidney, James
Ten Million Ghosts 1936,O 24,23:7
Sidney, Jean
Big Fight, The 1928,S 19,33:1
Street Scene 1929,Ja 11,20:4
Sidney, Jess
Transplanting Jean 1921,Ja 4,11:2
Jane-Our Stranger 1925,O 9,27:2
Machinal 1928,S 8,10:3
Broken Chain, The 1929,F 21,30:4
Playboy of the Western World, The 1930,Ja 3,20:4
General John Regan 1930,Ja 30,16:5
Sidney, P Jay
Androcles and the Lion 1938,D 17,10:5
Big White Fog 1940,O 23,26:2
Run, Little Chillun 1943,Ag 14,6:1
Carmen Jones 1943,D 3,26:2
Jeb 1946,F 22,20:2
Don't Go Away Mad 1949,My 10,28:2
Twentieth Century 1950,D 25,23:6

Sidney, P Jay—Cont
Winner, The 1954,F 18,34:1
Cool World, The 1960,F 23,38:2
Octoroon, The 1961,Ja 28,13:1
Playroom, The 1965,D 6,49:1
Sidney, Robert
On Your Toes 1936,Ap 13,14:4
This Is the Army 1942,Jl 5,28:2
Sidney, Robert (Choreographer)
Three to Make Ready 1946,Mr 8,16:2
Toplitzky of Notre Dame 1946,D 27,13:4
Along Fifth Avenue 1949,Ja 14,28:2
Dance Me a Song 1950,Ja 21,10:5
Sidney, Robert (Director)
Cocktails of 1934 1934,My 5,22:1
Along Fifth Avenue 1949,Ja 14,28:2
Sidney, Sylvia
Prunella; Love in a Garden 1926,Je 16,23:3
Crime 1927,F 23,27:3
Mirrors 1928,Ja 19,17:1
Gods of the Lightning 1928,O 25,27:2
Nice Women 1929,Je 11,27:4
Cross Roads 1929,N 12,34:2
Many a Slip 1930,F 4,29:2
Bad Girl 1930,O 3,30:2
To Quito and Back 1937,S 21,29:1
To Quito and Back 1937,S 26,XI,3:6
To Quito and Back 1937,O 7,30:4
Gentle People, The 1939,Ja 6,25:1
Sarah Adler Testimonial 1939,Mr 15,18:2
Very Special Baby, A 1956,N 15,43:2
Auntie Mame 1958,Ag 12,33:2
Enter Laughing 1963,Mr 15,8:1
Enter Laughing 1963,Je 16,II,1:1
All My Pretty Little Ones 1964,F 5,30:1
Damn You, Scarlett O'Hara 1964,F 5,30:1
She Stoops to Conquer 1968,Ap 1,58:3
Sidney, Sylvia (Miscellaneous)
Auntie Mame 1958,Ag 12,33:2
Siebert, Charles
Richard III 1966,Ag 11,26:1
Galileo 1967,Ap 14,31:1
Love's Labour's Lost 1968,Je 28,36:1
Jimmy Shine 1968,D 6,52:1
Colette 1970,My 17,II,1:1
Gingerbread Lady, The 1970,D 14,58:3
Sieburg, George
Squaring the Circle 1936,Ag 12,15:3
Siedel, Ehrhardt
Journey's End 1929,S 22,IX,4:1
Siedhoff, Joost
Nathan der Weise 1966,D 10,45:2
Minna von Barnhelm 1968,N 13,37:1
Schloss, Das 1968,N 20,35:3
Amphitryon 1970,N 18,40:1
Kurve, Die 1970,N 25,25:1
Siedhoff, Thomas (Director)
Amphitryon 1970,N 18,40:1
Kleinburgerhochzeit, Die 1970,N 25,25:1
Kurve, Die 1970,N 25,25:1
Siegal, Al
Vaudeville (Palace) 1930,S 15,29:2
Girl Crazy 1930,O 15,27:1
Wonder Bar, The 1931,Mr 18,23:4
Siegal, Frances
Medea 1965,N 29,46:1
Siegal, Mordecai (Producer)
Seven at Dawn, The 1961,Ap 18,43:1
Siegal, Mort
House Remembered, A 1957,F 7,20:2
Siegal, Mort (Miscellaneous)
Machinal 1960,Ap 8,27:1
Siegel, Arthur
Lovely Me 1946,D 26,30:4
Siegel, Arthur (Composer)
New Faces of 1952 1952,My 17,23:2
New Faces of 1952 1952,My 25,II,1:1
Shoestring Revue 1955,Mr 1,22:2
New Faces of 1956 1956,Je 15,32:1
Mask and Gown 1957,S 11,29:1
Not While I'm Eating 1961,D 20,37:1
New Faces of 1962 1962,F 2,25:1
Cats' Pajamas, The 1962,Je 1,16:2
Leonard Sillman's New Faces of 1968
   1968,My 3,43:1
American Hamburger League, The 1969,S 17,51:1
Siegel, Arthur (Lyricist)
New Faces of 1952 1952,My 17,23:2
New Faces of 1956 1956,Je 15,32:1
Mask and Gown 1957,S 11,29:1
New Faces of 1962 1962,F 2,25:1
Cats' Pajamas, The 1962,Je 1,16:2
Leonard Sillman's New Faces of 1968
   1968,My 3,43:1
Siegel, Arthur (Miscellaneous)
Lovely Me 1946,D 26,30:4
Laughs and Other Events 1960,O 11,57:1
Siegel, Arthur (Musical Director)
Cats' Pajamas, The 1962,Je 1,16:2
Siegel, Benjamin
Rosalinda; Fledermaus, Die 1942,O 29,26:5
Siegel, Charles
Does a Tiger Wear a Necktie? 1967,F 4,17:1
Crimes and Crimes 1970,Ja 19,35:1

Siegel, David W (Producer)
Blackouts of 1949 1949,S 7,39:2
Siegel, Eli
Brooklyn, U S A 1941,D 22,24:2
Siegel, Joseph S (Producer)
World War 2 1/2 1969,Mr 25,40:1
Siegel, Larry (Lyricist)
Mad Show, The 1966,Ja 10,16:1
Siegel, Larry (Playwright)
Mad Show, The 1966,Ja 10,16:1
Siegel, Larry (Scenic Designer)
Softly, and Consider the Nearness 1964,My 12,32:1
Home Movies 1964,My 12,32:1
Siegel, Marilyn
Hide and Seek 1957,Ap 3,26:1
Music Man, The 1957,D 20,31:1
Music Man, The 1958,S 28,II,1:1
Siegel, Martin
Drums in the Night 1967,My 18,54:1
Siegel, Max (Playwright)
We Americans 1926,O 13,20:4
Siegel, Max (Producer)
My Fair Ladies 1941,Mr 24,12:7
Three's a Family 1943,My 6,24:2
Siegel, Mort (Miscellaneous)
Romeo and Juliet 1965,Je 21,36:3
Siegel, Morton (Director)
Lulu; Earth Spirit 1970,Mr 28,32:1
Siegel, Sanford
Danton's Death 1938,N 3,26:2
Siegel, William (Costume Designer)
Bublitchki 1938,Ja 17,11:2
Siegel, William (Playwright)
Jolly Orphan, The 1929,D 23,18:6
Little Clown, The 1930,Mr 15,23:3
Village Wedding, A 1930,S 24,26:2
My Little Girl 1931,F 2,22:4
Night in the Woods, A 1931,Mr 2,19:3
Lucky Night, The 1931,S 14,15:5
Rich Paupers 1932,Mr 14,13:4
Song of the Ghetto, The 1932,O 3,15:5
Honeymoon for Three, A 1933,Ja 30,9:6
Happy Family, A 1934,S 24,15:2
What Girls Do 1935,Ja 14,10:4
East Side Wedding, An 1935,Ja 21,18:2
Itche Mayer of Warsaw 1935,Ja 31,22:4
Heaven on Earth 1935,O 8,26:2
Girls of Today 1935,N 20,26:5
Lucky Boy 1935,D 2,19:5
Souls for Sale 1936,S 21,27:6
Night in Budapest, A 1936,N 3,33:2
Let's Get Married 1937,Ja 11,16:2
Sins of Mothers 1937,Mr 30,20:2
My Malkele 1937,S 20,18:6
Warson at Night 1938,Ja 31,14:3
My Baby's Wedding 1938,O 10,15:3
Long Live America 1939,Ja 2,28:3
Polish Rabbi, The 1939,Mr 20,13:3
Her Great Mistake 1940,F 5,12:6
Wish Me Luck! 1954,N 1,37:2
Wedding March, The 1955,O 17,33:1
My Wife With Conditions 1963,O 21,39:1
Siegl, D
Penny Change 1963,O 25,37:1
Siegle, Larry
Lady in the Dark 1941,Ja 24,14:2
Siegle, Lawrence
Devil and Daniel Webster, The 1939,My 19,26:1
Siegler, Ivy
Greenwillow 1970,D 8,60:1
Siegmeister, Elie (Composer)
Maid in Japan 1939,F 20,12:5
Doodle Dandy of the U S A 1942,O 19,15:2
Sleepy Hollow 1948,Je 4,26:3
Siegmeister, Elie (Miscellaneous)
Sing Out, Sweet Land! 1944,D 28,24:2
Carnival in Flanders 1953,S 9,38:2
Kean 1961,N 3,28:2
Siemaszkowska
Women's House, The 1930,Ap 27,IX,3:1
Siemers, Friedrich
Ides of March, The 1962,N 17,16:4
Sienkiewicz, Henry (Original Author)
Quo Vadis 1932,O 17,18:2
Siepi, Cesare
Bravo Giovanni 1962,My 21,41:2
Bravo Giovanni 1962,My 27,II,1:1
Sierra, G Martinez (Original Author)
Spring in Autumn 1933,O 25,22:5
Sierra, G Martinez (Playwright)
Cradle Song 1921,Mr 1,18:2
Cradle Song 1926,N 21,VIII,4:1
Cradle Song 1927,Ja 25,18:2
Road to Happiness, The 1927,My 3,24:1
Romantic Young Lady, The 1927,My 5,30:2
Blind Heart, The 1927,My 8,30:2
Fragila Rosina 1927,My 10,24:4
Cradle Song 1927,My 10,24:4
Kingdom of God, The 1927,N 20,IX,2:7
Kingdom of God, The 1928,O 14,X,1:3
Kingdom of God, The 1928,D 21,30:2
Kingdom of God, The 1928,D 30,VIII,1:1
Mama 1930,Mr 30,VIII,4:8

Madame Pepita 1931,Mr 7,17:1
Take Two From One 1931,O 4,VIII,2:6
Two Shepherds, The 1935,F 12,25:4
Cradle Song 1936,Je 7,IX,1:1
Holy Night 1936,D 24,20:2
Cradle Song 1955,D 2,32:2
Sierra, Gregory
Measure for Measure 1966,Jl 14,27:1
King John 1967,Jl 14,19:1
Endecott and the Red Cross 1968,My 7,50:1
Que Vida de Perro 1968,Ag 2,24:1
Sierra, Manuel (Costume Designer)
Britannicus 1958,N 29,17:2
Sierra, Marie Martinez (Playwright)
Cradle Song 1927,Ja 25,18:2
Mama 1930,Mr 30,VIII,4:8
Take Two From One 1931,O 4,VIII,2:6
Cradle Song 1955,D 2,32:2
Sieveking, Alejandro (Playwright)
Remolienda, La; Bawdy Party 1968,F 3,20:1
Sievers, David
Any Day Now 1941,Je 10,28:2
Criminals, The 1941,D 22,24:3
Sievers, Harry F
Bombo 1921,O 7,20:2
Betty Lee 1924,D 26,18:2
Siff, Andrew (Producer)
Family Affair, A 1962,Ja 29,17:1
Sifton, Claire (Playwright)
In the Meantime 1930,D 7,IX,1:6
Midnight 1930,D 30,25:1
1931 1931,D 11,34:3
1931- 1931,D 20,VIII,1:1
Blood on the Moon 1934,S 30,IX,3:1
Sifton, Paul (Playwright)
Belt, The 1927,O 20,33:1
In the Meantime 1930,D 7,IX,1:6
Midnight 1930,D 30,25:1
1931 1931,D 11,34:3
1931- 1931,D 20,VIII,1:1
Blood on the Moon 1934,S 30,IX,3:1
Sigaloff, Eugene
Tenth Commandment, The 1926,N 18,27:1
Clear All Wires! 1932,S 15,19:1
Clear All Wires! 1932,S 25,IX,1:1
Body Beautiful, The 1935,N 1,24:3
Leave It to Me! 1938,N 10,32:2
Stranger, The 1945,F 13,21:2
Sigaux, Gilbert (Translator)
Hedda Gabler 1962,D 13,8:5
Sigel, David
Tragical Historie of Doctor Faustus, The
1964,O 6,34:2
Sigel, Michael
Sunny River 1941,D 5,28:2
Siggins, Jeff
Impossible Years, The 1965,O 14,55:1
Pousse-Cafe 1966,Mr 19,19:2
Biscuit 1966,My 17,51:2
Keep It in the Family 1967,S 28,59:1
Sigler, Victor
Is Zat So? 1925,Ap 25,18:2
Sigman, Carl (Composer)
Angel in the Wings 1947,D 12,36:4
Sigman, Carl (Lyricist)
Angel in the Wings 1947,D 12,36:4
Sigmond, Ainsley
Kwamina 1961,O 24,42:1
Signore, Don (Director)
Now You See It 1967,N 20,59:1
Beclch 1968,D 17,59:1
Signorelli, John (Miscellaneous)
Second Time Around, The 1962,Ap 21,14:1
Signoret, Gabriel
Locus Solus 1922,D 9,11:4
Moulin de la Galette, Le 1923,Ja 28,VII,2:7
Homme Qui Jouait du Banjo, L' 1926,O 24,VIII,2:1
Vacances de Paques, Les 1927,Ja 2,VII,2:1
Sexe Fort, Le 1927,F 13,VII,4:1
Mauvais Ange, Le 1927,Je 5,VII,2:1
Robe de Perles, La 1928,Ja 15,VIII,2:3
Je T'Attendais 1929,Ja 20,VIII,1:8
Avare, L' 1930,F 2,VIII,4:1
Signoret, Simone
Little Foxes, The 1962,D 6,56:1
Signoret, Simone (Miscellaneous)
Little Foxes, The 1962,D 6,56:1
Signoret (Director)
Robe de Perles, La 1928,Ja 15,VIII,2:3
Sigrist, Susan
Most Happy Fella, The 1966,My 12,55:1
Siguard, John (Producer)
Snookie 1941,Je 4,26:2
Sigurjonsson, Johann (Playwright)
Eyvind of the Hills 1921,F 2,14:1
Sigyn
Gay Divorce 1960,Ap 4,37:1
Sikelianos, Algelos (Producer)
Prometheus Unbound 1927,My 29,VII,6:7
Sikola, Zdenek (Composer)
Pierrot's Journey 1964,Ag 5,23:1
Sikora, Morris
Low Bridge 1933,F 10,13:4

Sil-Vara (Playwright)
Caprice 1929,Ja 1,61:1
Caprice 1929,Ja 13,VIII,1:1
Sila, Silva
Casa di Tutti, La; Everybody's Home 1932,D 5,21:4
Curioso Accidente, Un 1933,Mr 6,16:3
Romanticismo 1933,My 1,10:5
Silber, Don
Hamp 1967,Mr 10,32:1
Glorious Ruler, The 1969,Jl 1,31:1
Silberberg, Joseph
Enchanting Melody 1964,N 25,40:1
Silberberg, Sara
Jim Cooperkop 1930,O 18,23:1
Silberkasten, Morris
Tenth Commandment, The 1926,N 18,27:1
Gardener's Dog, The 1927,O 21,27:1
Gold Diggers, The 1927,D 3,19:2
On Foreign Soil 1927,D 24,8:2
Alexander Pushkin 1928,Ja 27,14:2
Major Noah 1929,F 23,17:2
Stempenu, the Fiddler 1929,Mr 9,24:7
Hello Grandpa! 1931,Ja 2,25:3
Women of New York 1931,Mr 23,24:3
Chayim Lederer 1932,N 15,24:4
Revolt 1933,Ja 12,21:3
Jacques Bergson 1936,O 31,24:6
Water Carrier, The 1936,D 25,20:2
Borderline 1937,F 10,18:6
Yoshe Kalb 1939,F 6,9:2
Silberman, David (Producer)
What Big Ears! 1942,Ap 21,18:5
R U R 1942,D 4,30:2
Silberman, David Jr (Producer)
Not While I'm Eating 1961,D 20,37:1
Silberman, Jerry
Twelfth Night 1959,Jl 11,10:2
Silbersher, Marvin
Once There Was a Russian 1961,F 20,32:2
Silberstein, Ira (Lighting Director)
Revolt of the Beavers, The 1937,My 21,19:2
Treasure Island 1938,My 15,II,2:3
Silberstein, Morris
Women of New York 1931,Mr 23,24:3
Silbert, Jacob
Three in Love 1931,S 26,25:5
Silbert, Lisa
Mendel, Inc 1929,N 26,28:5
Humpty Dumpty 1932,S 18,IX,2:1
Murder at the Vanities 1933,S 13,22:4
God Man and Devil 1935,Mr 62,22:3
Yoina Seeks a Bride 1936,O 20,31:1
In a Jewish Grocery 1939,O 2,15:2
Silcox, C E
Little Theatre Tournament; Shall We Join the
Ladies? 1929,My 9,34:3
Shall We Join the Ladies? 1929,My 12,28:3
Siler, Cinda
Elizabeth the Queen 1966,N 4,30:1
Siletti, Mario
Cena Delle Beffe, La; Jest, The 1930,N 24,26:4
Cardinale, Il; Cardinal, The 1931,Ja 12,24:2
Sansone; Samson 1931,F 9,25:1
Marchese di Priola, Il 1931,Mr 2,19:3
Arzigogolo, L'; Whim, The 1931,Ap 27,24:4
Alba, Il Gioro, La Notte, L'; Dawn, the Day, the
Night, The 1931,My 18,21:4
Giuochi di Prestigio 1931,N 2,26:1
Berretto a Songali, Il; Cap With Bells, The
1931,N 30,16:3
Piccolo Santo, Il; Little Saint, The 1931,D 14,16:4
Civil Death, The 1932,Ja 25,20:3
Ladro, Il; Thief, The 1932,F 22,23:4
T'Amo E Sarai Mia; I Love You and You'll Be
Mine 1932,Mr 21,19:4
Canto Della Vita, Il; Song of Life, The
1932,Ap 4,13:3
Casa di Tutti, La; Everybody's Home 1932,D 5,21:4
Cardinale, Il 1933,Ja 9,24:2
Istruttoria, L'; Judicial Inquiry, The 1933,F 13,11:3
Curioso Accidente, Un 1933,Mr 6,16:3
Romanticismo 1933,My 1,10:5
Liane, Le (Ties That Bind) 1933,Je 12,20:3
Promessi Sposi I,; Betrothed, The 1934,O 22,13:2
Safari! 1955,My 12,32:6
Out of This World 1955,N 10,44:2
Queen After Death 1956,Mr 13,33:2
Little Mary Sunshine 1959,N 19,49:3
Little Mary Sunshine 1959,N 29,II,1:1
Alchemist, The 1964,S 15,33:1
Siletti, Mario (Director)
Promessi Sposi I,; Betrothed, The 1934,O 22,13:2
Redemptor, The 1959,My 5,40:1
What Did You Say "What" For? 1959,My 5,40:1
Silich, L N (Scenic Designer)
Cherry Orchard, The 1965,F 10,46:1
Silju, Eigil
Julia, Jake, and Uncle Joe 1961,Ja 30,19:1
Silju, Erik
Goa 1968,F 23,46:1
Silk, Morton
Nights of Wrath; Nuits de la Colere, Les
1947,D 1,26:4

Sill, Alfreda
Broadway Shadows 1930,Ap 1,34:6
Native Ground 1937,Mr 24,28:4
Silliman, Maureen
Lend an Ear 1969,O 29,32:1
Sillings, John (Director)
Sound of Silence, A 1965,Mr 9,30:1
Sillman, June
Who's Who 1938,Mr 2,16:2
Sillman, June (Composer)
Fools Rush In 1934,D 26,19:2
All in Fun 1940,D 28,11:2
Sillman, June (Lyricist)
New Faces 1934,Mr 16,24:5
Fools Rush In 1934,D 26,19:2
New Faces of 1936 1936,My 20,24:5
Who's Who 1938,Mr 2,16:2
All in Fun 1940,D 28,11:2
Sillman, June (Playwright)
New Faces 1934,Mr 16,24:5
Sillman, Leonard
Merry-Go-Round 1927,Je 1,25:4
Vaudeville (Palace) 1928,Ag 28,27:3
New Faces 1934,Mr 16,24:5
Fools Rush In 1934,D 26,19:2
Ugly Runts, The 1935,Je 11,24:4
All in Fun 1940,N 22,26:2
New Faces of 1943 1942,D 23,22:2
Leonard Sillman's New Faces of 1968
1968,My 3,43:1
Madwoman of Chaillot, The 1970,Mr 23,48:3
Sillman, Leonard (Director)
New Faces 1934,Mr 16,24:5
Fools Rush In 1934,D 26,19:2
New Faces of 1936 1936,My 20,24:5
Who's Who 1938,Mr 2,16:2
Journey's End 1939,S 19,29:2
All in Fun 1940,D 28,11:2
Mask and Gown 1957,S 11,29:1
New Faces of 1962 1962,F 2,25:1
Leonard Sillman's New Faces of 1968
1968,My 3,43:1
New Faces of 1968 1968,My 12,II,7:1
Sillman, Leonard (Miscellaneous)
Who's Who 1938,Mr 2,16:2
New Faces of 1956 1956,Je 15,32:1
Leonard Sillman's New Faces of 1968
1968,My 3,43:1
Sillman, Leonard (Playwright)
New Faces 1934,Mr 16,24:5
Who's Who 1938,Mr 2,16:2
Mask and Gown 1957,S 11,29:1
Sillman, Leonard (Producer)
New Faces of 1936 1936,My 20,24:5
Journey's End 1939,S 19,29:2
Journey's End 1939,S 24,IX,1:1
They Knew What They Wanted 1939,O 3,19:1
All in Fun 1940,D 28,11:2
New Faces of 1943 1942,D 23,22:2
If the Shoe Fits 1946,D 6,29:4
Happy as Larry 1950,Ja 7,11:2
New Faces of 1952 1952,My 17,23:2
Mrs Patterson 1954,D 2,37:1
New Faces of 1956 1956,Je 15,32:1
Mask and Gown 1957,S 11,29:1
Miss Isobel 1957,D 27,22:1
Second String, A 1960,Ap 14,36:2
Family Way, The 1965,Ja 14,44:5
American Hamburger League, The 1969,S 17,51:1
Madwoman of Chaillot, The 1970,Mr 23,48:3
Hay Fever 1970,N 10,55:1
Silloway, Frank Fayette
This Mad Whirl 1937,Ja 10,II,4:8
Sills, Frank
Just Fancy! 1927,O 12,30:2
Sills, Paul (Director)
From the Second City 1961,S 27,32:1
Open Season at Second City 1964,Ja 23,25:1
Dynamite Tonight 1964,Mr 16,36:2
Dynamite Tonight 1967,Mr 16,52:2
Story Theater 1970,O 27,54:1
Story Theater 1970,N 8,II,1:1
Sills, Paul (Playwright)
Story Theater 1970,O 27,54:1
Sills, Paul (Producer)
From the Second City 1961,S 27,32:1
Sills, Pawnee
Raisin' Hell in the Son 1962,Jl 3,13:2
Electra 1969,Ag 8,14:1
Sills, Stephanie (Miscellaneous)
Exception and the Rule, The 1965,My 21,19:1
Prodigal Son, The 1965,My 21,19:1
Sills, Stephanie (Producer)
Lovers and Other Strangers 1968,S 19,63:1
Exchange 1970,F 9,47:2
Sillward, Edward
Tarzan of the Apes 1921,S 8,14:3
Silman, Joseph
Chivalry 1925,D 16,22:3
Silo, Jon
Springtime Folly 1951,F 27,23:4
Can-Can 1953,My 8,28:1
Passion of Josef D, The 1964,F 12,29:1

Tenth Man, The 1967,N 9,54:1
Silon, Carole
Caution: A Love Story 1969,Ap 4,45:1
Silone, Ignazio (Original Author)
Bitter Stream 1936,Mr 31,16:6
Silton, Charlotte
Girls in Uniform 1932,D 31,10:3
Blue Jeans 1933,Ap 9,31:5
Hate Planters 1933,My 26,24:5
Silva, Henry
Camino Real 1953,Mr 20,26:1
Hatful of Rain, A 1955,N 10,44:1
Hatful of Rain, A 1955,D 4,II,1:1
Silva, Hernando (Producer)
Leyenda del Beso, La 1942,N 20,26:4
Silva, Nino (Musical Director)
Darwin's Theories 1960,O 19,53:2
Silva, R (Playwright)
Affaire, Une 1931,D 13,VIII,2:2
Silveira, Mary
Venetian Glass Nephew, The 1931,F 24,26:3
Silver
Dance Me a Song 1950,Ja 21,10:5
Silver, Abner (Composer)
Song Writer, The 1928,Ag 14,15:2
Lew Leslie's Blackbirds of 1939 1939,F 13,12:2
Silver, Abner (Lyricist)
Song Writer, The 1928,Ag 14,15:2
Lew Leslie's Blackbirds of 1939 1939,F 13,12:2
Silver, Alma
Blue Butterfly, The 1929,F 17,29:3
Blue Butterfly, The 1929,My 4,17:2
Silver, Beau
Camino Real 1960,My 17,42:2
Silver, Borah
Penny Change 1963,O 25,37:1
Silver, Fred (Miscellaneous)
Fun City 1968,Mr 7,53:2
Silver, H Richard (Producer)
Ever Since Paradise 1957,Jl 12,18:4
Silver, Helen
Vamp, The 1955,N 11,30:1
Body Beautiful, The 1958,Ja 24,15:2
Silver, Ira
Precedent 1931,Ap 15,24:5
Silver, Joe
Annie Get Your Gun 1957,Mr 9,15:5
Nature's Way 1957,O 17,42:2
Gypsy 1959,My 22,31:6
O Marry Me 1961,O 28,13:1
Heroine, The 1963,F 21,5:5
Zulu and the Zayda, The 1965,N 11,59:1
You Know I Can't Hear You When the Water's
Running; Shock of Recognition, The
1967,Mr 14,54:1
Silver, Johnny
Guys and Dolls 1950,N 25,11:2
Guys and Dolls 1951,O 7,II,1:1
Silver, Joseph
Tobacco Road 1942,S 7,34:2
Heads or Tails 1947,My 3,10:6
Lamp at Midnight 1947,D 22,29:2
Victors, The 1948,D 27,17:2
Blood Wedding 1949,F 7,16:2
Sun and I, The 1949,Mr 21,18:4
Silver, Milton
Cherry Pie 1926,Ap 15,24:4
Silver, Milton (Playwright)
Mystery Ship, The 1927,Mr 15,28:2
Silver, Paul (Playwright)
Power and Glory 1938,My 1,X,2:5
Silver, Raphael (Producer)
Soldiers 1968,My 2,58:1
Silver, Reuben (Director)
Bless the Child 1968,My 5,II,16:1
Silver, Richard
Set My People Free 1948,N 4,38:2
Silver, Walter (Lighting Director)
Macbeth 1955,O 20,42:2
Midsummer Night's Dream, A 1956,Ja 14,12:2
Romeo and Juliet 1956,F 24,20:4
Silver, Zachary
Twisting Road, The; Jewel of the South, The
1957,N 18,36:5
Silvera, Frank
Anna Lucasta 1947,O 30,31:3
Camino Real 1953,Mr 20,26:1
Camino Real 1953,Mr 29,II,1:1
Mademoiselle Colombe 1954,Ja 7,26:1
Saint Joan 1954,S 18,12:1
Skin of Our Teeth, The 1955,Ag 18,16:1
Hatful of Rain, A 1955,N 10,44:1
Hatful of Rain, A 1955,D 4,II,1:1
For the Time Being 1957,D 18,42:7
Jane Eyre 1958,My 2,31:1
Semi-Detached 1960,Mr 11,20:2
King Lear 1962,Ag 14,35:1
Lady of the Camellias, The 1963,Mr 22,7:1
Amen Corner, The 1965,Ap 16,35:1
Amen Corner, The 1965,Ap 25,II,1:2
Silvera, Frank (Director)
Juno and the Paycock 1955,F 24,20:4
Amen Corner, The 1965,Ap 16,35:1

Silverberg, Sam
Aristocrats 1935,My 2,16:2
Silverberg, Sam (Producer)
Noontide 1961,Je 2,37:1
Silverberg, Sarah
Uriel Acosta 1939,D 31,18:3
Silverbush, Sam
Gods of the Lightning 1928,O 25,27:2
Mr Samuel 1930,N 11,28:4
Silverini, Armando
Rugantino 1964,F 7,34:1
Silverman, Ann (Costume Designer)
Stage Affair, A 1962,Ja 17,30:2
Silverman, Bill (Miscellaneous)
Burning Bright 1959,O 17,27:2
Silverman, Ernest (Playwright)
Sappho 1960,Ja 12,22:1
Silverman, Hy (Miscellaneous)
Burning, The 1963,D 4,57:1
Silverman, Hy (Producer)
Walk in Dark Places, A 1966,Ja 28,21:1
Better Luck Next Time 1966,Ja 28,21:1
Silverman, Jack H (Producer)
13 Daughters 1961,Mr 3,17:2
Silverman, Jerry
Rivalry, The 1959,F 9,24:2
Silverman, Jerry (Miscellaneous)
Laughs and Other Events 1960,O 11,57:1
Silverman, Maxwell (Producer)
Dumbbell People in a Barbell World 1962,F 15,25:1
Play That on Your Old Piano 1965,O 15,49:1
Silverman, Morton S
Purple Canary, The 1963,Ap 23,31:1
Burn Me to Ashes 1963,N 20,48:1
Silverman, Ruth
Mighty Nimrod, The 1931,My 13,23:1
Silverman, Stanley (Composer)
Golden Six, The 1958,O 27,31:2
Country Wife, The 1965,D 10,58:2
Yerma 1966,D 9,60:1
Richard III 1967,Je 14,43:1
Saint Joan 1968,Ja 5,42:1
Tiger at the Gates 1968,Mr 1,30:1
Midsummer Night's Dream, A 1968,Je 13,54:1
Beggar on Horseback 1970,My 15,47:2
Beggar on Horseback 1970,My 24,II,1:1
School for Scandal, The 1970,Je 11,51:1
Silverman, Stanley (Miscellaneous)
Galileo 1967,Ap 14,31:1
Silverman, Stanley (Musical Director)
Caucasian Chalk Circle, The 1966,Mr 25,35:1
Alchemist, The 1966,O 14,48:1
Silvern, Barrie (Original Author)
Limits 1968,F 19,52:1
Silvern, Charles
Taming of the Shrew, The 1940,F 6,17:2
Silvernail, Clarke
Nature's Nobleman 1921,N 15,23:2
Montmartre 1922,F 14,20:1
Fashions for Men 1922,D 6,22:1
Agent 666, L' 1923,My 30,10:5
Rust 1924,F 1,12:1
White Collars 1925,F 24,17:2
Jane-Our Stranger 1925,O 9,27:2
Not Herbert 1926,Ja 27,16:2
Silent House, The 1928,F 8,28:5
Silvernail, Clarke (Director)
Busybody, The 1924,S 30,27:5
Beau Gallant 1926,Ap 6,26:3
Head or Tail 1926,N 10,24:1
Such Is Life 1927,S 1,27:3
Hello, Yourself 1928,O 31,28:2
Squealer, The 1928,N 13,36:3
Silvernail, Clarke (Playwright)
Cafe de Danse 1929,Ja 16,22:2
Silvers, Julia
Greenwich Village Follies 1922,S 13,18:2
Greenwich Village Follies 1924,S 17,16:1
Silvers, Louis (Director)
1776 1926,Ap 24,11:2
Silvers, Phil
Yokel Boy 1939,Jl 7,12:2
High Button Shoes 1947,O 10,32:2
High Button Shoes 1947,N 23,II,1:1
Top Banana 1951,N 2,19:2
Top Banana 1951,N 18,II,1:1
Do Re Mi 1960,D 27,23:2
Do Re Mi 1961,Ja 8,II,1:1
Silvers, Sid
Artists and Models 1925,Je 25,16:2
Night in Spain, A 1927,My 4,28:2
Night in Spain, A 1927,My 22,VIII,1:1
Vaudeville (Palace) 1928,D 17,23:3
Vaudeville (Palace) 1928,D 24,10:8
Humpty Dumpty 1932,S 18,IX,2:1
Take a Chance 1932,N 28,11:2
Silvers, Sid (Composer)
Song Writer, The 1928,Ag 14,15:2
Silvers, Sid (Lyricist)
Song Writer, The 1928,Ag 14,15:2
Silvers, Sid (Miscellaneous)
High Kickers 1941,N 1,21:2

Silvers, Sid (Playwright)
You Said It 1931,Ja 20,21:3
Take a Chance 1932,N 28,11:2
Silverstein, Elliot (Director)
Maybe Tuesday 1958,Ja 30,18:3
Silverstein, Jerome
Rich Man, Poor Man 1950,F 13,15:4
Silvertown Cord Orchestra
Vaudeville (Palace) 1927,Ja 25,18:3
Silvestri, Aldo
Liane, Le (Ties That Bind); Ties That Bind (Le Liane) 1929,Ap 22,22:1
Silvestri, Richard
Petrified Forest, The 1942,Ag 19,14:3
Sim, Alastair
Venetian, The 1931,N 2,26:1
Cottage to Let 1940,Ag 11,IX,2:5
Mr Gillie 1950,Mr 10,31:2
Sima, Oskar
Italienische Nacht 1931,My 10,VIII,1:5
Simak, Clifford (Original Author)
How to Make a Man 1961,F 3,16:1
Simanek, Otto
Mikado, The 1942,F 4,22:2
Pirates of Penzance, The 1942,F 18,22:2
Iolanthe 1942,F 24,26:4
Gondoliers, The 1942,Mr 4,22:3
Stalag 17 1951,My 9,41:2
Simas, Eugene (2nd Lieut)
Swing Sister Wac Swing 1944,Ja 4,20:4
Simckes, Seymour (Playwright)
Seven Days of Mourning 1969,D 17,64:1
Seven Days of Mourning 1970,Ja 4,II,5:1
Simcox, Tom
Painted Days, The 1961,Ap 7,24:1
Simek, Vasek (Director)
Wicked Cooks, The 1967,Ja 24,42:1
Sondra 1967,My 10,39:1
Harold 1967,My 10,39:1
Simeone, Harry (Composer)
Hear! Hear! 1955,S 28,38:1
Simeone, Harry (Playwright)
Hear! Hear! 1955,S 28,38:1
Simetti, Otto (Director)
Mary Stuart 1956,Ap 28,10:2
Simkhovitch, Ben K (Playwright)
Playboy of Newark, The 1943,Mr 20,11:2
Simkhovitch, Helena
Caesar and Cleopatra 1925,Ap 14,27:1
Simkin, Edward R
Will, The 1930,My 6,33:1
Simmelkjaer, Harold E
Taboo 1922,Ap 5,22:1
Simmonds, Stanley
Li'l Abner 1956,N 16,24:2
Fiorello! 1959,N 24,45:3
Let It Ride 1961,O 13,27:4
How Now, Dow Jones 1967,D 8,53:1
Maggie Flynn 1968,O 24,52:1
Jimmy 1969,O 24,38:1
Simmons, Bartlett
Gay Paree 1925,Ag 19,14:3
Night in Spain, A 1927,My 4,28:2
Say When 1928,Je 27,29:3
Music in May 1929,Ap 2,29:1
Wonderful Night, A; Fledermaus, Die 1929,N 1,23:3
Laugh Parade, The 1931,N 3,31:2
Life Begins at 8:40 1934,Ag 28,24:2
Student Prince, The 1936,Jl 12,II,5:2
Rose Marie 1936,Jl 22,22:6
Blossom Time 1936,Jl 29,23:1
My Maryland 1936,Ag 12,14:2
Bitter Sweet 1936,Ag 26,17:3
Sally, Irene and Mary 1938,Jl 5,13:4
Simmons, Connie
Happy Time, The 1968,Ja 19,32:2
Simmons, Danny
Bringing Up Father 1925,Mr 31,16:1
Vaudeville (Palace) 1931,Mr 2,19:2
Scrap Book 1932,Ag 2,20:3
Simmons, Doree
King and the Duke, The 1955,Je 2,25:2
Simmons, Earl
Camels Are Coming, The 1931,O 3,20:4
Simmons, Georgia
Searching for the Sun 1936,F 20,22:6
Homecoming 1942,N 17,28:5
O'Daniel 1947,F 25,32:2
Traitor, The 1949,Ap 1,30:2
House of Breath, The 1957,Ap 15,23:2
All the Way Home 1960,D 1,42:1
Rose Tattoo, The 1966,O 21,36:2
Simmons, Harold
Lady in the Dark 1941,Ja 24,14:2
Simmons, Jacquie
Gay Divorce 1932,N 30,23:4
Simmons, Jamie
Mardi Gras! 1965,Je 28,33:2
Simmons, Junius
Promis' Lan', De 1930,My 28,31:2
Simmons, Kay
Artists and Models 1930,Je 11,33:2

Little Racketeer, The 1932,Ja 19,24:4
Bitter Sweet 1934,My 8,28:4
Simmons, Lydia
Last Pad, The 1970,D 8,61:1
Simmons, Maude
John Henry 1940,Ja 11,18:2
Run, Little Chillun 1943,Ag 14,6:1
Finian's Rainbow 1947,Ja 11,23:2
Wisteria Trees, The 1950,Mr 30,39:1
Simmons, Maurice L (Director)
Smyth With a Y 1937,Je 30,19:5
Simmons, Nat
You Can't Take It With You 1965,N 24,32:1
School for Scandal, The 1966,N 22,33:2
War and Peace 1967,Mr 22,42:1
Pantagleize 1967,D 1,54:1
Simmons, Nina
Audition of the Apprentice Theatre 1939,Je 2,26:2
Simmons, Ollie
Case of Philip Lawrence, The 1937,Je 9,31:1
Horse Play 1937,Ag 28,8:3
Simmons, Pat (Lighting Director)
All Kinds of Giants 1961,D 19,40:1
Cherry Orchard, The 1970,My 7,63:2
Simmons, Robert
Libel! 1935,D 8,X,5:8
Libel! 1935,D 21,10:5
Simmons, Roscoe
Ginger Snaps 1930,Ja 1,30:5
Simmons, Stanley
Allegro 1947,O 11,10:2
Rape of Lucretia, The 1948,D 30,24:2
Out of This World 1950,D 22,17:3
Simmons, Stanley (Costume Designer)
Qudrille 1954,N 4,39:2
Almost Crazy 1955,Je 21,37:1
Waiting for Godot 1956,Ap 20,21:2
Waiting for Godot 1957,Ja 22,25:1
Garden District; Something Unspoken 1958,Ja 8,23:4
Garden District; Suddenly Last Summer 1958,Ja 8,23:4
Finian's Rainbow 1960,Ap 28,31:1
King and I, The 1960,My 12,40:1
Come Blow Your Horn 1961,F 23,31:3
Show Boat 1961,Ap 13,32:1
Porgy and Bess 1961,My 18,40:1
Not While I'm Eating 1961,D 20,37:1
Can-Can 1962,My 17,32:2
Brigadoon 1962,My 31,21:4
Brigadoon 1963,F 1,6:2
Oklahoma! 1963,F 28,8:2
Oklahoma! 1963,My 16,40:1
White Rose and the Red, The 1964,Mr 17,31:1
West Side Story 1964,Ap 9,24:2
Porgy and Bess 1964,My 7,32:1
Brigadoon 1964,D 24,9:1
Kiss Me, Kate 1965,My 13,31:1
South Pacific 1965,Je 3,25:1
Carousel 1965,Ag 11,39:1
Oklahoma! 1965,D 16,62:1
How to Succeed in Business Without Really Trying 1966,Ap 21,45:1
Show Boat 1966,Jl 20,48:1
Elizabeth the Queen 1966,N 4,30:1
Carousel 1966,D 16,56:2
Sound of Music, The 1967,Ap 27,52:1
There's a Girl in My Soup 1967,O 19,58:1
Brigadoon 1967,D 14,59:2
Come Summer 1969,Mr 19,43:1
In the Bar of a Tokyo Hotel 1969,My 12,54:1
Exchange 1970,F 9,47:2
Boy Friend, The 1970,Ap 15,54:1
Simmons, Stanley (Miscellaneous)
Carmen Jones 1956,Je 1,28:2
South Pacific 1961,Ap 27,26:3
My Fair Lady 1964,My 21,43:2
My Fair Lady 1968,Je 14,42:1
Simmons, Ted (Musical Director)
Leonard Sillman's New Faces of 1968 1968,My 3,43:1
Simmons, W Bartlett
Laugh Parade, The 1931,S 20,VIII,3:1
Simmons, Willard Earl (Director)
Broadway Shadows 1930,Ap 1,34:6
Simmons, Willard Earl (Playwright)
Broadway Shadows 1930,Ap 1,34:6
Simmons, William
Retablo de Maese Pedro, El 1925,D 30,10:1
Tobias and the Angel 1937,Ap 29,16:5
Simms, Don
Three Men on a Horse 1969,O 17,35:1
Simms, Don (Lighting Director)
Ruddigore 1965,Ag 27,16:1
Simms, Hilda
Anna Lucasta 1944,Je 17,10:1
Anna Lucasta 1944,Ag 31,15:1
Anna Lucasta 1944,S 10,II,1:1
Anna Lucasta 1947,O 30,31:3
Anna Lucasta 1947,N 9,II,3:7
Desire Caught by the Tail 1950,F 18,9:8
Gentle People, The 1950,Ap 15,10:5
Cool World, The 1960,F 23,38:2

Simms, Hilda—Cont
Tambourines to Glory 1963,N 4,47:1
Madwoman of Chaillot, The 1970,Mr 23,48:3
Simms, Hilda (Miscellaneous)
Mandingo 1961,My 23,43:6
Simms, Laura
Moondreamers, The 1969,D 9,68:1
Simms, Lois
Hot Rhythm 1930,Ag 22,18:5
Simms, Margaret
Liza 1922,N 28,24:1
Hot Chocolates 1929,Je 21,17:4
Simms, William
Liza 1922,N 28,24:1
Simon, Alfred (Composer)
Canteen Show, The 1942,S 4,18:1
Simon, Arnold
Petrified Forest, The 1942,Ag 19,14:3
Simon, Barbara
High John De Conquer 1969,Ap 23,39:1
Simon, Barney (Director)
Hello and Goodbye 1968,N 13,36:2
Hello and Goodbye 1969,S 19,54:1
Simon, Connie (Producer)
Seven at Dawn, The 1961,Ap 18,43:1
Simon, Cyril (Director)
Song for a Certain Midnight 1959,S 17,49:1
Telemachus Clay 1963,N 16,17:2
Sarah and the Sax 1964,My 5,53:1
Dirty Old Man, The 1964,My 5,53:1
Great Western Union, The 1965,F 10,45:1
Medea 1965,N 29,46:1
Simon, Danny (Director)
Catch a Star! 1955,S 7,35:2
Simon, Danny (Playwright)
Catch a Star! 1955,S 7,35:2
Simon, Dave
Comrades 1956,Je 6,38:1
Simon, Douglas (Miscellaneous)
Nest, The 1970,Ap 10,46:1
Simon, E Francis
Dinny and the Witches 1959,D 10,53:3
Simon, Frances
Lady With a Lamp, The 1931,N 20,27:2
Simon, Linda
Medea 1965,N 29,46:1
Simon, Louis
Rose Girl, The 1921,F 12,11:1
What's Your Wife Doing? 1923,O 2,10:3
Moonlight 1924,Ja 31,13:7
Mercenary Mary 1925,Ap 14,27:3
Bye Bye Bonnie 1927,Ja 14,15:3
Simon, Louis (Playwright)
Bye Bye Bonnie 1927,Ja 14,15:3
Simon, Louis M
Jewel Robbery 1932,Ja 14,17:2
Simon, Louis M (Costume Designer)
Garrick Gaieties 1930,Je 5,29:2
Simon, Louis M (Director)
Thy People 1935,Ag 13,20:3
Good Men and True 1935,O 26,12:4
Trial of Dr Beck, The 1937,Ag 10,22:2
Simon, Louis M (Lyricist)
Garrick Gaieties 1930,Je 5,29:2
Simon, Louis M (Playwright)
Garrick Gaieties 1930,Je 5,29:2
Simon, Louis M (Producer)
Thy People 1935,Ag 13,20:3
Woman and the Blues, A 1966,Mr 29,35:2
Simon, Maia
Grand Vizir, Le 1970,Ap 8,38:3
Simon, Marcel
Epinard Gagne le Grand Steeple 1926,D 19,VII,3:3
Simon, Max (Original Author)
Hotel Alimony 1934,Ja 30,16:2
Simon, Max (Playwright)
Kiss Me! 1927,Jl 22,17:1
Storm Center 1927,D 1,33:2
Simon, Mayo (Playwright)
Walking to Waldheim 1967,N 11,25:2
Happiness 1967,N 11,25:2
Walking to Waldheim 1967,N 19,II,1:1
L A Under Siege 1970,Ag 16,II,1:7
Simon, Michel
Jean de la Lune 1929,My 12,IX,5:3
Bonheur 1933,My 14,IX,1:4
Joies du Capitole, Les 1935,Ap 21,IX,2:1
Fric Frac 1936,N 29,XII,2:4
Simon, Neil (Playwright)
Catch a Star! 1955,S 7,35:2
Come Blow Your Horn 1961,F 23,31:3
Come Blow Your Horn 1961,Mr 5,II,1:1
Little Me 1962,N 19,41:3
Little Me 1962,D 2,II,1:1
Barefoot in the Park 1963,O 24,36:2
Odd Couple, The 1965,Mr 11,36:1
Odd Couple, The 1965,Mr 21,II,1:1
Sweet Charity 1966,Ja 31,22:1
Star-Spangled Girl, The 1966,D 22,38:1
Star-Spangled Girl, The 1967,Ja 8,II,1:5
Plaza Suite; Visitor From Hollywood 1968,F 15,49:1
Plaza Suite; Visitor From Mamaroneck 1968,F 15,49:1

Simon, Neil (Playwright)—Cont

Plaza Suite; Visitor From Forest Hills
  1968,F 15,49:1
Plaza Suite 1968,F 25,II,1:1
Promises, Promises 1968,D 2,59:3
Plaza Suite 1968,D 14,61:2
Promises, Promises 1968,D 15,II,3:1
Last of the Red Hot Lovers 1969,D 29,37:1
Last of the Red Hot Lovers 1970,Ja 4,II,1:1
Plaza Suite 1970,Mr 22,90:3
Gingerbread Lady, The 1970,D 14,58:3
Gingerbread Lady, The 1970,D 20,II,3:7
Simon, Peter
Kicking the Castle Down 1967,Ja 19,43:1
Twelfth Night 1969,Ag 14,29:2
Simon, Richard
Life With Father 1939,Ag 15,14:4
Life With Father 1939,N 9,26:2
Years Ago 1946,D 4,44:2
Dear Judas 1947,O 6,26:4
Simon, Robert
No for an Answer 1941,Ja 6,10:6
Russian People, The 1942,D 30,17:2
Apology 1943,Mr 23,14:2
Brighten the Corner 1945,D 13,33:2
Truckline Cafe 1946,F 28,19:4
On Whitman Avenue 1946,My 9,28:2
Sundown Beach 1948,S 8,37:1
Simon, Robert A (Composer)
Hold Your Horses 1933,S 26,26:4
Simon, Robert A (Lyricist)
Ups-A-Daisy 1928,O 9,34:2
Gang's All Here, The 1931,F 19,21:3
Hold Your Horses 1933,S 26,26:4
Champagne, Sec 1933,O 16,20:2
Simon, Robert A (Playwright)
Ups-A-Daisy 1928,O 9,34:2
Simon, Robert F
Mrs January & Mr Ex 1944,Ap 1,10:2
Of Thee I Sing 1952,My 6,34:2
Nature of the Crime 1970,Mr 24,41:1
Simon, Roger Hendricks
Volpone 1967,Je 30,29:1
Henry IV 1968,F 7,40:1
Three Sisters, The 1968,Mr 18,56:1
Simon, Simone
Three After Three 1939,N 25,13:5
Simon-Girardi, Aime
Diable a Paris, Le 1927,N 13,IX,4:2
Simonds, Kenneth
Blue Blood 1924,Ap 3,21:2
Simone, Dorothy
Seventeen 1924,Ap 12,18:2
Simone, Michael (Director)
Dream of Swallows, A 1964,Ap 15,46:1
License, The 1969,Ap 23,42:1
Man With the Flower in His Mouth, The
  1969,Ap 23,42:1
Jar, The 1969,Ap 23,42:1
Simone, Mme
Vierge Folle, La; Foolish Virgin, The
  1924,Mr 22,12:2
Couturiere de Luneville, La 1924,Mr 26,16:2
Aiglon, L' 1924,O 21,21:1
Naked 1924,O 28,27:2
Naked 1924,N 2,VII,1:1
Madame Sans-Gene 1924,N 4,30:1
Parisienne 1924,N 25,26:2
Amoureuse 1924,N 28,13:1
Virgin With a Big Heart, The 1925,F 1,VII,2:1
Secret, Le 1928,Mr 25,IX,4:6
Vilaine Femme, Une 1933,Ja 1,IX,3:4
Roi, Deux Dames et un Valet, Un
  1935,Mr 3,VIII,2:3
Simone, Mme (Original Author)
Roi, Deux Dames et un Valet, Un
  1935,Mr 3,VIII,2:3
Simone, Nehem
Storm Operation 1944,Ja 12,28:2
Simone, Ralph
Honors Are Even 1921,Ag 11,8:2
Bulls, Bears and Asses 1932,My 7,11:3
I Loved You Wednesday 1932,O 12,27:1
Dodsworth 1934,F 26,20:4
French Touch, The 1945,D 10,18:2
Heads or Tails 1947,My 3,10:6
I Gotta Get Out 1947,S 26,27:2
Simonet, Lillian
P S I Love You 1964,N 20,40:1
Simoni, Renato (Producer)
Oedipus Rex 1937,My 9,XI,7:5
Simoni, Silvana
Awakening of Spring, The 1964,My 13,50:1
Simonian, George (Producer)
Marching Song 1959,D 29,20:1
Simonin, Vincent
Great Day! 1929,O 18,24:3
Simonini, Pierre (Costume Designer)
Avare, L', L'; Miser, The 1966,F 9,32:1
Reine Morte, La 1966,F 16,52:1
Simonini, Pierre (Scenic Designer)
Annonce Faite a Marie, L' 1965,Ap 6,33:2
Avare, L', L'; Miser, The 1966,F 9,32:1
Reine Morte, La 1966,F 16,52:1

Simonoff, Betty
Shulamith 1931,O 14,26:4
Mother's Son 1931,N 26,36:4
Pleasure 1931,D 28,20:2
Untitled-Benefit 1933,Ja 25,13:3
Simonov
Hamlet 1932,Je 26,IX,1:3
Simonov, Konstantin (Playwright)
Russian People, The 1942,Jl 18,8:2
Russian People, The 1942,D 16,21:3
Russian People, The 1942,D 30,17:2
Russian Question, The 1946,D 14,18:2
Whole World Over, The 1947,Ap 6,II,1:1
Russian Question, The 1947,My 4,I,54:3
Foreign Specter 1949,Je 5,15:3
Strange Shadow 1949,Jl 20,30:4
Alien Shadow 1949,Jl 22,16:5
Simonov, Konstantin (Translator)
Whole World Over, The 1947,Mr 28,28:2
Simonovic, Konstantin (Musical Director)
Oresteia 1966,Je 30,29:1
Birds, The 1966,Jl 1,40:1
Simons, Constance
Grass Is Always Greener, The 1955,F 16,25:2
Simons, Gus
Porgy and Bess 1935,O 11,30:2
Simons, Robert D (Director)
Toy for the Clowns, A 1962,S 13,31:2
Squat Betty 1964,F 25,24:1
Sponge Room, The 1964,F 25,24:1
Simons, Robert D (Producer)
Sponge Room, The 1964,F 25,24:1
Squat Betty 1964,F 25,24:1
Simons, Seymour (Composer)
Her Family Tree 1920,D 28,9:2
Simons, Seymour (Lyricist)
Her Family Tree 1920,D 28,9:2
Simons, Ted (Miscellaneous)
Sap of Life, The 1961,O 3,44:1
Anything Goes 1962,My 16,35:1
Simons, Ted (Musical Director)
Amorous Flea, The 1964,F 18,26:1
Simonson, Lee (Costume Designer)
Peer Gynt 1923,F 11,VII,1:1
Fata Morgana 1924,Mr 4,16:3
Glass Slipper, The 1925,O 20,29:1
Goat Song 1926,Ja 26,18:1
Juarez and Maximilian 1926,O 12,31:1
Road to Rome, The 1927,F 1,24:2
Volpone 1928,Ap 22,IX,1:1
Volpone 1930,Mr 11,24:5
Marco Millions 1930,Mr 4,24:4
Volpone 1930,Mr 11,24:5
Elizabeth the Queen 1930,N 4,37:1
Dream of Sganarelle, The 1933,O 17,26:5
School for Husbands, The 1933,O 17,26:5
School for Husbands, The 1933,D 3,IX,6:5
Sleeping Clergyman, A 1934,O 9,16:1
Simpleton of the Unexpected Isles, The
  1935,F 19,27:5
Prelude to Exile 1936,N 17,34:6
Prelude to Exile 1936,D 1,31:1
Masque of the Kings, The 1937,F 9,19:4
Joan of Lorraine 1946,N 19,40:2
Simonson, Lee (Director)
Man and the Masses 1924,Ap 15,25:1
Simonson, Lee (Lighting Director)
Peer Gynt 1923,F 11,VII,1:1
Joan of Lorraine 1946,N 19,40:2
Simonson, Lee (Miscellaneous)
Good Earth, The 1932,O 18,23:4
American Dream; 1650 1933,F 22,24:5
American Dream; 1849 1933,F 22,24:5
American Dream; 1933 1933,F 22,24:5
Both Your Houses 1933,Mr 7,20:3
They Shall Not Die 1934,F 22,24:4
Jig Saw 1934,My 1,26:3
Sleeping Clergyman, A 1934,O 9,16:1
Rain From Heaven 1934,D 25,28:4
Simonson, Lee (Producer)
Days Without End 1934,Ja 9,19:1
Simpleton of the Unexpected Isles, The
  1935,F 19,27:5
Simonson, Lee (Scenic Designer)
Liliom 1921,My 1,VII,1:1
From Morn to Midnight 1922,My 22,17:2
Adding Machine, The 1923,Mr 25,VIII,1:1
As You Like It 1923,Ap 29,VII,1:1
Fata Morgana 1924,Mr 4,16:3
Man and the Masses 1924,Ap 15,25:1
Bewitched 1924,O 2,26:3
Bewitched 1924,O 5,VIII,1:1
Mongrel, The 1924,D 16,28:2
Arms and the Man 1925,S 15,28:1
Glass Slipper, The 1925,O 20,29:1
Glass Slipper, The 1925,O 25,VIII,1:1
Goat Song 1926,Ja 26,18:1
Juarez and Maximilian 1926,O 12,31:1
Road to Rome, The 1927,F 1,24:2
Marco Millions 1928,Ja 10,28:2
Volpone 1928,Ap 10,32:1
Volpone 1928,Ap 22,IX,1:1
Faust 1928,O 9,34:1

Simonson, Lee (Scenic Designer)—Cont

Dynamo 1929,F 12,22:1
Camel Through the Needle's Eye, The
  1929,Ap 16,32:2
Damn Your Honor 1929,D 31,14:3
R U R 1930,F 18,28:1
Apple Cart, The 1930,F 25,30:1
Marco Millions 1930,Mr 4,24:4
Volpone 1930,Mr 11,24:5
Hotel Universe 1930,Ap 15,29:1
Roar China! 1930,O 28,23:1
Elizabeth the Queen 1930,N 4,37:1
Miracle at Verdun 1931,Mr 17,34:6
Lean Harvest 1931,O 14,26:3
Collision 1932,F 17,19:2
Good Earth, The 1932,O 18,23:4
Red Planet 1932,D 19,19:2
American Dream; 1933 1933,F 22,24:5
American Dream; 1650 1933,F 22,24:5
American Dream; 1849 1933,F 22,24:5
Mask and the Face, The 1933,My 9,20:2
Dream of Sganarelle, The 1933,O 17,26:5
School for Husbands, The 1933,O 17,26:5
School for Husbands, The 1933,D 3,IX,6:5
Days Without End 1934,Ja 9,19:1
They Shall Not Die 1934,F 22,24:4
They Shall Not Die 1934,Mr 4,IX,1:3
Jig Saw 1934,My 1,26:3
Sleeping Clergyman, A 1934,O 9,16:1
Rain From Heaven 1934,D 16,XI,2:1
Rain From Heaven 1934,D 18,26:4
Simpleton of the Unexpected Isles, The
  1935,F 19,27:5
Parade 1935,My 21,22:2
Parade 1935,My 26,XI,1:1
Love Is Not So Simple 1935,N 5,33:1
Call It a Day 1936,Ja 29,15:2
End of Summer 1936,Ja 31,17:1
End of Summer 1936,F 18,26:4
Idiot's Delight 1936,Mr 10,26:7
Idiot's Delight 1936,Mr 25,25:2
Prelude to Exile 1936,N 17,34:6
Prelude to Exile 1936,N 22,XI,3:2
Prelude to Exile 1936,D 1,31:1
Jane Eyre 1937,Ja 3,X,2:1
Masque of the Kings, The 1937,F 9,19:4
Amphitryon 38 1937,Je 24,30:2
Virginia 1937,S 3,13:2
Virginia 1937,S 12,XI,1:1
Virginia 1937,O 5,29:1
Madame Bovary 1937,O 6,28:4
Amphitryon 38 1937,N 7,XI,1:1
Lorelei 1938,N 30,21:2
Streets Are Guarded, The 1944,N 21,19:7
Foxhole in the Parlor 1945,My 24,15:4
Joan of Lorraine 1946,N 19,40:2
Joan of Lorraine 1946,N 24,II,1:1
Simont, Marc (Scenic Designer)
Pin Up 1966,Je 24,30:2
Miracle in Brooklyn 1966,Je 24,30:2
Venus-Shot 1966,Je 24,30:2
Child and the Dragon, The 1966,Je 24,30:2
Simonyi, Maria
Uri Muri 1928,Ap 15,IX,4:1
Simov, V A (Scenic Designer)
Dead Souls 1965,F 5,34:1
Simpson, Alan (Playwright)
Rockefeller and the Red Indians 1968,O 25,37:1
Simpson, Frances
Girl in the Coffin, The 1920,F 10,10:2
Suppressed Desires 1920,F 10,10:2
Magnanimous Lover, The 1920,F 10,10:2
Thank You 1921,O 4,10:2
Much Ado About Nothing 1927,N 19,14:6
Trip to Scarborough, A 1929,Mr 18,31:2
Dragon, The 1929,Mr 26,34:2
Simpson, Grant
Poor Little Ritz Girl 1920,Jl 29,7:1
Snapshots of 1921 1921,Je 3,19:2
Ziegfeld Follies 1922,Je 6,18:2
Passing Show of 1924, The 1924,S 4,13:4
Vaudeville (Palace) 1926,S 28,30:4
Peggy-Ann 1926,D 28,16:3
Simpson, Harold (Playwright)
9 O'Clock Revue 1923,O 5,22:1
Nine to Eleven, The 1925,Jl 12,VII,1:1
By the Way 1925,D 29,20:3
Cave Man, The 1928,Ja 1,VIII,1:3
Sentenced 1932,Mr 6,VIII,2:4
Without Witness 1933,D 28,25:1
Simpson, Helen (Playwright)
Gooseberry Fool 1929,N 2,14:8
Simpson, Ivan
Charm School, The 1920,Ag 3,12:1
Rollo's Wild Oat 1920,N 24,14:1
Green Goddess, The 1921,Ja 19,14:1
Way Things Happen, The 1924,Ja 29,17:5
Old English 1924,D 24,11:2
Julius Caesar 1927,Je 7,27:2
Garden of Eden, The 1927,S 28,28:1
Command Performance, The 1928,O 4,27:1
Perfect Alibi, The 1928,N 28,24:2
Kiss of Importance, A 1930,D 2,31:3
Male Animal, The 1940,Ja 10,17:2

Simpson, Ivan—Cont

Bright Boy 1944,Mr 3,19:5
Sleep, My Pretty One 1944,N 3,26:8
Barretts of Wimpole Street, The 1945,Mr 27,23:6
Secret Room, The 1945,N 8,16:2
Swan Song 1946,My 16,29:2
Haven, The 1946,N 14,39:4
Antony and Cleopatra 1947,N 27,49:2
Make Way for Lucia 1948,D 23,23:5
Caesar and Cleopatra 1949,D 22,28:2

Simpson, Kenneth (Playwright)
All That Glitters 1938,Ja 20,18:2

Simpson, Margaret
Gay Blades 1937,N 12,26:6

Simpson, Marie
Yellow Jacket, The 1928,N 8,27:3
Falstaff 1928,D 26,14:2
Boundry Line, The 1930,F 6,21:1

Simpson, N F (Playwright)
Resounding Tinkle, The 1961,Ap 4,42:2
Hole, The 1961,Ap 4,42:2
One Way Pendulum 1961,S 19,38:2

Simpson, Pamela
Enchantment 1927,Ap 28,27:3
Silver Cord, The 1928,F 19,VIII,2:1
Romeo and Juliet 1934,D 21,30:3
Barchester Towers 1937,D 1,27:1
Candida 1952,Ap 23,23:6
Arsenic and Old Lace 1970,N 5,59:1

Simpson, Peggy
Roof, The 1929,N 24,X,1:6
Bachelor Born 1938,Ja 26,26:3

Simpson, Reginald (Playwright)
Who Goes Next? 1931,Mr 8,VIII,2:4
Living Dangerously 1934,Je 8,19:3
Living Dangerously 1935,Ja 14,10:3

Simpson, Richard
Legend of Leonora, The 1927,Mr 30,22:4
Out of the Sea 1927,D 6,26:2

Simpson, Robert
Decameron, The 1961,Ap 13,32:1
Tiny Alice 1969,S 30,42:1

Simpson, Ronald
March Hares 1928,Ja 1,VIII,1:3
Toy Cart, The 1930,D 7,IX,2:7
Woman Kind 1933,S 28,25:2
And Be My Love 1934,Ja 19,25:2
Rocket to the Moon 1948,Mr 23,30:4

Simpson, Ronald (Playwright)
Those Naughty Nineties 1931,S 13,IX,2:7

Simpson, S L (Producer)
Babies a La Carte 1927,Ag 16,31:1
Lawyers' Dilemma, The 1928,Jl 10,17:2

Simpson, Sean
Woman Is My Idea 1968,S 26,61:1

Simpson, Sloan
Brigadoon 1957,Mr 28,37:1

Simpson, Sloan (Miscellaneous)
Bullfight 1954,Ja 13,25:2

Simpson, William
Passing Show of 1924, The 1924,S 4,13:4

Simpson Sisters
Gay Blades 1937,N 16,27:1

Sims, Charles J
Zeno 1923,Ag 27,14:2

Sims, Don (Miscellaneous)
Yeomen of the Guard, The 1965,Jl 8,34:1

Sims, Frederic
Romance 1921,Mr 1,18:2

Sims, Hilda
Scrapped 1927,O 16,IX,2:7

Sims, John
Singin' the Blues 1931,S 17,21:3

Sims, Patricia
Gypsy Lady 1946,S 18,25:6

Sims, Paul
Music Man, The 1963,Ag 15,24:1

Sims, Sandman
Hoofers, The 1969,Jl 30,23:4

Sims, Sylvia
Diamond Lil 1948,N 30,33:2

Sims, Varley
Knight of the Burning Pestle, The 1927,Ap 23,15:1

Sims, William
We Have Always Lived in the Castle
1966,O 20,53:1

Simson, Richard
Simon Called Peter 1924,N 11,20:2

Sinatra, Spencer
Rivalry, The 1959,F 9,24:2

Sincere, Jean
Razzle Dazzle 1951,F 20,21:1
Oh Captain! 1958,F 5,21:2
Mis-Guided Tour 1959,O 13,44:7
Life With Father 1967,O 20,53:2

Sinclair, Ada
Lassie 1920,Ap 7,9:2
Tyrant, The 1930,N 13,33:1
Passing of the Third Floor Back, The
1937,Ag 3,20:6

Sinclair, Archie
S S Glencairn 1924,N 4,31:4
S S Glencairn 1929,Ja 10,24:5

Sinclair, Arthur
White-Headed Boy, The 1921,S 16,20:1
Send for Dr O'Grady 1923,Jl 29,VI,1:6
Fanshastics 1924,Ja 17,13:2
Professor Tim 1927,Ap 17,VII,1:4
Shadow of a Gunman, The 1927,Je 26,VIII,1:3
Plough and the Stars, The 1927,N 29,30:2
Plough and the Stars, The 1927,D 4,X,1:1
Juno and the Paycock 1927,D 20,32:2
Real McCoy, The 1928,Jl 15,VIII,2:1
Mr Gilhooley 1930,O 1,26:1
Old Man Murphy 1931,My 19,25:2
Jumbo 1935,N 18,20:2
Spring Tide 1936,Ag 9,IX,1:5
Art and Craft 1936,D 1,30:4
Orchard Walls 1937,F 21,X,2:1
Taming of the Shrew, The 1937,Ap 11,XI,2:1
Juno and the Paycock 1937,Ag 29,X,2:1
Spring Meeting 1938,Je 19,IX,2:1
Finian's Rainbow 1947,N 9,II,3:7

Sinclair, Barry
Man and Boy 1963,S 5,28:1

Sinclair, Betty
Winslow Boy, The 1947,O 30,32:2
Deep Blue Sea, The 1952,N 6,38:3
Doctor's Dilemma, The 1955,Ja 12,22:1
Sleeping Prince, The 1956,N 2,31:1
Auntie Mame 1958,Ag 12,33:2
Port-Royal 1960,Ap 26,41:1
Lord Pengo 1962,N 20,41:2
Seagull, The 1964,Ap 6,36:1
Crucible, The 1964,Ap 7,30:2

Sinclair, Charles (Director)
Light Wines and Beer 1930,N 11,28:6
Firefly, The 1937,Ag 4,14:1

Sinclair, Diane
Too Many Girls 1939,O 19,26:2
Pal Joey 1940,D 26,22:2
Tempest, The 1945,Ja 26,17:2
Tempest, The 1945,N 13,24:6
Happy as Larry 1950,Ja 7,11:2

Sinclair, Dorothy
Sailor, Beware! 1935,My 7,28:4

Sinclair, Edward
Canteen Show, The 1942,S 4,18:1

Sinclair, Edward (Miscellaneous)
Canteen Show, The 1942,S 4,18:1

Sinclair, Eric
Legend of Lovers 1951,D 27,17:1
Much Ado About Nothing 1952,My 2,20:1

Sinclair, Ethel
Vaudeville (Palace) 1923,N 20,23:4
Vaudeville (Palace) 1924,Mr 18,25:1
Vaudeville (Palace) 1927,F 8,20:3

Sinclair, Frances (Translator)
Melody That Got Lost, The 1938,F 6,X,1:2

Sinclair, Frank
Battling Buttler 1923,O 9,17:2

Sinclair, George
Puppets of Passion 1927,F 25,24:4
If Booth Had Missed 1932,F 5,24:2
Processional 1937,O 14,23:1

Sinclair, Horace
Honors Are Even 1921,Ag 11,8:2
House Divided, The 1923,N 12,14:1
Bachelor's Brides 1925,My 29,20:2
Just Beyond 1925,D 2,22:4
Interference 1927,O 19,24:3
Woman Denied, A 1931,F 26,21:1
Payment Deferred 1931,O 1,24:2
Wild Waves 1932,F 20,11:4
School for Husbands, The 1933,O 17,26:5
Dream of Sganarelle, The 1933,O 17,26:5
Bridal Quilt 1934,O 11,28:5
Bishop Misbehaves, The 1935,F 21,22:4
Bishop Misbehaves, The 1935,Ag 27,23:4
Taming of the Shrew, The 1935,O 1,27:3
Ghosts 1936,My 12,26:8
And Now Goodbye 1937,F 3,26:4
Passing of the Third Floor Back, The
1937,Ag 3,20:6
To Quito and Back 1937,O 7,30:4
Merry Wives of Windsor, The 1938,Ap 15,22:3
Good Hunting 1938,N 22,26:5
Skylark 1939,O 12,32:2
Me and Harry 1942,Ap 3,24:6

Sinclair, Horace (Director)
Potiphar's Wife 1928,D 24,10:7
Tyrant, The 1930,N 13,33:1
There You Are! 1932,My 17,25:4
Personal Appearance 1936,Jl 9,17:4

Sinclair, Howard
Bully, The 1924,D 26,18:1

Sinclair, Hugh
Mariners 1927,Mr 29,22:2
Our Betters 1928,F 21,18:2
These Few Ashes 1928,O 31,28:1
Lady of the Orchids, The 1928,D 14,37:3
Serena Blandish 1929,Ja 24,30:3
Vaudeville (Palace) 1929,S 23,24:6
Her Friend the King 1929,O 8,34:5
Other Men's Wives 1929,N 13,24:4
Recapture 1930,Ja 19,VIII,2:6

Sinclair, Hugh—Cont
Recapture 1930,Ja 30,16:4
New Yorkers, The 1930,N 16,VIII,3:1
Getting Married 1931,Mr 31,25:5
Good Companions, The 1931,O 2,31:1
Good Companions, The 1931,O 11,VIII,1:1
Too True to Be Good 1932,Mr 1,19:2
Too True to Be Good 1932,Mr 6,VIII,1:1
Too True to Be Good 1932,Ap 5,27:5
Escape Me Not 1933,D 9,18:6
Escape Me Never! 1935,Ja 22,22:2
Something Gay 1935,Ap 30,12:2
Orchard Walls 1937,F 21,X,2:1
Fight's On, The; Uneasy Virtue; Pardon My Back
1937,Ag 4,14:1
Love of Women 1937,D 14,33:2
Goodness, How Sad 1938,N 6,IX,3:5

Sinclair, Jo (Playwright)
Long Moment, The 1950,My 22,16:6

Sinclair, Judy
Gentlemen Prefer Blondes 1949,D 9,35:3
Top Banana 1951,N 2,19:2

Sinclair, Madge
Mod Donna 1970,My 4,48:1

Sinclair, Mary
Journey With Strangers, A 1958,N 27,53:1

Sinclair, Maud
Advertising of Kate, The 1922,My 9,22:2
Six Characters in Search of an Author
1922,O 31,11:2
Other Rose, The 1923,D 16,IX,2:4
Other Rose, The 1923,D 21,15:2
Arabian Nightmare, The 1927,Ja 11,36:3
Salvation 1928,F 1,31:1
Town Boy 1929,O 5,22:4
Heat Lightning 1933,S 16,9:6
Page Miss Glory 1934,N 28,24:2

Sinclair, Michael (Miscellaneous)
Live Like Pigs 1965,Je 8,48:2

Sinclair, Nena
Locked Room, The 1933,D 26,18:5

Sinclair, Robert
Song Writer, The 1928,Ag 14,15:2
Veneer 1929,N 13,24:5
Once in a Lifetime 1931,F 1,VIII,1:3
High Button Shoes 1955,Mr 12,10:6

Sinclair, Robert B (Director)
Once in a Lifetime 1931,F 1,VIII,1:3
Life Begins 1932,Mr 29,23:2
For Services Rendered 1933,Ap 13,15:5
Peace on Earth 1933,N 30,39:2
Dodsworth 1934,F 26,20:4
Dance With Your Gods 1934,O 8,14:3
Journey by Night, A 1935,Ap 17,26:3
Long Frontier, The 1935,Jl 23,24:4
Pride and Prejudice 1935,N 6,32:4
Pride and Prejudice 1935,N 17,IX,1:1
Postman Always Rings Twice, The 1936,F 7,14:4
Postman Always Rings Twice, The 1936,F 26,17:2
St Helena 1936,O 7,32:1
Women, The 1936,D 28,13:1
Babes in Arms 1937,Ap 15,18:4
Save Me the Waltz 1938,Mr 1,19:2
Philadelphia Story, The 1939,Mr 29,21:1
Philadelphia Story, The 1939,Ap 2,X,1:1
Wookey, The 1941,S 11,20:5
Without Love 1942,N 11,28:1
My Name is Aquilon 1949,F 10,38:2
Never Say Never 1951,N 21,21:2

Sinclair, Tom
Get Thee to Canterbury 1969,Ja 26,74:1

Sinclair, Upton (Playwright)
Singing Jailbirds 1928,My 20,VIII,2:1
Singing Jailbirds 1928,D 5,34:4
Singing Jailbirds 1930,F 10,20:8
Giant's Strength, A 1948,Je 19,8:5
Giant's Strength, A 1948,D 13,18:6
Cicero 1961,F 9,37:2

Sinclaire, Honey
Fireman's Flame, The 1937,O 11,26:2

Sincoff, Abe
Love and Politics 1929,O 21,30:7
Slaves of Luxury 1930,F 8,13:3
Sonitchka 1930,Mr 8,21:3
Three in Love 1931,S 26,25:5
East of Broadway 1932,Ja 27,19:3

Sincoff, Al
Unwritten Chapter, The 1920,O 12,18:1

Sindbad (Playwright)
General Percy Gruendet ein Koenigreich
1932,N 6,IX,3:1

Sindelar, Pearl
Hospitality 1922,N 14,16:1
Wild Duck, The 1925,F 25,16:4

Sindelar, Ron (Composer)
Critic, The 1969,Jl 26,15:2

Sinden, Donald
Odd Man In 1957,Jl 17,21:3
Tempest, The 1963,Ap 3,43:1
Twelfth Night 1969,S 1,13:1
Henry VIII 1969,O 11,42:1
London Assurance 1970,Je 25,55:2
London Assurance 1970,Ag 7,26:1

Sinden, Frederick
Yeomen of the Guard, The 1955,O 4,39:2
Sinden, Leon
Semi-Detached 1963,O 8,49:1
Sindler, Merrill (Costume Designer)
All Kinds of Giants 1961,D 19,40:1
Sindler, Merrill (Scenic Designer)
Across the Board on Tomorrow Morning
1961,O 23,22:5
Talking to You 1961,O 23,22:5
All Kinds of Giants 1961,D 19,40:1
Laundry, The 1963,F 19,5:2
To Be Young Gifted and Black; World of Lorraine
Hansberry, The 1969,Ja 3,15:1
Tonight in Living Color; Golden Fleece, The
1969,Je 11,43:1
Tonight in Living Color; David Show, The
1969,Je 11,43:1
Sindral, Jacques (Alfred Fabre-Luce) (Playwright)
Double 1929,Ja 13,VIII,2:7
Transfuges, Les 1929,N 10,X,4:1
Sing, Fay
Love City, The 1926,Ja 26,18:2
Singelis, James (Scenic Designer)
Romeo and Jeanette 1969,D 16,53:1
Singer, Ada
Mother's Sabbath Days 1960,N 21,33:2
Backlane Center 1961,N 23,51:1
Eleventh Inheritor, The 1962,N 22,43:5
Enchanting Melody 1964,N 25,40:1
Singer, Alex (Miscellaneous)
Viva Madison Avenue 1960,Ap 7,42:1
Singer, Andre (Composer)
Reunion in New York 1940,F 22,28:4
Rip Van Winkle 1947,Jl 16,28:2
Eastward in Eden 1947,N 19,33:2
Lamp at Midnight 1947,D 22,29:2
Twelfth Night 1959,Jl 11,10:2
Singer, Arthur
Bitter Oleander 1935,F 12,24:3
Panic 1935,Mr 16,18:4
Singer, Campbell (Playwright)
Calculated Risk 1962,N 1,35:1
Singer, Dolph (Lyricist)
White Lights 1927,O 12,30:4
Summer Wives 1936,Ap 14,18:1
Singer, Dolph (Playwright)
Summer Wives 1936,Ap 14,18:1
Singer, G P
How Revolting! 1932,Mr 11,14:6
Singer, George
Bacchae, The 1969,Mr 15,24:1
Singer, Gerard (Playwright)
Frere Jacques 1968,Je 8,23:2
Singer, Harry
Seven Against One 1930,My 7,25·1
Singer, I J (Original Author)
Yoshe Kalb 1932,O 3,15:5
Yoshe Kalb 1932,N 6,IX,2:1
Yoshe Kalb 1932,D 18,X,3:1
Yoshe Kalb 1933,D 29,27:2
Brothers Ashkenazi, The 1937,S 21,28:6
Yoshe Kalb 1939,F 6,9:2
Chaver, Nachman 1939,O 2,15:2
Brothers Ashkenazi, The 1970,N 17,53:2
Singer, I J (Playwright)
Shabtai Tavi 1932,D 7,28:8
Brothers Ashkenazi, The 1937,S 21,28:6
Chaver, Nachman 1939,O 2,15:2
Family Carnovsky, The 1943,O 19,16:7
Brothers Ashkenazi, The 1955,N 12,24:4
Singer, Isaac
Brothers Ashkenazi, The 1955,N 12,24:4
Singer, Isaac Basheves (Original Author)
Story Theater Repertory; Gimpel the Food
1970,O 21,40:1
Singer, Isaac Basheves (Playwright)
Devil's Game, A 1959,N 9,35:6
Singer, Jacques (Miscellaneous)
Caesar and Cleopatra 1951,D 20,43:2
Antony and Cleopatra 1951,D 21,22:2
Singer, Joseph
Merchant of Venice, The 1920,D 30,16:2
Macbeth 1924,Mr 17,18:1
Crooked Friday, The 1925,O 9,27:3
Eight Bells 1933,O 30,14:2
Yoshe Kalb 1933,D 29,27:2
Tomorrow's a Holiday! 1935,D 31,10:2
Ten Million Ghosts 1936,O 24,23:7
Sunup to Sundown 1938,F 2,14:3
He Who Gets Slapped 1946,Mr 21,31:4
Singer, Louis J (Miscellaneous)
Ghosts 1948,F 17,31:2
Hedda Gabler 1948,F 25,27:2
Singer, Louis J (Producer)
Glass Menagerie, The 1945,Ap 2,15:5
Our Lan' 1947,S 29,16:5
Sundown Beach 1948,S 8,37:1
Singer, Margaret (Miscellaneous)
Patience 1967,O 13,32:1
Iolanthe 1967,O 18,40:1
Mikado, The 1967,O 25,42:2

Singer, Marshe
Thousand and One Nights 1959,D 16,53:2
Singer, Midgets
Vaudeville (Hippodrome) 1925,D 29,21:2
Keep Moving 1934,Ag 24,10:2
Singer, Morris
Walk Hard 1944,D 1,28:2
Singer, Mort H Jr (Producer)
Bees and the Flowers, The 1946,S 27,19:3
Singer, Norman (Director)
Story Theater 1970,O 27,54:1
Moon Walk 1970,N 27,52:1
Singer, Norman (Miscellaneous)
Carnival! 1968,D 13,58:1
But Never Jam Today 1969,Ap 24,40:1
Singer, Pearl
Susan Slept Here 1961,Jl 12,35:2
Singer, Philip
American Landscape 1938,D 5,19:2
Singer, Raymond
Disintegration of James Cherry, The
1970,Ja 30,33:3
Candyapple, The 1970,N 24,33:1
Singer, Reuben
Don Juan; Feast With the Statue, The
1956,Ja 4,21:4
River Line, The 1957,Ja 3,29:2
Girl of the Golden West, The 1957,N 6,44:1
Milk and Honey 1961,O 11,52:1
Fade Out--Fade In 1964,My 27,45:1
Singer, Robert
Pirates of Penzance, The 1970,Jl 26,49:5
Pirates of Penzance, The 1970,D 6,84:6
Singer, Ron (Miscellaneous)
All Women Are One 1965,Ja 8,21:1
Singer, Ron (Producer)
Call It Virtue 1963,Mr 28,8:2
Singer, Sylvia
Mikado, The 1942,F 4,22:2
Pirates of Penzance, The 1942,F 18,22:2
Iolanthe 1942,F 24,26:4
Singer, Sylvia (Miscellaneous)
Every Other Evil 1961,Ja 23,20:2
Singer Midgets
Racketty Packetty House 1931,N 7,16:1
Singerman, Paulina
Amor 1937,Ap 22,18:6
Cuando Los Hijos De Eva No Son Los Hijos De
Adan 1937,My 1,17:4
Singerman, Paulina (Director)
Amor 1937,Ap 22,18:6
Singerman, Paulina (Producer)
Amor 1937,Ap 22,18:6
Singh, W Wana
Congai 1928,N 28,24:3
Ghost Parade, The 1929,O 31,28:4
Heat Wave 1931,F 18,14:6
Sex Fable, The 1931,O 21,26:1
White Cargo 1941,My 14,24:3
Singha, Kumara
Love's Call 1925,S 11,20:1
Lucky 1927,Mr 23,28:3
Singing Bird
Arrow-Maker, The 1956,O 5,20:1
Singing Soldiers of Fortune
Vaudeville (Palace) 1932,Je 13,19:7
Single, Betty Jane
Annie Get Your Gun 1957,Mr 9,15:5
Singleton, David
Founders, The 1957,My 14,39:1
Singleton, Harry
Fortuna 1962,Ja 4,26:1
Singleton, Sam
Great Goodness of Life (A Coon Show)
1969,Ap 27,92:1
Great Goodness of Life (A Coon Show)
1969,Ap 27,92:1
Black Quartet, A; Great Goodness of Life (A Coon
Show) 1969,Jl 31,28:1
Sinkler, Arthur B
East Lynne Goes West 1931,My 3,I,26:5
Sinn, Steven (Miscellaneous)
Indians 1969,O 14,51:1
Sinne
Lucky Break 1925,Ag 12,16:2
Sinne, Frank
Roar China! 1930,O 28,23:1
Sinnott, Frank
Countess Maritza 1926,S 20,21:1
Sinnott, Helene
Fair Circassian, The 1921,D 7,22:3
Old Soak, The 1922,Ag 23,14:5
Made for Each Other 1924,S 30,27:2
Rat, The 1925,F 11,19:3
Treat 'Em Rough 1926,O 5,26:2
Synthetic Sin 1927,O 11,26:2
That's the Woman 1930,S 4,27:2
Five Star Final 1930,D 31,11:1
Sinnott, Patricia
Elizabeth the Queen 1966,N 4,30:1
Sintae, Evelyn
Her Family Tree 1920,D 28,9:2

Sipavina, Yekaterina
Aladdin and His Wonderful Lamp 1963,O 21,39:1
Sipperly, Ralph
Meanest Man in the World, The 1920,O 13,18:2
Six-Cylinder Love 1921,Ag 26,8:2
Deep Tangled Wildwood, The 1923,N 6,22:1
New Poor, The 1924,Ja 8,26:1
Schemers 1924,S 16,27:1
Fall Guy, The 1925,Mr 11,19:1
Canary Dutch 1925,S 9,22:1
Sirat
World of Suzie Wong, The 1958,O 15,47:1
Siravo, George (Musical Director)
Mrs Patterson 1954,D 2,37:1
Sircom, Arthur
Straw Hat, The 1926,O 15,20:2
Trumpet Shall Sound, The 1926,D 11,15:2
Granite 1927,F 12,13:1
Sorcerer, The 1928,Je 24,VIII,1:1
Much Ado About Nothing 1929,N 17,30:4
Penny Wise 1935,Jl 2,24:2
Sircom, Arthur (Director)
Springtime for Henry 1931,D 10,29:2
Money in the Air 1932,Mr 8,19:3
Men Must Fight 1932,O 15,13:4
Good Woman, Poor Thing, A 1933,Ja 10,27:3
Sailor, Beware! 1933,S 29,24:4
Give Us This Day 1933,O 28,20:6
All Good Americans 1933,D 6,29:2
Whatever Possessed Her 1934,Ja 26,21:2
Battleship Gertie 1935,Ja 19,9:2
Penny Wise 1935,Jl 2,24:2
All Bow Down 1935,Ag 6,20:4
Whatever Goes Up 1935,N 26,28:2
I Want a Policeman! 1936,Ja 15,15:5
Seen But Not Heard 1936,S 18,19:2
Tide Rising 1937,Ja 26,17:2
Penny Wise 1937,Ap 20,28:6
Western Union 1937,Ag 10,22:7
Damn Deborah 1937,Ag 17,23:1
Tell Me Pretty Maiden 1937,D 17,33:5
Window Shopping 1938,D 24,13:2
Day in the Sun 1939,My 17,29:2
Case of Youth, A 1940,Mr 25,10:3
Romantic Mr Dickens 1940,D 3,33:2
Your Loving Son 1941,Ap 5,13:2
All the Comforts of Home 1942,My 26,24:5
Ramshackle Inn 1944,Ja 6,17:5
Mrs January & Mr Ex 1944,Ap 1,10:2
Odds on Mrs Oakley, The 1944,O 3,18:8
Sircom, Arthur (Miscellaneous)
Springtime for Henry 1931,D 10,29:2
Siregyol, Robert
Ecole des Femmes, L' 1961,Ap 28,23:1
Siretta, Dan
Coco 1969,D 19,66:1
Sireygeol, Robert
Annonce Faite a Marie, L' 1965,Ap 6,33:2
Sirmay, Albert (Composer)
Ripples 1930,F 2,VIII,2:7
Ripples 1930,F 12,26:1
Prince Charming 1930,O 14,31:1
Sirola, Anthony
Madre, La 1959,F 12,24:1
Sirola, Joseph
Song for a Certain Midnight 1959,S 17,49:1
Unsinkable Molly Brown, The 1960,N 4,28:1
Golden Rainbow 1968,F 5,27:1
Golden Rainbow 1968,Mr 3,II,3:1
Sirola, Joyce
Goose for the Gander, A 1945,Ja 24,16:4
Siron, Louis
Once in a Lifetime 1931,F 1,VIII,1:3
Sirota, Linda Mae
Long Days, The 1951,Ap 21,10:5
Sirota, Sylvia
Suddenly a Stranger 1936,Ag 4,15:2
Man From Cairo, The 1938,My 5,26:5
Sirovich, William Irving (Dr) (Playwright)
Schemers 1924,S 16,27:1
Sirvent, Fernando (Miscellaneous)
Blood Wedding 1958,Ap 1,35:1
Sisco, Jeanne
Solo 1962,Ap 27,26:1
Sisco, Jeanne (Miscellaneous)
Solo 1962,Ap 27,26:1
Night Is Black Bottles, The 1962,D 5,56:1
Sisco, Jimmy
New Faces of 1956 1956,Je 15,32:1
Sisk, George
War and Peace 1942,My 22,26:3
Sisk, James
Icetime 1947,My 29,28:2
Howdy Mr Ice 1948,Je 25,28:5
Sisk, Lewis
Trojan Horse, The 1940,O 31,28:3
Sisk, Max
Misanthrope, The 1956,N 13,44:1
Sisk, Michael
This Way to the Tomb 1961,D 9,21:1
Sissle, Noble
Chocolate Dandies, The 1924,S 2,22:2
Shuffle Along of 1933 1932,D 27,11:3

Sissle, Noble—Cont
Harlem Cavalcade 1942,My 2,11:2
Shuffle Along 1952,My 9,20:5
Sissle, Noble (Composer)
Chocolate Dandies, The 1924,S 2,22:2
Sissle, Noble (Director)
Harlem Cavalcade 1942,My 2,11:2
Sissle, Noble (Lyricist)
Chocolate Dandies, The 1924,S 2,22:2
Shuffle Along of 1933 1932,D 27,11:3
Shuffle Along 1952,My 9,20:5
Sissle, Noble (Miscellaneous)
In Bamville 1924,Mr 16,VIII,2:1
Sissle, Noble (Playwright)
Shuffle Along 1921,My 23,16:2
Chocolate Dandies, The 1924,S 2,22:2
Sissle, Noble and His Band
Vaudeville (Palace) 1931,F 16,16:3
Sisson, Richard
Master of the Revels 1935,Ag 14,16:2
Blind Alley 1940,O 16,28:2
Sisters G
Vaudeville (Hollywood) 1932,Ap 19,25:5
Siston, Louis
Thomas Paine 1930,Mr 21,30:7
Sitgreaves, Beverly
Square Peg, A 1923,Ja 29,10:2
Square Peg, A 1923,F 11,VII,1:1
Devil's Disciple, The 1923,Ap 24,24:1
Devil's Disciple, The 1923,My 6,VII,1:1
Agent 666, L' 1923,My 30,10:5
Royal Fandango, A 1923,N 13,25:1
Untitled-Recital 1923,D 29,8:2
Weak Woman, A 1926,Ja 27,16:3
2 Girls Wanted 1926,S 10,25:3
Now-A-Days 1929,Ag 6,29:3
Fiesta 1929,S 18,35:1
Seven 1929,D 28,10:5
One Chaste Man 1930,Je 11,33:5
Country Wife, The 1931,Ap 19,31:5
Guest Room, The 1931,O 7,29:2
Housewarming 1932,Ag 8,25:1
Shooting Star 1933,Je 13,22:2
I Was Waiting for You 1933,N 14,23:3
Moor Born 1934,Ap 4,26:4
Moor Born 1934,Ap 8,X,2:7
Bride of Torozko, The 1934,Jl 10,24:7
De Luxe 1935,Mr 6,22:2
Laughing Woman, The 1936,O 14,30:1
Sitters, Jake
Handful of Fire 1958,O 2,45:3
Sittler, Marion
Ringside Seat 1938,N 23,24:5
Audition of the Apprentice Theatre 1939,Je 2,26:2
Billy Draws a Horse 1939,D 22,14:5
Sitwell, Osbert
Follow the Sun 1936,F 5,15:8
Sitwell, Osbert (Playwright)
Elsa Lanchester-Herself 1961,F 6,28:1
Sivaraman, Kottakkal
Mahabharata 1970,N 28,22:1
Sivy, Michael
Temper the Wind 1946,D 28,10:2
Bathsheba 1947,Mr 27,40:2
Julia, Jake, and Uncle Joe 1961,Ja 30,19:1
Siwertz, Sigurd (Playwright)
Trio's Wedding, The 1930,Jl 13,VIII,2:1
Six, Jack
Thurber Carnival, A 1960,F 27,13:2
Six Dixie Vamps
Plantation Revue, The 1922,Jl 18,18:4
Six Mighty Atoms
Pardon Our French 1950,O 6,22:4
Sizemore, Arthur (Composer)
Brown Buddies 1930,O 8,29:1
Sjoberg, Alf (Director)
Miss Julie 1962,My 17,31:1
Skaar, Perry
Sunrise at Campobello 1958,Ja 31,25:1
Giants, Sons of Giants 1962,Ja 8,26:2
Skaff, George (Producer)
Vintage '60 1960,S 13,41:1
Skala, Lilia
Letters to Lucerne 1941,D 24,14:2
Many Moons 1947,D 15,35:2
Rumpelstiltskin 1948,Mr 15,27:3
Indian Captive, The 1949,Ja 31,15:2
With a Silk Thread 1950,Ap 13,34:3
Call Me Madam 1950,O 13,25:1
Dreigroschenoper, Die 1965,Mr 12,24:1
Zelda 1969,Mr 6,38:1
Skalet, Arthur
Mascaiada 1929,D 28,10:6
Skapik, Martin
Chicken Every Sunday 1944,Ap 6,27:2
Skariatina, Irina (Translator)
Cherry Orchard, The 1944,Ja 26,22:1
Skavlan, Olaf
Virgin, The 1926,F 23,26:1
Skeen, Martha
Help Yourself! 1936,Jl 15,15:1
Skeete, Yolande
Endecott and the Red Cross 1968,My 7,50:1

Skelly, Ann
Vaudeville (Palace) 1929,O 7,22:4
Skelly, Hal
Night Boat, The 1920,F 3,18:1
Girl in the Spotlight, The 1920,Jl 13,9:3
Orange Blossoms 1922,S 20,18:1
Mary Jane McKane 1923,D 26,13:2
Betty Lee 1924,D 26,18:2
Lambs Gambol 1925,Ap 27,15:1
Vaudeville (Palace) 1925,D 29,21:2
Vaudeville (Palace) 1926,Ag 3,19:2
Burlesque 1927,S 2,15:3
Burlesque 1927,S 11,VIII,1:1
Roamin' Gentleman, A 1930,F 23,VIII,2:5
Vaudeville (Palace) 1930,Mr 7,21:2
Manhattan Medley 1932,S 25,IX,1:6
Melody 1933,F 15,17:4
Lambs Gambol 1933,Ap 24,10:1
Ghost Writer, The 1933,Je 20,22:4
Queer People 1934,F 16,16:2
Come What May 1934,My 16,23:4
Skelly, Hal (Producer)
Come What May 1934,My 16,23:4
Skelly, Hazel
Vaudeville (Hippodrome) 1925,D 29,21:2
Skelly, Hugh (Miscellaneous)
Popsy 1941,F 11,26:2
Skelly, Madge
Lady Behave 1943,N 17,30:1
Skelly, Monica
Vaudeville (Palace) 1929,O 7,22:4
Skelly, Robert
Last Man In, The 1930,My 8,32:5
Skelton, Geoffrey (Playwright)
Persecution and Assassination of Marat As
Performed by the Inmates of the Asylum of
Charenton Under the Direction of the Marquis de
Sade, The 1965,D 28,35:1
Persecution and Assassination of Marat As
Performed by the Inmates of the Asylum of
Charenton Under the Direction of the Marquis de
Sade, The 1967,Ja 4,34:1
Skelton, Geoffrey (Translator)
Persecution and Assassination of Marat As
Performed by the Inmates of the Asylum of
Charenton Under the Direction of the Marquis de
Sade, The 1966,Ja 9,II,1:1
Skelton, George
Gentle People, The 1939,Ja 6,25:1
Skelton, Henry
Dancers, The 1923,O 18,17:2
Skelton, Thomas (Director)
Come Slowly, Eden 1966,D 7,56:1
Skelton, Thomas (Lighting Director)
Enchanted, The 1958,Ap 23,41:1
Calvary 1960,Jl 22,13:1
Santa Claus 1960,Jl 22,13:1
Escurial 1960,Jl 22,13:1
Misalliance 1961,S 26,32:2
Oh Dad, Poor Dad, Mamma's Hung You in the
Closet and I'm Feelin' So Sad 1962,F 27,28:1
Oh Dad, Poor Dad, Mamma's Hung You in the
Closet and I'm Feelin' So Sad 1963,Ag 28,28:2
In the Summer House 1964,Mr 26,43:1
Wiener Blut 1964,S 12,14:1
Zizi 1964,N 23,51:1
Sing to Me Through Open Windows
1965,Mr 16,45:1
Day the Whores Came Out to Play Tennis, The
1965,Mr 16,45:1
Your Own Thing 1968,Ja 15,33:1
Mike Downstairs 1968,Ap 19,35:1
Jimmy Shine 1968,D 6,52:1
Big Time Buck White 1968,D 9,58:1
Does a Tiger Wear a Necktie? 1969,F 26,38:1
Come Summer 1969,Mr 19,43:1
Henry V 1969,Je 9,57:1
Much Ado About Nothing 1969,Je 16,57:1
Hamlet 1969,Je 30,33:1
Three Sisters, The 1969,Ag 4,29:1
Patriot for Me, A 1969,O 6,58:1
Indians 1969,O 14,51:1
Henry V 1969,N 11,43:1
Coco 1969,D 19,66:1
Purlie 1970,Mr 16,53:1
Mahagonny 1970,Ap 29,51:1
Bob and Ray-The Two and Only 1970,S 25,36:1
Lovely Ladies, Kind Gentlemen 1970,D 29,38:1
Skelton, Thomas (Miscellaneous)
Peh Shuh Tchuwan; White Snake, The 1963,Ja 4,5:2
Skelton, Thomas (Scenic Designer)
Tio Ch'an; Beautiful Bait, The 1962,N 13,44:1
Skelton, William
Catherine Was Great 1944,Ag 3,16:1
Skeptics, The
Fun With Music 1946,N 25,38:5
Skidmore, Hobart
Masque of the Kings, The 1937,F 9,19:4
Good Hunting 1938,N 22,26:5
Skidmore, Katherine
Nina Rosa 1930,My 31,19:3
Nina Rosa 1930,S 22,22:5
Marching By 1932,Mr 4,17:1

Skiles, Steve
Now Is the Time for all Good Men 1967,S 27,42:1
Skilling, William (Scenic Designer)
Lady From Maxim's, The 1970,Je 1,41:1
Skillingns, Doris
Ice Follies 1963,Ja 10,5:2
Skillings, Charles (Lighting Director)
Ice Follies 1959,Ja 14,30:1
Ice Follies 1961,Ja 11,25:2
Ice Follies 1963,Ja 10,5:2
Skillman, R J
It's the Valet 1933,D 15,25:4
Skinner, Cornelia Otis
Blood and Sand 1921,S 21,16:2
Will Shakespeare 1923,Ja 2,14:1
Tweedles 1923,Ag 14,10:1
Wild Westcotts, The 1923,D 25,26:2
In His Arms 1924,O 14,23:1
White Collars 1925,F'24,17:2
Untitled-Revue 1928,N 19,16:2
Untitled-One Woman Show 1928,D 17,25:3
Untitled-One Woman Show 1929,N 18,22:6
After Holbein 1931,Je 17,32:3
Wives of Henry VIII, The 1931,N 16,22:3
Empress Eugenie, The 1932,N 23,15:4
Loves of Charles II, The 1933,D 28,25:2
Mansion on the Hudson 1935,Ap 3,20:4
Candida 1935,Ag 20,25:1
Loves of Charles II, The 1937,Mr 29,15:1
Edna His Wife 1937,D 8,30:3
Love for Love 1940,Je 4,19:5
Theatre 1941,O 26,IX,2:3
Theatre 1941,N 13,34:2
Searching Wind, The 1944,Ap 13,25:2
Searching Wind, The 1944,Ap 23,II,1:1
Lady Windermere's Fan 1946,O 15,29:2
Untitled-One Woman Show 1949,Je 29,33:5
Paris '90 1952,Mr 5,33:2
Paris '90 1952,Mr 16,II,1:1
Paris '90 1954,Mr 5,14:4
Characters and Chicanery 1956,Ja 24,26:2
Major Barbara 1956,O 31,27:1
Fun and Magic 1957,D 30,19:4
Pleasure of His Company, The 1958,O 23,36:1
Pleasure of His Company, The 1958,N 2,II,1:1
Skinner, Cornelia Otis (Composer)
Edna His Wife 1937,D 8,30:3
Skinner, Cornelia Otis (Playwright)
Mansion on the Hudson 1935,Ap 3,20:4
Edna His Wife 1937,D 8,30:3
Paris '90 1952,Mr 5,33:2
Pleasure of His Company, The 1958,O 23,36:1
Pleasure of His Company, The 1958,N 2,II,1:1
Pleasure of His Company, The 1959,Ap 24,22:3
Skinner, Edith W (Miscellaneous)
Hamlet 1957,Ja 29,27:1
Skinner, Edwin L (Playwright)
Book of Job, The 1936,Mr 5,24:6
Skinner, Harold
Mecca 1920,O 5,12:2
Skinner, Jack
Green Table, The 1942,Ja 22,12:2
Prodigal Son, The 1942,F 18,22:2
Skinner, Joseph
Gang War 1928,Ag 21,27:2
Skinner, Lauralee
Men Must Fight 1932,O 15,13:4
Skinner, Maud (Playwright)
Pietro 1920,Ja 20,10:2
Skinner, Mildred
Parisiana 1928,F 10,26:3
Skinner, Neil
Love for Love 1940,Je 4,19:5
Mr Peebles and Mr Hooker 1946,O 11,29:2
Skinner, Nell
What's Your Number? 1929,Ag 16,18:3
Skinner, Otis
Pietro 1920,Ja 20,10:2
Pietro 1920,Ja 25,VIII,2:2
Blood and Sand 1921,S 21,16:2
Blood and Sand 1921,S 25,VI,1:4
Sancho Panza 1923,O 21,VIII,2:1
Sancho Panza 1923,N 27,23:1
Sancho Panza 1923,D 2,VIII,1:1
Henry IV, Part I 1926,Je 1,29:1
Henry IV, Part I 1926,Je 6,VIII,1:1
Honor of the Family, The 1926,D 27,21:1
Merry Wives of Windsor, The 1928,Mr 20,20:1
Hundred Years Old, A 1929,Ap 19,27:5
Hundred Years Old, A 1929,O 2,28:2
Merchant of Venice, The 1931,N 4,31:1
Merchant of Venice, The 1931,N 9,22:2
Troilus and Cressida 1932,Je 7,22:3
Uncle Tom's Cabin 1933,My 30,13:4
Noble Prize, The 1933,Jl 4,16:4
Uncle Tom's Cabin 1933,O 10,24:3
Seven Keys to Baldpate 1935,My 28,30:2
Skinner, Richard
Hamlet 1922,N 17,14:1
Taming of the Shrew, The 1925,D 19,14:1
Straw Hat, The 1926,O 15,20:2
Rapid Transit 1927,Ap 8,21:2
Taming of the Shrew, The 1927,O 26,26:4

Skinner, Richard—Cont

Sorcerer, The 1928,Je 24,VIII,1:1
Wild Duck, The 1928,N 19,17:1
Money in the Air 1932,Mr 8,19:3

Skinner, Richard (Miscellaneous)
Family Portrait 1939,Mr 9,18:4
Charley's Aunt 1940,O 18,24:2
Wonderful Journey 1946,D 26,30:2

Skinner, Richard (Producer)
Front Page, The 1935,Jl 9,24:4
Patsy, The 1935,Jl 16,24:1
Post Road 1935,Jl 23,24:3
Smiling Through 1935,Jl 30,17:2
Hay Fever 1935,Ag 6,20:3
Caste 1935,Ag 13,20:3
Patience 1935,S 3,24:4
Personal Appearance 1936,Je 16,23:4
Personal Appearance 1936,Je 23,27:3
Fresh Fields 1936,Je 23,27:3
They Knew What They Wanted 1936,Jl 28,23:4
Elizabeth the Queen 1936,Ag 4,15:2
Pomeroy's Past 1936,Ag 4,15:2
Be So Kindly 1937,F 9,19:4
I Know What I Like 1939,N 25,13:5
School for Scandal, The 1940,Je 18,29:5
Signature 1945,F 15,25:2

Skinner, Robert (Scenic Designer)
Puntila 1959,My 15,26:2
Happy Haven, The 1963,My 10,40:6

Skinner, Roland
Finian's Rainbow 1947,Ja 11,23:2

Skipitaris, Loukas
Zorba 1968,N 18,58:1

Skipper, William
Banjo Eyes 1941,D 26,20:2
Park Avenue 1946,N 5,31:2
Almost Crazy 1955,Je 21,37:1
Not While I'm Eating 1961,D 20,37:1

Skipper, William (Choreographer)
Almost Crazy 1955,Je 21,37:1

Skipper and Kate
Star and Garter 1942,Je 25,26:2

Skipworth, Alison
Torch Bearers, The 1922,Ag 30,10:2
Swan, The 1923,O 24,15:3
Enchanted April, The 1925,Ag 25,12:3
Grand Duchess and the Waiter, The 1925,O 14,31:1
Port O' London 1926,F 10,20:2
Ashes of Love 1926,Mr 23,24:3
Buy, Buy Baby 1926,O 8,26:2
New York Exchange 1926,D 31,11:2
Julie 1927,My 10,24:4
Garden of Eden, The 1927,S 28,28:1
Spellbound 1927,N 15,26:2
Los Angeles 1927,D 20,32:3
Mrs Dane's Defense 1928,F 7,30:1
Say When 1928,Je 27,29:3
Angela 1928,D 4,28:2
Cafe de Danse 1929,Ja 16,22:2
Button, Button 1929,O 24,26:1
Primer for Lovers, A 1929,N 19,26:5
Marseilles; Marius 1930,N 9,IX,3:2
Marseilles 1930,N 18,28:2
30 Days Hath September 1938,O 1,10:5
When We Are Married 1939,N 21,19:5
When We Are Married 1939,D 10,X,5:6
When We Are Married 1939,D 26,22:3
First Stop to Heaven 1941,Ja 6,10:7

Skirball, Jack H (Miscellaneous)
Jacobowsky and the Colonel 1944,Mr 15,17:2

Skirball, Jack H (Producer)
Jacobowsky and the Colonel 1944,Mr 19,II,1:1

Skitch, Jeffrey
Mikado, The 1955,S 30,20:2
Princess Ida 1955,O 14,22:3
H M S Pinafore 1955,O 18,48:1
Mikado, The 1962,N 14,43:1
Trial by Jury 1962,N 23,32:4
H M S Pinafore 1962,N 23,32:4
Iolanthe 1962,N 28,42:1
Iolanthe 1964,N 18,52:1
H M S Pinafore 1964,N 20,40:1
Trial by Jury 1964,N 20,40:1

Sklar, Alan
Deirdre of the Sorrows 1959,O 15,46:1

Sklar, George (Lyricist)
Parade 1935,My 21,22:2

Sklar, George (Playwright)
Merry-Go-Round 1932,Ap 23,11:2
Merry-Go-Round 1932,My 1,VIII,1:1
Peace on Earth 1933,N 30,39:2
Stevedore 1934,Ap 19,33:2
Stevedore 1934,Ap 29,IX,1:1
Stevedore 1934,O 2,18:2
Parade 1935,My 7,26:1
Parade 1935,My 12,X,2:5
Parade 1935,My 21,22:2
Parade 1935,My 26,XI,1:1
Life and Death of an American 1939,My 20,11:2
Laura 1947,Je 27,16:1
Stevedore 1949,F 23,30:2
And People All Around 1966,Ag 7,II,1:1
And People All Around 1968,F 12,46:1

Sklar, Irving
Tin Pan Alley 1928,N 2,29:1

Sklar, Martin
Evening With the Times Square Two, An 1967,My 21,83:6

Sklar, Paul
Whatever Goes Up 1935,N 26,28:2

Sklar, Roberta (Director)
Have I Got One for You 1968,Ja 8,32:1
Terminal 1970,Ap 15,51:2
Endgame 1970,My 6,47:1
Terminal 1970,My 24,II,3:1

Sklar, Roberta (Miscellaneous)
Serpent, The 1970,Je 2,35:1

Skloot, Robert
Harpers Ferry 1967,Je 6,52:2

Skner, Berthe
Montmartre 1922,F 14,20:1

Skoda, Albin
Hamlet in Wittenberg 1936,N 15,XI,2:4

Skodak, Edna
White Lights 1927,O 12,30:4

Skodik, Leo (Director)
Don Carlos 1964,N 25,40:1
Captain of Koepenick, The 1964,D 2,60:1

Skolnik, Peter (Director)
Nobody Hears A Broken Drum 1970,Mr 20,55:1

Skolnik, Peter (Producer)
Nobody Hears A Broken Drum 1970,Mr 20,55:1

Skolovsky, Zadel
Polonaise 1945,O 8,20:2

Skonald, Florence
Vaudeville (Palace) 1928,O 9,35:2

Skulnick, Broche
Going to America 1961,O 30,33:7

Skulnik, Menasha
In a Tenement House 1932,Ja 25,20:4
Pioneers 1932,F 26,22:5
Wedding Chains 1932,Mr 28,10:5
Untitled-Benefit 1933,Ja 25,13:3
God Man and Devil 1935,Mr 6,22:3
Perfect Fishel, The 1935,S 30,12:4
Laugh Night 1936,S 14,25:1
Schlemihl 1936,S 19,20:4
Straw Hero, The 1936,N 24,35:1
Galician Rabbi, The 1937,F 13,9:7
Yossel and His Wives 1937,S 19,II,8:3
Jolly Village, The 1937,N 15,15:5
Warson at Night 1938,Ja 31,14:3
Little Tailor, The 1938,Mr 21,18:2
Wise Fool, The 1938,O 10,15:3
Mazel Tov, Rabbi 1938,N 28,10:4
Jewish Heart, The 1939,Ja 25,16:6
Three Men and a Girl 1939,F 6,9:3
Fifth Season, The 1953,Ja 24,13:2
Flowering Peach, The 1954,D 29,19:2
Flowering Peach, The 1955,Ja 9,II,1:1
Uncle Willie 1956,D 21,17:1
49th Cousin, The 1960,O 28,22:1
Zulu and the Zayda, The 1965,N 11,59:1

Skulnik, Menasha (Producer)
Schlemihl 1936,S 19,20:4

Skulnik, Sarah
One Woman 1931,D 14,16:4
Yossel and His Wives 1937,S 19,II,8:3
Warson at Night 1938,Ja 31,14:3
Little Tailor, The 1938,Mr 21,18:2

Skutch, Ira (Producer)
Whitman Portrait, A 1966,O 12,37:1

Sky, Don (Choreographer)
Bella 1961,N 17,40:1

Sky, Don (Miscellaneous)
Bella 1961,N 17,40:1

Skylar, Joy
Top Banana 1951,N 2,19:2

Skylarks, The
Vaudeville (Palace) 1952,Ap 14,23:2
Vaudeville (Palace) 1952,Ap 27,II,1:1
Vaudeville (Palace) 1953,O 15,42:1

Slack, Benjamin Hess
Stephen D 1966,Ag 5,17:1
Jungle of Cities 1970,Mr 1,75:2

Slack, Bunty
Green Table, The 1942,Ja 22,12:2
Prodigal Son, The 1942,F 18,22:2

Slack, Edith
Up She Goes 1922,N 7,14:2

Slack, Forman R
His Majesty the Queen 1926,Mr 9,8:1
Betty Behave 1927,Mr 9,28:4

Slack, Gertrude
Gordon Reilly 1952,N 26,20:5

Slade, Julian (Composer)
Salad Days 1958,N 11,24:1

Slade, Julian (Lyricist)
Salad Days 1958,N 11,24:1

Slade, Julian (Playwright)
Salad Days 1958,N 11,24:1

Slade, Marie
White-Headed Boy, The 1921,S 16,20:1

Slade, Mark
There Was a Little Girl 1960,Mr 1,28:1

Slade, Martin
Anna Lucasta 1944,Je 17,10:1

Slade, Martin C
Big Deal, The 1953,Mr 7,13:6

Slade, Martin de C
Brown Sugar 1937,D 3,29:2

Slade, Stuart (Scenic Designer)
Sweet Miani 1962,S 26,33:2

Slade, Susan (Miscellaneous)
Natural Look, The 1967,Mr 13,45:2

Slade, Susan (Playwright)
Ready When You Are, C. B.! 1964,D 8,55:1

Sladen-Smith, F (Playwright)
Little Theatre Tournament; St Simeon Stylites 1926,My 7,12:2

Slagel, Donald
From Here to There; Slow Dusk 1958,Ap 24,37:3
From Here to There; Otherwise Engaged 1958,Ap 24,37:3

Slagle, A Russell
Fatal Lady, The 1936,Mr 19,23:7
Chocolate Soldier, The 1942,Je 24,22:2

Slagle, Charles
It Happens on Ice 1941,Ap 5,13:2
Stars on Ice 1942,Jl 3,12:2
Ice Capades 1952,S 12,18:1

Slagle, Jake
Samarkand 1926,D 22,24:4

Slaiman, Marjorie (Costume Designer)
Great White Hope, The 1967,D 14,58:1
Iceman Cometh, The 1968,Ap 1,58:1
Indians 1969,My 27,43:1
Indians 1969,O 14,51:1
Indians 1969,O 19,II,1:1
Night Thoreau Spent in Jail, The 1970,N 2,66:1

Slane, E S
Peg o' My Heart 1948,Ag 25,29:2

Slane, Stephan (Producer)
Lend an Ear 1959,S 25,20:5

Slate, Barbara
Kismet 1953,D 4,2:4

Slate, Henry
You Said It 1931,Ja 20,21:3
Winged Victory 1943,N 22,24:1
South Pacific 1949,Ap 8,30:2
South Pacific 1949,Ap 17,II,1:1
South Pacific 1955,My 5,39:5

Slate, Jack
You Said It 1931,Ja 20,21:3
Winged Victory 1943,N 22,24:1

Slate, Syd
You Said It 1931,Ja 20,21:3

Slate Brothers
Vaudeville (Palace) 1929,Je 24,27:4
Vanities 1931,Ag 16,VIII,1:1
Earl Carroll's Vanities 1931,Ag 28,18:7

Slater, B J
1776 1969,Mr 17,46:2

Slater, Barton (Producer)
Broadway Boy 1932,My 4,23:5

Slater, Daphne
Romeo and Juliet 1947,Ap 7,18:5

Slater, Harold
Whole Town's Talking, The 1923,S 9,VII,1:1

Slater, James
Caukey 1944,F 18,15:4

Slater, Maximilan (Director)
Fools Are Passing Through 1958,Ap 3,24:2

Slater, Maximilan (Playwright)
Fools Are Passing Through 1958,Ap 3,24:2

Slater, Montagu (Playwright)
Stay Down Miner 1936,My 11,16:4

Slater, Thomas
Henry V 1964,My 13,52:1
Saint Joan 1964,My 14,41:1
Richard III 1965,Je 3,26:1

Slatner, Eve
Herne's Egg, The 1960,S 20,48:1

Slaton, Don
Best Foot Forward 1963,Ap 3,43:1

Slattery, Anne Hamilton
Little Theatre Tournament; House With the Twisty Windows, The 1929,My 8,34:4

Slattery, Charles
Piker, The 1925,Ja 16,14:1
Chicago 1926,D 31,11:1
Black Velvet 1927,S 28,28:1
Clutching Claw, The 1928,F 15,20:1
Mr Moneypenny 1928,O 17,26:2
Crooks' Convention, The 1929,S 19,37:4
City Haul 1929,D 31,14:4
Just to Remind You 1931,S 8,39:1
Of Mice and Men 1937,N 24,20:5

Slattery, John
Pleasure Bound 1929,F 19,22:4

Slattery, May
George White's Scandals 1926,Je 15,23:2

Slattery, Richard X
King's Standards, The 1958,F 14,19:1
Child of the Morning 1958,Ap 22,40:2
Listen to the Quiet 1958,O 28,40:2
Cook for Mr General, A 1961,O 20,39:1

Slaughter, Tod
Wolves of Tanner's Close, or the Crimes of Burke and Hare, The; Crimes of Burke and Hare, The 1932,Ja 10,VIII,2:4

Slaughter, Tod (Producer)
Wolves of Tanner's Close, or the Crimes of Burke and Hare, The; Crimes of Burke and Hare, The 1932,Ja 10,VIII,2:4

Slausen, Janet
Hamlet 1945,D 14,25:2

Slava, Lyda
Awake and Sing! 1938,D 23,16:6

Slavenska, Mia
Arabian Nights 1954,Je 25,15:2

Slaviansky, Agreneva (Princess) and the Royal /Russian Choir
Vaudeville (Palace) 1929,Je 17,29:3

Slaviansky Russian Choir
Passion Play, The 1929,My 5,IX,1:1

Slavin, Arthur
Partition 1948,O 29,31:2

Slavin, Eugene
Wonder World 1964,My 18,32:1

Slavin, L (Playwright)
Intervention 1936,O 11,X,1:4

Slavin, Mildred
Night Music 1951,Ap 9,29:6
South Pacific 1957,Ap 25,35:1

Slavin, Millie
To Broadway With Love 1964,Ap 30,28:6
Promises, Promises 1968,D 2,59:3

Slavin, Susan
Dark of the Moon 1970,Ap 4,21:2

Slavina, Norma
Chauve-Souris of 1943 1943,Ag 13,13:2

Slavsky, Otto
Blue Butterfly, The 1929,F 17,29:3

Slayter, Marcus
Yeah-Man 1932,My 27,27:3

Slayter, Marcus (Choreographer)
Yeah-Man 1932,My 27,27:3

Slayton, Helen
Finian's Rainbow 1953,Mr 7,13:2

Slaytor, Dorothy
Fata Morgana 1931,D 26,15:3

Slaytor, Joseph
Good Old Days, The 1923,Ag 15,21:2

Slear, Ralph
Marching By 1932,Mr 4,17:1

Slebert, Charles
As You Like It 1968,Je 24,42:3

Sledge, Eddie
Kiss Me, Kate 1948,D 31,10:3

Sleeper, Donald
On the Level 1937,Mr 26,24:4

Sleeper, Kenneth
Shrike, The 1953,N 26,51:2

Sleeper, Martha
Stepping Out 1929,My 21,29:1
Dinner at Eight 1933,Ap 9,IX,1:7
Good Men and True 1935,De 26,12:4
Russet Mantle 1936,Ja 17,15:5
Russet Mantle 1936,Ja 26,IX,1:1
Double Dummy 1936,N 12,30:1
Save Me the Waltz 1938,Mr 1,19:2
I Must Love Someone 1939,F 8,18:7
Cream in the Well, The 1941,Ja 21,19:2
Land Is Bright, The 1941,O 21,28:5
Land Is Bright, The 1941,O 29,26:2
Land Is Bright, The 1941,N 9,IX,1:1
Perfect Marriage, The 1944,O 27,17:6
Rugged Path, The 1945,N 12,17:2
Christopher Blake 1946,D 2,33:2
Christopher Blake 1946,D 8,II,5:1

Sleigh, T W
Middle Watch, The 1929,O 17,27:1

Slemons, Fredrica
Bridal Quilt 1934,O 11,28:5
Plumes in the Dust 1936,N 7,14:2
House in the Country, A 1937,Ja 12,18:3
Beautiful People, The 1941,Ap 22,27:2
Show Boat 1946,Ja 7,17:2

Sletzer, Meyer
It Is to Laugh 1927,D 27,24:2

Slevers, David
King Lear 1940,D 16,27:2

Slevin, Doc
Ballad of John Ogilvie, The 1968,O 9,42:4

Slevin, James M (Producer)
Howie 1958,S 18,35:2

Sleysin, Jeanne
Intermezzo 1957,F 15,20:4

Slezak, Leo
Blue Beard 1929,Jl 7,VIII,2:1

Slezak, Walter
Meet My Sister 1930,D 31,11:1
Frau Die Weiss Was Sie Will, Eine 1932,O 9,IX,3:7
Music in the Air 1932,O 23,IX,3:3
Music in the Air 1932,N 9,28:2
Music in the Air 1932,N 20,IX,1:1
Ode to Liberty 1934,D 22,20:2
May Wine 1935,D 6,30:3
Doll's House, A 1937,Jl 18,II,6:8

Doll's House, A 1937,Jl 25,X,2:3
I Married an Angel 1938,My 12,26:2
I Married an Angel 1938,My 22,XI,1:1
Trojan Women, The 1941,Ap 9,32:5
Somewhere in France 1941,Ap 29,16:8
Little Dark Horse 1941,N 17,14:4
My 3 Angels 1953,Mr 12,23:2
Fanny 1954,N 5,16:1
Fanny 1954,N 21,II,1:1
First Gentleman, The 1957,Ap 26,22:2
First Gentleman, The 1957,My 5,II,1:1
Gazebo, The 1958,D 13,2:7

Slipper Revue
Vaudeville (Palace) 1930,Mr 31,24:2

Sloan, Anthony (Playwright)
Oedipus 1970,F 23,30:1

Sloan, Claude
Natural Man 1941,My 8,20:4

Sloan, Estelle
Toplitzky of Notre Dame 1946,D 27,13:4

Sloan, Fern
Susie Is a Good Girl 1968,N 5,53:2
Subscriber, The 1968,N 5,53:2
Grab Bag, The 1968,N 5,53:2
Mourning Becomes Electra 1969,S 7,II,1:2
Play by Aleksandr Solzhenitsyn, A 1970,O 18,94:1

Sloan, Grena
It Happened Tomorrow 1933,My 6,11:5
Let 'Em Eat Cake 1933,O 23,18:1
Stage Door 1936,O 23,26:3

Sloan, Kathe
Wretched the Lionhearted 1962,S 13,31:2

Sloan, Kay
Jubilee 1935,O 14,20:1

Sloan, Kenneth Cooper
Steel 1939,D 20,30:2

Sloan, Mary Jane
My Romance 1948,O 20,38:5

Sloan, Michael (Producer)
Rumple 1957,N 7,42:2

Sloan, Mimi
Education of H*Y*M*A*N K*A*P*L*A*N, The 1968,Ap 5,57:1

Sloan, Robert
Heat Lightning 1933,S 16,9:6

Sloan, Robin
Sleepy Hollow 1948,Je 4,26:3

Sloane, A Baldwin (Composer)
Greenwich Village Follies 1920,Ag 31,7:3
China Rose 1925,Ja 20,18:1

Sloane, Christy
Cradle Snatchers 1932,N 17,23:2

Sloane, Everett
Playing With Love 1929,F 27,16:4
Boy Meets Girl 1935,N 28,38:2
All That Glitters 1938,Ja 20,18:2
Native Son 1941,Mr 25,26:5
Men in Shadow 1943,Mr 11,16:2
Bell for Adano, A 1944,N 10,24:6
Bell for Adano, A 1944,D 7,21:2
How I Wonder 1947,O 1,34:2
Room Service 1953,Ap 7,34:1
Black-Eyed Susan 1954,D 24,7:5

Sloane, Everett (Director)
Dancer, The 1946,Je 6,16:5

Sloane, Gerard
Schoolhouse on the Lot 1938,Mr 23,18:4

Sloane, Jerry
Page Miss Glory 1934,N 28,24:2
Paths of Glory 1935,S 27,24:2
All Editions 1936,D 23,17:2

Sloane, Joyce (Miscellaneous)
Borstal Boy 1970,Ap 1,38:1

Sloane, Martin (Scenic Designer)
Joy of Serpents 1930,Ap 4,22:4

Sloane, Michael (Miscellaneous)
Sweethearts 1947,Ja 22,31:2

Sloane, Michael (Producer)
Top Banana 1951,N 2,19:2
Carnival in Flanders 1953,S 9,38:2

Sloane, Nancy
Variations of 1940 1940,Ja 29,12:1

Sloane, Robert
Locked Room, The 1933,D 26,18:5
Come What May 1934,My 16,23:4
Ladies' Money 1934,N 2,26:6
Substitute for Murder 1935,O 23,18:6
May Wine 1935,D 6,30:3
Much Ado About Nothing 1963,Jl 15,25:2
As You Like It 1966,Je 4,19:1

Sloane, Robert (Playwright)
Howdy Stranger 1937,Ja 15,17:5

Sloane, Sydney
This Side of Paradise 1962,F 22,19:6

Sloane, Sydney (Playwright)
This Side of Paradise 1962,F 22,19:6

Slocum, Alma
Men of Distinction 1953,My 1,18:4
Sappho 1960,Ja 12,22:1

Slocum, Earl (Prof) (Musical Director)
Shroud My Body Down 1934,D 9,II,1:6

Slocum, Joseph
One-Act Plays of the Sea; In the Zone 1937,O 30,23:2
One-Act Plays of the Sea; Bound East for Cardiff 1937,O 30,23:2

Sloninsky, Philip
Wooden Idol, The 1930,My 13,27:2

Slorance, Stan
Indian Captive, The 1949,Ja 31,15:2

Slotoroff, Marvin (Playwright)
Destiny Rag 1968,My 28,41:1

Slough, Sue
Off Your Marx 1936,Ap 2,28:2

Slout, Bill
Born Yesterday 1958,Mr 22,12:6

Sloux, Guy
Printemps 1929,Ap 21,X,2:7

Slowacki, Julius
Constant Prince, The 1969,O 18,36:1

Slowacki, Julius (Playwright)
Constant Prince, The 1969,O 26,II,1:1

Slowik, Joseph (Director)
Mother Courage and Her Children 1964,My 12,32:2

Sloyan, James J
Henry V 1965,Je 29,27:2
Hamlet 1967,D 27,45:1
Spiro Who? 1969,My 19,55:1
Spiro Who? 1969,Je 15,II,3:6
Indians 1969,O 14,51:1
Dream Out of Time, A 1970,N 9,52:1

Sloyan, James J (Lighting Director)
Wars of the Roses, The (Part II) 1970,Jl 3,15:1

Sloyan, James J (Miscellaneous)
Troilus and Cressida 1965,Ag 13,17:1
Richard III 1966,Ag 11,26:1
King John 1967,Jl 14,19:1
Romeo and Juliet 1968,Ag 16,19:1
Wars of the Roses, The (Part I) 1970,Jl 2,30:1
Richard III 1970,Jl 4,11:1

Slutsker, Bertha
Burmese Pwe, A 1926,Mr 17,28:1

Slvy, Michael
Richard III 1949,F 9,33:2

Slyde, Jimmy
Hoofers, The 1969,Jl 30,23:4

Smaill, Edith M (Director)
Jonah and the Whale 1940,My 5,II,8:4

Small, Allan (Miscellaneous)
Arms and the Girl 1950,F 3,28:2
Make a Wish 1951,Ap 19,38:1

Small, Bennie
Louisiana 1933,F 28,15:5

Small, Danny Trio
Vaudeville (Palace) 1930,F 17,18:4

Small, David R
What a Relief 1935,D 14,10:6

Small, Dorothy (Pvt)
Swing Sister Wac Swing 1944,Ja 4,20:4

Small, Edgar
Survivors, The 1948,Ja 20,27:2

Small, Hazel Lee
Cocktails of 1934 1934,My 5,22:1

Small, Jack (Director)
Allah Be Praised! 1944,Ap 21,14:2

Small, Jack (Miscellaneous)
All You Need Is One Good Break 1950,F 10,20:3
Conscience 1952,My 16,17:6

Small, Jack (Producer)
Burning Deck, The 1940,Mr 2,9:2

Small, Jules
Ruddigore 1965,Ag 27,16:1

Small, Margot
House of Flowers 1954,D 31,11:2

Small, Mary
Early to Bed 1943,Je 18,16:2

Small, Mary E
South Pacific 1965,Je 3,25:1

Small, Neva
Something More! 1964,N 11,36:1
Impossible Years, The 1965,O 14,55:1
Henry, Sweet Henry 1967,O 24,51:2
Ballad for a Firing Squad 1968,D 12,64:2
Show Me Where the Good Times Are 1970,Mr 6,32:1
How Much, How Much? 1970,Ap 21,49:1

Small, Oggie
Guys and Dolls 1955,Ap 21,32:2
Finian's Rainbow 1955,My 19,25:1

Small, Paul (Producer)
Laugh Time 1943,S 9,35:2
Star Time 1944,S 13,16:2

Small, Richard
Shylock and His Daughter 1947,S 30,22:2

Small, Robert
Hershel, The Jester 1948,D 14,39:2

Small, Sally (Lighting Director)
To Be or Not to Be-What Kind of a Question Is That? 1970,O 20,39:1

Small, Victor R (Original Author)
All the Living 1938,Mr 25,14:4

Smallens, Alexander (Miscellaneous)
Porgy and Bess 1935,O 11,30:2
Porgy and Bess 1942,Ja 23,16:2

Smallens, Alexander (Musical Director)
Porgy and Bess 1935,O 1,27:2
Porgy and Bess 1935,O 11,30:2
Porgy and Bess 1952,S 8,18:2
Porgy and Bess 1952,O 10,21:4
Porgy and Bess 1953,F 17,21:1
Porgy and Bess 1953,Mr 10,25:5
Porgy and Bess 1953,Mr 15,II,1:1
Porgy and Bess 1954,S 23,42:6
Porgy and Bess 1954,D 17,36:7
Porgy and Bess 1955,Ag 5,14:5
Porgy and Bess 1956,Ja 15,II,3:1
Smalley, Harold
Kick Back, The 1936,Je 23,27:3
Smalls, Joseph
They Shall Not Die 1934,F 22,24:4
Smart, Dick
Bloomer Girl 1947,Ja 7,33:2
All for Love 1949,Ja 24,16:5
Smart, Gino (Miscellaneous)
Wonderful Town 1958,Mr 6,32:4
Smart, J Scott
Bell for Adano, A 1944,D 7,21:2
Smart, Jack
New Faces of 1936 1936,My 20,24:5
Seperate Rooms 1940,Mr 25,10:3
Smart, Richard
Two for the Show 1940,F 9,14:2
Smart, Verta
Mandingo 1961,My 23,43:6
Smaulding, Laurline
Rain 1948,F 2,15:2
Smedley, Roy
Oh! Oh! Nurse 1925,D 8,28:4
Smidt, Bertha
Sonya's Search for the Christmas Star
1929,D 14,24:6
Smidt, Friede
Sonya's Search for the Christmas Star
1929,D 14,24:6
Smight, Jack (Director)
49th Cousin, The 1960,O 28,22:1
Smiles & Smiles
Hairpin Harmony 1943,O 2,18:5
Smiley, Brenda
TV 1966,N 7,66:1
Motel 1966,N 7,66:1
Interview 1966,N 7,66:1
Scuba Duba 1967,O 11,36:1
Scuba Duba 1969,Ap 7,51:1
Smiley, Enid (Costume Designer)
How Long Till Summer 1949,D 28,30:3
Smiley, Faye
Choice, The 1930,My 9,20:5
Smiley, Joseph
All-Star Jamboree 1921,Jl 14,18:1
Talk About Girls 1927,Je 15,31:3
Skin of Our Teeth, The 1942,N 19,29:5
Smiley, Polly
Girl From Wyoming, The 1938,O 31,12:1
Summer Night 1939,N 3,17:1
Smiley, Pril (Miscellaneous)
Bananas 1968,D 5,60:1
Inner Journey, The 1969,Mr 21,42:1
Smiley, Ralph
Assassin, The 1945,O 18,20:2
I Gotta Get Out 1947,S 26,27:2
Madwoman of Chaillot, The 1950,Je 14,41:2
Smiley, Robert
Pietro 1920,Ja 20,10:2
Ruint 1925,Ap 8,24:2
Smillie, F B
Somebody's Lion 1921,Ap 13,20:1
Smink, Peter
Zizi 1964,N 23,51:1
Smirnov, Boris
Kremlin Chimes 1965,F 25,23:1
Smirnova, Olga
Revue Russe, The 1922,O 6,28:1
Merry World, The 1926,Je 9,18:3
Smirnova, Viktoriya
Aladdin and His Wonderful Lamp 1963,O 21,39:1
Smisko, Patricia (Miscellaneous)
To Be or Not to Be-What Kind of a Question Is
That? 1970,O 20,39:1
Smissaert, Leonard
Seven Keys to Baldpate 1930,Ja 8,25:2
Smit, Leo (Composer)
Sunset 1966,My 13,34:1
Smith, Adele
Manhattan Mary 1927,S 27,30:3
Whoopee 1928,D 5,34:3
Smith, Alan
Saint of Bleecker Street, The 1954,D 28,21:1
Smith, Alex
Richard III 1953,Jl 15,22:2
Smith, Alexander
Lost Boy 1932,Ja 6,24:4
Smith, Alfred E
Friars Club Frolic 1933,My 15,16:4
Smith, Allie
Pleasure Bound 1929,F 19,22:4

Smith, Alma
Brown Buddies 1930,O 8,29:1
Smith, Anthony Patric (Playwright)
Alcestis Comes Back 1962,Ap 24,33:1
Smith, Archie
Harriet 1944,S 28,26:1
Show-Off, The 1950,Je 1,24:5
Troublemakers, The 1954,D 31,11:3
Tempest, The 1955,S 3,8:6
Brothers Karamazov, The 1957,D 9,39:4
Brothers Karamazov, The 1957,D 22,II,3:1
Idiot, The 1960,S 26,38:1
Emmanuel 1960,D 5,42:2
Firebugs, The 1963,N 22,41:1
King Lear 1963,N 23,22:1
Smith, Art
Broken Dishes 1929,N 6,28:3
House of Connelly, The 1931,S 29,22:4
1931 1931,D 11,34:3
Night Over Taos 1932,Mr 10,25:3
Success Story 1932,S 27,24:4
Men in White 1933,S 27,24:2
Waiting for Lefty 1935,F 11,14:5
Awake and Sing! 1935,F 20,23:2
Weep for the Virgins 1935,D 2,18:1
Case of Clyde Griffiths 1936,Mr 14,10:4
Johnny Johnson 1936,N 20,26:3
Golden Boy 1937,N 5,18:5
Rocket to the Moon 1938,N 25,18:2
Rocket to the Moon 1938,D 4,X,5:1
Awake and Sing! 1939,Mr 8,18:2
My Heart's in the Highlands 1939,Ap 14,29:2
My Heart's in the Highlands 1939,My 7,X,1:1
Thunder Rock 1939,N 15,18:1
Night Music 1940,F 23,18:2
Heavenly Express 1940,Ap 19,24:2
Heavenly Express 1940,Ap 28,IX,1:1
Retreat to Pleasure 1940,D 18,32:2
Tanyard Street 1941,F 5,16:2
Clash by Night 1941,D 29,20:2
Johnny Doodle 1942,Mr 19,28:2
Strings, My Lord, Are False, The 1942,My 20,24:2
Silk Hat Harry 1943,Ag 22,II,1:6
Next Half Hour, The 1945,O 30,14:6
Oedipus Rex 1945,D 17,16:7
Enemy of the People, An 1950,D 29,14:1
Anna Christie 1952,Ja 10,33:1
Anna Christie 1952,Ja 20,II,1:1
Golden Boy 1952,Mr 13,24:3
Golden Boy 1952,Mr 23,II,1:1
Home Is the Hero 1954,S 23,42:2
High Named Today 1954,D 11,11:2
Master Builder, The 1955,Mr 2,23:2
Anna Christie 1955,N 22,41:1
Volpone 1957,Ja 8,27:1
Volpone 1957,Ja 13,II,10:1
West Side Story 1957,S 27,14:4
Touch of the Poet, A 1958,O 3,23:2
Machinal 1960,Ap 8,27:1
All the Way Home 1960,D 1,42:1
Diff'rent 1961,O 18,52:1
Smith, Arthur (Playwright)
Nether-World 1938,O 22,15:2
Boom-Boom Clopper 1940,Ja 6,8:7
Smith, Ascher
Mrs O'Brien Entertains 1939,F 9,16:3
Smith, Aubrey
Mary, Mary, Quite Contrary 1923,S 12,14:1
Constant Wife, The 1926,N 30,26:3
Smith, Augustus
On Whitman Avenue 1946,My 9,28:2
Long Way From Home, A 1948,F 9,25:2
Grandma's Diary 1948,S 23,36:2
Smith, Augustus (Director)
Conjur' Man Dies 1936,Mr 12,18:5
Turpentine 1936,Je 27,21:6
Smith, Augustus Jr
Finian's Rainbow 1947,Ja 11,23:2
Our Lan' 1947,S 29,16:5
Smith, Augustus Sr
Our Lan' 1947,S 29,16:5
Smith, Barbara Lee
Me and Juliet 1953,My 29,17:1
Smith, Basil
Mecca 1920,O 5,12:2
No Trespassing! 1926,S 8,19:1
Smith, Ben
Field God, The 1927,Ap 22,18:2
Field God, The 1927,My 1,VIII,1:1
John 1927,N 5,16:4
Carry On 1928,Ja 24,26:1
Rope 1928,F 23,18:3
Rope 1928,Mr 4,IX,1:1
Holiday 1928,N 27,36:1
As Good As New 1930,N 4,37:3
Colonel Satan 1931,Ja 12,24:1
Brass Ankle 1931,Ap 24,26:4
Sentinels 1931,D 26,15:1
They Shall Not Die 1934,F 22,24:4
Dance With Your Gods 1934,O 8,14:3
Rain From Heaven 1934,D 25,28:4
County Chairman, The 1936,My 26,26:5
As We Forgive Our Debtors 1936,Ag 11,24:6

Smith, Ben—Cont
Russet Mantle 1936,Ag 18,15:2
And Stars Remain 1936,O 13,32:2
Days to Come 1936,D 16,35:1
Good Hunting 1938,N 22,26:5
Distant City, The 1941,S 23,27:5
Solitaire 1942,Ja 28,22:2
Apology 1943,Mr 23,14:2
Smith, Benny
Hooray!! It's a Glorious Day. . .And All That
1966,Mr 10,28:1
Smith, Bert
City of Kings 1949,F 18,27:2
Smith, Bessie
Pansy 1929,My 15,36:3
Smith, Betsy
Much Ado About Nothing 1964,Jl 24,15:2
Smith, Betty
Miser, The 1950,Mr 27,19:5
Smith, Betty (Original Author)
Tree Grows in Brooklyn, A 1951,Ap 29,II,1:1
Smith, Betty (Playwright)
First in Heart, The 1947,N 14,29:2
Tree Grows in Brooklyn, A 1951,Ap 20,24:3
Smith, Betty Jane
On Your Toes 1936,Ap 13,14:4
Snookie 1941,Je 4,26:2
High Kickers 1941,N 1,21:2
Smith, Bill
Show Boat 1954,My 6,44:1
Smith, Bill (Costume Designer)
At Home at the Palace 1967,Ag 1,23:1
Smith, Bob
Criminals, The 1941,D 22,24:3
Smith, Boyd (Playwright)
Patriarch, The 1926,D 11,15:1
Patriarch, The 1929,N 26,28:5
Smith, Burrell
Texas Town 1941,Ap 30,22:3
Out of My House 1942,Ja 8,28:6
Smith, C Aubrey
Bachelor Father, The 1928,F 29,28:2
Bachelor Father, The 1929,O 20,IX,1:4
Spring Again 1941,O 28,28:3
Spring Again 1941,N 11,28:2
Smith, C Aubrey (Director)
Mixed Doubles 1927,Ap 27,22:3
Smith, C E
Racket, The 1927,N 23,28:3
City Haul 1929,D 31,14:4
Tyrant, The 1930,N 13,33:1
Man Who Reclaimed His Head 1932,S 9,17:3
Hold Your Horses 1933,S 26,26:4
All Rights Reserved 1934,N 7,33:5
What a Relief 1935,D 14,10:6
What a Relief 1935,D 19,34:4
Smith, Carl Beitell (Director)
Side-Show 1931,My 16,13:1
Smith, Carl Beitell (Playwright)
Side-Show 1931,My 16,13:1
Smith, Caryl
Return Engagement 1940,N 2,19:2
Smith, Cedric
Bourgeois Gentilhomme, Le 1964,Je 18,28:2
Smith, Charles
Marching Song 1937,F 18,18:2
Pirates of Penzance, The 1942,F 20,20:2
Smith, Charles (Miscellaneous)
Carousel 1957,S 12,38:2
Mahagonny 1970,Ap 29,51:1
Smith, Charlson
Sonya 1921,Ag 16,18:3
Smith, Christopher
Anna Kleiber 1965,Ja 20,33:1
Smith, Chuck
Threepenny Opera, The 1954,Mr 11,26:5
Smith, Ciel
Dionysus in 69 1968,Je 7,35:3
Macbeth 1969,N 21,51:1
Macbeth 1969,N 30,II,3:1
Gertrude 1970,N 13,29:1
Smith, Clara
Sweet Chariot 1930,O 24,30:2
Smith, Clarence
Carry Nation 1932,O 31,18:2
Porgy and Bess 1935,O 11,30:2
Smith, Clifford
Madcap, The 1928,F 1,31:2
Luckee Girl 1928,S 17,28:6
Good Morning 1937,D 4,20:7
Smith, Conrad S (Playwright)
Trial Honeymoon 1947,N 4,31:2
Smith, Cora
Audition of the Apprentice Theatre 1939,Je 2,26:2
Wookey, The 1941,S 11,20:5
Heart of a City 1942,F 13,24:6
World's Full of Girls, The 1943,D 7,31:2
Lower North 1944,Ag 26,15:4
I Remember Mama 1944,O 20,16:2
Smith, Cornelia
Low Bridge 1933,F 10,13:4
Smith, Cyrena
Prunella; Love in a Garden 1926,Je 16,23:3
Escape 1927,O 27,33:1

Smith, Cyrena—Cont

Blind Mice 1930,O 16,28:2
Cloudy With Showers 1931,S 2,17:5
$25 an Hour 1933,My 11,14:4
Fools Rush In 1934,D 26,19:2

Smith, Cyril

Provincetown Follies, The 1935,N 4,24:3
Viva O'Brien 1941,O 10,27:2

Smith, D P

Rules of the Game, The 1960,D 20,44:1

Smith, David

Show Boat 1956,Je 22,16:1
H M S Pinafore 1964,Mr 21,13:4
Patience 1964,Mr 26,42:1
Dreigroschenoper, Die 1965,Mr 12,24:1
Saint of Bleecker Street, The 1965,Mr 19,28:1
Patience 1965,Ap 16,34:1
Mikado, The 1965,Ap 17,11:3
Where's Charley? 1966,My 26,57:1

Smith, Delos V Jr

Making of Moo, The 1958,Je 12,34:1
Secret Concubine, The 1960,Mr 22,29:2
Tiger Rag, The 1961,F 17,20:2
Fun Couple, The 1962,O 27,15:2
Winter Journey 1968,Mr 13,39:1
Front Page, The 1968,O 20,85:5
Our Town 1969,N 28,50:1

Smith, Dick (Miscellaneous)

Baker Street 1965,F 17,36:1
Zorba 1968,N 18,58:1

Smith, Dinnie

Miss Isobel 1957,D 27,22:1
Only in America 1959,N 20,35:1

Smith, Dodie (Original Author)

I Capture the Castle 1954,Ap 11,II,2:1

Smith, Dodie (Playwright)

Autumn Crocus 1932,N 21,20:2
Call It a Day 1935,N 24,IX,1:2
Call It a Day 1936,Ja 21,26:7
Call It a Day 1936,Ja 29,15:2
Call It a Day 1936,F 9,X,1:1
Bonnet Over the Windmill 1937,S 9,19:4
Bonnet Over the Windmill 1937,S 26,XI,2:5
Dear Octopus 1938,O 2,IX,2:1
Dear Octopus 1939,Ja 12,22:2
Dear Octopus 1939,N 12,IX,2:5
Dear Octopus 1940,My 19,IX,1:4
Lovers and Friends 1943,D 5,II,5:1
Letter From Paris 1952,O 11,17:8
Letter From Paris 1952,N 9,II,3:1
I Capture the Castle 1954,Ap 11,II,2:1
Autumn Crocus 1954,Je 22,24:7

Smith, Dolly

Blue Butterfly, The 1929,F 17,29:3

Smith, Don

Founders, The 1957,My 14,39:1

Smith, Don (Miscellaneous)

Eccentricities of Davy Crockett, The 1961,Ja 4,26:1
Riding Hood Revisited 1961,Ja 4,26:1
Willie the Weeper 1961,Ja 4,26:1
Brigadoon 1962,My 31,21:4
Brigadoon 1963,F 1,6:2

Smith, Don (Musical Director)

Willie the Weeper 1961,Ja 4,26:1
Eccentricities of Davy Crockett, The 1961,Ja 4,26:1
Riding Hood Revisited 1961,Ja 4,26:1

Smith, Donald

Jayhawker 1934,N 6,34:2

Smith, Donald (Playwright)

Lovers and Friends 1943,N 30,23:2

Smith, Donegan

Night Thoreau Spent in Jail, The 1970,N 2,66:1

Smith, Doris

Pink String and Sealing Wax 1957,S 6,13:1

Smith, Dorothy Alberta (Producer)

39 Steps 1938,Mr 12,13:1

Smith, E A (Scenic Designer)

Grab Bag, The 1968,N 5,53:2
Susie Is a Good Girl 1968,N 5,53:2
Subscriber, The 1968,N 5,53:2

Smith, E W (Playwright)

Drunkard, The; Fallen Saved, The 1959,Je 24,37:2

Smith, Ed

Chalked Out 1937,Mr 26,24:2

Smith, Eddy

Texas Li'l Darlin' 1949,N 26,10:5
Hayride 1954,S 14,24:2

Smith, Edgar (Playwright)

Whirl of New York, The 1921,Je 14,18:1
Red Pepper 1922,My 30,8:3
Broadway Nights 1929,Jl 16,23:2
Street Singer, The 1929,Jl 28,VIII,1:6
Street Singer, The 1929,S 18,35:2
So This Is Paris 1930,Ap 27,IX,2:3
Hello Paris 1930,N 17,29:3

Smith, Edith

Star-Wagon, The 1937,S 30,18:5

Smith, Edward C (Playwright)

Little Theatre Tournament; Release 1926,My 4,30:2

Smith, Eileen

Street Scene 1929,Ja 11,20:4
Would-Be Gentleman, The 1930,Ap 30,29:2

Smith, Eleanor (Lady) (Original Author)

Ballerina 1933,O 11,26:3

Smith, Eleanor (Lady) (Playwright)

Ballerina 1933,O 29,IX,1:6
Goose-Feather Bed 1935,D 17,30:7

Smith, Ellis

Clerambard 1957,N 8,22:3

Smith, Elwood

Home Is the Hunter 1945,D 21,25:4
St Louis Woman 1946,Ap 1,22:2
City of Kings 1949,F 18,27:2
Four Saints in Three Acts 1952,Ap 17,35:1
Finian's Rainbow 1955,My 19,25:1
Fly Blackbird 1962,F 6,26:2

Smith, Elwood (Director)

Medal for Willie, A 1951,O 16,35:2

Smith, Emerson

Sonya's Search for the Christmas Star
1929,D 14,24:6

Smith, Emery

Faith of Our Fathers 1950,Ag 6,72:2

Smith, Esther

Strange Fruit 1945,N 30,18:6

Smith, Esther (Miscellaneous)

Strange Fruit 1945,N 30,18:6

Smith, Ethel

Season of Choice 1959,Ap 14,40:1
Beyond Desire 1967,O 11,36:1

Smith, Eugene

Fragile Fox 1954,O 13,27:1
Buck White 1969,D 3,63:1

Smith, Eva Vaughan

Cat on a Hot Tin Roof 1955,Mr 25,18:2

Smith, Evelyn

Would-Be Gentleman, The 1930,Ap 30,29:2
Partition 1948,O 29,31:2

Smith, Everett F

Lady's Not for Burning, The 1959,Ja 31,13:2

Smith, F Kent

Fiesta 1928,D 13,25:2

Smith, Frances

Green Pastures, The 1935,F 27,16:2
Father, The 1937,Ap 21,18:5
Case of Philip Lawrence, The 1937,Je 9,31:1
Aries Is Rising 1939,N 22,16:5

Smith, Francesca

How Now, Dow Jones 1967,D 8,53:1

Smith, Francis

Conjur' Man Dies 1936,Mr 12,18:5

Smith, Frank

Peter and the Wolf 1969,N 30,85:5

Smith, Frederick

Blue Blood 1924,Ap 3,21:2
Dope 1926,Ja 4,16:3
Triple Crossed 1927,My 6,21:2
Porgy 1929,S 14,17:3
Wrong Number 1934,Mr 14,23:6
Jefferson Davis 1936,F 19,17:2
Madam Will You Walk 1953,D 2,2:4

Smith, G Albert

Rita Coventry 1923,F 20,12:2
Holy Terror, A 1925,S 29,31:2
Love 'Em and Leave 'Em 1926,F 4,20:4
Chicago 1926,D 31,11:1
Coquette 1927,N 9,23:1
Coquette 1927,N 13,IX,1:1
Those We Love 1930,F 20,22:2
Wiser They Are, The 1931,Ap 7,31:1
Animal Kingdom, The 1932,Ja 13,26:4
Party's Over, The 1933,Mr 28,23:3
Curtain Rises, The 1933,O 20,15:2
Small Miracle 1934,S 27,24:3
Ceiling Zero 1935,Ap 11,26:2
Katy Did So What? 1935,N 6,32:3
Double Dummy 1936,N 12,30:1
Farewell Summer 1937,Mr 30,20:2
Love in My Fashion 1937,D 4,21:4
If You Get It, Do You Want It? 1938,D 1,28:2
Michael Drops In 1938,D 28,24:3
Off to Buffalo! 1939,F 22,18:2
Out From Under 1940,My 6,13:2
More the Merrier, The 1941,S 16,19:3
Land Is Bright, The 1941,O 29,26:2
Alice in Arms 1945,F 1,18:4
State of the Union 1945,N 15,25:2
Wisteria Trees, The 1950,Mr 30,39:1
Chase, The 1952,Ap 16,30:2
Debut 1956,F 23,32:1

Smith, Garland

Let Freedom Ring 1935,N 7,26:2
Prelude 1936,Ap 20,17:4
Bury the Dead 1936,Ap 20,17:4

Smith, Garnett

Feast of Panthers 1961,Mr 21,32:1
Shoemaker's Holiday, The 1967,Mr 3,25:1
Canterbury Tales; Merchant's Tale, The
1969,F 4,34:1
Canterbury Tales; Pilgrims, The 1969,F 4,34:1

Smith, Gary (Lighting Director)

Electra 1959,F 14,15:1
Harlequinade 1959,F 14,15:1

Smith, Gary (Scenic Designer)

Saturday Night Kid, The 1958,My 16,22:1
Innocents, The 1959,Ap 21,41:2
All the King's Men 1959,O 17,27:2

Smith, Gary (Scenic Designer)—Cont

Parade 1960,Ja 21,27:4
Eccentricities of Davy Crockett, The 1961,Ja 4,26:1
Willie the Weeper 1961,Ja 4,26:1
Riding Hood Revisited 1961,Ja 4,26:1

Smith, Geddeth

Golden Six, The 1958,O 27,31:2
Henry V 1963,Je 14,37:1
Caesar and Cleopatra 1963,Ag 1,18:2
Much Ado About Nothing 1964,Je 11,26:2
Richard III 1964,Je 12,44:2
Hamlet 1964,Jl 4,9:1
Imaginary Invalid, The 1967,My 2,53:1
Touch of the Poet, A 1967,My 3,38:2
Ways and Means 1967,My 4,34:1
Still Life 1967,My 4,34:1

Smith, Geoffrey

Midsummer Night Scream, A 1960,D 16,45:1

Smith, George

Wonderful Night, A; Fledermaus, Die
1929,N 1,23:3
Tragedy of the Ages, The 1933,Ap 7,22:7
Body Beautiful, The 1935,N 1,24:3
Good Morning 1937,D 4,20:7
Unconquered, The 1940,F 14,25:2
Wedding in Japan 1949,N 11,29:1
Scapegoat, The 1950,Ap 20,36:5

Smith, George (Director)

Leave It to Me! 1938,N 10,32:2

Smith, George C (Mrs) (Costume Designer)

Twelfth Disciple, The 1930,My 17,21:4

Smith, George H

Tragedy of the Ages, The 1933,Ap 7,22:7

Smith, George W

Rendezvous 1932,O 13,22:3
Paths of Glory 1935,S 27,24:2
Boy Meets Girl 1935,N 28,38:2
Brown Sugar 1937,D 3,29:2
All That Glitters 1938,Ja 20,18:2
Return of the Vagabond, The 1940,My 14,27:2

Smith, Gerald (Playwright)

Now 1968,Je 6,53:1

Smith, Gerald Oliver

Wait Till We're Married 1921,S 27,14:1
Mike Angelo 1923,Ja 9,26:2
Whole Town's Talking, The 1923,Ag 30,8:2
Lady Be Good 1924,D 2,23:4
Oh, Kay! 1926,N 9,31:3
Silent House, The 1928,F 8,28:5
What a Question 1930,F 23,VIII,2:5
I Want My Wife 1930,Mr 21,30:7
Pardon My English 1933,Ja 21,11:4
Beginner's Luck 1935,Jl 23,24:4

Smith, Glenn Allen (Playwright)

Home Away From, A 1969,Ap 29,40:3

Smith, Gloria

Blue Butterfly, The 1929,F 17,29:3
Lost in the Stars 1949,O 31,21:2
Top Banana 1951,N 2,19:2
By the Beautiful Sea 1954,Ap 9,20:1
Almost Crazy 1955,Je 21,37:1

Smith, Gordon

Strike Up the Band 1930,Ja 15,29:1
Americana 1932,O 6,19:3
What a Relief 1935,D 14,10:6

Smith, Gordon (Miscellaneous)

Tango 1968,Ja 1,11:1
Serjeant Musgrave's Dance 1968,Je 16,52:4
Resistible Rise of Arturo Ui, The 1968,Ag 8,25:1

Smith, Gouverneur E Jr

Laugh It Off 1925,Ap 25,18:4

Smith, Grace

Vaudeville (Palace) 1929,N 11,20:5
Vaudeville (Palace) 1932,Jl 4,14:5

Smith, Gus

Walk Together Chillun 1936,F 5,15:2
Turpentine 1936,Je 27,21:6

Smith, Guy Jr

Mother, The 1935,N 20,26:3

Smith, H Ben

First Flight 1925,S 18,26:2
Nirvana 1926,Mr 4,19:1
In Abraham's Bosom 1926,D 31,10:2

Smith, H C

Hamlet 1923,N 27,23:6

Smith, H Reeves

Sporting Thing to Do, The 1923,F 20,12:2

Smith, H V (Playwright)

Drunkard, The 1934,Ap 1,X,1:1

Smith, Hank

Brown Buddies 1930,O 8,29:1

Smith, Hardy W (Miscellaneous)

Hotel Paradiso 1957,Ap 12,22:2

Smith, Hardy W (Producer)

Island of Goats 1955,O 5,40:1
Rashomon 1959,Ja 28,36:2

Smith, Harold

Vegetable, The, or From President to Postman
1929,Ap 11,32:3

Smith, Harry

Vaudeville (Hippodrome) 1926,Mr 16,22:2
New Faces of 1936 1936,My 20,24:5
My Mother, My Father and Me 1963,Mr 25,5:5

Smith, Harry B (Lyricist)
Betty, Be Good 1920,My 5,14:2
Fashions of 1924 1923,Jl 19,18:2
Love Song, The 1925,Ja 14,19:4
Natja 1925,F 17,19:2
Princess Flavia 1925,N 3,34:3
Naughty Riquette 1926,S 14,25:2
Naughty Riquette 1926,S 19,IX,1:1
Countess Maritza 1926,S 20,21:1
Cherry Blossoms 1927,Mr 29,22:3
Half a Widow 1927,S 13,37:3
Love Call, The 1927,O 25,33:1
White Lilacs 1928,S 11,31:2
Red Robe, The 1928,D 26,15:1
Robin Hood 1929,N 20,26:5
Serenade, The 1930,Mr 5,26:7
Three Little Girls 1930,Mr 30,VIII,2:7
Three Little Girls 1930,Ap 15,29:1
Robin Hood 1932,Ja 28,25:4
Circus Princess, The 1937,Ag 31,26:6
Robin Hood 1944,N 8,28:2
Smith, Harry B (Original Author)
Piggy 1927,Ja 12,22:2
Robin Hood 1932,Ja 28,25:4
Smith, Harry B (Playwright)
Caroline 1923,F 1,13:2
Love Song, The 1925,Ja 14,19:4
Princess Flavia 1925,N 3,34:3
Sweetheart Time 1926,Ja 20,23:2
Countess Maritza 1926,Mr 30,20:3
Naughty Riquette 1926,S 14,25:2
Naughty Riquette 1926,S 19,IX,1:1
Countess Maritza 1926,S 20,21:1
Cherry Blossoms 1927,Mr 29,22:3
Circus Princess, The 1927,Ap 26,32:2
Half a Widow 1927,S 13,37:3
Love Call, The 1927,O 25,33:1
White Lilacs 1928,S 11,31:2
Red Robe, The 1928,D 26,15:1
Sweethearts 1929,S 23,25:1
Fortune Teller, The 1929,N 5,32:3
Serenade, The 1930,Mr 5,26:7
Rogues and Vagabonds 1930,My 8,32:5
Fencing Master, The 1936,Ap 1,29:1
Circus Princess, The 1937,Ag 31,26:6
Robin Hood 1944,N 8,28:2
Sweethearts 1947,Ja 22,31:2
Smith, Harry B (Translator)
Marching By 1932,Mr 4,17:1
Smith, Harry James (Playwright)
Mrs Bumpstead-Leigh 1929,Ap 2,28:3
Tailor-Made Man, A 1929,O 22,26:3
Smith, Harry K
I Gotta Get Out 1947,S 26,27:2
Smith, Hay
Cock-A-Doodle Dandy 1955,N 4,26:5
Smith, Haydon
Sherry! 1967,Mr 29,39:1
Smith, Helen Zenna (Original Author)
Stepdaughters of War 1930,O 7,27:1
Smith, Helene (Costume Designer)
Johnny Johnson 1941,My 3,20:2
Smith, Henry Clapp
What Next 1920,Ja 27,7:2
Man About Town, A 1921,Mr 22,15:1
Untitled-Pantomime 1921,Ap 3,VII,1:1
Nantucket Follies 1927,Jl 30,13:2
Smith, Henry Clapp (Playwright)
Punk, or the Amateur Rehearsal 1923,My 10,22:3
Life Begins at 8:40 1934,Ag 28,24:2
Smith, Howard
Miss Quis 1937,Ap 8,20:5
Solitaire 1942,Ja 28,22:2
Life of Reilly, The 1942,Ap 30,13:2
Manhattan Nocturne 1943,O 27,26:2
Decision 1944,F 3,23:2
Dear Ruth 1944,D 14,29:2
Dear Ruth 1944,D 31,II,1:1
Mr Peebles and Mr Hooker 1946,O 11,29:2
Magic Touch, The 1947,S 4,30:1
Death of a Salesman 1949,F 11,27:2
Mid-Summer 1953,Ja 22,19:1
Pink Elephant, The 1953,Ap 23,37:2
Red Rainbow, A 1953,S 15,37:4
Anniversary Waltz 1954,Ap 8,34:1
Gang's All Here, The 1959,O 2,23:1
Smith, Howard I
Finian's Rainbow 1967,Ap 6,44:1
Smith, Hugh
Ice Follies 1966,Ja 12,27:6
Smith, Izetta
Hamlet 1968,Je 10,59:1
Flea in Her Ear, A 1969,O 4,25:1
Smith, J A (Director)
Case of Philip Lawrence, The 1937,Je 9,31:1
Smith, J A (Playwright)
Turpentine 1936,Je 27,21:6
Smith, J Ascher
Ringside 1928,Ag 30,13:2
Holiday 1928,N 27,36:1
Those We Love 1930,F 20,22:2
Sweet Stranger 1930,O 22,23:3
20th Century 1932,D 30,15:1

Drums Begin, The 1933,N 25,10:5
John Brown 1934,Ja 23,22:3
Ladies' Money 1934,N 2,26:6
Three Men on a Horse 1935,Ja 31,22:3
Unconquered, The 1940,F 14,25:2
Case of Youth, A 1940,Mr 25,10:3
Love for Love 1940,Je 4,19:5
Three Men on a Horse 1942,O 10,10:2
Smith, J Augustus
Louisiana 1933,F 28,15:5
Smith, J Augustus (Playwright)
Louisiana 1933,F 28,15:5
Smith, J Dayton
Susannah 1955,F 25,18:4
Smith, J English
Dream Girl 1951,My 10,39:1
Smith, J Marshall
Ripples 1930,F 12,26:1
Smith, J Sebastian
Sacred and Profane Love 1920,F 24,11:1
Smith, J Walter
Becky Sharp 1929,Je 4,29:1
All's Well That Ends Well 1966,Je 17,39:1
Harpers Ferry 1967,Je 6,52:2
Smith, Jack
Vaudeville (Palace) 1926,S 28,30:4
Processional 1937,O 14,23:1
Big Blow 1938,O 3,11:2
Smith, Jack (Scenic Designer)
Treatment, The 1968,My 10,54:7
Soap Opera 1968,My 10,54:7
Smith, James
Hotel Mouse, The 1922,Mr 14,11:3
Smith, Jamie
Coriolanus 1954,Ja 20,34:2
Miss Julie 1956,F 22,23:2
Stronger, The 1956,F 22,23:2
Tall Story 1959,Ja 30,33:2
Smith, Jane
London, Paris and New York 1926,Je 8,23:1
Vaudeville (Palace) 1926,Je 8,23:1
Grass Harp, The 1952,Mr 28,26:2
Smith, Jeanine
Lend an Ear 1948,D 17,38:2
Smith, Jeanne Perkins
Great Big Doorstep, The 1942,N 27,26:2
Smith, Jess
In White America 1965,F 9,42:5
Smith, Jess (Producer)
Web, The 1932,Je 28,24:4
Barber Had Two Sons, The 1943,F 2,22:2
Smith, Jimmie
Slightly Married 1943,O 26,19:2
Smith, Jimmy
You'll See Stars 1943,Ja 1,26:6
Smith, Jo Jo
Joyful Noise, A 1966,D 16,57:1
Smith, Joan
Lady Comes Across, The 1942,Ja 10,10:2
Garden of Time 1945,Mr 10,13:7
Smith, Joe
Whirl of New York, The 1921,Je 14,18:1
Sidewalks of New York 1927,O 4,33:1
Synthetic Sin 1927,O 11,26:2
Vaudeville (Palace) 1929,Jl 8,17:6
Mendel, Inc 1929,S 1,VIII,1:1
Mendel, Inc 1929,N 26,28:5
Vaudeville (Palace) 1930,Jl 7,22:2
Sky's the Limit, The 1934,D 18,25:5
Summer Wives 1936,Ap 14,18:1
Laugh, Town, Laugh! 1942,Je 20,9:1
Laugh, Town, Laugh! 1942,Je 23,22:2
Brights Lights of 1944 1943,S 17,27:4
Smith, Joe Bates
Moral Fabric 1932,N 22,25:3
Tea for Three 1935,Jl 9,24:4
Rain Before Seven 1935,Ag 13,20:3
Squaring the Circle 1935,O 4,24:6
One Thing After Another 1937,D 29,17:2
Smith, Joe Bates (Playwright)
Devil Takes a Bride, The 1938,O 8,10:3
Smith, John
Tragedy of Nan, The 1920,F 18,9:1
Fair Circassian, The 1921,D 7,22:3
Porgy and Bess 1964,My 7,32:1
Smith, John J
Utopia, Limited; Flowers of Progress, The 1957,F 27,21:1
Yeomen of the Guard, The 1957,My 22,28:3
Gondoliers, The 1957,My 29,34:2
From Here to There; Real Strange One, A 1958,Ap 24,37:3
From Here to There; Otherwise Engaged 1958,Ap 24,37:3
Smith, John W
Our Lan' 1947,Ap 19,11:2
Smith, Joseph S
Vagabond King, The 1925,S 22,23:3
Smith, Josephine
Processional 1937,O 14,23:1
Smith, Judith (Miscellaneous)
Much Ado About Nothing 1963,Jl 15,25:2

Smith, Justine
Common Sin, The 1928,O 16,28:2
Smith, Karen
Best Foot Forward 1963,Ap 3,43:1
Smith, Kate
Honeymoon Lane 1926,S 21,32:3
Vaudeville (Palace) 1929,Ap 8,32:7
Flying High 1930,Mr 4,24:4
Vaudeville (Palace) 1931,Ja 19,25:3
Vaudeville (Palace) 1931,Ag 3,15:7
Vaudeville (Palace) 1931,S 7,19:2
Vaudeville (Palace) 1931,S 28,17:5
Vaudeville (Palace) 1932,Ag 1,11:5
Smith, Kegan (Costume Designer)
King Lear 1964,My 19,43:2
Smith, Kenneth
Prunella 1929,Ap 10,23:3
Smith, Kent
Men Must Fight 1932,O 15,13:4
Spring in Autumn 1933,O 25,22:5
Drums Begin, The 1933,N 25,10:5
Dodsworth 1934,F 26,20:4
Dodsworth 1934,Ag 21,12:3
Mad Morning 1935,Je 25,14:1
Lambent Flame, The 1935,Jl 16,24:2
Caesar and Cleopatra 1935,Ag 22,21:1
Saint Joan 1936,Mr 10,27:4
Seen But Not Heard 1936,S 18,19:2
Wingless Victory, The 1936,N 25,17:5
Wingless Victory, The 1936,D 24,20:2
Candida 1937,Mr 11,20:2
Idiot's Delight 1937,Ag 10,22:7
Star-Wagon, The 1937,S 30,18:5
How to Get Tough About It 1938,F 9,16:2
Herod and Mariamne 1938,O 27,27:2
Jeremiah 1939,F 4,11:2
Christmas Eve 1939,D 28,17:2
International Incident, An 1940,Ap 3,18:2
Old Acquaintance 1940,D 24,18:3
Story of Mary Surratt, The 1947,F 10,25:2
Antony and Cleopatra 1947,N 27,49:2
Antony and Cleopatra 1947,D 7,II,5:1
Good Housekeeping 1949,Ag 17,19:3
Wisteria Trees, The 1950,Mr 30,39:1
Wisteria Trees, The 1950,Ap 9,II,1:1
Burning Bright 1950,O 19,40:2
Richard II 1951,Ja 25,21:2
Autumn Garden, The 1951,Mr 8,36:2
Autumn Garden, The 1951,Mr 18,II,1:1
Wild Duck, The 1951,D 27,17:1
Charley's Aunt 1953,D 23,22:2
What Every Woman Knows 1954,D 23,16:2
Measure for Measure 1956,Je 29,16:1
Saint Joan 1956,S 12,42:1
Saint Joan 1956,S 16,II,1:1
Child Buyer, The 1962,My 14,35:1
Smith, Kirby
Kismet 1953,D 4,2:4
Sound of Music, The 1959,N 17,40:2
Smith, Lane
Borak 1960,D 14,51:1
Leader, The 1969,Ap 22,40:2
Honest-to-God Schnozzola, The 1969,Ap 22,40:2
Nest, The 1970,Ap 10,46:1
Children in the Rain 1970,O 3,14:1
Smith, Larry
No More Peace 1937,F 27,9:1
Smith, Le Roy Symphonic Band
Vaudeville (Winter Garden) 1922,F 14,21:1
Smith, Lee
Dawn 1924,N 25,27:1
Sure Fire! 1926,O 21,23:1
Lady Alone 1927,Ja 21,12:5
Mr Moneypenny 1928,O 17,26:2
Bedfellows 1929,Jl 3,19:2
Paid Companions 1931,Je 23,28:4
Jim Dandy 1941,N 8,10:5
Smith, Lee (Costume Designer)
Kicking the Castle Down 1967,Ja 19,43:1
Smith, Len Jr
Naughty-Naught '00 1946,O 21,27:5
Mister Roberts 1948,F 19,27:2
Smith, Leon
Trojan Horse, The 1940,O 31,28:3
Smith, Lester Al (Producer)
No Mother to Guide Her 1933,D 26,18:5
Smith, Lew
World's My Oyster, The 1956,Ag 10,10:4
Smith, Lew (Costume Designer)
World's My Oyster, The 1956,Ag 10,10:4
Smith, Lillian
Pins and Needles 1922,F 2,20:1
Smith, Lillian (Original Author)
Strange Fruit 1945,N 30,18:6
Smith, Lillian (Playwright)
Strange Fruit 1945,N 30,18:6
Smith, Lillian Adele
No Foolin' 1926,Je 25,25:1
Smith, Lois
Time Out for Ginger 1952,N 27,50:4
Wisteria Trees, The 1955,F 3,20:2
Young and Beautiful, The 1955,O 3,23:2
Young and Beautiful, The 1956,Ag 16,30:6

Smith, Lois—Cont

Glass Menagerie, The 1956,N 22,50:1
Glass Menagerie, The 1956,D 2,II,1:1
Orpheus Descending 1957,Mr 22,28:1
Orpheus Descending 1957,Mr 31,II,1:1
Edwin Booth 1958,N 25,37:1
Bicycle Ride to Nevada 1963,S 25,38:1
Uncle Vanya 1969,Ag 31,II,4:1
Sunday Dinner 1970,N 3,28:1

Smith, Loring
Glamour Preferred 1940,N 16,13:2
Not in Our Stars 1941,Ap 26,20:5
Life of Reilly, The 1942,Ap 30,13:2
All for All 1943,S 30,25:2
Over Twenty-One 1944,Ja 4,20:2
Joy Forever, A 1946,Ja 8,20:2
John Loves Mary 1947,F 5,29:2
Happiest Years, The 1949,Ap 26,29:8
Texas Li'l Darlin' 1949,N 26,10:5
Captain Brassbound's Conversion 1950,D 28,21:1
Of Thee I Sing 1952,My 6,34:2
Be Your Age 1953,Ja 15,24:2
Solid Gold Cadillac, The 1953,N 6,24:2
Solid Gold Cadillac, The 1953,N 15,II,1:1
Matchmaker, The 1955,D 6,45:6
Matchmaker, The 1955,D 18,II,3:1
Twelfth Night 1960,Je 9,29:4
Tempest, The 1960,Je 20,35:1
Gay Life, The 1961,N 20,38:1
Murderer Among Us, A 1964,Mr 26,43:1
Hello, Dolly! 1965,S 11,17:1
Hello, Dolly! 1965,O 10,3:3

Smith, Louis
Haiti 1938,Mr 3,16:1
Ring Two 1939,N 23,38:2

Smith, Louise
Eden End 1935,O 22,17:1

Smith, Louise (Costume Designer)
New York Idea, The 1963,Jl 13,12:2

Smith, Maggie
New Faces of 1956 1956,Je 15,32:1
Othello 1964,Ap 22,56:1
Master Builder, The 1964,Je 10,50:2
Othello 1964,Jl 23,18:4
Country Wife, The 1969,Ag 30,10:3
Beaux' Stratagem, The 1970,F 10,50:2
Three Sisters, The 1970,F 12,30:1
Beaux' Stratagem, The 1970,F 22,II,1:1
Three Sisters, The 1970,F 22,II,1:1
Hedda Gabler 1970,Jl 18,12:1

Smith, Marc (Playwright)
Mattathias of Modin 1968,Ap 15,41:1

Smith, Margaret
New Freedom, The 1930,My 15,32:4
New Freedom, The 1930,My 17,21:4

Smith, Marjorie
Can-Can 1959,Ag 26,25:4
Camelot 1960,D 5,42:1

Smith, Mark
Cave Girl, The 1920,Ag 19,12:2
Up in the Clouds 1922,Ja 3,20:3
Lollipop 1924,Ja 22,15:3
Something to Brag About 1925,Ag 14,14:3
Monkey Talks, The 1925,D 29,20:1
Kitty's Kisses 1926,My 7,12:2
White Eagle, The 1927,D 27,24:4
Love, Honor and Betray 1930,Mr 13,22:2
Stork Is Dead, The 1932,S 24,18:2
Knickerbocker Holiday 1938,O 20,26:2
Twelfth Night 1940,O 27,IX,1:5
Twelfth Night 1940,N 20,26:3

Smith, Marshall
Girl Crazy 1930,O 15,27:1
Anything Goes 1934,N 22,26:1

Smith, Marvin
Tragicomedy of Don Cristobita and Dona Rosita,
  The 1958,My 30,12:2

Smith, Mary
Crime 1927,F 23,27:3

Smith, Matthew
Trelawney of the 'Wells' 1927,F 1,24:4
Houseparty 1929,S 10,26:5
Climax, The 1933,Je 14,22:2
Order Please 1934,O 10,21:2
Weather Permitting 1935,My 24,24:5
Ah, Wilderness! 1935,Ag 20,25:1
London Assurance 1937,F 19,14:5
Bat, The 1937,Je 1,27:5
Cat and the Canary, The 1937,Je 15,26:3
Places, Please 1937,N 13,10:6
That Old Devil 1944,Je 6,14:2

Smith, Merritt
John Henry 1940,Ja 11,18:2
St Louis Woman 1946,Ap 1,22:2
Set My People Free 1948,N 4,38:2
Sherry! 1967,Mr 29,39:1

Smith, Michael
Life With Mother 1948,O 21,32:2

Smith, Mildred
Men on the Sea 1944,O 4,25:2
Lysistrata 1946,O 18,27:5
Beggar's Holiday 1946,D 27,13:3
Beggar's Holiday 1947,Ja 26,II,1:1
Long Way From Home, A 1948,F 9,25:2

S S Glencairn; Moon of the Caribbees
  1948,My 21,21:2
Insect Comedy, The 1948,Je 4,26:3
Set My People Free 1948,N 4,38:2
Set My People Free 1948,N 14,II,1:1
Forward the Heart 1949,Ja 29,9:2

Smith, Milton (Director)
Prima Donna 1929,D 12,36:4
New Freedom, The 1930,My 15,32:4
New Freedom, The 1930,My 17,21:4
If Booth Had Missed 1931,My 14,27:1
If Booth Had Missed 1932,F 5,24:2
Fields Beyond, The 1933,F 14,19:5
Sun and I, The 1933,Ap 4,15:2
Fields Beyond, The 1936,Mr 7,11:2
Paul Bunyan 1941,My 6,25:1
Two Misers, The 1943,D 9,30:5
Belle of New York, The 1948,D 2,36:6

Smith, Milton (Scenic Designer)
Prima Donna 1929,D 12,36:4
New Freedom, The 1930,My 15,32:4
New Freedom, The 1930,My 17,21:4

Smith, Muriel
Carmen Jones 1943,D 3,26:2
Carmen Jones 1945,My 3,26:5
Carmen Jones 1946,Ap 8,32:2
Carmen Jones 1946,Ap 14,II,1:2
Our Lan' 1947,Ap 19,11:2
Our Lan' 1947,S 29,16:5
Cradle Will Rock, The 1947,N 25,38:3
Cradle Will Rock, The 1947,D 27,11:2
Sojourner Truth 1948,Ap 22,35:2
Hippolytus 1948,N 22,25:5
South Pacific 1951,N 2,19:1
South Pacific 1951,N 11,II,3:1
King and I, The 1953,O 9,33:3
King and I, The 1955,My 17,33:4
King and I, The 1956,Ap 19,35:4
Carmen Jones 1956,Je 1,28:2

Smith, Neil (Lighting Director)
Don Juan; Feast With the Statue, The
  1956,Ja 4,21:4

Smith, Neil (Producer)
Deathwatch 1958,O 10,34:2
Deirdre of the Sorrows 1959,O 15,46:1

Smith, Nick
Romeo and Juliet 1965,Je 21,36:3
Coriolanus 1965,Je 21,36:1
Romeo and Juliet 1965,Je 21,36:3
Taming of the Shrew, The 1965,Je 24,32:2
King Lear 1965,Je 25,39:1
Portrait of a Queen 1968,F 29,29:1

Smith, Noreen
Picture of Dorian Gray, The 1956,Ag 18,15:5

Smith, Norwood
Show Boat 1948,S 9,33:2
Night in Venice, A 1952,Je 27,18:6
Night in Venice, A 1952,Jl 13,II,1:1

Smith, Oliver (Costume Designer)
Sail Away 1961,O 4,48:5
Daughter of Silence 1961,D 1,28:1

Smith, Oliver (Miscellaneous)
West Side Story 1964,Ap 9,24:2
Certain Young Man, A 1967,D 27,45:1

Smith, Oliver (Producer)
On the Town 1944,D 29,11:4
Million Dollar Baby 1945,D 22,17:2
No Exit 1946,N 27,21:1
Me and Molly 1948,F 27,27:2
Gentlemen Prefer Blondes 1949,D 9,35:3
Bless You All 1950,D 15,42:2
In the Summer House 1953,D 30,17:1
Clearing in the Woods, A 1957,Ja 11,20:2
My Fair Lady 1958,Mr 9,II,1:1
Juno 1959,Mr 10,41:1
Show Girl 1961,Ja 13,37:1
Tiger Tiger Burning Bright 1962,D 24,5:2
Natural Affection 1963,F 2,5:2
Stephen D 1967,S 25,58:1
Niggerlovers, The; Man and Dog 1967,O 2,54:2
Niggerlovers, The; Demonstration, The
  1967,O 2,54:2
Exercise, The 1968,Ap 25,54:1
Collision Course; Rats 1968,My 9,55:2
Collision Course; Tour 1968,My 9,55:2
Collision Course; Thoughts on the Instant of
  Greeting a Friend on the Street 1968,My 9,55:2
Collision Course; Camera Obscura 1968,My 9,55:2
Collision Course; Jew! 1968,My 9,55:2
Collision Course; Unexpurgated Memoirs of
  Bernard Mergendeiler, The 1968,My 9,55:2
Collision Course; Metaphors 1968,My 9,55:2
Collision Course; Stars and Stripes 1968,My 9,55:2
Collision Course; Chuck 1968,My 9,55:2
Collision Course; Skywriting 1968,My 9,55:2
Collision Course; Wandering 1968,My 9,55:2
Next 1969,F 11,27:1
Adaptation 1969,F 11,27:1
Indians 1969,O 14,51:1
Alice in Wonderland 1970,O 9,43:1

Smith, Oliver (Scenic Designer)
Rosalinda; Fledermaus, Die 1942,O 29,26:5
Wind Remains, The 1943,Mr 31,16:6

Smith, Oliver (Scenic Designer)—Cont

New Moon, The 1944,My 18,16:2
Perfect Marriage, The 1944,O 27,17:6
Perfect Marriage, The 1944,N 5,II,1:2
Rhapsody 1944,N 23,37:2
On the Town 1944,D 29,11:4
Million Dollar Baby 1945,D 22,17:2
Billion Dollar Baby 1945,D 30,II,1:1
Beggar's Holiday 1946,D 27,13:3
Beggar's Holiday 1947,Ja 26,II,1:1
Brigadoon 1947,Mr 14,28:2
High Button Shoes 1947,O 10,32:2
Topaze 1947,D 29,21:5
Look, Ma, I'm Dancin' 1948,Ja 30,20:2
Along Fifth Avenue 1949,Ja 14,28:2
Miss Liberty 1949,Je 14,26:6
Miss Liberty 1949,Jl 16,6:5
Miss Liberty 1949,Jl 24,II,1:1
Gentlemen Prefer Blondes 1949,D 9,35:3
Brigadoon 1950,My 3,36:2
Bless You All 1950,D 15,42:2
Bless You All 1951,My 20,II,1:1
Paint Your Wagon 1951,N 13,32:2
Pal Joey 1952,Ja 4,17:6
Carnival in Flanders 1953,S 9,38:2
At Home With Ethel Waters 1953,S 23,36:1
In the Summer House 1953,D 30,17:1
Burning Glass, The 1954,Mr 5,15:2
Carousel 1954,Je 3,32:2
On Your Toes 1954,O 12,24:4
Will Success Spoil Rock Hunter? 1955,O 14,22:2
My Fair Lady 1956,Mr 16,20:2
Mr Wonderful 1956,Mr 23,23:2
My Fair Lady 1956,Mr 25,II,1:1
My Fair Lady 1956,Ap 29,II,17:1
Auntie Mame 1956,N 1,47:2
Auntie Mame 1956,N 11,II,1:1
Candide 1956,D 3,40:2
Candide 1956,D 9,II,5:1
Clearing in the Woods, A 1957,Ja 11,20:2
Clearing in the Woods, A 1957,Ja 20,II,1:1
Eugenia 1957,Ja 31,20:1
Visit to a Small Planet 1957,F 8,18:1
Brigadoon 1957,Mr 28,37:1
Carousel 1957,S 12,38:2
West Side Story 1957,S 27,14:4
West Side Story 1957,O 27,II,15:3
Jamaica 1957,N 1,32:2
Jamaica 1957,N 10,II,1:1
Time Remembered 1957,N 13,41:2
Nude With Violin 1957,N 15,36:1
Time Remembered 1957,N 24,II,1:1
Winesburg, Ohio 1958,F 6,22:2
Say Darling 1958,Ap 4,17:1
Auntie Mame 1958,Ag 12,33:2
Flower Drum Song 1958,D 2,44:1
Flower Drum Song 1958,D 7,II,5:1
Say Darling 1959,F 26,38:2
Juno 1959,Mr 10,41:1
Destry Rides Again 1959,Ap 24,24:1
Destry Rides Again 1959,My 3,II,1:1
Cheri 1959,O 13,44:1
Take Me Along 1959,O 23,22:2
Sound of Music, The 1959,N 17,40:2
Five Finger Exercise 1959,D 3,45:4
Five Finger Exercise 1959,D 13,II,3:1
Goodbye Charlie 1959,D 17,50:1
West Side Story 1960,Ap 28,31:1
Taste of Honey, A 1960,O 5,46:1
Becket 1960,O 6,50:1
Unsinkable Molly Brown, The 1960,N 4,28:1
Under the Yum-Yum Tree 1960,N 17,45:1
Camelot 1960,D 5,42:1
Camelot 1960,D 11,II,5:1
Show Girl 1961,Ja 13,37:1
Mary, Mary 1961,Mr 9,24:2
Becket 1961,My 9,44:1
Sail Away 1961,O 4,48:5
Gay Life, The 1961,N 20,38:1
Daughter of Silence 1961,D 1,28:1
Night of the Iguana, The 1961,D 29,10:1
Romulus 1962,Ja 11,27:1
Brigadoon 1962,My 31,21:4
My Fair Lady 1962,Je 14,24:1
Eddie Fisher at the Winter Garden 1962,O 3,47:1
Come on Strong 1962,O 5,29:1
Lord Pengo 1962,N 20,41:2
Tiger Tiger Burning Bright 1962,D 24,5:2
Brigadoon 1963,F 1,6:2
Natural Affection 1963,F 2,5:2
Children From Their Games 1963,Ap 12,33:1
On the Town 1963,My 31,30:7
Barefoot in the Park 1963,O 24,36:2
110 in the Shade 1963,O 25,37:1
Girl Who Came to Supper, The 1963,D 9,49:1
Chinese Prime Minister, The 1964,Ja 3,14:1
Hello, Dolly! 1964,Ja 17,22:1
Dylan 1964,Ja 20,18:1
Hello, Dolly! 1964,Ja 26,II,1:1
In the Summer House 1964,Mr 26,43:1
My Fair Lady 1964,My 21,43:2
Beekman Place 1964,O 8,50:1
Ben Franklin in Paris 1964,O 28,52:1
I Was Dancing 1964,N 9,40:4

Smith, Oliver (Scenic Designer)—Cont
Luv 1964,N 12,43:1
Luv 1964,N 22,II,1:1
Bajour 1964,N 24,42:1
Slow Dance on the Killing Ground 1964,D 1,50:1
Poor Richard 1964,D 3,59:1
Brigadoon 1964,D 24,9:1
Kelly 1965,F 8,28:2
Baker Street 1965,F 17,36:1
Odd Couple, The 1965,Mr 11,36:1
On a Clear Day You Can See Forever
  1965,O 18,44:1
Cactus Flower 1965,D 9,60:2
Best Laid Plans, The 1966,Mr 26,15:2
Show Boat 1966,Jl 20,48:1
I Do! I Do! 1966,D 6,58:1
Breakfast at Tiffany's 1966,D 15,60:1
I Do! I Do! 1966,D 18,II,3:1
Star-Spangled Girl, The 1966,D 22,38:1
Illya Darling 1967,Ap 12,37:1
Sound of Music, The 1967,Ap 27,52:1
Song of the Grasshopper 1967,S 29,52:2
Illya Darling 1967,N 2,58:1
Hello, Dolly! 1967,N 13,61:1
How Now, Dow Jones 1967,D 8,53:1
Brigadoon 1967,D 14,59:2
Darling of the Day 1968,Ja 29,26:2
Plaza Suite; Visitor From Forest Hills
  1968,F 15,49:1
Plaza Suite; Visitor From Hollywood
  1968,F 15,49:1
Plaza Suite; Visitor From Mamaroneck
  1968,F 15,49:1
Plaza Suite 1968,F 25,II,1:1
Weekend 1968,Mr 14,50:2
Weekend 1968,Mr 31,II,1:1
Exercise, The 1968,Ap 25,54:1
My Fair Lady 1968,Je 14,42:1
West Side Story 1968,Je 25,32:1
Plaza Suite 1968,D 14,61:2
Dear World 1969,F 7,33:1
Dear World 1969,F 16,II,1:1
But, Seriously... 1969,F 28,29:1
Come Summer 1969,Mr 19,43:1
Patriot for Me, A 1969,O 6,58:1
Indians 1969,O 14,51:1
Indians 1969,O 19,II,1:1
Jimmy 1969,O 24,38:1
Last of the Red Hot Lovers 1969,D 29,37:1
Last of the Red Hot Lovers 1970,Ja 4,II,1:1
Hello, Dolly! 1970,Ap 12,II,3:7
Lovely Ladies, Kind Gentlemen 1970,D 29,38:1
Smith, Orlando
Way Things Happen, The 1924,Ja 29,17:5
Smith, Osborne
Irma la Douce 1960,S 30,31:2
Smith, P Lloyd
They Never Come Back 1920,D 19,I,22:3
Smith, Pat
Live Life Again 1945,O 1,14:7
Smith, Pat (Miscellaneous)
Widowers' Houses 1959,Mr 3,39:2
Smith, Patricia
Point of No Return 1951,D 14,35:2
Maybe Tuesday 1958,Ja 30,18:3
Howie 1958,S 18,35:2
Smith, Paul
Look After Lulu 1959,Mr 4,35:1
Smith, Paul Gerard (Director)
Shuffle Along 1952,My 9,20:5
Smith, Paul Gerard (Lyricist)
Keep Kool 1924,My 23,16:4
Smith, Paul Gerard (Playwright)
Keep Kool 1924,My 23,16:4
Padlocks of 1927 1927,Jl 6,23:4
White Lights 1927,O 12,30:4
Funny Face 1927,N 23,28:2
Here's Howe! 1928,My 2,19:3
Earl Carroll's Vanities 1928,Ag 7,25:2
Funny Face 1928,N 9,22:3
Murray Anderson's Almanac 1929,Ag 15,20:3
Heads Up! 1929,N 12,34:1
Nine Fifteen Revue, The 1930,F 12,26:2
Shuffle Along 1952,My 9,20:5
Smith, Paul John
Macbeth 1968,N 30,49:3
Smith, Paula Bowers
Any Woman 1934,Ag 28,24:4
Smith, Peggy
Clarence 1923,My 14,18:4
Blue Butterfly, The 1929,My 4,17:2
Smith, Peter Kite
Lady Comes Across, The 1942,Ja 10,10:2
Smith, Pinkham
What a Relief 1935,D 14,10:6
Smith, Puddy
Banjo Eyes 1941,D 26,20:2
Smith, Quaid
Dracula Sabbat 1970,O 2,28:2
Smith, Queenie
Just Because 1922,Mr 23,11:1
Orange Blossoms 1922,S 20,18:1
Cinders 1923,Ap 4,22:1
Helen of Troy, New York 1923,Je 20,22:6

Sitting Pretty 1924,Mr 30,VIII,2:7
Sitting Pretty 1924,Ap 9,24:2
Be Yourself! 1924,Ag 24,VII,1:8
Be Yourself! 1924,S 4,13:3
Tip-Toes 1925,D 29,20:2
Judy 1927,F 8,20:2
Street Singer, The 1929,Jl 28,VIII,1:6
Street Singer, The 1929,S 18,35:2
Little Racketeer, The 1931,O 11,VIII,4:7
Little Racketeer, The 1932,Ja 19,24:4
Vaudeville (Palace) 1932,My 23,18:7
Blue Widow, The 1933,Ag 31,20:2
Uncle Tom's Cabin 1933,O 10,24:3
Every Thursday 1934,My 11,25:5
Marie Antoinette in Pennsylvania 1949,My 12,26:2
Smith, R B (Lyricist)
Kid Himself, The 1925,D 25,23:2
Smith, R B (Playwright)
Kid Himself, The 1925,D 25,23:2
Smith, Ralph
Big Fight, The 1928,S 19,33:1
Smith, Raymond
Hayride 1954,S 14,24:2
Caucasian Chalk Circle, The 1961,N 1,35:1
Smith, Reed
So Proudly We Hail 1936,S 23,28:4
Smith, Reginald
Babes in the Zoo 1930,F 26,22:3
Smith, Robert
One for the Money 1939,F 6,9:2
Two for the Show 1940,F 9,14:2
Family Affair, A 1946,N 28,41:2
Gramercy Ghost 1951,Ap 27,20:2
Girl in Pink Tights, The 1954,Mr 6,13:2
Venice Preserv'd 1955,D 13,54:4
Auntie Mame 1956,N 1,47:2
Laundry, The 1963,F 19,5:2
Smith, Robert B (Lyricist)
Sweethearts 1925,S 23,25:1
Smith, Robert B (Playwright)
Sweethearts 1947,Ja 22,31:2
Smith, Robert Paul (Playwright)
Tender Trap, The 1954,O 14,37:2
Tender Trap, The 1961,Ag 26,15:1
Smith, Robinson (Producer)
Parnell 1935,N 12,24:2
Parnell 1936,My 5,26:2
Richard II 1937,F 6,14:2
Richard II 1937,S 16,28:2
Escape This Night 1938,Ap 23,18:1
Outward Bound 1938,D 23,16:5
Smith, Rollin
Beggar's Holiday 1946,D 27,13:3
Smith, Rome
Threepenny Opera, The 1955,S 21,38:1
Smith, Rome (Miscellaneous)
Cave Dwellers, The 1957,O 21,29:2
Smith, Roxanne
Drums in the Night 1967,My 18,54:1
Smith, Roy
It's a Bird . . . It's a Plane . . . It's Superman
  1966,Mr 30,34:1
Smith, Rufus
Knickerbocker Holiday 1938,O 20,26:2
Paint Your Wagon 1951,N 13,32:2
Pipe Dream 1955,D 1,44:1
Gift of Time, A 1962,F 23,34:1
Come on Strong 1962,O 5,29:1
3 Bags Full 1966,Mr 7,22:1
Annie Get Your Gun 1966,Je 1,42:2
Education of H*Y*M*A*N K*A*P*L*A*N, The
  1968,Ap 5,57:1
Smith, S Ascher
Little Father of the Wilderness, The 1930,Je 3,27:1
Smith, S M
Tiger Smiles, The 1930,D 18,29:1
It's the Valet 1933,D 15,25:4
Smith, Salees
Bedrock 1934,N 18,II,6:3
Smith, Sally
Roar of the Greasepaint-the Smell of the Crowd
  1965,My 17,46:2
Smith, Sammy
Wish You Were Here 1952,Je 26,26:6
Plain and Fancy 1955,Ja 28,14:2
How to Succeed in Business Without Really Trying
  1961,O 16,34:1
Oklahoma! 1965,D 16,62:1
How Now, Dow Jones 1967,D 8,53:1
Goodbye People, The 1968,D 4,52:1
Wrong Way Light Bulb, The 1969,Mr 5,40:1
Smith, Sarah B (Playwright)
Piper Paid 1934,D 26,19:1
Smith, Sarah H (Miscellaneous)
Curate's Play, The 1961,D 18,41:3
Tableaux 1961,D 18,41:3
Smith, Sarah Jane
Brigadoon 1967,D 14,59:2
South Pacific 1968,Je 30,54:2
South Pacific 1969,Jl 7,27:1
Smith, Seba (Playwright)
Half Horse, Half Alligator 1966,Mr 14,37:2

Smith, Selma
Ginger Snaps 1930,Ja 1,30:5
Smith, Sheila
Best Foot Forward 1956,Mr 3,16:1
Fiorello! 1962,Je 14,24:1
Sweet Miani 1962,S 26,33:2
Hot Spot 1963,Ap 20,17:2
Smith, Sherry
Crime and Punishment 1947,D 23,29:3
Smith, Shevlin (Mrs)
Variations of 1940 1940,Ja 29,12:1
Smith, Shirley
Winkelberg 1958,Ja 15,26:2
Highest Tree, The 1959,N 5,41:1
Smith, Sid (Producer)
Ice Capades 1964,Ag 27,27:2
Ice Capades 1966,Je 2,50:2
Smith, Sidney
Buckaroo 1929,Mr 18,31:1
Richelieu 1934,My 22,28:1
Horse Eats Hat 1936,S 28,14:2
Smith, Speedy
Change Your Luck 1930,Je 7,10:2
Hummin' Sam 1933,Ap 10,8:8
Blackbirds 1933,D 4,22:3
Smith, Speedy (Choreographer)
Change Your Luck 1930,Je 7,10:2
Smith, Stanley
You Said It 1931,Ja 20,21:3
Hold Your Horses 1933,Ag 31,20:4
Hold Your Horses 1933,S 26,26:4
Satellite 1935,N 21,27:5
Black Widow 1936,F 13,24:3
Smith, Susan
Neighbors 1966,N 15,51:4
Smith, Susan A
Villa of Madame Vidac, The 1959,O 1,40:1
Smith, Sydney
Taps 1925,Ap 15,16:2
Present Arms 1928,Ap 27,16:2
Allure 1934,O 30,22:6
Richard II 1937,S 16,28:2
Hamlet 1938,O 13,28:1
Henry IV, Part I 1939,Ja 31,17:2
Hamlet 1939,D 5,35:2
Richard II 1940,Ap 2,31:2
R U R 1942,D 4,30:2
Harriet 1943,Mr 4,24:2
Curious Savage, The 1950,O 25,44:3
Edwin Booth 1958,N 25,37:1
Smith, Sydney Goodser (Playwright)
Wallace, The 1960,Ag 23,26:4
Smith, T Burton
Brown Sugar 1937,D 3,29:2
Smith, Theodore
Dover Road, The 1924,D 20,18:2
Anna Lucasta 1944,Ag 31,15:1
Power of Darkness, The 1948,O 11,28:2
Smith, Thorne (Original Author)
If I Were You 1938,Ja 25,24:2
Smith, Tom
Cinderella on Broadway 1920,Je 25,18:1
Vaudeville (Palace) 1926,O 26,24:2
Smith, Trixie
Brass Ankle 1931,Ap 24,26:4
Constant Sinner, The 1931,S 15,30:1
Louisiana 1933,F 28,15:5
Big White Fog 1940,O 23,26:2
Smith, Truman
Boyd's Daughter 1940,O 12,20:2
Twelfth Night 1949,O 4,33:2
Innkeepers, The 1956,F 3,19:1
Drink to Me Only 1958,O 9,47:4
Dr Willy Nilly 1959,Je 5,18:2
Kean 1961,N 3,28:2
Best Foot Forward 1963,Ap 3,43:1
Smith, Ursula
Honor and Offer 1969,My 14,36:1
Smith, Viola
Cabaret 1966,N 21,62:1
Smith, Virginia
Dice of the Gods, The 1923,Ap 6,20:2
Lollipop 1924,Ja 22,15:3
Schemers 1924,S 16,27:1
Peter Pan 1924,N 7,16:2
Merry Merry 1925,S 25,24:3
Virgin Man, The 1927,Ja 19,20:4
Padlocks of 1927 1927,Jl 6,23:4
Happy 1927,D 6,26:3
Merry Wives of Windsor, The 1928,Mr 20,20:1
Just a Minute 1928,O 9,34:3
Shoot the Works! 1931,Jl 22,19:5
Petticoat Fever 1935,Je 25,14:5
Try and Get It 1943,Ag 3,13:2
Smith, W H
Goat Alley 1921,Je 21,20:2
Man From Earth, The 1923,Ja 3,6:2
Fiesta 1933,D 16,12:2
What a Relief 1935,D 14,10:6
What a Relief 1935,D 19,34:4
Smith, W H (Composer)
Drake's Drum 1923,D 26,17:7

mith, W H (Playwright)
Drunkard, The; Fallen Saved, The 1959,Je 24,37:2
Drunkard, The 1970,Ap 14,54:1
mith, Waldron
Merchant of Venice, The 1920,D 30,16:2
mith, Wallace (Original Author)
May Wine 1935,N 23,23:1
May Wine 1935,D 6,30:3
mith, Wallace H
Drake's Drum 1923,D 26,17:7
mith, Wallace H (Playwright)
Drake's Drum 1923,D 26,17:7
mith, Walter
Now-A-Days 1929,Ag 6,29:3
mith, Walter Reed
Girl From Wyoming, The 1938,O 31,12:1
mith, Whiz
When the Roll Is Called Up Yonder
1930,My 9,20:5
mith, William
Mountain, The 1933,S 12,28:6
Porgy and Bess 1942,Ja 23,16:2
Porgy and Bess 1943,S 14,26:2
Porgy and Bess 1944,F 8,13:2
Memphis Bound 1945,My 25,23:2
Show Boat 1946,Ja 7,17:2
Show Boat 1948,S 9,33:2
Lost in the Stars 1949,O 31,21:2
Show Boat 1956,Je 22,16:1
Show Boat 1957,Je 28,30:2
Smith, William B
What Price Glory 1924,S 6,14:3
Smith, William Fletcher
Poisoned Kiss, The 1937,Ap 22,19:1
Smith, William P (Playwright)
Oh, Hector! 1929,Mr 6,33:2
Smith, Wilson
Park Avenue 1946,N 5,31:2
Street Scene 1947,Ja 10,17:2
Allegro 1947,O 11,10:2
Smith, Winchell (Director)
Holy Terror, A 1925,S 29,31:2
These Charming People 1925,O 7,31:2
Last of Mrs Cheyney, The 1925,N 10,23:5
Wisdom Tooth, The 1926,F 16,22:2
2 Girls Wanted 1926,S 10,25:3
Night Hostess 1928,S 13,31:2
Waterloo Bridge 1930,Ja 7,29:2
Vinegar Tree, The 1930,N 20,30:3
Vinegar Tree, The 1930,D 7,IX,1:1
Tadpole, The 1931,D 6,VIII,2:7
Smith, Winchell (Playwright)
Wheel, The 1921,My 8,VI,1:1
Wheel, The 1921,Ag 30,10:1
Thank You 1921,O 4,10:2
Thank You 1921,O 16,VI,1:1
Lightnin' 1925,F 1,VII,2:1
Holy Terror, A 1925,S 29,31:2
City Chap, The 1925,O 27,21:1
Zoo, The 1927,O 9,VIII,1:3
Tadpole, The 1931,D 6,VIII,2:7
Lightnin' 1938,S 16,17:2
Smith, Winfield
Good Neighbor 1941,O 22,26:2
Snafu 1944,O 26,19:5
Smith and Dale
Vaudeville (Palace) 1932,F 15,13:3
Frank Fay's Vaudeville 1939,Mr 3,20:4
Laugh, Town, Laugh! 1942,Jl 23,15:3
Vaudeville (Palace) 1950,My 25,36:2
Vaudeville (Palace) 1951,O 17,36:6
Old Bucks and New Wings 1962,N 6,39:4
Smith Kids, The
Caribbean Carnival 1947,D 6,12:2
Smith-Payne, Anna
Dear Brutus 1926,Jl 15,21:3
Smithers, Thomas H
Father, The 1937,Ap 21,18:5
Smithers, William
Romeo and Juliet 1951,Mr 12,21:2
Romeo and Juliet 1951,Mr 25,II,1:1
Legend of Lovers 1951,D 27,17:1
End as a Man 1953,S 16,39:1
End As a Man 1953,S 27,II,1:1
Troublemakers, The 1954,D 31,11:3
Sea Gull, The 1956,O 23,38:1
Square Root of Wonderful, The 1957,O 31,40:1
Shadow of a Gunman, The 1958,N 21,26:1
Shadow of a Gunman, The 1958,N 30,II,1:1
Romeo and Juliet 1959,Je 15,31:1
Romeo and Juliet 1959,Je 21,II,1:1
Who'll Save the Plowboy? 1962,Ja 10,24:2
Man and Boy 1963,N 13,34:1
Smithfield, George
Two Fellows and a Girl 1923,Jl 20,8:2
Up the Alley 1931,Jl 24,20:3
Tragedy of the Ages, The 1933,Ap 7,22:7
Chalk Dust 1936,Mr 5,24:5
Doctor Faustus 1937,Ja 9,21:2
Cradle Will Rock, The 1937,D 6,19:4
Cradle Will Rock, The 1938,Ja 4,19:3
White Cargo 1941,My 14,24:3

Smithfield, George (Director)
One Man's Woman 1926,My 26,25:1
Trial Marriage 1927,F 1,24:3
Marriage on Approval 1928,Mr 2,28:2
Black Scandals 1928,O 27,23:2
Chippies 1929,My 30,23:3
Smithfield, George (Playwright)
Black Scandals 1928,O 27,23:2
Up the Alley 1931,Jl 24,20:3
Smithfield, George (Producer)
When in Rome 1934,F 28,22:6
Smithies, Richard
Hamlet 1964,Je 17,49:1
Smithies, Richard H R (Director)
Poker Session, The 1967,S 20,42:2
Smithies, Richard H R (Producer)
Poker Session, The 1967,S 20,42:2
Smithies, Thomas H (Director)
Importance of Being Earnest, The 1936,O 22,31:2
Smithson, Frank (Director)
Honest Liars 1926,Jl 20,17:2
Artists and Models 1930,Je 11,33:2
Smithson, Laura
Matriarch, The 1930,Mr 19,24:5
Smock, Jim
Oklahoma! 1958,Mr 8,15:2
Smolden, W L (Miscellaneous)
Visitatio Sepulchri; Peregrinus 1968,Ap 29,49:1
Planctus Mariae 1968,Ap 29,49:1
Smolin, Dmitry (Playwright)
Lysistrata 1925,D 15,28:2
Smolko, John
Kaleidoscope 1957,Je 14,20:2
Mask and Gown 1957,S 11,29:1
On the Town 1959,Ja 16,36:1
It's a Bird . . . It's a Plane . . . It's Superman
1966,Mr 30,34:1
Smoller, Dorothy
Checkerboard, The 1920,Ag 20,7:2
Bachelor's Night, A 1921,O 18,20:1
Up in the Clouds 1922,Ja 3,20:3
Smyth, Carleton J
Upon My Soul 1927,Ap 22,19:1
Smyth, Craig
What a Relief 1935,D 14,10:6
Smythe, Betty Jean
Day Before Spring, The 1945,N 23,27:2
Smythe, George
Gods of the Lightning 1928,O 25,27:2
Smythe, J Emerson (Miscellaneous)
Elizabeth Sleeps Out 1936,Ap 21,27:6
Smythe, Kit
Put It in Writing 1963,My 14,31:1
Smythe, Paul (Director)
Evensong 1933,F 1,13:4
Smythe, Robert
Lassie 1920,Ap 7,9:2
Snader, Edward L
Welcome Stranger 1920,S 14,12:1
Snaith, William (Scenic Designer)
Thomas Paine 1930,Mr 21,30:7
Snapper, Kitty
Wisteria Trees, The 1950,Mr 30,39:1
Snare, George
Taming of the Shrew, The 1935,O 1,27:3
Snead, Kitty-Alice
Golden Streets, The 1970,Ag 14,21:1
Snedeker, Lendon
Laugh It Off 1925,Ap 25,18:4
Sneed, Harold
Run, Little Chillun! 1933,Mr 2,21:3
Sneed, Ray
Policy Kings 1938,D 31,6:2
Sneed, Sherman
Porgy and Bess 1953,Mr 10,25:5
Carmen Jones 1956,Je 1,28:2
Belafonte at the Palace 1959,D 16,55:1
Snegoff, Leonid
First Law, The 1929,My 7,28:4
Riverside Drive 1931,Ja 6,24:2
Man With the Portfolio, The 1931,F 12,24:6
Armored Train No 1469 1931,N 28,20:3
Snegoff, Leonid (Director)
Right to Kill, The 1926,F 16,22:2
First Law, The 1929,My 7,28:4
Armored Train No 1469 1931,N 28,20:3
Snegoff, Leonid (Playwright)
First Law, The 1929,My 7,28:4
Sneider, Vern (Original Author)
Teahouse of the August Moon, The 1953,O 16,32:1
Teahouse of the August Moon, The
1954,Mr 10,30:2
Teahouse of the August Moon, The
1954,My 2,II,3:1
Teahouse of the August Moon, The
1955,My 10,24:1
Teahouse of the August Moon, The 1956,N 9,33:2
Lovely Ladies, Kind Gentlemen 1970,D 29,38:1
Snell, Bruce (Miscellaneous)
Salad Days 1958,N 11,24:1
Snell, Christopher
Wisteria Trees, The 1955,F 3,20:2
Most Happy Fella, The 1956,My 4,20:1

Snell, David
Wars of the Roses, The (Part I) 1970,Jl 2,30:1
Wars of the Roses, The (Part II) 1970,Jl 3,15:1
Richard III 1970,Jl 4,11:1
Snell, Eugenie (Miscellaneous)
Song of the Grasshopper 1967,S 29,52:2
Snelling, Stuart
Crow's Nest, The 1923,My 10,22:3
Snevellicci, Miss
George Barnwell; London Merchant, The
1928,O 2,34:3
Snevellicci, Mr
George Barnwell; London Merchant, The
1928,O 2,34:3
Snider, Michael
All the Living 1938,Mr 25,14:4
Snider, Richard
Desire Under the Elms 1951,N 22,45:1
Tall Kentuckian, The 1953,Je 17,30:1
Snider, Sherry Lee
Greenwillow 1970,D 8,60:1
Snitman, Sam (Pvt)
Swing Sister Wac Swing 1944,Ja 4,20:4
Snitow, Charles
Paul Bunyan 1941,My 6,25:1
Snitt, A E (Playwright)
Phantoms 1930,Ja 14,24:3
Snitzer, Henrietta
Silent Forces 1920,Ag 30,12:1
Snively, A B
Drake's Drum 1923,D 26,17:7
Snodgrass, James (Playwright)
Marie Antoinette in Pennsylvania 1949,My 12,26:2
Snodgrass, Quincy
Hayride 1954,S 14,24:2
Snodgrass, Wilder M (Miscellaneous)
Square in the Eye 1965,My 20,54:1
Snook, John B
York Nativity Play, The 1956,D 5,49:2
Snookums
Howdy Mr Ice 1948,Je 25,28:5
Snoozer Jr (Dog)
Vaudeville (Palace) 1929,My 20,22:8
Vaudeville (Palace) 1932,Je 13,19:7
Snow, C P (Original Author)
New Men, The 1962,S 7,35:2
Affair, The 1962,S 21,34:2
Affair, The 1962,O 7,II,1:1
Masters, The 1963,Je 1,16:8
Snow, Davis (Playwright)
Long Days, The 1951,Ap 21,10:5
Snow, E P
Dover Road, The 1924,D 20,18:2
Snow, Edward F
Casanova 1923,S 27,10:2
Snow, Harry
Once Upon a Mattress 1959,My 12,40:1
Brigadoon 1962,My 31,21:4
Brigadoon 1963,F 1,6:2
Brigadoon 1964,D 24,9:1
Snow, Julie
Inside Story 1942,O 30,22:2
From Morn Till Midnight 1948,D 7,41:6
Snow, Leslie
Mime Theatre of Etienne Decroux, The
1959,D 24,15:1
Snow, Lida
Prologue to Glory 1938,Mr 18,22:2
Snow, Marjorie L
Clarence 1923,My 14,18:4
Snow, Marvee
Main Street 1921,O 6,21:1
Snow, Nelson
Music Box Revue 1923,S 24,5:3
Oh, Please! 1926,D 22,24:3
Fioretta 1929,F 6,30:3
Snow, Ross
Paging Danger 1931,F 27,19:2
Snow, Thomas J (Miscellaneous)
Marching Song 1959,D 29,20:1
Snow, Valada
Chocolate Dandies, The 1924,S 2,22:2
Snow, Virginia (Producer)
Candida 1970,Ap 7,41:1
Snow and Columbus
Vaudeville (Palace) 1926,S 21,32:5
Snowden, Elmer
Moon Vine, The 1943,F 12,22:2
Snowden, Van
Poupees de Paris, Les 1962,D 13,8:2
Poupees de Paris, Les 1964,My 16,11:1
Snowden, William
Sound of Music, The 1959,N 17,40:2
Snyden, Betta
Henri Christophe 1945,Je 7,24:5
Snyder, A A (Producer)
Veils 1928,Mr 14,28:5
Snyder, Alice
Green Pastures, The 1935,F 27,16:2
Snyder, Arlen Dean
Family Way, The 1965,Ja 14,44:5
Open 24 Hours 1969,F 12,31:1
Brightower 1970,Ja 29,32:1

Snyder, Arlen Dean—Cont

Candyapple, The 1970,N 24,33:1

Snyder, Bozo
What Does the Public Want? 1923,Jl 16,14:3
Michael Todd's Peep Show 1950,Je 29,37:2
Peep Show 1950,Jl 9,II,1:1

Snyder, Carleton (Lighting Director)
Skits-Oh-Frantics 1967,Ap 3,39:2

Snyder, Carleton (Scenic Designer)
Skits-Oh-Frantics 1967,Ap 3,39:2

Snyder, Charles
Father, The 1949,N 17,36:2

Snyder, Dan (Scenic Designer)
Visit, The 1967,S 13,41:1

Snyder, Drew
Cock-A-Doodle Dandy 1969,Ja 21,40:1
Hamlet 1969,Mr 4,34:1
Wars of the Roses, The (Part I) 1970,Jl 2,30:1
Wars of the Roses, The (Part II) 1970,Jl 3,15:1
Richard III 1970,Jl 4,11:1
Henry VI, Parts I, II, III 1970,Jl 5,II,3:1

Snyder, Dwight
Ripples 1930,F 12,26:1
Girl Crazy 1930,O 15,27:1
Anything Goes 1934,N 22,26:1

Snyder, Frederick N
Little Town of Bethlehem, The 1920,D 27,11:1

Snyder, Frieda
Boutique Fantasque, La 1929,D 28,10:6

Snyder, Gene (Choreographer)
At Home Abroad 1935,S 20,17:4
Yokel Boy 1939,Jl 7,12:2

Snyder, Glen
Moon Is a Gong, The 1926,Mr 13,21:3

Snyder, J E (Rev) (Composer)
Quo Vadis 1932,O 17,18:2
Passion Play 1934,F 12,15:1

Snyder, Kathe
Doctor Faustus Lights the Lights 1951,D 3,23:4
Lovers 1956,My 11,23:1

Snyder, Louise
Out of the Frying Pan 1941,F 12,24:2

Snyder, Philip
Enchanted Isle 1927,S 20,33:2
Blue and the Gray, The; War Is Hell Gray, The 1929,D 27,26:4

Snyder, Richard
John Turner Davis 1958,Jl 2,25:1

Snyder, Ronald (Miscellaneous)
Boy Friend, The 1970,Ap 15,54:1

Snyder, Ted (Composer)
Fashions of 1924 1923,Jl 19,18:2

Snyder, Tommy (Bozo)
New Americana 1928,N 30,32:4

Snyder, William (Playwright)
Days and Nights of Beebee Fenstermaker, The 1962,S 18,33:1

Snyder, William (Producer)
Conversation Piece 1957,N 19,38:2

Snyder, William H Jr
Merry Wives of Windsor, The 1954,F 17,27:1

Snyder, William H Jr (Miscellaneous)
Gift of Time, A 1962,F 23,34:1

Soanes, Jack
Deep Channels 1929,O 19,22:3
Dear Old England 1930,Mr 26,24:6
Order Please 1934,O 10,21:2
Lord Blesses the Bishop, The 1934,N 28,24:5
Satellite 1935,N 21,27:5
Granite 1936,Ja 14,24:6
Call Me Ziggy 1937,F 13,9:6
To Quito and Back 1937,O 7,30:4

Soanlon, Walter
County Chairman, The 1936,My 26,26:5

Soans, Jacqueline
Cyrano de Bergerac 1946,O 9,33:2
Cyrano de Bergerac 1947,Ja 17,27:2
Dear Judas 1947,O 6,26:4
Bear, The 1948,F 6,29:2
Wedding, The 1948,F 6,29:2
Tragedian in Spite of Himself, A 1948,F 6,29:2
On the Harmfulness of Tobacco 1948,F 6,29:2

Soans, Paula
Beautiful Changes, The 1956,Mr 24,15:2
Mrs Warren's Profession 1956,Je 7,35:2

Soans, Paula (Costume Designer)
Candida 1957,F 9,14:1

Soares, Sylvia
Gentleman Caller, The 1969,Ap 27,92:1
Black Quartet, A; Gentleman Caller, The 1969,Jl 31,28:1
Gentleman Caller, The 1969,Ag 3,II,1:4

Sobel, Billy
Hit the Deck! 1927,Ap 26,32:1

Sobel, Eva
Irving Berlin's New Music Box Revue 1922,O 24,18:1

Sobel, Jack
Anathema 1923,Ap 11,16:2

Sobel, Louis
Vaudeville (Palace) 1932,Jl 11,11:6

Sobel, Stephen (Miscellaneous)
Crimes of Passion; Erpingham Camp, The 1969,O 27,54:1

Crimes of Passion; Ruffian on the Stair, The 1969,O 27,54:1

Sobell, Jack (Playwright)
30 Days Hath September 1938,O 1,10:5

Sobell, Martin
Merry Duchess, The 1943,Je 24,25:1

Soberg, Joe
Savage Rhythm 1932,Ja 1,30:4

Sobie, Stanley
Tragical Historie of Doctor Faustus, The 1964,O 6,34:2

Sobienieniowski, Florjan (Translator)
On the Rocks 1933,N 25,10:1

Sobieniopski, Alfred (Translator)
Apple Cart, The 1929,Je 15,6:2

Sobko, Vadim (Playwright)
Behind the Second Front 1949,My 9,3:3

Soble, Ron
King and the Duke, The 1955,Je 2,25:2
Venice Preserv'd 1955,D 13,54:4

Sobol, Edward (Director)
Spring Song 1934,O 2,18:2
Dodsworth 1938,F 23,26:2
High Kickers 1941,N 1,21:2

Sobol, Louis (Playwright)
High Hatters, The 1928,My 11,28:2

Soboloff, Arnold
By Hex 1956,Je 19,25:1
Escurial 1956,O 3,29:2
Brothers Karamazov, The 1957,D 9,39:4
Vincent 1959,O 1,40:1
Mandingo 1961,My 23,43:6
Egg, The 1962,Ja 9,23:2
Bravo Giovanni 1962,My 21,41:2
Beauty Part, The 1962,D 28,5:2
One Flew Over the Cuckoo's Nest 1963,N 14,40:2
Anyone Can Whistle 1964,Ap 6,36:1
Gogo Loves You 1964,O 10,19:2
Sweet Charity 1966,Ja 31,22:1
Mike Downstairs 1968,Ap 19,35:1
Bananas 1968,D 5,60:1
Papp 1969,My 6,39:1
Camino Real 1970,Ja 9,42:1
Show Me Where the Good Times Are 1970,Mr 6,32:1
Architect and the Emperor of Assyria, The 1970,Jl 24,17:2
Architect and the Emperor of Assyria, The 1970,Ag 9,II,1:5

Soboloff, Arnold (Miscellaneous)
Escurial 1956,O 3,29:2
Lesson, The 1956,O 3,29:2

Sobotka, Ruth
Cherry Orchard, The 1962,N 15,46:2
Firebugs, The 1963,N 22,41:1
King Lear 1963,N 23,22:1

Socolow, Al
Tragicomedy of Don Cristobita and Dona Rosita, The 1958,My 30,12:2

Socolow, Frank
Taste of Honey, A 1960,O 5,46:1

Soden, Frank P
Simon's Wife 1945,Mr 9,16:4

Soderling, Walter
Circle, The 1921,S 13,12:1
Casanova 1923,S 27,10:2
Judy Drops In 1924,O 6,24:2
Undercurrent, The 1925,F 4,18:2
Command Performance, The 1928,O 4,27:1

Sodero, Cesare (Musical Director)
Paese del Campanelli, Il; Land of Bells, The 1935,My 10,25:4

Soderstrom, Ellen
Little Old New York 1920,S 9,9:2

Soederbaum, Ulla
Green Table, The 1942,Ja 22,12:2
Prodigal Son, The 1942,F 18,22:2

Soeneland, Senta
Chicago 1927,D 18,IX,1:8

Sofaer, Abraham
Matriarch, The 1930,Mr 19,24:5
Love's Labour's Lost 1932,Ag 7,IX,1:7
Richard II 1934,N 4,IX,3:1
Professor Bernhardi 1936,Je 12,IX,1:8
Victoria Regina 1936,S 1,24:5
Merchant of Venice, The 1938,Ja 15,18:8
Victoria Regina 1938,O 4,20:2
Gentle People, The 1939,Jl 30,IX,1:3
Macbeth 1942,Jl 26,VIII,1:7
In the Matter of J Robert Oppenheimer 1968,Je 7,31:1

Sofaer, Ruth (Scenic Designer)
Crucible, The 1958,Mr 17,21:1

Soffer, Sam (Composer)
Night Is Black Bottles, The 1962,D 5,56:1

Soffer, Sam (Playwright)
Night Is Black Bottles, The 1962,D 5,56:1

Soffer, Sheldon (Miscellaneous)
Iphigenia in Aulis 1967,N 22,40:2

Sofia, Marilyn
Ruddigore 1954,Ap 21,36:4
Sorcerer, The 1954,My 26,34:3

Soglow, Otto
Illustrators' Show, The 1936,Ja 23,25:3

Soglow, Otto (Playwright)
Illustrators' Show, The 1936,Ja 23,25:3
Russell Patterson's Sketch-Book 1960,F 8,35:1

Sohmers, Barbara
Trial, The 1955,Je 15,35:2
Spring's Awakening 1955,O 10,30:2
An Evening With G B S; Press Cuttings 1957,F 19,35:7

Sokal, Dennis
Gloria and Esperanza 1970,F 5,32:1

Sokic, Ruzica
Progress of Bora, The Tailor, The 1968,Je 27,49:2
Who's Afraid of Virginia Woolf? 1968,Jl 4,13:1
Victor, or The Children Take Over 1968,Jl 10,22:4

Sokol, Gloria
Threepenny Opera, The 1954,Mr 11,26:5

Sokol, Marilyn
Year Boston Won the Pennant, The 1969,My 23,38:1
Universal Nigger, The 1970,Mr 21,18:1

Sokoler, Bob (Producer)
Kataki 1959,Ap 10,24:1

Sokoloff, Ivan (Playwright)
Passion of Judas, The 1930,D 2,31:2

Sokoloff, Nikolai (Musical Director)
Neighborhood Playhouse Program 1930,F 21,23:1

Sokoloff, Nikolas and The Cleveland Orchestra
Heldenleben, Ein 1929,Ap 27,16:4

Sokoloff, Vladimir
Miracle, The 1927,Je 8,23:2
Midsummer Night's Dream, A 1927,N 18,21:1
Midsummer Night's Dream, A 1927,D 4,X,6:1
Jedermann 1927,D 8,33:2
Jedermann 1927,D 18,IX,6:1
Dantons Tod 1927,D 21,28:3
Danton's Death 1928,Ja 1,VIII,1:1
Dantons Tod 1928,Ja 1,VIII,3:1
Peripherie 1928,Ja 3,29:1
Diener Zweier Herren; Servant of Two Masters, The 1928,Ja 10,28:3
Kabale und Liebe 1928,Ja 17,22:3
Servant of Two Masters, The 1928,Ja 22,VIII,6:1
Lebende Leichnam, Der, Der; Living Corpse, The 1928,Ja 24,26:2
Gespenster, Die; Ghosts 1928,F 8,28:6
Burlesque; Artisten 1928,Je 10,17:2
Artisten; Burlesque 1928,S 23,IX,2:2
Faiseur, Le 1936,Ja 12,IX,3:7
Danton's Death 1938,N 3,26:2
Flowers of Virtue, The 1942,F 6,22:2
Crime and Punishment 1947,D 23,29:3
Crime and Punishment 1948,Ja 4,II,1:1
Madwoman of Chaillot, The 1949,Ja 9,II,1:1
Power of Darkness, The 1959,S 30,33:1

Sokoloff, Vladimir (Director)
Lottie Dundass 1941,Ag 22,19:5

Sokoloff, Vladimir (Producer)
Cry Havoc 1942,N 8,VIII,1:7

Sokolow, Anna
Mascaiada 1929,D 28,10:6
Iron Flowers 1933,Je 13,22:2
You Can't Sleep Here 1941,My 11,I,42:6

Sokolow, Anna (Choreographer)
Noah 1935,F 14,25:2
Sing for Your Supper 1939,Ap 25,18:6
Street Scene 1947,Ja 10,17:2
Great Campaign, The 1947,Ap 1,33:2
Sleepy Hollow 1948,Je 4,26:3
Regina 1949,N 1,32:2
Happy as Larry 1950,Ja 7,11:2
Robin Hood 1950,N 6,32:2
Madam Will You Walk 1953,D 2,2:4
Red Roses for Me 1955,D 29,15:2
Candide 1956,D 9,II,5:1
Copper and Brass 1957,O 18,19:2
On Baile's Strand 1959,Ap 13,34:4
Death of Cuchulain, The 1959,Ap 13,34:4

Sokolow, Anna (Director)
Robin Hood 1950,N 6,32:2
Metamorphosis 1957,F 20,38:1
Metamorphosis 1957,Mr 17,II,8:5

Sokolow, Anna (Playwright)
Bananas 1968,D 5,60:1

Sola, Leonor
Too Many Girls 1939,O 19,26:2

Soladar, Ward
Getting Even 1929,Ag 20,31:1

Solanke, Jimi
Madmen and Specialists 1970,Ag 3,38:1

Solann, Evelyn
Frugal Noon 1964,My 23,15:2

Solano, Joanne
Three Sisters, The 1959,S 22,46:1

Solano, Solita (Playwright)
Face Value 1921,D 27,10:2

Solar, Willie
Vaudeville (Palace) 1926,Jl 20,17:4
Vaudeville (Palace) 1926,D 7,24:3

Soldano, Pietro
Abisso 1920,O 10,VI,1:8

Mati, Oscar
Fuerza Ciega, La 1927,D 6,26:1

Ado, Sally
Up Eden 1968,N 27,42:1

Meri, Ferruccio
Servant of Two Masters, The 1960,F 24,42:2

Meng, Ingrid
Century Revue and the Midnight Rounders, The
1920,Jl 13,9:1
Passing Show of 1921, The 1920,D 30,16:2
Blue Bird, The 1923,D 26,13:3

Mieri, Cesare (Playwright)
Tombola, La; Lottery, The 1936,N 9,23:4

Min, Harvey
Sign of Jonah, The 1960,S 9,35:1
Worm in Horseradish, A 1961,Mr 14,32:3
Man's a Man, A 1962,S 20,30:2
Firebugs, The 1963,N 22,41:1
King Lear 1963,N 23,22:1

Mitode Solis, Luchino
Waiting for Godot 1956,Ap 29,II,1:2

Milberg, Harvey (Composer)
Antigone 1967,Ja 14,18:1

Milers, John (Scenic Designer)
God Innis 1937,Ag 25,24:3

Mily, Mildred
Pal Joey 1940,D 26,22:2

Mims, Kenny (Composer)
Leonard Sillman's New Faces of 1968
1968,My 3,43:1

Mims, Kenny (Lyricist)
Leonard Sillman's New Faces of 1968
1968,My 3,43:1

Mims, Kenny (Playwright)
Leonard Sillman's New Faces of 1968
1968,My 3,43:1

Milness, Howard
Ten Million Ghosts 1936,O 24,23:7

Olnick, Brenda
Caucasian Chalk Circle, The 1961,N 1,35:1

Olodar, Cesar (Composer)
Dollar Princess 1949,Je 2,32:1

Olodar, Cesar (Lyricist)
Dollar Princess 1949,Je 2,32:1

Olomon, Ely
First Mortgage 1929,O 11,36:1

Olomon, Lewis (Playwright)
Saturday Night 1928,Jl 31,13:5
Snafu 1944,O 26,19:5

Olomon, Renee (Miscellaneous)
Don't Worry Brother! 1963,O 14,35:2
Let's Sing Yiddish 1966,N 10,63:1
Sing Israel Sing 1967,My 12,50:1
From Israel With Laughter 1969,O 17,34:1

Olomon, Renee (Musical Director)
Honeymoon in Israel, A 1962,O 15,33:5
Light, Lively and Yiddish 1970,O 28,58:1

Olomon, Roger
Smyth With a Y 1937,Je 30,19:5

Olomon, Simon
Brothers Ashkenazi, The 1955,N 12,24:4

Olomon, Sol
Pickwick 1927,S 6,35:2
Tinguely Machine Mystery, or the Love Suicide at
Kaluka, The 1965,D 24,15:5

Solomon, Steve
Courtyard 1960,Mr 1,28:1

Solomon, Steve (Producer)
Courtyard 1960,Mr 1,28:1

Solomon, Syd
Tinguely Machine Mystery, or the Love Suicide at
Kaluka, The 1965,D 24,15:5

Solomos, Alexis (Costume Designer)
Oresteia 1966,Je 30,29:1

Solomos, Alexis (Director)
Oresteia 1966,Je 30,29:1
Birds, The 1966,Jl 1,40:1

Solorzano, Carlos (Playwright)
Cruce de Vias 1969,N 2,86:5

Solorzano, Consuela
Mexicana 1939,Ap 22,14:4

Solotaroff, M (Scenic Designer)
Dostigayev 1935,Ja 14,10:5
Recruits 1935,Ja 20,X,3:1
Haunch, Paunch and Jowl 1935,D 27,22:4
Hirsh Lekert 1936,Mr 11,23:2
200,000 1936,O 14,30:2
Outlaw, The 1937,O 6,28:1
Good Soldier Schweik, The 1937,D 22,33:2

Solov, Zachary
Lady Comes Across, The 1942,Ja 10,10:2
Along Fifth Avenue 1949,Ja 14,28:2

Solov, Zachary (Choreographer)
King of the Whole Damn World 1962,Ap 16,32:2
Merry Widow, The 1964,Ag 18,24:2

Solovieva, V
Revisor; Inspector General, The 1935,F 18,19:6
Poverty Is No Crime 1935,F 21,22:5
Enemies 1935,Mr 19,24:7

Soloway, Leonard (Producer)
Mark Twain Tonight! 1966,Mr 24,48:2
Philosophy in the Boudoir 1969,My 22,55:2

Soltan, Malcolm
Scarlet Sister Mary 1930,N 26,19:2
Payment Deferred 1931,O 1,24:2
Come of Age 1934,Ja 13,16:6
Sleeping Clergyman, A 1934,O 9,16:1

Solte, Salvatore
Trumpeter of Sakkingen 1921,Ja 15,11:3

Soltes, Bess
Wooden Idol, The 1930,My 13,27:2

Soltesz, Eva
Sweethearts 1947,Ja 22,31:2

Soltez, Chase
Silver Whistle, The 1948,N 25,49:2

Soltis, Mona
Nina Rosa 1930,S 22,22:5

Solveg, Maria
Midsummer Night's Dream, A 1927,Ag 8,6:1
Midsummer Night's Dream, A 1927,N 18,21:1
Midsummer Night's Dream, A 1927,D 4,X,6:1
Jedermann 1927,D 8,33:2
Jedermann 1927,D 18,IX,6:1
Dantons Tod 1927,D 21,28:3
Dantons Tod 1928,Ja 1,VIII,3:1
Er Ist an Allem Schuld; He Is to Blame for
Everything 1928,Ja 10,28:3
Diener Zweier Herren; Servant of Two Masters,
The 1928,Ja 10,28:3
Kabale und Liebe 1928,Ja 17,22:3
Servant of Two Masters, The 1928,Ja 22,VIII,6:1
Lebende Leichnam, Der, Der; Living Corpse, The
1928,Ja 24,26:2
Gespenster, Die; Ghosts 1928,F 8,28:6

Solveig, Esther
Tenth Man, The 1929,Mr 21,29:2
Lingering Past, The 1932,Je 30,26:5

Solway, Betty
Ladies Night in a Turkish Bath 1961,Mr 22,38:1

Solzhenitsyn, Aleksandr (Playwright)
Play by Aleksandr Solzhenitsyn, A 1970,O 18,94:1
Play by Aleksandr Solzhenitsyn, A 1970,O 25,II,1:3

Somack, Jack
Country Girl, The 1966,S 30,55:1
Cannibals, The 1968,N 4,60:1

Somerfeld, Robert (Playwright)
Projection Room, The 1969,Ja 15,38:2

Somers, Albert
Pickwick 1927,S 6,35:2

Somers, Brett
Maybe Tuesday 1958,Ja 30,18:3

Somers, D Benton
Pigeon, The 1930,O 15,26:2

Somers, Donald
Sinbad the Sailor 1929,D 27,26:5
Midsummer Night's Dream, A 1932,N 18,22:2
Merchant of Venice, The 1932,N 24,34:5
Ghosts 1933,My 24,24:5
Miser, The 1950,Mr 27,19:5
Major Barbara 1951,F 24,10:2
Babes in Arms 1951,Mr 10,7:3
Pygmalion 1952,F 9,11:2
Little Glass Clock, The 1956,Mr 27,40:2
Secret Concubine, The 1960,Mr 22,29:2
Brother to Dragons 1968,D 8,86:1
Wilson in the Promise Land 1970,Ja 11,78:1
Wilson in the Promise Land 1970,My 27,41:1

Somers, Esther
Easy Terms 1925,S 23,22:2

Somers, Harry
Midsummer Night's Dream, A 1960,Je 30,23:5

Somers, Harry (Composer)
Midsummer Night's Dream, A 1960,Je 30,23:5

Somers, Jimsey
Violet 1944,O 25,16:1
Apple of His Eye 1946,F 6,18:2
Virginia Reel 1947,Ap 15,28:2
Rip Van Winkle 1947,Jl 16,28:2

Somers, Martin A
Squealer, The 1928,N 13,36:3

Somerset, C W
Double-Or Quit 1922,O 8,VI,1:7

Somerset, David
Sunset 1966,My 13,34:1

Somerset, Pat
Orange Blossoms 1922,S 20,18:1
Dancers, The 1923,O 18,17:2
Outsider, The 1924,Mr 4,16:4
Mid-Channel 1928,S 16,IX,1:4

Somerset (Playwright)
Lady Frederick 1970,S 17,57:1

Somerside, Judith
Crime at Blossoms, The 1937,Jl 17,12:8
To Tell You the Truth 1948,Ap 19,28:6

Somerville, Baxter (Director)
Rose and Glove 1934,S 9,35:5

Somerville, Randolph (Director)
Dover Road, The 1924,D 20,18:2
Seventeen 1926,My 1,10:1
As You Like It 1936,Ap 24,18:4

Somerville, Randolph (Miscellaneous)
Champion, The 1925,Ap 24,16:4

Somerville, Randolph (Producer)
Ship, The 1929,N 21,24:7
Magic 1929,D 17,28:5
Seven Keys to Baldpate 1930,Ja 8,25:2
Round Table, The 1930,F 28,20:5

Somial
Letter, The 1927,O 30,IX,4:1

Somin, W O (Original Author)
Close Quarters 1937,Ap 18,II,3:5
Close Quarters 1939,Mr 7,19:2

Somlay
Postmistress, The 1928,Ja 15,VIII,2:1
Uri Muri 1928,Ap 15,IX,4:1
Trial of Mary Dugan, The 1928,S 30,IX,4:4

Somlyo, Roy A (Miscellaneous)
Dear World 1969,F 7,33:1
Home 1970,N 18,41:1

Somme, John
Tia Juana 1927,N 16,28:4

Sommer, Edith (Playwright)
Roomful of Roses, A 1955,O 18,48:1

Sommer, Jimmy
Star Spangled Family 1945,Ap 11,18:6

Sommer, Josef
Caesar and Cleopatra 1963,Ag 1,18:2
Much Ado About Nothing 1964,Je 11,26:2
Richard III 1964,Je 12,44:2
Hamlet 1964,Jl 4,9:1
Romeo and Juliet 1965,Je 21,36:3
Coriolanus 1965,Je 21,36:1
King Lear 1965,Je 25,39:1
Falstaff 1966,Je 20,27:1
Murder in the Cathedral 1966,Je 21,38:1
Twelfth Night 1966,Je 23,28:1
Julius Caesar 1966,Je 24,29:2
Richard II 1968,Je 24,42:3
Androcles and the Lion 1968,Je 27,47:1
Love's Labour's Lost 1968,Je 28,36:1
All's Well That Ends Well 1970,Je 16,53:1
Othello 1970,Je 22,43:1
Othello 1970,S 15,51:1

Sommer, Sally
Dirtiest Show in Town, The 1970,My 2,21:1

Sommers, Chet
Meet Peter Grant 1961,My 11,41:4

Sommers, Floyd
Nights of Wrath; Nuits de la Colere, Les
1947,D 1,26:4

Sommers, Gordon
Right of Possession 1930,My 9,20:5
Twelfth Disciple, The 1930,My 17,21:4

Sommers, Helene
Yellow Jacket, The 1923,Ap 20,20:3

Sommers, Marian
Little Father of the Wilderness, The 1930,Je 3,27:1

Sommers, Maurice
Opportunity 1920,Jl 31,5:1
De Luxe 1935,Mr 6,22:2
Boy Meets Girl 1935,N 28,38:2
Boy Meets Girl 1937,Jl 6,23:1
Boy Meets Girl 1943,Je 23,15:5

Sommers, Shelley
Hair 1970,Ja 13,39:1

Somner, Pearl (Costume Designer)
Summer of the Seventeenth Doll 1959,O 14,52:1
Guitar 1959,N 11,42:5
Oh, Kay! 1960,Ap 18,37:2
Ninety Day Mistress, The 1967,N 7,49:1
But, Seriously... 1969,F 28,29:1
Bill Noname 1970,Mr 3,37:1

Somnes, George
Wild Justice 1935,Jl 9,24:3

Somnes, George (Director)
Ladies of Creation 1931,S 9,25:1
Reprise 1935,My 2,16:2
With All My Heart 1935,Jl 30,17:1
Sun Kissed 1937,Mr 11,20:2
Greatest Show on Earth, The 1938,Ja 6,22:2
Brown Danube, The 1939,My 18,30:4
Pastoral 1939,N 2,26:2

Somnes, George (Miscellaneous)
Land's End 1946,D 12,37:5

Somnes, George (Producer)
Sun Kissed 1937,Mr 11,20:2
Greatest Show on Earth, The 1938,Ja 6,22:2
Brown Danube, The 1939,My 18,30:4
Pastoral 1939,N 2,26:2

Somogi, Judith (Miscellaneous)
Iolanthe 1965,My 19,42:1
Yeomen of the Guard, The 1965,Jl 8,34:1

Somogi, Judith (Musical Director)
Pirates of Penzance, The 1966,My 24,54:1
Trial by Jury 1966,Je 8,41:2
H M S Pinafore 1966,Je 8,41:2
Amahl and the Night Visitors 1970,D 26,11:1

Somogyi, Erzsi
Uri Muri 1928,Ap 15,IX,4:1

Somogyi, Miss
Nem Elhetek Muzsikaszo Nelkul
1928,D 30,VIII,4:4

Somr, Josef
Whose Turn Next? 1970,Ap 19,74:3

Sondergaard, Gale
Faust 1928,O 9,34:1

Sondergaard, Gale—Cont
Major Barbara 1928,N 20,28:4
Karl and Anna 1929,O 8,34:1
Red Rust 1929,D 18,31:1
American Dream; 1933 1933,F 22,24:5
American Dream; 1650 1933,F 22,24:5
Iron Flowers 1933,Je 13,22:2
Doctor Monica 1933,N 7,29:3
Invitation to a Murder 1934,My 18,26:3
Cue for Passion 1940,D 20,33:4
Woman, The 1965,O 21,56:1
Kicking the Castle Down 1967,Ja 19,43:1
Visit, The 1967,S 13,41:1
Tango 1968,Ja 1,11:1
Uncle Vanya 1969,Ag 31,II,4:1
Sondergaard, Hester
Black Pit 1935,Mr 21,26:6
Mother, The 1935,N 20,26:3
Bitter Stream 1936,Mr 31,16:6
Marching Song 1937,F 18,18:2
My Heart's in the Highlands 1939,Ap 14,29:2
My Heart's in the Highlands 1939,My 7,X,1:1
No for an Answer 1941,Ja 6,10:6
Private Life of the Master Race, The
 1945,Je 13,28:3
Galileo 1947,D 8,34:2
Church Street 1948,F 10,27:2
Sonderskov, Robert
Every Other Evil 1961,Ja 23,20:2
Sonderskov, Robert (Miscellaneous)
Every Other Evil 1961,Ja 23,20:2
Sonderson, Lora
Our Nell 1922,D 5,24:1
Go-Go 1923,Mr 13,19:4
Music Box Revue 1923,S 24,5:3
Sondheim, Stephen (Composer)
Girls of Summer 1956,N 20,45:1
Invitation to a March 1960,O 31,27:2
Funny Thing Happened on the Way to the Forum,
 A 1962,My 9,49:1
Anyone Can Whistle 1964,Ap 6,36:1
Company 1970,Ap 27,40:1
Company 1970,My 3,II,1:4
Company 1970,Jl 29,31:1
Sondheim, Stephen (Lyricist)
West Side Story 1957,S 27,14:4
West Side Story 1957,O 6,II,1:1
Gypsy 1959,My 22,31:6
Gypsy 1959,My 31,II,1:1
Gypsy 1959,Je 7,II,1:3
West Side Story 1960,Ap 28,31:1
West Side Story 1960,My 8,II,1:1
Funny Thing Happened on the Way to the Forum,
 A 1962,My 9,49:1
Funny Thing Happened on the Way to the Forum,
 A 1962,My 20,II,1:1
Anyone Can Whistle 1964,Ap 6,36:1
West Side Story 1964,Ap 9,24:2
Do I Hear a Waltz? 1965,Mr 19,28:1
Do I Hear a Waltz? 1965,Mr 28,II,1:1
Leonard Bernstein's Theater Songs 1965,Je 29,27:2
West Side Story 1968,Je 25,32:1
Company 1970,Ap 27,40:1
Sondheimer, Hans (Lighting Director)
Criminals, The 1941,D 22,24:3
Nathan the Wise 1944,F 22,26:3
All the King's Men 1948,Ja 19,19:2
E=MC2 1948,Je 16,36:2
Outside the Door 1949,Mr 2,33:2
House in Berlin, A (Als der Kreig zu Ende War);
 Als der Krieg zu Ende War (A House in Berlin)
 1950,D 27,32:3
Pirates of Penzance, The 1968,Ap 26,32:1
H M S Pinafore 1968,Ap 29,47:2
Yeomen of the Guard, The 1968,My 9,53:1
Patience 1968,My 16,52:1
Fiesta in Madrid 1969,My 29,49:1
Song, Sooh Ah
Teahouse of the August Moon, The
 1955,My 10,24:1
Sonino, Max (Producer)
No More Frontier 1931,O 22,27:1
Sonnenburg, Walter (Scenic Designer)
Curtains Up! 1959,N 3,26:3
Sonner, Pierre
Hamlet 1952,D 2,39:1
Sonnesbeck, Lujah
Miss Temple Is Willing 1936,Jl 21,13:1
Sonnier, Pierre
Baptiste 1952,N 13,34:2
Amphitryon 1952,N 21,21:2
Fourberies de Scapin, Les 1952,N 21,21:2
Occupe-Toi d'Amelie; Keep Your Eyes on Amelie
 1952,N 25,35:2
Sontag, Hedy
Electronic Nigger, The 1968,Mr 9,23:2
Patriot for Me, A 1969,O 6,58:1
Sontagg, Hildegard
Smyth With a Y 1937,Je 30,19:5
Soo, Jack
Flower Drum Song 1958,D 2,44:1
Soper, Gay
Canterbury Tales 1968,S 7,23:3

Sophocles (Miscellaneous)
Elder Statesman, The 1958,Ag 31,II,3:1
Sophocles (Original Author)
Electra 1927,My 4,28:3
Electra 1927,D 2,20:6
King Oedipus 1933,Ja 16,12:4
Electra 1959,F 14,15:1
Oedipus Rex 1959,Ap 30,36:1
Antigone 1959,S 16,46:2
Electra 1965,S 8,33:1
Wives, The 1965,Je 6,II,1:1
Electra 1969,Ag 8,14:1
Sophocles (Playwright)
Antigone 1923,My 4,18:4
Antigone 1923,My 25,28:1
Oedipus Rex 1923,O 26,14:1
Oedipe a Colone 1924,S 7,III,12:4
Oedipus the King 1926,D 26,VII,4:8
Electra 1927,My 15,VIII,1:1
Oedipus Rex 1929,Mr 24,X,2:3
Antigone 1930,Ap 25,28:4
Electra 1930,D 27,16:1
Trachiniae 1931,Ja 27,21:2
Electra 1931,My 24,VIII,3:5
Electra 1932,Ja 9,21:4
Oedipus Rex 1936,O 18,X,3:8
Oedipus Rex 1937,My 9,XI,7:5
Electra 1939,Jl 9,IX,1:6
Oedipus Tyrannus 1941,My 10,13:8
Oedipus Rex 1945,N 11,II,2:5
Oedipus Rex 1945,D 17,16:7
Antigone 1946,F 24,II,1:1
Oedipus Rex 1948,My 24,23:2
Electra 1952,N 20,38:2
Oedipus Tyrannus 1952,N 25,35:2
Oedipus Rex 1954,Jl 17,6:6
Oedipus Rex 1956,S 4,32:6
Philoctetes 1959,Ja 14,28:1
Oedipus Rex 1960,Ap 30,15:2
Electra 1961,S 20,23:4
Electra 1962,Ag 30,34:1
Electra 1964,Ag 12,42:1
Philoctetes 1964,Ag 19,29:1
Oedipus Rex 1965,Jl 9,17:1
Antigone 1968,O 11,36:1
Soraghan, Edmund
Squaw Man, The 1921,D 27,10:3
Soraghan, Joseph Edmond (Director)
Deep Channels 1929,O 19,22:3
Sorano, Daniel
Lorenzaccio 1958,O 15,44:2
Marie Tudor 1958,O 22,39:1
Don Juan 1958,O 29,29:1
Sorbets, Gaston (Original Author)
Princess in the Cage, The 1933,Mr 19,IX,2:2
Sorel, Ann
Damaged Goods 1937,My 18,27:2
Sorel, Cecile
Aventuriere, L' 1922,N 14,16:1
Demi-Monde, Le 1922,N 15,22:3
Dame aux Camelias, La 1922,N 16,22:2
Dame aux Camelias, La 1922,N 19,VII,1:1
Megere Apprivoisee, La 1922,N 20,21:2
Misanthrope, Le 1922,N 22,18:2
Tartuffe 1922,N 23,21:3
Maitresse de Roi 1926,D 1,24:1
Dame aux Camelias, La 1926,D 7,24:2
Misanthrope, Le 1926,D 10,31:2
Aventuriere, L' 1926,D 17,27:3
Sorel, Eve
Red, Hot and Blue! 1936,O 30,26:3
Sorel, Felicia
Rose of Stamboul, The 1922,Mr 8,11:2
Pinwheel Revel 1922,Je 16,20:6
Pinwheel Revel 1922,Ag 1,14:2
Earl Carroll's Vanities 1925,Jl 7,24:1
White Peacock, The 1929,Ap 27,16:4
Sunday Nights at Nine 1933,N 13,20:7
After Such Pleasures 1934,F 8,15:2
Sunday Nights at Nine 1934,Mr 5,18:5
Saluta 1934,Ag 29,13:4
Sunday Nights at Nine 1934,N 19,12:1
Ugly Runts, The 1935,Je 11,24:4
Sunday Nights at 9 1935,N 11,21:1
Sorel, Felicia (Choreographer)
Cabbages and Kings 1933,Je 28,24:5
Everywhere I Roam 1938,D 30,10:4
Everywhere I Roam 1939,Ja 8,IX,1:1
Everywhere I Roam 1939,Ja 22,IX,8:1
Jeremiah 1939,F 4,11:2
Trojan Women, The 1941,Ap 9,32:5
Belle Helene, La 1941,Jl 8,14:1
Johnny Doodle 1942,Mr 19,28:2
Pirate, The 1942,N 26,39:2
Run, Little Chillun 1943,Ag 14,6:1
My Dear Public 1943,S 10,28:1
Lysistrata 1946,O 18,27:5
Henry VIII 1946,N 7,42:2
Louisiana Lady 1947,Je 3,35:2
Sorel, Felicia (Director)
Pins and Needles 1939,Ap 21,26:2
Sorel, Felicia (Miscellaneous)
Cock-A-Doodle-Doo 1949,F 28,16:5

Sorel, Guy
In Time to Come 1941,D 29,20:2
Winter Soldiers 1942,N 30,19:2
Harriet 1943,Mr 4,24:2
Patriots, The 1943,D 21,22:5
Assassin, The 1945,O 18,20:2
Monique 1957,O 23,38:1
Face of a Hero 1960,O 21,29:5
Gift of Time, A 1962,F 23,34:1
Burning, The 1963,D 4,57:1
Sorel, Louise
Take Her, She's Mine 1961,D 22,19:1
Lorenzo 1963,F 16,5:2
Dragon, The 1963,Ap 10,32:1
Man and Boy 1963,N 13,34:1
Sorel, Sonia
Duchess of Malfi, The 1946,O 16,35:2
Leading Lady 1948,O 19,33:1
Rose Tattoo, The 1951,F 5,19:2
Long Watch, The 1952,Mr 21,19:5
Sorel, Theodore
Much Ado About Nothing 1964,Je 11,26:2
Richard III 1964,Je 12,44:2
Hamlet 1964,Jl 4,9:1
Coriolanus 1965,Je 21,36:1
Romeo and Juliet 1965,Je 21,36:3
Taming of the Shrew, The 1965,Je 24,32:2
King Lear 1965,Je 25,39:1
Arms and the Man 1967,Je 23,44:2
Sorel, Toni
Hamlet 1936,N 11,54:2
George Washington Slept Here 1940,O 19,20:3
Sorell, Annette
Cherry Orchard, The 1944,Ja 26,22:1
Therese 1945,O 10,24:2
Sorell, Doris
Hamlet 1951,Jl 20,13:6
Sorell, Walter (Playwright)
Everyman Today 1958,Ja 16,32:4
Sorensen, Holger
Sally 1948,My 7,31:2
Rape of Lucretia, The 1948,D 30,24:2
Sorfing, Ingrid
Vaudeville (Hippodrome) 1924,Ap 29,12:2
Sorg, Ann
Young and Fair, The 1948,N 23,35:2
Springtime Folly 1951,F 27,23:4
Soria, Madeleine
Maitre Bolbec et son Mari 1926,N 14,VIII,2:1
Ma Soeur et Moi 1928,Ap 29,IX,2:3
Untitled-Play 1928,N 11,X,2:7
Manquait un Homme, Il 1929,Ap 14,X,2:1
Belle de Nuit, La 1932,Ap 10,VIII,2:5
Sorian, Jack
All the King's Men 1948,Ja 19,19:2
Beaver Coat, The 1956,Mr 29,22:5
Soriano, Pepe
Projimos, Los 1966,Je 29,38:5
Sorin, David
Yoshe Kalb 1933,D 29,27:2
Sorin, Louis
God of Vengeance, The 1922,D 20,22:5
Humoresque 1923,F 28,13:2
Constant Nymph, The 1926,D 10,31:1
Footlights 1927,Ag 20,8:2
Los Angeles 1927,D 20,32:3
Money Lender, The 1928,Ag 28,27:3
Animal Crackers 1928,O 24,26:2
Well of Romance, The 1930,N 8,21:2
Shoot the Works! 1931,Ag 21,20:2
Bulls, Bears and Asses 1932,My 7,11:3
Keeping Expenses Down 1932,O 21,25:2
Anybody's Game 1932,D 22,21:4
Howdy Stranger 1937,Ja 15,17:5
Three Waltzes 1937,D 27,10:2
Scene of the Crime, The 1940,Mr 29,24:1
Glamour Preferred 1940,N 16,13:2
Night Before Christmas, The 1941,Mr 30,I,48:2
Night Before Christmas, The 1941,Ap 11,25:2
Rosalinda; Fledermaus, Die 1942,O 29,26:5
Sophie 1944,D 26,22:7
Swan Song 1946,My 16,29:2
Me and Molly 1948,F 27,27:2
Madwoman of Chaillot, The 1949,S 11,II,1:1
Madwoman of Chaillot, The 1950,Je 14,41:2
Collector's Item 1952,F 9,11:2
Sorkin, Joel
Here Be Dragons 1970,D 21,52:1
Sorlisi, Simona
Rugantino 1964,F 7,34:1
Soroka, Morris
Passing of Chow-Chow, The 1929,O 4,24:4
Sorokin, Dosi (Costume Designer)
Peter and the Wolf 1969,N 30,85:5
Soroko, Oskar
Mary of Magdala 1946,Mr 26,24:5
Sorrell, Ruth
Mrs Patterson 1957,F 6,20:2
Sorrentino, Vincent (Lighting Director)
Trouble in Mind 1955,N 5,23:2
Beaver Coat, The 1956,Mr 29,22:5
Sorrentino, Vincent (Miscellaneous)
Beaver Coat, The 1956,Mr 29,22:5

Sorrentino, Vincent (Miscellaneous)—Cont

All Women Are One 1965,Ja 8,21:1
Sorrentino, Vincent (Scenic Designer)
Trouble in Mind 1955,N 5,23:2
Private Life of the Master Race, The
1956,Ja 31,33:3
Sorsby, Lenore
Great Music 1924,O 6,24:1
Devil Within, The 1925,Mr 17,19:4
Loose Ankles 1926,Ag 17,15:1
What Ann Brought Home 1927,F 22,22:2
Behold This Dreamer 1927,N 1,20:4
Red Dust 1928,Ja 3,29:2
Get Me in the Movies 1928,My 22,18:3
Patsy, The 1929,Ja 6,VIII,1:4
Death Takes a Holiday 1929,D 27,26:4
In The Best of Families 1931,F 3,29:1
Social Register, The 1931,N 10,28:2
Heat Lightning 1933,S 16,9:6
Loose Moments 1935,F 5,22:3
For Valor 1935,N 19,27:5
Coriolanus 1937,O 10,VI,4:7
Young Mr Disraeli 1937,N 10,30:5
Diff'rent 1937,N 21,II,10:7
Diff'rent 1938,Ja 26,26:4
Captain Jinks of the Horse Marines 1938,Ja 28,16:2
No More Peace 1938,Ja 29,13:2
Coriolanus 1938,F 2,14:5
Sorsky, John (Original Author)
Day of Judgement, The 1941,O 9,27:3
Sorte, Joseph Della
Ross 1961,D 27,20:2
Jar, The 1969,Ap 23,42:1
Sorvino, Paul
Bajour 1964,N 24,42:1
Mating Dance 1965,N 4,58:1
Sosa, Dana
New Faces of 1956 1956,Je 15,32:1
Sostek, Edward
Liliom 1956,F 18,12:5
Sable Brush, The 1956,N 28,41:1
Sostek, Edward (Miscellaneous)
Annie Get Your Gun 1957,Mr 9,15:5
Sotelo, Sam
Across the Board on Tomorrow Morning
1942,Ag 18,17:1
Sother, Joaquin
Lady With a Lamp, The 1931,N 20,27:2
Sothern, Ann
Faithfully Yours 1951,O 19,22:5
Sothern, E H
Twelfth Night 1921,N 1,17:1
Twelfth Night 1921,N 6,VI,1:1
Merchant of Venice, The 1921,N 22,17:1
Cymbeline 1923,O 3,12:1
Cymbeline 1923,O 14,VIII,1:1
Taming of the Shrew, The 1923,O 16,19:3
Twelfth Night 1923,O 23,17:1
Hamlet 1923,O 31,12:1
Merchant of Venice, The 1923,N 6,22:2
Romeo and Juliet 1923,N 13,25:2
Accused 1925,S 20,VIII,2:4
Accused 1925,S 30,20:1
Accused 1925,O 11,VIII,1:1
What Never Dies 1926,D 19,VII,6:1
What Never Dies 1926,D 29,24:2
Untitled-One Man Show 1928,D 12,34:5
Sothern, E H (Producer)
Cymbeline 1923,O 14,VIII,1:1
Taming of the Shrew, The 1923,O 16,19:3
Twelfth Night 1923,O 23,17:1
Hamlet 1923,O 31,12:1
Merchant of Venice, The 1923,N 6,22:2
Romeo and Juliet 1923,N 13,25:2
Sothern, Georgia
Star and Garter 1942,Je 25,26:2
Star and Garter 1942,S 13,VIII,1:1
Naked Genius, The 1943,O 22,20:5
Sothern, Guy
Sign of Jonah, The 1960,S 9,35:1
To Damascus 1961,F 15,40:2
Square, The 1961,Mr 24,37:1
Sothern, Harry
Constant Nymph, The 1926,D 10,31:1
Good Hope, The 1927,O 19,24:2
2 + 2 = 5 1927,N 29,30:3
First Stone, The 1928,Ja 14,12:2
Twelfth Night 1930,O 16,28:2
Lean Harvest 1931,O 14,26:3
Lady With a Lamp, The 1931,N 20,27:2
Midsummer Night's Dream, A 1932,Jl 13,15:1
Scorpion, The 1933,N 28,28:4
Murder in the Cathedral 1936,Mr 21,13:5
Hero Is Born, A 1937,O 2,18:6
Robin Landing 1937,N 19,26:4
Leave Her to Heaven 1940,F 28,16:2
Wookey, The 1941,S 11,20:5
Bird in Hand 1942,O 20,24:2
Sheppey 1944,Ap 19,27:2
Devils Galore 1945,S 13,27:2
Swan Song 1946,My 16,29:2
Harlequinade 1949,O 13,32:2
Gramercy Ghost 1951,Ap 27,20:2
Hook'n Ladder 1952,Ap 30,31:2

Sothern, Henry
Shadow and Substance 1938,Ja 27,16:2
Sothern, Sara
Fool, The 1922,O 24,18:1
Arabesque 1925,O 21,20:2
Fool's Bells 1925,D 24,8:3
Mama Loves Papa 1926,F 23,26:2
Sotoconi, Ruben
Remolienda, La; Bawdy Party 1968,F 3,20:1
Soudeikin, A (Scenic Designer)
Gardener's Dog, The 1927,O 21,27:1
Soudeikina, Jeanne
Chauve-Souris of 1943 1943,Ag 13,13:2
Soudeikine, Serge (Costume Designer)
Chief Thing, The 1926,Mr 23,24:2
New Faces 1934,Mr 16,24:5
Chinese Nightingale, The 1934,O 6,20:4
Chauve-Souris of 1943 1943,Ag 13,13:2
Soudeikine, Serge (Scenic Designer)
Chauve-Souris 1922,O 11,22:2
Chief Thing, The 1926,Mr 23,24:2
New Faces 1934,Mr 16,24:5
Chinese Nightingale, The 1934,O 6,20:4
Porgy and Bess 1935,O 1,27:2
Porgy and Bess 1935,O 11,30:2
Forbidden Melody 1936,O 13,30:3
Forbidden Melody 1936,N 3,33:1
Chauve-Souris of 1943 1943,Ag 13,13:2
Soudek, Ann (Miscellaneous)
Annie Get Your Gun 1957,Mr 9,15:5
Souer, Bernard (Miscellaneous)
Bronx Express, 1968 1968,N 16,43:3
Souffront, Blanche
Medea 1960,Jl 26,25:2
Soukop, Boris (Scenic Designer)
Pierrot's Journey 1964,Ag 5,23:1
Soulat, Robert (Playwright)
Baby-Foot 1962,O 11,48:5
Soule, Betty
Jack in the Pulpit 1925,Ja 7,33:1
Soule, Donald (Scenic Designer)
Tree Witch, The 1961,Je 5,39:4
New York Idea, The 1963,Jl 13,12:2
Soule, Ralph
Merry Widow, The 1921,S 6,13:1
Soule, Robert (Costume Designer)
Long Gallery, The 1958,Mr 7,17:2
Enchanted, The 1958,Ap 23,41:1
Journey With Strangers, A 1958,N 27,53:1
Trip to Bountiful, The 1959,F 27,20:4
Orpheus Descending 1959,O 6,45:2
Fly Blackbird 1962,F 6,26:2
Riverwind 1962,D 14,5:5
Soule, Robert (Lighting Director)
Elsa Lanchester-Herself 1961,F 6,28:1
Soule, Robert (Scenic Designer)
Time of Storm 1954,F 26,14:2
Kiss Me, Kate 1954,Mr 27,13:2
Garden District; Suddenly Last Summer
1958,Ja 8,23:4
Garden District; Something Unspoken
1958,Ja 8,23:4
Garden District; Suddenly Last Summer
1958,Ja 19,II,1:1
Long Gallery, The 1958,Mr 7,17:2
Enchanted, The 1958,Ap 23,41:1
Golden Six, The 1958,O 27,31:2
Journey With Strangers, A 1958,N 27,53:1
Trip to Bountiful, The 1959,F 27,20:4
Widowers' Houses 1959,Mr 3,39:2
Chic 1959,My 19,28:2
Orpheus Descending 1959,O 6,45:2
Pretender, The 1960,My 25,42:1
Greenwich Village U S A 1960,S 29,30:5
Donogoo 1961,Ja 19,25:3
Elsa Lanchester-Herself 1961,F 6,28:1
Tiger Rag, The 1961,F 17,20:2
Tattooed Countess, The 1961,My 4,40:2
Red Roses for Me 1961,N 28,41:1
Fly Blackbird 1962,F 6,26:2
Deuces Wild; Thus 1962,Ap 25,31:1
Deuces Wild; It's All Yours 1962,Ap 25,31:1
Charlatans; On Circe's Island 1962,Ap 27,26:1
Charlatans; Summer Ghost, A 1962,Ap 27,26:1
Riverwind 1962,D 14,5:5
Soulias, Christina
Earth Journey 1944,Ap 28,24:2
Soulier (Playwright)
Quand Je Voudrais 1924,Je 29,VII,1:8
Soumagne, Henry (Playwright)
Terminus 1928,S 30,IX,2:1
Soupault, Pierre
Age of Innocence, The 1928,N 28,24:2
Sour, Robert (Lyricist)
Sing for Your Supper 1939,Ap 25,18:6
Morning Star 1940,Ap 17,26:4
Mr Strauss Goes to Boston 1945,S 7,20:2
Sousa, John Philip (Musical Director)
Lambs Gambol 1925,Ap 27,15:1
Sousa, Leone
Who's Who 1938,Mr 2,16:2
Sousa, Margaret
Elsie Janis and Her Gang 1922,Ja 17,13:2

Soussanin, Nicholas
Vaudeville (Palace) 1929,My 20,22:8
Gather Ye Rosebuds 1934,N 29,33:2
Idiot's Delight 1937,Ag 10,22:7
Soussanin, Nicholas (Director)
House of Remsen 1934,Ap 3,26:4
Soussanin, Nicholas (Playwright)
House of Remsen 1934,Ap 3,26:4
Soussanin, Nicholas (Producer)
House of Remsen 1934,Ap 3,26:4
Soussanin, Nikita
Bridal Crown, The 1938,F 7,11:2
Soutar, Agnes
So's Your Old Manhattan 1927,My 5,30:5
South, Dorothy
Wildcat, The 1921,N 28,16:2
Wrong Number 1934,Mr 14,23:6
Southard, Bennett
On the Stairs 1922,S 26,18:2
Woman on the Jury, The 1923,Ag 16,10:4
Man Who Died Twice, The 1925,D 14,19:1
Wooden Kimono 1926,D 28,16:2
She Means Business 1931,Ja 27,21:2
Foolscap 1933,Ja 12,21:2
Kultur 1933,S 27,24:3
Southard, Carol
Season of the Beast 1958,Mr 14,29:2
Southard, Harry D
Fall and Rise of Susan Lenox, The 1920,Je 11,11:2
Cat and the Canary, The 1922,F 8,13:1
Gorilla, The 1925,Ap 29,24:2
Pyramids 1926,Jl 20,17:2
Black Cockatoo, The 1926,D 31,11:1
Tia Juana 1927,N 16,28:4
Adventure 1928,S 26,25:2
Damn Your Honor 1929,D 31,14:3
Grand Hotel 1930,N 14,30:4
Chrysalis 1932,N 16,15:2
Crime and Punishment 1935,Ja 23,20:3
All the Living 1938,Mr 25,14:4
Southard, Henry
Cock Robin 1928,Ja 13,26:6
Southbrook, Ellen
Shore Leave 1922,Ag 9,20:2
King Can Do No Wrong, The 1927,N 17,28:4
Paris Bound 1927,D 28,26:3
Paris Bound 1929,Jl 20,8:3
Your Uncle Dudley 1929,N 19,26:4
Bellamy Trial, The 1931,Ap 23,28:6
Souther, Joaquin
Paddy the Next Best Thing 1920,Ag 28,5:5
Tyrants 1924,Mr 5,14:1
Tangletoes 1925,F 18,17:1
School for Scandal, The 1925,O 24,19:1
Friend Indeed 1926,Ap 27,22:3
Much Ado About Nothing 1927,N 19,14:6
At the Gate of the Kingdom 1927,D 9,28:5
Box Seats 1928,Ap 20,27:2
Lean Harvest 1931,O 14,26:3
Lady With a Lamp, The 1931,N 20,27:2
Money in the Air 1932,Mr 8,19:3
Give Us This Day 1933,O 28,20:6
Pure in Heart, The 1934,Mr 21,24:3
Petticoat Fever 1935,Mr 5,22:2
Tide Rising 1937,Ja 26,17:2
Many Mansions 1937,O 28,28:6
All the Living 1938,Mr 25,14:4
Souther, John
First Million, The 1943,Ap 29,27:4
Boy Meets Girl 1943,Je 23,15:5
Naked Genius, The 1943,O 22,20:5
Take It As It Comes 1944,F 11,17:2
Snafu 1944,O 26,19:5
You Can't Take It With You 1945,Mr 27,23:7
Southerland, Yvonne
Life and Times of J Walter Smintheus, The
1970,D 10,59:1
Southern, Alice
Pickwick 1927,S 6,35:2
Southern, Dora
Bitter Oleander 1935,F 12,24:3
Southern, Ernest (Scenic Designer)
She Gave Him All She Had 1939,D 2,20:7
Southern, Georgia
International Playgirls '64 1964,My 22,40:2
Southern, Sara
Dagger, The 1925,S 10,28:1
Southerne (Playwright)
Oroonoko 1932,Ag 28,IX,1:1
Southgate, Betsy Jane
Garden of Eden, The 1927,S 28,28:1
Southgate, Harold (Director)
Park Avenue, Ltd 1932,Mr 4,17:1
Southwick, Leslie
King Lear 1964,My 19,43:2
Southwick, Mildred
Fatal Wedding, The 1924,Je 3,22:3
Desert Flower, The 1924,N 19,18:2
Brother Elks 1925,S 15,29:2
Julie 1927,My 10,24:4
Babies a La Carte 1927,Ag 16,31:1
Southwick, Raymond
Jefferson Davis 1936,F 19,17:2

861

Southwick, Raymond—Cont
It Can't Happen Here 1936,O 28,30:1
Sun and I, The 1937,F 27,9:5
Southwick, Victor
Patriots, The 1943,Ja 30,11:2
Soutollo (Composer)
Leyenda del Beso, La 1942,N 20,26:4
Soutter, R
Gentlemen, the Queen 1927,Ap 23,14:3
Soutzo
Vierge Folle, La; Foolish Virgin, The 1924,Mr 22,12:2
Souvaine, Henry (Composer)
Americana 1926,Jl 27,15:3
Merry-Go-Round 1927,Je 1,25:4
Souvaine, Henry (Producer)
Spring Tonic 1936,My 11,16:1
Sovey, Raymond
Hamlet 1920,Mr 17,14:2
Sovey, Raymond (Costume Designer)
Brothers Karamazov, The 1927,Ja 4,20:1
Mikado, The; Town of Titipu, The 1927,S 19,30:1
Month in the Country, A 1930,Mr 18,30:5
Second Little Show, The 1930,S 3,36:1
Twelfth Night 1930,O 16,28:2
Third Little Show, The 1931,Je 2,34:3
Way of the World, The 1931,Je 2,34:3
Gay Divorce 1932,N 13,IX,1:7
Oscar Wilde 1938,O 11,20:2
Damask Cheek, The 1942,O 23,24:2
Therese 1945,O 10,24:2
All the Way Home 1960,D 1,42:1
Sovey, Raymond (Director)
Prunella 1929,Ap 10,23:3
Vagabond King, The 1943,Je 30,24:2
Sovey, Raymond (Lighting Director)
Grandma's Diary 1948,S 23,36:2
Edward, My Son 1948,O 1,30:2
Cocktail Party, The 1950,Ja 23,17:2
Green Bay Tree, The 1951,F 2,18:2
Look After Lulu 1959,Mr 4,35:1
Sovey, Raymond (Scenic Designer)
Glory Hallelujah 1926,Ap 7,26:2
Ladder, The 1926,O 23,15:1
Proud Woman, A 1926,N 16,24:1
Brothers Karamazov, The 1927,Ja 4,20:1
Mikado, The; Town of Titipu, The 1927,S 19,30:1
Coquette 1927,N 9,23:1
Front Page, The 1928,Ag 15,19:2
Goin' Home 1928,Ag 24,23:2
Command Performance, The 1928,O 4,27:1
Little Accident 1928,O 10,32:3
Three Cheers 1928,O 16,28:1
Animal Crackers 1928,O 24,26:2
Tonight at 12 1928,N 16,28:1
Wings Over Europe 1928,D 11,35:1
Scarlet Pages 1929,S 10,26:3
Strictly Dishonorable 1929,S 19,37:1
Other Men's Wives 1929,N 13,24:4
Meteor 1929,D 24,15:1
Top Speed 1929,D 26,20:1
Strike Up the Band 1930,Ja 15,29:1
Month in the Country, A 1930,Mr 18,30:5
That's the Woman 1930,S 4,27:2
Twelfth Night 1930,O 16,28:2
As Good As New 1930,N 4,37:3
Art and Mrs Bottle 1930,N 19,19:3
Vinegar Tree, The 1930,N 20,30:3
Green Grow the Lilacs 1930,D 14,IX,3:1
Inspector General, The 1930,D 24,19:2
Green Grow the Lilacs 1931,Ja 27,21:2
Green Grow the Lilacs 1931,F 8,VIII,1:1
Wiser They Are, The 1931,Ap 7,31:1
Way of the World, The 1931,Je 2,34:3
Cloudy With Showers 1931,S 2,17:5
Left Bank, The 1931,O 6,35:3
Wonder Boy 1931,O 24,20:1
Counsellor-at-Law 1931,N 7,17:2
Fast Service 1931,N 18,26:3
After All 1931,D 4,28:4
Wild Waves 1932,F 20,11:4
Hey, Nonny, Nonny! 1932,Je 7,22:3
Here Today 1932,S 7,14:2
I Loved You Wednesday 1932,O 12,27:1
Black Sheep 1932,O 14,22:6
Men Must Fight 1932,O 15,13:4
Honeymoon 1932,D 24,11:2
Conquest 1933,F 20,11:3
Lone Valley 1933,Mr 11,18:6
Shooting Star 1933,Je 13,22:2
Blue Widow, The 1933,Ag 31,20:2
Her Master's Voice 1933,O 24,24:3
Doctor Monica 1933,N 7,29:3
She Loves Me Not 1933,N 21,22:4
She Loves Me Not 1933,N 26,IX,1:1
Wooden Slipper, The 1934,Ja 4,16:3
Oliver Oliver 1934,Ja 6,18:5
Ragged Army 1934,F 27,16:5
Distaff Side, The 1934,S 26,17:2
Post Road 1934,D 5,28:3
Portrait of Gilbert 1934,D 29,11:5
Petrified Forest, The 1935,Ja 8,26:1
Petrified Forest, The 1935,Ja 13,IX,1:1
Fly Away Home 1935,Ja 16,20:4

Eldest, The 1935,F 12,24:3
Distant Shore, The 1935,F 22,26:2
Dominant Sex, The 1935,Ap 2,24:5
Life's Too Short 1935,S 21,18:5
Most of the Game 1935,O 2,27:4
Bright Star 1935,O 16,26:2
May Wine 1935,D 6,30:3
Libel! 1935,D 21,10:5
Light Behind the Shadow, The 1936,Ja 21,26:6
Alice Takat 1936,F 11,19:2
Sweet Aloes 1936,Mr 5,24:5
Star Spangled 1936,Mr 11,23:1
Tovarich 1936,O 16,31:4
Promise 1936,D 31,20:4
And Now Goodbye 1937,F 3,26:4
Yes, My Darling Daughter 1937,F 10,19:2
Amazing Dr. Clitterhouse, The 1937,Mr 3,26:4
Babes in Arms 1937,Ap 15,18:4
French Without Tears 1937,S 29,19:1
Love of Women 1937,D 14,33:2
If I Were You 1938,Ja 25,24:2
Once Is Enough 1938,F 16,16:2
Oscar Wilde 1938,O 11,20:2
Dance Night 1938,O 15,20:5
Knights of Song 1938,O 18,29:2
Miss Swan Expects 1939,F 21,15:2
Woman Brown, The 1939,D 9,18:5
Ladies in Retirement 1940,Mr 27,24:3
Grey Farm 1940,My 4,12:7
Jupiter Laughs 1940,S 10,27:1
Delicate Story 1940,D 5,32:2
Arsenic and Old Lace 1941,Ja 11,13:2
Boudoir 1941,F 8,18:4
Your Loving Son 1941,Ap 5,13:2
Happy Days 1941,My 14,24:2
Village Green 1941,S 4,24:4
Walrus and the Carpenter, The 1941,N 10,20:2
Ring Around Elizabeth 1941,N 18,32:2
Letters to Lucerne 1941,D 24,14:2
Guest in the House 1942,F 25,25:2
Broken Journey 1942,Je 24,22:2
Strip for Action 1942,O 1,26:2
Damask Cheek, The 1942,O 23,24:2
Counsellor-at-Law 1942,N 25,17:2
Flare Path 1942,D 24,20:2
Tomorrow the World 1943,Ap 15,22:2
Murder Without Crime 1943,Ag 19,24:6
Another Love Story 1943,O 13,29:2
Outrageous Fortune 1943,N 4,28:5
Feathers in a Gale 1943,D 22,26:2
Over Twenty-One 1944,Ja 4,20:2
Jackpot 1944,Ja 14,15:2
For Keeps 1944,Je 15,17:5
Lower North 1944,Ag 26,15:4
Soldier's Wife 1944,O 5,18:6
Sleep, My Pretty One 1944,N 3,26:8
Hasty Heart, The 1945,Ja 4,14:2
And Be My Love 1945,F 22,30:4
Place of Our Own, A 1945,Ap 3,23:7
Ryan Girl, The 1945,S 25,28:2
Therese 1945,O 10,24:2
Rich Full Life, The 1945,N 10,9:2
State of the Union 1945,N 15,25:2
Mermaids Singing, The 1945,N 29,26:6
Apple of His Eye 1946,F 6,18:2
Antigone 1946,F 19,21:3
This, Too, Shall Pass 1946,My 1,32:4
Wonderful Journey 1946,D 26,30:2
Love Goes to Press 1947,Ja 2,22:2
Parlor Story 1947,Mr 5,29:2
I Gotta Get Out 1947,S 26,27:2
Heiress, The 1947,S 30,22:2
Heiress, The 1947,O 5,II,1:1
For Love or Money 1947,N 5,36:2
Harvest of Years 1948,Ja 13,29:2
Hallams, The 1948,Mr 5,18:2
Grandma's Diary 1948,S 23,36:2
Edward, My Son 1948,O 1,30:2
Traitor, The 1949,Ap 1,30:2
Traitor, The 1949,Ap 10,II,1:1
Cocktail Party, The 1950,Ja 23,17:2
Ring Around the Moon 1950,N 24,30:1
Four Twelves Are 48 1951,Ja 18,30:2
Green Bay Tree, The 1951,F 2,18:2
Gramercy Ghost 1951,Ap 27,20:2
Remains to Be Seen 1951,O 4,37:1
Gigi 1951,N 26,20:4
Come of Age 1952,Ja 24,22:2
One Bright Day 1952,Mr 20,37:2
Living Room, The 1954,N 18,41:1
Living Room, The 1954,N 28,II,1:1
Witness for the Prosecution 1954,D 17,35:2
Great Sebastians, The 1956,Ja 5,27:1
Reluctant Debutante, The 1956,O 11,50:1
Reluctant Debutante, The 1956,O 21,II,1:1
Under Milk Wood 1957,O 16,42:5
Sowande, Fela (Miscellaneous)
Sponono 1964,Ap 3,28:1
Sowerby, Githa (Playwright)
Rutherford and Son 1927,Ap 13,29:2
Sowersby, Lenore
Suicide Love 1924,S 7,VII,1:4

Sowka, Nick
Doctor Faustus 1957,F 19,35:7
Sowka, Nick (Miscellaneous)
Parade at the Devil's Bridge 1957,F 19,35:7
Doctor Faustus 1957,F 19,35:7
Soy, Ming
Queer People 1934,F 16,16:2
Soyer, Moses (Costume Designer)
Golem, The 1931,N 6,28:5
Soyfer, Jura (Playwright)
From Vienna 1939,Je 21,26:2
Soyinka, Wole (Director)
Madmen and Specialists 1970,Ag 3,38:1
Soyinka, Wole (Playwright)
Trials of Brother Jero, The 1967,N 10,60:1
Strong Breed, The 1967,N 10,60:1
Trials of Brother Jero, The; Strong Breed, The 1967,N 26,II,1:1
Kongi's Harvest 1968,Ap 21,II,5:3
Madmen and Specialists 1970,Ag 3,38:1
Sozio, Peter
Dear Judas 1947,O 6,26:4
Spaak, Charles (Original Author)
Carnival in Flanders 1953,S 9,38:2
Spacey, John G
Other Men's Wives 1929,N 13,24:4
There's Always Juliet 1932,O 28,23:2
Spadaro
Palace aux Femmes 1926,O 10,VIII,2:1
Vive la Femme 1927,My 29,VII,2:1
Spaeth, Anton
Fig Leaf in Her Bonnet, A 1961,Je 15,50:1
Spaeth, Michael
Armor of Light 1950,F 24,26:4
Spaeth, Sigmund
Sunday Nights at Nine 1933,N 13,20:7
Sunday Nights at Nine 1934,Mr 5,18:5
Sunday Nights at Nine 1934,N 19,12:1
Spagnuolo, Joseph
As You Like It 1955,O 29,12:2
Romeo and Juliet 1955,D 16,36:3
Spagnuolo, Joseph (Miscellaneous)
Romeo and Juliet 1955,D 16,36:3
Spaisman, Zipora
Thousand and One Nights 1959,D 16,53:2
Sage of Rottenburg, The 1963,N 20,48:1
Enchanting Melody 1964,N 25,40:1
Fifth Commandment, The 1965,N 15,48:4
Prince Reuvaini 1967,N 19,83:1
Bronx Express, 1968 1968,N 16,43:3
Melody Lingers On, The 1969,N 17,55:1
Brothers Ashkenazi, The 1970,N 17,53:2
Spalding, Albert
Variations of 1940 1940,Ja 29,12:1
Spalding, Charles (Playwright)
Small Wonder 1948,S 16,33:5
Spalding, Charles F (Miscellaneous)
Of Thee I Sing 1952,My 6,34:2
Spalding, Kim
Tobacco Road 1943,S 6,21:3
Lower North 1944,Ag 26,15:4
Stranger, The 1945,F 13,21:2
Spalding, Sid
Hollywood Ice Revue 1953,Ja 16,17:2
Spalding, Tony
Bamboo Cross 1955,F 22,17:2
Spalding, Wells
Night Call, The 1922,Ap 27,12:2
Spanabel, Robert
Henry V 1964,My 13,52:1
Spance, Eulalie (Playwright)
Fool's Errand, The 1927,My 3,24:3
Spangenberg, Bill
Music Man, The 1957,D 20,31:1
Spangler, Jack
Vaudeville (Palace) 1930,F 10,20:3
Spangler, Kay
Earl Carroll's Vanities 1927,Ja 5,18:1
Vaudeville (Palace) 1930,F 10,20:3
Spangler, Sheldon
Man Who Married a Dumb Wife, The 1930,My 9,20:5
Spanky the Skating Chimp
Ice Capades 1969,Ja 8,42:1
Ice Capades 1970,Ja 7,35:1
Spann, James
Merry Widow, The 1961,O 27,28:2
Gondoliers, The 1963,Je 5,33:2
Spann, James B
Walking Happy 1966,N 28,47:1
Lovely Ladies, Kind Gentlemen 1970,D 29,38:1
Spanos, Nick C (Producer)
U S A 1959,O 29,38:1
Spar, Vincent (Miscellaneous)
Idiot, The 1960,S 26,38:1
Man and Superman 1960,N 7,46:2
Emmanuel 1960,D 5,42:2
Spar, Vincent (Producer)
Mandragola 1958,My 29,23:2
Sparer, Paul
Love's Labour's Lost 1953,F 5,20:3
Merchant of Venice, The 1953,Mr 5,20:2
Moby Dick 1955,Ap 26,25:3

parer, Paul—Cont
Othello 1955,S 8,27:2
Othello 1955,S 18,II,1:1
Henry IV, Part I 1955,S 22,34:2
Saint Joan 1956,S 12,42:1
King Lear 1959,Ja 3,11:2
Philoctetes 1959,Ja 14,28:1
Much Ado About Nothing 1959,S 18,25:2
Cut of the Axe 1960,F 2,38:2
Rules of the Game, The 1960,D 20,44:1
As You Like It 1961,Je 17,13:2
Macbeth 1961,Je 19,31:1
Cook for Mr General, A 1961,O 20,39:1
Ross 1961,D 27,20:2
Seagull, The 1962,Mr 22,42:1
Tavern, The 1962,Ap 5,29:1
Right You Are (If You Think You Are)
   1964,Mr 5,37:1
Impromptu at Versailles 1964,Mr 10,43:1
Lower Depths, The 1964,Mr 31,30:1
Man and Superman 1964,D 7,45:2
War and Peace 1965,Ja 12,32:1
Judith 1965,Mr 25,42:2
Judith 1965,Ap 4,II,1:1
World of Ray Bradbury, The; Pedestrian, The;
   Veldt, The; To the Chicago Abyss 1965,O 10,11:1
Falstaff 1966,Je 20,27:1
Murder in the Cathedral 1966,Je 21,38:1
Julius Caesar 1966,Je 24,29:2
After the Rain 1967,O 10,54:1
Tea Party 1968,O 16,40:1
Operation Sidewinder 1970,Mr 13,33:1
Wars of the Roses, The (Part I) 1970,Jl 2,30:1
Wars of the Roses, The (Part II) 1970,Jl 3,15:1
Henry VI, Parts I, II, III 1970,Jl 5,II,3:1
Happiness Cage, The 1970,O 5,56:4
Happiness Cage, The 1970,O 11,II,1:1
Sparios, Jason
Finis for Oscar Wilde 1964,F 15,15:1
Spark, Muriel (Original Author)
Prime of Miss Jean Brodie, The 1968,Ja 17,39:1
Prime of Miss Jean Brodie, The 1968,Ja 25,32:4
Prime of Miss Jean Brodie, The 1968,Ja 28,II,1:1
Spark, Muriel (Playwright)
Doctors of Philosophy 1962,O 3,46:8
Sparks, Arthur
Nobody's Business 1923,O 23,17:1
Sparks, Daniel
Good Morning, Dearie 1921,N 2,20:2
Sparks, Dee
Oedipus 1946,My 21,19:2
Sparks, James
Sweet River 1936,O 29,30:2
Sparks, Jane
Corn Is Green, The 1954,F 27,10:2
Sparks, Jeanni
Lady of Mexico 1962,O 20,13:2
Sparks, John J
Smooth as Silk 1921,F 23,18:3
Sparks, Ned
My Golden Girl 1920,F 3,18:2
Jim Jam Jems 1920,O 5,13:2
Sparks, Randy
Tom Sawyer 1958,Jl 15,21:8
Sparks, Robert (Director)
Monkey 1932,F 12,25:2
Sparks, Robert (Miscellaneous)
Lysistrata 1930,Je 6,20:1
Sparks, Robert (Producer)
Never No More 1932,Ja 8,27:1
Monkey 1932,F 12,25:2
Sparks, Sonny
Catch a Star! 1955,S 7,35:2
Sparling, Herbert
Half-Moon, The 1920,N 2,15:2
Sparrow, Wilma
Beautiful Changes, The 1956,Mr 24,15:2
Spasojevic, Neda
Ubu Roi 1968,Je 29,20:1
Victor, or The Children Take Over 1968,Jl 10,22:4
Spater, Richard
Noah 1935,F 14,25:2
Robin Landing 1937,N 19,26:4
Spaul, Guy
Plan M 1942,F 21,15:2
Spaulding, Bruce (Playwright)
Greater Love 1931,Mr 3,39:1
Spaulding, Elaine
Guys and Dolls 1955,Ap 21,32:2
Spaulding, George
Mrs Jimmie Thompson 1920,Mr 30,9:1
Valley Forge 1934,D 11,28:3
Othello 1937,Ja 7,16:4
Farewell Summer 1937,Mr 30,20:2
On Location 1937,S 28,19:1
Window Shopping 1938,D 24,13:2
Walking Gentleman, The 1942,My 8,26:2
Cat Screams, The 1942,Je 17,26:5
Follow the Girls 1944,Ap 10,15:2
Spaulding, George L
Soliloquy 1938,N 29,26:4
Spaulding, Kenneth
As the Girls Go 1948,N 15,21:2

Spaulding, Louis F
Right Girl, The 1921,Mr 16,12:1
Spaulding, Sid
Stars on Ice 1942,Jl 3,12:2
Spaulding, Wells
Hail and Farewell 1923,F 20,12:1
Spaull, Guy
Good Hunting 1938,N 22,26:5
Importance of Being Earnest, The 1939,Ja 13,16:2
Family Portrait 1939,Mr 9,18:4
Leave Her to Heaven 1940,F 28,16:2
Lady in Waiting 1940,Mr 28,19:1
Sarah Simple 1940,N 18,22:5
All the Comforts of Home 1942,My 26,24:5
I Killed the Count 1942,S 4,18:1
Innocent Voyage, The 1943,N 16,27:2
Around the World 1946,Je 1,9:5
Duchess of Malfi, The 1946,O 16,35:2
Vigil, The 1948,My 22,8:6
Leading Lady 1948,O 19,33:1
Make Way for Lucia 1948,D 23,23:5
Lost in the Stars 1949,O 31,21:2
Billy Budd 1951,F 12,18:3
Getting Married 1951,My 14,28:5
Music in the Air 1951,O 9,32:2
First Lady 1952,My 29,18:5
Seagulls Over Sorrento 1952,S 12,18:4
Heel, The 1954,My 27,33:2
Apollo of Bellac, The 1954,My 29,12:1
Purification, The 1954,My 29,12:1
Witness for the Prosecution 1954,D 17,35:2
Apple Cart, The 1956,O 19,23:1
First Gentleman, The 1957,Ap 26,22:2
Under Milk Wood 1957,O 16,42:5
Entertainer, The 1958,F 13,22:2
Hidden Stranger 1963,Ja 10,5:5
Lion in Love, The 1963,Ap 26,28:3
Ivanov 1966,My 4,50:1
Spavin, George
Bachelor's Brides 1925,My 29,20:2
Speaight, Robert
Brass Paperweight, The 1928,N 4,IX,2:4
Journey's End 1929,Jl 14,IX,5:1
Murder in the Cathedral 1935,N 2,12:2
Agamemnon 1936,N 2,25:6
Murder in the Cathedral 1938,F 17,16:2
Five Kings 1939,Mr 5,X,3:1
Speakman, Walter
Taming of the Shrew, The 1927,O 26,26:4
Exceeding Small 1928,O 23,32:2
Lady From the Sea, The 1929,Mr 19,36:1
Charm 1929,N 29,24:5
Speaks, Margaret
Greenwich Villagers, The 1927,Ag 19,20:2
Spear, Bob
Mystery Ship, The 1927,Mr 15,28:2
Spear, Fred
Jumbo 1935,N 18,20:2
Spear, George
This One Man 1930,O 22,32:3
Spear, Valerie
Venice Preserv'd 1955,D 13,54:4
Spear, Winifred
Carolinian, The 1925,N 3,34:2
Spearman, James A
I Never Sang for My Father 1968,Ja 26,30:1
Spearman, Rawn
Let's Make an Opera 1950,D 14,50:2
Four Saints in Three Acts 1952,Ap 17,35:1
House of Flowers 1954,D 31,11:2
Porgy and Bess 1961,My 18,40:1
Spears, Dorothy (Playwright)
Prima Donna 1929,S 22,IX,2:6
Spears, Patti (Playwright)
Strange Play, A 1944,Je 2,20:3
Specht, Bobby
Ice Capades 1952,S 12,18:1
Ice Capades 1953,S 11,25:1
Ice Capades 1954,S 16,37:1
Ice Capades 1955,S 15,38:1
Ice Capades 1956,S 13,41:2
Ice Capades 1957,S 5,33:2
Ice Capades 1958,S 4,33:2
Ice Capades 1959,S 4,12:1
Ice Capades 1960,S 1,30:1
Ice Capades 1961,Ag 31,24:4
Specht, Carl
Catherine Was Great 1944,Ag 3,16:1
Sky Drift 1945,N 14,25:2
He Who Gets Slapped 1946,Mr 21,31:4
Specht, E E (Mrs)
One Woman's Husband 1920,Mr 23,9:3
Speck, Samuel
House Divided, The 1923,N 12,14:1
Spector, Arnold
Grand Duchess 1929,D 17,29:2
Gypsy Baron, The 1930,Ap 22,22:8
Orpheus in Hades 1930,D 16,30:1
Chocolate Soldier, The 1932,F 9,30:3
Fledermaus, Die 1933,My 14,II,3:8
They Should Have Stood in Bed 1942,F 14,18:5
Merry Widow, The 1943,Ag 5,19:2
Yours Is My Heart 1946,S 6,16:5

Spector, Arnold (Director)
Paradise Island 1962,Je 28,22:1
Around the World in 80 Days 1963,Je 24,22:1
Mardi Gras! 1965,Je 28,33:2
Spector, Arnold (Miscellaneous)
Paradise Island 1961,Je 24,11:1
Around the World in 80 Days 1964,Je 29,33:2
Mardi Gras! 1966,Jl 11,32:2
Arabian Nights 1967,Jl 3,12:1
South Pacific 1968,Je 30,54:2
South Pacific 1969,Jl 7,27:1
Sound of Music, The 1970,Jl 3,13:1
Spector, Chana
His Wife's Lover 1929,O 21,30:6
God's Thieves 1930,O 27,17:4
Spector, Joel (Composer)
Nathan the Wise 1944,F 22,26:3
Spector, Joel (Producer)
Barrier, The 1950,N 3,32:2
Make a Million 1958,O 24,39:2
Let It Ride 1961,O 13,27:4
Spector, Lawrence
Hamlet 1956,O 29,34:1
Susannah and the Elders 1959,O 19,37:3
Spector, Renee
King And the Cobbler, The 1954,D 13,33:6
Spector, Sue (Costume Designer)
All the King's Men 1959,O 17,27:2
Here Come the Clowns 1960,S 20,48:1
Philoktetes 1961,Ap 25,41:1
Speechley, Billy
After Dark 1926,O 10,VIII,2:1
Speer, Bernice
Rise of Rosie O'Reilly, The 1923,D 26,13:4
Earl Carroll's Vanities 1926,Ag 25,19:4
Speer, Maggi
Me, Candido! 1956,O 16,36:2
Speer, Maggi (Costume Designer)
Obbligato 1958,F 19,22:2
Speer, Maggi (Miscellaneous)
Me, Candido! 1956,O 16,36:2
Speer, Richard (Scenic Designer)
Meet the Prince 1935,Jl 9,24:5
Speidel, Thomas
Three Sisters, The 1939,O 16,23:1
Charley's Aunt 1940,O 18,24:2
Speirs, Ruth (Translator)
In the Matter of J Robert Oppenheimer
   1968,My 27,55:1
In the Matter of J Robert Oppenheimer
   1968,Je 7,31:1
In the Matter of J Robert Oppenheimer
   1969,Mr 7,28:1
Speiser, Frank
Story Theater Repertory; Saint Julian the
   Hospitaler 1970,O 21,40:1
Story Theater Repertory; Gimpel the Food
   1970,O 21,40:1
Revenger's Tragedy, The 1970,D 2,58:1
Spellman, George
Show Boat 1948,S 9,33:2
Spelvin, Abraham J
Cafe Crown 1942,Ja 24,12:5
Spelvin, Charles
New York 1927,N 15,26:2
Spelvin, Chong
First Wife, The 1945,N 28,21:5
Spelvin, Frank
War Song, The 1928,S 25,29:3
Spelvin, Fred
Petrified Forest, The 1943,N 2,30:6
Spelvin, George
Broken Wing, The 1920,N 30,14:1
Dear Me 1921,Ja 18,14:1
Wheel, The 1921,Ag 30,10:1
Thank You 1921,O 4,10:2
Merton of the Movies 1922,N 14,16:2
Polly Preferred 1923,Ja 12,13:3
Anathema 1923,Ap 11,16:2
Chicken Feed 1923,S 25,10:2
What's Your Wife Doing? 1923,O 2,10:3
Deep Tangled Wildwood, The 1923,N 6,22:1
Sitting Pretty 1924,Ap 9,24:2
Ashes 1924,O 21,21:2
Big Boy 1925,Ja 8,28:2
Hell's Bells! 1925,Ja 27,14:2
Houses of Sand 1925,F 18,17:1
Gorilla, The 1925,Ap 29,24:2
Lady of the Rose 1925,My 20,26:4
Love's Call 1925,S 11,20:1
Merry Merry 1925,S 25,24:3
Holy Terror, A 1925,S 29,31:2
Moon Is a Gong, The 1926,Mr 13,21:3
Hearts Are Trumps! 1927,Ap 8,21:1
Gossipy Sex, The 1927,Ap 20,28:3
Shannons of Broadway, The 1927,S 27,30:4
Ringside 1928,Ag 30,13:2
Command Performance, The 1928,O 4,27:1
Waterloo Bridge 1930,Ja 7,29:2
Room 349 1930,Ap 23,24:5
Through the Night 1930,Ag 19,19:1
On the Spot 1930,O 30,33:3
Meet My Sister 1930,D 31,11:1

Spelvin, George—Cont

Rap, The 1931,Ap 7,31:2
Broadway Boy 1932,My 4,23:5
Marathon 1933,Ja 28,8:8
Hilda Cassidy 1933,My 5,18:3
Spring in Autumn 1933,O 25,22:5
All Good Americans 1933,D 6,29:2
Let Freedom Ring 1935,N 7,26:2
Conjur' Man Dies 1936,Mr 12,18:5
Lightnin' 1938,S 16,17:2
Window Shopping 1938,D 24,13:2
Night of Love 1941,Ja 8,14:2
Savonarola 1942,Ap 24,20:2
Vickie 1942,S 23,28:1
Tinker's Dam 1943,Ja 29,22:2
Petrified Forest, The 1943,N 2,30:6
Take It As It Comes 1944,F 11,17:2
Broken Hearts of Broadway 1944,Je 13,16:2
Naughty-Naught '00 1946,O 21,27:5
High Button Shoes 1947,O 10,32:2
Me and Molly 1948,F 27,27:2
Dinosaur Wharf 1951,N 9,23:2
In the Summer House 1953,D 30,17:1
Edward II 1958,F 12,32:5
Jane Eyre 1958,My 2,31:1
Purple Canary, The 1963,Ap 23,31:1
Spelvin, George (Director)
Beaver Coat, The 1956,Mr 29,22:5
Spelvin, George Jr
Don Q Jr 1926,Ja 28,16:3
Gentlemen of the Press 1928,Ag 28,27:2
Kibitzer, The 1929,F 19,22:5
Salt Water 1929,N 27,30:3
All in Favor 1942,Ja 21,20:6
Spelvin, George Sr
Kibitzer, The 1929,F 19,22:5
Spelvin, Georgette
Riddle Me This! 1932,F 26,22:5
Forsaking All Others 1933,Mr 2,21:2
American, Very Early 1934,Ja 31,21:2
Spelvin, Georsianna
Indian Captive, The 1949,Ja 31,15:2
Spelvin, James
Light Wines and Beer 1930,N 11,28:6
Spelvin, Jean
Mary of Magdala 1946,Mr 26,24:5
Spelvin, M
Girofle-Girofla 1926,N 23,26:3
Spelvin, Milton
In Bed We Cry 1944,N 15,20:2
Spelvin, Walter
If Love Were All 1931,N 14,14:5
Spelvino, Giorgio
In Any Language 1952,O 9,40:2
Spelvinsky, George
They All Come to Moscow 1933,My 12,20:6
Spence, Chenault (Lighting Director)
Dames at Sea 1970,S 24,60:1
Spence, Doralyne
Stigma 1927,F 11,19:1
Spence, Eulalie (Playwright)
Divina Pastora, La 1931,Mr 4,33:2
Spence, Joseph
Gypsy Jim 1924,Ja 15,17:4
Spence, Ralph (Playwright)
Ziegfeld Follies 1921,Je 22,10:1
Ziegfeld Follies 1922,Je 6,18:2
Gorilla, The 1925,Ap 19,IX,2:1
Gorilla, The 1925,Ap 29,24:2
Earl Carroll's Vanities 1931,Ag 28,18:7
Spence, Wall
Drift 1925,N 25,15:3
Subway Express 1929,S 25,34:3
Spence, Wall (Playwright)
House of Fear, The 1929,O 8,34:2
Spencer, Arthur
Doctor Faustus 1937,Ja 9,21:2
Tell My Story 1939,Mr 16,26:6
Spencer, Beatrice
Shylock and His Daughter 1947,S 30,22:2
Spencer, Betty
Prunella; Love in a Garden 1926,Je 16,23:3
Spencer, Bob
Sing Muse 1961,D 7,52:1
Gingham Dog, The 1968,O 13,II,18:6
Spencer, Christine
Carmen Jones 1959,Ag 18,25:1
Ballad for Bimshire 1963,O 16,54:1
Spencer, Colin (Playwright)
Spitting Image 1968,S 11,42:1
Spitting Image 1969,Mr 3,28:1
Spencer, Edith
For Better or Worse 1927,F 1,24:3
Spencer, Everett
Life and Death of an American 1939,My 20,11:2
Spencer, Frank
Miles of Heaven, The 1937,Ag 31,27:4
Spencer, Frank (Costume Designer)
Little Dark Horse 1941,N 17,14:4
Tonight in Samarkand 1955,F 17,22:2
Guys and Dolls 1955,Ap 21,32:2
Ponder Heart, The 1956,F 17,14:2
Jane Eyre 1958,My 2,31:1

Spencer, Frank (Miscellaneous)
Point of No Return 1951,D 14,35:2
Spencer, Frank G
Hamlet 1920,Mr 17,14:2
Spencer, Frank M
Roof, The 1930,Je 14,9:2
Spencer, Frank M (Director)
Orphee 1935,Mr 23,10:3
Spencer, Frank M (Producer)
Orphee 1935,Mr 23,10:3
Spencer, Franklyn
Borak 1960,D 14,51:1
Spencer, Franz (Playwright)
Villa of Madame Vidac, The 1959,O 1,40:1
Spencer, Fred Jr
Poupees de Paris, Les 1964,My 16,11:1
Spencer, Gage (Costume Designer)
Lady in the Dark 1952,Mr 8,11:3
Spencer, Gillian
Top Secret 1960,S 6,40:1
Spencer, Gordon
Women at the Tomb, The 1961,Ap 25,41:1
Spencer, Helen
Home Chat 1927,N 13,IX,2:1
Girl's Best Friend, A 1929,N 10,X,2:1
To See Ourselves 1930,D 28,VIII,2:6
Avalanche 1932,F 14,VIII,1:8
Rats of Norway, The 1933,Ap 30,IX,1:7
Spencer, Herbert
Frankie and Johnny 1930,S 26,16:5
Spencer, J De Witt
John Henry 1940,Ja 11,18:2
Trojan Horse, The 1940,O 31,28:3
Spencer, Jack (Original Author)
Modern Statuary 1968,My 28,41:1
Spencer, Janet
Tragical Historie of Doctor Faustus, The
1964,O 6,34:2
Spencer, Joan
Guest in the House 1942,F 25,25:2
Spencer, John
East of Suez 1922,S 22,16:3
Spencer, Katherine
Peg o' My Dreams 1924,My 6,25:3
Spencer, Kenneth
John Henry 1940,Ja 11,18:2
Show Boat 1946,Ja 7,17:2
Show Boat 1946,Ja 13,II,1:1
Spencer, Lillian
Imaginary Invalid, The 1922,Jl 26,26:2
Old Bill, M P 1926,N 11,22:2
Spencer, Louis
Doctor Faustus Lights the Lights 1951,D 3,23:4
Spencer, Margaret
Robin Hood 1944,N 8,28:2
Spencer, Marian
Alien Corn 1939,Jl 23,IX,2:3
Old Acquaintance 1941,D 28,IX,2:3
Love for Love 1947,My 27,30:2
Quadrille 1953,Ap 5,II,1:1
Someone to Talk To 1956,Jl 19,30:2
Spencer, Page
Up in the Clouds 1922,Ja 3,20:3
Signature 1945,F 15,25:2
Spencer, Peter
Age of Innocence, The 1928,N 28,24:2
Spencer, Peter (Playwright)
Third Little Show, The 1931,Je 14,VIII,1:2
Spencer, R E (Original Author)
Lady Who Came to Stay, The 1941,Ja 3,13:2
Spencer, Richard
Hotbed 1928,N 10,20:7
Fata Morgana 1931,D 26,15:3
Spencer, Ritchie (Costume Designer)
Slow Dance on the Killing Ground
1970,My 14,43:1
Spencer, Robert
Present Arms 1928,Ap 27,16:2
How's Your Health? 1929,N 27,30:3
Pardon My English 1933,Ja 21,11:4
Untitled-Recital 1970,S 3,36:1
Spencer, Sandy
Carmilla 1970,D 1,61:2
Spencer, T J (Playwright)
Jonah! 1967,S 22,52:2
Spencer, Thomas
Ziegfeld Follies 1922,Je 6,18:2
Spencer, William (Miscellaneous)
House of Bernarda Alba, The 1963,N 25,23:2
Spencer, Zynaid
Let's Face It 1941,O 30,26:2
Spender, Stephen (Translator)
Mary Stuart 1958,S 3,38:1
Lulu 1958,S 30,24:1
Spender-Clay, Paul
Bitter Sweet 1929,N 6,30:2
Spengeman, Carl G
Vagabond King, The 1935,N 29,22:7
Spengler, Thomas
Red Mill, The 1945,O 17,16:2
Spengler, Thomas (Miscellaneous)
Front Page, The 1946,S 5,22:4

Spenser, Jeremy
Innocents, The 1952,Jl 4,9:7
Spera, Mitchell
Rothschilds, The 1970,O 20,40:1
Sperantseva, (Mme)
Chauve-Souris 1925,Ja 15,25:1
Sperduto, Al
Enemy of the People, An 1959,F 5,24:4
Sperduto, Al (Producer)
Enemy of the People, An 1959,F 5,24:4
Sperling, Milton (Miscellaneous)
Time Remembered 1957,N 13,41:2
Spero, Arete (Producer)
Happy Hypocrite, The 1968,S 6,38:1
Sperrin, Paul
Processional 1937,O 14,23:1
Speth, Myron
Around the World 1946,Je 1,9:5
Spette, Augusta
Princess Ida 1925,Ap 14,27:2
Spevlin, Dummy
Pal Joey 1940,D 26,22:2
Spewack, Bella (Original Author)
Leave It to Me! 1938,N 10,32:2
Kiss Me, Kate 1948,D 31,10:3
Spewack, Bella (Playwright)
Poppa 1928,D 25,31:1
Poppa 1928,D 30,VIII,1:1
Spring Song 1932,Ag 14,IX,1:6
Clear All Wires! 1932,S 15,19:1
Clear All Wires! 1932,S 25,IX,1:1
Spring Song 1934,O 2,18:2
Boy Meets Girl 1935,N 19,27:2
Boy Meets Girl 1935,N 28,38:2
Boy Meets Girl 1935,D 15,XI,3:1
Boy Meets Girl 1937,Jl 6,23:1
Miss Swan Expects 1939,F 21,15:2
Boy Meets Girl 1943,Je 23,15:5
Woman Bites Dog 1946,Ap 18,21:2
Kiss Me, Kate 1949,Ja 16,II,1:1
Golden State, The 1950,N 27,29:3
Kiss Me, Kate 1952,Ja 9,24:6
My 3 Angels 1953,Mr 12,23:2
Kiss Me, Kate 1954,Mr 27,13:2
Festival 1955,Ja 19,22:1
My 3 Angels 1956,F 4,24:2
Kiss Me, Kate 1956,My 10,27:2
Kiss Me, Kate 1959,Ag 10,24:1
Kiss Me, Kate 1964,F 16,29:1
Kiss Me, Kate 1965,My 13,31:1
Kiss Me, Kate 1966,F 5,32:1
Kiss Me, Kate 1970,D 26,10:4
Spewack, Sam (Director)
Leave It to Me! 1938,N 10,32:2
Miss Swan Expects 1939,F 21,15:2
Two Blind Mice 1949,Mr 3,32:2
Golden State, The 1950,N 27,29:3
Spewack, Sam (Original Author)
Leave It to Me! 1938,N 10,32:2
Kiss Me, Kate 1948,D 31,10:3
Spewack, Sam (Playwright)
War Song, The 1928,S 25,29:3
Poppa 1928,D 25,31:1
Poppa 1928,D 30,VIII,1:1
Clear All Wires! 1932,S 15,19:1
Clear All Wires! 1932,S 25,IX,1:1
Spring Song 1934,O 2,18:2
Boy Meets Girl 1935,N 19,27:2
Boy Meets Girl 1935,N 28,38:2
Boy Meets Girl 1935,D 15,XI,3:1
Boy Meets Girl 1936,My 28,18:8
Boy Meets Girl 1937,Jl 6,23:1
Leave It to Me! 1938,O 23,IX,3:5
Miss Swan Expects 1939,F 21,15:2
Boy Meets Girl 1943,Je 23,15:5
Woman Bites Dog 1946,Ap 18,21:2
Kiss Me, Kate 1949,Ja 16,II,1:1
Two Blind Mice 1949,Mr 3,32:2
Two Blind Mice 1949,Mr 20,II,1:1
Golden State, The 1950,N 27,29:3
Kiss Me, Kate 1952,Ja 9,24:6
Under the Sycamore Tree 1952,Ap 24,38:4
Under the Sycamore Tree 1952,My 11,II,3:7
My 3 Angels 1953,Mr 12,23:2
Kiss Me, Kate 1954,Mr 27,13:2
Festival 1955,Ja 19,22:1
My 3 Angels 1956,F 4,24:2
Kiss Me, Kate 1956,My 10,27:2
Kiss Me, Kate 1959,Ag 10,24:1
Under the Sycamore Tree 1960,Mr 8,37:2
Once There Was a Russian 1961,F 20,32:2
Kiss Me, Kate 1964,F 16,29:1
Kiss Me, Kate 1965,My 13,31:1
Kiss Me, Kate 1966,F 5,32:1
Kiss Me, Kate 1970,D 26,10:4
Spewack, Sam (Producer)
Under the Sycamore Tree 1952,Ap 24,38:4
Spewack, Samuel (Lyricist)
Golden State, The 1950,N 27,29:3
Speyer, Erica
Circle of Chalk, The 1950,D 2,8:3
Touch of the Poet, A 1961,My 15,34:6

Speyer, Wilhelm (Playwright)
Hat, a Coat, a Glove, A 1934,F 1,15:2
Speyser, Paul
Hamlet 1967,D 27,45:1
Spialek, Hans (Composer)
Where's Charley? 1948,O 12,33:2
Spialek, Hans (Miscellaneous)
My Darlin' Aida 1952,O 28,36:4
Spialek, Hans (Musical Director)
Louisiana Lady 1947,Je 3,35:2
Hold It! 1948,My 6,31:5
Sleepy Hollow 1948,Je 4,26:3
Spickers, Reed Hutchins (Playwright)
Sable Brush, The 1956,N 28,41:1
Spiegel, Ivan (Scenic Designer)
Republic, The 1970,Ap 28,49:1
Spiegel, Lawrence (Miscellaneous)
Local Stigmatic, The; Trouble in the Works
1969,N 4,55:2
Local Stigmatic, The; Request Stop 1969,N 4,55:2
Local Stigmatic, The; Applicant 1969,N 4,55:2
Local Stigmatic, The 1969,N 4,55:2
Local Stigmatic, The; Last to Go 1969,N 4,55:2
Local Stigmatic, The; That's Your Trouble
1969,N 4,55:2
Local Stigmatic, The; Interview 1969,N 4,55:2
Local Stigmatic, The; That's All 1969,N 4,55:2
Spielberg, David
Two Executioners, The 1964,Mr 25,46:2
MacBird! 1967,F 23,38:1
Bacchae, The 1969,Mr 15,24:1
Bacchae, The 1969,Mr 23,II,11:1
Narrow Road to the Deep North 1969,D 2,64:1
Persians, The 1970,Ap 16,53:1
Persians, The 1970,Ap 26,II,1:3
Spielman, Fred (Composer)
Lady Says Yes, A 1945,Ja 11,18:5
Spielter, William (Composer)
One Glorious Hour 1927,Ap 15,27:2
Spiering, Frank (Playwright)
Exhibition 1969,My 16,41:1
Spiering, Frank Jr (Lyricist)
Plot Against the Chase Manhattan Bank, The
1963,N 27,29:1
Spigelgass, Leonard (Playwright)
Majority of One, A 1959,F 17,28:2
Majority of One, A 1959,F 22,II,1:1
Majority of One, A 1960,Mr 10,37:5
Dear Me, the Sky Is Falling 1963,Mr 4,9:1
Wrong Way Light Bulb, The 1969,Mr 5,40:1
Look to the Lilies 1970,Mr 30,59:1
Spigner, Brenda
Life and Times of J Walter Smintheus, The
1970,D 10,59:1
Spiliopoulos, Char
Electra 1930,D 27,16:1
Spiliopoulos, X
Iphigenia 1931,Ja 6,24:1
Spillane, Francis
Veronica's Veil 1934,F 19,20:7
Spiller, Joanne
Gay Life, The 1961,N 20,38:1
Spiller, Leslie J (Producer)
One Sunday Afternoon 1933,F 16,23:5
One Sunday Afternoon 1933,S 17,X,2:4
Amourette 1933,S 28,25:2
Night Remembers, The 1934,N 28,24:3
Hook-Up, The 1935,My 9,24:6
Spiller, Marshall (Lighting Director)
Men and Dreams 1966,S 7,51:2
Funny Kind of Evening With David Kossoff, A
1967,Ja 31,52:1
Go Fly a Kite! 1969,O 20,60:1
Spina, Harold (Composer)
Rally 'Round The Girls 1942,Mr 29,VIII,2:2
Spindelman, Alfred
Dreaming Dust, The 1955,D 8,46:5
Curious Savage, The 1956,Mr 17,12:3
Drat! the Cat! 1965,O 11,54:2
Spinedi, Goffredo
Rugantino 1964,F 7,34:1
Spinelli
Untitled-Revue 1924,My 25,VIII,1:8
Spinelli, Andree
Ziegfeld Midnight Frolic 1920,Mr 17,14:2
Spinelly
Lion et la Poule, Le 1923,N 21,23:2
Diable 1926,O 31,VIII,2:4
Lelia 1928,D 2,X,2:1
Amoureuse Aventure, L' 1929,F 10,IX,4:6
Femme Sous la Pluie, Llne 1929,My 26,IX,4:1
Amour a l'Americaine, L' 1930,Ap 13,X,2:7
Folle de son Corps 1932,My 1,VIII,2:6
Frenetiques, Les 1935,Ja 13,IX,2:1
Spinelly, Mlle
Marriage of Fredaine, The 1924,Mr 2,VIII,1:3
Dompteur, Le, ou L'Anglais Tel Qu' On La Mange
1926,Ja 10,VII,1:3
Spinetti, Victor
Hostage, The 1960,S 21,42:1
Oh What a Lovely War 1964,O 1,30:1
Grosse Valise, La 1965,D 15,52:1

Spinetti, Victor (Director)
In His Own Write 1968,Je 20,50:5
In His Own Write 1968,Jl 9,30:2
In His Own Write 1968,Jl 14,II,4:5
Spingarn, Hope
Hamlet 1936,N 11,54:2
Spingler, Doug
From A to Z 1960,Ap 21,23:2
Show Boat 1966,Jl 20,48:1
How Now, Dow Jones 1967,D 8,53:1
Minnie's Boys 1970,Mr 27,27:1
Spinney, Brad
Cave Dwellers, The 1957,O 21,29:2
Spira, Camilla
Escape 1928,My 20,VIII,2:1
Journalisten, Die 1932,Jl 17,IX,1:1
Spira, Francoise
Miracle Worker, The 1961,O 8,II,3:4
Spirella, Antony
Gang War 1928,Ag 21,27:2
Spiro, Lenoria
Naughty Riquette 1926,S 14,25:2
Spitalny, Phil
Spring Tonic 1936,My 11,16:1
Spitz, Arthur (Producer)
Yours Is My Heart 1946,S 6,16:5
Spitz, Marjorie (Lighting Director)
Doctor Faustus Lights the Lights 1951,D 3,23:4
Spitzer, Robert (Playwright)
Homme de Joie, L' 1929,Mr 17,X,2:7
Amour a l'Americaine, L' 1930,Ap 13,X,2:7
Son Mari 1936,Ap 17,17:3
Si Je Voulais; If I Wished to 1937,Ja 28,22:5
Spivak, Alice
Take Me to Bed 1969,Je 14,24:1
Time for Bed 1969,Je 14,24:1
Spivak, Alice (Director)
Life and Times of J Walter Smintheus, The
1970,D 10,59:1
Spivey, Cordelia
Forest Ring, The 1930,Ap 26,11:2
Little Princess, The 1931,F 7,11:3
Splendids, Les
Vaudeville (Palace) 1923,My 15,22:2
Spohn, Patrick
Fig Leaves Are Falling, The 1969,Ja 3,19:1
Spoliansky, Mischa (Composer)
Two Neck-Ties 1929,O 13,IX,4:7
Wie Werde Ich Reich und Gluecklich?
1930,Ag 31,VIII,2:1
Alles Schwindel 1931,Je 7,VIII,2:5
Haus Dazwischen, Das 1933,F 19,IX,3:1
Hundert Meter Glueck 1933,F 19,IX,3:1
Spolidoro, Ascanio
Puppets 1925,Mr 10,19:1
Spolinasky, Mischa (Composer)
Es Liegt in der Luft 1928,S 23,IX,2:2
Sponder, Wanda
Suds in Your Eye 1944,Ja 13,15:5
Hickory Stick 1944,My 9,15:6
Spong, Hilda
Fan, The 1921,O 4,10:1
Fedora 1922,F 11,18:1
Manhattan 1922,Ag 16,7:5
Humming Bird, The 1923,Ja 16,16:2
Pride 1923,My 3,22:3
Swan, The 1923,O 24,15:3
Harvest 1925,S 21,16:2
Lucky Sam McCarver 1925,O 22,22:1
Right Age to Marry, The 1926,F 16,22:3
What Never Dies 1926,D 29,24:2
Caste 1927,D 24,8:1
Veils 1928,Mr 14,28:5
He Understood Women 1928,Ag 16,25:1
High Road, The 1928,S 11,31:1
Young Sinners 1929,N 29,24:4
Stella Brady 1931,O 11,VIII,4:3
Only the Young 1932,S 22,25:2
Evensong 1933,F 1,13:4
Young Sinners 1933,Mr 7,20:4
Thoroughbred 1933,N 7,29:2
These Two 1934,My 8,28:3
Birthday 1934,D 27,24:2
One Good Year 1935,N 28,38:3
Lady Has a Heart, The 1937,S 27,24:1
Higher and Higher 1940,Ap 5,24:3
Spooner, Cecil
House of Fear, The 1929,O 8,34:2
Paid Companions 1931,Je 23,28:4
Lady Refuses, The 1933,Mr 8,18:6
Spooner, Edna May
Babbling Brookes 1927,F 26,13:2
Spooner, Gilbert
Sale and a Sailor, A, or Glory! What Price!
1926,Ap 25,30:4
Sposta, Phyllis
Sound of Music, The 1970,Jl 3,13:1
Spotton, Rhanda Elizabeth (Costume Designer)
Sacco-Vanzetti 1969,F 9,78:1
Spottswood, James
Wait Till We're Married 1921,S 27,14:1
Deluge, The 1922,Ja 28,14:2
Partners Again 1922,My 2,22:2

Spottswood, James—Cont
Robert E Lee 1923,N 21,23:1
New Toys 1924,F 19,12:1
Close Harmony 1924,D 2,23:1
Out of the Night 1927,O 18,32:3
Rock Me, Julie 1931,F 4,21:1
Company's Coming! 1931,Ap 21,35:5
Take My Tip 1932,Ap 12,25:2
20th Century 1932,D 30,15:1
Between Two Worlds 1934,O 26,24:2
Eldest, The 1935,F 12,24:3
Knock on Wood 1935,My 29,16:2
If This Be Treason 1935,S 24,28:2
Season Changes, The 1935,D 24,10:2
Bright Honor 1936,S 28,14:1
Spradling, Grant
Kismet 1965,Je 23,45:1
Annie Get Your Gun 1966,Je 1,42:2
Sprague, Nora
Opportunity 1920,Jl 31,5:1
Sprague, Ralph
Ghosts 1925,D 2,23:2
Great Gatsby, The 1926,F 3,22:1
Such Is Life 1927,S 1,27:3
Sprague, Sidney (Choreographer)
Blackberries of 1932 1932,Ap 5,27:5
Spraight, Robert
Salome 1931,Je 21,VIII,1:4
Spratley, Tom
Transgressor Rides Again, The 1969,My 21,42:1
Sprechchor, Berlin University
Persians, The 1927,F 27,VII,2:3
Spreder, Michael
Johnny 2X4 1942,Mr 17,24:6
Spree, Joseph
Artists and Models 1924,O 16,33:3
Naughty Riquette 1926,S 14,25:2
Lace Petticoat 1927,Ja 5,18:2
Sons o' Guns 1929,N 27,30:4
Wiser They Are, The 1931,Ap 7,31:1
Here Goes the Bride 1931,N 4,31:2
Sprigge, Elisabeth (Playwright)
Elisabeth of Austria 1938,N 20,IX,1:8
Sprigge, Elisabeth (Producer)
Elisabeth of Austria 1938,N 20,IX,1:8
Sprigge, Elisabeth (Translator)
Easter 1957,Ja 17,35:2
Crime and Crime 1963,D 17,51:2
Sprigge, Katriona (Playwright)
Elisabeth of Austria 1938,N 20,IX,1:8
Sprigge, Katriona (Producer)
Elisabeth of Austria 1938,N 20,IX,1:8
Spriggs, Elizabeth
Comedy of Errors, The 1964,My 21,43:1
Hamlet 1965,Ag 20,18:2
London Assurance 1970,Ag 7,26:1
Sprinchorn, Evert (Translator)
Crimes and Crimes 1970,Ja 19,35:1
Spring, Helen
Mud 1924,Jl 4,14:3
Dearest Enemy 1925,S 19,9:2
She Couldn't Say No! 1926,S 1,27:3
Mr Moneypenny 1928,O 17,26:2
Deep Channels 1929,O 19,22:3
Springer, Abraham (Director)
Cowboy in Israel, A 1962,O 29,36:2
Springer, Benson
Mr Big 1941,O 1,24:2
Springer, Philip (Composer)
Shoestring '57 1956,N 6,31:1
Ziegfeld Follies 1957,Mr 2,19:2
Hotel Passionato 1965,O 23,16:1
Springer, Philip (Lyricist)
Ziegfeld Follies 1957,Mr 2,19:2
Springer, Thomas Grant (Playwright)
Poppy God, The 1921,Ag 30,10:1
Springer, Wilbur C Jr (Composer)
Take It Away 1936,D 15,30:5
Springer, Wilbur C Jr (Lyricist)
Take It Away 1936,D 15,30:5
Springhorn, Harold F
You'll Never Know 1921,Ap 21,9:2
Sproston, F Manning
Hunky Dory 1922,S 5,21:2
Spruill, James
Toilet, The 1964,D 17,51:1
Coop, The 1966,Mr 2,48:1
This Here Nice Place 1966,N 2,35:2
Niggerlovers, The; Demonstration, The
1967,O 2,54:2
Niggerlovers, The; Man and Dog 1967,O 2,54:2
Trials of Brother Jero, The 1967,N 10,60:1
Strong Breed, The 1967,N 10,60:1
Spruill, W Robert
Boeuf sur le Toit, Le 1930,Ap 25,28:4
Antigone 1930,Ap 25,28:4
Sprung, Sandy
Of Thee I Sing 1969,Mr 8,19:1
Ben Bagley's Shoestring Revues 1970,O 24,22:1
Spurfeld, Ewald (Miscellaneous)
Don Carlos 1964,N 25,40:1
Captain of Koepenick, The 1964,D 2,60:1
Spurin, Joseph
Pietro 1920,Ja 20,10:2

Spurin, Joseph—Cont
Broken Wing, The 1920,N 30,14:1
Zander the Great 1923,Ap 10,24:2
Princess Flavia 1925,N 3,34:3
Spurin-Calleia, Joseph
Broadway 1926,S 17,19:3
Front Page, The 1928,Ag 15,19:2
Last Mile, The 1930,F 14,21:2
Grand Hotel 1930,N 14,30:4
Honeymoon 1932,D 24,11:2
Ten Minute Alibi 1933,O 18,24:3
Bride of Torozko, The 1934,Jl 10,24:7
Small Miracle 1934,S 27,24:3
Spurr, Horton
Ramblers, The 1926,S 21,32:2
Squarey, Gilbert
Pleased to Meet You 1928,O 30,27:2
Roadside 1930,S 27,21:1
Lost Boy 1932,Ja 6,24:4
Late One Evening 1933,Ja 10,27:3
Shooting Star 1933,Je 13,22:2
Shatter'd Lamp, The 1934,Mr 22,26:3
Merrily We Roll Along 1934,O 1,14:1
Squarzina, Luigi (Director)
Venetian Twins, The 1968,My 29,23:1
Squibb, June
Best Foot Forward 1956,Mr 3,16:1
Sable Brush, The 1956,N 28,41:1
Annie Get Your Gun 1957,Mr 9,15:5
Boy Friend, The 1958,Ja 27,24:4
Lend an Ear 1959,S 25,20:5
Happy Time, The 1968,Ja 19,32:2
Squire, J C (Playwright)
Berkeley Square 1926,O 7,19:6
Berkeley Square 1926,O 24,VIII,2:1
Berkeley, Square 1929,Mr 24,X,4:5
Squire, Jack
Dew Drop Inn 1923,My 18,26:4
Battling Buttler 1923,O 9,17:2
Matinee Girl, The 1926,F 2,20:3
Rainbow Rose 1926,Mr 17,28:2
Squire, Jacqueline
Champ-Blays, The 1936,O 9,30:4
Squire, Katherine
At the Gate of the Kingdom 1927,D 9,28:5
Black Tower 1932,Ja 12,29:2
Goodbye Again 1932,D 29,16:4
Hipper's Holiday 1934,O 19,26:2
Lady of Letters 1935,Mr 29,26:6
Life's Too Short 1935,S 21,18:5
Many Mansions 1937,O 28,28:6
As You Like It 1939,My 9,28:4
Liberty Jones 1941,F 6,24:2
Family, The 1943,Mr 31,22:4
Chicken Every Sunday 1944,Ap 6,27:2
Throng o' Scarlet 1947,D 2,37:2
Cock-A-Doodle-Doo 1949,F 28,16:5
Traveling Lady 1954,O 28,45:2
Six Characters in Search of an Author
1955,D 12,38:1
Six Characters in Search of an Author
1955,D 25,II,3:1
Sin of Pat Muldoon, The 1957,Mr 14,35:1
Shadow of a Gunman, The 1958,N 21,26:1
Shadow of a Gunman, The 1958,N 30,II,1:1
Roots 1961,Mr 7,40:2
Roots 1961,Mr 19,II,1:1
This Here Nice Place 1966,N 2,35:2
Thieves' Carnival 1967,Je 5,52:1
Harpers Ferry 1967,Je 6,52:2
Visit, The 1967,S 13,41:1
Boy on the Straight-Back Chair 1969,Mr 18,36:1
Squire, Mr (Playwright)
Our Vivid Rustics 1922,Ap 30,VII,1:1
Squire, Robert
Lady's Gentleman, A 1937,D 24,20:5
Squire, Ronald
On Approval 1927,My 15,VIII,2:6
By Candle Light 1928,O 7,IX,2:7
Canaries Sometimes Sing 1929,N 10,X,2:1
Breadwinner, The 1930,O 1,26:3
Breadwinner, The 1930,O 19,IX,4:1
Sex Fable, The 1931,O 21,26:1
Dr Pygmalion 1932,Ap 24,VIII,1:1
Springtime for Henry 1932,D 4,IX,3:8
Tread Softly 1935,N 8,19:6
Tread Softly 1935,D 8,X,5:1
Laughter in Court 1936,S 10,29:4
Laughter in Court 1936,S 27,X,3:5
Plan for a Hostess 1938,Mr 27,X,1:3
Sugar Plum 1939,Ap 2,X,1:7
His Wife's Castle 1939,O 1,IX,2:2
Ducks and Drakes 1941,D 14,IX,4:3
Jane 1947,Ja 30,19:6
Jane 1947,F 9,II,3:7
Squire, William
Henry IV, Part I 1946,My 7,25:2
Henry IV, Part II 1946,My 8,33:4
Oedipus; Critic, The 1946,My 21,19:2
Elder Statesman, The 1958,Ag 31,II,3:1
Elizabethans, The 1962,Ja 22,19:1
Squires, Gil
Golden Dawn 1927,D 1,32:3
Spring Is Here 1929,Mr 12,26:1

Simple Simon 1931,Mr 10,23:2
Squires, Irving (Producer)
Garden of Sweets, The 1961,N 1,35:1
Squires, Jack
Marjorie 1924,Ag 12,12:2
Happy-Go-Lucky 1926,O 1,27:2
Yours Truly 1927,Ja 26,16:5
Artists and Models 1927,N 16,28:2
Woof, Woof 1929,D 26,20:4
Sari 1930,Ja 29,27:1
Simple Simon 1931,Mr 10,23:2
Squires, Lynda
Hair 1970,Ja 13,39:1
Srnec, Jiri
Apparition Theater of Prague, The 1966,N 17,56:2
Srnec, Jiri (Director)
Apparition Theater of Prague, The 1966,N 17,56:2
Staal, Herta
Ides of March, The 1962,N 17,16:4
Stabava, Yuri (Playwright)
Colleagues, The 1962,Je 21,26:1
Stabile, James (Producer)
Stop-Over 1938,Ja 12,16:5
Stabin, Sara
King And the Cobbler, The 1954,D 13,33:6
Thousand and One Nights 1959,D 16,53:2
Mother's Sabbath Days 1960,N 21,33:2
Backlane Center 1961,Mr 23,51:1
Eleventh Inheritor, The 1962,N 22,43:5
Enchanting Melody 1964,N 25,40:1
Bronx Express, 1968 1968,N 16,43:3
Melody Lingers On, The 1969,N 17,55:1
Brothers Ashkenazi, The 1970,N 17,53:2
Stabler, Ben (Miscellaneous)
Holiday on Ice 1969,Ag 28,44:1
Stabler, Ben (Musical Director)
Holiday on Ice 1965,S 2,38:4
Holiday on Ice 1966,S 1,30:1
Holiday on Ice 1967,Ag 31,29:2
Holiday on Ice 1968,Ag 29,44:1
Holiday on Ice 1969,Ag 28,44:1
Stabler, Jerry
Judy Garland's New Variety Show 1956,S 27,43:2
Stachelczyk, Tony (Scenic Designer)
Overruled 1959,My 27,32:2
Buoyant Billions 1959,My 27,32:2
Getting Married 1959,Je 5,18:2
Stack, James
Engaged! or Cheviot's Choice 1965,Ap 24,19:2
Pirates of Penzance, The 1970,D 6,84:6
Stack, Maurice (Dr)
Veronica's Veil 1936,F 10,19:6
Stack, Richard
Of Thee I Sing 1969,Mr 8,19:1
Stackpole, Lyle
Jade God, The 1929,My 14,28:3
Blue Ghost, The 1930,Mr 11,24:5
Stacpoole, H De Vere (Original Author)
Blue Lagoon, The 1921,S 15,16:1
Stacpoole, H De Vere (Playwright)
Monsieur le Comte 1933,F 12,IX,3:4
Stacy, Lee
Lend an Ear 1948,D 17,38:2
Stacy, Neil
Enemy 1969,D 19,65:6
Stadlen, Lewis J
Minnie's Boys 1970,F 15,II,1:1
Minnie's Boys 1970,Mr 27,27:1
Minnie's Boys 1970,Ap 5,II,1:1
Happiness Cage, The 1970,O 5,56:4
Happiness Cage, The 1970,O 11,II,1:1
Staehle, Cyrus
Antony and Cleopatra 1924,F 20,22:1
Rat, The 1925,F 11,19:3
Gods of the Lightning 1931,F 19,21:4
Cyrano de Bergerac 1932,D 27,11:2
Feathers in a Gale 1943,D 22,26:2
Signature 1945,F 15,25:2
Staerk, Ludwig
Dreimal Hochzeit 1929,Ap 28,IX,1:4
Staff, Frank (Choreographer)
Wait a Minim! 1966,Mr 8,43:1
Staffa, Mary Ann
H M S Pinafore 1960,Ja 29,14:1
Utopia, Limited 1960,Ag 8,27:2
Yeomen of the Guard, The 1961,Ap 28,23:1
Mikado, The 1961,My 5,23:1
Grand Duke, The 1961,My 12,24:1
Princess Ida 1961,My 19,23:1
Iolanthe 1961,My 26,29:6
H M S Pinafore 1961,Je 9,29:5
Student Prince, The 1961,Jl 14,14:1
Merry Widow, The 1961,O 27,28:2
Vagabond King, The 1961,N 24,36:1
Gondoliers, The 1961,D 8,44:1
Iolanthe 1962,Ag 8,34:2
Gondoliers, The 1963,Je 5,33:2
Stafford, Ann
Silhouettes 1969,S 9,41:1
Stafford, Anna
Danton's Death 1938,N 3,26:2
Stafford, Curt
As the Girls Go 1948,N 15,21:2

Stafford, Curt—Cont
Gentlemen Prefer Blondes 1949,D 9,35:3
Stafford, Eleanor
Don't, George! 1944,N 4,18:6
Stafford, Grace
Rat, The 1925,F 11,19:3
Stafford, Grey
Make Yourself at Home 1945,S 14,21:2
Magnificent Yankee, The 1946,Ja 23,21:2
Stafford, Hanley
Double Dummy 1936,N 12,30:1
Stafford, Harry (Miscellaneous)
Transatlantic Rhythm 1936,O 2,16:3
Stafford, Joseph
Peter Pan 1954,O 21,30:2
Stafford, Lesley
Let Freedom Ring 1935,N 7,26:2
Prelude 1936,Ap 20,17:4
Bury the Dead 1936,Ap 20,17:4
200 Were Chosen 1936,N 21,21:1
Washington Jitters 1938,My 3,19:1
Stafford, Marie
Cinderella on Broadway 1920,Je 25,18:1
Stafford, W H Jr
Tiger Smiles, The 1930,D 18,29:1
Stafford, Yvonne
Electra 1969,Ag 8,14:1
Stafford-Clark, Max (Director)
Jakey Fat Boy 1970,Ap 6,46:1
Dear Janet Rosenberg, Dear Mr Kooning
1970,Ap 6,46:1
Stages, Current (Producer)
Climate of Eden, The 1953,N 21,11:2
Stagg, Madge (Costume Designer)
Drunkard, The; Fallen Saved, The 1959,Je 24,37:2
Staggers, Elaine
Hot Money 1931,N 9,22:2
Staheli, Paul (Scenic Designer)
Three Sisters, The 1969,O 10,38:1
Stahl, Dick
Career 1957,My 1,42:6
Androcles and the Lion 1958,F 22,8:3
Committee, The 1964,S 17,53:1
Committee, The 1964,S 27,II,1:1
Critic, The 1965,Jl 26,15:2
Stahl, Irwin (Miscellaneous)
Sotoba Komachi 1961,F 1,15:1
Damask Drum, The 1961,F 4,15:1
Hans's Crime 1961,F 4,15:1
Electra 1962,Mr 22,42:1
Stahl, Isobel
Loud Speaker 1927,Mr 3,27:2
Stahl, William
This Fine-Pretty World 1923,D 27,11:1
Emperor Jones, The 1924,My 7,18:1
Saint, The 1924,O 13,20:3
S S Glencairn 1924,N 4,31:4
Desire Under the Elms 1924,N 12,20:7
Fountain, The 1925,D 11,26:1
Stahl-Nachbauer
Constant Nymph, The 1927,Ap 24,VII,2:1
Stahle, Cyrus
As We Forgive Our Debtors 1947,Mr 11,37:2
Stahli, Edgar
S S Glencairn 1924,N 4,31:4
Stahlnachbaur, Ernst (Director)
Unentbehrliche, Der 1937,O 24,XI,3:1
Staiger, Dorothy
Medium, The 1950,Jl 20,22:5
Medium, The 1950,S 3,II,1:1
Staiger, Libi
Most Happy Fella, The 1959,F 11,50:2
Destry Rides Again 1959,Ap 24,24:1
Most Happy Fella, The 1960,Ap 22,25:3
Sophie 1963,Ap 16,32:1
Stainbrook, Richard D (Producer)
Kaleidoscope 1957,Je 14,20:2
Staisey, George
Best Foot Forward 1941,O 2,28:2
Stalewa, Iwa
Wiener Blut 1964,S 12,14:1
Staley, Christine (Miscellaneous)
Persecution and Assassination of Marat As
Performed by the Inmates of the Asylum of
Charenton Under the Direction of the Marquis de
Sade, The 1965,D 28,35:1
Stall, Karl
Lancelot and Elaine 1921,S 13,12:1
Lollipop 1924,Ja 22,15:3
Princess Ida 1925,Ap 14,27:2
Charley's Aunt 1925,Je 2,16:2
Drift 1925,N 25,15:3
Katy Did 1927,My 10,24:3
Room in Red and White, A 1936,Ja 20,23:3
Stall, Kurt
Ten Million Ghosts 1936,O 24,23:7
Stallard, Ernest
Bluebeard's Eighth Wife 1921,S 20,12:2
Other Rose, The 1923,D 21,15:2
Habitual Husband, The 1924,D 25,27:3
Grand Duchess and the Waiter, The
1925,O 14,31:1
Weak Woman, A 1926,Ja 27,16:3
Her Cardboard Lover 1927,Mr 22,30:5

tallard, Ernest—Cont
Midsummer Night's Dream, A 1927,Je 27,25:1
People Don't Do Such Things 1927,N 24,28:3
Furies, The 1928,Mr 8,23:1
Perfect Alibi, The 1928,N 28,24:2
tallard, Margaret
Merchant of Venice, The 1947,F 24,16:2
tallings, Clifford
Remember the Day 1935,S 26,19:3
tallings, Laurence (Lyricist)
Deep River 1926,O 5,26:2
Rainbow 1928,N 22,25:1
Rainbow 1928,D 16,IX,1:1
tallings, Laurence (Original Author)
Virginia 1937,S 3,13:2
Virginia 1937,O 5,29:1
Stallings, Laurence (Playwright)
What Price Glory 1924,S 6,14:3
What Price Glory 1924,S 21,VII,1:1
What Price Glory 1924,S 28,VII,1:1
First Flight 1925,S 18,26:2
Buccaneer, The 1925,S 20,VIII,2:4
First Flight 1925,S 27,VII,1:1
Buccaneer, The 1925,O 3,10:2
Deep River 1926,O 5,26:2
Deep River 1926,O 10,VIII,1:1
Deep River 1926,O 10,VIII,4:8
Rainbow 1928,N 4,IX,1:3
Rainbow 1928,N 22,25:1
Rainbow 1928,D 16,IX,1:1
What Price Glory 1929,Ap 28,IX,1:4
Farewell to Arms, A 1930,S 23,30:3
Eldorado 1931,O 25,VIII,2:5
Virginia 1937,S 12,XI,1:1
Streets Are Guarded, The 1944,N 21,19:7
Streets Are Guarded, The 1944,N 26,II,1:1
What Price Glory 1949,Mr 3,33:2
Stallone, Nick
Three Plays of the Sea 1970,Ag 20,39:1
Stallone, Sylvester E
Score 1970,O 29,57:4
Stallwitz, Erika
Anna Kleiber 1965,Ja 20,33:1
Stamer, Fred (Composer)
Buttrio Square 1952,O 15,40:2
Stamer, Fred (Miscellaneous)
Maurice Chevalier 1963,Ja 30,7:2
Maurice Chevalier at 77 1965,Ap 2,26:1
Stamford, John
Girl in Pink Tights, The 1954,Mr 6,13:2
H M S Pinafore 1965,Ap 15,39:1
Yeomen of the Guard, The 1965,Ap 22,26:1
Stamford, Paul (Playwright)
Girl From Nantucket, The 1945,N 9,17:2
Stamm, Bill
Anything Goes 1934,N 22,26:1
Stamm, Max
Second Best Bed 1946,Je 4,20:2
Stamm, William
Anything Goes 1934,N 22,26:1
Stamos, Martino
Wiener Blut 1964,S 12,14:1
Stamp, Terence
Alfie 1964,D 18,27:1
Stamp-Taylor, Enid
To Kill a Cat 1939,Jl 2,IX,1:6
Stamper, Dave
Vaudeville (Palace) 1923,F 13,25:1
Ziegfeld Follies 1923,O 22,17:2
Follies 1925,Jl 7,24:3
Stamper, Dave (Composer)
Ziegfeld Follies 1920,Je 23,14:1
Ziegfeld Follies 1921,Je 22,10:1
Ziegfeld Follies 1922,Je 6,18:2
Ziegfeld Follies 1924,Je 25,26:1
Take the Air 1927,N 23,28:2
Lovely Lady 1927,D 30,22:1
Ziegfeld Follies 1931,Jl 2,30:5
Provincetown Follies, The 1935,N 4,24:3
Orchids Preferred 1937,My 12,26:5
Stamper, Dave (Lyricist)
Ziegfeld Follies 1920,Je 23,14:1
Orchids Preferred 1937,Ap 29,16:6
Stamper, Dave (Playwright)
Ziegfeld Follies 1920,Je 23,14:1
Ziegfeld Follies 1931,Jl 2,30:5
Orchids Preferred 1937,Ap 29,16:6
Stamper, George
Runnin' Wild 1923,O 30,17:3
Stamper, George (Choreographer)
Americana 1928,O 31,28:2
Ginger Snaps 1930,Ja 1,30:5
Stamps, Philip A
Prodigal Son, The 1965,My 21,19:1
Stanborough, Reginald
Country Wife, The 1936,D 2,34:1
Stanbury, Douglas
Vaudeville (Palace) 1929,S 30,22:3
Simple Simon 1930,F 19,22:1
Stanbury, Henry
Untitled-Passion Play 1926,Mr 30,20:2
Stancill, Mary
Second Man, The 1930,My 2,23:2

Stanczak, Marian (Scenic Designer)
Mirele Efros 1967,O 20,55:1
Standard, Jack
Young and Beautiful, The 1959,My 29,13:1
Stander, Hollice
Nighthawks 1967,D 30,14:2
Stander, Lionel
Final Balance, The 1928,O 31,28:3
Singing Jailbirds 1928,D 5,34:4
S S Glencairn 1929,Ja 10,24:5
Red Rust 1929,D 18,31:1
With Privileges 1930,S 16,30:2
House Beautiful, The 1931,Mr 13,20:4
Little Ol' Boy 1933,Ap 25,15:5
Drums Begin, The 1933,N 25,10:5
Bride of Torozko, The 1934,S 14,24:2
Summer Night 1939,N 3,17:1
Banjo Eyes 1941,N 8,10:6
Banjo Eyes 1941,D 26,20:2
Pal Joey 1952,Ja 4,17:6
Pal Joey 1952,Ja 13,II,1:1
Pal Joey 1952,F 17,II,13:5
Plough and the Stars, The 1956,Ap 6,14:1
Conquering Hero, The 1961,Ja 17,40:2
Policemen, The 1961,N 22,24:2
Arturo Ui 1963,N 12,49:1
St Joan of the Stockyards 1964,Je 12,45:1
Stander, Lionel (Producer)
Brooklyn, U S A 1941,D 22,24:2
Stander, Matthew (Producer)
Helen 1964,D 11,55:4
Standing, Gordon
Hamlet 1925,N 10,23:1
Standing, Guy
Clair de Lune 1921,Ap 19,15:1
Carolinian, The 1925,N 3,34:2
Diversion 1928,Ja 6,26:3
Diversion 1928,Ja 12,25:1
Money Lender, The 1928,Ag 28,27:3
Jealous Moon, The 1928,N 21,32:2
Paolo and Francesca 1929,Ap 2,28:2
Jenny 1929,O 9,34:4
Mrs Moonlight 1930,S 30,24:3
Come Easy 1933,Ag 30,22:5
Halfway to Hell 1934,Ja 3,22:3
Jefferson Davis 1936,F 19,17:2
Summer Night 1939,N 3,17:1
Up in Central Park 1945,Ja 29,17:2
Up in Central Park 1947,My 20,29:2
Standing, Herbert
Outrageous Mrs Palmer, The 1920,O 13,18:1
Queen Victoria 1923,N 16,15:1
Leap, The 1924,My 23,16:5
Taps 1925,Ap 15,16:2
Man or Devil 1925,My 22,22:4
Napoleon 1928,Mr 9,21:1
So Was Napoleon 1930,Ja 9,22:2
His Majesty's Car 1930,O 24,30:1
Silent Witness, The 1931,Mr 24,31:5
Lady Windermere's Fan 1932,Ja 27,19:3
Living Dangerously 1935,Ja 14,10:3
Happy Ending 1936,Jl 15,14:3
Black Limelight 1936,N 10,31:1
Storm Over Patsy 1937,Mr 9,26:4
Father Malachy's Miracle 1937,N 18,26:4
Standing, John
Importance of Being Earnest, The 1968,Jl 6,9:1
Ring Around the Moon 1968,N 2,28:1
Girlfriend 1970,F 19,59:1
Arms and the Man 1970,Jl 10,18:1
Arms and the Man 1970,Ag 26,36:1
Alchemist, The 1970,Ag 26,36:1
Standing, Katherine
Transplanting Jean 1921,Ja 4,11:2
What Never Dies 1926,D 29,24:2
Money Lender, The 1928,Ag 28,27:3
Michael and Mary 1929,D 14,23:3
Mrs Moonlight 1930,S 30,24:3
Chalk Dust 1936,Mr 5,24:5
Lady Has a Heart, The 1937,S 27,24:1
Standing, Michael
Chips With Everything 1963,O 2,49:1
Standish, Helene
Yokel Boy 1939,Jl 7,12:2
Standish, Jane
More the Merrier, The 1941,S 16,19:3
Standish, Miles (Playwright)
I Dream of Jeanie 1963,Je 25,23:1
Standish, Pamela
Touch Wood 1934,Jl 1,X,1:3
Standlee, Shirley
Good Housekeeping 1949,Ag 17,19:3
Stane, Walter
Lady in the Dark 1943,Mr 1,14:2
Lute Song 1946,F 7,29:2
Staneks Six, The
Aquacircus 1958,Je 30,24:6
Stanely, William
Good Times 1920,Ag 10,10:1
Staneska, Kamila
Antony and Cleopatra 1937,N 11,30:2
Stanfield, Regina
Holiday 1930,F 6,21:2

Stanford, Antony
Charley's Aunt 1925,Je 2,16:2
He Walked in Her Sleep 1929,Ap 5,28:2
Come-On Man, The 1929,Ap 23,26:2
Stanford, Jack
Greenwich Village Follies 1928,Ap 10,32:2
Panama Hattie 1943,D 5,II,5:1
Stanford, Mabel
Broadway Whirl, The 1921,Je 9,10:4
Stang, Arnold
All in Favor 1942,Ja 21,20:6
You'll See Stars 1943,Ja 1,26:6
Front Page, The 1969,My 12,54:2
Front Page, The 1969,My 25,II,1:1
Stange, Freddie
Open House 1925,D 15,28:3
Light of Asia, The 1928,O 10,32:2
Thunder in the Air 1929,N 12,34:3
Topaze 1930,F 13,25:3
Peter Ibbetson 1931,Ap 9,30:3
Young Sinners 1933,Mr 7,20:4
Stange, Frederic
Bright Honor 1936,S 28,14:1
Stange, Hugh (Director)
Veneer 1929,N 13,24:5
Long Road, The 1930,S 10,30:2
After Tomorrow 1931,Ag 27,22:4
Mother Sings 1935,N 13,24:1
Stange, Hugh (Miscellaneous)
Mother Sings 1935,N 13,24:1
Stange, Hugh (Playwright)
Dawn of Ireland, The 1920,O 1,14:2
Hello, Lola! 1926,Ja 13,30:1
Fog-Bound 1927,Ap 2,21:2
Tin Pan Alley 1928,N 2,29:1
Veneer 1929,N 13,24:5
Veneer 1929,N 24,X,1:1
Headquarters 1929,N 24,X,4:5
Headquarters 1929,D 5,32:4
Long Road, The 1930,Jl 20,VIII,2:1
After Tomorrow 1930,Ag 10,VIII,2:3
Long Road, The 1930,S 10,30:2
After Tomorrow 1931,Ag 27,22:4
False Dreams, Farewell 1934,Ja 16,18:3
Mother Sings 1935,N 13,24:1
Stange, Stanislaus (Lyricist)
Chocolate Soldier, The 1930,Ja 28,28:1
Stange, Stanislaus (Miscellaneous)
Chocolate Soldier, The 1947,Mr 13,34:2
Stange, Stanislaus (Playwright)
Chocolate Soldier, The 1921,D 13,24:2
Chocolate Soldier, The 1931,S 22,33:3
Chocolate Soldier, The 1942,Je 24,22:2
Stanhope, Frank
Paradise Alley 1924,Ap 2,17:3
Stanhope, Frederick (Director)
Stork, The 1925,Ja 27,14:2
Florida Girl 1925,N 3,34:1
Stronger Than Love 1925,D 29,20:2
Wooden Kimono 1926,D 28,16:2
Behold This Dreamer 1927,N 1,20:4
Jenny 1929,O 9,34:4
Little Orchard Annie 1930,Ap 22,33:1
She Means Business 1931,Ja 27,21:2
Stanhope, Frederick (Producer)
Faithful Heart, The 1922,O 15,VIII,1:1
Wooden Kimono 1926,D 28,16:2
Stanhope, Jane (Costume Designer)
Man of Destiny, The 1957,Ap 1,21:2
Portrait of a Madonna 1957,Ap 1,21:2
Bedtime Story 1957,Ap 1,21:2
Stanhope, Lawrence
Jefferson Davis 1936,F 19,17:2
Stanislaus, Sidney
Nocturne 1925,F 17,19:1
Stanislavsky, Constantin
Lower Depths, The 1923,Ja 16,16:1
Lower Depths, The 1923,Ja 21,VII,1:1
Cherry Orchard, The 1923,Ja 23,18:1
Cherry Orchard, The 1923,Ja 28,VII,1:1
Three Sisters, The 1923,Ja 30,12:2
Lady From the Provinces, The 1923,F 27,14:2
Tsar Fyodor Ivanovitch 1923,My 22,14:3
Mistress of the Inn, The; Locandiera, La
   1923,N 22,16:1
Ivanoff 1923,N 27,23:2
Enough Stupidity in Every Wise Man
   1923,D 6,23:1
Uncle Vanya 1924,Ja 29,16:2
Moscow Art Theatre 1924,My 13,25:2
Stanislavsky, Constantin (Director)
Tsar Fyodor Ivanovitch 1923,Ja 11,25:1
Tsar Fyodor Ivanovitch 1923,Ja 14,VII,1:1
Lower Depths, The 1923,Ja 21,VII,1:1
Cherry Orchard, The 1923,Ja 28,VII,1:1
Cherry Orchard, The; Three Sisters, The
   1923,F 4,VII,1:1
Brothers Karamazov, The 1923,Mr 4,VII,1:1
Lady From the Provinces, The 1923,Mr 4,VII,1:1
Locandiera, La 1923,D 9,IX,1:1
Lower Depths, The 1923,D 9,IX,1:1
In the Claws of Life 1923,D 9,IX,1:1

Stanislavsky, Constantin (Miscellaneous)
  Lodging for the Night, A 1922,O 2,10:2
  Czar Feodor 1922,O 22,VIII,1:6
Stanislavsky, Constantin (Original Author)
  Tsar Fyodor Ivanovitch 1923,Ja 11,25:1
Stanislavsky, Constantin (Playwright)
  Brothers Karamazov, The 1923,F 27,14:2
Stanislavsky, Constantin (Producer)
  Dead Souls 1965,F 5,34:1
Stanislavsky Opera Players
  Porgy and Bess 1945,Je 17,II,4:3
Stanislawski, Edward
  Russian Isba 1920,Mr 12,18:4
Stanislovsky, Mordecai (Miscellaneous)
  Talent '54 1954,Ap 13,40:1
Stanitsyn, Victor
  Dead Souls 1965,F 5,34:1
Stanitsyn, Victor (Director)
  Cherry Orchard, The 1965,F 10,46:1
Stankovic, Srboliub (Miscellaneous)
  Victor, or The Children Take Over 1968,Jl 10,22:4
Stanley, Aileen
  Silks and Satins 1920,Jl 16,19:1
  Vaudeville (Palace) 1926,Mr 23,24:3
  Pleasure Bound 1929,F 19,22:4
  Artists and Models 1930,Je 11,33:2
  Vaudeville (Palace) 1930,Ag 18,24:3
  Vaudeville (Palace) 1931,Ja 26,21:5
Stanley, Alida
  Our Town 1944,Ja 11,24:5
Stanley, Alvah
  Henry V 1964,My 13,52:1
  Richard III 1965,Je 3,26:1
  Cherry Orchard, The 1965,Ag 2,17:2
Stanley, Art
  Hit the Deck 1960,Je 24,32:1
Stanley, Arthur (Lyricist)
  Fritzi 1935,D 21,10:3
Stanley, Bert
  Vagabond King, The 1943,Je 30,24:2
Stanley, Beth
  Mimic World of 1921, The 1921,Ag 18,9:2
Stanley, Bette
  Young and Fair, The 1948,N 23,35:2
Stanley, Earle
  Electra 1927,My 4,28:3
Stanley, Edwin
  Donovan Affair, The 1926,Ag 31,15:2
  Marriage Bed, The 1929,Ja 8,35:1
  This Man's Town 1930,Mr 11,24:4
Stanley, Eric
  Journey's End 1929,Mr 23,23:1
  Journey's End 1930,Ja 27,24:7
Stanley, Florence
  Machinal 1960,Ap 8,27:1
  Electra 1964,Ag 12,42:1
  Fiddler on the Roof 1970,F 28,20:1
Stanley, Helene
  Pardon Our French 1950,O 6,22:4
Stanley, Jack
  Yours Truly 1927,Ja 26,16:5
Stanley, Jack (Lyricist)
  Passing Show of 1922, The 1922,S 21,18:2
Stanley, John W
  Lost in the Stars 1949,O 31,21:2
Stanley, Joseph B
  Vaudeville (Palace) 1924,O 21,21:2
  Vaudeville (Palace) 1926,Ap 20,24:6
Stanley, Kim
  Yes is for a Very Young Man 1949,Je 7,27:2
  House of Bernarda Alba, The 1951,Ja 8,14:6
  Chase, The 1952,Ap 16,30:2
  Picnic 1953,F 20,14:7
  Picnic 1953,Mr 1,II,1:1
  Traveling Lady 1954,O 28,45:2
  Bus Stop 1955,Mr 3,23:2
  Bus Stop 1955,Mr 13,II,1:1
  Clearing in the Woods, A 1957,Ja 11,20:2
  Clearing in the Woods, A 1957,Ja 20,II,1:1
  Cat on a Hot Tin Roof 1958,Ja 31,24:2
  Touch of the Poet, A 1958,O 3,23:2
  Touch of the Poet, A 1958,O 12,II,1:1
  Cheri 1959,O 13,44:1
  Far Country, A 1961,Ap 5,32:1
  Far Country, A 1961,Ap 16,II,1:1
  Natural Affection 1963,F 2,5:2
  Three Sisters, The 1964,Je 23,24:1
  Three Sisters, The 1964,Jl 5,II,1:1
  Three Sisters, The 1965,My 15,19:4
Stanley, Lane
  Headquarters 1929,D 5,32:4
Stanley, Lee
  Slightly Delinquent 1954,O 26,32:5
Stanley, Louise
  Distant City, The 1941,S 23,27:5
Stanley, Martha (Playwright)
  Scrambled Wives 1920,Ag 6,16:1
  Teaser, The 1921,Jl 28,8:3
  My Son 1924,S 18,18:2
  Puppy Love 1925,O 4,IX,2:1
  Puppy Love 1926,Ja 28,16:3
  Wasp's Nest, The 1927,O 26,26:3
  Let and Sub-Let 1930,My 20,32:2

Stanley, Minnie
  Busybody, The 1924,S 30,27:5
  Weak Sisters 1925,O 14,31:3
  Cafe de Danse 1929,Ja 16,22:2
  Subway Express 1929,S 25,34:3
  Murder in the Cathedral 1936,Mr 21,13:5
  It Can't Happen Here 1936,O 28,30:1
Stanley, Pamela
  As Bad as I Am 1935,S 29,X,1:6
  Hamlet 1936,O 20,31:3
  Hamlet 1936,N 11,54:2
  Victoria Regina 1937,Je 22,26:2
  Victoria Regina 1937,Jl 11,X,1:7
Stanley, Pat
  Carnival in Flanders 1953,S 9,38:2
  Pajama Game, The 1957,My 16,27:1
  Pajama Game, The 1957,My 26,II,1:1
  Carousel 1957,S 12,38:2
  Blue Denim 1958,F 28,17:1
  Blue Denim 1958,Ap 20,II,1:1
  Goldilocks 1958,O 13,33:1
  Goldilocks 1958,O 19,II,1:1
  Fiorello! 1959,N 24,45:3
  Fiorello! 1959,N 29,II,1:1
  Sunday in New York 1961,N 10,40:1
Stanley, Paul
  Brighten the Corner 1945,D 13,33:2
Stanley, Ralph
  Tall Story 1959,Ja 30,33:2
Stanley, Robert J
  Zombie 1932,F 11,17:2
Stanley, Roy
  Detective Story 1954,F 13,11:2
Stanley, S Victor
  Journey's End 1929,Mr 23,23:1
  Journey's End 1929,Jl 14,IX,5:1
  Journey's End 1930,Ja 27,24:7
  Payment Deferred 1931,O 1,24:2
Stanley, Truman
  O'Brien Girl, The 1921,O 4,10:2
Stanley, William
  Hamlet 1936,O 9,30:2
Stanley Twins
  Vaudeville (Palace) 1931,Je 15,23:5
  George White's Scandals 1935,D 26,20:2
Stannard, Heather
  Venus Observed 1950,Ja 19,35:2
  Richard II 1951,Mr 25,75:3
Stanovitch, Anna
  Midsummer Night's Dream, A 1967,Je 30,23:1
Stansbury, Hope
  Chocolates 1967,Ap 11,51:1
Stantley, Ralph
  Harriet 1944,S 28,26:1
  Assassin, The 1945,O 18,20:2
  Mr Peebles and Mr Hooker 1946,O 11,29:2
  Golden Fleecing 1959,O 16,24:5
  Sing Muse 1961,D 7,52:1
  What Makes Sammy Run? 1964,F 28,19:1
Stanton, Arthur (Miscellaneous)
  Veronica's Veil 1950,F 12,II,1:5
Stanton, Babe
  Lady Billy 1920,D 15,18:2
Stanton, Barbara
  Mary of Magdala 1946,Mr 26,24:5
  Blithe Spirit 1952,F 23,7:5
  Crucible, The 1953,Ja 23,15:2
  Crucible, The 1953,Jl 2,20:2
  Dandy Dick 1956,Ja 11,37:2
  House of Breath, The 1957,Ap 15,23:2
  Crucible, The 1958,Mr 12,36:1
  Mousetrap, The 1960,N 7,46:1
  Crucible, The 1964,Ap 7,30:2
Stanton, Bebe
  June Days 1925,Ag 7,12:5
  Earl Carroll's Vanities 1926,Ag 25,19:4
  Earl Carroll's Vanities 1927,Ja 5,18:1
Stanton, Bill
  Mame 1966,My 25,41:1
Stanton, Ernie
  Billie 1928,O 2,34:2
  Vaudeville (Broadway) 1932,D 27,11:4
Stanton, George (Producer)
  Carib Song 1945,S 28,17:2
Stanton, Gertrude
  There You Are! 1932,My 17,25:4
Stanton, Harry
  Madame Aphrodite 1961,D 30,13:1
Stanton, Helen
  Merry Duchess, The 1943,Je 24,25:1
Stanton, Jack
  Du Barry Was a Lady 1939,D 7,34:2
  Top-Notchers 1942,My 30,8:5
  Up in Central Park 1947,My 20,29:2
Stanton, Josephine
  Boudoir 1941,F 8,18:4
Stanton, Mable
  Honors Are Even 1921,Ag 11,8:2
Stanton, Mary
  Drink to Me Only 1958,O 9,47:4
Stanton, Merle
  Skirt, The 1921,N 8,28:1
  Schemers 1924,S 16,27:1

Stanton, Merle—Cont
  Donovan Affair, The 1926,Ag 31,15:2
  Humbug, The 1929,N 28,34:5
Stanton, Olive
  Class of '29 1936,My 16,10:3
  Cradle Will Rock, The 1937,D 6,19:4
  Cradle Will Rock, The 1938,Ja 4,19:3
Stanton, Paul
  Devils 1926,Mr 18,26:4
  Manhattan Mary 1927,S 27,30:3
  Simple Simon 1930,F 19,22:1
  Anybody's Game 1932,D 22,21:4
Stanton, Ray
  Vaudeville (Palace) 1926,Mr 23,24:3
  Vaudeville (Palace) 1926,Jl 20,17:4
Stanton, Robert
  Angel in the Wings 1947,D 12,36:4
  Confederacy, The 1958,Jl 3,20:1
Stanton, Sandra
  Woman's a Fool-To Be Clever, A 1938,O 19,18:6
Stanton, Sanford E (Director)
  Star of Bengal 1929,S 26,27:2
Stanton, Sanford E (Producer)
  Scarlet Lily, The 1927,Ja 31,12:3
Stanton, Todd
  Hand in Glove 1944,D 5,19:1
Stanton, Val
  Billie 1928,O 2,34:2
  Vaudeville (Broadway) 1932,D 27,11:4
Stantons, The
  Tattle Tales 1930,Jl 20,VIII,2:1
Stanwell, Ann
  Skin of Our Teeth, The 1955,Ag 18,16:1
  Jane Eyre 1958,My 2,31:1
Stanwood, Sheldon
  Scaramouche 1923,O 25,14:2
Stanwyck, Barbara
  Noose, The 1926,O 21,23:3
  Burlesque 1927,S 2,15:3
  Burlesque 1927,S 11,VIII,1:1
  Vaudeville (Palace) 1929,F 4,21:4
  Conflict, The 1929,F 11,26:2
  Vaudeville (Palace) 1929,F 11,26:2
  Vaudeville (Palace) 1929,Mr 18,30:5
  Vaudeville (Palace) 1932,Mr 7,13:4
  Tattle Tales 1933,Je 2,22:6
Stanwyck, Barbara (Producer)
  Tattle Tales 1933,Je 2,22:6
Stanwyck, Jay (Miscellaneous)
  Here Come the Clowns 1960,S 20,48:1
  Evening's Frost, An 1965,O 12,56:1
  Serjeant Musgrave's Dance 1966,Mr 9,44:1
Stanwyck, Jay (Producer)
  Sponge Room, The 1964,F 25,24:1
  Squat Betty 1964,F 25,24:1
  World of Illusion 1964,Je 25,26:2
  That 5 A.M. Jazz 1964,O 20,42:2
Stanyon, Bryan
  Semi-Detached 1963,O 8,49:1
Staples, Everett (Costume Designer)
  Hidden Horizon 1946,S 20,42:2
Stapleton, Allen
  Respectfully Yours 1947,My 14,29:4
Stapleton, Jean
  American Gothic 1953,N 11,35:6
  In the Summer House 1953,D 30,17:1
  Damn Yankees 1955,My 6,17:1
  Bells Are Ringing 1956,N 29,43:4
  Bells Are Ringing 1956,N 30,18:2
  Juno 1959,Mr 10,41:1
  Rhinoceros 1961,Ja 10,27:1
  Funny Girl 1964,Mr 27,15:1
Stapleton, Katharine
  Wuziz! 1970,O 2,25:2
Stapleton, Maureen
  Playboy of the Western World, The 1946,O 28,18:3
  Antony and Cleopatra 1947,N 27,49:2
  Bird Cage, The 1950,F 23,32:2
  Rose Tattoo, The 1951,F 5,19:2
  Rose Tattoo, The 1951,F 11,II,1:1
  Emperor's Clothes, The 1953,F 10,24:2
  Crucible, The 1953,Jl 2,20:2
  Richard III 1953,D 10,65:2
  Sea Gull, The 1954,My 12,38:1
  Sea Gull, The 1954,My 23,II,1:1
  27 Wagons Full of Cotton 1955,Ja 19,23:2
  All in One; 27 Wagons Full of Cotton
    1955,Ap 20,40:3
  All in One 1955,Ap 24,II,1:1
  Orpheus Descending 1957,Mr 22,28:1
  Orpheus Descending 1957,Mr 31,II,1:1
  Cold Wind and the Warm, The 1958,D 9,55:1
  Cold Wind and the Warm, The 1959,Ja 18,II,1:1
  Toys in the Attic 1960,F 26,23:2
  Toys in the Attic 1960,Mr 6,II,1:1
  Glass Menagerie, The 1965,My 5,53:2
  Glass Menagerie, The 1965,My 16,II,1:1
  Rose Tattoo, The 1966,O 21,36:2
  Rose Tattoo, The 1966,N 20,II,1:1
  Plaza Suite; Visitor From Mamaroneck
    1968,F 15,49:1
  Plaza Suite; Visitor From Forest Hills
    1968,F 15,49:1

Stapleton, Maureen—Cont

Plaza Suite; Visitor From Hollywood
1968,F 15,49:1
Plaza Suite 1968,F 25,II,1:1
Plaza Suite 1968,D 14,61:2
Norman, Is That You? 1970,F 20,30:1
Gingerbread Lady, The 1970,D 14,58:3
Gingerbread Lady, The 1970,D 20,II,3:7
Stapleton, Willamae
Ring Two 1939,N 23,38:2
Stapleton, William
Ring Two 1939,N 23,38:2
Stapp, John
Little Theatre Tournament; Rain 1929,My 11,22:2
Star, Dolores
Alive and Kicking 1950,Ja 18,25:5
Star, George
White Cargo 1960,D 30,12:1
Star, June
Spring Fever 1925,Ag 4,14:2
Starbird, Charlotte (Miscellaneous)
What Shall We Tell Caroline? 1961,N 22,24:2
Dock Brief, The 1961,N 22,24:2
Starbuck, Betty
Garrick Gaieties 1925,My 18,12:2
Garrick Gaieties 1926,My 11,25:2
Peggy-Ann 1926,D 28,16:3
Chee-Chee 1928,S 26,25:1
Hello, Daddy! 1928,D 27,26:5
Me for You 1929,S 22,IX,2:6
Heads Up! 1929,N 12,34:1
Wild Waves 1932,Ja 24,VIII,3:3
Wild Waves 1932,F 20,11:4
Gay Divorce 1932,N 30,23:4
All the King's Horses 1934,Ja 31,21:3
Love on an Island 1934,Jl 24,20:5
Starbuck, Fred
Time Remembered 1957,N 13,41:2
Starbuck, James
Merry Widow, The 1943,Ag 5,19:2
Winter's Tale, The 1946,Ja 16,18:6
Music in My Heart 1947,O 3,30:2
Sleepy Hollow 1948,Je 4,26:3
Starbuck, James (Choreographer)
Michael Todd's Peep Show 1950,Je 29,37:2
Oh Captain! 1958,F 5,21:2
Starbuck, James (Miscellaneous)
Thurber Carnival, A 1960,F 27,13:2
Starbuck, Larry
Bad Habits of 1926 1926,My 1,11:1
Starbuck, Wilson (Playwright)
Sea Dogs 1939,N 7,30:3
Starck, Edna
Love Song, The 1925,Ja 14,19:4
Starcke, Walter (Miscellaneous)
I Am a Camera 1951,N 29,39:6
Starcke, Walter (Producer)
I've Got Sixpence 1952,D 3,44:2
Starer, Robert (Miscellaneous)
Gay Life, The 1961,N 20,38:1
Starer, Ronald (Composer)
Cherry Orchard, The 1962,N 15,46:2
Starita, Gloria
Candida 1969,F 3,29:1
Lady From Maxim's, The 1970,Je 1,41:1
Stark, Bruce W (Miscellaneous)
Moon Is Blue, The 1961,Ag 9,29:1
Utbu 1966,Ja 5,24:1
Stark, Bruce W (Producer)
Sweet Enemy, The 1965,F 16,39:1
Four Seasons, The 1968,Mr 15,32:1
Billy 1969,Mr 24,56:1
Stark, C Nick
Bronx Express 1922,Ap 27,12:2
Stark, Douglas
Everywhere I Roam 1938,D 30,10:4
Fireworks on the James 1940,My 15,30:2
Trial of Lee Harvey Oswald, The 1967,N 6,64:1
Stark, James
Singin' the Blues 1931,S 17,21:3
Stark, John
If This Be Treason 1935,S 24,28:2
Magistrate, The 1959,My 14,30:6
Cut of the Axe 1960,F 2,38:2
Stark, Joy
People vs Ranchman, The 1968,O 28,56:1
Stark, Julius
Alt Heidelberg 1926,My 31,10:5
Stark, Larry
Sniper, The 1959,O 28,40:4
Stark, Leighton
Hole in the Wall, The 1920,Mr 27,11:1
Beware of Dogs 1921,O 4,10:1
Bootleggers, The 1922,N 28,24:1
Square Peg, A 1923,Ja 29,10:2
Cold Feet 1923,My 22,14:2
In the Next Room 1923,N 28,14:1
Stark, Leo
Three Musketeers, The 1921,My 20,18:5
Sweet Nell of Old Drury 1923,My 19,16:4
Jealous Moon, The 1928,N 21,32:2
Stark, Leslie J
Uncommon Denominator, The 1963,My 8,35:2

Stark, Leslie J (Playwright)
Uncommon Denominator, The 1963,My 8,35:2
Stark, Leslie J (Producer)
Exercise, The 1968,Ap 25,54:1
Stark, Michael
Infinite Shoeblack, The 1930,F 18,28:1
Stark, Mr
Merry Wives of West Point, The 1932,Mr 20,II,7:7
Stark, Nick
Poppy God, The 1921,Ag 30,10:1
Stark, Ray (Producer)
Funny Girl 1964,Mr 27,15:1
Stark, Richard
Symphony 1935,Ap 27,20:3
Stark, Sally
Dames at Sea 1968,D 21,46:1
Dames at Sea 1970,Ja 5,46:3
Stark, Sheldon (Playwright)
Time of Storm 1954,F 26,14:2
Starkand, Martin
Brownstone Urge, The 1969,D 18,63:1
Starke, Pauline
Zombie 1932,F 11,17:2
Starkey, Walter
Mermaids Singing, The 1945,N 29,26:6
This, Too, Shall Pass 1946,My 1,32:4
Druid Circle, The 1947,O 23,29:5
Starkie, Ben
Young Alexander 1929,Mr 13,28:2
House of Remsen 1934,Ap 3,26:4
Prisoners of War 1935,Ja 29,24:1
Ceiling Zero 1935,Ap 11,26:2
This Our House 1935,D 12,33:3
It Can't Happen Here 1936,O 28,30:1
Hero Is Born, A 1937,O 2,18:6
Starkie, Martin (Director)
Canterbury Tales 1968,S 7,23:3
Canterbury Tales; Merchant's Tale, The
1969,F 4,34:1
Canterbury Tales; Steward's Tale, The
1969,F 4,34:1
Canterbury Tales; Pilgrims, The 1969,F 4,34:1
Canterbury Tales; Wife of Bath's Tale, The
1969,F 4,34:1
Canterbury Tales; Miller's Tale, The 1969,F 4,34:1
Starkie, Martin (Playwright)
Canterbury Tales 1968,S 7,23:3
Canterbury Tales; Steward's Tale, The
1969,F 4,34:1
Canterbury Tales; Pilgrims, The 1969,F 4,34:1
Canterbury Tales; Wife of Bath's Tale, The
1969,F 4,34:1
Canterbury Tales; Miller's Tale, The 1969,F 4,34:1
Canterbury Tales; Merchant's Tale, The
1969,F 4,34:1
Starkle, Ben
Class of '29 1936,My 16,10:3
Empress of Destiny 1938,Mr 10,16:2
Starkman, Mr
Something Different 1967,N 29,52:1
Starkweather, John
Camelot 1960,D 5,42:1
Starkweather, John (Miscellaneous)
Big Man 1966,My 20,41:1
Duet for Three 1966,My 20,41:1
Starkweather, Mildred
Achilles Had a Heel 1935,O 14,20:2
Cyrano de Bergerac 1936,Ap 28,17:1
Starling, Lynn
Three Showers 1920,Ap 6,18:1
Imaginary Invalid, The 1922,Jl 26,26:2
Starling, Lynn (Director)
Weak Sisters 1925,O 14,31:3
Starling, Lynn (Playwright)
Underwrite Your Husband 1923,O 14,VIII,2:4
Meet the Wife 1923,N 27,23:4
Meet the Wife 1923,D 16,IX,1:1
In His Arms 1924,O 14,23:1
Weak Sisters 1925,O 14,31:3
Meet the Wife 1927,Jl 3,VII,1:4
Skin Deep 1927,O 18,32:1
Meet the Wife 1928,D 3,30:6
First Apple, The 1933,D 28,25:1
Meet the Wife 1937,Jl 6,23:1
Beverly Hills 1940,N 8,24:2
Starlings, The
Hellzapoppin 1938,S 23,34:2
Starmer, Garrett
Growing Pains 1933,N 24,24:2
Starner, Marie
Hello Paris 1930,N 17,29:3
Blossom Time 1931,Mr 5,32:1
Starnes, Darrell
Henry-Behave 1926,Ag 24,19:4
Starowieska, Eva (Miscellaneous)
Tango 1969,Ja 20,33:1
Starr, Adelaide
Genius and the Crowd 1920,S 7,20:1
Starr, Ben (Playwright)
Family Way, The 1965,Ja 14,44:5
Starr, Bill
All American 1962,Mr 20,44:1

Starr, Bill—Cont

It's a Bird . . . It's a Plane . . . It's Superman
1966,Mr 30,34:1
Starr, Blaze
Burlesque on Parade 1963,D 12,48:1
Starr, Dave
Hot Corner, The 1956,Ja 26,25:2
Starr, Frances
One 1920,S 15,12:2
Easiest Way, The 1921,S 7,14:1
Easiest Way, The 1921,S 11,VI,1:1
Shore Leave 1922,Ag 9,20:2
Vaudeville (Palace) 1925,Ap 7,16:3
Vaudeville (Palace) 1925,S 29,31:2
Colette 1925,S 29,31:2
Shelf, The 1926,Jl 4,VII,3:2
Shelf, The 1926,S 28,31:1
Vaudeville (Palace) 1927,My 24,23:1
Immoral Isabella 1927,O 28,20:3
Diplomacy 1928,My 29,16:3
Diplomacy 1928,Je 3,VIII,1:1
Autumn Violins 1929,F 10,IX,2:1
Lake, The 1933,D 19,26:3
Lake, The 1933,D 27,24:2
Lake, The 1934,Ja 7,X,1:1
Moor Born 1934,Ap 4,26:4
Moor Born 1934,Ap 8,X,2:7
Lady Jane 1934,S 11,24:2
Field of Ermine 1935,F 9,10:4
Stardust 1935,Jl 17,22:4
Good, The 1938,O 6,27:2
Claudia 1941,F 13,24:2
Claudia 1942,My 25,11:3
Young and Fair, The 1948,N 23,35:2
Long Days, The 1951,Ap 21,10:5
Sacred Flame, The 1952,O 8,35:2
Ladies of the Corridor, The 1953,O 22,33:5
Ladies of the Corridor, The 1953,N 1,II,1:1
Starr, Frances (Playwright)
Autumn Violins 1929,F 10,IX,2:1
Starr, Jack
Vaudeville (Loew's State) 1932,Jl 18,9:7
Starr, Jane
It Pays to Sin 1933,N 4,18:6
Starr, Jean
Keep Shufflin' 1928,F 28,18:3
Starr, John
All's Well That Ends Well 1966,Je 17,39:1
Richard III 1966,Ag 11,26:1
Starr, Manya (Producer)
Whisper to Me 1960,N 22,38:6
Starr, Mark
Mill Shadows 1932,F 29,20:7
Starr, Monique (Costume Designer)
Wonderful World of Burlesque, The
1965,Ap 29,38:1
Starr, Muriel
John Hawthorne 1921,Ja 24,16:1
Dream Child 1934,Jl 31,20:2
Star-Wagon, The 1937,S 30,18:5
On the Rocks 1938,Je 16,20:2
Case History 1938,O 22,15:2
Velvet Glove, The 1949,O 27,26:2
Starr, Robert
Adrienne 1923,My 29,10:4
Starr, Roger
Macbeth 1955,O 20,42:2
Midsummer Night's Dream, A 1956,Ja 14,12:2
Twelfth Night 1957,Ja 5,12:2
Julius Caesar 1957,O 24,39:1
Mandragola 1958,My 29,23:2
Starr, Sally
Scandals 1924,Jl 1,16:1
LeMaire's Affairs 1927,Mr 29,22:4
Optimists, The 1928,Ja 31,28:2
Angels Don't Kiss 1932,Ap 6,22:5
One More Honeymoon 1934,Ap 2,13:5
Broadway Interlude 1934,Ap 20,16:3
Starr, Vicki
Dear Judas 1947,O 6,26:4
Starrett, Charles
Star of Bengal 1929,S 26,27:2
Claire Adams 1929,N 20,26:3
Starrett, Ken (Costume Designer)
Hobo 1961,Ap 11,41:2
Starrett, Ken (Lighting Director)
Hedda Gabler 1960,N 10,61:1
Starrit, Charles
Courage 1927,Ja 20,20:1
Stasheff, Mr
Man Without Money, A 1929,N 3,27:4
Stasney, Dorothy
Me, Candido! 1956,O 16,36:2
Staten, George (Producer)
Stepping Sisters 1930,Ap 23,24:2
Paging Danger 1931,F 27,19:2
Devil's Host, The 1931,N 20,27:2
Stathatou, N
Screwball, The 1957,My 25,24:7
Statler Twins
Sons o' Fun 1941,D 2,28:2
Stattel, Robert
Cherry Orchard, The 1960,Je 4,17:2
Man and Superman 1960,Ag 17,35:3

Stattel, Robert—Cont

When I Was a Child 1960,D 9,38:1
Don Carlos 1962,F 28,27:5
Storm, The 1962,Mr 31,17:2
Knight From Olmedo, The 1962,N 26,36:2
Taming of the Shrew, The 1963,Mr 8,9:1
Alchemist, The 1964,S 15,33:1
Danton's Death 1965,O 22,46:1
Country Wife, The 1965,D 10,58:2
Titus Andronicus 1967,Ag 10,43:2
Iphigenia in Aulis 1967,N 22,40:2
Ergo 1968,Mr 4,29:1
Henry IV, Part I 1968,Je 30,54:7
Henry IV, Part II 1968,Jl 2,33:1
Romeo and Juliet 1968,Ag 16,19:1
King Lear 1968,N 8,43:1
Patriot for Me, A 1969,O 6,58:1
Persians, The 1970,Ap 16,53:1

Statz, Mary
Tree Grows in Brooklyn, A 1951,Ap 20,24:3

Stauber, Mary
Americana 1928,O 31,28:2
Black Crook, The 1929,Mr 12,26:5

Stauch, George
Henry V 1965,Je 29,27:2
Sunset 1966,My 13,34:1
Drums in the Night 1967,My 18,54:1

Stauffer, Blaire
Fortuna 1962,Ja 4,26:1
As You Like It 1963,Jl 17,19:2

Stauffer, Richard
Fantasticks, The 1960,My 4,55:2

Staunton, Pamela
Unto Such Glory 1937,My 7,28:2

Staup, Jacqueline
Cantatrice Chauve, La 1962,Ja 16,30:1

Stavers, William
Critic, The 1965,Jl 26,15:2

Stavianik, Edd
Professor Bernhardi 1968,Mr 20,38:1

Stavis, Barrie (Playwright)
Sun and I, The 1933,Ap 4,15:2
Sun and I, The 1937,F 27,9:5
Lamp at Midnight 1947,D 22,29:2
Sun and I, The 1949,Mr 21,18:4
Man Who Never Died, The 1958,N 22,27:2
Harpers Ferry 1967,Je 6,52:2

Stavis, Leona (Playwright)
Sun and I, The 1933,Ap 4,15:2
Sun and I, The 1937,F 27,9:5
Sun and I, The 1949,Mr 21,18:4

Stavisky, Lotte
Joan of Lorraine 1946,N 19,40:2
Harry, Noon and Night 1965,My 6,44:1

Stavro, Sidney
War 1929,S 19,37:3
Miracle at Verdun 1931,Mr 17,34:6
One More Genius 1936,Ag 11,24:6

Stavro, Sidney (Director)
War 1929,S 19,37:3
Enchanted Prince, The: A 1932 Musical Fantasy 1931,D 29,27:1

Stavro, Sidney (Playwright)
Enchanted Prince, The: A 1932 Musical Fantasy 1931,D 29,27:1

Staw, Ryzard
Labyrinth, The 1965,Ja 6,32:1
Woman, The 1965,Ja 6,32:1
Nightmare, The 1965,Ja 6,32:1
Book, The 1965,Ja 6,32:1
Kernel and the Shell, The 1965,Ja 6,32:1
Jacob and the Angel 1965,Ja 6,32:1
Post Office, The 1965,Ja 6,32:1
Jaselka 1965,Ja 6,32:1

Staw, Sala
Mary Stuart 1956,Ap 28,10:2
Tonight We Improvise 1959,N 7,27:4
Five Posts in the Market Place 1961,Mr 6,30:1
Five Queens 1963,S 11,46:2

Staw, Sala (Playwright)
Five Queens 1963,S 11,46:2

Stayman, G B
Shannons of Broadway, The 1927,S 27,30:4

Stayton, Frank (Playwright)
Mixed Doubles 1927,Ap 27,22:3

Stead, Emily
Little Jessie James 1923,Ag 16,10:4

Steadman, Ross
Seven Mirrors 1945,O 26,17:2

Stearne, Eric (Scenic Designer)
Gift of Fury, A 1958,Mr 24,21:4

Stearns, Bessie
Bursting the Barriers 1930,My 7,25:1

Stearns, Elizabeth (Lighting Director)
Five Queens 1963,S 11,46:2

Stearns, Elizabeth (Miscellaneous)
Secret Concubine, The 1960,Mr 22,29:2
Five Evenings 1963,My 10,37:3

Stearns, Elizabeth Winslow (Director)
Immortality, Ltd 1938,Mr 6,II,2:3

Stearns, George
Electra 1932,Ja 9,21:4

Stearns, James Hart (Costume Designer)
Danton's Death 1965,O 22,46:1

Country Wife, The 1965,D 10,58:2
Caucasian Chalk Circle, The 1966,Mr 25,35:1
Alchemist, The 1966,O 14,48:1
Yerma 1966,O 9,60:1
East Wind, The 1967,F 10,30:1
Galileo 1967,Ap 14,31:1
Galileo 1967,Ap 23,II,1:1
Halfway up the Tree 1967,N 8,52:1
Cyrano de Bergerac 1968,Ap 26,30:1
Miser, The 1969,My 9,35:1
Disintegration of James Cherry, The 1970,Ja 30,33:3
Amphitryon 1970,My 29,13:1

Stearns, James Hart (Miscellaneous)
Amphitryon 1970,My 29,13:1

Stearns, James Hart (Scenic Designer)
Country Wife, The 1965,D 10,58:2
Caucasian Chalk Circle, The 1966,Mr 25,35:1
Alchemist, The 1966,O 14,48:1
Alchemist, The 1969,Je 12,51:1
Amphitryon 1970,My 29,13:1

Stearns, John
Night Music 1940,F 23,18:2
Good Neighbor 1941,O 22,26:2

Stearns, Johnny
One Touch of Venus 1943,O 8,14:1
Are You With It? 1945,N 12,17:3

Stearns, L Lawrence
Bursting the Barriers 1930,My 7,25:1

Stearns, Roger
New Faces 1934,Mr 16,24:5
You Never Know 1938,S 22,26:3
Stars in Your Eyes 1939,F 10,18:2
Barretts of Wimpole Street, The 1945,Mr 27,23:6

Stebbins, Rowland (Miscellaneous)
On Stage 1935,O 30,16:6
White Horse Inn 1936,O 2,28:5

Stebbins, Rowland (Playwright)
Green Pastures, The 1935,Mr 24,VIII,1:1

Stebbins, Rowland (Producer)
Green Pastures, The 1931,Mr 1,VIII,1:1
Mr Whistler 1931,D 6,VIII,2:6
Red Planet 1932,D 19,19:2
Green Pastures, The 1933,O 5,24:5
Green Pastures, The 1933,O 22,IX,1:6
Tight Britches 1934,S 12,26:2
Lost Horizons 1934,O 16,31:2
Green Pastures, The 1935,F 27,16:2
Antony and Cleopatra 1937,N 11,30:2
Merely Murder 1937,D 4,21:4
Patriots, The 1943,Ja 30,11:2
Patriots, The 1943,F 7,II,1:1
Patriots, The 1943,D 21,22:5
Flamingo Road 1946,Mr 20,18:2

Steber, Eleanor
Where's Charley? 1966,My 26,57:1
Sound of Music, The 1967,Ap 27,52:1

Stebert, Charles
Colette 1970,My 7,60:1

Steck, Hazel
Maggie Flynn 1968,O 24,52:1

Steck, Olga
Fables 1922,F 7,12:2
Sue, Dear 1922,Jl 11,16:2
Springtime of Youth 1922,O 27,15:1
Ziegfeld Follies 1923,O 22,17:2
China Rose 1925,Ja 20,18:1
Matinee Girl, The 1926,F 2,20:3
Vaudeville (Palace) 1926,Mr 23,24:3
Robin Hood 1929,N 20,26:5
Serenade, The 1930,Mr 5,26:7

Steckel, Leonhard
Mississippi 1931,Ja 11,VIII,1:6

Steckler, Roy P (Miscellaneous)
Laura 1947,Je 27,16:1

Steckler, S P (Miscellaneous)
Laura 1947,Je 27,16:1

Stecko, Joseph (Miscellaneous)
Leave It to Jane 1959,My 26,30:2

Stecko, Joseph (Musical Director)
Leave It to Jane 1959,My 26,30:2
Kittiwake Island 1960,O 13,43:1
Hi, Paisano 1961,O 2,36:2
Riverwind 1962,D 14,5:5
Secret Life of Walter Mitty, The 1964,O 27,44:5

Stedhoff, Joost
Kleinburgerhochzeit, Die 1970,N 25,25:1

Stedman, Al
Vaudeville (Palace) 1923,O 30,16:1

Stedman, Fanny
Vaudeville (Palace) 1923,O 30,16:1

Steeger, Henry
Fratricide Punished 1925,Ap 21,19:1
Romio and Julietta 1925,Ap 21,19:1

Steel, Amanda
Love's Labour's Lost 1953,F 5,20:3
Cretan Woman, The 1954,Jl 8,18:2
Clandestine Marriage, The 1954,O 4,23:2

Steel, John
Ziegfeld Follies 1920,Je 23,14:1
Irving Berlin's New Music Box Revue 1922,O 24,18:1
Music Box Revue 1923,S 24,5:3

Steel, John—Cont

Vaudeville (Palace) 1927,N 1,20:3
Vaudeville (Palace) 1928,O 23,32:5

Steel, Lewis (Lighting Director)
Orpheus Descending 1959,O 6,45:2

Steele, Amanda
Evening With G B S, An; O'Flaherty, V C 1957,F 19,35:7
An Evening With G B S; Press Cuttings 1957,F 19,35:7

Steele, Arthur
Makropoulos Secret, The 1926,Ja 22,12:4

Steele, Bernard (Director)
House Unguarded 1929,Ja 16,22:2
Devil's Host, The 1931,N 20,27:2
Scorpion, The 1933,N 28,28:4

Steele, Bernard (Producer)
House Unguarded 1929,Ja 16,22:2

Steele, Bill
Noah 1954,O 11,32:2
Open 24 Hours 1969,F 12,31:1
Satisfaction Guaranteed 1969,F 12,31:1

Steele, Bobbie
Sweet Land of Liberty 1929,S 24,29:2

Steele, Byron
Singing Girl, The 1952,Je 4,31:8

Steele, Cathy
Ice Capades 1957,S 5,33:2
Ice Capades 1960,S 1,30:1
Ice Capades 1961,Ag 31,24:4
Ice Capades 1962,Ag 30,34:1
Ice Capades 1963,Ag 29,37:2
Ice Capades 1964,Ag 27,27:2
Ice Capades 1966,Je 2,50:2
Ice Capades 1967,Je 2,33:1
Ice Capades 1969,Ja 8,42:1

Steele, David
Lovely Ladies, Kind Gentlemen 1970,D 29,38:1

Steele, Dorothy
Tinker's Dam 1943,Ja 29,22:2
Miser, The 1950,Mr 27,19:5

Steele, Eleanor
Orpheus in Hades 1930,D 16,30:1
Chocolate Soldier, The 1932,F 9,30:3

Steele, George S (Miscellaneous)
Fresh Fields 1936,F 11,19:2

Steele, Helen
Veils 1928,Mr 14,28:5

Steele, Jean
Passing Show of 1923, The 1923,Je 15,24:6

Steele, John
Midnight Frolic 1920,Ag 4,7:1

Steele, John William
This Mad Whirl 1937,Ja 10,II,4:8

Steele, Lewis
R U R 1942,D 4,30:2

Steele, Marjorie
Sabrina Fair 1954,Ag 5,18:1

Steele, Michael
Sabrina Fair 1953,N 12,37:1

Steele, Owen (Playwright)
Trouble in July 1949,D 2,36:2

Steele, Porter (Composer)
Falstaff 1928,D 26,14:2

Steele, Richard
Wilson in the Promise Land 1970,Ja 11,78:1
Wilson in the Promise Land 1970,My 27,41:1

Steele, Robert L (Lighting Director)
Penny Friend, The 1966,D 27,46:1
By Jupiter 1967,Ja 20,28:2

Steele, Robert L (Producer)
Spiro Who? 1969,My 19,55:1

Steele, Susan
World We Live In, The 1922,N 1,16:1

Steele, Tommy
Half a Sixpence 1965,Ap 26,38:2

Steele, Vernon
Hole in the Wall, The 1920,Mr 27,11:1
In His Arms 1924,O 14,23:1
Ladies of the Evening 1924,D 24,11:2
Importance of Being Earnest, The 1926,My 4,30:1
Ladder, The 1926,O 23,15:1
So Am I 1928,Ja 28,9:1
Pirate, The 1929,Ap 21,IX,1:4
Wonder Bar, The 1931,Mr 18,23:4
Roof, The 1931,O 31,22:4

Steele, Wes
Tarot 1970,D 12,19:1

Steele, Wilbur Daniel (Original Author)
When Hell Froze 1930,O 5,IX,4:6

Steele, Wilbur Daniel (Playwright)
Giant's Stair, The 1927,My 4,29:1
When Hell Froze 1930,O 5,IX,4:6
Any Woman 1934,Ag 28,24:4
Post Road 1934,D 5,28:3
Post Road 1935,Jl 23,24:3
How Beautiful With Shoes 1935,N 29,24:1
Post Road 1936,Ag 5,15:4
Post Road 1949,Ap 28,27:3

Steele, William
Alexander Hamilton 1949,Mr 30,29:2

Steele-Reed, Richard
Cuban Thing, The 1968,S 25,36:2

teell, Susan
If You Get It, Do You Want It? 1938,D 1,28:2
On the Town 1944,D 29,11:4
Cellar and the Well, The 1950,D 11,30:2
Music in the Air 1951,O 9,32:2
Grass Harp, The 1952,Mr 28,26:2
Madam Will You Walk 1953,D 2,2:4
Madam Will You Walk 1953,D 20,II,3:1
All That Fall 1957,O 8,41:2
teelman, Ronald
Prince of Peasantmania 1970,F 22,88:1
teen, Jan (Director)
Get Thee to Canterbury 1969,Ja 26,74:1
teen, Jan (Playwright)
Get Thee to Canterbury 1969,Ja 26,74:1
teen, Mike
Desk Set, The 1955,O 25,36:7
teen, Sam
Doodle Dandy of the U S A 1942,O 19,15:2
Allegro 1947,O 11,10:2
teenshorne, Aage
Judgment Day 1934,S 13,26:4
Big Blow 1938,O 3,11:2
American Landscape 1938,D 5,19:2
Sea Dogs 1939,N 7,30:3
Two on an Island 1940,Ja 23,17:2
teep, Miriam
Candida 1925,D 19,14:2
teere, Clifton
Merry Widow, The 1961,O 27,28:2
Vagabond King, The 1961,N 24,36:1
Gondoliers, The 1961,D 8,44:1
teers, Carol
Twilight Walk 1951,S 25,25:4
teeve, Marion
Comedy of Women, A 1929,S 14,17:4
Stefan, Bronia
Don Juan; Feast With the Statue, The 1956,Ja 4,21:4
Too Late the Phalarope 1956,O 12,35:1
Trial of Dmitri Karamazov, The 1958,Ja 28,30:1
Stefan, Marina
Dracula Sabbat 1970,O 2,28:2
Stefani, Roger (Choreographer)
Vie Parisienne, La 1964,Mr 11,34:2
Stefanidou, Smaro
Screwball, The 1957,My 25,24:7
Stefanini, Niska
Meet My Sister 1930,D 31,11:1
Steffan, Ernst (Composer)
Toni aus Wien, Die 1931,Ag 30,VIII,2:2
Katharina 1932,O 2,IX,3:1
Steffan, Geary Jr
Hollywood Ice Revue 1943,Ja 24,II,1:1
Steffan, Sophia
Mikado, The 1959,O 2,24:1
Pirates of Penzance, The 1960,O 7,29:1
Pirates of Penzance, The 1961,Ja 20,24:5
Gondoliers, The 1961,Ja 26,33:2
Steffans, Peggy
Red Roses for Me 1961,N 28,41:1
Steffe, Edwin
Happy Town 1959,O 8,49:2
Anya 1965,N 30,48:1
Canterbury Tales; Pilgrims, The 1969,F 4,34:1
Cry for Us All 1970,Ap 9,48:2
Steffen, Albert (Playwright)
Friedens Tragoedie 1936,N 17,34:4
Peace Tragedy 1937,Ja 3,X,3:1
Steger, Carlton
Keating 1927,D 26,26:6
Steger, Julia
Earl Carroll's Vanities 1925,Jl 7,24:1
Stegman, Diana
Orange Blossoms 1922,S 20,18:1
Kid Boots 1924,Ja 1,21:3
Stegmeyer, William (Miscellaneous)
Ziegfeld Follies 1957,Mr 2,19:2
Joyful Noise, A 1966,D 16,57:1
Stehl, George
Adding Machine, The 1923,Mr 20,24:1
Stehli, Edgar
Treasure, The 1920,O 5,13:1
John Hawthorne 1921,Ja 24,16:1
Liliom 1921,Ap 21,18:1
Cloister, The 1921,Je 6,16:3
He Who Gets Slapped 1922,Ja 10,15:1
From Morn to Midnight 1922,My 22,17:2
Hamlet 1922,N 17,14:1
Launzi 1923,O 11,16:3
Hamlet 1923,N 27,23:6
Crime in the Whistler Room, The 1924,O 10,22:2
S S Glencairn 1924,N 4,31:4
Patience 1924,D 30,15:1
Michel Auclair 1925,Mr 5,23:1
Love for Love 1925,Ap 5,IX,1:2
Love for Love 1925,S 15,29:3
Last Night of Don Juan, The 1925,N 10,23:2
Fountain, The 1925,D 11,26:1
You Can't Win 1926,F 17,12:1
East Lynne 1926,Mr 11,18:4
Ladder, The 1926,O 23,15:1
Strange Prince, The 1926,D 8,24:2

Ladder, The 1927,O 7,24:2
Mystery Square 1929,Ap 5,28:3
Channel Road, The 1929,O 18,24:2
At the Bottom 1930,Ja 10,24:3
Ada Beats the Drum 1930,My 9,20:4
Venetian Glass Nephew, The 1931,F 24,26:3
Pillars of Society, The 1931,O 15,19:1
Steel 1931,N 19,26:5
Papavert 1931,D 30,25:1
Mr Papavert 1932,Ja 23,18:6
Birthright 1933,N 22,22:3
House of Remsen 1934,Ap 3,26:4
Daughters of Atreus 1936,O 15,33:1
Blow Ye Winds 1937,S 24,17:4
Something for Nothing 1937,D 10,33:5
Greatest Show on Earth, The 1938,Ja 6,22:2
Eye on the Sparrow 1938,My 4,26:3
Brown Danube, The 1939,My 18,30:4
Passenger to Bali, A 1940,Mr 15,26:2
Love for Love 1940,Je 4,19:5
Arsenic and Old Lace 1941,Ja 11,13:2
Duke in Darkness, The 1944,Ja 25,15:2
Church Street 1948,F 10,27:2
Bravo! 1948,N 12,31:2
Happy Time, The 1950,Ja 25,24:1
Mid-Summer 1953,Ja 22,19:1
Wooden Dish, The 1955,O 7,20:1
Sin of Pat Muldoon, The 1957,Mr 14,35:1
Semi-Detached 1960,Mr 11,20:2
Devils, The 1965,N 17,51:2
Those That Play the Clowns 1966,N 25,48:1
Stehli, Edgar (Playwright)
Ladder, The 1927,O 7,24:2
Steidman, Joel
Tom Paine 1969,Mr 30,71:2
Steiger, Jimmy
Scandals 1920,Je 8,9:1
Passing Show of 1924, The 1924,S 4,13:4
White Lights 1927,O 12,30:4
Steiger, Rod
Stevedore 1949,F 23,30:2
John Brown 1950,My 4,32:7
Night Music 1951,Ap 9,29:6
Seagulls Over Sorrento 1952,S 12,18:4
Rashomon 1959,Ja 28,36:2
Rashomon 1959,F 8,II,1:1
Moby Dick 1962,N 4,82:6
Moby Dick 1962,N 29,45:1
Steimann, Viola
Myself and I 1929,Ag 31,13:6
Stein, Abe
Of Thee I Sing 1952,My 6,34:2
Stein, Ben (Producer)
Jade God, The 1929,My 14,28:3
Black Tower 1932,Ja 12,29:2
Invitation to a Murder 1934,My 18,26:3
Bet Your Life 1937,Ap 6,20:2
Stein, Geoffrey
Hedda Gabler 1920,O 5,12:2
Fool, The 1922,O 24,18:1
Stein, Gertrude
Street Singers 1938,D 12,25:6
Queen Mother 1938,D 26,29:4
Schwartse Mamme 1939,Ja 16,11:3
Farblondjete Honeymoon 1955,S 27,42:1
Stein, Gertrude (Lyricist)
Four Saints in Three Acts 1952,Ap 17,35:1
Stein, Gertrude (Playwright)
Yes is for a Very Young Man 1949,Je 7,27:2
Doctor Faustus Lights the Lights 1951,D 3,23:4
Yes is for a Very Young Man 1963,Mr 6,7:5
In Circles 1967,O 14,12:1
In Circles 1967,N 5,II,1:7
In Circles 1968,Je 28,36:1
Gertrude Stein's First Reader 1969,D 16,56:1
Stein, Gisela
Don Carlos 1964,N 25,40:1
Stein, Henrietta (Producer)
Exception and the Rule, The 1965,My 21,19:1
Prodigal Son, The 1965,My 21,19:1
Stein, Irving (Miscellaneous)
Cocktails of 1934 1934,My 5,22:1
Stein, Joseph (Miscellaneous)
Lend an Ear 1948,D 17,38:2
Alive and Kicking 1950,Ja 18,25:5
Stein, Joseph (Playwright)
Mrs Gibsons' Boys 1949,My 5,35:2
Plain and Fancy 1955,Ja 28,14:2
Plain and Fancy 1955,F 6,II,1:1
Mr Wonderful 1956,Mr 23,23:2
Body Beautiful, The 1958,Ja 24,15:2
Juno 1959,Mr 10,41:1
Juno 1959,Mr 15,II,1:1
Take Me Along 1959,O 23,22:2
Enter Laughing 1963,Mr 15,8:1
Enter Laughing 1963,Je 16,II,1:1
Fiddler on the Roof 1964,S 23,56:2
Fiddler on the Roof 1964,O 4,II,1:1
Fiddler on the Roof 1965,Je 9,40:1
Fiddler on the Roof 1967,F 17,50:1
Fiddler on the Roof 1967,S 7,50:1
Fiddler on the Roof 1967,S 28,59:2
Zorba 1968,N 18,58:1

Stein, Joseph (Playwright)—Cont
Fiddler on the Roof 1969,Je 26,47:1
Fiddler on the Roof 1969,Ag 8,10:2
Fiddler on the Roof 1969,N 16,82:6
Fiddler on the Roof 1970,F 28,20:1
Stein, Joseph (Producer)
We Bombed in New Haven 1968,O 17,51:1
Stein, Julian
Fantasticks, The 1960,My 4,55:2
Stein, Julian (Composer)
Chic 1959,My 19,28:2
Pimpernel! 1964,Ja 7,26:6
Stein, Julian (Miscellaneous)
Smiling the Boy Fell Dead 1961,Ap 20,28:1
Sap of Life, The 1961,O 3,44:1
Fortuna 1962,Ja 4,26:1
Stein, Julian (Musical Director)
She Shall Have Music 1959,Ja 23,18:4
Fantasticks, The 1960,My 4,55:2
Valmouth 1960,O 7,29:1
Smiling the Boy Fell Dead 1961,Ap 20,28:1
Sap of Life, The 1961,O 3,44:1
Half-Past Wednesday 1962,Ap 7,16:2
Anything Goes 1962,My 16,35:1
Yearling, The 1965,D 11,25:1
How to Be a Jewish Mother 1967,D 29,18:1
Education of H*Y*M*A*N K*A*P*L*A*N, The 1968,Ap 5,57:1
Blood Red Roses 1970,Mr 23,48:1
Stein, Kenneth J (Producer)
Dumbbell People in a Barbell World 1962,F 15,25:1
Stein, Leo (Lyricist)
Wiener Blut 1964,S 12,14:1
Stein, Leo (Original Author)
Merry Widow, The 1964,Ag 18,24:2
Stein, Leo (Playwright)
Merry Widow, The 1929,D 3,29:1
Merry Widow, The 1931,S 8,39:1
Merry Widow, The 1932,F 21,VIII,23:3
Wiener Blut 1932,S 4,IX,2:2
Merry Widow, The 1942,Jl 16,22:1
Merry Widow, The 1961,O 27,28:2
Stein, Leonard (Miscellaneous)
Fashion 1959,Ja 21,27:1
Stein, Michael
Falstaff 1966,Je 20,27:1
Murder in the Cathedral 1966,Je 21,38:1
Julius Caesar 1966,Je 24,29:2
Stein, Monroe
Alt Heidelberg 1926,My 31,10:5
Stein, Muriel (Costume Designer)
Shadow Years, The 1957,Ja 9,26:2
Stein, Paul
Peace on Earth 1933,N 30,39:2
Sailors of Cattaro 1934,D 11,28:4
Take a Giant Step 1956,S 26,30:1
Stein, Phil
Wonderful Journey 1946,D 26,30:2
Stein, Phil (Miscellaneous)
Belafonte at the Palace 1959,D 16,55:1
Stein, Sol (Playwright)
Shadow of My Enemy, A 1957,D 12,35:4
Stein, Susan
Take Her, She's Mine 1961,D 22,19:1
Stein, William
When in Rome 1934,F 28,22:6
War and Peace 1942,My 22,26:3
Steinbart, Kurt
Romeo and Juliet 1935,D 24,10:2
Saint Joan 1936,Mr 10,27:4
Hamlet 1936,O 9,30:2
Steinbeck, Jayson
Yeomen of the Guard, The 1961,Ap 28,23:1
Mikado, The 1961,My 5,23:1
Grand Duke, The 1961,My 12,24:1
Iolanthe 1961,My 26,29:6
Steinbeck, John (Original Author)
Of Mice and Men 1937,N 24,20:5
Of Mice and Men 1937,D 12,XI,3:1
Tortilla Flat 1938,Ja 13,16:2
Moon Is Down, The 1942,Ap 8,22:2
Pipe Dream 1955,D 1,44:1
Pipe Dream 1955,D 11,II,5:1
Of Mice and Men 1958,D 5,38:1
Steinbeck, John (Playwright)
Of Mice and Men 1937,N 24,20:5
Of Mice and Men 1937,D 12,XI,3:1
Of Mice and Men 1939,Ap 30,XI,3:5
Moon Is Down, The 1942,Ap 8,22:2
Moon Is Down, The 1942,Ap 12,VIII,1:1
Moon Is Down, The 1942,My 10,VIII,1:1
Moon Is Down, The 1943,Jl 11,II,1:5
Burning Bright 1950,O 19,40:2
Burning Bright 1950,O 29,II,1:1
Burning Bright 1959,O 17,27:2
Moon Is Down, The 1963,N 15,5:2
Here's Where I Belong 1968,Mr 4,32:1
Steinberg, Ben (Musical Director)
Peter Pan 1950,Ap 25,27:2
Sandhog 1954,N 24,17:1
Steinberg, Bert (Producer)
Nobody Hears A Broken Drum 1970,Mr 20,55:1

Steinberg, David
Return of Second City in "20,000 Frozen Grenadiers," The 1966,Ap 22,36:1
Little Murders 1967,Ap 26,38:1
Carry Me Back to Morningside Heights 1968,F 28,41:1

Steinberg, Deborah
Tree Witch, The 1961,Je 5,39:4
Richard II 1961,Ag 30,25:1
Francesca da Rimini 1967,S 12,54:1

Steinberg, Harold (Playwright)
Trial of Lee Harvey Oswald, The 1967,N 6,64:1

Steinberg, Harold (Producer)
Women at the Tomb, The 1961,Ap 25,41:1
Philoktetes 1961,Ap 25,41:1

Steinberg, Herbert (Scenic Designer)
Family Portrait 1959,My 6,48:2

Steinberg, Herman
Mascaiada 1929,D 28,10:6

Steinberg, Mollie B (Director)
Sellout, The 1933,S 7,17:2

Steinberg, Mollie B (Miscellaneous)
All the Comforts of Home 1942,My 26,24:5

Steinberg, Morton
Gianni Schicci 1969,F 25,36:1

Steinberg, Mr (Playwright)
Galician Rabbi, The 1937,F 13,9:7

Steinberg, S
Oy, Is Dus a Leben!; Oh, What a Life! 1942,O 13,19:2

Steinberg, S (Playwright)
Little Cantor, The 1930,S 24,26:2

Steinberg, Samuel (Playwright)
Little Bandit 1935,Ap 19,24:2
Matinee Wife 1936,Ap 25,21:3

Steinbock, Rudolf (Director)
Maria Stuart 1968,Mr 27,38:1

Steinbrecher, Alexander (Composer)
Jux Will Er Sich Machen, Einen 1968,Ap 3,41:1

Steinbrecher, Alexander (Musical Director)
Jux Will Er Sich Machen, Einen 1968,Ap 3,41:1

Steinbrenner, George M 3d (Miscellaneous)
Applause 1970,Mr 31,35:1

Steinbrenner, George M 3d (Producer)
Not Now Darling 1970,O 30,33:1

Steinbrenner, Karl
Cradle of Willow, A 1961,D 16,20:2

Steiner, Edward G Jr (Director)
Beaux' Stratagem, The 1935,Jl 17,22:5

Steiner, Eugene
Truckline Cafe 1946,F 28,19:4
All My Sons 1947,Ja 30,21:2
Survivors, The 1948,Ja 20,27:2
As the Girls Go 1948,N 15,21:2
Season in the Sun 1950,S 29,31:2

Steiner, Goldye M
Lulu Belle 1926,F 10,20:1

Steiner, Gretchen H
Patriarch, The 1926,D 11,15:1

Steiner, Herbert
Merrily We Roll Along 1934,O 1,14:1

Steiner, Hilda
Johannes Kreisler 1922,D 25,20:3

Steiner, John
Persecution and Assassination of Marat As Performed by the Inmates of the Asylum of Charenton Under the Direction of the Marquis de Sade, The 1965,D 28,35:1

Steiner, Ludwig
Alien Corn 1933,F 21,17:2

Steiner, Max
Song of Dnieper 1946,O 26,10:5

Steiner, Paul
Henri Christophe 1945,Je 7,24:5
Captain Brassbound's Conversion 1950,D 28,21:1

Steiner, Robert (Director)
Escape This Night 1938,Ap 23,18:1

Steiner, Robert (Playwright)
Escape This Night 1938,Ap 23,18:1

Steiner, Rose
Truckline Cafe 1946,F 28,19:4

Steiner, Sigfrit
Wozzeck 1966,Ap 6,34:1
Minna von Barnhelm 1968,N 13,37:1
Schloss, Das 1968,N 20,35:3

Steinert, Alexander (Composer)
Wetward Ho 1921,Ap 22,13:2
It's Only Natural 1922,Ap 21,13:2
Romeo and Juliet 1940,My 10,27:1
Sherlock Holmes 1953,O 31,11:2

Steinfeld, Roslee
Bad Habits of 1925 1925,F 9,17:1

Steinharter, Walter (Scenic Designer)
Doctored Wife, The 1950,Jl 12,33:2
Son, The 1950,Ag 16,24:6

Steinhorn, William
Living Corpse, The 1929,D 7,19:1

Steininger, Franz (Composer)
Music in My Heart 1947,O 3,30:2

Steininger, Franz (Musical Director)
Music in My Heart 1947,O 3,30:2
Lady From Paris, The 1950,S 27,36:1

Steinkamp, Dawn
Witness for the Prosecution 1954,D 17,35:2

Steinmann, Herbert (Miscellaneous)
All in Love 1961,N 11,15:2

Steinmetz, Edward
Streets of New York, The 1934,Jl 21,14:5
Camille 1935,Jl 31,21:1
Earth Journey 1944,Ap 28,24:2
Seven Mirrors 1945,O 26,17:2

Steinmetz, Edward (Director)
Double Door 1935,Ag 21,22:2
Royal Family, The 1936,Ag 12,15:1
Whiteheaded Boy, The 1937,Ag 11,27:3

Steinmetz, Edward (Miscellaneous)
Coquette 1935,Jl 10,24:1

Steinway, Fred
One Sunday Afternoon 1933,F 16,23:5
Slight Case of Murder, A 1935,S 12,28:5

Steinway, John
Variations of 1940 1940,Ja 29,12:1

Steinway, Theodore
Variations of 1940 1940,Ja 29,12:1

Steinway, Theodore (Mrs)
Passing of the Third Floor Back, The 1924,F 8,19:4

Steinway, Theodore E
Passing of the Third Floor Back, The 1924,F 8,19:4
Nantucket Follies 1927,Jl 30,13:2

Steinwurzel, Meyer
Kibbetzers, Inc 1935,My 13,18:5

Stell, Joseph (Lighting Director)
Fourth Avenue North 1961,S 28,50:2
Backlane Center 1961,N 23,51:1
Whisper in God's Ear, A 1962,O 12,27:2
Eleventh Inheritor, The 1962,N 22,43:5

Stell, Joseph (Scenic Designer)
Fourth Avenue North 1961,S 28,50:2
Backlane Center 1961,N 23,51:1
Whisper in God's Ear, A 1962,O 12,27:2
Eleventh Inheritor, The 1962,N 22,43:5

Stembler, Sallie
Wonderful Night, A; Fledermaus, Die 1929,N 1,23:3

Stemler, Clarence
Good as Gold 1957,Mr 8,22:2

Stempel, Desiree
Champion, The 1921,Ja 4,11:1

Stenberg, Enar (Scenic Designer)
West Side Story 1965,Je 25,37:2

Stenborg, Helen
Month in the Country, A 1963,My 29,39:2
Say Nothing 1965,Ja 28,21:2
Rimers of Eldritch, The 1967,F 21,53:1

Stenerson, Cristian (Scenic Designer)
Abraham's Offering 1938,D 18,IX,4:2

Stengel, Anton
Dark Tower, The 1933,N 27,20:3

Stengel, Leni
Princess Turandot 1926,N 13,14:2
These Few Ashes 1928,O 31,28:1
Shoestring Revue 1929,N 23,19:2
Tovarich 1936,O 16,31:4
Swan Song 1946,My 16,29:2

Stenn, Mia
My Heart's in the Highlands 1950,F 18,8:4

Stenner, Stanley
Peter Pan 1954,O 21,30:2

Stenning, Arthur
Silver Box, The 1928,Ja 18,23:1
Made in France 1930,N 12,21:1
Heat Wave 1931,F 18,14:6
Melo 1931,Ap 17,26:6
Cyrano de Bergerac 1932,D 27,11:2
False Dreams, Farewell 1934,Ja 16,18:3
Hamlet 1934,D 26,19:3
Richard III 1934,D 28,24:3
Libel! 1935,D 21,10:5
Story of Mary Surratt, The 1947,F 10,25:2
Sherlock Holmes 1953,O 31,11:2

Stensel, Glenn
Sweet Bird of Youth 1959,Mr 11,39:2

Stenuf, Hedi
It Happens on Ice 1940,O 11,24:3
It Happens on Ice 1941,Ap 5,13:2
It Happens on Ice 1941,Ag 31,IX,1:1

Stenzel, Eleanor
Blue Butterfly, The 1929,F 17,29:3

Stepan, M J
Betty Behave 1927,Mr 9,28:4

Stepanek, Charles
Hot Pan 1928,F 16,14:1
Thoroughbred 1933,N 7,29:2

Stepanek, Charles (Scenic Designer)
If Love Were All 1931,N 14,14:5

Stepanek, Karel
Close Quarters 1941,Ag 17,IX,1:8
Moon Is Down, The 1943,Jl 11,II,1:5
Jacobowsky and the Colonel 1945,Je 24,II,1:3
Makropoulos Secret, The 1957,D 4,52:4

Stepanek, Karel (Scenic Designer)
Millionairess, The 1938,Ag 16,22:5

Stepanek, Lily
Jux Will Er Sich Machen, Einen 1968,Ap 3,41:1

Stepanek, M
Mr Pickwick 1931,Ja 11,VIII,3:5

Stepankowsky, W J (Translator)
Zaporogetz Za Dunayem 1937,My 9,II,5:3

Stepanova, Angelina
Cherry Orchard, The 1965,F 10,46:1
Kremlin Chimes 1965,F 25,23:1

Stephan, Atlee (Lighting Director)
Sold to the Movies; Crossing the Gap 1970,Je 18,54:2
Sold to the Movies; Life Size 1970,Je 18,54:2
Sold to the Movies; Type 424 Meet Type Oh-Oh, No! 1970,Je 18,54:2

Stephan, Frances
Little Town of Bethlehem, The 1920,D 27,11:1
Little Town of Bethlehem, The 1922,D 26,15:4

Stephana, Lian
Treasure, The 1920,O 5,13:1
John Hawthorne 1921,Ja 24,16:1

Stephani, Frederick (Playwright)
Hickory Stick 1944,My 9,15:6

Stephanya (Costume Designer)
All by Myself 1964,Je 16,47:1

Stephen
Vaudeville (Palace) 1931,Jl 13,13:4

Stephen, Atlee 3d (Lighting Director)
Getting Married 1970,Ja 20,46:1

Stephen, Edith (Choreographer)
Dream Play 1960,N 23,22:1

Stephen, John
Patriots, The 1943,Ja 30,11:2
Patriots, The 1943,D 21,22:5
Catherine Was Great 1944,Ag 3,16:1

Stephen, Robert
As You Like It 1968,Jl 6,9:1

Stephens, Billy
Vanderbilt Revue, The 1930,N 6,22:6

Stephens, Dick
Merry Widow, The 1961,O 27,28:2

Stephens, George
Runnin' Wild 1923,O 30,17:3
To Tell You the Truth 1948,Ap 19,28:6

Stephens, Grace
Roseanne 1923,D 31,9:5

Stephens, Harvey
Other Men's Wives 1929,N 13,24:4
Dishonored Lady 1930,F 5,27:1
Tomorrow and Tomorrow 1931,Ja 14,26:3
Tomorrow and Tomorrow 1931,Ja 25,VIII,1:1
Animal Kingdom, The 1932,Ja 13,26:4
Best Years 1932,S 8,16:2
Conquest 1933,F 20,11:3
Party's Over, The 1933,Mr 28,23:3
Wife Insurance 1934,Ap 13,24:5
Over Twenty-One 1944,Ja 4,20:2
Violet 1944,O 25,16:1
South Pacific 1949,Ap 8,30:2
South Pacific 1949,Ap 17,II,1:1
South Pacific 1951,Jl 10,30:5
Time Limit! 1956,Ja 25,27:2

Stephens, Jean
King and the Duke, The 1955,Je 2,25:2

Stephens, Jeanne
Wind Remains, The 1943,Mr 31,16:6

Stephens, Jerome (Miscellaneous)
Iolanthe 1955,S 28,38:1
Mikado, The 1955,S 30,20:2
Pirates of Penzance, The 1955,O 7,21:1

Stephens, John
Winter Soldiers 1942,N 30,19:2

Stephens, Kelley
Happy Hunting 1956,D 7,30:1

Stephens, Leona
Right This Way 1938,Ja 6,22:3

Stephens, Leona (Playwright)
Morning After, The 1925,Jl 28,24:2

Stephens, Murray
People on the Hill 1931,S 26,25:5
Constant Wife, The 1935,Jl 3,20:2
Holmeses of Baker Street, The 1936,D 10,34:3

Stephens, Nan Bagby (Playwright)
Roseanne 1923,D 31,9:5
Roseanne 1924,Mr 11,16:3

Stephens, Nancy Jane
Possibilities 1968,D 5,60:1

Stephens, Oatis
Joyful Noise, A 1966,D 16,57:1

Stephens, Peter John (Playwright)
Power of Dreams, A 1958,Mr 11,33:1

Stephens, Robert
Epitaph for George Dillon 1958,N 5,44:1
Epitaph for George Dillon 1958,N 16,II,1:1
Royal Hunt of the Sun, The 1964,Jl 8,40:6
Armstrong's Last Goodnight 1965,Jl 7,26:1
As You Like It 1967,O 15,II,9:3
Beaux' Stratagem, The 1970,F 10,50:2
Three Sisters, The 1970,F 12,30:1
Beaux' Stratagem, The 1970,F 22,II,1:1
Three Sisters, The 1970,F 22,II,1:1
Hedda Gabler 1970,Jl 18,12:1

Stephens, Scott
Days of Our Youth, The 1941,N 29,15:2

Stephens, Sheila
Trojan Horse, The 1940,O 31,28:3
Stephens, William
Jolly Roger, The 1923,Ag 31,10:4
Wake Up and Dream 1929,D 31,14:3
Stephens, William (Producer)
Two Seconds 1931,O 10,20:6
Stephenson, Adelbert
Tom Sawyer 1931,D 26,15:3
Stephenson, Edwin
Troilus and Cressida 1963,Je 19,40:2
Richard II 1964,Je 17,47:1
Bourgeois Gentilhomme, Le 1964,Je 18,28:2
Stephenson, Henry
Spanish Love 1920,Ag 18,6:1
Fool, The 1922,O 24,18:1
Dancing Mothers 1924,Ag 12,12:2
Pelican, The 1925,S 22,23:2
Magda 1925,D 22,18:4
Magda 1926,Ja 27,16:2
Adorable Liar, The 1926,Ag 31,15:2
Crown Prince, The 1927,Mr 24,23:2
Command to Love, The 1927,S 21,27:1
Love Duel, The 1929,Ap 16,32:3
Dancing Partner 1930,Jl 27,VIII,2:3
Dancing Partner 1930,Ag 6,24:2
Petticoat Influence 1930,D 16,34:6
Cynara 1931,N 3,31:1
Firebird 1932,N 22,25:2
Astonished Heart, The; Tonight at Eight
    1940,Ag 6,15:3
That Lady 1949,O 20,38:8
That Lady 1949,N 23,18:4
That Lady 1949,D 4,II,5:1
Stephenson, Jean
Victoria Regina 1935,D 27,15:2
Stephenson, John
Jitta's Atonement 1935,Ja 31,22:3
Stephenson, John (Producer)
Jitta's Atonement 1935,Ja 31,22:3
Stephenson, Lee
Between the Devil 1937,D 23,24:5
Stephenson, Marion
Starlight 1925,Mr 4,17:2
Antonia 1925,O 21,20:1
Man From Toronto, The 1926,Je 18,27:2
What Ann Brought Home 1927,F 22,22:2
Iron Men 1936,O 20,30:6
Stephenson, Paul
Camille 1932,N 2,23:3
Stephenson, Paul (Director)
Tomorrow's Monday 1936,Jl 16,15:6
Man Who Ate the Popomack, The 1937,Jl 28,15:1
Steplight, Randall
Texas Town 1941,Ap 30,22:3
Stepowski, Junosza
Apple Cart, The 1929,Je 15,6:2
Steppat, Ilse
Iphigenia in Aulis; Agamemnon's Death; Electra;
    Iphigenia in Delphi 1962,N 11,82:4
Steppe, Harry
O K 1925,My 4,16:1
Stept, Sam H (Composer)
Music Hall Varieties 1932,N 23,15:3
Shady Lady 1933,Jl 6,26:3
Yokel Boy 1939,Jl 7,12:2
Stept, Sam H (Lyricist)
Music Hall Varieties 1932,N 23,15:3
Shady Lady 1933,Jl 6,26:3
Stept, Sammy (Composer)
Michael Todd's Peep Show 1950,Je 29,37:2
Stept, Sammy (Lyricist)
Michael Todd's Peep Show 1950,Je 29,37:2
Sterbini, Alessandro A
Casa di Tutti, La; Everybody's Home 1932,D 5,21:4
Sterck, Wilhelm (Playwright)
Experience Unnecessary 1931,D 31,16:2
Steris, Dimitra
Electra 1958,My 10,17:7
Electra 1962,Mr 22,42:1
Trojan Women, The 1963,D 24,7:6
Sterling, Ada (Playwright)
Nica 1926,Ja 26,19:1
Sterling, Dolly
Bunk of 1926 1926,Ap 23,25:2
Sterling, G L
Monkey's Paw, The 1922,D 30,13:4
Sterling, George
Shakespeare's Merchant 1939 1939,Ja 10,16:3
Sterling, George (Translator)
Everyman 1941,My 9,19:2
Sterling, Harriet
Woman of Bronze, The 1920,S 8,9:2
Great Music 1924,O 6,24:1
Woman of Bronze, The 1927,Je 16,25:4
American, Very Early 1934,Ja 31,21:2
Field of Ermine 1935,F 9,10:4
Sterling, J Warren
Master Builder, The 1925,N 11,27:1
Sterling, Jan
Rugged Path, The 1945,N 12,17:2
Dunnigan's Daughter 1945,D 27,16:1
This, Too, Shall Pass 1946,My 1,32:4

Present Laughter 1946,O 30,31:2
Two Blind Mice 1949,Mr 3,32:2
Small War on Murray Hill 1957,Ja 4,19:1
Small War on Murray Hill 1957,Ja 13,II,1:1
Perfect Setup, The 1962,O 25,47:1
Once for the Asking 1963,N 21,42:2
Friday Night; Mary Agnes Is Thirty-Five
    1965,F 9,42:5
Friday Night; River, The 1965,F 9,42:5
Sterling, Jane
Bachelor Born 1938,Ja 26,26:3
When We Are Married 1939,D 26,22:3
Grey Farm 1940,My 4,12:7
This Rock 1943,F 19,23:2
Sterling, Joseph
Bronx Express 1922,Ap 27,12:2
Sterling, Julie
Orchids Preferred 1937,My 12,26:5
Sterling, L
Chivalry 1925,D 16,22:3
Sterling, Margot
Father Malachy's Miracle 1937,N 18,26:4
Sterling, Mary (Miscellaneous)
Wuziz! 1970,O 2,25:2
Sterling, Nora
School for Scandal, The 1925,O 24,19:1
Sterling, Oscar
Guest in the House 1942,F 25,25:2
Sterling, Philip
Silk Stockings 1955,F 25,17:3
Victims of Duty 1960,Ja 20,26:1
Much Ado About Nothing 1961,Jl 7,17:1
Richard II 1961,Ag 30,25:1
Opening of a Window, The 1961,S 26,32:2
Henry IV, Part I 1962,Je 18,20:4
Richard II 1962,Je 18,20:2
Party for Divorce, A 1966,O 12,37:1
Party on Greenwich Avenue, The 1967,My 11,52:1
Peddler, The 1967,D 9,62:1
Summertree 1968,Mr 4,29:1
Sterling, Richard
My Aunt From Ypsilanti 1923,My 2,22:6
Expressing Willie 1924,Ap 17,22:1
Something to Brag About 1925,Ag 14,14:3
Triumphant Bachelor, The 1927,S 16,21:1
Mirrors 1928,Ja 19,17:1
My Girl Friday! 1929,F 13,20:2
Ladies Don't Lie 1929,O 11,36:3
Alien Corn 1933,F 21,17:2
Alien Corn 1933,F 26,IX,1:1
Ah, Wilderness! 1933,O 3,28:2
Touch of Brimstone, A 1935,S 23,20:1
Co-Respondent Unknown 1936,F 12,24:4
Happy Ending 1936,Jl 15,14:3
Behind the Red Lights 1937,Ja 14,17:4
On Borrowed Time 1938,F 4,16:4
Life With Father 1939,N 9,26:2
That Lady 1949,N 23,18:4
First Lady 1952,My 29,18:5
Sterling, Robert
Gramercy Ghost 1951,Ap 27,20:2
Roman Candle 1960,F 4,34:2
Sterling, Robert (Producer)
Decision 1929,My 28,37:3
Lady Luck 1936,Ap 16,21:2
Sterling, Roy
Wind Is Ninety, The 1945,Je 22,12:2
Young Man's Fancy, A 1947,Ap 30,33:2
Sterling, S Suissabell
Mikado, The; Town of Titipu, The 1927,S 19,30:1
Sterling, Susan
Mister Malatesta 1923,F 27,14:2
Sterling, Sybil
Iolanthe 1926,Ap 20,24:2
Pirates of Penzance, The; Slave of Duty, The
    1926,D 7,25:1
Sterling, Thomas (Original Author)
Mr Fox of Venice 1959,Ap 16,28:1
Sterling, Warren
Sex 1926,Ap 27,22:4
Tales of Rigo 1927,My 31,25:3
Nona 1932,O 5,26:4
Stern, Alan (Composer)
Whistling Wizard and the Sultan of Tuffet
    1970,F 1,70:1
Stern, Alan (Playwright)
Whistling Wizard and the Sultan of Tuffet
    1970,F 1,70:1
Ali Baba and the Forty Thieves 1970,D 29,40:1
Stern, Alfred (Costume Designer)
I Must Love Someone 1939,F 8,18:7
Stern, Alfred (Producer)
Dinny and the Witches 1959,D 10,53:3
Stern, Allan (Miscellaneous)
Delightful Season, A 1960,S 29,30:1
Stern, Allan (Playwright)
Bil and Cora Baird's Marionette Theater
    1955,D 27,29:2
Bil and Cora Baird's Marionette Theater; Ali Baba
    and the Forty Thieves 1956,S 3,10:1
Stern, Arthur
Seven Against One 1930,My 7,25:1

Stern, Arthur (Playwright)
Henry's Harem 1926,S 14,25:2
Stern, August L (Playwright)
Hired Husband 1932,Je 4,9:5
Stern, August L (Producer)
Hired Husband 1932,Je 4,9:5
Stern, Bill
Sun Field, The 1942,D 10,33:2
Stern, Charles H
One on the House 1941,Mr 30,I,47:3
Stern, Elma (Lyricist)
Bathsheba 1947,Mr 27,40:2
Stern, Ernest (Costume Designer)
Casanova 1928,N 4,IX,2:1
Merry Widow, The 1929,F 17,IX,2:3
Three Musketeers 1929,O 13,IX,4:7
Bitter Sweet 1929,N 6,30:2
Boy David, The 1936,N 22,VI,7:1
King Lear 1947,F 19,32:2
As You Like It 1947,F 21,16:2
Stern, Ernest (Scenic Designer)
Casanova 1928,N 4,IX,2:1
Merry Widow, The 1929,F 17,IX,2:3
Three Musketeers 1929,O 13,IX,4:7
Bitter Sweet 1929,N 6,30:2
Evergreen 1930,D 21,VIII,1:6
Im Weissen Roessel 1930,D 28,VIII,2:4
White Horse Inn 1931,Ap 9,30:2
Casanova 1932,Je 19,IX,2:1
Flying Trapeze, The 1935,Je 2,IX,2:3
Young Madame Conti 1937,Ap 1,18:4
Paganini 1937,My 21,18:6
King Lear 1947,F 19,32:2
As You Like It 1947,F 21,16:2
Stern, Ernst
Paganini 1937,Je 6,XI,1:2
Stern, Eva
School for Scandal, The 1953,Je 24,29:2
Climate of Eden, The 1953,N 21,11:2
Purification, The 1959,D 9,57:5
Between Two Thieves 1960,F 12,23:1
Secret Concubine, The 1960,Mr 22,29:2
Stern, G B (Original Author)
Matriarch, The 1930,Ja 26,VIII,2:1
Matriarch, The 1930,Mr 19,24:5
Debonair 1930,Ap 24,29:2
Stern, G B (Playwright)
Tents of Israel; Matriarch, The 1929,My 26,IX,1:3
Matriarch, The 1930,Ja 26,VIII,2:1
Matriarch, The 1930,Mr 19,24:5
Man Who Pays the Piper, The 1931,Mr 1,VIII,2:4
Middle Man 1936,S 8,23:1
Stern, G B (Producer)
Debonair 1930,Ap 24,29:2
Stern, Harold (Composer)
Artists and Models 1930,Je 11,33:2
Stern, Henry (Miscellaneous)
Three Men on a Horse 1969,O 17,35:1
Place for Polly, A 1970,Ap 20,45:1
Stern, Henry R (Producer)
Brain Sweat 1934,Ap 5,24:4
Stern, Joseph
Henry IV, Part I 1968,Je 30,54:7
Henry IV, Part II 1968,Jl 2,33:1
Stern, Joseph (Playwright)
Fiddler on the Roof 1965,Ag 15,II,2:5
Stern, Lawrence
Gandhi 1970,O 21,37:1
Stern, Lee
Shadow Years, The 1957,Ja 9,26:2
Stern, Leni (Playwright)
In the Nick of Time 1967,Je 2,36:1
Stern, Leon
Mother Sings 1935,N 13,24:1
Tomorrow's a Holiday! 1935,D 31,10:2
Cross-Town 1937,Mr 18,21:5
Censored 1938,F 28,18:2
Stern, Lionel (Miscellaneous)
Local Stigmatic, The; Last to Go 1969,N 4,55:2
Local Stigmatic, The; That's Your Trouble
    1969,N 4,55:2
Local Stigmatic, The; Request Stop 1969,N 4,55:2
Local Stigmatic, The 1969,N 4,55:2
Local Stigmatic, The; That's All 1969,N 4,55:2
Local Stigmatic, The; Applicant 1969,N 4,55:2
Local Stigmatic, The; Interview 1969,N 4,55:2
Local Stigmatic, The; Trouble in the Works
    1969,N 4,55:2
Stern, Maurice
Pirates of Penzance, The 1961,Ja 20,24:5
Gondoliers, The 1961,Ja 26,33:2
Stern, Milton (Miscellaneous)
Ziegfeld Follies 1957,Mr 2,19:2
Stern, Nancy (Miscellaneous)
It's All Yours 1942,Mr 26,26:2
Stern, Nancy (Playwright)
Now I Lay Me Down to Sleep 1950,Mr 3,21:2
Stern, Nancy (Producer)
Eastward in Eden 1947,N 19,33:2
Macbeth 1948,Ap 1,30:2
Stern, Peter (Miscellaneous)
1776 1969,Mr 17,46:2

Stern, Philip Van Doren (Original Author)
Man Who Killed Lincoln, The 1939,D 30,9:1
Man Who Killed Lincoln, The 1940,Ja 18,26:4
Stern, Philip Van Doren (Playwright)
Man Who Killed Lincoln, The 1940,Ja 18,26:4
Stern, Rudi (Miscellaneous)
Reincarnation of Christ Show, The 1966,D 4,II,5:1
Stern, Stewart
French Touch, The 1945,D 10,18:2
Stern, Tom
Never Too Late 1963,S 25,48:1
Stern, William
Ladies Leave 1929,O 2,28:3
Stern (Scenic Designer)
Bitter Sweet 1929,O 27,IX,2:1
Sterna, Katta
Midsummer Night's Dream, A 1927,Ag 8,6:1
Sternard, Ralph
Page Miss Glory 1934,N 28,24:2
Sternberg, A
Untitled-Revue 1935,S 23,20:2
Sternberg, Ann
Gertrude Stein's First Reader 1969,D 16,56:1
Sternberg, Ann (Composer)
Gertrude Stein's First Reader 1969,D 16,56:1
Sternberg, Anne (Choreographer)
All in Love 1961,N 11,15:2
Sternberg, Julius Von Jr
Betty Behave 1927,Mr 9,28:4
Sterndale-Bennett, J (Playwright)
Gift Horse, The 1926,N 21,VIII,4:1
Sterndale-Bennett, Joan
Time Gentlemen Please! 1961,N 9,40:4
Sterne, Emma Gelders (Playwright)
Reluctant Dragon, The 1931,D 12,23:5
Sterne, Gordon
Trial, The 1955,Je 15,35:2
Spring's Awakening 1955,O 10,30:2
Sterne, Morgan
Good Soup, The 1960,Mr 3,26:4
I Am a Camera 1961,Jl 10,26:1
Miss Julie 1961,Jl 10,26:1
Garden of Sweets, The 1961,N 1,35:1
Seidman and Son 1962,O 16,32:2
Sterne, Richard
Beyond Desire 1967,O 11,36:1
Sterner, Lawrence
Farmer's Wife, The 1924,O 10,22:3
Old Bill, M P 1926,N 11,22:2
Sternhagen, Frances
Thieves' Carnival 1955,F 2,21:1
Skin of Our Teeth, The 1955,Ag 18,16:1
Carefree Tree, The 1955,O 12,37:2
Admirable Bashville, The 1956,F 21,38:1
Country Wife, The 1957,Je 27,22:1
Saintliness of Margery Kempe, The 1959,F 3,35:6
Viva Madison Avenue 1960,Ap 7,42:1
Misalliance 1961,S 26,32:2
Great Day in the Morning 1962,Mr 29,29:1
Matter of Like Life and Death, A 1963,O 3,28:2
Play 1964,Ja 6,35:1
Slight Ache, A 1964,D 10,62:1
Room, The 1964,D 10,62:1
Right Honourable Gentleman, The 1965,O 20,50:2
Displaced Person, The 1966,D 30,15:1
Cocktail Party, The 1968,O 8,42:1
Cocktail Party, The 1968,O 20,II,1:1
Cock-A-Doodle Dandy 1969,Ja 21,40:1
Cock-A-Doodle Dandy 1969,F 2,II,1:1
Sternheim, Carl (Playwright)
Mask of Virtue, The 1935,My 16,20:1
Mask of Virtue, The 1935,Je 9,IX,1:1
Tabula Rasa 1970,O 13,52:2
Sterni, Giuseppe
Potenza, La 1926,Je 29,21:3
Attore, L' 1929,Mr 11,29:5
Piacere Dell 'Onesta, Il 1929,Mr 25,33:1
Serata D'Inverno; Winter Evening, A
1929,Ap 8,32:5
Liane, Le (Ties That Bind); Ties That Bind (Le
Liane) 1929,Ap 22,22:1
Man of Gold, A; Uomo d'Oro, Un 1929,My 6,30:2
Assalto, L' 1929,My 20,23:2
Tutto Per Bene; All's Well That Ends Well
1929,Je 3,27:1
Oh, Professor 1930,My 2,19:6
Tristi Amori; Unhappy Loves 1930,O 27,17:6
Strana Avventura, Una; Queer Adventure, A
1930,O 27,17:6
Piacere Del'Onesta, Il; Happiness of Probity, The
1930,N 10,16:4
Cena Delle Beffe, La; Jest, The 1930,N 24,26:4
In Fondo Al Cuore; Depths of the Heart, The
1930,D 8,27:1
Gli Spettri 1930,D 22,16:4
Cardinale, Il; Cardinal, The 1931,Ja 12,24:2
Delitto e Castigo; Crime and Punishment
1931,Ja 26,20:5
Sansone; Samson 1931,F 9,25:1
Marchese di Priola, Il 1931,Mr 2,19:3
Cantico dei Cantici, Il; Song of Songs
1931,Ap 13,17:3

Onda e lo Scoglio, L'; Wave and the Rock, The
1931,Ap 13,17:3
Arzigogolo, L'; Whim, The 1931,Ap 27,24:4
Alba, Il Gioro, La Notte, L'; Dawn, the Day, the
Night, The 1931,My 18,21:4
Cantico dei Cantici, Il; Song of Songs
1931,My 18,21:4
Giuochi di Prestigio 1931,N 2,26:1
Sing High, Sing Low 1931,N 13,26:4
Incendio Doloso, L'; False Flame, The
1931,N 16,22:4
Berretto a Songali, Il; Cap With Bells, The
1931,N 30,16:3
Zia Morta, La; Dead Aunt, The 1931,N 30,16:3
Piccolo Santo, Il; Little Saint, The 1931,D 14,16:4
Profumo di Mia Moglie, Il; My Wife's Perfume
1932,Ja 11,29:5
Civil Death, The 1932,Ja 25,20:3
Trio 1932,F 8,21:1
Ladro, Il; Thief, The 1932,F 22,23:4
T'Amo E Sarai Mia; I Love You and You'll Be
Mine 1932,Mr 21,19:4
Canto Della Vita, Il; Song of Life, The
1932,Ap 4,13:3
Casa di Tutti, La; Everybody's Home 1932,D 5,21:4
Cardinale, Il 1933,Ja 9,24:2
Zia Morta, La; Dead Aunt, The 1933,F 13,11:3
Istruttoria, L'; Judicial Inquiry, The 1933,F 13,11:3
Curioso Accidente, Un 1933,Mr 6,16:3
Romanticismo 1933,My 1,10:5
Liane, Le (Ties That Bind) 1933,Je 12,20:3
Ingeborg 1933,D 11,23:3
Conte di Monte Cristo, Il 1934,Ja 22,13:2
Padrone Delle Ferriere, Il 1934,Mr 19,13:5
Colonello Bridall, L' 1934,Ap 16,20:3
Romanticismo 1934,My 14,20:2
Miserabili I, 1934,S 24,15:1
Miserabili I, 1934,O 1,14:2
Signora Dalle Camelie, La; Camille 1934,O 22,13:2
Processo dei Veleni, Il; Case of Poisons, The
1935,Ja 21,18:2
Romanzo di un Giovane Povero, Il 1935,F 25,12:3
Signo Della Croce, Il 1935,O 7,11:1
Adventurer, The 1935,N 11,21:1
Cardinale Giovanni de Medici, Il 1935,D 9,24:8
Three Guardsmen, The 1936,F 17,21:3
Religione e Patria 1936,Mr 23,22:4
Due Orfanelle, Le; Two Orphans, The
1936,O 5,24:4
Morte Civile, La; Civic Death 1936,N 9,23:4
Sansone; Samson 1936,N 30,25:2
Feudalismo Oppure La Terra Bassa; Feudalism or
the Lowland 1937,Mr 8,22:2
Fantasmi 1937,Mr 22,26:5
Medico Delle Pazze, Il; Physician of Mad Woman,
The 1937,S 27,24:2
Signora Dalle Camelie, La; Dame aux Camelias, La
1937,O 9,16:3
Please, Mrs. Garibaldi 1939,Mr 17,24:3
They Knew What They Wanted 1939,O 3,19:1
Sterni, Giuseppe (Director)
Attore, L' 1929,Mr 11,29:5
Piacere Dell 'Onesta, Il 1929,Mr 25,33:1
Serata D'Inverno; Winter Evening, A
1929,Ap 8,32:5
Liane, Le (Ties That Bind); Ties That Bind (Le
Liane) 1929,Ap 22,22:1
Man of Gold, A; Uomo d'Oro, Un 1929,My 6,30:2
Assalto, L' 1929,My 20,23:2
Tutto Per Bene; All's Well That Ends Well
1929,Je 3,27:1
Oh, Professor 1930,My 2,19:6
Tristi Amori; Unhappy Loves 1930,O 27,17:6
Piacere Del'Onesta, Il; Happiness of Probity, The
1930,N 10,16:4
Cena Delle Beffe, La; Jest, The 1930,N 24,26:4
In Fondo Al Cuore; Depths of the Heart, The
1930,D 8,27:1
Gli Spettri 1930,D 22,16:4
Cardinale, Il; Cardinal, The 1931,Ja 12,24:2
Delitto e Castigo; Crime and Punishment
1931,Ja 26,20:5
Sansone; Samson 1931,F 9,25:1
Marchese di Priola, Il 1931,Mr 2,19:3
Cantico dei Cantici, Il; Song of Songs
1931,Ap 13,17:3
Onda e lo Scoglio, L'; Wave and the Rock, The
1931,Ap 13,17:3
Arzigogolo, L'; Whim, The 1931,Ap 27,24:4
Alba, Il Gioro, La Notte, L'; Dawn, the Day, the
Night, The 1931,My 18,21:4
Cantico dei Cantici, Il; Song of Songs
1931,My 18,21:4
Giuochi di Prestigio 1931,N 2,26:1
Incendio Doloso, L'; False Flame, The
1931,N 16,22:4
Berretto a Songali, Il; Cap With Bells, The
1931,N 30,16:3
Zia Morta, La; Dead Aunt, The 1931,N 30,16:3
Piccolo Santo, Il; Little Saint, The 1931,D 14,16:4
Profumo di Mia Moglie, Il; My Wife's Perfume
1932,Ja 11,29:5
Civil Death, The 1932,Ja 25,20:3

Sterni, Giuseppe (Director)—Cont

Trio 1932,F 8,21:1
Ladro, Il; Thief, The 1932,F 22,23:4
T'Amo E Sarai Mia; I Love You and You'll Be
Mine 1932,Mr 21,19:4
Canto Della Vita, Il; Song of Life, The
1932,Ap 4,13:3
Casa di Tutti, La; Everybody's Home 1932,D 5,21:4
Cardinale, Il 1933,Ja 9,24:2
Zia Morta, La; Dead Aunt, The 1933,F 13,11:3
Istruttoria, L'; Judicial Inquiry, The 1933,F 13,11:3
Curioso Accidente, Un 1933,Mr 6,16:3
Tragedy of the Ages, The 1933,Ap 7,22:7
Romanticismo 1933,My 1,10:5
Liane, Le (Ties That Bind) 1933,Je 12,20:3
Ingeborg 1933,D 11,23:3
Conte di Monte Cristo, Il 1934,Ja 22,13:2
Padrone Delle Ferriere, Il 1934,Mr 19,13:5
Colonello Bridall, L' 1934,Ap 16,20:3
Romanticismo 1934,My 14,20:2
Miserabili I, 1934,S 24,15:1
Miserabili I, 1934,O 1,14:2
Signora Dalle Camelie, La; Camille 1934,O 22,13:2
Processo dei Veleni, Il; Case of Poisons, The
1935,Ja 21,18:2
Romanzo di un Giovane Povero, Il 1935,F 25,12:3
Signo Della Croce, Il 1935,O 7,11:1
Adventurer, The 1935,N 11,21:1
Testamento della Zia d'America, Il; American
Aunt's Will, The 1936,Mr 23,22:4
Religione e Patria 1936,Mr 23,22:4
Due Orfanelle, Le; Two Orphans, The
1936,O 5,24:4
Morte Civile, La; Civic Death 1936,N 9,23:4
Sansone; Samson 1936,N 30,25:2
Asino di Buridano, L' 1936,N 30,25:2
Lucrezia Borgia 1937,Mr 8,22:2
Feudalismo Oppure La Terra Bassa; Feudalism or
the Lowland 1937,Mr 8,22:2
Sposa e la Cavalla, La 1937,Mr 22,26:5
Fantasmi 1937,Mr 22,26:5
Signora Dalle Camelie, La; Dame aux Camelias, La
1937,O 9,16:3
Sterni, Giuseppe (Playwright)
Conte di Monte Cristo, Il 1934,Ja 22,13:2
Conte di Monte Cristo, Il 1935,Ap 1,17:6
Signo Della Croce, Il 1935,O 7,11:1
Three Guardsmen, The 1936,F 17,21:3
Due Orfanelle, Le; Two Orphans, The
1936,O 5,24:4
Medico Delle Pazze, Il; Physician of Mad Woman,
The 1937,S 27,24:2
Sterni, Giuseppe (Producer)
Civil Death, The 1932,Ja 25,20:3
Sternroyd, Vincent
Cymbeline 1923,O 3,12:1
Sterns, Roger
Garrick Gaieties 1930,Je 5,29:2
Forsaking All Others 1933,Mr 2,21:2
Sterrett, Lee
Tavern, The 1920,S 28,14:1
Stetson, Claire
Jazz a La Carte 1922,Je 3,8:3
Stetson, Dale (Scenic Designer)
New Yorkers, The 1930,D 9,31:1
You Said It 1931,Ja 20,21:3
Three Times the Hour 1931,Ag 26,15:5
Here Goes the Bride 1931,N 4,31:2
Fatal Alibi, The 1932,F 10,26:6
Christopher Comes Across 1932,Je 1,19:2
Stettheimer, Florine (Miscellaneous)
Four Saints in Three Acts 1952,Ap 17,35:1
Steuart-Tavant, E (Miscellaneous)
All the King's Horses 1934,Ja 31,21:3
Steuer, Arthur
Tea and Sympathy 1953,O 1,35:1
Steuer, Arthur (Playwright)
Terrible Swift Sword, The 1955,N 16,42:1
Steurer, Ralph
One Woman's Husband 1920,Mr 23,9:3
Stevans, William H
Cyrano de Bergerac 1923,N 2,14:1
Stevens, Barclay
Seven Mirrors 1945,O 26,17:2
Stevens, Charles
What a Relief 1935,D 14,10:6
Stevens, Clifford (Miscellaneous)
Front Page, The 1968,O 20,85:5
Place Without Doors, A 1970,D 1,60:1
Stevens, Connie
Hilarities 1948,S 10,20:2
Star-Spangled Girl, The 1966,D 22,38:1
Stevens, Craig
Here's Love 1963,O 4,28:1
Stevens, Cuyler
Fortuno 1925,D 23,22:1
Stevens, Dana
Horse Eats Hat 1936,S 28,14:2
Stevens, Donald
Libel! 1935,D 21,10:5
Country Wife, The 1936,D 2,34:1
Idiot's Delight 1937,Ag 10,22:7
Dream Girl 1945,D 15,13:2
Relapse, The 1950,N 23,54:2

evens, Edmond
Woman Brown, The 1939,D 9,18:5
Leave Her to Heaven 1940,F 28,16:2
Golden Wings 1941,D 9,46:6
evens, Edmond (Scenic Designer)
Imaginary Invalid, The 1968,My 28,41:1
evens, Emilie
Bonds of Interest, The 1951,D 1,7:2
Yerma 1952,F 8,18:4
Summer and Smoke 1952,Ap 25,19:5
American Gothic 1953,N 11,35:6
Girl on the Via Flaminia, The 1954,F 10,37:1
evens, Emily
Sophie 1920,Mr 3,12:2
Foot-Loose 1920,My 11,12:1
Foot-Loose 1920,Ag 15,VI,1:1
Sporting Thing to Do, The 1923,F 20,12:2
Sporting Thing to Do, The 1923,F 25,VII,1:1
Captain Briquet 1923,S 16,VII,2:8
Lesson in Love, A 1923,S 25,10:1
Lesson in Love, A 1923,S 30,II,1:1
Fata Morgana 1924,Mr 4,16:3
Fata Morgana 1924,Mr 9,VIII,1:1
Fata Morgana 1924,Ag 24,VII,1:1
Hedda Gabler 1926,Ja 27,16:5
evens, Ethel
Camille 1956,S 19,33:1
evens, Fran
Most Happy Fella, The 1966,My 12,55:1
How Now, Dow Jones 1967,D 8,53:1
Paradise Gardens East 1969,Mr 11,39:1
Cry for Us All 1970,Ap 9,48:2
Stevens, Frank Shaw
Firebird of Florence 1945,Mr 23,13:4
Midsummer Night's Dream, A 1950,Je 22,33:2
Antony and Cleopatra 1963,Je 21,33:1
Stevens, Frankie
Just a Minute 1928,O 9,34:3
Stevens, Geoffe
Stars on Ice 1942,Jl 3,12:2
Stars on Ice (2d Edition) 1943,Je 25,13:2
Hats Off to Ice 1944,Je 23,15:2
Hollywood Ice Revue 1953,Ja 16,17:2
Hollywood Ice Revue 1955 1955,Ja 14,16:1
Stevens, George
H M S Pinafore 1935,Ag 13,20:6
Stevens, Gil (Composer)
Elliott Murphy's Aquashow 1956,Je 20,26:2
Ice Capades 1970,Ja 7,35:1
Stevens, Gil (Lyricist)
Ice Capades 1970,Ja 7,35:1
Stevens, Gil (Musical Director)
Elliott Murphy's Aquashow 1956,Je 20,26:2
Stevens, Ginny
Aquacircus 1958,Je 30,24:6
Stevens, Goger L (Producer)
Tiger Tiger Burning Bright 1962,D 24,5:2
Stevens, Gould (Scenic Designer)
War 1929,S 19,37:3
Stevens, H C G (Playwright)
Immortal Garden 1934,O 19,26:3
Stevens, Houseley Jr
Black Eye, The 1938,Mr 8,22:4
On the Rocks 1938,Je 16,20:2
If You Get It, Do You Want It? 1938,D 1,28:2
Shakespeare's Merchant 1939 1939,Ja 10,16:3
Stop Press 1939,Mr 20,13:2
Journey's End 1939,S 19,29:2
Stevens, Houseley Sr
Time of Your Life, The 1939,O 26,26:2
Time of Your Life, The 1940,S 24,27:2
Stevens, Howard
Sign of the Leopard 1928,D 12,34:4
Stevens, Inger
Debut 1956,F 23,32:1
Roman Candle 1960,F 4,34:2
Stevens, Jane Kip (Costume Designer)
O Say Can You See! 1962,O 9,45:1
Stevens, Janet
Green Pastures, The 1935,F 27,16:2
Stevens, Jeremy
Fourth Wall, The 1968,S 5,53:1
Stevens, Jeremy (Director)
Fourth Wall, The 1968,S 5,53:1
Stevens, Jerry (Composer)
Champagne Complex 1955,Ap 13,33:1
Stevens, John B
On the Level 1937,Mr 26,24:4
Stevens, John Wright (Scenic Designer)
Millionairess, The 1969,Mr 3,28:1
Stevens, Josephine
Go-Go 1923,Mr 13,19:4
Forbidden 1923,O 2,10:2
Myrtie 1924,F 5,21:2
Stevens, Julie
Snookie 1941,Je 4,26:2
Brooklyn, U S A 1941,D 22,24:2
Proof Thro' the Night 1942,D 26,14:2
World's Full of Girls, The 1943,D 7,31:2
Sleep, My Pretty One 1944,N 3,26:8
Stevens, June (Miscellaneous)
Forensic and the Navigators 1970,Ap 2,43:1

Stevens, June (Producer)
Unseen Hand, The 1970,Ap 2,43:1
Stevens, K T
Man Who Came to Dinner, The 1940,F 10,19:5
Land Is Bright, The 1941,O 29,26:2
Yankee Point 1942,N 24,28:2
Nine Girls 1943,Ja 14,26:2
Voice of the Turtle, The 1944,D 10,II,6:4
Laura 1947,Je 27,16:1
Stevens, Kelly
Brigadoon 1963,F 1,6:2
Stevens, Knox
Jason 1942,Ja 22,12:2
Stevens, Larry
Annie Get Your Gun 1957,Mr 9,15:5
Stevens, Larry (Choreographer)
On the Town 1959,F 14,15:1
Stevens, Leila
Fashion 1937,Mr 21,II,7:8
Stevens, Leon B
Here Come the Clowns 1954,My 5,36:2
Misalliance 1955,F 12,10:6
Geranium Hat, The 1959,Mr 18,45:1
Hasty Heart, The 1959,S 15,45:2
Burning Bright 1959,O 17,27:2
Between Two Thieves 1960,F 12,23:1
Wall, The 1960,O 12,44:4
Night Is Black Bottles, The 1962,D 5,56:1
Place for Chance, The 1964,My 15,44:2
Diamond Orchid 1965,F 11,44:4
Investigation, The 1966,O 5,40:1
Stevens, Leslie
Sarah Simple 1940,N 18,22:5
Stevens, Leslie (Playwright)
Bullfight 1954,Ja 13,25:2
Champagne Complex 1955,Ap 13,33:1
Lovers 1956,My 11,23:1
Marriage-Go-Round, The 1958,O 30,37:1
Marriage-Go-Round, The 1958,N 9,II,1:1
Stevens, Lydia F
Little Town of Bethlehem, The 1922,D 26,15:4
Stevens, Lynda
John Brown's Body 1953,F 16,17:2
Stevens, Marilyn
Six Characters in Search of an Author
1955,D 12,38:1
Stevens, Mark
Mid-Summer 1953,Ja 22,19:1
Stevens, Marti
Buttrio Square 1952,O 15,40:2
First Impressions 1959,Mr 20,28:1
Oh, Kay! 1960,Ap 18,37:2
No Strings 1964,Ja 1,17:1
High Spirits 1964,N 4,46:4
Stevens, Merle
Marjolaine 1922,Ja 25,16:1
Vagabond King, The 1925,S 22,23:3
O'Flynn, The 1934,D 28,24:1
Stevens, Miss
Hedda Gabler 1926,F 21,VII,1:2
Stevens, Morton
Kind Lady 1937,Jl 6,23:1
Stevens, Morton (Miscellaneous)
Mr Wonderful 1956,Mr 23,23:2
Stevens, Morton (Musical Director)
Mr Wonderful 1956,Mr 23,23:2
Stevens, Morton L
New Poor, The 1924,Ja 8,26:1
Farmer Takes a Wife, The 1934,O 31,17:1
Winterset 1935,S 26,19:2
Love for Love 1936,Je 30,15:4
Night of January 16 1937,Jl 20,19:3
Idiot's Delight 1937,Ag 10,22:7
Robin Landing 1937,N 19,26:4
Western Waters 1937,D 29,17:1
I Married an Angel 1938,My 12,26:2
Pastoral 1939,N 2,26:2
Romeo and Juliet 1940,My 10,27:1
Lady Who Came to Stay, The 1941,Ja 3,13:2
Lady Comes Across, The 1942,Ja 10,10:2
Great Big Doorstep, The 1942,N 27,26:2
Jackpot 1944,Ja 14,15:2
Odds on Mrs Oakley, The 1944,O 3,18:8
Streets Are Guarded, The 1944,N 21,19:7
Stranger, The 1945,F 13,21:2
Round Trip 1945,My 30,16:4
Iceman Cometh, The 1946,O 10,31:3
Kathleen 1948,F 4,26:2
Oh, Mr Meadowbrook! 1948,D 27,17:2
Four Twelves Are 48 1951,Ja 18,30:2
Stevens, Murray
Reunion in Vienna 1931,N 17,31:1
Stevens, Naomi
Son, The 1950,Ap 1,12:4
Stevens, Nat (Producer)
Legend of Lizzie, The 1959,F 10,39:1
Stevens, Onslow
Stage Door 1936,S 29,35:1
Stage Door 1936,O 23,26:3
Schoolhouse on the Lot 1938,Mr 23,18:4
Millionairess, The 1938,Ag 16,22:5
Dame Nature 1938,S 27,24:3
Michael Drops In 1938,D 28,24:3

Stevens, Onslow—Cont
Burning Deck, The 1940,Mr 2,9:2
Return of Ulysses, The 1943,Ja 28,22:2
Return of Ulysses, The 1943,F 7,II,1:6
Eastward in Eden 1947,N 19,33:2
Ghost of Elsinore, The 1949,Ap 16,10:2
Clearing in the Woods, A 1957,Ja 11,20:2
Stevens, Onslow (Director)
Return of Ulysses, The 1943,Ja 28,22:2
Return of Ulysses, The 1943,F 7,II,1:6
Ghost of Elsinore, The 1949,Ap 16,10:2
Stevens, Paul
My Heart's in the Highlands 1949,N 22,36:7
My Heart's in the Highlands 1950,F 18,8:4
Desire Under the Elms 1951,N 22,45:1
Merchant of Venice, The 1953,Mr 5,20:2
Moon in Capricorn 1953,O 28,37:2
As You Like It 1955,O 29,12:2
Romeo and Juliet 1955,D 16,36:3
Antigone 1956,Ap 3,32:2
Two Gentlemen of Verona 1957,Jl 23,21:5
Compulsion 1957,O 25,21:1
Ivanov 1958,O 8,42:1
Ivanov 1958,O 19,II,1:1
Jeannette 1960,Mr 25,20:2
General Seeger 1962,Mr 1,26:2
Tempest, The 1962,Jl 17,18:2
Andorra 1963,F 11,5:5
Advocate, The 1963,O 15,46:7
Love's Labour's Lost 1965,Je 16,46:1
Troilus and Cressida 1965,Ag 13,17:1
White Devil, The 1965,D 7,56:1
Memorandum, The 1968,My 6,55:1
Stevens, R L (Miscellaneous)
Peer Gynt 1951,Ja 29,15:2
Mary Rose 1951,Mr 5,25:2
Ecole des Femmes, L'; School for Wives
1951,Mr 19,22:1
Night Music 1951,Ap 9,29:6
Stevens, R L (Playwright)
Peter Pan 1950,Ap 25,27:2
Stevens, R L (Producer)
Getting Married 1950,Je 14,41:2
Stevens, Ramse (Costume Designer)
Come Play With Me 1959,My 1,33:5
Thurber Carnival, A 1960,F 27,13:2
Stevens, Richard
Heart of a City 1942,F 13,24:6
All the Comforts of Home 1942,My 26,24:5
Stevens, Rise
Chocolate Soldier, The 1932,F 9,30:3
Variations of 1940 1940,Ja 29,12:1
King and I, The 1964,Jl 7,26:1
Stevens, Rita
South 1955,My 2,17:4
Stevens, Robert
Hole in the Wall, The 1920,Mr 27,11:1
Merchant of Venice, The 1921,Ap 2,14:2
Stevens, Robert L (Producer)
Milk Train Doesn't Stop Here Anymore, The
1963,Ja 18,7:1
Stevens, Roger
Remarkable Mr Pennypacker, The 1953,D 31,11:2
Stevens, Roger L (Miscellaneous)
Tamburlaine the Great 1956,Ja 20,19:1
Major Barbara 1956,O 31,27:1
Sleeping Prince, The 1956,N 2,31:1
West Side Story 1957,S 27,14:4
Boy Growing Up, A 1957,O 8,41:1
Visit, The 1958,My 6,40:1
Oh Dad, Poor Dad, Mamma's Hung You in the
Closet and I'm Feelin' So Sad 1962,F 27,28:1
Stevens, Roger L (Producer)
Twelfth Night 1949,O 4,33:2
Cellar and the Well, The 1950,D 11,30:2
Escapade 1953,N 19,40:1
Remarkable Mr Pennypacker, The 1953,D 31,11:2
Dark Is Light Enough, The 1955,F 24,20:1
Bus Stop 1955,Mr 3,23:2
Memory of Two Mondays, A 1955,S 30,21:1
View From the Bridge, A 1955,S 30,21:1
Island of Goats 1955,O 5,40:1
Clearing in the Woods, A 1957,Ja 11,20:2
Sin of Pat Muldoon, The 1957,Mr 14,35:1
Under Milk Wood 1957,O 16,42:5
Time Remembered 1957,N 13,41:2
Rope Dancers, The 1957,N 21,39:1
Joyce Grenfell 1958,Ap 8,32:1
Firstborn, The 1958,My 1,35:1
Firstborn, The 1958,Jl 4,16:3
Goldilocks 1958,O 13,33:1
Cold Wind and the Warm, The 1958,D 9,55:1
Much Ado About Nothing 1959,S 18,25:2
Tumbler, The 1960,F 25,32:2
Duel of Angels 1960,Ap 20,42:2
Rosemary 1960,N 15,47:1
Alligators, The 1960,N 15,47:1
Under the Yum-Yum Tree 1960,N 17,45:1
Conquering Hero, The 1961,Ja 17,40:2
Julia, Jake, and Uncle Joe 1961,Ja 30,19:1
Midgie Purvis 1961,F 2,25:3
Mary, Mary 1961,Mr 9,24:2
Importance of Being Oscar, The 1961,Mr 15,45:2
Far Country, A 1961,Ap 5,32:1

Stevens, Roger L (Producer)—Cont
Caretaker, The 1961,O 5,42:3
Blood, Sweat & Stanley Poole 1961,O 6,31:1
Everybody Loves Opal 1961,O 12,40:2
Man for All Seasons, A 1961,N 23,51:1
First Love 1961,D 26,20:2
Romulus 1962,Ja 11,27:1
Father, The 1962,My 15,49:1
Long Day's Journey Into Night 1962,My 16,35:4
Miss Julie 1962,My 17,31:1
Step on a Crack 1962,O 18,48:1
Calculated Risk 1962,N 1,35:1
Andorra 1963,F 11,5:5
Children From Their Games 1963,Ap 12,33:1
Oh Dad, Poor Dad, Mamma's Hung You in the
  Closet and I'm Feelin' So Sad 1963,Ag 28,28:2
Bicycle Ride to Nevada 1963,S 25,38:1
Private Ear, The 1963,O 10,51:1
Public Eye, The 1963,O 10,51:1
Case of Libel, A 1963,O 11,43:2
Rainy Day in Newark, A 1963,O 23,35:1
Chinese Prime Minister, The 1964,Ja 3,14:1
Man for All Seasons, A 1964,Ja 28,24:2
Dirty Old Man, The 1964,My 5,53:1
Sarah and the Sax 1964,My 5,53:1
Indians 1969,O 14,51:1
Sheep on the Runway 1970,F 2,28:3
Conduct Unbecoming 1970,O 13,50:1
Stevens, Rose
Orpheus in Hades 1930,D 16,30:1
Stevens, Rowena (Producer)
Swan, The 1954,Ag 17,16:6
Stevens, Roy K
Fire! 1968,My 12,II,7:1
Fire! 1969,Ja 29,26:1
Stevens, Ruth
If This Be Treason 1935,S 24,28:2
Stevens, Ruthelma
Blonde Sinner, The 1926,Jl 15,21:2
Speakeasy 1927,S 27,30:1
Jarnegan 1928,S 25,29:2
Hotel Universe 1930,Ap 15,29:1
Roadside 1930,S 27,21:1
Anatol 1931,Ja 17,23:3
Life Begins 1932,Mr 29,23:2
Man of Wax, The 1933,Ag 6,X,1:6
Red Rainbow, A 1953,S 15,37:4
Stevens, Sandra
Girls of Summer 1956,N 20,45:1
Stevens, Sandy
Have You Heard This One 1953,N 9,23:4
Stevens, Sharlene
Go Show Me a Dragon 1961,O 28,18:1
Stevens, Susan
King Lear 1968,Je 3,55:4
Stevens, Sydney G
Yerma 1952,F 8,18:4
Summer and Smoke 1952,Ap 25,19:5
Stevens, Terri
Stiffkey Scandals of 1932, The 1969,Je 14,24:3
Stevens, Thomas Wood (Director)
Anatomist, The 1932,O 25,24:3
Stevens, Toby
Under Milk Wood 1957,O 16,42:5
Stevens, Tony
Boy Friend, The 1970,Ap 15,54:1
Stevens, Ursula
'Tis Pity She's a Whore 1958,D 6,21:1
Stevens, Valerie
Treasure, The 1920,O 5,13:1
Stevens, Van
Song of Norway 1958,Je 23,19:2
Song of Norway 1959,Je 26,16:2
Music Man, The 1965,Je 17,26:4
Stevens, Virginia
Macbeth 1930,Mr 26,24:6
Richard III 1930,Mr 31,24:1
As You Like It 1930,Ap 3,32:5
Julius Caesar 1930,Ap 4,22:3
Merchant of Venice, The 1931,N 17,31:1
Julius Caesar 1931,N 18,26:3
Little Black Book, The 1932,D 27,11:2
Riddle Me This! 1933,Mr 15,21:3
Ship Comes in, A 1934,S 20,21:1
Weep for the Virgins 1935,D 2,18:1
Case of Clyde Griffiths 1936,Mr 14,10:4
All the Living 1938,Mr 25,14:4
Night Music 1940,F 23,18:2
Stevens, Warren
Celebration 1948,Ap 12,24:2
Sundown Beach 1948,S 8,37:1
Smile of the World, The 1949,Ja 13,26:5
Detective Story 1949,Mr 24,34:2
Detective Story 1949,Ap 3,II,1:1
Stevens Brothers, The
Night in Venice, A 1929,My 22,30:2
Stevenson, Allan
Savonarola 1942,Ap 24,20:2
R U R 1942,D 4,30:2
Family Affair, A 1946,N 28,41:2
Anne of the Thousand Days 1948,D 9,49:2
Angels Kiss Me 1951,Ap 18,37:6
Dance of Death, The 1960,S 14,51:1

Stevenson, Ann
Abe Lincoln in Illinois 1938,O 17,12:2
Stevenson, Berton E (Original Author)
In the Next Room 1923,O 3,15:3
Stevenson, Bill
Espanola 1921,D 30,13:1
Stevenson, Bob
Signature 1945,F 15,25:2
Oh What a Lovely War 1964,O 1,30:1
Stevenson, Bob (Choreographer)
Oh What a Lovely War 1964,O 1,30:1
Romeo and Juliet 1967,F 22,18:1
Stevenson, Burton E (Original Author)
In the Next Room 1923,N 28,14:1
Stevenson, Charles A
Merchant of Venice, The 1921,Ap 2,14:2
Stevenson, David
As You Like It 1937,N 1,25:2
Stevenson, Douglas
Hitchy-Koo, 1920 1920,O 20,11:3
Blue Kitten, The 1922,Ja 14,9:3
Sun Showers 1923,F 6,14:2
Stevenson, Elizabeth
Carolinian, The 1925,N 3,34:2
Stevenson, Geff
Hair 1970,Ja 13,39:1
Stevenson, James (Miscellaneous)
Boys From Syracuse, The 1963,Ap 16,31:1
Stevenson, James (Producer)
Local Stigmatic, The; Last to Go 1969,N 4,55:2
Local Stigmatic, The; That's Your Trouble
  1969,N 4,55:2
Local Stigmatic, The; Trouble in the Works
  1969,N 4,55:2
Local Stigmatic, The; Applicant 1969,N 4,55:2
Local Stigmatic, The; That's All 1969,N 4,55:2
Local Stigmatic, The 1969,N 4,55:2
Local Stigmatic, The; Interview 1969,N 4,55:2
Local Stigmatic, The; Request Stop 1969,N 4,55:2
Stevenson, Janet (Playwright)
Counterattack 1943,F 4,27:2
Counterattack 1943,F 14,II,1:1
Stevenson, Jim
Goodbye Again 1956,Ap 25,38:1
Stevenson, Karole Kaye
Caution: A Love Story 1969,Ap 4,45:1
Stevenson, Lyall
Ice Capades 1954,S 16,37:1
Ice Capades 1955,S 15,38:1
Stevenson, Margot
Firebird 1932,N 22,25:2
Party, A 1933,Ag 24,18:4
Barretts of Wimpole Street, The 1935,F 26,16:2
Symphony 1935,Ap 27,20:3
Truly Valiant 1936,Ja 10,17:3
Stage Door 1936,O 23,26:3
You Can't Take It With You 1936,D 15,31:1
Golden Wings 1941,N 25,33:3
Golden Wings 1941,D 9,46:6
Little Women 1944,D 13,29:2
Leading Lady 1948,O 19,33:1
Young and Beautiful, The 1955,O 3,23:2
Portrait of a Madonna 1959,Ap 16,28:1
Pound on Demand, A 1959,Ap 16,28:1
One by One 1964,D 2,60:1
Hostile Witness 1966,F 18,26:1
Stevenson, Mim (Miscellaneous)
War Games 1969,Ap 18,37:1
Stevenson, Paul
Moon in the Yellow River, The 1932,Mr 1,19:3
Stevenson, Philip (Playwright)
Counterattack 1943,F 4,27:2
Counterattack 1943,F 14,II,1:1
Stevenson, R L (Playwright)
Beau Austin 1929,N 17,IX,2:4
Stevenson, Richard
It Is the Law 1922,N 30,28:2
Square Peg, A 1923,Ja 29,10:2
White Cargo 1926,Ap 6,22:2
Kongo 1926,Mr 31,20:5
Cock Robin 1928,Ja 13,26:6
Hotbed 1928,N 10,20:7
Coastwise 1931,D 1,23:1
Lady Windermere's Fan 1932,Ja 27,19:3
White Cargo 1941,My 14,24:3
Spring Again 1941,O 28,28:3
Spring Again 1941,N 11,28:2
Stevenson, Robert
Poppa Is Home 1961,D 20,37:1
Stevenson, Robert (Costume Designer)
Closing Door, The 1949,D 2,36:2
Stevenson, Robert (Miscellaneous)
Country Scandal, A 1960,My 6,21:8
Delightful Season, A 1960,S 29,30:1
Behind the Wall 1960,N 1,47:1
When I Was a Child 1960,D 9,38:1
Anniversary, The 1961,Ap 21,26:2
On the High Road 1961,Ap 21,26:2
Wedding, The 1961,Ap 21,26:2
Buskers, The 1961,O 31,28:1
Poppa Is Home 1961,D 20,37:1
Beyond the Horizon 1962,O 26,27:2
Call It Virtue 1963,Mr 28,8:2

Stevenson, Robert (Miscellaneous)—Cont
Cat and the Canary, The 1965,Ja 5,26:1
Time for Bed 1969,Je 14,24:1
Take Me to Bed 1969,Je 14,24:1
Nest, The 1970,Ap 10,46:1
Stevenson, Robert Louis (Original Author)
Suicide Club, The 1929,Mr 10,X,4:5
Mystery Square 1929,Ap 5,28:3
Traitor, The 1930,My 3,23:4
Treasure Island 1938,My 15,II,2:3
Stevenson, Robert Louis (Playwright)
Dr Jeckyll and Mr Hyde 1927,Ap 24,VII,2:3
Stevenson, Robert Ten Eyck (Costume Designer)
Pardon My English 1933,Ja 21,11:4
Stevenson, Tom
Symphony 1935,Ap 27,20:3
Stevenson, William (Director)
White Cargo 1941,My 14,24:3
Stevenson, William Adell III
Five on the Black Hand Side 1970,Ja 2,32:2
Stever, Aletta
Bridal Crown, The 1938,F 7,11:2
Stever, Letty
Of V We Sing 1942,F 16,20:3
Stever, Willis
Birthday Party, The 1961,My 15,34:6
Stevlingson, Edward
Our Town 1969,N 28,50:1
Getting Married 1970,Ja 20,46:1
Steward, Erwin (Miscellaneous)
J B 1958,Ap 24,37:1
Steward, Frank
Gondoliers, The 1934,S 4,23:1
Trial by Jury 1934,S 14,24:3
Yeomen of the Guard, The 1934,S 21,28:3
Patience 1934,O 12,32:2
Gondoliers, The 1936,S 8,23:1
Yeomen of the Guard, The 1936,S 15,37:2
Patience 1936,O 6,28:6
Steward, Parker
School for Husbands, The 1933,O 17,26:5
Chocolate Soldier, The 1934,My 3,15:3
Steward, Ron
Sambo 1969,D 22,42:1
Sambo 1970,Jl 23,24:1
Steward, Ron (Composer)
Believers, The 1968,My 10,57:4
Five on the Black Hand Side 1970,Ja 11,II,1:1
Sambo 1970,Ja 11,II,3:7
Sambo 1970,Jl 23,24:1
Steward, Ron (Lyricist)
Believers, The 1968,My 10,57:4
Sambo 1970,Jl 23,24:1
Steward, Ron (Playwright)
Sambo 1969,D 22,42:1
Stewart, Al
Cave Dwellers, The 1957,O 21,29:2
Stewart, Alan
Devil and Daniel Webster, The 1939,My 19,26:1
Stewart, Alexander
Macbeth 1928,N 20,28:3
Back Fire 1932,Je 14,26:3
Stewart, Allen
Gondoliers, The 1940,O 1,29:2
Trojan Women, The 1941,Ap 9,32:5
Mikado, The 1944,F 12,11:3
Trial by Jury 1944,F 15,14:4
Cox and Box 1944,F 18,15:5
Pirates of Penzance, The 1944,F 18,15:5
Gondoliers, The 1944,F 22,26:3
Iolanthe 1944,F 23,17:1
Patience 1944,F 26,11:4
Ruddigore 1944,Mr 3,19:5
Yeomen of the Guard, The 1944,Mr 5,34:3
Stewart, Anita
My House Is Your House 1970,O 16,53:2
Stewart, Athole
Skin Game, The 1920,My 23,VI,1:3
Canaries Sometimes Sing 1929,N 10,X,2:1
Canaries Sometimes Sing 1930,O 21,34:2
O H M S 1931,Mr 29,VIII,2:1
Flat to Let 1931,D 20,VIII,3:6
Conversation Piece 1934,O 24,24:1
Stewart, Athole (Director)
On Approval 1926,O 19,27:1
Canaries Sometimes Sing 1930,O 21,34:2
Evensong 1933,F 1,13:4
Stewart, Betty
Her Family Tree 1920,D 28,9:2
Stewart, Billy
Belafonte at the Palace 1959,D 16,55:1
Stewart, C G (Miscellaneous)
Green Pastures, The 1933,O 5,24:5
Stewart, Carolyn Hill
Jeb 1946,F 22,20:2
Hamlet 1951,Jl 20,13:6
Stewart, Charles (Producer)
Love on Leave 1944,Je 21,23:4
Stewart, Charles Conger (Playwright)
Gasoline Gypsies 1931,Je 8,21:3
Stewart, Darrell
Heel, The 1954,My 27,33:2
Egoists, The 1959,O 14,52:2

Stewart, David (Playwright)
Mutiny 1936,My 11,16:2
Stewart, David J
Walking Gentleman, The 1942,My 8,26:2
Antigone 1946,F 19,21:3
Antony and Cleopatra 1947,N 27,49:2
That Lady 1949,N 23,18:4
Rose Tattoo, The 1951,F 5,19:2
Barefoot in Athens 1951,N 1,35:2
Camino Real 1953,Mr 20,26:1
Camino Real 1953,Mr 29,II,1:1
School for Scandal, The 1953,Je 24,29:2
Immoralist, The 1954,F 2,18:7
Immoralist, The 1954,F 9,22:1
Immoralist, The 1954,F 14,II,1:1
Anastasia 1954,D 30,13:1
Anastasia 1955,Ja 16,II,1:1
Making of Moo, The 1958,Je 12,34:1
Man for All Seasons, A 1961,N 23,51:1
Man for All Seasons, A 1961,D 3,II,1:1
Man for All Seasons, A 1962,S 23,II,1:1
After the Fall 1964,Ja 24,18:1
Marco Millions 1964,F 21,33:1
Changeling, The 1964,O 30,32:2
Incident at Vichy 1964,D 4,44:1
Danton's Death 1965,O 22,46:1
Come Slowly, Eden 1966,D 7,56:1
Stewart, Devida
Small Wonder 1948,S 16,33:5
Stewart, Dink
My Magnolia 1926,Jl 13,19:2
Stewart, Dixie
Oklahoma! 1969,Je 24,37:1
Stewart, Don
Kilgo Run, The 1953,D 13,105:1
Student Gypsy, The; Prince of Liederkranz, The 1963,O 1,34:1
Jo 1964,F 13,25:1
Babes in the Wood 1964,D 29,21:2
Stewart, Donald Ogden
Holiday 1928,N 27,36:1
Rebound 1930,F 4,29:1
Social Register, The 1931,N 10,28:2
Ballyhoo of 1932 1932,S 7,14:2
Sun and I, The 1937,F 27,9:5
Stewart, Donald Ogden (Playwright)
Los Angeles 1927,D 20,32:3
Rebound 1930,F 4,29:1
Rebound 1930,F 16,IX,1:1
Fine and Dandy 1930,S 24,26:1
Rebound 1931,N 1,VIII,4:1
How I Wonder 1947,O 1,34:2
Kidders, The 1957,N 13,40:6
Stewart, Dorothy
Tom Sawyer 1931,D 26,15:3
Stewart, Eleanor
Romeo and Juliet 1968,Ag 16,19:1
Stewart, Ellen (Director)
Caution: A Love Story 1969,Ap 4,45:1
Homo 1969,Ap 12,40:2
Queen of Greece, The 1969,Ap 12,40:2
Ubu Roi 1970,F 17,33:1
Dirtiest Show in Town, The 1970,My 2,21:1
Golden Bat 1970,Je 27,18:2
Stewart, Ellen (Miscellaneous)
Constant Prince, The 1969,O 18,36:1
Acropolis 1969,N 5,40:1
Apocalypsis cum Figuris 1969,N 20,60:2
Stewart, Ellen (Producer)
Give My Regards to Off Off Broadway 1966,D 9,57:1
Stewart, Elliott
Madame Pompadour 1924,N 12,20:6
Stewart, Frances
Red, Hot and Blue! 1936,O 30,26:3
Stewart, Francis
Three Times the Hour 1931,Ag 26,15:5
Stewart, Fred
Ladies of Creation 1931,S 9,25:1
Experience Unnecessary 1931,D 31,16:2
Stork Is Dead, The 1932,S 24,18:2
Over Here 1936,Mr 16,21:2
200 Were Chosen 1936,N 21,21:1
Excursion 1937,Ap 10,11:4
Robin Landing 1937,N 19,26:4
Washington Jitters 1938,My 3,19:1
Devil and Daniel Webster, The 1939,My 19,26:1
Night Music 1940,F 23,18:2
Retreat to Pleasure 1940,D 18,32:2
Heart of a City 1942,F 13,24:6
Land's End 1946,D 12,37:5
Whole World Over, The 1947,Mr 28,28:2
Galileo 1947,D 8,34:2
Volpone 1948,Ja 9,24:6
Afternoon Storm 1948,Ap 12,24:2
Home Life of a Buffalo; Hope's the Thing 1948,My 12,34:6
Gone Tomorrow; Hope's the Thing 1948,My 12,34:6
Hope Is the Thing With Feathers; Hope's the Thing 1948,My 12,34:6
Magnolia Alley 1949,Ap 19,29:2
Brigadoon 1950,My 3,36:2

Arms and the Man 1950,O 20,34:2
Enemy of the People, An 1950,D 29,14:1
Flight Into Egypt 1952,Mr 19,33:2
Crucible, The 1953,Ja 23,15:2
Cat on a Hot Tin Roof 1955,Mr 25,18:2
Cat on a Hot Tin Roof 1955,Ap 3,II,1:1
Girls in 509, The 1958,O 16,47:1
Gang's All Here, The 1959,O 2,23:1
Conquering Hero, The 1961,Ja 17,40:2
Coming Forth by Day of Osiris Jones, The; Kid, The 1961,Mr 15,45:2
Romulus 1962,Ja 11,27:1
Deputy, The 1964,F 27,26:1
Galileo 1967,Ap 14,31:1
More Stately Mansions 1967,N 1,40:1
Memory Bank, The 1970,Ja 12,24:3
Memory Bank, The 1970,Ja 25,II,1:4
Room Service 1970,My 13,49:1
Stewart, Fred (Composer)
Prelude 1936,Ap 20,17:4
Bury the Dead 1936,Ap 20,17:4
Everywhere I Roam 1939,Ja 8,IX,1:1
Stewart, Fred (Director)
Madame Is Served 1949,F 15,28:1
Coming Forth by Day of Osiris Jones, The; Kid, The 1961,Mr 15,45:2
Stewart, Fred (Lyricist)
Everywhere I Roam 1938,D 30,10:4
Stewart, Fred (Miscellaneous)
Marathon '33 1963,D 23,20:1
Stewart, Fred (Playwright)
Town and Country Jig, A 1937,D 13,22:8
Stewart, Fred (Producer)
Celebration 1948,Ap 12,24:2
Afternoon Storm 1948,Ap 12,24:2
Hope Is the Thing With Feathers 1948,Ap 12,24:2
Stewart, Fred M (Composer)
Malice in Wonderland 1953,D 17,51:3
Stewart, Fred M (Lyricist)
Malice in Wonderland 1953,D 17,51:3
Stewart, Gordon (Producer)
Pirates of Penzance, The 1967,Ag 7,34:2
Stewart, Grant
Cave Girl, The 1920,Ag 19,12:2
Survival of the Fittest 1921,Mr 15,14:1
Married Woman, The 1921,D 26,21:1
Mike Angelo 1923,Ja 9,26:2
Children of the Moon 1923,Ag 18,10:3
In His Arms 1924,O 14,23:1
Undercurrent, The 1925,F 4,18:2
Bride Retires, The 1925,My 18,12:3
Young Woodley 1925,N 3,34:1
Veils 1928,Mr 14,28:5
Money Lender, The 1928,Ag 28,27:3
Olympia 1928,O 17,26:1
Wings Over Europe 1928,D 11,35:1
Stewart, Helen
Pot-Luck 1921,S 30,10:1
Pinch Hitter, A 1922,Je 2,20:4
Busybody, The 1924,S 30,27:5
Play Without a Name, A 1928,N 26,30:5
Guest in the House 1942,F 25,25:2
Stewart, Henry S (Composer)
Half Moon Inn 1923,Mr 21,19:2
Old King's 1924,Mr 12,19:3
Half Moon Inn 1925,Mr 10,14:1
Stewart, James
Tiger Smiles, The 1930,D 18,29:1
Carry Nation 1932,O 31,18:2
Goodbye Again 1932,D 29,16:4
Spring in Autumn 1933,O 25,22:5
All Good Americans 1933,D 6,29:2
Yellow Jack 1934,Mr 7,22:6
Divided by Three 1934,O 3,24:2
Page Miss Glory 1934,N 28,24:2
Journey by Night 1935,Ap 7,IX,2:1
Journey by Night, A 1935,Ap 17,26:3
Harvey 1947,Jl 15,27:3
Harvey 1970,F 25,41:1
Stewart, Jean-Pierre
Henry IV, Part II 1968,Jl 2,33:1
King Lear 1968,N 8,43:1
In the Matter of J Robert Oppenheimer 1969,Mr 7,28:1
Miser, The 1969,My 9,35:1
Stewart, Jeb
Oklahoma! 1958,Mr 8,15:2
Stewart, Jimmy
Harvey 1970,Mr 8,II,1:1
Stewart, Job
Romeo and Juliet 1956,O 25,41:1
Macbeth 1956,O 30,42:2
Troilus and Cressida 1956,D 27,21:1
Hamlet 1958,D 17,2:7
Henry V 1958,D 26,2:7
Romeo and Juliet 1962,F 14,39:1
Saint Joan 1962,F 21,57:4
Astrakhan Coat, The 1967,Ja 13,18:1
Stewart, Joe
Shadow Years, The 1957,Ja 9,26:2
Stewart, Johnny
High Button Shoes 1947,O 10,32:2
Love Life 1948,O 8,31:2

Stewart, Johnny—Cont
Happy Time, The 1950,Ja 25,24:1
King and I, The 1951,Mr 30,26:2
King and I, The 1951,Ap 8,II,1:1
Grass Harp, The 1952,Mr 28,26:2
Bernardine 1952,O 17,33:4
Bernardine 1952,N 9,II,1:1
Sleeping Prince, The 1956,N 2,31:1
Waltz of the Toreadors, The 1957,Ja 18,17:2
Waltz of the Toreadors, The 1957,Ja 27,II,1:1
Waltz of the Toreadors, The 1958,Mr 5,37:1
Crystal Heart, The 1960,F 16,31:2
Tattooed Countess, The 1961,My 4,40:2
Stewart, Joseph
Sound of Music, The 1959,N 17,40:2
Stewart, June
Comes the Revelation 1942,My 27,26:2
Stewart, Katherine
Trimmed in Scarlet 1920,F 3,18:1
Genius and the Crowd 1920,S 7,20:1
Love Letter, The 1921,O 5,20:1
Farmer's Wife, The 1924,O 10,22:3
Jane-Our Stranger 1925,O 9,27:2
Sport of Kings, The 1926,My 5,24:2
Strange Prince, The 1926,D 8,24:2
Constant Nymph, The 1926,D 10,31:1
Pickwick 1927,Mr 13,VII,1:1
Pickwick 1927,S 6,35:2
Age of Innocence, The 1928,N 28,24:2
Recapture 1930,Ja 19,VIII,2:6
Tonight or Never 1930,N 19,19:3
Money in the Air 1932,Mr 8,19:3
Shatter'd Lamp, The 1934,Mr 22,26:3
Ode to Liberty 1934,D 22,20:2
Yr Obedient Husband 1938,Ja 11,26:5
I Married an Angel 1938,My 12,26:2
Stewart, Larry
Lend an Ear 1948,D 17,38:2
Stewart, Lesley
Skyscraper 1965,N 15,48:1
Stewart, Lila Agnew (Director)
In the Land of the Midnight Sun 1930,Ja 7,27:4
Stewart, Louis
Advertising of Kate, The 1922,My 9,22:2
Stewart, Mac (Miscellaneous)
Disney on Parade 1970,S 24,63:1
Stewart, Margaret
Knickerbocker Holiday 1938,O 20,26:2
Stewart, Marianne
You Touched Me! 1945,S 26,27:2
You Touched Me! 1945,S 30,II,1:1
Swan Song 1946,My 16,29:2
Survivors, The 1948,Ja 20,27:2
Stewart, Martha
Park Avenue 1946,N 5,31:2
Guys and Dolls 1951,O 7,II,1:1
Stewart, Martin
Once Over Lightly 1942,N 20,26:2
Stewart, Mary
Bedrock 1934,N 18,II,6:3
Fuente Ovejuna; Sheep Well, The 1936,My 3,II,4:1
No More Peace 1937,F 27,9:1
Stewart, Melvin
Wedding in Japan 1957,Mr 12,37:7
Simply Heavenly 1957,My 22,28:2
Cool World, The 1960,F 23,38:2
Brouhaha 1960,Ap 27,31:2
Hostage, The 1960,S 21,42:1
Moon on a Rainbow Shawl 1962,Ja 16,30:1
In the Counting House 1962,D 15,5:5
My Mother, My Father and Me 1963,Mr 25,5:5
Last Minstrel, The 1963,My 9,40:2
Stewart, Michael (Playwright)
Bye Bye Birdie 1960,Ap 15,13:4
Carnival! 1961,Ap 14,22:2
Hello, Dolly! 1964,Ja 17,22:1
Hello, Dolly! 1964,Ja 26,II,1:1
Those That Play the Clowns 1966,N 25,48:1
Hello, Dolly! 1967,N 13,61:1
George M! 1968,Ap 11,48:1
Carnival! 1968,D 13,58:1
Stewart, Mickey
Alice in Arms 1945,F 1,18:4
Stewart, Mike (Lyricist)
Razzle Dazzle 1951,F 20,21:1
Shoestring Revue 1955,Mr 1,22:2
Shoestring '57 1956,N 6,31:1
Stewart, Mike (Playwright)
Razzle Dazzle 1951,F 20,21:1
Shoestring Revue 1955,Mr 1,22:2
Littlest Revue, The 1956,My 23,37:2
Stewart, Murray C
Young American, A 1946,Ja 18,14:5
Stewart, Nonie
My Beginning 1962,Ja 31,21:1
Lion in Love, The 1963,Ap 26,28:3
Stewart, Norman
Under the Gaslight 1929,Ap 3,27:1
Getting Even 1929,Ag 20,31:1
Stewart, Owen
New Faces of 1936 1936,My 20,24:5
Stewart, Parker
School for Husbands, The 1933,O 17,26:5

Stewart, Patricia
  Best Foot Forward 1963,Ap 3,43:1
Stewart, Patrick
  Troilus and Cressida 1969,Jl 31,26:1
  King John 1970,Je 19,27:2
Stewart, Paul
  Fall and Rise of Susan Lenox, The 1920,Je 11,11:2
  Two Seconds 1931,O 10,20:6
  East of Broadway 1932,Ja 27,19:3
  Bulls, Bears and Asses 1932,My 7,11:3
  Wine of Choice 1938,F 22,18:4
  Native Son 1941,Mr 25,26:5
  Mister Roberts 1950,My 21,II,1:1
Stewart, Paul (Director)
  Alternate Current 1939,D 23,8:3
  Twilight Walk 1951,S 25,25:4
  Sing Me No Lullaby 1954,O 15,17:2
Stewart, Paul (Playwright)
  Miss Temple Is Willing 1936,Jl 21,13:1
Stewart, Paula
  Most Happy Fella, The 1959,F 11,50:2
  From A to Z 1960,Ap 21,23:2
  Wildcat 1960,D 17,20:2
  Let It Ride 1961,O 13,27:4
Stewart, Princess
  Black Nativity 1961,D 12,54:2
Stewart, Ray
  Play 1964,Mr 25,46:2
  Experiment, The 1967,My 9,54:2
  King Lear 1968,N 8,43:1
  Cry of Players, A 1968,N 15,40:1
  Inner Journey, The 1969,Mr 21,42:1
  Postcards 1970,Mr 17,36:1
  Early Morning 1970,N 26,57:1
Stewart, Rey
  Guns 1928,Ag 7,25:2
Stewart, Robert
  Daughters of Atreus 1936,O 15,33:1
  Othello 1937,Ja 7,16:4
  Last Stop 1944,S 6,17:2
Stewart, Robert T
  Oedipus Tyrannus 1941,My 10,13:8
Stewart, Robin
  Camelot 1960,D 5,42:1
Stewart, Rodney
  Mr Big 1941,O 1,24:2
  Heart of a City 1942,F 13,24:6
Stewart, Ron (Composer)
  Sambo 1969,D 22,42:1
Stewart, Rosalie (Producer)
  Show-Off, The 1924,O 21,21:1
  Enchanted April, The 1925,Ag 25,12:3
  Craig's Wife 1925,O 13,21:2
  Daisy Mayme 1926,O 26,24:2
  A la Carte 1927,Ag 18,25:3
  Behold the Bridegroom 1927,D 27,24:1
  Precious 1929,Ja 15,22:5
Stewart, Rosemarie (Choreographer)
  Ice Capades 1952,S 12,18:1
  Ice Capades 1953,S 11,25:1
  Ice Capades 1955,S 15,38:1
  Ice Capades 1957,S 5,33:2
  Ice Capades 1960,S 1,30:1
  Ice Capades 1961,Ag 31,24:4
Stewart, Rosemarie (Director)
  Ice Capades 1964,Ag 27,27:2
Stewart, Rosemarie (Miscellaneous)
  Ice Capades 1958,S 4,33:2
  Ice Capades 1959,S 4,12:1
  Ice Capades 1960,S 1,30:1
  Ice Capades 1962,Ag 30,34:1
Stewart, Sada
  Under Milk Wood 1953,My 29,17:1
Stewart, Slam
  Holiday on Broadway 1948,Ap 28,33:3
Stewart, Sophie
  Marigold 1930,O 9,23:1
  Marriage Is No Joke 1934,F 7,16:2
  Young Mr Disraeli 1934,N 13,22:2
  Emperor of Make-Believe, The 1936,Mr 17,25:5
  Young Mr Disraeli 1937,N 10,30:5
  Twelfth Night 1940,O 27,IX,1:5
  Twelfth Night 1940,N 20,26:3
  Life With Father 1947,Je 6,27:3
Stewart, Therese
  Adding Machine, The 1923,Mr 20,24:1
Stewart, Vance (Mrs)
  Prunella 1929,Ap 10,23:3
Stewart, Virginia (Playwright)
  Emperor's New Clothes, The 1950,Je 20,23:2
Stewart, William
  Trumpets of the Lord 1963,D 23,22:3
  Trumpets of the Lord 1969,Ap 30,37:1
Stewer, Jan (Playwright)
  Barnet's Folly 1935,F 15,22:2
  Barnet's Folly 1935,Mr 10,VIII,2:1
Steyaert, Francois
  As Husbands Go 1931,Mr 6,26:5
Steytler, Henrietta
  Iolanthe 1951,F 16,22:1
Stibbs, Ruth
  39 Steps 1938,Mr 12,13:1

Stiber, Nancy
  Nights of Wrath; Nuits de la Colere, Les 1947,D 1,26:4
  Silver Tassie, The 1949,Jl 22,16:5
  Silver Tassle, The 1949,S 4,II,1:1
Stickley, Grace
  Burmese Pwe, A 1926,Mr 17,28:1
  Romantic Young Lady, The 1926,My 5,24:3
  Pinwheel 1927,F 4,16:4
Stickney, Dorothy
  Squall, The 1926,N 12,20:1
  Chicago 1926,D 31,11:1
  March Hares 1928,Ap 3,32:6
  Beaux' Stratagem, The 1928,Je 5,20:1
  Beaux' Stratagem, The 1928,Je 10,VIII,1:1
  Front Page, The 1928,Ag 15,19:2
  Front Page, The 1928,Ag 26,VII,1:1
  Milestones 1930,Je 3,27:1
  Philip Goes Forth 1931,Ja 4,VIII,2:2
  Philip Goes Forth 1931,Ja 13,35:4
  Way of the World, The 1931,Je 2,34:3
  Another Language 1932,Ap 26,25:3
  Another Language 1932,My 15,VIII,1:1
  Another Language 1933,My 9,20:2
  County Chairman, The 1936,My 26,26:5
  On Borrowed Time 1938,F 4,16:4
  Life With Father 1939,Ag 15,14:4
  Life With Father 1939,N 9,26:2
  Life With Father 1939,N 19,X,1:1
  Life With Mother 1948,Je 9,36:3
  Life With Mother 1948,O 21,32:2
  Life With Mother 1948,O 31,II,1:1
  Life With Mother 1949,Mr 27,II,1:1
  Small Hours, The 1951,F 16,22:1
  To Be Continued 1952,Ap 24,37:2
  Kind Sir 1953,S 28,21:2
  Kind Sir 1953,N 5,41:2
  Honeys, The 1955,Ap 29,26:1
  Lovely Light, A 1960,F 9,27:4
  Riot Act, The 1963,Mr 9,5:2
  Lovely Light, A 1964,Ja 21,24:2
  Life With Father 1967,O 20,53:2
  Mundy Scheme, The 1969,D 12,75:1
Stickney, Dorothy (Playwright)
  Lovely Light, A 1960,F 9,27:4
Stickney, Grace
  Dybbuk, The 1925,D 16,22:2
Stiebel, Victor (Scenic Designer)
  Joyce Grenfell Requests the Pleasure 1955,O 11,48:1
Stiefel, Milton
  Taps 1925,Ap 15,16:2
  Man or Devil 1925,My 22,22:4
Stiefel, Milton (Director)
  First Night 1930,N 27,32:3
  Unexpected Husband 1931,Je 3,29:4
  Her Tin Soldier 1933,Ap 7,22:6
  Another Love 1934,Mr 20,26:3
  Post Road 1935,Jl 23,24:3
  Jazz Age 1937,Jl 20,19:3
  Horse Fever 1940,N 25,21:2
Stiefel, Milton (Producer)
  Another Love 1934,Mr 20,26:3
  Ah, Wilderness! 1935,Ag 20,25:1
Stieglitz, Perry (Playwright)
  Fall 1957,N 22,19:1
Stiegmeister, Elie (Composer)
  Swing Out, Sweet Land! 1944,N 10,24:6
Stiehl, Claude Albon (Playwright)
  Royal Koko 1937,Ja 10,X,2:5
Stiffler, Ledru
  I'll Say She Is 1924,My 20,15:1
Stiller, Jerry
  Coriolanus 1954,Ja 20,34:2
  Golden Apple, The 1954,Mr 12,15:2
  Clandestine Marriage, The 1954,O 4,23:2
  Men in White 1955,F 26,13:2
  Julius Caesar 1955,Jl 13,20:1
  Tempest, The 1955,Ag 2,18:2
  Tempest, The 1955,Ag 7,II,1:1
  Carefree Tree, The 1955,O 12,37:2
  Three Times Three; Merrye Playe, A 1956,My 24,27:2
  Three Times Three; Box and Cox 1956,My 24,27:2
  Three Times Three; How He Lied to Her Husband 1956,My 24,27:2
  Diary of a Scoundrel 1956,N 5,41:1
  Good Woman of Setzuan, The 1956,D 19,41:2
  Measure for Measure 1957,Ja 23,24:1
  Taming of the Shrew, The 1957,F 21,30:2
  Romeo and Juliet 1957,Je 28,30:2
  Two Gentlemen of Verona 1957,Jl 23,21:5
  Macbeth 1957,Ag 16,11:2
  Richard III 1957,N 26,41:1
  As You Like It 1958,Ja 21,33:6
  Power and the Glory, The 1958,D 12,2:7
  Secret Concubine, The 1960,Mr 22,29:2
Stiller, Nikki
  Antigone 1962,D 29,5:5
Stiller, Paul
  Paths of Glory 1935,S 27,24:2
  Richard II 1961,Ag 30,25:1

Stilley, Walter (Scenic Designer)
  Cretan Woman, The 1954,My 21,17:2
Stillman, Al (Composer)
  Star and Garter 1942,Je 25,26:2
  Icetime 1947,My 29,28:2
  Howdy Mr Ice 1948,Je 25,28:5
  Howdy, Mr Ice of 1950 1949,My 27,24:2
Stillman, Al (Lyricist)
  Virginia 1937,S 3,13:2
  It Happens on Ice 1940,O 11,24:3
  Star and Garter 1942,Je 25,26:2
  Stars on Ice 1942,Jl 3,12:2
  Howdy, Mr Ice of 1950 1949,My 27,24:2
Stillman, C D
  Gentlemen, the Queen 1927,Ap 23,14:3
Stillman, George Schley
  In the Days of the Turbins 1934,Mr 7,22:5
Stillman, Henry
  Power of Darkness, The 1920,Ja 22,22:1
  Medea 1920,Mr 23,12:2
  Henry IV, Part I 1926,Je 1,29:1
  Aiglon, L' 1927,D 27,24:3
  Yellow Jacket, The 1928,N 8,27:3
Stillman, Henry (Director)
  Open House 1925,D 15,28:3
  Number 7 1926,S 9,21:3
  Bottom of the Cup, The 1927,F 1,24:2
  Forbidden Roads 1928,Ap 17,26:4
  Falstaff 1928,D 26,14:2
  Milestones 1930,Je 3,27:1
  With Privileges 1930,S 16,30:2
  Jefferson Davis 1936,F 19,17:2
Stillman, Henry (Playwright)
  Nocturne 1925,F 17,19:1
  Lally 1927,F 9,16:3
  Technique 1931,My 15,21:1
Stillman, Jack
  Jonica 1930,Ap 8,27:1
Stillman, John Jr (Miscellaneous)
  All the Living 1938,Mr 25,14:4
Stillman, Keith
  Fiesta 1929,S 18,35:1
  Blue and the Gray, The; War Is Hell Gray, The 1929,D 27,26:4
Stillman, Marcia
  Antigone 1959,S 16,46:2
Stills, Mary
  Potters, The 1923,D 10,21:4
  Patsy, The 1925,D 24,8:5
  Take My Advice 1927,N 2,24:3
  Be Your Age 1929,F 5,27:1
Stillwagon, William
  Little Theatre Tournament; Father Returns, The 1929,My 7,28:1
Stillwell, Charles (Miscellaneous)
  Man With the Portfolio, The 1931,F 12,24:6
Stillwell, Charles B (Scenic Designer)
  Chains 1930,F 23,29:2
  Riverside Drive 1931,Ja 6,24:2
Stillwell, Elizabeth
  Happy Valley, Limited 1936,Je 30,15:1
Stillwell, George
  Ambush 1921,O 11,22:1
  Tales of Rigo 1927,My 31,25:3
  Machinal 1928,S 8,10:3
  Machinal 1928,S 16,IX,1:1
Stilphen, Louise
  Hansel and Gretel 1929,D 25,21:1
Stimac, Anthony J (Director)
  Rip Van Wrinkle 1967,D 23,28:1
  Papers 1968,D 3,54:1
Stimmel, George L
  His Majesty the Queen 1926,Mr 9,8:1
Stimpson, Harry F
  Foemen of the Yard 1935,Ap 6,10:4
Stinchfeld, George
  Fireman's Flame, The 1937,O 11,26:2
Stine, Gayle (Producer)
  Champagne Complex 1955,Ap 13,33:1
  Lovers 1956,My 11,23:1
Stine, Harold
  Without the Walls 1922,Ap 17,17:1
Stinnes, Daisy (Playwright)
  Sons, The 1922,D 13,28:3
Stinnett, Macleary
  Design for Living 1933,Ja 3,19:5
  Design for Living 1933,Ja 25,13:2
Stinnette, Dorothy
  Out of This World 1955,O 13,35:2
  Out of This World 1955,N 10,44:2
  New Girl in Town 1957,My 15,40:1
  Leave It to Jane 1959,My 26,30:2
  Queen and the Rebels, The 1965,F 26,16:1
Stinnette, Juanita
  Deep Harlem 1929,Ja 8,35:2
  Sugar Hill 1931,D 26,15:2
Stipo, Carmine
  Awakening of Spring, The 1964,My 13,50:1
  One Is a Lonely Number 1964,Je 19,37:3
Stirling, Edward
  Speckled Band, The 1926,N 14,VIII,2:1
  Escape 1926,D 12,VIII,3:4

rling, Edward—Cont
Where There's a Will 1939,Ja 18,16:6
rling, Edward (Director)
Where There's a Will 1939,Ja 18,16:6
rling, Edward (Playwright)
Rag Picker of Paris, The: or, Modest Modiste 1935,N 12,23:7
Where There's a Will 1939,Ja 18,16:6
rling, Edward (Producer)
Importance of Being Earnest, The 1926,O 3,VIII,2:1
Where There's a Will 1939,Ja 18,16:6
rling, Luzerne L
Coriolanus 1927,Je 18,8:3
rling, Nora
Age of Innocence, The 1928,N 28,24:2
rling, Nora (Playwright)
My Name Is Legion 1952,Ap 21,23:7
rling, Oscar
Hamlet 1923,N 20,23:3
Interference 1927,O 19,24:3
Getting Married 1931,Mr 31,25:5
Chinese Nightingale, The 1934,O 6,20:4
Dorian Gray 1936,Jl 21,13:3
Don't Look Now! 1936,N 4,41:3
Kind Lady 1940,S 4,28:3
rling, Richard
Places, Please 1937,N 13,10:6
rling, William
Let Freedom Ring 1935,N 7,26:2
ites, Julane
Happy Time, The 1968,Ja 19,32:2
ith, Michael
Tall Kentuckian, The 1953,Je 17,30:1
ix, John (Director)
Shoemaker's Prodigious Wife, The 1949,Je 15,38:2
Father, The 1949,Ag 21,II,1:1
Earth Spirit 1950,Je 7,33:4
Mary Rose 1951,Mr 5,25:2
Mary Rose 1951,Mr 11,II,1:1
Take a Giant Step 1953,O 4,II,1:1
What Every Woman Knows 1954,D 23,16:2
Wisteria Trees, The 1955,F 3,20:2
Othello 1955,S 8,27:2
Too Late the Phalarope 1956,O 12,35:1
Park 1970,Ap 23,47:1
Slow Dance on the Killing Ground 1970,My 14,43:1
rober, Anita
Antony and Cleopatra 1959,Ja 14,28:1
robitzer (Playwright)
Liselott 1932,My 22,VIII,2:3
robrawa, Renee
Singing Jailbirds 1928,My 20,VIII,2:1
rock, David
Front Page, The 1968,O 20,85:5
rock, Elwin
Sleeping Prince, The 1956,N 2,31:1
rock, Mary Michol
Stephen D 1966,Ag 5,17:1
rock, Nigel
You Never Can Tell 1948,Mr 17,31:2
Caine Mutiny Court-Martial, The 1956,Je 14,40:1
Mixed Doubles 1969,Ap 12,43:2
rock, Ralph (Playwright)
Habit 1926,N 4,VIII,4:7
Quest 1928,Ja 8,VIII,2:3
rockbridge, Dorothy (Playwright)
Mistletoe Bough, The 1923,My 12,15:4
rockdale, Ann
Hail Scrawdyke! 1966,N 29,50:1
rocker, Leonard
Paul Bunyan 1941,My 6,25:1
Rosalinda; Fledermaus, Die 1942,O 29,26:5
rocker, Stewart
Zaporogetz Za Dunayem 1937,My 9,II,5:3
rockhausen, Karlheinz (Playwright)
Originale 1964,S 9,46:1
rocking, Robert
Rat's Mass, A 1969,N 1,39:1
Candaules, Commissioner 1970,My 29,15:1
Street Sounds 1970,O 23,32:1
rocking, Sybil
Bees and the Flowers, The 1946,S 27,19:3
rockley, Martha
Last Enemy, The 1934,Jl 13,14:4
Stockton, Billy
Pied Piper of Hamelin, The 1950,Ap 3,19:2
Stockton, Chuck (Miscellaneous)
Love Is a Time of Day 1969,D 23,21:3
Stockton, Esther
God of Vengeance, The 1922,D 20,22:5
Jealous Moon, The 1928,N 21,32:2
Stockton, Frank R (Playwright)
Lady or the Tiger?, The 1966,O 19,53:1
Stockton, Miriam (Playwright)
Scarlet Letter, The 1926,Ja 8,16:5
Stockton, Roberta
Importance of Being Earnest, The 1936,O 22,31:2
Stockton, Sadie
Shake Hands With the Devil 1949,O 21,30:4
Stockwell, Dean
Innocent Voyage, The 1943,N 16,27:2
Compulsion 1957,O 25,21:1
Compulsion 1957,N 3,II,1:1

Stockwell, Guy
Innocent Voyage, The 1943,N 16,27:2
Chicken Every Sunday 1944,Ap 6,27:2
Stockwell, Harry
Earl Carroll's Vanities 1930,Jl 2,28:3
As Thousands Cheer 1933,O 2,22:1
Scandals 1939,Ag 29,17:2
Oklahoma! 1943,N 14,II,1:1
Marinka 1945,Jl 19,19:2
Can-Can 1959,Ag 26,25:4
Stockwell, Jeremy
Fortune and Men's Eyes 1969,O 23,55:1
Stockwell, Jock (Costume Designer)
Carricknabauna 1967,Mr 31,30:1
Stockwell, Jock (Lighting Director)
Cry of the Raindrop 1961,Mr 8,38:1
Carricknabauna 1967,Mr 31,30:1
Stockwell, Jock (Scenic Designer)
Cry of the Raindrop 1961,Mr 8,38:1
Carricknabauna 1967,Mr 31,30:1
Stoddard, Brandon
J B 1958,Ap 24,37:1
Stoddard, Eunice
Revolt 1928,N 1,25:3
Meet the Prince 1929,F 26,30:5
Red Rust 1929,D 18,31:1
Month in the Country, A 1930,Mr 18,30:5
Puppet Show 1930,O 29,26:5
Life Line, The 1930,D 29,19:3
House of Connelly, The 1931,S 29,22:4
1931 1931,D 11,34:3
Night Over Taos 1932,Mr 10,25:3
Big Night 1933,Ja 18,16:2
Three-Cornered Moon 1933,Mr 17,20:6
Men in White 1933,S 27,24:2
Till the Day I Die 1935,Mr 27,24:5
Weep for the Virgins 1935,D 2,18:1
Case of Clyde Griffiths 1936,Mr 14,10:4
Casey Jones 1938,F 21,14:2
Stoddard, George E (Playwright)
Jim Jam Jems 1920,O 5,13:2
Go-Go 1923,Mr 13,19:4
Sharlee 1923,N 23,20:1
China Rose 1925,Ja 20,18:1
Oh! Oh! Nurse 1925,D 8,28:4
Stoddard, Haila
Jazz Age 1937,Jl 20,19:3
Woman's a Fool-To Be Clever, A 1938,O 19,18:6
I Know What I Like 1939,N 25,13:5
Kindred 1939,D 27,17:2
Susannah and the Elders 1940,O 13,47:7
Susannah and the Elders 1940,O 30,28:2
Rivals, The 1941,N 18,32:2
Rivals, The 1942,Ja 15,24:2
Moon Vine, The 1943,F 12,22:2
Blithe Spirit 1943,S 12,II,1:1
Rip Van Winkle 1947,Jl 16,28:2
Doctor Social 1948,F 12,29:5
Springtime for Henry 1951,Mr 15,36:2
Glad Tidings 1951,O 12,33:2
Frogs of Spring, The 1953,O 21,36:2
One Eye Closed 1954,N 25,45:2
Ever Since Paradise 1957,Jl 12,18:4
Dark Corners 1964,My 6,43:1
Stoddard, Haila (Director)
Round With Ring, A 1969,O 30,56:1
Stoddard, Haila (Miscellaneous)
Secret Room, The 1945,N 8,16:2
Stoddard, Haila (Playwright)
Come Play With Me 1959,My 1,33:5
Beast in Me, The 1963,My 17,29:1
Round With Ring, A 1969,O 30,56:1
Stoddard, Haila (Producer)
Dead Pigeon 1953,D 24,10:2
One Eye Closed 1954,N 25,45:2
Come Play With Me 1959,My 1,33:5
Thurber Carnival, A 1960,F 27,13:2
Birthday Party, The 1967,O 4,40:2
Private Lives 1968,My 20,59:1
Gingham Dog, The 1969,Ap 24,41:1
Last Sweet Days of Isaac, The 1970,Ja 27,49:1
Lemon Sky 1970,My 18,40:1
Stoddard, Henry H
Lady of the Lamp, The 1920,Ag 18,6:4
Stoddard, Lothrop (Miscellaneous)
R U R 1922,O 15,VIII,1:1
Stoddard, Marie
Topics of 1923 1923,N 21,23:2
Artists and Models 1924,O 16,33:3
My Princess 1927,O 7,24:2
Student Prince, The 1931,Ja 30,18:1
Stoddard, Michael
Narrow Road to the Deep North 1969,D 2,64:1
Stoddard, Miriam
Don Juan 1921,S 8,14:2
Stoddart, J H
Gentlemen of the Press 1928,Ag 28,27:2
Ladies of the Jury 1929,O 22,26:2
Louder, Please! 1931,N 13,26:4
Stodelle, Ernestine
Russian Bank 1940,My 25,20:2
Stoeber, Orville
Boy on the Straight-Back Chair 1969,Mr 18,36:1

Stoeber, Orville (Composer)
Boy on the Straight-Back Chair 1969,Mr 18,36:1
Tonight in Living Color; David Show, The 1969,Je 11,43:1
Tonight in Living Color; Golden Fleece, The 1969,Je 11,43:1
Stoessel, Albert (Musical Director)
Hansel and Gretel 1929,D 25,21:1
Poisoned Kiss, The 1937,Ap 22,19:1
Stoessel, Ludwig
Street Scene 1930,Mr 16,IX,4:1
Stoianovsky
Chauve-Souris 1922,Je 6,17:4
Chauve-Souris 1925,Ja 15,25:1
Stoiber, Rudolf (Producer)
Amen Corner, The 1965,Je 13,82:4
Stojkovic, Danilo
Progress of Bora, The Tailor, The 1968,Je 27,49:2
Ubu Roi 1968,Je 29,20:1
Victor, or The Children Take Over 1968,Jl 10,22:4
Stoker, Bram (Original Author)
Dracula 1927,Mr 11,24:3
Dracula 1927,O 6,29:1
Dracula 1931,Ap 14,33:3
Dracula Sabbat 1970,O 2,28:2
Stoker, Bram (Playwright)
Cops and Horrors; Dracula 1970,Ag 11,27:1
Stoker, H G
Loyalties 1922,S 28,18:1
Journey's End 1928,D 30,VIII,4:1
Journey's End 1929,Jl 14,IX,5:1
Man Who Pays the Piper, The 1931,Mr 1,VIII,2:4
Man of Yesterday 1935,Mr 17,VIII,1:4
Flashing Stream, The 1938,S 2,21:4
Flashing Stream, The 1938,S 18,X,1:4
Stoker, H G (Playwright)
Below the Surface 1932,Ja 31,VIII,2:1
Stoker, Willard (Director)
Don't Listen, Ladies 1948,D 29,16:2
Thurber Carnival, A 1962,Ap 12,42:1
Stokes, Al
They Shall Not Die 1934,F 22,24:4
Too Many Boats 1934,S 12,26:3
Dance With Your Gods 1934,O 8,14:3
Conjur 1938,N 1,27:2
Mamba's Daughters 1939,Ja 4,24:2
Mamba's Daughters 1940,Mr 25,10:4
Cabin in the Sky 1940,O 26,19:2
Stokes, Desmond
Measure for Measure 1967,F 15,37:1
Hamlet 1967,F 17,44:1
Romeo and Juliet 1967,F 22,18:1
Stokes, Dorothy
Camel's Back, The 1923,N 4,19:2
Stokes, Eric (Miscellaneous)
Way of the World, The 1965,Je 2,40:1
Stokes, Fritz
Mercy Street 1969,O 28,43:1
Stokes, I Newton Phelps 2d
Coriolanus 1927,Je 18,8:3
Stokes, John
Lawful Larceny 1922,Ja 3,20:2
Silence 1924,N 13,18:2
City Haul 1929,D 31,14:4
Those We Love 1930,F 20,22:2
Stokes, Leslie (Playwright)
Laura Garnett 1934,Jl 17,24:4
Oscar Wilde 1936,S 30,29:4
Oscar Wilde 1936,O 18,X,3:8
Out of Sight 1937,Mr 5,17:6
Out of Sight 1937,Mr 28,XI,2:2
Frozen Glory 1938,F 11,27:6
Oscar Wilde 1938,O 11,20:2
Oscar Wilde 1938,O 16,IX,1:1
Oscar Wilde 1957,Ap 20,21:3
Stokes, Marian
That French Lady 1927,Mr 16,29:3
Stokes, Melvin
Parisiana 1928,F 10,26:3
Stokes, Sewell (Playwright)
Laura Garnett 1934,Jl 17,24:4
Oscar Wilde 1936,S 30,29:4
Oscar Wilde 1936,O 18,X,3:8
Out of Sight 1937,Mr 5,17:6
Out of Sight 1937,Mr 28,XI,2:2
Frozen Glory 1938,F 11,27:6
Oscar Wilde 1938,O 11,20:2
Oscar Wilde 1938,O 16,IX,1:1
Oscar Wilde 1957,Ap 20,21:3
Stokesberry, Lauren
Cotton Stockings 1923,D 19,16:2
Stokman, Abraham
World of Kurt Weill in Song, The 1964,My 13,53:1
Stokowski, Leopold (Musical Director)
Midsummer Night's Dream, A 1956,Jl 20,9:5
Stokowski, Sonya
White Haired Boy, The 1940,O 29,32:6
Letters to Lucerne 1941,D 9,47:6
Letters to Lucerne 1941,D 24,14:2
Kiss Them for Me 1945,Mr 21,27:2
Dream Girl 1945,D 15,13:2
Stoler, Shirley
Breaking Wall, The 1960,Ja 26,27:5

Stoler, Shirley—Cont
Balls 1965,F 11,45:1
Stoll, Oswald (Sir) (Miscellaneous)
Casanova 1932,Je 19,IX,2:1
Stoll, Oswald (Sir) (Producer)
Twenty to One 1935,N 13,24:3
Stoll, Silvia
Half-Caste, The 1926,Mr 30,20:4
Stoller, Maurice (Playwright)
Maid in Japan 1939,F 20,12:5
Stoller, Mike (Miscellaneous)
Hail Scrawdyke! 1966,N 29,50:1
Stollery, David John
On Borrowed Time 1953,F 11,34:1
Stollery, Dick
Jotham Valley 1951,F 7,37:2
Stoloff, Michaela
Ist Geraldine ein Engel? 1946,N 4,33:4
Stoltz, Robert (Composer)
Im Weissen Roessel 1931,Ja 4,VIII,3:5
Stolz, Robert
Merry Widow, The 1943,Ag 5,19:2
Stolz, Robert (Composer)
Sky High 1925,Mr 3,21:4
Rise and Shine 1936,My 8,21:4
Night of Love 1941,Ja 8,14:2
Mr Strauss Goes to Boston 1945,S 7,20:2
Eisrevue 1969,O 23,55:1
Stolz, Robert (Miscellaneous)
Vienna at Night 1945,Ap 30,12:4
Stolz, Robert (Musical Director)
Gypsy Baron, The 1942,Je 20,8:5
Gypsy Baron, The 1942,Ag 7,12:4
Beggar Student, The 1942,S 26,11:4
Merry Widow, The 1943,Ag 22,II,5:1
Mr Strauss Goes to Boston 1945,S 7,20:2
Stolz, Robert (Playwright)
Merry Widow, The 1943,Ag 5,19:2
Merry Widow, The 1944,O 9,17:1
Stolzenberg, Sidney
Seven Against One 1930,My 7,25:1
Stone, Alfred
Stone for Danny Fisher, A 1954,O 22,24:2
Stone, Allen
Criss Cross 1926,O 13,20:2
Stone, Allene
Stepping Stones 1923,N 7,14:3
Stone, Alma (Original Author)
Bible Salesman, The 1961,F 21,40:1
Stone, Alma (Playwright)
Bible Salesman, The 1960,F 22,12:2
Stone, Barton
Show Boat 1966,Jl 20,48:1
Trial of Lee Harvey Oswald, The 1967,N 6,64:1
Stone, Ben
Detective Story 1954,F 13,11:2
Thunder Rock 1956,F 27,18:1
Girl of the Golden West, The 1957,N 6,44:1
Stone, Bentley
Street Singer, The 1929,S 18,35:2
Stone, Bernice
Vaudeville Marches On 1938,D 30,11:1
Stone, Betty
Night in Venice, A 1952,Je 27,18:6
Stone, Billy
High Hatters, The 1928,My 11,28:2
Stone, C
Lady of the Lamp, The 1920,Ag 18,6:4
Stone, Carol
Mackerel Skies 1934,Ja 24,20:4
Jayhawker 1934,O 16,31:4
Jayhawker 1934,N 6,34:2
Her Week-End 1936,Mr 20,28:5
Book of Charm, The 1936,Je 30,15:1
White Horse Inn 1936,O 2,28:5
Spring in Autumn 1937,Ag 17,23:1
As You Like It 1941,O 21,29:2
Lady Behave 1943,N 17,30:1
Dark of the Moon 1945,Mr 15,27:2
Dark of the Moon 1945,Mr 25,II,1:1
They Knew What They Wanted 1949,F 17,28:2
Desire Under the Elms 1952,Ja 17,23:4
Desire Under the Elms 1952,Ja 20,II,1:1
Kilgo Run, The 1953,D 13,105:1
Stone, Clement (Miscellaneous)
Riot Act, The 1963,Mr 9,5:2
Stone, Clifford
Spider, The 1927,Mr 23,29:1
Stone, Clyde
Camels Are Coming, The 1931,O 3,20:4
Stone, David
Merchant of Venice, The 1931,N 9,22:2
Rugged Path, The 1945,N 12,17:2
Stone, Dorothy
Stepping Stones 1923,N 7,14:3
Criss Cross 1926,O 13,20:2
Three Cheers 1928,O 7,IX,2:3
Three Cheers 1928,O 16,28:1
Three Cheers 1928,O 21,IX,1:1
Show Girl 1929,Ag 8,29:4
Show Girl 1929,Ag 25,VIII,1:1
Ripples 1930,F 2,VIII,2:7
Ripples 1930,F 12,26:1
Vaudeville (Palace) 1931,S 28,17:5

Smiling Faces 1932,Ag 31,12:3
As Thousands Cheer 1934,Jl 10,24:2
Sea Legs 1937,My 19,26:5
Gay Divorce 1937,Jl 20,19:4
Gay Divorce 1937,Ag 11,27:2
You Can't Take It With You 1945,Mr 27,23:7
Red Mill, The 1945,O 17,16:2
Stone, Dorothy (Lyricist)
Front Page Stuff 1926,D 29,24:4
Stone, Douglas
Moondreamers, The 1969,D 9,68:1
Stone, Edward D (Scenic Designer)
Can-Can 1959,Ag 26,25:4
Stone, Elly
Valmouth 1960,O 7,29:1
O, Oysters! 1961,Ja 31,23:1
O Marry Me 1961,O 28,13:1
Jacques Brel Is Alive and Well and Living in Paris 1968,Ja 23,25:2
Jacques Brel Is Alive and Well and Living in Paris 1970,Ja 21,34:1
Jacques Brel Is Alive and Well and Living in Paris 1970,F 15,II,1:1
Stone, Ernest
Lamp at Midnight 1947,D 22,29:2
Victors, The 1948,D 27,17:2
Stone, Ezra
Tom Sawyer 1931,D 26,15:3
O Evening Star 1936,Ja 9,24:6
Brother Rat 1936,D 17,34:5
What a Life 1938,Ap 14,26:2
Horse Fever 1940,N 25,21:2
This Is the Army 1942,Jl 5,28:2
This Is the Army 1942,Ag 16,VIII,1:1
Alchemist, The 1948,My 7,31:4
She Stoops to Conquer 1949,D 29,21:3
Stone, Ezra (Director)
See My Lawyer 1939,S 28,29:1
Reunion in New York 1940,F 22,28:4
This Is the Army 1942,Jl 5,28:2
January Thaw 1946,F 5,18:2
Me and Molly 1948,F 27,27:2
To Tell You the Truth 1948,Ap 19,28:6
At War With the Army 1949,Mr 9,32:2
Wake Up, Darling 1956,My 3,34:2
Curtains Up! 1959,N 3,26:3
Stone, Ezra (Miscellaneous)
Reunion in New York 1940,F 22,28:4
Pink Elephant, The 1953,Ap 23,37:2
Stone, Florence
Will Morrissey's Newcomers 1923,Ag 9,16:2
Stone, Fred
Tip-Top 1920,O 6,13:2
Stepping Stones 1923,N 7,14:3
Criss Cross 1926,O 13,20:2
Three Cheers 1928,O 7,IX,2:3
Three Cheers 1928,O 21,IX,1:1
Ripples 1930,F 2,VIII,2:7
Ripples 1930,F 12,26:1
Smiling Faces 1932,Ag 31,12:3
Jayhawker 1934,O 16,31:4
Jayhawker 1934,N 6,34:2
Lightnin' 1938,S 16,17:2
You Can't Take It With You 1945,Mr 27,23:7
Time Gentlemen Please! 1961,N 9,40:4
Stone, Fred (Mrs)
Ripples 1930,F 12,26:1
Stone, Fred (Playwright)
Smiling Faces 1931,D 13,VIII,2:5
Stone, Gary
Earl Carroll's Vanities 1940,Ja 15,11:2
Stone, George
Hello, Lola! 1926,Ja 13,30:1
Stone, Gertrude
Bitter Oleander 1935,F 12,24:3
Stone, Greg
My Wife and I 1966,O 11,53:2
Earthlight Theater 1970,N 4,38:2
Stone, Harlan
This Rock 1943,F 19,23:2
Star Spangled Family 1945,Ap 11,18:6
Stone, Harold
World We Make, The 1939,N 21,19:1
Counterattack 1943,F 4,27:2
One Touch of Venus 1943,O 8,14:1
Stone, Harold (Director)
Ernest in Love 1960,My 5,39:4
In White America 1963,N 1,26:1
Ordinary Man, An 1968,S 10,39:1
Memory Bank, The 1970,Ja 24,23:3
Memory Bank, The 1970,Ja 25,II,1:4
Room Service 1970,My 13,49:1
Charley's Aunt 1970,Jl 6,38:1
Stone, Harold (Miscellaneous)
Abraham Cochrane 1964,F 18,26:1
Stone, Harold (Producer)
Honeymoon 1932,D 24,11:2
Stone, Harold J
Morning Star 1940,Ap 17,26:4
Apology 1943,Mr 23,14:2
Bell for Adano, A 1944,D 7,21:2
S S Glencairn; Moon of the Caribbees 1948,My 21,21:2

Stone, Harold J—Cont
S S Glencairn; Bound East for Cardiff 1948,My 21,21:2
S S Glencairn; Long Voyage Home, The 1948,My 21,21:2
S S Glencairn; In the Zone 1948,My 21,21:2
Stone, Harry
Till the Day I Die 1935,Mr 27,24:5
Waiting for Lefty 1935,Mr 27,24:5
Stone, Harvey
Guys and Dolls 1959,Jl 22,22:2
Pal Joey 1961,Je 1,32:1
Stone, Helen
Sonya's Search for the Christmas Star 1929,D 14,24:6
Stone, Howard
Side-Show 1931,My 16,13:1
Good Housekeeping 1949,Ag 17,19:3
Stone, Howard (Miscellaneous)
Look Back in Anger 1957,O 2,28:2
Vintage '60 1960,S 13,41:1
Stone, Irving (Playwright)
Truly Valiant 1936,Ja 10,17:3
Stone, Jack
Whistling in the Dark 1932,Ja 20,16:6
Man Bites Dog 1933,Ap 26,11:2
Stone, James
As You Like It 1936,Ap 24,18:4
Stone, Janet
Greenwich Village Follies 1920,Ag 31,7:3
Ziegfeld Follies 1921,Je 22,10:1
One Kiss 1923,N 28,14:2
Puzzles of 1925 1925,F 3,25:3
Stone, Janey
Lady Butterfly 1923,Ja 23,18:1
Stone, Jeff
Shylock and His Daughter 1947,S 30,22:2
Stone, Jerald B (Musical Director)
Get Thee to Canterbury 1969,Ja 26,74:1
Stone, Jerry
Seeds in the Wind 1948,Ap 26,27:2
Seeds in the Wind 1948,My 26,29:2
Stone, Jon
Golden Six, The 1958,O 27,31:2
Stone, Leete
Caesar and Cleopatra 1925,Ap 14,27:1
Call of Life, The 1925,O 10,10:1
Stone, Leonard
Titus Andronicus 1956,D 3,40:2
Look Homeward, Angel 1957,N 29,33:1
Redhead 1959,F 6,21:1
Stone, Lester B
Off the Record; Mayor Answers the Newspapers! Wow! 1935,Je 19,23:3
Stone, Lew (Musical Director)
On Your Toes 1937,F 6,15:2
Stone, Marcia
In a Jewish Grocery 1939,O 2,15:2
Stone, Mark
Daphne Laureola 1950,S 19,38:6
Cindy 1964,Mr 20,24:1
Stone, Michael (Miss)
Black Widow 1936,F 13,24:3
Stone, Milburn
Jayhawker 1934,N 6,34:2
Around the Corner 1936,D 29,17:2
Stone, Mimi (Composer)
Pimpernel! 1964,Ja 7,26:6
Stone, Miriam
Once Upon a Time 1939,D 21,28:2
Stone, Muriel
Greater Love 1931,Mr 3,39:1
Stone, Neil
Wild Rose, The 1926,O 21,23:1
Good Boy 1928,S 6,23:2
Gambling 1929,Ag 27,31:2
Frankie and Johnny 1930,S 26,16:5
Midnight 1930,D 30,25:1
Stone, Paddy
Joyce Grenfell Requests the Pleasure 1955,O 11,48:1
Stone, Paddy (Choreographer)
Joyce Grenfell Requests the Pleasure 1955,O 11,48:1
Stone, Patt (Producer)
Kreutzer Sonata, The 1961,F 16,24:2
Stone, Paula
Ripples 1930,F 2,VIII,2:7
Ripples 1930,F 12,26:1
Smiling Faces 1931,D 13,VIII,2:5
Church Mouse, A 1933,Je 27,13:7
Stone, Paula (Miscellaneous)
Sweethearts 1947,Ja 22,31:2
Stone, Paula (Producer)
Red Mill, The 1945,O 17,16:2
Top Banana 1951,N 2,19:2
Carnival in Flanders 1953,S 9,38:2
Rumple 1957,N 7,42:2
Stone, Peggy
Jimmie's Women 1927,S 27,30:3
Stone, Peter (Lighting Director)
To Damascus 1961,F 15,40:2
Stone, Peter (Playwright)
Kean 1961,N 3,28:2

Stone, Peter (Playwright)—Cont
Kean 1961,N 12,II,1:1
Skyscraper 1965,N 15,48:1
1776 1969,Mr 17,46:2
1776 1969,Mr 23,II,1:1
1776 1970,Je 18,54:4
Two by Two 1970,N 11,37:1
Two by Two 1970,N 22,II,1:1

Stone, Peter (Scenic Designer)
To Damascus 1961,F 15,40:2
Seven Scenes for Yeni 1963,My 13,36:2

Stone, Philip
Ten Million Ghosts 1936,O 24,23:7
Contractor, The 1970,Ag 17,32:1

Stone, Robert
Merrily We Roll Along 1934,O 1,14:1

Stone, Robinson
Othello 1945,My 23,25:4
Strange Fruit 1945,N 30,18:6
Cyrano de Bergerac 1946,O 9,33:2
Alchemist, The 1948,My 7,31:4
Insect Comedy, The 1948,Je 4,26:3
She Stoops to Conquer 1949,D 29,21:3
Devil's Disciple, The 1950,Ja 26,23:2
Twentieth Century 1950,D 25,23:6
Cyrano de Bergerac 1953,N 13,24:3
Richard III 1953,D 10,65:2
Boy With a Cart, The 1954,Ap 5,19:2
Noah 1954,O 11,32:2
Hour Glass, The 1955,O 17,33:1
Thunder Rock 1956,F 27,18:1
Thor, With Angels 1956,O 15,29:4
Marvellous History of Saint Bernard, The 1958,F 24,16:3

Stone, Robinson (Producer)
Country Wife, The 1955,Ap 6,35:1

Stone, Samuel
Walk Hard 1944,D 1,28:2

Stone, Sidney
Three Musketeers, The 1921,My 20,18:5
Summer Night 1939,N 3,17:1
International Incident, An 1940,Ap 3,18:2
Mr Big 1941,O 1,24:2
Three Men on a Horse 1942,O 10,10:2
Allah Be Praised! 1944,Ap 21,14:2
Hilarities 1948,S 10,20:2

Stone, Sydney (Director)
Barrister, The 1932,N 22,25:2

Stone, Sydney (Playwright)
Love Scandal, A 1923,N 7,14:1
Restless Women 1927,D 27,24:1
Barrister, The 1932,N 22,25:2

Stone, Sydney (Producer)
Barrister, The 1932,N 22,25:2

Stone, Sylvia
I Married an Angel 1938,My 12,26:2
As We Forgive Our Debtors 1947,Mr 11,37:2
Deuces Wild; Thus 1962,Ap 25,31:1
Deuces Wild; It's All Yours 1962,Ap 25,31:1

Stone, Thomas
Peter Flies High 1931,N 10,28:3

Stone, Thomas (Miscellaneous)
Oh Dad, Poor Dad, Mamma's Hung You in the Closet and I'm Feelin' So Sad 1962,F 27,28:1
Oh Dad, Poor Dad, Mamma's Hung You in the Closet and I'm Feelin' So Sad 1962,Ap 29,II,3:1

Stone, Virginia
Blind Mice 1930,O 16,28:2
Schoolgirl 1930,N 21,31:1

Stone, W Clement (Miscellaneous)
On an Open Roof 1963,Ja 30,7:3

Stone, W Leete
Two by Two 1925,F 24,17:1

Stone, William
Sinner 1927,F 8,20:2
Queen Bee 1929,N 13,25:1
Juno and the Paycock 1940,Ja 17,24:2

Stone, William (Playwright)
Adrienne 1923,My 29,10:4

Stone and Gibbons
Vaudeville (Palace) 1932,Jl 18,9:7

Stone and Hays
Passing Show of 1921, The 1920,D 30,16:2

Stoneburne, Miss
Blushing Bride, The 1922,F 7,12:1

Stoneburner, Sam
Foreplay 1970,D 11,58:2

Stoneham, Norman C (Miscellaneous)
Lally 1927,F 9,16:3

Stoneman, Bob
Life and Times of J Walter Smintheus, The 1970,D 10,59:1

Stoneman, Donnell
Eleventh Hour, The 1956,Jl 10,26:7

Stoner, Donald M (Producer)
Hotel Alimony 1934,Ja 30,16:2

Stoner, Frederick (Scenic Designer)
Hamlet 1945,D 23,II,3:1

Stoner, Joe
Hold On to Your Hats 1940,S 12,30:3

Stoner, Lou
Hold On to Your Hats 1940,S 12,30:3

Stonleys
Jumbo 1935,N 18,20:2

Stonorov, Andrea
Cherry Orchard, The 1970,My 7,63:2

Stonzek, Morris (Miscellaneous)
Merry Widow, The 1943,Ag 29,II,5:3

Stoock, Geraldine
Follow the Girls 1944,Ap 10,15:2

Stooges, Three
Scandals 1939,Ag 20,IX,2:1
Scandals 1939,Ag 29,17:2

Stopka, Andrzej (Scenic Designer)
Story of the Glorious Resurrection of Our Lord, The 1962,Je 10,II,1:1

Stopp, Gerald
Liliom 1921,Ap 21,18:1

Stoppard, Tom (Playwright)
Rosencrantz and Guildenstern Are Dead 1967,O 17,53:1
Rosencrantz and Guildenstern Are Dead 1967,O 29,II,1:1
Enter a Free Man 1968,Ap 7,II,8:1
Real Inspector Hound, The 1968,Je 19,38:2
Real Inspector Hound, The 1968,Jl 8,45:1
Real Inspector Hound, The 1968,Jl 14,II,4:5
Rosencrantz and Guildenstern Are Dead 1970,N 19,39:3

Stor, Adrian
Bride Got Farblondjet, The 1967,N 6,61:6

Storch, Arthur
End as a Man 1953,S 16,39:1
End As a Man 1953,S 27,II,1:1
Time Limit! 1956,Ja 25,27:2
Girls of Summer 1956,N 20,45:1
Look Homeward, Angel 1957,N 29,33:1
Night Circus, The 1958,D 3,44:1
Long Dream, The 1960,F 18,36:2

Storch, Arthur (Director)
Across the Board on Tomorrow Morning 1961,O 23,22:5
Talking to You 1961,O 23,22:5
Three Times Three; George Washington Crossing the Delaware 1962,Mr 2,24:1
Three Times Three; Twenty-Five Cent White Cap, The 1962,Mr 2,24:1
Typists, The 1963,F 6,5:2
Tiger, The 1963,F 6,5:2
Owl and the Pussycat, The 1964,N 19,48:1
Impossible Years, The 1965,O 14,55:1
Best Laid Plans, The 1966,Mr 26,15:2
Orange Souffle; Wen, The; Out From Under 1966,Jl 16,14:6
Under the Weather 1966,O 28,35:1
Golden Rainbow 1968,F 5,27:1
Golden Rainbow 1968,Mr 3,II,3:1
Local Stigmatic, The; Interview 1969,N 4,55:2
Local Stigmatic, The; That's Your Trouble 1969,N 4,55:2
Local Stigmatic, The 1969,N 4,55:2
Local Stigmatic, The; That's All 1969,N 4,55:2
Local Stigmatic, The; Request Stop 1969,N 4,55:2
Local Stigmatic, The; Applicant 1969,N 4,55:2
Local Stigmatic, The; Last to Go 1969,N 4,55:2
Local Stigmatic, The; Trouble in the Works 1969,N 4,55:2
Chinese, The 1970,Mr 11,42:2
Dr Fish 1970,Mr 11,42:2

Storch, Larry
Red White and Blue 1950,O 8,64:5
Littlest Revue, The 1956,My 23,37:2
Who Was That Lady I Saw You With? 1958,Mr 4,33:2

Storer, Edward (Translator)
Six Characters in Search of an Author 1922,O 31,11:2
Six Characters in Search of an Author 1931,Ap 16,29:2

Storer, Llyon
Doctor Faustus 1961,Ap 26,36:1
Candida 1961,Ap 27,26:1

Storey, Belle
Vaudeville (Forty-Fourth Street Theatre) 1921,S 20,12:2

Storey, Bobbie
Garden of Weeds 1924,Ap 29,12:3

Storey, David (Playwright)
Home 1970,Je 20,23:1
Home 1970,Ag 17,32:1
Contractor, The 1970,Ag 17,32:1
Home 1970,N 18,41:1
Home 1970,N 29,II,1:1

Storey, Rex
Spice of 1922 1922,Jl 7,12:4

Storie, A Henderson
And So to Bed 1927,N 10,23:1
Cherry Orchard, The 1928,Mr 6,20:1

Stork, Clifford
Triumph 1935,O 15,18:5

Stork, Clyde
Machinal 1928,S 8,10:3

Storke, Charles A
Yanqui and the Senorita, The 1952,Ag 8,8:7

Storm, James
School for Scandal, The 1966,N 22,33:2
Wild Duck, The 1967,Ja 12,49:1

Storm, James—Cont
War and Peace 1967,Mr 22,42:1
Unknown Soldier and His Wife, The 1967,Jl 7,22:1

Storm, Joan
Try It With Alice 1924,Je 24,18:4
Eve's Leaves 1925,Mr 27,22:2
Henry's Harem 1926,S 14,25:2
Damn the Tears 1927,Ja 22,11:1
Box Seats 1928,Ap 20,27:2
Merry Wives of Windsor, The 1938,Ap 15,22:3

Storm, John
Carolinian, The 1925,N 3,34:2

Storm, Lesley (Playwright)
Dark Horizon 1934,Ap 21,13:3
Wise Woman, The 1934,N 9,24:3
Follow Your Saint 1936,S 25,20:3
Follow Your Saint 1936,O 11,X,3:1
Billy Draws a Horse 1939,D 22,14:5
Heart of a City 1942,F 13,24:6
Heart of a City 1942,Mr 1,VIII,1:1
Great Day 1945,Mr 25,II,2:4
Black Chiffon 1949,Je 12,II,3:1
Black Chiffon 1950,S 28,39:2
Black Chiffon 1950,O 15,II,1:1
Roar Like a Dove 1964,My 22,40:2

Storm, Lucy
Pygmalion 1945,D 27,16:1

Storm, Wayne
Fourth Avenue North 1961,S 28,50:2

Storoshenko, Vadim
Uncle Vanya 1960,F 13,13:4

Story, Belle
Good Times 1920,Ag 10,10:1
Vaudeville (Palace) 1924,S 30,27:5

Story, Bill
Be Your Age 1953,Ja 15,24:2
Three by Thurber; Imperturbable Spirit, The 1955,Mr 8,23:2
Three by Thurber; Middle Years, The 1955,Mr 8,23:2

Story, Gloria
Rhapsody 1944,N 23,37:2
Firebird of Florence 1945,Mr 23,13:4
Sweethearts 1947,Ja 22,31:2

Story, Rex
Vaudeville (Winter Garden) 1922,F 14,21:1

Story, Ted
Me and Juliet 1970,My 15,42:1

Storye, Fabian (Composer)
Right This Way 1938,Ja 6,22:3

Storye, Fabian (Miscellaneous)
Right This Way 1938,Ja 6,22:3

Stoska, Polyna
Gypsy Baron, The 1944,N 15,20:3
Street Scene 1947,Ja 10,17:2
Street Scene 1947,Ja 19,II,1:1

Stoss, F (Director)
Rendezvous in Wien 1956,S 5,23:1

Stoss, Franz (Producer)
10th Man, The 1966,Ap 23,15:6

Stothart, Herbert (Composer)
Always You 1920,Ja 6,18:2
Tickle Me 1920,Ag 18,9:1
Jimmie 1920,N 18,15:3
Daffy Dill 1922,Ag 23,14:5
Wildflower 1923,F 9,10:1
Mary Jane McKane 1923,D 26,13:2
Vogues of 1924 1924,Mr 28,14:3
Marjorie 1924,Ag 12,12:2
Rose Marie 1924,Ag 24,VII,1:8
Rose Marie 1924,S 3,12:2
Song of the Flame 1925,D 11,26:4
Song of the Flame 1925,D 31,10:2
Golden Dawn 1927,O 2,VIII,4:6
Golden Dawn 1927,D 1,32:3
Rose Marie 1928,Mr 31,23:2
Rose Marie 1928,Ap 29,IX,2:8
Good Boy 1928,S 6,23:2
Polly 1929,Ja 9,28:3

Stothart, Herbert (Lyricist)
Good Boy 1928,S 6,23:2
Polly 1929,Ja 9,28:3

Stothart, Herbert (Musical Director)
Rose Marie 1928,Mr 31,23:2

Stott, Judith
Chalk Garden, The 1956,My 13,II,3:1

Stott, Mike (Playwright)
Erogenous Zones 1969,Ap 8,41:1

Stott, Monty
Stars on Ice 1942,Jl 3,12:2
Hollywood Ice Revue 1953,Ja 16,17:2
Hollywood Ice Revue 1955,Ja 14,16:1
Ice Capades 1963,Ag 29,37:2

Stou, Oswald (Sir) (Producer)
White Horse Inn 1931,Ap 27,24:5

Stoudnour, David
Touch 1970,N 9,52:1

Stoudnour, David (Miscellaneous)
Touch 1970,N 9,52:1

Stoudt, Paul (Producer)
Kitchen, The 1966,Je 14,50:1

Stough, Raymond
Anvil, The 1962,O 31,33:3

Stout, Gordon
Greeks Had a Word for It, The 1930,S 26,16:5
Stout, Loren
Becky Sharp 1929,Je 4,29:1
Little Father of the Wilderness, The 1930,Je 3,27:1
Stout, M L
Who's Who 1924,Ap 18,19:2
Stout, Royal C
Blue Flame, The 1920,Mr 16,18:1
Near Santa Barbara 1921,F 1,14:1
Smooth as Silk 1921,F 23,18:3
Your Woman and Mine 1922,F 28,17:2
Wasp, The 1923,Mr 28,14:3
Cousin Sonia 1925,D 8,28:3
Wisdom Tooth, The 1926,F 16,22:2
Wild Man of Borneo, The 1927,S 14,29:2
High Gear 1927,O 7,24:3
Royal Family, The 1927,D 29,26:4
Among the Married 1929,O 4,24:3
Overture 1930,D 8,26:4
Enemy Within 1931,O 6,35:3
Divine Moment, A 1934,Ja 8,21:8
Are You Decent? 1934,Ap 20,16:2
Yesterday's Orchids 1934,O 6,20:4
Black Pit 1935,Mr 21,26:6
Mother Sings 1935,N 13,24:1
Tomorrow's a Holiday! 1935,D 31,10:2
Howdy Stranger 1937,Ja 15,17:5
Too Many Heroes 1937,N 16,26:2
Stoutenburgh, Larry
Vaudeville (Palace) 1926,Je 1,29:5
Stovall, Miriam
Man and Superman 1947,O 9,31:2
Stover, Frederick (Lighting Director)
Browning Version, The 1949,O 13,32:2
Harlequinade 1949,O 13,32:2
Stover, Frederick (Scenic Designer)
Meet the People 1940,D 26,22:2
Hamlet 1945,D 14,25:2
Man and Superman 1947,O 9,31:2
Browning Version, The 1949,O 13,32:2
Harlequinade 1949,O 13,32:2
Browning Version, The 1949,O 23,II,1:1
Stover, Harry
Vaudeville (Palace) 1921,Jl 5,15:1
Stover, Helen
Vaudeville (Hippodrome) 1924,Ja 1,21:1
Stover, James
Golden Age, The 1963,N 19,49:2
Stover, Maud Ream
Poppy 1923,S 4,14:2
Stowe, Harriet Beecher (Original Author)
Uncle Tom's Cabin 1933,My 30,13:4
Sweet River 1936,O 29,30:2
Uncle Tom's Cabin 1949,Ap 18,13:3
Stowe, Harriet Beecher (Playwright)
Uncle Tom's Cabin 1933,O 10,24:3
Stowe, Leslie
Pasteur 1923,Mr 13,19:1
Go West, Young Man 1923,N 13,25:2
Babes in Toyland 1930,D 22,17:1
Stowell, E (Composer)
Pudding on the Ritz 1932,Ap 9,18:3
Stowell, E (Lyricist)
Pudding on the Ritz 1932,Ap 9,18:3
Stowell, Faye Smiley
Little Town of Bethlehem, The 1920,D 27,11:1
Without the Walls 1921,Mr 28,8:1
Without the Walls 1922,Ap 17,17:1
Little Town of Bethlehem, The 1922,D 26,15:4
Stowell, Thomas C
Without the Walls 1920,Je 7,20:1
Little Town of Bethlehem, The 1920,D 27,11:1
Without the Walls 1921,Mr 28,8:1
Without the Walls 1922,Ap 17,17:1
Little Town of Bethlehem, The 1922,D 26,15:4
Choice, The 1930,My 9,20:5
Stowell, Thomas C (Playwright)
Choice, The 1930,My 9,20:5
Stowitts, William Seabury
Irving Berlin's New Music Box Revue
1922,O 24,18:1
Stowski, Sonya
Patriots, The 1943,D 21,22:5
Stoyanovsky, Arcadi
Russian Bank 1940,My 25,20:2
Chauve-Souris of 1943 1943,Ag 13,13:2
Straasberg, M
Wise Men of Chelm, The 1933,O 18,24:4
Straat, Hans
Father, The 1962,My 15,49:1
Strachan, Alan
Twelfth Night 1970,Ja 1,18:1
Strachan, John
Porgy and Bess 1935,O 11,30:2
Strachan, Mary
Green Stick 1934,O 10,21:2
Strachey, Lytton (Original Author)
Queen Victoria 1923,N 25,VIII,1:1
Stradley, John (Playwright)
Stop Press 1939,Mr 20,13:2
Stradley, John Duff (Director)
Wayside 1957,Ap 18,34:1

Alley of the Sunset 1959,D 31,11:1
Stradley, John Duff (Playwright)
Wayside 1957,Ap 18,34:1
Alley of the Sunset 1959,D 31,11:1
Stradner, Frau
Love Is Not So Simple 1935,N 20,26:7
Strahl, Juliet
Cinderella on Broadway 1920,Je 25,18:1
Passing Show of 1921, The 1920,D 30,16:2
Strahl, Max
Mother's Sabbath Days 1960,N 21,33:2
Backlane Center 1961,N 23,51:1
Strahlman, William
Sweetheart Shop, The 1920,S 1,13:4
Straight, Beatrice
Possessed, The 1939,O 25,26:2
Twelfth Night 1941,D 3,32:2
Story of Miss N N, The 1942,S 28,13:1
Witch, The 1942,S 28,13:1
Land of Fame 1943,S 22,31:5
Wanhope Building, The 1947,F 11,36:5
Eastward in Eden 1947,N 19,33:2
Innocents, The 1950,F 2,30:2
Innocents, The 1950,F 12,II,1:1
Grand Tour, The 1951,D 11,45:2
Crucible, The 1953,Ja 23,15:2
Crucible, The 1953,F 1,II,1:1
Sing Me No Lullaby 1954,O 15,17:2
Sing Me No Lullaby 1954,O 24,II,1:1
River Line, The 1957,Ja 3,29:2
Phedre 1966,F 11,36:1
Everything in the Garden 1967,N 30,60:1
Everything in the Garden 1967,D 10,II,5:1
Straight, C Jay Jr
Hook-Up, The 1935,My 9,24:6
Straight, Sidney F
Rainbow's End 1928,D 26,14:6
Straight, Willard (Composer)
Legend of Lizzie, The 1959,F 10,39:1
Athenian Touch, The 1964,Ja 15,25:4
Strain, Drucilla
Anything Goes 1934,N 22,26:1
Lady Comes Across, The 1942,Ja 10,10:2
Jackpot 1944,Ja 14,15:2
Hollywood Pinafore 1945,Je 1,20:1
Nellie Bly 1946,Ja 22,32:2
Strain, Vincent
Honest Liars 1926,Jl 20,17:2
Kibitzer, The 1929,F 19,22:5
Strait, Ross
Betty Behave 1927,Mr 9,28:4
Strand, Judith
Tom Sawyer - Ballad of the Mississippi
1947,D 27,11:3
Strand, Oscar (Miscellaneous)
Miracle, The 1932,Ap 10,I,18:1
Strand, Oscar (Scenic Designer)
Kingdom of God in Bohemia, The
1931,Mr 8,VIII,2:7
Tales of Hoffmann 1932,Ja 10,VIII,1:6
Grosses Welttheater 1933,Ap 16,IX,2:5
Much Ado About Nothing 1933,Ap 30,IX,2:2
Strane, Robert
Here Comes Santa Claus 1962,My 18,34:1
Strang, Franc C
Paolo and Francesca 1929,Ap 2,28:2
Strang, Vicki (Miscellaneous)
Macbeth 1969,N 21,51:1
Strange, Freddy
Ah, Wilderness! 1934,O 30,23:1
Strange, Hugh Stanislaus (Playwright)
Decoy, The 1927,Ag 21,VII,1:8
Strange, James
Rang Tang 1927,Jl 13,20:1
Strange, John Stephen (Original Author)
Strangler Fig, The 1940,My 7,31:2
Strange, Leslie
Vaudeville (Palace) 1930,F 17,18:4
Strange, Michael
Easter 1926,Mr 19,24:3
Electra 1927,My 4,28:3
Aiglon, L' 1927,D 27,24:3
Variations of 1940 1940,Ja 29,12:1
Strange, Michael (Miscellaneous)
One Day More 1926,Mr 19,24:3
Easter 1926,Mr 19,24:3
Liberace's Variety Bill 1957,Ap 22,29:5
Strange, Michael (Playwright)
Clair de Lune 1921,Ap 10,VI,1:1
Clair de Lune 1921,Ap 19,15:1
Clair de Lune 1921,Ap 24,VI,1:1
Strange, Robert
Nobody's Money 1921,Ag 18,9:3
Wait Till We're Married 1921,S 27,14:1
Straw, The 1921,N 11,16:2
Banco 1922,S 21,18:1
Mike Angelo 1923,Ja 9,26:2
Dice of the Gods, The 1923,Ap 6,20:2
In Love With Love 1923,Ag 7,20:1
Dust Heap, The 1924,Ap 25,20:2
Little Angel, The 1924,S 29,10:3
Youngest, The 1924,D 23,17:1
Good Bad Woman, A 1925,F 10,21:1

Strange, Robert—Cont
Gorilla, The 1925,Ap 29,24:2
Sandalwood 1926,S 23,23:1
Heavy Traffic 1928,S 6,23:3
Most Immoral Lady, A 1928,N 27,36:1
Strong Man's House, A 1929,S 17,34:3
Seven 1929,D 28,10:5
Virtue's Bed 1930,Ap 16,26:5
Midnight 1930,D 30,25:1
Three Times the Hour 1931,Ag 26,15:5
Marathon 1933,Ja 28,8:8
Both Your Houses 1933,Mr 7,20:3
Both Your Houses 1933,My 23,22:2
Strange, Stanislaus (Translator)
Chocolate Soldier, The 1934,My 3,15:3
Strano, Carl
Richard II 1968,Je 24,42:3
Love's Labour's Lost 1968,Je 28,36:1
Much Ado About Nothing 1969,Je 16,57:1
Hamlet 1969,Je 30,33:1
Henry V 1969,N 11,43:1
Strasberg, John
Five Evenings 1963,My 10,37:3
Marathon '33 1963,D 23,20:1
Strasberg, John (Miscellaneous)
Blues for Mister Charlie 1964,Ap 24,24:1
Strasberg, Lee
Processional 1925,Ja 13,17:1
Chief Thing, The 1926,Mr 23,24:2
Garrick Gaieties 1926,My 11,25:2
Four Walls 1927,S 20,33:1
Red Rust 1929,D 18,31:1
Green Grow the Lilacs 1931,Ja 27,21:2
Strasberg, Lee (Director)
Vegetable, The, or From President to Postman
1929,Ap 11,32:3
House of Connelly, The 1931,S 29,22:4
1931 1931,D 11,34:3
1931- 1931,D 20,VIII,1:1
Night Over Taos 1932,Mr 10,25:3
Success Story 1932,S 27,24:4
Hilda Cassidy 1933,My 5,18:3
Men in White 1933,S 27,24:2
Men in White 1933,O 1,IX,1:1
Gentlewoman 1934,Mr 23,28:4
Gold Eagle Guy 1934,N 29,33:4
Gold Eagle Guy 1934,D 9,X,1:1
Case of Clyde Griffiths 1936,Mr 14,10:4
Johnny Johnson 1936,N 20,26:3
Roosty 1938,F 15,21:2
All the Living 1938,Mr 25,14:4
Dance Night 1938,O 15,20:5
Flight Into China 1939,S 12,28:1
Summer Night 1939,N 3,17:1
Fifth Column, The 1940,Ja 27,9:1
Fifth Column, The 1940,Mr 7,18:2
Fifth Column, The 1940,Mr 17,X,1:1
Clash by Night 1941,D 29,20:2
Kiss for Cinderella, A 1942,Mr 11,22:2
R U R 1942,D 4,30:2
Apology 1943,Mr 23,14:2
South Pacific 1943,D 30,11:2
Skipper Next to God 1948,Ja 5,14:5
Big Knife, The 1949,F 25,27:5
Big Knife, The 1949,Mr 6,II,1:1
Closing Door, The 1949,D 2,36:2
Peer Gynt 1951,Ja 29,15:2
Peer Gynt 1951,F 4,II,1:1
Strange Interlude 1963,Je 18,34:6
Three Sisters, The 1964,Je 23,24:1
Three Sisters, The 1964,Jl 5,II,1:1
Three Sisters, The 1964,Jl 28,26:7
Blues for Mister Charlie 1965,My 5,52:1
Three Sisters, The 1965,My 15,19:4
Strasberg, Lee (Miscellaneous)
Marathon '33 1963,D 23,20:1
Strasberg, Lee (Producer)
Apology 1943,Mr 23,14:2
Country Girl, The 1966,S 30,55:1
Strasberg, Susan
Maya 1953,Je 10,35:1
Diary of Anne Frank, The 1955,O 6,24:2
Diary of Anne Frank, The 1955,O 16,II,1:1
Time Remembered 1957,N 13,41:2
Time Remembered 1957,N 24,II,1:1
Shadow of a Gunman, The 1958,N 21,26:1
Shadow of a Gunman, The 1958,N 30,II,1:1
Lady of the Camellias, The 1963,Mr 22,7:1
Strasfogel, Ignace (Composer)
Duchess of Malfi, The 1946,O 16,35:2
Strasfogel, Ignace (Musical Director)
Brigadoon 1950,My 3,36:2
Strassberg, M
Gardener's Dog, The 1927,O 21,27:1
Strassberg, Morris
Merchant of Venice, The 1922,D 22,13:1
Wolves 1924,D 31,9:4
We Americans 1926,O 13,20:4
Gold Diggers, The 1927,D 3,19:2
On Foreign Soil 1927,D 24,8:2
Alexander Pushkin 1928,Ja 27,14:2
Othello 1929,F 4,21:2
Major Noah 1929,F 23,17:2
Jew Suss 1929,O 19,22:3

Strassberg, Morris—Cont
Angels on Earth 1929,D 11,34:7
Roaming Stars 1930,Ja 25,12:2
Chains 1930,F 23,29:2
Spring Song 1934,O 2,18:2
Professor Mamlock 1937,Ap 14,30:3
Song of Dnieper 1946,O 26,10:5
Shylock and His Daughter 1947,S 30,22:2
Shepherd King, The 1955,O 13,36:2
Brothers Ashkenazi, The 1955,N 12,24:4
Hole in the Head, A 1957,Mr 1,15:1
World of Mrs Solomon, The; Another Chance 1969,Je 4,37:1
Awake and Sing! 1970,My 28,35:1
Awake and Sing! 1970,Je 7,II,1:1
Strassberg, Morris (Director)
Shepherd King, The 1955,O 13,36:2
Brothers Ashkenazi, The 1955,N 12,24:4
Bride Got Farblondjet, The 1967,N 6,61:6
Strasser, Robin
Country Girl, The 1966,S 30,55:1
Strater, Christopher
Journey of the Fifth Horse, The 1966,Ap 22,36:1
Carricknabauna 1967,Mr 31,30:1
Strater, Nicholas A (Miscellaneous)
Folies Bergere 1964,Je 3,36:1
Strater, Nicholas A (Producer)
Semi-Detached 1963,O 8,49:1
Stratford, Gwyn
Young Sinners 1929,N 29,24:4
Hobo 1931,F 12,24:4
Strathmore, Violette
As You Were 1920,Ja 28,22:3
Blushing Bride, The 1922,F 7,12:1
Artists and Models 1924,O 16,33:3
Strathy, Margaret
We're All in the Gutter 1927,Mr 5,12:2
Strattin, Maria
Illya Darling 1967,Ap 12,37:1
Stratton, Albert
Twelfth Night 1969,Ag 14,29:2
Colette 1970,O 15,58:1
Stratton, Anna
Fall and Rise of Susan Lenox, The 1920,Je 11,11:2
Stratton, Chester
Tomorrow's Harvest 1934,D 6,26:5
Red Harvest 1937,Mr 31,29:2
Scene of the Crime, The 1940,Mr 29,24:1
Canteen Show, The 1942,S 4,18:1
Connecticut Yankee, A 1943,N 18,30:2
Barretts of Wimpole Street, The 1945,Mr 27,23:6
Man and Superman 1947,O 9,31:2
Man and Superman 1949,My 17,28:6
Live Wire, The 1950,Ag 18,16:2
Richard II 1951,Ja 25,21:2
Idiot's Delight 1951,My 24,46:3
Sherlock Holmes 1953,O 31,11:2
Stratton, Clare
Top Hole 1924,S 2,22:3
He Walked in Her Sleep 1929,Ap 5,28:2
Blue Widow, The 1933,Ag 31,20:2
Stratton, Elbridge
Henry IV 1920,Je 20,II,9:2
Stratton, Gil Jr
Best Foot Forward 1941,O 2,28:2
Stratton, John
Hidden River, The 1959,Ap 14,41:2
Sweet Charity 1966,Ja 31,22:1
Stratton, Mike (Lyricist)
Of V We Sing 1942,F 16,20:3
Stratton, Ron
Happiest Girl in the World, The 1961,Ap 4,42:1
Finian's Rainbow 1967,Ap 6,44:1
Straub, Agnes
Elisabeth von England 1930,D 14,IX,4:1
Heilige aus U.S.A, Die; Saint From USA, The 1931,D 13,VIII,3:5
Straub, John
Male Animal, The 1941,Jl 9,24:6
Holiday 1941,Jl 23,15:2
Drifting Apart: or, The Fisherman's Child 1941,Ag 20,16:6
Macbeth 1941,N 12,30:2
Henry VIII 1946,N 7,42:2
Androcles and the Lion 1946,D 20,29:2
Yellow Jack 1947,F 28,26:2
Alice in Wonderland 1947,Ap 7,19:2
Galileo 1947,D 8,34:2
Tower Beyond Tragedy, The 1950,N 27,29:1
Richard II 1951,Ja 25,21:2
Taming of the Shrew, The 1951,Ap 26,35:2
Saint Joan 1951,O 5,23:2
Strong Are Lonely, The 1953,S 30,38:3
Richard III 1953,D 10,65:2
Potting Shed, The 1958,N 3,49:2
Imaginary Invalid, The 1967,My 2,53:1
Touch of the Poet, A 1967,My 3,38:2
Ways and Means 1967,My 4,34:1
Straub, John E
Hippolytus 1935,Je 15,20:4
Straub, Laura
Game of Love and Death, The 1929,N 26,28:4

Straus, Barnard (Producer)
Temper the Wind 1946,D 28,10:2
Temper the Wind 1947,Ja 12,II,1:1
For Love or Money 1947,N 5,36:2
Double in Hearts 1956,O 17,41:7
Straus, Ivan
Laterna Magika 1964,Ag 4,21:1
Straus, Jack (Composer)
Wetward Ho 1921,Ap 22,13:2
Straus, Oscar (Composer)
Last Waltz, The 1921,My 11,20:3
Chocolate Soldier, The 1921,D 13,24:2
Naughty Riquette 1926,S 14,25:2
Theresina 1927,My 8,II,1:8
Mariette 1928,O 21,IX,5:6
Marietta 1929,D 8,X,4:4
Chocolate Soldier, The 1930,Ja 28,28:1
Farmer General, The 1931,Mr 31,24:8
Bauerngeneral, Der 1931,Ap 19,VIII,2:4
Chocolate Soldier, The 1931,S 22,33:3
Chocolate Soldier, The 1932,F 9,30:3
Frau Die Weiss Was Sie Will, Eine 1932,O 9,IX,3:7
Mother of Pearl 1933,F 26,IX,3:1
Chocolate Soldier, The 1934,My 3,15:3
Mariette 1937,Je 29,18:3
Three Waltzes 1937,N 15,15:6
Three Waltzes 1937,D 27,10:2
Three Waltzes 1938,Je 26,II,7:5
Mes Amours 1940,My 3,16:5
Chocolate Soldier, The 1942,Je 24,22:2
Chocolate Soldier, The 1947,Mr 13,34:2
Straus, Oscar (Musical Director)
Theresina 1927,My 8,II,1:8
Straus, Sylvie
Walking to Waldheim 1967,N 11,25:2
Inquest 1970,Ap 24,38:1
Straus, Victor (Miscellaneous)
Carry Me Back to Morningside Heights 1968,F 28,41:1
Strauss, Bernard (Miscellaneous)
Fragile Fox 1954,O 13,27:1
Strauss, Bob
Having Wonderful Time 1937,F 22,12:5
Strauss, Edward (Musical Director)
Me Nobody Knows, The 1970,My 19,42:1
Strauss, Helda
Good Times 1920,Ag 10,10:1
Strauss, Johann Jr (Composer)
Fruehlingsluft 1921,N 29,17:4
Casanova 1928,N 4,IX,2:1
Fledermaus, Die 1929,Jl 14,IX,2:1
Wonderful Night, A; Fledermaus, Die 1929,N 1,23:3
Fledermaus, Die 1930,Ap 20,VIII,7:7
Gypsy Baron, The 1930,Ap 22,22:8
Lied der Liebe, Das 1932,F 7,VIII,1:3
Casanova 1932,Je 19,IX,2:1
Wiener Blut 1932,S 4,IX,2:2
Fledermaus, Die 1933,My 14,II,3:8
Great Waltz, The 1934,S 24,14:4
Wonderful Night, A; Fledermaus, Die 1937,Jl 14,17:1
Three Waltzes 1937,N 15,15:6
Three Waltzes 1937,D 27,10:2
Three Waltzes 1938,Je 26,II,7:5
Gypsy Baron, The 1942,Je 20,8:5
Gypsy Baron, The 1942,Ag 7,12:4
Rosalinda; Fledermaus, Die 1942,O 29,26:5
Rosalinda 1943,F 14,II,1:4
Merry Duchess, The 1943,Je 24,25:1
Gypsy Baron, The 1944,Je 15,17:3
Gypsy Baron, The 1944,N 15,20:3
Vienna at Night 1945,Ap 30,12:4
Night in Venice, A 1952,Jl 13,II,1:1
Fledermaus, Die 1954,My 20,38:5
Wiener Blut 1964,S 12,14:1
Strauss, Johann Jr (Original Author)
Champagne, Sec 1933,O 16,20:2
Strauss, Johann Jr (Playwright)
Night in Venice, A 1952,Je 27,18:6
Night in Venice, A 1953,Je 26,15:2
Strauss, Johann Sr (Composer)
Three Waltzes 1937,N 15,15:6
Three Waltzes 1937,D 27,10:2
Three Waltzes 1938,Je 26,II,7:5
Strauss, John (Composer)
Littlest Revue, The 1956,My 23,37:2
Strauss, John (Lyricist)
Littlest Revue, The 1956,My 23,37:2
Strauss, John (Miscellaneous)
Littlest Revue, The 1956,My 23,37:2
Strauss, John (Musical Director)
Morning Sun 1963,O 7,36:2
Dynamite Tonight 1967,Mr 16,52:2
Strauss, Marcel (Director)
We All Do 1927,Mr 1,30:3
Hilda Cassidy 1933,My 5,18:3
Tell My Story 1939,Mr 16,26:6
Strauss, Marcel (Miscellaneous)
Invitation to a Murder 1934,My 18,26:3
Strauss, Marcel (Playwright)
We All Do 1927,Mr 1,30:3

Strauss, Richard (Composer)
Rosenkavalier, Der 1927,Mr 6,VII,4:4
Heldenleben, Ein 1929,Ap 27,16:4
Strauss, Robert
Merchant of Venice, The 1920,D 30,16:2
Roseanne 1923,D 31,9:5
Book of Charm, The 1925,S 4,26:3
Hamlet 1930,Mr 25,34:4
Macbeth 1930,Mr 26,24:6
Twelfth Night 1930,Mr 27,24:7
Taming of the Shrew, The 1930,Mr 28,22:8
Richard III 1930,Mr 31,24:1
King Lear 1930,Ap 1,34:6
As You Like It 1930,Ap 3,32:5
Julius Caesar 1930,Ap 4,22:3
King Lear 1930,D 26,18:2
Casey Jones 1938,F 21,14:2
Catherine Was Great 1944,Ag 3,16:1
Down to Miami 1944,S 12,23:5
Nellie Bly 1946,Ja 22,32:2
Detective Story 1949,Mr 24,34:2
Twentieth Century 1950,D 25,23:6
Stalag 17 1951,My 9,41:2
Portofino 1958,F 22,8:3
Strauss, Trudi
Merry Duchess, The 1943,Je 24,25:1
Strauss, Wally
Fanny 1954,N 5,16:1
Strauss, Walter
Here Come the Clowns 1960,S 20,48:1
Strauss Dancing Troupe, Sara Mildred
Ziegfeld Follies 1934,Ja 5,24:3
Calling All Stars 1934,N 22,26:1
Calling All Stars 1934,D 14,28:2
Stravinsky, Igor (Composer)
Tale of the Soldier, The 1927,Ag 14,VII,1:7
Soldier's Tale, A 1955,Jl 13,21:2
Renard 1970,Ap 26,II,1:3
Stravinsky, Igor (Playwright)
Renard 1970,Mr 25,36:4
Strawbridge, Edwin
Rubicon, The 1922,F 22,13:1
Strawbridge, Edwin (Choreographer)
Chocolate Soldier, The 1932,F 9,30:3
Fools Rush In 1934,D 26,19:2
Strawbridge, Lawrence
Faith of Our Fathers 1950,Ag 6,72:2
Strawn, Arthur (Playwright)
Sleep No More 1944,S 1,11:5
Strawn, C J (Costume Designer)
Arden of Faversham 1970,F 17,33:1
Ubu Roi 1970,F 17,33:1
Streader, Norma
Beaux' Stratagem, The 1970,F 10,50:2
Three Sisters, The 1970,F 12,30:1
Stream, Eloise
Butter and Egg Man, The 1925,S 24,28:1
Broadway 1926,S 26,VIII,1:1
Paradise 1927,D 26,26:4
Streatfield, Noel (Playwright)
Wisdom Teeth 1936,Mr 3,25:2
Streator, Edward J Jr (Playwright)
Never Say Horses 1951,D 7,34:4
Strebig, Donald
Poppy God, The 1921,Ag 30,10:1
Street, Anthony W (Scenic Designer)
International Revue 1930,F 26,22:2
Zombie 1932,F 11,17:2
Furnished Rooms 1934,My 30,14:6
Satellite 1935,N 21,27:5
Street, Austin
Bare Facts 1927,Je 30,35:1
Street, George
Under the Counter 1947,O 4,10:2
Street, James (Original Author)
Hazel Flagg 1953,F 12,22:2
Street, Julian
Scarlet Coat, The 1924,D 24,11:1
Street, Julian (Lyricist)
Scarlet Coat, The 1924,D 24,11:1
Street, Julian (Original Author)
Rita Coventry 1923,F 20,12:2
Street, Julian (Playwright)
Scarlet Coat, The 1924,D 24,11:1
Street, Walter (Scenic Designer)
Late Wisdom 1934,Ap 24,27:4
Street, William
Trial of Joan of Arc, The 1921,Mr 28,8:2
Streeter, Rhoden
King John 1956,Je 28,33:5
Fighting Cock, The 1959,D 9,57:3
Streett, William (Director)
Lady Beyond the Moon 1931,Ap 1,36:5
Streett, William (Producer)
School for Scandal, The 1925,O 24,19:1
Master of the Inn, The 1925,D 23,22:2
Streger, Paul (Director)
Jewel Robbery 1932,Ja 14,17:2
Streger, Paul (Producer)
Celebrity 1927,D 27,24:3
Jarnegan 1928,S 25,29:2
Sweet Stranger 1930,O 22,23:3
Jewel Robbery 1932,Ja 14,17:2

Streger, Paul (Producer)—Cont
  Parlor Story 1947,Mr 5,29:2
Strehler, Giorgio (Director)
  Servant of Two Masters, The 1960,F 24,42:2
  Servant of Two Masters, The 1960,F 29,31:5
Strehlow, John
  Passion Play, The 1929,Ap 30,32:1
Streich, Evelyn
  Steps Leading Up 1941,Ap 19,20:6
Streicher, M M
  Hop, Signor! 1962,My 8,45:2
  Coriolanus 1965,Jl 15,23:1
Streicher, M M (Miscellaneous)
  Collision Course; Unexpurgated Memoirs of
    Bernard Mergendeiler, The 1968,My 9,55:2
  Collision Course; Rats 1968,My 9,55:2
  Collision Course; Camera Obscura 1968,My 9,55:2
  Collision Course; Thoughts on the Instant of
    Greeting a Friend on the Street 1968,My 9,55:2
  Collision Course; Tour 1968,My 9,55:2
  Collision Course; Metaphors 1968,My 9,55:2
  Collision Course; Wandering 1968,My 9,55:2
  Collision Course; Jew! 1968,My 9,55:2
  Collision Course; Skywriting 1968,My 9,55:2
  Collision Course; Stars and Stripes 1968,My 9,55:2
  Collision Course; Chuck 1968,My 9,55:2
Streiner, Sydell
  Alexander Hamilton 1949,Mr 30,29:2
Streisand, Barbra
  Another Evening With Harry Stoones
    1961,O 23,22:2
  I Can Get It for You Wholesale 1962,Mr 23,29:1
  Funny Girl 1964,Mr 27,15:1
  Funny Girl 1966,Ap 15,46:1
Strelitzer, Hugo (Dr) (Musical Director)
  Return of Ulysses, The 1943,F 7,II,1:6
Strelsky, Nikander
  Lady From the Sea, The 1935,D 14,11:3
Stremel, Henry
  Dancing Girl, The 1923,Ja 25,16:2
  Will Morrissey's Newcomers 1923,Ag 9,16:2
Strengell, Sara
  Winter Soldiers 1942,N 30,19:2
  French Touch, The 1945,D 10,18:2
Strenkovsky, S
  Revisor; Inspector General, The 1935,F 18,19:6
  Poverty Is No Crime 1935,F 21,22:5
  White Guard, The; Days of the Turbins
    1935,Mr 7,27:5
  Enemies 1935,Mr 19,24:7
Streshney, Valery
  On Your Toes 1936,Ap 13,14:4
Stribling, T S (Original Author)
  Rope 1928,Mr 4,IX,1:1
Stribling, T S (Playwright)
  Rope 1928,F 23,18:3
  Rope 1928,Mr 4,IX,1:1
Strick, Doris
  Mikado, The 1935,Ag 24,17:5
Strickland, Carolyn
  Twisting Road, The; One Tuesday Morning
    1957,N 18,36:5
  Moon on a Rainbow Shawl 1962,Ja 16,30:1
Strickland, Dwight
  Joy of Serpents 1930,Ap 4,22:4
Strickland, Ethel
  Devil to Pay, The 1925,D 4,26:2
  What's the Big Idea? 1926,Mr 24,20:3
  Half-Naked Truth, The 1926,Je 8,23:1
  Great Scott! 1929,S 3,25:1
  Berlin 1931,D 31,16:1
  Another Love 1934,Mr 20,26:3
  Window Shopping 1938,D 24,13:2
Strickland, F Cowles (Director)
  Thunder in the Air 1929,N 12,34:3
  Patriarch, The 1929,N 26,28:5
  Best Sellers 1933,My 4,20:2
Strickland, Helen
  Neighbors 1923,D 27,11:1
  New Englander, The 1924,F 8,22:2
  Macbeth 1924,Mr 17,18:1
  Dawn 1924,N 25,27:1
  Stolen Fruit 1925,O 8,31:4
  At Mrs Beam's 1926,Ap 26,24:3
  Uninvited Guest, The 1927,S 28,28:2
  Courage 1928,O 9,34:2
  Passing Present, The 1931,D 8,36:2
  Child of Manhattan 1932,Mr 2,15:1
  Girl Outside, The 1932,O 25,24:3
  Dark Victory 1934,N 10,18:2
  Love on the Dole 1936,F 25,23:3
  In Clover 1937,O 14,23:1
Strickland, Peggy
  Gondoliers, The 1935,Ag 6,20:5
Strickler, Jerry
  Mr President 1962,O 22,34:2
  Rate of Exchange 1968,Ap 2,50:1
Stricklin, Dean
  Dance of Death, The 1966,Je 3,31:1
  As You Like It 1966,Je 4,19:1
Stricklyn, Ray
  Climate of Eden, The 1952,N 7,20:2
  Grass Harp, The 1953,Ap 28,32:2
  Grass Harp, The 1953,My 24,II,1:1

Long Day's Journey Into Night 1963,Je 27,25:1
Stride, John
  Macbeth 1962,F 7,32:2
  Romeo and Juliet 1962,F 14,39:1
  Romeo and Juliet 1962,F 25,II,1:1
  Lady of the Camellias, The 1963,Mr 22,7:1
  Love for Love 1967,O 21,17:1
  Dance of Death 1967,O 29,II,5:1
  Flea in Her Ear, A 1967,O 30,59:1
  Love for Love 1967,O 30,59:1
Strider, Marje
  Originale 1964,S 9,46:1
Strike, Maurice (Scenic Designer)
  Heartbreak House 1968,Jl 6,9:1
Striker, Joseph
  Mendel, Inc 1929,N 26,28:5
  East of Broadway 1932,Ja 27,19:3
  Saturday Night 1933,Mr 1,13:2
  It's a Wise Child 1933,My 17,15:2
  Satellite 1935,N 21,27:5
Strimpell, Stephen
  Twelfth Night 1960,Je 9,29:4
  Tempest, The 1960,Je 20,35:1
  Antony and Cleopatra 1960,Ag 1,19:1
  Dumbbell People in a Barbell World 1962,F 15,25:1
  Candida 1962,N 12,35:5
  Sunday Man, The 1964,My 14,41:3
  On the Necessity of Being Polygamous
    1964,D 9,61:1
  Good Day 1965,O 19,51:1
  To Be Young Gifted and Black; World of Lorraine
    Hansberry, The 1969,Ja 3,15:1
  Disintegration of James Cherry, The
    1970,Ja 30,33:3
Strindberg, August (Original Author)
  Road to Damascus, The; Nach Damaskus
    1937,My 30,X,2:5
  Last Dance, The 1948,Ja 28,27:2
  Stronger, The 1965,N 11,59:1
  Miss Julie 1965,N 11,59:1
Strindberg, August (Playwright)
  Christus 1922,My 28,VI,1:6
  Dance of Death, The; Totentanz 1923,D 17,23:3
  Spook Sonata, The 1924,Ja 7,23:3
  Spook Sonata, The 1924,Ja 13,VII,1:1
  Dream Play 1926,Ja 21,18:2
  Easter 1926,Mr 19,24:3
  Spook Sonata, The 1927,Jl 10,VII,2:3
  Father, The 1927,S 4,VII,2:1
  Father, The 1927,S 11,VIII,2:4
  Miss Julie 1927,O 30,IX,2:1
  Pariah 1927,O 30,IX,2:1
  Dance of Death, The 1928,F 5,VIII,4:7
  Father, The 1928,My 12,9:4
  Easter 1928,O 28,IX,1:3
  Pelican, The 1929,N 14,25:1
  Gustav Vasa 1930,N 2,VIII,3:2
  Father, The 1931,O 9,21:1
  Dream Play 1933,Ap 23,X,1:3
  To Damascus 1933,N 12,IX,1:1
  Dream Play 1935,D 8,X,4:5
  Dream Play 1936,Je 28,IX,1:6
  Father, The 1937,Ap 21,18:5
  Queen Christina 1937,N 29,18:1
  Bridal Crown, The 1938,F 7,11:2
  Stronger, The 1949,Je 15,38:2
  Father, The 1949,Ag 21,II,1:1
  Father, The 1949,N 17,36:2
  Creditors 1949,N 22,36:5
  Father, The 1949,N 27,II,1:1
  Creditors 1949,N 27,II,1:1
  Mistress of the House, The 1950,Ja 31,19:1
  Miss Julie 1954,Mr 29,24:3
  Stronger, The 1956,F 22,23:2
  Miss Julie 1956,F 22,23:2
  Miss Julie 1956,Mr 4,II,1:1
  Comrades 1956,Je 6,38:1
  Easter 1957,Ja 17,35:2
  Easter 1957,F 3,II,1:1
  Dance of Death, The 1960,S 14,51:1
  Dream Play 1960,N 23,22:1
  To Damascus 1961,F 15,40:2
  Miss Julie 1961,Jl 10,26:1
  Creditors 1962,Ja 26,19:1
  Father, The 1962,My 15,49:1
  Miss Julie 1962,My 17,31:1
  Crime and Crime 1963,D 17,51:2
  Miss Julie 1965,Jl 29,19:1
  Dance of Death, The 1966,Je 3,31:1
  Dance of Death, The 1967,O 20,50:1
  Dance of Death 1967,O 29,II,5:1
  Dance of Death, The 1969,My 26,53:1
  Crimes and Crimes 1970,Ja 19,35:1
  Dream Play 1970,Ap 17,45:1
Strindberg, Mme (Translator)
  Lovers and Enemies 1927,S 21,27:1
Stringer, Lewis
  Power Without Glory 1948,Ja 14,30:2
Stringfellow, Frank
  First Night 1930,N 27,32:3
  Sophisticrats, The 1933,F 14,19:5
  Yellow Jack 1934,Mr 7,22:6

Stringfellow, James
  Three Plays of the Sea 1970,Ag 20,39:1
Stringfield, Lamar (Composer)
  Tread the Green Grass 1932,Jl 24,IX,1:3
  Shroud My Body Down 1934,D 9,II,1:6
Stritch, Elaine
  Private Life of the Master Race, The
    1945,Je 13,28:3
  Loco 1946,O 17,29:2
  Angel in the Wings 1947,D 12,36:4
  Yes, M'Lord 1949,O 5,35:2
  Pal Joey 1952,Ja 4,17:6
  Pal Joey 1952,Ja 13,II,1:1
  On Your Toes 1954,O 12,24:4
  Bus Stop 1955,Mr 3,23:2
  Bus Stop 1955,Mr 13,II,1:1
  Sin of Pat Muldoon, The 1957,Mr 14,35:1
  Goldilocks 1958,O 13,33:1
  Goldilocks 1958,O 19,II,1:1
  Sail Away 1961,O 4,48:5
  Sail Away 1962,Je 23,14:3
  Wonderful Town 1967,My 18,50:1
  Private Lives 1968,My 20,59:1
  Company 1970,Ap 27,40:1
  Company 1970,My 3,II,1:4
Strobach, Ben (Miscellaneous)
  Stop the World-I Want to Get Off 1962,O 4,45:4
Strobbe, William
  Amedee: or, How to Disentangle Yourself
    1955,N 1,27:3
Strobbe, William (Lighting Director)
  Amedee: or, How to Disentangle Yourself
    1955,N 1,27:3
Strode, Hudson (Playwright)
  Little Theatre Tournament; End of the Dance, The
    1929,My 11,22:2
Strode, W Chetham (Playwright)
  Heart's Content 1936,D 24,22:2
  Heart's Content 1937,Ja 24,X,3:1
Stroeva, Dora (Mme)
  Music Box Revue 1923,S 24,5:3
Strom, A William (Lighting Director)
  Diversions 1958,N 8,14:4
Strom, A William (Scenic Designer)
  Diversions 1958,N 8,14:4
Strom, Myrna
  Corner of the Bed, A 1969,F 27,35:2
Stromberg, Hunt Jr (Miscellaneous)
  Front Page, The 1946,S 5,22:4
  Sally 1948,My 7,31:2
Stromberg, Hunt Jr (Producer)
  Red Mill, The 1945,O 17,16:2
Strome, Edwin
  Nights of Wrath; Nuits de la Colere, Les
    1947,D 1,26:4
  Miser, The 1950,Mr 27,19:5
  Stalag 17 1951,My 9,41:2
Strommen, Robert
  Sign of Jonah, The 1957,My 2,27:1
Strong, Austin
  Man About Town, A 1921,Mr 22,15:1
  Henry IV, Part I 1926,Je 1,29:1
Strong, Austin (Director)
  Nantucket Follies 1927,Jl 30,13:2
  Play Without a Name, A 1928,N 26,30:5
  Little Father of the Wilderness, The 1930,Je 3,27:1
  Three Wise Fools 1936,Mr 2,12:2
Strong, Austin (Playwright)
  Heaven 1920,Je 13,VI,1:8
  Untitled-Pantomime 1921,Ap 3,VII,1:1
  Seventh Heaven 1922,O 31,11:1
  Drums of Oude, The 1927,My 3,24:3
  Seventh Heaven 1927,S 3,13:1
  Play Without a Name, A 1928,N 26,30:5
  Little Father of the Wilderness, The 1930,Je 3,27:1
  Three Wise Fools 1936,Ja 14,25:2
  Three Wise Fools 1936,Mr 2,12:2
  Seventh Heaven 1955,My 27,16:2
Strong, Austin (Producer)
  Nantucket Follies 1927,Jl 30,13:2
Strong, Austin (Scenic Designer)
  Play Without a Name, A 1928,N 26,30:5
Strong, Charles
  Good Times 1920,Ag 10,10:1
  Page Miss Glory 1934,N 28,24:2
Strong, Craig
  Midsummer Night's Dream, A 1963,Jl 1,19:2
Strong, Fred E
  Breakfast in Bed 1920,F 4,12:1
  Gentle Grafters 1926,O 28,23:1
  Out of the Night 1927,O 18,32:3
Strong, H L
  Espanola 1921,D 30,13:1
Strong, Harold L (Lighting Director)
  Man From Earth, The 1923,Ja 3,6:2
Strong, Harold L (Scenic Designer)
  Man From Earth, The 1923,Ja 3,6:2
Strong, Jack
  Vaudeville (Hippodrome) 1926,Mr 16,22:2
Strong, Jay
  Home Fires 1923,Ag 21,12:1
Strong, Jay (Director)
  Fascist's Holiday, The 1943,Ja 26,14:2

Strong, Jay (Playwright)
Nine O'Clock Revue 1936,Jl 8,14:3
Strong, Julia
Katja 1926,O 19,27:3
Strong, Marliene
Memphis Bound 1945,My 25,23:2
Strong, Michael
Spring Again 1941,N 11,28:2
Russian People, The 1942,D 30,17:2
I'll Take the High Road 1943,N 10,28:3
Thank You Svoboda 1944,Mr 2,13:2
Men to the Sea 1944,O 4,25:2
It's A Gift 1945,Mr 13,18:7
Whole World Over, The 1947,Mr 28,28:2
Detective Story 1949,Mr 24,34:2
Enemy of the People, An 1950,D 29,14:1
Emperor's Clothes, The 1953,F 10,24:2
Anastasia 1954,D 30,13:1
Anastasia 1955,Ja 16,II,1:1
Month in the Country, A 1956,Ap 4,23:1
Firstborn, The 1958,My 1,35:1
Firstborn, The 1958,My 11,II,1:1
Rhinoceros 1961,Ja 10,27:1
Rhinoceros 1961,Ja 22,II,1:1
After the Fall 1964,Ja 24,18:1
Marco Millions 1964,F 21,33:1
But for Whom Charlie 1964,Mr 13,42:2
Changeling, The 1964,O 30,32:2
Incident at Vichy 1964,D 4,44:1
Strong, Nellie
Marjolaine 1922,Ja 25,16:1
Strong, Rod
New Faces of 1956 1956,Je 15,32:1
Mask and Gown 1957,S 11,29:1
Strong, Sarah
Four O'Clock 1933,F 14,19:6
Strong, Tac (Choreographer)
She Shall Have Music 1959,Ja 23,18:4
Strong, Tao
Plain and Fancy 1955,F 6,II,6:6
Strong, Wayland
Pygmalion 1938,Ja 27,16:3
Captain Jinks of the Horse Marines 1938,Ja 28,16:2
No More Peace 1938,Ja 29,13:2
Coriolanus 1938,F 2,14:5
Strongin, Mimi
Seeds in the Wind 1948,Ap 26,27:2
Seeds in the Wind 1948,My 26,29:2
Enchanted, The 1950,Ja 19,34:2
Cry of the Peacock 1950,Ap 12,33:2
Johnny Summit 1957,S 25,23:4
Stroock, Bianca (Costume Designer)
Counsellor-at-Law 1942,N 25,17:2
Wallflower 1944,Ja 27,14:2
Calico Wedding 1945,Mr 8,18:6
Round Trip 1945,My 30,16:4
Fatal Witness, The 1946,N 20,43:2
Christopher Blake 1946,D 2,33:2
Wonderful Journey 1946,D 26,30:2
Parlor Story 1947,Mr 5,29:2
Hallams, The 1948,Mr 5,18:2
Metropole 1949,D 7,43:2
Sabrina Fair 1953,N 12,37:1
Stroock, Bianca (Miscellaneous)
Big Two, The 1947,Ja 9,21:2
Stroock, Geraldine
Winter's Tale, The 1946,Ja 16,18:6
Stroock, Gloria
Oh, Herbert! 1945,Je 20,26:3
Little Women 1945,D 24,18:2
Truckline Cafe 1946,F 28,19:4
Gayden 1949,My 11,34:4
Stroom, Eric (Playwright)
One Flight Down 1937,D 14,32:4
Stroube, Juan
Pygmalion 1952,F 9,11:2
Stroud, Claude
Heaven on Earth 1948,S 17,29:2
Stroud, Richard
Midsummer Night's Dream, A 1968,D 9,59:1
Strouse, Alexander Jr
Blue Jeans 1933,Ap 9,31:5
Strouse, Charles (Composer)
Shoestring Revue 1955,Mr 1,22:2
Littlest Revue, The 1956,My 23,37:2
Sixth Finger in a Five Finger Glove 1956,O 9,31:4
Shoestring '57 1956,N 6,31:1
Bye Bye Birdie 1960,Ap 15,13:4
All American 1962,Mr 20,44:1
Golden Boy 1964,O 21,56:1
Golden Boy 1964,N 1,II,1:1
It's a Bird . . . It's a Plane . . . It's Superman
1966,Mr 30,34:1
Applause 1970,Mr 31,35:1
Applause 1970,Ap 5,II,1:1
Strouse, Charles (Lyricist)
Littlest Revue, The 1956,My 23,37:2
Golden Boy 1964,N 1,II,1:1
Strouse, Charles (Musical Director)
Shoestring Revue 1955,Mr 1,22:2
Strouse, Irving (Playwright)
Thorntons, The 1956,F 15,26:1

Strouse, Irving (Producer)
Bad Habits of 1926 1926,My 1,11:1
Man Who Never Died, The 1958,N 22,27:2
Strouse, Irving S (Director)
Bad Habits of 1925 1925,F 9,17:1
Strouse, Irving S (Playwright)
Bad Habits of 1925 1925,F 9,17:1
Strouse, Jack
Century Revue and the Midnight Rounders, The
1920,Jl 13,9:1
Strouse, Sandy
Achilles Had a Heel 1935,O 14,20:2
How Beautiful With Shoes 1935,N 29,24:1
Tide Rising 1937,Ja 26,17:2
Chalked Out 1937,Mr 26,24:2
Eye on the Sparrow 1938,My 4,26:3
Lorelei 1938,N 30,21:2
Sea Dogs 1939,N 7,30:3
Stroux, Hans (Director)
All God's Chillun Got Wings 1932,Mr 27,VIII,3:3
Stroux, Karl-Heinz (Director)
Rhinoceros 1959,N 2,41:1
Nathan the Wise 1962,Mr 7,29:1
Before Sundown 1962,Mr 14,43:1
Stroux, Karl-Heinz (Miscellaneous)
Nathan the Wise 1962,Mr 7,29:1
Before Sundown 1962,Mr 14,43:1
Strozzi, Kay
Living Mask, The 1924,Ja 22,15:1
Flame of Love 1924,Ap 22,19:2
Ladies of the Evening 1924,D 24,11:2
Jane-Our Stranger 1925,O 9,27:2
Crown Prince, The 1927,Mr 24,23:2
Matrimonial Bed, The 1927,O 13,23:2
Ink 1927,N 2,24:2
Heavy Traffic 1928,S 6,23:3
Humbug, The 1929,N 28,34:5
Silent Witness, The 1931,Mr 24,31:5
Silent Witness, The 1931,My 10,VIII,3:5
Animal Kingdom, The 1932,Ja 3,VIII,3:1
These Two 1934,My 8,28:3
Alley Cat 1934,S 18,18:1
Tomorrow's Harvest 1934,D 6,26:5
Moroni 1936,Ag 19,19:1
St Helena 1936,S 29,35:1
St Helena 1936,O 7,32:1
Madwoman of Chaillot, The 1970,Mr 23,48:3
Struck, Brenda
More the Merrier, The 1941,S 16,19:3
Strudwick, Lucille
Small Miracle 1934,S 27,24:3
Panic 1935,Mr 16,18:4
Let Freedom Ring 1935,N 7,26:2
Prelude 1936,Ap 20,17:4
200 Were Chosen 1936,N 21,21:1
Strudwick, Shepperd
Falstaff 1928,D 26,14:2
Life Line, The 1930,D 29,19:3
Both Your Houses 1933,Mr 7,20:3
Both Your Houses 1933,My 23,22:2
Biography 1934,F 6,24:4
Jig Saw 1934,My 1,26:3
Tight Britches 1934,S 12,26:2
Lady of Letters 1935,Mr 29,26:6
Trelawney of the 'Wells' 1935,Jl 16,24:1
Let Freedom Ring 1935,N 7,26:2
Private Hicks 1936,Ja 13,14:4
End of Summer 1936,F 18,26:4
As You Like It 1937,N 1,25:2
As You Like It 1937,N 8,18:2
Great Lady 1938,D 2,26:6
Three Sisters, The 1939,O 16,23:1
Christopher Blake 1946,D 2,33:2
Christopher Blake 1946,D 8,II,5:1
Affairs of State 1950,S 26,37:2
Bat, The 1953,Ja 21,28:2
Ladies of the Corridor, The 1953,O 22,33:5
Ladies of the Corridor, The 1953,N 1,II,1:1
Doctor's Dilemma, The 1955,Ja 12,22:1
Sea Gull, The 1956,O 23,38:1
Night Circus, The 1958,D 3,44:1
Desert Incident, A 1959,Mr 25,40:1
Only in America 1959,N 20,35:1
Who's Afraid of Virginia Woolf? 1962,N 1,34:1
Devils, The 1965,N 17,51:2
Measure for Measure 1966,Jl 14,27:1
Galileo 1967,Ap 14,31:1
Price, The 1968,O 30,39:1
Strunk, William Jr (Playwright)
Antony and Cleopatra 1937,N 11,30:2
Strunsky, Sheba
Princess Turandot 1926,N 13,14:2
Centuries, The 1927,N 30,23:1
Hoboken Blues 1928,F 18,10:1
Struthers, James (Producer)
Eight O'Clock Tuesday 1941,Ja 7,18:2
Struwel, Peter
Merchant of Yonkers, The 1938,D 29,14:2
Stryker, G A
Opportunity 1920,Jl 31,5:1
Little Poor Man, The 1925,Ag 6,14:1
Half-Naked Truth, The 1926,Je 8,23:1

Stryker, Helen
Paolo and Francesca 1924,D 3,24:2
Stryker, Muriel
Sun-Kist 1921,My 24,20:2
Ziegfeld Follies 1922,Je 6,18:2
Magnolia Lady, The 1924,N 26,17:2
Vaudeville (Palace) 1926,Je 29,21:3
Strzelecki, Zenobius (Scenic Designer)
Mother Courage 1967,N 17,55:1
Stuart, Aimee (Playwright)
Clara Gibbings 1928,D 9,X,2:1
Her Shop 1929,F 24,IX,4:3
Meet Lady Clara 1930,Mr 30,VIII,2:7
Lady Clara 1930,Ap 18,28:7
Nine Till Six 1930,S 29,17:2
Birthday 1934,D 27,24:2
Nine Till Six 1936,Mr 14,10:3
Indian Summer 1936,Ap 20,17:5
Indian Summer 1936,My 17,IX,2:2
Love of Women 1937,D 14,33:2
Jeannie 1940,F 18,IX,2:5
Jeannie 1940,Ap 14,IX,1:7
Jeannie 1940,N 13,29:2
Lace on Her Petticoat 1951,S 5,40:3
Stuart, Aleen
Lady Comes Across, The 1942,Ja 10,10:2
Stuart, Allan
Tragedy of the Ages, The 1933,Ap 7,22:7
Stuart, Avon
Lonesome Train, The 1965,Je 17,25:1
Stuart, Betty
Jackpot 1944,Ja 14,15:2
Stuart, D E (Composer)
It's the Valet 1933,D 15,25:4
Stuart, D E (Lyricist)
It's the Valet 1933,D 15,25:4
Stuart, Dick
Crucible, The 1958,Mr 17,21:1
Stuart, Donald
Love in Our Time 1952,O 4,14:3
Streetcar Named Desire, A 1955,Mr 4,18:2
Stuart, Donald Clive (Director)
Man From Earth, The 1923,Ja 3,6:2
Drake's Drum 1923,D 26,17:7
Fortuno 1925,D 23,22:1
Samarkand 1926,D 22,24:4
It's the Valet 1933,D 15,25:4
Stuart, Eddie (Composer)
Old Bucks and New Wings 1962,N 6,39:4
Stuart, Edward
Partition 1948,O 29,31:2
Stuart, Eleanor
Death Takes a Holiday 1931,F 17,29:1
All's Well That Ends Well 1953,Jl 16,18:2
Measure for Measure 1954,Je 30,23:1
Oedipus Rex 1954,Jl 17,6:6
Julius Caesar 1955,Je 29,23:3
Henry V 1956,Je 20,27:2
Coriolanus 1961,Je 21,31:2
Stuart, Francis (Playwright)
Glory 1936,Ja 27,20:1
Stuart, Frank S (Composer)
Before I Wake 1968,O 14,56:1
Stuart, Frank S (Producer)
Before I Wake 1968,O 14,56:1
Stuart, George
Drunkard, The 1936,S 20,IX,3:4
Stuart, Geraldine
Annie Get Your Gun 1957,Mr 9,15:5
Stuart, Harvey (Director)
Fallout 1959,My 21,36:2
Stuart, Harvey (Miscellaneous)
Pigeon, The 1957,My 17,19:2
Stuart, Harvey (Producer)
Fallout 1959,My 21,36:2
Stuart, Igene
Noah 1935,F 14,25:2
Stuart, Isabel
First Man, The 1922,Mr 6,9:2
Stuart, J Marberger (Playwright)
Make Me Disappear 1969,My 14,34:1
Stuart, J Marberger (Producer)
Make Me Disappear 1969,My 14,34:1
Stuart, James
Lord Byron's Love Letter 1955,Ja 19,23:2
Stuart, Jane
Sambo 1970,Jl 23,24:1
Stuart, Jay
Cry for Us All 1970,Ap 9,48:2
Stuart, Jeanne
Nine Till Six 1930,S 29,17:2
Rats of Norway, The 1948,Ap 16,27:6
Stuart, Jeff
Life With Father 1967,O 20,53:2
Stuart, Joel
Merchant of Venice, The 1962,F 3,13:2
Exhaustion of Our Son's Love, The 1965,O 19,51:1
Winterset 1966,F 10,32:2
School for Scandal, The 1966,N 22,33:2
Wild Duck, The 1967,Ja 12,49:1
Stuart, Jonathan (Lighting Director)
Cage, The 1970,Je 19,25:1

Stuart, Jonathan (Miscellaneous)
Cage, The 1970,Je 19,25:1
Stuart, Jonathan (Scenic Designer)
Cage, The 1970,Je 19,25:1
Stuart, Julia
Respect for Riches, The 1920,My 12,9:1
Paddy the Next Best Thing 1920,Ag 28,5:5
Stuart, Katherine
Kid Boots 1924,Ja 1,21:3
Stuart, Kerry
Trojan Horse, The 1940,O 31,28:3
Stuart, Larry
Nellie Bly 1946,Ja 22,32:2
Stuart, Laura
Women at the Tomb, The 1961,Ap 25,41:1
Electra 1962,Mr 22,42:1
Stuart, Leslie (Composer)
Florodora 1920,Ap 6,18:1
Florodora 1936,Ag 23,II,8:2
Stuart, Loraine
Texas Town 1941,Ap 30,22:3
Out of My House 1942,Ja 8,28:6
Stuart, Marguerite
My Son 1924,S 18,18:2
Stuart, Marie
Don't Tell 1920,S 29,12:1
Taboo 1922,Ap 5,22:1
Stuart, Marion
Houseboat on the Styx, The 1928,D 26,14:3
Stuart, Marjorie L (Miscellaneous)
Make Me Disappear 1969,My 14,34:1
Stuart, Marjorie L (Playwright)
Make Me Disappear 1969,My 14,34:1
Stuart, Mark
Old Bucks and New Wings 1962,N 6,39:4
To Be or Not to Be-What Kind of a Question Is
That? 1970,O 20,39:1
Stuart, Mary
Electra 1932,Ja 9,21:4
Women, The 1936,D 28,13:1
Stuart, Maxine
Western Waters 1937,D 29,17:1
Sunup to Sundown 1938,F 2,14:3
Ring Two 1939,N 23,38:2
Nine Girls 1943,Ja 14,26:2
Goose for the Gander, A 1945,Ja 24,16:4
At War With the Army 1949,Mr 9,32:2
Child Buyer, The 1962,My 14,35:1
Stuart, Michael
Too True to Be Good 1937,Jl 27,24:2
Stuart, Michael (Miscellaneous)
Alive and Kicking 1950,Ja 18,25:5
Stuart, Miriam
Madame X 1927,Jl 7,29:3
Ledge, A 1929,N 19,26:3
Did I Say No? 1931,S 23,19:4
Boy Friend, The 1932,Je 8,22:3
Stuart, Morgan
Pre-Honeymoon 1936,My 1,19:4
Utopia, Limited; Flowers of Progress, The
1957,F 27,21:1
Mikado, The 1957,Ap 24,28:2
H M S Pinafore 1957,My 1,42:6
Pirates of Penzance, The 1957,My 8,43:1
Yeomen of the Guard, The 1957,My 22,28:3
Gondoliers, The 1957,My 29,34:2
H M S Pinafore 1960,Ja 29,14:1
Utopia, Limited 1960,Ap 8,27:2
Stuart, Morna (Playwright)
Traitor's Gate 1938,D 4,X,7:5
Stuart, Norman
Biography 1934,F 6,24:4
Spring Song 1934,O 2,18:2
Paths of Glory 1935,S 27,24:2
Lady Precious Stream 1936,Ja 28,15:2
Bat, The 1937,Je 1,27:5
Siege 1937,D 9,31:4
Family Portrait 1939,Mr 9,18:4
Taming of the Shrew, The 1940,F 6,17:2
Land Is Bright, The 1941,O 29,26:2
Stuart, Patricia Quinn (Costume Designer)
In White America 1963,N 1,26:1
Burning, The 1963,D 4,57:1
Cindy 1964,Mr 20,24:1
Diary of a Madman 1964,Ap 17,29:2
Princess Rebecca Birnbaum 1966,Mr 7,22:1
Young Marrieds Play Monopoly 1966,Mr 7,22:1
Suburban Tragedy 1966,Mr 7,22:1
Make Like a Dog 1966,Mr 7,22:1
Beyond Desire 1967,O 11,36:1
Cuban Thing, The 1968,S 25,36:2
Cry of Players, A 1968,N 15,40:1
Me Nobody Knows, The 1970,My 19,42:1
Stuart, Peggy (Composer)
Red Roses for Me 1961,N 28,41:1
Stuart, Peter
Parasite, The 1965,D 17,43:2
Falstaff 1966,Je 20,27:1
Twelfth Night 1966,Je 23,28:1
Julius Caesar 1966,Je 24,29:2
Don't Shoot Mable It's Your Husband
1968,O 23,34:1

Stuart, Philip (Playwright)
Clara Gibbings 1928,D 9,X,2:1
Her Shop 1929,F 24,IX,4:3
Meet Lady Clara 1930,Mr 30,VIII,2:7
Lady Clara 1930,Ap 18,28:7
Nine Till Six 1930,S 29,17:2
Birthday 1934,D 27,24:2
Nine Till Six 1936,Mr 14,10:3
Indian Summer 1936,Ap 20,17:5
Indian Summer 1936,My 17,IX,2:2
Love of Women 1937,D 14,33:2
Stuart, Ralph
New Sin, The 1923,My 28,18:3
Rat, The 1925,F 11,19:3
Come of Age 1934,Ja 13,16:6
Stuart, Ralph (Director)
Man Who Died Twice, The 1925,D 14,19:1
Stuart, Richard
Two Orphans, The 1926,Ap 6,26:2
Stuart, Robert C
On the Level 1937,Mr 26,24:4
Stuart, Roy
Best People, The 1933,Mr 16,21:5
Beg, Borrow or Steal 1960,F 11,39:4
Cafe Crown 1964,Ap 18,32:1
Stuart, Sybil
Sun-Kist 1921,My 24,20:2
Stuart, Wally
Royal Family, The 1927,D 29,26:4
Stubblefield, Thomas J
My Kinsman, Major Molineux 1964,N 2,62:2
Stubbs, Bill
Jotham Valley 1951,F 7,37:2
Stubbs, Harry
Endless Chain, The 1922,S 5,21:2
Listening In 1922,D 5,24:1
Dice of the Gods, The 1923,Ap 6,20:2
Butter and Egg Man, The 1925,S 24,28:1
Nightstick 1927,N 11,20:4
Big Fight, The 1928,S 19,33:1
Stubbs, Herbert
Carmen Jones 1956,Je 1,28:2
Carmen Jones 1959,Ag 18,25:1
Stubbs, Louise
Trial of Lee Harvey Oswald, The 1967,N 6,64:1
Americana Pastoral 1968,D 11,51:1
Open 24 Hours 1969,F 12,31:1
Satisfaction Guaranteed 1969,F 12,31:1
Reckoning, The 1969,S 5,28:1
Contributions; Contribution 1970,Mr 10,53:1
Stubbs, Ray
Romeo and Juliet 1961,F 24,24:1
Antony and Cleopatra 1963,Je 21,33:1
Hamlet 1964,Je 17,49:1
Henry V 1965,Je 29,27:2
Stucchio, Jeanne
Paradise 1931,My 12,29:2
Stuchkoff, N (Lyricist)
If the Rabbi Wants 1929,D 23,18:5
Love Thief, The 1931,Ja 19,24:5
Stuchkoff, N (Playwright)
If the Rabbi Wants 1929,D 23,18:5
Stuck, Goodloe (Scenic Designer)
Master of the Revels 1935,Ag 14,16:2
Stucker, Gilbert (Lighting Director)
Way of the World, The 1950,Ap 9,73:5
Stuckmann, Eugene
Cat and the Canary, The 1935,Ag 13,20:3
Richard III 1943,Mr 27,8:3
Othello 1943,O 20,18:1
Tempest, The 1945,Ja 26,17:2
Henry VIII 1946,N 7,42:2
Androcles and the Lion 1946,D 20,29:2
Pound on Demand 1946,D 20,29:3
Yellow Jack 1947,F 28,26:2
Alice in Wonderland 1947,Ap 7,19:2
Skipper Next to God 1948,Ja 5,14:5
Richard III 1953,D 10,65:2
Stuckmann, Eugene (Miscellaneous)
Fools Are Passing Through 1958,Ap 3,24:2
Rosmersholm 1962,Ap 12,42:1
Cherry Orchard, The 1962,N 15,46:2
Doll's House, A 1963,F 4,5:6
Stucky, William (Playwright)
Touchstone 1953,F 4,33:2
Studds, Harry O
Lady for a Night, A 1928,Ap 17,26:4
Studer, Hal
Lamp at Midnight 1947,D 22,29:2
Church Street 1948,F 10,27:2
Family Portrait 1959,My 6,48:2
Studholme, Marion
H M S Pinafore 1960,S 8,41:1
Pirates of Penzance, The 1961,S 7,41:1
Pirates of Penzance, The 1961,S 17,II,1:1
Studley, Julien J (Producer)
World War 2 1/2 1969,Mr 25,40:1
Candaules, Commissioner 1970,My 29,15:1
Stuewe, Hans
Victoria Regina 1938,Ap 17,X,2:1
Stuhler, William R Jr (Composer)
Man From Earth, The 1923,Ja 3,6:2

Stulik, Lincoln John (Lighting Director)
Emperor, The 1963,Ap 17,30:1
Month in the Country, A 1963,My 29,39:2
Stulik, Lincoln John (Miscellaneous)
Crystal Heart, The 1960,F 16,31:2
Brouhaha 1960,Ap 27,31:2
Stumvoll, Walter
Professor Bernhardi 1968,Mr 20,38:1
Maria Stuart 1968,Mr 27,38:1
Sturdivant, Brian
Patriot for Me, A 1969,O 6,58:1
Sturdy, Hugh
Wretched the Lionhearted 1962,S 13,31:2
Birds, The 1967,My 7,67:1
Sturez, Louis
Miracle, The 1924,Ja 16,17:1
Sturez, Maurice
Mima 1928,D 13,24:2
Sturgeon, George
Wookey, The 1941,S 11,20:5
Sturgeon, Jean
Hats Off to Ice 1944,Je 23,15:2
Sturges, Preston
Hotbed 1928,N 10,20:7
Sturges, Preston (Composer)
Well of Romance, The 1930,N 8,21:2
Sturges, Preston (Director)
Carnival in Flanders 1953,S 9,38:2
Sturges, Preston (Lyricist)
Well of Romance, The 1930,N 8,21:2
Sturges, Preston (Original Author)
Conquering Hero, The 1961,Ja 17,40:2
Sturges, Preston (Playwright)
Guinea Pig, The 1929,Ja 8,35:1
Strictly Dishonorable 1929,S 19,37:1
Strictly Dishonorable 1929,S 29,IX,1:1
Recapture 1930,Ja 19,VIII,2:6
Recapture 1930,Ja 30,16:4
Strictly Dishonorable 1931,Mr 11,23:5
Strictly Dishonorable 1931,Ap 12,IX,1:3
Child of Manhattan 1932,Mr 2,15:1
Make a Wish 1951,Ap 19,38:1
Carnival in Flanders 1953,S 9,38:2
Sturges, Preston (Producer)
Guinea Pig, The 1929,Ja 8,35:1
Sturges, Thyrza
This Thing Called Love 1935,Jl 2,24:4
Sturgess, Sydney
Winter's Tale, The 1958,Jl 23,34:3
King John 1960,Je 29,26:2
Romeo and Juliet 1960,Jl 1,14:1
Hadrian VII 1969,Ja 9,22:1
Sturgess, Ted
Country Wife, The 1955,Ap 6,35:1
Sturgis, Ann
Glad Tidings 1951,O 12,33:2
Sturgis, Norman R
Without the Walls 1922,Ap 17,17:1
Choice, The 1930,My 9,20:5
Sturm, Emmy
Morgen Wieder Lustig 1921,Je 5,VI,1:3
Braut von Lucullus, Die 1921,D 11,VI,1:4
Casanova 1928,N 4,IX,2:1
Sturm, Justin (Miscellaneous)
Once There Was a Russian 1961,F 20,32:2
That Hat! 1964,S 24,45:1
Sturm, Justin (Playwright)
I Know What I Like 1939,N 25,13:5
One Eye Closed 1954,N 25,45:2
Sturm, Justin (Producer)
Debut 1956,F 23,32:1
Sturm, Katherine (Miscellaneous)
That Hat! 1964,S 24,45:1
Sturrey, Waldo
Edward, My Son 1948,O 1,30:2
Sturridge, Charles
Hamlet 1970,D 28,40:1
Stutchkoff, Misha
'Round the Family Table 1938,O 8,10:3
Stutchkoff, Nuchim (Playwright)
'Round the Family Table 1938,O 8,10:3
In a Jewish Grocery 1939,O 2,15:2
Stuthman, Fred
Hamlet 1970,O 19,51:1
Stutz, Richard (Composer)
Along Fifth Avenue 1949,Ja 14,28:2
Stutz, Richard (Lyricist)
Along Fifth Avenue 1949,Ja 14,28:2
Styers, Glen
Here Come the Clowns 1954,My 5,36:2
Styler, Alan
Mikado, The 1951,Ja 30,21:2
Trial by Jury 1951,F 6,24:2
Gondoliers, The 1951,F 13,27:2
Iolanthe 1951,F 16,22:1
Cox and Box 1951,F 20,21:2
Iolanthe 1955,S 28,38:1
Yeomen of the Guard, The 1955,O 4,39:2
Trial by Jury 1955,O 18,48:1
Gondoliers, The 1962,N 16,25:2
Pirates of Penzance, The 1962,N 21,28:1
Trial by Jury 1962,N 23,32:4
Trial by Jury 1964,N 20,40:1

Styler, Alan—Cont
Mikado, The 1964,N 27,43:1
H M S Pinafore 1966,N 24,64:1

Styles, Buddy
Best Foot Forward 1941,O 2,28:2

Styles, Edwin
Vanities 1932,S 18,IX,2:1
Vanities 1932,S 28,22:4
Dark Eyes 1948,Mr 25,34:4

Stylists, The
Anything Goes 1934,N 22,26:1

Styne, Jule (Composer)
High Button Shoes 1947,O 10,32:2
High Button Shoes 1948,D 23,23:7
Gentlemen Prefer Blondes 1949,D 9,35:3
Michael Todd's Peep Show 1950,Je 29,37:2
Two on the Aisle 1951,Jl 20,13:6
Two on the Aisle 1951,Jl 29,II,1:1
Hazel Flagg 1953,F 12,22:2
Peter Pan 1954,O 21,30:2
High Button Shoes 1955,Mr 12,10:6
Bells Are Ringing 1956,N 29,43:4
Bells Are Ringing 1956,N 30,18:2
Miss Lonelyhearts 1957,O 4,26:2
Say Darling 1958,Ap 4,17:1
Say Darling 1958,Ap 13,II,1:1
Party With Betty Comden and Adolph Green, A
    1958,D 24,2:7
Say Darling 1959,F 26,38:2
Gypsy 1959,My 22,31:6
Gypsy 1959,My 31,II,1:1
Do Re Mi 1960,D 27,23:2
Do Re Mi 1961,Ja 8,II,1:1
Subways Are for Sleeping 1961,D 28,22:1
Arturo Ui 1963,N 12,49:1
Arturo Ui 1963,N 24,II,1:1
Funny Girl 1964,Mr 27,15:1
Wonder World 1964,My 18,32:1
Fade Out--Fade In 1964,My 27,45:1
Hallelujah, Baby! 1967,Ap 27,51:1
Hallelujah, Baby! 1967,My 7,II,1:1
Darling of the Day 1968,Ja 29,26:2
Darling of the Day 1968,F 11,II,3:1
Look to the Lilies 1970,Mr 30,59:1
Look to the Lilies 1970,Ap 12,II,3:7

Styne, Jule (Costume Designer)
Gentlemen Prefer Blondes 1949,D 18,II,3:1

Styne, Jule (Director)
Something More! 1964,N 11,36:1

Styne, Jule (Lyricist)
High Button Shoes 1947,O 10,32:2
High Button Shoes 1948,D 23,23:7
Michael Todd's Peep Show 1950,Je 29,37:2
High Button Shoes 1955,Mr 12,10:6
Say Darling 1958,Ap 13,II,1:1

Styne, Jule (Miscellaneous)
Mr Wonderful 1956,Mr 23,23:2
First Impressions 1959,Mr 20,28:1

Styne, Jule (Producer)
Make a Wish 1951,Ap 19,38:1
Pal Joey 1952,Ja 4,17:6
In Any Language 1952,O 9,40:2
Hazel Flagg 1953,F 12,22:2
Will Success Spoil Rock Hunter? 1955,O 14,22:2
Mr Wonderful 1956,Mr 23,23:2
Say Darling 1958,Ap 4,17:1
Fade Out--Fade In 1964,My 27,45:1
Fade Out--Fade In 1965,F 16,40:2

Styne, Stanley (Lyricist)
Wonder World 1964,My 18,32:1

Suarez, Hilda
Projimos, Los 1966,Je 29,38:5

Suarez, Ilka (Costume Designer)
Jacques Brel Is Alive and Well and Living in Paris
    1968,Ja 23,25:2

Suarez, Olga
Lady Comes Across, The 1942,Ja 10,10:2
Music in My Heart 1947,O 3,30:2

Suarez, Roberto Rodriguez (Director)
Crossroads 1969,Ag 7,28:1

Suberville, Jean (Playwright)
Don Juan 1932,N 13,IX,2:5

Subotnick, Morton (Composer)
Galileo 1963,Ja 5,5:2
Milk Train Doesn't Stop Here Anymore, The
    1965,Jl 27,25:1
Danton's Death 1965,O 22,46:1
Caucasian Chalk Circle, The 1966,Mr 25,35:1

Subotnick, Morton (Lyricist)
Caucasian Chalk Circle, The 1966,Mr 25,35:1

Subramanya, Shireen
Guide, The 1968,Mr 7,50:1

Such, Georginna
Fall and Rise of Susan Lenox, The 1920,Je 11,11:2

Suchy, Margit
Blaue Hemd von Ithaka, Das 1931,Mr 15,IX,2:4

Sudakov, Ilya (Producer)
Ivan the Terrible 1944,N 12,II,1:6

Sudana, Philip
Hamlet 1936,N 11,54:2

Sudek, Ann
Shadow Years, The 1957,Ja 9,26:2

Sudermann, Hermann (Playwright)
Rosen 1921,My 15,VI,1:6
Glueck im Winkel 1921,Jl 24,VI,1:7
Magda 1925,D 22,18:4
Magda 1926,Ja 27,16:2
Magda 1930,Je 1,VIII,2:8

Sudlow, Joan
Carry On 1928,Ja 24,26:1
Tomorrow 1928,D 29,20:2
Town Boy 1929,O 5,22:4
Red Harvest 1937,Mr 31,29:2

Sudman, Arnold
For Valor 1935,N 19,27:5

Sudraka (Original Author)
Toy Cart, The 1930,D 7,IX,2:7

Sudrow, Irving (Miscellaneous)
World of Carl Sandburg, The 1960,S 15,44:1

Sue, Lyda
Higher and Higher 1940,Ap 5,24:3

Sue, Nitza
Midsummer Night's Dream, A 1967,Je 30,23:1

Sue Hasting's Marionettes
At Home Abroad 1935,S 20,17:4

Sues, Alan
Tea and Sympathy 1953,O 1,35:1

Sues, Leonard
Johnny 2X4 1942,Mr 17,24:6
Beat the Band 1942,O 15,26:1
Sons and Soldiers 1943,My 5,22:2

Suess, Oscar
Veronica's Veil 1936,Mr 2,4:3
Passion Play 1938,Mr 7,11:2

Suesse, Dana (Composer)
Let's Play Fair 1938,Ja 19,26:4
Case of Youth, A 1940,Mr 25,10:3
Seven Year Itch, The 1952,N 21,21:2
Come Play With Me 1959,My 1,33:5
Golden Fleecing 1959,O 16,24:5

Suesse, Dana (Lyricist)
Ziegfeld Follies 1934,Ja 5,24:3
Come Play With Me 1959,My 1,33:5

Suesse, Dana (Playwright)
Ziegfeld Follies 1934,Ja 5,24:3
It Takes Two 1947,F 4,33:4

Suessenguth, Arnim
Unentbehrliche, Der 1937,O 24,XI,3:1

Sufrin, Herb (Director)
Cats' Pajamas, The 1962,Je 1,16:2

Sufrin, Herb (Playwright)
In the Nick of Time 1967,Je 2,36:1

Sufrin, Herbert
Nights of Wrath; Nuits de la Colere, Les
    1947,D 1,26:4

Suga, Reo
Red Dust 1928,Ja 3,29:2
Mystery Man, The 1928,Ja 27,14:2

Suga, Sensuke (Playwright)
Greengrocer's Daughter, The 1966,Mr 16,50:1

Sugah-Turner, Charles
Show-Off, The 1932,D 13,25:4

Sugarman, Harold
Champion, The 1925,Ap 24,16:4

Sugden, Peter
Trial by Jury 1962,N 23,32:4

Sugerman, Louis
Jazz a La Carte 1922,Je 3,8:3

Sugihara, William
Fly Blackbird 1962,F 6,26:2

Sugimoto, Kazuo (Scenic Designer)
Fishing for Wives 1966,Mr 16,50:1
General's Daughter, The 1966,Mr 16,50:1
Greengrocer's Daughter, The 1966,Mr 16,50:1

Sugrue, Frank (Director)
Jungle of Cities 1970,Mr 1,75:2

Sugrue, Frank (Producer)
Narrow Road to the Deep North 1969,D 2,64:1
Jungle of Cities 1970,Mr 1,75:2
In 3 Zones 1970,N 3,28:1

Suhl, Yuri
Untitled-Poetry Reading 1967,Jl 18,29:1

Suhl, Yuri (Miscellaneous)
Untitled-Poetry Reading 1967,Jl 18,29:1

Suhr, Edward (Scenic Designer)
Bergbahn 1929,My 26,IX,2:3

Suiter, Bobra
Carousel 1949,Ja 26,28:2

Sukmen, Harry (Musical Director)
Pardon Our French 1950,O 6,22:4

Sulc (Playwright)
Petit Choc, Le 1928,O 28,IX,2:1
Jolly Joker, The 1928,O 28,IX,2:1

Sulcova, Jana
Matter of Days, A 1969,My 20,40:1

Suleman
Ali Baba 1951,Mr 27,34:2

Sulic, Vassili
Folies Bergere 1964,Je 3,36:1

Suling, Helen R
Vagabond King, The 1935,N 29,22:7

Sullavan, Joseph
Rainmaker, The 1954,O 29,28:1

Sullavan, Margaret
Modern Virgin, A 1931,My 21,33:4
Chrysalis 1932,N 16,15:2
Bad Manners 1933,Ja 31,15:5

Sullavan, Margaret—Cont
Stage Door 1936,S 29,35:1
Stage Door 1936,O 4,IX,2:1
Stage Door 1936,O 23,26:3
Stage Door 1936,N 1,X,1:1
Voice of the Turtle 1943,D 9,30:3
Voice of the Turtle, The 1943,D 19,II,3:1
Voice of the Turtle, The 1947,Jl 10,17:1
Voice of the Turtle, The 1947,Ag 24,II,1:5
Deep Blue Sea, The 1952,N 6,38:3
Deep Blue Sea, The 1952,D 7,II,7:2
Deep Blue Sea, The 1952,D 14,II,3:1
Deep Blue Sea, The 1953,Ap 4,8:6
Sabrina Fair 1953,N 12,37:1
Sabrina Fair 1953,N 22,II,1:1
Janus 1955,N 25,37:2

Sullivan, A S (Composer)
Thespis 1953,Ja 17,13:5

Sullivan, Alan (Original Author)
Jade God, The 1929,My 14,28:3

Sullivan, Ann
Wonderful Journey 1946,D 26,30:2
Temporary Island, A 1948,Mr 15,27:3
Hilda Crane 1950,N 2,38:2

Sullivan, Arthur
Good Boy 1928,S 6,23:2

Sullivan, Arthur (Composer)
Iolanthe 1920,Ja 6,13:3
H M S Pinafore 1920,Ja 13,10:2
Ruddigore 1920,Ja 20,11:2
Ruddigore 1920,F 1,VIII,2:2
Mikado, The 1924,Jl 29,9:1
Patience 1924,D 30,15:1
Patience 1925,Ja 4,VII,1:1
Patience 1925,F 1,VII,1:1
H M S Pinafore 1926,Ap 7,26:3
Iolanthe 1926,Ap 20,24:2
Iolanthe 1926,Ap 25,VIII,1:1
Mikado, The 1926,S 22,13:1
Mikado, The 1926,O 10,VIII,2:1
Pirates of Penzance, The; Slave of Duty, The
    1926,D 7,25:1
Pirates of Penzance, The 1926,D 12,VIII,3:1
Mikado, The; Town of Titipu, The 1927,S 19,30:1
Mikado, The 1927,S 25,VIII,1:1
Mikado, The 1927,O 30,IX,4:6
Iolanthe 1927,N 15,26:3
So.cerer, The 1928,Je 24,VIII,1:1
Gondoliers 1929,O 22,26:3
Patience 1929,D 16,34:5
Mikado, The; Town of Titipu, The 1931,My 5,33:2
H M S Pinafore 1931,My 19,25:2
H M S Pinafore 1931,My 31,II,1:2
Ruddigore 1931,Ag 18,28:3
Mikado, The 1931,Ag 25,17:7
Iolanthe 1932,Ja 5,20:2
Gondoliers, The 1932,Ja 12,29:1
Mikado, The 1932,Jl 29,18:4
Mikado, The 1933,Ap 18,13:4
Yeomen of the Guard, The 1933,My 2,20:4
H M S Pinafore 1933,My 9,20:3
Trial by Jury 1933,My 9,20:3
Yeomen of the Guard, The 1933,Ag 15,20:5
Mikado, The 1934,Ap 3,26:3
Pirates of Penzance, The 1934,Ap 10,26:5
Mikado, The 1934,Ap 24,27:5
Iolanthe 1934,My 1,26:4
Mikado, The 1934,My 22,28:2
Gondoliers, The 1934,S 4,23:1
Gondoliers, The 1934,S 9,IX,1:1
Iolanthe 1934,S 11,24:3
H M S Pinafore 1934,S 14,24:3
Trial by Jury 1934,S 14,24:3
Mikado, The; Town of Titipu, The 1934,S 18,18:1
Yeomen of the Guard, The 1934,S 21,28:3
Ruddigore 1934,S 25,25:2
Princess Ida; Castle Adamant 1934,S 28,26:3
Patience 1934,O 12,32:2
Rose of Persia 1935,Mr 1,17:4
H M S Pinafore 1935,Ag 17,18:4
Mikado, The 1935,Ag 24,17:5
Patience 1935,S 3,24:4
Mikado, The 1936,Ap 11,18:4
Pirates of Penzance, The 1936,Ap 21,27:5
Trial by Jury 1936,Ap 28,17:2
H M S Pinafore 1936,Ap 28,17:2
Iolanthe 1936,My 5,26:2
Utopia, Limited 1936,My 23,10:6
Gondoliers, The 1936,Jl 19,12:5
Gondoliers, The 1936,S 8,23:1
Yeomen of the Guard, The 1936,S 15,37:2
Iolanthe 1936,S 22,30:3
Patience 1936,O 6,28:6
Princess Ida 1936,O 13,32:2
Ruddigore 1936,O 23,26:4
Knights of Song 1938,O 18,29:2
Pirates of Penzance, The 1939,Ja 6,25:1
Trial by Jury 1939,Ja 6,25:1
Mikado, The 1939,Ja 10,16:3
Iolanthe 1939,Ja 13,16:3
H. M. S. Pinafore 1939,Ja 17,27:5
Cox and Box 1939,Ja 17,27:5
Gondoliers, The 1939,Ja 20,14:2
Yeomen of the Guard, The 1939,Ja 24,17:1

Sullivan, Arthur (Composer)—Cont

Patience 1939,Ja 27,16:3
Swing Mikado, The 1939,Mr 2,18:2
Mikado, The 1939,Mr 11,15:6
Swing Mikado, The 1939,Mr 12,XI,1:1
Hot Mikado, The 1939,Mr 24,26:2
Hot Mikado, The 1939,Ap 2,X,1:3
Hot Mikado, The 1939,Je 23,23:4
Yeomen of the Guard, The 1939,Jl 16,30:4
Yeomen of the Guard, The 1939,Jl 23,IX,2:1
Gondoliers, The 1940,O 1,29:2
Yeomen of the Guard, The 1941,D 19,34:3
H M S Pinafore 1942,Ja 22,12:2
Mikado, The 1942,F 4,22:2
Pirates of Penzance, The 1942,F 18,22:2
Pirates of Penzance, The 1942,F 20,20:2
Iolanthe 1942,F 24,26:4
Gondoliers, The 1942,Mr 4,22:3
Mikado, The 1944,F 12,11:3
Trial by Jury 1944,F 15,14:4
Gondoliers, The 1944,F 22,26:3
Iolanthe 1944,F 23,17:1
Ruddigore 1944,Mr 3,19:5
Yeomen of the Guard, The 1944,Mr 5,34:3
Hollywood Pinafore 1945,Je 1,20:1
Memphis Bound 1945,Je 10,II,1:1
Hollywood Pinafore 1945,Je 10,II,1:1
Pirates of Penzance, The 1946,My 17,14:6
Mikado, The 1946,Ag 12,9:2
Pirates of Penzance, The 1946,S 21,19:2
Mikado, The 1947,D 30,18:2
Pirates of Penzance, The 1948,Ja 6,27:2
Trial by Jury 1948,Ja 6,27:2
Pirates of Penzance, The 1948,Ja 11,II,1:1
Iolanthe 1948,Ja 13,29:3
H M S Pinafore 1948,Ja 20,26:2
Gondoliers, The 1948,Ja 27,31:2
Yeomen of the Guard, The 1948,F 3,30:2
Patience 1948,F 10,27:2
H M S Pinafore 1949,Jl 29,13:2
Mikado, The 1949,O 5,35:2
Pirates of Penzance, The 1949,O 11,41:2
H M S Pinafore 1949,O 18,34:2
Trial by Jury 1949,O 18,34:2
Mikado, The 1951,Ja 30,21:2
Mikado, The 1952,O 21,35:2
Pirates of Penzance, The 1952,O 28,36:4
Trial by Jury 1952,N 4,32:2
H M S Pinafore 1952,N 4,32:2
Iolanthe 1952,N 11,26:3
Mikado, The 1954,Mr 24,31:1
Pirates of Penzance, The 1954,Mr 31,32:5
Patience 1954,Ap 7,41:1
Ruddigore 1954,Ap 21,36:4
Iolanthe 1954,Ap 28,36:8
Yeomen of the Guard, The 1954,My 5,36:2
H M S Pinafore 1954,My 19,36:8
Sorcerer, The 1954,My 26,34:3
Iolanthe 1955,S 28,38:1
Mikado, The 1955,S 30,20:2
Yeomen of the Guard, The 1955,O 4,39:2
Pirates of Penzance, The 1955,O 7,21:1
Princess Ida 1955,O 14,22:3
H M S Pinafore 1955,O 18,48:1
Trial by Jury 1955,O 18,48:1
Ruddigore 1955,O 21,32:2
Utopia, Limited; Flowers of Progress, The
   1957,F 27,21:1
Utopia, Limited 1957,Mr 17,II,1:1
Mikado, The 1957,Ap 24,28:2
Pirates of Penzance, The 1957,My 8,43:1
Yeomen of the Guard, The 1957,My 22,28:3
Gondoliers, The 1957,My 29,34:2
H M S Pinafore; Trial by Jury 1957,Jl 29,16:1
Mikado, The 1959,O 2,24:1
H M S Pinafore 1960,Ja 29,14:1
Gondoliers, The 1960,F 7,II,1:1
H M S Pinafore 1960,Jl 17,51:1
Pirates of Penzance, The 1960,O 7,29:1
Mikado, The 1961,Ja 18,26:1
Pirates of Penzance, The 1961,Ja 20,24:5
Gondoliers, The 1961,Ja 26,33:2
H M S Pinafore 1961,F 2,26:6
Yeomen of the Guard, The 1961,Ap 28,23:1
Mikado, The 1961,My 5,23:1
Grand Duke, The 1961,My 12,24:1
Princess Ida 1961,My 19,23:1
Iolanthe 1961,My 26,29:6
H M S Pinafore 1961,Je 9,29:5
Pirates of Penzance, The 1961,S 7,41:1
Pirates of Penzance, The 1961,S 17,II,1:1
Gondoliers, The 1961,D 8,44:1
Iolanthe 1962,Ap 12,42:4
Gondoliers, The 1962,Ap 19,34:2
Gondoliers, The 1962,Jl 7,9:4
Yeomen of the Guard, The 1962,Jl 11,28:1
H M S Pinafore 1964,Mr 21,13:4
Gondoliers, The 1964,Mr 28,14:1
Yeomen of the Guard, The 1964,Ag 3,16:1
H M S Pinafore 1965,Ap 15,39:1
Patience 1965,Ap 16,34:1
Mikado, The 1965,Ap 17,11:3
Pirates of Penzance, The 1965,Ap 21,50:6
Engaged! or Cheviot's Choice 1965,Ap 24,19:2

Yeomen of the Guard, The 1965,Jl 8,34:1
Princess Ida 1967,Ap 17,46:2
Pirates of Penzance, The 1967,Ag 7,34:2
H M S Pinafore 1967,N 1,40:1
Mikado, The 1967,D 4,65:3
Pirates of Penzance, The 1968,Ap 26,32:1
H M S Pinafore 1968,Ap 29,47:2
Yeomen of the Guard, The 1968,My 9,53:1
Patience 1968,My 16,52:1
H M S Pinafore 1968,O 30,35:1
Patience 1968,N 1,34:1
Mikado, The 1968,N 2,29:4
Pirates of Penzance, The 1968,N 7,54:1
Iolanthe 1968,N 9,37:3
Gondoliers, The 1969,My 10,35:1
H M S Pinafore 1969,D 8,61:2
Patience 1970,My 10,72:4
Pirates of Penzance, The 1970,Jl 26,49:5
Pirates of Penzance, The 1970,D 6,84:6
Sullivan, Arthur (Director)
Yeomen of the Guard, The 1935,Jl 30,16:4
Sullivan, Arthur (Lyricist)
Gondoliers, The 1931,Je 2,34:4
Pirates of Penzance, The 1938,Je 3,16:2
Iolanthe 1962,Ag 8,34:2
Mikado, The 1962,N 14,43:1
Gondoliers, The 1962,N 16,25:2
Pirates of Penzance, The 1962,N 21,28:1
H M S Pinafore 1962,N 23,32:4
Trial by Jury 1962,N 23,32:4
Iolanthe 1962,N 28,42:1
Sullivan, Arthur (Miscellaneous)
Memphis Bound 1945,My 25,23:2
Sullivan, Arthur (Original Author)
Pirates of Penzance, The 1936,S 1,24:4
Trial by Jury 1936,S 1,24:4
H M S Pinafore 1936,S 29,34:2
Hollywood Pinafore 1945,Je 1,20:1
Iolanthe 1965,My 19,42:1
Sullivan, Arthur (Playwright)
Mikado, The 1925,Ap 13,25:1
Princess Ida 1925,Ap 14,27:2
Garrick Gaieties 1925,My 18,12:2
Ruddigore 1927,My 21,25:2
Patience 1927,My 24,23:2
Patience 1928,Je 26,29:3
Patience 1931,Je 16,30:4
Pirates of Penzance, The; Slave of Duty, The
   1931,Je 30,23:6
Iolanthe 1931,Jl 14,21:5
Patience 1933,My 23,22:6
Pirates of Penzance, The 1933,Ag 8,22:4
Trial by Jury 1934,Ap 17,27:2
H M S Pinafore 1934,Ap 17,27:2
Cox and Box 1934,S 7,24:3
Pirates of Penzance, The; Slave of Duty, The
   1934,S 7,24:3
Mikado, The 1935,Jl 16,24:4
Pirates of Penzance, The 1935,Jl 23,24:2
Gondoliers, The 1935,Ag 6,20:5
H M S Pinafore 1935,Ag 13,20:6
Trial by Jury 1935,Ag 13,20:6
Mikado, The 1936,Ag 21,13:2
Cox and Box 1936,S 29,34:2
Cox and Box 1942,F 20,20:2
Cox and Box 1948,Ja 20,26:2
H M S Pinafore 1951,F 6,24:2
Trial by Jury 1951,F 6,24:2
Gondoliers, The 1951,F 13,27:2
Iolanthe 1951,F 16,22:1
Cox and Box 1951,F 20,21:2
Pirates of Penzance, The 1951,F 20,21:2
Utopia, Limited 1960,Ap 8,27:2
H M S Pinafore 1960,S 8,41:1
Gondoliers, The 1963,Je 5,33:2
Yeomen of the Guard, The 1964,Mr 19,29:2
Patience 1964,Mr 26,42:1
Iolanthe 1964,N 18,52:1
H M S Pinafore 1964,N 20,40:1
Trial by Jury 1964,N 20,40:1
Pirates of Penzance, The 1964,N 27,43:1
Mikado, The 1964,N 27,43:1
Ruddigore 1964,D 4,44:1
Ruddigore 1965,Ag 27,16:1
Pirates of Penzance, The 1966,My 24,54:1
Trial by Jury 1966,Je 8,41:2
H M S Pinafore 1966,Je 8,41:2
Pirates of Penzance, The 1966,N 16,54:1
Mikado, The 1966,N 18,36:1
Ruddigore 1966,N 23,28:1
H M S Pinafore 1966,N 24,64:1
Patience 1966,N 30,58:1
Patience 1967,O 13,32:1
Iolanthe 1967,O 18,40:1
Mikado, The 1967,O 25,42:2
Gondoliers, The 1967,O 29,83:1
Sullivan, Barry
I Want a Policeman! 1936,Ja 15,15:5
St Helena 1936,O 7,32:1
All That Glitters 1938,Ja 20,18:2
Eye on the Sparrow 1938,My 4,26:3
Mr Big 1941,S 14,IX,2:5
Mr Big 1941,O 1,24:2

Sullivan, Barry—Cont

Ring Around Elizabeth 1941,N 18,32:2
Johnny 2X4 1942,Mr 17,24:6
Too Late the Phalarope 1956,O 12,35:1
Sullivan, Brad
Recruiting Officer, The 1958,F 8,12:2
Red Roses for Me 1961,N 28,41:1
Coriolanus 1965,Jl 15,23:1
Junebug Graduates Tonight! 1967,F 27,35:1
South Pacific 1967,Je 13,56:1
Memorandum, The 1968,My 6,55:1
South Pacific 1968,Je 30,54:2
South Pacific 1969,Jl 7,27:1
Universal Nigger, The 1970,Mr 21,18:1
Sullivan, Brian
Street Scene 1947,Ja 10,17:2
Sullivan, Charles
Exception and the Rule, The 1965,My 21,19:1
Sullivan, Charles E (Producer)
Fly by Night 1933,Je 3,16:2
Sullivan, D J
Sally, Irene and Mary 1922,S 5,21:2
Honeymoon Lane 1926,S 21,32:3
Hobo 1931,F 12,24:4
Little Racketeer, The 1932,Ja 19,24:4
Ardele 1958,Ap 9,39:4
Winter's Tale, The 1963,Je 29,13:1
Midsummer Night's Dream, A 1963,Jl 1,19:2
Measure for Measure 1964,Jl 27,22:3
Sullivan, Dan
Tiger at the Gates 1968,Mr 1,30:1
Camino Real 1970,Ja 9,42:1
Amphitryon 1970,My 29,13:1
Good Woman of Setzuan, The 1970,N 6,51:1
Sullivan, David
Condemned of Altona, The 1966,F 4,21:1
Sullivan, Deidre
Beyond Desire 1967,O 11,36:1
Sullivan, Doris
South Pacific 1969,Jl 7,27:1
Sullivan, Ed (Director)
Harlem Cavalcade 1942,My 2,11:2
Sullivan, Ed (Miscellaneous)
Crazy With the Heat 1941,Ja 31,15:2
Sullivan, Ed (Producer)
Harlem Cavalcade 1942,My 2,11:2
Sullivan, Elizabeth
Side-Show 1931,My 16,13:1
Sullivan, Elizabeth Higgins (Costume Designer)
Carry Nation 1932,O 31,18:2
Sullivan, Elliott
Red Rust 1929,D 18,31:1
Lysistrata 1930,Je 6,20:1
Winged Victory 1943,N 22,24:1
Sky Drift 1945,N 14,25:2
Brigadoon 1947,Mr 14,28:2
Victim, The 1952,My 3,17:5
Brigadoon 1957,Mr 28,37:1
Compulsion 1957,O 25,21:1
Power and the Glory, The 1958,D 12,2:7
Great God Brown, The 1959,O 7,48:1
Lysistrata 1959,N 25,19:4
Peer Gynt 1960,Ja 13,21:1
Henry IV 1960,Mr 2,42:1
Henry IV 1960,Ap 19,41:1
She Stoops to Conquer 1960,N 2,42:5
Plough and the Stars, The 1960,D 7,56:2
Sullivan, Fania
Whistling Wizard and the Sultan of Tuffet
   1970,F 1,70:1
Sullivan, Fania (Costume Designer)
Wizard of Oz, The 1968,N 28,69:2
Sullivan, Francis L
Many Waters 1929,S 26,27:1
Judgment of Dr Johnson, The 1932,F 7,VIII,2:4
Tovarich 1935,Ap 25,19:8
Duet for Two Hands 1947,O 8,28:3
ANTA Album 1950,Ja 30,13:2
Witness for the Prosecution 1954,D 17,35:2
Witness for the Prosecution 1954,D 26,II,1:1
Sullivan, Frank
Davy Jones's Locker 1959,Mr 30,25:1
Davy Jones's Locker 1966,D 25,48:5
People Is the Thing That the World Is Fullest Of
   1967,F 21,53:1
Wizard of Oz, The 1968,N 28,69:2
Whistling Wizard and the Sultan of Tuffet
   1970,F 1,70:1
Sullivan, Frank (Playwright)
Hey, Nonny, Nonny! 1932,Je 7,22:3
Sullivan, Fred
Room of Dreams 1930,N 6,22:4
Midnight 1930,D 30,25:1
Greater Love 1931,Mr 3,39:1
Sullivan, Gayne
Great Campaign, The 1947,Ap 1,33:2
Lovers 1956,My 11,23:1
Sullivan, George
Light Wines and Beer 1930,N 11,28:6
Wild Duck, The 1951,D 27,17:1
Sullivan, Gloria
Sally 1948,My 7,31:2
Sullivan, Grant
Auntie Mame 1956,N 1,47:2

Sullivan, Henry (Composer)
Blue Blood 1924,Ap 3,21:2
Murray Anderson's Almanac 1929,Ag 15,20:3
Little Racketeer, The 1931,O 11,VIII,4:7
Ballerina 1933,O 11,26:3
Keep Moving 1934,Ag 24,10:2
Thumbs Up! 1934,D 28,24:1
Home and Beauty 1937,F 3,26:2
John Murray Anderson's Almanac 1953,D 11,42:2
Sullivan, Henry (Lyricist)
John Murray Anderson's Almanac 1953,D 11,42:2
Sullivan, Howard
Naughty-Naught '00 1937,Ja 25,23:2
Sullivan, Hugh
Persecution and Assassination of Marat As
Performed by the Inmates of the Asylum of
Charenton Under the Direction of the Marquis de
Sade, The 1965,D 28,35:1
Sullivan, Isobel
Sonya's Search for the Christmas Star
1929,D 14,24:6
Sullivan, J J
Billy Budd 1959,F 28,13:3
Sullivan, James
Bringing Up Father 1925,Mr 31,16:1
Tartuffe 1957,O 9,39:1
Oh, Kay! 1960,Ap 18,37:2
Ladies Night in a Turkish Bath 1961,Mr 22,38:1
Sullivan, James E
Love Birds 1921,Mr 16,12:1
Chiffon Girl, The 1924,F 20,23:2
Sullivan, Jean
Lazarus Laughed 1948,Ap 9,27:4
Sullivan, Jean (Choreographer)
Lazarus Laughed 1948,Ap 9,27:4
Sullivan, Jeremiah
Scent of Flowers, A 1969,O 21,42:1
Scent of Flowers, A 1969,N 2,II,3:1
Sullivan, Jeremiah (Miscellaneous)
Scent of Flowers, A 1970,F 15,II,1:1
Sullivan, Jo
Sleepy Hollow 1948,Je 4,26:3
Let's Make an Opera 1950,D 14,50:2
Threepenny Opera, The 1954,Mr 11,26:5
Threepenny Opera, The 1954,Mr 21,II,1:1
Threepenny Opera, The 1954,Ap 4,II,7:1
Carousel 1954,Je 3,32:2
Threepenny Opera, The 1955,S 21,38:1
Most Happy Fella, The 1956,My 4,20:1
Most Happy Fella, The 1956,My 13,II,1:1
Wonderful Town 1958,Mr 6,32:4
Of Mice and Men 1958,D 5,38:1
Show Boat 1961,Ap 13,32:1
Sullivan, Joan
Playboy of the Western World, The 1932,O 21,25:1
Church Street 1934,N 20,24:5
Sullivan, Joe
Sundown Beach 1948,S 8,37:1
Sullivan, John
Last Man In, The 1930,My 8,32:5
Sullivan, John (Lighting Director)
Henry IV, Part I 1946,My 7,25:2
Henry IV, Part II 1946,My 8,33:4
Uncle Vanya 1946,My 14,18:2
Oedipus 1946,My 21,19:2
Oedipus; Critic, The 1946,My 21,19:2
Sullivan, John M
Bootleggers, The 1922,N 28,24:1
Thrills 1925,Ap 17,24:3
When You Smile 1925,O 6,31:2
Move On 1926,Ja 19,30:1
New York 1927,N 15,26:2
Aiglon, L' 1927,D 27,24:3
Sullivan, Joseph
Texas Town 1941,Ap 30,22:3
Live Wire, The 1950,Ag 18,16:2
Country Girl, The 1950,N 11,10:6
Child of the Morning 1951,N 17,9:7
Rainmaker, The 1954,N 7,II,1:1
Winesburg, Ohio 1958,F 6,22:2
Saturday Night Kid, The 1958,My 16,22:1
Best Man, The 1960,Ap 1,39:1
Captains and the Kings, The 1962,Ja 3,25:2
Fiddler on the Roof 1964,S 23,56:2
Sullivan, Joyce
Red Roses for Me 1951,Ap 26,35:8
Red Roses for Me 1955,D 29,15:2
Red Roses for Me 1956,Ja 8,II,1:1
Little Moon of Alban 1960,D 2,34:1
Sullivan, Kate
Coriolanus 1965,Jl 15,23:1
Sullivan, Katherine
Way, The 1940,O 12,20:3
Sullivan, Kathleen
Baal 1965,My 7,33:2
Sullivan, Kathleen A (Miscellaneous)
Indians 1969,O 14,51:1
Sullivan, Knute
Body Beautiful, The 1958,Ja 24,15:2
Sullivan, Lee
Walk With Music 1940,Je 5,33:2
High Kickers 1941,N 1,21:2
Let Freedom Sing 1942,O 6,18:2

Time, Place and the Girl, The 1942,O 22,24:3
Brigadoon 1947,Mr 14,28:2
Sullivan, Liam
From Morn Till Midnight 1948,D 7,41:6
Constant Wife, The 1951,D 10,34:3
Love's Labour's Lost 1953,F 5,20:3
Sullivan, Margaret
Hello, Lola! 1926,Ja 13,30:1
Side-Show 1931,My 16,13:1
If Love Were All 1931,N 14,14:5
Happy Landing 1932,Mr 28,10:5
Sullivan, Mark
Wisdom Tooth, The 1926,F 16,22:2
Elmer the Great 1928,S 25,29:1
Vermont 1929,Ja 9,28:1
Gambling 1929,Ag 27,31:2
Sullivan, Mary
Taming of the Shrew, The 1925,D 19,14:1
Sullivan, Maxine
Swingin' the Dream 1939,N 30,24:2
Sullivan, Mike
On the Spot 1930,O 30,33:3
Sullivan, Neil
Guests of the Nation 1958,My 21,40:1
Sullivan, Newt
Foxy 1964,F 17,26:1
Sullivan, Pania
Wizard of Oz, The 1968,N 28,69:2
Sullivan, Patrick
Sweet Enemy, The 1965,F 16,39:1
Golden Screw, The 1967,Ja 31,52:1
Sullivan, Paul (Lighting Director)
Leonard Sillman's New Faces of 1968
1968,My 3,43:1
American Hamburger League, The 1969,S 17,51:1
Memory Bank, The 1970,Ja 12,24:3
Nature of the Crime 1970,Mr 24,41:1
Sullivan, Richard
Up She Goes 1922,N 7,14:2
Outside Looking In 1925,S 8,28:1
Sullivan, Robert Patrick
Chief Thing, The 1963,Ap 30,27:2
Sullivan, Roger
Right Next to Broadway 1944,F 22,26:2
Sullivan, Roger (Director)
Meet Peter Grant 1961,My 11,41:4
Penny Change 1963,O 25,37:1
Sullivan, Roger (Miscellaneous)
Macbeth 1955,O 8,12:6
Sullivan, Sheila
How to Succeed in Business Without Really Trying
1966,Ap 21,45:1
By Jupiter 1967,Ja 20,28:2
Play It Again, Sam 1969,F 13,52:3
Play It Again, Sam 1969,Jl 13,II,1:1
Sullivan, Susan
She Stoops to Conquer 1968,Ap 1,58:3
Jimmy Shine 1968,D 6,52:1
Sullivan, Thomas
What Price Glory 1924,S 6,14:3
Sullivan, Vere (Playwright)
Village, The 1927,Ag 14,VII,1:7
Sully, Eve
Vaudeville (Palace) 1930,Ag 4,13:2
Vaudeville (Palace) 1930,O 20,29:1
Sully, Robert
Marriage Is for Single People 1945,N 22,38:2
Sully, Ruby (Playwright)
Hot Corner, The 1956,Ja 26,25:2
Sully, William
Broadway Brevities, 1920 1920,S 30,12:2
No Other Girl 1924,Ag 14,10:4
Ramblers, The 1926,S 21,32:2
Sulmonetti, Julian
Candida 1969,F 3,29:1
Dance of Death, The 1969,My 26,53:1
Trumpets and Drums 1969,O 13,52:1
Sumac, Yma
Flahooley 1951,My 15,39:1
Flahooley 1951,My 20,II,1:1
Sumdsten, Kaja
Sleepy Hollow 1948,Je 4,26:3
Summa, Shirley
Have You Heard This One 1953,N 9,23:4
Summers, Caley (Costume Designer)
Slight Ache, A 1964,D 10,62:1
Room, The 1964,D 10,62:1
Last Sweet Days of Isaac, The 1970,Ja 27,49:1
Summers, Cecil
Molly Darling 1922,S 2,10:2
Summers, Charles
Cyrano de Bergerac 1946,O 9,33:2
Cyrano de Bergerac 1947,Ja 17,27:2
Insect Comedy, The 1948,Je 4,26:3
Twentieth Century 1950,D 25,23:6
Cyrano de Bergerac 1953,N 13,24:3
Richard III 1953,D 10,65:2
Summers, Darby
Haven, The 1946,N 14,39:4
Summers, Eileen
Pink String and Sealing Wax 1957,S 6,13:1
Summers, Elaine
In Circles 1967,O 14,12:1

Summers, Elizabeth
Midsummer Night's Dream, A 1931,Ag 19,19:3
Summers, Lydia
Consul, The 1950,Mr 16,41:1
Consul, The 1950,Mr 26,II,1:1
Consul, The 1957,S 4,40:3
Summers, Michael
Rose in the Wilderness 1949,Ja 5,21:2
Summers, Robert N (Director)
Parasite, The 1965,D 17,43:2
Summers, Robert N (Playwright)
Parasite, The 1965,D 17,43:2
Summers, Sam
Nic-Nax of 1926 1926,Ag 5,19:1
Summers, Sam (Playwright)
Woof, Woof 1929,D 26,20:4
Summers, Vikki
Warning, The-A Theme for Linda 1969,Ap 27,92:1
Black Quartet, A; Warning, The-A Theme for
Linda 1969,Jl 31,28:1
Warning, The-A Theme for Linda 1969,Ag 3,II,1:4
Summerville, Ada
Red Pepper 1922,My 30,8:3
Summerville, Amelia
Gingham Girl, The 1922,Ag 29,15:5
Glass Slipper, The 1925,O 20,29:1
Summerville, Randolph (Prof) (Director)
Candida 1925,D 19,14:2
Sumner, Engel
Kreutzer Sonata, The 1924,My 15,22:3
Taming of the Shrew, The 1927,O 26,26:4
Shooting Star 1933,Je 13,22:2
Sumner, Fred
Amourette 1933,S 28,25:2
Mrs O'Brien Entertains 1939,F 9,16:3
Sumner, George (Producer)
Greater Lust, The 1936,Jl 14,22:4
Amateur Hour 1936,Jl 21,13:1
Sumner, James
Beggar on Horseback 1924,F 13,17:2
Sumner, John (Director)
Summer of the Seventeenth Doll 1958,Ja 23,23:2
Sumner, Marnel
Jackknife 1958,S 23,36:2
Sumner, Marnel (Miscellaneous)
All in Good Time 1965,F 19,25:1
Man of La Mancha 1965,N 23,52:1
Sumner, William
Trial by Jury 1939,Ja 6,25:1
Cox and Box 1939,Ja 17,27:5
Gondoliers, The 1939,Ja 20,14:2
Yeomen of the Guard, The 1939,Ja 24,17:1
Patience 1939,Ja 27,16:3
Peter Pan 1950,Ap 25,27:2
Sumonds, Robert
Camino Real 1970,Ja 9,42:1
Sumpter, Ralph
Squaw Man, The 1921,D 27,10:3
Major Barbara 1928,N 20,28:4
Young Sinners 1933,Mr 7,20:4
Within the Gates 1934,O 23,23:1
Jubilee 1935,O 14,20:1
Amazing Dr. Clitterhouse, The 1937,Mr 3,26:4
Between the Devil 1937,D 23,24:5
Millionairess, The 1938,Ag 16,22:5
Journey's End 1939,S 19,29:2
Woman Brown, The 1939,D 9,18:5
At the Stroke of Eight 1940,My 21,29:2
Second Best Bed 1946,Je 4,20:2
S S Glencairn; Bound East for Cardiff
1948,My 21,21:2
Day After Tomorrow 1950,O 27,25:2
Too Late the Phalarope 1956,O 12,35:1
Redhead 1959,F 6,21:1
Sun Fong-lin Company, The
Vaudeville (Hippodrome) 1925,S 1,18:3
Sundberg, Clinton
Nine Pine Street 1933,Ap 28,15:5
I Want a Policeman! 1936,Ja 15,15:5
Stars in Your Eyes 1939,F 10,18:2
Beverly Hills 1940,N 8,24:2
Arsenic and Old Lace 1941,Mr 25,26:7
Rugged Path, The 1945,N 12,17:2
Diary of Anne Frank, The 1955,O 6,24:2
Man in the Dog Suit, The 1958,O 31,34:2
Midgie Purvis 1961,F 2,25:3
Sunder, James (Playwright)
Mixed Doubles 1969,Ap 12,43:2
Sunderland, Nan
Easy Street 1924,Ag 15,16:4
Four Flusher, The 1925,Ap 14,27:4
Easy Come, Easy Go 1925,O 27,20:2
Baby Cyclone, The 1927,S 13,37:4
Elmer the Great 1928,S 25,29:1
Lady Lies, The 1928,N 27,36:2
Dodsworth 1934,F 26,20:4
Othello 1934,Jl 22,23:4
Othello 1934,Jl 29,IX,1:3
Dodsworth 1934,Ag 21,12:3
Othello 1936,N 27,26:5
Othello 1936,D 6,XII,6:1
Othello 1937,Ja 7,16:4
Miles of Heaven, The 1937,Ag 31,27:4

Sunderland, Nan—Cont
Robin Landing 1937,N 19,26:4
Sunderland, Netta
George Washington 1920,Mr 2,9:1
Taming of the Shrew, The 1921,My 12,20:2
Merchant of Venice, The 1921,My 14,10:4
Sunderland, Scott
Barretts of Wimpole Street, The 1930,Ag 21,13:4
Sunderman, Florence
Master of the Revels 1935,Ag 14,16:2
Sunderman, William
Belmont Varieties 1932,S 29,17:2
Sunderman, William F (Director)
Second Comin', The 1931,D 9,32:4
Sunderskov, Robert (Miscellaneous)
Merry Widow, The 1961,O 27,28:2
Sunderstrom, Frank
Six Flights Up 1939,F 26,IX,2:3
Sundgaard, Arnold (Lyricist)
Promised Valley 1947,Jl 23,18:3
Kittiwake Island 1960,O 13,43:1
Sundgaard, Arnold (Miscellaneous)
Young Abe Lincoln 1961,Ap 26,36:1
Sundgaard, Arnold (Playwright)
Everywhere I Roam 1938,Ap 22,15:1
Everywhere I Roam 1938,D 30,10:4
Everywhere I Roam 1939,Ja 8,IX,1:1
First Crocus, The 1942,Ja 3,14:6
Rhapsody 1944,N 23,37:2
Great Campaign, The 1947,Ap 1,33:2
Promised Valley 1947,Jl 23,18:3
Kilgo Run, The 1953,D 13,105:1
Kittiwake Island 1960,O 13,43:1
Of Love Remembered 1967,F 20,46:5
Sundgaard, Marge (Producer)
Great Western Union, The 1965,F 10,45:1
Sundmark, Betty
You Said It 1931,Ja 20,21:3
Sundquist, Ed (Scenic Designer)
Weather Permitting 1935,My 24,24:5
Sundstrom, Florence
Bright Honor 1936,S 28,14:1
Good, The 1938,O 6,27:2
Retreat to Pleasure 1940,D 18,32:2
Johnny on the Spot 1942,Ja 9,24:2
They Should Have Stood in Bed 1942,F 14,18:5
Sun Field, The 1942,D 10,33:2
Mr Strauss Goes to Boston 1945,S 7,20:2
Marriage Is for Single People 1945,N 22,38:2
Happy Birthday 1946,N 1,31:2
Rose Tattoo, The 1951,F 5,19:2
Faithfully Yours 1951,O 19,22:5
See the Jaguar 1952,D 4,46:2
Look Homeward, Angel 1957,N 29,33:1
Look Homeward, Angel 1958,Ag 31,II,1:1
Sundstrom, Frank
Assassin, The 1945,O 18,20:2
Ghost of Elsinore, The 1949,Ap 16,10:2
On Trial 1949,D 9,35:5
Trial, The 1950,Ap 13,34:3
Hilda Crane 1950,N 2,38:2
Sundstrom, Frank (Director)
Trial, The 1950,Ap 13,34:3
Sundstrom, Frank (Translator)
On Trial 1949,D 9,35:5
Trial, The 1950,Ap 13,34:3
Sundstrom, Jacqueline
Trial, The 1950,Ap 13,34:3
Sundstrom, Jacqueline (Translator)
On Trial 1949,D 9,35:5
Trial, The 1950,Ap 13,34:3
Sundt, Jacqueline
Oklahoma! 1951,My 30,15:2
Sunshine, Louis (Dr) (Producer)
This Woman Business 1926,D 8,25:1
Sunshine, Marion
Girl From Home, The 1920,My 4,9:2
Blue Kitten, The 1922,Ja 14,9:3
Daffy Dill 1922,Ag 23,14:5
Captain Jinks 1925,S 9,22:1
Vaudeville (Palace) 1926,N 23,27:3
Vaudeville (Palace) 1928,Mr 20,20:2
Vaudeville (Palace) 1929,O 21,31:2
Vaudeville (Palace) 1930,S 22,23:2
Vaudeville (Palace) 1931,Ap 13,17:2
Sunshine, Sue
Hayride 1954,S 14,24:2
Sunshine Girls, The
Good Morning, Dearie 1921,N 2,20:2
Suoboda, M
Blue Bird, The 1925,Ja 30,10:2
Supervielle, Jules (Playwright)
Belle au Bois, La 1932,Ap 3,VIII,2:1
Supinski, Donald
House Remembered, A 1957,F 7,20:2
Suraci, Patrick
Another City, Another Land 1968,O 9,42:1
Suragina, Alla
West Side Story 1965,Je 25,37:2
Suratt, Valeska
Spice of 1922 1922,Jl 7,12:4
Vaudeville (Palace) 1923,Mr 6,26:1
Surface, Herb
Oklahoma! 1965,D 16,62:1

Surona, Anthony
Passing of Chow-Chow, The 1929,O 4,24:4
Surovy, Nicolas
Helen 1964,D 11,55:4
Surratt, Everett
Elmer the Great 1928,S 25,29:1
Surtees, Madge
Out of Step 1925,Ja 30,12:1
Susa, Conrad (Composer)
Borak 1960,D 14,51:1
Moby Dick 1961,Ap 11,41:2
School for Scandal, The 1962,Mr 19,36:1
Richard II 1962,Je 18,20:2
King Lear 1963,Je 10,37:1
Winter's Tale, The 1963,Je 29,13:1
Midsummer Night's Dream, A 1963,Jl 1,19:2
Right You Are (If You Think You Are)
  1964,Mr 5,37:1
Tavern, The 1964,Mr 6,39:2
Much Ado About Nothing 1964,Je 11,26:2
Richard III 1964,Je 12,44:2
Man and Superman 1964,D 7,45:2
Judith 1965,Mr 25,42:2
Coriolanus 1965,Je 21,36:1
Romeo and Juliet 1965,Je 21,36:3
King Lear 1965,Je 25,39:1
Twelfth Night 1966,Je 23,28:1
Julius Caesar 1966,Je 24,29:2
Midsummer Night's Dream, A 1967,Je 19,42:1
Exit the King 1968,Ja 10,48:1
Twelfth Night 1968,Je 15,40:1
Serjeant Musgrave's Dance 1968,Je 16,52:4
Master Builder, The 1968,Je 22,26:1
As You Like It 1968,Je 24,42:3
Misanthrope, The 1968,O 10,59:1
Hamlet 1969,Mr 4,34:1
Hamlet 1969,Je 30,33:1
Three Sisters, The 1969,Ag 4,29:1
Local Stigmatic, The; That's Your Trouble
  1969,N 4,55:2
Local Stigmatic, The; Applicant 1969,N 4,55:2
Local Stigmatic, The; That's All 1969,N 4,55:2
Local Stigmatic, The; Last to Go 1969,N 4,55:2
Local Stigmatic, The; Request Stop 1969,N 4,55:2
Local Stigmatic, The; Interview 1969,N 4,55:2
Local Stigmatic, The; Trouble in the Works
  1969,N 4,55:2
Local Stigmatic, The 1969,N 4,55:2
All's Well That Ends Well 1970,Je 16,53:1
Othello 1970,Je 22,43:1
Devil's Disciple, The 1970,Je 30,48:1
Othello 1970,S 15,51:1
Susa, Conrad (Lighting Director)
Right You Are (If You Think You Are)
  1966,N 23,34:2
Susa, Conrad (Lyricist)
Richard II 1962,Je 18,20:2
Winter's Tale, The 1963,Je 29,13:1
Midsummer Night's Dream, A 1963,Jl 1,19:2
Twelfth Night 1966,Je 23,28:1
Julius Caesar 1966,Je 24,29:2
As You Like It 1968,Je 24,42:3
Susa, Conrad (Miscellaneous)
Cherry Orchard, The 1968,Mr 20,41:1
Susa, Conrad (Musical Director)
Seagull, The 1962,Mr 22,42:1
Henry V 1969,Je 9,57:1
Crimes of Passion; Ruffian on the Stair, The
  1969,O 27,54:1
Crimes of Passion; Erpingham Camp, The
  1969,O 27,54:1
All's Well That Ends Well 1970,Je 16,53:1
Othello 1970,Je 22,43:1
Devil's Disciple, The 1970,Je 30,48:1
Othello 1970,S 15,51:1
Susan, Black-Eyed
Bluebeard 1970,My 5,58:1
Susann, Jacqueline
Girl From Wyoming, The 1938,O 31,12:1
She Gave Him All She Had 1939,D 2,20:7
My Fair Ladies 1941,Mr 24,12:7
Banjo Eyes 1941,D 26,20:2
Blossom Time 1943,S 6,21:2
Jackpot 1944,Ja 14,15:2
Lady Says Yes, A 1945,Ja 11,18:5
Madwoman of Chaillot, The 1970,Mr 23,48:3
Susann, Jacqueline (Playwright)
Lovely Me 1946,D 26,30:4
Susanoff, Jacob
In-Laws 1960,O 17,32:4
Susanoff, Yaacob
Farblondjete Honeymoon 1955,S 27,42:1
Sushkewitch, B M (Director)
Jacob's Dream 1927,Ja 4,20:2
Suski, Thaddeus
Anne of England 1941,O 8,26:2
Seventh Trumpet, The 1941,N 22,10:6
God Strikes Back 1943,F 27,11:2
Suskind, Milton (Composer)
Florida Girl 1925,N 3,34:1
Susman, Bernard
Mima 1928,D 13,24:2
Nona 1932,O 5,26:4

Susoeff, Linda
Bead-Tangle 1970,Jl 16,38:1
Susov, Nina
Great Temptations, The 1926,My 19,29:1
Suss, Bernard W (Director)
Bedfellows 1929,Jl 3,19:2
Sussanoff, Jack
My Wife With Conditions 1963,O 21,39:1
Sussanoff, Yacob
My Malkele 1937,S 20,18:6
Sussel, Deborah
Phaedra 1967,My 22,50:2
Flea in Her Ear, A 1969,O 4,25:1
Flea in Her Ear, A 1969,O 12,II,9:1
Susskind, David (Miscellaneous)
Royal Hunt of the Sun, The 1965,O 27,36:2
Susskind, David (Producer)
Very Special Baby, A 1956,N 15,43:2
Handful of Fire 1958,O 2,45:3
Rashomon 1959,Ja 28,36:2
Kelly 1965,F 8,28:2
All in Good Time 1965,F 19,25:1
Brief Lives 1967,D 19,60:4
Sussman, Bernard
Shore Leave 1922,Ag 9,20:2
Sussman, Don (Lighting Director)
Widowers' Houses 1959,Mr 3,39:2
Jack in the Box 1960,My 19,43:3
'Toinette 1961,N 21,46:1
Theater of Peretz, The 1963,N 6,35:2
Sussman, Sadie
Dybbuk, The 1925,D 16,22:2
Burmese Pwe, A 1926,Mr 17,28:1
Grand Street Follies, The 1927,My 20,22:3
Sut-Tai, Jue
Vaudeville (Palace) 1929,D 16,34:4
Sutcliffe, Irene
Romeo and Juliet 1962,F 14,39:1
Suter, Ann
Vaudeville (Palace) 1926,N 16,24:3
Suter, Carrie
Gospel Glow 1962,O 28,87:5
Suter, Sandy
Gogo Loves You 1964,O 10,19:2
Sutherland, Alan
Peter Pan 1954,O 21,30:2
Sutherland, Alec (Costume Designer)
We Bombed in New Haven 1967,D 7,58:1
Whistle in the Dark, A 1968,F 17,32:2
Sutherland, Anne
Fall and Rise of Susan Lenox, The 1920,Je 11,11:2
Elton Case, The 1921,S 12,16:2
Serpent's Tooth, A 1922,Ag 25,8:5
Ruint 1925,Ap 8,24:2
Craig's Wife 1925,O 13,21:2
Intruder, The 1928,Jl 26,25:4
Houseparty 1929,S 10,26:5
They Never Grow Up 1930,Ap 8,27:1
London Calling 1930,S 28,VIII,4:1
London Calling 1930,O 20,29:1
Right of Happiness 1931,Ap 3,34:2
Divorce Me, Dear 1931,O 7,29:2
Lady of Letters 1935,Mr 29,26:6
Sutherland, Claudette
How to Succeed in Business Without Really Trying
  1961,O 16,34:1
Sutherland, Dan (Playwright)
Breach of Marriage 1949,Ja 27,20:5
Sutherland, Don
Hamlet 1969,Je 11,37:1
Merchant of Venice, The 1970,Je 10,39:1
School for Scandal, The 1970,Je 11,51:1
Sutherland, Elizabeth
Autumn Hill 1942,Ap 14,17:4
Haven, The 1946,N 14,39:4
Sutherland, Hope
Deburau 1920,D 24,14:3
Two Blocks Away 1921,Ag 31,8:3
Bronx Express 1922,Ap 27,12:2
Wild Oats Lane 1922,S 7,12:1
Potash and Perlmutter, Detectives; Poisoned by
  Pictures 1926,S 1,27:3
Sutherland, Jean (Costume Designer)
Robin Landing 1937,N 19,26:4
Sutherland, Margaret
Purple Mask, The 1920,Ja 6,18:1
Sutherland, Mildred
Saint's Parade 1930,N 1,23:4
Sutherland, Mildred (Costume Designer)
Tread the Green Grass 1932,Jl 24,IX,1:3
Temporary Island, A 1948,Mr 15,27:3
Story for Strangers, A 1948,S 22,39:2
Detective Story 1949,Mr 24,34:2
Pride's Crossing 1950,N 21,37:5
Sutherland, Nancy
Bead-Tangle 1970,Jl 16,38:1
Sutherland, Victor
New Sin, The 1923,My 28,18:3
Mud Turtle, The 1925,Ag 21,8:2
It Pays to Sin 1933,N 4,18:6
Arsenic and Old Lace 1941,Ja 11,13:2
State of the Union 1945,N 15,25:2
Man and Superman 1947,O 9,31:2

Sutherland, Victor—Cont
Man and Superman 1949,My 17,28:6
Southern Exposure 1950,S 27,36:3
Sutherland, William
New Moon, The 1944,My 18,16:2
Sutorius, James
Cherry Orchard, The 1970,My 7,63:2
Sutphen, D Arthur
Kind Lady 1938,Jl 11,14:2
Sutphen, Joy
Yours Truly 1927,Ja 26,16:5
Sutro, Alfred (Playwright)
Laughing Lady, The 1923,F 13,25:1
Laughing Lady, The 1923,F 18,VII,1:1
Desperate Lovers, The 1927,F 20,VII,1:4
Open Door, The 1928,Je 26,29:4
Little Theatre Tournament; Man in the Stalls, The
1929,My 8,34:4
Open Door, The 1930,Ja 28,28:1
Sutro, Victor H
Coriolanus 1927,Je 18,8:3
Sutton, Alma
Zunguru 1938,Ag 3,14:5
Zunguru 1938,Ag 7,IX,8:2
Zunguru 1940,Mr 21,30:5
Show Boat 1946,Ja 7,17:2
Sutton, Brent
Cyrano de Bergerac 1968,Ap 26,30:1
Sutton, Brent (Miscellaneous)
Saint Joan 1968,Ja 5,42:1
Sutton, Dolores
Man With the Golden Arm, The 1956,My 22,28:1
Machinal 1960,Ap 8,27:1
Machinal 1960,Ap 17,II,1:1
General Seeger 1962,Mr 1,26:2
Sutton, Dudley
Hostage, The 1960,S 21,42:1
Entertaining Mr Sloane 1965,O 13,41:1
Sutton, Elizabeth
Bird in Hand 1942,O 20,24:2
Sutton, Frank
Andersonville Trial, The 1959,D 30,15:1
Sutton, Fred
Ladies' Night 1920,Ag 10,10:1
Masked Woman, The 1922,D 23,14:2
Spring Fever 1925,Ag 4,14:2
Matrimonial Bed, The 1927,O 13,23:2
Scotland Yard 1929,S 28,16:6
Tobacco Road 1942,S 7,34:2
Tobacco Road 1943,S 6,21:3
Sutton, George W Jr (Playwright)
Little Theatre Tournament; Yellow Triangle, The
1929,My 10,32:2
Sutton, Henry
Comedian, The 1956,O 18,36:4
Ticket-of-Leave Man, The 1961,D 23,15:1
Sutton, Henry (Miscellaneous)
King of the Whole Damn World 1962,Ap 16,32:2
Kiss Mama 1964,O 2,30:1
Sutton, Jvotte
On Strivers' Row 1946,Mr 1,17:2
Sutton, Kay
Du Barry Was a Lady 1939,D 7,34:2
Sutton, Ken
G-II 1948,My 28,27:3
Uniform of Flesh 1949,Ja 31,15:2
Sutton, Susie
Meek Mose 1928,F 7,30:1
Green Pastures, The 1930,F 27,26:1
Stevedore 1934,Ap 19,33:2
Green Pastures, The 1935,F 27,16:2
Haiti 1938,Mr 3,16:1
Sutton, Virginia
Shake Hands With the Devil 1949,O 21,30:4
Suydan, Nancy (Miscellaneous)
Cold Wind and the Warm, The 1958,D 9,55:1
Suydenham, George
Rotters, The 1922,My 23,12:4
Suzman, Janet
Merchant of Venice, The 1965,Ap 17,9:1
Much Ado About Nothing 1968,O 16,33:1
Much Ado About Nothing 1969,S 1,13:1
Suzuki, Pat
Flower Drum Song 1958,D 2,44:1
Flower Drum Song 1958,D 7,II,5:1
Svalbe, Einar
Mother Lode 1934,D 24,16:5
Svar, John
Invitation to a Beheading 1969,Mr 18,36:1
Three Men on a Horse 1969,O 17,35:1
Svecenski, Louise
Big Two, The 1947,Ja 9,21:2
Svehla, Zdenek
Laterna Magika 1964,Ag 4,21:1
Svendsen, Johan
Journey's End 1930,Mr 30,VIII,3:4
Svensen, Sunja
Purification, The 1959,D 9,57:5
Mime Theatre of Etienne Decroux, The
1959,D 24,15:1
Santa Claus 1960,Jl 22,13:1
Ordinary Man, An 1968,S 10,39:1
Sverdloff, Isaac
Wise Men of Chelm, The 1933,O 18,24:2

Svetlik, Gisella
Kiss Me, Kate 1949,Ja 30,II,6:5
Out of This World 1950,D 22,17:3
Paint Your Wagon 1951,N 13,32:2
Svetlik, Susan
Allegro 1947,O 11,10:2
Svoboda, G
Revisor; Inspector General, The 1935,F 18,19:6
Svoboda, Josef (Scenic Designer)
Hamlet 1965,Ja 23,15:4
Three Sisters, The 1970,F 12,30:1
Three Sisters, The 1970,F 22,II,1:1
Swackhamer, E W
Time Remembered 1957,N 13,41:2
Swackhamer, E W (Director)
Rules of the Game, The 1960,D 20,44:1
Swados, Kim (Costume Designer)
Three by Thurber; Imperturbable Spirit, The
1955,Mr 8,23:2
Three by Thurber; Middle Years, The
1955,Mr 8,23:2
Three by Thurber; Mr Montoe Holds the Fort
1955,Mr 8,23:2
Swados, Kim (Lighting Director)
Bullfight 1954,Ja 13,25:2
Three by Thurber; Imperturbable Spirit, The
1955,Mr 8,23:2
Three by Thurber; Middle Years, The
1955,Mr 8,23:2
Three by Thurber; Mr Montoe Holds the Fort
1955,Mr 8,23:2
Swados, Kim (Scenic Designer)
Bullfight 1954,Ja 13,25:2
Three by Thurber; Middle Years, The
1955,Mr 8,23:2
Three by Thurber; Imperturbable Spirit, The
1955,Mr 8,23:2
Three by Thurber; Mr Montoe Holds the Fort
1955,Mr 8,23:2
Deirdre of the Sorrows 1959,O 15,46:1
Blacks, The 1961,My 5,23:1
Blacks, The 1961,My 14,II,1:1
Automobile Graveyard, The 1961,N 14,46:2
Shadow of Heroes 1961,D 6,59:1
Banker's Daughter, The 1962,Ja 23,37:1
Play With a Tiger 1964,D 31,14:2
Square in the Eye 1965,My 20,54:1
Sunset 1966,My 13,34:1
Swails, Wesley
Carnival in Flanders 1953,S 9,38:2
Swain, Charles
Holy Night 1941,D 22,23:3
Pirate, The 1942,N 26,39:2
Swain, Elizabeth
Tango 1969,Ja 20,33:1
Charley's Aunt 1970,Jl 6,38:1
Swain, G Bernard (Playwright)
Saint Joan 1940,Mr 11,10:6
Swain, Kenneth
Good Morning 1937,D 4,20:7
Swaine, Howard
Young American, A 1946,Ja 18,14:5
Swan, Bill
Pinocchio 1939,Ja 3,19:2
Swan, Boots
Ginger Snaps 1930,Ja 1,30:5
Swan, Buddy
World We Make, The 1939,N 21,19:1
Mr Sycamore 1942,N 14,13:2
You'll See Stars 1943,Ja 1,26:6
Swan, Elaine
My Mother, My Father and Me 1963,Mr 25,5:5
Swan, Harry
Eva the Fifth 1928,Ag 29,19:3
Swan, Jon (Playwright)
Investigation, The 1966,O 5,40:1
Fireworks; Football 1969,Je 12,51:1
Fireworks; Report, The 1969,Je 12,51:1
Fireworks; Fireworks for a Hot Fourth
1969,Je 12,51:1
Swan, Lea
Topsy and Eva 1924,D 24,11:1
Swan, Lynn
Score 1970,O 29,57:4
Swan, Mark
Vaudeville (Palace) 1926,Ag 31,15:3
Swan, Mark (Playwright)
Lady Butterfly 1923,Ja 23,18:1
Judy Drops In 1924,O 6,24:2
Howdy King 1926,O 17,VIII,2:4
Howdy King 1926,D 14,24:4
Judy 1927,F 8,20:2
Swanagan, Don (Scenic Designer)
Mrs Warren's Profession 1956,Je 7,35:2
Swander, Philip
Galileo 1947,D 8,34:2
Mystery of the Finding of the Cross, The
1959,Ja 16,35:2
Swanick, Anna (Translator)
Iphigenie in Tauris 1949,O 22,11:2
Swanlee (Producer)
Cafe Crown 1964,Ap 18,32:1

Swann, Caroline (Miscellaneous)
Tenth Man, The 1959,N 6,24:2
Swann, Caroline (Producer)
Hostage, The 1960,S 21,42:1
One Way Pendulum 1961,S 19,38:2
Dumbwaiter, The 1962,N 27,44:1
Collection, The 1962,N 27,44:1
Room, The 1964,D 10,62:1
Slight Ache, A 1964,D 10,62:1
Swann, DeFord (Composer)
Zuider Zee 1928,D 19,24:4
Swann, DeFord (Lyricist)
Zuider Zee 1928,D 19,24:4
Swann, Don Jr (Producer)
Sable Brush, The 1956,N 28,41:1
Swann, Donald
At the Drop of a Hat 1959,O 9,22:2
At the Drop of Another Hat 1966,D 28,30:2
At the Drop of Another Hat 1967,Ja 8,II,1:5
Swann, Donald (Composer)
At the Drop of a Hat 1959,O 9,22:2
At the Drop of Another Hat 1966,D 28,30:2
Swann, Elaine
Annie Get Your Gun 1957,Mr 9,15:5
Music Man, The 1957,D 20,31:1
Greenwillow 1960,Mr 9,38:1
Jennie 1963,O 18,35:2
Swann, Francis
Too Many Heroes 1937,N 16,26:2
Gloriana 1938,N 26,18:4
Bright Rebel 1938,D 28,24:2
Swann, Francis (Director)
Paradise Island 1961,Je 24,11:1
Swann, Francis (Playwright)
Out of the Frying Pan 1941,F 12,24:2
Follies of 1910, The 1960,Ja 15,37:3
Paradise Island 1961,Je 24,11:1
Paradise Island 1962,Je 28,22:1
Swann, Lynn (Miscellaneous)
Sable Brush, The 1956,N 28,41:1
Swanson, Alice
Come of Age 1934,Ja 13,16:6
Swanson, Beatrice
Florodora 1920,Ap 6,18:1
Rose Girl, The 1921,F 12,11:1
Last Waltz, The 1921,My 11,20:3
Blushing Bride, The 1922,F 7,12:1
Dew Drop Inn 1923,My 18,26:4
Vogues of 1924 1924,Mr 28,14:3
Parasites 1924,N 20,21:1
Artists and Models 1925,Je 25,16:2
First Apple, The 1933,D 28,25:1
Journey by Night, A 1935,Ap 17,26:3
Knock on Wood 1935,My 29,16:2
Swanson, Calvin (Miscellaneous)
Cock-A-Doodle Dandy 1958,N 13,39:2
On the Town 1959,Ja 16,36:1
Swanson, Douglas F
Mima 1928,D 13,24:2
Swanson, Gloria
Goose for the Gander, A 1945,Ja 24,16:4
Twentieth Century 1950,D 25,23:6
ANTA Album 1951,My 7,22:7
Nina 1951,D 6,44:3
Swanson, Gloria (Miscellaneous)
Nina 1951,D 6,44:3
Swanson, Jeanne
Come Out, Carlo! 1962,My 4,27:2
Swanson, Larry
Doctor Faustus Lights the Lights 1951,D 3,23:4
Taming of the Shrew, The 1956,Ag 11,11:2
Taming of the Shrew, The 1956,Ag 26,II,1:1
Camille 1956,S 19,33:1
Vincent 1959,O 1,40:1
Vincent 1959,O 11,II,1:1
Darker Flower, A 1963,Mr 11,7:2
Thistle in My Bed 1963,N 20,48:1
Those That Play the Clowns 1966,N 25,48:1
Sound of Music, The 1967,Ap 27,52:1
Unknown Soldier and His Wife, The 1967,Jl 7,22:1
Sound of Music, The 1970,Jl 3,13:1
Swanson, Marcella
Florodora 1920,Ap 6,18:1
Rose Girl, The 1921,F 12,11:1
Last Waltz, The 1921,My 11,20:3
Blushing Bride, The 1922,F 7,12:1
Dew Drop Inn 1923,My 18,26:4
Vogues of 1924 1924,Mr 28,14:3
Sky High 1925,Mr 3,21:4
Padre, The 1926,D 28,16:3
Mixed Doubles 1927,Ap 27,22:3
Madcap, The 1928,F 1,31:2
Boom Boom 1929,Ja 29,26:4
Babes in Toyland 1929,D 24,15:3
His Majesty's Car 1930,O 24,30:1
Purity 1930,D 26,18:2
Modern Virgin, A 1931,My 21,33:4
Good Companions, The 1931,O 2,31:1
Boy Friend, The 1932,Je 8,22:3
No More Ladies 1934,Ja 24,20:3
No More Ladies 1934,S 4,23:2
Night of January 16 1935,S 17,26:4
Show Is On, The 1937,S 20,18:4

Swanson, Paddy
Marie Vison, La 1970,Jl 15,29:1
Swanson, Susan (Miscellaneous)
Sextet 1958,N 27,53:1
Swanstrom, Arthur (Composer)
Carry On 1929,N 3,IX,1:7
Sons o' Guns 1929,N 27,30:4
Hold Your Horses 1933,S 26,26:4
Swanstrom, Arthur (Lyricist)
Greenwich Village Follies 1920,Ag 31,7:3
Greenwich Village Follies 1921,S 1,18:3
Sons o' Guns 1929,N 27,30:4
Prince Charming 1930,O 14,31:1
Hold Your Horses 1933,S 26,26:4
Sea Legs 1937,My 19,26:5
Swanstrom, Arthur (Original Author)
Sea Legs 1937,My 19,26:5
Swanstrom, Arthur (Playwright)
Greenwich Village Follies 1920,Ag 31,7:3
Swanstrom, Arthur (Producer)
Sons o' Guns 1929,N 27,30:4
Prince Charming 1930,O 14,31:1
Swanstrom, Bjorn I (Miscellaneous)
Blood Red Roses 1970,Mr 23,48:1
Swarbrick, Gene
Minstrel Boy, The 1948,O 15,28:2
Sward, Doris
Nellie Bly 1946,Ja 22,32:2
Respectfully Yours 1947,My 14,29:4
Swardson, Carole
Jack Jack 1968,Je 23,74:5
Swarthout, Gladys
Merry Widow, The 1933,Ag 13,IX,1:3
Swarthout, Glendon (Playwright)
O'Daniel 1947,F 25,32:2
Swartz, Anna Belle
Shunned 1960,D 21,39:1
Swartz, Jenie (Lighting Director)
Crimes and Crimes 1970,Ja 19,35:1
Swartz, Maurice
Dybbuk, The 1921,S 2,9:2
Rags 1922,Ja 29,VI,1:3
Anathema 1923,F 9,10:2
Anathema 1923,Ap 11,16:2
Inspector General, The 1923,My 1,24:1
Wolves 1924,D 31,9:4
Shakespeare and Company 1925,O 22,22:5
Swartz, Maurice (Director)
Dybbuk, The 1921,S 2,9:2
Dybbuk, The 1922,Ja 29,VI,1:3
Great Fortune, The 1922,D 9,11:1
Wolves 1924,D 31,9:4
Shakespeare and Company 1925,O 22,22:5
Swartz, Maurice (Scenic Designer)
Dybbuk, The 1922,Ja 29,VI,1:3
Smith's Daughters, The 1922,Ja 29,VI,1:3
Swartz, Tony
She Stoops to Conquer 1968,Ja 1,11:1
Twelfth Night 1968,Je 15,40:1
Serjeant Musgrave's Dance 1968,Je 16,52:4
Resistible Rise of Arturo Ui, The 1968,Ag 8,25:1
Merton of the Movies 1968,S 26,62:1
Resistible Rise of Arturo Ui, The 1968,D 23,44:1
Swayne, Eleanor
Johnny 2X4 1942,Mr 17,24:6
Magnificent Yankee, The 1946,Ja 23,21:2
When the Bough Breaks 1950,Mr 9,25:5
Swayne, Marian
Romance 1921,Mr 1,18:2
Clouds 1925,S 3,32:1
Mystery Ship, The 1927,Mr 15,28:2
Swayne, Viola
Too Much Party 1934,Mr 6,28:4
It Can't Happen Here 1936,O 28,30:1
Right You Are (If You Think You Are)
1957,Mr 5,37:1
Long Gallery, The 1958,Mr 7,17:2
Enchanted, The 1958,Ap 23,41:1
Play That on Your Old Piano 1965,O 15,49:1
Inherit the Wind 1967,Je 23,50:1
Swearingen, John
Man for All Seasons, A 1964,Ja 28,24:2
Me and Juliet 1970,My 15,42:1
Immaculate Misconception, The 1970,O 28,63:3
Swearingen, John (Miscellaneous)
Half Horse, Half Alligator 1966,Mr 14,37:2
Sweeney, John E
Merry Wives of Windsor, The 1954,F 17,27:1
Sweeney, Joseph
Near Santa Barbara 1921,F 1,14:1
Smooth as Silk 1921,F 23,18:3
Bewitched 1924,O 2,26:3
Appearances 1925,O 15,27:3
Vaudeville (Palace) 1926,S 21,32:5
Lily Sue 1926,N 17,22:2
Weather Clear, Track Fast 1927,O 19,24:5
Scarlet Fox, The 1928,Mr 28,31:1
Crooks' Convention, The 1929,S 19,37:4
White Flame 1929,N 5,32:7
Hobo 1931,F 12,24:4
Brass Ankle 1931,Ap 24,26:4
After Tomorrow 1931,Ag 27,22:4
Both Your Houses 1933,Mr 7,20:3

Farmer Takes a Wife, The 1934,O 31,17:1
Slight Case of Murder, A 1935,S 12,28:5
Dear Old Darling 1936,Mr 3,25:1
Days to Come 1936,D 16,35:1
Hitch Your Wagon! 1937,Ap 9,18:2
In Clover 1937,O 14,23:1
Too Many Heroes 1937,N 16,26:2
Missouri Legend 1938,S 20,27:2
Merchant of Yonkers, The 1938,D 29,14:2
Ladies and Gentlemen 1939,O 18,30:2
Johnny on the Spot 1942,Ja 9,24:2
Moon Is Down, The 1942,Ap 8,22:2
Apple of His Eye 1946,F 6,18:2
Story for Strangers, A 1948,S 22,39:2
Rat Race, The 1949,D 23,16:2
Legend of Sarah 1950,O 12,42:4
Courtin' Time 1951,Je 14,30:2
Crucible, The 1953,Ja 23,15:2
Crucible, The 1953,Jl 2,20:2
Sweeney, Margot
Chemmy Circle, The 1968,Ag 10,17:2
Sweeney, Paul
Wind Remains, The 1943,Mr 31,16:6
Sweeney, William J 4th
Cockeyed Kite 1961,S 14,27:1
Sweeny, Ann
De Sade Illustrated 1969,My 13,42:4
Mundy Scheme, The 1969,D 12,75:1
Sweeny, Pamela
Becky Sharp 1929,Je 4,29:1
Sweeny, Thompson
Becky Sharp 1929,Je 4,29:1
Sweet, A J
Don Juan in the Russian Manner 1954,Ap 23,23:2
Sweet, A J (Director)
Don Juan in the Russian Manner 1954,Ap 23,23:2
Sweet, Blanche
Petrified Forest, The 1934,D 21,31:6
Petrified Forest, The 1935,S 8,26:1
There's Always a Breeze 1938,Mr 3,16:2
Aries Is Rising 1939,N 22,16:5
Those Endearing Young Charms 1943,Je 17,16:3
Sweet, Dolph
Legend of Lovers 1959,O 28,40:3
Rhinoceros 1961,Ja 10,27:1
Romulus 1962,Ja 11,27:1
Dragon, The 1963,Ap 10,32:1
Advocate, The 1963,O 15,46:7
Too Much Johnson 1964,Ja 16,29:1
Sign in Sidney Brustein's Window, The
1964,O 16,32:1
Great Indoors, The 1966,F 2,23:1
Natural Look, The 1967,Mr 13,45:2
Ceremony of Innocence, The 1968,Ja 2,33:1
Billy 1969,Mr 24,56:1
Penny Wars, The 1969,O 16,52:1
Sweet, Gene
Don Juan in the Russian Manner 1954,Ap 23,23:2
Sweet, George
Dear Sir 1924,S 24,21:3
Betty Lee 1924,D 26,18:2
Footlights 1927,Ag 20,8:2
Who Cares 1930,Jl 9,27:1
Lambs Gambol 1932,Ap 25,18:2
On the Make 1932,My 24,23:2
Ghost Writer, The 1933,Je 20,22:4
Sweet, John
Truckline Cafe 1946,F 28,19:4
How I Wonder 1947,O 1,34:2
Sweet, Marion
Egghead, The 1957,O 10,39:1
Sweet, Robert W
Tableaux 1961,D 18,41:3
Sweet, Sam
Rugged Path, The 1945,N 12,17:2
Sweet, Sidney
Whispering Gallery, The 1935,D 1,II,12:6
Sweetland, Lee
Regina 1949,N 1,32:2
Sweetser, Norman
Beggar on Horseback 1924,F 13,17:2
Mayflowers 1925,N 25,14:2
Vaudeville (Palace) 1926,Ap 13,28:3
Swem, Margery
Phantoms 1930,Ja 14,24:3
Oh, Professor 1930,My 2,19:6
Swenning, Richard
Ice Capades 1960,S 1,30:1
Swensen, Arthur
Alice in Wonderland 1932,D 12,18:3
Swenson, Alfred
That Day 1922,O 4,27:3
Wall Street 1927,Ap 21,24:4
Great Power, The 1928,S 12,25:1
One Way Street 1928,D 25,31:2
Swenson, David
Phaedra 1967,My 22,50:2
Swenson, Inga
Twelfth Night 1954,N 10,42:2
Twelfth Night 1954,D 12,II,3:1
New Faces of 1956 1956,Je 15,32:1
First Gentleman, The 1957,Ap 26,22:2
First Gentleman, The 1957,My 5,II,1:1

Swenson, Inga—Cont
Hamlet 1958,Je 21,11:1
Midsummer Night's Dream, A 1958,Je 23,19:1
Winter's Tale, The 1958,Jl 21,17:4
Winter's Tale, The 1958,Jl 27,II,1:1
Romeo and Juliet 1959,Je 15,31:1
Romeo and Juliet 1959,Je 21,II,1:1
Peer Gynt 1960,Ja 13,21:1
110 in the Shade 1963,S 12,33:2
110 in the Shade 1963,O 25,37:1
Baker Street 1965,F 17,36:1
Baker Street 1965,F 28,II,1:1
My Fair Lady 1968,Je 14,42:1
Swenson, Joel
Apothecary, The 1926,Mr 17,28:1
Swenson, Karl
Three Sisters, The 1930,Ja 9,22:2
Glass of Water, A 1930,Mr 6,16:3
Antigone 1930,Ap 25,28:4
Boeuf sur le Toit, Le 1930,Ap 25,28:4
Carry Nation 1932,O 31,18:2
One Sunday Afternoon 1933,F 16,23:5
House of Remsen 1934,Ap 3,26:4
Fools Rush In 1934,D 26,19:2
Panic 1935,Mr 16,18:4
Just Suppose 1935,Jl 2,24:3
New Faces of 1936 1936,My 20,24:5
Highland Fling, A 1944,Ap 29,13:2
Man Who Had All the Luck, The 1944,N 24,18:5
Doll's House, A 1954,N 15,32:2
In the Matter of J Robert Oppenheimer
1968,Je 7,31:1
Swenson, Sven
Ulysses in Nighttown 1958,Je 6,30:1
Destry Rides Again 1959,Ap 24,24:1
Wildcat 1960,D 17,20:2
Golden Apple, The 1962,F 13,38:2
Little Me 1962,N 19,41:3
Joyful Noise, A 1966,D 16,57:1
Swenson, Sven (Producer)
And Puppy Dog Tails 1969,O 20,60:1
Swerdfager, Bruce
Taming of the Shrew, The 1954,Jl 1,22:2
Merchant of Venice, The 1955,Jl 1,13:1
Tamburlaine the Great 1956,Ja 20,19:1
Henry V 1956,Je 20,27:2
Merry Wives of Windsor, The 1956,Je 21,34:4
Love and Libel 1960,D 8,44:1
Swerdlow, Irwin
Belt, The 1927,O 20,33:1
Centuries, The 1927,N 30,23:1
Swerdlow, Irwin (Director)
Machine Wreckers, The 1937,Ap 12,14:2
Swerdlow, Stanley (Miscellaneous)
Firebugs, The 1963,F 13,7:2
Viet Rock 1966,N 11,38:1
Swerdlow, Stanley (Producer)
Toilet, The 1964,D 17,51:1
Slave, The 1964,D 17,51:1
Swerling, Jo (Playwright)
One Heluva Night 1924,Je 5,18:1
New Yorkers, The 1927,Mr 11,24:3
Kibitzer, The 1929,F 19,22:5
Guys and Dolls 1950,N 25,11:2
Guys and Dolls 1950,D 3,II,1:1
Guys and Dolls 1951,O 7,II,1:1
Guys and Dolls 1955,Ap 21,32:2
Guys and Dolls 1959,Jl 22,22:2
Guys and Dolls 1965,Ap 29,39:1
Guys and Dolls 1966,Je 9,55:2
Swete, E Lyall
Clair de Lune 1921,Ap 19,15:1
Swete, E Lyall (Director)
Old English 1924,D 24,11:2
Swetland, William
Parnell 1936,My 5,26:2
Saturday's Children 1936,Jl 7,22:5
Having Wonderful Time 1937,F 22,12:5
At the Theatre 1937,Ag 4,14:1
Room Service 1937,D 16,35:4
Ring Two 1939,N 23,38:2
Goodbye in the Night 1940,Mr 19,31:2
Our Town 1944,Ja 11,24:5
Who Was That Lady I Saw You With?
1958,Mr 4,33:2
Fashion 1959,Ja 21,27:1
Borak 1960,D 14,51:1
Call on Kuprin, A 1961,My 26,29:3
Captains and the Kings, The 1962,Ja 3,25:2
All the King's Men 1963,Jl 12,12:1
Whistle in the Dark, A 1968,F 17,32:2
Country People 1970,Ja 19,35:1
Swift, Allen
How to Make a Man 1961,F 3,16:1
Barroom Monks, The 1962,My 29,21:1
Portrait of the Artist as a Young Man, A
1962,My 29,21:1
Student Gypsy, The; Prince of Liederkranz, The
1963,O 1,34:1
Month of Sundays 1968,S 17,50:1
Swift, Allen (Producer)
Whores, Wars & Tin Pan Alley 1969,Je 17,37:1
Swift, Barbara
Pirates of Penzance, The 1970,Jl 26,49:5

Swift, Clive
Cymbeline 1962,Jl 18,21:2
Swift, Edgar (Lighting Director)
Story Theater Repertory; Saint Julian the
Hospitaler 1970,O 21,40:1
Story Theater Repertory; Gimpel the Food
1970,O 21,40:1
Swift, Frank
White Man 1936,O 19,22:4
Swift, G Patrick
It's the Valet 1933,D 15,25:4
Fiesta 1933,D 16,12:2
Swift, Hamilton
Junk 1927,Ja 6,25:1
Swift, James
Show Boat 1932,My 20,22:2
Swift, Kay (Composer)
Nine Fifteen Revue, The 1930,F 12,26:2
Garrick Gaieties 1930,Je 5,29:2
Fine and Dandy 1930,S 24,26:1
Paris '90 1952,Mr 5,33:2
Paris '90 1952,Mr 16,II,1:1
Swift, Kay (Lyricist)
Nine Fifteen Revue, The 1930,F 12,26:2
Paris '90 1952,Mr 5,33:2
Swift, Lucy Weston
Culbin Sands 1935,Mr 23,10:3
Swift, Michael (Playwright)
Hot Pan 1928,F 16,14:1
Hot Pan 1928,F 26,VIII,1:1
Swift, Thomas
Chippies 1929,My 30,23:3
Swifts, The Three
Vaudeville (Palace) 1929,S 16,30:4
Swig, Franklin M (Scenic Designer)
Ice Capades 1962,Ag 30,34:1
Swimmer, Saul (Director)
Follies of 1910, The 1960,Ja 15,37:3
Swimmer, Saul (Miscellaneous)
Follies of 1910, The 1960,Ja 15,37:3
Swinarski, Artur Marya (Playwright)
Alcestis Comes Back 1962,Ap 24,33:1
Swinburne, Mercia
Crooked Billet, The 1927,N 6,IX,2:5
Mulberry Bush, The 1930,My 18,VIII,2:6
Gioconda Smile, The 1950,O 9,21:2
Swinburne, Nora
Mountebank, The 1923,My 8,22:2
Mary, Mary, Quite Contrary 1923,S 12,14:1
Out Goes She 1928,D 30,VIII,4:1
Fame 1929,Mr 10,X,4:6
Lady Clara 1930,Ap 18,28:7
Lucky Dip 1930,N 16,VIII,4:1
King's Leisure, The 1936,My 31,II,6:8
Honor and Obey 1947,N 20,40:1
Red Letter Day 1952,Mr 16,II,3:7
Swinley, Ion
12 Miles Out 1927,F 20,VII,1:4
Rudolph of Austria 1932,Ap 10,VIII,3:7
Peer Gynt 1935,S 24,28:2
Swinnerton, Frank (Original Author)
Nocturne 1925,F 17,19:1
Swinsky, Jerry
El Cristo 1926,My 9,II,1:4
Swinstead, Joan
Astonished Heart, The 1936,N 25,17:2
Hands Across the Sea 1936,N 25,17:2
Shadow Play 1936,N 28,13:1
Still Life 1936,D 1,31:1
Family Album 1936,D 1,31:1
Ways and Means 1936,D 1,31:1
Swinton, Nerene
Tangerine 1921,Ag 10,8:2
Swire, R Derek
Hidden Stranger 1963,Ja 10,5:5
Swire, R Derek (Miscellaneous)
Man Out Loud, Girl Quiet 1962,Ap 4,38:1
Spanish Armada, The 1962,Ap 4,38:1
We're Civilized? 1962,N 9,30:1
Exit the King 1968,Ja 10,48:1
Much Ado About Nothing 1969,Je 16,57:1
Wars of the Roses, The (Part I) 1970,Jl 2,30:1
Wars of the Roses, The (Part II) 1970,Jl 3,15:1
Richard III 1970,Jl 4,11:1
Opium 1970,O 6,58:1
Swire, Willard
Lamp at Midnight 1947,D 22,29:2
Respectful Prostitute, The 1948,F 10,27:2
Swissler, Mary
Bedrock 1934,N 18,II,6:3
Switkes, Willy
Mime and Me, The 1960,Ap 8,27:3
Country Scandal, A 1960,My 6,21:8
Information Bureau, The 1962,Ja 31,21:1
Lovers in the Metro, The 1962,Ja 31,21:1
Firebugs, The 1963,F 13,7:2
Conerico Was Here to Stay 1965,Mr 4,37:1
Swoboda, G
Strange Child 1935,F 26,16:1
Enemies 1935,Mr 19,24:7
Swoboda, T
White Guard, The; Days of the Turbins
1935,Mr 7,27:5

Deluge, The 1935,Mr 26,23:7
Swoboda, Vecheslav (Choreographer)
Chauve-Souris of 1943 1943,Ag 13,13:2
Swope, Herbert Jr (Director)
Fragile Fox 1954,O 13,27:1
Step on a Crack 1962,O 18,48:1
Swope, Herbert Jr (Producer)
Step on a Crack 1962,O 18,48:1
Fair Game for Lovers 1964,F 11,43:2
Swope, Margaret
I Was Waiting for You 1933,N 14,23:3
Days Without End 1934,Ja 9,19:1
Swope, Tracy Brooks
Woman Is My Idea 1968,S 26,61:1
Swor, Bert
Brass Ankle 1931,Ap 24,26:4
Swor, Irene
Jonica 1930,Ap 8,27:1
Swor, Mabelle
Merry World, The 1926,Je 9,18:3
Sword, Charles H (Composer)
Cotton Stockings 1923,D 19,16:2
Sword, Charles H (Lyricist)
Cotton Stockings 1923,D 19,16:2
Sword, Charles H (Playwright)
Cotton Stockings 1923,D 19,16:2
Swymer, Gayle
Of Thee I Sing 1969,Mr 8,19:1
Sycamore Players, Indiana State University
Neighbors 1966,D 3,45:3
Sydell, Paul
Carnival! 1961,Ap 14,22:2
Sydell, Paul and Spotty
Vaudeville (Hippodrome) 1926,My 8,29:2
Vaudeville (Palace) 1926,Je 1,29:5
Vaudeville (Palace) 1926,S 28,30:4
Sydell Sisters
Vaudeville (Palace) 1931,Ja 19,25:3
Sydenham, George
Peg o' My Heart 1921,F 15,7:1
Fedora 1922,F 11,18:1
Sweeney Todd 1924,Jl 19,10:4
Bombasters Furioso 1924,Jl 19,10:4
Charley's Aunt 1925,Je 2,16:2
Old Bill, M P 1926,N 11,22:2
Sydmeth, Louise
Adding Machine, The 1923,Mr 20,24:1
Mad Honeymoon, The 1923,Ag 8,10:1
God Loves Us 1926,O 20,22:2
Wasp's Nest, The 1927,O 26,26:3
Sydney, Basil
Romance 1921,Mr 1,18:2
Romance 1921,Mr 6,VI,1:2
R U R 1922,O 10,16:1
Romeo and Juliet 1922,D 28,20:1
Sandro Botticelli 1923,Mr 27,24:2
Sandro Botticelli 1923,Ap 1,VII,1:1
Devil's Disciple, The 1923,Ap 24,24:1
Devil's Disciple, The 1923,My 6,VII,1:1
She Stoops to Conquer 1924,Je 10,24:3
Hamlet 1925,N 10,23:1
Hamlet 1925,N 22,VIII,1:1
Jest, The 1926,F 5,22:2
Jest, The 1926,F 14,VIII,1:1
Henry IV, Part I 1926,Je 1,29:1
Humble, The 1926,O 14,22:2
Crown Prince, The 1927,F 27,VII,4:6
Crown Prince, The 1927,Mr 24,23:2
Taming of the Shrew, The 1927,O 26,26:4
Taming of the Shrew, The 1927,N 13,IX,1:1
Twelve Thousand 1928,Mr 13,23:1
Twelve Thousand 1928,Mr 18,IX,1:1
Meet the Prince 1929,F 26,30:5
Meet the Prince 1929,Mr 10,X,1:1
Becky Sharp 1929,Je 4,29:1
Children of Darkness 1930,Ja 8,25:1
Children of Darkness 1930,Ja 19,VIII,1:1
Strange Interlude 1931,F 4,21:2
Strange Interlude 1931,F 22,VIII,1:3
Jewel Robbery 1932,Ja 14,17:2
Jewel Robbery 1932,F 10,27:1
Dinner at Eight 1933,Ja 7,11:5
Dinner at Eight 1933,Ja 29,IX,1:3
Dark Tower, The 1933,N 27,20:3
Dark Tower, The 1934,Je 10,IX,1:1
Flood Tide 1938,Mr 24,20:8
Traitor's Gate 1938,D 4,X,7:5
Sydney, Eric
In the Summer House 1964,Mr 26,43:1
Sydney, Howard
Strip Girl 1935,O 21,22:6
Sydney, Jess
Precedent 1931,Ap 15,24:5
Sydney, Midge
Broadway Boy 1932,My 4,23:5
Sydnor, Earl
Trial of Dr Beck, The 1937,Ag 10,22:2
Two on an Island 1940,Ja 23,17:2
Cabin in the Sky 1940,O 26,19:2
Skin of Our Teeth, The 1942,N 19,29:5
Set My People Free 1948,N 4,38:2
Shuffle Along 1952,My 9,20:5
Sweet Bird of Youth 1959,Mr 11,39:2

Sydnor, Earl—Cont
Emperor Jones, The 1964,Ag 6,20:4
I Never Sang for My Father 1968,Ja 26,30:1
Sydor, William
Alt Heidelberg 1926,My 31,10:5
Sydow, Jack
Major Barbara 1954,Je 30,23:2
Brothers Karamazov, The 1957,D 9,39:4
Leper, The 1970,Ap 24,40:1
Sydow, Jack (Director)
2 for Fun; Switch in Time, A 1955,My 26,34:1
2 for Fun; Anniversary, The 1955,My 26,34:1
Sudden End of Anne Cinquefoil, The
1961,Ja 11,25:2
Sophie 1963,Ap 16,32:1
Amorous Flea, The 1964,F 18,26:1
Crucible, The 1964,Ap 7,30:2
Midsummer Night's Dream, A 1964,Je 30,23:2
Giants' Dance, The 1964,N 17,48:2
Major Barbara 1965,My 18,33:1
Annie Get Your Gun 1966,Je 1,42:2
Imaginary Invalid, The 1967,My 2,53:1
Touch of the Poet, A 1967,My 3,38:2
Still Life 1967,My 4,34:1
John Brown's Body 1968,F 13,49:2
Sydow, Jack (Miscellaneous)
John Brown's Body 1968,F 13,49:2
Sydow, Jack (Playwright)
Brothers Karamazov, The 1957,D 9,39:4
Brothers Karamazov, The 1957,D 22,II,3:1
Idiot, The 1960,S 26,38:1
Sydow, John
First in Heart, The 1947,N 14,29:2
Sykes, Dama
Florodora 1920,Ap 6,18:1
Sykes, Dick
Touch and Go 1949,O 14,34:2
Cretan Woman, The 1954,My 21,17:2
Sykes, Judith
This Way to the Tomb 1961,D 9,21:1
Sykes, Nelson (Director)
Aunt Caroline's Will 1954,Ag 11,21:1
Dark Sonnet 1958,Mr 12,36:1
Sykes, Nelson (Musical Director)
Doctor Cupid 1952,Ag 14,19:6
Sylber, Charley
Madcap, The 1928,F 1,31:2
Sylbert, Paul (Costume Designer)
Passion of Gross, The 1955,Ja 24,20:2
Making of Moo, The 1958,Je 12,34:1
O, Oysters! 1961,Ja 31,23:1
Sylbert, Paul (Lighting Director)
Passion of Gross, The 1955,Ja 24,20:2
O, Oysters! 1961,Ja 31,23:1
Sylbert, Paul (Scenic Designer)
Passion of Gross, The 1955,Ja 24,20:2
Making of Moo, The 1958,Je 12,34:1
O, Oysters! 1961,Ja 31,23:1
Sylbert, Richard (Scenic Designer)
Egghead, The 1957,O 10,39:1
Sylovna, Sydelle
Lute Song 1946,F 7,29:2
Sylphe, Le
Scandals 1920,Je 8,9:1
Sylva, Daphne
Hamlet 1936,N 11,54:2
Two Time Mary 1937,Ag 3,20:5
Sylva, Marguerita
Skylark 1921,Jl 26,10:6
Cousin Sonia 1925,D 8,28:3
Golden Dawn 1927,D 1,32:3
Luana 1930,S 18,28:1
Great Lover, The 1932,O 12,27:3
Two Time Mary 1937,Ag 3,20:5
Three Waltzes 1937,D 27,10:2
Sylva, Marita
Romantic Mr Dickens 1940,D 3,33:2
Sylva, Vesta
Bitter Sweet 1929,N 6,30:2
Sylvain, Jules (Composer)
Autumn Manoeuvers 1938,N 27,IX,3:6
Sylvaine, Vernon
Courting 1925,S 14,17:1
Sylvaine, Vernon (Playwright)
Aren't Men Beasts? 1936,My 15,29:1
Spot of Bother 1937,Jl 7,26:2
Nap Hand 1940,Mr 10,XI,2:6
Women Aren't Angels 1941,Ap 27,IX,1:6
All Men Are Alike 1941,O 7,27:2
Warn That Man 1942,Ja 4,IX,1:4
As Long as They're Happy 1953,Ag 9,II,1:2
Sylvan, Jerry
Bitter Stream 1936,Mr 31,16:6
Sylvania, Ida
Greenwich Village Follies 1925,D 25,23:3
Sylvere, Jules
Nuit au Bouge, Une 1923,O 16,18:1
Alcide Pepis 1923,O 30,17:2
Crucifies, Les 1923,O 30,17:2
Peu de Musique, Un 1923,N 6,22:1
Laboratoire des Hallucinations, Le 1923,N 20,23:3
Fiole, La 1923,N 20,23:3
Sol Hyam's Brocanteur 1923,N 27,23:5

Sylvester
Ragged Edge, The 1927,F 13,VII,1:4
Sylvester, Frank
Macbeth 1921,F 18,16:1
Fan, The 1921,O 4,10:1
Lawbreaker, The 1922,F 7,12:1
Fool, The 1922,O 24,18:1
Backslapper, The 1925,Ap 13,25:2
Black Velvet 1927,S 28,28:1
Gringa, La 1928,F 2,17:1
Mr Moneypenny 1928,O 17,26:2
Oh, Promise Me 1930,N 25,31:1
Sylvester, Frederick
Vaudeville (Palace) 1924,Ap 1,18:1
Sylvester, George
Blue Bird, The 1923,D 26,13:3
Sitting Pretty 1924,Ap 9,24:2
Sylvester, Hannah
Hummin' Sam 1933,Ap 10,8:8
Sylvester, John
Sundown Beach 1948,S 8,37:1
All You Need Is One Good Break 1950,F 10,20:3
Sylvester, Murray
Laugh It Off 1934,Ap 5,24:2
Sylvester, William
Teahouse of the August Moon, The
1954,Ap 23,23:5
Teahouse of the August Moon, The
1954,My 2,II,3:1
Teahouse of the August Moon, The
1955,My 10,24:1
Mister Johnson 1956,Mr 30,11:1
As You Like It 1959,Jl 1,27:1
Othello 1959,Jl 2,17:2
Macbeth 1962,F 7,32:2
Saint Joan 1962,F 21,57:4
Sylvestre, Jerry
Devil's Little Game, The 1932,Ag 2,20:4
Sylvia
Sun Kissed 1937,Mr 11,20:2
New Faces of 1962 1962,F 2,25:1
Sylvia, Belle
Nina Rosa 1930,My 31,19:3
Nina Rosa 1930,S 22,22:5
Sylvia, Kenneth (Playwright)
Shadow Years, The 1957,Ja 9,26:2
Sylvie, Mme
Vocation, La 1926,D 19,VII,3:3
Dans l'Ombre du Harem 1927,My 29,VII,2:7
Amants de Paris, Les 1927,N 6,IX,4:1
Trouble, Le 1928,Ap 29,IX,2:3
Whisky 1929,Ja 13,VIII,2:7
Ennemie, L' 1929,Ap 28,IX,2:4
Amis Comme Avant 1930,Ja 26,VIII,2:1
Cyclone, Le 1931,O 25,VIII,1:6
Sylvon, Jerry
Chinese Nightingale, The 1934,O 6,20:4
Milky Way, The 1943,Je 10,17:2
Mexican Hayride 1944,Ja 29,9:6
Syme, Franklin T
Flahooley 1951,My 15,39:1
Symington, Donald
Galileo 1947,D 8,34:2
Dream Girl 1951,My 10,39:1
Pygmalion 1952,F 9,11:2
Girl Can Tell, A 1953,O 30,28:2
Lute Song 1959,Mr 13,24:1
Death of Satan, The 1960,Ap 6,49:1
Delightful Season, A 1960,S 29,30:1
Rate of Exchange 1968,Ap 2,50:1
Possibilities 1968,D 5,60:1
Symington, James
Wall Street 1927,Ap 21,24:4
Symon, Burk (Director)
Warrior's Husband, The 1932,Mr 12,19:4
Nona 1932,O 5,26:4
Red Planet 1932,D 19,19:2
Symonds, Barry
Summertree 1968,Mr 4,29:1
Symonds, Hall
Woman Disputed, A 1926,S 29,23:2
Symonds, Rebecca
Good Woman of Setzuan, The 1970,N 6,51:1
Symonds, Robert
Waiting for Godot 1958,Ag 6,22:1
Birthday Party, The 1961,My 15,34:6
Galileo 1963,Ja 5,5:2
Caretaker, The 1963,N 25,23:2
Danton's Death 1965,O 22,46:1
Caucasian Chalk Circle, The 1966,Mr 25,35:1
Alchemist, The 1966,O 14,48:1
Galileo 1967,Ap 14,31:1
Saint Joan 1968,Ja 5,42:1
Tiger at the Gates 1968,Mr 1,30:1
Cyrano de Bergerac 1968,Ap 26,30:1
Cry of Players, A 1968,N 15,40:1
Inner Journey, The 1969,Mr 21,42:1
Miser, The 1969,My 9,35:1
Miser, The 1969,My 25,II,1:1
Time of Your Life, The 1969,N 7,37:1
Time of Your Life, The 1969,N 16,II,1:4
Disintegration of James Cherry, The
1970,Ja 30,33:3

Silence 1970,Ap 3,43:1
Landscape 1970,Ap 3,43:1
Symonds, Robert (Director)
Country Wife, The 1965,D 10,58:2
East Wind, The 1967,F 10,30:1
Bananas 1968,D 5,60:1
Amphitryon 1970,My 29,13:1
Good Woman of Setzuan, The 1970,N 6,51:1
Good Woman of Setzuan, The 1970,N 15,II,1:5
Symonds, Robert (Miscellaneous)
Yerma 1966,D 9,60:1
Symonds, Vic (Scenic Designer)
Rattle of a Simple Man 1963,Ap 18,39:1
Symonette, Lys Bert (Composer)
Brecht on Brecht 1962,Ja 4,26:1
Symonette, Randolph
Rhapsody 1944,N 23,37:2
Firebird of Florence 1945,Mr 23,13:4
Street Scene 1947,Ja 10,17:2
Let's Make an Opera 1950,D 14,50:2
Regina 1952,Je 2,25:4
Symons, Arthur (Playwright)
Toy Cart, The 1930,D 7,IX,2:7
Symons, James
Shakuntala 1959,S 10,41:2
Syms, A
Royal Box, The 1928,N 21,32:3
Syms, Sylvia
Diamond Lil 1949,F 7,16:2
Dream Girl 1951,My 10,39:1
South Pacific 1955,My 5,39:5
Whoop-Up 1958,D 23,2:7
13 Daughters 1961,Mr 3,17:2
Camino Real 1970,Ja 9,42:1
Camino Real 1970,Ja 18,II,1:1
Much Ado About Nothing 1970,S 4,19:1
Boswell's Life of Johnson 1970,S 4,19:1
Syncopators, The
Sex 1926,Ap 27,22:4
Syndor, Earl
Long Way From Home, A 1948,F 9,25:2
Detective Story 1949,Mr 24,34:2
Synge, John Millington (Original Author)
Heart's a Wonder, The 1958,S 19,23:2
Synge, John Millington (Playwright)
Deirdre of the Sorrows 1920,S 26,VI,1:4
Playboy of the Western World, The 1930,Ja 3,20:4
Well of the Saints, The 1932,Ja 22,15:2
Playboy of the Western World, The 1932,O 21,25:1
Shadow of the Glen, The 1932,N 4,25:1
Well of the Saints, The 1934,N 22,26:2
Riders to the Sea 1937,F 15,13:2
Playboy of the Western World, The 1937,N 22,14:5
Playboy of the Western World, The 1946,O 28,18:3
Freight 1949,F 4,30:2
Riders to the Sea 1949,F 4,30:2
Deirdre of the Sorrows 1949,D 15,51:2
In the Shadow of the Glen 1957,Mr 7,24:1
Tinker's Wedding, The 1957,Mr 7,24:1
Riders to the Sea 1957,Mr 7,24:1
Riders to the Sea 1957,Mr 17,II,1:1
In the Shadow of the Glen; Tinker's Wedding, The
1957,Mr 17,II,1:1
Playboy of the Western World, The 1958,My 9,19:2
God and Kate Murphy 1959,F 27,21:2
Well of the Saints, The 1959,Ap 11,15:4
Deirdre of the Sorrows 1959,O 15,46:1
Playboy of the Western World, The 1968,S 4,40:1
Well of the Saints, The 1970,Ag 10,34:1
Synthesizer, Arp (Miscellaneous)
Forensic and the Navigators 1970,Ap 2,43:1
Unseen Hand, The 1970,Ap 2,43:1
Sypher, Harold (Producer)
Chief Thing, The 1963,Ap 30,27:2
Syrakos, Takis
Electra 1930,D 27,16:1
Syril, Jenny
Cloches de Cornville, Les; Chimes of Normandy,
The 1926,D 14,24:4
Perichole, La 1926,D 28,12:2
Perichole, La 1926,D 29,24:4
Syrjala, S
Stairs, The 1927,N 8,32:7
Syrjala, S (Miscellaneous)
Children's Hour, The 1934,N 21,23:2
Syrjala, S (Scenic Designer)
Precedent 1931,Ap 15,24:5
Devil in the Mind 1931,My 2,23:2
Far Away Horses 1933,Mr 22,21:6
Amourette 1933,S 28,25:2
Stevedore 1934,Ap 19,33:2
Milky Way, The 1934,My 9,23:2
Blind Alley 1935,S 25,19:6
Remember the Day 1935,S 26,19:3
Stork Mad 1936,O 1,28:4
Swing Your Lady 1936,O 19,22:4
Double Dummy 1936,N 12,30:1
Pins and Needles 1939,Ap 21,26:2
New Pins and Needles 1939,N 21,19:2
Fourposter, The 1951,O 25,34:2
Fourposter, The 1951,N 25,II,1:1
Syrotiak, David
Poupees de Paris, Les 1964,My 16,11:1

Szabo, Helen (Costume Designer)
Ice Capades 1954,S 16,37:1
Szabo, Sandor
Kek Roka; Blue Fox 1957,D 5,47:2
Egerfogo; Mousetrap, The 1958,Ja 30,18:6
Three Sisters, The 1959,S 22,46:1
Three Sisters, The 1959,O 4,II,1:1
First Love 1961,D 26,20:2
Oh Dad, Poor Dad, Mamma's Hung You in the
Closet and I'm Feelin' So Sad 1962,F 27,28:1
Oh Dad, Poor Dad, Mamma's Hung You in the
Closet and I'm Feelin' So Sad 1963,Ag 28,28:2
My Fair Lady 1964,My 21,43:2
Szabo, Sandor (Director)
Kek Roka; Blue Fox 1957,D 5,47:2
Egerfogo; Mousetrap, The 1958,Ja 30,18:6
Szaboles, Erno (Director)
Broadway 1927,O 23,VIII,2:4
Szaina-Lewandowska, Jadwiga (Musical Director)
Woman, The 1965,Ja 6,32:1
Jacob and the Angel 1965,Ja 6,32:1
Nightmare, The 1965,Ja 6,32:1
Labyrinth, The 1965,Ja 6,32:1
Book, The 1965,Ja 6,32:1
Post Office, The 1965,Ja 6,32:1
Kernel and the Shell, The 1965,Ja 6,32:1
Jaselka 1965,Ja 6,32:1
Szajna, Jozef (Costume Designer)
Acropolis 1969,N 5,40:1
Szajna, Jozef (Miscellaneous)
Acropolis 1969,N 5,40:1
Szajna, Jozef (Scenic Designer)
Acropolis 1969,N 5,40:1
Szakall, Szoeke
Countess Maritza 1927,Ja 30,VII,4:3
Szalay, Alexander
Antonia 1925,O 21,20:1
Szandrowsky, Myron
Once Over Lightly 1942,N 20,26:2
Szczepkowska, Marja M (Original Author)
Doctor Monica 1933,N 7,29:3
Szczuzewski, Andrzei
Jacob and the Angel 1965,Ja 6,32:1
Book, The 1965,Ja 6,32:1
Jaselka 1965,Ja 6,32:1
Kernel and the Shell, The 1965,Ja 6,32:1
Post Office, The 1965,Ja 6,32:1
Woman, The 1965,Ja 6,32:1
Labyrinth, The 1965,Ja 6,32:1
Nightmare, The 1965,Ja 6,32:1
Sze, Julia (Costume Designer)
Angel in the Wings 1947,D 12,36:4
Hold It! 1948,My 6,31:5
Death of a Salesman 1949,F 11,27:2
Man, The 1950,Ja 20,28:2
Drink to Me Only 1958,O 9,47:4
Help Stamp Out Marriage 1966,S 30,50:1
Love in E Flat 1967,F 14,38:1
Girl in the Freudian Slip, The 1967,My 19,34:3
Sze, Julia (Miscellaneous)
Command Decision 1947,O 2,30:2
Sze, Mai-Mai
Lady Precious Stream 1936,Ja 28,15:2
Lady Precious Stream 1936,F 23,X,1:1
Szekeley, Andrew (Director)
Ruy Blas 1957,D 14,16:3
Szekely, Louisa
Abie's Irish Rose 1928,Je 10,VIII,2:8
Szemere, Laslo
Consul, The 1951,S 8,9:3
Szenes, Istvan
Ice Follies 1963,Ja 10,5:2
Ice Follies 1965,Ja 13,35:1
Ice Follies 1966,Ja 12,27:6
Szifman, Arnold (Producer)
Women's House, The 1930,Ap 27,IX,3:1
Szilagi (Playwright)
My Fiddle Is Broken 1928,D 2,X,4:7
Szilard, Paul (Producer)
Greengrocer's Daughter, The 1966,Mr 16,50:1
Fishing for Wives 1966,Mr 16,50:1
General's Daughter, The 1966,Mr 16,50:1
Szilasi, Alix (Playwright)
Beggar Student, The 1942,S 26,11:4
Szinpad, Petofi (Producer)
Kek Roka; Blue Fox 1957,D 5,47:2
Szirmai, A (Dr) (Composer)
Ziegfeld Follies 1924,Je 25,26:1
Szogyi, Alex (Playwright)
Country Scandal, A 1960,My 15,II,1:1
Szogyi, Alex (Translator)
Country Scandal, A 1960,My 6,21:8
Seagull, The 1960,Je 2,26:4
Seagull, The 1962,Mr 22,42:1
Seagull, The 1962,Ap 1,II,1:1
Lower Depths, The 1964,Mr 31,30:1
Lower Depths, The 1964,Ap 12,II,1:1
Philosophy in the Boudoir 1969,My 22,55:2
Szomory, Dezso (Original Author)
Light Behind the Shadow, The 1936,Ja 21,26:6
Szomory, Dezso (Playwright)
A Nagyasszony 1927,O 30,IX,4:1
Alice Takat 1930,F 23,III,7:2

Szomory, Dezso (Translator)
Alice Takat 1936,F 11,19:2
Szony, Francois
Vaudeville (Palace) 1951,O 17,36:6
Szony, Giselle
Vaudeville (Palace) 1951,O 17,36:6
Szony and Claire
Wonder World 1964,My 18,32:1
Szonys, The
Red White and Blue 1950,O 8,64:5
Szorenyi, Eva
Kek Roka; Blue Fox 1957,D 5,47:2
Egerfogo; Mousetrap, The 1958,Ja 30,18:6
Szulc, Joseph (Composer)
Divin Mensonge 1926,N 14,VIII,2:1
Szurmiel, Szymon
Mother Courage 1967,N 17,55:1
Szwejlich, Michael
Mirele Efros 1967,O 20,55:1
Mother Courage 1967,N 17,55:1
Szyfman, Arnold (Director)
Julius Caesar 1928,Ap 8,VIII,4:3
Apple Cart, The 1929,Je 15,6:2
On the Rocks 1933,N 25,10:1
Saint Joan 1956,D 15,20:3

T

Ta-chun, Chien (Miscellaneous)
Peh Shuh Tchuwan; White Snake, The 1963,Ja 4,5:2
Tabbert, William
What's Up 1943,N 12,24:6
Follow the Girls 1944,Ap 10,15:2
Seven Lively Arts 1944,D 8,26:6
Million Dollar Baby 1945,D 22,17:2
Billion Dollar Baby 1945,D 30,II,1:1
South Pacific 1949,Ap 8,30:2
South Pacific 1949,Ap 17,II,1:1
South Pacific 1949,Je 5,II,1:1
South Pacific 1951,Jl 10,30:5
South Pacific 1951,S 2,II,1:1
Fanny 1954,N 5,16:1
Fanny 1954,N 21,II,1:1
Tabbitt, Michael (Miscellaneous)
Heartbreak House 1968,Jl 6,9:1
Chemmy Circle, The 1968,Ag 10,17:2
Taber, Benjamin C
East Lynne Goes West 1931,My 3,I,26:5
Taber, Joan
Elton Case, The 1921,S 12,16:2
Taber, Richard
Mrs Jimmie Thompson 1920,Mr 30,9:1
Blue Bonnet 1920,Ap 30,12:1
Ringside 1928,Ag 30,13:2
Parade 1929,S 1,VIII,1:1
Nigger Rich 1929,S 21,16:7
Life Begins 1932,Mr 29,23:2
Lambs Gambol 1932,Ap 25,18:2
Lambs Gambol 1933,Ap 24,10:1
Battleship Gertie 1935,Ja 19,9:2
Journey by Night, A 1935,Ap 17,26:3
Knock on Wood 1935,My 29,16:2
Slight Case of Murder, A 1935,S 12,28:5
Mid-West 1936,Ja 8,22:4
Come Angel Band 1936,F 19,17:1
Iron Men 1936,O 20,30:6
Behind the Red Lights 1937,Ja 14,17:4
Something for Nothing 1937,D 10,33:5
Come Across 1938,S 15,28:3
Window Shopping 1938,D 24,13:2
Off to Buffalo! 1939,F 22,18:2
Wind in the Sails 1940,Ag 1,24:6
Lily of the Valley 1942,Ja 27,25:2
Tomorrow the World 1943,Ap 15,22:2
Wonderful Journey 1946,D 26,30:2
Mrs Gibsons' Boys 1949,My 5,35:2
Taber, Richard (Playwright)
Is Zat So? 1925,Ja 6,23:4
Taberna, Juliana
Private Lives 1931,My 12,29:3
We the People 1933,Ja 23,9:5
Crime and Punishment 1935,Ja 23,20:3
Taboada, Josefina
Tambor y Cascabel; Drum and Bell 1932,Ap 21,25:4
Taboada, Maria
Pluma en el Viento; Feather in the Wind 1932,Ap 2,13:4
De Muy Buena Familia; Of Very Good Family 1932,Ap 29,13:3
Tabor, David
Crime and Crime 1963,D 17,51:2
My Sweet Charlie 1966,D 7,56:1
Frere Jacques 1968,Je 8,23:2
Tabor, Desiree
Earl Carroll's Vanities 1924,S 11,23:6
Circus Princess, The 1927,Ap 26,32:2
Gala Night 1930,F 26,22:4
Marching By 1932,Mr 4,17:1
Tabor, Guenther
Stellvertreter, Der 1963,F 23,7:8

Tabor, Mary
Veils 1928,Mr 14,28:5
Tabor, Robert
Mandarin, The 1920,N 10,18:2
Tabor, S L (Miscellaneous)
Late Wisdom 1934,Ap 24,27:4
Tabori, George (Director)
Stronger, The 1956,F 22,23:2
Miss Julie 1956,F 22,23:2
Miss Julie 1956,Mr 4,II,1:1
Tabori, George (Lyricist)
Niggerlovers, The; Man and Dog 1967,O 2,54:2
Niggerlovers, The; Demonstration, The 1967,O 2,54:2
Tabori, George (Miscellaneous)
Brecht on Brecht 1962,Ja 4,26:1
Resistible Rise of Arturo Ui, The 1969,Ag 18,28:1
Tabori, George (Playwright)
Flight Into Egypt 1952,Mr 19,33:2
Flight Into Egypt 1952,Mr 30,II,1:1
Emperor's Clothes, The 1953,F 10,24:2
Emperor's Clothes, The 1953,O 23,19:7
Miss Julie 1956,F 22,23:2
Stronger, The 1956,F 22,23:2
Brouhaha 1958,Ag 28,18:8
Brouhaha 1960,Ap 27,31:2
Miss Julie 1961,Jl 10,26:1
Brecht on Brecht 1961,N 15,52:2
Brecht on Brecht 1962,Ja 14,II,1:1
Arturo Ui 1963,N 12,49:1
Niggerlovers, The; Man and Dog 1967,O 2,54:2
Niggerlovers, The; Demonstration, The 1967,O 2,54:2
Niggerlovers, The 1967,O 15,II,3:1
Niggerlovers, The 1968,Jl 7,II,1:1
Cannibals, The 1968,N 4,60:1
Cannibals, The 1968,N 10,II,5:1
Whores, Wars & Tin Pan Alley 1969,Je 17,37:1
Tabori, George (Translator)
Andorra 1963,F 11,5:5
Resistible Rise of Arturo Ui, The 1968,Ag 8,25:1
Resistible Rise of Arturo Ui, The 1968,Ag 30,22:2
Guns of Carrar, The 1968,D 10,53:1
Resistible Rise of Arturo Ui, The 1968,D 23,44:1
Tabori, Kristoffer
Cry of Players, A 1968,N 15,40:1
Guns of Carrar, The 1968,D 10,53:1
Henry V 1969,Je 9,57:1
Henry V 1969,Je 15,II,3:1
Much Ado About Nothing 1969,Je 16,57:1
Hamlet 1969,Je 30,33:1
Penny Wars, The 1969,O 16,52:1
Henry V 1969,N 11,43:1
Dream of a Blacklisted Actor 1969,D 18,64:1
How Much, How Much? 1970,F 15,II,1:1
How Much, How Much? 1970,Ap 21,49:1
Tachau, Jean
Kiss Me, Kate 1949,Ja 30,II,6:5
Tachibana, Sahomi
Majority of One, A 1959,F 17,28:2
Tachna, Edith
American, Very Early 1934,Ja 31,21:2
In Gold We Trust 1936,S 1,24:1
Be So Kindly 1937,F 9,19:4
Stop Press 1939,Mr 20,13:2
Tackney, Stanley
Afternoon Storm 1948,Ap 12,24:2
Point of No Return 1951,D 14,35:2
High Named Today 1954,D 11,11:2
Tackney, Stanley (Director)
Lady's Not for Burning, The 1959,Ja 31,13:2
Tacy, John
March March, The 1966,N 15,51:4
Tadlock, Bob (Costume Designer)
Egg and I, The 1958,S 11,43:4
Tadlock, Thelma
Pal Joey 1952,Ja 4,17:6
Me and Juliet 1953,My 29,17:1
Taeb-Boucar
Infinite Shoeblack, The 1930,F 18,28:1
Tafel, Suzanne
Hay-Fever, Straw-Foot 1942,O 24,11:6
Carousel 1945,Ap 20,24:2
Taffe, Patricia
Skin of Our Teeth, The 1955,Ag 18,16:1
Tafler, Sidney
Henry IV, Part I 1946,My 7,25:2
Henry IV, Part II 1946,My 8,33:4
Henry IV 1946,My 12,II,1:1
Oedipus; Critic, The 1946,My 21,19:2
Taft, Bertha
Little Theatre Tournament; Fancy Free 1929,My 9,34:3
Taft, Frank
Doughgirls, The 1942,D 31,19:2
Taft, Richard C
Little Theatre Tournament; Fancy Free 1929,My 9,34:3
Taft, Sara
Jenny Kissed Me 1948,D 24,12:2
Talent '49 1949,Ap 13,39:4
Tager, Arnold
Richard III 1957,N 26,41:1

Tager, Arnold (Director)
When I Was a Child 1960,D 9,38:1
Tager, Arnold (Producer)
When I Was a Child 1960,D 9,38:1
Tagewell, Charles
Peer Gynt 1923,F 6,14:1
Tagg, Alan (Costume Designer)
Black Comedy 1967,F 13,42:1
Black Comedy; White Lies 1967,F 13,42:1
Tagg, Alan (Scenic Designer)
Look Back in Anger 1957,O 2,28:2
Entertainer, The 1958,F 13,22:2
All in Good Time 1965,F 19,25:1
Black Comedy; White Lies 1967,F 13,42:1
Black Comedy 1967,F 13,42:1
Come as You Are 1970,Ag 12,32:1
Tagg, Nick (Miscellaneous)
Best of Burlesque 1957,S 30,27:2
Taggart, Ben
What Women Do? 1925,Jl 21,26:4
Taggart, Hall
Woman of Bronze, The 1927,Je 16,25:4
Taggart, Millee
Possibilities 1968,D 5,60:1
Taggart, Vince
Golden Screw, The 1967,Ja 31,52:1
Tagger, Theodor (Ferdinand Bruckner) (Playwright)
Kreatur, Die 1930,My 25,IX,1:8
Elisabeth von England 1930,D 14,IX,4:1
Tagore, Rabindranath (Playwright)
Sacrifice 1920,D 11,11:2
Post Office, The 1920,D 11,11:2
When I Was a Child 1960,D 9,38:1
King of the Dark Chamber 1961,F 10,21:1
King of the Dark Chamber 1961,Ap 9,II,1:1
Taguese
Kykunkor 1934,D 22,21:3
Tahmin, Mary
Walk-Up 1961,F 24,24:1
Tahse, Martin (Producer)
Laughs and Other Events 1960,O 11,57:1
Morning Sun 1963,O 7,36:2
Tai, Ada
Dybbuk, The 1964,F 4,30:2
Tai, Ju Quon
Silks and Satins 1920,Jl 16,19:1
Taibi, Joseph
Dead End 1935,O 29,17:2
Taibi, Rose
Dead End 1935,O 29,17:2
Taie, John
Anna Lucasta 1944,Ag 31,15:1
Taintor, Melinda (Choreographer)
Utopia! 1963,My 7,47:4
Tairoff, Alexander
Desire Under the Elms 1930,Ag 3,23:4
Tairov (Producer)
Saint Joan 1925,Ja 11,VII,2:7
Tait, George
Porgy and Bess 1935,O 11,30:2
Taiz, Lillian
God of Vengeance, The 1922,D 20,22:5
Spring Is Here 1929,Mr 12,26:1
Duchess of Chicago, The 1929,N 17,IX,4:1
So This Is Paris 1930,Ap 27,IX,2:3
Tajo, Italo
Kiss Me, Kate 1959,Ag 10,24:1
Takahashi, Yasuyo (Costume Designer)
Marie Vison, La 1970,Jl 15,29:1
Takahashi, Sandra (Costume Designer)
Emerald Slippers, The 1970,S 2,31:2
Takahasi, Masaya
Othello 1960,S 11,II,7:1
Takamatsu, Prince (Producer)
Chushingura; Treasury of Loyal Retainers, The 1969,S 11,53:1
Kagami-Jishi; Mirror Lion Dance, The 1969,S 11,53:1
Momiji-Gari 1969,S 18,64:1
Kumagai Jinya 1969,S 18,64:1
Takamoto, E
If This Be Treason 1935,S 24,28:2
Takarada, Akira
Kiss Me, Kate 1966,F 5,32:1
Takashima, Tadao
My Fair Lady 1963,S 2,19:4
Takayama
Jumbo 1935,N 18,20:2
Takayo
World of Suzie Wong, The 1958,O 15,47:1
Takemoto, Harukodayu (Miscellaneous)
Greengrocer's Daughter, The 1966,Mr 16,50:1
Fishing for Wives 1966,Mr 16,50:1
General's Daughter, The 1966,Mr 16,50:1
Takemoto, Moiidayu (Miscellaneous)
Fishing for Wives 1966,Mr 16,50:1
General's Daughter, The 1966,Mr 16,50:1
Greengrocer's Daughter, The 1966,Mr 16,50:1
Takemoto, Oritayu (Miscellaneous)
Fishing for Wives 1966,Mr 16,50:1
General's Daughter, The 1966,Mr 16,50:1
Greengrocer's Daughter, The 1966,Mr 16,50:1

Takemoto, Tsudaiyu (Miscellaneous)
Greengrocer's Daughter, The 1966,Mr 16,50:1
General's Daughter, The 1966,Mr 16,50:1
Fishing for Wives 1966,Mr 16,50:1
Taketas
Vaudeville (Hippodrome) 1926,Mr 23,24:3
Takeuchi, Henry
Family, The 1943,Mr 31,22:4
Takezawa, Danroku (Miscellaneous)
Greengrocer's Daughter, The 1966,Mr 16,50:1
Fishing for Wives 1966,Mr 16,50:1
General's Daughter, The 1966,Mr 16,50:1
Takezawa, Tsudzawa (Miscellaneous)
Fishing for Wives 1966,Mr 16,50:1
Greengrocer's Daughter, The 1966,Mr 16,50:1
General's Daughter, The 1966,Mr 16,50:1
Tal, Ada
Each Had Six Wings 1964,Mr 12,39:1
Talankina, Lilya (Choreographer)
West Side Story 1965,Je 25,37:2
Talas, Mary
Seven Mirrors 1945,O 26,17:2
Talbert, Wen (Musical Director)
Bassa Moona 1936,D 9,35:4
Talbert, Wen and His Choir
Singin' the Blues 1931,S 17,21:3
Talbot, Ada May
Right of Happiness 1931,Ap 3,34:2
Talbot, Dorothy
Once in a Lifetime 1930,S 25,22:3
Talbot, Earl
O Evening Star 1936,Ja 9,24:6
Talbot, Edward
Fall and Rise of Susan Lenox, The 1920,Je 11,11:2
Talbot, F Story (Director)
Sometime Jam Today 1967,F 13,41:1
Talbot, F Story (Playwright)
Sometime Jam Today 1967,F 13,41:1
Talbot, Harris
Mr Jiggins of Jigginstown 1936,D 18,30:2
Talbot, Hayden (Playwright)
It Is the Law 1922,N 30,28:2
Murder on Account 1936,My 25,23:1
Murder on Account 1936,S 26,11:2
Talbot, John
Piper, The 1920,Mr 20,14:2
Talbot, Juliet
Journey to Jerusalem 1940,O 7,21:2
Talbot, Lilian
Fresh Fields 1936,F 11,19:2
Talbot, Lyle
Seperate Rooms 1940,Mr 25,10:3
South Pacific 1967,Je 13,56:1
Talbot, Mary
Jackson White 1935,Ap 22,14:6
Talbot, Nelly
Idiot, The 1960,S 26,38:1
Talbot, Nita
Never Say Never 1951,N 21,21:2
Fifth Season, The 1953,Ja 24,13:2
Uncle Willie 1956,D 21,17:1
Zelda 1969,Mr 6,38:1
Talbot, Paul
Steps Leading Up 1941,Ap 19,20:6
Talbot, Sharon
Don't Drink the Water 1966,N 18,37:1
Talbot, Story
Tragicomedy of Don Cristobita and Dona Rosita,
The 1958,My 30,12:2
Talbot, Story (Director)
Tragicomedy of Don Cristobita and Dona Rosita,
The 1958,My 30,12:2
Talbot, Winifred
Bitter Sweet 1929,N 6,30:2
Talbot-Martin, Elizabeth
Meet the People 1940,O 20,IX,3:3
Meet the People 1940,D 26,22:2
Meet the People 1941,Ja 12,IX,1:1
Talcott, Michael
Winterset 1966,F 10,32:2
Seven Days of Mourning 1969,D 17,64:1
Talens, Gwenda
Seven Mirrors 1945,O 26,17:2
Shake Hands With the Devil 1949,O 21,30:4
Taliafero, William
Lulu Belle 1926,F 10,20:1
Taliaferro, Clay
Beclch 1968,D 17,59:1
Taliaferro, Edith
Kissing Time 1920,O 12,18:2
Fashions of 1924 1923,Jl 19,18:2
Love Scandal, A 1923,N 7,14:1
Hook-Up, The 1935,My 9,24:6
Taliaferro, John
Girl in Pink Tights, The 1954,Mr 6,13:2
All in One; Trouble in Tahiti 1955,Ap 20,40:3
Foxy 1964,F 17,26:1
Ben Franklin in Paris 1964,O 28,52:1
Flora, the Red Menace 1965,My 12,41:2
Mame 1966,My 25,41:1
Dear World 1969,F 7,33:1
Taliaferro, Julian
Mr Jiggins of Jigginstown 1936,D 18,30:2

Processional 1937,O 14,23:1
Big Blow 1938,O 3,11:2
Taliaferro, Mabel
Piper, The 1920,Mr 20,14:2
Alice in Wonderland 1920,Ap 13,12:1
Back Fire 1932,Je 14,26:3
Ann Adams, Spinster 1933,Mr 27,12:4
Man Who Came to Dinner, The 1940,F 10,19:5
Man Who Came to Dinner, The 1940,F 18,IX,3:6
George Washington Slept Here 1940,O 19,20:3
Victory Belles 1943,O 27,26:3
Bloomer Girl 1944,O 6,18:5
Bloomer Girl 1947,Ja 7,33:2
Springtime Folly 1951,F 27,23:4
Talkov, Lew
Love Is No Heaven 1943,Mr 16,15:3
Talley
Yankee Point 1942,N 24,28:2
Talley, Norman
Midsummer Night's Dream, A 1959,Jl 29,34:1
Tallichet, Margaret
Virginian, The 1937,Ag 10,22:7
Every Man for Himself 1940,D 10,32:3
Tallman, Buell Jr
Man Who Married a Dumb Wife, The
1930,My 9,20:5
Tallman, Joseph
Going to America 1961,O 30,33:7
Tallmon, Ward
Between the Devil 1937,D 23,24:5
Lady in the Dark 1941,Ja 24,14:2
Lady in the Dark 1941,S 3,26:6
Tallon, Ninon (Producer)
Do You Know the Milky Way? 1961,O 17,45:1
Tally, Paul (Costume Designer)
York Nativity Play, The 1956,D 5,49:2
Talma, Zolya
Checkerboard, The 1920,Ag 20,7:2
Near Santa Barbara 1921,F 1,14:1
Morning After, The 1925,Jl 28,24:2
Stronger Than Love 1925,D 29,20:2
Mama Loves Papa 1926,F 23,26:2
Kept 1926,S 18,13:3
Where's Your Husband? 1927,Ja 15,10:3
Lally 1927,F 9,16:3
Great Necker, The 1928,Mr 7,28:2
Zeppelin 1929,Ja 15,22:3
Evensong 1933,F 1,13:4
Prisoners of War 1935,Ja 29,24:1
World We Make, The 1939,N 21,19:1
Romantic Mr Dickens 1940,D 3,33:2
For Keeps 1944,Je 15,17:5
Sadie Thompson 1944,N 17,25:2
Bravo! 1948,N 12,31:2
Diamond Lil 1951,S 15,8:2
Foenix in Choir 1958,O 28,40:2
Top Secret 1960,S 6,40:1
Talmadge, Irving DeW (Miscellaneous)
Path of Flowers, The 1936,S 18,19:3
Talmadge, Ray
Tip-Top 1920,O 6,13:2
Talman, William
Beverly Hills 1940,N 8,24:2
Spring Again 1941,N 11,28:2
Young Man's Fancy, A 1947,Ap 30,33:2
Talmud, Blanche
Critic, The 1925,My 9,12:4
Dybbuk, The 1925,D 16,22:2
Burmese Pwe, A 1926,Mr 17,28:1
Lion Tamer, The 1926,O 8,26:1
Grand Street Follies, The 1927,My 20,22:3
White Peacock, The 1929,Ap 27,16:4
Neighborhood Playhouse Program 1930,F 21,23:1
Talon, Jack
Shylock and His Daughter 1947,S 30,22:2
Talus, Pamela
Exchange 1970,F 9,47:2
Talva, Galina
Crime and Punishment 1947,D 23,29:3
Call Me Madam 1950,O 13,25:1
Tamamoto, T
Near Santa Barbara 1921,F 1,14:1
Gold 1921,Je 2,14:2
Thin Ice 1922,O 2,20:1
Crooked Square, The 1923,S 11,10:2
Tamanosuke, Kagaya
Kagotsurube; Courtesan, The 1960,Je 3,26:1
Tamantini, Franca
Rugantino 1964,F 7,34:1
Tamara
Cochran's 1930 Revue 1930,Ap 13,X,1:6
Vaudeville (Palace) 1930,D 22,16:5
Free for All 1931,S 9,25:1
They All Come to Moscow 1933,My 12,20:6
Roberta 1933,N 20,18:4
Tide Rising 1937,Ja 26,17:2
Roberta 1937,Je 27,II,6:1
Right This Way 1938,Ja 6,22:3
Leave It to Me! 1938,O 23,IX,3:5
Leave It to Me! 1938,N 10,32:2
Leave It to Me! 1938,N 20,IX,1:1
Leave It to Me! 1939,S 10,IX,1:1

Tamara, Florenz
Lollipop 1924,Ja 22,15:3
Tamari, Shimon (Composer)
Ping-Pong 1959,Ap 17,22:1
Tamaroff, Marsha
Zorba 1968,N 18,58:1
Tamas, Jack
Thieves' Carnival 1955,F 2,21:1
Tamayo, Jose (Director)
Knight From Olmedo, The 1962,N 26,36:2
Tamber, Selma (Miscellaneous)
See the Jaguar 1952,D 4,46:2
Square Root of Wonderful, The 1957,O 31,40:1
Tenth Man, The 1959,N 6,24:2
Loss of Roses, A 1959,N 30,27:1
Perfect Setup, The 1962,O 25,47:1
Tamber, Selma (Producer)
Viva Madison Avenue 1960,Ap 7,42:1
Decameron, The 1961,Ap 13,32:1
Possibilities 1968,D 5,60:1
Tamer, Christopher (Miscellaneous)
Othello 1970,S 15,51:1
Tamiris, Helen
Trojan Incident 1938,Ap 22,15:2
It's About Time 1942,Mr 31,28:3
It's Up to You 1943,Ap 1,19:1
Tamiris, Helen (Choreographer)
Fiesta 1929,S 18,35:1
Gold Eagle Guy 1934,N 29,33:4
Trojan Incident 1938,My 1,X,8:3
It's About Time 1942,Mr 31,28:3
Up in Central Park 1945,Ja 29,17:2
Show Boat 1946,Ja 7,17:2
Show Boat 1946,Ja 13,II,1:1
Annie Get Your Gun 1946,My 17,14:2
Annie Get Your Gun 1946,My 26,II,1:1
Park Avenue 1946,N 5,31:2
Up in Central Park 1947,My 20,29:2
Promised Valley 1947,Jl 23,18:3
Inside U S A 1948,My 1,19:2
Inside U S A 1948,My 23,II,1:1
Inside U S A 1948,Je 13,II,6:6
Inside U S A 1948,Ag 29,II,1:1
Show Boat 1948,S 9,33:2
Touch and Go 1949,O 14,34:2
Touch and Go 1949,O 30,II,1:1
Great to Be Alive! 1950,Mr 24,28:2
Bless You All 1950,D 15,42:2
Flahooley 1951,My 15,39:1
Flahooley 1951,My 20,II,1:1
By the Beautiful Sea 1954,Ap 9,20:1
By the Beautiful Sea 1954,Ap 18,II,1:1
Fanny 1954,N 5,16:1
Fanny 1954,N 21,II,1:1
Plain and Fancy 1955,Ja 28,14:2
Plain and Fancy 1955,F 6,II,6:6
Annie Get Your Gun 1958,F 20,29:2
Tamiris, Helen (Director)
Trojan Incident 1938,Ap 22,15:2
Trojan Incident 1938,My 1,X,8:3
Great Campaign, The 1947,Ap 1,33:2
Tamiris, Helen (Miscellaneous)
Park Avenue 1946,N 5,31:2
Carnival in Flanders 1953,S 9,38:2
Tamiris and Margarita
Music Box Revue 1924,D 2,23:3
Tamiroff, Akim
Tsar Fyodor Ivanovitch 1923,Ja 9,26:1
Brothers Karamazov, The 1923,N 20,23:4
Mistress of the Inn, The; Locandiera, La
1923,N 22,16:1
In the Claws of Life 1923,N 30,23:4
Enough Stupidity in Every Wise Man
1923,D 6,23:1
Death of Pazukhin, The 1924,F 12,20:1
Life Line, The 1930,D 29,19:3
Now I Lay Me Down to Sleep 1949,Jl 23,7:3
Rashomon 1959,Ja 28,36:2
Rashomon 1959,F 8,II,1:1
Tamiya, Jun
Scarlett 1970,Ja 3,19:1
Tammamoto, T
Man's Name, The 1921,N 16,22:1
Tammi, Tom V V
Patriot for Me, A 1969,O 6,58:1
Tammy, Jack
Awake and Sing! 1938,D 23,16:6
Tampio, Vince
Valmouth 1960,O 7,29:1
Tana, Cayetano Luca de (Playwright)
Gone With the Wind 1941,O 21,28:3
Tancock, Blanch
Trumpet Shall Sound, The 1926,D 11,15:2
Granite 1927,F 12,13:1
Much Ado About Nothing 1927,N 19,14:6
Tandberg, Rolfe
It's an Ill Wind 1957,Ap 24,28:1
Tandet, Joseph (Miscellaneous)
Blood Wedding 1958,Ap 1,35:1
Tandou, Jean-Roger
Andromaque 1964,F 29,13:2
Tandy, Jessica
Matriarch, The 1930,Mr 19,24:5

Tandy, Jessica—Cont

Last Enemy, The 1930,O 31,21:1
Maedchen in Uniform 1932,N 6,IX,1:3
Hamlet 1934,N 15,25:1
Hamlet 1934,D 2,X,3:6
Anthony and Anna 1935,D 8,X,5:1
Time and the Conways 1938,Ja 4,19:2
Glorious Morning 1938,Je 12,X,2:4
White Steed, The 1939,Ja 11,16:2
Geneva 1940,Ja 31,15:2
King Lear 1940,Ap 28,IX,1:7
Jupiter Laughs 1940,S 10,27:1
Anne of England 1941,O 8,26:2
Yesterday's Magic 1942,Ap 15,27:2
Streetcar Named Desire, A 1947,D 4,42:2
Streetcar Named Desire, A 1947,D 14,II,3:1
Streetcar Named Desire, A 1949,Je 12,II,1:1
Now I Lay Me Down to Sleep 1949,Jl 23,7:3
Fourposter, The 1951,O 25,34:2
Fourposter, The 1951,N 25,II,1:1
Madam Will You Walk 1953,D 2,2:4
Madam Will You Walk 1953,D 20,II,3:1
Fourposter, The 1955,Ja 6,23:3
Honeys, The 1955,Ap 29,26:1
Day by the Sea, A 1955,S 27,42:1
Day by the Sea, A 1955,O 2,II,1:1
Man in the Dog Suit, The 1958,O 31,34:2
Bedtime Story 1959,Ap 16,28:1
Portrait of a Madonna 1959,Ap 16,28:1
Pound on Demand, A 1959,Ap 16,28:1
Portrait of a Madonna 1959,Ap 26,II,1:1
Triple Play 1959,Ap 26,II,1:1
Five Finger Exercise 1959,D 3,45:4
Five Finger Exercise 1959,D 13,II,3:1
Macbeth 1961,Je 19,31:1
Macbeth 1961,Je 25,II,1:1
Troilus and Cressida 1961,Jl 24,15:1
Hamlet 1963,My 9,41:1
Hamlet 1963,My 19,II,1:1
Three Sisters, The 1963,Je 20,30:7
Death of a Salesman 1963,Jl 20,11:2
Three Sisters, The 1963,Jl 22,19:2
Physicists, The 1964,O 14,52:1
Physicists, The 1964,O 25,II,1:1
Way of the World, The 1965,Je 2,40:1
Cherry Orchard, The 1965,Ag 2,17:2
Delicate Balance, A 1966,S 23,44:1
Delicate Balance, A 1966,O 2,II,1:1
Heartbreak House 1968,Jl 6,9:1
Camino Real 1970,Ja 9,42:1
Camino Real 1970,Ja 18,II,1:1

Tandy, Victor

Loyalties 1922,S 28,18:1
Hassan 1924,S 23,23:1
Peter Pan 1924,N 7,16:2

Tanguay, Eva

Vaudeville (Palace) 1924,Ja 15,17:3
Vaudeville (Palace) 1926,Ap 27,22:3

Tania, Sholom

Untitled-Revue 1935,N 11,21:2

Tanin, Sholom

Dybbuk, The 1924,Ja 29,17:7

Tanina, Mlle

Revue Russe, The 1922,O 6,28:1

Tankersley, Robert

Barrier, The 1950,N 3,32:2

Tannebring, Tracy

In 3 Zones 1970,N 3,28:1

Tannehill, Frances

Purity 1930,D 26,18:2
Roof, The 1931,O 31,22:4
Inside Story, The 1932,F 23,23:2
Lingering Past, The 1932,Je 30,26:5
Field of Ermine 1935,F 9,10:4
Anne of England 1941,O 8,26:2
Heart of a City 1942,F 13,24:6
Counsellor-at-Law 1942,N 25,17:2
Murder Without Crime 1943,Ag 19,24:6
Right Next to Broadway 1944,F 22,26:2
Good Morning, Corporal 1944,Ag 9,13:7
First Mrs Fraser, The 1947,N 6,36:2
Not for Children 1951,F 14,35:2

Tannehill, Myrtle

Bonehead, The 1920,Ap 13,12:1
Broken Wing, The 1920,N 30,14:1
Dream Maker, The 1921,N 22,17:1
Dodsworth 1934,F 26,20:4
Philadelphia Story, The 1939,Mr 29,21:1
Pygmalion 1945,D 27,16:1

Tannen, Julius

Her Family Tree 1920,D 28,9:2
Round the Town 1924,My 22,14:3
Earl Carroll's Vanities 1925,Jl 7,24:1
Earl Carroll's Vanities 1925,D 29,20:3
Earl Carroll's Vanities 1926,Ag 25,19:4
Earl Carroll's Vanities 1927,Ja 5,18:1
Vanities 1927,F 22,19:1
New Americana 1928,N 30,32:4
Vaudeville (Palace) 1929,Jl 8,17:6
Vaudeville (Palace) 1929,O 21,31:2

Tannen, Julius (Playwright)

Her Family Tree 1920,D 28,9:2
Earl Carroll's Vanities 1925,Jl 7,24:1

Tannen, William

Garrick Gaieties 1930,Je 5,29:2
School for Scandal, The 1931,N 11,26:4
Keeping Expenses Down 1932,O 21,25:2
Lucrece 1932,D 21,22:2
Evensong 1933,F 1,13:4
Return of Hannibal, The 1937,F 2,21:1

Tannenbaum, Ida

Beau Brummell 1924,Ap 4,19:2

Tannenbaum, Max

Hershel, The Jester 1948,D 14,39:2

Tannenbaum, Murray

Roar of the Greasepaint-the Smell of the Crowd 1965,My 17,46:2

Tanner, Betty

Hold On to Your Hats 1940,S 12,30:3

Tanner, Christopher

Enemy of the People, An 1958,F 26,24:2

Tanner, Christopher (Choreographer)

Coriolanus 1965,Jl 15,23:1

Tanner, Christopher (Director)

Coriolanus 1965,Je 21,36:1
Julius Caesar 1966,Je 24,29:2

Tanner, Christopher (Miscellaneous)

Richard III 1964,Je 12,44:2
Hamlet 1964,Jl 4,9:1
Romeo and Juliet 1965,Je 21,36:3
King Lear 1965,Je 25,39:1
Hamlet 1969,Je 30,33:1

Tanner, Gordon

Wooden Dish, The 1955,O 7,20:1

Tanner, Jean

Showboat Revue 1935,Ag 18,13:2

Tanner, Kenneth

From Morn Till Midnight 1948,D 7,41:6
Great Magician, The 1951,N 22,45:1

Tanner, Marion

Tobacco Road 1960,My 11,44:2

Tanner, Martha

Hold On to Your Hats 1940,S 12,30:3

Tanner, Mickey

Hold On to Your Hats 1940,S 12,30:3

Tanner, Mister

Everybody Loves Opal 1961,O 12,40:2

Tanner, Tony

Little Boxes; Coffee Lace, The 1969,D 4,71:2
Little Boxes; Trevor 1969,D 4,71:2
Little Boxes 1970,F 15,II,1:1

Tanner, Tony (Director)

I Only Want an Answer 1968,F 6,36:1
Happy Hypocrite, The 1968,S 6,38:1

Tanner, Tony (Miscellaneous)

Happy Hypocrite, The 1968,S 6,38:1

Tanner, Vernon

Jubilee 1935,O 14,20:1
Hamlet 1936,N 11,54:2

Tanner, W P (Producer)

Penny Arcade 1930,Mr 11,24:5
Royal Virgin, The 1930,Mr 18,30:5

Tanno, Guy

Shakespeare's Merchant 1939 1939,Ja 10,16:3
Ghost for Sale 1941,S 30,27:4
Uniform of Flesh 1949,Ja 31,15:2

Tanno, Louis

Silent House, The 1932,N 9,28:3
Red Cat, The 1934,S 20,21:1
If a Body 1935,My 1,25:3
This Thing Called Love 1935,Jl 2,24:4
Triumph 1935,O 15,18:5

Tanno, Rita

Pal Joey 1952,Ja 4,17:6
I Feel Wonderful 1954,O 19,22:5
Almost Crazy 1955,Je 21,37:1

Tanny, Arno

Happy Valley, Limited 1936,Je 30,15:1
'Tis of Thee 1940,O 28,21:3

Tansley, Derek

Mr Pickwick 1952,S 18,36:3

Tanswell, Bertram

Bachelor Born 1938,Ja 26,26:3
As You Like It 1939,My 9,28:4
As You Like It; Midsummer Night's Dream, A; Comedy of Errors, The; Taming of the Shrew, The 1939,My 9,28:4
Jeannie 1940,N 13,29:2
Heart of a City 1942,F 13,24:6
I Killed the Count 1942,S 4,18:1
Harlequinade 1949,O 13,32:2
Billy Budd 1951,F 12,18:3

Tanya, Sonia

Priorities of 1942 1942,Mr 13,23:2

Tanya (Little)

Hello Solly! 1967,Ap 6,44:3

Tanzi, Ricki

Let's Face It 1941,O 30,26:2

Tanzillo, Janice

Enchanted, The 1958,Ap 23,41:1

Tanzy, Jan

In the Summer House 1964,Mr 26,43:1

Tanzy, Jeanne

Once for the Asking 1963,N 21,42:2
Anyone Can Whistle 1964,Ap 6,36:1
Bajour 1964,N 24,42:1

Tanzy, Jeanne—Cont

Annie Get Your Gun 1966,Je 1,42:2

Taormina, Fran

Hungerers, The 1955,D 22,19:1
Floydada to Matador 1955,D 22,19:1

Taormina, Salvatore

Rose Tattoo, The 1951,F 5,19:2

Tapia, Blanca

Amor 1937,Ap 22,18:6
Todo un Hombre 1937,Ap 28,19:2
Cuando Los Hijos De Eva No Son Los Hijos De Adan 1937,My 1,17:4
Tierra Baja 1937,My 8,22:4
Sirena Varada, La 1937,O 23,15:3

Tapley, Rose

Satellite 1935,N 21,27:5

Taplin, Frank E (Composer)

What a Relief 1935,D 14,10:6
Take It Away 1936,D 15,30:5

Taplin, Frank E (Lyricist)

What a Relief 1935,D 14,10:6
Take It Away 1936,D 15,30:5

Taplin, Frank E (Musical Director)

What a Relief 1935,D 14,10:6
Take It Away 1936,D 22,32:3

Taplin, Terence

Chips With Everything 1963,O 2,49:1

Tappan, Barbara Bruce

So's Your Old Antique 1930,My 8,32:5

Tappen, Frederick

Winter Soldiers 1942,N 30,19:2

Tapps, Georgie

Americana 1932,S 25,IX,1:6
Americana 1932,O 6,19:3
I'd Rather Be Right 1937,N 3,28:2
My Dear Public 1943,S 10,28:1
Duchess Misbehaves, The 1946,F 14,32:2
Hilarities 1948,S 10,20:2

Tapps, Georgie (Choreographer)

Duchess Misbehaves, The 1946,F 14,32:2
Hilarities 1948,S 10,20:2

Taradash, Daniel (Playwright)

Red Gloves 1948,D 6,28:2
There Was a Little Girl 1960,Mr 1,28:1

Taran, Alexandra

Three Sisters, The 1939,O 16,23:1
Tinker's Dam 1943,Ja 29,22:2

Taras, John

As You Like It 1936,Ap 24,18:4
Kiss for Cinderella, A 1942,Mr 11,22:2

Tarasova, Alla

Cherry Orchard, The 1923,Ja 23,18:1
Brothers Karamazov, The 1923,N 20,23:4
Ivanoff 1923,N 27,23:2
In the Claws of Life 1923,N 30,23:4
Uncle Vanya 1924,Ja 29,16:2
Brothers Karamazov, The 1924,My 6,25:2
Miracle, The 1924,My 22,14:3
Cherry Orchard, The 1964,Je 18,29:5
Cherry Orchard, The 1965,F 10,46:1
Kremlin Chimes 1965,F 25,23:1

Tarasova, Nina

Sunday Nights at Nine 1933,N 13,20:7
Sunday Nights at Nine 1934,N 19,12:1
Ugly Runts, The 1935,Je 11,24:4

Tarassova

Chauve-Souris 1929,Ja 23,20:2

Taravella, Jimmy

Kiss Me, Kate 1954,Mr 27,13:2

Tarbell, Albert

Orphee 1935,Mr 23,10:3
Empress of Destiny 1938,Mr 10,16:2

Tarbell, Albert (Director)

Yes, My Darling Daughter 1938,Je 14,17:1

Tarbell, Albert (Miscellaneous)

Importance of Being Earnest, The 1939,Ja 13,16:2

Tarbox, Russell (Composer)

So This Is Paris 1930,Ap 27,IX,2:3
Hello Paris 1930,N 17,29:3

Tarbuck, Barbara

Silence 1970,Ap 3,43:1

Tarbutton, James

Paint Your Wagon 1951,N 13,32:2
Paint Your Wagon 1951,N 18,II,1:1
Buttrio Square 1952,O 15,40:2

Tarby, Martin

Hobo 1931,F 12,24:4
Hot Money 1931,N 9,22:2
Audition of the Apprentice Theatre 1939,Je 2,26:2
Lamp at Midnight 1947,D 22,29:2
Respectful Prostitute, The 1948,F 10,27:2
Sun and I, The 1949,Mr 21,18:4
Pink Elephant, The 1953,Ap 23,37:2

Tarcai, Mary

Panic 1935,Mr 16,18:4
Sunup to Sundown 1938,F 2,14:3

Tardell, David Archer

Reunion of Sorts 1969,O 15,40:1

Tardieu, Jean (Playwright)

Information Bureau, The 1962,Ja 31,21:1
Lovers in the Metro, The 1962,Ja 31,21:1
Keyhole, The 1962,Ja 31,21:1

Tarkhanoff, Mikhail

Brothers Karamazov, The 1923,N 20,23:4

Tarkhanoff, Mikhail—Cont

Ivanoff 1923,N 27,23:2
Enemy of the People, An 1923,D 4,25:1
Death of Pazukhin, The 1924,F 12,20:1
Tarkington, Booth (Original Author)
Plutocrat, The 1930,F 21,23:3
Alice Adams 1946,Mr 9,9:4
Alice Adams 1947,Ag 5,26:1
Seventeen 1951,Je 22,16:6
Seventeen 1951,Jl 1,II,1:1
Tarkington, Booth (Playwright)
Poldekin 1920,S 10,12:1
Poldekin 1920,S 19,VI,1:1
Wren, The 1921,S 25,VI,1:8
Wren, The 1921,O 11,22:1
Wren, The 1921,O 16,VI,1:1
Intimate Strangers, The 1921,N 8,28:1
Rose Briar 1922,D 26,11:3
Trysting Place, The 1923,My 8,22:3
Clarence 1923,My 14,18:4
Magnolia 1923,Je 24,VII,1:4
Tweedles 1923,Ag 14,10:1
Tweedles 1923,Ag 19,VI,1:1
Magnolia 1923,Ag 28,12:3
Magnolia 1923,S 2,VI,1:1
Monsieur Beaucaire 1924,Mr 2,VIII,2:7
Seventeen 1924,Ap 12,18:2
Hello, Lola! 1926,Ja 13,30:1
Seventeen 1926,My 1,10:1
Hoosiers Abroad; Man From Home, The 1927,O 2,VIII,4:6
How's Your Health? 1929,N 27,30:3
Colonel Satan 1931,Ja 12,24:1
Colonel Satan 1931,Ja 18,I,28:6
Colonel Satan 1931,Ja 19,25:2
Colonel Satan 1931,F 8,VIII,3:3
Karabash 1939,Ag 27,IX,3:1
Alice Adams 1947,Ag 5,26:1
Tarkington, Rockne
Mandingo 1961,My 23,43:6
Tarla, Chana
In-Laws 1960,O 17,32:4
Tarle, Ann
Women at the Tomb, The 1961,Ap 25,41:1
Life Is a Dream 1962,Ja 15,22:3
Eternal Sabbath 1963,O 19,17:2
Tarle, Gertrude (Producer)
Many Mansions 1937,O 28,28:6
Tarleton, Diane
Time for the Gentle People, A 1967,My 26,50:1
Tarloff, Frank (Playwright)
They Should Have Stood in Bed 1942,F 14,18:5
Heroine, The 1963,F 21,5:5
Tarlow, Florence
Red Cross 1968,Ap 29,47:2
Man in the Glass Booth, The 1968,S 27,41:1
Promenade 1969,Je 5,56:1
Dracula Sabbat 1970,O 2,28:2
Good Woman of Setzuan, The 1970,N 6,51:1
Tarlowski, Morris
It Can't Happen Here 1936,O 28,30:1
Second Marriage 1953,O 12,30:1
Wish Me Luck! 1954,N 1,37:2
Wedding March, The 1955,O 17,33:1
Nice People 1958,O 20,36:1
Tarlowski, Morris (Miscellaneous)
Wedding March, The 1955,O 17,33:1
It's a Funny World 1956,O 22,24:1
It Could Happen to You 1957,O 28,30:5
Nice People 1958,O 20,36:1
Tarnay, Erno (Producer)
Dorottya 1929,F 3,VIII,2:1
Tarnoff, Anne
Fast Life 1928,S 27,35:2
Taros, George (Miscellaneous)
Have I Got One for You 1968,Ja 8,32:1
Just for Love 1968,O 18,40:1
Taros, George (Musical Director)
Harold Arlen Songbook, The 1967,Mr 1,48:1
Just for Love 1968,O 18,40:1
Hair 1970,Ja 13,39:1
Tarpey, Tom
Milk Train Doesn't Stop Here Anymore, The 1965,Jl 27,25:1
Glorious Ruler, The 1969,Jl 1,31:1
Crimes of Passion; Erpingham Camp, The 1969,O 27,54:1
All's Well That Ends Well 1970,Je 16,53:1
Devil's Disciple, The 1970,Je 30,48:1
Tarpoff, Arsen
Chauve-Souris of 1943 1943,Ag 13,13:2
Tarr, William (Producer)
Decameron, The 1961,Ap 13,32:1
Tarr, Yvonne (Lyricist)
Decameron, The 1961,Ap 13,32:1
Tarr, Yvonne (Playwright)
Decameron, The 1961,Ap 13,32:1
Tarrach, Walter
Don Carlos 1964,N 25,40:1
Tarranova, Dino
Rose Tattoo, The 1966,O 21,36:2
Tarrant, Larry (Director)
United States vs Julius and Ethel Rosenberg, The 1969,Ap 20,II,3:1

United States vs Julius and Ethel Rosenberg, The 1969,Ap 27,92:1
Tarride, Abel
Facon de Se Donner, La 1925,D 27,VII,2:1
Tarry, Mary
Nancy Ann 1924,Ap 1,18:1
Tarshis, Anne
Puppets of Passion 1927,F 25,24:4
Tarso, Ignacio Lopez
Macbeth 1966,Ag 29,23:4
Tartaglia, Alex
He Who Gets Slapped 1956,F 2,18:1
Tartaglia, Felix
Five Little Peppers, The 1952,My 19,13:1
Tartar, Mara
Peace on Earth 1933,N 30,39:2
Tartel, Michael
Billy 1969,Mr 24,56:1
Tarter, Shirley
Winter's Tale, The 1963,Je 29,13:1
Tartt, Peter
Tableaux 1961,D 18,41:3
Tarver, Ben (Director)
Cicero 1961,F 9,37:2
Go Show Me a Dragon 1961,O 28,18:1
David Show, The 1968,N 1,34:2
Tarver, Ben (Lyricist)
Man With a Load of Mischief, The 1966,N 7,65:1
Tarver, Ben (Miscellaneous)
Stage Affair, A 1962,Ja 17,30:2
Witches' Sabbath 1962,Ap 20,22:2
Tarver, Ben (Playwright)
Man With a Load of Mischief, The 1966,N 7,65:1
Tarver, Ben (Producer)
Cicero 1961,F 9,37:2
Vida es Sueno, La 1964,Mr 18,49:1
Life Is a Dream 1964,Mr 20,24:1
Tarver, Charlene (Miscellaneous)
Witches' Sabbath 1962,Ap 20,22:2
Tarvey, Edward
Man in Possession, The 1939,S 26,21:4
Tarvin, Harry F (Playwright)
Goodwill Ambassador 1959,Mr 3,39:2
Tarzan
Cinderella on Broadway 1920,Je 25,18:1
Tas, Marjorie
Gloriana 1938,N 26,18:4
Russian Bank 1940,My 25,20:2
Tasco, Rai
Big Knife, The 1959,N 13,25:1
Goose, The 1960,Mr 16,44:1
Cage, The 1961,Mr 6,30:1
Tashamira
Second Little Show, The 1930,S 3,36:1
Iron Flowers 1933,Je 18,VIII,5:2
Tashamira (Choreographer)
Iron Flowers 1933,Je 13,22:2
Iron Flowers 1933,Je 18,VIII,5:2
Tashman, Lilyan
Bachelor's Night, A 1921,O 18,20:1
Lady Bug 1922,Ap 18,15:3
I Will IF You Will 1922,Ag 30,10:4
Barnum Was Right 1923,Mr 13,19:3
Garden of Weeds 1924,Ap 29,12:3
Tashman, Richard
Shoemaker's Prodigious Wife, The 1949,Je 15,38:2
Task, Maggie
Anya 1965,N 30,48:1
Coco 1969,D 19,66:1
Look to the Lilies 1970,Mr 30,59:1
Tasker, Fred
Sherlock Holmes 1929,N 26,28:3
Tass, Marilyn
Babes Don't Cry Anymore 1968,F 21,55:1
Tassle
Ladies of the Corridor, The 1953,O 22,33:5
Tassone, Ron
Brigadoon 1964,D 24,9:1
Billy 1969,Mr 24,56:1
Tassoni, Beverly
Guys and Dolls 1950,N 25,11:2
Taswell, Mildred
Harriet 1943,Mr 4,24:2
Harriet 1944,S 28,26:1
Tatasciore, Alfred (Producer)
Big Knife, The 1959,N 13,25:1
Tate, Carroll
Brown Buddies 1930,O 8,29:1
Tate, Charles
Adventures of Marco Polo, The 1941,D 28,I,31:7
Show Boat 1946,Ja 7,17:2
Allegro 1947,O 11,10:2
Tate, Charles (Director)
Great Scot! 1965,N 12,56:3
Tate, Dennis
Black Monday 1962,Mr 7,29:1
Along Came a Spider 1963,My 28,33:1
Bohikee Creek 1966,Ap 29,39:1
Strong Breed, The 1967,N 10,60:1
Goa 1968,F 23,46:1
Bungler, The 1968,Ag 2,24:1
Blancs, Les 1970,N 16,48:4

Tate, John
Caukey 1944,F 18,15:4
Tobacco Road 1950,Mr 7,23:2
Faith of Our Fathers 1950,Ag 6,72:2
Tate, Neal (Composer)
Sambo 1969,D 22,42:1
Five on the Black Hand Side 1970,Ja 11,II,1:1
Sambo 1970,Jl 23,24:1
Tate, Neal (Musical Director)
Sambo 1969,D 22,42:1
Tate, Reginald
House of Borgia, The 1935,S 10,26:1
House of Borgia, The 1935,O 6,XI,3:1
Saint Joan 1936,Jl 26,II,1:3
Jane Eyre 1936,O 14,31:3
Jane Eyre 1936,N 8,X,3:4
Bridge of Sighs 1939,Jl 2,IX,1:4
Tatsunosuke
Chushingura; Treasury of Loyal Retainers, The 1969,S 11,53:1
Kumagai Jinya 1969,S 18,64:1
Momiji-Gari 1969,S 18,64:1
Tatterman Marionettes
Pan Pipes and Donkeys' Ears 1929,D 27,26:5
Stringing Broadway 1932,Mr 7,13:2
Tatterman Troupe
Peer Gynt 1937,Mr 14,II,7:8
Tattermuschova, Helena
Laterna Magika 1964,Ag 4,21:1
Tattersall, Viva
Escape 1927,O 27,33:1
Tattersall, Viva (Playwright)
Ritzy 1930,F 11,30:4
Tattnall, Benny
Haiti 1938,Mr 3,16:1
Mamba's Daughters 1953,Mr 21,12:6
Tatum, Cliff
Hot Corner, The 1956,Ja 26,25:2
Tatyana
Moscow Circus on Ice 1970,D 9,63:1
Taubenslag, Elliott
Pinocchio 1968,Ap 15,41:1
Rapunzel and the Wicked Witch 1968,Ap 15,41:1
Taubenslag, Elliott (Director)
Scarlet Lullaby 1968,Mr 11,48:1
Taubenslag, Elliott (Miscellaneous)
Three by Ferlinghetti; Alligation, The 1970,S 23,43:1
Three by Ferlinghetti; Three Thousand Red Ants 1970,S 23,43:1
Three by Ferlinghetti; Victims of Amnesia, The 1970,S 23,43:1
Taubenslag, Elliott (Playwright)
Scarlet Lullaby 1968,Mr 11,48:1
Tauber, Chaim
Life Is a Dream 1962,Ja 15,22:3
My Wife With Conditions 1963,O 21,39:1
Tauber, Chaim (Director)
Life Is a Dream 1962,Ja 15,22:3
Tauber, Chaim (Lyricist)
Happy Family, A 1934,S 24,15:2
Wedding March, The 1955,O 17,33:1
Tauber, Chaim (Miscellaneous)
My Wife With Conditions 1963,O 21,39:1
Tauber, Chaim (Playwright)
Golden Ring, The 1930,F 1,14:7
Life Is a Dream 1962,Ja 15,22:3
Good Luck 1964,O 19,38:3
Tauber, Chaim (Producer)
Life Is a Dream 1962,Ja 15,22:3
Tauber, Doris (Composer)
Star and Garter 1942,Je 25,26:2
Tauber, Doris (Lyricist)
Star and Garter 1942,Je 25,26:2
Tauber, Richard
Zarewitsch, Der 1927,Ap 3,VIII,2:1
Friederike 1929,F 17,IX,2:3
Land des Laechelns, Das 1929,D 8,X,4:4
Schoen ist die Welt 1931,Ja 11,VIII,1:8
Land of Smiles 1931,My 9,15:2
Lied der Liebe, Das 1932,F 7,VIII,1:3
Giuditta 1934,Ja 21,30:1
Paganini 1937,My 21,18:6
Paganini 1937,Je 6,XI,1:2
Land of Smiles 1942,Jl 5,VIII,1:7
Yours Is My Heart 1946,S 6,16:5
Tauber, Richard (Miscellaneous)
X Has No Value 1970,F 17,35:1
Tauber, Richard (Producer)
Land of Smiles 1942,Jl 5,VIII,1:7
Taubin, Amy
Dirty Old Man, The 1964,My 5,53:1
Measure for Measure 1966,Jl 14,27:1
Rimers of Eldritch, The 1967,F 21,53:1
Prime of Miss Jean Brodie, The 1968,Ja 17,39:1
Prime of Miss Jean Brodie, The 1968,Ja 28,II,1:1
All's Well That Ends Well 1970,Je 16,53:1
All's Well That Ends Well 1970,Je 21,II,3:2
Taubin, Sonny
Incubator 1932,N 2,23:3
Taubman, Milton
On the Town 1944,D 29,11:4

Taulane, Joseph
Marching Song 1937,F 18,18:2
Wise Tomorrow 1937,O 16,22:5
Tauman, Joseph
Don't Worry Brother! 1963,O 14,35:2
Tauritz, Frank (Translator)
Six Characters in Search of an Author
1955,D 12,38:1
Tausig, Ruth
Rubicon, The 1922,F 22,13:1
Tausing, Otto (Director)
Kleinburgerhochzeit, Die 1970,N 25 25:1
Kurve, Die 1970,N 25,25:1
Taussig, F B
It's Only Natural 1922,Ap 21,13:2
Tavares, Eric
Mummers and Men 1962,Mr 27,41:6
Macbeth 1962,N 17,16:2
Butterfly Dream, The 1966,My 20,41:1
Tavel, Ronald (Playwright)
Gorilla Queen 1967,Mr 20,26:1
Gorilla Queen 1967,Mr 26,II,1:2
Gorilla Queen 1967,Ap 25,36:1
Arenas of Lutetia 1968,D 1,II,3:5
Boy on the Straight-Back Chair 1969,Mr 18,36:1
Tavenner, Teddy
Courtin' Time 1951,Je 14,30:2
Tavernia, Patrick (Miscellaneous)
Hello Out There 1955,D 22,19:1
Hungerers, The 1955,D 22,19:1
Opera Opera 1955,D 22,19:1
Floydada to Matador 1955,D 22,19:1
Tavernier, Albert
Masked Woman, The 1922,D 23,14:2
Morphia 1923,Mr 7,20:2
Queen Victoria 1923,N 16,15:1
Dust Heap, The 1924,Ap 25,20:2
White Wings 1926,O 16,15:1
Beyond the Horizon 1926,D 1,24:2
Out of the Night 1927,O 18,32:3
Age of Innocence, The 1928,N 28,24:2
Tawde, George
Don't Tell 1920,S 29,12:1
Bunch and Judy, The 1922,N 29,20:1
If Winter Comes 1923,Ap 3,26:1
Aren't We All? 1923,My 22,14:2
Main Line, The 1924,Mr 26,19:4
She Stoops to Conquer 1928,My 15,17:1
S S Glencairn 1929,Ja 10,24:5
Ladies of the Jury 1929,O 22,26:2
Rivals, The 1930,Mr 14,24:4
Anatomist, The 1932,O 25,24:3
Foolscap 1933,Ja 12,21:2
Tawde, George (Director)
Well of the Saints, The 1932,Ja 22,15:2
Taweel, Maria
Desert Song, The 1946,Ja 9,20:2
Tawney, Ria
Hang Down Your Head and Die 1964,O 19,38:1
Tawse, Jocelyn (Miscellaneous)
Luther 1963,S 26,41:1
Taxiarchis, Ph
Electra 1961,S 20,23:4
Choephori 1961,S 27,32:4
Tay, Gracia
Teahouse of the August Moon, The
1955,My 10,24:1
Tayes, Brydon
Romeo and Juliet 1933,F 3,21:5
Taygun, Alvin
Crimes and Crimes 1970,Ja 19,35:1
Taygun, Meral
Don Juan 1970,My 26,32:1
Tayl, John
Fountain, The 1925,D 11,26:1
Taylor, Albert D (Miscellaneous)
Damn Yankees 1955,My 6,17:1
Taylor, Andrew
Porgy and Bess 1935,O 11,30:2
Run, Little Chillun 1943,Ag 14,6:1
Carmen Jones 1946,Ap 8,32:2
Taylor, Ann Ellen
Passing of the Third Floor Back, The 1924,F 8,19:4
Taylor, Athene
Ladies Leave 1929,O 2,28:3
Taylor, Banfield
Happy Landing 1932,Mr 28,10:5
Taylor, Billy
Molly Darling 1922,S 2,10:2
Magnolia Lady, The 1924,N 26,17:2
China Rose 1925,Ja 20,18:1
Hello, Daddy! 1928,D 27,26:5
Great Day! 1929,O 18,24:3
Smiling Faces 1931,D 13,VIII,2:5
Americana 1932,S 25,IX,1:6
Only Girl, The 1934,My 22,28:2
Keep Moving 1934,Ag 24,10:2
Sally, Irene and Mary 1938,Jl 5,13:4
Taylor, Catherine
Congai 1928,N 28,24:3
Taylor, Charles
Coriolanus 1927,Je 18,8:3
Walk Together Chillun 1936,F 5,15:2

Turpentine 1936,Je 27,21:6
Horse Play 1937,Ag 28,8:3
How Long Till Summer 1949,D 28,30:3
Peter Pan 1950,Ap 25,27:2
Richard III 1953,D 10,65:2
Magic and the Loss, The 1954,Ap 10,10:3
Taylor, Charlotte
Sweetheart Shop, The 1920,S 1,13:4
Taylor, Christopher (Playwright)
Wings of the Dove, The 1963,D 4,53:6
Taylor, Clarence
Harlem 1929,F 21,30:3
Taylor, Clarence (Miscellaneous)
Blind Alley 1940,O 16,28:2
Taylor, Clarence (Producer)
Sea Dogs 1939,N 7,30:3
Brooklyn Biarritz 1941,F 28,16:2
Taylor, Clarice
Home Is the Hunter 1945,D 21,25:4
Rain 1948,F 2,15:2
Medal for Willie, A 1951,O 16,35:2
In Splendid Error 1954,O 27,33:6
Trouble in Mind 1955,N 5,23:2
Twisting Road, The; Housekeeper, The
1957,N 18,36:5
Twisting Road, The; One Tuesday Morning
1957,N 18,36:5
Egg and I, The 1958,S 11,43:4
Summer of the Seventeenth Doll 1968,F 21,59:1
Summer of the Seventeenth Doll 1968,Mr 3,II,3:1
Kongi's Harvest 1968,Ap 15,49:1
Daddy Goodness 1968,Je 5,37:1
God Is a (Guess What?) 1968,D 18,56:1
Contribution 1969,Ap 2,37:1
String 1969,Ap 2,37:1
Contribution 1969,Ap 13,II,1:1
Song of the Lusitanian Bogey, The 1969,My 13,41:1
Man Better Man 1969,Jl 3,22:1
Five on the Black Hand Side 1970,Ja 2,32:2
Day of Absence 1970,Mr 18,39:1
Akokawe 1970,Je 5,21:1
Taylor, Clarice (Director)
Trouble in Mind 1955,N 5,23:2
Taylor, Deems
Man About Town, A 1921,Mr 22,15:1
Spring Tonic 1936,My 11,16:1
Concert Varieties 1945,Je 2,10:7
Taylor, Deems (Composer)
What Next 1920,Ja 27,7:2
Liliom 1921,My 1,VII,1:1
Casanova 1923,S 16,VII,2:8
Beggar on Horseback 1924,F 13,17:2
Beggar on Horseback 1924,F 17,VII,1:1
Bunk of 1926 1926,F 17,12:3
Liliom 1932,O 27,23:2
Lucrece 1932,N 30,22:8
Lucrece 1932,D 4,IX,3:3
Lucrece 1932,D 21,22:2
Liliom 1940,Mr 26,17:2
Alchemist, The 1948,My 7,31:4
Fashion 1959,Ja 21,27:1
Old Tune, The 1961,Mr 24,37:1
Taylor, Deems (Miscellaneous)
Smiling Through 1932,Ja 3,VIII,3:1
Taylor, Deems (Musical Director)
Variations of 1940 1940,Ja 29,12:1
Taylor, Dianne
Carmilla 1970,D 1,61:2
Taylor, Don
Winged Victory 1943,N 22,24:1
Fragile Fox 1954,O 13,27:1
Taylor, Dorothy
Peg o' My Heart 1948,Ag 25,29:2
Taylor, Doug
Detective Story 1954,F 13,11:2
Taylor, Douglas (Director)
Oh, Pioneers 1969,N 12,41:1
Taylor, Douglas (Lighting Director)
Simple Life, A 1964,My 18,36:1
Taylor, Douglas (Playwright)
Sudden and Accidental Re-education of Horse
Johnson, The 1968,D 19,63:1
Oh, Pioneers 1969,N 12,41:1
Taylor, Dwight (Miscellaneous)
Out of This World 1955,O 13,35:2
Taylor, Dwight (Original Author)
Gay Divorce 1932,N 13,IX,1:7
Gay Divorce 1937,Jl 20,19:4
Taylor, Dwight (Playwright)
Don't Tell George 1928,Jl 22,VII,1:1
Gay Divorce 1932,N 30,23:4
Out of This World 1950,D 22,17:3
Out of This World 1955,N 10,44:2
Gay Divorce 1960,Ap 4,37:1
Taylor, Dwight (Producer)
Where Do We Go From Here? 1938,N 16,26:2
Taylor, Edward
Naughty Marietta 1929,O 22,26:2
Fortune Teller, The 1929,N 5,32:3
Show Boat 1966,Jl 20,48:1
Wonderful Town 1967,My 18,50:1
Taylor, Edwin
Hottentot, The 1920,Mr 2,9:1

Taylor, Edwin—Cont
New Sin, The 1923,My 28,18:3
Last of Mrs Cheyney, The 1925,N 10,23:5
Taylor, Elizabeth
Little Angel, The 1924,S 29,10:3
Puppets 1925,Mr 10,19:1
Masque of Venice, The 1926,Mr 3,27:3
Women Go on Forever 1927,S 8,25:1
Pansy 1929,My 15,36:3
Those We Love 1930,F 20,22:2
Up and Up, The 1930,S 9,25:2
Schoolgirl 1930,N 21,31:1
Social Register, The 1931,N 10,28:2
Here Today 1932,S 7,14:2
West Side Story 1957,S 27,14:4
Taylor, Elizabeth (Mrs Richard Burton)
Untitled-Poetry Reading 1964,Je 22,23:4
Dr Faustus 1966,F 16,49:1
Taylor, Elliott
Hotel Mouse, The 1922,Mr 14,11:3
Taylor, Ernest
Hollywood Pinafore 1945,Je 1,20:1
Taylor, Estelle
Big Fight, The 1928,Ag 31,23:1
Big Fight, The 1928,S 19,33:1
Vaudeville (Palace) 1929,D 30,16:3
Taylor, Ethel
Shipwrecked 1924,N 13,18:1
Three Doors 1925,Ap 24,16:4
Harvest 1925,S 21,16:2
Good Fellow, The 1926,O 6,22:1
Miss Gulliver Travels 1931,N 26,36:4
Sunny River 1941,D 5,28:2
Taylor, Ethel (Playwright)
Miss Gulliver Travels 1931,N 26,36:4
Taylor, Eva
Bottomland 1927,Je 28,29:3
Mr Jiggins of Jigginstown 1936,D 18,30:2
Taylor, Evelyn
Allegro 1947,O 11,10:2
Small Wonder 1948,S 16,33:5
Carousel 1957,S 12,38:2
110 in the Shade 1963,O 25,37:1
Come Summer 1969,Mr 19,43:1
Minnie's Boys 1970,Mr 27,27:1
Taylor, Forrest Jr
Shooting Star 1933,Je 13,22:2
Ragged Army 1934,F 27,16:5
Tenting Tonight 1947,Ap 3,32:2
Open House 1947,Je 4,33:4
Taylor, Frank W
Easy Come, Easy Go 1925,O 27,20:2
Donovan Affair, The 1926,Ag 31,15:2
Gala Night 1930,F 26,22:4
Grand Hotel 1930,N 14,30:4
Dodsworth 1934,F 26,20:4
Taylor, G C
Magnanimous Lover, The 1933,F 1,13:5
Jayhawker 1934,N 6,34:2
Let Freedom Ring 1935,N 7,26:2
Prelude 1936,Ap 20,17:4
Bury the Dead 1936,Ap 20,17:4
Journeyman 1938,Ja 31,14:2
Washington Jitters 1938,My 3,19:1
Taylor, G O
Anna Christie 1921,N 3,22:1
Shame Woman, The 1923,O 17,14:1
Move On 1926,Ja 19,30:1
Juno and the Paycock 1926,Mr 16,22:1
Black Boy 1926,O 7,30:2
Hot Water 1929,Ja 22,22:3
Sun-Up 1929,F 19,22:6
One Day More 1933,F 1,13:5
Taylor, George
Marilyn's Affairs 1933,Mr 16,21:5
Natural Man 1941,My 8,20:4
Taylor, George E
Too Many Heroes 1937,N 16,26:2
Taylor, George L
Now You've Done It 1937,Mr 6,10:4
Taylor, George R
Double Door 1933,S 22,15:5
Battleship Gertie 1935,Ja 19,9:2
Sketch Book 1935,Je 5,22:2
Puritan, The 1936,Ja 24,14:3
Come Angel Band 1936,F 19,17:1
Taylor, Harold
Carmen Jones 1946,Ap 8,32:2
Taylor, Helen
Hamlet 1956,O 29,34:1
Taylor, Hilda
Frankie and Johnny 1952,O 29,37:2
Taylor, Hilda (Composer)
Frankie and Johnny 1952,O 29,37:2
Taylor, Holland
Poker Session, The 1967,S 20,42:2
David Show, The 1968,N 1,34:2
Tonight in Living Color; David Show, The
1969,Je 11,43:1
Taylor, Irene
Diff'rent 1937,N 21,II,10:7
Diff'rent 1938,Ja 26,26:4
Pygmalion 1938,Ja 27,16:3
Captain Jinks of the Horse Marines 1938,Ja 28,16:2

Taylor, Irving (Composer)
Lew Leslie's Blackbirds of 1939 1939,F 13,12:2
Taylor, Irving (Lyricist)
Lew Leslie's Blackbirds of 1939 1939,F 13,12:2
Taylor, J C
Man From Earth, The 1923,Ja 3,6:2
Taylor, Jackie
Captain Jinks 1925,S 9,22:1
Taylor, James
Possessed, The 1939,O 25,26:2
Taylor, James A (Lighting Director)
Time of the Key, A 1963,S 12,33:3
Taylor, James A (Miscellaneous)
Hang Down Your Head and Die 1964,O 19,38:1
Walk Down Mah Street! 1968,Je 13,54:1
Taylor, James A (Scenic Designer)
Goose, The 1960,Mr 16,44:1
Cats' Pajamas, The 1962,Je 1,16:2
Time of the Key, A 1963,S 12,33:3
Glass Menagerie, The 1965,My 5,53:2
Summertree 1968,Mr 4,29:1
Taylor, Jane
Pins and Needles 1922,F 2,20:1
My Girl 1924,N 25,27:2
Talk About Girls 1927,Je 15,31:3
Mystery Moon 1930,Je 24,23:4
Trojan Incident 1938,Ap 22,15:2
Big Blow 1938,O 3,11:2
Taylor, Joanne
My Darlin' Aida 1952,O 28,36:4
Mademoiselle Colombe 1954,Ja 7,26:1
Taylor, John
Emperor Jones, The 1924,My 7,18:1
All God's Chillun Got Wings 1924,Ag 19,9:1
Saint, The 1924,O 13,20:3
Diff'rent 1925,F 11,19:3
Triumph of the Egg, The 1925,F 11,19:3
Romio and Julietta 1925,Ap 21,19:1
Fratricide Punished 1925,Ap 21,19:1
Fountain, The 1925,D 11,26:1
Fortuno 1925,D 23,22:1
Trigger 1927,D 7,32:1
Sing High, Sing Low 1931,N 13,26:4
Society Girl 1931,D 31,16:1
Book of Job, The 1962,F 10,13:1
Taylor, John (Miscellaneous)
Orpheus Descending 1959,O 6,45:2
Taylor, John C
Chalked Out 1937,Mr 26,24:2
Taylor, John Jr
Sweet River 1936,O 29,30:2
Taylor, Jonathan
Delightful Season, A 1960,S 29,30:1
Donogoo 1961,Ja 19,25:3
Taylor, Julie
Wonderful World of Burlesque, The
1965,Ap 29,38:1
Taylor, June (Choreographer)
Paradise Island 1961,Je 24,11:1
Paradise Island 1962,Je 28,22:1
Around the World in 80 Days 1963,Je 24,22:1
Around the World in 80 Days 1964,Je 29,33:2
Mardi Gras! 1965,Je 28,33:2
Mardi Gras! 1966,Jl 11,32:2
Taylor, June (Director)
Paradise Island 1961,Je 24,11:1
Around the World in 80 Days 1964,Je 29,33:2
Mardi Gras! 1966,Jl 11,32:2
Taylor, Kathleen
Blue Butterfly, The 1929,F 17,29:3
Taylor, Keith
Devil's Disciple, The 1950,Ja 26,23:2
Macbeth 1956,O 30,42:2
Troilus and Cressida 1956,D 27,21:1
Child Buyer, The 1962,My 14,35:1
Taylor, Key
Too Many Girls 1939,O 19,26:2
Taylor, King
Naughty-Naught '00 1946,O 21,27:5
Taylor, Lance
Freight 1949,F 4,30:2
Freight 1950,Ap 27,36:2
In Splendid Error 1954,O 27,33:6
One More River 1960,Mr 19,12:2
Taylor, Lark
Trial of Joan of Arc, The 1921,Mr 28,8:2
Bronx Express 1922,Ap 27,12:2
Imaginary Invalid, The 1922,Jl 26,26:2
Hamlet 1922,N 17,14:1
Launzi 1923,O 11,16:3
Hamlet 1923,N 27,23:6
Man in Evening Clothes, The 1924,D 6,13:4
Plutocrat, The 1930,F 21,23:3
Taylor, Laurette
One Night in Rome 1920,Ap 30,1:2
One Night in Rome 1920,My 4,14:1
Peg o' My Heart 1921,F 15,7:1
Peg o' My Heart 1921,F 20,VI,1:1
Untitled-Benefit 1921,My 2,12:3
National Anthem, The 1922,Ja 24,16:3
National Anthem, The 1922,F 5,VI,1:1
Humoresque 1923,F 28,13:2
Humoresque 1923,Mr 4,VII,1:1

Sweet Nell of Old Drury 1923,My 19,16:4
Pierrot the Prodigal; Enfant Prodigue, L'
1925,Mr 7,8:1
Trelawney of the 'Wells' 1925,Je 2,16:2
In a Garden 1925,N 17,29:1
In a Garden 1925,N 22,VIII,1:1
Vaudeville (Palace) 1926,D 28,12:3
Delicate Justice 1927,N 27,IX,2:1
Furies, The 1928,Mr 8,23:1
Furies, The 1928,Mr 18,IX,1:1
Don't Tell George 1928,Jl 22,VII,1:1
Alice Sit-By-The-Fire 1932,Mr 8,19:3
Old Lady Shows Her Medals, The 1932,Mr 8,19:3
At the Theatre 1937,Ag 4,14:1
Candida 1938,Ag 31,13:2
Outward Bound 1938,D 23,16:5
Outward Bound 1939,Ja 1,IX,1:1
Glass Menagerie, The 1945,Ja 14,II,2:4
Glass Menagerie, The 1945,Ap 2,15:5
Glass Menagerie, The 1945,Ap 8,II,1:1
Taylor, Laurette (Playwright)
At the Theatre 1937,Ag 4,14:1
Taylor, Leila (Playwright)
Voltaire 1922,Mr 21,17:1
Taylor, Lloyd
Tyrant, The 1930,N 13,33:1
Peter Ibbetson 1931,Ap 9,30:3
Taylor, Lola
Opportunity 1920,Jl 31,5:1
Taylor, Mabel
This Rock 1943,F 19,23:2
Boy Meets Girl 1943,Je 23,15:5
Outrageous Fortune 1943,N 4,28:5
Gently Does It 1953,O 29,43:4
Taylor, Marguerite
Queen's Husband, The 1928,Ja 26,17:2
Taylor, Marie
Roseanne 1923,D 31,9:5
Master of the Inn, The 1925,D 23,22:2
Round-Up, The 1932,Mr 8,19:4
Taylor, Marion
Salome 1923,My 8,22:2
Chip Woman's Fortune, The 1923,My 8,22:2
Comedy of Errors, The 1923,My 16,22:5
Taylor, Marvin C
Clarence 1923,My 14,18:4
Taylor, Mary Lou
Possessed, The 1939,O 25,26:2
Twelfth Night 1941,D 3,32:2
Moon Vine, The 1943,F 12,22:2
Great Campaign, The 1947,Ap 1,33:2
Ivy Green, The 1949,Ap 6,37:2
Taylor, Matt (Playwright)
Stop-Over 1938,Ja 12,16:5
Taylor, Maxine S (Miscellaneous)
Rendezvous at Senlis 1961,F 28,39:2
Emperor, The 1963,Ap 17,30:1
Taylor, Merlin (Producer)
Hangman's Whip 1933,F 25,20:2
Taylor, Mitch
Maggie Flynn 1968,O 24,52:1
Taylor, Myron
Eternal Road, The 1937,Ja 8,14:2
Taylor, Nell
Mime Theatre of Etienne Decroux, The
1959,D 24,15:1
Taylor, Nettie
Little Theatre Tournament; Old Lady Shows Her
Medals, The 1928,My 11,28:1
Taylor, Noel
Reunion in Vienna 1931,N 17,31:1
Cross Ruff 1935,F 20,23:3
Taylor, Noel (Costume Designer)
Alice in Wonderland 1947,Ap 7,19:2
Alice in Wonderland 1947,Ap 13,II,1:1
Twentieth Century 1950,D 25,23:6
Stalag 17 1951,My 9,41:2
Wild Duck, The 1951,D 27,17:1
Come of Age 1952,Ja 24,22:2
One Bright Day 1952,Mr 20,37:2
Male Animal, The 1952,My 1,35:1
Tovarich 1952,My 15,39:2
First Lady 1952,My 29,18:5
Bernardine 1952,O 17,33:4
Dial 'M' for Murder 1952,O 30,41:2
Grey-Eyed People, The 1952,D 18,41:2
Teahouse of the August Moon, The 1953,O 16,32:1
Ladies of the Corridor, The 1953,O 22,33:5
In the Summer House 1953,D 30,17:1
Burning Glass, The 1954,Mr 5,15:2
Teahouse of the August Moon, The 1954,S 12,II,1:1
Festival 1955,Ja 19,22:1
Teahouse of the August Moon, The
1955,My 10,24:1
No Time for Sergeants 1955,O 21,32:2
Time Limit! 1956,Ja 25,27:2
Apple Cart, The 1956,O 19,23:1
Auntie Mame 1956,N 1,47:2
Teahouse of the August Moon, The 1956,N 9,33:2
Good as Gold 1957,Mr 8,22:2
Square Root of Wonderful, The 1957,O 31,40:1
Body Beautiful, The 1958,Ja 24,15:2
Auntie Mame 1958,Ag 12,33:2

Taylor, Noel (Costume Designer)—Cont
Comes a Day 1958,N 7,22:1
Tall Story 1959,Ja 30,33:2
Wall, The 1960,O 12,44:4
Little Moon of Alban 1960,D 2,34:1
Everybody Loves Opal 1961,O 12,40:2
Shot in the Dark, A 1961,O 19,40:1
Write Me a Murder 1961,O 27,28:2
Night of the Iguana, The 1961,D 29,10:1
General Seeger 1962,Mr 1,26:2
Great Day in the Morning 1962,Mr 29,29:1
Pullman Car Hiawatha 1962,D 4,46:2
Desire Under the Elms 1963,Ja 11,5:6
Riot Act, The 1963,Mr 9,5:2
Strange Interlude 1963,Mr 13,5:2
One Flew Over the Cuckoo's Nest 1963,N 14,40:2
Marathon '33 1963,D 23,21:2
What Makes Sammy Run? 1964,F 28,19:1
Hughie 1964,D 23,21:2
Matty and the Moron and Madonna
1965,Mr 30,53:1
And Things That Go Bump in the Night
1965,Ap 27,27:5
Baal 1965,My 7,33:2
Play That on Your Old Piano 1965,O 15,49:1
White Devil, The 1965,D 7,56:1
Great Indoors, The 1966,F 2,23:1
Mutilated, The 1966,F 23,42:1
Gnadiges Fraulein, The 1966,F 23,42:1
Loves of Cass McGuire, The 1966,O 7,36:1
We Have Always Lived in the Castle
1966,O 20,53:1
Dr Cook's Garden 1967,S 26,52:1
Song of the Grasshopper 1967,S 29,52:2
Lovers; Winners 1968,Jl 26,21:4
Lovers; Losers 1968,Jl 26,21:4
We Bombed in New Haven 1968,O 17,51:1
Possibilities 1968,D 5,60:1
Mundy Scheme, The 1969,D 12,75:1
Brightower 1970,Ja 29,32:1
Taylor, Noel (Playwright)
Cross Ruff 1935,F 20,23:3
Taylor, Norma
Here Goes the Bride 1931,N 4,31:2
Taylor, Otis Chatfield (Producer)
Fledgling 1940,N 28,29:2
Taylor, Paul H
Grey Heir, The 1926,Ap 6,29:2
Taylor, Philip
Measure for Measure 1967,F 15,37:1
Hamlet 1967,F 17,44:1
Romeo and Juliet 1967,F 22,18:1
Taylor, Raymond (Composer)
Almost Crazy 1955,Je 21,37:1
Taylor, Raymond (Lyricist)
Almost Crazy 1955,Je 21,37:1
Taylor, Rebecca
Tom Paine 1969,Mr 30,71:2
Tempest, The 1970,F 15,67:1
Taylor, Reese
Lucky Sam McCarver 1950,Ap 15,10:6
Taylor, Renee
Rehearsal, The 1952,My 27,30:5
Dinny and the Witches 1959,D 10,53:3
Machinal 1960,Ap 8,27:1
Third Ear, The 1964,My 29,16:1
Agatha Sue, I Love You 1966,D 15,61:1
Willie Doesn't Live Here Anymore 1967,F 8,20:2
Lovers and Other Strangers 1968,S 19,63:1
Taylor, Renee (Playwright)
Lovers and Other Strangers 1968,S 19,63:1
Lovers and Other Strangers 1968,S 29,II,1:1
Taylor, Robert H
Hamlet 1927,Ap 7,23:3
Taylor, Robert Lewis (Original Author)
All American 1962,Mr 20,44:1
Taylor, Robert U (Scenic Designer)
We Bombed in New Haven 1967,D 7,58:1
Henry IV 1968,F 7,40:1
Bench, The 1968,Mr 5,35:2
Nest, The 1970,Ap 10,46:1
Touch 1970,N 9,52:1
Taylor, Robin
He Who Gets Slapped 1946,Mr 21,31:4
Taylor, Rosemary (Original Author)
Chicken Every Sunday 1944,Ap 6,27:2
Chicken Every Sunday 1944,Ap 16,II,1:1
Taylor, Royston
Marigold 1930,O 9,23:1
Taylor, Ruth
Taboo 1922,Ap 5,22:1
Four Twelves Are 48 1951,Ja 18,30:2
Taylor, Samuel (Director)
Beekman Place 1964,O 8,50:1
Taylor, Samuel (Miscellaneous)
First Love 1961,D 26,20:2
No Strings 1962,Mr 16,24:1
Taylor, Samuel (Playwright)
Stop-Over 1938,Ja 12,16:5
Happy Time, The 1950,Ja 25,24:1
Nina 1951,D 6,44:3
Happy Time, The 1952,F 10,II,2:1
Sabrina Fair 1953,N 12,37:1
Sabrina Fair 1953,N 22,II,1:1

Taylor, Samuel (Playwright)—Cont
Sabrina Fair 1954,Ag 5,18:1
Pleasure of His Company, The 1958,O 23,36:1
Pleasure of His Company, The 1958,N 2,II,1:1
Pleasure of His Company, The 1959,Ap 24,22:3
First Love 1961,D 26,20:2
No Strings 1962,Mr 16,24:1
No Strings 1962,Mr 25,II,1:1
Beekman Place 1964,O 8,50:1
Avanti 1968,F 1,29:1
Taylor, Samuel (Producer)
Beekman Place 1964,O 8,50:1
Taylor, Shelby
Walk-Up 1961,F 24,24:1
Intimate Relations 1962,N 2,27:1
Taylor, Shiela
Escape Me Never! 1935,Ja 22,22:2
Taylor, Simon Watson (Translator)
Empire Builders, The 1968,O 2,34:1
Taylor, Theda (Lighting Director)
Failures, The 1959,Ja 6,30:2
Lend an Ear 1959,S 25,20:5
Great Scot! 1965,N 12,56:3
Taylor, Timothy
Comedy of Errors, The 1968,F 28,40:2
She Stoops to Conquer 1968,Ap 1,58:3
Futz 1968,O 22,37:1
Taylor, Tom (Playwright)
Ticket-of-Leave Man, The 1961,D 23,15:1
Taylor, Tony
Trojan Women, The 1938,Ja 25,24:2
Taylor, Trix
Flossie 1924,Je 4,25:2
Taylor, Valerie
On Approval 1927,My 15,VIII,2:6
Berkeley Square 1929,N 5,32:4
Petticoat Influence 1930,D 16,34:6
Peter Ibbetson 1931,Ap 9,30:3
Good Companions, The 1931,O 2,31:1
Good Companions, The 1931,O 11,VIII,1:1
Red Planet 1932,D 19,19:2
Call It a Day 1935,N 24,IX,1:2
Children's Hour, The 1936,N 13,27:3
Children's Hour, The 1936,N 29,XII,2:1
Orchard Walls 1937,F 4,17:3
Orchard Walls 1937,F 21,X,2:1
Fight's On, The; Uneasy Virtue; Pardon My Back
  1937,Ag 4,14:1
Love of Women 1937,D 14,33:2
Dear Octopus 1938,O 2,IX,2:1
Gioconda Smile, The 1950,O 9,21:2
Gioconda Smile, The 1950,O 15,II,1:1
Living Room, The 1953,Ap 17,29:5
Taylor, Vaughn
Home Life of a Buffalo; Hope's the Thing
  1948,My 12,34:6
Hope Is the Thing With Feathers; Hope's the
  Thing 1948,My 12,34:6
Gone Tomorrow; Hope's the Thing
  1948,My 12,34:6
Doctor's Dilemma, The 1955,Ja 12,22:1
Taylor, W B
Uncle Tom's Cabin 1933,My 30,13:4
Taylor, Wade
Detective Story 1954,F 13,11:2
Taylor, Wallace
Riot 1968,D 20,64:1
Taylor, William S (Miscellaneous)
Firebugs, The 1963,N 22,41:1
King Lear 1963,N 23,22:1
Taylor, William T
Fly With Me 1920,Mr 25,11:4
Riff-Raff 1926,F 9,18:6
Taylor, Willie
Hot Rhythm 1930,Ag 22,18:5
Taylor, Yvonne
Kid Boots 1924,Ja 1,21:3
Taylor-Young, Leigh
3 Bags Full 1966,Mr 7,22:1
Taynton, David (Producer)
Fallout 1959,My 21,36:2
Tayor, Terry
Rivals, The 1969,O 18,37:1
Tazewell, Charles
Man and the Masses 1924,Ap 15,25:1
They Knew What They Wanted 1924,N 25,27:1
Lucky Sam McCarver 1925,O 22,22:1
Tazewell, Charles (Playwright)
Sugar Hill 1931,D 26,15:2
Tchaikowsky, Peter Ilitch (Composer)
Catherine 1923,S 30,II,1:6
Music in My Heart 1947,O 3,30:2
Lady From Paris, The 1950,S 27,36:1
Tchechik-Efrati, G
Golem, The 1927,F 5,13:2
Tchemerinsky, B
Golem, The 1927,F 5,13:2
Tcherepnine, Serge (Composer)
Burn Me to Ashes 1963,N 20,48:1
Tchereskaya, Ljuba
Help! Help! the Globolinks 1970,D 24,10:2
Tcherkarsky, M
1860: or, Aris; 1860, or an Interrupted Festival
  1931,O 22,27:1

Tcherkassky, Alexei
Chauve-Souris 1929,Ja 23,20:2
Chauve-Souris; Queen of Spades, The
  1931,O 22,27:1
Tcherkassky, Marianna
Peter and the Wolf 1969,N 30,85:5
Tcherniavsky
Chauve-Souris 1925,Ja 15,25:1
Chauve-Souris 1929,Ja 23,20:2
Tchor, Ludmilla
Julia, Jake, and Uncle Joe 1961,Ja 30,19:1
Tchoukleva, (Mme)
Chauve-Souris 1925,Ja 15,25:1
Tckero, Suezo
On the Spot 1930,O 30,33:3
Te-kwei, Wu (Director)
Peh Shuh Tchuwan; White Snake, The 1963,Ja 4,5:2
Tead, Phillips
Tavern, The 1920,S 28,14:1
Children's Tragedy, The 1921,O 12,18:2
Teagarden, Geraldine
Sunset 1966,My 13,34:1
Nighthawks 1967,D 30,14:2
Teague, Scooter
110 in the Shade 1963,O 25,37:1
Teague, Terri
Young Master Dante, The 1968,D 31,19:1
Tearle, Conway
Mad Dog, The 1921,N 9,20:1
Mid-Channel 1928,S 16,IX,1:4
Dinner at Eight 1932,O 24,18:2
Living Dangerously 1935,Ja 14,10:3
Hey Diddle Diddle 1937,Ja 22,24:2
Antony and Cleopatra 1937,O 14,23:2
Antony and Cleopatra 1937,N 11,30:2
Tearle, David
Still Waters 1926,Mr 2,23:1
Scotch Mist 1926,S 21,32:3
Tearle, David (Playwright)
Arabian Nightmare, The 1927,Ja 11,36:3
Tearle, Godfrey
Garden of Allah, The 1920,Ag 29,VI,1:1
Card Players, The 1922,Ap 27,17:4
Card Players, The 1922,My 21,VI,1:6
Fake, The 1924,Mr 23,VIII,1:3
Fake, The 1924,O 7,26:3
White Assegai, The 1930,Ja 22,21:1
Hamlet 1931,Mr 22,VIII,2:1
Faithful Heart, The 1932,Ja 17,VIII,2:6
Julius Caesar 1932,F 9,30:7
Julius Caesar 1932,F 28,VIII,2:4
Road House 1932,O 30,IX,2:3
Key, The 1933,S 7,17:5
Henry V 1934,Ja 28,II,3:4
Living Dangerously 1934,Je 8,19:3
Hyde Park Corner 1934,O 28,IX,3:4
Fugitive, The 1936,Je 28,IX,1:8
Boy David, The 1936,N 22,VI,7:1
Boy David, The 1936,D 13,XI,5:3
Boy David, The 1936,D 15,30:6
Island, The 1938,F 11,27:5
Othello 1938,F 27,X,1:4
Flashing Stream, The 1938,S 2,21:4
Flashing Stream, The 1938,S 18,X,1:4
Flashing Stream, The 1939,Ap 11,19:2
Light of Heart, The 1940,Mr 3,X,3:4
Antony and Cleopatra 1947,N 27,49:2
Antony and Cleopatra 1947,D 7,II,5:1
His House in Order 1951,Ag 12,II,1:4
Hanging Judge 1952,S 24,40:4
Hanging Judge 1952,O 12,II,3:8
Tearle, Godfrey (Producer)
Flashing Stream, The 1938,S 2,21:4
Tearle, Noel
French Leave 1920,N 9,13:1
Title, The 1921,N 15,23:3
Enchanted Cottage, The 1923,Ap 2,22:3
Enchanted Cottage, The 1923,Ap 8,VIII,1:1
Love for Love 1925,Ap 1,21:2
Through the Night 1930,Ag 19,19:1
Laura Garnett 1934,Jl 17,24:4
Any Woman 1934,Ag 28,24:4
Teasdale, Verree
Youngest, The 1924,D 23,17:1
Morning After, The 1925,Jl 28,24:2
Master of the Inn, The 1925,D 23,22:2
Buy, Buy Baby 1926,O 8,26:2
Constant Wife, The 1926,N 30,26:3
By Request 1928,S 28,30:2
Precious 1929,Ja 15,22:5
Nice Women 1929,Je 11,27:4
Soldiers and Women 1929,Ag 25,VIII,3:1
Soldiers and Women 1929,S 3,25:1
Elizabeth and Essex 1930,Mr 2,IX,4:7
Royal Virgin, The 1930,Mr 18,30:5
Greeks Had a Word for It, The 1930,S 26,16:5
Marriage for Three 1931,N 12,30:5
Experience Unnecessary 1931,D 31,16:2
Experience Unnecessary 1932,Mr 28,10:2
Teaton, Lorraine
Abie's Irish Rose 1937,My 13,30:2
Teaton, Vera
Canteen Show, The 1942,S 4,18:1

Teatro dei Piccoli
Untitled-Marionettes 1932,D 23,22:2
Tebbetts, James
Merry Duchess, The 1943,Je 24,25:1
Tebeau, Marguerite
Eyvind of the Hills 1921,F 2,14:1
Night Hawk 1926,D 27,21:3
Triplets 1932,S 22,25:2
Merry Wives of Windsor, The 1938,Ap 15,22:3
Techner, Joseph (Scenic Designer)
Junk 1927,Ja 6,25:1
Teddy, Gerald
They Knew What They Wanted 1949,F 17,28:2
Teddy (Dog)
Vaudeville (Palace) 1926,Jl 6,19:3
Tedeschi, Gianrico
Servant of Two Masters, The 1960,F 24,42:2
My Fair Lady 1963,N 16,16:1
Tedesco, Viveca
Matty and the Moron and Madonna
  1965,Mr 30,53:1
Tedick, Feodore
Hit the Deck 1960,Je 24,32:1
Show Boat 1961,Ap 13,32:1
Tedrow, Irene
Richard II 1937,F 6,14:2
Richard II 1937,S 16,28:2
Hamlet 1938,O 13,28:1
Henry IV, Part I 1939,Ja 31,17:2
Our Town 1969,N 28,50:1
Our Town 1969,D 7,II,7:1
Teear, Graham
Hair 1970,Ja 13,39:1
Teed, Rose
High Kickers 1941,N 1,21:2
Teegel, Joachim
Rhinoceros 1959,N 2,41:1
Teele, Ernie
Adventure 1928,S 26,25:2
Teeman, Anne
Joseph 1930,F 13,25:3
Sex Fable, The 1931,O 21,26:1
Counsellor-at-Law 1932,S 13,17:2
Too Many Boats 1934,S 12,26:3
Women, The 1936,D 28,13:1
Teene, Edward
Kingdom of God, The 1928,D 21,30:2
Teer, Barbara Ann
Raisin' Hell in the Son 1962,Jl 3,13:2
Home Movies 1964,My 12,32:1
Day of Absence 1965,N 16,56:1
Where's Daddy? 1966,Mr 3,27:1
Who's Got His Own 1966,O 13,52:1
Does a Tiger Wear a Necktie? 1967,F 4,17:1
Experiment, The 1967,My 9,54:2
Teer, Barbara Ann (Director)
Believers, The 1968,N 10,57:4
Five on the Black Hand Side 1970,Ja 2,32:2
Teevy, T (Miss) (Playwright)
Reapers, The 1930,Ap 6,IX,2:1
Tefler, Ronald
Thank You Svoboda 1944,Mr 2,13:2
Tegeder, Earle (Costume Designer)
Sable Brush, The 1956,N 28,41:1
Tegeder, Earle (Scenic Designer)
Sable Brush, The 1956,N 28,41:1
Teichmann, Howard (Playwright)
Solid Gold Cadillac, The 1953,N 6,24:2
Solid Gold Cadillac, The 1953,N 15,II,1:1
Solid Gold Cadillac, The 1954,Ag 16,13:4
Miss Lonelyhearts 1957,O 4,26:2
Girls in 509, The 1958,O 16,47:1
Julia, Jake, and Uncle Joe 1961,Ja 30,19:1
Rainy Day in Newark, A 1963,O 23,35:1
Teichner, Charles (Scenic Designer)
Dora Mobridge 1930,Ap 21,20:2
Teichner, Joseph (Scenic Designer)
What Do We Know 1927,D 24,8:1
Teifer, Jerry (Composer)
Tall Story 1959,Ja 30,33:2
Teijelo, Gerald
Hot Spot 1963,Ap 20,17:2
Love's Labour's Lost 1965,Je 16,46:1
On a Clear Day You Can See Forever
  1965,O 18,44:1
Teijelo, Gerald (Choreog-apher)
Jo 1964,F 13,25:1
Teitel, Carol
Billy the Kid 1951,Ag 21,23:2
Anatomist, The 1957,F 27,21:5
Dark Lady of the Sonnets, The 1959,Ag 21,13:1
Passion, Poison and Petrifaction 1959,Ag 21,13:1
Shewing-Up of Blanco Posnet, The 1959,S 19,26:7
Country Scandal, A 1960,My 6,21:8
Country Scandal, A 1960,My 15,II,1:1
Under Milk Wood 1961,Mr 30,25:1
Under Milk Wood 1962,O 6,13:4
Pullman Car Hiawatha 1962,D 4,46:2
Much Ado About Nothing 1963,Jl 15,25:2
Colombe 1965,F 24,33:1

Teitel, Carol—Cont
Persecution and Assassination of Marat As Performed by the Inmates of the Asylum of Charenton Under the Direction of the Marquis de Sade, The 1967,Ja 4,34:1
Bench, The 1968,Mr 5,35:2
Flea in Her Ear, A 1969,O 4,25:1
Seven Days of Mourning 1969,D 17,64:1

Teitel, Lou
Caucasian Chalk Circle, The 1961,N 1,35:1

Teitel, N R (Playwright)
Bench, The 1968,Mr 5,35:2
Round With Ring, A 1969,O 30,56:1

Teitelbaum, Abraham
Wolves 1924,D 31,9:4
Tenth Commandment, The 1926,N 18,27:1
Gardener's Dog, The 1927,O 21,27:1
Gold Diggers, The 1927,D 3,19:2
Alexander Pushkin 1928,Ja 27,14:2
American Chasidim 1928,Mr 17,8:8
Golden Ring, The 1930,F 1,14:7
Soul of a Woman, The 1930,F 22,13:1
Longing for Home 1933,S 22,15:1
Slaves of the Public 1934,Mr 10,18:6
Secret of Love, The 1936,F 24,15:2
Souls for Sale 1936,S 21,27:6
Stepsisters 1936,O 13,32:3
Of One Mother 1937,Ja 18,21:3
Song of Dnieper 1946,O 26,10:5
Wandering Stars 1946,D 14,18:2
Shylock and His Daughter 1947,S 30,22:2

Teitelbaum, Anna
Tenth Commandment, The 1926,N 18,27:1
Gold Diggers, The 1927,D 3,19:2
Alexander Pushkin 1928,Ja 27,14:2
Stempenu, the Fiddler 1929,Mr 9,24:7
Soul of a Woman, The 1930,F 22,13:1
Hello Grandpa! 1931,Ja 2,25:3
New Man, The 1932,Ap 22,23:2
Happy Family, A 1934,S 24,15:2
East Side Wedding, An 1935,Ja 21,18:2
Itche Mayer of Warsaw 1935,Ja 31,22:4
Jacques Bergson 1936,O 31,24:6
Water Carrier, The 1936,D 25,20:2
Her Great Mistake 1940,F 5,12:6

Teitelbaum, Maurice (Lyricist)
Hooray!! It's a Glorious Day. . .And All That 1966,Mr 10,28:1

Teitelbaum, Maurice (Playwright)
Hooray!! It's a Glorious Day. . .And All That 1966,Mr 10,28:1

Teitelbaum, Mayme
Psychological Moment, The 1931,Mr 4,33:2
Divina Pastora, La 1931,Mr 4,33:2
Sparkin' 1931,Mr 4,33:2
Old Maid, The 1949,Ja 27,20:6
Post Road 1949,Ap 28,27:3
This Happy Breed 1952,Ap 4,23:2

Teitsworth, Dorothy
Myself and I 1929,Ag 31,13:6

Teitsworth, Dorothy (Choreographer)
Myself and I 1929,Ag 31,13:6

Tejada, Miguel Lerdo de
Vaudeville (Palace) 1928,Mr 13,23:2
Vaudeville (Palace) 1928,Mr 20,20:2

Teje, Tora
Macbeth 1931,O 11,VIII,4:5
Mourning Becomes Electra 1933,My 7,IX,2:3
Desire Under the Elms 1933,N 12,IX,1:1
Dream Play 1935,D 8,X,4:5
Gosta Berling's Saga 1936,Je 28,IX,1:6

Telasko, Ralf
Vienna at Night 1945,Ap 30,12:4

Teleshava, E S (Miscellaneous)
Dead Souls 1965,F 5,34:1

Telfer, Ronald
Career Angel 1944,My 24,23:7
Too Much for Maneuvers 1945,My 3,26:5
Caesar and Cleopatra 1949,D 22,28:2
Getting Married 1951,My 14,28:5

Telfer, Ronald (Playwright)
Oh, Mr Meadowbrook! 1948,D 27,17:2

Tell, Alma
Fall and Rise of Susan Lenox, The 1920,Je 11,11:2
When We Are Young 1920,N 23,11:1
Main Street 1921,O 6,21:1
It Is the Law 1922,N 30,28:2
Aren't We All? 1923,My 22,14:2
Kelly's Vacation 1924,Mr 16,VIII,2:1
Lass O' Laughter 1925,Ja 9,13:2
Odd Man Out 1925,My 26,24:3
These Charming People 1925,O 7,31:2

Tell, Arthur
My Sister Eileen 1940,D 27,23:2
Finian's Rainbow 1947,Ja 11,23:2
Pink Elephant, The 1953,Ap 23,37:2

Tell, Olive
Nemesis 1921,Ap 5,24:3
Whispering Wires 1922,Ag 8,26:2
Morphia 1923,Mr 7,20:2

Tell, P William (Playwright)
Pressing Business 1930,N 18,28:5

Tellegen, Lou
Don Juan 1921,S 8,14:2
Homme a la Rose, L' 1921,S 11,VI,1:1
Vaudeville (Palace) 1927,Mr 29,22:6
Anna 1928,My 17,25:2
Cortez 1929,N 5,32:2
Great Lover, The 1932,O 12,27:3
Lady Refuses, The 1933,Mr 8,18:6

Teller, Frank L (Producer)
Lady Do 1927,Ap 19,24:2

Telman, Steve
Fisherman, The 1965,Ja 27,24:6
Fourth Pig, The 1965,Ja 27,24:6

Telzel, Joan
Audition of the Apprentice Theatre 1939,Je 2,26:2

Temperley, Stephen
Henry IV, Part II 1968,Jl 2,33:1
Invitation to a Beheading 1969,Mr 18,36:1

Tempest, Diane
Satellite 1935,N 21,27:5
Kick Back, The 1936,Je 23,27:3

Tempest, Florenz
Vaudeville (Palace) 1929,O 21,31:2

Tempest, Marie
Serpent's Tooth, A 1922,Ag 25,8:5
Good Gracious, Annabelle 1923,F 15,23:2
Good Gracious, Annabelle 1923,F 25,VII,1:7
Marriage of Kitty, The 1923,Mr 18,VII,1:1
Midsummer Madness 1923,Jl 13,VII,1:6
Scarlet Lady, The 1926,O 17,VIII,2:1
Marquise, The 1927,Mr 20,VIII,2:7
Spot on the Sun, The 1927,Jl 24,VII,1:7
Masque of Venice, The 1928,F 12,VIII,2:1
Passing Brompton Road 1928,Ag 5,VII,1:1
Her Shop 1929,F 24,IX,4:3
First Mrs Fraser, The 1929,Jl 21,VIII,1:4
Little Catherine 1931,N 19,27:2
Little Catherine 1931,D 6,VIII,2:7
So Far and No Father 1932,F 17,19:4
So Far and No Father 1932,Mr 6,VIII,2:4
Vinegar Tree, The 1932,Je 9,27:7
Vinegar Tree, The 1932,Jl 10,IX,1:3
Tomorrow Will Be Friday 1932,S 18,IX,1:1
When Ladies Meet 1933,Ap 27,15:4
When Ladies Meet 1933,My 14,IX,2:2
Old Folks at Home 1934,Ja 14,IX,1:8
Theatre Royal; Royal Family, The 1934,O 24,24:2
Theatre Royal 1934,N 11,IX,1:1
Players' Masque for Marie Tempest, The 1935,Je 23,IX,1:3
Untitled-Benefit 1935,Je 23,IX,1:3
Short Story 1935,N 5,33:2
Short Story 1935,D 1,XI,5:3
Retreat From Folly 1937,F 25,18:2
Mary Goes to See 1938,Mr 6,XI,3:6
Dear Octopus 1938,O 2,IX,2:1

Tempest, Nina
Ten Nights in a Barroom 1928,Mr 28,31:2

Tempest, Tom
She Means Business 1931,Ja 27,21:2
Happy Landing 1932,Mr 28,10:5
Lady Detained, A 1935,Ja 10,23:3
Stag at Bay, The 1935,Jl 30,17:1
Little Inn, The 1935,Ag 20,25:1
Ethan Frome 1936,Ja 22,15:2
Virginia 1937,S 3,13:2
Be Your Age 1953,Ja 15,24:2

Tempest, Winnie
Yellow Sands 1927,S 12,29:3

Temple, Edna
Blossom Time 1922,O 24,18:2

Temple, Elaine
Helena's Boys 1924,Ap 8,22:2
Bit o' Love, A 1925,My 13,24:2
Pickwick 1927,S 6,35:2
Merry Wives of Windsor, The 1928,Mr 20,20:1
Hawk Island 1929,S 17,34:7
Family Affairs 1929,D 11,34:6
Mayfair 1930,Mr 18,30:5
People on the Hill 1931,S 26,25:5
Fresh Fields 1934,Jl 15,X,1:1

Temple, Jeanne
Summer Wives 1936,Ap 14,18:1
Sun Kissed 1937,Mr 11,20:2
Cat and the Canary, The 1937,Je 15,26:3

Temple, Joan
Charles and Mary 1930,F 23,VIII,2:1
Mrs Fischer's War 1931,Ag 9,VIII,1:3

Temple, Joan (Playwright)
Aspidistras 1927,Ja 2,VII,2:5
Hen Upon a Steeple 1927,Ap 24,VII,2:3
Cage, The; Aspidistras 1927,Ag 14,VII,1:7
Charles and Mary 1930,F 23,VIII,2:1
Mrs Fischer's War 1931,Ag 9,VIII,1:3

Temple, Leah
Musk 1920,Mr 15,13:1

Temple, Maria
Grey Farm 1940,My 4,12:7

Temple, Olive
Wonderful Thing, The 1920,F 18,9:1

Temple, Paula
Three Musketeers, The 1921,My 20,18:5

Temple, Ray (Costume Designer)
Safari! 1955,My 12,32:6

Temple, Ray (Lighting Director)
Salvation on a String; Chair Endowed 1954,Jl 7,23:1
Salvation on a String; Supper for the Dead 1954,Jl 7,23:1
Salvation on a String; No Count Boy, The 1954,Jl 7,23:1
Safari! 1955,My 12,32:6

Temple, Ray (Scenic Designer)
Salvation on a String; Supper for the Dead 1954,Jl 7,23:1
Salvation on a String; No Count Boy, The 1954,Jl 7,23:1
Salvation on a String; Chair Endowed 1954,Jl 7,23:1
Safari! 1955,My 12,32:6

Temple, Richard
Hotel Mouse, The 1922,Mr 14,11:3
Top Hole 1924,S 2,22:3
Pearl of Great Price, The 1926,N 2,34:3
Padre, The 1926,D 28,16:3
Sinner 1927,F 8,20:2
Woman of Bronze, The 1927,Je 16,25:4
Sons o' Guns 1929,N 27,30:4
Fata Morgana 1931,D 26,15:3
Let 'Em Eat Cake 1933,O 23,18:1
Florodora 1936,Ag 23,II,8:2
Between the Devil 1937,O 15,19:1
Journey's End 1939,S 19,29:2
Rebecca 1945,Ja 19,17:2
Wonderful Journey 1946,D 26,30:2
She Stoops to Conquer 1949,D 29,21:3

Temple, Richard W
Three Musketeers, The 1921,My 20,18:5

Temple, Richard W (Composer)
Three Musketeers, The 1921,My 20,18:5

Temple, Richard W (Playwright)
Three Musketeers, The 1921,My 20,18:5

Templeman, Louis
Naughty Marietta 1929,O 22,26:2
Naughty Marietta 1931,N 17,31:2
Firefly, The 1931,D 1,23:2

Templeton, Betty
Pirates of Penzance, The 1942,F 20,20:2

Templeton, Fay
Vaudeville (Palace) 1925,Je 28,VIII,1:1
H M S Pinafore 1926,Ap 7,26:3
H M S Pinafore 1931,My 19,25:2
H M S Pinafore 1931,My 31,II,1:2
H M S Pinafore 1931,Jl 28,17:6
Roberta 1933,N 20,18:4

Templeton, James
Vaudeville (Palace) 1926,Jl 27,15:4
Merry Malones, The 1927,S 27,30:2
Who Cares 1930,Jl 9,27:1

Templeton, Mercer
Honey Girl 1920,My 4,9:1
Little Nellie Kelly 1922,N 14,16:1
Vaudeville (Palace) 1926,Jl 27,15:4
Merry Malones, The 1927,S 27,30:2
Who Cares 1930,Jl 9,27:1

Templeton, Olive
Swan, The 1954,Ag 17,16:6
Uncle Vanya 1956,F 1,25:2
Uncle Vanya 1956,F 12,II,1:1
Happy Hunting 1956,D 7,30:1

Templeton, William P (Playwright)
Painted Smile, The 1938,My 8,X,1:7

Templey
Femme Dans un Lit, Une 1928,Ja 15,VIII,2:3

Templey, Marguerite
Attachee, L' 1929,My 19,IX,2:1

Tems, Robert
Appearances 1925,O 15,27:3

Ten-Brook, Harro
Colonel Satan 1931,Ja 12,24:1

Ten Eyck, Melissa
Up in the Clouds 1922,Ja 3,20:3

Ten Eyck (Costume Designer)
Forbidden Melody 1936,N 3,33:1

Tenen, Laiyle
Mr Strauss Goes to Boston 1945,S 7,20:2

Tenenholtz, Alex
Unwritten Chapter, The 1920,O 12,18:1
Jacques Bergson 1936,O 31,24:6
Jacques Bergson 1936,N 29,XII,3:3
Water Carrier, The 1936,D 25,20:2

Tenenholtz, Elias
Wolves 1924,D 31,9:4

Teney, Caryl
I'm Solomon 1968,Ap 24,51:1

Tenley, Theodore
Saint Joan 1940,Mr 11,10:6
Henry VIII 1946,N 7,42:2
Alice in Wonderland 1947,Ap 7,19:2
Dream Girl 1951,My 10,39:1
Idiot's Delight 1951,My 24,46:3
Lysistrata 1959,My 20,40:2

Tennant, Bill
Biff, Bing, Bang 1921,My 10,20:1

Tennant, Dorothy
Peacock 1932,O 12,27:1

Tennant, Frederick
Fuente Ovejuna; Sheep Well, The 1936,My 3,II,4:1
Tennant, H M (Miscellaneous)
Love for Love 1947,My 27,30:2
Tennant, H M (Producer)
Jane 1947,Ja 30,19:6
Touch of the Poet, A 1962,S 30,85:8
Tennant, H M, Ltd of London (Miscellaneous)
Importance of Being Earnest, The 1947,Mr 4,30:2
Tenney, Del
View From the Bridge, A 1956,N 9,34:4
Portrait of a Madonna 1957,Ap 1,21:2
Bedtime Story 1957,Ap 1,21:2
Philanderer, The 1958,My 13,26:2
You Never Can Tell 1958,Je 17,25:1
Prodigal, The 1960,F 12,23:1
Prodigal, The 1960,F 21,II,1:1
Tenney, Del (Producer)
Philanderer, The 1958,My 13,26:2
You Never Can Tell 1958,Je 17,25:1
Tenney, Helen
Peter Ibbetson 1931,Ap 9,30:3
Tenney, James
Originale 1964,S 9,46:1
Tenney, James (Miscellaneous)
Maids, The 1963,N 15,29:1
Tenney, Walter
Cherry Blossoms 1927,Mr 29,22:3
Tennis, Eleanor
Champagne, Sec 1933,O 16,20:2
Babes in Arms 1937,Ap 15,18:4
Mexican Hayride 1944,Ja 29,9:6
Tennyson, Alfred (Lord) (Playwright)
Harold 1928,Ap 29,IX,1:3
Launcelot and Elaine 1930,Mr 10,24:3
Devil and the Lady, The 1930,Ag 10,VIII,1:3
Tennyson, Arthur C
Sancho Panza 1923,N 27,23:1
Tennyson, Jean
Earl Carroll's Vanities 1928,Ag 7,25:2
Tennyson, William
Made in America 1925,O 15,27:2
Nightstick 1927,N 11,20:4
Tenowsky, Simon (Composer)
Voice of Israel, The 1948,O 26,40:2
Teper, Frederick (Dude)
Bluebeard 1970,My 5,58:1
Teplitsky, Grigory (Composer)
Obratsov Russian Pupper Theater in an Unusual
Concert 1963,O 3,28:1
Aladdin and His Wonderful Lamp 1963,O 21,39:1
Tepper, Morris
Good Boy 1928,S 6,23:2
Ter-Arutunian, Rouben (Costume Designer)
King John 1956,Je 28,33:5
Measure for Measure 1956,Je 29,16:1
Measure for Measure 1957,Ja 23,24:1
New Girl in Town 1957,My 26,II,1:1
Othello 1957,Je 24,19:2
Othello 1957,Je 30,II,1:1
Much Ado About Nothing 1957,Ag 8,15:2
Much Ado About Nothing 1957,Ag 18,II,1:1
Hot Spot 1963,Ap 20,17:2
Last Minstrel, The 1963,My 9,40:2
Save Me a Place at Forest Lawn 1963,My 9,40:2
Play of Herod, The 1963,D 10,55:2
Play of Herod, The 1965,D 29,24:2
Ivanov 1966,My 4,50:1
Eh? 1966,O 17,47:1
Macbeth 1967,Jl 31,21:1
Ter-Arutunian, Rouben (Director)
Taming of the Shrew, The 1957,F 21,30:2
Ter-Arutunian, Rouben (Scenic Designer)
King John 1956,Je 28,33:5
Measure for Measure 1956,Je 29,16:1
Taming of the Shrew, The 1956,Ag 6,20:1
Measure for Measure 1957,Ja 23,24:1
Measure for Measure 1957,F 3,II,1:1
Duchess of Malfi, The 1957,Mr 20,33:1
New Girl in Town 1957,My 15,40:1
New Girl in Town 1957,My 26,II,1:1
Othello 1957,Je 24,19:2
Othello 1957,Je 30,II,1:1
Merchant of Venice, The 1957,Jl 11,19:5
Merchant of Venice, The 1957,Ag 18,II,1:1
Much Ado About Nothing 1957,Ag 18,II,1:1
Who Was That Lady I Saw You With?
1958,Mr 4,33:2
Maria Golovin 1958,N 6,43:1
Redhead 1959,F 6,21:1
Redhead 1959,F 15,II,1:1
Twelfth Night 1960,Je 9,29:4
Tempest, The 1960,Je 26,II,1:1
Antony and Cleopatra 1960,Ag 1,19:1
Advise and Consent 1960,N 18,25:1
Donnybrook! 1961,My 19,23:1
Donnybrook! 1961,My 28,II,1:1
Passage to India, A 1962,F 1,23:1
Hot Spot 1963,Ap 20,17:2
Save Me a Place at Forest Lawn 1963,My 9,40:2
Last Minstrel, The 1963,My 9,40:2
Arturo Ui 1963,N 12,49:1

Milk Train Doesn't Stop Here Anymore, The
1964,Ja 2,33:1
Deputy, The 1964,F 27,26:1
Merry Widow, The 1964,Ag 18,24:2
Devils, The 1965,N 17,51:2
Ivanov 1966,My 4,50:1
Eh? 1966,O 17,47:1
Eh? 1966,N 6,II,1:1
Medea 1966,D 21,42:1
Party on Greenwich Avenue, The 1967,My 11,52:1
Macbeth 1967,Jl 31,21:1
Exit the King 1968,Ja 10,48:1
I'm Solomon 1968,Ap 24,51:1
Dozens, The 1969,Mr 14,51:1
Promenade 1969,Je 5,56:1
Terayama, Shuii (Director)
Marie Vison, La 1970,Jl 15,29:1
Terayama, Shuii (Lighting Director)
Marie Vison, La 1970,Jl 15,29:1
Terayama, Shuii (Playwright)
Marie Vison, La 1970,Jl 15,29:1
Terayama, Shuii (Scenic Designer)
Marie Vison, La 1970,Jl 15,29:1
Terbell, James
Merchants of Venus 1920,S 28,14:2
Terekhova, Vera (Scenic Designer)
Obratsov Russian Pupper Theater in an Unusual
Concert 1963,O 3,28:1
Terel, Charles (Scenic Designer)
Street Sounds 1970,O 23,32:1
Teres, Tevesa
Proof Thro' the Night 1942,D 26,14:2
Teresa (Choreographer)
Fiesta in Madrid 1969,My 29,49:1
Terheyden, Jerry
Hamlet 1957,Ja 29,27:1
Much Ado About Nothing 1961,Jl 7,17:1
Terieson, Arthur (Lighting Director)
Autumn's Here 1966,O 26,40:1
Terkel, Studs (Playwright)
Amazing Grace 1967,D 10,82:1
Termacic, Svetlana (Translator)
Ubu Roi 1968,Je 29,20:1
Termine, Ben
Noah 1954,O 11,32:2
Termine, Ben (Director)
Birds, The 1967,My 7,67:1
Termini, Joe
Vaudeville (Palace) 1926,S 21,32:5
Tern, Frances
Bedrock 1934,N 18,II,6:3
Ternent, Billy (Miscellaneous)
Plume de Ma Tante, La 1958,N 12,42:1
Terracciano, Flore
Lazarus Laughed 1948,Ap 9,27:4
Terrace, Mike
Safari! 1955,My 12,32:6
Terranova, Aldo
Lucrezia Borgia 1937,Mr 8,22:2
Feudalismo Oppure La Terra Bassa; Feudalism or
the Lowland 1937,Mr 8,22:2
Sposa e la Cavalla, La 1937,Mr 22,26:5
Terranova, Dino
Medico Delle Pazze, Il; Physician of Mad Woman,
The 1937,S 27,24:2
Signora Dalle Camelie, La; Dame aux Camelias, La
1937,O 9,16:3
Dark Legend 1952,Mr 25,24:2
In Any Language 1952,O 9,40:2
Becket 1961,My 9,44:1
Daughter of Silence 1961,D 1,28:1
Terrell, Barbara
Places, Please 1937,N 13,10:6
Terrell, Betty
Around the World in 80 Days 1964,Je 29,33:2
Terrell, Elwin Charles 2d (Scenic Designer)
Triumph of Robert Emmet, The 1969,My 8,54:1
Terrell, John (Playwright)
Nine O'Clock Revue 1936,Jl 8,14:3
Terrell, St John
Judgment Day 1934,S 13,26:4
Winterset 1935,S 26,19:2
Days of Our Youth, The 1941,N 29,15:2
Terrell, St John (Playwright)
Three by Thurber; Imperturbable Spirit, The
1955,Mr 8,23:2
Three by Thurber; Middle Years, The
1955,Mr 8,23:2
Three by Thurber; Mr Montoe Holds the Fort
1955,Mr 8,23:2
Terrell, St John (Producer)
Song of Norway 1951,Ja 11,28:5
Carmen Jones 1951,S 22,8:6
Allegro 1952,S 18,36:3
Three by Thurber; Imperturbable Spirit, The
1955,Mr 8,23:2
Three by Thurber; Middle Years, The
1955,Mr 8,23:2
Three by Thurber; Mr Montoe Holds the Fort
1955,Mr 8,23:2
I Must Be Talking to My Friends 1967,N 17,59:1
Terrill, Elizabeth
Liza 1922,N 28,24:1

Terris, Malcolm
Hamlet 1969,My 2,38:1
Terris, Norma
Queen O' Hearts 1922,O 11,22:1
Night in Paris, A 1926,Ja 6,16:3
Night in Paris, A 1926,Jl 27,15:4
Vaudeville (Palace) 1927,Ap 5,30:2
Vaudeville (Palace) 1927,Ap 12,25:4
Night in Spain, A 1927,My 4,28:2
Vaudeville (Palace) 1927,Je 14,33:3
Show Boat 1927,D 28,26:1
Show Boat 1928,Ja 8,VIII,1:1
Well of Romance, The 1930,N 8,21:2
Vaudeville (Palace) 1931,O 19,28:5
Vaudeville (Palace) 1931,O 26,22:3
Smiling Through 1932,Ja 3,VIII,3:1
Radio Carnival 1932,Mr 14,13:3
Show Boat 1932,My 20,22:2
Climax, The 1933,Je 14,22:2
So Many Paths 1934,D 7,26:5
Private Lives 1935,Je 26,18:3
Smiling Through 1935,Jl 30,17:2
Hands Across the Sea 1937,Ag 24,24:5
Still Life 1937,Ag 24,24:5
Fumed Oak 1937,Ag 24,24:5
Great Lady 1938,D 2,26:6
Terriss, Ellaline
Miracle Man, The 1935,My 14,17:5
Terron, Thelma
Mourners' Bench, The 1950,S 22,35:7
Terry, Albert
Ship, The 1929,N 21,24:7
Magic 1929,D 17,28:5
As You Like It 1936,Ap 24,18:4
Terry, Beatrice
Mary the 3d 1923,F 6,14:2
Mary the 3d 1923,F 11,VII,1:1
Children of the Moon 1923,Ag 18,10:3
Children of the Moon 1923,Ag 26,VI,1:1
Children of the Moon 1923,S 9,VII,1:1
Children of the Moon 1923,S 16,VII,1:1
Her Way Out 1924,Je 24,18:3
School for Scandal, The 1925,O 24,19:1
Saturday Night 1926,O 26,25:1
Three Sisters, The 1926,O 27,24:1
Locandiera, La; Mistress of the Inn, The
1926,N 23,26:1
Twelfth Night 1926,D 21,21:4
Cradle Song 1927,Ja 25,18:2
Jimmie's Women 1927,S 27,30:3
Carry On 1928,Ja 24,26:1
Command Performance, The 1928,O 4,27:1
Freddy 1929,Jl 17,23:4
Your Uncle Dudley 1929,N 19,26:4
Nancy's Private Affair 1930,Ja 14,24:3
Scarlet Sister Mary 1930,N 26,19:2
School for Scandal, The 1931,N 11,26:4
Liliom 1932,O 27,23:2
Camille 1932,O 28,23:2
Dear Jane 1932,N 15,24:3
Twelve Pound Look, The 1934,F 6,24:4
For Valor 1935,N 12,24:4
For Valor 1935,N 19,27:5
White Christmas 1936,Jl 7,22:2
Bright Rebel 1938,D 28,24:2
Terry, Bill
Great White Hope, The 1967,D 14,58:1
Terry, Brewster
Bedrock 1934,N 18,II,6:3
Terry, David (Miscellaneous)
New Faces of 1962 1962,F 2,25:1
Terry, David (Musical Director)
Seventh Heaven 1955,My 27,16:2
Terry, Don
Please Do Not Disturb 1936,Je 23,27:1
Terry, Eleanor
Out of a Blue Sky 1930,F 10,20:6
Terry, Ethel Grey
Honor Be Damned! 1927,Ja 27,13:1
Terry, Ethelind
Honeydew 1920,S 7,20:1
Kid Boots 1924,Ja 1,21:3
Rio Rita 1927,F 3,18:3
Nina Rosa 1930,S 22,22:5
Vaudeville (Palace) 1932,My 16,19:2
Terry, Frank
Gods of the Mountain, The 1950,My 25,36:2
Terry, Fred
Borderer, The 1923,Mr 18,VII,1:1
Terry, George
Cannibals, The 1968,N 4,60:1
Terry, Hazel
Time and the Conways 1938,Ja 4,19:2
Terry, J Harold (Playwright)
Carolinian, The 1925,N 3,34:2
Insult 1930,S 16,30:2
Terry, J Seymour
Loves of Lulu, The 1925,My 12,26:1
Terry, Jack
What Every Woman Knows 1926,Ap 14,20:2
Terry, Kathleen
Parisiana 1928,F 10,26:3
Back Here 1928,N 27,36:3

Terry, Kathleen—Cont
Solitaire 1929,Mr 13,28:3
Terry, Ken
On Whitman Avenue 1946,My 9,28:2
Seeds in the Wind 1948,Ap 26,27:2
Home Life of a Buffalo; Hope's the Thing
1948,My 12,34:6
Hope Is the Thing With Feathers; Hope's the
Thing 1948,My 12,34:6
Gone Tomorrow; Hope's the Thing
1948,My 12,34:6
Seeds in the Wind 1948,My 26,29:2
Terry, Mary Ellen
Arsenic and Old Lace 1943,D 13,18:6
Shoestring '57 1956,N 6,31:1
Terry, Megan (Director)
Viet Rock 1966,O 12,34:1
Viet Rock 1966,N 11,38:1
Terry, Megan (Playwright)
Viet Rock 1966,O 12,34:1
Viet Rock 1966,N 11,38:1
Viet Rock 1966,N 27,II,1:1
Jack Jack 1968,Je 23,74:5
Massachusetts Trust 1968,S 1,II,1:1
People vs Ranchman, The 1968,O 28,56:1
People vs Ranchman, The 1968,N 10,II,5:1
Approaching Simone 1970,Mr 9,43:1
Terry, Mike (Miscellaneous)
Buck White 1969,D 3,63:1
Terry, Nigel
She Stoops to Conquer 1969,Ag 18,28:1
Terry, Phil
Pardon Our French 1950,O 6,22:4
Terry, Renee
Bright Honor 1936,S 28,14:1
Terry, Richard
We Never Learn 1928,Ja 24,26:1
Pagan Lady 1930,O 21,34:2
Terry, Robert N
Captains and the Kings, The 1962,Ja 3,25:2
Terry, Sonny
Finian's Rainbow 1947,Ja 11,23:2
Finian's Rainbow 1948,Ag 29,II,1:1
Cat on a Hot Tin Roof 1955,Mr 25,18:2
Terry, Sylvia
Prodigal Son, The 1965,My 21,19:1
Terry, W Benson
Someone's Comin' Hungry 1969,Ap 1,51:1
Terry, Wilkins
Secret Garden, The 1931,N 8,31:4
Terry, William
I Like It Here 1946,Mr 23,8:6
Magic Touch, The 1947,S 4,30:1
Big Knife, The 1949,F 25,27:5
Terry, William A
Straw Hat, The 1937,D 31,8:2
Terry, William T
Brother Cain 1941,S 13,21:5
Terry, William W
Out of the Frying Pan 1941,F 12,24:2
Terry Girls, The
Trois Jeunes Filles Nues; Three Young Maids From
the Folies Bergere 1929,Mr 5,28:2
Terry-Lewis, Mabel
If Winter Comes 1923,Ap 3,26:1
Aren't We All? 1923,My 22,14:2
Aren't We All? 1923,My 27,VII,1:1
Constant Wife, The 1926,N 30,26:3
Stag, The 1929,Ap 21,IX,2:1
Importance of Being Earnest, The
1930,Jl 27,VIII,1:8
Victoria Regina 1937,Jl 11,X,1:7
Terson, Peter (Playwright)
Mooney and His Caravans 1968,My 17,50:3
Apprentices, The 1968,Ag 21,40:5
Spring-Heeled Jack 1970,Ag 27,41:2
Terwin, Johanna
Dantons Tod 1927,D 21,28:3
Er Ist an Allem Schuld; He Is to Blame for
Everything 1928,Ja 10,28:3
Kabale und Liebe 1928,Ja 17,22:3
Lebende Leichnam, Der, Der; Living Corpse, The
1928,Ja 24,26:2
Redemption: Lebende Leichnam, Der; Living
Corpse, The 1928,N 20,28:2
Ghosts; Gespenster 1929,F 6,30:3
Tery, Simone (Playwright)
Comme les Autres 1932,Jl 3,IX,1:1
Terzieff, Laurent
Luv 1965,N 16,56:4
Terzo, Jody (Scenic Designer)
Sold to the Movies; Crossing the Gap
1970,Je 18,54:2
Sold to the Movies; Life Size 1970,Je 18,54:2
Sold to the Movies; Type 424 Meet Type Oh-Oh,
No! 1970,Je 18,54:2
Tesich, Steven (Playwright)
Carpenters, The 1970,D 22,40:1
Carpenters, The 1970,D 27,II,1:1
Tesser, Ted
Enemy of the People, An 1959,F 5,24:4
Tessier, Valentine
Siegfried 1928,My 20,VIII,1:3
Suzanne 1929,F 17,IX,4:2

Jean de la Lune 1929,My 12,IX,5:3
Amphitryon 38 1929,D 1,X,4:1
Prof' d'Anglais, Le 1930,My 25,IX,2:8
Eau Fraiche, L' 1931,Je 7,VIII,3:5
Taciturne, Un 1931,N 22,VIII,1:6
Intermezzo 1933,Mr 26,IX,2:1
Homme, L' 1934,F 25,IX,2:3
Femme en Fleur, La 1936,F 23,X,2:3
Voyage, Le 1937,F 28,XI,2:1
Testa, Henry P (Producer)
Emerald Slippers, The 1970,S 2,31:2
Tester, Desmond
Touch Wood 1934,Jl 1,X,1:3
Tester, Ruth
Lucky Break 1925,Ag 12,16:2
Bunk of 1926 1926,F 17,12:3
Ramblers, The 1926,S 21,32:2
Second Little Show, The 1930,Ag 17,VIII,2:2
Second Little Show, The 1930,S 3,36:1
Gang's All Here, The 1931,F 19,21:3
Tether, Ellen
Little Poor Man, The 1925,Ag 6,14:1
Tetley, Dorothy
Bulldog Drummond 1921,D 27,10:2
Mulberry Bush, The 1930,My 18,VIII,2:6
Tetley, Glen
Great Campaign, The 1947,Ap 1,33:2
Kiss Me, Kate 1949,Ja 30,II,6:5
Out of This World 1950,D 22,17:3
Willie the Weeper 1961,Ja 4,26:1
Tetley, Glen (Choreographer)
Eccentricities of Davy Crockett, The 1961,Ja 4,26:1
Tetley, Glen (Director)
Fortuna 1962,Ja 4,26:1
Tetzel, Joan
Lorelei 1938,N 30,21:2
Liliom 1940,Mr 26,17:2
Happy Days 1941,My 14,24:2
Damask Cheek, The 1942,O 23,24:2
Harriet 1943,Mr 4,24:2
Peepshow 1944,F 4,12:2
Pretty Little Parlor 1944,Ap 18,24:8
I Remember Mama 1944,O 20,16:2
I Remember Mama 1944,O 29,II,1:1
Strange Bedfellows 1948,Ja 15,27:3
Red Gloves 1948,D 6,28:2
Winner, The 1954,F 18,34:1
Master Builder, The 1955,Mr 2,23:2
Master Builder, The 1955,Mr 20,II,1:1
U S A 1959,O 29,38:1
U S A 1959,N 8,II,1:1
One Flew Over the Cuckoo's Nest 1963,N 14,40:2
How the Other Half Loves 1970,Ag 7,23:1
Teuber, Max
Good Times 1920,Ag 10,10:1
Tewkesbury, Joan
Peter Pan 1954,O 21,30:2
Tewksbury, Ann
Pillars of Society, The 1931,O 15,19:1
Tews, Adolph
Quiet, Please! 1940,N 9,20:3
Texas, Marie
Folly Town 1920,My 18,9:2
Texas, Temple
It Takes Two 1947,F 4,33:4
Pipe Dream 1955,D 1,44:1
Texas Rhythm Boys, The
Texas Li'l Darlin' 1949,N 26,10:5
Thacher, John H
Hamlet 1927,Ap 7,23:3
Thacher, John S Jr
Orestes 1926,Je 20,II,3:6
Thacker, Rusty
Midsummer Night's Dream, A 1967,Je 19,42:1
Life With Father 1967,O 20,53:2
Your Own Thing 1968,Ja 15,33:1
Your Own Thing 1968,Ja 28,II,3:1
Your Own Thing 1969,Mr 29,39:1
Thackeray, William Makepeace (Original Author)
Becky Sharp 1929,Je 4,29:1
Rose and the Ring, The 1931,D 24,20:7
Vanity Fair 1946,N 3,I,54:6
Vanity Fair 1946,N 10,II,3:1
Vanity Fair 1962,N 28,44:8
Thackrey, Helen
Little Theatre Tournament; Joint Owners in Spain
1929,My 7,28:1
Thaddeus, Frances
Hickory Stick 1944,My 9,15:6
Thaell, Cliff
It Happens on Ice 1941,Ap 5,13:2
Thaell, Rona
It Happens on Ice 1941,Ap 5,13:2
Thaells, Cliff
Stars on Ice 1942,Jl 3,12:2
Thaler, Al
When the Bough Breaks 1950,Mr 9,25:5
Thaler, Harry
Wooden Idol, The 1930,My 13,27:2
Thall, Lenore
Canteen Show, The 1942,S 4,18:1
Thalmore, Claude
Tobias and the Angel 1937,Ap 29,16:5

Thames, Judy
Arms and the Man 1965,Je 24,32:5
X Has No Value 1970,F 17,35:1
Thames, Pravis
Miracle, The 1927,Ap 15,27:1
Thane, Elswyth (Playwright)
Tudor Wench, The 1933,N 12,IX,3:6
Young Mr Disraeli 1934,N 13,22:2
Young Mr Disraeli 1937,N 10,30:5
Tharnae, Charles
Journey's End 1930,Mr 30,VIII,3:4
Tharne, Mabel
Nativity Play, The 1937,D 21,29:1
Thatcher, Edwin
Siege 1937,D 9,31:4
Thatcher, Heather
Thy Name Is Woman 1926,Ag 22,VII,1:2
Lucky Break 1934,O 3,25:3
Full House 1935,Ag 22,20:3
Full House 1935,S 22,X,3:3
Thatcher, Leora
One Bright Day 1952,Mr 20,37:2
Children's Hour, The 1952,D 19,35:2
Thatcher, Torin
Edward, My Son 1948,O 1,30:2
That Lady 1949,O 20,38:8
That Lady 1949,N 23,18:4
That Lady 1949,D 4,II,5:1
Billy Budd 1951,F 12,18:3
Billy Budd 1951,F 18,II,1:1
Firstborn, The 1958,My 1,35:1
Firstborn, The 1958,My 11,II,1:1
Miracle Worker, The 1959,O 20,44:1
Miracle Worker, The 1959,N 1,II,1:1
Write Me a Murder 1961,O 27,28:2
Hidden Stranger 1963,Ja 10,5:5
Hidden Stranger 1963,Ja 15,8:5
Thatcher-Shreve, Adele
Mask and the Face, The 1924,S 11,27:3
Thater, Al
She Stoops to Conquer 1949,D 29,21:3
Thaw, Lawrence Copley (Mrs)
Riff-Raff 1926,F 9,18:6
Thawl, Beverly
Joy to the World 1948,Mr 19,28:2
Thawl, Evelyn
Show Is On, The 1936,D 26,14:2
Very Warm for May 1939,N 18,23:2
Thaxter, Phyllis
There Shall Be No Night 1940,Ap 30,25:2
Sundown Beach 1948,S 8,37:1
Take Her, She's Mine 1961,D 22,19:1
Thayer, Alonzo
Adams' Wife 1931,D 29,27:1
Thayer, Bettina
Show Boat 1946,Ja 7,17:2
Thayer, Forrest (Costume Designer)
Smile of the World, The 1949,Ja 13,26:5
Cock-A-Doodle-Doo 1949,F 28,16:5
Nineteenth Hole of Europe, The 1949,Mr 28,16:2
Live Wire, The 1950,Ag 18,16:2
Thayer, Joseph
Adam Solitaire 1925,N 7,19:2
Dream Play 1926,Ja 21,18:2
Moon Is a Gong, The 1926,Mr 13,21:3
Lady for a Night, A 1928,Ap 17,26:4
Pleased to Meet You 1928,O 30,27:2
Thayer, Jurien
Elsie Janis and Her Gang 1922,Ja 17,13:2
Thayer, Lorna
Comes a Day 1958,N 7,22:1
Never Live Over a Pretzel Factory 1964,Mr 30,37:1
Thayer, Mary
Lolly 1929,O 17,26:2
Solid South 1930,My 11,IX,2:6
Thayer, Raymond
Becky Sharp 1929,Je 4,29:1
Little Father of the Wilderness, The 1930,Je 3,27:1
County Chairman, The 1936,My 26,26:5
Thayer, Richard (Director)
Your Own Thing 1968,Ja 15,33:1
Thayer, Richard (Miscellaneous)
Blood Red Roses 1970,Mr 23,48:1
Thayer, Robert (Scenic Designer)
Naked 1950,S 7,39:2
Thayer, Royal
Woman Disputed, A 1926,S 29,23:2
Headquarters 1929,D 5,32:4
Thayer, Russell
Chrysalis 1932,N 16,15:2
All Rights Reserved 1934,N 7,33:5
Thayer, Sigourney (Director)
Beau-Strings 1926,Ap 27,22:2
Damn the Tears 1927,Ja 22,11:1
Keeper of the Keys 1933,O 19,23:2
Thayer, Sigourney (Producer)
Beau-Strings 1926,Ap 27,22:2
Men Must Fight 1931,Ap 12,IX,2:1
Bridal Wise 1932,My 31,15:5
Keeper of the Keys 1933,O 19,23:2
Thayer, Sigourney (Translator)
Pilgrimage, The; Pelerin, Le 1925,N 10,23:2

Thayer, Tanagra
Lady Windermere's Fan 1946,O 15,29:2
Thayer, Tina
Out From Under 1940,My 6,13:2
Thayr, Forrest Jr (Scenic Designer)
Sarah Simple 1940,N 18,22:5
The-Mathis, Marie
Lady Windermere's Fan 1927,F 27,VII,2:3
Theodore, Ralph
Devil Within, The 1925,Mr 17,19:4
Gossipy Sex, The 1927,Ap 20,28:3
Burlesque 1927,S 2,15:3
Burlesque 1927,S 11,VIII,1:1
Sweet Land of Liberty 1929,S 24,29:2
Last Mile, The 1930,F 14,21:2
Whistling in the Dark 1932,Ja 20,16:6
We the People 1933,Ja 23,9:5
Strange Gods 1933,Ap 17,16:6
Give Us This Day 1933,O 28,20:6
They Shall Not Die 1934,F 22,24:4
Jayhawker 1934,N 6,34:2
Mother Sings 1935,N 13,24:1
Seen But Not Heard 1936,S 18,19:2
Call Me Ziggy 1937,F 13,9:6
Cream in the Well, The 1941,Ja 21,19:2
Land Is Bright, The 1941,O 21,28:5
Land Is Bright, The 1941,O 29,26:2
Uncle Harry 1942,My 21,24:1
Ramshackle Inn 1944,Ja 6,17:5
Strange Fruit 1945,N 30,18:6
Truckline Cafe 1946,F 28,19:4
Happy Birthday 1946,N 1,31:2
Summer and Smoke 1948,O 7,33:2
Summer and Smoke 1948,O 17,II,1:1
Long Days, The 1951,Ap 21,10:5
Theatre des Quatre Saisons
Roi Cerf, Le 1937,O 27,28:7
Theatre du Peuple
Mother, The 1937,Ag 29,X,1:3
Theatre Today
Plough and the Stars, The 1950,Ap 2,II,1:1
Thedy and Family Group
Judy Garland's New Variety Show 1956,S 27,43:2
Theilade, Nina
Midsummer Night's Dream, A 1934,S 19,15:1
Theiss, Ernest
Mr Sycamore 1942,N 14,13:2
Thellman, Erika von
Madonna Wo Bist Du? 1932,Jl 17,IX,1:3
Victoria Regina 1938,Ap 17,X,2:1
Theman, Carl
Grand Duchess 1929,D 17,29:2
Themerson, Franciszka (Scenic Designer)
Threepenny Opera, The 1966,O 28,33:1
Thenstead, Adolph (Composer)
Caribbean Carnival 1947,D 6,12:2
Thenstead, Adolph (Lyricist)
Caribbean Carnival 1947,D 6,12:2
Thenstead, Adolph (Producer)
Caribbean Carnival 1947,D 6,12:2
Theobold, Neil
Foursome 1965,Mr 8,34:1
Leader, The 1965,Mr 8,34:1
Bedlam Galore, for Two or More 1965,Mr 8,34:1
Theodor
Florida Girl 1925,N 3,34:1
Theodor, Pan
God Strikes Back 1943,F 27,11:2
Theodore, Flavio
Just a Minute 1928,O 9,34:3
Theodore, Lee (Choreographer)
Baker Street 1965,F 17,36:1
Flora, the Red Menace 1965,My 12,41:2
Diary of Adam and Eve, The 1966,O 19,53:1
Passionella 1966,O 19,53:1
Lady or the Tiger?, The 1966,O 19,53:1
Darling of the Day 1968,Ja 29,26:2
West Side Story 1968,Je 25,32:1
Theodore, Lee (Director)
West Side Story 1968,Je 25,32:1
Noel Coward's Sweet Potato 1968,S 30,59:1
Noel Coward's Sweet Potato 1968,O 13,II,5:1
Park 1970,Ap 23,47:1
Theodore, Lee (Miscellaneous)
Electra 1964,Ag 12,42:1
Theodore, Luke (Miscellaneous)
Frankenstein 1968,O 3,54:1
Theodore, Paris
Peter Pan 1954,O 21,30:2
Theodore, Ralph
Wandering Jew, The 1921,O 27,22:1
Singin' the Blues 1931,S 17,21:3
Key Largo 1939,O 31,26:6
Key Largo 1939,N 28,30:2
Theopold, P H
Who's Who 1924,Ap 18,19:2
Therry, Michael
Pirates of Penzance, The 1942,F 20,20:2
H M S Pinafore 1949,Jl 29,13:2
Thery, Jacques (Original Author)
Dompteur, Le, ou L'Anglais Tel Qu' On La Mange
1926,Ja 10,VII,1:3

Thery, Jacques (Playwright)
Diable 1926,O 31,VIII,2:4
Knock Out 1927,Mr 27,VII,4:8
Thery, Jules (Playwright)
Fresh Fruit 1927,S 11,VIII,2:4
Thesiger, Ernest
Scarlet Lady, The 1926,O 17,VIII,2:1
Excelsior 1928,S 30,IX,1:3
Devil, The 1930,F 2,VIII,2:4
Devil Passes, The 1932,Ja 5,20:3
Devil Passes, The 1932,Ja 10,VIII,1:1
Sleeping Clergyman, A 1934,O 9,16:1
Saint Joan 1936,Jl 26,II,1:3
Country Wife, The 1936,O 7,32:3
Madame Bovary 1937,O 6,28:4
Madame Bovary 1937,N 17,26:2
In Good King Charles's Golden Days
1939,Ag 13,28:1
Big Ben 1939,S 10,IX,2:2
As You Like It 1950,Ja 27,27:2
As You Like It 1950,F 19,II,1:1
Country Wife, The 1957,N 28,56:1
Theslof, Gene
Holiday on Ice 1967,Ag 31,29:2
Theslof, Sara
Holiday on Ice 1967,Ag 31,29:2
Thestino, Manola
Spanish Love 1920,Ag 18,6:1
Theurer, J P
It's the Valet 1933,D 15,25:4
Fiesta 1933,D 16,12:2
Stags at Bay 1934,D 15,9:2
Theyard, Harry
Man of La Mancha 1965,N 23,52:1
Time for Singing, A 1966,My 23,48:2
Thibault, Claude
Twelfth Night 1957,Jl 4,16:4
Thie, Sharon (Playwright)
Collision Course; Thoughts on the Instant of
Greeting a Friend on the Street 1968,My 9,55:2
Thoughts on the Instant of Greeting a Friend on
the Street 1968,My 19,II,1:1
Thieberger, Richard (Original Author)
Strong Are Lonely, The 1953,S 30,38:3
Thiele, Herta
Egmont 1932,Je 19,IX,1:3
Thigpen, Helen
Porgy and Bess 1953,Mr 10,25:5
Thimar, David (Director)
No Hard Feelings 1965,Ap 5,33:8
Thimig, Hans
Midsummer Night's Dream, A 1927,Ag 8,6:1
Midsummer Night's Dream, A 1927,N 18,21:1
Jedermann 1927,D 8,33:2
Dantons Tod 1927,D 21,28:3
Peripherie 1928,Ja 3,29:1
Diener Zweier Herren; Servant of Two Masters,
The 1928,Ja 10,28:3
Er Ist an Allem Schuld; He Is to Blame for
Everything 1928,Ja 10,28:3
Servant of Two Masters, The 1928,Ja 22,VIII,6:1
Lebende Leichnam, Der, Der; Living Corpse, The
1928,Ja 24,26:2
Kyrill Reist ins Abendland 1933,Ja 8,IX,2:1
Harvey 1949,Mr 24,34:1
Thimig, Helene
Kabale und Liebe 1928,Ja 17,22:3
Lebende Leichnam, Der, Der; Living Corpse, The
1928,Ja 24,26:2
Dorothea Angermann 1928,F 19,VIII,2:1
Everyman 1929,Ag 5,25:1
Kreatur, Die 1930,My 25,IX,1:8
Schwierige, Der 1930,N 30,IX,2:1
Vor Sonnenuntergang; Before Sunset
1932,Mr 13,VIII,2:7
Thimig, Hermann
Midsummer Night's Dream, A 1925,Mr 8,VII,2:1
Peripherie 1926,D 19,VII,4:4
Midsummer Night's Dream, A 1927,Ag 8,6:1
Midsummer Night's Dream, A 1927,N 18,21:1
Jedermann 1927,D 8,33:2
Jedermann 1927,D 18,IX,6:1
Dantons Tod 1927,D 21,28:3
Peripherie 1928,Ja 3,29:1
Diener Zweier Herren; Servant of Two Masters,
The 1928,Ja 10,28:3
Servant of Two Masters, The 1928,Ja 22,VIII,6:1
Lebende Leichnam, Der, Der; Living Corpse, The
1928,Ja 24,26:2
Fledermaus, Die 1929,Jl 14,IX,2:1
Tales of Hoffmann 1932,Ja 10,VIII,1:6
Thimig, Hugo
Kyrill Reist ins Abendland 1933,Ja 8,IX,2:1
Thirkield, Rob
Tom Paine 1968,Mr 26,38:1
Thirkield, Robert (Scenic Designer)
Little Eyolf 1964,Mr 17,31:1
Thirlwell, George
Via Crucis 1923,N 13,25:2
Hamlet 1923,N 20,23:3
Thiveos, Nicos
Electra 1930,D 27,16:1

Thiveou, Maria
Electra 1930,D 27,16:1
Thom, Michael
King and I, The 1968,My 24,39:1
Thom, Norman F
Parson's Bride, The 1929,Ja 22,22:3
Thom, Norman F (Producer)
Parson's Bride, The 1929,Ja 22,22:3
Thom, Robert (Miscellaneous)
Compulsion 1957,O 25,21:1
Compulsion 1957,N 3,II,1:1
Thom, Robert (Playwright)
Bicycle Ride to Nevada 1963,S 25,38:1
Thom, Vie Von
World of Suzie Wong, The 1958,O 15,47:1
Thoma, Carl
Me Nobody Knows, The 1970,My 19,42:1
Me Nobody Knows, The 1970,My 31,II,1:6
Thoma, Helge (Miscellaneous)
Captain of Koepenick, The 1964,D 2,60:1
Thoma, Ludwig (Playwright)
Morals 1925,D 1,22:2
Morals 1925,D 6,VIII,5:1
Thoma, Maralyn
Sophie 1963,Ap 16,32:1
Thoma, Michael
No Time for Sergeants 1955,O 21,32:2
Thoma, Michael (Miscellaneous)
Tall Story 1959,Ja 30,33:2
Only in America 1959,N 20,35:1
Bye Bye Birdie 1960,Ap 15,13:4
Dear Me, the Sky Is Falling 1963,Mr 4,9:1
Bicycle Ride to Nevada 1963,S 25,38:1
What Makes Sammy Run? 1964,F 28,19:1
Golden Boy 1964,O 21,56:1
Best Laid Plans, The 1966,Mr 26,15:2
Sherry! 1967,Mr 29,39:1
Happy Time, The 1968,Ja 19,32:2
Oh! Calcutta! 1969,Je 18,33:1
Rothschilds, The 1970,O 20,40:1
Thomajan, Guy
Red Gloves 1948,D 6,28:2
Number, The 1951,O 31,33:2
Camino Real 1953,Mr 20,26:1
Thomajan, Guy (Director)
Harbor Lights 1956,O 5,20:1
Thoman, Milton J
Peter Pan 1924,N 7,16:2
Thomas, A E
Vermont 1928,D 30,VIII,1:6
Just Suppose 1935,Jl 2,24:3
Thomas, A E (Lyricist)
Our Nell 1922,D 5,24:1
Thomas, A E (Miscellaneous)
Mr Whistler 1931,D 6,VIII,2:6
Uncle Tom's Cabin 1933,My 30,13:4
Thomas, A E (Original Author)
Just Fancy! 1927,O 12,30:2
Thomas, A E (Playwright)
Come Out of the Kitchen 1920,Mr 16,17:7
Just Suppose 1920,N 2,15:1
Just Suppose 1920,N 7,VII,1:1
Champion, The 1921,Ja 4,11:1
Champion, The 1921,Ja 9,VI,1:1
Turn in the Road, A 1921,Je 12,VI,1:6
Only 38 1921,S 14,22:2
French Doll, The 1922,F 21,20:2
Our Nell 1922,D 5,24:1
Jolly Roger, The 1923,Ag 31,10:4
Jolly Roger, The 1923,S 9,VII,1:1
Magnolia Lady, The 1924,N 26,17:2
Fool's Bells 1925,D 24,8:3
Embers 1926,F 2,20:3
Lost 1927,Mr 29,22:2
Big Pond, The 1928,Ag 22,25:1
Vermont 1928,D 30,VIII,1:6
Vermont 1929,Ja 9,28:1
Her Friend the King 1929,O 8,34:5
No More Ladies 1934,Ja 24,20:3
No More Ladies 1934,S 4,23:2
No More Ladies 1934,S 19,14:4
Just Suppose 1935,Jl 2,24:3
Merely Murder 1937,D 4,21:4
Thomas, Ailene
Mrs Patterson 1957,F 6,20:2
Thomas, Allen
George Washington 1920,Mr 2,9:1
Hamlet 1920,Mr 17,14:2
Taming of the Shrew, The 1921,My 12,20:2
Merchant of Venice, The 1921,My 14,10:4
Earl Carroll's Vanities 1923,Jl 6,8:2
Jolly Roger, The 1923,Ag 31,10:4
Cyrano de Bergerac 1923,N 2,14:1
Thomas, Ann
Is Zat So? 1925,Ap 25,18:2
Wild Man of Borneo, The 1927,S 14,29:2
Lady Lies, The 1928,N 11,X,2:4
Lady Lies, The 1928,N 27,36:2
Love Expert, The 1929,S 24,29:1
Charm 1929,N 29,24:5
Challenge of Youth 1930,Ja 21,28:5
Lost Boy 1932,Ja 6,24:4
Sailor, Beware! 1933,S 29,24:4

Thomas, Ann—Cont
Symphony 1935,Ap 27,20:3
Stork Mad 1936,O 1,28:4
Having Wonderful Time 1937,F 22,12:5
Tell Me Pretty Maiden 1937,D 17,33:5
Man From Cairo, The 1938,My 5,26:5
Window Shopping 1938,D 24,13:2
Two on an Island 1940,Ja 23,17:2
Five Alarm Waltz 1941,Mr 14,16:2
Counsellor-at-Law 1942,N 25,17:2
New Life, A 1943,S 16,26:6
Doctors Disagree 1943,D 29,15:2
Chicken Every Sunday 1944,Ap 6,27:2
Would-Be Gentleman, The 1946,Ja 10,29:2
Made in Heaven 1946,O 25,28:2
Dance Me a Song 1950,Ja 21,10:5
Not for Children 1951,F 14,35:2
Home Is the Hero 1954,S 23,42:2
Adding Machine, The 1956,F 10,17:1
Dr Willy Nilly 1959,Je 5,18:2
Thomas, Arlette
Pique-Nique en Campagne 1969,My 1,50:1
Guernica 1969,My 1,50:1
Thomas, Audrey
Messin' Around 1929,Ap 23,26:3
Thomas, Augustus
Lambs Gambol 1925,Ap 27,15:1
Still Waters 1925,S 8,21:5
Thomas, Augustus (Director)
Lambs Gambol 1925,Ap 27,15:1
Still Waters 1926,Mr 2,23:1
Thomas, Augustus (Original Author)
Love Call, The 1927,O 25,33:1
Thomas, Augustus (Playwright)
Nemesis 1921,Ap 5,24:3
Nemesis 1921,Ap 10,VI,1:1
Still Waters 1925,S 8,21:5
Still Waters 1926,F 26,24:2
Still Waters 1926,Mr 2,23:1
Still Waters 1926,Mr 7,VIII,1:2
Thomas, Augustus (Producer)
Still Waters 1926,F 26,24:2
Still Waters 1926,Mr 2,23:1
Thomas, Beatrix
Magnolia Street 1934,Mr 9,22:6
Thomas, Bernard
Story of Mary Surratt, The 1947,F 10,25:2
Thomas, Bernard (Director)
Love Is a Time of Day 1969,D 23,21:3
Thomas, Bill
Ice Follies 1966,Ja 12,27:6
Ice Follies 1969,My 23,38:1
Thomas, Brandon (Original Author)
Where's Charley? 1948,O 12,33:2
Where's Charley? 1950,Ag 20,II,1:1
Thomas, Brandon (Playwright)
Charley's Aunt 1925,Je 2,16:2
Charley's Aunt 1940,O 18,24:2
Charley's Aunt 1941,Jl 31,12:4
Charley's Aunt 1953,D 23,22:2
Where's Charley? 1966,My 26,57:1
Charley's Aunt 1970,Jl 6,38:1
Thomas, C C
Galloper, The 1924,D 19,26:2
Thomas, C Fabian
Career Angel 1943,N 19,24:2
Thomas, Calvin
Hottentot, The 1920,Mr 2,9:1
Six-Cylinder Love 1921,Ag 26,8:2
Thoroughbreds 1924,S 9,12:1
Hush Money 1926,Mr 16,22:3
Phantom Ship, The 1926,Je 27,VII,3:1
Junk 1927,Ja 6,25:1
Set a Thief 1927,F 22,22:1
Trapped 1928,S 12,25:3
Show Girl 1929,Jl 3,19:3
Just to Remind You 1931,S 8,39:1
Anybody's Game 1932,D 22,21:4
We the People 1933,Ja 23,9:5
Ship Comes in, A 1934,S 20,21:1
Lady Detained, A 1935,Ja 10,23:3
Knock on Wood 1935,My 29,16:2
Night of January 16 1935,S 17,26:4
Mimie Scheller 1936,O 1,28:4
Miss Quis 1937,Ap 8,20:5
Wise Tomorrow 1937,O 16,22:5
Stop-Over 1938,Ja 12,16:5
Escape This Night 1938,Ap 23,18:1
Abe Lincoln in Illinois 1938,O 17,12:2
Village Green 1941,S 4,24:4
Sweet Charity 1942,D 29,26:4
Kiss and Tell 1943,Mr 18,22:1
Ryan Girl, The 1945,S 25,28:2
Carousel 1949,Ja 26,28:2
Carousel 1949,F 6,II,1:1
Angels Kiss Me 1951,Ap 18,37:6
Traveling Lady 1954,O 28,45:2
Pipe Dream 1955,D 1,44:1
Thomas, Calvin (Director)
Launcelot and Elaine 1930,Mr 10,24:3
Thomas, Calvin Jr
It Can't Happen Here 1938,Jl 26,22:2
Thomas, Campbell
Macbeth 1968,N 30,49:3

Thomas, Caroline
Trumpets and Drums 1969,O 13,52:1
Macbeth 1969,D 23,25:1
Thomas, Charles
Fireworks on the James 1940,My 15,30:2
Thomas, Charles Columbus
High John De Conquer 1969,Ap 23,39:1
Thomas, Charline
Fall and Rise of Susan Lenox, The 1920,Je 11,11:2
Thomas, Christine
Matchmaker, The 1955,D 6,45:6
Under Milk Wood 1957,O 16,42:5
Family Reunion, The 1958,O 21,39:1
Epitaph for George Dillon 1960,D 29,17:1
Complaisant Lover, The 1961,N 2,43:2
Thomas, Clara Fargo (Scenic Designer)
Grounds for Divorce 1924,O 5,VIII,1:1
Second Mrs Tanqueray, The 1924,O 28,27:1
High Road, The 1928,S 11,31:1
Thomas, Cleveland
Cure for Matrimony 1939,O 26,26:3
Thomas, Danny
Untitled-Revue 1950,Mr 29,36:2
Thomas, David
Night at an Inn, A 1930,My 10,25:1
Million Dollar Baby 1945,D 22,17:2
Street Scene 1947,Ja 10,17:2
Cradle Will Rock, The 1947,N 25,38:3
Cradle Will Rock, The 1947,D 27,11:2
Love Life 1948,O 8,31:2
Regina 1949,N 1,32:2
Courtin' Time 1951,Je 14,30:2
Paint Your Wagon 1951,N 13,32:2
Regina 1952,Je 2,25:4
Can-Can 1953,My 8,28:1
My Fair Lady 1956,Mr 16,20:2
All American 1962,Mr 20,44:1
Moby Dick 1962,N 29,45:1
Sophie 1963,Ap 16,32:1
Morning Sun 1963,O 7,36:2
Deputy, The 1964,F 27,26:1
On a Clear Day You Can See Forever
1965,O 18,44:1
Time for Singing, A 1966,My 23,48:2
Show Boat 1966,Jl 20,48:1
Soldiers 1968,My 2,58:1
Canterbury Tales; Pilgrims, The 1969,F 4,34:1
Coco 1969,D 19,66:1
Lovely Ladies, Kind Gentlemen 1970,D 29,38:1
Thomas, Debbie
My Wife and I 1966,O 11,53:2
Thomas, Dorleen
Annie Get Your Gun 1958,F 20,29:2
Thomas, Dorothy
Lady Comes Across, The 1942,Ja 10,10:2
Thomas, Dylan
Under Milk Wood 1953,My 29,17:1
Thomas, Dylan (Original Author)
Doctor and the Devils, The 1959,Ja 21,27:8
Thomas, Dylan (Playwright)
Under Milk Wood 1953,My 29,17:1
Under Milk Wood 1956,Ag 22,25:3
Boy Growing Up, A 1957,O 8,41:1
Under Milk Wood 1957,O 16,42:5
Under Milk Wood 1957,N 10,II,1:1
When I Was a Child 1960,D 9,38:1
Under Milk Wood 1961,Mr 30,25:1
Under Milk Wood 1961,Ap 9,II,1:1
Doctor and the Devils, The 1962,Ag 22,28:1
Under Milk Wood 1962,O 6,13:4
Songs From Milk Wood 1970,Ja 13,41:1
Thomas, E D (Playwright)
Babbling Brookes 1927,F 26,13:2
Thomas, E T Jr
Man From Earth, The 1923,Ja 3,6:2
Thomas, Eb
Macbeth 1957,Ag 16,11:2
Richard III 1957,N 26,41:1
Recruiting Officer, The 1958,F 8,12:2
Thomas, Edna
Lulu Belle 1926,F 10,20:1
Vaudeville (Palace) 1927,My 24,23:1
Ol' Man Satan 1932,O 4,26:3
Run, Little Chillun! 1933,Mr 2,21:3
Stevedore 1934,Ap 19,33:2
Macbeth 1936,Ap 15,25:4
Androcles and the Lion 1938,D 17,10:5
Harriet 1943,Mr 4,24:2
Harriet 1944,S 28,26:1
Strange Fruit 1945,N 30,18:6
Streetcar Named Desire, A 1947,D 4,42:2
Streetcar Named Desire, A 1950,My 24,36:1
Streetcar Named Desire, A 1956,F 16,24:1
Thomas, Edward (Composer)
Ballad for a Firing Squad 1968,D 12,64:2
Thomas, Edward (Miscellaneous)
Tall Story 1959,Ja 30,33:2
Thomas, Edward (Producer)
Ballad for a Firing Squad 1968,D 12,64:2
Thomas, Elise
Harlem 1929,F 21,30:3
Thomas, Elwood K
Keeper of the Keys 1933,O 19,23:2

Thomas, Evan
Anne-One Hundred 1927,Je 26,VIII,1:3
Ghost Parade, The 1929,O 31,28:4
Merry Widow, The 1929,D 3,29:1
Ghost for Sale 1941,S 30,27:4
Golden Wings 1941,D 9,46:6
Lady Windermere's Fan 1946,O 15,29:2
Much Ado About Nothing 1952,My 2,20:1
Sherlock Holmes 1953,O 31,11:2
Brigadoon 1967,D 14,59:2
H M S Pinafore 1968,Ap 29,47:2
Yeomen of the Guard, The 1968,My 9,53:1
My Fair Lady 1968,Je 14,42:1
Thomas, Frank M
Back Pay 1921,Ag 31,8:2
National Anthem, The 1922,Ja 24,16:3
Red Light Annie 1923,Ag 22,10:3
Aloma of the South Seas 1925,Ap 21,18:1
Little Spitfire, The 1926,Ag 17,15:2
Night Hawk 1926,D 27,21:3
Praying Curve 1927,Ja 25,18:2
House of Fear, The 1929,O 8,34:2
Launcelot and Elaine 1930,Mr 10,24:3
Louder, Please! 1931,N 13,26:4
Inside Story, The 1932,F 23,23:2
Carry Nation 1932,O 31,18:2
Tragedy of the Ages, The 1933,Ap 7,22:7
Gods We Make, The 1934,Ja 4,16:4
Remember the Day 1935,Jl 9,24:3
Remember the Day 1935,S 26,19:3
Chicken Every Sunday 1944,Ap 6,27:2
Chicken Every Sunday 1944,Ap 16,II,1:1
Rich Full Life, The 1945,N 10,9:2
Jeb 1946,F 22,20:2
Christopher Blake 1946,D 2,33:2
Hallams, The 1948,Mr 5,18:2
End as a Man 1953,S 16,39:1
End As a Man 1953,S 27,II,1:1
Legend of Lizzie, The 1959,F 10,39:1
Thomas, Frank M (Producer)
Digging for Apples 1962,S 28,29:4
Thomas, Frank M Jr
Little Ol' Boy 1933,Ap 25,15:5
Thunder on the Left 1933,N 1,25:2
Wednesday's Child 1934,Ja 17,23:2
Wednesday's Child 1934,Ja 28,IX,1:1
First Legion, The 1934,O 2,18:2
Remember the Day 1935,O 13,IX,1:1
Seen But Not Heard 1936,Jl 22,23:4
Thomas, Frankie
Remember the Day 1935,Jl 9,24:3
Remember the Day 1935,S 26,19:3
Seen But Not Heard 1936,S 18,19:2
Your Loving Son 1941,Ap 5,13:2
Thomas, Franklyn
Rain 1948,F 2,15:2
Thomas, Fred
Caribbean Carnival 1947,D 6,12:2
Thomas, Galvin
Abe Lincoln in Illinois 1938,O 4,20:1
Thomas, George
Lulu Belle 1926,F 10,20:1
Macbeth 1936,Ap 15,25:4
Thomas, Gerald (Miscellaneous)
Warm Body, A 1967,Ap 17,44:2
Thomas, Gregory
Flying Blind 1930,My 16,20:2
Thomas, H B
Her Salary Man 1921,N 29,20:1
Thomas, Hank
Streetcar Named Desire, A 1955,Mr 4,18:2
Thomas, Harold
School for Scandal, The 1925,D 7,18:2
Gentlemen Prefer Blondes 1926,S 29,23:1
She Stoops to Conquer 1928,My 15,17:1
Macbeth 1928,N 20,28:3
Falstaff 1928,D 26,14:2
One, Two, Three! 1930,S 30,24:2
Julius Caesar 1931,N 18,26:3
Good Earth, The 1932,O 18,23:4
Pride and Prejudice 1935,N 6,32:4
Black Limelight 1936,N 10,31:1
Yr Obedient Husband 1938,Ja 11,26:5
Come Across 1938,S 15,28:3
Thomas, Hazel
Young American, A 1946,Ja 18,14:5
Thomas, Henry
And People All Around 1968,F 12,46:1
Waltz Invention, The 1969,Ja 12,II,20:4
Thomas, Henry (Director)
Tell Her the Truth 1932,O 29,18:2
Thomas, Hugh
Chicken Every Sunday 1944,Ap 6,27:2
Earth Journey 1944,Ap 28,24:2
Misalliance 1955,F 12,10:6
Fantasticks, The 1960,My 4,55:2
Twelfth Night 1970,Ja 1,18:1
Hamlet 1970,D 28,40:1
Thomas, Hugh (Playwright)
Maggie 1953,F 19,20:2
Thomas, Hugh Jr
Mary of Magdala 1946,Mr 26,24:5

Thomas, Ian (Playwright)
Boswell's Life of Johnson 1970,S 4,19:1
Thomas, Ifor
Sing High, Sing Low 1931,N 13,26:4
Thomas, Irma
Ice Capades 1953,S 11,25:1
Ice Capades 1954,S 16,37:1
Ice Capades 1955,S 15,38:1
Ice Capades 1957,S 5,33:2
Ice Capades 1961,Ag 31,24:4
Thomas, Jackie
My Beginning 1962,Ja 31,21:1
Thomas, Jamie
South Pacific 1969,Jl 7,27:1
Thomas, Jane
Gambling 1929,Ag 27,31:2
Song and Dance Man, The 1930,Je 17,25:5
Song of Bernadette 1946,Mr 27,22:2
Thomas, Jean
Silks and Satins 1920,Jl 16,19:1
Last Waltz, The 1921,My 11,20:3
Thomas, Jean (Original Author)
Plum Hollow 1935,Je 16,II,6:7
Thomas, Jevan Brandon (Playwright)
Passing Brompton Road 1928,Ag 5,VII,1:1
Thomas, Jimmy
Change Your Luck 1930,Je 7,10:2
Thomas, Joel
Trial Honeymoon 1947,N 4,31:2
Eastward in Eden 1956,Ap 18,25:4
Ardele 1958,Ap 9,39:4
Vincent 1959,O 1,40:1
Vincent 1959,O 11,II,1:1
Thomas, John
Not in Our Stars 1941,Ap 26,20:5
Comes the Revelation 1942,My 27,26:2
Counterattack 1943,F 4,27:2
Golden Fleecing 1959,O 16,24:5
Cut of the Axe 1960,F 2,38:2
Thomas, John Charles
Love Letter, The 1921,O 5,20:1
Vaudeville (Palace) 1929,My 20,22:8
Vaudeville (Palace) 1929,Ag 19,23:1
Thomas, Joseph
Variations of 1940 1940,Ja 29,12:1
Wish You Were Here 1952,Je 26,26:6
Thomas, Joseph B (Mrs)
Variations of 1940 1940,Ja 29,12:1
Thomas, Lenore
Best Foot Forward 1941,O 2,28:2
Day Will Come, The 1944,S 8,17:2
Family Affair, A 1946,N 28,41:2
Thomas, Leo (Playwright)
Slightly Delinquent 1954,O 26,32:5
Thomas, Linda
Displaced Person, The 1966,D 30,15:1
Thomas, Lowell
Ryan Girl, The 1945,S 25,28:2
Thomas, Lucy
Bedrock 1934,N 18,II,6:3
Thomas, Margaret
Highland Fling, A 1944,Ap 29,13:2
Thomas, Marie
But Never Jam Today 1969,Ap 24,40:1
Moon on a Rainbow Shawl 1970,D 18,52:1
Thomas, Marilyn
Slave Ship 1969,N 22,46:1
Thomas, Martina
Women, The 1936,D 28,13:1
Thomas, Mary (Director)
Night in Spring, A 1935,Ag 7,22:2
Thomas, May
Delicate Story 1940,D 5,32:2
Thomas, Millard
Belafonte at the Palace 1959,D 16,55:1
Thomas, Millard (Composer)
Brown Buddies 1930,O 8,29:1
Thomas, Milo (Playwright)
Rate of Exchange 1968,Ap 2,50:1
Thomas, Milo 1st (Producer)
Story for a Sunday Evening, A 1950,N 18,10:5
Thomas, Miss
Pirates of Penzance, The 1926,D 12,VIII,3:1
Thomas, Mitch
Fiddler on the Roof 1964,S 23,56:2
Thomas, Mona
Blue Bonnet 1920,Ag 30,12:1
Thomas, Nicholas
Criminals, The 1941,D 22,24:3
Thomas, Norman Jr
Vaudeville (Palace) 1931,S 28,17:5
Thomas, Norman Quintette
Vaudeville (Palace) 1928,My 15,17:1
Vaudeville (Palace) 1930,My 5,27:5
Vaudeville (Palace) 1932,My 30,16:7
Thomas, Paul
That's That 1924,Ap 30,19:2
Thomas, Phil
Conjur' Man Dies 1936,Mr 12,18:5
Thomas, Philandre
Macbeth 1936,Ap 15,25:4
Thomas, Piri (Playwright)
Golden Streets, The 1970,Ag 14,21:1

Thomas, Powys
Measure for Measure 1957,Ja 23,24:1
Hamlet 1957,Jl 3,15:2
Under Milk Wood 1957,O 16,42:5
Two Gentlemen of Verona 1958,Mr 19,35:1
Broken Jug, The 1958,Ap 2,36:1
Henry IV, Part I 1958,Je 25,23:3
Much Ado About Nothing 1958,Je 26,22:1
Winter's Tale, The 1958,Jl 23,34:3
Salad Days 1958,N 11,24:1
Othello 1959,Jl 2,17:2
Henry IV, Part I 1965,Je 30,42:1
Julius Caesar 1965,Jl 2,18:1
Cherry Orchard, The 1965,Ag 2,17:2
Henry V 1966,Je 8,38:1
Henry VI 1966,Je 9,55:2
Romeo and Juliet 1968,Je 11,55:2
Three Musketeers, The 1968,Jl 24,49:2
Hamlet 1969,Je 11,37:1
Alchemist, The 1969,Je 12,51:1
Alchemist, The 1969,Je 22,II,1:7
Hamlet 1969,Je 22,II,1:7
Merchant of Venice, The 1970,Je 10,39:1
School for Scandal, The 1970,Je 11,51:1
Cymbeline 1970,Ag 23,II,1:6
Thomas, R Scott
Falstaff 1966,Je 20,27:1
Julius Caesar 1966,Je 24,29:2
Thomas, Ralph
Judas 1929,Ja 25,20:4
Thomas, Rhys
Yeomen of the Guard, The 1948,F 3,30:2
Thomas, Richard
Million Dollar Baby 1945,D 22,17:2
Strange Interlude 1963,Mr 13,5:2
Richard III 1964,Je 12,44:2
Playroom, The 1965,D 6,49:1
Richard III 1966,Ag 11,26:1
Everything in the Garden 1967,N 30,60:1
Thomas, Ring
Vermont 1929,Ja 9,28:1
Thomas, Robert
Confederacy, The 1958,Jl 3,20:1
Thomas, Robert (Original Author)
Catch Me if You Can 1965,Mr 10,50:1
Thomas, Robert John
This Mad Whirl 1937,Ja 10,II,4:8
Thomas, Royston
Sing to Me Through Open Windows
1965,Mr 16,45:1
Thomas, Rudolph (Director)
Patience 1929,D 16,34:5
Thomas, Rudolph (Musical Director)
Chocolate Soldier, The 1932,F 9,30:3
Thomas, Ruth
Toto 1921,Mr 22,15:2
Across the Street 1924,Mr 25,24:1
Pirates of Penzance, The; Slave of Duty, The
1926,D 7,25:1
Kidding Kidders 1928,Ap 24,28:3
Guinea Pig, The 1929,Ja 8,35:1
Merry-Go-Round 1932,Ap 23,11:2
Threepenny Opera, The 1933,Ap 14,22:4
Sellout, The 1933,S 7,17:2
As the Girls Go 1948,N 15,21:2
Thomas, Samuel
Bitter Sweet 1934,My 8,28:4
Thomas, Scott
Winter's Tale, The 1963,Je 29,13:1
Midsummer Night's Dream, A 1963,Jl 1,19:2
Thomas, Shirl
Banjo Eyes 1941,D 26,20:2
Thomas, T F
Sidewalks of New York 1927,O 4,33:1
Thomas, Timothy
Dancing Mothers 1924,Ag 12,12:2
Thomas, Tony
Comedy of Errors, The 1968,F 28,40:2
Henry V 1969,N 11,43:1
Immaculate Misconception, The 1970,O 28,63:3
Thomas, Tsay
She Stoops to Conquer 1968,Ap 1,58:3
Thomas, Vickie
Junebug Graduates Tonight! 1967,F 27,35:1
Street Sounds 1970,O 23,32:1
Thomas, W H
Witness for the Prosecution 1954,D 17,35:2
Thomas, Walter
Malinda 1929,D 4,37:2
Thomas, William (Lighting Director)
Lady Says Yes, A 1945,Ja 11,18:5
Thomas, William (Scenic Designer)
Capacity for Wings 1957,Ja 10,25:2
Thomas (Mr) (Original Author)
Bonita 1927,S 4,VII,2:4
Thomas and Covera
Vogues of 1924 1924,Mr 28,14:3
Thomas and Smith
Ice Follies 1965,Ja 13,35:1
Thomas Sisters
Parisiana 1928,F 10,26:3
Thomashefsky, Annie
Girl From Warsaw, The 1931,S 14,15:5

Thomashefsky, Annie—Cont
Mother's Son 1931,N 26,36:4
Under One Roof 1932,F 8,21:2
Big Surprise, The 1932,O 17,18:3
Traveling Salesman, The 1932,N 1,24:4
Jewish Melody, The 1933,Mr 27,12:4
Once Upon a Time 1933,S 22,15:1
Germany Aflame 1933,O 28,20:5
Three in Love 1933,N 8,32:5
Organ Grinder, The 1934,Ja 1,28:3
Happy Days 1934,Ap 2,12:5
Here Runs the Bride 1934,N 4,IX,2:1
One in a Million 1934,N 17,13:2
Lost Paradise 1934,D 14,28:3
What Girls Do 1935,Ja 14,10:4
Holiday in Town, A 1935,S 30,12:3
Secret of Love, The 1936,F 24,15:2
Yoina Seeks a Bride 1936,O 20,31:1
Little Tailor, The 1938,Mr 21,18:2
In a Jewish Grocery 1939,O 2,15:2
Her Great Mistake 1940,F 5,12:6
Thomashefsky, Bessie
Women of New York 1931,Mr 23,24:3
Lost Paradise 1934,D 14,28:3
Thomashefsky, Boris
Three Little Business Men, The 1923,S 4,12:1
Jolly Tailors, The 1923,N 3,13:3
Eretz Israel 1930,N 27,32:3
Singing Rabbi, The 1931,S 11,24:4
Mother's Son 1931,N 26,36:4
Lost Paradise 1934,D 14,28:3
Boris and Bessie 1937,D 23,24:6
Thomashefsky, Boris (Original Author)
Boris and Bessie 1937,D 23,24:6
Thomashefsky, Boris (Playwright)
Jolly Tailors, The 1923,N 3,13:3
Eretz Israel 1930,N 27,32:3
Singing Rabbi, The 1931,S 11,24:4
Mother's Son 1931,N 26,36:4
Thomashefsky, Boris (Producer)
Dybbuk, The 1924,Ja 29,17:7
Thomashefsky, Harry
Slaves of Luxury 1930,F 8,13:3
Hello Grandpa! 1931,Ja 2,25:3
Jolly World, A 1931,Ja 24,15:3
Thomashefsky, Harry (Playwright)
Singing Rabbi, The 1931,S 11,24:4
Thomashefsky, Harry (Producer)
Dybbuk, The 1924,Ja 29,17:7
Singing Rabbi, The 1931,S 11,24:4
Thomasin, Adelina
Treasure, The 1920,O 5,13:1
Thomassen, Jess
Good Hunting 1938,N 22,26:5
Thomps, Theon, U S
Plantation Revue, The 1922,Jl 18,18:4
Thompson, Alice
New Life, A 1943,S 16,26:6
Thompson, Ann
Strange Bedfellows 1948,Ja 15,27:3
Thompson, Arthur
Salome 1923,My 8,22:2
Thompson, Arthur C
Yerma 1966,D 9,60:1
Thompson, Audrey
Last of Mrs Cheyney, The 1925,N 10,23:5
Thompson, Charles
Holka Polka 1925,O 15,27:2
Belt, The 1927,O 20,33:1
Hot Pan 1928,F 16,14:1
Hobo 1931,F 12,24:4
Man on Stilts, The 1931,S 10,23:2
Lancashire Lass, The 1931,D 31,16:3
Peace on Earth 1933,N 30,39:2
Sailors of Cattaro 1934,D 11,28:4
Hymn to the Rising Sun 1937,My 7,28:2
Casey Jones 1938,F 21,14:2
Night Music 1940,F 23,18:2
Heavenly Express 1940,Ap 19,24:2
Mr Peebles and Mr Hooker 1946,O 11,29:2
Rosmersholm 1946,N 23,11:5
Season in the Sun 1950,S 29,31:2
Out West of Eighth 1951,S 21,20:3
Inherit the Wind 1955,Ap 22,20:2
Thompson, Charlotte (Playwright)
June Love 1921,Ap 26,20:1
Thompson, Clare
Artists and Models 1923,Ag 21,12:2
Thompson, Cleve
Black Nativity 1961,D 12,54:2
Thompson, Creighton
St Louis Woman 1946,Ap 1,22:2
Street Scene 1947,Ja 10,17:2
Gentleman From Athens, The 1947,D 10,42:4
Thompson, D J
Day Will Come, The 1944,S 8,17:2
Thompson, Dana (Director)
Hopalong--Freud 1953,Je 18,38:5
Brandy Is My True Love's Name 1953,Je 18,38:5
Thompson, David
Birds, The 1966,Jl 1,40:1
Thompson, DeKoven
Ol' Man Satan 1932,O 4,26:3

Thompson, Donald
 Killers 1928,Mr 14,28:3
 Getting Even 1929,Ag 20,31:1
Thompson, Dorothy (Playwright)
 Another Sun 1940,F 24,8:6
Thompson, Drew
 Heavenly Twins, The 1955,N 5,23:2
Thompson, Ed
 Rang Tang 1927,Jl 13,20:1
Thompson, Edgar
 Plain and Fancy 1955,Ja 28,14:2
Thompson, Edward
 Lulu Belle 1926,F 10,20:1
 Goat Alley 1927,Ap 21,24:3
 Trojan Horse, The 1940,O 31,28:3
 Our Lan' 1947,S 29,16:5
Thompson, Edward (Playwright)
 King's Pirate, The 1937,Je 11,26:1
 King's Pirate, The 1937,Je 27,X,1:3
Thompson, Edwin
 Caravan 1928,Ag 30,13:3
Thompson, El
 Cherry Blossoms 1927,Mr 29,22:3
Thompson, Ella
 Electra 1969,Ag 8,14:1
Thompson, Evan
 Littlest Crown, The 1968,Ap 15,41:1
 Jimmy 1969,O 24,38:1
 Mahagonny 1970,Ap 29,51:1
Thompson, Evelyn (Costume Designer)
 Sunset 1966,My 13,34:1
 Junebug Graduates Tonight! 1967,F 27,35:1
Thompson, Francis
 Don Juan; Feast With the Statue, The
 1956,Ja 4,21:4
Thompson, Frank (Costume Designer)
 Linden Tree, The 1948,Mr 3,28:2
 Rape of Lucretia, The 1948,D 30,24:2
 Late Love 1953,O 14,35:2
 His and Hers 1954,Ja 8,18:2
 Nature's Way 1957,O 17,42:2
 Nude With Violin 1957,N 15,36:1
 Moonbirds 1959,O 10,13:1
 Tenth Man, The 1959,N 6,24:2
 Viva Madison Avenue 1960,Ap 7,42:1
 How to Make a Man 1961,F 3,16:1
 Decameron, The 1961,Ap 13,32:1
 Pal Joey 1961,Je 1,32:1
 Perfect Setup, The 1962,O 25,47:1
 Harold 1962,N 30,27:1
 Photo Finish 1963,F 14,5:2
 Pal Joey 1963,My 30,21:1
 Irregular Verb to Love, The 1963,S 19,22:2
 Never Live Over a Pretzel Factory 1964,Mr 30,37:1
 Guys and Dolls 1965,Ap 29,39:1
 Kismet 1965,Je 23,45:1
 Zulu and the Zayda, The 1965,N 11,59:1
 Most Happy Fella, The 1966,My 12,55:1
 Where's Charley? 1966,My 26,57:1
 Annie Get Your Gun 1966,Je 1,42:2
 Guys and Dolls 1966,Je 9,55:2
 Rose Tattoo, The 1966,O 21,36:2
 Finian's Rainbow 1967,Ap 6,44:1
 Wonderful Town 1967,My 18,50:1
 Tenth Man, The 1967,N 9,54:1
 Place for Polly, A 1970,Ap 20,45:1
 Gingerbread Lady, The 1970,D 14,58:3
Thompson, Fred
 Romeo and Juliet 1935,D 24,10:2
 Saint Joan 1936,Mr 10,27:4
 Shoemaker's Holiday, The 1938,Ja 3,17:2
 Danton's Death 1938,N 3,26:2
Thompson, Fred (Costume Designer)
 Louisiana Lady 1947,Je 3,35:2
Thompson, Fred (Lyricist)
 Vogues of 1924 1924,Mr 28,14:3
 Marjorie 1924,Ag 12,12:2
Thompson, Fred (Original Author)
 Lady Comes Across, The 1942,Ja 10,10:2
 Girl From Nantucket, The 1945,N 9,17:2
Thompson, Fred (Playwright)
 Afgar 1920,N 9,13:2
 Vogues of 1924 1924,Mr 28,14:3
 Marjorie 1924,Ag 12,12:2
 Lady Be Good 1924,D 2,23:4
 Tell Me More 1925,Ap 14,27:3
 Tip-Toes 1925,D 29,20:2
 Stylish Stouts 1926,S 19,IX,1:3
 Rio Rita 1927,F 3,18:3
 Five O'Clock Girl, The 1927,O 11,26:3
 Funny Face 1927,N 23,28:2
 Here's Howe! 1928,My 2,19:3
 Treasure Girl 1928,N 9,22:1
 Funny Face 1928,N 9,22:3
 Carry On 1929,N 3,IX,1:7
 Sons o' Guns 1929,N 27,30:4
 Seeing Stars 1935,N 1,25:5
 Going Places 1936,O 9,30:5
 Follow the Girls 1944,Ap 10,15:2
Thompson, George
 Brook 1923,Ag 20,14:3
 Devil Within, The 1925,Mr 17,19:4
 Holy Terror, A 1925,S 29,31:2

 Noose, The 1926,O 21,23:3
 Great Adventure, The 1926,D 23,23:1
 Courage 1927,Ja 20,20:1
Thompson, H S
 Monkey's Paw, The 1922,D 30,13:4
Thompson, Hal
 Great Necker, The 1928,Mr 7,28:2
 Ada Beats the Drum 1930,My 9,20:4
 Smile at Me 1935,Ag 24,18:4
 Assorted Nuts 1940,Ap 7,I,44:6
 One Eye Closed 1954,N 25,45:2
Thompson, Hal (Director)
 Family Portrait 1959,My 6,48:2
 Jonah! 1967,S 22,52:2
Thompson, Hal (Producer)
 Family Portrait 1959,My 6,48:2
 Jonah! 1967,S 22,52:2
Thompson, Hallem (Playwright)
 Transplanting Jean 1921,Ja 4,11:2
Thompson, Hallett
 Extra 1923,Ja 24,22:3
 Move On 1926,Ja 19,30:1
Thompson, Harlan (Director)
 Merry Merry 1925,S 25,24:3
 Blessed Event 1932,F 13,23:2
 Blessed Event 1932,F 21,VIII,1:1
Thompson, Harlan (Lyricist)
 Little Jessie James 1923,Ag 16,10:4
 My Girl 1924,N 25,27:2
 Merry Merry 1925,S 25,24:3
 Twinkle Twinkle 1926,N 17,22:2
Thompson, Harlan (Playwright)
 Little Jessie James 1923,Ag 16,10:4
 My Girl 1924,N 25,27:2
 Merry Merry 1925,S 25,24:3
 Twinkle Twinkle 1926,N 17,22:2
 Lucky Break 1934,O 3,25:3
Thompson, Harlan (Producer)
 Blessed Event 1932,F 13,23:2
Thompson, Harrison
 Howdy Mr Ice 1948,Je 25,28:5
 Howdy, Mr Ice of 1950 1949,My 27,24:2
Thompson, Harry
 Green Pastures, The 1935,F 27,16:2
 Candida 1938,Ag 31,13:2
Thompson, Helen
 Blossom Time 1943,S 6,21:2
Thompson, Helen (Director)
 Shadow Play 1939,Ag 15,14:5
Thompson, Henry Larue
 This Mad Whirl 1937,Ja 10,II,4:8
Thompson, Hie
 New Faces of 1943 1942,D 23,22:2
Thompson, Hugh
 Guns 1928,Ag 7,25:2
 Noble Experiment, The 1930,O 28,21:4
 Vie Parisienne, La 1941,N 6,20:3
 Two Misers, The 1943,D 9,30:5
Thompson, I W
 Scarlet Coat, The 1924,D 24,11:1
Thompson, Irwin
 Scarlet Coat, The 1924,D 24,11:1
 Fortuno 1925,D 23,22:1
 Hamlet 1927,Ap 7,23:3
 Napoleon Passes 1927,D 21,29:2
Thompson, Irwin (Composer)
 Napoleon Passes 1927,D 21,29:2
Thompson, Irwin (Lyricist)
 Fortuno 1925,D 23,22:1
 Samarkand 1926,D 22,24:4
 Napoleon Passes 1927,D 21,29:2
Thompson, Irwin (Playwright)
 Fortuno 1925,D 23,22:1
Thompson, Irwin William
 Caesar and Cleopatra 1927,N 6,IX,2:1
Thompson, Irwin William (Director)
 Caesar and Cleopatra 1927,N 6,IX,2:1
Thompson, J Elmer
 Nervous Wreck, The 1923,O 10,16:1
Thompson, J Lee (Playwright)
 Murder Without Crime 1942,Ag 9,VIII,1:8
 Murder Without Crime 1943,Ag 19,24:6
Thompson, Jack
 Two Little Girls in Blue 1921,My 4,10:3
 Peggy-Ann 1926,D 28,16:3
 Crime 1927,F 23,27:3
 Connecticut Yankee, A 1927,N 4,24:2
 Fifty Million Frenchmen 1929,N 28,34:4
Thompson, James
 Pleasure Bound 1929,F 19,22:4
 Messin' Around 1929,Ap 23,26:3
Thompson, Jane
 Charlatan, The 1922,Ap 25,14:2
Thompson, Jay (Composer)
 Annie Get Your Gun 1957,Mr 9,15:5
 Bible Salesman, The 1961,F 21,40:1
 Oldest Trick in the World, The 1961,F 21,40:1
 Put It in Writing 1963,My 14,31:1
Thompson, Jay (Lyricist)
 Bible Salesman, The 1961,F 21,40:1
 Oldest Trick in the World, The 1961,F 21,40:1
Thompson, Jay (Miscellaneous)
 Annie Get Your Gun 1957,Mr 9,15:5

Thompson, Jay (Musical Director)
 Oldest Trick in the World, The 1961,F 21,40:1
 Bible Salesman, The 1961,F 21,40:1
Thompson, Jay (Playwright)
 Once Upon a Mattress 1959,My 12,40:1
 Once Upon a Mattress 1959,My 17,II,1:1
 Bible Salesman, The 1960,F 22,12:2
 Bible Salesman, The 1961,F 21,40:1
 Oldest Trick in the World, The 1961,F 21,40:1
 Put It in Writing 1963,My 14,31:1
Thompson, Jeska
 Subway Express 1929,S 25,34:3
Thompson, John
 Miss Liberty 1949,Jl 16,6:5
Thompson, Julian
 What Next 1920,Ja 27,7:2
Thompson, Julian (Playwright)
 Warrior's Husband, The 1932,Mr 12,19:4
 Man of Wax, The 1933,Ag 6,X,1:6
 Her Man of Wax 1933,O 12,32:3
 By Jupiter 1942,Je 4,22:1
 By Jupiter 1967,Ja 20,28:2
Thompson, Julie
 Jack and the Beanstalk 1947,N 3,28:2
Thompson, Julie (Director)
 Jack and the Beanstalk 1947,N 3,28:2
 Many Moons 1947,D 15,35:2
Thompson, Kay
 Hooray for What! 1937,N 7,XI,2:4
Thompson, Kay (Miscellaneous)
 Judy Garland's New Variety Show 1956,S 27,43:2
Thompson, Keith
 Royal Family, The 1936,Ag 12,15:1
Thompson, Kenneth
 Five Star Saint 1970,F 11,41:2
Thompson, Mabel
 Babes in Toyland 1930,D 22,17:1
 Gondoliers, The 1931,Je 2,34:4
 Mikado, The 1933,Ap 18,13:4
 Pirates of Penzance, The 1933,Ag 8,22:4
Thompson, Marshall
 Girl Can Tell, A 1953,O 30,28:2
Thompson, Mary
 Century Review, The 1920,Jl 22,9:5
Thompson, Mary-Ellen
 Mikado, The 1954,Mr 24,31:1
 Pirates of Penzance, The 1954,Mr 31,32:5
 Patience 1954,Ap 7,41:1
 Gondoliers, The 1954,Ap 14,24:3
 Iolanthe 1954,Ap 28,36:8
 Yeomen of the Guard, The 1954,My 5,36:2
 Sorcerer, The 1954,My 26,34:3
Thompson, Maurice
 Rain 1948,F 2,15:2
 Freight 1949,F 4,30:2
 Freight 1950,Ap 27,36:2
Thompson, May
 Century Revue and the Midnight Rounders, The
 1920,Jl 13,9:1
 Half-Moon, The 1920,N 2,15:2
Thompson, Michael
 Seven Days of Mourning 1969,D 17,64:1
Thompson, Natalie
 Delicate Story 1940,D 5,32:2
 Popsy 1941,F 11,26:2
 January Thaw 1946,F 5,18:2
Thompson, Norvell (Director)
 Drunkard, The; Fallen Saved, The 1929,D 31,14:6
Thompson, Norvell (Scenic Designer)
 Drunkard, The; Fallen Saved, The 1929,D 31,14:6
Thompson, Pat
 Joy of Serpents 1930,Ap 4,22:4
Thompson, Pete
 Brown Buddies 1930,O 8,29:1
Thompson, Peter
 All's Well That Ends Well 1970,Je 16,53:1
 All's Well That Ends Well 1970,Je 21,II,3:2
 Othello 1970,Je 22,43:1
 Othello 1970,Je 28,II,1:1
 Othello 1970,S 15,51:1
Thompson, Peter (Director)
 Slow Dance on the Killing Ground 1968,N 3,87:1
Thompson, Philip B
 Man and Superman 1960,Ag 17,35:3
Thompson, Polly
 Night of January 16 1935,D 16,22:5
Thompson, Ralph
 Three Cheers 1928,O 16,28:1
Thompson, Randall (Composer)
 Grand Street Follies, The 1926,Je 16,23:2
 Straw Hat, The 1926,O 15,20:2
Thompson, Ray
 Simply Heavenly 1957,My 22,28:2
Thompson, Rebecca
 Red Roses for Me 1961,N 28,41:1
 White Rose and the Red, The 1964,Mr 17,31:1
 Hedda Gabler 1970,Ja 18,78:1
 Hedda Gabler 1970,Ja 25,II,3:1
Thompson, Rex
 Alive and Kicking 1950,Ja 18,25:5
 Escapade 1953,N 19,40:1
 King of Hearts 1954,Ap 2,23:1
 King of Hearts 1954,Ap 11,II,1:1

Thompson, Rex—Cont
First Love 1961,D 26,20:2
Charley's Aunt 1970,Jl 6,38:1
Thompson, Robert
Richelieu 1934,My 22,28:1
Hamlet 1934,D 26,19:3
Good Morning 1937,D 4,20:7
Thompson, Robert J (Playwright)
Susie Is a Good Girl 1968,N 5,53:2
Grab Bag, The 1968,N 5,53:2
Subscriber, The 1968,N 5,53:2
Thompson, Rodney
Wheel, The 1921,Ag 30,10:1
Thompson, Ronnie
No Place to Be Somebody 1969,My 5,53:3
No Place to Be Somebody 1969,My 18,II,1:1
No Place to Be Somebody 1969,D 31,17:1
Thompson, Roy
Too Late the Phalarope 1956,O 12,35:1
Jamaica 1957,N 1,32:2
Belafonte at the Palace 1959,D 16,55:1
Thompson, Russell
Crime at Blossoms, The 1937,Jl 17,12:8
Thompson, S Iden
Golden Days 1921,N 2,20:1
Adam Solitaire 1925,N 7,19:2
Thompson, Sada
Clandestine Marriage, The 1954,O 4,23:2
White Devil, The 1955,Mr 15,32:5
Carefree Tree, The 1955,O 12,37:2
Misanthrope, The 1956,N 13,44:1
U S A 1956,D 19,41:4
River Line, The 1957,Ja 3,29:2
Othello 1957,Je 24,19:2
Much Ado About Nothing 1957,Ag 8,15:2
Ivanov 1958,O 8,42:1
Ivanov 1958,O 19,II,1:1
Juno 1959,Mr 10,41:1
Merry Wives of Windsor, The 1959,Jl 9,23:2
All's Well That Ends Well 1959,Ag 3,20:4
U S A 1959,O 29,38:1
U S A 1959,N 8,II,1:1
Twelfth Night 1960,Je 9,29:4
Tempest, The 1960,Je 20,35:1
Antony and Cleopatra 1960,Ag 1,19:1
Under Milk Wood 1961,Mr 30,25:1
Richard II 1962,Je 18,20:2
Henry IV, Part I 1962,Je 18,20:4
Last Minstrel, The 1963,My 9,40:2
Othello 1964,Jl 15,29:1
Tartuffe 1965,Ja 15,23:1
Johnny No-Trump 1967,O 9,60:2
American Dream, The 1968,O 3,55:1
Happy Days 1968,O 14,54:1
Evening for Merlin Finch, An 1968,D 30,25:1
Evening for Merlin Finch, An 1969,Ja 26,II,1:1
Effect of Gamma Rays on Man-in-the-Moon
  Marigolds, The 1970,Ap 8,32:1
Effect of Gamma Rays on Man-in-the-Moon
  Marigolds, The 1970,Ap 19,II,1:1
Thompson, Sheldon
Jack and the Beanstalk 1947,N 3,28:2
Many Moons 1947,D 15,35:2
Thompson, Sheldon (Director)
Little Red Riding Hood 1948,Ja 12,15:3
Rumpelstiltskin 1948,Mr 15,27:3
Thompson, Sheldon (Scenic Designer)
Jack and the Beanstalk 1947,N 3,28:2
Many Moons 1947,D 15,35:2
Rumpelstiltskin 1948,Mr 15,27:3
Thompson, Slim
Petrified Forest, The 1935,Ja 8,26:1
Petrified Forest, The 1943,N 2,30:6
Thompson, Sonny
Swing It 1937,Jl 23,17:2
Thompson, Steve
Brig, The 1963,My 16,40:1
Antigone 1968,O 11,36:1
Thompson, Sydney
Clouds of the Sun 1922,My 6,11:2
Tiger Cats 1924,O 22,18:1
Nocturne 1925,F 17,19:1
Nica 1926,Ja 26,19:1
Abraham; Dulcitus; Callimachus 1926,Mr 29,24:2
Thompson, Tazewell
Goa 1968,F 23,46:1
Thompson, Thedosia (Playwright)
King's Pirate, The 1937,Je 11,26:1
King's Pirate, The 1937,Je 27,X,1:3
Thompson, Tom
Two Little Girls in Blue 1921,My 4,10:3
Sweet Adeline 1929,S 4,33:1
Trial of Dr Beck, The 1937,Ag 10,22:2
Thompson, True
El Cristo 1926,My 9,II,1:4
Thompson, U S
Woof, Woof 1929,D 26,20:4
Thompson, Victoria
If Five Years Pass 1962,My 11,37:1
Thompson, W H
Night Lodging 1920,Ap 18,VI,2:1
Wildcat, The 1921,N 28,16:2
Thompson, Walter
Uniform of Flesh 1949,Ja 31,15:2

Saint Joan 1950,Mr 4,10:6
Thompson, Watson
It's About Time 1942,Mr 31,28:3
Thompson, Wendy
Pied Piper of Hamelin, The 1950,Ap 3,19:2
Thompson, Willard L
Made in Heaven 1946,O 25,28:2
Thompson, William
Bottom of the Cup, The 1927,F 1,24:2
Crooks' Convention, The 1929,S 19,37:4
Unsophisticates, The 1929,D 31,14:5
Happily Ever After 1945,Mr 16,21:2
Thompson, William C (Playwright)
Man Who Washed His Hands, The 1967,F 16,33:1
Thompson, William H
Guest of Honor, The 1920,S 21,12:1
Sonya 1921,Ag 16,18:3
Czarina, The 1922,F 1,22:1
Thompson, Wilma
Chicago 1926,D 31,11:1
What Do We Know 1927,D 24,8:1
Thompson, Woodman (Costume Designer)
Beggar on Horseback 1924,F 13,17:2
Firebrand, The 1924,O 16,33:1
Iolanthe 1926,Ap 20,24:2
Warrior's Husband, The 1932,Mr 12,19:4
Candida 1942,Ap 28,24:4
Magnificent Yankee, The 1946,Ja 23,21:2
Thompson, Woodman (Miscellaneous)
Plumes in the Dust 1936,N 7,14:2
Thompson, Woodman (Scenic Designer)
Beggar on Horseback 1924,F 13,17:2
Macbeth 1924,Mr 23,VIII,1:1
What Price Glory 1924,S 6,14:3
Minick 1924,S 25,20:1
Minick 1924,O 5,VIII,1:1
Firebrand, The 1924,O 16,33:1
Close Harmony 1924,D 2,23:1
Candida 1924,D 13,12:3
Habitual Husband, The 1924,D 25,27:3
Cocoanuts, The 1925,D 9,30:1
Hedda Gabler 1926,Ja 27,16:5
Wisdom Tooth, The 1926,F 16,22:2
Iolanthe 1926,Ap 20,24:2
Importance of Being Earnest, The 1926,My 4,30:1
Shelf, The 1926,S 28,31:1
Deep River 1926,O 5,26:2
White Wings 1926,O 16,15:1
God Loves Us 1926,O 20,22:2
Desert Song, The 1926,D 1,24:2
Pirates of Penzance, The; Slave of Duty, The
  1926,D 7,25:1
Merchant of Venice, The 1928,Ja 17,22:2
These Few Ashes 1928,O 31,28:1
Primer for Lovers, A 1929,N 19,26:5
This One Man 1930,O 22,32:3
Merchant of Venice, The 1930,N 16,VIII,3:1
Midnight 1930,D 30,25:1
Warrior's Husband, The 1932,Mr 12,19:4
Dangerous Corner 1932,O 28,23:1
Lady Jane 1934,S 11,24:2
Bishop Misbehaves, The 1935,F 21,22:4
Tomorrow's a Holiday! 1935,D 31,10:2
Candida 1937,Mr 11,20:2
Ghost of Yankee Doodle, The 1937,N 23,26:3
Candida 1942,Ap 28,24:4
Magnificent Yankee, The 1946,Ja 23,21:2
Hear That Trumpet 1946,O 8,19:2
Thomsen, Robert
They Shall Not Die 1934,F 22,24:4
Valley Forge 1934,D 11,28:3
It's You I Want 1935,F 6,23:3
Let Freedom Ring 1935,N 7,26:2
Bury the Dead 1936,Ap 20,17:4
Prelude 1936,Ap 20,17:4
Stage Door 1936,O 23,26:3
Excursion 1937,Ap 10,11:4
Western Waters 1937,D 29,17:1
Stop-Over 1938,Ja 12,16:5
Washington Jitters 1938,My 3,19:1
Jeremiah 1939,F 4,11:2
Mamba's Daughters 1940,Mr 25,10:4
Thomson, Alice
Country Wife, The 1936,D 2,34:1
Audition of the Apprentice Theatre 1939,Je 2,26:2
Inside Story 1942,O 30,22:2
Thomson, Archie
Just Fancy! 1927,O 12,30:2
Thomson, Archie (Miscellaneous)
If the Shoe Fits 1946,D 6,29:4
Thomson, Archie (Producer)
Joy Forever, A 1946,Ja 8,20:2
My 3 Angels 1953,Mr 12,23:2
Thomson, Arline
Vagabond King, The 1943,Je 30,24:2
Thomson, Barry
Taming of the Shrew, The 1935,S 22,X,3:2
Taming of the Shrew, The 1935,O 1,27:3
Idiot's Delight 1936,Mr 25,25:2
Amphitryon 38 1937,Je 24,30:2
Amphitryon 38 1937,N 2,32:2
Millionairess, The 1938,Ag 16,22:5
Second Best Bed 1946,Je 4,20:2

Thomson, Beatrice
Another Part of the Forest 1946,N 21,42:2
Thomson, Beatrix
Constant Nymph, The 1926,D 10,31:1
Constant Nymph, The 1926,D 19,VII,3:1
Out of the Sea 1927,D 6,26:2
Unknown Warrior, The 1928,O 30,26:6
Tents of Israel; Matriarch, The 1929,My 26,IX,1:3
Subway, The 1929,Jl 15,25:4
Artist and the Shadow, The 1930,Ap 6,IX,2:1
Monsieur Brotonneau 1930,O 5,IX,2:4
Princess in the Cage, The 1933,Mr 19,IX,2:2
Wisdom Teeth 1936,Mr 3,25:2
Duet by Accident 1938,Mr 27,X,1:3
Thomson, Beatrix (Playwright)
Duet by Accident 1938,Mr 27,X,1:3
Thomson, Bruce
Month in the Country, A 1959,Mr 2,32:2
Thomson, Carolyn
Right Girl, The 1921,Mr 16,12:1
Love Letter, The 1921,O 5,20:1
Vagabond King, The 1925,S 22,23:3
Thomson, Gladys
New York Exchange 1926,D 31,11:2
Thomson, Joy (Producer)
Clerambard 1957,N 8,22:3
American Mime Theatre 1958,S 25,28:4
Thomson, Kenneth
Great Broxopp, The 1921,N 16,22:1
Czarina, The 1922,F 1,22:1
School for Scandal, The 1923,Mr 13,19:2
Hush Money 1926,Mr 16,22:3
Thomson, Margaret
Fly Away Home 1937,Jl 28,15:1
Elizabeth the Queen 1937,Ag 25,24:3
Blithe Spirit 1946,Je 5,17:3
Thomson, Norman (Director)
Kiss Me, Kate 1963,D 1,184:3
Thomson, Ralph
Criss Cross 1926,O 13,20:2
Thomson, Virgil (Composer)
Bride for the Unicorn, A 1934,My 3,15:5
Injunction Granted! 1936,Jl 25,16:3
Horse Eats Hat 1936,S 28,14:2
Hamlet 1936,O 20,31:3
Hamlet 1936,O 25,X,1:5
Hamlet 1936,N 11,54:2
Antony and Cleopatra 1937,N 11,30:2
Oedipus Tyrannus 1941,My 10,13:8
Grass Harp, The 1952,Mr 28,26:2
Grass Harp, The 1952,Ap 6,II,1:1
Four Saints in Three Acts 1952,Ap 17,35:1
Ondine 1954,F 19,23:1
Ondine 1954,F 28,II,1:1
King John 1956,Je 28,33:5
Measure for Measure 1956,Je 29,16:1
Measure for Measure 1957,Ja 23,24:1
Othello 1957,Je 24,19:2
Merchant of Venice, The 1957,Jl 11,19:5
Much Ado About Nothing 1957,Ag 8,15:2
Hamlet 1958,Je 21,11:1
Bertha 1962,F 12,27:1
Thomson, Virgil (Musical Director)
Four Saints in Three Acts 1952,Ap 17,35:1
Thomson, Walter
Candida 1957,F 9,14:1
Oscar Wilde 1957,Ap 20,21:3
Under Milk Wood 1957,O 16,42:5
Hostile Witness 1966,F 18,26:1
Thor, Jerome
Bitter Oleander 1935,F 12,24:3
Panic 1935,Mr 16,18:4
Case of Clyde Griffiths 1936,Mr 14,10:4
Infernal Machine, The 1937,D 13,22:7
World We Make, The 1939,N 21,19:1
Doughgirls, The 1942,D 31,19:2
Get Away Old Man 1943,N 25,40:2
No Way Out 1944,O 31,23:1
Calico Wedding 1945,Mr 8,18:6
French Touch, The 1945,D 10,18:2
He Who Gets Slapped 1946,Mr 21,31:4
Thoreux, Therese
Zizi 1964,N 23,51:1
Thorley, Victor
Danton's Death 1938,N 3,26:2
Taming of the Shrew, The 1940,F 6,17:2
Moon Is Down, The 1942,Ap 8,22:2
Hamlet 1945,D 14,25:2
Volpone 1948,Ja 9,24:6
Angel Street 1948,Ja 23,26:6
Tragedian in Spite of Himself, A 1948,F 6,29:2
On the Harmfulness of Tobacco 1948,F 6,29:2
Wedding, The 1948,F 6,29:2
Bear, The 1948,F 6,29:2
Saint Joan 1950,Mr 4,10:6
Barrier, The 1950,N 3,32:2
Caligula 1960,F 17,31:1
Becket 1960,O 6,50:1
Becket 1961,My 9,44:1
Thormsen, Greta
Show Boat 1954,My 6,44:1
Thorn, Bertram
Advertising of Kate, The 1922,My 9,22:2

Thorn, Bertram—Cont

Caught Wet 1931,N 5,29:1
Curtain Rises, The 1933,O 20,15:2
Elizabeth Sleeps Out 1935,Ag 27,23:4
Prelude 1936,Ap 20,17:4
Bury the Dead 1936,Ap 20,17:4
Lend Me Your Ears! 1936,O 6,28:5
200 Were Chosen 1936,N 21,21:1
Penny Wise 1937,Ap 20,28:6
In Clover 1937,S 21,29:1
In Clover 1937,O 14,23:1
Washington Jitters 1938,My 3,19:1
Here Come the Clowns 1938,D 8,36:2
Foreigners 1939,D 6,30:2
Case of Youth, A 1940,Mr 25,10:3
Brooklyn Biarritz 1941,F 28,16:2
Alchemist, The 1948,My 7,31:4
I've Got Sixpence 1952,D 3,44:2
Thorn, George (Composer)
Sextet 1958,N 27,53:1
Thorn, George (Miscellaneous)
Dinny and the Witches 1959,D 10,53:3
Snow Maiden, The 1960,Ap 5,43:3
King of the Dark Chamber 1961,F 10,21:1
Drat! the Cat! 1965,O 11,54:2
Time for Singing, A 1966,My 23,48:2
Thorn, George (Producer)
Crimes of Passion; Erpingham Camp, The
   1969,O 27,54:1
Crimes of Passion; Ruffian on the Stair, The
   1969,O 27,54:1
Thorn, John
All Soul's Eve 1920,My 13,9:1
Plot Thickens, The 1922,S 6,16:1
Thorn, Olive Harper
Lights Out 1922,Ag 18,8:4
Thorndike, B A G
1776 1926,Ap 24,11:2
Thorndike, Daniel
Midsummer Night's Dream, A 1954,S 22,33:1
Thorndike, Eileen (Director)
Ding and Company 1934,N 20,24:2
Thorndike, Oliver
Night Must Fall 1947,F 13,33:6
Mary Rose 1951,Mr 5,25:2
Mary Rose 1951,Mr 11,II,1:1
Thorndike, Russell
Much Ado About Nothing 1929,N 17,30:4
Hamlet 1931,Ap 24,26:4
House of Borgia, The 1935,S 10,26:1
House of Borgia, The 1935,O 6,XI,3:1
Thorndike, Sybil
Macbeth 1921,Je 7,20:2
Cymbeline 1923,O 7,IX,2:2
Lie, The 1923,O 21,VIII,2:2
Saint Joan 1924,Mr 27,16:2
Macbeth 1927,Ja 2,30:1
Macbeth 1927,Ja 16,VII,4:3
Greater Love, The 1927,Ap 3,VIII,1:4
Judith of Israel 1928,F 17,24:2
Judith of Israel 1928,Mr 18,IX,4:8
Making of an Immortal, The 1928,Ap 29,IX,1:3
Mariners 1929,My 19,IX,1:8
Madame Plays Nap 1929,D 18,31:2
Devil, The 1930,F 2,VIII,2:4
Phedre 1930,Mr 23,IX,2:3
Fire in the Opera House 1930,Ap 6,IX,2:1
Othello 1930,My 20,33:1
Dark Hester 1931,My 17,VIII,1:3
Marriage by Purchase 1931,Je 21,VIII,1:3
All-Star Special 1931,Jl 18,16:4
Dark Saint, The; Envers d'une Sainte, L'
   1932,F 21,VIII,1:6
Distaff Side, The 1933,S 6,24:5
Distaff Side, The 1933,S 24,X,1:6
Nineties; Double Door 1934,Mr 22,24:6
Double Door 1934,Ap 15,X,2:2
Distaff Side, The 1934,S 26,17:2
Grief Goes Over 1935,Je 7,24:5
Grief Goes Over 1935,Jl 28,X,1:1
Cenci, The 1935,Ag 18,IX,1:4
Short Story 1935,N 5,33:2
Short Story 1935,D 1,XI,5:3
Time and the Conways 1938,Ja 4,19:2
Corn Is Green, The 1938,O 9,X,3:1
Medea 1941,Ag 3,IX,2:2
King John 1941,Ag 3,IX,2:2
Jacob 1942,Je 14,VIII,1:7
Peer Gynt 1944,O 1,II,1:3
Richard III 1944,O 1,II,1:3
Arms and the Man 1944,O 1,II,1:3
Call Home the Heart 1947,Ap 13,I,54:2
Linden Tree, The 1947,S 14,II,3:7
Foolish Gentlewoman, The 1949,Ap 3,II,3:1
Douglas Once 1950,S 10,II,3:1
Waters of the Moon 1951,My 6,II,3:7
Waters of the Moon 1953,Ap 2,34:3
Day by the Sea, A 1953,N 27,22:3
Day by the Sea, A 1953,D 20,II,4:2
Family Reunion, The 1956,Je 9,13:6
Potting Shed, The 1957,Ja 30,32:1
Potting Shed, The 1957,F 10,II,1:1
Untitled-Reading 1957,Ap 17,35:1
Waiting in the Wings 1960,Ag 9,31:4

Waiting in the Wings 1960,S 8,40:3
Teresa of Avila 1961,S 13,55:1
Uncle Vanya 1962,Jl 17,18:4
Vanity Fair 1962,N 28,44:8
Uncle Vanya 1963,Jl 2,16:2
Reluctant Peer, The 1964,Ja 16,30:2
There Was an Old Woman... 1969,O 16,56:4
Thorndike, Sybil (Producer)
Advertising April 1923,F 4,VII,1:4
Cymbeline 1923,O 7,IX,2:2
Saint Joan 1924,Mr 27,16:2
Henry VIII 1926,Ja 3,VII,2:8
Thorne, Charles
Lucrece 1932,D 21,22:2
Romeo and Juliet 1934,D 21,30:3
Thorne, David (Playwright)
Beyond Evil 1926,Je 8,23:2
Dorian Gray 1928,My 22,18:4
Thorne, David (Producer)
Beyond Evil 1926,Je 8,23:2
Thorne, Francis (Composer)
Fortuna 1962,Ja 4,26:1
Thorne, Franklin
Hamlet 1920,Mr 17,14:2
Thorne, Jack
It Is the Law 1922,N 30,28:2
Thorne, John
Up in Central Park 1947,My 20,29:2
Thorne, Kay
Howdy Stranger 1937,Ja 15,17:5
Thorne, Mabel
Case of Philip Lawrence, The 1937,Je 9,31:1
Thorne, Michael
Tower Beyond Tragedy, The 1950,N 27,29:1
Thorne, Nellie
If This Be Treason 1935,S 24,28:2
Excursion 1937,Ap 10,11:4
Girl From Wyoming, The 1938,O 31,12:1
Thorne, Raymond
Man With a Load of Mischief, The 1966,N 7,65:1
Papers 1968,D 3,54:1
Rose 1969,O 29,30:1
Dames at Sea 1970,S 24,60:1
Thorne, Raymond (Miscellaneous)
Baby With a Knife 1969,My 15,41:2
Pets 1969,My 15,41:2
Silver Grey Toy Poodle 1969,My 15,41:2
Thorne, Robert
In the Night Watch 1921,Ja 31,10:1
Extra 1923,Ja 24,22:3
Othello 1925,Ja 12,11:1
Taps 1925,Ap 15,16:2
Virgin, The 1926,F 23,26:1
Distant Drum, A 1928,Ja 21,13:1
Mother Lode 1934,D 24,16:5
Thirsty Soil 1937,F 4,16:2
Thorne, S J (Mrs)
One Woman's Husband 1920,Mr 23,9:3
Thorne, Samuels Jr
Coriolanus 1927,Je 8,8:3
Thorne, William L
Try It With Alice 1924,Je 24,18:4
Big Boy 1925,Ja 8,28:2
Thrills 1925,Ap 17,24:3
Love Call, The 1927,O 25,33:1
Thorne, Worley (Producer)
Conversation at Midnight 1964,N 13,27:1
Thornett, Keneth
Visit, The 1958,My 6,40:1
Thornley, Victor
Tower Beyond Tragedy, The 1950,N 27,29:1
Thornton, Angela
Little Glass Clock, The 1956,Mr 27,40:2
Nude With Violin 1957,N 15,36:1
Mousetrap, The 1960,N 7,46:1
Hostile Witness 1966,F 18,26:1
Thornton, Bernard
Seventh Heaven 1922,O 31,11:1
Play Without a Name, A 1928,N 26,30:5
Young Alexander 1929,Mr 13,28:2
Subway Express 1929,S 25,34:3
Constant Sinner, The 1931,S 15,30:1
Thornton, Charles
Sextet 1958,N 27,53:1
Thornton, Charles (Miscellaneous)
Sextet 1958,N 27,53:1
Thornton, Cherokee
Innocent Voyage, The 1943,N 16,27:2
Eagle Has Two Heads, The 1947,Mr 20,39:2
Tobacco Road 1950,Mr 7,23:2
Too Late the Phalarope 1956,O 12,35:1
Thornton, Drake
Doctor Social 1948,F 12,29:5
Thornton, Eric
H M S Pinafore 1951,F 6,24:2
Iolanthe 1951,F 16,22:1
Cox and Box 1951,F 20,21:2
Thornton, Evans
Love Life 1948,O 8,31:2
Miss Liberty 1949,Jl 16,6:5
Finian's Rainbow 1955,My 19,25:1
Show Boat 1956,Je 22,16:1
Show Boat 1957,Je 28,30:2

Thornton, Evans—Cont

Carousel 1957,S 12,38:2
Thornton, George
Arabesque 1925,O 21,20:2
Jeweled Tree, The 1926,O 8,26:2
Caravan 1928,Ag 30,13:3
Revenge With Music 1934,N 29,33:5
Return of the Vagabond, The 1940,My 14,27:2
Thornton, Jack
Pierrot the Prodigal; Enfant Prodigue, L'
   1925,Mr 7,8:1
Thornton, James
Vaudeville (Palace) 1926,Jl 27,15:4
Sidewalks of New York 1927,O 4,33:1
Thornton, James (Mrs)
Lady Who Came to Stay, The 1941,Ja 3,13:2
Thornton, Jim
Sweet Adeline 1929,S 4,33:1
Thornton, Joan
New Faces of 1962 1962,F 2,25:1
Thornton, Naomi
Live Like Pigs 1965,Je 8,48:2
Thornton, Norma
Me and Juliet 1953,My 29,17:1
Thornton, Richard
Henry IV, Part I 1926,Je 1,29:1
Three Musketeers, The 1928,Mr 14,28:1
Adam's Apple 1929,Je 11,27:5
Devil's Host, The 1931,N 20,27:2
Thornton, Sandra
Gertrude Stein's First Reader 1969,D 16,56:1
Thornton, Walker
Dark Hours, The 1932,N 15,24:2
Thornton, William
Light of Asia, The 1928,O 10,32:2
Infernal Machine, The 1937,D 13,22:7
Comes the Revelation 1942,My 27,26:2
Othello 1953,O 30,28:2
Hamlet 1954,Ap 24,15:2
Thorpe, George
White Peacock, The 1921,D 27,10:2
Faithful Heart, The 1922,O 11,22:1
New Poor, The 1924,Ja 8,26:1
Far Cry, The 1924,O 1,24:1
Hay Fever 1925,O 5,25:1
Port O' London 1926,F 10,20:2
Ashes of Love 1926,Mr 23,24:3
That Sort 1926,Ap 20,24:6
Vaudeville (Palace) 1926,Ap 20,24:6
This Woman Business 1926,D 8,25:1
Legend of Leonora, The 1927,Mr 30,22:4
Love Nest, The 1927,D 23,17:1
Behavior of Mrs Crane, The 1928,Mr 21,30:1
Happy Husband, The 1928,My 8,25:2
Potiphar's Wife 1928,D 24,10:7
Cyrano de Bergerac 1932,D 27,11:2
Cyrano de Bergerac 1936,Ap 28,17:1
Thorpe, Josie
Run Sheep Run 1938,N 4,26:2
Thorpe, Richard
Bitter Sweet 1929,N 6,30:2
Thorpe, Ted
Mr Adam 1949,My 26,34:6
Thorpe-Bates, Peggy
Young Elizabeth, The 1952,Ap 3,45:1
Thorr, Susan
Faust 1947,N 29,9:2
Thorsell, Karen
Delightful Season, A 1960,S 29,30:1
Have I Got a Girl for You! 1963,D 3,53:2
Thorson, Barbara
I Gotta Get Out 1947,S 26,27:2
Thorson, Marilyn (Miscellaneous)
God, Man & You, Baby! 1963,O 30,47:1
Thorson, Marilyn (Producer)
Fig Leaf in Her Bonnet, A 1961,Je 15,50:1
Thorson, Russell
Trojan Women, The 1938,Ja 25,24:2
Thortelson, Yngvo
Marching Song 1937,F 18,18:2
Thourlby, William
Stockade 1954,F 5,14:2
Will Success Spoil Rock Hunter? 1955,O 14,22:2
Visit, The 1958,My 6,40:1
Jackknife 1958,S 23,36:2
Threadgill, Leon
Porgy and Bess 1935,O 11,30:2
Three Arnauts, The
Vaudeville (Palace) 1924,Mr 18,25:1
Three Black Aces
Will Morrissey's Folies Bergere Revue
   1930,Ap 16,26:6
Three Bobs, The
Get Together 1921,S 5,12:2
Three Bruises, The
Ice Capades 1959,S 4,12:1
Ice Capades 1960,S 1,30:1
Three Business Men
Artists and Models 1943,N 6,16:6
Three Crackerjacks, The
Sketch Book 1935,Je 5,22:2
Three Giersdorf Sisters, The
Vaudeville (Palace) 1927,My 17,27:4

Three Golfers
O K 1925,My 4,16:1
Three Jays, The
Sketch Book 1935,Je 5,22:2
Three Meyakos
Ed Wynn's Carnival 1920,Ap 6,18:2
Three Nitos, The
Vaudeville (Hippodrome) 1926,Mr 16,22:2
Three Rhythm Dancers
Vaudeville (Palace) 1930,D 29,19:3
Three Rookies, The
Stars on Ice 1942,Jl 3,12:2
Three Sailors, The
Vaudeville (Palace) 1928,Mr 27,30:5
Vaudeville (Palace) 1928,O 9,35:2
Sketch Book 1929,Jl 2,33:5
Vaudeville (Palace) 1930,S 15,29:2
Three Slate Brothers
Ballyhoo 1930,D 23,24:1
Three Swifts, The
Vaudeville (Palace) 1930,D 8,27:2
Thress, Frances
Five O'Clock Girl, The 1927,O 11,26:3
Once in a Lifetime 1930,S 25,22:3
All the King's Horses 1934,Ja 31,21:3
Tomorrow's a Holiday! 1935,D 31,10:2
Orchids Preferred 1937,My 12,26:5
Thrift, Bea
Song Writer, The 1928,Ag 14,15:2
New Faces of 1936 1936,My 20,24:5
Throckmorton, Cleon (Producer)
Black Crook, The 1929,Mr 12,26:5
Star of Bengal 1929,S 26,27:2
Shoestring Revue 1929,N 23,19:2
Blue and the Gray, The; War Is Hell Gray, The 1929,D 27,26:4
Change Your Luck 1930,Je 7,10:2
Throckmorton, Cleon (Scenic Designer)
Saturday Night 1924,F 11,18:1
All God's Chillun Got Wings 1924,My 16,22:3
All God's Chillun Got Wings 1924,Ag 19,9:1
Crime in the Whistler Room, The 1924,O 10,22:2
S S Glencairn 1924,N 4,31:4
Patience 1924,D 30,15:1
Blue Peter, The 1925,Mr 25,25:3
Rosmersholm 1925,My 6,27:2
Engaged! or Cheviot's Choice 1925,Je 19,24:2
Outside Looking In 1925,S 8,28:1
Weak Sisters 1925,O 14,31:3
Man's Man, A 1925,O 14,31:2
Adam Solitaire 1925,N 7,19:2
Adam Solitaire 1925,N 15,VIII,1:1
Devil to Pay, The 1925,D 4,26:2
Man Who Died Twice, The 1925,D 14,19:1
Wise-Crackers, The 1925,D 17,26:1
Dream Play 1926,Ja 21,18:2
Makropoulos Secret, The 1926,Ja 22,12:4
East Lynne 1926,Mr 11,18:4
Bride of the Lamb 1926,Mr 31,20:3
Beyond Evil 1926,Je 8,23:2
Sandalwood 1926,S 23,23:1
Beyond the Horizon 1926,D 1,24:2
In Abraham's Bosom 1926,D 31,10:2
Earth 1927,Mr 10,23:1
Menace 1927,Mr 15,28:2
Rapid Transit 1927,Ap 8,21:2
Wall Street 1927,Ap 21,24:4
Triple Crossed 1927,My 6,21:2
Burlesque 1927,S 2,15:3
Triumphant Bachelor, The 1927,S 16,21:1
Jacob Slovak 1927,O 6,28:4
Porgy 1927,O 11,26:2
Good Hope, The 1927,O 19,24:2
Ivory Door, The 1927,O 19,24:5
Stairs, The 1927,N 8,32:7
Paradise 1927,D 26,26:4
These Modern Women 1928,F 14,26:2
Hot Pan 1928,F 16,14:1
Rope 1928,F 23,18:3
Napoleon 1928,Mr 9,21:1
Scarlet Fox, The 1928,Mr 28,31:1
Would-Be Gentleman, The 1928,O 2,34:1
Pleased to Meet You 1928,O 30,27:2
On Call 1928,N 10,20:7
After Dark 1928,D 11,35:2
After Dark: or, Neither Maid, Wife nor Widow 1929,F 10,IX,1:1
Man's Estate 1929,Ap 2,28:2
Mystery Square 1929,Ap 5,28:3
Getting Even 1929,Ag 20,31:1
Fiesta 1929,S 18,35:1
Red Rust 1929,D 18,31:1
Inspector Kennedy 1929,D 21,16:3
Tempest, The 1929,D 30,16:2
Unsophisticates, The 1929,D 31,14:5
Penny Arcade 1930,Mr 11,24:5
Old Rascal, The 1930,Mr 25,34:4
Stepping Sisters 1930,Ap 23,24:2
Torch Song 1930,Ag 28,23:1
She Means Business 1931,Ja 27,21:2
Hobo 1931,F 12,24:4
Gray Shadow 1931,Mr 11,23:4

Six Characters in Search of an Author 1931,Ap 16,29:2
Brass Ankle 1931,Ap 24,26:4
Just to Remind You 1931,S 8,39:1
Did I Say No? 1931,S 23,19:4
House of Connelly, The 1931,S 29,22:4
Two Seconds 1931,O 10,20:6
Hot Money 1931,N 9,22:2
Louder, Please! 1931,N 13,26:4
Widow in Green, A 1931,N 21,21:4
Springtime for Henry 1931,D 10,29:2
Sentinels 1931,D 26,15:1
Bride the Sun Shines On, The 1931,D 28,20:2
Monkey 1932,F 12,25:2
Moon in the Yellow River, The 1932,Mr 1,19:3
Moon in the Yellow River, The 1932,Mr 13,VIII,1:1
Truth About Blayds, The 1932,Ap 12,25:2
Another Language 1932,Ap 26,25:3
Bulls, Bears and Asses 1932,My 7,11:3
Hired Husband 1932,Je 4,9:5
Back Fire 1932,Je 14,26:3
Page Pygmalion 1932,Ag 4,17:5
Other One, The 1932,O 4,26:3
Criminal at Large 1932,O 11,26:3
Rendezvous 1932,O 13,22:3
Dark Hours, The 1932,N 15,24:2
Chrysalis 1932,N 16,15:2
Take a Chance 1932,N 28,11:2
Alien Corn 1933,F 21,17:2
Run, Little Chillun! 1933,Mr 2,21:3
Threepenny Opera, The 1933,Ap 14,22:4
Comic Artist, The 1933,Ap 20,20:3
Another Language 1933,My 9,20:2
Eight Bells 1933,O 30,14:2
Is Life Worth Living? 1933,N 10,24:6
Peace on Earth 1933,N 30,39:2
Gods We Make, The 1934,Ja 4,16:4
Sing and Whistle 1934,F 12,18:3
Lord Blesses the Bishop, The 1934,N 28,24:5
Ode to Liberty 1934,D 22,20:2
Kykunkor 1934,D 22,21:3
Creeping Fire 1935,Ja 17,22:3
Prisoners of War 1935,Ja 29,24:1
Bitter Oleander 1935,F 12,24:3
Noah 1935,F 14,25:2
I Want a Policeman! 1936,Ja 15,15:5
Jefferson Davis 1936,F 19,17:2
Searching for the Sun 1936,F 20,22:6
Woman of Destiny, A 1936,Mr 3,25:2
Bitter Stream 1936,Mr 31,16:6
Curtain Call 1937,Ap 23,24:7
Love in My Fashion 1937,D 4,21:4
Circle of Chalk, The 1941,Mr 27,28:4
Ghost for Sale 1941,S 30,27:4
Days of Our Youth, The 1941,N 29,15:2
Nathan the Wise 1942,Ap 4,18:4
Talking to You 1942,Ag 18,17:1
Across the Board on Tomorrow Morning 1942,Ag 18,17:1
Circle of Chalk, The 1950,D 2,8:3
Throne, Mal
Iceman Cometh, The 1956,My 8,38:1
Courageous One, The 1958,Ja 21,33:6
Legend of Lizzie, The 1959,F 10,39:1
Thronton, Barney
Elmer the Great 1928,S 25,29:1
Thropp, Clara
Little Jessie James 1923,Ag 16,10:4
Faust 1927,Ja 4,20:1
Babbling Brookes 1927,F 26,13:2
Field God, The 1927,Ap 22,18:2
Atlas and Eva 1928,F 7,30:2
Get Me in the Movies 1928,My 22,18:3
Jonica 1930,Ap 8,27:1
Girls in Uniform 1932,D 31,10:3
Mountain, The 1933,S 12,28:6
Thrower, Edna
Lulu Belle 1926,F 10,20:1
Women Go on Forever 1927,S 8,25:1
Box Seats 1928,Ap 20,27:2
Thuler, G (Composer)
Roaming Stars 1930,Ja 25,12:2
Thulin, Ingrid
Of Love Remembered 1967,F 20,46:5
Thumhart, Frank
Golden Screw, The 1967,Ja 31,52:1
Thumin, Cecilia
Arena Conta Zumbi 1969,Ag 19,31:1
Thuna, Lee (Playwright)
Natural Look, The 1967,Mr 13,45:2
Show Me Where the Good Times Are 1970,Mr 6,32:1
Thunhurst, William Jr
Traitor, The 1949,Ap 1,30:2
Thurau, Annie
Anneliese von Dessau 1926,F 26,24:3
Thurber, Francis B (Mrs)
Kind Lady 1938,Jl 11,14:2
Thurber, J Kent
Rain 1922,N 8,18:2
Ballyhoo 1927,Ja 5,18:1
Footlights 1927,Ag 20,8:2

Thurber, J Kent—Cont
Second Mate, The 1930,Mr 25,34:5
Rain 1935,F 13,24:1
Something Gay 1935,Ap 30,12:2
Devil of Pei-Ling 1936,F 21,20:4
Something for Nothing 1937,D 10,33:5
Thurber, J Kent (Director)
Second Mate, The 1930,Mr 25,34:5
Dora Mobridge 1930,Ap 21,20:2
Ebb Tide 1931,Je 9,33:6
Thurber, James (Original Author)
Beast in Me, The 1963,My 17,29:1
Secret Life of Walter Mitty, The 1964,O 27,44:5
Thurber, James (Playwright)
Male Animal, The 1940,Ja 10,17:2
Male Animal, The 1940,Ja 21,IX,1:1
Male Animal, The 1941,Jl 9,24:6
Many Moons 1947,D 15,35:2
Male Animal, The 1952,My 1,35:1
Male Animal, The 1952,My 18,II,1:1
Three by Thurber; Imperturbable Spirit, The 1955,Mr 8,23:2
Three by Thurber; Middle Years, The 1955,Mr 8,23:2
Three by Thurber; Mr Montoe Holds the Fort 1955,Mr 8,23:2
Thurber Carnival, A 1960,F 27,13:2
Thurber Carnival, A 1960,Mr 6,II,1:1
Thurber Carnival, A 1960,S 13,41:1
Thurber Carnival, A 1960,S 13,41:1
Thurber, Le G L
Pudding on the Ritz 1932,Ap 9,18:3
Thurgood, Reginald
Conversation Piece 1934,O 24,24:1
Thurm, Joel (Miscellaneous)
Umbrella, The 1965,My 27,31:1
Thurman, Beverly (Translator)
Asmodee 1958,Mr 26,42:2
Thurman, Elizabeth
Colombe 1965,F 24,33:1
Thurman, Mary
Sweethearts 1929,S 23,25:1
Merry Widow, The 1929,D 3,29:1
Babes in Toyland 1929,D 24,15:3
Thurman, Wallace (Playwright)
Harlem 1929,F 21,30:3
Harlem 1929,Mr 3,VIII,1:1
Thurschwell, Harry (Playwright)
Young Man's Fancy, A 1947,Ap 30,33:2
Thurston, Andrew
Polonaise 1945,O 8,20:2
Thurston, E Temple (Playwright)
Wandering Jew, The 1921,O 27,22:1
Roof and Four Walls, A 1923,Ja 21,VII,1:3
Blue Peter, The 1925,Mr 25,25:3
Wandering Jew, The 1927,F 2,22:4
Thurston, Frederick
Little Theatre Tournament; Another Room for Rent 1929,My 7,28:1
Thurston, Howard
Untitled-Magician 1927,Ap 19,25:2
Thurston, Robert
Nude With Violin 1957,N 15,36:1
Thurston, Ted
Big White Fog 1940,O 23,26:2
Paint Your Wagon 1951,N 13,32:2
Buttrio Square 1952,O 15,40:2
Girl in Pink Tights, The 1954,Mr 6,13:2
Li'l Abner 1956,N 16,24:2
Li'l Abner 1956,N 25,II,1:1
Bible Salesman, The 1960,F 22,12:2
Happiest Girl in the World, The 1961,Ap 4,42:1
Let It Ride 1961,O 13,27:4
Sophie 1963,Ap 16,32:1
Luther 1963,S 26,41:1
Cafe Crown 1964,Ap 18,32:1
I Had a Ball 1964,D 16,50:1
Wonderful Town 1967,My 18,50:1
Celebration 1969,Ja 23,55:2
Gantry 1970,F 16,44:1
Thurston, Temple (Playwright)
Wandering Jew, The 1921,O 30,VI,1:1
Blue Peter, The 1924,O 19,VIII,2:7
Emma Hamilton 1929,O 13,IX,4:1
Son of Man 1933,O 22,IX,2:2
Thweatt, Ann
Ship, The 1929,N 21,24:7
Magic 1929,D 17,28:5
Seven Keys to Baldpate 1930,Ja 8,25:2
Round Table, The 1930,F 28,20:5
Thys, Mado
Trois Jeunes Filles Nues; Three Young Maids From the Folies Bergere 1929,Mr 5,28:2
Passionement; Passionately 1929,Mr 8,31:4
Comte Obligado 1929,Mr 12,26:2
Bon Garcon, Un 1929,Mr 19,36:2
Pas Sur La Bouche; Not on the Lips 1929,Mr 26,34:3
Tiano, Lou
Penny Wars, The 1969,O 16,52:1
Tibbals, Cyrus
Caesar and Cleopatra 1935,Ag 22,21:1
Tibbett, Lawrence
King Lear 1923,Mr 10,9:4

Tibbett, Lawrence—Cont
Emperor Jones, The 1933,Mr 15,21:4
Miracle in the Mountains 1947,Ap 26,10:2
Barrier, The 1950,N 3,32:2
ANTA Album 1951,My 7,22:7
Tibbetts, Walter
Gondoliers, The 1940,O 1,29:2
Tiberghien, Jerome
Romeo and Juliet 1968,Je 11,55:2
Tiberio, Alba
Vaudeville (Hippodrome) 1925,S 1,18:3
Tiblad, Inga
Long Day's Journey Into Night 1956,F 19,II,1:6
Tibor, Yvonne
Rosalinda; Fledermaus, Die 1942,O 29,26:5
Tice, David
Peace 1969,Ja 28,49:1
Dracula Sabbat 1970,O 2,28:2
Tichacek, Stephen Jan (Miscellaneous)
Pinocchio 1939,Ja 3,19:2
Tichacek, Stephen Jan (Scenic Designer)
Danton's Death 1938,N 3,26:2
Danton's Death 1938,N 13,IX,1:1
Tichenor, Billy
Rainbow Rose 1926,Mr 17,28:2
Tichenor, Joseph (Scenic Designer)
Bottom of the Cup, The 1927,F 1,24:2
Tichenor, Tom (Miscellaneous)
Carnival! 1961,Ap 14,22:2
Ticholas, Rosemarie (Miscellaneous)
Empire Builders, The 1968,O 2,34:1
Tichy, Curth A
Professor Bernhardi 1968,Mr 20,38:1
Maria Stuart 1968,Mr 27,38:1
Jux Will Er Sich Machen, Einen 1968,Ap 3,41:1
Tidblad, Inga
Long Day's Journey Into Night 1962,My 16,35:4
Miss Julie 1962,My 17,31:1
Tiden, Fred
Wonderful Thing, The 1920,F 18,9:1
Respect for Riches, The 1920,My 12,9:1
Bad Man, The 1920,Ag 31,7:1
Charlatan, The 1922,Ap 25,14:2
Pride 1923,My 3,22:3
Sancho Panza 1923,N 27,23:1
Mismates 1925,Ap 14,27:2
Me 1925,N 24,28:1
Scotch Mist 1926,S 21,32:3
Sherlock Holmes 1928,F 21,18:4
Within the Law 1928,Mr 6,20:1
Hundred Years Old, A 1929,O 2,28:2
Dishonored Lady 1930,F 5,27:1
Tiden, Zelma
Steam Roller, The 1924,N 11,20:2
Baby Mine 1927,Je 10,21:2
Pure in Heart, The 1934,Mr 21,24:3
Tidmarsh, Vivian (Playwright)
Is Your Honeymoon Really Necessary?
1944,S 10,II,2:6
Tieck (Translator)
Taming of the Shrew, The 1933,N 5,IX,3:1
Richard III 1937,My 30,X,2:2
Tiedtke, Jacob
Three Sisters, The 1927,Mr 13,VII,2:4
Troilus and Cressida 1927,N 20,IX,4:7
Tienkler, Alfred
Gay Blades 1937,N 12,26:6
Tiernan, Junior (Master)
Taboo 1922,Ap 5,22:1
Tiernan, William (Miscellaneous)
Of Thee I Sing 1952,My 6,34:2
Tierney, Bill
Lady's Not for Burning, The 1959,Ja 31,13:2
Courtyard 1960,Mr 1,28:1
Tiger Rag, The 1961,F 17,20:2
Tierney, C A
It's Only Natural 1922,Ap 21,13:2
Tierney, Dorothy
My Golden Girl 1920,F 3,18:2
Checkerboard, The 1920,Ag 20,7:2
Rubicon, The 1922,F 22,13:1
Scaramouche 1923,O 25,14:2
Dawn 1924,N 25,27:1
Storm Center 1927,D 1,33:2
Tierney, Edward
Keep Kool 1924,My 23,16:4
Tierney, Gene
Mrs O'Brien Entertains 1939,F 9,16:3
Ring Two 1939,N 23,38:2
Male Animal, The 1940,Ja 10,17:2
Male Animal, The 1940,Ja 21,IX,1:1
Tierney, Grant (Producer)
Rag Picker of Paris, The: or, Modest Modiste
1935,N 12,23:7
Kind Lady 1935,N 19,27:3
Tulips Are Blooming, The 1935,D 4,27:6
Tierney, Harry (Composer)
Ziegfeld Follies 1920,Je 23,14:1
Up She Goes 1922,N 7,14:2
Glory 1922,D 26,10:1
Kid Boots 1924,Ja 1,21:3
Ziegfeld Follies 1924,Je 25,26:1
Rio Rita 1927,F 3,18:3
Cross My Heart 1928,S 18,32:7

Beau Brummell 1933,Ag 9,20:6
Moon Over Mulberry Street 1935,S 5,24:6
Tierney, Harry (Lyricist)
Ziegfeld Follies 1920,Je 23,14:1
Rio Rita 1927,F 3,18:3
Tierney, Harry (Playwright)
Ziegfeld Follies 1920,Je 23,14:1
Nekros 1960,O 26,44:1
Tierney, Harry Jr (Playwright)
Blood Bugle, The 1961,Je 29,26:1
Tierney, Lawrence J
Man's House, A 1943,Ap 3,10:4
Tierney, William
Born Yesterday 1958,Mr 22,12:6
Oklahoma! 1963,F 28,8:2
Oklahoma! 1963,My 16,40:1
Tiers, Alexander
Devil to Pay, The 1925,D 4,26:2
Garrick Gaieties 1926,My 11,25:2
Tietenbaum, Herbert (Miscellaneous)
Cocktails of 1934 1934,My 5,22:1
Tietjens, Eunice (Playwright)
Arabesque 1925,O 21,20:2
Tietjens, Walter
Woman of Bronze, The 1927,Je 16,25:4
Tiffany, Cameron (Mrs)
Variations of 1940 1940,Ja 29,12:1
Tiffany, Christy
Father Malachy's Miracle 1937,N 18,26:4
Tiffany, Lylah
All the Way Home 1960,D 1,42:1
Tiffany, Mary
Demon Mirror, The 1968,Mr 13,42:1
Tiffault, Leighton (Composer)
Story for a Sunday Evening, A 1950,N 18,10:5
Tiffin, Pamela
Dinner at Eight 1966,S 28,38:1
Uncle Vanya 1969,Ag 31,II,4:1
Tigar, Ken
Proposition, The 1968,Ap 20,25:3
Tigar, Merry (Miscellaneous)
Prince of Peasantmania 1970,F 22,88:1
Tigerman, Gary
Paris Is Out! 1970,F 3,35:1
Dream Out of Time, A 1970,N 9,52:1
Tigges, Byron
Bare Facts 1927,Je 30,35:1
Greenwich Villagers, The 1927,Ag 19,20:2
Tighe, Amy
In 3 Zones 1970,N 3,28:1
Tighe, Harry
Smiles 1930,N 19,19:2
Tighe, Harry (Playwright)
Insult 1930,S 16,30:2
Tighe, Kathleen
Go, Go, Go, God is Dead! 1966,O 12,37:1
Tighe, Milton
Bloody Laughter 1931,D 5,20:6
Tihmar, David (Choreographer)
William Had the Words! 1964,Mr 30,36:1
Tihmar, David (Director)
William Had the Words! 1964,Mr 30,36:1
Tihmar, David (Miscellaneous)
New Faces of 1956 1956,Je 15,32:1
Tilbury, Gladys
We're All in the Gutter 1927,Mr 5,12:2
Tilbury, Zeffie
Letter of the Law, The; Robe Rouge, La
1920,F 24,11:1
My Aunt From Ypsilanti 1923,My 2,22:6
Breaking Point, The 1923,Ag 17,8:4
Way Things Happen, The 1924,Ja 29,17:5
Red Falcon, The 1924,O 8,22:1
Tilden
Vierge Folle, La; Foolish Virgin, The
1924,Mr 22,12:2
Tilden, Anne
Partition 1948,O 29,31:2
Tilden, Beau
On Your Toes 1936,Ap 13,14:4
Johnny Belinda 1940,S 19,26:2
Annie Get Your Gun 1946,My 17,14:2
Orpheus Descending 1957,Mr 22,28:1
Goldilocks 1958,O 13,33:1
Tilden, Franziska
Konzert, Das 1968,Mr 25,52:1
Maria Stuart 1968,Mr 27,38:1
Jux Will Er Sich Machen, Einen 1968,Ap 3,41:1
Tilden, Georgina
Man or Devil 1925,My 22,22:4
Offence, The 1925,N 16,25:1
Schweiger 1926,Mr 24,20:4
Kitty's Kisses 1926,My 7,12:2
Tilden, Helen
French Leave 1920,N 9,13:1
Bronx Express 1922,Ap 27,12:2
Failures, The 1923,N 23,20:1
Candida 1925,N 10,23:4
Old Bill, M P 1926,N 11,22:2
Maya 1928,F 22,19:1
Yellow Jacket, The 1928,N 8,27:3
Falstaff 1928,D 26,14:2
R U R 1930,F 18,28:1

Tilden, Helen—Cont
Marco Millions 1930,Mr 4,24:4
Volpone 1930,Mr 11,24:5
Tilden, I E
They Never Come Back 1920,D 19,I,22:3
Tilden, Jane
Konzert, Das 1968,Mr 25,52:1
Jux Will Er Sich Machen, Einen 1968,Ap 3,41:1
Tilden, L E
Espanola 1921,D 30,13:1
Tilden, L E (Composer)
Espanola 1921,D 30,13:1
Tilden, L E (Lyricist)
Espanola 1921,D 30,13:1
Tilden, L E (Playwright)
Espanola 1921,D 30,13:1
Tilden, Milano
Cymbeline 1923,O 3,12:1
Fatal Wedding, The 1924,Je 3,22:3
Out of Step 1925,Ja 30,12:1
Sapphire Ring, The 1925,Ap 16,25:2
Man or Devil 1925,My 22,22:4
What Women Do? 1925,Jl 21,26:4
Great God Brown, The 1926,Ja 25,26:1
Chicago 1926,D 31,11:1
Silent Witness, The 1931,Mr 24,31:5
Sentinels 1931,D 26,15:1
June Moon 1933,My 16,15:5
Birthright 1933,N 22,22:3
Richard of Bordeaux 1934,F 15,16:2
Geraniums in My Window 1934,O 27,20:6
Potash and Perlmutter 1935,Ap 6,11:3
Call Me Ziggy 1937,F 13,9:6
Fabulous Invalid, The 1938,O 10,15:1
Tilden, Milano (Director)
June Moon 1933,My 16,15:5
Tilden, William T 2d
Clarence 1923,My 14,18:4
Don Q Jr 1926,Ja 28,16:3
They All Want Something 1926,O 13,20:2
Tillbury, Zeffie
Just Beyond 1925,D 2,22:4
Tiller, John
Vaudeville (Palace) 1930,Mr 3,18:5
Tiller, John Girls
Duchess of Chicago, The 1929,N 17,IX,4:1
Joker Wild 1955,My 20,19:4
Tiller, Lawrence Girls
An und Aus 1926,D 5,VIII,8:7
Tiller, Ted
Sing Out, Sweet Land! 1944,D 28,24:2
Grey-Eyed People, The 1952,D 18,41:2
Call It Virtue 1963,Mr 28,8:2
Amorous Flea, The 1964,F 18,26:1
Tiller Girls, The
Ziegfeld Follies 1922,Je 6,18:2
George White's Scandals 1923,Je 19,22:5
Ziegfeld Follies 1924,Je 25,26:1
Schoen und Schick 1928,Ag 26,II,1:2
Schoen und Schick 1928,N 4,IX,2:1
Tout Paris 1928,N 18,IX,2:1
Vaudeville (Palace) 1928,D 24,10:8
Tillinger, John
How's the World Treating You? 1966,O 25,50:1
Halfway up the Tree 1967,N 8,52:1
Tea Party 1968,O 16,40:1
Pequod 1969,Je 30,33:1
Crimes of Passion; Erpingham Camp, The
1969,O 27,54:1
Othello 1970,Je 22,43:1
Devil's Disciple, The 1970,Je 30,48:1
Othello 1970,S 15,51:1
Hay Fever 1970,N 10,55:1
Hay Fever 1970,N 22,II,18:6
Tillinghast, John K
Merry Wives of Windsor, The 1954,F 17,27:1
Tillio, M
Ziegfeld Follies 1921,Je 22,10:1
Tillisch, Ingeborg
Drums Begin, The 1933,N 25,10:5
Tillman, Daisy
Conjur 1938,N 1,27:2
Tillman, Henrietta
You Can't Win 1926,F 17,12:1
Tillman, Hunter
This Way to the Tomb 1961,D 9,21:1
Tillman, Judith
Young and Beautiful, The 1959,My 29,13:1
Darker Flower, A 1963,Mr 11,7:2
Tillsbury, Zeffie
Blood on the Moon 1934,S 30,IX,3:1
Tillstrom, Burr
Kukla, Burr and Ollie 1960,N 1,47:2
Tillstrom, Burr (Playwright)
Kukla, Burr and Ollie 1960,N 1,47:2
Tillus and Larue
Rainbow Rose 1926,Mr 17,28:2
Tilston, Jennifer
Black Comedy 1967,O 19,58:1
Little Boxes; Coffee Lace, The 1969,D 4,71:2
Little Boxes; Trevor 1969,D 4,71:2
Tilton, Elizabeth
Liliom 1956,F 18,12:5

Tilton, George (Playwright)
Odd Man Out 1925,My 26,24:3
Soldiers and Women 1929,Ag 25,VIII,3:1
Soldiers and Women 1929,S 3,25:1
Foreign Affairs 1932,Ap 14,25:5
Tilton, James (Lighting Director)
You Can't Take It With You 1965,N 24,32:1
Pantagleize 1967,D 1,54:1
Show-Off, The 1967,D 6,40:2
Exit the King 1968,Ja 10,48:1
Cherry Orchard, The 1968,Mr 20,41:1
Cocktail Party, The 1968,O 8,42:1
Misanthrope, The 1968,O 10,59:1
Ballad for a Firing Squad 1968,D 12,64:2
Cock-A-Doodle Dandy 1969,Ja 21,40:1
Hamlet 1969,Mr 4,34:1
Private Lives 1969,D 5,52:1
Harvey 1970,F 25,41:1
Criminals, The 1970,F 26,33:2
Tilton, James (Scenic Designer)
Right You Are (If You Think You Are)
1964,Mr 5,37:1
Impromptu at Versailles 1964,Mr 10,43:1
Scapin 1964,Mr 10,43:1
Lower Depths, The 1964,Mr 31,30:1
You Can't Take It With You 1965,N 24,32:1
School for Scandal, The 1966,N 22,33:2
Right You Are (If You Think You Are)
1966,N 23,34:2
We Comrades Three 1966,D 21,46:1
Wild Duck, The 1967,Ja 12,49:1
War and Peace 1967,Mr 22,42:1
Pantagleize 1967,D 1,54:1
Show-Off, The 1967,D 6,40:2
Cherry Orchard, The 1968,Mr 20,41:1
Misanthrope, The 1968,O 10,59:1
Ballad for a Firing Squad 1968,D 12,64:2
Cock-A-Doodle Dandy 1969,Ja 21,40:1
Hamlet 1969,Mr 4,34:1
Oh! Calcutta! 1969,Je 18,33:1
Doctor's Dilemma, The 1969,Je 24,37:1
Private Lives 1969,D 5,52:1
Harvey 1970,F 25,41:1
Criminals, The 1970,F 26,33:2
Tilton, Thomas
Grand Street Follies, The 1925,Je 19,24:1
Apothecary, The 1926,Mr 17,28:1
Tilton, Webb
Portofino 1958,F 22,8:3
South Pacific 1969,Jl 7,27:1
Timberg, Herman
Tick-Tack-Toe 1920,F 24,11:2
Vaudeville (Hippodrome) 1925,O 20,29:2
Vaudeville (Palace) 1929,Je 10,22:6
Vaudeville (Palace) 1931,Ja 19,25:3
Vaudeville (Palace) 1932,Ap 18,19:5
Timberg, Herman (Composer)
Tick-Tack-Toe 1920,F 24,11:2
Timberg, Herman (Director)
You'll See Stars 1943,Ja 1,26:6
Timberg, Herman (Lyricist)
You'll See Stars 1943,Ja 1,26:6
Timberg, Herman (Playwright)
Tick-Tack-Toe 1920,F 24,11:2
Crazy Quilt 1931,My 20,28:4
You'll See Stars 1943,Ja 1,26:6
Timberg, Sam (Composer)
Merry World, The 1926,Je 9,18:3
Broadway Nights 1929,Jl 16,23:2
Street Singer, The 1929,Jl 28,VIII,1:6
Street Singer, The 1929,S 18,35:2
Timberg, Sammy
Vaudeville (Hippodrome) 1924,O 21,21:2
Vaudeville (Hippodrome) 1925,O 20,29:2
Vaudeville (Hippodrome) 1926,Ap 13,28:2
Vaudeville (Palace) 1927,D 20,33:4
Vaudeville (Palace) 1929,Je 10,22:6
Timberlake, Craig
Mikado, The 1949,O 5,35:2
H M S Pinafore 1949,O 18,34:2
Trial by Jury 1949,O 18,34:2
As You Like It 1950,Ja 27,27:2
Timberlake, Leon C
Lost 1927,Mr 29,22:2
Timberlake, Ralph (Playwright)
Apple a Day, An 1936,My 25,23:5
Timberman, Elizabeth
Panic 1935,Mr 16,18:4
Timberry, Snittle
George Barnwell; London Merchant, The
1928,O 2,34:3
Timbers, Herman
Vaudeville (Hippodrome) 1926,Ap 13,28:2
Timblin, Charles
Vaudeville (Palace) 1930,Mr 24,24:5
Vaudeville (Palace) 1931,Je 29,20:1
Vaudeville (Palace) 1932,Jl 18,9:7
Tobacco Road 1940,D 5,32:3
Timmerman, Francois
Boys in the Band, The 1969,S 20,21:2
Timmins, Harry
Fashion 1937,Mr 21,II,7:8

Timmis, Walter
Scaramouche 1923,O 25,14:2
Timmons, Georgia Ann
Memphis Bound 1945,My 25,23:2
Timmons, Rodester
Native Son 1941,Mr 25,26:5
Native Son 1942,O 24,10:6
Finian's Rainbow 1953,Mr 7,13:2
Sandhog 1954,N 24,17:1
Finian's Rainbow 1955,My 19,25:1
Timmons, Ruth
Idiot's Delight 1936,Mr 25,25:2
Idiot's Delight 1937,Ag 10,22:7
Timoney, Alice (Playwright)
Bottled 1928,Ap 11,25:1
Timony, James (Producer)
Clean Beds 1939,My 26,21:2
Timothy, Christopher
Chips With Everything 1963,O 2,49:1
Timothy, Paul
South Pacific 1969,Jl 7,27:1
Timpson, Charles
Virginia 1937,S 3,13:2
Tinberg, Herman
Vaudeville (Palace) 1927,D 20,33:4
Tindal, Muriel
Hole in the Wall, The 1920,Mr 27,11:1
Phoebe of Quality Street 1921,My 10,20:1
Tinling, Ted
Along Came a Spider 1963,My 28,33:1
Once in a Lifetime 1964,Ja 29,20:1
Fun City 1968,Mr 7,53:2
Tinmer, David (Director)
Aqua Carnival 1962,Je 29,15:1
Tinn, John A
Teahouse of the August Moon, The
1955,My 10,24:1
Tinney, Allen
Porgy and Bess 1935,O 11,30:2
Brown Sugar 1937,D 3,29:2
Tinney, Frank
Tickle Me 1920,Ag 18,9:1
All-Star Jamboree 1921,Jl 14,18:1
Friar's Club Frolic 1922,Je 5,16:1
Daffy Dill 1922,Ag 23,14:5
Daffy Dill 1922,Ag 27,VI,1:1
Vaudeville (Palace) 1923,Mr 13,19:2
Music Box Revue 1923,S 24,5:3
Earl Carroll's Vanities 1925,D 29,20:3
Vanities 1926,Ja 10,VII,1:1
Tinney, William
Porgy and Bess 1935,O 11,30:2
Brown Sugar 1937,D 3,29:2
Tinnin, Glenna S (Director)
Tom Sawyer 1931,D 26,15:3
Tinova and Baikoft
Vaudeville (Palace) 1929,N 25,22:4
Tinsley, Joe
Phoebe of Quality Street 1921,My 10,20:1
Marjorie 1924,Ag 12,12:2
Tinsley, Robert
My Kinsman, Major Molineux 1964,N 2,62:2
Tiomkin, Dimitri
Vaudeville (Hippodrome) 1926,My 8,29:2
Tiomkin, Dimitri (Composer)
Ziegfeld Follies 1931,Jl 2,30:5
Tiomkin, Dimitri (Playwright)
Ziegfeld Follies 1931,Jl 2,30:5
Tiomkin, Dmitri (Producer)
Keeping Expenses Down 1932,O 21,25:2
Tiomkin and Kharlton
Vaudeville (Palace) 1925,D 8,28:6
Tionco, Maureen
South Pacific 1965,Je 3,25:1
Make Me Disappear 1969,My 14,34:1
Tip and Tow
Crazy With the Heat 1941,Ja 31,15:2
Tip Top Four
George White's Scandals 1923,Je 19,22:5
Tippett, Tom (Director)
Mill Shadows 1932,F 29,20:7
Tippett, Tom (Playwright)
Mill Shadows 1932,F 29,20:7
Tippit, Wayne
Comedian, The 1956,O 18,36:4
Parade at the Devil's Bridge 1957,F 19,35:7
Doctor Faustus 1957,F 19,35:7
Tall Story 1959,Ja 30,33:2
Only in America 1959,N 20,35:1
Under the Sycamore Tree 1960,Mr 8,37:2
Misalliance 1961,S 26,32:2
Alchemist, The 1964,S 15,33:1
Young Master Dante, The 1968,D 31,19:1
Gantry 1970,F 16,44:1
Tipson, Thelma
Garrick Gaieties 1930,Je 5,29:2
Free for All 1931,S 9,25:1
Blessed Event 1932,F 13,23:2
Tipton, Ben (Scenic Designer)
Blackouts of 1949 1949,S 7,39:2
Tipton, Jennifer (Lighting Director)
Macbeth 1967,Jl 31,21:1
Richard II 1968,Je 24,42:3

Tipton, Jennifer (Lighting Director)—Cont
Love's Labour's Lost 1968,Je 28,36:1
Susie Is a Good Girl 1968,N 5,53:2
Subscriber, The 1968,N 5,53:2
Grab Bag, The 1968,N 5,53:2
Horseman, Pass By 1969,Ja 16,46:4
Our Town 1969,N 28,50:1
Tirado, Nelson
White Cargo 1960,D 30,12:1
Tirella, Eddie
Diamond Lil 1948,N 30,33:2
Tiroff, James
Brig, The 1963,My 16,40:1
Tirrell, Donald Bailey (Costume Designer)
Marching Song 1959,D 29,20:1
Tirrell, Donald Bailey (Lighting Director)
Fashion 1959,Ja 21,27:1
Tirrell, Donald Bailey (Scenic Designer)
Fashion 1959,Ja 21,27:1
Marching Song 1959,D 29,20:1
Tisdale, Harry
Moon Is a Gong, The 1926,Mr 13,21:3
Tisen, Paul and His Orchestra
Vaudeville (Palace) 1926,S 21,32:5
Vaudeville (Palace) 1927,Jl 19,27:6
Tishman, Herbert
Threepenny Opera, The 1955,S 21,38:1
Tishman, Jerry (Miscellaneous)
Much Ado About Nothing 1952,My 2,20:1
Titakis, Nick
Utopia, Limited 1960,Ap 8,27:2
Yeomen of the Guard, The 1961,Ap 28,23:1
Grand Duke, The 1961,My 12,24:1
H M S Pinafore 1961,Je 9,29:5
Student Prince, The 1961,Jl 14,14:1
Titcomb, Caldwell (Composer)
Henry V 1956,Jl 7,11:2
Saint Joan 1956,S 12,42:1
Puntila 1959,My 15,26:2
Titheradge, Dion
Loose Ends 1926,N 2,34:2
Titheradge, Dion (Director)
Loose Ends 1926,N 2,34:2
Titheradge, Dion (Playwright)
Loose Ends 1926,N 2,34:2
Dear Love 1930,My 18,VIII,3:1
Frailties 1931,Ja 30,18:3
Man of Yesterday 1935,F 20,22:5
Man of Yesterday 1935,Mr 17,VIII,1:4
Titheradge, Madge
Garden of Allah, The 1920,Ag 29,VI,1:1
To Have the Honor 1924,My 11,VIII,2:7
Happy Husband, The 1927,Jl 10,VII,2:3
Home Chat 1927,N 13,IX,2:1
Patriot, The 1928,Ja 20,15:1
Patriot, The 1928,Ja 29,VIII,1:1
Business With America 1933,Ja 1,IX,1:3
Theatre Royal; Royal Family, The 1934,O 24,24:2
Theatre Royal 1934,N 11,IX,1:1
Promise 1936,Mr 22,XI,1:7
Mademoiselle 1936,O 4,IX,3:7
Titkos, Ilona
Road to Rome, The 1928,Je 10,VIII,2:8
Titmuss, Phyllis
Half a Loaf 1926,N 28,VIII,1:4
Love at Second Sight 1927,S 11,VIII,2:4
Titolo, Theodore S (Scenic Designer)
Rat's Mass, A 1969,N 1,39:1
Titsworth, Frances
Straw Hat, The 1926,O 15,20:2
Trumpet Shall Sound, The 1926,D 11,15:2
Tittoni, Tommaso
Idiot's Delight 1936,Mr 25,25:2
Titus, Kay
Creoles 1927,S 23,33:3
Titus, Mary
Of V We Sing 1942,F 16,20:3
Titzell, Josiah (Lyricist)
Garrick Gaieties 1930,Je 5,29:2
Tlhotlhalemaie, Cocky
Sponono 1964,Ap 3,28:1
Toback, Anna
Village Wedding, A 1930,S 24,26:2
Russian Love 1930,N 27,32:3
Night in the Woods, A 1931,Mr 2,19:3
Berl and Shmerl Corporation 1934,Ap 2,12:5
Holiday in Town, A 1935,S 30,12:3
Secret of Love, The 1936,F 24,15:2
Yoina Seeks a Bride 1936,O 20,31:1
Mazel Tov, Rabbi 1938,N 28,10:4
Jewish Heart, The 1939,Ja 25,16:6
Toback, Hannah
Mecca 1920,O 5,12:2
Bitter Sweet 1934,My 8,28:4
Bitter Sweet 1936,Ag 26,17:3
Cellar and the Well, The 1950,D 11,30:2
Tober, Marie
Call It a Day 1935,N 24,IX,1:2
Tobey, Cliff (Miscellaneous)
Beclch 1968,D 17,59:1
Tobey, Clifford
Girl From Samos, The 1954,N 24,17:1
Tobey, Kenneth
As You Like It 1941,O 21,29:2

Tobey, Kenneth—Cont
Sunny River 1941,D 5,28:2
Johnny on the Spot 1942,Ja 9,24:2
Mexican Mural; Patio With Flamingo 1942,Ap 27,19:2
Janie 1942,S 11,24:2
New Life, A 1943,S 16,26:6
Suds in Your Eye 1944,Ja 13,15:5
Truckline Cafe 1946,F 28,19:4
Joan of Lorraine 1946,N 19,40:2
As We Forgive Our Debtors 1947,Mr 11,37:2
Survivors, The 1948,Ja 20,27:2
Golden Boy 1964,O 21,56:1
Tobias, Aurelio
Processional 1937,O 14,23:1
Tobias, Charles (Composer)
Keep It Clean 1929,Je 25,35:5
Sketch Book 1935,Je 5,22:2
Yokel Boy 1939,Jl 7,12:2
New Hellzapoppin, The 1939,D 12,36:4
Tobias, Charles (Lyricist)
Keep It Clean 1929,Je 25,35:5
Sketch Book 1935,Je 5,22:2
Hellzapoppin 1938,S 23,34:2
Tobias, Fred (Lyricist)
Pousse-Cafe 1966,Mr 19,19:2
Gantry 1970,F 16,44:1
Tobias, George
What Price Glory 1924,S 6,14:3
International, The 1928,Ja 16,24:4
Grey Fox, The 1928,O 23,32:3
S S Glencairn 1929,Ja 10,24:5
Fiesta 1929,S 18,35:1
Red Rust 1929,D 18,31:1
Sailors of Cattaro 1934,D 11,28:4
Black Pit 1935,Mr 21,26:6
Drums Professor, The 1935,Jl 30,17:2
Paths of Glory 1935,S 19,29:1
Paths of Glory 1935,S 27,24:2
Hell Freezes Over 1935,D 30,14:2
Name Your Poison 1936,Ja 21,27:4
Star Spangled 1936,Mr 11,23:1
Emperor Jones, The 1936,Ag 11,24:6
You Can't Take It With You 1936,D 6,XII,6:2
You Can't Take It With You 1936,D 15,31:1
You Can't Take It With You 1937,Ag 29,X,1:1
Good Hunting 1938,N 22,26:5
Silk Stockings 1955,F 25,17:3
Tobias, Henry
Off to Buffalo! 1939,F 22,18:2
Tobias, Henry H (Composer)
Padlocks of 1927 1927,Jl 6,23:4
Tobias, Jerry
Diamond Lil 1949,F 7,16:2
Tobias, John
Sweeney Todd 1957,Ag 28,21:4
Tobias, Oliver
Hair 1969,S 13,30:1
Tobias, S B
Claw, The 1921,O 18,20:1
Tobias, Willard
Jack in the Pulpit 1925,Ja 7,33:1
Bad Habits of 1926 1926,My 1,11:1
God Loves Us 1926,O 20,22:2
Say It With Flowers 1926,D 6,29:1
Tobin, Dan
American Holiday 1936,F 22,13:3
Philadelphia Story, The 1939,Mr 29,21:1
Tobin, Gene
Love Life 1948,O 8,31:2
Tobin, Genevieve
Little Old New York 1920,S 9,9:2
Little Old New York 1920,S 19,VI,1:1
Untitled-Benefit 1921,My 2,12:3
Polly Preferred 1923,Ja 12,13:3
King Lear 1923,Mr 10,9:4
Dear Sir 1924,S 24,21:3
Youngest, The 1924,D 23,17:1
Treat 'Em Rough 1926,O 5,26:2
This Woman Business 1926,D 8,25:1
Murray Hill 1927,Ag 21,VII,1:8
Murray Hill 1927,S 30,29:1
Trial of Mary Dugan, The 1928,Mr 7,28:3
Fifty Million Frenchmen 1929,N 28,34:4
Tobin, Lawrence (Director)
Purple Canary, The 1963,Ap 23,31:1
Tobin, Lawrence (Producer)
Purple Canary, The 1963,Ap 23,31:1
Tobin, Matthew
Hour Glass, The 1955,O 17,33:1
Hasty Heart, The 1959,S 15,45:2
Boys From Syracuse, The 1963,Ap 16,31:1
Empire Builders, The 1968,O 2,34:1
Boys in the Band, The 1969,F 18,36:1
Lyle 1970,Mr 21,16:2
Tobin, Matthew (Miscellaneous)
Royal Gambit 1959,Mr 5,34:2
Tobin, Niall
Borstal Boy 1967,O 11,39:2
Tobin, Patricia
Two on the Aisle 1951,Jl 20,13:6
Tobin, Richard L (Director)
Shunned 1960,D 21,39:1

Tobin, Rick
Ronde, La 1960,My 10,44:2
Nathan the Wise 1962,Mr 23,29:1
Tobin, Ruth
Sunup to Sundown 1938,F 2,14:3
Flight Into China 1939,S 12,28:1
Tobin, Vivian
Shavings 1920,F 17,18:1
Grand Duke, The 1921,N 2,20:1
Give and Take 1923,Ja 19,13:1
Rivals, The 1923,My 9,14:2
We've Got to Have Money 1923,Ag 21,12:1
Just Life 1926,S 15,33:3
Padre, The 1926,D 28,16:3
Take My Advice 1927,N 2,24:3
March Hares 1928,Ap 3,32:6
Perfect Alibi, The 1928,N 28,24:2
Toby, Mark
Marching Song 1937,F 18,18:2
Tobias and the Angel 1937,Ap 29,16:5
Toca, Elisa
Wisteria Trees, The 1950,Mr 30,39:1
Tocher, E W (Playwright)
Old Lady Says No!, The 1929,Ag 11,VIII,2:1
Moon in the Yellow River, The 1931,My 17,VIII,3:3
Moon in the Yellow River, The 1931,S 27,VIII,2:8
Tochey, John Peter (Original Author)
Jonesy 1929,Ap 10,32:2
Tochey, John Peter (Playwright)
Jonesy 1929,Ap 10,32:2
Todd, Abbie
Flora, the Red Menace 1965,My 12,41:2
Todd, Ann
No More Ladies 1934,O 7,IX,3:7
Man of Yesterday 1935,Mr 17,VIII,1:4
Promise 1936,Mr 22,XI,1:7
She, Too, Was Young 1938,S 4,X,2:1
Love in a Mist 1941,N 30,IX,3:1
Lottie Dundass 1943,Ag 22,II,1:8
Four Winds 1957,S 26,21:2
Todd, Beverly
Deep Are the Roots 1960,O 4,47:1
No Strings 1964,Ja 1,17:1
Todd, Clarence (Composer)
Keep Shufflin' 1928,F 28,18:3
Todd, Dick
New Moon, The 1944,My 18,16:2
Todd, Donna
Don Carlos 1962,F 28,27:5
Storm, The 1962,Mr 31,17:2
Todd, George
All Good Americans 1933,D 6,29:2
Todd, James
John 1927,N 5,16:4
Cock Robin 1928,Ja 13,26:6
Strange Interlude 1928,D 18,37:3
Bridal Quilt 1934,O 11,28:5
Ceiling Zero 1935,Ap 11,26:2
Curse You, Jack Dalton 1935,Jl 16,24:1
She Cried for the Moon 1935,Jl 23,24:3
O Evening Star 1936,Ja 9,24:6
Farewell Summer 1937,Mr 30,20:2
Work Is for Horses 1937,N 22,14:6
Sunup to Sundown 1938,F 2,14:3
Michael Drops In 1938,D 28,24:3
Day in the Sun 1939,My 17,29:2
Sea Dogs 1939,N 7,30:3
Strangler Fig, The 1940,My 7,31:2
Blind Alley 1940,O 16,28:2
Brooklyn Biarritz 1941,F 28,16:2
Let's Face It 1941,O 30,26:2
Yankee Point 1942,N 24,28:2
Apology 1943,Mr 23,14:2
Perfect Marriage, The 1944,O 27,17:6
Todd, John
Mask of Hamlet, The 1921,Ag 23,10:3
Money in the Air 1932,Mr 8,19:3
Todd, Judson (Miscellaneous)
Shoestring Revue 1955,Mr 1,22:2
Todd, Judson (Mrs) (Miscellaneous)
Shoestring Revue 1955,Mr 1,22:2
Anything Goes 1962,My 16,35:1
Todd, Lorraine
Million Dollar Baby 1945,D 22,17:2
Todd, Michael (Miscellaneous)
Up in Central Park 1947,My 20,29:2
Todd, Michael (Playwright)
Live Wire, The 1950,Ag 18,16:2
Todd, Michael (Producer)
Call Me Ziggy 1937,F 13,9:6
Man From Cairo, The 1938,My 5,26:5
Hot Mikado, The 1939,Mr 24,26:2
Hot Mikado, The 1939,Ap 2,X,1:3
Hot Mikado, The 1939,Je 23,23:4
Star and Garter 1942,Je 25,26:2
Star and Garter 1942,S 13,VIII,1:1
Something for the Boys 1943,Ja 17,VIII,1:1
Naked Genius, The 1943,O 22,20:5
Naked Genius, The 1943,O 31,II,1:1
Naked Genius, The 1943,N 7,II,1:6
Mexican Hayride 1944,Ja 29,9:6
Pick-Up Girl 1944,My 4,25:2

Todd, Michael (Producer)—Cont
Catherine Was Great 1944,Jl 11,18:2
Catherine Was Great 1944,Ag 3,16:1
Up in Central Park 1945,Ja 29,17:2
Hamlet 1945,D 14,25:2
Would-Be Gentleman, The 1946,Ja 20,II,1:1
January Thaw 1946,F 5,18:2
Hamlet 1946,Je 4,18:4
As the Girls Go 1948,N 15,21:2
Peep Show 1950,Je 7,34:5
Peep Show 1950,Jl 9,II,1:1
Live Wire, The 1950,Jl 19,26:2
Peep Show 1950,Ag 27,II,1:1
Night in Venice, A 1952,Je 27,18:6
Night in Venice, A 1952,Jl 13,II,1:1
Night in Venice, A 1953,Je 26,15:2
Todd, Michael Jr (Miscellaneous)
Around the World in 80 Days 1964,Je 29,33:2
Todd, Michael Jr (Producer)
And I Met a Man 1970,Ap 11,20:3
Todd, Mildred
New Faces 1934,Mr 16,24:5
Fools Rush In 1934,D 26,19:2
Squaring the Circle 1935,O 4,24:6
Who's Who 1938,Mr 2,16:2
What Big Ears! 1942,Ap 21,18:5
Sweet Charity 1942,D 29,26:4
Todd, Nick
Delightful Season, A 1960,S 29,30:1
Todd, Stella
Stranger, The 1945,F 13,21:2
Todd, Thomas
Howdy Stranger 1937,Ja 15,17:5
Todd, William N Jr
What a Relief 1935,D 14,10:6
Todorovic, Bora
Progress of Bora, The Tailor, The 1968,Je 27,49:2
Ubu Roi 1968,Je 29,20:1
Victor, or The Children Take Over 1968,Jl 10,22:4
Todrina, T
Yegor Bulevitch 1934,Ja 8,21:7
Aristocrats 1935,My 2,16:2
Tofano, Gloria
Flies, The 1954,S 10,18:2
Rose Tattoo, The 1966,O 21,36:2
Jar, The 1969,Ap 23,42:1
Tofferson, Chris (Costume Designer)
Concept, The 1968,My 7,51:1
Toia, Jacques
Amphitryon 1970,F 4,38:1
Malade Imaginaire, Le 1970,F 18,40:2
Toibin, Niall
Borstal Boy 1967,O 12,55:2
Death and Resurrection of Mr Roche, The 1968,O 11,44:4
Borstal Boy 1970,Ap 1,38:1
Borstal Boy 1970,Ap 12,II,9:6
Toigo, Alfred
Valmouth 1960,O 7,29:1
Kean 1961,N 3,28:2
Giants, Sons of Giants 1962,Ja 8,26:2
Hidden Stranger 1963,Jl 10,5:5
Kismet 1965,Je 23,45:1
Those That Play the Clowns 1966,N 25,48:1
Toja, Jacques
Bourgeois Gentilhomme, Le 1955,O 26,26:1
Barbier de Seville, Le 1955,N 9,40:1
Arlequin Poli par l'Amour 1955,N 9,40:1
Jeu de l'Amour et du Hasard, Le 1955,N 16,42:4
Avare, L', L'; Miser, The 1966,F 9,32:1
Cid, Le 1966,F 12,17:1
Reine Morte, La 1966,F 16,52:1
Fil a la Paite, Un 1966,F 18,25:1
Troupe Du Roi, La 1970,F 4,38:1
Don Juan 1970,F 7,24:2
Femmes Savaantes, Les 1970,F 14,12:1
Tokar, Norman
Revisor; Inspector General, The 1935,F 18,19:6
Poverty Is No Crime 1935,F 21,22:5
Strange Child 1935,F 26,16:1
See My Lawyer 1939,S 28,29:1
Delicate Story 1940,D 5,32:2
Days of Our Youth, The 1941,N 29,15:2
Life of Reilly, The 1942,Ap 30,13:2
Magic Touch, The 1947,S 4,30:1
Tokarskaya, S
Enemies 1935,Mr 19,24:7
Tokatyan, Leon (Playwright)
13 Daughters 1961,Mr 3,17:2
Tokayer, Sheindi
Home Movies 1964,My 12,32:1
Tokizo, Nakamura
Kagotsurube; Courtesan, The 1960,Je 3,26:1
Kanjincho; Subscription List, The 1960,Je 3,26:1
Kagotsurube; Courtesan, The 1960,Je 3,26:1
Musume Dojoji; Maiden at the Dojo Temple, The 1960,Je 10,37:1
Chushingura; Forty-Seven Ronin, The 1960,Je 10,37:1
Migawari Zazen; Substitute, The 1960,Je 10,37:1
Chushingura; Forty-Seven Ronin, The 1960,Je 17,35:4
Musume Dojoji; Maiden at the Dojo Temple, The 1960,Je 17,35:4

Tokyo Kid Brothers
Golden Bat 1970,Ag 16,II,1:1
Tolan, Michael
Grass Is Always Greener, The 1955,F 16,25:2
Miser, The 1955,Mr 18,34:2
Will Success Spoil Rock Hunter? 1955,O 14,22:2
Genius and the Goddess, The 1957,D 11,41:1
Majority of One, A 1959,F 17,28:2
Journey of the Fifth Horse, The 1966,Ap 22,36:1
Tolan, Michael (Producer)
Walk Together Children 1968,N 12,54:1
Toland, John
That Hat! 1964,S 24,45:1
Persecution and Assassination of Marat As
    Performed by the Inmates of the Asylum of
    Charenton Under the Direction of the Marquis de
    Sade, The 1967,Ja 4,34:1
Tolaydo, Michael
Cherry Orchard, The 1970,My 7,63:2
Tolbert, Ann (Choreographer)
Tree Witch, The 1961,Je 5,39:4
Tolbert-Hewitt, Owen
Tin Top Valley 1947,Mr 1,11:2
Devil's Disciple, The 1950,Ja 26,23:2
Wild Duck, The 1951,D 27,17:1
No Time for Sergeants 1955,O 21,32:2
Toledano, Jose
Cabalgata 1949,Jl 8,14:2
Toledo, Julio
Cabalgata 1949,Jl 8,14:2
Tolentino, Joan
In 3 Zones 1970,N 3,28:1
Toler, Harrison
Lady of the Lamp, The 1920,Ag 18,6:4
Toler, Morris
Brothers Ashkenazi, The 1955,N 12,24:4
Toler, Sidney
Sophie 1920,Mr 3,12:2
Foot-Loose 1920,Ag 15,VI,1:1
Poldekin 1920,S 10,12:1
Deburau 1920,D 24,14:3
Kiki 1921,N 30,13:1
49ers, The 1922,N 7,14:1
Laugh, Clown, Laugh! 1923,N 29,30:1
Dove, The 1925,F 12,17:3
Canary Dutch 1925,S 9,22:1
Tommy 1927,Ja 11,36:4
Tommy 1927,Mr 27,VII,1:1
Mrs Bumpstead-Leigh 1929,Ap 2,28:3
It's a Wise Child 1929,Jl 28,VIII,1:6
It's a Wise Child 1929,Ag 7,29:1
It's a Wise Child 1929,Ag 25,VIII,1:1
Toler, Sidney (Director)
Ritzy 1930,F 11,30:4
Toler, Sidney (Playwright)
Golden Days 1921,N 2,20:1
Exile, The 1923,Ap 10,24:2
Bye Bye, Barbara 1924,Ag 26,6:3
Ritzy 1930,F 11,30:4
Tolkan, James
Between Two Thieves 1960,F 12,23:1
Shoemaker and the Peddler, The 1960,O 15,27:4
Once in a Lifetime 1964,Ja 29,20:1
Cannibals, The 1968,N 4,60:1
Tolkin, Mel (Composer)
Tickets, Please! 1950,Ap 28,25:2
Tolkin, Mel (Lyricist)
Tickets, Please! 1950,Ap 28,25:2
Tolkin, Mel (Playwright)
Of V We Sing 1942,F 16,20:3
Maybe Tuesday 1958,Ja 30,18:3
Toll, David
Me and Juliet 1970,My 15,42:1
Toll, John
Escape This Night 1938,Ap 23,18:1
Tolle, Mildred
Ups-A-Daisy 1928,O 9,34:2
Hey, Nonny, Nonny! 1932,Je 7,22:3
Tollefsen, Merald
Excess Baggage 1927,D 27,24:2
Toller, Ernest (Lyricist)
Pepper Mill 1937,Ja 6,19:4
Toller, Ernest (Playwright)
Masse Mensch 1922,Ap 2,VI,1:2
Maschinenstuermer, Die 1922,Jl 23,VI,1:1
Machine Wreckers, The 1923,My 13,VIII,3:5
Hinkeman 1924,Mr 2,VIII,2:1
Man and the Masses 1924,Ap 15,25:1
Masse Mensch; Man and the Masses
    1924,Ap 20,VIII,1:1
Man and the Masses 1924,My 25,VIII,1:8
Hoppla, Wir Leben! 1927,D 11,IX,4:1
Hoopla! 1929,Mr 10,X,4:6
Bourgeois Gentilhomme, Le 1929,Mr 24,X,2:3
Feuer aus Den Kesseln 1930,O 19,IX,2:4
Bloody Laughter 1931,D 5,20:6
Miracle in America 1934,O 2,18:4
Draw the Fires 1935,Je 9,IX,1:1
No More Peace 1936,Je 12,19:4
Pepper Mill 1937,Ja 6,19:4
No More Peace 1937,F 27,9:1
Machine Wreckers, The 1937,Ap 12,14:2
No More Peace 1937,Je 4,26:7

No More Peace 1938,Ja 29,13:2
Blind Man's Buff 1953,N 15,II,3:1
Toller, Lillian
Poppa 1928,D 25,31:1
Mr Papavert 1932,Ja 23,18:6
Tolliver, Jon
Ruy Blas 1957,D 14,16:3
Tolman, C H
Countess Maritza 1926,S 20,21:1
Tolstoy, Alexis (Playwright)
Czar Feodor 1922,O 22,VIII,1:6
Tsar Fyodor Ivanovitch 1923,Ja 9,26:1
Golden Book of Love, The 1923,N 22,21:4
Rasputin 1927,N 11,6:5
Tsar Fyodor 1929,F 19,22:3
Rasputin 1929,My 12,IX,2:3
Ivan the Terrible 1944,N 12,II,1:6
Tolstoy, Leo (Original Author)
Anna Karenina 1937,Ap 25,IV,4:5
War and Peace 1942,My 22,26:3
War and Peace 1943,Ag 22,II,1:8
Power of Darkness, The 1948,O 11,28:2
Kreutzer Sonata, The 1961,F 16,24:2
War and Peace 1962,Je 16,10:1
War and Peace 1965,Ja 12,32:1
War and Peace 1965,Ja 31,II,1:1
War and Peace 1967,Mr 22,42:1
War and Peace 1967,Ap 2,II,1:1
Tolstoy, Leo (Playwright)
Power of Darkness, The 1920,Ja 22,22:1
Power of Darkness, The 1920,Ja 25,VIII,2:1
Chauve-Souris 1922,O 11,22:2
Tsar Fyodor Ivanovitch 1923,Ja 14,VII,1:1
Tsar Fyodor Ivanovitch 1923,My 22,14:3
Living Corpse, The 1924,Mr 18,25:2
Er Ist an Allem Schuld; He Is to Blame for
    Everything 1928,Ja 10,28:3
Lebende Leichnam, Der, Der; Living Corpse, The
    1928,Ja 24,26:2
Redemption: Lebende Leichnam, Der; Living
    Corpse, The 1928,N 20,28:2
Fruits of Englightenment, The 1928,N 25,X,2:3
Redemption 1929,F 5,27:2
Living Corpse, The 1929,D 7,19:1
Resurrection 1930,Je 8,IX,3:1
Power of Darkness, The 1959,S 30,33:1
Power of Darkness, The 1962,Je 21,26:1
Tom Jones and his orchestra
Boom Boom 1929,Ja 29,26:4
Tomanec, Joyce
Oklahoma! 1969,Je 24,37:1
Tomaroff, Aron
East Wind 1931,O 28,19:1
Tomas, Donna (Costume Designer)
Candaules, Commissioner 1970,My 29,15:1
Tomas, Salvadore
Almost Faithful 1948,Je 5,9:2
As You Like It 1955,O 29,12:2
Romeo and Juliet 1955,D 16,36:3
Tomaszewski, Henryk (Director)
Jaselka 1965,Ja 6,32:1
Kernel and the Shell, The 1965,Ja 6,32:1
Woman, The 1965,Ja 6,32:1
Post Office, The 1965,Ja 6,32:1
Book, The 1965,Ja 6,32:1
Nightmare, The 1965,Ja 6,32:1
Labyrinth, The 1965,Ja 6,32:1
Jacob and the Angel 1965,Ja 6,32:1
Tomaszewski, Henryk (Producer)
Labyrinth, The 1965,Ja 6,32:1
Kernel and the Shell, The 1965,Ja 6,32:1
Woman, The 1965,Ja 6,32:1
Nightmare, The 1965,Ja 6,32:1
Book, The 1965,Ja 6,32:1
Post Office, The 1965,Ja 6,32:1
Jacob and the Angel 1965,Ja 6,32:1
Jaselka 1965,Ja 6,32:1
Tombardi, Robert
Take a Gander 1956,D 14,36:4
Tombes, Andrew
Poor Little Ritz Girl 1920,Jl 29,7:1
Blue Eyes 1921,F 22,11:2
O'Brien Girl, The 1921,O 4,10:2
Ziegfeld Follies 1922,Je 6,18:2
Ziegfeld Follies 1923,Je 5,24:3
Marjorie 1924,Ag 12,12:2
Tell Me More 1925,Ap 14,27:3
Tip-Toes 1925,D 29,20:2
Talk About Girls 1927,Je 15,31:3
Ziegfeld Follies 1927,Ag 17,27:3
Three Cheers 1928,O 16,28:1
Street Singer, The 1929,S 18,35:2
Ripples 1930,F 2,VIII,2:7
Ripples 1930,F 12,26:1
Face the Music 1932,F 18,24:5
Tell Her the Truth 1932,O 29,18:2
All the King's Horses 1934,Ja 31,21:3
Music Hath Charms 1934,D 31,8:2
Tomer, Ben-Zion (Playwright)
Children of the Shadows 1964,F 27,26:1
Tomes, Joseph
Romeo and Juliet 1940,My 10,27:1
Bathsheba 1947,Mr 27,40:2

Tomkins, Don
Good News 1927,Ag 14,VII,2:1
Good News 1927,S 7,35:4
Follow Thru 1929,Ja 10,24:3
Ballyhoo 1930,D 23,24:1
Free for All 1931,S 9,25:1
Wildcat 1960,D 17,20:2
Tomkins, William
Bringing Up Father 1925,Mr 31,16:1
Tomlan, Gwynne
Beclch 1968,D 17,59:1
Electra 1969,Ag 8,14:1
Tomlin, Lily
World of Illusion 1964,Je 25,26:2
Great Airplane Snatch, The 1969,My 28,36:1
Tomlinson, Charles
Tiger Rag, The 1961,F 17,20:2
Tomlinson, Charles (Costume Designer)
Papers 1968,D 3,54:1
Madwoman of Chaillot, The 1970,Mr 23,48:3
Tomlinson, Kate
Eastward in Eden 1947,N 19,33:2
Guys and Dolls 1955,Ap 21,32:2
Tomlinson, Ruth
Inspector General, The 1923,My 1,24:1
Between Two Worlds 1934,O 26,24:2
Tomney, John
Nina Rosa 1930,My 31,19:3
Nina Rosa 1930,S 22,22:5
Tompkins, Florence Aitken
Little Theatre Tournament; Little Italy
    1928,My 10,31:1
Tompkins, Joan
Fly Away Home 1935,Ja 16,20:4
Caste 1935,Ag 13,20:3
Elizabeth Sleeps Out 1935,Ag 27,23:4
Pride and Prejudice 1935,N 3,X,1:5
Pride and Prejudice 1935,N 6,32:4
Golden Journey, The 1936,S 16,28:6
My Sister Eileen 1940,D 27,23:2
Church Street 1948,F 10,27:2
Blood Wedding 1949,F 7,16:2
Blood Wedding 1949,F 13,II,1:1
Bruno and Sidney 1949,My 4,38:2
Tompkins, Toby
Much Ado About Nothing 1969,Je 16,57:1
Hamlet 1969,Je 30,33:1
Cherry Orchard, The 1970,My 7,63:2
Tompkins, Tomie
Trouble in July 1949,D 2,36:2
Tompkins, Vera
Man Who Ate the Popomack, The 1924,Mr 25,24:1
Way of the World, The 1924,N 18,23:4
Shanghai Gesture, The 1926,F 2,20:2
Woman Disputed, A 1926,S 29,23:2
Toms, Archie
Brown Buddies 1930,O 8,29:1
Toms, Carl (Scenic Designer)
Love's Labour's Lost 1968,D 22,54:3
Vivat! Vivat Regina! 1970,Jl 20,21:2
Sleuth 1970,N 13,25:1
Toms, Richard
Battleship Gertie 1935,Ja 19,9:2
Toms, Robert
Scalawag, The 1927,Mr 30,22:3
Triple Crossed 1927,My 6,21:2
Lawyers' Dilemma, The 1928,Jl 10,17:2
Fast Life 1928,S 27,35:2
Congai 1928,N 28,24:3
Headquarters 1929,D 5,32:4
If Booth Had Missed 1932,F 5,24:2
When in Rome 1934,F 28,22:6
Order Please 1934,O 10,21:2
Jefferson Davis 1936,F 19,17:2
Prologue to Glory 1938,Mr 18,22:2
Yours, A Lincoln 1942,Jl 10,12:3
Manhattan Nocturne 1943,O 27,26:2
Ramshackle Inn 1944,Ja 6,17:5
State of the Union 1945,N 15,25:2
Tonde, Edwin
Bottomland 1927,Je 28,29:3
Tone, Aileen
Clouds of the Sun 1922,My 6,11:2
Tone, Bernard
Thieves' Carnival 1955,F 2,21:1
Typewriter, The 1955,Jl 29,8:3
Venice Preserv'd 1955,D 13,54:4
Power of Dreams, A 1958,Mr 11,33:1
Tone, Franchot
Belt, The 1927,O 20,33:1
Centuries, The 1927,N 30,23:1
International, The 1928,Ja 16,24:4
Age of Innocence, The 1928,N 28,24:2
Uncle Vanya 1929,My 25,17:1
Cross Roads 1929,N 12,34:2
Red Rust 1929,D 18,31:1
Hotel Universe 1930,Ap 15,29:1
Pagan Lady 1930,S 28,VIII,4:1
Pagan Lady 1930,O 21,34:2
Green Grow the Lilacs 1931,Ja 27,21:2
Green Grow the Lilacs 1931,F 8,VIII,1:1
House of Connelly, The 1931,S 29,22:4
1931 1931,D 11,34:3

Tone, Franchot—Cont
1931- 1931,D 20,VIII,1:1
Night Over Taos 1932,Mr 10,25:3
Thousand Summers, A 1932,My 25,23:4
Success Story 1932,S 27,24:4
Gentle People, The 1939,Ja 6,25:1
Fifth Column, The 1940,Ja 27,9:1
Fifth Column, The 1940,F 4,IX,1:6
Fifth Column, The 1940,Mr 7,18:2
Fifth Column, The 1940,Mr 17,X,1:1
Hope for the Best 1945,F 8,14:4
Hope for the Best 1945,F 18,II,1:1
ANTA Album 1951,My 7,22:7
Oh, Men! Oh, Women! 1953,D 18,37:2
Time of Your Life, The 1955,Ja 20,34:1
Time of Your Life, The 1955,Ja 30,II,1:1
Uncle Vanya 1956,F 1,25:2
Uncle Vanya 1956,F 12,II,1:1
Moon for the Misbegotten, A 1957,My 3,21:2
Moon for the Misbegotten, A 1957,My 12,II,1:1
Mandingo 1961,My 23,43:6
Strange Interlude 1963,Mr 13,5:2
Bicycle Ride to Nevada 1963,S 25,38:1
Dirty Old Man, The 1964,My 5,53:1
Beyond Desire 1967,O 11,36:1
Tone, Richard
I Feel Wonderful 1954,O 19,22:5
Parade 1960,Ja 21,27:4
13 Daughters 1961,Mr 3,17:2
Pousse-Cafe 1966,Mr 19,19:2
Tone, Richard (Choreographer)
Parade 1960,Ja 21,27:4
Tone, Rudy
Make Mine Manhattan 1948,Ja 16,26:2
Kiss Me, Kate 1949,Ja 30,II,6:5
Toner, Don (Miscellaneous)
Pilgrim's Progress 1962,Mr 21,36:2
Toner, Joseph
Passing Show of 1921, The 1920,D 30,16:2
Vogues of 1924 1924,Mr 28,14:3
Circus Princess, The 1927,Ap 26,32:2
Music in May 1929,Ap 2,29:1
Prince of Pilsen, The 1930,Ja 14,24:3
Blossom Time 1931,Mr 5,32:1
Countess Maritza 1936,Ag 19,18:2
Naughty Marietta 1936,S 2,19:5
Blossom Time 1938,D 27,12:2
Fiorello! 1959,N 24,45:3
Toner, Tom
Friends and Lovers; In the Zone; Bound East for
  Cardiff 1961,My 11,43:1
Six Characters in Search of an Author
  1961,My 11,43:1
Friends and Lovers; End of the Beginning, The
  1961,My 11,43:1
Once in a Lifetime 1962,O 30,30:1
Devils, The 1963,N 5,25:1
Galileo 1968,D 1,88:4
Murderous Angels 1970,F 8,70:1
Tonetti, Anne
Cyrano de Bergerac 1923,N 2,14:1
Green Hat, The 1925,S 16,23:2
Cyrano de Bergerac 1928,D 26,14:4
Roadside 1930,S 27,21:1
Between Two Worlds 1934,O 26,24:2
Toney, Jim
Vaudeville (Palace) 1924,Ap 29,12:2
Vaudeville (Palace) 1928,S 4,21:3
Tong, Yo Hay (Princess)
Little Racketeer, The 1932,Ja 19,24:4
Tonga, Lillian Brennard (Choreographer)
Becky Sharp 1929,Je 4,29:1
Tonge, Ashton
Skin Game, The 1920,O 21,11:1
Mask and the Face, The 1924,S 11,27:3
Peter Pan 1924,N 7,16:2
Pelican, The 1925,S 22,23:2
Tonge, Lillian Brennard
Meet the Prince 1929,F 26,30:5
Becky Sharp 1929,Je 4,29:1
His Majesty's Car 1930,O 24,30:1
Good Companions, The 1931,O 2,31:1
After All 1931,D 4,28:4
There's Always Juliet 1932,O 28,23:2
Distaff Side, The 1934,S 26,17:2
Point Valaine 1935,Ja 17,22:2
Call It a Day 1936,Ja 21,26:7
Call It a Day 1936,Ja 29,15:2
At Mrs Beam's 1937,Jl 27,24:2
Father Malachy's Miracle 1937,N 18,26:4
Millionairess, The 1938,Ag 16,22:5
Tonge, Philip
Bluebeard's Eighth Wife 1921,S 20,12:2
Bunch and Judy, The 1922,N 29,20:1
School for Scandal, The 1925,D 7,18:2
Lombardi, Ltd 1927,Je 7,27:3
Interference 1927,O 19,24:3
Bellamy Trial, The 1931,Ap 23,28:6
Lady With a Lamp, The 1931,N 20,27:2
Clear All Wires! 1932,S 15,19:1
Design for Living 1933,Ja 3,19:5
Design for Living 1933,Ja 25,13:2
Eight Bells 1933,O 30,14:2
Lake, The 1933,D 27,24:2
Point Valaine 1935,Ja 17,22:2

Fresh Fields 1936,F 11,19:2
When We Are Married 1939,N 21,19:5
When We Are Married 1939,D 26,22:3
Jupiter Laughs 1940,S 10,27:1
Jeannie 1940,N 13,29:2
Eight O'Clock Tuesday 1941,Ja 7,18:2
Blithe Spirit 1941,N 6,26:2
Two Mrs Carrolls, The 1943,Ag 4,14:1
Duchess Misbehaves, The 1946,F 14,32:2
Tonight at 8:30; Red Peppers 1948,F 21,8:2
Tonight at 8:30; Family Album 1948,F 21,8:2
Tonight at 8:30; Ways and Means 1948,F 21,8:2
Tonight at 8:30; Shadow Play 1948,F 24,20:4
Tonight at 8:30; Fumed Oak 1948,F 24,20:4
Tonight at 8:30; Hands Across the Sea
  1948,F 24,20:4
Cup of Trembling, The 1948,Ap 21,33:5
Make Way for Lucia 1948,D 23,23:5
Twelfth Night 1949,O 4,33:2
Twelfth Night 1949,O 9,II,1:1
ANTA Album 1950,Ja 30,13:2
Cry of the Peacock 1950,Ap 12,33:2
Ring Around the Moon 1950,N 24,30:1
ANTA Album 1951,My 7,22:7
Tonken, Mischa
Catherine Was Great 1944,Ag 3,16:1
Big Two, The 1947,Ja 9,21:2
Tonken, Murray
Theatre of the Soul 1942,Mr 21,13:5
Across the Board on Tomorrow Morning
  1942,Mr 21,13:5
Tonkonogy, Gertrude (Playwright)
Three-Cornered Moon 1933,Mr 17,20:6
Three-Cornered Moon 1934,N 27,27:2
Town House 1948,S 24,31:2
Tonks, Bruce
Right You Are (If You Think You Are)
  1950,Je 29,37:2
Tonley, Toni
Hall of Healing 1952,My 8,35:6
Too, Lou
Republic, The 1970,Ap 28,49:1
Toohey, John Peter (Playwright)
Swifty 1922,O 17,14:1
Jonesy 1929,F 24,IX,4:1
Toole, Letitia
Natural Man 1941,My 8,20:4
Anna Lucasta 1944,Je 17,10:1
On Strivers' Row 1946,Mr 1,17:2
Toombes, Andrew
No Foolin' 1926,Je 25,25:1
Toombs, Alfred (Original Author)
Good as Gold 1957,Mr 8,22:2
Toombs, Rudolph
Constant Sinner, The 1931,S 15,30:1
Never No More 1932,Ja 8,27:1
Too Many Boats 1934,S 12,26:3
Toomey, Regis
Sailor, Beware! 1934,Ja 21,X,1:6
Topa, John A
Private Life of the Master Race, The
  1945,Je 13,28:3
Vincent 1959,O 1,40:1
Vincent 1959,O 11,II,1:1
Come Share My House 1960,F 19,20:2
Walk-Up 1961,F 24,24:1
Mandingo 1961,My 23,43:6
Little Private World of Arthur Morton Fenwick,
  The 1967,O 31,38:2
Topa, John A (Director)
Little Private World of Arthur Morton Fenwick,
  The 1967,O 31,38:2
Topa, John A (Playwright)
Little Private World of Arthur Morton Fenwick,
  The 1967,O 31,38:2
Topart, Jean
Lorenzaccio 1958,O 15,44:2
Marie Tudor 1958,O 22,39:1
Don Juan 1958,O 29,29:1
Topol
Fiddler on the Roof 1967,F 17,50:1
Topping, Susan
Only Jealousy of Emer, The 1970,Mr 25,36:4
Only Jealousy of Emer, The 1970,Ap 26,II,1:3
Carmilla 1970,D 1,61:2
Torbay
Better Times 1922,S 4,14:2
Torbet, Bruce
Shewing-Up of Blanco Posnet, The 1959,S 19,26:7
Torbet, Bruce (Scenic Designer)
Shewing-Up of Blanco Posnet, The 1959,S 19,26:7
Torchiana, Frances
Marseilles 1930,N 18,28:2
Tordy, Christa
Midsummer Night's Dream, A 1927,Ag 8,6:1
Torelli, Giacomo (Miscellaneous)
Amphitryon 1970,F 4,38:1
Tores, Andy
Bill Noname 1970,Mr 3,37:1
Toretzka, Ludmilla
White Peacock, The 1921,D 27,10:2

Toretzka, Ludmilla—Cont
Lady, The 1923,D 5,23:2
Nirvana 1926,Mr 4,19:1
Uncle Vanya 1929,My 25,17:1
Diana 1929,D 10,37:1
Clear All Wires! 1932,S 15,19:1
Jayhawker 1934,N 6,34:2
Bitter Oleander 1935,F 12,24:3
Path of Flowers, The 1936,S 18,19:3
Romance 1937,Ag 17,23:1
Sunup to Sundown 1938,F 2,14:3
Merry Wives of Windsor, The 1938,Ap 15,22:3
Unconquered, The 1940,F 14,25:2
Dark Eyes 1943,Ja 15,20:2
Dark Eyes 1943,Ja 31,II,1:1
Rose Tattoo, The 1951,F 5,19:2
Horses in Midstream 1953,Ap 3,18:7
Four Winds 1957,S 26,21:2
Call on Kuprin, A 1961,My 26,29:3
Torffield, Marvin (Miscellaneous)
Steambath 1970,Jl 1,49:1
Torgerson, Ulita
Philadelphia 1929,S 17,34:5
Frederika 1937,F 5,16:5
Torgeson, Sonia
Ondine 1954,F 19,23:1
Torigi, Richard
Consul, The 1952,O 30,41:2
Torlonia, Donna Marina
Variations of 1940 1940,Ja 29,12:1
Tormey, John
Persecution and Assassination of Marat As
  Performed by the Inmates of the Asylum of
  Charenton Under the Direction of the Marquis de
  Sade, The 1967,Ja 4,34:1
Mike Downstairs 1968,Ap 19,35:1
Our Town 1969,N 28,50:1
Tormsen, Norval
My Romance 1948,O 20,38:5
Torn, Jesse (Playwright)
Fig Leaf in Her Bonnet, A 1961,Je 15,50:1
Torn, Rip
Chaparral 1958,S 10,38:2
Sweet Bird of Youth 1959,Mr 11,39:2
Sweet Bird of Youth 1959,Mr 22,II,1:1
Daughter of Silence 1961,D 1,28:1
Desire Under the Elms 1963,Ja 11,5:6
Strange Interlude 1963,Je 18,34:6
Blues for Mister Charlie 1964,Ap 24,24:1
Kitchen, The 1966,Je 14,50:1
Country Girl, The 1966,S 30,55:1
Deer Park, The 1967,F 1,27:2
Deer Park, The 1967,F 12,II,1:4
Cuban Thing, The 1968,S 25,36:2
Dream of a Blacklisted Actor 1969,D 18,64:1
Torn, Rip (Director)
Beard, The 1967,O 25,40:1
Leader, The 1969,Ap 22,40:2
Honest-to-God Schnozzola, The 1969,Ap 22,40:2
Torner, Luis
Don Juan Tenorio 1953,N 20,18:5
El Alcalde De Zalamea 1953,N 23,32:5
Torok, Frank S (Miscellaneous)
Rate of Exchange 1968,Ap 2,50:1
Crimes and Crimes 1970,Ja 19,35:1
Story Theater Repertory; Gimpel the Food
  1970,O 21,40:1
Story Theater Repertory; Saint Julian the
  Hospitaler 1970,O 21,40:1
Revenger's Tragedy, The 1970,D 2,58:1
Torok (Playwright)
Romance of Ida, The 1929,F 3,VIII,2:1
Torpey, Joseph
Melody Man, The 1924,My 14,14:2
Torpey, William
Stepping Stones 1923,N 7,14:3
Three Cheers 1928,O 16,28:1
Roberta 1933,N 20,18:4
Show Boat 1946,Ja 7,17:2
Torpey, William and Londell, Joan
Naked Genius, The 1943,O 22,20:5
Torpy, Joe
Snapshots of 1921 1921,Je 3,19:2
Torralba, Pilar
Wildcat, The 1921,N 28,16:2
Torrance, Barbara
Come of Age 1952,Ja 24,22:2
Torrance, Robert (Translator)
Philoctetes 1964,Ag 19,29:1
Torre, Madja
Broadway Shadows 1930,Ap 1,34:6
Torre, Rosario
Don Juan Tenorio 1953,N 20,18:5
Torren, Frank
Brownstone Urge, The 1969,D 18,63:1
Torrence, David
Right to Strike, The 1921,O 25,20:1
Torrence, Ernest
Night Boat, The 1920,F 3,18:1
Torrence, George
Treat 'Em Rough 1926,O 5,26:2
Torrence, Katchie
Thesmophoriazusae, The; Goddesses of Athens,
  The 1955,D 14,52:4

Torres, Henry (Translator)
Trial of Mary Dugan, The 1929,F 24,IX,1:8
Torres, Jose
Shore Leave 1922,Ag 9,20:2
Torres, Jose (Choreographer)
Mariage de Figaro, Le 1964,F 26,41:2
Torres, Raquel
Adam Had Two Sons 1932,Ja 17,VIII,3:5
Adam Had Two Sons 1932,Ja 21,17:1
Torres, Victor
Cabalgata 1949,Jl 8,14:2
Torrey, Susan
Look Homeward, Angel 1957,N 29,33:1
Torriani, Aimee
Topsy and Eva 1924,D 24,11:1
Torrillo, Don
Judy Garland's New Variety Show 1956,S 27,43:2
Torrup, Ingeborg
Light of Asia, The 1928,O 10,32:2
Bonds of Interest, The 1929,O 15,34:2
Richelieu 1929,D 26,20:3
King Lear 1930,D 26,18:2
Torrup, Ingeborg (Miscellaneous)
Hippolytus 1948,N 22,25:5
Tors, Jan
Ice Capades 1961,Ag 31,24:4
Ice Capades 1963,Ag 29,37:2
Tortfield, Mildred (Producer)
Another City, Another Land 1968,O 9,42:1
Tory, Peter
King Lear 1964,My 19,43:2
Tory, Rosemary
Antigone 1962,D 29,5:5
Orthee 1962,D 29,5:5
Medea 1965,N 29,46:1
When We Dead Awaken 1966,Ap 19,37:2
Deer Park, The 1967,F 1,27:2
Torzs
Trial of Mary Dugan, The 1928,S 30,IX,4:4
A Farkas 1928,O 28,IX,2:1
Toser, David (Costume Designer)
Great White Hope, The 1968,O 4,40:1
Shoot Anything With Hair That Moves
1969,F 3,29:1
Does a Tiger Wear a Necktie? 1969,F 26,38:1
Our Town 1969,N 28,50:1
Tosha, Rosen
Azuma Kabuki Dancers and Musicians
1954,F 19,22:3
Tost, William
Trial by Jury 1966,Je 8,41:2
H M S Pinafore 1966,Je 8,41:2
Patience 1967,O 13,32:1
Iolanthe 1967,O 18,40:1
Mikado, The 1967,O 25,42:2
Gondoliers, The 1967,O 29,83:1
H M S Pinafore 1967,N 1,40:1
Blood Red Roses 1970,Mr 23,48:1
Totero, Charles A (Producer)
Giants, Sons of Giants 1962,Ja 8,26:2
Totheroh, Dan (Director)
Wind in the Sails 1940,Ag 1,24:6
Totheroh, Dan (Playwright)
Wild Birds 1925,Ap 10,16:1
Wild Birds 1925,Ap 26,VIII,1:1
Daughters of Music 1926,S 26,VIII,2:7
Wild Birds 1929,Je 23,VIII,2:3
Distant Drums 1932,Ja 19,24:3
Distant Drums 1932,Ja 31,VIII,1:1
Moor Born 1934,Ap 4,26:4
Moor Born 1934,Ap 8,X,2:7
Mother Lode 1934,D 24,16:5
Searching for the Sun 1936,F 20,22:6
Wind in the Sails 1940,Ag 1,24:6
Live Life Again 1945,O 1,14:7
Toto
Vaudeville (Hippodrome) 1924,F 12,20:2
Greenwich Village Follies 1924,N 25,26:2
Vaudeville (Hippodrome) 1926,Ap 20,24:6
Vaudeville (Hippodrome) 1926,Ap 27,22:3
Vaudeville (Palace) 1926,Je 1,29:5
Vaudeville (Palace) 1929,S 2,16:3
Vaudeville (Palace) 1932,Je 13,19:7
Totten, Edyth
Babbling Brookes 1927,F 26,13:2
Totten, Joe Byron
Patriots, The 1943,D 21,22:5
Totten, Joe Byron (Director)
So That's That 1925,D 15,28:3
Spook House 1930,Je 4,33:3
To My Husband 1936,My 2,35:2
Totten, Joe Byron (Playwright)
Love's Call 1925,S 11,20:1
So That's That 1925,D 15,28:3
Spook House 1930,My 25,IX,3:1
Spook House 1930,Je 4,33:3
Totten, Joe Byron (Producer)
To My Husband 1936,My 2,35:2
Totten, Parker
Belt, The 1927,O 20,33:1
Tottenham, Merle
Nine Till Six 1930,S 29,17:2

Toubin, William
Judgment Day 1934,S 13,26:4
Crime and Punishment 1935,Ja 23,20:3
Dead End 1935,O 29,17:2
Tell My Story 1939,Mr 16,26:6
Petrified Forest, The 1943,N 2,30:6
Touche
Cherry Orchard, The 1944,Ja 26,22:1
Touchnoff, (Messr)
Chauve-Souris 1925,Ja 15,25:1
Toudouze, Georges G- (Playwright)
Parmi les Loups 1926,N 7,VIII,2:7
Toumanova, Tamara
Stars in Your Eyes 1939,F 10,18:2
Tounda, Mina
Hippolytus 1968,N 20,38:3
Tourag, Vincent (Producer)
Pilgrim's Progress 1962,Mr 21,36:2
Touret, Gisele
Misanthrope, Le 1960,Mr 9,38:3
Tourison, E R (Composer)
Don Quixote, Esquire 1920,My 7,12:6
Tourneur, Cyril (Playwright)
Revenger's Tragedy, The 1966,O 7,37:1
Revenger's Tragedy, The 1970,D 2,58:1
Revenger's Tragedy, The 1970,D 6,II,5:1
Tours, Frank (Composer)
Taming of the Shrew, The 1935,O 1,27:3
Taming of the Shrew, The 1940,F 6,17:2
Tours, Frank (Miscellaneous)
Mayflowers 1925,N 25,14:2
Great Waltz, The 1934,S 24,14:4
Jubilee 1935,O 14,20:1
Tours, Frank (Musical Director)
Tonight at 8:30; Ways and Means 1948,F 21,8:2
Tonight at 8:30; Family Album 1948,F 21,8:2
Tonight at 8:30; Red Peppers 1948,F 21,8:2
Tonight at 8:30; Shadow Play 1948,F 24,20:4
Tonight at 8:30; Hands Across the Sea
1948,F 24,20:4
Tonight at 8:30; Fumed Oak 1948,F 24,20:4
Tourso, Ronnie
Desert Incident, A 1959,Mr 25,40:1
Semi-Detached 1960,Mr 11,20:2
Behind the Wall 1960,N 1,47:1
Tousley, Bennett E
What a Relief 1935,D 14,10:6
Toussaint, Mari
God Is a (Guess What?) 1968,D 18,56:1
Malcochon 1969,Ap 2,37:1
Man Better Man 1969,Jl 3,22:1
Toussant, Theodore
Beclch 1968,D 17,59:1
Toustonogov, Egrogy (Producer)
Henry IV 1969,My 11,4:1
Toustonogov, Egrogy (Scenic Designer)
Henry IV 1969,My 11,4:1
Toutain, Blanche
Robe de Perles, La 1928,Ja 15,VIII,2:3
Tovatt, Patrick
Hamlet 1968,Je 10,59:1
Tovell, Albert
Clair de Lune 1921,Ap 19,15:1
Mama Loves Papa 1926,F 23,26:2
Tow, William
Tom Sawyer - Ballad of the Mississippi
1947,D 27,11:3
Towb, Harry
Under the Weather 1966,O 28,35:1
Towber, Chaim
Two Hearts 1935,My 6,22:2
Cowboy in Israel, A 1962,O 29,36:2
Trees Die Standing, The 1969,O 13,52:1
Towber, Chaim (Lyricist)
Uncle Sam in Israel 1952,D 8,38:5
Towber, Chaim (Miscellaneous)
Cowboy in Israel, A 1962,O 29,36:2
Trees Die Standing, The 1969,O 13,52:1
Towber, Chaim (Playwright)
Two Hearts 1935,My 6,22:2
Cowboy in Israel, A 1962,O 29,36:2
Hello Charlie 1965,O 25,47:2
Towbin, Beryl
Girl in Pink Tights, The 1954,Mr 6,13:2
From A to Z 1960,Ap 21,23:2
Family Affair, A 1962,Ja 29,17:1
Education of H*Y*M*A*N K*A*P*L*A*N, The
1968,Ap 5,57:1
Towbin, Cyril
Jazz a La Carte 1922,Je 3,8:3
Towell, Bernard A
Sale and a Sailor, A, or Glory! What Price!
1926,Ap 25,30:4
Tower, Allan
Lady Screams, The 1927,My 3,24:2
Sex Fable, The 1931,O 21,26:1
In Heaven and Earth 1936,Mr 27,24:8
Dark of the Moon 1945,Mr 15,27:2
Tower, Ken
Trio 1944,D 30,13:4
From Morn Till Midnight 1948,D 7,41:6
Tower, Robert
New Moon, The 1942,Ag 19,14:2

Tower, Robert—Cont
Rosalinda; Fledermaus, Die 1942,O 29,26:5
Follow the Girls 1944,Ap 10,15:2
Towers, Charles
Personal Appearance 1936,Jl 9,17:4
Towers, Constance
Anya 1965,N 30,48:1
Show Boat 1966,Jl 20,48:1
Carousel 1966,D 16,56:2
Sound of Music, The 1967,Ap 27,52:1
King and I, The 1968,My 24,39:1
Engagement Baby, The 1970,My 22,40:1
Sound of Music, The 1970,Jl 3,13:1
Towers, Cynthia (Miscellaneous)
Black Monday 1962,Mr 7,29:1
Towers, Don
Steps Leading Up 1941,Ap 19,20:6
Towers, Harry
Tobacco Road 1942,S 7,34:2
Towers, Richard
Almost Crazy 1955,Je 21,37:1
Towers, Susan
Jane Eyre 1958,My 2,31:1
Childhood 1962,Ja 12,28:1
Shout From the Rooftops 1964,O 29,40:1
Happy Journey to Trenton and Camden, The
1966,S 7,53:1
Towey, John
Dream Out of Time, A 1970,N 9,52:1
Towle, Hannibal S
Roof, The 1930,Je 14,9:2
Towle, J A
Orpheus in Hades 1930,D 16,30:1
Towle, Joseph
Silks and Satins 1920,Jl 16,19:1
Towne, Barbara
I Married an Angel 1938,My 12,26:2
Towne, Charles Hanson (Miscellaneous)
Love for Love 1940,Je 4,19:5
Towne, Harriet
Vaudeville (Palace) 1923,My 15,22:2
Vaudeville (Hippodrome) 1926,Mr 30,20:4
Vaudeville (Palace) 1926,Ap 27,22:3
Vaudeville (Palace) 1926,D 28,12:3
Towne, Lester
Catherine Was Great 1944,Ag 3,16:1
Would-Be Gentleman, The 1946,Ja 10,29:2
Towne, Red
Innocent Voyage, The 1943,N 16,27:2
Towneley, Jane
Kingdom of God, The 1928,D 21,30:2
Towner, Neil
Storm Operation 1944,Ja 12,28:2
Towner, Wesley
Bridal Crown, The 1938,F 7,11:2
Towner, Wesley (Playwright)
Case of Youth, A 1940,Mr 25,10:3
Townes, Harry
Mr Sycamore 1942,N 14,13:2
Twelfth Night 1949,O 4,33:2
Dawn's Early Light 1950,O 25,44:3
Gramercy Ghost 1951,Ap 27,20:2
In the Matter of J Robert Oppenheimer
1968,Je 7,31:1
In the Matter of J Robert Oppenheimer
1969,Mr 7,28:1
Townley, Barry
Only the Young 1932,S 22,25:2
It Happened Tomorrow 1933,My 6,11:5
Townley, Harry
Angels Don't Kiss 1932,Ap 6,22:5
Towns, Cynthia
But Never Jam Today 1969,Ap 24,40:1
Old Judge Mose Is Dead 1969,Ag 29,25:1
Townsen, Paul (Costume Designer)
Idiot's Delight 1957,F 23,14:2
Townsend, Barbara
As You Like It 1937,N 1,25:2
Rumpelstiltskin 1948,Mr 15,27:3
Rose Tattoo, The 1966,O 21,36:2
Townsend, Bebe
Walk Together Chillun 1936,F 5,15:2
Case of Philip Lawrence, The 1937,Je 9,31:1
Townsend, Cynthia
Reunion in Vienna 1931,N 17,31:1
Townsend, Dwight
I Want You 1961,S 15,29:1
Townsend, Elizabeth
Lake, The 1933,D 27,24:2
Camille 1956,S 19,33:1
Trojan Women, The 1957,Mr 19,42:7
Townsend, Genevieve
Trojan Horse, The 1940,O 31,28:3
Townsend, Jill
Inadmissible Evidence 1965,D 1,52:1
Townsend, K C
I Want You 1961,S 15,29:1
As You Like It 1963,Jl 17,19:2
One Flew Over the Cuckoo's Nest 1963,N 14,40:2
Henry, Sweet Henry 1967,O 24,51:2
Townsend, Newton
Night at an Inn, A 1930,My 10,25:1
Townsend, Puritan
Manhattan 1922,Ag 16,7:5

Townsend, Puritan—Cont
Butter and Egg Man, The 1925,S 24,28:1
Townsend, Reynolds K
Choice, The 1930,My 9,20:5
Townsend, Theresa
Prunella 1929,Ap 10,23:3
Townsend, W J
Thumbs Down 1923,Ag 7,20:1
Townsend, William
Earth 1927,Mr 10,23:1
Townsend, Willis
Harlequinade 1959,F 14,15:1
Townshend, Claire
Stairs, The 1927,N 8,32:7
Wild Duck, The 1928,N 19,17:1
Hedda Gabler 1929,F 4,20:3
Townshend, Marchioness (Producer)
Murder on Account 1936,S 26,11:2
Townshend, Peter
Tommy 1969,O 26,82:1
Townshend, William
Gray Shadow 1931,Mr 11,23:4
Townsley, Barry
Bootleggers, The 1922,N 28,24:1
Apache, The 1923,My 9,14:3
Toy, Mary Mon
House of Flowers 1954,D 31,11:2
World of Suzie Wong, The 1958,O 15,47:1
Toy, Noel
Wine, Women and Song 1942,S 29,18:3
Toye, Jennifer
Princess Ida 1955,O 14,22:3
Mikado, The 1962,N 14,43:1
Gondoliers, The 1962,N 16,25:2
Iolanthe 1962,N 28,42:1
Trial by Jury 1964,N 20,40:1
Mikado, The 1964,N 27,43:1
Ruddigore 1964,D 4,44:1
Toye, Wendy
Ballerina 1933,O 29,IX,1:6
Toye, Wendy (Choreographer)
Joyce Grenfell Requests the Pleasure
1955,O 11,48:1
Toye, Wendy (Director)
Big Ben 1946,Ag 4,II,1:4
Peter Pan 1950,Ap 25,27:2
Peter Pan 1950,Ap 30,II,1:1
Toyomatsu, Seitjuro (Miscellaneous)
Fishing for Wives 1966,Mr 16,50:1
General's Daughter, The 1966,Mr 16,50:1
Greengrocer's Daughter, The 1966,Mr 16,50:1
Toyotake, Tsubamedayu (Miscellaneous)
Fishing for Wives 1966,Mr 16,50:1
General's Daughter, The 1966,Mr 16,50:1
Greengrocer's Daughter, The 1966,Mr 16,50:1
Toyser, Ronald (Miscellaneous)
Athenian Touch, The 1964,Ja 15,25:4
Tozer, J R
Lass O' Laughter 1925,Ja 9,13:2
Tozere, Frederic
Stepping Sisters 1930,Ap 23,24:2
Betty, Be Careful 1931,My 5,33:3
Blue Monday 1932,Je 3,23:2
Murder in the Cathedral 1936,Mr 21,13:5
It Can't Happen Here 1936,O 28,30:1
Sun and I, The 1937,F 27,9:5
Red Harvest 1937,Mr 31,29:2
Mistress of the Inn, The 1937,Je 22,26:3
Princess Turandot 1937,Ag 3,20:5
Hero Is Born, A 1937,O 2,18:6
As You Like It 1937,N 1,25:2
Shoemaker's Holiday, The 1938,Ja 3,17:2
Shoemaker's Holiday, The 1938,Ja 9,X,1:1
Madame Capet 1938,O 26,26:2
Waltz in Goose Step 1938,N 2,26:2
Glorious Morning 1938,N 28,10:3
Key Largo 1939,O 31,26:6
Key Largo 1939,N 28,30:2
Journey to Jerusalem 1940,O 7,21:2
Gabrielle 1941,Mr 26,26:2
Trojan Women, The 1941,Ap 9,32:5
Cuckoos on the Hearth 1941,S 17,26:2
Solitaire 1942,Ja 28,22:2
Outrageous Fortune 1943,N 4,28:5
In Bed We Cry 1944,N 15,20:2
Signature 1945,F 15,25:2
Rich Full Life, The 1945,N 10,9:2
Oedipus Rex 1945,D 17,16:7
Miracle in the Mountains 1947,Ap 26,10:2
Tower Beyond Tragedy, The 1950,N 27,29:1
King of Friday's Men, The 1951,F 22,26:2
First Lady 1952,My 29,18:5
Saint Joan 1956,S 12,42:1
Happy Town 1959,O 8,49:2
Caligula 1960,F 17,31:1
Daughter of Silence 1961,D 1,28:1
Hidden Stranger 1963,Ja 10,5:5
Mr Simian 1963,O 22,44:1
Little Boxes; Coffee Lace, The 1969,D 4,71:2
Little Boxes; Trevor 1969,D 4,71:2
Tozzi, George
Rape of Lucretia, The 1948,D 30,24:2
Tough at the Top 1949,Jl 17,58:5

Yozzi, Giorgio
South Pacific 1967,Je 13,56:1
Trabert, Elvira
Colonel Satan 1931,Ja 12,24:1
Wonder Bar, The 1931,Mr 18,23:4
Three Times the Hour 1931,Ag 26,15:5
Trabert, George
My Golden Girl 1920,F 3,18:2
Lady Butterfly 1923,Ja 23,18:1
Champagne, Sec 1933,O 16,20:2
Gypsy Blonde 1934,Je 26,22:5
Florodora 1936,Ag 23,II,8:2
Blossom Time 1936,Ag 30,II,5:8
Frederika 1937,F 5,16:5
Trabue, Marion
Go West, Young Man 1923,N 13,25:2
Peggy-Ann 1926,D 28,16:3
Trabue, Virginia
Czarina, The 1922,F 1,22:1
Tracey, Andrew
Wait a Minim! 1966,Mr 8,43:1
Tracey, Andrew (Musical Director)
Wait a Minim! 1966,Mr 8,43:1
Tracey, Fay
Playboy of the Western World, The 1958,My 9,19:2
Tracey, Kathlyn
Night Hawk 1925,F 25,16:4
Tracey, Paul
Wait a Minim! 1966,Mr 8,43:1
Rothschilds, The 1970,O 20,40:1
Tracey, Royal Dana
Smooth as Silk 1921,F 23,18:3
All-Star Jamboree 1921,Jl 14,18:1
Yankee Princess, The 1922,O 3,22:1
Inspector General, The 1923,My 1,24:1
Woman on the Jury, The 1923,Ag 16,10:4
Diff'rent 1925,F 11,19:3
Playboy of the Western World, The 1930,Ja 3,20:4
Midnight 1930,D 30,25:1
Precedent 1931,Ap 15,24:5
Steel 1931,N 19,26:5
If Booth Had Missed 1932,F 5,24:2
Mountain, The 1933,S 12,28:6
False Dreams, Farewell 1934,Ja 16,18:3
Kill That Story 1934,Ag 30,22:2
Page Miss Glory 1934,N 28,24:2
Sap Runs High, The 1936,F 5,15:3
Man's House, A 1943,Ap 3,10:4
Sons and Soldiers 1943,My 5,22:2
Land of Fame 1943,S 22,31:5
Ramshackle Inn 1944,Ja 6,17:5
Tracey, Thomas F
Ever Green Lady, The 1922,O 12,25:2
Mister Malatesta 1923,F 27,14:2
Cyrano de Bergerac 1923,N 2,14:1
Othello 1925,Ja 12,11:1
Hamlet 1925,O 12,19:2
Old Bill, M P 1926,N 11,22:2
Honor Be Damned! 1927,Ja 27,13:1
Gang's All Here, The 1931,F 19,21:3
Merry-Go-Round 1932,Ap 23,11:2
Passionate Pilgrim, The 1932,O 20,24:3
We the People 1933,Ja 23,9:5
Kill That Story 1934,Ag 30,22:2
Sweet Mystery of Life 1935,O 12,13:3
Damaged Goods 1937,My 18,27:2
Schoolhouse on the Lot 1938,Mr 23,18:4
Abe Lincoln in Illinois 1938,O 17,12:2
Doughgirls, The 1942,D 31,19:2
Tract, Jo
Catch Me if You Can 1965,Mr 10,50:1
Mame 1966,My 25,41:1
Tracy, Arthur
Hook-Up, The 1935,My 9,24:6
Tracy, Cora
Iolanthe 1920,Ja 6,13:3
Ruddigore 1920,Ja 20,11:2
Ruddigore 1920,F 1,VIII,2:2
Tracy, Edward
Cradle Snatchers 1932,N 17,23:2
Tracy, Helen
Romance 1921,Mr 1,18:2
Tracy, John
Telemachus Clay 1963,N 16,17:2
Tracy, Katherine
Sentinels 1931,D 26,15:1
Come of Age 1934,Ja 13,16:6
Tracy, Lee
Show-Off, The 1924,F 6,16:2
Book of Charm, The 1925,S 4,26:3
Glory Hallelujah 1926,Ap 7,26:2
Broadway 1926,S 17,19:3
Broadway 1926,S 26,VIII,1:1
Front Page, The 1928,Ag 15,19:2
Front Page, The 1928,Ag 26,VII,1:1
Oh, Promise Me 1930,N 25,31:1
Louder, Please! 1931,N 13,26:4
Bright Star 1935,O 13,IX,1:6
Bright Star 1935,O 16,26:2
Every Man for Himself 1940,D 10,32:3
Traitor, The 1949,Ap 1,30:2
Traitor, The 1949,Ap 10,II,1:1
Metropole 1949,D 7,43:2

Tracy, Lee—Cont
Mr Barry's Etchings 1950,F 1,26:2
Show-Off, The 1950,Je 1,24:5
Show-Off, The 1950,Je 11,II,1:1
ANTA Album 1951,My 7,22:7
Idiot's Delight 1951,My 24,46:3
Best Man, The 1960,Ap 1,39:1
Best Man, The 1960,Ap 10,II,1:1
Minor Miracle 1965,O 8,4:3
Tracy, Lisa
Dark of the Moon 1970,Ap 4,21:2
Tracy, Matt (Lighting Director)
Latent Heterosexual, The 1968,Mr 22,52:1
Tracy, Spencer
Royal Fandango, A 1923,N 13,25:1
Yellow 1926,S 22,30:1
Baby Cyclone, The 1927,S 13,37:4
Conflict 1929,Mr 7,22:4
Conflict 1929,Mr 24,X,1:1
Parade 1929,S 1,VIII,1:1
Nigger Rich 1929,S 21,16:7
Dread 1929,O 27,IX,2:1
Last Mile, The 1930,F 14,21:2
Rugged Path, The 1945,N 12,17:2
Rugged Path, The 1945,N 18,II,1:1
Tracy, Virginia
Lady With a Lamp, The 1931,N 20,27:2
Bulls, Bears and Asses 1932,My 7,11:3
Lone Valley 1933,Mr 11,18:6
And Be My Love 1934,Ja 19,25:2
Jig Saw 1934,My 1,26:3
Post Road 1934,D 5,28:3
Sweet Mystery of Life 1935,O 12,13:3
Empress of Destiny 1938,Mr 10,16:2
Escape This Night 1938,Ap 23,18:1
Tracy, William
Hitch Your Wagon! 1937,Ap 9,18:2
Tracy and Hay
Passing Show of 1924, The 1924,S 4,13:4
Trader, George Henry
Steadfast 1923,O 31,12:1
Bride, The 1924,My 6,25:1
Pigs 1924,S 2,22:5
Lost 1927,Mr 29,22:2
One, Two, Three! 1930,S 30,24:2
Social Register, The 1931,N 10,28:2
Life Begins 1932,Mr 29,23:2
Come Easy 1933,Ag 30,22:5
Whatever Possessed Her 1934,Ja 26,21:2
Woman of Destiny, A 1936,Mr 3,25:2
It Can't Happen Here 1936,O 28,30:1
Trado, Frank
Passing Show of 1923, The 1923,Je 15,24:6
Passing Show of 1924, The 1924,S 4,13:4
Harry Delmar's Revels 1927,N 29,30:2
Trado, Peter
Harry Delmar's Revels 1927,N 29,30:2
Traeger, Ralph
Thomas Paine 1930,Mr 21,30:7
Trahan, Al
Vaudeville (Palace) 1928,O 30,27:3
Vaudeville (Palace) 1928,N 6,35:2
Vaudeville (Palace) 1929,N 4,29:1
Vaudeville (Palace) 1929,D 30,16:3
Second Little Show, The 1930,Ag 17,VIII,2:2
Second Little Show, The 1930,S 3,36:1
Vaudeville (Palladium) 1931,My 12,28:4
Vaudeville (Palace) 1931,Je 8,21:2
Vaudeville (New Amsterdam Theatre)
1931,Je 22,17:3
Variety Anthology 1932,Mr 21,19:4
Vaudeville Marches On 1938,D 30,11:1
Top-Notchers 1942,My 30,8:5
Trahan and Wallace
Vaudeville (Palace) 1927,Ap 26,33:1
Vaudeville (Palace) 1927,My 3,25:2
Vaudeville (Palace) 1927,My 10,25:3
Vaudeville (Proctor's) 1927,My 17,27:4
Trail Blazers
Hayride 1954,S 14,24:2
Traill, Peter (Playwright)
Guilty One, The 1922,Ag 13,VI,1:3
Guilty One, The 1923,Mr 21,19:1
Tread Softly 1935,N 8,19:6
Tread Softly 1935,D 8,X,5:1
Trailovic, Mira (Director)
Who's Afraid of Virginia Woolf? 1968,Jl 4,13:1
Train, A K
It's Only Natural 1922,Ap 21,13:2
Trainer, David (Playwright)
Acquisition, The 1968,D 31,19:1
Acquisition, The 1969,Ja 12,II,1:1
Trainer, Jack
Spice of 1922 1922,Jl 7,12:4
Trainor, George
Night in Spain, A 1927,My 4,28:2
Trainor, Jimmie
Night in Spain, A 1927,My 4,28:2
Trama, Johnny
Laughter Over Broadway 1939,Ja 16,10:3
Top Banana 1951,N 2,19:2
Tramel
Monsieur Qui Se Regrette, Un 1928,D 9,X,2:7

Trammel, Nolia
  Sweet Genevieve 1945,Mr 21,27:3
  Billy the Kid 1951,Ag 21,23:2
Trammell, Lynn
  Days Between, The 1965,Je 4,39:1
Trangman, Michael (Scenic Designer)
  Under Milk Wood 1956,Ag 22,25:3
Transwell, Bertram
  Richard III 1943,Mr 27,8:3
  Storm Operation 1944,Ja 12,28:2
Trantum, Francesca
  Auntie Mame 1958,Ag 12,33:2
Trapani, Louis G
  Hamlet 1970,O 19,51:1
Trapp, Maria Augusta (Original Author)
  Sound of Music, The 1959,N 17,40:2
Trapp, Maria Augusta (Playwright)
  Sound of Music, The 1967,Ap 27,52:1
  Sound of Music, The 1970,Jl 3,13:1
Trares, Mildred
  Country Wife, The 1955,Ap 6,35:1
  Thor, With Angels 1956,O 15,29:4
Trask, C Hooper
  Breakfast in Bed 1920,F 4,12:1
Trask, C Hooper (Producer)
  Cradle Snatchers 1927,Ap 15,27:2
  Sign of the Leopard 1928,D 24,17:7
Trask, Katrina (Playwright)
  Without the Walls 1920,Je 7,20:1
  Little Town of Bethlehem, The 1920,D 27,11:1
Trask, Richard
  Enemy of the People, An 1950,D 29,14:1
Trask, Willard
  Spots of the Leopard, The 1963,S 25,38:1
Trasker, Harold
  Tiger Smiles, The 1930,D 18,29:1
Traub, Bessie
  Inspector General, The 1930,D 24,19:2
Traub, Zelde
  Shylock and His Daughter 1947,S 30,22:2
Traube, Shepard (Director)
  No More Frontier 1931,O 22,27:1
  Thousand Summers, A 1932,My 25,23:4
  Sophisticrats, The 1933,F 14,19:5
  But Not for Love 1934,N 27,26:2
  Sailor, Beware! 1935,My 7,28:4
  Angel Street 1941,D 6,15:2
  Winter Soldiers 1942,N 30,19:2
  Patriots, The 1943,Ja 30,11:2
  Patriots, The 1943,F 7,II,1:1
  Patriots, The 1943,D 21,22:5
  Stranger, The 1945,F 13,21:2
  Gioconda Smile, The 1950,O 9,21:2
  Green Bay Tree, The 1951,F 2,18:2
  Time Out for Ginger 1952,N 27,50:4
  Girl in Pink Tights, The 1954,Mr 6,13:2
  Grand Prize, The 1955,Ja 27,17:1
  Goodbye Again 1956,Ap 25,38:1
  Holiday for Lovers 1957,F 15,20:1
  Monique 1957,O 23,38:1
  Carnival 1962,Je 6,37:1
Traube, Shepard (Miscellaneous)
  Thousand Summers, A 1932,My 25,23:4
Traube, Shepard (Producer)
  No More Frontier 1931,O 22,27:1
  Sophisticrats, The 1933,F 14,19:5
  But Not for Love 1934,N 27,26:2
  Sailor, Beware! 1935,My 7,28:4
  Angel Street 1941,D 6,15:2
  Stranger, The 1945,F 13,21:2
  Green Bay Tree, The 1951,F 2,18:2
  Time Out for Ginger 1952,N 27,50:4
  Grand Prize, The 1955,Ja 27,17:1
  Goodbye Again 1956,Ap 25,38:1
  Holiday for Lovers 1957,F 15,20:1
  Monique 1957,O 23,38:1
  Fun and Magic 1957,D 30,19:4
  Undercover Man 1966,Je 3,30:2
Traubel, Helen
  Pipe Dream 1955,D 1,44:1
  Pipe Dream 1955,D 11,II,5:1
Trautvetter, Paul (Scenic Designer)
  Merry-Go-Rounders, The 1956,N 22,50:1
Traux, Harry
  Mikado, The 1924,Jl 29,9:1
Traux, Harry (Director)
  Mikado, The 1924,Jl 29,9:1
Travalena, Fred
  Caution: A Love Story 1969,Ap 4,45:1
Travanti, Daniel
  Here Comes Santa Claus 1962,My 18,34:1
  Othello 1964,Jl 15,29:1
Travell, George
  Love's Old Sweet Song 1940,My 3,16:3
Travelyan, Hilda
  March Hares 1928,Ja 1,VIII,1:3
Travelyan, Raleigh (Original Author)
  Next Time I'll Sing to You 1963,N 28,69:2
Traver, Martin C
  What a Relief 1935,D 14,10:6
Travers, Barbara
  Family Mishmash, A 1958,O 20,36:1

Travers, Ben (Playwright)
  Plunder 1928,Jl 22,VII,1:3
  Mischief 1928,Ag 5,VII,1:1
  Night Like This, A 1930,Mr 9,IX,4:1
  Ladies' Night 1933,N 19,IX,3:7
  Chastity, My Brother 1936,My 9,27:3
  O Mistress Mine 1936,D 4,30:3
  O Mistress Mine 1936,D 20,XI,3:3
Travers, Bill
  Cook for Mr General, A 1961,O 20,39:1
  Taming of the Shrew, The 1962,Ap 24,33:3
  Macbeth 1962,Je 6,35:2
  Abraham Cochrane 1964,F 18,26:1
Travers, Courtney
  One Shot Fired 1927,N 8,32:5
Travers, Helen
  Bluffing Bluffers 1924,D 23,17:2
Travers, Henry
  Power of Darkness, The 1920,Ja 22,22:1
  Jane Clegg 1920,F 25,14:1
  Jane Clegg 1920,Mr 28,V,6:1
  Treasure, The 1920,O 5,13:1
  Heartbreak House 1920,N 11,11:1
  Liliom 1921,Ap 21,18:1
  Cloister, The 1921,Je 6,16:3
  He Who Gets Slapped 1922,Ja 10,15:1
  From Morn to Midnight 1922,My 22,17:2
  R U R 1922,O 10,16:1
  Windows 1923,O 9,17:2
  Failures, The 1923,N 23,20:1
  Saint Joan 1923,D 29,8:4
  Saint Joan 1924,Ja 6,VII,1:1
  Caesar and Cleopatra 1925,Ap 14,27:1
  Arms and the Man 1925,S 15,28:1
  Arms and the Man 1925,O 4,IX,1:1
  Androcles and the Lion 1925,N 24,28:1
  Arms and the Man 1926,Ja 21,18:3
  Chief Thing, The 1926,Mr 23,24:2
  At Mrs Beam's 1926,Ap 26,24:3
  Pygmalion 1926,N 16,24:1
  Pygmalion 1926,N 21,VIII,1:1
  Brothers Karamazov, The 1927,Ja 4,20:1
  Right You Are (If You Think You Are)
    1927,F 24,27:1
  Doctor's Dilemma, The 1927,N 22,33:1
  Marco Millions 1928,Ja 10,28:2
  Volpone 1928,Ap 10,32:1
  Volpone 1928,Ap 22,IX,1:1
  Camel Through the Needle's Eye, The
    1929,Ap 16,32:2
  Camel Through the Needle's Eye, The
    1929,Ap 28,IX,1:1
  R U R 1930,F 18,28:1
  Marco Millions 1930,Mr 4,24:4
  Month in the Country, A 1930,Mr 18,30:5
  Getting Married 1931,Mr 31,25:5
  Reunion in Vienna 1931,N 17,31:1
  Good Earth, The 1932,O 18,23:4
  You Can't Take It With You 1936,D 1,30:8
  You Can't Take It With You 1936,D 6,XII,6:2
  You Can't Take It With You 1936,D 15,31:1
  You Can't Take It With You 1936,D 20,XI,3:1
  You Can't Take It With You 1937,Ag 29,X,1:1
Travers, Jean
  Parade 1935,My 21,22:2
Travers, Julie
  Fencing Master, The 1936,Ap 1,29:1
Travers, Margot
  Coco 1969,D 19,66:1
Travers, Mary Lou
  Ice Capades 1954,S 16,37:1
  Ice Capades 1955,S 15,38:1
Travers, Mazie
  Paradise 1931,My 12,29:2
Travers, Michael (Costume Designer)
  Show Boat 1956,Je 22,16:1
Travers, Reginald
  Man Who Ate the Popomack, The 1924,Mr 25,24:1
Travers, Sally
  Skin of Our Teeth, The 1945,N 18,II,2:5
Travers, Sy
  Johnny Doodle 1942,Mr 19,28:2
  Winners and Losers 1947,F 27,27:2
  Little Clay Cart, The 1953,Jl 1,25:1
  Montserrat 1954,My 26,34:2
  Arms and the Man 1956,O 2,39:4
  Time of Vengeance 1959,D 11,39:1
  Time of Vengeance 1959,D 27,II,1:1
  Coggerers, The 1960,Mr 23,33:1
  Time to Go 1960,Mr 23,33:1
  Miracle, The 1960,D 5,42:3
  Old Tune, The 1961,Mr 24,37:1
  Don Carlos 1962,F 28,27:5
  Storm, The 1962,Mr 31,17:2
  Corruption in the Palace of Justice 1963,O 9,49:2
  Play That on Your Old Piano 1965,O 15,49:1
  Wicked Cooks, The 1967,Ja 24,42:1
Travers, Vincent (Musical Director)
  Seventeen 1951,Je 22,16:6
Travers, Walter
  Spider, The 1927,Mr 23,29:1
Traverse, Claude
  All the King's Men 1948,Ja 19,19:2

Traverse, Claude—Cont
  Chameleon, The 1949,F 7,16:2
  Burning Bush, The 1949,D 17,15:5
  All the King's Men 1950,Jl 19,25:6
Traversi, Camillo Antona (Playwright)
  Cardinale, Il; Cardinal, The 1931,Ja 12,24:2
  Cardinale, Il 1933,Ja 9,24:2
Travis, Barbara
  Farblondjete Honeymoon 1955,S 27,42:1
  Music Man, The 1957,D 20,31:1
Travis, Douglas
  Infantry, The 1966,N 15,51:1
Travis, Edward
  Oh, Hector! 1929,Mr 6,33:2
Travis, Edward (Composer)
  Oh, Hector! 1929,Mr 6,33:2
Travis, Michael (Costume Designer)
  Show Boat 1957,Je 28,30:2
  Portofino 1958,F 22,8:3
  Song of Norway 1958,Je 23,19:2
  Once More With Feeling 1958,O 22,39:1
  Third Best Sport 1958,D 31,15:3
  Song of Norway 1959,Je 26,16:2
  Happy Town 1959,O 8,49:2
  Hit the Deck 1960,Je 24,32:1
  Rape of the Belt, The 1960,N 7,46:1
  Rhinoceros 1961,Ja 10,27:1
  Blood, Sweat & Stanley Poole 1961,O 6,31:1
  Cook for Mr General, A 1961,O 20,39:1
  Come on Strong 1962,O 5,29:1
  Advocate, The 1963,O 15,46:7
  Roar Like a Dove 1964,My 22,40:2
  I Was Dancing 1964,N 9,40:4
  Promises to Keep 1965,Jl 22,25:1
  How to Be a Jewish Mother 1967,D 29,18:1
Travis, Warren (Costume Designer)
  Milk Train Doesn't Stop Here Anymore, The
    1965,Jl 27,25:1
Travis, Warren (Miscellaneous)
  Crucible, The 1958,Mr 12,36:1
Travis, Warren (Scenic Designer)
  Milk Train Doesn't Stop Here Anymore, The
    1965,Jl 27,25:1
Travolta, Ellen
  Tom Paine 1969,Mr 30,71:2
Traylor, Rudy
  Carmen Jones 1951,S 22,8:6
Traylor, William
  Nude With Violin 1957,N 15,36:1
  Cry of the Raindrop 1961,Mr 8,38:1
  Show Boat 1966,Jl 20,48:1
  Of Love Remembered 1967,F 20,46:5
Trazenfeld, William
  Don Juan; Feast With the Statue, The
    1956,Ja 4,21:4
Tre, A
  Piacere Dell 'Onesta, Il 1929,Mr 25,33:1
Treacher, Arthur
  Great Temptations, The 1926,My 19,29:1
  Madcap, The 1928,F 1,31:2
  Colonel Satan 1931,Ja 12,24:1
  Wonder Bar, The 1931,Mr 18,23:4
  School for Scandal, The 1931,N 11,26:4
  Panama Hattie 1940,O 4,28:4
  Panama Hattie 1940,O 31,28:2
  Ziegfeld Follies 1943,Ap 2,16:2
  Ziegfeld Follies 1943,Ap 11,II,1:1
  Caesar and Cleopatra 1949,D 22,28:2
  Getting Married 1950,Je 14,41:2
  Getting Married 1951,My 14,28:5
  Back to Methuselah 1958,Mr 27,41:5
  Back to Methuselah 1958,Ap 6,II,1:1
  Fighting Cock, The 1959,D 9,57:3
  Paradise Island 1961,Je 24,11:1
  Paradise Island 1962,Je 28,22:1
Treacy, Emerson
  Searching for the Sun 1936,F 20,22:6
Treadwell, Irene
  Wisteria Trees, The 1950,Mr 30,39:1
Treadwell, Laura
  Men Must Fight 1932,O 15,13:4
Treadwell, Louise
  Pigeon, The 1922,F 3,13:1
  Chains of Dew 1922,Ap 28,20:2
Treadwell, Sophie (Director)
  Lone Valley 1933,Mr 11,18:6
Treadwell, Sophie (Playwright)
  Gringo 1922,D 15,26:3
  Gringo 1922,D 24,VII,1:1
  Lonely Lee 1923,N 11,VIII,2:6
  O Nightingale 1925,Ap 16,25:2
  Machinal 1928,S 8,10:3
  Machinal 1928,S 16,IX,1:1
  Ladies Leave 1929,O 2,28:3
  Lone Valley 1933,Mr 11,18:6
  Plumes in the Dust 1936,O 26,21:3
  Plumes in the Dust 1936,N 7,14:2
  Plumes in the Dust 1936,N 15,XI,1:1
  Hope for a Harvest 1941,Ap 5,18:4
  Hope for a Harvest 1941,N 27,28:2
  Hope for a Harvest 1941,D 7,X,5:1
  Machinal 1960,Ap 8,27:1
  Machinal 1960,Ap 17,II,1:1

Treadwell, Sophie (Producer)
Lone Valley 1933,Mr 11,18:6
Treat, Roger
On the Town 1944,D 29,11:4
Trebbi, Attilio
Serata D'Inverno; Winter Evening, A
1929,Ap 8,32:5
Liane, Le (Ties That Bind); Ties That Bind (Le
Liane) 1929,Ap 22,22:1
Assalto, L' 1929,My 20,23:2
Tutto Per Bene; All's Well That Ends Well
1929,Je 3,27:1
Trebitsch, Paul (Producer)
Sunshine 1926,Ag 18,15:2
Trebitsch, Siegfried (Playwright)
Jitta's Atonement 1923,Ja 18,16:3
Jitta's Atonement 1925,F 1,VII,2:1
Frau Jitta's Suehne 1930,My 18,VIII,2:6
Jitta's Atonement 1935,Ja 31,22:3
Trebitsch, Siegfried (Translator)
Saint Joan 1924,N 9,VII,2:3
Trebor, Haynes (Playwright)
Dawn's Early Light 1950,O 25,44:3
Trebor, Mildred (Costume Designer)
Legend of Lovers 1951,D 27,17:1
Venus Observed 1952,F 14,24:2
Seagulls Over Sorrento 1952,S 12,18:4
Picnic 1953,F 20,14:7
Treco, E A
I Love an Actress 1931,S 18,29:2
Trecu, Pirmin (Choreographer)
Romeo and Juliet 1962,F 14,39:1
Tree, Dorothy
Cherry Pie 1926,Ap 15,24:4
Strange Prince, The 1926,D 8,24:2
Triumphant Bachelor, The 1927,S 16,21:1
Marquise, The 1927,N 15,26:4
Holiday 1928,N 27,36:1
Merchant of Venice, The 1930,D 3,29:2
Clear All Wires! 1932,S 15,19:1
Clear All Wires! 1932,S 25,IX,1:1
Bright Honor 1936,S 28,14:1
Tree, Iris
Miracle, The 1925,S 29,31:6
Miracle, The 1927,F 1,24:5
Tree, Iris (Playwright)
Cock-A-Doodle-Doo 1949,F 28,16:5
Tree, Joanne
Truckline Cafe 1946,F 28,19:4
Tree, Lady
Unknown, The 1920,Ag 29,VI,1:4
Indoor Fireworks 1934,Mr 30,26:6
Josephine 1934,S 26,17:5
Tree, Viola
Truth Game, The 1928,O 21,IX,1:3
Truth Game, The 1930,D 29,19:1
Tree, Viola (Playwright)
Dancers, The 1923,F 25,VII,1:7
Tree, Viola (Producer)
Unknown, The 1920,Ag 10,17:7
Trees, Amanda
Month of Sundays 1968,S 17,50:1
Trees, Carl
Higher and Higher 1940,Ap 5,24:3
Treffry, Joan
Anything Might Happen 1923,F 21,22:3
Treglown, Jeremy
Midsummer Night's Dream, A 1968,D 9,59:1
Tregoe, William
Virginia Reel 1947,Ap 15,28:2
Thorntons, The 1956,F 15,26:1
Tregoe, William (Director)
My House Is Your House 1970,O 16,53:2
Trehy, Robert
Iolanthe 1962,Ap 12,42:4
Yeomen of the Guard, The 1968,My 9,53:1
Treiber, Eleonore
Nowhere to Go But Up 1962,N 12,36:2
Anyone Can Whistle 1964,Ap 6,36:1
Half a Sixpence 1965,Ap 26,38:2
Treichler, Paul F (Playwright)
Cure for Matrimony 1939,O 26,26:3
Treil, H W
Nowhere Bound 1935,Ja 23,20:2
Treister, Leizer (Playwright)
Shepherd King, The 1955,O 13,36:2
Treitel, Herbert
Cyrano de Bergerac 1936,Ap 28,17:1
Trekman, Emma
Walking Happy 1966,N 28,47:1
Trelease, Ruby
Genius and the Crowd 1920,S 7,20:1
Sancho Panza 1923,N 27,23:1
Trelfell, John (Miscellaneous)
Guys and Dolls 1959,Jl 22,22:2
Trelor and Harris
Vaudeville (Palace) 1927,Jl 5,19:3
Tremaine, Ann
Everyman Today 1958,Ja 16,32:4
Tremaine, Beatrice
Scarlet Man, The 1921,Ag 23,10:3
Tremaine, Bobbie
Nikki 1931,S 30,23:4

Tremaine, Paul
Friends and Lovers; In the Zone; Bound East for
Cardiff 1961,My 11,43:1
Tremaine, Paul (Scenic Designer)
Six Characters in Search of an Author
1961,My 11,43:1
Tremayne, Les
Heads or Tails 1947,My 3,10:6
Detective Story 1949,Mr 24,34:2
Tremor, Georges
Homme Qui Assassina, L' 1924,N 11,20:1
Procureur Hallers, Le 1924,N 13,18:1
Homme et Ses Fantomes, L' 1924,N 14,16:1
Merchant of Venice, The 1924,N 18,23:2
Bourgeois Gentilhomme, Le 1924,N 20,21:2
Trenaman, John
Hamlet 1969,My 2,38:1
Trench, Fred
Achilles Had a Heel 1935,O 14,20:2
Trenerry, Walter N (Producer)
Interlock 1958,F 7,18:1
Trenholm, Cissy
Howdy Mr Ice 1948,Je 25,28:5
Howdy, Mr Ice of 1950 1949,My 27,24:2
Trenholme, Helen
Strange Orchestra 1933,N 29,23:2
To See Ourselves 1935,My 1,25:2
Victoria Regina 1935,D 27,15:2
Country Wife, The 1936,D 2,34:1
Amazing Dr. Clitterhouse, The 1937,Mr 3,26:4
Bachelor Born 1938,Ja 26,26:3
Come Across 1938,S 15,28:3
Importance of Being Earnest, The 1939,Ja 13,16:2
Woman Brown, The 1939,D 9,18:5
Boyd's Daughter 1940,O 12,20:2
Watch on the Rhine 1941,Ap 2,26:2
Proof Thro' the Night 1942,D 26,14:2
Trenk, William (Director)
My L A 1951,D 9,87:1
Trenk, William (Producer)
My L A 1951,D 9,87:1
Trenkler, Freddie
Gay Blades 1937,N 16,27:1
It Happens on Ice 1941,Ap 5,13:2
Stars on Ice 1942,Jl 3,12:2
Hollywood Ice Revue 1943,Ja 24,II,1:1
Stars on Ice (2d Edition) 1943,Je 25,13:2
Hats Off to Ice 1944,Je 23,15:2
Icetime 1946,Je 21,20:5
Icetime 1947,My 29,28:2
Howdy Mr Ice 1948,Je 25,28:5
Howdy, Mr Ice of 1950 1949,My 27,24:2
Hollywood Ice Revue 1950,Ja 21,13:4
Hollywood Ice Revue 1953,Ja 16,17:2
Hollywood Ice Revue 1954,Ja 15,16:2
Hollywood Ice Revue 1955 1955,Ja 14,16:1
Hollywood Ice Revue 1956,Ja 13,17:1
Ice Capades 1956,S 13,41:2
Ice Capades 1957,S 5,33:2
Ice Capades 1958,S 4,33:2
Ice Capades 1961,Ag 31,24:4
Ice Capades 1962,Ag 30,34:1
Ice Capades 1967,Je 2,33:1
Ice Capades 1969,Ja 8,42:1
Trenour, Robert
Emperor, The 1963,Ap 17,30:1
Trenour, Robert (Miscellaneous)
Tour De Four 1963,Je 19,41:1
Colombe 1965,F 24,33:1
Trent, Bruce
Wish You Were Here 1953,O 11,83:5
Trent, Charles
Henri Christophe 1945,Je 7,24:5
Trent, Jo (Lyricist)
Rang Tang 1927,Jl 13,20:1
Fioretta 1929,F 6,30:3
Sugar Hill 1931,D 26,15:2
Trent, Joey
Comic Strip 1958,My 15,26:2
Trent, Karen Sue
Six Characters in Search of an Author
1955,D 12,38:1
Trent, Lee
Tidbits of 1946 1946,Jl 9,17:2
Trent, Sheila
Mister Romeo 1927,S 6,35:3
We Never Learn 1928,Ja 24,26:1
Get Me in the Movies 1928,My 22,18:3
Eva the Fifth 1928,Ag 29,19:3
Bidding High 1932,S 29,17:2
False Dreams, Farewell 1934,Ja 16,18:3
Every Thursday 1934,My 11,25:5
Sleeping Clergyman, A 1934,O 9,16:1
Tomorrow's Harvest 1934,D 6,26:5
This Thing Called Love 1935,Jl 2,24:4
Dead End 1935,O 29,17:2
All the Living 1938,Mr 25,14:4
Clean Beds 1939,My 26,21:2
Scene of the Crime, The 1940,Mr 29,24:1
Embezzled Heaven 1944,N 1,20:2
Diamond Lil 1948,N 30,33:2
Diamond Lil 1949,F 7,16:2
Diamond Lil 1951,S 15,8:2

Trent, Warren
I Myself 1934,My 10,24:6
Old Maid, The 1935,Ja 8,26:1
Trentini, Emma
Vaudeville (Palace) 1925,Ap 21,18:1
Vaudeville (Hippodrome) 1926,F 23,26:2
Treseder, Kenneth
Mademoiselle 1932,O 19,22:4
Best People, The 1933,Mr 16,21:5
Party, A 1933,Ag 24,18:4
Distant Shore, The 1935,F 22,26:2
Springtime for Henry 1936,Je 30,15:1
Middle Man 1936,S 8,23:1
Oscar Wilde 1938,O 11,20:2
My Dear Children 1940,F 1,16:2
Rebecca 1945,Ja 19,17:2
S S Glencairn; In the Zone 1948,My 21,21:2
S S Glencairn; Moon of the Caribbees
1948,My 21,21:2
S S Glencairn; Bound East for Cardiff
1948,My 21,21:2
S S Glencairn; Long Voyage Home, The
1948,My 21,21:2
S S Glencairn; Long Voyage Home, The; Moon of
the Caribbees; In the Zone; Bound East for
Cardiff 1948,My 30,II,1:1
Tresko, Elsa
Give My Regards to Off Off Broadway
1966,D 9,57:1
Caution: A Love Story 1969,Ap 4,45:1
Dirtiest Show in Town, The 1970,My 2,21:1
Dirtiest Show in Town, The 1970,Je 29,43:2
Treskoff, Olga
Marjolaine 1922,Ja 25,16:1
Sancho Panza 1923,N 27,23:1
Vagabond King, The 1925,S 22,23:3
Tresnay, Pierre
Ligne du Coeur, La 1931,O 25,VIII,1:7
Tress, David
Midsummer Night's Dream, A 1967,Je 30,23:1
Tress, David (Miscellaneous)
Picture of Dorian Gray, The 1956,Ag 18,15:5
Tressider, Edythe
Rollo's Wild Oat 1920,N 24,14:1
Fashions for Men 1922,D 6,22:1
Major Barbara 1928,N 20,28:4
Diana 1929,D 10,37:1
Tressler, Otto
Abraham Lincoln 1934,D 1,8:6
Treston, Pat
Beautiful Jailer, The 1957,My 17,19:2
Season of the Beast 1958,Mr 14,29:2
Tretiakow, S (Playwright)
Roar China! 1930,O 28,23:1
Trett, Vera
Five O'Clock Girl, The 1927,O 11,26:3
Trevathan, Sue
Riders to the Sea 1957,Mr 7,24:1
Heloise 1958,S 25,28:4
Heloise 1958,O 5,II,1:1
Trevathan, Sue (Lighting Director)
Fall 1957,N 22,19:1
Trevelyan, H B (Playwright)
Dark Angel, The 1925,F 11,19:2
Trevelyan, Hilda
Lad, The 1929,Ja 13,VIII,4:5
Trevelyan, R C (Playwright)
Angel 1933,D 24,IX,2:2
Trevieres, Michel
Overcoat, The 1960,S 7,45:1
Treville, Roger
Felix 1926,O 10,VIII,2:1
Mes Amours 1940,My 3,16:5
Trevis, Bob
Vintage '60 1960,S 13,41:1
Trevor, Ann
Captive, The 1926,S 30,23:1
Happy Husband, The 1927,Jl 10,VII,2:3
Symphony in Two Flats 1930,S 17,30:4
Trevor, Austin
Escape 1927,O 27,33:1
Escape 1927,N 6,IX,1:1
Patriot, The 1928,Ja 20,15:1
Patriot, The 1928,Ja 29,VIII,1:1
Roulette 1935,Je 16,X,1:1
Call It a Day 1935,N 24,IX,1:2
Once Is Enough 1938,F 16,16:2
Don't Listen, Ladies 1948,D 29,16:2
Trevor, Claire
Whistling in the Dark 1932,Ja 20,16:6
Party's Over, The 1933,Mr 28,23:3
Big Two, The 1947,Ja 9,21:2
Trevor, Constance
Sex Fable, The 1931,O 21,26:1
Trevor, Edward
Roar China! 1930,O 28,23:1
Mary of Scotland 1933,N 28,28:3
Valley Forge 1934,D 11,28:3
Among Those Sailing 1936,F 12,24:4
Daughters of Atreus 1936,O 15,33:1
Hedda Gabler 1936,N 17,34:4
God Innis 1937,Ag 25,24:3
Oscar Wilde 1938,O 11,20:2

Trevor, Edward—Cont
Attack 1942,S 8,13:4
Trevor, John
Cyrano de Bergerac 1923,N 2,14:1
Rope's End 1929,S 20,34:5
Black Limelight 1936,N 10,31:1
Wookey, The 1941,S 11,20:5
Trevor, John (Playwright)
Red Light 1931,D 6,VIII,2:7
Trevor, Norman
Foot-Loose 1920,My 11,12:1
Enter Madame 1920,Ag 17,11:2
Lilies of the Field 1921,O 5,20:1
Married Woman, The 1921,D 26,21:1
Married Woman, The 1922,F 5,VI,1:1
Desert Sands 1922,F 14,20:1
Manhattan 1922,Ag 16,7:5
To Love 1922,O 18,16:2
Mountebank, The 1923,My 8,22:2
Mountebank, The 1923,My 13,VIII,1:1
Love Scandal, A 1923,N 7,14:1
Goose Hangs High, The 1924,Ja 30,16:1
Goose Hangs High, The 1924,F 3,VII,1:1
It All Depends 1925,Ag 11,16:4
All Dressed Up 1925,S 10,28:1
Young Blood 1925,N 25,15:1
Young Blood 1925,N 29,VIII,1:1
Captive, The 1926,S 30,23:1
Trevor, Norman (Producer)
Married Woman, The 1922,F 5,VI,1:1
Trevor, Ted
Vaudeville (Palace) 1926,Ap 20,24:6
Vaudeville (Palace) 1926,Jl 6,19:3
Trew, Grafton
They Shall Not Die 1934,F 22,24:4
Trexler, Charles
Parnell 1935,N 12,24:2
Parnell 1936,My 5,26:2
Aged 26 1936,D 22,32:1
School for Scandal, The 1940,Je 23,IX,1:1
Treynor, Blair (Playwright)
Broadway Brevities, 1920 1920,S 30,12:2
Treyz, Russell (Director)
Knack With Horses, A 1970,D 21,52:1
Here Be Dragons 1970,D 21,52:1
Tria, Carmelina
'Il Tesoro D'Isacco; Treasure of Isaac, The 1928,Ja 26,17:1
Triana, Jose (Playwright)
Criminals, The 1967,O 15,II,9:3
Criminals, The 1970,F 26,33:2
Triand, Louis
Across the Board on Tomorrow Morning 1942,Mr 21,13:5
Theatre of the Soul 1942,Mr 21,13:5
Tribble, Andrew
Put and Take 1921,Ag 24,12:3
Brown Buddies 1930,O 8,29:1
Brain Sweat 1934,Ap 5,24:4
Tribush, Nancy
Hang Down Your Head and Die 1964,O 19,38:1
Oh! Calcutta! 1969,Je 18,33:1
Trichter, Jerry
Nathan the Wise 1962,Mr 23,29:1
Mrs Warren's Profession 1963,Ap 25,39:1
Trick, Ormal B
Everyman Today 1958,Ja 16,32:4
Tricot, Georges
Procureur Hallers, Le 1924,N 13,18:1
Bourgeois Gentilhomme, Le 1924,N 20,21:2
Taming of the Shrew, The 1924,N 25,27:3
Trierweller, James
Winners and Losers 1947,F 27,27:2
Deputy of Paris, The 1947,Mr 22,9:5
Triesalt, John
First Flight 1925,S 18,26:2
Triesault, Ivan
Jeweled Tree, The 1926,O 8,26:2
Marathon 1933,Ja 28,8:8
Divine Drudge 1933,O 27,22:3
Star Spangled 1936,Mr 11,23:1
Hamlet 1936,O 9,30:2
Foreigners 1939,D 6,30:2
Burning Deck, The 1940,Mr 2,9:2
Walrus and the Carpenter, The 1941,N 10,20:2
Triesch, Irene
Dance of Death, The; Totentanz 1923,D 17,23:3
Rosmersholm 1924,F 8,22:3
Triest, Frank
Airways, Inc 1929,F 21,30:5
Triest, William
Battle Hymn 1936,My 23,12:1
Path of Flowers, The 1936,S 18,19:3
Trigere, Pauline (Costume Designer)
Exercise, The 1968,Ap 25,54:1
Trigg, Barclay
Lulu Belle 1926,F 10,20:1
Harlem 1929,F 21,30:3
Dance With Your Gods 1934,O 8,14:3
Nativity Play, The 1937,D 21,29:1
Trigg, Zenaide
Comedy of Errors, The 1963,Je 13,28:1
Triggs, Harold
Spring Tonic 1936,My 11,16:1

Triggs, John
Two on an Island 1940,Ja 23,17:2
Flight to the West 1940,D 31,19:1
Trikonis, Gus
Bajour 1964,N 24,42:1
Trilby
Horse Fever 1940,N 25,21:2
Trilling, Ilya
Lucky Night, The 1931,S 14,15:5
Trilling, Ilya (Choreographer)
Once Upon a Time 1933,S 22,15:1
Trilling, Ilya (Composer)
Yoina Seeks a Bride 1936,O 20,31:1
Give Me Back My Heart 1937,O 4,17:6
Semele's Bar Mitzvah 1938,Ja 17,11:2
Queen Mother 1938,D 26,29:4
Schwartse Mamme 1939,Ja 16,11:3
Trilling, Ilya (Director)
Here Runs the Bride 1934,S 20,21:3
Trilling, Ilya (Lyricist)
Queen Mother 1938,D 26,29:4
Trilling, Ilya (Musical Director)
Street Singers 1938,D 12,25:6
Trilling, Ilya (Playwright)
Jolly Wedding, The 1937,N 17,26:3
David and Esther 1938,O 12,34:3
Trimble, Jessy (Playwright)
Leap, The 1924,My 23,16:5
Immoral Support 1935,S 3,24:3
Trimble, Lester (Composer)
Little Clay Cart, The 1953,Jl 1,25:1
Trimble, Theodore
Samarkand 1926,D 22,24:4
Trimble, Thomas H
Fiesta 1933,D 16,12:2
Trimble, Walden
I Will IF You Will 1922,Ag 30,10:4
Trini
Dancing Girl, The 1923,Ja 25,16:2
Artists and Models 1924,O 16,33:3
Vaudeville (Palace) 1925,D 29,21:2
Vaudeville (Palace) 1926,Je 1,29:5
Vaudeville (Palace) 1926,N 16,24:3
Vaudeville (Palace) 1926,N 23,27:3
Take the Air 1927,N 23,28:2
Cafe de Danse 1929,Ja 16,22:2
Wonder Bar, The 1931,Mr 18,23:4
Vaudeville (Palace) 1932,Ja 4,27:4
Trinidad, Arsenio
Majority of One, A 1959,F 17,28:2
Trinnier, Vaughn
New Moon, The 1944,My 18,16:2
Bloomer Girl 1944,O 6,18:5
Trintzius, Rene (Playwright)
Poudre d'Or, La 1928,Je 17,VIII,1:4
Trinz, William (Producer)
My Fair Lady 1959,F 21,25:6
Trio, Dickens
Pickwick 1927,S 6,35:2
Trio, Lime
American Jubilee 1940,My 13,20:5
Trio Fatima, The
Wonder World 1964,My 18,32:1
Triola, Anne
My L A 1951,D 9,87:1
Triplett, William
Legal Murder 1934,F 16,16:2
Revolt of the Beavers, The 1937,My 21,19:2
Too Many Heroes 1937,N 16,26:2
Tripolino, Joseph
Light, Lively and Yiddish 1970,O 28,58:1
Tripolitoff, Nicholas
Merry World, The 1926,Je 9,18:3
Tripp, Burton
Our Town 1944,Ja 11,24:5
Jacobowsky and the Colonel 1944,Mr 15,17:2
Tripp, James
Midsummer Night's Dream, A 1964,Je 30,23:2
Hamlet 1969,Mr 4,34:1
Conduct Unbecoming 1970,O 13,50:1
Tripp, Michael
Nine Fifteen Revue, The 1930,F 12,26:2
Tripp, Paul
Cyrano de Bergerac 1936,Ap 28,17:1
Enemy of the People, An 1937,F 16,19:1
Temper the Wind 1946,D 28,10:2
49th Cousin, The 1960,O 28,22:1
Tripp, Paul (Director)
Seeds in the Wind 1948,Ap 26,27:2
Seeds in the Wind 1948,My 26,29:2
Trisler, Joyce (Choreographer)
Everyman Today 1958,Ja 16,32:4
Put It in Writing 1963,My 14,31:1
Titus Andronicus 1967,Ag 10,43:2
Romeo and Juliet 1968,Ag 16,19:1
King Arthur 1968,N 3,87:1
Peer Gynt 1969,Jl 17,56:1
Trisler, Joyce (Miscellaneous)
Great Scot! 1965,N 12,56:3
Henry IV, Part I 1968,Je 30,54:7
Tristan, Dorothy
Tragical Historie of Doctor Faustus, The 1964,O 6,34:2

Tristan, Dorothy—Cont
Midsummer Night's Dream, A 1967,Je 19,42:1
Macbeth 1967,Jl 31,21:1
Tristani, Marcel
Phedre 1963,O 21,39:1
Berenice 1963,O 30,46:1
Troupe Du Roi, La 1970,F 4,38:1
Amphitryon 1970,F 4,38:1
Troupe Du Roi, La 1970,F 4,38:1
Don Juan 1970,F 7,24:2
Femmes Savaantes, Les 1970,F 14,12:1
Malade Imaginaire, Le 1970,F 18,40:2
Tristjansky, Olga
Grand Duchess and the Waiter, The 1925,O 14,31:1
Trisvan, Thomas
Lulu Belle 1926,F 10,20:1
Tritippo, James (Scenic Designer)
Ice Capades 1963,Ag 29,37:2
Tritsch, Mona
High Button Shoes 1955,Mr 12,10:6
Trittipo, James (Costume Designer)
Captains and the Kings, The 1962,Ja 3,25:2
Trittipo, James (Lighting Director)
Captains and the Kings, The 1962,Ja 3,25:2
Trittipo, James (Scenic Designer)
Captains and the Kings, The 1962,Ja 3,25:2
Ice Capades 1969,Ja 8,42:1
Trivas, Victor (Playwright)
Crime and Punishment 1935,Ja 23,20:3
Trivas, Victor (Scenic Designer)
Bourgeois Gentilhomme, Le 1929,Mr 24,X,2:3
Trivers, Barry (Composer)
Ziegfeld Follies 1931,Jl 2,30:5
Trivers, Barry (Lyricist)
Heaven on Earth 1948,S 17,29:2
Trivers, Barry (Original Author)
Heaven on Earth 1948,S 17,29:2
Trivers, Barry (Playwright)
Ziegfeld Follies 1931,Jl 2,30:5
Trivers, Benn
New Yorkers, The 1927,Mr 11,24:3
Trivers, Edith
Red Cat, The 1934,S 20,21:1
Trix, Helen
Vaudeville (Palace) 1926,S 7,24:6
Trix, Mattie
Vaudeville (Palace) 1926,S 7,24:6
Trixie
Howdy, Mr Ice of 1950 1949,My 27,24:2
Ice Capades 1952,S 12,18:1
Trochman, Saul
Little Theatre Tournament; Man in the Stalls, The 1929,My 8,34:4
Seven Against One 1930,My 7,25:1
Trockmorton, Cleon (Scenic Designer)
Give Us This Day 1933,O 28,20:6
Trockowna, Anna
O'Flynn, The 1934,D 28,24:1
Troie, Robert (Scenic Designer)
Before I Wake 1968,O 14,56:1
Trollope, Anthony (Original Author)
Barchester Towers 1937,N 19,26:6
Barchester Towers 1937,D 1,27:1
Trombetta, Robert
Gondoliers, The 1967,O 29,83:1
Tronto, Rudy
She Shall Have Music 1959,Ja 23,18:4
Irma la Douce 1960,S 30,31:2
Boys From Syracuse, The 1963,Ap 16,31:1
Boys From Syracuse, The 1963,Je 2,II,1:1
Secret Life of Walter Mitty, The 1964,O 27,44:5
Tronto, Rudy (Choreographer)
Wet Paint 1965,Ap 13,33:1
Tronto, Rudy (Miscellaneous)
Persecution and Assassination of Marat As Performed by the Inmates of the Asylum of Charenton Under the Direction of the Marquis de Sade, The 1967,Ja 4,34:1
Troobnick, Eugene
From the Second City 1961,S 27,32:1
Untitled-Revue; Second City 1962,Ja 12,30:2
Dynamite Tonight 1967,Mr 16,52:2
Before You Go 1968,Ja 12,20:1
Androcles and the Lion 1968,Je 27,47:1
Time of Your Life, The 1969,N 7,37:1
Don Juan 1970,My 26,32:1
Don Juan 1970,My 31,II,1:6
Trotman, Jim
Egg and I, The 1958,S 11,43:4
Ballad for Bimshire 1963,O 16,54:1
Trotman, William
Red, White and Maddox 1969,Ja 27,27:1
Narrow Road to the Deep North 1969,D 2,64:1
Trotman, William (Scenic Designer)
Jungle of Cities 1970,Mr 1,75:2
Trott, Pat
Fig Leaves Are Falling, The 1969,Ja 3,19:1
Trott, Richard
Sancho Panza 1923,N 27,23:1
Trotter, Alan
Escape 1927,O 27,33:1
Trotter, Elizabeth (Playwright)
Alice Adams 1946,Mr 9,9:4

Trotter, Elizabeth (Playwright)—Cont
Alice Adams 1947,Ag 5,26:1
Trotter Brothers, The
Folies Bergere 1964,Je 3,36:1
Troubetzkoy, Princess (Amelie Rives) (Playwright)
Love in a Mist 1926,Ap 13,28:3
Troubetzkoy, Youka
If the Shoe Fits 1946,D 6,29:4
Troubridge, St Vincent (Playwright)
Kindertragoedie; Children's Tragedy, The 1931,D 27,VIII,3:1
Troughton, John
Richard III 1920,Mr 8,7:1
Nemesis 1921,Ap 5,24:3
Great Broxopp, The 1921,N 16,22:1
So This Is London 1922,Ag 31,18:2
Alarm Clock, The 1923,D 25,26:2
Plain Jane 1924,My 13,24:2
American Born 1925,O 6,31:3
Padre, The 1926,D 28,16:3
Wrecker, The 1928,F 28,18:2
When Crummles Played 1928,O 2,34:3
Lost Sheep 1930,My 6,33:2
Old Man Murphy 1931,My 19,25:2
If Love Were All 1931,N 14,14:5
Mother Lode 1934,D 24,16:5
First Lady 1935,N 27,17:4
Troughton, Patrick
Caesar and Cleopatra 1951,D 20,43:2
Trouncer, Cecil
Gooseberry Fool 1929,N 2,14:8
Saint Joan 1936,Jl 26,II,1:3
Apple Cart, The 1953,My 8,29:3
Troup, James (Producer)
Case History 1938,O 22,15:2
Troupe, Tom
Trial of the Catonsville Nine, The 1970,Ag 16,II,1:7
Trout, Charles
Polly 1925,O 12,19:1
Trout, Dink
Wild Rose, The 1926,O 21,23:1
Troutman, Doris E
Singing Jailbirds 1928,D 5,34:4
Airways, Inc 1929,F 21,30:5
Troutman, Ivy
Road Together, The 1924,Ja 18,21:2
De Luxe 1935,Mr 6,22:2
Room in Red and White, A 1936,Ja 20,23:3
Tell Me Pretty Maiden 1937,D 17,33:5
Dear Octopus 1939,Ja 12,22:2
Kind Lady 1940,S 4,28:3
Kiss for Cinderella, A 1942,Mr 11,22:2
Late George Apley, The 1944,O 20,16:4
Late George Apley, The 1944,N 22,26:2
Trovaioli, Armando (Composer)
Rugantino 1964,F 7,34:1
Trovato, Carmelina
'Il Tesoro D'Isacco; Treasure of Isaac, The 1928,Ja 26,17:1
Trovato, Giuseppe
'Il Tesoro D'Isacco; Treasure of Isaac, The 1928,Ja 26,17:1
Trow, George (Playwright)
William Had the Words! 1964,Mr 30,36:1
Trowbridge, Charles
Broken Wing, The 1920,N 30,14:1
Just Because 1922,Mr 23,11:1
Night Call, The 1922,Ap 27,12:2
Last Warning, The 1922,O 25,23:1
Sweet Seventeen 1924,Mr 18,24:2
Locked Door, The 1924,Je 20,17:2
Backslapper, The 1925,Ap 13,25:2
It All Depends 1925,Ag 11,16:4
Craig's Wife 1925,O 13,21:2
We Never Learn 1928,Ja 24,26:1
Behavior of Mrs Crane, The 1928,Mr 21,30:1
Congai 1928,N 28,24:3
Stripped 1929,Je 9,VIII,1:2
Ladies Leave 1929,O 2,28:3
Boundry Line, The 1930,F 6,21:1
Ladies of Creation 1931,S 9,25:1
Mackerel Skies 1934,Ja 24,20:4
I Myself 1934,My 10,24:6
Trowbridge, Saint Vincent (Translator)
Betrayal 1931,Ja 25,VIII,2:7
Trowbridge, Una Lady (Playwright)
Cheri 1930,N 16,VIII,4:1
Trowsdale, Campbell
Twelfth Night 1957,Jl 4,16:4
Troy, Ella
Jolly Tailors, The 1923,N 3,13:3
Troy, Hector
Waiting for Lefty 1967,D 19,58:2
Does a Tiger Wear a Necktie? 1969,F 26,38:1
Summertree 1969,D 10,60:1
Troy, Henry
Black Boy 1926,O 7,30:2
Kilpatrick's Old-Time Minstrels 1930,Ap 21,20:2
Troy, Louise
Infernal Machine, The 1954,Mr 22,22:2
Merchant of Venice, The 1955,Ja 8,9:7
Conversation Piece 1957,N 19,38:2
Camelot 1960,D 5,42:1
O, Oysters! 1961,Ja 31,23:1

Shot in the Dark, A 1961,O 19,40:1
Doll's House, A 1963,F 4,5:6
Tovarich 1963,Mr 20,5:1
High Spirits 1964,Ap 8,34:1
Walking Happy 1966,N 28,47:1
Walking Happy 1966,D 18,II,3:1
Troy, Mary
Amedee: or, How to Disentangle Yourself 1955,N 1,27:3
Don Juan; Feast With the Statue, The 1956,Ja 4,21:4
Troy, Michael
Ardele 1958,Ap 9,39:4
Antigone 1959,S 16,46:2
Truax, Ernest
Lysistrata 1930,Je 6,20:1
Truax, James (Producer)
If Five Years Pass 1962,My 11,37:1
One-Woman Show, A 1962,My 22,31:1
Truax, Maude
Fool, The 1922,O 24,18:1
Silence 1924,N 13,18:2
Truax, Sarah
Man Who Ate the Popomack, The 1924,Mr 25,24:1
My Son 1924,S 18,18:2
Trubin, Sybil (Miscellaneous)
Dandy Dick 1956,Ja 11,37:2
Trubin, Sybil (Producer)
Thieves' Carnival 1955,F 2,21:1
Morning's at Seven 1955,Je 23,25:1
Trucco, Juanita
Tragedy of the Ages, The 1933,Ap 7,22:7
True, Geraldyn
Dover Road, The 1926,Ap 29,20:3
True, Gertrude
Candida 1926,Mr 17,28:3
True, Lois
Tall Kentuckian, The 1953,Je 17,30:1
True, Mary
Power of Darkness, The 1920,Ja 22,22:1
Chief Thing, The 1926,Mr 23,24:2
Stairs, The 1927,N 8,32:7
True Brethren, The
Story Theater 1970,O 27,54:1
Truell, Augusta
Beau Brummell 1924,Ap 4,19:2
Trueman, Paula
Green Ring, The 1922,Ap 5,22:1
Little Clay Cart, The 1924,D 6,13:3
Fratricide Punished 1925,Ap 21,19:1
Romio and Julietta 1925,Ap 21,19:1
Critic, The 1925,My 9,12:4
Grand Street Follies, The 1925,Je 19,24:1
Dybbuk, The 1925,D 16,22:2
Burmese Pwe, A 1926,Mr 17,28:1
Romantic Young Lady, The 1926,My 5,24:3
Grand Street Follies, The 1926,Je 16,23:2
Dybbuk, The 1926,D 17,27:2
Pinwheel 1927,F 4,16:4
Commedia Dell' Arte 1927,Ap 6,24:3
Grand Street Follies, The 1927,My 20,22:3
Lovers and Enemies 1927,S 21,27:1
If 1927,O 26,26:2
Love Nest, The 1927,D 23,17:1
Maya 1928,F 22,19:1
Grand Street Follies, The 1928,My 29,16:2
Grand Street Follies, The 1929,My 2,20:4
Grand Street Follies, The 1929,My 12,IX,1:2
Grand Street Follies, The 1929,Je 19,34:3
Sweet and Low 1930,N 18,28:5
Ladies of Creation 1931,S 9,25:1
Midsummer Night's Dream, A 1932,N 18,22:2
Merchant of Venice, The 1932,N 24,34:5
Sunday Nights at Nine 1933,N 13,20:7
Panic 1935,Mr 16,18:4
You Can't Take It With You 1936,D 15,31:1
George Washington Slept Here 1940,O 19,20:3
As You Like It 1941,O 21,29:2
Kiss and Tell 1943,Mr 18,22:1
Kiss and Tell 1943,Mr 28,II,1:1
Feathers in a Gale 1943,D 22,26:2
Violet 1944,O 25,16:1
For Love or Money 1947,N 5,36:2
Mrs McThing 1952,F 21,22:1
Wake Up, Darling 1956,My 3,34:2
Family Affair, A 1962,Ja 29,17:1
Wonderful Town 1963,F 15,10:2
Sunday Man, The 1964,My 14,41:3
Music Man, The 1965,Je 17,26:4
Happy Journey to Trenton and Camden, The 1966,S 7,53:1
Queens of France 1966,S 7,53:1
Long Christmas Dinner, The 1966,S 7,53:1
Sherry! 1967,Mr 29,39:1
Postcards 1967,D 6,41:1
Dr Fish 1970,Mr 11,42:2
Truesdale, Ernest
Freight 1950,Ap 27,36:2
Truesdell, Frederick
Voltaire 1922,Mr 21,17:1
That Day 1922,Jl 9,VI,1:4
That Day 1922,O 4,27:3
Gorilla, The 1925,Ap 29,24:2

Truesdell, Frederick—Cont
Shelf, The 1926,S 28,31:1
Our Betters 1928,F 21,18:2
Crashing Through 1928,O 30,26:5
Apple Cart, The 1930,F 25,30:1
Truesdell, Frederick (Playwright)
Lambs Gambol 1925,Ap 27,15:1
Truesdell, Howard
Jimmie 1920,N 18,15:3
Near Santa Barbara 1921,F 1,14:1
Smooth as Silk 1921,F 23,18:3
Extra 1923,Ja 24,22:3
Truex, Ernest
No More Blondes 1920,Ja 8,22:1
Blue Bonnet 1920,Ag 30,12:1
Six-Cylinder Love 1921,Jl 24,VI,1:1
Six-Cylinder Love 1921,Ag 26,8:2
New Toys 1924,Ja 20,VII,2:8
New Toys 1924,F 19,12:1
New Toys 1924,F 24,VII,1:1
Annie 1924,O 12,VIII,2:1
Annie Dear 1924,N 5,25:3
Fall Guy, The 1925,Mr 11,19:1
Lambs Gambol 1925,Ap 27,15:1
Pomeroy's Past 1926,Ap 20,24:4
Pomeroy's Past 1926,My 2,VIII,1:1
Fall Guy, The 1926,O 10,VIII,2:1
First Year, The 1926,D 19,VII,6:4
Good Morning, Bill! 1927,D 25,VIII,1:4
Call Me Georges 1928,Je 10,VIII,1:3
Patsy, The 1929,Ja 6,VIII,1:4
Many Waters 1929,S 26,27:1
Many Waters 1929,O 6,IX,1:1
Ritzy 1930,F 11,30:4
Lysistrata 1930,Ap 29,30:5
Lysistrata 1930,Je 1,VIII,1:1
Napi 1931,Mr 12,22:5
Third Little Show, The 1931,My 10,VIII,2:4
Third Little Show, The 1931,Je 2,34:3
Whistling in the Dark 1932,Ja 20,16:6
Lambs Gambol 1932,Ap 25,18:2
Best Sellers 1933,My 4,20:2
Love and Babies 1933,Ag 23,21:4
Sing and Whistle 1934,F 12,18:3
Jig Saw 1934,My 1,26:3
Gather Ye Rosebuds 1934,N 29,33:2
Gather Ye Rosebuds 1934,D 2,X,1:1
Hook-Up, The 1935,My 9,24:6
Prodigal Father, The 1935,Jl 2,24:2
Whatever Goes Up 1935,N 26,28:2
Larger Than Life 1936,Mr 17,25:3
Middle Man 1936,S 8,23:1
Frederika 1937,F 5,16:5
George Washington Slept Here 1940,S 24,27:3
George Washington Slept Here 1940,O 19,20:3
George Washington Slept Here 1940,O 27,IX,1:1
Helen Goes to Troy 1944,Ap 25,17:2
Helen Goes to Troy 1944,Ap 30,II,1:1
Henry VIII 1946,N 7,42:2
What Every Woman Knows 1946,N 9,13:2
John Gabriel Borkman 1946,N 13,33:2
Pound on Demand 1946,D 20,29:3
Androcles and the Lion 1946,D 20,29:2
Temporary Island, A 1948,Mr 15,27:3
Oh, Mr Meadowbrook! 1948,D 27,17:2
Golden State, The 1950,N 27,29:3
Four Twelves Are 48 1951,Ja 18,30:2
Flahooley 1951,My 15,39:1
Good Soup, The 1960,Mr 3,26:4
Venus at Large 1962,Ap 13,30:1
Very Rich Woman, A 1965,O 5,5:8
Truex, Ernest (Director)
Pomeroy's Past 1926,Ap 20,24:4
Curtain Rises, The 1933,O 20,15:2
Sing and Whistle 1934,F 12,18:3
Truex, Ernest (Producer)
Out Goes She 1928,D 30,VIII,4:1
Sing and Whistle 1934,F 12,18:3
Truex, James
Return to Folly 1935,Jl 23,24:3
Blind Alley 1935,S 25,19:6
Tovarich 1936,O 16,31:4
Worse Things Happen at Sea 1937,S 1,15:3
Where Do We Go From Here? 1938,N 16,26:2
Day in the Sun 1939,My 17,29:2
Three Men on a Horse 1942,O 10,10:2
Truex, Philip
World Waits, The 1933,O 26,22:5
Too Much Party 1934,Mr 6,28:4
Battleship Gertie 1935,Ja 19,9:2
Hook-Up, The 1935,My 9,24:6
Prodigal Father, The 1935,Jl 2,24:2
Return to Folly 1935,Jl 23,24:3
Richard II 1937,F 6,14:2
Richard II 1937,S 16,28:2
Fabulous Invalid, The 1938,O 10,15:1
Family Portrait 1939,Mr 9,18:4
Man Who Came to Dinner, The 1940,F 10,19:5
This Is the Army 1942,Jl 5,28:2
This Is the Army 1942,Ag 16,VIII,1:1
Magnificent Yankee, The 1946,Ja 23,21:2
Finian's Rainbow 1948,Ag 29,II,1:1
Truffiger, Jules (Playwright)
Chatiment, Un 1929,My 5,IX,2:4

uhill, Lee
Young and Fair, The 1948,N 23,35:2

uitt, Birney B
Sale and a Sailor, A, or Glory! What Price!
1926,Ap 25,30:4
Hoot Mon, or Clans Across the Sea 1927,My 8,29:4

rull, Monford
Relapse, The 1950,N 23,54:2

ruman, Garrick (Playwright)
Head or Tail 1926,N 10,24:1

ruman, Margaret
Autumn Crocus 1954,Je 22,24:7
Autumn Crocus 1954,Jl 7,23:7

ruman, Ralph
Josef Suss 1930,Ja 21,28:5

rumbo, Dalton (Original Author)
Washington Jitters 1938,My 3,19:1

rumbo, Dalton (Playwright)
Biggest Thief in Town 1949,Mr 31,31:2

rump, Donald J (Miscellaneous)
Paris Is Out! 1970,F 3,35:1

rundy, Natalie
Girl Can Tell, A 1953,O 30,28:2

ruppo, Mildred
World We Make, The 1939,N 21,19:1

ruscott, John (Costume Designer)
Camelot 1964,Ag 20,34:1

ruscott, John (Scenic Designer)
Camelot 1964,Ag 20,34:1

ruscott, Mark
Dearest Enemy 1925,S 19,9:2
Criss Cross 1926,O 13,20:2

russel, Jack
Cry for Us All 1970,Ap 9,48:2

rustman, Susan
Mrs Warren's Profession 1963,Ap 25,39:1

ryanos, John
Henry V 1965,Je 29,27:2

rybom, Jean
Let's Face It 1941,O 30,26:2

rybom, Jeanne C
Pal Joey 1940,D 26,22:2

ryon, Tom
Cyrano de Bergerac 1953,N 13,24:3
Richard III 1953,D 10,65:2

rytler, Peter
Cold Wind and the Warm, The 1958,D 9,55:1
Moonbirds 1959,O 10,13:1

rzcinski, Edmund (Playwright)
Stalag. 17 1951,My 9,41:2
Stalag 17 1953,Ap 6,24:2

saganeas, Christos
Electra 1930,D 27,16:1
Iphigenia 1931,Ja 6,24:1

sakrali, Olga
Hippolytus 1968,N 20,38:3

Sani, Nolan
Peter and the Wolf 1969,N 30,85:5

schechow, Michael
Phaea 1930,Ag 31,VIII,2:1

schemerinsky, B
Dybbuk, The 1926,D 14,24:2
Eternal Jew, The 1926,D 21,21:2

schudin, Mike (Composer)
No Hard Feelings 1965,Ap 5,33:8

schunko, Maxi (Costume Designer)
Professor Bernhardi 1968,Mr 20,38:1

shura
Holiday in Israel 1968,O 14,55:2

siang, H T
War and Peace 1942,My 22,26:3

siang, H T (Playwright)
China Marches On 1939,O 22,IX,2:1

soutsouvas, Sam
Twelfth Night 1969,Ag 14,29:2

surusuke, Kagaya
Kagotsurube; Courtesan, The 1960,Je 3,26:1

Tubbs, William C
Patriots, The 1943,D 21,22:5
Happily Ever After 1945,Mr 16,21:2

Tubby, Gertrude Ogden (Playwright)
Boy Who Lived Twice, A 1945,S 12,31:2

Tubens, Joe (Miscellaneous)
Drat! the Cat! 1965,O 11,54:2
Minnie's Boys 1970,Mr 27,27:1
One Night Stands of a Noisy Passenger; Noisy
Passenger, The 1970,D 31,8:3
One Night Stands of a Noisy Passenger; Passage,
Un 1970,D 31,8:3
One Night Stands of a Noisy Passenger; Last
Stand 1970,D 31,8:3

Tucci, Maria
Twelfth Night 1958,Ag 7,21:4
Jackhammer, The 1962,F 6,26:2
Milk Train Doesn't Stop Here Anymore, The
1963,Ja 18,7:1
Five Evenings 1963,My 10,37:3
Corruption in the Palace of Justice 1963,O 9,49:2
Trojan Women, The 1963,D 24,7:6
Deputy, The 1964,F 27,26:1
Coriolanus 1965,Je 21,36:1
Romeo and Juliet 1965,Je 21,36:3
White Devil, The 1965,D 7,56:1

Rose Tattoo, The 1966,O 21,36:2
Rose Tattoo, The 1966,N 20,II,1:1
Yerma 1966,D 9,60:1
Antigone 1967,Je 19,43:1
Merchant of Venice, The 1967,Je 22,46:2
Little Foxes, The 1967,O 27,53:1
Little Foxes, The 1967,N 5,II,1:1
Cuban Thing, The 1968,S 25,36:2
Horseman, Pass By 1969,Ja 16,46:4
Hamlet 1969,Je 30,33:1
Three Sisters, The 1969,Ag 4,29:1
Three Sisters, The 1969,Ag 10,II,3:1
Great White Hope, The 1969,S 27,26:1
Shepherd of Avenue B, The 1970,My 16,30:1

Tucci, Toni
Rat Race, The 1949,D 23,16:2

Tuck, Alice May
Junk 1927,Ja 6,25:1
Murray Hill 1927,S 30,29:1
Alice Sit-By-The-Fire 1932,Mr 8,19:3
Old Lady Shows Her Medals, The 1932,Mr 8,19:3
Back Fire 1932,Je 14,26:3
Late One Evening 1933,Ja 10,27:3
Double Door 1933,S 22,15:5

Tucker, Al
Old Bucks and New Wings 1962,N 6,39:4

Tucker, Arline
Polly Preferred 1923,Ja 12,13:3
Deacon, The 1925,N 25,14:3

Tucker, Bobby Quintet
Holiday on Broadway 1948,Ap 28,33:3

Tucker, Carl (Composer)
Fritzi 1935,D 21,10:3

Tucker, Charlene
Red, Hot and Blue! 1936,O 30,26:3

Tucker, Don (Composer)
Red, White and Maddox 1968,O 5,71:4

Tucker, Don (Director)
Red, White and Maddox 1969,Ja 27,27:1

Tucker, Don (Playwright)
Red, White and Maddox 1968,N 3,87:1
Red, White and Maddox 1969,Ja 27,27:1

Tucker, Dorothy
Pins and Needles 1939,Ap 21,26:2

Tucker, Duane
Dracula Sabbat 1970,O 2,28:2

Tucker, Earl (Snake Hips)
Vaudeville (Hollywood) 1932,F 16,24:3

Tucker, Ethel
Road Together, The 1924,Ja 18,21:2

Tucker, Eugenia
Chinese Nightingale, The 1934,O 6,20:4

Tucker, Forrest
Fair Game for Lovers 1964,F 11,43:2

Tucker, Harland
Indiscretion 1929,Mr 5,28:1
Made in France 1930,N 12,21:1
Inside Story, The 1932,F 23,23:2
Move on, Sister 1933,O 25,22:4
First Legion, The 1934,O 2,18:2
Valley Forge 1934,D 11,28:3
If This Be Treason 1935,S 24,28:2

Tucker, Helen
Pearl of Great Price, The 1926,N 2,34:3
He Loved the Ladies 1927,My 11,29:2
Social Register, The 1931,N 10,28:2

Tucker, Hobart
Romio and Julietta 1925,Ap 21,19:1
Fratricide Punished 1925,Ap 21,19:1
Dr Faustus 1926,O 27,25:5

Tucker, Ian
Peter Pan 1954,O 21,30:2
Greenwillow 1960,Mr 9,38:1
Midsummer Night's Dream, A 1967,Je 19,42:1
Antigone 1967,Je 19,43:1
Macbeth 1967,Jl 31,21:1
West Side Story 1968,Je 25,32:1

Tucker, Lorenzo
Make Me Know It 1929,N 5,32:5
Constant Sinner, The 1931,S 15,30:1
Ol' Man Satan 1932,O 4,26:3
Hummin' Sam 1933,Ap 10,8:8

Tucker, Marc (Lighting Director)
Here Comes Santa Claus 1962,My 18,34:1

Tucker, Michael
Prince of Peasantmania 1970,F 22,88:1
Night Thoreau Spent in Jail, The 1970,N 2,66:1

Tucker, Queenell
Don't Look Now! 1936,N 4,41:3

Tucker, Robert
Peter Pan 1954,O 21,30:2

Tucker, Robert (Choreographer)
Ice Capades 1955,S 15,38:1
Midsummer Night's Dream, A 1967,Je 19,42:1
Merchant of Venice, The 1967,Je 22,46:2

Tucker, Sophie
Vaudeville (Palace) 1923,Ap 3,26:4
Earl Carroll's Vanities 1924,S 11,23:6
Vaudeville (Palace) 1926,Ap 13,28:3
Rufus Le Maire's Affairs 1926,Jl 18,VII,1:7
Gay Paree 1927,Mr 22,31:1
Vaudeville (Palace) 1928,Ap 10,32:4
Vaudeville (Palace) 1928,O 9,35:2

Tucker, Sophie—Cont
Vaudeville (Palace) 1929,Je 17,29:3
Vaudeville (Palace) 1929,Je 24,27:4
Follow a Star 1930,S 18,28:2
Vaudeville (Palace) 1932,F 15,13:3
Vaudeville (Palace) 1932,F 6,18:2
Leave It to Me! 1938,O 23,IX,3:5
Leave It to Me! 1938,N 10,32:2
Leave It to Me! 1938,N 20,IX,1:1
Vacation Follies 1939,Ag 30,15:6
Leave It to Me! 1939,S 10,IX,1:1
Leave It to Me! 1940,Ja 18,27:2
High Kickers 1941,O 12,I,54:3
High Kickers 1941,N 1,21:2

Tucker, Theta
Cities in Bezique; Beast's Story, A 1969,Ja 13,26:1

Tucker, Wayne
Cradle Will Rock, The 1964,N 9,40:4
Cradle Will Rock, The 1964,N 9,40:4

Tucker, William
Nightingale, The 1927,Ja 4,20:4

Tuckerman, Maury
House of Fear, The 1929,O 8,34:2
Journey's End 1930,Ag 5,26:4
Merchant of Venice, The 1930,D 3,29:2
Widow in Green, A 1931,N 21,21:4
Alice Sit-By-The-Fire 1932,Mr 8,19:3
Cradle Snatchers 1932,N 17,23:2
May Wine 1935,D 6,30:3
Merry Wives of Windsor, The 1938,Ap 15,22:3
Hamlet 1938,O 13,28:1
Henry IV, Part I 1939,Ja 31,17:2
Hamlet 1939,D 5,35:2
In Bed We Cry 1944,N 15,20:2
Woman Bites Dog 1946,Ap 18,21:2
Grand Tour, The 1951,D 11,45:2

Tuckerman, Maury (Director)
Bernard Shaw Story, The 1965,N 19,31:1

Tuckerman, Maury (Miscellaneous)
Importance of Being Oscar, The 1961,Mr 15,45:2

Tuckinoff, David
Russian People, The 1942,D 30,17:2

Tudela, Alfonso
Road to Happiness, The 1927,My 3,24:1
Blind Heart, The 1927,My 8,30:2
Pygmalion 1927,My 12,25:2

Tuden, Fred
White Eagle, The 1927,D 27,24:4

Tuden, William T
That Smith Boy 1926,F 20,13:1

Tudor, Anthony (Choreographer)
Hollywood Pinafore 1945,Je 1,20:1
Hollywood Pinafore 1945,Je 17,II,4:5
Day Before Spring, The 1945,N 23,27:2
Day Before Spring, The 1945,D 2,II,1:1

Tudor, Henry O
Watched Pot, The 1933,My 5,13:7

Tudor, Jennifer
Hamlet 1969,My 2,38:1

Tudor, Ray
Leave It to Jane 1959,My 26,30:2
Madame Aphrodite 1961,D 30,13:1

Tudor, Roland
Sweethearts 1929,S 23,25:1
Mlle Modiste 1929,O 8,34:1

Tudor, Rowan
Well of Romance, The 1930,N 8,21:2
Up in Central Park 1945,Ja 29,17:2
Up in Central Park 1947,My 20,29:2
Flahooley 1951,My 15,39:1
Allegro 1952,S 18,36:3

Tudor-Barnes, Michael
Love for Love 1967,O 21,17:1

Tueller, George (Composer)
Angels on Earth 1929,D 11,34:7

Tuerk, John (Miscellaneous)
Command to Love, The 1927,S 21,27:1
Cafe 1930,Ag 29,11:1
Mackerel Skies 1934,Ja 24,20:4

Tuerk, John (Producer)
One of the Family 1925,D 23,22:3
Baby Mine 1927,Je 10,21:2
Furies, The 1928,Mr 8,23:1
Golden Age, The 1928,Ap 25,31:3
Strong Man's House, A 1929,Je 30,VIII,1:2
Strong Man's House, A 1929,S 17,34:3
Moor Born 1934,Ap 4,26:4
Moor Born 1934,Ap 8,X,2:7
Order Please 1934,O 10,21:2
Within the Gates 1934,O 23,23:1
Mother Lode 1934,D 24,16:5
Dominant Sex, The 1935,Ap 2,24:5
Crime Marches on 1935,O 24,19:1
Black Limelight 1936,N 10,31:1
Tell Me Pretty Maiden 1937,D 17,33:5
Come Across 1938,S 15,28:3
Romantic Mr Dickens 1940,D 3,33:2
Distant City, The 1941,S 23,27:5

Tuerk, Spencer
Free Soul, A 1928,Ja 13,26:5

Tufts, Jeanne
Out of My House 1942,Ja 8,28:6
Only the Heart 1942,D 7,22:3

Tufts, Jeanne—Cont
Relapse, The 1950,N 23,54:2
Tufts, Warner
Julius Caesar 1923,F 9,10:4
Tugend, Harry (Lyricist)
Ziegfeld Follies 1934,Ja 5,24:3
Tugend, Harry (Playwright)
Ziegfeld Follies 1934,Ja 5,24:3
Wayward Stork, The 1966,Ja 20,27:1
Tuite, Cyrilla
Geisha, The 1931,O 6,35:4
Tulane, Paul (Playwright)
Straw Hat, The 1926,O 15,20:2
Tull, Maurice C (Playwright)
Second Act, The 1927,My 5,30:1
Tull, Patrick
Astrakhan Coat, The 1967,Ja 13,18:1
Tuller, Joseph
Cornered 1920,D 9,18:2
Tuller, Morton
Dead End 1936,S 20,IX,3:7
Tulley, Tom
Chalked Out 1937,Mr 26,24:2
Tullman, Eleanor
Stronger, The 1949,Je 15,38:2
Tulloch, Jake
Hayride 1954,S 14,24:2
Tulloch, Lawrence
Way of the World, The 1924,N 18,23:4
Wild Birds 1925,Ap 10,16:1
Edgar Allan Poe 1925,O 6,31:1
Hamlet 1925,N 10,23:1
Tully, Gene
Recruiting Officer, The 1958,F 8,12:2
Tully, George
Meet the Wife 1927,Jl 3,VII,1:4
Tully, Jim (Original Author)
Outside Looking In 1925,S 13,VIII,1:1
Jarnegan 1928,S 25,29:2
Tully, Jim (Playwright)
Outside Looking In 1925,S 8,28:1
Black Boy 1926,S 26,VIII,2:7
Black Boy 1926,O 7,30:2
Tully, Milton
Merry Widow, The 1931,S 8,39:1
Geisha, The 1931,O 6,35:4
Tully, Phillip
Four O'Clock 1933,F 14,19:6
Iolanthe 1942,F 24,26:4
Gondoliers, The 1942,Mr 4,22:3
Tully, Richard Walton (Playwright)
Luana 1930,S 18,28:1
Tully, Tom
Call Me Ziggy 1937,F 13,9:6
White Steed, The 1939,Ja 11,16:2
Time of Your Life, The 1939,O 26,26:2
Night Music 1940,F 23,18:2
Time of Your Life, The 1940,S 24,27:2
Ah, Wilderness! 1941,O 3,26:2
Jason 1942,Ja 22,12:2
Strings, My Lord, Are False, The 1942,My 20,24:2
Sun Field, The 1942,D 10,33:2
Tulman, Eleanor
King Midas and the Golden Touch 1948,O 25,28:3
Tulmann, Alec
Low Bridge 1933,F 10,13:4
Tumarin, Boris
Emperor's New Clothes, The 1941,D 27,15:5
Winter Soldiers 1942,N 30,19:2
Family, The 1943,Mr 31,22:4
Victors, The 1948,D 27,17:2
Prescott Proposals, The 1953,D 17,53:1
Anastasia 1954,D 30,13:1
Anastasia 1955,Ja 16,II,1:1
Innkeepers, The 1956,F 3,19:1
Three Sisters, The 1959,S 22,46:1
Three Sisters, The 1959,O 4,II,1:1
Devil's Advocate, The 1961,Mr 10,20:1
Garden of Sweets, The 1961,N 1,35:1
Merchant of Venice, The 1962,F 3,13:2
Venus at Large 1962,Ap 13,30:1
Whisper Into My Good Ear 1962,O 2,47:1
Firebugs, The 1963,F 13,7:2
Traveller Without Luggage 1964,S 18,26:2
Giants' Dance, The 1964,N 17,48:2
Tenth Man, The 1967,N 9,54:1
Man in the Glass Booth, The 1968,S 27,41:1
Tumarin, Boris (Director)
Emperor's New Clothes, The 1941,D 27,15:5
Lamp at Midnight 1947,D 22,29:2
Blood Wedding 1949,F 7,16:2
Blood Wedding 1949,F 13,II,1:1
Sun and I, The 1949,Mr 21,18:4
House of Bernarda Alba, The 1951,Ja 8,14:6
Sands of the Negev 1954,O 20,32:1
Brothers Karamazov, The 1957,D 9,39:4
Idiot, The 1960,S 26,38:1
Montserrat 1961,Ja 9,30:5
Merchant of Venice, The 1962,F 3,13:2
Tumarin, Boris (Miscellaneous)
House of Bernarda Alba, The 1951,Ja 8,14:6
Tumarin, Boris (Playwright)
Brothers Karamazov, The 1957,D 9,39:4
Brothers Karamazov, The 1957,D 22,II,3:1

Idiot, The 1960,S 26,38:1
Tun, Tun
Saratoga 1959,D 8,59:4
Tunbridge, Joseph (Composer)
Dear Love 1930,My 18,VIII,3:1
Tell Her the Truth 1932,O 29,18:2
Big Business 1937,F 19,15:3
Tunbridge, Joseph (Lyricist)
Dear Love 1930,My 18,VIII,3:1
Tune, Tommy
Baker Street 1965,F 17,36:1
Joyful Noise, A 1966,D 16,57:1
How Now, Dow Jones 1967,D 8,53:1
Tunezi, Gene (Lighting Director)
Signs Along the Cynic Route 1961,D 15,49:5
Put It in Writing 1963,My 14,31:1
Tour De Four 1963,Je 19,41:1
Tunick, Jonathan (Miscellaneous)
All in Love 1961,N 11,15:2
Promises, Promises 1968,D 2,59:3
Tunick, Jonathan (Musical Director)
Company 1970,Ap 27,40:1
Tunisse, Bernard
Rosalinda; Fledermaus, Die 1942,O 29,26:5
Tunkel, Joseph (Playwright)
Jesters, The 1938,Mr 14,13:3
Tunkeler, Der (Playwright)
Should I Marry, or Shouldn't I? 1936,S 28,14:3
Tunnard, Peter
Possessed, The 1939,O 25,26:2
Tunney, Kieran (Playwright)
God and Kate Murphy 1959,F 27,21:2
Tuotti, Joseph Dolan (Original Author)
Buck White 1969,D 3,63:1
Tuotti, Joseph Dolan (Playwright)
Big Time Buck White 1968,D 9,58:1
Big Time Buck White 1968,D 15,II,5:1
Tupou, Manu
Indians 1969,My 27,43:1
Indians 1969,O 14,51:1
Indians 1969,O 19,II,1:1
Madwoman of Chaillot, The 1970,Mr 23,48:3
Tupper, Mary
Say It With Flowers 1926,D 6,29:1
Turash, Stephanie
Sunny River 1941,D 5,28:2
Jonah! 1966,F 16,52:1
Turaue, Mimi
Man of La Mancha 1965,N 23,52:1
Turegano, Ethel
Blue Butterfly, The 1929,F 17,29:3
Blue Butterfly, The 1929,My 4,17:2
Turenne, Louis
Devils, The 1965,N 17,51:2
Happy Birthday, Wanda June 1970,O 8,58:2
Happy Birthday, Wanda June 1970,O 18,II,1:1
Turgell, Edith
Let's Face It 1941,O 30,26:2
Jackpot 1944,Ja 14,15:2
Turgenev, Ivan (Original Author)
Journey of the Fifth Horse, The 1966,My 8,II,1:1
Turgenev, Ivan (Playwright)
Lady From the Provinces, The 1923,F 27,14:2
Lady From the Provinces, The 1923,Mr 4,VII,1:1
Month in the Country, A 1930,Mr 18,30:5
Month in the Country, A 1956,Ap 4,23:1
Month in the Country, A 1956,Ap 15,II,1:1
Month in the Country, A 1959,Mr 2,32:2
Month in the Country, A 1963,My 29,39:2
Turgeon, Peter
Brigadoon 1950,My 3,36:2
Live Wire, The 1950,Ag 18,16:2
Beggar's Opera, The 1957,Mr 14,35:1
Thurber Carnival, A 1960,F 27,13:2
Send Me No Flowers 1960,D 6,54:1
Little Me 1962,N 19,41:3
Turi, Yashi
Merton of the Movies 1922,N 14,16:2
Turk, David
Living Corpse, The 1929,D 7,19:1
Romeo and Juliet 1930,Ap 22,33:1
Liliom 1932,O 27,23:2
Dear Jane 1932,N 15,24:3
Tell My Story 1939,Mr 16,26:6
Turk, Lee
Arms for Venus 1937,Mr 12,18:7
Turk, Muriel
Point of No Return 1957,Mr 23,17:2
Turk, Philip (Miscellaneous)
Mike Downstairs 1968,Ap 19,35:1
I'm Solomon 1968,Ap 24,51:1
Turk, Robert (Choreographer)
Ice Capades 1967,Je 2,33:1
Ice Capades 1969,Ja 8,42:1
Ice Capades 1970,Ja 7,35:1
Turk, Robert (Director)
Ice Capades 1967,Je 2,33:1
Ice Capades 1969,Ja 8,42:1
Ice Capades 1970,Ja 7,35:1
Turk, Robert (Miscellaneous)
Ice Capades 1970,Ja 7,35:1
Turke, Roy (Composer)
Plantation Revue, The 1922,Jl 18,18:4

Turke, Roy (Lyricist)
Plantation Revue, The 1922,Jl 18,18:4
Dixie to Broadway 1924,O 30,22:1
Turkenich, Sylvia (Miscellaneous)
Cocktails of 1934 1934,My 5,22:1
Turkewitz, Bernice (Miscellaneous)
Jackass, The 1960,Mr 24,39:2
Turkil, Lou
Stop Press 1939,Mr 20,13:2
Turkington, Brian
Journey of the Fifth Horse, The 1966,Ap 22,36:1
Richard III 1966,Ag 11,26:1
Turkoff, Jonas (Director)
House on Grand Street, A 1953,O 10,12:6
Devil's Game, A 1959,N 9,35:6
Turl, Carfax
And So to Bed 1927,N 10,23:1
Turleigh, Veronica
Laughing Woman, The 1934,Ap 8,33:6
Laughing Lady, The 1934,My 6,IX,2:5
Dog Beneath the Skin, The 1936,F 23,X,1:3
Agamemnon 1936,N 2,25:6
Turley, Dianne
Corruption in the Palace of Justice 1963,O 9,49:2
Turmail, R
Connelly vs Connelly 1961,F 18,11:3
Turman, Glynn
Raisin in the Sun, A 1959,Mr 12,27:1
Who's Got His Own 1966,O 13,52:1
Junebug Graduates Tonight! 1967,F 27,35:1
Harpers Ferry 1967,Je 6,52:2
Visit, The 1967,S 13,41:1
Turn, David
Spring in Autumn 1937,Ag 17,23:1
Turnage, Wayne
Help! Help! the Globolinks 1970,D 24,10:2
Turnbull, Alexander
Gypsy Baron, The 1944,Je 15,17:3
Turnbull, Deborah
Winter's Tale, The 1958,Jl 23,34:3
Turnbull, Glenn
Call Me Mister 1946,Ap 19,26:2
Turnbull, John R
Crooked Friday, The 1925,O 9,27:3
Offence, The 1925,N 16,25:1
Murder on the Second Floor 1929,S 12,35:1
Geneva 1940,Ja 31,15:2
Turnbull, John R (Director)
Offence, The 1925,N 16,25:1
Turnby, Otto
Sign of the Leopard 1928,D 12,34:4
Turnell, Edythia
Three to Make Ready 1946,Mr 8,16:2
Turner, Alden
Present Laughter 1946,O 30,31:2
Druid Circle, The 1947,O 23,29:5
Turner, Ann
School for Brides 1944,Ag 2,19:4
Turner, Bridget
Semi-Detached 1963,O 8,49:1
Erb 1970,Ap 9,49:1
Turner, Bunty
My Fair Lady 1959,Ja 27,26:1
Turner, Charles
Revenger's Tragedy, The 1970,D 2,58:1
Turner, Charles (Lyricist)
Sweeney Todd 1957,Ag 28,21:4
Turner, Charles (Miscellaneous)
Electra 1969,Ag 8,14:1
Turner, Charles (Musical Director)
Dynamite Tonight 1964,Mr 16,36:2
Turner, Claramae
Mikado, The 1959,O 2,24:1
Iolanthe 1962,Ap 12,42:4
Gondoliers, The 1962,Ap 19,34:2
Patience 1964,Mr 26,42:1
Gondoliers, The 1965,Mr 28,14:1
Patience 1965,Ap 16,34:1
Mikado, The 1965,Ap 17,11:3
Patience 1968,My 16,52:1
Fiesta in Madrid 1969,My 29,49:1
Turner, Clyde
Conjur 1938,N 1,27:2
Annie Get Your Gun 1946,My 17,14:2
Four Saints in Three Acts 1952,Ap 17,35:1
Carmen Jones 1956,Je 1,28:2
Porgy and Bess 1964,My 7,32:1
Turner, David (Playwright)
Semi-Detached 1962,D 6,54:3
Semi-Detached 1963,O 8,49:1
Semi-Detached 1963,O 20,II,1:1
Turner, David Anthony (Translator)
Oedipus 1968,Ap 2,54:1
Oedipus 1968,Jl 31,29:1
Turner, Dorothy
Swing It 1937,Jl 23,17:2
Turner, Douglas
Raisin in the Sun, A 1959,Mr 12,27:1
Pullman Car Hiawatha 1962,D 4,46:2
Coriolanus 1965,Jl 15,23:1
Happy Ending 1965,N 16,56:1
Day of Absence 1965,N 16,56:1
Kongi's Harvest 1968,Ap 15,49:1

Turner, Douglas—Cont
Daddy Goodness 1968,Je 5,37:1
Ceremonies in Dark Old Men 1969,F 6,33:1
Ceremonies in Dark Old Men 1969,F 23,II,5:1
Reckoning, The 1969,S 5,28:1
Harangues, The 1970,Ja 14,42:1
Harangues, The 1970,Ja 25,II,1:4

Turner, Eva
Hoofers, The 1969,Jl 30,23:4

Turner, Eve
Escape Me Not 1933,D 9,18:6
Escape Me Never! 1935,Ja 22,22:2

Turner, Florence
Sign of the Leopard 1928,D 12,34:4

Turner, Frances
Elizabeth Sleeps Out 1936,Ap 21,27:6

Turner, Gene
Hollywood Ice Revue 1942,Ja 20,26:4

Turner, George
Old Maid, The 1949,Ja 27,20:6
Dandy Dick 1956,Ja 11,37:2
Apple Cart, The 1956,O 19,23:1
Flowering Cherry 1959,O 22,46:1
Complaisant Lover, The 1961,N 2,43:2
Crucible, The 1964,Ap 7,30:2
Entertaining Mr Sloane 1965,O 13,41:1
Sambo 1969,D 22,42:1
Sambo 1970,Jl 23,24:1

Turner, Holly
Generation 1965,O 8,5:6

Turner, Jerry (Director)
Henry VI, Part I 1964,Jl 23,18:1

Turner, John
Scaramouche 1923,O 25,14:2
Taming of the Shrew, The 1927,O 26,26:4
Twelfth Night 1966,Je 10,51:2

Turner, John (Playwright)
Two by Two 1925,F 24,17:1
Queen Mab 1925,My 3,VIII,2:1
His Queen 1925,My 12,26:1
Scarlet Lady, The 1926,O 17,VIII,2:1
Spot on the Sun, The 1927,Jl 24,VII,1:7
Spot on the Sun, The 1927,D 25,VIII,2:3
Lord of the Manor, The 1928,O 14,X,2:1
Wake Up and Dream 1929,Ap 14,X,1:8
Wake Up and Dream 1929,D 31,14:3
Plus ca Change 1930,F 26,22:3
To Account Rendered 1931,Ja 24,15:3
To Account Rendered 1931,F 15,VIII,2:5
Punchinello 1932,Mr 27,VIII,2:1
This Inconstancy 1933,Mr 25,13:6
This Inconstancy 1933,Ap 16,IX,1:3
For the Defense 1935,F 27,17:3
For the Defense; There Go All of Us
 1935,Mr 24,VIII,2:3

Turner, Lavina
Turpentine 1936,Je 27,21:6

Turner, Lily (Miscellaneous)
House of Bernarda Alba, The 1951,Ja 8,14:6
Brothers Karamazov, The 1957,D 9,39:4

Turner, Lily (Producer)
O Marry Me 1961,O 28,13:1
Dodo Bird, The 1967,D 9,62:1
Peddler, The 1967,D 9,62:1

Turner, Lou
Spring Fever 1925,Ag 4,14:2
Free Soul, A 1928,Ja 13,26:5

Turner, Maidel
Martinique 1920,Ap 27,18:2
Varying Shore, The 1921,D 6,24:1
Egotist, The 1922,D 27,12:1
Book of Charm, The 1925,S 4,26:3
Book of Charm, The 1925,S 13,VIII,1:1
Tommy 1927,Ja 11,36:4
Spring Is Here 1929,Mr 12,26:1
Apron Strings 1930,F 18,28:2
Angel Island 1937,O 21,26:2
What a Life 1938,Ap 14,26:2
Mrs O'Brien Entertains 1939,F 9,16:3
Glamour Preferred 1940,N 16,13:2
By Jupiter 1942,Je 4,22:1
Dark of the Moon 1945,Mr 15,27:2
State of the Union 1945,N 15,25:2

Turner, Martha
Babes in Arms 1951,Mr 10,7:3

Turner, Maud
Hobo 1931,F 12,24:4
Before Morning 1933,F 10,13:4

Turner, Michael
Noye's Fludde 1959,Mr 17,41:2

Turner, Myrtle
Peter Rabbit 1928,D 27,26:4
Sinbad the Sailor 1929,D 27,26:5

Turner, Nelson
Creoles 1927,S 23,33:3

Turner, Pat
Can-Can 1953,My 8,28:1
Can-Can 1959,Ag 26,25:4
Fiorello! 1959,N 24,45:3
Wonderful Town 1963,F 15,10:2
Pal Joey 1963,My 30,21:1

Turner, Peter (Miscellaneous)
Universal Nigger, The 1970,Mr 21,18:1

Turner, Ret (Costume Designer)
Vintage '60 1960,S 13,41:1

Turner, Robert
Summer Wives 1936,Ap 14,18:1
Lute Song 1946,F 7,29:2

Turner, Roland (Miscellaneous)
In Circles 1967,O 14,12:1

Turner, Roland (Scenic Designer)
In Circles 1967,O 14,12:1
In Circles 1968,Je 28,36:1

Turner, Sanders (Sandy)
Mister Roberts 1948,F 19,27:2

Turner, Stanley
Around the World 1946,Je 1,9:5

Turner, Susanne
Geneva 1940,Ja 31,15:2
Good Neighbor 1941,O 22,26:2

Turner, Terri
Henry V 1965,Je 29,27:2
Taming of the Shrew, The 1965,Jl 3,10:5
White Devil, The 1965,D 7,56:1
Bungler, The 1968,Ag 2,24:1

Turner, Violet
Peter Rabbit 1928,D 27,26:4
Sinbad the Sailor 1929,D 27,26:5

Turner, W J (Playwright)
Man Who Ate the Popomack, The 1924,Mr 25,24:1
Man Who Ate the Popomack, The
 1924,Mr 30,VIII,1:1
Man Who Ate the Popomack, The
 1924,Ap 6,VIII,1:1

Turner, William H
Reflected Glory 1936,S 18,19:5
Reflected Glory 1936,S 22,30:2

Turney, Catherine (Playwright)
Bitter Harvest 1936,Mr 1,IX,3:6
Bitter Harvest 1936,My 13,28:1
My Dear Children 1939,Mr 25,19:6
My Dear Children 1940,F 1,16:2

Turney, Hazel
Six-Fifty, The 1921,O 25,20:1

Turney, Katherine (Playwright)
One More Genius 1936,Ag 11,24:6

Turney, Nadyne
Rose 1969,O 29,30:1

Turney, Robert
Streets of New York, The 1931,O 7,29:1

Turney, Robert (Miscellaneous)
Trojan Women, The 1941,Ap 9,32:5

Turney, Robert (Playwright)
Daughters of Atreus 1936,O 15,33:1
Secret Room, The 1945,N 8,16:2

Turnley, Peggy
Street Scene 1947,Ja 10,17:2
Regina 1949,N 1,32:2
Under Milk Wood 1957,O 16,42:5

Turoff, Robert (Director)
Madame Aphrodite 1961,D 30,13:1
Golden Apple, The 1962,F 13,38:2

Turpin, Allan (Playwright)
Turn of the Screw 1946,O 28,19:2

Turpin, Harry
Bombo 1921,O 7,20:2

Tury, Bill (Director)
Ice Follies 1969,My 23,38:1
Ice Follies 1970,My 23,27:1

Tushar, James
All in One; Trouble in Tahiti 1955,Ap 20,40:3

Tushinsky, Joseph S (Musical Director)
New Moon, The 1942,Ag 19,14:2

Tushinsky, Joseph S (Producer)
Chocolate Soldier, The 1942,Je 24,22:2
Merry Widow, The 1942,Jl 16,22:1

Tuso, Frederick
Emerald Slippers, The 1970,S 2,31:2

Tutin, Dorothy
Living Room, The 1953,Ap 17,29:5
I Am a Camera 1954,Mr 13,11:1
I Am a Camera 1954,Ap 11,II,2:1
Lark, The 1955,My 13,21:2
Lark, The 1955,My 29,II,1:1
Wild Duck, The 1956,Ja 8,II,3:1
Lark, The 1956,Ja 8,II,3:1
Once More With Feeling 1959,Jl 10,30:1
Merchant of Venice, The 1960,Ap 13,46:5
Twelfth Night 1960,My 18,48:6
Romeo and Juliet 1961,Ag 16,36:3
Othello 1961,O 11,53:6
Hollow Crown, The 1963,Ja 31,5:1
Portrait of a Queen 1965,My 7,35:5
Portrait of a Queen 1968,F 29,29:1
Play on Love 1970,Ja 16,31:1

Tutt, Dorothy (Miscellaneous)
Pictures in the Hallway 1956,S 17,23:2

Tutt, J Homer
Deep Harlem 1929,Ja 8,35:2
Ginger Snaps 1930,Ja 1,30:5
Green Pastures, The 1930,F 27,26:1
Green Pastures, The 1930,F 27,26:1
Green Pastures, The 1935,F 27,16:2
How Come Lawd? 1937,O 1,18:5
Zunguru 1938,Ag 7,IX,8:2

Tutt, J Homer (Director)
Ginger Snaps 1930,Ja 1,30:5

Tutt, J Homer (Lyricist)
Deep Harlem 1929,Ja 8,35:2
Deep Harlem 1929,Ja 8,35:2
Ginger Snaps 1930,Ja 1,30:5

Tutt, J Homer (Playwright)
Ginger Snaps 1930,Ja 1,30:5

Tutt, Steve
Marie Vison, La 1970,Jl 15,29:1

Tuttle, Anthony
Winesburg, Ohio 1958,F 6,22:2

Tuttle, Anthony (Miscellaneous)
Antigone 1959,S 16,46:2

Tuttle, Barbara (Miscellaneous)
Scent of Flowers, A 1969,O 21,42:1
One Night Stands of a Noisy Passenger; Noisy
 Passenger, The 1970,D 31,8:3
One Night Stands of a Noisy Passenger; Passage,
 Un 1970,D 31,8:3
One Night Stands of a Noisy Passenger; Last
 Stand 1970,D 31,8:3

Tuttle, Barry C (Lighting Director)
Stage Affair, A 1962,Ja 17,30:2

Tuttle, Barry C (Producer)
Stage Affair, A 1962,Ja 17,30:2

Tuttle, Barry C (Scenic Designer)
Stage Affair, A 1962,Ja 17,30:2

Tuttle, Bess
Two Orphans, The 1926,Ap 6,26:2

Tuttle, Dave (Producer)
Personal Appearance 1936,Je 16,23:4

Tuttle, Day
Bad Habits of 1926 1926,My 1,11:1
Orphee 1935,Mr 23,10:3
Candida 1938,Ag 31,13:2
Book of Job, The 1962,F 10,13:1

Tuttle, Day (Director)
Front Page, The 1935,Jl 9,24:4
Patience 1935,S 3,24:4
Deputy of Paris, The 1947,Mr 22,9:5
In Good King Charles's Golden Days
 1957,Ja 25,16:1
In Good King Charles's Golden Days
 1957,F 3,II,1:1
Lysistrata 1959,My 20,40:2

Tuttle, Day (Miscellaneous)
Retreat From Folly 1937,Je 29,18:3
Family Portrait 1939,Mr 9,18:4
Charley's Aunt 1940,O 18,24:2
E-MC2 1948,Je 16,36:2
Curtains Up! 1959,N 3,26:3

Tuttle, Day (Producer)
Front Page, The 1935,Jl 9,24:4
Patsy, The 1935,Jl 16,24:1
Post Road 1935,Jl 23,24:3
Hay Fever 1935,Ag 6,20:3
Caste 1935,Ag 13,20:3
Patience 1935,S 3,24:4
Personal Appearance 1936,Je 23,27:3
Fresh Fields 1936,Je 23,27:3
They Knew What They Wanted 1936,Jl 28,23:4
Pomeroy's Past 1936,Ag 4,15:2
Elizabeth the Queen 1936,Ag 4,15:2
School for Scandal, The 1940,Je 18,29:5
Life of Reilly, The 1942,Ap 30,13:2
Lysistrata 1959,My 20,40:2
Book of Job, The 1962,F 10,13:1

Tuttle, Evelyn
Veronica's Veil 1950,F 12,II,1:5

Tuttle, F Day
Faun, The 1924,F 6,19:2
Faun, The 1924,Mr 28,17:2
Galloper, The 1924,D 19,26:2
Murder in the Cathedral 1935,D 21,11:3

Tuttle, F W
Successful Calamity, A 1921,Mr 19,11:2

Tuttle, Jay (Producer)
Smiling Through 1935,Jl 30,17:2

Tuttle, Preston
Lady Precious Stream 1936,Ja 28,15:2

Tuzlukov, Boris (Scenic Designer)
Aladdin and His Wonderful Lamp 1963,O 21,39:1

Twachtman, David M (Scenic Designer)
Shadow and Substance 1938,Ja 27,16:2

Twain, Joan
Red Poppy, The 1922,D 21,18:2

Twain, Mark (Original Author)
Prince and the Pauper, The 1920,N 2,15:1
Prince and the Pauper, The 1920,N 7,VII,1:1
Prince and the Pauper, The 1920,N 21,VI,1:4
Joan of Arc 1926,Ap 24,21:2
Joan of Arc 1927,Ap 15,26:2
Connecticut Yankee, A 1927,O 9,VIII,1:3
Connecticut Yankee, A 1927,N 4,24:2
Tom Sawyer 1931,D 26,15:3
Connecticut Yankee, A 1943,N 18,30:2
Tom Sawyer - Ballad of the Mississippi
 1947,D 27,11:3
Livin' the Life 1957,Ap 29,20:1
Tom Sawyer 1958,Jl 15,21:8
Mark Twain Tonight! 1960,S 2,17:6
Mark Twain Tonight! 1960,N 13,1:2

Twain, Mark (Original Author)—Cont
Huckleberry 1962,Je 3,43:1
Twain, Mark (Playwright)
Mark Twain Tonight! 1959,Ap 7,40:2
Half Horse, Half Alligator 1966,Mr 14,37:2
Diary of Adam and Eve, The 1966,O 19,53:1
Twain, Michael
Kill the One-Eyed Man 1965,O 21,56:1
Empire Builders, The 1968,O 2,34:1
Twain, Michael (Producer)
Empire Builders, The 1968,O 2,34:1
Twain, Norman (Producer)
Golden Six, The 1958,O 27,31:2
Distant Bell, A 1960,Ja 14,29:1
Roots 1961,Mr 7,40:2
Lady of the Camellias, The 1963,Mr 22,7:1
Traveller Without Luggage 1964,S 18,26:2
Bajour 1964,N 24,42:1
Peterpat 1965,Ja 7,27:1
World of Charles Aznavour, The 1965,O 15,49:1
Gilbert Becaud on Broadway 1966,N 1,35:1
Apparition Theater of Prague, The 1966,N 17,56:2
Henry, Sweet Henry 1967,O 24,51:2
Gilbert Becaud Sings Love 1968,O 7,53:5
Cop-Out 1969,Ap 8,42:1
Home Fires 1969,Ap 8,42:1
Hamlet 1969,My 2,38:1
Charles Aznavour 1970,F 5,32:4
Twamley, Mark
Arsenic and Old Lace 1943,D 13,18:6
Twardowski, Hans Von
Hetaerengespraeche 1927,Ja 9,VII,4:1
Anne of England 1941,O 8,26:2
Twardowski, Hans Von (Director)
Shakespeare's Merchant 1939 1939,Ja 10,16:3
Twardowski, Hans Von (Playwright)
Shakespeare's Merchant 1939 1939,Ja 10,16:3
Twardy, Ray
Viva O'Brien 1941,O 10,27:2
Tweddell, Frank
Peace Palace 1933,Je 6,30:2
Peace on Earth 1933,N 30,39:2
White Hell 1935,Ag 13,20:3
Let Freedom Ring 1935,N 7,26:2
Hell Freezes Over 1935,D 30,14:2
Prelude 1936,Ap 20,17:4
Bury the Dead 1936,Ap 20,17:4
200 Were Chosen 1936,N 21,21:1
Around the Corner 1936,D 29,17:2
Abe Lincoln in Illinois 1938,O 17,12:2
Claudia 1941,F 13,24:2
Suds in Your Eye 1944,Ja 13,15:5
Thank You Svoboda 1944,Mr 2,13:2
Pick-Up Girl 1944,My 4,25:2
Strange Fruit 1945,N 30,18:6
Iceman Cometh, The 1946,O 10,31:3
Our Lan' 1947,S 29,16:5
Story for Strangers, A 1948,S 22,39:2
Two Blind Mice 1949,Mr 3,32:2
Mr Barry's Etchings 1950,F 1,26:2
Borned in Texas 1950,Ag 22,30:6
Golden State, The 1950,N 27,29:3
Southwest Corner, The 1955,F 4,18:2
Legend of Lizzie, The 1959,F 10,39:1
Whisper to Me 1960,N 22,38:6
Calculated Risk 1962,N 1,35:1
Fade Out--Fade In 1964,My 27,45:1
Tweed, Barbette
King Lear 1968,N 8,43:1
Tweed, Frank
Windows 1923,O 9,17:2
Saint Joan 1923,D 29,8:4
Tweeddell, Frank
Petrified Forest, The 1935,Ja 8,26:1
Twelve Paraders
Laugh Parade, The 1931,S 20,VIII,3:1
Twelvetrees, Clark
Hot Money 1931,N 9,22:2
Iron Men 1936,O 20,30:6
Twelvetrees, Helen
Boudoir 1941,F 8,18:4
Arsenic and Old Lace 1941,Mr 25,26:7
Arsenic and Old Lace 1944,Jl 3,7:3
Twelvetrees, Jason
Hamlet 1969,My 2,38:1
Twiner, Clyde
Porgy and Bess 1961,My 18,40:1
Twiss, J O (Playwright)
Heritage 1933,Je 4,IX,1:3
Twitchell, Arthur C Jr (Miscellaneous)
First Gentleman, The 1957,Ap 26,22:2
Love Me Little 1958,Ap 15,42:2
Twombley, Roland
Juarez and Maximilian 1926,O 12,31:1
Rapid Transit 1927,Ap 8,21:2
Ten Nights in a Barroom 1928,Mr 28,31:2
Twomey, Kay (Composer)
Girl From Nantucket, The 1945,N 9,17:2
Twomey, Neil (Playwright)
No More Women 1926,Ag 4,17:2
That French Lady 1927,Mr 16,29:3
Twyman, Louise
Porgy and Bess 1935,O 11,30:2
Sweet River 1936,O 29,30:2

Tyana, Olivette
Jumbo 1935,N 18,20:2
Tyeerof
Bagrovyostrov 1928,D 16,III,3:5
Tyen, Joan (Lighting Director)
Shake Hands With the Devil 1949,O 21,30:4
Tyers, John
Vie Parisienne, La 1941,N 6,20:3
Winged Victory 1943,N 22,24:1
Gypsy Lady 1946,S 18,25:6
Inside U S A 1948,Mr 30,27:3
Inside U S A 1948,My 1,19:2
Old Maid and the Thief, The 1949,N 7,32:4
Fledermaus, Die 1954,My 20,38:5
All in One; Trouble in Tahiti 1955,Ap 20,40:3
Tylbor, Sylvia
Trees Die Standing, The 1969,O 13,52:1
Mirele Efros 1969,D 26,41:1
Tyler, Betty Jane
County Chairman, The 1936,My 26,26:5
Tyler, Beverly
Firebird of Florence 1945,Mr 23,13:4
Tyler, Converse
Hell's Bells! 1925,Ja 27,14:2
Grand Duchess and the Waiter, The
1925,O 14,31:1
Cradle Snatchers 1932,N 17,23:2
Tyler, Dallas
Out of Step 1925,Ja 30,12:1
Tyler, E Royall (Playwright)
Contrast, The 1940,Mr 26,17:2
Tyler, Ed (Composer)
Sweet Miani 1962,S 26,33:2
Tyler, Ed (Lyricist)
Sweet Miani 1962,S 26,33:2
Tyler, Edward
Porgy and Bess 1943,S 14,26:2
Carmen Jones 1943,D 3,26:2
Tyler, Elizabeth
At the Gate of the Kingdom 1927,D 9,28:5
People on the Hill 1931,S 26,25:5
Tyler, Francis
Girofle-Girofla 1926,N 24,26:2
Falstaff 1928,D 26,14:2
Mikado, The 1932,Jl 29,18:4
School for Husbands, The 1933,O 17,26:5
Tyler, Franklin
Assorted Nuts 1940,Ap 7,I,44:6
Tyler, Franklin (Composer)
Assorted Nuts 1940,Ap 7,I,44:6
Tyler, Franklin (Lyricist)
Assorted Nuts 1940,Ap 7,I,44:6
Tyler, George C (Director)
Plough and the Stars, The 1927,N 29,30:2
Out of the Sea 1927,D 6,26:2
Juno and the Paycock 1927,D 20,32:2
Tyler, George C (Miscellaneous)
She Stoops to Conquer 1928,My 20,VIII,1:1
Tyler, George C (Playwright)
Admirable Crichton, The 1931,Mr 10,23:2
Tyler, George C (Producer)
Foot-Loose 1920,Ag 15,VI,1:1
We Moderns 1924,Mr 12,17:2
Young Woodley 1925,N 3,34:1
School for Scandal, The 1925,D 7,18:2
School for Scandal, The 1925,D 13,IX,3:1
Constant Nymph, The 1926,D 10,31:1
Tommy 1927,Ja 11,36:4
Trelawney of the 'Wells' 1927,F 1,24:4
Adventurous Age, The 1927,F 8,20:1
Behold This Dreamer 1927,N 1,20:4
Spellbound 1927,N 15,26:2
Spellbound 1927,N 20,IX,1:1
She Stoops to Conquer 1928,My 15,17:1
Diplomacy 1928,My 29,16:3
Diplomacy 1928,Je 3,VIII,1:1
Macbeth 1928,N 20,28:3
Jim the Penman 1928,D 2,X,4:2
Mrs Bumpstead-Leigh 1929,Ap 2,28:3
Houseparty 1929,S 10,26:5
Sweet Land of Liberty 1929,S 24,29:2
Ladies of the Jury 1929,O 6,IX,1:4
Ladies of the Jury 1929,O 22,26:2
Your Uncle Dudley 1929,N 19,26:4
Sherlock Holmes 1929,N 26,28:3
It's a Grand Life 1930,F 11,30:3
Rivals, The 1930,Mr 14,24:4
Mr Samuel 1930,O 26,VIII,3:5
Mr Samuel 1930,N 11,28:4
Colonel Satan 1931,Ja 12,24:1
For Valor 1935,N 19,27:5
Tyler, Harry
Shannons of Broadway, The 1927,S 27,30:4
Privilege Car 1931,Mr 4,33:1
Collision 1932,F 17,19:2
Lambs Gambol 1932,Ap 25,18:2
Clear All Wires! 1932,S 15,19:1
Clear All Wires! 1932,S 25,IX,1:1
American, Very Early 1934,Ja 31,21:2
Whatever Goes Up 1935,N 26,28:2

Tyler, Jack
Man on Stilts, The 1931,S 10,23:2
Children's Hour, The 1934,N 21,23:2
Now You've Done It 1937,Mr 6,10:4
Our Betters 1937,Jl 22,16:2
Escape This Night 1938,Ap 23,18:1
Tyler, James
Golden Age, The 1963,N 19,49:2
Tyler, Janet
Suds in Your Eye 1944,Ja 13,15:5
Harvey 1944,N 2,23:2
Tyler, Jeanne
Lady Comes Across, The 1942,Ja 10,10:2
Tyler, Jim (Miscellaneous)
Half a Sixpence 1965,Ap 26,38:2
Celebration 1969,Ja 23,55:2
Gantry 1970,F 16,44:1
Tyler, Judy
Pipe Dream 1955,D 1,44:1
Pipe Dream 1955,D 11,II,5:1
Tyler, Lelah
30 Days Hath September 1938,O 1,10:5
Heads or Tails 1947,My 3,10:6
Tyler, Maurice
Blossom Time 1931,Mr 5,32:1
Tyler, Mel
Killers 1928,Mr 14,28:3
Troika 1930,Ap 2,32:6
Man on Stilts, The 1931,S 10,23:2
Merry-Go-Round 1932,Ap 23,11:2
Sojourner Truth 1948,Ap 22,35:2
Tyler, Phyllis
Coquette 1927,N 9,23:1
Moon Vine, The 1943,F 12,22:2
Tyler, Richard
Macbeth 1941,N 12,30:2
Moon Vine, The 1943,F 12,22:2
Tomorrow the World 1943,Ap 15,22:2
Christopher Blake 1946,D 2,33:2
Christopher Blake 1946,D 8,II,5:1
Tyler, Royall (Playwright)
Contrast, The 1926,O 1,26:2
Tyler, Veronica
Porgy and Bess 1964,My 7,32:1
Tyman, Joseph (Miscellaneous)
Hero of Santa Maria, The 1926,My 1,10:1
Man of Destiny, The 1926,My 1,10:1
Tynan, Brandon
Purple Mask, The 1920,Ja 6,18:1
Purple Mask, The 1920,Ja 11,VIII,2:1
Ziegfeld Midnight Frolic 1920,Mr 17,14:2
Mandarin, The 1920,N 10,18:2
Tyranny of Love, The 1921,My 3,20:2
Tyranny of Love, The 1921,My 8,VI,1:1
Ziegfeld Follies 1922,Je 6,18:2
Ziegfeld Follies 1923,Ja 30,12:2
Ziegfeld Follies 1924,Je 25,26:1
Lambs Gambol 1925,Ap 27,15:1
Human Nature 1925,S 25,24:3
That French Lady 1927,Mr 16,29:3
Interference 1928,My 8,25:4
Devil's Mistress, The 1929,Mr 10,X,4:5
Night Remembers, The 1934,N 28,24:3
Three Wise Fools 1936,Ja 14,25:2
Three Wise Fools 1936,Mr 2,12:2
Tynan, Brandon (Playwright)
Tavern, The 1921,Ja 23,VI,1:1
Tynan, Kenneth (Miscellaneous)
Soldiers 1968,My 2,58:1
Oh! Calcutta! 1969,Je 18,33:1
Oh! Calcutta! 1970,Jl 29,30:1
Tynan, Kenneth (Playwright)
Oh! Calcutta! 1969,Je 18,33:1
Oh! Calcutta! 1969,Je 29,II,1:7
Tynan, Kenneth (Producer)
Soldiers 1968,D 14,62:5
Tynan, Leonard J (Playwright)
Lingering Past, The 1932,Je 30,26:5
Tyne, George
Sound of Hunting, A 1945,N 21,16:6
See the Jaguar 1952,D 4,46:2
Threepenny Opera, The 1954,Mr 11,26:5
Lunatics and Lovers 1954,D 14,44:2
Lovers 1956,My 11,23:1
Too Late the Phalarope 1956,O 12,35:1
Hotel Paradiso 1957,Ap 12,22:2
Country Wife, The 1957,N 28,56:1
Tyne, Joan (Lighting Director)
City of Kings 1949,F 18,27:2
Tyner, Charles
Johnny Johnson 1956,O 22,24:1
Orpheus Descending 1957,Mr 22,28:1
Under Milk Wood 1957,O 16,42:5
Bed Time 1958,Ap 11,20:2
Sweet Bird of Youth 1959,Mr 11,39:2
Sweet Bird of Youth 1959,Mr 22,II,1:1
One Flew Over the Cuckoo's Nest 1963,N 14,40:2
Tyra, Dan
Where People Gather 1967,O 26,56:1
Tyre, Virginia
Gondoliers, The 1944,F 22,26:3
Tyrrell, Ann
Infernal Machine, The 1937,D 13,22:7
Elizabeth the Queen 1941,O 17,27:2

Tyrrell, Dave
R U R 1942,D 4,30:2
Night Watch In Syria 1943,Ja 5,15:5
Goose for the Gander, A 1945,Ja 24,16:4
Love Goes to Press 1947,Ja 2,22:2
Open House 1947,Je 4,33:4
Tyrrell, Norman
Sappho 1961,Ag 23,28:5
Tyrrell, Rose
Jubilee 1935,O 14,20:1
Tyrrell, Susan
In the Summer House 1964,Mr 26,43:1
Until the Monkey Comes 1966,Je 21,38:1
Rimers of Eldritch, The 1967,F 21,53:1
Cry of Players, A 1968,N 15,40:1
Invitation to a Beheading 1969,Mr 18,36:1
Time of Your Life, The 1969,N 7,37:1
Camino Real 1970,Ja 9,42:1
Tyrrell, Tom
Country Wife, The 1955,Ap 6,35:1
Tyrrell, William J
Laugh It Off 1934,Ap 5,24:2
Tysick, Sylvia
Stop the World-I Want to Get Off 1962,O 4,45:4
Tyson, Cicely
Blacks, The 1961,My 5,23:1
Moon on a Rainbow Shawl 1962,Ja 16,30:1
Tiger Tiger Burning Bright 1962,D 24,5:2
Blue Boy in Black, The 1963,My 1,32:1
Trumpets of the Lord 1963,D 23,22:3
Hand Is on the Gate, A 1966,S 22,54:1
Carry Me Back to Morningside Heights 1968,F 28,41:1
To Be Young Gifted and Black; World of Lorraine Hansberry, The 1969,Ja 3,15:1
Trumpets of the Lord 1969,Ap 30,37:1
Tyson, Joan
Bugs 1965,N 19,31:1
Elizabeth the Queen 1966,N 4,30:1
Tyson, Ruth (Director)
Holiday on Ice 1966,S 1,30:1
Holiday on Ice 1967,Ag 31,29:2
Tyson, Ruth (Playwright)
Holiday on Ice 1967,Ag 31,29:2
Tyson, Ruth (Producer)
Holiday on Ice 1965,S 2,38:4
Tyson, Tara
Foreplay 1970,D 11,58:2
Tyszka, Walter
Shunned 1960,D 21,39:1
Tzesler, Samuel (Translator)
King And the Cobbler, The 1954,D 13,33:6

U

Ucci, Toni
Rugantino 1964,F 7,34:1
Uchin, Jerry
War and Peace 1942,My 22,26:3
Udall (Playwright)
Ralph Roister Doister 1932,Ag 28,IX,1:1
Udane, Edythe
Lotte Goslar's Pantomime Circus-For Humans Only 1957,D 17,45:1
Udell, Peggy
Wonderful Night, A; Fledermaus, Die 1929,N 1,23:3
Udell, Peter (Lyricist)
Purlie 1970,Mr 16,53:1
Udo, Eric
All Editions 1936,D 23,17:2
Udovik, Victoria
Groove Tube 1969,O 12,88:3
Udvardy, Lillian
Idiot's Delight 1951,My 24,46:3
Misalliance 1955,F 12,10:6
Ugarte, Eduardo (Playwright)
Max and Mr Max 1932,Ja 24,VIII,3:5
Ugarte, Yolanda
Public Relations 1944,Ap 7,23:3
Uggams, Elois
Pirate, The 1942,N 26,39:2
Uggams, Leslie
Hallelujah, Baby! 1967,Ap 27,51:1
Hallelujah, Baby! 1967,My 7,II,1:1
Her First Roman 1968,O 21,53:3
Her First Roman 1968,N 3,II,1:1
Uhl, Jerome
Princess Ida 1925,Ap 14,27:2
Uhl, Richard R
Hamlet 1938,N 8,26:1
Once Over Lightly 1938,D 10,13:4
Uhl, Richard R (Composer)
Once Over Lightly 1938,D 10,13:4
Uhl, Richard R (Lyricist)
Once Over Lightly 1926,D 10,13:4
Uhl, Richard R (Playwright)
Once Over Lightly 1938,D 10,13:4
Once Over Lightly 1938,D 17,10:8
Uhler, Gertrude Ennis (Choreographer)
Confederacy, The 1958,Jl 3,20:1

Uhry, Alfred (Lyricist)
Here's Where I Belong 1968,Mr 4,32:1
Ukena, Paul
Maggie 1953,F 19,20:2
Sandhog 1954,N 24,17:1
Yeomen of the Guard, The 1964,Mr 19,29:2
H M S Pinafore 1964,Mr 21,13:4
H M S Pinafore 1965,Ap 15,39:1
H M S Pinafore 1968,Ap 29,47:2
Mikado, The 1968,My 2,59:1
Yeomen of the Guard, The 1968,My 9,53:1
Cry for Us All 1970,Ap 9,48:2
Uksila, Gretel
Stars on Ice (2d Edition) 1943,Je 25,13:2
Hats Off to Ice 1944,Je 23,15:2
Uksila, Richard
Stars on Ice (2d Edition) 1943,Je 25,13:2
Uksila, Robert
Hats Off to Ice 1944,Je 23,15:2
Ula, Mekk
Kongo 1926,Mr 31,20:5
Ulano, Sam
Safari! 1955,My 12,32:6
Ulbrich, Franz (Director)
Schlageter 1933,My 28,IX,1:3
Hundred Days 1934,Ap 29,IX,2:3
Ulbricht, Otto
All for Love 1938,Ap 5,19:4
Ullbright
Straw Hat, The 1939,S 30,10:6
Ullett, Nic
Love and Let Love 1968,Ja 4,30:1
Ullman, Claudia
Man Who Married a Dumb Wife, The 1923,My 10,22:3
Ullman, Claudia (Director)
Broken Engagement, The 1921,My 12,20:2
Ullman, Furth (Lighting Director)
Dark of the Moon 1958,F 27,22:2
Ullman, Furth (Scenic Designer)
Lady From Paris, The 1950,S 27,36:1
Dark of the Moon 1958,F 27,22:2
Ullman, James R (Miscellaneous)
Men in White 1933,S 27,24:2
On the Rocks 1938,Je 16,20:2
Ullman, James R (Producer)
Far Away Horses 1933,Mr 22,21:6
Milky Way, The 1934,My 9,23:2
Birthday 1934,D 27,24:2
Blind Alley 1935,S 25,19:6
Eastwood Ho 1936,Jl 8,14:2
All Desirable Young Men 1936,Jl 22,22:5
So Proudly We Hail 1936,S 23,28:4
Stork Mad 1936,O 1,28:4
Laughing Woman, The 1936,O 14,30:1
Double Dummy 1936,N 12,30:1
Ullman, Morton
Hot Money 1931,N 9,22:2
Ulloa, Alejandro
Don Juan Tenorio 1953,N 20,18:5
El Alcalde De Zalamea 1953,N 23,32:5
Ulloa, Alejandro (Director)
Don Juan Tenorio 1953,N 20,18:5
El Alcalde De Zalamea 1953,N 23,32:5
Ullock, Harry
Simon Called Peter 1924,N 11,20:2
Ullrich, Jan
Picnic 1934,My 3,15:2
Hipper's Holiday 1934,O 19,26:2
Play's the Thing, The 1935,Jl 24,20:4
Class of '29 1936,My 16,10:3
Ten Million Ghosts 1936,O 24,23:7
To Quito and Back 1937,O 7,30:4
Ullrich, Luise
Roulette 1932,Mr 27,VIII,3:1
Ulm, Fritz
Farewell to Arms, A 1930,S 23,30:3
Ulmar, Boris
Cyrano de Bergerac 1936,Ap 28,17:1
Enemy of the People, An 1937,F 16,19:1
Ulmer, Georges
Folies Bergere 1964,Je 3,36:1
Ulmer, Joan
Night Thoreau Spent in Jail, The 1970,N 2,66:1
Ulmer, John
Curious Savage, The 1956,Mr 17,12:3
Ulmer, John (Director)
Rope Dancers, The 1959,Mr 14,26:1
Ulric, Ginger
Inside Story 1942,O 30,22:2
Ulric, Joanne
From Morn Till Midnight 1948,D 7,41:6
Ulric, Lenore
Kiki 1921,N 30,13:1
Kiki 1921,D 4,VII,1:2
Harem, The 1924,N 16,VIII,2:8
Harem, The 1924,D 3,24:1
Lulu Belle 1926,F 10,20:1
Lulu Belle 1926,F 14,VIII,1:1
Vaudeville (Palace) 1927,Mr 29,22:6
Wolf's Cub, The 1927,Ag 30,21:2
Vaudeville (Palace) 1928,My 8,25:2
Mima 1928,D 13,24:2

Ulric, Lenore—Cont
Mima 1928,D 23,VIII,1:1
Sandy Hooker, The 1929,N 10,X,4:8
Pagan Lady 1930,S 28,VIII,4:1
Pagan Lady 1930,O 21,34:2
Social Register, The 1931,O 4,VIII,2:3
Social Register, The 1931,N 10,28:2
Nona 1932,S 18,IX,2:1
Nona 1932,O 5,26:4
Her Man of Wax 1933,O 12,32:3
Naked Man, The 1935,Jl 2,24:3
Road to Paradise, The 1935,Jl 16,24:2
Name Your Poison 1936,Ja 21,27:4
Faust 1938,Ag 28,IX,2:5
Fifth Column, The 1940,Ja 27,9:1
Fifth Column, The 1940,F 4,IX,1:6
Fifth Column, The 1940,Mr 7,18:2
Fifth Column, The 1940,Mr 17,X,1:1
Antony and Cleopatra 1947,N 27,49:2
Ulrich, Louise
Rauhnacht 1932,F 21,VIII,2:1
Uman, Adolf (Scenic Designer)
Steppe Around 1922,Mr 29,17:4
Umani, Sam
Increased Difficulty of Concentration, The 1969,D 5,48:1
Camino Real 1970,Ja 9,42:1
Umeii
Kagami-Jishi; Mirror Lion Dance, The 1969,S 11,53:1
Umeki, Myoshi
Flower Drum Song 1958,D 2,44:1
Flower Drum Song 1958,D 7,II,5:1
Umesuke
Kagami-Jishi; Mirror Lion Dance, The 1969,S 11,53:1
Unamuno, Miguel De (Playwright)
Todo un Hombre 1937,Ap 28,19:2
Difunta, La 1969,N 2,86:5
Unda, Emilie
Redemption: Lebende Leichnam, Der; Living Corpse, The 1928,N 20,28:2
Gestern und Heute 1931,My 24,VIII,2:1
Underdown, Edward
Hands Across the Sea 1936,N 25,17:2
Astonished Heart, The 1936,N 25,17:2
We Were Dancing 1936,N 28,13:1
Shadow Play 1936,N 28,13:1
Still Life 1936,D 1,31:1
Ways and Means 1936,D 1,31:1
Family Album 1936,D 1,31:1
Underhill, Berry
Fashion 1937,Mr 21,II,7:8
Underhill, Edwin
Conversation Piece 1934,O 24,24:1
Underhill, John Garrett (Musical Director)
Cradle Song 1955,D 2,32:2
Underhill, John Garrett (Playwright)
Cradle Song 1921,Mr 1,18:2
Field of Ermine 1935,F 9,10:4
Cradle Song 1955,D 2,32:2
Underhill, John Garrett (Producer)
Field of Ermine 1935,F 9,10:4
Underhill, John Garrett (Translator)
Passion Flower, The 1920,Ja 14,12:1
Evil Doers of Good, The 1923,Ja 17,22:2
Cradle Song 1927,Ja 25,18:2
Bonds of Interest, The 1929,O 15,34:2
Underhill, Margaret
Antigone 1923,My 4,18:4
Underwood, Claude
Misalliance 1955,F 12,10:6
Underwood, Doris
Head or Tail 1926,N 10,24:1
New York Exchange 1926,D 31,11:2
Puppet Show 1930,O 29,26:5
News Item 1935,Ag 6,20:3
Money Mad 1937,My 25,32:5
Sleep No More 1944,S 1,11:5
Underwood, Frances
Toto 1921,Mr 22,15:2
Face Value 1921,D 27,10:2
Home Fires 1923,Ag 21,12:1
White Collars 1925,F 24,17:2
Deacon, The 1925,N 25,14:3
Good Fellow, The 1926,O 6,22:1
Veils 1928,Mr 14,28:5
Underwood, Franklin (Composer)
Lovely Ladies, Kind Gentlemen 1970,D 29,38:1
Underwood, Franklin (Lyricist)
Lovely Ladies, Kind Gentlemen 1970,D 29,38:1
Underwood, Franklin (Miscellaneous)
Fun City 1968,Mr 7,53:2
Underwood, Franklyn (Director)
Synthetic Sin 1927,O 11,26:2
Underwood, John (Lighting Director)
Tenth of an Inch Makes the Difference, A 1962,N 13,44:1
Underwood, John (Miscellaneous)
Utopia! 1963,My 7,47:4
Underwood, Josephine
Schoolmaster, The 1928,Mr 21,30:1
Underwood, Marios
Kiss in a Taxi, The 1925,Ag 26,14:1

Underwood, Marios—Cont
Everything's Jake 1930,Ja 17,20:4
Underwood, Maurice
Playing With Love 1929,F 27,16:4
Underwood, Robert
Hummin' Sam 1933,Ap 10,8:8
Unger, Gladys (Playwright)
Fair Circassian, The 1921,D 7,22:3
Goldfish, The 1922,Ap 18,15:3
Love Habit, The 1923,Mr 15,17:1
Business Widow, The 1923,D 11,27:1
Werewolf, The 1924,Je 8,VII,1:8
Werewolf, The 1924,Ag 26,6:1
Werewolf, The 1924,Ag 31,VII,1:1
Top Hole 1924,S 2,22:3
Starlight 1924,O 5,VIII,1:3
Virgin of Bethulia, The 1925,F 24,17:2
Starlight 1925,Mr 4,17:2
Starlight 1925,Mr 15,VIII,1:1
Stolen Fruit 1925,O 8,31:4
Monkey Talks, The 1925,D 29,20:1
2 Girls Wanted 1926,S 10,25:3
Lovely Lady 1927,D 30,22:1
Madcap, The 1928,F 1,31:2
Ladies of Creation 1931,Ag 30,VIII,1:7
Ladies of Creation 1931,S 9,25:1
Experience Unnecessary 1931,D 31,16:2
Experience Unnecessary 1932,Mr 28,10:2
Nona 1932,S 18,IX,2:1
Nona 1932,O 5,26:4
$25 an Hour 1933,My 11,14:4
Unger, Gladys (Translator)
Werewolf, The 1924,Ag 31,VII,1:1
Unger, Hermann (Playwright)
Rote General, Der 1928,D 23,VIII,4:1
Gartenlaube, Die 1930,Mr 30,VIII,4:1
Unger, Jean
Good Boy 1928,S 6,23:2
Unger, Katherine
Her Majesty the Widow 1937,Jl 14,16:2
Unger, Maurice A
Petticoat Fever 1937,Mr 21,II,7:3
Unger, Robert (Lyricist)
Bohikee Creek 1966,Ap 29,39:1
Unger, Robert (Playwright)
Bohikee Creek 1966,Ap 29,39:1
Unger, Roberta
Family Reunion, The 1947,N 29,9:2
Unger, Stella
Papavert 1931,D 30,25:1
Mr Papavert 1932,Ja 23,18:6
Unger, Stella (Lyricist)
Seventh Heaven 1955,My 27,16:2
Unger, Stella (Playwright)
Seventh Heaven 1955,My 27,16:2
Rosalie 1957,Je 26,28:2
Uni
Cranmer of Canterbury 1959,D 4,36:1
Unkel, William C
Tableaux 1961,D 18,41:3
Unkelbach, Kurt (Playwright)
Straw Hat, The 1937,D 31,8:2
Unruh, Fritz von (Playwright)
Bonaparte 1927,My 15,VIII,1:3
Unterhauser, Oswald (Musical Director)
Wiener Blut 1964,S 12,14:1
Untermeyer, Louis H (Translator)
Man and the Masses 1924,Ap 15,25:1
Upham, Eva
Bivouac at Lucca 1957,O 30,26:1
Upham, T C (Playwright)
Lost Boy 1932,Ja 6,24:4
Uppman, John
Eternal Road, The 1937,Ja 8,14:2
Uppman, Theodor
Courtin' Time 1951,Je 14,30:2
Upright, Blanche (Playwright)
Valley of Content, The 1925,Ja 14,19:2
Upstarts, The
Tickets, Please! 1950,Ap 28,25:2
Upthegrove, Betty
Lady With a Lamp, The 1931,N 20,27:2
Raw Meat 1933,Mr 23,13:2
Upthegrove, Elizabeth
Infinite Shoeblack, The 1930,F 18,28:1
Girls in Uniform 1932,D 31,10:3
Upton, Frances
Little Jessie James 1923,Ag 16,10:4
My Girl 1924,N 25,27:2
Twinkle Twinkle 1926,N 17,22:2
Lady Do 1927,Ap 19,24:2
Talk About Girls 1927,Je 15,31:3
Ziegfeld Follies 1927,Ag 17,27:3
Whoopee 1928,D 5,34:3
Vaudeville (Palace) 1931,Je 15,23:5
Hold Your Horses 1933,S 26,26:4
Upton, Leonard
Sorry You've Been Troubled 1929,O 13,IX,4:1
Upton, Lucille
Rat, The 1925,F 11,19:3
Uraneff, Vadim
Musk 1920,Mr 15,13:1
Uraneff, Vadim (Director)
Clean Beds 1939,My 26,21:2

Uraneff, Vadini
Hamlet 1922,N 17,14:1
Hamlet 1923,N 27,23:6
Urashima, Chikako
How to Succeed in Business Without Really Trying 1964,Jl 18,10:1
Urbach, Leslie
False Dreams, Farewell 1934,Ja 16,18:3
Urban, Alfred
War and Peace 1942,My 22,26:3
Urban, Gretl (Scenic Designer)
Season Changes, The 1935,D 24,10:2
Urban, Joseph (Scenic Designer)
Midnight Frolic 1920,Ag 4,7:1
Midnight Frolic 1921,N 19,11:3
Tale of the Wolf, The 1925,O 8,31:2
Song of the Flame 1925,D 31,10:2
No Foolin' 1926,Je 25,25:1
Wild Rose, The 1926,O 21,23:1
Yours Truly 1927,Ja 26,16:5
Rio Rita 1927,F 3,18:3
Rio Rita 1927,F 13,VII,1:1
Follies 1927,Ag 7,VII,1:8
Ziegfeld Follies 1927,Ag 17,27:3
Follies 1927,Ag 28,VII,1:1
Golden Dawn 1927,D 1,32:3
Rosalie 1927,D 18,IX,2:3
Show Boat 1927,D 28,26:1
Show Boat 1928,Ja 8,VIII,1:1
Rosalie 1928,Ja 11,26:3
Three Musketeers, The 1928,Mr 4,IX,2:3
Three Musketeers, The 1928,Mr 14,28:1
Treasure Girl 1928,N 9,22:1
Polly 1928,N 11,X,2:4
Whoopee 1928,D 5,34:3
Polly 1929,Ja 9,28:3
Show Girl 1929,Jl 3,19:3
Sons o' Guns 1929,N 27,30:4
Sons o' Guns 1930,Ja 12,VIII,1:1
Ripples 1930,F 12,26:1
Simple Simon 1930,F 19,22:1
Flying High 1930,Mr 4,24:4
Prince Charming 1930,O 14,31:1
Smiles 1930,N 19,19:2
Simple Simon 1931,Mr 10,23:2
Ziegfeld Follies 1931,Jl 2,30:5
George White's Scandals 1931,S 15,30:1
Good Fairy, The 1931,N 25,17:1
Hot-Cha! 1932,Mr 9,17:3
Show Boat 1932,My 20,22:2
Music in the Air 1932,O 23,IX,3:3
Music in the Air 1932,N 9,28:2
Good Fairy, The 1932,N 18,22:3
Melody 1933,F 15,17:4
Urban, Lola
Friedens Tragoedie 1936,N 17,34:4
Urban, Ruth
Pardon My English 1933,Ja 21,11:4
Rose Marie 1936,Jl 22,22:6
Salute to Spring 1937,Jl 14,16:2
I Married an Angel 1938,My 12,26:2
Urbano, Tony
Poupees de Paris, Les 1962,D 13,8:2
Poupees de Paris, Les 1964,My 16,11:1
Urbano, Tony (Miscellaneous)
Poupees de Paris, Les 1962,D 13,8:2
Poupees de Paris, Les 1964,My 16,11:1
Urbant Schitsch, Rudolf (Playwright)
This for Remembrance 1937,Mr 17,31:1
Urbont, Carl
Tomorrow's a Holiday! 1935,D 31,10:2
Urbont, Jacques (Composer)
Livin' the Life 1957,Ap 29,20:1
All in Love 1961,N 11,15:2
Great Indoors, The 1966,F 2,23:1
Urbont, Jacques (Miscellaneous)
All in Love 1961,N 11,15:2
Urbont, Jacques (Musical Director)
All in Love 1961,N 11,15:2
Urbont, Jacques (Producer)
All in Love 1961,N 11,15:2
Ure, Mary
Time Remembered 1955,My 4,35:1
Crucible, The 1956,Ap 11,28:3
View From the Bridge, A 1956,O 12,35:3
Look Back in Anger 1957,O 2,28:2
Look Back in Anger 1957,O 13,II,1:1
Othello 1959,Ap 8,41:3
Othello 1959,Ap 12,II,3:1
Midsummer Night's Dream, A 1959,Je 3,30:1
Duel of Angels 1960,Ap 20,42:2
Duel of Angels 1960,My 1,II,1:1
Two Character Play, The 1967,D 13,54:5
U'Ren, Bertram
Advertising of Kate, The 1922,My 9,22:2
Urhausen, Roy
Show Boat 1954,O 29,28:4
Urich, Tom
Shoemaker's Holiday, The 1967,Mr 3,25:1
Applause 1970,Mr 31,35:1
Uridge, Francis
No More Peace 1937,F 27,9:1

Uris, Roland
Love, Honor and Oh Baby 1940,Mr 29,25:2
Urmancis, Henry F (Sgt)
Swing Sister Wac Swing 1944,Ja 4,20:4
Urmston, Ken
Greenwich Village U S A 1960,S 29,30:5
Urmy, Ralph
Philip Goes Forth 1931,Ja 13,35:4
Adams' Wife 1931,D 29,27:1
Urquhardt, David
Tragedy of Nan, The 1920,F 18,9:1
Clubs Are Trumps 1924,O 15,27:1
Urquhart, Philippa
Tempest, The 1963,Ap 3,43:1
Urtula, Lucrecia Reyes (Choreographer)
Ice Capades 1960,S 1,30:1
Urvantzov, Leo (Playwright)
Right to Kill, The 1926,F 16,22:2
Urwin, Sue
Hamlet 1970,D 28,40:1
Uryga, Jan
Jaselka 1965,Ja 6,32:1
Post Office, The 1965,Ja 6,32:1
Book, The 1965,Ja 6,32:1
Nightmare, The 1965,Ja 6,32:1
Kernel and the Shell, The 1965,Ja 6,32:1
Jacob and the Angel 1965,Ja 6,32:1
Labyrinth, The 1965,Ja 6,32:1
Woman, The 1965,Ja 6,32:1
Urylee, Leonardos
Our Lan' 1947,S 29,16:5
Usandizaga, Rondalla (Composer)
Romantic Young Lady, The 1927,My 5,30:2
Usha, Screemati
Ramayana 1931,Ja 13,35:4
Usher, May
Vaudeville (Palace) 1928,D 3,30:6
Usigli, Rudolfo (Director)
Amphitryon 38 1939,Jl 16,IX,1:1
Uspenskaya, Maria
Lower Depths, The 1923,Ja 16,16:1
Cherry Orchard, The 1923,Ja 23,18:1
Cherry Orchard, The 1923,Ja 28,VII,1:1
Three Sisters, The 1923,Ja 30,12:2
Ivanoff 1923,N 27,23:2
Enough Stupidity in Every Wise Man 1923,D 6,23:1
Uncle Vanya 1924,Ja 29,16:2
Death of Pazukhin, The 1924,F 12,20:1
Ussachevsky, Vladimir (Miscellaneous)
King Lear 1956,Ja 13,17:1
Back to Methuselah 1958,Mr 27,41:5
Cannibals, The 1968,N 4,60:1
Ustinov, Peter
Frenzy 1948,Ap 22,35:2
Romanoff and Juliet 1956,My 19,12:5
Romanoff and Juliet 1957,O 11,24:1
Photo Finish 1962,Mr 28,35:3
Photo Finish 1962,Ap 26,23:7
Photo Finish 1963,F 14,5:2
Ustinov, Peter (Composer)
Romanoff and Juliet 1957,O 11,24:1
Ustinov, Peter (Director)
Photo Finish 1962,Mr 28,35:3
Photo Finish 1963,F 14,5:2
Halfway up the Tree 1967,N 8,52:1
Ustinov, Peter (Playwright)
House of Regrets 1942,O 18,VIII,1:5
Blow Your Own Trumpet 1943,S 19,II,1:6
House of Regrets 1948,Mr 14,II,2:4
Indifferent Shepherd, The 1948,Mr 14,II,2:4
Frenzy 1948,Ap 22,35:2
Man in the Raincoat, The 1949,S 11,II,2:1
Moment of Truth 1951,D 9,II,7:7
Love of Four Colonels, The 1953,Ja 16,17:2
No Sign of a Dove 1953,D 20,II,4:2
Romanoff and Juliet 1956,My 19,12:5
Romanoff and Juliet 1956,Jl 1,II,1:6
Romanoff and Juliet 1957,O 11,24:1
Photo Finish 1962,Mr 28,35:3
Photo Finish 1962,Ap 26,23:7
Photo Finish 1963,Ja 23,5:5
Photo Finish 1963,F 14,5:2
Unknown Soldier and His Wife, The 1967,Jl 7,22:1
Halfway up the Tree 1967,N 8,52:1
Halfway up the Tree 1967,N 19,II,1:1
Halfway up the Tree 1967,N 24,60:4
Utae, Kagaya
Kagotsurube; Courtesan, The 1960,Je 3,26:1
Utaemon, Nakamura VI
Kagotsurube; Courtesan, The 1960,Je 3,26:1
Tsubosaka Reigenki; Miracle at Tsubosaka Temple, The 1960,Je 3,26:1
Musume Dojoji; Maiden at the Dojo Temple, The 1960,Je 10,37:1
Chushingura; Forty-Seven Ronin, The 1960,Je 10,37:1
Musume Dojoji; Maiden at the Dojo Temple, The 1960,Je 17,35:4
Chushingura; Forty-Seven Ronin, The 1960,Je 17,35:4
Utazo, Kagaya
Kagotsurube; Courtesan, The 1960,Je 3,26:1

Utazo, Kagaya—Cont
Chushingura; Forty-Seven Ronin, The 1960,Je 10,37:1
Chushingura; Forty-Seven Ronin, The 1960,Je 17,35:4
Utmore, Betty
Quicksand 1928,F 14,26:3
Utt, Kenneth (Pfc)
Yellow Jack 1944,Ap 7,23:3
Uttal, Ivan (Miscellaneous)
Play With a Tiger 1964,D 31,14:2
Utting, Francis A
Betty Behave 1927,Mr 9,28:4
Uttry, Arthur
Lady Billy 1920,D 15,18:2
Queen O' Hearts 1922,O 11,22:1
Mystery Moon 1930,Je 24,23:4
Dodsworth 1934,F 26,20:4
Personal Appearance 1936,Jl 9,17:4
Howdy Stranger 1937,Ja 15,17:5
Uvillier, Kalman
God Man and Devil 1935,Mr 6,22:3
Uyeno Japanese Troupe
Untitled-Revue 1930,Ap 22,33:2
Uziel, Phyllis (Costume Designer)
Old Bucks and New Wings 1962,N 6,39:4

V

Vaad, Ron
Make Me Disappear 1969,My 14,34:1
Vaccarella, Joe
Babes Don't Cry Anymore 1968,F 21,55:1
Vaccaro, Brenda
Everybody Loves Opal 1961,O 12,40:2
Affair, The 1962,S 21,34:2
Children From Their Games 1963,Ap 12,33:1
Cactus Flower 1965,D 9,60:2
Natural Look, The 1967,Mr 13,45:2
How Now, Dow Jones 1967,D 8,53:1
How Now, Dow Jones 1967,D 24,II,3:2
Goodbye People, The 1968,D 4,52:1
Goodbye People, The 1968,D 15,II,3:1
Vaccaro, Frank
Rivalry, The 1959,F 9,24:2
Vaccaro, John (Director)
Conquest of the Universe 1967,N 27,60:1
Moke Eaters, The 1968,O 28,55:3
Vaccaro, Vilma
Utopia! 1963,My 7,47:4
Vachell, Horace Annesley (Playwright)
Count X 1921,My 29,VI,1:7
Vachon, Kate (Costume Designer)
Firebugs, The 1968,Jl 2,36:1
Vachtangov, Eugene (Director)
Dybbuk, The 1926,N 21,VIII,1:3
Dybbuk, The 1926,D 14,24:2
Dybbuk, The 1926,D 26,VII,1:1
Dybbuk, The 1948,My 3,26:3
Dybbuk, The 1964,F 4,30:2
Vacic, Mira
Victor, or The Children Take Over 1968,Jl 10,22:4
Vadie, Maryon
Cinderella on Broadway 1920,Je 25,18:1
Vaudeville (Palace) 1926,My 11,25:3
Vaudeville (Palace) 1927,Je 28,29:2
Vadie and Gygi
Vaudeville (Palace) 1928,Ja 3,29:3
Vagliano, Stephen (Playwright)
Strange Rhythm 1937,Ap 20,29:2
Vahanian, Marc L
Time of Your Life, The 1969,N 7,37:1
Vail, Amanda (Playwright)
Love Me Little 1958,Ap 15,42:2
Vail, Bobby
Number, The 1951,O 31,33:2
Bernardine 1952,O 17,33:4
Carnival in Flanders 1953,S 9,38:2
Vail, Edward (Director)
Woman of Destiny, A 1936,Mr 3,25:2
Vail, Edwin
Man Who Killed Lincoln, The 1940,Ja 18,26:4
Journey to Jerusalem 1940,O 7,21:2
Vail, Edwin (Director)
Blonde Sinner, The 1926,Jl 15,21:2
Vail, Lester
Caught 1925,O 6,31:2
Makropoulos Secret, The 1926,Ja 22,12:4
Good Fellow, The 1926,O 6,22:1
Behold the Bridegroom 1927,D 27,24:1
Unknown Warrior, The 1928,O 30,26:6
Gypsy 1929,Ja 15,22:2
Marry the Man! 1929,Ap 23,26:3
Strong Man's House, A 1929,Je 30,VIII,1:2
Strong Man's House, A 1929,S 17,34:3
Top O' the Hill 1929,N 27,30:4
Nancy's Private Affair 1930,Ja 14,24:3
Border-Land 1932,Mr 30,15:5
Hat, a Coat, a Glove, A 1934,F 1,15:2
Are You Decent? 1934,Ap 20,16:2
Bridal Quilt 1934,O 11,28:5
Tomorrow's Harvest 1934,D 6,26:5

Vail, Lester (Director)
Hope for a Harvest 1941,N 27,28:2
Mr Sycamore 1942,N 14,13:2
Chicken Every Sunday 1944,Ap 6,27:2
Vail, Mildred
Cyrano de Bergerac 1932,D 27,11:2
Cyrano de Bergerac 1936,Ap 28,17:1
Vail, Robert
Henry V 1960,Je 30,23:1
Taming of the Shrew, The 1960,Ag 20,17:1
Vail, Seymour (Producer)
Adaptation 1969,F 11,27:1
Next 1969,F 11,27:1
Vail, Tom
King Lear 1964,Jl 23,18:1
Henry VI, Part I 1964,Jl 23,18:1
Merchant of Venice, The 1964,Jl 23,18:1
Vaile, Isla
What a Life 1938,Ap 14,26:2
Vaill, Arthur E
Chiffon Girl, The 1924,F 20,23:2
Vaitl, Eva
Ratten, Die 1966,Ap 13,36:1
Vajda, Ernest (Original Author)
Grounds for Divorce 1924,Mr 2,VIII,2:7
Viens Avec Nous Petit! 1927,F 20,VII,2:1
Vajda, Ernest (Playwright)
Fata Morgana 1924,Mr 4,16:3
Fata Morgana 1924,Mr 9,VIII,1:1
Fata Morgana 1924,Ag 24,VII,1:1
Grounds for Divorce 1924,S 24,20:1
Little Angel, The 1924,S 29,10:3
Little Angel, The 1924,O 5,VIII,1:1
Fata Morgana 1924,O 12,VIII,1:1
Little Angel, The 1924,O 12,VIII,1:1
Harem, The 1924,D 3,24:1
Crown Prince, The 1927,F 27,VII,4:6
Crown Prince, The 1927,Mr 24,23:2
Fata Morgana 1931,D 26,15:3
Vajda, John S (Translator)
Little Angel, The 1924,S 29,10:3
Vakalo, Georges (Costume Designer)
Paix, La 1933,Ja 15,IX,2:1
Vakalo, Georges (Scenic Designer)
Paix, La 1933,Ja 15,IX,2:1
Val, Una
Strip Girl 1935,O 21,22:6
Idiot's Delight 1936,Mr 25,25:2
Val-Norton, Dennis
Evensong 1933,F 1,13:4
Valadin, Brigitte
Grosse Valise, La 1965,D 15,52:1
Valaida
Rhapsody in Black 1931,My 5,33:2
Blackbirds 1934,Ag 26,II,6:5
Valaire, Valerie
It Is the Law 1922,N 30,28:2
Humming Bird, The 1923,Ja 16,16:2
Connie Goes Home 1923,S 7,10:1
Kept 1926,S 18,13:3
Synthetic Sin 1927,O 11,26:2
Mrs Bumpstead-Leigh 1929,Ap 2,28:3
Third Day, The 1929,Ag 13,23:4
Frankie and Johnny 1930,S 26,16:5
Great Man, The 1931,Ap 8,20:6
Wooden Soldier, The 1931,De 23,28:4
We the People 1933,Ja 23,9:5
Arsenic and Old Lace 1944,Jl 3,7:3
Little Women 1944,D 13,29:2
Anybody Home 1949,F 26,10:5
Valando, Tommy (Miscellaneous)
Agatha Sue, I Love You 1966,D 15,61:1
Valare, Lorna
Marie Antoinette 1921,N 23,16:1
Valbel, Henry
Aiglon, L' 1924,O 21,21:1
Madame Sans-Gene 1924,N 4,30:1
Valcourt, Gaston
Prelude 1935,Je 27,17:4
Valcourt, Gaston (Playwright)
Private Affair, A 1936,My 15,28:7
Valdes
Pearl of Great Price, The 1926,N 2,34:3
Valdes-Blain, Rolando (Composer)
Bullfight 1954,Ja 13,25:2
Valdes-Blain, Rolando (Musical Director)
Bullfight 1954,Ja 13,25:2
Valdes-Blain, Rolondo
Bullfight 1954,Ja 13,25:2
Valdez, Corrinne
Michael Todd's Peep Show 1950,Je 29,37:2
Valdez, Fred (Playwright)
Egg in Your Beer 1945,My 13,II,1:3
Valdez, Marie
Mikado, The 1942,F 4,22:2
Pirates of Penzance, The 1942,F 18,22:2
Iolanthe 1942,F 24,26:4
Gondoliers, The 1942,Mr 4,22:3
Mikado, The 1944,F 12,11:3
H M S Pinafore 1944,F 15,14:4
Pirates of Penzance, The 1944,F 18,15:5
Gondoliers, The 1944,F 22,26:3
Iolanthe 1944,F 23,17:1

Valdez, Marie—Cont
Patience 1944,F 26,11:4
Yeomen of the Guard, The 1944,Mr 5,34:3
Valdez, Tito
Michael Todd's Peep Show 1950,Je 29,37:2
Valdy, Regine
Frankie and Johnny 1930,S 26,16:5
Adam Had Two Sons 1932,Ja 21,17:1
International Incident, An 1940,Ap 3,18:2
Vale, Eugene (Playwright)
Devils Galore 1945,S 13,27:2
Vale, Martin (Playwright)
Two Mrs Carrolls, The 1935,Je 13,26:1
Two Mrs Carrolls, The 1943,Ag 4,14:1
Two Mrs Carrolls, The 1943,Ag 8,II,1:1
Vale, Michael
Red Eye of Love 1961,Je 13,28:1
Egg, The 1962,Ja 9,23:2
Cafe Crown 1964,Ap 18,32:1
Last Analysis, The 1964,O 2,30:1
Impossible Years, The 1965,O 14,55:1
Treatment, The 1968,My 10,54:7
Autograph Hound, The 1968,D 14,60:1
Moths, The 1970,My 12,46:1
Vale, Rita
Wall Street 1927,Ap 21,24:4
Lombardi, Ltd 1927,Je 7,27:3
Creoles 1927,S 23,33:3
Faust 1928,O 9,34:1
Let Us Be Gay 1929,F 22,19:1
Candle-Light 1929,O 1,28:2
Going Gay 1933,Ag 4,18:5
And Be My Love 1934,Ja 19,25:2
Simpleton of the Unexpected Isles, The 1935,F 19,27:5
All This While 1935,Jl 30,17:2
Accent on Youth 1935,Ag 13,20:3
First Lady 1935,N 27,17:4
Tonight in Samarkand 1955,F 17,22:2
Lark, The 1955,N 18,20:1
Vale, Violet
Yankee Princess, The 1922,O 3,22:1
Valency, Maurice (Composer)
Dance Me a Song 1950,Ja 21,10:5
Valency, Maurice (Playwright)
Madwoman of Chaillot, The 1949,Ja 9,II,1:1
Enchanted, The 1950,Ja 19,34:2
Madwoman of Chaillot, The 1950,Je 14,41:2
Ondine 1954,F 28,II,1:1
Virtuous Island, The 1957,Ap 10,39:1
Apollo of Bellac, The 1957,Ap 10,39:1
Apollo of Bellac, The 1958,Mr 7,17:2
Enchanted, The 1958,Ap 23,41:1
Visit, The 1958,My 6,40:1
Visit, The 1958,My 18,II,1:1
Visit, The 1960,Mr 9,38:3
Thracian Horses, The 1961,S 28,58:2
Visit, The 1967,S 13,41:1
Dear World 1969,F 7,33:1
Madwoman of Chaillot, The 1970,Mr 23,48:3
Valency, Maurice (Translator)
Ondine 1954,F 19,23:1
Valency, Morris (Playwright)
All Desirable Young Men 1936,Jl 22,22:5
Valeninoff, Val
Gypsy Lady 1946,S 18,25:6
Valente, Jack
Penny Wars, The 1969,O 16,52:1
Valente, Maria
Vaudeville (Palace) 1928,S 4,21:3
Vaudeville (Palace) 1929,Jl 15,25:4
Valenti, Alfredo (Director)
Hansel and Gretel 1929,D 25,21:1
Valenti, Michael
Your Own Thing 1968,Ja 15,33:1
Valenti, Michael (Composer)
Just for Love 1968,O 18,40:1
Blood Red Roses 1970,Mr 23,48:1
Valenti, Michael (Lighting Director)
Time for the Gentle People, A 1967,My 26,50:1
Valenti, Tino
Farewell to Arms, A 1930,S 23,30:3
Singing Rabbi, The 1931,S 11,24:4
Fast Service 1931,N 18,26:3
Chicken Every Sunday 1944,Ap 6,27:2
Valentin, Amedee (Playwright)
Poudre d'Or, La 1928,Je 17,VIII,1:4
Valentin, Hermann
Saint Joan 1924,N 9,VII,2:3
Hokus Pokus 1928,Ja 29,VIII,4:1
Valentin, Maria
Pluma en el Viento; Feather in the Wind 1932,Ap 2,13:4
Tambor y Cascabel; Drum and Bell 1932,Ap 21,25:4
Cuando Los Hijos De Eva No Son Los Hijos De Adan; When Eve's Children Are Not Adam's 1932,Ap 23,11:2
Valentina (Costume Designer)
Amphitryon 38 1937,Je 24,30:2
Amphitryon 38 1937,N 22,32:2
No Time for Comedy 1939,Ap 18,26:4
No Time for Comedy 1939,Ap 30,XI,1:1
There Shall Be No Night 1940,Ap 30,25:2

Valentina (Costume Designer)—Cont

Rugged Path, The 1945,N 12,17:2
Antony and Cleopatra 1947,N 27,49:2
Antony and Cleopatra 1947,D 7,II,5:1
My Name is Aquilon 1949,F 10,38:2
Bell, Book and Candle 1950,N 15,37:4
Ondine 1954,F 28,II,1:1
Chinese Prime Minister, The 1964,Ja 3,14:1
High Spirits 1964,Ap 8,34:1

Valentine

Dream Play 1960,N 23,22:1

Valentine, Albert

Dybbuk, The 1954,O 27,33:6
Three Sisters, The 1955,F 26,13:2
Threepenny Opera, The 1955,S 21,38:1

Valentine, Don

O'Flynn, The 1934,D 28,24:1
Savonarola 1942,Ap 24,20:2
Hairpin Harmony 1943,O 2,18:5
Embezzled Heaven 1944,N 1,20:2

Valentine, Edith

Man's a Man, A 1962,S 20,30:2

Valentine, Edith (Musical Director)

Man's a Man, A 1962,S 20,30:2

Valentine, Elizabeth

Love Set, The 1923,Mr 20,24:2
Laughing Woman, The 1936,O 14,30:1
Lady Windermere's Fan 1946,O 15,29:2

Valentine, Ethel

Glass Slipper, The 1925,O 20,29:1

Valentine, Grace

Cave Girl, The 1920,Ag 19,12:2
Chivalry 1925,D 16,22:3
Trial Marriage 1927,F 1,24:3
Kidding Kidders 1928,Ap 24,28:3
Hook-Up, The 1935,My 9,24:6
Fabulous Invalid, The 1938,O 10,15:1
American Way, The 1939,Ja 23,9:2
George Washington Slept Here 1940,O 19,20:3
Last Stop 1944,S 6,17:2
Happy Birthday 1946,N 1,31:2
Story for Strangers, A 1948,S 22,39:2
Season in the Sun 1950,S 29,31:2
Anna Christie 1952,Ja 10,33:1
Anna Christie 1952,Ja 20,II,1:1
Palm Tree in a Rose Garden, A 1957,N 27,26:2

Valentine, Gwendolyn

Trimmed in Scarlet 1920,F 3,18:1

Valentine, J W

Gentlemen, the Queen 1927,Ap 23,14:3

Valentine, James

Conversation Piece 1957,N 19,38:2
Cloud 7 1958,F 15,15:2
Epitaph for George Dillon 1958,N 5,44:1
Duel of Angels 1960,Ap 20,42:2
Ross 1961,D 27,20:2
Henry IV, Part I 1962,Je 18,20:4
Richard II 1962,Je 18,20:2
Six Characters in Search of an Author 1963,Mr 11,7:2
Beyond the Fringe, '65 1964,D 16,49:2
Major Barbara 1965,My 18,33:1
Falstaff 1966,Je 20,27:1
Twelfth Night 1966,Je 23,28:1
Julius Caesar 1966,Je 24,29:2
Midsummer Night's Dream, A 1967,Je 19,42:1
Heartbreak House 1968,Jl 6,9:1
Chemmy Circle, The 1968,Ag 10,17:2

Valentine, John

All's Well That Ends Well 1966,Je 17,39:1
Richard III 1966,Ag 11,26:1
Jonah! 1967,S 22,52:2

Valentine, Judith

Abortion 1959,O 28,40:4
Dance of Death, The 1960,S 14,51:1
Lulu; Earth Spirit 1970,Mr 28,32:1

Valentine, Paul

Wish You Were Here 1952,Je 26,26:6
Hit the Trail 1954,D 3,31:2
Oh Captain! 1958,F 5,21:2
Shoemaker's Holiday, The 1967,Je 3,19:1

Valentine, Ralph (Director)

Ice Capades 1966,Je 2,50:2

Valentine, Richard

Cock-A-Doodle Dandy 1955,N 4,26:5

Valentine, Richard (Lighting Director)

Dance of Death, The 1960,S 14,51:1

Valentine, Ruth

Clouds of the Sun 1922,My 6,11:2

Valentine, William

9 O'Clock Revue 1923,O 5,22:1
Best People, The 1924,Ag 20,8:1
Mayflowers 1925,N 25,14:2
Three Cheers 1928,O 16,28:1
Invitation to a Murder 1934,My 18,26:3
Dooley Cashes In 1935,Ag 17,18:6
Call Me Ziggy 1937,F 13,9:6
Bet Your Life 1937,Ap 6,20:2
Money Mad 1937,My 25,32:5
All Men Are Alike 1941,O 7,27:2
Make Yourself at Home 1945,S 14,21:2

Valentine (Playwright)

Tons of Money 1922,My 21,VI,1:6
Compromising Daphne 1927,O 2,II,7:2

Compromising Daphne 1927,O 16,IX,2:7

Valentini, Octavio

Puppet Show 1930,O 29,26:5

Valentini, Vincent (Director)

Parisiana 1928,F 10,26:3

Valentini, Vincent (Playwright)

Parisiana 1928,F 10,26:3

Valentinoff, Val

Rainbow 1928,N 22,25:1
Virginia 1937,S 3,13:2
Sons o' Fun 1941,D 2,28:2
Follow the Girls 1944,Ap 10,15:2

Valenty, Lili

Bitter Stream 1936,Mr 31,16:6
Cue for Passion 1940,D 20,33:4
Land Is Bright, The 1941,O 29,26:2
Pick-Up Girl 1944,My 4,25:2
Sky Drift 1945,N 14,25:2
Now I Lay Me Down to Sleep 1950,Mr 3,21:2

Valenza, Frank

Bernardine 1952,O 17,33:4

Valeo, Val (Miscellaneous)

Cocktails of 1934 1934,My 5,22:1

Valere, Simone

Baptiste 1952,N 13,34:2
Fausses Confidences, Les 1952,N 13,34:2
Baptiste 1952,N 13,34:2
Fourberies de Scapin, Les 1952,N 21,21:2
Occupe-Toi d'Amelie; Keep Your Eyes on Amelie 1952,N 25,35:2
Repetition, La; Rehearsal, The 1952,N 28,22:2
Hamlet 1952,D 2,39:1
Volpone 1957,F 5,27:2
Misanthrope, Le 1957,F 8,19:1
Intermezzo 1957,F 15,20:4
Chien du Jardinier, Le; Gardener's Dog, The 1957,F 19,36:1
Adieux, Les 1957,F 19,36:1
Repetition, La 1957,S 3,23:2
Mariage de Figaro, Le 1964,F 26,41:2
Vie Parisienne, La 1964,Mr 11,34:2

Valeri, Mme

Blue Bird, The 1925,Ja 30,10:2

Valerie, Olive

In the Next Room 1923,N 28,14:1
Assumption of Hannele, The 1924,F 16,16:2
Jeweled Tree, The 1926,O 8,26:2
Maid of All Work 1927,Ja 13,28:4
Lady Beyond the Moon 1931,Ap 1,36:5

Valerio, Don

Vaudeville (Palace) 1923,O 23,18:2
Vaudeville (Palace) 1929,Jl 8,17:6

Valerio, Frederico (Composer)

Hit the Trail 1954,D 3,31:2

Valerio, Theresa

Tip-Top 1920,O 6,13:2
Black and White Revue, The 1923,O 28,VIII,2:1

Valero, Roslyn

Pink Elephant, The 1953,Ap 23,37:2
When We Dead Awaken 1966,Ap 19,37:2

Valery, Dana

Wait a Minim! 1966,Mr 8,43:1

Valetti, Rosa

Fremde Frau, Die 1921,D 11,VI,1:4
Broadway 1928,Ap 15,IX,4:7
Threepenny Opera, The 1928,D 2,X,4:4
Street Scene 1930,Mr 16,IX,4:1
Ich Tanze um die Welt mit Dir 1930,Ag 31,VIII,2:1
Sturm im Wasserglas 1930,D 28,VIII,2:4
Royal Family, The 1931,Ap 12,IX,1:3
Vinegar Tree, The 1931,N 15,VIII,4:1

Valez, Amalia

Polonaise 1945,O 8,20:2

Valguarnera, Marguerite

Don Juan in the Russian Manner 1954,Ap 23,23:2

Valie, Jay

Diff'rent 1938,Ja 26,26:4

Valina

Chauve-Souris 1929,Ja 23,20:2

Valk, Frederick

Othello 1942,Ag 9,VIII,1:7
Merchant of Venice, The 1955,Jl 1,13:1

Valk, Fritz

Alien Corn 1939,Jl 23,IX,2:3

Vall, Jon-Lee (Producer)

How to Be a Jewish Mother 1967,D 29,18:1

Vall, Seymour (Playwright)

How to Be a Jewish Mother 1967,D 29,18:1

Vall, Seymour (Producer)

How to Be a Jewish Mother 1967,D 29,18:1
How to Steal an Election 1968,O 14,56:1
Just for Love 1968,O 18,40:1
Shoot Anything With Hair That Moves 1969,F 3,29:1
World War 2 1/2 1969,Mr 25,40:1
Blood Red Roses 1970,Mr 23,48:1

Vallaro, Vic

Jack in the Box 1960,My 19,43:3

Valle, Helga

Holiday on Ice 1967,Ag 31,29:2
Holiday on Ice 1968,Ag 29,44:1

Valle, Jorge

Holiday on Ice 1967,Ag 31,29:2

Valle, Jorge—Cont

Holiday on Ice 1968,Ag 29,44:1

Valle, Mario

Vaudeville (Palace) 1926,Je 15,23:3
Vaudeville (Palace) 1926,D 7,24:3

Vallee, Ernie

Mystery Moon 1930,Je 24,23:4

Vallee, Marcel

Onzieme Commandement 1932,My 15,VIII,2:2
French Without Tears 1937,S 26,II,4:3
French Without Tears 1937,S 29,19:1

Vallee, Mary

Wisteria Trees, The 1950,Mr 30,39:1

Vallee, Rudy

Vaudeville (Palace) 1929,Mr 11,22:5
Scandals 1931,Ag 11,28:4
Scandals 1931,Ag 16,VIII,1:1
George White's Scandals 1931,S 15,30:1
George White's Scandals 1935,D 26,20:2
Man in Possession, The 1939,S 26,21:4
How to Succeed in Business Without Really Trying 1961,O 16,34:1

Vallen, Leslie

Pajama Tops 1963,Je 1,15:1

Valli, Nina

Longing for Home 1933,S 22,15:1

Vallier, Jo Anne

Eagle Has Two Heads, The 1956,D 14,37:2
Here Come the Clowns 1960,S 20,48:1
Seven at Dawn, The 1961,Ap 18,43:1

Vallmer, Lula (Playwright)

Sun-Up 1923,My 25,28:1

Vallon, Michael

Bell for Adano, A 1944,D 7,21:2
Song of Bernadette 1946,Mr 27,22:2

Vallon, Nenette

Heure du Berger, L'; Propitious Moment, The 1936,N 12,30:1
Sexe Fort, Le; Strong Sex, The 1937,Ja 14,17:4
Si Je Voulais; If I Wished to 1937,Ja 28,22:5
Christian 1937,F 25,18:6

Valmond, Marguerite

As-tu du Coeur? 1926,O 31,VIII,2:4

Valori, Bice

Rugantino 1964,F 7,34:1

Valray, Marie

Breaking Point, The 1923,Ag 17,8:4
Vagabond, The 1923,D 28,13:4

Vals, Francois (Miscellaneous)

Maurice Chevalier 1963,Ja 30,7:2

Valsamaki, Mme (Producer)

Mandragola 1930,F 2,VIII,4:1

Valsch, Wilbur

Reunion 1938,Ap 12,26:4

Valsy, Lucette

Cat and the Fiddle, The 1931,O 16,26:4

Van, Billy

Diamond Lil 1948,N 30,33:2
Diamond Lil 1949,F 7,16:2
Diamond Lil 1951,S 15,8:2

Van, Billy B

Adrienne 1923,My 29,10:4
Dream Girl, The 1924,Ag 21,12:2
Artists and Models 1925,Je 25,16:2
Gay Paree 1925,Ag 19,14:3
Great Temptations, The 1926,My 19,29:1
Great Temptations, The 1926,My 23,VIII,1:1
Sunny Days 1928,F 9,29:1

Van, Bobby

Alive and Kicking 1950,Ja 18,25:5
On Your Toes 1954,O 12,24:4

Van, Earl

Wonderful World of Burlesque, The 1965,Ap 29,38:1

Van, Gus

Vaudeville (Palace) 1930,S 15,29:2
Vaudeville (Palace) 1931,F 16,3:5
Vaudeville (Palace) 1932,S 12,13:5
Toplitzky of Notre Dame 1946,D 27,13:4
Old Bucks and New Wings 1962,N 6,39:4

Van, Madeline

Hitchy-Koo, 1920 1920,O 20,11:3

Van, Samye

Goldilocks 1958,O 13,33:1

Van, Shirley

Million Dollar Baby 1945,D 22,17:2
Barefoot Boy With Cheek 1947,Ap 4,20:2

Van, Vera

May Wine 1935,D 6,30:3

Van, Vinnie

Digging for Apples 1962,S 28,29:4

Van Ackerman, E (Scenic Designer)

Tia Juana 1927,N 16,28:4

Van Aken, Gretchen

Walking Happy 1966,N 28,47:1

Van Aken, Gretchen (Choreographer)

Digging for Apples 1962,S 28,29:4

Van Alst, Dorothy

Bye Bye Bonnie 1927,Ja 14,15:3

Van Alstyne, Dutton

Tartuffe 1957,O 9,39:1
Power of Dreams, A 1958,Mr 11,33:1
Jack 1958,Je 4,39:2
'Tis Pity She's a Whore 1958,D 6,21:1

Van and Schenck
Ziegfeld Follies 1920,Je 23,14:1
Ziegfeld Follies 1921,Je 22,10:1
Nifties of 1923 1923,S 26,10:1
Vaudeville (Palace) 1924,Ja 1,21:1
Vaudeville (Palace) 1928,Ag 7,25:5
Vaudeville (Palace) 1928,Ag 14,15:5
Vaudeville (Palace) 1929,Mr 11,22:5
Van Antwerp, John (Original Author)
Naughty-Naught '00 1946,O 21,27:5
Van Antwerp, John (Playwright)
Girl From Wyoming, The 1938,O 31,12:1
Van Ark, Joan
Death of a Salesman 1963,Jl 20,11:2
Van Arsdale, Lillie
Honeymooning 1927,Mr 18,25:3
Van Auken, Betty
Dodsworth 1934,F 26,20:4
Van Auker, Grace
Fata Morgana 1931,D 26,15:3
Van Benschoten, Steve
King John 1967,Jl 14,19:1
Rivals, The 1969,O 18,37:1
Crimes and Crimes 1970,Ja 19,35:1
Don Juan 1970,My 26,32:1
Three Philip Roth Stories; Defender of the Faith 1970,Jl 31,14:1
Three Philip Roth Stories; Conversion of the Jews 1970,Jl 31,14:1
Cops and Horrors; Fly Paper 1970,Ag 11,27:1
Cops and Horrors; Dracula 1970,Ag 11,27:1
Story Theater Repertory; Saint Julian the Hospitaler 1970,O 21,40:1
Story Theater Repertory; Gimpel the Food 1970,O 21,40:1
Revenger's Tragedy, The 1970,D 2,58:1
Van Biene, Eileen
Cinderella on Broadway 1920,Je 25,18:1
Go Easy Mabel 1922,My 9,22:2
Nightingale, The 1927,Ja 4,20:4
Van Bridge, Tony
Tamburlaine the Great 1956,Ja 20,19:1
Henry V 1956,Je 20,27:2
Merry Wives of Windsor, The 1956,Je 21,34:4
Henry V 1956,Je 24,II,1:1
Hamlet 1957,Jl 3,15:2
Twelfth Night 1957,Jl 4,16:4
Henry IV, Part I 1958,Je 25,23:3
Much Ado About Nothing 1958,Je 26,22:1
As You Like It 1959,Jl 1,27:1
Othello 1959,Jl 2,17:2
Midsummer Night's Dream, A 1960,Je 30,23:5
Romeo and Juliet 1960,Jl 1,14:1
Love and Libel 1960,D 8,44:1
Troilus and Cressida 1963,Je 19,40:2
Comedy of Errors, The 1963,Je 21,35:3
Timon of Athens 1963,Jl 31,19:2
Richard II 1964,Je 17,47:1
King Lear 1964,Je 19,36:1
Henry IV, Part I 1965,Je 30,42:1
Falstaff; Henry IV, Part II 1965,Jl 1,35:1
Henry V 1966,Je 8,38:1
Henry VI 1966,Je 9,55:2
Government Inspector, The 1967,Je 15,55:1
Merry Wives of Windsor, The 1967,Ag 4,18:1
Government Inspector, The 1967,O 28,34:1
Saint Joan 1968,Ja 5,42:1
Tiger at the Gates 1968,Mr 1,30:1
Tiger at the Gates 1968,Mr 10,II,1:1
Heartbreak House 1968,Jl 6,9:1
Galileo 1968,D 1,88:4
In the Matter of J Robert Oppenheimer 1969,Mr 7,28:1
Henry V 1969,Je 9,57:1
Much Ado About Nothing 1969,Je 16,57:1
Hamlet 1969,Je 30,33:1
Hamlet 1969,Jl 6,II,1:1
Van Brugh, Violet
Evensong 1932,Jl 1,19:6
Van Bruten, John (Playwright)
London Wall 1931,My 2,23:2
Van Bruten, John (Producer)
London Wall 1931,My 2,23:2
Van Buren, A H
Her Salary Man 1921,N 29,20:1
It Is the Law 1922,N 30,28:2
Time 1923,N 27,23:3
Saint Joan 1923,D 29,8:4
Saint Joan 1924,Ja 6,VII,1:1
Sap, The 1924,D 16,28:3
Morning After, The 1925,Jl 28,24:2
Little Spitfire, The 1926,Ag 17,15:2
Stag at Bay, The 1935,Jl 30,17:1
Little Inn, The 1935,Ag 20,25:1
Black Widow 1936,F 13,24:3
Two Time Mary 1937,Ag 3,20:5
Reno 1937,Ag 10,22:7
Here Come the Clowns 1938,D 8,36:2
Life With Father 1939,Ag 15,14:4
Life With Father 1939,N 9,26:2
Life With Mother 1948,O 21,32:2
Van Buren, A H (Director)
Gypsy Fires 1925,D 8,28:3

Jay Walker, The 1926,F 9,23:1
Little Spitfire, The 1926,Ag 17,15:2
Crime 1927,F 23,27:3
Tightwad, The 1927,Ap 18,18:2
Trial of Mary Dugan, The 1927,S 20,33:1
Trial of Mary Dugan, The 1927,O 9,VIII,1:1
Fast Life 1928,S 27,35:2
Widow in Green, A 1931,N 21,21:4
Inside Story, The 1932,F 23,23:2
Stork Is Dead, The 1932,S 24,18:2
Nine Pine Street 1933,Ap 28,15:5
Move on, Sister 1933,O 25,22:4
Invitation to a Murder 1934,My 18,26:3
Nowhere Bound 1935,Ja 23,20:2
Rain 1935,Ag 27,23:4
Ragged Edge, The 1935,N 26,28:3
Behind the Red Lights 1937,Ja 14,17:4
Bet Your Life 1937,Ap 6,20:2
Van Buren, Peter
Howdy Stranger 1937,Ja 15,17:5
Many Mansions 1937,O 28,28:6
Van Buskirk, Evelyn
Pirates of Penzance, The 1942,F 20,20:2
Van Cello and Mary
Vaudeville (Palace) 1923,Mr 13,19:2
Vaudeville (Palace) 1926,S 28,30:4
Van Cleva, Virgil
Nativity Play, The 1937,D 21,29:1
Van Cleve, Edith
Malvaloca 1922,O 3,22:1
Antony and Cleopatra 1924,F 20,22:1
Depths, The 1925,Ja 28,15:3
New Gallantry, The 1925,S 25,24:2
Broadway 1926,S 17,19:3
Channel Road, The 1929,O 18,24:2
Wild Waves 1932,F 20,11:4
American Dream; 1933 1933,F 22,24:5
June Moon 1933,My 16,15:5
Three and One 1933,O 26,22:6
Three Men on a Horse 1935,Ja 31,22:3
Angel Island 1937,O 21,26:2
All That Glitters 1938,Ja 20,18:2
What a Life 1938,Ap 14,26:2
Ring Two 1939,N 23,38:2
Goodbye in the Night 1940,Mr 19,31:2
Van De Plasch, Kristin
Visit, The 1967,S 13,41:1
Van De Plasch, Raedell
Visit, The 1967,S 13,41:1
Van De Velde Troupe
Vaudeville (Hippodrome) 1925,D 8,28:6
Van Dekker, Albert
Marco Millions 1928,Ja 10,28:2
Volpone 1928,Ap 10,32:1
Conflict 1929,Mr 7,22:4
R U R 1930,F 18,28:1
Marco Millions 1930,Mr 4,24:4
Volpone 1930,Mr 11,24:5
Doctor X 1930,Jl 31,12:4
Sisters of the Chorus 1930,O 21,34:3
Napi 1931,Mr 12,22:5
Blue Widow, The 1933,Ag 31,20:2
First Apple, The 1933,D 28,25:1
House of Remsen 1934,Ap 3,26:4
Brittle Heaven 1934,N 14,22:5
Fly Away Home 1935,Ja 16,20:4
Journey by Night, A 1935,Ap 17,26:3
Knock on Wood 1935,My 29,16:2
Squaring the Circle 1935,O 4,24:6
Laughing Woman, The 1936,Jl 8,14:7
Johnny Johnson 1936,N 20,26:3
Enemy of the People, An 1937,F 16,19:1
van Delden, Egbert H
Betty Behave 1927,Mr 9,28:4
Van Den Heuvel, Albert
York Nativity Play, The 1956,D 5,49:2
Sign of Jonah, The 1957,My 2,27:1
Van Der Vlis, Diana
Happiest Millionaire, The 1956,N 21,21:3
Happiest Millionaire, The 1956,D 2,II,1:1
Comes a Day 1958,N 7,22:1
Mighty Man Is He, A 1960,Ja 7,25:2
Shot in the Dark, A 1961,O 19,40:1
On an Open Roof 1963,Ja 30,7:3
As You Like It 1968,Je 24,42:3
Love's Labour's Lost 1968,Je 28,36:1
Van Devere, Trish
Kicking the Castle Down 1967,Ja 19,43:1
Van Domlin, John (Miscellaneous)
Children in the Rain 1970,O 3,14:1
Van Doren, Harmon
Bernardine 1952,O 17,33:4
Van Doren, Mark (Playwright)
Last Days of Lincoln, The 1961,O 19,39:7
Van Dorn, Mildred
Get Me in the Movies 1928,My 22,18:3
Few Wild Oats, A 1932,Mr 25,22:6
Sophisticrats, The 1933,F 14,19:5
Yoshe Kalb 1933,D 29,27:2
Weep for the Virgins 1935,D 2,18:1
Tapestry in Gray 1935,D 28,10:2
Van Dorpe, Gloria
Arabian Nights 1954,Je 25,15:2

Van Dorpe, Gloria—Cont
Arabian Nights 1955,Je 24,16:1
Van Dreelan, John
Daphne Laureola 1950,S 19,38:6
Daphne Laureola 1950,S 24,II,1:1
Van Drouten, Gretchen
Right You Are (If You Think You Are) 1950,Je 29,37:2
Van Druten, John (Director)
There's Always Juliet 1932,O 28,23:2
Damask Cheek, The 1942,O 23,24:2
Voice of the Turtle 1943,D 9,30:3
I Remember Mama 1944,O 20,16:2
Mermaids Singing, The 1945,N 29,26:6
Druid Circle, The 1947,O 23,29:5
Make Way for Lucia 1948,D 23,23:5
Bell, Book and Candle 1950,N 15,37:4
Bell, Book and Candle 1950,D 17,II,3:1
King and I, The 1951,Mr 30,26:2
King and I, The 1951,Ap 8,II,1:1
I Am a Camera 1951,N 29,39:6
I've Got Sixpence 1952,D 3,44:2
I've Got Sixpence 1952,D 7,II,5:1
King and I, The 1953,O 9,33:3
King and I, The 1953,O 18,II,3:1
Van Druten, John (Miscellaneous)
Cabaret 1966,D 4,II,5:1
Van Druten, John (Original Author)
Cabaret 1968,Ja 12,19:1
Van Druten, John (Playwright)
Young Woodley 1925,N 3,34:1
Young Woodley 1925,N 8,VIII,1:1
Diversion 1927,Ag 14,VII,2:1
Chance Acquaintance 1927,N 27,IX,4:1
Diversion 1928,Ja 6,26:3
Diversion 1928,Ja 12,25:1
Young Woodley 1928,Mr 11,VIII,1:3
Return of the Soldier, The 1928,Jl 8,VIII,1:7
After All 1929,My 26,IX,1:3
Third Day, The 1929,Ag 13,23:4
Destinies 1929,D 29,VIII,2:6
After All 1930,Mr 12,32:7
London Wall 1931,My 24,VIII,1:6
All-Star Special 1931,Jl 18,16:4
There's Always Juliet 1931,O 13,26:5
Hollywood Holiday 1931,N 8,VIII,4:1
After All 1931,D 4,28:4
There's Always Juliet 1932,F 16,24:2
There's Always Juliet 1932,F 28,VIII,1:1
Somebody Knows 1932,My 29,VIII,1:1
Behold We Live 1932,Ag 17,13:2
Behold We Live 1932,S 11,IX,1:1
There's Always Juliet 1932,O 28,23:2
Distaff Side, The 1933,S 6,24:5
Distaff Side, The 1933,S 24,X,1:6
All Paris Knows 1934,Jl 24,20:1
Distaff Side, The 1934,S 26,17:2
Flowers of the Forest 1934,N 21,23:2
Flowers of the Forest 1934,D 9,X,3:1
Flowers of the Forest 1935,Ap 5,21:6
Flowers of the Forest 1935,Ap 9,25:2
Flowers of the Forest 1935,Ap 14,IX,1:1
Most of the Game 1935,O 2,27:4
Gertie Maude 1937,Ag 18,14:5
Gertie Maude 1937,S 5,X,2:1
Leave Her to Heaven 1940,F 28,16:2
Old Acquaintance 1940,D 10,33:5
Old Acquaintance 1940,D 24,18:3
Old Acquaintance 1941,D 28,IX,2:3
Solitaire 1942,Ja 28,22:2
Solitaire 1942,F 8,IX,1:1
Damask Cheek, The 1942,O 23,24:2
Damask Cheek, The 1942,N 8,VIII,1:1
Voice of the Turtle 1943,D 9,30:3
Voice of the Turtle, The 1943,D 19,II,3:1
I Remember Mama 1944,O 20,16:2
I Remember Mama 1944,O 29,II,1:1
Voice of the Turtle, The 1944,D 10,II,6:4
Voice of the Turtle, The 1944,D 19,27:2
Mermaids Singing, The 1945,N 29,26:6
Mermaids Singing, The 1945,D 9,II,5:1
Voice of the Turtle, The 1947,Jl 10,17:1
Voice of the Turtle, The 1947,Ag 24,II,1:5
Druid Circle, The 1947,O 23,29:5
Druid Circle, The 1947,N 16,II,1:1
I Remember Mama 1948,Ap 11,II,3:1
Make Way for Lucia 1948,D 23,23:5
Bell, Book and Candle 1950,N 15,37:4
Bell, Book and Candle 1950,D 17,II,3:1
I Am a Camera 1951,N 29,39:6
I Am a Camera 1951,D 9,II,5:1
I've Got Sixpence 1952,D 3,44:2
I've Got Sixpence 1952,D 7,II,5:1
I Am a Camera 1954,Mr 13,11:1
I Am a Camera 1954,Ap 11,II,2:1
Bell, Book and Candle 1954,O 6,30:8
I Am a Camera 1956,O 10,47:2
Voice of the Turtle, The 1961,Je 28,41:1
I Am a Camera 1961,Jl 10,26:1
Cabaret 1966,N 21,62:1
Van Dusen, Elizabeth
Everyman Today 1958,Ja 16,32:4
Family Reunion, The 1960,D 10,26:1

Van Dusen, Granville
Harpers Ferry 1967,Je 6,52:2
Visit, The 1967,S 13,41:1
She Stoops to Conquer 1968,Ja 1,11:1
Twelfth Night 1968,Je 15,40:1
Resistible Rise of Arturo Ui, The 1968,Ag 8,25:1
Merton of the Movies 1968,S 26,62:1
Resistible Rise of Arturo Ui, The 1968,D 23,44:1
Van Duser, Jane
Corn Is Green, The 1943,My 4,18:3
Harvey 1944,N 2,23:2
Bernardine 1952,O 17,33:4
Midgie Purvis 1961,F 2,25:3
Van Dycke, Tom (Producer)
Six Characters in Search of an Author
1931,Ap 16,29:2
Van Dyk, James
Traitor, The 1949,Ap 1,30:2
Van Dyke, Caroline
Pastorale 1936,Mr 5,24:6
Van Dyke, Dick
Girls Against the Boys, The 1959,N 3,26:1
Girls Against the Boys, The 1959,N 8,II,1:1
Bye Bye Birdie 1960,Ap 15,13:4
Van Dyke, John H
Fiesta 1933,D 16,12:2
Van Dyke, Marcia
Tree Grows in Brooklyn, A 1951,Ap 20,24:3
Tree Grows in Brooklyn, A 1951,Ap 29,II,1:1
Van Dyke, Rudy
Stars on Ice (2d Edition) 1943,Je 25,13:2
Van Dyke, Samuel
Nativity Play, The 1937,D 21,29:1
Van Emburgh, Norman
Yeomen of the Guard, The 1933,My 2,20:4
Bohemian Girl, The 1933,Jl 28,18:5
Yeomen of the Guard, The 1933,Ag 15,20:5
Jubilee 1935,O 14,20:1
Pirates of Penzance, The 1936,Ap 21,27:5
This Is the Army 1942,Jl 5,28:2
Van Eyck, Tony
Kreatur, Die 1930,My 25,IX,1:8
Van Felton, Bostic
Toilet, The 1964,D 17,51:1
Van Fleet, Jo
Winter's Tale, The 1946,Ja 16,18:6
Whole World Over, The 1947,Mr 28,28:2
Closing Door, The 1949,D 2,36:2
King Lear 1950,D 26,18:1
Flight Into Egypt 1952,Mr 19,33:2
Camino Real 1953,Mr 20,26:1
Camino Real 1953,Mr 29,II,1:1
Trip to Bountiful, The 1953,N 4,30:3
Trip to Bountiful, The 1953,N 15,II,1:1
Look Homeward, Angel 1957,N 29,33:1
Look Homeward, Angel 1957,D 8,II,5:1
Rosemary 1960,N 15,47:1
Alligators, The 1960,N 15,47:1
Oh Dad, Poor Dad, Mamma's Hung You in the
Closet and I'm Feelin' So Sad 1962,F 27,28:1
Oh Dad, Poor Dad, Mamma's Hung You in the
Closet and I'm Feelin' So Sad 1962,Ap 29,II,3:1
Our Town 1968,S 29,77:4
Van Fleet, Mary
Ivanov 1958,O 8,42:1
All the King's Men 1959,O 17,27:2
Van Geldern, Charlotte (Costume Designer)
Electra 1958,My 10,17:7
Van Geldern, George (Scenic Designer)
Electra 1958,My 10,17:7
Van Gilder, Lydia
Naughty Marietta 1929,O 22,26:2
Music in the Air 1932,N 9,28:2
Van Gluck, Stephen (Director)
Surgeon, The 1932,O 28,23:1
Van Gluck, Stephen (Playwright)
Jane Brady-Editor 1935,Jl 2,24:3
Point of Honor, A 1937,Ja 31,II,10:4
Point of Honor, A 1937,F 12,26:2
Van Griethuysen, Ted
Failures, The 1959,Ja 6,30:2
Purification, The 1959,D 9,57:5
She Stoops to Conquer 1960,N 2,42:5
Plough and the Stars, The 1960,D 7,56:2
Hamlet 1961,Mr 17,17:1
As You Like It 1961,Je 17,13:2
Macbeth 1961,Je 19,31:1
Troilus and Cressida 1961,Jl 24,15:1
O Marry Me 1961,O 28,13:1
Red Roses for Me 1961,N 28,41:1
Romulus 1962,Ja 11,27:1
Moon Besieged, The 1962,D 6,54:1
White Rose and the Red, The 1964,Mr 17,31:1
Midsummer Night's Dream, A 1964,Je 30,23:2
Galileo 1967,Ap 14,31:1
Basement, The 1968,O 16,40:1
Van Griethuysen, Ted (Costume Designer)
Crystal Heart, The 1960,F 16,31:2
Javelin 1966,N 10,63:1
Van Griethuysen, Ted (Director)
Hedda Gabler 1970,Ja 18,78:1
Van Grona, Eugene (Choreographer)
Lew Leslie's Blackbirds of 1939 1939,F 13,12:2

Van Grona, Eugene (Director)
'Tis Pity She's a Whore 1958,D 6,21:1
Van Grove, Isaac (Miscellaneous)
Eternal Road, The 1937,Ja 8,14:2
Beautiful Dreamer 1960,D 28,22:1
Van Grove, Isaac (Musical Director)
Flag Is Born, A 1946,S 7,10:6
Van Gundy, William
Daughters of Atreus 1936,O 15,33:1
Van Gyseghem, Andre
All God's Chillun Got Wings 1933,Mr 14,19:4
Forty-Eight Hour's Leave 1941,S 28,IX,1:4
Macbeth 1962,F 7,32:2
Romeo and Juliet 1962,F 14,39:1
Saint Joan 1962,F 21,57:4
Van Hekle, Eugene
Capacity for Wings 1957,Ja 10,25:2
Fam and Yam 1960,O 26,44:1
Nekros 1960,O 26,44:1
Van Heusen, James (Composer)
Swingin' the Dream 1939,N 30,24:2
New Aquacade Revue, The 1940,My 13,20:5
Nellie Bly 1946,Ja 22,32:2
Nellie Bly 1946,Ja 27,II,1:1
Carnival in Flanders 1953,S 9,38:2
Eddie Fisher at the Winter Garden 1962,O 3,47:1
Poupees de Paris, Les 1964,My 16,11:1
Skyscraper 1965,N 15,48:1
Walking Happy 1966,N 28,47:1
Van Heusen, James (Lyricist)
Eddie Fisher at the Winter Garden 1962,O 3,47:1
Van Heusen, James (Producer)
Carnival in Flanders 1953,S 9,38:2
Van Holland, Dudley (Mrs)
One Woman's Husband 1920,Mr 23,9:3
Van Hook, Robert S
Teahouse of the August Moon, The
1954,Ap 23,23:6
Van Hoose, Helen
Only 38 1921,S 14,22:2
Roger Bloomer 1923,Mr 2,18:3
Macbeth 1924,Mr 17,18:1
Hedda Gabler 1924,My 17,18:4
Hedda Gabler 1926,Ja 27,16:5
Van Hooton, Robert
Captain Brassbound's Conversion 1950,D 28,21:1
Ladies of the Corridor, The 1953,O 22,33:5
Van Horn, Earl
Yours Truly 1927,Ja 26,16:5
Van Horn, Franklin
White Lilacs 1928,S 11,31:2
Van Horn, Inez
Yours Truly 1927,Ja 26,16:5
Van Hoven, Frank
Vaudeville (Palace) 1926,Ag 17,21:2
Vaudeville (Palace) 1927,Ag 2,19:1
Van Itallie, Jean-Claude (Playwright)
War 1966,Ap 13,36:1
TV 1966,N 7,66:1
Interview 1966,N 7,66:1
Motel 1966,N 7,66:1
America Hurrah; Interview; TV; Motel
1967,Ag 13,II,3:6
America Hurrah; Interview; TV; Motel
1967,O 10,55:2
Collision Course; Thoughts on the Instant of
Greeting a Friend on the Street 1968,My 9,55:2
Thoughts on the Instant of Greeting a Friend on
the Street 1968,My 19,II,1:1
Serpent, The 1969,F 9,II,1:4
Serpent, The 1970,My 24,II,3:1
Serpent, The 1970,Je 2,35:1
Van Leer, Wim (Playwright)
Final Solution, The 1964,N 21,32:4
Van Lein, Charlotte
Solid Gold Cadillac, The 1953,N 6,24:2
Van Lieu, Ron
Coop, The 1966,Mr 2,48:1
Prince of Peasantmania 1970,F 22,88:1
Van Liew, Willard
It's the Valet 1933,D 15,25:4
Van Liew, Willard (Playwright)
It's the Valet 1933,D 15,25:4
Van Loan, H H (Original Author)
Noose, The 1926,O 21,23:3
Blood Money 1927,Ag 23,29:2
Romance, Inc 1929,Mr 24,X,4:7
Van Loan, Paul (Composer)
Icetime 1947,My 29,28:2
Howdy Mr Ice 1948,Je 25,28:5
Howdy, Mr Ice of 1950 1949,My 27,24:2
Van Loan, Paul (Musical Director)
Hollywood Ice Revue 1953,Ja 16,17:2
Hollywood Ice Revue 1954,Ja 15,16:2
Hollywood Ice Revue 1955 1955,Ja 14,16:1
Van Loon, James
Blue Blood 1924,Ap 3,21:2
Van Marr, Feon
Vaudeville (Palace) 1927,Mr 1,31:2
Van Martens, Valerie
It's A Gift 1945,Mr 13,18:7

Van Nardroff, Elizabeth
New Freedom, The 1930,My 17,21:4
Van Nardroff, Elizabeth (Director)
New Freedom, The 1930,My 17,21:4
Van Nuys, Ed
No Place to Be Somebody 1969,My 5,53:3
No Place to Be Somebody 1969,D 31,17:1
Van Nuys, Eric
Feast of Panthers 1961,Mr 21,32:1
Ross 1961,D 27,20:2
Van Orden, Philip S
Little Town of Bethlehem, The 1922,D 26,15:4
Van Ore, Harry
Lulu; Earth Spirit 1970,Mr 28,32:1
Van Oss, Katrina
Allegro 1947,O 11,10:2
Van Parys (Composer)
Lulu 1927,O 2,VIII,2:4
Van Patten, Dickie
Home Sweet Home 1936,Jl 1,29:2
On Borrowed Time 1938,F 4,16:4
Woman Brown, The 1939,D 9,18:5
Lady Who Came to Stay, The 1941,Ja 3,13:2
Land Is Bright, The 1941,O 29,26:2
Skin of Our Teeth, The 1942,N 19,29:5
Snark Was a Boojum, The 1943,S 2,14:4
Decision 1944,F 3,23:2
Too Hot for Maneuvers 1945,My 3,26:5
Wind Is Ninety, The 1945,Je 22,12:2
O Mistress Mine 1946,Ja 24,25:2
Have I Got a Girl for You! 1963,D 3,53:2
But, Seriously... 1969,F 28,29:1
Van Patten, Joyce
Popsy 1941,F 11,26:2
This Rock 1943,F 19,23:2
Tomorrow the World 1943,Ap 15,22:2
Tomorrow the World 1943,Ap 25,II,1:1
Perfect Marriage, The 1944,O 27,17:6
Wind Is Ninety, The 1945,Je 22,12:2
Bees and the Flowers, The 1946,S 27,19:3
They Knew What They Wanted 1949,F 17,28:2
Desk Set, The 1955,O 25,36:7
Hole in the Head, A 1957,Mr 1,15:1
Hole in the Head, A 1957,Mr 10,II,1:1
Between Two Thieves 1960,F 12,23:1
Spoon River Anthology 1963,My 2,40:5
Spoon River Anthology 1963,S 30,23:2
Van Pelt, Katherine
Vogues of 1924 1924,Mr 28,14:3
Van Prague, Martha (Costume Designer)
Fashion 1937,Mr 21,II,7:8
Van Putten, Carlos
Carmen Jones 1945,My 3,26:5
Van Rein, Jane
Flossie 1924,Je 4,25:2
Van Rensselaer, Hal
Broadway Brevities, 1920 1920,S 30,12:2
Up in the Clouds 1922,Ja 3,20:3
Sally, Irene and Mary 1922,S 5,21:2
Passing Show of 1923, The 1923,Je 15,24:6
Vogues of 1924 1924,Mr 28,14:3
Van Rensselaer, Raymond
Squaw Man, The 1921,D 27,10:3
Van Rijn, Nancy
Show Boat 1966,Jl 20,48:1
Van Ritter, Frances
Jumbo 1935,N 18,20:2
Van Ronkel, Alford (Director)
Pre-Honeymoon 1936,My 1,19:4
Van Ronkel, Alford (Playwright)
Pre-Honeymoon 1936,My 1,19:4
Van Rooten, Luis
Dancer, The 1946,Je 6,16:5
Number, The 1951,O 31,33:2
Touch of the Poet, A 1958,O 3,23:2
Candida 1962,N 12,35:5
Luther 1963,S 26,41:1
Van Rosen, Robert (Costume Designer)
Princess Turandot 1926,N 13,14:2
Bloody Laughter 1931,D 5,20:6
Water Carrier, The 1936,D 25,20:2
Empress of Destiny 1938,Mr 10,16:2
Van Rosen, Robert (Scenic Designer)
Princess Turandot 1926,N 13,14:2
Man With the Portfolio, The 1931,F 12,24:6
Bloody Laughter 1931,D 5,20:6
Wolves 1932,Ja 7,26:3
Wise Men of Chelm, The 1933,O 18,24:4
Josephus 1933,D 1,22:5
Jacques Bergson 1936,O 31,24:6
Water Carrier, The 1936,D 25,20:2
Empress of Destiny 1938,Mr 10,16:2
Van Ryn, Karen
Johnny 2X4 1942,Mr 17,24:6
Van Santen, Jamie (Miscellaneous)
God Is Back, Black and Singing Gospel at the
Fortune Theater 1969,N 19,48:1
Van Saun, Michele (Costume Designer)
Subscriber, The 1968,N 5,53:2
Grab Bag, The 1968,N 5,53:2
Susie Is a Good Girl 1968,N 5,53:2
Van Scott, Glory
Fly Blackbird 1962,F 6,26:2

Van Scott, Glory—Cont
Prodigal Son, The 1965,My 21,19:1
Who's Who, Baby? 1968,Ja 30,36:1
Bill Noname 1970,Mr 3,37:1
Don't Bother Me, I Can't Cope 1970,O 8,60:3
Van Scoyk, Bob (Playwright)
Littlest Revue, The 1956,My 23,37:2
Van Sickle, Edward
Much Ado About Nothing 1952,My 2,20:1
Van Sickle, Raymond
Mad Dog, The 1921,N 9,20:1
Zander the Great 1923,Ap 10,24:2
Dawn 1924,N 25,27:1
One of the Family 1925,D 23,22:3
Kidding Kidders 1928,Ap 24,28:3
It's a Grand Life 1930,F 11,30:3
Journeyman 1938,Ja 31,14:2
Victory Belles 1943,O 27,26:3
Chicken Every Sunday 1944,Ap 6,27:2
Farther Off From Heaven 1947,Je 4,33:3
Summer and Smoke 1947,Ag 10,II,1:1
Summer and Smoke 1948,O 7,33:2
Summer and Smoke 1948,O 17,II,1:1
One Bright Day 1952,Mr 20,37:2
Cut of the Axe 1960,F 2,38:2
Van Sickle, Raymond (Playwright)
Best Years 1932,S 8,16:2
Sun Kissed 1937,Mr 11,20:2
Van Sise, Joan
Master Builder, The 1957,D 18,42:7
Van Sloan, Edward
Polly Preferred 1923,Ja 12,13:3
Morals 1925,D 1,22:2
Schweiger 1926,Mr 24,20:4
Juarez and Maximilian 1926,O 12,31:1
Lost 1927,Mr 29,22:2
Dracula 1927,O 6,29:1
Remote Control 1929,S 11,24:5
Vigil, The 1948,My 22,8:6
Van Slyke, Arthur
Guns 1928,Ag 7,25:2
Van Slyke, Harriet
Legend of Leonora, The 1926,My 1,10:1
Van Stark, E R
It's the Valet 1933,D 15,25:4
Van Tassel, Philip
Three Times the Hour 1931,Ag 26,15:5
Van Tassle, Theo
Merry Widow, The 1931,S 8,39:1
Geisha, The 1931,O 6,35:4
Chimes of Normandy, The 1931,N 3,31:3
Naughty Marietta 1931,N 17,31:2
Chocolate Soldier, The 1934,My 3,15:3
Van Vechten, Carl (Original Author)
Tattooed Countess, The 1961,My 4,40:2
Van Vechten, Ed
Ghosts 1925,D 2,23:2
Van Vechten, Karl
Something to Brag About 1925,Ag 14,14:3
Van Veen, Henry
Dear Brutus 1926,Jl 15,21:3
Van Vlack, Donald
Fuente Ovejuna; Sheep Well, The 1936,My 3,II,4:1
Van Vleet, Peggy
All the Comforts of Home 1942,My 26,24:5
I Gotta Get Out 1947,S 26,27:2
Van Vlijman, Jan (Composer)
Reconstruction 1969,Jl 8,36:1
Van Volkenburg, Ellen
Medea 1920,Mr 23,12:2
Candida 1922,Mr 23,11:1
Cheapside 1938,F 28,18:2
Van Volkenburg, Ellen (Director)
Bird Cage, The 1925,Je 3,26:2
Unknown Warrior, The 1931,O 23,28:4
Venetian, The 1931,N 2,26:1
Tobias and the Angel 1937,Ap 29,16:5
Eastward in Eden 1947,N 19,33:2
Van Volkenburg, Ellen (Scenic Designer)
Venetian, The 1931,N 2,26:1
Van Vooren, Monique
Merry Widow, The 1957,Ap 11,36:6
Van Voorhis, C T
Great Adventure, The 1926,D 23,23:1
Van Voorhis, C W
Crown Prince, The 1927,Mr 24,23:2
Sisters 1927,D 26,26:5
Quicksand 1928,F 14,26:3
Skull, The 1928,Ap 24,28:3
Zeppelin 1929,Ja 15,22:3
Ladies of the Jury 1929,O 22,26:2
Van Way, Nolan
Oh Captain! 1958,F 5,21:2
Wonderful Town 1967,My 18,50:1
South Pacific 1969,Jl 7,27:1
Van Wey, Adelaide
Paul Bunyan 1941,My 6,25:1
Van Wie, Harmanus
Field of Ermine 1935,F 9,10:4
Van Winkle, David
Mermaids Singing, The 1945,N 29,26:6
Van Winkle, Dorothy (Costume Designer)
Smile at Me 1935,Ag 24,18:4

Van Witsen, Leo (Costume Designer)
Beast in Me, The 1963,My 17,29:1
Van-Wolfe, Ian
Camille 1932,N 2,23:3
Van Wyck, Robert
Hamlet 1968,Jl 4,15:1
Van Zandt, Forest
Exiles 1957,Mr 13,27:1
Van Zandt, Leona
Orpheus Descending 1959,O 6,45:2
Van Zandt, Philip
Joy of Serpents 1930,Ap 4,22:4
American Tragedy, An 1931,F 21,15:5
Regular Guy, A; Man's Man, A 1931,Je 5,27:1
I Loved You Wednesday 1932,O 12,27:1
Shooting Star 1933,Je 13,22:2
Ragged Army 1934,F 27,16:5
Night Remembers, The 1934,N 28,24:3
Hook-Up, The 1935,My 9,24:6
Good Men and True 1935,O 26,12:4
Whatever Goes Up 1935,N 26,28:2
In the Bag 1936,D 18,30:2
Van Zandt, Porter
Richard II 1951,Ja 25,21:2
Dial 'M' for Murder 1952,O 30,41:2
Van Zandt, Porter (Director)
Warm Body, A 1967,Ap 17,44:2
Van Zandt, Porter (Miscellaneous)
Egghead, The 1957,O 10,39:1
Two for the Seesaw 1958,Ja 17,15:1
Miracle Worker, The 1959,O 20,44:1
All the Way Home 1960,D 1,42:1
Gideon 1961,N 10,38:1
Thousand Clowns, A 1962,Ap 6,31:2
Mother Courage and Her Children 1963,Mr 30,5:5
Any Wednesday 1964,F 19,34:1
Daphne in Cottage D 1967,O 16,56:1
Brief Lives 1967,D 19,60:4
Goodbye People, The 1968,D 4,52:1
Georgy 1970,F 27,26:1
Van Zandt, Roland (Playwright)
Wilson in the Promise Land 1970,Ja 11,78:1
Wilson in the Promise Land 1970,My 27,41:1
Van Zanten, John
Cyrano de Bergerac 1936,Ap 28,17:1
Van Zee, Bertha
Steel 1939,D 20,30:2
Vanarelli, Mario (Scenic Designer)
Hi, Paisano 1961,O 2,36:2
Vanasse, O J
Captain Jinks 1925,S 9,22:1
No More Women 1926,Ag 4,17:2
Desert Song, The 1926,D 1,24:2
America's Sweetheart 1931,F 11,23:1
East Wind 1931,O 28,19:1
Page Miss Glory 1934,N 28,24:2
Vanbrugh, Irene
Truth About Blayds, The 1922,Ja 15,VI,1:7
Eileen 1922,Je 18,VI,1:6
Belinda 1922,Jl 30,VI,1:7
Desperate Lovers, The 1927,F 20,VII,1:4
Art and Mrs Bottle 1929,N 13,25:2
Art and Mrs Bottle 1929,D 8,X,2:5
Swan, The 1930,Jl 27,VIII,1:8
Hamlet 1931,Mr 22,VIII,2:1
Prince of Wisdom, The 1932,Jl 10,IX,1:4
Dinner at Eight 1933,Ja 7,11:5
Dinner at Eight 1933,Ja 29,IX,1:3
Viceroy Sarah 1935,F 13,27:4
Viceroy Sarah 1935,Mr 10,VIII,2:1
Orchard Walls 1937,F 21,X,2:1
Operette 1938,Mr 17,17:4
Operette 1938,Ap 3,XI,1:8
In Good King Charles's Golden Days
1939,Ag 13,28:1
Vanbrugh, John (Sir) (Playwright)
Relapse, The 1948,F 15,II,3:2
Relapse, The 1950,N 23,54:2
Vanbrugh, Prudence
This Way to Paradise 1930,Ja 31,24:2
Frau Jitta's Suehne 1930,My 18,VIII,2:6
Vanbrugh, Violet
This Way to Paradise 1930,Ja 31,24:2
Frau Jitta's Suehne 1930,My 18,VIII,2:6
Vanbrugh (Playwright)
Provoked Wife, The 1936,O 25,X,2:4
Vance, Dick (Miscellaneous)
Ballad for Bimshire 1963,O 16,54:1
Vance, Dorothy
Solid Ivory 1925,N 17,29:3
Vance, Herbert
Letter of the Law, The; Robe Rouge, La
1920,F 24,11:1
Vance, J H (Composer)
Kid Himself, The 1925,D 25,23:2
Vance, Leta Nicholson (Playwright)
Blue Flame, The 1920,Mr 16,18:1
Vance, Mary
Tired Business Man, The 1929,Je 5,32:5
Dear Old England 1930,Mr 26,24:6
Vance, Nina (Director)
Three Love Affairs; Phoenix Too Frequent, A
1958,Mr 11,33:1

Vance, Nina (Director)—Cont
Three Love Affairs; Bedtime Story 1958,Mr 11,33:1
Three Love Affairs; Still Life 1958,Mr 11,33:1
Friends and Lovers; End of the Beginning, The
1961,My 11,43:1
Friends and Lovers; Proposal, The 1961,My 11,43:1
Six Characters in Search of an Author
1961,My 11,43:1
Friends and Lovers; In the Zone; Bound East for
Cardiff 1961,My 11,43:1
Long Day's Journey Into Night 1963,Je 27,25:1
Effect of Gamma Rays on Man-in-the-Moon
Marigolds, The 1965,Je 7,48:1
Galileo 1968,D 1,88:4
Vance, Nina (Producer)
Effect of Gamma Rays on Man-in-the-Moon
Marigolds, The 1965,Je 27,II,1:1
Galileo 1968,D 1,88:4
Vance, Ray
Her Family Tree 1920,D 28,9:2
Vance, Tari
Dream With Music 1944,My 19,15:2
Vance, Vivian
Anything Goes 1934,N 22,26:1
Red, Hot and Blue! 1936,O 30,26:3
Hooray for What! 1937,D 2,32:5
Skylark 1939,O 12,32:2
Out From Under 1940,My 6,13:2
Let's Face It 1941,O 30,26:2
It Takes Two 1947,F 4,33:4
Cradle Will Rock, The 1947,D 27,11:2
My Daughter, Your Son 1969,My 14,36:2
Vancourt, Gaston
Carrida 1935,Ag 2,22:2
Vandegrift, George
Little Father of the Wilderness, The 1930,Je 3,27:1
Vander Noot, Edwin H (Scenic Designer)
One-Act Variety Theatre; Devil Is a Good Man,
The 1940,Mr 20,36:2
Vanderbilt, Gertrude
Oh! Oh! Nurse 1925,D 8,28:4
Vaudeville (Palace) 1926,Ap 27,22:3
Tabloid 1929,S 29,IX,5:1
Vanderbilt, Gloria
Swan, The 1954,Ag 17,16:6
Time of Your Life, The 1955,Ja 20,34:1
Time of Your Life, The 1955,Ja 30,II,1:1
Vanderbilt, Jeanne Murray
Brigadoon 1967,D 14,59:2
Vandergriff, Robert
Idiot, The 1960,S 26,38:1
Emmanuel 1960,D 5,42:2
Montserrat 1961,Ja 9,30:5
Vandergrift, J Montayne
Bootleggers, The 1922,N 28,24:1
Vanderhurst, Sam
Dixie to Broadway 1924,O 30,22:1
Vanderlip, Frank (Mrs) (Miscellaneous)
Mu Lan 1921,F 25,16:2
Vandermeir, Carol
Trojan Women, The 1957,Mr 19,42:7
Obbligato 1958,F 19,22:2
Vanderneers, Gerda (Costume Designer)
Meet the People 1940,D 26,22:2
Vandernoot, Edwin H (Scenic Designer)
This Earth Is Ours 1940,Ap 26,24:2
Vandervort, Philip
Zulu and the Zayda, The 1965,N 11,59:1
Vanderwall, Joan
Hill Between, The 1938,Mr 12,12:5
Vandever, Michael
There Was a Little Girl 1960,Mr 1,28:1
Vandis, Titos
On a Clear Day You Can See Forever
1965,O 18,44:1
Illya Darling 1967,Ap 12,37:1
Illya Darling 1967,N 2,58:1
Guide, The 1968,Mr 7,50:1
Look to the Lilies 1970,Mr 30,59:1
Vandiver, Mary
Roseanne 1923,D 31,9:5
Vane, Amy
Midsummer Night's Dream, A 1967,Je 30,23:1
Vane, Daphne
Keep Off the Grass 1940,My 24,22:6
Dybbuk, The 1954,O 27,33:6
Vane, Denton
Excess Baggage 1927,D 27,24:2
Vane, Gerald
Geneva 1940,Ja 31,15:2
Vane, Nancy
Small Miracle 1934,S 27,24:3
Vane, Norman (Playwright)
Harbor Lights 1956,O 5,20:1
Vane, Sutton (Playwright)
Outward Bound 1924,Ja 8,26:1
Outward Bound 1924,Ja 13,VII,1:1
Falling Leaves 1924,N 3,VIII,2:1
Overture 1925,My 3,VIII,2:1
Outward Bound 1927,Ja 30,VII,2:4
Outward Bound 1927,Mr 16,28:3
Regatta 1928,F 5,VIII,4:7
Outward Bound 1938,D 23,16:5
Outward Bound 1939,Ja 1,IX,1:1

Vaneck, Pierre
Possessed, The 1959,Ja 31,13:7
Vanee, Jerri
Laugh Time 1943,S 9,35:2
Vanel, Charles
Homme Qui Assassina, L' 1924,N 11,20:1
Procureur Hallers, Le 1924,N 13,18:1
Merchant of Venice, The 1924,N 18,23:2
Bourgeois Gentilhomme, Le 1924,N 20,21:2
Taming of the Shrew, The 1924,N 25,27:3
Shock Troops 1969,F 22,36:1
Vanel, Peter (Translator)
Don Juan; Feast With the Statue, The
1956,Ja 4,21:4
Vanessi
Innocent Eyes 1924,My 21,22:2
Sky High 1925,Mr 3,21:4
Night in Paris, A 1926,Ja 6,16:3
Vaudeville (Palace) 1927,Jl 12,29:3
Vaudeville (Palace) 1928,N 19,16:3
Vaudeville (Palace) 1929,Jl 1,31:4
Great Day! 1929,O 18,24:3
Vanet, Mabel
Ghosts 1925,D 2,23:2
Vanison, Dolores
Greenwillow 1970,D 8,60:1
Vankin, Maurice
Career 1943,O 29,22:6
Vanloo (Playwright)
Girofle-Girofla 1926,N 23,26:3
Vann, Barbara
Terminal 1970,Ap 15,51:2
Serpent, The 1970,Je 2,35:1
Vann, Dorothy
Geese 1969,Ja 13,26:6
Vanna, Della
Love Is Like That 1927,Ap 19,24:1
Vanne, Marda
Easy Virtue 1925,D 8,28:2
Constant Wife, The 1927,My 1,VIII,2:7
Many Waters 1929,S 26,27:1
To See Ourselves 1930,D 28,VIII,2:6
Present From Margate, The 1933,D 15,28:1
Genius at Home 1934,Ja 16,18:3
Genius at Home 1934,F 11,IX,3:1
Parnell 1936,My 24,IX,1:7
King of Nowhere, The 1938,Ap 3,XI,1:8
Flashing Stream, The 1938,S 2,21:4
Vanneman, Marie
Pal Joey 1940,D 26,22:2
Banjo Eyes 1941,D 26,20:2
Vanni, Alfred (Playwright)
Onda e lo Scoglio, L'; Wave and the Rock, The
1931,Ap 13,17:3
Vanni, Lola
Before You're 25 1929,Ap 17,30:2
Vanoff, Nicholas (Producer)
Of Love Remembered 1967,F 20,46:5
Vanoni, Ornella
Rugantino 1964,F 2,II,1:4
Rugantino 1964,F 7,34:1
Vanselow, Robert
Peter Pan 1954,O 21,30:2
Vansittart, Sir Robert (Playwright)
Dead Heat 1939,Ag 27,IX,1:6
Vanterpool, Audrey
Carmen Jones 1946,Ap 8,32:2
Carmen Jones 1956,Je 1,28:2
Vanti, Lela
Storm Operation 1944,Ja 12,28:2
Vantine, Marion
Seeing Things 1920,Je 18,19:2
His Queen 1925,My 12,26:1
Head First 1926,Ja 7,22:4
Vaon Gontard, Gert (Producer)
Faust, Part I; Prelude in the Theater 1961,F 5,27:2
Vaquer, Pascual
Billy 1969,Mr 24,56:1
Varady (Costume Designer)
As Thousands Cheer 1933,O 15,IX,1:1
Varca, Louis
Daughters of Atreus 1936,O 15,33:1
Varconi, Victor
Russian People, The 1942,D 16,21:3
Russian People, The 1942,D 30,17:2
Varden, Beth
Miss Lulu Bett 1920,D 28,9:1
Texas Nightingale, The 1922,N 21,15:2
Varden, Evelyn
Alley Cat 1934,S 18,18:1
Woman of the Soil, A 1935,Mr 26,23:6
Is This a Zither? 1935,Je 11,24:3
Life's Too Short 1935,S 21,18:5
Weep for the Virgins 1935,D 2,18:1
Russet Mantle 1936,Ja 17,15:5
Russet Mantle 1936,Ja 26,IX,1:1
Prelude to Exile 1936,N 17,34:6
Prelude to Exile 1936,N 22,XI,3:2
Prelude to Exile 1936,D 1,31:1
Now You've Done It 1937,Mr 6,10:4
Western Union 1937,Ag 10,22:7
To Quito and Back 1937,S 21,29:1
To Quito and Back 1937,O 7,30:4

Our Town 1938,Ja 23,II,10:6
Our Town 1938,Ja 26,27:4
Our Town 1938,Ja 30,X,3:1
Our Town 1938,F 5,18:3
Our Town 1938,F 13,X,1:1
Family Portrait 1939,Mr 9,18:4
Ladies and Gentlemen 1939,O 18,30:2
Grey Farm 1940,My 4,12:7
Return Engagement 1940,N 2,19:2
Lady Who Came to Stay, The 1941,Ja 3,13:2
Candle in the Wind 1941,S 16,19:6
Candle in the Wind 1941,O 23,26:2
Family, The 1943,Mr 31,22:4
Our Town 1944,Ja 11,24:5
Dream Girl 1945,D 15,13:2
Present Laughter 1946,O 30,31:2
She Stoops to Conquer 1949,D 29,21:3
Hilda Crane 1950,N 2,38:2
Romeo and Juliet 1951,Ja 23,24:8
Romeo and Juliet 1951,Mr 12,21:2
Romeo and Juliet 1951,Mr 25,II,1:1
Date With April, A 1953,Ap 16,36:2
Bad Seed, The 1954,D 9,42:1
Bad Seed, The 1954,D 19,II,3:1
Varden, Norma
When in Rome 1929,Je 16,VIII,2:1
Varden, Venita
Melody 1933,F 15,17:4
Vardi, David
Lenin's Dowry 1932,My 13,17:3
Untitled-Dramatic Reading 1933,Mr 6,16:4
Dybbuk, The 1948,My 3,26:3
David's Crown 1948,My 10,26:2
Oedipus Rex 1948,My 24,23:2
Tenth Man, The 1959,N 6,24:2
Tenth Man, The 1959,N 15,II,1:1
Vardi, David (Director)
Dybbuk, The 1925,D 16,22:2
Lenin's Dowry 1932,My 13,17:3
Vardi, David (Playwright)
Lenin's Dowry 1932,My 13,17:3
Vardi, David (Producer)
Lenin's Dowry 1932,My 13,17:3
Varela, Nina
Student Prince, The 1943,Je 9,16:2
Heaven on Earth 1948,S 17,29:2
Nineteenth Hole of Europe, The 1949,Mr 28,16:2
Pardon Our French 1950,O 6,22:4
Plough and the Stars, The 1956,Ap 6,14:1
Rose Tattoo, The 1966,O 21,36:2
Wicked Cooks, The 1967,Ja 24,42:1
Varenne, Mauricet (Playwright)
Ca, C'Est Montmartre! 1927,F 6,VII,4:1
Varenne, Pierre (Playwright)
Paris-Boulevards 1926,N 21,VIII,2:1
Ca, C'Est Montmartre! 1927,F 6,VII,4:1
Affaire, Une 1931,D 13,VIII,2:2
Varennes, Andre
Homme Qui Assassina, L' 1924,N 11,20:1
Procureur Hallers, Le 1924,N 13,18:1
Homme et Ses Fantomes, L' 1924,N 14,16:1
Merchant of Venice, The 1924,N 18,23:2
Taming of the Shrew, The 1924,N 25,27:3
Varesi, Gilda
Jest, The 1920,F 1,VIII,2:2
Night Lodging 1920,Ap 18,VI,2:1
Heaven 1920,Je 13,VI,1:8
Enter Madame 1920,Ag 17,11:2
Enter Madame 1920,Ag 22,VI,1:1
Enter Madame 1920,O 17,VI,1:1
Varesi, Gilda (Playwright)
Enter Madame 1920,O 17,VI,1:1
Enter Madame 1921,Mr 6,VI,1:2
Varesi, Nina
Carry Nation 1932,O 31,18:2
Vargas
Lac Sale, Le 1926,O 3,VIII,2:1
Vocation, La 1926,D 19,VII,3:3
Vargas, Fernando
Cabalgata 1949,Jl 8,14:2
Vargas, Tomy
Golden Streets, The 1970,Ag 14,21:1
Vargas (M)
Rain 1927,Mr 3,23:2
Rain 1927,Mr 27,VII,4:8
Vari, John
Right You Are (If You Think You Are)
1957,Mr 5,37:1
No Trifling With Love 1959,N 10,55:3
Incident at Vichy 1964,D 4,44:1
Vari, John (Playwright)
Farewell, Farewell Eugene 1960,S 28,35:1
Vario, Si
Moon Vine, The 1943,F 12,22:2
Loco 1946,O 17,29:2
Brigadoon 1964,D 24,9:1
Varis, Aldo
Paese dei Campanelli, Il; Land of Bells, The
1935,My 10,25:4
Varley, Vezey
Young Madame Conti 1937,Ap 1,18:4

Varnel, Marcel (Director)
As You Desire Me 1931,Ja 29,21:2
Melo 1931,Ap 17,26:6
Varnel, Marcel (Producer)
Assassin, The 1945,Mr 23,13:6
Varner, Van (Producer)
Cockeyed Kite 1961,S 14,27:1
Varney, Amedeo
Paese dei Campanelli, Il; Land of Bells, The
1935,My 10,25:4
Varney, Amelia
Cindy 1964,Mr 20,24:1
Music Man, The 1965,Je 17,26:4
Varney, Edwin
Three Doors 1925,Ap 24,16:4
Varney, Isabel
Patience 1935,S 3,24:4
Varney, Lindley H (Musical Director)
Patience 1935,S 3,24:4
Varny, E J
Her Man of Wax 1933,O 12,32:3
Varon, Benjamin (Playwright)
Letter to the Times, A 1966,D 5,63:1
Varon, Lisa
Motke Ganef 1932,D 30,15:2
It Can't Happen Here 1936,O 28,30:1
Varon, Miriam
Letter to the Times, A 1966,D 5,63:1
Varon, Miriam (Playwright)
Letter to the Times, A 1966,D 5,63:1
Varona, Jose (Costume Designer)
Macbeth 1966,Ag 29,23:4
Merchant of Venice, The 1967,Je 22,46:2
Volpone 1967,Je 30,29:1
Fiesta in Madrid 1969,My 29,49:1
Varona, Jose (Scenic Designer)
Fiesta in Madrid 1969,My 29,49:1
Varrato, Edmond
Persecution and Assassination of Marat As
Performed by the Inmates of the Asylum of
Charenton Under the Direction of the Marquis de
Sade, The 1967,Ja 4,34:1
Mike Downstairs 1968,Ap 19,35:1
Varrelle, M
Wonderful Night, A; Fledermaus, Die
1929,N 1,23:3
Varro, Juan
Great Magoo, The 1932,D 3,20:7
Our Wife 1933,Mr 3,13:2
Crucible 1933,S 5,22:4
Drums Begin, The 1933,N 25,10:5
Invitation to a Murder 1934,My 18,26:3
Small Miracle 1934,S 27,24:3
Boy Meets Girl 1937,Jl 6,23:1
Varro, Paul
Path of Flowers, The 1936,S 18,19:3
Man Who Killed Lincoln, The 1940,Ja 18,26:4
Varron, Allegra
My Romance 1948,O 20,38:5
Varrone, Gene
Goldilocks 1958,O 13,33:1
Take Me Along 1959,O 23,22:2
Subways Are for Sleeping 1961,D 28,22:1
Bravo Giovanni 1962,My 21,41:2
Tovarich 1963,Mr 20,5:1
Drat! the Cat! 1965,O 11,54:2
Don't Drink the Water 1966,N 18,37:1
Dear World 1969,F 7,33:1
Coco 1969,D 19,66:1
Varrone, Joe
Aquashow 1953,Je 24,29:2
Aquashow 1954,Je 23,20:4
Varrone, Lou
Aquashow 1953,Je 24,29:2
Aquashow 1954,Je 23,20:4
Varsanyi, Irene
Postmistress, The 1928,Ja 15,VIII,2:1
Trial of Mary Dugan, The 1928,S 30,IX,4:4
Varshilov, B (Director)
Golem, The 1948,My 17,22:3
Vasco
Better Times 1922,S 4,14:2
Vaselle, Renata
By Jupiter 1967,Ja 20,28:2
Ballad for a Firing Squad 1968,D 12,64:2
Vasil, Art
Calvary 1960,Jl 22,13:1
Golden Streets, The 1970,Ag 14,21:1
Vasiliev, V N (Composer)
Dollar Princess 1949,Je 2,32:1
Vasiliev, V N (Lyricist)
Dollar Princess 1949,Je 2,32:1
Vasilievsky
Vaudeville (Palace) 1929,My 13,26:3
Vasiloff, Thomas S
Yeomen of the Guard, The 1961,Ap 28,23:1
Mikado, The 1961,My 5,23:1
Grand Duke, The 1961,My 12,24:1
Iolanthe 1961,My 26,29:6
H M S Pinafore 1961,Je 9,29:5
Student Prince, The 1961,Jl 14,14:1

Vasiloff, Thomas S—Cont
Merry Widow, The 1961,O 27,28:2
Vagabond King, The 1961,N 24,36:1
Iolanthe 1962,Ag 8,34:2
Vasnick, Andrew
Gianni Schicci 1969,F 25,36:1
Tale of Kasane, The 1969,F 25,36:1
Vasquez, Bill
Streetcar Named Desire, A 1955,Mr 4,18:2
Vasquezel, Carol Lynn
West Side Story 1968,Je 25,32:1
Vass, Virginia
Three's a Family 1943,My 6,24:2
Vassalou, J
Electra 1952,N 20,38:2
Vasseux, Jean-Claude
War Games 1969,Ap 18,37:1
Vassilious, M
Choephori 1961,S 27,32:4
Vassilkova
Chauve-Souris 1922,Je 6,17:4
Vasta, Dolly
Scarlet Lullaby 1968,Mr 11,48:1
Vasta, Joe
Scarlet Lullaby 1968,Mr 11,48:1
Pinocchio 1968,Ap 15,41:1
Vasudevan, P
Mahabharata 1970,N 28,22:1
Vaszari, Piroska
Nem Elhetek Muzsikaszo Nelkul
1928,D 30,VIII,4:4
Vaszary, Johann (Original Author)
It Pays to Sin 1933,N 4,18:6
Vaszary, John (Playwright)
Girl of Good Family, The 1932,N 13,IX,3:7
I Married an Angel 1938,My 12,26:2
Vaszary, Miss
Be Good Till You Die 1929,D 29,VIII,4:1
Vatgas, Marcella
Ice Follies 1966,Ja 12,27:6
Vath, Richard
Pajama Tops 1963,Je 1,15:1
Vath, Richard (Director)
Pajama Tops 1963,Je 1,15:1
Vatske, Roberta
Carnival! 1968,D 13,58:1
Vattier
Voie Lactee, La 1933,F 26,IX,2:2
Vauchez, Henri J
Nautical but Nice 1931,Ap 19,31:6
Vaugham, Gladys (Director)
Othello 1964,O 13,48:1
Vaughan, Allan
They Shall Not Die 1934,F 22,24:4
Steel 1939,D 20,30:2
Merry Widow, The 1944,O 9,17:1
Vaughan, Beryl
Every Man for Himself 1940,D 10,32:3
Vaughan, David
Country Wife, The 1957,N 28,56:1
Boy Friend, The 1958,Ja 27,24:4
Epitaph for George Dillon 1958,N 5,44:1
In Circles 1967,O 14,12:1
Peace 1968,N 10,87:1
Minnie's Boys 1970,Mr 27,27:1
Boy Friend, The 1970,Ap 15,54:1
Vaughan, David (Choreographer)
Cherry Orchard, The 1962,N 15,46:2
Vaughan, Denis (Director)
Flies, The 1954,S 10,18:2
Trial, The 1955,Je 15,35:2
Spring's Awakening 1955,O 10,30:2
Summer of Daisy Miller, The 1963,My 28,33:1
Vaughan, Dorothy
Slightly Scandalous 1944,Je 14,16:2
Vaughan, Edna
Tale of the Wolf, The 1925,O 8,31:2
Vaughan, Elizabeth
Fashion 1937,Mr 21,II,7:8
Vaughan, Gladys (Director)
Richard II 1961,Ag 30,25:1
Merchant of Venice, The 1962,Je 22,1:4
Macbeth 1962,N 17,16:2
Winter's Tale, The 1963,Ag 16,14:1
Baal 1965,My 7,33:2
Baal 1965,Je 6,II,1:1
Coriolanus 1965,Jl 15,23:1
Macbeth 1966,Je 29,38:1
Vaughan, Gladys (Miscellaneous)
Much Ado About Nothing 1961,Jl 7,17:1
King Lear 1962,Ag 14,35:1
Vaughan, Helen (Playwright)
Tristram 1962,O 29,36:1
Vaughan, Jack (Director)
Best of Burlesque 1957,S 30,27:2
Vaughan, Jack (Miscellaneous)
Best of Burlesque 1957,S 30,27:2
Russell Patterson's Sketch-Book 1960,F 8,35:1
Vaughan, Jack (Musical Director)
These Are My Loves 1960,Ap 19,41:2
Vaughan, Jack (Playwright)
Best of Burlesque 1957,S 30,27:2
Vaughan, Jane
Escape Me Never! 1935,Ja 22,22:2

Vaughan, Jean (Costume Designer)
Man and Superman 1953,F 21,11:2
Villa of Madame Vidac, The 1959,O 1,40:1
Vaughan, Katharine
Shewing-Up of Blanco Posnet, The 1959,S 19,26:7
Kittiwake Island 1960,O 13,43:1
Vaughan, Robert
Bat, The 1920,Ag 24,6:1
John Brown's Body 1953,F 16,17:2
Vaughan, Stuart
Strong Are Lonely, The 1953,S 30,38:3
Clandestine Marriage, The 1954,O 4,23:2
Thieves' Carnival 1955,F 2,21:1
Vaughan, Stuart (Director)
I Knock at the Door 1956,Mr 19,27:5
Pictures in the Hallway 1956,My 28,23:1
Taming of the Shrew, The 1956,Ag 11,11:2
Taming of the Shrew, The 1956,Ag 26,II,1:1
Pictures in the Hallway 1956,S 17,23:2
Pictures in the Hallway 1956,S 23,II,1:1
River Line, The 1957,Ja 3,29:2
Romeo and Juliet 1957,Je 28,30:2
Two Gentlemen of Verona 1957,Jl 23,21:5
Macbeth 1957,Ag 16,11:2
I Know at the Door 1957,S 30,27:2
Richard III 1957,N 26,41:1
As You Like It 1958,Ja 21,33:6
Othello 1958,Jl 4,16:1
Family Reunion, The 1958,O 21,39:1
Family Reunion, The 1958,O 26,II,1:1
Power and the Glory, The 1958,D 12,2:7
Beaux' Stratagem, The 1959,F 25,35:4
Julius Caesar 1959,Ag 4,30:1
Julius Caesar 1959,Ag 16,II,1:1
Great God Brown, The 1959,O 7,48:1
Great God Brown, The 1959,O 18,II,1:1
Pictures in the Hallway 1959,D 28,19:1
Peer Gynt 1960,Ja 24,II,1:1
Henry IV 1960,Mr 2,42:1
Henry IV 1960,Mr 13,II,1:1
Henry IV 1960,Ap 19,41:1
Henry IV, Part II 1960,Ap 24,II,1:1
She Stoops to Conquer 1960,N 2,42:5
She Stoops to Conquer 1960,N 13,II,1:1
She Stoops to Conquer 1960,N 15,36:3
Plough and the Stars, The 1960,D 7,56:2
Octoroon, The 1961,Ja 28,13:1
Hamlet 1961,Mr 17,17:1
Hamlet 1961,Mr 26,II,1:1
Hamlet 1961,Ap 30,II,1:1
Abe Lincoln in Illinois 1963,Ja 23,5:2
Taming of the Shrew, The 1963,Mr 8,9:1
Firebugs, The 1963,N 22,41:1
King Lear 1963,N 23,22:1
Wars of the Roses, The (Part I) 1970,Jl 2,30:1
Wars of the Roses, The (Part II) 1970,Jl 3,15:1
Richard III 1970,Jl 4,11:1
Henry VI, Parts I, II, III 1970,Jl 5,II,3:1
Vaughan, Stuart (Miscellaneous)
Lysistrata 1959,N 25,19:4
Vaughan, Stuart (Playwright)
Tristram 1962,O 29,36:1
Vaughan, Stuart (Scenic Designer)
Romeo and Juliet 1957,Je 28,30:2
Two Gentlemen of Verona 1957,Jl 23,21:5
Macbeth 1957,Ag 16,11:2
Richard III 1957,N 26,41:1
Vaughan, William
Piper, The 1920,Mr 20,14:2
Counsellor-at-Law 1942,N 25,17:2
Vaughan, Williams (Composer)
Poisoned Kiss, The 1936,Je 7,IX,5:1
Poisoned Kiss, The 1937,Ap 22,19:1
Vaughn, Bill
Camels Are Coming, The 1931,O 3,20:4
Vaughn, David
Peace 1969,Ja 28,49:1
Vaughn, Dona D
Company 1970,Ap 27,40:1
Vaughn, Edna
Blood and Sand 1921,S 21,16:2
Vaughn, Eric
Poet's Follies of 1955 1955,My 15,II,3:1
Vaughn, Gerald
Satellite 1935,N 21,27:5
Vaughn, Gladys (Director)
Othello 1964,Jl 15,29:1
Vaughn, Heidi
What Did We Do Wrong? 1967,O 23,56:1
Vaughn, Hilda
Lady Bug 1922,Ap 18,15:3
Glory Hallelujah 1926,Ap 7,26:2
Seed of the Brute 1926,N 2,34:3
Prisoner, The 1927,D 30,22:2
Only the Heart 1942,D 7,22:3
It's Up to You 1943,Ap 1,19:1
Get Away Old Man 1943,N 25,40:2
Jacobowsky and the Colonel 1944,Mr 15,17:2
On Whitman Avenue 1946,My 9,28:2
Temporary Island, A 1948,Mr 15,27:3
Celebration 1948,Ap 12,24:2
Medea 1949,My 3,31:2

Vaughn, Hilda—Cont
Devil's Disciple, The 1950,Ja 26,23:2
Devil's Disciple, The 1950,F 5,II,1:1
River Line, The 1957,Ja 3,29:2
Vaughn, Hilda (Original Author)
Soldier and the Gentlewoman, The
1933,My 7,IX,1:4
Vaughn, Hilda (Playwright)
She, Too, Was Young 1938,S 4,X,2:1
Vaughn, Jack
Way, The 1940,O 12,20:3
Vaughn, Madelaine
Red Planet 1932,D 19,19:2
Vaughn, Olive
Ziegfeld Follies 1920,Je 23,14:1
George White's Scandals 1921,Jl 12,14:1
George White's Scandals 1922,Ag 29,10:1
George White's Scandals 1923,Je 19,22:5
Scandals 1924,Jl 1,16:1
Vaughn, Peter
Twist of Sand, A 1969,F 22,36:1
Vaughn, Robert
Breaking Point, The 1923,Ag 17,8:4
Vaughn, Ross
House in Berlin, A (Als der Kreig zu Ende War);
Als der Kreig zu Ende War (A House in Berlin)
1950,D 27,32:3
Simpleton of the Unexpected Isles, The
1954,Ja 12,19:1
Vaughn, Ruth
Temporary Island, A 1948,Mr 15,27:3
Vaughn, Sanne
Jack Jack 1968,Je 23,74:5
Vaughn, Sharon
Funny Girl 1964,Mr 27,15:1
Vaughn, Stuart (Director)
Peer Gynt 1960,Ja 13,21:1
Vaughn, W E
Master of the Revels 1935,Ag 14,16:2
Vaughn, Walter
Bad Girl 1930,O 3,30:2
Old Man Murphy 1931,My 19,25:2
Trick for Trick 1932,F 19,14:2
Creeping Fire 1935,Ja 17,22:3
Vaughn, William
Counsellor-at-Law 1931,N 7,17:2
Help Yourself! 1936,Jl 15,15:1
Treasure Island 1938,My 15,II,2:3
Vaughns, Laura
Mamba's Daughters 1940,Mr 25,10:4
Vaux, William
By Jupiter 1942,Je 4,22:1
Firebird of Florence 1945,Mr 23,13:4
Vavra, Mr
Man Platonof, The 1929,Mr 3,VIII,3:1
Vayzatha
Megilla of Itzik Manger, The 1968,O 10,60:1
Vazquez, Carmen
Cabalgata 1949,Jl 8,14:2
Vea, Katina
Everyman 1953,O 12,30:2
Veakis, D
Oedipus Tyrannus 1952,N 25,35:2
Electra 1961,S 20,23:4
Choephori 1961,S 27,32:4
Eumenides 1961,S 27,32:4
Veale, Carrington
Fifty-Fifty 1937,N 20,21:1
Veale, Thomas C
Fifty-Fifty 1937,D 5,II,3:4
Veasey, William
Our Lan' 1947,Ap 19,11:2
Our Lan' 1947,S 29,16:5
Green Pastures, The 1951,Mr 16,35:2
Porgy and Bess 1953,Mr 10,25:5
Veaux, Clyde
Toto 1921,Mr 22,15:2
Desert Flower, The 1924,N 19,18:2
Deacon, The 1925,N 25,14:3
Gang War 1928,Ag 21,27:2
Cortez 1929,N 5,32:2
Room 349 1930,Ap 23,24:5
Girl Crazy 1930,O 15,27:1
On the Make 1932,My 24,23:2
Great Lover, The 1932,O 12,27:3
Whistling in the Dark 1932,N 4,25:2
Slight Case of Murder, A 1935,S 12,28:5
Veber, Pierre (Original Author)
Oh, Please! 1926,D 22,24:3
Veber, Pierre (Playwright)
Monsieur de Cinq Heures 1924,O 12,VIII,1:6
Kiss in a Taxi, The 1925,Ag 26,14:1
Divin Mensonge 1926,N 14,VIII,2:1
Epinard Gagne le Grand Steeple 1926,D 19,VII,3:3
On Ne Roule pas Antoinette 1927,Ap 10,VIII,2:7
Rejouissance, La 1929,F 24,IX,1:8
Femme au Chat, La 1929,Je 9,VIII,2:4
Madame Est Avec Moi 1937,My 16,X,2:6
Veber, Serge (Playwright)
Bonheur, Le 1923,N 20,23:3
Lulu 1927,O 2,VIII,2:4
Lulu 1928,O 28,IX,2:1
Veber (Playwright)
Passionement 1928,Ja 15,VIII,2:1

Veber (Playwright)—Cont

Sunny Days 1928,F 9,29:1
Vecchio, Alberto
Lute Song 1946,F 7,29:2
Vechetova, Bozena
Pierrot's Journey 1964,Ag 5,23:1
Button, Button 1970,O 20,41:1
Vecsey, Armand (Composer)
Hotel Mouse, The 1922,Mr 14,11:3
Nightingale, The 1927,Ja 4,20:4
Veda, Louis
Volpone 1928,Ap 10,32:1
Man's Estate 1929,Ap 2,28:2
R U R 1930,F 18,28:1
Marco Millions 1930,Mr 4,24:4
Month in the Country, A 1930,Mr 18,30:5
Farewell to Arms, A 1930,S 23,30:3
Midnight 1930,D 30,25:1
Vedder, Barbara (Translator)
Dossier, The 1961,Ja 14,15:2
Vedura, Duc di
Variations of 1940 1940,Ja 29,12:1
Veechio, Albert
Lute Song 1946,F 7,29:2
Veere, Rod (Miscellaneous)
Frankenstein 1968,O 3,54:1
Vees, Albert
Sing High, Sing Low 1931,N 13,26:4
World We Make, The 1939,N 21,19:1
Good Neighbor 1941,O 22,26:2
Vega, Jose (Miscellaneous)
Chalk Garden, The 1955,O 27,29:1
Very Special Baby, A 1956,N 15,43:2
Genius and the Goddess, The 1957,D 11,41:1
Handful of Fire 1958,O 2,45:3
Rashomon 1959,Ja 28,36:2
Aspern Papers, The 1962,F 8,26:1
Night Life 1962,O 24,44:1
Semi-Detached 1963,O 8,49:1
High Spirits 1964,Ap 8,34:1
Something More! 1964,N 11,36:1
Lion in Winter, The 1966,Mr 4,23:1
Those That Play the Clowns 1966,N 25,48:1
Natural Look, The 1967,Mr 13,45:2
To Clothe the Naked 1967,Ap 28,30:1
Something Different 1967,N 29,52:1
George M! 1968,Ap 11,48:1
Fire! 1969,Ja 29,26:1
Vega, Leslie
Dark Legend 1952,Mr 25,24:2
Vega, Lope de (Original Author)
Villana, La 1928,Ja 1,VIII,8:3
Esta Noche... Teatro 1968,O 15,40:1
Vega, Lope de (Playwright)
Dama Boba, La; Villano En Su Rincon, El;
　Fuenteovejuna 1935,S 22,X,2:5
Knight From Olmedo, The 1962,N 26,36:2
Veglia, Paul
Kismet 1965,Je 23,45:1
Vehr, Bill
Bluebeard 1970,My 5,58:1
Veide, Miriam
Dybbuk, The 1924,Ja 29,17:7
Veile, Joy
Captain Jinks of the Horse Marines 1938,Ja 28,16:2
Veiller, Anthony (Playwright)
Polonaise 1945,O 8,20:2
Veillers, Bayard (Director)
Damn Your Honor 1929,D 31,14:3
Veillers, Bayard (Mrs) (Playwright)
Two Mrs Carrolls, The 1935,Je 13,26:1
Veillers, Bayard (Playwright)
Trial of Mary Dugan, The 1927,S 20,33:1
Trial of Mary Dugan, The 1927,O 9,VIII,1:1
Within the Law 1928,Mr 6,20:1
Trial of Mary Dugan, The 1928,Mr 7,28:3
Trial of Mary Dugan, The 1928,Je 24,VIII,1:4
Trial of Mary Dugan, The 1928,S 30,IX,4:4
Damn Your Honor 1929,D 31,14:3
That's the Woman 1930,S 4,27:2
Veit, Martha
Untitled-Passion Play 1922,My 10,21:3
Veitch, Jack
Savages Under the Skin 1927,Mr 25,25:2
Vejar, Rudy
King and I, The 1964,Jl 7,26:1
Merry Widow, The 1964,Ag 18,24:2
Kismet 1965,Je 23,45:1
Velasco, Vi
Ballad for a Firing Squad 1968,D 12,64:2
Velasquez, Juan
Bamboo Cross 1955,F 22,17:2
Highway Robbery 1955,N 8,36:1
Velden, Kaj (Scenic Designer)
Take a Bow 1944,Je 16,15:3
Velebny, Karel (Composer)
Pierrot's Journey 1964,Ag 5,23:1
Velez, Frank
Pleasure Bound 1929,F 19,22:4
Velez, Joe
Gianni Schicci 1969,F 25,36:1
Tale of Kasane, The 1969,F 25,36:1
Critic, The 1969,Mr 9,76:5

Velez, Lupe
Vaudeville (Palace) 1931,Je 22,17:2
Hot-Cha! 1932,Mr 9,17:3
Strike Me Pink 1933,Mr 6,16:3
Transatlantic Rhythm 1936,O 2,16:3
You Never Know 1938,Mr 4,16:3
You Never Know 1938,S 22,26:3
Velie, Janet
Mary 1920,O 19,12:1
Perfect Fool, The 1921,N 8,28:2
Round the Town 1924,My 22,14:3
Bye Bye, Barbara 1924,Ag 26,6:3
Grab Bag, The 1924,O 7,26:2
Cocoanuts, The 1925,D 9,30:1
Rain or Shine 1928,F 10,26:3
Three Cheers 1928,O 16,28:1
Heads Up! 1929,N 12,34:1
Velie, Jay
Round the Town 1924,My 22,14:3
Grab Bag, The 1924,O 7,26:2
Vaudeville (Palace) 1926,O 26,24:2
A la Carte 1927,Ag 18,25:3
Vaudeville (Palace) 1932,O 3,15:5
Diff'rent 1937,N 21,II,10:7
Pygmalion 1938,Ja 27,16:3
No More Peace 1938,Ja 29,13:2
Fabulous Invalid, The 1938,O 10,15:1
Counsellor-at-Law 1942,N 25,17:2
Our Town 1944,Ja 11,24:5
Carousel 1945,Ap 20,24:2
Carousel 1949,Ja 26,28:2
Call Me Madam 1950,O 13,25:1
Happy Hunting 1956,D 7,30:1
Jennie 1963,O 18,35:2
Carousel 1966,D 16,56:2
Sound of Music, The 1967,Ap 27,52:1
Beyond Desire 1967,O 11,36:1
Sound of Music, The 1970,Jl 3,13:1
Velie, John D
Roof, The 1930,Je 14,9:2
Velie, Sheldon (Scenic Designer)
Fake, The 1924,O 7,26:3
Velinskaya, Helen
Bonfire to Glory 1936,Jl 28,23:4
Vellie, Jay
Coriolanus 1938,F 2,14:5
Carousel 1954,Je 3,32:2
Veloz, Frank (Director)
For Your Pleasure 1943,F 6,9:2
Veloz and Yolanda
Love Call, The 1927,O 25,33:1
Vaudeville (Palace) 1929,Ag 19,23:1
For Your Pleasure 1943,F 6,9:2
Velsey, Graham
Night Hostess 1928,S 13,31:2
Nut Farm, The 1929,O 15,34:3
London Calling 1930,O 20,29:1
Meet My Sister 1930,D 31,11:1
No More Frontier 1931,O 22,27:1
Food for Midas 1942,Ja 31,12:7
Savonarola 1942,Ap 24,20:2
Native Son 1942,O 24,10:6
Man's House, A 1943,Ap 3,10:4
Othello 1943,O 20,18:1
War President 1944,Ap 25,17:3
Embezzled Heaven 1944,N 1,20:2
And Be My Love 1945,F 22,30:4
As We Forgive Our Debtors 1947,Mr 11,37:2
Our Lan' 1947,S 29,16:5
Crucible, The 1953,Ja 23,15:2
Crucible, The 1953,Jl 2,20:2
Mummers and Men 1962,Mr 27,41:6
Velton, James
Dancers, The 1923,O 18,17:2
Velty, Juliette
Potiphar's Wife 1928,D 24,10:7
Ven, Johnnie
Arsenic and Old Lace 1943,D 13,18:6
Venable, Evelyn
Midsummer Night's Dream, A 1934,S 19,15:1
Venable, Jimmy
Three to Make Ready 1946,Mr 8,16:2
Venable, Lucy
Merry-Go-Rounders, The 1956,N 22,50:1
Venable, Lucy (Choreographer)
Merry-Go-Rounders, The 1956,N 22,50:1
Venable, Virginia
Fiesta 1929,S 18,35:1
It's a Grand Life 1930,F 11,30:3
Venables, Marcy (Miscellaneous)
People Is the Thing That the World Is Fullest Of
　1967,F 21,53:1
Venantonio, John
Our Town 1969,N 28,50:1
Vendenberg, Bram
'Tis of Thee 1940,O 28,21:3
Vendig, Laurie
Twelfth Night 1954,N 10,42:2
Merchant of Venice, The 1955,F 23,23:2
Macbeth 1955,O 20,42:2
Venditti, Nick
Jar, The 1969,Ap 23,42:1

Vendroff, Reuben
Town Lunatics 1933,F 6,11:4
Vene, Roger P
Robin Hood 1944,N 8,28:2
Veness, Amy
Bird in Hand 1929,Ap 5,28:2
Veney, Norma
Skin of Our Teeth, The 1955,Ag 18,16:1
Veneziani, Rossetta
Rose Tattoo, The 1966,O 21,36:2
Vengay, Anita
Barber Had Two Sons, The 1943,F 2,22:2
Venkstern, N (Playwright)
Pikvikski Klub; Pickwick Club, The 1936,O 4,IX,1:8
Venn, Johnnie
Alice in Arms 1945,F 1,18:4
Vennegut, Marjorie
First Man, The 1922,Mr 6,9:2
Venneri, Darwin
Darwin's Theories 1960,O 19,53:2
Venneri, Darwin (Composer)
Darwin's Theories 1960,O 19,53:2
Venneri, Darwin (Lyricist)
Darwin's Theories 1960,O 19,53:2
Venning, Una
Symphony in Two Flats 1930,S 17,30:4
Venoig, Laurie
Twelfth Night 1954,D 12,II,3:1
Venora, Lee
Happy Town 1959,O 8,49:2
Kean 1961,N 3,28:2
Kean 1961,N 12,II,1:1
Patience 1964,Mr 26,42:1
King and I, The 1964,Jl 7,26:1
Kismet 1965,Je 23,45:1
Ventantonio, John
All's Well That Ends Well 1970,Je 16,53:1
Othello 1970,Je 22,43:1
Othello 1970,S 15,51:1
Ventura, Clyde
Milk Train Doesn't Stop Here Anymore, The
　1963,Ja 18,7:1
Saint of Bleecker Street, The 1965,Mr 19,28:1
Ventura, Elinor
Ist Geraldine ein Engel? 1946,N 4,33:4
Ventura, Toni
Rugantino 1964,F 7,34:1
Ventura, William
Gondoliers, The 1935,Ag 6,20:5
Ventura (Mme)
Fiaccola Sotto il Moggio, La 1927,D 25,VIII,4:3
Carnaval des Enfants, Le 1930,Mr 2,IX,4:2
Venture, Dick
This Happy Breed 1952,Ap 4,23:2
Venture, H (Producer)
Tambourines to Glory 1963,N 4,47:1
Venture, Richard
Rose in the Wilderness 1949,Ja 5,21:2
Don't Go Away Mad 1949,My 10,28:2
Edge of the Sword, The 1949,N 10,40:3
Deirdre of the Sorrows 1949,D 15,51:2
Once Around the Block 1950,My 25,36:2
Dinosaur Wharf 1951,N 9,23:2
Merchant of Venice, The 1953,Mr 5,20:2
Child Buyer, The 1962,My 14,35:1
Winter's Tale, The 1963,Je 29,13:1
Midsummer Night's Dream, A 1963,Jl 1,19:2
Great White Hope, The 1967,D 14,58:1
Iceman Cometh, The 1968,Ap 1,58:1
Country People 1970,Ja 19,35:1
Venture, S (Producer)
Tambourines to Glory 1963,N 4,47:1
Venturi, Aldo
Trial, The 1955,Je 15,35:2
Venturo, William
Yeomen of the Guard, The 1935,Jl 30,16:4
Venus, William
Sancho Panza 1923,N 27,23:1
Venuta, Benay
Anything Goes 1935,S 15,IX,1:1
Orchids Preferred 1937,Ap 29,16:6
Orchids Preferred 1937,My 12,26:5
Kiss the Boys Goodbye 1938,S 29,30:2
By Jupiter 1942,Je 4,22:1
By Jupiter 1942,Ag 30,VIII,1:1
Nellie Bly 1946,Ja 22,32:2
Nellie Bly 1946,Ja 27,II,1:1
Hazel Flagg 1953,F 12,22:2
Copper and Brass 1957,O 18,19:2
Carousel 1965,Ag 11,39:1
Annie Get Your Gun 1966,Je 1,42:2
Venza, Jac (Costume Designer)
Cretan Woman, The 1954,Jl 8,18:2
Comic Strip 1958,My 15,26:2
Venza, Jac (Scenic Designer)
Cretan Woman, The 1954,Jl 8,18:2
Comic Strip 1958,My 15,26:2
On the Town 1959,Ja 16,36:1
On the Town 1959,Ja 25,II,1:1
Vera, Rosa
Clinging Vine, The 1922,D 25,20:2
Vera-Ellen
By Jupiter 1942,Je 4,22:1

Vera-Ellen—Cont
By Jupiter 1942,Ag 16,VIII,2:1
Connecticut Yankee, A 1943,N 18,30:2

Verat, Pierre
Maitresse de Roi 1926,D 1,24:1

Verba, Vahrah
Five O'Clock Girl, The 1927,O 11,26:3

Verberkmoes, Robert (Miscellaneous)
Taming of the Shrew, The 1956,Ag 11,11:2

Verberkmoes, Robert (Scenic Designer)
Camille 1956,S 19,33:1
Trojan Women, The 1957,Mr 19,42:7
Shakuntala 1959,S 10,41:2
Mister Roberts 1962,O 12,27:2

Verbit, Helen
Fiorello! 1959,N 24,45:3
Call It Virtue 1963,Mr 28,8:2
Fiddler on the Roof 1964,S 23,56:2
Lovers and Other Strangers 1968,S 19,63:1

Verceil Sisters
Earl Carroll's Vanities 1928,Ag 7,25:2

Vercors (Playwright)
Zoo 1964,F 15,15:3

Vercourt, A (Playwright)
Alcide Pepis 1923,O 30,17:2

Verdera, Clara
Breakfast in Bed 1920,F 4,12:1

Verdi, Francis M
Enter Madame 1920,Ag 17,11:2
Square Crooks 1926,Mr 2,23:2
Sh! The Octopus 1928,F 22,19:2

Verdi, Francis M (Playwright)
Inside Story, The 1932,F 23,23:2

Verdi, Fred
Blood and Sand 1921,S 21,16:2
Gang War 1928,Ag 21,27:2

Verdi, Giuseppe (Composer)
My Darlin' Aida 1952,O 28,36:4

Verdi, Joe
My Country 1926,Ag 10,19:1
I'd Rather Be Right 1937,N 3,28:2
Return of the Vagabond, The 1940,My 14,27:2
Men to the Sea 1944,O 4,25:2
Bell for Adano, A 1944,D 7,21:2
In Any Language 1952,O 9,40:2

Verdie, Negro
Cantatrice Chauve, La 1962,Ja 16,30:1
Laundry, The 1963,F 19,5:2

Verdier, Paul (Director)
Nuns, The 1970,Je 2,35:1

Verdier, Paul (Playwright)
Nuns, The 1970,Je 2,35:1

Verdon, Gwen
Alive and Kicking 1950,Ja 18,25:5
Can-Can 1953,My 8,28:1
Can-Can 1953,My 17,II,1:1
Damn Yankees 1955,My 6,17:1
New Girl in Town 1957,My 15,40:1
New Girl in Town 1957,My 26,II,1:1
Redhead 1959,F 6,21:1
Redhead 1959,F 15,II,1:1
Sweet Charity 1966,Ja 31,22:1

Verdun, Paula
Dark Hours, The 1932,N 15,24:2

Verea, Lisette
Merry Widow, The 1943,Ag 5,19:2
Merry Widow, The 1943,Ag 22,II,5:1
Merry Widow, The 1944,O 9,17:1

Verebes, Ernst
Lied der Liebe, Das 1932,F 7,VIII,1:3

Vereker, Sidney
Battle Hymn 1936,My 23,12:1
Hymn to the Rising Sun 1937,My 7,28:2

Verga, Giovanni (Playwright)
Lupa, La 1969,Je 5,54:1

Vergi, Elsa
Medea 1964,S 1,31:1
Iphigenia in Aulis 1968,N 13,40:1
Hippolytus 1968,N 20,38:3

Verhaeren, Emile (Playwright)
Cloister, The 1921,Je 6,16:3
Clotture, Le 1927,Ja 23,VII,2:1

Verhey, Keith
Gondoliers, The 1954,Ap 14,24:3

Verigun, Frank
Holy Terror, A 1925,S 29,31:2
Broadway 1926,S 17,19:3
Ringside 1928,Ag 30,13:2
Sing High, Sing Low 1931,N 13,26:4
Wild Waves 1932,F 20,11:4
American Dream; 1933 1933,F 22,24:5
American Dream; 1650 1933,F 22,24:5
I Myself 1934,My 10,24:6
Bride of Torozko, The 1934,Jl 10,24:7
Bride of Torozko, The 1934,S 14,24:2
Woman of Destiny, A 1936,Mr 3,25:2

Verikaitis, Vaclovas
H M S Pinafore 1960,S 8,41:1

Verina, Pola
Dagmar 1923,Ja 23,18:2

Verina, Winifrede
Three Musketeers, The 1921,My 20,18:5
Jack and Jill 1923,Mr 23,17:2
Ramblers, The 1926,S 21,32:2

Veritch, Robert
Case of Philip Lawrence, The 1937,Je 9,31:1

Verity, Amy
Pins and Needles 1922,F 2,20:1

Verkade, Edward
Hamlet 1925,D 8,29:2

Verklas, Bruce
Sextet 1958,N 27,53:1

Verley, Bernard
Hamlet 1965,Ja 23,15:4

Verly, Michele
Knock 1937,N 17,26:3
Jean de la Lune 1937,D 14,33:3
Jalousie du Barbouille, La 1937,D 28,28:7
Medecin Malgre Lui, Le 1937,D 28,28:7
Y'Avait un Prisonnier 1938,Ja 25,24:3

Vermeil, Henry
Avare, L'; Miser, The 1924,Mr 12,17:3

Vermel, Anne (Costume Designer)
Don Juan; Feast With the Statue, The 1956,Ja 4,21:4

Vermell, Henry
Affaires Son les Affaires, Les 1924,Mr 11,17:1

Vermilyea, Harold
Pagans 1921,Ja 5,11:1
Captain Applejack 1921,D 31,14:2
Alarm Clock, The 1923,D 25,26:2
Lady Killer, The 1924,Mr 13,14:2
Enemy, The 1925,O 21,20:1
Loose Ankles 1926,Ag 17,15:1
Los Angeles 1927,D 20,32:3
Killers 1928,Mr 14,28:3
Anna 1928,My 17,25:2
Man With Red Hair, A 1928,N 9,22:2
Midnight 1930,D 30,25:1
We Are No Longer Children 1932,Ap 1,17:2
Bad Manners 1933,Ja 31,15:5
Pure in Heart, The 1934,Mr 21,24:3
Fulton of Oak Falls 1937,Ja 2,15:3
Fulton of Oak Falls 1937,F 11,18:2
Madame Bovary 1937,O 6,28:4
Madame Bovary 1937,N 17,26:2
If I Were You 1938,Ja 9,II,3:2
If I Were You 1938,Ja 25,24:2
Gloriana 1938,N 26,18:4
Gabrielle 1941,Mr 26,26:2
Not in Our Stars 1941,Ap 26,20:5
Jacobowsky and the Colonel 1944,Mr 15,17:2
Jacobowsky and the Colonel 1944,Mr 19,II,1:1
Deep Are the Roots 1945,S 27,24:4
Deadfall 1955,O 28,20:1

Vermont, Ted (Director)
Pilgrim's Progress 1962,Mr 21,36:2

Vermonti, Edward
Eternal Road, The 1937,Ja 8,14:2

Vernay, Joseph
Duke in Darkness, The 1944,Ja 25,15:2

Verne, Adela
Vaudeville (Palace) 1926,Je 29,21:3
Vaudeville (Palace) 1927,My 31,25:1
Vaudeville (Palace) 1928,Mr 6,20:5
Vaudeville (Palace) 1928,Je 26,29:4
Vaudeville (Palace) 1930,Jl 7,22:2

Verne, Jules (Original Author)
Around the World 1946,Je 1,9:5
Around the World 1946,Je 9,II,1:1

Vernel, Marcel (Director)
Ladies All 1930,Jl 29,25:2

Verneuic, Louis (Playwright)
Lady-in-Law, The 1927,O 23,VIII,4:1
Satan 1927,N 27,IX,4:7

Verneuil, Juliette
Aiglon, L' 1924,O 21,21:1
Madame Sans-Gene 1924,N 4,30:1
Caprice, Un 1924,N 25,26:2
Parisienne 1924,N 25,26:2
Amoureuse 1924,N 28,13:1

Verneuil, Louis
Amant de Madame Vidal, L' 1928,Mr 25,IX,4:6

Verneuil, Louis (Director)
Affaires of State 1950,S 26,37:2
Love and Let Love 1951,O 20,11:2

Verneuil, Louis (Original Author)
No Ordinary Lady 1936,O 1,28:3
Matrimony, PFD 1936,N 13,26:3

Verneuil, Louis (Playwright)
Traite d'Auteuil, Le 1921,Jl 17,VI,1:8
Love Habit, The 1923,Mr 15,17:1
Love Habit, The 1923,Mr 25,VIII,1:1
Women and Ladies 1925,My 10,VIII,4:4
Oh! Mama 1925,Ag 20,22:2
Oh! Mama 1925,Ag 30,VII,1:1
Cousin Sonia 1925,D 8,28:3
First Love 1926,N 9,31:2
Maitre Bolbec et son Mari 1926,N 14,VIII,2:1
Tu m'ePouseras 1927,Mr 13,VII,2:7
Mademoiselle Flute 1927,Je 12,VII,2:1
Amant de Madame Vidal, L' 1928,Mr 25,IX,4:6
Ma Soeur et Moi 1928,Ap 29,IX,2:3
Jealousy 1928,O 23,32:2
Course a l'Etoile, La 1928,D 9,X,2:7
Boom Boom 1929,Ja 29,26:4
He's Mine 1929,N 17,IX,2:4
Guignol 1930,Mr 30,VIII,2:4

Verneuil, Louis (Playwright)—Cont
Miss France 1930,Ap 13,X,2:7
Meet My Sister 1930,D 31,11:1
Banque Nemo, La 1931,D 13,VIII,2:2
T'Amo E Sarai Mia; I Love You and You'll Be Mine 1932,Mr 21,19:4
Avril 1932,O 16,IX,2:2
Mari Que J'ai Voulu, Le 1934,Ap 29,IX,2:2
Ecole des Contribuables, L' 1934,Ap 29,IX,2:2
Homme au Foulard Bleu, L' 1935,My 26,XI,2:2
Vive le Roi 1935,N 24,IX,3:7
Fontaines Lumineuses, Les 1935,D 29,IX,2:1
Pile ou Face 1936,Jl 5,IX,1:8
Difficulty of Getting Married, The 1936,Jl 7,22:1
Matrimony, PFD 1936,N 6,28:4
Vie Parisienne, La 1936,N 22,13,14:5
Affairs of State 1950,S 26,37:2
Affairs of State 1950,O 1,II,1:1
Love and Let Love 1951,O 20,11:2
Affairs of State 1952,Ag 22,12:2

Verney, Richard
Threepenny Opera, The 1955,S 21,38:1
Threepenny Opera, The 1956,Mr 11,II,1:1
Threepenny Opera, The 1960,S 15,44:3

Vernick, Isidore
Awake and Sing! 1938,D 23,16:6

Vernier, Robert
Dark of the Moon 1958,F 27,22:2

Vernille, Nitza
Go-Go 1923,Mr 13,19:4
Vaudeville (Palace) 1927,Jl 26,16:5
Vaudeville (Palace) 1928,My 15,17:1
Vaudeville (Palace) 1929,N 11,20:5
Forbidden Melody 1936,N 3,33:1

Vernille and Donaldson
Revels of 1936 1935,S 30,12:4

Verno, Jerry
Alfie 1964,D 18,27:1

Vernon, Anne
Little Hut, The 1953,O 8,37:2

Vernon, Claire
Trial of Dr Beck, The 1937,Ag 10,22:2

Vernon, Dorothy
Hot Money 1931,N 9,22:2
No Questions Asked 1934,F 6,24:3
Hide and Seek 1934,Ag 7,20:2
Room Service 1935,N 17,II,7:7
Red, Hot and Blue! 1936,O 30,26:3

Vernon, Elmer
Best Foot Forward 1941,O 2,28:2

Vernon, Frank (Director)
Matriarch, The 1930,Mr 19,24:5

Vernon, Frank (Original Author)
Matriarch, The 1930,Mr 19,24:5

Vernon, Frank (Playwright)
Red Rust 1929,D 18,31:1
Matriarch, The 1930,Mr 19,24:5

Vernon, Frank (Translator)
Maya 1927,D 11,IX,2:1
Little Catherine 1931,N 19,27:2
Little Catherine 1931,D 6,VIII,2:7

Vernon, Gilbert
Cranks 1956,My 14,23:1
Cranks 1956,N 27,32:1

Vernon, Grenville (Playwright)
Menagerie 1935,Jl 2,24:3

Vernon, Gwynedd
Lucky One, The 1922,N 21,15:2
As You Like It 1923,Ap 24,24:1

Vernon, Harry M (Playwright)
By the Way 1926,Ap 16,20:3

Vernon, Hope
Florida Girl 1925,N 3,34:1

Vernon, Isabel
Opportunity 1920,Jl 31,5:1
Cafe de Danse 1929,Ja 16,22:2
Tired Business Man, The 1929,Je 5,32:5
Uncle Vanya 1930,Ap 16,26:5

Vernon, Jackie
At Home at the Palace 1967,Ag 1,23:1

Vernon, John
As You Like It 1959,Jl 1,27:1
King John 1960,Je 29,26:2
Romeo and Juliet 1960,Jl 1,14:1
Coriolanus 1961,Je 21,31:2
Henry VIII 1961,Je 22,22:1
Taming of the Shrew, The 1962,Je 21,25:1
Troilus and Cressida 1965,Ag 13,17:1
Royal Hunt of the Sun, The 1965,O 27,36:2

Vernon, Lou
Green Pastures, The 1930,F 27,26:1

Vernon, Margaret (Playwright)
Yellow 1926,S 22,30:1

Vernon, Marie
Fall and Rise of Susan Lenox, The 1920,Je 11,11:2

Vernon, Olga
Fools Rush In 1934,D 26,19:2

Vernon, Shirley
Puzzles of 1925 1925,F 3,25:3
Good News 1927,Ag 14,VII,2:1
Good News 1927,S 7,35:4
Sons o' Guns 1929,N 27,30:4

Vernon, Valentine
Audition of the Apprentice Theatre 1939,Je 2,26:2
Johnny Belinda 1940,S 19,26:2

Vernon, Valentine—Cont

As You Like It 1941,O 21,29:2
Vernon, Virginia (Playwright)
Red Rust 1929,D 18,31:1
Little Catherine 1931,N 19,27:2
Vernon, Virginia (Translator)
Maya 1927,D 11,IX,2:1
Little Catherine 1931,D 6,VIII,2:7
Vernon, Vivian
Sally 1920,D 22,16:1
Du Barry 1932,N 23,15:2
Shady Lady 1933,Jl 6,26:3
Vernon, Wally
Vaudeville (Palace) 1932,My 2,13:2
Vernon, Ward
Overture 1930,D 8,26:4
Vernon, Whit
Song of Bernadette 1946,Mr 27,22:2
Vero, Marie
Vaudeville (Palace) 1927,Ja 4,21:2
Verola, Paul (Translator)
Outward Bound 1927,Ja 30,VII,2:4
Verona
Gay Paree 1926,N 10,24:2
Cherry Blossoms 1927,Mr 29,22:3
Veronica
Artists and Models 1923,Ag 21,12:2
Half-Caste, The 1926,Mr 30,20:4
Veronica, Ann
Neighbors 1969,Ja 15,38:2
Veronica, Betty
Earl Carroll's Vanities 1930,Jl 2,28:3
Verry, Pierre
Evening of Pantomime, An 1955,S 21,38:1
Marcel Marceau 1956,F 2,18:1
Untitled-Pantomime 1958,Ja 22,23:1
Overcoat, The 1960,S 7,45:1
Marcel Marceau 1963,Ja 3,5:7
Marcel Marceau 1965,N 18,56:1
Vershinin, Ilya (Playwright)
Counterattack 1943,F 4,27:2
Vert, Bernice
Boyd's Daughter 1940,O 12,20:2
Vert (Composer)
Leyenda del Beso, La 1942,N 20,26:4
Vertes, Marcel (Costume Designer)
Seventh Heaven 1955,My 27,16:2
Vertes, Marcel (Scenic Designer)
Seventh Heaven 1955,My 27,16:2
Verwayne, Percy
Black Boy 1926,O 7,30:2
Porgy 1927,O 11,26:2
Sweet Chariot 1930,O 24,30:2
Singin' the Blues 1931,S 17,21:3
Scrap Book 1932,Ag 2,20:3
Too Many Boats 1934,S 12,26:3
Walk Together Chillun 1936,F 5,15:2
Conjur' Man Dies 1936,Mr 12,18:5
Androcles and the Lion 1938,D 17,10:5
Jeb 1946,F 22,20:2
Vesely, Pavel
Laterna Magika 1964,Ag 4,21:1
Vesselli, Judith
Ladies' Night 1920,Ag 10,10:1
Vest, Bud
Sweet Charity 1966,Ja 31,22:1
Hallelujah, Baby! 1967,Ap 27,51:1
Vestel, Guy de
Atout... Coeur 1936,Mr 27,25:4
Son Mari 1936,Ap 17,17:3
Vestel, Guy de (Director)
Atout... Coeur 1936,Mr 27,25:4
Son Mari 1936,Ap 17,17:3
Vestoff, Floria
Ballyhoo 1930,D 23,24:1
Vestoff, Floria (Lyricist)
Russell Patterson's Sketch-Book 1960,F 8,35:1
Vestoff, Marian
Vaudeville (Palace) 1929,F 4,21:4
Vestoff, Valodia
Artists and Models 1924,O 16,33:3
Katja 1926,O 19,27:3
Allez-Opp! 1927,Ag 3,29:3
Vaudeville (Palace) 1929,F 4,21:4
Vaudeville (Palace) 1929,Mr 11,22:5
Anything Goes 1934,N 22,26:1
Vestoff, Virginia
Fallout 1959,My 21,36:2
Crystal Heart, The 1960,F 16,31:2
From A to Z 1960,Ap 21,23:2
Baker Street 1965,F 17,36:1
Ben Bagley's New Cole Porter Revue
1965,D 23,20:1
Man With a Load of Mischief, The 1966,N 7,65:1
Love and Let Love 1968,Ja 4,30:1
1776 1969,Mr 17,46:2
Vetchor, (Mlle)
1860: or, Aris; 1860, or an Interrupted Festival
1931,O 22,27:1
Veviorke (Playwright)
Philosopher, A - A Drunkard 1936,S 28,14:3
Veynes, Francois de (Playwright)
Chagrins d'Amour 1926,N 14,VIII,2:1
Grandee Penitence, La 1926,N 14,VIII,2:1

Vezin, Cornelius
Gentlemen of the Press 1928,Ag 28,27:2
Topaze 1930,F 13,25:3
Sing High, Sing Low 1931,N 13,26:4
Via, Dick
Lovers, Villains and Fools: A Shakespearean
Variety Show 1956,O 24,44:7
Via, Richard A
Great Magician, The 1951,N 22,45:1
Vialar, Paul (Original Author)
Obbligato 1958,F 19,22:2
Vialar, Paul (Playwright)
Homme Qui Jouait du Banjo, L' 1926,O 24,VIII,2:1
Coeur Tout Neuf, Un 1928,F 12,VIII,1:3
Vialle, Max
Grosse Valise, La 1965,D 15,52:1
Vian, Boris (Playwright)
Empire Builders, The 1968,O 2,34:1
Vianna, Oduvaldo (Playwright)
Amor 1937,Ap 22,18:6
Viau, Joseph
Good Morning, Dearie 1921,N 2,20:2
Vibach, Karl
Faust, Part I; Play, The 1961,F 5,27:2
Viber, Nene
Time of Your Life, The 1939,O 26,26:2
Time of Your Life, The 1940,S 24,27:2
Vichey, Luben (Producer)
Men and Dreams 1966,S 7,51:2
Vick, Hal
Sambo 1970,Jl 23,24:1
Vickers, John
Visit, The 1960,Mr 9,38:3
Vickers, Yvette
Gang's All Here, The 1959,O 2,23:1
Vickery, Edward
Merry-Go-Round 1932,Ap 23,11:2
Vickery, Edwin
Caught 1925,O 6,31:2
Henry's Harem 1926,S 14,25:2
Criminal Code, The 1929,O 3,28:2
Rap, The 1931,Ap 7,31:2
Murder at the Vanities 1933,S 13,22:4
Ragged Army 1934,F 27,16:5
If This Be Treason 1935,S 24,28:2
Vickery, James
Story Teller, The 1951,D 15,11:3
Joan of Lorraine 1955,Mr 26,12:2
Macbeth 1955,O 20,42:2
Titus Andronicus 1956,D 3,40:2
Clearing in the Woods, A 1959,F 13,32:1
Vickery (Costume Designer)
Redemptor, The 1959,My 5,40:1
Vicory, Frances
Blind Mice 1930,O 16,28:2
Victor, Charles
Jane 1947,F 9,II,3:7
Victor, Dee
Way of the World, The 1954,S 30,38:2
Way of the World, The 1954,O 17,II,1:1
White Devil, The 1955,Mr 15,32:5
Carefree Tree, The 1955,O 12,37:2
Dandy Dick 1956,Ja 11,37:2
Diary of a Scoundrel 1956,N 5,41:1
Right You Are (If You Think You Are)
1957,Mr 5,37:1
Fashion 1959,Ja 21,27:1
Child Buyer, The 1964,D 22,35:1
Judith 1965,Mr 25,42:2
You Can't Take It With You 1965,N 24,32:1
School for Scandal, The 1966,N 22,33:2
Right You Are (If You Think You Are)
1966,N 23,34:2
War and Peace 1967,Mr 22,42:1
Victor, Dorothy Dee
Moon in the Yellow River, The 1961,F 7,40:2
Victor, Eric
You'll See Stars 1943,Ja 1,26:6
Inside U S A 1948,My 1,19:2
Inside U S A 1948,My 23,II,1:1
Inside U S A 1948,Je 13,II,6:6
Inside U S A 1948,Ag 29,II,1:1
Victor, Eric (Choreographer)
You'll See Stars 1943,Ja 1,26:6
All for Love 1949,Ja 24,16:5
Victor, Josephine
Martinique 1920,Ap 27,18:2
Martinique 1920,My 2,VI,2:2
Skin Game, The 1920,O 21,11:1
Juliet and Romeo 1921,My 17,20:3
Vaudeville (Palace) 1921,My 17,20:3
Dolly Jordan 1922,O 4,26:1
Cup, The 1923,N 13,25:1
Pelican, The 1924,O 26,VIII,1:1
Judgment Day 1934,S 13,26:4
Wise Tomorrow 1937,O 5,29:2
Wise Tomorrow 1937,O 16,22:5
Summer Night 1939,N 3,17:1
Victor, Josephine (Director)
Doctor X 1931,F 10,25:1
Victor, Lucia
This Rock 1943,F 19,23:2

Victor, Lucia (Director)
Hello, Dolly! 1967,N 13,61:1
Bill Noname 1970,Mr 3,37:1
Hello, Dolly! 1970,Mr 30,52:1
Victor, Lucia (Miscellaneous)
Rope Dancers, The 1957,N 21,39:1
Take Me Along 1959,O 23,22:2
Becket 1960,O 6,50:1
Becket 1961,My 9,44:1
Rehearsal, The 1963,S 24,45:2
Hello, Dolly! 1964,Ja 17,22:1
Victor, Lucia (Playwright)
Detour After Dark 1959,Je 9,11:4
Victor, Lucia (Producer)
Milky Way, The 1943,Je 10,17:2
Boy Meets Girl 1943,Je 23,15:5
Victor, Marc
Sunset 1966,My 13,34:1
Victor, Paula
Dumbbell People in a Barbell World 1962,F 15,25:1
Victor, Robert (Playwright)
Peter Petrolus 1937,Ap 5,16:5
Peter Petrolus 1937,Ap 25,X,1:1
Victor, Thomas
Cave at Machpelah, The 1959,Jl 1,25:1
Victor, Victor (Playwright)
Unwritten Chapter, The 1920,O 12,18:1
Flight 1929,F 19,22:3
Flight 1929,Mr 24,X,1:1
Soliloquy 1938,N 29,26:4
Victoria, Vesta
Vaudeville (Palace) 1927,Ap 5,30:2
Victory, Frances
Daddy's Gone A-Hunting 1921,S 1,18:3
Letty Pepper 1922,Ap 11,22:2
Uptown West 1923,Ap 4,22:2
Strawberry Blonde, The 1927,F 8,20:3
Victory, Thomas Master
Phoebe of Quality Street 1921,My 10,20:1
Vicuna, Pablo
Amor 1937,Ap 22,18:6
Tierra Baja 1937,My 8,22:4
Vidal, Gore (Playwright)
Visit to a Small Planet 1957,F 8,18:1
Visit to a Small Planet 1957,F 24,II,1:1
Best Man, The 1960,Ap 1,39:1
Best Man, The 1960,Ap 10,II,1:1
Best Man, The 1960,O 5,44:6
Fire to the Sea 1961,N 15,20:5
Romulus 1962,Ja 11,27:1
Weekend 1968,Mr 14,50:2
Weekend 1968,Mr 31,II,1:1
Vidali, (Mme)
Night in Spain, A 1927,My 4,28:2
Vidiella, Tomas
Remolienda, La; Bawdy Party 1968,F 3,20:1
Vidor, Doris (Miscellaneous)
I Never Sang for My Father 1968,Ja 26,30:1
Viebrock, John
Trojan Horse, The 1940,O 31,28:3
Viehmann, Theodore (Director)
Final Balance, The 1928,O 31,28:3
Every Thursday 1934,My 11,25:5
Drums Professor, The 1935,Jl 30,17:2
Viele, Sheldon K (Scenic Designer)
Rising Son, The 1924,O 28,27:2
Servant in the House, The 1925,Ap 8,24:2
Enchanted April, The 1925,Ag 25,12:3
Jane-Our Stranger 1925,S 9,27:2
Craig's Wife 1925,O 13,21:2
One of the Family 1925,D 23,22:3
Wasp's Nest, The 1927,O 26,26:3
Three Cheers 1928,O 16,28:1
Vielhaber, Werner
Why Do I Deserve This? 1966,Ja 19,31:2
Viera, Robert
Dantons Tod 1927,D 21,28:3
Viereck, Peter (Playwright)
Tree Witch, The 1961,Je 5,39:4
Vierengle, Bob
Rules of the Game, The 1960,D 20,44:1
Viergol (Playwright)
Pibe de Corralon, El 1927,D 23,16:4
Viertel, Berthold (Director)
Grey Farm 1940,My 4,12:7
They Walk Alone 1941,Mr 13,24:2
Private Life of the Master Race, The
1945,Je 13,28:3
Private Life of the Master Race, The
1945,Je 17,II,1:1
Viertel, Joseph M (Playwright)
So Proudly We Hail 1936,S 23,28:4
Viertel, Peter (Playwright)
Survivors, The 1948,Ja 20,27:2
Survivors, The 1948,Ja 25,II,1:1
Vieuille, Jean-Paul (Costume Designer)
Pique-Nique en Campagne 1969,My 1,50:1
Guernica 1969,My 1,50:1
Vieuille, Jean-Paul (Scenic Designer)
Guernica 1969,My 1,50:1
Pique-Nique en Campagne 1969,My 1,50:1
Vieville, Andrew
Homme et Ses Fantomes, L' 1924,N 14,16:1

Vieville, Andrew—Cont
Bourgeois Gentilhomme, Le 1924,N 20,21:2
Taming of the Shrew, The 1924,N 25,27:3
Vigal, Al
Hot Rhythm 1930,Ag 22,18:5
Vigal, John
Keep Shufflin' 1928,F 28,18:3
Vigarez, Senorita
Mission Play, The 1925,F 1,IV,20:3
Viglione, Gina
13 Daughters 1961,Mr 3,17:2
Vigny, Alfred de (Playwright)
Chatterton 1926,O 3,VIII,2:1
Vigoda, Abe
Dance of Death, The 1960,S 14,51:1
Feast of Panthers 1961,Mr 21,32:1
Richard II 1961,Ag 30,25:1
Shadow of Heroes 1961,D 6,59:1
Witches' Sabbath 1962,Ap 20,22:2
Tempest, The 1962,Jl 17,18:2
Cherry Orchard, The 1962,N 15,46:2
Darker Flower, A 1963,Mr 11,7:2
Mrs Warren's Profession 1963,Ap 25,39:1
Cat and the Canary, The 1965,Ja 5,26:1
Persecution and Assassination of Marat As
Performed by the Inmates of the Asylum of
Charenton Under the Direction of the Marquis de
Sade, The 1967,Ja 4,34:1
Man in the Glass Booth, The 1968,S 27,41:1
Inquest 1970,Ap 24,38:1
Vigoda, Bob (Composer)
Political Party, A 1963,S 27,17:5
Vigoda, Bob (Lyricist)
Political Party, A 1963,S 27,17:5
Vigoda, Bob (Playwright)
Political Party, A 1963,S 27,17:5
Vigor, George
Tomorrow's a Holiday! 1935,D 31,10:2
Farewell Summer 1937,Mr 30,20:2
Vigran, Herbert
Achilles Had a Heel 1935,O 14,20:2
Cyrano de Bergerac 1936,Ap 28,17:1
Happy Valley, Limited 1936,Je 30,15:1
Having Wonderful Time 1937,F 22,12:5
Vigszinhaz (Producer)
Siege of Besztercze, The 1929,F 3,VIII,2:1
Viharo, Robert
Malcolm 1966,Ja 12,29:1
Winter Journey 1968,Mr 13,39:1
Vikas
Guide, The 1968,Mr 7,50:1
Viken, Brett
Miss Julie 1956,F 22,23:2
Vikings, The
Ziegfeld Follies 1934,Ja 5,24:3
Ziegfeld Follies 1943,Ap 2,16:2
Vilan, Demetrios
Gala Night 1930,F 26,22:4
Saluta 1934,Ag 29,13:4
Sunday Nights at Nine 1934,N 19,12:1
Ugly Runts, The 1935,Je 11,24:4
End of Summer 1936,Ja 31,17:1
On Your Toes 1936,Ap 13,14:4
On Your Toes 1937,Ag 3,21:2
Show Is On, The 1937,S 20,18:4
Vilan, Demetrios (Choreographer)
Belle Helene, La 1941,Jl 8,14:1
Vilan, Demetrios (Director)
On Borrowed Time 1953,Ja 1,19:1
Jane Eyre 1958,My 2,31:1
Vilan, Demetrios (Producer)
Belle Helene, La 1941,Jl 8,14:1
Vilar, Jean
Triomphe de l'Amour, Le 1958,O 17,32:1
Don Juan 1958,O 29,29:1
Cid, Le 1958,O 31,35:2
Resistible Rise of Arturo Ui, The 1960,N 16,51:2
Resistable Ascension of Arturo Ui, The
1960,D 25,II,5:1
Man for All Seasons, A 1963,My 11,15:1
Vilar, Jean (Director)
Triomphe de l'Amour, Le 1958,O 17,32:1
Marie Tudor 1958,O 22,39:1
Don Juan 1958,O 29,29:1
Cid, Le 1958,O 31,35:2
Antigone 1960,D 14,52:1
Resistable Ascension of Arturo Ui, The
1960,D 25,II,5:1
Red Roses for Me 1961,F 11,26:5
Man for All Seasons, A 1963,My 11,15:1
Vilar, Jean (Miscellaneous)
Resistible Rise of Arturo Ui, The 1960,N 16,51:2
Vilar, Jean (Playwright)
Oppenheimer File, The 1964,D 15,56:1
Vilar, Jean (Producer)
Lettre Morte 1960,Mr 29,47:6
Krapp's Last Tape 1960,Mr 29,47:6
Vilbert, Henri
Marius 1956,F 6,27:4
Vildrac, Charles (Playwright)
Paquebot Tenacity, Le 1920,Ag 15,VI,1:1
Steamship Tenacity 1922,Ja 3,20:2
Michel Auclair 1925,Mr 5,23:1
Pilgrimage, The; Pelerin, Le 1925,N 10,23:2

Paquebot Tenacity, Le 1930,Mr 9,IX,2:7
Return to Yesterday 1936,Ap 29,19:1
Return to Yesterday 1936,My 31,X,1:5
Paquebot Tenacity, Le 1939,Ja 10,16:4
Vilhon, Gilbert
Three Musketeers, The 1968,Je 26,43:1
Villa, Consuelo
Variations of 1940 1940,Ja 29,12:1
Villa, Danny
Billy 1969,Mr 24,56:1
Villa-Lobos, Heitor (Composer)
Magdalena 1948,Jl 28,27:2
Magdalena 1948,S 21,31:2
Magdalena 1948,S 26,II,7:1
Magdalena 1948,S 26,II,1:1
Villairs, Arthur
One Heluva Night 1924,Je 5,18:1
Villamil, Jaclynn
Annie Get Your Gun 1966,Je 1,42:2
Passionella 1966,O 19,53:1
Lady or the Tiger?, The 1966,O 19,53:1
Villani, Anthony
Magistrate, The 1959,My 14,30:6
Villani, Anthony (Miscellaneous)
Magistrate, The 1959,My 14,30:6
Villani, Fredd
Bonds of Interest, The 1951,D 1,7:2
Villani, Mario
Fifty Million Frenchmen 1929,N 28,34:4
Villar, Paco (Miscellaneous)
Vida es Sueno, La 1964,Mr 18,49:1
Villarias, Carlos
Wildcat, The 1921,N 28,16:2
Villars, Andree
Social Register, The 1931,N 10,28:2
Villars, Arthur
Innocent Idea, An 1920,My 26,9:4
Dr David's Dad 1924,Ag 14,10:3
Within the Gates 1934,O 23,23:1
Villars, Jessie
Why Men Leave Home 1922,Jl 30,VI,1:3
Why Men Leave Home 1922,S 13,18:2
Villasana, Juan
Rio Rita 1927,F 3,18:3
Cortez 1929,N 5,32:2
Room 349 1930,Ap 23,24:5
Farewell to Arms, A 1930,S 23,30:3
Villaz, Paul
Untitled-Revue 1968,O 21,55:4
Cabaret Rive Gauche 1969,S 5,30:1
Villechaize, Herve
Young Master Dante, The 1968,D 31,19:1
Honest-to-God Schnozzola, The 1969,Ap 22,40:2
Moondreamers, The 1969,D 9,68:1
Gloria and Esperanza 1970,F 5,32:1
Marie Vison, La 1970,Jl 15,29:1
Villella, Edward
Annie Get Your Gun 1958,F 20,29:2
Brigadoon 1962,My 31,21:4
Brigadoon 1963,F 1,6:2
Brigadoon 1964,D 24,9:1
Brigadoon 1967,D 14,59:2
Villemain
Vierge Folle, La; Foolish Virgin, The
1924,Mr 22,12:2
Villiers, George (Duke of Buckingham) (Playwright)
Rehearsal, The 1952,My 27,30:5
Villiers, James
Tomorrow With Pictures 1960,Je 3,26:3
Villiers, Mavis
Philadelphia, Here I Come! 1966,F 17,28:1
Vilna Troupe
Neveile, The 1924,F 9,16:2
Dybbuk, The 1937,F 24,18:4
Vilner, David
Cyrano de Bergerac 1968,Ap 26,30:1
Vilon, Una
Murder at the Vanities 1933,S 13,22:4
Vimes, Madeleine
Annonce Faite a Marie, L' 1965,Ap 6,33:2
Vimnera, August (Scenic Designer)
Hearts Are Trumps! 1927,Ap 8,21:1
Footlights 1927,Ag 20,8:2
Red Dust 1928,Ja 3,29:2
Silver Box, The 1928,Ja 18,23:1
Vimtour, Richard
Liliom 1940,Mr 26,17:2
Vinaver, Chemjo (Composer)
Jeremiah 1939,F 4,11:2
Vinaver, Steven (Director)
Diversions 1958,N 8,14:4
Divorce Me, Darling 1965,F 2,29:6
Vinaver, Steven (Lyricist)
Mad Show, The 1966,Ja 10,16:1
Vinaver, Steven (Playwright)
Diversions 1958,N 8,14:4
Vinay, Ramon
Streets of Paris, The 1939,Je 20,25:2
Vincent, Allen
Starlight 1925,Mr 4,17:2
Spread Eagle 1927,Ap 5,30:2
Vinegar Tree, The 1930,N 20,30:3

Vincent, Allen (Playwright)
Letters to Lucerne 1941,D 9,47:6
Letters to Lucerne 1941,D 24,14:2
Vincent, Charles
Casanova 1923,S 27,10:2
Vincent, Chuck (Lighting Director)
Love Your Crooked Neighbor 1969,D 30,40:1
Vincent, Chuck (Miscellaneous)
Parents and Children 1969,Ja 13,26:6
Geese 1969,Ja 13,26:6
Vincent, Chuck (Scenic Designer)
Harangues, The 1970,Ja 14,42:1
Day of Absence 1970,Mr 18,39:1
Brotherhood 1970,Mr 18,39:1
Akokawe 1970,Je 5,21:1
Vincent, Claude (Translator)
Conscience 1952,My 16,17:6
Vincent, Edgar
Reunion in New York 1940,F 22,28:4
Vincent, Frances
Side-Show 1931,My 16,13:1
Vincent, Frank
Liliom 1940,Mr 26,17:2
Vincent, George
Hamlet 1936,O 9,30:2
Rosalinda; Fledermaus, Die 1942,O 29,26:5
Vincent, Helen
Diamond Lil 1928,Ap 10,32:1
Vincent, Henry
Little Miss Charity 1920,S 3,6:3
Macbeth 1921,F 18,16:1
Red Light Annie 1923,Ag 22,10:3
Madame Pompadour 1924,N 12,20:6
Her Cardboard Lover 1927,Mr 22,30:5
Flight 1929,F 19,22:3
Diana 1929,D 10,37:1
Suspense 1930,Ag 13,22:3
Petticoat Influence 1930,D 16,34:6
Oliver Oliver 1934,Ja 6,18:5
Lady Jane 1934,S 11,24:2
O'Flynn, The 1934,D 28,24:1
Times Have Changed 1935,F 26,16:1
Tapestry in Gray 1935,D 28,10:2
Sweet Aloes 1936,Mr 5,24:5
Promise 1936,D 31,20:4
London Assurance 1937,F 19,14:5
Barchester Towers 1937,D 1,27:1
Bright Rebel 1938,D 28,24:2
Glamour Preferred 1940,N 16,13:2
My Fair Ladies 1941,Mr 24,12:7
Mrs January & Mr Ex 1944,Ap 1,10:2
Catherine Was Great 1944,Ag 3,16:1
Vincent, Irving (Director)
Prayer Meeting: or, The First Militant Minister
1969,Ap 27,92:1
Great Goodness of Life (A Coon Show)
1969,Ap 27,92:1
Black Quartet, A; Great Goodness of Life (A Coon
Show) 1969,Jl 31,28:1
Black Quartet, A; Prayer Meeting or The First
Militant Minister 1969,Jl 31,28:1
Prayer Meeting: or, The First Militant Minister
1969,Ag 3,II,1:4
Vincent, Irving (Miscellaneous)
At the Drop of a Hat 1959,O 9,22:2
Vincent, J J (Director)
Kultur 1933,S 27,24:3
Vincent, J J (Producer)
Kultur 1933,S 27,24:3
Vincent, Jack
Kissing Time 1920,O 12,18:2
Vincent, James
Letter, The 1927,S 27,30:1
Insult 1930,S 16,30:2
Criminal at Large 1932,O 11,26:3
Alien Corn 1933,F 21,17:2
Vincent, Jerry
Alice in Arms 1945,F 1,18:4
Vincent, Lawrence
Darker Flower, A 1963,Mr 11,7:2
Vincent, Marshall
Richard III 1920,Mr 8,7:1
Pigeon, The 1922,F 3,13:1
Malvaloca 1922,O 3,22:1
Number 7 1926,S 9,21:3
Cocktail Impromptu 1927,Ja 13,28:4
Last Torture, The 1927,Ja 13,28:4
Maid of All Work 1927,Ja 13,28:4
John 1927,N 5,16:4
Potiphar's Wife 1928,D 24,10:7
Vincent, Millard
Jest, The 1926,F 5,22:2
Vincent, Nat (Lyricist)
Liza 1922,N 28,24:1
Vincent, Nell
Iphigenia in Aulis 1921,Ap 8,18:2
Vincent, Paul
White Devil, The 1965,D 7,56:1
Vincent, Ralph
Sherlock Holmes 1928,F 21,18:4
Vincent, Romo
Beat the Band 1942,O 15,26:1
Marinka 1945,Jl 19,19:2

Vincent, Romo—Cont
Whoop-Up 1958,D 23,2:7
Vincent, Sean (Playwright)
Up the Rebels 1941,O 31,21:1
Audition, The 1968,Je 19,38:2
Vincent, Sean Patrick (Playwright)
Audition, The 1968,Jl 8,45:1
Audition, The 1968,Jl 14,II,4:5
Vincent, Virginia
Twilight Walk 1951,S 25,25:4
Wedding Breakfast 1954,N 22,29:2
Wedding Breakfast 1954,D 5,II,5:1
Vincent, Walter (Producer)
Headquarters 1929,D 5,32:4
Vincent, Yves
Streetcar Named Desire, A 1949,O 19,36:6
Turlututu 1962,S 29,14:2
Vincent Lopez and his band
Greenwich Village Follies 1924,S 17,16:1
Vinci, Nino
Aria del Continente, L' 1927,O 5,30:2
Vinciguerra, Frank (Composer)
Lysistrata 1968,N 15,42:1
Vincuna, Pablo
Todo un Hombre 1937,Ap 28,19:2
Vine, Billy
High Kickers 1941,N 1,21:2
Vine, Richard
Kismet 1953,D 4,2:4
Vine, Sam
World's a Stage, The 1969,My 13,42:1
Vines, Margaret
Take Two From One 1931,O 4,VIII,2:6
Faithful Heart, The 1932,Ja 17,VIII,2:6
Rudolph of Austria 1932,Ap 10,VIII,3:7
Party, A 1932,Jl 10,IX,1:2
Dinner at Eight 1933,Ja 7,11:5
Dinner at Eight 1933,Ja 29,IX,1:3
Richard of Bordeaux 1934,F 15,16:2
Night Arrival 1938,D 25,IX,5:4
Trip to Bountiful, The 1956,Jl 5,25:1
Vines, Murray
Guys and Dolls 1955,Ap 21,32:2
Vines, William
Hamlet 1964,Jl 4,9:1
Tempest, The 1970,F 15,67:1
Viney, Virginia
Commedia Dell' Arte 1957,Jl 5,13:2
Vinmera, August (Scenic Designer)
Mulberry Bush, The 1927,O 27,33:1
Vinnera (Scenic Designer)
Intruder, The 1928,Jl 26,25:4
Vinogradoff, Anatol
Witch of Castile, The 1930,O 25,21:1
Man With the Portfolio, The 1931,F 12,24:6
New Man, The 1932,Ap 22,23:2
Bread 1932,D 14,27:3
Wise Men of Chelm, The 1933,O 18,24:4
Vinogradoff, Anatol (Playwright)
Man With the Portfolio, The 1931,F 12,24:6
Vinroot, Fred
Make Me Disappear 1969,My 14,34:1
Vinson, Helen
Los Angeles 1927,D 20,32:3
Death Takes a Holiday 1931,F 17,29:1
Berlin 1931,D 31,16:1
Fatal Alibi, The 1932,F 10,26:6
Vinson, Helene (Miscellaneous)
Elliott Murphy's Aquashow 1956,Je 20,26:2
Vinson, Marc
Love Me Little 1958,Ap 15,42:2
Vinson, Maribel Y
Gay Blades 1937,N 12,26:6
Gay Blades 1937,N 16,27:1
Vinson, Maribel Y (Choreographer)
Gay Blades 1937,N 16,27:1
Vinson, Maribel Y (Director)
Gay Blades 1937,N 16,27:1
Vinsont, Gil
Madre, La 1959,F 12,24:1
Vinton, Arthur
Clubs Are Trumps 1924,O 15,27:1
Aloma of the South Seas 1925,Ap 21,18:1
Chicago 1926,D 31,11:1
Speakeasy 1927,S 27,30:1
Veils 1928,Mr 14,28:5
Big Fight, The 1928,S 19,33:1
Indiscretion 1929,Mr 5,28:1
On the Spot 1930,O 30,33:3
Constant Sinner, The 1931,S 15,30:1
Whistling in the Dark 1932,Ja 20,16:6
Libel! 1935,D 8,X,5:8
Libel! 1935,D 21,10:5
Forbidden Melody 1936,N 3,33:1
Frederika 1937,F 5,16:5
Come Across 1938,S 15,28:3
Day Will Come, The 1944,S 8,17:2
Arms and the Girl 1950,F 3,28:2
Vinton, Doris
Artists and Models 1924,O 16,33:3
Manhatters, The 1927,Ag 4,25:4
Say When 1928,Je 27,29:3
Luckee Girl 1928,S 17,28:6
Orchids Preferred 1937,Ap 29,16:6

Vinton, George
Papavert 1931,D 30,25:1
Vintour, Richard
She Stoops to Conquer 1949,D 29,21:3
Viol, W C
It's the Valet 1933,D 15,25:4
Viola, Al
Enemy of the People, An 1959,F 5,24:4
Come Share My House 1960,F 19,20:2
Viola, Al (Producer)
After the Angels 1961,F 11,27:5
Viola, Dolores
Oedipus Rex 1959,Ap 30,36:1
Viola, John
When Differences Disappear 1941,Je 3,17:4
Violett, Ellen (Playwright)
Copper and Brass 1957,O 18,19:2
Color of Darkness: An Evening in the World of
James Purdy; Cracks 1963,O 1,24:1
Color of Darkness: An Evening in the World of
James Purdy; Encore 1963,O 1,34:1
Color of Darkness: An Evening in the World of
James Purdy; You Reach for Your Hat
1963,O 1,34:1
Color of Darkness: An Evening in the World of
James Purdy; Sermon 1963,O 1,34:1
Color of Darkness: An Evening in the World of
James Purdy; Everything Under the Sun
1963,O 1,34:1
Color of Darkness: An Evening in the World of
James Purdy; Don't Call Me By My Right Name
1963,O 1,34:1
Violino, Terry
Bajour 1964,N 24,42:1
Violinsky (Composer)
Keep It Clean 1929,Je 25,35:5
Violinsky (Lyricist)
Keep It Clean 1929,Je 25,35:5
Vipond, Neil
Measure for Measure 1954,Je 30,23:1
Taming of the Shrew, The 1954,Jl 1,22:2
Merchant of Venice, The 1955,Jl 1,13:1
Tamburlaine the Great 1956,Ja 20,19:1
Hamlet 1957,Jl 3,15:2
Edward II 1958,F 12,32:5
Cicero 1961,F 9,37:2
Orthee 1962,D 29,5:5
Antigone 1962,D 29,5:5
Burn Me to Ashes 1963,N 20,48:1
Possibilities 1968,D 5,60:1
Viracola, Fiddle
Clerambard 1957,N 8,22:3
Lend an Ear 1959,S 25,20:5
Damask Drum, The 1961,F 4,15:1
Hans's Crime 1961,F 4,15:1
Beauty Part, The 1962,D 28,5:2
Wives, The 1965,My 18,35:4
Virdon, Leslie
Springboard, The 1927,O 13,23:1
Virginia and West
Greenwich Village Follies 1923,S 21,4:6
Virginians, The
Sing Out the News 1938,S 26,12:5
????? 1939,Ja 2,28:2
Virta, Nikolai (Playwright)
Conspiracy of the Doomed, The: or, In a Certain
Country 1949,Ap 10,6:1
Visaroff, Michael
Star Spangled 1936,Mr 11,23:1
Vischer, Joanna
Sacred Flame, The 1952,O 8,35:2
Full Moon in March, A 1960,S 20,48:1
Visco, Philip
Childhood 1962,Ja 12,28:1
Visconti, Luchino (Director)
After the Fall 1965,Ja 25,21:6
Visconti, Vera
Red Velvet Goat, The 1939,Ja 21,18:4
Mr Banks of Birmingham 1939,Ja 21,18:4
Viscusi, Anthony
Don Juan in the Russian Manner 1954,Ap 23,23:2
Vishnevsky, Alexander
Tsar Fyodor Ivanovitch 1923,Ja 9,26:1
Lower Depths, The 1923,Ja 16,16:1
Three Sisters, The 1923,Ja 30,12:2
Brothers Karamazov, The 1923,N 20,23:4
Mistress of the Inn, The; Locandiera, La
1923,N 22,16:1
In the Claws of Life 1923,N 30,23:4
Enemy of the People, An 1923,D 4,25:1
Uncle Vanya 1924,Ja 29,16:2
Vishnevsky (Playwright)
Last Defensive, The 1931,S 27,VIII,3:2
Viskovsky, Vladimir (Director)
Inspector General, The 1922,O 9,15:4
Vita, Michael
Promises, Promises 1968,D 2,59:3
Vitacco, Lou
Drunkard, The 1970,Ap 14,54:1
Ben Bagley's Shoestring Revues 1970,O 24,22:1
Vitak, Albertina
Peg o' My Dreams 1924,My 6,25:3
Hassard Short's Ritz Revue 1924,S 18,19:1

Vitak, Albertina—Cont
This Year of Grace 1928,N 8,27:1
Vitale, Adriano
Arabian Nights 1954,Je 25,15:2
Vitale, Gary
Doctor Faustus 1961,Ap 26,36:1
Vitale, Joseph
Music Hall Varieties 1932,N 23,15:3
Page Miss Glory 1934,N 28,24:2
One Good Year 1935,N 28,38:3
All Editions 1936,D 23,17:2
Common Ground 1945,Ap 26,27:2
Vitale, Lorenzo
Three Musketeers, The 1921,My 20,18:5
Vitali, Billi
Patriot for Me, A 1969,O 6,58:1
Vitalin, Freda
Dybbuk, The 1924,Ja 29,17:7
Vitalis, Roy
Circus Princess, The 1927,Ap 26,32:2
Marching By 1932,Mr 4,17:1
Vitelli, Joseph
Fuente Ovejuna; Sheep Well, The 1936,My 3,II,4:1
Vitez, Joan
Violet 1944,O 25,16:1
Vitez, Miklos (Playwright)
Overzealous Youth, The 1928,D 2,X,4:7
Viti, Geraldine
Golden Apple, The 1954,Mr 12,15:2
Vitiello, Peter
Emerald Slippers, The 1970,S 2,31:2
Vito, Frank
Cage, The 1961,Mr 6,30:1
Vitold, Michel
Bal des Voleurs, Le 1938,N 29,26:4
Precieuses Ridicules, Les 1938,D 13,30:3
Fourberies de Scapin, Les 1938,D 13,30:3
Faiseur, Le; Promoter, The 1938,D 27,12:3
Chacun Sa Verite 1939,Ja 24,17:1
37 Sous de M Montaudoin, Les 1939,F 7,17:2
Enterrement, L' 1939,F 7,17:2
37 Sous de M Montaudoin, Les 1939,F 7,17:2
Siegfried 1939,F 21,15:2
Barbier de Seville, Le 1939,Mr 7,19:2
Vitold, Michel (Director)
Britannicus 1961,Mr 3,17:1
Vitrac, Roger (Playwright)
Victor, or The Children Take Over 1968,Jl 10,22:4
Vits, Kathryn
Patience 1929,D 16,34:5
Vittes, Louis (Playwright)
Comes the Revelation 1942,My 27,26:2
Vittes, Michael (Playwright)
Limits 1968,F 19,52:1
Vitulli, Kenneth
Cave Dwellers, The 1961,O 16,34:2
Vivanco, Moises (Miscellaneous)
Flahooley 1951,My 15,39:1
Vivara
Dream Girl, The 1924,Ag 21,12:2
Vives, Amadeo (Composer)
Villana, La 1928,Ja 1,VIII,8:3
Vivian, Ann
Lyle 1970,Mr 21,16:2
Vivian, Daisy
Sophie 1920,Mr 3,12:2
Vivian, David
Ivory Door, The 1927,O 19,24:5
Peter Pan; Boy Who Would Not Grow Up, The
1928,N 27,36:3
Would-Be Gentleman, The 1930,Ap 30,29:2
Counsellor-at-Law 1931,N 7,17:2
Romeo and Juliet 1934,D 21,30:3
Barretts of Wimpole Street, The 1935,F 26,16:2
Romeo and Juliet 1935,D 24,10:2
Saint Joan 1936,Mr 10,27:4
Vivian, George
Rubicon, The 1922,F 22,13:1
Midsummer Night's Dream, A 1932,Jl 13,15:1
Vivian, George (Director)
Autumn Fire 1926,O 27,25:3
Who Cares 1930,Jl 9,27:1
Merchant of Venice, The 1931,N 17,31:1
Julius Caesar 1931,N 18,26:3
Hamlet 1931,N 19,26:6
Vivian, Lawrence
Would-Be Gentleman, The 1930,Ap 30,29:2
Give Me Yesterday 1931,Mr 5,32:1
Vivian, Leonard
So This Is London 1922,Ag 31,18:2
Vivian, Percival
Lassie 1920,Ap 7,9:2
Merchant of Venice, The 1922,D 22,13:1
As You Like It 1923,Ap 24,24:1
Lulu Belle 1926,F 10,20:1
Macbeth 1928,N 20,28:3
Rivals, The 1930,Mr 14,24:4
Midsummer Night's Dream, A 1932,Jl 13,15:1
Passionate Pilgrim, The 1932,O 20,24:3
Midsummer Night's Dream, A 1932,N 18,22:2
Twelfth Night 1932,N 19,20:5
Comedy of Errors, The 1932,N 22,25:3
Merchant of Venice, The 1932,N 24,34:5

ivian, Percival—Cont
Romeo and Juliet 1933,F 3,21:5
Chinese Nightingale, The 1934,O 6,20:4
ivian, Percival (Director)
Midsummer Night's Dream, A 1932,N 18,22:2
Twelfth Night 1932,N 19,20:5
Comedy of Errors, The 1932,N 22,25:3
Merchant of Venice, The 1932,N 24,34:5
Romeo and Juliet 1933,F 3,21:5
Love Kills 1934,My 2,25:3
Henrietta the Eighth 1935,Je 25,15:4
ivian, Robert
Personality 1921,Ag 29,14:3
Sweeney Todd 1924,Jl 19,10:4
High Stakes 1924,S 10,21:3
These Charming People 1925,O 7,31:2
Potash and Perlmutter, Detectives; Poisoned by
    Pictures 1926,S 1,27:3
Taming of the Shrew, The 1927,O 26,26:4
Twelve Thousand 1928,Mr 13,23:1
Mr Moneypenny 1928,O 17,26:2
Lady Dedlock 1929,Ja 1,61:2
Mystery Square 1929,Ap 5,28:3
Scotland Yard 1929,S 28,16:6
Michael and Mary 1929,D 14,23:3
9th Street Guest, The 1930,Ag 26,24:3
Give Me Yesterday 1931,Mr 5,32:1
Divorce Me, Dear 1931,O 7,29:2
Jewel Robbery 1932,Ja 14,17:2
Intimate Relations 1932,Mr 29,23:2
Stork Is Dead, The 1932,S 24,18:2
Best People, The 1933,Mr 16,21:5
Drunkard, The 1934,Ap 1,X,1:1
Taming of the Shrew, The 1935,O 1,27:3
Murder in the Old Red Barn, The 1936,F 3,20:4
Madame Bovary 1937,N 17,26:2
I Am My Youth 1938,Mr 8,22:4
Bright Rebel 1938,D 28,24:2
Brown Danube, The 1939,My 18,30:4
She Gave Him All She Had 1939,D 2,20:7
Distant City, The 1941,S 23,27:5
ivian, Ruth
Farmer's Wife, The 1924,O 10,22:3
Sport of Kings, The 1926,My 5,24:2
Great Adventure, The 1926,D 23,23:1
Possibilities 1927,F 19,13:3
Escape 1927,O 27,33:1
Much Ado About Nothing 1929,N 17,30:4
They Don't Mean Any Harm 1932,F 24,25:2
Midsummer Night's Dream, A 1932,Jl 13,15:1
Midsummer Night's Dream, A 1932,N 18,22:2
Twelfth Night 1932,N 19,20:5
Comedy of Errors, The 1932,N 22,25:3
Romeo and Juliet 1933,F 3,21:5
Chinese Nightingale, The 1934,O 6,20:4
Distant Shore, The 1935,F 22,26:2
Eden End 1935,O 22,17:1
Sweet Aloes 1936,Mr 5,24:5
And Now Goodbye 1937,F 3,26:4
Young Madame Conti 1937,Ap 1,18:4
Man Who Came to Dinner, The 1939,O 17,31:1
Strings, My Lord, Are False, The 1942,My 20,24:2
Damask Cheek, The 1942,O 23,24:2
Duet for Two Hands 1947,O 8,28:3
Hope Is the Thing With Feathers; Hope's the
    Thing 1948,My 12,34:6
Home Life of a Buffalo; Hope's the Thing
    1948,My 12,34:6
Gone Tomorrow; Hope's the Thing
    1948,My 12,34:6
Vivian-Reis, Joan
Adventurous Age, The 1927,F 8,20:1
Vizard, Harold
My Golden Girl 1920,F 3,18:2
Little Nellie Kelly 1922,N 14,16:1
When You Smile 1925,O 6,31:2
Luckee Girl 1928,S 17,28:6
Launcelot and Elaine 1930,Mr 10,24:3
Lambs Gambol 1933,Ap 24,10:1
Vizari, Mrs
Nem Elhetek Muzsikaszo Nelkul
    1928,D 30,VIII,4:4
Vizy, Evan M
Three Sisters, The 1968,Mr 18,56:1
Vlassoff, Leo
Chauve-Souris of 1943 1943,Ag 13,13:2
Vlay, J S (Playwright)
Take It Away 1936,D 22,32:3
Vocalis, Charles
Julius Caesar 1950,Je 21,30:1
Vocovitch, St
Oedipus Tyrannus 1952,N 25,35:2
Vodnoy, M
Strike Me Pink 1933,Mr 6,16:3
Voehl, Charles
Little Poor Man, The 1925,Ag 6,14:1
Voelkel, Elda
Schoolgirl 1930,N 21,31:1
She Lived Next to the Firehouse 1931,F 11,23:1
Voelpel, Fred (Costume Designer)
On the Town 1959,F 14,15:1
Fallout 1959,My 21,36:2
From A to Z 1960,Ap 21,23:2

Sudden End of Anne Cinquefoil, The
    1961,Ja 11,25:2
Young Abe Lincoln 1961,Ap 26,36:1
No Strings 1962,Mr 16,24:1
Milk Train Doesn't Stop Here Anymore, The
    1963,Ja 18,7:1
Sophie 1963,Ap 16,32:1
Play 1964,Ja 6,35:1
Lover, The 1964,Ja 6,35:1
Murderer Among Us, A 1964,Mr 26,43:1
Absence of a Cello 1964,S 22,45:1
Sign in Sidney Brustein's Window, The
    1964,O 16,32:1
Giants' Dance, The 1964,N 17,48:2
Peterpat 1965,Ja 7,27:1
Major Barbara 1965,My 18,33:1
That Thing at the Cherry Lane 1965,My 19,42:1
Drat! the Cat! 1965,O 11,54:2
South Pacific 1967,Je 13,56:1
Tiger at the Gates 1968,Mr 1,30:1
Merton of the Movies 1968,S 26,62:1
Spitting Image 1969,Mr 3,28:1
Critic, The 1969,Mr 9,76:5
Home Fires 1969,Ap 8,42:1
Cop-Out 1969,Ap 8,42:1
Oh! Calcutta! 1969,Je 18,33:1
Memory Bank, The 1970,Ja 12,24:3
Sganarelle 1970,Ja 13,41:1
Songs From Milk Wood 1970,Ja 13,41:1
Two by Two 1970,N 11,37:1
Voelpel, Fred (Lighting Director)
Fallout 1959,My 21,36:2
From A to Z 1960,Ap 21,23:2
That Thing at the Cherry Lane 1965,My 19,42:1
Voelpel, Fred (Miscellaneous)
Vintage '60 1960,S 13,41:1
Voelpel, Fred (Scenic Designer)
Born Yesterday 1958,Mr 22,12:6
Fallout 1959,My 21,36:2
From A to Z 1960,Ap 21,23:2
Vintage '60 1960,S 13,41:1
Alligators, The 1960,N 15,47:1
Rosemary 1960,N 15,47:1
Young Abe Lincoln 1961,Ap 26,36:1
Hang Down Your Head and Die 1964,O 19,38:1
That Thing at the Cherry Lane 1965,My 19,42:1
South Pacific 1967,Je 13,56:1
Indian Wants the Bronx, The 1968,Ja 18,47:2
It's Called the Sugar Plum 1968,Ja 18,47:2
South Pacific 1968,Je 30,54:2
Gianni Schicci 1969,F 25,36:1
Tale of Kasane, The 1969,F 25,36:1
Blueprints 1969,F 25,36:1
Critic, The 1969,Mr 9,76:5
Cop-Out 1969,Ap 8,42:1
Home Fires 1969,Ap 8,42:1
South Pacific 1969,Jl 7,27:1
Memory Bank, The 1970,Ja 12,24:3
Sganarelle 1970,Ja 13,41:1
Memory Bank, The 1970,Ja 25,II,1:4
Effect of Gamma Rays on Man-in-the-Moon
    Marigolds, The 1970,Ap 8,32:1
Voeth, Harold
Between the Devil 1937,D 23,24:5
Voeth, Jack
Between the Devil 1937,D 23,24:5
Nellie Bly 1946,Ja 22,32:2
Vogeding, Frederick
Light of the World, The 1920,Ja 7,17:1
Fool, The 1922,O 24,18:1
Starlight 1925,Mr 4,17:2
Vogel, Arthur (Playwright)
Cage, The 1961,Mr 6,30:1
Vogel, Fred
Little Clay Cart, The 1953,Jl 1,25:1
Montserrat 1954,My 26,34:2
Men in White 1955,F 26,13:2
Miser, The 1955,Mr 18,34:2
Vogel, Frederic (Miscellaneous)
Oscar Wilde 1957,Ap 20,21:3
Vogel, George
Apollo of Bellac, The 1958,Mr 7,17:2
Beyond the Horizon 1962,O 26,27:2
King Lear 1963,N 23,22:1
Vogel, George (Miscellaneous)
Chic 1959,My 19,28:2
Summer of the Seventeenth Doll 1959,O 14,52:1
Vogel, John G
Nautical but Nice 1931,Ap 19,31:6
Vogel, Marvin
Bad Habits of 1926 1926,My 1,11:1
Vogel, Michael F (Producer)
Utopia, Limited 1960,Ap 8,27:2
Vogel, Richard
End as a Man 1953,S 16,39:1
Vogel, Wesley
Santa Claus 1960,Jl 22,13:1
Vogt, Richard
Play of Daniel, The 1960,D 27,23:6

Vohs, Frank
'Tis Pity She's a Whore 1958,D 6,21:1
Meet Peter Grant 1961,My 11,41:4
Pilgrim's Progress 1962,Mr 21,36:2
Vohs, Joan
Parlor Story 1947,Mr 5,29:2
Voight, Bernhard (Playwright)
Friend Indeed 1926,Ap 27,22:3
Voight, Charles
Untitled-Revue 1923,My 12,15:4
Voight, Fred
Drunkard, The; Fallen Saved, The 1929,D 31,14:6
Voight, Frederic
Barretts of Wimpole Street, The 1931,F 10,25:1
Best Sellers 1933,My 4,20:2
She Loves Me Not 1933,N 21,22:4
Page Miss Glory 1934,N 28,24:2
Old Maid, The 1935,Ja 8,26:1
Black Limelight 1936,N 10,31:1
Antony and Cleopatra 1937,N 11,30:2
Voight, Jon
O, Oysters! 1961,Ja 31,23:1
View From the Bridge, A 1965,Ja 29,24:1
That Summer-That Fall 1967,Mr 17,33:1
Voiz, Valerie von
Phedre 1966,F 11,36:1
Vokes, Harry
Woman on the Jury, The 1923,Ag 16,10:4
Sweet Adeline 1929,S 4,33:1
Queer People 1934,F 16,16:2
Vokes, May
Bat, The 1920,Ag 24,6:1
Cold Feet 1923,My 22,14:2
Cold Feet 1923,My 22,14:3
Annie 1924,O 12,VIII,2:1
Annie Dear 1924,N 5,25:3
Holka Polka 1925,O 15,27:2
Matrimonial Bed, The 1927,O 13,23:2
Doctor X 1931,F 10,25:1
It's a Wise Child 1933,My 17,15:2
Bat, The 1937,Je 1,27:5
Thanks for Tomorrow 1938,S 28,28:2
Voketaitis, Arnold
Pirates of Penzance, The 1960,O 7,29:1
Vol Janin, Mischa
George White's Scandals 1923,Je 19,22:5
Volanakis, Minos (Director)
Oresteia 1961,N 8,43:5
Bacchae, The 1963,Ap 25,39:5
Volanakis, Minos (Playwright)
Iphigenia in Aulis 1967,N 22,40:2
Volanakis, Minos (Translator)
Bacchae, The 1963,Ap 25,39:5
Voland, Herbert
Men in White 1955,F 26,13:2
voland, Herbert
Song Out of Sorrow 1955,N 1,27:3
Voland, Herbert
Someone Waiting 1956,F 15,26:1
Wayside 1957,Ap 18,34:1
Fools Are Passing Through 1958,Ap 3,24:2
Farewell, Farewell Eugene 1960,S 28,35:1
Write Me a Murder 1961,O 27,28:2
Giants' Dance, The 1964,N 17,48:2
In the Matter of J Robert Oppenheimer
    1968,Je 7,31:1
Voland, Mark
Praise Of Folly 1954,F 24,23:2
Volare, Lorna
Blue Lagoon, The 1921,S 15,16:1
Alias Jimmy Valentine 1921,D 9,20:3
Royal Fandango, A 1923,N 13,25:1
Volavkova (Costume Designer)
Man With a Load of Mischief, The 1966,N 7,65:1
Volin, Bob (Miscellaneous)
Golden Streets, The 1970,Ag 14,21:1
Voljanin, M
Revue Russe, The 1922,O 6,28:1
Volk, George
Hamlet 1936,N 11,54:2
Behind the Red Lights 1937,Ja 14,17:4
There's Always a Breeze 1938,Mr 3,16:2
Volk, Hilde
Rape of the Sabine Women, The 1949,F 5,10:5
Volkenburg, Ellen Van
Possessed, The 1939,O 25,26:2
Volkman, Lois
Lady in the Dark 1941,Ja 24,14:2
This Rock 1943,F 19,23:2
Volkman, Nancy
Three...With Women in Mind; How a Nice Girl
    Named Janet Contracted Syphilis 1970,N 28,22:1
Three...With Women in Mind; I Hear It Kissing Me
    Ladies 1970,N 28,22:1
Three...With Women in Mind; Jeff Chandler
    1970,N 28,22:1
Volkoff, Chris
Merry Widow, The 1943,Ag 5,19:2
Merry Widow, The 1943,Ag 22,II,5:1
Sadie Thompson 1944,N 17,25:2
Volksbuehne
200,000 1966,F 15,33:5

Volland, Virginia
Come of Age 1934,Ja 13,16:6
Volland, Virginia (Costume Designer)
Infernal Machine, The 1937,D 13,22:7
Gently Does It 1953,O 29,43:4
One Eye Closed 1954,N 25,45:2
Grand Prize, The 1955,Ja 27,17:1
Hot Corner, The 1956,Ja 26,25:2
Tunnel of Love, The 1957,F 14,31:4
Hide and Seek 1957,Ap 3,26:1
Genius and the Goddess, The 1957,D 11,41:1
Two for the Seesaw 1958,Ja 17,15:1
Sunrise at Campobello 1958,Ja 31,25:1
Gazebo, The 1958,D 13,2:7
Raisin in the Sun, A 1959,Mr 12,27:1
Mighty Man Is He, A 1960,Ja 7,25:2
Volland, Virginia (Miscellaneous)
Time Out for Ginger 1952,N 27,50:4
Volle, Danielle
Phedre 1963,O 21,39:1
Vollee, Phyllis
Nativity Play, The 1937,D 21,29:1
Vollmar, Patricia (Producer)
Satisfaction Guaranteed 1969,F 12,31:1
Open 24 Hours 1969,F 12,31:1
Vollmer, Frank
Royal Family, The 1927,D 29,26:4
Vollmer, Lula (Playwright)
Shame Woman, The 1923,O 17,14:1
Shame Woman, The 1923,O 21,VIII,1:1
Dunce Boy, The 1925,Ap 4,20:2
Sun-Up 1925,Ag 14,13:4
Trigger 1927,D 7,32:1
Sun-Up 1928,S 18,34:6
Sun-Up 1928,O 23,33:1
Troika 1930,Ap 2,32:6
Sun-Up 1930,My 10,25:1
Sentinels 1931,D 26,15:1
Hill Between, The 1938,Mr 12,12:5
Vollmoeller, Karl (Playwright)
Miracle, The 1924,Ja 16,17:1
Miracle, The 1924,Ag 19,9:1
Miracle, The 1925,Ag 17,10:4
Miracle, The 1926,D 28,16:2
Miracle, The 1927,Ap 15,27:1
Passion Play, The 1929,Ap 30,32:1
Cocktail 1931,F 15,VIII,3:2
Volmer, Lulu (Playwright)
Sun-Up 1925,My 5,25:1
Volner, Ruth
Legend of Lovers 1951,D 27,17:1
Little Clay Cart, The 1953,Jl 1,25:1
2 for Fun; Anniversary, The 1955,My 26,34:1
2 for Fun; Switch in Time, A 1955,My 26,34:1
Drunkard, The; Fallen Saved, The 1959,Je 24,37:2
Funnyhouse of a Negro 1964,Ja 15,25:3
Oresteia 1966,Je 30,29:1
Birds, The 1966,Jl 1,40:1
Volodin, Alexander (Playwright)
Five Evenings 1963,My 10,37:3
Volsch, Wilbur
Arms for Venus 1937,Mr 12,18:7
Voltaire, Dante
He Who Gets Slapped 1922,Ja 10,15:1
Voltaire (Original Author)
Candide 1933,My 16,15:6
Candide 1956,D 9,II,5:1
Candide 1959,My 1,35:4
Volterra, Leon (Producer)
1927 1927,Mr 6,VII,4:4
Amant de Madame Vidal, L' 1928,Mr 25,IX,4:6
Vom Lehn, Elgar F
Once Over Lightly 1938,D 10,13:4
Vomacka, Jirl Miler-Milan (Lighting Director)
Pierrot's Journey 1964,Ag 5,23:1
Von Ambesser, Alex
Konzert, Das 1968,Mr 25,52:1
Von Ambesser, Alex (Director)
Jux Will Er Sich Machen, Einen 1968,Ap 3,41:1
Minna von Barnhelm 1968,N 13,37:1
Von Antalffy, Dezzo (Composer)
Passion Play, The 1929,Ap 30,32:1
Von Aspe, John
Mikado, The 1924,Jl 29,9:1
Von Barre, J W (Playwright)
Deep Channels 1929,O 19,22:3
Von Barre, J W (Producer)
Deep Channels 1929,O 19,22:3
Von Bernuth, Frances (Costume Designer)
Mighty Nimrod, The 1931,My 13,23:1
Von Bernuth, Frances (Scenic Designer)
Mighty Nimrod, The 1931,My 13,23:1
Von Brandenstein, Patrizia (Costume Designer)
Front Page, The 1968,O 20,85:5
Don't Shoot Mable It's Your Husband 1968,O 23,34:1
Trumpets and Drums 1969,O 13,52:1
Von Buelow, Eda
Checkerboard, The 1920,Ag 20,7:2
Wild Oats Lane 1922,S 7,12:1
Inspector General, The 1923,My 1,24:1
Love Song, The 1925,Ja 14,19:4

Gypsy Fires 1925,D 8,28:3
Sex 1926,Ap 27,22:4
57 Bowery 1928,Ja 27,14:3
Incubator 1932,N 2,23:3
One Sunday Afternoon 1933,F 16,23:5
Von Busing, Fritzi
Bombo 1921,O 7,20:2
Von Dekker, Albert
Lysistrata 1930,Ap 29,30:5
Von Der Hude, Arnd
Mystery of the Finding of the Cross, The 1959,Ja 16,35:2
Von Eicken, Hlega
Country Wife, The 1957,Je 27,22:1
Von Essen, Medha (Choreographer)
Shakuntala 1959,S 10,41:2
von Furstenberg, Betsy
Second Threshold 1951,Ja 3,23:2
Second Threshold 1951,Ja 14,II,1:1
Dear Barbarians 1952,F 22,15:2
Oh, Men! Oh, Women! 1953,D 18,37:2
What Every Woman Knows 1954,D 23,16:2
Chalk Garden, The 1955,O 27,29:1
Chalk Garden, The 1955,N 13,II,1:1
Child of Fortune 1956,N 14,41:1
Nature's Way 1957,O 17,42:2
Wonderful Town 1958,Mr 6,32:4
Making of Moo, The 1958,Je 12,34:1
Say Darling 1959,F 26,38:2
Season of Choice 1959,Ap 14,40:1
Much Ado About Nothing 1959,S 18,25:2
Mary, Mary 1961,Mr 9,24:2
Paisley Convertible, The 1967,F 13,42:1
Wonderful Town 1967,My 18,50:1
Beyond Desire 1967,O 11,36:1
Avanti 1968,F 1,29:1
Private Lives 1968,My 20,59:1
Gingerbread Lady, The 1970,D 14,58:3
Gingerbread Lady, The 1970,D 20,II,3:7
Von Golisch, Fred
Red Robe, The 1928,D 26,15:1
Von Gontard, Gert (Miscellaneous)
Nathan the Wise 1962,Mr 7,29:1
Before Sundown 1962,Mr 14,43:1
Nathan der Weise 1966,D 10,45:2
Konzert, Das 1968,Mr 25,52:1
Jux Will Er Sich Machen, Einen 1968,Ap 3,41:1
Von Gontard, Gert (Producer)
Faust, Part I; Prologue in Heaven 1961,F 5,27:2
Faust, Part I; Play, The 1961,F 5,27:2
Satiric Evening 1963,O 24,36:2
Don Carlos 1964,N 25,40:1
Captain of Koepenick, The 1964,D 2,60:1
Wozzeck 1966,Ap 6,34:1
Mitschuldigen, Die 1966,Ap 6,34:1
Ratten, Die 1966,Ap 13,36:1
Minna von Barnhelm 1968,N 13,37:1
Schloss, Das 1968,N 20,35:3
Amphitryon 1970,N 18,40:1
Kurve, Die 1970,N 25,25:1
Kleinburgerhochzeit, Die 1970,N 25,25:1
Von Grona's Ten Dancers
Vaudeville (Palace) 1932,My 16,19:2
Von Gross, Erwin
Wiener Blut 1964,S 12,14:1
Von Hallberg, Sven
Maya 1928,F 22,19:1
Von Halmay, Tibor
Menschen im Hotel 1930,Mr 16,IX,4:1
Von Hessen, Gizalt (Translator)
Chameleon, The 1932,Jl 19,20:4
Von Hofmannsthal, Hugo (Playwright)
Via Crucis 1923,N 13,25:2
Jedermann 1927,D 8,33:2
Schwierige, Der 1930,N 30,IX,2:1
Everyman 1931,Jl 19,III,8:6
Everyman 1941,My 9,19:2
Von Jany, Tabor
De Luxe 1935,Mr 6,22:2
Von Kantzow, Elfi (Costume Designer)
Edwina Black 1950,N 22,20:5
Jane 1952,F 2,10:2
Brass Ring, The 1952,Ap 11,19:2
Von Kantzow, Elfi (Lighting Director)
Brass Ring, The 1952,Ap 11,19:2
Von Kantzow, Elfi (Scenic Designer)
Jane 1952,F 2,10:2
Brass Ring, The 1952,Ap 11,19:2
von Kleist, Heinrich (Playwright)
Broken Jug, The 1958,Ap 2,36:1
Amphitryon 1970,N 18,40:1
Von Kracke, Louis
No More Peace 1937,F 27,9:1
Von Liebenfels, Jorg
Nathan der Weise 1966,D 10,45:2
Von Mendelssohn, Francesco (Director)
Eternal Road, The 1937,Ja 8,14:2
Von Mertens, Valerie
Hokus Pokus 1928,Ja 29,VIII,4:1
Von Mitzel, Max
Shipwrecked 1924,N 13,18:1
Jack in the Pulpit 1925,Ja 7,33:1
Gang War 1928,Ag 21,27:2

Von Mitzel, Max—Cont
Street Wolf, The 1929,Ja 1,61:1
Broken Chain, The 1929,F 21,30:4
Congratulations 1929,My 1,28:4
Patriarch, The 1929,N 26,28:5
Oh, Professor 1930,My 2,19:6
Von Nardroff, Elizabeth
New Freedom, The 1930,My 15,32:4
Life Begins 1932,Mr 29,23:2
Von Nardroff, Elizabeth (Director)
New Freedom, The 1930,My 15,32:4
Von Orbok, Attila (Playwright)
His Majesty's Car 1930,O 24,30:1
Von Patten, Richard
Tapestry in Gray 1935,D 28,10:2
Von Reith, Inge
Patriot for Me, A 1969,O 6,58:1
Von Reznick, E H (Composer)
Johannes Kreisler 1922,D 25,20:3
Von Rhau, Henry
Shanghai Gesture, The 1926,F 2,20:2
Woman Disputed, A 1926,S 29,23:2
Von Rhau, Lee (Director)
Boy on the Straight-Back Chair 1969,Mr 18,36:1
Von Rheinhold, Cal
Annie Get Your Gun 1957,Mr 9,15:5
Von Rigel, Robert
Let Freedom Ring 1935,N 7,26:2
Victoria Regina 1935,D 27,15:2
Victoria Regina 1938,O 4,20:2
Von Salis, Guido
Firebugs, The 1969,N 27,52:1
Philipp Hotz 1969,N 27,52:1
Von Scherler, Sasha
Comedian, The 1956,O 18,36:4
In Good King Charles's Golden Days 1957,Ja 25,16:1
In Good King Charles's Golden Days 1957,F 3,II,1:1
Conversation Piece 1957,N 19,38:2
As You Like It 1958,Ja 21,33:6
Look After Lulu 1959,Mr 4,35:1
Great God Brown, The 1959,O 7,48:1
Lysistrata 1959,N 25,19:4
Good Soup, The 1960,Mr 3,26:4
Under Milk Wood 1961,Mr 30,25:1
First Love 1961,D 26,20:2
Alfie 1964,D 18,27:1
Willie Doesn't Live Here Anymore 1967,F 8,20:2
Sondra 1967,My 10,39:1
Cyrano de Bergerac 1968,Ap 26,30:1
Stop, You're Killing Me; Laughs, Etc 1969,Mr 20,53:1
Twelfth Night 1969,Ag 14,29:2
Crimes of Passion; Ruffian on the Stair, The 1969,O 27,54:1
Crimes of Passion; Erpingham Camp, The 1969,O 27,54:1
Crimes of Passion; Erpingham Camp, The; Ruffian on the Stair, The 1969,N 9,II,1:1
Wars of the Roses, The (Part I) 1970,Jl 2,30:1
Trelawny of the 'Wells' 1970,O 12,48:1
Von Schiller, Friedlich (Playwright)
Kabale und Liebe 1928,Ja 17,22:3
Mary Stuart 1956,Ap 28,10:2
Don Carlos 1964,N 25,40:1
Maria Stuart 1968,Mr 27,38:1
Von Scholz, Wilhelm (Playwright)
Race With the Shadow, The 1924,Ja 21,20:5
Von Shillagh, Arthur
Shakespeare's Merchant 1939 1939,Ja 10,16:3
Von Stroheim, Eric (Original Author)
May Wine 1935,N 23,23:1
May Wine 1935,D 6,30:3
Von Stroheim, Erich
Arsenic and Old Lace 1941,Mr 25,26:7
Von Tassel, Theo
Chocolate Soldier, The 1931,S 22,33:3
Von Thellmann, Eirka
All's Well That Ends Well 1928,Ap 1,IX,2:4
Von Tilzer, Albert (Composer)
Gingham Girl, The 1922,Ag 29,15:5
Adrienne 1923,My 29,10:4
Bye Bye Bonnie 1927,Ja 14,15:3
Von Tornow, Georgiana
Naked 1926,N 9,31:2
Von Twardowski, Hans (Director)
If You Get It, Do You Want It? 1938,D 1,28:2
Von Unruh, Fritz (Playwright)
Phaea 1930,Ag 31,VIII,2:1
Von Volkenburg, Ellen (Producer)
Othello 1930,My 20,33:1
Von Volz, Valerie
Make Me Disappear 1969,My 14,34:1
Von Weber, Roland
Infernal Machine, The 1954,Mr 22,22:2
Doll's House, A 1954,N 15,32:2
Von Winterstein, Eduard
Midsummer Night's Dream, A 1927,N 18,21:1
Jedermann 1927,D 8,33:2
Dantons Tod 1927,D 21,28:3
Er Ist an Allem Schuld; He Is to Blame for Everything 1928,Ja 10,28:3

Von Winterstein, Eduard—Cont
Diener Zweier Herren; Servant of Two Masters, The 1928,Ja 10,28:3
Kabale und Liebe 1928,Ja 17,22:3
Lebende Leichnam, Der, Der; Living Corpse, The 1928,Ja 24,26:2
Gespenster, Die; Ghosts 1928,F 8,28:6
Robbers, The 1928,Ag 10,9:2

Von Zerneck, Frank (Miscellaneous)
Bring Me a Warm Body 1962,Ap 17,29:3

Von Zerneck, Peter
Land of Fame 1943,S 22,31:5
Common Ground 1945,Ap 26,27:2
Palm Tree in a Rose Garden, A 1957,N 27,26:2

Vonderheid, Louis
Murder in the Cathedral 1958,Mr 22,12:4

Vonne, Virginia
Firefly, The 1938,Jl 12,15:4
Blossom Time 1938,D 27,12:2

Vonnegut, Kurt (Playwright)
Happy Birthday, Wanda June 1970,O 8,58:2
Happy Birthday, Wanda June 1970,O 18,II,1:1

Vonnegut, Marjorie
Power of Darkness, The 1920,Ja 22,22:1
Harem, The 1924,D 3,24:1
Blue Peter, The 1925,Mr 25,25:3
Engaged! or Cheviot's Choice 1925,Je 19,24:2

Vonnegut, Ruth
Dark Hours, The 1932,N 15,24:2

Vonnegut, Walter
Faust 1928,O 9,34:1
Strange Interlude 1928,D 18,37:3
Everything's Jake 1930,Ja 17,20:4
Grand Hotel 1930,N 14,30:4
Ah, Wilderness! 1933,O 3,28:2
Peace on Earth 1933,N 30,39:2
Petrified Forest, The 1935,Ja 8,26:1
Postman Always Rings Twice, The 1936,F 26,17:2

Vonoskoff, Les
Illusioniste, L' 1927,Ja 11,36:5

Vool-Ellin, Ruth
Eleventh Inheritor, The 1962,N 22,43:5
Fifth Commandment, The 1965,N 15,48:4

Voorhees, Don (Musical Director)
Swingin' the Dream 1939,N 30,24:2
American Jubilee 1940,My 13,20:5

Voorhees, Don and His Orchestra
Nine Fifteen Revue, The 1930,F 12,26:2

Voorheis, Rousseau
Immodest Violet 1920,Ag 25,6:2

Voorhis, C W Van
It's a Grand Life 1930,F 11,30:3

Vorenberg, William (Director)
Faith of Our Fathers 1950,Ag 6,72:2

Vorgrin, Beulah
Slightly Delinquent 1954,O 26,32:5

Vorno, Antony
Rehearsal, The 1952,My 27,30:5
Camino Real 1953,Mr 20,26:1
View From the Bridge, A 1955,S 30,21:1
Memory of Two Mondays, A 1955,S 30,21:1
Comrades 1956,Je 6,38:1
Eagle Has Two Heads, The 1956,D 14,37:2

Vornoff
Chauve-Souris 1929,Ja 23,20:2

Vorse, Mary Heaton (Playwright)
First Stone, The 1928,Ja 14,12:2

Vos, Richard
Cannibals, The 1968,N 4,60:1
Young Master Dante, The 1968,D 31,19:1
Boy on the Straight-Back Chair 1969,Mr 18,36:1

Vosberg, John
Bedfellows 1929,Jl 3,19:2

Vosburg, Harold
All-Star Jamboree 1921,Jl 14,18:1
Man Who Died Twice, The 1925,D 14,19:1

Vosburg, Peter
As You Like It 1936,Ap 24,18:4

Vosburgh, David
1776 1969,Mr 17,46:2

Vosburgh, John
Guinea Pig, The 1929,Ja 8,35:1
Whirlpool 1929,D 4,37:3
Sap Runs High, The 1936,F 5,15:3
Mimie Scheller 1936,O 1,28:4
Miss Quis 1937,Ap 8,20:5

Vosburgh, William Wallace (Playwright)
Your Young Men 1935,Ag 8,13:2

Vose, Carl H
Arabian, The 1927,N 1,20:5
Royal Box, The 1928,N 21,32:3
Sakura 1928,D 26,14:4
Three Men and a Woman 1932,Ja 12,29:2

Vose, Carl H (Costume Designer)
Sakura 1928,D 26,14:4

Vose, Carl H (Scenic Designer)
Sakura 1928,D 26,14:4

Vose, Robert
Getting Even 1929,Ag 20,31:1

Voskovec, George
North and South 1930,O 5,IX,4:1
Golem, The 1931,D 13,VIII,3:4
Tempest, The 1945,Ja 26,17:2
Tempest, The 1945,F 4,II,1:1

Hortense, to Bed With You 1949,Jl 9,9:2
Happy Journey to Trenton and Camden, The 1949,Jl 9,9:2
Lady of Larkspur Lotion, The 1949,Jl 9,9:2
Love of Four Colonels, The 1953,Ja 16,17:2
His and Hers 1954,Ja 8,18:2
Sea Gull, The 1954,My 12,38:1
Festival 1955,Ja 19,22:1
Uncle Vanya 1956,F 1,25:2
Uncle Vanya 1956,F 12,II,1:1
Tenth Man, The 1959,N 6,24:2
Tenth Man, The 1959,N 15,II,1:1
Big Fish, Little Fish 1961,Mr 16,42:2
Big Fish, Little Fish 1961,Mr 26,II,1:1
Call on Kuprin, A 1961,My 26,29:3
Do You Know the Milky Way? 1961,O 17,45:1
Jewish Wife 1961,N 15,52:2
Brecht on Brecht 1961,N 15,52:2
Brecht on Brecht 1962,Ja 4,26:1
Brecht on Brecht 1962,Ja 14,II,1:1
Caesar and Cleopatra 1963,Ag 1,18:2
Hamlet 1964,Ap 10,30:1
Physicists, The 1964,O 14,52:1
Physicists, The 1964,O 25,II,1:1
World of Ray Bradbury, The; Pedestrian, The; Veldt, The; To the Chicago Abyss 1965,O 10,11:1
Alchemist, The 1966,O 14,48:1
East Wind, The 1967,F 10,30:1
Galileo 1967,Ap 14,31:1
Other Man, The 1968,F 9,50:1
Oh, Say Can You See L A 1968,F 9,50:1
Cabaret 1969,F 2,74:2
Penny Wars, The 1969,O 16,52:1
Murderous Angels 1970,F 8,70:1
Murderous Angels 1970,Mr 15,II,1:4
Slow Dance on the Killing Ground 1970,My 14,43:1

Vosper, Frank
Colonel Satan 1931,Ja 18,I,28:6
Colonel Satan 1931,F 8,VIII,3:3
Elizabeth of England 1931,O 18,VIII,1:3
Rose Without a Thorn 1932,Ap 3,VIII,1:5
Josephine 1934,S 26,17:5
Josephine 1934,O 14,X,3:1
Hamlet 1934,N 15,25:1
Hamlet 1934,D 2,X,3:6
Hangman, The 1935,O 23,18:6
Love From a Stranger 1936,F 3,20:7
Love From a Stranger 1936,Ap 1,28:7
Love From a Stranger 1936,Ap 26,IX,2:2
Love From a Stranger 1936,S 22,31:5
Love From a Stranger 1936,S 30,28:1

Vosper, Frank (Playwright)
Surmise 1927,O 23,VIII,1:3
Spellbound 1927,N 15,26:2
Spellbound 1927,N 20,IX,1:1
Murder on the Second Floor 1929,S 12,35:1
Murder on the Second Floor 1929,S 22,IX,1:1
Debonair 1930,Ap 24,29:2
Lucky Dip 1930,N 16,VIII,4:1
Spellbound 1931,F 22,VIII,4:1
Love From a Stranger 1936,F 3,20:7
Love From a Stranger 1936,Ap 1,28:7
Love From a Stranger 1936,Ap 26,IX,2:2
Love From a Stranger 1936,S 22,31:5
Love From a Stranger 1936,S 30,28:1

Vosper, Frank (Producer)
Debonair 1930,Ap 24,29:2

Voss, Arnold
Flight to the West 1940,D 15,I,59:5

Voss, Grace
Charley's Aunt 1925,Je 2,16:2
Her First Affaire 1927,Ag 23,29:2

Voss, Herbert (Miscellaneous)
Moon in the Yellow River, The 1961,F 7,40:2

Voss, Peter
Ice Capades 1964,Ag 27,27:2
Ice Capades 1966,Je 2,50:2
Ice Capades 1967,Je 2,33:1

Voss, Stephanie
Fantasticks, The 1961,S 8,36:5

Vosseler, Heidi
Boys From Syracuse, The 1938,N 24,36:1

Vosselli, Judith
Back Pay 1921,Ag 31,8:2
Wild Oats Lane 1922,S 7,12:1
Casanova 1923,S 27,10:2
Fanshastics 1924,Ja 17,13:2
Louie the 14th 1925,Mr 4,17:1
Forbidden Roads 1928,Ap 17,26:4
Crashing Through 1928,O 30,26:5
It Happened Tomorrow 1933,My 6,11:5

Vostra, Alena (Playwright)
Matter of Days, A 1969,My 20,40:1
Whose Turn Next? 1970,Ap 19,74:3

Votava, Antonin
Laterna Magika 1964,Ag 4,21:1

Votos, Christopher
110 in the Shade 1963,O 25,37:1
Child Buyer, The 1964,D 22,35:1
Do I Hear a Waltz? 1965,Mr 19,28:1

Votrian, Peter
Harbor Lights 1956,O 5,20:1

Voutsinas, Andreas
Lulu 1958,S 30,24:1
J B 1958,D 12,2:7
Come Share My House 1960,F 19,20:2
Secret Concubine, The 1960,Mr 22,29:2
Coop, The 1966,Mr 2,48:1
Natural Look, The 1967,Mr 13,45:2

Voutsinas, Andreas (Director)
Fun Couple, The 1962,O 27,15:2

Voutsinas, Evangelos
Macbeth 1968,N 30,49:3

Vowles, Kenneth (Lighting Director)
Measure for Measure 1967,F 15,37:1
Hamlet 1967,F 17,44:1
Romeo and Juliet 1967,F 22,18:1

Vox, Helen
Maitresse de Roi 1926,D 1,24:1

Vox, Valentine
Vaudeville (Palace) 1927,My 10,25:3

Voyer, Guy
Battling Buttler 1923,O 9,17:2

Voysey, Michael (Playwright)
By George 1967,O 13,33:1

Vozikiadou, E
Electra 1952,N 20,38:2

Voznesensky, Andrei (Playwright)
Save Your Face 1970,My 28,28:1

Vraz, Victor
It's A Gift 1945,Mr 13,18:7
Minstrel Boy, The 1948,O 15,28:2

Vreeland, Albert
What's Your Number? 1929,Ag 16,18:3

Vroom, Anna
Inspector General, The 1923,My 1,24:1

Vroom, Edward
Cyrano de Bergerac 1920,Mr 20,14:3
Merchant of Venice, The 1921,Ap 2,14:2

Vroom, Edward (Producer)
Cyrano de Bergerac 1920,Mr 20,14:3
Merchant of Venice, The 1921,Ap 2,14:2

Vroom, Florence
Milestones 1930,Je 3,27:1
Stepdaughters of War 1930,O 7,27:1
Other One, The 1932,O 4,26:3
30 Days Hath September 1938,O 1,10:5

Vroom, Lodewick (Producer)
Dark Hours, The 1932,N 15,24:2
Mikado, The 1935,Jl 16,24:4
Pirates of Penzance, The 1935,Jl 23,24:2
Yeomen of the Guard, The 1935,Jl 30,16:4
Gondoliers, The 1935,Ag 6,20:5
Trial by Jury 1935,Ag 13,20:6
H M S Pinafore 1935,Ag 13,20:6
Around the Corner 1936,D 29,17:2
That Old Devil 1944,Je 6,14:2

Vroom, Paul (Miscellaneous)
My Darlin' Aida 1952,O 28,36:4

Vroom, Paul (Producer)
Number, The 1951,O 31,33:2
Fragile Fox 1954,O 13,27:1
Double in Hearts 1956,O 17,41:7
Rape of the Belt, The 1960,N 7,46:1
Too True to Be Good 1963,Mr 14,8:2
Never Live Over a Pretzel Factory 1964,Mr 30,37:1

Vrooman, A H
It's the Valet 1933,D 15,25:4

Vrooman, F E
Don Quixote, Esquire 1920,My 7,12:6

Vucci, Ralph
Guys and Dolls 1955,Ap 21,32:2
Song of Norway 1958,Je 23,19:2
Can-Can 1959,Ag 26,25:4
Paradise Island 1961,Je 24,11:1
What Makes Sammy Run? 1964,F 28,19:1
Golden Boy 1964,O 21,56:1

Vuillemetz, Mr (Playwright)
Roi Pausole, Le 1931,Ja 25,VIII,8:8

Vulpius, Paul (Original Author)
Youth at the Helm 1934,N 25,IX,3:1
Help Yourself! 1936,Jl 15,15:1

Vuolo, Louis
Sweeney Todd 1957,Ag 28,21:4
Parasite, The 1965,D 17,43:2

Vuolo, Tito
World We Make, The 1939,N 21,19:1
World We Make, The 1939,D 3,IX,5:1
Mr and Mrs North 1941,Ja 13,11:2
Johnny on the Spot 1942,Ja 9,24:2
Take It As It Comes 1944,F 11,17:2
Bell for Adano, A 1944,N 10,24:6
Bell for Adano, A 1944,D 7,21:2
Bell for Adano, A 1944,D 17,II,3:2

Vydra, Vaclav
Abraham Lincoln 1927,Ja 21,12:3

Vye, Christopher (Playwright)
Death Asks a Verdict 1937,Ja 10,X,1:8

Vye, Murvyn
Hamlet 1936,O 9,30:2
As You Like It 1941,O 21,29:2
Carousel 1945,Ap 20,24:2
Carousel 1945,Ap 29,II,1:1
Live Wire, The 1950,Ag 18,16:2
Live Wire, The 1950,Ag 27,II,1:1

Vye, Murvyn—Cont
Number, The 1951,O 31,33:2
Carousel 1953,My 6,38:1
Arturo Ui 1963,N 12,49:1
South Pacific 1965,Je 3,25:1
Caucasian Chalk Circle, The 1966,Mr 25,35:1
Vyner, Margaret
Once Is Enough 1938,F 16,16:2

W

Waaser, Carol (Lighting Director)
Rivals, The 1969,O 18,37:1
Cops and Horrors; Fly Paper 1970,Ag 11,27:1
Cops and Horrors; Dracula 1970,Ag 11,27:1
Waber, Bernard (Original Author)
Lyle 1970,Mr 21,16:2
Wachob, J F (Scenic Designer)
Jim Dandy 1941,N 8,10:5
Wachsberger, Clyde (Scenic Designer)
Last Pad, The 1970,D 8,61:1
Wachter, F M
Tiger Smiles, The 1930,D 18,29:1
Wachthausen, Rene (Playwright)
Purity 1930,D 26,18:2
Wack, Glorya
Squaring the Circle 1936,Ag 12,15:3
Wack, Richard (Scenic Designer)
Forever This Land 1952,Je 30,14:6
Wacker, Bob
Between the Devil 1937,D 23,24:5
Wada, Mann
We Americans 1926,O 13,20:4
Letter, The 1927,S 27,30:1
Waddell, Clyde
Season of the Beast 1958,Mr 14,29:2
Waddell, Joan Carter
Ups-A-Daisy 1928,O 9,34:2
Waddington, Patrick
First Episode 1934,S 18,18:1
Magnificent Hugo, The 1961,Ap 8,12:2
Kean 1961,N 3,28:2
Rosmersholm 1962,Ap 12,42:1
Rosmersholm 1962,Ap 22,II,1:1
Affair, The 1962,S 21,34:2
Darker Flower, A 1963,Mr 11,7:2
Wade, Albert
Hamlet 1927,Ap 7,23:3
Caesar and Cleopatra 1927,N 6,IX,2:1
Napoleon Passes 1927,D 21,29:2
Golden Dog, The 1929,D 25,21:2
Second Man, The 1930,My 2,23:2
Wade, Albert (Director)
Caesar and Cleopatra 1927,N 6,IX,2:1
Wade, Allan
Last Enemy, The 1930,O 31,21:1
Wade, Allan (Translator)
Machine Infernale, La 1935,Ap 21,IX,2:2
Wade, Beatrice
Long Way From Home, A 1948,F 9,25:2
Wade, Betty
Harriet 1943,Mr 4,24:2
Wade, Dick
Pastoral 1939,N 2,26:2
Wade, Edith
Time to Go 1952,My 8,35:6
Wade, Evelyn
School for Virtue 1931,Ap 22,29:2
Dooley Cashes In 1935,Ag 17,18:6
Wade, Frances
Pirates of Penzance, The 1936,Ap 21,27:5
Wade, James (Costume Designer)
Princess Ida 1955,O 14,22:3
Wade, James (Scenic Designer)
Princess Ida 1955,O 14,22:3
Wade, Jeanne
Minskey the Magnificent 1936,D 26,14:3
Wade, Lenore
Harriet 1943,Mr 4,24:2
Harriet 1944,S 28,26:1
Wade, Leroy
Enemy of the People, An 1927,O 4,32:5
Wade, Maurice
Inside Story 1942,O 30,22:2
Wade, Percy
Singin' the Blues 1931,S 17,21:3
Wade, Randolph
Too Many Heroes 1937,N 16,26:2
Brown Danube, The 1939,My 18,30:4
Time of Your Life, The 1939,O 26,26:2
Heavenly Express 1940,Ap 19,24:2
Brooklyn Biarritz 1941,F 28,16:2
Wade, Robert
Life With Mother 1948,O 21,32:2
Wade, Sherman
Within Four Walls 1923,Ap 18,24:1
Wade, Stuart
Tickets, Please! 1950,Ap 28,25:2
Wade, Warren
Smiling the Boy Fell Dead 1961,Ap 20,28:1
Captains and the Kings, The 1962,Ja 3,25:2
Anything Goes 1962,My 16,35:1
Winterset 1966,F 10,32:2

Measure for Measure 1966,Jl 14,27:1
Galileo 1967,Ap 14,31:1
Wade, Willie
Country Wife, The 1957,N 28,56:1
Wadimoff, E
Blue Bird, The 1932,Ap 22,23:2
Wadsworth, Henry
Lady Lies, The 1928,N 27,36:2
Flight 1929,F 19,22:3
First Night 1930,N 27,32:3
Wadsworth, Wheeler
All-Star Jamboree 1921,Jl 14,18:1
Wadsworth, William
Seeing Things 1920,Je 18,19:2
Zander the Great 1923,Ap 10,24:2
Wisdom Tooth, The 1926,F 16,22:2
Eva the Fifth 1928,Ag 29,19:3
Heat Lightning 1933,S 16,9:6
Drums Begin, The 1933,N 25,10:5
Small Miracle 1934,S 27,24:3
On Your Toes 1936,Ap 13,14:4
Our Town 1938,F 5,18:3
Three's a Family 1943,My 6,24:2
Waechter, Herman P
You'll Never Know 1921,Ap 21,9:2
Waelder, Frederick J
Advertising of Kate, The 1922,My 9,22:2
Waescher, Aribert
All's Well That Ends Well 1928,Ap 1,IX,2:4
Outside Looking In 1929,Je 23,VIII,2:1
Heilige Crispin, Der 1933,Je 25,IX,1:2
Wagener, Hilde
Maria Stuart 1968,Mr 27,38:1
Wagenheim, Charles
Holy Terror, A 1925,S 29,31:2
Devil to Pay, The 1925,D 4,26:2
Four Walls 1927,S 20,33:1
Ringside 1928,Ag 30,13:2
20th Century 1932,D 30,15:1
Drums Begin, The 1933,N 25,10:5
Hook-Up, The 1935,My 9,24:6
American Holiday 1936,F 22,13:3
Schoolhouse on the Lot 1938,Mr 23,18:4
Wagenheim, Charles (Playwright)
East of Broadway 1932,Ja 27,19:3
Wager, Michael
Small Hours, The 1951,F 16,22:1
Bernardine 1952,O 17,33:4
Merchant of Venice, The 1953,Mr 5,20:2
Remarkable Mr Pennypacker, The 1953,D 31,11:2
Othello 1955,S 8,27:2
Othello 1955,S 18,II,1:1
Henry IV, Part I 1955,S 22,34:2
Six Characters in Search of an Author
   1955,D 12,38:1
Six Characters in Search of an Author
   1955,D 25,II,3:1
Henry V 1956,Jl 7,11:2
Saint Joan 1956,S 12,42:1
Hamlet 1957,Ja 29,27:1
Prometheus Bound 1957,Ag 9,11:6
Courageous One, The 1958,Ja 21,33:6
Firstborn, The 1958,My 1,35:1
Twelfth Night 1959,Jl 11,10:2
Macbeth 1959,Ag 1,9:2
Noontide 1961,Je 2,37:1
Brecht on Brecht 1961,N 15,52:2
Brecht on Brecht 1962,Ja 4,26:1
Brecht on Brecht 1962,Ja 14,II,1:1
Sunset 1966,My 13,34:1
Penny Friend, The 1966,D 27,46:1
Cuban Thing, The 1968,S 25,36:2
Trelawny of the 'Wells' 1970,O 12,48:1
Wager, Michael (Miscellaneous)
Henry V 1956,Jl 7,11:2
Saint Joan 1956,S 12,42:1
Twelfth Night 1959,Jl 11,10:2
Macbeth 1959,Ag 1,9:2
Dynamite Tonight 1964,Mr 16,36:2
Wager, Michael (Playwright)
Six Characters in Search of an Author
   1955,D 12,38:1
Wager, Michael (Producer)
Henry IV, Part I 1955,S 22,34:2
Where's Daddy? 1966,Mr 3,27:1
Wagg, Kenneth (Producer)
Four Winds 1957,S 26,21:2
Waggoner, Don
Eastward in Eden 1956,Ap 18,25:4
Waggoner, George (Composer)
Tattle Tales 1933,Je 2,22:6
Waggoner, George (Lyricist)
Tattle Tales 1933,Je 2,22:6
Waglin, Eddie
Lower North 1944,Ag 26,15:4
Wagner, Al (Lighting Director)
Lady's Not for Burning, The 1959,Ja 31,13:2
Wagner, Arthur (Miscellaneous)
Wonder World 1964,My 18,32:1
Wagner, Barbara
Ice Capades 1960,S 1,30:1
Ice Capades 1962,Ag 30,34:1

Wagner, Charles
This Fine-Pretty World 1923,D 27,11:1
Small Timers, The 1925,Ja 28,15:3
S S Glencairn 1929,Ja 10,24:5
Airways, Inc 1929,F 21,30:5
Wagner, Charles L (Miscellaneous)
Prelude to Exile 1936,D 1,31:1
Wagner, Charles L (Producer)
Helena's Boys 1924,Ap 8,22:2
Quarantine 1924,D 17,19:7
Carolinian, The 1925,N 3,34:2
Love in a Mist 1926,Ap 13,28:3
Barker, The 1927,Ja 19,20:6
Window Panes 1927,F 22,22:2
Springboard, The 1927,O 13,23:1
Ink 1927,O 23,VIII,1:3
Ink 1927,N 2,24:2
March Hares 1928,Ap 3,32:6
George Barnwell; London Merchant, The
   1928,O 2,34:3
When Crummles Played 1928,O 2,34:3
Man With Red Hair, A 1928,N 9,22:2
Prima Donna 1929,S 22,IX,2:6
Tyrant, The 1930,N 13,33:1
Wagner, Clifford
Sport of Kings, The 1926,My 5,24:2
Wagner, Daniel
Little Theatre Tournement; Where The Cross Is
   Made 1928,My 10,31:1
Wagner, Erica V
Rape of the Sabine Women, The 1949,F 5,10:5
Wagner, Frank (Choreographer)
I Feel Wonderful 1954,O 19,22:5
Ziegfeld Follies 1957,Mr 2,19:2
Leonard Sillman's New Faces of 1968
   1968,My 3,43:1
Wagner, Frank (Director)
Leonard Sillman's New Faces of 1968
   1968,My 3,43:1
Wagner, Frank (Miscellaneous)
How to Steal an Election 1968,O 14,56:1
Wagner, Franklin
Sleepy Hollow 1948,Je 4,26:3
Wagner, George
Hollywood Ice Revue 1953,Ja 16,17:2
Macbeth 1955,O 20,42:2
Wagner, George (Miscellaneous)
Macbeth 1955,O 20,42:2
Midsummer Night's Dream, A 1956,Ja 14,12:2
Romeo and Juliet 1956,F 24,20:4
Hamlet 1956,O 29,34:1
Wagner, Helen
Sunny River 1941,D 5,28:2
Winter's Tale, The 1946,Ja 16,18:6
Wagner, Irma
Little Theatre Tournament; Shall We Join the
   Ladies? 1929,My 9,34:3
Shall We Join the Ladies? 1929,My 12,28:3
Wagner, Janyce
Pal Joey 1952,Ja 4,17:6
Say Darling 1959,F 26,38:2
Saratoga 1959,D 8,59:4
Wagner, John (Scenic Designer)
Great Music 1924,O 6,24:1
Wagner, Leonard T
Macbeth 1968,N 30,49:3
Wagner, Lillian
Rose of Stamboul, The 1922,Mr 8,11:2
Wagner, Marsha
Wildcat 1960,D 17,20:2
Wagner, Merry
This Our House 1935,D 12,33:3
Wagner, Nathaniel
Clinging Vine, The 1922,D 25,20:2
Princess April 1924,D 2,23:2
Countess Maritza 1926,Mr 30,20:3
Countess Maritza 1926,S 20,21:1
My Maryland 1927,S 13,37:2
Nikki 1931,S 30,23:4
Wagner, Paul
Winter Soldiers 1942,N 30,19:2
Don Carlos 1964,N 25,40:1
Wagner, Peggy
Hippolytus 1948,N 22,25:5
Wagner, Richard (Miscellaneous)
World of Gunter Grass, The 1966,Ap 27,38:1
Wagner, Robin (Lighting Director)
Waiting for Godot 1958,Ag 6,22:1
Between Two Thieves 1960,F 12,23:1
Delightful Season, A 1960,S 29,30:1
Borak 1960,D 14,51:1
Worm in Horseradish, A 1961,Mr 14,32:3
Entertain a Ghost 1962,Ap 10,48:1
Days and Nights of Beebee Fenstermaker, The
   1962,S 18,33:1
Burning, The 1963,D 4,57:1
Wagner, Robin (Scenic Designer)
Waiting for Godot 1958,Ag 6,22:1
And the Wind Blows 1959,Ap 29,28:1
Between Two Thieves 1960,F 12,23:1
Prodigal, The 1960,F 12,23:1
Prodigal, The 1960,F 21,II,1:1
Delightful Season, A 1960,S 29,30:1

Wagner, Robin (Scenic Designer)—Cont
Borak 1960,D 14,51:1
Worm in Horseradish, A 1961,Mr 14,32:3
Entertain a Ghost 1962,Ap 10,48:1
Days and Nights of Beebee Fenstermaker, The 1962,S 18,33:1
Cages; Snowangel; Epiphany 1963,Je 14,36:1
In White America 1963,N 1,26:1
Burning, The 1963,D 4,57:1
White Rose and the Red, The 1964,Mr 17,31:1
View From the Bridge, A 1965,Ja 29,24:1
Hard Travelin' 1965,Je 17,25:1
Lonesome Train, The 1965,Je 17,25:1
Evening's Frost, An 1965,O 12,56:1
Condemned of Altona, The 1966,F 4,21:1
Galileo 1967,Ap 14,31:1
Galileo 1967,Ap 23,II,1:1
Phaedra 1967,My 22,50:2
Trial of Lee Harvey Oswald, The 1967,N 6,64:1
Certain Young Man, A 1967,D 27,45:1
Hair 1968,Ap 30,40:2
Lovers and Other Strangers 1968,S 19,63:1
Cuban Thing, The 1968,S 25,36:2
Great White Hope, The 1968,O 4,40:1
Promises, Promises 1968,D 2,59:3
Watering Place, The 1969,Mr 13,51:1
My Daughter, Your Son 1969,My 14,36:2
Hair 1970,Ja 13,39:1
Gantry 1970,F 16,44:1
Mahagonny 1970,Ap 29,51:1
Engagement Baby, The 1970,My 22,40:1
Wagner, Ruth (Costume Designer)
Another Evening With Harry Stoones 1961,O 23,22:2
Spanish Armada, The 1962,Ap 4,38:1
Man Out Loud, Girl Quiet 1962,Ap 4,38:1
Wagner, Shirley Jac
King Lear 1961,My 15,34:6
House of Bernarda Alba, The 1963,N 25,23:2
Danton's Death 1965,O 22,46:1
Country Wife, The 1965,D 10,58:2
Caucasian Chalk Circle, The 1966,Mr 25,35:1
Alchemist, The 1966,O 14,48:1
East Wind, The 1967,F 10,30:1
Saint Joan 1968,Ja 5,42:1
Tiger at the Gates 1968,Mr 1,30:1
Cyrano de Bergerac 1968,Ap 26,30:1
Wagner, Thomas (Composer)
Lion in Winter, The 1966,Mr 4,23:1
Wagner, Walter
Slight Case of Murder, A 1935,S 12,28:5
Crime Marches on 1935,O 24,19:1
Brother Rat 1936,D 17,34:5
See My Lawyer 1939,S 28,29:1
Wagoner, Walter
Come Angel Band 1936,F 19,17:1
Wagstaff, Elsie
Diversion 1928,Ja 12,25:1
Wrecker, The 1928,F 28,18:2
Wagstaff, Joe
Billie 1928,O 2,34:2
Fine and Dandy 1930,S 24,26:1
Wagstaffe, Alice (Playwright)
Voyageur Sans Bagage, Le 1938,Ja 2,X,3:5
Wahl, Anders de
Markurells in Wadkoeping 1930,N 2,VIII,3:2
Wahl, Lois (Producer)
Love Your Crooked Neighbor 1969,D 30,40:1
Wahl, Marylin
They Knew What They Wanted 1939,O 3,19:1
Wahl, Walter Dare
Vaudeville (Palace) 1929,S 16,30:4
Blossom Time 1931,Mr 5,32:1
Life Begins at 8:40 1934,Ag 28,24:2
Life Begins at 8:40 1934,S 2,IX,1:1
Laughter Over Broadway 1939,Ja 16,10:3
Top Banana 1951,N 2,19:2
Wahle, Evelyn
Danton's Death 1938,N 3,26:2
Margin for Error 1939,N 4,11:3
Wahlert, William
Knickerbocker Holiday 1938,O 20,26:2
Waide, Barbara
Cretan Woman, The 1954,Jl 8,18:2
Dark Lady of the Sonnets, The 1956,F 21,38:1
Dark Lady of the Sonnets, The 1956,Mr 4,II,1:1
Mrs Patterson 1957,F 6,20:2
King Lear 1959,Ja 3,11:2
Wailez, Gus
Zizi 1964,N 23,51:1
Waine, Allen
Kiss Me, Kate 1954,Mr 27,13:2
Waine, Allen (Choreographer)
Kiss Me, Kate 1954,Mr 27,13:2
Wainer, Lee (Composer)
1935 1936,My 13,28:2
Power 1937,F 24,18:5
Some of the People 1937,Mr 11,20:1
One-Third of a Nation 1938,Ja 18,27:2
Sing for Your Supper 1939,Ap 25,18:6
Life Begins in '40 1940,Ap 5,24:2
Hit the Road 1941,Ap 4,18:3
New Faces of 1943 1942,D 23,22:2

Wainer, Lee (Lyricist)
Morning Star 1940,Ap 17,26:4
Wainer, Lee (Miscellaneous)
New Faces of 1943 1942,D 23,22:2
Wainer, Lee (Musical Director)
Life Begins in '40 1940,Ap 5,24:2
Hit the Road 1941,Ap 4,18:3
Wainsztain, Schaia
Dracula Sabbat 1970,O 2,28:2
Wainwright, Helen
Vaudeville (Hippodrome) 1926,My 4,31:2
Vaudeville (Hippodrome) 1926,My 8,29:2
Vaudeville (Hippodrome) 1926,My 11,25:3
Wainwright, Jeanne
Wife With a Smile, The 1921,N 29,20:1
Wainwright, Lennal
Man Better Man 1969,Jl 3,22:1
Wainwright, Marie
Captain Applejack 1921,D 31,14:2
Wainwright, Ralph
All's Well That Ends Well 1966,Je 17,39:1
Wainwright Sisters
Two Seconds 1931,O 10,20:6
Waisberg, Louis
Roaming Stars 1930,Ja 25,12:2
Waissman, Kenneth (Producer)
Fortune and Men's Eyes 1969,O 23,55:1
Wait, Donald
Laugh It Off 1934,Ap 5,24:2
Wait, Robert R
My Wife and I 1966,O 11,53:2
Waite, Eric
Ice Capades 1955,S 15,38:1
Ice Capades 1956,S 13,41:2
Ice Capades 1957,S 5,33:2
Ice Capades 1958,S 4,33:2
Ice Capades 1959,S 4,12:1
Ice Capades 1960,S 1,30:1
Ice Capades 1961,Ag 31,24:4
Holiday on Ice 1965,S 2,38:4
Waite, Franklin
Storm Center 1927,D 1,33:2
Waite, Ozzie
Kongi's Harvest 1968,Ap 15,49:1
Waite, Ralph
Blues for Mister Charlie 1964,Ap 24,24:1
Hogan's Goat 1965,N 12,56:1
Mutilated, The 1966,F 23,42:1
Drums in the Night 1967,My 18,54:1
Trial of Lee Harvey Oswald, The 1967,N 6,64:1
Hamlet 1967,D 27,45:1
Hamlet 1968,Jl 4,15:1
Watering Place, The 1969,Mr 13,51:1
Twelfth Night 1969,Ag 14,29:2
Waithe, Allan
Cape Smoke 1925,F 17,19:1
Lulu Belle 1926,F 10,20:1
Waits, Fred
Sambo 1970,Jl 23,24:1
Waizman, Max
Like a King 1921,O 4,10:1
Partners Again 1922,My 2,22:2
Shelter 1926,Ja 26,18:2
Potash and Perlmutter, Detectives; Poisoned by Pictures 1926,S 1,27:3
Scalawag, The 1927,Mr 30,22:3
Wakatake, Fuemi (Playwright)
General's Daughter, The 1966,Mr 16,50:1
Greengrocer's Daughter, The 1966,Mr 16,50:1
Wakefield, Ann
Boy Friend, The 1954,O 1,20:1
Wakefield, Ed
Magic Ring, The 1923,O 2,10:1
Wakefield, Gilbert (Playwright)
Garey Divorce Case, The 1929,My 12,IX,2:3
Counsel's Opinion 1931,S 13,IX,2:5
Wakefield, Henrietta
Robin Hood 1935,Jl 15,20:6
Wakefield, Hugh
Louie the 14th 1925,Mr 4,17:1
Service for Two 1926,Ag 31,15:1
Service for Two 1926,S 5,VII,1:1
On Approval 1926,O 19,27:1
Quest 1928,Ja 8,VIII,2:3
Knight Errant 1928,S 2,VII,2:1
Sorry You've Been Troubled 1929,O 13,IX,4:1
Money! Money! 1931,Mr 15,IX,2:8
This Inconstancy 1933,Ap 16,IX,1:3
Springtime for Henry 1951,Mr 15,36:2
Wakefield, Hugh (Playwright)
Let Us Divorce; Counsel's Opinion 1932,Ap 17,VIII,2:6
Wakefield, Jack
Catch a Star! 1955,S 7,35:2
I Had a Ball 1964,D 16,50:1
Wakefield, John
Yeomen of the Guard, The 1962,Jl 11,28:1
Wakefield, Oliver
Ziegfeld Follies 1934,Ja 5,24:3
Two's Company 1952,D 16,43:5
Wakeling, Alan (Playwright)
Disney on Parade 1970,S 24,63:1

Wakeman, Frederic (Original Author)
Kiss Them for Me 1945,Mr 25,II,1:1
Kiss Them for Me 1945,MR 21,27:2
Wakeman, Maurice (Miscellaneous)
Spring 3100 1928,F 16,14:2
Wakhevitch, Georges (Scenic Designer)
Ring Around the Moon 1950,N 24,30:1
Fanny 1956,D 2,II,3:1
Walberg, Betty (Choreographer)
Anyone Can Whistle 1964,Ap 6,36:1
Walberg, Betty (Composer)
Metamorphosis 1957,F 20,38:1
Walberg, Betty (Miscellaneous)
Gypsy 1959,My 22,31:6
Fiddler on the Roof 1964,S 23,56:2
On a Clear Day You Can See Forever 1965,O 18,44:1
It's a Bird . . . It's a Plane . . . It's Superman 1966,Mr 30,34:1
Walberg, Bety (Miscellaneous)
Kelly 1965,F 8,28:2
Walberg, Gerry
Silver Tassie, The 1949,Jl 22,16:5
There Is No End 1950,F 17,27:4
Cellar and the Well, The 1950,D 11,30:2
Walbridge, Elsa
Jubilee 1935,O 14,20:1
Walbrookon, Anton
Watch on the Rhine 1942,My 3,VIII,1:7
Call Me Madam 1952,Mr 16,84:3
Walburg, Otto
Jedermann 1927,D 8,33:2
Walburn, Raymond
Manhattan 1922,Ag 16,7:5
Awful Truth, The 1922,S 19,14:3
Tyrants 1924,Mr 5,14:1
Show-Off, The 1924,O 26,VIII,1:1
If I Was Rich 1926,S 3,15:2
Sinner 1927,F 8,20:2
Triumphant Bachelor, The 1927,S 16,21:1
Take My Advice 1927,N 2,24:3
Great Necker, The 1928,Mr 7,28:2
On Call 1928,N 10,20:7
Zeppelin 1929,Ja 15,22:3
Freddy 1929,Jl 17,23:4
Three Little Girls 1930,Ap 15,29:1
House Beautiful, The 1931,Mr 13,20:4
Bridal Wise 1932,My 31,15:5
Budget, The 1932,S 21,26:4
Tell Her the Truth 1932,O 29,18:2
Show-Off, The 1932,D 13,25:4
Man Bites Dog 1933,Ap 26,11:2
Pursuit of Happiness, The 1933,O 10,24:4
Another Love 1934,Mr 20,26:3
Park Avenue 1946,N 5,31:2
Funny Thing Happened on the Way to the Forum, A 1962,My 9,49:1
Very Rich Woman, A 1965,O 5,5:8
Walburn, Raymond (Director)
Show-Off, The 1932,D 13,25:4
Walcott, Derek (Playwright)
Malcochon 1969,Ap 2,37:1
Walcott, Florence
Assumption of Hannele, The 1924,F 16,16:2
Tommy 1927,Ja 11,36:4
Re-Echo 1934,Ja 12,28:4
Walcott, George
Piper, The 1920,Mr 20,14:2
Swan, The 1923,O 24,15:3
Old English 1924,D 24,11:2
Young Woodley 1925,N 3,34:1
It's a Wise Child 1929,Ag 7,29:1
It's a Wise Child 1933,My 17,15:2
Going Gay 1933,Ag 4,18:5
Re-Echo 1934,Ja 12,28:4
Walcott, Jackie
Carmen Jones 1959,Ag 18,25:1
Walcott, Marie
As Husbands Go 1935,Jl 10,24:1
Walcott, William
Song and Dance Man, The 1924,Ja 1,21:2
Home Towners, The 1926,Ag 24,19:3
Philadelphia 1929,S 17,34:5
White Flame 1929,N 5,32:7
Cloudy With Showers 1931,S 2,17:5
Wald, Lester
Excursion 1937,Ap 10,11:4
Waldau, Gustav
Midsummer Night's Dream, A 1925,Mr 8,VII,2:1
Schwierige, Der 1930,N 30,IX,2:1
Weaker Sex, The 1931,Mr 1,VIII,1:3
Roulette 1932,Ja 17,VIII,2:2
Konjunktur 1933,D 10,X,5:1
Waldbrunn, Ernst
Rendezvous in Wien 1956,S 5,23:1
Waldeck, Fred
Rainbow Rose 1926,Mr 17,28:2
Walden, Bertha
Wonder Bar, The 1931,Mr 18,23:4
Spring Song 1934,O 2,18:2
Potash and Perlmutter 1935,Ap 6,11:3
Abie's Irish Rose 1937,My 13,30:2

Walden, Bertha—Cont
Me and Molly 1948,F 27,27:2
Walden, Claudia
Our Town 1940,Je 30,35:5
Soft Shoulders 1940,Jl 18,22:5
In Bed We Cry 1944,N 15,20:2
Walden, Don
In April Once 1955,Mr 14,29:3
Walden, Elsa (Miscellaneous)
Under the Yum-Yum Tree 1964,My 29,18:1
Walden, Grant
Best Foot Forward 1963,Ap 3,43:1
Walden, Henry
Journey to Jerusalem 1940,O 7,21:2
Walden, Robert
Hey You, Light Man! 1963,Mr 2,5:2
Meeting, The 1967,D 13,55:1
Lime Green 1969,Mr 27,54:2
Walden, Stanley
Oh! Calcutta! 1969,Je 18,33:1
Walden, Stanley (Composer)
Scuba Duba 1967,O 11,36:1
Walden, Stanley (Miscellaneous)
Serpent, The 1970,Je 2,35:1
Walden, Stanley (Musical Director)
Horseman, Pass By 1969,Ja 16,46:4
Walden, Vilma
Intruder, The 1928,Jl 26,25:4
Walden, Walter (Costume Designer)
At the Bottom 1930,Ja 10,24:3
Walden, Walter (Scenic Designer)
Subway, The 1929,Ja 26,15:1
Vegetable, The, or From President to Postman
1929,Ap 11,32:3
At the Bottom 1930,Ja 10,24:3
Life Line, The 1930,D 29,19:3
Lost Boy 1932,Ja 6,24:4
Jayhawker 1934,N 6,34:2
Swing It 1937,Jl 23,17:2
Story Teller, The 1951,D 15,11:3
Walden, William (Playwright)
Metropole 1949,D 7,43:2
Waldheim, Aloha
One Man's Woman 1926,My 26,25:1
Waldis, Otto
Proud Accent 1949,Ap 23,10:2
Waldman, Al
Vaudeville (Palace) 1927,Jl 5,19:3
Vaudeville (Palace) 1929,Mr 25,33:2
Waldman, Honey
Way of the World, The 1950,Ap 9,73:5
Waldman, Lorraine
Show Boat 1948,S 9,33:2
Waldman, Robert (Composer)
Here's Where I Belong 1968,Mr 4,32:1
Waldman, Ted
Vaudeville (Palace) 1927,Jl 5,19:3
Vaudeville (Palace) 1929,Mr 25,33:2
Waldmueller, Lizzi
Victoria and Her Hussar 1930,S 21,IX,2:6
Glueckliche Reise 1933,Ja 1,IX,1:1
Bezauberndes Fraeulein 1933,N 19,IX,3:1
Hamlet in Wittenberg 1936,N 15,XI,2:4
Dominant Sex, The 1937,O 24,XI,3:2
Waldo, Earl
Vagabond King, The 1925,S 22,23:3
Waldock, Denis (Playwright)
Jam Today 1942,Mr 1,VIII,1:3
Waldon, Gertrude
Babes in Toyland 1930,D 22,17:1
Iolanthe 1931,Jl 14,21:5
Pirates of Penzance, The 1936,Ap 21,27:5
Iolanthe 1936,My 5,26:2
Waldon, Henry
Miser, The 1950,Mr 27,19:5
Master Builder Solness 1950,My 26,19:3
Waldon, Louis
Ballad of the Sad Cafe, The 1963,O 31,27:1
Great Western Union, The 1965,F 10,45:1
Line of Least Existence, The 1968,Mr 25,53:1
Waldon, Walter (Scenic Designer)
Prologue to Glory 1938,Mr 18,22:2
Waldorf
Music in the Air 1951,O 9,32:2
Waldorf, Claire
Von Mund zu Mund 1926,D 5,VIII,8:7
Waldrige, Harold
Wheel, The 1921,Ag 30,10:1
Polly Preferred 1923,Ja 12,13:3
Love 'Em and Leave 'Em 1926,F 4,20:4
Poppa 1928,D 25,31:1
Poppa 1928,D 30,VIII,1:1
Veneer 1929,N 13,24:5
Geraniums in My Window 1934,O 27,20:6
Without Warning 1937,My 3,23:2
Snark Was a Boojum, The 1943,S 2,14:4
Waldrip, Gladstone
East Wind 1931,O 28,19:1
Forbidden Melody 1936,N 3,33:1
Knights of Song 1938,O 18,29:2
Waldron, Charles
Passion Flower, The 1920,Ja 14,12:1
Mary Stuart 1921,Mr 22,15:1
Elton Case, The 1921,Jl 5,15:1

Swords 1921,S 2,9:3
Elton Case, The 1921,S 12,16:2
Bill of Divorcement, A 1921,O 11,22:2
Pinch Hitter, A 1922,Je 2,20:4
Guilty One, The 1923,Mr 21,19:1
Mrs Partridge Presents 1925,Ja 6,23:3
Hamlet 1925,N 10,23:1
Magda 1925,D 22,18:4
Magda 1926,Ja 27,16:2
Pyramids 1926,Jl 20,17:2
Heaven-Tappers, The 1927,Mr 9,28:3
Madame X 1927,Jl 7,29:3
Coquette 1927,N 9,23:1
Coquette 1927,N 13,IX,1:1
Those We Love 1930,F 20,22:2
Vikings, The 1930,My 13,27:3
Schoolgirl 1930,N 21,31:1
Barretts of Wimpole Street, The 1931,F 10,25:1
Barretts of Wimpole Street, The 1931,F 22,VIII,1:1
Electra 1932,Ja 9,21:4
Lucrece 1932,N 30,22:8
Lucrece 1932,D 21,22:2
Lucrece 1933,Ja 1,IX,1:1
Alien Corn 1933,F 21,17:2
Alien Corn 1933,F 26,IX,1:1
Pursuit of Happiness, The 1933,O 10,24:4
Dance With Your Gods 1934,O 8,14:3
Aiglon, L' 1934,N 5,22:2
Romeo and Juliet 1934,D 4,23:2
Romeo and Juliet 1934,D 21,30:3
Romeo and Juliet 1934,D 30,IX,1:1
Barretts of Wimpole Street, The 1935,F 26,16:2
Flowers of the Forest 1935,Ap 9,25:2
Romeo and Juliet 1935,D 24,10:2
Saint Joan 1936,Mr 10,27:4
I Am My Youth 1938,Mr 8,22:4
American Landscape 1938,D 5,19:2
Deep Are the Roots 1945,S 27,24:4
Deep Are the Roots 1945,O 7,II,1:1
Waldron, Donnee
Sure Fire! 1926,O 21,23:1
Waldron, Gertrude
Pirates of Penzance, The 1936,Ap 21,27:5
Waldron, Jack
Flossie 1924,Je 4,25:2
Great Temptations, The 1926,My 19,29:1
Pal Joey 1952,Ja 4,17:6
Pajama Game, The 1954,My 14,20:2
Vamp, The 1955,N 11,30:1
Pajama Game, The 1957,My 16,27:1
Say Darling 1959,F 26,38:2
Pal Joey 1961,Je 1,32:1
Waldron, Jack (Original Author)
What a Killing 1961,Mr 28,41:1
Waldron, Marga
George White's Scandals 1923,Je 19,22:5
Vaudeville (Hippodrome) 1924,Mr 18,25:1
Enchanted Isle 1927,S 20,33:2
Hot Water 1929,Ja 22,22:3
Waldron, Martin
Saint Joan 1950,Mr 4,10:6
King Lear 1950,D 26,18:1
Sleeping Prince, The 1956,N 2,31:1
Trial of Dmitri Karamazov, The 1958,Ja 28,30:1
Fools Are Passing Through 1958,Ap 3,24:2
Merchant of Venice, The 1962,F 3,13:2
Waldrop, Oza
Quiet, Please! 1940,N 9,20:3
Waldrup, Gladstone
Show Boat 1954,My 20,22:2
Waldt, Irving (Director)
Mikado, The 1935,Ag 24,17:5
Walduck, Ann
Ice Capades 1958,S 4,33:2
Walenta, Edmund
Around the World in 80 Days 1964,Je 29,33:2
Wales, Amy (Playwright)
Rockbound 1929,Ap 20,23:2
Wales, Bettie
Marie Antoinette 1921,N 23,16:1
Wales, Gary
Celebration 1969,Ja 23,55:2
Wales, Minna
Present Arms 1928,Ap 27,16:2
Wales, Pauline
Pirates of Penzance, The 1962,N 21,28:1
Iolanthe 1962,N 28,42:1
Iolanthe 1964,N 18,52:1
H M S Pinafore 1964,N 20,40:1
Pirates of Penzance, The 1964,N 27,43:1
Pirates of Penzance, The 1966,N 16,54:1
Mikado, The 1966,N 18,36:1
Ruddigore 1966,N 23,28:1
Patience 1966,N 30,58:1
H M S Pinafore 1966,N 24,64:1
H M S Pinafore 1968,O 30,35:1
Mikado, The 1968,N 2,29:4
Pirates of Penzance, The 1968,N 7,54:1
Iolanthe 1968,N 9,37:3
Walford, Ann
Midsummer Night's Dream, A 1954,S 22,33:1
Walken, Christopher
Baker Street 1965,F 17,36:1

Walken, Christopher—Cont
Lion in Winter, The 1966,Mr 4,23:1
Measure for Measure 1966,Jl 14,27:1
Rose Tattoo, The 1966,O 21,36:2
Rose Tattoo, The 1966,N 20,II,1:1
Unknown Soldier and His Wife, The 1967,Jl 7,22:1
Iphigenia in Aulis 1967,N 22,40:2
Iphigenia in Aulis 1967,D 3,II,1:1
Romeo and Juliet 1968,Je 11,55:2
Midsummer Night's Dream, A 1968,Je 13,54:1
Romeo and Juliet 1968,Je 23,II,1:1
Three Musketeers, The 1968,Jl 24,49:2
Chronicles of Hell, The 1969,O 19,II,12:1
Lemon Sky 1970,My 18,40:1
Walken, Glenn
Giants, Sons of Giants 1962,Ja 8,26:2
Best Foot Forward 1963,Ap 3,43:1
Carpenters, The 1970,D 22,40:1
Walken, Ken
Climate of Eden, The 1952,N 7,20:2
Visit, The 1958,My 6,40:1
Walken, Ronald
Best Foot Forward 1963,Ap 3,43:1
Walker, Adele
Becky Sharp 1929,Je 4,29:1
Little Father of the Wilderness, The 1930,Je 3,27:1
Walker, Albert B
Coriolanus 1927,Je 18,8:3
Walker, Alixe
Doctor X 1931,F 10,25:1
Walker, Allen (Miscellaneous)
Right You Are (If You Think You Are)
1957,Mr 5,37:1
Walker, Andrew
Big White Fog 1940,O 23,26:2
Walker, Antoinette
Innocent Idea, An 1920,My 26,9:4
Walker, Arlene
Wayward Stork, The 1966,Ja 20,27:1
Walker, Bernice
Blue Butterfly, The 1929,F 17,29:3
Walker, Betty
Springtime Folly 1951,F 27,23:4
Middle of the Night 1956,F 9,39:1
Middle of the Night 1956,F 19,II,1:1
Passion of Josef D, The 1964,F 12,29:1
Ready When You Are, C. B.! 1964,D 8,55:1
Walker, Bonnie
Cabaret 1966,N 21,62:1
Walker, C P
Amen Corner, The 1965,Ap 16,35:1
Walker, Charles (Playwright)
Third Parade, The 1933,O 23,18:2
Walker, Charlotte
Call the Doctor 1920,S 1,14:1
Skylark 1921,Jl 26,10:6
Trilby 1921,D 24,7:2
School for Scandal, The 1923,Je 5,24:3
Comedienne 1924,O 22,18:1
Two by Two 1925,F 24,17:1
Roof, The 1931,O 31,22:4
If Booth Had Missed 1932,F 5,24:2
Boy Friend, The 1932,Je 8,22:3
Girls in Uniform 1932,D 31,10:3
Any Woman 1934,Ag 28,24:4
Sleeping Clergyman, A 1934,O 9,16:1
Walker, Clara
God Is Back, Black and Singing Gospel at the
Fortune Theater 1969,N 19,48:1
Walker, Clifford
School for Scandal, The 1925,O 24,19:1
Aiglon, L' 1927,D 27,24:3
Wrecker, The 1928,F 28,18:2
Becky Sharp 1929,Je 4,29:1
Soldiers and Women 1929,S 3,25:1
Peter Ibbetson 1931,Ap 9,30:3
Walker, Clyde
Show Boat 1966,Jl 20,48:1
Walker, Dan
Elsie Janis and Her Gang 1922,Ja 17,13:2
Agent 666, L' 1923,My 30,10:5
This Fine-Pretty World 1923,D 27,11:1
Juarez and Maximilian 1926,O 12,31:1
No Trifling With Love 1959,N 10,55:3
Walker, David (Composer)
Mira 1970,Je 3,51:1
Walker, David (Miscellaneous)
Criss-Crossing 1970,Ja 22,30:1
Watercolor 1970,Ja 22,30:1
Walker, Diana
Fourth Pig, The 1965,Ja 27,24:6
Mame 1966,My 25,41:1
Play It Again, Sam 1969,F 13,52:3
Walker, Don (Composer)
Allah Be Praised! 1944,Ap 21,14:2
Memphis Bound 1945,My 25,23:2
Memphis Bound 1945,Je 10,II,1:1
Heaven on Earth 1948,S 17,29:2
Great to Be Alive! 1950,Mr 24,28:2
Courtin' Time 1951,Je 14,30:2
Beauty Part, The 1962,D 28,5:2
Music Man, The 1965,Je 17,26:4
Walker, Don (Lyricist)
Memphis Bound 1945,My 25,23:2

Walker, Don (Lyricist)—Cont
Courtin' Time 1951,Jl 1,II,1:1
Walker, Don (Miscellaneous)
Beat the Band 1942,O 15,26:1
Park Avenue 1946,N 5,31:2
Finian's Rainbow 1947,Ja 11,23:2
Miss Liberty 1949,Je 14,26:6
Call Me Madam 1950,O 13,25:1
Bless You All 1950,D 15,42:2
Courtin' Time 1951,Je 14,30:2
Top Banana 1951,N 2,19:2
Pal Joey 1952,Ja 4,17:6
Of Thee I Sing 1952,My 6,34:2
Wish You Were Here 1952,Je 26,26:6
Buttrio Square 1952,O 15,40:2
Hazel Flagg 1953,F 12,22:2
Maggie 1953,F 19,20:2
Wonderful Town 1953,F 26,22:3
Me and Juliet 1953,My 29,17:1
Carnival in Flanders 1953,S 9,38:2
Most Happy Fella, The 1956,My 4,20:1
Pajama Game, The 1957,My 16,27:1
Music Man, The 1957,D 20,31:1
Wonderful Town 1958,Mr 6,32:4
First Impressions 1959,Mr 20,28:1
Greenwillow 1960,Mr 9,38:1
Finian's Rainbow 1960,Ap 28,31:1
Unsinkable Molly Brown, The 1960,N 4,28:1
Gay Life, The 1961,N 20,38:1
She Loves Me 1963,Ap 24,39:1
Here's Love 1963,O 4,28:1
What Makes Sammy Run? 1964,F 28,19:1
Anyone Can Whistle 1964,Ap 6,36:1
Fiddler on the Roof 1964,S 23,56:2
Baker Street 1965,F 17,36:1
Flora, the Red Menace 1965,My 12,41:2
Anya 1965,N 30,48:1
Time for Singing, A 1966,My 23,48:2
Cabaret 1966,N 21,62:1
Happy Time, The 1968,Ja 19,32:2
Her First Roman 1968,O 21,53:3
Zorba 1968,N 18,58:1
Walker, Don (Musical Director)
Connecticut Yankee, A 1943,N 18,30:2
Up in Central Park 1945,Ja 29,17:2
Carousel 1945,Ap 20,24:2
Up in Central Park 1947,My 20,29:2
Look, Ma, I'm Dancin' 1948,Ja 30,20:2
My Romance 1948,O 20,38:5
Miss Liberty 1949,Jl 16,6:5
Touch and Go 1949,O 14,34:2
Gentlemen Prefer Blondes 1949,D 9,35:3
Girl in Pink Tights, The 1954,Mr 6,13:2
Pajama Game, The 1954,My 14,20:2
On Your Toes 1954,O 12,24:4
Hit the Trail 1954,D 3,31:2
Silk Stockings 1955,F 25,17:3
Ankles Aweigh 1955,Ap 19,27:1
Damn Yankees 1955,My 6,17:1
Finian's Rainbow 1955,My 19,25:1
Greenwillow 1960,Mr 20,II,1:1
Cabaret 1966,D 4,II,5:1
Rothschilds, The 1970,O 20,40:1
Walker, E A
Matriarch, The 1930,Mr 19,24:5
Walker, Edith Campbell
Wild Westcotts, The 1923,D 25,26:2
Mask and the Face, The 1924,S 11,27:3
Walker, Elizabeth
Summertree 1969,D 10,60:1
Walker, Ernest
Capacity for Wings 1957,Ja 10,25:1
Walker, Ethel Jane
Fioretta 1929,F 6,30:3
Walker, Fay
Six-Cylinder Love 1921,Ag 26,8:2
Beggar on Horseback 1924,F 13,17:2
Walker, Finette
Jubilee 1935,O 14,20:1
Walker, Francis
Footlights 1927,Ag 20,8:2
Walker, Gertrude
Weather Clear, Track Fast 1927,O 19,24:5
Show Boat 1932,My 20,22:2
Clean Beds 1939,My 26,21:2
Walker, Gillian (Director)
Little Murders 1969,Ja 6,38:1
Walker, Gillian (Miscellaneous)
Iphigenia in Aulis 1967,N 22,40:2
Moon for the Misbegotten, A 1968,Je 13,55:2
Morning 1968,N 29,52:1
Night 1968,N 29,52:1
Noon 1968,N 29,52:1
Trumpets of the Lord 1969,Ap 30,37:1
Ah, Wilderness! 1969,N 9,86:1
Walker, Helen
Jason 1942,Ja 22,12:2
Walker, Ivan
Merry Duchess, The 1943,Je 24,25:1
Walker, James
Hollow Crown, The 1963,Ja 31,5:1
Walker, James (Miscellaneous)
Gondoliers, The 1962,N 16,25:2
Pirates of Penzance, The 1964,N 27,43:1

Pirates of Penzance, The 1966,N 16,54:1
Mikado, The 1966,N 18,36:1
Ruddigore 1966,N 23,28:1
H M S Pinafore 1966,N 24,64:1
Patience 1966,N 30,58:1
Walker, James (Musical Director)
Trial by Jury 1964,N 20,40:1
H M S Pinafore 1968,O 30,35:1
Mikado, The 1968,N 2,29:4
Pirates of Penzance, The 1968,N 7,54:1
Iolanthe 1968,N 9,37:3
Walker, James J (Mayor) (Composer)
Say When 1928,Je 27,29:3
Walker, James J (Mayor) (Lyricist)
Say When 1928,Je 27,29:3
Walker, Jewel
Mime Theatre of Etienne Decroux, The
  1959,D 24,15:1
Walker, Joel (Miscellaneous)
Hawk, The 1968,Ap 18,54:1
Walker, John
Ten Million Ghosts 1936,O 24,23:7
Walker, Johnnie (Director)
Make Yourself at Home 1945,S 14,21:2
Walker, Johnnie (Producer)
Make Yourself at Home 1945,S 14,21:2
Haven, The 1946,N 14,39:4
Walker, Johnny
Folly Town 1920,My 18,9:2
Walker, Joseph A (Choreographer)
Ododo 1970,N 25,26:1
Walker, Joseph A (Director)
Ododo 1970,N 25,26:1
Walker, Joseph A (Lyricist)
Believers, The 1968,My 10,57:4
Walker, Joseph A (Playwright)
Believers, The 1968,My 10,57:4
Harangues, The 1970,Ja 14,42:1
Harangues, The 1970,Ja 25,II,1:4
Harangues, The 1970,S 13,II,1:1
Ododo 1970,N 25,26:1
Ododo 1970,D 6,II,5:1
Walker, Joyce
Kongi's Harvest 1968,Ap 15,49:1
Walker, June
Six-Cylinder Love 1921,Ag 26,8:2
Nervous Wreck, The 1923,O 10,16:1
Nervous Wreck, The 1923,O 21,VIII,1:1
Processional 1925,Ja 13,17:1
Glass Slipper, The 1925,O 20,29:1
Glass Slipper, The 1925,O 25,VIII,1:1
Glory Hallelujah 1926,Ap 7,26:2
Glory Hallelujah 1926,Ap 11,VIII,1:1
Gentlemen Prefer Blondes 1926,S 29,23:1
Gentlemen Prefer Blondes 1926,O 3,VIII,1:1
Our Little Wife 1927,My 10,25:3
Love Nest, The 1927,D 23,17:1
Bachelor Father, The 1928,F 29,28:2
Waterloo Bridge 1929,D 1,X,4:7
Waterloo Bridge 1930,Ja 7,29:2
Green Grow the Lilacs 1931,Ja 27,21:2
Collision 1932,F 17,19:2
We Are No Longer Children 1932,Ap 1,17:2
Pure in Heart, The 1932,O 9,IX,3:7
Chrysalis 1932,N 16,15:2
Our Wife 1933,Mr 3,13:2
School for Husbands, The 1933,O 17,26:5
Farmer Takes a Wife, The 1934,O 9,17:2
Farmer Takes a Wife, The 1934,O 28,IX,3:1
Farmer Takes a Wife, The 1934,O 31,17:1
Farmer Takes a Wife, The 1934,N 11,IX,1:1
Just Suppose 1935,Jl 2,24:3
For Valor 1935,N 12,24:4
For Valor 1935,N 19,27:5
They Knew What They Wanted 1936,Jl 7,17:2
They Knew What They Wanted 1936,Jl 21,13:1
They Knew What They Wanted 1936,Jl 28,23:4
Girl From Wyoming, The 1938,O 31,12:1
Merchant of Yonkers, The 1938,D 13,30:1
Merchant of Yonkers, The 1938,D 18,IX,3:2
Merchant of Yonkers, The 1938,D 29,14:2
They Knew What They Wanted 1939,O 3,19:1
Ring Two 1939,N 14,20:3
Ring Two 1939,N 23,38:2
Twelfth Night 1940,O 27,IX,1:5
Twelfth Night 1940,N 20,26:3
Twelfth Night 1940,N 24,IX,1:1
Only the Heart 1944,Ap 5,17:2
Round Trip 1945,My 30,16:4
Truckline Cafe 1946,F 28,19:4
Hallams, The 1948,Mr 5,18:2
Happiest Years, The 1949,Ap 26,29:8
Ladies of the Corridor, The 1953,O 22,33:5
Ladies of the Corridor, The 1953,N 1,II,1:1
Sea Gull, The 1954,My 12,38:1
All Summer Long 1954,S 24,26:2
All Summer Long 1954,O 3,II,1:1
Morning's at Seven 1955,Je 23,25:1
Middle of the Night 1956,F 9,39:1
Middle of the Night 1956,F 19,II,1:1
Blue Denim 1958,F 28,17:1
Blue Denim 1958,Ap 20,II,1:1
Girls Against the Boys, The 1959,N 3,26:1

Follies of 1910, The 1960,Ja 15,37:3
Walker, Laura
Ghost Between, The 1921,Mr 23,11:2
Mask of Hamlet, The 1921,Ag 23,10:3
Walker, Laura (Playwright)
Doctor Monica 1933,N 7,29:3
Among Those Sailing 1936,F 12,24:4
Walker, Lillian
Mating Season, The 1927,Jl 19,27:6
Banshee, The 1927,D 6,26:2
Mother Lode 1934,D 24,16:5
Walker, Mabel
Swing Mikado, The 1939,Mr 2,18:2
Walker, Margaret
Lucky Break 1925,Ag 12,16:2
Rainbow Rose 1926,Mr 17,28:2
Honest Liars 1926,Jl 20,17:2
Geisha, The 1931,O 6,35:4
Green Stick 1934,O 10,21:2
In Heaven and Earth 1936,Mr 27,24:8
Stop Press 1939,Mr 20,13:2
Babes in Arms 1951,Mr 10,7:3
Walker, Marie Louise
We've Got to Have Money 1923,Ag 21,12:1
Steadfast 1923,O 31,12:1
High Hatters, The 1928,My 11,28:2
Walker, Martin
Silver Box, The 1928,Ja 18,23:1
Our Betters 1928,F 21,18:2
Painted Veil, The 1931,O 11,VIII,2:4
Laying the Devil 1933,Jl 23,IX,1:3
Indian Summer 1936,Ap 20,17:5
Indian Summer 1936,My 17,IX,2:2
Flare Path 1942,Ag 23,VIII,1:6
Walker, Mickey
Walk Hard 1946,Mr 28,34:2
Walker, Mildred (Original Author)
Southwest Corner, The 1955,F 4,18:2
Southwest Corner, The 1955,F 13,II,1:1
Walker, Millard (Composer)
Bureau-Crazy 1935,Ag 29,25:4
Walker, Nancy
Best Foot Forward 1941,S 12,24:4
Best Foot Forward 1941,O 2,28:2
Best Foot Forward 1941,O 26,IX,1:3
On the Town 1944,D 29,11:4
On the Town 1945,Ja 7,II,1:1
Barefoot Boy With Cheek 1947,Ap 4,20:2
Look, Ma, I'm Dancin' 1948,Ja 30,20:2
Along Fifth Avenue 1949,Ja 14,28:2
ANTA Album 1950,Ja 30,13:2
Phoenix '55 1955,Ap 25,20:2
Fallen Angels 1956,Ja 18,27:1
Copper and Brass 1957,O 18,19:2
Wonderful Town 1958,Mr 6,32:4
Girls Against the Boys, The 1959,N 3,26:1
Girls Against the Boys, The 1959,N 8,II,1:1
Do Re Mi 1960,D 27,23:2
Do Re Mi 1961,Ja 8,II,1:1
Cherry Orchard, The 1968,Mr 20,41:1
Cherry Orchard, The 1968,Ap 7,II,3:7
Cocktail Party, The 1968,O 8,42:1
Cocktail Party, The 1968,O 20,II,1:1
Walker, Nancy (Director)
Utbu 1966,Ja 5,24:1
Walker, Natalie Barth (Costume Designer)
First Mrs Fraser, The 1947,N 6,36:2
Cup of Trembling, The 1948,Ap 21,33:5
Two Blind Mice 1949,Mr 3,32:2
Black Chiffon 1950,S 28,39:2
Season in the Sun 1950,S 29,31:2
Double in Hearts 1956,O 17,41:7
Walker, Nina
Money Lender, The 1928,Ag 28,27:3
Find the Fox 1930,Je 21,20:4
Pressing Business 1930,N 18,28:5
Walker, Norman
Pelleas and Melisande 1957,F 20,38:1
Walker, Pax
Lottie Dundass 1941,Ag 22,19:5
Highland Fling, A 1944,Ap 29,13:2
Walker, Phyllis
Hello Out There 1941,S 11,20:6
Member of the Wedding, The 1950,Ja 6,26:6
Walker, Polly
No Foolin' 1926,Je 25,25:1
Merry Malones, The 1927,S 27,30:2
Billie 1928,O 2,34:2
Hello Paris 1930,N 17,29:3
Lovely Lady 1932,Mr 20,VIII,1:8
Walker, Ralph
Rainbow 1928,N 22,25:1
Walker, Rhoderick
Tonight at 8:30; Ways and Means 1948,F 21,8:2
Tonight at 8:30; Family Album 1948,F 21,8:2
Tonight at 8:30; Red Peppers 1948,F 21,8:2
Tonight at 8:30; Hands Across the Sea
  1948,F 24,20:4
Tonight at 8:30; Shadow Play 1948,F 24,20:4
Qudrille 1954,N 4,39:2

Walker, Richard
Gondoliers, The 1934,S 4,23:1
Pirates of Penzance, The; Slave of Duty, The 1934,S 7,24:3
Trial by Jury 1934,S 14,24:3
H M S Pinafore 1934,S 14,24:3
Princess Ida; Castle Adamant 1934,S 28,26:3
Pirates of Penzance, The 1936,S 1,24:4
Trial by Jury 1936,S 1,24:4
H M S Pinafore 1936,S 29,34:2
Cox and Box 1936,S 29,34:2
Princess Ida 1936,O 13,32:2
Pirates of Penzance, The 1939,Ja 6,25:1
Trial by Jury 1939,Ja 6,25:1
H. M. S. Pinafore 1939,Ja 17,27:5
Cox and Box 1939,Ja 17,27:5
Trial by Jury 1948,Ja 6,27:2
Pirates of Penzance, The 1948,Ja 6,27:2
Pirates of Penzance, The 1948,Ja 11,II,1:1
Iolanthe 1948,Ja 13,29:3
H M S Pinafore 1948,Ja 20,26:2
Cox and Box 1948,Ja 20,26:2
Yeomen of the Guard, The 1948,F 3,30:2
Patience 1948,F 10,27:2
My Fair Lady 1959,Ja 27,26:1
Walker, Robert
Chameleon, The 1932,Jl 19,20:4
I Knock at the Door 1964,N 26,52:2
Pictures in the Hallway 1964,D 17,51:1
Beaux' Stratagem, The 1970,F 10,50:2
Three Sisters, The 1970,F 12,30:1
Walker, Robert (Scenic Designer)
Devil Came From Dublin, The! 1955,Je 3,27:2
Believers, The 1968,My 10,57:4
Walker, Rudolph
Tempest, The 1970,Ag 29,14:1
Walker, Sally
Small War on Murray Hill 1957,Ja 4,19:1
Walker, Sid
Keep Off the Grass 1940,My 24,22:6
Walker, Stuart (Director)
Book of Job, The 1922,O 31,11:1
Love City, The 1926,Ja 26,18:2
Walker, Stuart (Miscellaneous)
Love Is Like That 1927,Ap 19,24:1
Walker, Stuart (Playwright)
Nevertheless 1920,D 28,9:1
Walker, Stuart (Producer)
Main Street 1921,Jl 24,VI,1:1
Judith 1924,Mr 2,VIII,2:7
Walker, Sydney
Julius Caesar 1957,O 24,39:1
King Lear 1959,Ja 3,11:2
Becket 1960,O 6,50:1
Becket 1961,My 9,44:1
Right You Are (If You Think You Are) 1964,Mr 5,37:1
Tavern, The 1964,Mr 6,39:2
Scapin 1964,Mr 10,43:1
Lower Depths, The 1964,Mr 31,30:1
War and Peace 1965,Ja 12,32:1
War and Peace 1965,Ja 31,II,1:1
Judith 1965,Mr 25,42:2
You Can't Take It With You 1965,N 24,32:1
School for Scandal, The 1966,N 22,33:2
Right You Are (If You Think You Are) 1966,N 23,34:2
School for Scandal, The 1966,D 11,II,3:1
We Comrades Three 1966,D 21,46:1
Wild Duck, The 1967,Ja 12,49:1
War and Peace 1967,Mr 22,42:1
Pantagleize 1967,D 1,54:1
Cherry Orchard, The 1968,Mr 20,41:1
Cherry Orchard, The 1968,Ap 7,II,3:7
Cocktail Party, The 1968,O 8,42:1
Misanthrope, The 1968,O 10,59:1
Cocktail Party, The 1968,O 20,II,1:1
Cock-A-Doodle Dandy 1969,Ja 21,40:1
Cock-A-Doodle Dandy 1969,F 2,II,1:1
Scent of Flowers, A 1969,O 21,42:1
Blood Red Roses 1970,Mr 23,48:1
Nuns, The 1970,Je 2,35:1
Good Woman of Setzuan, The 1970,N 6,51:1
Good Woman of Setzuan, The 1970,N 15,II,1:5
Walker, Sydney (Playwright)
Nathan the Wise 1962,Mr 23,29:1
Walker, Thomas
Bacchae, The 1969,Mr 15,24:1
Walker, Turnley
Waltz in Goose Step 1938,N 2,26:2
Walker, Ula
Junebug Graduates Tonight! 1967,F 27,35:1
Murderous Angels 1970,F 8,70:1
Walker, Vincent
Lady From the Sea, The 1935,D 14,11:3
Fuente Ovejuna; Sheep Well, The 1936,My 3,II,4:1
Walker, Walter
Fall and Rise of Susan Lenox, The 1920,Je 11,11:2
In the Night Watch 1921,Ja 31,10:1
Up in the Clouds 1922,Ja 3,20:3
I Will IF You Will 1922,Ag 30,10:4
It Is the Law 1922,N 30,28:2
Roger Bloomer 1923,Mr 2,18:3

Blue Bird, The 1923,D 26,13:3
Top Hole 1924,S 2,22:3
Crooked Friday, The 1925,O 9,27:3
Joker, The 1925,N 17,29:1
American Tragedy, An 1926,O 12,31:2
Great Power, The 1928,S 12,25:1
Holiday 1928,N 27,36:1
Half Gods 1929,D 23,18:5
Rebound 1930,F 4,29:1
Rebound 1930,F 16,IX,1:1
Walker, William
Wandering Jew, The 1927,F 2,22:4
Ringside 1928,Ag 30,13:2
White Man 1936,O 19,22:4
Black Rhythm 1936,D 21,19:2
Confederacy, The 1958,Jl 3,20:1
Wildcat 1960,D 17,20:2
Walker, William (Producer)
Spread It Abroad 1936,Ap 2,29:5
Walker, Zena
South 1955,My 2,17:4
Joe Egg 1968,F 2,26:1
Joe Egg 1968,F 11,II,1:1
Joe Egg 1968,Ap 27,43:2
Walkly, Beryl
Josef Suss 1930,Ja 21,28:5
Walkup, Fairfax (Costume Designer)
Forever This Land 1952,Je 30,14:6
Wilderness Road 1955,Je 30,20:4
Wall, Bill
Ice Follies 1959,Ja 14,30:1
Ice Follies 1961,Ja 11,25:2
Ice Follies 1962,Ja 10,24:6
Ice Follies 1966,Ja 12,27:6
Wall, Evelyn
Quiet, Please! 1940,N 9,20:3
Wall, Fred (Playwright)
Handy Man, The 1925,Mr 10,19:2
Wall, Geraldine
Love Nest, The 1927,D 23,17:1
Little Accident 1928,O 10,32:3
Blind Mice 1930,O 16,28:2
Child of Manhattan 1932,Mr 2,15:1
Domino 1932,Ag 7,IX,1:1
Domino 1932,Ag 17,13:2
Heat Lightning 1933,S 16,9:6
Merrily We Roll Along 1934,O 1,14:1
Wall, Harry (Playwright)
Havoc 1924,Ja 27,VII,2:4
Havoc 1924,S 2,22:2
Wall, Jack
Gang's All Here, The 1931,F 19,21:3
Wall, James E
Shuffle Along 1952,My 9,20:5
Mister Johnson 1956,Mr 30,11:1
Jamaica 1957,N 1,32:2
Wall, James E (Miscellaneous)
Kwamina 1961,O 24,42:1
Wall, Jean
Masque et Visage 1927,Ap 3,VIII,4:7
Robe de Perles, La 1928,Ja 15,VIII,2:3
Bapteme, Le 1928,Mr 11,VIII,2:7
Ludo 1932,Je 12,X,1:3
Trois et Une 1933,Ja 1,IX,3:4
Voyage, Le 1937,F 28,XI,2:1
Wall, Lucile
Montmartre 1922,F 14,20:1
Wall, Margery
Clinging Vine, The 1922,D 25,20:2
Wall, Marion
Low Bridge 1933,F 10,13:4
Wall, Mary
Just Life 1926,S 15,33:3
Hidden 1927,O 5,30:4
Come-On Man, The 1929,Ap 23,26:2
Wall, Max
Vanities 1932,S 18,IX,2:1
Vanities 1932,S 28,22:4
Panama Hattie 1943,D 5,II,5:1
Wall, Mervin (Original Author)
Fursey 1962,O 3,47:2
Wall, Mildred
Carnaval 1924,D 30,15:1
Appearances 1925,O 15,27:3
Broadway 1926,S 17,19:3
Up Pops the Devil 1930,S 2,19:1
Louder, Please! 1931,N 13,26:4
Blessed Event 1932,F 13,23:2
Blessed Event 1932,F 21,VIII,1:1
Dark Victory 1934,N 10,18:2
Penny Wise 1935,Jl 2,24:2
Return to Folly 1935,Jl 23,24:3
Whatever Goes Up 1935,N 26,28:2
Penny Wise 1937,Ap 20,28:6
Hallams, The 1948,Mr 5,18:2
Wall, William James (Costume Designer)
Prince of Peasantmania 1970,F 22,88:1
Wall, William James (Scenic Designer)
Mr Grossman 1964,My 6,43:1
Dark Corners 1964,My 6,43:1
Prince of Peasantmania 1970,F 22,88:1
Wall and Dova
Ice Follies 1958,Ja 15,26:2

Wall and Dova—Cont
Ice Follies 1960,Ja 13,20:1
Ice Follies 1965,Ja 13,35:1
Wallace, Alan
Doctor X 1930,Jl 31,12:4
Social Register, The 1931,N 10,28:2
Passionate Pilgrim, The 1932,O 20,24:3
Your Young Men 1935,Ag 8,13:2
American Holiday 1936,F 22,13:3
Wallace, Alfreda
Men in White 1955,F 26,13:2
Wallace, Alice
Roof, The 1930,Je 14,9:2
Wallace, Andree
Derryowen 1946,O 29,34:2
Kathleen 1948,F 4,26:2
Wallace, Ann
Golden Days 1921,N 2,20:1
Wallace, Art
Nowhere to Go But Up 1962,N 12,36:2
Music Man, The 1965,Je 17,26:4
Joyful Noise, A 1966,D 16,57:1
Now Is the Time for all Good Men 1967,S 27,42:1
Perfect Party, The 1969,Mr 21,42:1
Wallace, Augusta
Fly Away Home 1937,Ap 27,18:1
Lightnin' 1938,S 16,17:2
Wallace, Basil
Front Page, The 1968,O 20,85:5
Wallace, Ben (Costume Designer)
Take a Bow 1944,Je 16,15:3
Wallace, Bentley
Whirlpool 1929,D 4,37:3
Wisteria Trees, The 1950,Mr 30,39:1
Wallace, Bernard
Joy of Serpents 1930,Ap 4,22:4
Seven Against One 1930,My 7,25:1
Wallace, Beryl
Vanities 1932,S 28,22:4
Murder at the Vanities 1933,S 13,22:4
Sketch Book 1935,Je 5,22:2
Women, The 1936,D 28,13:1
Earl Carroll's Vanities 1940,Ja 15,11:2
Wallace, Betty
Sorcerer, The 1928,Je 24,VIII,1:1
Wallace, Billie
Burlesk 1927,S 4,VII,1:1
Wallace, Blanche
Drifting 1922,Ja 3,20:3
Wallace, Carl
Miracle in the Mountains 1947,Ap 26,10:2
Wallace, Cedric Trio
Beggars Are Comming to Town 1945,O 29,16:2
Wallace, Charles Ray
Bavu 1922,F 27,16:1
Monster, The 1922,Ag 10,20:3
Wallace, Coley
Mandingo 1961,My 23,43:6
Wallace, Connie
Six Characters in Search of an Author 1961,My 11,43:1
Wallace, David (Miscellaneous)
Lady Alone 1927,Ja 21,12:5
Rope 1928,F 23,18:3
Wallace, David (Playwright)
Rope 1928,F 23,18:3
Rope 1928,Mr 4,IX,1:1
Wallace, David Alexander
This Mad Whirl 1937,Ja 10,II,4:8
Wallace, Dick
Hold Your Horses 1933,S 26,26:4
Strip Girl 1935,O 21,22:6
Enemy of the People, An 1937,F 16,19:1
Wallace, Donald
Mummers and Men 1962,Mr 27,41:6
Wallace, Donald (Miscellaneous)
Mummers and Men 1962,Mr 27,41:6
Wallace, Douglas (Miscellaneous)
Gertrude Stein's First Reader 1969,D 16,56:1
Wallace, Edgar
All-Star Special 1931,Jl 18,16:4
Wallace, Edgar (Miscellaneous)
On the Spot 1930,O 30,33:3
Wallace, Edgar (Original Author)
Frog, The 1936,Ap 12,II,8:4
Sun Never Sets, The 1938,Je 26,IX,2:1
Wallace, Edgar (Playwright)
Pins and Needles 1922,F 2,20:1
Double Dan 1927,Je 5,VII,2:1
Squeaker, The 1928,Je 24,VIII,4:2
Sign of the Leopard 1928,D 2,X,4:2
Sign of the Leopard 1928,D 12,34:4
Sign of the Leopard 1928,D 24,17:7
Lad, The 1929,Ja 13,VIII,4:5
Ringer, The 1929,Mr 24,X,4:7
Persons Unknown 1929,Je 2,VIII,2:7
On the Spot 1930,Ap 3,32:6
On the Spot 1930,Ap 20,VIII,2:1
On the Spot 1930,O 30,33:3
Smoky Cell 1930,D 17,30:2
On the Spot 1931,Ja 18,VIII,3:1
Case of the Frightened Lady, The 1931,S 6,VIII,2:1
Man Who Changed His Name, The 1932,My 3,25:3
Criminal at Large 1932,O 11,26:3

Wallace, Edgar (Producer)
Sign of the Leopard 1928,D 12,34:4
Wallace, Eleanor
Roll Sweet Chariot 1934,O 3,24:3
Wallace, Emmett Babe
Lysistrata 1946,O 18,27:5
Wallace, Frances
Music Hath Charms 1934,D 31,8:2
Wallace, Frank K
Topsy and Eva 1924,D 24,11:1
Wallace, Fred
Brown Sugar 1937,D 3,29:2
Wallace, G D
Pipe Dream 1955,D 1,44:1
Wallace, George
Last Man In, The 1930,My 8,32:5
New Girl in Town 1957,My 15,40:1
New Girl in Town 1957,My 26,II,1:1
Jennie 1963,O 18,35:2
Wallace, Gordon
Living Corpse, The 1929,D 7,19:1
Lady of the Camellias, The 1931,Ja 27,21:2
Wallace, Harry
Silver Tassie, The 1929,O 25,26:1
Long Road, The 1930,S 10,30:2
Wallace, J C
Casanova 1923,S 27,10:2
Wallace, James
Skin of Our Teeth, The 1966,Je 2,51:1
As You Like It 1966,Je 4,19:1
Harpers Ferry 1967,Je 6,52:2
House of Atreus, The; Furies, The 1967,Jl 24,23:1
Visit, The 1967,S 13,41:1
Wallace, James G (Judge)
Off the Record; Mayor Answers the Newspapers!
Wow! 1935,Je 19,23:3
Wallace, James W
Caesar and Cleopatra 1925,Ap 14,27:1
House of Shadows, The 1927,Ap 22,18:4
Wallace, Janice
My Dear Public 1943,S 10,28:1
Wallace, Janice (Costume Designer)
Make Yourself at Home 1945,S 14,21:2
Wallace, Jerome H (Producer)
Second Comin', The 1931,D 9,32:4
Wallace, Jerry
By Hex 1956,Je 19,25:1
Wallace, Jo
Golden Days 1921,N 2,20:1
National Anthem, The 1922,Ja 24,16:3
Main Line, The 1924,Mr 26,19:4
Is Zat So? 1925,Ja 6,23:4
Wallace, John
Bystander 1937,S 15,27:1
Hi, Paisano 1961,O 2,36:2
Wallace, Kathleen
Bright Honor 1936,S 28,14:1
Wallace, Laura
Silver Grey Toy Poodle 1969,My 15,41:2
Pets 1969,My 15,41:2
Wallace, Lee
Journey of the Fifth Horse, The 1966,Ap 22,36:1
Journey of the Fifth Horse, The 1966,My 8,II,1:1
Saturday Night 1968,F 26,43:1
Shepherd of Avenue B, The 1970,My 16,30:1
Wallace, Marcia
Fourth Wall, The 1968,S 5,53:1
Calling in Crazy 1969,O 7,42:2
Dark of the Moon 1970,Ap 4,21:2
Wallace, Margaret
Janie 1942,S 11,24:2
Wallace, Marie
Harlequinade 1959,F 14,15:1
Beauty Part, The 1962,D 28,5:2
Nobody Loves an Albatross 1963,D 20,20:1
Right Honourable Gentleman, The 1965,O 20,50:2
Wallace, Mike
Reclining Figure 1954,O 8,26:5
Wallace, Milton
Puppet Show 1930,O 29,26:5
Enemy Within 1931,O 6,35:3
Blessed Event 1932,F 13,23:2
Wallace, Morgan
Acquittal, The 1920,Ja 6,18:2
Tavern, The 1920,S 28,14:1
Nature's Nobleman 1921,N 15,23:2
Lawbreaker, The 1922,F 7,12:1
Stork, The 1925,Ja 27,14:2
Gentle Grafters 1926,O 28,23:1
Ballyhoo 1927,Ja 5,18:1
Women Go on Forever 1927,S 8,25:1
Loco 1946,O 17,29:2
Wallace, Morgan (Playwright)
Congratulations 1929,My 1,28:4
Wallace, Norman
Miracle in the Mountains 1947,Ap 26,10:2
Wallace, Paul
Gypsy 1959,My 22,31:6
Wallace, Phoebe
Everybody's Welcome 1931,O 14,26:3
Wallace, Ramsey
Valley of Content, The 1925,Ja 14,19:2
Thrills 1925,Ap 17,24:3

Clouds 1925,S 3,32:1
Open House 1925,D 15,28:3
90 Horse Power 1926,Mr 16,22:4
Lost 1927,Mr 29,22:2
Wallace, Ramsey (Producer)
Lost 1927,Mr 29,22:2
Wallace, Regina
Ouija Board, The 1920,Mr 30,9:1
Pagans 1921,Ja 5,11:1
Nobody's Money 1921,Ag 18,9:3
Your Woman and Mine 1922,F 28,17:2
Breaking Point, The 1923,Ag 17,8:4
Show-Off, The 1924,F 6,16:2
Divorce a la Carte 1928,Mr 27,30:3
Housewarming 1932,Ap 8,25:1
I Myself 1934,My 10,24:6
First Lady 1935,N 27,17:4
Antony and Cleopatra 1937,N 11,30:2
Run Sheep Run 1938,N 4,26:2
Male Animal, The 1940,Ja 10,17:2
Male Animal, The 1952,My 1,35:1
Male Animal, The 1952,My 18,II,1:1
First Lady 1952,My 29,18:5
Wallace, Robert F (Playwright)
There Was a Young Man 1940,F 27,17:4
Wallace, Rona
Lady Butterfly 1923,Ja 23,18:1
Wallace, Ronald (Lighting Director)
Whistle in the Dark, A 1969,O 9,55:1
Country People 1970,Ja 19,35:1
Place Without Doors, A 1970,D 1,60:1
Wallace, Royce
Beggar's Holiday 1946,D 27,13:3
Happy as Larry 1950,Ja 7,11:2
Mamba's Daughters 1953,Mr 21,12:6
Year Round, The 1953,My 6,38:7
Once Over Lightly 1955,Mr 16,39:1
God's Trombones 1960,F 10,43:4
Shakespeare in Harlem 1960,F 10,43:4
Pretender, The 1960,My 25,42:1
Funny Girl 1964,Mr 27,15:1
Wallace, Ruby
Natural Man 1941,My 8,20:4
Wallace, Sarah
Let's Laugh Again 1937,Ag 24,24:5
Wallace, Slappy
Blackbirds 1933,D 4,22:3
Wallace, Stanley
What a Relief 1935,D 14,10:6
Wallace, Trudy
Show Boat 1966,Jl 20,48:1
Henry, Sweet Henry 1967,O 24,51:2
Wallace, Vernon
Vaudeville (Palace) 1927,Mr 1,31:2
A la Carte 1927,Ag 18,25:3
Wallace, Virginia
Boy Meets Girl 1937,Jl 6,23:1
Wallace and Cappo
Vaudeville (Hippodrome) 1926,Mr 23,24:3
Wallace Sisters
Jonica 1930,Ap 8,27:1
Wallach, D Bryan
Three Men on a Horse 1969,O 17,35:1
Wallach, Eli
Sky Drift 1945,N 14,25:2
Henry VIII 1946,N 7,42:1
Androcles and the Lion 1946,D 20,29:2
Yellow Jack 1947,F 28,26:2
Alice in Wonderland 1947,Ap 7,19:2
Antony and Cleopatra 1947,N 27,49:2
Lady From the Sea, The 1950,Ag 8,23:2
Rose Tattoo, The 1951,F 5,19:2
Rose Tattoo, The 1951,F 11,II,1:1
Camino Real 1953,Mr 20,26:1
Camino Real 1953,Mr 29,II,1:1
Scarecrow, The 1953,Je 17,31:1
Mademoiselle Colombe 1954,Ja 7,26:1
Teahouse of the August Moon, The
  1954,Ap 23,23:5
Teahouse of the August Moon, The
  1954,My 2,II,3:1
Major Barbara 1956,O 31,27:1
Chairs, The 1958,Ja 10,20:3
Chairs, The; Lesson, The 1958,F 16,II,1:1
Cold Wind and the Warm, The 1958,D 9,55:1
Cold Wind and the Warm, The 1959,Ja 18,II,1:1
Rhinoceros 1961,Ja 10,27:1
Rhinoceros 1961,Ja 22,II,1:1
Brecht on Brecht 1961,N 15,52:2
Typists, The 1963,F 6,5:2
Tiger, The 1963,F 6,5:2
Luv 1964,N 12,43:1
Luv 1964,N 22,II,1:1
Staircase 1968,Ja 11,41:2
Staircase 1968,Ja 21,II,3:7
Wallach, George
Audition of the Apprentice Theatre 1939,Je 2,26:2
Man With Blonde Hair, The 1941,N 5,30:2
Wallach, Ira (Playwright)
These Are the Times 1950,My 11,37:2
Hopalong--Freud 1953,Je 18,38:5
Once Over Lightly 1955,Mr 16,39:1
Phoenix '55 1955,Ap 25,20:2

Wallach, Ira (Playwright)—Cont
Drink to Me Only 1958,O 9,47:4
Hit the Deck 1960,Je 24,32:1
Smiling the Boy Fell Dead 1961,Ap 20,28:1
Absence of a Cello 1964,S 22,45:1
That Thing at the Cherry Lane 1965,My 19,42:1
Absence of a Cello; Mal de Test, Le 1965,S 9,36:3
Wallach, Michael (Playwright)
Sweet Mystery of Life 1935,O 12,13:3
Wallach, Samuel (Producer)
Deacon, The 1925,N 25,14:3
Climax, The 1926,My 18,29:3
Strange Gods 1933;Ap 17,16:6
Wallack, Susan
Junebug Graduates Tonight! 1967,F 27,35:1
Wallack, William
Young Alexander 1929,Mr 13,28:2
Wallburg
Servant of Two Masters, The 1928,Ja 22,VIII,6:1
Wallburg, Otto
Neidhardt von Gneisenau 1927,Ja 23,VII,4:5
Baby Mine 1927,Ap 3,VIII,2:1
Midsummer Night's Dream, A 1927,N 18,21:1
Dantons Tod 1927,D 21,28:3
Peripherie 1928,Ja 3,29:1
Diener Zweier Herren; Servant of Two Masters,
  The 1928,Ja 10,28:3
Kabale und Liebe 1928,Ja 17,22:3
Lebende Leichnam, Der, Der; Living Corpse, The
  1928,Ja 24,26:2
Fledermaus, Die 1929,Jl 14,IX,2:1
Little Accident 1929,S 22,IX,4:1
Im Weissen Roessel 1930,D 28,VIII,2:4
Fair Helen 1931,Ag 30,VIII,2:1
Journalisten, Die 1932,Jl 17,IX,1:1
Rosse 1933,My 7,IX,2:5
Walle, Alma
Friedens Tragoedie 1936,N 17,34:4
Wallen, George C
Waterloo Bridge 1930,Ja 7,29:2
Wallenda Troupe
Vaudeville (Palace) 1933,Ja 16,13:2
Wallenius, Etta
Blue Butterfly, The 1929,F 17,29:3
Wallenius, Heddie
Blue Butterfly, The 1929,F 17,29:3
Waller, Bert (Miscellaneous)
Irma la Douce 1960,S 30,31:2
Waller, David
Hamlet 1965,Ag 20,18:2
Much Ado About Nothing 1968,O 16,33:1
Landscape 1969,Jl 13,II,8:1
Troilus and Cressida 1969,Jl 31,26:1
Silver Tassle, The 1969,S 12,35:2
Hamlet 1970,Je 5,23:1
Hamlet 1970,Ag 3,37:3
Midsummer Night's Dream, A 1970,Ag 28,15:1
Midsummer Night's Dream, A 1970,S 13,II,7:1
Waller, Dorothy
Face the Music 1932,F 18,24:5
Gay Divorce 1932,N 30,23:4
Waller, Edmund
Buccaneer, The 1925,O 3,10:2
Waller, F (Composer)
Keep Shufflin' 1928,F 28,18:3
Waller, Fats
Vaudeville Marches On 1938,D 30,11:1
Waller, Frances
Wonderful Journey 1946,D 26,30:2
Great Campaign, The 1947,Ap 1,33:2
Throng o' Scarlet 1947,D 2,37:2
Coast of Illyria, The 1949,Ap 5,37:4
Metropole 1949,D 7,43:2
Show-Off, The 1950,Je 1,24:5
Waller, Jack (Composer)
Dear Love 1930,My 18,VIII,3:1
Tell Her the Truth 1932,O 29,18:2
Big Business 1937,F 19,15:3
Waller, Jack (Lyricist)
Dear Love 1930,My 18,VIII,3:1
Waller, Jack (Playwright)
Certainly, Sir 1936,S 18,19:5
Waller, Jack (Producer)
Command Performance 1933,O 18,24:3
Waller, John
Dragon, The 1922,D 27,12:1
Red Light Annie 1923,Ag 22,10:3
Rain 1935,F 13,24:1
Lysistrata 1959,N 25,19:4
Foxy 1964,F 17,26:1
Waller, John (Choreographer)
Lysistrata 1959,N 25,19:4
Peer Gynt 1960,Ja 13,21:1
Waller, Lewis
Dancing Mothers 1924,Ag 12,12:2
Gray Shadow 1931,Mr 11,23:4
Waller, Lewis (Playwright)
Cocktail Impromptu 1927,Ja 13,28:4
Waller, Louise
Joker, The 1925,N 17,29:1
Waller, Margaret
What Never Dies 1926,D 29,24:2
See Naples and Die 1929,S 27,30:4
Between Two Worlds 1934,O 26,24:2

Waller, Margaret—Cont
Doll's House, A 1937,Jl 25,X,2:3
Doll's House, A 1937,D 28,28:6
Cafe Crown 1942,Ja 24,12:5
Russian People, The 1942,D 30,17:2
Waller, Nancy Lewis
Respect for Riches, The 1920,My 12,9:1
Peter Ibbetson 1931,Ap 9,30:3
Waller, Oscar (Composer)
Revolt of the Beavers, The 1937,My 21,19:2
Waller, Sydney Schubert (Director)
Blind Angel, The 1965,Ap 2,26:1
Bitch of Waverly Place, The 1965,Ap 2,26:1
Waller, Thomas (Composer)
Hot Chocolates 1929,Je 21,17:4
Waller, Thomas (Fats) (Composer)
Early to Bed 1943,Je 18,16:2
Waller, Tod
Red Planet 1932,D 19,19:2
Waller, Tod (Director)
Cabbages and Kings 1933,Je 28,24:5
Waller, William Oden (Scenic Designer)
Take the Air 1927,N 23,28:2
Song Writer, The 1928,Ag 14,15:2
June Moon 1929,O 10,34:5
Suspense 1930,Ag 13,22:3
Social Register, The 1931,N 10,28:2
Rain 1935,F 13,24:1
Seven Keys to Baldpate 1935,My 28,30:2
Dear Old Darling 1936,Mr 3,25:1
County Chairman, The 1936,My 26,26:5
Bright Honor 1936,S 28,14:1
Fulton of Oak Falls 1937,F 11,18:2
Return of the Vagabond, The 1940,My 14,27:2
Boys and Girls Together 1940,O 2,19:2
Wallerstein, Liebert
Nathan the Wise 1942,Ap 4,18:4
Wallerstein, Margaret
Jugend im Mai 1927,Ja 23,VII,4:5
Rose Marie 1928,Mr 31,23:2
Rose Marie 1928,Ap 29,IX,2:8
Wallerstein, Rolf
Dybbuk, The 1954,O 27,33:6
Wallerstein, Rose
Two Hearts 1935,My 6,22:2
Walley, H R (Composer)
They Never Come Back 1920,D 19,I,22:3
Walley, Nathan
International Ice Frolics, The 1938,My 7,18:3
Wallgren, Gunn
Six Flights Up 1939,F 26,IX,2:3
Wallin, Bengt-Arne (Composer)
Sangen om Skrapuken 1967,Ap 9,II,1:3
Walling, Roy
Lilies of the Field 1921,O 5,20:1
Love Child, The 1922,N 15,22:1
Blue Bandanna, The 1924,Je 24,18:4
Walling, Roy (Director)
Laff That Off 1925,N 3,34:2
High Gear 1927,O 7,24:3
Cyclone Lover, The 1928,Je 6,23:3
Enemy Within 1931,O 6,35:3
Walling, Roy (Playwright)
Manhattan Nocturne 1943,O 27,26:2
Walling, Roy (Producer)
Cyclone Lover, The 1928,Je 6,23:3
Back Seat Drivers 1928,D 26,14:4
Come-On Man, The 1929,Ap 23,26:2
Walling, Stratton
Barefoot in Athens 1951,N 1,35:2
Merchant of Venice, The 1955,Ja 8,9:7
Candida 1957,Mr 29,18:5
Rate of Exchange 1968,Ap 2,50:1
Wallingford, Katrina
Comedy of Good and Evil, A 1938,Ap 8,16:3
Wallingford, L
1776 1926,Ap 24,11:2
Wallis, Charles
Man's House, A 1943,Ap 3,10:4
Happily Ever After 1945,Mr 16,21:2
Wallis, David
Mummers and Men 1962,Mr 27,41:6
Wallis, Francis
Hamlet 1967,F 17,44:1
Wallis, J Kendall
Caesar and Cleopatra 1927,N 6,IX,2:1
Wallis, Keene (Translator)
Sailors of Cattaro 1934,D 11,28:4
Wallis, Shani
Call Me Madam 1952,Mr 16,84:3
Wish You Were Here 1953,O 11,83:5
Wonderful Town 1955,Mr 6,II,3:1
Time for Singing, A 1966,My 23,48:2
Walliser, Blair (Producer)
Pink Elephant, The 1953,Ap 23,37:2
Wallman, Ruth
Three Sisters, The 1968,Mr 18,56:1
Man and Superman 1970,F 24,48:1
Wallner, Helmut
Wiener Blut 1964,S 12,14:1
Wallop, Douglass (Original Author)
Damn Yankees 1955,My 6,17:1
Wallop, Douglass (Playwright)
Damn Yankees 1955,My 6,17:1

Wallowitch, John (Miscellaneous)
Curtains Up! 1959,N 3,26:3
Sweet Miani 1962,S 26,33:2
Wallrich, Charles
Song for a Certain Midnight 1959,S 17,49:1
Walls, Tom
Thark 1927,Jl 24,VII,1:7
Plunder 1928,Jl 22,VII,1:3
Night Like This, A 1930,Mr 9,IX,4:1
Ladies' Night 1933,N 19,IX,3:7
Wallsten, Robert
Fiesta 1928,D 13,25:2
I Loved You Wednesday 1932,O 12,27:1
Foolscap 1933,Ja 12,21:2
Old Maid, The 1935,Ja 8,26:1
Thy People 1935,Ag 13,20:3
Most of the Game 1935,O 2,27:4
Eastwood Ho 1936,Jl 8,14:2
Spring Thaw 1938,Mr 22,18:1
Coggerers, The 1939,Ja 21,18:4
Mr Banks of Birmingham 1939,Ja 21,18:4
Rivals, The 1941,N 18,32:2
Rivals, The 1942,Ja 15,24:2
Wallsten, Robert (Playwright)
Marriage Royal 1937,Jl 15,16:2
Eight O'Clock Tuesday 1941,Ja 7,18:2
Wally
Just Beyond 1925,D 2,22:4
Wally the Harper (Composer)
Sensations 1970,O 26,48:2
Walmer, Max (Miscellaneous)
Luther 1963,S 26,41:1
Walpole, Helen
Brief Moment 1931,N 10,28:2
Truth about Blayds, The 1932,Ap 12,25:2
Dangerous Corner 1933,Jl 18,20:4
Spring in Autumn 1933,O 25,22:5
Errant Lady 1934,S 18,18:2
Aiglon, L' 1934,N 5,22:2
Case of Clyde Griffiths 1936,Mr 14,10:4
Daughters of Atreus 1936,O 15,33:1
Walpole, Hugh (Original Author)
Man With Red Hair, A 1928,Mr 25,IX,1:3
Man With Red Hair, A 1928,Je 17,VIII,1:6
Cathedral, The 1930,D 28,VIII,2:6
Cathedral, The 1932,D 18,X,5:6
Old Ladies, The 1935,Ap 4,21:2
Kind Lady 1935,Ap 28,X,1:1
Old Ladies, The 1935,Ap 28,X,2:3
Kind Lady 1935,Jl 23,24:4
Night in the House 1935,N 8,19:5
Kind Lady 1935,N 19,27:3
Kind Lady 1940,S 4,28:3
Walpole, Hugh (Playwright)
Man With Red Hair, A 1928,N 9,22:2
Cathedral, The 1932,D 18,X,5:6
Young Huntress, The 1933,F 19,IX,1:3
Kind Lady 1935,Ap 24,24:5
Walpole, John
Greeks Had a Word for It, The 1930,S 26,16:5
Walser, Harry
Bursting the Barriers 1930,My 7,25:1
Walser, Martin (Playwright)
Rabbit Race, The 1963,Ag 28,39:3
Walsh, Alixandria
Nathan Weinstein, Mystic, Connecticut 1966,F 26,15:2
Walsh, Arnold
Much Ado About Nothing 1929,N 17,30:4
Walsh, Arthur
Stalag 17 1951,My 9,41:2
Walsh, Barry
19th Hole, The 1927,O 12,30:3
Sons o' Guns 1929,N 27,30:4
Walsh, Betty Jane
Oklahoma! 1947,My 1,35:3
Walsh, Billy
Five O'Clock Girl, The 1927,O 11,26:3
Walsh, Brownie
Five O'Clock Girl, The 1927,O 11,26:3
Walsh, Christopher
Hamlet 1969,My 2,38:1
Walsh, Clare
Ice Capades 1958,S 4,33:2
Walsh, Edward
Wise Have Not Spoken, The 1954,F 11,35:2
Walsh, Enid
Pirates of Penzance, The 1948,Ja 6,27:2
Trial by Jury 1948,Ja 6,27:2
Gondoliers, The 1948,Ja 27,31:2
Trial by Jury 1951,F 6,24:2
Gondoliers, The 1951,F 13,27:2
Iolanthe 1951,F 16,22:1
Pirates of Penzance, The 1951,F 20,21:2
Walsh, Grace
Paese dei Campanelli, Il; Land of Bells, The 1935,My 10,25:4
Walsh, Helen
Simple Simon 1930,F 19,22:1
Walsh, J D
We've Got to Have Money 1923,Ag 21,12:1
Walsh, Jack
Katja 1926,O 19,27:3

Walsh, James
Last Man In, The 1930,My 8,32:5
Saint Joan 1950,Mr 4,10:6
Walsh, James (Producer)
Matty and the Moron and Madonna 1965,Mr 30,53:1
Beard, The 1967,O 25,40:1
Hawk, The 1968,Ap 18,54:1
Riot 1968,D 20,64:1
Watering Place, The 1969,Mr 13,51:1
Walsh, James A Jr
Once Over Lightly 1938,D 10,13:4
Walsh, Jane
Dooley Cashes In 1935,Ag 17,18:6
Summer Wives 1936,Ap 14,18:1
Walsh, John
Peg o' My Dreams 1924,My 6,25:3
You Said It 1931,Ja 20,21:3
Marching By 1932,Mr 4,17:1
Caviar 1934,Je 8,19:2
Howdy, Mr Ice of 1950 1949,My 27,24:2
Trouble in July 1949,D 2,36:2
Walsh, Joseph Lee (Playwright)
Empress of Destiny 1938,Mr 10,16:2
Walsh, Joyce
St Helena 1936,O 7,32:1
Walsh, Julia
Tomorrow's a Holiday! 1935,D 31,10:2
Walsh, Katharine
Music Box Revue 1924,D 2,23:3
Far Away Horses 1933,Mr 22,21:6
Walsh, Louis
On Your Toes 1936,Ap 13,14:4
Walsh, M Emmet
Death of the Well-Loved Boy, The 1967,My 16,48:1
Does a Tiger Wear a Necktie? 1969,F 26,38:1
Walsh, Marie-Beth (Lighting Director)
Simpleton of the Unexpected Isles, The 1954,Ja 12,19:1
Walsh, Mary
Book of Charm, The 1925,S 4,26:3
Henry-Behave 1926,Ag 24,19:4
Merry Wives of Windsor, The 1928,Mr 20,20:1
Walsh, Mary Jane
I'd Rather Be Right 1937,N 3,28:2
Sing Out the News 1938,S 26,12:5
Sing Out the News 1938,O 2,IX,1:1
Too Many Girls 1939,O 19,26:2
Let's Face It 1941,O 10,27:1
Let's Face It 1941,O 30,26:2
Allah Be Praised! 1944,Ap 21,14:2
Walsh, Mary Rose
Cape Cod Follies 1929,S 19,37:2
Walsh, Maurice (Original Author)
Donnybrook! 1961,My 19,23:1
Walsh, Mavis
Roberta 1933,N 20,18:4
Tomorrow's a Holiday! 1935,D 31,10:2
Walsh, Neil
Chicago 70 1970,My 26,33:1
Walsh, Norman
York Nativity Play, The 1956,D 5,49:2
Walsh, Norman (Director)
Servant of Two Masters, The 1958,F 11,35:2
Walsh, Pat
As You Were 1920,Ja 28,22:3
Jeweled Tree, The 1926,O 8,26:2
Walsh, Percy
Journey's End 1929,Jl 14,IX,5:1
Walsh, Richard
Lazarus Laughed 1948,Ap 9,27:4
Walsh, Thomas
Cornered 1920,D 9,18:2
Letty Pepper 1922,Ap 11,22:2
Hell's Bells! 1925,Ja 27,14:2
Laura 1947,Je 27,16:1
Design For A Stained Glass Window 1950,Ja 24,26:2
Walsh, Thomas deWitt (Playwright)
Certain Young Man, A 1967,D 27,45:1
Walsh, Valerie
Oh What a Lovely War 1964,O 1,30:1
Walsh, William
Lazarus Laughed 1948,Ap 9,27:4
Macbeth 1955,O 8,12:6
Idiot's Delight 1957,F 23,14:2
Steambath 1970,Jl 1,49:1
Walsh, William (Composer)
Tattle Tales 1933,Je 2,22:6
Walsh, William (Lyricist)
Tattle Tales 1933,Je 2,22:6
Walsh, Winifred
Our Town 1944,Ja 11,24:5
Walshe, Pat
Fine and Dandy 1930,S 24,26:1
Walska, Ganna
Castiglione, La 1929,Je 2,26:5
Walston, Ray
Hamlet 1945,D 14,25:2
Front Page, The 1946,S 5,22:4
Survivors, The 1948,Ja 20,27:2
Alchemist, The 1948,My 7,31:4

Walston, Ray—Cont

S S Glencairn; Bound East for Cardiff
1948,My 21,21:2
S S Glencairn; In the Zone 1948,My 21,21:2
S S Glencairn; Moon of the Caribbees
1948,My 21,21:2
S S Glencairn; Long Voyage Home, The; Moon of
the Caribbees; In the Zone; Bound East for
Cardiff 1948,My 30,II,1:1
Insect Comedy, The 1948,Je 4,26:3
Summer and Smoke 1948,O 7,33:2
Richard III 1949,F 9,33:2
Mrs Gibsons' Boys 1949,My 5,35:2
Rat Race, The 1949,D 23,16:2
South Pacific 1950,Ap 26,36:5
South Pacific 1951,N 11,II,3:1
Me and Juliet 1953,My 29,17:1
Me and Juliet 1953,Je 7,II,1:1
House of Flowers 1954,D 31,11:2
Damn Yankees 1955,My 6,17:1
Who Was That Lady I Saw You With?
1958,Mr 4,33:2
Agatha Sue, I Love You 1966,D 15,61:1

Walte, Sarita
Passing Show of 1924, The 1924,S 4,13:4

Walter, Bruno (Musical Director)
Fledermaus, Die 1930,Ap 20,VIII,7:7

Walter, Charles
New Faces 1934,Mr 16,24:5
Fools Rush In 1934,D 26,19:2

Walter, Dorothy
Paradise Alley 1924,Ap 2,17:3
Big Hearted Herbert 1934,Ja 2,17:3

Walter, Edwin
No More Blondes 1920,Ja 8,22:1
Oh, Henry! 1920,My 6,14:2
Man in the Making, The 1921,S 21,16:2
Exciters, The 1922,S 23,10:4
Potters, The 1923,D 10,21:4
Easy Come, Easy Go 1925,O 27,20:2
Potash and Perlmutter, Detectives; Poisoned by
Pictures 1926,S 1,27:3
Kidding Kidders 1928,Ap 24,28:3
Elmer the Great 1928,S 25,29:1
Lady Fingers 1929,F 1,22:4
Woof, Woof 1929,D 26,20:4
She Means Business 1931,Ja 27,21:2
Tobacco Road 1933,D 5,31:2
Tobacco Road 1940,D 5,32:3
Tobacco Road 1942,S 7,34:2
Tobacco Road 1943,S 6,21:3

Walter, Elizabeth
Blackouts of 1949 1949,S 7,39:2

Walter, Eugene (Playwright)
Easiest Way, The 1921,S 7,14:1
Easiest Way, The 1921,S 11,VI,1:1
Man's Name, The 1921,N 16,22:1
Jealousy 1928,O 23,32:2

Walter, Eugene (Producer)
Come Angel Band 1936,F 19,17:1

Walter, Eugene (Scenic Designer)
Master Builder Solness 1950,My 26,19:3

Walter, Jessica
Severed Head, A 1964,O 29,40:1

Walter, Lou (Miscellaneous)
Poupees de Paris, Les 1964,My 16,11:1

Walter, Louis Verneuil-Eugene (Playwright)
Obsession 1946,O 2,39:2

Walter, Manny (Miscellaneous)
Poupees de Paris, Les 1964,My 16,11:1

Walter, Margaret
Russian People, The 1942,D 16,21:3

Walter, Nancy
Everyman Today 1958,Ja 16,32:4

Walter, Paula
Poppa 1928,D 25,31:1

Walter, Pola
Dybbuk, The 1924,Ja 29,17:7

Walter, Richard
Macbeth 1955,O 8,12:6

Walter, Serge (Composer)
Grand Street Follies, The 1928,My 29,16:2
Belmont Varieties 1932,S 29,17:2

Walter, Serge (Lyricist)
Belmont Varieties 1932,S 29,17:2

Walter, Serge (Playwright)
Grand Street Follies, The 1929,My 2,20:4

Walter, Sydney Schubert (Director)
Balls 1965,F 11,45:1
Jack Jack 1968,Je 23,74:5

Walter, Wilfrid
Venetian, The 1931,Mr 15,IX,4:3
Venetian, The 1931,N 2,26:1
Happy and Glorious 1931,N 21,21:4
Genius at Home 1934,Ja 16,18:3
Genius at Home 1934,F 11,IX,3:1
Hamlet 1936,O 20,31:3
Hamlet 1936,N 11,54:2

Walter, Wilfrid (Playwright)
Happy and Glorious 1931,N 21,21:4

Walter, Wilfrid (Producer)
Happy and Glorious 1931,N 21,21:4

Walter, Wilfrid (Scenic Designer)
Happy and Glorious 1931,N 21,21:4

Walter, Wilmer
For Better or Worse 1927,F 1,24:3

Walter and Ellis
Harry Delmar's Revels 1927,N 29,30:2

Walter and Irene
Ice Follies 1958,Ja 15,26:2

Walters, Casey
Texas Town 1941,Ap 30,22:3
Out of My House 1942,Ja 8,28:6
Mister Roberts 1948,F 19,27:2
Red Roses for Me 1955,D 29,15:2
Red Roses for Me 1956,Ja 8,II,1:1

Walters, Charles
Tale of the Wolf, The 1925,O 8,31:2
Strange Interlude 1928,Ja 31,28:1
No More Frontier 1931,O 22,27:1
Parade 1935,My 21,22:2
Jubilee 1935,S 23,20:3
Jubilee 1935,O 14,20:1
Jubilee 1935,N 24,IX,8:1
So Proudly We Hail 1936,S 23,28:4
Show Is On, The 1936,D 26,14:2
Between the Devil 1937,O 15,19:1
Between the Devil 1937,D 23,24:5
I Married an Angel 1938,My 12,26:2
I Married an Angel 1938,My 22,XI,1:1
Du Barry Was a Lady 1939,D 7,34:2

Walters, Charles (Choreographer)
Let's Face It 1941,O 30,26:2
Banjo Eyes 1941,D 26,20:2
St Louis Woman 1946,Ap 1,22:2

Walters, Charles (Director)
Vaudeville (Palace) 1951,O 17,36:6

Walters, Dorothy
Desert Flower, The 1924,N 19,18:2
Devil Within, The 1925,Mr 17,19:4
Kosher Kitty Kelly 1925,Je 16,24:2
Judge's Husband, The 1926,S 28,31:1
Manhattan Mary 1927,S 27,30:3
First Mortgage 1929,O 11,36:1
Whirlpool 1929,D 4,37:3
Mr Gilhooley 1930,O 1,26:1
Warrior's Husband, The 1932,Mr 12,19:4
Dinner at Eight 1932,O 24,18:2

Walters, Edward
Free for All 1931,S 9,25:1
It Pays to Sin 1933,N 4,18:6

Walters, Emily
Vaudeville (Palace) 1925,O 6,31:3
Vaudeville (Palace) 1927,My 10,25:3

Walters, Ethel
As Thousands Cheer 1934,Jl 10,24:2

Walters, Frank
Katja 1926,O 19,27:3

Walters, Gwendolyn
Porgy and Bess 1964,My 7,32:1

Walters, Harry
Spice of 1922 1922,Jl 7,12:4
I'll Say She Is 1924,My 20,15:1

Walters, Harvey
In Times Square 1931,N 24,29:3

Walters, Henry
Cape Smoke 1925,F 17,19:1
Othello 1937,Ja 7,16:4

Walters, Hillis
Harlem 1929,F 21,30:3

Walters, Jack
Processional 1937,O 14,23:1

Walters, Jessica
Photo Finish 1963,F 14,5:2

Walters, Letha
White Peacock, The 1921,D 27,10:2

Walters, Lillian
They All Come to Moscow 1933,My 12,20:6

Walters, Lou (Director)
Artists and Models 1943,N 6,16:6

Walters, Lou (Miscellaneous)
Artists and Models 1943,N 6,16:6

Walters, Lou (Producer)
Ziegfeld Follies 1943,Ap 2,16:2
Artists and Models 1943,N 6,16:6
Take a Bow 1944,Je 16,15:3

Walters, Marrian
Made in Heaven 1946,O 25,28:2
Under the Yum-Yum Tree 1964,My 29,18:1

Walters, Mavis
Dybbuk, The 1954,O 27,33:6

Walters, Miss
Tattle Tales 1930,Jl 20,VIII,2:1

Walters, Nancy
Ankles Aweigh 1955,Ap 19,27:1

Walters, Pat
Well of Romance, The 1930,N 8,21:2

Walters, Polly
She Loves Me Not 1933,N 21,22:4
She Loves Me Not 1933,N 26,IX,1:1
Body Beautiful, The 1935,N 1,24:3
Red, Hot and Blue! 1936,O 8,26:1
Red, Hot and Blue! 1936,O 30,26:3
Life of Reilly, The 1942,Ap 30,13:2

Walters, Rex
Hamlet 1931,Ap 24,26:4

Walters, Sidney
Respectful Prostitute, The 1948,F 10,27:2
Insect Comedy, The 1948,Je 4,26:3
Victors, The 1948,D 27,17:2
Blood Wedding 1949,F 7,16:2

Walters, Sidney (Director)
Me, Candido! 1956,O 16,36:2
Five Posts in the Market Place 1961,Mr 6,30:1
Walk in Darkness 1963,O 29,30:2
Dodo Bird, The 1967,D 9,62:1
Peddler, The 1967,D 9,62:1
Love Your Crooked Neighbor 1969,D 30,40:1

Walters, Susan
Good Luck 1964,O 19,38:3
Hello Charlie 1965,O 25,47:2
Untitled-Revue 1966,O 3,62:5
Let's Sing Yiddish 1966,N 10,63:1
Sing Israel Sing 1967,My 12,50:1
Megilla of Itzik Manger, The 1968,O 10,60:1

Walters, Teddy
Vanderbilt Revue, The 1930,N 6,22:6

Walters, Thorley
Under the Counter 1947,O 4,10:2

Walters, Tim
Scaramouche 1923,O 25,14:2

Walters, Walter
Vaudeville (Palace) 1925,O 6,31:3

Walthall, Winona
Kansas City Kitty 1929,S 26,27:4

Walther, Elaine
Marinka 1945,Jl 19,19:2

Walther, Gretchen
Something About a Soldier 1962,Ja 5,36:2
Not a Way of Life 1967,Mr 23,28:1

Walther, M Clark (Composer)
East Lynne Goes West 1931,My 3,I,26:5

Walther, Michael (Costume Designer)
Hamlet 1970,O 27,54:2
Rosencrantz and Guildenstern Are Dead
1970,N 19,39:3

Walthers, Mimi
Banjo Eyes 1941,D 26,20:2

Walton, Arnold
Time to Go 1952,My 8,35:6

Walton, Bert
Look Who's Here 1932,O 31,18:5

Walton, Charles
Man Bites Dog 1933,Ap 26,11:2
Remember the Day 1935,S 26,19:3
Tomorrow's a Holiday! 1935,D 31,10:2
Chalked Out 1937,Mr 26,24:2

Walton, Douglas
Billy Draws a Horse 1939,D 22,14:5

Walton, Edna
Passion Flower, The 1920,Ja 14,12:1
Gringo 1922,D 15,26:3

Walton, Edward
Back Pay 1921,Ag 31,8:2
Red Light Annie 1923,Ag 22,10:3

Walton, Fred
Passing Show of 1922, The 1922,S 21,18:2
Song Writer, The 1928,Ag 14,15:2
Cat and the Fiddle, The 1931,O 16,26:4

Walton, Georgina Jones (Playwright)
Light of Asia, The 1928,O 10,32:2

Walton, Gladys
Century Revue and the Midnight Rounders, The
1920,Jl 13,9:1
Last Waltz, The 1921,My 11,20:3
Lady in Ermine, The 1922,O 3,22:2
June Days 1925,Ag 7,12:5

Walton, Gladys Hastings (Playwright)
Wolves of Tanner's Close, or the Crimes of Burke
and Hare, The; Crimes of Burke and Hare, The
1932,Ja 10,VIII,2:4

Walton, Helen
Flying Blind 1930,My 16,20:2

Walton, John
Black Eye, The 1938,Mr 8,22:4

Walton, Joseph
Sex Fable, The 1931,O 21,26:1

Walton, Kraft
Great Way, The 1921,N 8,28:2
Mima 1928,D 13,24:2

Walton, Lester A (Producer)
Meek Mose 1928,F 7,30:1

Walton, Tony (Costume Designer)
Valmouth 1960,O 7,29:1
Once There Was a Russian 1961,F 20,32:2
Funny Thing Happened on the Way to the Forum,
A 1962,My 9,49:1
Rehearsal, The 1963,S 24,45:2
Golden Boy 1964,O 21,56:1
Diary of Adam and Eve, The 1966,O 19,53:1
Passionella 1966,O 19,53:1
Lady or the Tiger?, The 1966,O 19,53:1

Walton, Tony (Lighting Director)
Conversation Piece 1957,N 19,38:2
One Over the Eight 1961,Je 25,II,3:5

Walton, Tony (Miscellaneous)
Golden Boy 1964,O 21,56:1

Walton, Tony (Scenic Designer)
Conversation Piece 1957,N 19,38:2

Walton, Tony (Scenic Designer)—Cont

Valmouth 1960,O 7,29:1
Once There Was a Russian 1961,F 20,32:2
One Over the Eight 1961,Je 25,II,3:5
Funny Thing Happened on the Way to the Forum,
A 1962,My 9,49:1
Golden Boy 1964,O 21,56:1
Golden Boy 1964,N 1,II,1:1
Apple Tree, The 1966,O 30,II,1:1
In His Own Write 1968,Jl 9,30:2

Walton, Vera

Blue Monday 1932,Je 3,23:2
Whoop-Up 1958,D 23,2:7

Walton, William (Composer)

Boy David, The 1936,N 22,VI,7:1

Walton and O'Rourke

Sons o' Fun 1941,D 2,28:2

Waltuch, Barbara

Thistle in My Bed 1963,N 20,48:1

Waltz, Pat

Caine Mutiny Court-Martial, The 1953,O 14,35:1

Waltzer, Bernard (Producer)

Ballad for Bimshire 1963,O 16,54:1

Waltzer, Jack

Taming of the Shrew, The 1956,Ag 6,20:1
Johnny Johnson 1956,O 22,24:1
Secret Concubine, The 1960,Mr 22,29:2
To Damascus 1961,F 15,40:2
After the Fall 1964,Ja 24,18:1
Marco Millions 1964,F 21,33:1
Changeling, The 1964,O 30,32:2
Incident at Vichy 1964,D 4,44:1

Walworth, James C (Lighting Director)

Mikado, The 1967,D 4,65:3

Walz, Erik

Mahogany Hall 1934,Ja 18,18:5
Panic 1935,Mr 16,18:4
Let Freedom Ring 1935,N 7,26:2
Bury the Dead 1936,Ap 20,17:4
Prelude 1936,Ap 20,17:4
Bury the Dead 1936,Ap 20,17:4
200 Were Chosen 1936,N 21,21:1
Arms for Venus 1937,Mr 12,18:7
Excursion 1937,Ap 10,11:4
Washington Jitters 1938,My 3,19:1
Woman Brown, The 1939,D 9,18:5
Fireworks on the James 1940,My 15,30:2
First Stop to Heaven 1941,Ja 6,10:7

Walzer, W (Playwright)

Holka Polka 1925,O 15,27:2

Wamboldt, M P

Flying Blind 1930,My 16,20:2

Wamboldt, M P (Director)

Flying Blind 1930,My 16,20:2

Wamboldt, Virginia

Flying Blind 1930,My 16,20:2

Wamen, James

Carmen Jones 1956,Je 1,28:2
Kismet 1965,Je 23,45:1

Wampler, Ben (Director)

Deadly Game, The 1966,F 14,34:1

Wanamaker, Nicholas (Producer)

School for Wives 1957,Je 20,23:4

Wanamaker, Olive

Savage Rhythm 1932,Ja 1,30:4

Wanamaker, Sam

Cafe Crown 1942,Ja 24,12:5
Counterattack 1943,F 4,27:2
This, Too, Shall Pass 1946,My 1,32:4
Joan of Lorraine 1946,N 19,40:2
Goodbye My Fancy 1948,N 18,35:2
Arms and the Man 1950,O 20,34:2
Winter Journey; Country Girl, The 1952,Ap 4,21:1
Winter Journey; Country Girl, The
1952,Ap 13,II,3:7
Big Knife, The 1954,Ja 17,II,4:4
Rainmaker, The 1956,Je 1,26:7
Othello 1959,Ap 8,41:3
Othello 1959,Ap 12,II,3:1
Far Country, A 1961,Ap 5,32:1
Far Country, A 1961,Ap 16,II,1:1

Wanamaker, Sam (Director)

Gentleman From Athens, The 1947,N 30,I,78:2
Gentleman From Athens, The 1947,D 10,42:4
Goodbye My Fancy 1948,N 18,35:2
Goodbye My Fancy 1948,N 28,II,1:1
Parisienne 1950,Jl 25,24:2
Lady From the Sea, The 1950,Ag 8,23:2
Borned in Texas 1950,Ag 22,30:6
Winter Journey; Country Girl, The
1952,Ap 13,II,3:7
Big Knife, The 1954,Ja 17,II,4:4
World of Sholom Aleichem, The 1955,Ja 12,22:4
Threepenny Opera, The 1956,F 12,83:1
Rainmaker, The 1956,Je 1,26:7
Children From Their Games 1963,Ap 12,33:1
Case of Libel, A 1963,O 11,43:2
Murderer Among Us, A 1964,Mr 26,43:1

Wanamaker, Sam (Producer)

Parisienne 1950,Jl 25,24:2
Lady From the Sea, The 1950,Ag 8,23:2
Borned in Texas 1950,Ag 22,30:6
Big Knife, The 1954,Ja 17,II,4:4
Children From Their Games 1963,Ap 12,33:1

Wanatabe, Miyoko (Miscellaneous)

Mikado, The 1967,D 4,65:3

Wand, Billy (Lighting Director)

Groove Tube 1969,O 12,88:3

Wanderman, Walt

Enter Laughing 1963,Mr 15,8:1

Wandrey, Donna

Brownstone Urge, The 1969,D 18,63:1

Wandrey, Eduard

Don Carlos 1964,N 25,40:1
Captain of Koepenick, The 1964,D 2,60:1

Wang, Cilli

World of Cilli Wang, The 1957,O 15,38:4

Wang, Cilli (Playwright)

World of Cilli Wang, The 1957,O 15,38:4

Wang, Richard

Veneer 1929,N 13,24:5
Singapore 1932,N 15,24:2
Her Tin Soldier 1933,Ap 7,22:6
Anything Goes 1934,N 22,26:1
Sea Dogs 1939,N 7,30:3

Wang, T C

Roar China! 1930,O 28,23:1

Wangel, Hedwig

Little Accident 1929,S 22,IX,4:1

Wanger, Donna

Hello Out There 1955,D 22,19:1
Floydada to Matador 1955,D 22,19:1

Wanger, Wally (Director)

Take a Bow 1944,Je 16,15:3

Wangler, Marguerite Jane (Miscellaneous)

On Stage 1935,Jl 23,24:4

Wanick, Buck (Musical Director)

Artists and Models 1943,N 6,16:6

Wank, Jesse (Producer)

Yeah-Man 1932,My 27,27:3

Wanless, Barrie

Waltz in Goose Step 1938,N 2,26:2
Audition of the Apprentice Theatre 1939,Je 2,26:2
Counsellor-at-Law 1942,N 25,17:2

Wanshel, Jeff (Playwright)

Disintegration of James Cherry, The
1970,Ja 30,33:3
Disintegration of James Cherry, The 1970,F 8,II,1:6

Wanzer and Palmer

Vaudeville (Palace) 1924,Mr 18,25:1

Waram, Percy

Married Woman, The 1921,D 26,21:1
Shadow, The 1922,Ap 25,14:2
Lucky One, The 1922,N 21,15:2
Tidings Brought to Mary, The 1922,D 25,20:1
Love Scandal, A 1923,N 7,14:1
Cape Smoke 1925,F 17,19:1
Hamlet 1925,N 10,23:1
Hangman's House 1926,D 17,27:2
Major Barbara 1928,N 20,28:4
Major Barbara 1928,D 2,X,1:1
Camel Through the Needle's Eye, The
1929,Ap 16,32:2
Elizabeth the Queen 1930,N 4,37:1
Du Barry 1932,N 23,15:2
For Services Rendered 1933,Ap 13,15:5
Ruy Blas 1933,O 10,24:4
Picnic 1934,My 3,15:2
Living Dangerously 1935,Ja 14,10:3
Pride and Prejudice 1935,N 3,X,1:5
Pride and Prejudice 1935,N 6,32:4
Pride and Prejudice 1935,N 17,IX,1:1
St Helena 1936,S 29,35:1
St Helena 1936,O 7,32:1
Country Wife, The 1936,D 2,34:1
Pride and Prejudice 1937,Ag 3,20:5
Ruy Blas 1938,Jl 24,IX,2:1
Merchant of Yonkers, The 1938,D 13,30:1
Merchant of Yonkers, The 1938,D 18,IX,3:2
Merchant of Yonkers, The 1938,D 29,14:2
Life With Father 1940,Mr 3,X,2:5
Late George Apley, The 1944,O 20,16:4
Late George Apley, The 1944,N 22,26:2
Late George Apley, The 1944,D 3,II,1:1
Another Part of the Forest 1946,N 21,42:2
Another Part of the Forest 1946,D 1,II,1:1
Anne of the Thousand Days 1948,D 9,49:2
Gambler, The 1952,O 14,40:1
Reclining Figure 1954,O 8,26:5
Chalk Garden, The 1955,N 13,II,1:1
Monique 1957,O 23,38:1

Warburg, Gerald (Composer)

Jazz a La Carte 1922,Je 3,8:3

Warburg, Kay (Composer)

Say When 1928,Je 27,29:3

Warburg, Kay (Lyricist)

Say When 1928,Je 27,29:3

Warburton, Charles

March Hares 1921,Ag 12,8:3
Macbeth 1924,Mr 17,18:1
Critic, The 1925,My 9,12:4
Little Poor Man, The 1925,Ag 6,14:1
Carolinian, The 1925,N 3,34:2
Whispering Gallery, The 1929,F 12,22:2

Warburton, Sean

Man Is Man 1962,S 19,31:1

Warburton, William John

Riff-Raff 1926,F 9,18:6

Warburton, William John (Mrs)

Riff-Raff 1926,F 9,18:6

Warchoff, Milton

Paul Bunyan 1941,My 6,25:1

Ward, Aida

Blackbirds 1928,My 10,31:3

Ward, Al

Top Secret 1960,S 6,40:1

Ward, Al (Director)

No Laughter in Heaven 1938,My 17,26:5

Ward, Alan

K Guy, The 1928,O 16,28:4
That Ferguson Family 1928,D 24,10:7
Paris Bound 1929,Jl 20,8:3
Holiday 1930,F 6,21:2
On the Spot 1930,O 30,33:3
It Happened Tomorrow 1933,My 6,11:5
Kultur 1933,S 27,24:3
Lucky Sam McCarver 1950,Ap 15,10:6

Ward, Albert

Henry's Harem 1926,S 14,25:2

Ward, Albert E Jr (Scenic Designer)

Black Eye, The 1938,Mr 8,22:4
Conjur 1938,N 1,27:2
If You Get It, Do You Want It? 1938,D 1,28:2

Ward, Alice

Rose Bernd 1922,S 27,17:1

Ward, Allan

Processional 1925,Ja 13,17:1
Androcles and the Lion 1925,N 24,28:1

Ward, Andre (Costume Designer)

Vincent 1959,O 1,40:1

Ward, Audrey

Emperor Jones, The 1945,Ja 17,18:4
Deirdre of the Sorrows 1959,O 15,46:1
Seidman and Son 1962,O 16,32:2
Abraham Cochrane 1964,F 18,26:1
Live Like Pigs 1965,Je 8,48:2

Ward, Barney

Polly of Hollywood 1927,F 22,22:3

Ward, Bernard

Trumpets of the Lord 1969,Ap 30,37:1

Ward, Bernard (Miscellaneous)

Trials of Brother Jero, The 1967,N 10,60:1
Strong Breed, The 1967,N 10,60:1

Ward, Billee

Love in Our Time 1952,O 4,14:3

Ward, Cecilia

Lord Byron's Love Letter 1955,Ja 19,23:2
Gondoliers, The 1961,Ja 26,33:2
H M S Pinafore 1961,F 2,26:6

Ward, Clara

Jack Benny 1963,Mr 1,10:5
Tambourines to Glory 1963,N 4,47:1

Ward, Clara (Miscellaneous)

Tambourines to Glory 1963,N 4,47:1

Ward, Colleen

New Life, A 1943,S 16,26:6

Ward, Craig

Puppets of Passion 1927,F 25,24:4
Miss Gulliver Travels 1931,N 26,36:4
Kultur 1933,S 27,24:3
Henrietta the Eighth 1935,Je 25,15:4
Devil of Pei-Ling 1936,F 21,20:4

Ward, David (Playwright)

Knack With Horses, A 1970,D 21,52:1
Here Be Dragons 1970,D 21,52:1

Ward, Diana

Anything Goes 1937,Ag 17,23:4
Anything Goes 1937,Ag 26,24:3

Ward, Dorothy

Phoebe of Quality Street 1921,My 10,20:1
Whirl of New York, The 1921,Je 14,18:1

Ward, Douglas Turner

Reckoning, The 1969,S 14,II,1:3
Reckoning, The 1969,S 14,II,1:1

Ward, Douglas Turner (Director)

Kongi's Harvest 1968,Ap 15,49:1
Daddy Goodness 1968,Je 5,37:1
Contribution 1969,Ap 2,37:1
Man Better Man 1969,Jl 3,22:1
Man Better Man 1969,Jl 13,II,3:6
Brotherhood 1970,Mr 18,39:1
Day of Absence 1970,Mr 18,39:1
Brotherhood 1970,Mr 18,39:1

Ward, Douglas Turner (Original Author)

Contribution 1969,Ap 13,II,1:1

Ward, Douglas Turner (Playwright)

Day of Absence 1965,Mr 16,56:1
Happy Ending 1965,N 16,56:1
Reckoning, The 1969,S 5,28:1
Reckoning, The 1969,S 14,II,1:3
Reckoning, The 1969,S 14,II,1:1
Reckoning, The 1969,S 22,36:1
Brotherhood 1970,Mr 18,39:1
Day of Absence 1970,Mr 18,39:1
Brotherhood 1970,Mr 29,II,1:1

Ward, Douglas Turner (Producer)

Song of the Lusitanian Bogey, The 1968,Ja 3,52:1

Ward, Ed

Sniper, The 1959,O 28,40:4

Ward, Edward (Composer)
Tattle Tales 1933,Je 2,22:6
Ward, Edward (Lyricist)
Tattle Tales 1933,Je 2,22:6
Ward, Eva
Episode 1925,F 5,23:2
Ward, Evelyn
Early to Bed 1943,Je 18,16:2
Ward, Fannie
Vaudeville (Palace) 1926,D 7,24:3
Vaudeville (Palace) 1927,N 15,27:2
Vaudeville (Palace) 1928,F 21,19:2
Ward, Fleming
He and She 1920,F 13,16:3
Martinique 1920,Ap 27,18:2
Wake Up, Jonathan 1921,Ja 18,14:1
Lady Bug 1922,Ap 18,15:3
Woman on the Jury, The 1923,Ag 16,10:4
Gypsy Jim 1924,Ja 15,17:4
High Stakes 1924,S 10,21:3
One of the Family 1925,D 23,22:3
Romancing 'Round 1927,O 4,32:4
Carry On 1928,Ja 24,26:1
Little Accident 1928,O 10,32:3
Keeper of the Keys 1933,O 19,23:2
Ragged Army 1934,F 27,16:5
Three Men on a Horse 1935,Ja 31,22:3
See My Lawyer 1939,S 28,29:1
Best Foot Forward 1941,O 2,28:2
Three Men on a Horse 1942,O 10,10:2
Snark Was a Boojum, The 1943,S 2,14:4
Chicken Every Sunday 1944,Ap 6,27:2
Too Hot for Maneuvers 1945,My 3,26:5
Magnificent Yankee, The 1946,Ja 2,23:6
Magnificent Yankee, The 1946,Ja 23,21:2
Ward, Francis
Hero of Santa Maria, The 1926,My 1,10:1
If 1927,O 26,26:2
Ward, Frank (Musical Director)
Pudding on the Ritz 1932,Ap 9,18:3
Ward, George
Battle Hymn 1936,My 23,12:1
Lady in the Dark 1941,Ja 24,14:2
Ward, Hap
Ziegfeld Follies 1923,O 22,17:2
Ward, Harry
Good Times 1920,Ag 10,10:1
Gorilla, The 1925,Ap 29,24:2
Ward, Helen
Orphee 1935,Mr 23,10:3
Holiday 1941,Jl 23,15:2
Ward, Henry (Composer)
Midsummer Night's Dream, A 1968,D 9,59:1
Twelfth Night 1970,Ja 1,18:1
Ward, Herbert (Scenic Designer)
Caste 1927,D 24,8:1
Mr Papavert 1932,Ja 23,18:6
It Happened Tomorrow 1933,My 6,11:5
Ship Comes in, A 1934,S 20,21:1
Ward, James
All God's Chillun Got Wings 1924,My 16,22:3
All God's Chillun Got Wings 1924,Ag 19,9:1
Is Zat So? 1925,Ap 25,18:2
Pursuit of Happiness, The 1952,Mr 22,9:2
Ward, Jane (Miscellaneous)
Increased Difficulty of Concentration, The
1969,D 5,48:1
Amphitryon 1970,My 29,13:1
Ward, Janet
King of Friday's Men, The 1951,F 22,26:2
Middle of the Night 1956,F 9,39:1
Volpone 1957,Ja 8,27:1
Volpone 1957,Ja 13,II,10:1
Miss Lonelyhearts 1957,O 4,26:2
Chaparral 1958,S 10,38:2
J B 1958,D 12,2:7
Deep Are the Roots 1960,O 4,47:1
Roots 1961,Mr 7,40:2
Egg, The 1962,Ja 9,23:2
Play With a Tiger 1964,D 31,14:2
Impossible Years, The 1965,O 14,55:1
Of Love Remembered 1967,F 20,46:5
Summertree 1969,D 10,60:1
Dream of a Blacklisted Actor 1969,D 18,64:1
Cruising Speed 600 MPH 1970,Ja 6,48:3
Ward, Jean
Lulu Belle 1926,F 10,20:1
Ward, John
Little Old New York 1920,S 9,9:2
World We Live In, The 1922,N 1,16:1
Shame Woman, The 1923,O 17,14:1
Crime 1927,F 23,27:3
Family Reunion, The 1947,N 29,9:2
Sleepy Hollow 1948,Je 4,26:3
Faith of Our Fathers 1950,Ag 6,72:2
Ward, John (Scenic Designer)
Electra 1959,F 14,15:1
Harlequinade 1959,F 14,15:1
Ward, Judy Peyton (Costume Designer)
Glass Cage, The 1957,Mr 11,21:2
Ward, Kerry
Play, A 1925,F 11,19:2

Ward, Larry
Here Come the Clowns 1954,My 5,36:2
Saint Joan 1954,S 18,12:1
Ward, Laurel
Hair 1970,Ja 13,39:1
Ward, Lem (Director)
Processional 1937,O 14,23:1
One-Third of a Nation 1938,Ja 18,27:2
Clinton Street 1939,O 13,27:2
Brooklyn, U S A 1941,D 22,24:2
Brooklyn, U S A 1941,D 28 X,1:1
Uncle Harry 1942,My 21,24:1
Eve of St Mark, The 1942,O 8,30:2
Ward, Lem (Miscellaneous)
Listen Professor! 1943,D 23,22:1
Ward, Lem (Producer)
Awake and Sing! 1938,D 23,16:6
Ward, Lulu Mae
Walk Hard 1946,Mr 28,34:2
Power of Darkness, The 1948,O 11,28:2
Ward, Mackenzie
Red Blinds 1926,O 1,27:1
This Was a Man 1926,N 24, 27:1
Pickwick 1927,S 6,35:2
Happy Husband, The 1928,My 8,25:2
High Road, The 1928,S 11,3 1
Heat Wave 1931,F 18,14:6
Barchester Towers 1937,D 1,27:1
Ward, Margaret (Miscellaneous)
This Way to the Tomb 1961,D 9,21:1
Ward, Mary
Cradle Song 1927,Ja 25,18:2
Good Hope, The 1927,O 19,24:2
Peter Pan; Boy Who Would Not Grow Up, The
1928,N 27,36:3
Living Corpse, The 1929,D 7,19:1
Women Have Their Way, The 1930,Ja 28,28:1
Romeo and Juliet 1930,Ap 22,33:1
Alison's House 1930,D 2,31:2
Ward, Morris J
Poppa 1928,D 25,31:1
Ward, Mr
Marching By 1931,N 15,VII,4:2
Ward, Nancee
Best of Burlesque 1957,S 30,27:2
Ward, Palmer
Plumes in the Dust 1936,N 7,14:2
Waltz in Goose Step 1938,N 2,26:2
Ward, Pamela
Caribbean Carnival 1947,D 6,12:2
Ward, Penelope
French Without Tears 1937,S 26,II,4:3
French Without Tears 1937,S 29,19:1
Set to Music 1939,Ja 19,16:2
Lady Windermere's Fan 1946,O 15,29:2
Ward, Polly
Top Banana 1951,N 2,19:2
Ward, Richard
Marry the Man! 1929,Ap 23,26:3
Land Beyond the River, A 1957,Mr 29,15:7
John Turner Davis 1958,Jl 2,25:1
Man Who Never Died, The 1958,N 22,27:2
Ballad of Jazz Street, The 1959,N 12,28:1
God's Trombones 1960,F 10,43:4
Shakespeare in Harlem 1960,F 10,43:4
Nat Turner 1960,N 7,46:3
Walk in Darkness 1963,O 29,30:2
Sweet Enemy, The 1965,F 16,39:1
Amen Corner, The 1965,Je 13,82:4
Firebugs, The 1968,Jl 2,36:1
Ceremonies in Dark Old Men 1969,O 11,42:1
Ward, Ronald
Charlot's Revue 1924,Ja 10,18:1
These Two 1933,Mr 5,IX,1:6
Ward, Royce
Low Bridge 1933,F 10,13:4
Ward, Sam
All-Star Jamboree 1921,Jl 1 ,18:1
Ward, Sandra
Rose Marie 1936,Jl 22,22:6
Florodora 1936,Ag 23,II,8:2
Firefly, The 1937,Ag 4,14:1
Ward, Smothers
Lulu Belle 1926,F 10,20:1
Ward, Solly
Vaudeville (Palace) 1921,Jl 5,15:1
Music Box Revue 1923,My 20,VII,1:3
Music Box Revue 1923,S 24,5:3
Vaudeville (Proctor's) 1927,My 17,27:4
Vaudeville (Palace) 1928,Mr 6,20:5
Music in May 1929,Ap 2,29:1
Vaudeville (Palace) 1929,S 9,30:5
Wonderful Night, A; Fledermaus, Die
1929,N 1,23:3
Vaudeville (New Amsterdam Theatre)
1931,Je 22,17:3
Marching By 1932,Mr 4,17:1
Keeping Expenses Down 1932,O 21,25:2
Great Waltz, The 1934,S 24,14:4
Fabulous Invalid, The 1938,O 10,15:1
Ward, Stella
Folly Town 1920,My 18,9:2

Ward, Stewart
Trial of Dr Beck, The 1937,Ag 10,22:2
Ward, Susan
Tom Sawyer - Ballad of the Mississippi
1947,D 27,11:3
Ward, Theodore
Smell the Sweet Savor 1940,F 3,8:4
Ward, Theodore (Playwright)
Big White Fog 1940,O 23,26:2
Our Lan' 1947,Ap 19,11:2
Our Lan' 1947,S 29,16:5
John Brown 1950,My 4,32:7
Ward, Tim (Director)
Year Boston Won the Pennant, The
1969,My 23,38:1
Ward, Tim (Miscellaneous)
Yerma 1966,D 9,60:1
Galileo 1967,Ap 14,31:1
Cyrano de Bergerac 1968,Ap 26,30:1
King Lear 1968,N 8,43:1
Camino Real 1970,Ja 9,42:1
Ward, Tommy (Director)
Goose for the Gander, A 1945,Ja 24,16:4
Ward, Toni (Costume Designer)
Eve of St Mark, The 1942,O 8,30:2
Patriots, The 1943,Ja 30,11:2
Ward, Toni (Miscellaneous)
Listen Professor! 1943,D 23,22:1
Ward, Trevor
Power Without Glory 1948,Ja 14,30:2
Ward, W Bradley
Woman Disputed, A 1926,S 29,23:2
Ward, Walter
Bright Honor 1936,S 28,14:1
Enemy of the People, An 1937,F 16,19:1
Once Upon a Time 1939,D 21,28:2
Ward, Wayne
Music Man, The 1957,D 20,31:1
Music Man, The 1965,Je 17,26:4
Ward & Harvey Studios, Inc (Scenic Designer)
Enemy Within 1931,O 6,35:3
Ward and Diamond
Vaudeville (Palace) 1926,Ag 31,15:3
Ward and Harvey (Scenic Designer)
Unexpected Husband 1931,Je 3,29:4
Ward and Lane
Crazy With the Heat 1941,Ja 31,15:2
Ward and Van
Vaudeville (Palace) 1924,Ap 1,18:1
Streets of Paris, The 1939,Je 20,25:2
Ward Family, The Flying
Vaudeville (Hippodrome) 1923,D 18,16:1
Ward Singers, The
Jack Benny 1963,Mr 1,10:5
Warda, Arnold
Mother Courage and Her Children 1964,My 12,32:2
Warde, Angela
Erminie 1921,Ja 4,11:1
49ers, The 1922,N 7,14:1
Deep Tangled Wildwood, The 1923,N 6,22:1
Play, A 1925,F 11,19:2
Warde, Shirley
Smooth as Silk 1921,F 23,18:3
Goose Hangs High, The 1924,Ja 30,16:1
Yellow 1926,S 22,30:1
Money From Home 1927,Mr 1,30:2
Lady Lies, The 1928,N 11,X,2:4
Lady Lies, The 1928,N 27,36:2
House Unguarded 1929,Ja 16,22:2
Maggie, the Magnificent 1929,O 22,26:1
Warde, Shirley (Playwright)
Queen at Home 1930,N 2,VIII,3:5
Queen at Home 1930,D 30,25:2
Trick for Trick 1932,F 19,14:2
Wardell, Michel
Cyrano de Bergerac 1936,Ap 28,17:1
Warden, Chancellor
Drift 1925,N 25,15:3
Warden, Gentry (Composer)
Swing Mikado, The 1939,Mr 2,18:2
Warden, Jack
Golden Boy 1952,Mr 13,24:3
Lullaby 1954,F 4,21:2
Sing Me No Lullaby 1954,O 15,17:2
View From the Bridge, A 1955,S 30,21:1
Memory of Two Mondays, A 1955,S 30,21:1
Very Special Baby, A 1956,N 15,43:2
Body Beautiful, The 1958,Ja 24,15:2
Cages; Snowangel; Epiphany 1963,Je 14,36:1
Orange Souffle; Wen, The; Out From Under
1966,Jl 16,14:6
Man in the Glass Booth, The 1969,Ap 17,58:1
Man in the Glass Booth, The 1969,Ap 18,37:3
Warden, Jerry (Costume Designer)
Power of Dreams, A 1958,Mr 11,33:1
Warden, Yvonne
Trials of Brother Jero, The 1967,N 10,60:1
Wardlaw, Wick
Hero of Santa Maria, The 1926,My 1,10:1
Wardley, Jeanne
Daddy's Gone A-Hunting 1921,S 1,18:3
Kreutzer Sonata, The 1924,My 15,22:3
Rat, The 1925,F 11,19:3

Wardley, Jeanne—Cont
Mr Samuel 1930,N 11,28:4
Hilda Cassidy 1933,My 5,18:3
Yoshe Kalb 1933,D 29,27:2
Fabulous Invalid, The 1938,O 10,15:1
American Way, The 1939,Ja 23,9:2
Wardwell, Geoffrey
Goose Hangs High, The 1924,Ja 30,16:1
Merry Wives of Windsor, The 1928,Mr 20,20:1
Broken Chain, The 1929,F 21,30:4
Merchant of Venice, The 1930,D 3,29:2
As Husbands Go 1931,Mr 6,26:5
Criminal at Large 1932,O 11,26:3
Lake, The 1933,D 27,24:2
Wardwell, John
Nathan Weinstein, Mystic, Connecticut
1966,F 26,15:2
Fire! 1969,Ja 29,26:1
Fireworks; Football 1969,Je 12,51:1
Fireworks; Fireworks for a Hot Fourth
1969,Je 12,51:1
Ware, Allan
Ruddigore 1931,Ag 11,28:3
Ware, Dick
Kid Boots 1924,Ja 1,21:3
Ware, Evelyn
Macbeth 1924,Mr 17,18:1
Ware, Florence
Ziegfeld Follies 1920,Je 23,14:1
Ware, Francis
Big Blow 1938,O 3,11:2
Ware, Harlan (Playwright)
Return to Folly 1935,Jl 23,24:3
Ware, Helen
Pagans 1921,Ja 5,11:1
Wandering Jew, The 1921,O 27,22:1
Montmartre 1922,F 14,20:1
Within Four Walls 1923,Ap 18,24:1
Her Dearest Friend 1923,My 15,22:2
Vaudeville (Palace) 1923,My 15,22:2
Great Music 1924,O 6,24:1
Paolo and Francesca 1924,D 3,24:2
Vaudeville (Palace) 1926,Ap 27,22:3
Thou Desperate Pilot 1927,Mr 8,23:1
Candida 1927,Ag 31,19:4
Salvation 1928,F 1,31:1
Ware, Herta
Let Freedom Ring 1935,N 7,26:2
Bury the Dead 1936,Ap 20,17:4
Prelude 1936,Ap 20,17:4
200 Were Chosen 1936,N 21,21:1
Journeyman 1938,Ja 31,14:2
Alice Adams 1947,Ag 5,26:1
Afternoon Storm 1948,Ap 12,24:2
Ware, John
Goodbye My Fancy 1948,N 18,35:2
Caesar and Cleopatra 1949,D 22,28:2
Ware, Marguerite
Trojan Women, The 1941,Ap 9,32:5
Ware, Midge
Fifth Season, The 1953,Ja 24,13:2
Mandragola 1956,Mr 1,36:4
Maybe Tuesday 1958,Ja 30,18:3
Ware, Sylvia
Merchant of Venice, The 1930,D 3,29:2
Ware, William
Blancs, Les 1970,N 16,48:4
Warem, Percy
Chalk Garden, The 1955,O 27,29:1
Waren, Flori
Parade at the Devil's Bridge 1957,F 19,35:7
Doctor Faustus 1957,F 19,35:7
Waren, Helen
Flossie 1924,Je 4,25:2
Yoshe Kalb 1933,D 29,27:2
Black Pit 1935,Mr 21,26:6
Walk Into My Parlor 1941,N 20,38:2
Richard III 1943,Mr 27,8:3
Moonbirds 1959,O 10,13:1
Waren, Helen (Playwright)
Music Shop, The 1962,F 16,35:2
Witch, The 1962,F 16,35:2
Vagrant, The 1962,F 16,35:2
Waren, Helen (Producer)
Vagrant, The 1962,F 16,35:2
Music Shop, The 1962,F 16,35:2
Witch, The 1962,F 16,35:2
Waren, Stanley (Director)
Vagrant, The 1962,F 16,35:2
Music Shop, The 1962,F 16,35:2
Witch, The 1962,F 16,35:2
Love of Two Hours, The 1962,O 27,16:2
Waren, Stanley (Producer)
Witch, The 1962,F 16,35:2
Vagrant, The 1962,F 16,35:2
Music Shop, The 1962,F 16,35:2
Warfel, William B (Lighting Director)
Route 1 1964,N 18,52:3
Don Juan 1970,My 26,32:1
Revenger's Tragedy, The 1970,D 2,58:1
Warfield, Chris
Cradle Will Rock, The 1964,N 9,40:4
Warfield, David
Return of Peter Grimm, The 1921,S 22,12:2
Merchant of Venice, The 1922,D 22,13:1
Merchant of Venice, The 1923,Ja 7,VII,1:1
Warfield, Donald
Comedy of Errors, The 1967,Je 15,58:4
King John 1967,Jl 14,19:1
Titus Andronicus 1967,Ag 10,43:2
We Bombed in New Haven 1967,D 7,58:1
Henry IV, Part II 1968,Jl 2,33:1
People vs Ranchman, The 1968,O 28,56:1
War Games 1969,Ap 18,37:1
Love Your Crooked Neighbor 1969,D 30,40:1
Watercolor 1970,Ja 22,30:1
Saved 1970,O 29,57:1
Warfield, Joel
O Say Can You See! 1962,O 9,45:1
Jimmy Shine 1968,D 6,52:1
Warfield, Mariene
Great White Hope, The 1968,O 13,II,1:1
Warfield, Marjorie
It Never Rains 1931,D 25,29:3
Legal Murder 1934,F 16,16:2
Warfield, Marlene
Matter of Like Life and Death, A 1963,O 3,28:2
All's Well That Ends Well 1966,Je 17,39:1
Volpone 1967,Je 30,29:1
Great White Hope, The 1968,O 4,40:1
Warfield, Ruth (Composer)
Arabesque 1925,O 21,20:2
Damn the Tears 1927,Ja 22,11:1
Warfield, William
Set My People Free 1948,N 4,38:2
Regina 1949,N 1,32:2
Porgy and Bess 1952,Ag 6,17:7
Porgy and Bess 1952,S 8,18:2
Porgy and Bess 1952,S 18,36:5
Porgy and Bess 1952,O 10,21:4
Porgy and Bess 1961,My 18,40:1
Porgy and Bess 1964,My 7,32:1
Porgy and Bess 1965,O 20,53:3
Show Boat 1966,Jl 20,48:1
Warg, Rea (Miscellaneous)
Shout From the Rooftops 1964,O 29,40:1
Wargo, George
Dark of the Moon 1970,Ap 4,21:2
Warik, Josef
Crimes of Passion; Erpingham Camp, The
1969,O 27,54:1
Othello 1970,S 15,51:1
Waring, Alfred (Miscellaneous)
Life I Gave You, The 1931,My 12,29:3
Waring, Claire
Annie Get Your Gun 1958,F 20,29:2
Guys and Dolls 1959,Jl 22,22:2
My Fair Lady 1964,My 21,43:2
Guys and Dolls 1965,Ap 29,39:1
Guys and Dolls 1966,Je 9,55:2
Wonderful Town 1967,My 18,50:1
My Fair Lady 1968,Je 14,42:1
Waring, Clara
Once in a Lifetime 1930,S 25,22:3
Waring, Derek
Portrait of a Queen 1968,F 29,29:1
Waring, Fred
Hello, Yourself 1928,O 31,28:2
Hear! Hear! 1955,S 28,38:1
Waring, Fred (Choreographer)
New Yorkers, The 1930,D 9,31:1
Waring, Fred (Producer)
Hear! Hear! 1955,S 28,38:1
Waring, Fred and his Pennsylvanians
Vaudeville (Palace) 1928,F 7,30:5
Vaudeville (Palace) 1928,F 14,26:2
Vaudeville (Palace) 1928,F 21,19:2
Hello, Yourself 1928,O 31,28:2
Waring, Fred and His Pennsylvanians
Vaudeville (Palace) 1929,D 2,28:6
Waring, Fred and his Pennsylvanians
New Yorkers, The 1930,N 16,VIII,3:1
New Yorkers, The 1930,D 9,31:1
Waring, Fred Glee Club
New Aquacade Revue, The 1940,My 13,20:5
Actors Fund Fete 1942,F 23,24:5
Waring, Herbert
Green Goddess, The 1921,Ja 19,14:1
Waring, James D (Director)
Stephen D 1966,Ag 5,17:1
Stephen D 1967,S 25,58:1
Stephen D 1967,O 8,II,1:6
She Stoops to Conquer 1968,Ap 1,58:3
Waring, James D (Lighting Director)
Faith of Our Fathers 1950,Ag 6,72:2
Oedipus Rex 1959,Ap 30,36:1
Stephen D 1966,Ag 5,17:1
Waring, James D (Scenic Designer)
Oedipus Rex 1959,Ap 30,36:1
Stephen D 1966,Ag 5,17:1
Waring, Jeanette
What of It? 1929,Mr 9,24:2
Waring, Richard
Lady of the Camellias, The 1931,Ja 27,21:2
Liliom 1932,O 27,23:2
Camille 1932,O 28,23:2
Dear Jane 1932,N 15,24:3

Waring, Richard—Cont
Alice in Wonderland 1932,D 12,18:3
Aiglon, L' 1934,N 5,22:2
Come Across 1938,S 15,28:3
Frank Fay's Vaudeville 1939,Mr 3,20:4
Man Who Killed Lincoln, The 1939,D 30,9:1
Man Who Killed Lincoln, The 1940,Ja 18,26:4
To What Red Hell 1940,My 5,I,54:8
At the Stroke of Eight 1940,My 21,29:2
Corn Is Green, The 1940,N 27,27:2
Corn Is Green, The 1943,My 4,18:3
Corn Is Green, The 1943,My 9,II,1:1
Truckline Cafe 1946,F 28,19:4
Henry VIII 1946,N 7,42:2
What Every Woman Knows 1946,N 9,13:2
Androcles and the Lion 1946,D 20,29:2
Alice in Wonderland 1947,Ap 7,19:2
Corn Is Green, The 1950,Ja 12,33:2
Gramercy Ghost 1951,Ap 27,20:2
Little Clay Cart, The 1953,Jl 1,25:1
Measure for Measure 1957,Ja 23,24:1
Measure for Measure 1957,F 3,II,1:1
Othello 1957,Je 24,19:2
Merchant of Venice, The 1957,Jl 11,19:5
Much Ado About Nothing 1957,Ag 8,15:2
Hamlet 1958,Je 21,11:1
Midsummer Night's Dream, A 1958,Je 23,19:1
Winter's Tale, The 1958,Jl 21,17:4
Edwin Booth 1958,N 25,37:1
Merry Wives of Windsor, The 1959,Jl 9,23:2
All's Well That Ends Well 1959,Ag 3,20:4
Twelfth Night 1960,Je 9,29:4
Tempest, The 1960,Je 20,35:1
Antony and Cleopatra 1960,Ag 1,19:1
As You Like It 1961,Je 17,13:2
Macbeth 1961,Je 19,31:1
Richard II 1962,Je 18,20:2
Henry IV, Part I 1962,Je 18,20:4
Cherry Orchard, The 1962,N 15,46:2
Doll's House, A 1963,F 4,5:6
Life Is a Dream 1964,Mr 20,24:1
Portrait of a Queen 1968,F 29,29:1
Waring, Sandra
Howdy Stranger 1937,Ja 15,17:5
Waring, Tom (Composer)
Hear! Hear! 1955,S 28,38:1
Waring, Tom (Playwright)
Hear! Hear! 1955,S 28,38:1
Wark, Robert
Wanhope Building, The 1947,F 11,36:5
Nude With Violin 1957,N 15,36:1
Warmington, Stanley
Trimmed in Scarlet 1920,F 3,18:1
Richard III 1920,Mr 8,7:1
Warne, Sidney
Murder in the Cathedral 1938,F 17,16:2
Warner, Ardelle
Once Over Lightly 1942,N 20,26:2
Warner, Daniel
Tambourine 1925,D 30,10:2
Warner, David
Wars of the Roses, The 1963,Jl 18,14:1
Hamlet 1965,Ag 20,18:2
Tiny Alice 1970,Ja 17,24:1
Warner, Ellen B
Mud Turtle, The 1925,Ag 21,8:2
Warner, H B
Danger 1921,D 23,18:3
You and I 1923,F 20,12:1
You and I 1923,F 25,VII,1:1
Silence 1924,N 13,18:2
Warner, Jack
Garrison Theatre 1940,My 26,IX,2:1
Hold It! 1948,My 6,31:5
Happy as Larry 1950,Ja 7,11:2
Warner, Jack L (Producer)
Jimmy 1969,O 24,38:1
Warner, Jackie
Rumple 1957,N 7,42:2
Whoop-Up 1958,D 23,2:7
Warner, Jean
Love Dreams 1921,O 11,22:2
Warner, Jethro
Oh, Ernest! 1927,My 10,24:3
Killers 1928,Mr 14,28:3
Whoopee 1928,D 5,34:3
Gold Braid 1930,My 14,31:2
Warner, John
Anna Ascends 1920,S 23,14:1
True to Form 1921,S 13,12:1
Wall Street 1927,Ap 21,24:4
Pirate, The 1929,Ap 21,IX,1:4
Mrs Mouse Are You Within? 1968,Je 2,II,3:6
Mrs Mouse Are You Within? 1968,Jl 8,45:1
Warner, Maurice
Color of Darkness: An Evening in the World of
James Purdy; You Reach for Your Hat
1963,O 1,34:1
Warner, Neil (Musical Director)
Man of La Mancha 1965,N 23,52:1
Warner, Oscar
Solid Ivory 1925,N 17,29:3
Warner, Richard
Room 349 1930,Ap 23,24:5

Warner, Richard—Cont
Dark Hours, The 1932,N 15,24:2
Late One Evening 1933,Ja 10,27:3
Mountain, The 1933,S 12,28:6
George and Margaret 1937,S 23,32:2
Warner, Richard D
First Lady 1952,My 29,18:5
Warner, Robert
What Price Glory 1924,S 6,14:3
Warner, Sturgis (Lyricist)
Foemen of the Yard 1935,Ap 6,10:4
Warner, Thomas (Director)
Henry VIII 1930,Jl 13,VIII,2:1
Warner, Tom
John Brown 1950,My 4,32:7
Warner, William
As You Like It 1936,Ap 24,18:4
Warner Brothers (Producer)
Jupiter Laughs 1940,S 10,27:1
Warnes, Marion
Let Freedom Sing 1942,O 6,18:2
Warnick, Clay (Composer)
Dream With Music 1944,My 19,15:2
Memphis Bound 1945,My 25,23:2
Tickets, Please! 1950,Ap 28,25:2
Warnick, Clay (Lyricist)
Memphis Bound 1945,My 25,23:2
Tickets, Please! 1950,Ap 28,25:2
Warnick, Clay (Miscellaneous)
Park Avenue 1946,N 5,31:2
Hold It! 1948,My 6,31:5
Donnybrook! 1961,My 19,23:1
Little Me 1962,N 19,41:3
Warnick, Clay (Musical Director)
Hold It! 1948,My 6,31:5
Heaven on Earth 1948,S 17,29:2
All for Love 1949,Ja 24,16:5
Michael Todd's Peep Show 1950,Je 29,37:2
Donnybrook! 1961,My 19,23:1
Ice Capades 1961,Ag 31,24:4
Warnick, Geoffry
Rapid Transit 1927,Ap 8,21:2
Warnk, Josef
Othello 1970,Je 22,43:1
Warnow, Mark (Producer)
What's Up 1943,N 12,24:6
Warnshuis, Lois
Tom Sawyer - Ballad of the Mississippi
1947,D 27,11:3
Warre, Michael
Henry IV, Part I 1946,My 7,25:2
Henry IV, Part II 1946,My 8,33:4
Henry IV 1946,My 12,II,1:1
Oedipus; Critic, The 1946,My 21,19:2
Oedipus 1946,My 21,19:2
King Lear 1946,O 13,II,2:3
Warren, Alaina
In 3 Zones 1970,N 3,28:1
Warren, Barnett (Director)
Blue Monday 1932,Je 3,23:2
Warren, Barnett (Producer)
Blue Monday 1932,Je 3,23:2
Warren, Betty
Dear Ruth 1946,Mr 1,17:3
Warren, Billie
Three Plays of the Sea 1970,Ag 20,39:1
Warren, Brett (Director)
Power 1937,F 24,18:5
Wanhope Building, The 1947,F 11,36:5
House in Berlin, A (Als der Kreig zu Ende War);
Als der Krieg zu Ende War (A House in Berlin)
1950,D 27,32:3
Warren, Bruce
She Cried for the Moon 1935,Jl 23,24:3
Warren, Chandler (Producer)
Thracian Horses, The 1961,S 28,58:2
My Daughter, Your Son 1969,My 14,36:2
Jumping Fool, The 1970,F 10,53:1
Warren, Charles
Merrily We Roll Along 1936,Je 30,15:1
Warren, David
Joan of Lorraine 1955,Mr 26,12:2
Warren, Edith
Black Boy 1926,O 7,30:2
Warren, Edna (Playwright)
Right of Possession 1930,My 9,20:5
Warren, Eleanor
What's the Use? 1926,S 7,19:1
Warren, Elton J
Carmen Jones 1943,D 3,26:2
Carmen Jones 1945,My 3,26:5
Carmen Jones 1946,Ap 8,32:2
Carmen Jones 1946,Ap 14,II,1:2
Carmen Jones 1951,S 22,8:6
Phoenix '55 1955,Ap 25,20:2
Warren, Ernest
Finian's Rainbow 1953,Mr 7,13:2
Warren, Fay
Marry the Man! 1929,Ap 23,26:3
Warren, Florence
Mr Jiggins of Jigginstown 1936,D 18,30:2
Warren, Flori
Razzle Dazzle 1951,F 20,21:1

Warren, Fran
Danny Kaye's International Show 1953,Ja 19,20:2
Warren, George
Diamond Lil 1948,N 30,33:2
Diamond Lil 1949,F 7,16:2
Warren, George (Miscellaneous)
Cocktails of 1934 1934,My 5,22:1
Warren, Gloria
What's Up 1943,N 12,24:6
What's Up 1943,N 21,II,1:1
Warren, H C
War Song, The 1928,S 25,29:3
Warren, Harry
Diamond Lil 1948,N 30,33:2
Diamond Lil 1949,F 7,16:2
Warren, Harry (Composer)
Laugh Parade, The 1931,N 3,31:2
Shangri-La 1956,Je 14,40:1
Warren, Harvey (Scenic Designer)
Ice Capades 1955,S 15,38:1
Ice Capades 1956,S 13,41:2
Ice Capades 1957,S 5,33:2
Ice Capades 1958,S 4,33:2
Warren, Heppie
Antonia 1925,O 21,20:1
Warren, Herbert
Light Wines and Beer 1930,N 11,28:6
Honor Code, The 1931,My 19,25:3
Guest Room, The 1931,O 7,29:2
Four O'Clock 1933,F 14,19:6
Birthright 1933,N 22,22:3
Brittle Heaven 1934,N 14,22:5
Symphony 1935,Ap 27,20:3
Sweet Mystery of Life 1935,O 12,13:3
Summer Wives 1936,Ap 14,18:1
Mimie Scheller 1936,O 1,28:4
Cross-Town 1937,Mr 18,21:5
Warren, Howard
Cranmer of Canterbury 1959,D 4,36:1
Warren, Jack
Searching for the Sun 1936,F 20,22:6
Spring Dance 1936,Ag 26,17:4
Work Is for Horses 1937,N 22,14:6
Warren, Jay
High Named Today 1954,D 11,11:2
It's an Ill Wind 1957,Ap 24,28:1
Warren, Jeff
Brigadoon 1950,My 3,36:2
Call Me Madam 1952,Mr 16,84:3
Lend an Ear 1959,S 25,20:5
Warren, Jennifer
Scuba Duba 1967,O 11,36:1
Scuba Duba 1969,Ap 7,51:1
Warren, Joseph
Barefoot in Athens 1951,N 1,35:2
One Bright Day 1952,Mr 20,37:2
Detective Story 1954,F 13,11:2
Third Person 1955,D 30,13:4
Lovers, Villains and Fools: A Shakespearean
Variety Show 1956,O 24,44:7
Enemy of the People, An 1959,F 5,24:4
Night of the Auk 1963,My 22,35:2
Advocate, The 1963,O 15,46:7
Philadelphia, Here I Come! 1966,F 17,28:1
Jonah! 1967,S 22,52:2
Borstal Boy 1970,Ap 1,38:1
Warren, Julie
Connecticut Yankee, A 1943,N 18,30:2
For Keeps 1944,Je 15,17:5
Around the World 1946,Je 1,9:5
Warren, Katharine
Farewell to Arms, A 1930,S 23,30:3
As You Desire Me 1931,Ja 29,21:2
Three Times the Hour 1931,Ag 26,15:5
Cyrano de Bergerac 1932,D 27,11:2
Thunder on the Left 1933,N 1,25:2
Wednesday's Child 1934,Ja 17,23:2
Piper Paid 1934,D 26,19:1
Blind Alley 1935,S 25,19:6
Cyrano de Bergerac 1936,Ap 28,17:1
Romeo and Juliet 1940,My 10,27:1
Warren, Kenneth
Summer of the Seventeenth Doll 1958,Ja 23,23:2
Luther 1963,S 26,41:1
Warren, Kenneth J
Canterbury Tales 1968,S 7,23:3
Warren, Leon R (Scenic Designer)
Incubator 1932,N 2,23:3
Warren, Lesley Ann
110 in the Shade 1963,O 25,37:1
Drat! the Cat! 1965,O 11,54:2
Warren, Lloyd
Green Pastures, The 1935,F 27,16:2
Native Son 1941,Mr 25,26:5
Warren, Marcia
Measure for Measure 1967,F 15,37:1
Hamlet 1967,F 17,44:1
Romeo and Juliet 1967,F 22,18:1
Warren, Marietta
White Man 1936,O 19,22:4
Warren, Paul
Marjolaine 1922,Ja 25,16:1
Hayride 1954,S 14,24:2

Warren, Pete
Many Waters 1929,S 26,27:1
Warren, Peter (Producer)
Oh, Herbert! 1945,Je 20,26:3
Warren, Richard
We've Got to Have Money 1923,Ag 21,12:1
Plough and the Stars, The 1956,Ap 6,14:1
Warren, Robert Penn (Original Author)
All the King's Men 1959,O 17,27:2
Warren, Robert Penn (Playwright)
All the King's Men 1948,Ja 19,19:2
All the King's Men 1950,Jl 19,25:6
All the King's Men 1959,O 17,27:2
All the King's Men 1959,O 25,II,1:1
All the King's Men 1963,Jl 12,12:1
Brother to Dragons 1968,D 8,86:1
Warren, Ruth
Sweet Little Devil 1924,Ja 22,15:4
Kitty's Kisses 1926,My 7,12:2
Warren, S W
Singin' the Blues 1931,S 17,21:3
Warren, Salley
Music Hath Charms 1934,D 31,8:2
Warren, Verna
Streetcar Named Desire, A 1955,Mr 4,18:2
Warren, Vincent
Crystal Heart, The 1960,F 16,31:2
Warren, William (Scenic Designer)
Thoroughbred 1933,N 7,29:2
Warren and O'Brien
Vaudeville (Palace) 1926,Ap 13,28:3
Warren-Wilson, Daphne
No More Ladies 1934,S 4,23:2
Warrender, Harold
Earl Carroll's Vanities 1927,Ja 5,18:1
Anthony and Anna 1935,N 9,18:2
Anthony and Anna 1935,D 8,X,5:1
Warrenton, Lule
Heaven-Tappers, The 1927,Mr 9,28:3
Warrick, Ruth
Thorntons, The 1956,F 15,26:1
Miss Lonelyhearts 1957,O 4,26:2
Single Man at a Party 1959,Ap 22,30:4
Warrier, Govinda (Costume Designer)
Mahabharata 1970,N 28,22:1
Warrier, Govinda (Miscellaneous)
Mahabharata 1970,N 28,22:1
Warrilow, David
Red Horse Animation, The 1970,N 20,32:1
Warriner, Frederic
Shakespeare's Merchant 1939 1939,Ja 10,16:3
Circle, The 1939,Jl 12,17:2
White Steed, The 1939,Ag 16,21:3
Blind Alley 1939,Ag 23,18:8
King Lear 1950,D 26,18:1
Taming of the Shrew, The 1951,Ap 26,35:2
Getting Married 1951,My 14,28:5
Saint Joan 1951,O 5,23:2
Pin to See the Peepshow, A 1953,S 18,17:2
Clandestine Marriage, The 1954,O 4,23:2
Clandestine Marriage, The 1954,O 17,II,1:1
Doctor's Dilemma, The 1955,Ja 12,22:1
Wayward Saint, The 1955,F 18,17:1
White Devil, The 1955,Mr 15,32:5
Tempest, The 1955,S 3,8:6
Carefree Tree, The 1955,O 12,37:2
Six Characters in Search of an Author
1955,D 12,38:1
Major Barbara 1956,O 31,27:1
Time Remembered 1957,N 13,41:2
Fashion 1959,Ja 21,27:1
Romeo and Juliet 1959,Je 15,31:1
Romeo and Juliet 1959,Je 21,II,1:1
Merry Wives of Windsor, The 1959,Jl 9,23:2
All's Well That Ends Well 1959,Ag 3,20:4
Caligula 1960,F 17,31:1
Henry V 1960,Je 30,23:1
Measure for Measure 1960,Jl 27,33:1
Taming of the Shrew, The 1960,Ag 20,17:1
She Stoops to Conquer 1960,N 2,42:5
Plough and the Stars, The 1960,D 7,56:2
Hamlet 1961,Mr 17,17:1
Androcles and the Lion 1961,N 22,24:2
Dark Lady of the Sonnets, The 1961,D 15,48:1
Man for All Seasons, A 1964,Ja 28,24:2
Coriolanus 1965,Je 21,36:1
Taming of the Shrew, The 1965,Je 24,32:2
White Devil, The 1965,D 7,56:1
Oresteia 1966,Je 30,29:1
Birds, The 1966,Jl 1,40:1
Volpone 1967,Je 30,29:1
Hamlet 1967,D 27,45:1
Portrait of a Queen 1968,F 29,29:1
Romeo and Juliet 1968,Ag 16,19:1
Invitation to a Beheading 1969,Mr 18,36:1
Trelawny of the 'Wells' 1970,O 12,48:1
Trelawney of the 'Wells' 1970,O 25,II,16:1
Warriner, Kate
Mother Lode 1934,D 24,16:5
Caesar and Cleopatra 1935,Ag 22,21:1
Black Limelight 1936,N 10,31:1
Merchant of Venice, The 1938,Ja 15,18:8
Victoria Regina 1938,O 4,20:2

Warriner, Kate—Cont

As You Like It 1939,My 9,28:4
Another Sun 1940,F 24,8:6
Your Loving Son 1941,Ap 5,13:2

Warring-Manley, Marian
Home Fires 1923,Ag 21,12:1
Morals 1925,D 1,22:2
John Gabriel Borkman 1926,Ja 30,13:1
Constant Nymph, The 1926,D 10,31:1
Constant Nymph, The 1926,D 19,VII,3:1
Skin Deep 1927,O 18,32:1
In The Best of Families 1931,F 3,29:1
American, Very Early 1934,Ja 31,21:2
Shoemaker's Holiday, The 1938,Ja 3,17:2
Shoemaker's Holiday, The 1938,Ja 9,X,1:1

Warrington, Ann
Guest of Honor, The 1920,S 21,12:1

Warrington, George
Black Crook, The 1929,Mr 12,26:5

Warrington, Jane
Cat and the Canary, The 1922,F 8,13:1

Warsaw Jewish Troupe
Untitled-Revue 1939,Ap 5,31:2

Warschawer, Ari
Dybbuk, The 1948,My 3,26:3
Golem, The 1948,My 17,22:3

Warshaw, Leon
Off Your Marx 1936,Ap 2,28:2

Warshawer, L
Dybbuk, The 1926,D 14,24:2
Jacob's Dream 1927,Ja 4,20:2
Golem, The 1927,F 5,13:2

Warshawski, Mark
Both Kooney Lemels 1964,O 12,37:2
Melody Lingers On, The 1969,N 17,55:1

Warshawsky, Ruth
Our Town 1968,D 14,62:1

Warshawsky, Samuel Jesse (Playwright)
Steadfast 1923,O 31,12:1
Woman of Destiny, A 1936,Mr 3,25:2

Warszawski, Merek
Brothers Ashkenazi, The 1970,N 17,53:2

Warthin, A Scott
Lady From the Sea, The 1935,D 14,11:3

Warwas, Ewa
Nightmare, The 1965,Ja 6,32:1
Kernel and the Shell, The 1965,Ja 6,32:1
Labyrinth, The 1965,Ja 6,32:1
Woman, The 1965,Ja 6,32:1
Post Office, The 1965,Ja 6,32:1
Book, The 1965,Ja 6,32:1
Jacob and the Angel 1965,Ja 6,32:1
Jaselka 1965,Ja 6,32:1

Warwick, Betty
Hearts Are Trumps! 1927,Ap 8,21:1

Warwick, Henry
Champion, The 1921,Ja 4,11:1
Rose of Stamboul, The 1922,Mr 8,11:2
Guilty One, The 1923,Mr 21,19:1
Swan, The 1923,O 24,15:3
Assumption of Hannele, The 1924,F 16,16:2
Shanghai Gesture, The 1926,F 2,20:2
Potiphar's Wife 1928,D 24,10:7
Murder on the Second Floor 1929,S 12,35:1
Berkeley Square 1929,N 5,32:4
Peace Palace 1933,Je 6,30:2

Warwick, James
Arms and the Man 1970,Jl 10,18:1
Arms and the Man 1970,Ag 26,36:1

Warwick, James (Playwright)
Blind Alley 1935,S 25,19:6
Blind Alley 1939,Ag 23,18:8
Blind Alley 1940,O 16,28:2

Warwick, Margaretta
Gioconda Smile, The 1950,O 9,21:2
Brass Ring, The 1952,Ap 11,19:2
Pin to See the Peepshow, A 1953,S 18,17:2
Corn Is Green, The 1954,F 27,10:2
Will and the Way, The 1957,D 3,46:5
Apollo of Bellac, The 1958,Mr 7,17:2
Family Reunion, The 1958,O 21,39:1
Summer of the Seventeenth Doll 1959,O 14,52:1
Mousetrap, The 1960,N 7,46:1
One Way Pendulum 1961,S 19,38:2

Warwick, Nicholas
Othello 1937,Ja 7,16:4

Warwick, Noel
Find the Fox 1930,Je 21,20:4

Warwick, Robert
In the Night Watch 1921,Ja 31,10:1
Drifting 1922,Ja 3,20:3
Drifting 1922,Ja 22,VI,1:1
Rivals, The 1922,Je 6,18:2
To Love 1922,O 18,16:2
Cheaper to Marry 1924,Ap 16,26:1
His Queen 1925,My 12,26:1
Lady's Virtue, A 1925,N 24,28:2
Two Orphans, The 1926,Ap 6,26:2
Two Orphans, The 1926,Ap 11,VIII,1:1
Vaudeville (Palace) 1927,My 31,25:1
Mrs Dane's Defense 1928,F 7,30:1
Sherlock Holmes 1928,F 21,18:4
Within the Law 1928,Mr 6,20:1
Nice Women 1929,Je 11,27:4

Primer for Lovers, A 1929,N 19,26:5

Warwick Dancers, Six
Two Seconds 1931,O 10,20:6

Warzycki, Helen
Trojan Women, The 1923,My 27,10:2

Wasadayu, Toyotake
Chushingura; Treasury of Loyal Retainers, The 1969,S 11,53:1
Kumagai Jinya 1969,S 18,64:1

Wascher, Aribert
Twelfth Night 1932,O 23,IX,3:1

Washbourne, Mona
Nude With Violin 1957,N 15,36:1
Home 1970,Ag 17,32:1
Home 1970,N 18,41:1
Home 1970,N 29,II,1:1

Washburn, Charles (Playwright)
All Editions 1936,D 23,17:2
She Gave Him All She Had 1939,D 2,20:7

Washburn, Conway
Machinal 1928,S 8,10:3

Washburn, Deric (Playwright)
Love Nest, The 1963,Ja 28,7:6

Washburn, Gloria
Man Who Killed Lincoln, The 1940,Ja 18,26:4

Washburn, Gloria (Miscellaneous)
Joan of Lorraine 1955,Mr 26,12:2

Washburn, Jack
Fanny 1954,N 5,16:1
Paradise Island 1961,Je 24,11:1
Mr President 1962,O 22,34:2

Washburn, John
Macbeth 1921,F 18,16:1
Four Flusher, The 1925,Ap 14,27:4
Damn the Tears 1927,Ja 22,11:1

Washburn, John (Playwright)
They All Come to Moscow 1933,My 12,20:6

Washburn, John Larry (Producer)
Answered the Flute 1960,Mr 10,37:4

Washburn, John M
Spring 3100 1928,F 16,14:2

Washburn, Martin (Scenic Designer)
Full Moon in March, A 1960,S 20,48:1

Washburn, Mary
Vaudeville (Palace) 1925,O 6,31:3

Washburne, Conway
Killers 1928,Mr 14,28:3
Street Scene 1929,Ja 11,20:4
Counsellor-at-Law 1931,N 7,17:2
Between Two Worlds 1934,O 26,24:2
Excursion 1937,Ap 10,11:4

Washburne, Mae
Her Salary Man 1921,N 29,20:1

Washcoe, Wil (Lighting Director)
They Walk Alone 1941,Mr 13,24:2
Mexican Mural; Patio With Flamingo 1942,Ap 27,19:2
Mexican Mural; Miracle Painting 1942,Ap 27,19:2
Mexican Mural; Moonlight Scene 1942,Ap 27,19:2
Mexican Mural; Vera Cruz Interior 1942,Ap 27,19:2

Washington, Benveneta
Green Pastures, The 1935,F 27,16:2
John Henry 1940,Ja 11,18:2

Washington, Dorothy
Trial of Dr Beck, The 1937,Ag 10,22:2

Washington, Ernestine
Gospel Glow 1962,O 28,87:5

Washington, Fredi
Sweet Chariot 1930,O 24,30:2
Singin' the Blues 1931,S 17,21:3
Run, Little Chillun! 1933,Mr 2,21:3
Mamba's Daughters 1939,Ja 4,24:2
Mamba's Daughters 1939,Ja 15,IX,1:1
Mamba's Daughters 1940,Mr 25,10:4
Lysistrata 1946,O 18,27:5
Long Way From Home, A 1948,F 9,25:2
How Long Till Summer 1949,D 28,30:3

Washington, Geneva
Black Rhythm 1936,D 21,19:2

Washington, George Dewey
Strike Me Pink 1933,Mr 6,16:3

Washington, Isabell
Harlem 1929,F 21,30:3
Bomboola 1929,Je 27,17:3
Singin' the Blues 1931,Ap 12,IX,2:1
Singin' the Blues 1931,S 17,21:3

Washington, James (Scenic Designer)
Kill the One-Eyed Man 1965,O 21,56:1

Washington, Joseph
Pirate, The 1942,N 26,39:2

Washington, King
Hot Rhythm 1930,Ag 22,18:5

Washington, Lamont
Twisting Road, The; One Tuesday Morning 1957,N 18,36:5
Hair 1968,Ap 30,40:2

Washington, Margo
Our Lan' 1947,Ap 19,11:2
Our Lan' 1947,S 29,16:5

Washington, Mattie
Carmen Jones 1951,S 22,8:6

Washington, Ned (Composer)
Blackbirds 1933,D 4,22:3

Washington, Ned (Lyricist)
Blackbirds 1933,D 4,22:3

Washington, Sally
Lost Horizons 1934,O 16,31:2
Prelude 1936,Ap 20,17:4

Washington, Vernon
Cabin in the Sky 1964,Ja 22,32:1
Trials of Brother Jero, The 1967,N 10,60:1
Scuba Duba 1969,Ap 7,51:1

Wasinsky, Gertrude
Revolt of the Beavers, The 1937,My 21,19:2

Wasko, George
Point of No Return 1957,Mr 23,17:2

Wasserman, Dale (Playwright)
Livin' the Life 1957,Ap 29,20:1
One Flew Over the Cuckoo's Nest 1963,N 14,40:2
One Flew Over the Cuckoo's Nest 1963,D 1,II,1:1
Man of La Mancha 1965,N 23,52:1

Wasserman, Dale (Producer)
Man of La Mancha 1966,O 5,42:5

Wasserman, Don
Caucasian Chalk Circle, The 1961,N 1,35:1

Wasserman, Herb
Me and Juliet 1953,My 29,17:1

Wassermann, Charles U (Playwright)
Time of Vengeance 1959,D 11,39:1

Wasson, Greear
Dance of Death, The 1969,My 26,53:1

Watanabe, Miyoko
Mikado, The 1968,My 2,59:1

Waterbury, Adrian B
Grey Heir, The 1926,Ap 6,29:2

Waterbury, Francelia
Mystery Square 1929,Ap 5,28:3
It Pays to Sin 1933,N 4,18:6

Waterfield, Phoebe
Murder in the Cathedral 1938,F 17,16:2

Waterhouse, Keith (Playwright)
Sponge Room, The 1964,F 25,24:1
Squat Betty 1964,F 25,24:1
Billy Liar 1965,Mr 18,26:1
Help Stamp Out Marriage 1966,S 30,50:1
Whoops-A-Daisy 1968,D 13,61:1

Waterman, Dennis
Carving a Statue 1964,S 18,25:1
Enemy 1969,D 19,65:6

Waterman, Dorothy
Yes, Yes, Yvette 1927,O 4,32:3

Waterman, Ida
Martinique 1920,Ap 27,18:2
Lawful Larceny 1922,Ja 3,20:2

Waterman, Willard
Mame 1966,My 25,41:1

Waterous, Allen
Castles in the Air 1926,S 7,19:2
Mikado, The 1931,Ag 25,17:7
Iolanthe 1932,Ja 5,20:2
Gondoliers, The 1932,Ja 12,29:1
Robin Hood 1932,Ja 28,25:4
Mikado, The 1933,Ap 18,13:4
Lambs Gambol 1933,Ap 24,10:1
Yeomen of the Guard, The 1933,My 2,20:4
Trial by Jury 1933,My 9,20:3
H M S Pinafore 1933,My 9,20:3
Patience 1933,My 23,22:6
Bohemian Girl, The 1933,Jl 28,18:5
Pirates of Penzance, The 1933,Ag 8,22:4
Yeomen of the Guard, The 1933,Ag 15,20:5
Mikado, The 1934,Ap 3,26:3
Pirates of Penzance, The 1934,Ap 10,26:5
H M S Pinafore 1934,Ap 17,27:2
Trial by Jury 1934,Ap 17,27:2
Iolanthe 1934,My 1,26:4

Waterous, Herbert
H M S Pinafore 1920,Ja 13,10:2
Ruddigore 1920,Ja 20,11:2
Ruddigore 1920,F 1,VIII,2:2
Some Party 1922,Ap 17,22:1
Lady Fingers 1929,F 1,22:4
Naughty Marietta 1929,O 22,26:2
Mikado, The; Town of Titipu, The 1931,My 5,33:2
Iolanthe 1931,Jl 14,21:5
Ruddigore 1931,Ag 11,28:3
Mikado, The 1931,Ag 25,17:7
Iolanthe 1932,Ja 5,20:2
Mikado, The 1933,Ap 18,13:4
Yeomen of the Guard, The 1933,My 2,20:4
Pirates of Penzance, The 1933,Ag 8,22:4
Yeomen of the Guard, The 1933,Ag 15,20:5
Mikado, The 1934,Ap 3,26:3
Pirates of Penzance, The 1934,Ap 10,26:5
H M S Pinafore 1934,Ap 17,27:2
Trial by Jury 1934,Ap 17,27:2
Iolanthe 1934,My 1,26:4
Mikado, The 1935,Jl 16,24:4
Pirates of Penzance, The 1935,Jl 23,24:2
Yeomen of the Guard, The 1935,Jl 30,16:4
Trial by Jury 1935,Ag 13,20:6
H M S Pinafore 1935,Ag 13,20:6
Mikado, The 1936,Ap 11,18:4
Pirates of Penzance, The 1936,Ap 21,27:5
H M S Pinafore 1936,Ap 28,17:2
Trial by Jury 1936,Ap 28,17:2

Waterous, Herbert—Cont
Iolanthe 1936,My 5,26:2
Waterous, Herbett (Mrs)
Firefly, The 1931,D 1,23:2
Waterous, Jayne
Babes in Toyland 1929,D 24,15:3
Babes in Toyland 1930,D 22,17:1
Waters, Ada
Polly Preferred 1923,Ja 12,13:3
Waters, Bunny
Between the Devil 1937,D 23,24:5
Waters, Edna
Mamba's Daughters 1940,Mr 25,10:4
Waters, Ethel
Africana 1927,Jl 12,29:2
Africana 1927,S 4,VII,1:1
Vaudeville (Palace) 1927,S 20,33:3
Vaudeville (Palace) 1928,Ag 28,27:3
Lew Leslie's Blackbirds of 1930 1930,O 23,34:5
Rhapsody in Black 1931,My 5,33:2
As Thousands Cheer 1933,S 10,II,5:3
As Thousands Cheer 1933,O 2,22:1
As Thousands Cheer 1933,O 15,IX,1:1
At Home Abroad 1935,S 4,22:3
At Home Abroad 1935,S 8,IX,1:1
At Home Abroad 1935,S 20,17:4
At Home Abroad 1935,O 27,IX,1:1
Mamba's Daughters 1939,Ja 4,24:2
Mamba's Daughters 1939,Ja 15,IX,1:1
Mamba's Daughters 1940,Mr 25,10:4
Cabin in the Sky 1940,O 26,19:2
Cabin in the Sky 1940,N 3,IX,1:1
Cabin in the Sky 1940,N 10,IX,2:1
Laugh Time 1943,S 9,35:2
Laugh Time 1943,S 19,II,1:1
Blue Holiday 1945,My 22,13:3
Member of the Wedding, The 1950,Ja 6,26:6
Member of the Wedding, The 1950,Ja 15,II,1:1
ANTA Album 1950,Ja 30,13:2
Member of the Wedding, The 1950,My 14,II,1:1
Member of the Wedding, The 1950,S 17,II,1:1
At Home With Ethel Waters 1953,S 23,36:1
Evening With Ethel Waters, An 1959,Ap 9,36:1
Waters, Hadley (Playwright)
Ghost Parade, The 1929,O 31,28:4
Little Orchard Annie 1930,Ap 22,33:1
She Cried for the Moon 1935,Jl 23,24:3
Waters, Hal
Hobo 1961,Ap 11,41:2
Waters, Helen
Trial Honeymoon 1947,N 4,31:2
Diamond Lil 1951,S 15,8:2
Winkelberg 1958,Ja 15,26:2
Jack 1958,Je 4,39:2
J B 1958,D 12,2:7
Waters, James R
Detour, The 1921,Ag 24,12:2
Bronx Express 1922,Ap 27,12:2
It's a Boy! 1922,S 20,18:3
Jarnegan 1928,S 25,29:2
Wonder Boy 1931,O 24,20:1
East of Broadway 1932,Ja 27,19:3
Jezebel 1933,D 20,26:3
Excursion 1937,Ap 10,11:4
Excursion 1937,Ap 18,XI,1:1
Pastoral 1939,N 2,26:2
All in Favor 1942,Ja 21,20:6
Waters, Jan
Young Visitors, The 1968,D 26,48:1
Waters, Jimmy
Porgy and Bess 1935,O 11,30:2
Brown Sugar 1937,D 3,29:2
Porgy and Bess 1942,Ja 23,16:2
Way of the World, The 1950,Ap 9,73:5
Waters, John
Machinal 1928,S 8,10:3
Waters, Keane
What Price Glory 1924,S 6,14:3
Waters, Marianne Brown (Lyricist)
Right This Way 1938,Ja 6,22:1
Waters, Marianne Brown (Original Author)
Right This Way 1938,Ja 6,22:3
Waters, Marianne Brown (Playwright)
Blue Widow, The 1933,Ag 31,20:2
Waters, Patricia
Laughing Woman, The 1936,O 14,30:1
Empress of Destiny 1938,Mr 10,16:2
My Dear Children 1940,F 1,16:2
Waters, Paulette
You Can't Take It With You 1965,N 24,32:1
School for Scandal, The 1966,N 22,33:2
Waters, Tom (Director)
Laughwind 1966,Mr 3,27:1
Waters, Tom (Playwright)
Laughwind 1966,Mr 3,27:1
Waterston, Sam
As You Like It 1963,Jl 17,19:2
Oh Dad, Poor Dad, Mamma's Hung You in the Closet and I'm Feelin' So Sad 1963,Ag 28,28:2
Thistle in My Bed 1963,N 20,48:1
Fitz 1966,My 17,51:2
Halfway up the Tree 1967,N 8,52:1
Ergo 1968,Mr 4,29:1
Muzeeka 1968,Ap 29,47:2

Red Cross 1968,Ap 29,47:2
Henry IV, Part I 1968,Je 30,54:7
Henry IV, Part II 1968,Jl 2,33:1
Henry IV, Part II 1968,Jl 14,II,1:1
Spitting Image 1969,Mr 3,28:1
Indians 1969,O 14,51:1
Indians 1969,O 19,II,1:1
Brass Butterfly, The 1970,Ja 31,34:1
And I Met a Man 1970,Ap 11,20:3
Hay Fever 1970,N 10,55:1
Hay Fever 1970,N 22,II,18:6
Waterstreet, Edmund
Gianni Schicci 1969,F 25,36:1
Tale of Kasane, The 1969,F 25,36:1
Songs From Milk Wood 1970,Ja 13,41:1
Sganarelle 1970,Ja 13,41:1
Watford, Gwendoline
Women of Twilight 1952,Mr 4,22:2
Watkin, Lawrence Edward (Original Author)
On Borrowed Time 1953,F 11,34:1
Watkin, Pierre
Possession 1928,O 3,35:1
Scrap Book 1932,Ag 2,20:3
Mad Hopes, The 1932,D 2,26:3
We the People 1933,Ja 23,9:5
Whatever Possessed Her 1934,Ja 26,21:2
Too Much Party 1934,Mr 6,28:4
Watkins, Frances
Vie Parisienne, La 1945,Ja 13,14:5
Watkins, Gordon
Porgy and Bess 1965,Mr 6,17:1
Junebug Graduates Tonight! 1967,F 27,35:1
Watkins, Gordon (Composer)
Electronic Nigger, The 1968,Mr 9,23:2
Son, Come Home, A 1968,Mr 9,23:2
Electronic Nigger, The 1968,Mr 9,23:2
Clara's Ole Man 1968,Mr 9,23:2
Watkins, John P
Paradise Island 1961,Je 24,11:1
Watkins, Lawrence Edward (Original Author)
On Borrowed Time 1938,F 4,16:4
Watkins, Linda
Prunella; Love in a Garden 1926,Je 16,23:3
Devil in the Cheese, The 1926,D 30,22:4
Ivory Door, The 1927,O 19,24:5
Wild Duck, The 1928,N 19,17:1
Hedda Gabler 1929,F 4,20:3
Lady From the Sea, The 1929,Mr 19,36:1
June Moon 1929,Ag 4,VIII,1:6
June Moon 1929,O 10,34:5
Sweet Stranger 1930,O 22,23:3
In the Meantime 1930,D 7,IX,1:6
Midnight 1930,D 30,25:1
Love and Babies 1933,Ag 23,21:4
Give Us This Day 1933,O 28,20:6
They Shall Not Die 1934,F 22,24:4
They Shall Not Die 1934,Mr 4,IX,1:3
They Shall Not Die 1934,Mr 11,X,1:1
Say When 1934,O 28,IX,3:1
Say When 1934,N 9,24:2
County Chairman, The 1936,My 26,26:5
Aged 26 1936,D 22,32:1
Penny Wise 1937,Ap 20,28:6
I Am My Youth 1938,Mr 8,22:4
Janie 1942,S 11,24:2
Watkins, M W (Composer)
Half Moon Inn 1923,Mr 21,19:2
Watkins, Mary Jane
Ol' Man Satan 1932,O 4,26:3
Watkins, Maurine (Playwright)
Chicago 1926,D 31,11:1
Chicago 1927,Ja 9,VII,1:1
Revelry 1927,S 4,VII,2:4
Revelry 1927,S 13,37:1
Chicago 1927,D 18,IX,1:8
Chicago 1935,Mr 14,19:6
Watkins, Morris W (Composer)
Old King's 1924,Mr 12,19:3
Half Moon Inn 1925,Mr 10,14:1
Watkins, Perry (Costume Designer)
One-Act Plays of the Sea; In the Zone 1937,O 30,23:2
One-Act Plays of the Sea; Bound East for Cardiff 1937,O 30,23:2
One-Act Plays of the Sea; Moon of the Caribbees 1937,O 30,23:2
One-Act Plays of the Sea; Long Voyage Home, The 1937,O 30,23:2
Androcles and the Lion 1938,D 17,10:5
Run, Little Chillun 1943,Ag 14,6:1
Brights Lights of 1944 1943,S 17,27:4
Watkins, Perry (Lighting Director)
Big White Fog 1940,O 23,26:2
Forward the Heart 1949,Ja 29,9:2
Johnny Summit 1957,S 25,23:4
Watkins, Perry (Miscellaneous)
You'll See Stars 1943,Ja 1,26:6
Blue Holiday 1945,My 22,13:3
Watkins, Perry (Producer)
Beggar's Holiday 1946,D 27,13:3
Watkins, Perry (Scenic Designer)
Horse Play 1937,Ag 28,8:3

Watkins, Perry (Scenic Designer)—Cont
One-Act Plays of the Sea; Long Voyage Home, The 1937,O 30,23:2
One-Act Plays of the Sea; In the Zone 1937,O 30,23:2
One-Act Plays of the Sea; Moon of the Caribbees 1937,O 30,23:2
One-Act Plays of the Sea; Bound East for Cardiff 1937,O 30,23:2
Haiti 1938,Mr 3,16:1
Pinocchio 1939,Ja 3,19:2
Mamba's Daughters 1939,Ja 4,24:2
Mamba's Daughters 1939,Ja 15,IX,1:1
Mamba's Daughters 1940,Mr 25,10:4
Big White Fog 1940,O 23,26:2
Run, Little Chillun 1943,Ag 14,6:1
Brights Lights of 1944 1943,S 17,27:4
Manhattan Nocturne 1943,O 27,26:2
Take It As It Comes 1944,F 11,17:2
Blue Holiday 1945,My 22,13:3
Forward the Heart 1949,Ja 29,9:2
Harbor Lights 1956,O 5,20:1
Johnny Summit 1957,S 25,23:4
Watkins, William J (Composer)
Rainbow's End 1928,D 26,14:6
Watkins, William J (Lyricist)
Rainbow's End 1928,D 26,14:6
Watkinson, Eve
Lady of the Sea 1945,S 9,II,1:5
Watkyn, Arthur (Playwright)
Muted Strings 1936,N 11,54:4
Watling, Dilys
Georgy 1970,F 27,26:1
Watling, John
Flare Path 1942,Ag 23,VIII,1:6
Day After Tomorrow 1950,O 27,25:2
Watrous, David (Miscellaneous)
Signs Along the Cynic Route 1961,D 15,49:5
Watrous, Herbert
Pirates of Penzance, The; Slave of Duty, The 1931,Je 30,23:6
Watsky, Leon
Detour, The 1921,Ag 24,12:2
Watson, Al Jr
Bunch and Judy, The 1922,N 29,20:1
Watson, Alfred
Ramblers, The 1926,S 21,32:2
Watson, Ann
Women, The 1936,D 28,13:1
Watson, Arthur
Dreaming Dust, The 1955,D 8,46:5
Richard III 1957,N 26,41:1
As You Like It 1958,Ja 21,33:6
Othello 1958,Jl 4,16:1
Twelfth Night 1958,Ag 7,21:4
Julius Caesar 1959,Ag 4,30:1
Watson, Betty Jane
Toplitzky of Notre Dame 1946,D 27,13:4
Sleepy Hollow 1948,Je 4,26:3
Hilarities 1948,S 10,20:2
As the Girls Go 1948,N 15,21:2
ANTA Album 1951,My 7,22:7
Annie Get Your Gun 1958,F 20,29:2
Sail Away 1961,O 4,48:5
Watson, Bobby
Rise of Rosie O'Reilly, The 1923,D 26,13:4
Annie 1924,O 12,VIII,2:1
Annie Dear 1924,N 5,25:3
American Born 1925,S 27,VII,2:1
American Born 1925,O 6,31:3
Allez-Opp! 1927,Ag 3,29:3
Optimists, The 1928,Ja 31,28:2
Greenwich Village Follies 1928,Ap 10,32:2
Cross My Heart 1928,S 18,32:7
Vaudeville (Palace) 1929,Mr 11,22:5
Watson, Brian
Plot Against the Chase Manhattan Bank, The 1963,N 27,29:1
Watson, Chester
Consul, The 1950,Mr 16,41:1
Happy Town 1959,O 8,49:2
Watson, Clay (Lighting Director)
From Morn Till Midnight 1948,D 7,41:6
Don't Go Away Mad 1949,My 10,28:2
Watson, Clay (Scenic Designer)
From Morn Till Midnight 1948,D 7,41:6
Don't Go Away Mad 1949,My 10,28:2
Edge of the Sword, The 1949,N 10,40:3
Watson, Donald (Translator)
Chairs, The 1958,Ja 10,20:3
Lesson, The 1958,Ja 10,20:3
Victims of Duty 1960,Ja 20,26:1
Killer, The 1960,Mr 23,33:1
Shepherd's Chameleon, The 1960,N 30,41:1
New Tenant, The 1964,My 28,40:2
Victims of Duty 1964,My 28,40:2
Exit the King 1968,Ja 10,48:1
Victims; The; Victims of Duty 1968,Mr 6,34:1
Watson, Dorothy
American Tragedy, An 1931,F 21,15:5
Watson, Douglas
Antony and Cleopatra 1947,N 27,49:2
Leading Lady 1948,O 19,33:1
Richard III 1949,F 9,33:2

Watson, Douglas—Cont

Happiest Years, The 1949,Ap 26,29:8
That Lady 1949,O 20,38:8
That Lady 1949,N 23,18:4
Wisteria Trees, The 1950,Mr 30,39:1
Romeo and Juliet 1951,Ja 23,24:8
Romeo and Juliet 1951,Mr 12,21:2
Romeo and Juliet 1951,Mr 25,II,1:1
Desire Under the Elms 1952,Ja 17,23:4
Desire Under the Elms 1952,Ja 20,II,1:1
Brass Ring, The 1952,Ap 11,19:2
Sunday Breakfast 1952,My 30,12:2
Scarecrow, The 1953,Je 17,31:1
Cyrano de Bergerac 1953,N 13,24:3
Richard III 1953,D 10,65:2
Confidential Clerk, The 1954,F 12,22:1
Portrait of a Lady 1954,D 22,27:6
Miser, The 1955,Mr 18,34:2
Young and Beautiful, The 1955,O 3,23:2
Little Glass Clock, The 1956,Mr 27,40:2
Henry V 1956,Jl 7,11:2
Metamorphosis 1957,F 20,38:1
Pelleas and Melisande 1957,F 20,38:1
Metamorphosis 1957,Mr 17,II,8:5
Pale Horse, Pale Rider 1957,O 30,26:1
Season of Choice 1959,Ap 14,40:1
Antony and Cleopatra 1960,Ag 1,19:1
Merchant of Venice, The 1962,F 3,13:2
Man for All Seasons, A 1962,S 23,II,1:1
King Lear 1963,Je 10,37:1
Comedy of Errors, The 1963,Je 13,28:1
Henry V 1963,Je 14,37:1
Chinese Prime Minister, The 1964,Ja 3,14:1
Much Ado About Nothing 1964,Je 11,26:2
Richard III 1964,Je 12,44:2
Falstaff 1966,Je 20,27:1
Murder in the Cathedral 1966,Je 21,38:1
Julius Caesar 1966,Je 24,29:2
Come Slowly, Eden 1966,D 7,56:1
Persecution and Assassination of Marat As
 Performed by the Inmates of the Asylum of
 Charenton Under the Direction of the Marquis de
 Sade, The 1967,Ja 4,34:1
Prime of Miss Jean Brodie, The 1968,Ja 17,39:1
Pirates of Penzance, The 1968,Ap 26,32:1
Watson, Douglas (Playwright)
Metamorphosis 1957,F 20,38:1
Watson, Douglas (Producer)
Pale Horse, Pale Rider 1957,O 30,26:1
Watson, Edna (Costume Designer)
Don't Bother Me, I Can't Cope 1970,O 8,60:3
Watson, Edward
Mecca 1920,O 5,12:2
Watson, Gaile
Potash and Perlmutter 1935,Ap 6,11:3
Watson, George
Goat Alley 1927,Ap 21,24:3
Watson, Harry
Passing Show of 1921, The 1920,D 30,16:2
Vaudeville (Hippodrome) 1924,F 19,12:1
Tip-Toes 1925,D 29,20:2
Watson, Helen
Variations of 1940 1940,Ja 29,12:1
Watson, Horace (Producer)
Hamlet 1931,Mr 22,VIII,2:1
Watson, Jack
Try It With Alice 1924,Je 24,18:4
Watson, James R
Glory for All 1937,F 9,18:2
Watson, Jane
Variations of 1940 1940,Ja 29,12:1
Watson, Joan
Major Barbara 1951,F 24,10:2
Dark of the Moon 1958,F 27,22:2
Watson, John
Narrow Road to the Deep North 1969,D 2,64:1
Jungle of Cities 1970,Mr 1,75:2
Watson, Joseph K
Potash and Perlmutter 1935,Ap 6,11:3
Watson, Justice
Duchess of Malfi, The 1957,Mr 20,33:1
Watson, Laurence
Barrier, The 1950,N 3,32:2
Shuffle Along 1952,My 9,20:5
Annie Get Your Gun 1958,F 20,29:2
Watson, Lee (Lighting Director)
View From the Bridge, A 1955,S 30,21:1
Memory of Two Mondays, A 1955,S 30,21:1
Diary of Anne Frank, The 1955,O 6,24:2
Harbor Lights 1956,O 5,20:1
Girls of Summer 1956,N 20,45:1
Protective Custody 1956,D 29,8:7
Moon for the Misbegotten, A 1957,My 3,21:2
Cave Dwellers, The 1957,O 21,29:2
Miss Isobel 1957,D 27,22:1
Garden District; Something Unspoken
 1958,Ja 8,23:4
Garden District; Suddenly Last Summer
 1958,Ja 8,23:4
Garden District; Suddenly Last Summer
 1958,Ja 19,II,1:1
Portofino 1958,F 22,8:3
Next President, The 1958,Ap 10,34:3
Comic Strip 1958,My 15,26:2

Golden Six, The 1958,O 27,31:2
Night Circus, The 1958,D 3,44:1
On the Town 1959,Ja 16,36:1
On the Town 1959,Ja 25,II,1:1
Legend of Lizzie, The 1959,F 10,39:1
U S A 1959,O 29,38:1
Lovely Light, A 1960,F 9,27:4
Jackass, The 1960,Mr 24,39:2
Machinal 1960,Ap 8,27:1
Machinal 1960,Ap 17,II,1:1
Port-Royal 1960,Ap 26,41:1
Pretender, The 1960,My 25,42:1
Shoemaker and the Peddler, The 1960,O 15,27:4
Blacks, The 1961,My 5,23:1
Do You Know the Milky Way? 1961,O 17,45:1
Madame Aphrodite 1961,D 30,13:1
Cherry Orchard, The 1962,N 15,46:2
Night Thoreau Spent in Jail, The 1970,N 2,66:1
Watson, Lee (Miscellaneous)
Mask and Gown 1957,S 11,29:1
Importance of Being Oscar, The 1961,Mr 15,45:2
Watson, Lee (Scenic Designer)
Next President, The 1958,Ap 10,34:3
Lovely Light, A 1960,F 9,27:4
Moby Dick 1961,Ap 11,41:2
Watson, Leo
At Home Abroad 1935,S 20,17:4
Watson, Lucile
Respect for Riches, The 1920,My 12,9:1
Unwritten Chapter, The 1920,O 12,18:1
Heartbreak House 1920,N 11,11:1
Heartbreak House 1920,N 21,VI,1:2
White Villa, The 1921,F 15,7:1
White Villa, The 1921,F 20,VI,1:1
March Hares 1921,Ag 12,8:3
Everyday 1921,N 17,15:1
Nest, The 1922,F 2,20:1
Fools Errant 1922,Ag 22,12:3
Dragon, The 1922,D 27,12:1
You and I 1923,F 20,12:1
You and I 1923,F 25,VII,1:1
Far Cry, The 1924,O 1,24:1
Ghosts 1926,Mr 17,28:2
Importance of Being Earnest, The 1926,My 4,30:1
Mozart 1926,N 23,26:2
Off Key 1927,F 9,16:2
Love Is Like That 1927,Ap 19,24:1
Zoo, The 1927,O 9,VIII,1:3
That's the Woman 1930,S 4,27:2
No More Ladies 1934,Ja 24,20:3
Post Road 1934,D 5,28:3
Pride and Prejudice 1935,O 23,19:2
Pride and Prejudice 1935,N 3,X,1:5
Pride and Prejudice 1935,N 6,32:4
Pride and Prejudice 1935,N 10,IX,2:5
Pride and Prejudice 1935,N 17,IX,1:1
Prelude to Exile 1936,N 17,34:6
Prelude to Exile 1936,N 22,XI,3:2
Prelude to Exile 1936,D 1,31:1
Yes, My Darling Daughter 1937,F 10,19:2
Yes, My Darling Daughter 1937,F 28,XI,1:1
Dear Octopus 1939,Ja 12,22:2
Watch on the Rhine 1941,Ap 2,26:2
Watch on the Rhine 1941,Ap 13,IX,1:1
Watch on the Rhine 1941,Ag 24,IX,1:1
Family, The 1943,Mr 31,22:4
Ring Around the Moon 1950,N 24,30:1
Bat, The 1953,Ja 21,28:2
Late Love 1953,O 14,35:2
Watson, MacDonald
Hunky Dory 1921,My 29,VI,1:7
Hunky Dory 1922,S 5,21:2
Watson, MacDonald (Playwright)
Hunky Dory 1921,My 29,VI,1:7
Hunky Dory 1922,S 5,21:2
Watson, Malcolm
King Lear 1947,F 19,32:2
As You Like It 1947,F 21,16:2
Merchant of Venice, The 1947,F 24,16:2
Volpone 1947,F 25,32:2
Hamlet 1947,F 27,27:2
Watson, Margaret
Town Boy 1929,O 5,22:4
Cyrano de Bergerac 1932,D 27,11:2
Cyrano de Bergerac 1936,Ap 28,17:1
Watson, Marriott (Mrs)
Mrs Fischer's War 1931,Ag 9,VIII,1:3
Watson, Martha Emma
Polonaise 1945,O 8,20:2
Sweethearts 1947,Ja 22,31:2
Watson, Milton
Animal Crackers 1928,O 24,26:2
Sons o' Guns 1929,N 27,30:4
Vanities 1931,Ag 11,28:4
Earl Carroll's Vanities 1931,Ag 28,18:7
Strike Me Pink 1933,Mr 6,16:3
Saluta 1934,Ag 29,13:4
Viva O'Brien 1941,O 10,27:2
Count Me In 1942,O 9,24:2
Music in the Air 1951,O 9,32:2
Watson, Minor
Why Men Leave Home 1922,S 13,18:2
That Awful Mrs Eaton! 1924,S 30,27:1

Watson, Minor—Cont

Magnolia Lady, The 1924,N 26,17:2
Two Married Men 1925,Ja 14,19:1
Mismates 1925,Ap 14,27:2
Howdy King 1926,D 14,24:4
Trigger 1927,D 7,32:1
These Modern Women 1928,F 14,26:2
This Thing Called Love 1928,S 18,32:7
It's a Wise Child 1929,Jl 28,VIII,1:6
It's a Wise Child 1929,Ag 7,29:1
It's a Wise Child 1929,Ag 25,VIII,1:1
Friendship 1931,My 10,VIII,2:5
Friendship 1931,S 1,30:2
Friendship 1931,S 13,IX,1:1
Reunion in Vienna 1931,N 17,31:1
Divine Drudge 1933,O 27,22:3
Theodora, the Queen 1934,F 1,15:3
Tapestry in Gray 1935,D 28,10:2
End of Summer 1936,Ja 31,17:1
End of Summer 1936,F 9,X,2:3
End of Summer 1936,F 18,26:4
State of the Union 1945,N 7,21:3
State of the Union 1945,N 15,25:2
State of the Union 1945,N 25,II,1:1
State of the Union 1946,S 8,II,1:1
Watson, Monk
Elsie Janis and Her Gang 1922,Ja 17,13:2
Watson, Moray
Public Eye, The 1963,O 10,51:1
Semi-Detached 1963,O 20,II,1:1
Watson, Morris (Miscellaneous)
1935 1936,My 13,28:2
Injunction Granted! 1936,Jl 25,16:3
Power 1937,F 24,18:5
Watson, Nan Marriott
Lass O' Laughter 1922,My 21,VI,1:6
Watson, Nan Marriott (Playwright)
Lass O' Laughter 1922,My 21,VI,1:6
Lass O' Laughter 1925,Ja 9,13:2
Watson, Peggy
Caribbean Carnival 1947,D 6,12:2
Watson, Ray
Front Page, The 1968,O 20,85:5
Watson, Richard
Mikado, The 1947,D 30,18:2
Gondoliers, The 1948,Ja 27,31:2
Yeomen of the Guard, The 1948,F 3,30:2
Mikado, The 1951,Ja 30,21:2
Trial by Jury 1951,F 6,24:2
Gondoliers, The 1951,F 13,27:2
Iolanthe 1951,F 16,22:1
Pirates of Penzance, The 1951,F 20,21:2
Watson, Robert
Conjur 1938,N 1,27:2
Watson, Rosabel (Composer)
King Lear 1947,F 19,32:2
As You Like It 1947,F 21,16:2
Merchant of Venice, The 1947,F 24,16:2
Volpone 1947,F 25,32:2
Hamlet 1947,F 27,27:2
Watson, Rudolph
Saint Joan 1940,Mr 11,10:6
Pygmalion 1945,D 27,16:1
Antony and Cleopatra 1947,N 27,49:2
Watson, Ruth-Ann
Night in Paris, A 1926,Jl 27,15:4
Watson, Sam
Does a Tiger Wear a Necktie? 1969,F 26,38:1
Watson, Susan
Lend an Ear 1959,S 25,20:5
Bye Bye Birdie 1960,Ap 15,13:4
Ben Franklin in Paris 1964,O 28,52:1
Carousel 1965,Ag 11,39:1
Oklahoma! 1965,D 16,62:1
Where's Charley? 1966,My 26,57:1
Joyful Noise, A 1966,D 16,57:1
Celebration 1969,Ja 23,55:2
Beggar on Horseback 1970,My 15,47:2
Beggar on Horseback 1970,My 24,II,1:1
Watson, Virginia
New Americana 1928,N 30,32:4
Vaudeville (Palace) 1930,Mr 7,21:2
Watson, W J (Playwright)
Take It Away 1936,D 15,30:5
Take It Away 1936,D 22,32:3
Watson, W W
This Is New York 1930,N 29,21:1
Watson, Walter
Inspector Kennedy 1929,D 21,16:3
Watson, Walter (Costume Designer)
Tiny Alice 1969,S 30,42:1
Watson, William J
Cape Cod Follies 1929,S 19,37:2
What a Relief 1935,D 14,10:6
Take It Away 1936,D 15,30:5
Fol-De-Rol 1937,D 11,22:4
Watson Sisters (Fanny and Kitty)
Vaudeville (Palace) 1930,N 17,21:2
Watt, Al F
Savage Rhythm 1932,Ja 1,30:4
Watt, Billie Lou
Little Women 1945,D 24,18:2
Barefoot Boy With Cheek 1947,Ap 4,20:2
E-MC2 1948,Je 16,36:2

Watt, Ethel (Producer)
Riding Hood Revisited 1961,Ja 4,26:1
Willie the Weeper 1961,Ja 4,26:1
Eccentricities of Davy Crockett, The 1961,Ja 4,26:1
Watt, Hannah
Kreutzer Sonata, The 1961,F 16,24:2
Watt, Hannah (Playwright)
Kreutzer Sonata, The 1961,F 16,24:2
Watt, Stan
Point of No Return 1957,Mr 23,17:2
All the King's Men 1959,O 17,27:2
Roman Candle 1960,F 4,34:2
Borak 1960,D 14,51:1
Blue Boy in Black, The 1963,My 1,32:1
Playroom, The 1965,D 6,49:1
Watters, Elizabeth
Little Theatre Tournament; Another Room for
Rent 1929,My 7,28:1
Watters, George Manker (Playwright)
Burlesque 1927,S 2,15:3
Burlesque 1946,D 26,30:3
Burlesque 1947,Ja 5,II,1:1
Watters, Hal
Celebration 1969,Ja 23,55:2
Watton, Edward
Immodest Violet 1920,Ag 25,6:2
Watts, Al
Marriage of Cana, The 1932,F 3,22:4
Hummin' Sam 1933,Ap 10,8:8
Stevedore 1934,Ap 19,33:2
Walk Together Chillun 1936,F 5,15:2
Macbeth 1936,Ap 15,25:4
Watts, Dodo
Middle Watch, The 1929,O 17,27:1
Watts, Ed
H M S Pinafore 1957,My 1,42:6
On the Town 1959,F 14,15:1
Watts, Elizabeth
Italian Straw Hat, The 1957,O 1,37:2
Destry Rides Again 1959,Ap 24,24:1
Watts, Frank
Crime Marches on 1935,O 24,19:1
Watts, George
Jumbo 1935,N 18,20:2
Babes in Arms 1937,Ap 15,18:4
Knickerbocker Holiday 1938,O 20,26:2
Ladies and Gentlemen 1939,O 18,30:2
Watts, Irene
Green Pastures, The 1935,F 27,16:2
Watts, James
Greenwich Village Follies 1921,S 1,18:3
Vaudeville (Winter Garden) 1922,F 14,21:1
Spice of 1922 1922,Jl 7,12:4
Passing Show of 1923, The 1923,Je 15,24:6
Patience 1927,My 24,23:2
Watts, Jeanne
Beaux' Stratagem, The 1970,F 10,50:2
Three Sisters, The 1970,F 12,30:1
Watts, Lyman
Wrecker, The 1928,F 28,18:2
Watts, Lyonel
Dover Road, The 1921,D 24,7:2
Outward Bound 1924,Ja 8,26:1
Shall We Join the Ladies? 1925,Ja 14,19:1
Isabel 1925,Ja 14,19:1
O Nightingale 1925,Ap 16,25:2
Enemy, The 1925,O 21,20:1
Beau-Strings 1926,Ap 27,22:2
Watts, Muriel
Unto Such Glory 1937,My 7,28:2
Watts, Nancy
Macbeth 1962,N 17,16:2
Watts, Peggy
My Girl 1924,N 25,27:2
Watts, Schuyler (Director)
Wind Remains, The 1943,Mr 31,16:6
Watts, Schuyler (Miscellaneous)
Hamlet 1936,O 25,X,1:5
Ondine 1954,F 19,23:1
Watts, Schuyler (Playwright)
Hamlet 1936,N 11,54:2
Watts, Twinkle
Stars on Ice 1942,Jl 3,12:2
Stars on Ice (2d Edition) 1943,Je 25,13:2
Watts, Virginia
Houseboat on the Styx, The 1928,D 26,14:3
Mystery Moon 1930,Je 24,23:4
Watts, W E
Bellamy Trial, The 1928,Ag 20,21:1
Watts, William E (Director)
No for an Answer 1941,Ja 6,10:6
Watts-Weston, Victor
Hamlet 1931,Ap 24,26:4
Waugh, Anne
Bed Time 1958,Ap 11,20:2
Wavitch
Chauve-Souris 1922,Je 6,17:4
Waxler, Steven (Lighting Director)
'Tis Pity She's a Whore 1967,O 21,15:2
Waxman, A P (Producer)
Sadie Thompson 1944,N 17,25:2
Duchess Misbehaves, The 1946,F 14,32:2

Waxman, Bob (Musical Director)
Ben Bagley's Shoestring Revues 1970,O 24,22:1
Waxman, Herschel (Producer)
Moondreamers, The 1969,D 9,68:1
Waxman, Percy (Lyricist)
Bunk of 1926 1926,F 17,12:3
Waxman, Percy (Playwright)
Bunk of 1926 1926,F 17,12:3
Waxman, Philip A (Producer)
Star Spangled Family 1945,Ap 11,18:6
Strange Bedfellows 1948,Ja 15,27:3
Waybe, Rollo (Scenic Designer)
Double Door 1933,S 22,15:5
Wayburn, Ned
Vaudeville (Palace) 1924,F 19,12:1
Vaudeville (Proctor's) 1927,My 17,27:4
Wayburn, Ned (Director)
Ned Wayburn's Gambols 1929,Ja 16,22:3
Smiles 1930,N 19,19:2
Wayburn, Ned (Miscellaneous)
Drake's Drum 1923,D 26,17:7
Wayburn, Ned (Playwright)
Buds of 1927 1927,F 22,22:5
Wayburn, Ned (Producer)
Ned Wayburn's Gambols 1929,Ja 16,22:3
Waycoff, Leon
It Pays to Sin 1933,N 4,18:6
Wayland, Len
Long Day's Journey Into Night 1963,Je 27,25:1
Wayland, Mickey
New Faces of 1962 1962,F 2,25:1
Wayne, Bernie (Composer)
Skits-Oh-Frantics 1967,Ap 3,39:2
Wayne, Bernie (Lyricist)
Skits-Oh-Frantics 1967,Ap 3,39:2
Wayne, Charles
Turpentine 1936,Je 27,21:6
Wayne, Chuck (Composer)
Orpheus Descending 1957,Mr 22,28:1
Wayne, David
Escape This Night 1938,Ap 23,18:1
Yes, My Darling Daughter 1938,Jl 13,19:2
Animal Kingdom, The 1938,Jl 27,14:5
Biography 1938,Ag 3,14:7
Arms and the Man 1938,Ag 10,14:1
Bachelor Born 1938,Ag 17,23:1
Dance Night 1938,O 15,20:5
Scene of the Crime, The 1940,Mr 29,24:1
Merry Widow, The 1943,Ag 5,19:2
Peepshow 1944,F 4,12:2
Park Avenue 1946,N 5,31:2
Finian's Rainbow 1947,Ja 11,23:2
Finian's Rainbow 1947,Ja 26,II,1:1
Mister Roberts 1948,F 19,27:2
Mister Roberts 1948,F 29,II,1:1
Teahouse of the August Moon, The 1953,O 16,32:1
Teahouse of the August Moon, The
1953,O 25,II,1:1
Teahouse of the August Moon, The 1954,S 12,II,1:1
Ponder Heart, The 1956,F 17,14:2
Ponder Heart, The 1956,F 26,II,1:1
Loud Red Patrick, The 1956,O 4,28:1
Loud Red Patrick, The 1956,O 14,II,1:1
Say Darling 1958,Ap 4,17:1
Say Darling 1958,Ap 13,II,1:1
Send Me No Flowers 1960,D 6,54:1
Venus at Large 1962,Ap 13,30:1
Too True to Be Good 1963,Mr 14,8:2
Too True to Be Good 1963,Mr 23,5:6
Too True to Be Good 1963,Ap 9,28:1
After the Fall 1964,Ja 24,18:1
Marco Millions 1964,F 21,33:1
But for Whom Charlie 1964,Mr 13,42:2
Incident at Vichy 1964,D 4,44:1
Incident at Vichy 1964,D 20,II,3:1
Yearling, The 1965,D 11,25:1
Show Boat 1966,Jl 20,48:1
Happy Time, The 1968,Ja 19,32:2
Happy Time, The 1968,Ja 28,II,3:1
Wayne, David (Producer)
Loud Red Patrick, The 1956,O 4,28:1
Wayne, Francis
Hamlet 1936,O 9,30:2
Wayne, Fredd
Texas Li'l Darlin' 1949,N 26,10:5
Not for Children 1951,F 14,35:2
Go Fly a Kite! 1969,O 20,60:1
Wayne, Fredd (Playwright)
Go Fly a Kite! 1969,O 20,60:1
Wayne, Iris
Hold On to Your Hats 1940,S 12,30:3
Wayne, Jeff (Composer)
Two Cities 1969,Mr 1,22:1
Wayne, Jerry
Vaudeville (Palace) 1949,My 20,32:4
Guys and Dolls 1953,Je 7,II,1:3
Wayne, John
What Price Glory 1949,Mr 3,33:2
Wayne, Justina
Henry-Behave 1926,Ag 24,19:4
Reunion in Vienna 1931,N 17,31:1
Ragged Army 1934,F 27,16:5

Wayne, Marjorie
Rose of Stamboul, The 1922,Mr 8,11:2
Wayne, Marshall
Aquashow 1952,Je 25,25:1
Wayne, Mildred
Demi-Virgin, The 1921,O 19,22:1
Milgrim's Progress 1924,D 23,17:1
Lulu Belle 1926,F 10,20:1
Wayne, Naunton
1066 and All That 1935,My 26,XI,2:5
All Wave 1936,N 25,18:3
Wise Tomorrow 1937,O 5,29:2
Wise Tomorrow 1937,O 16,22:5
Arsenic and Old Lace 1943,Ja 1,26:5
Honor and Obey 1947,N 20,40:1
Reluctant Peer, The 1964,Ja 16,30:2
Wayne, Paula
Wonderful Town 1958,Mr 6,32:4
Say Darling 1959,F 26,38:2
Hi, Paisano 1961,O 2,36:2
Best Foot Forward 1963,Ap 3,43:1
Golden Boy 1964,O 21,56:1
Wayne, Peter
Miracle at Verdun 1931,Mr 17,34:6
Wayne, Robert
That Awful Mrs Eaton! 1924,S 30,27:1
Lily Sue 1926,N 17,22:2
19th Hole, The 1927,O 12,30:3
Wayne, Rollo
Artists and Models 1923,Ag 21,12:2
Wayne, Rollo (Scenic Designer)
Crooked Friday, The 1925,O 9,27:3
Offence, The 1925,N 16,25:1
H M S Pinafore 1926,Ap 7,26:3
Ruddigore 1927,My 21,25:2
Murray Hill 1927,S 30,29:1
Great Necker, The 1928,Mr 7,28:2
Gang War 1928,Ag 21,27:2
White Lilacs 1928,S 11,31:2
Common Sin, The 1928,O 16,28:2
Exceeding Small 1928,O 23,32:2
Sign of the Leopard 1928,D 12,34:4
Security 1929,Mr 29,20:1
Jonesy 1929,Ap 10,32:2
Congratulations 1929,My 1,28:4
First Law, The 1929,My 7,28:4
Rope's End 1929,S 20,34:5
Nigger Rich 1929,S 21,16:7
Stripped 1929,O 22,26:1
Young Sinners 1929,N 29,24:4
Death Takes a Holiday 1929,D 27,26:4
Prince of Pilsen, The 1930,Ja 14,24:3
Chocolate Soldier, The 1930,Ja 28,28:1
Topaze 1930,F 13,25:3
Infinite Shoeblack, The 1930,F 18,28:1
Count of Luxembourg, The 1930,F 18,28:2
Serenade, The 1930,Mr 5,26:7
Lady Clara 1930,Ap 18,28:7
Ladies All 1930,Jl 29,25:2
Up Pops the Devil 1930,S 2,19:1
Insult 1930,S 16,30:2
Nine Till Six 1930,S 29,17:2
His Majesty's Car 1930,O 24,30:1
On the Spot 1930,O 30,33:3
Last Enemy, The 1930,O 31,21:1
Man in Possession, The 1930,N 3,19:1
Babes in Toyland 1930,D 22,17:1
Purity 1930,D 26,18:2
Truth Game, The 1930,D 29,19:1
Silent Witness, The 1931,Mr 24,31:5
Melo 1931,Ap 17,26:6
Modern Virgin, A 1931,My 21,33:4
Constant Sinner, The 1931,S 15,30:1
Good Companions, The 1931,O 2,31:1
Marriage for Three 1931,N 12,30:5
If Booth Had Missed 1932,F 5,24:2
Blessed Event 1932,F 13,23:2
Happy Landing 1932,Mr 28,10:5
Boy Friend, The 1932,Je 8,22:3
Best Years 1932,S 8,16:2
Peacock 1932,O 12,27:1
Perfect Marriage, The 1932,N 17,23:2
Autumn Crocus 1932,N 21,20:2
Best Sellers 1933,My 4,20:2
First Episode 1934,S 18,18:1
Spring Freshet 1934,O 5,28:3
Journey by Night, A 1935,Ap 17,26:3
If a Body 1935,Ap 21,II,8:3
If a Body 1935,My 1,25:3
In Heaven and Earth 1936,Mr 27,24:8
Kick Back, The 1936,Je 23,27:3
Trial of Dr Beck, The 1937,Ag 10,22:2
Treasure Island 1938,My 15,II,2:3
Wayne, Sherman (Miscellaneous)
Meet Peter Grant 1961,My 11,41:4
Fourth Avenue North 1961,S 28,50:2
Cantilevered Terrace, The 1962,Ja 18,24:1
Wayne, Sherman (Producer)
Penny Change 1963,O 25,37:1
White Rose and the Red, The 1964,Mr 17,31:1
Wayne, Shirley
Hellzapoppin 1938,S 23,34:2
New Hellzapoppin, The 1939,D 12,36:4

Wayne, William
Sweet Little Devil 1924,Ja 22,15:4
Kitty's Kisses 1926,My 7,12:2
Jimmie's Women 1927,S 27,30:3
Wayne & Warren
Passing Show of 1922, The 1922,S 21,18:2
Wayne and Marlin
Star and Garter 1942,Je 25,26:2
Wayne Sisters
Ice Capades 1960,S 1,30:1
Wazzan Troupe
Judy Garland's New Variety Show 1956,S 27,43:2
Wead, Frank (Playwright)
Ceiling Zero 1935,Ap 2,24:3
Ceiling Zero 1935,Ap 11,26:2
Ceiling Zero 1935,Ap 21,IX,1:1
Weale, Emma De
Little Black Book, The 1932,D 27,11:2
Weamer, Ray
Banjo Eyes 1941,D 26,20:2
Wearing, Michael (Director)
Isabel's a Jezebel 1970,D 27,II,3:1
Weatherford, Charles (Miscellaneous)
Apple, The 1961,D 8,44:1
Weatherford, Earl
Girofle-Girofla 1926,N 24,26:2
Eternal Road, The 1937,Ja 8,14:2
Everywhere I Roam 1938,D 30,10:4
Weatherford, Skip
Mountain Giants, The 1961,Ap 5,32:3
Weatherford, Skip (Lighting Director)
Mountain Giants, The 1961,Ap 5,32:3
Weatherly, Tom (Miscellaneous)
Little Show, The 1929,My 1,28:5
Second Little Show, The 1930,S 3,36:1
Third Little Show, The 1931,Je 2,34:3
Weatherly, Tom (Producer)
Untitled-Revue 1928,N 19,16:2
Undertow 1929,N 10,X,4:8
Claire Adams 1929,N 20,26:3
Second Little Show, The 1930,Ag 17,VIII,2:2
Gay Divorce 1932,N 30,23:4
She Loves Me Not 1933,N 21,22:4
Illustrators' Show, The 1936,Ja 23,25:3
Little Darling 1942,O 28,26:2
Murder Without Crime 1943,Ag 19,24:6
Weathersby, Helen
New Brooms 1924,N 18,23:5
Weathersby, Jennie
Erminie 1921,Ja 4,11:1
Up She Goes 1922,N 7,14:2
Weaver, Alice
Scandals 1924,Jl 1,16:1
George White's Scandals 1925,Je 23,24:2
My Girl Friday! 1929,F 13,20:2
Weaver, Barbara
Out of This World 1950,D 22,17:3
Weaver, Beverly
Meet the People 1940,D 26,22:2
Weaver, Crawford
Song of the Bridge 1942,Ap 7,27:5
Weaver, Dennis
Out West of Eighth 1951,S 21,20:3
Weaver, Doodles
Meet the People 1940,D 26,22:2
Meet the People 1941,Ja 12,IX,1:1
Weaver, E H
They Never Come Back 1920,D 19,I,22:3
Fan, The 1921,O 4,10:1
Weaver, E H (Lyricist)
They Never Come Back 1920,D 19,I,22:3
Weaver, E H (Playwright)
They Never Come Back 1920,D 19,I,22:3
Weaver, Elviry
Vaudeville (Palace) 1929,N 18,22:4
Vaudeville (Palace) 1929,N 25,22:4
Vaudeville (Palace) 1931,Ja 19,25:3
Weaver, Erenay
Noose, The 1926,O 21,23:3
Weaver, Fritz
Way of the World, The 1954,S 30,38:2
Way of the World, The 1954,O 17,II,1:1
Doctor's Dilemma, The 1955,Ja 12,22:1
White Devil, The 1955,Mr 15,32:5
Julius Caesar 1955,Jl 13,20:1
Tempest, The 1955,Ag 2,18:2
Chalk Garden, The 1955,O 27,29:1
Chalk Garden, The 1955,N 13,II,1:1
King John 1956,Je 28,33:5
Taming of the Shrew, The 1956,Ag 6,20:1
Protective Custody 1956,D 29,8:7
Miss Lonelyhearts 1957,O 4,26:2
Hamlet 1958,Je 21,11:1
Family Reunion, The 1958,O 21,39:1
Family Reunion, The 1958,O 26,II,1:1
Power and the Glory, The 1958,D 12,2:7
Twelfth Night 1959,Jl 11,10:2
Great God Brown, The 1959,O 7,48:1
Great God Brown, The 1959,O 18,II,1:1
Peer Gynt 1960,Ja 13,21:1
Peer Gynt 1960,Ja 24,II,1:1
Henry IV 1960,Mr 2,42:1
Henry IV 1960,Mr 13,II,1:1

Henry IV 1960,Ap 19,41:1
Henry IV, Part II 1960,Ap 24,II,1:1
All American 1962,Mr 20,44:1
Lorenzo 1963,F 16,5:2
Around the World in 80 Days 1963,Je 24,22:1
White House, The 1964,My 20,39:1
Baker Street 1965,F 17,36:1
Baker Street 1965,F 28,II,1:1
Sorrow of Frederick, The 1967,Jl 8,14:2
My Fair Lady 1968,Je 14,42:1
Child's Play 1970,F 18,39:1
Child's Play 1970,Mr 1,II,1:4
Weaver, Harriett (Playwright)
Virginia Reel 1947,Ap 15,28:2
Weaver, Jane
Paul Bunyan 1941,My 6,25:1
Weaver, Jeffrie
Family Reunion, The 1947,N 29,9:2
Weaver, John (Miscellaneous)
Deathwatch 1958,O 10,34:2
Weaver, John (Playwright)
Virginia Reel 1947,Ap 15,28:2
Weaver, John V A (Playwright)
Love 'Em and Leave 'Em 1926,F 4,20:4
Love 'Em and Leave 'Em 1926,F 14,VIII,1:1
Weaver, Neal (Playwright)
War Games 1969,Ap 18,37:1
Weaver, Paul
Steel 1939,D 20,30:2
Weaver, Ray
Kiss Me, Kate 1956,My 10,27:2
Weaver, William
Silver Tassie, The 1949,Jl 22,16:5
Weaver, William (Costume Designer)
Frederika 1937,F 5,16:5
Weaver, William (Miscellaneous)
Red Roses for Me 1955,D 29,15:2
Happiest Millionaire, The 1956,N 21,21:3
Cock-A-Doodle Dandy 1958,N 13,39:2
Mighty Man Is He, A 1960,Ja 7,25:2
More Stately Mansions 1967,N 1,40:1
Weaver Brothers, The
Vaudeville (Palace) 1926,Mr 23,24:3
Vaudeville (Palace) 1928,Ap 10,32:4
Vaudeville (Palace) 1929,N 18,22:4
Vaudeville (Palace) 1929,N 25,22:4
Vaudeville (Palace) 1931,Ja 19,25:3
Webb, Alan
Hands Across the Sea 1936,N 25,17:2
Astonished Heart, The 1936,N 25,17:2
Red Peppers 1936,N 25,17:2
Shadow Play 1936,N 28,13:1
We Were Dancing 1936,N 28,13:1
Ways and Means 1936,D 1,31:1
Family Album 1936,D 1,31:1
Still Life 1936,D 1,31:1
George and Margaret 1937,S 23,32:2
Winslow Boy, The 1947,O 30,32:2
Winslow Boy, The 1947,N 9,II,1:1
Nina 1951,D 6,44:3
Deep Blue Sea, The 1952,N 6,38:3
Twelfth Night 1955,Je 7,37:4
Genius and the Goddess, The 1957,D 11,41:1
Heartbreak House 1959,O 19,37:1
Heartbreak House 1959,O 25,II,1:1
Night of the Iguana, The 1961,D 29,10:1
Night of the Iguana, The 1962,Ja 7,II,1:1
Chinese Prime Minister, The 1964,Ja 3,14:1
Chinese Prime Minister, The 1964,Ja 12,II,1:1
Chinese Prime Minister, The 1965,My 21,21:1
Utbu 1966,Ja 5,24:1
We Have Always Lived in the Castle
  1966,O 20,53:1
I Never Sang for My Father 1968,Ja 26,30:1
I Never Sang for My Father 1968,F 4,II,1:1
Webb, Alyce
Ballad for Bimshire 1963,O 16,54:1
Porgy and Bess 1964,My 7,32:1
Kiss Me, Kate 1965,My 13,31:1
Webb, Arthur B
Solid Ivory 1925,N 17,29:3
Webb, Aston (Sir) (Scenic Designer)
Via Crucis 1923,F 11,VII,1:4
Webb, Barbara
Christine 1960,Ap 29,27:1
Porgy and Bess 1961,My 18,40:1
Mardi Gras! 1965,Je 28,33:2
Sherry! 1967,Mr 29,39:1
Here's Where I Belong 1968,Mr 4,32:1
I'm Solomon 1968,Ap 24,51:1
Webb, Byron (Lighting Director)
Haiti 1938,Mr 3,16:1
Androcles and the Lion 1938,D 17,10:5
Webb, Clifton
As You Were 1920,Ja 28,22:3
Jack and Jill 1923,Mr 23,17:2
Meet the Wife 1923,N 27,23:4
Parasites 1924,N 20,21:1
Sunny 1925,S 23,22:1
She's My Baby 1928,Ja 4,22:2
Treasure Girl 1928,N 9,22:1
Vaudeville (Palace) 1929,Ja 21,18:3
Little Show, The 1929,My 1,28:5

Webb, Clifton—Cont
Little Show, The 1929,My 12,IX,1:2
Three's a Crowd 1930,O 5,IX,4:6
Three's a Crowd 1930,O 16,28:3
Three's a Crowd 1930,O 26,VIII,1:1
Flying Colors 1932,S 16,24:2
Flying Colors 1932,O 9,IX,1:1
As Thousands Cheer 1933,S 10,II,5:3
As Thousands Cheer 1933,O 2,22:1
As Thousands Cheer 1933,O 15,IX,1:1
And Stars Remain 1936,S 29,35:2
And Stars Remain 1936,O 4,IX,2:1
And Stars Remain 1936,O 13,32:2
You Never Know 1938,Mr 4,16:3
You Never Know 1938,S 22,26:3
Importance of Being Earnest, The 1939,Ja 13,16:2
Blithe Spirit 1941,N 6,26:2
Blithe Spirit 1941,N 16,IX,1:1
Actors Fund Fete 1942,F 23,24:5
Blithe Spirit 1943,S 12,II,1:1
Present Laughter 1946,O 30,31:2
Webb, Danny (Staff Sgt)
Swing Sister Wac Swing 1944,Ja 4,20:4
Webb, Danny (Staff Sgt) (Director)
Swing Sister Wac Swing 1944,Ja 4,20:4
Webb, Denis (Playwright)
Swing Sister Wac Swing 1944,Ja 4,20:4
Miss Isobel 1957,D 27,22:1
Webb, Douglass
Ladies Night in a Turkish Bath 1961,Mr 22,38:1
Webb, Elmon (Lighting Director)
Her Master's Voice 1964,D 28,33:2
Kicking the Castle Down 1967,Ja 19,43:1
Whistle in the Dark, A 1968,F 17,32:2
Webb, Elmon (Scenic Designer)
Her Master's Voice 1964,D 28,33:2
Laughwind 1966,Mr 3,27:1
Kicking the Castle Down 1967,Ja 19,43:1
Whistle in the Dark, A 1968,F 17,32:2
Country People 1970,Ja 19,35:1
Webb, Eugenie
Cymbeline 1923,O 3,12:1
Yellow Jacket, The 1928,N 8,27:3
Webb, Franklyn
Cyrano de Bergerac 1936,Ap 28,17:1
Daughters of Atreus 1936,O 15,33:1
Webb, Geoffrey
Trigon, The 1965,O 11,62:2
Webb, George W (Producer)
Nature of the Crime 1970,Mr 24,41:1
Webb, Harry
Vaudeville (Palace) 1928,D 24,10:8
Webb, Hazel
Silks and Satins 1920,Jl 16,19:1
Webb, Janet
Gondoliers, The 1940,O 1,29:2
Webb, Jethro
Trial of Dr Beck, The 1937,Ag 10,22:2
Webb, Joe
Honor Code, The 1931,My 19,25:3
Webb, Josephine
Great Music 1924,O 6,24:1
Webb, Kenneth (Composer)
Steppe Around 1922,Mr 29,17:4
Gay Divorce 1932,N 30,23:4
Webb, Kenneth (Director)
Room of Dreams 1930,N 6,22:4
Laugh It Off 1934,Ap 5,24:2
Webb, Kenneth (Miscellaneous)
Gay Divorce 1960,Ap 4,37:1
Webb, Kenneth (Playwright)
One of the Family 1925,D 23,22:3
Houseboat on the Styx, The 1928,D 26,14:3
Who Cares 1930,Jl 9,27:1
Zombie 1932,F 11,17:2
Lambs Gambol 1932,Ap 25,18:2
Gay Divorce 1932,N 13,IX,1:7
Illustrators' Show, The 1936,Ja 23,25:3
Gay Divorce 1937,Jl 20,19:4
Webb, Lizbeth
Bless the Bride 1947,My 5,31:2
Guys and Dolls 1953,My 29,17:5
Guys and Dolls 1953,Je 7,II,1:3
Webb, M Tello
Drums of Jeopardy, The 1922,My 30,8:4
Whispering Wires 1922,Ag 8,26:2
Badges 1924,D 4,25:1
Baby Mine 1927,Je 10,21:2
Airways, Inc 1929,F 21,30:5
Webb, Margaret
Latent Heterosexual, The 1968,Mr 22,52:1
Webb, Mary (Original Author)
Precious Bane 1932,Ap 24,VIII,1:1
Webb, Mildred
Show Is On, The 1937,S 20,18:4
Webb, Richard
Three Little Business Men, The 1923,S 4,12:1
Swing It 1937,Jl 23,17:2
Webb, Robb
Galileo 1968,D 1,88:4
Webb, Roy (Composer)
Steppe Around 1922,Mr 29,17:4
Old King's 1924,Mr 12,19:3

Webb, Roy (Composer)—Cont
Half Moon Inn 1925,Mr 10,14:1

Webb, Roy (Lyricist)
Steppe Around 1922,Mr 29,17:4

Webb, Ruth
Early to Bed 1943,Je 18,16:2
Marinka 1945,Jl 19,19:2
Kiss Me, Kate 1954,Mr 27,13:2

Webb, Sherrill (Playwright)
Honest Liars 1926,Jl 20,17:2

Webb, Teddy
Make It Snappy 1922,Ap 14,20:2
Blossom Time 1922,O 24,18:2
Blossom Time 1923,My 22,14:4
Blossom Time 1923,Je 1,22:2

Webb, Theodore
Prince Charlie and Flora 1931,Ag 29,16:5

Webb, William
Whispering Wires 1922,Ag 8,26:2

Webber, Bob
Royal Family, The 1951,Ja 11,28:2

Webber, Florence
Poor Little Ritz Girl 1920,Jl 29,7:1
Lollipop 1924,Ja 22,15:3

Webber, Frederick
Mister Pitt 1924,Ja 23,15:3

Webber, Gene
Barefoot 1925,O 20,29:2
Monkey Talks, The 1925,D 29,20:1
What Every Woman Knows 1926,Ap 14,20:2
Near to the Stars 1932,F 23,23:2
Boy Friend, The 1932,Je 8,22:3
Four O'Clock 1933,F 14,19:6
Diff'rent 1937,N 21,II,10:7
Diff'rent 1938,Ja 26,26:4
Pygmalion 1938,Ja 27,16:3
Captain Jinks of the Horse Marines 1938,Ja 28,16:2
No More Peace 1938,Ja 29,13:2
Coriolanus 1938,F 2,14:5

Webber, James Plaisted (Playwright)
Falstaff 1928,D 26,14:2

Webber, John F
Return of Peter Grimm, The 1921,S 22,12:2

Webber, Robert
Two Blind Mice 1949,Mr 3,32:2
No Time for Sergeants 1955,O 21,32:2
Orpheus Descending 1957,Mr 22,28:1
Fair Game 1957,N 4,39:1
Loss of Roses, A 1959,N 30,27:1
Period of Adjustment 1960,N 11,34:1
Period of Adjustment 1960,N 20,II,1:1

Weber, Bernard M (Producer)
Teaspoon Every Four Hours, A 1969,Je 16,57:1

Weber, Carl (Director)
Hofmeister, Der 1963,Ag 10,9:1
Henry IV 1968,F 7,40:1
Cyrano de Bergerac 1968,Ap 26,30:1
Miser, The 1969,My 9,35:1

Weber, Florence (Costume Designer)
Sketch Book 1929,Jl 2,33:5

Weber, Franz
Love in the Country 1930,S 28,VIII,4:4
Blaue Boll, Der 1931,Ja 25,VIII,4:1
Heilige Crispin, Der 1933,Je 25,IX,1:2

Weber, Fredricka
Those That Play the Clowns 1966,N 25,48:1
Last Sweet Days of Isaac, The 1970,Ja 27,49:1
Last Sweet Days of Isaac, The 1970,F 8,II,1:6
Last Sweet Days of Isaac, The 1970,F 15,II,1:1

Weber, Herbert
Ballyhoo 1930,D 23,24:1
When in Rome 1934,F 28,22:6
Bitter Sweet 1934,My 8,28:4

Weber, Joe
Friar's Club Frolic 1922,Je 5,16:1
Vaudeville (Central) 1922,S 19,14:1

Weber, Joe (Producer)
Caste 1927,D 24,8:1

Weber, Johnny
High Flyers 1927,Je 26,VIII,1:1

Weber, Joseph H
Room 349 1930,Ap 23,24:5

Weber, Karl
Land of Fame 1943,S 22,31:5
Lady Behave 1943,N 17,30:1
Lamp at Midnight 1947,D 22,29:2
Respectful Prostitute, The 1948,F 10,27:2
Respectful Prostitute, The 1948,F 15,II,1:1
Sun and I, The 1949,Mr 21,18:4
Best Man, The 1960,Ap 1,39:1

Weber, L Lawrence (Miscellaneous)
Love Call, The 1927,O 25,33:1

Weber, L Lawrence (Producer)
Nobody's Money 1921,My 22,VI,1:6

Weber, Lawrence
Man Who Killed Lincoln, The 1940,Ja 18,26:4
Steps Leading Up 1941,Ap 19,20:6
Snookie 1941,Je 4,26:2
My Romance 1948,O 20,38:5
Hazel Flagg 1953,F 12,22:2
She Shall Have Music 1959,Ja 23,18:4
Guitar 1959,N 11,42:5

Weber, Lawrence (Producer)
Sea Woman, The 1925,Ag 25,12:2

Dagger, The 1925,S 10,28:1
Cowboy Crazy 1926,Ag 1,VII,4:1
Bye Bye Bonnie 1927,Ja 14,15:3
Lady Alone 1927,Ja 21,12:5
Crown Prince, The 1927,Mr 24,23:2
Romancing 'Round 1927,O 4,32:4
Nice Women 1929,Je 11,27:4
Her Friend the King 1929,O 8,34:5
Diana 1929,D 10,37:1
Family Affairs 1929,D 11,34:6
Ritzy 1930,F 11,30:4
She Lived Next to the Firehouse 1931,F 11,23:1
Napi 1931,Mr 12,22:5
Man Who Reclaimed His Head 1932,S 9,17:3
Strip Girl 1935,O 21,22:6
Angels of Anadarko 1962,O 11,47:1

Weber, Rex
Vaudeville (Palace) 1928,Jl 24,13:4
Americana 1932,S 25,IX,1:6
Americana 1932,O 6,19:3
Threepenny Opera, The 1933,Ap 14,22:4
Hold Your Horses 1933,S 26,26:4
Old Bucks and New Wings 1962,N 6,39:4

Weber, Richard
Pierrot's Journey 1964,Ag 5,23:1
Button, Button 1970,O 20,41:1

Weber, Shirley
Icetime 1946,Je 21,20:5

Weber, William
Susan and God 1943,D 14,30:2
Dream With Music 1944,My 19,15:2
Hamlet 1945,D 14,25:2

Weber and Fields
Vaudeville (Central) 1922,S 24,VI,1:1
Vaudeville (Palace) 1925,Ap 21,18:1
Lambs Gambol 1925,Ap 27,15:1
Vaudeville (Palace) 1925,Je 7,VIII,1:1
Variety Anthology 1932,Mr 21,19:4

Webley, John
Pirates of Penzance, The 1968,N 7,54:1

Webster, Adrian
Twelfth Night 1970,Ja 1,18:1
Hamlet 1970,D 28,40:1

Webster, Al
Murder at the Vanities 1933,S 13,22:4
On Borrowed Time 1938,F 4,16:4

Webster, Al (Director)
Mum's the Word 1940,D 6,28:5

Webster, Albert
Star of Bengal 1929,S 26,27:2

Webster, Alfred
Road to Rome, The 1927,F 1,24:2
Grey Fox, The 1928,O 23,32:3
Incubator 1932,N 2,23:3
20th Century 1932,D 30,15:1
John Brown 1934,Ja 23,22:3
Kill That Story 1934,Ag 30,22:2
Creeping Fire 1935,Ja 17,22:3

Webster, Ben
Night Must Fall 1936,S 29,34:1
Young Mr Disraeli 1937,N 10,30:5
Romeo and Juliet 1940,My 10,27:1

Webster, Ben (Costume Designer)
Merchants of Glory 1925,D 15,28:3

Webster, Ben (Scenic Designer)
Merchants of Glory 1925,D 15,28:3

Webster, Bruce
Quadrille 1954,N 4,39:2
Song Out of Sorrow 1955,N 1,27:3

Webster, Byron
Connelly vs Connelly 1961,F 18,11:3
Feast of Panthers 1961,Mr 21,32:1
Ticket-of-Leave Man, The 1961,D 23,15:1
My Fair Lady 1964,My 21,43:2
Ben Franklin in Paris 1964,O 28,52:1
On a Clear Day You Can See Forever 1965,O 18,44:1
Sherry! 1967,Mr 29,39:1
My Fair Lady 1968,Je 14,42:1
Murderous Angels 1970,F 8,70:1

Webster, Charles
George Washington 1920,Mr 2,9:1
Cyrano de Bergerac 1920,Mr 20,14:3
Man of the People, A 1920,S 8,9:2
Trial of Joan of Arc, The 1921,Mr 28,8:2
Candida 1922,Mr 23,11:1
Roger Bloomer 1923,Mr 2,18:3
Nobody's Business 1923,O 23,17:1
Critic, The 1925,My 9,12:4
Juno and the Paycock 1926,Mr 16,22:1

Webster, Charles (Playwright)
Man Who Died Twice, The 1925,D 14,19:1

Webster, Cleveland (Lighting Director)
Fashion 1937,Mr 21,II,7:8

Webster, E S
It's Only Natural 1922,Ap 21,13:2

Webster, Elizabeth
Ship, The 1929,N 21,24:7
Round Table, The 1930,F 28,20:5

Webster, Frank
Merry Widow, The 1921,S 6,13:1

Webster, Gladys
Civilian Clothes 1923,Jl 26,13:2

Webster, H McRae (Director)
Air-Minded 1932,F 11,17:3
Angels Don't Kiss 1932,Ap 6,22:5

Webster, Harold
Prince and the Pauper, The 1920,N 2,15:1
Twelfth Night 1921,N 1,17:1
Merchant of Venice, The 1921,N 22,17:1
School for Scandal 1923,Mr 13,19:2
Untitled-Revue 1923,My 12,15:4
Floriani's Wife 1923,O 1,10:1
Royal Fandango, A 1923,N 13,25:1
Antony and Cleopatra 1924,F 20,22:1
Second Mrs Tanqueray, The 1924,O 28,27:1
Scotch Mist 1926,S 21,32:3
Come-On Man, The 1929,Ap 23,26:2
Diana 1929,D 10,37:1
Josef Suss 1930,Ja 21,28:5
Philip Goes Forth 1931,Ja 13,35:4
Mad Hopes, The 1932,D 2,26:3
Shady Lady 1933,Jl 6,26:3
Come of Age 1934,Ja 13,16:6
Witness for the Prosecution 1954,D 17,35:2

Webster, Harry R
Lady Billy 1920,D 15,18:2

Webster, Hugh
Taming of the Shrew, The 1962,Je 21,25:1
Tempest, The 1962,Je 22,14:1
Cyrano de Bergerac 1962,Ag 1,21:1
Moby Dick 1962,N 29,45:1
Troilus and Cressida 1963,Je 19,40:2
Cyrano de Bergerac 1963,Je 20,30:1
Comedy of Errors, The 1963,Je 21,35:3
Timon of Athens 1963,Jl 31,19:2
Richard II 1964,Je 17,47:1
Bourgeois Gentilhomme, Le 1964,Je 18,28:2
King Lear 1964,Je 19,36:1
Henry IV, Part I 1965,Je 30,42:1
Julius Caesar 1965,Jl 2,18:1
Cherry Orchard, The 1965,Ag 2,17:2

Webster, Jean B (Miscellaneous)
My Kinsman, Major Molineux 1964,N 2,62:2
Benito Cereno 1964,N 2,62:2

Webster, Joan
School for Brides 1944,Ag 2,19:4
From Morn Till Midnight 1948,D 7,41:6

Webster, John
Sophie 1920,Mr 3,12:2
Foot-Loose 1920,My 11,12:1
In the Night Watch 1921,Ja 31,10:1
Beware of Dogs 1921,O 4,10:1
Merton of the Movies 1922,N 14,16:2
Poor Nut, The 1925,Ap 28,18:1

Webster, John (Playwright)
Duchess of Malfi, The 1946,O 16,35:2
White Devil, The 1955,Mr 15,32:5
Duchess of Malfi, The 1957,Mr 20,33:1
Duchess of Malfi, The 1962,Mr 5,27:1
White Devil, The 1965,D 7,56:1
White Devil, The 1969,N 14,38:2

Webster, June
Simon Called Peter 1924,N 11,20:2
Back Here 1928,N 27,36:3
Saturday Night 1933,Mr 1,13:2
Call Me Ziggy 1937,F 13,9:6

Webster, Lucille
Merton of the Movies 1922,N 14,16:2
Lady Killer, The 1924,Mr 13,14:2
Butter and Egg Man 1925,S 24,28:1
Shannons of Broadway, The 1927,S 27,30:4
Shannons of Broadway, The 1927,O 9,VIII,1:1

Webster, M Coates
Bloodstream 1932,Mr 31,25:1

Webster, Margaret
Sea Gull, The 1938,Mr 29,19:2
Sea Gull, The 1938,Ap 3,XI,1:1
Family Portrait 1939,Mr 9,18:4
Trojan Women, The 1941,Ap 9,32:5
Othello 1942,Ag 16,VIII,1:7
Othello 1943,O 20,18:1
Othello 1943,O 24,II,1:1
Henry VIII 1946,N 7,42:2
John Gabriel Borkman 1946,N 13,33:2
Pound on Demand 1946,D 20,29:3
Alice in Wonderland 1947,Ap 7,19:2
High Ground, The 1951,F 21,31:2
Brontes, The 1963,D 21,17:2

Webster, Margaret (Director)
Richard II 1937,F 6,14:2
Richard II 1937,F 14,X,1:1
Richard II 1937,S 16,28:2
Richard II 1937,S 26,XI,1:1
Young Mr Disraeli 1937,N 10,30:5
Hamlet 1938,O 13,28:1
Hamlet 1938,O 30,IX,1:1
Henry IV, Part I 1939,Ja 31,17:2
Henry IV 1939,F 5,IX,1:1
Family Portrait 1939,Mr 9,18:4
As You Like It 1939,My 9,28:4
As You Like It; Midsummer Night's Dream, A; Comedy of Errors, The; Taming of the Shrew, The 1939,My 9,28:4
Viceroy Sarah 1939,Ag 15,14:4
Hamlet 1939,D 5,35:2

Webster, Margaret (Director)—Cont

Hamlet 1939,D 10,X,3:1
Richard II 1940,Ap 2,31:2
Twelfth Night 1940,O 27,IX,1:5
Twelfth Night 1940,N 20,26:3
Twelfth Night 1940,N 24,IX,1:1
Battle of Angels 1941,Ja 5,IX,1:7
Trojan Women, The 1941,Ap 9,32:5
Macbeth 1941,N 12,30:2
Macbeth 1941,N 23,IX,1:1
Othello 1942,Ag 16,VIII,1:7
Flare Path 1942,D 24,20:2
Counterattack 1943,F 4,27:2
Counterattack 1943,F 14,II,1:1
Othello 1943,O 20,18:1
Othello 1943,O 24,II,1:1
Cherry Orchard, The 1944,Ja 26,22:1
Cherry Orchard, The 1944,F 6,II,1:1
Tempest, The 1945,F 4,II,1:1
Therese 1945,O 10,24:2
Therese 1945,O 28,II,1:1
Henry VIII 1946,N 7,42:2
What Every Woman Knows 1946,N 9,13:2
Androcles and the Lion 1946,D 20,29:2
Ghosts 1948,F 17,31:2
Devil's Disciple, The 1950,Ja 26,23:2
Devil's Disciple, The 1950,F 5,II,1:1
Richard II 1951,Ja 25,21:2
Taming of the Shrew, The 1951,Ap 26,35:2
Saint Joan 1951,O 5,23:2
Saint Joan 1951,O 14,II,1:1
Evening With Will Shakespeare, An 1952,D 7,86:5
Strong Are Lonely, The 1953,S 30,38:3
Richard III 1953,D 10,65:2
Measure for Measure 1957,N 20,42:8
Back to Methuselah 1958,Mr 27,41:5
Back to Methuselah 1958,Ap 6,II,1:1
Aspern Papers, The 1962,F 8,26:1
Aspern Papers, The 1962,F 18,II,1:1
Antony and Cleopatra 1963,S 14,12:4
Carving a Statue 1968,My 1,43:1

Webster, Margaret (Miscellaneous)
Hedda Gabler 1948,F 25,27:2

Webster, Margaret (Playwright)
Girl Unknown 1936,S 17,18:2
Girl Unknown 1936,O 4,IX,3:7
Tempest, The 1945,Ja 26,17:2
Three to Make Ready 1946,Mr 8,16:2
Royal Highness 1949,Ap 14,29:3
Brontes, The 1963,D 21,17:2

Webster, Margaret (Producer)
Lovers' Meeting 1937,Je 3,23:1
Cherry Orchard, The 1944,Ja 26,22:1
Othello 1945,My 23,25:4
Tempest, The 1945,N 13,24:6

Webster, Mary
Dear Charles 1954,S 16,37:2

Webster, Paul (Composer)
My L A 1951,D 9,87:1

Webster, Paul (Lyricist)
Alive and Kicking 1950,Ja 18,25:5
Catch a Star! 1955,S 7,35:2
Christine 1960,Ap 29,27:1

Webster, Sandy
Seagull, The 1968,Jl 25,27:2

Webster, Tom (Miscellaneous)
Streamline 1934,S 29,13:1
Streamline 1934,O 21,IX,1:3

Webster, Tony (Playwright)
Greatest Man Alive!, The 1957,My 9,37:2

Webster, William
Timon of Athens 1963,Jl 31,19:2

Wechsberg, Peter
Sganarelle 1970,Ja 13,41:1

Wechsler, Bard
Bronx Express, 1968 1968,N 16,43:3

Wechsler, Gil (Choreographer)
Viet Rock 1966,N 11,38:1

Wechsler, Gil (Lighting Director)
Staircase 1968,Ja 11,41:2

Weck, Peter
Rendezvous in Wien 1956,S 5,23:1
Konzert, Das 1968,Mr 25,52:1
Songs From Milk Wood 1970,Ja 13,41:1

Weddle, Vernon
Five Evenings 1963,My 10,37:3
King Lear 1963,N 23,22:1

Wedekind, Frank (Playwright)
Loves of Lulu, The 1925,My 12,26:1
Franziska 1927,Ja 30,VII,4:3
Liebestrank 1927,Ja 30,VII,4:3
Lulu 1927,Ja 30,VII,4:3
Earth Spirit 1950,Je 7,33:4
Spring's Awakening 1955,O 10,30:2
Lulu 1958,S 30,24:1
Awakening of Spring, The 1964,My 13,50:1
Lulu; Earth Spirit 1970,Mr 28,32:1

Wedell, Ellen Jaine
Tartuffe 1957,O 9,39:1

Wedge, Maura K
Happiest Girl in the World, The 1961,Ap 4,42:1

Wedgeworth, Ann
Crucible, The 1958,Mr 12,36:1
Crucible, The 1958,Je 1,II,1:1

Chaparral 1958,S 10,38:2
Make a Million 1958,O 24,39:2
Glory in the Flower 1959,D 9,57:5
Days and Nights of Beebee Fenstermaker, The 1962,S 18,33:1
Blues for Mister Charlie 1964,Ap 24,24:1
Last Analysis, The 1964,O 2,30:1
Ludlow Fair 1966,Mr 23,42:1
Leader, The 1969,Ap 22,40:2
Honest-to-God Schnozzola, The 1969,Ap 22,40:2

Wee, De Sangpur
Brouhaha 1960,Ap 27,31:2

Wee, O E (Playwright)
Dangerous Corner 1933,Jl 18,20:4

Wee, O E (Producer)
Dracula 1931,Ap 14,33:3
Great Lover, The 1932,O 12,27:3
Whistling in the Dark 1932,N 4,25:2
Good Fairy, The 1932,N 18,22:3
Show-Off, The 1932,D 13,25:4
As Husbands Go 1933,Ja 20,20:5
Monster, The 1933,F 11,11:5
Riddle Me This! 1933,Mr 15,21:3
Best People, The 1933,Mr 16,21:5
It's a Wise Child 1933,My 17,15:2
John Ferguson 1933,Jl 11,15:7
Perfumed Lady, The 1934,Mr 13,27:2
Every Thursday 1934,My 11,25:5
Nowhere Bound 1935,Ja 23,20:2
Devil of Pei-Ling 1936,F 21,20:4
Something for Nothing 1937,D 10,33:5

Weed, Garner
Jealous Moon, The 1928,N 21,32:2

Weed, Mary
Herne's Egg, The 1960,S 20,48:1
Storm, The 1962,Mr 31,17:2

Weede, Robert
Most Happy Fella, The 1956,My 4,20:1
Most Happy Fella, The 1956,My 13,II,1:1
Milk and Honey 1961,O 11,52:1
Cry for Us All 1970,Ap 9,48:2

Weede, Stanley
Skin of Our Teeth, The 1942,N 19,29:5

Weeden, Bill (Miscellaneous)
I'm Solomon 1968,Ap 24,51:1

Week, Ahne
Tobias and the Angel 1937,Ap 29,16:5

Weekes, A Hathaway
Variations of 1940 1940,Ja 29,12:1

Weeks, Ada Mae
Jim Jam Jems 1920,O 5,13:2
O'Brien Girl, The 1921,O 4,10:2

Weeks, Al (Playwright)
Her Family Tree 1920,D 28,9:2

Weeks, Alan
Body Beautiful, The 1958,Ja 24,15:2
Funny Girl 1964,Mr 27,15:1
Hallelujah, Baby! 1967,My 7,II,1:1
George M! 1968,Ap 11,48:1
George M! 1968,Ap 21,II,1:5
Take One Step 1968,Jl 5,17:1
Fig Leaves Are Falling, The 1969,Ja 3,19:1
Billy 1969,Mr 24,56:1
Baby With a Knife 1969,My 15,41:2
Bill Noname 1970,Mr 3,37:1
Don't Bother Me, I Can't Cope 1970,O 8,60:3

Weeks, Barbara
Seventh Heart, The 1927,My 3,24:4
Lombardi, Ltd 1927,Je 7,27:3
Absent Father 1932,O 18,23:5
Satellite 1935,N 21,27:5
Double Dummy 1936,N 12,30:1

Weeks, Bobbe
Ringside 1928,Ag 30,13:2

Weeks, John (Miscellaneous)
Me and Juliet 1970,My 15,42:1

Weeks, Larry
This Is the Army 1942,Jl 5,28:2

Weeks, Madison
Leap, The 1924,My 23,16:5

Weeks, Marion
Student Prince, The 1931,Ja 30,18:1
Strange Bedfellows 1948,Ja 15,27:3

Weeks, Mildred
Fatal Lady, The 1936,Mr 19,23:7

Weeks, Walter Scott
Tragedy of the Ages, The 1933,Ap 7,22:7
Body Beautiful, The 1935,N 1,24:3
Woman of Destiny, A 1936,Mr 3,25:2
Kick Back, The 1936,Je 23,27:3
Howdy Stranger 1937,Ja 15,17:5

Weems, John T (Producer)
Clandestine on the Morning Line 1961,O 31,28:1
Thistle in My Bed 1963,N 20,48:1
Caretaker, The 1964,Ja 31,16:1

Weenolsen, Robert (Playwright)
Honest Liars 1926,Jl 20,17:2

Weenolsen, Robert (Producer)
Lend Me Your Ears! 1936,O 6,28:5

Weerth, Ernest (Costume Designer)
King Lear 1925,O 12,18:1

Weerth, Ernest (Scenic Designer)
King Lear 1925,O 12,18:1

Weese, Edna
Myself and I 1929,Ag 31,13:6

Weese, Edna (Musical Director)
Myself and I 1929,Ag 31,13:6

Wegener, Paul
Liebestrank 1927,Ja 30,VII,4:3

Weglyn, Michi (Miscellaneous)
Collector's Item 1952,F 9,11:2

Wegman, Dorothy
No Foolin' 1926,Je 25,25:1
Rio Rita 1927,F 3,18:3

Wegman, Myron E
Hero of Santa Maria, The 1926,My 1,10:1

Wegner, Wally
Threepenny Opera, The 1955,S 21,38:1

Wehn, Josephine
Letter of the Law, The; Robe Rouge, La 1920,F 24,11:1
Chains of Dew 1922,Ap 28,20:2
We Americans 1926,O 13,20:4
Four Walls 1927,S 20,33:1
Maya 1928,F 22,19:1
Congai 1928,N 28,24:3
If Love Were All 1931,N 14,14:5

Wehrle, Helen
George White's Scandals 1925,Je 23,24:2
Nic-Nax of 1926 1926,Ag 5,19:1
Gay Paree 1926,N 10,24:2
Wann und Wo 1927,D 18,IX,1:8

Weichert, Richard (Director)
Brest-Litovsk 1930,N 30,IX,2:1

Weichman, Harry
Princess Flavia 1925,N 3,34:3

Weidenbacher, William (Miscellaneous)
Carmilla 1970,D 1,61:2

Weidenbacher, William (Scenic Designer)
Gertrude 1970,N 13,29:1

Weidenfeld, Jay
Night Watch In Syria 1943,Ja 5,15:5

Weidhaas, Oscar (Costume Designer)
Horse Play 1937,Ag 28,8:3

Weidhaas, Ralph
Woman of Bronze, The 1920,S 8,9:2
Master of the Inn, The 1925,D 23,22:2
Ten Nights in a Barroom 1928,Mr 28,31:2

Weidhaas, Ted (Costume Designer)
Life Begins at 8:40 1934,S 2,IX,1:1

Weidhaas, Ted (Scenic Designer)
Thumbs Up! 1934,D 28,24:1

Weidhaas, Wynn (Costume Designer)
Life Begins at 8:40 1934,S 2,IX,1:1

Weidinger, Helen
Jazz a La Carte 1922,Je 3,8:3

Weidler, Virginia
Rich Full Life, The 1945,N 10,9:2

Weidman, Charles
Heldenleben, Ein 1929,Ap 27,16:4
Neighborhood Playhouse Program 1930,F 21,23:1
Candide 1933,My 16,15:6
School for Husbands, The 1933,O 17,26:5
Dream of Sganarelle, The 1933,O 17,26:5
School for Husbands, The 1933,O 17,26:5
School for Husbands, The 1933,D 3,IX,6:5

Weidman, Charles (Choreographer)
Lysistrata 1930,Ap 29,30:5
Lysistrata 1930,Je 6,20:1
Americana 1932,O 6,19:3
Americana 1932,O 16,IX,11:2
Candide 1933,My 16,15:6
As Thousands Cheer 1933,O 2,22:1
School for Husbands, The 1933,O 17,26:5
Dream of Sganarelle, The 1933,O 17,26:5
School for Husbands, The 1933,D 3,IX,6:5
Good Girl, The 1934,Je 26,22:5
I'd Rather Be Right 1937,O 17,XI,2:1
I'd Rather Be Right 1937,N 3,28:2
New Faces of 1943 1942,D 23,22:2
Jackpot 1944,Ja 14,15:2
New Moon, The 1944,My 18,16:2
Sing Out, Sweet Land! 1944,D 28,24:2
Barrier, The 1950,N 3,32:2
Littlest Revue, The 1956,My 23,37:2
Portofino 1958,F 22,8:3

Weidman, Charles Dancers
Americana 1932,O 6,19:3
Hold Your Horses 1933,Ag 31,20:4
As Thousands Cheer 1933,S 10,II,5:3
Life Begins at 8:40 1934,Ag 12,IX,1:1
Life Begins at 8:40 1934,S 2,IX,1:1

Weidman, Jean
Dole Brothers 1932,Mr 26,17:7

Weidman, Jerome (Original Author)
I Can Get It for You Wholesale 1962,Mr 23,29:1

Weidman, Jerome (Playwright)
Fiorello! 1959,N 24,45:3
Fiorello! 1959,N 29,II,1:1
Tenderloin 1960,O 18,47:2
I Can Get It for You Wholesale 1962,Mr 23,29:1
Fiorello! 1962,Je 14,24:1
Pousse-Cafe 1966,Mr 19,19:2
Mother Lover, The 1969,F 3,28:1

Weidner, Paul
  Magistrate, The 1959,My 14,30:6
Weidner, Paul (Director)
  Waltz Invention, The 1969,Ja 12,II,20:4
  Take Me to Bed 1969,Je 14,24:1
  Time for Bed 1969,Je 14,24:1
Weigel, Helene
  Frau Flinz 1962,Jl 8,II,1:1
Weigel, Helene (Director)
  Frau Flinz 1962,Jl 8,II,1:1
Weigel, Jean
  Country People 1970,Ja 19,35:1
Weigel, Jean (Miscellaneous)
  Whistle in the Dark, A 1968,F 17,32:2
Weigert, Hans (Miscellaneous)
  No Exit 1956,Ag 15,23:1
  Don Carlos 1962,F 28,27:5
  Storm, The 1962,Mr 31,17:2
Weigert, Hans (Playwright)
  From Vienna 1939,Je 21,26:2
Weigert, Hans (Producer)
  Mrs Patterson 1957,F 6,20:2
  Obbligato 1958,F 19,22:2
Weigert, Hans (Translator)
  Ronde, La 1960,My 10,44:2
Weigert, Rene (Miscellaneous)
  Ziegfeld Follies 1957,Mr 2,19:2
  Oklahoma! 1963,F 28,8:2
Weight, Michael (Scenic Designer)
  Winslow Boy, The 1947,O 30,32:2
  Separate Tables 1956,O 26,33:1
Weil, Beulah
  Texas Town 1941,Ap 30,22:3
  Out of My House 1942,Ja 8,28:6
Weil, Duke
  Caution: A Love Story 1969,Ap 4,45:1
Weil, Gilbert
  Nautical but Nice 1931,Ap 19,31:6
Weil, Kurt (Composer)
  Threepenny Opera, The 1928,D 2,X,4:4
Weil, Leonard D (Playwright)
  If You Get It, Do You Want It? 1938,D 1,28:2
Weil, Leroy
  Zaporogetz Za Dunayem 1937,My 9,II,5:3
Weil, Robert
  New Faces of 1943 1942,D 23,22:2
  Burlesque 1946,D 26,30:3
  Once Upon a Mattress 1959,My 12,40:1
  Becket 1960,O 6,50:1
  Blood, Sweat & Stanley Poole 1961,O 6,31:1
  Night Life 1962,O 24,44:1
  Skits-Oh-Frantics 1967,Ap 3,39:2
  Love Your Crooked Neighbor 1969,D 30,40:1
Weil, T Elliot
  Technique 1931,My 15,21:1
Weiler, Bernice (Producer)
  Carving a Statue 1968,My 1,43:1
  Othello 1970,S 15,51:1
Weill, Gus (Playwright)
  To Bury a Cousin 1967,My 17,38:3
  Parents and Children 1969,Ja 13,26:6
  Geese 1969,Ja 13,26:6
Weill, Kurt
  Threepenny Opera, The 1928,D 2,X,4:4
Weill, Kurt (Composer)
  Zar Laesst Sich Photographieren, Der
    1928,Ap 22,IX,6:7
  Happy End 1929,O 27,IX,4:1
  Threepenny Opera, The 1933,Ap 14,22:4
  Johnny Johnson 1936,N 19,XII,1:1
  Johnny Johnson 1936,N 20,26:3
  Eternal Road, The 1937,Ja 8,14:2
  Eternal Road, The 1937,Ja 24,X,1:1
  Knickerbocker Holiday 1938,O 2,IX,3:3
  Knickerbocker Holiday 1938,O 20,26:2
  Knickerbocker Holiday 1938,N 20,IX,1:1
  Railroads on Parade 1939,My 14,XI,1:2
  Two on an Island 1940,Ja 23,17:2
  Lady in the Dark 1940,D 31,18:6
  Lady in the Dark 1941,Ja 5,IX,1:7
  Lady in the Dark 1941,Ja 24,14:2
  Lady in the Dark 1941,F 2,IX,1:1
  Lady in the Dark 1941,S 3,26:6
  Lady in the Dark 1941,S 7,IX,1:1
  Lady in the Dark 1943,Mr 1,14:2
  One Touch of Venus 1943,O 8,14:1
  One Touch of Venus 1943,O 17,II,1:1
  Firebird of Florence 1945,Mr 23,13:4
  Flag Is Born, A 1946,S 7,10:6
  Flag Is Born, A 1946,S 15,II,21:1
  Street Scene 1947,Ja 10,17:2
  Street Scene 1947,Ja 19,II,1:1
  Love Life 1948,O 8,31:2
  Lost in the Stars 1949,O 31,21:2
  Lost in the Stars 1949,N 6,II,1:1
  Lady in the Dark 1952,Mr 8,11:3
  Threepenny Opera, The 1954,Mr 11,26:5
  Threepenny Opera, The 1954,Mr 21,II,1:1
  Threepenny Opera, The 1954,Ap 4,II,7:1
  Threepenny Opera, The 1955,S 21,38:1
  Threepenny Opera, The 1956,F 12,83:1
  Threepenny Opera, The 1956,Mr 11,II,1:1
  Dreigroschenoper, Die 1965,Mr 21,II,13:1

Threepenny Opera, The 1966,O 28,33:1
  Flight of Lindbergh, The 1969,My 26,55:2
  Whores, Wars & Tin Pan Alley 1969,Je 17,37:1
  Mahagonny 1970,My 10,II,1:1
  Mahagonny 1970,My 10,II,15:1
Weill, Kurt (Miscellaneous)
  Street Scene 1947,Ja 10,17:2
Weill, Kurt (Musical Director)
  Threepenny Opera, The 1955,S 21,38:1
Weill, Kurt (Playwright)
  Johnny Johnson 1956,O 22,24:1
  Dreigroschenoper, Die 1965,Mr 12,24:1
  Mahagonny 1970,Ap 29,51:1
Weille, Blair (Composer)
  Man and Superman 1960,Ag 17,35:3
Weiman, Rita (Original Author)
  Acquittal, The 1920,Ja 11,VIII,2:1
Weiman, Rita (Playwright)
  Acquittal, The 1920,Ja 6,18:2
  Acquittal, The 1920,Ja 11,VIII,2:1
  King's Breakfast, The 1937,D 13,22:8
Weimar, Lorraine
  Gay Paree 1925,Ag 19,14:3
  Gay Paree 1926,N 10,24:2
  Luckee Girl 1928,S 17,28:6
  Three Little Girls 1930,Ap 15,29:1
  Little Racketeer, The 1932,Ja 19,24:4
Weinberg, Charles
  Ode to Liberty 1937,Ag 18,15:2
  Goodbye Again 1937,S 1,15:1
Weinberg, Charles (Composer)
  Yeah-Man 1932,My 27,27:3
Weinberg, Charles (Lyricist)
  Yeah-Man 1932,My 27,27:3
Weinberg, Frances
  Yo Ho Hum 1927,My 7,15:1
Weinberg, Gus (Playwright)
  Ned Wayburn's Gambols 1929,Ja 16,22:3
Weinberg, Lawrence (Playwright)
  Big Man 1966,My 20,41:1
  Duet for Three 1966,My 20,41:1
  And I Met a Man 1970,Ap 11,20:3
Weinberg, Myron (Miscellaneous)
  Tevya and His Daughters 1957,S 17,38:2
Weinberg, Myron (Producer)
  Best of Burlesque 1957,S 30,27:2
  All That Fall 1957,O 8,41:2
  Quare Fellow, The 1958,N 28,34:1
  Jeannette 1960,Mr 25,20:2
Weinberg, Tobi
  Tragical Historie of Doctor Faustus, The
    1964,O 6,34:2
  Troilus and Cressida 1965,Ag 13,17:1
Weinberger, Alf
  Fall Guy, The 1925,Mr 11,19:1
  Drums Begin, The 1933,N 25,10:5
Weinberger, Jaromir (Composer)
  Bed of Roses, A 1934,Ap 1,X,7:5
Weinberger, Mildred
  Flying Blind 1930,My 16,20:2
Weinburg, Gus C
  Spanish Love 1920,Ag 18,6:1
Weinburg, Gustave
  Tell Me Pretty Maiden 1937,D 17,33:5
Weine, Max G (Playwright)
  Love of Two Hours, The 1962,O 27,16:2
Weiner, Arne
  Madame Lafayette 1960,Mr 4,21:1
  On the High Road 1961,Ap 21,26:2
  Come Out, Carlo! 1962,My 4,27:2
  Saving Grace, The 1963,Ap 19,28:1
  Those That Play the Clowns 1966,N 25,48:1
  To Bury a Cousin 1967,My 17,38:3
Weiner, Boris
  Wolves 1924,D 31,9:4
  Tenth Commandment, The 1926,N 18,27:1
  Major Noah 1929,F 23,17:2
  Roaming Stars 1930,Ja 25,12:2
  Chains 1930,F 23,29:2
Weiner, George (Producer)
  Her First Roman 1968,O 21,53:3
Weiner, Jack (Lighting Director)
  Oedipus Rex 1960,Ap 30,15:2
Weiner, Jack (Scenic Designer)
  Oedipus Rex 1960,Ap 30,15:2
Weiner, Lazar (Composer)
  Once Upon a Time 1933,S 22,15:1
Weiner, Leslie (Playwright)
  In the Counting House 1962,D 15,5:5
Weiner, Robert (Miscellaneous)
  Shangri-La 1956,Je 14,40:1
  Spoon River Anthology 1963,S 30,23:2
  What Makes Sammy Run? 1964,F 28,19:1
  Gantry 1970,F 16,44:1
Weiner, Robert (Producer)
  Tall Story 1959,Ja 30,33:2
  Her First Roman 1968,O 21,53:3
Weiner, Stuart (Producer)
  Cindy 1964,Mr 20,24:1
Weingarten, Leo
  Mirele Efros 1969,D 26,41:1
Weingartner, Felix (Director)
  Children of the Don, The 1923,Mr 30,14:2

Weinheber, Josef (Playwright)
  After-Dinner Evening With Oskar Werner, An
    1967,Mr 27,39:1
Weinrib, Len
  Billy Barnes Revue, The 1959,Je 10,42:2
Weinrich, David
  His Wife's Lover 1929,O 21,30:6
Weinrich, H
  My Little Girl 1931,F 2,22:4
Weinstein, Arnold
  Tinguely Machine Mystery, or the Love Suicide at
    Kaluka, The 1965,D 24,15:5
Weinstein, Arnold (Director)
  Dynamite Tonight 1964,Mr 16,36:2
Weinstein, Arnold (Lyricist)
  Fortuna 1962,Ja 4,26:1
  Three Sisters, The 1968,Mr 18,56:1
  Metamorphoses 1969,D 12,69:1
Weinstein, Arnold (Miscellaneous)
  Open Season at Second City 1964,Ja 23,25:1
Weinstein, Arnold (Playwright)
  Red Eye of Love 1961,Je 13,28:1
  Fortuna 1962,Ja 4,26:1
  Three Times Three; Not Enough Rope
    1962,Mr 2,24:1
  Three Times Three; Twenty-Five Cent White Cap,
    The 1962,Mr 2,24:1
  Dynamite Tonight 1964,Mr 16,36:2
  Dynamite Tonight 1967,Mr 16,52:2
  Greatshot 1969,My 18,II,3:1
  Whores, Wars & Tin Pan Alley 1969,Je 17,37:1
  Metamorphoses 1969,D 12,69:1
  Mahagonny 1970,Ap 29,51:1
  Mahagonny 1970,My 10,II,1:1
Weinstein, Arnold (Translator)
  Metamorphoses 1969,D 12,69:1
Weinstein, Charlotte
  Subway Express 1929,S 25,34:3
Weinstein, Henry T (Director)
  Antigone 1956,Ap 3,32:2
Weinstein, Henry T (Miscellaneous)
  River Line, The 1957,Ja 3,29:2
  Third Best Sport 1958,D 31,15:3
  Pound on Demand, A 1959,Ap 16,28:1
  Portrait of a Madonna 1959,Ap 16,28:1
  On the Harmful Effects of Tobacco
    1959,Ap 16,28:1
  Bedtime Story 1959,Ap 16,28:1
Weinstein, Henry T (Producer)
  Zoo Story, The 1961,Jl 10,26:1
  Miss Julie 1961,Jl 10,26:1
  I Am a Camera 1961,Jl 10,26:1
Weinstein, Robert S (Miscellaneous)
  Touch 1970,N 9,52:1
Weinstock, Davis (Producer)
  Saturday Night 1968,F 26,43:1
  Memory Bank, The 1970,Ja 12,24:3
Weinstock, Jack (Playwright)
  How to Succeed in Business Without Really Trying
    1961,O 16,34:1
  Hot Spot 1963,Ap 20,17:2
  Catch Me if You Can 1965,Mr 10,50:1
  How to Succeed in Business Without Really Trying
    1966,Ap 21,45:1
Weintraub, Frances
  Radio Girl, The 1929,O 19,22:4
  Jolly Orphan, The 1929,D 23,18:6
  Little Clown, The 1930,Mr 15,23:3
  Longing for Home 1933,S 22,15:1
  He, She and the Ox 1934,F 21,22:7
Weintraub, Fred (Director)
  Gogo Loves You 1964,O 10,19:2
Weintraub, Milton
  Mikado, The 1935,Ag 24,17:5
Weintraub, Rebecca
  His Wife's Lover 1929,O 21,30:6
  Women of New York 1931,Mr 23,24:3
  Girl From Warsaw, The 1931,S 14,15:5
  Kibitzer, The 1931,N 7,17:3
  Under One Roof 1932,F 8,21:2
  New Man, The 1932,Ap 22,23:2
  God Man and Devil 1935,Mr 6,22:3
  Oy, Is Dus a Leben!; Oh, What a Life!
    1942,O 13,19:2
  Family Carnovsky, The 1943,O 19,16:7
Weintraub, Sam
  Wooden Idol, The 1930,My 13,27:2
Weintraub, Sigmund (Producer)
  Wild Man, The 1930,My 17,21:5
Weir, Beverlee
  Hello, Dolly! 1965,S 11,17:1
Weir, Ellyce
  Big Deal, The 1953,Mr 7,13:6
Weir, Gregg
  Five Posts in the Market Place 1961,Mr 6,30:1
  Six Characters in Search of an Author
    1963,Mr 11,7:2
  Matty and the Moron and Madonna
    1965,Mr 30,53:1
Weir, Helen
  Strong, The 1924,F 27,15:3
  Gossipy Sex, The 1927,Ap 20,28:3

Weir, Murray A
  When We Dead Awaken 1926,My 18,29:3
Weir, Richard (Miscellaneous)
  Caesar and Cleopatra 1927,N 6,IX,2:1
Weir, Robert
  Sale and a Sailor, A, or Glory! What Price!
  1926,Ap 25,30:4
Weirich, Ingeborg
  Before Sundown 1962,Mr 14,43:1
Weir's Elephants
  Vaudeville (Hippodrome) 1923,D 18,16:1
  Vaudeville (Palace) 1926,Ap 13,28:3
Weirum, Howard
  Hamlet 1937,Ag 24,24:4
Weisbecker, James F (Rev) (Director)
  Untitled-Passion Play 1925,Mr 2,5:6
Weisberg, Joan
  Prometheus Bound 1967,My 11,52:1
Weisberg, Louis
  Jew Suss 1929,O 19,22:3
  Angels on Earth 1929,D 11,34:7
  Chains 1930,F 23,29:2
  Verdict, The 1934,S 22,12:5
  In-Laws 1934,O 25,28:2
  60,000 Heroes 1935,Ja 28,11:5
  Parnosseh 1935,F 16,8:8
  Sappho 1935,Mr 22,26:4
Weisburd, Abe (Miscellaneous)
  Postmark Zero 1965,N 2,28:1
Weise, Moe (Miscellaneous)
  Whistle in the Dark, A 1969,O 9,55:1
Weise, Norman
  Arms and the Girl 1950,F 3,28:2
  Paint Your Wagon 1951,N 13,32:2
  Carnival in Flanders 1953,S 9,38:2
Weiseman, George H
  Decision 1929,My 28,37:3
Weiseman, Joseph
  King Lear 1950,D 26,18:1
Weisenfreund, Muni
  Anathema 1923,F 9,10:2
  Wolves 1924,D 31,9:4
Weiser, Jacob
  Treasure, The 1920,O 5,13:1
  John Hawthorne 1921,Ja 24,16:1
Weiser, Jacob (Director)
  Right Age to Marry, The 1926,F 16,22:3
  Broadway Boy 1932,My 4,23:5
Weiser, Jacob (Playwright)
  First American Dictator 1939,Mr 15,18:2
Weiser, Max (Composer)
  Valley Forge 1934,D 11,28:3
Weiser, Mel (Director)
  Brightower 1970,Ja 29,32:1
Weiser, Mel (Producer)
  Brightower 1970,Ja 29,32:1
Weisgal, Meyer W (Musical Director)
  Eternal Road, The 1937,Ja 8,14:2
Weisgerber, Antje
  Faust, Part I; Play, The 1961,F 5,27:2
  Minna von Barnhelm 1968,N 13,37:1
  Schloss, Das 1968,N 20,35:3
Weishar, Joseph (Lighting Director)
  Antigone 1959,S 16,46:2
Weishar, Joseph (Scenic Designer)
  Antigone 1959,S 16,46:2
  Power of Darkness, The 1959,S 30,33:1
  Miss Emily Adam 1960,Mr 30,43:1
Weiskopf, D K (Producer)
  Hat, a Coat, a Glove, A 1934,F 1,15:2
Weisman, Alfred
  Abie's Irish Rose 1922,My 24,22:4
Weisman, Lorenzo
  Macbeth 1966,Ag 29,23:4
Weismantel, Leo (Playwright)
  Untitled-Passion Play 1933,Jl 16,II,4:7
Weiss, Anne
  Tobias and the Angel 1937,Ap 29,16:5
Weiss, Arthur
  Merry Widow, The 1961,O 27,28:2
Weiss, Charles (Miscellaneous)
  Second Time Around, The 1962,Ap 21,14:1
  House of Flowers 1968,Ja 29,26:2
Weiss, David (Scenic Designer)
  Thy Kingdom Come 1957,Je 25,24:6
Weiss, Ernest Raoul (Playwright)
  Room of Dreams 1930,N 6,22:4
Weiss, Estelle
  Revolt of the Beavers, The 1937,My 21,19:2
Weiss, Evelyn
  Banjo Eyes 1941,D 26,20:2
Weiss, Fred (Playwright)
  What's Up 1953,O 28,37:2
Weiss, George
  Marriage of Mr Mississippi, The 1969,N 20,60:5
  Philipp Hotz 1969,N 27,52:1
Weiss, George (Composer)
  Mr Wonderful 1956,Mr 23,23:2
  First Impressions 1959,Mr 20,28:1
  Maggie Flynn 1968,O 24,52:1
  Maggie Flynn 1968,N 3,II,1:1
Weiss, George (Lyricist)
  Mr Wonderful 1956,Mr 23,23:2

First Impressions 1959,Mr 20,28:1
  Maggie Flynn 1968,O 24,52:1
Weiss, George (Playwright)
  Maggie Flynn 1968,O 24,52:1
Weiss, Harris
  Cave at Machpelah, The 1959,Jl 1,25:1
Weiss, Jeff
  Spofford 1967,D 15,54:3
  Gloria and Esperanza 1969,Ap 5,30:1
Weiss, Jerry
  Emperor's New Clothes, The 1950,Je 20,23:2
  Enemy of the People, An 1958,F 26,24:2
  When I Was a Child 1960,D 9,38:1
Weiss, Louis
  Little Cantor, The 1930,S 24,26:2
Weiss, Noel (Miscellaneous)
  Laundry, The 1963,F 19,5:2
Weiss, Noel (Producer)
  All Kinds of Giants 1961,D 19,40:1
  Guide, The 1968,Mr 7,50:1
  Philosophy in the Boudoir 1969,My 22,55:2
Weiss, Paul
  January Thaw 1946,F 5,18:2
Weiss, Peter (Playwright)
  Persecution and Assassination of Marat As
  Performed by the Inmates of the Asylum of
  Charenton Under the Direction of the Marquis de
  Sade, The 1964,My 1,42:1
  Investigation, The 1965,O 21,55:3
  Persecution and Assassination of Marat As
  Performed by the Inmates of the Asylum of
  Charenton Under the Direction of the Marquis de
  Sade, The 1965,D 28,35:1
  Persecution and Assassination of Marat As
  Performed by the Inmates of the Asylum of
  Charenton Under the Direction of the Marquis de
  Sade, The 1966,Ja 9,II,1:1
  Investigation, The 1966,O 5,40:1
  Investigation, The 1966,N 13,II,1:1
  Persecution and Assassination of Marat As
  Performed by the Inmates of the Asylum of
  Charenton Under the Direction of the Marquis de
  Sade, The 1967,Ja 4,34:1
  Persecution and Assassination of Marat As
  Performed by the Inmates of the Asylum of
  Charenton Under the Direction of the Marquis de
  Sade, The 1967,Ja 15,II,1:1
  Sangen om Skrapuken 1967,Ap 9,II,1:3
  Song of the Lusitanian Bogey, The 1968,Ja 3,52:1
  Song of the Lusitanian Bogey, The 1968,Ja 14,II,1:1
  Vietnam Discourse 1968,Mr 31,II,22:6
  Song of the Lusitanian Bogey, The 1969,My 13,41:1
  Trotsky in Exile 1970,F 1,II,5:1
Weiss, Robert
  Gideon 1961,N 10,38:1
Weiss, Rosilyn
  Sweet Genevieve 1945,Mr 21,27:3
Weiss, Rudolf
  Two on an Island 1940,Ja 23,17:2
  Flight to the West 1940,D 31,19:1
  Earth Spirit 1950,Je 7,33:4
  Naked 1950,S 7,39:2
  Potting Shed, The 1957,Ja 30,32:1
  Three Sisters, The 1959,S 22,46:1
  Shadow of Heroes 1961,D 6,59:1
  Kiss Mama 1964,O 2,30:1
  Deadly Game, The 1966,F 14,34:1
Weiss, Stanley G (Producer)
  Miss Emily Adam 1960,Mr 30,43:1
Weiss, Stephen (Lyricist)
  Hellzapoppin 1938,S 23,34:2
Weissberg, Eric
  Joyful Noise, A 1966,D 16,57:1
Weissberg, Louis
  Othello 1929,F 4,21:2
  Major Noah 1929,F 23,17:2
Weissberger, Felix (Director)
  Symphony 1935,Ap 27,20:3
Weissberger, Jose A (Translator)
  Bitter Oleander 1935,F 12,24:3
Weisse, Hermann
  Before Sundown 1962,Mr 14,43:1
Weissenbach, Charles H
  Seven Against One 1930,My 7,25:1
Weissenborn, Guenther (Playwright)
  Submarine S-4 1929,My 26,IX,2:3
Weissman, Deborah (Scenic Designer)
  Ever Since Paradise 1957,Jl 12,18:4
Weissman, Dora
  Hitch Your Wagon! 1937,Ap 9,18:2
  Two on an Island 1940,Ja 23,17:2
  Man With Blonde Hair, The 1941,N 5,30:2
  Oy, Is Dus a Leben!; Oh, What a Life!
  1942,O 13,19:2
  New Life, A 1943,S 16,26:6
  Down to Miami 1944,S 12,23:5
Weissmann, Henry (Producer)
  Soliloquy 1938,N 29,26:4
Weissmann, Polaire
  This Fine-Pretty World 1923,D 27,11:1
  Time Is a Dream 1924,Ap 23,24:2
Weissmann, Polaire (Costume Designer)
  Bitter Oleander 1935,F 12,24:3

Weissmann, Rita H (Scenic Designer)
  Ben Bagley's Shoestring Revues 1970,O 24,22:1
Weissmuller, Don
  What's Up 1943,N 12,24:6
  Pipe Dream 1955,D 1,44:1
Weissmuller, Johnny
  Aquacade 1939,My 5,26:2
Weist, Dwight
  Sunday Nights at 9 1935,N 11,21:1
  Peepshow 1944,F 4,12:2
  Jimmy 1969,O 24,38:1
Weist, George
  Vaudeville (Palace) 1926,Mr 23,24:3
Weitz, Millie
  Pins and Needles 1939,Ap 21,26:2
  New Pins and Needles 1939,N 21,19:2
  To Bury a Cousin 1967,My 17,38:3
Weitzenkorn, Louis (Director)
  Name Your Poison 1936,Ja 21,27:4
Weitzenkorn, Louis (Playwright)
  First Mortgage 1929,O 11,36:1
  Five Star Final 1930,D 31,11:1
  Late Night Final 1931,Je 26,26:3
  Five-Star Final 1931,Jl 18,16:4
  Name Your Poison 1936,Ja 21,27:4
Weizenfreud, Munie
  Andersh; New Worlds 1922,S 26,18:2
  Inspector General, The 1922,O 9,15:4
  Great Fortune, The 1922,D 9,11:1
Weizman, Morris
  It Can't Happen Here 1936,O 28,30:1
Welber, Dolores
  Man and Superman 1960,Ag 17,35:3
Welber, Robert (Producer)
  Saintliness of Margery Kempe, The 1959,F 3,35:6
  Geranium Hat, The 1959,Mr 18,45:1
Welbes, George
  Oh, Say Can You See L A 1968,F 9,50:1
  Other Man, The 1968,F 9,50:1
  Oh! Calcutta! 1969,Je 18,33:1
Welborn, Irma (Musical Director)
  Ah! Wah! 1932,My 11,15:2
Welch, Barry
  Vaudeville (Palace) 1930,D 1,19:1
Welch, Ben
  Jimmie 1920,N 18,15:3
Welch, Bess
  Hamlet 1954,Ap 24,15:2
Welch, Charles
  Sweet River 1936,O 29,30:2
  Porgy and Bess 1942,Ja 23,16:2
  Porgy and Bess 1943,S 14,26:2
  Porgy and Bess 1944,F 8,13:2
  Memphis Bound 1945,My 25,23:2
  St Louis Woman 1946,Ap 1,22:2
  Kiss Me, Kate 1954,Mr 27,13:2
  Cloud 7 1958,F 15,15:2
  Make a Million 1958,O 24,39:2
  Donnybrook! 1961,My 19,23:1
  Half-Past Wednesday 1962,Ap 7,16:2
  Billygoat Eddie 1964,Ap 21,43:2
  Golden Boy 1964,O 21,56:1
  Darling of the Day 1968,Ja 29,26:2
  Dear World 1969,F 7,33:1
Welch, Eddie (Playwright)
  Earl Carroll's Vanities 1930,Jl 2,28:3
  Earl Carroll's Vanities 1931,Ag 28,18:7
Welch, Edgar
  Half a Widow 1927,S 13,37:3
  Rosalie 1928,Ja 11,26:3
Welch, Elizabeth
  Nymph Errant 1933,O 7,18:2
  Let's Raise the Curtain 1936,S 29,34:3
Welch, Harriett
  Seven Mirrors 1945,O 26,17:2
Welch, Harry
  Vanities 1927,F 22,19:1
Welch, Howard
  Cotton Stockings 1923,D 19,16:2
Welch, J M (Producer)
  Sh! The Octopus 1928,F 22,19:2
Welch, James
  Clean Beds 1939,My 26,21:2
Welch, Jean
  Importance of Being Earnest, The 1936,O 22,31:2
Welch, Ken (Composer)
  Shoestring Revue 1955,Mr 1,22:2
Welch, Ken (Miscellaneous)
  Skits-Oh-Frantics 1967,Ap 3,39:2
Welch, Lew
  Bulls, Bears and Asses 1932,My 7,11:3
Welch, Loren
  Are You With It? 1945,N 12,17:3
  Barefoot Boy With Cheek 1947,Ap 4,20:2
  Look, Ma, I'm Dancin' 1948,Ja 30,20:2
Welch, Margot
  Dr Willy Nilly 1959,Je 5,18:2
  What Shall We Tell Caroline? 1961,N 22,24:2
Welch, Mary
  Little Women 1944,D 13,29:2
  Moon for the Misbegotten, A 1947,F 21,16:2
  Joy to the World 1948,Mr 19,28:2
  House of Bernarda Alba, The 1951,Ja 8,14:6

Welch, Mary—Cont

Dream Girl 1951,My 10,39:1
Solid Gold Cadillac, The 1953,N 6,24:2
Purple Dust 1956,D 28,15:1
Sunrise at Campobello 1958,Ja 31,25:1

Welch, Melba

Icetime 1947,My 29,28:2

Welch, Miriam

Zorba 1968,N 18,58:1
Lend an Ear 1969,O 29,32:1

Welch, Mitzie

Student Gypsy, The; Prince of Liederkranz, The 1963,O 1,34:1

Welch, Nelson

Liliom 1932,O 27,23:2
Camille 1932,O 28,23:2
Dear Jane 1932,N 15,24:3
Alice in Wonderland 1932,D 12,18:3
Cherry Orchard, The 1933,Mr 7,20:3
Winter's Tale, The 1963,Je 29,13:1
Midsummer Night's Dream, A 1963,Jl 1,19:2

Welch, Niles

Donovan Affair, The 1926,Ag 31,15:2

Welch, Patrick

On Your Toes 1954,O 12,24:4

Welch, Phyllis

Prodigal Father, The 1935,Jl 2,24:2
Stardust 1935,Jl 17,22:4
Slight Case of Murder, A 1935,S 12,28:5
Granite 1936,Ja 14,24:6
High Tor 1937,Ja 11,15:2
Lysistrata 1937,Jl 20,19:3

Welch, Sidney

Slice It Thin 1945,My 11,22:5

Welch, William

Lady in the Dark 1941,Ja 24,14:2

Welch, William (Playwright)

How to Make a Man 1961,F 3,16:1

Welchman, Harry

Desert Song, The 1927,My 8,VII,1:5

Weld, Gordon

That's the Woman 1930,S 4,27:2
Chauve-Souris; Queen of Spades, The 1931,O 22,27:1
Dead End 1935,O 29,17:2

Weld, Sylvia

Ethan Frome 1936,Ja 22,15:2
Excursion 1937,Ap 10,11:4
I Am My Youth 1938,Mr 8,22:4
American Landscape 1938,D 5,19:2
Royal Family, The 1940,Ag 13,15:3
Fledgling 1940,N 28,29:2

Weld (Costume Designer)

Laugh Parade, The 1931,N 3,31:2

Weld (Scenic Designer)

Laugh Parade, The 1931,N 3,31:2

Weldanos, The

Vaudeville (Palace) 1926,O 26,24:2
Vaudeville (Palace) 1927,O 11,27:2

Welden, Ben

Nica 1926,Ja 26,19:1
Tin Pan Alley 1928,N 2,29:1
Quitter, The 1934,F 6,24:4

Weldman, Charles (Choreographer)

If the Shoe Fits 1946,D 6,29:4

Weldon, Ann

Flea in Her Ear, A 1969,O 4,25:1

Weldon, Bunny (Choreographer)

Radio Girl, The 1929,O 19,22:4
If the Rabbi Wants 1929,D 23,18:5
Motke From Slobodke 1930,Ap 12,23:3
Mystery Moon 1930,Je 24,23:4

Weldon, Bunny (Director)

Footlights 1927,Ag 20,8:2

Weldon, Charles

Buck White 1969,D 3,63:1
Ododo 1970,N 25,26:1

Weldon, Clare

Intimate Strangers, The 1921,N 8,28:1
Rita Coventry 1923,F 20,12:2
Nancy Ann 1924,Ap 1,18:1
Nancy Ann 1924,Ap 6,VIII,1:1

Weldon, Jane

Cyrano de Bergerac 1936,Ap 28,17:1

Weldon, Joan

Kean 1961,N 3,28:2
Merry Widow, The 1964,Ag 18,24:2

Weldon, Leslie

Kitchen, The 1966,Je 14,50:1

Weldon, Mortimer

First Love 1926,N 9,31:2
Farewell to Arms, A 1930,S 23,30:3
As You Desire Me 1931,Ja 29,21:2
Her Man of Wax 1933,O 12,32:3
Wooden Slipper, The 1934,Ja 4,16:3
Achilles Had a Heel 1935,O 14,20:2
Cyrano de Bergerac 1936,Ap 28,17:1
Enemy of the People, An 1937,F 16,19:1
Curtain Call 1937,Ap 23,24:7
Window Shopping 1938,D 24,13:2

Weldy, Max (Costume Designer)

Student Prince, The 1936,Jl 12,II,5:2
Bitter Sweet 1936,Ag 26,17:3
Student Prince, The 1937,Jl 28,15:1

Weldy, Max (Scenic Designer)

George White's Scandals 1928,Jl 3,19:1

Welfard, Darry

Scandals 1920,Je 8,9:1

Welford, Christine

Scandals 1920,Je 8,9:1
George White's Scandals 1921,Jl 12,14:1

Welford, Dallas

No More Blondes 1920,Ja 8,22:1
Oh, Henry! 1920,My 6,14:2
Girl With Carmine Lips, The 1920,Ag 11,6:1
French Leave 1920,N 9,13:1
Blue Kitten, The 1922,Ja 14,9:3
Shadow, The 1922,Ap 25,14:2
Plot Thickens, The 1922,S 6,16:1
Blossom Time 1923,My 22,14:3
Mary Jane McKane 1923,D 26,13:2
Mrs Bumpstead-Leigh 1929,Ap 2,28:3
London Calling 1930,O 20,29:1
Napi 1931,Mr 12,22:5

Welford, Darry

George White's Scandals 1921,Jl 12,14:1

Welford, Nancy

Orange Blossoms 1922,S 20,18:1
Cinders 1923,Ap 4,22:1
Twinkle Twinkle 1926,N 17,22:2
Lady Do 1927,Ap 19,24:2
Rain or Shine 1928,F 10,26:3

Welichansky, Israel

Aristocrats 1935,My 2,16:2
Chains 1937,Ja 22,25:1
Clinton Street 1939,O 13,27:2

Welisch, Ernest (Lyricist)

Spanische Nachtigall, Die 1920,D 12,VI,1:4
Madame Pompadour 1924,N 12,20:6

Welisch, Ernest (Playwright)

Spanische Nachtigall, Die 1920,D 12,VI,1:4
Lady in Ermine, The 1922,O 3,22:2
Madame Pompadour 1924,N 12,20:6
Naughty Riquette 1926,S 14,25:2
Jugend im Mai 1927,Ja 23,VII,4:5
Casanova 1928,N 4,IX,2:1
Three Musketeers 1929,O 13,IX,4:7
Casanova 1932,Je 19,IX,2:1
Alt Heidelberg; Student Prince, The 1932,N 20,IX,3:3

Welk, Ehm (Playwright)

Kreuzabnahme 1929,My 26,IX,2:3

Well, A W

Whispering Gallery, The 1935,D 1,II,12:6

Well, West

Vaudeville (Palace) 1923,Ja 16,16:3

Weller, Carrie

Henry-Behave 1926,Ag 24,19:4
Marriage on Approval 1928,Mr 2,28:2
Front Page, The 1928,Ag 15,19:2
Lost Boy 1932,Ja 6,24:4
Music in the Air 1932,N 9,28:2
O Evening Star 1936,Ja 9,24:6
Love on the Dole 1936,F 25,23:3
Double Dummy 1936,N 12,30:1
Our Town 1938,F 5,18:3
Merchant of Yonkers, The 1938,D 29,14:2

Weller, Cedric

Cyrano de Bergerac 1923,N 2,14:1
Cyrano de Bergerac 1926,F 19,18:1
Henry IV, Part I 1926,Je 1,29:1
Midsummer Night's Dream, A 1927,Je 27,25:1

Weller, Fritz

Conjur' Man Dies 1936,Mr 12,18:5
Case of Philip Lawrence, The 1937,Je 9,31:1

Weller, Ted

Lady Billy 1920,D 15,18:2
Be Yourself! 1924,S 4,13:3

Welles, Benjamin (Playwright)

Come Across 1937,Ap 10,10:7
So Proudly We Hail 1938,Mr 30,18:5
So Proudly We Hail 1938,Ap 9,11:1

Welles, Halsted

Saint's Parade 1930,N 1,23:4
King's Coat, The 1933,Ja 12,21:4

Welles, Halsted (Director)

Hippolytus 1935,Je 15,20:4
Murder in the Cathedral 1936,Mr 21,13:5
Murder in the Cathedral 1936,Mr 29,IX,1:1
Robin Landing 1937,N 19,26:4
Everywhere I Roam 1938,Ap 22,15:1
First Crocus, The 1942,Ja 3,14:6
Temporary Island, A 1948,Mr 15,27:3

Welles, Halsted (Playwright)

Temporary Island, A 1948,Mr 15,27:3

Welles, Jay

Mary of Magdala 1946,Mr 26,24:5

Welles, Metro

Hostage, The 1960,S 21,42:1

Welles, Orson

Jew Suss 1931,N 8,VIII,4:4
Dead Ride Fast, The 1931,D 6,VIII,4:5
Archdupe 1931,D 27,VIII,4:1
Romeo and Juliet 1934,D 4,23:2
Romeo and Juliet 1934,D 21,30:3
Romeo and Juliet 1934,D 21,30:3
Panic 1935,Mr 16,18:4

Welles, Orson—Cont

Horse Eats Hat 1936,S 28,14:2
Ten Million Ghosts 1936,O 24,23:7
Doctor Faustus 1937,Ja 9,21:2
Tragical Historie of Doctor Faustus, The 1937,Ja 31,XI,1:1
Julius Caesar 1937,N 12,26:6
Heartbreak House 1938,Ap 30,18:2
Danton's Death 1938,N 3,26:2
Danton's Death 1938,N 13,IX,1:1
Five Kings 1939,F 28,16:4
Five Kings 1939,Mr 5,X,3:1
Around the World 1946,Je 1,9:5
Around the World 1946,Je 9,II,1:1
Macbeth 1947,My 30,25:1
Moby Dick 1955,Je 17,18:8
Moby Dick 1955,Jl 24,II,1:6
King Lear 1956,Ja 13,17:1
King Lear 1956,Ja 22,II,1:1

Welles, Orson (Director)

Macbeth 1936,Ap 5,IX,1:4
Macbeth 1936,Ap 15,25:3
Macbeth 1936,Ap 15,25:4
Horse Eats Hat 1936,S 28,14:2
Doctor Faustus 1937,Ja 9,21:2
Tragical Historie of Doctor Faustus, The 1937,Ja 31,XI,1:1
Julius Caesar 1937,N 12,26:6
Shoemaker's Holiday, The 1938,Ja 3,17:2
Cradle Will Rock, The 1938,Ja 4,19:3
Shoemaker's Holiday, The 1938,Ja 9,X,1:1
Shoemaker's Holiday, The 1938,Ja 23,XI,1:6
Heartbreak House 1938,Ap 30,18:2
Danton's Death 1938,N 3,26:2
Five Kings 1939,F 28,16:4
Native Son 1941,Mr 25,26:5
Native Son 1941,Ap 6,IX,1:1
Native Son 1942,O 24,10:6
Native Son 1942,N 1,VIII,1:1
Around the World 1946,Je 1,9:5
King Lear 1956,Ja 13,17:1
King Lear 1956,Ja 22,II,1:1
Rhinoceros 1960,Ap 30,15:3

Welles, Orson (Miscellaneous)

Macbeth 1936,Ap 15,25:4
Moby Dick 1955,Je 17,18:8
Moby Dick 1955,Jl 24,II,1:6

Welles, Orson (Playwright)

Horse Eats Hat 1936,S 28,14:2
Around the World 1946,Je 1,9:5
Around the World 1946,Je 9,II,1:1
Moby Dick 1962,N 4,82:6
Moby Dick 1962,N 29,45:1

Welles, Orson (Producer)

Julius Caesar 1937,N 28,XI,1:1
Julius Caesar 1938,Ja 30,X,3:1
Five Kings 1939,F 28,16:4
Five Kings 1939,Mr 5,X,3:1
Native Son 1941,Mr 25,26:5
Native Son 1941,Ap 6,IX,1:1
Around the World 1946,Je 9,II,1:1
Macbeth 1947,My 30,25:1

Welles, Virginia

Panic 1935,Mr 16,18:4
Horse Eats Hat 1936,S 28,14:2

Wellesley, Alfred

Middle Watch, The 1929,O 17,27:1

Wellesley, Arthur

Scarlet Fox, The 1928,Mr 28,31:1

Wellesley, Charles

Mad Hopes, The 1932,D 2,26:3
Baby Pompadour 1934,D 28,24:2
Slight Case of Murder, A 1935,S 12,28:5
Libel! 1935,D 21,10:5
Young Madame Conti 1937,Ap 1,18:4
Woman Brown, The 1939,D 9,18:5

Wellesley, Eugene

Oedipus Rex 1923,O 26,14:1
Via Crucis 1923,N 13,25:2
Burgomaster of Stilemonde, The 1923,N 16,15:3
Saturday Night 1926,O 26,25:1

Wellesz, Egon (Composer)

Scherz, List und Rache 1928,Ap 22,IX,6:7

Wellford, William

Lucky Sam McCarver 1925,O 22,22:1

Wellington, Arthur

Veils 1928,Mr 14,28:5
Man Who Came to Dinner, The 1940,F 10,19:5

Wellington, George

Return of Peter Grimm, The 1921,S 22,12:2

Wellington, Guy

Charm 1929,N 29,24:5

Wellington, Winifred

Daddy's Gone A-Hunting 1921,S 1,18:3
Nervous Wreck, The 1923,O 10,16:1

Welliver, Ralph

Bright Honor 1936,S 28,14:1

Wellman, Alice

Prince of Pilsen, The 1930,Ja 14,24:3

Wellman, Edward

Desert Song, The 1946,Ja 9,20:2

Wellman, Emily Ann

Wasp, The 1923,Mr 28,14:3
Dagger, The 1925,S 10,28:1

Wellman, Emily Ann—Cont
Rockbound 1929,Ap 20,23:2
Miss Quis 1937,Ap 8,20:5
Wells, Bee
Black Scandals 1928,O 27,23:2
Wells, Ben
Little Miss Charity 1920,S 3,6:3
Sweet Adeline 1929,S 4,33:1
Wells, Billy
Greenwich Village Follies 1923,S 21,4:6
Vaudeville (Loew's State) 1932,O 3,15:5
Wells, Billy (Playwright)
Sky's the Limit, The 1934,D 18,25:5
Michael Todd's Peep Show 1950,Je 29,37:2
Wells, Caroline
Bamboo Cross 1955,F 22,17:2
Wells, Charles B
Paddy the Next Best Thing 1920,Ag 28,5:5
Wells, David (Playwright)
Paganini 1935,F 10,VIII,3:1
Wells, Deering
Loyalties 1922,S 28,18:1
Hassan 1924,S 23,23:1
Old English 1924,D 24,11:2
Wells, Edna (Miscellaneous)
Peter Ibbetson 1926,Mr 26,24:7
Wells, Eleanor
Two by Two 1925,F 24,17:1
Whirlpool 1929,D 4,37:3
Thanks for Tomorrow 1938,S 28,28:2
Wells, Eleanor (Playwright)
Viva O'Brien 1941,O 10,27:2
Wells, Emma (Playwright)
By Your Leave 1934,Ja 25,15:3
Wells, F B
Moon Is a Gong, The 1926,Mr 13,21:3
Wells, George
Magic 1929,D 17,28:5
Seven Keys to Baldpate 1930,Ja 8,25:2
Round Table, The 1930,F 28,20:5
Wells, Gilbert
Earl Carroll's Vanities 1926,Ag 25,19:4
Vaudeville (Palace) 1930,Mr 24,24:5
Wells, H G (Original Author)
Wonderful Visit, The 1921,Ap 3,VII,1:3
Ann Veronica 1949,My 21,9:2
Half a Sixpence 1965,Ap 26,38:2
Wells, H G (Playwright)
Wonderful Visit, The 1924,F 13,17:3
Wonderful Visit, The 1924,My 18,VII,1:1
Wells, John
George White's Scandals 1926,Je 15,23:2
Wells, John (Playwright)
Great Day! 1929,O 18,24:3
Mrs Wilson's Diary 1967,O 8,II,13:5
Wells, Lawrence
Student Prince, The 1924,D 3,25:3
Wells, Leigh Burton (Playwright)
Allure 1934,O 30,22:6
Wells, M B
1776 1926,Ap 24,11:2
Gentlemen, the Queen 1927,Ap 23,14:3
Wells, Mack
Sun Showers 1923,F 6,14:2
Wells, Malcolm
Anne of the Thousand Days 1948,D 9,49:2
Wells, Malcolm (Miscellaneous)
Clearing in the Woods, A 1957,Ja 11,20:2
Sin of Pat Muldoon, The 1957,Mr 14,35:1
Wells, Malcolm (Producer)
Country Wife, The 1957,N 28,56:1
Wells, Marie
Florodora 1920,Ap 6,18:1
Merry Widow, The 1921,S 6,13:1
Wells, Marion
Long Road, The 1930,S 10,30:2
Melo 1931,Ap 17,26:6
Wells, Mary K
Everything in the Garden 1967,N 30,60:1
Wells, Maurice
Major Barbara 1928,N 20,28:4
We the People 1933,Ja 23,9:5
Between Two Worlds 1934,O 26,24:2
Creeping Fire 1935,Ja 17,22:3
Woman of the Soil, A 1935,Mr 26,23:6
Hallowe'en 1936,F 21,20:3
Spring Thaw 1938,Mr 22,18:1
Escape This Night 1938,Ap 23,18:1
Glorious Morning 1938,N 28,10:3
Only the Heart 1944,Ap 5,17:2
Wells, Metro
Scapegoat, The 1950,Ap 20,36:5
Wells, Niles
Policy Kings 1938,D 31,6:2
Wells, Peavey
Blue Peter, The 1925,Mr 25,25:3
Engaged! or Cheviot's Choice 1925,Je 19,24:2
Wells, Rhea (Scenic Designer)
Cherry Pie 1926,Ap 15,24:4
Wells, Robert (Lyricist)
3 for Tonight 1955,Ap 7,23:2
Wells, Robert (Playwright)
3 for Tonight 1955,Ap 7,23:2

Wells, Staring (Costume Designer)
Romio and Julietta 1925,Ap 21,19:1
Fratricide Punished 1925,Ap 21,19:1
Wells, Tomlinson
Wings Over Europe 1936,Mr 4,24:7
Wells, Virginia
Cinderella on Broadway 1920,Je 25,18:1
Vaudeville (Palace) 1923,Ja 16,16:3
Wells, William K (Composer)
Manhattan Mary 1927,S 27,30:3
Wells, William K (Director)
Folly Town 1920,My 18,9:2
Viva O'Brien 1941,O 10,27:2
Wells, William K (Lyricist)
Manhattan Mary 1927,S 27,30:3
Wells, William K (Miscellaneous)
Ziegfeld Follies 1943,Ap 2,16:2
Wells, William K (Playwright)
Folly Town 1920,My 18,9:2
George White's Scandals 1923,Je 19,22:5
Scandals 1924,Jl 1,16:1
Tell Me More 1925,Ap 14,27:3
George White's Scandals 1925,Je 23,24:2
George White's Scandals 1926,Je 15,23:2
Manhattan Mary 1927,S 27,30:3
Harry Delmar's Revels 1927,N 29,30:2
George White's Scandals 1928,Jl 3,19:1
George White's Scandals 1929,S 24,29:1
Music Hall Varieties 1932,N 23,15:3
George White's Scandals 1935,D 26,20:2
Viva O'Brien 1941,O 10,27:2
Wells and the Four Fays
Vaudeville (Palace) 1952,F 27,22:2
Elliott Murphy's Aquashow 1956,Je 20,26:2
Wellsley, Eugene
Hamlet 1923,N 20,23:3
Wellwarth, George (Translator)
Lovers in the Metro, The 1962,Ja 31,21:1
Keyhole, The 1962,Ja 31,21:1
Information Bureau, The 1962,Ja 31,21:1
Welly, Max
Up in the Clouds 1922,Ja 3,20:3
Welsh, Anna
Faraway Princess, The 1922,D 6,3:2
Welsh, Betty
Dove, The 1925,F 12,17:3
Welsh, Eddie (Playwright)
Ned Wayburn's Gambols 1929,Ja 16,22:3
Welsh, Elizabeth
Runnin' Wild 1923,O 30,17:3
Chocolate Dandies, The 1924,S 2,22:2
Welsh, Harry
Boom Boom 1929,Ja 29,26:4
Broadway Nights 1929,Jl 16,23:2
Artists and Models 1930,Je 11,33:2
Meet My Sister 1930,D 31,11:1
Welsh, Katherine
Master of the Revels 1935,Ag 14,16:2
Welsh, Kenneth
Henry V 1966,Je 8,38:1
Henry VI 1966,Je 9,55:2
Antony and Cleopatra 1967,Ag 2,25:1
Merry Wives of Windsor, The 1967,Ag 4,18:1
Antony and Cleopatra 1967,O 29,83:4
Tartuffe 1968,Je 12,39:1
Midsummer Night's Dream, A 1968,Je 13,54:1
Three Musketeers, The 1968,Jl 24,49:2
Hamlet 1969,Je 11,37:1
Measure for Measure 1969,Je 13,41:3
Hamlet 1969,Je 22,II,1:7
Merchant of Venice, The 1970,Je 10,39:1
School for Scandal, The 1970,Je 11,51:1
Cymbeline 1970,Jl 24,17:2
Cymbeline 1970,Ag 23,II,1:6
Welsh, Lew J
Marry the Man! 1929,Ap 23,26:3
Welsh, Norman
Taming of the Shrew, The 1962,Je 21,25:1
Tempest, The 1962,Je 22,14:1
Cyrano de Bergerac 1962,Ag 1,21:1
Welsh, Ron
Take Her, She's Mine 1961,D 22,19:1
Welsh, Scott
Tip-Top 1920,O 6,13:2
Some Party 1922,Ap 17,22:1
Princess Ida 1925,Ap 14,27:2
Play Without a Name, A 1928,N 26,30:5
Welsh-Homer, Charles
Tyrants 1924,Mr 5,14:1
Man Who Ate the Popomack, The 1924,Mr 25,24:1
Welting, Patricia
Patience 1965,Ap 16,34:1
Weltshko, Johann
Untitled-Passion Play 1927,Jl 31,VII,1:6
Welty, Eudora (Original Author)
Ponder Heart, The 1956,F 26,II,1:1
Welty, Eudora (Playwright)
Ponder Heart, The 1956,F 17,14:2
Littlest Revue, The 1956,My 23,37:2
Welty, Jeanne
Mystery of Theodosia Burr, The 1947,Mr 10,24:7
Welty, Ruth (Playwright)
With Privileges 1930,S 16,30:2

Welty, Ruth (Playwright)—Cont
White Dress, The 1932,D 14,27:3
Wen, Tsu Yin
Mu Lan 1921,F 25,16:2
Wences, Senor
Laugh, Town, Laugh! 1942,Je 23,22:2
Laugh, Town, Laugh! 1942,Jl 23,15:3
Danny Kaye Show 1963,Ap 11,28:2
Wenclawska, Ruza
Fashion 1924,F 5,21:2
Wendall, Eleanor
Searching for the Sun 1936,F 20,22:6
Wendel, Beth (Playwright)
Genius and the Goddess, The 1957,D 11,41:1
Wendel, Elmarie
Foenix in Choir 1958,O 28,40:2
Little Mary Sunshine 1959,N 19,49:3
Little Mary Sunshine 1959,N 29,II,1:1
Hobo 1961,Ap 11,41:2
O Say Can You See! 1962,O 9,45:1
That Hat! 1964,S 24,45:1
Babes in the Wood 1964,D 29,21:2
Decline and Fall of the Entire World As Seen
Through the Eyes of Cole Porter Revisited, The
1965,Mr 31,24:2
Wendel, Paul
New Moon, The 1942,Ag 19,14:2
Wendell, Dorothy Day (Playwright)
Tell Me Pretty Maiden 1937,D 17,33:5
Wendell, Howard
Great Campaign, The 1947,Ap 1,33:2
Show-Off, The 1950,Je 1,24:5
Julius Caesar 1950,Je 21,30:1
Curious Savage, The 1950,O 25,44:3
Make a Wish 1951,Ap 19,38:1
Wendell, Ingrid
Eisrevue 1969,O 23,55:1
Wendell, Lynn
Kiss Me, Kate 1965,My 13,31:1
Wending, George
Twelfth Disciple, The 1930,My 17,21:4
Wendler, Otto Bernhard (Playwright)
Liebe, Mord und Alkohol 1931,Mr 29,VIII,3:2
Wendley, Richard
Sherlock Holmes 1953,O 31,11:2
Wendling, George
Twelfth Disciple, The 1930,My 17,21:4
Wendorf, Reuben
Verdict, The 1934,S 22,12:5
In-Laws 1934,O 25,28:2
Treasure, The 1934,D 18,25:5
60,000 Heroes 1935,Ja 28,11:5
Parnosseh 1935,F 16,8:8
Madame Pagliacci 1935,S 30,12:3
Stranger, The 1935,N 7,26:2
Saint and Sinners 1935,D 30,15:2
Freidel Becomes a Bride 1936,F 10,14:3
Who Is Who? 1938,D 24,13:3
Yoshe Kalb 1939,F 6,9:2
All You Need Is One Good Break 1950,F 10,20:3
In-Laws 1960,O 17,32:4
World Is a Stage, The 1962,N 5,37:4
Country Boy, The 1963,O 28,20:1
Wendt, William
Hamlet 1959,S 11,21:4
South Pacific 1965,Ap 3,25:1
Wendy, Peter (Playwright)
Room V 1941,S 28,IX,1:4
Wenerholm, Wana
Lady in the Dark 1941,Ja 24,14:2
By Jupiter 1942,Je 4,22:1
Wenger, John (Lighting Director)
Walk Hard 1946,Mr 28,34:2
Wenger, John (Scenic Designer)
Bridge of Distances, The 1925,S 29,30:1
Bridge of Distances, The 1925,O 4,IX,1:1
Master of the Inn, The 1925,D 23,22:2
Tip-Toes 1925,D 29,20:2
Monkey Talks, The 1925,D 29,20:1
No Foolin' 1926,Je 25,25:1
Oh, Kay! 1926,N 9,31:3
Piggy 1927,Ja 12,22:2
Hit the Deck! 1927,Ap 26,32:1
Funny Face 1927,N 23,28:2
Spring Song 1927,D 22,26:3
Here's Howe! 1928,My 2,19:3
Good Boy 1928,S 6,23:2
Ups-A-Daisy 1928,O 9,34:2
Spring Is Here 1929,Mr 12,26:1
Pardon My English 1933,Ja 21,11:4
Walk Hard 1946,Mr 28,34:2
Wengraf, John
Candle in the Wind 1941,S 16,19:6
Candle in the Wind 1941,O 23,26:2
Candle in the Wind 1941,N 2,IX,1:1
French Touch, The 1945,D 10,18:2
Ist Geraldine ein Engel? 1946,N 4,33:4
Traitor, The 1949,Ap 1,30:2
Wenham, Jane
Oedipus; Critic, The 1946,My 21,19:2
Oedipus 1946,My 21,19:2
Wenitsky, Harry
Alt Heidelberg 1926,My 31,10:5

Wenkstern (Playwright)
Pickwick Club, The 1936,S 27,X,1:1
Wenman, Diana (Miscellaneous)
Salad Days 1958,N 11,24:1
Wenman, Henry
Journey's End 1929,Mr 23,23:1
Journey's End 1929,Jl 14,IX,5:1
Journey's End 1930,Ja 27,24:7
Wenneman, Klaus
Dallas-November 22d 1965,N 12,54:1
Wenning, A T
This Fine-Pretty World 1923,D 27,11:1
Wenrich, Percy (Composer)
Right Girl, The 1921,Mr 16,12:1
Some Party 1922,Ap 17,22:1
Lambs Gambol 1925,Ap 27,15:1
Fool's Bells 1925,D 24,8:3
Castles in the Air 1926,S 7,19:2
Who Cares 1930,Jl 9,27:1
Wenrich, Percy (Lyricist)
Lambs Gambol 1925,Ap 27,15:1
Wensydler, Hans (Composer)
Romio and Julietta 1925,Ap 21,19:1
Fratricide Punished 1925,Ap 21,19:1
Wente, William Wray
Merry Wives of Windsor, The 1954,F 17,27:1
Wentler, Fred
Play's the Thing, The 1948,Ap 29,19:2
Wentworth, John
Drunkard, The; Fallen Saved, The 1929,D 31,14:6
Audition of the Apprentice Theatre 1939,Je 2,26:2
Wentworth, Philip
King and I, The 1956,Ap 19,35:4
Kiss Me, Kate 1956,My 10,27:2
Wentworth, Richard
Once Over Lightly 1942,N 20,26:2
Show Boat 1954,O 29,28:4
Show Boat 1957,Je 28,30:2
Mikado, The 1968,My 2,59:1
Wenzel, Arthur
Born Yesterday 1958,Mr 22,12:6
Wenzel, Helen
Priorities of 1942 1942,Mr 13,23:2
What's Up 1943,N 12,24:6
Wenzel, Marcin (Costume Designer)
Jaselka 1965,Ja 6,32:1
Book, The 1965,Ja 6,32:1
Woman, The 1965,Ja 6,32:1
Post Office, The 1965,Ja 6,32:1
Labyrinth, The 1965,Ja 6,32:1
Kernel and the Shell, The 1965,Ja 6,32:1
Jacob and the Angel 1965,Ja 6,32:1
Nightmare, The 1965,Ja 6,32:1
Wepman, Helen
Breaking Wall, The 1960,Ja 26,27:5
Werba, Louis (Producer)
Barnum Was Right 1922,N 12,VIII,1:6
Twinkle Twinkle 1926,N 17,22:2
Passing of the Third Floor Back, The
1937,Ag 3,20:6
Dead End 1937,Ag 17,23:1
Werbek, Henry
From Vienna 1939,Je 21,26:2
Werbezirk, Gisela
Abie's Irish Rose 1927,O 23,VIII,2:4
Dreimal Hochzeit 1929,Ap 28,IX,1:4
Queen Mother 1938,D 26,29:4
Proud Accent 1949,Ap 23,10:2
Werbing, Teja (Playwright)
Little Theatre Tournament; Aristocrat, The
1929,My 8,34:4
Werfel, Franz (Original Author)
Song of Bernadette 1944,Jl 27,15:3
Embezzled Heaven 1944,N 1,20:2
Embezzled Heaven 1944,N 5,II,1:2
Jacobowsky and the Colonel 1945,Je 24,II,1:3
Song of Bernadette 1946,Mr 27,22:2
Werfel, Franz (Playwright)
Juarez and Maximilian 1925,My 27,26:3
Goat Song 1926,Ja 26,18:1
Goat Song 1926,F 7,VII,1:1
Schweiger 1926,Mr 24,20:4
Schweiger 1926,Mr 28,VIII,1:1
Juarez and Maximilian 1926,O 12,31:1
Juarez and Maximilian 1926,O 17,VIII,1:1
Paul Among the Jews 1928,Ag 5,VII,1:1
Kingdom of God in Bohemia, The
1931,Mr 8,VIII,2:7
Eternal Road, The 1937,Ja 8,14:2
Eternal Road, The 1937,Ja 24,X,1:1
Jacobowsky and the Colonel 1944,Mr 15,17:2
Jacobowsky and the Colonel 1944,Mr 19,II,1:1
Jacobowsky and the Colonel 1944,My 21,II,1:1
Werich, Jan
North and South 1930,O 5,IX,4:1
Golem, The 1931,D 13,VIII,3:4
Tempest, The 1945,Ja 26,17:2
Tempest, The 1945,F 4,II,1:1
Finian's Rainbow 1949,O 19,36:3
Werkwerth, Manfred (Director)
Frau Flinz 1962,Jl 8,II,1:1
Werner, Don (Scenic Designer)
Drunkard, The; Fallen Saved, The 1959,Je 24,37:2

Werner, Fred
Would-Be Gentleman, The 1946,Ja 10,29:2
Howdy Mr Ice 1948,Je 25,28:5
Werner, Fred (Miscellaneous)
Conquering Hero, The 1961,Ja 17,40:2
Sail Away 1961,O 4,48:5
Little Me 1962,N 19,41:3
Leonard Bernstein's Theater Songs 1965,Je 29,27:2
Skyscraper 1965,N 15,48:1
Werner, Fred (Musical Director)
Gay Divorce 1960,Ap 4,37:1
High Spirits 1964,Ap 8,34:1
Sweet Charity 1966,Ja 31,22:1
Werner, Oskar
After-Dinner Evening With Oskar Werner, An
1967,Mr 27,39:1
Werner, Paul
Fedora 1924,Ja 24,14:2
Werner, Phil (Producer)
Praying Curve 1927,Ja 25,18:2
Werner, Walter
Heilige Crispin, Der 1933,Je 25,IX,1:2
Wernher, Hilda (Playwright)
Christine 1960,Ap 29,27:1
Wernick, Richard (Composer)
Saintliness of Margery Kempe, The 1959,F 3,35:6
Geranium Hat, The 1959,Mr 18,45:1
Wernicke, Annemarie
Wozzeck 1966,Ap 6,34:1
Ratten, Die 1966,Ap 13,36:1
Wernimont, Marguerite
Man Who Died Twice, The 1925,D 14,19:1
Wernli, Rick
Comforter, The 1964,O 22,42:1
Werrenrath, Reinald
School for Scandal, The 1923,Je 5,24:3
Music in the Air 1932,O 23,IX,3:3
Music in the Air 1932,N 9,28:2
Music in the Air 1932,N 20,IX,1:1
Werris, Sam E (Playwright)
Crazy With the Heat 1941,Ja 15,18:2
Werteimer, Sidney Jr
Great Guns 1939,N 18,23:4
Wertenbaker, Lael Tucker (Original Author)
Gift of Time, A 1962,F 23,34:1
Gift of Time, A 1962,Mr 4,II,1:1
Werth, Anna
Bitter Sweet 1934,My 8,28:4
Wertham, Fredric (Dr) (Original Author)
Dark Legend 1952,Mr 25,24:2
Wertheim, L (Scenic Designer)
With Privileges 1930,S 16,30:2
Wertheim, Maurice (Miscellaneous)
Mourning Becomes Electra; Homecoming
1931,O 27,22:1
Mourning Becomes Electra; Haunted, The
1931,O 27,22:1
Mourning Becomes Electra; Hunted, The
1931,O 27,22:1
Mourning Becomes Electra; Homecoming
1932,My 10,25:2
Mourning Becomes Electra; Haunted, The
1932,My 10,25:2
Mourning Becomes Electra; Hunted, The
1932,My 10,25:2
Wertheim, Ruth White (Composer)
Hamlet 1931,N 6,28:4
Hamlet 1931,N 22,VIII,8:3
Wertimer, Ned
Texas Li'l Darlin' 1949,N 26,10:5
Live Wire, The 1950,Ag 18,16:2
Best Foot Forward 1956,Mr 3,16:1
Disenchanted, The 1958,D 4,53:4
Hobo 1961,Ap 11,41:2
Emperor, The 1963,Ap 17,30:1
Family Way, The 1965,Ja 14,44:5
Hotel Passionato 1965,O 23,16:1
Wescott, Marcy
Two Bouquets, The 1938,Je 1,19:2
Boys From Syracuse, The 1938,N 24,36:1
Too Many Girls 1939,O 19,26:2
Wesier, Jacob A (Producer)
Broken Chain, The 1929,F 21,30:4
Wesker, Arnold (Director)
Friends, The 1970,My 22,41:2
Wesker, Arnold (Playwright)
Roots 1961,Mr 7,40:2
Roots 1961,Mr 19,II,1:1
Chips With Everything 1963,O 2,49:1
Kitchen, The 1966,Je 14,50:1
Four Seasons, The 1968,Mr 15,32:1
Friends, The 1970,My 22,41:2
Friends, The 1970,Jl 24,17:2
Friends, The 1970,Ag 30,II,1:1
Wesley, Donald (Miscellaneous)
Sing to Me Through Open Windows
1965,Mr 16,45:1
Day the Whores Came Out to Play Tennis, The
1965,Mr 16,45:1
Henry V 1965,Je 29,27:2
Butter and Egg Man, The 1966,O 18,49:1
Night of the Dunce 1966,D 29,21:1

Wesley, Joel
Pink Elephant, The 1953,Ap 23,37:2
Wesley, Tallulah
It Never Rains 1929,N 20,26:4
Penal Law 2010 1930,Ap 19,14:2
Wild Waves 1932,F 20,11:4
Weslin, Louis (Lyricist)
Silks and Satins 1920,Jl 16,19:1
Weslow, William
Plain and Fancy 1955,Ja 28,14:2
Plain and Fancy 1955,F 6,II,6:6
Wesoly, Luba
Off to Buffalo! 1939,F 22,18:2
Wess, Norman
Danton's Death 1938,N 3,26:2
Wesselhoeft, Eleanor
Great God Brown, The 1926,Ja 25,26:1
Beyond the Horizon 1926,D 1,24:2
Stairs, The 1927,N 8,32:7
Street Scene 1929,Ja 11,20:4
Wessels, Florence
Security 1929,Mr 29,20:1
Wessely, Paula
Roulette 1932,Ja 17,VIII,2:2
Rose Bernd 1932,D 4,IX,1:3
Wesson, Gene
Happy Hunting 1956,D 7,30:1
Wesson Brothers
Wine, Women and Song 1942,S 29,18:3
West, Abe
Seven Against One 1930,My 7,25:1
West, Albert
Cyrano de Bergerac 1923,N 2,14:1
Merchant of Venice, The 1925,D 28,12:1
Cyrano de Bergerac 1926,F 19,18:1
Joan of Arc 1926,Ap 24,21:2
John 1927,N 5,16:4
See Naples and Die 1929,S 27,30:4
Last Mile, The 1930,F 14,21:2
Lady Beyond the Moon 1931,Ap 1,36:5
Experience Unnecessary 1931,D 31,16:2
Blind Alley 1935,S 25,19:6
Double Dummy 1936,N 12,30:1
Off to Buffalo! 1939,F 22,18:2
Weak Link, The 1940,Mr 5,19:2
Royal Family, The 1940,Ag 13,15:3
Porgy and Bess 1942,Ja 23,16:2
West, Alfred
Nobody's Business 1923,O 23,17:1
West, Alvy (Composer)
Whistling Wizard and the Sultan of Tuffet
1970,F 1,70:1
West, Alvy (Miscellaneous)
Davy Jones's Locker 1959,Mr 30,25:1
Davy Jones's Locker 1966,D 25,48:5
West, Alvy (Musical Director)
Wizard of Oz, The 1968,N 28,69:2
Ali Baba and the Forty Thieves 1970,D 29,40:1
West, Arthur
Sun-Kist 1921,My 24,20:2
All-Star Jamboree 1921,Jl 14,18:1
Ziegfeld Follies 1923,O 22,17:2
Paradise Alley 1924,Ap 2,17:3
Captain Jinks 1925,S 9,22:1
Young Alexander 1929,Mr 13,28:2
Aries Is Rising 1939,N 22,16:5
West, Barbara (Miscellaneous)
Return of Ulysses, The 1943,F 7,II,1:6
West, Basil
Sophie 1920,Mr 3,12:2
Marie Antoinette 1921,N 23,16:1
Busybody, The 1924,S 30,27:5
West, Bernie
Bells Are Ringing 1956,N 29,43:4
Bells Are Ringing 1956,N 30,18:2
Oh, Kay! 1960,Ap 18,37:2
Hit the Deck 1960,Je 24,32:1
All American 1962,Mr 20,44:1
Beauty Part, The 1962,D 28,5:2
Children From Their Games 1963,Ap 12,33:1
Poor Bitos 1964,N 16,40:2
Wayward Stork, The 1966,Ja 20,27:1
Teaspoon Every Four Hours, A 1969,Je 16,57:1
West, Bert
Chicken Feed 1923,S 25,10:2
Spellbound 1927,F 16,17:2
West, Bonnie
Rumple 1957,N 7,42:2
West, Brooks
Taming of the Shrew, The 1940,F 6,17:2
There Shall Be No Night 1940,Ap 30,25:2
Joan of Lorraine 1946,N 19,40:2
West, Buster
Vaudeville (Palace) 1925,O 20,29:2
George White's Scandals 1926,Je 15,23:2
Scandals 1927,Jl 3,VII,1:1
Ups-A-Daisy 1928,O 9,34:2
Vaudeville (Palace) 1931,My 4,15:2
Vaudeville (Palace) 1932,Je 6,18:2
White Horse Inn 1936,O 2,28:5
Follow the Girls 1944,Ap 10,15:2
Follow the Girls 1944,Ap 16,II,1:2

West, Charles
  Romeo and Juliet 1956,O 25,41:1
West, Claude (Miscellaneous)
  Brothers Karamazov, The 1957,D 9,39:4
  Drunkard, The; Fallen Saved, The 1959,Je 24,37:2
  Idiot, The 1960,S 26,38:1
  Man and Superman 1960,N 7,46:2
  Emmanuel 1960,D 5,42:2
  Montserrat 1961,Ja 9,30:5
  Five Posts in the Market Place 1961,Mr 6,30:1
  Merchant of Venice, The 1962,F 3,13:2
West, Clifford
  Respectfully Yours 1947,My 14,29:4
West, Donald
  Way of the World, The 1965,Je 2,40:1
  Richard III 1965,Je 3,26:1
  Skin of Our Teeth, The 1966,Je 2,51:1
  As You Like It 1966,Je 4,19:1
West, Dorothy
  Crooked Square, The 1923,S 11,10:2
West, Edna
  Jack in the Pulpit 1925,Ja 7,33:1
  Society Girl 1931,D 31,16:1
  All the King's Horses 1934,Ja 31,21:3
  Strip Girl 1935,O 21,22:6
  Alice Takat 1936,F 11,19:2
  Ladies and Gentlemen 1939,O 18,30:2
  Old Acquaintance 1940,D 24,18:3
  Jason 1942,Ja 22,12:2
West, Edwin (Producer)
  She Shall Have Music 1959,Ja 23,18:4
West, Eric
  Eight Bells 1933,O 30,14:2
West, Everett
  Knights of Song 1938,O 18,29:2
  New Moon, The 1942,Ag 19,14:2
  Rosalinda; Fledermaus, Die 1942,O 29,26:5
West, Fay
  Ed Wynn's Carnival 1920,Ap 6,18:2
  Fair Circassian, The 1921,D 7,22:3
  Bye Bye, Barbara 1924,Ag 26,6:3
West, Frances
  Puntila 1959,My 15,26:2
West, Frederick
  Pageant of the Nativity of Christ 1948,D 25,6:7
West, Gene
  Front Page, The 1928,Ag 15,19:2
  Nigger Rich 1929,S 21,16:7
West, Gordon
  Around the World 1946,Je 1,9:5
West, Harold
  Mob, The 1920,O 11,18:1
  Great Adventure, The 1921,F 26,9:2
  Verge, The 1921,N 15,23:2
  Hairy Ape, The 1922,Mr 10,18:2
  Salome 1922,My 23,12:4
  Stepping Stones 1923,N 7,14:3
  His Queen 1925,My 12,26:1
  Dybbuk, The 1925,D 16,22:2
  Aiglon, L' 1927,D 27,24:3
  Mademoiselle 1932,O 19,22:4
  Field of Ermine 1935,F 9,10:4
  Meet the Prince 1935,Ag 6,20:4
  Tell Me Pretty Maiden 1937,D 17,33:5
West, Isabel
  Paddy the Next Best Thing 1920,Ag 28,5:5
  Romance 1921,Mr 1,18:2
  Seventh Heaven 1922,O 31,11:1
  What Women Do? 1925,Jl 21,26:4
West, J Royer
  Friars Club Frolic 1933,My 15,16:4
West, James
  Born Yesterday 1954,Ja 1,16:6
West, Jennifer
  Dutchman 1964,Mr 25,46:2
  Diamond Orchid 1965,F 11,44:4
  Malcolm 1966,Ja 12,29:1
  Sondra 1967,My 10,39:1
  Harold 1967,My 10,39:1
  Tiger at the Gates 1968,Mr 1,30:1
West, John
  Ups-A-Daisy 1928,O 9,34:2
  Prologue to Glory 1938,Mr 18,22:2
West, Joseph
  Seven Against One 1930,My 7,25:1
West, Joyce
  Man and Superman 1960,N 7,46:2
  Emmanuel 1960,D 5,42:2
  Five Posts in the Market Place 1961,Mr 6,30:1
West, Judi
  Shoot Anything With Hair That Moves 1969,F 3,29:1
West, Julius (Translator)
  Wedding, The 1961,Ap 21,26:2
  On the High Road 1961,Ap 21,26:2
  Anniversary, The 1961,Ap 21,26:2
West, Kathleen
  Trial by Jury 1955,O 18,48:1
West, Laura (Playwright)
  Night Before Christmas, The 1941,Ap 11,25:2
West, Madge
  Dreaming Dust, The 1955,D 8,46:5
  Age and Grace 1956,F 21,38:2

You Never Can Tell 1958,Je 17,25:1
  Lysistrata 1959,My 20,40:2
  Living Room, The 1962,N 22,43:5
West, Mae
  Mimic World of 1921, The 1921,Ag 18,9:2
  Sex 1926,Ap 27,22:4
  Wicked Age, The 1927,O 2,VIII,4:6
  Wicked Age, The 1927,N 5,16:6
  Diamond Lil 1928,Ap 10,32:1
  Sex 1930,S 28,VIII,2:5
  Constant Sinner, The 1931,Ag 30,VIII,1:6
  Constant Sinner, The 1931,S 15,30:1
  Catherine Was Great 1944,Ag 3,16:1
  Diamond Lil 1948,Ja 26,16:6
  Diamond Lil 1948,F 15,II,3:2
  Diamond Lil 1948,N 30,33:2
  Diamond Lil 1949,F 7,16:2
  Diamond Lil 1951,S 15,8:2
West, Mae (Original Author)
  Constant Sinner, The 1931,Ag 30,VIII,1:6
  Constant Sinner, The 1931,S 15,30:1
West, Mae (Playwright)
  Wicked Age, The 1927,N 5,16:6
  Diamond Lil 1928,Ap 10,32:1
  Pleasure Man 1928,O 2,34:7
  Diamond Lil 1929,Ja 27,IX,1:3
  Constant Sinner, The 1931,Ag 30,VIII,1:6
  Catherine Was Great 1944,Jl 11,18:2
  Catherine Was Great 1944,Ag 3,16:1
  Diamond Lil 1948,Ja 26,16:6
  Diamond Lil 1948,N 30,33:2
  Diamond Lil 1949,F 7,16:2
  Diamond Lil 1951,S 15,8:2
West, Martha (Costume Designer)
  One-Woman Show, A 1962,My 22,31:1
West, Morris L (Original Author)
  Devil's Advocate, The 1961,Mr 10,20:1
  Devil's Advocate, The 1961,Mr 19,II,1:1
  Daughter of Silence 1961,D 1,28:1
West, Morris L (Playwright)
  Daughter of Silence 1961,D 1,28:1
West, Nathanael (Original Author)
  Miss Lonelyhearts 1957,O 4,26:2
West, Nathanael (Playwright)
  Good Hunting 1938,N 22,26:5
West, Nelson
  She Loves Me Not 1933,N 21,22:4
West, Olive
  Arabesque 1925,O 21,20:2
  Glory Hallelujah 1926,Ap 7,26:2
West, Ollie
  Let's Face It 1941,O 30,26:2
West, Pat
  Vaudeville (Palace) 1929,Jl 15,25:4
West, Paul
  Rosalinda; Fledermaus, Die 1942,O 29,26:5
  This Was Burlesque 1965,Mr 17,55:3
West, Percita
  Blind Mice 1930,O 16,28:2
West, Rebecca (Original Author)
  Return of the Soldier, The 1928,Jl 8,VIII,1:7
West, Robert
  Take It As It Comes 1944,F 11,17:2
West, Rowena
  Weak Sisters 1925,O 14,31:3
West, Solon
  Yeomen of the Guard, The 1935,Jl 30,16:4
  Gondoliers, The 1935,Ag 6,20:5
West, Starr
  News Item 1935,Ag 6,20:3
West, Timothy
  Italian Girl, The 1968,Jl 4,14:1
  Richard II 1969,S 4,50:1
  Edward II 1969,S 4,50:1
  Much Ado About Nothing 1970,S 4,19:1
  Boswell's Life of Johnson 1970,S 4,19:1
  Exiles 1970,N 19,42:4
West, Vivian
  Lady of the Lamp, The 1920,Ag 18,6:4
West, Will
  Love Letter, The 1921,O 5,20:1
West, Willie
  Laffing Room Only 1944,D 25,15:4
Westbay, Annette (Miscellaneous)
  Madame Alias 1927,S 4,VII,2:4
Westbay, Annette (Playwright)
  Heaven-Tappers, The 1927,Mr 9,28:3
Westberg, Margaret
  Lady in the Dark 1941,Ja 24,14:2
  Lady in the Dark 1941,S 3,26:6
Westbrook, Frank
  Shoemaker's Holiday, The 1938,Ja 3,17:2
  On the Town 1944,D 29,11:4
  Allegro 1947,O 11,10:2
Westbrook, Frank (Choreographer)
  Song of Norway 1958,Je 23,19:2
  Song of Norway 1959,Je 26,16:2
Westbrook, Frank (Director)
  Skits-Oh-Frantics 1967,Ap 3,39:2
Westbrook, Frank (Miscellaneous)
  Song of Norway 1959,Je 26,16:2
Westbrook, John
  Play of Daniel, The 1961,D 28,22:6

Westbrook, John—Cont

  Untitled-Recital 1970,S 3,36:1
Westcott, Gordon
  Great Necker, The 1928,Mr 7,28:2
  House of Fear, The 1929,O 8,34:2
  Short Cut, The 1930,Ja 28,28:2
  Room 349 1930,Ap 23,24:5
  Paging Danger 1931,F 27,19:2
Westcott, Harry
  Little Theatre Tournament; Monkey's Paw, The 1929,My 10,32:2
  Contrast, The 1940,Mr 26,17:2
Westcott, Lester
  Patience 1935,S 3,24:4
Westcott, Lynda
  No Place to Be Somebody 1969,My 5,53:3
  No Place to Be Somebody 1969,D 31,17:1
Westcott, Netta
  Symphony in Two Flats 1930,S 17,30:4
Westerfield, James
  Sing Out, Sweet Land! 1944,D 28,24:2
  Madwoman of Chaillot, The 1949,Ja 9,II,1:1
  Detective Story 1949,Mr 24,34:2
  Venus Observed 1952,F 14,24:2
  Wooden Dish, The 1955,O 7,20:1
  Cut of the Axe 1960,F 2,38:2
Westergren, Haakan
  Dear Octopus 1939,N 12,IX,2:5
Westerlund, Catrin
  Father, The 1962,My 15,49:1
  Long Day's Journey Into Night 1962,My 16,35:4
Westerman, Dale
  Great Scot! 1965,N 12,56:3
  Most Happy Fella, The 1966,My 12,55:1
  Show Boat 1966,Jl 20,48:1
Westermeier, Paul
  Lauf ins Glueck 1935,My 19,IX,2:5
Western, Burke
  Molly Darling 1922,S 2,10:2
  Paradise Alley 1924,Ap 2,17:3
Westerton, Frank
  Champion, The 1921,Ja 4,11:1
  It Is the Law 1922,N 30,28:2
Westervelt, Conrad (Playwright)
  Not so Fast 1923,My 23,18:4
  Romancing 'Round 1927,O 4,32:4
  Mongolia 1927,D 27,24:5
  Down to Miami 1944,S 12,23:5
Westervelt, L (Playwright)
  Sweet Seventeen 1924,Mr 18,24:2
  Made for Each Other 1924,S 30,27:2
Westfield, Earl B (Composer)
  Malinda 1929,D 4,37:2
Westfield, Earl B (Lyricist)
  Malinda 1929,D 4,37:2
Westheimer, David (Playwright)
  My Sweet Charlie 1966,D 7,56:1
  My Sweet Charlie 1966,D 25,II,1:1
Westland, Mary
  Faith and Prudence 1952,O 15,40:2
Westley, Ethel
  Glass Slipper, The 1925,O 20,29:1
  Strange Interlude 1928,Ja 31,28:1
Westley, Helen
  Power of Darkness, The 1920,Ja 22,22:1
  Jane Clegg 1920,F 25,14:1
  Treasure, The 1920,O 5,13:1
  Heartbreak House 1920,N 11,11:1
  Mr Pim Passes By 1921,Mr 1,18:1
  Liliom 1921,Ap 21,18:1
  He Who Gets Slapped 1922,Ja 10,15:1
  From Morn to Midnight 1922,My 22,17:2
  R U R 1922,O 10,16:1
  Lucky One, The 1922,N 21,15:2
  Tidings Brought to Mary, The 1922,D 25,20:1
  Peer Gynt 1923,F 6,14:1
  Adding Machine, The 1923,Mr 20,24:1
  Windows 1923,O 9,17:2
  Failures, The 1923,N 23,20:1
  Race With the Shadow, The 1924,Ja 21,20:5
  Fata Morgana 1924,Mr 4,16:3
  Guardsman, The 1924,O 14,23:1
  Caesar and Cleopatra 1925,Ap 14,27:1
  Glass Slipper, The 1925,O 20,29:1
  Glass Slipper, The 1925,O 25,VIII,1:1
  Merchants of Glory 1925,D 15,28:3
  Goat Song 1926,Ja 26,18:1
  Chief Thing, The 1926,Mr 23,24:2
  At Mrs Beam's 1926,Ap 26,24:3
  Pygmalion 1926,N 16,24:1
  Right You Are (If You Think You Are) 1927,F 24,27:1
  Mr Pim Passes By 1927,Ap 19,24:1
  Doctor's Dilemma, The 1927,N 22,33:1
  Strange Interlude 1928,Ja 31,28:1
  Volpone 1928,Ap 10,32:1
  Faust 1928,O 9,34:1
  Major Barbara 1928,N 20,28:4
  Major Barbara 1928,D 2,X,1:1
  Dynamo 1929,F 12,22:1
  Camel Through the Needle's Eye, The 1929,Ap 16,32:2
  Camel Through the Needle's Eye, The 1929,Ap 28,IX,1:1

Westley, Helen—Cont
Apple Cart, The 1930,F 25,30:1
Green Grow the Lilacs 1931,Ja 27,21:2
Green Grow the Lilacs 1931,F 8,VIII,1:1
Getting Married 1931,Mr 31,25:5
Reunion in Vienna 1931,N 17,31:1
American Dream; 1933 1933,F 22,24:5
American Dream; 1849 1933,F 22,24:5
They Shall Not Die 1934,F 22,24:4
Jig Saw 1934,My 1,26:3
Sleeping Clergyman, A 1934,O 9,16:1
Love Is Not So Simple 1935,N 5,33:1
Love Is Not So Simple 1935,N 10,IX,1:6
Primrose Path, The 1939,Ja 5,16:3
Primrose Path, The 1939,Ja 16,11:2
Westley, Helen (Miscellaneous)
Moon in the Yellow River, The 1932,Mr 1,19:3
American Dream; 1849 1933,F 22,24:5
American Dream; 1650 1933,F 22,24:5
American Dream; 1933 1933,F 22,24:5
Mask and the Face, The 1933,My 9,20:2
Jig Saw 1934,My 1,26:3
Westley, Jay
Goodbye Again 1943,N 10,28:4
Westley, John
Seeing Things 1920,Je 18,19:2
Dulcy 1921,Ag 15,14:1
Ice-Bound 1923,F 12,16:2
Twelve Miles Out 1925,N 17,29:2
Henry IV, Part I 1926,Je 1,29:1
Beaux' Stratagem, The 1928,Je 5,20:1
Button, Button 1929,O 24,26:1
Through the Night 1930,Ag 19,19:1
Great Man, The 1931,Ap 8,20:6
Bad Penny, A 1931,Ag 23,VIII,2:4
Work Is for Horses 1937,N 22,14:6
Westleyans, Nimble
Hello, Yourself 1928,O 31,28:2
Westman, Bernard (Composer)
Brothers Karamazov, The 1957,D 9,39:4
Idiot, The 1960,S 26,38:1
Sudden End of Anne Cinquefoil, The
1961,Ja 11,25:2
Westman, Herbert
Bewitched 1924,O 2,26:3
Westman, Neville
Bit o' Love, A 1925,My 13,24:2
Regular Guy, A; Man's Man, A 1931,Je 5,27:1
Anybody's Game 1932,D 22,21:4
Moroni 1936,Ag 19,19:1
Westman, Nydia
Pigs 1924,S 2,22:5
2 Girls Wanted 1926,S 10,25:3
Jonesy 1929,F 24,IX,4:1
Buckaroo 1929,Mr 18,31:1
Jonesy 1929,Ap 10,32:2
Unsophisticates, The 1929,D 31,14:5
Ada Beats the Drum 1930,My 9,20:4
American Primitive 1937,Ag 13,12:5
Merchant of Yonkers, The 1938,D 29,14:2
Strange Bedfellows 1948,Ja 15,27:3
Madwoman of Chaillot, The 1949,Ja 9,II,1:1
Madwoman of Chaillot, The 1949,S 11,II,1:1
Madwoman of Chaillot, The 1950,Je 14,41:2
Mr Pickwick 1952,S 18,36:3
Mr Pickwick 1952,S 28,II,1:1
Emperor's Clothes, The 1953,F 10,24:2
Sleeping Prince, The 1956,N 2,31:1
Endgame 1958,Ja 29,32:4
Endgame 1958,F 16,II,1:1
Distant Bell, A 1960,Ja 14,29:1
Rape of the Belt, The 1960,N 7,46:1
Midgie Purvis 1961,F 2,25:3
I Am a Camera 1961,Jl 10,26:1
Westman, Theodore
Thank You 1921,O 4,10:2
Not so Fast 1923,My 23,18:4
Brook 1923,Ag 20,14:3
Houses of Sand 1925,F 18,17:1
Family Upstairs, The 1925,Ag 18,14:2
Romancing 'Round 1927,O 4,32:4
Westman, Theodore (Playwright)
Solid Ivory 1925,N 17,29:3
Westmoreland, Lillian
Rang Tang 1927,Jl 13,20:1
Weston, Ann
Subway Express 1929,S 25,34:3
Our Town 1944,Ja 11,24:5
Weston, Bert
Processional 1937,O 14,23:1
Cradle Will Rock, The 1937,D 6,19:4
Cradle Will Rock, The 1938,Ja 4,19:3
Weston, Betty
Henky 1924,Ap 27,VIII,2:3
Melody Man, The 1924,My 14,14:2
Gorilla, The 1925,Ap 29,24:2
Lady Screams, The 1927,My 3,24:2
Weston, Beverly
Top Banana 1951,N 2,19:2
Wish You Were Here 1952,Je 26,26:6
Weston, Bill (Miscellaneous)
Come on Strong 1962,O 5,29:1
Weston, David
Founders, The 1957,My 14,39:1

Weston, Eddie
Gentlemen Prefer Blondes 1949,D 9,35:3
Rumple 1957,N 7,42:2
Weston, Ellen
Far Country, A 1961,Ap 5,32:1
Weston, Emanuel
Bottomland 1927,Je 28,29:3
Weston, Eric
Days of Our Youth, The 1941,N 29,15:2
Weston, Geo
Sellout, The 1933,S 7,17:2
Weston, Graham
Home 1970,N 18,41:1
Weston, Hal
Star of Bengal 1929,S 26,27:2
Second Mate, The 1930,Mr 25,34:5
Weston, Helen
Babbling Brookes 1927,F 26,13:2
Weston, Horace
Opportunity 1920,Jl 31,5:1
Weston, Huntly
Bulls, Bears and Asses 1932,My 7,11:3
Furnished Rooms 1934,My 30,14:6
Help Yourself! 1936,Jl 15,15:1
Doctor Faustus 1937,Ja 9,21:2
Weston, Jack
Season in the Sun 1950,S 29,31:2
Bells Are Ringing 1956,N 29,43:4
Bells Are Ringing 1956,N 30,18:2
Weston, James
Red, White and Maddox 1969,Ja 27,27:1
Lovely Ladies, Kind Gentlemen 1970,D 29,38:1
Weston, Jay (Miscellaneous)
Does a Tiger Wear a Necktie? 1969,F 26,38:1
Weston, Maggie
Dice of the Gods, The 1923,Ap 6,20:2
Weston, Mark
Billy Budd 1955,My 4,35:1
Time Limit! 1956,Ja 25,27:2
Weston, Melissa
School for Scandal, The 1953,Je 24,29:2
Weston, R P (Lyricist)
Tell Her the Truth 1932,O 29,18:2
Weston, R P (Playwright)
Tell Her the Truth 1932,O 29,18:2
Weston, Robert
Winners and Losers 1947,F 27,27:2
Weston, Ruth
Love and Babies 1933,Ag 23,21:4
No More Ladies 1934,Ja 24,20:3
Red Cat, The 1934,S 20,21:1
Dominant Sex, The 1935,Ap 2,24:5
Seven Keys to Baldpate 1935,My 28,30:2
Country Wife, The 1935,Jl 2,24:2
There's Wisdom in Women 1935,Jl 16,24:1
If This Be Treason 1935,Jl 30,17:1
There's Wisdom in Women 1935,O 31,17:1
Among Those Sailing 1936,F 12,24:4
Eastwood Ho 1936,Jl 8,14:2
Would-Be Gentleman, The 1936,Ag 4,15:1
Forbidden Melody 1936,N 3,33:1
Double Exposure 1937,Ag 18,15:2
Run Sheep Run 1938,N 4,26:2
American Way, The 1939,Ja 23,9:2
Pastoral 1939,N 2,26:2
Out From Under 1940,My 6,13:2
George Washington Slept Here 1940,O 19,20:3
Night Before Christmas, The 1941,Mr 30,I,48:2
Night Before Christmas, The 1941,Ap 11,25:2
Lady Comes Across, The 1942,Ja 10,10:2
What Big Ears! 1942,Ap 21,18:5
Three's a Family 1943,My 6,24:2
Weston, Scotty
Vaudeville (Palace) 1929,Jl 15,25:4
Weston, Victor Watts
Burgomaster of Stilemonde, The 1923,N 16,15:3
Hamlet 1923,N 20,23:3
Weston, William
Good Times 1920,Ag 10,10:1
Westphal, Audrey
Banjo Eyes 1941,D 26,20:2
Wetherall, Frances
At Mrs Beam's 1923,Mr 11,VIII,2:4
Wetherell, Nancy
New Faces of 1936 1936,My 20,24:5
Wetmore, Donald (Director)
Fireworks on the James 1940,My 15,30:2
Wetmore, Joan
Two Bouquets, The 1938,Je 1,19:2
Two on an Island 1940,Ja 23,17:2
Kind Lady 1940,S 4,28:3
Counsellor-at-Law 1942,N 25,17:2
New Life, A 1943,S 16,26:6
For Keeps 1944,Je 15,17:5
Hope for the Best 1945,F 8,14:4
Small Hours, The 1951,F 16,22:1
Girl Can Tell, A 1953,O 30,28:2
Last Love of Don Juan, The 1955,N 24,40:1
Harlequinade 1959,F 14,15:1
Electra 1959,F 14,15:1
Overruled 1959,My 27,32:2
Buoyant Billions 1959,My 27,32:2
Getting Married 1959,Je 5,18:2

Wetmore, Joan—Cont
Advise and Consent 1960,N 18,25:1
Very Rich Woman, A 1965,O 5,5:8
Great Indoors, The 1966,F 2,23:1
Wetson, Richard
Trial by Jury 1948,Ja 6,27:2
Wettach, Dolores
Shakuntala 1959,S 10,41:2
Wettergren, Eric (Dr) (Miscellaneous)
Green Pastures, The 1932,O 30,IX,2:4
Wetzel, Arleen
Pequod 1969,Je 30,33:1
Wetzel, Donald (Original Author)
All Summer Long 1954,S 24,26:2
All Summer Long 1954,O 3,II,1:1
Wetzel, Edward
Veronica's Veil 1936,F 10,19:6
Wever, Edward H
Merchant of Venice, The 1922,D 22,13:1
Rita Coventry 1923,F 20,12:2
Sweet Seventeen 1924,Mr 18,24:2
Nerves 1924,S 2,22:2
Judy Drops In 1924,O 6,24:2
She Had to Know 1925,F 3,25:3
Lucky Break 1925,Ag 12,16:2
Great Gatsby, The 1926,F 3,22:1
Lady Alone 1927,Ja 21,12:5
Love Is Like That 1927,Ap 19,24:1
Tonight at 12 1928,N 16,28:1
Wever, G De Wolf
Espanola 1921,D 30,13:1
Wever, Ned
Second Little Show, The 1930,Ag 17,VIII,2:2
Second Little Show, The 1930,S 3,36:1
Days to Come 1936,D 16,35:1
Case History 1938,O 22,15:2
Wexler, Gil (Lighting Director)
Viet Rock 1966,O 12,34:1
Wexler, Irving (Producer)
Cage, The 1961,Mr 6,30:1
417 1961,Mr 6,30:1
Wexler, Jacob
Twice 100,000 1934,N 23,22:6
Wexler, Joan
Shylock and His Daughter 1947,S 30,22:2
Wexler, Peter (Costume Designer)
Taming of the Shrew, The 1963,Mr 8,9:1
Camino Real 1970,Ja 9,42:1
Wexler, Peter (Lighting Director)
Portrait of the Artist as a Young Man, A
1962,My 29,21:1
Barroom Monks, The 1962,My 29,21:1
Abe Lincoln in Illinois 1963,Ja 23,5:2
Taming of the Shrew, The 1963,Mr 8,9:1
Joyful Noise, A 1966,D 16,57:1
Wexler, Peter (Miscellaneous)
In the Matter of J Robert Oppenheimer
1968,Je 7,31:1
In the Matter of J Robert Oppenheimer
1969,Mr 7,28:1
Wexler, Peter (Scenic Designer)
Antony and Cleopatra 1959,Ja 14,28:1
Big Knife, The 1959,N 13,25:1
Brecht on Brecht 1961,N 15,52:2
Curate's Play, The 1961,D 18,41:3
Tableaux 1961,D 18,41:3
Portrait of the Artist as a Young Man, A
1962,My 29,21:1
Barroom Monks, The 1962,My 29,21:1
Abe Lincoln in Illinois 1963,Ja 23,5:2
Taming of the Shrew, The 1963,Mr 8,9:1
War and Peace 1965,Ja 12,32:1
White Devil, The 1965,D 7,56:1
Joyful Noise, A 1966,D 16,57:1
Happy Time, The 1968,Ja 19,32:2
In the Matter of J Robert Oppenheimer
1968,Je 7,31:1
In the Matter of J Robert Oppenheimer
1969,Mr 7,28:1
Uncle Vanya 1969,Ag 31,II,4:1
Camino Real 1970,Ja 9,42:1
Camino Real 1970,Ja 18,II,1:1
Murderous Angels 1970,F 8,70:1
Minnie's Boys 1970,Mr 27,27:1
Wexler, Yale
Tea and Sympathy 1953,O 1,35:1
Best House in Naples, The 1956,O 27,16:2
Wexler, Yale (Producer)
Sound of Hunting, A 1954,Ap 7,41:1
Once Over Lightly 1955,Mr 16,39:1
Wexley, John
At the Bottom 1930,Ja 10,24:3
Yoshe Kalb 1933,D 29,27:2
Wexley, John (Director)
Steel 1931,N 19,26:5
Wexley, John (Original Author)
Rapide de Minuit, Le; Last Mile, The
1932,Ap 3,VIII,2:1
Wexley, John (Playwright)
Last Mile, The 1930,F 14,21:2
Last Mile, The 1930,Mr 2,IX,1:1
Last Mile, The 1930,D 21,VIII,3:1
Steel 1931,N 19,26:5
They Shall Not Die 1934,F 22,24:4

Wexley, John (Playwright)—Cont
They Shall Not Die 1934,Mr 4,IX,1:3
They Shall Not Die 1934,Mr 11,X,1:1
Weyand, Ronald
Cave Dwellers, The 1957,O 21,29:2
Golem, The 1959,F 26,38:2
Country Scandal, A 1960,My 6,21:8
Becket 1960,O 6,50:1
Firebugs, The 1963,F 13,7:2
Chief Thing, The 1963,Ap 30,27:2
Lesson, The 1963,S 18,35:4
Great Western Union, The 1965,F 10,45:1
Danton's Death 1965,O 22,46:1
Alchemist, The 1966,O 14,48:1
East Wind, The 1967,F 10,30:1
Galileo 1967,Ap 14,31:1
Saint Joan 1968,Ja 5,42:1
Tiger at the Gates 1968,Mr 1,30:1
King Lear 1968,N 8,43:1
Cry of Players, A 1968,N 15,40:1
Miser, The 1969,My 9,35:1
Weyl, Michael
Father, The 1937,Ap 21,18:5
Weyman, Stanley (Original Author)
Red Robe, The 1928,D 26,15:1
Red Robe, The 1929,Ja 13,VIII,1:1
Weyse, Bill
Assassin, The 1945,O 18,20:2
Whale, James (Director)
Journey's End 1929,Mr 23,23:1
Hundred Years Old, A 1929,O 2,28:2
Journey's End 1930,Ag 5,26:4
Violet, The 1930,S 30,24:2
Hand in Glove 1944,D 5,19:1
Whale, James (Producer)
Journey's End 1928,D 30,VIII,4:1
Whale, James (Scenic Designer)
Hundred Years Old, A 1929,O 2,28:2
Whalen, Dick
Dixie to Broadway 1924,O 30,22:1
Whalen, Grover
Off the Record; Mayor Answers the Newspapers!
Wow! 1935,Je 19,23:3
Down in the Dumps 1937,Mr 7,II,1:1
Whalen, Harold
Luana 1930,S 18,28:1
Off to Buffalo! 1939,F 22,18:2
Scandals 1939,Ag 29,17:2
Whalen, Michael
Ten Little Indians 1944,Je 28,21:2
Kiss Me, Kate 1965,My 13,31:1
Whaley, Charlotte
Only in America 1959,N 20,35:1
Wharton, Carly (Mrs) (Producer)
Too Many Heroes 1937,N 16,26:2
Medicine Show 1940,Ap 13,20:6
Wharton, Carly (Producer)
Cream in the Well, The 1941,Ja 21,19:2
Cafe Crown 1942,Ja 24,12:5
Cherry Orchard, The 1944,Ja 26,22:1
Assassin, The 1945,O 18,20:2
Wharton, Edith (Original Author)
Age of Innocence, The 1928,N 18,IX,2:6
Age of Innocence, The 1928,N 28,24:2
Old Maid, The 1935,Ja 8,26:1
Ethan Frome 1936,Ja 7,24:7
Ethan Frome 1936,Ja 22,15:2
Ethan Frome 1936,F 2,IX,1:1
Wharton, John F (Producer)
Many Mansions 1937,O 28,28:6
Time Remembered 1957,N 13,41:2
Rope Dancers, The 1957,N 21,39:1
Wharton, Leigh
John Gabriel Borkman 1959,N 26,57:4
Death of Satan, The 1960,Ap 6,49:1
To Damascus 1961,F 15,40:2
French Way, The; Grand Vizier, The
1962,Mr 21,36:2
French Way, The; Edward and Agrippina
1962,Mr 21,36:2
Antigone 1962,D 29,5:5
Orthee 1962,D 29,5:5
Lorenzo 1963,F 16,5:2
Serjeant Musgrave's Dance 1966,Mr 9,44:1
Wharton, Mr (Playwright)
Heart of Cellini, The 1923,O 21,VIII,2:1
Whatmore, Mr
Sarah Simple 1937,My 23,X,2:1
Wheatley, Alan
House of Borgia, The 1935,O 6,XI,3:1
St Helena 1936,O 7,32:1
Wheatley, Jane
Oh, Henry! 1920,My 6,14:2
Merchant of Venice, The 1921,Ap 2,14:2
Ambush 1921,O 11,22:1
Voltaire 1922,Mr 21,17:1
What the Public Wants 1922,My 2,22:3
Second Mrs Tanqueray, The 1924,O 28,27:1
Arms and the Man 1925,S 15,28:1
Arms and the Man 1925,O 4,IX,1:1
Yellow 1926,S 22,30:1
Warrior's Husband, The 1932,Mr 12,19:4
Dangerous Corner 1932,O 28,23:1

Wheatley, Jane (Director)
Dangerous Corner 1933,Jl 18,20:4
Wheatley, Joan
New Moon, The 1942,Ag 19,14:2
Rosalinda; Fledermaus, Die 1942,O 29,26:5
Wheatley, John Illingworth
This Mad Whirl 1937,Ja 10,II,4:8
Wheatley, Tom
Ping-Pong 1959,Ap 17,22:1
Measure for Measure 1960,Jl 27,33:1
All the Way Home 1960,D 1,42:1
Cat and the Canary, The 1965,Ja 5,26:1
Wheaton, Anna
Three Showers 1920,Ap 6,18:1
Nine O'Clock Revue 1921,F 9,7:5
Vaudeville (Palace) 1922,F 14,21:1
Wheaton, Edna
Ziegfeld Follies 1921,Je 22,10:1
Wheaton, Gladys
Artists and Models 1927,N 16,28:2
Whedon, John (Lyricist)
1776 1926,Ap 24,11:2
Not Now-Later 1928,Ap 14,25:1
Whedon, John (Original Author)
Texas Li'l Darlin' 1949,N 26,10:5
Whedon, John (Playwright)
Gentlemen, the Queen 1927,Ap 23,14:3
Not Now-Later 1928,Ap 14,25:1
Life's Too Short 1935,S 21,18:5
Whedon, Spencer
Man Who Married a Dumb Wife, The
1930,My 9,20:5
Whedon, Tom (Lyricist)
All Kinds of Giants 1961,D 19,40:1
Whedon, Tom (Playwright)
All Kinds of Giants 1961,D 19,40:1
Wheel, Patricia
Tempest, The 1945,Ja 26,17:2
Cyrano de Bergerac 1946,O 9,33:2
Cyrano de Bergerac 1947,Ja 17,27:2
Harlequinade 1949,O 13,32:2
Browning Version, The 1949,O 13,32:2
Cry of the Peacock 1950,Ap 12,33:2
Gertie 1952,Ja 31,23:1
Sacred Flame, The 1952,O 8,35:2
Charley's Aunt 1953,D 23,22:2
Soldiers 1968,My 2,58:1
Wheeldin, Aurelia
Messin' Around 1929,Ap 23,26:3
Change Your Luck 1930,Je 7,10:2
Wheeler, A C (Miss) (Translator)
Mama 1930,Mr 30,VIII,4:8
Wheeler, Bert
Ziegfeld Follies 1923,O 22,17:2
Vaudeville (Hippodrome) 1924,S 30,27:5
Vaudeville (Palace) 1925,D 8,28:6
Vaudeville (Palace) 1926,Je 22,21:3
Rio Rita 1927,F 3,18:3
Vaudeville (Palace) 1929,D 2,28:6
Vaudeville (New Amsterdam Theatre)
1931,Je 22,17:3
Scandals 1931,S 27,VIII,3:7
New Priorities of 1943 1942,S 16,28:2
Laugh Time 1943,S 9,35:2
Laugh Time 1943,S 19,II,1:1
Three Wishes for Jamie 1952,Mr 22,9:2
Gang's All Here, The 1959,O 2,23:1
Seven Scenes for Yeni 1963,My 13,36:2
Wheeler, Betty
Ziegfeld Follies 1923,O 22,17:2
Vaudeville (Hippodrome) 1924,S 30,27:5
Vaudeville (Palace) 1925,D 8,28:6
Vaudeville (Palace) 1926,Je 22,21:3
Wheeler, Billy Edd (Playwright)
Hatfields & McCoys 1970,Je 23,34:1
Wheeler, Burt
All for Love 1949,Ja 24,16:5
Wheeler, Byron
West Side Story 1968,Je 25,32:1
Wheeler, C E (Dr) (Translator)
Via Crucis 1923,N 13,25:2
Wheeler, Carlstadt
Miracle, The 1924,Ja 16,17:1
Wheeler, Carol
Parlor Story 1947,Mr 5,29:2
Gayden 1949,My 11,34:4
Ladies of the Corridor, The 1953,O 22,33:5
Wheeler, Charles
Yours Truly 1927,Ja 26,16:5
Wheeler, Claudia Carlstadt
Miracle, The 1924,Ag 19,9:1
Wheeler, Curtis
Tall Kentuckian, The 1953,Je 17,30:1
Don't Drink the Water 1966,N 18,37:1
Wheeler, David (Director)
Live Like Pigs 1965,Je 8,48:2
Plebeians Rehearse the Uprising, The
1968,S 8,II,11:1
Stop, You're Killing Me; Bad Bad Jo-Jo
1969,Mr 20,53:1
Stop, You're Killing Me; Terrible Jim Fitch
1969,Mr 20,53:1

Wheeler, David (Director)—Cont
Stop, You're Killing Me; Laughs, Etc
1969,Mr 20,53:1
Criminals, The 1970,F 26,33:2
Wheeler, Frankie
Friars Club Frolic 1933,My 15,16:4
Slight Case of Murder, A 1935,S 12,28:5
Wheeler, Harold (Choreographer)
Coco 1969,D 19,66:1
Wheeler, Harold (Miscellaneous)
Promises, Promises 1968,D 2,59:3
Wheeler, Harold (Musical Director)
Promises, Promises 1968,D 2,59:3
Wheeler, Hugh (Playwright)
Big Fish, Little Fish 1961,Mr 16,42:2
Big Fish, Little Fish 1961,Mr 26,II,1:1
Look: We've Come Through 1961,O 26,40:1
We Have Always Lived in the Castle
1966,O 20,53:1
Wheeler, Jerry (Director)
Wonderful World of the Brothers Grimm, The
1967,D 23,28:1
Wheeler, Jerry (Producer)
Wonderful World of the Brothers Grimm, The
1967,D 23,28:1
Wheeler, Joan
Growing Pains 1933,N 24,24:2
Strangers at Home 1934,S 15,20:5
Achilles Had a Heel 1935,Ap 28,X,1:1
Western Waters 1937,D 29,17:1
Wheeler, John
Century Revue and the Midnight Rounders, The
1920,Jl 13,9:1
Guest of Honor, The 1920,S 21,12:1
American Tragedy, An 1926,O 12,31:2
On the Spot 1930,O 30,33:3
Crucible 1933,S 5,22:4
Her Man of Wax 1933,O 12,32:3
Summer Wives 1936,Ap 14,18:1
Blossom Time 1938,D 27,12:2
Mikado, The 1942,F 4,22:2
Pirates of Penzance, The 1942,F 18,22:2
Iolanthe 1942,F 24,26:4
Strings, My Lord, Are False, The 1942,My 20,24:2
Happiest Girl in the World, The 1961,Ap 4,42:1
Sweet Charity 1966,Ja 31,22:1
Wheeler, Josh
Paint Your Wagon 1951,N 13,32:2
Wheeler, Kenneth
Patience 1924,D 30,15:1
Wheeler, Lois
Innocent Voyage, The 1943,N 16,27:2
Pick-Up Girl 1944,My 4,25:2
Trio 1944,D 30,13:4
All My Sons 1947,Ja 30,21:2
All My Sons 1947,F 9,II,1:1
Young and Fair, The 1948,N 23,35:2
Dinosaur Wharf 1951,N 9,23:2
Fifth Season, The 1953,Ja 24,13:2
Troublemakers, The 1954,D 31,11:3
Trial of Dmitri Karamazov, The 1958,Ja 28,30:1
Wheeler, Mike
Macbeth 1968,N 30,49:3
Wheeler, Raymond
Little Theatre Tournament; End of the Dance, The
1929,My 11,22:2
Wheeler, Roger
Bellamy Trial, The 1928,Ag 20,21:1
Wheeler, Roger (Playwright)
Gray Shadow 1931,Mr 11,23:4
Wheeler, Ron (Miscellaneous)
John Gabriel Borkman 1959,N 26,57:4
Wheeler, Ruth
Footlights 1927,Ag 20,8:2
Whelan, Arleen
Doughgirls, The 1942,D 31,19:2
Doughgirls, The 1943,Ja 10,VIII,1:1
Oh, Herbert! 1945,Je 20,26:3
Whelan, Christopher (Composer)
World of Paul Slickey, The 1959,My 6,48:7
Whelan, Ken
Lady Comes Across, The 1942,Ja 10,10:2
Whelan, Ken (Choreographer)
Let Freedom Sing 1942,O 6,18:2
Whelan, Martin
Greenwillow 1970,D 8,60:1
Whelan, Ray
Chicago 70 1970,My 26,33:1
Whelan, Thomas
View From the Bridge, A 1956,N 9,34:4
Whelen, Christopher (Composer)
Richard II 1956,O 24,44:1
Much Ado About Nothing 1958,Ag 27,34:6
Wheller, Steve
Earthlight Theater 1970,N 4,38:2
Whiffen, John
Dancers, The 1923,O 18,17:2
Whiffen, Peggy
Trelawney of the 'Wells' 1927,F 1,24:4
Just Fancy! 1927,O 12,30:2
Whiffen, Thomas (Mrs)
Just Suppose 1920,N 2,15:1
Untitled-Benefit 1922,My 8,14:5
Advertising of Kate, The 1922,My 9,22:2

Whiffen, Thomas (Mrs)—Cont
Goose Hangs High, The 1924,Ja 30,16:1
Goose Hangs High, The 1924,F 3,VII,1:1
Trelawney of the 'Wells' 1925,Je 2,16:2
Jane-Our Stranger 1925,O 9,27:2
Two Orphans, The 1926,Ap 6,26:2
Two Orphans, The 1926,Ap 11,VIII,1:1
Trelawney of the 'Wells' 1927,F 1,24:4
Trelawney of the 'Wells' 1927,F 6,VII,1:1
Just Fancy! 1927,O 12,30:2
Whight, Bob
Stars on Ice 1942,Jl 3,12:2
Stars on Ice (2d Edition) 1943,Je 25,13:2
Whight, Peggy
Stars on Ice 1942,Jl 3,12:2
Hats Off to Ice 1944,Je 23,15:2
Whipper, Leigh
Porgy 1927,O 11,26:2
Change Your Luck 1930,Je 7,10:2
Never No More 1932,Ja 8,27:1
Yeah-Man 1932,My 27,27:3
Stevedore 1934,Ap 19,33:2
White Man 1936,O 19,22:4
How Come Lawd? 1937,O 1,18:5
Of Mice and Men 1937,N 24,20:5
Medicine Show 1940,Ap 13,20:6
Lysistrata 1946,O 18,27:5
Volpone 1948,Ja 9,24:6
Set My People Free 1948,N 4,38:2
How Long Till Summer 1949,D 28,30:3
Child of the Morning 1951,N 17,9:7
Shrike, The 1952,Ja 16,20:2
Shrike, The 1953,N 26,51:2
Whipper, Leigh (Miscellaneous)
Yeah-Man 1932,My 27,27:3
Whipple, Carol
Tragedian in Spite of Himself, A 1948,F 6,29:2
Wedding, The 1948,F 6,29:2
Bear, The 1948,F 6,29:2
On the Harmfulness of Tobacco 1948,F 6,29:2
Whipple, Sidney B (Original Author)
Mr Banks of Birmingham 1939,Ja 21,18:4
Red Velvet Goat, The 1939,Ja 21,18:4
Coggerers, The 1939,Ja 21,18:4
Whipple, Waldo
Breakfast in Bed 1920,F 4,12:1
Whisonant, Lawrence
Belle Helene, La 1941,Jl 8,14:1
Porgy and Bess 1942,Ja 23,16:2
Whistler, Edna
Little Nellie Kelly 1922,N 14,16:1
No, No, Nanette 1925,S 17,20:2
Whistler, Rex (Costume Designer)
Victoria Regina 1936,Ja 5,IX,1:1
Whistler, Rex (Playwright)
Baronet and the Butterfly, The 1924,Je 8,VII,1:8
Whistler, Rex (Scenic Designer)
Streamline 1934,O 21,IX,1:3
Victoria Regina 1935,D 27,15:2
Victoria Regina 1936,Ja 5,IX,1:1
Pride and Prejudice 1936,Ag 30,IX,1:1
Victoria Regina 1937,Jl 11,X,1:7
Old Music 1937,S 5,X,2:1
Victoria Regina 1938,O 4,20:2
Love for Love 1947,My 27,30:2
Whitaker, David
Tempest, The 1970,F 15,67:1
Whitaker, R
What a Relief 1935,D 19,34:4
Little Dark Horse 1941,N 17,14:4
Native Son 1942,O 24,10:6
Whitaker, Robert
Cock-A-Doodle Dandy 1955,N 4,26:5
Whitaker, Rudolph
South Pacific 1943,D 30,11:2
Jeb 1946,F 22,20:2
Whitaker, Valentine
Loyalties 1928,Ag 26,VII,1:3
Whitbrook, Mary
Crime and Punishment 1935,Ja 23,20:3
Whitby, Gwynne
Women of Twilight 1952,Mr 4,22:2
Whitcomb, Barry
Sport of Kings, The 1926,My 5,24:2
Arabian, The 1927,N 1,20:5
Napoleon 1928,Mr 9,21:1
Whitcomb, Beverly
Thracian Horses, The 1961,S 28,58:2
Whitcombe, Cliff
Hit the Deck! 1927,Ap 26,32:1
Saluta 1934,Ag 29,13:4
White, A Courtney
Once Upon a Time 1939,D 21,28:2
White, A M
Who's Who 1924,Ap 18,19:2
White, Aaron
Carmen Jones 1956,Je 1,28:2
White, Al
Vaudeville (Palace) 1928,Ag 28,27:3
White, Al Jr (Choreographer)
Star and Garter 1942,Je 25,26:2
Connecticut Yankee, A 1943,N 18,30:2
Memphis Bound 1945,My 25,23:2

Texas Li'l Darlin' 1949,N 26,10:5
White, Al Jr (Director)
Mr Winkle's Holliday 1946,Je 24,27:6
White, Alfred
Pressing Business 1930,N 18,28:5
Cafe Crown 1942,Ja 24,12:5
Assassin, The 1945,O 18,20:2
White, Alfred (Director)
Hired Husband 1932,Je 4,9:5
White, Alfred H
Abie's Irish Rose 1937,My 13,30:2
White, Alfred H (Playwright)
Pressing Business 1930,N 18,28:5
Sap Runs High, The 1936,F 1,9:4
Sap Runs High, The 1936,F 5,15:3
White, Alice
Dinner at Eight 1933,Ap 9,IX,1:7
White, Anna
King Lear 1968,Je 3,55:4
White, Arthur Corning (Playwright)
Virgin, The 1926,F 23,26:1
Julie 1927,My 10,24:4
Love in the Tropics 1927,O 19,24:3
White, Barbara
Holiday 1928,N 27,36:1
White, Beatrice
It Never Rains 1931,D 25,29:3
White, Bernard (Scenic Designer)
Via Crucis 1923,F 11,VII,1:4
White, Bertram
Julius Caesar 1930,Ap 4,22:3
White, Bishop
Once Over Lightly 1938,D 10,13:4
White, Bobby
Love's Old Sweet Song 1940,My 3,16:3
My Sister Eileen 1940,D 27,23:2
Lifeline 1942,D 1,20:3
Flare Path 1942,D 24,20:2
Sleepy Hollow 1948,Je 4,26:3
White, Carl
Pony Cart, The 1954,S 15,39:2
White, Carmel
All That Glitters 1938,Ja 20,18:2
Kiss the Boys Goodbye 1938,S 29,30:2
White, Charles
Letter of the Law, The; Robe Rouge, La
   1920,F 24,11:1
Napoleon 1928,Mr 9,21:1
Career 1957,My 1,42:6
Cloud 7 1958,F 15,15:2
Comes a Day 1958,N 7,22:1
Cockeyed Kite 1961,S 14,27:1
Front Page, The 1968,O 20,85:5
Front Page, The 1969,My 12,54:2
Front Page, The 1969,N 2,86:1
White, Christine
Long Watch, The 1952,Mr 21,19:5
Hatful of Rain, A 1955,N 10,44:1
White, Courtney
Myrtie 1924,F 5,21:2
Main Line, The 1924,Mr 26,19:4
Fatal Wedding, The 1924,Je 3,22:3
Honor of the Family, The 1926,D 27,21:1
Get Me in the Movies 1928,My 22,18:3
Dracula 1931,Ap 14,33:3
Her Man of Wax 1933,O 12,32:3
Birthright 1933,N 22,22:3
Field of Ermine 1935,F 9,10:4
If a Body 1935,My 1,25:3
This Our House 1935,D 12,33:3
White, Crystal
Blackouts of 1949 1949,S 7,39:2
White, Dan (Miscellaneous)
Ziegfeld Follies 1943,Ap 2,16:2
White, Dana
Happiest Millionaire, The 1956,N 21,21:3
Love Me Little 1958,Ap 15,42:2
White, David
Leaf and Bough 1949,Ja 22,10:2
Great Big Doorstep, The 1950,Mr 18,8:6
Earth Spirit 1950,Je 7,33:4
Pink Elephant, The 1953,Ap 23,37:2
Roomful of Roses, A 1955,O 18,48:1
White, Deborah
Princess Rebecca Birnbaum 1966,Mr 7,22:1
Suburban Tragedy 1966,Mr 7,22:1
White, Deede
Safari! 1955,My 12,32:6
White, Donald
Make Yourself at Home 1945,S 14,21:2
Ivy Green, The 1949,Ap 6,37:2
White, E B (Playwright)
Hey, Nonny, Nonny! 1932,Je 7,22:3
White, Earl
Dark Hours, The 1932,N 15,24:2
White, Eddie (Producer)
Family Way, The 1965,Ja 14,44:5
Summertree 1969,D 10,60:1
White, Edgar (Playwright)
Life and Times of J Walter Smintheus, The
   1970,D 10,59:1
White, Edith
Pressing Business 1930,N 18,28:5

White, Edmund (Playwright)
Blue Boy in Black, The 1963,My 1,32:1
White, Edna
Nightstick 1927,N 11,20:4
White, Edward
Music in My Heart 1947,O 3,30:2
White, Eric
Something More! 1964,N 11,36:1
White, Ethel
Carmen Jones 1943,D 3,26:2
White, F Fitzpatrick (Producer)
Buffalo Skinner, The 1959,F 20,18:1
White, Flo
Would-Be Gentleman, The 1930,Ap 30,29:2
White, Frances
Jimmie 1920,N 18,15:3
Vaudeville (Forty-Fourth Street Theatre)
   1921,S 20,12:2
Hotel Mouse, The 1922,Mr 14,11:3
Vaudeville (Palace) 1924,Ap 29,29:2
White, G Harris (Composer)
Round With Ring, A 1969,O 30,56:1
White, George
Scandals 1920,Je 8,9:1
Friars Club Frolic 1921,Je 13,16:2
George White's Scandals 1921,Jl 12,14:1
George White's Scandals 1922,Ag 29,10:1
Manhattan Mary 1927,S 27,30:3
George White's Scandals 1929,S 24,29:1
John Brown 1950,My 4,32:7
White, George (Composer)
Manhattan Mary 1927,S 27,30:3
George White's Scandals 1929,S 24,29:1
White, George (Director)
George White's Scandals 1926,Je 15,23:2
Manhattan Mary 1927,S 27,30:3
George White's Scandals 1928,Jl 3,19:1
George White's Scandals 1929,S 24,29:1
George White's Scandals 1931,S 15,30:1
Music Hall Varieties 1932,N 23,15:3
Melody 1933,F 15,17:4
George White's Scandals 1935,D 26,20:2
Scandals 1939,Ag 20,IX,2:1
Scandals 1939,Ag 29,17:2
White, George (Lyricist)
Manhattan Mary 1927,S 27,30:3
George White's Scandals 1929,S 24,29:1
White, George (Miscellaneous)
Jackass, The 1960,Mr 24,39:2
Marcus in the High Grass 1960,N 22,38:6
White, George (Playwright)
Scandals 1920,Je 8,9:1
George White's Scandals 1921,Jl 12,14:1
George White's Scandals 1922,Ag 29,10:1
George White's Scandals 1923,Je 19,22:5
Scandals 1924,Jl 1,16:1
George White's Scandals 1925,Je 23,24:2
George White's Scandals 1926,Je 15,23:2
Manhattan Mary 1927,S 27,30:3
George White's Scandals 1928,Jl 3,19:1
George White's Scandals 1929,S 24,29:1
George White's Scandals 1931,S 15,30:1
Music Hall Varieties 1932,N 23,15:3
George White's Scandals 1935,D 26,20:2
Scandals 1939,Ag 29,17:2
Royal Gambit 1959,Mr 5,34:2
Royal Gambit 1959,Mr 15,II,1:1
Jackass, The 1960,Mr 24,39:2
Sign of Jonah, The 1960,S 9,35:1
Emperor, The 1963,Ap 17,30:1
Murderer Among Us, A 1964,Mr 26,43:1
White, George (Producer)
Scandals 1920,Je 8,9:1
George White's Scandals 1926,Je 15,23:2
Scandals 1927,Jl 3,VII,1:1
Manhattan Mary 1927,S 4,VII,2:4
Manhattan Mary 1927,S 27,30:3
George White's Scandals 1928,Jl 3,19:1
George White's Scandals 1929,S 24,29:1
Flying High 1930,F 9,VIII,1:1
Flying High 1930,Mr 4,24:4
Scandals 1931,Ag 11,28:4
Scandals 1931,Ag 16,VIII,1:1
George White's Scandals 1931,S 15,30:1
Scandals 1931,S 27,VIII,3:7
Music Hall Varieties 1932,N 23,15:3
Music Hall Varieties 1933,Ja 3,19:4
Melody 1933,F 15,17:4
Scandals 1935,O 30,17:1
George White's Scandals 1935,D 26,20:2
Scandals 1939,Ag 20,IX,2:1
Scandals 1939,Ag 29,17:2
Scandals 1939,S 3,IX,1:1
White, Gil
Simple Simon 1930,F 19,22:1
Smiles 1930,N 19,19:2
Jubilee 1935,O 14,20:1
White, Gladys
Deep River 1926,O 5,26:2
White, Gordon
City of Kings 1949,F 18,27:2
White, H Fisher
Cymbeline 1923,O 3,12:1

White, H Mortimer
Drifting 1922,Ja 3,20:3
White, Harold
Serena Blandish 1929,Ja 24,30:3
White, Harriet
Take It As It Comes 1944,F 11,17:2
White, Harry
Artists and Models 1924,O 16,33:3
Vaudeville (Palace) 1930,Mr 3,18:5
Vaudeville (Palace) 1930,D 1,19:1
Don Carlos 1962,F 28,27:5
Storm, The 1962,Mr 31,17:2
Walk in Darkness 1963,O 29,30:2
White, Harvey
Mississippi 1929,Ap 14,X,2:1
White, Helen
Polly 1925,O 12,19:1
Porgy and Bess 1935,O 11,30:2
White, Henry
Love Letter, The 1921,O 5,20:1
White, Henry C (Playwright)
Sunshine 1926,Ag 18,15:2
White, Hub
Wicked Age, The 1927,N 5,16:6
White, Hugh (Playwright)
Little A 1947,Ja 16,31:2
White, Irving (Playwright)
Fly Away Home 1935,Ja 16,20:4
Fly Away Home 1936,Jl 21,13:1
Fly Away Home 1937,Jl 27,24:3
Fly Away Home 1937,Jl 28,15:1
White, J Andrew (Major)
Black Boy 1926,O 7,30:2
White, J Fisher
Thunder in the Air 1929,N 12,34:3
White, J Irving
Arabian, The 1927,N 1,20:5
White, J J (Director)
Rap, The 1931,Ap 7,31:2
It Never Rains 1931,D 25,29:3
Angeline Moves In 1932,Ap 20,27:5
In Heaven and Earth 1936,Mr 27,24:8
White, J J (Producer)
House of Doom, The 1932,Ja 26,20:4
White, Jack
Betsy 1926,D 29,24:3
George White's Scandals 1929,S 24,29:1
White, James
Brigadoon 1950,My 3,36:2
Peter Pan 1954,O 21,30:2
White, Jane
Secret Garden, The 1931,N 8,31:4
Rosalinda; Fledermaus, Die 1942,O 29,26:5
Strange Fruit 1945,N 30,18:6
Insect Comedy, The 1948,Je 4,26:3
Razzle Dazzle 1951,F 20,21:1
Climate of Eden, The 1952,N 7,20:2
Take a Giant Step 1953,O 4,II,1:1
Time of Storm 1954,F 26,14:2
Jane Eyre 1958,My 2,31:1
Power and the Glory, The 1958,D 12,2:7
Once Upon a Mattress 1959,My 12,40:1
Taming of the Shrew, The 1960,Ag 20,17:1
Hop, Signor! 1962,My 8,45:2
Trojan Women, The 1963,D 24,7:6
Love's Labour's Lost 1965,Je 16,46:1
Coriolanus 1965,Jl 15,23:1
Troilus and Cressida 1965,Ag 13,17:1
Iphigenia in Aulis 1968,Ap 6,43:1
Cuban Thing, The 1968,S 25,36:2
White, Jane (Costume Designer)
Living Room, The 1962,N 22,43:5
White, Jane Douglas (Musical Director)
Jo 1964,F 13,25:1
White, Jean
Snapshots of 1921 1921,Je 3,19:2
White, Jesse
Sons and Soldiers 1943,My 5,22:2
My Dear Public 1943,S 10,28:1
Mrs Kimball Presents 1944,Mr 1,17:3
Helen Goes to Troy 1944,Ap 25,17:2
Harvey 1944,N 2,23:2
Cradle Will Rock, The 1947,D 27,11:2
Red Gloves 1948,D 6,28:2
Kelly 1965,F 8,28:2
Kiss Me, Kate 1965,My 13,31:1
Harvey 1970,F 25,41:1
White, Joan
Susannah and the Elders 1937,N 21,XI,3:6
Junior Miss 1943,Ap 18,II,1:1
Passage to India, A 1962,F 1,23:1
Stephen D 1967,S 25,58:1
White, Joan (Director)
Madrigal of Shakespeare, A 1968,F 14,56:2
White, Joe
Let and Sub-Let 1930,My 20,32:2
White, John (Playwright)
Bugs 1965,N 19,31:1
Veronica 1965,N 19,31:1
Bananas 1968,D 5,60:1
White, John C
Mama Loves Papa 1926,F 23,26:2

White, John Jr
How Long Till Summer 1949,D 28,30:3
White, John Reeves (Miscellaneous)
Play of Risen Christ, The 1970,Mr 9,44:1
White, Jonathan
Measure for Measure 1954,Je 30,23:1
Antony and Cleopatra 1967,Ag 2,25:1
Government Inspector, The 1967,O 28,34:1
White, Joseph (Playwright)
Old Judge Mose Is Dead 1969,Ag 29,25:1
White, Josh
John Henry 1939,D 17,IX,5:6
John Henry 1940,Ja 11,18:2
Blue Holiday 1945,My 22,13:3
Long Way From Home, A 1948,F 9,25:2
How Long Till Summer 1949,D 28,30:3
Man, The 1950,Ja 20,28:2
Touchstone 1953,F 4,33:2
Only in America 1959,N 20,35:1
Long Dream, The 1960,F 18,36:2
White, Joyce
Clinging Vine, The 1922,D 25,20:2
Passing Show of 1924, The 1924,S 4,13:4
Castles in the Air 1926,S 7,19:2
Satellite 1935,N 21,27:5
White, Judy
Saving Grace, The 1963,Ap 19,28:1
Sambo 1970,Jl 23,24:1
White, June
Little Theatre Tournament; Man in the Stalls, The
1929,My 8,34:4
Achilles Had a Heel 1935,O 14,20:2
White, Kenneth (Playwright)
Who Fights This Battle? 1936,S 21,26:3
Lady Who Came to Stay, The 1941,Ja 3,13:2
Visitor, The 1944,O 18,24:5
Freight 1949,F 4,30:2
Riders to the Sea 1949,F 4,30:2
Freight 1950,Ap 27,36:2
White, Lawrence
Happy-Go-Lucky 1920,Ag 25,6:1
White, Lee
Come In 1924,My 11,VIII,1:4
White, Leonard
Sleep of Prisoners, A 1951,O 17,36:2
White, Leonard (Playwright)
Wooden Idol, The 1930,My 13,27:2
White, Les (Director)
Too Hot for Maneuvers 1945,My 3,26:5
White, Les (Miscellaneous)
Ziegfeld Follies 1943,Ap 2,16:2
White, Les (Playwright)
Cocktails of 1934 1934,My 5,22:1
Too Hot for Maneuvers 1945,My 3,26:5
White, Lewis
Swing Mikado, The 1939,Mr 2,18:2
White, Lillian
Little Miss Charity 1920,S 3,6:3
Good Morning, Dearie 1921,N 2,20:2
Bunch and Judy, The 1922,N 29,20:1
Stepping Stones 1923,N 7,14:3
White, Lilly
Best of Burlesque 1957,S 30,27:2
White, Livinia
Pirate, The 1942,N 26,39:2
White, Louise
Precedent 1931,Ap 15,24:5
White, Ludlow
New Moon, The 1944,My 18,16:2
White, Madelyn
Sing Out the News 1938,S 26,12:5
White, Marjorie
Hello, Lola! 1926,Ja 13,30:1
Lady Fingers 1929,F 1,22:4
Hot-Cha! 1932,F 21,VIII,2:1
Hot-Cha! 1932,Mr 9,17:3
White, Mark
Man and Superman 1964,D 7,45:2
War and Peace 1965,Ja 12,32:1
Judith 1965,Mr 25,42:2
White, Michael (Miscellaneous)
Philadelphia, Here I Come! 1966,F 17,28:1
Loot 1968,Mr 19,40:2
Tom Paine 1968,Mr 26,38:1
Oh! Calcutta! 1969,Je 18,33:1
White, Michael (Producer)
Cambridge Circus 1964,O 7,53:1
Tom Paine 1967,N 12,II,17:6
Sleuth 1970,N 13,25:1
White, Miles (Costume Designer)
Right This Way 1938,Ja 6,22:3
Best Foot Forward 1941,O 2,28:2
Best Foot Forward 1941,O 26,IX,1:3
Pirate, The 1942,N 26,39:2
Oklahoma! 1943,Ap 1,27:1
Ziegfeld Follies 1943,Ap 2,16:2
Ziegfeld Follies 1943,Ap 11,II,1:1
Oklahoma! 1943,Ap 11,II,1:1
Early to Bed 1943,Je 18,16:2
Get Away Old Man 1943,N 25,40:2
Allah Be Praised! 1944,Ap 21,14:2
Dream With Music 1944,My 19,15:2
Bloomer Girl 1944,O 6,18:5

White, Miles (Costume Designer)—Cont
Bloomer Girl 1944,O 8,II,1:1
Carousel 1945,Ap 20,24:2
Day Before Spring, The 1945,N 23,27:2
Gypsy Lady 1946,S 18,25:6
Duchess of Malfi, The 1946,O 16,35:2
Carousel 1949,Ja 26,28:2
Gentlemen Prefer Blondes 1949,D 9,35:3
Bless You All 1950,D 15,42:2
Bless You All 1951,My 20,II,1:1
Oklahoma! 1951,My 30,15:2
Pal Joey 1952,Ja 4,17:6
Three Wishes for Jamie 1952,Mr 22,9:2
Two's Company 1952,D 16,43:5
Two's Company 1952,D 21,II,3:1
Hazel Flagg 1953,F 12,22:2
Oklahoma! 1953,S 1,19:1
Girl in Pink Tights, The 1954,Mr 6,13:2
Ankles Aweigh 1955,Ap 19,27:1
Eugenia 1957,Ja 31,20:1
Jamaica 1957,N 1,32:2
Jamaica 1957,N 10,II,1:1
Time Remembered 1957,N 13,41:2
Time Remembered 1957,N 24,II,1:1
Oh Captain! 1958,F 5,21:2
Cheri 1959,O 13,44:1
Take Me Along 1959,O 23,22:2
Bye Bye Birdie 1960,Ap 15,13:4
Unsinkable Molly Brown, The 1960,N 4,28:1
Show Girl 1961,Ja 13,37:1
Milk and Honey 1961,O 11,52:1
Ice Capades 1966,Je 2,50:2
Ice Capades 1967,Je 2,33:1
Oklahoma! 1969,Je 24,37:1
Candida 1970,Ap 7,41:1
White, Miles (Director)
Ice Capades 1966,Je 2,50:2
White, Miles (Miscellaneous)
High Button Shoes 1947,O 10,32:2
White, Mortimer
Yankee Princess, The 1922,O 3,22:1
Madre 1923,D 31,9:6
Wonderful Visit, The 1924,F 13,17:3
Second Mrs Tanqueray, The 1924,O 28,27:1
Small Timers, The 1925,Ja 28,15:3
Nocturne 1925,F 17,19:1
White, Murray
Wine, Women and Song 1942,S 29,18:3
White, Myrna
Funny Thing Happened on the Way to the Forum
A 1962,My 9,49:1
White, Natalie (Playwright)
Emperor's New Clothes, The 1950,Je 20,23:2
White, Nathaniel
Liliom 1956,F 18,12:5
Wedding in Japan 1957,Mr 12,37:7
Marching Song 1959,D 29,20:1
White, Newt
Cock-A-Doodle Dandy 1955,N 4,26:5
White, Newton (Miscellaneous)
Much Ado About Nothing 1961,Jl 7,17:1
Midsummer Night's Dream, A 1961,Ag 3,13:1
White, Newton (Scenic Designer)
Time to Go 1960,Mr 23,33:1
Coggerers, The 1960,Mr 23,33:1
White, Nora
Song of Norway 1944,Ag 22,20:2
White, Norman H Jr (Playwright)
Reunion 1938,Ap 12,26:4
White, Norman H Jr (Producer)
Reunion 1938,Ap 12,26:4
White, Onna (Choreographer)
Guys and Dolls 1955,Ap 21,32:2
Finian's Rainbow 1955,My 19,25:1
Carmen Jones 1956,Je 1,28:2
Music Man, The 1957,D 20,31:1
Music Man, The 1958,S 28,II,1:1
Whoop-Up 1958,D 23,2:7
Take Me Along 1959,O 23,22:2
Irma la Douce 1960,S 30,31:2
Irma la Douce 1960,O 16,II,1:1
Let It Ride 1961,O 13,27:4
I Had a Ball 1964,D 16,50:1
Half a Sixpence 1965,Ap 26,38:2
Mame 1966,My 25,41:1
Illya Darling 1967,Ap 12,37:1
Illya Darling 1967,N 2,58:1
White, Onna (Director)
1776 1969,Mr 17,46:2
Gantry 1970,F 16,44:1
White, Onna (Miscellaneous)
Music Man, The 1965,Je 17,26:4
White, Patricia
Calico Wedding 1945,Mr 8,18:6
Minstrel Boy, The 1948,O 15,28:2
Rumple 1957,N 7,42:2
White, Pearlie
Little Cantor, The 1930,S 24,26:2
White, Peter
Boys in the Band, The 1968,Ap 15,48:1
White, Philip
Blue Eyes 1921,F 22,11:2
Snapshots of 1921 1921,Je 3,19:2
Partners Again 1923,Mr 1,10:3

White, Philip—Cont

Tantrum, The 1924,S 5,20:2
Menagerie 1935,Jl 2,24:3
Candle in the Wind 1941,O 23,26:2
Patriots, The 1943,Ja 30,11:2
Patriots, The 1943,D 21,22:5
Song of Norway 1944,Ag 22,20:2
White, Reeta
Slave Ship 1969,N 22,46:1
White, Richard
Streetcar Named Desire, A 1955,Mr 4,18:2
Macbeth 1955,O 20,42:2
White, Richard (Musical Director)
John Brown's Body 1953,F 16,17:2
White, Robert
Kiss and Tell 1943,Mr 18,22:1
Kiss and Tell 1943,Mr 28,II,1:1
Skipper Next to God 1948,Ja 5,14:5
Magnolia Alley 1949,Ap 19,29:2
Play of Daniel, The 1960,D 27,23:6
Play of Daniel, The 1961,D 28,22:6
Elizabethans, The 1962,Ja 22,19:1
White, Robertson
Streets Are Guarded, The 1944,N 21,19:7
White, Robin
Hair 1970,Ja 13,39:1
White, Ronald
Confederacy, The 1958,Jl 3,20:1
White, Rosa
Deep Harlem 1929,Ja 8,35:2
White, Ruth
Snapshots of 1921 1921,Je 3,19:2
Bunch and Judy, The 1922,N 29,20:1
Stepping Stones 1923,N 7,14:3
War 1929,S 19,37:3
Mascaiada 1929,D 28,10:6
Caukey 1944,F 18,15:4
Ivy Green, The 1949,Ap 6,37:2
Noah 1954,O 11,32:2
Troublemakers, The 1954,D 31,11:3
Ponder Heart, The 1956,F 17,14:2
Happiest Millionaire, The 1956,N 21,21:3
Happiest Millionaire, The 1956,D 2,II,1:1
Chaparral 1958,S 10,38:2
Maidens and Mistresses at Home at the Zoo
    1958,O 29,31:1
Rashomon 1959,Ja 28,36:2
Warm Peninsula, The 1959,O 21,46:2
Whisper to Me 1960,N 22,38:6
Big Fish, Little Fish 1961,Mr 16,42:2
Big Fish, Little Fish 1961,Mr 26,II,1:1
Happy Days 1961,S 18,36:1
Lord Pengo 1962,N 20,41:2
Sarah and the Sax 1964,My 5,53:1
Absence of a Cello 1964,S 22,45:1
Malcolm 1966,Ja 12,29:1
Motel 1966,N 7,66:1
Little Murders 1967,Ap 26,38:1
Birthday Party, The 1967,O 4,40:2
Birthday Party, The 1967,O 15,II,1:1
Box-Mao-Box; Box 1968,Mr 8,48:1
Box 1968,O 1,39:1
Box 1968,O 13,II,5:1
White, Ruth (Voice)
America Hurrah; Interview; TV; Motel
    1967,O 10,55:2
White, Sammy
Passing Show of 1921, The 1920,D 30,16:2
Polly Preferred 1923,Ja 12,13:3
Greenwich Village Follies 1923,S 21,4:6
Melody Man, The 1924,My 14,14:2
Girl Friend, The 1926,Mr 18,26:5
Show Boat 1927,D 28,26:1
Show Boat 1928,Ja 8,VIII,1:1
Vaudeville (Palace) 1929,Ag 19,23:1
Vaudeville (Palace) 1931,O 19,28:5
Show Boat 1932,My 20,22:2
Yours Is My Heart 1946,S 6,16:5
Show Boat 1948,S 9,33:2
White, Schuyler
Right to Strike, The 1921,O 25,20:1
White, Sheldon (Playwright)
Right to Love, The 1925,Je 9,16:4
White, Shirley
Straw Hat, The 1926,O 15,20:2
White, Steve
County Chairman, The 1936,My 26,26:5
White, Sybil
Clearing in the Woods, A 1957,Ja 11,20:2
White, T H (Original Author)
Camelot 1960,O 3,35:1
Camelot 1960,D 5,42:1
White, T J
Front Page, The 1937,N 12,27:2
White, Ted (Miscellaneous)
Clandestine on the Morning Line 1961,O 31,28:1
White, Thelma
Earl Carroll's Vanities 1926,Ag 25,19:4
Spring Is Here 1929,Mr 12,26:1
Earl Carroll's Vanities 1930,Jl 2,28:3
Tell Her the Truth 1932,O 29,18:2
Saluta 1934,Ag 29,13:4
Right This Way 1938,Ja 6,22:3

White, Tommy
Hole in the Head, A 1957,Mr 1,15:1
Hole in the Head, A 1957,Mr 10,II,1:1
White, Tony
Hoofers, The 1969,Jl 30,23:4
White, Valerie
Call Home the Heart 1947,Ap 13,I,54:2
Winslow Boy, The 1947,O 30,32:2
Winslow Boy, The 1947,N 9,II,1:1
White, Victoria
My Golden Girl 1920,F 3,18:2
Clinging Vine, The 1922,D 25,20:2
White, W H
Student Prince, The 1924,D 3,25:3
White, W L (Playwright)
1776 1926,Ap 24,11:2
White, Wally
Hamlet 1954,Ap 24,15:2
White, Walter
Bombo 1921,O 7,20:2
Salome 1923,My 8,22:2
White, Watson
Yours, A Lincoln 1942,Jl 10,12:3
Lower North 1944,Ag 26,15:4
Up in Central Park 1945,Ja 29,17:2
Christopher Blake 1946,D 2,33:2
Gentleman From Athens, The 1947,D 10,42:4
Hilda Crane 1950,N 2,38:2
White, Wilfrid Hyde
Under the Counter 1947,O 4,10:2
Caesar and Cleopatra 1951,D 20,43:2
Antony and Cleopatra 1951,D 21,22:2
Reluctant Debutante, The 1956,O 11,50:1
Reluctant Debutante, The 1956,O 21,II,1:1
White, William
Merry Widow, The 1921,S 6,13:1
Serenade, The 1930,Mr 5,26:7
Simple Simon 1931,Mr 10,23:2
Merry Widow, The 1931,S 8,39:1
Pirates of Penzance, The 1938,Je 3,16:2
White, William L (Playwright)
Who's Who 1924,Ap 18,19:2
White, Wilson
Little Red Riding Hood 1948,Ja 12,15:3
White, Wylma Lynn
Merry Wives of Windsor, The 1954,F 17,27:1
White and Tierney
Vaudeville (Palace) 1927,Ag 23,29:3
Vaudeville (Palace) 1928,Jl 10,17:3
White Deer, Princess
Tip-Top 1920,O 6,13:2
Nine O'Clock Revue 1921,F 9,7:5
Nine O'Clock Revue 1921,F 9,7:5
Yankee Princess, The 1922,O 3,22:1
Lucky 1927,Mr 23,28:3
White Hawk, Chief
Bad Man, The 1920,Ag 31,7:1
Whitecar, W A
Inspector General, The 1923,My 1,24:1
Whitehawk, Bhana
Rain 1922,N 8,18:2
Whitehead, Bea
I Am a Camera 1956,O 10,47:2
Whitehead, Martha
Boy on the Straight-Back Chair 1969,Mr 18,36:1
Whitehead, O Z
Watched Pot, The 1933,My 5,13:7
Lake, The 1933,D 27,24:2
New Faces 1934,Mr 16,24:5
Jayhawker 1934,N 6,34:2
Fools Rush In 1934,D 26,19:2
O Evening Star 1936,Ja 9,24:6
As We Forgive Our Debtors 1936,Ag 11,24:6
Hamlet 1936,N 11,54:2
Farewell Summer 1937,Mr 30,20:2
Madame Bovary 1937,O 6,28:4
Madame Bovary 1937,N 17,26:2
Sea Gull, The 1938,Mr 29,19:2
Miss Swan Expects 1939,F 21,15:2
Life With Father 1940,Mr 3,X,2:5
Twelfth Night 1960,Je 9,29:4
Tempest, The 1960,Je 20,35:1
Whitehead, Paxton
Hole, The 1961,Ap 4,42:2
Gallows Humor 1961,Ap 19,35:1
One Way Pendulum 1961,S 19,38:2
Electra 1962,Mr 22,42:1
Affair, The 1962,S 21,34:2
Doll's House, A 1963,F 4,5:6
King Lear 1963,Je 10,37:1
Beyond the Fringe 1964 1964,Ja 10,18:1
Heartbreak House 1968,Jl 6,9:1
Chemmy Circle, The 1968,Ag 10,17:2
Doctor's Dilemma, The 1969,Je 24,37:1
Guardsman, The 1969,Ag 17,II,5:1
Rondelay 1969,N 6,55:1
Brass Butterfly, The 1970,Ja 31,34:1
Candida 1970,Ap 7,41:1
Forty Years On 1970,Ag 30,II,1:1
Whitehead, Paxton (Director)
Chemmy Circle, The 1968,Ag 10,17:2
Forty Years On 1970,Ag 30,II,1:1

Whitehead, Paxton (Miscellaneous)
Heartbreak House 1968,Jl 6,9:1
Chemmy Circle, The 1968,Ag 10,17:2
Whitehead, Ralph
Big Boy 1925,Ja 8,28:2
Happy-Go-Lucky 1926,O 1,27:2
Betsy 1926,D 29,24:3
Lady Do 1927,Ap 19,24:2
Kiss Me! 1927,Jl 22,17:1
Vaudeville (Palace) 1928,F 14,26:2
Whitehead, Robert
Mr Big 1941,O 1,24:2
Heart of a City 1942,F 13,24:6
Whitehead, Robert (Director)
Desire Under the Elms 1952,Ja 17,23:4
Mrs McThing 1952,F 21,22:1
Golden Boy 1952,Mr 13,24:3
Four Saints in Three Acts 1952,Ap 17,35:1
Sunday Breakfast 1952,My 30,12:2
After the Fall 1964,Ja 24,18:1
Marco Millions 1964,F 21,33:1
But for Whom Charlie 1964,Mr 13,42:2
Changeling, The 1964,O 30,32:2
Incident at Vichy 1964,D 4,44:1
Whitehead, Robert (Miscellaneous)
Medea 1949,My 3,31:2
Mrs McThing 1952,Mr 2,II,1:1
Tamburlaine the Great 1956,Ja 20,19:1
Major Barbara 1956,O 31,27:1
Sleeping Prince, The 1956,N 2,31:1
Visit, The 1958,My 6,40:1
Physicists, The 1964,O 14,52:1
Where's Daddy? 1966,Mr 3,27:1
Sorrow of Frederick, The 1967,Jl 8,14:2
Whitehead, Robert (Producer)
Medea 1947,O 21,27:2
Crime and Punishment 1947,D 23,29:3
Member of the Wedding, The 1950,Ja 6,26:6
Night Music 1951,Ap 9,29:6
Time of the Cuckoo, The 1952,O 16,37:4
Emperor's Clothes, The 1953,F 10,24:2
Remarkable Mr Pennypacker, The 1953,D 31,11:2
Saint Joan 1954,S 18,12:1
Flowering Peach, The 1954,D 29,19:2
Bus Stop 1955,Mr 3,23:2
Skin of Our Teeth, The 1955,Ag 18,16:1
Memory of Two Mondays, A 1955,S 30,21:1
View From the Bridge, A 1955,S 30,21:1
Waltz of the Toreadors, The 1956,D 22,14:8
Waltz of the Toreadors, The 1957,Ja 18,17:2
Hole in the Head, A 1957,Mr 1,15:1
Orpheus Descending 1957,Mr 22,28:1
Waltz of the Toreadors, The 1958,Mr 5,37:1
Touch of the Poet, A 1958,O 3,23:2
Goldilocks 1958,O 13,33:1
Cold Wind and the Warm, The 1958,D 9,55:1
Much Ado About Nothing 1959,S 18,25:2
Conquering Hero, The 1961,Ja 17,40:2
Midgie Purvis 1961,F 2,25:3
Man for All Seasons, A 1961,N 23,51:1
Man for All Seasons, A 1964,Ja 28,24:2
Prime of Miss Jean Brodie, The 1968,Ja 17,39:1
Prime of Miss Jean Brodie, The 1968,Ja 25,32:4
Price, The 1968,F 8,37:1
Sheep on the Runway 1970,F 2,28:3
Whitehead, William
Penny Arcade 1930,Mr 11,24:5
Barretts of Wimpole Street, The 1931,F 10,25:1
Chauve-Souris; Queen of Spades, The
    1931,O 22,27:1
Musical Chairs 1934,Jl 31,20:7
Aiglon, L' 1934,N 5,22:2
Aged 26 1936,D 22,32:1
Greatest Show on Earth, The 1938,Ja 6,22:2
Rivals, The 1942,Ja 15,24:2
Affair of Honor 1956,Ap 7,12:3
Whitehill, Jane
People vs Ranchman, The 1968,O 28,56:1
Young Master Dante, The 1968,D 31,19:1
War Games 1969,Ap 18,37:1
Whitehill, Lou
Abortion 1959,O 28,40:4
Movie Man 1959,O 28,40:4
Whitehouse, Robert
Richard III 1920,Mr 8,7:1
Whitehurst, George (Costume Designer)
Confederacy, The 1958,Jl 3,20:1
Whitelaw, Arthur (Producer)
Best Foot Forward 1963,Ap 3,43:1
Cabin in the Sky 1964,Ja 22,32:1
Woman and the Blues, A 1966,Mr 29,35:2
You're a Good Man, Charlie Brown 1967,Mr 8,51:1
Butterflies Are Free 1969,O 22,30:1
Minnie's Boys 1970,Mr 27,27:1
Whitelaw, John Biddle (Scenic Designer)
Bridal Quilt 1934,O 11,28:5
Reprise 1935,My 2,16:2
Whiteley, Larry
Of Thee I Sing 1969,Mr 8,19:1
Whiteley, Larry (Miscellaneous)
Now 1968,Je 6,53:1
Of Thee I Sing 1969,Mr 8,19:1
Promenade 1969,Je 5,56:1

Whiteley, Larry (Miscellaneous)—Cont
To Be or Not to Be-What Kind of a Question Is That? 1970,O 20,39:1
Whitely, Thelma
Semi-Detached 1963,O 8,49:1
Life Price 1969,Ja 14,36:2
Whitely, Thomas
Sky High 1925,Mr 3,21:4
Nightingale, The 1927,Ja 4,20:4
Whiteman, Edith
Henri Christophe 1945,Je 7,24:5
Anna Lucasta 1947,O 30,31:3
Whiteman, Leonard
Family Mishmash, A 1958,O 20,36:1
Mirele Efros 1969,D 26,41:1
Whiteman, Madge
Middle Watch, The 1929,O 17,27:1
Whiteman, Paul
Ziegfeld Follies 1923,O 22,17:2
Variety Anthology 1932,Mr 21,19:4
Whiteman, Paul (Musical Director)
Jumbo 1935,N 24,IX,1:1
Whiteman, Paul and His Orchestra
George White's Scandals 1922,Ag 29,10:1
Brighter London 1923,Ap 8,VIII,1:7
Vaudeville (Hippodrome) 1925,S 1,18:3
Lucky 1927,Mr 23,28:3
Vaudeville (Palace) 1928,D 31,9:3
Ziegfeld's Midnight Frolic 1929,F 19,22:4
Jumbo 1935,N 18,20:2
Whitesell, Lila
Pelleas and Melisande 1957,F 20,38:1
Whiteside
Untitled-Benefit 1922,My 8,14:5
Whiteside, Ann
Roomful of Roses, A 1955,O 18,48:1
Wake Up, Darling 1956,My 3,34:2
Night Is Black Bottles, The 1962,D 5,56:1
Way of the World, The 1965,Je 2,40:1
Jumping Fool, The 1970,F 10,53:1
Whiteside, Edward (Producer)
Katy Did 1927,My 10,24:3
Whiteside, Rosamond
Erminie 1921,Ja 4,11:1
Princess Ida 1925,Ap 14,27:2
Engaged! or Cheviot's Choice 1925,Je 19,24:2
Whiteside, Walker
Hindu, The 1922,Mr 22,13:3
Arabian, The 1927,N 1,20:5
Royal Box, The 1928,N 21,32:3
Sakura 1928,D 26,14:4
Three Men and a Woman 1932,Ja 12,29:2
Whiteside, Walker (Director)
Royal Box, The 1928,N 21,32:3
Sakura 1928,D 26,14:4
Three Men and a Woman 1932,Ja 12,29:2
Whiteside, Walker (Playwright)
Arabian, The 1926,Ap 25,VIII,1:8
Whiteside, Walker (Producer)
Arabian, The 1926,Ap 25,VIII,1:8
Royal Box, The 1928,N 21,32:3
Sakura 1928,D 26,14:4
Whitey (Dog)
Vaudeville (Palace) 1929,N 4,29:1
Whitey's Steppers
Hellzapoppin 1938,S 23,34:2
Whitfield, Alice
Jacques Brel Is Alive and Well and Living in Paris 1968,Ja 23,25:2
Whitfield, Arthur
Jack in the Box 1960,My 19,43:3
Whitfield, Booth
Let Freedom Ring 1935,N 7,26:2
Prelude 1936,Ap 20,17:4
Bury the Dead 1936,Ap 20,17:4
Whitfield, Howard
Mr Barry's Etchings 1950,F 1,26:2
Whitfield, Howard (Miscellaneous)
Blue Denim 1958,F 28,17:1
There Was a Little Girl 1960,Mr 1,28:1
Little Moon of Alban 1960,D 2,34:1
Subways Are for Sleeping 1961,D 28,22:1
Deputy, The 1964,F 27,26:1
Zelda 1969,Mr 6,38:1
Whitfield, Hugh
Ivanov 1958,O 8,42:1
Saintliness of Margery Kempe, The 1959,F 3,35:6
Whitfield, Hugh (Costume Designer)
What a Killing 1961,Mr 28,41:1
Whitfield, Hugh (Director)
Man and Superman 1960,Ag 17,35:3
Don Juan in Hell 1960,O 4,47:3
Whitfield, James
John Brown 1950,My 4,32:7
Whitfield, June
Women of Twilight 1952,Mr 4,22:2
Whitfield, Philip
Zaporogetz Za Dunayem 1937,My 9,II,5:3
Devil and Daniel Webster, The 1939,My 19,26:1
Whitfield, Vantile (Scenic Designer)
Amen Corner, The 1965,Ap 16,35:1
Whithorne, Emerson (Composer)
Marco Millions 1930,Mr 4,24:4

Whiting, Byron
Wizard of Oz, The 1968,N 28,69:2
Whistling Wizard and the Sultan of Tuffet 1970,F 1,70:1
Whiting, George
Vaudeville (Palace) 1927,Ap 26,33:1
Whiting, Jack
Ziegfeld Follies 1922,Je 6,18:2
Orange Blossoms 1922,S 20,18:1
Aren't We All? 1923,My 22,14:2
Stepping Stones 1923,N 7,14:3
Annie Dear 1924,N 5,25:3
When You Smile 1925,O 6,31:2
Rainbow Rose 1926,Mr 17,28:2
Ramblers, The 1926,S 21,32:2
Yes, Yes, Yvette 1927,O 4,32:3
She's My Baby 1928,Ja 4,22:2
Hold Everything 1928,O 11,24:2
Me for You 1929,S 22,IX,2:6
Heads Up! 1929,N 12,34:1
America's Sweetheart 1931,Ja 25,VIII,2:4
America's Sweetheart 1931,F 11,23:1
Vaudeville (Palace) 1932,F 15,13:3
Vaudeville (Palace) 1932,My 23,18:7
Take a Chance 1932,N 28,11:2
Calling All Stars 1934,N 22,26:1
Calling All Stars 1934,N 14,28:2
Anything Goes 1935,Je 15,20:5
Rise and Shine 1936,My 8,21:4
On Your Toes 1937,F 6,15:2
Very Warm for May 1939,N 18,23:2
Walk With Music 1940,Je 5,33:2
Hold On to Your Hats 1940,Jl 17,25:3
Hold On to Your Hats 1940,S 12,30:3
Beat the Band 1942,O 15,26:1
Overtons, The 1945,F 7,16:6
Springtime Folly 1951,F 27,23:4
Of Thee I Sing 1952,My 6,34:2
Hazel Flagg 1953,F 12,22:2
Girl Can Tell, A 1953,O 30,28:2
Golden Apple, The 1954,Mr 12,15:2
Golden Apple, The 1954,Mr 21,II,1:1
Annie Get Your Gun 1958,F 20,29:2
Whiting, Jere
Tree Witch, The 1961,Je 5,39:4
Whiting, John (Playwright)
Marching Song 1959,D 29,20:1
Devils, The 1961,F 21,41:1
Devils, The 1963,N 5,25:1
Devils, The 1963,N 17,II,1:1
Devils, The 1965,N 17,51:2
Devils, The 1965,N 28,II,1:1
Gates of Summer, The 1970,Je 16,53:2
Whiting, Margaret
Moon for the Misbegotten, A 1960,Ja 22,14:8
Whiting, Napoleon
Make Me Know It 1929,N 5,32:5
Whiting, Richard (Composer)
Free for All 1931,Ag 16,VIII,1:1
Free for All 1931,S 9,25:1
Take a Chance 1932,N 28,11:2
Whiting, William
California 1953,Je 18,38:5
Brandy Is My True Love's Name 1953,Je 18,38:5
Hopalong--Freud 1953,Je 18,38:5
Where There's a Will 1953,Je 18,38:5
Legitimate Steal, The 1958,Ap 1,35:1
Sign of Jonah, The 1960,S 9,35:1
Whiting, William (Director)
Hi Ho Figaro 1947,Jl 23,18:8
Thorntons, The 1956,F 15,26:1
Ivory Branch, The 1956,My 25,27:1
Legitimate Steal, The 1958,Ap 1,35:1
Whiting, William (Playwright)
Hi Ho Figaro 1947,Jl 23,18:8
Sextet 1958,N 27,53:1
Whiting, William (Producer)
Brandy Is My True Love's Name 1953,Je 18,38:5
Where There's a Will 1953,Je 18,38:5
California 1953,Je 18,38:5
Hopalong--Freud 1953,Je 18,38:5
Whiting and Burt
Vaudeville (Palace) 1928,F 28,18:7
Vaudeville (Palace) 1928,Jl 31,13:5
Whitlaw, Billie
Touch of the Poet, A 1962,S 30,85:8
Whitlege, Orval
Vaudeville (Palace) 1926,Je 1,29:5
Vaudeville (Palace) 1928,Jl 31,13:5
Vaudeville (Palace) 1929,Ja 21,18:3
Vaudeville (Palace) 1930,S 29,19:1
Whitley, Albert
Wind and the Rain, The 1934,F 2,20:6
Fools Rush In 1934,D 26,19:2
Lady Precious Stream 1936,Ja 28,15:2
Cyrano de Bergerac 1953,N 13,24:3
Time of Your Life, The 1955,Ja 20,34:1
Whitley, Bert
Cyrano de Bergerac 1946,O 9,33:2
Cyrano de Bergerac 1947,Ja 17,27:2
Insect Comedy, The 1948,Je 4,26:3
Richard III 1953,D 10,65:2

Whitley, Clifford (Miscellaneous)
Stop Press 1935,F 22,26:4
Whitley, Edward
Censored 1938,F 28,18:2
Whitley, Thomas
Merry World, The 1926,Je 9,18:3
Whitlock, Bache McEvers (Playwright)
Triumph of Robert Emmet, The 1969,My 8,54:1
Whitlock, Kenneth N (Producer)
Arms and the Man 1965,Je 24,32:5
Whitlock, Vic
Front Page, The 1946,S 5,22:4
Whitly, May
There's Always Juliet 1932,F 16,24:2
Whitman, Dale (Miscellaneous)
Home Away From, A 1969,Ap 29,40:3
Whitman, Edith
Garden of Time 1945,Mr 10,13:7
Whitman, Ernest
Harlem 1929,F 21,30:3
Last Mile, The 1930,F 14,21:2
Savage Rhythm 1932,Ja 1,30:4
Bloodstream 1932,Mr 31,25:1
Scrap Book 1932,Ag 2,20:3
Monster, The 1933,F 11,11:5
John Brown 1934,Ja 23,22:3
Whitman, Gladys
Crucible, The 1958,Mr 17,21:1
Whitman, Peter
Broadway Interlude 1934,Ap 20,16:3
Whitman, Stanley
Getting Even 1929,Ag 20,31:1
Every Other Evil 1961,Ja 23,20:2
Whitman, Walt (Original Author)
Whitman Portrait, A 1966,O 12,37:1
Whitman, Walt (Playwright)
We Comrades Three 1962,O 12,26:1
We Comrades Three 1966,D 21,46:1
Whitman, William
Shakespeare's Merchant 1939 1939,Ja 10,16:3
Talent '49 1949,Ap 13,39:4
Jane 1952,F 2,10:2
Way of the World, The 1954,S 30,38:2
Six Characters in Search of an Author 1955,D 12,38:1
I Am a Camera 1956,O 10,47:2
Buoyant Billions 1959,My 27,32:2
Getting Married 1959,Je 5,18:2
Magnificent Hugo, The 1961,Ap 8,12:2
Whitman, William (Producer)
I Am a Camera 1956,O 10,47:2
Whitman, William C (Miscellaneous)
Comic Strip 1958,My 15,26:2
Whitmore, Dean
Captain Brassbound's Conversion 1950,D 28,21:1
Whitmore, Dorothy
Blossom Time 1921,S 30,10:1
Rise of Rosie O'Reilly, The 1923,D 26,13:4
Be Yourself! 1924,S 4,13:3
Merry World, The 1926,Je 9,18:3
Katja 1926,O 19,27:3
Merry Malones, The 1927,S 27,30:2
Whitmore, James
Command Decision 1947,O 2,30:2
Command Decision 1947,O 12,II,1:1
Winesburg, Ohio 1958,F 6,22:2
Inquest 1970,Ap 24,38:1
Inquest 1970,My 3,II,3:1
Whitmore, John J (Costume Designer)
Castro Complex, The 1970,N 19,40:1
Whitmore, Virginia
Roberta 1933,N 20,18:4
Whitner, Edwin
Enemy Within 1931,O 6,35:3
Fireworks on the James 1940,My 15,30:2
Magnificent Yankee, The 1946,Ja 23,21:2
I Gotta Get Out 1947,S 26,27:2
Coast of Illyria, The 1949,Ap 5,37:4
Coast of Illyria, The 1949,Ap 13,39:2
Only in America 1959,N 20,35:1
Whitney, Ann
Yesterday's Orchids 1934,O 6,20:4
Whitney, Beatrice
Three Musketeers, The 1921,My 20,18:5
Whitney, Beverly
Let's Face It 1941,O 30,26:2
Faithfully Yours 1951,O 19,22:5
Whitney, Chuck (Costume Designer)
Sextet 1958,N 27,53:1
Whitney, Claire
Innocent Idea, An 1920,My 26,9:4
Vaudeville (Palace) 1924,S 16,26:5
Buds of 1927 1927,F 22,22:5
Vaudeville (Palace) 1930,F 17,18:4
Page Pygmalion 1932,Ag 4,17:5
Broadway Interlude 1934,Ap 20,16:3
Whitney, Dale (Miscellaneous)
Brig, The 1963,My 16,40:1
Whitney, Don (Miscellaneous)
Pajama Tops 1963,Je 1,15:1
Whitney, Donald
Tempest, The 1959,D 28,19:2

Whitney, Dorothy
Julius Caesar 1955,Jl 13,20:1
Tempest, The 1955,Ag 2,18:2
King Lear 1959,Ja 3,11:2
Ping-Pong 1959,Ap 17,22:1
Good Soup, The 1960,Mr 3,26:4
Happy as Larry 1961,Ap 26,36:1
Duchess of Malfi, The 1962,Mr 5,27:1
Whitney, Eleanor
Would-Be Gentleman, The 1946,Ja 10,29:2
Whitney, Emmet
Wandering Jew, The 1921,O 27,22:1
Whitney, George Jr
Foemen of the Yard 1935,Ap 6,10:4
Whitney, H McAlpin
Arms for Venus 1937,Mr 12,18:7
Whitney, Helene
Yours Is My Heart 1946,S 6,16:5
Whitney, Iris
I Was Waiting for You 1933,N 14,23:3
John Brown 1934,Ja 23,22:3
Another Love 1934,Mr 20,26:3
Petrified Forest, The 1935,N 24,II,9:3
Come Angel Band 1936,F 19,17:1
Plumes in the Dust 1936,N 7,14:2
Passing of the Third Floor Back, The
1937,Ag 3,20:6
Abe Lincoln in Illinois 1938,O 17,12:2
Juno and the Paycock 1940,Ja 17,24:2
Flying Gerardos, The 1940,D 30,21:4
Dark of the Moon 1945,Mr 15,27:2
Awakening of Spring, The 1964,My 13,50:1
3 Bags Full 1966,Mr 7,22:1
Whitney, J H
Galloper, The 1924,D 19,26:2
Whitney, Jack
Jubilee 1935,O 14,20:1
Jubilee 1935,N 24,IX,8:1
Nellie Bly 1946,Ja 22,32:2
Whitney, John (Miscellaneous)
World of Ray Bradbury, The; Pedestrian, The;
Veldt, The; To the Chicago Abyss 1965,O 10,11:1
Whitney, Lee
School for Husbands, The 1933,O 17,26:5
Great Waltz, The 1935,Ag 6,20:5
Whitney, Louise
Hard Travelin' 1965,Je 17,25:1
Whitney, Lynn
Farewell Summer 1937,Mr 30,20:2
Whitney, Mac
Twisting Road, The; Jewel of the South, The
1957,N 18,36:5
Twisting Road, The; One Tuesday Morning
1957,N 18,36:5
Confederates, The 1959,S 29,45:1
Top Secret 1960,S 6,40:1
Whitney, Marjorie
Earl Carroll's Vanities 1927,Ja 5,18:1
Whitney, Mildred
Mirage, The 1920,O 1,14:1
Launzi 1923,O 11,16:3
Wild Birds 1925,Ap 10,16:1
Whitney, Nina
Music Hath Charms 1934,D 31,8:2
At Home Abroad 1935,S 20,17:4
At Home Abroad 1935,O 27,IX,8:1
Roberta 1937,Je 27,II,6:1
Maytime 1937,Jl 6,23:4
Wonderful Night, A; Fledermaus, Die
1937,Jl 14,17:1
Sally, Irene and Mary 1938,Jl 5,13:4
Whitney, Peter D
Hippolytus 1935,Je 15,20:4
Whitney, Salem
Deep Harlem 1929,Ja 8,35:2
Whitney, Salem (Playwright)
Deep Harlem 1929,Ja 8,35:2
Whitney, Shirley
School for Brides 1944,Ag 2,19:4
Whitney, Tutt
Green Pastures, The 1930,F 27,26:1
Whitridge, Jack
Circus Princess, The 1937,Ag 31,26:6
Whitson, George
For Valor 1935,N 19,27:5
Whitson, Pauline
Little Old New York 1920,S 9,9:2
Spring Cleaning 1923,N 10,16:3
Fake, The 1924,O 7,26:3
Whitson, Steve (Lighting Director)
Dirtiest Show in Town, The 1970,Je 29,43:2
Here Be Dragons 1970,D 21,52:1
Whitson Brothers
Take a Bow 1944,Je 16,15:3
Star Time 1944,S 13,16:2
Whitsun-Jones, Paul
Country Wife, The 1957,N 28,56:1
Whitt, Dale (Miscellaneous)
Terminal 1970,Ap 15,51:2
Endgame 1970,My 6,47:1
Serpent, The 1970,Je 2,35:1
Whitt, Dale E (Miscellaneous)
Leonard Bernstein's Theater Songs 1965,Je 29,27:2

Whittaker, Ella
Aunt Caroline's Will 1954,Ag 11,21:1
Whittaker, James
Kibitzer, The 1929,F 19,22:5
Whittaker, Jean
Vaudeville (Palace) 1926,Je 15,23:3
Whittaker, Ralph R
What a Relief 1935,D 14,10:6
Whittell, Josephine
Betty, Be Good 1920,My 5,14:2
One Kiss 1923,N 28,14:2
Busybody, The 1924,S 30,27:5
No, No, Nanette 1925,S 17,20:2
Whittemore, Henry
Nerves 1924,S 2,22:2
Spring Fever 1925,Ag 4,14:2
Cocoanuts, The 1925,D 9,30:1
Free Soul, A 1928,Ja 13,26:5
This Thing Called Love 1928,S 18,32:7
Flying High 1930,Mr 4,24:4
Too Many Boats 1934,S 12,26:3
Whittemore, R M (Composer)
Not Now-Later 1928,Ap 14,25:1
Whitten, Wayne
Great Adventure, The 1926,D 23,23:1
Whitten, Wendell
Secret Garden, The 1931,N 8,31:4
Career Angel 1944,My 24,23:7
Captain Brassbound's Conversion 1950,D 28,21:1
Royal Family, The 1951,Ja 11,28:2
Richard II 1951,Ja 25,21:2
Wild Duck, The 1951,D 27,17:1
Whitteridge, Jack
Orchids Preferred 1937,Ap 29,16:6
Orchids Preferred 1937,My 12,26:5
Firefly, The 1937,Ag 4,14:1
Gay Divorce 1937,Ag 11,27:2
Anything Goes 1937,Ag 17,23:4
Anything Goes 1937,Ag 26,24:3
Whittfield, Arthur
Great Scot! 1965,N 12,56:3
Whittfield, Howard (Miscellaneous)
Mr President 1962,O 22,34:2
Whittier, Robert
Enemy of the People, An 1920,S 7,19:3
Father, The 1928,My 12,9:4
Fuente Ovejuna; Sheep Well, The 1936,My 3,II,4:1
Whittier, Robert (Playwright)
Father, The 1928,My 12,9:4
Whittier, Robert (Producer)
Enemy of the People, An 1920,S 7,19:3
Father, The 1928,My 12,9:4
Whitting, Byron
People Is the Thing That the World Is Fullest Of
1967,F 21,53:1
Whittington, Alease
Cool World, The 1960,F 23,38:2
Whittington, George
Battle Hymn 1936,My 23,12:1
Hymn to the Rising Sun 1937,My 7,28:2
Whittington, Padye
Mistress of the House, The 1950,Ja 31,19:1
Whittle, James
Pantagleize 1967,D 1,54:1
Cocktail Party, The 1968,O 8,42:1
Misanthrope, The 1968,O 10,59:1
Whittle, Robert
Make Me Disappear 1969,My 14,34:1
Whittleweed, Ralph
Honest Liars 1926,Jl 20,17:2
Whittmore, R M
Gentlemen, the Queen 1927,Ap 23,14:3
Whitty, May (Dame)
Behold We Live 1932,S 11,IX,1:1
Maitlands, The 1934,Jl 22,IX,1:3
It Happened to Adam 1934,N 10,18:6
Night Must Fall 1935,Jl 7,IX,1:7
Farm of Three Echoes 1935,D 2,19:4
Night Must Fall 1936,S 29,34:1
Yr Obedient Husband 1937,N 27,21:2
Yr Obedient Husband 1938,Ja 11,26:5
Viceroy Sarah 1939,Ag 15,14:4
Romeo and Juliet 1940,My 10,27:1
Trojan Women, The 1941,Ap 9,32:5
Lottie Dundass 1941,Ag 22,19:5
Therese 1945,O 10,24:2
Therese 1945,O 28,II,1:1
Night Must Fall 1947,F 13,33:6
Whitty, Neta
Eastward in Eden 1956,Ap 18,25:4
Who, The
Tommy 1969,O 26,82:1
Whomsley, Iola
Angelic Doctor 1953,Ap 14,30:2
Whorf, Richard
Banshee, The 1927,D 6,26:2
Bellamy Trial, The 1928,Ag 20,21:1
Monkey 1932,F 12,25:2
Red Planet 1932,D 19,19:2
Foolscap 1933,Ja 12,21:2
Three-Cornered Moon 1933,Mr 17,20:6
Ticket-of-Leave Man, The 1933,Jl 4,16:4
Whatever Possessed Her 1934,Ja 26,21:2

Whorf, Richard—Cont
Lady From the Sea, The 1934,My 2,25:2
Spring Freshet 1934,O 5,28:3
Fools Rush In 1934,D 26,19:2
Panic 1935,Mr 16,18:4
Taming of the Shrew, The 1935,Ap 23,24:1
Taming of the Shrew, The 1935,S 22,X,3:2
Taming of the Shrew, The 1935,O 1,27:3
Taming of the Shrew, The 1935,O 20,X,1:1
Idiot's Delight 1936,Mr 10,26:7
Idiot's Delight 1936,Mr 25,25:2
Dr Knock 1936,Jl 14,22:1
Amphitryon 38 1937,Je 24,30:2
Amphitryon 38 1937,N 2,32:2
Amphitryon 38 1937,N 7,XI,1:1
Sea Gull, The 1938,Mr 29,19:2
Amphitryon 38 1938,Je 5,IX,2:6
Taming of the Shrew, The 1940,F 6,17:2
There Shall Be No Night 1940,Ap 30,25:2
There Shall Be No Night 1940,S 10,27:3
Volpone 1948,Ja 9,24:6
Wedding, The 1948,F 6,29:2
Bear, The 1948,F 6,29:2
On the Harmfulness of Tobacco 1948,F 6,29:2
Tragedian in Spite of Himself, A 1948,F 6,29:2
Richard III 1949,F 9,33:2
Richard III 1949,F 13,II,1:1
Season in the Sun 1950,S 29,31:2
Season in the Sun 1950,O 8,II,1:1
Fifth Season, The 1953,Ja 24,13:2
Whorf, Richard (Costume Designer)
Richard III 1949,F 9,33:2
Richard III 1949,F 13,II,1:1
Ondine 1954,F 19,23:1
Ondine 1954,F 28,II,1:1
Whorf, Richard (Director)
Fireman's Flame, The 1937,O 11,26:2
But Not Goodbye 1944,Ap 12,19:2
Royal Family, The 1951,Ja 11,28:2
Seventeen 1951,Je 22,16:6
Seventeen 1951,Jl 1,II,1:1
Faithfully Yours 1951,O 19,22:5
Genius and the Goddess, The 1957,D 11,41:1
Julia, Jake, and Uncle Joe 1961,Ja 30,19:1
Whorf, Richard (Miscellaneous)
Volpone 1948,Ja 9,24:6
Whorf, Richard (Playwright)
Fools Rush In 1934,D 26,19:2
Whorf, Richard (Scenic Designer)
Ticket-of-Leave Man, The 1933,Jl 4,16:4
On Stage 1935,Jl 23,24:4
There Shall Be No Night 1940,Ap 30,25:2
Fledgling 1940,N 28,29:2
Old Acquaintance 1940,D 24,18:3
But Not Goodbye 1944,Ap 12,19:2
Richard III 1949,F 9,33:2
Richard III 1949,F 13,II,1:1
Cyrano de Bergerac 1953,N 13,24:3
Richard III 1953,D 10,65:2
Genius and the Goddess, The 1957,D 11,41:1
Whytal, Russ
Letter of the Law, The; Robe Rouge, La
1920,F 24,11:1
Spanish Love 1920,Ag 18,6:1
Mary Stuart 1921,Mr 22,15:1
Romeo and Juliet 1922,D 28,20:1
Sancho Panza 1923,N 27,23:1
Enemy, The 1925,O 21,20:1
Garden of Eden, The 1927,S 28,28:1
Whytall, Russ (Mrs)
Tarnish 1923,O 2,10:1
Whyte, Donn
Brownstone Urge, The 1969,D 18,63:1
Foreplay 1970,D 11,58:2
Whyte, Eileen
There Is a Play Tonight 1961,F 16,24:2
Whyte, Ian (Musical Director)
Practical Cats 1954,Ag 27,11:5
Whyte, Jerome
Pal Joey 1940,D 26,22:2
Whyte, Jerome (Director)
Three Waltzes 1938,Je 26,II,7:5
Sally, Irene and Mary 1938,Jl 5,13:4
Sound of Music, The 1961,My 19,22:6
Whyte, Jerome (Miscellaneous)
Sweet Charity 1942,D 29,26:4
Oklahoma! 1951,My 30,15:2
Me and Juliet 1953,My 29,17:1
Oklahoma! 1953,S 1,19:1
Pipe Dream 1955,D 1,44:1
Bells Are Ringing 1956,N 30,18:2
Flower Drum Song 1958,D 2,44:1
Whyte, Jerome (Producer)
Avanti 1968,F 1,29:1
Wiata, Inia
Most Happy Fella, The 1960,Ap 22,25:3
Wiberg, Knud (Playwright)
We All Do 1927,Mr 1,30:3
Wiberg, Solven
Great Campaign, The 1947,Ap 1,33:2
Wiborg, Mary Hoyt (Playwright)
Taboo 1922,Ap 5,22:1

Wicheler, Fernand (Playwright)
Histoire du Crocodile, L' 1926,O 3,VIII,2:1
Wichfeld, A (Producer)
Round-Up, The 1932,Mr 8,19:4
Wick, Andre (Mme)
Annonce Faite a Marie, L'; Tidings Brought to
  Mary, The 1942,My 21,24:1
Wick, Bruno
This Is New York 1930,N 29,21:1
As Husbands Go 1931,Mr 6,26:5
Blue Monday 1932,Je 3,23:2
As Husbands Go 1933,Ja 20,20:5
Suds in Your Eye 1944,Ja 13,15:5
I Remember Mama 1944,O 20,16:2
Tree Grows in Brooklyn, A 1951,Ap 20,24:3
Wick, Dodee
Reunion 1938,Ap 12,26:4
Blind Alley 1940,O 16,28:2
Homeward Look, The 1954,Je 4,26:2
Wick, Evelyn
Vagabond King, The 1943,Je 30,24:2
Wick, Myron
Foemen of the Yard 1935,Ap 6,10:4
Wick, Otto (Musical Director)
Trumpeter of Sakkingen 1921,Ja 15,11:3
Wicke, Gus
Ballyhoo 1930,D 23,24:1
Wicke, Hal (Director)
Moon Walk 1970,N 27,52:1
Wicker, John F
Engaged! or Cheviot's Choice 1965,Ap 24,19:2
Wickes, Elbert A (Miscellaneous)
Resurrection 1934,N 20,24:5
Church Street 1934,N 20,24:5
Well of the Saints, The 1934,N 22,26:2
Coiner, The 1934,N 22,26:2
Wickes, Elbert A (Producer)
Plough and the Stars, The 1934,N 13,22:2
Drama at Inish 1934,N 15,24:2
Look at the Heffernans 1934,N 17,13:2
Wickes, Joseph (Scenic Designer)
Home Towners, The 1926,Ag 24,19:3
Lily Sue 1926,N 17,22:2
What Never Dies 1926,D 29,24:2
Hidden 1927,O 5,30:4
Bachelor Father, The 1928,F 29,28:2
Mima 1928,D 13,24:2
It's a Wise Child 1929,Ag 7,29:1
Tonight or Never 1930,N 19,19:3
Wickes, Kenneth
Heartbreak House 1968,Jl 6,9:1
Chemmy Circle, The 1968,Ag 10,17:2
Wickes, Mary
Cat and the Canary, The 1935,Jl 9,24:4
All This While 1935,Jl 30,17:2
Declassee 1935,Ag 6,20:3
Accent on Youth 1935,Ag 13,20:3
In Old Kentucky 1935,Ag 27,23:4
Spring Dance 1936,Jl 7,22:2
Spring Dance 1936,Ag 26,17:4
Stage Door 1936,O 23,26:3
Hitch Your Wagon! 1937,Ap 9,18:2
Father Malachy's Miracle 1937,N 18,26:4
Danton's Death 1938,N 3,26:2
Stars in Your Eyes 1939,F 10,18:2
Man Who Came to Dinner, The 1939,O 17,31:1
Jackpot 1944,Ja 14,15:2
Dark Hammock 1944,D 12,27:8
Hollywood Pinafore 1945,Je 1,20:1
Apple of His Eye 1946,F 6,18:2
Park Avenue 1946,N 5,31:2
Town House 1948,S 24,31:2
Show Boat 1952,Je 6,19:5
Wickham, Ann
Dial 'M' for Murder 1958,F 8,12:2
Wickham, Glynne (Director)
Birthday Party, The 1961,My 15,34:6
Wickland, Lyons
Sylvia 1923,Ap 26,22:1
Undercurrent, The 1925,F 4,18:2
Sex 1926,Ap 27,22:4
He Loved the Ladies 1927,My 11,29:2
Mr Moneypenny 1928,O 17,26:2
Judas 1929,Ja 25,20:4
Wicklund, Richard
Child Buyer, The 1962,My 14,35:1
Wicks, Frank (Director)
Orange Souffle; Wen, The; Out From Under
  1966,Jl 16,14:6
Wicks, Frank (Lighting Director)
Yeomen of the Guard, The 1961,Ap 28,23:1
Mikado, The 1961,My 5,23:1
Grand Duke, The 1961,My 12,24:1
Princess Ida 1961,My 19,23:1
Iolanthe 1961,My 26,29:6
H M S Pinafore 1961,Je 9,29:5
Student Prince, The 1961,Jl 14,14:1
Wicks, Frank (Miscellaneous)
Yeomen of the Guard, The 1961,Ap 28,23:1
Mikado, The 1961,My 5,23:1
Grand Duke, The 1961,My 12,24:1
Princess Ida 1961,My 19,23:1
Iolanthe 1961,My 26,29:6

H M S Pinafore 1961,Je 9,29:5
Student Prince, The 1961,Jl 14,14:1
Wicks, Frank (Scenic Designer)
Yeomen of the Guard, The 1961,Ap 28,23:1
Mikado, The 1961,My 5,23:1
Grand Duke, The 1961,My 12,24:1
Princess Ida 1961,My 19,23:1
Iolanthe 1961,My 26,29:6
H M S Pinafore 1961,Je 9,29:5
Student Prince, The 1961,Jl 14,14:1
Wickwire, Martha
Flying Blind 1930,My 16,20:2
Wickwire, Nancy
Under Milk Wood 1953,My 29,17:1
Way of the World, The 1954,S 30,38:2
Way of the World, The 1954,O 17,II,1:1
Grand Prize, The 1955,Ja 27,17:1
White Devil, The 1955,Mr 15,32:5
Cherry Orchard, The 1955,O 19,38:1
Midsummer Night's Dream, A 1956,Jl 20,9:5
Measure for Measure 1957,Ja 23,24:1
Girl of the Golden West, The 1957,N 6,44:1
As You Like It 1958,Ja 21,33:6
Midsummer Night's Dream, A 1958,Je 23,19:1
Winter's Tale, The 1958,Jl 21,17:4
Winter's Tale, The 1958,Jl 27,II,1:1
Clearing in the Woods, A 1959,F 13,32:1
Romeo and Juliet 1959,Je 15,31:1
Romeo and Juliet 1959,Je 21,II,1:1
Merry Wives of Windsor, The 1959,Jl 9,23:2
All's Well That Ends Well 1959,Ag 3,20:4
Thracian Horses, The 1961,S 28,58:2
Elizabethans, The 1962,Ja 22,19:1
Rosmersholm 1962,Ap 12,42:1
Rosmersholm 1962,Ap 22,II,1:1
Seidman and Son 1962,O 16,32:2
Golden Age, The 1963,N 19,49:2
Abraham Cochrane 1964,F 18,26:1
Traveller Without Luggage 1964,S 18,26:2
Way of the World, The 1965,Je 2,40:1
Richard III 1965,Je 3,26:1
Cherry Orchard, The 1965,Ag 2,17:2
Skin of Our Teeth, The 1966,Je 2,51:1
Dance of Death, The 1966,Je 3,31:1
Here's Where I Belong 1968,Mr 4,32:1
Coriolanus 1968,My 26,II,7:1
Widdecombe, Wallace
So This Is London 1922,Ag 31,18:2
Queen's Husband, The 1928,Ja 26,17:2
First Night 1930,N 27,32:3
Red Planet 1932,D 19,19:2
Lost Horizons 1934,O 16,31:2
White Christmas 1936,Jl 7,22:2
Middle Man 1936,S 8,23:1
Victoria Regina 1938,O 4,20:2
Sheppey 1944,Ap 19,27:2
Hand in Glove 1944,D 5,19:1
Mermaids Singing, The 1945,N 29,26:6
Cyrano de Bergerac 1946,O 9,33:2
Cyrano de Bergerac 1947,Ja 17,27:2
Cyrano de Bergerac 1953,N 13,24:3
Richard III 1953,D 10,65:2
Widder, Robert (Scenic Designer)
Doctor Cupid 1952,Ag 14,19:6
Widder, William (Scenic Designer)
Corn Is Green, The 1954,F 27,10:2
Widdicombe, Wallace
Old Bill, M P 1926,N 11,22:2
We Are No Longer Children 1932,Ap 1,17:2
Widdoes, Kathleen
Firstborn, The 1958,My 1,35:1
Firstborn, The 1958,My 11,II,1:1
Three Sisters, The 1959,S 22,46:1
Three Sisters, The 1959,O 4,II,1:1
Notes From the Underground 1960,Ja 20,26:1
Henry V 1960,Je 30,23:1
Measure for Measure 1960,Jl 27,33:1
Idiot, The 1960,S 26,38:1
Romeo and Juliet 1961,F 24,24:1
Midsummer Night's Dream, A 1961,Ag 3,13:1
Richard II 1961,Ag 30,25:1
Tempest, The 1962,Jl 17,18:2
Maids, The 1963,N 15,29:1
To Clothe the Naked 1967,Ap 28,30:1
'Tis Pity She's a Whore 1967,O 21,15:2
Henry IV 1968,F 7,40:1
Three Sisters, The 1968,Mr 18,56:1
World War 2 1/2 1969,Mr 25,40:1
Wideman, Beverly
House of Leather, The 1970,Mr 19,56:1
Wideman, Henry
Don Juan in the Russian Manner 1954,Ap 23,23:2
Wideman, Max
Kosher Kitty Kelly 1925,Je 16,24:2
Widgren, Olof
Kyskhet 1939,Jl 9,IX,2:1
Widman, Anne
Dear Judas 1947,O 6,26:4
Widman, Anneliese
Next President, The 1958,Ap 10,34:3
Widman, Marilyn
Shoemaker's Prodigious Wife, The 1949,Je 15,38:2

Widmark, Richard
Kiss and Tell 1943,Mr 18,22:1
Get Away Old Man 1943,N 25,40:2
Trio 1944,D 30,13:4
Kiss Them for Me 1945,Mr 21,27:2
Kiss Them for Me 1945,N 25,II,1:1
Dunnigan's Daughter 1945,D 27,16:1
Dunnigan's Daughter 1946,Ja 6,II,1:1
Widney, Stone (Director)
Month of Sundays 1968,S 17,50:1
Widney, Stone (Producer)
Coco 1969,D 19,66:1
Wieck, Dorothea
Raetzel um Beate 1936,N 8,X,2:1
Wied, Gustav (Original Author)
2 + 2 = 5 1927,N 29,30:3
Wieder, Emanuel
Kith and Kin 1930,My 14,31:1
Wiedhaas, Ralph
Good Old Days, The 1923,Ag 15,21:2
Wiegert, Rene (Miscellaneous)
Can-Can 1959,Ag 26,25:4
Wiegert, Rene (Musical Director)
Boys From Syracuse, The 1963,Ap 16,31:1
Joyful Noise, A 1966,D 16,57:1
Wieland, Alice
Aunt Caroline's Will 1954,Ag 11,21:1
Wiemann, Matthias
Troilus and Cressida 1927,N 20,IX,4:7
Verbrecher, Die 1928,D 23,VIII,4:1
Journey's End 1929,S 15,IX,2:6
Journey's End 1929,S 22,IX,4:1
Waterloo Bridge 1931,N 29,VIII,4:1
Wiener, George (Miscellaneous)
Who's Who, Baby? 1968,Ja 30,36:1
Wiener, Jack
Backlane Center 1961,N 23,51:1
Eleventh Inheritor, The 1962,N 22,43:5
Wiener, Norbert (Prof) (Miscellaneous)
R U R 1950,My 7,IV,13:6
Wiensko, Robert H
Body Beautiful, The 1958,Ja 24,15:2
Mating Dance 1965,N 4,58:1
Wier, Leonard
My Fair Lady 1958,My 1,34:5
Wier, R R
Hoot Mon, or Clans Across the Sea 1927,My 8,29:4
Wiere Brothers
Vaudeville Marches On 1938,D 30,11:1
Laughter Over Broadway 1939,Ja 16,10:3
Jerry Lewis' Variety Show 1957,F 8,18:5
Wiernik, Bertha (Playwright)
Destruction 1932,Jl 1,19:5
Hate Planters 1933,My 26,24:5
Wiers-Jenssen, H (Playwright)
Witch, The 1926,N 19,22:5
Wierum, Howard
As You Like It 1939,My 9,28:4
Hamlet 1939,D 5,35:2
Richard II 1940,Ap 2,31:2
Elizabeth the Queen 1941,O 17,27:2
Cyrano de Bergerac 1946,O 9,33:2
Cyrano de Bergerac 1947,Ja 17,27:2
Insect Comedy, The 1948,Je 4,26:3
First Lady 1952,My 29,18:5
Emperor's Clothes, The 1953,O 23,19:7
In Splendid Error 1954,O 27,33:6
Troublemakers, The 1954,D 31,11:3
Juno and the Paycock 1955,F 24,20:4
Beaver Coat, The 1956,Mr 29,22:5
Doll's House, A 1956,My 8,29:2
Protective Custody 1956,D 29,8:7
Land Beyond the River, A 1957,Mr 29,15:7
Shadow of My Enemy, A 1957,D 12,35:4
Third Best Sport 1958,D 31,15:3
Only in America 1959,N 20,35:1
Andersonville Trial, The 1959,D 30,15:1
Cage, The 1961,Mr 6,30:1
Wiest, Dianne
Country People 1970,Ja 19,35:1
Wiest, George
Vaudeville (Palace) 1926,Jl 20,17:4
Wiger, Nick
Ladies' Money 1934,N 2,26:6
Three Men on a Horse 1935,Ja 31,22:3
Wigert, Knut
Abraham's Offering 1938,D 18,IX,4:2
Wigfield, Erma
Eleventh Hour, The 1956,Jl 10,26:7
Wigg, Ray
Bedrock 1934,N 18,II,6:3
Wiggam, Lionel
Jim Dandy 1941,N 8,10:5
Wiggins, Chris
King John 1960,Je 29,26:2
Soldiers 1968,Mr 3,88:2
Wiggins, Russell Garland
Henry IV, Part II 1968,Jl 2,33:1
Romeo and Juliet 1968,Ag 16,19:1
Wight, Evelyn
Simon Called Peter 1924,N 11,20:2
Shanghai Gesture, The 1926,F 2,20:2

Wight, Read
New York Exchange 1926,D 31,11:2
Wightman, Gordon E
Vagabond King, The 1935,N 29,22:7
Wightman, Harold
Little Theatre Tournament; Old Lady Shows Her
Medals, The 1928,My 11,28:1
Wightman, Marian (Playwright)
Dagger, The 1925,S 10,28:1
Wightman, Robert (Lighting Director)
Asmodee 1958,Mr 26,42:2
What a Killing 1961,Mr 28,41:1
Wightman, Robert (Scenic Designer)
Scrapbooks 1953,N 6,24:2
Trial of Dmitri Karamazov, The 1958,Ja 28,30:1
Sign of Winter 1958,My 8,35:1
American Mime Theatre 1958,S 25,28:4
What a Killing 1961,Mr 28,41:1
Wigwam Players (Costume Designer)
Side-Show 1931,My 16,13:1
Wigwam Players (Scenic Designer)
Side-Show 1931,My 16,13:1
Wiklinski, Stanley
Bacchae, The 1969,Mr 15,24:1
Crimes and Crimes 1970,Ja 19,35:1
Don Juan 1970,My 26,32:1
Wiland, Steve
Wish You Were Here 1952,Je 26,26:6
Wilbanks, Marion
Hitchy-Koo, 1920 1920,O 20,11:3
Wilbert, Harlan
Corn Is Green, The 1954,F 27,10:2
Wilbourn, Phyllis
Peter Ibbetson 1931,Ap 9,30:3
Wilbraham, Edward (Playwright)
Ostriches 1925,Mr 31,16:1
Wilbur, Claire
Score 1970,O 29,57:4
Wilbur, Crane
Ouija Board, The 1920,Mr 30,9:1
Easy Terms 1925,S 23,22:2
Fountain, The 1925,D 11,26:1
Nirvana 1926,Mr 4,19:1
Bride of the Lamb 1926,Mr 31,20:3
Bride of the Lamb 1926,Ap 4,VIII,1:1
Woman Disputed, A 1926,S 29,23:2
Vaudeville (Palace) 1927,My 3,25:2
Celebrity 1927,D 27,24:3
Rope 1928,F 23,18:3
Rope 1928,Mr 4,IX,1:1
Fast Life 1928,S 27,35:2
Jealousy 1928,D 6,31:2
Farewell to Arms, A 1930,S 23,30:3
On the Spot 1930,O 30,33:3
Mourning Becomes Electra; Hunted, The
1932,My 10,25:2
Mourning Becomes Electra; Homecoming
1932,My 10,25:2
Wilbur, Crane (Director)
Woman Disputed, A 1926,S 29,23:2
Halfway to Hell 1934,Ja 3,22:3
Happily Ever After 1945,Mr 16,21:2
Wilbur, Crane (Playwright)
Ouija Board, The 1920,Mr 30,9:1
Monster, The 1922,Ag 10,20:3
I Will IF You Will 1922,Ag 30,10:4
Easy Terms 1925,S 23,22:2
Song Writer, The 1928,Ag 14,15:2
Romance, Inc 1929,Mr 24,X,4:7
Border-Land 1932,Mr 30,15:5
Monster, The 1933,F 11,11:5
Halfway to Hell 1934,Ja 3,22:3
Are You Decent? 1934,Ap 20,16:2
Wilbur, Jane
Child Buyer, The 1962,My 14,35:1
Wilbur, Keith
Vaudeville (Palace) 1929,D 2,28:6
Wilbur, Richard (Lyricist)
Candide 1956,D 3,40:2
Candide 1956,D 9,II,5:1
Leonard Bernstein's Theater Songs 1965,Je 29,27:2
Wilbur, Richard (Playwright)
Misanthrope, The 1968,O 10,59:1
Wilbur, Richard (Translator)
Misanthrope, The 1968,N 13,44:1
Tartuffe 1965,Ja 15,23:1
Tartuffe 1968,Je 12,39:1
Tartuffe 1968,Je 23,II,1:1
Misanthrope, The 1968,O 20,II,1:1
Wilbur, Victor
Chicago 1926,D 31,11:1
Wilbur DeParis and his New Orleans Orchestra
Mardi Gras! 1966,Jl 11,32:2
Wilck, Laura (Producer)
Geraniums in My Window 1934,O 27,20:6
Wilck, Laura D (Miscellaneous)
Thunder in the Air 1929,N 12,34:3
Wilck, Laura D (Producer)
Get Me in the Movies 1928,My 22,18:3
Flight 1929,F 19,22:3
Troika 1930,Ap 2,32:6
Made in France 1930,O 19,IX,3:4
Made in France 1930,N 12,21:1

Wilck, Lillian
Phoebe of Quality Street 1921,My 10,20:1
Three Doors 1925,Ap 24,16:4
Nirvana 1926,Mr 4,19:1
Wilcox, Bert
American Tragedy, An 1926,O 12,31:2
One Way Street 1928,D 25,31:2
Buckaroo 1929,Mr 18,31:1
American Tragedy, An 1931,F 21,15:5
Hotel Alimony 1934,Ja 30,16:2
American Holiday 1936,F 22,13:3
Case of Youth, A 1940,Mr 25,10:3
Arsenic and Old Lace 1944,Jl 3,7:3
Louisiana Lady 1947,Je 3,35:2
Sleepy Hollow 1948,Je 4,26:3
Wilcox, Collin
Day the Money Stopped, The 1958,F 21,19:4
Season of Choice 1959,Ap 14,40:1
Camino Real 1960,My 17,42:2
Look: We've Come Through 1961,O 26,40:1
Period of Adjustment 1962,Je 4,24:2
Family Way, The 1965,Ja 14,44:5
Wilcox, Constance (Playwright)
Heart of Frances, The 1923,Ja 29,11:2
Wilcox, Emma
Rose of Stamboul, The 1922,Mr 8,11:2
Rain 1922,N 8,18:2
Rain 1926,O 12,27:1
Rain 1935,F 13,24:1
Wilcox, Frank
Little Orchard Annie 1930,Ap 22,33:1
Napi 1931,Mr 12,22:5
Monkey 1932,F 12,25:2
Life Begins 1932,Mr 29,23:2
Uncle Tom's Cabin 1933,My 30,13:4
Shooting Star 1933,Je 13,22:2
I Myself 1934,My 10,24:6
Little Shot 1935,Ja 18,28:4
Journey by Night, A 1935,Ap 17,26:3
Curse You, Jack Dalton 1935,Jl 16,24:1
Rain 1935,Ag 27,23:4
Mid-West 1936,Ja 8,22:4
Come Angel Band 1936,F 19,17:1
You Can't Take It With You 1936,D 15,31:1
Mr and Mrs North 1941,Ja 13,11:2
Village Green 1941,S 4,24:4
Snark was a Boojum, The 1943,S 2,14:4
Take It As It Comes 1944,F 11,17:2
But Not Goodbye 1944,Ap 12,19:2
Parlor Story 1947,Mr 5,29:2
Wilcox, Irwin
Mr Big 1941,O 1,24:2
Wilcox, Joan
Merchant of Venice, The 1955,Ja 8,9:7
Wilcox, Larry (Miscellaneous)
Boys From Syracuse, The 1963,Ap 16,31:1
Yearling, The 1965,D 11,25:1
Pousse-Cafe 1966,Mr 19,19:2
Walking Happy 1966,N 28,47:1
Education of H*Y*M*A*N K*A*P*L*A*N, The
1968,Ap 5,57:1
Ballad for a Firing Squad 1968,D 12,64:2
Wilcox, Larry (Musical Director)
Look to the Lilies 1970,Mr 30,59:1
Wilcox, Lee
Minnie and Mr Williams 1948,O 28,37:2
Liar, The 1950,My 19,30:2
Wilcox, Lee (Miscellaneous)
My Heart's in the Highlands 1950,F 18,8:4
Wilcox, Lee (Musical Director)
My Heart's in the Highlands 1949,N 22,36:7
Wilcox, Nina
Time of Your Life, The 1955,Ja 20,34:1
Tall Story 1959,Ja 30,33:2
Wilcox, Pansy
Lightnin' 1938,S 16,17:2
Wilcox, Ruth
These Days 1928,N 13,36:2
Wilcox, Vivian
Moroni 1936,Ag 19,19:1
Wilcoxon, Henry
We Were Dancing; Tonight at Eight 1940,Ag 6,15:3
Vigil, The 1948,My 22,8:6
Wild, Earl (Composer)
Stone for Danny Fisher, A 1954,O 22,24:2
Wildberg, John (Miscellaneous)
Porgy and Bess 1944,F 8,13:2
Wildberg, John (Playwright)
Gas Light 1939,Ag 30,20:8
Wildberg, John (Producer)
Woman's a Fool-To Be Clever, A 1938,O 19,18:6
Porgy and Bess 1943,S 14,26:2
One Touch of Venus 1943,O 8,14:1
Anna Lucasta 1944,Ag 31,15:1
Anna Lucasta 1944,S 10,II,1:1
Memphis Bound 1945,My 25,23:2
Black Chiffon 1950,S 28,39:2
Wilde, Al (Producer)
Holiday on Broadway 1948,Ap 28,33:3
Wilde, Cornell
They All Come to Moscow 1933,My 12,20:6
Moon Over Mulberry Street 1935,S 5,24:6
Daughters of Atreus 1936,O 15,33:1

Wilde, Cornell—Cont
Jeremiah 1939,F 4,11:2
Pastoral 1939,N 2,26:2
Romeo and Juliet 1940,My 10,27:1
Western Wind 1949,Ag 9,20:6
Wilde, David (Producer)
Ninety Day Mistress, The 1967,N 7,49:1
Wilde, Elizabeth
How Beautiful With Shoes 1935,N 29,24:1
New Faces of 1936 1936,My 20,24:5
Who's Who 1938,Mr 2,16:2
30 Days Hath September 1938,O 1,10:5
Wilde, Gene
Mother Courage and Her Children 1963,Mr 30,5:5
Wilde, Hagar (Playwright)
Fight's On, The; Uneasy Virtue; Pardon My Back
1937,Ag 4,14:1
Guest in the House 1942,F 25,25:2
Made in Heaven 1946,O 25,28:2
Honor and Obey 1947,N 20,40:1
Wilde, Oscar (Original Author)
Oh, Ernest! 1927,My 10,24:3
Dorian Gray 1936,Jl 21,13:3
After The Ball 1954,Jl 18,II,1:6
Picture of Dorian Gray, The 1956,Ag 18,15:5
Untitled-Reading 1957,Ja 23,24:6
Wilde, Oscar (Playwright)
Ideal Husband, An 1921,Mr 6,VI,1:7
Salome 1923,My 23,12:4
Salome 1923,My 8,22:2
Salome 1923,My 20,VII,1:1
Importance of Being Earnest, The 1925,Jl 28,24:2
Importance of Being Earnest, The 1926,My 4,30:1
Importance of Being Earnest, The 1926,O 3,VIII,2:1
Florentine Tragedy, A 1927,F 2,22:4
Lady Windermere's Fan 1927,F 27,VII,2:3
Dorian Gray 1928,My 22,18:4
Lady Windermere's Fan 1930,Jl 27,VIII,1:8
Importance of Being Earnest, The
1930,Jl 27,VIII,1:8
Salome 1931,Je 21,VIII,1:4
Lady Windermere's Fan 1932,Ja 27,19:3
Importance of Being Earnest, The 1936,O 22,31:2
Importance of Being Earnest, The 1939,Ja 13,16:2
Importance of Being Earnest, The 1939,S 17,X,2:3
Ideal Husband, An 1946,Ap 14,II,2:1
Lady Windermere's Fan 1946,O 15,29:2
Importance of Being Earnest, The 1947,Ja 24,18:6
Importance of Being Earnest, The 1947,Mr 4,30:2
Importance of Being Earnest, The 1947,Mr 9,II,1:1
After The Ball 1954,Je 11,19:3
Florentine Tragedy, The 1956,F 14,24:4
Salome 1956,F 14,24:4
Ernest in Love 1960,My 5,39:4
Delightful Season, A 1960,S 29,30:1
Importance of Being Oscar, The 1961,Mr 15,45:2
Importance of Being Earnest, The 1963,F 27,5:2
Picture of Dorian Gray, The 1963,Ag 29,37:4
Importance of Being Earnest, The 1968,Jl 6,9:1
Wilde, Pamela
Lute Song 1946,F 7,29:2
Wilde, Percival (Playwright)
Crooked Gamblers 1920,Ag 2,12:1
Little Shot 1935,Ja 18,28:4
Wilde, Peter
Plough and the Stars, The 1956,Ap 6,14:1
Wilde, R (Translator)
Little Racketeer, The 1932,Ja 19,24:4
Wilde, Renee
He Who Gets Slapped 1922,Ja 10,15:1
Wilder, Alec (Composer)
Bird Cage, The 1950,F 23,32:2
See the Jaguar 1952,D 4,46:2
Once Over Lightly 1955,Mr 16,39:1
Kittiwake Island 1960,O 13,43:1
Wilder, Alec (Lyricist)
Once Over Lightly 1955,Mr 16,39:1
Wilder, Billy (Original Author)
Promises, Promises 1968,D 2,59:3
Promises, Promises 1968,D 15,II,3:1
Wilder, Bolton (Lighting Director)
Once Upon a Time 1939,D 21,28:2
Wilder, Clinton (Miscellaneous)
Regina 1949,N 1,32:2
Six Characters in Search of an Author
1955,D 12,38:1
Happy Journey to Trenton and Camden, The
1966,S 7,53:1
Queens of France 1966,S 7,53:1
Long Christmas Dinner, The 1966,S 7,53:1
Delicate Balance, A 1966,S 23,44:1
Party for Divorce 1966,O 12,37:1
Match-Play 1966,O 12,37:1
Butter and Egg Man, The 1966,O 18,49:1
Night of the Dunce 1966,D 29,21:1
Rimers of Eldritch, The 1967,F 21,53:1
Party on Greenwich Avenue, The 1967,My 11,52:1
Johnny No-Trump 1967,O 9,60:2
Everything in the Garden 1967,N 30,60:1
Home 1970,N 18,41:1
Wilder, Clinton (Producer)
Tender Trap, The 1954,O 14,37:2
Visit to a Small Planet 1957,F 8,18:1
American Dream, The 1961,Ja 25,28:1

Wilder, Clinton (Producer)—Cont

Bartleby 1961,Ja 25,28:1
Death of Bessie Smith, The 1961,Mr 2,19:1
Gallows Humor 1961,Ap 19,35:1
Happy Days 1961,S 18,36:1
Bertha 1962,F 12,27:1
Endgame 1962,F 12,27:1
Whisper Into My Good Ear 1962,O 2,47:1
Mrs Dally Has a Lover 1962,O 2,47:1
Who's Afraid of Virginia Woolf? 1962,O 15,33:1
Who's Afraid of Virginia Woolf? 1962,N 1,34:1
American Dream, The 1963,My 29,39:6
Zoo Story, The 1963,My 29,39:6
Corruption in the Palace of Justice 1963,O 9,49:2
Play 1964,Ja 6,35:1
Lover, The 1964,Ja 6,35:1
Funnyhouse of a Negro 1964,Ja 15,25:3
Play 1964,Mr 25,46:2
Dutchman 1964,Mr 25,46:2
Two Executioners, The 1964,Mr 25,46:2
Giants' Dance, The 1964,N 17,48:2
Tiny Alice 1964,D 30,14:2
Home Free! 1965,F 11,45:1
Up to Thursday 1965,F 11,45:1
Balls 1965,F 11,45:1
Pigeons 1965,Mr 4,37:1
Conerico Was Here to Stay 1965,Mr 4,37:1
Lovey 1965,Mr 26,27:1
Hunting the Jingo Birds 1965,Mr 26,27:1
Do Not Pass Go 1965,Ap 20,44:1
Happy Days 1965,S 14,45:2
Malcolm 1966,Ja 12,29:1
Wilder, David
Billy Budd 1955,My 4,35:1
Zorba 1968,N 18,58:1
Wilder, Duane (Miscellaneous)
Birthday Party, The 1967,O 4,40:2
Wilder, Duane (Producer)
Private Lives 1968,My 20,59:1
Gingham Dog, The 1969,Ap 24,41:1
Last Sweet Days of Isaac, The 1970,Ja 27,49:1
Lemon Sky 1970,My 18,40:1
Wilder, Frank (Playwright)
Sweet Chariot 1930,O 24,30:2
Wilder, Gene
Roots 1961,Mr 7,40:2
Complaisant Lover, The 1961,N 2,43:2
One Flew Over the Cuckoo's Nest 1963,N 14,40:2
Dynamite Tonight 1964,Mr 16,36:2
White House, The 1964,My 20,39:1
Wilder, Jo
Threepenny Opera, The 1956,Mr 11,II,1:1
Threepenny Opera, The 1960,S 15,44:3
She Loves Me 1963,Ap 24,39:1
Wilder, Lilyan
Noah 1954,O 11,32:2
Hour Glass, The 1955,O 17,33:1
Thunder Rock 1956,F 27,18:1
Box of Watercolors, A 1957,F 18,22:2
Tango 1969,Ja 20,33:1
Wilder, Marc
Kismet 1953,D 4,2:4
Vintage '60 1960,S 13,41:1
Wilder, Nancy
Curious Savage, The 1956,Mr 17,12:3
Milk Train Doesn't Stop Here Anymore, The
1963,S 18,32:1
Wilder, R H
Bunch and Judy, The 1922,N 29,20:1
Wilder, Rex (Musical Director)
Aunt Caroline's Will 1954,Ag 11,21:1
Wilder, Richard
Harriet 1944,S 28,26:1
Julius Caesar 1950,Je 21,30:1
Wilder, Robert (Original Author)
Flamingo Road 1946,Mr 20,18:2
Wilder, Robert (Playwright)
Sweet Chariot 1930,O 12,VIII,4:1
Stardust 1935,Jl 17,22:4
Flamingo Road 1946,Mr 20,18:2
Wilder, Sally (Playwright)
Stardust 1935,Jl 17,22:4
Flamingo Road 1946,Mr 20,18:2
Wilder, Thornton
Our Town 1938,S 16,17:3
ANTA Album 1951,My 7,22:7
Wilder, Thornton (Original Author)
Ides of March, The 1962,N 17,16:4
Ides of March, The 1963,Ag 9,12:1
Hello, Dolly! 1964,Ja 17,22:1
Hello, Dolly! 1964,Ja 26,II,1:1
Wilder, Thornton (Playwright)
Trumpet Shall Sound, The 1926,D 11,15:2
Lucrece 1933,Ja 1,IX,1:1
Love and How to Cure It 1937,F 11,19:3
Doll's House, A 1937,Jl 25,X,2:3
Doll's House, A 1937,D 28,28:6
Our Town 1938,Ja 23,II,10:6
Our Town 1938,Ja 26,27:4
Our Town 1938,Ja 30,X,3:1
Our Town 1938,F 5,18:3
Our Town 1938,F 13,X,1:1
Our Town 1938,S 16,17:3
Merchant of Yonkers, The 1938,D 13,30:1

Merchant of Yonkers, The 1938,D 18,IX,3:2
Merchant of Yonkers, The 1938,D 29,14:2
Our Town 1940,Je 30,35:5
Skin of Our Teeth, The 1942,N 19,29:5
Skin of Our Teeth, The 1942,N 22,VIII,1:1
Skin of Our Teeth, The 1943,Ja 3,VIII,1:1
Skin of Our Teeth, The 1943,My 9,II,1:1
Our Town 1944,Ja 11,24:5
Skin of Our Teeth, The 1945,Mr 20,22:8
Skin of Our Teeth, The 1945,My 27,II,1:3
Skin of Our Teeth, The 1945,N 18,II,2:5
Our Town 1946,My 2,27:3
Our Town 1946,O 27,II,2:4
Happy Journey to Trenton and Camden, The
 1948,Mr 21,II,1:1
Victors, The 1948,D 27,17:2
Victors, The 1949,Ja 2,II,1:1
Happy Journey to Trenton and Camden, The
 1949,Jl 9,9:2
Matchmaker, The 1954,Ag 24,18:1
Matchmaker, The 1954,S 5,II,3:7
Matchmaker, The 1954,N 5,16:4
Matchmaker, The 1954,N 14,II,3:1
Our Town 1955,Mr 18,32:8
Matchmaker, The 1955,My 8,II,1:1
Skin of Our Teeth, The 1955,Je 29,25:3
Skin of Our Teeth, The 1955,Ag 18,16:1
Life in the Sun, A 1955,Ag 24,24:7
Life in the Sun, A 1955,Ag 28,II,1:6
Skin of Our Teeth, The 1955,Ag 28,II,1:1
Matchmaker, The 1955,D 6,45:6
Matchmaker, The 1955,D 18,II,3:1
Alcestiade 1957,Je 29,11:5
Tipsy Sisters, The 1957,Je 29,11:5
Alcestiade 1957,N 6,43:1
Our Town 1959,Mr 24,46:2
Our Town 1959,Ap 5,II,1:1
Skin of Our Teeth, The 1960,O 14,24:1
Skin of Our Teeth, The 1961,Mr 6,30:1
Skin of Our Teeth, The 1961,Mr 20,32:6
Skin of Our Teeth, The 1961,Mr 28,40:2
Skin of Our Teeth, The 1961,Ap 1,11:2
Our Town 1961,Ap 4,34:3
Skin of Our Teeth, The 1961,Ap 11,43:5
Skin of Our Teeth, The 1961,Ap 21,29:1
Skin of Our Teeth, The 1961,My 1,35:3
Skin of Our Teeth, The 1961,My 19,22:2
Skin of Our Teeth, The 1961,My 31,28:1
Our Town 1961,N 4,14:7
Plays for Bleecker Street 1962,Ja 12,28:1
Infancy 1962,Ja 12,28:1
Someone From Assisi 1962,Ja 12,28:1
Childhood 1962,Ja 12,28:1
Plays for Bleecker Street; Infancy; Childhood;
 Someone From Assisi 1962,Ja 21,II,1:1
Pullman Car Hiawatha 1962,D 4,46:2
Hello, Dolly! 1965,Ag 10,17:2
Skin of Our Teeth, The 1966,Je 2,51:1
Happy Journey to Trenton and Camden, The
 1966,S 7,53:1
Long Christmas Dinner, The 1966,S 7,53:1
Queens of France 1966,S 7,53:1
Hello, Dolly! 1967,N 13,61:1
Skin of Our Teeth, The 1968,S 12,55:1
Our Town 1968,S 29,77:4
Our Town 1968,D 14,62:1
Our Town 1969,N 28,50:1
Our Town 1969,D 7,II,7:1
Wilder, Thornton (Translator)
Lucrece 1932,N 30,22:8
Lucrece 1932,D 4,IX,3:3
Lucrece 1932,D 21,22:2
Alcestiade 1957,Je 29,11:5
Wilderman, William
Regina 1949,N 1,32:2
Regina 1952,Je 2,25:4
My Darlin' Aida 1952,O 28,36:4
Wildhack, Robert
Life Begins at 8:40 1934,Ag 28,24:2
Life Begins at 8:40 1934,S 2,IX,1:1
Wildman, Carl (Playwright)
Infernal Machine, The 1937,D 13,22:7
Wildman, Carl (Translator)
Antigone 1962,D 29,5:5
Orthee 1962,D 29,5:5
Wilds, Sophie
Swords 1921,S 2,9:3
Dagmar 1923,Ja 23,18:2
Wile, Everett (Producer)
Five Alarm Waltz 1941,Mr 14,16:2
Wile, Joan
Can-Can 1959,Ag 26,25:4
Wilee, Cornel
Having Wonderful Time 1937,F 22,12:5
Wilenchick, Clement
House of Connelly, The 1931,S 29,22:4
1931 1931,D 11,34:3
Night Over Taos 1932,Mr 10,25:3
Rendezvous 1932,O 13,22:3
Little Ol' Boy 1933,Ap 25,15:5
Jezebel 1933,D 20,26:3
Lady From the Sea, The 1934,My 2,25:2
Geraniums in My Window 1934,O 27,20:6

Wilenchick, Clement—Cont

Paths of Glory 1935,S 27,24:2
Petrified Forest, The 1935,N 24,II,9:3
Devil of Pei-Ling 1936,F 21,20:4
Dead End 1936,S 20,IX,3:7
But for the Grace of God 1937,Ja 13,21:4
Wilenchick, Clement (Costume Designer)
Doctor Knock 1928,F 24,15:2
Wilenchick, Clement (Scenic Designer)
Doctor Knock 1928,F 24,15:2
Wilensky, Mary
Love and Politics 1929,O 21,30:7
Slaves of Luxury 1930,F 8,13:3
Stranger, The 1935,N 7,26:2
Golden Stream, The 1936,F 13,25:1
Wilensky, Michael
Radio Girl, The 1929,O 19,22:4
Kibitzer, The 1931,N 7,17:3
Under One Roof 1932,F 8,21:2
Traveling Salesman, The 1932,N 1,24:4
Honeymoon for Three, A 1933,Ja 30,9:6
Oy, Is Dus a Leben!; Oh, What a Life!
 1942,O 13,19:2
Wilensky, Stephen
Twelfth Night 1969,Ag 14,29:2
Wiles, Sylvia
Cradle Song 1921,Mr 1,18:2
Roger Bloomer 1923,Mr 2,18:3
Wiley, Charles Jr
Our Town 1938,F 5,18:3
Our Town 1944,Ja 11,24:5
Wiley, Charles Sr
Arrest That Woman 1936,S 19,20:4
Wiley, Jackson (Musical Director)
High Button Shoes 1955,Mr 12,10:6
Wiley, Kent (Director)
On Location 1937,S 28,19:1
Wiley, Kent (Playwright)
On Location 1937,S 28,19:1
Wiley, Major
Harold Arlen Songbook, The 1967,Mr 1,48:1
Wilford (Miss)
Garden of Eden, The 1927,O 26,26:2
Wilfred, Thomas (Composer)
Vikings, The 1930,My 13,27:3
Wilfred, Thomas (Director)
Vikings, The 1930,My 13,27:3
Wilfred, Thomas (Miscellaneous)
Vikings, The 1930,My 13,27:3
Wilhelm, Frank (Playwright)
Louie the 14th 1925,Mr 4,17:1
Wilhelm, George
Midsummer Night's Dream, A 1931,Ag 19,19:3
Did I Say No? 1931,S 23,19:4
Bloody Laughter 1931,D 5,20:6
Wolves 1932,Ja 7,26:3
Park Avenue, Ltd 1932,Mr 4,17:1
Wilhelm, Jean (Choreographer)
High Button Shoes 1955,Mr 12,10:6
Wilhelm, Jean (Lighting Director)
Hasty Heart, The 1954,Mr 13,10:1
Wilhelm, Julius (Playwright)
Louie the 14th 1925,Mr 4,17:1
Sari 1930,Ja 29,27:1
Wilhelm, Prince of Sweden (Miscellaneous)
Kinangozi 1924,F 10,II,3:7
On Board 1927,Mr 16,28:6
Wilis, Frances
Vaudeville (Palace) 1932,Jl 11,11:6
Wilk, Max (Playwright)
Small Wonder 1948,S 16,33:5
Cloud 7 1958,F 15,15:2
Wilk, Ruth
Schoolhouse on the Lot 1938,Mr 23,18:4
Hamlet 1938,O 13,28:1
Wilk, Ruth (Miscellaneous)
It's All Yours 1942,Mr 26,26:2
Wilke, Hubert
Sophie 1920,Mr 3,12:2
Poldekin 1920,S 10,12:1
Humoresque 1923,F 28,13:2
Queen Victoria 1923,N 16,15:1
Leah Kleschna 1924,Ap 22,19:2
Aiglon, L' 1927,D 27,24:3
Wilkens, Verna
Romance 1921,Mr 1,18:2
True to Form 1921,S 13,12:1
Wilkenson, Biddy
Five O'Clock Girl, The 1927,O 11,26:3
Wilkerson, Arnold
Hair 1967,O 30,55:1
Jimmy Shine 1968,D 6,52:1
Fireworks; Football 1969,Je 12,51:1
Fireworks; Fireworks for a Hot Fourth
 1969,Je 12,51:1
Wilkerson, Frederick
Hamlet 1951,Jl 20,13:6
Wilkes, Allen Tupper (Original Author)
Creaking Chair, The 1924,Jl 27,VII,1:8
Wilkes, Allene Tupper (Playwright)
Creaking Chair, The 1926,F 23,26:1
Wilkes, Alton
As You Like It 1936,Ap 24,18:4

Wilkes, Alton (Director)
Deadly Game, The 1966,F 14,34:1
Wilkes, Alton (Producer)
Deadly Game, The 1960,F 3,27:2
Deadly Game, The 1966,F 14,34:1
Wilkes, Jocelyn
Princess Ida 1967,Ap 17,46:2
H M S Pinafore 1969,D 8,61:2
Pirates of Penzance, The 1970,D 6,84:6
Wilkes, Mattie
Runnin' Wild 1923,O 30,17:3
Lulu Belle 1926,F 10,20:1
Wilkes, Pat
On Your Toes 1954,O 12,24:4
Once Over Lightly 1955,Mr 16,39:1
Mr Wonderful 1956,Mr 23,23:2
Bells Are Ringing 1956,N 30,18:2
Wilkes, Robert
Walk Hard 1944,D 1,28:2
Mamba's Daughters 1953,Mr 21,12:6
Wilkes, Thomas (Producer)
Topsy and Eva 1924,D 24,11:1
Downstream 1926,Ja 12,28:1
Wilkin, Barbara
Howie 1958,S 18,35:2
Wilkin, Jeremy
Hamlet 1957,Jl 3,15:2
Twelfth Night 1957,Jl 4,16:4
Broken Jug, The 1958,Ap 2,36:1
Much Ado About Nothing 1958,Je 26,22:1
Winter's Tale, The 1958,Jl 23,34:3
As You Like It 1959,Jl 1,27:1
Long and the Short and the Tall, The
  1962,Mr 30,28:2
Wilkin, Jeremy (Miscellaneous)
As You Like It 1959,Jl 1,27:1
Wilkins, Charlotte
Veils 1928,Mr 14,28:5
Wilkins, Claire
Hats Off to Ice 1944,Je 23,15:2
Wilkins, Enid
Porgy and Bess 1935,O 11,30:2
Wilkins, George
Ten Nights in a Barroom 1928,Mr 28,31:2
Wilkins, Jean
Three Musketeers, The 1921,My 20,18:5
Wilkins, Jerry
Cindy 1964,S 25,33:1
Wilkins, Joseph
Blossom Time 1931,Mr 5,32:1
Wilkins, Kenneth
Babes in Arms 1937,Ap 15,18:4
Wilkins, Marion
Vaudeville (Palace) 1930,N 17,21:2
Wilkins, Mary
Blossom Time 1931,Mr 5,32:1
Wilkins, Robert
Midsummer Night's Dream, A 1957,Je 27,21:3
Philoctetes 1959,Ja 14,28:1
Wilkins, Robin Davis
Simple Life, A 1964,My 18,36:1
Wilkins, Wilbur
Tiger Smiles, The 1930,D 18,29:1
Wilkinson, Bert
Biff, Bing, Bang 1921,My 10,20:1
Wilkinson, Dudley
Her Family Tree 1920,D 28,9:2
Queen O' Hearts 1922,O 11,22:1
Wilkinson, Dudley (Composer)
Queen O' Hearts 1922,O 11,22:1
Wilkinson, Geoffrey
King Lear 1947,F 19,32:2
As You Like It 1947,F 21,16:2
Merchant of Venice, The 1947,F 24,16:2
Volpone 1947,F 25,32:2
Hamlet 1947,F 27,27:2
Wilkinson, James
Boys From Syracuse, The 1938,N 24,36:1
Wilkinson, June
Pajama Tops 1963,Je 1,15:1
Wilkinson, Kate
Madre, La 1959,F 12,24:1
Rimers of Eldritch, The 1967,F 21,53:1
Watercolor 1970,Ja 22,30:1
Postcards 1970,Mr 17,36:1
Wilkinson, Leslie
Autumn's Here 1966,O 26,40:1
Wilkinson, Marc (Composer)
As You Like It 1967,O 15,II,9:3
Rosencrantz and Guildenstern Are Dead
  1967,O 17,53:1
Love for Love 1967,O 21,17:1
Love for Love 1967,O 30,59:1
Three Sisters, The 1970,F 12,30:1
Wilkinson, Marc (Miscellaneous)
Royal Hunt of the Sun, The 1965,O 27,36:2
Wilkinson, Norman (Costume Designer)
Iphigenie in Tauris 1915,Je 1,15:5
Iolanthe 1948,Ja 13,29:3
Wilkinson, Norman (Scenic Designer)
Tempest, The 1934,Ap 17,26:6
Wilkinson, Robert Sheldon
This Mad Whirl 1937,Ja 10,II,4:8

Will
Sweet Adeline 1929,S 4,33:1
Will Vodery Singers
Strike Me Pink 1933,Mr 6,16:3
Will Vodery's Plantation Orchestra
Plantation Revue, The 1922,Jl 18,18:4
Dixie to Broadway 1924,O 30,22:1
Willa, Suzanne
Barnum Was Right 1923,Mr 13,19:3
O Nightingale 1925,Ap 16,25:2
Excess Baggage 1927,D 27,24:2
Queen at Home 1930,D 30,25:2
Tell Me Pretty Maiden 1937,D 17,33:5
Willan, Healey (Dr) (Composer)
Prince Charlie and Flora 1931,Ag 29,16:5
Willard, Angela
I'll Take the High Road 1943,N 10,28:3
Willard, Catherine
Mask and the Face, The 1924,S 11,27:3
Simon Called Peter 1924,N 11,20:2
Great Gatsby, The 1926,F 3,22:1
Arabian Nightmare, The 1927,Ja 11,36:3
Love Is Like That 1927,Ap 19,24:1
Young Love 1928,O 31,28:1
Seven Year Love 1929,O 27,IX,2:1
Everything's Jake 1930,Ja 17,20:4
Milestones 1930,Je 3,27:1
Snark Was a Boojum, The 1943,S 2,14:4
Deep Mrs Sykes, The 1945,Mr 20,22:6
Deep Mrs Sykes, The 1945,Mr 25,II,1:1
You Touched Me! 1945,S 26,27:2
You Touched Me! 1945,S 30,II,1:1
Make Way for Lucia 1948,D 23,23:5
I Am a Camera 1951,N 29,39:6
Willard, Charles (Director)
Me and Juliet 1970,My 15,42:1
Willard, Charles (Mrs)
Puppets of Passion 1927,F 25,24:4
Machinal 1928,S 8,10:3
Escape This Night 1938,Ap 23,18:1
Willard, Dorothy (Producer)
Signature 1945,F 15,25:2
Liar, The 1950,My 19,30:2
Willard, Edmund
Machines 1930,N 23,IX,2:4
Arsenic and Old Lace 1943,Ja 1,26:5
Willard, Fred
Return of Second City in "20,000 Frozen
  Grenadiers," The 1966,Ap 22,36:1
Little Murders 1969,Ja 6,38:1
Arf 1969,My 28,36:1
Great Airplane Snatch, The 1969,My 28,36:1
Willard, George
Commedia Dell' Arte 1957,Jl 5,13:2
Master Builder, The 1957,D 18,42:7
Willard, Harold
George White's Scandals 1935,D 26,20:2
Willard, John
Cat and the Canary, The 1922,F 8,13:1
Helena's Boys 1924,Ap 8,22:2
Natja 1925,F 17,19:2
Mikado, The 1925,Ap 13,25:1
Lambs Gambol 1925,Ap 27,15:1
Love in a Mist 1926,Ap 13,28:3
On the Make 1932,My 24,23:2
Triplets 1932,S 22,25:2
Bohemian Girl, The 1933,Jl 28,18:5
Pirates of Penzance, The 1936,Ap 21,27:5
Julius Caesar 1937,N 12,26:6
Shoemaker's Holiday, The 1938,Ja 3,17:2
Willard, John (Director)
Sisters 1927,D 26,26:5
Willard, John (Playwright)
Blue Flame, The 1920,Mr 16,18:1
Cat and the Canary, The 1922,F 8,13:1
Green Beetle, The 1924,Jl 20,VII,1:7
Green Beetle, The 1924,S 3,12:3
Fog 1927,F 8,20:1
Sisters 1927,D 11,IX,2:5
Sisters 1927,D 26,26:5
Adventure 1928,S 26,25:2
Cat and the Canary, The 1935,Jl 9,24:4
Cat and the Canary, The 1937,Je 15,26:3
Cat and the Canary, The 1965,Ja 5,26:1
Willard, Marion
Move on, Sister 1933,O 25,22:4
Willard, Ralph
Street Scene 1929,Ja 11,20:4
Willard, Thomas
Hitch Your Wagon! 1937,Ap 9,18:2
Willemetz, Albert (Lyricist)
Trois Jeunes Filles Nues; Three Young Maids From
  the Folies Bergere 1929,Mr 5,28:2
Passionement; Passionately 1929,Mr 8,31:4
Ta Bouche 1929,Mr 15,28:5
Joies du Capitole, Les 1935,Ap 21,IX,2:1
Willemetz, Albert (Miscellaneous)
Springtime 1924,My 11,VIII,1:4
Willemetz, Albert (Playwright)
One Kiss 1923,N 28,14:2
A Vol d'Oiseau 1926,D 5,VIII,8:7
J'Aime 1927,Ja 23,VII,2:1
1927 1927,Mr 6,VII,4:4

Willemetz, Albert (Playwright)—Cont
Trois Jeunes Filles Nues; Three Young Maids From
  the Folies Bergere 1929,Mr 5,28:2
Passionement; Passionately 1929,Mr 8,31:4
Ta Bouche 1929,Mr 15,28:5
IIIe Chambre, La 1929,N 24,X,2:1
Mes Amours 1940,My 3,16:5
Willeminsky, J M (Composer)
Du Barry 1932,N 23,15:2
Willeminsky, J M (Playwright)
Du Barry 1931,S 20,VIII,1:6
Du Barry 1932,My 8,VIII,1:6
Willems, Eleanor
Passing Show of 1924, The 1924,S 4,13:4
Artists and Models 1925,Je 25,16:2
Willemsen, Madeline
Soles Truncos, Los; House on Cristo Street, The
  1959,Ag 31,15:2
Willens, Dot
Cyrano de Bergerac 1926,F 19,18:1
Willenz, Maria (Costume Designer)
A la Carte 1927,Ag 18,25:3
Willenz, Max
Miracle at Verdun 1931,Mr 17,34:6
Merchant of Yonkers, The 1938,D 29,14:2
Willer, Alicia (Miscellaneous)
John Gabriel Borkman 1959,N 26,57:4
Willerman, Susan
Perfect Party, The 1969,Mr 21,42:1
Willet, Chase
Pigeon, The 1930,O 15,26:2
Willett, Charles
Revolt of the Beavers, The 1937,My 21,19:2
Willett, Jack
Sons and Soldiers 1943,My 5,22:2
Doctors Disagree 1943,D 29,15:2
Willey, Alan
Swan, The 1923,O 24,15:3
Merchant of Venice, The 1928,Ja 17,22:2
Game of Love and Death, The 1929,N 26,28:4
Michael and Mary 1929,D 14,23:3
Death Takes a Holiday 1931,F 17,29:1
Willey, Leonard
Opportunity 1920,Jl 31,5:1
Teaser, The 1921,Jl 28,8:3
Six-Fifty, The 1921,O 25,20:1
Lady, The 1923,D 5,23:2
Simon Called Peter 1924,N 11,20:2
Legend of Leonora, The 1927,Mr 30,22:4
Merchant of Venice, The 1928,Ja 17,22:2
Becky Sharp 1929,Je 4,29:1
Thunder in the Air 1929,N 12,34:3
Michael and Mary 1929,D 14,23:3
Red Planet 1932,D 19,19:2
Mary of Scotland 1933,N 28,28:3
Willey, Richard
Hamlet 1970,D 28,40:1
Willey, Robert
Junior Miss 1941,N 19,28:2
Winged Victory 1943,N 22,24:1
Little A 1947,Ja 16,31:2
Men We Marry, The 1948,Ja 17,11:2
Willey, Robert A (Producer)
Greenwillow 1960,Mr 9,38:1
William, Clarence 3d
Party on Greenwich Avenue, The 1967,My 11,52:1
William, David
Midsummer Night's Dream, A 1962,Jl 2,22:2
William, David (Director)
King Lear 1950,Ag 30,26:2
Midsummer Night's Dream, A 1962,Jl 2,22:2
Twelfth Night 1966,Je 10,51:2
Merry Wives of Windsor, The 1967,Ag 4,18:1
William, Earl
Alive and Kicking 1950,Ja 18,25:5
Courtin' Time 1951,Je 14,30:2
H M S Pinafore 1952,N 4,32:2
Trial by Jury 1952,N 4,32:2
Iolanthe 1952,N 11,26:3
Carousel 1953,My 6,38:1
William, Warren
Wonderful Visit, The 1924,F 13,17:3
Nocturne 1925,F 17,19:1
Blue Peter, The 1925,Mr 25,25:3
Rosmersholm 1925,My 6,27:2
Twelve Miles Out 1925,N 17,29:2
Fanny 1926,S 22,30:1
Paradise 1927,D 26,26:4
Veils 1928,Mr 14,28:5
Golden Age, The 1928,Ap 25,31:3
Sign of the Leopard 1928,D 12,34:4
Let Us Be Gay 1929,F 22,19:1
Week-end 1929,O 23,26:4
Out of a Blue Sky 1930,F 10,20:6
Vikings, The 1930,My 13,27:3
Stepdaughters of War 1930,O 7,27:1
Vinegar Tree, The 1930,N 20,30:3
Williams, Addie
Don Juan 1921,S 8,14:2
Williams, Alan
For Charity 1937,Ag 25,24:3
Williams, Alan (Director)
Hipper's Holiday 1934,O 19,26:2

Williams, Alan (Playwright)
It's a Grand Life 1930,F 2,VIII,2:7
It's a Grand Life 1930,F 11,30:3
Williams, Angela
Wedding, The 1961,Ap 21,26:2
Williams, Ann
Two Seconds 1931,O 10,20:6
Mimie Scheller 1936,O 1,28:4
Between Two Thieves 1960,F 12,23:1
Six Characters in Search of an Author
1961,My 11,43:1
Milk Train Doesn't Stop Here Anymore, The
1963,Ja 18,7:1
Applause 1970,Mr 31,35:1
Applause 1970,Ap 5,II,1:1
Williams, Annabelle
It Never Rains 1931,D 25,29:3
Crucible 1933,S 5,22:4
Naked Man, The 1935,Jl 2,24:3
Williams, Arnold
Big Time Buck White 1968,D 9,58:1
Williams, Art
Best Foot Forward 1941,O 2,28:2
Williams, Art (Director)
Snow Maiden, The 1960,Ap 5,43:3
Williams, Arthur
In Circles 1967,O 14,12:1
In Circles 1968,Je 28,36:1
Williams, Barbara
Midsummer Night's Dream, A 1931,Ag 19,19:3
Smiling Faces 1932,Ag 31,12:3
Fiorello! 1962,Je 14,24:1
Streets of New York, The 1963,O 30,47:1
Williams, Bert
Broadway Brevities, 1920 1920,S 30,12:2
Williams, Betty
Sally 1920,D 22,16:1
Lady, The 1923,D 5,23:2
X Has No Value 1970,F 17,35:1
Williams, Betty (Costume Designer)
Nat Turner 1960,N 7,46:3
Long Christmas Dinner, The 1966,S 7,53:1
Queens of France 1966,S 7,53:1
Happy Journey to Trenton and Camden, The
1966,S 7,53:1
Williams, Billie
Babes in Toyland 1930,D 22,17:1
Williams, Billy
Firebird of Florence 1945,Mr 23,13:4
Williams, Billy Dee
Cool World, The 1960,F 23,38:2
Taste of Honey, A 1960,O 5,46:1
Taste of Honey, A 1960,N 6,II,1:1
Taste of Honey, A 1961,My 17,43:1
Blue Boy in Black, The 1963,My 1,32:1
Firebugs, The 1968,Jl 2,36:1
Slow Dance on the Killing Ground
1970,My 14,43:1
Williams, Buck
Naughty Marietta 1931,N 17,31:2
Williams, C J
Kibitzer, The 1929,F 19,22:5
Wonder Bar, The 1931,Mr 18,23:4
Williams, C Leonard
Volpone 1967,Je 30,29:1
Williams, C M (Scenic Designer)
Puritan, The 1936,Ja 24,14:3
Williams, Castle
Jubilee 1935,O 14,20:1
Williams, Charles
Student Prince, The 1924,D 3,25:3
Kitty's Kisses 1926,My 7,12:2
Temperance Town, A 1929,Ag 11,VIII,2:1
Porgy and Bess 1935,O 11,30:2
Every Man for Himself 1940,D 10,32:3
Confederacy, The 1958,Jl 3,20:1
Williams, Charles (Playwright)
Cranmer of Canterbury 1959,D 4,36:1
Williams, Christola
Sailor, Beware! 1935,My 7,28:4
Mad Morning 1935,Je 25,14:1
Satellite 1935,N 21,27:5
Walk Together Chillun 1936,F 5,15:2
Brown Sugar 1937,D 3,29:2
Williams, Clarence
Bottomland 1927,Je 28,29:3
Our Lan' 1947,Ap 19,11:2
Belafonte at the Palace 1959,D 16,55:1
Williams, Clarence (Composer)
Bottomland 1927,Je 28,29:3
Williams, Clarence (Playwright)
Bottomland 1927,Je 28,29:3
Williams, Clarence (Producer)
Bottomland 1927,Je 28,29:3
Williams, Clarence 3d
Egg and I, The 1958,S 11,43:4
Long Dream, The 1960,F 18,36:2
Walk in Darkness 1963,O 29,30:2
Sarah and the Sax 1964,My 5,53:1
Slow Dance on the Killing Ground 1964,D 1,50:1
Great Indoors, The 1966,F 2,23:1
Does a Tiger Wear a Necktie? 1967,F 4,17:1
King John 1967,Jl 14,19:1

Williams, Clark
One More Genius 1936,Ag 11,24:6
Little Women 1944,D 13,29:2
Little Women 1945,D 24,18:2
Angel in the Pawnshop 1951,Ja 19,20:3
Williams, Clement M (Scenic Designer)
Come What May 1934,My 16,23:4
Williams, Clifford
Antony and Cleopatra 1951,D 21,22:2
Williams, Clifford (Director)
Comedy of Errors, The 1962,S 12,34:2
Tempest, The 1963,Ap 3,43:1
Comedy of Errors, The 1964,My 21,43:1
Our Man Crichton 1964,D 23,21:1
Jew of Malta, The 1965,Ap 17,9:1
Merchant of Venice, The 1965,Ap 17,9:1
As You Like It 1967,O 6,33:4
As You Like It 1967,O 15,II,9:3
Soldiers 1968,Mr 3,88:2
Soldiers 1968,My 2,58:1
Dr Faustus 1968,Je 29,20:1
As You Like It 1968,Jl 6,9:1
Edward II 1969,Ja 19,II,30:5
Back to Methuselah 1969,Ag 31,46:3
Sleuth 1970,N 13,25:1
Williams, Clifford (Lighting Director)
Comedy of Errors, The 1964,My 21,43:1
Williams, Clifford (Producer)
Afore Night Come 1964,Je 26,34:1
Soldiers 1968,Mr 3,88:2
Soldiers 1969,Ja 5,II,3:1
Williams, Clifford (Scenic Designer)
Comedy of Errors, The 1964,My 21,43:1
Williams, Clyde
Blues for Mister Charlie 1964,Ap 24,24:1
Utbu 1966,Ja 5,24:1
Williams, Craig
Lucky Sam McCarver 1925,O 22,22:1
Window Panes 1927,F 22,22:2
Ringside 1928,Ag 30,13:2
Rhapsody, The 1930,S 16,30:3
Du Barry 1932,N 23,15:2
Play, Genius, Play! 1935,O 31,17:2
Williams, Curt
Macbeth 1962,N 17,16:2
Inherit the Wind 1967,Je 23,50:1
Williams, D A
Take a Brace 1923,Ap 20,20:3
Williams, Dale
We Bombed in New Haven 1968,O 17,51:1
Williams, Dan
Paradise 1931,My 12,29:2
Williams, David (Miscellaneous)
Romeo and Juliet 1962,Ap 3,42:1
Williams, Debbie
Ice Follies 1966,Ja 12,27:6
Williams, Dennis (Costume Designer)
Recruiting Officer, The 1958,F 8,12:2
Williams, Derek
Journey's End 1929,Mr 23,23:1
Journey's End 1929,Mr 31,VIII,1:1
Journey's End 1929,Jl 14,IX,5:1
Journey's End 1930,Ja 27,24:7
Sex Fable, The 1931,O 21,26:1
Shining Hour, The 1934,F 14,22:6
Jubilee 1935,S 23,20:3
Jubilee 1935,O 14,20:1
Good Hunting 1938,N 22,26:5
Importance of Being Earnest, The 1939,Ja 13,16:2
Williams, Dick
Copper and Brass 1957,O 18,19:2
Big Time Buck White 1968,D 9,58:1
Williams, Dick (Director)
Big Time Buck White 1968,D 9,58:1
Pig Pen, The 1970,My 21,47:1
Williams, Dick Singers
Untitled-Judy Garland 1967,D 26,45:1
Williams, Dolores
Abe Lincoln in Illinois 1938,O 17,12:2
Williams, Drid (Choreographer)
Electra 1962,Mr 22,42:1
Williams, Dudley
Pelleas and Melisande 1957,F 20,38:1
Williams, Duke
Wedding in Japan 1949,N 11,29:1
Wisteria Trees, The 1950,Mr 30,39:1
Williams, E Crawshay (Playwright)
This Marriage 1924,My 18,VII,2:8
Williams, Earl
Parson's Bride, The 1929,Ja 22,22:3
Night at an Inn, A 1930,My 10,25:1
Williams, Edmund
Scarecrow, The 1953,Je 17,31:1
Little Clay Cart, The 1953,Jl 1,25:1
Cyanamide 1954,Mr 26,17:6
Juno and the Paycock 1955,F 24,20:4
Inherit the Wind 1955,Ap 22,20:2
Tall Story 1959,Ja 30,33:2
Only in America 1959,N 20,35:1
Room Service 1970,My 13,49:1
Williams, Edmund (Miscellaneous)
When We Dead Awaken 1966,Ap 19,37:2

Williams, Elaine
Sappho 1960,Ja 12,22:1
Williams, Eleanor
Love Child, The 1922,N 15,22:1
Desert Flower, The 1924,N 19,18:2
Kiss in a Taxi, The 1925,Ag 26,14:1
Barker, The 1927,Ja 19,20:6
By Request 1928,S 28,30:2
Enemy Within 1931,O 6,35:3
New York to Cherbourg 1932,F 20,11:4
On Your Toes 1954,O 12,24:4
Williams, Eliot Crawshay (Playwright)
E & O E 1935,Jl 12,15:3
Williams, Elizabeth
Lulu Belle 1926,F 10,20:1
Goat Alley 1927,Ap 21,24:3
Williams, Elwoodson
Adding Machine, The 1970,D 5,40:1
Williams, Emlyn
And So to Bed 1927,N 10,23:1
Case of the Frightened Lady, The 1931,S 6,VIII,2:1
Criminal at Large 1932,O 11,26:3
Rose and Glove 1934,S 9,35:5
Josephine 1934,S 26,17:5
Night Must Fall 1935,Jl 7,IX,1:7
Night Must Fall 1936,S 29,34:1
Light of Heart, The 1941,Je 15,IX,2:5
Morning Star, The 1942,S 20,VIII,1:1
Wind of Heaven, The 1945,Ap 22,II,2:3
Montserrat 1949,O 31,21:4
Untitled-Reading 1952,Ja 30,20:2
Emlyn Williams 1952,F 5,25:2
Untitled-Reading 1952,F 17,II,1:1
Bleak House 1952,S 4,24:7
Bleak House 1953,Ap 21,33:2
Someone Waiting 1953,N 26,51:7
Boy Growing Up, A 1957,O 8,41:1
Daughter of Silence 1961,D 1,28:1
Man for All Seasons, A 1962,S 23,II,1:1
Deputy, The 1964,F 27,26:1
Emlyn Williams as Charles Dickens 1970,N 4,41:1
Williams, Emlyn (Director)
Night Must Fall 1936,S 29,34:1
Watch on the Rhine 1942,My 3,VIII,1:7
Little Foxes, The 1942,N 1,VIII,2:1
Williams, Emlyn (Playwright)
Murder Has Been Arranged, A 1930,N 30,IX,1:8
Port Said 1931,N 22,VIII,2:1
Murder Has Been Arranged, A 1931,D 12,23:5
Spring, 1600 1934,F 1,14:1
Spring, 1600 1934,Mr 4,IX,3:8
Josephine 1934,S 26,17:5
Josephine 1934,O 14,X,3:1
Night Must Fall 1935,Jl 7,IX,1:7
Night Must Fall 1936,S 29,34:1
He Was Born Gay 1937,My 27,20:5
He Was Born Gay 1937,Je 13,XI,1:7
Corn Is Green, The 1938,O 9,X,3:1
Light of Heart, The 1940,Mr 3,X,3:4
Corn Is Green, The 1940,N 27,27:2
Corn Is Green, The 1940,D 1,X,1:1
Light of Heart, The 1941,Je 15,IX,2:5
Morning Star, The 1941,D 28,IX,2:3
Morning Star 1942,F 15,VIII,3:6
Yesterday's Magic 1942,Ap 15,27:2
Morning Star, The 1942,S 15,18:4
Morning Star, The 1942,S 20,VIII,1:1
Corn Is Green, The 1943,My 4,18:3
Corn Is Green, The 1943,My 9,II,1:1
Wind of Heaven, The 1945,Ap 22,II,2:3
Trespass 1947,Ag 24,II,1:7
Corn Is Green, The 1950,Ja 12,33:2
Bleak House 1953,Ap 21,33:2
Someone Waiting 1953,N 26,51:7
Corn Is Green, The 1954,F 27,10:2
Someone Waiting 1956,F 15,26:1
Williams, Emlyn (Translator)
Month in the Country, A 1956,Ap 4,23:1
Month in the Country, A 1956,Ap 15,II,1:1
Month in the Country, A 1959,Mr 2,32:2
Master Builder, The 1964,Je 10,50:2
Master Builder, The 1968,Je 22,26:1
Williams, Enid
Hilarities 1948,S 10,20:2
Williams, Eugene
Brothers 1928,D 26,14:3
Williams, Eva
Old Soak, The 1922,Ag 23,14:5
Commodore Marries, The 1929,S 5,26:3
Commodore Marries, The 1929,S 15,IX,1:1
Williams, Florence
Lady Windermere's Fan 1932,Ja 27,19:3
Girls in Uniform 1932,D 31,10:3
Joyous Season, The 1934,Ja 30,16:3
Closed Room, The 1934,Jl 24,20:2
Allure 1934,O 30,22:6
Old Maid, The 1935,Ja 8,26:1
Call It a Day 1936,Ja 21,26:7
Call It a Day 1936,Ja 29,15:2
Call It a Day 1936,F 9,X,1:1
Little Foxes, The 1939,F 16,16:2
Little Foxes, The 1939,F 26,IX,1:1
Trojan Women, The 1941,Ap 9,32:5

Williams, Florence—Cont
All the Comforts of Home 1942,My 26,24:5
Williams, Foster
Crime Marches on 1935,O 24,19:1
O Evening Star 1936,Ja 9,24:6
Bright Honor 1936,S 28,14:1
Sweet River 1936,O 29,30:2
Williams, Frances
Madre 1923,D 31,9:6
Innocent Eyes 1924,My 21,22:2
Cocoanuts, The 1925,D 9,30:1
George White's Scandals 1926,Je 15,23:2
Big Lake 1927,Ap 9,17:2
Scandals 1927,Jl 3,VII,1:1
Martine 1928,Ap 5,19:3
George White's Scandals 1928,Jl 3,19:1
Lady From Alfaqueque, The; Consulesa, La
  1929,Ja 15,22:3
Katerina 1929,F 26,30:3
George White's Scandals 1929,S 24,29:1
Three Sisters, The 1930,Ja 9,22:2
Glass of Water, A 1930,Mr 6,16:3
Antigone 1930,Ap 25,28:4
Vaudeville (Palace) 1930,Ag 4,13:2
New Yorkers, The 1930,N 16,VIII,3:1
New Yorkers, The 1930,D 9,31:1
Everybody's Welcome 1931,O 14,26:3
Gentlewoman 1934,Mr 23,28:4
Life Begins at 8:40 1934,Ag 28,24:2
Life Begins at 8:40 1934,S 2,IX,1:1
Beaux' Stratagem, The 1935,Jl 17,22:5
Camille 1935,Jl 31,21:1
Double Door 1935,Ag 21,22:2
Late Christopher Bean, The 1935,Ag 28,13:1
Call It a Day 1936,Ja 21,26:7
Call It a Day 1936,Ja 29,15:2
Casey Jones 1938,F 21,14:2
Aquacade 1939,My 5,26:2
Three After Three 1939,N 25,13:5
Walk With Music 1940,Je 5,33:2
Let's Face It 1941,O 30,26:2
Brights Lights of 1944 1943,S 17,27:4
Enchanted, The 1950,Ja 19,34:2
Son, The 1950,Ap 1,12:4
Williams, Frank
Heaven-Tappers, The 1927,Mr 9,28:3
Williams, Fred
Flight Into Egypt 1952,Mr 19,33:2
Williams, Fritz
Fools Errant 1922,Ag 22,12:3
Rain 1922,N 8,18:2
Human Nature 1925,S 25,24:3
Makropoulos Secret, The 1926,Ja 22,12:4
Spread Eagle 1927,Ap 5,30:2
Before You're 25 1929,Ap 17,30:2
Berkeley Square 1929,N 5,32:4
Williams, Genevieve
Katy Did 1927,My 10,24:3
Forbidden Roads 1928,Ap 17,26:4
Hedda Gabler 1929,F 4,20:3
Becky Sharp 1929,Je 4,29:1
Williams, George
Up She Goes 1922,N 7,14:2
Bewitched 1924,O 2,26:3
Williams, George C
Trial of Dr Beck, The 1937,Ag 10,22:2
Williams, George J
Schemers 1924,S 16,27:1
Holy Terror, A 1925,S 29,31:2
Killers 1928,Mr 14,28:3
Ringside 1928,Ag 30,13:2
Williams, George W
Out of Step 1925,Ja 30,12:1
Brother Elks 1925,S 15,29:2
Gray Shadow 1931,Mr 11,23:4
If Booth Had Missed 1932,F 5,24:2
Hat, a Coat, a Glove, A 1934,F 1,15:2
Williams, Gerald
Sweet River 1936,O 29,30:2
Williams, Gilman
Black Crook, The 1929,Mr 12,26:5
Williams, Grif (Costume Designer)
Connelly vs Connelly 1961,F 18,11:3
Williams, Gus
Funnyhouse of a Negro 1964,Ja 15,25:3
Williams, Guy
Midsummer Night's Dream, A 1963,Jl 1,19:2
Williams, Gwendoline
Fields Beyond, The 1936,Mr 7,11:2
Williams, Gwilym
Corn Is Green, The 1943,My 4,18:3
Minnie and Mr Williams 1948,O 28,37:2
Corn Is Green, The 1950,Ja 12,33:2
Williams, Hannah
Sweet and Low 1930,N 18,28:5
Hooray for What! 1937,N 7,XI,2:4
Williams, Harcourt
Cornelius 1935,Ap 14,IX,1:1
Devil to Pay, The 1939,Jl 21,11:1
King Lear 1947,Ap 28,IX,1:7
Williams, Harcourt (Director)
Antony and Cleopatra 1930,D 14,IX,3:1
Voysey Inheritance, The 1934,Je 3,IX,2:5

Williams, Harcourt (Producer)
Devil to Pay, The 1939,Jl 21,11:1
Williams, Harold
Richelieu 1929,D 26,20:3
Cyrano de Bergerac 1932,D 27,11:2
Williams, Harriet
Deep Harlem 1929,Ja 8,35:2
Williams, Heathcote (Playwright)
Local Stigmatic, The; Applicant 1969,N 4,55:2
Local Stigmatic, The 1969,N 4,55:2
Local Stigmatic, The; Request Stop 1969,N 4,55:2
Local Stigmatic, The; That's All 1969,N 4,55:2
Local Stigmatic, The; Interview 1969,N 4,55:2
Local Stigmatic, The; Trouble in the Works
  1969,N 4,55:2
Local Stigmatic, The; That's Your Trouble
  1969,N 4,55:2
Local Stigmatic, The; Last to Go 1969,N 4,55:2
Williams, Helen (Playwright)
God Innis 1937,Ag 25,24:3
Williams, Henry B
Plain Dealer, The 1929,My 23,27:1
Saint's Parade 1930,N 1,23:4
Blackbirds 1933,D 4,22:3
Beaux' Stratagem, The 1935,Jl 17,22:5
Williams, Henry B (Scenic Designer)
Saint's Parade 1930,N 1,23:4
Coquette 1935,Jl 10,24:1
Beaux' Stratagem, The 1935,Jl 17,22:5
Hay Fever 1935,Jl 24,20:4
Camille 1935,Jl 31,21:1
Williams, Herb
Vaudeville (Palace) 1926,D 21,20:5
Vaudeville (Palace) 1929,F 18,29:1
Vaudeville (Palace) 1929,D 23,19:1
Earl Carroll's Vanities 1930,Jl 2,28:3
Vaudeville (Palace) 1931,Ja 26,21:5
Vaudeville (Palace) 1931,Jl 6,24:6
Vaudeville (Palace) 1932,Jl 4,14:5
Farmer Takes a Wife, The 1934,O 28,IX,3:1
Farmer Takes a Wife, The 1934,O 31,17:1
Farmer Takes a Wife, The 1934,N 11,IX,1:1
At Home Abroad 1935,S 4,22:3
At Home Abroad 1935,S 8,IX,1:1
At Home Abroad 1935,S 20,17:4
Williams, Herb (Translator)
Cousin Sonia 1925,D 8,28:3
Williams, Herman
Forbidden Melody 1936,N 3,33:1
Williams, Hermanos
Vaudeville (Palace) 1927,D 6,26:3
Williams, Hermanos Trio
Laugh, Town, Laugh! 1942,Je 23,22:2
Laugh, Town, Laugh! 1942,Jl 23,15:3
Williams, Herschel (Original Author)
Janie 1942,S 11,24:2
Williams, Herschel (Playwright)
Janie 1942,S 11,24:2
Men We Marry, The 1948,Ja 17,11:2
Williams, Herschel (Producer)
John Brown's Body 1960,Je 22,31:1
Williams, Herschel V Jr
Patriarch, The 1926,D 11,15:1
Williams, Hope
What Next 1920,Ja 27,7:2
Paris Bound 1927,D 28,26:3
Paris Bound 1928,Ja 15,VIII,1:1
Holiday 1928,N 27,36:1
Holiday 1928,D 9,X,1:1
Rebound 1930,F 4,29:1
Rebound 1930,F 16,IX,1:1
New Yorkers, The 1930,N 16,VIII,3:1
New Yorkers, The 1930,D 9,31:1
New Yorkers, The 1930,D 28,VIII,1:1
Passing Present, The 1931,N 29,VIII,2:2
Passing Present, The 1931,D 8,36:2
Too True to Be Good 1932,Mr 1,19:2
Too True to Be Good 1932,Mr 6,VIII,1:1
Too True to Be Good 1932,Ap 5,27:5
Strike Me Pink 1933,Mr 6,16:3
All Good Americans 1933,D 6,29:2
Amphitryon 38 1937,Je 24,30:2
Importance of Being Earnest, The 1939,Ja 13,16:2
Williams, Hugh
Grand Hotel 1931,S 27,VIII,1:4
Flowers of the Forest 1935,Ap 9,25:2
Pride and Prejudice 1936,Ag 30,IX,1:1
Old Music 1937,Ag 19,22:2
Old Music 1937,S 5,X,2:1
Once Is Enough 1938,F 16,16:2
Williams, Hugh (Playwright)
Irregular Verb to Love, The 1963,S 19,22:2
Irregular Verb to Love, The 1963,S 29,II,1:1
Flip Side, The 1968,O 11,36:1
Williams, Hunter (Producer)
Gala Night 1930,F 26,22:4
Williams, Ina
Century Revue and the Midnight Rounders, The
  1920,Jl 13,9:1
Keep Kool 1924,My 23,16:4
City Chap, The 1925,O 27,21:1
Yours Truly 1927,Ja 26,16:5
Vaudeville (Palace) 1929,O 21,31:2

Williams, Irene
H M S Pinafore 1920,Ja 13,10:2
Erminie 1921,Ja 4,11:1
Girofle-Girofla 1926,N 24,26:2
Free and Easy 1959,D 15,51:4
Free and Easy 1959,D 20,II,3:2
Williams, Irma
Sweet River 1936,O 29,30:2
Williams, J Lister
Symphony in Two Flats 1930,S 17,30:4
Williams, James
Case of Philip Lawrence, The 1937,Je 9,31:1
Williams, Jane
Fall and Rise of Susan Lenox, The 1920,Je 11,11:2
39 Steps 1938,Mr 12,13:1
Williams, Janis
Hold On to Your Hats 1940,S 12,30:3
Williams, Jay
R U R 1942,D 4,30:2
Nathan the Wise 1944,F 22,26:3
Williams, Jazzbo
Searching for the Sun 1936,F 20,22:6
Williams, Jean
Sweet River 1936,O 29,30:2
Williams, Jeanne
Seven Mirrors 1945,O 26,17:2
Safari! 1955,My 12,32:6
Williams, Jennifer
Geese 1969,Ja 13,26:6
Williams, Jesse Lynch (Playwright)
Why Not? 1922,D 25,20:1
Why Not? 1922,D 31,VII,1:1
Lovely Lady 1925,S 20,VIII,2:4
Lovely Lady 1925,O 15,27:1
Williams, Jill
Charlot's Revue 1924,Ja 10,18:1
Williams, John
Fake, The 1924,O 7,26:3
Dark Angel, The 1925,F 11,19:2
Kiss in a Taxi, The 1925,Ag 26,14:1
Ghost Train, The 1926,Ag 26,17:2
Mixed Doubles 1927,Ap 27,22:3
Ten Per Cent 1927,S 14,29:3
Interference 1927,O 19,24:3
Happy Husband, The 1928,My 8,25:2
High Road, The 1928,S 11,31:1
Elmer the Great 1928,S 25,29:1
Vermont 1929,Ja 9,28:1
Gambling 1929,Ag 27,31:2
Tavern, The 1930,My 20,32:1
Song and Dance Man, The 1930,Je 17,25:5
Once in a Lifetime 1930,S 25,22:3
One, Two, Three! 1930,S 30,24:2
Petticoat Influence 1930,D 16,34:6
I Love an Actress 1931,S 18,29:2
East of Broadway 1932,Ja 27,19:3
Good Woman, Poor Thing, A 1933,Ja 10,27:3
Ten Minute Alibi 1933,O 18,24:3
Peace on Earth 1933,N 30,39:2
Dodsworth 1934,F 26,20:4
Stevedore 1934,Ap 19,33:2
Dance With Your Gods 1934,O 8,14:3
Dear Old Darling 1936,Mr 3,25:1
White Christmas 1936,Jl 7,22:2
Barchester Towers 1937,D 1,27:1
Right This Way 1938,Ja 6,22:3
Once Is Enough 1938,F 16,16:2
Miss Swan Expects 1939,F 21,15:2
No Time for Comedy 1939,Ap 18,26:4
Scandals 1939,Ag 29,17:2
Meet the People 1940,D 26,22:2
Meet the People 1941,Ja 12,IX,1:1
Claudia 1941,F 13,24:2
Let's Face It 1941,O 30,26:2
Family Affair, A 1946,N 28,41:2
If the Shoe Fits 1946,D 6,29:4
Barefoot Boy With Cheek 1947,Ap 4,20:2
Men We Marry, The 1948,Ja 17,11:2
Anne of the Thousand Days 1948,D 9,49:2
Velvet Glove, The 1949,D 27,26:2
Venus Observed 1952,F 14,24:2
Venus Observed 1952,F 24,II,1:1
Singing Girl, The 1952,Je 4,31:8
Dial 'M' for Murder 1952,O 30,41:2
Dial 'M' for Murder 1952,N 30,II,1:1
On Your Toes 1954,O 12,24:4
Dark Is Light Enough, The 1955,F 24,20:1
Ross 1961,D 27,20:2
New York Idea, The 1963,Jl 13,12:2
Chinese Prime Minister, The 1964,Ja 3,14:1
Chinese Prime Minister, The 1964,Ja 12,II,1:1
Hay Fever 1970,N 10,55:1
Hay Fever 1970,N 22,II,18:6
Williams, John D (Director)
Lally 1927,F 9,16:3
Savages Under the Skin 1927,Mr 25,25:2
Aiglon, L' 1927,D 27,24:3
Man With Red Hair, A 1928,N 9,22:2
Pagan Lady 1930,S 28,VIII,4:1
Pagan Lady 1930,O 21,34:2
Williams, John D (Producer)
Assumption of Hannele, The 1924,F 16,16:2
Aiglon, L' 1927,D 27,24:3

Williams, John J
Late Arrival 1953,O 20,35:5
Williams, John S (Miscellaneous)
B J One 1931,My 7,21:3
Williams, Johnee
Maid in the Ozarks 1946,Jl 16,20:3
Williams, Johnny
Ice Follies 1966,Ja 12,27:6
Williams, Josephine
Wheel, The 1921,Ag 30,10:1
Serpent's Tooth, A 1922,Ag 25,8:5
Craig's Wife 1925,O 13,21:2
Royal Family, The 1927,D 29,26:4
Moon in the Yellow River, The 1932,Mr 1,19:3
Moon in the Yellow River, The 1932,Mr 13,VIII,1:1
Tiara, The 1932,D 12,18:3
Far Away Horses 1933,Mr 22,21:6
Her Master's Voice 1933,O 24,24:3
Macbeth 1936,Ap 15,25:4
Williams, Judith
J B 1958,Ap 24,37:1
Williams, Karl
Song Out of Sorrow 1955,N 1,27:3
Taming of the Shrew, The 1956,Ag 11,11:2
Anatomist, The 1957,F 27,21:5
Romeo and Juliet 1957,Je 28,30:2
Two Gentlemen of Verona 1957,Jl 23,21:5
Richard III 1957,N 26,41:1
Electra 1958,My 10,17:7
Measure for Measure 1960,Jl 27,33:1
Darker Flower, A 1963,Mr 11,7:2
Williams, Kay
Song of Norway 1959,Je 26,16:2
House of Bernarda Alba, The 1963,N 25,23:2
Williams, Ken
Top Speed 1929,D 26,20:1
Trio 1944,D 30,13:4
One Over the Eight 1961,Je 25,II,3:5
Three Plays of the Sea 1970,Ag 20,39:1
Williams, Ken (Producer)
Follies of 1910, The 1960,Ja 15,37:3
Williams, L A Jr
Coriolanus 1927,Je 18,8:3
Williams, Larry
This Our House 1935,D 12,33:3
O Evening Star 1936,Ja 9,24:6
Middle Man 1936,S 8,23:1
Lysistrata 1946,O 18,27:5
Williams, Lawrence
Mad Honeymoon, The 1923,Ag 8,10:1
Williams, Lillian
How Beautiful With Shoes 1935,N 29,24:1
Williams, Liz
Born Yesterday 1958,Mr 22,12:6
Follies of 1910, The 1960,Ja 15,37:3
Williams, Louise
Shuffle Along of 1933 1932,D 27,11:3
Williams, Luther
Carry Nation 1932,O 31,18:2
Williams, Malcolm
Mirage, The 1920,O 1,14:1
Magnolia 1923,Ag 28,12:3
Wisdom Tooth, The 1926,F 16,22:2
God Loves Us 1926,O 20,22:2
Beyond the Horizon 1926,D 1,24:2
Comic, The 1927,Ap 20,28:2
Breaks, The 1928,Ap 17,26:3
Little Accident 1928,O 10,32:3
Purity 1930,D 26,18:2
Williams, Margaret
Wheel, The 1921,Ag 30,10:1
Outrageous Fortune 1943,N 4,28:5
Green Pastures, The 1951,Mr 16,35:2
Midsummer Night's Dream, A 1964,Je 30,23:2
Williams, Margaret (Playwright)
Irregular Verb to Love, The 1963,S 19,22:2
Irregular Verb to Love, The 1963,S 29,II,1:1
Flip Side, The 1968,O 11,36:1
Williams, Margery (Playwright)
Out of the Night 1927,O 18,32:3
Williams, Marian
Dearest Enemy 1925,S 19,9:2
Williams, Marshall (Lighting Director)
Song of the Lusitanian Bogey, The 1968,Ja 3,52:1
God Is a (Guess What?) 1968,D 18,56:1
Satisfaction Guaranteed 1969,F 12,31:1
Open 24 Hours 1969,F 12,31:1
High John De Conquer 1969,Ap 23,39:1
But Never Jam Today 1969,Ap 24,40:1
Black Quartet, A; Great Goodness of Life (A Coon Show) 1969,Jl 31,28:1
Black Quartet, A; Warning, The-A Theme for Linda 1969,Jl 31,28:1
Black Quartet, A; Prayer Meeting or The First Militant Minister 1969,Jl 31,28:1
Black Quartet, A; Gentleman Caller, The 1969,Jl 31,28:1
Williams, Mary Lou
Blue Holiday 1945,My 22,13:3
Williams, Mervin
Streets of New York, The 1931,O 7,29:1
Bride the Sun Shines On, The 1931,D 28,20:2

Dodsworth 1934,F 26,20:4
Arrest That Woman 1936,S 19,20:4
Comedy of Good and Evil, A 1938,Ap 8,16:3
On the Rocks 1938,Je 16,20:2
Jeremiah 1939,F 4,11:2
Cafe Crown 1942,Ja 24,12:5
Proud Accent 1949,Ap 23,10:2
Anna Christie 1955,N 22,41:1
Six Characters in Search of an Author 1955,D 12,38:1
Comrades 1956,Je 6,38:1
Good Woman of Setzuan, The 1956,D 19,41:2
Richard III 1957,N 26,41:1
Courageous One, The 1958,Ja 21,33:6
Macbeth 1962,N 17,16:2
Passion of Josef D, The 1964,F 12,29:1
Medea 1965,N 29,46:1
Does a Tiger Wear a Necktie? 1967,F 4,17:1
Williams, Mervin (Director)
Infernal Machine, The 1937,D 13,22:7
No Laughter in Heaven 1938,My 17,26:5
Williams, Michael
King Lear 1964,My 19,43:2
Comedy of Errors, The 1964,My 21,43:1
Persecution and Assassination of Marat As Performed by the Inmates of the Asylum of Charenton Under the Direction of the Marquis de Sade, The 1965,D 28,35:1
Troilus and Cressida 1969,Jl 31,26:1
London Assurance 1970,Ag 7,26:1
Williams, Milton
Green Pastures, The 1930,F 27,26:1
Green Pastures, The 1935,F 27,16:2
Sailor, Beware! 1935,My 7,28:4
Cabin in the Sky 1940,O 26,19:2
St Louis Woman 1946,Ap 1,22:2
How Long Till Summer 1949,D 28,30:3
You Can't Take It With You 1951,Ap 7,8:6
Pursuit of Happiness, The 1952,Mr 22,9:2
Hole in the Head, A 1957,Mr 1,15:1
Sweet Bird of Youth 1959,Mr 11,39:2
One Flew Over the Cuckoo's Nest 1963,N 14,40:2
Williams, Minnie
Trial of Dr Beck, The 1937,Ag 10,22:2
Williams, Murial
Merrily We Roll Along 1934,O 1,14:1
Co-Respondent Unknown 1936,Ag 19,18:5
Lorelei 1938,N 30,21:2
Intimate Relations 1962,N 2,27:1
We Have Always Lived in the Castle 1966,O 20,53:1
Williams, Musa
Dance With Your Gods 1934,O 8,14:3
Porgy and Bess 1935,O 11,30:2
Sweet River 1936,O 29,30:2
John Henry 1939,D 17,IX,5:6
John Henry 1940,Ja 11,18:2
Strangler Fig, The 1940,My 7,31:2
Porgy and Bess 1942,Ja 23,16:2
Porgy and Bess 1943,S 14,26:2
Porgy and Bess 1944,F 8,13:2
Happy Birthday 1946,N 1,31:2
Set My People Free 1948,N 4,38:2
South Pacific 1951,S 2,II,1:1
Cat on a Hot Tin Roof 1955,Mr 25,18:2
Williams, Nancy
Amahl and the Night Visitors 1970,D 24,10:2
Williams, Noel
Ponder Heart, The 1956,F 17,14:2
Williams, Nora
Vaudeville (Palace) 1932,Ap 25,18:3
Vaudeville (Palace) 1932,My 2,13:2
Williams, Norman
These Modern Women 1928,F 14,26:2
Camel Through the Needle's Eye, The 1929,Ap 16,32:2
House Beautiful, The 1931,Mr 13,20:4
As Husbands Go 1933,Ja 20,20:5
Big Hearted Herbert 1934,Ja 2,17:3
Achilles Had a Heel 1935,O 14,20:2
How Beautiful With Shoes 1935,N 29,24:1
So Proudly We Hail 1936,S 23,28:4
Days of Our Youth, The 1941,N 29,15:2
Williams, Olena
Swing It 1937,Jl 23,17:2
Williams, Pat
Blackouts of 1949 1949,S 7,39:2
Ice Follies 1966,Ja 12,27:6
Williams, Pat (Miscellaneous)
Golden Rainbow 1968,F 5,27:1
Williams, Peter
Daphne Laureola 1950,S 19,38:6
Williams, Phyllis (Composer)
Hear! Hear! 1955,S 28,38:1
Williams, Phyllis (Playwright)
Hear! Hear! 1955,S 28,38:1
Williams, R Davis
Willow and I, The 1942,D 11,32:2
Williams, Ralph
King and the Duke, The 1955,Je 2,25:2
Ronde, La 1955,Je 28,24:2
Saint Joan 1956,S 12,42:1
Bonds of Interest, The 1958,My 7,43:1

Williams, Ralph—Cont
Look: We've Come Through 1961,O 26,40:1
She Loves Me 1963,Ap 24,39:1
She Loves Me 1963,My 5,II,1:1
Cocktail Party, The 1968,O 8,42:1
Misanthrope, The 1968,O 10,59:1
Cocktail Party, The 1968,O 20,II,1:1
Cock-A-Doodle Dandy 1969,Ja 21,40:1
Remote Asylum 1970,D 13,II,3:1
Williams, Ramsay
Love on Leave 1944,Je 21,23:4
Williams, Regina
Porgy and Bess 1935,O 11,30:2
Sweet River 1936,O 29,30:2
Williams, Rex
Too Many Heroes 1937,N 16,26:2
Knights of Song 1938,O 18,29:2
Man With Blonde Hair, The 1941,N 5,30:2
Rugged Path, The 1945,N 12,17:2
Rat Race, The 1949,D 23,16:2
Live Wire, The 1950,Ag 18,16:2
Men of Distinction 1953,My 1,18:4
Once More With Feeling 1958,O 22,39:1
Williams, Rex (Director)
Sappho 1960,Ja 12,22:1
Williams, Rex (Playwright)
Sappho 1960,Ja 12,22:1
Williams, Rex (Producer)
Sappho 1960,Ja 12,22:1
Williams, Rhys
Richard II 1937,F 6,14:2
Richard II 1937,S 16,28:2
Hamlet 1938,O 13,28:1
Henry IV, Part I 1939,Ja 31,17:2
Henry IV 1939,F 5,IX,1:1
Hamlet 1939,D 5,35:2
Richard II 1940,Ap 2,31:2
Corn Is Green, The 1940,N 27,27:2
Morning Star, The 1942,S 15,18:4
Morning Star, The 1942,S 20,VIII,1:1
Lifeline 1942,D 1,20:3
Harriet 1943,Ja 29,22:1
Harriet 1943,Mr 4,24:2
Chicken Every Sunday 1944,Ap 6,27:2
Chicken Every Sunday 1944,Ap 16,II,1:1
Mr Peebles and Mr Hooker 1946,O 11,29:2
Biggest Thief in Town 1949,Mr 31,31:2
Williams, Richard
Strange Fruit 1945,N 30,18:6
On Whitman Avenue 1946,My 9,28:2
Earthlight Theater 1970,N 4,38:2
Williams, Richard (Miscellaneous)
Lady or the Tiger?, The 1966,O 19,53:1
Diary of Adam and Eve, The 1966,O 19,53:1
Passionella 1966,O 19,53:1
Williams, Rico
Good Woman of Setzuan, The 1970,N 6,51:1
Williams, Robbie
Ice Follies 1966,Ja 12,27:6
Williams, Robert
Abie's Irish Rose 1922,My 24,22:4
Milgrim's Progress 1924,D 23,17:1
Kept 1926,S 18,13:3
That French Lady 1927,Mr 16,29:3
Jimmie's Women 1927,S 27,30:3
Soldiers and Women 1929,S 3,25:1
Scarlet Pages 1929,S 10,26:3
Half Gods 1929,D 23,18:5
Rebound 1930,F 4,29:1
Rebound 1930,F 16,IX,1:1
Fatal Woman, The 1930,Mr 2,IX,4:7
Love, Honor and Betray 1930,Mr 13,22:2
Little Orchard Annie 1930,Ap 22,33:1
Halfway to Hell 1934,Ja 3,22:3
Nowhere Bound 1935,Ja 23,20:2
Country Wife, The 1935,Jl 2,24:2
Coward, The 1935,Jl 16,24:1
If This Be Treason 1935,Jl 30,17:1
If This Be Treason 1935,S 24,28:2
Porgy and Bess 1935,O 11,30:2
Let Freedom Ring 1935,N 7,26:2
Prelude 1936,Ap 20,17:4
Bury the Dead 1936,Ap 20,17:4
Russet Mantle 1936,Ag 18,15:2
Lend Me Your Ears! 1936,O 6,28:5
Ten Million Ghosts 1936,O 24,23:7
200 Were Chosen 1936,N 21,21:1
Call Me Ziggy 1937,F 13,9:6
Hitch Your Wagon! 1937,Ap 9,18:2
Excursion 1937,Ap 10,11:4
Thanks for Tomorrow 1938,S 28,28:2
Mrs O'Brien Entertains 1939,F 9,16:3
Sea Dogs 1939,N 7,30:3
Two on an Island 1940,Ja 23,17:2
Man With Blonde Hair, The 1941,N 5,30:2
Johnny on the Spot 1942,Ja 9,24:2
They Should Have Stood in Bed 1942,F 14,18:5
Autumn Hill 1942,Ap 14,17:4
Show Time 1942,S 17,20:2
Eve of St Mark, The 1942,O 8,30:2
Judy Garland's New Variety Show 1956,S 27,43:2
Williams, Robert (Costume Designer)
Athenian Touch, The 1964,Ja 15,25:4

Williams, Robert T (Lighting Director)
Warm Body, A 1967,Ap 17,44:2
Williams, Robert T (Scenic Designer)
Plot Against the Chase Manhattan Bank, The
1963,N 27,29:1
Cindy 1964,Mr 20,24:1
Girl Could Get Lucky, A 1964,S 21,36:1
Glass Menagerie, The 1965,My 5,53:2
Warm Body, A 1967,Ap 17,44:2
Month of Sundays 1968,S 17,50:1
Charley's Aunt 1970,Jl 6,38:1
Williams, Rodney
Beautiful Changes, The 1956,Mr 24,15:2
Williams, Roger
Vaudeville (Palace) 1926,My 8,29:2
Vaudeville (Palace) 1927,Je 28,29:2
Williams, Roy
Sunny River 1941,D 5,28:2
Williams, Roy (Playwright)
Disney on Parade 1970,S 24,63:1
Williams, Rudy
Viva O'Brien 1941,O 10,27:2
Williams, Ruth
Allegro 1952,S 18,36:3
Williams, Sally
Woman of Bronze, The 1920,S 8,9:2
Williams, Sharon
Come Share My House 1960,F 19,20:2
Williams, Spencer (Composer)
Put and Take 1921,Ag 24,12:3
Williams, Stanley
Hymn to the Rising Sun 1937,My 7,28:2
Williams, Teddy
Prodigal Son, The 1965,My 21,19:1
Williams, Tennessee (Lyricist)
Orpheus Descending 1957,Mr 22,28:1
Williams, Tennessee (Playwright)
Battle of Angels 1940,D 31,18:6
Battle of Angels 1941,Ja 5,IX,1:7
You Touched Me! 1943,O 17,II,2:4
Glass Menagerie, The 1945,Ap 2,15:5
Glass Menagerie, The 1945,Ap 8,II,1:1
You Touched Me! 1945,S 26,27:2
You Touched Me! 1945,S 30,II,1:1
Stairs to the Roof 1947,F 26,35:4
Summer and Smoke 1947,Jl 9,18:5
Summer and Smoke 1947,Ag 10,II,1:1
Streetcar Named Desire, A 1947,D 4,42:2
Streetcar Named Desire, A 1947,D 14,II,3:1
Glass Menagerie, The 1948,Jl 29,17:2
Summer and Smoke 1948,O 7,33:2
Summer and Smoke 1948,O 17,II,1:1
Streetcar Named Desire, A 1949,Je 12,II,1:1
Lady of Larkspur Lotion, The 1949,Jl 9,9:2
Streetcar Named Desire, A 1949,S 29,38:1
Streetcar Named Desire, A 1949,O 13,33:6
Streetcar Named Desire, A 1949,O 19,36:6
Streetcar Named Desire, A 1949,D 11,II,3:1
Streetcar Named Desire, A 1950,My 24,36:1
Summer and Smoke 1950,O 29,II,3:7
Rose Tattoo, The 1951,F 5,19:2
Rose Tattoo, The 1951,F 11,II,1:1
Summer and Smoke 1951,N 23,32:7
Summer and Smoke 1952,Ja 25,13:5
Summer and Smoke 1952,F 10,II,2:3
Summer and Smoke 1952,Ap 25,19:5
Summer and Smoke 1952,My 4,II,1:1
Camino Real 1953,Mr 20,26:1
Camino Real 1953,Mr 29,II,1:1
Purification, The 1954,My 29,12:1
Purification, The 1954,Je 6,II,1:1
Lord Byron's Love Letter 1955,Ja 19,23:2
27 Wagons Full of Cotton 1955,Ja 19,23:2
Streetcar Named Desire, A 1955,Mr 4,18:2
Camino Real 1955,Mr 21,21:3
Cat on a Hot Tin Roof 1955,Mr 25,18:2
Cat on a Hot Tin Roof 1955,Ap 3,II,1:1
All in One; 27 Wagons Full of Cotton
1955,Ap 20,40:3
All in One 1955,Ap 24,II,1:1
Streetcar Named Desire, A 1956,F 16,24:1
Sweet Bird of Youth 1956,Ap 17,27:2
This Property Is Condemned 1956,O 29,34:1
Glass Menagerie, The 1956,N 22,50:1
Glass Menagerie, The 1956,D 2,II,1:1
Orpheus Descending 1957,Mr 22,28:1
Orpheus Descending 1957,Mr 31,II,1:1
Portrait of a Madonna 1957,Ap 1,21:2
Camino Real 1957,Ap 9,41:1
Garden District; Suddenly Last Summer
1958,Ja 8,23:4
Garden District; Something Unspoken
1958,Ja 8,23:4
Garden District; Suddenly Last Summer
1958,Ja 19,II,1:1
Cat on a Hot Tin Roof 1958,Ja 31,24:2
Garden District 1958,S 17,44:2
Sweet Bird of Youth 1959,Mr 11,39:2
Orpheus Descending 1959,Mr 18,44:6
Sweet Bird of Youth 1959,Mr 22,II,1:1
I Rise in Flame, Cried the Phoenix 1959,Ap 15,30:1
Portrait of a Madonna 1959,Ap 16,28:1
Portrait of a Madonna 1959,Ap 26,II,1:1

Orpheus Descending 1959,My 15,23:3
Orpheus Descending 1959,O 6,45:2
Purification, The 1959,D 9,57:5
Camino Real 1960,My 17,42:2
Camino Real 1960,My 29,II,1:1
This Property Is Condemned 1960,Ag 26,13:1
Period of Adjustment 1960,N 11,34:1
Period of Adjustment 1960,N 20,II,1:1
Glass Menagerie, The 1961,Mr 6,30:1
Glass Menagerie, The 1961,Ap 1,11:2
Glass Menagerie, The 1961,Ap 11,43:5
Glass Menagerie, The 1961,Ap 21,29:1
Glass Menagerie, The 1961,My 1,35:3
Glass Menagerie, The 1961,My 19,22:2
Glass Menagerie, The 1961,My 31,28:1
Glass Menagerie, The 1961,Je 16,27:3
Glass Menagerie, The 1961,Ag 21,20:7
Orpheus Descending 1961,Ag 28,21:2
Night of the Iguana, The 1961,D 29,10:1
Period of Adjustment 1962,Ja 3,25:1
Night of the Iguana, The 1962,Ja 7,II,1:1
Period of Adjustment 1962,Je 4,24:2
Milk Train Doesn't Stop Here Anymore, The
1962,Jl 12,19:8
Milk Train Doesn't Stop Here Anymore, The
1963,Ja 18,7:1
Milk Train Doesn't Stop Here Anymore, The
1963,S 18,32:1
Milk Train Doesn't Stop Here Anymore, The
1964,Ja 2,33:1
Glass Menagerie, The 1964,Jl 20,18:3
Streetcar Named Desire, A 1965,F 19,27:1
Glass Menagerie, The 1965,My 5,53:2
Glass Menagerie, The 1965,My 16,II,1:1
Milk Train Doesn't Stop Here Anymore, The
1965,Ja 27,25:1
Mutilated, The 1966,F 23,42:1
Gnadiges Fraulein, The 1966,F 23,42:1
Slapstick Tragedy; Mutilated, The; Gnadiges
Fraulein, The 1966,Mr 6,II,1:1
Rose Tattoo, The 1966,O 21,36:2
Rose Tattoo, The 1966,N 20,II,1:1
Two Character Play, The 1967,D 13,54:5
Seven Descents of Myrtle, The 1968,Mr 28,54:1
Seven Descents of Myrtle, The 1968,Ap 7,II,1:5
In the Bar of a Tokyo Hotel 1969,My 12,54:1
In the Bar of a Tokyo Hotel 1969,My 25,II,5:4
Camino Real 1970,Ja 9,42:1
Camino Real 1970,Ja 18,II,1:1
Williams, Thyra
Medea 1960,Jl 26,25:2
Williams, Tom
Champion, The 1921,Ja 4,11:1
Bronx Express 1922,Ap 27,12:2
Springtime of Youth 1922,O 27,15:1
Jane-Our Stranger 1925,O 9,27:2
O'Flynn, The 1934,D 28,24:1
Corn Is Green, The 1943,My 4,18:3
Lute Song 1946,F 7,29:2
Flag Is Born, A 1946,S 7,10:6
Twelfth Night 1949,O 4,33:2
Madwoman of Chaillot, The 1950,Je 14,41:2
Tall Story 1959,Ja 30,33:2
Lute Song 1959,Mr 13,24:1
Happy Town 1959,O 8,49:2
Williams, Troy
Amedee: or, How to Disentangle Yourself
1955,N 1,27:3
Williams, Valentine (Original Author)
Berlin 1931,D 31,16:1
Williams, Valentine (Playwright)
Berlin 1931,D 31,16:1
Williams, Van
No Time for Sergeants 1955,O 21,32:2
Williams, Van (Composer)
Rehearsal, The 1952,My 27,30:5
Williams, Vernon G
Stepping Sisters 1930,Ap 23,24:2
Williams, Virginia
We All Do 1927,Mr 1,30:3
Merry Andrew 1929,Ja 22,22:2
Williams, Wade
Confederacy, The 1958,Jl 3,20:1
Williams, Waldine
Black Scandals 1928,O 27,23:2
Run, Little Chillun! 1933,Mr 2,21:3
Belle Helene, La 1941,Jl 8,14:1
Williams, Walter
Kit Marlowe 1936,My 24,35:1
Hamlet 1939,D 5,35:2
Richard II 1940,Ap 2,31:2
Macbeth 1941,N 12,30:2
Dragon, The 1963,Ap 10,32:1
Last Analysis, The 1964,O 2,30:1
Williams, Warren
Expressing Willie 1924,Ap 17,22:1
Easter 1926,Mr 19,24:3
One Day More 1926,Mr 19,24:3
Williams, Wes
Moondreamers, The 1969,D 9,68:1
Williams, Wilhelmina
Walk Together Chillun 1936,F 5,15:2
Macbeth 1936,Ap 15,25:4

Williams, Wilhelmina—Cont
Nativity Play, The 1937,D 21,29:1
Williams, Willard
Belt, The 1927,O 20,33:1
Williams, William
Cat-Bird, The 1920,F 17,18:1
Piper, The 1920,Mr 20,14:2
Good Times 1920,Ag 10,10:1
Checkerboard, The 1920,Ag 20,7:2
Mirage, The 1920,O 1,14:1
French Doll, The 1922,F 21,20:2
Virtue (?) 1922,N 17,14:1
Dragon, The 1922,D 27,12:1
All Gummed Up 1923,Ja 29,11:2
As You Like It 1923,Ap 24,24:1
New Poor, The 1924,Ja 8,26:1
Dawn 1924,N 25,27:1
Complex, The 1925,Mr 4,17:2
Solid Ivory 1925,N 17,29:3
You Can't Win 1926,F 17,12:1
Iolanthe 1926,Ap 20,24:2
Pirates of Penzance, The; Slave of Duty, The
1926,D 7,25:1
Pirates of Penzance, The 1926,D 12,VIII,3:1
Mikado, The; Town of Titipu, The 1927,S 19,30:1
Chee-Chee 1928,S 26,25:1
East Wind 1931,O 28,19:1
Lady of Letters 1935,Mr 29,26:6
Williams, William A (Director)
Raw Meat 1933,Mr 23,13:2
Williams, William Carlos (Playwright)
Many Loves 1959,Ja 14,28:1
Many Loves 1961,Je 16,29:1
Williams, William T (Scenic Designer)
X Has No Value 1970,F 17,35:1
Williams and Keene
Vaudeville (Palace) 1926,My 11,25:3
Williams and Wolfus
What's in a Name? 1920,Mr 20,14:2
Vaudeville (Palace) 1923,Ap 3,26:4
Williams Family, The
Ice Follies 1967,Ja 11,51:1
Williams Sisters
Scandals 1924,Jl 1,16:1
Americana 1928,O 31,28:2
New Americana 1928,N 30,32:4
Vaudeville (Palace) 1929,F 11,26:2
Williamsom, Laird
Henry VI, Part I 1964,Jl 23,18:1
Williamson, Anne
Will Shakespeare 1923,Ja 2,14:1
Williamson, Bruce
John Brown 1950,My 4,32:7
Williamson, Bud
Greenwich Village Follies 1924,S 17,16:1
Williamson, Charles
Joan of Lorraine 1955,Mr 26,12:2
Williamson, Howard
Iolanthe 1968,N 9,37:3
Williamson, Hugh
Doughgirls, The 1942,D 31,19:2
Williamson, Hugh Ross (Playwright)
Rose and Glove 1934,S 9,35:5
Various Heavens 1936,Mr 8,IX,1:1
Mr Gladstone 1937,O 1,18:4
Mr Gladstone 1937,O 17,XI,3:5
Pilgrim's Progress 1948,Jl 20,27:5
Teresa of Avila 1961,S 13,55:1
Williamson, J C (Producer)
Three Men on a Horse 1936,Mr 24,26:4
Williamson, Mary
Cynara 1931,N 3,31:1
Williamson, Nicol
Inadmissible Evidence 1964,S 10,31:1
Inadmissible Evidence 1965,D 1,52:1
Hamlet 1969,F 19,38:1
Hamlet 1969,Mr 2,II,3:1
Hamlet 1969,My 2,38:1
Hamlet 1969,My 11,II,1:1
Williamson, Robert
Champion, The 1921,Ja 4,11:1
Shipwrecked 1924,N 13,18:1
Jack in the Pulpit 1925,Ja 7,33:1
Castles in the Air 1926,S 7,19:2
Music in the Air 1932,N 9,28:2
Berkeley Square 1935,Ag 20,25:1
Murder in the Cathedral 1936,Mr 21,13:5
White Horse Inn 1936,O 2,28:5
Antony and Cleopatra 1937,N 11,30:2
Pinocchio 1939,Ja 3,19:2
Williamson, Rosemary
As the Girls Go 1948,N 15,21:2
Williamson, Ruth
Good Morning, Dearie 1921,N 2,20:2
Just Because 1922,Mr 23,11:1
Williamson, Susan
Persecution and Assassination of Marat As
Performed by the Inmates of the Asylum of
Charenton Under the Direction of the Marquis de
Sade, The 1965,D 28,35:1
Williamson, W W (Mrs)
One Woman's Husband 1920,Mr 23,9:3
Williard, Matilda (Corp)
Swing Sister Wac Swing 1944,Ja 4,20:4

Williard, Matilda (Wac Corp) (Costume Designer)
Swing Sister Wac Swing 1944,Ja 4,20:4
Willie, Charles
Hitchy-Koo, 1920 1920,O 20,11:3
Willie, Jose
Flowers of Virtue, The 1942,F 6,22:2
Willie, West and McGinty
Vaudeville (Palace) 1926,Jl 20,17:4
Vaudeville (Palace) 1929,F 4,21:4
Vaudeville (Palace) 1930,F 17,18:4
Aquacade 1939,My 5,26:2
Willingham, Annot
Schoolgirl 1930,N 21,31:1
Willingham, Calder (Original Author)
End as a Man 1953,S 16,39:1
End As a Man 1953,S 27,II,1:1
Willingham, Calder (Playwright)
End as a Man 1953,S 16,39:1
End As a Man 1953,S 27,II,1:1
Willis, Arthur
Billy Budd 1959,F 28,13:3
Willis, Austin
Man and Boy 1963,N 13,34:1
Minor Adjustment, A 1967,O 7,33:3
Willis, Carter
Injury Sustained 1940,O 24,30:3
Willis, Eddie
Vaudeville (Palace) 1928,Jl 31,13:5
Willis, George
Robert E Lee 1923,N 21,23:1
Carmen Jones 1943,D 3,26:2
Carmen Jones 1945,My 3,26:5
Carmen Jones 1946,Ap 8,32:2
Carmen Jones 1951,S 22,8:6
Willis, Gloria
Take It As It Comes 1944,F 11,17:2
Her Master's Voice 1964,D 28,33:2
Willis, Harold (Playwright)
Sound of Silence, A 1965,Mr 9,30:1
Willis, Henry
Much Ado About Nothing 1929,N 17,30:4
Willis, Horton
And Puppy Dog Tails 1969,O 20,60:1
Willis, Jack
Furnished Rooms 1934,My 30,14:6
Willis, Jill
Pickwick 1927,S 6,35:2
Vaudeville (Palace) 1928,Ap 3,32:5
Willis, Joseph
Brown Buddies 1930,O 8,29:1
Shuffle Along of 1933 1932,D 27,11:3
Noah 1935,F 14,25:2
Willis, Josephine
Old Bill, M P 1926,N 11,22:2
Willis, Keith
Brigadoon 1957,Mr 28,37:1
Can-Can 1959,Ag 26,25:4
Willis, Lynn
Ever Since Paradise 1957,Jl 12,18:4
Willis, Lynn (Musical Director)
Ever Since Paradise 1957,Jl 12,18:4
Willis, Marion
How Beautiful With Shoes 1935,N 29,24:1
Stork Mad 1936,O 1,28:4
Sweet River 1936,O 29,30:2
Howdy Stranger 1937,Ja 15,17:5
Too Many Heroes 1937,N 16,26:2
All the Living 1938,Mr 25,14:4
Goodbye in the Night 1940,Mr 19,31:2
Willis, Mervyn
Arden of Faversham 1970,F 17,33:1
Willis, Morton
Alt Heidelberg 1926,My 31,10:5
Willis, S
Vaudeville (Palace) 1931,O 19,28:5
Willis, Susan
Little Clay Cart, The 1953,Jl 1,25:1
Macbeth 1955,O 8,12:6
Last Love of Don Juan, The 1955,N 24,40:1
Thesmophoriazusae, The; Goddesses of Athens,
The 1955,D 14,52:4
Winter's Tale, The 1963,Je 29,13:1
Midsummer Night's Dream, A 1963,Jl 1,19:2
Love and Let Love 1968,Ja 4,30:1
Willis, Susanne
Come Seven 1920,Jl 20,10:1
Man in the Making, The 1921,S 21,16:2
Willison, Barbara
Sing High, Sing Low 1931,N 13,26:4
Broadway Boy 1932,My 4,23:5
Willison, Walter
Norman, Is That You? 1970,F 20,30:1
Two by Two 1970,N 11,37:1
Two by Two 1970,N 22,II,1:1
Willman, Elwil (Director)
All's Well That Ends Well 1955,Je 7,37:4
Willman, Noel
Legend of Lovers 1951,D 27,17:1
Rashomon 1959,Ja 28,36:2
Rashomon 1959,F 8,II,1:1
Hamlet 1961,Ap 12,46:1
Isle of Children 1962,Mr 17,16:2

Willman, Noel (Director)
Man for All Seasons, A 1961,N 23,51:1
Man for All Seasons, A 1961,D 3,II,1:1
Beauty Part, The 1962,D 28,5:2
Man for All Seasons, A 1964,Ja 28,24:2
Lion in Winter, The 1966,Mr 4,23:1
Darling of the Day 1968,Ja 29,26:2
Ring Around the Moon 1968,N 2,28:1
Willman, Noel (Producer)
Lion in Winter, The 1966,Mr 13,II,1:1
Willmore, Lydia
Up the Line 1926,N 23,26:1
Willner, A M (Original Author)
Blossom Time 1923,My 22,14:3
Blossom Time 1931,Mr 5,32:1
Great Waltz, The 1934,S 24,14:4
Blossom Time 1938,D 27,12:2
Willner, A M (Playwright)
Blossom Time 1921,S 30,10:1
Count of Luxembourg, The 1930,F 18,28:2
Blossom Time 1943,S 6,21:2
Willon, Carl V
Romio and Julietta 1925,Ap 21,19:1
Willoughby, Deane
Mary of Scotland 1933,N 28,28:3
Willoughby, Hugh (Scenic Designer)
Earl Carroll's Vanities 1928,Ag 7,25:2
Earl Carroll's Vanities 1931,Ag 28,18:7
Saluta 1934,Ag 29,13:4
Tide Rising 1937,Ja 26,17:2
Where Do We Go From Here? 1938,N 16,26:2
Willoughby, Lewis
Hurricane 1923,D 26,13:4
Willoughby, Marlene
Dracula Sabbat 1970,O 2,28:2
Willoughby, Peggy
Charlot's Revue 1924,Ja 10,18:1
Willoughby, Ronald
Walk in Darkness 1963,O 29,30:2
Little Eyolf 1964,Mr 17,31:1
Wills, Carolyn
Surgeon, The 1932,O 28,23:1
Wills, Drusilla
Murder on the Second Floor 1929,S 12,35:1
Wills, Gloria
Allegro 1947,O 11,10:2
Wills, Helen
Come of Age 1934,Ja 13,16:6
Wills, Lou
Best Foot Forward 1941,O 2,28:2
One Touch of Venus 1943,O 8,14:1
Laffing Room Only 1944,D 25,15:4
Are You With It? 1945,N 12,17:3
Louisiana Lady 1947,Je 3,35:2
Tree Grows in Brooklyn, A 1951,Ap 20,24:3
South Pacific 1957,Ap 25,35:1
Show Boat 1957,Je 28,30:2
What a Killing 1961,Mr 28,41:1
Lovely Ladies, Kind Gentlemen 1970,D 29,38:1
Wills, Mary (Costume Designer)
Ice Follies 1963,Ja 10,5:2
Ice Follies 1964,Ja 8,41:2
Ice Follies 1965,Ja 13,35:1
Ice Follies 1966,Ja 12,27:6
Ice Follies 1967,Ja 11,51:1
Wills, Michael
Bright Rebel 1938,D 28,24:2
Wills, Si
Vaudeville (Palace) 1932,S 12,13:5
Wills, Walter
Humming Bird, The 1923,Ja 16,16:2
Willshire, Gerard
Cape Smoke 1925,F 17,19:1
Monkey Talks, The 1925,D 29,20:1
90 Horse Power 1926,Mr 16,22:4
Willson, A Leslie (Translator)
Wicked Cooks, The 1967,Ja 24,42:1
Willson, Donald
Passionate Pilgrim, The 1932,O 20,24:3
Plumes in the Dust 1936,N 7,14:2
Willson, Meredith (Composer)
Music Man, The 1957,D 20,31:1
Unsinkable Molly Brown, The 1960,N 4,28:1
Music Man, The 1963,Ag 15,24:1
Here's Love 1963,S 20,28:3
Here's Love 1963,O 4,28:1
Music Man, The 1965,Je 17,26:4
Willson, Meredith (Lyricist)
Music Man, The 1957,D 20,31:1
Unsinkable Molly Brown, The 1960,N 4,28:1
Music Man, The 1963,Ag 15,24:1
Here's Love 1963,S 20,28:3
Here's Love 1963,O 4,28:1
Music Man, The 1965,Je 17,26:4
Willson, Meredith (Original Author)
Music Man, The 1957,D 20,31:1
Music Man, The 1965,Je 17,26:4
Willson, Meredith (Playwright)
Music Man, The 1957,D 20,31:1
Music Man, The 1958,S 28,II,1:1
Music Man, The 1961,Mr 18,17:3
Music Man, The 1963,Ag 15,24:1
Here's Love 1963,S 20,28:3

Willson, Meredith (Playwright)—Cont
Here's Love 1963,O 4,28:1
Music Man, The 1965,Je 17,26:4
Willys, Six
Boys and Girls Together 1940,O 2,19:2
Top-Notchers 1942,My 30,8:5
Wilman, Marilyn
Right You Are (If You Think You Are)
1950,Je 29,37:2
Wilmarth, Louise
Sun-Up 1930,My 10,25:1
Wilmer, Sidney (Producer)
Headquarters 1929,D 5,32:4
Wilmerton, Lincoln
Streets of Paris, The 1939,Je 20,25:2
Wilmore, Lydia
Getting Even 1929,Ag 20,31:1
Wilmot, Pat (Playwright)
Truce of the Bear 1957,O 24,39:1
Wilmot, Thomas A
Roof, The 1930,Je 14,9:2
Racket, The 1930,N 20,30:6
Wilmshurst, Carolyn
John Gabriel Borkman 1959,N 26,57:4
Wilmurt, Arthur (Playwright)
Guest Room, The 1931,O 7,29:2
Noah 1935,F 14,25:2
Young Couple Wanted 1940,Ja 25,16:2
Young Couple Wanted 1940,F 4,IX,1:1
Wilmurt, Arthur (Scenic Designer)
Doctor X 1930,Jl 31,12:4
Wilner, Max
Radio Girl, The 1929,O 19,22:4
Jolly Orphan, The 1929,D 23,18:6
Little Clown, The 1930,Mr 15,23:3
Girl From Warsaw, The 1931,S 14,15:5
Shulamith 1931,O 14,26:4
Mother's Son 1931,N 26,36:4
Pleasure 1931,D 28,20:2
Under One Roof 1932,F 8,21:2
Happy Family, A 1934,S 24,15:2
Game of Love, A 1934,O 25,26:6
Twice 100,000 1934,N 23,22:6
East Side Wedding, An 1935,Ja 21,18:2
Itche Mayer of Warsaw 1935,Ja 31,22:4
Lovka Maladetz 1935,Mr 27,25:5
Matinee Wife 1936,Ap 25,21:3
Wilner, Sis (Composer)
Star and Garter 1942,Je 25,26:2
Wilner, Sis (Lyricist)
Star and Garter 1942,Je 25,26:2
Wilsea, Bertha
Chalk Dust 1936,Mr 5,24:5
Wilsey, Mary
Beware of the Bull 1933,My 30,13:7
Wilshin, Sunday
Earl Carroll's Vanities 1927,Ja 5,18:1
Wilson, Adelaide
Roger Bloomer 1923,Mr 2,18:3
Lady, The 1923,D 5,23:2
Great Music 1924,O 6,24:1
Wilson, Adin
Fall and Rise of Susan Lenox, The 1920,Je 11,11:2
Dancing Mothers 1924,Ag 12,12:2
Damn Your Honor 1929,D 31,14:3
Launcelot and Elaine 1930,Mr 10,24:3
Wilson, Adrian
Poet's Follies of 1955 1955,My 15,II,3:1
Wilson, Al (Composer)
Yeah-Man 1932,My 27,27:3
Wilson, Al (Lyricist)
Yeah-Man 1932,My 27,27:3
Wilson, Alan
Help Yourself! 1936,Jl 15,15:1
It Can't Happen Here 1936,O 28,30:1
Wilson, Alex
Young American, A 1946,Ja 18,14:5
Wilson, Alice Bromley
Square Peg, A 1923,Ja 29,10:2
Wilson, Alma (Playwright)
Company's Coming! 1931,Ap 21,35:5
Wilson, Andi (Miscellaneous)
Shepherd's Chameleon, The 1960,N 30,41:1
Wilson, Angus (Playwright)
Mulberry Bush, The 1955,S 28,38:3
Wilson, Anita
Man Better Man 1969,Jl 3,22:1
Day of Absence 1970,Mr 18,39:1
Ododo 1970,N 25,26:1
Wilson, Anne (Choreographer)
Moon Walk 1970,N 27,52:1
Wilson, Arthur
One-Act Plays of the Sea; Long Voyage Home,
The 1937,O 30,23:2
Androcles and the Lion 1938,D 17,10:5
Wilson, Audree
Oklahoma! 1951,My 30,15:2
Wilson, Barry
My 3 Angels 1956,F 4,24:2
Shadow Years, The 1957,Ja 9,26:2
Wilson, Beatrice
Caroline 1923,F 1,13:2
Wilson, Ben
Score 1970,O 29,57:4

Wilson, Bertha
Woman of Bronze, The 1920,S 8,9:2
Wilson, Betty
Play of Daniel, The 1959,Ja 6,30:2
Play of Daniel, The 1959,D 28,17:6
Play of Daniel, The 1960,D 27,23:6
Golden Age, The 1963,N 19,49:2
Wilson, Bradford
Blue Blood 1924,Ap 3,21:2
Wilson, Carl
Jonah! 1966,F 16,52:1
Moondreamers, The 1969,D 9,68:1
Wilson, Carol
Pirate, The 1942,N 26,39:2
Wilson, Carrie
Promenade 1969,Je 5,56:1
Wilson, Charles
Adrienne 1923,My 29,10:4
Lazybones 1924,S 23,23:1
Donovan Affair, The 1926,Ag 31,15:2
War Song, The 1928,S 25,29:3
This Man's Town 1930,Mr 11,24:4
Up and Up, The 1930,S 9,25:2
Three Times the Hour 1931,Ag 26,15:5
Wilson, Charles (Musical Director)
Much Ado About Nothing 1964,Je 11,26:2
Richard III 1964,Je 12,44:2
Hamlet 1964,Jl 4,9:1
Mikado, The 1965,Ap 17,11:3
Wilson, Charles G
Louder, Please! 1931,N 13,26:4
Wilson, Chris
Effect of Gamma Rays on Man-in-the-Moon
Marigolds, The 1965,Je 7,48:1
Wilson, Claggett (Costume Designer)
Taming of the Shrew, The 1935,O 1,27:3
Taming of the Shrew, The 1940,F 6,17:2
Wilson, Claggett (Producer)
Taming of the Shrew, The 1940,F 6,17:2
Wilson, D S (Miscellaneous)
Sweet Enemy, The 1965,F 16,39:1
Wilson, Daphne
Shannons of Broadway, The 1927,S 27,30:4
Mystery Square 1929,Ap 5,28:3
Ten Minute Alibi 1933,O 18,24:3
Invitation to a Murder 1934,My 18,26:3
Wilson, Demond
Five on the Black Hand Side 1970,Ja 2,32:2
Wilson, Derby
Hoofers, The 1969,Jl 30,23:4
Wilson, Dolores
Yearling, The 1965,D 11,25:1
Cry for Us All 1970,Ap 9,48:2
Wilson, Don
Make a Million 1958,O 24,39:2
Wilson, Don (Playwright)
Beggar Student, The 1942,S 26,11:4
Wilson, Donald
Passionate Pilgrim, The 1932,O 20,24:3
Wilson, Dooley
Conjur' Man Dies 1936,Mr 12,18:5
Strangler Fig, The 1940,My 7,31:2
Cabin in the Sky 1940,O 26,19:2
Cabin in the Sky 1940,N 3,IX,1:1
Bloomer Girl 1944,O 6,18:5
Wilson, Dore
Lazarus Laughed 1928,Ap 10,33:1
Wilson, Doreen
Song of Norway 1944,Ag 22,20:2
Gypsy Lady 1946,S 18,25:6
Wilson, Douglas
Ladies Night in a Turkish Bath 1961,Mr 22,38:1
Wilson, Edith
Plantation Revue, The 1922,Jl 18,18:4
Hot Chocolates 1929,Je 21,17:4
Hot Rhythm 1930,Ag 22,18:5
Shuffle Along of 1933 1932,D 27,11:3
Hummin' Sam 1933,Ap 10,8:8
Blackbirds 1933,D 4,22:3
Memphis Bound 1945,My 25,23:2
Wilson, Edmund (Playwright)
Crime in the Whistler Room, The 1924,O 10,22:2
Little Blue Light, The 1951,Ap 30,17:2
Wilson, Edwin
Passing of the Third Floor Back, The
1928,Ja 17,22:7
Passing of the Third Floor Back, The
1928,F 21,18:2
Tenth Man, The 1929,Mr 21,29:2
War 1929,S 19,37:3
Second Mate, The 1930,Mr 25,34:5
Wilson, Edwin (Producer)
Burning, The 1963,D 4,57:1
Better Luck Next Time 1966,Ja 28,21:1
Walk in Dark Places, A 1966,Ja 28,21:1
Agatha Sue, I Love You 1966,D 15,61:1
Wilson, Eileen
No More Blondes 1920,Ja 8,22:1
Lady of the Lamp, The 1920,Ag 18,6:4
Night Duel, The 1926,F 16,22:3
Little Spitfire, The 1926,Ag 17,15:2
Burlesque 1927,S 2,15:3
Peter Flies High 1931,N 10,28:3

Wilson, Eleanor
Eagle Has Two Heads, The 1947,Mr 20,39:2
Silver Whistle, The 1948,N 25,49:2
Wayward Saint, The 1955,F 18,17:1
Villa of Madame Vidac, The 1959,O 1,40:1
Weekend 1968,Mr 14,50:2
Prince of Peasantmania 1970,F 22,88:1
Wilson, Elizabeth
Picnic 1953,F 20,14:7
Desk Set, The 1955,O 25,36:7
Tunnel of Love, The 1957,F 14,31:4
Big Fish, Little Fish 1961,Mr 16,42:2
Big Fish, Little Fish 1961,Mr 26,II,1:1
Yes is for a Very Young Man 1963,Mr 6,7:5
Eh? 1966,O 17,47:1
Little Murders 1969,Ja 6,38:1
Sheep on the Runway 1970,F 2,28:3
Good Woman of Setzuan, The 1970,N 6,51:1
Wilson, Ethel
Tyranny of Love, The 1921,Mr 2,7:3
Magnolia 1923,Ag 28,12:3
Gypsy Jim 1924,Ja 15,17:4
Spooks 1925,Je 2,16:4
Monkey Talks, The 1925,D 29,20:1
Just Life 1926,S 15,33:3
Her First Affaire 1927,Ag 23,29:2
Spring Song 1927,D 22,26:3
Song Writer, The 1928,Ag 14,15:2
So This Is Paris 1930,Ap 27,IX,2:3
Hello Paris 1930,N 17,29:3
Yoshe Kalb 1933,D 29,27:2
Tight Britches 1934,S 12,26:2
Portrait of Gilbert 1934,D 29,11:5
Rain 1935,F 13,24:1
Is This a Zither? 1935,Je 11,24:3
Lambent Flame, The 1935,Jl 16,24:2
Drums Professor, The 1935,Jl 30,17:2
Meet the Prince 1935,Ag 6,20:4
Bishop Misbehaves, The 1935,Ag 27,23:4
Life's Too Short 1935,S 21,18:5
First Lady 1935,N 27,17:4
Happiest Days, The 1939,Ap 12,26:2
Doughgirls, The 1942,D 31,19:2
Wilson, Evelyn
George White's Scandals 1929,S 24,29:1
Wilson, F H
Taboo 1922,Ap 5,22:1
Wilson, Fay
Madame Lafayette 1960,Mr 4,21:1
Wilson, Flip
Old Bucks and New Wings 1962,N 6,39:4
Wilson, Forrest (Playwright)
Bloody Laughter 1931,D 5,20:6
Blessed Event 1932,Ja 31,VIII,1:6
Blessed Event 1932,F 13,23:2
Blessed Event 1932,F 21,VIII,1:1
Wilson, Francis
Erminie 1921,Ja 4,11:1
Rivals, The 1922,Je 6,18:2
Rivals, The 1923,My 9,14:2
School for Scandal, The 1923,Je 5,24:3
She Stoops to Conquer 1924,Je 10,24:3
Rip Van Winkle 1925,N 24,28:5
Rip Van Winkle 1925,D 6,VIII,5:1
Straw Hat, The 1926,O 15,20:2
Granite 1927,F 12,13:1
Much Ado About Nothing 1927,N 19,14:6
Doctor Knock 1928,F 24,15:2
Little Father of the Wilderness, The 1930,Je 3,27:1
Wilson, Frank
All God's Chillun Got Wings 1924,My 16,22:3
All God's Chillun Got Wings 1924,Ag 19,9:1
All God's Chillun Got Wings 1924,Ag 24,VII,1:1
In Abraham's Bosom 1926,D 31,10:2
In Abraham's Bosom 1927,F 20,VII,1:1
Porgy 1927,O 11,26:2
Porgy 1929,S 14,17:3
Sweet Chariot 1930,O 12,VIII,4:1
Sweet Chariot 1930,O 24,30:2
Singin' the Blues 1931,Ap 12,IX,2:1
Singin' the Blues 1931,S 17,21:3
Bloodstream 1932,Mr 31,25:1
We the People 1933,Ja 23,9:5
They Shall Not Die 1934,F 22,24:4
Roll Sweet Chariot 1934,O 3,24:3
Roll Sweet Chariot 1934,O 14,X,1:1
Green Pastures, The 1935,F 27,16:2
Sailor, Beware! 1935,My 7,28:4
Emperor Jones, The 1936,Ag 11,24:6
Journeyman 1938,Ja 31,14:2
All the Living 1938,Mr 25,14:4
Kiss the Boys Goodbye 1938,S 29,30:2
Emperor Jones, The 1939,Je 20,25:2
Watch on the Rhine 1941,Ap 2,26:2
South Pacific 1943,D 30,11:2
Memphis Bound 1945,My 25,23:2
Set My People Free 1948,N 4,38:2
Set My People Free 1948,N 14,II,1:1
Big Knife, The 1949,F 25,27:5
How Long Till Summer 1949,D 28,30:3
Moby Dick 1955,Ap 26,25:3
And People All Around 1968,F 12,46:1

Wilson, Frank (Director)
Walk Together Chillun 1936,F 5,15:2
Wilson, Frank (Playwright)
Meek Mose 1928,F 7,30:1
Walk Together Chillun 1936,F 5,15:2
Wilson, Fred
Student Prince, The 1924,D 3,25:3
Wilson, Garnay
Ringside Seat 1938,N 23,24:5
Johnny on the Spot 1942,Ja 9,24:2
Detective Story 1949,Mr 24,34:2
Wilson, George
Fanshastics 1924,Ja 17,13:2
Wookey, The 1941,S 11,20:5
Wilson, Georges
Lorenzaccio 1958,O 15,44:2
Triomphe de l'Amour, Le 1958,O 17,32:1
Marie Tudor 1958,O 22,39:1
Don Juan 1958,O 29,29:1
Cid, Le 1958,O 31,35:2
Resistable Ascension of Arturo Ui, The
1960,D 25,II,5:1
Man for All Seasons, A 1963,My 11,15:1
Wilson, Georges (Director)
Children of the Sun 1963,D 11,56:3
Master Puntila and His Valet, Matti 1964,N 21,34:1
Wilson, Georges (Producer)
Romulus the Great 1964,Ap 30,29:1
Wilson, Georgiana
Adding Machine, The 1923,Mr 20,24:1
Wilson, Gilbert
Jubilee 1935,O 14,20:1
Set to Music 1939,Ja 19,16:2
Wilson, Gladys
Tangerine 1921,Ag 10,8:2
Dumb-Bell 1923,N 27,23:2
Grounds for Divorce 1924,S 24,20:1
Hush Money 1926,Mr 16,22:3
One Glorious Hour 1927,Ap 15,27:2
Tales of Rigo 1927,My 31,25:3
Six Characters in Search of an Author
1931,Ap 16,29:2
Wilson, Glenn
Richard III 1949,F 9,33:2
Wilson, Grace
Return Journey, The 1928,S 23,IX,1:3
Wilson, Gretchen
Wonderful Night, A; Fledermaus, Die
1929,N 1,23:3
Wilson, Hansford
Night Boat, The 1920,F 3,18:1
City Chap, The 1925,O 27,21:1
Rainbow Rose 1926,Mr 17,28:2
Enchanted Isle 1927,S 20,33:2
If Booth Had Missed 1932,F 5,24:2
Cradle Will Rock, The 1937,D 6,19:4
Sing for Your Supper 1939,Ap 25,18:6
Wilson, Harry
Red Rust 1929,D 18,31:1
Up and Up, The 1930,S 9,25:2
Four O'Clock 1933,F 14,19:6
Anything Goes 1934,N 22,26:1
Chalked Out 1937,Mr 26,24:2
Wilson, Harry Leon (Original Author)
Merton of the Movies 1922,N 14,16:2
Wilson, Harry Leon (Playwright)
Tweedles 1923,Ag 14,10:1
Tweedles 1923,Ag 19,VI,1:1
How's Your Health? 1929,N 27,30:3
Wilson, Helen
Paolo and Francesca 1929,Ap 2,28:2
Wilson, Henriette
Her Family Tree 1920,D 28,9:2
Wilson, Henry
According to Law 1944,Je 2,20:3
Wilson, Herbert
Sherlock Holmes 1929,N 26,28:3
Wilson, Horace
Promis' Lan', De 1930,My 28,31:2
Wilson, Inez Richardson
Green Pastures, The 1930,F 27,26:1
Wilson, Isabelle
Louisiana Lady 1947,Je 3,35:2
Wilson, J P
Hamlet 1925,O 12,19:2
Merchant of Venice, The 1925,D 28,12:1
Cyrano de Bergerac 1926,F 19,18:1
Escape 1927,O 27,33:1
When Crummles Played 1928,O 2,34:3
Potiphar's Wife 1928,D 24,10:7
Maggie, the Magnificent 1929,O 22,26:1
Headquarters 1929,D 5,32:4
One, Two, Three! 1930,S 30,24:2
Lake, The 1933,D 27,24:2
Say When 1934,N 9,24:2
Puritan, The 1936,Ja 24,14:3
Spring Thaw 1938,Mr 22,18:1
Good Hunting 1938,N 22,26:5
Mr Banks of Birmingham 1939,Ja 21,18:4
Boyd's Daughter 1940,O 12,20:2
Corn Is Green, The 1943,My 4,18:3
While the Sun Shines 1944,S 20,21:3
While the Sun Shines 1944,S 24,II,1:1

Wilson, J P—Cont

Pygmalion 1945,D 27,16:1
I Know My Love 1949,N 3,36:1
Prescott Proposals, The 1953,D 17,53:1

Wilson, Jack

Vaudeville (Palace) 1923,Mr 6,26:1
Vaudeville (Palace) 1924,Ja 22,15:6
Earl Carroll's Vanities 1925,D 29,20:3
Oh, Please! 1926,D 22,24:3
Footlights 1927,Ag 20,8:2
Beaux' Stratagem, The 1957,Jl 9,25:4
Man Who Never Died, The 1958,N 22,27:2

Wilson, Jack (Director)

Blithe Spirit 1941,N 16,IX,1:1

Wilson, Jack (Playwright)

Vintage '60 1960,S 13,41:1

Wilson, James

Sunny 1925,S 23,22:1
Merry Widow, The 1961,O 27,28:2
Vagabond King, The 1961,N 24,36:1
Gondoliers, The 1961,D 8,44:1
Iolanthe 1962,Ag 8,34:2
Gondoliers, The 1963,Je 5,33:2
Patience 1964,Mr 26,42:1
Patience 1965,Ap 16,34:1
Patience 1967,O 13,32:1
Iolanthe 1967,O 18,40:1
Mikado, The 1967,O 25,42:2
Gondoliers, The 1967,O 29,83:1
H M S Pinafore 1967,N 1,40:1

Wilson, Janice

Donogoo 1961,Ja 19,25:3

Wilson, Jay

Seeing Things 1920,Je 18,19:2
Nervous Wreck, The 1923,O 10,16:1
Her Way Out 1924,Je 24,18:3
Be Yourself! 1924,S 4,13:3
Honest Liars 1926,Jl 20,17:2
Front Page, The 1928,Ag 15,19:2
Band Wagon, The 1931,Je 4,31:3
Flying Colors 1932,S 16,24:2
Dodsworth 1934,F 26,20:4
Revenge With Music 1934,N 29,33:5
For Valor 1935,N 19,27:5

Wilson, Jean Douglas

Courting 1925,S 14,17:1

Wilson, Jeanette

Betty, Be Good 1920,My 5,14:2

Wilson, Jeffrey

Prodigal Son, The 1965,My 21,19:1

Wilson, Jennifer

Romeo and Juliet 1956,O 25,41:1
Macbeth 1956,O 30,42:2
Troilus and Cressida 1956,D 27,21:1

Wilson, Jessie

Ethan Frome 1936,Ja 22,15:2

Wilson, John

Bachelor Born 1938,Ag 17,23:1

Wilson, John (Composer)

Everyman Today 1958,Ja 16,32:4

Wilson, John (Playwright)

Hamp 1964,Ag 18,25:1
Hamp 1967,Mr 10,32:1

Wilson, John (Producer)

Set to Music 1939,Ja 19,16:2

Wilson, John C

Variations of 1940 1940,Ja 29,12:1

Wilson, John C (Director)

Blithe Spirit 1941,N 6,26:2
Pirate, The 1942,N 26,39:2
Connecticut Yankee, A 1943,N 18,30:2
In Bed We Cry 1944,N 15,20:2
Foolish Notion 1945,Mr 14,23:2
Foolish Notion 1945,Mr 18,II,1:1
Day Before Spring, The 1945,N 23,27:2
Present Laughter 1946,O 30,31:2
Eagle Has Two Heads, The 1947,Mr 20,39:2
Kiss Me, Kate 1948,D 31,10:3
Gentlemen Prefer Blondes 1949,D 9,35:3
Bless You All 1950,D 15,42:2
Make a Wish 1951,Ap 19,38:1
Kiss Me, Kate 1952,Ja 9,24:6
Late Love 1953,O 14,35:2
Starcross Story, The 1954,Ja 14,25:2
Seventh Heaven 1955,My 27,16:2

Wilson, John C (Miscellaneous)

Taming of the Shrew, The 1935,O 1,27:3
Taming of the Shrew, The 1940,F 6,17:2
Importance of Being Earnest, The 1947,Mr 4,30:2
Love for Love 1947,My 27,30:2
Private Lives 1948,O 5,30:2

Wilson, John C (Mrs)

Variations of 1940 1940,Ja 29,12:1

Wilson, John C (Producer)

Point Valaine 1935,Ja 17,22:2
Hands Across the Sea 1936,N 25,17:2
Astonished Heart, The 1936,N 25,17:2
Red Peppers 1936,N 25,17:2
We Were Dancing 1936,N 28,13:1
Fumed Oak 1936,N 28,13:1
Shadow Play 1936,N 28,13:1
Still Life 1936,D 1,31:1
Ways and Means 1936,D 1,31:1
Family Album 1936,D 1,31:1

Excursion 1937,Ap 10,11:4
George and Margaret 1937,S 23,32:2
Dear Octopus 1939,Ja 12,22:2
Blithe Spirit 1941,N 6,26:2
Blithe Spirit 1943,S 12,II,1:1
Lovers and Friends 1943,N 30,23:2
Lovers and Friends 1943,D 5,II,5:1
Bloomer Girl 1944,O 6,18:5
In Bed We Cry 1944,N 15,20:2
Streets Are Guarded, The 1944,N 21,19:7
Day Before Spring, The 1945,N 23,27:2
Day Before Spring, The 1945,D 2,II,1:1
O Mistress Mine 1946,Ja 24,25:2
Present Laughter 1946,O 30,31:2
Bloomer Girl 1947,Ja 7,33:2
Eagle Has Two Heads, The 1947,Mr 20,39:2
Winslow Boy, The 1947,O 30,32:2
Children's Party, A 1947,D 29,21:5
In County Kerry 1947,D 29,21:5
At an Art Exhibition 1947,D 29,21:5
Actress, The 1947,D 29,21:5
Three Breakfasts 1947,D 29,21:5
Power Without Glory 1948,Ja 14,30:2
I Know My Love 1949,N 3,36:1
Lady's Not for Burning, The 1950,N 9,42:2
Nina 1951,D 6,44:3
Deep Blue Sea, The 1952,N 6,38:3
Little Hut, The 1953,O 8,37:2
Starcross Story, The 1954,Ja 14,25:2
Burning Glass, The 1954,Mr 5,15:2
Quadrille 1954,N 4,39:2
Eugenia 1957,Ja 31,20:1
Garden District; Suddenly Last Summer 1958,Ja 8,23:4
Garden District; Something Unspoken 1958,Ja 8,23:4

Wilson, Joseph N P

Moral Fabric 1932,N 22,25:3

Wilson, Josephine

Invitation au Voyage, L' 1930,Ja 26,VIII,1:8

Wilson, Judy

Beaux' Stratagem, The 1970,F 10,50:2
Three Sisters, The 1970,F 12,30:1

Wilson, Julie

Kiss Me, Kate 1951,Mr 9,30:5
Jimmy 1969,O 24,38:1
Jimmy 1969,N 9,II,1:1
Park 1970,Ap 23,47:1

Wilson, June

Love on Leave 1944,Je 21,23:4
Bet Your Life 1952,F 19,26:6

Wilson, K C

Cherry Orchard, The 1970,My 7,63:2

Wilson, Karen

Brother to Dragons 1968,D 8,86:1

Wilson, Katherine

He Who Gets Slapped 1922,Ja 10,15:1
Devil's Disciple, The 1923,Ap 24,24:1
Chicken Feed 1923,S 25,10:2
Cock o' the Roost 1924,O 14,23:1
Guardsman, The 1924,O 14,23:1
Paid 1925,N 26,32:1
Love 'Em and Leave 'Em 1926,F 4,20:4
Love 'Em and Leave 'Em 1926,F 14,VIII,1:1
American Tragedy, An 1926,O 12,31:2
American Tragedy, An 1926,O 24,VIII,1:1
Distant Drum, A 1928,Ja 21,13:1
Play Without a Name, A 1928,N 26,30:5
Among the Married 1929,O 4,24:3
Top O' the Hill 1929,N 27,30:4
Out of a Blue Sky 1930,F 10,20:6
Vinegar Tree, The 1930,N 20,30:3
Berlin 1931,D 31,16:1
Housewarming 1932,Ap 8,25:1
Criminal at Large 1932,O 11,26:3
Ruy Blas 1933,O 10,24:4
Yellow Jack 1934,Mr 7,22:6

Wilson, Kendrick

Audition of the Apprentice Theatre 1939,Je 2,26:2

Wilson, Keppel and Betty

Vaudeville (Palace) 1930,S 15,29:2

Wilson, Lanford (Playwright)

Home Free! 1965,F 11,45:1
Madness of Lady Bright, The 1966,Mr 23,42:1
Ludlow Fair 1966,Mr 23,42:1
This Is the Rill Speaking 1966,Ap 12,43:1
Rimers of Eldritch, The 1967,F 21,53:1
Collision Course; Wandering 1968,My 9,55:2
Gingham Dog, The 1968,O 13,II,18:6
Gingham Dog, The 1969,Ap 24,41:1
Gingham Dog, The 1969,My 4,II,1:5
Lemon Sky 1970,My 18,40:1

Wilson, Lee

Here's Where I Belong 1968,Mr 4,32:1
Sound of Music, The 1970,Jl 3,13:1

Wilson, Lena

Deep Harlem 1929,Ja 8,35:2

Wilson, Leone

Heart of a City 1942,F 13,24:6
Medea 1947,O 21,27:2

Wilson, Lester

Anyone Can Whistle 1964,Ap 6,36:1
Golden Boy 1964,O 21,56:1

Wilson, Letitia (Producer)

Asmodee 1958,Mr 26,42:2
Sign of Winter 1958,My 8,35:1

Wilson, Lewis

R U R 1942,D 4,30:2

Wilson, Lionel

Good Morning, Corporal 1944,Ag 9,13:7
Fragile Fox 1954,O 13,27:1
Once in a Lifetime 1964,Ja 29,20:1

Wilson, Lisle

Volpone 1967,Je 30,29:1
Hamlet 1967,D 27,45:1
Hamlet 1968,Jl 4,15:1
Death of Bessie Smith, The 1968,O 3,55:1
Five on the Black Hand Side 1970,Ja 2,32:2

Wilson, Lizzie

Vaudeville (Palace) 1931,Mr 2,19:2

Wilson, Lohr

Bluebeard 1970,My 5,58:1

Wilson, Lohr (Costume Designer)

Her Master's Voice 1964,D 28,33:2
Death of the Well-Loved Boy, The 1967,My 16,48:1

Wilson, Lois

Farewell Summer 1937,Mr 30,20:2
Mermaids Singing, The 1945,N 29,26:6
Madwoman of Chaillot, The 1970,Mr 23,48:3

Wilson, Margaret

Gay Paree 1925,Ag 19,14:3
Vaudeville (Palace) 1926,Ag 31,15:3
Black Eye, The 1938,Mr 8,22:4

Wilson, Marie

Music Hath Charms 1934,D 31,8:2

Wilson, Mark (Playwright)

Disney on Parade 1970,S 24,63:1

Wilson, Marriott

Surgeon, The 1932,O 28,23:1
Mayor of Zalamea, The 1946,Ja 28,15:5
Wise Have Not Spoken, The 1954,F 11,35:2
Pink String and Sealing Wax 1957,S 6,13:1

Wilson, Martha

Boo Hoo! East Lynne 1959,S 9,50:4

Wilson, Mary

Babes in Toyland 1930,D 22,17:1

Wilson, Mary Jane

All in Love 1961,N 11,15:2

Wilson, Mary Louise

Bonds of Interest, The 1958,My 7,43:1
Our Town 1959,Mr 24,46:2
Hot Spot 1963,Ap 20,17:2
Flora, the Red Menace 1965,My 12,41:2
Great Career, A 1968,D 30,25:1
Evening for Merlin Finch, An 1969,Ja 26,II,1:1
Criss-Crossing 1970,Ja 22,30:1
Whispers on the Wind 1970,Je 4,50:1

Wilson, Master A

Under the Gaslight 1929,Ap 3,27:1

Wilson, Morgan (Miscellaneous)

Evening of Rare Pleasures, An 1959,Je 4,26:2
Kataki 1959,D 16,55:1

Wilson, Nathaniel (Director)

Getting Even 1929,Ag 20,31:1

Wilson, Nathaniel (Playwright)

Getting Even 1929,Ag 20,31:1

Wilson, Nathaniel (Producer)

Getting Even 1929,Ag 20,31:1

Wilson, Odin

Corn Is Green, The 1954,F 27,10:2

Wilson, Parker

Magic 1929,D 17,28:5
Seven Keys to Baldpate 1930,Ja 8,25:2
Round Table, The 1930,F 28,20:5
As You Like It 1936,Ap 24,18:4
Lady in the Dark 1941,Ja 24,14:2
Dream With Music 1944,My 19,15:2
Camino Real 1953,Mr 20,26:1

Wilson, Parker (Director)

Seven Keys to Baldpate 1930,Ja 8,25:2

Wilson, Patricia

Fiorello! 1959,N 24,45:3
Fiorello! 1959,N 29,II,1:1

Wilson, Paul

Shore Leave 1922,Ag 9,20:2
Beggar on Horseback 1924,F 13,17:2
Bridge of Distances, The 1925,S 29,30:1
Song of the Flame 1925,D 31,10:2
Tia Juana 1927,N 16,28:4
Fast Life 1928,S 27,35:2
Man Who Reclaimed His Head 1932,S 9,17:3
Janie 1942,S 11,24:2
Cyrano de Bergerac 1946,O 9,33:2
Cyrano de Bergerac 1947,Ja 17,27:2
Skipper Next to God 1948,Ja 5,14:5

Wilson, Perry

Trojan Women, The 1938,Ja 25,24:2
Cream in the Well, The 1941,Ja 21,19:2
Trojan Women, The 1941,Ap 9,32:5
Village Green 1941,S 14,IX,1:1
First Crocus, The 1942,Ja 3,14:6
Mexican Mural; Vera Cruz Interior 1942,Ap 27,19:2
Corn Is Green, The 1943,My 4,18:3
Stranger, The 1945,F 13,21:2
Celebration 1948,Ap 12,24:2

Wilson, Perry—Cont
His and Hers 1954,Ja 8,18:2
Wilson, Perry (Miss)
Village Green 1941,S 4,24:4
Pillar to Post 1943,D 11,11:2
On Whitman Avenue 1946,My 9,28:2
Wilson, Ray
We Girls 1921,N 10,26:3
National Anthem, The 1922,Ja 24,16:3
Advertising of Kate, The 1922,My 9,22:2
Wilson, Richard
Shoemaker's Holiday, The 1938,Ja 3,17:2
Danton's Death 1938,N 3,26:2
Wilson, Robert
Gondoliers, The 1934,S 4,23:1
Trial by Jury 1934,S 14,24:3
Yeomen of the Guard, The 1934,S 21,28:3
Trial by Jury 1936,S 1,24:4
Gondoliers, The 1936,S 8,23:1
Yeomen of the Guard, The 1936,S 15,37:2
Kiss for Cinderella, A 1942,Mr 11,22:2
Teahouse of the August Moon, The
1954,Ap 23,23:6
Wilson, Robin
Henry, Sweet Henry 1967,O 24,51:2
Wilson, Roy
Happy Town 1959,O 8,49:2
Wilson, Sandy (Composer)
Boy Friend, The 1954,O 1,20:1
Boy Friend, The 1954,O 10,II,1:1
Boy Friend, The 1958,Ja 27,24:4
Valmouth 1960,O 7,29:1
Boy Friend, The 1970,Ap 15,54:1
Wilson, Sandy (Lyricist)
Boy Friend, The 1954,O 1,20:1
Boy Friend, The 1954,O 10,II,1:1
Boy Friend, The 1958,Ja 27,24:4
Valmouth 1960,O 7,29:1
Boy Friend, The 1970,Ap 15,54:1
Wilson, Sandy (Original Author)
Boy Friend, The 1954,O 1,20:1
Wilson, Sandy (Playwright)
Boy Friend, The 1954,O 10,II,1:1
Boy Friend, The 1958,Ja 27,24:4
Valmouth 1960,O 7,29:1
Divorce Me, Darling 1965,F 2,29:6
Boy Friend, The 1970,Ap 15,54:1
Wilson, Sarah
Penny Friend, The 1966,D 27,46:1
Wilson, Scott
Laugh It Off 1925,Ap 25,18:4
Wilson, Scott (Costume Designer)
As You Like It 1937,N 1,25:2
Great Lady 1938,D 2,26:6
Wilson, Sona
Cherry Orchard, The 1955,O 19,38:1
Wilson, Speedy
Pansy 1929,My 15,36:3
Black Rhythm 1936,D 21,19:2
Wilson, Stewart
Ouija Board, The 1920,Mr 30,9:1
All-Star Idlers of 1921, The 1921,Jl 16,5:2
Letty Pepper 1922,Ap 11,22:2
Good Old Days, The 1923,Ag 15,21:2
Wilson, Ted
Hate Planters 1933,My 26,24:5
Wilson, Theodore
Daddy Goodness 1968,Je 5,37:1
God Is a (Guess What?) 1968,D 18,56:1
Malcochon 1969,Ap 2,37:1
Night Thoreau Spent in Jail, The 1970,N 2,66:1
Wilson, Ural
Ballad for Bimshire 1963,O 16,54:1
Who's Who, Baby? 1968,Ja 30,36:1
Wilson, Viola
Mikado, The 1939,Ja 10,16:3
Iolanthe 1939,Ja 13,16:3
Gondoliers, The 1939,Ja 20,14:2
Patience 1939,Ja 27,16:3
Wilson, Virginia
Imaginary Invalid, The 1922,Jl 26,26:2
Gypsy Jim 1924,Ja 15,17:4
All God's Chillun Got Wings 1924,My 16,22:3
All God's Chillun Got Wings 1924,Ag 19,9:1
Wilson, W J (Director)
Padlocks of 1927 1927,Jl 6,23:4
Wilson, Walter
Three Showers 1920,Ap 6,18:1
Buzzin' Around 1920,Jl 7,14:1
Zeno 1923,Ag 27,14:2
Family Upstairs, The 1925,Ag 18,14:2
Family Upstairs, The 1925,Ag 23,VII,1:1
1776 1926,Ap 24,11:2
Ghost Train, The 1926,Ag 26,17:2
Gentlemen, the Queen 1927,Ap 23,14:3
Kidding Kidders 1928,Ap 24,28:3
Street Wolf, The 1929,Ja 1,61:1
Room 349 1930,Ap 23,24:5
London Calling 1930,O 20,29:1
Young Sinners 1931,Ap 21,35:5
Berlin 1931,D 31,16:1
Round-Up, The 1932,Mr 8,19:4
Knock on Wood 1935,My 29,16:2

Wilson, Walter (Director)
90 Horse Power 1926,Mr 16,22:4
Rainbow Rose 1926,Mr 17,28:2
Triplets 1932,S 22,25:2
Wilson, Ward
Vaudeville (Loew's State) 1932,O 3,15:5
Wilson, Wayne
Humoresque 1923,F 28,13:2
Eastward in Eden 1956,Ap 18,25:4
Crucible, The 1958,Mr 12,36:1
Captains and the Kings, The 1962,Ja 3,25:2
Merchant of Venice, The 1962,Je 22,1:4
Henry V 1965,Je 29,27:2
All's Well That Ends Well 1966,Je 17,39:1
Measure for Measure 1966,Jl 14,27:1
Richard III 1966,Ag 11,26:1
Wilson, William J (Director)
Mayflowers 1925,N 25,14:2
Wild Rose, The 1926,O 21,23:1
Oh, Ernest! 1927,My 10,24:3
Wilson, William J (Producer)
Fountania 1926,Ja 17,II,8:8
Wilson, Woodrow
Black Rhythm 1936,D 21,19:2
Wilsrud, Astrid
Lady's Not for Burning, The 1957,F 22,26:2
Apollo of Bellac, The 1958,Mr 7,17:2
Browning Version, The 1958,Mr 7,17:2
Month in the Country, A 1959,Mr 2,32:2
Skin of Our Teeth, The 1961,My 1,35:3
Doll's House, A 1963,F 4,5:6
One Flew Over the Cuckoo's Nest 1963,N 14,40:2
Wilstach, Paul (Playwright)
Her Happiness 1922,O 8,VI,1:6
Wilten, Ruth (Choreographer)
Alice in Wonderland 1947,Ap 7,19:2
Wilton, Charles
New York Exchange 1926,D 31,11:2
Wilton, Herbert
Kit Marlowe 1936,My 24,35:1
Wilton, Joe
Vaudeville (Palace) 1928,Jl 24,13:4
Wilton, Ruth
Master Builder, The 1925,N 11,27:1
Saturday Night 1926,O 26,25:1
Three Sisters, The 1926,O 27,24:1
Cradle Song 1927,Ja 25,18:2
Inheritors 1927,Mr 8,23:1
2 + 2 = 5 1927,N 29,30:3
These Days 1928,N 13,36:2
Living Corpse, The 1929,D 7,19:1
Aiglon, L' 1934,N 5,22:2
Wilton and Weber
Vaudeville (Palace) 1928,Ja 3,29:3
Vaudeville (Palace) 1929,My 20,22:8
Vaudeville (Palace) 1930,Mr 7,21:2
Vaudeville (Palace) 1931,Je 8,21:2
Wiltshire, George
Hot Rhythm 1930,Ag 22,18:5
Wiltshire, Margaret
Like a King 1921,O 4,10:1
Beau-Strings 1926,Ap 27,22:2
Wiman, Anna
Rosalinda; Fledermaus, Die 1942,O 29,26:5
Chocolate Soldier, The 1947,Mr 13,34:2
Wiman, Dwight Deere (Director)
Most Immoral Lady, A 1928,N 27,36:1
Second Little Show, The 1930,S 3,36:1
Wiman, Dwight Deere (Miscellaneous)
Two Orphans, The 1926,Ap 6,26:2
As You Like It 1937,N 1,25:2
Wiman, Dwight Deere (Playwright)
Champagne, Sec 1933,O 16,20:2
Higher and Higher 1940,Ag 6,15:4
Wiman, Dwight Deere (Producer)
Lucky Sam McCarver 1925,O 22,22:1
Little Eyolf 1926,F 3,22:1
Masque of Venice, The 1926,Mr 3,27:3
Devils 1926,Mr 18,26:4
Seed of the Brute 1926,N 2,34:3
Hangman's House 1926,D 17,27:2
Road to Rome, The 1927,F 1,24:2
Dark, The 1927,F 2,22:5
House of Shadows, The 1927,Ap 22,18:4
Women Go on Forever 1927,S 8,25:1
Command to Love, The 1927,S 21,27:1
Queen's Husband, The 1928,Ja 26,17:2
Grey Fox, The 1928,O 23,32:3
Jealous Moon, The 1928,N 21,32:2
Most Immoral Lady, A 1928,N 27,36:1
Judas 1929,Ja 25,20:4
Paolo and Francesca 1929,Ap 2,28:2
Little Show, The 1929,My 1,28:5
Jenny 1929,O 9,34:4
Second Little Show, The 1930,S 3,36:1
Vinegar Tree, The 1930,N 20,30:3
Third Little Show, The 1931,Je 2,34:3
After All 1931,D 4,28:4
Gay Divorce 1932,N 30,23:4
Bad Manners 1933,Ja 31,15:5
She Loves Me Not 1933,N 21,22:4
Wooden Slipper, The 1934,Ja 4,16:3
Oliver Oliver 1934,Ja 6,18:5

Wiman, Dwight Deere (Producer)—Cont
Distaff Side, The 1934,S 26,17:2
Distant Shore, The 1935,F 22,26:2
Most of the Game 1935,O 2,27:4
Room in Red and White, A 1936,Ja 20,23:3
On Your Toes 1936,Ap 13,14:4
Babes in Arms 1937,Ap 15,18:4
On Borrowed Time 1938,F 4,16:4
I Married an Angel 1938,My 12,26:2
I Married an Angel 1938,My 22,XI,1:1
Great Lady 1938,D 2,26:6
Stars in Your Eyes 1939,F 10,18:2
Three Sisters, The 1939,O 16,23:1
Morning's at Seven 1939,N 7,30:2
Morning's at Seven 1939,N 12,IX,2:3
Morning's at Seven 1939,D 1,26:2
Leave Her to Heaven 1940,F 28,16:2
Higher and Higher 1940,Mr 17,X,2:5
Higher and Higher 1940,Ap 5,24:3
Higher and Higher 1940,Ag 6,15:4
Old Acquaintance 1940,D 10,33:5
Old Acquaintance 1940,D 24,18:3
They Can't Get You Down 1941,N 2,IX,3:5
Letters to Lucerne 1941,D 9,47:6
Letters to Lucerne 1941,D 24,14:2
Solitaire 1942,Ja 28,22:2
By Jupiter 1942,Je 4,22:1
Damask Cheek, The 1942,O 23,24:2
Damask Cheek, The 1942,N 8,VIII,1:1
Street Scene 1947,Ja 10,17:2
Story for Strangers, A 1948,S 22,39:2
Big Knife, The 1949,F 25,27:5
Dance Me a Song 1950,Ja 21,10:5
Romeo and Juliet 1951,Ja 23,24:8
Romeo and Juliet 1951,Mr 12,21:2
Wiman, Katherine
Charley's Aunt 1940,O 18,24:2
Wiman, Nancy
Stars in Your Eyes 1939,F 10,18:2
Letters to Lucerne 1941,D 9,47:6
Letters to Lucerne 1941,D 24,14:2
Wimberly, Jerry
Comic Strip 1958,My 15,26:2
Only in America 1959,N 20,35:1
Wimmer, Maria
Ratten, Die 1966,Ap 13,36:1
Wimperis, Arthur (Lyricist)
As You Were 1920,Ja 28,22:3
Louie the 14th 1925,Mr 4,17:1
Wimperis, Arthur (Original Author)
Prince Charming 1930,O 14,31:1
Wimperis, Arthur (Playwright)
As You Were 1920,Ja 28,22:3
Elopement, The 1923,S 2,VI,1:7
Louie the 14th 1925,Mr 4,17:1
By the Way 1926,Ap 16,20:3
Lovely Lady 1932,Mr 20,VIII,1:8
Winant, Forrest
His Chinese Wife 1920,My 18,9:3
Winant, Haim
Never Say Never 1951,N 21,21:2
Teahouse of the August Moon, The 1953,O 16,32:1
Winborne, Gertrude
Exceeding Small 1928,O 23,32:2
Winburg, Pearle
Marshall 1930,My 10,25:1
Winburn, Bess
One Bright Day 1952,Mr 20,37:2
Winburn, Janet
Pirates of Penzance, The 1968,Ap 26,32:1
H M S Pinafore 1968,Ap 29,47:2
Mikado, The 1968,My 2,59:1
Wincelberg, Shimon (Playwright)
Kataki 1959,Ap 10,24:1
Kataki 1959,D 16,55:1
Wincelberg, Shimon (Translator)
Sands of the Negev 1954,O 20,32:1
Wincere, Helene
Lady Refuses, The 1933,Mr 8,18:6
Winchell, Rod
Mrs January & Mr Ex 1944,Ap 1,10:2
Calico Wedding 1945,Mr 8,18:6
Aria Da Capo 1958,My 21,40:1
Winchell, Walter
Vaudeville (New Amsterdam Theatre) 1931,Je 22,17:3
Winchester, Barbara
Caukey 1944,F 18,15:4
Many Loves 1959,Ja 14,28:1
Connection, The 1959,Jl 16,30:2
Women of Trachis 1960,Je 23,18:3
Cockeyed Kite 1961,S 14,27:1
Winchester, Eugene
Hold Your Horses 1933,S 26,26:4
Winckler, Carlton (Lighting Director)
Duchess Misbehaves, The 1946,F 14,32:2
Wincott, Rosalie
Booster, The 1929,O 25,26:2
Windberger, Ferry (Scenic Designer)
Wiener Blut 1964,S 12,14:1
Winde, Beatrice
Junebug Graduates Tonight! 1967,F 27,35:1
Windel, Hans
For Valor 1935,N 19,27:5

Windell, Charles
Out West of Eighth 1951,S 21,20:3
Windhager, Eduard
Untitled-Passion Play 1927,Jl 31,VII,1:6
Windham, Amasa
Last Enemy, The 1934,Jl 13,14:4
Windham, Donald (Playwright)
You Touched Me! 1943,O 17,II,2:4
You Touched Me! 1945,S 26,27:2
You Touched Me! 1945,S 30,II,1:1
Windheim, Marek
Good Girl, The 1934,Je 26,22:5
Windingstad, Ole (Musical Director)
In the Land of the Midnight Sun 1930,Ja 7,27:4
Windisch, Ilka
Chameleon, The 1949,F 7,16:2
Windom, William
Henry VIII 1946,N 7,42:2
John Gabriel Borkman 1946,N 13,33:2
Androcles and the Lion 1946,D 20,29:2
Yellow Jack 1947,F 28,26:2
Alice in Wonderland 1947,Ap 7,19:2
When the Bough Breaks 1950,Mr 9,25:5
Girl Can Tell, A 1953,O 30,28:2
Mademoiselle Colombe 1954,Ja 7,26:1
Grand Prize, The 1955,Ja 27,17:1
Fallen Angels 1956,Ja 18,27:1
Greatest Man Alive!, The 1957,My 9,37:2
Twelfth Night 1958,Ag 7,21:4
U S A 1959,O 29,38:1
U S A 1959,N 8,II,1:1
Viva Madison Avenue 1960,Ap 7,42:1
Drums Under the Windows 1960,O 14,26:1
Rules of the Game, The 1960,D 20,44:1
Child Buyer, The 1962,My 14,35:1
Windsor, Adele
Naughty Cinderella 1925,N 10,23:6
Sh! The Octopus 1928,F 22,19:2
Windsor, Barbara
Oh What a Lovely War 1964,O 1,30:1
Windsor, Claire
Boy Who Lived Twice, A 1945,S 12,31:2
Windsor, David
Dorian Gray 1936,Jl 21,13:3
Windsor, Helen
Lady Comes Across, The 1942,Ja 10,10:2
Windsor, Judith
Old Rascal, The 1930,Mr 25,34:4
Windsor, Laura
How Beautiful With Shoes 1935,N 29,24:1
Cyrano de Bergerac 1936,Ap 28,17:1
Having Wonderful Time 1937,F 22,12:5
Windsor, Nancy
Happiest Girl in the World, The 1961,Ap 4,42:1
Windsor, Peter (Composer)
Safari! 1955,My 12,32:6
Windsor, Ruth
As Husbands Go 1931,Mr 6,26:5
Windt, Valentine (Director)
Twelfth Night 1949,O 4,33:2
Twelfth Night 1949,O 9,II,1:1
Windust, Bretaigne
Hamlet 1927,Ap 7,23:3
Tsar Fyodor 1929,F 19,22:3
Old Timer 1929,Ap 30,33:4
I Was Waiting for You 1933,N 14,23:3
Oliver Oliver 1934,Ja 6,18:5
Distaff Side, The 1934,S 26,17:2
Taming of the Shrew, The 1935,S 22,X,3:2
Taming of the Shrew, The 1935,O 1,27:3
Idiot's Delight 1936,Mr 25,25:2
Murder Without Crime 1943,Ag 19,24:6
Hasty Heart, The 1945,Ja 14,II,1:1
Windust, Bretaigne (Composer)
Idiot's Delight 1936,Mr 25,25:2
Windust, Bretaigne (Director)
Spring in Autumn 1933,O 25,22:5
Little Shot 1935,Ja 18,28:4
Caesar and Cleopatra 1935,Ag 22,21:1
Idiot's Delight 1936,Mr 10,26:7
Amphitryon 38 1937,Je 24,30:2
Amphitryon 38 1937,N 2,32:2
Circle, The 1938,Ap 19,24:2
What Every Woman Knows 1938,Ag 30,14:5
Great Lady 1938,D 2,26:6
Life With Father 1939,N 9,26:2
Arsenic and Old Lace 1941,Ja 11,13:2
Strip for Action 1942,O 1,26:2
Family, The 1943,Mr 31,22:4
Murder Without Crime 1943,Ag 19,24:6
Trio 1944,D 30,13:4
Hasty Heart, The 1945,Ja 4,14:2
Oh, Herbert! 1945,Je 20,26:3
State of the Union 1945,N 15,25:2
Finian's Rainbow 1947,Ja 11,23:2
Parlor Story 1947,Mr 5,29:2
Remains to Be Seen 1951,O 4,37:1
Gently Does It 1953,O 29,43:4
Great Sebastians, The 1956,Ja 5,27:1
Girls in 509, The 1958,O 16,47:1
Windust, Bretaigne (Producer)
Murder Without Crime 1943,Ag 19,24:6

Windust, Ernest B
Candida 1926,Mr 17,28:3
Windust, Penelope
Spofford 1967,D 15,54:3
Wineburgh, Harold
Bursting the Barriers 1930,My 7,25:1
Wines, Christopher
Home Away From, A 1969,Ap 29,40:3
Winfield, Hemsley
Lulu Belle 1926,F 10,20:1
Earth 1927,Mr 10,23:1
Harlem 1929,F 21,30:3
Wade in de Water 1929,S 14,17:2
Promis' Lan', De 1930,My 28,31:2
Winfield, Hemsley (Director)
Promis' Lan', De 1930,My 28,31:2
Winfield, Sonia
Oh, Ernest! 1927,My 10,24:3
Winfield, Virgie
Lulu Belle 1926,F 10,20:1
Winfindale, Joan
Business With America 1933,Ja 1,IX,1:3
Winfree, Sarah
Trojan Women, The 1938,Ja 25,24:2
Wing, Anna
Merry Wives of Windsor, The 1967,Ag 4,18:1
Wing, Edward
Forty-Four Below 1935,Jl 23,24:3
Night of January 16 1935,S 17,26:4
Wing, Ted
Tickle Me 1920,Ag 18,9:1
Wing, Toby
You Never Know 1938,Mr 4,16:3
You Never Know 1938,S 22,26:3
Wing, Tom (Composer)
Sometime Jam Today 1967,F 13,41:1
Wing-Davey, Mark
Midsummer Night's Dream, A 1968,D 9,59:1
Wingate, Peter (Costume Designer)
She Stoops to Conquer 1960,N 2,42:5
Plough and the Stars, The 1960,D 7,56:2
Octoroon, The 1961,Ja 28,13:1
Hamlet 1961,Mr 17,17:1
Androcles and the Lion 1961,N 22,24:2
Rate of Exchange 1968,Ap 2,50:1
In 3 Zones 1970,N 3,28:1
Wingate, Peter (Scenic Designer)
She Stoops to Conquer 1960,N 2,42:5
Plough and the Stars, The 1960,D 7,56:2
Octoroon, The 1961,Ja 28,13:1
Hamlet 1961,Mr 17,17:1
Caucasian Chalk Circle, The 1961,N 1,35:1
Androcles and the Lion 1961,N 22,24:2
Firebugs, The 1963,F 13,7:2
Emperor, The 1963,Ap 17,30:1
Month in the Country, A 1963,My 29,39:2
Crime and Crime 1963,D 17,51:2
Prodigal Son, The 1965,My 21,19:1
Exception and the Rule, The 1965,My 21,19:1
Rate of Exchange 1968,Ap 2,50:1
Winge, Torsten
Tattar-Adel 1939,S 17,X,2:4
Wingfield, Conway
Poppy God, The 1921,Ag 30,10:1
White Cargo 1923,N 6,22:2
Banshee, The 1927,D 6,26:2
Mrs Dane's Defense 1928,F 7,30:1
Sherlock Holmes 1928,F 21,18:4
Within the Law 1928,Mr 6,20:1
Great Power, The 1928,S 12,25:1
Holiday 1930,F 6,21:2
Holmeses of Baker Street, The 1936,D 10,34:3
Wingo, Eva
Black Scandals 1928,O 27,23:2
Wingreen, Jason
Bonds of Interest, The 1951,D 1,7:2
Summer and Smoke 1952,Ap 25,19:5
Girl on the Via Flaminia, The 1954,F 10,37:1
Fragile Fox 1954,O 13,27:1
Winiar-Katchur, E
Dybbuk, The 1926,D 14,24:2
Eternal Jew, The 1926,D 21,21:2
Jacob's Dream 1927,Ja 4,20:2
Golem, The 1927,F 5,13:2
Winifred, Henry
Africana 1927,Jl 12,29:2
Winkelman, Clifford S (Composer)
How Revolting! 1932,Mr 11,14:6
Winkler, Carlton (Lighting Director)
New Faces of 1943 1942,D 23,22:2
Winkler, Gretchen
Jayhawker 1934,N 6,34:2
Winkler, Henry
Bacchae, The 1969,Mr 15,24:1
Don Juan 1970,My 26,32:1
Three Philip Roth Stories; Defender of the Faith
1970,Jl 31,14:1
Three Philip Roth Stories; Conversion of the Jews
1970,Jl 31,14:1
Three Philip Roth Stories; Epstein 1970,Jl 31,14:1
Cops and Horrors; Fly Paper 1970,Ag 11,27:1
Cops and Horrors; Dracula 1970,Ag 11,27:1
Cops and Horrors; Fly Paper 1970,Ag 11,27:1

Winkler, Henry—Cont
Story Theater Repertory; Saint Julian the
Hospitaler 1970,O 21,40:1
Story Theater Repertory; Gimpel the Food
1970,O 21,40:1
Revenger's Tragedy, The 1970,D 2,58:1
Winkler, Herbert (Musical Director)
Vienna at Night 1945,Ap 30,12:4
Winkler, Leonora
Green Pastures, The 1935,F 27,16:2
Winkler, Margaret
Hill Between, The 1938,Mr 12,12:5
Winkler, Mel
Electra 1969,Ag 8,14:1
Penny Wars, The 1969,O 16,52:1
Winkler, Norbert
Singing Girl, The 1952,Je 4,31:8
Winkler, Robert (Scenic Designer)
Macbeth 1969,D 23,25:1
Winkler, Ruthie
Schwartse Mamme 1939,Ja 16,11:3
Winkler, Ted
Constant Wife, The 1935,Jl 3,20:2
Winkler, Viola
Round Table, The 1930,F 28,20:5
As You Like It 1936,Ap 24,18:4
Winkler, Zoe
Seven Mirrors 1945,O 26,17:2
Winkoop, Paul (Lyricist)
Flair-Flair the Idol of Paree 1935,Mr 13,16:1
Winkopp, Paul
Piggy 1927,Ja 12,22:2
Winkopp, Paul (Choreographer)
Laugh It Off 1934,Ap 5,24:2
Winkopp, Paul (Composer)
Flair-Flair the Idol of Paree 1935,Mr 13,16:1
Life Begins in '40 1940,Ap 5,24:2
Winkopp, Paul (Director)
Off Your Marx 1936,Ap 2,28:2
Some of the People 1937,Mr 11,20:1
Life Begins in '40 1940,Ap 5,24:2
Hit the Road 1941,Ap 4,18:3
Winlocke, Isabelle
Man or Devil 1925,My 22,22:4
Clouds 1925,S 3,32:1
Chicago 1926,D 31,11:1
Dora Mobridge 1930,Ap 21,20:2
Winn, George D
Mystery Ship, The 1927,Mr 15,28:2
Winn, Katherine
Our Town 1968,S 29,77:4
Three Sisters, The 1969,O 10,38:1
Three Sisters, The 1969,O 19,II,3:1
Winn, Lynn
Cabaret 1966,N 21,62:1
Coco 1969,D 19,66:1
Winn, Rella
Geisha, The 1931,O 6,35:4
Winn, Tyler
Alchemist, The 1948,My 7,31:4
Winnall, Elsie
Princess Ida 1936,O 13,32:2
Winne, Jack
Three Times the Hour 1931,Ag 26,15:5
Hot Money 1931,N 9,22:2
Winnerstrands, Olof
Six Flights Up 1939,F 26,IX,2:3
Winninger, Charles
Ziegfeld Follies 1920,Je 23,14:1
Broadway Whirl, The 1921,Je 9,10:4
Good Old Days, The 1923,Ag 15,21:2
Good Old Days, The 1923,Ag 19,VI,1:1
Vaudeville (Palace) 1924,F 19,12:1
Vaudeville (Hippodrome) 1924,Ap 29,12:2
No, No, Nanette 1925,S 17,20:2
Oh, Please! 1926,D 22,24:3
Yes, Yes, Yvette 1927,O 4,32:3
Show Boat 1927,D 28,26:1
Show Boat 1928,Ja 8,VIII,1:1
Smiling Through 1932,Ja 3,VIII,3:1
Through the Years 1932,Ja 29,13:3
Show Boat 1932,My 20,22:2
Lambs Gambol 1933,Ap 24,10:1
Revenge With Music 1934,N 29,33:5
Music in the Air 1951,O 9,32:2
Music in the Air 1951,O 21,II,1:1
Winogradoff, Anatole
Othello 1929,F 4,21:2
Major Noah 1929,F 23,17:2
Riverside Drive 1931,Ja 6,24:2
Motke Ganef 1932,D 30,15:2
Revolt 1933,Ja 12,21:3
Josephus 1933,D 1,22:5
Winterset 1935,S 26,19:2
Winterset 1935,O 6,XI,1:1
They Knew What They Wanted 1936,Jl 8,14:2
Jacques Bergson 1936,O 31,24:6
Water Carrier, The 1936,D 25,20:2
Chaver, Nachman 1939,O 2,15:2
Day of Judgement, The 1941,O 9,27:3
Family Affair, A 1946,N 28,41:2
Shylock and His Daughter 1947,S 30,22:2
Voice of Israel, The 1948,O 26,40:2
Hershel, The Jester 1948,D 14,39:2

Winogradoff, Anatole—Cont
Yosele the Nightingale 1949,O 21,30:4
Number, The 1951,O 31,33:2
Grass Is Always Greener, The 1955,F 16,25:2
Winogradoff, Anatole (Director)
Othello 1929,F 4,21:2
Where Do We Go From Here? 1938,N 16,26:2
Winogron, Blanche
Elizabethans, The 1962,Ja 22,19:1
Golden Age, The 1963,N 19,49:2
Winona
Gang's All Here, The 1931,F 19,21:3
Winsett, Betty
Lady in the Dark 1952,Mr 8,11:3
Winsloe, Christa (Playwright)
Maedchen in Uniform 1932,N 6,IX,1:3
Girls in Uniform 1932,D 31,10:3
Winslow, Ann
Dover Road, The 1921,D 24,7:2
Last Warning, The 1922,O 25,23:1
Minick 1924,S 25,20:1
Seen But Not Heard 1936,S 18,19:2
Winslow, Barbara
Trojan Horse, The 1940,O 31,28:3
Winslow, Charles Edward Amory (Translator)
Magda 1926,Ja 27,16:2
Winslow, Christa (Playwright)
Gestern und Heute 1931,My 24,VIII,2:1
Schicksal Nach Wunsch 1932,O 23,IX,3:1
Winslow, Elsie
Earth 1927,Mr 10,23:1
Nativity Play, The 1937,D 21,29:1
Winslow, Herbert Hall (Playwright)
Broken Branches 1922,Mr 7,11:1
What's Your Wife Doing? 1923,O 2,10:3
Common Sense 1923,D 2,VIII,2:1
Mercenary Mary 1925,Ap 14,27:3
He Loved the Ladies 1927,My 11,29:2
Winslow, James
Hamlet 1948,D 4,9:2
Trouble in July 1949,D 2,36:2
Pajama Tops 1963,Je 1,15:1
Winslow, John C
Fiesta 1933,D 16,12:2
Winslow, Leah
His Chinese Wife 1920,My 18,9:3
Mask of Hamlet, The 1921,Ag 23,10:3
Man in the Making, The 1921,S 21,16:2
So This Is London 1922,Ag 31,18:2
Top Hole 1924,S 2,22:3
Right to Love, The 1925,Je 9,16:4
Dagger, The 1925,S 10,28:1
Joker, The 1925,N 17,29:1
Puppy Love 1926,Ja 28,16:3
Shelf, The 1926,S 28,31:1
Tightwad, The 1927,Ap 18,18:2
Winslow, Rain
Annie Get Your Gun 1958,F 20,29:2
Lute Song 1959,Mr 13,24:1
Winslow, Warren
Final Balance, The 1928,O 31,28:3
Winstan, Nadine
Fall of Eve, The 1925,S 1,18:1
Winston, Alan
Rosalinda; Fledermaus, Die 1942,O 29,26:5
Winston, Alice
Cellar and the Well, The 1950,D 11,30:2
Fortress of Glass 1952,S 5,19:2
Johnny Johnson 1956,O 22,24:1
Winston, Ann
Mask and the Face, The 1924,S 11,27:3
Man in Evening Clothes, The 1924,D 6,13:4
Sure Fire! 1926,O 21,23:1
Free Soul, A 1928,Ja 13,26:5
City Haul 1929,D 31,14:4
Winston, Bess
Dead End 1935,O 29,17:2
Winston, Billy
Dead End 1935,O 29,17:2
Winston, Bruce
Katja 1926,O 19,27:3
Pickwick 1927,Mr 13,VII,1:1
Pickwick 1927,S 6,35:2
Pickwick 1927,S 11,VIII,1:1
Winston, Doris
Nathan the Wise 1944,F 22,26:3
Winston, Emily
Triumph 1935,O 15,18:5
I Take Care of My Friends 1936,Jl 21,13:2
Winston, Florence
As You Like It 1941,O 21,29:2
Winston, Harold
Macbeth 1921,F 18,16:1
Claw, The 1921,O 18,20:1
Children of the Moon 1923,Ag 18,10:3
Bridge of Distances, The 1925,S 29,30:1
Damn the Tears 1927,Ja 22,11:1
Winston, Harold (Director)
Uncle Vanya 1929,My 25,17:1
Brass Ankle 1931,Ap 24,26:4
Other One, The 1932,O 4,26:3
Blue Widow, The 1933,Ag 31,20:2
Winston, Hattie
Prodigal Son, The 1965,My 21,19:1

Song of the Lusitanian Bogey, The 1968,Ja 3,52:1
Summer of the Seventeenth Doll 1968,F 21,59:1
Kongi's Harvest 1968,Ap 15,49:1
God Is a (Guess What?) 1968,D 18,56:1
Man Better Man 1969,Jl 3,22:1
Man Better Man 1969,Jl 13,II,3:6
Sambo 1969,D 22,42:1
Me Nobody Knows, The 1970,F 15,II,1:1
Bill Noname 1970,Mr 3,37:1
Me Nobody Knows, The 1970,My 19,42:1
Winston, Helene
Henry V 1956,Je 20,27:2
Time of Your Life, The 1969,N 7,37:1
Winston, Irene
Veils 1928,Mr 14,28:5
Having Wonderful Time 1937,F 22,12:5
Brooklyn, U S A 1941,D 22,24:2
Winston, Jacqueline
Subway Express 1929,S 25,34:3
Child of Manhattan 1932,Mr 2,15:1
Winston, John
Candida 1935,Ag 20,25:1
Winston, Marian
Song Writer, The 1928,Ag 14,15:2
Winston, Martha
Babes in Arms 1951,Mr 10,7:3
Winston, Martha (Playwright)
To Damascus 1961,F 15,40:2
Winston, Morton
Cabin in the Sky 1964,Ja 22,32:1
Winston, Natalie
Mikado, The 1942,F 4,22:2
Pirates of Penzance, The 1942,F 18,22:2
Iolanthe 1942,F 24,26:4
Gondoliers, The 1942,Mr 4,22:3
Winston, Paulette
Oh, Kay! 1926,N 9,31:3
Winston, Ronald (Director)
Farewell, Farewell Eugene 1960,S 28,35:1
Winston, Ross
Affair of Honor 1956,Ap 7,12:3
Winter, Bernard
Doughgirls, The 1942,D 31,19:2
Winter, Carola
Sonya's Search for the Christmas Star
1929,D 14,24:6
Winter, Cecil
Henry IV, Part I 1946,My 7,25:2
Henry IV, Part II 1946,My 8,33:4
Oedipus 1946,My 21,19:2
Winter, Charles
Green Pastures, The 1935,F 27,16:2
Winter, Claude
Cid, Le 1963,N 8,36:2
Troupe Du Roi, La 1970,F 4,38:1
Winter, Doris
Ice Capades 1963,Ag 29,37:2
Winter, Edward
Galileo 1963,Ja 5,5:2
Country Wife, The 1965,D 10,58:2
Condemned of Altona, The 1966,F 4,21:1
Caucasian Chalk Circle, The 1966,Mr 25,35:1
Cabaret 1966,N 21,62:1
Birthday Party, The 1967,O 4,40:2
Promises, Promises 1968,D 2,59:3
Winter, Eleanor
Bloomer Girl 1944,O 6,18:5
Peter Pan 1950,Ap 25,27:2
Winter, Elma
Well of the Saints, The 1959,Ap 11,15:4
Winter, Hal (Lighting Director)
Grand Vizier, The 1961,D 13,55:5
Cayenne Pepper 1961,D 13,55:5
Winter, Hal (Miscellaneous)
Victims of Duty 1960,Ja 20,26:1
Coming Forth by Day of Osiris Jones, The; Kid,
The 1961,Mr 15,45:2
Winter, Harrison
Jacobowsky and the Colonel 1944,Mr 15,17:2
Winter, Irving
Handful of Fire 1958,O 2,45:3
Winter, Janice
Jubilee 1935,O 14,20:1
Winter, Jessie
Tread Softly 1935,N 8,19:6
Tread Softly 1935,D 8,X,5:1
Winter, Julian
Vagabond King, The 1925,S 22,23:3
Winter, Keith (Original Author)
Rats of Norway, The 1933,Ap 30,IX,1:7
Winter, Keith (Playwright)
Rats of Norway, The 1933,Ap 30,IX,1:7
Shining Hour, The 1934,F 14,22:6
Shining Hour, The 1934,F 25,IX,1:1
Shining Hour, The 1934,S 25,25:4
Shining Hour, The 1934,S 23,X,3:6
Ringmaster, The 1935,Mr 12,24:5
Ringmaster, The 1935,Ap 7,IX,1:6
Worse Things Happen at Sea 1935,Ap 21,IX,2:2
Old Music 1937,Ag 19,22:2
Worse Things Happen at Sea 1937,S 1,15:3
Old Music 1937,S 5,X,2:1
We at the Cross Roads 1939,Mr 26,X,3:1

Winter, Keith (Playwright)—Cont
Rats of Norway, The 1948,Ap 16,27:6
Winter, Lester W
Final Balance, The 1928,O 31,28:3
Winter, Lois Wales
Hearts Are Trumps! 1927,Ap 8,21:1
Winter, Nigel M
Noye's Fludde 1959,Mr 17,41:2
Winter, Percy
Hearts Are Trumps! 1927,Ap 8,21:1
Winter, Richard
Happiest Girl in the World, The 1961,Ap 4,42:1
Winter, Rose
Teaser, The 1921,Jl 28,8:3
Montmartre 1922,F 14,20:1
Comedian, The 1923,Mr 14,14:1
Forbidden 1923,O 2,10:2
Rain 1935,Ag 27,23:4
Frederika 1937,F 5,16:5
Winter, Valentine
Yankee Princess, The 1922,O 3,22:1
Winter, Vera
Chinese Lily, A 1925,Mr 24,26:5
Winter, Winona
Broadway Whirl, The 1921,Je 9,10:4
Winter-Berger, Robert N (Producer)
Dark Legend 1952,Mr 25,24:2
Victim, The 1952,My 3,17:5
Winter Sisters
Edith Piaf 1947,O 30,30:2
Winterberg, Robert (Playwright)
Anneliese von Dessau 1926,F 26,24:3
Winterbottom, Goddard (Director)
After the Angels 1961,F 11,27:5
Winterbottom, Goddard (Miscellaneous)
Herne's Egg, The 1960,S 20,48:1
Winterburn, Alan
Veils 1928,Mr 14,28:5
Winters, Anne
It's a Funny World 1956,O 22,24:1
It Could Happen to You 1957,O 28,30:5
Kosher Widow, The 1959,N 2,40:2
Go Fight City Hall 1961,N 3,28:5
Country Boy, The 1963,O 28,20:1
Winters, Arthur
Who Is Who? 1938,D 24,13:3
Winters, Charles
Vaudeville (Palace) 1926,Mr 16,22:2
Winters, Clark
Oklahoma! 1955,Je 21,37:7
Winters, David
On Your Toes 1954,O 12,24:4
Sandhog 1954,N 24,17:1
Shinbone Alley 1957,Ap 15,23:2
West Side Story 1957,S 27,14:4
Gypsy 1959,My 22,31:6
One More River 1960,Mr 19,12:2
Half-Past Wednesday 1962,Ap 7,16:2
Winters, Elaine
Great Magician, The 1951,N 22,45:1
Winters, Jeanne
On the Spot 1930,O 30,33:3
Winters, Joan
Bad Girl 1930,O 3,30:2
Garrison Theatre 1940,My 26,IX,2:1
Winters, Julian
Mecca 1920,O 5,12:2
Winters, June
New Hellzapoppin, The 1939,D 12,36:4
Winters, Lawrence
Call Me Mister 1946,Ap 19,26:2
Call Me Mister 1946,Ap 28,II,1:1
Show Boat 1954,My 6,44:1
Show Boat 1954,O 29,28:4
Long Dream, The 1960,F 18,36:2
Winters, Lucille
Empress of Destiny 1938,Mr 10,16:2
Winters, Marian
E-MC2 1948,Je 16,36:2
Hippolytus 1948,N 22,25:5
Dream Girl 1951,My 10,39:1
I Am a Camera 1951,N 29,39:6
I Am a Camera 1951,D 9,II,5:1
Sing Me No Lullaby 1954,O 15,17:2
Dark Is Light Enough, The 1955,F 24,20:1
Auntie Mame 1956,N 1,47:2
Tall Story 1959,Ja 30,33:2
49th Cousin, The 1960,O 28,22:1
Cherry Orchard, The 1962,N 15,46:2
Nobody Loves an Albatross 1963,D 20,20:1
Nobody Loves an Albatross 1964,Ja 5,II,1:1
Mating Dance 1965,N 4,58:1
King John 1967,Jl 14,19:1
Winters, Maurice
Hall of Healing 1952,My 8,35:6
Winters, Norma
Lady Behave 1943,N 17,30:1
Knight of the Burning Pestle, The 1953,O 24,13:2
Moon in Capricorn 1953,O 28,37:2
Journey With Strangers, A 1958,N 27,53:1
Winters, Percy
Bomboola 1929,Je 27,17:3
Winters, Renee
Best Foot Forward 1963,Ap 3,43:1

Winters, Roland
Who Was That Lady I Saw You With?
1958,Mr 4,33:2
Cook for Mr General, A 1961,O 20,39:1
Calculated Risk 1962,N 1,35:1
Minnie's Boys 1970,Mr 27,27:1
Minnie's Boys 1970,Ap 5,II,3:1
Winters, Shelley
Night Before Christmas, The 1941,Ap 11,25:2
Rosalinda; Fledermaus, Die 1942,O 29,26:5
Hatful of Rain, A 1955,N 10,44:1
Hatful of Rain, A 1955,D 4,II,1:1
Girls of Summer 1956,N 20,45:1
Cages; Snowangel; Epiphany 1963,Je 14,36:1
Orange Souffle; Wen, The; Out From Under
1966,Jl 16,14:6
Under the Weather 1966,O 28,35:1
Minnie's Boys 1970,Mr 27,27:1
Minnie's Boys 1970,Ap 5,II,3:1
Winters, Shelley (Playwright)
One Night Stands of a Noisy Passenger; Noisy
Passenger, The 1970,D 31,8:3
One Night Stands of a Noisy Passenger; Last
Stand 1970,D 31,8:3
One Night Stands of a Noisy Passenger; Passage,
Un 1970,D 31,8:3
Winters, Stephanie
Stop the World-I Want to Get Off 1962,O 4,45:4
Winters, Verna (Miscellaneous)
Master Builder, The 1957,D 18,42:7
Winterstein, Eduard von
Persians, The 1927,F 27,VII,2:3
Winther, Robert
Midsummer Night's Dream, A 1956,Ja 14,12:2
Winthorp, Ethel
Sporting Thing to Do, The 1923,F 20,12:2
Winthrop, Ann
Lend Me Your Ears! 1936,O 6,28:5
Father Malachy's Miracle 1937,N 18,26:4
Winthrop, Eddie
Sun Showers 1923,F 6,14:2
Winthrop, Ethel
Nemesis 1921,Ap 5,24:3
Dumb-Bell 1923,N 27,23:2
Winthrop, Jan
Boy Meets Girl 1937,Jl 6,23:1
Winthrop, John
Short Cut, The 1930,Ja 28,28:2
Ethan Frome 1936,Ja 22,15:2
Seen But Not Heard 1936,S 18,19:2
Wingless Victory, The 1936,N 25,17:5
Wingless Victory, The 1936,D 24,20:2
Virginian, The 1937,Ag 10,22:7
Missouri Legend 1938,S 20,27:2
Wintle, Sylvia (Costume Designer)
Sweeney Todd 1957,Ag 28,21:4
Winton, Don (Miscellaneous)
Story Theater 1970,O 27,54:1
Winton, Lily
Having Wonderful Time 1937,F 22,12:5
Journeyman 1938,Ja 31,14:2
Wintz, George (Producer)
She Got What She Wanted 1929,Mr 5,28:1
Apron Strings 1931,Je 7,VIII,8:1
Ten Nights in a Barroom 1932,Ja 21,17:1
Shuffle Along of 1933 1932,D 27,11:3
Winwood, Estelle
Tyranny of Love, The 1921,Mr 2,7:3
Tyranny of Love, The 1921,Mr 6,VI,1:2
Tyranny of Love, The 1921,My 3,20:2
Tyranny of Love, The 1921,My 8,VI,1:1
Circle, The 1921,S 13,12:1
Madame Pierre 1922,F 16,11:1
Madame Pierre 1922,F 19,VI,1:1
Go Easy Mabel 1922,My 9,22:2
Red Poppy, The 1922,D 21,18:2
Anything Might Happen 1923,F 21,22:3
Anything Might Happen 1923,F 25,VII,1:1
But for the Grace of God 1923,S 9,VII,2:4
Spring Cleaning 1923,N 10,16:3
Spring Cleaning 1923,N 18,VIII,1:1
Buccaneer, The 1925,O 3,10:2
Taming of the Shrew, The 1925,D 19,14:1
Taming of the Shrew, The 1925,D 27,VII,1:1
Weak Woman, A 1926,Ja 27,16:3
Chief Thing, The 1926,Mr 23,24:2
Beau-Strings 1926,Ap 27,22:2
Beau-Strings 1926,My 2,VIII,1:1
Head or Tail 1926,N 10,24:1
Trelawney of the 'Wells' 1927,F 1,24:4
Fallen Angels 1927,D 2,20:4
We Never Learn 1928,Ja 24,26:1
Furies, The 1928,Mr 8,23:1
Scarlet Sister Mary 1930,N 26,19:2
Admirable Crichton, The 1931,Mr 10,23:2
Admirable Crichton, The 1931,Mr 29,VIII,1:1
Distaff Side, The 1934,S 26,17:2
Ugly Runts, The 1935,Je 11,24:4
Pursuit of Happiness, The 1935,Jl 16,24:2
Eden End 1935,O 22,17:1
I Want a Policeman! 1936,Ja 15,15:5
Reflected Glory 1936,Jl 22,23:1
Merry Wives of Windsor, The 1938,Ap 15,22:3

On the Rocks 1938,Je 16,20:2
Good Hunting 1938,N 22,26:5
Importance of Being Earnest, The 1939,Ja 13,16:2
When We Are Married 1939,N 21,19:5
When We Are Married 1939,D 10,X,5:6
When We Are Married 1939,D 26,22:3
Ladies in Retirement 1940,Mr 27,24:3
Pirate, The 1942,N 26,39:2
Ten Little Indians 1944,Je 28,21:2
Lady Windermere's Fan 1946,O 15,29:2
Madwoman of Chaillot, The 1949,Ja 9,II,1:1
Madwoman of Chaillot, The 1949,S 11,II,1:1
Madwoman of Chaillot, The 1950,Je 14,41:2
Mrs Warren's Profession 1950,O 26,39:2
Mr Pickwick 1952,S 18,36:3
Mr Pickwick 1952,S 28,II,1:1
Speaking of Murder 1956,D 20,37:1
Lute Song 1959,Mr 13,24:1
Nathan Weinstein, Mystic, Connecticut
1966,F 26,15:2
Winwood, Estelle (Director)
Importance of Being Earnest, The 1939,Ja 13,16:2
Winwood, Estelle (Producer)
Merry Wives of Windsor, The 1938,Ap 15,22:3
Winyar, E
Golem, The 1927,F 5,13:2
Wipf, Alex
Ah, Wilderness! 1969,N 9,86:1
Wird, Edward (Musical Director)
Red Mill, The 1945,O 17,16:2
Wirl, Erik
Countess Maritza 1927,Ja 30,VII,4:3
Wirth, May
Vaudeville (Palace) 1928,N 26,31:2
Vaudeville (Broadway) 1932,D 27,11:4
Wirth Family, The
Vaudeville (Palace) 1927,Mr 1,31:2
Wirtz, Arthur (Producer)
It Happens on Ice 1940,O 11,24:3
It Happens on Ice 1941,Ap 5,13:2
Stars on Ice 1942,Jl 3,12:2
Hollywood Ice Revue 1943,Ja 24,II,1:1
Stars on Ice (2d Edition) 1943,Je 25,13:2
Hats Off to Ice 1944,Je 23,15:2
Icetime 1946,Je 21,20:5
Icetime 1947,My 29,28:2
Howdy Mr Ice 1948,Je 25,28:5
Howdy, Mr Ice of 1950 1949,My 27,24:2
Funzapoppin 1949,Jl 1,16:2
Hollywood Ice Revue 1953,Ja 16,17:2
Hollywood Ice Revue 1954,Ja 15,16:2
Hollywood Ice Revue 1955 1955,Ja 14,16:1
Hollywood Ice Revue 1956,Ja 13,17:1
Wirtz, Benjamin (Rev) (Producer)
Veronica's Veil 1950,F 12,II,1:5
Veronica's Veil 1954,F 28,I,78:5
Wirwill, Sandy
Holiday on Ice 1965,S 2,38:4
Holiday on Ice 1966,S 1,30:1
Wisbar, Tania
Journey With Strangers, A 1958,N 27,53:1
Wisdom, Norman
Walking Happy 1966,N 28,47:1
Walking Happy 1966,D 18,II,3:1
Not Now Darling 1970,O 30,33:1
Wise, Aldeah
Passion Flower, The 1920,Ja 14,12:1
Topaze 1930,F 13,25:3
Violet, The 1930,S 30,24:2
One, Two, Three! 1930,S 30,24:2
Country Wife, The 1931,Ap 19,31:5
Wise, Alvea
God of Vengeance, The 1922,D 20,22:5
Wise, Blanche (Miscellaneous)
Hide and Seek 1957,Ap 3,26:1
Wise, Edwina
Pride and Prejudice 1935,N 6,32:4
Wise, Emma
Minick 1924,S 25,20:1
Morning After, The 1925,Jl 28,24:2
Kept 1926,S 18,13:3
Salvation 1928,F 1,31:1
Wise, Harry
Marco Millions 1930,Mr 4,24:4
Wise, Jim (Composer)
Dames at Sea 1968,D 21,46:1
Dames at Sea 1970,S 24,60:1
Wise, Patricia
Pirates of Penzance, The 1968,Ap 26,32:1
Wise, Thomas (Mrs)
Richard III 1920,Mr 8,7:1
Call the Doctor 1920,S 1,14:1
Becky Sharp 1929,Je 4,29:1
Wise, Thomas A
School for Scandal, The 1923,Je 5,24:3
Adorable Liar, The 1926,Ag 31,15:2
Nightingale, The 1927,Ja 4,20:4
Behold This Dreamer 1927,N 1,20:4
Wisehart, Fredreika
Yeomen of the Guard, The 1968,My 9,53:1
Wisehart, Peter (Composer)
Comedy of Errors, The 1962,S 12,34:2

Wisely, Edward B
Caesar and Cleopatra 1927,N 6,IX,2:1
Wiseman, George H
Master of the Inn, The 1925,D 23,22:2
Legend of Leonora, The 1927,Mr 30,22:4
Wiseman, Joseph
Abe Lincoln in Illinois 1938,O 17,12:2
Journey to Jerusalem 1940,O 7,21:2
Candle in the Wind 1941,O 23,26:2
Joan of Lorraine 1946,N 19,40:2
Antony and Cleopatra 1947,N 27,49:2
Detective Story 1949,Mr 24,34:2
Detective Story 1949,Ap 3,II,1:1
That Lady 1949,O 20,38:8
That Lady 1949,N 23,18:4
Golden Boy 1952,Mr 13,24:3
Golden Boy 1952,Mr 23,II,1:1
Lark, The 1955,N 18,20:1
Lark, The 1955,N 27,II,1:1
Duchess of Malfi, The 1957,Mr 20,33:1
Marco Millions 1964,F 21,33:1
Incident at Vichy 1964,D 4,44:1
Incident at Vichy 1964,D 20,II,3:1
Murder in the Cathedral 1966,Je 21,38:1
In the Matter of J Robert Oppenheimer
1968,My 27,55:1
In the Matter of J Robert Oppenheimer
1968,Je 7,31:1
In the Matter of J Robert Oppenheimer
1968,Je 9,II,1:1
In the Matter of J Robert Oppenheimer
1969,Mr 7,28:1
In the Matter of J Robert Oppenheimer
1969,Mr 16,II,1:3
Uncle Vanya 1969,Ag 31,II,4:1
Wiseman, Philip (Director)
Conversation Piece 1957,N 19,38:2
Wiseman, Philip (Producer)
Conversation Piece 1957,N 19,38:2
Wisenfrend, Muni
We Americans 1926,O 13,20:4
Four Walls 1927,S 20,33:1
Four Walls 1927,O 2,VIII,1:1
Wishard, Scoville
Jotham Valley 1951,F 7,37:2
Wishart, Fredreika
Patience 1968,My 16,52:1
Wishart, Harris
Iron Men 1936,O 20,30:6
Wishart, Peter (Composer)
Comedy of Errors, The 1964,My 21,43:1
Wishengrad, Morton (Playwright)
Rope Dancers, The 1957,N 21,39:1
Rope Dancers, The 1957,D 1,II,1:1
Rope Dancers, The 1957,D 22,II,3:1
Rope Dancers, The 1959,Mr 14,26:1
Rope Dancers, The 1959,Jl 15,26:2
Wishon, Rosalind
Pleasure Bound 1929,F 19,22:4
Wonderful Night, A; Fledermaus, Die
1929,N 1,23:3
Wishy, Joseph (Miscellaneous)
Time for Singing, A 1966,My 23,48:2
Orlando Furioso 1970,N 5,59:1
Wiskind, Kenneth
Don Juan in the Russian Manner 1954,Ap 23,23:2
Wisner, Rene (Playwright)
Untitled-Play 1927,D 18,IX,4:4
Wisniak, Kazimierz (Costume Designer)
Post Office, The 1965,Ja 6,32:1
Kernel and the Shell, The 1965,Ja 6,32:1
Woman, The 1965,Ja 6,32:1
Jacob and the Angel 1965,Ja 6,32:1
Nightmare, The 1965,Ja 6,32:1
Book, The 1965,Ja 6,32:1
Jaselka 1965,Ja 6,32:1
Labyrinth, The 1965,Ja 6,32:1
Wister, Malcolm L
Fiesta 1933,D 16,12:2
Wister, Owen (Playwright)
Virginian, The 1937,Ag 10,22:7
Wister, William R
Laugh It Off 1925,Ap 25,18:4
Witbeck, B F (Producer)
Jay Walker, The 1926,F 9,23:1
Little Spitfire, The 1926,Ag 17,15:2
Jimmie's Women 1927,S 27,30:3
Witchie, Katharine
Oh, Ernest! 1927,My 10,24:3
Witcover, Walt
Saint Joan 1950,Mr 4,10:6
Captain Brassbound's Conversion 1950,D 28,21:1
Royal Family, The 1951,Ja 11,28:2
Finian's Rainbow 1953,Mr 7,13:2
Witcover, Walt (Director)
Hasty Heart, The 1954,Mr 13,10:1
Three Times Three; Box and Cox 1956,My 24,27:2
Three Times Three; How He Lied to Her Husband
1956,My 24,27:2
Three Times Three; Merrye Playe, A
1956,My 24,27:2
Exiles 1957,Mr 13,27:1
Hanjo 1960,N 16,51:4

Witcover, Walt (Director)—Cont
Lady Akane, The 1960,N 16,51:4
Signs Along the Cynic Route 1961,D 15,49:5
Exhaustion of Our Son's Love, The 1965,O 19,51:1
Good Day 1965,O 19,51:1
Witcover, Walt (Miscellaneous)
Three Plays of the Sea 1970,Ag 20,39:1
Witcover, Walt (Producer)
Three Times Three; Box and Cox 1956,My 24,27:2
Three Times Three; How He Lied to Her Husband 1956,My 24,27:2
Three Times Three; Merrye Playe, A 1956,My 24,27:2
Witham, Arthur
Biff, Bing, Bang 1921,My 10,20:1
Withe, Will
Good Boy 1928,S 6,23:2
Withee, Mabel
Rose Girl, The 1921,F 12,11:1
Sonny 1921,Ag 17,12:2
Rose of Stamboul, The 1922,Mr 8,11:2
Lady Butterfly 1923,Ja 23,18:1
Dew Drop Inn 1923,My 18,26:4
Artists and Models 1924,O 16,33:3
Cocoanuts, The 1925,D 9,30:1
Witherbee, Lysle
Silence 1924,N 13,18:2
Witherill, Val
Embezzled Heaven 1944,N 1,20:2
Withers, Charles
Hitchy-Koo, 1920 1920,O 20,11:3
Vaudeville (Palace) 1923,F 13,25:1
Vaudeville (Palace) 1926,Ag 10,19:4
Vaudeville (Palace) 1927,Jl 5,19:3
New Hellzapoppin, The 1939,D 12,36:4
Withers, Goldie
They Came to a City 1943,Je 6,II,1:6
Withers, Googie
Winter Journey; Country Girl, The 1952,Ap 4,21:1
Deep Blue Sea, The 1953,Ap 4,8:6
Waiting For Gillian 1954,Ap 22,36:2
Janus 1957,Ap 25,34:2
Much Ado About Nothing 1958,Ag 27,34:6
Complaisant Lover, The 1961,N 2,43:2
Withers, Grant
American Primitive 1937,Ag 13,12:5
Withers, Helen
Mima 1928,D 13,24:2
Du Barry 1932,N 23,15:2
Withers, Isabelle
Wild Westcotts, The 1923,D 25,26:2
Haunted House, The 1924,S 3,12:1
Her Majesty the Widow 1934,Je 19,24:5
Withers, Iva
Carousel 1949,Ja 26,28:2
Carousel 1949,F 6,II,1:1
Show Boat 1952,Je 6,19:5
Guys and Dolls 1959,Jl 22,22:2
Forty Carats 1968,D 27,45:1
Witherspoon, Cora
Lilies of the Field 1921,O 5,20:1
Awful Truth, The 1922,S 19,14:3
Grounds for Divorce 1924,S 24,20:1
Fall of Eve, The 1925,S 1,18:1
Hush Money 1926,Mr 16,22:3
Constant Wife, The 1926,N 30,26:3
Olympia 1928,O 17,26:1
Precious 1929,Ja 15,22:5
Waterloo Bridge 1929,D 1,X,4:7
Waterloo Bridge 1930,Ja 7,29:2
Philip Goes Forth 1931,Ja 4,VIII,2:2
Philip Goes Forth 1931,Ja 13,35:4
Philip Goes Forth 1931,Ja 18,VIII,1:1
Way of the World, The 1931,Je 2,34:3
Jewel Robbery 1932,Ja 14,17:2
Camille 1932,N 2,23:3
Forsaking All Others 1933,Mr 2,21:2
Shooting Star 1933,Je 13,22:2
Jezebel 1933,D 20,26:3
Mackerel Skies 1934,Ja 24,20:4
Jig Saw 1934,My 1,26:3
Say When 1934,N 9,24:2
It's You I Want 1935,F 6,23:3
De Luxe 1935,Mr 6,22:2
All Bow Down 1935,Ag 6,20:4
Touch of Brimstone, A 1935,S 23,20:1
All Men Are Alike 1941,O 7,27:2
Willow and I, The 1942,D 11,32:2
Front Page, The 1946,S 5,22:4
Profile 1947,Ag 12,26:1
Withington, Lillian
Up in Central Park 1947,My 20,29:2
Withrow, William
Hero of Santa Maria, The 1926,My 1,10:1
Witler, Ben-Zion
Uncle Sam in Israel 1952,D 8,38:5
Witliams, Frances
Vaudeville (Palace) 1931,Je 8,21:2
Witmark, Julius P Jr
Half Moon Inn 1925,Mr 10,14:1
Witney, Frederick (Playwright)
Adventurous Age, The 1927,F 8,20:1
Witsch, Christa
Tenth Man, The 1962,O 3,46:1

Witsen, Leo Van (Costume Designer)
Seven at Dawn, The 1961,Ap 18,43:1
Witt, Howard
Richard III 1957,N 26,41:1
As You Like It 1958,Ja 21,33:6
Indians 1969,My 27,43:1
Night Thoreau Spent in Jail, The 1970,N 2,66:1
Wittenborn, Paul
Moon Walk 1970,N 27,52:1
Wittler, Therese
Eyes 1930,My 10,25:1
Hill Between, The 1938,Mr 12,12:5
Not in Our Stars 1941,Ap 26,20:5
Wittlinger, Karl (Playwright)
Do You Know the Milky Way? 1961,O 17,45:1
Wittly, Bert
Papavert 1931,D 30,25:1
Wittman, Ellen (Miscellaneous)
Man Is Man 1962,S 19,31:1
Xmas in Las Vegas 1965,N 5,31:1
Wait Until Dark 1966,F 3,21:1
Goodbye People, The 1968,D 4,52:1
Arsenic and Old Lace 1970,N 5,59:1
Wittman, Morris (Playwright)
Sacrilege, The 1921,My 3,20:1
Wittop, Freddy (Costume Designer)
Count Me In 1942,O 9,24:2
Beat the Band 1942,O 15,26:1
Heartbreak House 1959,O 19,37:1
Two for Fun 1961,F 14,45:3
Carnival! 1961,Ap 14,22:2
Subways Are for Sleeping 1961,D 28,22:1
Hello, Dolly! 1964,Ja 17,22:1
Hello, Dolly! 1964,Ja 26,II,1:1
To Broadway With Love 1964,Ap 30,28:6
Bajour 1964,N 24,42:1
Kelly 1965,F 8,28:2
Roar of the Greasepaint-the Smell of the Crowd 1965,My 17,46:2
Holiday on Ice 1965,S 2,38:4
On a Clear Day You Can See Forever 1965,O 18,44:1
3 Bags Full 1966,Mr 7,22:1
Holiday on Ice 1966,S 1,30:1
I Do! I Do! 1966,D 6,58:1
Breakfast at Tiffany's 1966,D 15,60:1
Holiday on Ice 1967,Ag 31,29:2
Hello, Dolly! 1967,N 13,61:1
Happy Time, The 1968,Ja 19,32:2
George M! 1968,Ap 11,48:1
Holiday on Ice 1968,Ag 29,44:1
Dear World 1969,F 7,33:1
Holiday on Ice 1969,Ag 28,44:1
Patriot for Me, A 1969,O 6,58:1
Lovely Ladies, Kind Gentlemen 1970,D 29,38:1
Wittop, Freddy (Miscellaneous)
Carnival! 1968,D 13,58:1
Wittop, Freddy (Scenic Designer)
Beat the Band 1942,O 15,26:1
Holiday on Ice 1966,S 1,30:1
Witts, Jack
George White's Scandals 1922,Ag 29,10:1
Wittstein, Ed (Costume Designer)
Gondoliers, The 1961,Ja 26,33:2
Kean 1961,N 3,28:2
Bravo Giovanni 1962,My 21,41:2
Ginger Man, The 1963,N 22,42:1
White House, The 1964,My 20,39:1
Yearling, The 1965,D 11,25:1
As You Like It 1968,Je 24,42:3
Celebration 1969,Ja 23,55:2
Wittstein, Ed (Director)
Happy Journey to Trenton and Camden, The 1966,S 7,53:1
Wittstein, Ed (Lighting Director)
Legend of Lovers 1959,O 28,40:3
Celebration 1969,Ja 23,55:2
Wittstein, Ed (Miscellaneous)
Fantasticks, The 1960,My 4,55:2
Chips With Everything 1963,O 2,49:1
Wittstein, Ed (Scenic Designer)
Dr Willy Nilly 1959,Je 5,18:2
Legend of Lovers 1959,O 28,40:3
Gondoliers, The 1961,Ja 26,33:2
Kean 1961,N 3,28:2
Love Nest, The 1963,Ja 28,7:6
Enter Laughing 1963,Mr 15,8:1
Rainy Day in Newark, A 1963,O 23,35:1
Ginger Man, The 1963,N 22,42:1
Trumpets of the Lord 1963,D 23,22:3
Once in a Lifetime 1964,Ja 29,20:1
White House, The 1964,My 20,39:1
New Tenant, The 1964,My 28,40:2
Knack, The 1964,My 28,42:2
Victims of Duty 1964,My 28,40:2
Tragical Historie of Doctor Faustus, The 1964,O 6,34:2
Room, The 1964,D 10,62:1
Slight Ache, A 1964,D 10,62:1
Sing to Me Through Open Windows 1965,Mr 16,45:1
Day the Whores Came Out to Play Tennis, The 1965,Mr 16,45:1

Wittstein, Ed (Scenic Designer)—Cont
And Things That Go Bump in the Night 1965,Ap 27,27:5
Yearling, The 1965,D 11,25:1
Serjeant Musgrave's Dance 1966,Mr 9,44:1
Kitchen, The 1966,Je 14,50:1
Falstaff 1966,Je 20,27:1
Long Christmas Dinner, The 1966,S 7,53:1
Queens of France 1966,S 7,53:1
Natural Look, The 1967,Mr 13,45:2
You Know I Can't Hear You When the Water's Running; I'm Herbert 1967,Mr 14,54:1
You Know I Can't Hear You When the Water's Running; Shock of Recognition, The 1967,Mr 14,54:1
You Know I Can't Hear You When the Water's Running; I'll Be Home for Christmas 1967,Mr 14,54:1
You Know I Can't Hear You When the Water's Running; Footsteps of Doves, The 1967,Mr 14,54:1
Merchant of Venice, The 1967,Je 22,46:2
Before You Go 1968,Ja 12,20:1
Richard II 1968,Je 24,42:3
As You Like It 1968,Je 24,42:3
Man in the Glass Booth, The 1968,S 27,41:1
Tea Party 1968,O 16,40:1
Basement, The 1968,O 16,40:1
Tea Party 1968,N 3,II,7:4
Honor and Offer 1968,D 1,II,3:1
Little Murders 1969,Ja 6,38:1
Celebration 1969,Ja 23,55:2
Much Ado About Nothing 1969,Je 16,57:1
Scent of Flowers, A 1969,O 21,42:1
Last Sweet Days of Isaac, The 1970,Ja 27,49:1
I Dreamt I Dwelt in Bloomingdale's 1970,F 13,26:1
Blood Red Roses 1970,Mr 23,48:1
Happy Birthday, Wanda June 1970,O 8,58:2
Wittstein, Edwin (Lighting Director)
Yes is for a Very Young Man 1949,Je 7,27:2
Wittstein, Edwin (Scenic Designer)
Yes is for a Very Young Man 1949,Je 7,27:2
Wittstein, Hortense
Gods Are Wise, The 1930,My 6,33:1
Wittstein, Hyman
Jazz a La Carte 1922,Je 3,8:3
Witty, Frank (Playwright)
No Exit 1936,Ja 22,15:3
Woddell, Barbara
Audition of the Apprentice Theatre 1939,Je 2,26:2
Wode, Ed (Director)
Che! 1969,Mr 24,56:1
Republic, The 1970,Ap 28,49:1
Wode, Ed (Playwright)
Republic, The 1970,Ap 28,49:1
Wode, Ed (Producer)
Che! 1969,Mr 24,56:1
Wodehouse, P G (Lyricist)
Nightingale, The 1927,Ja 4,20:4
Rosalie 1928,Ja 11,26:3
Three Musketeers, The 1928,Mr 14,28:1
Sally 1948,My 7,31:2
Rosalie 1957,Je 26,28:2
Leave It to Jane 1959,My 26,30:2
Wodehouse, P G (Original Author)
Who's Who 1934,S 21,28:4
Anything Goes 1934,N 18,IX,1:7
Anything Goes 1937,Ag 26,24:3
From Here to There; Otherwise Engaged 1958,Ap 24,37:3
Wodehouse, P G (Playwright)
Sitting Pretty 1924,Mr 30,VIII,2:7
Sitting Pretty 1924,Ap 9,24:2
Play's the Thing, The 1926,N 4,25:1
Oh, Kay! 1926,N 9,31:3
Her Cardboard Lover 1927,Mr 22,30:5
Good Morning, Bill! 1927,D 25,VIII,1:4
Damsel in Distress, A 1928,S 2,VII,2:1
Her Cardboard Lover 1928,S 9,IX,2:7
Play's the Thing, The 1928,D 23,VIII,4:7
Baa, Baa, Black Sheep 1929,My 12,IX,2:3
Candle-Light 1929,O 1,28:2
Who's Who 1934,S 21,28:4
Anything Goes 1934,N 22,26:1
Inside Stand, The 1935,N 22,18:1
Leave It to Jane 1959,My 26,30:2
Oh, Kay! 1960,Ap 18,37:2
Anything Goes 1962,My 16,35:1
Wodehouse, P G (Translator)
Candle Light 1929,S 22,IX,2:6
Play's the Thing, The 1948,Ap 29,19:2
Wodetzky, Christine
Nathan der Weise 1966,D 10,45:2
Wodson, Elaine
Alien Corn 1935,Ja 20,X,3:8
Woegerer, Otto
Hamlet in Wittenberg 1936,N 15,XI,2:4
Woehl, Arthur L
Traffic Signals 1937,Ag 7,7:4
Woelffer, Hans (Director)
Bezauberndes Fraeulein 1933,N 19,IX,3:1
Woelffer, Hans (Producer)
Raetzel um Beate 1936,N 8,X,2:1
Woellhaf, Richard
Front Page Stuff 1926,D 29,24:4

Woerner, Marcena
As You Like It 1945,Jl 4,10:4
Woester, Heinz
Elizabeth and Essex 1935,N 9,18:8
Wohl, David (Scenic Designer)
Twisting Road, The; Jewel of the South, The
1957,N 18,36:5
Twisting Road, The; Housekeeper, The
1957,N 18,36:5
Twisting Road, The; One Tuesday Morning
1957,N 18,36:5
Hasty Heart, The 1959,S 15,45:2
Wohl, Herman
Untitled-Benefit 1933,Ja 25,13:3
Wohl, Herman (Composer)
Love and Politics 1929,O 21,30:7
Sonitchka 1930,Mr 8,21:3
Russian Love 1930,N 27,32:3
Great Miracle, The 1931,D 12,23:5
Big Surprise, The 1932,O 17,18:3
Traveling Salesman, The 1932,N 1,24:4
Jewish Melody, The 1933,Mr 27,12:4
Love for Sale 1936,Ja 24,14:2
Wohl, Herman (Lyricist)
Traveling Salesman, The 1932,N 1,24:4
Wohl, Herman (Musical Director)
Night in the Woods, A 1931,Mr 2,19:3
Wohl, Herman (Playwright)
Village Wedding, A 1930,S 24,26:2
Rich Paupers 1932,Mr 14,13:4
Love for Sale 1932,D 5,21:4
Honeymoon for Three, A 1933,Ja 30,9:6
Wohlbruck, Adolf
Royal Family, The 1931,Ap 12,IX,1:3
Jewel Robbery; Juwelenraub am Kurfurstendamm
1932,F 21,VIII,2:3
Wohlman, Al
Sun-Kist 1921,My 24,20:2
Gay Paree 1926,N 10,24:2
Woisky, Albert (Costume Designer)
Pousse-Cafe 1966,Mr 19,19:2
Woitasik, George (Miscellaneous)
Gondoliers, The 1963,Je 5,33:2
Wojak, Regina (Miscellaneous)
Sea Gull, The 1956,O 23,38:1
Wojak, Regina (Playwright)
Italian Straw Hat, The 1957,O 1,37:2
Wojcikowska, Sonia
Oklahoma! 1943,N 14,II,1:1
Wojewodka, Jan (Producer)
Visit With the Family, A 1957,O 17,42:5
Wolas, Edith
Rose in the Wilderness 1949,Ja 5,21:2
Wolas, Eva (Playwright)
Respectful Prostitute, The 1948,F 15,II,1:1
Respectful Prostitute, The 1948,Mr 21,II,1:1
To Tell You the Truth 1948,Ap 19,28:6
Wolas, Eva (Translator)
Respectful Prostitute, The 1948,F 10,27:2
Wolaski, Barry
Give My Regards to Off Off Broadway
1966,D 9,57:1
Wolcott, Geri
Persecution and Assassination of Marat As
Performed by the Inmates of the Asylum of
Charenton Under the Direction of the Marquis de
Sade, The 1967,Ja 4,34:1
Wolcott, Helen
Hottentot, The 1920,Mr 2,9:1
Guest of Honor, The 1920,S 21,12:1
Wolcott, Jean
Burning Bush, The 1949,D 17,15:5
Scapegoat, The 1950,Ap 20,36:5
Wolder, Herrmann
Vielgeliebte, Die 1935,My 19,IX,2:5
Woldin, Judd (Choreographer)
Beast in Me, The 1963,My 17,29:1
Woldron, Al
Howdy Stranger 1937,Ja 15,17:5
Woleschak, Metro
Outside the Door 1949,Mr 2,33:2
Wolf, Andreas
Professor Bernhardi 1968,Mr 20,38:1
Maria Stuart 1968,Mr 27,38:1
Wolf, Anne
Red, Hot and Blue! 1936,O 30,26:3
Wolf, Carl
Mikado, The 1942,F 4,22:2
Pirates of Penzance, The 1942,F 18,22:2
Iolanthe 1942,F 24,26:4
Gondoliers, The 1942,Mr 4,22:3
Wolf, Claire
Boys From Syracuse, The 1938,N 24,36:1
Wolf, Daisy (Playwright)
We Never Learn 1927,D 25,VIII,2:3
We Never Learn 1928,Ja 24,26:1
Wolf, Daniel
Port O' London 1926,F 10,20:2
Gentlemen Prefer Blondes 1926,S 29,23:1
Garden of Eden, The 1927,S 28,28:1
Los Angeles 1927,D 20,32:3
Wolf, Eugene (Original Author)
Case of Youth, A 1940,Mr 25,10:3

Wolf, Friedrich (Playwright)
Cyankali 1929,N 24,X,2:4
Sailors of Cattaro 1934,D 11,28:4
Professor Mamlock 1937,Ap 14,30:3
Wolf, Gusti
Konzert, Das 1968,Mr 25,52:1
Wolf, Hal
Tenth Avenue 1927,Ag 16,31:1
Wolf, Hank
All in Favor 1942,Ja 21,20:6
Wolf, Helen
Nautical but Nice 1931,Ap 19,31:6
Wolf, James
Fall and Rise of Susan Lenox, The 1920,Je 11,11:2
Wolf, Joan
Noah 1954,O 11,32:2
Wolf, Peter (Lighting Director)
Corn Is Green, The 1950,Ja 12,33:2
Devil's Disciple, The 1950,Ja 26,23:2
Heiress, The 1950,F 9,34:2
Wolf, Peter (Scenic Designer)
Sweethearts 1947,Ja 22,31:2
Linden Tree, The 1948,Mr 3,28:2
Corn Is Green, The 1950,Ja 12,33:2
Devil's Disciple, The 1950,Ja 26,23:2
Heiress, The 1950,F 9,34:2
West Side Story 1964,Ap 9,24:2
To Broadway With Love 1964,Ap 30,28:6
Guys and Dolls 1965,Ap 29,39:1
Guys and Dolls 1966,Je 9,55:2
Sound of Music, The 1970,Jl 3,13:1
Wolf, Pierre (Playwright)
Embers 1926,F 2,20:3
Wolf, Richard R (Composer)
Plot Against the Chase Manhattan Bank, The
1963,N 27,29:1
Wolf, Simon
Love and Politics 1929,O 21,30:7
Slaves of Luxury 1930,F 8,13:3
Sonitchka 1930,Mr 8,21:3
Wolf, Tommy (Composer)
Nervous Set, The 1959,My 13,43:1
Wolf, Tommy (Miscellaneous)
Nervous Set, The 1959,My 13,43:1
Wolf, Tommy (Musical Director)
Nervous Set, The 1959,My 13,43:1
Wolf, Van (Miscellaneous)
Sunset 1966,My 13,34:1
Wolf, Willi (Playwright)
Zur Goldnen Liebe 1932,Ja 24,VIII,1:4
Wolf-Ferrari (Composer)
Secret of Suzanne, The 1920,Ja 13,10:2
Doctor Cupid 1952,Ag 14,19:6
Wolfe, Carol
Gondoliers, The 1940,O 1,29:2
Wolfe, Edwin
All the Way Home 1960,D 1,42:1
Wolfe, Edwin R
Ambush 1921,O 11,22:1
Boubouroche 1921,N 29,20:1
Wife With a Smile, The 1921,N 29,20:1
He Who Gets Slapped 1922,Ja 10,15:1
You and I 1925,O 20,29:1
Wolfe, Edwin R (Director)
Field God, The 1927,Ap 22,18:2
Mongolia 1927,D 27,24:5
Wolfe, Humbert (Playwright)
Silent Knight, The 1937,N 17,26:4
Silent Knight, The 1937,D 5,XII,5:8
Wolfe, Ian
Claw, The 1921,O 18,20:1
Gods of the Lightning 1928,O 25,27:2
Sea Gull, The 1929,Ap 10,32:2
At the Bottom 1930,Ja 10,24:3
Lysistrata 1930,Ap 29,30:5
Lysistrata 1930,Je 6,20:1
Devil in the Mind 1931,My 2,23:2
Lone Valley 1933,Mr 11,18:6
Winesburg, Ohio 1958,F 6,22:2
Deputy, The 1964,F 27,26:1
Murderous Angels 1970,F 8,70:1
Wolfe, Jacques (Composer)
John Henry 1939,D 12,36:4
John Henry 1939,D 17,IX,5:6
John Henry 1940,Ja 11,18:2
Wolfe, Joel
Room Service 1970,My 13,49:1
Wolfe, Jutta
Circle of Chalk, The 1941,Mr 27,28:4
Any Day Now 1941,Je 10,28:2
Oh, Herbert! 1945,Je 20,26:3
Truckline Cafe 1946,F 28,19:4
Desire Under the Elms 1952,Ja 17,23:4
Exiles 1957,Mr 13,27:1
Wolfe, Karin
Third Person 1955,D 30,13:4
Bye Bye Birdie 1960,Ap 15,13:4
Best Foot Forward 1963,Ap 3,43:1
Jo 1964,F 13,25:1
Autumn's Here 1966,O 26,40:1
Wolfe, Thomas (Original Author)
Web and the Rock, The 1950,Ag 20,II,1:1
Look Homeward, Angel 1957,N 29,33:1

Wolfe, Thomas (Original Author)—Cont
Look Homeward, Angel 1957,D 8,II,5:1
Look Homeward, Angel 1958,Ag 31,II,1:1
Look Homeward, Angel 1962,Ap 4,38:3
Wolfe, Thomas (Playwright)
Manor House 1953,D 27,53:4
Elsa Lanchester-Herself 1961,F 6,28:1
Welcome to Our City 1962,O 13,17:1
Wolfe, William
Lido Girl, The 1928,Ag 24,23:2
Wolferman, Barbara (Producer)
Blue Denim 1958,F 28,17:1
Wolfert, Pat
Sweet Bird of Youth 1956,Ap 17,27:2
Wolff, Art (Director)
Scaffold for Marionettes, A 1968,Mr 24,II,16:5
Wolff, Art (Miscellaneous)
Toilet, The 1964,D 17,51:1
Slave, The 1964,D 17,51:1
Veronica 1965,N 19,31:1
Bugs 1965,N 19,31:1
Wolff, Beverly
Saint of Bleecker Street, The 1965,Mr 19,28:1
Wolff, Colette
Evening With G B S, An; O'Flaherty, V C
1957,F 19,35:7
Christmas in the Market Place 1960,D 10,26:1
Resounding Tinkle, The 1961,Ap 4,42:2
Wolff, Egon (Playwright)
Invasores, Los 1970,D 12,20:1
Wolff, F Richard
Seven Against One 1930,My 7,25:1
Wolff, Frank
Billy Budd 1955,My 4,35:1
Highway Robbery 1955,N 8,36:1
Crucible, The 1958,Mr 17,21:1
Wolff, Frederic
Student Prince, The 1924,D 3,25:3
Wolff, Hank
Mexican Hayride 1944,Ja 29,9:6
Wolff, Joseph
Bury the Dead 1936,Ap 20,17:4
Prelude 1936,Ap 20,17:4
Wolff, Keinert
Barretts of Wimpole Street, The 1945,Mr 27,23:6
Song of Bernadette 1946,Mr 27,22:2
Wolff, Learned (Director)
Friedens Tragoedie 1936,N 17,34:4
Wolff, Marguerite (Translator)
Night Arrival 1938,D 25,IX,5:4
Wolff, Pierre (Playwright)
Chimin de Damas, Le 1921,N 20,VI,1:3
Apres l'Amour 1924,N 2,VIII,1:3
Temps d'Aimer, Le 1926,D 12,VIII,3:4
Belle de Nuit, La 1932,Ap 10,VIII,2:5
Wolff, Roger
Blue and the Gray, The; War Is Hell Gray, The
1929,D 27,26:4
Wolff, Ruth Rehrer (Translator)
Golem, The 1959,F 26,38:2
Wolff, William Almon (Playwright)
Broadway Interlude 1934,Ap 20,16:3
Wolff-Ferrari, Ermanno (Composer)
Four Brawlers, The 1928,Mr 4,IX,2:7
Wolffs, Hazel
King's Standards, The 1958,F 14,19:1
Reunion of Sorts 1969,O 15,40:1
Wolfgang, Roth (Costume Designer)
Androcles and the Lion 1946,D 20,29:2
Wolfgang, Roth (Scenic Designer)
Androcles and the Lion 1946,D 20,29:2
Wolfington, Iggie
Mrs McThing 1952,F 21,22:1
Mrs McThing 1952,Mr 2,II,1:1
One Eye Closed 1954,N 25,45:2
Music Man, The 1957,D 20,31:1
Music Man, The 1958,S 28,II,1:1
Can-Can 1962,My 17,32:2
Marathon '33 1963,D 23,20:1
Bedlam Galore, for Two or More 1965,Mr 8,34:1
Impromptu, L' 1965,Mr 8,34:1
Wolfit, Donald
Pirate Mallory 1935,O 8,26:3
Catiline 1936,Ja 28,14:6
Antony and Cleopatra 1936,N 1,X,3:7
Hamlet 1947,Ja 8,26:2
King Lear 1947,F 19,32:2
As You Like It 1947,F 21,16:2
Merchant of Venice, The 1947,F 24,16:2
Volpone 1947,F 25,32:2
Hamlet 1947,F 27,27:2
Tamburlaine the Great 1951,O 14,II,3:7
Strong Are Lonely, The 1956,F 5,II,3:1
All in Good Time 1965,F 19,25:1
Wolfit, Donald (Director)
King Lear 1947,F 19,32:2
As You Like It 1947,F 21,16:2
Merchant of Venice, The 1947,F 24,16:2
Volpone 1947,F 25,32:2
Hamlet 1947,F 27,27:2
Wolfit, Donald (Playwright)
Tamburlaine the Great 1956,Ja 20,19:1
Wolfit, Donald (Scenic Designer)
Volpone 1947,F 25,32:2

Wolfit, Donald (Scenic Designer)—Cont

Hamlet 1947,F 27,27:2
Wolfson, Bernice
Boutique Fantasque, La 1929,D 28,10:6
Wolfson, D S (Producer)
Summer Wives 1936,Ap 14,18:1
Wolfson, John (Playwright)
Route 1 1964,N 18,52:3
Wolfson, Martin
Little Clay Cart, The 1924,D 6,13:3
Critic, The 1925,My 9,12:4
Glass Slipper, The 1925,O 20,29:1
Goat Song 1926,Ja 26,18:1
Bad Habits of 1926 1926,My 1,11:1
Enchanted Isle 1927,S 20,33:2
Stairs, The 1927,N 8,32:7
Faust 1928,O 9,34:1
Marco Millions 1930,Mr 4,24:4
Did I Say No? 1931,S 23,19:4
Counsellor-at-Law 1931,N 7,17:2
Stevedore 1934,O 2,18:2
Sailors of Cattaro 1934,D 11,28:4
Black Pit 1935,Mr 21,26:6
Mother, The 1935,N 20,26:3
Co-Respondent Unknown 1936,F 12,24:4
Marching Song 1937,F 18,18:2
Yr Obedient Husband 1938,Ja 11,26:5
Ladies and Gentlemen 1939,O 18,30:2
No for an Answer 1941,Ja 6,10:6
Gabrielle 1941,Mr 26,26:2
Brooklyn, U S A 1941,D 22,24:2
Brooklyn, U S A 1941,D 28,IX,1:1
Cat Screams, The 1942,Je 17,26:5
Counterattack 1943,F 4,27:2
Counterattack 1943,F 14,II,1:1
Oedipus Rex 1945,D 17,16:7
Rip Van Winkle 1947,Jl 16,28:2
Cup of Trembling, The 1948,Ap 21,33:5
South Pacific 1949,Ap 8,30:2
South Pacific 1949,Ap 17,II,1:1
South Pacific 1949,Je 5,II,1:1
South Pacific 1951,Jl 10,30:5
South Pacific 1951,S 2,II,1:1
Guys and Dolls 1955,Ap 21,32:2
South Pacific 1955,My 5,39:5
Month in the Country, A 1956,Ap 4,23:1
South Pacific 1957,Ap 25,35:1
Goldilocks 1958,O 13,33:1
Guys and Dolls 1955,Jl 22,25:2
Cafe Crown 1964,Ap 18,32:1
Baker Street 1965,F 17,36:1
West Side Story 1968,Je 25,32:1
Great White Hope, The 1969,S 27,26:1
Wolfson, Martin (Director)
Tailor Becomes a Storekeeper, The 1938,Ap 14,26:3
Wolfson, Rosebud
Boutique Fantasque, La 1929,D 28,10:6
Wolfson, Steve
Absalom 1956,My 17,37:2
Heloise 1958,S 25,28:4
Sweet Confession 1959,Ap 15,30:1
Wolfson, Vera
Some of the People 1937,Mr 11,20:1
Wolfson, Victor
Counsellor-at-Law 1931,N 7,17:2
Wolfson, Victor (Director)
Crime and Punishment 1935,Ja 23,20:3
Mother, The 1935,N 20,26:3
Wolfson, Victor (Miscellaneous)
Brown Danube, The 1939,My 18,30:4
Wolfson, Victor (Original Author)
American Gothic 1953,N 11,35:6
Wolfson, Victor (Playwright)
Bitter Stream 1936,Mr 31,16:6
Excursion 1937,Ap 10,11:4
Excursion 1937,Ap 18,XI,1:1
Excursion 1937,Jl 27,24:3
Pastoral 1939,N 2,26:2
Family, The 1943,Mr 31,22:4
Pride's Crossing 1950,N 21,37:5
American Gothic 1953,N 11,35:6
Seventh Heaven 1955,My 27,16:2
Wolfson, Victor (Producer)
Crime and Punishment 1935,Ja 23,20:3
Wolheim, Louis
Letter of the Law, The; Robe Rouge, La 1920,F 24,11:1
Broken Wing, The 1920,N 30,14:1
Fair Circassian, The 1921,D 7,22:3
Idle Inn, The 1921,D 21,26:2
Hairy Ape, The 1922,Mr 10,18:2
Hairy Ape, The 1922,Ap 16,VI,1:1
Macbeth 1924,Mr 17,18:1
Catskill Dutch 1924,My 7,18:1
What Price Glory 1924,S 6,14:3
Lambs Gambol 1925,Ap 27,15:1
Pardon My Glove 1926,My 23,VIII,1:1
Wolheim, Louis (Playwright)
Claw, The 1921,O 18,20:1
Idle Inn, The 1921,D 21,26:2
Wolin, Donald (Producer)
Brass Ring, The 1952,Ap 11,19:2
Wolin, Donald M (Miscellaneous)
Enemy of the People, An 1950,D 29,14:1

Wolin, Doris
Jack in the Box 1960,My 19,43:3
Wolk, Jesse
Smile at Me 1935,Ag 24,18:4
Wolkind, Dorothy
Paradise 1931,My 12,29:2
Wolkoff, Hyman
Roaming Stars 1930,Ja 25,12:2
Chains 1930,F 23,29:2
Wollencott, Eric
Judgment Day 1934,S 13,26:4
Between Two Worlds 1934,O 26,24:2
Little Shot 1935,Ja 18,28:4
Times Have Changed 1935,F 26,16:1
I Want a Policeman! 1936,Ja 15,15:5
Crab Apple 1936,Jl 8,14:2
Daughters of Atreus 1936,O 15,33:1
Angel Island 1937,O 21,26:2
Wolman, Martin
Boutique Fantasque, La 1929,D 28,10:6
Wolmark, May
New Freedom, The 1930,My 15,32:4
New Freedom, The 1930,My 17,21:4
Wolmer, Phyllis
Pins and Needles 1922,F 2,20:1
Wolpe, Stefan (Composer)
Baal 1965,My 7,33:2
Exception and the Rule, The 1965,My 21,19:1
Wolper, Dave (Producer)
Follow the Girls 1944,Ap 10,15:2
Follow the Girls 1944,Ap 16,II,1:2
Men to the Sea 1944,O 4,25:2
Wolrond, Edward (Costume Designer)
Strong Breed, The 1967,N 10,60:1
Trials of Brother Jero, The 1967,N 10,60:1
Wolser, Harris
Lazarus Laughed 1948,Ap 9,27:4
Wolsk, Eugene (Producer)
Chaparral 1958,S 10,38:2
Lion in Winter, The 1966,Mr 4,23:1
Mark Twain Tonight! 1966,Mr 24,48:2
Investigation, The 1966,O 5,40:1
Something Different 1967,N 29,52:1
Wolsky, Albert (Costume Designer)
Your Own Thing 1968,Ja 15,33:1
Little Murders 1969,Ja 6,38:1
White House Murder Case, The 1970,F 19,59:1
Wolston-Hallett, Mary
Rutherford and Son 1927,Ap 13,29:2
Wolveridge, Carol
Innocents, The 1952,Jl 4,9:7
Bad Seed, The 1955,My 1,II,3:1
Wolvin, Roy
Naughty-Naught '00 1946,O 21,27:5
Womack, Joyce
Liliom 1956,F 18,12:5
Womble, Andre
Little Foxes, The 1967,O 27,53:1
To Be Young Gifted and Black; World of Lorraine Hansberry, The 1969,Ja 3,15:1
Akokawe 1970,Je 5,21:1
Womrath, G Fred (Producer)
Joy of Living 1931,Ap 7,31:1
Wonder, Tommy
Two for the Show 1940,F 9,14:2
Two for the Show 1940,F 18,IX,2:1
Banjo Eyes 1941,D 26,20:2
Ziegfeld Follies 1943,Ap 2,16:2
Tickets, Please! 1950,Ap 28,25:2
Wong, Anna May
Circle of Chalk, The 1929,Mr 31,VIII,2:6
On the Spot 1930,O 30,33:3
Princess Turandot 1937,Ag 3,20:5
Wong, Irene
Roar China! 1930,O 28,23:1
Wong, Joe
Vaudeville (Palace) 1931,My 25,17:4
Vaudeville (Palace) 1932,Je 6,18:2
Blackouts of 1949 1949,S 7,39:2
Wonn, Edward
Alias Jimmy Valentine 1921,D 9,20:3
Paradise Alley 1924,Ap 2,17:3
Wontner, Arthur
Love in Pawn 1923,Ap 8,VIII,1:7
Captive, The 1926,S 30,23:1
Captive, The 1926,O 10,VIII,1:1
Mariners 1927,Mr 29,22:2
Interference 1927,O 19,24:3
This Way to Paradise 1930,Ja 31,24:2
Napoleon: The Hundred Days 1932,My 8,VIII,1:3
Twelfth Night 1932,Ag 7,IX,1:6
Philomel 1932,D 4,IX,3:8
Great Experiment, The 1936,Ap 22,28:4
Woo, Helen
Master of the Inn, The 1925,D 23,22:2
Wood, Alice
Animal Crackers 1928,O 24,26:2
It's the Valet 1933,D 15,25:4
Wood, Allan (Playwright)
Weak Link, The 1940,Mr 5,19:2
Wood, Angela
John Brown's Body 1960,Je 22,31:1
Friends and Lovers; Proposal, The 1961,My 11,43:1

Wood, Angela—Cont

Six Characters in Search of an Author 1961,My 11,43:1
Hidden Stranger 1963,Ja 10,5:5
Six Characters in Search of an Author 1963,Mr 11,7:2
Hamlet 1969,Je 11,37:1
Hamlet 1969,Je 22,II,1:7
Wood, Arthur
Dream Maker, The 1921,N 22,17:1
Barnum Was Right 1923,Mr 13,19:3
Money Business 1926,Ja 21,18:1
Ghost Train, The 1926,Ag 26,17:2
Wonderful Night, A; Fledermaus, Die 1929,N 1,23:3
On the Make 1932,My 24,23:2
Ghost Writer, The 1933,Je 20,22:4
Fiesta 1933,D 16,12:2
Wood, Austin
Laugh It Off 1925,Ap 25,18:4
Wood, Barbara (Miscellaneous)
I Dreamt I Dwelt in Bloomingdale's 1970,F 13,26:1
Sensations 1970,O 26,48:2
Wood, Beatrice
Great Way, The 1921,N 8,28:2
Wood, Bert
Annie Get Your Gun 1958,F 20,29:2
Wood, Bert (Miscellaneous)
Drink to Me Only 1958,O 9,47:4
Paris Is Out! 1970,F 3,35:1
Wood, Bert C
Dark Hours, The 1932,N 15,24:2
If This Be Treason 1935,S 24,28:2
Wood, Bertram
Trojan Horse, The 1940,O 31,28:3
On Your Toes 1954,O 12,24:4
Wood, Britt
Vaudeville (Palace) 1932,My 30,16:7
Wood, Charles
Sally 1948,My 7,31:2
Kiss Me, Kate 1948,D 31,10:3
Song of Norway 1958,Je 23,19:2
Wood, Charles (Director)
Anvil, The 1961,Ag 8,32:2
Wood, Charles (Playwright)
H 1969,F 14,34:2
Wood, Charles H Jr
Romeo and Juliet 1940,Ap 16,28:4
Wood, Charles R (Director)
Anvil, The 1962,O 31,33:3
Wood, Charles R (Producer)
God and Kate Murphy 1959,F 27,21:2
Anvil, The 1962,O 31,33:3
Wood, Charles Winter
Green Pastures, The 1935,F 27,16:2
Green Pastures, The 1935,Mr 24,VIII,1:1
Wood, Cyrus (Lyricist)
Blushing Bride, The 1922,F 7,12:1
Lady in Ermine, The 1922,O 3,22:2
Springtime of Youth 1922,O 27,15:1
Lovely Lady 1927,D 30,22:1
Wood, Cyrus (Playwright)
Blushing Bride, The 1922,F 7,12:1
Sally, Irene and Mary 1922,S 5,21:2
Lady in Ermine, The 1922,O 3,22:2
June Days 1925,Ag 7,12:5
Lovely Lady 1927,D 30,22:1
Street Singer, The 1929,Jl 28,VIII,1:6
Street Singer, The 1929,S 18,35:2
Woof, Woof 1929,D 26,20:4
Good Night Ladies 1945,Ja 18,16:2
Ladies Night in a Turkish Bath 1961,Mr 22,38:1
Wood, David (Playwright)
Stiffkey Scandals of 1932, The 1969,Je 14,24:3
Wood, Deedee (Choreographer)
Do Re Mi 1960,D 27,23:2
Wood, Dorothy (Director)
Mikado, The 1935,Ag 24,17:5
Wood, Douglas
Little Old New York 1920,S 9,9:2
Marie Antoinette 1921,N 23,16:1
Wild Oats Lane 1922,S 7,12:1
Give and Take 1923,Ja 19,13:1
Wild Westcotts, The 1923,S 25,26:2
Sweet Seventeen 1924,Mr 18,24:2
Milgrim's Progress 1924,D 23,17:1
Trelawney of the 'Wells' 1925,Je 2,16:2
Sandalwood 1926,S 23,23:1
Bye Bye Bonnie 1927,Ja 14,15:3
Madame X 1927,Jl 7,29:3
Gods of the Lightning 1928,O 25,27:2
Old Rascal, The 1930,Mr 25,34:4
Marseilles 1930,N 18,28:2
She Means Business 1931,Ja 27,21:2
Good Fairy, The 1931,N 25,17:1
Take a Chance 1932,N 28,11:2
Good-Bye to Love 1940,Je 8,18:1
Jane Eyre 1958,My 2,31:1
Wood, Douglas (Director)
Half-Naked Truth, The 1926,Je 8,23:1
Wood, Edythe
Bruno and Sidney 1949,My 4,38:2
Wood, Elaine
Measure for Measure 1969,Je 13,41:3

993

Wood, Ellie
Buffalo Skinner, The 1959,F 20,18:1
'Toinette 1961,N 21,46:1
Wood, Ernest
Marriage Bed, The 1929,Ja 8,35:1
Wood, Eugene
Eyes 1930,My 10,25:1
Oscar Wilde 1957,Ap 20,21:3
Pajama Game, The 1957,My 16,27:1
Marvellous History of Saint Bernard, The
  1958,F 24,16:3
Courtyard 1960,Mr 1,28:1
Cherry Orchard, The 1960,Je 4,17:2
Borak 1960,D 14,51:1
Subways Are for Sleeping 1961,D 28,22:1
Bring Me a Warm Body 1962,Ap 17,29:3
Anvil, The 1962,O 31,33:3
Night of the Auk 1963,My 22,35:2
Dream of Swallows, A 1964,Ap 15,46:1
Kiss Me, Kate 1965,My 13,31:1
This Here Nice Place 1966,N 2,35:2
Great White Hope, The 1967,D 14,58:1
Iceman Cometh, The 1968,Ap 1,58:1
Great White Hope, The 1968,O 4,40:1
Good Woman of Setzuan, The 1970,N 6,51:1
Wood, Eugene (Director)
Lawrence of Arabia 1954,D 10,35:3
Wood, F Carter
Betty Behave 1927,Mr 9,28:4
Wood, Forrest
Career 1957,My 1,42:6
Golden Six, The 1958,O 27,31:2
Wood, Frank J
Immodest Violet 1920,Ag 25,6:2
Wood, Freeman
Ruined Lady, The 1920,Ja 21,10:2
Wood, G
Cyrano de Bergerac 1953,N 13,24:3
Richard III 1953,D 10,65:2
King and the Duke, The 1955,Je 2,25:2
Ronde, La 1955,Je 28,24:2
Cradle Song 1955,D 2,32:2
Thunder Rock 1956,F 27,18:1
Lesson, The 1956,O 3,29:2
Thor, With Angels 1956,O 15,29:4
Box of Watercolors, A 1957,F 18,22:2
Tobias and the Angel 1957,O 21,29:5
Potting Shed, The 1958,N 3,49:2
Kittiwake Island 1960,O 13,43:1
Seagull, The 1964,Ap 6,36:1
Crucible, The 1964,Ap 7,30:2
Major Barbara 1965,My 18,33:1
Imaginary Invalid, The 1967,My 2,53:1
Touch of the Poet, A 1967,My 3,38:2
Still Life 1967,My 4,34:1
John Brown's Body 1968,F 13,49:2
Comedy of Errors, The 1968,F 28,40:2
She Stoops to Conquer 1968,Ap 1,58:3
Henry V 1969,N 11,43:1
Wood, G (Composer)
Rose in the Wilderness 1949,Ja 5,21:2
King and the Duke, The 1955,Je 2,25:2
Ronde, La 1955,Je 28,24:2
Cradle Song 1955,D 2,32:2
Box of Watercolors, A 1957,F 18,22:2
Wood, G (Director)
Fumed Oak 1967,My 4,34:1
Comedy of Errors, The 1968,F 28,40:2
Wood, G (Lyricist)
Shoestring '57 1956,N 6,31:1
Box of Watercolors, A 1957,F 18,22:2
Wood, G (Miscellaneous)
Imaginary Invalid, The 1967,My 2,53:1
Wood, G (Musical Director)
Rose in the Wilderness 1949,Ja 5,21:2
Wood, G (Playwright)
Box of Watercolors, A 1957,F 18,22:2
Wood, Gar
My Sweet Charlie 1966,D 7,56:1
Wood, Gordon B
John Brown's Body 1953,F 16,17:2
Wood, Harlington Jr
Forever This Land 1951,Jl 29,II,1:1
Forever This Land 1952,Je 30,14:6
Forever This Land 1952,Jl 6,II,1:1
Wood, Harriet
Gala Night 1930,F 26,22:4
Wood, Harry
Good Earth, The 1932,O 18,23:4
Wood, Haydn (Composer)
Dear Love 1930,My 18,VIII,3:1
Wood, Haydn (Lyricist)
Dear Love 1930,My 18,VIII,3:1
Wood, Helen
Seventeen 1951,Je 22,16:6
Pal Joey 1952,Ja 4,17:6
Pal Joey 1952,F 17,II,13:5
Ziegfeld Follies 1957,Mr 2,19:2
Rosalie 1957,Je 26,28:2
Wonder World 1964,My 18,32:1
Wood, Henry (Mrs) (Original Author)
Boo Hoo! East Lynne 1959,S 9,50:4

Wood, Henry (Mrs) (Playwright)
East Lynne 1926,Mr 11,18:4
Royal Baggage 1934,O 27,20:5
Boo Hoo! East Lynne 1959,S 9,50:4
Wood, Ireland
Daphne Laureola 1950,S 19,38:6
Wood, Ireland (Playwright)
Up the Garden Path 1937,Jl 7,26:2
Wood, Jacquie (Costume Designer)
Fig Leaf in Her Bonnet, A 1961,Je 15,50:1
Wood, John
Rosencrantz and Guildenstern Are Dead
  1967,O 17,53:1
Rosencrantz and Guildenstern Are Dead
  1967,O 29,II,1:1
Exiles 1970,N 19,42:4
Wood, John (Miscellaneous)
Jungle of Cities 1970,Mr 1,75:2
Wood, Joseph (Composer)
Twelfth Night 1941,D 3,32:2
Land of Fame 1943,S 22,31:5
Wood, Judith
Dinner at Eight 1932,O 24,18:2
Play, Genius, Play! 1935,O 31,17:2
Wood, Kelly
Cindy 1964,S 25,33:1
Pequod 1969,Je 30,33:1
Wood, Larry
Springtime of Youth 1922,O 27,15:1
Billie 1928,O 2,34:2
Wood, Leo (Lyricist)
Letty Pepper 1922,Ap 11,22:2
Wood, Lillian
Ed Wynn's Carnival 1920,Ap 6,18:2
Wood, Lois
Hotel Mouse, The 1922,Mr 14,11:3
Wood, Lou
Three's a Crowd 1930,O 16,28:3
Wood, Marcia
Shoemaker's Holiday, The 1967,Mr 3,25:1
Wood, Marjorie
Madame Pierre 1922,F 16,11:1
Man in Evening Clothes, The 1924,D 6,13:4
Little Minister, The 1925,Mr 24,21:1
Something to Brag About 1925,Ag 14,14:3
Joker, The 1925,N 17,29:1
Yellow 1926,S 22,30:1
Happy Landing 1932,Mr 28,10:5
Good Earth, The 1932,O 18,23:4
Big Hearted Herbert 1934,Ja 2,17:3
Good-Bye Please 1934,O 25,26:6
Rain 1935,Ag 27,23:4
Alice Takat 1936,F 11,19:2
Bitter Stream 1936,Mr 31,16:6
Women, The 1936,D 28,13:1
Lady Windermere's Fan 1946,O 15,29:2
Wood, Maxine (Playwright)
On Whitman Avenue 1946,My 9,28:2
Wood, May
Hot Money 1931,N 9,22:2
Wood, Michael
Midsummer Night's Dream, A 1968,D 9,59:1
Wood, Mike
Twelfth Night 1970,Ja 1,18:1
Wood, Milton
St Louis Woman 1946,Ap 1,22:2
Wood, Norma Jean
House of Leather, The 1970,Mr 19,56:1
Wood, Peggy
Untitled-Benefit 1921,My 2,12:3
Main Street 1921,Jl 24,VI,1:1
Marjolaine 1922,Ja 25,16:1
Clinging Vine, The 1922,D 25,20:2
Clinging Vine, The 1922,D 31,VII,1:1
Bride, The 1924,My 6,25:1
Bride, The 1924,My 11,VIII,1:1
Candida 1925,Ap 5,IX,1:2
Candida 1925,Ap 26,VIII,1:1
Candida 1925,N 10,23:4
Henry IV, Part I 1926,Je 1,29:1
Lady in Love, A 1927,F 22,22:1
Lady in Love, A 1927,F 27,VII,1:1
Merchant of Venice, The 1928,Ja 10,38:6
Merchant of Venice, The 1928,Ja 17,22:2
Play Without a Name, A 1928,N 26,30:5
Bitter Sweet 1929,Jl 19,14:2
Saturday Night 1933,Mr 1,13:2
Saturday Night 1933,Mr 19,IX,1:1
Best Sellers 1933,My 4,20:2
Champagne, Sec 1933,O 16,20:2
Closed Room, The 1934,Jl 24,20:2
Birthday 1934,D 27,24:2
Miss Quis 1937,Ap 2,18:5
Miss Quis 1937,Ap 8,20:5
Never Trouble Trouble 1937,Ag 18,15:2
Operette 1938,F 18,22:3
Operette 1938,Mr 17,17:4
Operette 1938,Ap 3,XI,1:8
Love for Love 1940,Je 4,19:5
Old Acquaintance 1940,D 10,33:5
Old Acquaintance 1940,D 24,18:3
Blithe Spirit 1941,N 6,26:2
Blithe Spirit 1941,N 16,IX,1:1

Wood, Peggy—Cont
Actors Fund Fete 1942,F 23,24:5
Blithe Spirit 1943,S 12,II,1:1
Happiest Years, The 1949,Ap 26,29:8
ANTA Album 1950,Ja 30,13:2
Getting Married 1951,My 14,28:5
Charley's Aunt 1953,D 23,22:2
Candida 1957,Mr 29,18:5
Girls in 509, The 1958,O 16,47:1
Rape of the Belt, The 1960,N 7,46:1
Knight From Olmedo, The 1962,N 26,36:2
Opening Night 1963,O 3,28:2
Pictures in the Hallway 1964,D 17,51:1
Madrigal of Shakespeare, A 1968,F 14,56:2
Madwoman of Chaillot, The 1970,Mr 23,48:3
Passage to E M Forster, A 1970,O 28,62:1
Wood, Peter (Director)
Iceman Cometh, The 1958,Ja 30,18:3
As You Like It 1959,Jl 1,27:1
As You Like It 1959,Jl 5,II,1:1
Hamlet 1961,Ap 12,46:1
Beggar's Opera, The 1963,Jl 17,20:1
Public Eye, The 1963,O 10,51:1
Private Ear, The 1963,O 10,51:1
Semi-Detached 1963,O 20,II,1:1
Master Builder, The 1964,Je 10,50:2
Poor Richard 1964,D 3,59:1
Love for Love 1967,O 21,17:1
Love for Love 1967,O 30,59:1
Wood, Philip
John Hawthorne 1921,Ja 24,16:1
White Villa, The 1921,F 15,7:1
Liliom 1921,Ap 21,18:1
Cloister, The 1921,Je 6,16:3
Sandro Botticelli 1923,Mr 27,24:2
Casanova 1923,S 27,10:2
Starlight 1925,Mr 4,17:2
Hamlet 1925,O 12,19:2
Merchant of Venice, The 1925,D 28,12:1
Cyrano de Bergerac 1926,F 19,18:1
American Tragedy, An 1926,O 12,31:2
Celebrity 1927,D 27,24:3
Gentlemen of the Press 1928,Ag 28,27:2
House Unguarded 1929,Ja 16,22:2
Good Earth, The 1932,O 18,23:4
First Legion, The 1934,O 2,18:2
Battleship Gertie 1935,Ja 19,9:2
Jumbo 1935,N 18,20:2
Sweet River 1936,O 29,30:2
Sun Kissed 1937,Mr 11,20:2
Room Service 1937,My 20,16:1
Devil Takes a Bride, The 1938,O 8,10:3
Primrose Path, The 1939,Ja 5,16:3
Primrose Path, The 1939,Ja 16,11:2
Wood, Philip (Playwright)
Lend Me Your Ears! 1936,O 6,28:5
Wood, Robert M
Fiesta 1933,D 16,12:2
What a Relief 1935,D 14,10:6
Wood, Roland
Texas Town 1941,Ap 30,22:3
Two Blind Mice 1949,Mr 3,32:2
Enchanted, The 1950,Ja 19,34:2
Tree Grows in Brooklyn, A 1951,Ap 20,24:3
Time Out for Ginger 1952,N 27,50:4
Frogs of Spring, The 1953,O 21,36:2
Winesburg, Ohio 1958,F 6,22:2
Quare Fellow, The 1958,N 28,34:1
Our Town 1959,Mr 24,46:2
Dragon, The 1963,Ap 10,32:1
Hogan's Goat 1965,N 12,56:1
Wood, Stanley
Hindu, The 1922,Mr 22,13:3
Peer Gynt 1923,F 6,14:1
Glass Slipper, The 1925,O 20,29:1
Merchants of Glory 1925,D 15,28:3
Chief Thing, The 1926,Mr 23,24:2
Faust 1928,O 9,34:1
On the Spot 1930,O 30,33:3
Reunion in Vienna 1931,N 17,31:1
Within the Gates 1934,O 23,23:1
Mother, The 1935,N 20,26:3
Love on the Dole 1936,F 25,23:3
Marching Song 1937,F 18,18:2
Eve of St Mark, The 1942,O 8,30:2
Wood, Stuart Craig
Lovely Ladies, Kind Gentlemen 1970,D 29,38:1
Wood, Victor
Rats of Norway, The 1948,Ap 16,27:6
Faithfully Yours 1951,O 19,22:5
Wood, Wallace
Crooked Friday, The 1925,O 9,27:3
Easy Virtue 1925,D 8,28:2
Wood, Wee Georgie
Vaudeville (Palace) 1923,O 30,16:1
Vaudeville (Palace) 1927,O 18,32:4
Wood, William T S (Director)
Rose, The 1922,D 30,13:4
Monkey's Paw, The 1922,D 30,13:4
Why Not? 1922,D 30,13:4
Woodall, James
Walk in Darkness 1963,O 29,30:2
Woodard, Dolores
Our Lan' 1947,Ap 19,11:2

Woodard, Ernest
Confederacy, The 1958,Jl 3,20:1
Woodburn, Bill
Days Between, The 1965,Je 4,39:1
Woodburn, James
Victoria Regina 1935,D 27,15:2
Spring Meeting 1938,D 9,30:4
Woodburn, Joseph
Sweet Land of Liberty 1929,S 24,29:2
Woodburn, Robert
Round Trip 1945,My 30,16:4
Woodbury, Clare
Family Upstairs, The 1925,Ag 18,14:2
Broadway 1926,S 17,19:3
Little Accident 1928,O 10,32:3
Housewarming 1932,Ap 8,25:1
Lilly Turner 1932,S 20,26:1
20th Century 1932,D 30,15:1
Ghost Writer, The 1933,Je 20,22:4
Hat, a Coat, a Glove, A 1934,F 1,15:2
Fly Away Home 1935,Ja 16,20:4
Stick-in-the-Mud 1935,D 2,18:2
Russet Mantle 1936,Ja 17,15:5
Days to Come 1936,D 16,35:1
Missouri Legend 1938,S 20,27:2
Johnny Belinda 1940,S 19,26:2
Apple of His Eye 1946,F 6,18:2
Woodbury, David O (Playwright)
Escape Into Glory 1941,Mr 20,24:2
Woodbury, Frances
Maggie, the Magnificent 1929,O 22,26:1
It Pays to Sin 1933,N 4,18:6
This Thing Called Love 1935,Jl 2,24:4
Empress of Destiny 1938,Mr 10,16:2
Pillar to Post 1943,D 11,11:2
Wooddell, Barbara
Man Who Came to Dinner, The 1939,O 17,31:1
Mr and Mrs North 1941,Ja 13,11:2
Woodell, Pat
Untitled-Revue 1965,Je 25,38:1
Woodford, Jack (Playwright)
Two for Fun 1961,F 14,45:3
Woodford, Jennie
Rockefeller and the Red Indians 1968,O 25,37:1
Woodgate, Herbert (Major) (Playwright)
Tarzan of the Apes 1921,S 8,14:3
Woodhead, Ed
Androcles and the Lion 1946,D 20,29:2
Yellow Jack 1947,F 28,26:2
Woodhull, Daniel E Jr
Hamlet 1927,Ap 7,23:3
Caesar and Cleopatra 1927,N 6,IX,2:1
Woodhull, Harrison
Abe Lincoln in Illinois 1938,O 17,12:2
Woodhull, Harrison (Producer)
Miracle in the Mountains 1947,Ap 26,10:2
Two Blind Mice 1949,Mr 3,32:2
Woodhull, J W
Tiger Smiles, The 1930,D 18,29:1
Wooding, Grace
Dreams for Sale 1922,S 14,24:1
Wooding, Russell (Composer)
Promis' Lan', De 1930,My 28,31:2
Woodle, John C
What a Relief 1935,D 14,10:6
Woodley, Percy
Grand Duke, The 1921,N 2,20:1
Shore Leave 1922,Ag 9,20:2
Dearest Enemy 1925,S 19,9:2
Mima 1928,D 13,24:2
Dancing Partner 1930,Ag 6,24:2
I Love an Actress 1931,S 18,29:2
Woodlin, Haas
Sweet River 1936,O 29,30:2
Woodlock, Joanne
Idiot's Delight 1951,My 24,46:3
Woodman, Arthur
Tenth Man, The 1929,Mr 21,29:2
Woodman, David
Enemy of the People, An 1959,F 5,24:4
Woodman, Lorrine
On the Level 1937,Mr 26,24:4
Woodman, William (Miscellaneous)
Geranium Hat, The 1959,Mr 18,45:1
Deirdre of the Sorrows 1959,O 15,46:1
PS 193 1962,O 31,33:1
Woodner, Beverly (Costume Designer)
Joy to the World 1948,Mr 19,28:2
Woodring, Richard
Priest in the Cellar, The 1969,F 19,39:1
Woodruff, Betty
Little Poor Man, The 1925,Ag 6,14:1
Woodruff, Charlotte
Artists and Models 1923,Ag 21,12:2
Betty Lee 1924,D 26,18:2
Great Temptations, The 1926,My 19,29:1
White Lilacs 1928,S 11,31:2
Fortune Teller, The 1929,N 5,32:3
Woodruff, Eleanor
Nemesis 1921,Ap 5,24:3
Honors Are Even 1921,Ag 11,8:2

Back to Methuselah (Part II: The Gospel of the
  Brothers Barnabas); Gospel of the Brothers
  Barnabas, The (Back to Methuselah, Part II)
  1922,F 28,17:2
Back to Methuselah (Part IV: The Tragedy of an
  Elderly Gentleman); Tragedy of an Elderly
  Gentleman, The (Back to Methuselah, Part IV)
  1922,Mr 7,11:1
Back to Methuselah (Part V: As Far as Thought
  Can Reach); As Far as Thought Can Reach (Back
  to Methuselah, Part V) 1922,Mr 14,11:2
Six Characters in Search of an Author
  1922,O 31,11:2
Song and Dance Man, The 1924,Ja 1,21:2
Locked Door, The 1924,Je 20,17:2
Donovan Affair, The 1926,Ag 31,15:2
Revelry 1927,S 13,37:1
Crashing Through 1928,O 30,26:5
Flight 1929,F 19,22:3
Great Barrington, The 1931,F 20,18:1
Breadwinner, The 1931,S 23,19:4
Woodruff, Frank
Venetian, The 1931,N 2,26:1
Stork Is Dead, The 1932,S 24,18:2
They Shall Not Die 1934,F 22,24:4
Woodruff, Harriet
Hospitality 1922,N 14,16:1
Heart of Frances, The 1923,Ja 29,11:2
Woodruff, Helen S (Lyricist)
Just Because 1922,Mr 23,11:1
Woodruff, Helen S (Playwright)
Just Because 1922,Mr 23,11:1
Woodruff, Joane
Boutique Fantasque, La 1929,D 28,10:6
Mascaiada 1929,D 28,10:6
Woodruff, Kenneth
Trial of Dr Beck, The 1937,Ag 10,22:2
Woodruff, Roland
Yes, Yes, Yvette 1927,O 4,32:3
Woods, A H (Miscellaneous)
Melo 1931,Ap 17,26:6
Abide With Me 1935,N 22,19:2
Woods, A H (Producer)
Fake, The 1924,O 7,26:3
Green Hat, The 1925,Ap 5,IX,2:4
Kiss in a Taxi, The 1925,Ag 26,14:1
All Dressed Up 1925,S 10,28:1
Green Hat, The 1925,S 16,23:2
Pelican, The 1925,S 22,23:2
These Charming People 1925,O 7,31:2
Stolen Fruit 1925,O 8,31:4
Shanghai Gesture, The 1926,F 2,20:2
Untitled-Magic Show 1926,My 24,24:2
Ghost Train, The 1926,Ag 26,17:2
Potash and Perlmutter, Detectives; Poisoned by
  Pictures 1926,S 1,27:3
Woman Disputed, A 1926,S 29,23:2
Illusioniste, L' 1927,Ja 11,36:5
Crime 1927,F 23,27:3
Her Cardboard Lover 1927,Mr 22,30:5
Mr What's-His-Name 1927,S 4,VII,2:4
Trial of Mary Dugan, The 1927,S 20,33:1
Matrimonial Bed, The 1927,O 13,23:2
Mulberry Bush, The 1927,O 27,33:1
Fanatics, The 1927,N 8,32:4
Man With Red Hair, A 1928,Je 17,VIII,1:6
Fast Life 1928,S 27,35:2
Jealousy 1928,O 23,32:2
Scarlet Pages 1929,S 1,VIII,1:1
Scarlet Pages 1929,S 10,26:3
Murder on the Second Floor 1929,S 12,35:1
Scotland Yard 1929,S 28,16:6
Recapture 1930,Ja 30,16:4
Love, Honor and Betray 1930,Mr 13,22:2
9th Street Guest, The 1930,Ag 26,24:3
Farewell to Arms, A 1930,S 23,30:3
Five Star Final 1930,D 31,11:1
Inside Story, The 1932,F 23,23:2
Stork Is Dead, The 1932,S 24,18:2
Move on, Sister 1933,O 25,22:4
Red Cat, The 1934,S 20,21:1
Night of January 16 1935,S 17,26:4
Ragged Edge, The 1935,N 26,28:3
Name Your Poison 1936,Ja 21,27:4
Censored 1938,F 28,18:2
Good-Bye to Love 1940,Je 8,18:1
Nine Girls 1943,Ja 14,26:2
Try and Get It 1943,Ag 3,13:2
Woods, Al (Producer)
Good Old Days, The 1923,Ag 19,VI,1:1
Woods, Alfred
Bridge of Distances, The 1925,S 29,30:1
Woods, Allan (Director)
Black Quartet, A; Gentleman Caller, The
  1969,Jl 31,28:1
Woods, Allie
Song of the Lusitanian Bogey, The 1968,Ja 3,52:1
Kongi's Harvest 1968,Ap 15,49:1
Daddy Goodness 1968,Je 5,37:1
God Is a (Guess What?) 1968,D 18,56:1
Malcochon 1969,Ap 2,37:1
Contribution 1969,Ap 2,37:1
Man Better Man 1969,Jl 3,22:1

Woods, Allie—Cont
Day of Absence 1970,Mr 18,39:1
Akokawe 1970,Je 5,21:1
Woods, Allie (Director)
Gentleman Caller, The 1969,Ap 27,92:1
Gentleman Caller, The 1969,Ag 3,II,1:4
Woods, Barbara
Master Builder, The 1955,Mr 2,23:2
Woods, Bert (Miscellaneous)
Wonderful Town 1963,F 15,10:2
Pal Joey 1963,My 30,21:1
Woods, Carson
Under Milk Wood 1957,O 16,42:5
Woods, Cyrus (Lyricist)
Dew Drop Inn 1923,My 18,26:4
Woods, Donald
Singapore 1932,N 15,24:2
Quiet, Please! 1940,O 20,IX,2:3
Quiet, Please! 1940,N 9,20:3
Rosmersholm 1962,Ap 12,42:1
Rosmersholm 1962,Ap 22,II,1:1
Damn You, Scarlett O'Hara 1964,F 5,30:1
All My Pretty Little Ones 1964,F 5,30:1
One by One 1964,D 2,60:1
Woods, Edward
Speakeasy 1927,S 27,30:1
Trapped 1928,S 12,25:3
Zeppelin 1929,Ja 15,22:3
Houseparty 1929,S 10,26:5
Sky's the Limit, The 1934,D 18,25:5
White Hell 1935,Ag 13,20:3
One Good Year 1935,N 28,38:3
Tortilla Flat 1938,Ja 13,16:2
Woods, Edward (Producer)
Buttrio Square 1952,O 15,40:2
Woods, Eugenia
Chalk Dust 1936,Mr 5,24:5
Path of Flowers, The 1936,S 18,19:3
Big Blow 1938,O 3,11:2
Woods, F J
Skirt, The 1921,N 8,28:1
Woods, Forrest
Piper, The 1920,Mr 20,14:2
Woods, Franker
Queen O' Hearts 1922,O 11,22:1
Hit the Deck! 1927,Ap 26,32:1
Present Arms 1928,Ap 27,16:2
Vanderbilt Revue, The 1930,N 6,22:6
Woods, Jack
Moment Musical 1943,Je 1,18:1
Physicists, The 1964,O 14,52:1
Woods, Jack (Miscellaneous)
Debut 1956,F 23,32:1
Cranks 1956,N 27,32:1
Woods, James
South Pacific 1969,Jl 7,27:1
Borstal Boy 1970,Ap 1,38:1
Saved 1970,O 29,57:1
Saved 1970,N 1,II,10:1
Woods, Jill
Noah 1954,O 11,32:2
Woods, Johnny
Vaudeville (Palace) 1932,My 9,19:3
Earl Carroll's Vanities 1940,Ja 15,11:2
Woods, Josephine
Love in Our Time 1952,O 4,14:3
Simply Heavenly 1957,My 22,28:2
Goose, The 1960,Mr 16,44:1
Woods, Larry
Mystery Moon 1930,Je 24,23:4
Woods, Lesley
Double Dummy 1936,N 12,30:1
Excursion 1937,Ap 10,11:4
Comes the Revelation 1942,My 27,26:2
Assassin, The 1945,O 18,20:2
Infernal Machine, The 1954,Mr 22,22:2
Doll's House, A 1954,N 15,32:2
Merchant of Venice, The 1955,Ja 8,9:7
Entertain a Ghost 1962,Ap 10,48:1
Case of Libel, A 1963,O 11,43:2
Woods, Louise
Shuffle Along 1952,My 9,20:5
Woods, Margie
Schoolgirl 1930,N 21,31:1
Woods, Mr (Director)
Steam Roller, The 1924,O 26,VIII,2:1
Woods, Ralph
Caesar and Cleopatra 1935,Ag 22,21:1
Woods, Richard
My Heart's in the Highlands 1950,F 18,8:4
Captain Brassbound's Conversion 1950,D 28,21:1
American Gothic 1953,N 11,35:6
Eastward in Eden 1956,Ap 18,25:4
Long Gallery, The 1958,Mr 7,17:2
Beg, Borrow or Steal 1960,F 11,39:4
Sandbox, The 1960,My 17,42:2
Two Executioners, The 1960,My 17,42:2
Chip, The 1960,My 17,42:2
Miracle, The 1960,D 5,42:3
Donogoo 1961,Ja 19,25:3
Caesar and Cleopatra 1963,Ag 1,18:2
Right You Are (If You Think You Are)
  1964,Mr 5,37:1
Tavern, The 1964,Mr 6,39:2

Woods, Richard—Cont
Impromptu at Versailles 1964,Mr 10,43:1
Lower Depths, The 1964,Mr 31,30:1
Man and Superman 1964,D 7,45:2
War and Peace 1965,Ja 12,32:1
You Can't Take It With You 1965,N 24,32:1
School for Scandal, The 1966,N 22,33:2
Right You Are (If You Think You Are)
 1966,N 23,34:2
Wild Duck, The 1967,Ja 12,49:1
Pantagleize 1967,D 1,54:1
Exit the King 1968,Ja 10,48:1
Exit the King 1968,Ja 21,II,1:2
Cherry Orchard, The 1968,Mr 20,41:1
Cock-A-Doodle Dandy 1969,Ja 21,40:1
Hamlet 1969,Mr 4,34:1
Year Boston Won the Pennant, The
 1969,My 23,38:1
Coco 1969,D 19,66:1
Woods, Robert
Anathema 1923,Ap 11,16:2
Come Angel Band 1936,F 19,17:1
Young Madame Conti 1937,Ap 1,18:4
Woods, Robert (Miscellaneous)
Moby Dick 1955,Ap 26,25:3
Six Characters in Search of an Author
 1955,D 12,38:1
Miss Julie 1956,F 22,23:2
Stronger, The 1956,F 22,23:2
Queen After Death 1956,Mr 13,33:2
Month in the Country, A 1956,Ap 4,23:1
Littlest Revue, The 1956,My 23,37:2
Good Woman of Setzuan, The 1956,D 19,41:2
Duchess of Malfi, The 1957,Mr 20,33:1
Livin' the Life 1957,Ap 29,20:1
Makropoulos Secret, The 1957,D 4,52:4
Infernal Machine, The 1958,F 4,33:1
Family Reunion, The 1958,O 21,39:1
Power and the Glory, The 1958,D 12,2:7
Beaux' Stratagem, The 1959,F 25,35:4
Hey You, Light Man! 1963,Mr 2,5:2
Woods, Robert (Producer)
Macbeth 1948,Ap 1,30:2
Banquet for the Moon, A 1961,Ja 20,24:2
Woods, Ruth
Sabrina Fair 1953,N 12,37:1
Woods, Stanley
Kibitzer, The 1929,F 19,22:5
Out of a Blue Sky 1930,F 10,20:6
Woods, Tom
Victoria Regina 1935,D 27,15:2
Victoria Regina 1938,O 4,20:2
Infernal Machine, The 1954,Mr 22,22:2
Woods, Tommy
Runnin' Wild 1923,O 30,17:3
Woods, Walter (Playwright)
Billy the Kid 1951,Ag 21,23:2
Woods, Willie
Junebug Graduates Tonight! 1967,F 27,35:1
Woods and Wyde
Vaudeville (Palace) 1923,Mr 13,19:2
Woods Sisters
Rise of Rosie O'Reilly, The 1923,D 26,13:4
Woodside, Lorence M (Mrs) (Translator)
Sonya's Search for the Christmas Star
 1929,D 14,24:6
Woodson, Elaine
Catiline 1936,Ja 28,14:6
Woodson, James H
Runnin' Wild 1923,O 30,17:3
Woodson, William
Harriet 1943,Mr 4,24:2
Othello 1943,O 20,18:1
Cyrano de Bergerac 1946,O 9,33:2
Cyrano de Bergerac 1947,Ja 17,27:2
Three Sisters, The 1955,F 26,13:2
Moon for the Misbegotten, A 1957,My 3,21:2
Conversation Piece 1957,N 19,38:2
Woodthorpe, Peter
Visit, The 1958,My 6,40:1
Darling of the Day 1968,Ja 29,26:2
Woodvine, John
Richard II 1956,O 24,44:1
Romeo and Juliet 1956,O 25,41:1
Macbeth 1956,O 30,42:2
Woodward, Bliss
Paul Bunyan 1941,My 6,25:1
Woodward, Charles (Miscellaneous)
Johnny No-Trump 1967,O 9,60:2
Woodward, Charles (Producer)
Boys in the Band, The 1968,Ap 15,48:1
Front Page, The 1969,My 12,54:2
Watercolor 1970,Ja 22,30:1
Criss-Crossing 1970,Ja 22,30:1
What the Butler Saw 1970,My 5,56:1
Woodward, David
Unto Such Glory 1937,My 7,28:2
Hymn to the Rising Sun 1937,My 7,28:2
Woodward, Dolores
Our Lan' 1947,S 29,16:5
Woodward, Edward
Rattle of a Simple Man 1963,Ap 18,39:1
High Spirits 1964,Ap 8,34:1
Best Laid Plans, The 1966,Mr 26,15:2

Two Cities 1969,Mr 1,22:1
Woodward, Ernest
Comedienne 1924,O 22,18:1
Double Door 1933,S 22,15:5
Allure 1934,O 30,22:6
Battleship Gertie 1935,Ja 19,9:2
Whatever Goes Up 1935,N 26,28:2
Seen But Not Heard 1936,S 18,19:2
Too Many Heroes 1937,N 16,26:2
Roosty 1938,F 15,21:2
Eye on the Sparrow 1938,My 4,26:3
Rugged Path, The 1945,N 12,17:2
Woodward, Eugenie
Madras House, The 1921,O 31,18:2
Open House 1925,D 15,28:3
Honor of the Family, The 1926,D 27,21:1
Cyclone Lover, The 1928,Je 6,23:3
Personal Appearance 1936,Jl 9,17:4
Woodward, Eugenie (Mrs)
Dagger, The 1925,S 10,28:1
Woodward, Eugenie (Playwright)
Leap, The 1924,My 23,16:5
Two by Two 1925,F 24,17:1
Woodward, George
Straw, The 1921,N 11,16:2
Woodward, Harold
Nightingale, The 1927,Ja 4,20:4
Woodward, Jenny
Leap, The 1924,My 23,16:5
Woodward, Joanne
Lovers 1956,My 11,23:1
Baby Want a Kiss 1964,Ap 20,32:1
Woodward, Marjorie
Patience 1935,S 3,24:4
Woodward, Matthew C (Lyricist)
Springtime of Youth 1922,O 27,15:1
Woodward, Philip
Battle Hymn 1936,My 23,12:1
Woodward, Ruth M (Playwright)
Red Geranium, The 1922,My 9,22:3
Nude in Washington Square, The 1934,Ag 7,20:1
Woodworth, John
Missouri Legend 1938,S 20,27:2
Woodworth, Richard
Adventures of Marco Polo, The 1941,D 28,I,31:7
Woodworth, Samuel (Playwright)
Forest Rose, The 1928,F 26,VIII,2:7
Forest Rose, The 1928,Mr 18,IX,1:1
Wool, Walter
Countess Maritza 1926,S 20,21:1
Wooland, Norman
Time and the Conways 1938,Ja 4,19:2
Woolery, Pete
Vaudeville (Palace) 1928,Ag 28,27:3
Woolever, Harry
My Fair Lady 1964,My 21,43:2
Woolever, Harry (Choreographer)
'Toinette 1961,N 21,46:1
Woolever, Harry (Director)
My Fair Lady 1968,Je 14,42:1
Wooley, Edgar M (Director)
Out o' Luck 1925,D 19,15:1
Wooley, Janet
Vagabond King, The 1935,N 29,22:7
Wooley, Reginald (Costume Designer)
Boy Friend, The 1954,O 1,20:1
Wooley, Reginald (Scenic Designer)
Boy Friend, The 1954,O 1,20:1
Woolf, Edgar Allan (Playwright)
Love Birds 1921,Mr 16,12:1
Fate's Messenger 1927,Ja 4,21:2
Woman of the Earth, A 1927,F 1,24:6
Woman of the Earth, A 1927,My 31,25:1
Woman of the Earth, A 1927,S 27,31:3
India 1928,Ja 17,23:3
Woolf, Harold
Cyclone Lover, The 1928,Je 6,23:3
Night Hostess 1928,S 13,31:2
Congai 1928,N 28,24:3
Remote Control 1929,S 11,24:5
Fast Service 1931,N 18,26:3
Porgy and Bess 1935,O 11,30:2
Fulton of Oak Falls 1937,Ja 2,15:3
Fulton of Oak Falls 1937,F 11,18:2
Woolf, Henry
Persecution and Assassination of Marat As
 Performed by the Inmates of the Asylum of
 Charenton Under the Direction of the Marquis de
 Sade, The 1965,D 28,35:1
Hero Rises Up, The 1968,N 9,26:2
Woolf, Virginia (Playwright)
When I Was a Child 1960,D 9,38:1
Woolf, Walter
Florodora 1920,Ap 6,18:1
Century Revue and the Midnight Rounders, The
 1920,Jl 13,9:1
Last Waltz, The 1921,My 11,20:3
Lady in Ermine, The 1922,O 3,22:2
Passing Show of 1923, The 1923,Je 15,24:6
Dream Girl, The 1924,Ag 21,12:2
Artists and Models 1925,Je 25,16:2
Countess Maritza 1926,Mr 30,20:3
Red Robe, The 1928,My 2,18:5

Woolf, Walter—Cont
Red Robe, The 1928,D 26,15:1
Red Robe, The 1929,Ja 13,VIII,1:1
Duchess of Chicago, The 1929,N 17,IX,4:1
Dear Love 1930,My 18,VIII,3:1
Ladies All 1930,Jl 20,VIII,2:1
Ladies All 1930,Jl 29,25:2
Great Man, The 1931,Ap 8,20:6
Experience Unnecessary 1931,D 31,16:2
Experience Unnecessary 1932,Mr 28,10:2
Melody 1933,F 15,17:4
Woolfenden, Guy (Composer)
King Lear 1964,My 19,43:2
Woolfenden, Guy (Musical Director)
King Lear 1964,My 19,43:2
Woolfolk, Helen
Porgy and Bess 1942,Ja 23,16:2
Woolfolk, William
John Henry 1940,Ja 11,18:2
Carmen Jones 1943,D 3,26:2
Woolford, Guy
One Good Year 1935,N 28,38:3
Wooll, Edward (Playwright)
Libel! 1935,D 3,32:8
Libel! 1935,D 8,X,5:8
Libel! 1935,D 21,10:5
Wooll, Joseph
Doctor Faustus 1937,Ja 9,21:2
Woollcott, Alexander
Brief Moment 1931,O 25,VIII,2:1
Brief Moment 1931,N 10,28:2
Brief Moment 1932,F 28,VIII,1:1
Wine of Choice 1938,F 22,18:4
Wine of Choice 1938,F 27,X,1:1
Man Who Came to Dinner, The 1940,F 10,19:5
Man Who Came to Dinner, The 1940,F 18,IX,3:6
Man Who Came to Dinner, The 1941,Mr 23,IX,1:1
Woollcott, Alexander (Director)
Dark Tower, The 1933,N 27,20:3
Woollcott, Alexander (Playwright)
Channel Road, The 1929,O 18,24:2
Channel Road, The 1929,O 27,IX,1:1
Dark Tower, The 1933,N 27,20:3
Dark Tower, The 1934,Je 10,IX,1:1
Woolley, Edgar (Director)
Faun, The 1924,Mr 28,17:2
Galloper, The 1924,D 19,26:2
Aiglon, L' 1925,O 31,20:3
Orestes 1926,Je 20,II,3:6
Coriolanus 1927,Je 18,8:3
Fifty Million Frenchmen 1929,N 28,34:4
Woolley, Edgar (Producer)
Coriolanus 1927,Je 18,8:3
Woolley, Emily
Night in Paris, A 1926,Jl 27,15:4
Woolley, Jack
Reluctant Dragon, The 1931,D 12,23:5
Woolley, Keith Small
Village Wooing 1934,Ap 18,22:5
Woolley, Mary E
Mount Holyoke Milestones 1933,Ap 9,II,3:4
Woolley, Monty
On Your Toes 1936,Ap 13,14:4
Knights of Song 1938,O 18,29:2
Man Who Came to Dinner, The 1939,S 26,21:3
Man Who Came to Dinner, The 1939,O 1,IX,2:5
Man Who Came to Dinner, The 1939,O 17,31:1
Man Who Came to Dinner, The 1939,O 22,IX,1:1
Woolley, Monty (Director)
Second Little Show, The 1930,S 3,36:1
New Yorkers, The 1930,D 9,31:1
America's Sweetheart 1931,F 11,23:1
Walk a Little Faster 1932,D 8,24:4
Champagne, Sec 1933,O 16,20:2
Jubilee 1935,O 14,20:1
Woolley, Monty (Miscellaneous)
Frogs, The 1941,N 14,25:3
Woolman, Claude
Ivanov 1958,O 8,42:1
Philoctetes 1959,Ja 14,28:1
Twelfth Night 1960,Je 9,29:4
Tempest, The 1960,Je 20,35:1
Antony and Cleopatra 1960,Ag 1,19:1
Hamlet 1963,My 9,41:1
Miser, The 1963,My 10,39:1
Three Sisters, The 1963,Jl 22,19:2
Henry V 1964,My 13,52:1
Saint Joan 1964,My 14,41:1
Volpone 1964,Jl 20,18:3
Tartuffe 1965,Ja 15,23:1
Woolman, Dickie
Thank You 1921,O 4,10:2
Woolsey, Fred
Way of the Cross, The 1959,Ja 16,35:2
Mystery of the Finding of the Cross, The
 1959,Ja 16,35:2
Cranmer of Canterbury 1959,D 4,36:1
Woolsey, Robert
Right Girl, The 1921,Mr 16,12:1
All-Star Idlers of 1921, The 1921,Jl 16,5:2
Blue Kitten, The 1922,Ja 14,9:3
Lady in Ermine, The 1922,O 3,22:2
Poppy 1923,S 4,14:2
Mayflowers 1925,N 25,14:2

Woolsey, Robert—Cont
Honest Liars 1926,Jl 20,17:2
Rio Rita 1927,F 3,18:3
My Princess 1927,O 7,24:2
Scandals 1931,S 27,VIII,3:7
Woosley, Richard
Anna Christie 1955,N 22,41:1
Wooster, Boots
Purple Mask, The 1920,Ja 6,18:1
Honors Are Even 1921,Ag 11,8:2
Ice-Bound 1923,F 12,16:2
Mad Honeymoon, The 1923,Ag 8,10:1
Made for Each Other 1924,S 30,27:2
Wooten, Roberta
Long Moment, The 1950,My 22,16:6
Wootton, Miriam
My Princess 1927,O 7,24:2
Wor, Michael
Our Town 1940,Je 30,35:5
Face, The 1941,N 29,15:3
Worden, Frank
Chocolate Soldier, The 1934,My 3,15:3
Worden, Master J
Under the Gaslight 1929,Ap 3,27:1
Worden, Yvonne
Strong Breed, The 1967,N 10,60:1
Wordley, Ralph
Susannah and the Elders 1940,O 30,28:2
Wordsworth, Richard
Importance of Being Earnest, The 1947,Mr 4,30:2
Love for Love 1947,My 27,30:2
Richard II 1956,O 24,44:1
Romeo and Juliet 1956,O 25,41:1
Macbeth 1956,O 30,42:2
Troilus and Cressida 1956,D 27,21:1
Twelfth Night 1958,Ag 27,32:1
Twelfth Night 1958,D 10,54:2
Hamlet 1958,D 17,2:7
Henry V 1958,D 26,2:7
Worf, Richard
John Ferguson 1928,Ja 18,23:1
Work, Cecily
Becky Sharp 1929,Je 4,29:1
Workman, Audree
It Never Rains 1929,N 20,26:4
Virtue's Bed 1930,Ap 16,26:5
Workman, Jenny
Girl in Pink Tights, The 1954,Mr 6,13:2
Pipe Dream 1955,D 1,44:1
Brigadoon 1962,My 31,21:4
Brigadoon 1963,F 1,6:2
Carousel 1965,Ag 11,39:1
Carousel 1966,D 16,56:2
Worland, Deci
Republic, The 1970,Ap 28,49:1
World, Robert
Men and Dreams 1966,S 7,51:2
World, Sascha
Men and Dreams 1966,S 7,51:2
Worley, Jane (Miscellaneous)
Parade 1960,Ja 21,27:4
Worley, Jo Anne
Billy Barnes People, The 1961,Je 14,10:3
That Thing at the Cherry Lane 1965,My 19,42:1
Hotel Passionato 1965,O 23,16:1
Mad Show, The 1966,Ja 10,16:1
Worley, Lee
Terminal 1970,Ap 15,51:2
Serpent, The 1970,Je 2,35:1
Worlock, Frederic
Old House, The 1920,Jl 11,VI,1:6
Scaramouche 1923,O 25,14:2
Moon-Flower, The 1924,Ja 27,VII,2:7
Moon-Flower, The 1924,F 26,15:1
Far Cry, The 1924,O 1,24:1
She Had to Know 1925,F 3,25:3
Grand Duchess and the Waiter, The
1925,O 14,31:1
Julius Caesar 1927,Je 7,27:2
Furies, The 1928,Mr 8,23:1
Common Sin, The 1928,O 16,28:2
Hedda Gabler 1929,F 4,20:3
Scotland Yard 1929,S 28,16:6
Damn Your Honor 1929,D 31,14:3
Mayfair 1930,Mr 18,30:5
Greeks Had a Word for It, The 1930,S 26,16:5
Truth About Blayds, The 1932,Ap 12,25:2
Camille 1932,N 2,23:3
Foolscap 1933,Ja 12,21:2
Merry Widow, The 1933,Ag 13,IX,1:3
Jezebel 1933,D 20,26:3
Dodsworth 1934,F 26,20:4
Dodsworth 1934,Ag 21,12:3
On Stage 1935,O 30,16:6
Tovarich 1936,O 16,31:4
Amazing Dr. Clitterhouse, The 1937,Mr 3,26:4
Richard II 1937,S 16,28:2
Suspect 1940,Ap 10,30:4
Anne of England 1941,O 8,26:2
Medea 1949,My 3,31:2
Richard II 1951,Ja 25,21:2
Saint Joan 1951,O 5,23:2
Doctor's Dilemma, The 1955,Ja 12,22:1
Doctor's Dilemma, The 1955,Ja 23,II,1:1

Worman, Cliff
Opportunity 1920,Jl 31,5:1
Anna Ascends 1920,S 23,14:1
Dr David's Dad 1924,Ag 14,10:3
Worms, Jean
Mon Coeur au Ralenti 1927,Je 12,VII,2:1
Image, L' 1928,Ja 1,VIII,2:3
Worms, Robert A
Ticket-of-Leave Man, The 1961,D 23,15:1
Wormser, Andre (Composer)
Pierrot the Prodigal; Enfant Prodigue, L'
1925,Mr 7,8:1
Wornser, Janice
Logia a la Natividad de Nuestro Senor Jesucristo,
El 1937,D 14,33:4
Woronov, Mary
Conquest of the Universe 1967,N 27,60:1
Worrall, Dusty
Carousel 1949,Ja 26,28:2
Carousel 1949,F 6,II,1:1
Carousel 1954,Je 3,32:2
Music Man, The 1957,D 20,31:1
Music Man, The 1958,S 28,II,1:1
Worrall, Tom (Musical Director)
Disney on Parade 1970,S 24,63:1
Worrell, Devah
Shore Leave 1922,Ag 9,20:2
Rain or Shine 1928,F 10,26:3
Worsley, Pat
Conversation Piece 1934,O 24,24:1
Worsnopp, Andrew
As You Like It 1968,Je 24,42:3
Love's Labour's Lost 1968,Je 28,36:1
Worth, Alice
Demon Mirror, The 1968,Mr 13,42:1
Worth, Betty
East of Broadway 1932,Ja 27,19:3
Four O'Clock 1933,F 14,19:6
Green Stick 1934,O 10,21:2
Worth, Billie
Higher and Higher 1940,Ap 5,24:3
Brights Lights of 1944 1943,S 17,27:4
Jackpot 1944,Ja 14,15:2
Seven Lively Arts 1944,D 8,26:6
Courtin' Time 1951,Je 14,30:2
Call Me Madam 1952,Mr 16,84:3
Worth, Buddy
Sunny River 1941,D 5,28:2
Worth, Caroline
Kittiwake Island 1960,O 13,43:1
Worth, Coley
Fledermaus, Die 1954,My 20,38:5
Pirates of Penzance, The 1961,Ja 20,24:5
H M S Pinafore 1961,F 2,26:6
Pousse-Cafe 1966,Mr 19,19:2
Worth, Gracie
Let 'Em Eat Cake 1933,O 23,18:1
Music Hath Charms 1934,D 31,8:2
Blossom Time 1936,Jl 29,23:1
Show Boat 1938,Je 30,21:1
Blossom Time 1938,D 27,12:2
Worth, Harry
Steppe Around 1922,Mr 29,17:4
House of Fear, The 1929,O 8,34:2
Torch Song 1930,Ag 3,VIII,3:4
If I Were You 1931,S 24,21:1
Little Women 1931,D 8,36:2
We Are No Longer Children 1932,Ap 1,17:2
Too Many Boats 1934,S 12,26:3
Jayhawker 1934,N 6,34:2
Ten Little Indians 1944,Je 28,21:2
Leading Lady 1948,O 19,33:1
Detective Story 1949,Mr 24,34:2
Worth, Irene
Two Mrs Carrolls, The 1943,Ag 4,14:1
Love Goes to Press 1946,Ja 19,16:2
Cocktail Party, The 1949,Ag 23,28:6
Cocktail Party, The 1950,Ja 23,17:2
Cocktail Party, The 1950,Ja 29,II,1:1
Richard III 1953,Jl 15,22:2
All's Well That Ends Well 1953,Jl 16,18:2
Day by the Sea, A 1953,N 27,22:3
Day by the Sea, A 1953,D 20,II,4:2
Life in the Sun, A 1955,Ag 24,24:7
Life in the Sun, A 1955,Ag 28,II,1:6
Queen and the Rebels, The 1956,F 5,II,3:1
Mary Stuart 1957,O 9,39:1
Mary Stuart 1957,O 20,II,1:1
Mary Stuart 1958,S 3,38:1
As You Like It 1959,Jl 1,27:1
As You Like It 1959,Jl 5,II,1:1
Toys in the Attic 1960,F 26,23:2
Toys in the Attic 1960,Mr 6,II,1:1
Macbeth 1962,Je 6,35:2
Ides of March, The 1963,Ag 9,12:1
King Lear 1964,My 19,43:2
Tiny Alice 1964,D 30,14:2
Tiny Alice 1965,Ja 10,II,1:1
Song at Twilight, A 1966,Ap 17,86:5
Shadows of the Evening; Come Into the Garden,
Maud 1966,Ap 27,38:1
Prometheus Bound 1967,My 11,52:1
Prometheus Bound 1967,Je 11,II,1:1

Worth, Irene—Cont
Heartbreak House 1967,Ag 27,II,1:1
Oedipus 1968,Mr 31,II,5:1
Oedipus 1968,Ap 2,54:1
Oedipus 1968,Jl 31,29:1
Tiny Alice 1970,Ja 17,24:1
Hedda Gabler 1970,Je 12,28:1
Hedda Gabler 1970,Je 21,II,1:1
Worth, Jean
Man's Man, A 1925,O 14,31:2
Worth, John M (sic) (Director)
Eye on the Sparrow 1938,My 4,26:3
Worth, Joyce
New Faces of 1936 1936,My 20,24:5
Worth, Lee
Without Warning 1937,My 3,23:2
Worth, Maggie
Best Foot Forward 1956,Mr 3,16:1
Let It Ride 1961,O 13,27:4
Girl Who Came to Supper, The 1963,D 9,49:1
Around the World in 80 Days 1964,Je 29,33:2
My Fair Lady 1968,Je 14,42:1
Worth, Mary
Broken Wing, The 1920,N 30,14:1
Worth, Peggy
Find the Fox 1930,Je 21,20:4
Worth, Richard
Time, Place and the Girl, The 1942,O 22,24:3
Worth, Robert
Processional 1937,O 14,23:1
Worth, William
20th Century 1932,D 30,15:1
Worth, Winnie
Charm 1929,N 29,24:5
Worth Sisters
Artists and Models 1943,N 6,16:6
Worthing, Gerrie
She Loves Me Not 1933,N 21,22:4
First Episode 1934,S 18,18:1
Life's Too Short 1935,S 21,18:5
Naughty-Naught '00 1937,Ja 25,23:2
Worthing, Helen Lee
Greenwich Village Follies 1920,Ag 31,7:3
Ziegfeld Follies 1923,O 22,17:2
Worthington, Elizabeth
School for Brides 1944,Ag 2,19:4
Worthington, Tim
Plain and Fancy 1955,Ja 28,14:2
Worthington, W
Gentlemen, the Queen 1927,Ap 23,14:3
Worthington, William
Treasure, The 1920,O 5,13:1
Will Shakespeare 1923,Ja 2,14:1
Mrs Partridge Presents 1925,Ja 6,23:3
Shanghai Gesture, The 1926,F 2,20:2
Worthy and Thompson
Vaudeville (Palace) 1931,My 25,17:4
Blackbirds 1933,D 4,22:3
Woshak, Tamara
Let's Sing Yiddish 1966,N 10,63:1
Wouk, Herman (Composer)
Hit the Road 1941,Ap 4,18:3
Wouk, Herman (Lyricist)
Laugh It Off 1934,Ap 5,24:2
Wouk, Herman (Original Author)
Caine Mutiny Court-Martial, The 1953,O 14,35:1
Caine Mutiny Court-Martial, The 1953,D 15,52:8
Caine Mutiny Court-Martial, The 1954,Ja 21,27:2
Wouk, Herman (Playwright)
Laugh It Off 1934,Ap 5,24:2
Traitor, The 1949,Ap 1,30:2
Traitor, The 1949,Ap 10,II,1:1
Caine Mutiny Court-Martial, The 1953,O 14,35:1
Caine Mutiny Court-Martial, The 1953,D 15,52:8
Caine Mutiny Court-Martial, The 1954,Ja 21,27:2
Caine Mutiny Court-Martial, The 1954,Ja 31,II,1:1
Caine Mutiny Court-Martial, The 1956,Je 14,40:1
Nature's Way 1957,O 17,42:2
Woursell, A (Miscellaneous)
In the Shadow of the Glen 1957,Mr 7,24:1
Tinker's Wedding, The 1957,Mr 7,24:1
Riders to the Sea 1957,Mr 7,24:1
Woursell, A (Producer)
Lady From the Sea, The 1956,D 13,49:5
Wouters, Francene
Peer Gynt 1923,F 6,14:1
Blue Bird, The 1923,D 26,13:3
Is Zat So? 1925,Ap 25,18:2
Woykoff, I M (Playwright)
Love in the Country 1930,S 28,VIII,4:4
Wozniak, Zbyslaw
Porgy and Bess 1950,N 26,II,7:8
Wragge, Betty
Audition of the Apprentice Theatre 1939,Je 2,26:2
Wragge, Eddie
Glass Slipper, The 1925,O 20,29:1
Topaze 1930,F 13,25:3
Month in the Country, A 1930,Mr 18,30:5
Would-Be Gentleman, The 1930,Ap 30,29:2
Mr Samuel 1930,N 11,28:4
As Husbands Go 1931,Mr 6,26:5
Wragge, Edward
Bright Honor 1936,S 28,14:1

Wragge, Elizabeth
Up the Line 1926,N 23,26:1
Would-Be Gentleman, The 1930,Ap 30,29:2
Dead End 1935,O 29,17:2
Wray, Fay
Nikki 1931,S 30,23:4
Life With Father 1939,Ag 15,14:4
Mr Big 1941,S 7,I,51:3
Mr Big 1941,S 14,IX,2:5
Mr Big 1941,O 1,24:2
Golden Wings 1941,N 25,33:3
Golden Wings 1941,D 9,46:6
Wray, John
Ouija Board, The 1920,Mr 30,9:1
Nightcap, The 1921,Ag 16,18:3
Polly Preferred 1923,Ja 12,13:3
Silence 1924,N 13,18:2
Enemy, The 1925,O 21,20:1
Broadway 1926,S 17,19:3
Nightstick 1927,N 11,20:4
Tin Pan Alley 1928,N 2,29:1
Achilles Had a Heel 1935,Ap 28,X,1:1
Achilles Had a Heel 1935,O 14,20:2
Beat the Band 1942,O 15,26:1
Wray, John (Choreographer)
New Faces of 1943 1942,D 23,22:2
Call Me Mister 1946,Ap 19,26:2
Call Me Mister 1946,Ap 28,II,1:1
Wray, John (Director)
Wild Birds 1925,Ap 10,16:1
Wray, John (Playwright)
Nightstick 1927,N 11,20:4
So Was Napoleon 1930,Ja 9,22:2
Wray, Marshall
Achilles Had a Heel 1935,O 14,20:2
Wray, Rex D
Somebody's Lion 1921,Ap 13,20:1
Wrede, Casper (Original Author)
Hamlet 1968,Ag 21,40:2
Wrede, Gerda (Producer)
Hamlet 1947,Jl 13,I,47:2
Wreford, Reynell (Composer)
Enemy, The 1925,O 21,20:1
Wren, Jane
Peter Pan 1924,N 7,16:2
Wren, Jenny
Help Yourself! 1936,Jl 15,15:1
Wren, P C (Original Author)
Beau Geste 1929,F 17,IX,2:1
Wren, Sam
Women Go on Forever 1927,S 8,25:1
Skin Deep 1927,O 18,32:1
This Is New York 1930,N 29,21:1
Streets of New York, The 1931,O 7,29:1
Pillars of Society, The 1931,O 15,19:1
Bride the Sun Shines On, The 1931,D 28,20:2
Anybody's Game 1932,D 22,21:4
Unto the Third 1933,Ap 21,24:8
Blue Widow, The 1933,Ag 31,20:2
Sunday Nights at Nine 1933,N 13,20:7
Sunday Nights at Nine 1934,Mr 5,18:5
Sunday Nights at Nine 1934,N 19,12:1
Crime and Punishment 1935,Ja 23,20:3
Play, Genius, Play! 1935,O 31,17:2
Wren, William Gross
This Mad Whirl 1937,Ja 10,II,4:8
Wrenn, Edward
Faith and Prudence 1952,O 15,40:2
Wrenne, Val
Harriet 1944,S 28,26:1
Wrick, Mary
Bitter Sweet 1934,My 8,28:4
Wright, Bob
Merry Widow, The 1964,Ag 18,24:2
Kiss Me, Kate 1965,My 13,31:1
Sound of Music, The 1967,Ap 27,52:1
Man of La Mancha 1969,My 3,38:4
Wright, Cathy
Crimes of Passion; Erpingham Camp, The
1969,O 27,54:1
Wright, Charles
Henry V 1928,Mr 16,26:2
Wright, Charlynn
City of Kings 1949,F 18,27:2
Wright, Cobina
Spring Tonic 1936,My 11,16:1
Wright, Cobina Jr
Lorelei 1938,N 30,21:2
Wright, Crawford (Composer)
Heloise 1958,S 25,28:4
Wright, Crawford (Miscellaneous)
Colombe 1965,F 24,33:1
Wright, Dare
Pride and Prejudice 1935,N 6,32:4
Wright, David
Twelfth Night 1970,Ja 1,18:1
Wright, David (Playwright)
Hang Down Your Head and Die 1964,O 19,38:1
Stiffkey Scandals of 1932, The 1969,Je 14,24:3
Would You Look At Them Smashing All the
Lovely Windows! 1969,S 5,30:1
Wright, Dorothy
Spread Eagle 1935,N 5,33:6

Wright, Dorothy (Playwright)
Cradle of Willow, A 1961,D 16,20:2
Wright, Edith Mae
Oh, Ernest! 1927,My 10,24:3
Wright, Edward
Frankie and Johnny 1930,S 26,16:5
Processional 1937,O 14,23:1
Big Blow 1938,O 3,11:2
Wright, Ellsworth
Strange Fruit 1945,N 30,18:6
Long Way From Home, A 1948,F 9,25:2
John Brown 1950,My 4,32:7
Fancy Meeting You Again 1952,Ja 15,23:2
Shrike, The 1953,N 26,51:2
Wright, Ethel
His Chinese Wife 1920,My 18,9:3
Enchanted Cottage, The 1923,Ap 2,22:3
White Desert 1923,O 19,17:3
Mister Pitt 1924,Ja 23,15:3
Wright, Eugene P (Playwright)
Old King's 1924,Mr 12,19:3
Wright, Fred
Mikado, The; Town of Titipu, The 1927,S 19,30:1
Iolanthe 1927,N 15,26:3
Wright, Garth
Murder in the Cathedral 1958,Mr 22,12:4
Wright, Geoffrey (Composer)
Your Number's Up 1936,D 24,22:2
Wright, George
Fool, The 1922,O 24,18:1
Holy Terror, A 1925,S 29,31:2
Four Walls 1927,S 20,33:1
Let Us Be Gay 1929,F 22,19:1
That's Gratitude 1930,S 12,28:1
Bridal Wise 1932,My 31,15:5
Wright, George Sr
Kiss of Importance, A 1930,D 2,31:3
Wright, Ginger (Choreographer)
Galileo 1968,D 1,88:4
Wright, Haidee
Unknown, The 1920,Ag 29,VI,1:4
Will Shakespeare 1923,Ja 2,14:1
Will Shakespeare 1923,Ja 21,VII,1:1
What Never Dies 1926,D 19,VII,6:1
What Never Dies 1926,D 29,24:2
What Never Dies 1927,Ja 16,VII,1:1
Mariners 1927,Mr 29,22:2
Father, The 1927,S 4,VII,2:1
Royal Family, The 1927,D 29,26:4
Royal Family, The 1928,Ja 8,VII,1:1
Mrs Moonlight 1930,S 30,24:3
Barbara's Wedding 1931,O 9,21:1
Father, The 1931,O 9,21:1
Napoleon: The Hundred Days 1932,Ap 19,25:2
Napoleon: The Hundred Days 1932,My 8,VIII,1:3
Distaff Side, The 1933,S 24,X,1:6
Aunt of England 1935,Mr 28,25:4
Aunt of England 1935,Ap 21,IX,2:2
Gentle Rain 1936,S 20,IX,1:4
Wright, Hazel
Tangerine 1921,Ag 10,8:2
Wright, Helen
Unto Such Glory 1937,My 7,28:2
Wright, Hoxie
Squaring the Circle 1936,Ag 12,15:3
Wright, Hugh
Without Witness 1933,D 28,25:1
Wright, J H
Laugh It Off 1925,Ap 25,18:4
Wright, Jackson
Trojan Women, The 1941,Ap 9,32:5
Wright, James
Haiti 1938,Mr 3,16:1
If You Get It, Do You Want It? 1938,D 1,28:2
Mamba's Daughters 1939,Ja 4,24:2
Mamba's Daughters 1940,Mr 25,10:4
Stars on Ice (2d Edition) 1943,Je 25,13:2
Long Way From Home, A 1948,F 9,25:2
Tobacco Road 1950,Mr 7,23:2
Venice Preserv'd 1955,D 13,54:4
Servant of Two Masters, The 1958,F 11,35:2
Wright, Jerome
Black Monday 1962,Mr 7,29:1
Wright, Joyce
Pirates of Penzance, The 1948,Ja 6,27:2
Mikado, The 1951,Ja 30,21:2
Trial by Jury 1951,F 6,24:2
Gondoliers, The 1951,F 13,27:2
Iolanthe 1951,F 16,22:1
Iolanthe 1955,S 28,38:1
Mikado, The 1955,S 30,20:2
Yeomen of the Guard, The 1955,O 4,39:2
Pirates of Penzance, The 1955,O 7,21:1
H M S Pinafore 1955,O 18,48:1
Ruddigore 1955,O 21,32:2
Wright, Julann
Country Wife, The 1955,Ap 6,35:1
Wright, Kenneth
Trial of Dr Beck, The 1937,Ag 10,22:2
Wright, Mabel
What Do We Know 1927,D 24,8:1

Wright, Margaret
Last Triangle, The (An Embroidered Camp)
1968,Mr 19,41:1
Peace 1969,Ja 28,49:1
Wright, Mark (Miscellaneous)
Krapp's Last Tape 1960,Ja 15,37:2
Zoo Story, The 1960,Ja 15,37:2
Killer, The 1960,Mr 23,33:1
American Dream, The 1961,Ja 25,28:1
Bartleby 1961,Ja 25,28:1
Death of Bessie Smith, The 1961,Mr 2,19:1
Gallows Humor 1961,Ap 19,35:1
Who's Afraid of Virginia Woolf? 1962,O 15,33:1
Who's Afraid of Virginia Woolf? 1962,N 1,34:1
Tiny Alice 1964,D 30,14:2
Malcolm 1966,Ja 12,29:1
You Know I Can't Hear You When the Water's
  Running; I'm Herbert 1967,Mr 14,54:1
You Know I Can't Hear You When the Water's
  Running; I'll Be Home for Christmas
  1967,Mr 14,54:1
You Know I Can't Hear You When the Water's
  Running; Footsteps of Doves, The
  1967,Mr 14,54:1
You Know I Can't Hear You When the Water's
  Running; Shock of Recognition, The
  1967,Mr 14,54:1
Wright, Mark (Producer)
Birthday Party, The 1967,O 4,40:2
Private Lives 1968,My 20,59:1
Box 1968,O 1,39:1
Quotations From Chairman Mao Tse-Tung
  1968,O 1,39:1
American Dream, The 1968,O 3,55:1
Death of Bessie Smith, The 1968,O 3,55:1
Krapp's Last Tape 1968,O 11,41:1
Zoo Story, The 1968,O 11,41:1
Happy Days 1968,O 14,54:1
Gingham Dog, The 1969,Ap 24,41:1
Last Sweet Days of Isaac, The 1970,Ja 27,49:1
Lemon Sky 1970,My 18,40:1
Wright, Martha
Music in My Heart 1947,O 3,30:2
Great to Be Alive! 1950,Mr 24,28:2
South Pacific 1951,Jl 10,30:5
South Pacific 1951,S 2,II,1:1
Wright, Mary
All's Well That Ends Well 1970,Je 16,53:1
Devil's Disciple, The 1970,Je 30,48:1
Wright, Max
Great White Hope, The 1967,D 14,58:1
Iceman Cometh, The 1968,Ap 1,58:1
Wright, Michael
Doctor Faustus Lights the Lights 1951,D 3,23:4
Jamaica 1957,N 1,32:2
Wright, Michael (Scenic Designer)
Separate Tables 1955,My 22,II,1:1
Wright, Ned
World's My Oyster, The 1956,Ag 10,10:4
Belafonte at the Palace 1959,D 16,55:1
Porgy and Bess 1961,My 18,40:1
Wright, Pamela
Lady Windermere's Fan 1946,O 15,29:2
Wright, Patricia
Enchanted, The 1950,Ja 19,34:2
Wright, Paul
Tia Juana 1927,N 16,28:4
Gringa, La 1928,F 2,17:1
Wright, Pearl
Brain Sweat 1934,Ap 5,24:4
Wright, Peter
Will and the Way, The 1957,D 3,46:5
Wright, Richard (Original Author)
Native Son 1941,Mr 25,26:5
Native Son 1941,Ap 6,IX,1:1
Native Son 1942,O 24,10:6
Native Son 1942,N 1,VIII,1:1
Long Dream, The 1960,F 18,36:2
Wright, Richard (Playwright)
Native Son 1941,Mr 25,26:5
Native Son 1941,Ap 6,IX,1:1
Native Son 1942,O 24,10:6
Native Son 1942,N 1,VIII,1:1
Daddy Goodness 1968,Je 5,37:1
Wright, Robert
Kiss Me, Kate 1952,Ja 9,24:6
Hit the Trail 1954,D 3,31:2
South Pacific 1957,Ap 25,35:1
Tall Story 1959,Ja 30,33:2
Wright, Robert (Composer)
Song of Norway 1944,Ag 22,20:2
Song of Norway 1944,Ag 27,II,1:1
Kismet 1953,D 4,2:4
Song of Norway 1958,Je 23,19:2
At the Grand 1958,Ag 13,24:3
Song of Norway 1959,Je 26,16:2
Kean 1961,N 3,28:2
Kean 1961,N 12,II,1:1
Kismet 1965,Je 23,45:1
Anya 1965,N 30,48:1
Wright, Robert (Director)
Gypsy Lady 1946,S 18,25:6

Wright, Robert (Lyricist)
Song of Norway 1944,Ag 22,20:2
Song of Norway 1944,Ag 27,II,1:1
Gypsy Lady 1946,S 18,25:6
Magdalena 1948,S 21,31:2
Magdalena 1948,S 26,II,1:1
Kismet 1953,D 4,2:4
At the Grand 1958,Ag 13,24:3
Song of Norway 1959,Je 26,16:2
Kean 1961,N 3,28:2
Kean 1961,N 12,II,1:1
Kismet 1965,Je 23,45:1
Anya 1965,N 30,48:1
Wright, Robert (Miscellaneous)
Magdalena 1948,S 21,31:2
Wright, Robert (Playwright)
Love Doctor, The 1959,O 14,52:4
Wright, Russel
Loud Speaker 1927,Mr 3,27:2
Stairs, The 1927,N 8,32:7
Wright, Russel (Costume Designer)
Grand Street Follies, The 1925,Je 19,24:1
Wright, Russel (Director)
Romio and Julietta 1925,Ap 21,19:1
Fratricide Punished 1925,Ap 21,19:1
Wright, Russel (Scenic Designer)
Fratricide Punished 1925,Ap 21,19:1
Romio and Julietta 1925,Ap 21,19:1
Grand Street Follies, The 1925,Je 19,24:1
Wright, Sam
Booster, The 1929,O 25,26:2
Pudding on the Ritz 1932,Ap 9,18:3
Wright, Sheila
Midsummer Night's Dream, A 1954,S 22,33:1
Wright, Stephen
Purple Mask, The 1920,Ja 6,18:1
Pasteur 1923,Mr 13,19:1
Green Beetle, The 1924,S 3,12:3
Badges 1924,D 4,25:1
Bridge of Distances, The 1925,S 29,30:1
Arabian Nightmare, The 1927,Ja 11,36:3
Mountain Fury 1929,S 26,27:2
Peter Ibbetson 1931,Ap 9,30:3
Midsummer Night's Dream, A 1968,D 9,59:1
Twelfth Night 1970,Ja 1,18:1
Hamlet 1970,D 28,40:1
Wright, Teresa
Life With Father 1939,N 9,26:2
Life With Father 1939,N 19,X,1:1
King's Maid, The 1941,Ag 27,15:3
Dark at the Top of the Stairs, The 1957,D 6,38:1
Dark at the Top of the Stairs, The 1957,D 15,II,3:1
I Never Sang for My Father 1968,Ja 26,30:1
I Never Sang for My Father 1968,F 4,II,1:1
Who's Happy Now? 1969,N 18,39:1
Passage to E M Forster, A 1970,O 28,62:1
Wright, Tom
Trip to Bountiful, The 1959,F 27,20:4
Wright, U
Juno and the Paycock 1932,O 20,24:3
Playboy of the Western World, The 1932,O 21,25:1
Shadow of a Gunman, The 1932,O 31,18:1
Big House, The 1933,Ja 5,19:3
King Oedipus 1933,Ja 16,12:4
Plough and the Stars, The 1934,N 13,22:2
Drama at Inish 1934,N 15,24:2
Well of the Saints, The 1934,N 22,26:2
Playboy of the Western World, The 1937,N 22,14:5
Juno and the Paycock 1937,D 7,32:5
Drama at Inish 1937,D 14,33:2
Wright, Will
Happy Town 1959,O 8,49:2
Wright, William H (Playwright)
Man in the Dog Suit, The 1958,O 31,34:2
Wright, Wynn
Case of Libel, A 1963,O 11,43:2
Wright Brothers, The
Vaudeville (Palace) 1928,N 6,35:2
Wright Dancers
Sun-Kist 1921,My 24,20:2
Vaudeville (Palace) 1927,N 8,33:3
Wrightson, Earl
New Moon, The 1944,My 18,16:2
Firebird of Florence 1945,Mr 23,13:4
Wrightson, Olivia
Jamboree 1932,N 25,18:4
Wrigley, Ben
Arabian Nights 1955,Je 24,16:1
Wrigley, Gene
Ice Follies 1963,Ja 10,5:2
Wrobieski, Bronek
Sweethearts 1929,S 23,25:1
Wrought, Michael
Night Is Black Bottles, The 1962,D 5,56:1
Wu, Elsie
Roar China! 1930,O 28,23:1
Wu, Honorable
If a Body 1935,My 1,25:3
First Lady 1935,N 27,17:4
Wu, Mr
Vaudeville (Palace) 1929,D 16,34:4
Wuepper, Karl-Heinz
Faust, Part I; Play, The 1961,F 5,27:2

Wuest, Ida
Merry Wives of Windsor 1929,Mr 24,X,2:3
Wuestenhagen, Karl
Don Karlos 1935,Jl 28,X,1:6
Wukovich, Linda (Scenic Designer)
Hedda Gabler 1970,Ja 18,78:1
Wulff, Cecile
Lancashire Lass, The 1931,D 31,16:3
Twelfth Night 1934,Jl 17,24:5
County Chairman, The 1936,My 26,26:5
Wulff, Derick (Lyricist)
Kiss Me! 1927,Jl 22,17:1
Wulff, Derick (Playwright)
Kiss Me! 1927,Jl 22,17:1
Wulff, Derick (Translator)
Holka Polka 1925,O 15,27:2
Wully, Wee
Don't Tell 1920,S 29,12:1
Wulp, John (Director)
Red Eye of Love 1961,Je 13,28:1
Wulp, John (Playwright)
Saintliness of Margery Kempe, The 1959,F 3,35:6
Wulp, John (Producer)
Red Eye of Love 1961,Je 13,28:1
Fortuna 1962,Ja 4,26:1
Three Times Three; George Washington Crossing the Delaware 1962,Mr 2,24:1
Three Times Three; Not Enough Rope 1962,Mr 2,24:1
Three Times Three; Twenty-Five Cent White Cap, The 1962,Mr 2,24:1
Wulp, John (Scenic Designer)
Red Eye of Love 1961,Je 13,28:1
Three Times Three; Twenty-Five Cent White Cap, The 1962,Mr 2,24:1
Three Times Three; Not Enough Rope 1962,Mr 2,24:1
Three Times Three; George Washington Crossing the Delaware 1962,Mr 2,24:1
Endecott and the Red Cross 1968,My 7,50:1
Wunch, Fred (Miscellaneous)
Nights of Wrath; Nuits de la Colere, Les 1947,D 1,26:4
Wunderlich, Larry (Miscellaneous)
Time of Vengeance 1959,D 11,39:1
Whisper to Me 1960,N 22,38:6
Wuntch, Fred (Costume Designer)
John Brown 1950,My 4,32:7
Wuntch, Fred (Scenic Designer)
John Brown 1950,My 4,32:7
Great Magician, The 1951,N 22,45:1
Wuolijoki, Hella (Original Author)
Women of Property 1937,Ag 1,X,1:7
Wuolijoki, Hella (Playwright)
Women of Property 1937,Jl 9,18:3
Wupperman, Carlos (Playwright)
Triumph of X, The 1921,Ag 25,8:2
Wurger, Bernard F
Jo 1964,F 13,25:1
Wurtzel, Stuart (Scenic Designer)
Toy for the Clowns, A 1962,S 13,31:2
Wretched the Lionhearted 1962,S 13,31:2
Hamlet 1968,Je 10,59:1
Don't Shoot Mable It's Your Husband 1968,O 23,34:1
Tiny Alice 1969,S 30,42:1
Flea in Her Ear, A 1969,O 4,25:1
Trumpets and Drums 1969,O 13,52:1
Wurzel, (Messr)
Chauve-Souris 1925,Ja 15,25:1
Wussow, Klaus Jurgen
Maria Stuart 1968,Mr 27,38:1
Wyane, Rollo (Scenic Designer)
Silent Witness, The 1931,My 10,VIII,3:5
Wyart, Albert
Sitting Pretty 1924,Ap 9,24:2
Wyasht, Lydia
Ballerina 1933,O 29,IX,1:6
Wyatt, Alfred (Costume Designer)
Detective Story 1954,F 13,11:2
Wyatt, Don
Marathon 1933,Ja 28,8:8
Wyatt, Eustace
Old English 1924,D 24,11:2
Elmer Gantry 1928,Ag 10,9:4
Heartbreak House 1938,Ap 30,18:2
Danton's Death 1938,N 3,26:2
Emperor Jones, The 1939,Je 20,25:2
Wyatt, Jane
Give Me Yesterday 1931,Mr 5,32:1
Fatal Alibi, The 1932,F 10,26:6
Mad Hopes, The 1932,D 2,26:3
Evensong 1933,F 1,13:4
Conquest 1933,F 20,11:3
For Services Rendered 1933,Ap 13,15:5
Joyous Season, The 1934,Ja 30,16:3
Lost Horizons 1934,O 16,31:2
Bishop Misbehaves, The 1935,F 21,22:4
Save Me the Waltz 1938,Mr 1,19:2
Night Music 1940,F 23,18:2
Night Music 1940,Mr 3,X,1:1
Quiet, Please! 1940,O 20,IX,2:3
Quiet, Please! 1940,N 9,20:3

Wyatt, Jane—Cont
Hope for the Best 1945,F 8,14:4
Hope for the Best 1945,F 18,II,1:1
Autumn Garden, The 1951,Mr 8,36:2
Autumn Garden, The 1951,Mr 18,II,1:1
Wyatt, Jerry
Applause 1970,Mr 31,35:1
Wyatt, Kelley (Musical Director)
Threepenny Opera, The 1956,Mr 11,II,1:1
Wyatt, Marguerite
Lulu Belle 1926,F 10,20:1
Wyatt, Richard
Peter Pan 1954,O 21,30:2
Wyatt, Richard G
Green Table, The 1942,Ja 22,12:2
Prodigal Son, The 1942,F 18,22:2
Wyatt, Stephen
Midsummer Night's Dream, A 1968,D 9,59:1
Wyatt and Taylor
Holiday on Broadway 1948,Ap 28,33:3
Wycherley, William (Playwright)
Country Wife, The 1926,D 19,VII,6:4
Country Wife, The 1927,Ja 2,VII,2:5
Plain Dealer, The 1929,My 23,27:1
Country Wife, The 1931,Ap 19,31:5
Country Wife, The 1936,O 7,32:3
Country Wife, The 1936,O 25,X,2:4
Country Wife, The 1936,D 2,34:1
Country Wife, The 1936,D 13,XI,3:1
Country Wife, The 1940,Ap 21,IX,1:6
Country Wife, The 1957,Je 27,22:1
Country Wife, The 1957,N 28,56:1
Country Wife, The 1964,Ag 3,16:1
Country Wife, The 1965,D 10,58:2
Country Wife, The 1969,Ag 30,10:3
Wycherly, Margaret
Jane Clegg 1920,F 25,14:1
Mixed Marriage 1920,D 15,18:2
Eyvind of the Hills 1921,F 2,14:1
Verge, The 1921,N 15,23:2
Verge, The 1921,N 20,VI,1:1
Back to Methuselah (Part I: In the Beginning); In the Beginning (Back to Methuselah, Part I) 1922,F 28,17:2
Back to Methuselah (Part II: The Gospel of the Brothers Barnabas); Gospel of the Brothers Barnabas, The (Back to Methuselah, Part II) 1922,F 28,17:2
Back to Methuselah (Part IV: The Tragedy of an Elderly Gentleman); Tragedy of an Elderly Gentleman, The (Back to Methuselah, Part IV) 1922,Mr 7,11:1
Back to Methuselah (Part III: The Thing Happens); Thing Happens, The (Back to Methuselah, Part III) 1922,Mr 7,11:1
Back to Methuselah (Part V: As Far as Thought Can Reach); As Far as Thought Can Reach (Back to Methuselah, Part V) 1922,Mr 14,11:2
Taboo 1922,Ap 5,22:1
What the Public Wants 1922,My 2,22:3
Six Characters in Search of an Author 1922,O 31,11:2
Staircase, The 1923,Ja 29,11:2
Adding Machine, The 1923,Mr 20,24:1
Floriani's Wife 1923,O 1,10:1
Floriani's Wife 1923,O 7,IX,1:1
Blue Peter, The 1925,Mr 25,25:3
Rosmersholm 1925,My 6,27:2
Devil to Pay, The 1925,D 4,26:2
Devil to Pay, The 1925,D 13,IX,3:1
Proud Woman, A 1926,N 16,24:1
Set a Thief 1927,F 22,22:1
Mr Moneypenny 1928,O 17,26:2
Jade God, The 1929,My 14,28:3
Ship, The 1929,N 21,24:7
Round Table, The 1930,F 28,20:5
Getting Married 1931,Mr 31,25:5
Another Language 1932,Ap 26,25:3
Another Language 1932,My 15,VIII,1:1
Another Language 1932,My 9,20:2
Is Life Worth Living? 1933,N 10,24:6
Tobacco Road 1933,D 5,31:2
Hero Is Born, A 1937,O 2,18:6
Macbeth 1937,O 11,26:3
Liliom 1940,Mr 26,17:2
Hedda Gabler 1942,Ja 30,22:2
Dear Judas 1947,Ag 5,26:1
Dear Judas 1947,O 6,26:4
Nineteenth Hole of Europe, The 1949,Mr 28,16:2
Richard III 1953,D 10,65:2
Wycherly, Margaret (Director)
Unchastened Woman, The 1926,F 17,12:1
Ship, The 1929,N 21,24:7
Round Table, The 1930,F 28,20:5
Wyckham, John (Lighting Director)
Oliver 1963,Ja 8,5:5
Comedy of Errors, The 1964,My 21,43:1
Wyckham, John (Scenic Designer)
Beyond the Fringe 1962,O 29,36:1
Beyond the Fringe 1964,Ja 10,18:1
Comedy of Errors, The 1964,My 21,43:1
Wyckland, Lyons
Pasteur 1923,Mr 13,19:1

Wyckoff, Alexander (Scenic Designer)
When the Bough Breaks 1932,F 17,19:2
Anatomist, The 1932,O 25,24:3
Wyckoff, Eugene Thomas (Playwright)
Sonya 1921,Ag 16,18:3
Wyckoff, Evelyn
Lady in the Dark 1941,S 3,26:6
Lady Comes Across, The 1942,Ja 10,10:2
Johnny 2X4 1942,Mr 17,24:6
Hay-Foot, Straw-Foot 1942,O 24,11:6
Oklahoma! 1943,N 14,II,1:1
Wyckoff, Miss
Pickwick 1927,Mr 13,VII,1:1
Wyckoff, Virginia
Johnny 2X4 1942,Mr 17,24:6
Wye, Thomas
Brown Buddies 1930,O 8,29:1
Wyeth, W
Gentlemen, the Queen 1927,Ap 23,14:3
Wygant, Gordon
Blue Blood 1924,Ap 3,21:2
Wykes, Natalie
Love Expert, The 1929,S 24,29:1
Wylan, Sally
Many Loves 1959,Ja 14,28:1
Wylde, Cecil
Laugh It Off 1925,Ap 25,18:4
Wyler, Gretchen
Silk Stockings 1955,F 25,17:3
Silk Stockings 1955,Mr 27,II,1:1
Rumple 1957,N 7,42:2
Wonder World 1964,My 18,32:1
Wyler, Hillary
Trumpets and Drums 1969,O 13,52:1
Wyler, Hillary (Miscellaneous)
Macbeth 1969,D 23,25:1
Wyler, James
Long Watch, The 1952,Mr 21,19:5
Wyler, Jorie
Everyman 1953,O 12,30:2
Wyler, Margrit
Everyman 1941,My 9,19:2
All the King's Men 1948,Ja 19,19:2
Millionairess, The 1949,Ap 7,38:5
Sweet Bird of Youth 1956,Ap 17,27:2
Wyler, Mark
No Trifling With Love 1959,N 10,55:3
Answered the Flute 1960,Mr 10,37:4
Wyler, Michael
He Who Gets Slapped 1946,Mr 21,31:4
Iceman Cometh, The 1946,O 10,31:3
Twelfth Night 1949,O 4,33:2
Wyler, Trude
Quiet, Please! 1940,N 9,20:3
Wylie, Belle (Scenic Designer)
Your Young Men 1935,Ag 8,13:2
Wylie, Elinor (Original Author)
Venetian Glass Nephew, The 1931,F 24,26:3
Wylie, Frank
Chips With Everything 1963,O 2,49:1
Oedipus 1968,Mr 31,II,5:1
Wylie, John
Thumbs Down 1923,Ag 7,20:1
Three Love Affairs; Still Life 1958,Mr 11,33:1
Three Love Affairs; Bedtime Story 1958,Mr 11,33:1
Six Characters in Search of an Author
1961,My 11,43:1
Friends and Lovers; In the Zone; Bound East for
Cardiff 1961,My 11,43:1
Galileo 1968,D 1,88:4
Wylie, John (Director)
Friends and Lovers; In the Zone; Bound East for
Cardiff 1961,My 11,43:1
Friends and Lovers; End of the Beginning, The
1961,My 11,43:1
Friends and Lovers; Proposal, The 1961,My 11,43:1
Galileo 1968,D 1,88:4
Wylie, John (Miscellaneous)
Effect of Gamma Rays on Man-in-the-Moon
Marigolds, The 1965,Je 7,48:1
Wylie, Julian (Director)
Good Companions, The 1931,O 2,31:1
Wylie, Julian (Producer)
Good Companions, The 1931,My 15,20:8
Good Companions, The 1931,O 11,VIII,1:1
Wylie, Lauri (Playwright)
Dear Love 1930,My 18,VIII,3:1
John Murray Anderson's Almanac 1953,D 11,42:2
Almanac 1954,Ja 3,II,1:1
Wylie, Laurie (Original Author)
Prince Charming 1930,O 14,31:1
Wylie, Max (Playwright)
Fundamental George, The 1949,Ag 17,19:4
Wylie, Moira
Man for All Seasons, A 1964,Ja 28,24:2
Shoemaker's Holiday, The 1967,Je 3,19:1
Visit, The 1967,S 13,41:1
She Stoops to Conquer 1968,Ja 1,11:1
Wylie, Robert
Nineteenth Hole of Europe, The 1949,Mr 28,16:2
Wyllie, Meg
Corn Is Green, The 1954,F 27,10:2
First Gentleman, The 1957,Ap 26,22:2

Wylton, Tim
Saint Joan 1962,F 21,57:4
Wyman, Arthur
Blue and the Gray, The; War Is Hell Gray, The
1929,D 27,26:4
Wyman, Arthur E (Director)
Royal Koko 1937,Ja 10,X,2:5
Wyman, Florence
Lady in the Dark 1941,Ja 24,14:2
Wyman, Joel (Playwright)
Dinosaur Wharf 1951,N 9,23:2
Wyman, Kathryn
Man and Superman 1970,F 24,48:1
Hamlet 1970,O 27,54:2
Rosencrantz and Guildenstern Are Dead
1970,N 19,39:3
Wyman, Stephen
Midsummer Night's Dream, A 1967,Je 30,23:1
Endecott and the Red Cross 1968,My 7,50:1
Wymark, Patrick
Much Ado About Nothing 1958,Ag 27,34:6
Twelfth Night 1960,My 18,48:6
Midsummer Night's Dream, A 1962,Jl 2,22:2
Hamlet 1969,My 2,38:1
Wymbs, Luke
Hogan's Goat 1965,N 12,56:1
Wymonds, Robert
Country Wife, The 1965,D 10,58:2
Wymore, Patricia
Up in Central Park 1947,My 20,29:2
Hold It! 1948,My 6,31:5
All for Love 1949,Ja 24,16:5
Wynder, Gloria
Show Boat 1954,My 6,44:1
Show Boat 1954,O 29,28:4
Wyndham, Howard (Miscellaneous)
Taming of the Shrew, The 1937,Ap 11,XI,2:1
French Without Tears 1937,S 29,19:1
Wyndham, Lady (Producer)
Advertising April 1923,F 4,VII,1:4
Wyndham, Olive
Green Goddess, The 1921,Ja 19,14:1
Charlatan, The 1922,Ap 25,14:2
Thin Ice 1922,O 2,20:1
Vaudeville (Palace) 1924,Ap 1,18:1
Steam Roller, The 1924,N 11,20:2
Dinner at Eight 1932,O 24,18:2
Wyner, Yehudi
Johnny 2X4 1942,Mr 17,24:6
Wyner, Yehudi (Composer)
My Kinsman, Major Molineux 1964,N 2,62:2
Benito Cereno 1964,N 2,62:2
Wyngarde, Peter
Duel of Angels 1960,Ap 20,42:2
Two Character Play, The 1967,D 13,54:5
Wyngate, Valerie
Her Cardboard Lover 1927,Mr 22,30:5
Wyngate, Valerie (Playwright)
Her Cardboard Lover 1927,Mr 22,30:5
Her Cardboard Lover 1928,S 9,IX,2:7
Wynn, Ed
Ed Wynn's Carnival 1920,Ap 6,18:2
Ed Wynn's Carnival 1920,Ap 18,VI,2:3
All-Star Idlers of 1921, The 1921,Jl 16,5:2
Perfect Fool, The 1921,N 8,28:2
Perfect Fool, The 1921,N 27,VI,1:1
Lambs Gambol 1922,Ja 30,16:1
Grab Bag, The 1924,S 7,VII,1:4
Grab Bag, The 1924,O 7,26:2
Manhattan Mary 1927,S 4,VII,2:4
Manhattan Mary 1927,S 27,30:3
Manhattan Mary 1927,O 30,IX,1:1
Simple Simon 1930,F 2,VIII,2:7
Simple Simon 1930,F 19,22:1
Simple Simon 1930,Mr 2,IX,1:1
Simple Simon 1930,Mr 16,IX,1:1
Simple Simon 1930,N 23,IX,1:3
Simple Simon 1931,Mr 10,23:2
Vaudeville (Palace) 1931,My 4,15:2
Laugh Parade, The 1931,S 20,VIII,3:1
Laugh Parade, The 1931,N 3,31:2
Laugh Parade, The 1931,D 6,VIII,1:1
Lambs Gambol 1932,Ap 25,18:2
Light Behind the Shadow, The 1936,Ja 21,26:6
Hooray for What! 1937,N 7,XI,2:4
Hooray for What! 1937,D 2,32:5
Boys and Girls Together 1940,S 5,28:6
Boys and Girls Together 1940,O 2,19:2
Boys and Girls Together 1940,O 13,IX,1:1
Untitled-Revue 1941,My 18,IX,1:1
Laugh, Town, Laugh! 1942,Je 20,9:1
Laugh, Town, Laugh! 1942,Je 23,22:2
Laugh, Town, Laugh! 1942,Jl 23,15:3
Wynn, Ed (Composer)
Perfect Fool, The 1921,N 8,28:2
Grab Bag, The 1924,S 7,VII,1:4
Grab Bag, The 1924,O 7,26:2
Wynn, Ed (Director)
Laugh Parade, The 1931,N 3,31:2
Boys and Girls Together 1940,S 5,28:6
Boys and Girls Together 1940,O 2,19:2
Wynn, Ed (Lyricist)
Perfect Fool, The 1921,N 8,28:2

Wynn, Ed (Lyricist)—Cont
Grab Bag, The 1924,S 7,VII,1:4
Grab Bag, The 1924,O 7,26:2
Wynn, Ed (Playwright)
Ed Wynn's Carnival 1920,Ap 6,18:2
Perfect Fool, The 1921,N 8,28:2
Grab Bag, The 1924,S 7,VII,1:4
Grab Bag, The 1924,O 7,26:2
Simple Simon 1930,F 2,VIII,2:7
Simple Simon 1930,F 19,22:1
Simple Simon 1931,Mr 10,23:2
Laugh Parade, The 1931,N 3,31:2
Boys and Girls Together 1940,S 5,28:6
Boys and Girls Together 1940,O 2,19:2
Wynn, Ed (Producer)
Grab Bag, The 1924,S 7,VII,1:4
Laugh Parade, The 1931,S 20,VIII,3:1
Laugh Parade, The 1931,N 3,31:2
Light Behind the Shadow, The 1936,Ja 21,26:6
Alice Takat 1936,F 11,19:2
Boys and Girls Together 1940,S 5,28:6
Boys and Girls Together 1940,O 2,19:2
Laugh, Town, Laugh! 1942,Je 20,9:1
Laugh, Town, Laugh! 1942,Je 23,22:2
Laugh, Town, Laugh! 1942,Jl 23,15:3
Wynn, Helen
Hat, a Coat, a Glove, A 1934,F 1,15:2
Penny Wise 1935,Jl 2,24:2
As You Like It 1937,N 1,25:2
Three Sisters, The 1939,O 16,23:1
Wynn, Jack
Show Boat 1927,D 28,26:1
Wynn, Jess
Press Time 1938,N 28,10:4
Wynn, John
Of V We Sing 1942,F 16,20:3
Wynn, Keenan
Ten Minute Alibi 1935,Je 11,24:4
Remember the Day 1935,Jl 9,24:3
Stag at Bay, The 1935,Jl 30,17:1
Little Inn, The 1935,Ag 20,25:1
Remember the Day 1935,S 26,19:3
Feather in the Breeze 1936,Jl 14,22:2
Hitch Your Wagon! 1937,Ap 9,18:2
One for the Money 1939,F 6,9:2
Two for the Show 1940,F 9,14:2
Two for the Show 1940,F 18,IX,1:1
More the Merrier, The 1941,S 16,19:3
Johnny on the Spot 1942,Ja 9,24:2
Strip for Action 1942,O 1,26:2
Strip for Action 1942,O 11,VIII,1:1
Wynn, Linurte
World's My Oyster, The 1956,Ag 10,10:4
Wynn, Nan
Seven Lively Arts 1944,D 8,26:6
Wynn, Paul
Lady of the Lamp, The 1920,Ag 18,6:4
Wynn, Phyllis
Song of Songs 1958,O 29,31:1
Wynn, Virginia
Rose Girl, The 1921,F 12,11:1
Wynn-Evans, John
Philanderer, The 1958,My 13,26:2
Wynne, Angus G Jr (Miscellaneous)
To Broadway With Love 1964,Ap 30,28:6
Wynne, Hazel
Earl Carroll's Vanities 1927,Ja 5,18:1
Wynne, Jess
Lady Precious Stream 1936,Ja 28,15:2
Good Hunting 1938,N 22,26:5
Wynne, John
Silver Tassie, The 1929,O 25,26:1
Ah, Wilderness! 1933,O 3,28:2
Wynne, Ken
King Lear 1964,My 19,43:2
Comedy of Errors, The 1964,My 21,43:1
Wynne, Mabel (Composer)
Flying Trapeze, The 1935,Je 2,IX,2:3
Wynne, Patricia
Oh, Ernest! 1927,My 10,24:3
Wynne, Peggy
Tinker's Dam 1943,Ja 29,22:2
Hickory Stick 1944,My 9,15:6
Wynne, Shirley
Big Fight, The 1928,S 19,33:1
Wynne, Winifred
Barbara's Wedding 1931,O 9,21:1
Wynne, Wish
Double Dan 1927,Je 5,VII,2:1
Wynne-Evans, John
Will and the Way, The 1957,D 3,46:5
You Never Can Tell 1958,Je 17,25:1
Picnic on the Battlefield 1960,My 17,42:2
Escurial 1960,Jl 22,13:1
Calvary 1960,Jl 22,13:1
Mousetrap, The 1960,N 7,46:1
Happy as Larry 1961,Ap 26,36:1
Much Ado About Nothing 1963,Jl 15,25:2
Arms and the Man 1963,Ap 28,41:1
Wynne-Tyson, Esme (Playwright)
Security 1929,Mr 29,20:1
Wynroth, Alan
Moondreamers, The 1969,D 9,68:1
Marie Vison, La 1970,Jl 15,29:1

Wynroth, Alan—Cont
Coney Island Play 1970,O 31,34:2
Wynter, Dana
Black-Eyed Susan 1954,D 24,7:5
Wynter, Georgina
Matriarch, The 1930,Mr 19,24:5
Wynters, Charlotte
Bad Girl 1930,O 3,30:2
Wiser They Are, The 1931,Ap 7,31:1
Regular Guy, A; Man's Man, A 1931,Je 5,27:1
Air-Minded 1932,F 11,17:3
Her Tin Soldier 1933,Ap 7,22:6
Wynters, Wendy
Yes, Yes, No No 1969,Ja 1,16:1
Wynyard, Diana
Sorry You've Been Troubled 1929,O 13,IX,4:1
Man Who Pays the Piper, The 1931,Mr 1,VIII,2:4
Lean Harvest 1931,My 8,20:2
Devil Passes, The 1932,Ja 5,20:3
Devil Passes, The 1932,Ja 10,VIII,1:1
Wild December 1933,Je 25,IX,1:3
Sweet Aloes 1934,N 1,24:1
Players' Masque for Marie Tempest, The
1935,Je 23,IX,1:3
Anteroom, The 1936,Ag 15,6:7
Anteroom, The 1936,S 6,IX,1:1
Heart's Content 1936,D 24,22:2
Heart's Content 1937,Ja 24,X,3:1
Silent Knight, The 1937,N 17,26:4
Silent Knight, The 1937,D 5,XII,5:8
Watch on the Rhine 1942,My 3,VIII,1:7
Wind of Heaven, The 1945,Ap 22,II,2:3
Much Ado About Nothing 1952,F 10,II,2:1
Bad Seed, The 1955,My 1,II,3:1
Cue for Passion 1958,N 26,25:2
Cue for Passion 1958,D 7,II,5:1
Heartbreak House 1959,O 19,37:1
Heartbreak House 1959,O 25,II,1:1
Bird of Time 1961,Je 25,II,3:5
Hamlet 1963,O 23,37:2
Wynyard, John
King Lear 1947,F 19,32:2
As You Like It 1947,F 21,16:2
Merchant of Venice, The 1947,F 24,16:2
Volpone 1947,F 25,32:2
Hamlet 1947,F 27,27:2
Wypraechtiger, Hans
Before Sundown 1962,Mr 14,43:1
Wyse, John
Visit, The 1958,My 6,40:1
Visit, The 1960,Mr 9,38:3
Wyse, Ronald
Yours Truly 1927,Ja 26,16:5
Wyse, Ross Jr
Vaudeville (Palace) 1932,Jl 11,11:6
Scandals 1939,Ag 29,17:2
Wysocka, Lydia
Visit With the Family, A 1957,O 17,42:5
Wysor, Frances
Hansel and Gretel 1929,D 25,21:1
Wyspianski, Stanislaw (Playwright)
Acropolis 1969,N 5,40:1

X

Xaba, Douglas
Sponono 1964,Ap 3,28:1
Xant, Leyki
Cute Gata.....Oute Zhmia; Neither Cat . . . Nor
Damage 1957,D 20,31:1
Xantho, P A
But for the Grace of God 1937,Ja 13,21:4
Xantho, Peter
Bitter Stream 1936,Mr 31,16:6
Beautiful People, The 1941,Ap 22,27:2
Xantho, Peter (Lighting Director)
International Playgirls '64 1964,My 22,40:2
Wonderful World of Burlesque, The
1965,Ap 29,38:1
Xavier, Francis
Fencing Master, The 1936,Ap 1,29:1
Xeaakis, Iannis (Composer)
Oresteia 1966,Je 30,29:1
Xenakis, Antonis
Electra 1961,S 20,23:4
Choephori 1961,S 27,32:4
Eumenides 1961,S 27,32:4
Medea 1964,S 1,31:1
Electra 1964,S 8,33:1
Iphigenia in Aulis 1968,N 13,40:1
Hippolytus 1968,N 20,38:3
Xiegu, La
Student of Vich 1929,Ja 3,25:2
Ximenez, Chavo
Fiesta in Madrid 1969,My 29,49:1
Xirgu, Margarita
Dona Maria de Castilla 1933,Mr 19,IV,2:2
Dama Boba, La; Villano En Su Rincon, El;
Fuenteovejuna 1935,S 22,X,2:5

Y

Yablokoff, Herman
Papirossen 1936,S 18,19:3
Give Me Back My Heart 1937,O 4,17:6
Semele's Bar Mitzvah 1938,Ja 17,11:2
My Son and I 1960,O 24,24:2
Yablokoff, Herman (Director)
Give Me Back My Heart 1937,O 4,17:6
It's a Funny World 1956,O 22,24:1
It Could Happen to You 1957,O 28,30:5
My Son and I 1960,O 24,24:2
Yablokoff, Herman (Lyricist)
It's a Funny World 1956,O 22,24:1
Yablokoff, Herman (Playwright)
It's a Funny World 1956,O 22,24:1
My Son and I 1960,O 24,24:2
Yablokoff, Herman (Producer)
Uncle Sam in Israel 1952,D 8,38:5
Yablonovitz, Nahum (Producer)
Fools Are Passing Through 1958,Ap 3,24:2
Yablonski, Joseph (Playwright)
Shorty 1948,N 14,I,70:6
Yablonski, Margaret (Playwright)
Shorty 1948,N 14,I,70:6
Yablonsky, Yabo (Director)
Americana Pastoral 1968,D 11,51:1
Yablonsky, Yabo (Playwright)
Americana Pastoral 1968,D 11,51:1
Yachson, L
Oy, Is Dus a Leben!; Oh, What a Life!
1942,O 13,19:2
Yachson, Mordecai
In-Laws 1960,O 17,32:4
Bei Mir Bistu Schoen 1961,O 23,22:2
World Is a Stage, The 1962,N 5,37:4
Bride Got Farblondjet, The 1967,N 6,61:6
Yachson, Mordecai (Director)
Thousand and One Nights 1959,D 16,53:2
Yachson, Mordecai (Miscellaneous)
In-Laws 1960,O 17,32:4
Bei Mir Bistu Schoen 1961,O 23,22:2
It's Never Too Late for Happiness 1968,O 21,59:3
Oh What a Wedding! 1969,O 20,60:1
President's Daughter, The 1970,N 4,41:2
Yacht Club Boys
Vaudeville (Palace) 1932,Ap 4,13:4
Yacknowitz, Aron (Translator)
Lower Depths, The 1956,O 3,29:2
Yacopi Troupe
Vaudeville (Palace) 1929,F 11,26:2
Vaudeville (Palace) 1932,Ja 4,27:4
Yaeckel, Louis
Venetian Glass Nephew, The 1931,F 24,26:3
Yaeger, Rosetta
Don't Worry Brother! 1963,O 14,35:2
Yaeger, Sue
Sound of Music, The 1959,N 17,40:2
Yaenosuke, Bando
Kagotsurube; Courtesan, The 1960,Je 3,26:1
Musume Dojoji; Maiden at the Dojo Temple, The
1960,Je 10,37:1
Musume Dojoji; Maiden at the Dojo Temple, The
1960,Je 17,35:4
Yaffe, James (Playwright)
Deadly Game, The 1960,Ja 31,II,1:7
Deadly Game, The 1960,F 3,27:2
Dear Me, the Sky Is Falling 1963,Mr 4,9:1
Deadly Game, The 1966,F 14,34:1
Yaffe, Maury
Winter's Tale, The 1946,Ja 16,18:6
Yaffee, Ben
No for an Answer 1941,Ja 6,10:6
Fifth Horseman, The 1949,Je 14,26:6
Cock-A-Doodle Dandy 1950,F 1,26:2
My 3 Angels 1956,F 4,24:2
Compulsion 1957,O 25,21:1
Seagull, The 1964,Ap 6,36:1
Crucible, The 1964,Ap 7,30:2
Sondra 1967,My 10,39:1
Harold 1967,My 10,39:1
Beyond Desire 1967,O 11,36:1
Yager, Anita
Private Life of the Master Race, The
1956,Ja 31,33:3
Yager, Rosetta
Honeymoon in Israel, A 1962,O 15,33:5
Yago, Anne
Girofle-Girofla 1926,N 24,26:2
Patience 1931,Je 16,30:4
Pirates of Penzance, The; Slave of Duty, The
1931,Je 30,23:6
Yahya, Bennett
Trumpets and Drums 1969,O 13,52:1
Young Among Themselves, The 1970,Je 12,28:1
Yahya, Easter (Lyricist)
From Here to There; Real Strange One, A
1958,Ag 24,37:3
Yakim, Moni (Choreographer)
Henry V 1969,N 11,43:1

Yakim, Moni (Director)
Jacques Brel Is Alive and Well and Living in Paris
1968,Ja 23,25:2
Yakovleff, Alexander
O'Brien Girl, The 1921,O 4,10:2
Greenwich Village Follies 1922,S 13,18:2
Ziegfeld Follies 1923,O 22,17:2
East Wind 1931,O 28,19:1
Yakovleff, Alexander (Choreographer)
Music Hath Charms 1934,D 31,8:2
Yakovleva, Boris
Moscow Circus on Ice 1970,D 9,63:1
Yakovleva, Olga M
Romeo and Juliet 1970,My 28,28:1
Yakubowitz, Anna
Both Kooney Lemels 1964,O 12,37:2
Yakulow, N E (Scenic Designer)
Eternal Jew, The 1926,D 21,21:2
Yale Glee Club
Hay-Foot, Straw-Foot 1942,O 24,11:6
Yale Puppeteers
Pie-Eyed Piper, The 1932,D 5,21:4
Mister Noah 1933,Ja 18,16:2
Caesar Julius 1933,Mr 1,13:3
Sunday Nights at 9 1935,N 11,21:1
Sunday Nights at Nine 1936,D 7,27:3
Yalis, Grant (Playwright)
Night's Candles 1933,Je 25,IX,1:3
Yalman, Tunic (Director)
Trial of Lee Harvey Oswald, The 1967,N 6,64:1
Prince of Peasantmania 1970,F 22,88:1
Yama, Conrad
Flower Drum Song 1958,D 2,44:1
I Had a Ball 1964,D 16,50:1
Box-Mao-Box; Quotations From Chairman Mao
Tse-Tung 1968,Mr 8,48:1
Yamaguchi, Shirley
Shangri-La 1956,Je 14,40:1
Yamamota
Thrills 1925,Ap 17,24:3
Yamashige, George
Family, The 1943,Mr 31,22:4
Yanakopoulos, C (Playwright)
Cute Gata.....Oute Zhmia; Neither Cat . . . Nor
Damage 1957,D 20,31:1
Yancy, Emily
Hello, Dolly! 1967,N 13,61:1
Hello, Dolly! 1967,N 26,II,3:1
Yandell, L P
They Never Come Back 1920,D 19,I,22:3
Yanelli, Frank
Babes in Toyland 1929,D 24,15:3
Babes in Toyland 1930,D 22,17:1
Yanka, Ruzzka
Room of Dreams 1930,N 6,22:4
Yannelli, Francesco
Fortune Teller, The 1929,N 5,32:3
Merry Widow, The 1929,D 3,29:1
Yanni, Gene
Young Provincials, The 1958,S 19,22:4
Yano, Hiroji
Spider, The 1927,Mr 23,29:1
Play Without a Name, A 1928,N 26,30:5
Yanofsky, Nat
Seven Against One 1930,My 7,25:1
Yanover, David
One Woman 1931,D 14,16:4
Yanowitz, Sandra (Miscellaneous)
Postcards 1970,Mr 17,36:1
Grin and Bare It 1970,Mr 17,36:1
Yanowitz, Susan (Playwright)
Terminal 1970,Ap 15,51:2
Terminal 1970,My 24,II,3:1
Yanshin, Mikhail
Dead Souls 1965,F 5,34:1
Cherry Orchard, The 1965,F 10,46:1
Yantis, Luther (Playwright)
Chippies 1929,My 30,23:3
Yanuzzi, Laura
Veronica's Veil 1950,F 12,II,1:5
Yaple, Paul
Nobody's Business 1923,O 23,17:1
Yapp, Cecil
Prince and the Pauper, The 1920,N 2,15:1
Blue Lagoon, The 1921,S 15,16:1
Madame Pierre 1922,F 16,11:1
Why Not? 1922,D 25,20:1
Cyrano de Bergerac 1923,N 2,14:1
Wild Duck, The 1925,F 25,16:4
Hamlet 1925,O 12,19:2
Merchant of Venice, The 1925,D 28,12:1
Cyrano de Bergerac 1926,F 19,18:1
Immortal Thief, The 1926,O 4,21:1
Caponsacchi 1926,O 27,24:2
Enemy of the People, An 1927,O 4,32:5
Hamlet 1928,Ja 5,33:2
Henry V 1928,Mr 16,26:2
Light of Asia 1928,O 10,32:2
Enemy of the People, An 1928,N 6,34:3
Cyrano de Bergerac 1928,D 26,14:4
Bonds of Interest, The 1929,O 15,34:2
Richelieu 1929,D 26,20:3
He 1931,S 22,33:1

Yaray, Hans (Director)
Ist Geraldine ein Engel? 1946,N 4,33:4
Yaray, Hans (Playwright)
Ist Geraldine ein Engel? 1946,N 4,33:4
Yarborough, Bertram (Director)
These Tender Mercies 1948,Je 7,16:4
Three by Thurber; Imperturbable Spirit, The 1955,Mr 8,23:2
Three by Thurber; Middle Years, The 1955,Mr 8,23:2
Three by Thurber; Mr Montoe Holds the Fort 1955,Mr 8,23:2
Oh, Kay! 1960,Ap 18,37:2
Yarborough, Bertram (Miscellaneous)
Oh, Kay! 1960,Ap 18,37:2
Yarborough, Bertram (Playwright)
These Tender Mercies 1948,Je 7,16:4
Yarborough, Katherine
Runnin' Wild 1923,O 30,17:3
Yarbough, Billie
Keep Shufflin' 1928,F 28,18:3
Just a Minute 1928,O 9,34:3
Yarbrough, Camille
Cities in Bezique; Beast's Story, A 1969,Ja 13,26:1
Trumpets of the Lord 1969,Ap 30,37:1
Sambo 1969,D 22,42:1
Yarde, Margaret
Many Waters 1929,S 26,27:1
Poison Pen 1937,Ag 10,22:3
Yaretskaya, Rogneda
Uncle Vanya 1960,F 13,13:4
Yarick, Doris
Gondoliers, The 1961,Ja 26,33:2
H M S Pinafore 1961,F 2,26:6
Iolanthe 1962,Ap 12,42:4
Yarmis, Joseph
Mikado, The 1935,Ag 24,17:5
Yarmy, Dick
Adaptation 1970,Mr 12,46:1
Yarnell, Bruce
Hit the Deck 1960,Je 24,32:1
Camelot 1960,D 5,42:1
Happiest Girl in the World, The 1961,Ap 4,42:1
Annie Get Your Gun 1966,Je 1,42:2
Carousel 1966,D 16,56:2
Oklahoma! 1969,Je 24,37:1
Oklahoma! 1969,Jl 6,II,1:1
Yaroch, Greg
Night Thoreau Spent in Jail, The 1970,N 2,66:1
Yaron, Mira
Uncle Sam in Israel 1952,D 8,38:5
Yaroshevskaya, Kim
Henry V 1966,Je 8,38:1
Yarus, Buddy
Of V We Sing 1942,F 16,20:3
Let Freedom Sing 1942,O 6,18:2
Yaryan, Ted
Othello 1945,My 23,25:4
Strange Fruit 1945,N 30,18:6
Chase, The 1952,Ap 16,30:2
Yasunori, Saito
Golden Bat 1970,Je 27,18:2
Yates, Aubrey
Pirates of Penzance, The 1938,Je 3,16:2
Yates, Charles (Producer)
K Guy, The 1928,O 16,28:4
Yates, Christopher
Stephen D 1966,Ag 5,17:1
Yates, Clarence
Doctor Faustus 1937,Ja 9,21:2
Horse Play 1937,Ag 28,8:3
Yates, Dolores
Some of the People 1937,Mr 11,20:1
Yates, Elene
Trigger 1927,D 7,32:1
Yates, Gladys
Allez-Opp! 1927,Ag 3,29:3
Yates, Grant (Playwright)
Night's Candles 1933,S 21,22:1
Yates, Harold
Earl Carroll's Vanities 1925,Jl 7,24:1
Vaudeville (Palace) 1929,S 9,30:5
Yates, Irving (Producer)
K Guy, The 1928,O 16,28:4
Yates, Kathryn
Some Party 1922,Ap 17,22:1
Yates, Ruth
New Freedom, The 1930,My 15,32:4
New Freedom, The 1930,My 17,21:4
Yates and Lawley
Vaudeville (Palace) 1930,Ag 11,13:3
Yd, Jean d'
Brothers Karamazov, The 1926,D 12,VIII,3:4
Yeager, Edith
Launzi 1923,O 11,16:3
Yearsley, Wister
Poisoned Kiss, The 1937,Ap 22,19:1
Yeates, Ray
Jezebel 1933,D 20,26:3
Stevedore 1934,Ap 19,33:2
Porgy and Bess 1935,O 11,30:2
Sweet River 1936,O 29,30:2
John Henry 1940,Ja 11,18:2

Porgy and Bess 1953,Mr 10,25:5
Yeatman, R S (Original Author)
1066 and All That 1935,My 26,XI,2:5
Yeats, William Butler (Playwright)
Kathleen ni Houlihan 1920,Je 29,9:2
Player Queen, The 1923,O 17,14:2
Fighting the Waves 1929,Ag 11,15:6
Fighting the Waves 1929,S 22,IX,4:1
Hour Glass, The 1930,O 26,VIII,4:6
Words Upon the Window Pane, The 1930,N 19,19:5
Words Upon the Window Pane, The 1931,Ja 4,VIII,3:5
Cat and the Moon, The 1931,N 8,VIII,4:3
Words Upon the Window Pane, The 1932,O 29,18:2
Cathleen ni Houlihan 1932,O 31,18:1
King Oedipus 1933,Ja 16,12:4
Resurrection 1934,N 20,24:5
Oedipus Rex 1945,N 11,II,2:5
Oedipus 1946,My 21,19:2
Oedipus Rex 1954,Jl 17,6:6
Hour Glass, The 1955,O 17,33:1
Cat and the Moon, The 1959,Ja 27,27:5
Death of Cuchulain, The 1959,Ap 13,34:4
On Baile's Strand 1959,Ap 13,34:4
Calvary 1960,Jl 22,13:1
Full Moon in March, A 1960,S 20,48:1
Purgatory 1960,S 20,48:1
Herne's Egg, The 1960,S 20,48:1
Horseman, Pass By 1969,Ja 16,46:4
Only Jealousy of Emer, The 1970,Mr 25,36:4
Only Jealousy of Emer, The 1970,Ap 26,II,1:3
Yeats, William Butler (Translator)
Oedipus the King 1926,D 26,VII,4:8
Oedipus Rex 1945,D 17,16:7
Oedipus Rex 1956,S 4,32:6
Yeh, Ching
Hawk, The 1968,Ap 18,54:1
Moondreamers, The 1969,D 9,68:1
Yehuda, Meyer Ben (Composer)
Don't Worry Brother! 1963,O 14,35:2
Yehuda, Meyer Ben (Lyricist)
Honeymoon in Israel, A 1962,O 15,33:5
Yehuda, Meyer Ben (Playwright)
Honeymoon in Israel, A 1962,O 15,33:5
Yellanti, Nicholas (Scenic Designer)
Allure 1934,O 30,22:6
Yellen, Jack (Composer)
Sons o' Fun 1941,D 2,28:2
Yellen, Jack (Lyricist)
Spice of 1922 1922,Jl 7,12:4
Rain or Shine 1928,F 10,26:3
Murray Anderson's Almanac 1929,Ag 15,20:3
You Said It 1931,Ja 20,21:3
George White's Scandals 1935,D 26,20:2
Scandals 1939,Ag 29,17:2
Boys and Girls Together 1940,O 2,19:2
Ziegfeld Follies 1943,Ap 2,16:2
Yellen, Jack (Playwright)
You Said It 1931,Ja 20,21:3
Yellen, Jack (Producer)
You Said It 1931,Ja 20,21:3
Yellen, Sherman (Miscellaneous)
Oh! Calcutta! 1969,Je 18,33:1
Yellen, Sherman (Playwright)
Rothschilds, The 1970,O 20,40:1
Rothschilds, The 1970,N 1,II,1:1
Yellenti, Nicholas (Lighting Director)
Vigil, The 1948,My 22,8:6
Yellenti, Nicholas (Scenic Designer)
Easy Come, Easy Go 1925,O 27,20:2
Twelve Miles Out 1925,N 17,29:2
Solid Ivory 1925,N 17,29:3
Find Daddy 1926,Mr 9,21:3
Mirrors 1928,Ja 19,17:1
Mystery Man, The 1928,Ja 27,14:2
Quicksand 1928,F 14,26:3
Behavior of Mrs Crane, The 1928,Mr 21,30:1
Golden Age, The 1928,Ap 25,31:3
Happy Husband, The 1928,My 8,25:2
Get Me in the Movies 1928,My 22,18:3
War Song, The 1928,S 25,29:3
Adventure 1928,S 26,25:2
Tin Pan Alley 1928,N 2,29:1
Brothers 1928,D 26,14:3
Millions 1930,O 3,30:4
In The Best of Families 1931,F 3,29:1
Her Supporting Cast 1931,My 5,33:3
In Times Square 1931,N 24,29:3
Web, The 1932,Je 28,24:4
Curtain Rises, The 1933,O 20,15:2
American, Very Early 1934,Ja 31,21:2
Theodora, the Queen 1934,F 1,15:3
When in Rome 1934,F 28,22:6
Baby Pompadour 1934,D 28,24:2
Woman of the Soil, A 1935,Mr 26,23:6
Ragged Edge, The 1935,N 26,28:3
Love on the Dole 1936,F 25,23:3
Arrest That Woman 1936,S 19,20:4
Around the Corner 1936,D 29,17:2
Behind the Red Lights 1937,Ja 14,17:4
Something for Nothing 1937,D 10,33:5

Yellenti, Nicholas (Scenic Designer)—Cont
Censored 1938,F 28,18:2
Bright Rebel 1938,D 28,24:2
Aries Is Rising 1939,N 22,16:5
Vigil, The 1948,My 22,8:6
Yellin, Bill (Producer)
Nighthawks 1967,D 30,14:2
Yellin, Gleb (Composer)
Chauve-Souris of 1943 1943,Ag 13,13:2
Yelvington, Ramsey (Playwright)
Long Gallery, The 1958,Mr 7,17:2
Yeo, Mary Jane
It Happens on Ice 1940,O 11,24:3
It Happens on Ice 1941,Ap 5,13:2
Stars on Ice 1942,Jl 3,12:2
Stars on Ice (2d Edition) 1943,Je 25,13:2
Yerby, Lorees (Playwright)
Last Minstrel, The 1963,My 9,40:2
Save Me a Place at Forest Lawn 1963,My 9,40:2
Yerkes Flotilla Band
Vaudeville (Hippodrome) 1924,Mr 18,25:1
Yerkes Jazzy Six
Scandals 1920,Je 8,9:1
Yershoff, Vladimir
Tsar Fyodor Ivanovitch 1923,Ja 9,26:1
Brothers Karamazov, The 1923,N 20,23:4
In the Claws of Life 1923,N 30,23:4
Enemy of the People, An 1923,D 4,25:1
Death of Pazukhin, The 1924,F 12,20:1
Yerzy, David
Mountain, The 1933,S 12,28:6
Yessner, George
Chalk Dust 1936,Mr 5,24:5
Hymn to the Rising Sun 1937,My 7,28:2
Ygor and Tanya
Earl Carroll's Vanities 1940,Ja 15,11:2
Yiddish Art Company
Yoshe Kalb 1932,O 3,15:5
Yiddish Art Players
Day of Judgement, The 1941,O 9,27:3
Yiddishe Bande
Untitled-Revue 1939,Ap 5,31:2
Ying, Edwin Kim
Shangri-La 1956,Je 14,40:1
Ynes (Costume Designer)
Love and Let Love 1968,Ja 4,30:1
Yo-Hay-Tong
Nina Rosa 1930,S 22,22:5
Yoalit, Eva
Lenin's Dowry 1932,My 13,17:3
Untitled-Dramatic Reading 1933,Mr 6,16:4
Yochem, Valeria (Scenic Designer)
Seven Keys to Baldpate 1930,Ja 8,25:2
Yockel, Dorothy
Sea Gull, The 1929,Ap 10,32:2
Yoham, Jimmy
Affair of Honor 1956,Ap 7,12:3
Yohe, May and Her Orchestra
Vaudeville (Palace) 1923,My 15,22:2
Yohn, Erica
Alchemist, The 1966,O 14,48:1
Yerma 1966,D 9,60:1
Empire Builders, The 1968,O 2,34:1
Yokel, Alex (Producer)
Song Writer, The 1928,Ag 14,15:2
Under the Gaslight 1929,Ap 3,27:1
Three Men on a Horse 1935,Ja 22,22:7
Three Men on a Horse 1935,Ja 31,22:3
Julie the Great 1936,Ja 15,15:3
Three Men on a Horse 1936,Mr 24,26:4
Bury the Dead 1936,Ap 20,17:4
Prelude 1936,Ap 20,17:4
Bury the Dead 1936,Ap 26,IX,1:1
Love From a Stranger 1936,S 22,31:5
Love From a Stranger 1936,S 30,28:1
Young Mr Disraeli 1937,N 10,30:5
Horse Fever 1940,N 25,21:2
Three Men on a Horse 1942,O 10,10:2
Snark Was a Boojum, The 1943,S 2,14:4
Yokel, Dorothy
Caponsacchi 1928,Ja 25,20:3
Yokelson, Marshall (Scenic Designer)
All Summer Long 1953,Ja 29,23:1
Yoko, Shimoda
Golden Bat 1970,Je 27,18:2
Yokoyama, Elaine (Costume Designer)
Local Stigmatic, The; Trouble in the Works 1969,N 4,55:2
Local Stigmatic, The; Interview 1969,N 4,55:2
Local Stigmatic, The; Request Stop 1969,N 4,55:2
Local Stigmatic, The; That's All 1969,N 4,55:2
Local Stigmatic, The; Last to Go 1969,N 4,55:2
Local Stigmatic, The 1969,N 4,55:2
Local Stigmatic, The; That's Your Trouble 1969,N 4,55:2
Local Stigmatic, The; Applicant 1969,N 4,55:2
Yolanda
Pleasure Bound 1929,F 19,22:4
Yomen, Ben (Composer)
200,000 1936,O 14,30:2
Yong, Soo
House Unguarded 1929,Ja 16,22:2
Untitled-Recital 1930,Mr 10,24:4

Yong, Soo (Miss) (Miscellaneous)
Mei Lan-Fang 1930,F 17,18:2
Yongeyans, George
Consul, The 1950,Mr 2,32:3
Yonnel
Belle Mariniere, La 1929,D 8,X,2:2
Hamlet 1932,Je 12,X,1:1
Yordan, Philip (Playwright)
Any Day Now 1941,Je 10,28:2
Anna Lucasta 1944,Je 17,10:1
Anna Lucasta 1944,Ag 31,15:1
Anna Lucasta 1944,S 24,II,1:5
Anna Lucasta 1947,O 30,31:3
Anna Lucasta 1947,N 9,II,3:7
Anna Lucasta 1956,Ap 13,21:8
Bride Got Farblondjet, The 1967,N 6,61:6
York, Allen
Big Mogul, The 1925,My 12,26:3
York, Ann
Almost Crazy 1955,Je 21,37:1
York, Cameron
Bitter Sweet 1934,My 8,28:4
York, Chick
Vaudeville (Hippodrome) 1924,Ja 22,15:6
Vaudeville (Palace) 1926,N 16,24:3
A la Carte 1927,Ag 18,25:3
Take the Air 1927,N 23,28:2
Vaudeville (Palace) 1930,My 26,25:2
Vaudeville (Palace) 1931,Je 8,21:2
Show Is On, The 1937,S 20,18:4
High Kickers 1941,N 1,21:2
York, Dick
Tea and Sympathy 1953,O 1,35:1
Night of the Auk 1956,D 4,50:2
York, Doris
Best Foot Forward 1941,O 2,28:2
York, Harry
Riot 1968,D 20,64:1
York, Henrietta
Don Juan 1921,S 8,14:2
York, James
Jig Saw 1934,My 1,26:3
York, Melanie
Time to Go 1952,My 8,35:6
Hall of Healing 1952,My 8,35:6
York, Peter
Rondelay 1969,N 6,55:1
York, Powell
Wall Street 1927,Ap 21,24:4
York, Richard (Producer)
Boys From Syracuse, The 1963,Ap 16,31:1
York, Robert
Mad Morning 1935,Je 25,14:1
York, Robert (Playwright)
Ride a Cock Horse 1937,Ap 4,II,9:7
York, Sussanah
Wings of the Dove, The 1963,D 4,53:6
York, True
Vaudeville (Palace) 1930,My 26,25:2
York, Vincent
What Every Woman Knows 1926,Ap 14,20:2
Chicago 1926,D 31,11:1
Spread Eagle 1927,Ap 5,30:2
Front Page, The 1928,Ag 15,19:2
Up and Up, The 1930,S 9,25:2
Incubator 1932,N 2,23:3
Shooting Star 1933,Je 13,22:2
American, Very Early 1934,Ja 31,21:2
Brother Rat 1936,D 17,34:5
Best Foot Forward 1941,O 2,28:2
York, Vincent (Playwright)
Brittle Heaven 1934,N 14,22:5
York and King
Vaudeville (Palace) 1923,N 20,23:4
Vaudeville (Hippodrome) 1926,Mr 16,22:2
Vaudeville (Palace) 1930,S 22,23:2
York Players
Coming of Christ, The 1957,D 23,29:8
Yorke, Alan
Malcolm 1966,Ja 12,29:1
Yorke, Augustus
Glory Hallelujah 1926,Ap 7,26:2
Yorke, Bert
Vaudeville (Palace) 1923,O 23,18:2
Yorke, Gustave
Crime 1927,F 23,27:3
Yorke, Helen
Vaudeville (Palace) 1930,S 29,19:1
Yorke, John
Merry Widow, The 1921,S 6,13:1
Yorke, John (Producer)
Oh, Mr Meadowbrook! 1948,D 27,17:2
Boy Friend, The 1970,Ap 15,54:1
Yorke, Masie
Sunny Days 1928,F 9,29:1
Yorke, Oswald
Sophie 1920,Mr 3,12:2
Happy-Go-Lucky 1920,Ag 25,6:1
Talking Parrot, The 1923,D 4,25:3
That's the Woman 1930,S 4,27:2
Anatol 1931,Ja 17,23:3
Social Register, The 1931,N 10,28:2
Red Planet 1932,D 19,19:2

Ten Minute Alibi 1933,O 18,24:3
Lost Horizons 1934,O 16,31:2
Nowhere Bound 1935,Ja 23,20:2
Caesar and Cleopatra 1935,Ag 22,21:1
First Lady 1935,N 27,17:4
Barchester Towers 1937,D 1,27:1
Oscar Wilde 1938,O 11,20:2
Yorke, Ruth
Parnell 1935,N 12,24:2
Parnell 1936,My 5,26:1
Plumes in the Dust 1936,N 7,14:2
All the Living 1938,Mr 25,14:4
Morning Star 1940,Ap 17,26:4
Yorkshire, Charles
Love Dreams 1921,O 11,22:2
Yorku, Harry
First Wife, The 1945,N 28,21:5
Yorr, Leonard
Across the Board on Tomorrow Morning
1942,Mr 21,13:5
Theatre of the Soul 1942,Mr 21,13:5
Walk Hard 1944,D 1,28:2
Walk Hard 1946,Mr 28,34:2
Front Page, The 1946,S 5,22:4
Billy Budd 1951,F 12,18:3
Time to Go 1952,My 8,35:6
World of Mrs Solomon, The; Second Mrs Aarons,
The 1969,Je 4,37:1
Yoshida, Bunsho (Miscellaneous)
Fishing for Wives 1966,Mr 16,50:1
General's Daughter, The 1966,Mr 16,50:1
Greengrocer's Daughter, The 1966,Mr 16,50:1
Yoshida, Eiza (Miscellaneous)
Greengrocer's Daughter, The 1966,Mr 16,50:1
General's Daughter, The 1966,Mr 16,50:1
Fishing for Wives 1966,Mr 16,50:1
Yoshida, Fumiko (Producer)
Othello 1960,S 11,II,7:1
Yoshida, Minosuku (Miscellaneous)
Greengrocer's Daughter, The 1966,Mr 16,50:1
Fishing for Wives 1966,Mr 16,50:1
General's Daughter, The 1966,Mr 16,50:1
Greengrocer's Daughter, The 1966,Mr 16,50:1
General's Daughter, The 1966,Mr 16,50:1
Fishing for Wives 1966,Mr 16,50:1
Yoshida, Peter
Troilus and Cressida 1965,Ag 13,17:1
Yoshida, Tamako (Miscellaneous)
Greengrocer's Daughter, The 1966,Mr 16,50:1
General's Daughter, The 1966,Mr 16,50:1
Fishing for Wives 1966,Mr 16,50:1
General's Daughter, The 1966,Mr 16,50:1
Greengrocer's Daughter, The 1966,Mr 16,50:1
Fishing for Wives 1966,Mr 16,50:1
Yoshie, Matsuno
Golden Bat 1970,Je 27,18:2
Yoshiwara, Akihiko
Wine of Choice 1938,F 22,18:4
Foreigners 1939,D 6,30:2
Yoshiwara, Biscouren
Merrily We Roll Along 1934,O 1,14:1
If This Be Treason 1935,Jl 30,17:1
If This Be Treason 1935,S 24,28:2
O Evening Star 1936,Ja 9,24:6
Yoshiwara, Hanaki
Life Is Like That 1930,D 23,24:3
Yossiffon, Raquel
Brothers Ashkenazi, The 1970,N 17,53:2
Yost, Agnes Scott
Moon Vine, The 1943,F 12,22:2
Pillar to Post 1943,D 11,11:2
Man Who Had All the Luck, The 1944,N 24,18:5
Dark of the Moon 1945,Mr 15,27:2
Yost, Agnes Scott (Playwright)
You Can't Beat a Woman 1925,Mr 24,26:5
Yost, Ben
Artists and Models 1943,N 6,16:6
Yost, Ben and His Varsity Eight
Revels of 1936 1935,S 30,12:4
Ziegfeld Follies 1936,Ja 31,17:2
Sea Legs 1937,My 19,26:5
Yost, Donald K
It's the Valet 1933,D 15,25:4
Fiesta 1933,D 16,12:2
Yost, Herbert
Young Visitors, The 1920,N 30,14:1
Bachelor's Night, A 1921,O 18,20:1
Why Men Leave Home 1922,Jl 30,VI,1:3
Why Men Leave Home 1922,S 13,18:2
New Poor, The 1924,Ja 8,26:1
Comedienne 1924,O 22,18:1
Enchanted April, The 1925,Ag 25,12:3
Goat Song 1926,Ja 26,18:1
Proud Woman, A 1926,N 16,24:1
One Glorious Hour 1927,Ap 15,27:2
What the Doctor Ordered 1927,Ag 19,20:2
Take My Advice 1927,N 2,24:3
Congratulations 1929,My 1,28:4
What a Question 1930,F 23,VIII,2:5
I Want My Wife 1930,Mr 21,30:7
Rock Me, Julie 1931,Ja 4,VIII,2:3
Rock Me, Julie 1931,F 4,21:1
John Brown 1934,Ja 23,22:3

Yost, Herbert—Cont
Red Cat, The 1934,S 20,21:1
Battleship Gertie 1935,Ja 19,9:2
End of Summer 1936,Ja 31,17:1
End of Summer 1936,F 18,26:4
Home Sweet Home 1936,Jl 1,29:2
Masque of the Kings, The 1937,F 9,19:4
Wine of Choice 1938,F 22,18:4
Good, The 1938,O 6,27:2
Morning's at Seven 1939,N 7,30:2
Morning's at Seven 1939,D 1,26:2
My Fair Ladies 1941,Mr 24,12:7
Ring Around Elizabeth 1941,N 18,32:2
Cat Screams, The 1942,Je 17,26:5
Jacobowsky and the Colonel 1944,Mr 15,17:2
Jacobowsky and the Colonel 1944,Mr 19,II,1:1
Yost, Kenneth
Theatre of Angna Enters, The 1955,Ja 25,22:2
Yost, Paul
For Charity 1937,Ag 25,24:3
Youens, Frederic (Scenic Designer)
Bacchae, The 1963,Ap 25,39:5
Youmans, Robert
Pygmalion 1938,Ja 27,16:3
Captain Jinks of the Horse Marines 1938,Ja 28,16:2
No More Peace 1938,Ja 29,13:2
Coriolanus 1938,F 2,14:5
Youmans, Vincent (Composer)
Two Little Girls in Blue 1921,My 4,10:3
Wildflower 1923,F 9,10:1
Mary Jane McKane 1923,D 26,13:2
Lollipop 1924,Ja 22,15:3
No, No, Nanette 1925,S 17,20:2
Oh, Please! 1926,D 22,24:3
Hit the Deck! 1927,Ap 26,32:1
Rainbow 1928,N 22,25:1
Rainbow 1928,D 16,IX,1:1
Great Day! 1929,Je 9,VIII,1:2
Show Girl 1929,Ag 8,29:4
Show Girl 1929,Ag 25,VIII,1:1
Great Day! 1929,O 18,24:3
Nine Fifteen Revue, The 1930,F 12,26:2
Smiles 1930,N 19,19:2
Smiling Through 1932,Ja 3,VIII,3:1
Through the Years 1932,Ja 29,13:3
Round With Ring, A 1969,O 30,56:1
Youmans, Vincent (Lyricist)
Nine Fifteen Revue, The 1930,F 12,26:2
Youmans, Vincent (Miscellaneous)
Take a Chance 1932,N 28,11:2
Youmans, Vincent (Playwright)
Hit the Deck 1960,Je 24,32:1
Youmans, Vincent (Producer)
Hit the Deck! 1927,Ap 26,32:1
Great Day! 1929,O 18,24:3
Damn Your Honor 1929,D 31,14:3
Smiling Through 1932,Ja 3,VIII,3:1
Through the Years 1932,Ja 29,13:3
Youmi-Youmi
Kongi's Harvest 1968,Ap 15,49:1
Yound, Hobson
Naughty Marietta 1929,O 22,26:2
Young
High Kickers 1941,N 1,21:2
Young, Agnes
Carnival 1929,Ap 25,32:5
Mother, The 1939,Ap 26,26:2
Courageous One, The 1958,Ja 21,33:6
Hogan's Goat 1965,N 12,56:1
Young, Alan
Girl in the Freudian Slip, The 1967,My 19,34:3
Young, Alex
Caribbean Carnival 1947,D 6,12:2
Young, Allen
Swing It 1937,Jl 23,17:2
First Wife, The 1945,N 28,21:5
Young, Anthony (Director)
Surgeon, The 1932,O 28,23:1
Young, Anthony (Playwright)
Surgeon, The 1932,O 28,23:1
Young, Arden
I Am My Youth 1938,Mr 8,22:4
Young, Aston
Man Better Man 1969,Jl 3,22:1
X Has No Value 1970,F 17,35:1
Young, Barbara
Servant of Two Masters, The 1966,Je 28,51:1
Young, Bert
John Hawthorne 1921,Ja 24,16:1
Man Who Ate the Popomack, The 1924,Mr 25,24:1
Young, Betty
One Wife or Another 1933,F 7,23:6
Gloriana 1938,N 26,18:4
Young, Billy
Laffing Room Only 1944,D 25,15:4
Young, Blanche
Swing It 1937,Jl 23,17:2
Young, Boaz
Longing for Home 1933,S 22,15:1
Slaves of the Public 1934,Mr 10,18:6
It Can't Happen Here 1936,O 28,30:1
Young, Bryan
Love's Labour's Lost 1968,Je 28,36:1
Patriot for Me, A 1969,O 6,58:1

Young, Bryan—Cont

Madwoman of Chaillot, The 1970,Mr 23,48:3
Young, Carleton
Woman of Bronze, The 1927,Je 16,25:4
Sun-Up 1929,F 19,22:6
Page Pygmalion 1932,Ag 4,17:5
Man Who Reclaimed His Head 1932,S 9,17:3
Eight Bells 1933,O 30,14:2
Late Wisdom 1934,Ap 24,27:4
Yesterday's Orchids 1934,O 6,20:4
Two Story House 1941,S 2,20:3
Cuckoos on the Hearth 1941,S 17,26:2
Bathsheba 1947,Mr 27,40:2
Gentleman From Athens, The 1947,D 10,42:4
Young, Cathryn
Loyalties 1922,S 28,18:1
Young, Cy
Pajama Game, The 1957,My 16,27:1
Diversions 1958,N 8,14:4
Subways Are for Sleeping 1961,D 28,22:1
Divorce Me, Darling 1965,F 2,29:6
Young, Cy (Composer)
That Hat! 1964,S 24,45:1
Young, Cy (Lyricist)
That Hat! 1964,S 24,45:1
Young, Cy (Playwright)
That Hat! 1964,S 24,45:1
Young, David
Way of the World, The 1950,Ap 9,73:5
Young, David (Director)
Kicking the Castle Down 1967,Ja 19,43:1
Young, Don
Jack Jack 1968,Je 23,74:5
Young, Effie (Playwright)
Homeward Look, The 1954,Je 4,26:2
Young, Elizabeth
Child of Manhattan 1932,Mr 2,15:1
Only the Young 1932,S 22,25:2
Firebird 1932,N 22,25:2
Saturday Night 1933,Mr 1,13:2
Daughters of Atreus 1936,O 15,33:1
Masque of the Kings, The 1937,F 9,19:4
Ghost of Yankee Doodle, The 1937,O 28,28:5
All the Living 1938,Mr 25,14:4
Young, Emily M (Playwright)
Red Pepper 1922,My 30,8:3
Young, Ernest
Buzzin' Around 1920,Jl 7,14:1
Bombo 1921,O 7,20:2
Young, Estelle
Henri Christophe 1945,Je 7,24:5
Young, Eulalie
Naughty Marietta 1929,O 22,26:2
Naughty Marietta 1931,N 17,31:2
Firefly, The 1931,D 1,23:2
Young, Felix (Miscellaneous)
Marriage Bed, The 1929,Ja 8,35:1
Young, Felix (Producer)
Top O' the Hill 1929,N 27,30:4
Young, Frances
Marie Antoinette 1921,N 23,16:1
Young, Frederick
Cherry Orchard, The 1955,O 19,38:1
Death of Satan, The 1960,Ap 6,49:1
Man and Superman 1960,N 7,46:2
Hamlet 1961,Mr 17,17:1
Right Honourable Gentleman, The 1965,O 20,50:2
Young, George
On Your Toes 1936,Ap 13,14:4
Rhapsody 1944,N 23,37:2
Emperor's New Clothes, The 1950,Je 20,23:2
Flower Drum Song 1958,D 2,44:1
Young, Gig
Oh, Men! Oh, Women! 1953,D 18,37:2
Teahouse of the August Moon, The 1956,N 9,33:2
Under the Yum-Yum Tree 1960,N 17,45:1
There's a Girl in My Soup 1967,O 19,58:1
There's a Girl in My Soup 1967,N 12,II,5:6
Young, Halfred
Great Temptations, The 1926,My 19,29:1
Half a Widow 1927,S 13,37:3
Rosalie 1928,Ja 11,26:3
Night in Venice, A 1929,My 22,30:2
Artists and Models 1930,Je 11,33:2
Young, Harry
Black Eye, The 1938,Mr 8,22:4
Oscar Wilde 1938,O 11,20:2
Ringside Seat 1938,N 23,24:5
Shakespeare's Merchant 1939 1939,Ja 10,16:3
Woman Brown, The 1939,D 9,18:5
Kindred 1939,D 27,17:2
Juno and the Paycock 1940,Ja 17,24:2
To What Red Hell 1940,My 5,I,54:8
At the Stroke of Eight 1940,My 21,29:2
In Time to Come 1941,D 29,20:2
Richard III 1943,Mr 27,8:3
Beggars Are Comming to Town 1945,O 29,16:2
Young, Harry (Director)
First Mrs Fraser, The 1947,N 6,36:2
Young, Harry (Miscellaneous)
Ziegfeld Follies 1943,Ap 2,16:2
View From the Bridge, A 1955,S 30,21:1
Memory of Two Mondays, A 1955,S 30,21:1
Heartbreak House 1959,O 19,37:1

Face of a Hero 1960,O 21,29:5
Devil's Advocate, The 1961,Mr 10,20:1
Isle of Children 1962,Mr 17,16:2
Tovarich 1963,Mr 20,5:1
Rugantino 1964,F 7,34:1
Zulu and the Zayda, The 1965,N 11,59:1
Under the Weather 1966,O 28,35:1
South Pacific 1967,Je 13,56:1
Angela 1969,O 31,33:1
Brightower 1970,Ja 29,32:1
Two by Two 1970,N 11,37:1
Young, Harry (Playwright)
Open House 1947,Je 4,33:4
Young, Harry (Producer)
Wuthering Heights 1939,Ap 28,30:4
Young, Helene
Lady in the Dark 1943,Mr 1,14:2
Suds in Your Eye 1944,Ja 13,15:5
Young, Herbert
Porgy and Bess 1935,O 11,30:2
Young, Hobson
Fortune Teller, The 1929,N 5,32:3
Count of Luxembourg, The 1930,F 18,28:2
Serenade, The 1930,Mr 5,26:7
Ruddigore 1931,Ag 11,28:3
Yeomen of the Guard, The 1933,My 2,20:4
Bohemian Girl, The 1933,Jl 28,18:5
Yeomen of the Guard, The 1933,Ag 15,20:5
Young, Howard (Miscellaneous)
Desert Song, The 1946,Ja 9,20:2
Obsession 1946,O 2,39:2
Lady Windermere's Fan 1946,O 15,29:2
Tonight at 8:30; Ways and Means 1948,F 21,8:2
Tonight at 8:30; Red Peppers 1948,F 21,8:2
Tonight at 8:30; Family Album 1948,F 21,8:2
Tonight at 8:30; Hands Across the Sea
1948,F 24,20:4
Tonight at 8:30; Fumed Oak 1948,F 24,20:4
Tonight at 8:30; Shadow Play 1948,F 24,20:4
Young, Howard (Playwright)
Curious Savage, The 1950,O 25,44:3
Young, Howard (Producer)
Story of Mary Surratt, The 1947,F 10,25:2
Time for Elizabeth 1948,S 28,32:3
Young, Howard Irving (Director)
Hawk Island 1929,S 17,34:7
Young, Howard Irving (Playwright)
Not Herbert 1926,Ja 27,16:2
Hawk Island 1929,S 17,34:7
Drums Begin, The 1933,N 25,10:5
Young, Irene
Henry-Behave 1926,Ag 24,19:4
Young, Irwin
Game of Love and Death, The 1929,N 26,28:4
Young, J Arthur
Lancelot and Elaine 1921,S 13,12:1
Julius Caesar 1930,Ap 4,22:3
Tragedy of the Ages, The 1933,Ap 7,22:7
Queer People 1934,F 16,16:2
Lost Horizons 1934,O 16,31:2
Night of January 16 1935,S 17,26:4
Karl and Anna 1935,O 13,IX,3:1
Frederika 1937,F 5,16:5
Without Warning 1937,My 3,23:2
Night of January 16 1937,Jl 20,19:3
Star-Wagon, The 1937,S 30,18:5
Devil Takes a Bride, The 1938,O 8,10:3
Barber Had Two Sons, The 1943,F 2,22:2
Young, Jackie
Pansy 1929,My 15,36:3
Young, Jackson
Captain Brassbound's Conversion 1950,D 28,21:1
Lady in the Dark 1952,Mr 8,11:3
Wisteria Trees, The 1955,F 3,20:2
Salvage 1957,Ap 10,39:2
Young, James
Hobo 1931,F 12,24:4
Singin' the Blues 1931,S 17,21:3
Adam Had Two Sons 1932,Ja 21,17:1
Round-Up, The 1932,Mr 8,19:4
Reunion 1938,Ap 12,26:4
Life With Father 1939,Ag 15,14:4
Young, Janet
Medea 1920,Mr 23,12:2
Mr Faust 1922,Ja 31,11:2
Candida 1922,Mr 23,11:1
Mourning Becomes Electra; Hunted, The
1931,O 27,22:1
One Sunday Afternoon 1933,F 16,23:5
Nine Pine Street 1933,Ap 28,15:5
Pure in Heart, The 1934,Mr 21,24:3
Young, Janis
Don Carlos 1962,F 28,27:5
Storm, The 1962,Mr 31,17:2
Where People Gather 1967,O 26,56:1
Young, Jay
Furnished Rooms 1934,My 30,14:6
Farmer Takes a Wife, The 1934,O 31,17:1
Young, Jean
Round Table, The 1930,F 28,20:5
Young, Joan
Skin of Our Teeth, The 1945,Mr 20,22:8
South 1955,My 2,17:4

Young, Joe
Laffing Room Only 1944,D 25,15:4
Great Airplane Snatch, The 1969,My 28,36:1
Madwoman of Chaillot, The 1970,Mr 23,48:3
Young, Joe (Lyricist)
Lady Do 1927,Ap 19,24:2
Laugh Parade, The 1931,N 3,31:2
Young, John
Knickerbocker Holiday 1938,O 20,26:2
Career Angel 1943,N 19,24:2
If in the Green Wood 1947,Ja 17,27:6
Minstrel Boy, The 1948,O 15,28:2
Young, John (Director)
John Brown's Body 1964,Je 29,33:1
Young, John (Miscellaneous)
Cup of Trembling, The 1959,My 1,33:5
Cranmer of Canterbury 1959,D 4,36:1
Young, John (Producer)
Born Yesterday 1954,Ja 1,16:6
John Brown's Body 1964,Je 29,33:1
Young, Joseph (Composer)
Blackbirds 1933,D 4,22:3
Young, Joseph (Lyricist)
Blackbirds 1933,D 4,22:3
Young, Kathryn
Sidewalks and the Sound of Crying 1956,O 29,34:1
Young, Kirk R
What a Relief 1935,D 14,10:6
Young, Lawrence
Let's Make an Opera 1950,D 14,50:2
Young, Leonard
Biff, Bing, Bang 1921,My 10,20:1
Young, Lewis (Miscellaneous)
Desert Song, The 1946,Ja 9,20:2
Young, Lillian
Girl in the Spotlight, The 1920,Jl 13,9:3
Young, Marcel Prawy (Dr) (Translator)
Kiss Me, Kate 1956,F 15,27:6
Young, Marie
Earth 1927,Mr 10,23:1
Brain Sweat 1934,Ap 5,24:4
Macbeth 1936,Ap 15,25:4
Banjo Eyes 1941,D 26,20:2
Shuffle Along 1952,My 9,20:5
Love in Our Time 1952,O 4,14:3
Mamba's Daughters 1953,Mr 21,12:6
Porgy and Bess 1964,My 7,32:1
Young, Marshall (Miscellaneous)
Back to Methuselah 1958,Mr 27,41:5
Young, Marshall (Producer)
Answered the Flute 1960,Mr 10,37:4
Young, Martin
Midsummer Night's Dream, A 1968,D 9,59:1
Young, Mary
Outrageous Mrs Palmer, The 1920,O 13,18:1
Outrageous Mrs Palmer, The 1920,O 24,VI,1:2
We Girls 1921,N 10,26:3
Forbidden 1923,O 2,10:2
Dancing Mothers 1924,Ag 12,12:2
Julius Caesar 1927,Je 7,27:2
Porgy 1927,O 11,26:2
Restless Women 1927,D 27,24:1
Gypsy 1929,Ja 15,22:2
Lolly 1929,O 17,26:2
Katy Did So What? 1935,N 6,32:3
Storm Child 1936,Ap 18,18:4
Come Home to Roost 1936,O 11,X,3:1
At Your Service 1937,Ag 17,23:1
Young, Mary (Director)
Katy Did So What? 1935,N 6,32:3
Family Man, A 1936,Jl 8,14:2
Young, Mary (Playwright)
Katy Did So What? 1935,N 6,32:3
Young, Otis
Blues for Mister Charlie 1964,Ap 24,24:1
Young, Palmer
Business Widow, The 1923,D 11,27:1
Young, Pennington
Killers 1928,Mr 14,28:3
Near to the Stars 1932,F 23,23:2
Mikado, The 1932,Jl 29,18:4
Young, Ralph
Black Diamond 1933,F 24,12:2
Whoop-Up 1958,D 23,2:7
Young, Rida Johnson (Lyricist)
Dream Girl, The 1924,Ag 21,12:2
Naughty Marietta 1929,O 22,26:2
Naughty Marietta 1931,N 17,31:2
Naughty Marietta 1936,S 2,19:5
Young, Rida Johnson (Playwright)
Macushla 1920,My 18,9:3
Little Old New York 1920,S 9,9:2
Little Old New York 1920,S 19,VI,1:1
Front Seat, The 1921,My 22,VI,1:6
Rabbit's Foot, The 1924,Ap 27,VIII,2:3
Dream Girl, The 1924,Ag 21,12:2
Cock o' the Roost 1924,O 14,23:1
Naughty Marietta 1929,O 22,26:2
Naughty Marietta 1931,N 17,31:2
Naughty Marietta 1936,S 2,19:5
Young, Roland
Scrambled Wives 1920,Ag 6,16:1
Rollo's Wild Oat 1920,N 24,14:1

Young, Roland—Cont
Rollo's Wild Oat 1921,Ja 9,VI,1:1
Rollo's Wild Oat 1921,Ja 23,VI,1:1
Madame Pierre 1922,F 16,11:1
Madame Pierre 1922,F 19,VI,1:1
49ers, The 1922,N 7,14:1
Anything Might Happen 1923,F 21,22:3
Anything Might Happen 1923,F 25,VII,1:1
Devil's Disciple, The 1923,Ap 24,24:1
Devil's Disciple, The 1923,My 6,VII,1:1
Beggar on Horseback 1924,F 13,17:2
Beggar on Horseback 1924,F 17,VII,1:1
Hedda Gabler 1924,My 17,18:4
Tale of the Wolf, The 1925,O 8,31:2
Tale of the Wolf, The 1925,O 18,IX,1:2
Last of Mrs Cheyney, The 1925,N 1,VIII,2:4
Last of Mrs Cheyney, The 1925,N 10,23:5
Zoo, The 1927,O 9,VIII,1:3
Queen's Husband, The 1928,Ja 26,17:2
Queen's Husband, The 1928,F 12,VIII,1:1
Her Master's Voice 1933,O 24,24:3
Her Master's Voice 1933,D 10,X,3:1
Distant Shore, The 1935,F 22,26:2
All Bow Down 1935,Ag 6,20:4
Touch of Brimstone, A 1935,S 23,20:1
Spring Thaw 1938,Mr 22,18:1
Ask My Friend Sandy 1943,F 5,16:2
Another Love Story 1943,O 13,29:2
Young, Ronald
Mame 1966,My 25,41:1
George M! 1968,Ap 11,48:1
Boy Friend, The 1970,Ap 15,54:1
Young, Ross B (Costume Designer)
Cherry Orchard, The 1970,My 7,63:2
Young, Sharon (Choreographer)
Purification, The 1959,D 9,57:5
Young, Sharon (Composer)
Purification, The 1959,D 9,57:5
Young, Soo
Squealer, The 1928,N 13,36:3
Young, Stanley (Playwright)
Robin Landing 1937,N 19,26:4
Bright Rebel 1938,D 28,24:2
Ask My Friend Sandy 1943,F 5,16:2
Mr Pickwick 1952,S 18,36:3
Mr Pickwick 1952,S 28,II,1:1
Young, Stark (Director)
Welded 1924,Mr 18,24:1
George Dandin 1924,Ap 7,15:5
Young, Stark (Playwright)
Saint, The 1924,O 13,20:3
Colonnade, The 1925,My 3,VIII,2:1
Three Sisters, The 1955,Mr 20,II,1:1
Young, Stark (Translator)
Sea Gull, The 1938,Mr 29,19:2
Sea Gull, The 1938,Ap 3,XI,1:1
Three Sisters, The 1955,F 26,13:2
Cherry Orchard, The 1955,O 19,38:1
Uncle Vanya 1956,F 1,25:2
Uncle Vanya 1956,F 12,II,1:1
Three Sisters, The 1959,S 22,46:1
Three Sisters, The 1969,Ag 10,II,3:1
Young, Tammany
Wasp, The 1923,Mr 28,14:3
Lulu Belle 1926,F 10,20:1
White Lights 1927,O 12,30:4
Spring 3100 1928,F 16,14:2
Front Page, The 1928,Ag 15,19:2
Out of a Blue Sky 1930,F 10,20:6
New Yorkers, The 1930,D 9,31:1
Young, Tom
Biff, Bing, Bang 1921,My 10,20:1
Young, Victor
Marching By 1932,Mr 4,17:1
Winged Victory 1943,N 22,24:1
Arms and the Girl 1950,F 3,28:2
Young, Victor (Composer)
Blackbirds 1933,D 4,22:3
Seventh Heaven 1955,My 27,16:2
Around the World in 80 Days 1963,Je 24,22:1
Young, Victor (Lyricist)
Blackbirds 1933,D 4,22:3
Young, Victor (Miscellaneous)
Around the World in 80 Days 1964,Je 29,33:2
Young, Victor (Musical Director)
Pardon Our French 1950,O 6,22:4
Young, Virginia
Heel, The 1954,My 27,33:2
Young, Warren
This Our House 1935,D 12,33:3
Tide Rising 1937,Ja 26,17:2
Young, William
Channel Road, The 1929,O 18,24:2
Henry V 1958,D 26,2:7
Borak 1960,D 14,51:1
Plebeians Rehearse the Uprising, The
   1968,S 8,II,11:1
Stop, You're Killing Me; Bad Bad Jo-Jo
   1969,Mr 20,53:1
Young, Wynn
Novice and the Duke, The 1929,D 11,37:2
Young Circle Dramatic Studio
Squaring the Circle 1931,Ap 27,24:4

Younger, Judith
Laughwind 1966,Mr 3,27:1
Youngerman, Jack (Scenic Designer)
Deathwatch 1958,O 10,34:2
Youngers, The
Vaudeville (Palace) 1926,Je 1,29:5
Youngman, George
Red Pepper 1922,My 30,8:3
Youngman, Henny
New Priorities of 1943 1942,S 16,28:2
Aquashow 1954,Je 23,20:4
Rosalie 1957,Je 26,28:2
Youngman, Stanley
Gondoliers, The 1951,F 13,27:2
Youngs, Addeson
Marjolaine 1922,Ja 25,16:1
Youngstein, Max (Miscellaneous)
Playroom, The 1965,D 6,49:1
Younin, Sylvia (Lyricist)
Light, Lively and Yiddish 1970,O 28,58:1
Younin, Sylvia (Playwright)
Light, Lively and Yiddish 1970,O 28,58:1
Younin, Wolf (Lyricist)
Nice People 1958,O 20,36:1
Light, Lively and Yiddish 1970,O 28,58:1
Younin, Wolf (Miscellaneous)
Let's Sing Yiddish 1966,N 10,63:1
Younin, Wolf (Playwright)
Let's Sing Yiddish 1966,N 10,63:1
Sing Israel Sing 1967,My 12,50:1
Light, Lively and Yiddish 1970,O 28,58:1
Yousef, Tish
Daddy Come Home 1963,Ap 17,33:1
Youssoff, Ali
Squall, The 1926,N 12,20:1
Mima 1928,D 13,24:2
Smiling Faces 1932,Ag 31,12:3
Youtt, Gene (Lighting Director)
Woman and the Blues, A 1966,Mr 29,35:2
In the Nick of Time 1967,Je 2,36:1
Certain Young Man, A 1967,D 27,45:1
Victims, The; Escurial 1968,Mr 6,34:1
Victims, The; Victims of Duty 1968,Mr 6,34:1
Victims, The; On the Hazards of Smoking Tobacco
   1968,Mr 6,34:1
God Is Back, Black and Singing Gospel at the
   Fortune Theater 1969,N 19,48:1
Youtt, Gene (Scenic Designer)
God Is Back, Black and Singing Gospel at the
   Fortune Theater 1969,N 19,48:1
Yovin, Jose
Shore Leave 1922,Ag 9,20:2
Agent 666, L' 1923,My 30,10:5
Four in Hand 1923,S 7,10:2
Laugh, Clown, Laugh! 1923,N 29,30:1
Ladies of the Evening 1924,D 24,11:2
Yrven, Marcelle
Lulu 1927,O 2,VIII,2:4
Ysebaert, Michael (Lighting Director)
Last Pad, The 1970,D 8,61:1
Yselle, Elyne
Elsie 1923,Ap 3,26:1
Yu, Chin
Teahouse of the August Moon, The
   1955,My 10,24:1
Yubell, Eddie
Summer Wives 1936,Ap 14,18:1
Yuda, Michael
Shakuntala 1959,S 10,41:2
Yudelwitch, Tmima
Dybbuk, The 1926,D 14,24:2
Golem, The 1927,F 5,13:2
Yudkoff, Alvin S (Playwright)
Step a Little Closer 1948,My 28,26:6
Yuen, Lily
Yeah-Man 1932,My 27,27:3
Yuka, Blanche
Red Peppers; Tonight at Eight 1940,Ag 6,15:3
Yukiko, Kobayashi
Golden Bat 1970,Je 27,18:2
Yukimura, Izumi
No Strings 1964,Jl 18,10:1
Yule, Don
South Pacific 1965,Je 3,25:1
H M S Pinafore 1966,Je 8,41:2
Yule, Jack
Don't Throw Glass Houses 1938,D 28,24:4
Yule, Joe
Finian's Rainbow 1948,Ag 29,II,1:1
Yulin, Harris
Next Time I'll Sing to You 1963,N 28,69:2
Troubled Waters 1965,Je 4,40:2
Richard III 1966,Ag 11,26:1
King John 1967,Jl 14,19:1
Cannibals, The 1968,N 4,60:1
Yulin, Harris (Director)
Cuba Si 1968,D 10,53:1
Guns of Carrar, The 1968,D 10,53:1
Yun, Tom Chung
Strange Bedfellows 1948,Ja 15,27:3
Clutterbuck 1949,D 5,29:2
Yung, Shen
Mu Lan 1921,F 25,16:2

Yung, Wang
Put Down That Whip 1945,My 23,25:5
First Wife, The 1945,N 28,21:5
Yung, Wang (Director)
Put Down That Whip 1945,My 23,25:5
Yung, Wang (Translator)
Put Down That Whip 1945,My 23,25:5
Yurdin, Clay
Comes the Revelation 1942,My 27,26:2
Yurdin, Clay (Lighting Director)
Johnny Doodle 1942,Mr 19,28:2
Yurdin, Clay (Scenic Designer)
Johnny Doodle 1942,Mr 19,28:2
Yureva, Margarita
Blue Bird, The 1925,Ja 30,10:2
Three Sisters, The 1965,F 12,15:1
Kremlin Chimes 1965,F 25,23:1
Yuriko, Michiko
King and I, The 1951,Ap 8,II,1:1
Sandhog 1954,N 24,17:1
King and I, The 1960,My 12,40:1
Yuriko, Michiko (Choreographer)
King and I, The 1960,My 12,40:1
Yuriko, Michiko (Miscellaneous)
King and I, The 1963,Je 13,30:2
King and I, The 1964,Jl 7,26:1
Yurka, Blanche
Musk 1920,Mr 15,13:1
Americans in France, The 1920,Ag 4,14:1
Wife With a Smile, The 1921,N 29,20:1
Lawbreaker, The 1922,F 7,12:1
Hamlet 1922,N 17,14:1
Hamlet 1923,N 27,23:6
Man and the Masses 1924,Ap 15,25:1
Masse Mensch; Man and the Masses
   1924,Ap 20,VIII,1:1
Wild Duck, The 1925,F 25,16:4
Sea Woman, The 1925,Ag 25,12:2
Sea Woman, The 1925,Ag 30,VII,1:1
Goat Song 1926,Ja 26,18:1
Goat Song 1926,F 7,VII,1:1
Squall, The 1926,N 12,20:1
Wild Duck, The 1928,N 19,17:1
Hedda Gabler 1929,F 4,20:3
Lady From the Sea, The 1929,Mr 19,36:1
Vikings, The 1930,My 13,27:3
Electra 1931,My 24,VIII,3:5
Electra 1932,Ja 9,21:4
Troilus and Cressida 1932,Je 7,22:3
Lucrece 1932,N 30,22:8
Lucrece 1932,D 4,IX,3:3
Lucrece 1932,D 21,22:2
Lucrece 1933,Ja 1,IX,1:1
Comic Artist, The 1933,Ap 20,20:3
Spring in Autumn 1933,O 25,22:5
In the Days of the Turbins 1934,Mr 7,22:5
Yes, My Darling Daughter 1938,Je 14,17:1
Gloriana 1938,N 26,18:4
Tonight at 8:30 1940,Ag 11,IX,11:2
Barber Had Two Sons, The 1943,F 2,22:2
Wind Is Ninety, The 1945,Je 22,12:2
Oedipus Rex 1945,D 17,16:7
Temper the Wind 1946,D 28,10:2
Temper the Wind 1947,Ja 12,II,1:1
Untitled-One Woman Show 1951,Ap 23,20:2
Carefree Tree, The 1955,O 12,37:2
Diary of a Scoundrel 1956,N 5,41:1
Prometheus Bound 1957,Ag 9,11:6
Jane Eyre 1958,My 2,31:1
Dinner at Eight 1966,S 28,38:1
Madwoman of Chaillot, The 1970,Mr 23,48:3
Yurka, Blanche (Director)
Hedda Gabler 1929,F 4,20:3
Hedda Gabler 1929,F 17,IX,1:1
Carry Nation 1932,O 31,18:2
Yurka, George
Chauve-Souris of 1943 1943,Ag 13,13:2
Yuro, Charles D
Kith and Kin 1930,My 14,31:1
Yuro, Robert
Venus at Large 1962,Ap 13,30:1
Yurski, Sergei
Henry IV 1969,My 11,4:1
Yushkewitch, S (Original Author)
Mazal Darf Men; You Need Luck 1938,My 18,16:5
Yushny, Yascha
Blue Bird, The 1931,My 24,VIII,2:1
Blue Bird, The 1932,Ap 22,23:2
Yushny, Yascha (Playwright)
Seeniaya Ptitza 1924,D 29,11:1
Yushny, Yascha (Producer)
Blue Bird, The 1925,Ja 30,10:2
Blue Bird, The 1925,F 8,VII,1:1
Yutaka, Higashi (Director)
Golden Bat 1970,Je 27,18:2
Yutaka, Higashi (Playwright)
Golden Bat 1970,Je 27,18:2
Yuvelier, Kelman
Radio Girl, The 1929,O 19,22:4
Little Clown, The 1930,Mr 15,23:3
Yvain, Maurice (Composer)
One Kiss 1923,N 28,14:2
Untitled-Play 1925,D 27,VII,2:1

Yvain, Maurice (Composer)—Cont
Luckee Girl 1928,S 17,28:6
Ta Bouche 1929,Mr 15,28:5
Bon Garcon, Un 1929,Mr 19,36:2
Pas Sur La Bouche; Not on the Lips
1929,Mr 26,34:3
Yvain, Maurice (Lyricist)
Bon Garcon, Un 1929,Mr 19,36:2
Yvain, Maurice (Playwright)
Luckee Girl 1928,S 17,28:6
Bon Garcon, Un 1929,Mr 19,36:2
Yvan-Noe (Translator)
Man From Cairo, The 1938,My 5,26:5
Yvonne-Pothen
It's A Gift 1945,Mr 13,18:7

Z

Zaar, Maurice
World Is a Stage, The 1962,N 5,37:4
Zaar, Moishe
Both Kooney Lemels 1964,O 12,37:2
Zabelin, Elizabeth
Dead End 1935,O 29,17:2
Zabelle, Flora
Girl From Home, The 1920,My 4,9:2
Man on Stilts, The 1931,S 10,23:2
Zabrodina, Tatyana
Kremlin Chimes 1965,F 25,23:1
Zacharias, Steffen (Director)
Great Big Doorstep, The 1950,Mr 18,8:6
Zachary, Elizabeth
Peer Gynt 1923,F 6,14:1
Trip to Scarborough, A 1929,Mr 18,31:2
Dragon, The 1929,Mr 26,34:2
Zachary, George
Nautical but Nice 1931,Ap 19,31:6
Zachary, Rita
Nautical but Nice 1931,Ap 19,31:6
Zack, Sheftel
Sage of Rottenburg, The 1963,N 20,48:1
Zackey, Ruth
An und Aus 1926,D 5,VIII,8:7
Zackheim, Zalman
Brothers Ashkenazi, The 1955,N 12,24:4
Zacks, Lewis (Director)
Trial of Lee Harvey Oswald, The 1967,N 6,64:1
Zaconick, Bernice
Boutique Fantasque, La 1929,D 28,10:6
Zaconick, Dorothy
Boutique Fantasque, La 1929,D 28,10:6
Zadora, Michael (Composer)
Bridal Crown, The 1938,F 7,11:2
Zadora, Pia
Midgie Purvis 1961,F 2,25:3
Zafer, Jerry
As You Like It 1963,Jl 17,19:2
Zaferes, James
My Kinsman, Major Molineux 1964,N 2,62:2
Zaffaroni, Giorgio
Rugantino 1964,F 7,34:1
Zafiriou, H
Electra 1952,N 20,38:2
Zag (Ozark Mountain Boy)
Hayride 1954,S 14,24:2
Zagon, Istvan (Playwright)
One Can't Marry a Penniless Girl 1928,D 2,X,4:7
Land of Promises, The 1933,N 5,IX,2:2
Zagrebelsky, G
Revisor; Inspector General, The 1935,F 18,19:6
Poverty Is No Crime 1935,F 21,22:5
White Guard, The; Days of the Turbins
1935,Mr 7,27:5
Marriage 1935,Mr 12,24:8
Enemies 1935,Mr 19,24:7
Deluge, The 1935,Mr 26,23:7
Zahav, Menorah
Oh What a Wedding! 1969,O 20,60:1
Zahava
Untitled-Revue 1935,N 11,21:2
Zahn, Curtis (Playwright)
Conditioned Reflex 1967,Ja 11,51:1
Zahn, Mary
Boy Friend, The 1970,Ap 15,54:1
Zaidenworm, Chaim
Brothers Ashkenazi, The 1970,N 17,53:2
Zaino, Constantine
Alt Heidelberg 1926,My 31,10:5
Zaitzeff Brothers, The
Chauve-Souris 1923,S 4,12:1
Zaitzow, A (Scenic Designer)
Catiline 1936,Ja 28,14:6
Zak, John
O'Flynn, The 1934,D 28,24:1
Zak, Sheftel
Shepherd King, The 1955,O 13,36:2
Brothers Ashkenazi, The 1955,N 12,24:4
Devil's Game, A 1959,N 9,35:6
Fifth Commandment, The 1965,N 15,48:4
Zak, Sheftel (Producer)
Devil's Game, A 1959,N 9,35:6

Zak, Shirley
Boy Meets Girl 1937,Jl 6,23:1
Zakka, Kiki
Hippolytus 1968,N 20,38:3
Zakkai, Jamil
Cave at Machpelah, The 1959,Jl 1,25:1
Connection, The 1959,Jl 16,30:2
Tonight We Improvise 1959,N 7,27:4
Marrying Maiden, The 1960,Je 23,18:3
In the Jungle of Cities 1960,D 21,39:1
Jonah! 1966,F 16,52:1
Zakrzewski, Paul (Lyricist)
Sensations 1970,O 26,48:2
Zala, Nancy
Women at the Tomb, The 1961,Ap 25,41:1
In Circles 1967,O 14,12:1
Zaldivar, Gilberto (Producer)
Other Man, The 1968,F 9,50:1
Oh, Say Can You See L A 1968,F 9,50:1
Zaltzberg, Charlotte (Miscellaneous)
Blancs, Les 1970,N 16,48:4
Zaman, Rosalind (Miscellaneous)
World of Illusion 1964,Je 25,26:2
Zamar, Moshe
Yosele the Nightingale 1949,O 21,30:4
Zamboundi, Theodore
Century Revue and the Midnight Rounders, The
1920,Jl 13,9:1
Century Review, The 1920,Jl 22,9:5
Zamora, Antonio
Fuerza Ciega, La 1927,D 6,26:1
Zampese, Alan
Herne's Egg, The 1960,S 20,48:1
Zanbra (Tiger)
Mermaid's Holiday 1961,Jl 1,8:1
Zanders, Ingrid
Good Morning, Dearie 1921,N 2,20:2
Zandt, Philip Van
Hat, a Coat, a Glove, A 1934,F 1,15:2
Having Wonderful Time 1937,F 22,12:5
Zanetta, Tony
Lady From Maxim's, The 1970,Je 1,41:1
Zanetti, Giancarlo
Venetian Twins, The 1968,My 29,23:1
Zaneville, Bernard
Dead End 1935,O 29,17:2
Zang, Edward
Puntila 1959,My 15,26:2
Good Soldier Schweik, The 1963,Ap 9,57:1
Utopia! 1963,My 7,47:4
Measure for Measure 1964,Jl 27,22:3
Saint Joan 1968,Ja 5,42:1
Boys in the Band, The 1970,Ap 18,34:1
Early Morning 1970,N 26,57:1
Zanger, Jacob
Let's Get Married 1937,Ja 11,16:2
Bublitchki 1938,Ja 17,11:2
Yosele the Nightingale 1949,O 21,30:4
Shepherd King, The 1955,O 13,36:2
Brothers Ashkenazi, The 1955,N 12,24:4
In-Laws 1960,O 17,32:4
Honeymoon in Israel, A 1962,O 15,33:5
My Wife With Conditions 1963,O 21,39:1
Bride Got Farblondjet, The 1967,N 6,61:6
It's Never Too Late for Happiness 1968,O 21,59:3
Oh What a Wedding! 1969,O 20,60:1
Zangrilli, Jeannette
Vagabond King, The 1935,N 29,22:7
Zangwill, Israel (Playwright)
We Moderns 1923,D 30,VII,2:1
We Moderns 1924,Mr 12,17:2
We Moderns 1924,Mr 16,VIII,1:1
Zanides, Nick
Sweeney Todd 1957,Ag 28,21:4
As You Like It 1966,Je 4,19:1
Zanoff, Victor (Scenic Designer)
Swing It 1937,Jl 23,17:2
Zanova, Aja
Ice Capades 1964,Ag 27,27:2
Ice Capades 1966,Je 2,50:2
Ice Capades 1967,Je 2,33:1
Zanville, Bernard
Sailors of Cattaro 1934,D 11,28:4
Panic 1935,Mr 16,18:4
Till the Day I Die 1935,Mr 27,24:5
Waiting for Lefty 1935,Mr 27,24:5
Sweet Shadow 1935,Ag 7,22:2
Zapata, Carmen
Innkeepers, The 1956,F 3,19:1
Zapata, Sandra
Innkeepers, The 1956,F 3,19:1
Zapata, Sergio (Lighting Director)
Remolienda, La; Bawdy Party 1968,F 3,20:1
Zaphiropoulou, Miranda
Iphigenia in Aulis 1968,N 13,40:1
Hippolytus 1968,N 20,38:3
Zapolska, Gabryela (Playwright)
Sonya 1921,Ag 16,18:3
Three and the Man 1923,Ja 3,9:3
Zappa, Frank
Absolutely Freeee 1967,My 25,58:1
Zappa, Frank (Composer)
Absolutely Freeee 1967,My 25,58:1

Zappa, Frank (Lyricist)
Absolutely Freeee 1967,My 25,58:1
Zaranova, Erika
Jubilee 1935,O 14,20:1
Knickerbocker Holiday 1938,O 20,26:2
Variations of 1940 1940,Ja 29,12:1
Zardo, Eric
Vaudeville (Palace) 1925,Ap 21,18:1
Vaudeville (Palace) 1926,Je 15,23:3
Vaudeville (Palace) 1926,D 7,24:3
Zaret, Daniel
Cricket on the Hearth, The 1925,My 29,20:2
Zaret, H (Lyricist)
It's Up to You 1943,Ap 1,19:1
Zaret, Hy (Miscellaneous)
Let Freedom Sing 1942,O 6,18:2
Zaretzky, Herman (Composer)
Gold Diggers, The 1927,D 3,19:2
Zarit, Pam
Lend an Ear 1969,O 29,32:1
Zarkevitch, Theodore
Living Corpse, The 1929,D 7,19:1
Zarling, Beverly
An Evening With G B S; Press Cuttings
1957,F 19,35:7
Zaroubine, Alexander
Goin' Home 1928,Ag 24,23:2
Zaslavsky, Vera
Matinee Wife 1936,Ap 25,21:3
Zaslowski, Lenny
Hajj Malik, El 1970,O 4,II,5:1
Zasoek, Anna
Right to Kill, The 1926,F 16,22:2
Zatkin, Nathan (Producer)
Lady From the Sea, The 1934,My 2,25:2
Zavadski, Yuri (Director)
Cherry Orchard, The 1960,Je 4,17:2
Zavell, Lawrence
Young Alexander 1929,Mr 13,28:2
Zavin, Ben (Director)
Pigeon, The 1957,My 17,19:2
Johnny Summit 1957,S 25,23:4
Zavin, Ben (Playwright)
Johnny Summit 1957,S 25,23:4
Education of H*Y*M*A*N K*A*P*L*A*N, The
1968,Ap 5,57:1
Education of H*Y*M*A*N K*A*P*L*A*N, The
1968,Ap 14,II,1:1
Zavin, Mona
Broadway Shadows 1930,Ap 1,34:6
Zayas, Myrna
Movie Man 1959,O 28,40:4
Zayas, Paul
And the Wind Blows 1959,Ap 29,28:1
Homo 1969,Ap 12,40:2
Zayenda, Edmund
Shylock and His Daughter 1947,S 30,22:2
Second Marriage 1953,O 12,30:1
Shepherd King, The 1955,O 13,36:2
Brothers Ashkenazi, The 1955,N 12,24:4
Zayenda, Edmund (Producer)
Second Marriage 1953,O 12,30:1
Zebbs, Beecher
Money From Home 1927,Mr 1,30:2
19th Hole, The 1927,O 12,30:3
Zebrock, Stephen
Moon Is a Gong, The 1926,Mr 13,21:3
Window Panes 1927,F 22,22:2
Zechnoff, Irving
Medea 1920,Mr 23,12:2
Zee, Hope
Dear Judas 1947,O 6,26:4
Gentlemen Prefer Blondes 1949,D 9,35:3
Zee, John
Mandragola 1956,Mr 1,36:4
Changeling, The 1956,My 4,20:3
Confederates, The 1959,S 29,45:1
Ronde, La 1960,My 10,44:2
Rules of the Game, The 1960,D 20,44:1
Seven at Dawn, The 1961,Ap 18,43:1
Poppa Is Home 1961,D 20,37:1
Zeffirelli, Franco (Director)
Othello 1961,O 11,53:6
Romeo and Juliet 1962,F 14,39:1
Romeo and Juliet 1962,F 25,II,1:1
Lady of the Camellias, The 1963,Mr 22,7:1
Hamlet 1964,Je 2,32:8
Lupa, La 1965,N 12,57:1
Zeffirelli, Franco (Producer)
Lupa, La 1969,Je 5,54:1
Zeffirelli, Franco (Scenic Designer)
Othello 1961,O 11,53:6
Romeo and Juliet 1962,F 14,39:1
Lady of the Camellias, The 1963,Mr 22,7:1
Zeffron, Jerome
Will the Mail Train Run Tonight? 1964,Ja 10,18:1
Zeger, Julia
Trojan Women, The 1923,My 27,10:2
Zehner, Isobel
Sons o' Guns 1929,N 27,30:4

Zehner, Lili
 Steel 1931,N 19,26:5
 Growing Pains 1933,N 24,24:2
 Fly Away Home 1935,Ja 16,20:4
 Stage Door 1936,O 23,26:3
 Hill Between, The 1938,Mr 12,12:5
Zehren, Leroy (Director)
 In the Groove 1938,Ap 22,14:5
Zehringer, George
 Five Little Peppers, The 1952,My 19,13:1
Zeidenberg, Leon
 Wolves 1924,D 31,9:4
Zeidler, Frank (Playwright)
 Macbeth 1959,Je 7,124:3
Zeiger, Hal (Producer)
 Borscht Capades 1951,S 18,38:3
 Hello Solly! 1967,Ap 6,44:3
Zeigler, Larry (Miscellaneous)
 Of Thee I Sing 1969,Mr 8,19:1
 Dr Galley 1970,Ja 23,25:1
 Rooming House, The 1970,Ja 23,25:1
 Transfers 1970,Ja 23,25:1
 Early Morning 1970,N 26,57:1
Zeimann, Sonja
 My Fair Lady 1962,S 7,34:1
Zeiser, Hans Karl (Producer)
 Our Town 1955,Mr 18,32:8
Zeisl, Eric (Composer)
 Return of Ulysses, The 1943,Ja 28,22:2
 Return of Ulysses, The 1943,F 7,II,1:6
Zeisler, Alfred
 Barber Had Two Sons, The 1943,F 2,22:2
Zeisler, Peter (Miscellaneous)
 Candide 1956,D 3,40:2
 Hole in the Head, A 1957,Mr 1,15:1
 Juno 1959,Mr 10,41:1
 Sound of Music, The 1959,N 17,40:2
Zeislmeier, Josef
 Redemption: Lebende Leichnam, Der; Living
  Corpse, The 1928,N 20,28:2
Zeiss, Henry M
 Once Over Lightly 1938,D 10,13:4
Zeitgeist, The
 Last Sweet Days of Isaac, The 1970,Ja 27,49:1
Zeitlin, Aaron (Playwright)
 Wise Men of Chelm, The 1933,O 18,24:4
 Esterke 1940,O 18,24:2
Zeitlin, Frank
 Betty Behave 1927,Mr 9,28:4
Zeitlin, Ida
 Failures, The 1923,N 23,20:1
Zeitsoff, Elaine (Miscellaneous)
 Mulatto 1967,N 16,61:4
Zelaza, R
 Untitled-Revue 1935,N 11,21:2
Zelbis, Joshua
 Prince Reuvaini 1967,N 19,83:1
Zeldes, Shaye
 Germany Aflame 1933,O 28,20:5
Zeldis, Joshua
 King And the Cobbler, The 1954,D 13,33:6
 Thousand and One Nights 1959,D 16,53:2
 Mother's Sabbath Days 1960,N 21,33:2
 Backlane Center 1961,N 23,51:1
 Eleventh Inheritor, The 1962,N 22,43:5
 Sage of Rottenburg, The 1963,N 20,48:1
 Enchanting Melody 1964,N 25,40:1
 Fifth Commandment, The 1965,N 15,48:4
 Wandering Stars 1966,N 14,52:2
 Bronx Express, 1968 1968,N 16,43:3
 Melody Lingers On, The 1969,N 17,55:1
 Brothers Ashkenazi, The 1970,N 17,53:2
Zeldis, Lou
 Ubu Roi 1970,F 17,33:1
 Arden of Faversham 1970,F 17,33:1
Zelinka, Sidney (Miscellaneous)
 Hilarities 1948,S 10,20:2
Zelinskaya, Helen
 Cherry Orchard, The 1928,N 8,26:8
 God's Thieves 1930,O 27,17:4
 New Man, The 1932,Ap 22,23:2
 Yoshe Kalb 1932,N 6,IX,2:1
 Josephus 1933,D 1,22:5
 Spring Song 1934,O 2,18:2
 Wingless Victory, The 1936,D 24,20:2
 Five Alarm Waltz 1941,Mr 14,16:2
Zelitzkaya, S
 Poverty Is No Crime 1935,F 21,22:5
Zelitzky, V
 Revisor; Inspector General, The 1935,F 18,19:6
 Strange Child 1935,F 26,16:1
 White Guard, The; Days of the Turbins
  1935,Mr 7,27:5
 Marriage 1935,Mr 12,24:8
 Enemies 1935,Mr 19,24:7
Zell, Joan
 Grass Harp, The 1953,Ap 28,32:2
Zell, Joe E
 Sniper, The 1959,O 28,40:4
Zell, Violet
 Tip-Top 1920,O 6,13:2
Zeller, Gary (Lighting Director)
 Antigone 1962,D 29,5:5

 Orthee 1962,D 29,5:5
 Utopia! 1963,My 7,47:4
 Under the Yum-Yum Tree 1964,My 29,18:1
Zeller, Gary (Scenic Designer)
 Antigone 1962,D 29,5:5
 Orthee 1962,D 29,5:5
 Utopia! 1963,My 7,47:4
 Awakening of Spring, The 1964,My 13,50:1
Zeller, Kathy
 Hatfields & McCoys 1970,Je 23,34:1
Zeller, Mark
 Saratoga 1959,D 8,59:4
Zeller, Marvin
 High Button Shoes 1955,Mr 12,10:6
Zeller, Robert
 Paul Bunyan 1941,My 6,25:1
Zeller, Robert (Musical Director)
 Magdalena 1948,S 21,31:2
Zeller, Wolfgang (Composer)
 Faust 1928,O 9,34:1
Zelli, Joe (Producer)
 Papavert 1931,D 30,25:1
 Mr Papavert 1932,Ja 23,18:6
Zellias Sisters
 Vaudeville (Palace) 1927,Ja 25,18:3
Zemach, Benjamin
 Dybbuk, The 1926,D 14,24:2
 Eternal Jew, The 1926,D 21,21:2
 Jacob's Dream 1927,Ja 4,20:2
 Golem, The 1927,F 5,13:2
 Untitled-Recital 1931,Mr 23,24:3
 Eternal Road, The 1937,Ja 8,14:2
 Speak of the Devil! 1939,O 7,21:7
Zemach, Benjamin (Choreographer)
 Witch of Castile, The 1930,O 25,21:1
 200,000 1936,O 14,30:2
 Eternal Road, The 1937,Ja 8,14:2
Zemach, Benjamin (Director)
 Natural Man 1941,My 8,20:4
Zemach, Nahum
 Dybbuk, The 1926,D 14,24:2
 Eternal Jew, The 1926,D 21,21:2
 Jacob's Dream 1927,Ja 4,20:2
 Nowhere Bound 1935,Ja 23,20:2
Zemach, Nahum (Director)
 Heroic Years 1934,Ja 12,28:4
Zemel, Alan
 Matty and the Moron and Madonna
  1965,Mr 30,53:1
Zemmer, Jean
 Side-Show 1931,My 16,13:1
Zender, Marguerite
 Tickle Me 1920,Ag 18,9:1
 Elsie 1923,Ap 3,26:1
 Noble Rogue, A 1929,Ag 20,31:2
Zenni, Richard
 Little Theatre Tournament; Yellow Triangle, The
  1929,My 10,32:2
Zeno, Norman (Composer)
 Fools Rush In 1934,D 26,19:2
Zeno, Norman (Lyricist)
 Fools Rush In 1934,D 26,19:2
 Show Is On, The 1937,S 20,18:4
Zeno, Norman (Playwright)
 Fools Rush In 1934,D 26,19:2
Zentner, Matthew
 Shannons of Broadway, The 1927,S 27,30:4
Zeppilli, Alice
 Vaudeville (Palace) 1926,Ag 3,19:2
 Vaudeville (Palace) 1928,Ja 10,28:5
Zerbe, Anthony
 Cave Dwellers, The 1961,O 16,34:2
 Macbeth 1962,Je 20,41:1
 Moon Besieged, The 1962,D 6,54:1
 Devils, The 1963,N 5,25:1
 Trial of the Catonsville Nine, The 1970,Ag 16,II,1:7
Zerkowitz, B (Composer)
 Melusina 1930,My 11,IX,3:1
Zerkowitz, B (Playwright)
 My Fiddle Is Broken 1928,D 2,X,4:7
Zerneck, Peter Von
 Men in Shadow 1943,Mr 11,16:2
 Hidden Horizon 1946,S 20,42:2
Zerner, Maxwell
 Man Without Money, A 1929,N 3,27:4
 Seven Against One 1930,My 7,25:1
Zero, Jack
 Summer Wives 1936,Ap 14,18:1
Zerva, Eleni
 Eumenides 1961,S 27,32:4
 Medea 1964,S 1,31:1
Zervos, P
 Oedipus Tyrannus 1952,N 25,35:2
Zesch-Ballot, Hans
 Raetzel um Beate 1936,N 8,X,2:1
Zetlin, Erlinda (Miscellaneous)
 Me Nobody Knows, The 1970,My 19,42:1
 Castro Complex, The 1970,N 19,40:1
Zetter, Lois
 Blue Boy in Black, The 1963,My 1,32:1
Zetterling, Mai
 Restless Heart 1957,My 9,37:4

Zevin, Harry (Miscellaneous)
 Top Banana 1951,N 2,19:2
 Maggie 1953,F 19,20:2
Zhdanova, Maria
 In the Claws of Life 1923,N 30,23:4
 Death of Pazukhin, The 1924,F 12,20:1
Zhitsov, Aleksei
 Dead Souls 1965,F 5,34:1
 Kremlin Chimes 1965,F 25,23:1
Zhuarsvky, Jaslov (Playwright)
 Sabbati Zebi 1923,O 22,19:2
Zhuk, Tatyana
 Moscow Circus on Ice 1970,D 9,63:1
Zhulavsky, I (Original Author)
 Shabtai Tavi 1932,D 7,28:8
Zi, Henry (Composer)
 Circle of Chalk, The 1941,Mr 27,28:4
Zi, Ping Yuen
 Family, The 1943,Mr 31,22:4
Ziboran, George
 Sands of the Negev 1954,O 20,32:1
 Othello 1955,S 8,27:2
Ziccardi, Maria
 Blue Bonnet 1920,Ag 30,12:1
 Command Performance, The 1928,O 4,27:1
 Man's Estate 1929,Ap 2,28:2
 Ladies Don't Lie 1929,O 11,36:3
Ziceva, Olga
 Musk 1920,Mr 15,13:1
Zickel, Martin (Playwright)
 Zur Goldnen Liebe 1932,Ja 24,VIII,1:4
Ziebel, Ella
 Golden Ring, The 1930,F 1,14:7
Ziebel, Freda
 Three Little Business Men, The 1923,S 4,12:1
Zieder, Lili
 Karl Gerhard's Revue 1930,Jl 13,VIII,2:1
Ziegenthal, Herman (Scenic Designer)
 Faust 1933,Ja 22,IX,1:1
Ziegfeld, Florenz (Director)
 Rio Rita 1927,F 3,18:3
Ziegfeld, Florenz (Producer)
 Ziegfeld 9 o'clock Follies 1920,Mr 9,18:1
 Ziegfeld Midnight Frolic 1920,Mr 17,14:2
 Midnight Frolic 1920,Ag 4,7:1
 Midnight Frolic 1921,N 19,11:3
 Ziegfeld Follies 1923,Je 5,24:3
 Follies 1923,Je 26,14:5
 Kid Boots 1923,D 16,IX,2:4
 Follies, The 1923,D 23,VII,1:1
 Kid Boots 1924,Ja 1,21:3
 Follies 1924,Je 19,25:7
 Ziegfeld Follies 1924,Je 25,26:1
 Annie 1924,O 12,VIII,2:1
 Follies 1924,O 31,19:3
 Annie Dear 1924,N 5,25:3
 Louie the 14th 1925,Mr 4,17:1
 Follies 1925,Mr 11,19:2
 Follies 1925,Jl 7,24:3
 No Foolin' 1926,Je 25,25:1
 Betsy 1926,D 29,24:3
 Rio Rita 1927,F 3,18:3
 Rio Rita 1927,F 13,VII,1:1
 Follies 1927,Ag 7,VII,1:8
 Ziegfeld Follies 1927,Ag 17,27:3
 Follies 1927,Ag 28,VII,1:1
 Rosalie 1927,D 18,IX,2:3
 Show Boat 1927,D 28,26:1
 Rosalie 1928,Ja 11,26:3
 Three Musketeers, The 1928,Mr 4,IX,2:3
 Three Musketeers, The 1928,Mr 14,28:1
 Three Musketeers, The 1928,Mr 25,IX,1:1
 Whoopee 1928,N 11,X,2:4
 Whoopee 1928,D 5,34:3
 Ziegfeld's Midnight Frolic 1929,F 19,22:4
 Show Girl 1929,Jl 3,19:3
 Whoopee 1929,Ag 6,29:4
 Show Girl 1929,Ag 8,29:4
 Show Girl 1929,Ag 25,VIII,1:1
 Bitter Sweet 1929,N 6,30:2
 Simple Simon 1930,F 2,VIII,2:7
 Simple Simon 1930,F 19,22:1
 Smiles 1930,N 2,VIII,1:3
 Smiles 1930,N 19,19:2
 Ziegfeld Follies 1931,Jl 2,30:5
 Hot-Cha! 1932,F 21,VIII,2:1
 Hot-Cha! 1932,Mr 9,17:3
 Hot-Cha! 1932,Mr 20,VIII,1:1
 Show Boat 1932,My 20,22:2
Ziegfeld, Florenz, (Mrs) (Billie Burke) (Miscellaneous)
 Ziegfeld Follies 1934,Ja 5,24:3
Ziegfeld, Zenaide
 Clouds of the Sun 1922,My 6,11:2
 Los Angeles 1927,D 20,32:3
 Machinal 1928,S 8,10:3
Ziegler, Valerie
 Life Begins 1932,Mr 29,23:2
 Evensong 1933,F 1,13:4
Ziegler, William H (Composer)
 What a Relief 1935,D 14,10:6
Ziegler, William H (Lyricist)
 What a Relief 1935,D 14,10:6

Zierk, David (Lighting Director)
Bedlam Galore, for Two or More 1965,Mr 8,34:1
Impromptu, L' 1965,Mr 8,34:1
Leader, The 1965,Mr 8,34:1
Foursome 1965,Mr 8,34:1
Box-Mao-Box; Quotations From Chairman Mao
Tse-Tung 1968,Mr 8,48:1
Box-Mao-Box; Box 1968,Mr 8,48:1
Lemon Sky 1970,My 18,40:1

Ziese, Maxim (Playwright)
Siebenstein 1933,My 28,IX,1:3

Ziferstein, Gail
Fly Blackbird 1962,F 6,26:2

Ziffer, Frances (Composer)
Streetcar Named Desire, A 1955,Mr 4,18:2

Zigarelli, Salvatore
Servant of Two Masters, The 1958,F 11,35:2

Zigerlig, Agnes (Miscellaneous)
Veronica's Veil 1950,F 12,II,1:5

Zigouras, Arthur
Merry Wives of Windsor, The 1954,F 17,27:1

Zilahy, Lajos (Original Author)
Firebird 1932,S 25,IX,1:3
Farewell Performance 1936,S 11,28:3
Farewell Performance 1936,O 4,IX,1:1

Zilahy, Lajos (Playwright)
Siberia 1928,Ap 15,IX,4:1
A Tabornok 1928,D 2,X,4:7
In Command 1930,Mr 9,IX,4:3
Firebird 1932,Ap 17,VIII,3:8
Firebird 1932,N 22,25:2
Nacht zum 17. April, Die; Firebird 1932,D 18,X,4:5
Virgin and the Fawn, The 1949,Mr 18,33:2

Zilberkasten, Gertie
Love for Sale 1936,Ja 24,14:2

Zilberkasten, Morris
Motke Ganef 1932,D 30,15:2
Organ Grinder, The 1934,Ja 1,28:3

Zilberstein, Moishe
One in a Million 1934,N 17,13:2

Zilbert, Rosa
Fortune 1920,Ap 22,11:3

Zilinsky, A
Revisor; Inspector General, The 1935,F 18,19:6

Zilzer, Wolfgang
Barber Had Two Sons, The 1943,F 2,22:2

Ziman, Edward A (Composer)
International, The 1928,Ja 16,24:4
Hoboken Blues 1928,F 18,10:1

Ziman, Jerrold
Brass Butterfly, The 1970,Ja 31,34:1
Universal Nigger, The 1970,Mr 21,18:1
Arsenic and Old Lace 1970,N 5,59:1

Zimbalist, Efrem Jr
Variations of 1940 1940,Ja 29,12:1
Henry VIII 1946,N 7,42:2
What Every Woman Knows 1946,N 9,13:2
Androcles and the Lion 1946,D 20,29:2
Yellow Jack 1947,F 28,26:2
Hedda Gabler 1948,F 25,27:2
Fallen Angels 1956,Ja 18,27:1

Zimbalist, Efrem Jr (Composer)
Honeydew 1920,S 7,20:1

Zimbalist, Efrem Jr (Miscellaneous)
Telephone, The 1948,D 8,41:6
Medium, The 1948,D 8,41:6

Zimbalist, Efrem Jr (Producer)
Telephone, The 1947,My 2,28:2
Medium, The 1947,My 2,28:2
Consul, The 1950,Mr 16,41:1

Zimeleva, Vera
Russian Isba 1920,F 17,19:2
Russian Isba 1920,Mr 12,18:4

Zimet, Martin (Miscellaneous)
Come Out, Carlo! 1962,My 4,27:2
In the Penal Colony 1962,My 4,27:2

Zimet, Paul
Terminal 1970,Ap 15,51:2
Serpent, The 1970,Je 2,35:1

Zimet, Sidney (Miscellaneous)
Come Out, Carlo! 1962,My 4,27:2
In the Penal Colony 1962,My 4,27:2

Zimin, Mikhail
Cherry Orchard, The 1965,F 10,46:1

Zimmer, Bernard (Original Author)
Carnival in Flanders 1953,S 9,38:2

Zimmer, Bernard (Playwright)
Veau Gras, Le 1924,Mr 23,VIII,1:3
Birds, The 1928,F 19,VIII,4:4
Coup du Deux-Decembre, Le 1928,Ap 15,IX,2:2
Untitled-Play 1929,Mr 3,VIII,4:8
Printemps 1929,Ap 21,X,2:7
Pauvre Napoleon 1929,My 5,IX,2:4
Merry Wives of Windsor, The 1929,O 27,IX,2:4
Beau Danube Rouge 1931,My 17,VIII,1:5
Reseda 1933,Ja 15,IX,2:1

Zimmer, Edward
House With the Twisty Windows, The
1930,My 8,32:5

Zimmer, Forrest
Master of the Inn, The 1925,D 23,22:2
Good Fellow, The 1926,O 6,22:1

Mourning Becomes Electra; Hunted, The
1932,My 10,25:2
Mourning Becomes Electra; Haunted, The
1932,My 10,25:2

Zimmer, Irma (Playwright)
39 Steps 1938,Mr 12,13:1

Zimmerman, Al (Musical Director)
Assorted Nuts 1940,Ap 7,I,44:6

Zimmerman, Ed
Delightful Season, A 1960,S 29,30:1
Eccentricities of Davy Crockett, The 1961,Ja 4,26:1
Right Honourable Gentleman, The 1965,O 20,50:2
Patriot for Me, A 1969,O 6,58:1
Not Now Darling 1970,O 30,33:1

Zimmerman, Edwin
Arsenic and Old Lace 1943,D 13,18:6

Zimmerman, Floyd (Director)
Aquacade 1939,My 5,26:2

Zimmerman, Floyd (Miscellaneous)
New Aquacade Revue, The 1940,My 13,20:5

Zimmerman, Harry (Miscellaneous)
High Spirits 1964,Ap 8,34:1

Zimmerman, L I (Dr) (Director)
Cross and the Sword, The 1965,Je 28,32:6

Zimmerman, Ralph
Little Theatre Tournament; Edna 1929,My 11,22:2

Zimmerman, Ralph (Playwright)
Little Theatre Tournament; Edna 1929,My 11,22:2

Zimmermann, Jorg (Costume Designer)
Minna von Barnhelm 1968,N 13,37:1

Zimmermann, Jorg (Scenic Designer)
Minna von Barnhelm 1968,N 13,37:1

Zimmet, Marya
First One Asleep, Whistle 1966,F 28,19:1

Zinberg, Len (Original Author)
Walk Hard 1944,D 1,28:2
Walk Hard 1946,Mr 28,34:2

Zindel, Paul (Playwright)
Dream of Swallows, A 1964,Ap 15,46:1
Effect of Gamma Rays on Man-in-the-Moon
Marigolds, The 1965,Je 7,48:1
Effect of Gamma Rays on Man-in-the-Moon
Marigolds, The 1965,Je 27,II,1:1
Effect of Gamma Rays on Man-in-the-Moon
Marigolds, The 1970,Ap 8,32:1
Effect of Gamma Rays on Man-in-the-Moon
Marigolds, The 1970,Ap 19,II,1:1

Zingg, Peter F
Tableaux 1961,D 18,41:3

Zink, Ralph Spencer (Playwright)
Without Warning 1937,My 3,23:2

Zink, Russell
Infernal Machine, The 1937,D 13,22:7

Zinkeisen, Doris (Costume Designer)
Great Waltz, The 1934,S 24,14:4
Little Glass Clock, The 1954,D 12,II,5:1

Zinkeisen, Doris (Scenic Designer)
Nymph Errant 1933,O 29,IX,1:6
Streamline 1934,O 21,IX,1:3
Stop Press 1935,Mr 17,VIII,1:4
Taming of the Shrew, The 1937,Ap 11,XI,2:1
After the Ball 1954,Je 11,19:3
Little Glass Clock, The 1954,D 12,II,5:1

Zinn, Robert
Liliom 1956,F 18,12:5

Zipor, I B (Playwright)
Revolt 1933,Ja 12,21:3

Zipper, Gerald (Producer)
Plough and the Stars, The 1956,Ap 6,14:1

Zipper, Herbert (Miscellaneous)
Barrier, The 1950,N 3,32:2

Zipprodt, Patricia (Costume Designer)
Virtuous Island, The 1957,Ap 10,39:1
Apollo of Bellac, The 1957,Ap 10,39:1
Miss Lonelyhearts 1957,O 4,26:2
Rope Dancers, The 1957,N 21,39:1
Rope Dancers, The 1957,D 1,II,1:1
Crucible, The 1958,Mr 12,36:1
Back to Methuselah 1958,Mr 27,41:5
Night Circus, The 1958,D 3,44:1
Our Town 1959,Mr 24,46:2
Gang's All Here, The 1959,O 2,23:1
Balcony, The 1960,Mr 4,21:1
Camino Real 1960,My 17,42:2
Camino Real 1960,My 29,II,1:1
Period of Adjustment 1960,N 11,34:1
Blacks, The 1961,My 5,23:1
Garden of Sweets, The 1961,N 1,35:1
Sunday in New York 1961,N 10,40:1
Madame Aphrodite 1961,D 30,13:1
Oh Dad, Poor Dad, Mamma's Hung You in the
Closet and I'm Feelin' So Sad 1962,F 27,28:1
Man's a Man, A 1962,S 20,30:2
Step on a Crack 1962,O 18,48:1
Dragon, The 1963,Ap 10,32:1
She Loves Me 1963,Ap 24,39:1
Oh Dad, Poor Dad, Mamma's Hung You in the
Closet and I'm Feelin' So Sad 1963,Ag 28,28:2
Morning Sun 1963,O 7,36:2
Next Time I'll Sing to You 1963,N 28,69:2
Too Much Johnson 1964,Ja 16,29:1
Fiddler on the Roof 1964,S 23,56:2

Zipprodt, Patricia (Costume Designer)—Cont
Tragical Historie of Doctor Faustus, The
1964,O 6,34:2
Anya 1965,N 30,48:1
Pousse-Cafe 1966,Mr 19,19:2
Cabaret 1966,N 21,62:1
Little Foxes, The 1967,O 27,53:1
Plaza Suite; Visitor From Hollywood
1968,F 15,49:1
Plaza Suite; Visitor From Forest Hills
1968,F 15,49:1
Plaza Suite; Visitor From Mamaroneck
1968,F 15,49:1
Zorba 1968,N 18,58:1
Gianni Schicci 1969,F 25,36:1
Tale of Kasane, The 1969,F 25,36:1
Blueprints 1969,F 25,36:1
1776 1969,Mr 17,46:2
Georgy 1970,F 27,26:1

Zipprodt, Patricia (Miscellaneous)
Potting Shed, The 1957,Ja 30,32:1
Visit to a Small Planet 1957,F 8,18:1

Zipser, Arthur (Lyricist)
Of V We Sing 1942,F 16,20:3

Zipser, Stanley
Mr Moneypenny 1928,O 17,26:2

Zirlin, David
Othello 1958,Jl 4,16:1
Policemen, The 1961,N 22,24:2
Birds, The 1966,Jl 1,40:1

Ziskin, Victor (Composer)
Young Abe Lincoln 1961,Ap 26,36:1
Isle of Children 1962,Mr 17,16:2

Ziskind, Maggie
Storm, The 1962,Mr 31,17:2
Man's a Man, A 1962,S 20,30:2

Zito, Salvatore
First Night 1930,N 27,32:3
Bulls, Bears and Asses 1932,My 7,11:3

Zivanovic, Mihajlo
Progress of Bora, The Tailor, The 1968,Je 27,49:2

Zizak, John
Hunting the Jingo Birds 1965,Mr 26,27:1
World of Ray Bradbury, The; Pedestrian, The;
Veldt, The; To the Chicago Abyss 1965,O 10,11:1

Zizold, Carlos
Lenz 1926,Ap 29,20:4
Overture 1930,N 25,31:2
Overture 1930,D 8,26:4
Miracle at Verdun 1931,Mr 17,34:6

Zlatina, (Mme)
Chauve-Souris 1925,Ja 15,25:1

Znager, Jacob
With Open Eyes 1938,O 27,27:2

Zobel, Alvin
Censored 1938,F 28,18:2

Zoble, Vic
Hell'z-A-Splashin' 1959,Je 25,22:2
Ice Capades 1967,Je 2,33:1
Ice Capades 1970,Ja 7,35:1

Zobor, Elisa
Master Builder, The 1957,D 18,42:7

Zoeter, Fred
Kiss Me, Kate 1954,Mr 27,13:2

Zoffer, G (Playwright)
End of All Things Natural, The 1969,S 12,38:1

Zohar, Blanche
Lute Song 1946,F 7,29:2
Bathsheba 1947,Mr 27,40:2
Joy to the World 1948,Mr 19,28:2

Zola, Emile (Original Author)
Thou Shalt Not- 1938,S 25,IX,3:5
Therese 1945,O 10,24:2
Therese 1945,O 28,II,1:1

Zola, Emile (Playwright)
Assommoir, L' 1927,O 16,IX,4:7

Zoller, John
All Editions 1936,D 23,17:2

Zollinger, Jacob
They Knew What They Wanted 1924,N 25,27:1
Henry-Behave 1926,Ag 24,19:4

Zolna, Anna
Revolt of the Beavers, The 1937,My 21,19:2

Zolnay, Margaret
Sonya's Search for the Christmas Star
1929,D 14,24:6

Zolnay, Margo
Sonya's Search for the Christmas Star
1929,D 14,24:6

Zolotarefsky, I (Playwright)
Slaves of Luxury 1930,F 8,13:3

Zolotow, Morton (Miscellaneous)
Cantilevered Terrace, The 1962,Ja 18,24:1

Zolotow, Sam
Love on an Island 1934,Jl 24,20:5

Zolotukhin, Lev
Kremlin Chimes 1965,F 25,23:1

Zolt, Frank
Kid Boots 1924,Ja 1,21:3

Zomina, Sonia
Shepherd King, The 1955,O 13,36:2
Brothers Ashkenazi, The 1955,N 12,24:4
Bronx Express, 1968 1968,N 16,43:3
Zoob, David B (Composer)
Joan of Arkansas 1925,Ap 5,16:1
Sale and a Sailor, A, or Glory! What Price! 1926,Ap 25,30:4
Hoot Mon, or Clans Across the Sea 1927,My 8,29:4
Zook, Boyd
Merry Wives of Windsor, The 1928,Mr 20,20:1
Zorich, Louis
Henry V 1960,Je 30,23:1
Becket 1960,O 6,50:1
Becket 1961,My 9,44:1
Thracian Horses, The 1961,S 28,58:2
Shadow of Heroes 1961,D 6,59:1
Moby Dick 1962,N 29,45:1
Good Soldier Schweik, The 1963,Ap 9,57:1
Crime and Crime 1963,D 17,51:2
All Women Are One 1965,Ja 8,21:1
Danton's Death 1965,O 22,46:1
Condemned of Altona, The 1966,F 4,21:1
To Clothe the Naked 1967,Ap 28,30:1
Hadrian VII 1969,Ja 9,22:1
Zorina, Vera
On Your Toes 1937,F 6,15:2
I Married an Angel 1938,My 12,26:2
I Married an Angel 1938,My 22,XI,1:1
Louisiana Purchase 1940,My 29,19:2
Dream With Music 1944,My 19,15:2
Tempest, The 1945,Ja 26,17:2
Tempest, The 1945,F 4,II,1:1
Tempest, The 1945,N 13,24:6
Temporary Island, A 1948,Mr 15,27:3
On Your Toes 1954,O 12,24:4
Zoris, Les
Blackouts of 1949 1949,S 7,39:2
Zoritch, George
Early to Bed 1943,Je 18,16:2
Rhapsody 1944,N 23,37:2
Pardon Our French 1950,O 6,22:4
Zorn, George
Woman of Destiny, A 1936,Mr 3,25:2
Native Son 1941,Mr 25,26:5
Zorrilla, Jose (Playwright)
Don Juan Tenorio 1939,Jl 16,IX,1:1
Don Juan Tenorio 1953,N 20,18:5
Zorro
Aquacircus 1958,Je 30,24:6
Zortt, Mlle
Bourgeois Gentilhomme, Le 1955,O 26,26:1
Zorzi, Guglielmo (Playwright)
In Fondo Al Cuore; Depths of the Heart, The 1930,D 8,27:1
Zoska, Karin
Folies Bergere 1939,D 25,28:2
Zotoff, M
Chauve-Souris 1922,Je 6,17:4
Chauve-Souris 1925,Ja 15,25:1
Chauve-Souris 1929,Ja 23,20:2
1860: or, Aris; 1860, or an Interrupted Festival 1931,O 22,27:1
Zotto, Dante
Piacere Del'Onesta, Il; Happiness of Probity, The 1930,N 10,16:4
Zseto, Frederic Munn
Suds in Your Eye 1944,Ja 13,15:5
Zsolt, Bela (Playwright)
Untitled-Play 1929,D 29,VIII,4:1
Zube, Pete
Career 1943,O 29,22:6
Zucca, Jamie
Natja 1925,F 17,19:2
Zucca, Manna (Playwright)
Garrick Gaieties 1930,O 17,21:2
Zuccarello, Nino
Aria del Continente, L' 1927,O 5,30:2
Zucco, George
Journey's End 1928,D 30,VIII,4:1
Journey's End 1929,Jl 14,IX,5:1
Victoria Regina 1935,D 27,15:2
Zucco, George (Director)
Forty-Seven 1930,F 4,29:1
Zuccolo, Luigi
Piacere Dell 'Onesta, Il 1929,Mr 25,33:1
Serata D'Inverno; Winter Evening, A 1929,Ap 8,32:5
Zuch, Alan J (Miscellaneous)
My Daughter, Your Son 1969,My 14,36:2
Zucker, Gita
Commedia Dell' Arte 1927,Ap 6,24:3
Camels Are Coming, The 1931,O 3,20:4
Zucker, Milton
Dreaming Dust, The 1955,D 8,46:5
Italian Straw Hat, The 1957,O 1,37:2
Zucker, Stan (Producer)
Hilarities 1948,S 10,20:2

Zuckerberg, Regina
Three Little Business Men, The 1923,S 4,12:1
Jolly Tailors, The 1923,N 3,13:3
His Wife's Lover 1929,O 21,30:6
Singing Rabbi, The 1931,S 11,24:4
Mother's Son 1931,N 26,36:4
Zuckerman, Ira (Miscellaneous)
Five Queens 1963,S 11,46:2
Zuckerman, Lew (Playwright)
In the Groove 1938,Ap 22,14:5
Zuckert, Bill
Sixth Finger in a Five Finger Glove 1956,O 9,31:4
Shadow of My Enemy, A 1957,D 12,35:4
Family Portrait 1959,My 6,48:2
Gang's All Here, The 1959,O 2,23:1
Gay Apprentice, The 1960,F 3,27:2
Don Juan in Hell 1960,O 4,47:3
Zuckmayer, Carl (Playwright)
Katharina Knie 1929,Mr 10,X,2:1
What Price Glory 1929,Ap 28,IX,1:4
Hauptmann von Koeepenick, Der; Captain of Kopenick, The 1931,Ap 26,VIII,1:4
Kat 1931,O 4,VIII,4:1
Caravan 1932,My 1,VIII,2:2
Somewhere in France 1941,Ap 29,16:8
Devil's General, The 1953,O 11,II,3:7
Captain of Koepenick, The 1964,D 2,60:1
Zueva, Anastasia
Dead Souls 1965,F 5,34:1
Three Sisters, The 1965,F 12,15:1
Kremlin Chimes 1965,F 25,23:1
Zugsmith, Leane (Original Author)
Visitor, The 1944,O 18,24:5
Zuill, W E S
Tempest, The 1950,S 17,II,3:7
Zuker, Howard J (Producer)
Live Like Pigs 1965,Je 8,48:2
Zukor, Preston
Topaze 1947,D 29,21:5
Zullig, Hans
Green Table, The 1942,Ja 22,12:2
Prodigal Son, The 1942,F 18,22:2
Zungolo, Al
Hobo 1961,Ap 11,41:2
Zunser, Miriam Shomer (Playwright)
One of the Many 1921,O 4,10:3
Zur, Bomba
My Fair Lady 1964,F 20,24:4
Fiddler on the Roof 1965,Je 9,40:1
Fiddler on the Roof 1965,Ag 15,II,2:5
Zur, Menachen (Composer)
Unfair to Goliath 1970,Ja 26,27:1
Zur, Menachen (Musical Director)
Unfair to Goliath 1970,Ja 26,27:1
Zurer, Oscar (Miscellaneous)
Frying Pan, The 1966,N 8,45:1
Bridal Night, The 1966,N 8,45:1
Eternal Triangle 1966,N 8,45:1
Zurer, Oscar (Producer)
Play With a Tiger 1964,D 31,14:2
Zussin, Victoria
Something Different 1967,N 29,52:1
Zwack, Karl
Ice Follies 1937,D 22,29:1
Zweig, Eleanor
Cocktails of 1934 1934,My 5,22:1
Zweig, Fritz
Merry Widow, The 1944,O 9,17:1
Zweig, Stefan (Original Author)
Untitled-Play 1932,Ja 31,VIII,3:1
Zweig, Stefan (Playwright)
Volpone 1928,Ap 10,32:1
Volpone 1928,Ap 22,IX,1:1
Volpone 1928,D 9,X,2:7
Volpone 1930,Mr 11,24:5
Jeremiah 1939,F 4,11:2
Volpone 1957,Ja 8,27:1
Volpone 1957,Ja 13,II,10:1
Volpone 1957,F 5,27:2
Zweigbaum, Steven (Lighting Director)
This Was Burlesque 1970,F 12,31:1
Zweigbaum, Steven (Miscellaneous)
Memory Bank, The 1970,Ja 12,24:3
Room Service 1970,My 13,49:1
Zweighaft, James F B (Composer)
Steppe Around 1922,Mr 29,17:4
Zweighaft, James F B (Playwright)
Steppe Around 1922,Mr 29,17:4
Zweikoff, Peter (Composer)
Wozzeck 1966,Ap 6,34:1
Zweininger, Arthur (Playwright)
Armer Columbus 1928,Ap 22,IX,6:7
Zwerling, Arthur
Hamlet 1936,N 11,54:2
Zwerling, Barry
Cocktails of 1934 1934,My 5,22:1
Zwerling, Darrell
Along Came a Spider 1963,My 28,33:1
Room Service 1970,My 13,49:1
Zwerling, Ruby (Musical Director)
Hilarities 1948,S 10,20:2
Zwerling, Yetta
Golden Ring, The 1930,F 1,14:7

Soul of a Woman, The 1930,F 22,13:1
Motke From Slobodke 1930,Ap 12,23:3
Hello Grandpa! 1931,Ja 2,25:3
Jolly World, A 1931,Ja 24,15:3
Women of New York 1931,Mr 23,24:3
Song of the Ghetto, The 1932,O 3,15:5
Happy Family, A 1934,S 24,15:2
Twice 100,000 1934,N 23,22:6
East Side Wedding, An 1935,Ja 21,18:2
Itche Mayer of Warsaw 1935,Ja 31,22:4
Lovka Maladetz 1935,Mr 27,25:5
Heaven on Earth 1935,O 8,26:2
Love for Sale 1936,Ja 24,14:2
Pinye of Pinchev 1936,S 21,27:5
Night in Budapest, A 1936,N 3,33:2
His Jewish Girl 1936,D 9,34:1
Let's Get Married 1937,Ja 11,16:2
Give Me Back My Heart 1937,O 4,17:6
Semele's Bar Mitzvah 1938,Ja 17,11:2
My Baby's Wedding 1938,O 10,15:3
With Open Eyes 1938,O 27,27:2
Long Live America 1939,Ja 2,28:3
Polish Rabbi, The 1939,Mr 20,13:3
Family Mishmash, A 1958,O 20,36:1
Zwick, Joel
MacBird! 1967,F 23,38:1
Zwick, Joel (Miscellaneous)
Young Master Dante, The 1968,D 31,19:1
Zwick, Rene
Billy Budd 1955,My 4,35:1
Venice Preserv'd 1955,D 13,54:4
Children of Darkness 1958,Mr 1,11:4
Zwieback, H
My Little Girl 1931,F 2,22:4
Zwier, Hirsch (Original Author)
Madame Pagliacci 1935,S 30,12:3
Zwilinoff, Anna
Rose Bernd 1922,S 27,17:1
Zwink, Hans
Untitled-Passion Play 1934,My 18,12:1
Zwirling, Yetta
Eretz Israel 1930,N 27,32:3
Zybsko, Sasha
It's About Time 1942,Mr 31,28:3
Zylbecweig, Zalmon
Untitled-Revue 1935,N 11,21:2
Zynda, Henry von
Eight Bells 1933,O 30,14:2